Ingenix Has You Covered!

April ICD-9-CM Updates

With semi-annual ICD-9-CM changes effective April 1 and October 1, it is more important than ever to have up-to-date ICD-9-CM coding information in order to stay in compliance with HIPAA regulations. Ingenix is committed to providing you and your staff with the ICD-9-CM code update information you need to code accurately and efficiently. We are offering several ways to make sure you are always up-to-date.

- **Updateable *Expert* ICD-9-CM code books.**
  The February update will have any new April 1 codes.

- **Annual *Expert* and *Professional ICD-9-CM* editions.**
  Just visit *Ingenix Online* and look for the ICD-9, CPT® and HCPCS Alerts link under the Quick Access Resources menu.

  No extra charges for code changes. No additional cost for updated books. No hassle for you or your staff.

Revised Coding Guidelines

Revised official ICD-9-CM guidelines have been released and became effective December 1, 2005. Significant revisions were made to chapter-specific guidelines, the V code table and the use of terminology.

Only this set of guidelines, approved by the Cooperating Parties, is official. Adherence to these guidelines when assigning ICD-9-CM diagnosis and procedure codes is required under the Health Insurance Portability and Accountability Act (HIPAA).

Medicare Code Edits Notice

Not all Medicare edits for the new 2007 ICD-9-CM codes were released in time to be published in this edition. Once these edits are released we will post them on our Web site. Please visit www.ingenixonline.com and click on the ICD-9, CPT® and HCPCS Alerts link under the Quick Access Resources menu to view these edits.

Online Quick Access Resources

Ingenix is committed to providing you with current coding information. Ingenix hopes to assist you in correct application of coding conventions and guidelines in order to support your coding practices, training processes and ongoing quality and compliance initiatives. Included in these free resources are informative articles, regulatory updates and clinical coding scenarios that you can use to keep your facility, practice and staff informed on the latest changes.

Visit *Ingenix Online,* look for the Quick Access Resources menu and click on the Code This! and Ingenix Insights: Free eAlerts links to take advantage of the following free informative resources.

Code This!: Practical clinical coding scenarios demonstrate accurate classification of codes based on interpretation of documentation in compliance with official coding guidelines and conventions. These scenarios often reflect correct application of new codes and changes or updates of official coding guidelines in a clinical format. This feature is updated monthy.

Ingenix Insights: Free eAlerts: Access coding, billing and reimbursement analysis and breaking news that matters to you. These articles include regulatory, policy and other timely topics. Visit often for late-breaking news.

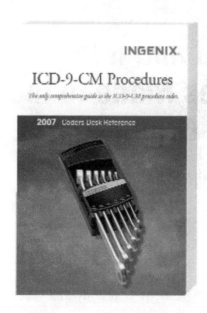

New! A comprehensive and informative guide to ICD-9-CM Procedures.

2007 Coders' Desk Reference for ICD-9-CM Procedures

Item No.: 1393 $129.95

Available: September 2006   ISBN: 978-1-56337-984-0

*C*oders' Desk Reference for ICD-9-CM Procedures provides coders, coding managers, medical staff, payers and health care professionals with a comprehensive and informative guide to the ICD-9-CM procedure code set. This reference will help to reduce the number of errors in code selection by giving detailed descriptions and coding advice for each procedure. The result is improved coding confidence and efficiency.

- **Ingenix Edge—Detailed descriptions of procedures using the common terminology found in the medical record.** Easy-to-understand terminology explains ICD-9-CM procedure codes, helping the user save time and reduce delayed claims by selecting the appropriate ICD-9-CM procedure code the first time.

- **Ingenix Edge— Master the intricacies of ICD-9-CM coding for procedures.** Special chapters provide detailed instructions on ICD-9-CM coding guidelines and conventions regarding Volume 3 Procedure coding.

- **Ingenix Edge—AHA's *Coding Clinic for ICD-9-CM* references and summary of advice.** Coding tips that reflect official coding advice found in *Coding Clinic* help you master correct coding practices.

- **Eponyms chapter.** In the medical record, procedures are often documented by their common name or eponym. This quick reference list is a convenient way to make the correct code selection.

- **Coding scenarios and coding tips.** The correct application of codes is demonstrated using coding scenarios that help improve overall coding accuracy and teach proper usage of specific ICD-9-CM procedure codes.

100% Money Back Guarantee

If our merchandise* ever fails to meet your expectations, please contact our Customer Service Department toll-free at 1.800.INGENIX (464.3649), option 1, for an immediate response. *Software: Credit will be granted for unopened packages only.

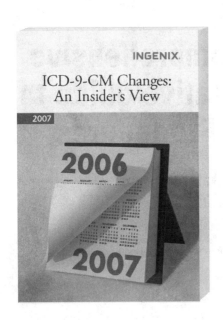

Understand and Interpret the Changes Made to the 2007 ICD-9-CM Code Set.

2007 ICD-9-CM Changes: An Insider's View

Item No.: 1077	$59.95
Available: September 2006	ISBN: 978-1-56337-920-8

A must-have resource for ICD-9-CM users! *ICD-9-CM Changes: An Insider's View* is a reference for understanding each of the code changes for 2007.

- **Ingenix Edge — Rationale for new and revised codes for 2007.** Knowing the reasons behind every new or revised code change is critical to adapting coding practices.

- **Ingenix Edge — Explanation of changes to indexes, conventions and instructional notes.** Understand what other changes will affect coding practices.

- **Ingenix Edge — Clinical presentation and treatment.** Coders must understand the clinical presentation of a condition or the intricacies of a procedure to code correctly to prevent "undercoding" or "overcoding."

- **Ingenix Edge — Clinical definitions of diagnoses and procedures.** Recognize terms in the medical records that pertain to new codes, ensuring correct application of the code changes.

- **Coding history and changes.** Understanding how the condition was coded in the past and how the change will impact coding practices.

- **Coding scenarios.** Examples of coding scenarios clarify application of the new codes.

- **Organized by chapter of ICD-9-CM.** Organizing the code changes in the context of their relationship to other codes provides insight into the rationale of the changes.

- **Detailed illustrations.** Illustrations are worth a thousand words and clarify some of the complex issues surrounding many of the code changes.

- **Annotated official addenda.** View the official addenda that contain all the changes with annotations to the three volumes of ICD-9-CM, including text deletions.

100% Money Back Guarantee

If our merchandise* ever fails to meet your expectations, please contact our Customer Service Department toll-free at 1.800.INGENIX (464.3649), option 1, for an immediate response. *Software: Credit will be granted for unopened packages only.

SAVE 5% when you order online—use source code FOBW7.

SAVE MORE and qualify for REWARDS when you order at IngenixOnline.com.

HERE ARE THE TOP THREE REASONS TO PLACE YOUR ORDER ONLINE:

1. Save an additional 5% when you order online*—use source **FOBW7**.

2. Get rewards for every $500 you spend at Ingenix Online with our eSmart program.**

3. Experience a quick, hassle-free purchase process with streamlined checkout options.

ingenix online frequent buyer program

Get rewards when you order online.

Ingenix eSmart is a program designed to reward our best Ingenix Online customers. If you are a registered online customer and qualify to participate**, all you have to do is use the returning customer checkout option for your web purchases every time you shop online. We keep track of your purchases. Once you reach $500, we send you a FREE product—it's that easy!

If you are not yet registered, go to IngenixOnline.com and register right away so we can get you started with the Ingenix eSmart program.

Are you part of our Medallion program?

Ingenix Online has enhanced options for you, for a hassle-free, streamlined purchase and account management experience!

To view your enhanced online account options, simply register with us at IngenixOnline.com. You will then be able to easily place orders from your Price List, get access to your purchase history, track shipments, change your profile, manage your address book and much more.

Could you benefit from an easy, quick way to consolidate orders for your company?

The Ingenix web-based consolidation tool is designed to streamline the purchasing process and enhance your productivity. For more information log into your account or visit www.ingenixonline.com/orderconsolidation.

(*) Additional 5% savings offer valid online, cannot be combined with any other offer and is not applicable to Partner accounts. Bookstore products, package items, eLearning products, Academy Credential Study Guides, online exams, Worker's Compensation items and conferences not included. For Medallion accounts, we compare the Price List discounts against the offer discounts and honor the better of the two.

(**) eSmart program valid for Ingenix customers who are NOT part of Medallion or Partner Accounts programs. You must be registered at Ingenix Online to have your online purchases tracked for rewards purposes. Shipping charges and taxes still apply and cannot be used for rewards. eSmart reward offers valid online only.

100% Money Back Guarantee

If our merchandise* ever fails to meet your expectations, please contact our Customer Service Department toll-free at 1.800.INGENIX (464.3649), option 1, for an immediate response. *Software and Data File: Credit will be granted for unopened packages only.

INGENIX.

Four simple ways to place an order.

Call
1.800.ingenix (464.3649), option 1. Mention source code FOBA7 when ordering.

Mail
PO Box 27116
Salt Lake City, UT 84127-0116
With payment and/or purchase order.

Fax
801.982.4033
With credit card information and/or purchase order.

Click
www.ingenixonline.com
Save 5% when you order online today—use source code FOBW7.

ingenix ℯ smart
ingenix online frequent buyer program

GET REWARDS FOR SHOPPING ONLINE!
To find out more, visit IngenixOnline.com

eSmart program available only to Ingenix customers who are not part of Medallion, Gold Medallion or Partner Accounts programs. You must be registered at Ingenix Online to have your online purchases tracked for rewards purposes. Shipping charges and taxes still apply and cannot be used for rewards. Offer valid online only.

100% Money Back Guarantee
If our merchandise* ever fails to meet your expectations, please contact our Customer Service Department toll-free at 1.800.ingenix (464.3649), option 1 for an immediate response.

*Software: Credit will be granted for unopened packages only.

Customer Service Hours
7:00 am - 5:00 pm Mountain Time
9:00 am - 7:00 pm Eastern Time

Shipping and Handling

no. of items	fee
1	$10.95
2-4	$12.95
5-7	$14.95
8-10	$19.95
11+	Call

Order Form

Information.

Customer No. _____ Contact No. _____

Source Code _____

Contact Name _____

Title _____ Specialty _____

Company _____

Street Address _____

City NO PO BOXES, PLEASE _____ State _____ Zip _____

Telephone ( ) _____ Fax ( ) _____
IN CASE WE HAVE QUESTIONS ABOUT YOUR ORDER

E-mail _____ @ _____
REQUIRED FOR ORDER CONFIRMATION AND SELECT PRODUCT DELIVERY.

Ingenix respects your right to privacy. We will not sell or rent your e-mail address or fax number to anyone outside Ingenix and its business partners. If you would like to remove your name from Ingenix promotion, please call 1.800.ingenix (464.3649), option 1.

Product

Item No.	Qty	Description	Price	Total

Subtotal _____

UT & VA residents, please add applicable Sales tax _____

(See chart on the left) Shipping & handling charges _____
All foreign orders, please call for shipping costs

Total _____

Payment

○ Please bill my credit card ○ MasterCard ○ VISA ○ Amex ○ Discover

Card No. | | | | | | | | | | | | | | | | | | | Expires | |
MONTH YEAR

Signature _____

○ Check enclosed, made payable to: Ingenix, Inc. ○ Please bill my office

Purchase Order No. _____
ATTACH COPY OF PURCHASE ORDER

2007

INGENIX®

ICD-9-CM
Expert

*for Hospitals
Volumes 1, 2 & 3*

*International Classification of Diseases
9th Revision
Clinical Modification*

Sixth Edition

*Edited by:
Anita C. Hart, RHIA, CCS, CCS-P
Beth Ford, RHIT, CCS*

Ingenix is committed to providing you with the ICD-9-CM code update information you need to code accurately and to be in compliance with HIPAA regulations. In the case of adoption of additional ICD-9-CM code changes effective April 1, 2007, Ingenix will provide these code changes to you at no additional cost! Just check back at http://www.IngenixOnline.com and look for the ICD-9, CPT® and HCPCS Alerts link under the Quick Access Resources menu to review the latest information concerning any new code changes.

Codes Valid October 1, 2006, through September 30, 2007

PUBLISHER'S NOTICE

All the codes, indexes and other material in the ICD-9-CM are compiled from official ICD-9-CM codes and instructions as well as the Medicare regulations and manuals issued or authorized by the Centers for Medicare and Medicaid Services. The code book is designed to provide accurate and authoritative information in regard to the subject covered, and every reasonable effort has been made to ensure the accuracy of the information within these pages. However, the ultimate responsibility for correct coding lies with the provider of services.

Ingenix, its employees, agents and staff make no representation, warranty or guarantee that this compilation of codes and narratives is error-free or that the use of this code book will prevent differences of opinion or disputes with Medicare or other third-party payers as to the codes that are accepted or the amounts that will be paid to providers of services, and will bear no responsibility or liability for the results or consequences of the use of this code book.

CONTINUING EDUCATION UNITS FOR CERTIFIED MEMBERS OF THE AMERICAN ACADEMY OF PROFESSIONAL CODERS

This publication has prior approval by the American Academy of Professional Coders for continuing education units (CEUs). Granting of prior approval in no way constitutes endorsement by the Academy of the publication content nor the publisher. Instructions to submit CEUs are available within the "Preapproved CEU Vendor List" file at www.aapc.com/education/CEUs/ceus.html.

OUR COMMITMENT TO ACCURACY

Ingenix is committed to producing accurate and reliable materials. To report corrections, please visit www.ingenixonline.com/accuracy or email accuracy@ingenix.com. You can also reach customer service by calling 1.800.INGENIX (464.3649), option 1.

SPECIAL REPORTS AND ANNOUNCEMENTS

Purchase of this publication entitles you to Special Reports and announcements via email. Please call customer service at 800 INGENIX (464-3649) or contact your bookstore to take advantage of this exciting free service that will keep you abreast of important code changes and regulatory developments.

Review, download, and print the Special Reports in .pdf format. Log on to http://www.ingenixonline.com/content/2007I9Expert

Preface

Since the federal government implemented diagnosis-related groups (DRGs) on October 1, 1983, medical record profes-sionals and others have had to refer to many sources for ICD-9-CM codes and coding and reimbursement principles.

ICD-9-CM for Hospitals, Volumes 1, 2 & 3, has been designed with the health information professional in mind. All three volumes of the most recent official government version of ICD-9-CM have been combined into one book.

Our technical experts have drawn upon their extensive hands-on experience to enhance the government's book with valuable features essential to correct coding and reimbursement. Without these enhancements, health information management departments would spend hours locating the information required to code each record accurately. Because of the thoroughness, accuracy, timeliness and ease of use of *ICD-9-CM for Hospitals,* health information departments nationwide have turned to them for their coding needs.

ICD-9-CM for Hospitals includes many of the enhancements described below in direct response to requests from our subscribers. As you review the content, you'll find the following:

- The complete ICD-9-CM official guidelines for coding and reporting, published by the U.S. Department of Health and Human Services and approved by the cooperating parties (American Hospital Association, American Health Information Management Association, Health Care Financing Administration and National Center for Health Statistics)
- All the official ICD-9-CM codes, indexes, notes, footnotes and symbols
- color-highlighted illustrations and clearly worded definitions integrated in the tabular, provide important clinical information
- Exclusive color coding, symbols, and footnotes that alert coders to coding and reimbursement issues, including the majority of the Medicare code edits and identification of conditions that significantly affect DRG assignment of cardiovascular and HIV cases.
- The complication and comorbidity (CC) exclusion list, integrated beneath the applicable codes makes it easier to determine complications and comorbidities excluded with a particular principal diagnosis
- The American Hospital Association (AHA's) *Coding Clinic for ICD-9-CM* references, integrated beneath the applicable codes to provide easy reference to official coding advice as designated by the four cooperating parties (AHA, AHIMA, CMS, and NCHS)
- Compliance symbol identifying diagnosis codes associated with DRGs targeted by the government for audit
- Check fourth- and fifth-digit symbols identify codes that require the addition of a fourth or fifth digit for code specificity and validity
- Symbols identify new codes and text revisions and pages are dated to indicate when the changes were made
- Synopsis of the code changes for the current year
- Color coding and symbol legend at the bottom of each page
- Exclusive QuickFlip Color Tabs for quick, easy location of terms and codes in the index and Tabular List

Please review "How to Use *ICD-9-CM for Hospitals (Volumes 1, 2 & 3)*" in this section to learn about the features that will help you assign and report correct codes, ensuring appropriate reimbursement.

USE OF OFFICIAL SOURCES

The *ICD-9-CM for Hospitals* contains the official U.S. Department of Health and Human Services, Ninth Revision, Sixth Edition ICD-9-CM codes, effective for the current year.

The color-coding, footnotes and symbols, which identify coding and reimbursement issues, are derived from official federal government sources, including the Medicare Code Edits (MCE), Version 24.0.

The American Hospital Association's (AHA) *Coding Clinic for ICD-9-CM* references are used with permission of the AHA.

IMPORTANT INFORMATION ABOUT YOUR SUBSCRIPTION SERVICE

If you have purchased the updateable *ICD-9-CM Expert for Hospitals,* your subscription includes an updating service throughout the year to keep the code book current and accurate. The February update includes new illustrations and definitions, *AHA Coding Clinic* references for third and fourth quarter, the latest MCEs, and official errata changes. In July you will receive a list of all new, revised, and invalid codes for the upcoming year.

TECHNICAL EDITORS

Anita C. Hart, RHIA, CCS, CCS-P
Product Manager, Ingenix
Ms. Hart's experience includes conducting and publishing research in clinical medicine and human genetics for Yale University, Massachusetts General Hospital, and Massachusetts Institute of Technology. In addition, Ms. Hart has supervised medical records management, health information management, coding and reimbursement, and worker's compensation issues as the office manager for a physical therapy rehabilitation clinic. Ms. Hart is an expert in physician and facility coding, reimbursement systems, and compliance issues. Ms. Hart developed *ICD-9-CM Changes: An Insider View,* and has served as technical consultant for numerous other publications for hospital and physician practices. Currrently, Ms. Hart is the Product Manager and Technical Editor for the ICD-9-CM and ICD-10-CM/PCS product lines.

Beth Ford, RHIT, CCS
Clinical/Technical Editor, Ingenix
Ms. Ford is a clinical/technical editor for Ingenix. She has extensive background in both the professional and technical components of CPT/HCPCS and ICD-9-CM coding. Ms. Ford has served as a coding supervisor and coding consultant, as well as a health information management director. She is an active member of the American Heath Information Management Association (AHIMA).

In addition to the editors, the following people have contributed to this book:

Michael E. Desposito, *Product Director and Client Relationships*
Lynn Speirs, *Senior Director, Editorial/Desktop Publishing*
Stacy Perry, *Manager, Desktop Publishing*
Tracy Betzler, *Desktop Publishing Specialist*
Irene Day, *Desktop Publishing Specialist*
Hope Dunn, *Desktop Publishing Specialist*
Kerrie Hornsby, *Desktop Publishing Specialist*
Kate Holden, *Editor*

WHAT TO DO IF YOU HAVE QUESTIONS

If you have any questions call our customer service department toll-free at 800-INGENIX (464-3649), option 1.

If you have comments on the content of this book, please email them to customerservice@ingenix.com or fax to 801-982-4033.

ADDITIONAL COPIES

Contact the customer service order department toll-free at 800-INGENIX (464-3649), option 1.

Introduction

HISTORY AND FUTURE OF ICD-9

The International Classification of Diseases, Ninth Revision, Clinical Modification (ICD-9-CM) is based on the official version of the World Health Organization's Ninth Revision, International Classification of Diseases (ICD-9). ICD-9 classifies morbidity and mortality information for statistical purposes, and for the indexing of hospital records by disease and operations, for data storage and retrieval.

This modification of ICD-9 supplants the Eighth Revision International Classification of Diseases, Adapted for Use in the United States (ICDA-8) and the Hospital Adaptation of ICDA (H-ICDA).

The concept of extending the International Classification of Diseases for use in hospital indexing was originally developed in response to a need for a more efficient basis for storage and retrieval of diagnostic data. In 1950, the U.S. Public Health Service and the Veterans Administration began independent tests of the International Classification of Diseases for hospital indexing purposes. The following year, the Columbia Presbyterian Medical Center in New York City adopted the International Classification of Diseases, Sixth Revision, with some modifications for use in its medical record department. A few years later, the Commission on Professional and Hospital Activities (CPHA) in Ann Arbor, Mich., adopted the International Classification of Diseases with similar modifications for use in hospitals participating in the Professional Activity Study.

The problem of adapting ICD for indexing hospital records was taken up by the U.S. National Committee on Vital and Health Statistics through its subcommittee on hospital statistics. The subcommittee reviewed the modifications made by the various users of ICD and proposed that uniform changes be made. This was done by a small working party.

In view of the growing interest in the use of the International Classification of Diseases for hospital indexing, a study was undertaken in 1956 by the American Hospital Association and the American Medical Record Association (then the American Association of Medical Record Librarians) of the relative efficiencies of coding systems for diagnostic indexing. This study indicated the International Classification of Diseases provided a suitable and efficient framework for indexing hospital records. The major users of the International Classification of Diseases for hospital indexing purposes then consolidated their experiences, and an adaptation was first published in December 1959. A revision was issued in 1962 and the first "Classification of Operations and Treatments" was included.

In 1966, the international conference for revising the International Classification of Diseases noted the eighth revision of ICD had been constructed with hospital indexing in mind and considered the revised classification suitable, in itself, for hospital use in some countries. However, it was recognized that the basic classification might provide inadequate detail for diagnostic indexing in other countries. A group of consultants was asked to study the eighth revision of ICD (ICD-8) for applicability to various users in the United States. This group recommended that further detail be provided for coding of hospital and morbidity data. The American Hospital Association was requested to develop the needed adaptation proposals. This was done by an advisory committee (the Advisory Committee to the Central Office on ICDA). In 1968 the United States Public Health Service published the product, Eighth Revision International Classification of Diseases, Adapted for Use in the United States. This became commonly known as ICDA-8, and beginning in 1968 it served as the basis for coding diagnostic data for both official morbidity and mortality statistics in the United States.

In 1968, the CPHA published the Hospital Adaptation of ICDA (H-ICDA) based on both the original ICD-8 and ICDA-8. In 1973, CPHA published a revision of H-ICDA, referred to as H-ICDA-2. Hospitals throughout the United States were divided in their use of these classifications until January 1979, when ICD-9-CM was made the single classification intended primarily for use in the United States, replacing these earlier related, but somewhat dissimilar, classifications.

Physicians have been required by law to submit diagnosis codes for Medicare reimbursement since the passage of the Medicare Catastrophic Coverage Act of 1988. This act requires physician offices to include the appropriate diagnosis codes when billing for services provided to Medicare beneficiaries on or after April 1, 1989. The Centers for Medicare and Medicaid Services (formerly known as Health Care Financing Administration) designated ICD-9-CM as the coding system physicians must use.

In 1993 the World Health Organization published the newest version of International Classification of Diseases, Tenth Revision, ICD-10. This version contains the greatest number of changes in the history of ICD. There are more codes (5,500 more than ICD-9) to allow more specific reporting of diseases and newly recognized conditions. ICD-10 consists of three volumes; Tabular List (volume I), instructions (volume 2) and the Alphabetic Index (volume 3). It contains 21 chapters including two supplementary ones. The codes are alphanumeric (A00–T98, V01–Y98 and Z00–Z99). Currently ICD-10 is being used in some European countries with implementation expected after the year 2009 in the United States.

ICD-9-CM BACKGROUND

In February 1977, a steering committee was convened by the National Center for Health Statistics to provide advice and counsel in developing a clinical modification of ICD-9. The organizations represented on the steering committee included the following:

- American Association of Health Data Systems
- American Hospital Association
- American Medical Record Association
- Association for Health Records
- Council on Clinical Classifications
- Centers for Medicare and Medicaid Services, Department of Health and Human Services
- WHO Center for Classification of Diseases for North America, sponsored by the National Center for Health Statistics, Department of Health and Human Services

The Council on Clinical Classifications was sponsored by the following:

- American Academy of Pediatrics
- American College of Obstetricians and Gynecologists
- American College of Physicians
- American College of Surgeons
- American Psychiatric Association
- Commission on Professional and Hospital Activities

The steering committee met periodically in 1977. Clinical guidance and technical input were provided by task forces on classification from the Council on Clinical Classification's sponsoring organizations.

ICD-9-CM is a clinical modification of the World Health Organization's ICD-9. The term "clinical" is used to emphasize the modification's intent: to serve as a useful tool to classify morbidity data for indexing medical records, medical care review, and ambulatory and other medical care programs, as well as for basic health statistics. To describe the clinical picture of the patient, the codes must be more precise than those needed only for statistical groupings and trend analysis.

CHARACTERISTICS OF ICD-9-CM

ICD-9-CM far exceeds its predecessors in the number of codes provided. The disease classification has been expanded to include health-related conditions and to provide greater specificity at the fifth-digit level of detail. These fifth digits are not optional; they are intended for use in recording the information substantiated in the clinical record.

Volume I (Tabular List) of ICD-9-CM contains four appendices:

Appendix A:	Morphology of Neoplasms
Appendix B:	Deleted Effective October 1, 2004
Appendix C:	Classification of Drugs by American Hospital Formulary Service List Number and Their ICD-9-CM Equivalents

These appendices are included as a reference to provide further information about the patient's clinical picture, to further define a diagnostic statement, to aid in classifying new drugs or to reference three-digit categories.

Volume 2 (Alphabetic Index) of ICD-9-CM contains many diagnostic terms that do not appear in Volume I since the index includes most diagnostic terms currently in use.

Volume 3 (Procedure Index and Procedure Tabular) of ICD-9-CM contains codes for operations and procedures. The format for the tabular is the same as Volume 1 disease tabular, except the codes consist of two digits with one or two digits following the decimal point. Conventions in the index follow Volume 2 conventions except some subterms appear immediately below the main term rather than following alphabetizing rules.

THE DISEASE CLASSIFICATION

ICD-9-CM is totally compatible with its parent system, ICD-9, thus meeting the need for comparability of morbidity and mortality statistics at the international level. A few fourth-digit codes were created in existing three-digit rubrics only when the necessary detail could not be accommodated by the use of a fifth-digit subclassification. To ensure that each rubric of ICD-9-CM collapses back to its ICD-9 counterpart the following specifications governed the ICD-9-CM disease classification:

Specifications for the Tabular List:

1. Three-digit rubrics and their contents are unchanged from ICD-9.

2. The sequence of three-digit rubrics is unchanged from ICD-9.

3. Three-digit rubrics are not added to the main body of the classification.

4. Unsubdivided three-digit rubrics are subdivided where necessary to
    •   add clinical detail
    •   isolate terms for clinical accuracy

5. The modification in ICD-9-CM is accomplished by adding a fifth digit to existing ICD-9 rubrics, except as noted under #7 below.

6. The optional dual classification in ICD-9 is modified.
    •   Duplicate rubrics are deleted:
        –   four-digit manifestation categories duplicating etiology entries
        –   manifestation inclusion terms duplicating etiology entries
    •   Manifestations of disease are identified, to the extent possible, by creating five-digit codes in the etiology rubrics.
    •   When the manifestation of a disease cannot be included in the etiology rubrics, provision for its identification is made by retaining the ICD-9 rubrics used for classifying manifestations of disease.

7. The format of ICD-9-CM is revised from that used in ICD-9.
    •   American spelling of medical terms is used.
    •   Inclusion terms are indented beneath the titles of codes.
    •   Codes not to be used for primary tabulation of disease are printed in italics with the notation, "code first underlying disease."

Specifications for the Alphabetic Index:

1. The format of the Alphabetic Index follows that of ICD-9.

2. When two codes are required to indicate etiology and manifestation, the manifestation code appears in brackets (e.g., diabetic cataract 250.5 [366.41]).

THE ICD-9-CM COORDINATION AND MAINTENANCE COMMITTEE

The four cooperating parties involved in maintaining the ICD-9-CM classification system include representatives of the American Hospital Association (AHA), the Centers for Medicare and Medicaid Services (CMS), the National Center for Health Statistics (NCHS), and the American Health Information Management Association (AHIMA).

Proposals for changes to the ICD-9-CM classification system are submitted and discussed in two open forum meetings held in April and October of each year at the Headquarters of the Centers for Medicare and Medicaid Services, Baltimore, Maryland. Comments received during and after the meetings are then discussed by the Committee. A notice of the new codes and code revisions approved by the Committee are published in the *Federal Register* as part of the proposed and final rule for the changes to the inpatient prospective payment system. The complete official document of changes to the classification system is released as the Addenda for the *International Classification of Diseases, Ninth Revision, Clinical Modification, Sixth Edition, Volumes 1, 2 and 3*.

How to Use the ICD-9-CM for Hospitals (Volumes 1, 2 & 3)

This *ICD-9-CM for Hospitals* is based on the official version of the International Classification of Diseases, Ninth Revision, Clinical Modification, Sixth Edition, issued by the U.S. Department of Health and Human Services. Annual code changes are implemented by the government and are effective Oct. 1 and valid through Sept. 30 of the following year.

The code book is totally compatible with its parent system, ICD-9, thus meeting the need for comparability of morbidity and mortality statistics at the international level.

This book is consistent with the content of the government's version of ICD-9-CM. However, to accommodate the coder's approach to coding, the Alphabetic Index has been placed before the Tabular List in both the disease and procedure classifications. This allows the user to locate the correct codes in a logical, natural manner by locating the term in the index, then confirming the accuracy of the code in the Tabular List.

STEPS TO CORRECT CODING

1. Look up the main term in the Alphabetic Index and scan the subterm entries as appropriate. Follow any cross-references such as "*see*" and "*see also*." Do not code from the Alphabetic Index without verifying the accuracy of the code in the Tabular List.

2. Locate the code in the numerically arranged Tabular List.

3. Observe the punctuation, footnotes, cross-references, color-coded prompts and other conventions described in the 'Conventions' section.

4. To determine the appropriateness of the code selection, read all instructional material:

   • "includes" and "*excludes*" notes
   • "*see*," "*see also*" and "*see category*" cross-references
   • "use additional code" and "*code first underlying disease*" instructions
   • "code also" and "*omit code*" notes
   • fourth- and fifth-digit requirements
   • CC exclusions

5. Consult definitions, relevant illustrations, CC exclusions, color coding and reimbursement prompts, the check fourth- and fifth-digit, age and sex symbols. Refer to the color/symbol legend at the bottom of each page for symbols. Refer to the list of footnotes that is included in the "Additional Conventions" section of this book for a full explanation of a footnote associated with a code.

6. Consult the official ICD-9-CM guidelines for coding and reporting, and refer to the AHA's *Coding Clinic for ICD-9-CM* for coding guidelines governing the use of specific codes.

7. Confirm and transcribe the correct code.

ORGANIZATION

Introduction
The introductory material in this book includes the history and future of ICD-9-CM as well as an overview of the classification system.

Official ICD-9-CM Conventions
This section provides a full explanation of all the official footnotes, symbols, instructional notes, and conventions found in the official government version.

Additional Conventions
Exclusive color-coding, symbols, and notations have been included in the *ICD-9-CM for Hospitals, Volumes 1, 2 & 3* to alert coders to important coding and reimbursement issues. This section provides a full explanation of the additional conventions used throughout this book.

Coding Guidelines
Included in this book are the official ICD-9-CM coding guidelines as approved by the four cooperating parties of the ICD-9-CM Coordination and Maintenance Committee. Failure to comply with the official coding guidelines may result in denied or delayed claims.

Summary of Code Changes
This section includes a complete listing of all new code changes for the current year.

Summary of AHA's Coding Clinic for ICD-9-CM Topics
This is a brief summary of the official advice concerning coding topics covered in the latest issues of AHA's *Coding Clinic for ICD-9-CM* and is found only in the *ICD-9-CM Expert for Hospitals* updateable edition.

Disease Classification: Alphabetic Index to Diseases
The Alphabetic Index to Diseases is separated by tabs labeled with the letters of the alphabet, contains diagnostic terms for illnesses, injuries and reasons for encounters with health care professionals. The Table of Drugs and Chemicals is easily located with the tab in this section.

The warning statement at the bottom of every page of the index, ▼ Subterms under main terms may continue to next column or page, is a reminder to always check for additional subterms before making final selection.

Disease Classification: Tabular List of Diseases
The Tabular List of Diseases arranges the ICD-9-CM codes and descriptors numerically. QuickFlip color tabs divide this section into chapters, identified by the code range on the tab.

The Tabular List includes two supplementary classifications:

• V Codes—Supplementary Classification of Factors Influencing Health Status and Contact with Health Services (V01–V86)
• E Codes—Supplementary Classification of External Causes of Injury and Poisoning (E800–E999)

ICD-9-CM includes four official appendixes.

• Appendix A   Morphology of Neoplasms
• Appendix B: Deleted Effective October 1, 2004
• Appendix C   Classification of Drugs by AHFS List
• Appendix D   Classification of Industrial Accidents According to Agency
• Appendix E   List of Three-digit Categories

These appendices are included as a reference to provide further information about the patient's circumstances, help further define a diagnostic statement, maintain a tumor registry and aid in classifying new drugs.

Procedure Classification: Alphabetic Index to Procedures
The Alphabetic Index to Procedures lists common surgical and procedural terminology.

The warning statement at the bottom of every page of the index, ▼ Subterms under main terms may continue to next column or page, is a reminder to always check for additional subterms before making final selection.

Procedure Classification: Tabular List of Procedures
The Tabular List of Procedures numerically arranges the procedure codes and their descriptors.

Resources

Listed below are the exclusive resources found ONLY in the *ICD-9-CM Expert for Hospitals, Volumes 1, 2 & 3* books.

Dx/MDC/DRG List

Provides the complete list of principal diagnosis codes and the MDC and DRG to which they group, with the exception of a combination of principal and secondary diagnosis affecting DRG assignment.

CC Condition List

A complete list of all codes considered CC (Complications and Comorbidities) that will affect DRG assignment. This an essential auditing tool for assigning the most appropriate DRG.

Pharmacological Listings

The most common generic and brand names of drugs are linked with the disease processes to assist in the identification of CC, thereby improving DRG assignment practices.

Valid Three-digit Code Table

ICD-9-CM is composed of codes with either 3, 4, or 5 digits. A code is invalid if it has not been coded to the full number of digits required for that code. There are a certain number codes that are valid for reporting as three digit codes. A list of the valid three-digit code is included as a convenient reference when auditing claims.

ICD-9-CM Official Conventions

ICD-9-CM FOOTNOTES, SYMBOLS, INSTRUCTIONAL NOTES AND CONVENTIONS

This *ICD-9-CM for Hospitals* preserves all the footnotes, symbols, instructional notes and conventions found in the government's official version. Accurate coding depends upon understanding the meaning of these elements.

The following appear in the disease Tabular List, unless otherwise noted.

OFFICIAL GOVERNMENT SYMBOLS

§   The section mark preceding a code denotes a footnote on the page. This symbol is used in the Tabular List of Diseases and in the Tabular List of Procedures.

ICD-9-CM CONVENTIONS USED IN THE TABULAR LIST

In addition to the symbols and footnotes above, the ICD-9-CM disease tabular has certain abbreviations, punctuation, symbols and other conventions. Our *ICD-9-CM for Hospitals* preserves these conventions. Proper use of the conventions will lead to efficient and accurate coding.

Abbreviations

NEC   Not elsewhere classifiable

This abbreviation is used when the ICD-9-CM system does not provide a code specific for the patient's condition.

NOS   Not otherwise specified

This abbreviation is the equivalent of 'unspecified' and is used only when the coder lacks the information necessary to code to a more specific four-digit subcategory.

[ ]   Brackets enclose synonyms, alternative terminology or explanatory phrases:

482.2   Pneumonia due to Hemophilus influenzae [H. influenzae]

Brackets that appear beneath a code indicate the fifth digits that are considered valid fifth digits for the code. This convention is applied for those instances in ICD-9-CM where not all common fifth digits are considered valid for each subcategory within a category.

715.0   Osteoarthrosis, generalized
[0,4,9]

Generalized arthrosis can only be assigned in cases for which the degenerative joint disease involves multiple joints. Therefore, this code is considered for arthrosis in the sites described as unspecified, hand (which consists of multiple joints), or multiple sites. Therefore, only fifth digits 0, 4, and 9 are valid with subcategory 715.0.

[ ]   Slanted brackets that appear in the Alphabetic Indexes indicate mandatory multiple coding. Both codes must be assigned to fully describe the condition and are sequenced in the order listed.

Tachycardia
ventricular (paroxysmal)
psychogenic 316 *[427.1]*

Psychogenic paroxysmal tachycardia is reported using both 316, Psychogenic factors associated with diseases classified elsewhere, and 427.1, Paroxysmal ventricular tachydcardia.

Diversion
biliopancratic (BPD) 43.7 *[45.51] [45.91]*

Code assignment of biliopancratic diversion is reported using all three codes 43.7, Partial gastrectomy with anastomosis to jejunum, 45.51, Isolation of segment of small intestine, and 45.91, Small-to-small intestinal anastomosis.

( )   Parentheses enclose supplementary words, called nonessential modifiers, that may be present in the narrative description of a disease without affecting the code assignment:

198.4   Other parts of nervous system
Meninges (cerebral) (spinal)

:   Colons are used in the Tabular List after an incomplete term that needs one or more of the modifiers that follow in order to make it assignable to a given category:

021.1   Enteric tularemia
Tularemia:
cryptogenic
intestinal
typhoidal

}   Braces enclose a series of terms, each of which is modified by the statement appearing to the right of the brace:

560.2   Volvulus
Knotting
Strangulation   } of intestine, bowel, or colon
Torsion
Twist

OTHER CONVENTIONS

Boldface   Boldface type is used for all codes and titles in the Tabular List.

Italicized   Italicized type is used for all exclusion notes and to identify codes that should not be used for describing the primary diagnosis.

INSTRUCTIONAL NOTES

These notes appear only in the Tabular List of Diseases:

Includes: An includes note further defines or clarifies the content of the chapter, subchapter, category, sub-category or subclassification. The includes note in the example below applies only to category 461.

Excludes: Terms following the word "*Excludes*" are not classified to the chapter, subchapter, category, subcategory or specific subclassification code under which it is found. The note also may provide the location of the excluded diagnosis. Excludes notes are italicized.

461   Acute sinusitis

INCLUDES   abscess
empyema
infection   } acute, of sinus
inflammation   (accessory)
suppuration   (nasal)

EXCLUDES   *chronic or unspecified sinusitis (473.0-473.9)*

Use additional code:
This instruction signals the coder that an additional code should be used if the information is available to provide a more complete picture of that diagnosis.

362.13   Changes in vascular appearance
Vascular sheathing of retina
Use additional code for any associated atherosclerosis (440.8)

There are coding circumstances outside of the etiology/manifestation convention when multiple coding for a single condition is required. The 'Use additional code' note will be found under the associated condition code in the tabular. In the index, the multiple coding requirement is indicated by the use of the slanted bracket. The two codes are to be sequenced as listed in the index. For example, retinal arterisosclerosis must be coded using two codes sequenced as listed in the index.

Arteriosclerosis, arteriosclerotic
  retinal (vascular) 440.8 *[362.13]*

Code first underlying disease:

The *Code first underlying disease* instructional note found under certain codes is a sequencing rule. Most often this sequencing rule applies to the etiology/manifestation convention and is found under at the manifestation code. The manifestation code may never be used alone or as a primary diagnosis (i.e., sequenced first). The instructional note, the code and its descriptor appear in italics in the Tabular List.

590.81 *Pyelitis or pyelonephritis in diseases classified elsewhere*

  Code first underlying disease as:
    tuberculosis (016.0)

Not all codes with a 'Code first underlying disease' instructional note are part of the etiology/manifestation convention. The 'Code first' note will appear, but the title of the code and the instructional note are not in italics. These codes may be reported alone or as the secondary diagnosis. For example, disseminated chorioretinitis may be reported as a principal diagnosis. However, if the underlying condition that caused disseminated chorioretinitis is known, such as tuberculous disseminated chorioretinitis, two codes are required and sequenced as listed in the index.

363.13 **Disseminated choroiditis and chorioretinitis, generalized**

  Code first underlying disease as:
    tuberculosis (017.3)

Code, if applicable, any causal condition first:

A code with this note indicates that this code may be assigned as a principal diagnosis when the causal condition is unknown or not applicable. If a causal condition is known, then the code for that condition should be sequenced as the principal or first-listed diagnosis.

590.0 **Chronic pyelonephritis**

  Chronic pyelitis
  Chronic pyonephrosis
  Code, if applicable, any causal condition first

Omit code:

"*Omit code*" is used to instruct the coder that no code is to be assigned. When this instruction is found in the Alphabetic Index to Diseases the medical term should not be coded as a diagnosis.

Metaplasia

  cervix — *omit code*

When used in Volume 3, '*omit code*' is meant to indicate procedures that do not merit separate code assignments, such as minor procedures preformed in conjunction with more extensive procedures or procedures that represent an operative approach.

Arthrotomy 80.10

  as operative approach — *omit code*

See Condition:

The "*see* condition" note found in the Alphabetic Index to Disease instructs the coder to refer to a main term for the condition. This note will follow index terms that are nouns for anatomical sites or adjectival forms of disease term. In the example below, the index terms 'Cervix' and 'Diffuse' are followed by the — *see* condition. Coders should search the index using a condition term such as atrophy or prolapse.

Cervix — *see* condition
Diffuse — *see* condition

Morphology Codes

For each neoplastic disease listed in the index, a morphology code is provided that identifies histological type and behavior.

Example:

Myelolipoma (M8870/0) — *see* Neoplasm, by site, benign

The histology is identified by the first four digits and the behavior is identified by the digit following the slash. Appendix A of Volume 1 contains a listing of morphology codes. This appendix is helpful when the pathology report identifies the neoplasm by using an M code. The coder may refer to Appendix A to determine the nomenclature of the neoplasm that will be the main term to search in the Index. The behavior classification is as follows:

  0   Benign
  1   Uncertain behavior
  2   Carcinoma in situ
  3   Malignant, primary site
  6   Malignant, secondary site.

Additional Conventions

NEW AND REVISED TEXT SYMBOLS

●   A bullet at a code or line of text indicates that that the entry is new.

▲   A triangle in the Tabular List indicates that the code title is revised. In the Alphabetic Index the triangle indicates that a code has changed.

►◄   These symbols appear at the beginning and at the end of a section of new or revised text.

When these symbols appear on a page there will be a date on the lower outside corner of the page indicating the date of the change, (e.g., October 2006).

ADDITIONAL DIGITS REQUIRED

√3rd   This symbol indicates that the code requires a third digit.

√4th   This symbol indicates that the code requires a fourth digit.

√5th   This symbol indicates that a code requires a fifth digit.

☑   This symbol found only in the Alphabetic Index sections and the Table of Drugs and Chemicals indicates that an additional digit is required. Referring to the tabular section is essential to locate the appropriate additional digit.

DEFINITIONS

DEF: This symbol indicates a definition of disease or procedure term. The definition will appear in blue type in the Disease and Procedure Tabular Lists.

AHA's *CODING CLINIC FOR ICD-9-CM* REFERENCES

The four cooperating parties have designated the AHA's *Coding Clinic for ICD-9-CM* as the official publication for coding guidelines. The references are identified by the notation **AHA:** followed by the issue, year and page number.

In the example below, AHA's *Coding Clinic for ICD-9-CM*, third quarter 1991, page 15, contains a discussion on code assignment for vitreous hemorrhage:

> **379.23**   **Vitreous hemorrhage**
> **AHA:** 3Q, '91, 15

The table below explains the abbreviations in the *Coding Clinic* references:

J-F	January/February
M-A	March/April
M-J	May/June
J-A	July/August
S-O	September/October
N-D	November/December
1Q	First quarter
2Q	Second quarter
3Q	Third quarter
4Q	Fourth quarter

MEDICARE CODE EDITS

Fiscal intermediaries use Medicare code edits (MCE) to check the coding accuracy on claims. The Medicare code edits are listed below:

1. Invalid diagnosis or procedure code
2. E-code as principal diagnosis
3. Duplicate of principal diagnosis (PDx) (as applied to a secondary diagnosis)
* 4. Age conflict
* 5. Sex conflict
* 6. Manifestation code as principal diagnosis
* 7. Nonspecific principal diagnosis
* 8. Questionable admission

*9. Unacceptable principal diagnosis
*10. Nonspecific OR procedure
*11. Noncovered procedure
12. Open biopsy check
*13. Bilateral procedure
14. Invalid age
15. Invalid sex
16. Invalid discharge status
*17. Limited coverage procedure

Starred edits are identified by colors, symbols or footnotes as described on the next page.

Age and Sex Edit Symbols

The age edits below address MCE edit 4 and are used to detect inconsistencies between the patient's age and diagnosis. They appear in the Tabular List of Diseases to the right of the code description.

Newborn Age: 0

> These diagnoses are intended for newborns and neonates and the patient's age must be 0 years

Pediatric Age: 0-17

> These diagnoses are intended for children and the patient's age must between 0 and 17 years

Maternity Age: 12-55

> These diagnoses are intended for the patients between the age of 12 and 55 years

Adult Age: 15-124

> These diagnoses are intended for the patients between the age of 15 and 124 years.

The sex symbols below address MCE edit 5 and are used to detect inconsistencies between the patient's sex and diagnosis or procedure. They appear in the Tabular Lists to the right of the code description:

♂   **Male diagnosis or procedure only**

> This symbol appears to the right of the code description. This reference appears in the disease and procedure Tabular List.

♀   **Female diagnosis or procedure only**

> This symbol appears to the right of the code description. This reference appears in the disease and procedure Tabular List.

Color Coding

For a quick reference to the color codes and their meaning, refer to the color/symbol legend located at the bottom of each page.

To alert the coder to important reimbursement issues affected by the code assignment, color bars have been added. The colors represent Medicare code edits as well as other reimbursement issues.

Color coding appears in both Tabular Lists. Some codes carry more than one color. Please note that the same color may appear in the disease and procedure Tabular Lists, but with different meanings.

Disease Tabular List
Manifestation Code

> These codes will appear in italic type as well as with a blue color bar over the code title. A manifestation code is not allowed to be reported as a primary diagnosis because each describes a manifestation of some other underlying disease, not the disease itself. This is referred to as mandatory multiple coding of etiology and manifestation. Code the underlying disease first. A 'Code first underlying disease' instructional note will appear with underlying disease codes identified. In the Alphabetic Index these codes are listed as the secondary code in slanted bracket with the code for the underlying disease listed first. Medicare code edit (MCE) 6

Unacceptable PDx

These codes will appear with a gray color bar over the code title. These codes do not describe a current illness or injury, but a circumstance which influences a patient's health status. These are considered an unacceptable principal diagnosis for inpatient admission. Medicare code edit (MCE) 9

Questionable Admission

These codes will also appear with a gray color bar over the code title. These codes identify a condition that usually is insufficient justification for hospital admission. Since these codes are considered an unacceptable principal diagnoses for inpatient admission, they are color coded in the same manner as the "unacceptable PDx codes". Medicare code edit (MCE) 8

Nonspecific PDx

These codes will have a yellow color bar over the code title. While these codes are considered valid ICD-9-CM codes, for inpatients discharged alive, a more specific principal diagnosis should be assigned. These codes are used when the neither the diagnostic statement nor the documentation provides enough information to assign a more specified diagnosis code. These codes may be stated as "Unspecified" or "Not otherwise specified (NOS)." Medicare code edit (MCE) 7

Procedure Tabular List
Nonspecific OR Procedure

While this code is a valid unspecific or not otherwise specified (NOS) procedure code, a more precise code should be used. The code is recognized as a nonspecific operating room procedure ONLY if ALL operating room procedures performed are coded NOS. Medicare code edit (MCE 10)

Valid OR

A procedure that triggers a change in DRG assignment.

Non-OR Procedure

A non-operating room procedure that affects DRG assignment.

Adjunct Codes

These codes are not to be reported alone and are indicated by the red color bar over the code title. Adjunct codes are assigned only in addition to a primary procedure. Their purpose is to provide supplemental information about the primary procedure performed. Adjunct codes are not procedure codes, but serve to provide additional detail about the primary procedure.

Example:

PTCA balloon inflation of two vessels, with insertion of one intravascular coronary stent.

Code assignment:

00.66 Percutaneous transluminal coronary angioplasty [PTCA] or athrectomy

00.41 Procedure on two vessels

00.45 Insertion of one vascular stent

In the above example, codes 00.41 and 00.45 are adjunct codes that provide specific detail about the PTCA procedure performed.

Footnotes

All footnotes are identified by a numerical superscript that appears to the upper left of the code:

[1]718.5 Ankylosis of joint

The footnote 1 indicates "Nonspecific PDx = 0". This means that when code 718.50, Ankylosis of the joint, site unspecified, the diagnosis is considered a nonspecific principal diagnosis. While this code may be valid according to ICD-9-CM, a more precise diagnosis should be used for the principal diagnosis for inpatient admission.

The following list identifies the meaning of each footnote number and the classification in which the footnote appears:

Disease Tabular

1 Diagnosis code with fifth digit of 0 is considered a 'Nonspecific' diagnosis when used as a principal diagnosis.

2 Diagnosis code with fifth digit of 9 is considered a 'Nonspecific' diagnosis when used as a principal diagnosis.

3 These V codes may be used as principal diagnosis on Medicare patients.

4 This V code, with the fourth digit of 1 or 2, is unacceptable as a principal diagnosis.

5 These codes, with the fourth digit of 0, may be used as a principal diagnosis for Medicare patients.

6 Rehabilitation codes acceptable as a principal diagnosis when accompanied by a secondary diagnosis reflecting the condition treated.

7 These V codes are acceptable as principal diagnosis when accompanied by a diagnosis of personal history of malignancy. These codes group to DRG 465.

8 Diagnosis code with fifth digit of 0 is considered a 'Questionable Admission' diagnosis when used as a principal diagnosis.

9 Diagnosis qualifies as a major cardiovascular condition for DRGs 551 and 553 only when assigned as either principal or secondary diagnosis.

10 Diagnosis qualifies as a major cardiovascular condition when assigned as a secondary diagnosis only.

11 Diagnosis qualifies as a major cardiovascular condition for DRGs 547, 549, 553, 555 and 557 only when assigned as either principal or secondary diagnosis.

Procedure Tabular

12 Valid OR procedure code if accompanied by one of the following codes: 37.80, 37.81, 37.82, 37.85, 37.86, 37.87.

13 Valid OR procedure code if accompanied by one of the following codes: 37.80, 37.83.

14 Valid OR procedure code if accompanied by one of the following codes: 37.80, 37.85, 37.86, 37.87.

15 Valid OR procedure code if accompanied by any one of the following codes: 37.80, 37.81, 37.82, 37.83, 37.85, 37.86, 37.87.

16 Valid OR procedure code if accompanied by any other pacemaker procedure except 37.72, 37.76.

17 Valid OR procedure code if accompanied by any other pacemaker procedure except 37.70, 37.71, 37.73, 37.76.

18 Procedure code with fourth digit of 0 is considered a 'Nonspecific' operating room procedure.

19 Non-covered procedure only when the following diagnoses are present as either a principal or secondary diagnosis: 204.00, 205.00, 205.10, 205.11, 206.00, 207.00, 208.00.

20 Non-covered procedure only when the following diagnoses are present as either a principal or secondary diagnosis: 203.00, 203.01.

21 Non-covered procedure except when there is at least one principal or secondary diagnosis from 250.00-250.93.

Other Notations

Alphabetic Indexes
▽ **Subterms under main terms may continue to next column or page.**

This warning statement is a reminder to always check for additional subterms and information that may continue onto the next page or column before making a final selection.

Disease Tabular
CC Condition

A complication or comorbidity diagnosis that may change DRG assignment. A complication is defined as a condition that arises during the hospital stay that extends the length of stay by at least one day in 75 percent of the cases. A comorbidity is a pre-existing condition that will, because of its presence with a specific principal diagnosis, that extends the length of stay by at least one day in 75 percent of the cases.

CC listed with a digit or range of digits indicates the fifth-digit assignments for that code that are considered CC conditions. Example: code 250.1 has a symbol CC 1-3 which means that only 250.11, 250.12, and 250.13 are considered CC conditions. Code 250.10 is not a CC condition.

CC Exclusion List

A exclusive feature of *ICD-9-CM for Hospitals* is the integration of the government's CC exclusion list with each affected code.

The CC exclusion list indicates secondary diagnosis codes that are excluded as CC conditions with certain principal diagnoses. This exclusion occurs because the cited conditions are inherent to the disease process of the principal diagnosis.

Listed below each code that is considered a complication or comorbidity (CC) diagnosis, are the codes or code ranges of principal diagnosis with which the CC code cannot be used.

In the example below, code 254.1 is considered a CC condition. However, the CC exclusion (CC Excl:) notation indicates that if a code from the listed code ranges is assigned as the principal diagnosis, the secondary diagnosis of 254.1 will not be recognized as a CC condition in DRG assignment.

254.1 Abscess of thymus `CC`
CC Excl: 254.0-254.1, 254.8-254.9, 259.8-259.9

Major Cardiovascular Complication Condition

A complication that causes the DRG to change from DRG 122 to DRG 121.

Complex Diagnosis

A diagnosis that causes the DRG assignment of a case to change from DRG 125 to DRG 124.

Medicare as Secondary Payer (MSP)

Note: The Medicare as Secondary Payer (MSP) alert identified trauma diagnoses that may be covered under automobile insurance, no-fault insurance, workmen's compensation or other types of liability insurance for which Medicare should be a secondary payer   Providers must verify MSP information prior to submitting the claim to Medicare. Therefore, this edit is no longer included in the official Medicare Code Editor (MCE) for the inpatient prospective payment system (IPPS).

▽ DRG

This symbol indicates the diagnosis is assigned to a diagnosis related group (DRG) that has been targeted for audit. The condition must be thoroughly documented in the medical record to prevent inappropriate coding or "upcoding."

HIV

This symbol indicates that the condition is considered a major HIV related diagnosis. When the condition is coded in combination with a diagnosis of human immunodeficiency virus (HIV), code 042, the case will move from DRG 490 to DRG 489.

Medicare as Secondary Payer (MSP)

Note: The Medicare as Secondary Payer (MSP) alert identified trauma diagnoses that may be covered under automobile insurance, no-fault insurance, workmen's compensation or other types of liability insurance for which Medicare should be a secondary payer Providers must verify MSP information prior to submitting the claim to Medicare. Therefore, this edit is no longer included in the official Medicare Code Editor (MCE) for the inpatient prospective payment system (IPPS).

V Code table

Note: Please note that while the official guidelines [Section 1. C.18.e.] include the V Code Table the reporting designations indicated by the Table are often in conflict with the Medicare code edits (MCE) for the inpatient prospective payment system (IPPS). Therefore, only the inpatient prospective payment system code edits are represented in this edition.

Procedure Tabular
Noncovered Procedure

A procedure not covered by Medicare. In some instances this procedure may also be identified as a valid operating room (OR) procedure that may trigger a DRG assignment. Even if a DRG assignment is made, Medicare may not reimburse for the noncovered procedure. Medicare code edit (MCE) 11.

Limited Coverage Procedure

A procedure whose medical complexity and serious nature incur associated costs that are deemed extraordinary and Medicare limits coverage to a portion of the cost. Medicare code edit (MCE) 17.

Bilateral Edit

Due to the lack of laterality in ICD-9-CM, there are certain lower extremity joint procedure codes that do not accurately reflect procedures that are performed in one admission on two or more different bilateral joints. To group to DRG 471, Bilateral or Multiple Joint Procedures of Lower Extremity, a case must be coded with a combination of two or more different major lower extremity joint procedures. The bilateral procedure symbol identifies those procedure codes that when coded twice represent the same procedure performed on both of the same bilateral joints of the lower extremity. Otherwise, a code edit will instruct the fiscal intermediary to verify that the two different procedures were performed on two different bilateral joints. Medicare code edit (MCE) 13.

Summary of Code Changes

DISEASE TABULAR LIST (VOLUME 1)

● 052.2 Postvaricella myelitis
Includes note added

● 053.14 Herpes zoster myelitis

● 054.74 Herpes simplex myelitis

136.3 Includes term added

151 Excludes note added

152 Excludes note added

171 Includes term added
Excludes term revised

174 Use additional code note added

175 Use additional code note added

202.1 Includes term deleted

211 Excludes note added

215.5 Includes term added

233.1 Includes term added
Excludes term revised

235 Excludes note added

238.1 Includes term added

238.7 Includes note deleted
Excludes terms added
Excludes note revised

● 238.71 Essential thrombocythemia
Includes note added

● 238.72 Low grade myelodysplastic syndrome lesions
Includes note added

● 238.73 High grade myelodysplastic syndrome lesions
Includes note added

● 238.74 Myelodysplastic syndrome with 5q deletion
Includes note added
Excludes note added

● 238.75 Myelodysplastic syndrome, unspecified

● 238.76 Myelofibrosis with myeloid metaplasia
Includes note added
Excludes note added

● 238.79 Other lymphatic and hematopoietic tissues
Includes note added

▲ 255.10 Primary Aldosteronism ►Hyperaldosteronism, unspecified◄
Includes term added
Includes term deleted

277.3 Includes note deleted

● 277.30 Amyloidosis, unspecified
Includes note added

● 277.31 Familial Mediterranean fever
Includes note added

● 277.39 Other amyloidosis
Includes note added

278.0 Use additional code note revised

▲ 284 Aplastic anemia and ►other bone marrow failure syndromes◄

284.0 Includes note deleted

● 284.01 Constitutional red blood cell aplasia
Includes note added

● 284.09 Other constitutional aplastic anemia
Includes note added

● 284.1 Pancytopenia
Excludes note added

● 284.2 Myelophthisis
Includes note added
Code first note added
Excludes note added

284.8 Includes term deleted
Excludes term deleted

284.9 Excludes term revised

285.0 Excludes term revised

▲ 285.2 Anemia in ►of◄ other chronic illness ►disease◄
Includes note added

▲ 285.29 Anemia of other chronic illness ►disease◄
Includes note added

285.8 Includes term deleted

287 Excludes term revised

▲ 288.0 Agranulocytosis ►Neutropenia◄
Includes term added
Includes terms deleted
Use additional code note deleted
Use additional code note added
Excludes term added

● 288.00 Neutropenia, unspecified

● 288.01 Congenital neutropenia
Includes note added

● 288.02 Cyclic neutropenia
Includes note added

● 288.03 Drug induced neutropenia
Use additional code note added

● 288.04 Neutropenia due to infection

● 288.09 Other neutropenia
Includes note added

● 288.4 Hemophagocytic syndromes
Includes note added

● 288.5 Decreased white blood cell count

● 288.50 Leukocytopenia, unspecified
Includes note added

● 288.51 Lymphocytopenia

● 288.59 Other decreased white blood cell count
Includes note added

● 288.6 Elevated white blood cell count
Excludes note added

● 288.60 Leukocytosis, unspecified
Includes note added

● 288.61 Lymphocytosis (symptomatic)
Includes note added

● 288.62 Leukemoid reaction
Includes note added

● 288.63 Monocytosis (symptomatic)
Includes note added

● 288.64 Plasmacytosis

● 288.65 Basophilia

● 288.69 Other elevated white blood cell count

288.8 Includes note deleted
Excludes terms added

289.4 Excludes term revised

● 289.53 Neutropenic splenomegaly

● 289.83 Myelofibrosis
Includes note added
Code first note added
Excludes note added

289.89 Includes term deleted

305.1 Excludes terms added

307.89 Code first note revised

309.81 Includes terms added

323 Includes terms revised
Excludes terms added

▲ 323.0 Encephalitis, ►myelitis, and encephalomyelitis◄ in viral diseases classified elsewhere
Includes note added

● 323.01 Encephalitis and encephalomyelitis in viral diseases classified elsewhere
Excludes note added

● 323.02 Myelitis in viral diseases classified elsewhere
Excludes note added

▲ 323.1 Encephalitis ►, myelitis, and encephalomyelitis◄ in rickettsial diseases classified elsewhere

▲ 323.2 Encephalitis ►, myelitis, and encephalomyelitis◄ in protozoal diseases classified elsewhere

▲ 323.4 Other encephalitis ►, myelitis, and encephalomyelitis◄ due to infection classified elsewhere
Excludes note deleted

● 323.41 Other encephalitis and encephalomyelitis due to infection classified elsewhere
Excludes note added

● 323.42 Other myelitis due to infection classified elsewhere
Excludes note added

▲ 323.5 Encephalitis ►, myelitis, and encephalomyelitis◄ following immunization procedures
Includes note deleted

● 323.51 Encephalitis and encephalomyelitis following immunization procedures
Includes note added

● 323.52 Myelitis following immunization procedures
Includes note added

▲ 323.6 Postinfectious encephalitis►, myelitis, and encephalomyelitis◄
Includes note deleted
Excludes note deleted

● 323.61 Infectious acute disseminated encephalomyelitis [ADEM]
Includes note added

● 323.62 Other postinfectious encephalitis and encephalomyelitis
Excludes note added

● 323.63 Postinfectious myelitis
Excludes note added

▲ 323.7 Toxic encephalitis►, myelitis, and encephalomyelitis◄

● 323.71 Toxic encephalitis and encephalomyelitis

● 323.72 Toxic myelitis

▲ 323.8 Other causes of encephalitis ►, myelitis, and encephalomyelitis◄
Excludes note deleted

● 323.81 Other causes of encephalitis and encephalomyelitis
Includes note added

● 323.82 Other causes of myelitis
Includes note added

▲ 323.9 Unspecified causes of encephalitis ►, myelitis, and encephalomyelitis◄

326 Instructional note revised

327 Section title added

327.5 Excludes term revised

● 331.83 Mild cognitive impairment, so stated
Excludes note added

▲ 333.6 Idiopathic ►Genetic◄ torsion dystonia

▲ 333.7 Symptomatic ►Acquired◄ torsion dystonia
Includes note deleted
Use additional code note deleted

● 333.71 Athetoid cerebral palsy
Includes note added
Excludes note added

● 333.72 Acute dystonia due to drugs
Includes note added
Use additional code note added
Excludes note added

● 333.79 Other acquired torsion dystonia

333.81 Excludes note added

333.82 Includes term deleted
Excludes note added

● 333.85 Subacute dyskinesia due to drugs
Includes note added
Use additional code note added
Excludes note added

333.92 Excludes note added

● 333.94 Restless legs syndrome [RLS]

333.99 Excludes term deleted

336.9 Excludes term revised

337.1 Code first note revised

338 Section title added

338 Pain, not elsewhere classified
Use additional code note added
Excludes note added

● 338.0 Central pain syndrome
Includes note added

● 338.1 Acute pain

● 338.11 Acute pain due to trauma

● 338.12 Acute post-thoracotomy pain
Includes note added

● 338.18 Other acute postoperative pain
Includes note added

● 338.19 Other acute pain
Excludes note added

● 338.2 Chronic pain
Excludes note added

● 338.21 Chronic pain due to trauma

● 338.22 Chronic post-thoracotomy pain

● 338.28 Other chronic postoperative pain

● 338.29 Other chronic pain

● 338.3 Neoplasm related pain (acute) (chronic)
Includes note added

● 338.4 Chronic pain syndrome
Includes note added
● 341.2 Acute (transverse) myelitis
Excludes note added
● 341.20 Acute (transverse) myelitis NOS
● 341.21 Acute (transverse) myelitis in conditions classified elsewhere
Code first note added
● 341.22 Idiopathic transverse myelitis
343 Excludes terms added
Excludes term revised
▲ 345 Epilepsy ▶and recurrent seizures◀
345.1 Excludes terms revised
▲ 345.4 ~~Partial epilepsy, with impairment of consciousness~~ ▶Localization-related (focal) (partial) epilepsy and epileptic syndromes with complex partial seizures◀
Includes terms added
▲ 345.40 ~~Partial epilepsy, with impairment of consciousness~~ ▶Localization-related (focal) (partial) epilepsy and epileptic syndromes with complex partial seizures◀, without mention of intractable epilepsy
▲ 345.41 ~~Partial epilepsy, with impairment of consciousness~~ ▶Localization-related (focal) (partial) epilepsy and epileptic syndromes with complex partial seizures◀, with intractable epilepsy
▲ 345.5 ~~Partial epilepsy, without impairment of consciousness~~ ▶Localization-related (focal) (partial) epilepsy and epileptic syndromes with simple partial seizures◀
Includes terms added
▲ 345.50 ~~Partial epilepsy, without impairment of consciousness~~ ▶Localization-related (focal) (partial) epilepsy and epileptic syndromes with simple partial seizures, without mention of intractable epilepsy
▲ 345.51 ~~Partial epilepsy, without impairment of consciousness~~ ▶Localization-related (focal) (partial) epilepsy and epileptic syndromes with simple partial seizures◀, with intractable epilepsy
▲ 345.8 Other forms of epilepsy ▶and recurrent seizures◀,
▲ 345.80 Other forms of epilepsy ▶and recurrent seizures◀, without mention of intractable epilepsy
▲ 345.81 Other forms of epilepsy ▶and recurrent seizures◀, with intractable epilepsy
345.9 Includes terms added
Excludes terms added
Excludes term revised
348.31 Excludes note added
349.82 Includes note added
357.4 Code first note added
Code first note revised
359.6 Code first note revised
360.0 Excludes note added
360.1 Excludes note added
● 377.43 Optic nerve hypoplasia
● 379.6 Inflammation (infection) of postprocedural bleb
Includes note added
● 379.60 Inflammation (infection) of postprocedural bleb, unspecified
● 379.61 Inflammation (infection) of postprocedural bleb, stage 1
● 379.62 Inflammation (infection) of postprocedural bleb, stage 2
● 379.63 Inflammation (infection) of postprocedural bleb, stage 3
Includes note added
▲ 389.11 Sensory hearing loss, ▶bilateral◀
▲ 389.12 Neural hearing loss, ▶bilateral◀
▲ 389.14 Central hearing loss, ▶bilateral◀
● 389.15 Sensorineural hearing loss, unilateral
● 389.16 Sensorineural hearing loss, asymmetrical
▲ 389.18 Sensorineural hearing loss of combined types, ▶bilateral◀
▲ 403 Hypertensive ▶chronic◀ kidney disease
Use additional code note deleted
▲ 403.0 Hypertensive ▶chronic◀ kidney disease, malignant
▲ 403.00 Hypertensive ▶chronic◀ kidney disease, malignant, ~~without~~ ▶with◀ chronic kidney disease ▶stage I through stage IV, or unspecified◀
Use additional code note added

▲ 403.01 Hypertensive ▶chronic◀ kidney disease, malignant, with chronic kidney disease ▶stage V or end stage renal disease◀
Use additional code note added
▲ 403.10 Hypertensive ▶chronic◀ kidney disease, benign, ~~without~~ ▶with◀ chronic kidney disease ▶stage I through stage IV, or unspecified◀
Use additional code note added
▲ 403.11 Hypertensive ▶chronic◀ kidney disease, benign, with chronic kidney disease ▶stage V or end stage renal disease◀
Use additional code note added
▲ 403.90 Hypertensive▶chronic◀ kidney disease, unspecified, ~~without~~ ▶with◀ chronic kidney disease ▶stage I through stage IV, or unspecified◀
Use additional code note added
▲ 403.91 Hypertensive ▶chronic◀ kidney disease, unspecified, with chronic kidney disease ▶stage I through stage IV, or unspecified◀
Use additional code note added
▲ 404 Hypertensive heart and ▶chronic◀ kidney disease
Use additional code note deleted
▲ 404.0 Hypertensive heart and ▶chronic◀ kidney disease, malignant
▲ 404.00 Hypertensive heart and ▶chronic◀ kidney disease, malignant, without heart failure ~~or~~ ▶and with◀ chronic kidney disease ▶stage I through stage IV, or unspecified◀
Use additional code note added
▲ 404.01 Hypertensive heart and ▶chronic◀ kidney disease, malignant, with heart failure ▶and with◀ chronic kidney disease stage I through stage IV, or unspecified◀
Use additional code note added
▲ 404.02 Hypertensive heart and ▶chronic◀ kidney disease, malignant,▶ without heart failure and◀ with chronic kidney disease ▶stage V or end stage renal disease◀
Use additional code note added
▲ 404.03 Hypertensive heart and ▶chronic◀ kidney disease, malignant, with heart failure ~~or~~ ▶and with◀ chronic kidney disease ▶stage V or end stage renal disease◀
Use additional code note added
▲ 404.1 Hypertensive heart and ▶chronic◀ kidney disease, benign
▲ 404.10 Hypertensive heart and ▶chronic◀ kidney disease, benign, without heart failure ~~or~~ ▶and with◀ chronic kidney disease ▶stage I through stage IV, or unspecified◀
Use additional code note added
▲ 404.11 Hypertensive heart and ▶chronic◀ kidney disease, benign, with heart failure ▶and◀ with chronic kidney disease stage I through stage IV, or unspecified◀
Use additional code note added
▲ 404.12 Hypertensive heart and ▶chronic◀ kidney disease, benign,▶ without heart failure and◀ with chronic kidney disease ▶stage V or end stage renal disease◀
Use additional code note added
▲ 404.13 Hypertensive heart and ▶chronic◀ kidney disease, benign, with heart failure ~~or~~ ▶and with◀ chronic kidney disease ▶stage V or end stage renal disease◀
Use additional code note added
▲ 404.9 Hypertensive heart and ▶chronic◀ kidney disease, unspecified
▲ 404.90 Hypertensive heart and ▶chronic◀ kidney disease, unspecified, without heart failure ~~or~~ ▶and with◀ chronic kidney disease ▶stage I through stage IV, or unspecified◀
Use additional code note added
▲ 404.91 Hypertensive heart and ▶chronic◀ kidney disease, unspecified, with heart failure ▶and with◀ chronic kidney disease stage I through stage IV, or unspecified◀
Use additional code note added
▲ 404.92 Hypertensive heart and ▶chronic◀ kidney disease, unspecified ,▶ without heart failure and◀ with chronic kidney disease ▶stage V or end stage renal disease◀
Use additional code note added
▲ 404.93 Hypertensive heart and ▶chronic◀ kidney disease, unspecified, with heart failure ~~or~~ ▶and with◀ chronic kidney disease ▶stage V or end stage renal disease◀
Use additional code note added

420.0 Code first note revised
425.7 Code first note revised
● 429.83 Takotsubo syndrome
Includes note added
440.24 Use additional code note added
445.81 Use additional code note revised
478.1 Includes note deleted
● 478.11 Nasal mucositis (ulcerative)
Use additional code note added
● 478.19 Other disease of nasal cavity and sinuses
Includes note added
496 Excludes term added
514 Excludes term added
517.8 Code first note revised
● 518.7 Transfusion related acute lung injury [TRALI]
519.1 Includes note deleted
● 519.11 Acute bronchospasm
Includes note added
Excludes note added
● 519.19 Other diseases of trachea and bronchus
Includes note added
520.6 Includes terms added
521.06 Includes note added
521.97 Includes note added
521.08 Includes note added
521.8 Includes note deleted
● 521.81 Cracked tooth
Excludes note added
● 521.89 Other specific diseases of hard tissues of teeth
Includes note added
● 523.00 Acute gingivitis, plaque induced
Includes note added
● 523.01 Acute gingivitis, non-plaque induced
523.1 Includes terms deleted
● 523.10 Chronic gingivitis, plaque induced
Includes note added
● 523.11 Chronic gingivitis, non-plaque induced
▲ 523.3 ▶Aggressive and◀ ~~A~~acute periodontitis
Excludes terms deleted
● 523.30 Aggressive periodontitis, unspecified
● 523.31 Aggressive periodontitis, localized
Includes note added
● 523.32 Aggressive periodontitis, generalized
● 523.33 Acute periodontitis
523.4 Excludes term deleted
● 523.40 Chronic periodontitis, unspecified
● 523.41 Chronic periodontitis, localized
● 523.42 Chronic periodontitis, generalized
524.07 Includes note added
524.2 Includes note added
▲ 524.21 ▶Malocclusion,◀ Angle's class I
▲ 524.22 ▶Malocclusion,◀, Angle's class II
▲ 524.23 ▶Malocclusion,◀ Angle's class III
524.24 Includes note added
524.25 Includes note added
524.26 Includes note added
524.27 Includes term added
524.28 Includes term added
524.29 Includes note added
524.33 Includes term added
524.34 Includes term added
▲ 524.35 Rotation of ▶tooth/◀teeth
524.36 Includes note added
524.37 Includes term added
524.54 Includes note added
524.55 Includes note added
524.56 Includes note added
● 525.6 Unsatisfactory restoration of tooth
Includes note added
Excludes note added
● 525.60 Unspecified unsatisfactory restoration of tooth
Includes note added
● 525.61 Open restoration margins
Includes note added
● 525.62 Unrepairable overhanging of dental restorative materials
Includes note added
● 525.63 Fractured dental restorative material without loss of material
Excludes note added
● 525.64 Fractured dental restorative material with loss of material
Excludes note added
● 525.65 Contour of existing restoration of tooth biologically incompatible with oral health
Includes note added

● 525.66 Allergy to existing dental restorative material
　　　　 Use additional code note added
● 525.67 Poor aesthetics of existing restoration
　　　　 Includes note added
● 525.69 Other unsatisfactory restoration of existing tooth
● 526.6 Periradicular pathology associated with previous endodontic treatment
● 526.61 Perforation of root canal space
● 526.62 Endodontic overfill
● 526.63 Endodontic underfill
● 526.69 Other periradicular pathology associated with previous endodontic treatment
▲ 528.0 Stomatitis ▶and mucositis (ulcerative)◀
　　　　 Includes note deleted
　　　　 Excludes terms added
● 528.00 Stomatitis and mucositis, unspecified
　　　　 Includes note added
● 528.01 Mucositis (ulcerative) due to antineoplastic therapy
　　　　 Use additional code note added
● 528.02 Mucositis (ulcerative) due to other drugs
　　　　 Use additional code note added
● 528.09 Other stomatitis and mucositis (ulcerative)
　528.3 Excludes term revised
　528.71 Includes note added
　528.72 Includes note added
　528.79 Includes term added
　530-538 Section title revised
　536.8 Includes note added
● 538 Gastrointestinal mucositis (ulcerative)
　　　　 Use additional code note added
　　　　 Excludes note added
　567 Excludes terms revised
　567.23 Excludes note added
　573 Excludes term revised
　580-589 Section title revised
　581.81 Code first note revised
　582.81 Code first note revised
　583.81 Code first note revised
　585 Excludes note deleted
　　　　 Code first note added
　585.5 Excludes note deleted
　585.6 Includes note added
　599.6 Excludes term deleted
　599.69 Code first note added
　600 Includes note added
　　　　 Use additional code note deleted
▲ 600.00 Hypertrophy (benign) of prostate without urinary obstruction ▶and other lower urinary tract symptoms [LUTS]◀
▲ 600.01 Hypertrophy (benign) of prostate with urinary obstruction ▶and other lower urinary tract symptoms [LUTS]◀
　　　　 Use additional code note added
▲ 600.20 Benign localized hyperplasia of prostate without urinary obstruction ▶and other lower urinary tract symptoms [LUTS]◀
▲ 600.21 Benign localized hyperplasia of prostate with urinary obstruction ▶and other lower urinary tract symptoms [LUTS]◀
　　　　 Use additional code note added
▲ 600.90 Hyperplasia of prostate, unspecified, without urinary obstruction ▶and other lower urinary tract symptoms [LUTS]◀
▲ 600.91 Hyperplasia of prostate, unspecified, with urinary obstruction ▶and other lower urinary tract symptoms [LUTS]◀
　　　　 Use additional code note added
　608.2 Includes note deleted
● 608.20 Torsion of testis, unspecified
● 608.21 Extravaginal torsion of spermatic cord
● 608.22 Intravaginal torsion of spermatic cord
● 608.23 Torsion of appendix testis
● 608.24 Torsion of appendix epididymis
　616.8 Includes note deleted
● 616.81 Mucositis (ulcerative) of cervix, vagina, and vulva
　　　　 Use additional code note added
● 616.89 Other inflammatory disease of cervix, vagina and vulva
● 618.84 Cervical stump prolapse
　629.2 Includes term added
　629.20 Includes term added
　629.21 Includes term added
　629.22 Includes term added
　629.23 Includes term added

● 629.29 Other female genital mutilation status
　　　　 Includes note added
● 629.81 Habitual aborter without current pregnancy
　　　　 Excludes note added
● 629.89 Other specified disorders of female genital organs
　629.9 Includes note deleted
　640-649 Section title revised
　　　　 Instructional note revised [5th digit box]
　641.3 Excludes note added
　642.2 Includes terms revised
　646.8 Excludes term deleted
　648.4 Instructional note revised
● 649 Other conditions or status of the mother complicating pregnancy, childbirth, or puerperium
● 649.0 Tobacco use disorder complicating pregnancy, childbirth, or puerperium
　　　　 Includes note added
● 649.00 Tobacco use disorder complicating pregnancy, childbirth, or the puerperium, unspecified as to episode of care or not applicable
● 649.01 Tobacco use disorder complicating pregnancy, childbirth, or the puerperium, delivered, with or without mention of antepartum condition
● 649.02 Tobacco use disorder complicating pregnancy, childbirth, or the puerperium, delivered, with mention of postpartum complication
● 649.03 Tobacco use disorder complicating pregnancy, childbirth, or the puerperium, antepartum condition or complication
● 649.04 Tobacco use disorder complicating pregnancy, childbirth, or the puerperium, postpartum condition or complication
● 649.1 Obesity complicating pregnancy, childbirth, or puerperium
　　　　 Use additional code note added
● 649.10 Obesity complicating pregnancy, childbirth, or the puerperium, unspecified as to episode of care or not applicable
● 649.11 Obesity complicating pregnancy, childbirth, or the puerperium, delivered, with or without mention of antepartum condition
● 649.12 Obesity complicating pregnancy, childbirth, or the puerperium, delivered, with mention of postpartum complication
● 649.13 Obesity complicating pregnancy, childbirth, or the puerperium, antepartum condition or complication
● 649.14 Obesity complicating pregnancy, childbirth, or the puerperium, postpartum condition or complication
● 649.2 Bariatric surgery complicating pregnancy, childbirth, or puerperium
　　　　 Includes note added
● 649.20 Bariatric surgery status complicating pregnancy, childbirth, or the puerperium, unspecified as to episode of care or not applicable
● 649.21 Bariatric surgery status complicating pregnancy, childbirth, or the puerperium, delivered, with or without mention of antepartum condition
● 649.22 Bariatric surgery status complicating pregnancy, childbirth, or the puerperium, delivered, with mention of postpartum complication
● 649.23 Bariatric surgery status complicating pregnancy, childbirth, or the puerperium, antepartum condition or complication
● 649.24 Bariatric surgery status complicating pregnancy, childbirth, or the puerperium, postpartum condition or complication
● 649.3 Coagulation defects complicating pregnancy, childbirth, or puerperium
　　　　 Use additional code note added
　　　　 Excludes note added
● 649.30 Coagulation defects complicating pregnancy, childbirth, or the puerperium, unspecified as to episode of care or not applicable
● 649.31 Coagulation defects complicating pregnancy, childbirth, or the puerperium, delivered, with or without mention of antepartum condition

● 649.32 Coagulation defects complicating pregnancy, childbirth, or the puerperium, delivered, with mention of postpartum complication
● 649.33 Coagulation defects complicating pregnancy, childbirth, or the puerperium, antepartum condition or complication
● 649.34 Coagulation defects complicating pregnancy, childbirth, or the puerperium, postpartum condition or complication
● 649.4 Epilepsy complicating pregnancy, childbirth, or puerperium
　　　　 Use additional code note added
　　　　 Excludes note added
● 649.40 Epilepsy complicating pregnancy, childbirth, or the puerperium, unspecified as to episode of care or not applicable
● 649.41 Epilepsy complicating pregnancy, childbirth, or the puerperium, delivered, with or without mention of antepartum condition
● 649.42 Epilepsy complicating pregnancy, childbirth, or the puerperium, delivered, with mention of postpartum complication
● 649.43 Epilepsy complicating pregnancy, childbirth, or the puerperium, antepartum condition or complication
● 649.44 Epilepsy complicating pregnancy, childbirth, or the puerperium, postpartum condition or complication
● 649.5 Spotting complicating pregnancy, childbirth, or puerperium
　　　　 Excludes note added
● 649.50 Spotting complicating pregnancy, unspecified as to episode of care or not applicable
● 649.51 Spotting complicating pregnancy, delivered, with or without mention of antepartum condition
● 649.53 Spotting complicating pregnancy, antepartum condition or complication
● 649.6 Uterine size date discrepancy complicating pregnancy, childbirth, or puerperium
● 649.60 Uterine size date discrepancy, unspecified as to episode of care or not applicable
● 649.61 Uterine size date discrepancy, delivered, with or without mention of antepartum condition
● 649.62 Uterine size date discrepancy, delivered, with mention of postpartum complication
● 649.63 Uterine size date discrepancy, antepartum condition or complication
● 649.64 Uterine size date discrepancy, postpartum condition or complication
　666.1 Includes term revised
　692.3 Excludes term revised
　693 Excludes term revised
　713.7 Code first note revised
● 729.7 Nontraumatic compartment syndrome
　　　　 Excludes note added
● 729.71 Nontraumatic compartment syndrome of upper extremity
　　　　 Includes note added
● 729.72 Nontraumatic compartment syndrome of lower extremity
　　　　 Includes note added
● 729.73 Nontraumatic compartment syndrome of abdomen
● 729.79 Nontraumatic compartment syndrome of other sites
　730.0 Use additional code note added
　730.1 Use additional code note added
　730.2 Use additional code note added
● 731.3 Major osseous defects
　　　　 Code first note added
　733.0 Use additional code note added
　733.4 Use additional code note added
　743.8 Excludes term added
　768 Excludes note added
▲ 768.3 Fetal distress first noted during labor ▶and delivery,◀ in liveborn infant
　　　　 Includes term revised
　768.5 Excludes note added
　768.6 Excludes note added
● 768.7 Hypoxic-ischemic encephalopathy [HIE]
　768.9 Excludes term deleted
　770.8 Excludes note added
● 770.87 Respiratory arrest of newborn
● 770.88 Hypoxemia of newborn
　　　　 Includes note added

▲ 775.8 Other transitory neonatal endocrine and metabolic disturbances
Excludes term deleted

● 775.81 Other acidosis of newborn
Includes note added

● 775.89 Other neonatal endocrine and metabolic disturbances
Includes note added

776.7 Excludes term revised

779.2 Includes term added
Excludes note added

● 779.85 Cardiac arrest of newborn

▲ 780.31 Febrile convulsions ▶(simple), unspecified◀
Includes term revised

● 780.32 Complex febrile convulsions
Includes note added
Excludes note added

780.39 Excludes term added

780.58 Excludes term revised

780.6 Code first note added

▲ 780.95 Excessive crying ▶of child, adolescent, or adult◀

● 780.96 Generalized pain
Includes note added

● 780.97 Altered mental status
Includes note added
Excludes note added

780.99 Excludes terms deleted

783.2 Use additional code note revised

784.3 Excludes term added

784.9 Includes note deleted

● 784.91 Postnasal drip

● 784.99 Other symptoms involving head and neck
Includes note added

785.52 Code first note deleted

788 Excludes term added

788.2 Excludes note deleted
Code first note added

788.3 Code first note added

788.4 Code first note added

788.6 Code first note added

● 788.64 Urinary hesitancy

● 788.65 Straining on urination

790 Excludes term revised

790.29 Includes term added

790.6 Includes term added
Excludes terms added

793.81 Excludes note added

793.89 Includes note added

793.9 Includes note deleted

● 793.91 Image test inconclusive due to excess body fat
Use additional code note added

● 793.99 Other nonspecific abnormal findings on radiological and other examinations of body structure
Includes note added

795.04 Includes note deleted

● 795.06 Papanicolaou smear of cervix with cytologic evidence of malignancy

795.7 Excludes terms added

● 795.8 Abnormal tumor markers
Includes note added
Excludes note added

● 795.81 Elevated carcinoembryonic antigen [CEA]

● 795.82 Elevated cancer antigen 125 [CA 125]

● 795.89 Other abnormal tumor markers

799.4 Code first note added
Excludes note deleted

▲ 873.63 Tooth (broken) ▶(fractured) (due to trauma) ◀
[Category 873.6 Internal structures of mouth, without mention of complications]
Excludes note added

▲ 873.73 Tooth (broken) ▶(fractured) (due to trauma) ◀
[Category 873.7 Internal structures of mouth, complicated]
Excludes note added

● 958.9 Traumatic compartment syndrome
Excludes note added

● 958.90 Compartment syndrome, unspecified

● 958.91 Traumatic compartment syndrome of upper extremity
Includes note added

● 958.92 Traumatic compartment syndrome of lower extremity
Includes note added

● 958.93 Traumatic compartment syndrome of abdomen

● 958.99 Traumatic compartment syndrome of other sites

960-979 Section Excludes note revised

▲ 995.2 ▶Other and◀ uUnspecified adverse effect of drug, medicinal and biological substance

● 995.20 Unspecified adverse effect of unspecified drug, medicinal and biological substance

● 995.21 Arthus phenomenon
Includes note added

● 995.22 Unspecified adverse effect of anesthesia

● 995.23 Unspecified adverse effect of insulin

● 995.27 Other drug allergy
Includes note added

● 995.29 Unspecified adverse effect of other drug, medicinal and biological substance

995.3 Excludes term added
Excludes term revised

995.4 Excludes term revised

995.9 Code first note deleted

▲ 995.91 ~~Systemic inflammatory response syndrome, unspecified~~ ▶Sepsis◀
Includes note added
Includes term deleted
Code first note added
Excludes note added

▲ 995.92 ~~Systemic inflammatory response syndrome due to infectious process without organ dysfunction~~ ▶Severe sepsis◀
Includes terms added
Includes term deleted
Code first note added
Use additional code note revised
Use additional code note added

▲ 995.93 Systemic inflammatory response syndrome due to noninfectious process without ▶acute◀ organ dysfunction
Code first note added
Excludes note added

▲ 995.94 Systemic inflammatory response syndrome due to noninfectious process with ▶acute◀ organ dysfunction
Code first note added
Use additional code note added
Use additional code note deleted
Excludes note added

996.45 Use additional code note added

996.7 Use additional code note added

997.3 Excludes terms added

998.5 Excludes terms added

999 Excludes terms revised

999.8 Excludes terms added

V01-V86 Section title revised

V07.39 Excludes terms revised

● V18.51 Colonic polyps
Excludes note added

● V18.59 Other digestive disorders

V20.2 Includes term added

V26.21 Excludes term revised

V26.3 Excludes term added

▲ V26.31 Testing ▶of female◀ for genetic disease carrier status

▲ V26.32 Other genetic testing ▶of female◀
Use additional code note added

● V26.34 Testing of male for genetic disease carrier status

● V26.35 Encounter for testing of male partner of habitual aborter

● V26.39 Other genetic testing of male

▲ V28 ▶Encounter for◀ Aantenatal screening ▶of mother◀

V45.3 Excludes note added

V45.77 Excludes term revised

● V45.86 Bariatric surgery status
Includes note added
Excludes note added

V54.1 Excludes note added

▲ V58.3 Attention to ~~surgical~~ dressings and sutures
Includes terms deleted
Includes term added
Excludes note added

● V58.30 Encounter for change or removal of nonsurgical wound dressing
Includes note added

● V58.31 Encounter for change or removal of surgical wound dressing

● V58.32 Encounter for removal of sutures

V58.41 Excludes term added

V58.49 Includes note added

V65.3 Use additional code note added

V65.4 Excludes terms revised

V70-V82 Section title revised

● V72.11 Encounter for hearing examination following failed hearing screening

● V72.19 Other examination of ears and hearing

● V82.7 Genetic screening
Excludes note added

● V82.71 Screening for genetic disease carrier status

● V82.79 Other genetic screening

V83-V84 Section title added

V85 Section title added

▲ V85 Body Mass Index ▶[BMI]◀

● V85.5 Body Mass Index, pediatric
Instructional note added

● V85.51 Body Mass Index, pediatric, less than 5th percentile for age

● V85.52 Body Mass Index, pediatric, 5th percentile to less than 85th percentile for age

● V85.53 Body Mass Index, pediatric, 85th percentile to less than 95th percentile for age

● V85.54 Body Mass Index, pediatric, greater than or equal to 95th percentile for age

V86 Section title added

● V86 Estrogen receptor status
Code first note added

● V86.0 Estrogen receptor positive status [ER+]

● V86.1 Estrogen receptor negative status [ER-]

PROCEDURE TABULAR (VOLUME 3)

● 00.44 Procedure on vessel bifurcation
Instructional note added

00.50 Instructional note added
Includes terms added

00.51 Instructional note added
Includes terms added

00.53 Instructional note added

00.54 Instructional note added

00.55 Code also note added

● 00.56 Insertion or replacement of implantable pressure sensor (lead) for intracardiac hemodynamic monitoring
Code also note added
Excludes note added

● 00.57 Implantation or replacement of subcutaneous device for intracardiac hemodynamic monitoring
Includes terms added
Code also note added

00.61 Code also note added

00.62 Code also note added

00.63 Code also note added

00.64 Code also note added

00.65 Code also note added

00.66 Code also note added

00.70 Code also note revised

00.71 Code also note revised

00.72 Code also note revised

00.73 Code also note revised

● 00.77 Hip replacement bearing surfaces, ceramic-on-polyethylene

▲ 00.8 Other knee ▶and hip◀ procedures

● 00.85 Resurfacing hip, total, acetabulum and femoral head
Includes note added

● 00.86 Resurfacing hip, partial, femoral head
Includes note added
Excludes note added

● 00.87 Resurfacing hip, partial, acetabulum
Includes note added
Excludes note added

▲ 01.26 Insertion of ▶catheter(s)◀ into cranial cavity ▶or tissue◀
Excludes note added

▲ 01.27 Removal of ▶catheter(s)◀ from cranial cavity ▶or tissue◀

● 01.28 Placement of intracranial catheter(s) via burr hole(s)
Includes note added
Code also note added
Excludes note added

02.93 Code also note revised

03.93 Code also note revised

04.92 Code also note revised

13.7 Excludes note added

● 13.90 Operations on lens, not elsewhere classified

● 13.91	Implantation of intraocular telescope Includes note added Excludes note added	37.75	Includes term revised	● 68.49	Other and unspecified total abdominal hysterectomy Includes note added
14.74	Includes note added	37.79	Includes terms added Excludes note added	▲ 68.59	Other ▶and unspecified◀ vaginal hysterectomy Excludes term revised

● 13.91   Implantation of intraocular telescope
       Includes note added
       Excludes note added
14.74   Includes note added
● 32.23   Open ablation of lung lesion or tissue
● 32.24   Percutaneous ablation of lung lesion or tissue
● 32.25   Thorascopic ablation of lung lesion or tissue
● 32.26   Other and unspecified ablation of lung lesion or tissue
32.28   Excludes terms added
32.29   Excludes terms added
● 33.7   Endoscopic insertion, replacement and removal of therapeutic device or substance in bronchus or lung
       Includes note added
       Excludes note added
● 33.71   Endoscopic insertion or replacement of bronchial valve(s)
       Includes note added
● 33.78   Endoscopic removal of bronchial device(s) or substances
● 33.79   Endoscopic insertion of other bronchial device(s) or substances
       Includes note added
34.92   Includes term added
▲ 35.53   Repair of ventricular septal defect with prosthesis, ▶open technique◀
● 35.55   Repair of ventricular septal defect with prosthesis, closed technique
36.03   Code also note added
36.06   Code also note added
36.07   Code also note added
36.09   Code also note added
36.32   Includes terms deleted
● 36.33   Endoscopic transmyocardial revascularization
       Includes note added
● 36.34   Percutaneous transmyocardial revascularization
       Includes note added
● 37.20   Noninvasive programmed electrical stimulation [NIPS]
       Excludes note added
▲ 37.26   ~~Cardiac~~ ▶Catheter based invasive◀ electrophysiologic ~~stimulation and recording studies~~ ▶testing◀
       Includes terms deleted
       Excludes terms added
37.66   Instructional note added
▲ 37.7   Insertion, revision, replacement, and removal of ~~pacemaker~~ leads; insertion of temporary pacemaker system,; or revision of cardiac device pocket

37.75   Includes term revised
37.79   Includes terms added
       Excludes note added
37.8   Instructional note added
● 39.74   Endovascular removal of obstruction from head and neck vessel(s)
       Instructional note added
       Excludes term deleted
37.96   Instructional note added
37.97   Excludes note added
37.98   Instructional note added
37.99   Includes terms deleted
       Excludes terms added
38   Excludes term revised
38.0   Excludes term added
38.1   Code also note added
38.4   Includes term added
39.50   Code also note added
39.72   Excludes note added
● 39.74   Endovascular removal of obstruction from head and neck vessel(s)
       Includes note added
       Code also note added
       Excludes note added
39.90   Code also note added
● 50.23   Open ablation of liver lesion or tissue
● 50.24   Percutaneous ablation of liver lesion or tissue
● 50.25   Laparoscopic ablation of liver lesion or tissue
● 50.26   Other and unspecified ablation of liver lesion or tissue
50.29   Excludes terms added
● 55.32   Open ablation of renal lesion or tissue
● 55.33   Percutaneous ablation of renal lesion or tissue
● 55.34   Laparoscopic ablation of renal lesion or tissue
● 55.35   Other and unspecified ablation of renal lesion or tissue
55.39   Excludes terms added
▲ 68.39   Other ▶and unspecified◀ subtotal abdominal hysterectomy
68.4   Includes note deleted
       Code also note revised
       Excludes note added
● 68.41   Laparoscopic total abdominal hysterectomy
       Includes note added

● 68.49   Other and unspecified total abdominal hysterectomy
       Includes note added
▲ 68.59   Other ▶and unspecified◀ vaginal hysterectomy
       Excludes term revised
68.6   Code also note revised
       Includes notes deleted
● 68.61   Laparoscopic radical abdominal hysterectomy
       Includes note added
● 68.69   Other and unspecified radical abdominal hysterectomy
       Includes note added
       Excludes note added
68.7   Code also note revised
       Excludes note revised
       Includes note deleted
● 68.71   Laparoscopic radical vaginal hysterectomy [LRVH]
● 68.79   Other and unspecified radical vaginal hysterectomy
       Includes note added
68.9   Excludes terms revised
80.51   Excludes term added
81.51   Code also note revised
81.52   Code also note revised
81.53   Code also note revised
84.59   Includes term added
84.73   Includes term added
86.28   Includes term added
89.45   Excludes terms revised
89.49   Excludes terms revised
89.6   Excludes terms added
93.59   Includes term added
96.05   Excludes note added
99.10   Includes terms added
99.28   Includes term added

▶◀ Revised Text   ● New Code   ▲ Revised Code Title

Coding Guidelines

ICD-9-CM OFFICIAL GUIDELINES FOR CODING AND REPORTING

Effective December 1, 2005
Narrative changes appear in bold text
The guidelines have been updated to include the V Code Table.

The Centers for Medicare and Medicaid Services (CMS) and the National Center for Health Statistics (NCHS), two departments within the U.S. Federal Government's Department of Health and Human Services (DHHS) provide the following guidelines for coding and reporting using the International Classification of Diseases, 9th Revision, Clinical Modification (ICD-9-CM). These guidelines should be used as a companion document to the official version of the ICD-9-CM as published on CD-ROM by the U.S. Government Printing Office (GPO).

These guidelines have been approved by the four organizations that make up the Cooperating Parties for the ICD-9-CM: the American Hospital Association (AHA), the American Health Information Management Association (AHIMA), CMS, and NCHS. These guidelines are included in the official government version of the ICD-9-CM and also appear in *Coding Clinic for ICD-9-CM*, published by the AHA.

These guidelines are a set of rules that have been developed to accompany and complement the official conventions and instructions provided within the ICD-9-CM itself. These guidelines are based on the coding and sequencing instructions in Volumes 1, 2, and 3 of ICD-9-CM, but provide additional instruction. Adherence to these guidelines when assigning ICD-9-CM diagnosis and procedure codes is required under the Health Insurance Portability and Accountability Act (HIPAA). The diagnosis codes (Volumes 1-2) have been adopted under HIPAA for all health care settings. Volume 3 procedure codes have been adopted for inpatient procedures reported by hospitals. A joint effort between the health care provider and the coder is essential to achieve complete and accurate documentation, code assignment, and reporting of diagnoses and procedures. These guidelines have been developed to assist both the health care provider and the coder in identifying those diagnoses and procedures that are to be reported. The importance of consistent, complete documentation in the medical record cannot be overemphasized. Without such documentation accurate coding cannot be achieved. The entire record should be reviewed to determine the specific reason for the encounter and the conditions treated.

The term "encounter" is used for all settings, including hospital admissions. In the context of these guidelines, the term "provider" is used throughout the guidelines to mean physician or any qualified health care practitioner who is legally accountable for establishing the patient's diagnosis. Only this set of guidelines, approved by the cooperating parties, is official.

The guidelines are organized into sections. Section I includes the structure and conventions of the classification and general guidelines that apply to the entire classification, and chapter-specific guidelines that correspond to the chapters as they are arranged in the classification. Section II includes guidelines for selection of principal diagnosis for non-outpatient settings. Section III includes guidelines for reporting additional diagnoses in non-outpatient settings. Section IV is for outpatient coding and reporting.

Section I. Conventions, general coding guidelines and chapter-specific guidelines

A. Conventions for the ICD-9-CM
 1. Format
 2. Abbreviations
   a. Index abbreviations
   b. Tabular abbreviations
 3. Punctuation
 4. Includes and excludes notes and inclusion terms
 5. Other and Unspecified codes
   a. "Other" codes
   b. "Unspecified" codes
 6. Etiology/manifestation convention ("code first," "use additional code," and "in diseases classified elsewhere" notes)
 7. "And"
 8. "With"
 9. "See" and "see also"
B. General coding guidelines
 1. Use of both Alphabetic Index and Tabular List

 2. Locate each term in the Alphabetic Index
 3. Level of detail in coding
 4. Code or codes from 001.0 through V86.1
 5. Selection of codes 001.0 through 999.9
 6. Signs and symptoms
 7. Conditions that are an integral part of a disease process
 8. Conditions that are not an integral part of a disease process
 9. Multiple coding for a single condition
 10. Acute and chronic conditions
 11. Combination code
 12. Late effects
 13. Impending or threatened condition
C. Chapter-specific coding guidelines
 1. Chapter 1: Infectious and Parasitic Diseases (001–139)
   a. Human immunodeficiency virus (HIV) infections
   b. Septicemia, systemic inflammatory response syndrome . . . (SIRS), sepsis, severe sepsis, and septic shock
 2. Chapter 2: Neoplasms (140–239)
   a. Treatment directed at the malignancy
   b. Treatment of secondary site
   c. Coding and sequencing of complications
   d. Primary malignancy previously excised
   e. Admissions/encounters involving chemotherapy and radiation therapy
   f. Admission/encounter to determine extent of malignancy
   g. Symptoms, signs, and ill-defined conditions listed in chapter 16
   h. Encounter for prophylactic organ removal
 3. Chapter 3: Endocrine, Nutritional, and Metabolic Diseases and Immunity Disorders (240–279)
   a. Diabetes mellitus
 4. Chapter 4: Diseases of Blood and Blood-Forming Organs (280–289)
   a. Anemia of chronic disease
 5. Chapter 5: Mental Disorders (290–319)
   Reserved for future guideline expansion
 6. Chapter 6: Diseases of Nervous System and Sense Organs (320–389)
   Reserved for future guideline expansion
 7. Chapter 7: Diseases of Circulatory System (390–459)
   a. Hypertension
   b. Cerebral infarction/stroke/cerebrovascular accident (CVA)
   c. Postoperative cerebrovascular accident
   d. Late effects of cerebrovascular disease
   e. Acute myocardial infarction (AMI)
 8. Chapter 8: Diseases of Respiratory System (460–519)
   a. Chronic obstructive pulmonary disease [COPD] and asthma
   b. Chronic obstructive pulmonary disease [COPD] and bronchitis
 9. Chapter 9: Diseases of Digestive System (520–579)
   Reserved for future guideline expansion
 10. Chapter 10: Diseases of Genitourinary System (580–629)
   a. Chronic kidney disease
 11. Chapter 11: Complications of Pregnancy, Childbirth, and the Puerperium (630–677)
   a. General rules for obstetric cases
   b. Selection of OB principal or first-listed diagnosis
   c. Fetal conditions affecting the management of the mother
   d. HIV infection in pregnancy, childbirth and the puerperium
   e. Current conditions complicating pregnancy
   f. Diabetes mellitus in pregnancy
   g. Gestational diabetes
   h. Normal delivery, code 650
   i. The postpartum and peripartum eriods
   j. Code 677 Late effect of complication of pregnancy
   k. Abortions
 12. Chapter 12: Diseases Skin and Subcutaneous Tissue (680–709)
   Reserved for future guideline expansion
 13. Chapter 13: Diseases of Musculoskeletal and Connective Tissue (710–739)
   Reserved for future guideline expansion

Section I. Conventions, general coding guidelines and chapter-specific guidelines
The conventions, general guidelines, and chapter-specific guidelines are applicable to all health care settings unless otherwise indicated.

A. Conventions for the ICD-9-CM
The conventions for the ICD-9-CM are the general rules for use of the classification independent of the guidelines. These conventions are incorporated within the index and tabular of the ICD-9-CM as instructional notes. The conventions are as follows:

1. **Format:**
   The ICD-9-CM uses an indented format for ease in reference

2. **Abbreviations**
   a. Index abbreviations
   NEC "Not elsewhere classifiable"—This abbreviation in the index represents "other specified." When a specific code is not available for a condition, the index directs the coder to the "other specified" code in the tabular.

   b. Tabular abbreviations
   NEC "Not elsewhere classifiable"—This abbreviation in the tabular represents "other specified." When a specific code is not available for a condition, the tabular includes an NEC entry under a code to identify the code as the "other specified" code (See section I.A.5.a.,"Other" codes).

   NOS "Not otherwise specified"—This abbreviation is the equivalent of unspecified. (See section I.A.5.b., "Unspecified" codes)

3. **Punctuation**
   [ ] Brackets are used in the Tabular List to enclose synonyms, alternative wording, or explanatory phrases. Brackets are used in the index to identify manifestation codes. (See section I.A.6., Etiology/manifestations)

   ( ) Parentheses are used in both the index and tabular to enclose supplementary words that may be present or absent in the statement of a disease or procedure without affecting the code number to which it is assigned. The terms within the parentheses are referred to as nonessential modifiers.

   : Colons are used in the Tabular List after an incomplete term needs one or more of the modifiers following the colon to make it assignable to a given category.

4. **Includes and excludes notes and inclusion terms**
   Includes: This note appears immediately under a three-digit code title to further define, or give examples of, the content of the category.

   Excludes: An excludes note under a code indicates that the terms excluded from the code are to be coded elsewhere. In some cases the codes for the excluded terms should not be used in conjunction with the code from which they are excluded. An example of this is a congenital condition excluded from an acquired form of the same condition. The congenital and acquired codes should not be used together. In other cases, the excluded terms may be used together with an excluded code. An example of this is when fractures of different bones are coded to different codes. Both codes may be used together if both types of fractures are present.

   Inclusion terms: List of terms included under certain four- and five-digit codes. These terms are the conditions for which that code number is to be used. The terms may be synonyms of the code title, or, in the case of "other specified" codes, the terms are a list of the various conditions assigned to that code. The inclusion terms are not necessarily exhaustive. Additional terms found only in the index may also be assigned to a code.

5. **Other and unspecified codes**
   a."Other" codes—Codes titled "other" or "other specified" (usually a code with a fourth digit of 8 or fifth digit of 9 for diagnosis codes) are for use when the information in the medical record provides detail for which a specific code does not exist. Index entries with NEC in the line designate "other" codes in the tabular. These index entries

represent specific disease entities for which no specific code exists so the term is included within an "other" code.

    b. **"Unspecified" codes**—Codes (usually a code with a fourth digit of 9 or fifth of 0 for diagnosis codes) titled "unspecified" are for use when the information in the medical record is insufficient to assign a more specific code.

6. **Etiology/manifestation convention ("code first," "use additional code," and "in diseases classified elsewhere" notes)**—Certain conditions have both an underlying etiology and multiple body system manifestations due to the underlying etiology. For such conditions, the ICD-9-CM has a coding convention that requires the underlying condition be sequenced first followed by the manifestation. Wherever such a combination exists, there is a "use additional code" note at the etiology code, and a "code first" note at the manifestation code. These instructional notes indicate the proper sequencing order of the codes, etiology followed by manifestation.

In most cases the manifestation codes will have in the code title, "in diseases classified elsewhere." Codes with this title are a component of the etiology/manifestation convention. The code title indicates that it is a manifestation code. "In diseases classified elsewhere," codes are never permitted to be used as first listed or principal diagnosis codes. They must be used in conjunction with an underlying condition code, and they must be listed following the underlying condition.

There are manifestation codes that do not have "in diseases classified elsewhere" in the title. For such codes a "use additional code" note will still be present and the rules for sequencing apply.

In addition to the notes in the tabular, these conditions also have a specific index entry structure. In the index both conditions are listed together with the etiology code first followed by the manifestation codes in brackets. The code in brackets is always to be sequenced second.

The most commonly used etiology/manifestation combinations are the codes for diabetes mellitus, category 250. For each code under category 250 there is a use additional code note for the manifestation that is specific for that particular diabetic manifestation. Should a patient have more than one manifestation of diabetes, more than one code from category 250 may be used with as many manifestation codes as are needed to fully describe the patient's complete diabetic condition. The category 250 diabetes codes should be sequenced first, followed by the manifestation codes.

"Code first" and "use additional code" notes are also used as sequencing rules in the classification for certain codes that are not part of an etiology/manifestation combination. See section I.B.9., "Multiple coding for a single condition."

7. **"And"**
The word "and" should be interpreted to mean either "and" or "or" when it appears in a title.

8. **"With"**
The word "with" in the Alphabetic Index is sequenced immediately following the main term, not in alphabetical order.

9. **"See" and "see also"**
The "see" instruction following a main term in the index indicates that another term should be referenced. It is necessary to go to the main term referenced with the "see" note to locate the correct code.

A "see also" instruction following a main term in the index instructs that there is another main term that may also be referenced that may provide additional index entries that may be useful. It is not necessary to follow the "see also" note when the original main term provides the necessary code.

B. General coding guidelines

1. **Use of both Alphabetic Index and Tabular List**—Use both the Alphabetic Index and the Tabular List when locating and assigning a code. Reliance on only the Alphabetic Index or the Tabular List leads to errors in code assignments and less specificity in code selection.

2. **Locate each term in the alphabetic index**—Locate each term in the Alphabetic Index and verify the code selected in the Tabular List. Read and be guided by instructional notations that appear in both the Alphabetic Index and the Tabular List.

3. **Level of detail in coding**—Diagnosis and procedure codes are to be used at their highest number of digits available.

ICD-9-CM diagnosis codes are composed of codes with either three, four, or five digits. Codes with three digits are included in ICD-9-CM as the heading of a category of codes that may be further subdivided by the use of four and/or fifth digits, which provide greater detail.

A three-digit code is to be used only if it is not further subdivided. Where fourth-digit subcategories and/or fifth-digit subclassifications are

provided, they must be assigned. A code is invalid if it has not been coded to the full number of digits required for that code. For example, acute myocardial infarction, code 410, has fourth digits that describe the location of the infarction (e.g., 410.2 Of inferolateral wall), and fifth digits that identify the episode of care. It would be incorrect to report a code in category 410 without a fourth and fifth digit.

ICD-9-CM Volume 3 procedure codes are composed of codes with either three or four digits. Codes with two digits are included in ICD-9-CM as the heading of a category of codes that may be further subdivided by the use of third and/or fourth digits, which provide greater detail.

4. **Code or codes from 001.0 through V86.1**—The appropriate code or codes from 001.0 through V86.1 must be used to identify diagnoses, symptoms, conditions, problems, complaints, or other reason(s) for the encounter/visit.

5. **Selection of codes 001.0 through 999.9**—The selection of codes 001.0 through 999.9 will frequently be used to describe the reason for the admission/encounter. These codes are from the section of ICD-9-CM for the classification of diseases and injuries (e.g., infectious and parasitic diseases; neoplasms; symptoms, signs, and ill-defined conditions, etc.).

6. **Signs and symptoms**—Codes that describe symptoms and signs, as opposed to diagnoses, are acceptable for reporting purposes when a related definitive diagnosis has not been established (confirmed) by the provider. Chapter 16 of ICD-9-CM, "Symptoms, Signs, and Ill-defined Conditions" (codes 780.0-799.9) contain many, but not all, codes for symptoms.

7. **Conditions that are an integral part of a disease process**—Signs and symptoms that are integral to the disease process should not be assigned as additional codes.

8. **Conditions that are not an integral part of a disease process**—Additional signs and symptoms that may not be associated routinely with a disease process should be coded when present.

9. **Multiple coding for a single condition**—In addition to the etiology/manifestation convention that requires two codes to fully describe a single condition that affects multiple body systems, there are other single conditions that also require more than one code. "Use additional code" notes are found in the tabular at codes that are not part of an etiology/manifestation pair where a secondary code is useful to fully describe a condition. The sequencing rule is the same as the etiology/manifestation pair where a secondary code is useful to fully describe a condition. The sequencing rule is the same; "use additional code" indicates that a secondary code should be added.

For example, for infections that are not included in chapter 1, a secondary code from category 041 Bacterial infection in conditions classified elsewhere and of unspecified site, may be required to identify the bacterial organism causing the infection. A "use additional code" note will normally be found at the infectious disease code, indicating a need for the organism code to be added as a secondary code.

"Code first" notes are also under certain codes that are not specifically manifestation codes but may be due to an underlying cause. When a "code first" note is present and an underlying condition is present, the underlying condition should be sequenced first.

"Code, if applicable, any causal condition first" notes indicate that this code may be assigned as a principal diagnosis when the causal condition is unknown or not applicable. If a causal condition is known, then the code for that condition should be sequenced as the principal or first-listed diagnosis.

Multiple codes may be needed for late effects, complication codes, and obstetric codes to more fully describe a condition. See the specific guidelines for these conditions for further instruction.

10. **Acute and chronic conditions**—If the same condition is described as both acute (subacute) and chronic, and separate subentries exist in the Alphabetic Index at the same indentation level, code both and sequence the acute (subacute) code first.

11. **Combination code**—A combination code is a single code used to classify:
   * Two diagnoses
   * A diagnosis with an associated secondary process (manifestation)
   * A diagnosis with an associated complication

Combination codes are identified by referring to subterm entries in the Alphabetic Index and by reading the inclusion and exclusion notes in the Tabular List.

Assign only the combination code when that code fully identifies the diagnostic conditions involved or when the Alphabetic Index so directs. Multiple coding should not be used when the classification provides a combination code that clearly identifies all of the elements documented in the diagnosis. When the combination code lacks necessary specificity in describing the manifestation or complication, an additional code should be used as a secondary code.

12. **Late effects**—A late effect is the residual effect (condition produced) after the acute phase of an illness or injury has terminated. There is no time limit on when a late effect code can be used. The residual may be apparent early, such as in cerebrovascular accident cases, or it may occur months or years later, such as that due to a previous injury. Coding of late effects generally requires two codes sequenced in the following order: The condition or nature of the late effect is sequenced first... The late effect code is sequenced second.

An exception to the above guidelines are those instances where the code for late effect is followed by a manifestation code identified in the Tabular List and title, or the late effect code has been expanded (at the fourth- and fifth-digit levels) to include the manifestation(s). The code for the acute phase of an illness or injury that led to the late effect is never used with a code for the late effect.

13. **Impending or threatened condition**—Code any condition described at the time of discharge as "impending" or "threatened" as follows:

If it did occur, code as confirmed diagnosis. If it did not occur, reference the Alphabetic Index to determine if the condition has a subentry term for "impending" or "threatened" and also reference main term entries for "Impending" and for "Threatened." If the subterms are listed, assign the given code. If the subterms are not listed, code the existing underlying condition(s) and not the condition described as impending or threatened.

C. Chapter-specific coding guidelines

In addition to general coding guidelines, there are guidelines for specific diagnoses and/or conditions in the classification. Unless otherwise indicated, these guidelines apply to all health care settings. Please refer to section II for guidelines on the selection of principal diagnosis.

1. **Chapter 1: Infectious and Parasitic Diseases (001-139)**
   a. **Human immunodeficiency virus (HIV) infections**

   1) **Code only confirmed cases**—Code only confirmed cases of HIV infection/illness. This is an exception to the hospital inpatient guideline section II, H.

   In this context, "confirmation" does not require documentation of positive serology or culture for HIV; the provider's diagnostic statement that the patient is HIV positive or has an HIV-related illness is sufficient.

   2) **Selection and sequencing of HIV codes**

   (a) Patient admitted for HIV-related condition—If a patient is admitted for an HIV-related condition, the principal diagnosis should be 042, followed by additional diagnosis codes for all reported HIV-related conditions.

   (b) Patient with HIV disease admitted for unrelated condition— If a patient with HIV disease is admitted for an unrelated condition (such as a traumatic injury), the code for the unrelated condition (e.g., the nature of injury code) should be the principal diagnosis. Other diagnoses would be 042 followed by additional diagnosis codes for all reported HIV-related conditions.

   (c) Whether the patient is newly diagnosed—Whether the patient is newly diagnosed or has had previous admissions/encounters for HIV conditions is irrelevant to the sequencing decision.

   (d) Asymptomatic human immunodeficiency virus—V08 Asymptomatic human immunodeficiency virus [HIV] infection, is to be applied when the patient without any documentation of symptoms is listed as being "HIV positive," "known HIV," "HIV test positive," or similar terminology. Do not use this code if the term "AIDS" is used or if the patient is treated for any HIV-related illness or is described as having any condition(s) resulting from his/her HIV positive status; use 042 in these cases.

   (e) Patients with inconclusive HIV serology—Patients with inconclusive HIV serology, but no definitive diagnosis or manifestations of the illness, may be assigned code 795.71 Inconclusive serologic test for human immunodeficiency virus [HIV].

   (f) Previously diagnosed HIV-related illness—Patients with any known prior diagnosis of an HIV-related illness should be coded to 042. Once a patient has developed an HIV-related illness, the patient should always be assigned code 042 on every subsequent admission/encounter. Patients previously diagnosed with any HIV illness (042) should never be assigned to 795.71 or V08.

   (g) HIV infection in pregnancy, childbirth and the puerperium— During pregnancy, childbirth, or the puerperium, a patient admitted (or presenting for a health care encounter) because of an HIV-related illness should receive a principal diagnosis code of 647.6x Other specified infectious and parasitic diseases in the mother classifiable elsewhere but complicating the pregnancy, childbirth or the

puerperium, followed by 042 and the code(s) for the HIV-related illness(es). Codes from chapter 15 always take sequencing priority.

Patients with asymptomatic HIV infection status admitted (or presenting for a health care encounter) during pregnancy, childbirth, or the puerperium should receive codes of 647.6x and V08.

   (h) Encounters for testing for HIV—If a patient is being seen to determine his/her HIV status, use code V73.89 Screening for other specified viral disease. Use code V69.8 Other problems related to lifestyle, as a secondary code if an asymptomatic patient is in a known high risk group for HIV. Should a patient with signs or symptoms or illness, or a confirmed HIV related diagnosis be tested for HIV, code the signs and symptoms or the diagnosis. An additional counseling code V65.44 may be used if counseling is provided during the encounter for the test.

   When a patient returns to be informed of his/her HIV test results, use code V65.44 HIV counseling, if the results of the test are negative.

   If the results are positive but the patient is asymptomatic, use code V08 Asymptomatic HIV infection. If the results are positive and the patient is symptomatic, use code 042 HIV infection, with codes for the HIV-related symptoms or diagnosis. The HIV counseling code may also be used if counseling is provided for patients with positive test results.

   b. **Septicemia, systemic inflammatory response syndrome (SIRS), sepsis, severe sepsis, and septic shock**

   1) **Sepsis as principal diagnosis or secondary diagnosis**

   (a) Sepsis as principal diagnosis—If sepsis is present on admission and meets the definition of principal diagnosis, the underlying systemic infection code (e.g., 038.xx, 112.5, etc.) should be assigned as the principal diagnosis, followed by code 995.91 Systemic inflammatory response syndrome due to infectious process without organ dysfunction, as required by the sequencing rules in the Tabular List. Codes from subcategory 995.9 can never be assigned as a principal diagnosis.

   (b) Sepsis as secondary diagnoses—When sepsis develops during the encounter (it was not present on admission), the sepsis codes may be assigned as secondary diagnoses, following the sequencing rules provided in the Tabular List.

   (c) Documentation unclear as to whether sepsis present on admission—If the documentation is not clear whether the sepsis was present on admission, the provider should be queried. After provider query, if sepsis is determined at that point to have met the definition of principal diagnosis, the underlying systemic infection (038.xx, 112.5, etc.) may be used as the principal diagnosis along with code 995.91 Systemic inflammatory response syndrome due to infectious process without organ dysfunction.

   2) **Septicemia/sepsis**—In most cases, it will be a code from category 038 Septicemia, that will be used in conjunction with a code from subcategory 995.9 such as the following:

   (a) Streptococcal sepsis—If the documentation in the record states streptococcal sepsis, codes 038.0 and code 995.91 should be used, in that sequence.

   (b) Streptococcal septicemia—If the documentation states streptococcal septicemia, only code 038.0 should be assigned; however, the provider should be queried whether the patient has sepsis, an infection with SIRS.

   (c) Sepsis or SIRS must be documented—Either the term sepsis or SIRS must be documented to assign a code from subcategory 995.9.

   3) **Terms "sepsis," " severe sepsis," or "SIRS"**—If the terms sepsis, severe sepsis, or SIRS are used with an underlying infection other than septicemia, such as pneumonia, cellulitis, or a nonspecified urinary tract infection, a code from category 038 should be assigned first, then code 995.91, followed by the code for the initial infection. The use of the terms sepsis or SIRS indicates that the patient's infection has advanced to the point of a systemic infection so the systemic infection should be sequenced before the localized infection. The instructional note under subcategory 995.9 instructs to assign the underlying systemic infection first.

   Note: The term "urosepsis" is a nonspecific term. If that is the only term documented then only code 599.0 should be assigned based on the default for the term in the ICD-9-CM index, in addition to the code for the causal organism if known.

   4) **Severe sepsis**—For patients with severe sepsis, the code for the systemic infection (e.g., 038.xx, 112.5, etc) or trauma should be sequenced first, followed by either code 995.92 Systemic inflammatory response syndrome due to infectious process with organ dysfunction, or code 995.94 Systemic inflammatory response syndrome due to noninfectious process with organ dysfunction. Codes for the specific organ dysfunctions should also be assigned.

5) Septic shock

(a) Sequencing of septic shock—Septic shock is a form of organ dysfunction associated with severe sepsis. A code for the initiating underlying systemic infection followed by a code for SIRS (code 995.92) must be assigned before the code for septic shock. As noted in the sequencing instructions in the Tabular List, the code for septic shock cannot be assigned as a principal diagnosis.

(b) Septic shock without documentation of severe sepsis—Septic shock cannot occur in the absence of severe sepsis. A code from subcategory 995.9 must be sequenced before the code for septic shock. The use additional code notes and the code first note provide sequencing instructions.

6) Sepsis and septic shock associated with abortion—Sepsis and septic shock associated with abortion, ectopic pregnancy, and molar pregnancy are classified to category codes in chapter 11 (630-639).

7) Negative or inconclusive blood cultures—Negative or inconclusive blood cultures do not preclude a diagnosis of septicemia or sepsis in patients with clinical evidence of the condition; however, the provider should be queried.

8) Newborn sepsis—See section I.C.15.j for information on the coding of newborn sepsis.

9) Sepsis due to a postprocedural infection—Sepsis resulting from a postprocedural infection is a complication of care. For such cases code 998.59 Other postoperative infections, should be coded first followed by the appropriate codes for the sepsis. The other guidelines for coding sepsis should then be followed for the assignment of additional codes.

10) External cause of injury codes with SIRS—An external cause code is not needed with codes 995.91 Systemic inflammatory response syndrome due to infectious process without organ dysfunction, or 995.92 Systemic inflammatory response syndrome due to infectious process with organ dysfunction.

Refer to section I.C.19.a.7 for instruction on the use of external cause of injury codes with codes for SIRS resulting from trauma.

2. Chapter 2: Neoplasms (140-239)
General guidelines

Chapter 2 of the ICD-9-CM contains the codes for most benign and all malignant neoplasms. Certain benign neoplasms, such as prostatic adenomas, may be found in the specific body system chapters. To properly code a neoplasm it is necessary to determine from the record if the neoplasm is benign, in situ, malignant, or of uncertain histologic behavior. If malignant, any secondary (metastatic) sites should also be determined.

The neoplasm table in the Alphabetic Index should be referenced first. However, if the histological term is documented, that term should be referenced first, rather than going immediately to the neoplasm table, in order to determine which column in the neoplasm table is appropriate. For example, if the documentation indicates "adenoma," refer to the term in the Alphabetic Index to review the entries under this term and the instructional note to "see also neoplasm, by site, benign." The table provides the proper code based on the type of neoplasm and the site. It is important to select the proper column in the table that corresponds to the type of neoplasm. The tabular should then be referenced to verify that the correct code has been selected from the table and that a more specific site code does not exist.

See section I. C. 18.d.4. for information regarding V codes for genetic susceptibility to cancer.

a. **Treatment directed at the malignancy**—If the treatment is directed at the malignancy, designate the malignancy as the principal diagnosis.

b. **Treatment of secondary site**—When a patient is admitted because of a primary neoplasm with metastasis and treatment is directed toward the secondary site only, the secondary neoplasm is designated as the principal diagnosis even though the primary malignancy is still present.

c. **Coding and sequencing of complications**—Coding and sequencing of complications associated with the malignancies or with the therapy thereof are subject to the following guidelines:

1) **Anemia associated with malignancy**—When admission/encounter is for management of an anemia associated with the malignancy, and the treatment is only for anemia, **the appropriate anemia code (such as code 285.22 Anemia in neoplastic disease)** is designated as the principal diagnosis and is followed by the appropriate code(s) for the malignancy.

Code 285.22 may also be used as a secondary code if the patient suffers from anemia and is being treated for the malignancy.

2) **Anemia associated with chemotherapy, immunotherapy and radiation therapy**—When the admission/encounter is for management of an anemia associated with chemotherapy, **immunotherapy,** or radiotherapy and the only treatment is for the anemia, the anemia is sequenced first followed by **code E933.1. The appropriate neoplasm code should be assigned as an additional code.**

3) **Management of dehydration due to the malignancy**—When the admission/encounter is for management of dehydration due to the malignancy or the therapy, or a combination of both, and only the dehydration is being treated (intravenous rehydration), the dehydration is sequenced first, followed by the code(s) for the malignancy.

4) **Treatment of a complication resulting from a surgical procedure**—When the admission/encounter is for treatment of a complication resulting from a surgical procedure, designate the complication as the principal or first-listed diagnosis if treatment is directed at resolving the complication.

d. **Primary malignancy previously excised**—When a primary malignancy has been previously excised or eradicated from its site and there is no further treatment directed to that site and there is no evidence of any existing primary malignancy, a code from category V10 Personal history of malignant neoplasm, should be used to indicate the former site of the malignancy. Any mention of extension, invasion, or metastasis to another site is coded as a secondary malignant neoplasm to that site. The secondary site may be the principal or first-listed with the V10 code used as a secondary code.

e. **Admissions/encounters involving chemotherapy, immunotherapy, and radiation therapy**

1) **Episode of care involves surgical removal of neoplasm**—When an episode of care involves the surgical removal of a neoplasm, primary or secondary site, followed by adjunct chemotherapy or radiation treatment **during the same episode of care,** the neoplasm code should be assigned as principal or first-listed diagnosis, using codes in the 140-198 series or where appropriate in the 200-203 series.

2) **Patient admission/encounter solely for administration of chemotherapy, immunotherapy, and radiation therapy**—If a patient admission/encounter is solely for the administration of chemotherapy, **immunotherapy** or radiation therapy, assign code V58.0 Encounter for radiation therapy, **V58.11 Encounter for antineoplastic chemotherapy, or V58.12 Encounter for antineoplastic immunotherapy as** the first-listed or principal diagnosis. If a patient receives **more than one of these therapies during the same admission, more than one of these codes may be assigned, in any sequence.**

3) **Patient admitted for radiotherapy/chemotherapy and immunotherapy and develops complications**—When a patient is admitted for the purpose of radiotherapy, **immunotherapy,** or chemotherapy and develops complications such as uncontrolled nausea and vomiting or dehydration, the principal or first-listed diagnosis is V58.0 Encounter for radiotherapy, **V58.11 Encounter for antineoplastic chemotherapy, or V58.12 Encounter for antineoplastic immunotherapy** followed by any codes for the complications.

See section I.C.18.d.8. for additional information regarding aftercare V codes.

f. **Admission/encounter to determine extent of malignancy**—When the reason for admission/encounter is to determine the extent of the malignancy, or for a procedure such as paracentesis or thoracentesis, the primary malignancy or appropriate metastatic site is designated as the principal or first-listed diagnosis, even though chemotherapy or radiotherapy is administered.

g. **Symptoms, signs, and ill-defined conditions listed in chapter 16**—Symptoms, signs, and ill-defined conditions listed in chapter 16 characteristic of, or associated with, an existing primary or secondary site malignancy cannot be used to replace the malignancy as principal or first-listed diagnosis, regardless of the number of admissions or encounters for treatment and care of the neoplasm.

h. See section I.C.18.d.14, Encounter for prophylactic organ removal

3. Chapter 3: Endocrine, Nutritional, and Metabolic Diseases and Immunity Disorders (240-279)

a. **Diabetes mellitus**—Codes under category 250 Diabetes mellitus, identify complications/manifestations associated with diabetes mellitus. A fifth-digit is required for all category 250 codes to identify the type of diabetes mellitus and whether the diabetes is controlled or uncontrolled.

1) Fifth digits for category 250: The following are the fifth digits for the codes under category 250:

0 type II or unspecified type, not stated as uncontrolled
1 type I, [juvenile type], not stated as uncontrolled
2 type II or unspecified type, uncontrolled
3 type I, [juvenile type], uncontrolled

The age of a patient is not the sole determining factor, though most type I diabetics develop the condition before reaching puberty. For this reason type I diabetes mellitus is also referred to as juvenile diabetes.

2) **Type of diabetes mellitus not documented**—If the type of diabetes mellitus is not documented in the medical record the default is type II.

3) **Diabetes mellitus and the use of insulin**—All type I diabetics must use insulin to replace what their bodies do not produce. However, the use of insulin does not mean that a patient is a type I diabetic. Some patients with type II diabetes mellitus are unable to control their blood sugar through diet and oral medication alone and do require insulin. If the documentation in a medical record does not indicate the type of diabetes but does indicate that the patient uses insulin, the appropriate fifth digit for type II must be used. For type II patients who routinely use insulin, code V58.67 Long-term (current) use of insulin, should also be assigned to indicate that the patient uses insulin. Code V58.67 should not be assigned if insulin is given temporarily to bring a type II patient's blood sugar under control during an encounter.

4) **Assigning and sequencing diabetes codes and associated conditions**—When assigning codes for diabetes and its associated conditions, the code(s) from category 250 must be sequenced before the codes for the associated conditions. The diabetes codes and the secondary codes that correspond to them are paired codes that follow the etiology/manifestation convention of the classification (See section I.A.6., Etiology/manifestation convention). Assign as many codes from category 250 as needed to identify all of the associated conditions that the patient has. The corresponding secondary codes are listed under each of the diabetes codes.

(a) **Diabetic retinopathy/diabetic macular edema—Diabetic macular edema, code 362.07, is only present with diabetic retinopathy. Another code from subcategory 362.0 Diabetic retinopathy, must be used with code 362.07. Codes under subcategory 362.0 are diabetes manifestation codes, so they must be used following the appropriate diabetes code.**

5) Diabetes mellitus in pregnancy and gestational diabetes

(a) For diabetes mellitus complicating pregnancy, see aection I.C.11.f., Diabetes mellitus in pregnancy.

(b) For gestational diabetes, see section I.C.11, g., Gestational diabetes.

6) **Insulin pump malfunction**

(a) Underdose of insulin due to insulin pump failure—An underdose of insulin due to an insulin pump failure should be assigned 996.57 Mechanical complication due to insulin pump, as the principal or first listed code, followed by the appropriate diabetes mellitus code based on documentation.

(b) Overdose of insulin due to insulin pump failure—The principal or first-listed code for an encounter due to an insulin pump malfunction resulting in an overdose of insulin should also be 996.57 Mechanical complication due to insulin pump, followed by code 962.3 Poisoning by insulins and antidiabetic agents, and the appropriate diabetes mellitus code based on documentation.

4. **Chapter 4: Diseases of Blood and Blood Forming Organs (280-289)**

a. **Anemia of chronic disease—Subcategory 285.2 Anemia in chronic illness, has codes for anemia in chronic kidney disease, code 285.21; anemia in neoplastic disease, code 285.22; and anemia in other chronic illness, code 285.29. These codes can be used as the principal/first-listed code if the reason for the encounter is to treat the anemia. They may also be used as secondary codes if treatment of the anemia is a component of an encounter but not the primary reason for the encounter. When using a code from subcategory 285 it is also necessary to use the code for the chronic condition causing the anemia.**

1) **Anemia in chronic kidney disease—When assigning code 285.21 Anemia in chronic kidney disease. It is also necessary to assign a code from category 585 Chronic kidney disease to indicate the stage of chronic kidney disease. See I.C.10.a., Chronic kidney disease (CKD).**

2) **Anemia in neoplastic disease—When assigning code 285.22 Anemia in neoplastic disease, it is also necessary to assign the neoplasm code that is responsible for the anemia. Code 285.22 is for use for anemia that is due to the malignancy, not for anemia due to antineoplastic chemotherapy drugs, which is an adverse effect.**

See I.C.2.c.1., Anemia associated with malignancy.

See I.C.2.c.2., Anemia associated with chemotherapy, immunotherapy and radiation therapy.

See I.C.17.e.1., Adverse effects.

5. **Chapter 5: Mental Disorders (290-319)**
Reserved for future guideline expansion

6. **Chapter 6: Diseases of Nervous System and Sense Organs (320-389)**
Reserved for future guideline expansion

7. **Chapter 7: Diseases of Circulatory System (390-459)**
a. Hypertension

Hypertension Table

The hypertension table, found under the main term, "Hypertension," in the Alphabetic Index, contains a complete listing of all conditions due to or associated with hypertension and classifies them according to malignant, benign, and unspecified.

1) **Hypertension, essential, or NOS**—Assign hypertension (arterial) (essential) (primary) (systemic) (NOS) to category code 401 with the appropriate fourth digit to indicate malignant (.0), benign (.1), or unspecified (.9). Do not use either .0 malignant or .1 benign unless medical record documentation supports such a designation.

2) **Hypertension with heart disease**—Heart conditions (425.8, 429.0–429.3, 429.8, 429.9) are assigned to a code from category 402 when a causal relationship is stated (due to hypertension) or implied (hypertensive). Use an additional code from category 428 to identify the type of heart failure in those patients with heart failure. More than one code from category 428 may be assigned if the patient has systolic or diastolic failure and congestive heart failure.

The same heart conditions (425.8, 429.0–429.3, 429.8, 429.9) with hypertension, but without a stated casual relationship, are coded separately. Sequence according to the circumstances of the admission/encounter.

3) **Hypertensive kidney disease with chronic renal failure**—Assign codes from category 403, Hypertensive **kidney** disease, when conditions classified to categories 585-587 are present. Unlike hypertension with heart disease, ICD-9-CM presumes a cause-and-effect relationship and classifies renal failure with hypertension as hypertensive renal disease.

4) **Hypertensive heart and kidney disease**—Assign codes from combination category 404, Hypertensive heart and **kidney** disease, when both hypertensive **kidney** disease and hypertensive heart disease are stated in the diagnosis. Assume a relationship between the hypertension and the **kidney** disease, whether or not the condition is so designated. Assign an additional code from category 428 to identify the type of heart failure. More than one code from category 428 may be assigned if the patient has systolic or diastolic failure and congestive heart failure.

5) **Hypertensive cerebrovascular disease**—First assign codes from 430–438 Cerebrovascular disease, then the appropriate hypertension code from categories 401–405.

6) **Hypertensive retinopathy**—Two codes are necessary to identify the condition. First assign the code from subcategory 362.11 Hypertensive retinopathy, then the appropriate code from categories 401–405 to indicate the type of hypertension.

7) **Hypertension, secondary**—Two codes are required: one to identify the underlying etiology and one from category 405 to identify the hypertension. Sequencing of codes is determined by the reason for admission/encounter.

8) **Hypertension, transient**—Assign code 796.2 Elevated blood pressure reading without diagnosis of hypertension, unless patient has an established diagnosis of hypertension. Assign code 642.3x for transient hypertension of pregnancy.

9) **Hypertension, controlled**—Assign appropriate code from categories 401–405. This diagnostic statement usually refers to an existing state of hypertension under control by therapy.

10) **Hypertension, uncontrolled**—Uncontrolled hypertension may refer to untreated hypertension or hypertension not responding to current therapeutic regimen. In either case, assign the appropriate code from categories 401-405 to designate the stage and type of hypertension. Code to the type of hypertension.

11) **Elevated blood pressure**—For a statement of elevated blood pressure without further specificity, assign code 796.2, Elevated blood pressure reading without diagnosis of hypertension, rather than a code from category 401.

b. **Cerebral infarction/stroke/cerebrovascular accident (CVA)**—The terms stroke and CVA are often used interchangeably to refer to a cerebral infarction. The terms stroke, CVA, and cerebral infarction NOS are all indexed to the default code 434.91, Cerebral artery occlusion, unspecified, with infarction. Code 436, Acute, but ill-defined, cerebrovascular disease, should not be used when the documentation states stroke or CVA.

c. **Postoperative cerebrovascular accident**—A cerebrovascular hemorrhage or infarction that occurs as a result of medical intervention is coded to 997.02, Iatrogenic cerebrovascular infarction or hemorrhage. Medical record documentation should clearly specify the cause- and-effect relationship between the medical intervention and the cerebrovascular accident in order to assign this code. A secondary code from the code range 430-432 or from a code from subcategories 433 or 434 with a fifth digit of "1" should also be used to identify the type of hemorrhage or infarct.

This guideline conforms to the use additional code note instruction at category 997. Code 436, Acute, but ill-defined, cerebrovascular disease, should not be used as a secondary code with code 997.02.

d. **Late effects of cerebrovascular disease**

1) **Category 438, late effects of cerebrovascular disease**—Category 438 is used to indicate conditions classifiable to categories 430–437 as the causes of late effects (neurologic deficits), themselves classified elsewhere. These "late effects" include neurologic deficits that persist after initial onset of conditions classifiable to 430–437. The neurologic deficits caused by cerebrovascular disease may be present from the onset or may arise at any time after the onset of the condition classifiable to 430-437.

2) **Codes from category 438 with codes from 430–437**—Codes from category 438 may be assigned on a health care record with codes from 430–437, if the patient has a current cerebrovascular accident (CVA) and deficits from an old CVA.

3) **Code V12.59**—Assign code V12.59 (and not a code from category 438) as an additional code for history of cerebrovascular disease when no neurologic deficits are present.

e. **Acute myocardial infarction (AMI)**

1) **ST elevation myocardial infarction (STEMI) and non-ST elevation myocardial infarction (NSTEMI)**—The ICD-9-CM codes for acute myocardial infarction (AMI) identify the site, such as anterolateral wall or true posterior wall. Subcategories 410.0-410.6 and 410.8 are used for ST elevation myocardial infarction (STEMI). Subcategory 410.7 Subendocardial infarction, is used for non-ST elevation myocardial infarction (NSTEMI) and nontransmural MIs.

2) **Acute myocardial infarction, unspecified**—Subcategory 410.9 is the default for the unspecified term acute myocardial infarction. If only STEMI or transmural MI without the site is documented, query the provider as to the site or assign a code from subcategory 410.9.

3) **AMI documented as nontransmural or subendocardial, but site provided**—If an AMI is documented as nontransmural or subendocardial but the site is provided, it is still coded as a subendocardial AMI. If NSTEMI evolves to STEMI, assign the STEMI code. If STEMI converts to NSTEMI due to thrombolytic therapy, it is still coded as STEMI.

8. Chapter 8: Diseases of Respiratory System (460-519)

a. **Chronic obstructive pulmonary disease [COPD] and asthma**

1) **Conditions that comprise COPD and asthma**—The conditions that comprise COPD are obstructive chronic bronchitis, subcategory 491.2, and emphysema, category 492. All asthma codes are under category 493 Asthma. Code 496 Chronic airway obstruction, not elsewhere classified, is a nonspecific code that should be used only when the documentation in a medical record does not specify the type of COPD being treated.

2) **Acute exacerbation of chronic obstructive bronchitis and asthma**—The codes for chronic obstructive bronchitis and asthma distinguish between uncomplicated cases and those in acute exacerbation. An acute exacerbation is a worsening or a decompensation of a chronic condition. An acute exacerbation is not equivalent to an infection superimposed on a chronic condition, though an exacerbation may be triggered by an infection.

3) **Overlapping nature of the conditions that comprise COPD and asthma**—Due to the overlapping nature of the conditions that make up COPD and asthma, there are many variations in the way these conditions are documented. Code selection must be based on the terms as documented. When selecting the correct code for the documented type of COPD and asthma, it is essential to first review the index and then verify the code in the Tabular List. There are many instructional notes under the different COPD subcategories and codes. It is important that all such notes be reviewed to ensure correct code assignment.

4) **Acute exacerbation of asthma and status asthmaticus**—An acute exacerbation of asthma is an increased severity of the asthma symptoms, such as wheezing and shortness of breath. Status asthmaticus refers to a patient's failure to respond to therapy administered during an asthmatic episode and is a life-threatening complication that requires emergency care. If status asthmaticus is documented by the provider with any type of COPD or with acute bronchitis, the status asthmaticus should be sequenced first. It supersedes any type of COPD, including that with acute exacerbation or acute bronchitis. It is inappropriate to assign an asthma code with fifth-digit 2, with acute exacerbation, together with an asthma code with fifth-digit 1, with status asthmaticus. Only the fifth-digit 1 should be assigned.

b. **Chronic obstructive pulmonary disease [COPD] and bronchitis**

1) **Acute bronchitis with COPD**—Acute bronchitis, code 466.0, is due to an infectious organism. When acute bronchitis is documented with COPD, code 491.22 Obstructive chronic bronchitis with acute bronchitis, should be assigned. It is not necessary to also assign code 466.0. If a medical record documents acute bronchitis with COPD with acute exacerbation, only code 491.22 should be assigned. The acute bronchitis included in code 491.22 supersedes the acute exacerbation. If a medical record documents COPD with acute exacerbation without mention of acute bronchitis, only code 491.21 should be assigned.

9. Chapter 9: Diseases of Digestive System (520-579)
Reserved for future guideline expansion

10. Chapter 10: Diseases of Genitourinary System (580-629)

a. **Chronic kidney disease**

1) **Stages of chronic kidney disease (CKD)**—The ICD-9-CM classifies CKD based on severity. The severity of CKD is designated by stages I-V. Stage II, code 585.2, equates to mild CKD; stage III, code 585.3, equates to moderate CKD; and stage IV, code 585.4, equates to severe CKD. Code 585.6 End-stage renal disease (ESRD), is assigned when the provider has documented end-stage renal disease (ESRD). If both a stage of CKD and ESRD are documented, assign code 585.6 only.

2) **Chronic kidney disease and kidney transplant status**—Patients who have undergone kidney transplant may still have some form of CKD because the kidney transplant may not fully restore kidney function. Code V42.0 may be assigned with the appropriate CKD code for patients who are status post kidney transplant, based on the patient's post-transplant stage. The use additional code note under category 585 provides this instruction.

Use of a 585 code with V42.0 does not necessarily indicate transplant rejection or failure. Patients with mild or moderate CKD following a transplant should not be coded as having transplant failure unless it is documented in the medical record. For patients with severe CKD or ESRD it is appropriate to assign code 996.81 Complications of transplanted organ, kidney transplant, when kidney transplant failure is documented. If a post kidney transplant patient has CKD and it is unclear from the documentation whether there is transplant failure or rejection, it is necessary to query the provider.

3) **Chronic kidney disease with other conditions**—Patients with CKD may also suffer from other serious conditions, most commonly diabetes mellitus and hypertension. The sequencing of the CKD code in relationship to codes for other contributing conditions is based on the conventions in the tabular list. See I.C.3.a.4. for sequencing instructions for diabetes.

See I.C.4.a.1. for anemia in CKD.

See I.C.7.a.3. for hypertensive kidney disease.

See I.C.17.f.1.b. Transplant complications, for instructions on coding of documented rejection or failure.

11. Chapter 11: Complications of Pregnancy, Childbirth, and the Puerperium (630-677)

a. General rules for obstetric cases

1) Codes from chapter 11 and sequencing priority—Obstetric cases require codes from chapter 11, codes in the range 630-677 Complications of pregnancy, childbirth, and the puerperium. Chapter 11 codes have sequencing priority over codes from other chapters. Additional codes from other chapters may be used in conjunction with chapter 11 codes to further specify conditions. Should the provider document that the pregnancy is incidental to the encounter, then code V22.2 should be used in place of any chapter 11 codes. It is the provider's responsibility to state that the condition being treated is not affecting the pregnancy.

2) Chapter 11 codes used only on the maternal record—Chapter 11 codes are to be used only on the maternal record, never on the record of the newborn.

3) Chapter 11 fifth digits—Categories 640-648, 651-676 have required fifth-digits, which indicate whether the encounter is antepartum, postpartum and whether a delivery has also occurred.

4) Fifth digits, appropriate for each code—The fifth digits, which are appropriate for each code number, are listed in brackets under each code. The fifth digits on each code should all be consistent with each other. That is, should a delivery occur all of the fifth digits should indicate the delivery.

b. Selection of OB principal or first-listed diagnosis

1) Routine outpatient prenatal visits—For routine outpatient prenatal visits when no complications are present, codes V22.0 Supervision of normal first pregnancy, and V22.1 Supervision of other normal pregnancy, should be used as the first-listed diagnoses. These codes should not be used in conjunction with chapter 11 codes.

2) Prenatal outpatient visits for high-risk patients—For prenatal outpatient visits for patients with high-risk pregnancies, a code from category V23 Supervision of high-risk pregnancy, should be used as the principal or first-listed diagnosis. Secondary chapter 11 codes may be used in conjunction with these codes if appropriate.

3) Episodes when no delivery occurs—In episodes when no delivery occurs, the principal diagnosis should correspond to the principal complication of the pregnancy, which necessitated the encounter. Should more than one complication exist, all of which are treated or monitored, any of the complication codes may be sequenced first.

4) When a delivery occurs—When a delivery occurs, the principal diagnosis should correspond to the main circumstances or complication of the delivery. In cases of cesarean delivery, the selection of the principal diagnosis should correspond to the reason the cesarean delivery was performed unless the reason for admission/encounter was unrelated to the condition resulting in the cesarean delivery.

5) Outcome of delivery—An outcome of delivery code, V27.0-V27.9, should be included on every maternal record when a delivery has occurred. These codes are not to be used on subsequent records or on the newborn record.

c. Fetal conditions affecting the management of the mother

1) Fetal condition responsible for modifying the management of the mother—Codes from category 655 Known or suspected fetal abnormality affecting management of the mother, and category 656 Other fetal and placental problems affecting the management of the mother, are assigned only when the fetal condition is actually responsible for modifying the management of the mother, i.e., by requiring diagnostic studies, additional observation, special care, or termination of pregnancy. The fact that the fetal condition exists does not justify assigning a code from this series to the mother's record.

2) In utero surgery—In cases when surgery is performed on the fetus, a diagnosis code from category 655 Known or suspected fetal abnormalities affecting management of the mother, should be assigned identifying the fetal condition. Procedure code 75.36 Correction of fetal defect, should be assigned on the hospital inpatient record.

No code from chapter 15, the perinatal codes, should be used on the mother's record to identify fetal conditions. Surgery performed in utero on a fetus is still to be coded as an obstetric encounter.

d. HIV infection in pregnancy, childbirth and the puerperium

During pregnancy, childbirth, or the puerperium, a patient admitted because of an HIV-related illness should receive a principal diagnosis of 647.6X Other specified infectious and parasitic diseases in the mother classifiable elsewhere, but complicating the pregnancy, childbirth, or the puerperium, followed by 042 and the code(s) for the HIV-related illness(es).

Patients with asymptomatic HIV infection status admitted during pregnancy, childbirth, or the puerperium should receive codes of 647.6X and V08.

e. Current conditions complicating pregnancy
—Assign a code from subcategory 648.x for patients that have current conditions when the condition affects the management of the pregnancy, childbirth, or the puerperium. Use additional secondary codes from other chapters to identify the conditions, as appropriate.

f. Diabetes mellitus in pregnancy
—Diabetes mellitus is a significant complicating factor in pregnancy. Pregnant women who are diabetic should be assigned code 648.0x Diabetes mellitus complicating pregnancy, and a secondary code from category 250 Diabetes mellitus, to identify the type of diabetes.

Code V58.67 Long-term (current) use of insulin, should also be assigned if the diabetes mellitus is being treated with insulin.

g. Gestational diabetes
—Gestational diabetes can occur during the second and third trimester of pregnancy in women who were not diabetic prior to pregnancy. Gestational diabetes can cause complications in the pregnancy similar to those of pre-existing diabetes mellitus. It also puts the woman at greater risk of developing diabetes after the pregnancy. Gestational diabetes is coded to 648.8x Abnormal glucose tolerance. Codes 648.0x and 648.8x should never be used together on the same record.

Code V58.67 Long-term (current) use of insulin, should also be assigned if the gestational diabetes is being treated with insulin.

h. Normal delivery, code 650

1) Normal delivery—Code 650 is for use in cases when a woman is admitted for a full-term normal delivery and delivers a single, healthy infant without any complications antepartum, during the delivery, or postpartum during the delivery episode. Code 650 is always a principal diagnosis. It is not to be used if any other code from chapter 11 is needed to describe a current complication of the antenatal, delivery, or perinatal period. Additional codes from other chapters may be used with code 650 if they are not related to or are in any way complicating the pregnancy.

2) Normal delivery with resolved antepartum complication—Code 650 may be used if the patient had a complication at some point during her pregnancy, but the complication is not present at the time of the admission for delivery.

3) V27.0 Single liveborn, outcome of delivery—V27.0 Single liveborn, is the only outcome of the delivery code appropriate for use with 650.

i. The postpartum and peripartum periods

1) Postpartum and peripartum periods—The postpartum period begins immediately after delivery and continues for six weeks following delivery. The peripartum period is defined as the last month of pregnancy to five months postpartum.

2) Postpartum complication—A postpartum complication is any complication occurring within the six-week period.

3) Pregnancy-related complications after six-week period—Chapter 11 codes may also be used to describe pregnancy-related complications after the six-week period should the provider document that a condition is pregnancy related.

4) Postpartum complications occurring during the same admission as delivery—Postpartum complications that occur during the same admission as the delivery are identified with a fifth digit of 2. Subsequent admissions/encounters for postpartum complications should be identified with a fifth digit of 4.

5) Admission for routine postpartum care following delivery outside hospital—When the mother delivers outside the hospital prior to admission and is admitted for routine postpartum care and no complications are noted, code V24.0 Postpartum care and examination immediately after delivery, should be assigned as the principal diagnosis.

Revised text in bold font

6) Admission following delivery outside hospital with postpartum conditions—A delivery diagnosis code should not be used for a woman who has delivered prior to admission to the hospital. Any postpartum conditions and/or postpartum procedures should be coded.

j. Code 677 Late effect of complication of pregnancy

1) Code 677—Code 677 Late effect of complication of pregnancy, childbirth, and the puerperium is for use in those cases when an initial complication of a pregnancy develops a sequelae requiring care or treatment at a future date.

2) After the initial postpartum period—This code may be used at any time after the initial postpartum period.

3) Sequencing of code 677—This code, like all late effect codes, is to be sequenced following the code describing the sequelae of the complication.

k. Abortions

1) Fifth digits required for abortion categories—Fifth digits are required for abortion categories 634-637. Fifth-digit 1, incomplete, indicates that all of the products of conception have not been expelled from the uterus. Fifth-digit 2, complete, indicates that all products of conception have been expelled from the uterus prior to the episode of care.

2) Code from categories 640-648 and 651-659—A code from categories 640-648 and 651-659 may be used as additional codes with an abortion code to indicate the complication leading to the abortion.

Fifth-digit 3 is assigned with codes from these categories when used with an abortion code because the other fifth digits will not apply. Codes from the 660-669 series are not to be used for complications of abortion.

3) Code 639 for complications—Code 639 is to be used for all complications following abortion. Code 639 cannot be assigned with codes from categories 634-638.

4) Abortion with liveborn fetus—When an attempted termination of pregnancy results in a liveborn fetus assign code 644.21 Early onset of delivery, with an appropriate code from category V27 Outcome of delivery. The procedure code for the attempted termination of pregnancy should also be assigned.

5) Retained products of conception following an abortion—Subsequent admissions for retained products of conception following a spontaneous or legally induced abortion are assigned the appropriate code from category 634 Spontaneous abortion, or 635 Legally induced abortion, with a fifth digit of 1 (incomplete). This advice is appropriate even when the patient was discharged previously with a discharge diagnosis of complete abortion.

12. Chapter 12: Diseases of Skin and Subcutaneous Tissue (680-709)
Reserved for future guideline expansion

13. Chapter 13: Diseases of Musculoskeletal and Connective Tissue (710-739)
Reserved for future guideline expansion

14. Chapter 14: Congenital Anomalies (740-759)

a. Codes in categories 740-759 Congenital anomalies—Assign an appropriate code(s) from categories 740-759, Congenital anomalies, when an anomaly is documented. A congenital anomaly may be the principal/first-listed diagnosis on a record or a secondary diagnosis. **When a congenital anomaly does not have a unique code assignment, assign additional code(s) for any manifestations that may be present.**

When the code assignment specifically identifies the congenital anomaly, manifestations that are an inherent component of the anomaly should not be coded separately. Additional codes should be assigned for manifestations that are not an inherent component.

Codes from Chapter 14 may be used throughout the life of the patient. If a congenital anomaly has been corrected, a personal history code should be used to identify the history of the anomaly. **Although present at birth, a congenital anomaly may not be identified until later in life. Whenever the condition is diagnosed by the physician, it is appropriate to assign a code from codes 740-759.**

For the birth admission, the appropriate code from category V30 Liveborn infants, according to type of birth should be sequenced as the principal diagnosis, followed by any congenital anomaly codes, 740-759.

15. Chapter 15: Newborn (Perinatal) Guidelines (760-779)
For coding and reporting purposes the perinatal period is defined as birth through the 28th day following birth. The following guidelines are provided for reporting purposes. Hospitals may record other diagnoses as needed for internal data use.

a. General perinatal rules

1) Chapter 15 codes—They are <u>never</u> for use on the maternal record. Codes from chapter 11, the obstetric chapter, are never permitted on the newborn record. Chapter 15 code may be used throughout the life of the patient if the condition is still present.

2) Sequencing of perinatal codes—Generally, codes from chapter 15 should be sequenced as the principal/first-listed diagnosis on the newborn record, with the exception of the appropriate V30 code for the birth episode, followed by codes from any other chapter that provide additional detail. The "use additional code" note at the beginning of the chapter supports this guideline. If the index does not provide a specific code for a perinatal condition, assign code 779.89 Other specified conditions originating in the perinatal period, followed by the code from another chapter that specifies the condition. Codes for signs and symptoms may be assigned when a definitive diagnosis has not been established.

3) Birth process or community acquired conditions—If a newborn has a condition that may be either due to the birth process or community acquired and the documentation does not indicate which it is, the default is due to the birth process and the code from chapter 15 should be used. If the condition is community acquired, a code from chapter 15 should not be assigned.

4) Code all clinically significant conditions—All clinically significant conditions noted on routine newborn examination should be coded. A condition is clinically significant if it requires:

- Clinical evaluation; or
- Therapeutic treatment; or
- Diagnostic procedures; or
- Extended length of hospital stay; or
- Increased nursing care and/or monitoring; or
- Has implications for future health care needs

Note: The perinatal guidelines listed above are the same as the general coding guidelines for "additional diagnoses," except for the final point regarding implications for future health care needs. Codes should be assigned for conditions that have been specified by the provider as having implications for future health care needs. Codes from the perinatal chapter should not be assigned unless the provider has established a definitive diagnosis.

b. Use of codes V30-V39—When coding the birth of an infant, assign a code from categories V30-V39, according to the type of birth. A code from this series is assigned as a principal diagnosis and assigned only once to a newborn at the time of birth.

c. Newborn transfers—If the newborn is transferred to another institution, the V30 series is not used at the receiving hospital.

d. Use of category V29

1) Assigning a code from category V29—Assign a code from category V29 Observation and evaluation of newborns and infants for suspected conditions not found, to identify those instances when a healthy newborn is evaluated for a suspected condition that is determined after study not to be present. Do not use a code from category V29 when the patient has identified signs or symptoms of a suspected problem; in such cases, code the sign or symptom.

A code from category V29 may also be assigned as a principal diagnosis for readmissions or encounters when the V30 code no longer applies. Codes from category V29 are for use only for healthy newborns and infants for which no condition after study is found to be present.

2) V29 code on a birth record—A V29 code is to be used as a secondary code after the V30 Outcome of delivery, code.

e. Use of other V codes on perinatal records—V codes other than V30 and V29 may be assigned on a perinatal or newborn record code. The codes may be used as a principal or first-listed diagnosis for specific types of encounters or for readmissions or encounters when the V30 code no longer applies.

See section I.C.18 for information regarding the assignment of V codes.

f. Maternal causes of perinatal morbidity—Codes from categories 760-763 Maternal causes of perinatal morbidity and mortality, are assigned only when the maternal condition has actually affected the fetus or newborn. The fact that the mother has an associated medical condition or experiences some complication of pregnancy, labor, or delivery does not justify the routine assignment of codes from these categories to the newborn record.

g. **Congenital anomalies in newborns**—For the birth admission, the appropriate code from category V30 Liveborn infants according to type of birth, should be used, followed by any congenital anomaly codes, categories 740-759. Use additional secondary codes from other chapters to specify conditions associated with the anomaly, if applicable.

Also, see section I.C.14 for information on the coding of congenital anomalies.

h. **Coding additional perinatal diagnoses**

1) **Assigning codes for conditions that require treatment**—Assign codes for conditions that require treatment or further investigation, prolong the length of stay, or require resource utilization.

2) **Codes for conditions specified as having implications for future health care needs**—Assign codes for conditions that have been specified by the provider as having implications for future health care needs.

Note: This guideline should not be used for adult patients.

3) **Codes for newborn conditions originating in the perinatal period**—Assign a code for newborn conditions originating in the perinatal period (categories 760-779), as well as complications arising during the current episode of care classified in other chapters, only if the diagnoses have been documented by the responsible provider at the time of transfer or discharge as having affected the fetus or newborn.

i. **Prematurity and fetal growth retardation**—Providers utilize different criteria in determining prematurity. A code for prematurity should not be assigned unless it is documented. The fift-digit assignment for codes from category 764 and subcategories 765.0 and 765.1 should be based on the recorded birth weight and estimated gestational age.

A code from subcategory 765.2 Weeks of gestation, should be assigned as an additional code with category 764 and codes from 765.0 and 765.1 to specify weeks of gestation as documented by the provider in the record.

j. **Newborn sepsis**—Code 771.81 Septicemia [sepsis] of newborn, should be assigned with a secondary code from category 041 Bacterial infections in conditions classified elsewhere and of unspecified site, to identify the organism. It is not necessary to use a code from subcategory 995.9 Systemic inflammatory response syndrome (SIRS), on a newborn record. A code from category 038 Septicemia, should not be used on a newborn record. Code 771.81 describes the sepsis.

16. **Chapter 16: Signs, Symptoms and Ill-Defined Conditions (780-799)**
Reserved for future guideline expansion

17. **Chapter 17: Injury and Poisoning (800-999)**

a. **Coding of injuries**—When coding injuries, assign separate codes for each injury unless a combination code is provided, in which case the combination code is assigned. Multiple injury codes are provided in ICD-9-CM but should not be assigned unless information for a more specific code is not available. These codes are not to be used for normal, healing surgical wounds or to identify complications of surgical wounds.

The code for the most serious injury, as determined by the provider and the focus of treatment, is sequenced first.

1) **Superficial injuries**—Superficial injuries such as abrasions or contusions are not coded when associated with more severe injuries of the same site.

2) **Primary injury with damage to nerves/blood vessels**—When a primary injury results in minor damage to peripheral nerves or blood vessels, the primary injury is sequenced first with additional code(s) from categories 950-957 Injury to nerves and spinal cord, and/or 900-904 Injury to blood vessels. When the primary injury is to the blood vessels or nerves, that injury should be sequenced first.

b. **Coding of fractures**—The principles of multiple coding of injuries should be followed in coding fractures. Fractures of specified sites are coded individually by site in accordance with both the provisions within categories 800-829 and the level of detail furnished by medical record content. Combination categories for multiple fractures are provided for use when there is insufficient detail in the medical record (such as trauma cases transferred to another hospital), when the reporting form limits the number of codes that can be used in reporting pertinent clinical data, or when there is insufficient specificity at the fourth-digit or fifth-digit level. More specific guidelines are as follows:

1) **Multiple fractures of same limb**—Multiple fractures of same limb classifiable to the same three-digit or four-digit category are coded to that category.

2) **Multiple unilateral or bilateral fractures of same bone**—Multiple unilateral or bilateral fractures of same bone(s) but classified to different fourth-digit subdivisions (bone part) within the same three-digit category are coded individually by site.

3) **Multiple fracture categories 819 and 828**—Multiple fracture categories 819 and 828 classify bilateral fractures of both upper limbs (819) and both lower limbs (828), but without any detail at the fourth-digit level other than open and closed type of fractures.

4) **Multiple fractures sequencing**—Multiple fractures are sequenced in accordance with the severity of the fracture. The provider should be asked to list the fracture diagnoses in the order of severity.

c. **Coding of burns**—Current burns (940-948) are classified by depth, extent, and by agent (E code). Burns are classified by depth as first degree (erythema), second degree (blistering), and third degree (full-thickness involvement).

1) **Sequencing of burn codes and related condition**—Sequence first the code that reflects the highest degree of burn when more than one burn is present.

(a) **When the reason for the admission or encounter is for treatment of external multiple burns, sequence first the code that reflects the burn of the highest degree.**

(b) **When a patient has both internal and external burns, the circumstances of admission govern the selection of the principal diagnosis or first-listed diagnosis.**

(c) **When a patient is admitted for burn injuries and other related conditions such as smoke inhalation and/or respiratory failure, the circumstances of admission govern the selection of the principal or first-listed diagnosis.**

2) **Burns of the same local site**—Classify burns of the same local site (three-digit category level, 940-947) but of different degrees to the subcategory identifying the highest degree recorded in the diagnosis.

3) **Non-healing burns**—Non-healing burns are coded as acute burns. Necrosis of burned skin should be coded as a non-healed burn.

4) **Code 958.3 Posttraumatic wound infection**—Assign code 958.3 Posttraumatic wound infection, not elsewhere classified, as an additional code for any documented infected burn site.

5) **Assign separate codes for each burn site**—When coding burns, assign separate codes for each burn site. Category 946 Burns of multiple specified sites, should only be used if the locations of the burns are not documented. Category 949 Burn, unspecified, is extremely vague and should rarely be used.

6) **Burns classified according to extent of body surface involved**—Assign codes from category 948 Burns, when the site of the burn is not specified or when there is a need for additional data. It is advisable to use category 948 as additional coding when needed to provide data for evaluating burn mortality, such as that needed by burn units. It is also advisable to use category 948 as an additional code for reporting purposes when there is mention of a third-degree burn involving 20 percent or more of the body surface.

In assigning a code from category 948:

• Fourth-digit codes are used to identify the percentage of total body surface involved in a burn (all degree).

• Fifth digits are assigned to identify the percentage of body surface involved in third-degree burn.

• Fifth-digit zero (0) is assigned when less than 10 percent or when no body surface is involved in a third-degree burn.

• Category 948 is based on the classic "rule of nines" in estimating body surface involved: head and neck are assigned 9 percent, each arm 9 percent, each leg 18 percent, the anterior trunk 18 percent, posterior trunk 18 percent, and genitalia 1 percent. Providers may change these percentage assignments where necessary to accommodate infants and children who have proportionately larger heads than adults and patients who have large buttocks, thighs, or abdomen that involve burns.

7) **Encounters for treatment of late effects of burns**—Encounters for the treatment of the late effects of burns (i.e., scars or joint contractures) should be coded to the residual condition (sequelae) followed by the appropriate late effect code (906.5-906.9). A late effect E code may also be used, if desired.

8) **Sequelae with a late effect code and current burn**—When appropriate, both a sequelae with a late effect code, and a current burn code may be assigned on the same record (when both a current burn and sequelae of an old burn exist).

d. Coding of debridement of wound, infection, or burn—Excisional debridement involves an excisional debridement (surgical removal or cutting away), as opposed to a mechanical (brushing, scrubbing, washing) debridement.

For coding purposes, excisional debridement is assigned to code 86.22.

Nonexcisional debridement is assigned to code 86.28.

e. Adverse effects, poisoning and toxic effects—The properties of certain drugs, medicinal and biological substances, or combinations of such substances, may cause toxic reactions. The occurrence of drug toxicity is classified in ICD-9-CM as follows:

   1) Adverse effect—When the drug was correctly prescribed and properly administered, code the reaction plus the appropriate code from the E930-E949 series. Codes from the E930-E949 series must be used to identify the causative substance for an adverse effect of drug, medicinal and biological substances, correctly prescribed and properly administered. The effect, such as tachycardia, delirium, gastrointestinal hemorrhaging, vomiting, hypokalemia, hepatitis, renal failure, or respiratory failure, is coded and followed by the appropriate code from the E930-E949 series.

Adverse effects of therapeutic substances correctly prescribed and properly administered (toxicity, synergistic reaction, side effect, and idiosyncratic reaction) may be due to (1) differences among patients, such as age, sex, disease, and genetic factors, and (2) drug-related factors, such as type of drug, route of administration, duration of therapy, dosage, and bioavailability.

   2) Poisoning

     (a) Error was made in drug prescription—Errors made in drug prescription or in the administration of the drug by provider, nurse, patient, or other person, use the appropriate poisoning code from the 960-979 series.

     (b) Overdose of a drug intentionally taken—If an overdose of a drug was intentionally taken or administered and resulted in drug toxicity, it would be coded as a poisoning (960-979 series).

     (c) Nonprescribed drug taken with correctly prescribed and properly administered drug—If a nonprescribed drug or medicinal agent was taken in combination with a correctly prescribed and properly administered drug, any drug toxicity or other reaction resulting from the interaction of the two drugs would be classified as a poisoning.

     (d) Sequencing of poisoning—When coding a poisoning or reaction to the improper use of a medication (e.g., wrong dose, wrong substance, wrong route of administration) the poisoning code is sequenced first, followed by a code for the manifestation. If there is also a diagnosis of drug abuse or dependence to the substance, the abuse or dependence is coded as an additional code.

See section I.C.3.a.6.b. if poisoning is the result of insulin pump malfunctions and section I.C.19 for general use of E codes.

   3) Toxic effects

     (a) Toxic effect codes—When a harmful substance is ingested or comes in contact with a person, this is classified as a toxic effect. The toxic effect codes are in categories 980-989.

     (b) Sequencing toxic effect codes—A toxic effect code should be sequenced first, followed by the codes that identify the result of the toxic effect.

     (c) External cause codes for toxic effects—An external cause code from categories E860-E869 for accidental exposure, code E950.6 or E950.7 for intentional self-harm, category E962 for assault, or categories E980-E982 for undetermined, should also be assigned to indicate intent.

f. Complications of care

   1) Transplant complications

     (a) Transplant complications other than kidney—Codes under subcategory 996.8 Complications of transplanted organ, are for use for both complications and rejection of transplanted organs. A transplant complication code is only assigned if the complication affects the function of the transplanted organ. Two codes are required to fully describe a transplant complication, the appropriate code from subcategory 996.8 and a secondary code that identifies the complication.

     Pre-existing conditions or conditions that develop after the transplant are not coded as complications unless they affect the function of the transplanted organ.

     Post-transplant surgical complications that do not relate to the function of the transplanted organ are classified to the specific complication. For example, a surgical wound dehiscence would

be coded as a wound dehiscence, not as a transplant complication.

Post-transplant patients who are seen for treatment unrelated to the transplanted organ should be assigned a code from category V42 Organ or tissue replaced by transplant, to identify the transplant status of the patient. A code from category V42 should never be used with a code from subcategory 996.8.

     (b) Kidney transplant and chronic kidney disease—Patients with chronic kidney disease (CKD) following a transplant should not be assumed to have transplant failure or rejection unless it is documented by the provider. If documentation supports the presence of failure or rejection, then it is appropriate to assign code 996.81 Complications of transplanted organs, kidney, followed by the appropriate CKD code.

18. Classification of Factors Influencing Health Status and Contact with Health Service (Supplemental V01-V86)
   Note: The chapter-specific guidelines provide additional information about the use of V codes for specified encounters.

a. Introduction—ICD-9-CM provides codes to deal with encounters for circumstances other than a disease or injury. The Supplementary Classification of Factors Influencing Health Status and Contact with Health Services (V01-V86) is provided to deal with occasions when circumstances other than a disease or injury (codes 001-999) are recorded as a diagnosis or problem.

There are four primary circumstances for the use of V codes:

   1) A person who is not currently sick encounters the health services for some specific reason, such as to act as an organ donor, to receive prophylactic care, such as inoculations or health screenings, or to receive counseling on health related issues.

   2) A person with a resolving disease or injury, or a chronic, long-term condition requiring continuous care, encounters the health care system for specific aftercare of that disease or injury (e.g., dialysis for renal disease; chemotherapy for malignancy; cast change). A diagnosis/symptom code should be used whenever a current, acute diagnosis is being treated or a sign or symptom is being studied.

   3) Circumstances or problems influence a person's health status but are not in themselves a current illness or injury.

   4) Newborns, to indicate birth status

b. V codes use in any health care setting—V codes are for use in any healthcare setting. V codes may be used as either a first-listed (principal diagnosis code in the inpatient setting) or secondary code, depending on the circumstances of the encounter. Certain V codes may only be used as first listed, others only as secondary codes. See section I.C.18.e, V code table.

c. V codes indicate a reason for an encounter—They are not procedure codes. A corresponding procedure code must accompany a V code to describe the procedure performed.

d. Categories of V codes

   1) Contact/exposure—Category V01 indicates contact with or exposure to communicable diseases. These codes are for patients who do not show any sign or symptom of a disease but have been exposed to it by close personal contact with an infected individual or are in an area where a disease is epidemic. These codes may be used as a first-listed code to explain an encounter for testing, or, more commonly, as a secondary code to identify a potential risk.

   2) Inoculations and vaccinations—Categories V03-V06 are for encounters for inoculations and vaccinations. They indicate that a patient is being seen to receive a prophylactic inoculation against a disease. The injection itself must be represented by the appropriate procedure code. A code from V03-V06 may be used as a secondary code if the inoculation is given as a routine part of preventive health care, such as a well-baby visit.

   3) Status—Status codes indicate that a patient is either a carrier of a disease or has the sequelae or residual of a past disease or condition. This includes such things as the presence of prosthetic or mechanical devices resulting from past treatment.

A status code is informative, because the status may affect the course of treatment and its outcome. A status code is distinct from a history code. The history code indicates that the patient no longer has the condition.

A status code should not be used with a diagnosis code from one of the body system chapters, if the diagnosis code includes the information provided by the status code. For example, code V42.1 Heart transplant status, should not be used with code 996.83 Complications of transplanted heart. The status code does not provide additional information. The complication code indicates that the patient is a heart transplant patient.

The status V codes/categories are:

V02   Carrier or suspected carrier of infectious diseases—Carrier status indicates that a person harbors the specific organisms of a disease without manifest symptoms and is capable of transmitting the infection.

V08   Asymptomatic HIV infection status—This code indicates that a patient has tested positive for HIV but has manifested no signs or symptoms of the disease.

V09   Infection with drug-resistant microorganisms—This category indicates that a patient has an infection that is resistant to drug treatment. Sequence the infection code first.

V21   Constitutional states in development

V22.2   Pregnant state, incidental—This code is a secondary code only for use when the pregnancy is in no way complicating the reason for visit. Otherwise, a code from the obstetric chapter is required.

V26.5x Sterilization status

V42   Organ or tissue replaced by transplant

V43   Organ or tissue replaced by other means

V44   Artificial opening status

V45   Other postsurgical states

V46   Other dependence on machines

V49.6   Upper limb amputation status

V49.7   Lower limb amputation status

V49.81 Postmenopausal status

V49.82 Dental sealant status

V49.83 Awaiting organ transplant status

V58.6   Long-term (current) drug use—This subcategory indicates a patient's continuous use of a prescribed drug (including such things as aspirin therapy) for the long-term treatment of a condition or for prophylactic use. It is not for use for patients who have addictions to drugs.

Assign a code from subcategory V58.6 Long-term (current) drug use, if the patient is receiving a medication for an extended period as a prophylactic measure (such as for the prevention of deep vein thrombosis) or as treatment of a chronic condition (such as arthritis) or a disease requiring a lengthy course of treatment (such as cancer). Do not assign a code from subcategory V58.6 for medication being administered for a brief period of time to treat an acute illness or injury (such as a course of antibiotics to treat acute bronchitis).

V83   Genetic carrier status—Genetic carrier status indicates that a person carries a gene, associated with a particular disease, which may be passed to offspring who may develop that disease. The person does not have the disease and is not at risk of developing the disease.

V84   Genetic susceptibility status—Genetic susceptibility indicates that a person has a gene that increases the risk of that person developing the disease.

Codes from category V84 Genetic susceptibility to disease, should not be used as principal or first-listed codes. If the patient has the condition to which he/she is susceptible and that condition is the reason for the encounter, the code for the current condition should be sequenced first. If the patient is being seen for follow-up after completed treatment for this condition and the condition no longer exists, a follow-up code should be sequenced first, followed by the appropriate personal history and genetic susceptibility codes. If the purpose of the encounter is genetic counseling associated with procreative management, a code from subcategory V26.3 Genetic counseling and testing, should be assigned as the first-listed code, followed by a code from category V84.

Additional codes should be assigned for any applicable family or personal history. See Section I.C.18.d.14. for information on prophylactic organ removal due to a genetic susceptibility.

Note: Categories V42-V46, and subcategories V49.6, V49.7 are for use only if there are no complications or malfunctions of the organ or tissue replaced, the amputation site, or the equipment on which the patient is dependent.

4) History (of)—There are two types of history V codes, personal and family. Personal history codes explain a patient's past medical condition that no longer exists and is not receiving any treatment but that has the potential for recurrence, and therefore may require continued monitoring. The exceptions to this general rule are category V14 Personal history of allergy to medicinal agents, and subcategory V15.0 Allergy, other than to medicinal agents. A person who has had an allergic episode to a substance or food in the past should always be considered allergic to the substance.

Family history codes are for use when a patient has a family member(s) who has had a particular disease that causes the patient to be at higher risk of also contracting the disease.

Personal history codes may be used in conjunction with follow-up codes and family history codes may be used in conjunction with screening codes to explain the need for a test or procedure. History codes are also acceptable on any medical record regardless of the reason for visit. A history of an illness, even if no longer present, is important information that may alter the type of treatment ordered.

The history V code categories are:

V10   Personal history of malignant neoplasm

V12   Personal history of certain other diseases

V13   Personal history of other diseases

     Except: V13.4 Personal history of arthritis, and V13.6 Personal history of congenital malformations. These conditions are life-long so are not true history codes.

V14   Personal history of allergy to medicinal agents

V15   Other personal history presenting hazards to health Except: V15.7 Personal history of contraception

V16   Family history of malignant neoplasm

V17   Family history of certain chronic disabling diseases

V18   Family history of certain other specific diseases

V19   Family history of other conditions

5) Screening—Screening is the testing for disease or disease precursors in seemingly well individuals so that early detection and treatment can be provided for those who test positive for the disease. Screenings that are recommended for many subgroups in a population include routine mammograms for women over 40, a fecal occult blood test for everyone over 50, an amniocentesis to rule out a fetal anomaly for pregnant women over 35, because the incidence of breast cancer and colon cancer in these subgroups is higher than in the general population, as is the incidence of Down's syndrome in older mothers.

The testing of a person to rule out or confirm a suspected diagnosis because the patient has some sign or symptom is a diagnostic examination, not a screening. In these cases, the sign or symptom is used to explain the reason for the test.

A screening code may be a first-listed code if the reason for the visit is specifically the screening exam. It may also be used as an additional code if the screening is done during an office visit for other health problems. A screening code is not necessary if the screening is inherent to a routine examination, such as a Pap smear done during a routine pelvic examination.

Should a condition be discovered during the screening then the code for the condition may be assigned as an additional diagnosis.

The V code indicates that a screening exam is planned. A procedure code is required to confirm that the screening was performed.

The screening V code categories:

V28   Antenatal screening

V73-V82 Special screening examinations

6) Observation—There are two observation V code categories. They are for use in very limited circumstances when a person is being observed for a suspected condition that is ruled out. The observation codes are not for use if an injury or illness or any signs or symptoms related to the suspected condition are present. In such cases the diagnosis/symptom code is used with the corresponding E code to identify any external cause.

The observation codes are to be used as principal diagnosis only. The only exception to this is when the principal diagnosis is required to be a code from the V30 Live born infant, category. Then the V29 observation code is sequenced after the V30 code. Additional codes may be used in addition to the observation code but only if they are unrelated to the suspected condition being observed.

The observation V code categories:

V29　Observation and evaluation of newborns for suspected condition not found
For the birth encounter, a code from category V30 should be sequenced before the V29 code.

V71　Observation and evaluation for suspected condition not found

7) Aftercare—Aftercare visit codes cover situations when the initial treatment of a disease or injury has been performed and the patient requires continued care during the healing or recovery phase, or for the long-term consequences of the disease. The aftercare V code should not be used if treatment is directed at a current, acute disease or injury, the diagnosis code is to be used in these cases. Exceptions to this rule are codes V58.0 Radiotherapy, and **codes from subcategory V58.1 Encounter for chemotherapy and immunotherapy for neoplastic conditions.** These codes are to be first listed, followed by the diagnosis code when a patient's encounter is solely to receive radiation therapy or chemotherapy for the treatment of a neoplasm. Should a patient receive both chemotherapy and radiation therapy during the same encounter, codes V58.0 and V58.1 may be used together on a record with either one being sequenced first.

The aftercare codes are generally first listed to explain the specific reason for the encounter. An aftercare code may be used as an additional code when some type of aftercare is provided in addition to the reason for admission and no diagnosis code is applicable. An example of this would be the closure of a colostomy during an encounter for treatment of another condition.

Certain aftercare V code categories need a secondary diagnosis code to describe the resolving condition or sequelae, for others, the condition is inherent in the code title.

Additional V code aftercare category terms include fitting and adjustment, and attention to artificial openings.

Status V codes may be used with aftercare V codes to indicate the nature of the aftercare. For example code V45.81 Aortocoronary bypass status, may be used with code V58.73 Aftercare following surgery of the circulatory system, NEC, to indicate the surgery for which the aftercare is being performed. Also, a transplant status code may be used following code V58.44 Aftercare following organ transplant, to identify the organ transplanted. A status code should not be used when the aftercare code indicates the type of status, such as using V55.0 Attention to tracheostomy with V44.0 Tracheostomy status.

The aftercare V category/codes:

V52　Fitting and adjustment of prosthetic device and implant
V53　Fitting and adjustment of other device
V54　Other orthopedic aftercare
V55　Attention to artificial openings
V56　Encounter for dialysis and dialysis catheter care
V57　Care involving the use of rehabilitation procedures
V58.0　Radiotherapy
V58.11 Encounter for antineoplastic chemotherapy
V58.12 Encounter for antineoplastic immunotherapy
V58.3　Attention to surgical dressings and sutures
V58.41　Encounter for planned post-operative wound closure
V58.42　Aftercare, surgery, neoplasm
V58.43　Aftercare, surgery, trauma
V58.44　Aftercare involving organ transplant
V58.49　Other specified aftercare following surgery
V58.7x　Aftercare following surgery
V58.81　Fitting and adjustment of vascular catheter
V58.82　Fitting and adjustment of non-vascular catheter
V58.83　Monitoring therapeutic drug
V58.89　Other specified aftercare

8) Follow-up—The follow-up codes are used to explain continuing surveillance following completed treatment of a disease, condition, or injury. They imply that the condition has been fully treated and no longer exists. They should not be confused with aftercare codes that explain current treatment for a healing condition or its sequelae. Follow-up codes may be used in conjunction with history codes to provide the full picture of the healed condition and its treatment. The follow-up code is sequenced first, followed by the history code.

A follow-up code may be used to explain repeated visits. Should a condition be found to have recurred on the follow-up visit, then the diagnosis code should be used in place of the follow-up code.

The follow-up V code categories:

V24　Postpartum care and evaluation
V67　Follow-up examination

9) Donor—Category V59 is the donor codes. They are used for living individuals who are donating blood or other body tissue. These codes are only for individuals donating for others, not for self-donations. They are not for use to identify cadaveric donations.

10) Counseling—Counseling V codes are used when a patient or family member receives assistance in the aftermath of an illness or injury, or when support is required in coping with family or social problems. They are not necessary for use in conjunction with a diagnosis code when the counseling component of care is considered integral to standard treatment.

The counseling V categories/codes:

V25.0　General counseling and advice for contraceptive management
V26.3　Genetic counseling
V26.4　General counseling and advice for procreative management
V61　Other family circumstances
V65.1　Person consulted on behalf of another person
V65.3　Dietary surveillance and counseling
V65.4　Other counseling, not elsewhere classified

11) Obstetrics and related conditions—See section I.C.11., the obstetrics guidelines for further instruction on the use of these codes.

V codes for pregnancy are for use in those circumstances when none of the problems or complications included in the codes from the obstetrics chapter exist (a routine prenatal visit or postpartum care). Codes V22.0 Supervision of normal first pregnancy, and V22.1 Supervision of other normal pregnancy, are always first listed and are not to be used with any other code from the OB chapter.

The outcome of delivery, category V27, should be included on all maternal delivery records. It is always a secondary code.

V codes for family planning (contraceptive) or procreative management and counseling should be included on an obstetric record either during the pregnancy or the postpartum stage, if applicable.

Obstetrics and related conditions V code categories:

V22　Normal pregnancy
V23　Supervision of high-risk pregnancy
Except: V23.2 Pregnancy with history of abortion. Code 646.3 Habitual aborter, from the OB chapter is required to indicate a history of abortion during a pregnancy.
V24　Postpartum care and evaluation
V25　Encounter for contraceptive management
Except V25.0x (See section I.C.18.d.11, Counseling)
V26　Procreative management
Except V26.5x Sterilization status, V26.3 and V26.4 (See section I.C.18.d.11., Counseling)
V27　Outcome of delivery
V28　Antenatal screening (See section I.C.18.d.6., Screening)

12) Newborn, infant and child—See section I.C.15, the newborn guidelines, for further instruction on the use of these codes.

Newborn V code categories:

V20　Health supervision of infant or child
V29　Observation and evaluation of newborns for suspected condition not found (See section I.C.18.d.7, Observation).
V30-V39 Liveborn infant according to type of birth

13) Routine and administrative examinations—The V codes allow for the description of encounters for routine examinations, such as a general check-up or, examinations for administrative purposes, such as a pre-employment physical. The codes are for use as first-listed codes only, and are not to be used if the examination is for diagnosis of a suspected condition or for treatment purposes. In such cases the diagnosis code is used. During a routine exam, should a diagnosis or condition be discovered, it should be coded as an additional code. Pre-existing and chronic conditions and history codes may also be included as additional codes as long as the examination is for administrative purposes and not focused on any particular condition.

Preoperative examination V codes are for use only in those situations when a patient is being cleared for surgery and no treatment is given.

The V code categories/code for routine and administrative examinations:

V20.2 Routine infant or child health check Any injections given should have a corresponding procedure code.

V70 General medical examination

V72 Special investigations and examinations Except V72.5 and V72.6

14) Miscellaneous V codes—The miscellaneous V codes capture a number of other health care encounters that do not fall into one of the other categories. Certain of these codes identify the reason for the encounter, others are for use as additional codes that provide useful information on circumstances that may affect a patient's care and treatment.

Prophylactic Organ Removal

For encounters specifically for prophylactic removal of breasts, ovaries, or another organ due to a genetic susceptibility to cancer or a family history of cancer, the principal or first-listed code should be a code from subcategory V50.4 Prophylactic organ removal, followed by the appropriate genetic susceptibility code and the appropriate family history code.

If the patient has a malignancy of one site and is having prophylactic removal at another site to prevent either a new primary malignancy or metastatic disease, a code for the malignancy should also be assigned in addition to a code from subcategory V50.4. A V50.4 code should not be assigned if the patient is having organ removal for treatment of a malignancy, such as the removal of the testes for the treatment of prostate cancer.

Miscellaneous V code categories/codes:

V07 Need for isolation and other prophylactic measures
V50 Elective surgery for purposes other than remedying health states
V58.5 Orthodontics
V60 Housing, household, and economic circumstances
V62 Other psychosocial circumstances
V63 Unavailability of other medical facilities for care
V64 Persons encountering health services for specific procedures, not carried out
V66 Convalescence and palliative care
V68 Encounters for administrative purposes
V69 Problems related to lifestyle

15) Nonspecific V codes—Certain V codes are so nonspecific, or potentially redundant with other codes in the classification, that there can be little justification for their use in the inpatient setting. Their use in the outpatient setting should be limited to those instances when there is no further documentation to permit more precise coding. Otherwise, any sign or symptom or any other reason for a visit that is captured in another code should be used.

Nonspecific V code categories/codes:

V11 Personal history of mental disorder—A code from the mental disorders chapter, with an in remission fifth digit, should be used.
V13.4 Personal history of arthritis
V13.6 Personal history of congenital malformations
V15.7 Personal history of contraception
V23.2 Pregnancy with history of abortion
V40 Mental and behavioral problems
V41 Problems with special senses and other special functions
V47 Other problems with internal organs
V48 Problems with head, neck, and trunk
V49 Problems with limbs and other problems
  Exceptions:
  V49.6 Upper limb amputation status
  V49.7 Lower limb amputation status
  V49.81 Postmenopausal status
  V49.82 Dental sealant status
V49.83 Awaiting organ transplant status
V51 Aftercare involving the use of plastic surgery
V58.2 Blood transfusion, without reported diagnosis
V58.9 Unspecified aftercare

V72.5 Radiological examination, NEC
V72.6 Laboratory examination
  Codes V72.5 and V72.6 are not to be used if any sign or symptoms, or reason for a test is documented. See section IV.K. and section IV.L. of the outpatient guidelines.

V Code Table
Items in bold indicate a change from the April 2005 table. Items underlined have been moved within the table since April 2005.

FIRST LISTED: V codes/categories/subcategories which are only acceptable as principal/first listed.

Codes:
V22.0 Supervision of normal first pregnancy
V22.1 Supervision of other normal pregnancy
V46.12 Encounter for respirator dependence during power failure
V46.13 Encounter for weaning from respirator [ventilator]
V56.0 Extracorporeal dialysis
V58.0 Radiotherapy
  V58.0 and **V58.1** may be used together on a record with either one being sequenced first, when a patient receives both chemotherapy and radiation therapy during the same encounter.
V58.11 Encounter for antineoplastic chemotherapy
  V58.0 and V58.11 may be used together on a record, with either one being sequenced first, when a patient receives both chemotherapy and radiation therapy during the same encounter.
V58.12 Encounter for antineoplastic immunotherapy

Categories/Subcategories:
V20 Health supervision of infant or child
V24 Postpartum care and examination
V29 Observation and evaluation of newborns for suspected condition not found
  Exception: A code from the V30-V39 may be sequenced before the V29 if it is the newborn record.
V30-V39 Liveborn infants according to type of birth
V57 Care involving use of rehabilitation procedures
V59 Donors
V66 Convalescence and palliative care
  Exception: V66.7 Palliative care
V68 Encounters for administrative purposes
V70 General medical examination
  Exception: V70.7 Examination of participant in clinical trial
V71 Observation and evaluation for suspected conditions not found
V72 Special investigations and examinations
  Exceptions:
  V72.4 Pregnancy examination or test
  V72.5 Radiological examination, NEC
  V72.6 Laboratory examination
  V72.86 Encounter for blood typing

FIRST OR ADDITIONAL: V code categories/subcategories which may be either principal/first-listed, or additional codes.

Codes:
V15.88 History of fall
V43.22 Fully implantable artificial heart status
V46.14 Mechanical complication of respirator [ventilator]
V49.81 Asymptomatic postmenopausal status (age-related) (natural)
V49.84 Bed confinement status
V49.89 Other specified conditions influencing health status
V70.7 Examination of participant in clinical trial
V72.5 Radiological examination, NEC
V72.6 Laboratory examination
V72.86 Encounter for blood typing

Categories/Subcategories:
V01 Contact with or exposure to communicable diseases
V02 Carrier or suspected carrier of infectious diseases
V03-V06 Need for prophylactic vaccination and inoculations
V07 Need for isolation and other prophylactic measures
V08 Asymptomatic HIV infection status
V10 Personal history of malignant neoplasm
V12 Personal history of certain other diseases
V13 Personal history of other diseases
  Exception:
  V13.4 Personal history of arthritis
  V13.69 Personal history of other congenital malformations

V16-V19	Family history of disease
V23	Supervision of high-risk pregnancy
V25	Encounter for contraceptive management
V26	Procreative management
	Exception: V26.5 Sterilization status
V28	Antenatal screening
V45.7	Acquired absence of organ
V49.6x	**Upper limb amputation status**
V49.7x	**Lower limb amputation status**
V50	Elective surgery for purposes other than remedying health states
V52	Fitting and adjustment of prosthetic device and implant
V53	Fitting and adjustment of other device
V54	Other orthopedic aftercare
V55	Attention to artificial openings
V56	Encounter for dialysis and dialysis catheter care
	Exception: V56.0 Extracorporeal dialysis
V58.3	Attention to surgical dressings and sutures
V58.4	Other aftercare following surgery
V58.7	Aftercare following surgery to specified body systems, not elsewhere classified
V58.8	Other specified procedures and aftercare
V61	Other family circumstances
V63	Unavailability of other medical facilities for care
V65	Other persons seeking consultation without complaint or sickness
V67	Follow-up examination
V69	Problems related to lifestyle
V72.4	**Pregnancy examination or test**
V73-V82	Special screening examinations
V83	Genetic carrier status

ADDITIONAL ONLY: V code categories/subcategories which may only be used as additional codes, not principal/first listed.

Codes:

V13.61	Personal history of hypospadias
V22.2	Pregnancy state, incidental
V46.11	**Dependence on respirator, status**
V49.82	Dental sealant status
V49.83	Awaiting organ transplant status
V66.7	Palliative care
V85	Body mass index

Categories/Subcategories:

V09	Infection with drug-resistant microorganisms
V14	Personal history of allergy to medicinal agents
V15	Other personal history presenting hazards to health
	Exception: V15.7 Personal history of contraception
V15.88	**History of fall**
V21	Constitutional states in development
V26.5	Sterilization status
V27	Outcome of delivery
V42	Organ or tissue replaced by transplant
V43	Organ or tissue replaced by other means
	Exception: V43.22 Fully implantable artificial heart status
V44	Artificial opening status
V45	Other postsurgical states
	Exception: Subcategory V45.7 Acquired absence of organ
V46	Other dependence on machines
	Exception: V46.12 Encounter for respirator dependence during power failure
V46.13	**Encounter for weaning from respirator [ventilator]**
~~V49.6x~~	~~Upper limb amputation status~~
~~V49.7x~~	~~Lower limb amputation status~~
V58.6	**Long-term current drug use**
V60	Housing, household, and economic circumstances
V62	Other psychosocial circumstances
V64	Persons encountering health services for specified procedure, not carried out
V84	Genetic susceptibility to disease
V85	**Body Mass Index**

NONSPECIFIC CODES AND CATEGORIES:

V11	Personal history of mental disorder
V13.4	Personal history of arthritis
V13.69	Personal history of congenital malformations
V15.7	Personal history of contraception
V40	Mental and behavioral problems
V41	Problems with special senses and other special functions
V47	Other problems with internal organs
V48	Problems with head, neck, and trunk
V49.0	**Deficiencies of limbs**
V49.1	**Mechanical problems with limbs**
V49.2	**Motor problems with limbs**
V49.3	**Sensory problems with limbs**
V49.4	**Disfigurements in limbs**
V49.5	**Other problems with limbs**
V49.9	**Unspecified condition influencing health status**
V51	Aftercare involving the use of plastic surgery
V58.2	Blood transfusion, without reported diagnosis
V58.5	Orthodontics
V58.9	Unspecified aftercare
V72.5	Radiological examination, NEC
V72.6	Laboratory examination

19. Supplemental Classification of External Causes of Injury and Poisoning (E-codes, E800-E999)

Introduction: These guidelines are provided for those who are currently collecting E codes in order that there will be standardization in the process. If your institution plans to begin collecting E codes, these guidelines are to be applied. The use of E codes is supplemental to the application of ICD-9-CM diagnosis codes. E codes are never to be recorded as principal diagnoses (first-listed in non-inpatient setting) and are not required for reporting to CMS.

External causes of injury and poisoning codes (E codes) are intended to provide data for injury research and evaluation of injury prevention strategies. E codes capture how the injury or poisoning happened (cause), the intent (unintentional or accidental; or intentional, such as suicide or assault), and the place where the event occurred.

Some major categories of E codes include:

- Transport accidents
- Poisoning and adverse effects of drugs, medicinal substances and biologicals
- Accidental falls
- Accidents caused by fire and flames
- Accidents due to natural and environmental factors
- Late effects of accidents, assaults or self injury
- Assaults or purposely inflicted injury
- Suicide or self inflicted injury

These guidelines apply to the coding and collection of E codes from records in hospitals, outpatient clinics, emergency departments, other ambulatory care settings and provider offices, and nonacute care settings, except when other specific guidelines apply.

a. General E code coding guidelines

1) Used with any code in the range of 001-V86.1—An E code may be used with any code in the range of 001-V86.1, which indicates an injury, poisoning, or adverse effect due to an external cause.

2) Assign the appropriate E code for all initial treatments—Assign the appropriate E code for the initial encounter of an injury, poisoning, or adverse effect of drugs, not for subsequent treatment.

3) Use the full range of E codes—Use the full range of E codes to completely describe the cause, the intent and the place of occurrence, if applicable, for all injuries, poisonings, and adverse effects of drugs.

4) Assign as many E codes as necessary
Assign as many E codes as necessary to fully explain each cause. If only one E code can be recorded, assign the E code most related to the principal diagnosis.

5) The selection of the appropriate E code—The selection of the appropriate E code is guided by the Index to External Causes, which is located after the Alphabetical Index to Diseases and by inclusion and exclusion notes in the Tabular List.

6) E code can never be a principal diagnosis—An E code can never be a principal (first-listed) diagnosis.

7) External cause code(s) with systemic inflammatory response syndrome (SIRS)—An external cause code(s) may be used with codes 995.93 Systemic inflammatory response syndrome due to noninfectious process without organ dysfunction, and 995.94 Systemic inflammatory response syndrome due to noninfectious process with organ dysfunction, if trauma was the initiating insult that precipitated the

SIRS. The external cause(s) code should correspond to the most serious injury resulting from the trauma. The external cause code(s) should only be assigned if the trauma necessitated the admission in which the patient also developed SIRS. If a patient is admitted with SIRS but the trauma has been treated previously, the external cause codes should not be used.

b. **Place of occurrence guideline**—Use an additional code from category E849 to indicate the place of occurrence for injuries and poisonings. The place of occurrence describes the place where the event occurred and not the patient's activity at the time of the event.

Do not use E849.9 if the place of occurrence is not stated.

c. **Adverse effects of drugs, medicinal and biological substances guidelines**

1) **Do not code directly from the Table of Drugs**—Do not code directly from the Table of Drugs and Chemicals. Always refer back to the Tabular List.

2) **Use as many codes as necessary to describe**—Use as many codes as necessary to describe completely all drugs, medicinal or biological substances.

3) **If the same E code would describe the causative agent**—If the same E code would describe the causative agent for more than one adverse reaction, assign the code only once.

4) **If two or more drugs, medicinal or biological substances**—If two or more drugs, medicinal or biological substances are reported, code each individually unless the combination code is listed in the Table of Drugs and Chemicals. In that case, assign the E code for the combination.

5) **When a reaction results from the interaction of a drug(s)**—When a reaction results from the interaction of a drug(s) and alcohol, use poisoning codes and E codes for both.

6) **If the reporting format limits the number of E codes**—If the reporting format limits the number of E codes that can be used in reporting clinical data, code the one most related to the principal diagnosis. Include at least one from each category (cause, intent, place) if possible.

If there are different fourth-digit codes in the same three-digit category, use the code for "other specified" of that category. If there is no "other specified" code in that category, use the appropriate "unspecified" code in that category.

If the codes are in different three-digit categories, assign the appropriate E code for other multiple drugs and medicinal substances.

7) **Codes from the E930-E949 series**—Codes from the E930-E949 series must be used to identify the causative substance for an adverse effect of drug, medicinal and biological substances, correctly prescribed and properly administered. The effect, such as tachycardia, delirium, gastrointestinal hemorrhaging, vomiting, hypokalemia, hepatitis, renal failure, or respiratory failure, is coded and followed by the appropriate code from the E930-E949 series.

d. **Multiple cause E code coding guidelines**—If two or more events cause separate injuries, an E code should be assigned for each cause. The first listed E code will be selected in the following order:

E codes for child and adult abuse take priority over all other E codes. See section I.C.19.e., Child and adult abuse guidelines.

E codes for terrorism events take priority over all other E codes except child and adult abuse.

E codes for cataclysmic events take priority over all other E codes except child and adult abuse and terrorism.

E codes for transport accidents take priority over all other E codes except cataclysmic events and child and adult abuse and terrorism.

The first-listed E code should correspond to the cause of the most serious diagnosis due to an assault, accident, or self-harm, following the order of hierarchy listed above.

e. **Child and adult abuse guideline**

1) **Intentional injury**—When the cause of an injury or neglect is intentional child or adult abuse, the first-listed E code should be assigned from categories E960-E968 Homicide and injury purposely inflicted by other persons, (except category E967). An E code from category E967 Child and adult battering and other maltreatment, should be added as an additional code to identify the perpetrator, if known.

2) **Accidental intent**—In cases of neglect when the intent is determined to be accidental E code E904.0 Abandonment or neglect of infant and helpless person, should be the first-listed E code.

f. **Unknown or suspected intent guideline**

1) **If the intent (accident, self-harm, assault) of the cause of an injury or poisoning is unknown**—If the intent (accident, self-harm, assault) of the cause of an injury or poisoning is unknown or unspecified, code the intent as undetermined, E980-E989.

2) **If the intent (accident, self-harm, assault) of the cause of an injury or poisoning is questionable**—If the intent (accident, self-harm, assault) of the cause of an injury or poisoning is questionable, probable or suspected, code the intent as undetermined, E980-E989.

g. **Undetermined cause**—When the intent of an injury or poisoning is known, but the cause is unknown, use codes E928.9 Unspecified accident, E958.9 Suicide and self-inflicted injury by unspecified means, and E968.9 Assault by unspecified means.

These E codes should rarely be used, as the documentation in the medical record, in both the inpatient outpatient and other settings, should normally provide sufficient detail to determine the cause of the injury.

h. **Late effects of external cause guidelines**

1) **Late effect E codes**—Late effect E codes exist for injuries and poisonings but not for adverse effects of drugs, misadventures, and surgical complications.

2) **Late effect E codes (E929, E959, E969, E977, E989, or E999.1)**—A late effect E code (E929, E959, E969, E977, E989, or E999.1) should be used with any report of a late effect or sequela resulting from a previous injury or poisoning (905-909).

3) **Late effect E code with a related current injury**—A late effect E code should never be used with a related current nature of injury code.

4) **Use of late effect E codes for subsequent visits**—Use a late effect E code for subsequent visits when a late effect of the initial injury or poisoning is being treated. There is no late effect E code for adverse effects of drugs. Do not use a late effect E code for subsequent visits for follow-up care (e.g., to assess healing, to receive rehabilitative therapy) of the injury or poisoning when no late effect of the injury has been documented.

i. **Misadventures and complications of care guidelines**

1) **Code range E870-E876**—Assign a code in the range of E870-E876 if misadventures are stated by the provider.

2) **Code range E878-E879**—Assign a code in the range of E878-E879 if the provider attributes an abnormal reaction or later complication to a surgical or medical procedure, but does not mention misadventure at the time of the procedure as the cause of the reaction.

j. **Terrorism guidelines**

1) **Cause of injury identified by the federal government (FBI) as terrorism**—When the cause of an injury is identified by the federal government (FBI) as terrorism, the first-listed E code should be a code from category E979 Terrorism. The definition of terrorism employed by the FBI is found at the inclusion note at E979. The terrorism E code is the only E code that should be assigned. Additional E codes from the assault categories should not be assigned.

2) **Cause of an injury is suspected to be the result of terrorism**—When the cause of an injury is suspected to be the result of terrorism a code from category E979 should not be assigned. Assign a code in the range of E codes based on the documentation of intent and mechanism.

3) **Code E979.9 Terrorism, secondary effects**—Assign code E979.9 Terrorism, secondary effects, for conditions occurring subsequent to the terrorist event. This code should not be assigned for conditions that are due to the initial terrorist act.

4) **Statistical tabulation of terrorism codes**—For statistical purposes these codes will be tabulated within the category for assault, expanding the current category from E960-E969 to include E979 and E999.1.

Section II. Selection of Principal Diagnosis

The circumstances of inpatient admission always govern the selection of principal diagnosis. The principal diagnosis is defined in the Uniform Hospital Discharge Data Set (UHDDS) as "that condition established after study to be chiefly responsible for occasioning the admission of the patient to the hospital for care."

The UHDDS definitions are used by hospitals to report inpatient data elements in a standardized manner. These data elements and their definitions can be found in the July 31, 1985, *Federal Register* (vol. 50, no. 147), pp. 31038-40.

Since that time the application of the UHDDS definitions has been expanded to include all non-outpatient settings (acute care, short-term, long-term care and psychiatric hospitals; home health agencies; rehab facilities; nursing homes, etc.).

In determining principal diagnosis the coding conventions in the ICD-9-CM, Volumes 1 and 2 take precedence over these official coding guidelines. (See section I.A., Conventions, for the ICD-9-CM).

The importance of consistent, complete documentation in the medical record cannot be overemphasized. Without such documentation the application of all coding guidelines is a difficult, if not impossible, task.

A. Codes for symptoms, signs, and ill-defined conditions

Codes for symptoms, signs, and ill-defined conditions from chapter 16 are not to be used as principal diagnosis when a related definitive diagnosis has been established.

B. Two or more interrelated conditions, each potentially meeting the definition for principal diagnosis.

When there are two or more interrelated conditions (such as diseases in the same ICD-9-CM chapter or manifestations characteristically associated with a certain disease) potentially meeting the definition of principal diagnosis, either condition may be sequenced first, unless the circumstances of the admission, the therapy provided, the Tabular List, or the Alphabetic Index indicate otherwise.

C. Two or more diagnoses that equally meet the definition for principal diagnosis

In the unusual instance when two or more diagnoses equally meet the criteria for principal diagnosis as determined by the circumstances of admission, diagnostic workup and/or therapy provided, and the Alphabetic Index, Tabular List, or another coding guidelines do not provide sequencing direction, any one of the diagnoses may be sequenced first.

D. Two or more comparative or contrasting conditions.

In those rare instances when two or more contrasting or comparative diagnoses are documented as "either/or" (or similar terminology), they are coded as if the diagnoses were confirmed and the diagnoses are sequenced according to the circumstances of the admission. If no further determination can be made as to which diagnosis should be principal, either diagnosis may be sequenced first.

E. A symptom(s) followed by contrasting/comparative diagnoses

When a symptom(s) is followed by contrasting/comparative diagnoses, the symptom code is sequenced first. All the contrasting/comparative diagnoses should be coded as additional diagnoses.

F. Original treatment plan not carried out

Sequence as the principal diagnosis the condition, which after study occasioned the admission to the hospital, even though treatment may not have been carried out due to unforeseen circumstances.

G. Complications of surgery and other medical care

When the admission is for treatment of a complication resulting from surgery or other medical care, the complication code is sequenced as the principal diagnosis. If the complication is classified to the 996-999 series and the code lacks the necessary specificity in describing the complication, an additional code for the specific complication should be assigned.

H. Uncertain diagnosis

If the diagnosis documented at the time of discharge is qualified as "probable," "suspected," "likely," "questionable," "possible," or "still to be ruled out," code the condition as if it existed or was established. The bases for these guidelines are the diagnostic workup, arrangements for further workup or observation, and initial therapeutic approach that correspond most closely with the established diagnosis.

Note: This guideline is applicable only to short-term, acute, long-term care and psychiatric hospitals.

I. Admission from observation unit

1. **Admission following medical observation—When a patient is admitted to an observation unit for a medical condition that either worsens or does not improve, and is subsequently admitted as an inpatient of the same hospital for this same medical condition, the principal diagnosis would be the medical condition that led to the hospital admission.**

2. **Admission following post-operative observation—When a patient is admitted to an observation unit to monitor a condition (or complication) that develops following outpatient surgery and then is subsequently admitted as an inpatient of the same hospital, hospitals should apply the Uniform Hospital Discharge Data Set (UHDDS) definition of principal diagnosis as "that condition established after study to be chiefly responsible for occasioning the admission of the patient to the hospital for care."**

J. Admission from outpatient surgery

When a patient receives surgery in the hospital's outpatient surgery department and is subsequently admitted for continuing inpatient care at the same hospital, the following guidelines should be followed in selecting the principal diagnosis for the inpatient admission:

- **If the reason for the inpatient admission is a complication, assign the complication as the principal diagnosis.**

- **If no complication, or other condition, is documented as the reason for the inpatient admission, assign the reason for the outpatient surgery as the principal diagnosis.**

- **If the reason for the inpatient admission is another condition unrelated to the surgery, assign the unrelated condition as the principal diagnosis.**

Section III. Reporting Additional Diagnoses

GENERAL RULES FOR OTHER (ADDITIONAL) DIAGNOSES

For reporting purposes the definition for "other diagnoses" is interpreted as additional conditions that affect patient care in terms of requiring:

- Clinical evaluation; or
- Therapeutic treatment; or
- Diagnostic procedures; or
- Extended length of hospital stay; or
- Increased nursing care and/or monitoring.

The UHDDS item #11-b defines other diagnoses as "all conditions that coexist at the time of admission, that develop subsequently, or that affect the treatment received and/or the length of stay. Diagnoses that relate to an earlier episode which have no bearing on the current hospital stay are to be excluded." UHDDS definitions apply to inpatients in acute care, short-term, long-term care and psychiatric hospital settings. The UHDDS definitions are used by acute care short-term hospitals to report inpatient data elements in a standardized manner. These data elements and their definitions can be found in the July 31, 1985, *Federal Register* (vol. 50, no. 147), pp. 31038-40.

Since that time the application of the UHDDS definitions has been expanded to include all non-outpatient settings (acute care, short-term, long-term care and psychiatric hospitals; home health agencies; rehab facilities; nursing homes, etc.).

The following guidelines are to be applied in designating other diagnoses when neither the Alphabetic Index nor the Tabular List in ICD-9-CM provides direction. The listing of the diagnoses in the patient record is the responsibility of the attending provider.

A. Previous conditions

If the provider has included a diagnosis in the final diagnostic statement, such as the discharge summary or the face sheet, it should ordinarily be coded. Some providers include in the diagnostic statement resolved conditions or diagnoses and status-post procedures from previous admission that have no bearing on the current stay. Such conditions are not to be reported and are coded only if required by hospital policy.

However, history codes (V10-V19) may be used as secondary codes if the historical condition or family history has an impact on current care or influences treatment.

B. Abnormal findings

Abnormal findings (laboratory, x-ray, pathologic, and other diagnostic results) are not coded and reported unless the provider indicates their clinical significance. If the findings are outside the normal range and the attending provider has ordered other tests to evaluate the condition or prescribed treatment, it is appropriate to ask the provider whether the abnormal finding should be added.

Please note: This differs from the coding practices in the outpatient setting for coding encounters for diagnostic tests that have been interpreted by a provider.

C. Uncertain Diagnosis

If the diagnosis documented at the time of discharge is qualified as "probable," "suspected," "likely," "questionable," "possible," or "still to be ruled out," code the condition as if it existed or was established. The bases for these guidelines are the diagnostic workup, arrangements for further workup or observation, and initial therapeutic approach that correspond most closely with the established diagnosis.

Note: This guideline is applicable only to short-term, acute, long-term care and psychiatric hospitals.

Section IV. Diagnostic Coding and Reporting Guidelines for Outpatient Services

These coding guidelines for outpatient diagnoses have been approved for use by hospitals/providers in coding and reporting hospital-based outpatient services and provider-based office visits.

Information about the use of certain abbreviations, punctuation, symbols, and other conventions used in the ICD-9-CM Tabular List (code numbers and titles), can be found in section IA of these guidelines, under "Conventions for the ICD-9-CM." Information about the correct sequence to use in finding a code is also described in section I.

The terms "encounter" and "visit" are often used interchangeably in describing outpatient service contacts and, therefore, appear together in these guidelines without distinguishing one from the other.

Though the conventions and general guidelines apply to all settings, coding guidelines for outpatient and provider reporting of diagnoses will vary in a number of instances from those for inpatient diagnoses, recognizing that:

- The Uniform Hospital Discharge Data Set (UHDDS) definition of principal diagnosis applies only to inpatients in acute, short-term, long-term care and psychiatric hospitals.

- Coding guidelines for inconclusive diagnoses (probable, suspected, rule out, etc.) were developed for inpatient reporting and do not apply to outpatients.

A. Selection of first-listed condition

In the outpatient setting, the term "first-listed diagnosis" is used in lieu of principal diagnosis.

In determining the first-listed diagnosis the coding conventions of ICD-9-CM, as well as the general and disease-specific guidelines take precedence over the outpatient guidelines.

Diagnoses often are not established at the time of the initial encounter/visit. It may take two or more visits before the diagnosis is confirmed.

The most critical rule involves beginning the search for the correct code assignment through the Alphabetic Index. Never begin searching initially in the Tabular List as this will lead to coding errors.

1. **Outpatient surgery—When a patient presents for outpatient surgery, code the reason for the surgery as the first-listed diagnosis (reason for the encounter), even if the surgery is not performed due to a contraindication.**

2. **Observation stay—When a patient is admitted for observation for a medical condition, assign a code for the medical condition as the first-listed diagnosis. When a patient presents for outpatient surgery and develops complications requiring admission to observation, code the reason for the surgery as the first reported diagnosis (reason for the encounter), followed by codes for the complications as secondary diagnoses.**

B. Codes from 001.0 through V86.1

The appropriate code or codes from 001.0 through V86.1 must be used to identify diagnoses, symptoms, conditions, problems, complaints, or other reason(s) for the encounter/visit.

C. Accurate reporting of ICD-9-CM diagnosis codes

For accurate reporting of ICD-9-CM diagnosis codes, the documentation should describe the patient's condition, using terminology which includes specific diagnoses as well as symptoms, problems, or reasons for the encounter. There are ICD-9-CM codes to describe all of these.

D. Selection of codes 001.0 through 999.9

The selection of codes 001.0 through 999.9 will frequently be used to describe the reason for the encounter. These codes are from the section of ICD-9-CM for the classification of diseases and injuries (e.g. infectious and parasitic diseases; neoplasms; symptoms, signs, and ill-defined conditions, etc.).

E. Codes that describe symptoms and signs

Codes that describe symptoms and signs, as opposed to diagnoses, are acceptable for reporting purposes when a diagnosis has not been established (confirmed) by the provider. Chapter 16 of ICD-9-CM, Symptoms, Signs, and Ill-defined Conditions (codes 780.0-799.9) contain many, but not all, codes for symptoms.

F. Encounters for circumstances other than a disease or injury

ICD-9-CM provides codes to deal with encounters for circumstances other than a disease or injury. The Supplementary Classification of Factors Influencing Health Status and Contact with Health Services (V01.0-V84.8) is provided to deal with occasions when circumstances other than a disease or injury are recorded as diagnosis or problems.

G. Level of Detail in Coding

1. **ICD-9-CM codes with three, four, or five digits**—ICD-9-CM is composed of codes with either three, four, or five digits. Codes with three digits are included in ICD-9-CM as the heading of a category of codes that may be further subdivided by the use of fourth and/or fifth digits, which provide greater specificity.

2. **Use of full number of digits required for a code**—A three-digit code is to be used only if it is not further subdivided. Where fourth-digit subcategories and/or fifth-digit subclassifications are provided, they must be assigned. A code is invalid if it has not been coded to the full number of digits required for that code. See also discussion under section I.b.3., General coding guidelines, Level of detail in coding.

H. ICD-9-CM code for the diagnosis, condition, problem, or other reason for encounter/visit

List first the ICD-9-CM code for the diagnosis, condition, problem, or other reason for encounter/visit shown in the medical record to be chiefly responsible for the services provided. List additional codes that describe any coexisting conditions. In some cases the first-listed diagnosis may be a symptom when a diagnosis has not been established (confirmed) by the physician.

I. "Probable," "suspected," "questionable," "rule out," or "working diagnosis"

Do not code diagnoses documented as "probable," "suspected," "questionable," "rule out," or "working diagnosis." Rather, code the condition(s) to the highest degree of certainty for that encounter/visit, such as symptoms, signs, abnormal test results, or other reason for the visit. **Please note:** This differs from the coding practices used by short-term, acute care, long-term care, and psychiatric hospitals.

J. Chronic diseases

Chronic diseases treated on an ongoing basis may be coded and reported as many times as the patient receives treatment and care for the condition(s).

K. Code all documented conditions that coexist

Code all documented conditions that coexist at the time of the encounter/visit, and require or affect patient care treatment or management. Do not code conditions that were previously treated and no longer exist. However, history codes (V10-V19) may be used as secondary codes if the historical condition or family history has an impact on current care or influences treatment.

L. Patients receiving diagnostic services only

For patients receiving diagnostic services only during an encounter/visit, sequence first the diagnosis, condition, problem, or other reason for encounter/visit shown in the medical record to be chiefly responsible for the outpatient services provided during the encounter/visit. Codes for other diagnoses (e.g., chronic conditions) may be sequenced as additional diagnoses.

For outpatient encounters for diagnostic tests that have been interpreted by a physician and the final report is available at the time of coding, code any confirmed or definitive diagnosis(es) documented in the interpretation. Do not code related signs and symptoms as additional diagnoses.

Please note: This differs from the coding practice in the hospital inpatient setting regarding abnormal findings on test results.

M. Patients receiving therapeutic services only

For patients receiving therapeutic services only during an encounter/visit, sequence first the diagnosis, condition, problem, or other reason for encounter/visit shown in the medical record to be chiefly responsible for the outpatient services provided during the encounter/visit. Codes for other diagnoses (e.g., chronic conditions) may be sequenced as additional diagnoses.

The only exception to this rule is that when the primary reason for the admission/encounter is chemotherapy, radiation therapy, or rehabilitation, the appropriate V code for the service is listed first, and the diagnosis or problem for which the service is being performed is listed second.

N. Patients receiving preoperative evaluations only

For patients receiving preoperative evaluations only, sequence first a code from category V72.8 Other specified examinations, to describe the pre-op consultations. Assign a code for the condition to describe the reason for the surgery as an additional diagnosis. Code also any findings related to the pre-op evaluation.

O. Ambulatory surgery

For ambulatory surgery, code the diagnosis for which the surgery was performed. If the postoperative diagnosis is known to be different from the preoperative diagnosis at the time the diagnosis is confirmed, select the postoperative diagnosis for coding, since it is the most definitive.

P. Routine outpatient prenatal visits

For routine outpatient prenatal visits when no complications are present, code V22.0 Supervision of normal first pregnancy, or V22.1 Supervision of other normal pregnancy, should be used as the principal diagnosis. These codes should not be used in conjunction with chapter 11 codes.

A

AAT (alpha-1 antitrypsin) deficiency 273.4
AAV (disease) (illness) (infection) —
   see Human immunodeficiency virus (disease) (illness) (infection)
Abactio — *see* Abortion, induced
Abactus venter — *see* Abortion, induced
Abarognosis 781.99
Abasia (-astasia) 307.9
   atactica 781.3
   choreic 781.3
   hysterical 300.11
   paroxysmal trepidant 781.3
   spastic 781.3
   trembling 781.3
   trepidans 781.3
Abderhalden-Kaufmann-Lignac syndrome (cystinosis) 270.0
Abdomen, abdominal — *see also* condition
   accordion 306.4
   acute 789.0 ☑
   angina 557.1
   burst 868.00
   convulsive equivalent (*see also* Epilepsy) 345.5 ☑
   heart 746.87
   muscle deficiency syndrome 756.79
   obstipum 756.79
Abdominalgia 789.0 ☑
   periodic 277.31   ▲
Abduction contracture, hip or other joint — *see* Contraction, joint
Abercrombie's syndrome (amyloid degeneration) 277.39   ▲
Aberrant (congenital) — *see also* Malposition, congenital
   adrenal gland 759.1
   blood vessel NEC 747.60
      arteriovenous NEC 747.60
      cerebrovascular 747.81
      gastrointestinal 747.61
      lower limb 747.64
      renal 747.62
      spinal 747.82
      upper limb 747.63
   breast 757.6
   endocrine gland NEC 759.2
   gastrointestinal vessel (peripheral) 747.61
   hepatic duct 751.69
   lower limb vessel (peripheral) 747.64
   pancreas 751.7
   parathyroid gland 759.2
   peripheral vascular vessel NEC 747.60
   pituitary gland (pharyngeal) 759.2
   renal blood vessel 747.62
   sebaceous glands, mucous membrane, mouth 750.26
   spinal vessel 747.82
   spleen 759.0
   testis (descent) 752.51
   thymus gland 759.2
   thyroid gland 759.2
   upper limb vessel (peripheral) 747.63
Aberratio
   lactis 757.6
   testis 752.51
Aberration — *see also* Anomaly
   chromosome — *see* Anomaly, chromosome(s)
   distantial 368.9
   mental (*see also* Disorder, mental, nonpsychotic) 300.9
Abetalipoproteinemia 272.5
Abionarce 780.79
Abiotrophy 799.89
Ablatio
   placentae — *see* Placenta, ablatio
   retinae (*see also* Detachment, retina) 361.9
Ablation
   pituitary (gland) (with hypofunction) 253.7

Ablation — *continued*
   placenta — *see* Placenta, ablatio
   uterus 621.8
Ablepharia, ablepharon, ablephary 743.62
Ablepsia — *see* Blindness
Ablepsy — *see* Blindness
Ablutomania 300.3
Abnormal, abnormality, abnormalities
   — *see also* Anomaly
   acid-base balance 276.4
      fetus or newborn — *see* Distress, fetal
   adaptation curve, dark 368.63
   alveolar ridge 525.9
   amnion 658.9 ☑
      affecting fetus or newborn 762.9
   anatomical relationship NEC 759.9
   apertures, congenital, diaphragm 756.6
   auditory perception NEC 388.40
   autosomes NEC 758.5
      13 758.1
      18 758.2
      21 or 22 758.0
      D_1 758.1
      E_3 758.2
      G 758.0
   ballistocardiogram 794.39
   basal metabolic rate (BMR) 794.7
   biosynthesis, testicular androgen 257.2
   blood level (of)
      cobalt 790.6
      copper 790.6
      iron 790.6
      lead 790.6   ●
      lithium 790.6
      magnesium 790.6
      mineral 790.6
      zinc 790.6
   blood pressure
      elevated (without diagnosis of hypertension) 796.2
      low (*see also* Hypotension) 458.9
         reading (incidental) (isolated) (nonspecific) 796.3
   bowel sounds 787.5
   breathing behavior — *see* Respiration
   caloric test 794.19
   cervix (acquired) NEC 622.9
      congenital 752.40
      in pregnancy or childbirth 654.6 ☑
         causing obstructed labor 660.2 ☑
            affecting fetus or newborn 763.1
   chemistry, blood NEC 790.6
   chest sounds 786.7
   chorion 658.9 ☑
      affecting fetus or newborn 762.9
   chromosomal NEC 758.89
      analysis, nonspecific result 795.2
      autosomes (*see also* Abnormal, autosomes NEC) 758.5
      fetal, (suspected) affecting management of pregnancy 655.1 ☑
      sex 758.81
   clinical findings NEC 796.4
   communication — *see* Fistula
   configuration of pupils 379.49
   coronary
      artery 746.85
      vein 746.9
   cortisol-binding globulin 255.8
   course, Eustachian tube 744.24
   dentofacial NEC 524.9
      functional 524.50
      specified type NEC 524.89
   development, developmental NEC 759.9
      bone 756.9
      central nervous system 742.9
      direction, teeth 524.30
   Dynia (*see also* Defect, coagulation) 286.9

Abnormal, abnormality, abnormalities
   — *see also* Anomaly —
   continued
   Ebstein 746.2
   echocardiogram 793.2
   echoencephalogram 794.01
   echogram NEC — *see* Findings, abnormal, structure
   electrocardiogram (ECG) (EKG) 794.31
   electroencephalogram (EEG) 794.02
   electromyogram (EMG) 794.17
      ocular 794.14
   electro-oculogram (EOG) 794.12
   electroretinogram (ERG) 794.11
   erythrocytes 289.9
      congenital, with perinatal jaundice 282.9 [774.0]
   Eustachian valve 746.9
   excitability under minor stress 301.9
   fat distribution 782.9
   feces 787.7
   fetal heart rate — *see* Distress, fetal
   fetus NEC
      affecting management of pregnancy — *see* Pregnancy, management affected by, fetal ☑
      causing disproportion 653.7 ☑
         affecting fetus or newborn 763.1
         causing obstructed labor 660.1 ☑
            affecting fetus or newborn 763.1
   findings without manifest disease — *see* Findings, abnormal
   fluid
      amniotic 792.3
      cerebrospinal 792.0
      peritoneal 792.9
      pleural 792.9
      synovial 792.9
      vaginal 792.9
   forces of labor NEC 661.9 ☑
      affecting fetus or newborn 763.7
   form, teeth 520.2
   function studies
      auditory 794.15
      bladder 794.9
      brain 794.00
      cardiovascular 794.30
      endocrine NEC 794.6
      kidney 794.4
      liver 794.8
      nervous system
         central 794.00
         peripheral 794.19
      oculomotor 794.14
      pancreas 794.9
      placenta 794.9
      pulmonary 794.2
      retina 794.11
      special senses 794.19
      spleen 794.9
      thyroid 794.5
      vestibular 794.16
   gait 781.2
      hysterical 300.11
   gastrin secretion 251.5
   globulin
      cortisol-binding 255.8
      thyroid-binding 246.8
   glucagon secretion 251.4
   glucose 790.29
      in pregnancy, childbirth, or puerperium 648.8 ☑
         fetus or newborn 775.0
      non-fasting 790.29
   gravitational (G) forces or states 994.9
   hair 704.2
   hard tissue formation in pulp 522.3
   head movement 781.0
   heart
      rate
         fetus, affecting liveborn infant
            before the onset of labor 763.81
            during labor 763.82

Abnormal, abnormality, abnormalities
   — *see also* Anomaly —
   continued
   heart — *continued*
      rate — *continued*
         fetus, affecting liveborn infant — *continued*
            unspecified as to time of onset 763.83
         intrauterine
            before the onset of labor 763.81
            during labor 763.82
            unspecified as to time of onset 763.83
         newborn
            before the onset of labor 763.81
            during labor 763.82
            unspecified as to time of onset 763.83
      shadow 793.2
      sounds NEC 785.3
   hemoglobin (*see also* Disease, hemoglobin) 282.7
      trait — *see* Trait, hemoglobin, abnormal
   hemorrhage, uterus — *see* Hemorrhage, uterus
   histology NEC 795.4
   increase
      in
         appetite 783.6
         development 783.9
   involuntary movement 781.0
   jaw closure 524.51
   karyotype 795.2
   knee jerk 796.1
   labor NEC 661.9 ☑
      affecting fetus or newborn 763.7
   laboratory findings — *see* Findings, abnormal
   length, organ or site, congenital — *see* Distortion
   loss of height 781.91
   loss of weight 783.21
   lung shadow 793.1
   mammogram 793.80
      calcification 793.89   ●
      calculus 793.89   ●
      microcalcification 793.81
   Mantoux test 795.5
   membranes (fetal)
      affecting fetus or newborn 762.9
      complicating pregnancy 658.8 ☑
   menstruation — *see* Menstruation
   metabolism (*see also* condition) 783.9
   movement 781.0
      disorder NEC 333.90
         sleep related, unspecified 780.58
         specified NEC 333.99
      head 781.0
      involuntary 781.0
         specified type NEC 333.99
   muscle contraction, localized 728.85
   myoglobin (Aberdeen) (Annapolis) 289.9
   narrowness, eyelid 743.62
   optokinetic response 379.57
   organs or tissues of pelvis NEC
      in pregnancy or childbirth 654.9 ☑
         affecting fetus or newborn 763.89
         causing obstructed labor 660.2 ☑
            affecting fetus or newborn 763.1
   origin — *see* Malposition, congenital
   palmar creases 757.2
   Papanicolaou (smear)
      cervix 795.00

☑ Additional Digit Required — Refer to the Tabular List for Digit Selection   ▽ Subterms under main terms may continue to next column or page

2007 ICD-9-CM   ▶◀ Revised Text   ● New Line   ▲ Revised Code   **October 2006 · Volume 2 — 1**

Abnormal, abnormality, abnormalities
— *see also* Anomaly —
continued
Papanicolaou — *continued*
  cervix — *continued*
    with
      atypical squamous cells
        cannot exclude high grade
          squamous intraep-
          ithelial lesion (ASC-
          H) 795.02
        of undetermined signifi-
          cance (ASC-US)
          795.01
      cytologic evidence of malig- ●
        nancy 795.06
      high grade squamous intraep-
        ithelial lesion (HGSIL)
        795.04
      low grade squamous intraep-
        ithelial lesion (LGSIL)
        795.03
      nonspecific finding NEC 795.09
  other site 795.1
parturition
  affecting fetus or newborn 763.9
  mother — *see* Delivery, complicat-
    ed
pelvis (bony) — *see* Deformity, pelvis
percussion, chest 786.7
periods (grossly) (*see also* Menstruation) 626.9
phonocardiogram 794.39
placenta — *see* Placenta, abnormal
plantar reflex 796.1
plasma protein — *see* Deficiency,
  plasma, protein
pleural folds 748.8
position (*see also* Malposition)
  gravid uterus 654.4 ☑
    causing obstructed labor
      660.2 ☑
      affecting fetus or newborn
        763.1
posture NEC 781.92
presentation (fetus) — *see* Presentation, fetus, abnormal
product of conception NEC 631
puberty — *see* Puberty
pulmonary
  artery 747.3
  function, newborn 770.89
  test results 794.2
  ventilation, newborn 770.89
    hyperventilation 786.01
pulsations in neck 785.1
pupil reflexes 379.40
quality of milk 676.8 ☑
radiological examination 793.99 ▲
  abdomen NEC 793.6
  biliary tract 793.3
  breast 793.89
    mammogram NOS 793.80
    mammographic
      calcification 793.89 ●
      calculus 793.89 ●
      microcalcification 793.81 ●
  gastrointestinal tract 793.4
  genitourinary organs 793.5
  head 793.0
  image test inconclusive due to ●
    excess body fat 793.91
  intrathoracic organ NEC 793.2
  lung (field) 793.1
  musculoskeletal system 793.7
  retroperitoneum 793.6
  skin and subcutaneous tissue
    793.99 ▲
  skull 793.0
red blood cells 790.09
  morphology 790.09
  volume 790.09
reflex NEC 796.1
renal function test 794.4
respiration signs — *see* Respiration
response to nerve stimulation 794.10

Abnormal, abnormality, abnormalities
— *see also* Anomaly —
continued
retinal correspondence 368.34
rhythm, heart (*see also* Arrhythmia)
  fetus — *see* Distress, fetal
saliva 792.4
scan
  brain 794.09
  kidney 794.4
  liver 794.8
  lung 794.2
  thyroid 794.5
secretion
  gastrin 251.5
  glucagon 251.4
semen 792.2
serum level (of)
  acid phosphatase 790.5
  alkaline phosphatase 790.5
  amylase 790.5
  enzymes NEC 790.5
  lipase 790.5
shape
  cornea 743.41
  gallbladder 751.69
  gravid uterus 654.4 ☑
    affecting fetus or newborn
      763.89
    causing obstructed labor
      660.2 ☑
      affecting fetus or newborn
        763.1
  head (*see also* Anomaly, skull)
    756.0
  organ or site, congenital NEC —
    see Distortion
sinus venosus 747.40
size
  fetus, complicating delivery
    653.5 ☑
    causing obstructed labor
      660.1 ☑
  gallbladder 751.69
  head (*see also* Anomaly, skull)
    756.0
  organ or site, congenital NEC —
    see Distortion
  teeth 520.2
skin and appendages, congenital NEC
  757.9
soft parts of pelvis — *see* Abnormal,
  organs or tissues of pelvis
spermatozoa 792.2
sputum (amount) (color) (excessive)
  (odor) (purulent) 786.4
stool NEC 787.7
  bloody 578.1
    occult 792.1
  bulky 787.7
  color (dark) (light) 792.1
  content (fat) (mucus) (pus) 792.1
  occult blood 792.1
synchondrosis 756.9
test results without manifest disease
  — *see* Findings, abnormal
thebesian valve 746.9
thermography — *see* Findings, abnormal, structure
threshold, cones or rods (eye) 368.63
thyroid-binding globulin 246.8
thyroid product 246.8
toxicology (findings) NEC 796.0
tracheal cartilage (congenital) 748.3
transport protein 273.8
ultrasound results — *see* Findings,
  abnormal, structure
umbilical cord
  affecting fetus or newborn 762.6
  complicating delivery 663.9 ☑
  specified NEC 663.8 ☑
union
  cricoid cartilage and thyroid carti-
    lage 748.3
  larynx and trachea 748.3

Abnormal, abnormality, abnormalities
— *see also* Anomaly —
continued
union — *continued*
  thyroid cartilage and hyoid bone
    748.3
urination NEC 788.69
  psychogenic 306.53
  stream
    intermittent 788.61
    slowing 788.62
    splitting 788.61
    weak 788.62
  urgency 788.63
urine (constituents) NEC 791.9
uterine hemorrhage (*see also* Hemorrhage, uterus) 626.9
  climacteric 627.0
  postmenopausal 627.1
vagina (acquired) (congenital)
  in pregnancy or childbirth 654.7 ☑
    affecting fetus or newborn
      763.89
    causing obstructed labor
      660.2 ☑
      affecting fetus or newborn
        763.1
vascular sounds 785.9
vectorcardiogram 794.39
visually evoked potential (VEP) 794.13
vulva (acquired) (congenital)
  in pregnancy or childbirth 654.8 ☑
    affecting fetus or newborn
      763.89
    causing obstructed labor
      660.2 ☑
      affecting fetus or newborn
        763.1
weight
  gain 783.1
    of pregnancy 646.1 ☑
      with hypertension — *see*
        Toxemia, of pregnancy
  loss 783.21
x-ray examination — *see* Abnormal,
  radiological examination
Abnormally formed uterus — *see*
  Anomaly, uterus
Abnormity (any organ or part) — *see*
  Anomaly
ABO
  hemolytic disease 773.1
  incompatibility reaction 999.6
Abocclusion 524.20
Abolition, language 784.69
Aborter, habitual or recurrent NEC
  without current pregnancy
    629.81 ▲
  current abortion (*see also* Abortion,
    spontaneous) 634.9 ☑
    affecting fetus or newborn 761.8
  observation in current pregnancy
    646.3 ☑
Abortion (complete) (incomplete) (in-
  evitable) (with retained products of
  conception) 637.9 ☑

Note — Use the following fifth-digit
subclassification with categories
634–637:

  0 unspecified

  1 incomplete

  2 complete

with
  complication(s) (any) following pre-
    vious abortion — *see* catego-
    ry 639 ☑
  damage to pelvic organ (laceration)
    (rupture) (tear) 637.2 ☑
  embolism (air) (amniotic fluid)
    (blood clot) (pulmonary)
    (pyemic) (septic) (soap)
    637.6 ☑
  genital tract and pelvic infection
    637.0 ☑

Abortion — *continued*
with — *continued*
  hemorrhage, delayed or excessive
    637.1 ☑
  metabolic disorder 637.4 ☑
  renal failure (acute) 637.3 ☑
  sepsis (genital tract) (pelvic organ)
    637.0 ☑
  urinary tract 637.7 ☑
  shock (postoperative) (septic)
    637.5 ☑
  specified complication NEC
    637.7 ☑
  toxemia 637.3 ☑
  unspecified complication(s)
    637.8 ☑
  urinary tract infection 637.7 ☑
accidental — *see* Abortion, spontaneous
artificial — *see* Abortion, induced
attempted (failed) — *see* Abortion,
  failed
criminal — *see* Abortion, illegal
early — *see* Abortion, spontaneous
elective — *see* Abortion, legal
failed (legal) 638.9
  with
    damage to pelvic organ (lacera-
      tion) (rupture) (tear) 638.2
    embolism (air) (amniotic fluid)
      (blood clot) (pulmonary)
      (pyemic) (septic) (soap)
      638.6
    genital tract and pelvic infection
      638.0
    hemorrhage, delayed or exces-
      sive 638.1
    metabolic disorder 638.4
    renal failure (acute) 638.3
    sepsis (genital tract) (pelvic or-
      gan) 638.0
    urinary tract 638.7
    shock (postoperative) (septic)
      638.5
    specified complication NEC
      638.7
    toxemia 638.3
    unspecified complication(s)
      638.8
    urinary tract infection 638.7
fetal indication — *see* Abortion, legal
fetus 779.6
following threatened abortion — *see*
  Abortion, by type
habitual or recurrent (care during
  pregnancy) 646.3 ☑
  with current abortion (*see also*
    Abortion, spontaneous)
    634.9 ☑
    affecting fetus or newborn 761.8
  without current pregnancy
    629.81 ▲
homicidal — *see* Abortion, illegal
illegal 636.9 ☑
  with
    damage to pelvic organ (lacera-
      tion) (rupture) (tear)
      636.2 ☑
    embolism (air) (amniotic fluid)
      (blood clot) (pulmonary)
      (pyemic) (septic) (soap)
      636.6 ☑
    genital tract and pelvic infection
      636.0 ☑
    hemorrhage, delayed or exces-
      sive 636.1 ☑
    metabolic disorder 636.4 ☑
    renal failure 636.3 ☑
    sepsis (genital tract) (pelvic or-
      gan) 636.0 ☑
    urinary tract 636.7 ☑
    shock (postoperative) (septic)
      636.5 ☑
    specified complication NEC
      636.7 ☑
    toxemia 636.3 ☑

Abnormal, abnormality, abnormalities — Abortion

☑ Additional Digit Required — Refer to the Tabular List for Digit Selection   ▼ Subterms under main terms may continue to next column or page

2 — Volume 2 · October 2006   ▶◀ Revised Text   ● New Line   ▲ Revised Code   *2007 ICD-9-CM*

Abortion — *continued*
  illegal — *continued*
    with — *continued*
      unspecified complication(s)
        636.8
      urinary tract infection 636.7 ☑
    fetus 779.6
  induced 637.9 ☑
    illegal — *see* Abortion, illegal
    legal indications — *see* Abortion,
      legal
    medical indications — *see* Abortion, legal
    therapeutic — *see* Abortion, legal
    late — *see* Abortion, spontaneous
  legal (legal indication) (medical indication) (under medical supervision) 635.9 ☑
    with
      damage to pelvic organ (laceration) (rupture) (tear)
        635.2 ☑
      embolism (air) (amniotic fluid)
        (blood clot) (pulmonary)
        (pyemic) (septic) (soap)
        635.6 ☑
      genital tract and pelvic infection
        635.0 ☑
      hemorrhage, delayed or excessive 635.1 ☑
      metabolic disorder 635.4 ☑
      renal failure (acute) 635.3 ☑
      sepsis (genital tract) (pelvic organ) 635.0 ☑
      urinary tract 635.7 ☑
      shock (postoperative) (septic)
        635.5 ☑
      specified complication NEC
        635.7 ☑
      toxemia 635.3 ☑
      unspecified complication(s)
        635.8 ☑
      urinary tract infection 635.7 ☑
    fetus 779.6
  medical indication — *see* Abortion,
    legal
  mental hygiene problem — *see* Abortion, legal
  missed 632
  operative — *see* Abortion, legal
  psychiatric indication — *see* Abortion,
    legal
  recurrent — *see* Abortion, spontaneous
  self-induced — *see* Abortion, illegal
  septic — *see* Abortion, by type, with
    sepsis
  spontaneous 634.9 ☑
    with
      damage to pelvic organ (laceration) (rupture) (tear)
        634.2 ☑
      embolism (air) (amniotic fluid)
        (blood clot) (pulmonary)
        (pyemic) (septic) (soap)
        634.6 ☑
      genital tract and pelvic infection
        634.0 ☑
      hemorrhage, delayed or excessive 634.1 ☑
      metabolic disorder 634.4 ☑
      renal failure 634.3 ☑
      sepsis (genital tract) (pelvic organ) 634.0 ☑
      urinary tract 634.7 ☑
      shock (postoperative) (septic)
        634.5 ☑
      specified complication NEC
        634.7 ☑
      toxemia 634.3 ☑
      unspecified complication(s)
        634.8 ☑
      urinary tract infection 634.7 ☑
    fetus 761.8
    threatened 640.0 ☑

Abortion — *continued*
  spontaneous — *continued*
    threatened — *continued*
      affecting fetus or newborn 762.1
  surgical — *see* Abortion, legal
  therapeutic — *see* Abortion, legal
  threatened 640.0 ☑
    affecting fetus or newborn 762.1
  tubal — *see* Pregnancy, tubal
  voluntary — *see* Abortion, legal
Abortus fever 023.9
Aboulomania 301.6
Abrachia 755.20
Abrachiatism 755.20
Abrachiocephalia 759.89
Abrachiocephalus 759.89
Abrami's disease (acquired hemolytic
  jaundice) 283.9
Abramov-Fiedler myocarditis (acute
  isolated myocarditis) 422.91
Abrasion — *see also* Injury, superficial,
  by site
  cornea 918.1
  dental 521.20
    extending into
      dentine 521.22
      pulp 521.23
    generalized 521.25
    limited to enamel 521.21
    localized 521.24
  teeth, tooth (dentifrice) (habitual)
    (hard tissues) (occupational)
    (ritual) (traditional) (wedge defect) (*see also* Abrasion, dental)
    521.20
Abrikossov's tumor (M9580/0) — *see
  also* Neoplasm, connective tissue,
  benign
    malignant (M9580/3) — *see* Neoplasm, connective tissue, malignant
Abrism 988.8
Abruption, placenta — *see* Placenta,
  abruptio
Abruptio placentae — *see* Placenta,
  abruptio
Abscess (acute) (chronic) (infectional)
  (lymphangitic) (metastatic) (multiple) (pyogenic) (septic) (with lymphangitis) — *see also* Cellulitis
  682.9
  abdomen, abdominal
    cavity 567.22
    wall 682.2
  abdominopelvic 567.22
  accessory sinus (chronic) (*see also* Sinusitis) 473.9
  adrenal (capsule) (gland) 255.8
  alveolar 522.5
    with sinus 522.7
  amebic 006.3
    bladder 006.8
    brain (with liver or lung abscess)
      006.5
    liver (without mention of brain or
      lung abscess) 006.3
      with
        brain abscess (and lung abscess) 006.5
        lung abscess 006.4
    lung (with liver abscess) 006.4
      with brain abscess 006.5
    seminal vesicle 006.8
    specified site NEC 006.8
    spleen 006.8
  anaerobic 040.0
  ankle 682.6
  anorectal 566
  antecubital space 682.3
  antrum (chronic) (Highmore) (*see also*
    Sinusitis, maxillary) 473.0
  anus 566
  apical (tooth) 522.5
    with sinus (alveolar) 522.7
  appendix 540.1

Abscess — *see also* Cellulitis —
  continued
  areola (acute) (chronic) (nonpuerperal)
    611.0
    puerperal, postpartum 675.1 ☑
  arm (any part, above wrist) 682.3
  artery (wall) 447.2
  atheromatous 447.2
  auditory canal (external) 380.10
  auricle (ear) (staphylococcal) (streptococcal) 380.10
  axilla, axillary (region) 682.3
    lymph gland or node 683
  back (any part) 682.2
  Bartholin's gland 616.3
    with
      abortion — *see* Abortion, by
        type, with sepsis
      ectopic pregnancy (*see also* categories 633.0–633.9)
        639.0
      molar pregnancy (*see also* categories 630–632) 639.0
    complicating pregnancy or puerperium 646.6 ☑
    following
      abortion 639.0
      ectopic or molar pregnancy
        639.0
  bartholinian 616.3
  Bezold's 383.01
  bile, biliary, duct or tract (*see also*
    Cholecystitis) 576.8
  bilharziasis 120.1
  bladder (wall) 595.89
    amebic 006.8
  bone (subperiosteal) (*see also* Osteomyelitis) 730.0 ☑
    accessory sinus (chronic) (*see also*
      Sinusitis) 473.9
    acute 730.0 ☑
    chronic or old 730.1 ☑
    jaw (lower) (upper) 526.4
    mastoid — *see* Mastoiditis, acute
    petrous (*see also* Petrositis) 383.20
    spinal (tuberculous) (*see also* Tuberculosis) 015.0 ☑ [730.88]
    nontuberculous 730.08
  bowel 569.5
  brain (any part) 324.0
    amebic (with liver or lung abscess)
      006.5
    cystic 324.0
    late effect — *see* category 326
    otogenic 324.0
    tuberculous (*see also* Tuberculosis)
      013.3 ☑
  breast (acute) (chronic) (nonpuerperal)
    611.0
    newborn 771.5
    puerperal, postpartum 675.1 ☑
    tuberculous (*see also* Tuberculosis)
      017.9 ☑
  broad ligament (chronic) (*see also*
    Disease, pelvis, inflammatory)
    614.4
    acute 614.3
  Brodie's (chronic) (localized) (*see also*
    Osteomyelitis) 730.1 ☑
  bronchus 519.19 ▲
  buccal cavity 528.3
  bulbourethral gland 597.0
  bursa 727.89
    pharyngeal 478.29
  buttock 682.5
  canaliculus, breast 611.0
  canthus 372.20
  cartilage 733.99
  cecum 569.5
    with appendicitis 540.1
  cerebellum, cerebellar 324.0
    late effect — *see* category 326
  cerebral (embolic) 324.0
    late effect — *see* category 326
  cervical (neck region) 682.1
    lymph gland or node 683

Abscess — *see also* Cellulitis —
  continued
  cervical — *continued*
    stump (*see also* Cervicitis) 616.0
  cervix (stump) (uteri) (*see also* Cervicitis) 616.0
  cheek, external 682.0
    inner 528.3
  chest 510.9
    with fistula 510.0
    wall 682.2
  chin 682.0
  choroid 363.00
  ciliary body 364.3
  circumtonsillar 475
  cold (tuberculous) (*see also* Tuberculosis, abscess)
    articular — *see* Tuberculosis, joint
  colon (wall) 569.5
  colostomy or enterostomy 569.61
  conjunctiva 372.00
  connective tissue NEC 682.9
  cornea 370.55
    with ulcer 370.00
  corpus
    cavernosum 607.2
    luteum (*see also* Salpingo-oophoritis) 614.2
  Cowper's gland 597.0
  cranium 324.0
  cul-de-sac (Douglas') (posterior) (*see
    also* Disease, pelvis, inflammatory) 614.4
    acute 614.3
  dental 522.5
    with sinus (alveolar) 522.7
  dentoalveolar 522.5
    with sinus (alveolar) 522.7
  diaphragm, diaphragmatic 567.22
  digit NEC 681.9
  Douglas' cul-de-sac or pouch (*see also*
    Disease, pelvis, inflammatory)
    614.4
    acute 614.3
  Dubois' 090.5
  ductless gland 259.8
  ear
    acute 382.00
    external 380.10
    inner 386.30
    middle — *see* Otitis media
  elbow 682.3
  endamebic — *see* Abscess, amebic
  entamebic — *see* Abscess, amebic
  enterostomy 569.61
  epididymis 604.0
  epidural 324.9
    brain 324.0
    late effect — *see* category 326
    spinal cord 324.1
  epiglottis 478.79
  epiploon, epiploic 567.22
  erysipelatous (*see also* Erysipelas) 035
  esophagostomy 530.86
  esophagus 530.19
  ethmoid (bone) (chronic) (sinus) (*see
    also* Sinusitis, ethmoidal) 473.2
  external auditory canal 380.10
  extradural 324.9
    brain 324.0
    late effect — *see* category 326
    spinal cord 324.1
  extraperitoneal — *see* Abscess, peritoneum
  eye 360.00
  eyelid 373.13
  face (any part, except eye) 682.0
  fallopian tube (*see also* Salpingo-oophoritis) 614.2
  fascia 728.89
  fauces 478.29
  fecal 569.5
  femoral (region) 682.6
  filaria, filarial (*see also* Infestation, filarial) 125.9

☑ Additional Digit Required — Refer to the Tabular List for Digit Selection   ▼ Subterms under main terms may continue to next column or page

2007 ICD-9-CM   ▶◀ Revised Text   ● New Line   ▲ Revised Code   **October 2006 · Volume 2 — 3**

Abscess — see also Cellulitis — continued

finger (any) (intrathecal) (periosteal) (subcutaneous) (subcuticular) 681.00
fistulous NEC 682.9
flank 682.2
foot (except toe) 682.7
forearm 682.3
forehead 682.0
frontal (sinus) (chronic) (see also Sinusitis, frontal) 473.1
gallbladder (see also Cholecystitis, acute) 575.0
gastric 535.0 ☑
genital organ or tract NEC
  female 616.9
    with
      abortion — see Abortion, by type, with sepsis
      ectopic pregnancy (see also categories 633.0–633.9) 639.0
      molar pregnancy (see also categories 630–632) 639.0
    following
      abortion 639.0
      ectopic or molar pregnancy 639.0
    puerperal, postpartum, childbirth 670.0 ☑
  male 608.4
genitourinary system, tuberculous (see also Tuberculosis) 016.9 ☑
gingival 523.30 ▲
gland, glandular (lymph) (acute) NEC 683
glottis 478.79
gluteal (region) 682.5
gonorrheal NEC (see also Gonococcus) 098.0
groin 682.2
gum 523.30 ▲
hand (except finger or thumb) 682.4
head (except face) 682.8
heart 429.89
heel 682.7
helminthic (see also Infestation, by specific parasite) 128.9
hepatic 572.0
  amebic (see also Abscess, liver, amebic) 006.3
  duct 576.8
hip 682.6
  tuberculous (active) (see also Tuberculosis) 015.1 ☑
ileocecal 540.1
ileostomy (bud) 569.61
iliac (region) 682.2
  fossa 540.1
iliopsoas 567.31
  nontuberculous 728.89
  tuberculous (see also Tuberculosis) 015.0 ☑ [730.88]
infraclavicular (fossa) 682.3
inguinal (region) 682.2
  lymph gland or node 683
intersphincteric (anus) 566
intestine, intestinal 569.5
  rectal 566
intra-abdominal (see also Abscess, peritoneum) 567.22
  postoperative 998.59
intracranial 324.0
  late effect — see category 326
intramammary — see Abscess, breast
intramastoid (see also Mastoiditis, acute) 383.00
intraorbital 376.01
intraperitoneal 567.22
intraspinal 324.1
  late effect — see category 326
intratonsillar 475
iris 364.3
ischiorectal 566

Abscess — see also Cellulitis — continued

jaw (bone) (lower) (upper) 526.4
  skin 682.0
joint (see also Arthritis, pyogenic) 711.0 ☑
  vertebral (tuberculous) (see also Tuberculosis) 015.0 ☑ [730.88]
  nontuberculous 724.8
kidney 590.2
  with
    abortion — see Abortion, by type, with urinary tract infection
    calculus 592.0
    ectopic pregnancy (see also categories 633.0–633.9) 639.8
    molar pregnancy (see also categories 630–632) 639.8
    complicating pregnancy or puerperium 646.6 ☑
    affecting fetus or newborn 760.1
  following
    abortion 639.8
    ectopic or molar pregnancy 639.8
knee 682.6
  joint 711.06
  tuberculous (active) (see also Tuberculosis) 015.2 ☑
labium (majus) (minus) 616.4
  complicating pregnancy, childbirth, or puerperium 646.6 ☑
lacrimal (passages) (sac) (see also Dacryocystitis) 375.30
  caruncle 375.30
  gland (see also Dacryoadenitis) 375.00
lacunar 597.0
larynx 478.79
lateral (alveolar) 522.5
  with sinus 522.7
leg, except foot 682.6
lens 360.00
lid 373.13
lingual 529.0
  tonsil 475
lip 528.5
Littre's gland 597.0
liver 572.0
  amebic 006.3
    with
      brain abscess (and lung abscess) 006.5
      lung abscess 006.4
    due to Entamoeba histolytica 006.3
    dysenteric (see also Abscess, liver, amebic) 006.3
  pyogenic 572.0
  tropical (see also Abscess, liver, amebic) 006.3
loin (region) 682.2
lumbar (tuberculous) (see also Tuberculosis) 015.0 ☑ [730.88]
  nontuberculous 682.2
lung (miliary) (putrid) 513.0
  amebic (with liver abscess) 006.4
    with brain abscess 006.5
lymphangitic, acute — see Cellulitis
lymph, lymphatic, gland or node (acute) 683
  any site, except mesenteric 683
  mesentery 289.2
malar 526.4
mammary gland — see Abscess, breast
marginal (anus) 566
mastoid (process) (see also Mastoiditis, acute) 383.00
  subperiosteal 383.01
maxilla, maxillary 526.4
  molar (tooth) 522.5
    with sinus 522.7
  premolar 522.5

Abscess — see also Cellulitis — continued

maxilla, maxillary — continued
  sinus (chronic) (see also Sinusitis, maxillary) 473.0
mediastinum 513.1
meibomian gland 373.12
meninges (see also Meningitis) 320.9
mesentery, mesenteric 567.22
mesosalpinx (see also Salpingo-oophoritis) 614.2
milk 675.1 ☑
Monro's (psoriasis) 696.1
mons pubis 682.2
mouth (floor) 528.3
multiple sites NEC 682.9
mural 682.2
muscle 728.89
  psoas 567.31
myocardium 422.92
nabothian (follicle) (see also Cervicitis) 616.0
nail (chronic) (with lymphangitis) 681.9
  finger 681.02
  toe 681.11
nasal (fossa) (septum) 478.19 ▲
  sinus (chronic) (see also Sinusitis) 473.9
nasopharyngeal 478.29
nates 682.5
navel 682.2
  newborn NEC 771.4
neck (region) 682.1
  lymph gland or node 683
nephritic (see also Abscess, kidney) 590.2
nipple 611.0
  puerperal, postpartum 675.0 ☑
nose (septum) 478.19 ▲
  external 682.0
omentum 567.22
operative wound 998.59
orbit, orbital 376.01
ossifluent — see Abscess, bone
ovary, ovarian (corpus luteum) (see also Salpingo-oophoritis) 614.2
oviduct (see also Salpingo-oophoritis) 614.2
palate (soft) 528.3
  hard 526.4
palmar (space) 682.4
pancreas (duct) 577.0
paradontal 523.30 ▲
parafrenal 607.2
parametric, parametrium (chronic) (see also Disease, pelvis, inflammatory) 614.4
  acute 614.3
paranephric 590.2
parapancreatic 577.0
parapharyngeal 478.22
pararectal 566
parasinus (see also Sinusitis) 473.9
parauterine (see also Disease, pelvis, inflammatory) 614.4
  acute 614.3
paravaginal (see also Vaginitis) 616.10
parietal region 682.8
parodontal 523.30 ▲
parotid (duct) (gland) 527.3
  region 528.3
parumbilical 682.2
  newborn 771.4
pectoral (region) 682.2
pelvirectal 567.22
pelvis, pelvic
  female (chronic) (see also Disease, pelvis, inflammatory) 614.4
    acute 614.3
  male, peritoneal (cellular tissue) — see Abscess, peritoneum
  tuberculous (see also Tuberculosis) 016.9 ☑
penis 607.2
  gonococcal (acute) 098.0

Abscess — see also Cellulitis — continued

penis — continued
  gonococcal — continued
    chronic or duration of 2 months or over 098.2
perianal 566
periapical 522.5
  with sinus (alveolar) 522.7
periappendiceal 540.1
pericardial 420.99
pericecal 540.1
pericemental 523.30 ▲
pericholecystic (see also Cholecystitis, acute) 575.0
pericoronal 523.30 ▲
peridental 523.30 ▲
perigastric 535.0 ☑
perimetric (see also Disease, pelvis, inflammatory) 614.4
  acute 614.3
perinephric, perinephritic (see also Abscess, kidney) 590.2
perineum, perineal (superficial) 682.2
  deep (with urethral involvement) 597.0
  urethra 597.0
periodontal (parietal) 523.31 ▲
  apical 522.5
periosteum, periosteal (see also Periostitis) 730.3 ☑
  with osteomyelitis (see also Osteomyelitis) 730.2 ☑
    acute or subacute 730.0 ☑
    chronic or old 730.1 ☑
peripleuritic 510.9
  with fistula 510.0
periproctic 566
periprostatic 601.2
perirectal (staphylococcal) 566
perirenal (tissue) (see also Abscess, kidney) 590.2
perisinuous (nose) (see also Sinusitis) 473.9
peritoneum, peritoneal (perforated) (ruptured) 567.22
  with
    abortion — see Abortion, by type, with sepsis
    appendicitis 540.1
    ectopic pregnancy (see also categories 633.0–633.9) 639.0
    molar pregnancy (see also categories 630–632) 639.0
  following
    abortion 639.0
    ectopic or molar pregnancy 639.0
  pelvic, female (see also Disease, pelvis, inflammatory) 614.4
    acute 614.3
  postoperative 998.59
  puerperal, postpartum, childbirth 670.0 ☑
  tuberculous (see also Tuberculosis) 014.0 ☑
peritonsillar 475
perityphlic 540.1
periureteral 593.89
periurethral 597.0
  gonococcal (acute) 098.0
    chronic or duration of 2 months or over 098.2
periuterine (see also Disease, pelvis, inflammatory) 614.4
  acute 614.3
perivesical 595.89
pernicious NEC 682.9
petrous bone — see Petrositis
phagedenic NEC 682.9
  chancroid 099.0
pharynx, pharyngeal (lateral) 478.29
phlegmonous NEC 682.9
pilonidal 685.0
pituitary (gland) 253.8

☑ Additional Digit Required — Refer to the Tabular List for Digit Selection
Subterms under main terms may continue to next column or page
4 — Volume 2 · October 2006
►◄ Revised Text
● New Line
▲ Revised Code
2007 ICD-9-CM

Abscess — *see also* Cellulitis — *continued*
- pleura 510.9
  - with fistula 510.0
- popliteal 682.6
- postanal 566
- postcecal 540.1
- postlaryngeal 478.79
- postnasal 478.19 ▲
- postpharyngeal 478.24
- posttonsillar 475
- posttyphoid 002.0
- Pott's (*see also* Tuberculosis) 015.0 ☑ *[730.88]*
- pouch of Douglas (chronic) (*see also* Disease, pelvis, inflammatory) 614.4
- premammary — *see* Abscess, breast
- prepatellar 682.6
- prostate (*see also* Prostatitis) 601.2
  - gonococcal (acute) 098.12
    - chronic or duration of 2 months or over 098.32
- psoas 567.31
  - nontuberculous 728.89
  - tuberculous (*see also* Tuberculosis) 015.0 ☑ *[730.88]*
- pterygopalatine fossa 682.8
- pubis 682.2
- puerperal — *see* Puerperal, abscess, by site
- pulmonary — *see* Abscess, lung
- pulp, pulpal (dental) 522.0
  - finger 681.01
  - toe 681.10
- pyemic — *see* Septicemia
- pyloric valve 535.0 ☑
- rectovaginal septum 569.5
- rectovesical 595.89
- rectum 566
- regional NEC 682.9
- renal (*see also* Abscess, kidney) 590.2
- retina 363.00
- retrobulbar 376.01
- retrocecal 567.22
- retrolaryngeal 478.79
- retromammary — *see* Abscess, breast
- retroperineal 682.2
- retroperitoneal 567.38
  - postprocedural 998.59 ●
- retropharyngeal 478.24
  - tuberculous (*see also* Tuberculosis) 012.8 ☑
- retrorectal 566
- retrouterine (*see also* Disease, pelvis, inflammatory) 614.4
  - acute 614.3
- retrovesical 595.89
- root, tooth 522.5
  - with sinus (alveolar) 522.7
- round ligament (*see also* Disease, pelvis, inflammatory) 614.4
  - acute 614.3
- rupture (spontaneous) NEC 682.9
- sacrum (tuberculous) (*see also* Tuberculosis) 015.0 ☑ *[730.88]*
  - nontuberculous 730.08
- salivary duct or gland 527.3
- scalp (any part) 682.8
- scapular 730.01
- sclera 379.09
- scrofulous (*see also* Tuberculosis) 017.2 ☑
- scrotum 608.4
- seminal vesicle 608.0
  - amebic 006.8
- septal, dental 522.5
  - with sinus (alveolar) 522.7
- septum (nasal) 478.19 ▲
- serous (*see also* Periostitis) 730.3 ☑
- shoulder 682.3
- side 682.2
- sigmoid 569.5
- sinus (accessory) (chronic) (nasal) (*see also* Sinusitis) 473.9
  - intracranial venous (any) 324.0

Abscess — *see also* Cellulitis — *continued*
- sinus (*see also* Sinusitis) — *continued*
  - intracranial venous — *continued*
    - late effect — *see* category 326
  - Skene's duct or gland 597.0
- skin NEC 682.9
  - tuberculous (primary) (*see also* Tuberculosis) 017.0 ☑
- sloughing NEC 682.9
- specified site NEC 682.8
  - amebic 006.8
- spermatic cord 608.4
- sphenoidal (sinus) (*see also* Sinusitis, sphenoidal) 473.3
- spinal
  - cord (any part) (staphylococcal) 324.1
    - tuberculous (*see also* Tuberculosis) 013.5 ☑
  - epidural 324.1
- spine (column) (tuberculous) (*see also* Tuberculosis) 015.0 ☑ *[730.88]*
  - nontuberculous 730.08
- spleen 289.59
  - amebic 006.8
- staphylococcal NEC 682.9
- stitch 998.59
- stomach (wall) 535.0 ☑
- strumous (tuberculous) (*see also* Tuberculosis) 017.2 ☑
- subarachnoid 324.9
  - brain 324.0
  - cerebral 324.0
  - late effect — *see* category 326
  - spinal cord 324.1
- subareolar (*see also* Abscess, breast)
  - puerperal, postpartum 675.1 ☑
- subcecal 540.1
- subcutaneous NEC 682.9
- subdiaphragmatic 567.22
- subdorsal 682.2
- subdural 324.9
  - brain 324.0
  - late effect — *see* category 326
  - spinal cord 324.1
- subgaleal 682.8
- subhepatic 567.22
- sublingual 528.3
  - gland 527.3
- submammary — *see* Abscess, breast
- submandibular (region) (space) (triangle) 682.0
  - gland 527.3
- submaxillary (region) 682.0
  - gland 527.3
- submental (pyogenic) 682.0
  - gland 527.3
- subpectoral 682.2
- subperiosteal — *see* Abscess, bone
- subperitoneal 567.22
- subphrenic (*see also* Abscess, peritoneum) 567.22
  - postoperative 998.59
- subscapular 682.2
- subungual 681.9
- suburethral 597.0
- sudoriparous 705.89
- suppurative NEC 682.9
- supraclavicular (fossa) 682.3
- suprahepatic 567.22
- suprapelvic (*see also* Disease, pelvis, inflammatory) 614.4
  - acute 614.3
- suprapubic 682.2
- suprarenal (capsule) (gland) 255.8
- sweat gland 705.89
- syphilitic 095.8
- teeth, tooth (root) 522.5
  - with sinus (alveolar) 522.7
  - supporting structures NEC 523.30 ▲
- temple 682.0
- temporal region 682.0

Abscess — *see also* Cellulitis — *continued*
- temporosphenoidal 324.0
  - late effect — *see* category 326
- tendon (sheath) 727.89
- testicle — *see* Orchitis
- thecal 728.89
- thigh (acquired) 682.6
- thorax 510.9
  - with fistula 510.0
- throat 478.29
- thumb (intrathecal) (periosteal) (subcutaneous) (subcuticular) 681.00
- thymus (gland) 254.1
- thyroid (gland) 245.0
- toe (any) (intrathecal) (periosteal) (subcutaneous) (subcuticular) 681.10
- tongue (staphylococcal) 529.0
- tonsil(s) (lingual) 475
- tonsillopharyngeal 475
- tooth, teeth (root) 522.5
  - with sinus (alveolar) 522.7
  - supporting structure NEC 523.30 ▲
- trachea 478.9
- trunk 682.2
- tubal (*see also* Salpingo-oophoritis) 614.2
- tuberculous — *see* Tuberculosis, abscess
- tubo-ovarian (*see also* Salpingo-oophoritis) 614.2
- tunica vaginalis 608.4
- umbilicus NEC 682.2
  - newborn 771.4
- upper arm 682.3
- upper respiratory 478.9
- urachus 682.2
- urethra (gland) 597.0
- urinary 597.0
- uterus, uterine (wall) (*see also* Endometritis) 615.9
  - ligament (*see also* Disease, pelvis, inflammatory) 614.4
    - acute 614.3
  - neck (*see also* Cervicitis) 616.0
- uvula 528.3
- vagina (wall) (*see also* Vaginitis) 616.10
- vaginorectal (*see also* Vaginitis) 616.10
- vas deferens 608.4
- vermiform appendix 540.1
- vertebra (column) (tuberculous) (*see also* Tuberculosis) 015.0 ☑ *[730.88]*
  - nontuberculous 730.0 ☑
- vesical 595.89
- vesicouterine pouch (*see also* Disease, pelvis, inflammatory) 614.4
- vitreous (humor) (pneumococcal) 360.04
- vocal cord 478.5
- von Bezold's 383.01
- vulva 616.4
  - complicating pregnancy, childbirth, or puerperium 646.6 ☑
- vulvovaginal gland (*see also* Vaginitis) 616.3
- web-space 682.4
- wrist 682.4

Absence (organ or part) (complete or partial)
- acoustic nerve 742.8
- adrenal (gland) (congenital) 759.1
  - acquired V45.79
- albumin (blood) 273.8
- alimentary tract (complete) (congenital) (partial) 751.8
  - lower 751.5
  - upper 750.8
- alpha-fucosidase 271.8
- alveolar process (acquired) 525.8
  - congenital 750.26

Absence — *continued*
- anus, anal (canal) (congenital) 751.2
- aorta (congenital) 747.22
- aortic valve (congenital) 746.89
- appendix, congenital 751.2
- arm (acquired) V49.60
  - above elbow V49.66
  - below elbow V49.65
  - congenital (*see also* Deformity, reduction, upper limb) 755.20
    - lower — *see* Absence, forearm, congenital
    - upper (complete) (partial) (with absence of distal elements, incomplete) 755.24
      - with
        - complete absence of distal elements 755.21
        - forearm (incomplete) 755.23
- artery (congenital) (peripheral) NEC (*see also* Anomaly, peripheral vascular system) 747.60
  - brain 747.81
  - cerebral 747.81
  - coronary 746.85
  - pulmonary 747.3
  - umbilical 747.5
- atrial septum 745.69
- auditory canal (congenital) (external) 744.01
- auricle (ear) (with stenosis or atresia of auditory canal), congenital 744.01
- bile, biliary duct (common) or passage (congenital) 751.61
- bladder (acquired) V45.74
  - congenital 753.8
- bone (congenital) NEC 756.9
  - marrow 284.9
    - acquired (secondary) 284.8
    - congenital 284.09 ▲
    - hereditary 284.09 ▲
    - idiopathic 284.9
  - skull 756.0
- bowel sounds 787.5
- brain 740.0
  - specified part 742.2
- breast(s) (acquired) V45.71
  - congenital 757.6
- broad ligament (congenital) 752.19
- bronchus (congenital) 748.3
- calvarium, calvaria (skull) 756.0
- canaliculus lacrimalis, congenital 743.65
- carpal(s) (congenital) (complete) (partial) (with absence of distal elements, incomplete) (*see also* Deformity, reduction, upper limb) 755.28
  - with complete absence of distal elements 755.21
- cartilage 756.9
- caudal spine 756.13
- cecum (acquired) (postoperative) (posttraumatic) V45.72
  - congenital 751.2
- cementum 520.4
- cerebellum (congenital) (vermis) 742.2
- cervix (acquired) (uteri) V45.77
  - congenital 752.49
- chin, congenital 744.89
- cilia (congenital) 743.63
  - acquired 374.89
- circulatory system, part NEC 747.89
- clavicle 755.51
- clitoris (congenital) 752.49
- coccyx, congenital 756.13
- cold sense (*see also* Disturbance, sensation) 782.0
- colon (acquired) (postoperative) V45.72
  - congenital 751.2
- congenital
  - lumen — *see* Atresia

☑ Additional Digit Required — Refer to the Tabular List for Digit Selection   ⱽᵉˢ Subterms under main terms may continue to next column or page

2007 ICD-9-CM   ▶◀ Revised Text   ● New Line   ▲ Revised Code   October 2006 · Volume 2 — 5

Absence — *continued*
  congenital — *continued*
    organ or site NEC — *see* Agenesis
    septum — *see* Imperfect, closure
  corpus callosum (congenital) 742.2
  cricoid cartilage 748.3
  diaphragm (congenital) (with hernia)
      756.6
    with obstruction 756.6
  digestive organ(s) or tract, congenital
      (complete) (partial) 751.8
    acquired V45.79
    lower 751.5
    upper 750.8
  ductus arteriosus 747.89
  duodenum (acquired) (postoperative)
      V45.72
    congenital 751.1
  ear, congenital 744.09
    acquired V45.79
    auricle 744.01
    external 744.01
    inner 744.05
    lobe, lobule 744.21
    middle, except ossicles 744.03
      ossicles 744.04
    ossicles 744.04
  ejaculatory duct (congenital) 752.89
  endocrine gland NEC (congenital)
      759.2
  epididymis (congenital) 752.89
    acquired V45.77
  epiglottis, congenital 748.3
  epileptic (atonic) (typical) (*see also*
      Epilepsy) 345.0 ☑
  erythrocyte 284.9
  erythropoiesis 284.9
    congenital 284.01 ▲
  esophagus (congenital) 750.3
  Eustachian tube (congenital) 744.24
  extremity (acquired)
    congenital (*see also* Deformity, re-
        duction) 755.4
    lower V49.70
    upper V49.60
  extrinsic muscle, eye 743.69
  eye (acquired) V45.78
    adnexa (congenital) 743.69
    congenital 743.00
    muscle (congenital) 743.69
  eyelid (fold), congenital 743.62
    acquired 374.89
  face
    bones NEC 756.0
    specified part NEC 744.89
  fallopian tube(s) (acquired) V45.77
    congenital 752.19
  femur, congenital (complete) (partial)
      (with absence of distal elements,
      incomplete) (*see also* Deformity,
      reduction, lower limb) 755.34
    with
      complete absence of distal ele-
          ments 755.31
      tibia and fibula (incomplete)
          755.33
  fibrin 790.92
  fibrinogen (congenital) 286.3
    acquired 286.6
  fibula, congenital (complete) (partial)
      (with absence of distal elements,
      incomplete) (*see also* Deformity,
      reduction, lower limb) 755.37
    with
      complete absence of distal ele-
          ments 755.31
      tibia 755.35
        with
          complete absence of distal
              elements 755.31
          femur (incomplete) 755.33
            with complete absence
                of distal ele-
                ments 755.31
  finger (acquired) V49.62

Absence — *continued*
  finger — *continued*
    congenital (complete) (partial) (*see
        also* Deformity, reduction,
        upper limb) 755.29
    meaning all fingers (complete)
        (partial) 755.21
    transverse 755.21
  fissures of lungs (congenital) 748.5
  foot (acquired) V49.73
    congenital (complete) 755.31
  forearm (acquired) V49.65
    congenital (complete) (partial) (with
        absence of distal elements,
        incomplete) (*see also* Deformi-
        ty, reduction, upper limb)
        755.25
    with
      complete absence of distal
          elements (hand and
          fingers) 755.21
      humerus (incomplete) 755.23
  fovea centralis 743.55
  fucosidase 271.8
  gallbladder (acquired) V45.79
    congenital 751.69
  gamma globulin (blood) 279.00
  genital organs
    acquired V45.77
    congenital
      female 752.89
        external 752.49
        internal NEC 752.89
      male 752.89
        penis 752.69
  genitourinary organs, congenital NEC
      752.89
  glottis 748.3
  gonadal, congenital NEC 758.6
  hair (congenital) 757.4
    acquired — *see* Alopecia
  hand (acquired) V49.63
    congenital (complete) (*see also* De-
        formity, reduction, upper
        limb) 755.21
  heart (congenital) 759.89
    acquired — *see* Status, organ re-
        placement
  heat sense (*see also* Disturbance,
      sensation) 782.0
  humerus, congenital (complete) (par-
      tial) (with absence of distal ele-
      ments, incomplete) (*see also*
      Deformity, reduction, upper
      limb) 755.24
    with
      complete absence of distal ele-
          ments 755.21
      radius and ulna (incomplete)
          755.23
  hymen (congenital) 752.49
  ileum (acquired) (postoperative) (post-
      traumatic) V45.72
    congenital 751.1
  immunoglobulin, isolated NEC 279.03
    IgA 279.01
    IgG 279.03
    IgM 279.02
  incus (acquired) 385.24
    congenital 744.04
  internal ear (congenital) 744.05
  intestine (acquired) (small) V45.72
    congenital 751.1
    large 751.2
    large V45.72
      congenital 751.2
  iris (congenital) 743.45
  jaw — *see* Absence, mandible
  jejunum (acquired) V45.72
    congenital 751.1
  joint, congenital NEC 755.8
  kidney(s) (acquired) V45.73
    congenital 753.0
  labium (congenital) (majus) (minus)
      752.49
  labyrinth, membranous 744.05

Absence — *continued*
  lacrimal apparatus (congenital) 743.65
  larynx (congenital) 748.3
  leg (acquired) V49.70
    above knee V49.76
    below knee V49.75
    congenital (partial) (unilateral) (*see
        also* Deformity, reduction,
        lower limb) 755.31
    lower (complete) (partial) (with
        absence of distal ele-
        ments, incomplete)
        755.35
      with
        complete absence of distal
            elements (foot and
            toes) 755.31
        thigh (incomplete) 755.33
          with complete absence
              of distal ele-
              ments 755.31
    upper — *see* Absence, femur
  lens (congenital) 743.35
    acquired 379.31
  ligament, broad (congenital) 752.19
  limb (acquired)
    congenital (complete) (partial) (*see
        also* Deformity, reduction)
        755.4
    lower 755.30
      complete 755.31
      incomplete 755.32
      longitudinal — *see* Deficien-
          cy, lower limb, longitu-
          dinal
      transverse 755.31
    upper 755.20
      complete 755.21
      incomplete 755.22
      longitudinal — *see* Deficien-
          cy, upper limb, longitu-
          dinal
      transverse 755.21
    lower NEC V49.70
    upper NEC V49.60
  lip 750.26
  liver (congenital) (lobe) 751.69
  lumbar (congenital) (vertebra) 756.13
    isthmus 756.11
    pars articularis 756.11
  lumen — *see* Atresia
  lung (bilateral) (congenital) (fissure)
      (lobe) (unilateral) 748.5
    acquired (any part) V45.76
  mandible (congenital) 524.09
  maxilla (congenital) 524.09
  menstruation 626.0
  metacarpal(s), congenital (complete)
      (partial) (with absence of distal
      elements, incomplete) (*see also*
      Deformity, reduction, upper
      limb) 755.28
    with all fingers, complete 755.21
  metatarsal(s), congenital (complete)
      (partial) (with absence of distal
      elements, incomplete) (*see also*
      Deformity, reduction, lower
      limb) 755.38
    with complete absence of distal el-
        ements 755.31
  muscle (congenital) (pectoral) 756.81
    ocular 743.69
  musculoskeletal system (congenital)
      NEC 756.9
  nail(s) (congenital) 757.5
  neck, part 744.89
  nerve 742.8
  nervous system, part NEC 742.8
  neutrophil 288.00   ▲
  nipple (congenital) 757.6
  nose (congenital) 748.1
    acquired 738.0
  nuclear 742.8
  ocular muscle (congenital) 743.69
  organ
    of Corti (congenital) 744.05

Absence — *continued*
  organ — *continued*
    or site
      acquired V45.79
      congenital NEC 759.89
  osseous meatus (ear) 744.03
  ovary (acquired) V45.77
    congenital 752.0
  oviduct (acquired) V45.77
    congenital 752.19
  pancreas (congenital) 751.7
    acquired (postoperative) (posttrau-
        matic) V45.79
  parathyroid gland (congenital) 759.2
  parotid gland(s) (congenital) 750.21
  patella, congenital 755.64
  pelvic girdle (congenital) 755.69
  penis (congenital) 752.69
    acquired V45.77
  pericardium (congenital) 746.89
  perineal body (congenital) 756.81
  phalange(s), congenital 755.4
    lower limb (complete) (intercalary)
        (partial) (terminal) (*see also*
        Deformity, reduction, lower
        limb) 755.39
      meaning all toes (complete)
          (partial) 755.31
      transverse 755.31
    upper limb (complete) (intercalary)
        (partial) (terminal) (*see also*
        Deformity, reduction, upper
        limb) 755.29
      meaning all digits (complete)
          (partial) 755.21
      transverse 755.21
  pituitary gland (congenital) 759.2
  postoperative — *see* Absence, by site,
      acquired
  prostate (congenital) 752.89
    acquired V45.77
  pulmonary
    artery 747.3
    trunk 747.3
    valve (congenital) 746.01
    vein 747.49
  punctum lacrimale (congenital) 743.65
  radius, congenital (complete) (partial)
      (with absence of distal elements,
      incomplete) 755.26
    with
      complete absence of distal ele-
          ments 755.21
      ulna 755.25
        with
          complete absence of distal
              elements 755.21
          humerus (incomplete)
              755.23
  ray, congenital 755.4
    lower limb (complete) (partial) (*see
        also* Deformity, reduction,
        lower limb) 755.38
      meaning all rays 755.31
      transverse 755.31
    upper limb (complete) (partial) (*see
        also* Deformity, reduction,
        upper limb) 755.28
      meaning all rays 755.21
      transverse 755.21
  rectum (congenital) 751.2
    acquired V45.79
  red cell 284.9
    acquired (secondary) 284.8
    congenital 284.01   ▲
    hereditary 284.01   ▲
    idiopathic 284.9
  respiratory organ (congenital) NEC
      748.9
  rib (acquired) 738.3
    congenital 756.3
  roof of orbit (congenital) 742.0
  round ligament (congenital) 752.89
  sacrum, congenital 756.13
  salivary gland(s) (congenital) 750.21
  scapula 755.59

☑ Additional Digit Required — Refer to the Tabular List for Digit Selection   ▽ Subterms under main terms may continue to next column or page

6 — Volume 2 · October 2006   ▶◀ Revised Text   ● New Line   ▲ Revised Code   *2007 ICD-9-CM*

Absence — *continued*
 scrotum, congenital 752.89
 seminal tract or duct (congenital)
  752.89
  acquired V45.77
 septum (congenital) (*see also* Imperfect, closure, septum)
  atrial 745.69
   and ventricular 745.7
  between aorta and pulmonary
   artery 745.0
  ventricular 745.3
   and atrial 745.7
 sex chromosomes 758.81
 shoulder girdle, congenital (complete)
  (partial) 755.59
 skin (congenital) 757.39
 skull bone 756.0
  with
   anencephalus 740.0
   encephalocele 742.0
   hydrocephalus 742.3
    with spina bifida (*see also*
     Spina bifida) 741.0 ☑
   microcephalus 742.1
 spermatic cord (congenital) 752.89
 spinal cord 742.59
 spine, congenital 756.13
 spleen (congenital) 759.0
  acquired V45.79
 sternum, congenital 756.3
 stomach (acquired) (partial) (postoperative) V45.75
  with postgastric surgery syndrome
   564.2
  congenital 750.7
 submaxillary gland(s) (congenital)
  750.21
 superior vena cava (congenital) 747.49
 tarsal(s), congenital (complete) (partial)
  (with absence of distal elements,
  incomplete) (*see also* Deformity,
  reduction, lower limb) 755.38
 teeth, tooth (congenital) 520.0
  with abnormal spacing 524.30
  acquired 525.10
   with malocclusion 524.30
   due to
    caries 525.13
    extraction 525.10
    periodontal disease 525.12
    trauma 525.11
 tendon (congenital) 756.81
 testis (congenital) 752.89
  acquired V45.77
 thigh (acquired) 736.89
 thumb (acquired) V49.61
  congenital 755.29
 thymus gland (congenital) 759.2
 thyroid (gland) (surgical) 246.8
  with hypothyroidism 244.0
  cartilage, congenital 748.3
  congenital 243
 tibia, congenital (complete) (partial)
  (with absence of distal elements,
  incomplete) (*see also* Deformity,
  reduction, lower limb) 755.36
  with
   complete absence of distal elements 755.31
   fibula 755.35
    with
     complete absence of distal
      elements 755.31
     femur (incomplete) 755.33
      with complete absence
       of distal elements 755.31
 toe (acquired) V49.72
  congenital (complete) (partial)
   755.39
   meaning all toes 755.31
   transverse 755.31
  great V49.71
 tongue (congenital) 750.11
 tooth, teeth (congenital) 520.0

Absence — *continued*
 tooth, teeth — *continued*
  with abnormal spacing 524.30
  acquired 525.10
   with malocclusion 524.30
   due to
    caries 525.13
    extraction 525.10
    periodontal disease 525.12
    trauma 525.11
 trachea (cartilage) (congenital) (rings)
  748.3
 transverse aortic arch (congenital)
  747.21
 tricuspid valve 746.1
 ulna, congenital (complete) (partial)
  (with absence of distal elements,
  incomplete) (*see also* Deformity,
  reduction, upper limb) 755.27
  with
   complete absence of distal elements 755.21
   radius 755.25
    with
     complete absence of distal
      elements 755.21
     humerus (incomplete)
      755.23
 umbilical artery (congenital) 747.5
 ureter (congenital) 753.4
  acquired V45.74
 urethra, congenital 753.8
  acquired V45.74
 urinary system, part NEC, congenital
  753.8
  acquired V45.74
 uterus (acquired) V45.77
  congenital 752.3
 uvula (congenital) 750.26
 vagina, congenital 752.49
  acquired V45.77
 vas deferens (congenital) 752.89
  acquired V45.77
 vein (congenital) (peripheral) NEC (*see
  also* Anomaly, peripheral vascular system) 747.60
  brain 747.81
  great 747.49
  portal 747.49
  pulmonary 747.49
 vena cava (congenital) (inferior) (superior) 747.49
 ventral horn cell 742.59
 ventricular septum 745.3
 vermis of cerebellum 742.2
 vertebra, congenital 756.13
 vulva, congenital 752.49
Absentia epileptica — *see also* Epilepsy
 345.0 ☑
Absinthemia — *see also* Dependence
 304.6 ☑
Absinthism — *see also* Dependence
 304.6 ☑
Absorbent system disease 459.89
Absorption
 alcohol, through placenta or breast
  milk 760.71
 antibiotics, through placenta or breast
  milk 760.74
 anticonvulsants, through placenta or
  breast milk 760.77
 antifungals, through placenta or
  breast milk 760.74
 anti-infective, through placenta or
  breast milk 760.74
 antimetabolics, through placenta or
  breast milk 760.78
 chemical NEC 989.9
  specified chemical or substance —
   see Table of Drugs and
   Chemicals
  through placenta or breast milk
   (fetus or newborn) 760.70
   alcohol 760.71
   anticonvulsants 760.77
   antifungals 760.74

Absorption — *continued*
 chemical — *continued*
  through placenta or breast milk —
   continued
   anti-infective agents 760.74
   antimetabolics 760.78
   cocaine 760.75
   "crack" 760.75
   diethylstilbestrol [DES] 760.76
   hallucinogenic agents 760.73
   medicinal agents NEC 760.79
   narcotics 760.72
   obstetric anesthetic or analgesic
    drug 763.5
   specified agent NEC 760.79
   suspected, affecting management of pregnancy
    655.5 ☑
 cocaine, through placenta or breast
  milk 760.75
 drug NEC (*see also* Reaction, drug)
  through placenta or breast milk
   (fetus or newborn) 760.70
   alcohol 760.71
   anticonvulsants 760.77
   antifungals 760.74
   anti-infective agents 760.74
   antimetabolics 760.78
   cocaine 760.75
   "crack" 760.75
   diethylstilbestrol [DES] 760.76
   hallucinogenic agents 760.73
   medicinal agents NEC 760.79
   narcotics 760.72
   obstetric anesthetic or analgesic
    drug 763.5
   specified agent NEC 760.79
   suspected, affecting management of pregnancy
    655.5 ☑
 fat, disturbance 579.8
 hallucinogenic agents, through placenta or breast milk 760.73
 immune sera, through placenta or
  breast milk 760.79
 lactose defect 271.3
 medicinal agents NEC, through placenta or breast milk 760.79
 narcotics, through placenta or breast
  milk 760.72
 noxious substance — *see* Absorption,
  chemical
 protein, disturbance 579.8
 pus or septic, general — *see* Septicemia
 quinine, through placenta or breast
  milk 760.74
 toxic substance — *see* Absorption,
  chemical
 uremic — *see* Uremia
Abstinence symptoms or syndrome
 alcohol 291.81
 drug 292.0
Abt-Letterer-Siwe syndrome (acute
 histiocytosis X) (M9722/3) 202.5 ☑
Abulia 799.89
Abulomania 301.6
Abuse
 adult 995.80
  emotional 995.82
  multiple forms 995.85
  neglect (nutritional) 995.84
  physical 995.81
  psychological 995.82
  sexual 995.83
 alcohol — *see also* Alcoholism
  305.0 ☑
  dependent 303.9 ☑
  non-dependent 305.0 ☑
 child 995.50
  counseling
   perpetrator
    non-parent V62.83
    parent V61.22
   victim V61.21
  emotional 995.51

Abuse — *continued*
 child — *continued*
  multiple forms 995.59
  neglect (nutritional) 995.52
  physical 995.54
   shaken infant syndrome 995.55
  psychological 995.51
  sexual 995.53
 drugs, nondependent 305.9 ☑

> *Note* — *Use the following fifth-digit
> subclassification with the following
> codes: 305.0, 305.2–305.9:*
>
> 0   *unspecified*
>
> 1   *continuous*
>
> 2   *episodic*
>
> 3   *in remission*

  amphetamine type 305.7 ☑
  antidepressants 305.8 ☑
  anxiolytic 305.4 ☑
  barbiturates 305.4 ☑
  caffeine 305.9 ☑
  cannabis 305.2 ☑
  cocaine type 305.6 ☑
  hallucinogens 305.3 ☑
  hashish 305.2 ☑
  hypnotic 305.4 ☑
  inhalant 305.9 ☑
  LSD 305.3 ☑
  marijuana 305.2 ☑
  mixed 305.9 ☑
  morphine type 305.5 ☑
  opioid type 305.5 ☑
  phencyclidine (PCP) 305.9 ☑
  sedative 305.4 ☑
  specified NEC 305.9 ☑
  tranquilizers 305.4 ☑
 spouse 995.80
 tobacco 305.1
Acalcerosis 275.40
Acalcicosis 275.40
Acalculia 784.69
 developmental 315.1
Acanthocheilonemiasis 125.4
Acanthocytosis 272.5
Acanthokeratodermia 701.1
Acantholysis 701.8
 bullosa 757.39
Acanthoma (benign) (M8070/0) — *see
 also* Neoplasm, by site, benign
 malignant (M8070/3) — *see* Neoplasm, by site, malignant
Acanthosis (acquired) (nigricans) 701.2
 adult 701.2
 benign (congenital) 757.39
 congenital 757.39
 glycogenic
  esophagus 530.89
 juvenile 701.2
 tongue 529.8
Acanthrocytosis 272.5
Acapnia 276.3
Acarbia 276.2
Acardia 759.89
Acardiacus amorphus 759.89
Acardiotrophia 429.1
Acardius 759.89
Acariasis 133.9
 sarcoptic 133.0
Acaridiasis 133.9
Acarinosis 133.9
Acariosis 133.9
Acarodermatitis 133.9
 urticarioides 133.9
Acarophobia 300.29
Acatalasemia 277.89
Acatalasia 277.89
Acatamathesia 784.69
Acataphasia 784.5
Acathisia 781.0
 due to drugs 333.99
Acceleration, accelerated
 atrioventricular conduction 426.7
 idioventricular rhythm 427.89

☑ Additional Digit Required — Refer to the Tabular List for Digit Selection   ⑂ Subterms under main terms may continue to next column or page

2007 ICD-9-CM   ▶◀ Revised Text   ● New Line   ▲ Revised Code   Volume 2 — 7

Accessory (congenital)
adrenal gland 759.1
anus 751.5
appendix 751.5
atrioventricular conduction 426.7
auditory ossicles 744.04
auricle (ear) 744.1
autosome(s) NEC 758.5
21 or 22 758.0
biliary duct or passage 751.69
bladder 753.8
blood vessels (peripheral) (congenital)
NEC (see also Anomaly, peripheral vascular system) 747.60
cerebral 747.81
coronary 746.85
bone NEC 756.9
foot 755.67
breast tissue, axilla 757.6
carpal bones 755.56
cecum 751.5
cervix 752.49
chromosome(s) NEC 758.5
13-15 758.1
16-18 758.2
21 or 22 758.0
autosome(s) NEC 758.5
D₁ 758.1
E₃ 758.2
G 758.0
sex 758.81
coronary artery 746.85
cusp(s), heart valve NEC 746.89
pulmonary 746.09
cystic duct 751.69
digits 755.00
ear (auricle) (lobe) 744.1
endocrine gland NEC 759.2
external os 752.49
eyelid 743.62
eye muscle 743.69
face bone(s) 756.0
fallopian tube (fimbria) (ostium) 752.19
fingers 755.01
foreskin 605
frontonasal process 756.0
gallbladder 751.69
genital organ(s)
female 752.89
external 752.49
internal NEC 752.89
male NEC 752.89
penis 752.69
genitourinary organs NEC 752.89
heart 746.89
valve NEC 746.89
pulmonary 746.09
hepatic ducts 751.69
hymen 752.49
intestine (large) (small) 751.5
kidney 753.3
lacrimal canal 743.65
leaflet, heart valve NEC 746.89
pulmonary 746.09
ligament, broad 752.19
liver (duct) 751.69
lobule (ear) 744.1
lung (lobe) 748.69
muscle 756.82
navicular of carpus 755.56
nervous system, part NEC 742.8
nipple 757.6
nose 748.1
organ or site NEC — see Anomaly, specified type NEC
ovary 752.0
oviduct 752.19
pancreas 751.7
parathyroid gland 759.2
parotid gland (and duct) 750.22
pituitary gland 759.2
placental lobe — see Placenta, abnormal
preauricular appendage 744.1
prepuce 605

Accessory — continued
renal arteries (multiple) 747.62
rib 756.3
cervical 756.2
roots (teeth) 520.2
salivary gland 750.22
sesamoids 755.8
sinus — see condition
skin tags 757.39
spleen 759.0
sternum 756.3
submaxillary gland 750.22
tarsal bones 755.67
teeth, tooth 520.1
causing crowding 524.31
tendon 756.89
thumb 755.01
thymus gland 759.2
thyroid gland 759.2
toes 755.02
tongue 750.13
tragus 744.1
ureter 753.4
urethra 753.8
urinary organ or tract NEC 753.8
uterus 752.2
vagina 752.49
valve, heart NEC 746.89
pulmonary 746.09
vertebra 756.19
vocal cords 748.3
vulva 752.49
Accident, accidental — see also condition
birth NEC 767.9
cardiovascular (see also Disease, cardiovascular) 429.2
cerebral (see also Disease, cerebrovascular, acute) 434.91
cerebrovascular (current) (CVA) (see also Disease, cerebrovascular, acute) 434.91
embolic 434.11
healed or old V12.59
hemorrhagic — see Hemorrhage, brain
impending 435.9
ischemic 434.91
late effect — see Late effect(s) (of) cerebrovascular disease
postoperative 997.02
thrombotic 434.01
coronary (see also Infarct, myocardium) 410.9 ☑
craniovascular (see also Disease, cerebrovascular, acute) 436
during pregnancy, to mother, affecting fetus or newborn 760.5
heart, cardiac (see also Infarct, myocardium) 410.9 ☑
intrauterine 779.89
vascular — see Disease, cerebrovascular, acute
Accommodation
disorder of 367.51
drug-induced 367.89
toxic 367.89
insufficiency of 367.4
paralysis of 367.51
hysterical 300.11
spasm of 367.53
Accouchement — see Delivery
Accreta placenta (without hemorrhage) 667.0 ☑
with hemorrhage 666.0 ☑
Accretio cordis (nonrheumatic) 423.1
Accretions on teeth 523.6
Accumulation secretion, prostate 602.8
Acephalia, acephalism, acephaly 740.0
Acephalic 740.0
Acephalobrachia 759.89
Acephalocardia 759.89
Acephalocardius 759.89
Acephalochiria 759.89
Acephalochirus 759.89
Acephalogaster 759.89

Acephalostomus 759.89
Acephalothorax 759.89
Acephalus 740.0
Acetonemia 790.6
diabetic 250.1 ☑
Acetonglycosuria 982.8
Acetonuria 791.6
Achalasia 530.0
cardia 530.0
digestive organs congenital NEC 751.8
esophagus 530.0
pelvirectal 751.3
psychogenic 306.4
pylorus 750.5
sphincteral NEC 564.89
Achard-Thiers syndrome (adrenogenital) 255.2
Ache(s) — see Pain
Acheilia 750.26
Acheiria 755.21
Achillobursitis 726.71
Achillodynia 726.71
Achlorhydria, achlorhydric 536.0
anemia 280.9
diarrhea 536.0
neurogenic 536.0
postvagotomy 564.2
psychogenic 306.4
secondary to vagotomy 564.2
Achloroblepsia 368.52
Achloropsia 368.52
Acholia 575.8
Acholuric jaundice (familial) (splenomegalic) — see also Spherocytosis 282.0
acquired 283.9
Achondroplasia 756.4
Achrestic anemia 281.8
Achroacytosis, lacrimal gland 375.00
tuberculous (see also Tuberculosis) 017.3 ☑
Achroma, cutis 709.00
Achromate (congenital) 368.54
Achromatopia 368.54
Achromatopsia (congenital) 368.54
Achromia
congenital 270.2
parasitica 111.0
unguium 703.8
Achylia
gastrica 536.8
neurogenic 536.3
psychogenic 306.4
pancreatica 577.1
Achylosis 536.8
Acid
burn (see also Burn, by site)
from swallowing acid — see Burn, internal organs
deficiency
amide nicotinic 265.2
amino 270.9
ascorbic 267
folic 266.2
nicotinic (amide) 265.2
pantothenic 266.2
intoxication 276.2
peptic disease 536.8
stomach 536.8
psychogenic 306.4
Acidemia 276.2
arginosuccinic 270.6
fetal
affecting management of pregnancy 656.3 ☑
before onset of labor, in liveborn infant 768.2
during labor ▶and delivery◀ in liveborn infant 768.3
intrauterine 656.3 ☑
unspecified as to time of onset, in liveborn infant 768.4
newborn 775.81 ●
pipecolic 270.7
Acidity, gastric (high) (low) 536.8
psychogenic 306.4

Acidocytopenia 288.59 ▲
Acidocytosis 288.3
Acidopenia 288.59 ▲
Acidosis 276.2
diabetic 250.1 ☑
fetal, affecting management of pregnancy 756.8 ☑
fetal, affecting newborn 775.81 ▲
kidney tubular 588.89
newborn 775.81 ●
lactic 276.2
metabolic NEC 276.2
with respiratory acidosis 276.4
of newborn 775.81 ●
late, of newborn 775.7
newborn 775.81 ●
renal
hyperchloremic 588.89
tubular (distal) (proximal) 588.89
respiratory 276.2
complicated by
metabolic acidosis 276.4
of newborn 775.81 ●
metabolic alkalosis 276.4
Aciduria 791.9
arginosuccinic 270.6
beta-aminoisobutyric (BAIB) 277.2
glutaric
type I 270.7
type II (type IIA, IIB, IIC) 277.85
type III 277.86
glycolic 271.8
methylmalonic 270.3
with glycinemia 270.7
organic 270.9
orotic (congenital) (hereditary) (pyrimidine deficiency) 281.4
Acladiosis 111.8
skin 111.8
Aclasis
diaphyseal 756.4
tarsoepiphyseal 756.59
Acleistocardia 745.5
Aclusion 524.4
Acmesthesia 782.0
Acne (pustular) (vulgaris) 706.1
agminata (see also Tuberculosis) 017.0 ☑
artificialis 706.1
atrophica 706.0
cachecticorum (Hebra) 706.1
conglobata 706.1
conjunctiva 706.1
cystic 706.1
decalvans 704.09
erythematosa 695.3
eyelid 706.1
frontalis 706.0
indurata 706.1
keloid 706.1
lupoid 706.0
necrotic, necrotica 706.0
miliaris 704.8
neonatal 706.1
nodular 706.1
occupational 706.1
papulosa 706.1
rodens 706.0
rosacea 695.3
scorbutica 267
scrofulosorum (Bazin) (see also Tuberculosis) 017.0 ☑
summer 692.72
tropical 706.1
varioliformis 706.0
Acneiform drug eruptions 692.3
Acnitis (primary) — see also Tuberculosis 017.0 ☑
Acomia 704.00
Acontractile bladder 344.61
Aconuresis — see also Incontinence 788.30
Acosta's disease 993.2 ●
Acousma 780.1
Acoustic — see condition
Acousticophobia 300.29

Acquired — see condition
Acquired immune deficiency syndrome
— see Human immunodeficiency
virus (disease) (illness) (infection)
Acquired immunodeficiency syndrome
— see Human immunodeficiency
virus (disease) (illness) (infection)
Acragnosis 781.99
Acrania 740.0
Acroagnosis 781.99
Acroasphyxia, chronic 443.89
Acrobrachycephaly 756.0
Acrobystiolith 608.89
Acrobystitis 607.2
Acrocephalopolysyndactyly 755.55
Acrocephalosyndactyly 755.55
Acrocephaly 756.0
Acrochondrohyperplasia 759.82
Acrocyanosis 443.89
  newborn 770.83
    meaning transient blue hands and
feet — omit code
Acrodermatitis 686.8
  atrophicans (chronica) 701.8
  continua (Hallopeau) 696.1
  enteropathica 686.8
  Hallopeau's 696.1
  perstans 696.1
  pustulosa continua 696.1
  recalcitrant pustular 696.1
Acrodynia 985.0
Acrodysplasia 755.55
Acrohyperhidrosis — see also Hyper-
hidrosis 780.8
Acrokeratosis verruciformis 757.39
Acromastitis 611.0
Acromegaly, acromegalia (skin) 253.0
Acromelalgia 443.82
Acromicria, acromikria 756.59
Acronyx 703.0
Acropachyderma 757.39
Acropachy, thyroid — see also Thyrotox-
icosis 242.9 ☑
Acroparesthesia 443.89
  simple (Schultz's type) 443.89
  vasomotor (Nothnagel's type) 443.89
Acropathy thyroid — see also Thyrotox-
icosis 242.9 ☑
Acrophobia 300.29
Acroposthitis 607.2
Acroscleriasis — see also Scleroderma
710.1
Acroscleroderma — see also Scleroder-
ma 710.1
Acrosclerosis — see also Scleroderma
710.1
Acrosphacelus 785.4
Acrosphenosyndactylia 755.55
Acrospiroma, eccrine (M8402/0) — see
Neoplasm, skin, benign
Acrostealgia 732.9
Acrosyndactyly — see also Syndactylism
755.10
Acrotrophodynia 991.4
Actinic — see also condition
  cheilitis (due to sun) 692.72
    chronic NEC 692.74
    due to radiation, except from sun
692.82
  conjunctivitis 370.24
  dermatitis (due to sun) (see also Dermatitis, actinic) 692.70
  due to
    roentgen rays or radioactive
substance 692.82
    ultraviolet radiation, except
from sun 692.82
    sun NEC 692.70
  elastosis solare 692.74
  granuloma 692.73
  keratitis 370.24
  ophthalmia 370.24
  reticuloid 692.73
Actinobacillosis, general 027.8
Actinobacillus
  lignieresii 027.8

Actinobacillus — continued
  mallei 024
  muris 026.1
Actinocutitis NEC — see also Dermatitis, actinic 692.70
Actinodermatitis NEC — see also Dermatitis, actinic 692.70
Actinomyces
  israelii (infection) — see Actinomycosis
  muris-ratti (infection) 026.1
Actinomycosis, actinomycotic 039.9
  with
    pneumonia 039.1
  abdominal 039.2
  cervicofacial 039.3
  cutaneous 039.0
  pulmonary 039.1
  specified site NEC 039.8
  thoracic 039.1
Actinoneuritis 357.89
Action, heart
  disorder 427.9
    postoperative 997.1
  irregular 427.9
    postoperative 997.1
    psychogenic 306.2
Active — see condition
Activity decrease, functional 780.99
Acute — see also condition
  abdomen NEC 789.0 ☑
  gallbladder (see also Cholecystitis,
acute) 575.0
Acyanoblepsia 368.53
Acyanopsia 368.53
Acystia 753.8
Acystinervia — see Neurogenic, bladder
Acystineuria — see Neurogenic, bladder
Adactylia, adactyly (congenital) 755.4
  lower limb (complete) (intercalary)
(partial) (terminal) (see also Deformity, reduction, lower limb)
755.39
    meaning all digits (complete) (par-
tial) 755.31
    transverse (complete) (partial)
755.31
  upper limb (complete) (intercalary)
(partial) (terminal) (see also Deformity, reduction, upper limb)
755.29
    meaning all digits (complete) (par-
tial) 755.21
    transverse (complete) (partial)
755.21
Adair-Dighton syndrome (brittle bones
and blue sclera, deafness) 756.51
Adamantinoblastoma (M9310/0) — see
Ameloblastoma
Adamantinoma (M9310/0) — see
Ameloblastoma
Adamantoblastoma (M9310/0) — see
Ameloblastoma
**Adams-Stokes (-Morgagni) disease or
syndrome** (syncope with heart
block) 426.9
Adaptation reaction — see also Reaction, adjustment 309.9
Addiction — see also Dependence
  absinthe 304.6 ☑
  alcoholic (ethyl) (methyl) (wood)
303.9 ☑
    complicating pregnancy, childbirth,
or puerperium 648.4 ☑
      affecting fetus or newborn
760.71
    suspected damage to fetus affecting
management of pregnancy
655.4 ☑
  drug (see also Dependence) 304.9 ☑
  ethyl alcohol 303.9 ☑
  heroin 304.0 ☑
  hospital 301.51
  methyl alcohol 303.9 ☑
  methylated spirit 303.9 ☑
  morphine (-like substances) 304.0 ☑
  nicotine 305.1

Addiction — see also Dependence —
continued
  opium 304.0 ☑
  tobacco 305.1
  wine 303.9 ☑
Addison's
  anemia (pernicious) 281.0
  disease (bronze) (primary adrenal insufficiency) 255.4
    tuberculous (see also Tuberculosis)
017.6 ☑
  keloid (morphea) 701.0
  melanoderma (adrenal cortical hypofunction) 255.4
Addison-Biermer anemia (pernicious)
281.0
Addison-Gull disease — see Xanthoma
Addisonian crisis or melanosis (acute
adrenocortical insufficiency) 255.4
Additional — see also Accessory
  chromosome(s) 758.5
    13-15 758.1
    16-18 758.2
    21 758.0
    autosome(s) NEC 758.5
    sex 758.81
**Adduction contracture, hip or other
joint** — see Contraction, joint
ADEM (acute disseminated encephalomyelitis) (postinfectious)
136.9 [323.61] ▲
  infectious 136.9 [323.61] ▲
  noninfectious 323.81 ▲
Adenasthenia gastrica 536.0
Aden fever 061
Adenitis — see also Lymphadenitis
289.3
  acute, unspecified site 683
    epidemic infectious 075
  axillary 289.3
    acute 683
    chronic or subacute 289.1
  Bartholin's gland 616.89 ▲
  bulbourethral gland (see also Urethritis) 597.89
  cervical 289.3
    acute 683
    chronic or subacute 289.1
  chancroid (Ducrey's bacillus) 099.0
  chronic (any lymph node, except
mesenteric) 289.1
    mesenteric 289.2
  Cowper's gland (see also Urethritis)
597.89
  epidemic, acute 075
  gangrenous 683
  gonorrheal NEC 098.89
  groin 289.3
    acute 683
    chronic or subacute 289.1
  infectious 075
  inguinal (region) 289.3
    acute 683
    chronic or subacute 289.1
  lymph gland or node, except mesenteric 289.3
    acute 683
    chronic or subacute 289.1
    mesenteric (acute) (chronic) (non-
specific) (subacute) 289.2
  mesenteric (acute) (chronic) (nonspecific) (subacute) 289.2
    due to Pasteurella multocida (P.
septica) 027.2
  parotid gland (suppurative) 527.2
  phlegmonous 683
  salivary duct or gland (any) (recurring)
(suppurative) 527.2
  scrofulous (see also Tuberculosis)
017.2 ☑
  septic 289.3
  Skene's duct or gland (see also Urethritis) 597.89
  strumous, tuberculous (see also Tuberculosis) 017.2 ☑
  subacute, unspecified site 289.1

Adenitis — see also Lymphadenitis —
continued
  sublingual gland (suppurative) 527.2
  submandibular gland (suppurative)
527.2
  submaxillary gland (suppurative)
527.2
  suppurative 683
  tuberculous — see Tuberculosis,
lymph gland
  urethral gland (see also Urethritis)
597.89
  venereal NEC 099.8
  Wharton's duct (suppurative) 527.2
Adenoacanthoma (M8570/3) — see
Neoplasm, by site, malignant
Adenoameloblastoma (M9300/0) 213.1
  upper jaw (bone) 213.0
Adenocarcinoma (M8140/3) — see also
Neoplasm, by site, malignant

Note — The list of adjectival modifiers
below is not exhaustive. A description
of adenocarcinoma that does not appear
in this list should be coded in the same
manner as carcinoma with that description. Thus, "mixed acidophil-basophil
adenocarcinoma," should be coded in
the same manner as "mixed acidophil-
basophil carcinoma," which appears in
the list under "Carcinoma."

Except where otherwise indicated, the
morphological varieties of adenocarcinoma in the list below should be coded by
site as for "Neoplasm, malignant."

---

  with
    apocrine metaplasia (M8573/3)
    cartilaginous (and osseous) meta-
plasia (M8571/3)
    osseous (and cartilaginous) meta-
plasia (M8571/3)
    spindle cell metaplasia (M8572/3)
    squamous metaplasia (M8570/3)
  acidophil (M8280/3)
    specified site — see Neoplasm, by
site, malignant
    unspecified site 194.3
  acinar (M8550/3)
  acinic cell (M8550/3)
  adrenal cortical (M8370/3) 194.0
  alveolar (M8251/3)
  and
    epidermoid carcinoma, mixed
(M8560/3)
    squamous cell carcinoma,
mixed (M8560/3)
  apocrine (M8401/3)
    breast — see Neoplasm, breast,
malignant
    specified site NEC — see Neoplasm,
skin, malignant
    unspecified site 173.9
  basophil (M8300/3)
    specified site — see Neoplasm, by
site, malignant
    unspecified site 194.3
  bile duct type (M8160/3)
    liver 155.1
    specified site NEC — see Neoplasm,
by site, malignant
    unspecified site 155.1
  bronchiolar (M8250/3) — see Neoplasm, lung, malignant
  ceruminous (M8420/3) 173.2
  chromophobe (M8270/3)
    specified site — see Neoplasm, by
site, malignant
    unspecified site 194.3
  clear cell (mesonephroid type)
(M8310/3)
  colloid (M8480/3)
  cylindroid type (M8200/3)
  diffuse type (M8145/3)
    specified site — see Neoplasm, by
site, malignant
    unspecified site 151.9

☑ Additional Digit Required — Refer to the Tabular List for Digit Selection   Subterms under main terms may continue to next column or page

2007 ICD-9-CM   ▶◀ Revised Text   ● New Line   ▲ Revised Code   **October 2006 · Volume 2 — 9**

Adenocarcinoma — *see also* Neoplasm, by site, malignant — *continued*
duct (infiltrating) (M8500/3)
  with Paget's disease (M8541/3) — *see* Neoplasm, breast, malignant
  specified site — *see* Neoplasm, by site, malignant
  unspecified site 174.9
embryonal (M9070/3)
endometrioid (M8380/3) — *see* Neoplasm, by site, malignant
eosinophil (M8280/3)
  specified site — *see* Neoplasm, by site, malignant
  unspecified site 194.3
follicular (M8330/3)
  and papillary (M8340/3) 193
  moderately differentiated type (M8332/3) 193
  pure follicle type (M8331/3) 193
  specified site — *see* Neoplasm, by site, malignant
  trabecular type (M8332/3) 193
  unspecified type 193
  well differentiated type (M8331/3) 193
gelatinous (M8480/3)
granular cell (M8320/3)
Hürthle cell (M8290/3) 193
in
  adenomatous
    polyp (M8210/3)
    polyposis coli (M8220/3) 153.9
  polypoid adenoma (M8210/3)
  tubular adenoma (M8210/3)
  villous adenoma (M8261/3)
infiltrating duct (M8500/3)
  with Paget's disease (M8541/3) — *see* Neoplasm, breast, malignant
  specified site — *see* Neoplasm, by site, malignant
  unspecified site 174.9
inflammatory (M8530/3)
  specified site — *see* Neoplasm, by site, malignant
  unspecified site 174.9
in situ (M8140/2) — *see* Neoplasm, by site, in situ
intestinal type (M8144/3)
  specified site — *see* Neoplasm, by site, malignant
  unspecified site 151.9
intraductal (noninfiltrating) (M8500/2)
  papillary (M8503/2)
    specified site — *see* Neoplasm, by site, in situ
    unspecified site 233.0
  specified site — *see* Neoplasm, by site, in situ
  unspecified site 233.0
islet cell (M8150/3)
  and exocrine, mixed (M8154/3)
    specified site — *see* Neoplasm, by site, malignant
    unspecified site 157.9
  pancreas 157.4
  specified site NEC — *see* Neoplasm, by site, malignant
  unspecified site 157.4
lobular (M8520/3)
  specified site — *see* Neoplasm, by site, malignant
  unspecified site 174.9
medullary (M8510/3)
mesonephric (M9110/3)
mixed cell (M8323/3)
mucinous (M8480/3)
mucin-producing (M8481/3)
mucoid (M8480/3) (*see also* Neoplasm, by site, malignant)
  cell (M8300/3)
    specified site — *see* Neoplasm, by site, malignant
    unspecified site 194.3

Adenocarcinoma — *see also* Neoplasm, by site, malignant — *continued*
nonencapsulated sclerosing (M8350/3) 193
oncocytic (M8290/3)
oxyphilic (M8290/3)
papillary (M8260/3)
  and follicular (M8340/3) 193
  intraductal (noninfiltrating) (M8503/2)
    specified site — *see* Neoplasm, by site, in situ
    unspecified site 233.0
  serous (M8460/3)
    specified site — *see* Neoplasm, by site, malignant
    unspecified site 183.0
papillocystic (M8450/3)
  specified site — *see* Neoplasm, by site, malignant
  unspecified site 183.0
pseudomucinous (M8470/3)
  specified site — *see* Neoplasm, by site, malignant
  unspecified site 183.0
renal cell (M8312/3) 189.0
sebaceous (M8410/3)
serous (M8441/3) (*see also* Neoplasm, by site, malignant)
  papillary
    specified site — *see* Neoplasm, by site, malignant
    unspecified site 183.0
signet ring cell (M8490/3)
superficial spreading (M8143/3)
sweat gland (M8400/3) — *see* Neoplasm, skin, malignant
trabecular (M8190/3)
tubular (M8211/3)
villous (M8262/3)
water-clear cell (M8322/3) 194.1
Adenofibroma (M9013/0)
clear cell (M8313/0) — *see* Neoplasm, by site, benign
endometrioid (M8381/0) 220
  borderline malignancy (M8381/1) 236.2
  malignant (M8381/3) 183.0
mucinous (M9015/0)
  specified site — *see* Neoplasm, by site, benign
  unspecified site 220
prostate 600.20
  with   ●
    other lower urinary tract   ●
      symptoms (LUTS)   ●
      600.21
    urinary   ●
      obstruction 600.21   ●
      retention 600.21   ●
serous (M9014/0)
  specified site — *see* Neoplasm, by site, benign
  unspecified site 220
specified site — *see* Neoplasm, by site, benign
unspecified site 220
Adenofibrosis
breast 610.2
endometrioid 617.0
Adenoiditis 474.01
acute 463
chronic 474.01
  with chronic tonsillitis 474.02
Adenoids (congenital) (of nasal fossa) 474.9
hypertrophy 474.12
vegetations 474.2
Adenolipomatosis (symmetrical) 272.8
Adenolymphoma (M8561/0)
specified site — *see* Neoplasm, by site, benign
unspecified 210.2

Adenomatosis (M8220/0)
endocrine (multiple) (M8360/1)
  single specified site — *see* Neoplasm, by site, uncertain behavior
  two or more specified sites 237.4
  unspecified site 237.4
erosive of nipple (M8506/0) 217
pluriendocrine — *see* Adenomatosis, endocrine
pulmonary (M8250/1) 235.7
  malignant (M8250/3) — *see* Neoplasm, lung, malignant
specified site — *see* Neoplasm, by site, benign
unspecified site 211.3
Adenomatous
cyst, thyroid (gland) — *see* Goiter, nodular
goiter (nontoxic) (*see also* Goiter, nodular) 241.9
  toxic or with hyperthyroidism 242.3 ☑
Adenoma (sessile) (M8140/0) — *see also* Neoplasm, by site, benign

> *Note — Except where otherwise indicated, the morphological varieties of adenoma in the list below should be coded by site as for "Neoplasm, benign."*

acidophil (M8280/0)
  specified site — *see* Neoplasm, by site, benign
  unspecified site 227.3
acinar (cell) (M8550/0)
acinic cell (M8550/0)
adrenal (cortex) (cortical) (functioning) (M8370/0) 227.0
  clear cell type (M8373/0) 227.0
  compact cell type (M8371/0) 227.0
  glomerulosa cell type (M8374/0) 227.0
  heavily pigmented variant (M8372/0) 227.0
  mixed cell type (M8375/0) 227.0
alpha cell (M8152/0)
  pancreas 211.7
  specified site NEC — *see* Neoplasm, by site, benign
  unspecified site 211.7
alveolar (M8251/0)
apocrine (M8401/0)
  breast 217
  specified site NEC — *see* Neoplasm, skin, benign
  unspecified site 216.9
basal cell (M8147/0)
basophil (M8300/0)
  specified site — *see* Neoplasm, by site, benign
  unspecified site 227.3
beta cell (M8151/0)
  pancreas 211.7
  specified site NEC — *see* Neoplasm, by site, benign
  unspecified site 211.7
bile duct (M8160/0) 211.5
black (M8372/0) 227.0
bronchial (M8140/1) 235.7
  carcinoid type (M8240/3) — *see* Neoplasm, lung, malignant
  cylindroid type (M8200/3) — *see* Neoplasm, lung, malignant
ceruminous (M8420/0) 216.2
chief cell (M8321/0) 227.1
chromophobe (M8270/0)
  specified site — *see* Neoplasm, by site, benign
  unspecified site 227.3
clear cell (M8310/0)
colloid (M8334/0)
  specified site — *see* Neoplasm, by site, benign
  unspecified site 226
cylindroid type, bronchus (M8200/3) — *see* Neoplasm, lung, malignant

Adenoma — *see also* Neoplasm, by site, benign — *continued*
duct (M8503/0)
embryonal (M8191/0)
endocrine, multiple (M8360/1)
  single specified site — *see* Neoplasm, by site, uncertain behavior
  two or more specified sites 237.4
  unspecified site 237.4
endometrioid (M8380/0) (*see also* Neoplasm, by site, benign)
  borderline malignancy (M8380/1) — *see* Neoplasm, by site, uncertain behavior
eosinophil (M8280/0)
  specified site — *see* Neoplasm, by site, benign
  unspecified site 227.3
fetal (M8333/0)
  specified site — *see* Neoplasm, by site, benign
  unspecified site 226
follicular (M8330/0)
  specified site — *see* Neoplasm, by site, benign
  unspecified site 226
hepatocellular (M8170/0) 211.5
Hürthle cell (M8290/0) 226
intracystic papillary (M8504/0)
islet cell (functioning) (M8150/0)
  pancreas 211.7
  specified site NEC — *see* Neoplasm, by site, benign
  unspecified site 211.7
liver cell (M8170/0) 211.5
macrofollicular (M8334/0)
  specified site NEC — *see* Neoplasm, by site, benign
  unspecified site 226
malignant, malignum (M8140/3) — *see* Neoplasm, by site, malignant
mesonephric (M9110/0)
microfollicular (M8333/0)
  specified site — *see* Neoplasm, by site, benign
  unspecified site 226
mixed cell (M8323/0)
monomorphic (M8146/0)
mucinous (M8480/0)
mucoid cell (M8300/0)
  specified site — *see* Neoplasm, by site, benign
  unspecified site 227.3
multiple endocrine (M8360/1)
  single specified site — *see* Neoplasm, by site, uncertain behavior
  two or more specified sites 237.4
  unspecified site 237.4
nipple (M8506/0) 217
oncocytic (M8290/0)
oxyphilic (M8290/0)
papillary (M8260/0) (*see also* Neoplasm, by site, benign)
  intracystic (M8504/0)
papillotubular (M8263/0)
Pick's tubular (M8640/0)
  specified site — *see* Neoplasm, by site, benign
  unspecified site
    female 220
    male 222.0
pleomorphic (M8940/0)
polypoid (M8210/0)
prostate (benign) 600.20   ●
  with   ●
    other lower urinary tract   ●
      symptoms (LUTS)   ●
      600.21
    urinary   ●
      obstruction 600.21   ●
      retention 600.21   ●
rete cell 222.0

☑ Additional Digit Required — Refer to the Tabular List for Digit Selection   ⓦ Subterms under main terms may continue to next column or page

10 — Volume 2 • October 2006   ▶◀ Revised Text   ● New Line   ▲ Revised Code   **2007 ICD-9-CM**

Adenoma — *see also* Neoplasm, by site, benign — *continued*
  sebaceous, sebaceum (gland) (senile) (M8410/0) (*see also* Neoplasm, skin, benign)
    disseminata 759.5
  Sertoli cell (M8640/0)
    specified site — *see* Neoplasm, by site, benign
    unspecified site
      female 220
      male 222.0
  skin appendage (M8390/0) — *see* Neoplasm, skin, benign
  sudoriferous gland (M8400/0) — *see* Neoplasm, skin, benign
  sweat gland or duct (M8400/0) — *see* Neoplasm, skin, benign
  testicular (M8640/0)
    specified site — *see* Neoplasm, by site, benign
    unspecified site
      female 220
      male 222.0
  thyroid 226
  trabecular (M8190/0)
  tubular (M8211/0) (*see also* Neoplasm, by site, benign)
    papillary (M8460/3)
    Pick's (M8640/0)
      specified site — *see* Neoplasm, by site, benign
      unspecified site
        female 220
        male 222.0
  tubulovillous (M8263/0)
  villoglandular (M8263/0)
  villous (M8261/1) — *see* Neoplasm, by site, uncertain behavior
  water-clear cell (M8322/0) 227.1
  wolffian duct (M9110/0)
Adenomyoma (M8932/0) — *see also* Neoplasm, by site, benign
  prostate 600.20
    with ●
      other lower urinary tract ●
        symptoms (LUTS) ●
          600.21 ●
      urinary ●
        obstruction 600.21 ●
        retention 600.21 ●
Adenomyometritis 617.0
Adenomyosis (uterus) (internal) 617.0
Adenopathy (lymph gland) 785.6
  inguinal 785.6
  mediastinal 785.6
  mesentery 785.6
  syphilitic (secondary) 091.4
  tracheobronchial 785.6
    tuberculous (*see also* Tuberculosis) 012.1 ☑
      primary, progressive 010.8 ☑
  tuberculous (*see also* Tuberculosis, lymph gland) 017.2 ☑
    tracheobronchial 012.1 ☑
      primary, progressive 010.8 ☑
Adenopharyngitis 462
Adenophlegmon 683
Adenosalpingitis 614.1
Adenosarcoma (M8960/3) 189.0
Adenosclerosis 289.3
Adenosis
  breast (sclerosing) 610.2
  vagina, congenital 752.49
Adentia (complete) (partial) — *see also* Absence, teeth 520.0
Adherent
  labium (minus) 624.4
  pericardium (nonrheumatic) 423.1
    rheumatic 393
  placenta 667.0 ☑
    with hemorrhage 666.0 ☑
  prepuce 605
  scar (skin) NEC 709.2
  tendon in scar 709.2

Adhesion(s), adhesive (postinfectional) (postoperative)
  abdominal (wall) (*see also* Adhesions, peritoneum) 568.0
  amnion to fetus 658.8 ☑
    affecting fetus or newborn 762.8
  appendix 543.9
  arachnoiditis — *see* Meningitis
  auditory tube (Eustachian) 381.89
  bands (*see also* Adhesions, peritoneum)
    cervix 622.3
    uterus 621.5
  bile duct (any) 576.8
  bladder (sphincter) 596.8
  bowel (*see also* Adhesions, peritoneum) 568.0
  cardiac 423.1
    rheumatic 398.99
  cecum (*see also* Adhesions, peritoneum) 568.0
  cervicovaginal 622.3
    congenital 752.49
    postpartal 674.8 ☑
    old 622.3
  cervix 622.3
  clitoris 624.4
  colon (*see also* Adhesions, peritoneum) 568.0
  common duct 576.8
  congenital (*see also* Anomaly, specified type NEC)
    fingers (*see also* Syndactylism, fingers) 755.11
    labium (majus) (minus) 752.49
    omental, anomalous 751.4
    ovary 752.0
    peritoneal 751.4
    toes (*see also* Syndactylism, toes) 755.13
    tongue (to gum or roof of mouth) 750.12
  conjunctiva (acquired) (localized) 372.62
    congenital 743.63
    extensive 372.63
  cornea — *see* Opacity, cornea
  cystic duct 575.8
  diaphragm (*see also* Adhesions, peritoneum) 568.0
  due to foreign body — *see* Foreign body
  duodenum (*see also* Adhesions, peritoneum) 568.0
    with obstruction 537.3
  ear, middle — *see* Adhesions, middle ear
  epididymis 608.89
  epidural — *see* Adhesions, meninges
  epiglottis 478.79
  Eustachian tube 381.89
  eyelid 374.46
    postoperative 997.99
      surgically created V45.69
  gallbladder (*see also* Disease, gallbladder) 575.8
  globe 360.89
  heart 423.1
    rheumatic 398.99
  ileocecal (coil) (*see also* Adhesions, peritoneum) 568.0
  ileum (*see also* Adhesions, peritoneum) 568.0
  intestine (postoperative) (*see also* Adhesions, peritoneum) 568.0
    with obstruction 560.81
      with hernia (*see also* Hernia, by site, with obstruction)
        gangrenous — *see* Hernia, by site, with gangrene
  intra-abdominal (*see also* Adhesions, peritoneum) 568.0
  iris 364.70
    to corneal graft 996.79
  joint (*see also* Ankylosis) 718.5 ☑
  kidney 593.89

Adhesion(s), adhesive — *continued*
  labium (majus) (minus), congenital 752.49
  liver 572.8
  lung 511.0
  mediastinum 519.3
  meninges 349.2
    cerebral (any) 349.2
      congenital 742.4
    congenital 742.8
    spinal (any) 349.2
      congenital 742.59
    tuberculous (cerebral) (spinal) (*see also* Tuberculosis, meninges) 013.0 ☑
  mesenteric (*see also* Adhesions, peritoneum) 568.0
  middle ear (fibrous) 385.10
    drum head 385.19
      to
        incus 385.11
        promontorium 385.13
        stapes 385.12
    specified NEC 385.19
  nasal (septum) (to turbinates) 478.19 ▲
  nerve NEC 355.9
    spinal 355.9
      root 724.9
        cervical NEC 723.4
        lumbar NEC 724.4
        lumbosacral 724.4
        thoracic 724.4
  ocular muscle 378.60
  omentum (*see also* Adhesions, peritoneum) 568.0
  organ or site, congenital NEC — *see* Anomaly, specified type NEC
  ovary 614.6
    congenital (to cecum, kidney, or omentum) 752.0
  parauterine 614.6
  parovarian 614.6
  pelvic (peritoneal)
    female (postoperative) (postinfection) 614.6
    male (postoperative) (postinfection) (*see also* Adhesions, peritoneum) 568.0
    postpartal (old) 614.6
    tuberculous (*see also* Tuberculosis) 016.9 ☑
  penis to scrotum (congenital) 752.69
  periappendiceal (*see also* Adhesions, peritoneum) 568.0
  pericardium (nonrheumatic) 423.1
    rheumatic 393
    tuberculous (*see also* Tuberculosis) 017.9 ☑ [420.0]
  pericholecystic 575.8
  perigastric (*see also* Adhesions, peritoneum) 568.0
  periovarian 614.6
  periprostatic 602.8
  perirectal (*see also* Adhesions, peritoneum) 568.0
  perirenal 593.89
  peritoneum, peritoneal (fibrous) (postoperative) 568.0
    with obstruction (intestinal) 560.81
      with hernia (*see also* Hernia, by site, with obstruction)
        gangrenous — *see* Hernia, by site, with gangrene
      duodenum 537.3
    congenital 751.4
    female (postoperative) (postinfective) 614.6
    pelvic, female 614.6
    pelvic, male 568.0
    postpartal, pelvic 614.6
    to uterus 614.6
  peritubal 614.6
  periureteral 593.89
  periuterine 621.5
  perivesical 596.8

Adhesion(s), adhesive — *continued*
  perivesicular (seminal vesicle) 608.89
  pleura, pleuritic 511.0
    tuberculous (*see also* Tuberculosis, pleura) 012.0 ☑
  pleuropericardial 511.0
  postoperative (gastrointestinal tract) (*see also* Adhesions, peritoneum) 568.0
    eyelid 997.99
      surgically created V45.69
    pelvic female 614.9
    pelvic male 568.0
    urethra 598.2
  postpartal, old 624.4
  preputial, prepuce 605
  pulmonary 511.0
  pylorus (*see also* Adhesions, peritoneum) 568.0
  Rosenmüller's fossa 478.29
  sciatic nerve 355.0
  seminal vesicle 608.89
  shoulder (joint) 726.0
  sigmoid flexure (*see also* Adhesions, peritoneum) 568.0
  spermatic cord (acquired) 608.89
    congenital 752.89
  spinal canal 349.2
    nerve 355.9
      root 724.9
        cervical NEC 723.4
        lumbar NEC 724.4
        lumbosacral 724.4
        thoracic 724.4
  stomach (*see also* Adhesions, peritoneum) 568.0
  subscapular 726.2
  tendonitis 726.90
    shoulder 726.0
  testicle 608.89
  tongue (congenital) (to gum or roof of mouth) 750.12
    acquired 529.8
  trachea 519.19 ▲
  tubo-ovarian 614.6
  tunica vaginalis 608.89
  ureter 593.89
  uterus 621.5
    to abdominal wall 614.6
      in pregnancy or childbirth 654.4 ☑
        affecting fetus or newborn 763.89
  vagina (chronic) (postoperative) (postradiation) 623.2
  vaginitis (congenital) 752.49
  vesical 596.8
  vitreous 379.29
Adie (-Holmes) syndrome (tonic pupillary reaction) 379.46
Adiponecrosis neonatorum 778.1
Adiposa dolorosa 272.8
Adiposalgia 272.8
Adiposis
  cerebralis 253.8
  dolorosa 272.8
  tuberosa simplex 272.8
Adiposity 278.02
  heart (*see also* Degeneration, myocardial) 429.1
  localized 278.1
Adiposogenital dystrophy 253.8
Adjustment
  prosthesis or other device — *see* Fitting of
  reaction — *see* Reaction, adjustment
Administration, prophylactic
  antibiotics V07.39
  antitoxin, any V07.2
  antivenin V07.2
  chemotherapeutic agent NEC V07.39
  chemotherapy NEC V07.39
  diphtheria antitoxin V07.2
  fluoride V07.31
  gamma globulin V07.2
  immune sera (gamma globulin) V07.2

☑ Additional Digit Required — Refer to the Tabular List for Digit Selection ▽ Subterms under main terms may continue to next column or page

2007 ICD-9-CM ▶◀ Revised Text ● New Line ▲ Revised Code October 2006 · Volume 2 — 11

Administration, prophylactic —
continued
  passive immunization agent V07.2
  RhoGAM V07.2
Admission (encounter)
  as organ donor — *see* Donor
  by mistake V68.9
  for
    adequacy testing (for)
      hemodialysis V56.31
      peritoneal dialysis V56.32
    adjustment (of)
      artificial
        arm (complete) (partial)
          V52.0
        eye V52.2
        leg (complete) (partial) V52.1
      brain neuropacemaker V53.02
      breast
        implant V52.4
        prosthesis V52.4
      cardiac device V53.39
        defibrillator, automatic im-
          plantable V53.32
        pacemaker V53.31
          carotid sinus V53.39
      catheter
        non-vascular V58.82
        vascular V58.81
      cerebral ventricle (communicat-
        ing) shunt V53.01
      colostomy belt V55.3
      contact lenses V53.1
      cystostomy device V53.6
      dental prosthesis V52.3
      device, unspecified type V53.90
        abdominal V53.5
        cardiac V53.39
          defibrillator, automatic
            implantable V53.32
          pacemaker V53.31
        carotid sinus V53.39
        cerebral ventricle (communi-
          cating) shunt V53.01
        insulin pump V53.91
        intrauterine contraceptive
          V25.1
        nervous system V53.09
        orthodontic V53.4
        other device V53.99
        prosthetic V52.9
          breast V52.4
          dental V52.3
          eye V52.2
          specified type NEC V52.8
        special senses V53.09
        substitution
          auditory V53.09
          nervous system V53.09
          visual V53.09
        urinary V53.6
      dialysis catheter
        extracorporeal V56.1
        peritoneal V56.2
      diaphragm (contraceptive)
        V25.02
      growth rod V54.02
      hearing aid V53.2
      ileostomy device V55.2
      intestinal appliance or device
        NEC V53.5
      intrauterine contraceptive de-
        vice V25.1
      neuropacemaker (brain) (periph-
        eral nerve) (spinal cord)
        V53.02
      orthodontic device V53.4
      orthopedic (device) V53.7
        brace V53.7
        cast V53.7
        shoes V53.7
      pacemaker
        brain V53.02
        cardiac V53.31
        carotid sinus V53.39
        peripheral nerve V53.02

Admission — *continued*
  for — *continued*
    adjustment — *continued*
      pacemaker — *continued*
        spinal cord V53.02
      prosthesis V52.9
        arm (complete) (partial)
          V52.0
        breast V52.4
        dental V52.3
        eye V52.2
        leg (complete) (partial) V52.1
        specified type NEC V52.8
      spectacles V53.1
      wheelchair V53.8
    adoption referral or proceedings
      V68.89
    aftercare (*see also* Aftercare) V58.9
      cardiac pacemaker V53.31
      chemotherapy V58.11
      dialysis
        extracorporeal (renal) V56.0
        peritoneal V56.8
        renal V56.0
      fracture (*see also* Aftercare,
        fracture) V54.9
      medical NEC V58.89
      organ transplant V58.44
      orthopedic V54.9
        specified care NEC V54.89
      pacemaker device
        brain V53.02
        cardiac V53.31
        carotid sinus V53.39
        nervous system V53.02
        spinal cord V53.02
      postoperative NEC V58.49
        wound closure, planned
          V58.41
      postpartum
        immediately after delivery
          V24.0
        routine follow-up V24.2
      postradiation V58.0
      radiation therapy V58.0
      removal of
        non-vascular catheter
          V58.82
        vascular catheter V58.81
      specified NEC V58.89
      surgical NEC V58.49
        wound closure, planned
          V58.41
    antineoplastic
      chemotherapy V58.11
      immunotherapy V58.12
    artificial insemination V26.1
    attention to artificial opening (of)
      V55.9
      artificial vagina V55.7
      colostomy V55.3
      cystostomy V55.5
      enterostomy V55.4
      gastrostomy V55.1
      ileostomy V55.2
      jejunostomy V55.4
      nephrostomy V55.6
      specified site NEC V55.8
        intestinal tract V55.4
        urinary tract V55.6
      tracheostomy V55.0
      ureterostomy V55.6
      urethrostomy V55.6
    battery replacement
      cardiac pacemaker V53.31
    blood typing V72.86
      Rh typing V72.86   ●
    boarding V65.0
    breast
      augmentation or reduction
        V50.1
      removal, prophylactic V50.41
    change of
      cardiac pacemaker (battery)
        V53.31
      carotid sinus pacemaker V53.39

Admission — *continued*
  for — *continued*
    change of — *continued*
      catheter in artificial opening —
        see Attention to, artificial,
        opening
      drains V58.49   ●
      dressing
        wound V58.30   ●
          nonsurgical V58.30   ●
          surgical V58.31   ●
      fixation device
        external V54.89
        internal V54.01
      Kirschner wire V54.89
      neuropacemaker device (brain)
        (peripheral nerve) (spinal
        cord) V53.02
      nonsurgical wound dressing ●
        V58.30   ●
      pacemaker device
        brain V53.02
        cardiac V53.31
        carotid sinus V53.39
        nervous system V53.02
      plaster cast V54.89
      splint, external V54.89
      Steinmann pin V54.89
      surgical ▶wound◀ dressing
        V58.31   ▲
      traction device V54.89
      wound packing V58.30   ●
        nonsurgical V58.30   ●
        surgical V58.31   ●
    checkup only V70.0
    chemotherapy, antineoplastic
      V58.11
    circumcision, ritual or routine (in
      absence of medical indica-
      tion) V50.2
    clinical research investigation
      (control) (normal comparison)
      (participant) V70.7
    closure of artificial opening — *see*
      Attention to, artificial, open-
      ing
    contraceptive
      counseling V25.09
        emergency V25.03
        postcoital V25.03
      management V25.9
        specified type NEC V25.8
    convalescence following V66.9
      chemotherapy V66.2
      psychotherapy V66.3
      radiotherapy V66.1
      surgery V66.0
      treatment (for) V66.5
        combined V66.6
        fracture V66.4
        mental disorder NEC V66.3
        specified condition NEC
          V66.5
    cosmetic surgery NEC V50.1
      following healed injury or opera-
      tion V51
    counseling (*see also* Counseling)
      V65.40
      without complaint or sickness
        V65.49
      contraceptive management
        V25.09
        emergency V25.03
        postcoital V25.03
      dietary V65.3
      exercise V65.41
      for
        nonattending third party
          V65.19
        pediatric pre-birth visit for
          expectant mother
          V65.11
      victim of abuse
        child V61.21
        partner or spouse V61.11
      genetic V26.33

Admission — *continued*
  for — *continued*
    counseling (*see also* Counseling) —
      continued
      gonorrhea V65.45
      HIV V65.44
      human immunodeficiency virus
        V65.44
      injury prevention V65.43
      insulin pump training V65.46
      procreative management V26.4
      sexually transmitted disease
        NEC V65.45
        HIV V65.44
      specified reason NEC V65.49
      substance use and abuse
        V65.42
      syphilis V65.45
      victim of abuse
        child V61.21
        partner or spouse V61.11
    desensitization to allergens V07.1
    dialysis V56.0
      catheter
        fitting and adjustment
          extracorporeal V56.1
          peritoneal V56.2
        removal or replacement
          extracorporeal V56.1
          peritoneal V56.2
      extracorporeal (renal) V56.0
      peritoneal V56.8
      renal V56.0
    dietary surveillance and counseling
      V65.3
    drug monitoring, therapeutic
      V58.83
    ear piercing V50.3
    elective surgery V50.9
      breast
        augmentation or reduction
          V50.1
        removal, prophylactic V50.41
      circumcision, ritual or routine
        (in absence of medical in-
        dication) V50.2
      cosmetic NEC V50.1
        following healed injury or
          operation V51
      ear piercing V50.3
      face-lift V50.1
      hair transplant V50.0
      plastic
        cosmetic NEC V50.1
        following healed injury or
          operation V51
      prophylactic organ removal
        V50.49
        breast V50.41
        ovary V50.42
      repair of scarred tissue (follow-
        ing healed injury or opera-
        tion) V51
      specified type NEC V50.8
    end-of-life care V66.7
    examination (*see also* Examination)
      V70.9
      administrative purpose NEC
        V70.3
      adoption V70.3
      allergy V72.7
      at health care facility V70.0
      athletic team V70.3
      camp V70.3
      cardiovascular, preoperative
        V72.81
      clinical research investigation
        (control) (participant)
        V70.7
      dental V72.2
      developmental testing (child)
        (infant) V20.2
      donor (potential) V70.8
      driver's license V70.3
      ear V72.19   ▲
      employment V70.5

☑ Additional Digit Required — Refer to the Tabular List for Digit Selection   ▽ Subterms under main terms may continue to next column or page

12 — Volume 2 • October 2006   ▶◀ Revised Text   ● New Line   ▲ Revised Code   **2007 ICD-9-CM**

Admission — *continued*
  for — *continued*
    examination (*see also* Examination)
      — *continued*
      eye V72.0
      follow-up (routine) — *see* Examination, follow-up
      for admission to
        old age home V70.3
        school V70.3
      general V70.9
        specified reason NEC V70.8
      gynecological V72.31
      health supervision (child) (infant) V20.2
      hearing V72.19 ▲
        following failed hearing ●
          screening V72.11 ●
      immigration V70.3
      infant, routine V20.2 ●
      insurance certification V70.3
      laboratory V72.6
      marriage license V70.3
      medical (general) (*see also* Examination, medical) V70.9
      medicolegal reasons V70.4
      naturalization V70.3
      pelvic (annual) (periodic) V72.31
      postpartum checkup V24.2
      pregnancy (possible) (unconfirmed) V72.40
        negative result V72.41
        positive result V72.42
      preoperative V72.84
        cardiovascular V72.81
        respiratory V72.82
        specified NEC V72.83
      preprocedural V72.84
        cardiovascular V72.81
        general physical V72.83
        respiratory V72.82
        specified NEC V72.83
      prison V70.3
      psychiatric (general) V70.2
        requested by authority V70.1
      radiological NEC V72.5
      respiratory, preoperative V72.82
      school V70.3
      screening — *see* Screening
      skin hypersensitivity V72.7
      specified type NEC V72.85
      sport competition V70.3
      vision V72.0
      well baby and child care V20.2
    exercise therapy V57.1
    face-lift, cosmetic reason V50.1
    fitting (of)
      artificial
        arm (complete) (partial) V52.0
        eye V52.2
        leg (complete) (partial) V52.1
      biliary drainage tube V58.82
      brain neuropacemaker V53.02
      breast V52.4
        implant V52.4
        prosthesis V52.4
      cardiac pacemaker V53.31
      catheter
        non-vascular V58.82
        vascular V58.81
      cerebral ventricle (communicating) shunt V53.01
      chest tube V58.82
      colostomy belt V55.2
      contact lenses V53.1
      cystostomy device V53.6
      dental prosthesis V52.3
      device, unspecified type V53.90
        abdominal V53.5
        cerebral ventricle (communicating) shunt V53.01
        insulin pump V53.91
        intrauterine contraceptive V25.1
        nervous system V53.09

Admission — *continued*
  for — *continued*
    fitting — *continued*
      device, unspecified type — *continued*
        orthodontic V53.4
        other device V53.99
        prosthetic V52.9
          breast V52.4
          dental V52.3
          eye V52.2
          special senses V53.09
        substitution
          auditory V53.09
          nervous system V53.09
          visual V53.09
      diaphragm (contraceptive) V25.02
      fistula (sinus tract) drainage tube V58.82
      growth rod V54.02
      hearing aid V53.2
      ileostomy device V55.2
      intestinal appliance or device NEC V53.5
      intrauterine contraceptive device V25.1
      neuropacemaker (brain) (peripheral nerve) (spinal cord) V53.02
      orthodontic device V53.4
      orthopedic (device) V53.7
        brace V53.7
        cast V53.7
        shoes V53.7
      pacemaker
        brain V53.02
        cardiac V53.31
        carotid sinus V53.39
        spinal cord V53.02
      pleural drainage tube V58.82
      prosthesis V52.9
        arm (complete) (partial) V52.0
        breast V52.4
        dental V52.3
        eye V52.2
        leg (complete) (partial) V52.1
        specified type NEC V52.8
      spectacles V53.1
      wheelchair V53.8
    follow-up examination (routine) (following) V67.9
      cancer chemotherapy V67.2
      chemotherapy V67.2
      high-risk medication NEC V67.51
      injury NEC V67.59
      psychiatric V67.3
      psychotherapy V67.3
      radiotherapy V67.1
      specified surgery NEC V67.09
      surgery V67.00
        vaginal pap smear V67.01
      treatment (for) V67.9
        combined V67.6
        fracture V67.4
        involving high-risk medication NEC V67.51
        mental disorder V67.3
        specified NEC V67.59
    hair transplant, for cosmetic reason V50.0
    health advice, education, or instruction V65.4 ☑
    hormone replacement therapy (postmenopausal) V07.4
    hospice care V66.7
    immunotherapy, antineoplastic V58.12
    insertion (of)
      subdermal implantable contraceptive V25.5
    insulin pump titration V53.91
    insulin pump training V65.46

Admission — *continued*
  for — *continued*
    intrauterine device
      insertion V25.1
      management V25.42
    investigation to determine further disposition V63.8
    isolation V07.0
    issue of
      medical certificate NEC V68.0
      repeat prescription NEC V68.1
        contraceptive device NEC V25.49
    kidney dialysis V56.0
    lengthening of growth rod V54.02
    mental health evaluation V70.2
      requested by authority V70.1
    nonmedical reason NEC V68.89
    nursing care evaluation V63.8
    observation (without need for further medical care) (*see also* Observation) V71.9
      accident V71.4
      alleged rape or seduction V71.5
      criminal assault V71.6
      following accident V71.4
        at work V71.3
      foreign body ingestion V71.89
      growth and development variations, childhood V21.0
      inflicted injury NEC V71.6
      ingestion of deleterious agent or foreign body V71.89
      injury V71.6
      malignant neoplasm V71.1
      mental disorder V71.09
      newborn — *see* Observation, suspected, condition, newborn
      rape V71.5
      specified NEC V71.89
      suspected disorder V71.9
        abuse V71.81
        accident V71.4
          at work V71.3
        benign neoplasm V71.89
        cardiovascular V71.7
        exposure
          anthrax V71.82
          biological agent NEC V71.83
          SARS V71.83
        heart V71.7
        inflicted injury NEC V71.6
        malignant neoplasm V71.1
        mental NEC V71.09
        neglect V71.81
        specified condition NEC V71.89
        tuberculosis V71.2
      tuberculosis V71.2
    occupational therapy V57.21
    organ transplant, donor — *see* Donor
    ovary, ovarian removal, prophylactic V50.42
    palliative care V66.7
    Papanicolaou smear
      cervix V76.2
        for suspected malignant neoplasm V76.2
          no disease found V71.1
        routine, as part of gynecological examination V72.31
        to confirm findings of recent normal smear following initial abnormal smear V72.32
      vaginal V76.47
        following hysterectomy for malignant condition V67.01
    passage of sounds or bougie in artificial opening — *see* Attention to, artificial, opening

Admission — *continued*
  for — *continued*
    paternity testing V70.4
    peritoneal dialysis V56.32
    physical therapy NEC V57.1
    plastic surgery
      cosmetic NEC V50.1
      following healed injury or operation V51
    postmenopausal hormone replacement therapy V07.4
    postpartum observation
      immediately after delivery V24.0
      routine follow-up V24.2
    poststerilization (for restoration) V26.0
    procreative management V26.9
      specified type NEC V26.8
    prophylactic
      administration of
        antibiotics V07.39
        antitoxin, any V07.2
        antivenin V07.2
        chemotherapeutic agent NEC V07.39
        chemotherapy NEC V07.39
        diphtheria antitoxin V07.2
        fluoride V07.31
        gamma globulin V07.2
        immune sera (gamma globulin) V07.2
        RhoGAM V07.2
        tetanus antitoxin V07.2
      breathing exercises V57.0
      chemotherapy NEC V07.39
      fluoride V07.31
      measure V07.9
        specified type NEC V07.8
      organ removal V50.49
        breast V50.41
        ovary V50.42
    psychiatric examination (general) V70.2
      requested by authority V70.1
    radiation management V58.0
    radiotherapy V58.0
    reforming of artificial opening — *see* Attention to, artificial, opening
    rehabilitation V57.9
      multiple types V57.89
      occupational V57.21
      orthoptic V57.4
      orthotic V57.81
      physical NEC V57.1
      specified type NEC V57.89
      speech V57.3
      vocational V57.22
    removal of
      cardiac pacemaker V53.31
      cast (plaster) V54.89
      catheter from artificial opening — *see* Attention to, artificial, opening
      cerebral ventricle (communicating) shunt V53.01
      cystostomy catheter V55.5
      device
        cerebral ventricle (communicating) shunt V53.01
        fixation
          external V54.89
          internal V54.01
        intrauterine contraceptive V25.42
        traction, external V54.89
      drains V58.49 ●
      dressing
        wound V58.30 ●
          nonsurgical V58.30 ●
          surgical V58.31 ●
      fixation device
        external V54.89
        internal V54.01
      intrauterine contraceptive device V25.42

☑ Additional Digit Required — Refer to the Tabular List for Digit Selection   ▽ Subterms under main terms may continue to next column or page

2007 ICD-9-CM   ►◄ Revised Text   ● New Line   ▲ Revised Code   **October 2006 • Volume 2 — 13**

Admission — *continued*
  for — *continued*
    removal of — *continued*
      Kirschner wire V54.89
      neuropacemaker (brain) (peripheral nerve) (spinal cord) V53.02
      nonsurgical wound dressing ● V58.30 ●
      orthopedic fixation device
        external V54.89
        internal V54.01
      pacemaker device
        brain V53.02
        cardiac V53.31
        carotid sinus V53.39
        nervous system V53.02
      plaster cast V54.89
      plate (fracture) V54.01
      rod V54.01
      screw (fracture) V54.01
      splint, traction V54.89
      staples V58.32 ●
      Steinmann pin V54.89
      subdermal implantable contraceptive V25.43
      surgical ►wound◄ dressing V58.31 ▲
      sutures V58.32 ▲
      traction device, external V54.89
      ureteral stent V53.6
      wound packing V58.30 ●
        nonsurgical V58.30 ●
        surgical V58.31 ●
    repair of scarred tissue (following healed injury or operation) V51
    reprogramming of cardiac pacemaker V53.31
    respirator [ventilator] dependence during
      mechanical failure V46.14
      power failure V46.12
      for weaning V46.13
    restoration of organ continuity (poststerilization) (tuboplasty) (vasoplasty) V26.0
    Rh typing V72.86 ●
    sensitivity test (*see also* Test, skin)
      allergy NEC V72.7
      bacterial disease NEC V74.9
      Dick V74.8
      Kveim V82.89
      Mantoux V74.1
      mycotic infection NEC V75.4
      parasitic disease NEC V75.8
      Schick V74.3
      Schultz-Charlton V74.8
    social service (agency) referral or evaluation V63.8
    speech therapy V57.3
    sterilization V25.2
    suspected disorder (ruled out) (without need for further care) — *see* Observation
    terminal care V66.7
    tests only — *see* Test
    therapeutic drug monitoring V58.83
    therapy
      blood transfusion, without reported diagnosis V58.2
      breathing exercises V57.0
      chemotherapy, antineoplastic V58.11
        prophylactic NEC V07.39
          fluoride V07.31
      dialysis (intermittent) (treatment)
        extracorporeal V56.0
        peritoneal V56.8
        renal V56.0
        specified type NEC V56.8
      exercise (remedial) NEC V57.1
        breathing V57.0

Admission — *continued*
  for — *continued*
    therapy — *continued*
      immunotherapy, antineoplastic V58.12
      long-term (current) drug use NEC V58.69
        antibiotics V58.62
        anticoagulants V58.61
        anti-inflammatories, non-steroidal (NSAID) V58.64
        antiplatelets V58.63
        antithrombotics V58.63
        aspirin V58.66
        insulin V58.67
        steroids V58.65
      occupational V57.21
      orthoptic V57.4
      physical NEC V57.1
      radiation V58.0
      speech V57.3
      vocational V57.22
    toilet or cleaning
      of artificial opening — *see* Attention to, artificial, opening
      of non-vascular catheter V58.82
      of vascular catheter V58.81
    tubal ligation V25.2
    tuboplasty for previous sterilization V26.0
    vaccination, prophylactic (against)
      arthropod-borne virus, viral NEC V05.1
        disease NEC V05.1
        encephalitis V05.0
      Bacille Calmette Guérin (BCG) V03.2
      BCG V03.2
      chickenpox V05.4
      cholera alone V03.0
        with typhoid-paratyphoid (cholera + TAB) V06.0
      common cold V04.7
      dengue V05.1
      diphtheria alone V03.5
      diphtheria-tetanus-pertussis (DTP) (DTaP) V06.1
        with
          poliomyelitis (DTP + polio) V06.3
          typhoid-paratyphoid (DTP + TAB) V06.2
      diphtheria-tetanus [Td] [DT] without pertussis V06.5
      disease (single) NEC V05.9
        bacterial NEC V03.9
          specified type NEC V03.89
        combinations NEC V06.9
          specified type NEC V06.8
        specified type NEC V05.8
        viral NEC V04.89
      encephalitis, viral, arthropod-borne V05.0
      Hemophilus influenzae, type B [Hib] V03.81
      hepatitis, viral V05.3
      immune sera (gamma globulin) V07.2
      influenza V04.81
        with
          Streptococcus pneumoniae [pneumococcus] V06.6
      Leishmaniasis V05.2
      measles alone V04.2
      measles-mumps-rubella (MMR) V06.4
      mumps alone V04.6
        with measles and rubella (MMR) V06.4
      not done because of contraindication V64.09
      pertussis alone V03.6
      plague V03.3
      pneumonia V03.82

Admission — *continued*
  for — *continued*
    vaccination, prophylactic — *continued*
      poliomyelitis V04.0
        with diphtheria-tetanus-pertussis (DTP+ polio) V06.3
      rabies V04.5
      respiratory syncytial virus (RSV) V04.82
      rubella alone V04.3
        with measles and mumps (MMR) V06.4
      smallpox V04.1
      specified type NEC V05.8
      Streptococcus pneumoniae [pneumococcus] V03.82
        with
          influenza V06.6
      tetanus toxoid alone V03.7
        with diphtheria [Td] [DT] V06.5
          and pertussis (DTP) (DTaP) V06.1
      tuberculosis (BCG) V03.2
      tularemia V03.4
      typhoid alone V03.1
        with diphtheria-tetanus-pertussis (TAB + DTP) V06.2
      typhoid-paratyphoid alone (TAB) V03.1
      typhus V05.8
      varicella (chicken pox) V05.4
      viral encephalitis, arthropod-borne V05.0
      viral hepatitis V05.3
      yellow fever V04.4
    vasectomy V25.2
    vasoplasty for previous sterilization V26.0
    vision examination V72.0
    vocational therapy V57.22
    waiting period for admission to other facility V63.2
      undergoing social agency investigation V63.8
    well baby and child care V20.2
    x-ray of chest
      for suspected tuberculosis V71.2
      routine V72.5
Adnexitis (suppurative) — *see also* Salpingo-oophoritis 614.2
Adolescence NEC V21.2
Adoption
  agency referral V68.89
  examination V70.3
  held for V68.89
Adrenal gland — *see* condition
Adrenalism 255.9
  tuberculous (*see also* Tuberculosis) 017.6 ☑
Adrenalitis, adrenitis 255.8
  meningococcal hemorrhagic 036.3
Adrenarche, precocious 259.1
Adrenocortical syndrome 255.2
Adrenogenital syndrome (acquired) (congenital) 255.2
  iatrogenic, fetus or newborn 760.79
Adrenoleukodystrophy 277.86
  neonatal 277.86
  x-linked 277.86
Adrenomyeloneuropathy 277.86
Adventitious bursa — *see* Bursitis
Adynamia (episodica) (hereditary) (periodic) 359.3
Adynamic
  ileus or intestine (*see also* Ileus) 560.1
  ureter 753.22
Aeration lung, imperfect, newborn 770.5
Aerobullosis 993.3
Aerocele — *see* Embolism, air

Aerodermectasia
  subcutaneous (traumatic) 958.7
    surgical 998.81
  surgical 998.81
Aerodontalgia 993.2
Aeroembolism 993.3
Aerogenes capsulatus infection — *see also* Gangrene, gas 040.0
Aero-otitis media 993.0
Aerophagy, aerophagia 306.4
  psychogenic 306.4
Aerosinusitis 993.1
Aerotitis 993.0
Affection, affections — *see also* Disease
  sacroiliac (joint), old 724.6
  shoulder region NEC 726.2
Afibrinogenemia 286.3
  acquired 286.6
  congenital 286.3
  postpartum 666.3 ☑
African
  sleeping sickness 086.5
  tick fever 087.1
  trypanosomiasis 086.5
    Gambian 086.3
    Rhodesian 086.4
Aftercare V58.9
  amputation stump V54.89 ●
  artificial openings — *see* Attention to, artificial, opening
  blood transfusion without reported diagnosis V58.2
  breathing exercise V57.0
  cardiac device V53.39
    defibrillator, automatic implantable V53.32
    pacemaker V53.31
      carotid sinus V53.39
  carotid sinus pacemaker V53.39
  cerebral ventricle (communicating) shunt V53.01
  chemotherapy session (adjunctive) (maintenance) V58.11
  defibrillator, automatic implantable cardiac V53.32
  exercise (remedial) (therapeutic) V57.1
    breathing V57.0
  extracorporeal dialysis (intermittent) (treatment) V56.0
  following surgery NEC V58.49
    for
      injury V58.43
      neoplasm V58.42
      organ transplant V58.44
      trauma V58.43
    joint replacement V54.81
    of
      circulatory system V58.73
      digestive system V58.75
      genital organs V58.76
      genitourinary system V58.76
      musculoskeletal system V58.78
      nervous system V58.72
      oral cavity V58.75
      respiratory system V58.74
      sense organs V58.71
      skin V58.77
      subcutaneous tissue V58.77
      teeth V58.75
      urinary system V58.76
    wound closure, planned V58.41
  fracture V54.9
    healing V54.89
    pathologic
      ankle V54.29
      arm V54.20
        lower V54.22
        upper V54.21
      finger V54.29
      foot V54.29
      hand V54.29
      hip V54.23
      leg V54.24
        lower V54.26
        upper V54.25
      pelvis V54.29

☑ Additional Digit Required — Refer to the Tabular List for Digit Selection   ☒ Subterms under main terms may continue to next column or page

Aftercare — *continued*
  fracture — *continued*
    healing — *continued*
      pathologic — *continued*
        specified site NEC V54.29
        toe(s) V54.29
        vertebrae V54.27
        wrist V54.29
      traumatic
        ankle V54.19
        arm V54.10
          lower V54.12
          upper V54.11
        finger V54.19
        foot V54.19
        hand V54.19
        hip V54.13
        leg V54.14
          lower V54.16
          upper V54.15
        pelvis V54.19
        specified site NEC V54.19
        toe(s) V54.19
        vertebrae V54.17
        wrist V54.19
    removal of
      external fixation device V54.89
      internal fixation device V54.01
    specified care NEC V54.89
  gait training V57.1
    for use of artificial limb(s) V57.81
  internal fixation device V54.09
  involving
    dialysis (intermittent) (treatment)
      extracorporeal V56.0
      peritoneal V56.8
      renal V56.0
    gait training V57.1
      for use of artificial limb(s)
        V57.81
    growth rod
      adjustment V54.02
      lengthening V54.02
    internal fixation device V54.09
    orthoptic training V57.4
    orthotic training V57.81
    radiotherapy session V58.0
    removal of
      drains V58.49   ●
      dressings   ●
        wound V58.30   ●
          nonsurgical V58.30   ●
          surgical V58.31   ●
      fixation device
        external V54.89
        internal V54.01
        fracture plate V54.01
      nonsurgical wound dressing   ●
        V58.30   ●
      pins V54.01
      plaster cast V54.89
      rods V54.01
      screws V58.32   ▲
      staples V58.32   ●
      surgical ▶wound◀ dressings
        V58.31   ▲
      sutures V58.32   ▲
      traction device, external V54.89
      wound packing V58.30   ●
        nonsurgical V58.30   ●
        surgical V58.31   ●
  neuropacemaker (brain) (peripheral
    nerve) (spinal cord) V53.02
  occupational therapy V57.21
  orthodontic V58.5
  orthopedic V54.9
    change of external fixation or trac-
      tion device V54.89
    following joint replacement V54.81
    internal fixation device V54.09
    removal of fixation device
      external V54.89
      internal V54.01
    specified care NEC V54.89
  orthoptic training V57.4
  orthotic training V57.81

Aftercare — *continued*
  pacemaker
    brain V53.02
    cardiac V53.31
    carotid sinus V53.39
    peripheral nerve V53.02
    spinal cord V53.02
  peritoneal dialysis (intermittent)
    (treatment) V56.8
  physical therapy NEC V57.1
    breathing exercises V57.0
  radiotherapy session V58.0
  rehabilitation procedure V57.9
    breathing exercises V57.0
    multiple types V57.89
    occupational V57.21
    orthoptic V57.4
    orthotic V57.81
    physical therapy NEC V57.1
    remedial exercises V57.1
    specified type NEC V57.89
    speech V57.3
    therapeutic exercises V57.1
    vocational V57.22
  renal dialysis (intermittent) (treatment)
    V56.0
  specified type NEC V58.89
    removal of non-vascular catheter
      V58.82
    removal of vascular catheter
      V58.81
  speech therapy V57.3
  stump, amputation V54.89   ●
  vocational rehabilitation V57.22
After-cataract 366.50
  obscuring vision 366.53
  specified type, not obscuring vision
    366.52
Agalactia 676.4 ☑
Agammaglobulinemia 279.00
  with lymphopenia 279.2
  acquired (primary) (secondary) 279.06
  Bruton's X-linked 279.04
  infantile sex-linked (Bruton's) (congen-
    ital) 279.04
  Swiss-type 279.2
Aganglionosis (bowel) (colon) 751.3
Age (old) — *see also* Senile 797
Agenesis — *see also* Absence, by site,
    congenital
  acoustic nerve 742.8
  adrenal (gland) 759.1
  alimentary tract (complete) (partial)
    NEC 751.8
    lower 751.2
    upper 750.8
  anus, anal (canal) 751.2
  aorta 747.22
  appendix 751.2
  arm (complete) (partial) (*see also* De-
    formity, reduction, upper limb)
    755.20
  artery (peripheral) NEC (*see also*
    Anomaly, peripheral vascular
    system) 747.60
    brain 747.81
    coronary 746.85
    pulmonary 747.3
    umbilical 747.5
  auditory (canal) (external) 744.01
  auricle (ear) 744.01
  bile, biliary duct or passage 751.61
  bone NEC 756.9
  brain 740.0
    specified part 742.2
  breast 757.6
  bronchus 748.3
  canaliculus lacrimalis 743.65
  carpus NEC (*see also* Deformity, reduc-
    tion, upper limb) 755.28
  cartilage 756.9
  cecum 751.2
  cerebellum 742.2
  cervix 752.49
  chin 744.89
  cilia 743.63

Agenesis — *see also* Absence, by site,
    congenital — *continued*
  circulatory system, part NEC 747.89
  clavicle 755.51
  clitoris 752.49
  coccyx 756.13
  colon 751.2
  corpus callosum 742.2
  cricoid cartilage 748.3
  diaphragm (with hernia) 756.6
  digestive organ(s) or tract (complete)
    (partial) NEC 751.8
    lower 751.2
    upper 750.8
  ductus arteriosus 747.89
  duodenum 751.1
  ear NEC 744.09
    auricle 744.01
    lobe 744.21
  ejaculatory duct 752.89
  endocrine (gland) NEC 759.2
  epiglottis 748.3
  esophagus 750.3
  Eustachian tube 744.24
  extrinsic muscle, eye 743.69
  eye 743.00
    adnexa 743.69
    eyelid (fold) 743.62
  face
    bones NEC 756.0
    specified part NEC 744.89
  fallopian tube 752.19
  femur NEC (*see also* Absence, femur,
    congenital) 755.34
  fibula NEC (*see also* Absence, fibula,
    congenital) 755.37
  finger NEC (*see also* Absence, finger,
    congenital) 755.29
  foot (complete) (*see also* Deformity,
    reduction, lower limb) 755.31
  gallbladder 751.69
  gastric 750.8
  genitalia, genital (organ)
    female 752.89
      external 752.49
      internal NEC 752.89
    male 752.89
      penis 752.69
  glottis 748.3
  gonadal 758.6
  hair 757.4
  hand (complete) (*see also* Deformity,
    reduction, upper limb) 755.21
  heart 746.89
    valve NEC 746.89
      aortic 746.89
      mitral 746.89
      pulmonary 746.01
  hepatic 751.69
  humerus NEC (*see also* Absence,
    humerus, congenital) 755.24
  hymen 752.49
  ileum 751.1
  incus 744.04
  intestine (small) 751.1
    large 751.2
  iris (dilator fibers) 743.45
  jaw 524.09
  jejunum 751.1
  kidney(s) (partial) (unilateral) 753.0
  labium (majus) (minus) 752.49
  labyrinth, membranous 744.05
  lacrimal apparatus (congenital) 743.65
  larynx 748.3
  leg NEC (*see also* Deformity, reduc-
    tion, lower limb) 755.30
  lens 743.35
  limb (complete) (partial) (*see also* De-
    formity, reduction) 755.4
    lower NEC 755.30
    upper 755.20
  lip 750.26
  liver 751.69
  lung (bilateral) (fissures) (lobe) (unilat-
    eral) 748.5
  mandible 524.09

Agenesis — *see also* Absence, by site,
    congenital — *continued*
  maxilla 524.09
  metacarpus NEC 755.28
  metatarsus NEC 755.38
  muscle (any) 756.81
  musculoskeletal system NEC 756.9
  nail(s) 757.5
  neck, part 744.89
  nerve 742.8
  nervous system, part NEC 742.8
  nipple 757.6
  nose 748.1
  nuclear 742.8
  organ
    of Corti 744.05
    or site not listed — *see* Anomaly,
      specified type NEC
  osseous meatus (ear) 744.03
  ovary 752.0
  oviduct 752.19
  pancreas 751.7
  parathyroid (gland) 759.2
  patella 755.64
  pelvic girdle (complete) (partial) 755.69
  penis 752.69
  pericardium 746.89
  perineal body 756.81
  pituitary (gland) 759.2
  prostate 752.89
  pulmonary
    artery 747.3
    trunk 747.3
    vein 747.49
  punctum lacrimale 743.65
  radioulnar NEC (*see also* Absence,
    forearm, congenital) 755.25
  radius NEC (*see also* Absence, radius,
    congenital) 755.26
  rectum 751.2
  renal 753.0
  respiratory organ NEC 748.9
  rib 756.3
  roof of orbit 742.0
  round ligament 752.89
  sacrum 756.13
  salivary gland 750.21
  scapula 755.59
  scrotum 752.89
  seminal duct or tract 752.89
  septum
    atrial 745.69
    between aorta and pulmonary
      artery 745.0
    ventricular 745.3
  shoulder girdle (complete) (partial)
    755.59
  skull (bone) 756.0
    with
      anencephalus 740.0
      encephalocele 742.0
      hydrocephalus 742.3
        with spina bifida (*see also*
          Spina bifida) 741.0 ☑
      microcephalus 742.1
  spermatic cord 752.89
  spinal cord 742.59
  spine 756.13
    lumbar 756.13
      isthmus 756.11
      pars articularis 756.11
  spleen 759.0
  sternum 756.3
  stomach 750.7
  tarsus NEC 755.38
  tendon 756.81
  testicular 752.89
  testis 752.89
  thymus (gland) 759.2
  thyroid (gland) 243
    cartilage 748.3
  tibia NEC (*see also* Absence, tibia,
    congenital) 755.36
  tibiofibular NEC 755.35
  toe (complete) (partial) (*see also* Ab-
    sence, toe, congenital) 755.39

Agenesis — *see also* Absence, by site, congenital — *continued*
  tongue 750.11
  trachea (cartilage) 748.3
  ulna NEC (*see also* Absence, ulna, congenital) 755.27
  ureter 753.4
  urethra 753.8
  urinary tract NEC 753.8
  uterus 752.3
  uvula 750.26
  vagina 752.49
  vas deferens 752.89
  vein(s) (peripheral) NEC (*see also* Anomaly, peripheral vascular system) 747.60
    brain 747.81
    great 747.49
    portal 747.49
    pulmonary 747.49
  vena cava (inferior) (superior) 747.49
  vermis of cerebellum 742.2
  vertebra 756.13
    lumbar 756.13
      isthmus 756.11
      pars articularis 756.11
  vulva 752.49
Ageusia — *see also* Disturbance, sensation 781.1
Aggressiveness 301.3
Aggressive outburst — *see also* Disturbance, conduct 312.0 ☑
  in children or adolescents 313.9
Aging skin 701.8
Agitated — *see* condition
Agitation 307.9
  catatonic (*see also* Schizophrenia) 295.2 ☑
Aglossia (congenital) 750.11
Aglycogenosis 271.0
Agnail (finger) (with lymphangitis) 681.02
Agnosia (body image) (tactile) 784.69
  verbal 784.69
    auditory 784.69
      secondary to organic lesion 784.69
    developmental 315.8
    secondary to organic lesion 784.69
    visual 784.69
      developmental 315.8
      secondary to organic lesion 784.69
  visual 368.16
    developmental 315.31
Agoraphobia 300.22
  with panic disorder 300.21
Agrammatism 784.69
Agranulocytopenia ▶— *see also* Agranulocytosis◀ 288.09   ▲
Agranulocytosis (angina) 288.09   ▲
  chronic 288.09   ●
  cyclical 288.02   ●
  genetic 288.01   ●
  infantile 288.01   ●
  periodic 288.02   ●
  pernicious 288.09   ●
Agraphia (absolute) 784.69
  with alexia 784.61
  developmental 315.39
Agrypnia — *see also* Insomnia 780.52
Ague — *see also* Malaria 084.6
  brass-founders' 985.8
  dumb 084.6
  tertian 084.1
Agyria 742.2
Ahumada-del Castillo syndrome (nonpuerperal galactorrhea and amenorrhea) 253.1
AIDS 042
AIDS-associated retrovirus (disease) (illness) 042
  infection — *see* Human immunodeficiency virus, infection
AIDS-associated virus (disease) (illness) 042

AIDS-associated virus — *continued*
  infection — *see* Human immunodeficiency virus, infection
AIDS-like disease (illness) (syndrome) 042
AIDS-related complex 042
AIDS-related conditions 042
AIDS-related virus (disease) (illness) 042
  infection — *see* Human immunodeficiency virus, infection
AIDS virus (disease) (illness) 042
  infection — *see* Human immunodeficiency virus, infection
Ailment, heart — *see* Disease, heart
Ailurophobia 300.29
Ainhum (disease) 136.0
Air
  anterior mediastinum 518.1
  compressed, disease 993.3
  embolism (any site) (artery) (cerebral) 958.0
    with
      abortion — *see* Abortion, by type, with embolism
      ectopic pregnancy (*see also* categories 633.0–633.9) 639.6
      molar pregnancy (*see also* categories 630–632) 639.6
    due to implanted device — *see* Complications, due to (presence of) any device, implant, or graft classified to 996.0–996.5 NEC
    following
      abortion 639.6
      ectopic or molar pregnancy 639.6
    infusion, perfusion, or transfusion 999.1
    in pregnancy, childbirth, or puerperium 673.0 ☑
    traumatic 958.0
  hunger 786.09
    psychogenic 306.1
  leak (lung) (pulmonary) (thorax) 512.8
    iatrogenic 512.1
    postoperative 512.1
  rarefied, effects of — *see* Effect, adverse, high altitude
  sickness 994.6
Airplane sickness 994.6
Akathisia, acathisia 781.0
  due to drugs 333.99
  neuroleptic-induced acute 333.99
Akinesia algera 352.6
Akiyami 100.89
Akureyri disease (epidemic neuromyasthenia) 049.8
Alacrima (congenital) 743.65
Alactasia (hereditary) 271.3
Alagille syndrome 759.89
Alalia 784.3
  developmental 315.31
    receptive-expressive 315.32
  secondary to organic lesion 784.3
Alaninemia 270.8
Alastrim 050.1
Albarrán's disease (colibacilluria) 791.9
Albers-Schönberg's disease (marble bones) 756.52
Albert's disease 726.71
Albinism, albino (choroid) (cutaneous) (eye) (generalized) (isolated) (ocular) (oculocutaneous) (partial) 270.2
Albinismus 270.2
Albright (-Martin) (-Bantam) disease (pseudohypoparathyroidism) 275.49
Albright (-McCune) (-Sternberg) syndrome (osteitis fibrosa disseminata) 756.59
Albuminous — *see* condition
Albuminuria, albuminuric (acute) (chronic) (subacute) 791.0
  Bence-Jones 791.0

Albuminuria, albuminuric — *continued*
  cardiac 785.9
  complicating pregnancy, childbirth, or puerperium 646.2 ☑
    with hypertension — *see* Toxemia, of pregnancy
    affecting fetus or newborn 760.1
  cyclic 593.6
  gestational 646.2 ☑
  gravidarum 646.2 ☑
    with hypertension — *see* Toxemia, of pregnancy
    affecting fetus or newborn 760.1
  heart 785.9
  idiopathic 593.6
  orthostatic 593.6
  postural 593.6
  pre-eclamptic (mild) 642.4 ☑
    affecting fetus or newborn 760.0
    severe 642.5 ☑
      affecting fetus or newborn 760.0
  recurrent physiologic 593.6
  scarlatinal 034.1
Albumosuria 791.0
  Bence-Jones 791.0
  myelopathic (M9730/3) 203.0 ☑
Alcaptonuria 270.2
Alcohol, alcoholic
  abstinence 291.81
  acute intoxication 305.0 ☑
    with dependence 303.0 ☑
  addiction (*see also* Alcoholism) 303.9 ☑
    maternal
      with suspected fetal damage affecting management of pregnancy 655.4 ☑
      affecting fetus or newborn 760.71
  amnestic disorder, persisting 291.1
  anxiety 291.89
  brain syndrome, chronic 291.2
  cardiopathy 425.5
  chronic (*see also* Alcoholism) 303.9 ☑
  cirrhosis (liver) 571.2
  delirium 291.0
    acute 291.0
    chronic 291.1
    tremens 291.0
    withdrawal 291.0
  dementia NEC 291.2
  deterioration 291.2
  drunkenness (simple) 305.0 ☑
  hallucinosis (acute) 291.3
  induced
    circadian rhythm sleep disorder 291.82
    hypersomnia 291.82
    insomnia 291.82
    mental disorder 291.9
      anxiety 291.89
      mood 291.89
      sexual 291.89
      sleep 291.82
      specified type 291.89
    parasomnia 291.82
    persisting
      amnestic disorder 291.1
      dementia 291.2
    psychotic disorder
      with
        delusions 291.5
        hallucinations 291.3
    sleep disorder 291.82
  insanity 291.9
  intoxication (acute) 305.0 ☑
    with dependence 303.0 ☑
    pathological 291.4
  jealousy 291.5
  Korsakoff's, Korsakov's, Korsakow's 291.1
  liver NEC 571.3
    acute 571.1
    chronic 571.2
  mania (acute) (chronic) 291.9

Alcohol, alcoholic — *continued*
  mood 291.89
  paranoia 291.5
  paranoid (type) psychosis 291.5
  pellagra 265.2
  poisoning, accidental (acute) NEC 980.9
    specified type of alcohol — *see* Table of Drugs and Chemicals
  psychosis (*see also* Psychosis, alcoholic) 291.9
    Korsakoff's, Korsakov's, Korsakow's 291.1
    polyneuritic 291.1
      with
        delusions 291.5
        hallucinations 291.3
  related disorder 291.9
  withdrawal symptoms, syndrome NEC 291.81
    delirium 291.0
    hallucinosis 291.3
Alcoholism 303.9 ☑

Note — *Use the following fifth-digit subclassification with category 303:*

  0   *unspecified*
  1   *continuous*
  2   *episodic*
  3   *in remission*

  with psychosis (*see also* Psychosis, alcoholic) 291.9
  acute 303.0 ☑
  chronic 303.9 ☑
    with psychosis 291.9
  complicating pregnancy, childbirth, or puerperium 648.4 ☑
    affecting fetus or newborn 760.71
  history V11.3
  Korsakoff's, Korsakov's, Korsakow's 291.1
  suspected damage to fetus affecting management of pregnancy 655.4 ☑
Alder's anomaly or syndrome (leukocyte granulation anomaly) 288.2
Alder-Reilly anomaly (leukocyte granulation) 288.2
Aldosteronism (primary) 255.10
  congenital 255.10
  familial type I 255.11
  glucocorticoid-remediable 255.11
  secondary 255.14
Aldosteronoma (M8370/1) 237.2
Aldrich (-Wiskott) syndrome (eczema-thrombocytopenia) 279.12
Aleppo boil 085.1
Aleukemic — *see* condition
Aleukia
  congenital 288.09   ▲
  hemorrhagica 284.9
    acquired (secondary) 284.8
    congenital 284.09   ▲
    idiopathic 284.9
  splenica 289.4
Alexia (congenital) (developmental) 315.01
  secondary to organic lesion 784.61
Algoneurodystrophy 733.7
Algophobia 300.29
Alibert-Bazin disease (M9700/3) 202.1 ☑
Alibert's disease (mycosis fungoides) (M9700/3) 202.1 ☑
Alice in Wonderland syndrome 293.89
Alienation, mental — *see also* Psychosis 298.9
Alkalemia 276.3
Alkalosis 276.3
  metabolic 276.3
    with respiratory acidosis 276.4
  respiratory 276.3
Alkaptonuria 270.2
Allen-Masters syndrome 620.6

☑ Additional Digit Required — Refer to the Tabular List for Digit Selection   Subterms under main terms may continue to next column or page

16 — Volume 2 • October 2006   ▶◀ Revised Text   ● New Line   ▲ Revised Code   *2007 ICD-9-CM*

Allergic bronchopulmonary aspergillosis 518.6
Allergy, allergic (reaction) 995.3
  air-borne substance — *see also* Fever, hay 477.9
    specified allergen NEC 477.8
  alveolitis (extrinsic) 495.9
    due to
      Aspergillus clavatus 495.4
      cryptostroma corticale 495.6
      organisms (fungal, thermophilic actinomyces, other) growing in ventilation (air conditioning systems) 495.7
    specified type NEC 495.8
  anaphylactic shock 999.4
    due to food — *see* Anaphylactic shock, due to, food
  angioneurotic edema 995.1
  animal (cat) (dog) (epidermal) 477.8
    dander 477.2
    hair 477.2
  arthritis (*see also* Arthritis, allergic) 716.2 ☑
  asthma — *see* Asthma
  bee sting (anaphylactic shock) 989.5
  biological — *see* Allergy, drug
  bronchial asthma — *see* Asthma
  conjunctivitis (eczematous) 372.14
  dander, animal (cat) (dog) 477.2
  dandruff 477.8
  dermatitis (venenata) — *see* Dermatitis
  diathesis V15.09
  drug, medicinal substance, and biological (any) (correct medicinal substance properly administered) (external) (internal) 995.27 ▲
    wrong substance given or taken NEC 977.9
    specified drug or substance — *see* Table of Drugs and Chemicals
  dust (house) (stock) 477.8
  eczema — *see* Eczema
  endophthalmitis 360.19
  epidermal (animal) 477.8
  existing dental restorative maerial ● 525.66 ●
  feathers 477.8
  food (any) (ingested) 693.1
    atopic 691.8
    in contact with skin 692.5
  gastritis 535.4 ☑
  gastroenteritis 558.3
  gastrointestinal 558.3
  grain 477.0
  grass (pollen) 477.0
    asthma (*see also* Asthma) 493.0 ☑
    hay fever 477.0
  hair, animal (cat) (dog) 477.2
  hay fever (grass) (pollen) (ragweed) (tree) (*see also* Fever, hay) 477.9
  history (of) V15.09
    to
      eggs V15.03
      food additives V15.05
      insect bite V15.06
      latex V15.07
      milk products V15.02
      nuts V15.05
        peanuts V15.01
      radiographic dye V15.08
      seafood V15.04
      specified food NEC V15.05
      spider bite V15.06
  horse serum — *see* Allergy, serum
  inhalant 477.9
    dust 477.8
    pollen 477.0
    specified allergen other than pollen 477.8
  kapok 477.8
  medicine — *see* Allergy, drug

Allergy, allergic — *continued*
  migraine 346.2 ☑
  milk protein 558.3
  pannus 370.62
  pneumonia 518.3
  pollen (any) (hay fever) 477.0
    asthma (*see also* Asthma) 493.0 ☑
  primrose 477.0
  primula 477.0
  purpura 287.0
  ragweed (pollen) (Senecio jacobae) 477.0
    asthma (*see also* Asthma) 493.0 ☑
    hay fever 477.0
  respiratory (*see also* Allergy, inhalant) 477.9
    due to
      drug — *see* Allergy, drug
      food — *see* Allergy, food
  rhinitis (*see also* Fever, hay) 477.9
    due to food 477.1
  rose 477.0
  Senecio jacobae 477.0
  serum (prophylactic) (therapeutic) 999.5
    anaphylactic shock 999.4
    shock (anaphylactic) (due to adverse effect of correct medicinal substance properly administered) 995.0
    food — *see* Anaphylactic shock, due to, food
    from serum or immunization 999.5
      anaphylactic 999.4
  sinusitis (*see also* Fever, hay) 477.9
  skin reaction 692.9
    specified substance — *see* Dermatitis, due to
  tree (any) (hay fever) (pollen) 477.0
    asthma (*see also* Asthma) 493.0 ☑
  upper respiratory (*see also* Fever, hay) 477.9
  urethritis 597.89
  urticaria 708.0
  vaccine — *see* Allergy, serum
Allescheriosis 117.6
Alligator skin disease (ichthyosis congenita) 757.1
  acquired 701.1
Allocheiria, allochiria — *see also* Disturbance, sensation 782.0
Almeida's disease (Brazilian blastomycosis) 116.1
Alopecia (atrophicans) (pregnancy) (premature) (senile) 704.00
  adnata 757.4
  areata 704.01
  celsi 704.01
  cicatrisata 704.09
  circumscripta 704.01
  congenital, congenitalis 757.4
  disseminata 704.01
  effluvium (telogen) 704.02
  febrile 704.09
  generalisata 704.09
  hereditaria 704.09
  marginalis 704.01
  mucinosa 704.09
  postinfectional 704.09
  seborrheica 704.09
  specific 091.82
  syphilitic (secondary) 091.82
  telogen effluvium 704.02
  totalis 704.09
  toxica 704.09
  universalis 704.09
  x-ray 704.09
Alpers' disease 330.8
Alpha-lipoproteinemia 272.4
Alpha thalassemia 282.49
Alphos 696.1
Alpine sickness 993.2
Alport's syndrome (hereditary hematuria-nephropathy-deafness) 759.89
Alteration (of), altered
  awareness 780.09

Alteration, altered — *continued*
  awareness — *continued*
    transient 780.02
  consciousness 780.09
    persistent vegetative state 780.03
    transient 780.02
  mental status 780.97 ▲
    amnesia (retrograde) 780.93
    memory loss 780.93
Alternaria (infection) 118
Alternating — *see* condition
Altitude, high (effects) — *see* Effect, adverse, high altitude
Aluminosis (of lung) 503
Alvarez syndrome (transient cerebral ischemia) 435.9
Alveolar capillary block syndrome 516.3
Alveolitis
  allergic (extrinsic) 495.9
    due to organisms (fungal, thermophilic actinomycete, other) growing in ventilation (air conditioning systems) 495.7
    specified type NEC 495.8
  due to
    Aspergillus clavatus 495.4
    Cryptostroma corticale 495.6
  fibrosing (chronic) (cryptogenic) (lung) 516.3
    idiopathic 516.3
    rheumatoid 714.81
  jaw 526.5
  sicca dolorosa 526.5
Alveolus, alveolar — *see* condition
Alymphocytosis (pure) 279.2
Alymphoplasia, thymic 279.2
Alzheimer's
  dementia (senile)
    with behavioral disturbance 331.0 [294.11]
    without behavioral disturbance 331.0 [294.10]
  disease or sclerosis 331.0
    with dementia — *see* Alzheimer's, dementia
Amastia — *see also* Absence, breast 611.8
Amaurosis (acquired) (congenital) — *see also* Blindness 369.00
  fugax 362.34
  hysterical 300.11
  Leber's (congenital) 362.76
  tobacco 377.34
  uremic — *see* Uremia
Amaurotic familial idiocy (infantile) (juvenile) (late) 330.1
Ambisexual 752.7
Amblyopia (acquired) (congenital) (partial) 368.00
  color 368.59
    acquired 368.55
  deprivation 368.02
  ex anopsia 368.00
  hysterical 300.11
  nocturnal 368.60
    vitamin A deficiency 264.5
  refractive 368.03
  strabismic 368.01
  suppression 368.01
  tobacco 377.34
  toxic NEC 377.34
  uremic — *see* Uremia
Ameba, amebic (histolytica) — *see also* Amebiasis
  abscess 006.3
    bladder 006.8
    brain (with liver and lung abscess) 006.5
    liver 006.3
      with
        brain abscess (and lung abscess) 006.5
        lung abscess 006.4
    lung (with liver abscess) 006.4
      with brain abscess 006.5

Ameba, amebic — *see also* Amebiasis — *continued*
  abscess — *continued*
    seminal vesicle 006.8
    spleen 006.8
  carrier (suspected of) V02.2
  meningoencephalitis
    due to Naegleria (gruberi) 136.2
    primary 136.2
Amebiasis NEC 006.9
  with
    brain abscess (with liver or lung abscess) 006.5
    liver abscess (without mention of brain or lung abscess) 006.3
    lung abscess (with liver abscess) 006.4
      with brain abscess 006.5
  acute 006.0
  bladder 006.8
  chronic 006.1
  cutaneous 006.6
  cutis 006.6
  due to organism other than Entamoeba histolytica 007.8
  hepatic (*see also* Abscess, liver, amebic) 006.3
  nondysenteric 006.2
  seminal vesicle 006.8
  specified
    organism NEC 007.8
    site NEC 006.8
Ameboma 006.8
Amelia 755.4
  lower limb 755.31
  upper limb 755.21
Ameloblastoma (M9310/0) 213.1
  jaw (bone) (lower) 213.1
    upper 213.0
  long bones (M9261/3) — *see* Neoplasm, bone, malignant
  malignant (M9310/3) 170.1
    jaw (bone) (lower) 170.1
      upper 170.0
  mandible 213.1
  tibial (M9261/3) 170.7
Amelogenesis imperfecta 520.5
  nonhereditaria (segmentalis) 520.4
Amenorrhea (primary) (secondary) 626.0
  due to ovarian dysfunction 256.8
  hyperhormonal 256.8
Amentia — *see also* Retardation, mental 319
  Meynert's (nonalcoholic) 294.0
    alcoholic 291.1
  nevoid 759.6
American
  leishmaniasis 085.5
  mountain tick fever 066.1
  trypanosomiasis — *see* Trypanosomiasis, American
Ametropia — *see also* Disorder, accommodation 367.9
Amianthosis 501
Amimia 784.69
Amino acid
  deficiency 270.9
    anemia 281.4
  metabolic disorder (*see also* Disorder, amino acid) 270.9
Aminoaciduria 270.9
  imidazole 270.5
Amnesia (retrograde) 780.93
  auditory 784.69
    developmental 315.31
    secondary to organic lesion 784.69
  dissociative 300.12
  hysterical or dissociative type 300.12
  psychogenic 300.12
  transient global 437.7
Amnestic (confabulatory) **syndrome** 294.0
  alcohol-induced persisting 291.1
  drug-induced persisting 292.83
  posttraumatic 294.0
Amniocentesis screening (for) V28.2

☑ Additional Digit Required — Refer to the Tabular List for Digit Selection   ⬛ Subterms under main terms may continue to next column or page

2007 ICD-9-CM   ▶◀ Revised Text   ● New Line   ▲ Revised Code   **October 2006 · Volume 2 — 17**

Amniocentesis screening —
continued
  alphafetoprotein level, raised V28.1
  chromosomal anomalies V28.0
Amnion, amniotic — *see also* condition
  nodosum 658.8 ☑
Amnionitis (complicating pregnancy)
  658.4 ☑
  affecting fetus or newborn 762.7
Amoral trends 301.7
Amotio retinae — *see also* Detachment,
  retina 361.9
Ampulla
  lower esophagus 530.89
  phrenic 530.89
Amputation
  any part of fetus, to facilitate delivery
    763.89
  cervix (supravaginal) (uteri) 622.8
    in pregnancy or childbirth 654.6 ☑
      affecting fetus or newborn
        763.89
  clitoris — *see* Wound, open, clitoris
  congenital
    lower limb 755.31
    upper limb 755.21
  neuroma (traumatic) (*see also* Injury,
    nerve, by site)
    surgical complication (late) 997.61
  penis — *see* Amputation, traumatic,
    penis
  status (without complication) — *see*
    Absence, by site, acquired
  stump (surgical) (posttraumatic)
    abnormal, painful, or with compli-
      cation (late) 997.60
    healed or old NEC (*see also* Ab-
      sence, by site, acquired)
      lower V49.70
      upper V49.60
  traumatic (complete) (partial)

> *Note* — "Complicated" includes traumat-
> ic amputation with delayed healing,
> delayed treatment, foreign body, or in-
> fection.

    arm 887.4
      at or above elbow 887.2
        complicated 887.3
      below elbow 887.0
        complicated 887.1
      both (bilateral) (any level(s))
        887.6
        complicated 887.7
      complicated 887.5
    finger(s) (one or both hands) 886.0
      with thumb(s) 885.0
        complicated 885.1
      complicated 886.1
    foot (except toe(s) only) 896.0
      and other leg 897.6
        complicated 897.7
      both (bilateral) 896.2
        complicated 896.3
      complicated 896.1
      toe(s) only (one or both feet)
        895.0
        complicated 895.1
    genital organ(s) (external) NEC
      878.8
      complicated 878.9
    hand (except finger(s) only) 887.0
      and other arm 887.6
        complicated 887.7
      both (bilateral) 887.6
        complicated 887.7
      complicated 887.1
      finger(s) (one or both hands)
        886.0
        with thumb(s) 885.0
          complicated 885.1
        complicated 886.1
      thumb(s) (with fingers of either
        hand) 885.0
        complicated 885.1
    head 874.9

Amputation — *continued*
  traumatic — *continued*
    late effect — *see* Late, effects (of),
      amputation
    leg 897.4
      and other foot 897.6
        complicated 897.7
      at or above knee 897.2
        complicated 897.3
      below knee 897.0
        complicated 897.1
      both (bilateral) 897.6
        complicated 897.7
      complicated 897.5
    lower limb(s) except toe(s) — *see*
      Amputation, traumatic, leg
    nose — *see* Wound, open, nose
    penis 878.0
      complicated 878.1
    sites other than limbs — *see*
      Wound, open, by site
    thumb(s) (with finger(s) of either
      hand) 885.0
      complicated 885.1
    toe(s) (one or both feet) 895.0
      complicated 895.1
    upper limb(s) — *see* Amputation,
      traumatic, arm
Amputee (bilateral) (old) — *see also* Absence, by site, acquired V49.70
Amusia 784.69
  developmental 315.39
  secondary to organic lesion 784.69
Amyelencephalus 740.0
Amyelia 742.59
Amygdalitis — *see* Tonsillitis
Amygdalolith 474.8
Amyloid disease or degeneration
  277.30   ▲
  heart 277.39 *[425.7]*   ▲
Amyloidosis (familial) (general) (generaliz-
  ized) (genetic) (primary)
  277.39   ▲
  with lung involvement
    277.39 *[517.8]*   ▲
  cardiac, hereditary 277.39   ●
  heart 277.39 *[425.7]*   ▲
  nephropathic 277.39 *[583.81]*   ▲
  neuropathic (Portuguese) (Swiss)
    277.39 *[357.4]*   ▲
  pulmonary 277.39 *[517.8]*   ▲
  secondary 277.39   ●
  systemic, inherited 277.39   ▲
Amylopectinosis (brancher enzyme deficiency) 271.0
Amylophagia 307.52
Amyoplasia, congenita 756.89
Amyotonia 728.2
  congenita 358.8
**Amyotrophia, amyotrophy, amyotroph-
ic** 728.2
  congenita 756.89
  diabetic 250.6 ☑ *[358.1]*
  lateral sclerosis (syndrome) 335.20
  neuralgic 353.5
  sclerosis (lateral) 335.20
  spinal progressive 335.21
Anacidity, gastric 536.0
  psychogenic 306.4
Anaerosis of newborn 770.88   ▲
Analbuminemia 273.8
Analgesia — *see also* Anesthesia 782.0
Analphalipoproteinemia 272.5
Anaphylactic shock or reaction (correct
  substance properly administered)
  995.0
  due to
    food 995.60
      additives 995.66
      crustaceans 995.62
      eggs 995.68
      fish 995.65
      fruits 995.63
      milk products 995.67
      nuts (tree) 995.64
      peanuts 995.61

Anaphylactic shock or reaction —
continued
  due to — *continued*
    food — *continued*
      seeds 995.64
      specified NEC 995.69
      tree nuts 995.64
      vegetables 995.63
    immunization 999.4
    overdose or wrong substance given
      or taken 977.9
      specified drug — *see* Table of
        Drugs and Chemicals
    serum 999.4
  following sting(s) 989.5
  purpura 287.0
  serum 999.4
Anaphylactoid shock or reaction — *see*
  Anaphylactic shock
Anaphylaxis — *see* Anaphylactic shock
Anaplasia, cervix 622.10
Anarthria 784.5
Anarthritic rheumatoid disease 446.5
Anasarca 782.3
  cardiac (*see also* Failure, heart) 428.0
  fetus or newborn 778.0
  lung 514
  nutritional 262
  pulmonary 514
  renal (*see also* Nephrosis) 581.9
Anaspadias 752.62
Anastomosis
  aneurysmal — *see* Aneurysm
  arteriovenous, congenital NEC (*see
    also* Anomaly, arteriovenous)
    747.60
    ruptured, of brain (*see also* Hemor-
      rhage, subarachnoid) 430
  intestinal 569.89
    complicated NEC 997.4
      involving urinary tract 997.5
  retinal and choroidal vessels 743.58
    acquired 362.17
Anatomical narrow angle (glaucoma)
  365.02
Ancylostoma (infection) (infestation)
  126.9
  americanus 126.1
  braziliense 126.2
  caninum 126.8
  ceylanicum 126.3
  duodenale 126.0
  Necator americanus 126.1
Ancylostomiasis (intestinal) 126.9
  ancylostoma
    americanus 126.1
    caninum 126.8
    ceylanicum 126.3
    duodenale 126.0
  braziliense 126.2
  Necator americanus 126.1
Anders' disease or syndrome (adiposis
  tuberosa simplex) 272.8
Andersen's glycogen storage disease
  271.0
Anderson's disease 272.7
Andes disease 993.2
Andrews' disease (bacterid) 686.8
Androblastoma (M8630/1)
  benign (M8630/0)
    specified site — *see* Neoplasm, by
      site, benign
    unspecified site
      female 220
      male 222.0
  malignant (M8630/3)
    specified site — *see* Neoplasm, by
      site, malignant
    unspecified site
      female 183.0
      male 186.9
  specified site — *see* Neoplasm, by site,
    uncertain behavior

Androblastoma — *continued*
  tubular (M8640/0)
    with lipid storage (M8641/0)
      specified site — *see* Neoplasm,
        by site, benign
      unspecified site
        female 220
        male 222.0
    specified site — *see* Neoplasm, by
      site, benign
    unspecified site
      female 220
      male 222.0
  unspecified site
    female 236.2
    male 236.4
Android pelvis 755.69
  with disproportion (fetopelvic) 653.3 ☑
    affecting fetus or newborn 763.1
    causing obstructed labor 660.1 ☑
      affecting fetus or newborn 763.1
Anectasis, pulmonary (newborn or fetus)
  770.5
Anemia 285.9
  with
    disorder of
      anaerobic glycolysis 282.3
      pentose phosphate pathway
        282.2
    koilonychia 280.9
  6-phosphogluconic dehydrogenase
    deficiency 282.2
  achlorhydric 280.9
  achrestic 281.8
  Addison's (pernicious) 281.0
  Addison-Biermer (pernicious) 281.0
  agranulocytic 288.09   ▲
  amino acid deficiency 281.4
  aplastic 284.9
    acquired (secondary) 284.8
    congenital 284.01   ▲
    constitutional 284.01   ▲
    due to
      chronic systemic disease 284.8
      drugs 284.8
      infection 284.8
      radiation 284.8
    idiopathic 284.9
    myxedema 244.9
    of or complicating pregnancy
      648.2 ☑
    red cell (acquired) (with thymoma)
      284.8
      congenital 284.01   ▲
      pure 284.01   ●
    specified type NEC 284.8
    toxic (paralytic) 284.8
  aregenerative 284.9
    congenital 284.01   ▲
  asiderotic 280.9
  atypical (primary) 285.9
  autohemolysis of Selwyn and Dacie
    (type I) 282.2
  autoimmune hemolytic 283.0
  Baghdad Spring 282.2
  Balantidium coli 007.0
  Biermer's (pernicious) 281.0
  blood loss (chronic) 280.0
    acute 285.1
  bothriocephalus 123.4
  brickmakers' (*see also* Ancylostomia-
    sis) 126.9
  cerebral 437.8
  childhood 282.9
  chlorotic 280.9
  chronica congenita aregenerativa
    284.01   ▲
  chronic simple 281.9
  combined system disease NEC
    281.0 *[336.2]*
    due to dietary deficiency
      281.1 *[336.2]*
  complicating pregnancy or childbirth
    648.2 ☑
  congenital (following fetal blood loss)
    776.5

☑ Additional Digit Required — Refer to the Tabular List for Digit Selection   ▽ Subterms under main terms may continue to next column or page

18 — Volume 2 · October 2006   ▶◀ Revised Text   ● New Line   ▲ Revised Code   *2007 ICD-9-CM*

Anemia — *continued*
congenital — *continued*
aplastic 284.01 ▲
due to isoimmunization NEC 773.2
Heinz-body 282.7
hereditary hemolytic NEC 282.9
nonspherocytic
Type I 282.2
Type II 282.3
pernicious 281.0
spherocytic (*see also* Spherocytosis) 282.0
Cooley's (erythroblastic) 282.49
crescent — *see* Disease, sickle-cell
cytogenic 281.0
Dacie's (nonspherocytic)
type I 282.2
type II 282.3
Davidson's (refractory) 284.9
deficiency 281.9
2, 3 diphosphoglycurate mutase 282.3
2, 3 PG 282.3
6-PGD 282.2
6-phosphogluronic dehydrogenase 282.2
amino acid 281.4
combined B_{12} and folate 281.3
enzyme, drug-induced (hemolytic) 282.2
erythrocytic glutathione 282.2
folate 281.2
dietary 281.2
drug-induced 281.2
folic acid 281.2
dietary 281.2
drug-induced 281.2
G-6-PD 282.2
GGS-R 282.2
glucose-6-phosphate dehydrogenase (G-6-PD) 282.2
glucose-phosphate isomerase 282.3
glutathione peroxidase 282.2
glutathione reductase 282.2
glyceraldehyde phosphate dehydrogenase 282.3
GPI 282.3
G SH 282.2
hexokinase 282.3
iron (Fe) 280.9
specified NEC 280.8
nutritional 281.9
with
poor iron absorption 280.9
specified deficiency NEC 281.8
due to inadequate dietary iron intake 280.1
specified type NEC 281.8
of or complicating pregnancy 648.2 ☑
pentose phosphate pathway 282.2
PFK 282.3
phosphofructo-aldolase 282.3
phosphofructokinase 282.3
phosphoglycerate kinase 282.3
PK 282.3
protein 281.4
pyruvate kinase (PK) 282.3
TPI 282.3
triosephosphate isomerase 282.3
vitamin B_{12} NEC 281.1
dietary 281.1
pernicious 281.0
Diamond-Blackfan (congenital hypoplastic) 284.01 ▲
dibothriocephalus 123.4
dimorphic 281.9
diphasic 281.8
diphtheritic 032.89
Diphyllobothrium 123.4
drepanocytic (*see also* Disease, sickle-cell) 282.60
due to
blood loss (chronic) 280.0
acute 285.1

Anemia — *continued*
due to — *continued*
defect of Embden-Meyerhof pathway glycolysis 282.3
disorder of glutathione metabolism 282.2
fetal blood loss 776.5
fish tapeworm (D. latum) infestation 123.4
glutathione metabolism disorder 282.2
hemorrhage (chronic) 280.0
acute 285.1
hexose monophosphate (HMP) shunt deficiency 282.2
impaired absorption 280.9
loss of blood (chronic) 280.0
acute 285.1
myxedema 244.9
Necator americanus 126.1
prematurity 776.6
selective vitamin B_{12} malabsorption with proteinuria 281.1
Dyke-Young type (secondary) (symptomatic) 283.9
dyserythropoietic (congenital) (types I, II, III) 285.8
dyshemopoietic (congenital) 285.8
Egypt (*see also* Ancylostomiasis) 126.9
elliptocytosis (*see also* Elliptocytosis) 282.1
enzyme deficiency, drug-induced 282.2
epidemic (*see also* Ancylostomiasis) 126.9
EPO resistant 285.21
erythroblastic
familial 282.49
fetus or newborn (*see also* Disease, hemolytic) 773.2
late 773.5
erythrocytic glutathione deficiency 282.2
erythropoietin-resistant (EPO resistant anemia) 285.21
essential 285.9
Faber's (achlorhydric anemia) 280.9
factitious (self-induced blood letting) 280.0
familial erythroblastic (microcytic) 282.49
Fanconi's (congenital pancytopenia) 284.09 ▲
favism 282.2
fetal, following blood loss 776.5
fetus or newborn
due to
ABO
antibodies 773.1
incompatibility, maternal/fetal 773.1
isoimmunization 773.1
Rh
antibodies 773.0
incompatibility, maternal/fetal 773.0
isoimmunization 773.0
following fetal blood loss 776.5
fish tapeworm (D. latum) infestation 123.4
folate (folic acid) deficiency 281.2
dietary 281.2
drug-induced 281.2
folate malabsorption, congenital 281.2
folic acid deficiency 281.2
dietary 281.2
drug-induced 281.2
G-6-PD 282.2
general 285.9
glucose-6-phosphate dehydrogenase deficiency 282.2
glutathione-reductase deficiency 282.2
goat's milk 281.2
granulocytic 288.09 ▲
Heinz-body, congenital 282.7
hemoglobin deficiency 285.9

Anemia — *continued*
hemolytic 283.9
acquired 283.9
with hemoglobinuria NEC 283.2
autoimmune (cold type) (idiopathic) (primary) (secondary) (symptomatic) (warm type) 283.0
due to
cold reactive antibodies 283.0
drug exposure 283.0
warm reactive antibodies 283.0
fragmentation 283.19
idiopathic (chronic) 283.9
infectious 283.19
autoimmune 283.0
non-autoimmune 283.10
toxic 283.19
traumatic cardiac 283.19
acute 283.9
due to enzyme deficiency NEC 282.3
fetus or newborn (*see also* Disease, hemolytic) 773.2
late 773.5
Lederer's (acquired infectious hemolytic anemia) 283.19
autoimmune (acquired) 283.0
chronic 282.9
idiopathic 283.9
cold type (secondary) (symptomatic) 283.0
congenital (spherocytic) (*see also* Spherocytosis) 282.0
nonspherocytic — *see* Anemia, hemolytic, nonspherocytic, congenital
drug-induced 283.0
enzyme deficiency 282.2
due to
cardiac conditions 283.19
drugs 283.0
enzyme deficiency NEC 282.3
drug-induced 282.2
presence of shunt or other internal prosthetic device 283.19
thrombotic thrombocytopenic purpura 446.6
elliptocytotic (*see also* Elliptocytosis) 282.1
familial 282.9
hereditary 282.9
due to enzyme deficiency NEC 282.3
specified NEC 282.8
idiopathic (chronic) 283.9
infectious (acquired) 283.19
mechanical 283.19
microangiopathic 283.19
non-autoimmune NEC 283.10
nonspherocytic
congenital or hereditary NEC 282.3
glucose-6-phosphate dehydrogenase deficiency 282.2
pyruvate kinase (PK) deficiency 282.3
type I 282.2
type II 282.3
type I 282.2
type II 282.3
of or complicating pregnancy 648.2 ☑
resulting from presence of shunt or other internal prosthetic device 283.19
secondary 283.19
autoimmune 283.0
sickle-cell — *see* Disease, sickle-cell

Anemia — *continued*
hemolytic — *continued*
Stransky-Regala type (Hb-E) (*see also* Disease, hemoglobin) 282.7
symptomatic 283.19
autoimmune 283.0
toxic (acquired) 283.19
uremic (adult) (child) 283.11
warm type (secondary) (symptomatic) 283.0
hemorrhagic (chronic) 280.0
acute 285.1
HEMPAS 285.8
hereditary erythroblast multinuclearity-positive acidified serum test 285.8
Herrick's (hemoglobin S disease) 282.61
hexokinase deficiency 282.3
high A_2 282.49
hookworm (*see also* Ancylostomiasis) 126.9
hypochromic (idiopathic) (microcytic) (normoblastic) 280.9
with iron loading 285.0
due to blood loss (chronic) 280.0
acute 285.1
familial sex linked 285.0
pyridoxine-responsive 285.0
hypoplasia, red blood cells 284.8
congenital or familial 284.01 ▲
hypoplastic (idiopathic) 284.9
congenital 284.01 ▲
familial 284.01 ▲
of childhood 284.09 ▲
idiopathic 285.9
hemolytic, chronic 283.9
in
chronic illness NEC 285.29
chronic kidney disease 285.21
end-stage renal disease 285.21
neoplastic disease 285.22
infantile 285.9
infective, infectional 285.9
intertropical (*see also* Ancylostomiasis) 126.9
iron (Fe) deficiency 280.9
due to blood loss (chronic) 280.0
acute 285.1
of or complicating pregnancy 648.2 ☑
specified NEC 280.8
Jaksch's (pseudoleukemia infantum) 285.8
Joseph-Diamond-Blackfan (congenital hypoplastic) 284.01 ▲
labyrinth 386.50
Lederer's (acquired infectious hemolytic anemia) 283.19
leptocytosis (hereditary) 282.49
leukoerythroblastic 284.2 ▲
macrocytic 281.9
nutritional 281.2
of or complicating pregnancy 648.2 ☑
tropical 281.2
malabsorption (familial), selective B_{12}
with proteinuria 281.1
malarial (*see also* Malaria) 084.6
malignant (progressive) 281.0
malnutrition 281.9
marsh (*see also* Malaria) 084.6
Mediterranean (with hemoglobinopathy) 282.49
megaloblastic 281.9
combined B_{12} and folate deficiency 281.3
nutritional (of infancy) 281.2
of infancy 281.2
of or complicating pregnancy 648.2 ☑
refractory 281.3
specified NEC 281.3
megalocytic 281.9
microangiopathic hemolytic 283.19

Anemia — *continued*
microcytic (hypochromic) 280.9
due to blood loss (chronic) 280.0
acute 285.1
familial 282.49
hypochromic 280.9
microdrepanocytosis 282.49
miners' (*see also* Ancylostomiasis)
126.9
myelopathic 285.8
myelophthisic (normocytic) 284.2 ▲
newborn (*see also* Disease, hemolytic)
773.2
due to isoimmunization (*see also*
Disease, hemolytic) 773.2
late, due to isoimmunization 773.5
posthemorrhagic 776.5
nonregenerative 284.9
nonspherocytic hemolytic — *see* Anemia, hemolytic, nonspherocytic
normocytic (infectional) (not due to
blood loss) 285.9
due to blood loss (chronic) 280.0
acute 285.1
myelophthisic 284.2 ▲
nutritional (deficiency) 281.9
with
poor iron absorption 280.9
specified deficiency NEC 281.8
due to inadequate dietary iron intake 280.1
megaloblastic (of infancy) 281.2
of childhood 282.9
of chronic ●
disease NEC 285.29 ●
illness NEC 285.29 ●
of or complicating pregnancy 648.2 ☑
affecting fetus or newborn 760.8
of prematurity 776.6
orotic aciduric (congenital) (hereditary)
281.4
osteosclerotic 289.89
ovalocytosis (hereditary) (*see also* Elliptocytosis) 282.1
paludal (*see also* Malaria) 084.6
pentose phosphate pathway deficiency
282.2
pernicious (combined system disease)
(congenital) (dorsolateral spinal
degeneration) (juvenile)
(myelopathy) (neuropathy) (posterior sclerosis) (primary) (progressive) (spleen) 281.0
of or complicating pregnancy
648.2 ☑
pleochromic 285.9
of sprue 281.8
portal 285.8
posthemorrhagic (chronic) 280.0
acute 285.1
newborn 776.5
postoperative
due to blood loss 285.1
other 285.9
postpartum 648.2 ☑
pressure 285.9
primary 285.9
profound 285.9
progressive 285.9
malignant 281.0
pernicious 281.0
protein-deficiency 281.4
pseudoleukemica infantum 285.8
puerperal 648.2 ☑
pure red cell 284.8
congenital 284.01 ▲
pyridoxine-responsive (hypochromic)
285.0
pyruvate kinase (PK) deficiency 282.3
refractoria sideroblastica 238.72 ▲
refractory (primary) 238.72 ▲
with
excess ●
blasts-1 (RAEB-1) 238.73 ●
blasts-2 (RAEB-2) 238.73 ●
hemochromatosis 238.72 ●

Anemia — *continued*
refractory — *continued*
with — *continued*
ringed sideroblasts (RARS) ●
238.72 ●
megaloblastic 281.3
sideroblastic 238.72 ▲
sideropenic 280.9
Rietti-Greppi-Micheli (thalassemia
minor) 282.49
scorbutic 281.8
secondary (to) 285.9
blood loss (chronic) 280.0
acute 285.1
hemorrhage 280.0
acute 285.1
inadequate dietary iron intake
280.1
semiplastic 284.9
septic 285.9
sickle-cell (*see also* Disease, sickle-cell) 282.60
sideroachrestic 285.0
sideroblastic (acquired) (any type)
(congenital) (drug-induced) (due
to disease) (hereditary) (primary)
(secondary) (sex-linked
hypochromic) (vitamin B_6 responsive) 285.0
refractory 238.72 ▲
sideropenic (refractory) 280.9
due to blood loss (chronic) 280.0
acute 285.1
simple chronic 281.9
specified type NEC 285.8
spherocytic (hereditary) (*see also*
Spherocytosis) 282.0
splenic 285.8
familial (Gaucher's) 272.7
splenomegalic 285.8
stomatocytosis 282.8
syphilitic 095.8
target cell (oval) 282.49
thalassemia 282.49
thrombocytopenic (*see also* Thrombocytopenia) 287.5
toxic 284.8
triosephosphate isomerase deficiency
282.3
tropical, macrocytic 281.2
tuberculous (*see also* Tuberculosis)
017.9 ☑
vegan's 281.1
vitamin
B_6-responsive 285.0
B_{12} deficiency (dietary) 281.1
pernicious 281.0
von Jaksch's (pseudoleukemia infantum) 285.8
Witts' (achlorhydric anemia) 280.9
Zuelzer (-Ogden) (nutritional megaloblastic anemia) 281.2
Anencephalus, anencephaly 740.0
fetal, affecting management of pregnancy 655.0 ☑
Anergasia — *see also* Psychosis, organic
294.9
senile 290.0
Anesthesia, anesthetic 782.0
complication or reaction NEC
995.22 ▲
due to
correct substance properly administered 995.22 ▲
overdose or wrong substance
given 968.4
specified anesthetic — *see*
Table of Drugs and
Chemicals
cornea 371.81
death from
correct substance properly administered 995.4
during delivery 668.9 ☑
overdose or wrong substance given
968.4

Anesthesia, anesthetic — *continued*
death from — *continued*
specified anesthetic — *see* Table of
Drugs and Chemicals
eye 371.81
functional 300.11
hyperesthetic, thalamic 338.0 ▲
hysterical 300.11
local skin lesion 782.0
olfactory 781.1
sexual (psychogenic) 302.72
shock
due to
correct substance properly administered 995.4
overdose or wrong substance
given 968.4
specified anesthetic — *see* Table
of Drugs and Chemicals
skin 782.0
tactile 782.0
testicular 608.9
thermal 782.0
Anetoderma (maculosum) 701.3
Aneuploidy NEC 758.5
Aneurin deficiency 265.1
Aneurysm (anastomotic) (artery) (cirsoid)
(diffuse) (false) (fusiform) (multiple)
(ruptured) (saccular) (varicose)
442.9
abdominal (aorta) 441.4
ruptured 441.3
syphilitic 093.0
aorta, aortic (nonsyphilitic) 441.9
abdominal 441.4
dissecting 441.02
ruptured 441.3
syphilitic 093.0
arch 441.2
ruptured 441.1
arteriosclerotic NEC 441.9
ruptured 441.5
ascending 441.2
ruptured 441.1
congenital 747.29
descending 441.9
abdominal 441.4
ruptured 441.3
ruptured 441.5
thoracic 441.2
ruptured 441.1
dissecting 441.00
abdominal 441.02
thoracic 441.01
thoracoabdominal 441.03
due to coarctation (aorta) 747.10
ruptured 441.5
sinus, right 747.29
syphilitic 093.0
thoracoabdominal 441.7
ruptured 441.6
thorax, thoracic (arch) (nonsyphilitic) 441.2
dissecting 441.01
ruptured 441.1
syphilitic 093.0
transverse 441.2
ruptured 441.1
valve (heart) (*see also* Endocarditis,
aortic) 424.1
arteriosclerotic NEC 442.9
cerebral 437.3
ruptured (*see also* Hemorrhage,
subarachnoid) 430
arteriovenous (congenital) (peripheral)
NEC (*see also* Anomaly, arteriovenous) 747.60
acquired NEC 447.0
brain 437.3
ruptured (*see also* Hemorrhage, subarachnoid)
430
coronary 414.11
pulmonary 417.0
brain (cerebral) 747.81

Aneurysm — *continued*
arteriovenous (*see also* Anomaly, arteriovenous) — *continued*
brain — *continued*
ruptured (*see also* Hemorrhage,
subarachnoid) 430
coronary 746.85
pulmonary 747.3
retina 743.58
specified site NEC 747.89
acquired 447.0
traumatic (*see also* Injury, blood
vessel, by site) 904.9
basal — *see* Aneurysm, brain
berry (congenital) (ruptured) (*see also*
Hemorrhage, subarachnoid) 430
brain 437.3
arteriosclerotic 437.3
ruptured (*see also* Hemorrhage,
subarachnoid) 430
arteriovenous 747.81
acquired 437.3
ruptured (*see also* Hemorrhage, subarachnoid)
430
ruptured (*see also* Hemorrhage,
subarachnoid) 430
berry (congenital) (ruptured) (*see
also* Hemorrhage, subarachnoid) 430
congenital 747.81
ruptured (*see also* Hemorrhage,
subarachnoid) 430
meninges 437.3
ruptured (*see also* Hemorrhage,
subarachnoid) 430
miliary (congenital) (ruptured) (*see
also* Hemorrhage, subarachnoid) 430
mycotic 421.0
ruptured (*see also* Hemorrhage,
subarachnoid) 430
nonruptured 437.3
ruptured (*see also* Hemorrhage,
subarachnoid) 430
syphilitic 094.87
syphilitic (hemorrhage) 094.87
traumatic — *see* Injury, intracranial
cardiac (false) (*see also* Aneurysm,
heart) 414.10
carotid artery (common) (external)
442.81
internal (intracranial portion) 437.3
extracranial portion 442.81
ruptured into brain (*see also*
Hemorrhage, subarachnoid) 430
syphilitic 093.89
intracranial 094.87
cavernous sinus (*see also* Aneurysm,
brain) 437.3
arteriovenous 747.81
ruptured (*see also* Hemorrhage,
subarachnoid) 430
congenital 747.81
ruptured (*see also* Hemorrhage,
subarachnoid) 430
celiac 442.84
central nervous system, syphilitic
094.89
cerebral — *see* Aneurysm, brain
chest — *see* Aneurysm, thorax
circle of Willis (*see also* Aneurysm,
brain) 437.3
congenital 747.81
ruptured (*see also* Hemorrhage,
subarachnoid) 430
ruptured (*see also* Hemorrhage,
subarachnoid) 430
common iliac artery 442.2
congenital (peripheral) NEC 747.60
brain 747.81
ruptured (*see also* Hemorrhage,
subarachnoid) 430

Aneurysm — *continued*
congenital — *continued*
cerebral — *see* Aneurysm, brain,
congenital
coronary 746.85
gastrointestinal 747.61
lower limb 747.64
pulmonary 747.3
renal 747.62
retina 743.58
specified site NEC 747.89
spinal 747.82
upper limb 747.63
conjunctiva 372.74
conus arteriosus (*see also* Aneurysm,
heart) 414.10
coronary (arteriosclerotic) (artery)
(vein) (*see also* Aneurysm, heart)
414.11
arteriovenous 746.85
congenital 746.85
syphilitic 093.89
cylindrical 441.9
ruptured 441.5
syphilitic 093.9
dissecting 442.9
aorta 441.00
abdominal 441.02
thoracic 441.01
thoracoabdominal 441.03
syphilitic 093.9
ductus arteriosus 747.0
embolic — *see* Embolism, artery
endocardial, infective (any valve) 421.0
femoral 442.3
gastroduodenal 442.84
gastroepiploic 442.84
heart (chronic or with a stated duration of over 8 weeks) (infectional)
(wall) 414.10
acute or with a stated duration of
8 weeks or less (*see also* Infarct, myocardium) 410.9 ☑
congenital 746.89
valve — *see* Endocarditis
hepatic 442.84
iliac (common) 442.2
infective (any valve) 421.0
innominate (nonsyphilitic) 442.89
syphilitic 093.89
interauricular septum (*see also*
Aneurysm, heart) 414.10
interventricular septum (*see also*
Aneurysm, heart) 414.10
intracranial — *see* Aneurysm, brain
intrathoracic (nonsyphilitic) 441.2
ruptured 441.1
syphilitic 093.0
jugular vein 453.8
lower extremity 442.3
lung (pulmonary artery) 417.1
malignant 093.9
mediastinal (nonsyphilitic) 442.89
syphilitic 093.89
miliary (congenital) (ruptured) (*see also* Hemorrhage, subarachnoid)
430
mitral (heart) (valve) 424.0
mural (arteriovenous) (heart) (*see also*
Aneurysm, heart) 414.10
mycotic, any site 421.0
without endocarditis — *see* ●
Aneurysm by site ●
ruptured, brain (*see also* Hemorrhage, subarachnoid) 430
myocardium (*see also* Aneurysm,
heart) 414.10
neck 442.81
pancreaticoduodenal 442.84
patent ductus arteriosus 747.0
peripheral NEC 442.89
congenital NEC (*see also*
Aneurysm, congenital)
747.60
popliteal 442.3
pulmonary 417.1

Aneurysm — *continued*
pulmonary — *continued*
arteriovenous 747.3
acquired 417.0
syphilitic 093.89
valve (heart) (*see also* Endocarditis,
pulmonary) 424.3
racemose 442.9
congenital (peripheral) NEC 747.60
radial 442.0
Rasmussen's (*see also* Tuberculosis)
011.2 ☑
renal 442.1
retinal (acquired) 362.17
congenital 743.58
diabetic 250.5 ☑ *[362.01]*
sinus, aortic (of Valsalva) 747.29
specified site NEC 442.89
spinal (cord) 442.89
congenital 747.82
syphilitic (hemorrhage) 094.89
spleen, splenic 442.83
subclavian 442.82
syphilitic 093.89
superior mesenteric 442.84
syphilitic 093.9
aorta 093.0
central nervous system 094.89
congenital 090.5
spine, spinal 094.89
thoracoabdominal 441.7
ruptured 441.6
thorax, thoracic (arch) (nonsyphilitic)
441.2
dissecting 441.01
ruptured 441.1
syphilitic 093.0
traumatic (complication) (early) — *see*
Injury, blood vessel, by site
tricuspid (heart) (valve) — *see* Endocarditis, tricuspid
ulnar 442.0
upper extremity 442.0
valve, valvular — *see* Endocarditis
venous 456.8
congenital NEC (*see also*
Aneurysm, congenital)
747.60
ventricle (arteriovenous) (*see also*
Aneurysm, heart) 414.10
visceral artery NEC 442.84
Angiectasis 459.89
Angiectopia 459.9
Angiitis 447.6
allergic granulomatous 446.4
hypersensitivity 446.20
Goodpasture's syndrome 446.21
specified NEC 446.29
necrotizing 446.0
Wegener's (necrotizing respiratory
granulomatosis) 446.4
Angina (attack) (cardiac) (chest) (effort)
(heart) (pectoris) (syndrome) (vasomotor) 413.9
abdominal 557.1
accelerated 411.1
agranulocytic 288.03   ▲
aphthous 074.0
catarrhal 462
crescendo 411.1
croupous 464.4
cruris 443.9
due to atherosclerosis NEC (*see*
also Arteriosclerosis, extremities) 440.20
decubitus 413.0
diphtheritic (membranous) 032.0
erysipelatous 034.0
erythematous 462
exudative, chronic 476.0
faucium 478.29
gangrenous 462
diphtheritic 032.0
infectious 462
initial 411.1
intestinal 557.1

Angina — *continued*
ludovici 528.3
Ludwig's 528.3
malignant 462
diphtheritic 032.0
membranous 464.4
diphtheritic 032.0
mesenteric 557.1
monocytic 075
nocturnal 413.0
phlegmonous 475
diphtheritic 032.0
preinfarctional 411.1
Prinzmetal's 413.1
progressive 411.1
pseudomembranous 101
psychogenic 306.2
pultaceous, diphtheritic 032.0
scarlatinal 034.1
septic 034.0
simple 462
stable NEC 413.9
staphylococcal 462
streptococcal 034.0
stridulous, diphtheritic 032.3
syphilitic 093.9
congenital 090.5
tonsil 475
trachealis 464.4
unstable 411.1
variant 413.1
Vincent's 101
Angioblastoma (M9161/1) — *see* Neoplasm, connective tissue, uncertain
behavior
Angiocholecystitis — *see also* Cholecystitis, acute 575.0
Angiocholitis — *see also* Cholecystitis,
acute 576.1
Angiodysgensis spinalis 336.1
Angiodysplasia (intestinalis) (intestine)
569.84
with hemorrhage 569.85
duodenum 537.82
with hemorrhage 537.83
stomach 537.82
with hemorrhage 537.83
Angioedema (allergic) (any site) (with
urticaria) 995.1
hereditary 277.6
Angioendothelioma (M9130/1) — *see*
also Neoplasm, by site, uncertain
behavior
benign (M9130/0) (*see also* Hemangioma, by site) 228.00
bone (M9260/3) — *see* Neoplasm,
bone, malignant
Ewing's (M9260/3) — *see* Neoplasm,
bone, malignant
nervous system (M9130/0) 228.09
Angiofibroma (M9160/0) — *see also*
Neoplasm, by site, benign
juvenile (M9160/0) 210.7
specified site — *see* Neoplasm, by
site, benign
unspecified site 210.7
Angiohemophilia (A) (B) 286.4
Angioid streaks (choroid) (retina) 363.43
Angiokeratoma (M9141/0) — *see also*
Neoplasm, skin, benign
corporis diffusum 272.7
Angiokeratosis
diffuse 272.7
Angioleiomyoma (M8894/0) — *see*
Neoplasm, connective tissue, benign
Angioleucitis 683
Angiolipoma (M8861/0) — *see also*
Lipoma, by site 214.9
infiltrating (M8861/1) — *see* Neoplasm, connective tissue, uncertain behavior
Angioma (M9120/0) — *see also* Heman-
gioma, by site 228.00
capillary 448.1
hemorrhagicum hereditaria 448.0

Angioma — *see also* Hemangioma, by
site — *continued*
malignant (M9120/3) — *see* Neoplasm, connective tissue, malignant
pigmentosum et atrophicum 757.33
placenta — *see* Placenta, abnormal
plexiform (M9131/0) — *see* Hemangioma, by site
senile 448.1
serpiginosum 709.1
spider 448.1
stellate 448.1
Angiomatosis 757.32
bacillary 083.8
corporis diffusum universale 272.7
cutaneocerebral 759.6
encephalocutaneous 759.6
encephalofacial 759.6
encephalotrigeminal 759.6
hemorrhagic familial 448.0
hereditary familial 448.0
heredofamilial 448.0
meningo-oculofacial 759.6
multiple sites 228.09
neuro-oculocutaneous 759.6
retina (Hippel's disease) 759.6
retinocerebellosa 759.6
retinocerebral 759.6
systemic 228.09
Angiomyolipoma (M8860/0)
specified site — *see* Neoplasm, connective tissue, benign
unspecified site 223.0
Angiomyoliposarcoma (M8860/3) — *see*
Neoplasm, connective tissue, malignant
Angiomyoma (M8894/0) — *see* Neoplasm, connective tissue, benign
Angiomyosarcoma (M8894/3) — *see*
Neoplasm, connective tissue, malignant
Angioneurosis 306.2
Angioneurotic edema (allergic) (any site)
(with urticaria) 995.1
hereditary 277.6
Angiopathia, angiopathy 459.9
diabetic (peripheral) 250.7 ☑ *[443.81]*
peripheral 443.9
diabetic 250.7 ☑ *[443.81]*
specified type NEC 443.89
retinae syphilitica 093.89
retinalis (juvenilis) 362.18
background 362.10
diabetic 250.5 ☑ *[362.01]*
proliferative 362.29
tuberculous (*see also* Tuberculosis)
017.3 ☑ *[362.18]*
Angiosarcoma (M9120/3) — *see* Neoplasm, connective tissue, malignant
Angiosclerosis — *see* Arteriosclerosis
Angioscotoma, enlarged 368.42
Angiospasm 443.9
brachial plexus 353.0
cerebral 435.9
cervical plexus 353.2
nerve
arm 354.9
axillary 353.0
median 354.1
ulnar 354.2
autonomic (*see also* Neuropathy,
peripheral, autonomic) 337.9
axillary 353.0
leg 355.8
plantar 355.6
lower extremity — *see* Angiospasm,
nerve, leg
median 354.1
peripheral NEC 355.9
spinal NEC 355.9
sympathetic (*see also* Neuropathy,
peripheral, autonomic) 337.9
ulnar 354.2

☑ Additional Digit Required — Refer to the Tabular List for Digit Selection   ▽ Subterms under main terms may continue to next column or page

2007 ICD-9-CM   ▶◀ Revised Text   ● New Line   ▲ Revised Code   October 2006 · Volume 2 — 21

Angiospasm — continued
nerve — continued
upper extremity — see Angiospasm, nerve, arm
peripheral NEC 443.9
traumatic 443.9
foot 443.9
leg 443.9
vessel 443.9
Angiospastic disease or edema 443.9
Angle's
class I 524.21
class II 524.22
class III 524.23
Anguillulosis 127.2
Angulation
cecum (see also Obstruction, intestine) 560.9
coccyx (acquired) 738.6
congenital 756.19
femur (acquired) 736.39
congenital 755.69
intestine (large) (small) (see also Obstruction, intestine) 560.9
sacrum (acquired) 738.5
congenital 756.19
sigmoid (flexure) (see also Obstruction, intestine) 560.9
spine (see also Curvature, spine) 737.9
tibia (acquired) 736.89
congenital 755.69
ureter 593.3
wrist (acquired) 736.09
congenital 755.59
Angulus infectiosus 686.8
Anhedonia 302.72
Anhidrosis (lid) (neurogenic) (thermogenic) 705.0
Anhydration 276.51
with
hypernatremia 276.0
hyponatremia 276.1
Anhydremia 276.52
with
hypernatremia 276.0
hyponatremia 276.1
Anidrosis 705.0
Aniridia (congenital) 743.45
Anisakiasis (infection) (infestation) 127.1
Anisakis larva infestation 127.1
Aniseikonia 367.32
Anisocoria (pupil) 379.41
congenital 743.46
Anisocytosis 790.09
Anisometropia (congenital) 367.31
Ankle — see condition
Ankyloblepharon (acquired) (eyelid) 374.46
filiforme (adnatum) (congenital) 743.62
total 743.62
Ankylodactly — see also Syndactylism 755.10
Ankyloglossia 750.0
Ankylosis (fibrous) (osseous) 718.50
ankle 718.57
any joint, produced by surgical fusion V45.4
cricoarytenoid (cartilage) (joint) (larynx) 478.79
dental 521.6
ear ossicle NEC 385.22
malleus 385.21
elbow 718.52
finger 718.54
hip 718.55
incostapedial joint (infectional) 385.22
joint, produced by surgical fusion NEC V45.4
knee 718.56
lumbosacral (joint) 724.6
malleus 385.21
multiple sites 718.59
postoperative (status) V45.4
sacroiliac (joint) 724.6

Ankylosis — continued
shoulder 718.51
specified site NEC 718.58
spine NEC 724.9
surgical V45.4
teeth, tooth (hard tissues) 521.6
temporomandibular joint 524.61
wrist 718.53
Ankylostoma — see Ancylostoma
Ankylostomiasis (intestinal) — see Ancylostomiasis
Ankylurethria — see also Stricture, urethra 598.9
Annular — see also condition
detachment, cervix 622.8
organ or site, congenital NEC — see Distortion
pancreas (congenital) 751.7
Anodontia (complete) (partial) (vera) 520.0
with abnormal spacing 524.30
acquired 525.10
causing malocclusion 524.30
due to
caries 525.13
extraction 525.10
periodontal disease 525.12
trauma 525.11
Anomaly, anomalous (congenital) (unspecified type) 759.9
abdomen 759.9
abdominal wall 756.70
acoustic nerve 742.9
adrenal (gland) 759.1
Alder (-Reilly) (leukocyte granulation) 288.2
alimentary tract 751.9
lower 751.5
specified type NEC 751.8
upper (any part, except tongue) 750.9
tongue 750.10
specified type NEC 750.19
alveolar 524.70
ridge (process) 525.8
specified NEC 524.79
ankle (joint) 755.69
anus, anal (canal) 751.5
aorta, aortic 747.20
arch 747.21
coarctation (postductal) (preductal) 747.10
cusp or valve NEC 746.9
septum 745.0
specified type NEC 747.29
aorticopulmonary septum 745.0
apertures, diaphragm 756.6
appendix 751.5
aqueduct of Sylvius 742.3
with spina bifida (see also Spina bifida) 741.0 ☑
arm 755.50
reduction (see also Deformity, reduction, upper limb) 755.20
arteriovenous (congenital) (peripheral) NEC 747.60
brain 747.81
cerebral 747.81
coronary 746.85
gastrointestinal 747.61
acquired — see Angiodysplasia
lower limb 747.64
renal 747.62
specified site NEC 747.69
spinal 747.82
upper limb 747.63
artery (see also Anomaly, peripheral vascular system) NEC 747.60
brain 747.81
cerebral 747.81
coronary 746.85
eye 743.9
pulmonary 747.3
renal 747.62
retina 743.9
umbilical 747.5

Anomaly, anomalous — continued
arytenoepiglottic folds 748.3
atrial
bands 746.9
folds 746.9
septa 746.9
atrioventricular
canal 745.69
common 745.69
conduction 426.7
excitation 426.7
septum 745.4
atrium — see Anomaly, atrial
auditory canal 744.3
specified type NEC 744.29
with hearing impairment 744.02
auricle
ear 744.3
causing impairment of hearing 744.02
heart 746.9
septum 745.5
autosomes, autosomal NEC 758.5
Axenfeld's 743.44
back 759.9
band
atrial 746.9
heart 746.9
ventricular 746.9
Bartholin's duct 750.9
biliary duct or passage 751.60
atresia 751.61
bladder (neck) (sphincter) (trigone) 753.9
specified type NEC 753.8
blood vessel 747.9
artery — see Anomaly, artery
peripheral vascular — see Anomaly, peripheral vascular system
vein — see Anomaly, vein
bone NEC 756.9
ankle 755.69
arm 755.50
chest 756.3
cranium 756.0
face 756.0
finger 755.50
foot 755.67
forearm 755.50
frontal 756.0
head 756.0
hip 755.63
leg 755.60
lumbosacral 756.10
nose 748.1
pelvic girdle 755.60
rachitic 756.4
rib 756.3
shoulder girdle 755.50
skull 756.0
with
anencephalus 740.0
encephalocele 742.0
hydrocephalus 742.3
with spina bifida (see also Spina bifida) 741.0 ☑
microcephalus 742.1
toe 755.66
brain 742.9
multiple 742.4
reduction 742.2
specified type NEC 742.4
vessel 747.81
branchial cleft NEC 744.49
cyst 744.42
fistula 744.41
persistent 744.41
sinus (external) (internal) 744.41
breast 757.9
broad ligament 752.10
specified type NEC 752.19
bronchus 748.3
bulbar septum 745.0
bulbus cordis 745.9

Anomaly, anomalous — continued
bulbus cordis — continued
persistent (in left ventricle) 745.8
bursa 756.9
canal of Nuck 752.9
canthus 743.9
capillary NEC (see also Anomaly, peripheral vascular system) 747.60
cardiac 746.9
septal closure 745.9
acquired 429.71
valve NEC 746.9
pulmonary 746.00
specified type NEC 746.89
cardiovascular system 746.9
complicating pregnancy, childbirth, or puerperium 648.5 ☑
carpus 755.50
cartilage, trachea 748.3
cartilaginous 756.9
caruncle, lacrimal, lachrymal 743.9
cascade stomach 750.7
cauda equina 742.59
cecum 751.5
cerebral (see also Anomaly, brain vessels) 747.81
cerebrovascular system 747.81
cervix (uterus) 752.40
with doubling of vagina and uterus 752.2
in pregnancy or childbirth 654.6 ☑
affecting fetus or newborn 763.89
causing obstructed labor 660.2 ☑
affecting fetus or newborn 763.1
Chédiak-Higashi (-Steinbrinck) (congenital gigantism of peroxidase granules) 288.2
cheek 744.9
chest (wall) 756.3
chin 744.9
specified type NEC 744.89
chordae tendineae 746.9
choroid 743.9
plexus 742.9
chromosomes, chromosomal 758.9
13 (13-15) 758.1
18 (16-18) 758.2
21 or 22 758.0
autosomes NEC (see also Abnormal, autosomes) 758.5
deletion 758.39
Christchurch 758.39
D_1 758.1
E_3 758.2
G 758.0
mitochondrial 758.9
mosaics 758.89
sex 758.81
complement, XO 758.6
complement, XXX 758.81
complement, XXY 758.7
complement, XYY 758.81
gonadal dysgenesis 758.6
Klinefelter's 758.7
Turner's 758.6
trisomy 21 758.0
cilia 743.9
circulatory system 747.9
specified type NEC 747.89
clavicle 755.51
clitoris 752.40
coccyx 756.10
colon 751.5
common duct 751.60
communication
coronary artery 746.85
left ventricle with right atrium 745.4
concha (ear) 744.3
connection
renal vessels with kidney 747.62
total pulmonary venous 747.41

Anomaly, anomalous — *continued*
- connective tissue 756.9
  - specified type NEC 756.89
- cornea 743.9
  - shape 743.41
  - size 743.41
  - specified type NEC 743.49
- coronary
  - artery 746.85
  - vein 746.89
- cranium — *see* Anomaly, skull
- cricoid cartilage 748.3
- cushion, endocardial 745.60
  - specified type NEC 745.69
- cystic duct 751.60
- dental arch 524.20 ●
  - specified NEC 524.29 ●
- dental arch relationship 524.20
  - angle's class I 524.21
  - angle's class II 524.22
  - angle's class III 524.23
  - articulation
    - anterior 524.27
    - posterior 524.27
    - reverse 524.27
  - disto-occlusion 524.22
    - division I 524.22
    - division II 524.22
  - excessive horizontal overlap 524.26
  - interarch distance (excessive) (inadequate) 524.28
  - mesio-occlusion 524.23
  - neutro-occlusion 524.21
  - open
    - anterior occlusal relationship 524.24
    - posterior occlusal relationship 524.25
  - specified NEC 524.29
- dentition 520.6
- dentofacial NEC 524.9
  - functional 524.50
  - specified type NEC 524.89
- dermatoglyphic 757.2
- Descemet's membrane 743.9
  - specified type NEC 743.49
- development
  - cervix 752.40
  - vagina 752.40
  - vulva 752.40
- diaphragm, diaphragmatic (apertures) NEC 756.6
- digestive organ(s) or system 751.9
  - lower 751.5
    - specified type NEC 751.8
  - upper 750.9
- distribution, coronary artery 746.85
- ductus
  - arteriosus 747.0
  - Botalli 747.0
- duodenum 751.5
- dura 742.9
  - brain 742.4
  - spinal cord 742.59
- ear 744.3
  - causing impairment of hearing 744.00
    - specified type NEC 744.09
  - external 744.3
    - causing impairment of hearing 744.02
    - specified type NEC 744.29
  - inner (causing impairment of hearing) 744.05
  - middle, except ossicles (causing impairment of hearing) 744.03
    - ossicles 744.04
  - ossicles 744.04
  - prominent auricle 744.29
  - specified type NEC 744.29
    - with hearing impairment 744.09
- Ebstein's (heart) 746.2
  - tricuspid valve 746.2
- ectodermal 757.9

Anomaly, anomalous — *continued*
- Eisenmenger's (ventricular septal defect) 745.4
- ejaculatory duct 752.9
  - specified type NEC 752.89
- elbow (joint) 755.50
- endocardial cushion 745.60
  - specified type NEC 745.69
- endocrine gland NEC 759.2
- epididymis 752.9
- epiglottis 748.3
- esophagus 750.9
  - specified type NEC 750.4
- Eustachian tube 744.3
  - specified type NEC 744.24
- eye (any part) 743.9
  - adnexa 743.9
    - specified type NEC 743.69
  - anophthalmos 743.00
  - anterior
    - chamber and related structures 743.9
      - angle 743.9
        - specified type NEC 743.44
      - specified type NEC 743.44
    - segment 743.9
      - combined 743.48
      - multiple 743.48
      - specified type NEC 743.49
  - cataract (*see also* Cataract) 743.30
  - glaucoma (*see also* Buphthalmia) 743.20
  - lid 743.9
    - specified type NEC 743.63
  - microphthalmos (*see also* Microphthalmos) 743.10
  - posterior segment 743.9
    - specified type NEC 743.59
    - vascular 743.58
    - vitreous 743.9
      - specified type NEC 743.51
  - ptosis (eyelid) 743.61
  - retina 743.9
    - specified type NEC 743.59
  - sclera 743.9
    - specified type NEC 743.47
  - specified type NEC 743.8
- eyebrow 744.89
- eyelid 743.9
  - specified type NEC 743.63
- face (any part) 744.9
  - bone(s) 756.0
  - specified type NEC 744.89
- fallopian tube 752.10
  - specified type NEC 752.19
- fascia 756.9
  - specified type NEC 756.89
- femur 755.60
- fibula 755.60
- finger 755.50
  - supernumerary 755.01
  - webbed (*see also* Syndactylism, fingers) 755.11
- fixation, intestine 751.4
- flexion (joint) 755.9
  - hip or thigh (*see also* Dislocation, hip, congenital) 754.30
- folds, heart 746.9
- foot 755.67
- foramen
  - Botalli 745.5
  - ovale 745.5
- forearm 755.50
- forehead (*see also* Anomaly, skull) 756.0
- form, teeth 520.2
- fovea centralis 743.9
- frontal bone (*see also* Anomaly, skull) 756.0
- gallbladder 751.60
- Gartner's duct 752.41
- gastrointestinal tract 751.9
  - specified type NEC 751.8
  - vessel 747.61
- genitalia, genital organ(s) or system
  - female 752.9

Anomaly, anomalous — *continued*
- genitalia, genital organ(s) or system — *continued*
  - female — *continued*
    - external 752.40
      - specified type NEC 752.49
    - internal NEC 752.9
  - male (external and internal) 752.9
    - epispadias 752.62
    - hidden penis 752.65
    - hydrocele, congenital 778.6
    - hypospadias 752.61
    - micropenis 752.64
    - testis, undescended 752.51
      - retractile 752.52
    - specified type NEC 752.89
- genitourinary NEC 752.9
- Gerbode 745.4
- globe (eye) 743.9
- glottis 748.3
- granulation or granulocyte, genetic 288.2
  - constitutional 288.2
  - leukocyte 288.2
- gum 750.9
- gyri 742.9
- hair 757.9
  - specified type NEC 757.4
- hand 755.50
- hard tissue formation in pulp 522.3
- head (*see also* Anomaly, skull) 756.0
- heart 746.9
  - auricle 746.9
  - bands 746.9
  - fibroelastosis cordis 425.3
  - folds 746.9
  - malposition 746.87
  - maternal, affecting fetus or newborn 760.3
  - obstructive NEC 746.84
  - patent ductus arteriosus (Botalli) 747.0
  - septum 745.9
    - acquired 429.71
    - aortic 745.0
    - aorticopulmonary 745.0
    - atrial 745.5
    - auricular 745.5
    - between aorta and pulmonary artery 745.0
    - endocardial cushion type 745.60
      - specified type NEC 745.69
    - interatrial 745.5
    - interventricular 745.4
      - with pulmonary stenosis or atresia, dextraposition of aorta, and hypertrophy of right ventricle 745.2
      - acquired 429.71
    - specified type NEC 745.8
    - ventricular 745.4
      - with pulmonary stenosis or atresia, dextraposition of aorta, and hypertrophy of right ventricle 745.2
      - acquired 429.71
  - specified type NEC 746.89
  - tetralogy of Fallot 745.2
  - valve NEC 746.9
    - aortic 746.9
      - atresia 746.89
      - bicuspid valve 746.4
      - insufficiency 746.4
      - specified type NEC 746.89
      - stenosis 746.3
        - subaortic 746.81
        - supravalvular 747.22
    - mitral 746.9
      - atresia 746.89
      - insufficiency 746.6
      - specified type NEC 746.89
      - stenosis 746.5
    - pulmonary 746.00

Anomaly, anomalous — *continued*
- heart — *continued*
  - valve — *continued*
    - pulmonary — *continued*
      - atresia 746.01
      - insufficiency 746.09
      - stenosis 746.02
        - infundibular 746.83
        - subvalvular 746.83
      - tricuspid 746.9
        - atresia 746.1
        - stenosis 746.1
  - ventricle 746.9
- heel 755.67
- Hegglin's 288.2
- hemianencephaly 740.0
- hemicephaly 740.0
- hemicrania 740.0
- hepatic duct 751.60
- hip (joint) 755.63
- hourglass
  - bladder 753.8
  - gallbladder 751.69
  - stomach 750.7
- humerus 755.50
- hymen 752.40
- hypersegmentation of neutrophils, hereditary 288.2
- hypophyseal 759.2
- ileocecal (coil) (valve) 751.5
- ileum (intestine) 751.5
- ilium 755.60
- integument 757.9
  - specified type NEC 757.8
- interarch distance (excessive) (inadequate) 524.28
- intervertebral cartilage or disc 756.10
- intestine (large) (small) 751.5
  - fixational type 751.4
- iris 743.9
  - specified type NEC 743.46
- ischium 755.60
- jaw NEC 524.9
  - closure 524.51
  - size (major) NEC 524.00
  - specified type NEC 524.89
- jaw-cranial base relationship 524.10
  - specified NEC 524.19
- jejunum 751.5
- joint 755.9
  - hip
    - dislocation (*see also* Dislocation, hip, congenital) 754.30
    - predislocation (*see also* Subluxation, congenital, hip) 754.32
    - preluxation (*see also* Subluxation, congenital, hip) 754.32
    - subluxation (*see also* Subluxation, congenital, hip) 754.32
  - lumbosacral 756.10
    - spondylolisthesis 756.12
    - spondylosis 756.11
  - multiple arthrogryposis 754.89
  - sacroiliac 755.69
- Jordan's 288.2
- kidney(s) (calyx) (pelvis) 753.9
  - vessel 747.62
- Klippel-Feil (brevicollis) 756.16
- knee (joint) 755.64
- labium (majus) (minus) 752.40
- labyrinth, membranous (causing impairment of hearing) 744.05
- lacrimal
  - apparatus, duct or passage 743.9
    - specified type NEC 743.65
  - gland 743.9
    - specified type NEC 743.64
- Langdon Down (mongolism) 758.0
- larynx, laryngeal (muscle) 748.3
  - web, webbed 748.2
- leg (lower) (upper) 755.60
  - reduction NEC (*see also* Deformity, reduction, lower limb) 755.30

☑ Additional Digit Required — Refer to the Tabular List for Digit Selection \u2003\u2003 ▽ Subterms under main terms may continue to next column or page

2007 ICD-9-CM \u2003 ▶◀ Revised Text \u2003 ● New Line \u2003 ▲ Revised Code \u2003 **October 2006 · Volume 2 — 23**

Anomaly, anomalous — *continued*
- lens 743.9
  - shape 743.36
  - specified type NEC 743.39
- leukocytes, genetic 288.2
  - granulation (constitutional) 288.2
- lid (fold) 743.9
- ligament 756.9
  - broad 752.10
  - round 752.9
- limb, except reduction deformity 755.9
  - lower 755.60
    - reduction deformity (*see also* Deformity, reduction, lower limb) 755.30
    - specified type NEC 755.69
  - upper 755.50
    - reduction deformity (*see also* Deformity, reduction, upper limb) 755.20
    - specified type NEC 755.59
- lip 750.9
  - harelip (*see also* Cleft, lip) 749.10
  - specified type NEC 750.26
- liver (duct) 751.60
  - atresia 751.69
- lower extremity 755.60
  - vessel 747.64
- lumbosacral (joint) (region) 756.10
- lung (fissure) (lobe) NEC 748.60
  - agenesis 748.5
  - specified type NEC 748.69
- lymphatic system 759.9
- Madelung's (radius) 755.54
- mandible 524.9
  - size NEC 524.00
- maxilla 524.9
  - size NEC 524.00
- May (-Hegglin) 288.2
- meatus urinarius 753.9
  - specified type NEC 753.8
- meningeal bands or folds, constriction of 742.8
- meninges 742.9
  - brain 742.4
  - spinal 742.59
- meningocele (*see also* Spina bifida) 741.9 ☑
  - acquired 349.2
- mesentery 751.9
- metacarpus 755.50
- metatarsus 755.67
- middle ear, except ossicles (causing impairment of hearing) 744.03
  - ossicles 744.04
- mitral (leaflets) (valve) 746.9
  - atresia 746.89
  - insufficiency 746.6
  - specified type NEC 746.89
  - stenosis 746.5
- mouth 750.9
  - specified type NEC 750.26
- multiple NEC 759.7
  - specified type NEC 759.89
- muscle 756.9
  - eye 743.9
    - specified type NEC 743.69
  - specified type NEC 756.89
- musculoskeletal system, except limbs 756.9
  - specified type NEC 756.9
- nail 757.9
  - specified type NEC 757.5
- narrowness, eyelid 743.62
- nasal sinus or septum 748.1
- neck (any part) 744.9
  - specified type NEC 744.89
- nerve 742.9
  - acoustic 742.9
    - specified type NEC 742.8
  - optic 742.9
    - specified type NEC 742.8
  - specified type NEC 742.8
- nervous system NEC 742.9
  - brain 742.9
    - specified type NEC 742.4

Anomaly, anomalous — *continued*
- nervous system — *continued*
  - specified type NEC 742.8
- neurological 742.9
- nipple 757.6
- nonteratogenic NEC 754.89
- nose, nasal (bone) (cartilage) (septum) (sinus) 748.1
- ocular muscle 743.9
- omphalomesenteric duct 751.0
- opening, pulmonary veins 747.49
- optic
  - disc 743.9
    - specified type NEC 743.57
  - nerve 742.9
- opticociliary vessels 743.9
- orbit (eye) 743.9
  - specified type NEC 743.66
- organ
  - of Corti (causing impairment of hearing) 744.05
  - or site 759.9
    - specified type NEC 759.89
- origin
  - both great arteries from same ventricle 745.11
  - coronary artery 746.85
  - innominate artery 747.69
  - left coronary artery from pulmonary artery 746.85
  - pulmonary artery 747.3
  - renal vessels 747.62
  - subclavian artery (left) (right) 747.21
- osseous meatus (ear) 744.03
- ovary 752.0
- oviduct 752.10
- palate (hard) (soft) 750.9
  - cleft (*see also* Cleft, palate) 749.00
- pancreas (duct) 751.7
- papillary muscles 746.9
- parathyroid gland 759.2
- paraurethral ducts 753.9
- parotid (gland) 750.9
- patella 755.64
- Pelger-Huët (hereditary hyposegmentation) 288.2
- pelvic girdle 755.60
  - specified type NEC 755.69
- pelvis (bony) 755.60
  - complicating delivery 653.0 ☑
    - rachitic 268.1
      - fetal 756.4
- penis (glans) 752.69
- pericardium 746.89
- peripheral vascular system NEC 747.60
  - gastrointestinal 747.61
  - lower limb 747.64
  - renal 747.62
  - specified site NEC 747.69
  - spinal 747.82
  - upper limb 747.63
- Peter's 743.44
- pharynx 750.9
  - branchial cleft 744.41
  - specified type NEC 750.29
- Pierre Robin 756.0
- pigmentation 709.00
  - congenital 757.33
  - specified NEC 709.09
- pituitary (gland) 759.2
- pleural folds 748.8
- portal vein 747.40
- position tooth, teeth 524.30
  - crowding 524.31
  - displacement 524.30
    - horizontal 524.33
    - vertical 524.34
  - distance
    - interocclusal
      - excessive 524.37
      - insufficient 524.36
  - excessive spacing 524.32
  - rotation 524.35
  - specified NEC 524.39

Anomaly, anomalous — *continued*
- preauricular sinus 744.46
- prepuce 752.9
- prostate 752.9
- pulmonary 748.60
  - artery 747.3
  - circulation 747.3
  - specified type NEC 748.69
  - valve 746.00
    - atresia 746.01
    - insufficiency 746.09
    - specified type NEC 746.09
    - stenosis 746.02
      - infundibular 746.83
      - subvalvular 746.83
  - vein 747.40
  - venous
    - connection 747.49
      - partial 747.42
      - total 747.41
    - return 747.49
      - partial 747.42
      - total (TAPVR) (complete) (subdiaphragmatic) (supradiaphragmatic) 747.41
- pupil 743.9
- pylorus 750.9
  - hypertrophy 750.5
  - stenosis 750.5
- rachitic, fetal 756.4
- radius 755.50
- rectovaginal (septum) 752.40
- rectum 751.5
- refraction 367.9
- renal 753.9
  - vessel 747.62
- respiratory system 748.9
  - specified type NEC 748.8
- rib 756.3
  - cervical 756.2
- Rieger's 743.44
- rings, trachea 748.3
- rotation (*see also* Malrotation)
  - hip or thigh (*see also* Subluxation, congenital, hip) 754.32
- round ligament 752.9
- sacroiliac (joint) 755.69
- sacrum 756.10
- saddle
  - back 754.2
  - nose 754.0
    - syphilitic 090.5
- salivary gland or duct 750.9
  - specified type NEC 750.26
- scapula 755.50
- sclera 743.9
  - specified type NEC 743.47
- scrotum 752.9
- sebaceous gland 757.9
- seminal duct or tract 752.9
- sense organs 742.9
  - specified type NEC 742.8
- septum
  - heart — *see* Anomaly, heart, septum
  - nasal 748.1
- sex chromosomes NEC (*see also* Anomaly, chromosomes) 758.81
- shoulder (girdle) (joint) 755.50
  - specified type NEC 755.59
- sigmoid (flexure) 751.5
- sinus of Valsalva 747.29
- site NEC 759.9
- skeleton generalized NEC 756.50
- skin (appendage) 757.9
  - specified type NEC 757.39
- skull (bone) 756.0
  - with
    - anencephalus 740.0
    - encephalocele 742.0
    - hydrocephalus 742.3
      - with spina bifida (*see also* Spina bifida) 741.0 ☑
    - microcephalus 742.1

Anomaly, anomalous — *continued*
- specified type NEC
  - adrenal (gland) 759.1
  - alimentary tract (complete) (partial) 751.8
    - lower 751.5
    - upper 750.8
  - ankle 755.69
  - anus, anal (canal) 751.5
  - aorta, aortic 747.29
    - arch 747.21
  - appendix 751.5
  - arm 755.59
  - artery (peripheral) NEC (*see also* Anomaly, peripheral vascular system) 747.60
    - brain 747.81
    - coronary 746.85
    - eye 743.58
    - pulmonary 747.3
    - retinal 743.58
    - umbilical 747.5
  - auditory canal 744.29
    - causing impairment of hearing 744.02
  - bile duct or passage 751.69
  - bladder 753.8
    - neck 753.8
  - bone(s) 756.9
    - arm 755.59
    - face 756.0
    - leg 755.69
    - pelvic girdle 755.69
    - shoulder girdle 755.59
    - skull 756.0
      - with
        - anencephalus 740.0
        - encephalocele 742.0
        - hydrocephalus 742.3
          - with spina bifida (*see also* Spina bifida) 741.0 ☑
        - microcephalus 742.1
  - brain 742.4
  - breast 757.6
  - broad ligament 752.19
  - bronchus 748.3
  - canal of Nuck 752.89
  - cardiac septal closure 745.8
  - carpus 755.59
  - cartilaginous 756.9
  - cecum 751.5
  - cervix 752.49
  - chest (wall) 756.3
  - chin 744.89
  - ciliary body 743.46
  - circulatory system 747.89
  - clavicle 755.51
  - clitoris 752.49
  - coccyx 756.19
  - colon 751.5
  - common duct 751.69
  - connective tissue 756.89
  - cricoid cartilage 748.3
  - cystic duct 751.69
  - diaphragm 756.6
  - digestive organ(s) or tract 751.8
    - lower 751.5
    - upper 750.8
  - duodenum 751.5
  - ear 744.29
    - auricle 744.29
      - causing impairment of hearing 744.02
    - causing impairment of hearing 744.09
    - inner (causing impairment of hearing) 744.05
    - middle, except ossicles 744.03
      - ossicles 744.04
  - ejaculatory duct 752.89
  - endocrine 759.2
  - epiglottis 748.3
  - esophagus 750.4
  - Eustachian tube 744.24
  - eye 743.8

☑ Additional Digit Required — Refer to the Tabular List for Digit Selection   ⚐ Subterms under main terms may continue to next column or page

24 — Volume 2   ▶◀ Revised Text   ● New Line   ▲ Revised Code   *2007 ICD-9-CM*

Anomaly, anomalous — *continued*
   specified type — *continued*
      eye — *continued*
         lid 743.63
         muscle 743.69
      face 744.89
         bone(s) 756.0
      fallopian tube 752.19
      fascia 756.89
      femur 755.69
      fibula 755.69
      finger 755.59
      foot 755.67
      fovea centralis 743.55
      gallbladder 751.69
      Gartner's duct 752.89
      gastrointestinal tract 751.8
      genitalia, genital organ(s)
         female 752.89
            external 752.49
            internal NEC 752.89
         male 752.89
            penis 752.69
            scrotal transposition 752.81
      genitourinary tract NEC 752.89
      glottis 748.3
      hair 757.4
      hand 755.59
      heart 746.89
         valve NEC 746.89
            pulmonary 746.09
      hepatic duct 751.69
      hydatid of Morgagni 752.89
      hymen 752.49
      integument 757.8
      intestine (large) (small) 751.5
         fixational type 751.4
      iris 743.46
      jejunum 751.5
      joint 755.8
      kidney 753.3
      knee 755.64
      labium (majus) (minus) 752.49
      labyrinth, membranous 744.05
      larynx 748.3
      leg 755.69
      lens 743.39
      limb, except reduction deformity
         755.8
         lower 755.69
            reduction deformity (see also
               Deformity, reduction,
               lower limb) 755.30
         upper 755.59
            reduction deformity (see also
               Deformity, reduction,
               upper limb) 755.20
      lip 750.26
      liver 751.69
      lung (fissure) (lobe) 748.69
      meatus urinarius 753.8
      metacarpus 755.59
      mouth 750.26
      muscle 756.89
         eye 743.69
      musculoskeletal system, except
         limbs 756.9
      nail 757.5
      neck 744.89
      nerve 742.8
         acoustic 742.8
         optic 742.8
      nervous system 742.8
      nipple 757.6
      nose 748.1
      organ NEC 759.89
         of Corti 744.05
      osseous meatus (ear) 744.03
      ovary 752.0
      oviduct 752.19
      pancreas 751.7
      parathyroid 759.2
      patella 755.64
      pelvic girdle 755.69
      penis 752.69
      pericardium 746.89

Anomaly, anomalous — *continued*
   specified type — *continued*
      peripheral vascular system NEC
         (see also Anomaly, peripheral
         vascular system) 747.60
      pharynx 750.29
      pituitary 759.2
      prostate 752.89
      radius 755.59
      rectum 751.5
      respiratory system 748.8
      rib 756.3
      round ligament 752.89
      sacrum 756.19
      salivary duct or gland 750.26
      scapula 755.59
      sclera 743.47
      scrotum 752.89
         transposition 752.81
      seminal duct or tract 752.89
      shoulder girdle 755.59
      site NEC 759.89
      skin 757.39
      skull (bone(s)) 756.0
         with
            anencephalus 740.0
            encephalocele 742.0
            hydrocephalus 742.3
               with spina bifida (see also
                  Spina bifida)
                  741.0 ☑
            microcephalus 742.1
      specified organ or site NEC 759.89
      spermatic cord 752.89
      spinal cord 742.59
      spine 756.19
      spleen 759.0
      sternum 756.3
      stomach 750.7
      tarsus 755.67
      tendon 756.89
      testis 752.89
      thorax (wall) 756.3
      thymus 759.2
      thyroid (gland) 759.2
         cartilage 748.3
      tibia 755.69
      toe 755.66
      tongue 750.19
      trachea (cartilage) 748.3
      ulna 755.59
      urachus 753.7
      ureter 753.4
         obstructive 753.29
      urethra 753.8
         obstructive 753.6
      urinary tract 753.8
      uterus 752.3
      uvula 750.26
      vagina 752.49
      vascular NEC (see also Anomaly,
         peripheral vascular system)
         747.60
         brain 747.81
      vas deferens 752.89
      vein(s) (peripheral) NEC (see also
         Anomaly, peripheral vascular
         system) 747.60
         brain 747.81
         great 747.49
         portal 747.49
         pulmonary 747.49
      vena cava (inferior) (superior)
         747.49
      vertebra 756.19
      vulva 752.49
   spermatic cord 752.9
   spine, spinal 756.10
      column 756.10
      cord 742.9
         meningocele (see also Spina bi-
            fida) 741.9 ☑
         specified type NEC 742.59
         spina bifida (see also Spina bifi-
            da) 741.9 ☑
         vessel 747.82

Anomaly, anomalous — *continued*
   spine, spinal — *continued*
      meninges 742.59
      nerve root 742.9
   spleen 759.0
   Sprengel's 755.52
   sternum 756.3
   stomach 750.9
      specified type NEC 750.7
   submaxillary gland 750.9
   superior vena cava 747.40
   talipes — see Talipes
   tarsus 755.67
      with complete absence of distal el-
         ements 755.31
   teeth, tooth NEC 520.9
      position 524.30
         crowding 524.31
         displacement 524.30
            horizontal 524.33
            vertical 524.34
         distance
            interocclusal
               excessive 524.37
               insufficient 524.36
         excessive spacing 524.32
         rotation 524.35
         specified NEC 524.39
         spacing 524.30
   tendon 756.9
      specified type NEC 756.89
   termination
      coronary artery 746.85
   testis 752.9
   thebesian valve 746.9
   thigh 755.60
      flexion (see also Subluxation, con-
         genital, hip) 754.32
   thorax (wall) 756.3
   throat 750.9
   thumb 755.50
      supernumerary 755.01
   thymus gland 759.2
   thyroid (gland) 759.2
      cartilage 748.3
   tibia 755.60
      saber 090.5
   toe 755.66
      supernumerary 755.02
      webbed (see also Syndactylism,
         toes) 755.13
   tongue 750.10
      specified type NEC 750.19
   trachea, tracheal 748.3
      cartilage 748.3
      rings 748.3
   tragus 744.3
   transverse aortic arch 747.21
   trichromata 368.59
   trichromatopsia 368.59
   tricuspid (leaflet) (valve) 746.9
      atresia 746.1
      Ebstein's 746.2
      specified type NEC 746.89
      stenosis 746.1
   trunk 759.9
   Uhl's (hypoplasia of myocardium, right
      ventricle) 746.84
   ulna 755.50
   umbilicus 759.9
      artery 747.5
   union, trachea with larynx 748.3
   unspecified site 759.9
   upper extremity 755.50
      vessel 747.63
   urachus 753.7
      specified type NEC 753.7
   ureter 753.9
      obstructive 753.20
      specified type NEC 753.4
         obstructive 753.29
   urethra (valve) 753.9
      obstructive 753.6
      specified type NEC 753.8
   urinary tract or system (any part, ex-
      cept urachus) 753.9

Anomaly, anomalous — *continued*
   urinary tract or system — *contin-
      ued*
      specified type NEC 753.8
      urachus 753.7
   uterus 752.3
      with only one functioning horn
         752.3
      in pregnancy or childbirth 654.0 ☑
         affecting fetus or newborn
            763.89
         causing obstructed labor
            660.2 ☑
            affecting fetus or newborn
               763.1
   uvula 750.9
   vagina 752.40
   valleculae 748.3
   valve (heart) NEC 746.9
      formation, ureter 753.29
      pulmonary 746.00
      specified type NEC 746.89
   vascular NEC (see also Anomaly, pe-
      ripheral vascular system)
      747.60
      ring 747.21
   vas deferens 752.9
   vein(s) (peripheral) NEC (see also
      Anomaly, peripheral vascular
      system) 747.60
      brain 747.81
      cerebral 747.81
      coronary 746.89
      great 747.40
         specified type NEC 747.49
      portal 747.40
      pulmonary 747.40
      retina 743.9
   vena cava (inferior) (superior) 747.40
   venous return (pulmonary) 747.49
      partial 747.42
      total 747.41
   ventricle, ventricular (heart) 746.9
      bands 746.9
      folds 746.9
      septa 745.4
   vertebra 756.10
   vesicourethral orifice 753.9
   vessels NEC (see also Anomaly, periph-
      eral vascular system) 747.60
      optic papilla 743.9
   vitelline duct 751.0
   vitreous humor 743.9
      specified type NEC 743.51
   vulva 752.40
   wrist (joint) 755.50
Anomia 784.69
Anonychia 757.5
   acquired 703.8
Anophthalmos, anophthalmus (clinical)
   (congenital) (globe) 743.00
   acquired V45.78
Anopsia (altitudinal) (quadrant) 368.46
Anorchia 752.89
Anorchism, anorchidism 752.89
Anorexia 783.0
   hysterical 300.11
   nervosa 307.1
Anosmia — see also Disturbance, sensation 781.1
   hysterical 300.11
   postinfectional 478.9
   psychogenic 306.7
   traumatic 951.8
Anosognosia 780.99
Anosphrasia 781.1
Anosteoplasia 756.50
Anotia 744.09
Anovulatory cycle 628.0
Anoxemia 799.02
   newborn 770.88   ▲
Anoxia 799.02
   altitude 993.2
   cerebral 348.1

Index — Anoxia — Apoplexia, apoplexy, apoplectic

Anoxia — continued
cerebral — continued
with
abortion — see Abortion, by type, with specified complication NEC
ectopic pregnancy (see also categories 633.0–633.9) 639.8
molar pregnancy (see also categories 630–632) 639.8
complicating
delivery (cesarean) (instrumental) 669.4 ☑
ectopic or molar pregnancy 639.8
obstetric anesthesia or sedation 668.2 ☑
during or resulting from a procedure 997.01
following
abortion 639.8
ectopic or molar pregnancy 639.8
newborn (see also Distress, fetal, liveborn infant) 770.88 ▲
due to drowning 994.1
fetal, affecting newborn 770.88 ▲
heart — see Insufficiency, coronary
high altitude 993.2
intrauterine
fetal death (before onset of labor) 768.0
during labor 768.1
liveborn infant — see Distress, fetal, liveborn infant
myocardial — see Insufficiency, coronary
newborn 768.9
mild or moderate 768.6
severe 768.5
pathological 799.02
Anteflexion — see Anteversion
Antenatal
care, normal pregnancy V22.1
first V22.0
screening of mother (for) V28.9
based on amniocentesis NEC V28.2
chromosomal anomalies V28.0
raised alphafetoprotein levels V28.1
chromosomal anomalies V28.0
fetal growth retardation using ultrasonics V28.4
isoimmunization V28.5
malformations using ultrasonics V28.3
raised alphafetoprotein levels in amniotic fluid V28.1
specified condition NEC V28.8
Streptococcus B V28.6
Antepartum — see condition
Anterior — see also condition
spinal artery compression syndrome 721.1
Antero-occlusion 524.24
Anteversion
cervix — ▶see◀ Anteversion, uterus
femur (neck), congenital 755.63
uterus, uterine (cervix) (postinfectional) (postpartal, old) 621.6
congenital 752.3
in pregnancy or childbirth 654.4 ☑
affecting fetus or newborn 763.89
causing obstructed labor 660.2 ☑
affecting fetus or newborn 763.1
Anthracosilicosis (occupational) 500
Anthracosis (lung) (occupational) 500
lingua 529.3
Anthrax 022.9
with pneumonia 022.1 [484.5]
colitis 022.2
cutaneous 022.0

Anthrax — continued
gastrointestinal 022.2
intestinal 022.2
pulmonary 022.1
respiratory 022.1
septicemia 022.3
specified manifestation NEC 022.8
Anthropoid pelvis 755.69
with disproportion (fetopelvic) 653.2 ☑
affecting fetus or newborn 763.1
causing obstructed labor 660.1 ☑
affecting fetus or newborn 763.1
Anthropophobia 300.29
Antibioma, breast 611.0
Antibodies
maternal (blood group) (see also Incompatibility) 656.2 ☑
anti-D, cord blood 656.1 ☑
fetus or newborn 773.0
Antibody deficiency syndrome
agammaglobulinemic 279.00
congenital 279.04
hypogammaglobulinemic 279.00
Anticoagulant, circulating — see also Circulating anticoagulants 286.5
Antimongolism syndrome 758.39
Antimonial cholera 985.4
Antisocial personality 301.7
Antithrombinemia — see also Circulating anticoagulants 286.5
Antithromboplastinemia — see also Circulating anticoagulants 286.5
Antithromboplastinogenemia — see also Circulating anticoagulants 286.5
Antitoxin complication or reaction — see Complications, vaccination
Anton (-Babinski) syndrome (hemiasomatognosia) 307.9
Antritis (chronic) 473.0
maxilla 473.0
acute 461.0
stomach 535.4 ☑
Antrum, antral — see condition
Anuria 788.5
with
abortion — see Abortion, by type, with renal failure
ectopic pregnancy (see also categories 633.0–633.9) 639.3
molar pregnancy (see also categories 630–632) 639.3
calculus (impacted) (recurrent) 592.9
kidney 592.0
ureter 592.1
congenital 753.3
due to a procedure 997.5
following
abortion 639.3
ectopic or molar pregnancy 639.3
newborn 753.3
postrenal 593.4
puerperal, postpartum, childbirth 669.3 ☑
specified as due to a procedure 997.5
sulfonamide
correct substance properly administered 788.5
overdose or wrong substance given or taken 961.0
traumatic (following crushing) 958.5
Anus, anal — see condition
Anusitis 569.49
Anxiety (neurosis) (reaction) (state) 300.00
alcohol-induced 291.89
depression 300.4
drug-induced 292.89
due to or associated with physical condition 293.84
generalized 300.02
hysteria 300.20
in
acute stress reaction 308.0
transient adjustment reaction 309.24

Anxiety — continued
panic type 300.01
separation, abnormal 309.21
syndrome (organic) (transient) 293.84
Aorta, aortic — see condition
Aortectasia 441.9
Aortitis (nonsyphilitic) 447.6
arteriosclerotic 440.0
calcific 447.6
Döhle-Heller 093.1
luetic 093.1
rheumatic (see also Endocarditis, acute, rheumatic) 391.1
rheumatoid — see Arthritis, rheumatoid
specific 093.1
syphilitic 093.1
congenital 090.5
Apathetic thyroid storm — see also Thyrotoxicosis 242.9 ☑
Apepsia 536.8
achlorhydric 536.0
psychogenic 306.4
Aperistalsis, esophagus 530.0
Apert-Gallais syndrome (adrenogenital) 255.2
Apertognathia 524.20
Apert's syndrome (acrocephalosyndactyly) 755.55
Aphagia 787.2
psychogenic 307.1
Aphakia (acquired) (bilateral) (postoperative) (unilateral) 379.31
congenital 743.35
Aphalangia (congenital) 755.4
lower limb (complete) (intercalary) (partial) (terminal) 755.39
meaning all digits (complete) (partial) 755.31
transverse 755.31
upper limb (complete) (intercalary) (partial) (terminal) 755.29
meaning all digits (complete) (partial) 755.21
transverse 755.21
Aphasia (amnestic) (ataxic) (auditory) (Broca's) (choreatic) (classic) (expressive) (global) (ideational) (ideokinetic) (ideomotor) (jargon) (motor) (nominal) (receptive) (semantic) (sensory) (syntactic) (verbal) (visual) (Wernicke's) 784.3
developmental 315.31
syphilis, tertiary 094.89
uremic — see Uremia
Aphemia 784.3
uremic — see Uremia
Aphonia 784.41
clericorum 784.49
hysterical 300.11
organic 784.41
psychogenic 306.1
Aphthae, aphthous — see also condition
Bednar's 528.2
cachectic 529.0
epizootic 078.4
fever 078.4
oral 528.2
stomatitis 528.2
thrush 112.0
ulcer (oral) (recurrent) 528.2
genital organ(s) NEC
female 629.89 ▲
male 608.89
larynx 478.79
Apical — see condition
Apical ballooning syndrome 429.83 ▲
Aplasia — see also Agenesis
alveolar process (acquired) 525.8
congenital 750.26
aorta (congenital) 747.22
aortic valve (congenital) 746.89
axialis extracorticalis (congenital) 330.0
bone marrow (myeloid) 284.9

Aplasia — see also Agenesis — continued
bone marrow — continued
acquired (secondary) 284.8
congenital 284.01 ▲
idiopathic 284.9
brain 740.0
specified part 742.2
breast 757.6
bronchus 748.3
cementum 520.4
cerebellar 742.2
congenital ▶(pure)◀ red cell 284.01 ▲
corpus callosum 742.2
erythrocyte 284.8
congenital 284.01 ▲
extracortical axial 330.0
eye (congenital) 743.00
fovea centralis (congenital) 743.55
germinal (cell) 606.0
iris 743.45
labyrinth, membranous 744.05
limb (congenital) 755.4
lower NEC 755.30
upper NEC 755.20
lung (bilateral) (congenital) (unilateral) 748.5
nervous system NEC 742.8
nuclear 742.8
ovary 752.0
Pelizaeus-Merzbacher 330.0
prostate (congenital) 752.89
red cell (with thymoma) 284.8
acquired (secondary) 284.8
congenital 284.01 ▲
hereditary 284.01 ▲
of infants 284.01 ▲
primary 284.01 ▲
pure 284.01 ●
round ligament (congenital) 752.89
salivary gland 750.21
skin (congenital) 757.39
spinal cord 742.59
spleen 759.0
testis (congenital) 752.89
thymic, with immunodeficiency 279.2
thyroid 243
uterus 752.3
ventral horn cell 742.59
Apleuria 756.3
Apnea, apneic (spells) 786.03
newborn, neonatorum 770.81
essential 770.81
obstructive 770.82
primary 770.81
sleep 770.81
specified NEC 770.82
psychogenic 306.1
sleep, unspecified 780.57
with
hypersomnia, unspecified 780.53
hyposomnia, unspecified 780.51
insomnia, unspecified 780.51
sleep disturbance 780.57
central, in conditions classified elsewhere 327.27
obstructive (adult) (pediatric) 327.23
organic 327.20
other 327.29
primary central 327.21
Apneumatosis newborn 770.4
Apodia 755.31
Aponeurosis 726.90
Apophysitis (bone) — see also Osteochondrosis 732.9
calcaneus 732.5
juvenile 732.6
Apoplectiform convulsions — see also Disease, cerebrovascular, acute 436
Apoplexia, apoplexy, apoplectic — see also Disease, cerebrovascular, acute 436

☑ Additional Digit Required — Refer to the Tabular List for Digit Selection   ▽ Subterms under main terms may continue to next column or page

26 — Volume 2 • October 2006   ▶◀ Revised Text   ● New Line   ▲ Revised Code   **2007 ICD-9-CM**

Apoplexia, apoplexy, apoplectic — *see also* Disease, cerebrovascular, acute — *continued*
abdominal 569.89
adrenal 036.3
attack 436
basilar (*see also* Disease, cerebrovascular, acute) 436
brain (*see also* Disease, cerebrovascular, acute) 436
bulbar (*see also* Disease, cerebrovascular, acute) 436
capillary (*see also* Disease, cerebrovascular, acute) 436
cardiac (*see also* Infarct, myocardium) 410.9 ☑
cerebral (*see also* Disease, cerebrovascular, acute) 436
chorea (*see also* Disease, cerebrovascular, acute) 436
congestive (*see also* Disease, cerebrovascular, acute) 436
newborn 767.4
embolic (*see also* Embolism, brain) 434.1 ☑
fetus 767.0
fit (*see also* Disease, cerebrovascular, acute) 436
healed or old V12.59
heart (auricle) (ventricle) (*see also* Infarct, myocardium) 410.9 ☑
heat 992.0
hemiplegia (*see also* Disease, cerebrovascular, acute) 436
hemorrhagic (stroke) (*see also* Hemorrhage, brain) 432.9
ingravescent (*see also* Disease, cerebrovascular, acute) 436
late effect — *see* Late effect(s) (of) cerebrovascular disease
lung — *see* Embolism, pulmonary
meninges, hemorrhagic (*see also* Hemorrhage, subarachnoid) 430
neonatorum 767.0
newborn 767.0
pancreatitis 577.0
placenta 641.2 ☑
progressive (*see also* Disease, cerebrovascular, acute) 436
pulmonary (artery) (vein) — *see* Embolism, pulmonary
sanguineous (*see also* Disease, cerebrovascular, acute) 436
seizure (*see also* Disease, cerebrovascular, acute) 436
serous (*see also* Disease, cerebrovascular, acute) 436
spleen 289.59
stroke (*see also* Disease, cerebrovascular, acute) 436
thrombotic (*see also* Thrombosis, brain) 434.0 ☑
uremic — *see* Uremia
uteroplacental 641.2 ☑
Appendage
fallopian tube (cyst of Morgagni) 752.11
intestine (epiploic) 751.5
preauricular 744.1
testicular (organ of Morgagni) 752.89
Appendicitis 541
with
perforation, peritonitis (generalized), or rupture 540.0
with peritoneal abscess 540.1
peritoneal abscess 540.1
acute (catarrhal) (fulminating) (gangrenous) (inflammatory) (obstructive) (retrocecal) (suppurative) 540.9
with
perforation, peritonitis, or rupture 540.0
with peritoneal abscess 540.1
peritoneal abscess 540.1

Appendicitis — *continued*
amebic 006.8
chronic (recurrent) 542
exacerbation — *see* Appendicitis, acute
fulminating — *see* Appendicitis, acute
gangrenous — *see* Appendicitis, acute
healed (obliterative) 542
interval 542
neurogenic 542
obstructive 542
pneumococcal 541
recurrent 542
relapsing 542
retrocecal 541
subacute (adhesive) 542
subsiding 542
suppurative — *see* Appendicitis, acute
tuberculous (*see also* Tuberculosis) 014.8 ☑
Appendiclausis 543.9
Appendicolithiasis 543.9
Appendicopathia oxyurica 127.4
Appendix, appendicular — *see also* condition
Morgagni (male) 752.89
fallopian tube 752.11
Appetite
depraved 307.52
excessive 783.6
psychogenic 307.51
lack or loss (*see also* Anorexia) 783.0
nonorganic origin 307.59
perverted 307.52
hysterical 300.11
Apprehension, apprehensiveness (abnormal) (state) 300.00
specified type NEC 300.09
Approximal wear 521.10
Apraxia (classic) (ideational) (ideokinetic) (ideomotor) (motor) 784.69
oculomotor, congenital 379.51
verbal 784.69
Aptyalism 527.7
Aqueous misdirection 365.83
Arabicum elephantiasis — *see also* Infestation, filarial 125.9
Arachnidism 989.5
Arachnitis — *see* Meningitis
Arachnodactyly 759.82
Arachnoidism 989.5
Arachnoiditis (acute) (adhesive) (basic) (brain) (cerebrospinal) (chiasmal) (chronic) (spinal) — *see also* Meningitis 322.9
meningococcal (chronic) 036.0
syphilitic 094.2
tuberculous (*see also* Tuberculosis, meninges) 013.0 ☑
Araneism 989.5
Arboencephalitis, Australian 062.4
Arborization block (heart) 426.6
Arbor virus, arbovirus (infection) NEC 066.9
ARC 042
Arches — *see* condition
Arcuatus uterus 752.3
Arcus (cornea)
juvenilis 743.43
interfering with vision 743.42
senilis 371.41
Arc-welders' lung 503
Arc-welders' syndrome (photokeratitis) 370.24
Areflexia 796.1
Areola — *see* condition
Argentaffinoma (M8241/1) — *see also* Neoplasm, by site, uncertain behavior
benign (M8241/0) — *see* Neoplasm, by site, benign
malignant (M8241/3) — *see* Neoplasm, by site, malignant
syndrome 259.2
Argentinian hemorrhagic fever 078.7
Arginosuccinicaciduria 270.6

Argonz-Del Castillo syndrome (nonpuerperal galactorrhea and amenorrhea) 253.1
Argyll-Robertson phenomenon, pupil, or syndrome (syphilitic) 094.89
atypical 379.45
nonluetic 379.45
nonsyphilitic 379.45
reversed 379.45
Argyria, argyriasis NEC 985.8
conjunctiva 372.55
cornea 371.16
from drug or medicinal agent
correct substance properly administered 709.09
overdose or wrong substance given or taken 961.2
Arhinencephaly 742.2
Arias-Stella phenomenon 621.30
Ariboflavinosis 266.0
Arizona enteritis 008.1
Arm — *see* condition
Armenian disease 277.31   ▲
Arnold-Chiari obstruction or syndrome — *see also* Spina bifida 741.0 ☑
type I 348.4
type II (*see also* Spina bifida) 741.0 ☑
type III 742.0
type IV 742.2
Arousals
confusional 327.41
Arrest, arrested
active phase of labor 661.1 ☑
affecting fetus or newborn 763.7
any plane in pelvis
complicating delivery 660.1 ☑
affecting fetus or newborn 763.1
bone marrow (*see also* Anemia, aplastic) 284.9
cardiac 427.5
with
abortion — *see* Abortion, by type, with specified complication NEC
ectopic pregnancy (*see also* categories 633.0–633.9) 639.8
molar pregnancy (*see also* categories 630–632) 639.8
complicating
anesthesia
correct substance properly administered 427.5
obstetric 668.1 ☑
overdose or wrong substance given 968.4
specified anesthetic — *see* Table of Drugs and Chemicals
delivery (cesarean) (instrumental) 669.4 ☑
ectopic or molar pregnancy 639.8
surgery (nontherapeutic) (therapeutic) 997.1
fetus or newborn 779.85   ▲
following
abortion 639.8
ectopic or molar pregnancy 639.8
postoperative (immediate) 997.1
long-term effect of cardiac surgery 429.4
cardiorespiratory (*see also* Arrest, cardiac) 427.5
deep transverse 660.3 ☑
affecting fetus or newborn 763.1
development or growth
bone 733.91
child 783.40
fetus 764.9 ☑
affecting management of pregnancy 656.5 ☑
tracheal rings 748.3
epiphyseal 733.91
granulopoiesis 288.09   ▲

Arrest, arrested — *continued*
heart — *see* Arrest, cardiac
respiratory 799.1
newborn 770.87   ▲
sinus 426.6
transverse (deep) 660.3 ☑
affecting fetus or newborn 763.1
Arrhenoblastoma (M8630/1)
benign (M8630/0)
specified site — *see* Neoplasm, by site, benign
unspecified site
female 220
male 222.0
malignant (M8630/3)
specified site — *see* Neoplasm, by site, malignant
unspecified site
female 183.0
male 186.9
specified site — *see* Neoplasm, by site, uncertain behavior
unspecified site
female 236.2
male 236.4
Arrhinencephaly 742.2
due to
trisomy 13 (13-15) 758.1
trisomy 18 (16-18) 758.2
Arrhythmia (auricle) (cardiac) (cordis) (gallop rhythm) (juvenile) (nodal) (reflex) (sinus) (supraventricular) (transitory) (ventricle) 427.9
bigeminal rhythm 427.89
block 426.9
bradycardia 427.89
contractions, premature 427.60
coronary sinus 427.89
ectopic 427.89
extrasystolic 427.60
postoperative 997.1
psychogenic 306.2
vagal 780.2
Arrillaga-Ayerza syndrome (pulmonary artery sclerosis with pulmonary hypertension) 416.0
Arsenical
dermatitis 692.4
keratosis 692.4
pigmentation 985.1
from drug or medicinal agent
correct substance properly administered 709.09
overdose or wrong substance given or taken 961.1
Arsenism 985.1
from drug or medicinal agent
correct substance properly administered 692.4
overdose or wrong substance given or taken 961.1
Arterial — *see* condition
Arteriectasis 447.8
Arteriofibrosis — *see* Arteriosclerosis
Arteriolar sclerosis — *see* Arteriosclerosis
Arteriolith — *see* Arteriosclerosis
Arteriolitis 447.6
necrotizing, kidney 447.5
renal — *see* Hypertension, kidney
Arteriolosclerosis — *see* Arteriosclerosis
Arterionephrosclerosis — *see also* Hypertension, kidney 403.90
Arteriopathy 447.9
Arteriosclerosis, arteriosclerotic (artery) (deformans) (diffuse) (disease) (endarteritis) (general) (obliterans) (obliterative) (occlusive) (senile) (with calcification) 440.9
with
gangrene 440.24
psychosis (*see also* Psychosis, arteriosclerotic) 290.40
ulceration 440.23
aorta 440.0

☑ Additional Digit Required — Refer to the Tabular List for Digit Selection   ▽ Subterms under main terms may continue to next column or page

Arteriosclerosis, arteriosclerotic — *continued*
arteries of extremities — *see* Arteriosclerosis, extremities
basilar (artery) (*see also* Occlusion, artery, basilar) 433.0 ☑
brain 437.0
bypass graft
  coronary artery 414.05
    autologous artery (gastroepiploic) (internal mammary) 414.04
    autologous vein 414.02
    nonautologous biological 414.03
    of transplanted heart 414.07
  extremity 440.30
    autologous vein 440.31
    nonautologous biological 440.32
cardiac — *see* Arteriosclerosis, coronary
cardiopathy — *see* Arteriosclerosis, coronary
cardiorenal (*see also* Hypertension, cardiorenal) 404.90
cardiovascular (*see also* Disease, cardiovascular) 429.2
carotid (artery) (common) (internal) (*see also* Occlusion, artery, carotid) 433.1 ☑
central nervous system 437.0
cerebral 437.0
  late effect — *see* Late effect(s) (of) cerebrovascular disease
cerebrospinal 437.0
cerebrovascular 437.0
coronary (artery) 414.00
  graft — *see* Arteriosclerosis, bypass graft
  native artery 414.01
    of transplanted heart 414.06
extremities (native artery) NEC 440.20
  bypass graft 440.30
    autologous vein 440.31
    nonautologous biological 440.32
  claudication (intermittent) 440.21
  and
    gangrene 440.24
    rest pain 440.22
    and
      gangrene 440.24
      ulceration 440.23
        and gangrene 440.24
    ulceration 440.23
      and gangrene 440.24
  gangrene 440.24
  rest pain 440.22
  and
    gangrene 440.24
    ulceration 440.23
      and gangrene 440.24
  specified site NEC 440.29
  ulceration 440.23
    and gangrene 440.24
heart (disease) (*see also* Arteriosclerosis, coronary)
valve 424.99
  aortic 424.1
  mitral 424.0
  pulmonary 424.3
  tricuspid 424.2
kidney (*see also* Hypertension, kidney) 403.90
labyrinth, labyrinthine 388.00
medial NEC (*see also* Arteriosclerosis, extremities) 440.20
mesentery (artery) 557.1
Mönckeberg's (*see also* Arteriosclerosis, extremities) 440.20
myocarditis 429.0
nephrosclerosis (*see also* Hypertension, kidney) 403.90
peripheral (of extremities) — *see* Arteriosclerosis, extremities
precerebral 433.9 ☑
  specified artery NEC 433.8 ☑

Arteriosclerosis, arteriosclerotic — *continued*
pulmonary (idiopathic) 416.0
renal (*see also* Hypertension, kidney) 403.90
  arterioles (*see also* Hypertension, kidney) 403.90
  artery 440.1
retinal (vascular) 440.8 [362.13]
specified artery NEC 440.8
  with gangrene 440.8 [785.4]
spinal (cord) 437.0
vertebral (artery) (*see also* Occlusion, artery, vertebral) 433.2 ☑
Arteriospasm 443.9
Arteriovenous — *see* condition
Arteritis 447.6
allergic (*see also* Angiitis, hypersensitivity) 446.20
aorta (nonsyphilitic) 447.6
  syphilitic 093.1
aortic arch 446.7
brachiocephalica 446.7
brain 437.4
  syphilitic 094.89
branchial 446.7
cerebral 437.4
  late effect — *see* Late effect(s) (of) cerebrovascular disease
  syphilitic 094.89
coronary (artery) (*see also* Arteriosclerosis, coronary)
  rheumatic 391.9
    chronic 398.99
  syphilitic 093.89
cranial (left) (right) 446.5
deformans — *see* Arteriosclerosis
giant cell 446.5
necrosing or necrotizing 446.0
nodosa 446.0
obliterans (*see also* Arteriosclerosis)
  subclaviocarotica 446.7
pulmonary 417.8
retina 362.18
rheumatic — *see* Fever, rheumatic
senile — *see* Arteriosclerosis
suppurative 447.2
syphilitic (general) 093.89
  brain 094.89
  coronary 093.89
  spinal 094.89
temporal 446.5
young female, syndrome 446.7
Artery, arterial — *see* condition
Arthralgia — *see also* Pain, joint 719.4 ☑
allergic (*see also* Pain, joint) 719.4 ☑
in caisson disease 993.3
psychogenic 307.89
rubella 056.71
Salmonella 003.23
temporomandibular joint 524.62
Arthritis, arthritic (acute) (chronic) (subacute) 716.9 ☑
  meaning Osteoarthritis — *see* Osteoarthrosis

Note — *Use the following fifth-digit subclassification with categories 711–712, 715–716:*

0	*site unspecified*
1	*shoulder region*
2	*upper arm*
3	*forearm*
4	*hand*
5	*pelvic region and thigh*
6	*lower leg*
7	*ankle and foot*
8	*other specified sites*
9	*multiple sites*

---

allergic 716.2 ☑
ankylosing (crippling) (spine) 720.0
  sites other than spine 716.9 ☑

Arthritis, arthritic — *continued*
atrophic 714.0
  spine 720.9
back (*see also* Arthritis, spine) 721.90
Bechterew's (ankylosing spondylitis) 720.0
blennorrhagic 098.50
cervical, cervicodorsal (*see also* Spondylosis, cervical) 721.0
Charcôt's 094.0 [713.5]
  diabetic 250.6 ☑ [713.5]
  syringomyelic 336.0 [713.5]
  tabetic 094.0 [713.5]
chylous (*see also* Filariasis) 125.9 [711.7] ☑
climacteric NEC 716.3 ☑
coccyx 721.8
cricoarytenoid 478.79
crystal (-induced) — *see* Arthritis, due to crystals
deformans (*see also* Osteoarthrosis) 715.9 ☑
  spine 721.90
    with myelopathy 721.91
degenerative (*see also* Osteoarthrosis) 715.9 ☑
  idiopathic 715.09
  polyarticular 715.09
  spine 721.90
    with myelopathy 721.91
dermatoarthritis, lipoid 272.8 [713.0]
due to or associated with
  acromegaly 253.0 [713.0]
  actinomycosis 039.8 [711.4] ☑
  amyloidosis 277.39 [713.7] ▲
  bacterial disease NEC 040.89 [711.4] ☑
  Behçet's syndrome 136.1 [711.2] ☑
  blastomycosis 116.0 [711.6] ☑
  brucellosis (*see also* Brucellosis) 023.9 [711.4] ☑
  caisson disease 993.3
  coccidioidomycosis 114.3 [711.6] ☑
  coliform (Escherichia coli) 711.0 ☑
  colitis, ulcerative (*see also* Colitis, ulcerative) 556.9 [713.1]
  cowpox 051.0 [711.5] ☑
  crystals (*see also* Gout)
    dicalcium phosphate 275.49 [712.1] ☑
    pyrophosphate 275.49 [712.2] ☑
    specified NEC 275.49 [712.8] ☑
  dermatoarthritis, lipoid 272.8 [713.0]
  dermatological disorder NEC 709.9 [713.3]
  diabetes 250.6 ☑ [713.5]
  diphtheria 032.89 [711.4] ☑
  dracontiasis 125.7 [711.7] ☑
  dysentery 009.0 [711.3] ☑
  endocrine disorder NEC 259.9 [713.0]
  enteritis NEC 009.1 [711.3] ☑
    infectious (*see also* Enteritis, infectious) 009.0 [711.3] ☑
    specified organism NEC 008.8 [711.3] ☑
    regional (*see also* Enteritis, regional) 555.9 [713.1]
    specified organism NEC 008.8 [711.3] ☑
  epiphyseal slip, nontraumatic (old) 716.8 ☑
  erysipelas 035 [711.4] ☑
  erythema
    epidemic 026.1
    multiforme 695.1 [713.3]
    nodosum 695.2 [713.3]
  Escherichia coli 711.0 ☑
  filariasis NEC 125.9 [711.7] ☑
  gastrointestinal condition NEC 569.9 [713.1]
  glanders 024 [711.4] ☑
  Gonococcus 098.50

Arthritis, arthritic — *continued*
due to or associated with — *continued*
  gout 274.0
  helminthiasis NEC 128.9 [711.7] ☑
  hematological disorder NEC 289.9 [713.2]
  hemochromatosis 275.0 [713.0]
  hemoglobinopathy NEC (*see also* Disease, hemoglobin) 282.7 [713.2]
  hemophilia (*see also* Hemophilia) 286.0 [713.2]
  Hemophilus influenzae (H. influenzae) 711.0 ☑
  Henoch (-Schönlein) purpura 287.0 [713.6]
  H. influenzae 711.0 ☑
  histoplasmosis NEC (*see also* Histoplasmosis) 115.99 [711.6] ☑
  hyperparathyroidism 252.00 [713.0]
  hypersensitivity reaction NEC 995.3 [713.6]
  hypogammaglobulinemia (*see also* Hypogamma-globulinemia) 279.00 [713.0]
  hypothyroidism NEC 244.9 [713.0]
  infection (*see also* Arthritis, infectious) 711.9 ☑
  infectious disease NEC 136.9 [711.8] ☑
  leprosy (*see also* Leprosy) 030.9 [711.4] ☑
  leukemia NEC (M9800/3) 208.9 [713.2]
  lipoid dermatoarthritis 272.8 [713.0]
  Lyme disease 088.81 [711.8] ☑
  Mediterranean fever, familial 277.31 [713.7] ▲
  meningococcal infection 036.82
  metabolic disorder NEC 277.9 [713.0]
  multiple myelomatosis (M9730/3) 203.0 [713.2]
  mumps 072.79 [711.5] ☑
  mycobacteria 031.8 [711.4] ☑
  mycosis NEC 117.9 [711.6] ☑
  neurological disorder NEC 349.9 [713.5]
  ochronosis 270.2 [713.0]
  O'Nyong Nyong 066.3 [711.5] ☑
  parasitic disease NEC 136.9 [711.8] ☑
  paratyphoid fever (*see also* Fever, paratyphoid) 002.9 [711.3] ☑
  Pneumococcus 711.0 ☑
  poliomyelitis (*see also* Poliomyelitis) 045.9 ☑ [711.5] ☑
  Pseudomonas 711.0 ☑
  psoriasis 696.0
  pyogenic organism (E. coli) (H. influenzae) (Pseudomonas) (Streptococcus) 711.0 ☑
  rat-bite fever 026.1 [711.4] ☑
  regional enteritis (*see also* Enteritis, regional) 555.9 [713.1]
  Reiter's disease 099.3 [711.1] ☑
  respiratory disorder NEC 519.9 [713.4]
  reticulosis, malignant (M9720/3) 202.3 [713.2]
  rubella 056.71
  salmonellosis 003.23
  sarcoidosis 135 [713.7]
  serum sickness 999.5 [713.6]
  Staphylococcus 711.0 ☑
  Streptococcus 711.0 ☑
  syphilis (*see also* Syphilis) 094.0 [711.4] ☑
  syringomyelia 336.0 [713.5]
  thalassemia 282.49 [713.2]
  tuberculosis (*see also* Tuberculosis, arthritis) 015.9 ☑ [711.4] ☑

☑ Additional Digit Required — Refer to the Tabular List for Digit Selection   ▽ Subterms under main terms may continue to next column or page

28 — Volume 2 · October 2006   ▶◀ Revised Text   ● New Line   ▲ Revised Code   **2007 ICD-9-CM**

Index

Arteriosclerosis, arteriosclerotic — Arthritis, arthritic

Arthritis, arthritic — *continued*
  due to or associated with — *continued*
    typhoid fever 002.0 *[711.3]* ☑
    ulcerative colitis (*see also* Colitis, ulcerative) 556.9 *[713.1]*
    urethritis
      nongonococcal (*see also* Urethritis, nongonococcal) 099.40 *[711.1]* ☑
      nonspecific (*see also* Urethritis, nongonococcal) 099.40 *[711.1]* ☑
      Reiter's 099.3
    viral disease NEC 079.99 *[711.5]* ☑
  erythema epidemic 026.1
  gonococcal 098.50
  gouty (acute) 274.0
  hypertrophic (*see also* Osteoarthrosis) 715.9 ☑
    spine 721.90
      with myelopathy 721.91
  idiopathic, blennorrheal 099.3
  in caisson disease 993.3 *[713.8]*
  infectious or infective (acute) (chronic) (subacute) NEC 711.9 ☑
    nonpyogenic 711.9 ☑
      spine 720.9
  inflammatory NEC 714.9
  juvenile rheumatoid (chronic) (polyarticular) 714.30
    acute 714.31
    monoarticular 714.33
    pauciarticular 714.32
  lumbar (*see also* Spondylosis, lumbar) 721.3
  meningococcal 036.82
  menopausal NEC 716.3 ☑
  migratory — *see* Fever, rheumatic
  neuropathic (Charcôt's) 094.0 *[713.5]*
    diabetic 250.6 ☑ *[713.5]*
    nonsyphilitic NEC 349.9 *[713.5]*
    syringomyelic 336.0 *[713.5]*
    tabetic 094.0 *[713.5]*
  nodosa (*see also* Osteoarthrosis) 715.9 ☑
    spine 721.90
      with myelopathy 721.91
  nonpyogenic NEC 716.9 ☑
    spine 721.90
      with myelopathy 721.91
  ochronotic 270.2 *[713.0]*
  palindromic (*see also* Rheumatism, palindromic) 719.3 ☑
  pneumococcal 711.0 ☑
  postdysenteric 009.0 *[711.3]* ☑
  postrheumatic, chronic (Jaccoud's) 714.4
  primary progressive 714.0
    spine 720.9
  proliferative 714.0
    spine 720.0
  psoriatic 696.0
  purulent 711.0 ☑
  pyogenic or pyemic 711.0 ☑
  rheumatic 714.0
    acute or subacute — *see* Fever, rheumatic
    chronic 714.0
      spine 720.9
  rheumatoid (nodular) 714.0
    with
      splenoadenomegaly and leukopenia 714.1
      visceral or systemic involvement 714.2
    aortitis 714.89
    carditis 714.2
    heart disease 714.2
    juvenile (chronic) (polyarticular) 714.30
      acute 714.31
      monoarticular 714.33
      pauciarticular 714.32
      spine 720.0
    rubella 056.71

Arthritis, arthritic — *continued*
  sacral, sacroiliac, sacrococcygeal (*see also* Spondylosis, sacral) 721.3
  scorbutic 267
  senile or senescent (*see also* Osteoarthrosis) 715.9 ☑
    spine 721.90
      with myelopathy 721.91
  septic 711.0 ☑
  serum (nontherapeutic) (therapeutic) 999.5 *[713.6]*
  specified form NEC 716.8 ☑
  spine 721.90
    with myelopathy 721.91
    atrophic 720.9
    degenerative 721.90
      with myelopathy 721.91
    hypertrophic (with deformity) 721.90
      with myelopathy 721.91
    infectious or infective NEC 720.9
    Marie-Strümpell 720.0
    nonpyogenic 721.90
      with myelopathy 721.91
    pyogenic 720.9
    rheumatoid 720.0
    traumatic (old) 721.7
    tuberculous (*see also* Tuberculosis) 015.0 ☑ *[720.81]*
  staphylococcal 711.0 ☑
  streptococcal 711.0 ☑
  suppurative 711.0 ☑
  syphilitic 094.0 *[713.5]*
    congenital 090.49 *[713.5]*
  syphilitica deformans (Charcôt) 094.0 *[713.5]*
  temporomandibular joint 524.69
  thoracic (*see also* Spondylosis, thoracic) 721.2
  toxic of menopause 716.3 ☑
  transient 716.4 ☑
  traumatic (chronic) (old) (post) 716.1 ☑
    current injury — *see* nature of injury
  tuberculous (*see also* Tuberculosis, arthritis) 015.9 ☑ *[711.4]* ☑
  urethritica 099.3 *[711.1]* ☑
  urica, uratic 274.0
  venereal 099.3 *[711.1]* ☑
  vertebral (*see also* Arthritis, spine) 721.90
  villous 716.8 ☑
  von Bechterew's 720.0
Arthrocele — *see also* Effusion, joint 719.0 ☑
Arthrochondritis — *see* Arthritis
Arthrodesis status V45.4
Arthrodynia — *see also* Pain, joint 719.4 ☑
  psychogenic 307.89
Arthrodysplasia 755.9
Arthrofibrosis joint — *see also* Ankylosis 718.5 ☑
Arthrogryposis 728.3
  multiplex, congenita 754.89
Arthrokatadysis 715.35
Arthrolithiasis 274.0
Arthro-onychodysplasia 756.89
Arthro-osteo-onychodysplasia 756.89

Arthropathy — *see also* Arthritis 716.9 ☑

> *Note* — Use the following fifth-digit subclassification with categories 711–712, 716:
>
> 0   site unspecified
> 1   shoulder region
> 2   upper arm
> 3   forearm
> 4   hand
> 5   pelvic region and thigh
> 6   lower leg
> 7   ankle and foot
> 8   other specified sites
> 9   multiple sites

  Behçet's 136.1 *[711.2]* ☑
  Charcôt's 094.0 *[713.5]*
    diabetic 250.6 ☑ *[713.5]*
    syringomyelic 336.0 *[713.5]*
    tabetic 094.0 *[713.5]*
  crystal (-induced) — *see* Arthritis, due to crystals
  gouty 274.0
  neurogenic, neuropathic (Charcôt's) (tabetic) 094.0 *[713.5]*
    diabetic 250.6 ☑ *[713.5]*
    nonsyphilitic NEC 349.9 *[713.5]*
    syringomyelic 336.0 *[713.5]*
  postdysenteric NEC 009.0 *[711.3]* ☑
  postrheumatic, chronic (Jaccoud's) 714.4
  psoriatic 696.0
  pulmonary 731.2
  specified NEC 716.8 ☑
  syringomyelia 336.0 *[713.5]*
  tabes dorsalis 094.0 *[713.5]*
    tabetic 094.0 *[713.5]*
  transient 716.4 ☑
  traumatic 716.1 ☑
  uric acid 274.0
Arthrophyte — *see also* Loose, body, joint 718.1 ☑
Arthrophytis 719.80
  ankle 719.87
  elbow 719.82
  foot 719.87
  hand 719.84
  hip 719.85
  knee 719.86
  multiple sites 719.89
  pelvic region 719.85
  shoulder (region) 719.81
  specified site NEC 719.88
  wrist 719.83
Arthropyosis — *see also* Arthritis, pyogenic 711.0 ☑
Arthroscopic surgical procedure converted to open procedure V64.43
Arthrosis (deformans) (degenerative) — *see also* Osteoarthrosis 715.9 ☑
  Charcôt's 094.0 *[713.5]*
  polyarticular 715.09
  spine (*see also* Spondylosis) 721.90
Arthus phenomenon 995.21 ▲
  due to
    correct substance properly administered 995.21 ▲
    overdose or wrong substance given or taken 977.9
      specified drug — *see* Table of Drugs and Chemicals
    serum 999.5
Articular — *see also* condition
  disc disorder (reducing or non-reducing) 524.63
  spondylolisthesis 756.12
Articulation
  anterior 524.27
  posterior 524.27
  reverse 524.27

Artificial
  device (prosthetic) — *see* Fitting, device
  insemination V26.1
  menopause (states) (symptoms) (syndrome) 627.4
  opening status (functioning) (without complication) V44.9
    anus (colostomy) V44.3
    colostomy V44.3
    cystostomy V44.50
      appendico-vesicostomy V44.52
      cutaneous-vesicostomy V44.51
      specified type NEC V44.59
    enterostomy V44.4
    gastrostomy V44.1
    ileostomy V44.2
    intestinal tract NEC V44.4
    jejunostomy V44.4
    nephrostomy V44.6
    specified site NEC V44.8
    tracheostomy V44.0
    ureterostomy V44.6
    urethrostomy V44.6
    urinary tract NEC V44.6
    vagina V44.7
    vagina status V44.7
ARV (disease) (illness) (infection) — *see* Human immunodeficiency virus (disease) (illness) (infection)
Arytenoid — *see* condition
Asbestosis (occupational) 501
Asboe-Hansen's disease (incontinentia pigmenti) 757.33
Ascariasis (intestinal) (lung) 127.0
Ascaridiasis 127.0
Ascaridosis 127.0
Ascaris 127.0
  lumbricoides (infestation) 127.0
  pneumonia 127.0
Ascending — *see* condition
ASC-H (atypical squamous cells cannot exclude high grade squamous intraepithelial lesion) 795.02
Aschoff's bodies — *see also* Myocarditis, rheumatic 398.0
Ascites 789.5
  abdominal NEC 789.5
  cancerous (M8000/6) 197.6
  cardiac 428.0
  chylous (nonfilarial) 457.8
    filarial (*see also* Infestation, filarial) 125.9
  congenital 778.0
  due to S. japonicum 120.2
  fetal, causing fetopelvic disproportion 653.7 ☑
  heart 428.0
  joint (*see also* Effusion, joint) 719.0 ☑
  malignant (M8000/6) 197.6
  pseudochylous 789.5
  syphilitic 095.2
  tuberculous (*see also* Tuberculosis) 014.0 ☑
Ascorbic acid (vitamin C) **deficiency** (scurvy) 267
ASC-US (atypical squamous cells of undetermined significance) 795.01
ASCVD (arteriosclerotic cardiovascular disease) 429.2
Aseptic — *see* condition
Asherman's syndrome 621.5
Asialia 527.7
Asiatic cholera — *see also* Cholera 001.9
Asocial personality or trends 301.7
Asomatognosia 781.8
Aspergillosis 117.3
  with pneumonia 117.3 *[484.6]*
  allergic bronchopulmonary 518.6
  nonsyphilitic NEC 117.3
Aspergillus (flavus) (fumigatus) (infection) (terreus) 117.3
Aspermatogenesis 606.0
Aspermia (testis) 606.0
Asphyxia, asphyxiation (by) 799.01
  antenatal — *see* Distress, fetal

☑ Additional Digit Required — Refer to the Tabular List for Digit Selection   ⋓ Subterms under main terms may continue to next column or page

2007 ICD-9-CM   ▶◀ Revised Text   ● New Line   ▲ Revised Code   October 2006 · Volume 2 — 29

Asphyxia, asphyxiation — *continued*
- bedclothes 994.7
- birth (*see also* Asphyxia, newborn) 768.9
- bunny bag 994.7
- carbon monoxide 986
- caul (*see also* Asphyxia, newborn) 768.9
- cave-in 994.7
  - crushing — *see* Injury, internal, intrathoracic organs
- constriction 994.7
- crushing — *see* Injury, internal, intrathoracic organs
- drowning 994.1
- fetal, affecting newborn 768.9
- food or foreign body (in larynx) 933.1
  - bronchioles 934.8
  - bronchus (main) 934.1
  - lung 934.8
  - nasopharynx 933.0
  - nose, nasal passages 932
  - pharynx 933.0
  - respiratory tract 934.9
    - specified part NEC 934.8
  - throat 933.0
  - trachea 934.0
- gas, fumes, or vapor NEC 987.9
  - specified — *see* Table of Drugs and Chemicals
- gravitational changes 994.7
- hanging 994.7
- inhalation — *see* Inhalation
- intrauterine
  - fetal death (before onset of labor) 768.0
    - during labor 768.1
  - liveborn infant — *see* Distress, fetal, liveborn infant
- local 443.0
- mechanical 994.7
  - during birth (*see also* Distress, fetal) 768.9
- mucus 933.1
  - bronchus (main) 934.1
  - larynx 933.1
  - lung 934.8
  - nasal passages 932
  - newborn 770.18
  - pharynx 933.0
  - respiratory tract 934.9
    - specified part NEC 934.8
  - throat 933.0
  - trachea 934.0
  - vaginal (fetus or newborn) 770.18
- newborn 768.9
  - with neurologic involvement 768.5
  - blue 768.6
  - livida 768.6
  - mild or moderate 768.6
  - pallida 768.5
  - severe 768.5
  - white 768.5
- pathological 799.01
- plastic bag 994.7
- postnatal (*see also* Asphyxia, newborn) 768.9
  - mechanical 994.7
- pressure 994.7
- reticularis 782.61
- strangulation 994.7
- submersion 994.1
- traumatic NEC — *see* Injury, internal, intrathoracic organs
- vomiting, vomitus — *see* Asphyxia, food or foreign body

Aspiration
- acid pulmonary (syndrome) 997.3
  - obstetric 668.0 ☑
- amniotic fluid 770.13
  - with respiratory symptoms 770.14
- bronchitis 507.0
- clear amniotic fluid 770.13
  - with
    - pneumonia 770.14
    - pneumonitis 770.14

Aspiration — *continued*
- clear amniotic fluid — *continued*
  - with — *continued*
    - respiratory symptoms 770.14
  - contents of birth canal 770.17
    - with respiratory symptoms 770.18
- fetal 770.10
  - blood 770.15
    - with
      - pneumonia 770.16
      - pneumonitis 770.16
    - pneumonitis 770.18
- food, foreign body, or gasoline (with asphyxiation) — *see* Asphyxia, food or foreign body
- meconium 770.11
  - with
    - pneumonia 770.12
    - pneumonitis 770.12
    - respiratory symptoms 770.12
  - below vocal cords 770.11
    - with respiratory symptoms 770.12
- mucus 933.1
  - into
    - bronchus (main) 934.1
    - lung 934.8
    - respiratory tract 934.9
      - specified part NEC 934.8
    - trachea 934.0
  - newborn 770.17
  - vaginal (fetus or newborn) 770.17
- newborn 770.10
  - with respiratory symptoms 770.18
  - blood 770.15
    - with
      - pneumonia 770.16
      - pneumonitis 770.16
      - respiratory symptoms 770.16
- pneumonia 507.0
  - fetus or newborn 770.18
    - meconium 770.12
- pneumonitis 507.0
  - fetus or newborn 770.18
    - meconium 770.12
  - obstetric 668.0 ☑
- postnatal stomach contents 770.85
  - with
    - pneumonia 770.86
    - pneumonitis 770.86
    - respiratory symptoms 770.86
- syndrome of newborn (massive) 770.18
  - meconium 770.12
- vernix caseosa 770.12
Asplenia 759.0
- with mesocardia 746.87
Assam fever 085.0
Assimilation, pelvis
- with disproportion 653.2 ☑
  - affecting fetus or newborn 763.1
  - causing obstructed labor 660.1 ☑
    - affecting fetus or newborn 763.1
Assmann's focus — *see also* Tuberculosis 011.0 ☑
Astasia (-abasia) 307.9
- hysterical 300.11
Asteatosis 706.8
- cutis 706.8
Astereognosis 780.99
Asterixis 781.3
- in liver disease 572.8
Asteroid hyalitis 379.22
Asthenia, asthenic 780.79
- cardiac (*see also* Failure, heart) 428.9
  - psychogenic 306.2
- cardiovascular (*see also* Failure, heart) 428.9
  - psychogenic 306.2
- heart (*see also* Failure, heart) 428.9
  - psychogenic 306.2
- hysterical 300.11
- myocardial (*see also* Failure, heart) 428.9
  - psychogenic 306.2
- nervous 300.5

Asthenia, asthenic — *continued*
- neurocirculatory 306.2
- neurotic 300.5
- psychogenic 300.5
- psychoneurotic 300.5
- psychophysiologic 300.5
- reaction, psychoneurotic 300.5
- senile 797
- Stiller's 780.79
- tropical anhidrotic 705.1
Asthenopia 368.13
- accommodative 367.4
- hysterical (muscular) 300.11
- psychogenic 306.7
Asthenospermia 792.2
Asthma, asthmatic (bronchial) (catarrh) (spasmodic) 493.9 ☑

> Note — Use the following fifth-digit subclassification with category 493:
> 0   without mention of status asthmaticus or acute exacerbation or unspecified
> 1   with status asthmaticus
> 2   with acute exacerbation

- with
  - chronic obstructive pulmonary disease (COPD) 493.2 ☑
  - hay fever 493.0 ☑
  - rhinitis, allergic 493.0 ☑
- allergic 493.9 ☑
  - stated cause (external allergen) 493.0 ☑
- atopic 493.0 ☑
- cardiac (*see also* Failure, ventricular, left) 428.1
- cardiobronchial (*see also* Failure, ventricular, left) 428.1
- cardiorenal (*see also* Hypertension, cardiorenal) 404.90
- childhood 493.0 ☑
- Colliers' 500
- cough variant 493.82
- croup 493.9 ☑
- detergent 507.8
- due to
  - detergent 507.8
  - inhalation of fumes 506.3
  - internal immunological process 493.0 ☑
- endogenous (intrinsic) 493.1 ☑
- eosinophilic 518.3
- exercise induced bronchospasm 493.81
- exogenous (cosmetics) (dander or dust) (drugs) (dust) (feathers) (food) (hay) (platinum) (pollen) 493.0 ☑
- extrinsic 493.0 ☑
- grinders' 502
- hay 493.0 ☑
- heart (*see also* Failure, ventricular, left) 428.1
- IgE 493.0 ☑
- infective 493.1 ☑
- intrinsic 493.1 ☑
- Kopp's 254.8
- late-onset 493.1 ☑
- meat-wrappers' 506.9
- Millar's (laryngismus stridulus) 478.75
- millstone makers' 502
- miners' 500
- Monday morning 504
- New Orleans (epidemic) 493.0 ☑
- platinum 493.0 ☑
- pneumoconiotic (occupational) NEC 505
- potters' 502
- psychogenic 316 *[493.9]* ☑
- pulmonary eosinophilic 518.3
- red cedar 495.8
- Rostan's (*see also* Failure, ventricular, left) 428.1

Asthma, asthmatic — *continued*
- sandblasters' 502
- sequoiosis 495.8
- stonemasons' 502
- thymic 254.8
- tuberculous (*see also* Tuberculosis, pulmonary) 011.9 ☑
- Wichmann's (laryngismus stridulus) 478.75
- wood 495.8
Astigmatism (compound) (congenital) 367.20
- irregular 367.22
- regular 367.21
Astroblastoma (M9430/3)
- nose 748.1
- specified site — *see* Neoplasm, by site, malignant
- unspecified site 191.9
Astrocytoma (cystic) (M9400/3)
- anaplastic type (M9401/3)
  - specified site — *see* Neoplasm, by site, malignant
  - unspecified site 191.9
- fibrillary (M9420/3)
  - specified site — *see* Neoplasm, by site, malignant
  - unspecified site 191.9
- fibrous (M9420/3)
  - specified site — *see* Neoplasm, by site, malignant
  - unspecified site 191.9
- gemistocytic (M9411/3)
  - specified site — *see* Neoplasm, by site, malignant
  - unspecified site 191.9
- juvenile (M9421/3)
  - specified site — *see* Neoplasm, by site, malignant
  - unspecified site 191.9
- nose 748.1
- pilocytic (M9421/3)
  - specified site — *see* Neoplasm, by site, malignant
  - unspecified site 191.9
- piloid (M9421/3)
  - specified site — *see* Neoplasm, by site, malignant
  - unspecified site 191.9
- protoplasmic (M9410/3)
  - specified site — *see* Neoplasm, by site, malignant
  - unspecified site 191.9
- specified site — *see* Neoplasm, by site, malignant
- subependymal (M9383/1) 237.5
  - giant cell (M9384/1) 237.5
- unspecified site 191.9
Astroglioma (M9400/3)
- nose 748.1
- specified site — *see* Neoplasm, by site, malignant
- unspecified site 191.9
Asymbolia 784.60
Asymmetrical breathing 786.09
Asymmetry — *see also* Distortion
- chest 786.9
- face 754.0
- jaw NEC 524.12
  - maxillary 524.11
- pelvis with disproportion 653.0 ☑
  - affecting fetus or newborn 763.1
  - causing obstructed labor 660.1 ☑
    - affecting fetus or newborn 763.1
Asynergia 781.3
Asynergy 781.3
- ventricular 429.89
Asystole (heart) — *see also* Arrest, cardiac 427.5
Ataxia, ataxy, ataxic 781.3
- acute 781.3
- brain 331.89
- cerebellar 334.3
  - hereditary (Marie's) 334.2
  - in
    - alcoholism 303.9 ☑ *[334.4]*

☑ Additional Digit Required — Refer to the Tabular List for Digit Selection   ℳ Subterms under main terms may continue to next column or page

30 — Volume 2   ►◄ Revised Text   ● New Line   ▲ Revised Code   **2007 ICD-9-CM**

Ataxia, ataxy, ataxic — *continued*
cerebellar — *continued*
in — *continued*
myxedema (*see also* Myxedema) 244.9 *[334.4]*
neoplastic disease NEC 239.9 *[334.4]*
cerebral 331.89
family, familial 334.2
cerebral (Marie's) 334.2
spinal (Friedreich's) 334.0
Friedreich's (heredofamilial) (spinal) 334.0
frontal lobe 781.3
gait 781.2
hysterical 300.11
general 781.3
hereditary NEC 334.2
cerebellar 334.2
spastic 334.1
spinal 334.0
heredofamilial (Marie's) 334.2
hysterical 300.11
locomotor (progressive) 094.0
diabetic 250.6 ☑ *[337.1]*
Marie's (cerebellar) (heredofamilial) 334.2
nonorganic origin 307.9
partial 094.0
postchickenpox 052.7
progressive locomotor 094.0
psychogenic 307.9
Sanger-Brown's 334.2
spastic 094.0
hereditary 334.1
syphilitic 094.0
spinal
hereditary 334.0
progressive locomotor 094.0
telangiectasia 334.8
Ataxia-telangiectasia 334.8
Atelectasis (absorption collapse) (complete) (compression) (massive) (partial) (postinfective) (pressure collapse) (pulmonary) (relaxation) 518.0
newborn (congenital) (partial) 770.5
primary 770.4
primary 770.4
tuberculous (*see also* Tuberculosis, pulmonary) 011.9 ☑
Ateleiosis, ateliosis 253.3
Atelia — *see* Distortion
Ateliosis 253.3
Atelocardia 746.9
Atelomyelia 742.59
Athelia 757.6
Atheroembolism
extremity
lower 445.02
upper 445.01
kidney 445.81
specified site NEC 445.89
Atheroma, atheromatous — *see also* Arteriosclerosis 440.9
aorta, aortic 440.0
valve (*see also* Endocarditis, aortic) 424.1
artery — *see* Arteriosclerosis
basilar (artery) (*see also* Occlusion, artery, basilar) 433.0 ☑
carotid (artery) (common) (internal) (*see also* Occlusion, artery, carotid) 433.1 ☑
cerebral (arteries) 437.0
coronary (artery) — *see* Arteriosclerosis, coronary
degeneration — *see* Arteriosclerosis
heart, cardiac — *see* Arteriosclerosis, coronary
mitral (valve) 424.0
myocardium, myocardial — *see* Arteriosclerosis, coronary
pulmonary valve (heart) (*see also* Endocarditis, pulmonary) 424.3
skin 706.2

Atheroma, atheromatous — *see also* Arteriosclerosis — *continued*
tricuspid (heart) (valve) 424.2
valve, valvular — *see* Endocarditis
vertebral (artery) (*see also* Occlusion, artery, vertebral) 433.2 ☑
Atheromatosis — *see also* Arteriosclerosis
arterial, congenital 272.8
Atherosclerosis — *see* Arteriosclerosis
Athetosis (acquired) 781.0
bilateral 333.79 ▲
congenital (bilateral) 333.6 ▲
double 333.71 ▲
unilateral 781.0
Athlete's
foot 110.4
heart 429.3
Athletic team examination V70.3
Athrepsia 261
Athyrea (acquired) — *see also* Hypothyroidism 244.9
congenital 243
Athyreosis (congenital) 243
acquired — *see* Hypothyroidism
Athyroidism (acquired) — *see also* Hypothyroidism 244.9
congenital 243
Atmospheric pyrexia 992.0
Atonia, atony, atonic
abdominal wall 728.2
bladder (sphincter) 596.4
neurogenic NEC 596.54
with cauda equina syndrome 344.61
capillary 448.9
cecum 564.89
psychogenic 306.4
colon 564.89
psychogenic 306.4
congenital 779.89
dyspepsia 536.3
psychogenic 306.4
intestine 564.89
psychogenic 306.4
stomach 536.3
neurotic or psychogenic 306.4
psychogenic 306.4
uterus
with hemorrhage 666.1 ☑ ●
without hemorrhage 669.8 ☑ ●
vesical 596.4
Atopy NEC V15.09
Atransferrinemia, congenital 273.8
Atresia, atretic (congenital) 759.89
alimentary organ or tract NEC 751.8
lower 751.2
upper 750.8
ani, anus, anal (canal) 751.2
aorta 747.22
with hypoplasia of ascending aorta and defective development of left ventricle (with mitral valve atresia) 746.7
arch 747.11
ring 747.21
aortic (orifice) (valve) 746.89
arch 747.11
aqueduct of Sylvius 742.3
with spina bifida (*see also* Spina bifida) 741.0 ☑
artery NEC (*see also* Atresia, blood vessel) 747.60
cerebral 747.81
coronary 746.85
eye 743.58
pulmonary 747.3
umbilical 747.5
auditory canal (external) 744.02
bile, biliary duct (common) or passage 751.61
acquired (*see also* Obstruction, biliary) 576.2
bladder (neck) 753.6
blood vessel (peripheral) NEC 747.60
cerebral 747.81

Atresia, atretic — *continued*
blood vessel — *continued*
gastrointestinal 747.61
lower limb 747.64
pulmonary artery 747.3
renal 747.62
spinal 747.82
upper limb 747.63
bronchus 748.3
canal, ear 744.02
cardiac
valve 746.89
aortic 746.89
mitral 746.89
pulmonary 746.01
tricuspid 746.1
cecum 751.2
cervix (acquired) 622.4
congenital 752.49
in pregnancy or childbirth 654.6 ☑
affecting fetus or newborn 763.89
causing obstructed labor 660.2 ☑
affecting fetus or newborn 763.1
choana 748.0
colon 751.2
cystic duct 751.61
acquired 575.8
with obstruction (*see also* Obstruction, gallbladder) 575.2
digestive organs NEC 751.8
duodenum 751.1
ear canal 744.02
ejaculatory duct 752.89
epiglottis 748.3
esophagus 750.3
Eustachian tube 744.24
fallopian tube (acquired) 628.2
congenital 752.19
follicular cyst 620.0
foramen of
Luschka 742.3
with spina bifida (*see also* Spina bifida) 741.0 ☑
Magendie 742.3
with spina bifida (*see also* Spina bifida) 741.0 ☑
gallbladder 751.69
genital organ
external
female 752.49
male NEC 752.89
penis 752.69
internal
female 752.89
male 752.89
glottis 748.3
gullet 750.3
heart
valve NEC 746.89
aortic 746.89
mitral 746.89
pulmonary 746.01
tricuspid 746.1
hymen 752.42
acquired 623.3
postinfective 623.3
ileum 751.1
intestine (small) 751.1
large 751.2
iris, filtration angle (*see also* Buphthalmia) 743.20
jejunum 751.1
kidney 753.3
lacrimal, apparatus 743.65
acquired — *see* Stenosis, lacrimal
larynx 748.3
ligament, broad 752.19
lung 748.5
meatus urinarius 753.6
mitral valve 746.89

Atresia, atretic — *continued*
mitral valve — *continued*
with atresia or hypoplasia of aortic orifice or valve, with hypoplasia of ascending aorta and defective development of left ventricle 746.7
nares (anterior) (posterior) 748.0
nasolacrimal duct 743.65
nasopharynx 748.8
nose, nostril 748.0
acquired 738.0
organ or site NEC — *see* Anomaly, specified type NEC
osseous meatus (ear) 744.03
oviduct (acquired) 628.2
congenital 752.19
parotid duct 750.23
acquired 527.8
pulmonary (artery) 747.3
valve 746.01
vein 747.49
pulmonic 746.01
pupil 743.46
rectum 751.2
salivary duct or gland 750.23
acquired 527.8
sublingual duct 750.23
acquired 527.8
submaxillary duct or gland 750.23
acquired 527.8
trachea 748.3
tricuspid valve 746.1
ureter 753.29
ureteropelvic junction 753.21
ureterovesical orifice 753.22
urethra (valvular) 753.6
urinary tract NEC 753.29
uterus 752.3
acquired 621.8
vagina (acquired) 623.2
congenital 752.49
postgonococcal (old) 098.2
postinfectional 623.2
senile 623.2
vascular NEC (*see also* Atresia, blood vessel) 747.60
cerebral 747.81
vas deferens 752.89
vein NEC (*see also* Atresia, blood vessel) 747.60
cardiac 746.89
great 747.49
portal 747.49
pulmonary 747.49
vena cava (inferior) (superior) 747.49
vesicourethral orifice 753.6
vulva 752.49
acquired 624.8
Atrichia, atrichosis 704.00
congenital (universal) 757.4
Atrioventricularis commune 745.69
At risk for falling V15.88
Atrophia — *see also* Atrophy
alba 709.09
cutis 701.8
idiopathica progressiva 701.8
senilis 701.8
dermatological, diffuse (idiopathic) 701.8
flava hepatis (acuta) (subacuta) (*see also* Necrosis, liver) 570
gyrata of choroid and retina (central) 363.54
generalized 363.57
senilis 797
dermatological 701.8
unguium 703.8
congenita 757.5
Atrophoderma, atrophodermia 701.9
diffusum (idiopathic) 701.8
maculatum 701.3
et striatum 701.3
due to syphilis 095.8
syphilitic 091.3
neuriticum 701.8

☑ Additional Digit Required — Refer to the Tabular List for Digit Selection   ▽ Subterms under main terms may continue to next column or page

2007 ICD-9-CM   ▶◀ Revised Text   ● New Line   ▲ Revised Code   October 2006 • Volume 2 — 31

Atrophoderma, atrophodermia —
    continued
    pigmentosum 757.33
    reticulatum symmetricum faciei 701.8
    senile 701.8
    symmetrical 701.8
    vermiculata 701.8
Atrophy, atrophic
    adrenal (autoimmune) (capsule) (cortex) (gland) 255.4
        with hypofunction 255.4
    alveolar process or ridge (edentulous) 525.20
        mandible 525.20
            minimal 525.21
            moderate 525.22
            severe 525.23
        maxilla 525.20
            minimal 525.24
            moderate 525.25
            severe 525.26
    appendix 543.9
    Aran-Duchenne muscular 335.21
    arm 728.2
    arteriosclerotic — *see* Arteriosclerosis
    arthritis 714.0
        spine 720.9
    bile duct (any) 576.8
    bladder 596.8
    blanche (of Milian) 701.3
    bone (senile) 733.99
        due to
            disuse 733.7
            infection 733.99
            tabes dorsalis (neurogenic) 094.0
        posttraumatic 733.99
    brain (cortex) (progressive) 331.9
        with dementia 290.10
        Alzheimer's 331.0
            with dementia — *see*
                Alzheimer's, dementia
        circumscribed (Pick's) 331.11
            with dementia
                with behavioral disturbance 331.11 *[294.11]*
                without behavioral disturbance 331.11 *[294.10]*
        congenital 742.4
        hereditary 331.9
        senile 331.2
    breast 611.4
        puerperal, postpartum 676.3 ☑
    buccal cavity 528.9
    cardiac (brown) (senile) (*see also* Degeneration, myocardial) 429.1
    cartilage (infectional) (joint) 733.99
    cast, plaster of Paris 728.2
    cerebellar — *see* Atrophy, brain
    cerebral — *see* Atrophy, brain
    cervix (endometrium) (mucosa) (myometrium) (senile) (uteri) 622.8
        menopausal 627.8
    Charcôt-Marie-Tooth 356.1
    choroid 363.40
        diffuse secondary 363.42
        hereditary (*see also* Dystrophy, choroid) 363.50
            gyrate
                central 363.54
                diffuse 363.57
                generalized 363.57
        senile 363.41
    ciliary body 364.57
    colloid, degenerative 701.3
    conjunctiva (senile) 372.89
    corpus cavernosum 607.89
    cortical (*see also* Atrophy, brain) 331.9
    Cruveilhier's 335.21
    cystic duct 576.8
    dacryosialadenopathy 710.2
    degenerative
        colloid 701.3
        senile 701.3
    Déjérine-Thomas 333.0

Atrophy, atrophic — *continued*
    diffuse idiopathic, dermatological 701.8
    disuse
        bone 733.7
        muscle 728.2
        pelvic muscles and anal sphincter 618.83
    Duchenne-Aran 335.21
    ear 388.9
    edentulous alveolar ridge 525.20
        mandible 525.20
            minimal 525.21
            moderate 525.22
            severe 525.23
        maxilla 525.20
            minimal 525.24
            moderate 525.25
            severe 525.26
    emphysema, lung 492.8
    endometrium (senile) 621.8
        cervix 622.8
    enteric 569.89
    epididymis 608.3
    eyeball, cause unknown 360.41
    eyelid (senile) 374.50
    facial (skin) 701.9
    facioscapulohumeral (Landouzy-Déjérine) 359.1
    fallopian tube (senile), acquired 620.3
    fatty, thymus (gland) 254.8
    gallbladder 575.8
    gastric 537.89
    gastritis (chronic) 535.1 ☑
    gastrointestinal 569.89
    genital organ, male 608.89
    glandular 289.3
    globe (phthisis bulbi) 360.41
    gum (*see also* Recession, gingival) 523.20
    hair 704.2
    heart (brown) (senile) (*see also* Degeneration, myocardial) 429.1
    hemifacial 754.0
        Romberg 349.89
    hydronephrosis 591
    infantile 261
        paralysis, acute (*see also* Poliomyelitis, with paralysis) 045.1 ☑
    intestine 569.89
    iris (generalized) (postinfectional) (sector shaped) 364.59
        essential 364.51
        progressive 364.51
        sphincter 364.54
    kidney (senile) (*see also* Sclerosis, renal) 587
        with hypertension (*see also* Hypertension, kidney) 403.90
        congenital 753.0
        hydronephrotic 591
        infantile 753.0
    lacrimal apparatus (primary) 375.13
        secondary 375.14
    Landouzy-Déjérine 359.1
    laryngitis, infection 476.0
    larynx 478.79
    Leber's optic 377.16
    lip 528.5
    liver (acute) (subacute) (*see also* Necrosis, liver) 570
        chronic (yellow) 571.8
        yellow (congenital) 570
            with
                abortion — *see* Abortion, by type, with specified complication NEC
                ectopic pregnancy (*see also* categories 633.0–633.9) 639.8
                molar pregnancy (*see also* categories 630–632) 639.8
            chronic 571.8
            complicating pregnancy 646.7 ☑

Atrophy, atrophic — *continued*
    liver (*see also* Necrosis, liver) — *continued*
        yellow — *continued*
            following
                abortion 639.8
                ectopic or molar pregnancy 639.8
            from injection, inoculation or transfusion (onset within 8 months after administration) — *see* Hepatitis, viral
            healed 571.5
            obstetric 646.7 ☑
            postabortal 639.8
            postimmunization — *see* Hepatitis, viral
            posttransfusion — *see* Hepatitis, viral
            puerperal, postpartum 674.8 ☑
    lung (senile) 518.89
        congenital 748.69
    macular (dermatological) 701.3
        syphilitic, skin 091.3
        striated 095.8
    muscle, muscular 728.2
        disuse 728.2
        Duchenne-Aran 335.21
        extremity (lower) (upper) 728.2
        familial spinal 335.11
        general 728.2
        idiopathic 728.2
        infantile spinal 335.0
        myelopathic (progressive) 335.10
        myotonic 359.2
        neuritic 356.1
        neuropathic (peroneal) (progressive) 356.1
        peroneal 356.1
        primary (idiopathic) 728.2
        progressive (familial) (hereditary) (pure) 335.21
            adult (spinal) 335.19
            infantile (spinal) 335.0
            juvenile (spinal) 335.11
            spinal 335.10
                adult 335.19
                hereditary or familial 335.11
                infantile 335.0
        pseudohypertrophic 359.1
        spinal (progressive) 335.10
            adult 335.19
            Aran-Duchenne 335.21
            familial 335.11
            hereditary 335.11
            infantile 335.0
            juvenile 335.11
        syphilitic 095.6
    myocardium (*see also* Degeneration, myocardial) 429.1
    myometrium (senile) 621.8
        cervix 622.8
    myotatic 728.2
    myotonia 359.2
    nail 703.8
        congenital 757.5
    nasopharynx 472.2
    nerve (*see also* Disorder, nerve)
        abducens 378.54
        accessory 352.4
        acoustic or auditory 388.5
        cranial 352.9
            first (olfactory) 352.0
            second (optic) (*see also* Atrophy, optic nerve) 377.10
            third (oculomotor) (partial) 378.51
                total 378.52
            fourth (trochlear) 378.53
            fifth (trigeminal) 350.8
            sixth (abducens) 378.54
            seventh (facial) 351.8
            eighth (auditory) 388.5
            ninth (glossopharyngeal) 352.2
            tenth (pneumogastric) (vagus) 352.3

Atrophy, atrophic — *continued*
    nerve (*see also* Disorder, nerve) — *continued*
        cranial — *continued*
            eleventh (accessory) 352.4
            twelfth (hypoglossal) 352.5
        facial 351.8
        glossopharyngeal 352.2
        hypoglossal 352.5
        oculomotor (partial) 378.51
            total 378.52
        olfactory 352.0
        peripheral 355.9
        pneumogastric 352.3
        trigeminal 350.8
        trochlear 378.53
        vagus (pneumogastric) 352.3
    nervous system, congenital 742.8
    neuritic (*see also* Disorder, nerve) 355.9
    neurogenic NEC 355.9
        bone
            tabetic 094.0
    nutritional 261
    old age 797
    olivopontocerebellar 333.0
    optic nerve (ascending) (descending) (infectional) (nonfamilial) (papillomacular bundle) (postretinal) (secondary NEC) (simple) 377.10
        associated with retinal dystrophy 377.13
        dominant hereditary 377.16
        glaucomatous 377.14
        hereditary (dominant) (Leber's) 377.16
        Leber's (hereditary) 377.16
        partial 377.15
        postinflammatory 377.12
        primary 377.11
        syphilitic 094.84
            congenital 090.49
            tabes dorsalis 094.0
    orbit 376.45
    ovary (senile), acquired 620.3
    oviduct (senile), acquired 620.3
    palsy, diffuse 335.20
    pancreas (duct) (senile) 577.8
    papillary muscle 429.81
    paralysis 355.9
    parotid gland 527.0
    patches skin 701.3
        senile 701.8
    penis 607.89
    pharyngitis 472.1
    pharynx 478.29
    pluriglandular 258.8
    polyarthritis 714.0
    prostate 602.2
    pseudohypertrophic 359.1
    renal (*see also* Sclerosis, renal) 587
    reticulata 701.8
    retina (*see also* Degeneration, retina) 362.60
        hereditary (*see also* Dystrophy, retina) 362.70
    rhinitis 472.0
    salivary duct or gland 527.0
    scar NEC 709.2
    sclerosis, lobar (of brain) 331.0
        with dementia
            with behavioral disturbance 331.0 *[294.11]*
            without behavioral disturbance 331.0 *[294.10]*
    scrotum 608.89
    seminal vesicle 608.89
    senile 797
        degenerative, of skin 701.3
        skin (patches) senile 701.8
    spermatic cord 608.89
    spinal (cord) 336.8
        acute 336.8
        muscular (chronic) 335.10
            adult 335.19
            familial 335.11

Atrophy, atrophic — *continued*
  spinal — *continued*
    muscular — *continued*
      juvenile 335.10
    paralysis 335.10
      acute (*see also* Poliomyelitis,
        with paralysis) 045.1 ☑
  spine (column) 733.99
  spleen (senile) 289.59
  spots (skin) 701.3
    senile 701.8
  stomach 537.89
  striate and macular 701.3
    syphilitic 095.8
  subcutaneous 701.9
    due to injection 999.9
  sublingual gland 527.0
  submaxillary gland 527.0
  Sudeck's 733.7
  suprarenal (autoimmune) (capsule)
    (gland) 255.4
    with hypofunction 255.4
  tarso-orbital fascia, congenital 743.66
  testis 608.3
  thenar, partial 354.0
  throat 478.29
  thymus (fat) 254.8
  thyroid (gland) 246.8
    with
      cretinism 243
      myxedema 244.9
    congenital 243
  tongue (senile) 529.8
    papillae 529.4
    smooth 529.4
  trachea 519.19   ▲
  tunica vaginalis 608.89
  turbinate 733.99
  tympanic membrane (nonflaccid)
    384.82
    flaccid 384.81
  ulcer (*see also* Ulcer, skin) 707.9
  upper respiratory tract 478.9
  uterus, uterine (acquired) (senile)
    621.8
    cervix 622.8
    due to radiation (intended effect)
      621.8
  vagina (senile) 627.3
  vascular 459.89
  vas deferens 608.89
  vertebra (senile) 733.99
  vulva (primary) (senile) 624.1
  Werdnig-Hoffmann 335.0
  yellow (acute) (congenital) (liver) (sub-
    acute) (*see also* Necrosis, liver)
    570
    chronic 571.8
    resulting from administration of
      blood, plasma, serum, or
      other biological substance
      (within 8 months of adminis-
      tration) — *see* Hepatitis, viral

Attack
  akinetic (*see also* Epilepsy) 345.0 ☑
  angina — *see* Angina
  apoplectic (*see also* Disease, cere-
    brovascular, acute) 436
  benign shuddering 333.93
  bilious — *see* Vomiting
  cataleptic 300.11
  cerebral (*see also* Disease, cerebrovas-
    cular, acute) 436
  coronary (*see also* Infarct, myocardi-
    um) 410.9 ☑
  cyanotic, newborn 770.83
  epileptic (*see also* Epilepsy) 345.9 ☑
  epileptiform 780.39
  heart (*see also* Infarct, myocardium)
    410.9 ☑
  hemiplegia (*see also* Disease, cere-
    brovascular, acute) 436
  hysterical 300.11
  jacksonian (*see also* Epilepsy) 345.5 ☑
  myocardium, myocardial (*see also* In-
    farct, myocardium) 410.9 ☑

Attack — *continued*
  myoclonic (*see also* Epilepsy) 345.1 ☑
  panic 300.01
  paralysis (*see also* Disease, cerebrovas-
    cular, acute) 436
  paroxysmal 780.39
  psychomotor (*see also* Epilepsy)
    345.4 ☑
  salaam (*see also* Epilepsy) 345.6 ☑
  schizophreniform (*see also*
    Schizophrenia) 295.4 ☑
  sensory and motor 780.39
  syncope 780.2
  toxic, cerebral 780.39
  transient ischemic (TIA) 435.9
  unconsciousness 780.2
    hysterical 300.11
  vasomotor 780.2
  vasovagal (idiopathic) (paroxysmal)
    780.2

Attention to
  artificial opening (of) V55.9
    digestive tract NEC V55.4
    specified site NEC V55.8
    urinary tract NEC V55.6
    vagina V55.7
  colostomy V55.3
  cystostomy V55.5
  dressing   ●
    wound V58.30   ●
      nonsurgical V58.30   ●
      surgical V58.31   ●
  gastrostomy V55.1
  ileostomy V55.2
  jejunostomy V55.4
  nephrostomy V55.6
  surgical dressings V58.31   ▲
  sutures V58.32   ▲
  tracheostomy V55.0
  ureterostomy V55.6
  urethrostomy V55.6

Attrition
  gum (*see also* Recession, gingival)
    523.20
  teeth (hard tissues) 521.10
    excessive 521.10
      extending into
        dentine 521.12
        pulp 521.13
      generalized 521.15
      limited to enamel 521.11
      localized 521.14

Atypical — *see also* condition
  cells
    endocervical 795.00
    endometrial 795.00
    glandular 795.00
  distribution, vessel (congenital) (pe-
    ripheral) NEC 747.60
  endometrium 621.9
  kidney 593.89

Atypism, cervix 622.10
Audible tinnitus — *see also* Tinnitus
  388.30
Auditory — *see* condition
Audry's syndrome (acropachyderma)
  757.39
Aujeszky's disease 078.89
Aura, jacksonian — *see also* Epilepsy
  345.5 ☑
Aurantiasis, cutis 278.3
Auricle, auricular — *see* condition
Auriculotemporal syndrome 350.8
Australian
  Q fever 083.0
  X disease 062.4
Autism, autistic (child) (infantile)
  299.0 ☑
Autodigestion 799.89
Autoerythrocyte sensitization 287.2
Autographism 708.3
Autoimmune
  cold sensitivity 283.0
  disease NEC 279.4
  hemolytic anemia 283.0
  thyroiditis 245.2

Autoinfection, septic — *see* Septicemia
Autointoxication 799.89
Automatism 348.8
  epileptic (*see also* Epilepsy) 345.4 ☑
  paroxysmal, idiopathic (*see also*
    Epilepsy) 345.4 ☑
Autonomic, autonomous
  bladder 596.54
    neurogenic 596.54
      with cauda equina 344.61
  dysreflexia 337.3
  faciocephalalgia (*see also* Neuropathy,
    peripheral, autonomic) 337.9
  hysterical seizure 300.11
  imbalance (*see also* Neuropathy, pe-
    ripheral, autonomic) 337.9
Autophony 388.40
Autosensitivity, erythrocyte 287.2
Autotopagnosia 780.99
Autotoxemia 799.89
Autumn — *see* condition
Avellis' syndrome 344.89
Aviators
  disease or sickness (*see also* Effect,
    adverse, high altitude) 993.2
  ear 993.0
  effort syndrome 306.2
Avitaminosis (multiple NEC) — *see also*
  Deficiency, vitamin 269.2
  A 264.9
  B 266.9
    with
      beriberi 265.0
      pellagra 265.2
  B_1 265.1
  B_2 266.0
  B_6 266.1
  B_{12} 266.2
  C (with scurvy) 267
  D 268.9
    with
      osteomalacia 268.2
      rickets 268.0
  E 269.1
  G 266.0
  H 269.1
  K 269.0
  multiple 269.2
  nicotinic acid 265.2
  P 269.1
Avulsion (traumatic) 879.8
  blood vessel — *see* Injury, blood ves-
    sel, by site
  cartilage (*see also* Dislocation, by site)
    knee, current (*see also* Tear,
      meniscus) 836.2
    symphyseal (inner), complicating
      delivery 665.6 ☑
  complicated 879.9
  diaphragm — *see* Injury, internal, di-
    aphragm
  ear — *see* Wound, open, ear
  epiphysis of bone — *see* Fracture, by
    site
  external site other than limb — *see*
    Wound, open, by site
  eye 871.3
  fingernail — *see* Wound, open, finger
  fracture — *see* Fracture, by site
  genital organs, external — *see* Wound,
    open, genital organs
  head (intracranial) NEC (*see also* In-
    jury, intracranial, with open in-
    tracranial wound)
    complete 874.9
    external site NEC 873.8
      complicated 873.9
  internal organ or site — *see* Injury,
    internal, by site
  joint (*see also* Dislocation, by site)
    capsule — *see* Sprain, by site
  ligament — *see* Sprain, by site
  limb (*see also* Amputation, traumatic,
    by site)

Avulsion — *continued*
  limb (*see also* Amputation, traumatic,
    by site) — *continued*
    skin and subcutaneous tissue —
      see Wound, open, by site
  muscle — *see* Sprain, by site
  nerve (root) — *see* Injury, nerve, by
    site
  scalp — *see* Wound, open, scalp
  skin and subcutaneous tissue — *see*
    Wound, open, by site
  symphyseal cartilage (inner), compli-
    cating delivery 665.6 ☑
  tendon (*see also* Sprain, by site)
    with open wound — *see* Wound,
      open, by site
  toenail — *see* Wound, open, toe(s)
  tooth 873.63
    complicated 873.73
Awaiting organ transplant status
  V49.83
Awareness of heart beat 785.1
Axe grinders' disease 502
Axenfeld's anomaly or syndrome
  743.44
Axilla, axillary — *see also* condition
  breast 757.6
Axonotmesis — *see* Injury, nerve, by site
Ayala's disease 756.89
Ayerza's disease or syndrome (pul-
  monary artery sclerosis with pul-
  monary hypertension) 416.0
Azoospermia 606.0
Azorean disease (of the nervous system)
  334.8
Azotemia 790.6
  meaning uremia (*see also* Uremia) 586
Aztec ear 744.29
Azygos lobe, lung (fissure) 748.69

B

Baader's syndrome (erythema multi-
  forme exudativum) 695.1
Baastrup's syndrome 721.5
Babesiasis 088.82
Babesiosis 088.82
Babington's disease (familial hemorrhag-
  ic telangiectasia) 448.0
Babinski-Fröhlich syndrome (adiposo-
  genital dystrophy) 253.8
Babinski-Nageotte syndrome 344.89
Babinski's syndrome (cardiovascular
  syphilis) 093.89
Bacillary — *see* condition
Bacilluria 791.9
  asymptomatic, in pregnancy or puer-
    perium 646.5 ☑
  tuberculous (*see also* Tuberculosis)
    016.9 ☑
Bacillus — *see also* Infection, bacillus
  abortus infection 023.1
  anthracis infection 022.9
  coli
    infection 041.4
      generalized 038.42
      intestinal 008.00
    pyemia 038.42
    septicemia 038.42
  Flexner's 004.1
  fusiformis infestation 101
  mallei infection 024
  Shiga's 004.0
  suipestifer infection (*see also* Infec-
    tion, Salmonella) 003.9
Back — *see* condition
Backache (postural) 724.5
  psychogenic 307.89
  sacroiliac 724.6
Backflow (pyelovenous) — *see also* Disease, renal 593.9
Backknee — *see also* Genu, recurvatum
  736.5
Bacteremia 790.7
  newborn 771.83
Bacteria
  in blood (*see also* Bacteremia) 790.7

☑ Additional Digit Required — Refer to the Tabular List for Digit Selection   ▽ Subterms under main terms may continue to next column or page

2007 ICD-9-CM   ▶◀ Revised Text   ● New Line   ▲ Revised Code   **October 2006 • Volume 2 — 33**

Bacteria — *continued*
in urine (*see also* Bacteriuria) 599.0
Bacterial — *see* condition
Bactericholia — *see also* Cholecystitis, acute 575.0
Bacterid, bacteride (Andrews' pustular) 686.8
Bacteriuria, bacteruria 791.9
with
urinary tract infection 599.0
asymptomatic 791.9
in pregnancy or puerperium 646.5 ☑
affecting fetus or newborn 760.1
Bad
breath 784.99 ▲
heart — *see* Disease, heart
trip (*see also* Abuse, drugs, nondependent) 305.3 ☑
Baehr-Schiffrin disease (thrombotic thrombocytopenic purpura) 446.6
Baelz's disease (cheilitis glandularis apostematosa) 528.5
Baerensprung's disease (eczema marginatum) 110.3
Bagassosis (occupational) 495.1
Baghdad boil 085.1
Bagratuni's syndrome (temporal arteritis) 446.5
Baker's
cyst (knee) 727.51
tuberculous (*see also* Tuberculosis) 015.2 ☑
itch 692.89
Bakwin-Krida syndrome (craniometaphyseal dysplasia) 756.89
Balanitis (circinata) (gangraenosa) (infectious) (vulgaris) 607.1
amebic 006.8
candidal 112.2
chlamydial 099.53
due to Ducrey's bacillus 099.0
erosiva circinata et gangraenosa 607.1
gangrenous 607.1
gonococcal (acute) 098.0
chronic or duration of 2 months or over 098.2
nongonococcal 607.1
phagedenic 607.1
venereal NEC 099.8
xerotica obliterans 607.81
Balanoposthitis 607.1
chlamydial 099.53
gonococcal (acute) 098.0
chronic or duration of 2 months or over 098.2
ulcerative NEC 099.8
Balanorrhagia — *see* Balanitis
Balantidiasis 007.0
Balantidiosis 007.0
Balbuties, balbutio 307.0
Bald
patches on scalp 704.00
tongue 529.4
Baldness — *see also* Alopecia 704.00
Balfour's disease (chloroma) 205.3 ☑
Balint's syndrome (psychic paralysis of visual fixation) 368.16
Balkan grippe 083.0
Ball
food 938
hair 938
Ballantyne (-Runge) syndrome (postmaturity) 766.22
Balloon disease — *see also* Effect, adverse, high altitude 993.2
Ballooning posterior leaflet syndrome 424.0
Balö's disease or concentric sclerosis 341.1
Bamberger's disease (hypertrophic pulmonary osteoarthropathy) 731.2
Bamberger-Marie disease (hypertrophic pulmonary osteoarthropathy) 731.2
Bamboo spine 720.0
Bancroft's filariasis 125.0

Band(s)
adhesive (*see also* Adhesions, peritoneum) 568.0
amniotic 658.8 ☑
affecting fetus or newborn 762.8
anomalous or congenital (*see also* Anomaly, specified type NEC)
atrial 746.9
heart 746.9
intestine 751.4
omentum 751.4
ventricular 746.9
cervix 622.3
gallbladder (congenital) 751.69
intestinal (adhesive) (*see also* Adhesions, peritoneum) 568.0
congenital 751.4
obstructive (*see also* Obstruction, intestine) 560.81
periappendiceal (congenital) 751.4
peritoneal (adhesive) (*see also* Adhesions, peritoneum) 568.0
with intestinal obstruction 560.81
congenital 751.4
uterus 621.5
vagina 623.2
Bandl's ring (contraction)
complicating delivery 661.4 ☑
affecting fetus or newborn 763.7
Bang's disease (Brucella abortus) 023.1
Bangkok hemorrhagic fever 065.4
Bannister's disease 995.1
Bantam-Albright-Martin disease (pseudohypoparathyroidism) 275.49
Banti's disease or syndrome (with cirrhosis) (with portal hypertension) — *see* Cirrhosis, liver
Bar
calcaneocuboid 755.67
calcaneonavicular 755.67
cubonavicular 755.67
prostate 600.90
with
other lower urinary tract symptoms (LUTS) 600.91 ●
● ●
urinary ●
obstruction 600.91 ●
retention 600.91 ●
talocalcaneal 755.67
Baragnosis 780.99
Barasheh, barashek 266.2
Barcoo disease or rot — *see also* Ulcer, skin 707.9
Bard-Pic syndrome (carcinoma, head of pancreas) 157.0
Bärensprung's disease (eczema marginatum) 110.3
Baritosis 503
Barium lung disease 503
Barlow (-Möller) disease or syndrome (meaning infantile scurvy) 267
Barlow's syndrome (meaning mitral valve prolapse) 424.0
Barodontalgia 993.2
Baron Münchausen syndrome 301.51
Barosinusitis 993.1
Barotitis 993.0
Barotrauma 993.2
odontalgia 993.2
otitic 993.0
sinus 993.1
Barraquer's disease or syndrome (progressive lipodystrophy) 272.6
Barré-Guillain syndrome 357.0
Barrel chest 738.3
Barré-Liéou syndrome (posterior cervical sympathetic) 723.2
Barrett's esophagus 530.85
Barrett's syndrome or ulcer (chronic peptic ulcer of esophagus) 530.85
Bársony-Polgár syndrome (corkscrew esophagus) 530.5
Bársony-Teschendorf syndrome (corkscrew esophagus) 530.5

Bartholin's
adenitis (*see also* Bartholinitis) 616.89 ▲
gland — *see* condition
Bartholinitis (suppurating) 616.89 ▲
gonococcal (acute) 098.0
chronic or duration of 2 months or over 098.2
Barth syndrome 759.89
Bartonellosis 088.0
Bartter's syndrome (secondary hyperaldosteronism with juxtaglomerular hyperplasia) 255.13
Basal — *see* condition
Basan's (hidrotic) **ectodermal dysplasia** 757.31
Baseball finger 842.13
Basedow's disease or syndrome (exophthalmic goiter) 242.0 ☑
Basic — *see* condition
Basilar — *see* condition
Bason's (hidrotic) **ectodermal dysplasia** 757.31
Basopenia 288.59 ▲
Basophilia 288.65 ▲
Basophilism (corticoadrenal) (Cushing's) (pituitary) (thymic) 255.0
Bassen-Kornzweig syndrome (abetalipoproteinemia) 272.5
Bat ear 744.29
Bateman's
disease 078.0
purpura (senile) 287.2
Bathing cramp 994.1
Bathophobia 300.23
Batten's disease, retina 330.1 [362.71]
Batten-Mayou disease 330.1 [362.71]
Batten-Steinert syndrome 359.2
Battered
adult (syndrome) 995.81
baby or child (syndrome) 995.54
spouse (syndrome) 995.81
Battey mycobacterium infection 031.0
Battledore placenta — *see* Placenta, abnormal
Battle exhaustion — *see also* Reaction, stress, acute 308.9
Baumgarten-Cruveilhier (cirrhosis) **disease, or syndrome** 571.5
Bauxite
fibrosis (of lung) 503
workers' disease 503
Bayle's disease (dementia paralytica) 094.1
Bazin's disease (primary) — *see also* Tuberculosis 017.1 ☑
Beach ear 380.12
Beaded hair (congenital) 757.4
Beals syndrome 759.82
Beard's disease (neurasthenia) 300.5
Bearn-Kunkel (-Slater) syndrome (lupoid hepatitis) 571.49
Beat
elbow 727.2
hand 727.2
knee 727.2
Beats
ectopic 427.60
escaped, heart 427.60
postoperative 997.1
premature (nodal) 427.60
atrial 427.61
auricular 427.61
postoperative 997.1
specified type NEC 427.69
supraventricular 427.61
ventricular 427.69
Beau's
disease or syndrome (*see also* Degeneration, myocardial) 429.1
lines (transverse furrows on fingernails) 703.8
Bechterew's disease (ankylosing spondylitis) 720.0
Bechterew-Strümpell-Marie syndrome (ankylosing spondylitis) 720.0

Becker's
disease (idiopathic mural endomyocardial disease) 425.2
dystrophy 359.1
Beck's syndrome (anterior spinal artery occlusion) 433.8 ☑
Beckwith (-Wiedemann) syndrome 759.89
Bedclothes, asphyxiation or suffocation by 994.7
Bed confinement status V49.84
Bednar's aphthae 528.2
Bedsore 707.00
with gangrene 707.00 [785.4]
Bedwetting — *see also* Enuresis 788.36
Beer-drinkers' heart (disease) 425.5
Bee sting (with allergic or anaphylactic shock) 989.5
Begbie's disease (exophthalmic goiter) 242.0 ☑
Behavior disorder, disturbance — *see also* Disturbance, conduct
antisocial, without manifest psychiatric disorder
adolescent V71.02
adult V71.01
child V71.02
dyssocial, without manifest psychiatric disorder
adolescent V71.02
adult V71.01
child V71.02
high risk — *see* Problem
Behçet's syndrome 136.1
Behr's disease 362.50
Beigel's disease or morbus (white piedra) 111.2
Bejel 104.0
Bekhterev's disease (ankylosing spondylitis) 720.0
Bekhterev-Strümpell-Marie syndrome (ankylosing spondylitis) 720.0
Belching — *see also* Eructation 787.3
Bell's
disease (*see also* Psychosis, affective) 296.0 ☑
mania (*see also* Psychosis, affective) 296.0 ☑
palsy, paralysis 351.0
infant 767.5
newborn 767.5
syphilitic 094.89
spasm 351.0
Bence-Jones albuminuria, albuminuria, or proteinuria 791.0
Bends 993.3
Benedikt's syndrome (paralysis) 344.89
Benign — *see also* condition
cellular changes, cervix 795.09
prostate
with
other lower urinary tract symptoms (LUTS) 600.21 ●
● ●
urinary ●
obstruction 600.21 ●
retention 600.21 ●
hyperplasia 600.20
neoplasm 222.2
Bennett's
disease (leukemia) 208.9 ☑
fracture (closed) 815.01
open 815.11
Benson's disease 379.22
Bent
back (hysterical) 300.11
nose 738.0
congenital 754.0
Bereavement V62.82
as adjustment reaction 309.0
Bergeron's disease (hysteroepilepsy) 300.11
Berger's paresthesia (lower limb) 782.0
Beriberi (acute) (atrophic) (chronic) (dry) (subacute) (wet) 265.0
with polyneuropathy 265.0 [357.4]

☑ Additional Digit Required — Refer to the Tabular List for Digit Selection ▽ Subterms under main terms may continue to next column or page

34 — Volume 2 · October 2006 ▶◀ Revised Text ● New Line ▲ Revised Code **2007 ICD-9-CM**

Beriberi — *continued*
  heart (disease) 265.0 *[425.7]*
  leprosy 030.1
  neuritis 265.0 *[357.4]*
Berlin's disease or edema (traumatic) 921.3
Berloque dermatitis 692.72
Bernard-Horner syndrome — *see also* Neuropathy, peripheral, autonomic 337.9
Bernard-Sergent syndrome (acute adrenocortical insufficiency) 255.4
Bernard-Soulier disease or thrombopathy 287.1
Bernhardt's disease or paresthesia 355.1
Bernhardt-Roth disease or syndrome (paresthesia) 355.1
Bernheim's syndrome — *see also* Failure, heart 428.0
Bertielliasis 123.8
Bertolotti's syndrome (sacralization of fifth lumbar vertebra) 756.15
Berylliosis (acute) (chronic) (lung) (occupational) 503
Besnier's
  lupus pernio 135
  prurigo (atopic dermatitis) (infantile eczema) 691.8
Besnier-Boeck disease or sarcoid 135
Besnier-Boeck-Schaumann disease (sarcoidosis) 135
Best's disease 362.76
Bestiality 302.1
Beta-adrenergic hyperdynamic circulatory state 429.82
Beta-aminoisobutyric aciduria 277.2
Beta-mercaptolactate-cysteine disulfiduria 270.0
Beta thalassemia (major) (minor) (mixed) 282.49
Beurmann's disease (sporotrichosis) 117.1
Bezoar 938
  intestine 936
  stomach 935.2
Bezold's abscess — *see also* Mastoiditis 383.01
Bianchi's syndrome (aphasia-apraxia-alexia) 784.69
Bicornuate or bicornis uterus 752.3
  in pregnancy or childbirth 654.0 ☑
    with obstructed labor 660.2 ☑
      affecting fetus or newborn 763.1
    affecting fetus or newborn 763.89
Bicuspid aortic valve 746.4
Biedl-Bardet syndrome 759.89
Bielschowsky's disease 330.1
Bielschowsky-Jansky
  amaurotic familial idiocy 330.1
  disease 330.1
Biemond's syndrome (obesity, polydactyly, and mental retardation) 759.89
Biermer's anemia or disease (pernicious anemia) 281.0
Biett's disease 695.4
Bifid (congenital) — *see also* Imperfect, closure
  apex, heart 746.89
  clitoris 752.49
  epiglottis 748.3
  kidney 753.3
  nose 748.1
  patella 755.64
  scrotum 752.89
  toe 755.66
  tongue 750.13
  ureter 753.4
  uterus 752.3
  uvula 749.02
    with cleft lip (*see also* Cleft, palate, with cleft lip) 749.20
Biforis uterus (suprasimplex) 752.3
Bifurcation (congenital) — *see also* Imperfect, closure
  gallbladder 751.69

Bifurcation — *see also* Imperfect, closure — *continued*
  kidney pelvis 753.3
  renal pelvis 753.3
  rib 756.3
  tongue 750.13
  trachea 748.3
  ureter 753.4
  urethra 753.8
  uvula 749.02
    with cleft lip (*see also* Cleft, palate, with cleft lip) 749.20
  vertebra 756.19
Bigeminal pulse 427.89
Bigeminy 427.89
Big spleen syndrome 289.4
Bilateral — *see* condition
Bile duct — *see* condition
Bile pigments in urine 791.4
Bilharziasis — *see also* Schistosomiasis 120.9
  chyluria 120.0
  cutaneous 120.3
  galacturia 120.0
  hematochyluria 120.0
  intestinal 120.1
  lipemia 120.9
  lipuria 120.0
  Oriental 120.2
  piarhemia 120.9
  pulmonary 120.2
  tropical hematuria 120.0
  vesical 120.0
Biliary — *see* condition
Bilious (attack) — *see also* Vomiting
  fever, hemoglobinuric 084.8
Bilirubinuria 791.4
Biliuria 791.4
Billroth's disease
  meningocele (*see also* Spina bifida) 741.9 ☑
Bilobate placenta — *see* Placenta, abnormal
Bilocular
  heart 745.7
  stomach 536.8
Bing-Horton syndrome (histamine cephalgia) 346.2 ☑
Binswanger's disease or dementia 290.12
Biörck (-Thorson) syndrome (malignant carcinoid) 259.2
Biparta, bipartite — *see also* Imperfect, closure
  carpal scaphoid 755.59
  patella 755.64
  placenta — *see* Placenta, abnormal
  vagina 752.49
Bird
  face 756.0
  fanciers' lung or disease 495.2
Bird's disease (oxaluria) 271.8
Birth
  abnormal fetus or newborn 763.9
  accident, fetus or newborn — *see* Birth, injury
  complications in mother — *see* Delivery, complicated
  compression during NEC 767.9
  defect — *see* Anomaly
  delayed, fetus 763.9
  difficult NEC, affecting fetus or newborn 763.9
  dry, affecting fetus or newborn 761.1
  forced, NEC, affecting fetus or newborn 763.89
  forceps, affecting fetus or newborn 763.2
  hematoma of sternomastoid 767.8
  immature 765.1 ☑
    extremely 765.0 ☑
  inattention, after or at 995.52
  induced, affecting fetus or newborn 763.89
  infant — *see* Newborn
  injury NEC 767.9

Birth — *continued*
  injury — *continued*
    adrenal gland 767.8
    basal ganglia 767.0
    brachial plexus (paralysis) 767.6
    brain (compression) (pressure) 767.0
    cerebellum 767.0
    cerebral hemorrhage 767.0
    conjunctiva 767.8
    eye 767.8
    fracture
      bone, any except clavicle or spine 767.3
      clavicle 767.2
      femur 767.3
      humerus 767.3
      long bone 767.3
      radius and ulna 767.3
      skeleton NEC 767.3
      skull 767.3
      spine 767.4
      tibia and fibula 767.3
    hematoma 767.8
      liver (subcapsular) 767.8
      mastoid 767.8
      skull 767.19
      sternomastoid 767.8
      testes 767.8
      vulva 767.8
    intracranial (edema) 767.0
    laceration
      brain 767.0
      by scalpel 767.8
      peripheral nerve 767.7
    liver 767.8
    meninges
      brain 767.0
      spinal cord 767.4
    nerves (cranial, peripheral) 767.7
      brachial plexus 767.6
      facial 767.5
    paralysis 767.7
      brachial plexus 767.6
      Erb (-Duchenne) 767.6
      facial nerve 767.5
      Klumpke (-Déjérine) 767.6
      radial nerve 767.6
      spinal (cord) (hemorrhage) (laceration) (rupture) 767.4
    rupture
      intracranial 767.0
      liver 767.8
      spinal cord 767.4
      spleen 767.8
      viscera 767.8
    scalp 767.19
    scalpel wound 767.8
    skeleton NEC 767.3
    specified NEC 767.8
    spinal cord 767.4
    spleen 767.8
    subdural hemorrhage 767.0
    tentorial, tear 767.0
    testes 767.8
    vulva 767.8
  instrumental, NEC, affecting fetus or newborn 763.2
  lack of care, after or at 995.52
  multiple
    affected by maternal complications of pregnancy 761.5
    healthy liveborn — *see* Newborn, multiple
  neglect, after or at 995.52
  newborn — *see* Newborn
  palsy or paralysis NEC 767.7
  precipitate, fetus or newborn 763.6
  premature (infant) 765.1 ☑
  prolonged, affecting fetus or newborn 763.9
  retarded, fetus or newborn 763.9
  shock, newborn 779.89
  strangulation or suffocation
    due to aspiration of clear amniotic fluid 770.13

Birth — *continued*
  strangulation or suffocation — *continued*
    due to aspiration of clear amniotic fluid — *continued*
      with respiratory symptoms 770.14
    mechanical 767.8
  trauma NEC 767.9
  triplet
    affected by maternal complications of pregnancy 761.5
    healthy liveborn — *see* Newborn, multiple
  twin
    affected by maternal complications of pregnancy 761.5
    healthy liveborn — *see* Newborn, twin
  ventouse, affecting fetus or newborn 763.3
Birthmark 757.32
Bisalbuminemia 273.8
Biskra button 085.1
Bite(s)
  with intact skin surface — *see* Contusion
  animal — *see* Wound, open, by site
    intact skin surface — *see* Contusion
  centipede 989.5
  chigger 133.8
  fire ant 989.5
  flea — *see* Injury, superficial, by site
  human (open wound) (*see also* Wound, open, by site)
    intact skin surface — *see* Contusion
  insect
    nonvenomous — *see* Injury, superficial, by site
    venomous 989.5
  mad dog (death from) 071
  open   ●
    anterior 524.24   ●
    posterior 524.25   ●
  poisonous 989.5
  red bug 133.8
  reptile 989.5
    nonvenomous — *see* Wound, open, by site
  snake 989.5
    nonvenomous — *see* Wound, open, by site
  spider (venomous) 989.5
    nonvenomous — *see* Injury, superficial, by site
  venomous 989.5
Biting
  cheek or lip 528.9
  nail 307.9
Black
  death 020.9
  eye NEC 921.0
  hairy tongue 529.3
  heel 924.20   ●
  lung disease 500
  palm 923.20   ●
Blackfan-Diamond anemia or syndrome (congenital hypoplastic anemia) 284.01   ▲
Blackhead 706.1
Blackout 780.2
Blackwater fever 084.8
Bladder — *see* condition
Blast
  blindness 921.3
  concussion — *see* Blast, injury
  injury 869.0
    with open wound into cavity 869.1
    abdomen or thorax — *see* Injury, internal, by site
    brain (*see also* Concussion, brain) 850.9
      with skull fracture — *see* Fracture, skull

☑ Additional Digit Required — Refer to the Tabular List for Digit Selection   ⊽ Subterms under main terms may continue to next column or page

2007 ICD-9-CM   ▶◀ Revised Text   ● New Line   ▲ Revised Code   **October 2006 · Volume 2 — 35**

Blast — continued

injury — continued

ear (acoustic nerve trauma) 951.5

with perforation, tympanic membrane — see Wound, open, ear, drum

lung (see also Injury, internal, lung) 861.20

otitic (explosive) 388.11

Blastomycosis, blastomycotic (chronic) (cutaneous) (disseminated) (lung) (pulmonary) (systemic) 116.0

Brazilian 116.1

European 117.5

keloidal 116.2

North American 116.0

primary pulmonary 116.0

South American 116.1

Bleb(s) 709.8

emphysematous (bullous) (diffuse) (lung) (ruptured) (solitary) 492.0

filtering, eye (postglaucoma) (status) V45.69

with complication 997.99

postcataract extraction (complication) 997.99

lung (ruptured) 492.0

congenital 770.5

subpleural (emphysematous) 492.0

Bleeder (familial) (hereditary) — see also Defect, coagulation 286.9

nonfamilial 286.9

Bleeding — see also Hemorrhage 459.0

anal 569.3

anovulatory 628.0

atonic, following delivery 666.1 ☑

capillary 448.9

due to subinvolution 621.1

puerperal 666.2 ☑

ear 388.69

excessive, associated with menopausal onset 627.0

familial (see also Defect, coagulation) 286.9

following intercourse 626.7

gastrointestinal 578.9

gums 523.8

hemorrhoids — see Hemorrhoids, bleeding

intermenstrual

irregular 626.6

regular 626.5

intraoperative 998.11

irregular NEC 626.4

menopausal 627.0

mouth 528.9

nipple 611.79

nose 784.7

ovulation 626.5

postclimacteric 627.1

postcoital 626.7

postmenopausal 627.1

following induced menopause 627.4

postoperative 998.11

preclimacteric 627.0

puberty 626.3

excessive, with onset of menstrual periods 626.3

rectum, rectal 569.3

tendencies (see also Defect, coagulation) 286.9

throat 784.8

umbilical stump 772.3

umbilicus 789.9

unrelated to menstrual cycle 626.6

uterus, uterine 626.9

climacteric 627.0

dysfunctional 626.8

functional 626.8

unrelated to menstrual cycle 626.6

vagina, vaginal 623.8

functional 626.8

vicarious 625.8

Blennorrhagia, blennorrhagic — see Blennorrhea

Blennorrhea (acute) 098.0

adultorum 098.40

alveolaris 523.40 ▲

chronic or duration of 2 months or over 098.2

gonococcal (neonatorum) 098.40

inclusion (neonatal) (newborn) 771.6

neonatorum 098.40

Blepharelosis — see also Entropion 374.00

Blepharitis (eyelid) 373.00

angularis 373.01

ciliaris 373.00

with ulcer 373.01

marginal 373.00

with ulcer 373.01

scrofulous (see also Tuberculosis) 017.3 ☑ [373.00]

squamous 373.02

ulcerative 373.01

Blepharochalasis 374.34

congenital 743.62

Blepharoclonus 333.81

Blepharoconjunctivitis — see also Conjunctivitis 372.20

angular 372.21

contact 372.22

Blepharophimosis (eyelid) 374.46

congenital 743.62

Blepharoplegia 374.89

Blepharoptosis 374.30

congenital 743.61

Blepharopyorrhea 098.49

Blepharospasm 333.81

due to drugs 333.85 ●

Blessig's cyst 362.62

Blighted ovum 631

Blind

bronchus (congenital) 748.3

eye (see also Blindness)

hypertensive 360.42

hypotensive 360.41

loop syndrome (postoperative) 579.2

sac, fallopian tube (congenital) 752.19

spot, enlarged 368.42

tract or tube (congenital) NEC — see Atresia

Blindness (acquired) (congenital) (both eyes) 369.00

blast 921.3

with nerve injury — see Injury, nerve, optic

Bright's — see Uremia

color (congenital) 368.59

acquired 368.55

blue 368.53

green 368.52

red 368.51

total 368.54

concussion 950.9

cortical 377.75

day 368.10

acquired 368.10

congenital 368.10

hereditary 368.10

specified type NEC 368.10

due to

injury NEC 950.9

refractive error — see Error, refractive

eclipse (total) 363.31

emotional 300.11

hysterical 300.11

legal (both eyes) (USA definition) 369.4

with impairment of better (less impaired) eye

near-total 369.02

with

lesser eye impairment 369.02

near-total 369.04

total 369.03

profound 369.05

with

lesser eye impairment 369.05

Blindness — continued

legal — continued

with impairment of better eye — continued

profound — continued

with — continued

lesser eye impairment — continued

near-total 369.07

profound 369.08

total 369.06

severe 369.21

with

lesser eye impairment 369.21

blind 369.11

near-total 369.13

profound 369.14

severe 369.22

total 369.12

total

with lesser eye impairment total 369.01

mind 784.69

moderate

both eyes 369.25

with impairment of lesser eye (specified as)

blind, not further specified 369.15

low vision, not further specified 369.23

near-total 369.17

profound 369.18

severe 369.24

total 369.16

one eye 369.74

with vision of other eye (specified as)

near-normal 369.75

normal 369.76

near-total

both eyes 369.04

with impairment of lesser eye (specified as)

blind, not further specified 369.02

total 369.03

one eye 369.64

with vision of other eye (specified as)

near-normal 369.65

normal 369.66

night 368.60

acquired 368.62

congenital (Japanese) 368.61

hereditary 368.61

specified type NEC 368.69

vitamin A deficiency 264.5

nocturnal — see Blindness, night

one eye 369.60

with low vision of other eye 369.10

profound

both eyes 369.08

with impairment of lesser eye (specified as)

blind, not further specified 369.05

near-total 369.07

total 369.06

one eye 369.67

with vision of other eye (specified as)

near-normal 369.68

normal 369.69

psychic 784.69

severe

both eyes 369.22

with impairment of lesser eye (specified as)

blind, not further specified 369.11

low vision, not further specified 369.21

near-total 369.13

profound 369.14

Blindness — continued

severe — continued

both eyes — continued

with impairment of lesser eye — continued

total 369.12

one eye 369.71

with vision of other eye (specified as)

near-normal 369.72

normal 369.73

snow 370.24

sun 363.31

temporary 368.12

total

both eyes 369.01

one eye 369.61

with vision of other eye (specified as)

near-normal 369.62

normal 369.63

transient 368.12

traumatic NEC 950.9

word (developmental) 315.01

acquired 784.61

secondary to organic lesion 784.61

Blister — see also Injury, superficial, by site

beetle dermatitis 692.89

due to burn — see Burn, by site, second degree

fever 054.9

multiple, skin, nontraumatic 709.8

Bloating 787.3

Bloch-Siemens syndrome (incontinentia pigmenti) 757.33

Bloch-Stauffer dyshormonal dermatosis 757.33

Bloch-Sulzberger disease or syndrome (incontinentia pigmenti) (melanoblastosis) 757.33

Block

alveolar capillary 516.3

arborization (heart) 426.6

arrhythmic 426.9

atrioventricular (AV) (incomplete) (partial) 426.10

with

2:1 atrioventricular response block 426.13

atrioventricular dissociation 426.0

first degree (incomplete) 426.11

second degree (Mobitz type I) 426.13

Mobitz (type) II 426.12

third degree 426.0

complete 426.0

congenital 746.86

congenital 746.86

Mobitz (incomplete)

type I (Wenckebach's) 426.13

type II 426.12

partial 426.13

auriculoventricular (see also Block, atrioventricular) 426.10

complete 426.0

congenital 746.86

congenital 746.86

bifascicular (cardiac) 426.53

bundle branch (complete) (false) (incomplete) 426.50

bilateral 426.53

left (complete) (main stem) 426.3

with right bundle branch block 426.53

anterior fascicular 426.2

with

posterior fascicular block 426.3

right bundle branch block 426.52

hemiblock 426.2

incomplete 426.2

with right bundle branch block 426.53

Block — *continued*
  bundle branch — *continued*
    left — *continued*
      posterior fascicular 426.2
        with
          anterior fascicular block
            426.3
          right bundle branch block
            426.51
      right 426.4
        with
          left bundle branch block (in-
            complete) (main stem)
            426.53
          left fascicular block 426.53
            anterior 426.52
            posterior 426.51
      Wilson's type 426.4
  cardiac 426.9
  conduction 426.9
    complete 426.0
  Eustachian tube (*see also* Obstruc-
    tion, Eustachian tube) 381.60
  fascicular (left anterior) (left posterior)
    426.2
  foramen Magendie (acquired) 331.3
    congenital 742.3
      with spina bifida (*see also* Spina
        bifida) 741.0 ☑
  heart 426.9
    first degree (atrioventricular)
      426.11
    second degree (atrioventricular)
      426.13
    third degree (atrioventricular)
      426.0
    bundle branch (complete) (false)
      (incomplete) 426.50
      bilateral 426.53
      left (*see also* Block, bundle
        branch, left) 426.3
      right (*see also* Block, bundle
        branch, right) 426.4
    complete (atrioventricular) 426.0
    congenital 746.86
    incomplete 426.13
    intra-atrial 426.6
    intraventricular NEC 426.6
    sinoatrial 426.6
    specified type NEC 426.6
  hepatic vein 453.0
  intraventricular (diffuse) (myofibrillar)
    426.6
    bundle branch (complete) (false)
      (incomplete) 426.50
      bilateral 426.53
      left (*see also* Block, bundle
        branch, left) 426.3
      right (*see also* Block, bundle
        branch, right) 426.4
  kidney (*see also* Disease, renal) 593.9
    postcystoscopic 997.5
  myocardial (*see also* Block, heart)
    426.9
  nodal 426.10
  optic nerve 377.49
  organ or site (congenital) NEC — *see*
    Atresia
  parietal 426.6
  peri-infarction 426.6
  portal (vein) 452
  sinoatrial 426.6
  sinoauricular 426.6
  spinal cord 336.9
  trifascicular 426.54
  tubal 628.2
  vein NEC 453.9
Blocq's disease or syndrome (astasia-
  abasia) 307.9
Blood
  constituents, abnormal NEC 790.6
  disease 289.9
    specified NEC 289.89
  donor V59.01
    other blood components V59.09
    stem cells V59.02

Blood — *continued*
  donor — *continued*
    whole blood V59.01
  dyscrasia 289.9
    with
      abortion — *see* Abortion, by
        type, with hemorrhage,
        delayed or excessive
      ectopic pregnancy (*see also* cat-
        egories 633.0–633.9)
        639.1
      molar pregnancy (*see also* cate-
        gories 630–632) 639.1
    fetus or newborn NEC 776.9
    following
      abortion 639.1
      ectopic or molar pregnancy
        639.1
    puerperal, postpartum 666.3 ☑
  flukes NEC (*see also* Infestation,
    Schistosoma) 120.9
  in
    feces (*see also* Melena) 578.1
      occult 792.1
    urine (*see also* Hematuria) 599.7
  mole 631
  occult 792.1
  poisoning (*see also* Septicemia) 038.9
  pressure
    decreased, due to shock following
      injury 958.4
    fluctuating 796.4
    high (*see also* Hypertension) 401.9
      incidental reading (isolated)
        (nonspecific), without diag-
        nosis of hypertension
        796.2
    low (*see also* Hypotension) 458.9
      incidental reading (isolated)
        (nonspecific), without diag-
        nosis of hypotension
        796.3
  spitting (*see also* Hemoptysis) 786.3
  staining cornea 371.12
  transfusion
    without reported diagnosis V58.2
    donor V59.01
      stem cells V59.02
    reaction or complication — *see*
      Complications, transfusion
  tumor — *see* Hematoma
  vessel rupture — *see* Hemorrhage
  vomiting (*see also* Hematemesis) 578.0
Blood-forming organ disease 289.9
Bloodgood's disease 610.1
Bloodshot eye 379.93
Bloom (-Machacek) (-Torre) syndrome
  757.39
Blotch, palpebral 372.55
Blount-Barber syndrome (tibia vara)
  732.4
Blount's disease (tibia vara) 732.4
Blue
  baby 746.9
  bloater 491.20
    with
      acute bronchitis 491.22
      exacerbation (acute) 491.21
  diaper syndrome 270.0
  disease 746.9
  dome cyst 610.0
  drum syndrome 381.02
  sclera 743.47
    with fragility of bone and deafness
      756.51
  toe syndrome 445.02
Blueness — *see also* Cyanosis 782.5
Blurring, visual 368.8
Blushing (abnormal) (excessive) 782.62
BMI (body mass index)
  adult
    25.0-25.9 V85.21
    26.0-26.9 V85.22
    27.0-27.9 V85.23
    28.0-28.9 V85.24
    29.0-29.9 V85.25

BMI — *continued*
  adult — *continued*
    30.0-30.9 V85.30
    31.0-31.9 V85.31
    32.0-32.9 V85.32
    33.0-33.9 V85.33
    34.0-34.9 V85.34
    35.0-35.9 V85.35
    36.0-36.9 V85.36
    37.0-37.9 V85.37
    38.0-38.9 V85.38
    39.0-39.9 V85.39
    40 and over V85.4
    between 19-24 V85.1
    less than 19 V85.0
  pediatric
    5th percentile to less than 85th ●
      percentile for age V85.52 ●
    85th percentile to less than 95th●
      percentile for age V85.53 ●
    greater than or equal to 95th ●
      percentile for age V85.54 ●
    less than 5th percentile for age ●
      V85.51 ●
Boarder, hospital V65.0
  infant V65.0
Bockhart's impetigo (superficial folliculitis) 704.8
Bodechtel-Guttmann disease (subacute
  sclerosing panencephalitis) 046.2
Boder-Sedgwick syndrome (ataxia-
  telangiectasia) 334.8
Body, bodies
  Aschoff (*see also* Myocarditis,
    rheumatic) 398.0
  asteroid, vitreous 379.22
  choroid, colloid (degenerative) 362.57
    hereditary 362.77
  cytoid (retina) 362.82
  drusen (retina) (*see also* Drusen)
    362.57
    optic disc 377.21
  fibrin, pleura 511.0
  foreign — *see* Foreign body
  Hassall-Henle 371.41
  loose
    joint (*see also* Loose, body, joint)
      718.1 ☑
      knee 717.6
    knee 717.6
    sheath, tendon 727.82
  Mallory's 034.1
  mass index (BMI)
    adult
      25.0-25.9 V85.21
      26.0-26.9 V85.22
      27.0-27.9 V85.23
      28.0-28.9 V85.24
      29.0-29.9 V85.25
      30.0-30.9 V85.30
      31.0-31.9 V85.31
      32.0-32.9 V85.32
      33.0-33.9 V85.33
      34.0-34.9 V85.34
      36.0-36.9 V85.36
      37.0-37.9 V85.37
      38.0-38.9 V85.38
      39.0-39.9 V85.39
      40 and over V85.4
      between 19-24 V85.1
      less than 19 V85.0
    pediatric
      5th percentile to less than ●
        85th percentile for age ●
        V85.52 ●
      85th percentile to less than ●
        95th percentile for age ●
        V85.53 ●
      greater than or equal to 95th ●
        percentile for age ●
        V85.54 ●
      less than 5th percentile for age●
        V85.51 ●
  Mooser 081.0
  Negri 071

Body, bodies — *continued*
  rice (joint) (*see also* Loose, body, joint)
    718.1 ☑
    knee 717.6
  rocking 307.3
Boeck's
  disease (sarcoidosis) 135
  lupoid (miliary) 135
  sarcoid 135
Boerhaave's syndrome (spontaneous
  esophageal rupture) 530.4
Boggy
  cervix 622.8
  uterus 621.8
Boil — *see also* Carbuncle 680.9
  abdominal wall 680.2
  Aleppo 085.1
  ankle 680.6
  anus 680.5
  arm (any part, above wrist) 680.3
  auditory canal, external 680.0
  axilla 680.3
  back (any part) 680.2
  Baghdad 085.1
  breast 680.2
  buttock 680.5
  chest wall 680.2
  corpus cavernosum 607.2
  Delhi 085.1
  ear (any part) 680.0
  eyelid 373.13
  face (any part, except eye) 680.0
  finger (any) 680.4
  flank 680.2
  foot (any part) 680.7
  forearm 680.3
  Gafsa 085.1
  genital organ, male 608.4
  gluteal (region) 680.5
  groin 680.2
  hand (any part) 680.4
  head (any part, except face) 680.8
  heel 680.7
  hip 680.6
  knee 680.6
  labia 616.4
  lacrimal (*see also* Dacryocystitis)
    375.30
    gland (*see also* Dacryoadenitis)
      375.00
    passages (duct) (sac) (*see also*
      Dacryocystitis) 375.30
  leg, any part, except foot 680.6
  multiple sites 680.9
  natal 085.1
  neck 680.1
  nose (external) (septum) 680.0
  orbit, orbital 376.01
  partes posteriores 680.5
  pectoral region 680.2
  penis 607.2
  perineum 680.2
  pinna 680.0
  scalp (any part) 680.8
  scrotum 608.4
  seminal vesicle 608.0
  shoulder 680.3
  skin NEC 680.9
  specified site NEC 680.8
  spermatic cord 608.4
  temple (region) 680.0
  testis 608.4
  thigh 680.6
  thumb 680.4
  toe (any) 680.7
  tropical 085.1
  trunk 680.2
  tunica vaginalis 608.4
  umbilicus 680.2
  upper arm 680.3
  vas deferens 608.4
  vulva 616.4
  wrist 680.4
Bold hives — *see also* Urticaria 708.9
Bolivian hemorrhagic fever 078.7
Bombé, iris 364.74

☑ Additional Digit Required — Refer to the Tabular List for Digit Selection   ▽ Subterms under main terms may continue to next column or page

2007 ICD-9-CM   ▶◀ Revised Text   ● New Line   ▲ Revised Code   **October 2006 • Volume 2 — 37**

Bomford-Rhoads anemia (refractory) 238.72 ▲

Bone — see condition

Bonnevie-Ullrich syndrome 758.6

Bonnier's syndrome 386.19

Bonvale Dam fever 780.79

Bony block of joint 718.80
- ankle 718.87
- elbow 718.82
- foot 718.87
- hand 718.84
- hip 718.85
- knee 718.86
- multiple sites 718.89
- pelvic region 718.85
- shoulder (region) 718.81
- specified site NEC 718.88
- wrist 718.83

Borderline
- intellectual functioning V62.89
- pelvis 653.1 ☑
    - with obstruction during labor 660.1 ☑
        - affecting fetus or newborn 763.1
- psychosis (see also Schizophrenia) 295.5 ☑
    - of childhood (see also Psychosis, childhood) 299.8 ☑
- schizophrenia (see also Schizophrenia) 295.5 ☑

Borna disease 062.9

Bornholm disease (epidemic pleurodynia) 074.1

Borrelia vincentii (mouth) (pharynx) (tonsils) 101

Bostock's catarrh — see also Fever, hay 477.9

Boston exanthem 048

Botalli, ductus (patent) (persistent) 747.0

Bothriocephalus latus infestation 123.4

Botulism 005.1
- wound — see Wound, open, by site, ● complicated ●

Bouba — see also Yaws 102.9

Bouffée délirante 298.3

Bouillaud's disease or syndrome (rheumatic heart disease) 391.9

Bourneville's disease (tuberous sclerosis) 759.5

Boutonneuse fever 082.1

Boutonniere
- deformity (finger) 736.21
- hand (intrinsic) 736.21

Bouveret (-Hoffmann) disease or syndrome (paroxysmal tachycardia) 427.2

Bovine heart — see Hypertrophy, cardiac

Bowel — see condition

Bowen's
- dermatosis (precancerous) (M8081/2) — see Neoplasm, skin, in situ
- disease (M8081/2) — see Neoplasm, skin, in situ
- epithelioma (M8081/2) — see Neoplasm, skin, in situ
- type
    - epidermoid carcinoma in situ (M8081/2) — see Neoplasm, skin, in situ
    - intraepidermal squamous cell carcinoma (M8081/2) — see Neoplasm, skin, in situ

Bowing
- femur 736.89
    - congenital 754.42
- fibula 736.89
    - congenital 754.43
- forearm 736.09
    - away from midline (cubitus valgus) 736.01
    - toward midline (cubitus varus) 736.02
- leg(s), long bones, congenital 754.44
- radius 736.09

Bowing — continued
- radius — continued
    - away from midline (cubitus valgus) 736.01
    - toward midline (cubitus varus) 736.02
- tibia 736.89
    - congenital 754.43

Bowleg(s) 736.42
- congenital 754.44
- rachitic 268.1

Boyd's dysentery 004.2

Brachial — see condition

Brachman-de Lange syndrome (Amsterdam dwarf, mental retardation, and brachycephaly) 759.89

Brachycardia 427.89

Brachycephaly 756.0

Brachymorphism and ectopia lentis 759.89

Bradley's disease (epidemic vomiting) 078.82

Bradycardia 427.89
- chronic (sinus) 427.81
- newborn 779.81
- nodal 427.89
- postoperative 997.1
- reflex 337.0
- sinoatrial 427.89
    - with paroxysmal tachyarrhythmia or tachycardia 427.81
    - chronic 427.81
- sinus 427.89
    - with paroxysmal tachyarrhythmia or tachycardia 427.81
    - chronic 427.81
    - persistent 427.81
    - severe 427.81
- tachycardia syndrome 427.81
- vagal 427.89

Bradypnea 786.09

Brailsford's disease 732.3
- radial head 732.3
- tarsal scaphoid 732.5

Brailsford-Morquio disease or syndrome (mucopolysaccharidosis IV) 277.5

Brain — see also condition
- death 348.8
- syndrome (acute) (chronic) (nonpsychotic) (organic) (with neurotic reaction) (with behavioral reaction) (see also Syndrome, brain) 310.9
    - with
        - presenile brain disease 290.10
        - psychosis, psychotic reaction (see also Psychosis, organic) 294.9
    - congenital (see also Retardation, mental) 319

Branched-chain amino-acid disease 270.3

Branchial — see condition

Brandt's syndrome (acrodermatitis enteropathica) 686.8

Brash (water) 787.1

Brass-founders' ague 985.8

Bravais-Jacksonian epilepsy — see also Epilepsy 345.5 ☑

Braxton Hicks contractions 644.1 ☑

Braziers' disease 985.8

Brazilian
- blastomycosis 116.1
- leishmaniasis 085.5

BRBPR (bright red blood per rectum) 569.3

Break
- cardiorenal — see Hypertension, cardiorenal
- retina (see also Defect, retina) 361.30

Breakbone fever 061

Breakdown
- device, implant, or graft — see Complications, mechanical

Breakdown — continued
- nervous (see also Disorder, mental, nonpsychotic) 300.9
- perineum 674.2 ☑

Breast — see condition

Breast feeding difficulties 676.8 ☑

Breath
- foul 784.99 ▲
- holder, child 312.81
- holding spells 786.9
- shortness 786.05

Breathing
- asymmetrical 786.09
- bronchial 786.09
- exercises V57.0
- labored 786.09
- mouth 784.99 ▲
    - causing malocclusion 524.59
- periodic 786.09
    - high altitude 327.22
- tic 307.20

Breathlessness 786.09

Breda's disease — see also Yaws 102.9

Breech
- delivery, affecting fetus or newborn 763.0
- extraction, affecting fetus or newborn 763.0
- presentation (buttocks) (complete) (frank) 652.2 ☑
    - with successful version 652.1 ☑
    - before labor, affecting fetus or newborn 761.7
    - during labor, affecting fetus or newborn 763.0

Breisky's disease (kraurosis vulvae) 624.0

Brennemann's syndrome (acute mesenteric lymphadenitis) 289.2

Brenner's
- tumor (benign) (M9000/0) 220
    - borderline malignancy (M9000/1) 236.2
    - malignant (M9000/3) 183.0
    - proliferating (M9000/1) 236.2

Bretonneau's disease (diphtheritic malignant angina) 032.0

Breus' mole 631

Brevicollis 756.16

Bricklayers' itch 692.89

Brickmakers' anemia 126.9

Bridge
- myocardial 746.85

Bright's
- blindness — see Uremia
- disease (see also Nephritis) 583.9
    - arteriosclerotic (see also Hypertension, kidney) 403.90

Bright red blood per rectum (BRBPR) 569.3

Brill's disease (recrudescent typhus) 081.1
- flea-borne 081.0
- louse-borne 081.1

Brill-Symmers disease (follicular lymphoma) (M9690/3) 202.0 ☑

Brill-Zinsser disease (recrudescent typhus) 081.1

Brinton's disease (linitis plastica) (M8142/3) 151.9

Brion-Kayser disease — see also Fever, paratyphoid 002.9

Briquet's disorder or syndrome 300.81

Brissaud's
- infantilism (infantile myxedema) 244.9
- motor-verbal tic 307.23

Brissaud-Meige syndrome (infantile myxedema) 244.9

Brittle
- bones (congenital) 756.51
- nails 703.8
    - congenital 757.5

Broad — see also condition
- beta disease 272.2
- ligament laceration syndrome 620.6

Brock's syndrome (atelectasis due to enlarged lymph nodes) 518.0

Brocq's disease 691.8
- atopic (diffuse) neurodermatitis 691.8
- lichen simplex chronicus 698.3
- parakeratosis psoriasiformis 696.2
- parapsoriasis 696.2

Brocq-Duhring disease (dermatitis herpetiformis) 694.0

Brodie's
- abscess (localized) (chronic) (see also Osteomyelitis) 730.1 ☑
- disease (joint) (see also Osteomyelitis) 730.1 ☑

Broken
- arches 734
    - congenital 755.67
- back — see Fracture, vertebra, by site
- bone — see Fracture, by site
- compensation — see Disease, heart
- heart syndrome 429.83 ●
- implant or internal device — see listing under Complications, mechanical
- neck — see Fracture, vertebra, cervical
- nose 802.0
    - open 802.1
- tooth, teeth 873.63
    - complicated 873.73

Bromhidrosis 705.89

Bromidism, bromism
- acute 967.3
    - correct substance properly administered 349.82
    - overdose or wrong substance given or taken 967.3
- chronic (see also Dependence) 304.1 ☑

Bromidrosiphobia 300.23

Bromidrosis 705.89

Bronchi, bronchial — see condition

Bronchiectasis (cylindrical) (diffuse) (fusiform) (localized) (moniliform) (postinfectious) (recurrent) (saccular) 494.0
- with acute exacerbation 494.1
- congenital 748.61
- tuberculosis (see also Tuberculosis) 011.5 ☑

Bronchiolectasis — see Bronchiectasis

Bronchiolitis (acute) (infectious) (subacute) 466.19
- with
    - bronchospasm or obstruction 466.19
    - influenza, flu, or grippe 487.1
- catarrhal (acute) (subacute) 466.19
- chemical 506.0
    - chronic 506.4
- chronic (obliterative) 491.8
- due to external agent — see Bronchitis, acute, due to
- fibrosa obliterans 491.8
- influenzal 487.1
- obliterans 491.8
    - with organizing pneumonia (B.O.O.P.) 516.8
    - status post lung transplant 996.84
- obliterative (chronic) (diffuse) (subacute) 491.8
    - due to fumes or vapors 506.4
- respiratory syncytial virus 466.11
- vesicular — see Pneumonia, broncho-

Bronchitis (diffuse) (hypostatic) (infectious) (inflammatory) (simple) 490
- with
    - emphysema — see Emphysema
    - influenza, flu, or grippe 487.1
    - obstruction airway, chronic 491.20
        - with
            - acute bronchitis 491.22
            - exacerbation (acute) 491.21
    - tracheitis 490
        - acute or subacute 466.0

☑ Additional Digit Required — Refer to the Tabular List for Digit Selection ▽ Subterms under main terms may continue to next column or page

38 — Volume 2 • October 2006   ▶◀ Revised Text   ● New Line   ▲ Revised Code   2007 ICD-9-CM

Bronchitis — *continued*
  with — *continued*
    tracheitis — *continued*
      acute or subacute — *continued*
        with bronchospasm or obstruction 466.0
      chronic 491.8
  acute or subacute 466.0
    with
      bronchospasm 466.0
      obstruction 466.0
      tracheitis 466.0
    chemical (due to fumes or vapors) 506.0
    due to
      fumes or vapors 506.0
      radiation 508.8
  allergic (acute) (*see also* Asthma) 493.9 ☑
  arachidic 934.1
  aspiration 507.0
    due to fumes or vapors 506.0
  asthmatic (acute) 493.90
    with
      acute exacerbation 493.92
      status asthmaticus 493.91
    chronic 493.2 ☑
  capillary 466.19
    with bronchospasm or obstruction 466.19
    chronic 491.8
  caseous (*see also* Tuberculosis) 011.3 ☑
  Castellani's 104.8
  catarrhal 490
    acute — *see* Bronchitis, acute
    chronic 491.0
  chemical (acute) (subacute) 506.0
    chronic 506.4
    due to fumes or vapors (acute) (subacute) 506.0
      chronic 506.4
  chronic 491.9
    with
      tracheitis (chronic) 491.8
    asthmatic 493.2 ☑
    catarrhal 491.0
    chemical (due to fumes and vapors) 506.4
    due to
      fumes or vapors (chemical) (inhalation) 506.4
      radiation 508.8
      tobacco smoking 491.0
    mucopurulent 491.1
    obstructive 491.20
      with
        acute bronchitis 491.22
        exacerbation (acute) 491.21
    purulent 491.1
    simple 491.0
    specified type NEC 491.8
  croupous 466.0
    with bronchospasm or obstruction 466.0
    due to fumes or vapors 506.0
  emphysematous 491.20
    with
      acute bronchitis 491.22
      exacerbation (acute) 491.21
  exudative 466.0
  fetid (chronic) (recurrent) 491.1
  fibrinous, acute or subacute 466.0
    with bronchospasm or obstruction 466.0
  grippal 487.1
  influenzal 487.1
  membranous, acute or subacute 466.0
    with bronchospasm or obstruction 466.0
  moulders' 502
  mucopurulent (chronic) (recurrent) 491.1
    acute or subacute 466.0

Bronchitis — *continued*
  obliterans 491.8
  obstructive (chronic) 491.20
    with
      acute bronchitis 491.22
      exacerbation (acute) 491.21
  pituitous 491.1
  plastic (inflammatory) 466.0
  pneumococcal, acute or subacute 466.0
    with bronchospasm or obstruction 466.0
  pseudomembranous 466.0
  purulent (chronic) (recurrent) 491.1
    acute or subacute 466.0
      with bronchospasm or obstruction 466.0
  putrid 491.1
  scrofulous (*see also* Tuberculosis) 011.3 ☑
  senile 491.9
  septic, acute or subacute 466.0
    with bronchospasm or obstruction 466.0
  smokers' 491.0
  spirochetal 104.8
  suffocative, acute or subacute 466.0
  summer (*see also* Asthma) 493.9 ☑
  suppurative (chronic) 491.1
    acute or subacute 466.0
  tuberculous (*see also* Tuberculosis) 011.3 ☑
  ulcerative 491.8
    Vincent's 101
  Vincent's 101
  viral, acute or subacute 466.0
Bronchoalveolitis 485
Bronchoaspergillosis 117.3
Bronchocele
  meaning
    dilatation of bronchus 519.19 ▲
    goiter 240.9
Bronchogenic carcinoma 162.9
Bronchohemisporosis 117.9
Broncholithiasis 518.89
  tuberculous (*see also* Tuberculosis) 011.3 ☑
Bronchomalacia 748.3
Bronchomoniliasis 112.89
Bronchomycosis 112.89
Bronchonocardiosis 039.1
Bronchopleuropneumonia — *see* Pneumonia, broncho-
Bronchopneumonia — *see* Pneumonia, broncho-
Bronchopneumonitis — *see* Pneumonia, broncho-
Bronchopulmonary — *see* condition
Bronchopulmonitis — *see* Pneumonia, broncho-
Bronchorrhagia 786.3
  newborn 770.3
  tuberculous (*see also* Tuberculosis) 011.3 ☑
Bronchorrhea (chronic) (purulent) 491.0
  acute 466.0
Bronchospasm 519.11 ▲
  with
    asthma — *see* Asthma
    bronchiolitis, acute 466.19
      due to respiratory syncytial virus 466.11
    bronchitis — *see* Bronchitis
    chronic obstructive pulmonary disease (COPD) 496
    emphysema — *see* Emphysema
  due to external agent — *see* Condition, respiratory, acute, due to
  acute 519.11 ●
  exercise induced 493.81
Bronchospirochetosis 104.8
Bronchostenosis 519.19 ▲
Bronchus — *see* condition
Bronze, bronzed
  diabetes 275.0

Bronze, bronzed — *continued*
  disease (Addison's) (skin) 255.4
    tuberculous (*see also* Tuberculosis) 017.6 ☑
Brooke's disease or tumor (M8100/0) — *see* Neoplasm, skin, benign
Brown enamel of teeth (hereditary) 520.5
Brown-Séquard's paralysis (syndrome) 344.89
Brown's tendon sheath syndrome 378.61
Brow presentation complicating delivery 652.4 ☑
Brucella, brucellosis (infection) 023.9
  abortus 023.1
  canis 023.3
  dermatitis, skin 023.9
  melitensis 023.0
  mixed 023.8
  suis 023.2
Bruck-de Lange disease or syndrome (Amsterdam dwarf, mental retardation, and brachycephaly) 759.89
Bruck's disease 733.99
Brugada syndrome 746.89
Brug's filariasis 125.1
Brugsch's syndrome (acropachyderma) 757.39
Bruhl's disease (splenic anemia with fever) 285.8
Bruise (skin surface intact) — *see also* Contusion
  with
    fracture — *see* Fracture, by site
    open wound — *see* Wound, open, by site
  internal organ (abdomen, chest, or pelvis) — *see* Injury, internal, by site
  umbilical cord 663.6 ☑
    affecting fetus or newborn 762.6
Bruit 785.9
  arterial (abdominal) (carotid) 785.9
  supraclavicular 785.9
Brushburn — *see* Injury, superficial, by site
Bruton's X-linked agammaglobulinemia 279.04
Bruxism 306.8
  sleep related 327.53
Bubbly lung syndrome 770.7
Bubo 289.3
  blennorrhagic 098.89
  chancroidal 099.0
  climatic 099.1
  due to Hemophilus ducreyi 099.0
  gonococcal 098.89
  indolent NEC 099.8
  inguinal NEC 099.8
    chancroidal 099.0
    climatic 099.1
    due to H. ducreyi 099.0
  scrofulous (*see also* Tuberculosis) 017.2 ☑
  soft chancre 099.0
  suppurating 683
  syphilitic 091.0
    congenital 090.0
  tropical 099.1
  venereal NEC 099.8
  virulent 099.0
Bubonic plague 020.0
Bubonocele — *see* Hernia, inguinal
Buccal — *see* condition
Buchanan's disease (juvenile osteochondrosis of iliac crest) 732.1
Buchem's syndrome (hyperostosis corticalis) 733.3
Buchman's disease (osteochondrosis, juvenile) 732.1
Bucket handle fracture (semilunar cartilage) — *see also* Tear, meniscus 836.2
Budd-Chiari syndrome (hepatic vein thrombosis) 453.0

Budgerigar-fanciers' disease or lung 495.2
Büdinger-Ludloff-Läwen disease 717.89
Buerger's disease (thromboangiitis obliterans) 443.1
Bulbar — *see* condition
Bulbus cordis 745.9
  persistent (in left ventricle) 745.8
Bulging fontanels (congenital) 756.0
Bulimia 783.6
  nervosa 307.51
  nonorganic origin 307.51
Bulky uterus 621.2
Bulla(e) 709.8
  lung (emphysematous) (solitary) 492.0
Bullet wound — *see also* Wound, open, by site
  fracture — *see* Fracture, by site, open
  internal organ (abdomen, chest, or pelvis) — *see* Injury, internal, by site, with open wound
  intracranial — *see* Laceration, brain, with open wound
Bullis fever 082.8
Bullying — *see also* Disturbance, conduct 312.0 ☑
Bundle
  branch block (complete) (false) (incomplete) 426.50
    bilateral 426.53
    left (*see also* Block, bundle branch, left) 426.3
      hemiblock 426.2
    right (*see also* Block, bundle branch, right) 426.4
  of His — *see* condition
  of Kent syndrome (anomalous atrioventricular excitation) 426.7
Bungpagga 040.81
Bunion 727.1
Bunionette 727.1
Bunyamwera fever 066.3
Buphthalmia, buphthalmos (congenital) 743.20
  associated with
    keratoglobus, congenital 743.22
    megalocornea 743.22
    ocular anomalies NEC 743.22
  isolated 743.21
  simple 743.21
Bürger-Grütz disease or syndrome (essential familial hyperlipemia) 272.3
Buried roots 525.3
Burke's syndrome 577.8
Burkitt's
  tumor (M9750/3) 200.2 ☑
  type malignant, lymphoma, lymphoblastic, or undifferentiated (M9750/3) 200.2 ☑

☑ Additional Digit Required — Refer to the Tabular List for Digit Selection   ▽ Subterms under main terms may continue to next column or page

2007 ICD-9-CM   ▶◀ Revised Text   ● New Line   ▲ Revised Code   **October 2006 · Volume 2 — 39**

Burn (acid) (cathode ray) (caustic) (chemical) (electric heating appliance) (electricity) (fire) (flame) (hot liquid or object) (irradiation) (lime) (radiation) (steam) (thermal) (x-ray) 949.0

Note — Use the following fifth-digit subclassification with category 948 to indicate the percent of body surface with third degree burn:

0	*Less than 10% or unspecified*
1	*10–19%*
2	*20–29%*
3	*30–39%*
4	*40–49%*
5	*50–59%*
6	*60–69%*
7	*70–79%*
8	*80–89%*
9	*90% or more of body surface*

with
    blisters — see Burn, by site, second degree
    erythema — see Burn, by site, first degree
    skin loss (epidermal) (see also Burn, by site, second degree)
    full thickness (see also Burn, by site, third degree)
        with necrosis of underlying tissues — see Burn, by site, third degree, deep
    first degree — see Burn, by site, first degree
    second degree — see Burn, by site, second degree
    third degree — see Burn, by site, third degree
        deep — see Burn, by site, third degree, deep
abdomen, abdominal (muscle) (wall) 942.03
    with
        trunk — see Burn, trunk, multiple sites
    first degree 942.13
    second degree 942.23
    third degree 942.33
        deep 942.43
            with loss of body part 942.53
ankle 945.03
    with
        lower limb(s) — see Burn, leg, multiple sites
    first degree 945.13
    second degree 945.23
    third degree 945.33
        deep 945.43
            with loss of body part 945.53
anus — see Burn, trunk, specified site NEC
arm(s) 943.00
    first degree 943.10
    second degree 943.20
    third degree 943.30
        deep 943.40
            with loss of body part 943.50
    lower — see Burn, forearm(s)
    multiple sites, except hand(s) or wrist(s) 943.09
        first degree 943.19
        second degree 943.29
        third degree 943.39
            deep 943.49
                with loss of body part 943.59
    upper 943.03
        first degree 943.13
        second degree 943.23
        third degree 943.33
            deep 943.43

Burn — continued
arm(s) — continued
    upper — continued
        third degree — continued
            deep — continued
                with loss of body part 943.53
auditory canal (external) — see Burn, ear
auricle (ear) — see Burn, ear
axilla 943.04
    with
        upper limb(s), except hand(s) or wrist(s) — see Burn, arm(s), multiple sites
    first degree 943.14
    second degree 943.24
    third degree 943.34
        deep 943.44
            with loss of body part 943.54
back 942.04
    with
        trunk — see Burn, trunk, multiple sites
    first degree 942.14
    second degree 942.24
    third degree 942.34
        deep 942.44
            with loss of body part 942.54
biceps
    brachii — see Burn, arm(s), upper
    femoris — see Burn, thigh
breast(s) 942.01
    with
        trunk — see Burn, trunk, multiple sites
    first degree 942.11
    second degree 942.21
    third degree 942.31
        deep 942.41
            with loss of body part 942.51
brow — see Burn, forehead
buttock(s) — see Burn, back
canthus (eye) 940.1
    chemical 940.0
cervix (uteri) 947.4
cheek (cutaneous) 941.07
    with
        face or head — see Burn, head, multiple sites
    first degree 941.17
    second degree 941.27
    third degree 941.37
        deep 941.47
            with loss of body part 941.57
chest wall (anterior) 942.02
    with
        trunk — see Burn, trunk, multiple sites
    first degree 942.12
    second degree 942.22
    third degree 942.32
        deep 942.42
            with loss of body part 942.52
chin 941.04
    with
        face or head — see Burn, head, multiple sites
    first degree 941.14
    second degree 941.24
    third degree 941.34
        deep 941.44
            with loss of body part 941.54
clitoris — see Burn, genitourinary organs, external
colon 947.3
conjunctiva (and cornea) 940.4
    chemical
        acid 940.3
        alkaline 940.2
cornea (and conjunctiva) 940.4
    chemical
        acid 940.3
        alkaline 940.2
costal region — see Burn, chest wall

Burn — continued
due to ingested chemical agent — see Burn, internal organs
ear (auricle) (canal) (drum) (external) 941.01
    with
        face or head — see Burn, head, multiple sites
    first degree 941.11
    second degree 941.21
    third degree 941.31
        deep 941.41
            with loss of a body part 941.51
elbow 943.02
    with
        hand(s) and wrist(s) — see Burn, multiple specified sites
        upper limb(s), except hand(s) or wrist(s) (see also Burn, arm(s), multiple sites)
    first degree 943.12
    second degree 943.22
    third degree 943.32
        deep 943.42
            with loss of body part 943.52
electricity, electric current — see Burn, by site
entire body — see Burn, multiple, specified sites
epididymis — see Burn, genitourinary organs, external
epigastric region — see Burn, abdomen
epiglottis 947.1
esophagus 947.2
extent (percent of body surface)
    less than 10 percent 948.0 ☑
    10-19 percent 948.1 ☑
    20-29 percent 948.2 ☑
    30-39 percent 948.3 ☑
    40-49 percent 948.4 ☑
    50-59 percent 948.5 ☑
    60-69 percent 948.6 ☑
    70-79 percent 948.7 ☑
    80-89 percent 948.8 ☑
    90 percent or more 948.9 ☑
extremity
    lower — see Burn, leg
    upper — see Burn, arm(s)
eye(s) (and adnexa) (only) 940.9
    with
        face, head, or neck 941.02
            first degree 941.12
            second degree 941.22
            third degree 941.32
                deep 941.42
                    with loss of body part 941.52
        other sites (classifiable to more than one category in 940–945) — see Burn, multiple, specified sites
        resulting rupture and destruction of eyeball 940.5
        specified part — see Burn, by site
eyeball (see also Burn, eye)
    with resulting rupture and destruction of eyeball 940.5
eyelid(s) 940.1
    chemical 940.0
face — see Burn, head
finger (nail) (subungual) 944.01
    with
        hand(s) — see Burn, hand(s), multiple sites
        other sites — see Burn, multiple, specified sites
        thumb 944.04
            first degree 944.14
            second degree 944.24
            third degree 944.34
                deep 944.44
                    with loss of body part 944.54

Burn — continued
finger — continued
    first degree 944.11
    second degree 944.21
    third degree 944.31
        deep 944.41
            with loss of body part 944.51
    multiple (digits) 944.03
        with thumb — see Burn, finger, with thumb
        first degree 944.13
        second degree 944.23
        third degree 944.33
            deep 944.43
                with loss of body part 944.53
flank — see Burn, abdomen
foot 945.02
    with
        lower limb(s) — see Burn, leg, multiple sites
    first degree 945.12
    second degree 945.22
    third degree 945.32
        deep 945.42
            with loss of body part 945.52
forearm(s) 943.01
    with
        upper limb(s), except hand(s) or wrist(s) — see Burn, arm(s), multiple sites
    first degree 943.11
    second degree 943.21
    third degree 943.31
        deep 943.41
            with loss of body part 943.51
forehead 941.07
    with
        face or head — see Burn, head, multiple sites
    first degree 941.17
    second degree 941.27
    third degree 941.37
        deep 941.47
            with loss of body part 941.57
fourth degree — see Burn, by site, third degree, deep
friction — see Injury, superficial, by site
from swallowing caustic or corrosive substance NEC — see Burn, internal organs
full thickness — see Burn, by site, third degree
gastrointestinal tract 947.3
genitourinary organs
    external 942.05
        with
            trunk — see Burn, trunk, multiple sites
        first degree 942.15
        second degree 942.25
        third degree 942.35
            deep 942.45
                with loss of body part 942.55
    internal 947.8
globe (eye) — see Burn, eyeball
groin — see Burn, abdomen
gum 947.0
hand(s) (phalanges) (and wrist) 944.00
    first degree 944.10
    second degree 944.20
    third degree 944.30
        deep 944.40
            with loss of body part 944.50
    back (dorsal surface) 944.06
        first degree 944.16
        second degree 944.26
        third degree 944.36
            deep 944.46
                with loss of body part 944.56
    multiple sites 944.08
        first degree 944.18
        second degree 944.28

☑ Additional Digit Required — Refer to the Tabular List for Digit Selection   ▽ Subterms under main terms may continue to next column or page

40 — Volume 2   ▶◀ Revised Text   ● New Line   ▲ Revised Code   *2007 ICD-9-CM*

Burn — continued
  hand(s) — continued
    multiple sites — continued
      third degree 944.38
        deep 944.48
          with loss of body part
            944.58
  head (and face) 941.00
    first degree 941.10
    second degree 941.20
    third degree 941.30
      deep 941.40
        with loss of body part 941.50
    eye(s) only 940.9
      specified part — see Burn, by
        site
    multiple sites 941.09
      with eyes — see Burn, eyes,
        with face, head, or neck
      first degree 941.19
      second degree 941.29
      third degree 941.39
        deep 941.49
          with loss of body part
            941.59
  heel — see Burn, foot
  hip — see Burn, trunk, specified site
    NEC
  iliac region — see Burn, trunk, speci-
    fied site NEC
  infected 958.3
  inhalation (see also Burn, internal
    organs) 947.9
  internal organs 947.9
    from caustic or corrosive substance
      (swallowing) NEC 947.9
    specified NEC (see also Burn, by
      site) 947.8
  interscapular region — see Burn, back
  intestine (large) (small) 947.3
  iris — see Burn, eyeball
  knee 945.05
    with
      lower limb(s) — see Burn, leg,
        multiple sites
    first degree 945.15
    second degree 945.25
    third degree 945.35
      deep 945.45
        with loss of body part 945.55
  labium (majus) (minus) — see Burn,
    genitourinary organs, external
  lacrimal apparatus, duct, gland, or
    sac 940.1
    chemical 940.0
  larynx 947.1
  late effect — see Late, effects (of), burn
  leg 945.00
    first degree 945.10
    second degree 945.20
    third degree 945.30
      deep 945.40
        with loss of body part 945.50
    lower 945.04
      with other part(s) of lower
        limb(s) — see Burn, leg,
        multiple sites
      first degree 945.14
      second degree 945.24
      third degree 945.34
        deep 945.44
          with loss of body part
            945.54
    multiple sites 945.09
      first degree 945.19
      second degree 945.29
      third degree 945.39
        deep 945.49
          with loss of body part
            945.59
    upper — see Burn, thigh
  lightning — see Burn, by site
  limb(s)
    lower (including foot or toe(s)) —
      see Burn, leg

Burn — continued
  limb(s) — continued
    upper (except wrist and hand) —
      see Burn, arm(s)
  lip(s) 941.03
    with
      face or head — see Burn, head,
        multiple sites
    first degree 941.13
    second degree 941.23
    third degree 941.33
      deep 941.43
        with loss of body part 941.53
  lumbar region — see Burn, back
  lung 947.1
  malar region — see Burn, cheek
  mastoid region — see Burn, scalp
  membrane, tympanic — see Burn, ear
  midthoracic region — see Burn, chest
    wall
  mouth 947.0
  multiple (see also Burn, unspecified)
    949.0
    specified sites classifiable to more
      than one category in
      940-945 ☑, 946.0
      first degree 946.1
      second degree 946.2
      third degree 946.3
        deep 946.4
          with loss of body part
            946.5
  muscle, abdominal — see Burn, ab-
    domen
  nasal (septum) — see Burn, nose
  neck 941.08
    with
      face or head — see Burn, head,
        multiple sites
    first degree 941.18
    second degree 941.28
    third degree 941.38
      deep 941.48
        with loss of body part 941.58
  nose (septum) 941.05
    with
      face or head — see Burn, head,
        multiple sites
    first degree 941.15
    second degree 941.25
    third degree 941.35
      deep 941.45
        with loss of body part 941.55
  occipital region — see Burn, scalp
  orbit region 940.1
    chemical 940.0
  oronasopharynx 947.0
  palate 947.0
  palm(s) 944.05
    with
      hand(s) and wrist(s) — see
        Burn, hand(s), multiple
        sites
    first degree 944.15
    second degree 944.25
    third degree 944.35
      deep 944.45
        with loss of a body part
          944.55
  parietal region — see Burn, scalp
  penis — see Burn, genitourinary or-
    gans, external
  perineum — see Burn, genitourinary
    organs, external
  periocular area 940.1
    chemical 940.0
  pharynx 947.0
  pleura 947.1
  popliteal space — see Burn, knee
  prepuce — see Burn, genitourinary
    organs, external
  pubic region — see Burn, genitouri-
    nary organs, external
  pudenda — see Burn, genitourinary
    organs, external
  rectum 947.3

Burn — continued
  sac, lacrimal 940.1
    chemical 940.0
  sacral region — see Burn, back
  salivary (ducts) (glands) 947.0
  scalp 941.06
    with
      face or neck — see Burn, head,
        multiple sites
    first degree 941.16
    second degree 941.26
    third degree 941.36
      deep 941.46
        with loss of body part 941.56
  scapular region 943.06
    with
      upper limb(s), except hand(s) or
        wrist(s) — see Burn,
        arm(s), multiple sites
    first degree 943.16
    second degree 943.26
    third degree 943.36
      deep 943.46
        with loss of body part 943.56
  sclera — see Burn, eyeball
  scrotum — see Burn, genitourinary
    organs, external
  septum, nasal — see Burn, nose
  shoulder(s) 943.05
    with
      hand(s) and wrist(s) — see
        Burn, multiple, specified
        sites
      upper limb(s), except hand(s) or
        wrist(s) — see Burn,
        arm(s), multiple sites
    first degree 943.15
    second degree 943.25
    third degree 943.35
      deep 943.45
        with loss of body part 943.55
  skin NEC (see also Burn, unspecified)
    949.0
  skull — see Burn, head
  small intestine 947.3
  sternal region — see Burn, chest wall
  stomach 947.3
  subconjunctival — see Burn, conjunc-
    tiva
  subcutaneous — see Burn, by site,
    third degree
  submaxillary region — see Burn, head
  submental region — see Burn, chin
  sun — see Sunburn
  supraclavicular fossa — see Burn,
    neck
  supraorbital — see Burn, forehead
  temple — see Burn, scalp
  temporal region — see Burn, scalp
  testicle — see Burn, genitourinary or-
    gans, external
  testis — see Burn, genitourinary or-
    gans, external
  thigh 945.06
    with
      lower limb(s) — see Burn, leg,
        multiple sites
    first degree 945.16
    second degree 945.26
    third degree 945.36
      deep 945.46
        with loss of body part 945.56
  thorax (external) — see Burn, chest
    wall
  throat 947.0
  thumb(s) (nail) (subungual) 944.02
    with
      finger(s) — see Burn, finger,
        with other sites, thumb
      hand(s) and wrist(s) — see
        Burn, hand(s), multiple
        sites
    first degree 944.12
    second degree 944.22
    third degree 944.32
      deep 944.42

Burn — continued
  thumb(s) — continued
    third degree — continued
      deep — continued
        with loss of body part 944.52
  toe (nail) (subungual) 945.01
    with
      lower limb(s) — see Burn, leg,
        multiple sites
    first degree 945.11
    second degree 945.21
    third degree 945.31
      deep 945.41
        with loss of body part 945.51
  tongue 947.0
  tonsil 947.0
  trachea 947.1
  trunk 942.00
    first degree 942.10
    second degree 942.20
    third degree 942.30
      deep 942.40
        with loss of body part 942.50
    multiple sites 942.09
      first degree 942.19
      second degree 942.29
      third degree 942.39
        deep 942.49
          with loss of body part
            942.59
    specified site NEC 942.09
      first degree 942.19
      second degree 942.29
      third degree 942.39
        deep 942.49
          with loss of body part
            942.59
  tunica vaginalis — see Burn, genitouri-
    nary organs, external
  tympanic membrane — see Burn, ear
  tympanum — see Burn, ear
  ultraviolet 692.82
  unspecified site (multiple) 949.0
    with extent of body surface in-
      volved specified
      less than 10 percent 948.0 ☑
      10-19 percent 948.1 ☑
      20-29 percent 948.2 ☑
      30-39 percent 948.3 ☑
      40-49 percent 948.4 ☑
      50-59 percent 948.5 ☑
      60-69 percent 948.6 ☑
      70-79 percent 948.7 ☑
      80-89 percent 948.8 ☑
      90 percent or more 948.9 ☑
    first degree 949.1
    second degree 949.2
    third degree 949.3
      deep 949.4
        with loss of body part 949.5
  uterus 947.4
  uvula 947.0
  vagina 947.4
  vulva — see Burn, genitourinary or-
    gans, external
  wrist(s) 944.07
    with
      hand(s) — see Burn, hand(s),
        multiple sites
    first degree 944.17
    second degree 944.27
    third degree 944.37
      deep 944.47
        with loss of body part 944.57
Burnett's syndrome (milk-alkali) 275.42
Burnier's syndrome (hypophyseal
  dwarfism) 253.3
Burning
  feet syndrome 266.2
  sensation (see also Disturbance, sen-
    sation) 782.0
  tongue 529.6
Burns' disease (osteochondrosis, lower
  ulna) 732.3
Bursa — see also condition
  pharynx 478.29

☑ Additional Digit Required — Refer to the Tabular List for Digit Selection   ▽ Subterms under main terms may continue to next column or page

2007 ICD-9-CM   ▶◀ Revised Text   ● New Line   ▲ Revised Code   Volume 2 — 41

Bursitis NEC 727.3
  Achilles tendon 726.71
  adhesive 726.90
    shoulder 726.0
  ankle 726.79
  buttock 726.5
  calcaneal 726.79
  collateral ligament
    fibular 726.63
    tibial 726.62
  Duplay's 726.2
  elbow 726.33
  finger 726.8
  foot 726.79
  gonococcal 098.52
  hand 726.4
  hip 726.5
  infrapatellar 726.69
  ischiogluteal 726.5
  knee 726.60
  occupational NEC 727.2
  olecranon 726.33
  pes anserinus 726.61
  pharyngeal 478.29
  popliteal 727.51
  prepatellar 726.65
  radiohumeral 727.3
  scapulohumeral 726.19
    adhesive 726.0
  shoulder 726.10
    adhesive 726.0
  subacromial 726.19
    adhesive 726.0
  subcoracoid 726.19
  subdeltoid 726.19
    adhesive 726.0
  subpatellar 726.69
  syphilitic 095.7
  Thornwaldt's, Tornwaldt's (pharyngeal) 478.29
  toe 726.79
  trochanteric area 726.5
  wrist 726.4
Burst stitches or sutures (complication of surgery) (external) 998.32
  internal 998.31
Buruli ulcer 031.1
Bury's disease (erythema elevatum diutinum) 695.89
Buschke's disease or scleredema (adultorum) 710.1
Busquet's disease (osteoperiostitis) — see also Osteomyelitis 730.1 ☑
Busse-Buschke disease (cryptococcosis) 117.5
Buttock — see condition
Button
  Biskra 085.1
  Delhi 085.1
  oriental 085.1
Buttonhole hand (intrinsic) 736.21
Bwamba fever (encephalitis) 066.3
Byssinosis (occupational) 504
Bywaters' syndrome 958.5

C

Cacergasia 300.9
Cachexia 799.4
  cancerous ▶(see also Neoplasm, by site, malignant)◀ 799.4 ▲
  cardiac — see Disease, heart
  dehydration 276.51
    with
      hypernatremia 276.0
      hyponatremia 276.1
  due to malnutrition 799.4 ▲
  exophthalmic 242.0 ☑
  heart — see Disease, heart
  hypophyseal 253.2
  hypopituitary 253.2
  lead 984.9
    specified type of lead — see Table of Drugs and Chemicals
  malaria 084.9
  malignant ▶(see also Neoplasm, by site, malignant)◀ 799.4 ▲

Cachexia — continued
  marsh 084.9
  nervous 300.5
  old age 797
  pachydermic — see Hypothyroidism
  paludal 084.9
  pituitary (postpartum) 253.2
  renal (see also Disease, renal) 593.9
  saturnine 984.9
    specified type of lead — see Table of Drugs and Chemicals
  senile 797
  Simmonds' (pituitary cachexia) 253.2
  splenica 289.59
  strumipriva (see also Hypothyroidism) 244.9
  tuberculous NEC (see also Tuberculosis) 011.9 ☑
Café au lait spots 709.09
Caffey's disease or syndrome (infantile cortical hyperostosis) 756.59
Caisson disease 993.3
Caked breast (puerperal, postpartum) 676.2 ☑
Cake kidney 753.3
Calabar swelling 125.2
Calcaneal spur 726.73
Calcaneoapophysitis 732.5
Calcaneonavicular bar 755.67
Calcareous — see condition
Calcicosis (occupational) 502
Calciferol (vitamin D) **deficiency** 268.9
  with
    osteomalacia 268.2
    rickets (see also Rickets) 268.0
Calcification
  adrenal (capsule) (gland) 255.4
    tuberculous (see also Tuberculosis) 017.6 ☑
  aorta 440.0
  artery (annular) — see Arteriosclerosis
  auricle (ear) 380.89
  bladder 596.8
    due to S. hematobium 120.0
  brain (cortex) — see Calcification, cerebral
  bronchus 519.19 ▲
  bursa 727.82
  cardiac (see also Degeneration, myocardial) 429.1
  cartilage (postinfectional) 733.99
  cerebral (cortex) 348.8
    artery 437.0
  cervix (uteri) 622.8
  choroid plexus 349.2
  conjunctiva 372.54
  corpora cavernosa (penis) 607.89
  cortex (brain) — see Calcification, cerebral
  dental pulp (nodular) 522.2
  dentinal papilla 520.4
  disc, intervertebral 722.90
    cervical, cervicothoracic 722.91
    lumbar, lumbosacral 722.93
    thoracic, thoracolumbar 722.92
  fallopian tube 620.8
  falx cerebri — see Calcification, cerebral
  fascia 728.89
  gallbladder 575.8
  general 275.40
  heart (see also Degeneration, myocardial) 429.1
    valve — see Endocarditis
  intervertebral cartilage or disc (postinfectional) 722.90
    cervical, cervicothoracic 722.91
    lumbar, lumbosacral 722.93
    thoracic, thoracolumbar 722.92
  intracranial — see Calcification, cerebral
  intraspinal ligament 728.89
  joint 719.80
    ankle 719.87
    elbow 719.82
    foot 719.87

Calcification — continued
  joint — continued
    hand 719.84
    hip 719.85
    knee 719.86
    multiple sites 719.89
    pelvic region 719.85
    shoulder (region) 719.81
    specified site NEC 719.88
    wrist 719.83
  kidney 593.89
    tuberculous (see also Tuberculosis) 016.0 ☑
  larynx (senile) 478.79
  lens 366.8
  ligament 728.89
    intraspinal 728.89
    knee (medial collateral) 717.89
  lung 518.89
    active 518.89
    postinfectional 518.89
    tuberculous (see also Tuberculosis, pulmonary) 011.9 ☑
  lymph gland or node (postinfectional) 289.3
    tuberculous (see also Tuberculosis, lymph gland) 017.2 ☑
  mammographic 793.89 ●
  massive (paraplegic) 728.10
  medial NEC (see also Arteriosclerosis, extremities) 440.20
  meninges (cerebral) 349.2
  metastatic 275.40
  Mönckeberg's — see Arteriosclerosis
  muscle 728.10
    heterotopic, postoperative 728.13
  myocardium, myocardial (see also Degeneration, myocardial) 429.1
  ovary 620.8
  pancreas 577.8
  penis 607.89
  periarticular 728.89
  pericardium (see also Pericarditis) 423.8
  pineal gland 259.8
  pleura 511.0
    postinfectional 518.89
    tuberculous (see also Tuberculosis, pleura) 012.0 ☑
  pulp (dental) (nodular) 522.2
  renal 593.89
  Rider's bone 733.99
  sclera 379.16
  semilunar cartilage 717.89
  spleen 289.59
  subcutaneous 709.3
  suprarenal (capsule) (gland) 255.4
  tendon (sheath) 727.82
    with bursitis, synovitis or tenosynovitis 727.82
  trachea 519.19 ▲
  ureter 593.89
  uterus 621.8
  vitreous 379.29
Calcified — see also Calcification
  hematoma NEC 959.9
Calcinosis (generalized) (interstitial) (tumoral) (universalis) 275.49
  circumscripta 709.3
  cutis 709.3
  intervertebralis 275.49 [722.90]
  Raynaud's phenomenonsclerodactylytelangiectasis (CRST) 710.1
Calciphylaxis — see also Calcification, ● by site 275.49 ●
Calcium
  blood
    high (see also Hypercalcemia) 275.42
    low (see also Hypocalcemia) 275.41
  deposits (see also Calcification, by site)
    in bursa 727.82
    in tendon (sheath) 727.82
      with bursitis, synovitis or tenosynovitis 727.82

Calcium — continued
  salts or soaps in vitreous 379.22
Calciuria 791.9
Calculi — see Calculus
Calculosis, intrahepatic — see Choledocholithiasis
Calculus, calculi, calculous 592.9
  ampulla of Vater — see Choledocholithiasis
  anuria (impacted) (recurrent) 592.0
  appendix 543.9
  bile duct (any) — see Choledocholithiasis
  biliary — see Cholelithiasis
  bilirubin, multiple — see Cholelithiasis
  bladder (encysted) (impacted) (urinary) 594.1
    diverticulum 594.0
  bronchus 518.89
  calyx (kidney) (renal) 592.0
    congenital 753.3
  cholesterol (pure) (solitary) — see Cholelithiasis
  common duct (bile) — see Choledocholithiasis
  conjunctiva 372.54
  cystic 594.1
    duct — see Cholelithiasis
  dental 523.6
    subgingival 523.6
    supragingival 523.6
  epididymis 608.89
  gallbladder (see also Cholelithiasis)
    congenital 751.69
  hepatic (duct) — see Choledocholithiasis
  intestine (impaction) (obstruction) 560.39
  kidney (impacted) (multiple) (pelvis) (recurrent) (staghorn) 592.0
    congenital 753.3
  lacrimal (passages) 375.57
  liver (impacted) — see Choledocholithiasis
  lung 518.89
  mammographic 793.89 ●
  nephritic (impacted) (recurrent) 592.0
  nose 478.19 ▲
  pancreas (duct) 577.8
  parotid gland 527.5
  pelvis, encysted 592.0
  prostate 602.0
  pulmonary 518.89
  renal (impacted) (recurrent) 592.0
    congenital 753.3
  salivary (duct) (gland) 527.5
  seminal vesicle 608.89
  staghorn 592.0
  Stensen's duct 527.5
  sublingual duct or gland 527.5
    congenital 750.26
  submaxillary duct, gland, or region 527.5
  suburethral 594.8
  tonsil 474.8
  tooth, teeth 523.6
  tunica vaginalis 608.89
  ureter (impacted) (recurrent) 592.1
  urethra (impacted) 594.2
  urinary (duct) (impacted) (passage) (tract) 592.9
    lower tract NEC 594.9
    specified site 594.8
  vagina 623.8
  vesical (impacted) 594.1
  Wharton's duct 527.5
Caliectasis 593.89
California
  disease 114.0
  encephalitis 062.5
Caligo cornea 371.03
Callositas, callosity (infected) 700
Callus (infected) 700
  bone 726.91

☑ Additional Digit Required — Refer to the Tabular List for Digit Selection ▼ Subterms under main terms may continue to next column or page

42 — Volume 2 · October 2006   ▶◀ Revised Text   ● New Line   ▲ Revised Code   *2007 ICD-9-CM*

Callus — *continued*
excessive, following fracture (*see also* Late, effect (of), fracture)
Calvé (-Perthes) disease (osteochondrosis, femoral capital) 732.1
Calvities — *see also* Alopecia 704.00
Cameroon fever — *see also* Malaria 084.6
Camptocormia 300.11
Camptodactyly (congenital) 755.59
Camurati-Engelmann disease (diaphyseal sclerosis) 756.59
Canal — *see* condition
Canaliculitis (lacrimal) (acute) 375.31
Actinomyces 039.8
chronic 375.41
Canavan's disease 330.0
Cancer (M8000/3) — *see also* Neoplasm, by site, malignant

Note — *The term "cancer" when modified by an adjective or adjectival phrase indicating a morphological type should be coded in the same manner as "carcinoma" with that adjective or phrase. Thus, "squamous-cell cancer" should be coded in the same manner as "squamous-cell carcinoma," which appears in the list under "Carcinoma."*

bile duct type (M8160/3), liver 155.1
hepatocellular (M8170/3) 155.0
Cancerous (M8000/3) — *see* Neoplasm, by site, malignant
Cancerphobia 300.29
Cancrum oris 528.1
Candidiasis, candidal 112.9
with pneumonia 112.4
balanitis 112.2
congenital 771.7
disseminated 112.5
endocarditis 112.81
esophagus 112.84
intertrigo 112.3
intestine 112.85
lung 112.4
meningitis 112.83
mouth 112.0
nails 112.3
neonatal 771.7
onychia 112.3
otitis externa 112.82
otomycosis 112.82
paronychia 112.3
perionyxis 112.3
pneumonia 112.4
pneumonitis 112.4
skin 112.3
specified site NEC 112.89
systemic 112.5
urogenital site NEC 112.2
vagina 112.1
vulva 112.1
vulvovaginitis 112.1
Candidiosis — *see* Candidiasis
Candiru infection or infestation 136.8
Canities (premature) 704.3
congenital 757.4
Canker (mouth) (sore) 528.2
rash 034.1
Cannabinosis 504
Canton fever 081.9
Cap
cradle 690.11
Capillariasis 127.5
Capillary — *see* condition
Caplan-Colinet syndrome 714.81
Caplan's syndrome 714.81
Capsule — *see* condition
Capsulitis (joint) 726.90
adhesive (shoulder) 726.0
hip 726.5
knee 726.60
labyrinthine 387.8
thyroid 245.9
wrist 726.4
Caput
crepitus 756.0

Caput — *continued*
medusae 456.8
succedaneum 767.19
Carapata disease 087.1
Carate — *see* Pinta
Carbohydrate-deficient glycoprotein syndrome (CGDS) 271.8
Carboxyhemoglobinemia 986
Carbuncle 680.9
abdominal wall 680.2
ankle 680.6
anus 680.5
arm (any part, above wrist) 680.3
auditory canal, external 680.0
axilla 680.3
back (any part) 680.2
breast 680.2
buttock 680.5
chest wall 680.2
corpus cavernosum 607.2
ear (any part) (external) 680.0
eyelid 373.13
face (any part, except eye) 680.0
finger (any part) 680.4
flank 680.2
foot (any part) 680.7
forearm 680.3
genital organ (male) 608.4
gluteal (region) 680.5
groin 680.2
hand (any part) 680.4
head (any part, except face) 680.8
heel 680.7
hip 680.6
kidney (*see also* Abscess, kidney) 590.2
knee 680.6
labia 616.4
lacrimal
gland (*see also* Dacryoadenitis) 375.00
passages (duct) (sac) (*see also* Dacryocystitis) 375.30
leg, any part except foot 680.6
lower extremity, any part except foot 680.6
malignant 022.0
multiple sites 680.9
neck 680.1
nose (external) (septum) 680.0
orbit, orbital 376.01
partes posteriores 680.5
pectoral region 680.2
penis 607.2
perineum 680.2
pinna 680.0
scalp (any part) 680.8
scrotum 608.4
seminal vesicle 608.0
shoulder 680.3
skin NEC 680.9
specified site NEC 680.8
spermatic cord 608.4
temple (region) 680.0
testis 608.4
thigh 680.6
thumb 680.4
toe (any) 680.7
trunk 680.2
tunica vaginalis 608.4
umbilicus 680.2
upper arm 680.3
urethra 597.0
vas deferens 608.4
vulva 616.4
wrist 680.4
Carbunculus — *see also* Carbuncle 680.9
Carcinoid (tumor) (M8240/1) — *see also* Neoplasm, by site, uncertain behavior
and struma ovarii (M9091/1) 236.2
argentaffin (M8241/1) — *see* Neoplasm, by site, uncertain behavior
malignant (M8241/3) — *see* Neoplasm, by site, malignant

Carcinoid — *see also* Neoplasm, by site, uncertain behavior — *continued*
benign (M9091/0) 220
composite (M8244/3) — *see* Neoplasm, by site, malignant
goblet cell (M8243/3) — *see* Neoplasm, by site, malignant
malignant (M8240/3) — *see* Neoplasm, by site, malignant
nonargentaffin (M8242/1) (*see also* Neoplasm, by site, uncertain behavior)
malignant (M8242/3) — *see* Neoplasm, by site, malignant
strumal (M9091/1) 236.2
syndrome (intestinal) (metastatic) 259.2
type bronchial adenoma (M8240/3) — *see* Neoplasm, lung, malignant
Carcinoidosis 259.2
Carcinomaphobia 300.29
Carcinomatosis
peritonei (M8010/6) 197.6
specified site NEC (M8010/3) — *see* Neoplasm, by site, malignant
unspecified site (M8010/6) 199.0
Carcinoma (M8010/3) — *see also* Neoplasm, by site, malignant

Note — *Except where otherwise indicated, the morphological varieties of carcinoma in the list below should be coded by site as for "Neoplasm, malignant."*

with
apocrine metaplasia (M8573/3)
cartilaginous (and osseous) metaplasia (M8571/3)
osseous (and cartilaginous) metaplasia (M8571/3)
productive fibrosis (M8141/3)
spindle cell metaplasia (M8572/3)
squamous metaplasia (M8570/3)
acidophil (M8280/3)
specified site — *see* Neoplasm, by site, malignant
unspecified site 194.3
acidophil-basophil, mixed (M8281/3)
specified site — *see* Neoplasm, by site, malignant
unspecified site 194.3
acinar (cell) (M8550/3)
acinic cell (M8550/3)
adenocystic (M8200/3)
adenoid
cystic (M8200/3)
squamous cell (M8075/3)
adenosquamous (M8560/3)
adnexal (skin) (M8390/3) — *see* Neoplasm, skin, malignant
adrenal cortical (M8370/3) 194.0
alveolar (M8251/3)
cell (M8250/3) — *see* Neoplasm, lung, malignant
anaplastic type (M8021/3)
apocrine (M8401/3)
breast — *see* Neoplasm, breast, malignant
specified site NEC — *see* Neoplasm, skin, malignant
unspecified site 173.9
basal cell (pigmented) (M8090/3) (*see also* Neoplasm, skin, malignant)
fibro-epithelial type (M8093/3) — *see* Neoplasm, skin, malignant
morphea type (M8092/3) — *see* Neoplasm, skin, malignant
multicentric (M8091/3) — *see* Neoplasm, skin, malignant
basaloid (M8123/3)
basal-squamous cell, mixed (M8094/3) — *see* Neoplasm, skin, malignant
basophil (M8300/3)
specified site — *see* Neoplasm, by site, malignant

Carcinoma — *see also* Neoplasm, by site, malignant — *continued*
basophil — *continued*
unspecified site 194.3
basophil-acidophil, mixed (M8281/3)
specified site — *see* Neoplasm, by site, malignant
unspecified site 194.3
basosquamous (M8094/3) — *see* Neoplasm, skin, malignant
bile duct type (M8160/3)
and hepatocellular, mixed (M8180/3) 155.0
liver 155.1
specified site NEC — *see* Neoplasm, by site, malignant
unspecified site 155.1
branchial or branchiogenic 146.8
bronchial or bronchogenic — *see* Neoplasm, lung, malignant
bronchiolar (terminal) (M8250/3) — *see* Neoplasm, lung, malignant
bronchiolo-alveolar (M8250/3) — *see* Neoplasm, lung, malignant
bronchogenic (epidermoid) 162.9
C cell (M8510/3)
specified site — *see* Neoplasm, by site, malignant
unspecified site 193
ceruminous (M8420/3) 173.2
chorionic (M9100/3)
specified site — *see* Neoplasm, by site, malignant
unspecified site
female 181
male 186.9
chromophobe (M8270/3)
specified site — *see* Neoplasm, by site, malignant
unspecified site 194.3
clear cell (mesonephroid type) (M8310/3)
cloacogenic (M8124/3)
specified site — *see* Neoplasm, by site, malignant
unspecified site 154.8
colloid (M8480/3)
cribriform (M8201/3)
cylindroid type (M8200/3)
diffuse type (M8145/3)
specified site — *see* Neoplasm, by site, malignant
unspecified site 151.9
duct (cell) (M8500/3)
with Paget's disease (M8541/3) — *see* Neoplasm, breast, malignant
infiltrating (M8500/3)
specified site — *see* Neoplasm, by site, malignant
unspecified site 174.9
ductal (M8500/3)
ductular, infiltrating (M8521/3)
embryonal (M9070/3)
and teratoma, mixed (M9081/3)
combined with choriocarcinoma (M9101/3) — *see* Neoplasm, by site, malignant
infantile type (M9071/3)
liver 155.0
polyembryonal type (M9072/3)
endometrioid (M8380/3)
eosinophil (M8280/3)
specified site — *see* Neoplasm, by site, malignant
unspecified site 194.3
epidermoid (M8070/3) (*see also* Carcinoma, squamous cell)
and adenocarcinoma, mixed (M8560/3)
in situ, Bowen's type (M8081/2) — *see* Neoplasm, skin, in situ
intradermal — *see* Neoplasm, skin, in situ

Carcinoma — *see also* Neoplasm, by site, malignant — *continued*
fibroepithelial type basal cell (M8093/3) — *see* Neoplasm, skin, malignant
follicular (M8330/3)
  and papillary (mixed) (M8340/3) 193
  moderately differentiated type (M8332/3) 193
  pure follicle type (M8331/3) 193
  specified site — *see* Neoplasm, by site, malignant
  trabecular type (M8332/3) 193
  unspecified site 193
  well differentiated type (M8331/3) 193
gelatinous (M8480/3)
giant cell (M8031/3)
  and spindle cell (M8030/3)
granular cell (M8320/3)
granulosa cell (M8620/3) 183.0
hepatic cell (M8170/3) 155.0
hepatocellular (M8170/3) 155.0
  and bile duct, mixed (M8180/3) 155.0
hepatocholangiolitic (M8180/3) 155.0
Hürthle cell (thyroid) 193
hypernephroid (M8311/3)
in
  adenomatous
    polyp (M8210/3)
    polyposis coli (M8220/3) 153.9
  pleomorphic adenoma (M8940/3)
  polypoid adenoma (M8210/3)
  situ (M8010/3) — *see* Carcinoma, in situ
  tubular adenoma (M8210/3)
  villous adenoma (M8261/3)
infiltrating duct (M8500/3)
  with Paget's disease (M8541/3) — *see* Neoplasm, breast, malignant
  specified site — *see* Neoplasm, by site, malignant
  unspecified site 174.9
inflammatory (M8530/3)
  specified site — *see* Neoplasm, by site, malignant
  unspecified site 174.9
in situ (M8010/2) (*see also* Neoplasm, by site, in situ)
  epidermoid (M8070/2) (*see also* Neoplasm, by site, in situ)
    with questionable stromal invasion (M8076/2)
    specified site — *see* Neoplasm, by site, in situ
    unspecified site 233.1
    Bowen's type (M8081/2) — *see* Neoplasm, skin, in situ
  intraductal (M8500/2)
    specified site — *see* Neoplasm, by site, in situ
    unspecified site 233.0
  lobular (M8520/2)
    specified site — *see* Neoplasm, by site, in situ
    unspecified site 233.0
  papillary (M8050/2) — *see* Neoplasm, by site, in situ
  squamous cell (M8070/2) (*see also* Neoplasm, by site, in situ)
    with questionable stromal invasion (M8076/2)
    specified site — *see* Neoplasm, by site, in situ
    unspecified site 233.1
  transitional cell (M8120/2) — *see* Neoplasm, by site, in situ
intestinal type (M8144/3)
  specified site — *see* Neoplasm, by site, malignant
  unspecified site 151.9

Carcinoma — *see also* Neoplasm, by site, malignant — *continued*
intraductal (noninfiltrating) (M8500/2)
  papillary (M8503/2)
    specified site — *see* Neoplasm, by site, in situ
    unspecified site 233.0
  specified site — *see* Neoplasm, by site, in situ
  unspecified site 233.0
intraepidermal (M8070/2) (*see also* Neoplasm, skin, in situ)
  squamous cell, Bowen's type (M8081/2) — *see* Neoplasm, skin, in situ
intraepithelial (M8010/2) (*see also* Neoplasm, by site, in situ)
  squamous cell (M8072/2) — *see* Neoplasm, by site, in situ
intraosseous (M9270/3) 170.1
  upper jaw (bone) 170.0
islet cell (M8150/3)
  and exocrine, mixed (M8154/3)
    specified site — *see* Neoplasm, by site, malignant
    unspecified site 157.9
  pancreas 157.4
  specified site NEC — *see* Neoplasm, by site, malignant
  unspecified site 157.4
juvenile, breast (M8502/3) — *see* Neoplasm, breast, malignant
Kulchitsky's cell (carcinoid tumor of intestine) 259.2
large cell (M8012/3)
  squamous cell, non-keratinizing type (M8072/3)
Leydig cell (testis) (M8650/3)
  specified site — *see* Neoplasm, by site, malignant
  unspecified site 186.9
    female 183.0
    male 186.9
liver cell (M8170/3) 155.0
lobular (infiltrating) (M8520/3)
  non-infiltrating (M8520/3)
    specified site — *see* Neoplasm, by site, in situ
    unspecified site 233.0
  specified site — *see* Neoplasm, by site, malignant
  unspecified site 174.9
lymphoepithelial (M8082/3)
medullary (M8510/3)
  with
    amyloid stroma (M8511/3)
      specified site — *see* Neoplasm, by site, malignant
      unspecified site 193
    lymphoid stroma (M8512/3)
      specified site — *see* Neoplasm, by site, malignant
      unspecified site 174.9
mesometanephric (M9110/3)
mesonephric (M9110/3)
metastatic (M8010/6) — *see* Metastasis, cancer
metatypical (M8095/3) — *see* Neoplasm, skin, malignant
morphea type basal cell (M8092/3) — *see* Neoplasm, skin, malignant
mucinous (M8480/3)
mucin-producing (M8481/3)
mucin-secreting (M8481/3)
mucoepidermoid (M8430/3)
mucoid (M8480/3)
  cell (M8300/3)
    specified site — *see* Neoplasm, by site, malignant
    unspecified site 194.3
mucous (M8480/3)
nonencapsulated sclerosing (M8350/3) 193

Carcinoma — *see also* Neoplasm, by site, malignant — *continued*
noninfiltrating
  intracystic (M8504/2) — *see* Neoplasm, by site, in situ
  intraductal (M8500/2)
    papillary (M8503/2)
      specified site — *see* Neoplasm, by site, in situ
      unspecified site 233.0
    specified site — *see* Neoplasm, by site, in situ
    unspecified site 233.0
  lobular (M8520/2)
    specified site — *see* Neoplasm, by site, in situ
    unspecified site 233.0
oat cell (M8042/3)
  specified site — *see* Neoplasm, by site, malignant
  unspecified site 162.9
odontogenic (M9270/3) 170.1
  upper jaw (bone) 170.0
onocytic (M8290/3)
oxyphilic (M8290/3)
papillary (M8050/3)
  and follicular (mixed) (M8340/3) 193
  epidermoid (M8052/3)
  intraductal (noninfiltrating) (M8503/2)
    specified site — *see* Neoplasm, by site, in situ
    unspecified site 233.0
  serous (M8460/3)
    specified site — *see* Neoplasm, by site, malignant
    surface (M8461/3)
      specified site — *see* Neoplasm, by site, malignant
      unspecified site 183.0
    unspecified site 183.0
  squamous cell (M8052/3)
  transitional cell (M8130/3)
papillocystic (M8450/3)
  specified site — *see* Neoplasm, by site, malignant
  unspecified site 183.0
parafollicular cell (M8510/3)
  specified site — *see* Neoplasm, by site, malignant
  unspecified site 193
pleomorphic (M8022/3)
polygonal cell (M8034/3)
prickle cell (M8070/3)
pseudoglandular, squamous cell (M8075/3)
pseudomucinous (M8470/3)
  specified site — *see* Neoplasm, by site, malignant
  unspecified site 183.0
pseudosarcomatous (M8033/3)
regaud type (M8082/3) — *see* Neoplasm, nasopharynx, malignant
renal cell (M8312/3) 189.0
reserve cell (M8041/3)
round cell (M8041/3)
Schmincke (M8082/3) — *see* Neoplasm, nasopharynx, malignant
Schneiderian (M8121/3)
  specified site — *see* Neoplasm, by site, malignant
  unspecified site 160.0
scirrhous (M8141/3)
sebaceous (M8410/3) — *see* Neoplasm, skin, malignant
secondary (M8010/6) — *see* Neoplasm, by site, malignant, secondary
secretory, breast (M8502/3) — *see* Neoplasm, breast, malignant
serous (M8441/3)
  papillary (M8460/3)
    specified site — *see* Neoplasm, by site, malignant

Carcinoma — *see also* Neoplasm, by site, malignant — *continued*
serous — *continued*
  papillary — *continued*
    unspecified site 183.0
  surface, papillary (M8461/3)
    specified site — *see* Neoplasm, by site, malignant
    unspecified site 183.0
Sertoli cell (M8640/3)
  specified site — *see* Neoplasm, by site, malignant
  unspecified site 186.9
signet ring cell (M8490/3)
  metastatic (M8490/6) — *see* Neoplasm, by site, secondary
simplex (M8231/3)
skin appendage (M8390/3) — *see* Neoplasm, skin, malignant
small cell (M8041/3)
  fusiform cell type (M8043/3)
  squamous cell, non-keratinizing type (M8073/3)
solid (M8230/3)
  with amyloid stroma (M8511/3)
    specified site — *see* Neoplasm, by site, malignant
    unspecified site 193
spheroidal cell (M8035/3)
spindle cell (M8032/3)
  and giant cell (M8030/3)
spinous cell (M8070/3)
squamous (cell) (M8070/3)
  adenoid type (M8075/3)
  and adenocarcinoma, mixed (M8560/3)
  intraepidermal, Bowen's type — *see* Neoplasm, skin, in situ
  keratinizing type (large cell) (M8071/3)
  large cell, non-keratinizing type (M8072/3)
  microinvasive (M8076/3)
    specified site — *see* Neoplasm, by site, malignant
    unspecified site 180.9
  non-keratinizing type (M8072/3)
  papillary (M8052/3)
  pseudoglandular (M8075/3)
  small cell, non-keratinizing type (M8073/3)
  spindle cell type (M8074/3)
  verrucous (M8051/3)
superficial spreading (M8143/3)
sweat gland (M8400/3) — *see* Neoplasm, skin, malignant
theca cell (M8600/3) 183.0
thymic (M8580/3) 164.0
trabecular (M8190/3)
transitional (cell) (M8120/3)
  papillary (M8130/3)
  spindle cell type (M8122/3)
tubular (M8211/3)
undifferentiated type (M8020/3)
urothelial (M8120/3)
ventriculi 151.9
verrucous (epidermoid) (squamous cell) (M8051/3)
villous (M8262/3)
water-clear cell (M8322/3) 194.1
wolffian duct (M9110/3)
Carcinosarcoma (M8980/3) — *see also* Neoplasm, by site, malignant
  embryonal type (M8981/3) — *see* Neoplasm, by site, malignant
Cardiac — *see also* condition
death — *see* Disease, heart
device
  defibrillator, automatic implantable V45.02
  in situ NEC V45.00
  pacemaker
    cardiac
      fitting or adjustment V53.31
      in situ V45.01

☑ Additional Digit Required — Refer to the Tabular List for Digit Selection   ▽ Subterms under main terms may continue to next column or page

Index

Carcinoma — Cardiac

Cardiac — *see also* condition — *continued*
  device — *continued*
    pacemaker — *continued*
      carotid sinus
        fitting or adjustment V53.39
        in situ V45.09
    pacemaker — *see* Cardiac, device, pacemaker
    tamponade 423.9
Cardia, cardial — *see* condition
Cardialgia — *see also* Pain, precordial 786.51
Cardiectasis — *see* Hypertrophy, cardiac
Cardiochalasia 530.81
Cardiomalacia — *see also* Degeneration, myocardial 429.1
Cardiomegalia glycogenica diffusa 271.0
Cardiomegaly — *see also* Hypertrophy, cardiac 429.3
  congenital 746.89
  glycogen 271.0
  hypertensive (*see also* Hypertension, heart) 402.90
  idiopathic 429.3
Cardiomyoliposis — *see also* Degeneration, myocardial 429.1
Cardiomyopathy (congestive) (constrictive) (familial) (infiltrative) (obstructive) (restrictive) (sporadic) 425.4
  alcoholic 425.5
  amyloid 277.39 *[425.7]* ▲
  beriberi 265.0 *[425.7]*
  cobalt-beer 425.5
  congenital 425.3
  due to
    amyloidosis 277.39 *[425.7]* ▲
    beriberi 265.0 *[425.7]*
    cardiac glycogenosis 271.0 *[425.7]*
    Chagas' disease 086.0
    Friedreich's ataxia 334.0 *[425.8]*
    hypertension — *see* Hypertension, with, heart involvement
    mucopolysaccharidosis 277.5 *[425.7]*
    myotonia atrophica 359.2 *[425.8]*
    progressive muscular dystrophy 359.1 *[425.8]*
    sarcoidosis 135 *[425.8]*
  glycogen storage 271.0 *[425.7]*
  hypertensive — *see* Hypertension, with, heart involvement
  hypertrophic
    nonobstructive 425.4
    obstructive 425.1
      congenital 746.84
  idiopathic (concentric) 425.4
  in
    Chagas' disease 086.0
    sarcoidosis 135 *[425.8]*
  ischemic 414.8
  metabolic NEC 277.9 *[425.7]*
    amyloid 277.39 *[425.7]* ▲
    thyrotoxic (*see also* Thyrotoxicosis) 242.9 ☑ *[425.7]*
    thyrotoxicosis (*see also* Thyrotoxicosis) 242.9 ☑ *[425.7]*
  newborn 425.4
    congenital 425.3
  nutritional 269.9 *[425.7]*
    beriberi 265.0 *[425.7]*
  obscure of Africa 425.2
  peripartum 674.5 ☑
  postpartum 674.5 ☑
  primary 425.4
  secondary 425.9
  stress inuced 429.83 ●
  takotsubo 429.83 ▲
  thyrotoxic (*see also* Thyrotoxicosis) 242.9 ☑ *[425.7]*
  toxic NEC 425.9
  tuberculous (*see also* Tuberculosis) 017.9 ☑ *[425.8]*
Cardionephritis — *see* Hypertension, cardiorenal

Cardionephropathy — *see* Hypertension, cardiorenal
Cardionephrosis — *see* Hypertension, cardiorenal
Cardioneurosis 306.2
Cardiopathia nigra 416.0
Cardiopathy — *see also* Disease, heart 429.9
  hypertensive (*see also* Hypertension, heart) 402.90
  idiopathic 425.4
  mucopolysaccharidosis 277.5 *[425.7]*
Cardiopericarditis — *see also* Pericarditis 423.9
Cardiophobia 300.29
Cardioptosis 746.87
Cardiorenal — *see* condition
Cardiorrhexis — *see also* Infarct, myocardium 410.9 ☑
Cardiosclerosis — *see* Arteriosclerosis, coronary
Cardiosis — *see* Disease, heart
Cardiospasm (esophagus) (reflex) (stomach) 530.0
  congenital 750.7
Cardiostenosis — *see* Disease, heart
Cardiosymphysis 423.1
Cardiothyrotoxicosis — *see* Hyperthyroidism
Cardiovascular — *see* condition
Carditis (acute) (bacterial) (chronic) (subacute) 429.89
  Coxsackie 074.20
  hypertensive (*see also* Hypertension, heart) 402.90
  meningococcal 036.40
  rheumatic — *see* Disease, heart, rheumatic
  rheumatoid 714.2
Care (of)
  child (routine) V20.1
  convalescent following V66.9
    chemotherapy V66.2
    medical NEC V66.5
    psychotherapy V66.3
    radiotherapy V66.1
    surgery V66.0
    surgical NEC V66.0
    treatment (for) V66.5
      combined V66.6
      fracture V66.4
      mental disorder NEC V66.3
      specified type NEC V66.5
  end-of-life V66.7
  family member (handicapped) (sick)
    creating problem for family V61.49
    provided away from home for holiday relief V60.5
    unavailable, due to
      absence (person rendering care) (sufferer) V60.4
      inability (any reason) of person rendering care V60.4
  holiday relief V60.5
  hospice V66.7
  lack of (at or after birth) (infant) (child) 995.52
    adult 995.84
  lactation of mother V24.1
  palliative V66.7
  postpartum
    immediately after delivery V24.0
    routine follow-up V24.2
  prenatal V22.1
    first pregnancy V22.0
    high-risk pregnancy V23.9
      specified problem NEC V23.89
  terminal V66.7
  unavailable, due to
    absence of person rendering care V60.4
    inability (any reason) of person rendering care V60.4
  well baby V20.1
Caries (bone) — *see also* Tuberculosis, bone 015.9 ☑ *[730.8]* ☑

Caries — *see also* Tuberculosis, bone — *continued*
  arrested 521.04
  cementum 521.03
  cerebrospinal (tuberculous) 015.0 ☑ *[730.88]*
  dental (acute) (chronic) (incipient) (infected) 521.00
    with pulp exposure 521.03
    extending to
      dentine 521.02
      pulp 521.03
    other specified NEC 521.09
    pit and fissure 521.06
    primary ●
      pit and fissure origin 521.06 ●
      root surface 521.08 ●
      smooth surface origin 521.07 ●
    root surface 521.08
    smooth surface 521.07
  dentin (acute) (chronic) 521.02
  enamel (acute) (chronic) (incipient) 521.01
  external meatus 380.89
  hip (*see also* Tuberculosis) 015.1 ☑ *[730.85]*
  initial 521.01
  knee 015.2 ☑ *[730.86]*
  labyrinth 386.8
  limb NEC 015.7 ☑ *[730.88]*
  mastoid (chronic) (process) 383.1
  middle ear 385.89
  nose 015.7 ☑ *[730.88]*
  orbit 015.7 ☑ *[730.88]*
  ossicle 385.24
  petrous bone 383.20
  sacrum (tuberculous) 015.0 ☑ *[730.88]*
  spine, spinal (column) (tuberculous) 015.0 ☑ *[730.88]*
  syphilitic 095.5
    congenital 090.0 *[730.8]* ☑
  teeth (internal) 521.00
    initial 521.01
  vertebra (column) (tuberculous) 015.0 ☑ *[730.88]*
Carini's syndrome (ichthyosis congenita) 757.1
Carious teeth 521.00
Carneous mole 631
Carnosinemia 270.5
Carotid body or sinus syndrome 337.0
Carotidynia 337.0
Carotinemia (dietary) 278.3
Carotinosis (cutis) (skin) 278.3
Carpal tunnel syndrome 354.0
Carpenter's syndrome 759.89
Carpopedal spasm — *see also* Tetany 781.7
Carpoptosis 736.05
Carrier (suspected) **of**
  amebiasis V02.2
  bacterial disease (meningococcal, staphylococcal) NEC V02.59
  cholera V02.0
  cystic fibrosis gene V83.81
  defective gene V83.89
  diphtheria V02.4
  dysentery (bacillary) V02.3
    amebic V02.2
  Endamoeba histolytica V02.2
  gastrointestinal pathogens NEC V02.3
  genetic defect V83.89
  gonorrhea V02.7
  group B streptococcus V02.51
  HAA (hepatitis Australian-antigen) V02.61
  hemophilia A (asymptomatic) V83.01
    symptomatic V83.02
  hepatitis V02.60
    Australian-antigen (HAA) V02.61
    B V02.61
    C V02.62
    serum V02.61
    specified type NEC V02.69
    viral V02.60

Carrier (suspected) **of** — *continued*
  infective organism NEC V02.9
  malaria V02.9
  paratyphoid V02.3
  Salmonella V02.3
    typhosa V02.1
  serum hepatitis V02.61
  Shigella V02.3
  Staphylococcus NEC V02.59
  Streptococcus NEC V02.52
    group B V02.51
  typhoid V02.1
  venereal disease NEC V02.8
Carrión's disease (Bartonellosis) 088.0
Car sickness 994.6
Carter's
  relapsing fever (Asiatic) 087.0
Cartilage — *see* condition
Caruncle (inflamed)
  abscess, lacrimal (*see also* Dacryocystitis) 375.30
  conjunctiva 372.00
    acute 372.00
  eyelid 373.00
  labium (majus) (minus) 616.89 ▲
  lacrimal 375.30
  urethra (benign) 599.3
  vagina (wall) 616.89 ▲
Cascade stomach 537.6
Caseation lymphatic gland — *see also* Tuberculosis 017.2 ☑
Caseous
  bronchitis — *see* Tuberculosis, pulmonary
  meningitis 013.0 ☑
  pneumonia — *see* Tuberculosis, pulmonary
Cassidy (-Scholte) syndrome (malignant carcinoid) 259.2
Castellani's bronchitis 104.8
Castleman's tumor or lymphoma (mediastinal lymph node hyperplasia) 785.6
Castration, traumatic 878.2
  complicated 878.3
Casts in urine 791.7
Catalepsy 300.11
  catatonic (acute) (*see also* Schizophrenia) 295.2 ☑
  hysterical 300.11
  schizophrenic (*see also* Schizophrenia) 295.2 ☑
Cataphasia 307.0
Cataplexy (idiopathic) — *see* Narcolepsy
Cataract (anterior cortical) (anterior polar) (black) (capsular) (central) (cortical) (hypermature) (immature) (incipient) (mature) 366.9
  anterior
    and posterior axial embryonal 743.33
    pyramidal 743.31
    subcapsular polar
      infantile, juvenile, or presenile 366.01
      senile 366.13
  associated with
    calcinosis 275.40 *[366.42]*
    craniofacial dysostosis 756.0 *[366.44]*
    galactosemia 271.1 *[366.44]*
    hypoparathyroidism 252.1 *[366.42]*
    myotonic disorders 359.2 *[366.43]*
    neovascularization 366.33
  blue dot 743.39
  cerulean 743.39
  complicated NEC 366.30
  congenital 743.30
    capsular or subcapsular 743.31
    cortical 743.32
    nuclear 743.33
    specified type NEC 743.39
    total or subtotal 743.34
    zonular 743.32
  coronary (congenital) 743.39
    acquired 366.12

☑ Additional Digit Required — Refer to the Tabular List for Digit Selection   ▽ Subterms under main terms may continue to next column or page

2007 ICD-9-CM   ►◄ Revised Text   ● New Line   ▲ Revised Code   **October 2006 • Volume 2 — 45**

Cataract — *continued*
cupuliform 366.14
diabetic 250.5 ☑ *[366.41]*
drug-induced 366.45
due to
  chalcosis 360.24 *[366.34]*
  chronic choroiditis (*see also*
    Choroiditis) 363.20 *[366.32]*
  degenerative myopia
    360.21 *[366.34]*
  glaucoma (*see also* Glaucoma)
    365.9 *[366.31]*
  infection, intraocular NEC 366.32
  inflammatory ocular disorder NEC
    366.32
  iridocyclitis, chronic
    364.10 *[366.33]*
  pigmentary retinal dystrophy
    362.74 *[366.34]*
  radiation 366.46
electric 366.46
glassblowers' 366.46
heat ray 366.46
heterochromic 366.33
in eye disease NEC 366.30
infantile (*see also* Cataract, juvenile)
  366.00
intumescent 366.12
irradiational 366.46
juvenile 366.00
  anterior subcapsular polar 366.01
  combined forms 366.09
  cortical 366.03
  lamellar 366.03
  nuclear 366.04
  posterior subcapsular polar 366.02
  specified NEC 366.09
  zonular 366.03
lamellar 743.32
  infantile, juvenile, or presenile
    366.03
morgagnian 366.18
myotonic 359.2 *[366.43]*
myxedema 244.9 *[366.44]*
nuclear 366.16
posterior, polar (capsular) 743.31
  infantile, juvenile, or presenile
    366.02
  senile 366.14
presenile (*see also* Cataract, juvenile)
  366.00
punctate
  acquired 366.12
  congenital 743.39
secondary (membrane) 366.50
  obscuring vision 366.53
  specified type, not obscuring vision
    366.52
senile 366.10
  anterior subcapsular polar 366.13
  combined forms 366.19
  cortical 366.15
  hypermature 366.18
  immature 366.12
  incipient 366.12
  mature 366.17
  nuclear 366.16
  posterior subcapsular polar 366.14
  specified NEC 366.19
  total or subtotal 366.17
snowflake 250.5 ☑ *[366.41]*
specified NEC 366.8
subtotal (senile) 366.17
  congenital 743.34
sunflower 360.24 *[366.34]*
tetanic NEC 252.1 *[366.42]*
total (mature) (senile) 366.17
  congenital 743.34
  localized 366.21
  traumatic 366.22
toxic 366.45
traumatic 366.20
  partially resolved 366.23
  total 366.22
zonular (perinuclear) 743.32

Cataract — *continued*
zonular — *continued*
  infantile, juvenile, or presenile
    366.03
Cataracta 366.10
brunescens 366.16
cerulea 743.39
complicata 366.30
congenita 743.30
coralliformis 743.39
coronaria (congenital) 743.39
  acquired 366.12
diabetic 250.5 ☑ *[366.41]*
floriformis 360.24 *[366.34]*
membranacea
  accreta 366.50
  congenita 743.39
nigra 366.16
Catarrh, catarrhal (inflammation) — *see
  also* condition 460
acute 460
asthma, asthmatic (*see also* Asthma)
  493.9 ☑
Bostock's (*see also* Fever, hay) 477.9
bowel — *see* Enteritis
bronchial 490
  acute 466.0
  chronic 491.0
  subacute 466.0
cervix, cervical (canal) (uteri) — *see*
  Cervicitis
chest (*see also* Bronchitis) 490
chronic 472.0
congestion 472.0
conjunctivitis 372.03
due to syphilis 095.9
  congenital 090.0
enteric — *see* Enteritis
epidemic 487.1
Eustachian 381.50
eye (acute) (vernal) 372.03
fauces (*see also* Pharyngitis) 462
febrile 460
fibrinous acute 466.0
gastroenteric — *see* Enteritis
gastrointestinal — *see* Enteritis
gingivitis 523.00 ▲
hay (*see also* Fever, hay) 477.9
infectious 460
intestinal — *see* Enteritis
larynx (*see also* Laryngitis, chronic)
  476.0
liver 070.1
  with hepatic coma 070.0
lung (*see also* Bronchitis) 490
  acute 466.0
  chronic 491.0
middle ear (chronic) — *see* Otitis media, chronic
mouth 528.00 ▲
nasal (chronic) (*see also* Rhinitis)
  472.0
  acute 460
nasobronchial 472.2
nasopharyngeal (chronic) 472.2
  acute 460
nose — *see* Catarrh, nasal
ophthalmia 372.03
pneumococcal, acute 466.0
pulmonary (*see also* Bronchitis) 490
  acute 466.0
  chronic 491.0
spring (eye) 372.13
suffocating (*see also* Asthma) 493.9 ☑
summer (hay) (*see also* Fever, hay)
  477.9
throat 472.1
tracheitis 464.10
  with obstruction 464.11
tubotympanal 381.4
  acute (*see also* Otitis media, acute,
    nonsuppurative) 381.00
  chronic 381.10
vasomotor (*see also* Fever, hay) 477.9
vesical (bladder) — *see* Cystitis

Catarrhus aestivus — *see also* Fever,
  hay 477.9
Catastrophe, cerebral — *see also* Disease, cerebrovascular, acute 436
Catatonia, catatonic (acute) 781.99
with
  affective psychosis — *see* Psy-
    chosis, affective
  agitation 295.2 ☑
  dementia (praecox) 295.2 ☑
  due to or associated with physical
    condition 293.89
  excitation 295.2 ☑
  excited type 295.2 ☑
  in conditions classified elsewhere
    293.89
  schizophrenia 295.2 ☑
  stupor 295.2 ☑
Cat's ear 744.29
Cat-scratch — *see also* Injury, superficial
disease or fever 078.3
Cauda equina — *see also* condition
syndrome 344.60
Cauliflower ear 738.7
Caul over face 768.9
Causalgia 355.9
lower limb 355.71
upper limb 354.4
Cause
external, general effects NEC 994.9
not stated 799.9
unknown 799.9
Caustic burn — *see also* Burn, by site
from swallowing caustic or corrosive
  substance — *see* Burn, internal
  organs
Cavare's disease (familial periodic
  paralysis) 359.3
Cave-in, injury
crushing (severe) (*see also* Crush, by
  site) 869.1
suffocation 994.7
Cavernitis (penis) 607.2
lymph vessel — *see* Lymphangioma
Cavernositis 607.2
Cavernous — *see* condition
Cavitation of lung — *see also* Tuberculosis 011.2 ☑
  nontuberculous 518.89
  primary, progressive 010.8 ☑
Cavity
lung — *see* Cavitation of lung
optic papilla 743.57
pulmonary — *see* Cavitation of lung
teeth 521.00
vitreous (humor) 379.21
Cavovarus foot, congenital 754.59
Cavus foot (congenital) 754.71
  acquired 736.73
Cazenave's
disease (pemphigus) NEC 694.4
lupus (erythematosus) 695.4
CDGS (carbohydrate-deficient glycoprotein syndrome) 271.8
Cecitis — *see* Appendicitis
Cecocele — *see* Hernia
Cecum — *see* condition
Celiac
artery compression syndrome 447.4
disease 579.0
infantilism 579.0
Cell, cellular — *see also* condition
anterior chamber (eye) (positive aqueous ray) 364.04
Cellulitis (diffuse) (with lymphangitis) —
  see also Abscess 682.9
abdominal wall 682.2
anaerobic (*see also* Gas gangrene)
  040.0
ankle 682.6
anus 566
areola 611.0
arm (any part, above wrist) 682.3
auditory canal (external) 380.10
axilla 682.3

Cellulitis — *see also* Abscess —
  continued
back (any part) 682.2
breast 611.0
  postpartum 675.1 ☑
broad ligament (*see also* Disease,
  pelvis, inflammatory) 614.4
  acute 614.3
buttock 682.5
cervical (neck region) 682.1
cervix (uteri) (*see also* Cervicitis) 616.0
cheek, external 682.0
  internal 528.3
chest wall 682.2
chronic NEC 682.9
colostomy 569.61
corpus cavernosum 607.2
digit 681.9
Douglas' cul-de-sac or pouch (chronic)
  (*see also* Disease, pelvis, inflammatory) 614.4
  acute 614.3
drainage site (following operation)
  998.59
ear, external 380.10
enterostomy 569.61
erysipelar (*see also* Erysipelas) 035
esophagostomy 530.86
eyelid 373.13
face (any part, except eye) 682.0
finger (intrathecal) (periosteal) (subcutaneous) (subcuticular) 681.00
flank 682.2
foot (except toe) 682.7
forearm 682.3
gangrenous (*see also* Gangrene) 785.4
genital organ NEC
  female (*see also* Abscess, genital or-
    gan, female
    male 608.4
glottis 478.71
gluteal (region) 682.5
gonococcal NEC 098.0
groin 682.2
hand (except finger or thumb) 682.4
head (except face) NEC 682.8
heel 682.7
hip 682.6
jaw (region) 682.0
knee 682.6
labium (majus) (minus) (*see also* Vulvitis) 616.10
larynx 478.71
leg, except foot 682.6
lip 528.5
mammary gland 611.0
mouth (floor) 528.3
multiple sites NEC 682.9
nasopharynx 478.21
navel 682.2
  newborn NEC 771.4
neck (region) 682.1
nipple 611.0
nose 478.19   ▲
  external 682.0
orbit, orbital 376.01
palate (soft) 528.3
pectoral (region) 682.2
pelvis, pelvic
with
  abortion — *see* Abortion, by
    type, with sepsis
  ectopic pregnancy (*see also* cat-
    egories 633.0–633.9)
    639.0
  molar pregnancy (*see also* cate-
    gories 630–632) 639.0
female (*see also* Disease, pelvis,
  inflammatory) 614.4
  acute 614.3
following
  abortion 639.0
  ectopic or molar pregnancy
    639.0
male 567.21

☑ Additional Digit Required — Refer to the Tabular List for Digit Selection   ▽ Subterms under main terms may continue to next column or page

46 — Volume 2 · October 2006   ▶◀ Revised Text   ● New Line   ▲ Revised Code   **2007 ICD-9-CM**

Cellulitis — see also Abscess — continued
pelvis, pelvic — continued
  puerperal, postpartum, childbirth 670.0 ☑
penis 607.2
perineal, perineum 682.2
perirectal 566
peritonsillar 475
periurethral 597.0
periuterine (see also Disease, pelvis, inflammatory) 614.4
  acute 614.3
pharynx 478.21
phlegmonous NEC 682.9
rectum 566
retromammary 611.0
retroperitoneal (see also Peritonitis) 567.38
round ligament (see also Disease, pelvis, inflammatory) 614.4
  acute 614.3
scalp (any part) 682.8
  dissecting 704.8
scrotum 608.4
seminal vesicle 608.0
septic NEC 682.9
shoulder 682.3
specified sites NEC 682.8
spermatic cord 608.4
submandibular (region) (space) (triangle) 682.0
  gland 527.3
submaxillary 528.3
  gland 527.3
submental (pyogenic) 682.0
  gland 527.3
suppurative NEC 682.9
testis 608.4
thigh 682.6
thumb (intrathecal) (periosteal) (subcutaneous) (subcuticular) 681.00
toe (intrathecal) (periosteal) (subcutaneous) (subcuticular) 681.10
tonsil 475
trunk 682.2
tuberculous (primary) (see also Tuberculosis) 017.0 ☑
tunica vaginalis 608.4
umbilical 682.2
  newborn NEC 771.4
vaccinal 999.3
vagina — see Vaginitis
vas deferens 608.4
vocal cords 478.5
vulva (see also Vulvitis) 616.10
wrist 682.4
Cementoblastoma, benign (M9273/0) 213.1
upper jaw (bone) 213.0
Cementoma (M9273/0) 213.1
gigantiform (M9276/0) 213.1
  upper jaw (bone) 213.0
upper jaw (bone) 213.0
Cementoperiostitis 523.40 ▲
Cephalgia, cephalalgia — see also Headache 784.0
histamine 346.2 ☑
nonorganic origin 307.81
psychogenic 307.81
tension 307.81
Cephalhematocele, cephalematocele
due to birth injury 767.19
fetus or newborn 767.19
traumatic (see also Contusion, head) 920
Cephalhematoma, cephalematoma (calcified)
due to birth injury 767.19
fetus or newborn 767.19
traumatic (see also Contusion, head) 920
Cephalic — see condition
Cephalitis — see Encephalitis
Cephalocele 742.0

Cephaloma — see Neoplasm, by site, malignant
Cephalomenia 625.8
Cephalopelvic — see condition
Cercomoniasis 007.3
Cerebellitis — see Encephalitis
Cerebellum (cerebellar) — see condition
Cerebral — see condition
Cerebritis — see Encephalitis
Cerebrohepatorenal syndrome 759.89
Cerebromacular degeneration 330.1
Cerebromalacia — see also Softening, brain 434.9 ☑
Cerebrosidosis 272.7
Cerebrospasticity — see Palsy, cerebral
Cerebrospinal — see condition
Cerebrum — see condition
Ceroid storage disease 272.7
Cerumen (accumulation) (impacted) 380.4
Cervical — see also condition
auricle 744.43
high risk human papillomavirus (HPV) DNA test positive 795.05
intraepithelial glandular neoplasia ● 233.1 ●
low risk human papillomavirus (HPV) DNA test positive 795.09
rib 756.2
Cervicalgia 723.1
Cervicitis (acute) (chronic) (nonvenereal) (subacute) (with erosion or ectropion) 616.0
with
  abortion — see Abortion, by type, with sepsis
  ectopic pregnancy (see also categories 633.0–633.9) 639.0
  molar pregnancy (see also categories 630–632) 639.0
  ulceration 616.0
chlamydial 099.53
complicating pregnancy or puerperium 646.6 ☑
  affecting fetus or newborn 760.8
following
  abortion 639.0
  ectopic or molar pregnancy 639.0
gonococcal (acute) 098.15
  chronic or duration of 2 months or more 098.35
senile (atrophic) 616.0
syphilitic 095.8
trichomonal 131.09
tuberculous (see also Tuberculosis) 016.7 ☑
Cervicoaural fistula 744.49
Cervicocolpitis (emphysematosa) — see also Cervicitis 616.0
Cervix — see condition
Cesarean delivery, operation or section NEC 669.7 ☑
affecting fetus or newborn 763.4
post mortem, affecting fetus or newborn 761.6
previous, affecting management of pregnancy 654.2 ☑
Céstan-Chenais paralysis 344.89
Céstan-Raymond syndrome 433.8 ☑
Céstan's syndrome 344.89
Cestode infestation NEC 123.9
specified type NEC 123.8
Cestodiasis 123.9
CGF (congenital generalized fibromatosis) 759.89 ●
Chabert's disease 022.9
Chacaleh 266.2
Chafing 709.8
Chagas' disease — see also Trypanosomiasis, American 086.2
with heart involvement 086.0
Chagres fever 084.0
Chalasia (cardiac sphincter) 530.81
Chalazion 373.2
Chalazoderma 757.39
Chalcosis 360.24

Chalcosis — continued
cornea 371.15
crystalline lens 360.24 [366.34]
retina 360.24
Chalicosis (occupational) (pulmonum) 502
Chancre (any genital site) (hard) (indurated) (infecting) (primary) (recurrent) 091.0
congenital 090.0
conjunctiva 091.2
Ducrey's 099.0
extragenital 091.2
eyelid 091.2
Hunterian 091.0
lip (syphilis) 091.2
mixed 099.8
nipple 091.2
Nisbet's 099.0
of
  carate 103.0
  pinta 103.0
  yaws 102.0
palate, soft 091.2
phagedenic 099.0
Ricord's 091.0
Rollet's (syphilitic) 091.0
seronegative 091.0
seropositive 091.0
simple 099.0
soft 099.0
  bubo 099.0
  urethra 091.0
  yaws 102.0
Chancriform syndrome 114.1
Chancroid 099.0
anus 099.0
penis (Ducrey's bacillus) 099.0
perineum 099.0
rectum 099.0
scrotum 099.0
urethra 099.0
vulva 099.0
Chandipura fever 066.8
Chandler's disease (osteochondritis dissecans, hip) 732.7
Change(s) (of) — see also Removal of
arteriosclerotic — see Arteriosclerosis
battery
  cardiac pacemaker V53.31
bone 733.90
  diabetic 250.8 ☑ [731.8]
  in disease, unknown cause 733.90
bowel habits 787.99
cardiorenal (vascular) (see also Hypertension, cardiorenal) 404.90
cardiovascular — see Disease, cardiovascular
circulatory 459.9
cognitive or personality change of other type, nonpsychotic 310.1
color, teeth, tooth
  during formation 520.8
  extrinsic 523.6
  intrinsic posteruptive 521.7
contraceptive device V25.42
cornea, corneal
  degenerative NEC 371.40
  membrane NEC 371.30
  senile 371.41
coronary (see also Ischemia, heart) 414.9
degenerative
  chamber angle (anterior) (iris) 364.56
  ciliary body 364.57
  spine or vertebra (see also Spondylosis) 721.90
dental pulp, regressive 522.2
drains V58.49
dressing
  wound V58.30 ●
    nonsurgical V58.30 ●
    surgical V58.31 ●
fixation device V54.89
  external V54.89

Change(s) — see also Removal of — continued
fixation device — continued
  internal V54.01
heart (see also Disease, heart)
hip joint 718.95
hyperplastic larynx 478.79
hypertrophic
  nasal sinus (see also Sinusitis) 473.9
  turbinate, nasal 478.0
  upper respiratory tract 478.9
inflammatory — see Inflammation
joint (see also Derangement, joint) 718.90
  sacroiliac 724.6
Kirschner wire V54.89
knee 717.9
macular, congenital 743.55
malignant (M — — /3) (see also Neoplasm, by site, malignant)

> Note — for malignant change occurring in a neoplasm, use the appropriate M code with behavior digit /3 e.g., malignant change in uterine fibroid — M8890/3. For malignant change occurring in a nonneoplastic condition (e.g., gastric ulcer) use the M code M8000/3.

mental (status) NEC 780.97 ▲
  due to or associated with physical condition — see Syndrome, brain
myocardium, myocardial — see Degeneration, myocardial
of life (see also Menopause) 627.2
pacemaker battery (cardiac) V53.31
peripheral nerve 355.9
personality (nonpsychotic) NEC 310.1
plaster cast V54.89
refractive, transient 367.81
regressive, dental pulp 522.2
retina 362.9
  myopic (degenerative) (malignant) 360.21
  vascular appearance 362.13
sacroiliac joint 724.6
scleral 379.19
  degenerative 379.16
senile (see also Senility) 797
sensory (see also Disturbance, sensation) 782.0
skin texture 782.8
spinal cord 336.9
splint, external V54.89
subdermal implantable contraceptive V25.5
suture V58.32 ▲
traction device V54.89
trophic 355.9
  arm NEC 354.9
  leg NEC 355.8
  lower extremity NEC 355.8
  upper extremity NEC 354.9
vascular 459.9
vasomotor 443.9
voice 784.49
  psychogenic 306.1
wound packing V58.30 ●
  nonsurgical V58.30 ●
  surgical V58.31 ●
Changing sleep-work schedule, affecting sleep 327.36
Changuinola fever 066.0
Chapping skin 709.8
Character
depressive 301.12
Charcôt's
arthropathy 094.0 [713.5]
cirrhosis — see Cirrhosis, biliary
disease 094.0
  spinal cord 094.0
fever (biliary) (hepatic) (intermittent) — see Choledocholithiasis
joint (disease) 094.0 [713.5]
  diabetic 250.6 ☑ [713.5]
  syringomyelic 336.0 [713.5]

☑ Additional Digit Required — Refer to the Tabular List for Digit Selection   ▽ Subterms under main terms may continue to next column or page

2007 ICD-9-CM   ▶◀ Revised Text   ● New Line   ▲ Revised Code   October 2006 • Volume 2 — 47

Charcôt's — continued
  syndrome (intermittent claudication) 443.9
    due to atherosclerosis 440.21
Charcôt-Marie-Tooth disease, paralysis, or syndrome 356.1
CHARGE association (syndrome) 759.89
Charleyhorse (quadriceps) 843.8
  muscle, except quadriceps — see Sprain, by site
Charlouis' disease — see also Yaws 102.9
Chauffeur's fracture — see Fracture, ulna, lower end
Cheadle (-Möller) (-Barlow) disease or syndrome (infantile scurvy) 267
Checking (of)
  contraceptive device (intrauterine) V25.42
  device
    fixation V54.89
      external V54.89
      internal V54.09
    traction V54.89
    Kirschner wire V54.89
    plaster cast V54.89
    splint, external V54.89
Checkup
  following treatment — see Examination
  health V70.0
  infant (not sick) V20.2
  newborn, routine ●
    initial V20.2 ●
    subsequent V20.2 ●
  pregnancy (normal) V22.1
    first V22.0
    high-risk pregnancy V23.9
      specified problem NEC V23.89
Chédiak-Higashi (-Steinbrinck) anomaly, disease, or syndrome (congenital gigantism of peroxidase granules) 288.2
Cheek — see also condition
  biting 528.9
Cheese itch 133.8
Cheese washers' lung 495.8
Cheilitis 528.5
  actinic (due to sun) 692.72
    chronic NEC 692.74
      due to radiation, except from sun 692.82
    due to radiation, except from sun 692.82
  acute 528.5
  angular 528.5
  catarrhal 528.5
  chronic 528.5
  exfoliative 528.5
  gangrenous 528.5
  glandularis apostematosa 528.5
  granulomatosa 351.8
  infectional 528.5
  membranous 528.5
  Miescher's 351.8
  suppurative 528.5
  ulcerative 528.5
  vesicular 528.5
Cheilodynia 528.5
Cheilopalatoschisis — see also Cleft, palate, with cleft lip 749.20
Cheilophagia 528.9
Cheiloschisis — see also Cleft, lip 749.10
Cheilosis 528.5
  with pellagra 265.2
  angular 528.5
  due to
    dietary deficiency 266.0
    vitamin deficiency 266.0
Cheiromegaly 729.89
Cheiropompholyx 705.81
Cheloid — see also Keloid 701.4
Chemical burn — see also Burn, by site
  from swallowing chemical — see Burn, internal organs

Chemodectoma (M8693/1) — see Paraganglioma, nonchromaffin
Chemoprophylaxis NEC V07.39
Chemosis, conjunctiva 372.73
Chemotherapy
  convalescence V66.2
  encounter (for) V58.11
  maintenance V58.11
  prophylactic NEC V07.39
    fluoride V07.31
Cherubism 526.89
Chest — see condition
Cheyne-Stokes respiration (periodic) 786.04
Chiari's
  disease or syndrome (hepatic vein thrombosis) 453.0
  malformation
    type I 348.4
    type II (see also Spina bifida) 741.0 ☑
    type III 742.0
    type IV 742.2
  network 746.89
Chiari-Frommel syndrome 676.6 ☑
Chicago disease (North American blastomycosis) 116.0
Chickenpox — see also Varicella 052.9
  exposure to V01.71
  vaccination and inoculation (prophylactic) V05.4
Chiclero ulcer 085.4
Chiggers 133.8 ●
Chignon 111.2 ●
  fetus or newborn (from vacuum extraction) 767.19
Chigoe disease 134.1
Chikungunya fever 066.3
Chilaiditi's syndrome (subphrenic displacement, colon) 751.4
Chilblains 991.5
  lupus 991.5
Child
  behavior causing concern V61.20
Childbed fever 670.0 ☑
Childbirth — see also Delivery
  puerperal complications — see Puerperal
Childhood, period of rapid growth V21.0
Chill(s) 780.99
  with fever 780.6
  congestive 780.99
    in malarial regions 084.6
  septic — see Septicemia
  urethral 599.84
Chilomastigiasis 007.8
Chin — see condition
Chinese dysentery 004.9
Chiropractic dislocation — see also Lesion, nonallopathic, by site 739.9
Chitral fever 066.0
Chlamydia, chlamydial — see condition
Chloasma 709.09
  cachecticorum 709.09
  eyelid 374.52
    congenital 757.33
    hyperthyroid 242.0 ☑
  gravidarum 646.8 ☑
  idiopathic 709.09
  skin 709.09
  symptomatic 709.09
Chloroma (M9930/3) 205.3 ☑
Chlorosis 280.9
  Egyptian (see also Ancylostomiasis) 126.9
  miners' (see also Ancylostomiasis) 126.9
Chlorotic anemia 280.9
Chocolate cyst (ovary) 617.1
Choked
  disk or disc — see Papilledema
  on food, phlegm, or vomitus NEC (see also Asphyxia, food) 933.1
  phlegm 933.1

Choked — continued
  while vomiting NEC (see also Asphyxia, food) 933.1
Chokes (resulting from bends) 993.3
Choking sensation 784.99 ▲
Cholangiectasis — see also Disease, gallbladder 575.8
Cholangiocarcinoma (M8160/3)
  and hepatocellular carcinoma, combined (M8180/3) 155.0
  liver 155.1
  specified site NEC — see Neoplasm, by site, malignant
  unspecified site 155.1
Cholangiohepatitis 575.8
  due to fluke infestation 121.1
Cholangiohepatoma (M8180/3) 155.0
Cholangiolitis (acute) (chronic) (extrahepatic) (gangrenous) 576.1
  intrahepatic 575.8
  paratyphoidal (see also Fever, paratyphoid) 002.9
  typhoidal 002.0
Cholangioma (M8160/0) 211.5
  malignant — see Cholangiocarcinoma
Cholangitis (acute) (ascending) (catarrhal) (chronic) (infective) (malignant) (primary) (recurrent) (sclerosing) (secondary) (stenosing) (suppurative) 576.1
  chronic nonsuppurative destructive 571.6
  nonsuppurative destructive (chronic) 571.6
Cholecystdocholithiasis — see Choledocholithiasis
Cholecystitis 575.10
  with
    calculus, stones in
      bile duct (common) (hepatic) — see Choledocholithiasis
      gallbladder — see Cholelithiasis
  acute 575.0
  acute and chronic 575.12
  chronic 575.11
  emphysematous (acute) (see also Cholecystitis, acute) 575.0
  gangrenous (see also Cholecystitis, acute) 575.0
  paratyphoidal, current (see also Fever, paratyphoid) 002.9
  suppurative (see also Cholecystitis, acute) 575.0
  typhoidal 002.0
Choledochitis (suppurative) 576.1
Choledocholith — see Choledocholithiasis
Choledocholithiasis 574.5 ☑

Note — Use the following fifth-digit subclassification with category 574:
  0   without mention of obstruction
  1   with obstruction

  with
    cholecystitis 574.4 ☑
      acute 574.3 ☑
      chronic 574.4 ☑
    cholelithiasis 574.9 ☑
      with
        cholecystitis 574.7 ☑
          acute 574.6 ☑
          and chronic 574.8 ☑
          chronic 574.7 ☑
Cholelithiasis (impacted) (multiple) 574.2 ☑

Note — Use the following fifth-digit subclassification with category 574:
  0   without mention of obstruction
  1   with obstruction

  with
    cholecystitis 574.1 ☑
      acute 574.0 ☑
      chronic 574.1 ☑

Cholelithiasis — continued
  with — continued
    choledocholithiasis 574.9 ☑
      with
        cholecystitis 574.7 ☑
          acute 574.6 ☑
          and chronic 574.8 ☑
          chronic cholecystitis 574.7 ☑
Cholemia — see also Jaundice 782.4
  familial 277.4
  Gilbert's (familial nonhemolytic) 277.4
Cholemic gallstone — see Cholelithiasis
Choleperitoneum, choleperitonitis — see also Disease, gallbladder 567.81
Cholera (algid) (Asiatic) (asphyctic) (epidemic) (gravis) (Indian) (malignant) (morbus) (pestilential) (spasmodic) 001.9
  antimonial 985.4
  carrier (suspected) of V02.0
  classical 001.0
  contact V01.0
  due to
    Vibrio
      cholerae (Inaba, Ogawa, Hikojima serotypes) 001.0
      El Tor 001.1
  El Tor 001.1
  exposure to V01.0
  vaccination, prophylactic (against) V03.0
Cholerine — see also Cholera 001.9
Cholestasis 576.8
  due to total parenteral nutrition (TPN) 573.8 ●
Cholesteatoma (ear) 385.30
  attic (primary) 385.31
  diffuse 385.35
  external ear (canal) 380.21
  marginal (middle ear) 385.32
    with involvement of mastoid cavity 385.33
    secondary (with middle ear involvement) 385.33
  mastoid cavity 385.30
  middle ear (secondary) 385.32
    with involvement of mastoid cavity 385.33
  postmastoidectomy cavity (recurrent) 383.32
  primary 385.31
  recurrent, postmastoidectomy cavity 383.32
  secondary (middle ear) 385.32
    with involvement of mastoid cavity 385.33
Cholesteatosis (middle ear) — see also Cholesteatoma 385.30
  diffuse 385.35
Cholesteremia 272.0
Cholesterin
  granuloma, middle ear 385.82
  in vitreous 379.22
Cholesterol
  deposit
    retina 362.82
    vitreous 379.22
  imbibition of gallbladder (see also Disease, gallbladder) 575.6
Cholesterolemia 272.0
  essential 272.0
  familial 272.0
  hereditary 272.0
Cholesterosis, cholesterolosis (gallbladder) 575.6
  with
    cholecystitis — see Cholecystitis
    cholelithiasis — see Cholelithiasis
  middle ear (see also Cholesteatoma) 385.30
Cholocolic fistula — see also Fistula, gallbladder 575.5
Choluria 791.4
Chondritis (purulent) 733.99

☑ Additional Digit Required — Refer to the Tabular List for Digit Selection   ▼ Subterms under main terms may continue to next column or page

48 — Volume 2 • October 2006   ▶◀ Revised Text   ● New Line   ▲ Revised Code   **2007 ICD-9-CM**

Chondritis — *continued*
auricle 380.03
costal 733.6
Tietze's 733.6
patella, posttraumatic 717.7
pinna 380.03
posttraumatica patellae 717.7
tuberculous (active) (*see also* Tuberculosis) 015.9 ☑
intervertebral 015.0 ☑ *[730.88]*
Chondroangiopathia calcarea seu punctate 756.59
Chondroblastoma (M9230/0) — *see also* Neoplasm, bone, benign
malignant (M9230/3) — *see* Neoplasm, bone, malignant
Chondrocalcinosis (articular) (crystal deposition) (dihydrate) — *see also* Arthritis, due to, crystals 275.49 *[712.3]* ☑
due to
calcium pyrophosphate 275.49 *[712.2]* ☑
dicalcium phosphate crystals 275.49 *[712.1]* ☑
pyrophosphate crystals 275.49 *[712.2]* ☑
Chondrodermatitis nodularis helicis 380.00
Chondrodysplasia 756.4
angiomatose 756.4
calcificans congenita 756.59
epiphysialis punctata 756.59
hereditary deforming 756.4
rhizomelic punctata 277.86
Chondrodystrophia (fetalis) 756.4
calcarea 756.4
calcificans congenita 756.59
fetalis hypoplastica 756.59
hypoplastica calcinosa 756.59
punctata 756.59
tarda 277.5
Chondrodystrophy (familial) (hypoplastic) 756.4
Chondroectodermal dysplasia 756.55
Chondrolysis 733.99
Chondroma (M9220/0) — *see also* Neoplasm cartilage, benign
juxtacortical (M9221/0) — *see* Neoplasm, bone, benign
periosteal (M9221/0) — *see* Neoplasm, bone, benign
Chondromalacia 733.92
epiglottis (congenital) 748.3
generalized 733.92
knee 717.7
larynx (congenital) 748.3
localized, except patella 733.92
patella, patellae 717.7
systemic 733.92
tibial plateau 733.92
trachea (congenital) 748.3
Chondromatosis (M9220/1) — *see* Neoplasm, cartilage, uncertain behavior
Chondromyxosarcoma (M9220/3) — *see* Neoplasm, cartilage, malignant
Chondro-osteodysplasia (Morquio-Brailsford type) 277.5
Chondro-osteodystrophy 277.5
Chondro-osteoma (M9210/0) — *see* Neoplasm, bone, benign
Chondropathia tuberosa 733.6
Chondrosarcoma (M9220/3) — *see also* Neoplasm, cartilage, malignant
juxtacortical (M9221/3) — *see* Neoplasm, bone, malignant
mesenchymal (M9240/3) — *see* Neoplasm, connective tissue, malignant
Chordae tendineae rupture (chronic) 429.5
Chordee (nonvenereal) 607.89
congenital 752.63
gonococcal 098.2

Chorditis (fibrinous) (nodosa) (tuberosa) 478.5
Chordoma (M9370/3) — *see* Neoplasm, by site, malignant
Chorea (gravis) (minor) (spasmodic) 333.5
with
heart involvement — *see* Chorea with rheumatic heart disease
rheumatic heart disease (chronic, inactive, or quiescent) (conditions classifiable to 393–398) (*see* rheumatic heart condition involved)
active or acute (conditions classifiable to 391) 392.0
acute — *see* Chorea, Sydenham's
apoplectic (*see also* Disease, cerebrovascular, acute) 436
chronic 333.4
electric 049.8
gravidarum — *see* Eclampsia, pregnancy
habit 307.22
hereditary 333.4
Huntington's 333.4
posthemiplegic 344.89
pregnancy — *see* Eclampsia, pregnancy
progressive 333.4
chronic 333.4
hereditary 333.4
rheumatic (chronic) 392.9
with heart disease or involvement — *see* Chorea, with rheumatic heart disease
senile 333.5
Sydenham's 392.9
with heart involvement — *see* Chorea, with rheumatic heart disease
nonrheumatic 333.5
variabilis 307.23
Choreoathetosis (paroxysmal) 333.5
Chorioadenoma (destruens) (M9100/1) 236.1
Chorioamnionitis 658.4 ☑
affecting fetus or newborn 762.7
Chorioangioma (M9120/0) 219.8
Choriocarcinoma (M9100/3)
combined with
embryonal carcinoma (M9101/3) — *see* Neoplasm, by site, malignant
teratoma (M9101/3) — *see* Neoplasm, by site, malignant
specified site — *see* Neoplasm, by site, malignant
unspecified site
female 181
male 186.9
Chorioencephalitis, lymphocytic (acute) (serous) 049.0
Chorioepithelioma (M9100/3) — *see* Choriocarcinoma
Choriomeningitis (acute) (benign) (lymphocytic) (serous) 049.0
Chorionepithelioma (M9100/3) — *see* Choriocarcinoma
Chorionitis — *see also* Scleroderma 710.1
Chorioretinitis 363.20
disseminated 363.10
generalized 363.13
in
neurosyphilis 094.83
secondary syphilis 091.51
peripheral 363.12
posterior pole 363.11
tuberculous (*see also* Tuberculosis) 017.3 ☑ *[363.13]*
due to
histoplasmosis (*see also* Histoplasmosis) 115.92
toxoplasmosis (acquired) 130.2
congenital (active) 771.2
focal 363.00

Chorioretinitis — *continued*
focal — *continued*
juxtapapillary 363.01
peripheral 363.04
posterior pole NEC 363.03
juxtapapillaris, juxtapapillary 363.01
progressive myopia (degeneration) 360.21
syphilitic (secondary) 091.51
congenital (early) 090.0 *[363.13]*
late 090.5 *[363.13]*
late 095.8 *[363.13]*
tuberculous (*see also* Tuberculosis) 017.3 ☑ *[363.13]*
Choristoma — *see* Neoplasm, by site, benign
Choroid — *see* condition
Choroideremia, choroidermia (initial stage) (late stage) (partial or total atrophy) 363.55
Choroiditis — *see also* Chorioretinitis 363.20
leprous 030.9 *[363.13]*
senile guttate 363.41
sympathetic 360.11
syphilitic (secondary) 091.51
congenital (early) 090.0 *[363.13]*
late 090.5 *[363.13]*
late 095.8 *[363.13]*
Tay's 363.41
tuberculous (*see also* Tuberculosis) 017.3 ☑ *[363.13]*
Choroidopathy NEC 363.9
degenerative (*see also* Degeneration, choroid) 363.40
hereditary (*see also* Dystrophy, choroid) 363.50
specified type NEC 363.8
Choroidoretinitis — *see* Chorioretinitis
Choroidosis, central serous 362.41
Choroidretinopathy, serous 362.41
Christian's syndrome (chronic histiocytosis X) 277.89
Christian-Weber disease (nodular nonsuppurative panniculitis) 729.30
Christmas disease 286.1
Chromaffinoma (M8700/0) — *see also* Neoplasm, by site, benign
malignant (M8700/3) — *see* Neoplasm, by site, malignant
Chromatopsia 368.59
Chromhidrosis, chromidrosis 705.89
Chromoblastomycosis 117.2
Chromomycosis 117.2
Chromophytosis 111.0
Chromotrichomycosis 111.8
Chronic — *see* condition
Churg-Strauss syndrome 446.4
Chyle cyst, mesentery 457.8
Chylocele (nonfilarial) 457.8
filarial (*see also* Infestation, filarial) 125.9
tunica vaginalis (nonfilarial) 608.84
filarial (*see also* Infestation, filarial) 125.9
Chylomicronemia (fasting) (with hyperprebetalipoproteinemia) 272.3
Chylopericardium (acute) 420.90
Chylothorax (nonfilarial) 457.8
filarial (*see also* Infestation, filarial) 125.9
Chylous
ascites 457.8
cyst of peritoneum 457.8
hydrocele 603.9
hydrothorax (nonfilarial) 457.8
filarial (*see also* Infestation, filarial) 125.9
Chyluria 791.1
bilharziasis 120.0
due to
Brugia (malayi) 125.1
Wuchereria (bancrofti) 125.0
malayi 125.1
filarial (*see also* Infestation, filarial) 125.9

Chyluria — *continued*
filariasis (*see also* Infestation, filarial) 125.9
nonfilarial 791.1
Cicatricial (deformity) — *see* Cicatrix
Cicatrix (adherent) (contracted) (painful) (vicious) 709.2
adenoid 474.8
alveolar process 525.8
anus 569.49
auricle 380.89
bile duct (*see also* Disease, biliary) 576.8
bladder 596.8
bone 733.99
brain 348.8
cervix (postoperative) (postpartal) 622.3
in pregnancy or childbirth 654.6 ☑
causing obstructed labor 660.2 ☑
chorioretinal 363.30
disseminated 363.35
macular 363.32
peripheral 363.34
posterior pole NEC 363.33
choroid — *see* Cicatrix, chorioretinal
common duct (*see also* Disease, biliary) 576.8
congenital 757.39
conjunctiva 372.64
cornea 371.00
tuberculous (*see also* Tuberculosis) 017.3 ☑ *[371.05]*
duodenum (bulb) 537.3
esophagus 530.3
eyelid 374.46
with
ectropion — *see* Ectropion
entropion — *see* Entropion
hypopharynx 478.29
knee, semilunar cartilage 717.5
lacrimal
canaliculi 375.53
duct
acquired 375.56
neonatal 375.55
punctum 375.52
sac 375.54
larynx 478.79
limbus (cystoid) 372.64
lung 518.89
macular 363.32
disseminated 363.35
peripheral 363.34
middle ear 385.89
mouth 528.9
muscle 728.89
nasolacrimal duct
acquired 375.56
neonatal 375.55
nasopharynx 478.29
palate (soft) 528.9
penis 607.89
prostate 602.8
rectum 569.49
retina 363.30
disseminated 363.35
macular 363.32
peripheral 363.34
posterior pole NEC 363.33
semilunar cartilage — *see* Derangement, meniscus
seminal vesicle 608.89
skin 709.2
infected 686.8
postinfectional 709.2
tuberculous (*see also* Tuberculosis) 017.0 ☑
specified site NEC 709.2
throat 478.29
tongue 529.8
tonsil (and adenoid) 474.8
trachea 478.9
tuberculous NEC (*see also* Tuberculosis) 011.9 ☑

☑ Additional Digit Required — Refer to the Tabular List for Digit Selection   ꜛ Subterms under main terms may continue to next column or page

2007 ICD-9-CM   ▶◀ Revised Text   ● New Line   ▲ Revised Code   **Volume 2 — 49**

Cicatrix — *continued*
- ureter 593.89
- urethra 599.84
- uterus 621.8
- vagina 623.4
  - in pregnancy or childbirth 654.7 ☑
    - causing obstructed labor 660.2 ☑
  - vocal cord 478.5
- wrist, constricting (annular) 709.2

CIN I [cervical intraepithelial neoplasia I] 622.11

CIN II [cervical intraepithelial neoplasia II] 622.12

CIN III [cervical intraepithelial neoplasia III] 233.1

Cinchonism
- correct substance properly administered 386.9
- overdose or wrong substance given or taken 961.4

Circine herpes 110.5

Circle of Willis — *see* condition

Circular — *see also* condition
- hymen 752.49

Circulating anticoagulants 286.5
- following childbirth 666.3 ☑
- postpartum 666.3 ☑

Circulation
- collateral (venous), any site 459.89
- defective 459.9
  - congenital 747.9
  - lower extremity 459.89
- embryonic 747.9
- failure 799.89
  - fetus or newborn 779.89
  - peripheral 785.59
- fetal, persistent 747.83
- heart, incomplete 747.9

Circulatory system — *see* condition

Circulus senilis 371.41

Circumcision
- in absence of medical indication V50.2
- ritual V50.2
- routine V50.2
- status (post), female 629.20

Circumscribed — *see* condition

Circumvallata placenta — *see* Placenta, abnormal

Cirrhosis, cirrhotic 571.5
- with alcoholism 571.2
- alcoholic (liver) 571.2
- atrophic (of liver) — *see* Cirrhosis, portal
- Baumgarten-Cruveilhier 571.5
- biliary (cholangiolitic) (cholangitic) (cholestatic) (extrahepatic) (hypertrophic) (intrahepatic) (nonobstructive) (obstructive) (pericholangiolitic) (posthepatic) (primary) (secondary) (xanthomatous) 571.6
  - due to
    - clonorchiasis 121.1
    - flukes 121.3
- brain 331.9
- capsular — *see* Cirrhosis, portal
- cardiac 571.5
  - alcoholic 571.2
- central (liver) — *see* Cirrhosis, liver
- Charcôt's 571.6
- cholangiolitic — *see* Cirrhosis, biliary
- cholangitic — *see* Cirrhosis, biliary
- cholestatic — *see* Cirrhosis, biliary
- clitoris (hypertrophic) 624.2
- coarsely nodular 571.5
- congestive (liver) — *see* Cirrhosis, cardiac
- Cruveilhier-Baumgarten 571.5
- cryptogenic (of liver) 571.5
  - alcoholic 571.2
- dietary (*see also* Cirrhosis, portal) 571.5
- due to
  - bronzed diabetes 275.0

Cirrhosis, cirrhotic — *continued*
- due to — *continued*
  - congestive hepatomegaly — *see* Cirrhosis, cardiac
  - cystic fibrosis 277.00
  - hemochromatosis 275.0
  - hepatolenticular degeneration 275.1
  - passive congestion (chronic) — *see* Cirrhosis, cardiac
  - Wilson's disease 275.1
  - xanthomatosis 272.2
- extrahepatic (obstructive) — *see* Cirrhosis, biliary
- fatty 571.8
  - alcoholic 571.0
- florid 571.2
- Glisson's — *see* Cirrhosis, portal
- Hanot's (hypertrophic) — *see* Cirrhosis, biliary
- hepatic — *see* Cirrhosis, liver
- hepatolienal — *see* Cirrhosis, liver
- hobnail — *see* Cirrhosis, portal
- hypertrophic (*see also* Cirrhosis, liver)
  - biliary — *see* Cirrhosis, biliary
    - Hanot's — *see* Cirrhosis, biliary
- infectious NEC — *see* Cirrhosis, portal
- insular — *see* Cirrhosis, portal
- intrahepatic (obstructive) (primary) (secondary) — *see* Cirrhosis, biliary
- juvenile (*see also* Cirrhosis, portal) 571.5
- kidney (*see also* Sclerosis, renal) 587
- Laennec's (of liver) 571.2
  - nonalcoholic 571.5
- liver (chronic) (hepatolienal) (hypertrophic) (nodular) (splenomegalic) (unilobar) 571.5
  - with alcoholism 571.2
    - alcoholic 571.2
  - congenital (due to failure of obliteration of umbilical vein) 777.8
  - cryptogenic 571.5
    - alcoholic 571.2
  - fatty 571.8
    - alcoholic 571.0
  - macronodular 571.5
    - alcoholic 571.2
  - micronodular 571.5
    - alcoholic 571.2
  - nodular, diffuse 571.5
    - alcoholic 571.2
  - pigmentary 275.0
  - portal 571.5
    - alcoholic 571.2
  - postnecrotic 571.5
    - alcoholic 571.2
  - syphilitic 095.3
- lung (chronic) (*see also* Fibrosis, lung) 515
- macronodular (of liver) 571.5
  - alcoholic 571.2
- malarial 084.9
- metabolic NEC 571.5
- micronodular (of liver) 571.5
  - alcoholic 571.2
- monolobular — *see* Cirrhosis, portal
- multilobular — *see* Cirrhosis, portal
- nephritis (*see also* Sclerosis, renal) 587
- nodular — *see* Cirrhosis, liver
- nutritional (fatty) 571.5
- obstructive (biliary) (extrahepatic) (intrahepatic) — *see* Cirrhosis, biliary
- ovarian 620.8
- paludal 084.9
- pancreas (duct) 577.8
- pericholangiolitic — *see* Cirrhosis, biliary
- periportal — *see* Cirrhosis, portal
- pigment, pigmentary (of liver) 275.0
- portal (of liver) 571.5
  - alcoholic 571.2

Cirrhosis, cirrhotic — *continued*
- posthepatitic (*see also* Cirrhosis, postnecrotic) 571.5
- postnecrotic (of liver) 571.5
  - alcoholic 571.2
- primary (intrahepatic) — *see* Cirrhosis, biliary
- pulmonary (*see also* Fibrosis, lung) 515
- renal (*see also* Sclerosis, renal) 587
- septal (*see also* Cirrhosis, postnecrotic) 571.5
- spleen 289.51
- splenomegalic (of liver) — *see* Cirrhosis, liver
- stasis (liver) — *see* Cirrhosis, liver
- stomach 535.4 ☑
- Todd's (*see also* Cirrhosis, biliary) 571.6
- toxic (nodular) — *see* Cirrhosis, postnecrotic
- trabecular — *see* Cirrhosis, postnecrotic
- unilobar — *see* Cirrhosis, liver
- vascular (of liver) — *see* Cirrhosis, liver
- xanthomatous (biliary) (*see also* Cirrhosis, biliary) 571.6
  - due to xanthomatosis (familial) (metabolic) (primary) 272.2

Cistern, subarachnoid 793.0

Citrullinemia 270.6

Citrullinuria 270.6

Ciuffini-Pancoast tumor (M8010/3) (carcinoma, pulmonary apex) 162.3

Civatte's disease or poikiloderma 709.09

Clam diggers' itch 120.3

Clap — *see* Gonorrhea

Clarke-Hadfield syndrome (pancreatic infantilism) 577.8

Clark's paralysis 343.9

Clastothrix 704.2

Claude Bernard-Horner syndrome — *see also* Neuropathy, peripheral, autonomic 337.9

Claude's syndrome 352.6

Claudication, intermittent 443.9
- cerebral (artery) (*see also* Ischemia, cerebral, transient) 435.9
- due to atherosclerosis 440.21
- spinal cord (arteriosclerotic) 435.1
  - syphilitic 094.89
- spinalis 435.1
- venous (axillary) 453.8

Claudicatio venosa intermittens 453.8

Claustrophobia 300.29

Clavus (infected) 700

Clawfoot (congenital) 754.71
- acquired 736.74

Clawhand (acquired) 736.06
- congenital 755.59

Clawtoe (congenital) 754.71
- acquired 735.5

Clay eating 307.52

Clay shovelers' fracture — *see* Fracture, vertebra, cervical

Cleansing of artificial opening — *see also* Attention to artificial opening V55.9

Cleft (congenital) — *see also* Imperfect, closure
- alveolar process 525.8
- branchial (persistent) 744.41
  - cyst 744.42
- clitoris 752.49
- cricoid cartilage, posterior 748.3
- facial (*see also* Cleft, lip) 749.10
- lip 749.10
  - with cleft palate 749.20
    - bilateral (lip and palate) 749.24
      - with unilateral lip or palate 749.25
        - complete 749.23
        - incomplete 749.24

Cleft — *see also* Imperfect, closure — *continued*
- lip — *continued*
  - with cleft palate — *continued*
    - unilateral (lip and palate) 749.22
      - with bilateral lip or palate 749.25
        - complete 749.21
        - incomplete 749.22
      - bilateral 749.14
        - with cleft palate, unilateral 749.25
          - complete 749.13
          - incomplete 749.14
      - unilateral 749.12
        - with cleft palate, bilateral 749.25
          - complete 749.11
          - incomplete 749.12
- nose 748.1
- palate 749.00
  - with cleft lip 749.20
    - bilateral (lip and palate) 749.24
      - with unilateral lip or palate 749.25
        - complete 749.23
        - incomplete 749.24
    - unilateral (lip and palate) 749.22
      - with bilateral lip or palate 749.25
        - complete 749.21
        - incomplete 749.22
    - bilateral 749.04
      - with cleft lip, unilateral 749.25
        - complete 749.03
        - incomplete 749.04
    - unilateral 749.02
      - with cleft lip, bilateral 749.25
        - complete 749.01
        - incomplete 749.02
- penis 752.69
- posterior, cricoid cartilage 748.3
- scrotum 752.89
- sternum (congenital) 756.3
- thyroid cartilage (congenital) 748.3
- tongue 750.13
- uvula 749.02
  - with cleft lip (*see also* Cleft, lip, with cleft palate) 749.20
- water 366.12

Cleft hand (congenital) 755.58

Cleidocranial dysostosis 755.59

Cleidotomy, fetal 763.89

Cleptomania 312.32

Clérambault's syndrome 297.8
- erotomania 302.89

Clergyman's sore throat 784.49

Click, clicking
- systolic syndrome 785.2

Clifford's syndrome (postmaturity) 766.22

Climacteric — *see also* Menopause 627.2
- arthritis NEC (*see also* Arthritis, climacteric) 716.3 ☑
- depression (*see also* Psychosis, affective) 296.2 ☑
- disease 627.2
  - recurrent episode 296.3 ☑
  - single episode 296.2 ☑
- female (symptoms) 627.2
- male (symptoms) (syndrome) 608.89
- melancholia (*see also* Psychosis, affective) 296.2 ☑
  - recurrent episode 296.3 ☑
  - single episode 296.2 ☑
- paranoid state 297.2
- paraphrenia 297.2
- polyarthritis NEC 716.39
  - male 608.89
- symptoms (female) 627.2

Clinical research investigation (control) (participant) V70.7

Clinodactyly 755.59

☑ Additional Digit Required — Refer to the Tabular List for Digit Selection   ▽ Subterms under main terms may continue to next column or page

50 — Volume 2   ▶◀ Revised Text   ● New Line   ▲ Revised Code   *2007 ICD-9-CM*

Clitoris — see condition
Cloaca, persistent 751.5
Clonorchiasis 121.1
Clonorchiosis 121.1
Clonorchis infection, liver 121.1
Clonus 781.0
Closed bite 524.20
Closed surgical procedure converted to open procedure
  arthroscopic V64.43
  laparoscopic V64.41
  thoracoscopic V64.42
Closure
  artificial opening (see also Attention to artificial opening) V55.9
  congenital, nose 748.0
  cranial sutures, premature 756.0
  defective or imperfect NEC — see Imperfect, closure
  fistula, delayed — see Fistula
  fontanelle, delayed 756.0
  foramen ovale, imperfect 745.5
  hymen 623.3
  interauricular septum, defective 745.5
  interventricular septum, defective 745.4
  lacrimal duct 375.56
    congenital 743.65
    neonatal 375.55
  nose (congenital) 748.0
    acquired 738.0
  vagina 623.2
  valve — see Endocarditis
  vulva 624.8
Clot (blood)
  artery (obstruction) (occlusion) (see also Embolism) 444.9
  atrial appendage 429.89 ●
  bladder 596.7
  brain (extradural or intradural) (see also Thrombosis, brain) 434.0 ☑
    late effect — see Late effect(s) (of) cerebrovascular disease
  circulation 444.9
  heart (see also Infarct, myocardium) 410.9 ☑
    without myocardial infarction 429.89 ●
  vein (see also Thrombosis) 453.9
Clotting defect NEC — see also Defect, coagulation 286.9
Clouded state 780.09
  epileptic (see also Epilepsy) 345.9 ☑
  paroxysmal (idiopathic) (see also Epilepsy) 345.9 ☑
Clouding
  corneal graft 996.51
Cloudy
  antrum, antra 473.0
  dialysis effluent 792.5
Clouston's (hidrotic) ectodermal dysplasia 757.31
Clubbing of fingers 781.5
Clubfinger 736.29
  acquired 736.29
  congenital 754.89
Clubfoot (congenital) 754.70
  acquired 736.71
  equinovarus 754.51
  paralytic 736.71
Club hand (congenital) 754.89
  acquired 736.07
Clubnail (acquired) 703.8
  congenital 757.5
Clump kidney 753.3
Clumsiness 781.3
  syndrome 315.4
Cluttering 307.0
Clutton's joints 090.5
Coagulation, intravascular (diffuse) (disseminated) — see also Fibrinolysis 286.6
  newborn 776.2
Coagulopathy — see also Defect, coagulation 286.9
  consumption 286.6

Coagulopathy — see also Defect, coagulation — continued
  intravascular (disseminated) NEC 286.6
  newborn 776.2
Coalition
  calcaneoscaphoid 755.67
  calcaneus 755.67
  tarsal 755.67
Coal miners'
  elbow 727.2
  lung 500
Coal workers' lung or pneumoconiosis 500
Coarctation
  aorta (postductal) (preductal) 747.10
  pulmonary artery 747.3
Coated tongue 529.3
Coats' disease 362.12
Cocainism — see also Dependence 304.2 ☑
Coccidioidal granuloma 114.3
Coccidioidomycosis 114.9
  with pneumonia 114.0
  cutaneous (primary) 114.1
  disseminated 114.3
  extrapulmonary (primary) 114.1
  lung 114.5
    acute 114.0
    chronic 114.4
    primary 114.0
  meninges 114.2
  primary (pulmonary) 114.0
    acute 114.0
  prostate 114.3
  pulmonary 114.5
    acute 114.0
    chronic 114.4
    primary 114.0
  specified site NEC 114.3
Coccidioidosis 114.9
  lung 114.5
    acute 114.0
    chronic 114.4
    primary 114.0
  meninges 114.2
Coccidiosis (colitis) (diarrhea) (dysentery) 007.2
Cocciuria 791.9
Coccus in urine 791.9
Coccydynia 724.79
Coccygodynia 724.79
Coccyx — see condition
Cochin-China
  diarrhea 579.1
    anguilluliasis 127.2
  ulcer 085.1
Cockayne's disease or syndrome (microcephaly and dwarfism) 759.89
Cockayne-Weber syndrome (epidermolysis bullosa) 757.39
Cocked-up toe 735.2
Cock's peculiar tumor 706.2
Codman's tumor (benign chondroblastoma) (M9230/0) — see Neoplasm, bone, benign
Coenurosis 123.8
Coffee workers' lung 495.8
Cogan's syndrome 370.52
  congenital oculomotor apraxia 379.51
  nonsyphilitic interstitial keratitis 370.52
Coiling, umbilical cord — see Complications, umbilical cord
Coitus, painful (female) 625.0
  male 608.89
  psychogenic 302.76
Cold 460
  with influenza, flu, or grippe 487.1
  abscess (see also Tuberculosis, abscess)
    articular — see Tuberculosis, joint
  agglutinin
    disease (chronic) or syndrome 283.0
    hemoglobinuria 283.0

Cold — continued
  agglutinin — continued
    hemoglobinuria — continued
      paroxysmal (cold) (nocturnal) 283.2
  allergic (see also Fever, hay) 477.9
  bronchus or chest — see Bronchitis
    with grippe or influenza 487.1
  common (head) 460
    vaccination, prophylactic (against) V04.7
  deep 464.10
  effects of 991.9
    specified effect NEC 991.8
  excessive 991.9
    specified effect NEC 991.8
  exhaustion from 991.8
  exposure to 991.9
    specified effect NEC 991.8
  grippy 487.1
  head 460
  injury syndrome (newborn) 778.2
  intolerance 780.99
  on lung — see Bronchitis
  rose 477.0
  sensitivity, autoimmune 283.0
  virus 460
Coldsore — see also Herpes, simplex 054.9
Colibacillosis 041.4
  generalized 038.42
Colibacilluria 791.9
Colic (recurrent) 789.0 ☑
  abdomen 789.0 ☑
    psychogenic 307.89
  appendicular 543.9
  appendix 543.9
  bile duct — see Choledocholithiasis
  biliary — see Cholelithiasis
  bilious — see Cholelithiasis
  common duct — see Choledocholithiasis
  Devonshire NEC 984.9
    specified type of lead — see Table of Drugs and Chemicals
  flatulent 787.3
  gallbladder or gallstone — see Cholelithiasis
  gastric 536.8
  hepatic (duct) — see Choledocholithiasis
  hysterical 300.11
  infantile 789.0 ☑
  intestinal 789.0 ☑
  kidney 788.0
  lead NEC 984.9
    specified type of lead — see Table of Drugs and Chemicals
  liver (duct) — see Choledocholithiasis
  mucous 564.9
    psychogenic 316 [564.9]
  nephritic 788.0
  painter's NEC 984.9
  pancreas 577.8
  psychogenic 306.4
  renal 788.0
  saturnine NEC 984.9
    specified type of lead — see Table of Drugs and Chemicals
  spasmodic 789.0 ☑
  ureter 788.0
  urethral 599.84
    due to calculus 594.2
  uterus 625.2
    menstrual 625.3
  vermicular 543.9
  virus 460
  worm NEC 128.9
Colicystitis — see also Cystitis 595.9
Colitis (acute) (catarrhal) (croupous) (cystica superficialis) (exudative) (hemorrhagic) (noninfectious) (phlegmonous) (presumed noninfectious) 558.9
  adaptive 564.9
  allergic 558.3

Colitis — continued
  amebic (see also Amebiasis) 006.9
    nondysenteric 006.2
  anthrax 022.2
  bacillary (see also Infection, Shigella) 004.9
  balantidial 007.0
  chronic 558.9
    ulcerative (see also Colitis, ulcerative) 556.9
  coccidial 007.2
  dietetic 558.9
  due to radiation 558.1
  functional 558.9
  gangrenous 009.0
  giardial 007.1
  granulomatous 555.1
  gravis (see also Colitis, ulcerative) 556.9
  infectious (see also Enteritis, due to, specific organism) 009.0
    presumed 009.1
  ischemic 557.9
    acute 557.0
    chronic 557.1
    due to mesenteric artery insufficiency 557.1
  membranous 564.9
    psychogenic 316 [564.9]
  mucous 564.9
    psychogenic 316 [564.9]
  necrotic 009.0
  polyposa (see also Colitis, ulcerative) 556.9
  protozoal NEC 007.9
  pseudomembranous 008.45
  pseudomucinous 564.9
  regional 555.1
  segmental 555.1
  septic (see also Enteritis, due to, specific organism) 009.0
  spastic 564.9
    psychogenic 316 [564.9]
  Staphylococcus 008.41
    food 005.0
  thromboulcerative 557.0
  toxic 558.2
  transmural 555.1
  trichomonal 007.3
  tuberculous (ulcerative) 014.8 ☑
  ulcerative (chronic) (idiopathic) (nonspecific) 556.9
    entero- 556.0
    fulminant 557.0
    ileo- 556.1
    left-sided 556.5
    procto- 556.2
    proctosigmoid 556.3
    psychogenic 316 [556] ☑
    specified NEC 556.8
    universal 556.6
Collagen disease NEC 710.9
  nonvascular 710.9
  vascular (allergic) (see also Angiitis, hypersensitivity) 446.20
Collagenosis — see also Collagen disease 710.9
  cardiovascular 425.4
  mediastinal 519.3
Collapse 780.2
  adrenal 255.8
  cardiorenal (see also Hypertension, cardiorenal) 404.90
  cardiorespiratory 785.51
    fetus or newborn 779.85 ▲
  cardiovascular (see also Disease, heart) 785.51
    fetus or newborn 779.85 ▲
  circulatory (peripheral) 785.59
    with
      abortion — see Abortion, by type, with shock
      ectopic pregnancy (see also categories 633.0–633.9) 639.5

☑ Additional Digit Required — Refer to the Tabular List for Digit Selection
▽ Subterms under main terms may continue to next column or page

2007 ICD-9-CM   ▶◀ Revised Text   ● New Line   ▲ Revised Code   **October 2006 · Volume 2 — 51**

Collapse — *continued*
  circulatory — *continued*
    with — *continued*
      molar pregnancy (*see also* categories 630–632) 639.5
      during or after labor and delivery 669.1 ☑
      fetus or newborn 779.85 ▲
      following
        abortion 639.5
        ectopic or molar pregnancy 639.5
      during or after labor and delivery 669.1 ☑
      fetus or newborn 779.89
  external ear canal 380.50
    secondary to
      inflammation 380.53
      surgery 380.52
      trauma 380.51
  general 780.2
  heart — *see* Disease, heart
  heat 992.1
  hysterical 300.11
  labyrinth, membranous (congenital) 744.05
  lung (massive) (*see also* Atelectasis) 518.0
    pressure, during labor 668.0 ☑
  myocardial — *see* Disease, heart
  nervous (*see also* Disorder, mental, nonpsychotic) 300.9
  neurocirculatory 306.2
  nose 738.0
  postoperative (cardiovascular) 998.0
  pulmonary (*see also* Atelectasis) 518.0
    fetus or newborn 770.5
      partial 770.5
      primary 770.4
  thorax 512.8
    iatrogenic 512.1
    postoperative 512.1
  trachea 519.19 ▲
  valvular — *see* Endocarditis
  vascular (peripheral) 785.59
    with
      abortion — *see* Abortion, by type, with shock
      ectopic pregnancy (*see also* categories 633.0–633.9) 639.5
      molar pregnancy (*see also* categories 630–632) 639.5
    cerebral (*see also* Disease, cerebrovascular, acute) 436
    during or after labor and delivery 669.1 ☑
    fetus or newborn 779.89
    following
      abortion 639.5
      ectopic or molar pregnancy 639.5
  vasomotor 785.59
  vertebra 733.13
Collateral — *see also* condition
  circulation (venous) 459.89
  dilation, veins 459.89
Colles' fracture (closed) (reversed) (separation) 813.41
  open 813.51
Collet-Sicard syndrome 352.6
Collet's syndrome 352.6
Colliculitis urethralis — *see also* Urethritis 597.89
Colliers'
  asthma 500
  lung 500
  phthisis (*see also* Tuberculosis) 011.4 ☑
Collodion baby (ichthyosis congenita) 757.1
Colloid milium 709.3
Coloboma NEC 743.49
  choroid 743.59
  fundus 743.52
  iris 743.46

Coloboma — *continued*
  lens 743.36
  lids 743.62
  optic disc (congenital) 743.57
    acquired 377.23
  retina 743.56
  sclera 743.47
Coloenteritis — *see* Enteritis
Colon — *see* condition
Coloptosis 569.89
Color
  amblyopia NEC 368.59
    acquired 368.55
  blindness NEC (congenital) 368.59
    acquired 368.55
Colostomy
  attention to V55.3
  fitting or adjustment V55.3
  malfunctioning 569.62
  status V44.3
Colpitis — *see also* Vaginitis 616.10
Colpocele 618.6
Colpocystitis — *see also* Vaginitis 616.10
Colporrhexis 665.4 ☑
Colpospasm 625.1
Column, spinal, vertebral — *see* condition
Coma 780.01
  apoplectic (*see also* Disease, cerebrovascular, acute) 436
  diabetic (with ketoacidosis) 250.3 ☑
    hyperosmolar 250.2 ☑
  eclamptic (*see also* Eclampsia) 780.39
  epileptic 345.3
  hepatic 572.2
  hyperglycemic 250.2 ☑
  hyperosmolar (diabetic) (nonketotic) 250.2 ☑
  hypoglycemic 251.0
    diabetic 250.3 ☑
  insulin 250.3 ☑
    hyperosmolar 250.2 ☑
    non-diabetic 250.3 ☑
    organic hyperinsulinism 251.0
  Kussmaul's (diabetic) 250.3 ☑
  liver 572.2
  newborn 779.2
  prediabetic 250.2 ☑
  uremic — *see* Uremia
Combat fatigue — *see also* Reaction, stress, acute 308.9
Combined — *see* condition
Comedo 706.1
Comedocarcinoma (M8501/3) — *see also* Neoplasm, breast, malignant
  noninfiltrating (M8501/2)
    specified site — *see* Neoplasm, by site, in situ
    unspecified site 233.0
Comedomastitis 610.4
Comedones 706.1
  lanugo 757.4
Comma bacillus, carrier (suspected) of V02.3
Comminuted fracture — *see* Fracture, by site
Common
  aortopulmonary trunk 745.0
  atrioventricular canal (defect) 745.69
  atrium 745.69
  cold (head) 460
    vaccination, prophylactic (against) V04.7
  truncus (arteriosus) 745.0
  ventricle 745.3
Commotio (current)
  cerebri (*see also* Concussion, brain) 850.9
    with skull fracture — *see* Fracture, skull, by site
  retinae 921.3
  spinalis — *see* Injury, spinal, by site
Commotion (current)
  brain (without skull fracture) (*see also* Concussion, brain) 850.9

Commotion — *continued*
  brain (*see also* Concussion, brain) — *continued*
    with skull fracture — *see* Fracture, skull, by site
  spinal cord — *see* Injury, spinal, by site
Communication
  abnormal (*see also* Fistula)
    between
      base of aorta and pulmonary artery 745.0
      left ventricle and right atrium 745.4
      pericardial sac and pleural sac 748.8
      pulmonary artery and pulmonary vein 747.3
    congenital, between uterus and anterior abdominal wall 752.3
      bladder 752.3
      intestine 752.3
      rectum 752.3
    left ventricular — right atrial 745.4
    pulmonary artery — pulmonary vein 747.3
Compartment syndrome — *see* Syndrome, compartment ●
Compensation
  broken — *see* Failure, heart
  failure — *see* Failure, heart
  neurosis, psychoneurosis 300.11
Complaint — *see also* Disease
  bowel, functional 564.9
    psychogenic 306.4
  intestine, functional 564.9
    psychogenic 306.4
  kidney (*see also* Disease, renal) 593.9
  liver 573.9
  miners' 500
Complete — *see* condition
Complex
  cardiorenal (*see also* Hypertension, cardiorenal) 404.90
  castration 300.9
  Costen's 524.60
  ego-dystonic homosexuality 302.0
  Eisenmenger's (ventricular septal defect) 745.4
  homosexual, ego-dystonic 302.0
  hypersexual 302.89
  inferiority 301.9
  jumped process
    spine — *see* Dislocation, vertebra
  primary, tuberculosis (*see also* Tuberculosis) 010.0 ☑
  Taussig-Bing (transposition, aorta and overriding pulmonary artery) 745.11
Complications
  abortion NEC — *see* categories 634-639 ☑
  accidental puncture or laceration during a procedure 998.2
  amputation stump (late) (surgical) 997.60
    traumatic — *see* Amputation, traumatic
  anastomosis (and bypass) (*see also* Complications, due to (presence of) any device, implant, or graft classified to 996.0–996.5 NEC)
    hemorrhage NEC 998.11
    intestinal (internal) NEC 997.4
      involving urinary tract 997.5
    mechanical — *see* Complications, mechanical, graft
    urinary tract (involving intestinal tract) 997.5
  anesthesia, anesthetic NEC (*see also* Anesthesia, complication) 995.22 ▲
    in labor and delivery 668.9 ☑
      affecting fetus or newborn 763.5
      cardiac 668.1 ☑

Complications — *continued*
  anesthesia, anesthetic (*see also* Anesthesia, complication) — *continued*
    in labor and delivery — *continued*
      central nervous system 668.2 ☑
      pulmonary 668.0 ☑
      specified type NEC 668.8 ☑
  aortocoronary (bypass) graft 996.03
    atherosclerosis — *see* Arteriosclerosis, coronary
    embolism 996.72
    occlusion NEC 996.72
    thrombus 996.72
  arthroplasty (*see also* Complications, prosthetic joint) 996.49
  artificial opening
    cecostomy 569.60
    colostomy 569.60
    cystostomy 997.5
    enterostomy 569.60
    esophagostomy 530.87
      infection 530.86
      mechanical 530.87
    gastrostomy 536.40
    ileostomy 569.60
    jejunostomy 569.60
    nephrostomy 997.5
    tracheostomy 519.00
    ureterostomy 997.5
    urethrostomy 997.5
  bariatric surgery 997.4
  bile duct implant (prosthetic) NEC 996.79
    infection or inflammation 996.69
    mechanical 996.59
  bleeding (intraoperative) (postoperative) 998.11
  blood vessel graft 996.1
    aortocoronary 996.03
      atherosclerosis — *see* Arteriosclerosis, coronary
      embolism 996.72
      occlusion NEC 996.72
      thrombus 996.72
    atherosclerosis — *see* Arteriosclerosis, extremities
    embolism 996.74
    occlusion NEC 996.74
    thrombus 996.74
  bone growth stimulator NEC 996.78
    infection or inflammation 996.67
  bone marrow transplant 996.85
  breast implant (prosthetic) NEC 996.79
    infection or inflammation 996.69
    mechanical 996.54
  bypass (*see also* Complications, anastomosis)
    aortocoronary 996.03
      atherosclerosis — *see* Arteriosclerosis, coronary
      embolism 996.72
      occlusion NEC 996.72
      thrombus 996.72
    carotid artery 996.1
      atherosclerosis — *see* Arteriosclerosis, extremities
      embolism 996.74
      occlusion NEC 996.74
      thrombus 996.74
  cardiac (*see also* Disease, heart) 429.9
    device, implant, or graft NEC 996.72
      infection or inflammation 996.61
      long-term effect 429.4
      mechanical (*see also* Complications, mechanical, by type) 996.00
      valve prosthesis 996.71
        infection or inflammation 996.61
    postoperative NEC 997.1
      long-term effect 429.4

☑ Additional Digit Required — Refer to the Tabular List for Digit Selection   ▼ Subterms under main terms may continue to next column or page

52 — Volume 2 • October 2006   ▶◀ Revised Text   ● New Line   ▲ Revised Code   *2007 ICD-9-CM*

Complications — *continued*
- cardiorenal (*see also* Hypertension, cardiorenal) 404.90
- carotid artery bypass graft 996.1
  - atherosclerosis — *see* Arteriosclerosis, extremities
  - embolism 996.74
  - occlusion NEC 996.74
  - thrombus 996.74
- cataract fragments in eye 998.82
- catheter device NEC (*see also* Complications, due to (presence of) any device, implant, or graft classified to 996.0–996.5 NEC)
  - mechanical — *see* Complications, mechanical, catheter
- cecostomy 569.60
- cesarean section wound 674.3 ☑
- chin implant (prosthetic) NEC 996.79
  - infection or inflammation 996.69
  - mechanical 996.59
- colostomy (enterostomy) 569.60
  - specified type NEC 569.69
- contraceptive device, intrauterine NEC 996.76
  - infection 996.65
  - inflammation 996.65
  - mechanical 996.32
- cord (umbilical) — *see* Complications, umbilical cord
- cornea
  - due to
    - contact lens 371.82
- coronary (artery) bypass (graft) NEC 996.03
  - atherosclerosis — *see* Arteriosclerosis, coronary
  - embolism 996.72
  - infection or inflammation 996.61
  - mechanical 996.03
  - occlusion NEC 996.72
  - specified type NEC 996.72
  - thrombus 996.72
- cystostomy 997.5
- delivery 669.9 ☑
  - procedure (instrumental) (manual) (surgical) 669.4 ☑
  - specified type NEC 669.8 ☑
- dialysis (hemodialysis) (peritoneal) (renal) NEC 999.9
  - catheter NEC (*see also* Complications, due to (presence of) any device, implant, or graft classified to 996.0–996.5 NEC)
    - infection or inflammation 996.62
      - peritoneal 996.68
    - mechanical 996.1
      - peritoneal 996.56
- due to (presence of) any device, implant, or graft classified to 996.0–996.5 NEC 996.70
  - with infection or inflammation — *see* Complications, infection or inflammation, due to (presence of) any device, implant, or graft classified to 996.0–996.5 NEC
  - arterial NEC 996.74
    - coronary NEC 996.03
      - atherosclerosis — *see* Arteriosclerosis, coronary
      - embolism 996.72
      - occlusion NEC 996.72
      - specified type NEC 996.72
      - thrombus 996.72
    - renal dialysis 996.73
  - arteriovenous fistula or shunt NEC 996.74
  - bone growth stimulator 996.78
  - breast NEC 996.79
  - cardiac NEC 996.72
    - defibrillator 996.72
    - pacemaker 996.72
    - valve prosthesis 996.71

Complications — *continued*
- due to any device, implant, or graft classified to 996.0–996.5 — *continued*
  - catheter NEC 996.79
    - spinal 996.75
    - urinary, indwelling 996.76
    - vascular NEC 996.74
      - renal dialysis 996.73
    - ventricular shunt 996.75
  - coronary (artery) bypass (graft) NEC 996.03
    - atherosclerosis — *see* Arteriosclerosis, coronary
    - embolism 996.72
    - occlusion NEC 996.72
    - thrombus 996.72
  - electrodes
    - brain 996.75
    - heart 996.72
  - esophagostomy 530.87
  - gastrointestinal NEC 996.79
  - genitourinary NEC 996.76
  - heart valve prosthesis NEC 996.71
  - infusion pump 996.74
  - insulin pump 996.57
  - internal
    - joint prosthesis 996.77
    - orthopedic NEC 996.78
    - specified type NEC 996.79
  - intrauterine contraceptive device NEC 996.76
  - joint prosthesis, internal NEC 996.77
  - mechanical — *see* Complications, mechanical
  - nervous system NEC 996.75
  - ocular lens NEC 996.79
  - orbital NEC 996.79
  - orthopedic NEC 996.78
    - joint, internal 996.77
  - renal dialysis 996.73
  - specified type NEC 996.79
  - urinary catheter, indwelling 996.76
  - vascular NEC 996.74
  - ventricular shunt 996.75
  - during dialysis NEC 999.9
  - ectopic or molar pregnancy NEC 639.9
  - electroshock therapy NEC 999.9
  - enterostomy 569.60
    - specified type NEC 569.69
  - esophagostomy 530.87
    - infection 530.86
    - mechanical 530.87
  - external (fixation) device with internal component(s) NEC 996.78
    - infection or inflammation 996.67
    - mechanical 996.49
  - extracorporeal circulation NEC 999.9
  - eye implant (prosthetic) NEC 996.79
    - infection or inflammation 996.69
    - mechanical
      - ocular lens 996.53
      - orbital globe 996.59
  - gastrointestinal, postoperative NEC (*see also* Complications, surgical procedures) 997.4
  - gastrostomy 536.40
    - specified type NEC 536.49
  - genitourinary device, implant or graft NEC 996.76
    - infection or inflammation 996.65
      - urinary catheter, indwelling 996.64
    - mechanical (*see also* Complications, mechanical, by type) 996.30
      - specified NEC 996.39
  - graft (bypass) (patch) (*see also* Complications, due to (presence of) any device, implant, or graft classified to 996.0–996.5 NEC)
    - bone marrow 996.85
    - corneal NEC 996.79
      - infection or inflammation 996.69

Complications — *continued*
- graft (*see also* Complications, due to any device, implant, or graft classified to 996.0–996.5) — *continued*
  - corneal — *continued*
    - rejection or reaction 996.51
    - mechanical — *see* Complications, mechanical, graft
  - organ (immune or nonimmune cause) (partial) (total) 996.80
    - bone marrow 996.85
    - heart 996.83
    - intestines 996.87
    - kidney 996.81
    - liver 996.82
    - lung 996.84
    - pancreas 996.86
    - specified NEC 996.89
  - skin NEC 996.79
    - infection or inflammation 996.69
    - rejection 996.52
      - artificial 996.55
      - decellularized allodermis 996.55
- heart (*see also* Disease, heart transplant (immune or nonimmune cause)) 996.83
- hematoma (intraoperative) (postoperative) 998.12
- hemorrhage (intraoperative) (postoperative) 998.11
- hyperalimentation therapy NEC 999.9
- immunization (procedure) — *see* Complications, vaccination
- implant (*see also* Complications, due to (presence of) any device, implant, or graft classified to 996.0–996.5 NEC)
  - mechanical — *see* Complications, mechanical, implant
- infection and inflammation
  - due to (presence of) any device, implant or graft classified to 996.0–996.5 NEC 996.60
    - arterial NEC 996.62
      - coronary 996.61
      - renal dialysis 996.62
    - arteriovenous fistula or shunt 996.62
    - artificial heart 996.61
    - bone growth stimulator 996.67
    - breast 996.69
    - cardiac 996.61
    - catheter NEC 996.69
      - peritoneal 996.68
      - spinal 996.63
      - urinary, indwelling 996.64
      - vascular NEC 996.62
      - ventricular shunt 996.63
    - coronary artery bypass 996.61
    - electrodes
      - brain 996.63
      - heart 996.61
    - gastrointestinal NEC 996.69
    - genitourinary NEC 996.65
      - indwelling urinary catheter 996.64
    - heart assist device 996.61
    - heart valve 996.61
    - infusion pump 996.62
    - insulin pump 996.69
    - intrauterine contraceptive device 996.65
    - joint prosthesis, internal 996.66
    - ocular lens 996.69
    - orbital (implant) 996.69
    - orthopedic NEC 996.67
      - joint, internal 996.66
    - specified type NEC 996.69
    - urinary catheter, indwelling 996.64
    - ventricular shunt 996.63
- infusion (procedure) 999.9

Complications — *continued*
- infusion — *continued*
  - blood — *see* Complications, transfusion
  - infection NEC 999.3
  - sepsis NEC 999.3
- inhalation therapy NEC 999.9
- injection (procedure) 999.9
  - drug reaction (*see also* Reaction, drug) 995.27 ▲
  - infection NEC 999.3
  - sepsis NEC 999.3
  - serum (prophylactic) (therapeutic) — *see* Complications, vaccination
  - vaccine (any) — *see* Complications, vaccination
- inoculation (any) — *see* Complications, vaccination
- insulin pump 996.57
- internal device (catheter) (electronic) (fixation) (prosthetic) (*see also* Complications, due to (presence of) any device, implant, or graft classified to 996.0–996.5 NEC)
  - mechanical — *see* Complications, mechanical
- intestinal transplant (immune or nonimmune cause) 996.87
- intraoperative bleeding or hemorrhage 998.11
- intrauterine contraceptive device (*see also* Complications, contraceptive device) 996.76
  - with fetal damage affecting management of pregnancy 655.8 ☑
  - infection or inflammation 996.65
- jejunostomy 569.60
- kidney transplant (immune or nonimmune cause) 996.81
- labor 669.9 ☑
  - specified condition NEC 669.8 ☑
- liver transplant (immune or nonimmune cause) 996.82
- lumbar puncture 349.0
- mechanical
  - anastomosis — *see* Complications, mechanical, graft
  - artificial heart 996.09
  - bypass — *see* Complications, mechanical, graft
  - catheter NEC 996.59
    - cardiac 996.09
    - cystostomy 996.39
    - dialysis (hemodialysis) 996.1
      - peritoneal 996.56
    - during a procedure 998.2
    - urethral, indwelling 996.31
  - colostomy 569.62
  - device NEC 996.59
    - balloon (counterpulsation), intra-aortic 996.1
    - cardiac 996.00
      - automatic implantable defibrillator 996.04
      - long-term effect 429.4
      - specified NEC 996.09
    - contraceptive, intrauterine 996.32
    - counterpulsation, intra-aortic 996.1
    - fixation, external, with internal components 996.49
    - fixation, internal (nail, rod, plate) 996.40
    - genitourinary 996.30
      - specified NEC 996.39
    - insulin pump 996.57
    - nervous system 996.2
    - orthopedic, internal 996.40
      - prosthetic joint (*see also* Complications, mechanical, device, orthopedic, prosthetic, joint) 996.47
      - prosthetic NEC 996.59

☑ Additional Digit Required — Refer to the Tabular List for Digit Selection   ⏚ Subterms under main terms may continue to next column or page

2007 ICD-9-CM   ▶◀ Revised Text   ● New Line   ▲ Revised Code   **October 2006 · Volume 2 — 53**

Complications — Complications

Complications — *continued*
mechanical — *continued*
device — *continued*
prosthetic — *continued*
joint (*see also* Complications, prosthetic joint) 996.47
articular bearing surface wear 996.46
aseptic loosening 996.41
breakage 996.43
dislocation 996.42
failure 996.43
fracture 996.43
around prosthetic 996.44
peri-prosthetic 996.44
instability 996.42
loosening 996.41
peri-prosthetic osteolysis 996.45
subluxation 996.42
wear 996.46
umbrella, vena cava 996.1
vascular 996.1
dorsal column stimulator 996.2
electrode NEC 996.59
brain 996.2
cardiac 996.01
spinal column 996.2
enterostomy 569.62
esophagostomy 530.87
fistula, arteriovenous, surgically created 996.1
gastrostomy 536.42
graft NEC 996.52
aortic (bifurcation) 996.1
aortocoronary bypass 996.03
blood vessel NEC 996.1
bone 996.49
cardiac 996.00
carotid artery bypass 996.1
cartilage 996.49
corneal 996.51
coronary bypass 996.03
decellularized allodermis 996.55
genitourinary 996.30
specified NEC 996.39
muscle 996.49
nervous system 996.2
organ (immune or nonimmune cause) 996.80
heart 996.83
intestines 996.87
kidney 996.81
liver 996.82
lung 996.84
pancreas 996.86
specified NEC 996.89
orthopedic, internal 996.49
peripheral nerve 996.2
prosthetic NEC 996.59
skin 996.52
artificial 996.55
specified NEC 996.59
tendon 996.49
tissue NEC 996.52
tooth 996.59
ureter, without mention of resection 996.39
vascular 996.1
heart valve prosthesis 996.02
long-term effect 429.4
implant NEC 996.59
cardiac 996.00
automatic implantable defibrillator 996.04
long-term effect 429.4
specified NEC 996.09
electrode NEC 996.59
brain 996.2
cardiac 996.01
spinal column 996.2
genitourinary 996.30
nervous system 996.2
orthopedic, internal 996.49
prosthetic NEC 996.59

Complications — *continued*
mechanical — *continued*
implant — *continued*
prosthetic — *continued*
in
bile duct 996.59
breast 996.54
chin 996.59
eye
ocular lens 996.53
orbital globe 996.59
vascular 996.1
insulin pump 996.57
nonabsorbable surgical material 996.59
pacemaker NEC 996.59
brain 996.2
cardiac 996.01
nerve (phrenic) 996.2
patch — *see* Complications, mechanical, graft
prosthesis NEC 996.59
bile duct 996.59
breast 996.54
chin 996.59
ocular lens 996.53
reconstruction, vas deferens 996.39
reimplant NEC 996.59
extremity (*see also* Complications, reattached, extremity) 996.90
organ (*see also* Complications, transplant, organ, by site) 996.80
repair — *see* Complications, mechanical, graft
respirator [ventilator] V46.14
shunt NEC 996.59
arteriovenous, surgically created 996.1
ventricular (communicating) 996.2
stent NEC 996.59
tracheostomy 519.02
vas deferens reconstruction 996.39
ventilator [respirator] V46.14
medical care NEC 999.9
cardiac NEC 997.1
gastrointestinal NEC 997.4
nervous system NEC 997.00
peripheral vascular NEC 997.2
respiratory NEC 997.3
urinary NEC 997.5
vascular
mesenteric artery 997.71
other vessels 997.79
peripheral vessels 997.2
renal artery 997.72
nephrostomy 997.5
nervous system
device, implant, or graft NEC 349.1
mechanical 996.2
postoperative NEC 997.00
obstetric 669.9 ☑
procedure (instrumental) (manual) (surgical) 669.4 ☑
specified NEC 669.8 ☑
surgical wound 674.3 ☑
ocular lens implant NEC 996.79
infection or inflammation 996.69
mechanical 996.53
organ transplant — *see* Complications, transplant, organ, by site
orthopedic device, implant, or graft
internal (fixation) (nail) (plate) (rod) NEC 996.78
infection or inflammation 996.67
joint prosthesis 996.77
infection or inflammation 996.66
mechanical 996.40
pacemaker (cardiac) 996.72
infection or inflammation 996.61
mechanical 996.01

Complications — *continued*
pancreas transplant (immune or nonimmune cause) 996.86
perfusion NEC 999.9
perineal repair (obstetrical) 674.3 ☑
disruption 674.2 ☑
pessary (uterus) (vagina) — *see* Complications, contraceptive device
phototherapy 990
postcystoscopic 997.5
postmastoidectomy NEC 383.30
postoperative — *see* Complications, surgical procedures
pregnancy NEC 646.9 ☑
affecting fetus or newborn 761.9
prosthetic device, internal (*see also* Complications, due to (presence of) any device, implant or graft classified to 996.0–996.5 NEC)
mechanical NEC (*see also* Complications, mechanical) 996.59
puerperium NEC (*see also* Puerperal) 674.9 ☑
puncture, spinal 349.0
pyelogram 997.5
radiation 990
radiotherapy 990
reattached
body part, except extremity 996.99
extremity (infection) (rejection) 996.90
arm(s) 996.94
digit(s) (hand) 996.93
foot 996.95
finger(s) 996.93
foot 996.95
forearm 996.91
hand 996.92
leg 996.96
lower NEC 996.96
toe(s) 996.95
upper NEC 996.94
reimplant NEC (*see also* Complications, due to (presence of) any device, implant, or graft classified to 996.0–996.5 NEC)
bone marrow 996.85
extremity (*see also* Complications, reattached, extremity) 996.90
due to infection 996.90
mechanical — *see* Complications, mechanical, reimplant
organ (immune or nonimmune cause) (partial) (total) (*see also* Complications, transplant, organ, by site) 996.80
renal allograft 996.81
renal dialysis — *see* Complications, dialysis
respirator [ventilator], mechanical V46.14
respiratory 519.9
device, implant or graft NEC 996.79
infection or inflammation 996.69
mechanical 996.59
distress syndrome, adult, following trauma or surgery 518.5
insufficiency, acute, postoperative 518.5
postoperative NEC 997.3
therapy NEC 999.9
sedation during labor and delivery 668.9 ☑
affecting fetus or newborn 763.5
cardiac 668.1 ☑
central nervous system 668.2 ☑
pulmonary 668.0 ☑
specified type NEC 668.8 ☑
seroma (intraoperative) (postoperative) (noninfected) 998.13
infected 998.51

Complications — *continued*
shunt (*see also* Complications, due to (presence of) any device, implant, or graft classified to 996.0–996.5 NEC)
mechanical — *see* Complications, mechanical, shunt
specified body system NEC
device, implant, or graft — *see* Complications, due to (presence of) any device, implant, or graft classified to 996.0–996.5 NEC
postoperative NEC 997.99
spinal puncture or tap 349.0
stomach banding 997.4
stomach stapling 997.4
stoma, external
gastrointestinal tract
colostomy 569.60
enterostomy 569.60
esophagostomy 530.87
infection 530.86
mechanical 530.87
gastrostomy 536.40
urinary tract 997.5
surgical procedures 998.9
accidental puncture or laceration 998.2
amputation stump (late) 997.60
anastomosis — *see* Complications, anastomosis
burst stitches or sutures (external) 998.32
internal 998.31
cardiac 997.1
long-term effect following cardiac surgery 429.4
cataract fragments in eye 998.82
catheter device — *see* Complications, catheter device
cecostomy malfunction 569.62
colostomy malfunction 569.62
cystostomy malfunction 997.5
dehiscence (of incision) (external) 998.32
internal 998.31
dialysis NEC (*see also* Complications, dialysis) 999.9
disruption
anastomosis (internal) — *see* Complications, mechanical, graft
internal suture (line) 998.31
wound (external) 998.32
internal 998.31
dumping syndrome (postgastrectomy) 564.2
elephantiasis or lymphedema 997.99
postmastectomy 457.0
emphysema (surgical) 998.81
enterostomy malfunction 569.62
esophagostomy malfunction 530.87
evisceration 998.32
fistula (persistent postoperative) 998.6
foreign body inadvertently left in wound (sponge) (suture) (swab) 998.4
from nonabsorbable surgical material (Dacron) (mesh) (permanent suture) (reinforcing) (Teflon) — *see* Complications, due to (presence of) any device, implant, or graft classified to 996.0–996.5 NEC
gastrointestinal NEC 997.4
gastrostomy malfunction 536.42
hematoma 998.12
hemorrhage 998.11
ileostomy malfunction 569.62
internal prosthetic device NEC (*see also* Complications, internal device) 996.70
hemolytic anemia 283.19

☑ Additional Digit Required — Refer to the Tabular List for Digit Selection   ▽ Subterms under main terms may continue to next column or page

54 — Volume 2   ▶◀ Revised Text   ● New Line   ▲ Revised Code   *2007 ICD-9-CM*

Complications — *continued*
surgical procedures — *continued*
  internal prosthetic device (*see also* Complications, internal device) — *continued*
    infection or inflammation 996.60
    malfunction — *see* Complications, mechanical
    mechanical complication — *see* Complications, mechanical
    thrombus 996.70
  jejunostomy malfunction 569.62
  nervous system NEC 997.00
  obstruction, internal anastomosis — *see* Complications, mechanical, graft
  other body system NEC 997.99
  peripheral vascular NEC 997.2
  postcardiotomy syndrome 429.4
  postcholecystectomy syndrome 576.0
  postcommissurotomy syndrome 429.4
  postgastrectomy dumping syndrome 564.2
  postmastectomy lymphedema syndrome 457.0
  postmastoidectomy 383.30
    cholesteatoma, recurrent 383.32
    cyst, mucosal 383.31
    granulation 383.33
    inflammation, chronic 383.33
  postvagotomy syndrome 564.2
  postvalvulotomy syndrome 429.4
  reattached extremity (infection) (rejection) (*see also* Complications, reattached, extremity) 996.90
  respiratory NEC 997.3
  seroma 998.13
  shock (endotoxic) (hypovolemic) (septic) 998.0
  shunt, prosthetic (thrombus) (*see also* Complications, due to (presence of) any device, implant, or graft classified to 996.0–996.5 NEC)
    hemolytic anemia 283.19
  specified complication NEC 998.89
  stitch abscess 998.59
  transplant — *see* Complications, graft
  ureterostomy malfunction 997.5
  urethrostomy malfunction 997.5
  urinary NEC 997.5
  vascular
    mesenteric artery 997.71
    other vessels 997.79
    peripheral vessels 997.2
    renal artery 997.72
  wound infection 998.59
therapeutic misadventure NEC 999.9
  surgical treatment 998.9
tracheostomy 519.00
transfusion (blood) (lymphocytes) (plasma) NEC 999.8
  acute lung injury (TRALI) 518.7 ●
  atrophy, liver, yellow, subacute (within 8 months of administration) — *see* Hepatitis, viral
  bone marrow 996.85
  embolism
    air 999.1
    thrombus 999.2
  hemolysis NEC 999.8
    bone marrow 996.85
  hepatitis (serum) (type B) (within 8 months after administration) — *see* Hepatitis, viral
  incompatibility reaction (ABO) (blood group) 999.6
    Rh (factor) 999.7
  infection 999.3

Complications — *continued*
transfusion — *continued*
  jaundice (serum) (within 8 months after administration) — *see* Hepatitis, viral
  sepsis 999.3
  shock or reaction NEC 999.8
    bone marrow 996.85
  subacute yellow atrophy of liver (within 8 months after administration) — *see* Hepatitis, viral
  thromboembolism 999.2
transplant NEC (*see also* Complications, due to (presence of) any device, implant, or graft classified to 996.0–996.5 NEC)
  bone marrow 996.85
  organ (immune or nonimmune cause) (partial) (total) 996.80
    bone marrow 996.85
    heart 996.83
    intestines 996.87
    kidney 996.81
    liver 996.82
    lung 996.84
    pancreas 996.86
    specified NEC 996.89
trauma NEC (early) 958.8
ultrasound therapy NEC 999.9
umbilical cord
  affecting fetus or newborn 762.6
  complicating delivery 663.9 ☑
    affecting fetus or newborn 762.6
    specified type NEC 663.8 ☑
urethral catheter NEC 996.76
  infection or inflammation 996.64
  mechanical 996.31
urinary, postoperative NEC 997.5
vaccination 999.9
  anaphylaxis NEC 999.4
  cellulitis 999.3
  encephalitis or encephalomyelitis 323.51 ▲
  hepatitis (serum) (type B) (within 8 months after administration) — *see* Hepatitis, viral
  infection (general) (local) NEC 999.3
  jaundice (serum) (within 8 months after administration) — *see* Hepatitis, viral
  meningitis 997.09 *[321.8]*
  myelitis 323.52 ▲
  protein sickness 999.5
  reaction (allergic) 999.5
    Herxheimer's 995.0
    serum 999.5
  sepsis 999.3
  serum intoxication, sickness, rash, or other serum reaction NEC 999.5
  shock (allergic) (anaphylactic) 999.4
  subacute yellow atrophy of liver (within 8 months after administration) — *see* Hepatitis, viral
  vaccinia (generalized) 999.0
    localized 999.3
vascular
  device, implant, or graft NEC 996.74
    infection or inflammation 996.62
    mechanical NEC 996.1
      cardiac (*see also* Complications, mechanical, by type) 996.00
  following infusion, perfusion, or transfusion 999.2
  postoperative NEC 997.2
    mesenteric artery 997.71
    other vessels 997.79
    peripheral vessels 997.2
    renal artery 997.72

Complications — *continued*
ventilation therapy NEC 999.9
ventilator [respirator], mechanical V46.14
Compound presentation, complicating delivery 652.8 ☑
  causing obstructed labor 660.0 ☑
Compressed air disease 993.3
Compression
with injury — *see* specific injury
arm NEC 354.9
artery 447.1
  celiac, syndrome 447.4
brachial plexus 353.0
brain (stem) 348.4
  due to
    contusion, brain — *see* Contusion, brain
    injury NEC (*see also* Hemorrhage, brain, traumatic)
      birth — *see* Birth, injury, brain
      laceration, brain — *see* Laceration, brain
  osteopathic 739.0
bronchus 519.19 ▲
by cicatrix — *see* Cicatrix
cardiac 423.9
cauda equina 344.60
  with neurogenic bladder 344.61
celiac (artery) (axis) 447.4
cerebral — *see* Compression, brain
cervical plexus 353.2
cord (umbilical) — *see* Compression, umbilical cord
cranial nerve 352.9
  second 377.49
  third (partial) 378.51
    total 378.52
  fourth 378.53
  fifth 350.8
  sixth 378.54
  seventh 351.8
divers' squeeze 993.3
duodenum (external) (*see also* Obstruction, duodenum) 537.3
during birth 767.9
esophagus 530.3
  congenital, external 750.3
Eustachian tube 381.63
facies (congenital) 754.0
fracture — *see* Fracture, by site
heart — *see* Disease, heart
intestine (*see also* Obstruction, intestine) 560.9
  with hernia — *see* Hernia, by site, with obstruction
laryngeal nerve, recurrent 478.79
leg NEC 355.8
lower extremity NEC 355.8
lumbosacral plexus 353.1
lung 518.89
lymphatic vessel 457.1
medulla — *see* Compression, brain
nerve NEC (*see also* Disorder, nerve)
  arm NEC 354.9
  autonomic nervous system (*see also* Neuropathy, peripheral, autonomic) 337.9
  axillary 353.0
  cranial NEC 352.9
  due to displacement of intervertebral disc 722.2
    with myelopathy 722.70
    cervical 722.0
      with myelopathy 722.71
    lumbar, lumbosacral 722.10
      with myelopathy 722.73
    thoracic, thoracolumbar 722.11
      with myelopathy 722.72
  iliohypogastric 355.79
  ilioinguinal 355.79
  leg NEC 355.8
  lower extremity NEC 355.8
  median (in carpal tunnel) 354.0
  obturator 355.79

Compression — *continued*
nerve (*see also* Disorder, nerve) — *continued*
  optic 377.49
  plantar 355.6
  posterior tibial (in tarsal tunnel) 355.5
  root (by scar tissue) NEC 724.9
    cervical NEC 723.4
    lumbar NEC 724.4
    lumbosacral 724.4
    thoracic 724.4
  saphenous 355.79
  sciatic (acute) 355.0
  sympathetic 337.9
  traumatic — *see* Injury, nerve
  ulnar 354.2
  upper extremity NEC 354.9
peripheral — *see* Compression, nerve
spinal (cord) (old or nontraumatic) 336.9
  by displacement of intervertebral disc — *see* Displacement, intervertebral disc
  nerve
    root NEC 724.9
      postoperative 722.80
        cervical region 722.81
        lumbar region 722.83
        thoracic region 722.82
      traumatic — *see* Injury, nerve, spinal
    traumatic — *see* Injury, nerve, spinal
  spondylogenic 721.91
    cervical 721.1
    lumbar, lumbosacral 721.42
    thoracic 721.41
  traumatic (*see also* Injury, spinal, by site)
    with fracture, vertebra — *see* Fracture, vertebra, by site, with spinal cord injury
spondylogenic — *see* Compression, spinal cord, spondylogenic
subcostal nerve (syndrome) 354.8
sympathetic nerve NEC 337.9
syndrome 958.5
thorax 512.8
  iatrogenic 512.1
  postoperative 512.1
trachea 519.19 ▲
  congenital 748.3
ulnar nerve (by scar tissue) 354.2
umbilical cord
  affecting fetus or newborn 762.5
    cord prolapsed 762.4
  complicating delivery 663.2 ☑
    cord around neck 663.1 ☑
    cord prolapsed 663.0 ☑
upper extremity NEC 354.9
ureter 593.3
urethra — *see* Stricture, urethra
vein 459.2
vena cava (inferior) (superior) 459.2
vertebral NEC — *see* Compression, spinal (cord)
Compulsion, compulsive
eating 307.51
neurosis (obsessive) 300.3
personality 301.4
states (mixed) 300.3
swearing 300.3
  in Gilles de la Tourette's syndrome 307.23
tics and spasms 307.22
water drinking NEC (syndrome) 307.9
Concato's disease (pericardial polyserositis) 423.2
peritoneal 568.82
pleural — *see* Pleurisy
Concavity, chest wall 738.3
Concealed
hemorrhage NEC 459.0
penis 752.65

☑ Additional Digit Required — Refer to the Tabular List for Digit Selection   ▼ Subterms under main terms may continue to next column or page

2007 ICD-9-CM   ▶◀ Revised Text   ● New Line   ▲ Revised Code   October 2006 • Volume 2 — 55

Concentric fading 368.12
Concern (normal) **about sick person in family** V61.49
Concrescence (teeth) 520.2
Concretio cordis 423.1
rheumatic 393
Concretion — *see also* Calculus
appendicular 543.9
canaliculus 375.57
clitoris 624.8
conjunctiva 372.54
eyelid 374.56
intestine (impaction) (obstruction) 560.39
lacrimal (passages) 375.57
prepuce (male) 605
female (clitoris) 624.8
salivary gland (any) 527.5
seminal vesicle 608.89
stomach 537.89
tonsil 474.8
Concussion (current) 850.9
with
loss of consciousness 850.5
brief (less than one hour)
30 minutes or less 850.11
31-59 minutes 850.12
moderate (1-24 hours) 850.2
prolonged (more than 24 hours)
(with complete recovery)
(with return to pre-existing conscious level) 850.3
without return to pre-existing conscious level
850.4
mental confusion or disorientation
(without loss of consciousness) 850.0
with loss of consciousness —
see Concussion, with, loss
of consciousness
without loss of consciousness 850.0
blast (air) (hydraulic) (immersion)
(underwater) 869.0
with open wound into cavity 869.1
abdomen or thorax — *see* Injury,
internal, by site
brain — *see* Concussion, brain
ear (acoustic nerve trauma) 951.5
with perforation, tympanic
membrane — *see* Wound,
open, ear drum
thorax — *see* Injury, internal, intrathoracic organs NEC
brain or cerebral (without skull fracture) 850.9
with
loss of consciousness 850.5
brief (less than one hour)
30 minutes or less 850.11
31-59 minutes 850.12
moderate (1-24 hours) 850.2
prolonged (more than 24
hours) (with complete
recovery) (with return
to pre-existing con-
scious level) 850.3
without return to pre-ex-
isting conscious lev-
el 850.4
mental confusion or disorientation (without loss of consciousness) 850.0
with loss of consciousness —
see Concussion, brain,
with, loss of conscious-
ness
skull fracture — *see* Fracture,
skull, by site
without loss of consciousness
850.0
cauda equina 952.4
cerebral — *see* Concussion, brain
conus medullaris (spine) 952.4
hydraulic — *see* Concussion, blast

Concussion — *continued*
internal organs — *see* Injury, internal,
by site
labyrinth — *see* Injury, intracranial
ocular 921.3
osseous labyrinth — *see* Injury, intracranial
spinal (cord) (*see also* Injury, spinal,
by site)
due to
broken
back — *see* Fracture, vertebra, by site, with
spinal cord injury
neck — *see* Fracture, vertebra, cervical, with
spinal cord injury
fracture, fracture dislocation, or
compression fracture of
spine or vertebra — *see*
Fracture, vertebra, by
site, with spinal cord injury
syndrome 310.2
underwater blast — *see* Concussion,
blast
Condition — *see also* Disease
psychiatric 298.9
respiratory NEC 519.9
acute or subacute NEC 519.9
due to
external agent 508.9
specified type NEC 508.8
fumes or vapors (chemical)
(inhalation) 506.3
radiation 508.0
chronic NEC 519.9
due to
external agent 508.9
specified type NEC 508.8
fumes or vapors (chemical)
(inhalation) 506.4
radiation 508.1
due to
external agent 508.9
specified type NEC 508.8
fumes or vapors (chemical) (inhalation) 506.9
Conduct disturbance — *see also* Disturbance, conduct 312.9
adjustment reaction 309.3
hyperkinetic 314.2
Condyloma NEC 078.10
acuminatum 078.11
gonorrheal 098.0
latum 091.3
syphilitic 091.3
congenital 090.0
venereal, syphilitic 091.3
Confinement — *see* Delivery
Conflagration — *see also* Burn, by site
asphyxia (by inhalation of smoke,
gases, fumes, or vapors) 987.9
specified agent — *see* Table of
Drugs and Chemicals
Conflict
family V61.9
specified circumstance NEC V61.8
interpersonal NEC V62.81
marital V61.10
involving divorce or estrangement
V61.0
parent-child V61.20
partner V61.10
Confluent — *see* condition
Confusional arousals 327.41
Confusion, confused (mental) (state) —
see also State, confusional 298.9
acute 293.0
epileptic 293.0
postoperative 293.9
psychogenic 298.2
reactive (from emotional stress, psychological trauma) 298.2
subacute 293.1
Congelation 991.9

Congenital — *see also* condition
aortic septum 747.29
generalized fibromatosis (CGF) ●
759.89 ●
intrinsic factor deficiency 281.0
malformation — *see* Anomaly
Congestion, congestive (chronic) (passive)
asphyxia, newborn 768.9
bladder 596.8
bowel 569.89
brain (*see also* Disease, cerebrovascular NEC) 437.8
malarial 084.9
breast 611.79
bronchi 519.19 ▲
bronchial tube 519.19 ▲
catarrhal 472.0
cerebral — *see* Congestion, brain
cerebrospinal — *see* Congestion, brain
chest 514
chill 780.99
malarial (*see also* Malaria) 084.6
circulatory NEC 459.9
conjunctiva 372.71
due to disturbance of circulation
459.9
duodenum 537.3
enteritis — *see* Enteritis
eye 372.71
fibrosis syndrome (pelvic) 625.5
gastroenteritis — *see* Enteritis
general 799.89
glottis 476.0
heart (*see also* Failure, heart) 428.0
hepatic 573.0
hypostatic (lung) 514
intestine 569.89
intracranial — *see* Congestion, brain
kidney 593.89
labyrinth 386.50
larynx 476.0
liver 573.0
lung 514
active or acute (*see also* Pneumonia) 486
congenital 770.0
chronic 514
hypostatic 514
idiopathic, acute 518.5
passive 514
malaria, malarial (brain) (fever) (*see
also* Malaria) 084.6
medulla — *see* Congestion, brain
nasal 478.19 ▲
orbit, orbital 376.33
inflammatory (chronic) 376.10
acute 376.00
ovary 620.8
pancreas 577.8
pelvic, female 625.5
pleural 511.0
prostate (active) 602.1
pulmonary — *see* Congestion, lung
renal 593.89
retina 362.89
seminal vesicle 608.89
spinal cord 336.1
spleen 289.51
chronic 289.51
stomach 537.89
trachea 464.11
urethra 599.84
uterus 625.5
with subinvolution 621.1
viscera 799.89
Congestive — *see* Congestion
Conical
cervix 622.6
cornea 371.60
teeth 520.2
Conjoined twins 759.4
causing disproportion (fetopelvic)
653.7 ☑
Conjugal maladjustment V61.10

Conjugal maladjustment —
continued
involving divorce or estrangement
V61.0
Conjunctiva — *see* condition
Conjunctivitis (exposure) (infectious)
(nondiphtheritic) (pneumococcal)
(pustular) (staphylococcal) (streptococcal) NEC 372.30
actinic 370.24
acute 372.00
atopic 372.05
contagious 372.03
follicular 372.02
hemorrhagic (viral) 077.4
adenoviral (acute) 077.3
allergic (chronic) 372.14
with hay fever 372.05
anaphylactic 372.05
angular 372.03
Apollo (viral) 077.4
atopic 372.05
blennorrhagic (neonatorum) 098.40
catarrhal 372.03
chemical 372.01
allergic 372.05
meaning corrosion — *see* Burn,
conjunctiva
chlamydial 077.98
due to
Chlamydia trachomatis — *see*
Trachoma
paratrachoma 077.0
chronic 372.10
allergic 372.14
follicular 372.12
simple 372.11
specified type NEC 372.14
vernal 372.13
diphtheritic 032.81
due to
dust 372.05
enterovirus type 70 077.4
erythema multiforme
695.1 [372.33]
filariasis (*see also* Filariasis)
125.9 [372.15]
mucocutaneous
disease NEC 372.33
leishmaniasis 085.5 [372.15]
Reiter's disease 099.3 [372.33]
syphilis 095.8 [372.10]
toxoplasmosis (acquired) 130.1
congenital (active) 771.2
trachoma — *see* Trachoma
dust 372.05
eczematous 370.31
epidemic 077.1
hemorrhagic 077.4
follicular (acute) 372.02
adenoviral (acute) 077.3
chronic 372.12
glare 370.24
gonococcal (neonatorum) 098.40
granular (trachomatous) 076.1
late effect 139.1
hemorrhagic (acute) (epidemic) 077.4
herpetic (simplex) 054.43
zoster 053.21
inclusion 077.0
infantile 771.6
influenzal 372.03
Koch-Weeks 372.03
light 372.05
medicamentosa 372.05
membranous 372.04
meningococcic 036.89
Morax-Axenfeld 372.02
mucopurulent NEC 372.03
neonatal 771.6
gonococcal 098.40
Newcastle's 077.8
nodosa 360.14
of Beal 077.3
parasitic 372.15

Conjunctivitis — *continued*
- parasitic — *continued*
  - filariasis (*see also* Filariasis) 125.9 *[372.15]*
  - mucocutaneous leishmaniasis 085.5 *[372.15]*
- Parinaud's 372.02
- petrificans 372.39
- phlyctenular 370.31
- pseudomembranous 372.04
  - diphtheritic 032.81
- purulent 372.03
- Reiter's 099.3 *[372.33]*
- rosacea 695.3 *[372.31]*
- serous 372.01
  - viral 077.99
- simple chronic 372.11
- specified NEC 372.39
- sunlamp 372.04
- swimming pool 077.0
- trachomatous (follicular) 076.1
  - acute 076.0
  - late effect 139.1
- traumatic NEC 372.39
- tuberculous (*see also* Tuberculosis) 017.3 ☑ *[370.31]*
- tularemic 021.3
- tularensis 021.3
- vernal 372.13
  - limbar 372.13 *[370.32]*
- viral 077.99
  - acute hemorrhagic 077.4
  - specified NEC 077.8

Conjunctivochalasis 372.81

Conjunctoblepharitis — *see* Conjunctivitis

Connective tissue — *see* condition

Conn (-Louis) syndrome (primary aldosteronism) 255.12

Conradi (-Hünermann) syndrome or disease (chondrodysplasia calcificans congenita) 756.59

Consanguinity V19.7

Consecutive — *see* condition

Consolidated lung (base) — *see* Pneumonia, lobar

Constipation 564.00
- atonic 564.09
- drug induced
  - correct substance properly administered 564.09
  - overdose or wrong substance given or taken 977.9
    - specified drug — *see* Table of Drugs and Chemicals
- neurogenic 564.09
- other specified NEC 564.09
- outlet dysfunction 564.02
- psychogenic 306.4
- simple 564.00
- slow transit 564.01
- spastic 564.09

Constitutional — *see also* condition
- arterial hypotension (*see also* Hypotension) 458.9
- obesity 278.00
  - morbid 278.01
- psychopathic state 301.9
- short stature in childhood 783.43
- state, developmental V21.9
  - specified development NEC V21.8
- substandard 301.6

Constitutionally substandard 301.6

Constriction
- anomalous, meningeal bands or folds 742.8
- aortic arch (congenital) 747.10
- asphyxiation or suffocation by 994.7
- bronchus 519.19 ▲
- canal, ear (*see also* Stricture, ear canal, acquired) 380.50
- duodenum 537.3
- gallbladder (*see also* Obstruction, gallbladder) 575.2
  - congenital 751.69

Constriction — *continued*
- intestine (*see also* Obstruction, intestine) 560.9
- larynx 478.74
  - congenital 748.3
- meningeal bands or folds, anomalous 742.8
- organ or site, congenital NEC — *see* Atresia
- prepuce (congenital) 605
- pylorus 537.0
  - adult hypertrophic 537.0
  - congenital or infantile 750.5
  - newborn 750.5
- ring (uterus) 661.4 ☑
  - affecting fetus or newborn 763.7
- spastic (*see also* Spasm)
  - ureter 593.3
  - urethra — *see* Stricture, urethra
- stomach 537.89
- ureter 593.3
- urethra — *see* Stricture, urethra
- visual field (functional) (peripheral) 368.45

Constrictive — *see* condition

Consultation
- without complaint or sickness V65.9
  - feared complaint unfounded V65.5
  - specified reason NEC V65.8
- medical (*see also* Counseling, medical)
  - specified reason NEC V65.8

Consumption — *see* Tuberculosis

Contact
- with
  - AIDS virus V01.79
  - anthrax V01.81
  - cholera V01.0
  - communicable disease V01.9
    - specified type NEC V01.89
    - viral NEC V01.79
  - Escherichia coli (E. coli) V01.83
  - German measles V01.4
  - gonorrhea V01.6
  - HIV V01.79
  - human immunodeficiency virus V01.79
  - meningococcus V01.84
  - parasitic disease NEC V01.89
  - poliomyelitis V01.2
  - rabies V01.5
  - rubella V01.4
  - SARS-associated coronavirus V01.82
  - smallpox V01.3
  - syphilis V01.6
  - tuberculosis V01.1
  - varicella V01.71
  - venereal disease V01.6
  - viral disease NEC V01.79
- dermatitis — *see* Dermatitis

Contamination, food — *see also* Poisoning, food 005.9

Contraception, contraceptive
- advice NEC V25.09
  - family planning V25.09
  - fitting of diaphragm V25.02
  - prescribing or use of
    - oral contraceptive agent V25.01
    - specified agent NEC V25.02
- counseling NEC V25.09
  - emergency V25.03
  - family planning V25.09
  - fitting of diaphragm V25.02
  - prescribing or use of
    - oral contraceptive agent V25.01
      - emergency V25.03
      - postcoital V25.03
    - specified agent NEC V25.02
- device (in situ) V45.59
  - causing menorrhagia 996.76
  - checking V25.42
  - complications 996.32
  - insertion V25.1
  - intrauterine V45.51
  - reinsertion V25.42
  - removal V25.42

Contraception, contraceptive — *continued*
- device — *continued*
  - subdermal V45.52
- fitting of diaphragm V25.02
- insertion
  - intrauterine contraceptive device V25.1
  - subdermal implantable V25.5
- maintenance V25.40
  - examination V25.40
    - oral contraceptive V25.41
    - specified method NEC V25.49
    - subdermal implantable V25.43
    - intrauterine device V25.42
  - intrauterine device V25.42
  - oral contraceptive V25.41
  - specified method NEC V25.49
  - subdermal implantable V25.43
- management NEC V25.49
- prescription
  - oral contraceptive agent V25.01
    - emergency V25.03
    - postcoital V25.03
    - repeat V25.41
  - specified agent NEC V25.02
    - repeat V25.49
- sterilization V25.2
- surveillance V25.40
  - intrauterine device V25.42
  - oral contraceptive agent V25.41
  - subdermal implantable V25.43
  - specified method NEC V25.49

Contraction, contracture, contracted
- Achilles tendon (*see also* Short, tendon, Achilles) 727.81
- anus 564.89
- axilla 729.9
- bile duct (*see also* Disease, biliary) 576.8
- bladder 596.8
  - neck or sphincter 596.0
- bowel (*see also* Obstruction, intestine) 560.9
- Braxton Hicks 644.1 ☑
- bronchus 519.19 ▲
- burn (old) — *see* Cicatrix
- cecum (*see also* Obstruction, intestine) 560.9
- cervix (*see also* Stricture, cervix) 622.4
  - congenital 752.49
- cicatricial — *see* Cicatrix
- colon (*see also* Obstruction, intestine) 560.9
- conjunctiva trachomatous, active 076.1
  - late effect 139.1
- Dupuytren's 728.6
- eyelid 374.41
- eye socket (after enucleation) 372.64
- face 729.9
- fascia (lata) (postural) 728.89
  - Dupuytren's 728.6
  - palmar 728.6
  - plantar 728.71
- finger NEC 736.29
  - congenital 755.59
  - joint (*see also* Contraction, joint) 718.44
- flaccid, paralytic
  - joint (*see also* Contraction, joint) 718.4 ☑
  - muscle 728.85
  - ocular 378.50
- gallbladder (*see also* Obstruction, gallbladder) 575.2
- hamstring 728.89
  - tendon 727.81
- heart valve — *see* Endocarditis
- Hicks' 644.1 ☑
- hip (*see also* Contraction, joint) 718.4 ☑
- hourglass
  - bladder 596.8
    - congenital 753.8

Contraction, contracture, contracted — *continued*
- hourglass — *continued*
  - gallbladder (*see also* Obstruction, gallbladder) 575.2
    - congenital 751.69
  - stomach 536.8
    - congenital 750.7
    - psychogenic 306.4
  - uterus 661.4 ☑
    - affecting fetus or newborn 763.7
- hysterical 300.11
- infantile (*see also* Epilepsy) 345.6 ☑
- internal os (*see also* Stricture, cervix) 622.4
- intestine (*see also* Obstruction, intestine) 560.9
- joint (abduction) (acquired) (adduction) (flexion) (rotation) 718.40
  - ankle 718.47
  - congenital NEC 755.8
    - generalized or multiple 754.89
      - lower limb joints 754.89
    - hip (*see also* Subluxation, congenital, hip) 754.32
    - lower limb (including pelvic girdle) not involving hip 754.89
    - upper limb (including shoulder girdle) 755.59
  - elbow 718.42
  - foot 718.47
  - hand 718.44
  - hip 718.45
  - hysterical 300.11
  - knee 718.46
  - multiple sites 718.49
  - pelvic region 718.45
  - shoulder (region) 718.41
  - specified site NEC 718.48
  - wrist 718.43
- kidney (granular) (secondary) (*see also* Sclerosis, renal) 587
  - congenital 753.3
  - hydronephritic 591
  - pyelonephritic (*see also* Pyelitis, chronic) 590.00
  - tuberculous (*see also* Tuberculosis) 016.0 ☑
- ligament 728.89
  - congenital 756.89
- liver — *see* Cirrhosis, liver
- muscle (postinfectional) (postural) NEC 728.85
  - congenital 756.89
    - sternocleidomastoid 754.1
  - extraocular 378.60
  - eye (extrinsic) (*see also* Strabismus) 378.9
    - paralytic (*see also* Strabismus, paralytic) 378.50
  - flaccid 728.85
  - hysterical 300.11
  - ischemic (Volkmann's) 958.6
  - paralytic 728.85
  - posttraumatic 958.6
  - psychogenic 306.0
    - specified as conversion reaction 300.11
- myotonic 728.85
- neck (*see also* Torticollis) 723.5
  - congenital 754.1
  - psychogenic 306.0
- ocular muscle (*see also* Strabismus) 378.9
  - paralytic (*see also* Strabismus, paralytic) 378.50
- organ or site, congenital NEC — *see* Atresia
- outlet (pelvis) — *see* Contraction, pelvis
- palmar fascia 728.6
- paralytic
  - joint (*see also* Contraction, joint) 718.4 ☑
  - muscle 728.85

☑ Additional Digit Required — Refer to the Tabular List for Digit Selection   ▼ Subterms under main terms may continue to next column or page

2007 ICD-9-CM   ▶◀ Revised Text   ● New Line   ▲ Revised Code   October 2006 · Volume 2 — 57

Contraction, contracture, contracted
— continued
paralytic — continued
muscle — continued
ocular (see also Strabismus, paralytic) 378.50
pelvis (acquired) (general) 738.6
affecting fetus or newborn 763.1
complicating delivery 653.1 ☑
causing obstructed labor 660.1 ☑
generally contracted 653.1 ☑
causing obstructed labor 660.1 ☑
inlet 653.2 ☑
causing obstructed labor 660.1 ☑
midpelvic 653.8 ☑
causing obstructed labor 660.1 ☑
midplane 653.8 ☑
causing obstructed labor 660.1 ☑
outlet 653.3 ☑
causing obstructed labor 660.1 ☑
plantar fascia 728.71
premature
atrial 427.61
auricular 427.61
auriculoventricular 427.61
heart (junctional) (nodal) 427.60
supraventricular 427.61
ventricular 427.69
prostate 602.8
pylorus (see also Pylorospasm) 537.81
rectosigmoid (see also Obstruction, intestine) 560.9
rectum, rectal (sphincter) 564.89
psychogenic 306.4
ring (Bandl's) 661.4 ☑
affecting fetus or newborn 763.7
scar — see Cicatrix
sigmoid (see also Obstruction, intestine) 560.9
socket, eye 372.64
spine (see also Curvature, spine) 737.9
stomach 536.8
hourglass 536.8
congenital 750.7
psychogenic 306.4
tendon (sheath) (see also Short, tendon) 727.81
toe 735.8
ureterovesical orifice (postinfectional) 593.3
urethra 599.84
uterus 621.8
abnormal 661.9 ☑
affecting fetus or newborn 763.7
clonic, hourglass or tetanic 661.4 ☑
affecting fetus or newborn 763.7
dyscoordinate 661.4 ☑
affecting fetus or newborn 763.7
hourglass 661.4 ☑
affecting fetus or newborn 763.7
hypotonic NEC 661.2 ☑
affecting fetus or newborn 763.7
incoordinate 661.4 ☑
affecting fetus or newborn 763.7
inefficient or poor 661.2 ☑
affecting fetus or newborn 763.7
irregular 661.2 ☑
affecting fetus or newborn 763.7
tetanic 661.4 ☑
affecting fetus or newborn 763.7
vagina (outlet) 623.2
vesical 596.8
neck or urethral orifice 596.0
visual field, generalized 368.45
Volkmann's (ischemic) 958.6
Contusion (skin surface intact) 924.9
with
crush injury — see Crush

Contusion — continued
with — continued
dislocation — see Dislocation, by site
fracture — see Fracture, by site
internal injury (see also Injury, internal, by site)
heart — see Contusion, cardiac
kidney — see Contusion, kidney
liver — see Contusion, liver
lung — see Contusion, lung
spleen — see Contusion, spleen
intracranial injury — see Injury, intracranial
nerve injury — see Injury, nerve
open wound — see Wound, open, by site
abdomen, abdominal (muscle) (wall) 922.2
organ(s) NEC 868.00
adnexa, eye NEC 921.9
ankle 924.21
with other parts of foot 924.20
arm 923.9
lower (with elbow) 923.10
upper 923.03
with shoulder or axillary region 923.09
auditory canal (external) (meatus) (and other part(s) of neck, scalp, or face, except eye) 920
auricle, ear (and other part(s) of neck, scalp, or face except eye) 920
axilla 923.02
with shoulder or upper arm 923.09
back 922.31
bone NEC 924.9
brain (cerebral) (membrane) (with hemorrhage) 851.8 ☑

Note — *Use the following fifth-digit subclassification with categories 851–854:*

0   *unspecified state of consciousness*

1   *with no loss of consciousness*

2   *with brief [less than one hour] loss of consciousness*

3   *with moderate [1–24 hours] loss of consciousness*

4   *with prolonged [more than 24 hours] loss of consciousness and return to pre–existing conscious level*

5   *with prolonged [more than 24 hours] loss of consciousness, without return to pre–existing conscious level*

Use fifth–digit 5 to designate when a patient is unconscious and dies before regaining consciousness, regardless of the duration of the loss of consciousness

6   *with loss of consciousness of unspecified duration*

9   *with concussion, unspecified*

---

with
open intracranial wound 851.9 ☑
skull fracture — see Fracture, skull, by site
cerebellum 851.4 ☑
with open intracranial wound 851.5 ☑
cortex 851.0 ☑
with open intracranial wound 851.1 ☑
occipital lobe 851.4 ☑
with open intracranial wound 851.5 ☑
stem 851.4 ☑
with open intracranial wound 851.5 ☑

Contusion — continued
breast 922.0
brow (and other part(s) of neck, scalp, or face, except eye) 920
buttock 922.32
canthus 921.1
cardiac 861.01
with open wound into thorax 861.11
cauda equina (spine) 952.4
cerebellum — see Contusion, brain, cerebellum
cerebral — see Contusion, brain
cheek(s) (and other part(s) of neck, scalp, or face, except eye) 920
chest (wall) 922.1
chin (and other part(s) of neck, scalp, or face, except eye) 920
clitoris 922.4
conjunctiva 921.1
conus medullaris (spine) 952.4
cornea 921.3
corpus cavernosum 922.4
cortex (brain) (cerebral) — see Contusion, brain, cortex
costal region 922.1
ear (and other part(s) of neck, scalp, or face except eye) 920
elbow 923.11
with forearm 923.10
epididymis 922.4
epigastric region 922.2
eye NEC 921.9
eyeball 921.3
eyelid(s) (and periocular area) 921.1
face (and neck, or scalp, any part, except eye) 920
femoral triangle 922.2
fetus or newborn 772.6
finger(s) (nail) (subungual) 923.3
flank 922.2
foot (with ankle) (excluding toe(s)) 924.20
forearm (and elbow) 923.10
forehead (and other part(s) of neck, scalp, or face, except eye) 920
genital organs, external 922.4
globe (eye) 921.3
groin 922.2
gum(s) (and other part(s) of neck, scalp, or face, except eye) 920
hand(s) (except fingers alone) 923.20
head (any part, except eye) (and face) (and neck) 920
heart — see Contusion, cardiac
heel 924.20
hip 924.01
with thigh 924.00
iliac region 922.2
inguinal region 922.2
internal organs (abdomen, chest, or pelvis) NEC — see Injury, internal, by site
interscapular region 922.33
iris (eye) 921.3
kidney 866.01
with open wound into cavity 866.11
knee 924.11
with lower leg 924.10
labium (majus) (minus) 922.4
lacrimal apparatus, gland, or sac 921.1
larynx (and other part(s) of neck, scalp, or face, except eye) 920
late effect — see Late, effects (of), contusion
leg 924.5
lower (with knee) 924.10
lens 921.3
lingual (and other part(s) of neck, scalp, or face, except eye) 920
lip(s) (and other part(s) of neck, scalp, or face, except eye) 920
liver 864.01

Contusion — continued
liver — continued
with
laceration — see Laceration, liver
open wound into cavity 864.11
lower extremity 924.5
multiple sites 924.4
lumbar region 922.31
lung 861.21
with open wound into thorax 861.31
malar region (and other part(s) of neck, scalp, or face, except eye) 920
mandibular joint (and other part(s) of neck, scalp, or face, except eye) 920
mastoid region (and other part(s) of neck, scalp, or face, except eye) 920
membrane, brain — see Contusion, brain
midthoracic region 922.1
mouth (and other part(s) of neck, scalp, or face, except eye) 920
multiple sites (not classifiable to same three-digit category) 924.8
lower limb 924.4
trunk 922.8
upper limb 923.8
muscle NEC 924.9
myocardium — see Contusion, cardiac
nasal (septum) (and other part(s) of neck, scalp, or face, except eye) 920
neck (and scalp or face, any part, except eye) 920
nerve — see Injury, nerve, by site
nose (and other part(s) of neck, scalp, or face, except eye) 920
occipital region (scalp) (and neck or face, except eye) 920
lobe — see Contusion, brain, occipital lobe
orbit (region) (tissues) 921.2
palate (soft) (and other part(s) of neck, scalp, or face, except eye) 920
parietal region (scalp) (and neck or face, except eye) 920
lobe — see Contusion, brain
penis 922.4
pericardium — see Contusion, cardiac
perineum 922.4
periocular area 921.1
pharynx (and other part(s) of neck, scalp, or face, except eye) 920
popliteal space (see also Contusion, knee) 924.11
prepuce 922.4
pubic region 922.4
pudenda 922.4
pulmonary — see Contusion, lung
quadriceps femoralis 924.00
rib cage 922.1
sacral region 922.32
salivary ducts or glands (and other part(s) of neck, scalp, or face, except eye) 920
scalp (and neck, or face any part, except eye) 920
scapular region 923.01
with shoulder or upper arm 923.09
sclera (eye) 921.3
scrotum 922.4
shoulder 923.00
with upper arm or axillar regions 923.09
skin NEC 924.9
skull 920
spermatic cord 922.4
spinal cord (see also Injury, spinal, by site)
cauda equina 952.4
conus medullaris 952.4
spleen 865.01

☑ Additional Digit Required — Refer to the Tabular List for Digit Selection
ᴺᴱᵂ Subterms under main terms may continue to next column or page
58 — Volume 2
▶◀ Revised Text   ● New Line   ▲ Revised Code
2007 ICD-9-CM

Contusion — *continued*
spleen — *continued*
with open wound into cavity 865.11
sternal region 922.1
stomach — *see* Injury, internal, stomach
subconjunctival 921.1
subcutaneous NEC 924.9
submaxillary region (and other part(s) of neck, scalp, or face, except eye) 920
submental region (and other part(s) of neck, scalp, or face, except eye) 920
subperiosteal NEC 924.9
supraclavicular fossa (and other part(s) of neck, scalp, or face, except eye) 920
supraorbital (and other part(s) of neck, scalp, or face, except eye) 920
temple (region) (and other part(s) of neck, scalp, or face, except eye) 920
testis 922.4
thigh (and hip) 924.00
thorax 922.1
organ — *see* Injury, internal, intrathoracic
throat (and other part(s) of neck, scalp, or face, except eye) 920
thumb(s) (nail) (subungual) 923.3
toe(s) (nail) (subungual) 924.3
tongue (and other part(s) of neck, scalp, or face, except eye) 920
trunk 922.9
multiple sites 922.8
specified site — *see* Contusion, by site
tunica vaginalis 922.4
tympanum (membrane) (and other part(s) of neck, scalp, or face, except eye) 920
upper extremity 923.9
multiple sites 923.8
uvula (and other part(s) of neck, scalp, or face, except eye) 920
vagina 922.4
vocal cord(s) (and other part(s) of neck, scalp, or face, except eye) 920
vulva 922.4
wrist 923.21
with hand(s), except finger(s) alone 923.20
Conus (any type) (congenital) 743.57
acquired 371.60
medullaris syndrome 336.8
Convalescence (following) V66.9
chemotherapy V66.2
medical NEC V66.5
psychotherapy V66.3
radiotherapy V66.1
surgery NEC V66.0
treatment (for) NEC V66.5
combined V66.6
fracture V66.4
mental disorder NEC V66.3
specified disorder NEC V66.5
Conversion
closed surgical procedure to open procedure
arthroscopic V64.43
laparoscopic V64.41
thoracoscopic V64.42
hysteria, hysterical, any type 300.11
neurosis, any 300.11
reaction, any 300.11
Converter, tuberculosis (test reaction) 795.5
Convulsions (idiopathic) 780.39
apoplectiform (*see also* Disease, cerebrovascular, acute) 436
brain 780.39
cerebral 780.39
cerebrospinal 780.39

Convulsions — *continued*
due to trauma NEC — *see* Injury, intracranial
eclamptic (*see also* Eclampsia) 780.39
epileptic (*see also* Epilepsy) 345.9 ☑
epileptiform (*see also* Seizure, epileptiform) 780.39
epileptoid (*see also* Seizure, epileptiform) 780.39
ether
anesthetic
correct substance properly administered 780.39
overdose or wrong substance given 968.2
other specified type — *see* Table of Drugs and Chemicals
febrile ▶(simple)◀ 780.31
complex 780.32   ●
generalized 780.39
hysterical 300.11
infantile 780.39
epilepsy — *see* Epilepsy
internal 780.39
jacksonian (*see also* Epilepsy) 345.5 ☑
myoclonic 333.2
newborn 779.0
paretic 094.1
pregnancy (nephritic) (uremic) — *see* Eclampsia, pregnancy
psychomotor (*see also* Epilepsy) 345.4 ☑
puerperal, postpartum — *see* Eclampsia, pregnancy
recurrent 780.39
epileptic — *see* Epilepsy
reflex 781.0
repetitive 780.39
epileptic — *see* Epilepsy
salaam (*see also* Epilepsy) 345.6 ☑
scarlatinal 034.1
spasmodic 780.39
tetanus, tetanic (*see also* Tetanus) 037
thymic 254.8
uncinate 780.39
uremic 586
Convulsive — *see also* Convulsions
disorder or state 780.39
epileptic — *see* Epilepsy
equivalent, abdominal (*see also* Epilepsy) 345.5 ☑
Cooke-Apert-Gallais syndrome (adrenogenital) 255.2
Cooley's anemia (erythroblastic) 282.49
Coolie itch 126.9
Cooper's
disease 610.1
hernia — *see* Hernia, Cooper's
Coordination disturbance 781.3
Copra itch 133.8
Coprolith 560.39
Coprophilia 302.89
Coproporphyria, hereditary 277.1
Coprostasis 560.39
with hernia (*see also* Hernia, by site, with obstruction)
gangrenous — *see* Hernia, by site, with gangrene
Cor
biloculare 745.7
bovinum — *see* Hypertrophy, cardiac
bovis (*see also* Hypertrophy, cardiac)
pulmonale (chronic) 416.9
acute 415.0
triatriatum, triatrium 746.82
triloculare 745.8
biatriatum 745.3
biventriculare 745.69
Corbus' disease 607.1
Cord — *see also* condition
around neck (tightly) (with compression)
affecting fetus or newborn 762.5
complicating delivery 663.1 ☑
without compression 663.3 ☑

Cord — *see also* condition — *continued*
around neck — *continued*
complicating delivery — *continued*
without compression — *continued*
affecting fetus or newborn 762.6
bladder NEC 344.61
tabetic 094.0
prolapse
affecting fetus or newborn 762.4
complicating delivery 663.0 ☑
Cord's angiopathy — *see also* Tuberculosis 017.3 ☑ *[362.18]*
Cordis ectopia 746.87
Corditis (spermatic) 608.4
Corectopia 743.46
Cori type glycogen storage disease — *see* Disease, glycogen storage
Cork-handlers' disease or lung 495.3
Corkscrew esophagus 530.5
Corlett's pyosis (impetigo) 684
Corn (infected) 700
Cornea — *see also* condition
donor V59.5
guttata (dystrophy) 371.57
plana 743.41
Cornelia de Lange's syndrome (Amsterdam dwarf, mental retardation, and brachycephaly) 759.89
Cornual gestation or pregnancy — *see* Pregnancy, cornual
Cornu cutaneum 702.8
Coronary (artery) — *see also* condition
arising from aorta or pulmonary trunk 746.85
Corpora — *see also* condition
amylacea (prostate) 602.8
cavernosa — *see* condition
Corpulence — *see* Obesity
Corpus — *see* condition
Corrigan's disease — *see* Insufficiency, aortic
Corrosive burn — *see* Burn, by site
Corsican fever — *see also* Malaria 084.6
Cortical — *see also* condition
blindness 377.75
necrosis, kidney (bilateral) 583.6
Corticoadrenal — *see* condition
Corticosexual syndrome 255.2
Coryza (acute) 460
with grippe or influenza 487.1
syphilitic 095.8
congenital (chronic) 090.0
Costen's syndrome or complex 524.60
Costiveness — *see also* Constipation 564.00
Costochondritis 733.6
Cotard's syndrome (paranoia) 297.1
Cot death 798.0
Cotugno's disease 724.3
Cough 786.2
with hemorrhage (*see also* Hemoptysis) 786.3
affected 786.2
bronchial 786.2
with grippe or influenza 487.1
chronic 786.2
epidemic 786.2
functional 306.1
hemorrhagic 786.3
hysterical 300.11
laryngeal, spasmodic 786.2
nervous 786.2
psychogenic 306.1
smokers' 491.0
tea tasters' 112.89
Counseling NEC V65.40
without complaint or sickness V65.49
abuse victim NEC V62.89
child V61.21
partner V61.11
spouse V61.11

Counseling — *continued*
child abuse, maltreatment, or neglect V61.21
contraceptive NEC V25.09
device (intrauterine) V25.02
maintenance V25.40
intrauterine contraceptive device V25.42
oral contraceptive (pill) V25.41
specified type NEC V25.49
subdermal implantable V25.43
management NEC V25.9
oral contraceptive (pill) V25.01
emergency V25.03
postcoital V25.03
prescription NEC V25.02
oral contraceptive (pill) V25.01
emergency V25.03
postcoital V25.03
repeat prescription V25.41
repeat prescription V25.40
subdermal implantable V25.43
surveillance NEC V25.40
dietary V65.3
exercise V65.41
expectant mother, pediatric pre-birth visit V65.11
explanation of
investigation finding NEC V65.49
medication NEC V65.49
family planning V25.09
for nonattending third party V65.19
genetic V26.33
gonorrhea V65.45
health (advice) (education) (instruction) NEC V65.49
HIV V65.44
human immunodeficiency virus V65.44
injury prevention V65.43
insulin pump training V65.46
marital V61.10
medical (for) V65.9
boarding school resident V60.6
condition not demonstrated V65.5
feared complaint and no disease found V65.5
institutional resident V60.6
on behalf of another V65.19
person living alone V60.3
parent-child conflict V61.20
specified problem NEC V61.29
partner abuse
perpetrator V61.12
victim V61.11
pediatric pre-birth visit for expectant mother V65.11
perpetrator of
child abuse V62.83
parental V61.22
partner abuse V61.12
spouse abuse V61.12
procreative V65.49
sex NEC V65.49
transmitted disease NEC V65.45
HIV V65.44
specified reason NEC V65.49
spousal abuse
perpetrator V61.12
victim V61.11
substance use and abuse V65.42
syphilis V65.45
victim (of)
abuse NEC V62.89
child abuse V61.21
partner abuse V61.11
spousal abuse V61.11
Coupled rhythm 427.89
Couvelaire uterus (complicating delivery) — *see* Placenta, separation
Cowper's gland — *see* condition
Cowperitis — *see also* Urethritis 597.89
gonorrheal (acute) 098.0
chronic or duration of 2 months or over 098.2
Cowpox (abortive) 051.0

Index — Cowpox — Cruz-Chagas disease

Cowpox — *continued*
  due to vaccination 999.0
  eyelid 051.0 *[373.5]*
    postvaccination 999.0 *[373.5]*
Coxa
  plana 732.1
  valga (acquired) 736.31
    congenital 755.61
    late effect of rickets 268.1
  vara (acquired) 736.32
    congenital 755.62
    late effect of rickets 268.1
Coxae malum senilis 715.25
Coxalgia (nontuberculous) 719.45
  tuberculous (*see also* Tuberculosis)
    015.1 ☑ *[730.85]*
Coxalgic pelvis 736.30
Coxitis 716.65
Coxsackie (infection) (virus) 079.2
  central nervous system NEC 048
  endocarditis 074.22
  enteritis 008.67
  meningitis (aseptic) 047.0
  myocarditis 074.23
  pericarditis 074.21
  pharyngitis 074.0
  pleurodynia 074.1
  specific disease NEC 074.8
Crabs, meaning pubic lice 132.2
Crack baby 760.75
Cracked   ●
  nipple 611.2   ●
    puerperal, postpartum 676.1 ☑   ●
  tooth 521.81   ●
Cradle cap 690.11
Craft neurosis 300.89
Craigiasis 007.8
Cramp(s) 729.82
  abdominal 789.0 ☑
  bathing 994.1
  colic 789.0 ☑
    psychogenic 306.4
  due to immersion 994.1
  extremity (lower) (upper) NEC 729.82
  fireman 992.2
  heat 992.2
  hysterical 300.11
  immersion 994.1
  intestinal 789.0 ☑
    psychogenic 306.4
  linotypist's 300.89
    organic 333.84
  muscle (extremity) (general) 729.82
    due to immersion 994.1
    hysterical 300.11
  occupational (hand) 300.89
    organic 333.84
  psychogenic 307.89
  salt depletion 276.1
  sleep related leg 327.52
  stoker 992.2
  stomach 789.0 ☑
  telegraphers' 300.89
    organic 333.84
  typists' 300.89
    organic 333.84
  uterus 625.8
    menstrual 625.3
  writers' 333.84
    organic 333.84
    psychogenic 300.89
Cranial — *see* condition
Cranioclasis, fetal 763.89
Craniocleidodysostosis 755.59
Craniofenestria (skull) 756.0
Craniolacunia (skull) 756.0
Craniopagus 759.4
Craniopathy, metabolic 733.3
Craniopharyngeal — *see* condition
Craniopharyngioma (M9350/1) 237.0
Craniorachischisis (totalis) 740.1
Cranioschisis 756.0
Craniostenosis 756.0
Craniosynostosis 756.0
Craniotabes (cause unknown) 733.3
  rachitic 268.1

Craniotabes — *continued*
  syphilitic 090.5
Craniotomy, fetal 763.89
Cranium — *see* condition
Craw-craw 125.3
Creaking joint 719.60
  ankle 719.67
  elbow 719.62
  foot 719.67
  hand 719.64
  hip 719.65
  knee 719.66
  multiple sites 719.69
  pelvic region 719.65
  shoulder (region) 719.61
  specified site NEC 719.68
  wrist 719.63
Creeping
  eruption 126.9
  palsy 335.21
  paralysis 335.21
Crenated tongue 529.8
Creotoxism 005.9
Crepitus
  caput 756.0
  joint 719.60
    ankle 719.67
    elbow 719.62
    foot 719.67
    hand 719.64
    hip 719.65
    knee 719.66
    multiple sites 719.69
    pelvic region 719.65
    shoulder (region) 719.61
    specified site NEC 719.68
    wrist 719.63
Crescent or conus choroid, congenital
  743.57
Cretin, cretinism (athyrotic) (congenital)
  (endemic) (metabolic) (nongoitrous)
  (sporadic) 243
  goitrous (sporadic) 246.1
  pelvis (dwarf type) (male type) 243
    with disproportion (fetopelvic)
      653.1 ☑
      affecting fetus or newborn 763.1
      causing obstructed labor
        660.1 ☑
        affecting fetus or newborn
          763.1
  pituitary 253.3
Cretinoid degeneration 243
Creutzfeldt-Jakob disease (syndrome)
  (new variant) 046.1
  with dementia
    with behavioral disturbance
      046.1 *[294.11]*
    without behavioral disturbance
      046.1 *[294.10]*
Crib death 798.0
Cribriform hymen 752.49
Cri-du-chat syndrome 758.31
Crigler-Najjar disease or syndrome
  (congenital hyperbilirubinemia)
  277.4
Crimean hemorrhagic fever 065.0
Criminalism 301.7
Crisis
  abdomen 789.0 ☑
  addisonian (acute adrenocortical insuf-
    ficiency) 255.4
  adrenal (cortical) 255.4
  asthmatic — *see* Asthma
  brain, cerebral (*see also* Disease,
    cerebrovascular, acute) 436
  celiac 579.0
  Dietl's 593.4
  emotional NEC 309.29
    acute reaction to stress 308.0
    adjustment reaction 309.9
    specific to childhood or adolescence
      313.9
  gastric (tabetic) 094.0
  glaucomatocyclitic 364.22
  heart (*see also* Failure, heart) 428.9

Crisis — *continued*
  hypertensive — *see* Hypertension
  nitritoid
    correct substance properly admin-
      istered 458.29
    overdose or wrong substance given
      or taken 961.1
  oculogyric 378.87
    psychogenic 306.7
  Pel's 094.0
  psychosexual identity 302.6
  rectum 094.0
  renal 593.81
  sickle cell 282.62
  stomach (tabetic) 094.0
  tabetic 094.0
  thyroid (*see also* Thyrotoxicosis)
    242.9 ☑
  thyrotoxic (*see also* Thyrotoxicosis)
    242.9 ☑
  vascular — *see* Disease, cerebrovascu-
    lar, acute
Crocq's disease (acrocyanosis) 443.89
Crohn's disease — *see also* Enteritis,
  regional 555.9
Cronkhite-Canada syndrome 211.3
Crooked septum, nasal 470
Cross
  birth (of fetus) complicating delivery
    652.3 ☑
    with successful version 652.1 ☑
    causing obstructed labor 660.0 ☑
  bite, anterior or posterior 524.27   ▲
  eye (*see also* Esotropia) 378.00
Crossed ectopia of kidney 753.3
Crossfoot 754.50
Croup, croupous (acute) (angina)
  (catarrhal) (infective) (inflammatory)
  (laryngeal) (membranous)
  (nondiphtheritic) (pseudomembranous) 464.4
  asthmatic (*see also* Asthma) 493.9 ☑
  bronchial 466.0
  diphtheritic (membranous) 032.3
  false 478.75
  spasmodic 478.75
    diphtheritic 032.3
  stridulous 478.75
    diphtheritic 032.3
Crouzon's disease (craniofacial dysostosis) 756.0
Crowding, teeth 524.31
CRST syndrome (cutaneous systemic
  sclerosis) 710.1
Cruchet's disease (encephalitis lethargica) 049.8
Cruelty in children — *see also* Disturbance, conduct 312.9
Crural ulcer — *see also* Ulcer, lower extremity 707.10
Crush, crushed, crushing (injury) 929.9
  with
    fracture — *see* Fracture, by site
  abdomen 926.19
    internal — *see* Injury, internal,
      abdomen
  ankle 928.21
    with other parts of foot 928.20
  arm 927.9
    lower (and elbow) 927.10
    upper 927.03
      with shoulder or axillary region
        927.09
  axilla 927.02
    with shoulder or upper arm 927.09
  back 926.11
  breast 926.19
  buttock 926.12
  cheek 925.1
  chest — *see* Injury, internal, chest
  ear 925.1
  elbow 927.11
    with forearm 927.10
  face 925.1
  finger(s) 927.3
    with hand(s) 927.20

Crush, crushed, crushing —
  continued
  finger(s) — *continued*
    with hand(s) — *continued*
      and wrist(s) 927.21
  flank 926.19
  foot, excluding toe(s) alone (with an-
    kle) 928.20
  forearm (and elbow) 927.10
  genitalia, external (female) (male)
    926.0
    internal — *see* Injury, internal,
      genital organ NEC
  hand, except finger(s) alone (and wrist)
    927.20
  head — *see* Fracture, skull, by site
  heel 928.20
  hip 928.01
    with thigh 928.00
  internal organ (abdomen, chest, or
    pelvis) — *see* Injury, internal,
    by site
  knee 928.11
    with leg, lower 928.10
  labium (majus) (minus) 926.0
  larynx 925.2
  late effect — *see* Late, effects (of),
    crushing
  leg 928.9
    lower 928.10
      and knee 928.11
    upper 928.00
  limb
    lower 928.9
      multiple sites 928.8
    upper 927.9
      multiple sites 927.8
  multiple sites NEC 929.0
  neck 925.2
  nerve — *see* Injury, nerve, by site
  nose 802.0
    open 802.1
  penis 926.0
  pharynx 925.2
  scalp 925.1
  scapular region 927.01
    with shoulder or upper arm 927.09
  scrotum 926.0
  shoulder 927.00
    with upper arm or axillary region
      927.09
  skull or cranium — *see* Fracture,
    skull, by site
  spinal cord — *see* Injury, spinal, by
    site
  syndrome (complication of trauma)
    958.5
  testis 926.0
  thigh (with hip) 928.00
  throat 925.2
  thumb(s) (and fingers) 927.3
  toe(s) 928.3
    with foot 928.20
      and ankle 928.21
  tonsil 925.2
  trunk 926.9
    chest — *see* Injury, internal, in-
      trathoracic organs NEC
    internal organ — *see* Injury, inter-
      nal, by site
    multiple sites 926.8
    specified site NEC 926.19
  vulva 926.0
  wrist 927.21
    with hand(s), except fingers alone
      927.20
Crusta lactea 690.11
Crusts 782.8
Crutch paralysis 953.4
**Cruveilhier-Baumgarten cirrhosis,
  disease, or syndrome** 571.5
Cruveilhier's disease 335.21
Cruz-Chagas disease — *see also* Try-
  panosomiasis 086.2

☑ Additional Digit Required — Refer to the Tabular List for Digit Selection   ▼ Subterms under main terms may continue to next column or page

60 — Volume 2 · October 2006   ▶◀ Revised Text   ● New Line   ▲ Revised Code   *2007 ICD-9-CM*

Crying ●
- constant, continuous ●
  - adolescent 780.95 ●
  - adult 780.95 ●
  - baby 780.92 ●
  - child 780.95 ●
  - infant 780.92 ●
  - newborn 780.92 ●
- excessive ●
  - adolescent 780.95 ●
  - adult 780.95 ●
  - baby 780.92 ●
  - child 780.95 ●
  - infant 780.92 ●
  - newborn 780.92 ●
Cryoglobulinemia (mixed) 273.2
Crypt (anal) (rectal) 569.49
Cryptitis (anal) (rectal) 569.49
Cryptococcosis (European) (pulmonary) (systemic) 117.5
Cryptococcus 117.5
- epidermicus 117.5
- neoformans, infection by 117.5
Cryptopapillitis (anus) 569.49
Cryptophthalmos (eyelid) 743.06
Cryptorchid, cryptorchism, cryptorchidism 752.51
Cryptosporidiosis 007.4
Cryptotia 744.29
Crystallopathy
- calcium pyrophosphate (see also Arthritis) 275.49 [712.2] ☑
- dicalcium phosphate (see also Arthritis) 275.49 [712.1] ☑
- gouty 274.0
- pyrophosphate NEC (see also Arthritis) 275.49 [712.2] ☑
- uric acid 274.0
Crystalluria 791.9
Csillag's disease (lichen sclerosis et atrophicus) 701.0
Cuban itch 050.1
Cubitus
- valgus (acquired) 736.01
  - congenital 755.59
  - late effect of rickets 268.1
- varus (acquired) 736.02
  - congenital 755.59
  - late effect of rickets 268.1
Cultural deprivation V62.4
Cupping of optic disc 377.14
Curling esophagus 530.5
Curling's ulcer — see Ulcer, duodenum
Curschmann (-Batten) (-Steinert) disease or syndrome 359.2
Curvature
- organ or site, congenital NEC — see Distortion
- penis (lateral) 752.69
- Pott's (spinal) (see also Tuberculosis) 015.0 ☑ [737.43]
- radius, idiopathic, progressive (congenital) 755.54
- spine (acquired) (angular) (idiopathic) (incorrect) (postural) 737.9
  - congenital 754.2
  - due to or associated with
    - Charcôt-Marie-Tooth disease 356.1 [737.40]
    - mucopolysaccharidosis 277.5 [737.40]
    - neurofibromatosis 237.71 [737.40]
    - osteitis
      - deformans 731.0 [737.40]
      - fibrosa cystica 252.01 [737.40]
    - osteoporosis (see also Osteoporosis) 733.00 [737.40]
    - poliomyelitis (see also Poliomyelitis) 138 [737.40]
    - tuberculosis (Pott's curvature) (see also Tuberculosis) 015.0 ☑ [737.43]
  - kyphoscoliotic (see also Kyphoscoliosis) 737.30

Curvature — continued
- spine — continued
  - kyphotic (see also Kyphosis) 737.10
    - late effect of rickets 268.1 [737.40]
    - Pott's 015.0 ☑ [737.40]
  - scoliotic (see also Scoliosis) 737.30
  - specified NEC 737.8
  - tuberculous 015.0 ☑ [737.40]
Cushing's
- basophilism, disease, or syndrome (iatrogenic) (idiopathic) (pituitary basophilism) (pituitary dependent) 255.0
- ulcer — see Ulcer, peptic
Cushingoid due to steroid therapy
- correct substance properly administered 255.0
- overdose or wrong substance given or taken 962.0
Cut (external) — see Wound, open, by site
Cutaneous — see also condition
- hemorrhage 782.7
- horn (cheek) (eyelid) (mouth) 702.8
- larva migrans 126.9
Cutis — see also condition
- hyperelastic 756.83
  - acquired 701.8
- laxa 756.83
  - senilis 701.8
- marmorata 782.61
- osteosis 709.3
- pendula 756.83
  - acquired 701.8
- rhomboidalis nuchae 701.8
- verticis gyrata 757.39
  - acquired 701.8
Cyanopathy, newborn 770.83
Cyanosis 782.5
- autotoxic 289.7
- common atrioventricular canal 745.69
- congenital 770.83
- conjunctiva 372.71
- due to
  - endocardial cushion defect 745.60
  - nonclosure, foramen botalli 745.5
  - patent foramen botalli 745.5
  - persistent foramen ovale 745.5
- enterogenous 289.7
- fetus or newborn 770.83
- ostium primum defect 745.61
- paroxysmal digital 443.0
- retina, retinal 362.10
Cycle
- anovulatory 628.0
- menstrual, irregular 626.4
Cyclencephaly 759.89
Cyclical vomiting 536.2
- psychogenic 306.4
Cyclitic membrane 364.74
Cyclitis — see also Iridocyclitis 364.3
- acute 364.00
  - primary 364.01
  - recurrent 364.02
- chronic 364.10
  - in
    - sarcoidosis 135 [364.11]
    - tuberculosis (see also Tuberculosis) 017.3 ☑ [364.11]
- Fuchs' heterochromic 364.21
- granulomatous 364.10
- lens induced 364.23
- nongranulomatous 364.00
- posterior 363.21
- primary 364.01
- recurrent 364.02
- secondary (noninfectious) 364.04
  - infectious 364.03
- subacute 364.00
  - primary 364.01
  - recurrent 364.02
Cyclokeratitis — see Keratitis
Cyclophoria 378.44
Cyclopia, cyclops 759.89
Cycloplegia 367.51

Cyclospasm 367.53
Cyclosporiasis 007.5
Cyclothymia 301.13
Cyclothymic personality 301.13
Cyclotropia 378.33
Cyesis — see Pregnancy
Cylindroma (M8200/3) — see also Neoplasm, by site, malignant
- eccrine dermal (M8200/0) — see Neoplasm, skin, benign
- skin (M8200/0) — see Neoplasm, skin, benign
Cylindruria 791.7
Cyllosoma 759.89
Cynanche
- diphtheritic 032.3
- tonsillaris 475
Cynorexia 783.6
Cyphosis — see Kyphosis
Cyprus fever — see also Brucellosis 023.9
Cyriax's syndrome (slipping rib) 733.99
Cyst (mucus) (retention) (serous) (simple)

> Note — In general, cysts are not neoplastic and are classified to the appropriate category for disease of the specified anatomical site. This generalization does not apply to certain types of cysts which are neoplastic in nature, for example, dermoid, nor does it apply to cysts of certain structures, for example, branchial cleft, which are classified as developmental anomalies.
>
> The following listing includes some of the most frequently reported sites of cysts as well as qualifiers which indicate the type of cyst. The latter qualifiers usually are not repeated under the anatomical sites. Since the code assignment for a given site may vary depending upon the type of cyst, the coder should refer to the listings under the specified type of cyst before consideration is given to the site.

- accessory, fallopian tube 752.11
- adenoid (infected) 474.8
- adrenal gland 255.8
  - congenital 759.1
- air, lung 518.89
- allantoic 753.7
- alveolar process (jaw bone) 526.2
- amnion, amniotic 658.8 ☑
- anterior chamber (eye) 364.60
  - exudative 364.62
  - implantation (surgical) (traumatic) 364.61
  - parasitic 360.13
- anterior nasopalatine 526.1
- antrum 478.19 ▲
- anus 569.49
- apical (periodontal) (tooth) 522.8
- appendix 543.9
- arachnoid, brain 348.0
- arytenoid 478.79
- auricle 706.2
- Baker's (knee) 727.51
  - tuberculous (see also Tuberculosis) 015.2 ☑
- Bartholin's gland or duct 616.2
- bile duct (see also Disease, biliary) 576.8
- bladder (multiple) (trigone) 596.8
- Blessig's 362.62
- blood, endocardial (see also Endocarditis) 424.90
- blue dome 610.0
- bone (local) 733.20
  - aneurysmal 733.22
  - jaw 526.2
    - developmental (odontogenic) 526.0
    - fissural 526.1
    - latent 526.89
  - solitary 733.21
  - unicameral 733.21

Cyst — continued
- brain 348.0
  - congenital 742.4
    - hydatid (see also Echinococcus) 122.9
  - third ventricle (colloid) 742.4
- branchial (cleft) 744.42
- branchiogenic 744.42
- breast (benign) (blue dome) (pedunculated) (solitary) (traumatic) 610.0
  - involution 610.4
  - sebaceous 610.8
- broad ligament (benign) 620.8
  - embryonic 752.11
- bronchogenic (mediastinal) (sequestration) 518.89
  - congenital 748.4
- buccal 528.4
- bulbourethral gland (Cowper's) 599.89
- bursa, bursal 727.49
  - pharyngeal 478.26
- calcifying odontogenic (M9301/0) 213.1
  - upper jaw (bone) 213.0
- canal of Nuck (acquired) (serous) 629.1
  - congenital 752.41
- canthus 372.75
- carcinomatous (M8010/3) — see Neoplasm, by site, malignant
- cartilage (joint) — see Derangement, joint
- cauda equina 336.8
- cavum septi pellucidi NEC 348.0
- celomic (pericardium) 746.89
- cerebellopontine (angle) — see Cyst, brain
- cerebellum — see Cyst, brain
- cerebral — see Cyst, brain
- cervical lateral 744.42
- cervix 622.8
  - embryonal 752.41
  - nabothian (gland) 616.0
- chamber, anterior (eye) 364.60
  - exudative 364.62
  - implantation (surgical) (traumatic) 364.61
  - parasitic 360.13
- chiasmal, optic NEC (see also Lesion, chiasmal) 377.54
- chocolate (ovary) 617.1
- choledochal (congenital) 751.69
  - acquired 576.8
- choledochus 751.69
- chorion 658.8 ☑
- choroid plexus 348.0
- chyle, mesentery 457.8
- ciliary body 364.60
  - exudative 364.64
  - implantation 364.61
  - primary 364.63
- clitoris 624.8
- coccyx (see also Cyst, bone) 733.20
- colloid
  - third ventricle (brain) 742.4
  - thyroid gland — see Goiter
- colon 569.89
- common (bile) duct (see also Disease, biliary) 576.8
- congenital NEC 759.89
  - adrenal glands 759.1
  - epiglottis 748.3
  - esophagus 750.4
  - fallopian tube 752.11
  - kidney 753.10
    - multiple 753.19
    - single 753.11
  - larynx 748.3
  - liver 751.62
  - lung 748.4
  - mediastinum 748.8
  - ovary 752.0
  - oviduct 752.11
  - pancreas 751.7
  - periurethral (tissue) 753.8

Cyst — *continued*
  congenital — *continued*
    prepuce NEC 752.69
      penis 752.69
    sublingual 750.26
    submaxillary gland 750.26
    thymus (gland) 759.2
    tongue 750.19
    ureterovesical orifice 753.4
    vulva 752.41
  conjunctiva 372.75
  cornea 371.23
  corpora quadrigemina 348.0
  corpus
    albicans (ovary) 620.2
    luteum (ruptured) 620.1
  Cowper's gland (benign) (infected) 599.89
  cranial meninges 348.0
  craniobuccal pouch 253.8
  craniopharyngeal pouch 253.8
  cystic duct (*see also* Disease, gallbladder) 575.8
  Cysticercus (any site) 123.1
  Dandy-Walker 742.3
    with spina bifida (*see also* Spina bifida) 741.0 ☑
  dental 522.8
    developmental 526.0
    eruption 526.0
    lateral periodontal 526.0
    primordial (keratocyst) 526.0
    root 522.8
  dentigerous 526.0
    mandible 526.0
    maxilla 526.0
  dermoid (M9084/0) (*see also* Neoplasm, by site, benign)
    with malignant transformation (M9084/3) 183.0
    implantation
      external area or site (skin) NEC 709.8
      iris 364.61
      skin 709.8
      vagina 623.8
      vulva 624.8
    mouth 528.4
    oral soft tissue 528.4
    sacrococcygeal 685.1
      with abscess 685.0
  developmental of ovary, ovarian 752.0
  dura (cerebral) 348.0
    spinal 349.2
  ear (external) 706.2
  echinococcal (*see also* Echinococcus) 122.9
  embryonal
    cervix uteri 752.41
    genitalia, female external 752.41
    uterus 752.3
    vagina 752.41
  endometrial 621.8
    ectopic 617.9
  endometrium (uterus) 621.8
    ectopic — *see* Endometriosis
  enteric 751.5
  enterogenous 751.5
  epidermal (inclusion) (*see also* Cyst, skin) 706.2
  epidermoid (inclusion) (*see also* Cyst, skin) 706.2
    mouth 528.4
    not of skin — *see* Cyst, by site
    oral soft tissue 528.4
  epididymis 608.89
  epiglottis 478.79
  epiphysis cerebri 259.8
  epithelial (inclusion) (*see also* Cyst, skin) 706.2
  epoophoron 752.11
  eruption 526.0
  esophagus 530.89
  ethmoid sinus 478.19 ▲
  eye (retention) 379.8
    congenital 743.03

Cyst — *continued*
  eye — *continued*
    posterior segment, congenital 743.54
  eyebrow 706.2
  eyelid (sebaceous) 374.84
    infected 373.13
    sweat glands or ducts 374.84
  falciform ligament (inflammatory) 573.8
  fallopian tube 620.8
  female genital organs NEC 629.89 ▲
  fimbrial (congenital) 752.11
  fissural (oral region) 526.1
  follicle (atretic) (graafian) (ovarian) 620.0
    nabothian (gland) 616.0
  follicular (atretic) (ovarian) 620.0
    dentigerous 526.0
  frontal sinus 478.19 ▲
  gallbladder or duct 575.8
  ganglion 727.43
  Gartner's duct 752.41
  gas, of mesentery 568.89
  gingiva 523.8
  gland of moll 374.84
  globulomaxillary 526.1
  graafian follicle 620.0
  granulosal lutein 620.2
  hemangiomatous (M9121/0) (*see also* Hemangioma) 228.00
  hydatid (*see also* Echinococcus) 122.9
    fallopian tube (Morgagni) 752.11
    liver NEC 122.8
    lung NEC 122.9
    Morgagni 752.89
      fallopian tube 752.11
    specified site NEC 122.9
  hymen 623.8
    embryonal 752.41
  hypopharynx 478.26
  hypophysis, hypophyseal (duct) (recurrent) 253.8
    cerebri 253.8
  implantation (dermoid)
    anterior chamber (eye) 364.61
    external area or site (skin) NEC 709.8
    iris 364.61
    vagina 623.8
    vulva 624.8
  incisor, incisive canal 526.1
  inclusion (epidermal) (epithelial) (epidermoid) (mucous) (squamous) (*see also* Cyst, skin) 706.2
    not of skin — *see* Neoplasm, by site, benign
  intestine (large) (small) 569.89
  intracranial — *see* Cyst, brain
  intraligamentous 728.89
    knee 717.89
  intrasellar 253.8
  iris (idiopathic) 364.60
    exudative 364.62
    implantation (surgical) (traumatic) 364.61
    miotic pupillary 364.55
    parasitic 360.13
  Iwanoff's 362.62
  jaw (bone) (aneurysmal) (extravasation) (hemorrhagic) (traumatic) 526.2
    developmental (odontogenic) 526.0
    fissural 526.1
  keratin 706.2
  kidney (congenital) 753.10
    acquired 593.2
    calyceal (*see also* Hydronephrosis) 591
    multiple 753.19
    pyelogenic (*see also* Hydronephrosis) 591
    simple 593.2
    single 753.11
    solitary (not congenital) 593.2

Cyst — *continued*
  labium (majus) (minus) 624.8
    sebaceous 624.8
  lacrimal
    apparatus 375.43
    gland or sac 375.12
  larynx 478.79
  lens 379.39
    congenital 743.39
  lip (gland) 528.5
  liver 573.8
    congenital 751.62
    hydatid (*see also* Echinococcus) 122.8
      granulosis 122.0
      multilocularis 122.5
  lung 518.89
    congenital 748.4
    giant bullous 492.0
  lutein 620.1
  lymphangiomatous (M9173/0) 228.1
  lymphoepithelial
    mouth 528.4
    oral soft tissue 528.4
  macula 362.54
  malignant (M8000/3) — *see* Neoplasm, by site, malignant
  mammary gland (sweat gland) (*see also* Cyst, breast) 610.0
  mandible 526.2
    dentigerous 526.0
    radicular 522.8
  maxilla 526.2
    dentigerous 526.0
    radicular 522.8
  median
    anterior maxillary 526.1
    palatal 526.1
  mediastinum (congenital) 748.8
  meibomian (gland) (retention) 373.2
    infected 373.12
  membrane, brain 348.0
  meninges (cerebral) 348.0
    spinal 349.2
  meniscus knee 717.5
  mesentery, mesenteric (gas) 568.89
    chyle 457.8
    gas 568.89
  mesonephric duct 752.89
  mesothelial
    peritoneum 568.89
    pleura (peritoneal) 568.89
  milk 611.5
  miotic pupillary (iris) 364.55
  Morgagni (hydatid) 752.89
    fallopian tube 752.11
  mouth 528.4
  mullerian duct 752.89
  multilocular (ovary) (M8000/1) 239.5
  myometrium 621.8
  nabothian (follicle) (ruptured) 616.0
  nasal sinus 478.19 ▲
  nasoalveolar 528.4
  nasolabial 528.4
  nasopalatine (duct) 526.1
    anterior 526.1
  nasopharynx 478.26
  neoplastic (M8000/1) (*see also* Neoplasm, by site, unspecified nature)
    benign (M8000/0) — *see* Neoplasm, by site, benign
    uterus 621.8
  nervous system — *see* Cyst, brain
  neuroenteric 742.59
  neuroepithelial ventricle 348.0
  nipple 610.0
  nose 478.19 ▲
    skin of 706.2
  odontogenic, developmental 526.0
  omentum (lesser) 568.89
    congenital 751.8
  oral soft tissue (dermoid) (epidermoid) (lymphoepithelial) 528.4
  ora serrata 361.19
  orbit 376.81

Cyst — *continued*
  ovary, ovarian (twisted) 620.2
    adherent 620.2
    chocolate 617.1
    corpus
      albicans 620.2
      luteum 620.1
    dermoid (M9084/0) 220
    developmental 752.0
    due to failure of involution NEC 620.2
    endometrial 617.1
    follicular (atretic) (graafian) (hemorrhagic) 620.0
    hemorrhagic 620.2
    in pregnancy or childbirth 654.4 ☑
      affecting fetus or newborn 763.89
      causing obstructed labor 660.2 ☑
        affecting fetus or newborn 763.1
    multilocular (M8000/1) 239.5
    pseudomucinous (M8470/0) 220
    retention 620.2
    serous 620.2
    theca lutein 620.2
    tuberculous (*see also* Tuberculosis) 016.6 ☑
    unspecified 620.2
  oviduct 620.8
  palatal papilla (jaw) 526.1
  palate 526.1
    fissural 526.1
    median (fissural) 526.1
  palatine, of papilla 526.1
  pancreas, pancreatic 577.2
    congenital 751.7
    false 577.2
    hemorrhagic 577.2
    true 577.2
  paranephric 593.2
  para ovarian 752.11
  paraphysis, cerebri 742.4
  parasitic NEC 136.9
  parathyroid (gland) 252.8
  paratubal (fallopian) 620.8
  paraurethral duct 599.89
  paroophoron 752.11
  parovarian 752.11
  pars planus 364.60
    exudative 364.64
    primary 364.63
  pelvis, female
    in pregnancy or childbirth 654.4 ☑
      affecting fetus or newborn 763.89
      causing obstructed labor 660.2 ☑
        affecting fetus or newborn 763.1
  penis (sebaceous) 607.89
  periapical 522.8
  pericardial (congenital) 746.89
    acquired (secondary) 423.8
  pericoronal 526.0
  perineural (Tarlov's) 355.9
  periodontal 522.8
    lateral 526.0
  peripancreatic 577.2
  peripelvic (lymphatic) 593.2
  peritoneum 568.89
    chylous 457.8
  pharynx (wall) 478.26
  pilonidal (infected) (rectum) 685.1
    with abscess 685.0
    malignant (M9084/3) 173.5
  pituitary (duct) (gland) 253.8
  placenta (amniotic) — *see* Placenta, abnormal
  pleura 519.8
  popliteal 727.51
  porencephalic 742.4

☑ Additional Digit Required — Refer to the Tabular List for Digit Selection

▶◀ Revised Text   ● New Line   ▲ Revised Code

▼ Subterms under main terms may continue to next column or page

Cyst — *continued*
porencephalic — *continued*
    acquired 348.0
postanal (infected) 685.1
    with abscess 685.0
posterior segment of eye, congenital 743.54
postmastoidectomy cavity 383.31
preauricular 744.47
prepuce 607.89
    congenital 752.69
primordial (jaw) 526.0
prostate 600.3
pseudomucinous (ovary) (M8470/0) 220
pudenda (sweat glands) 624.8
    sebaceous 624.8
pupillary, miotic 364.55
radicular (residual) 522.8
radiculodental 522.8
ranular 527.6
Rathke's pouch 253.8
rectum (epithelium) (mucous) 569.49
renal — *see* Cyst, kidney
residual (radicular) 522.8
retention (ovary) 620.2
retina 361.19
    macular 362.54
    parasitic 360.13
    primary 361.13
    secondary 361.14
retroperitoneal 568.89
sacrococcygeal (dermoid) 685.1
    with abscess 685.0
salivary gland or duct 527.6
    mucous extravasation or retention 527.6
Sampson's 617.1
sclera 379.19
scrotum (sebaceous) 706.2
    sweat glands 706.2
sebaceous (duct) (gland) 706.2
    breast 610.8
    eyelid 374.84
    genital organ NEC
        female 629.89 ▲
        male 608.89
        scrotum 706.2
semilunar cartilage (knee) (multiple) 717.5
seminal vesicle 608.89
serous (ovary) 620.2
sinus (antral) (ethmoidal) (frontal) (maxillary) (nasal) (sphenoidal) 478.19 ▲
Skene's gland 599.89
skin (epidermal) (epidermoid, inclusion) (epithelial) (inclusion) (retention) (sebaceous) 706.2
    breast 610.8
    eyelid 374.84
    genital organ NEC
        female 629.89 ▲
        male 608.89
    neoplastic 216.3
    scrotum 706.2
    sweat gland or duct 705.89
solitary
    bone 733.21
    kidney 593.2
spermatic cord 608.89
sphenoid sinus 478.19 ▲
spinal meninges 349.2
spine (*see also* Cyst, bone) 733.20
spleen NEC 289.59
    congenital 759.0
    hydatid (*see also* Echinococcus) 122.9
spring water (pericardium) 746.89
subarachnoid 348.0
    intrasellar 793.0
subdural (cerebral) 348.0
    spinal cord 349.2
sublingual gland 527.6
    mucous extravasation or retention 527.6

Cyst — *continued*
submaxillary gland 527.6
    mucous extravasation or retention 527.6
suburethral 599.89
suprarenal gland 255.8
suprasellar — *see* Cyst, brain
sweat gland or duct 705.89
sympathetic nervous system 337.9
synovial 727.40
    popliteal space 727.51
Tarlov's 355.9
tarsal 373.2
tendon (sheath) 727.42
testis 608.89
theca-lutein (ovary) 620.2
Thornwaldt's, Tornwaldt's 478.26
thymus (gland) 254.8
thyroglossal (duct) (infected) (persistent) 759.2
thyroid (gland) 246.2
    adenomatous — *see* Goiter, nodular
    colloid (*see also* Goiter) 240.9
thyrolingual duct (infected) (persistent) 759.2
tongue (mucous) 529.8
tonsil 474.8
tooth (dental root) 522.8
tubo-ovarian 620.8
    inflammatory 614.1
tunica vaginalis 608.89
turbinate (nose) (*see also* Cyst, bone) 733.20
Tyson's gland (benign) (infected) 607.89
umbilicus 759.89
urachus 753.7
ureter 593.89
ureterovesical orifice 593.89
    congenital 753.4
urethra 599.84
urethral gland (Cowper's) 599.89
uterine
    ligament 620.8
        embryonic 752.11
    tube 620.8
uterus (body) (corpus) (recurrent) 621.8
    embryonal 752.3
utricle (ear) 386.8
    prostatic 599.89
utriculus masculinus 599.89
vagina, vaginal (squamous cell) (wall) 623.8
    embryonal 752.41
    implantation 623.8
    inclusion 623.8
vallecula, vallecular 478.79
ventricle, neuroepithelial 348.0
verumontanum 599.89
vesical (orifice) 596.8
vitreous humor 379.29
vulva (sweat glands) 624.8
    congenital 752.41
    implantation 624.8
    inclusion 624.8
    sebaceous gland 624.8
vulvovaginal gland 624.8
wolffian 752.89
Cystadenocarcinoma (M8440/3) — *see also* Neoplasm, by site, malignant
bile duct type (M8161/3) 155.1
endometrioid (M8380/3) — *see* Neoplasm, by site, malignant
mucinous (M8470/3)
    papillary (M8471/3)
        specified site — *see* Neoplasm, by site, malignant
        unspecified site 183.0
    specified site — *see* Neoplasm, by site, malignant
    unspecified site 183.0

Cystadenocarcinoma — *see also* Neoplasm, by site, malignant — *continued*
papillary (M8450/3)
    mucinous (M8471/3)
        specified site — *see* Neoplasm, by site, malignant
        unspecified site 183.0
    pseudomucinous (M8471/3)
        specified site — *see* Neoplasm, by site, malignant
        unspecified site 183.0
    serous (M8460/3)
        specified site — *see* Neoplasm, by site, malignant
        unspecified site 183.0
    specified site — *see* Neoplasm, by site, malignant
    unspecified site 183.0
pseudomucinous (M8470/3)
    papillary (M8471/3)
        specified site — *see* Neoplasm, by site, malignant
        unspecified site 183.0
    specified site — *see* Neoplasm, by site, malignant
    unspecified site 183.0
serous (M8441/3)
    papillary (M8460/3)
        specified site — *see* Neoplasm, by site, malignant
        unspecified site 183.0
    specified site — *see* Neoplasm, by site, malignant
    unspecified site 183.0
Cystadenofibroma (M9013/0)
clear cell (M8313/0) — *see* Neoplasm, by site, benign
endometrioid (M8381/0) 220
    borderline malignancy (M8381/1) 236.2
    malignant (M8381/3) 183.0
mucinous (M9015/0)
    specified site — *see* Neoplasm, by site, benign
    unspecified site 220
serous (M9014/0)
    specified site — *see* Neoplasm, by site, benign
    unspecified site 220
specified site — *see* Neoplasm, by site, benign
unspecified site 220
Cystadenoma (M8440/0) — *see also* Neoplasm, by site, benign
bile duct (M8161/0) 211.5
endometrioid (M8380/0) (*see also* Neoplasm, by site, benign)
    borderline malignancy (M8380/1) — *see* Neoplasm, by site, uncertain behavior
    malignant (M8440/3) — *see* Neoplasm, by site, malignant
mucinous (M8470/0)
    borderline malignancy (M8470/1)
        specified site — *see* Neoplasm, uncertain behavior
        unspecified site 236.2
    papillary (M8471/0)
        borderline malignancy (M8471/1)
            specified site — *see* Neoplasm, by site, uncertain behavior
            unspecified site 236.2
        specified site — *see* Neoplasm, by site, benign
        unspecified site 220
    specified site — *see* Neoplasm, by site, benign
    unspecified site 220
papillary (M8450/0)
    borderline malignancy (M8450/1)
        specified site — *see* Neoplasm, by site, uncertain behavior

Cystadenoma — *see also* Neoplasm, by site, benign — *continued*
papillary — *continued*
    borderline malignancy — *continued*
        unspecified site 236.2
    lymphomatosum (M8561/0) 210.2
    mucinous (M8471/0)
        borderline malignancy (M8471/1)
            specified site — *see* Neoplasm, by site, uncertain behavior
            unspecified site 236.2
        specified site — *see* Neoplasm, by site, benign
        unspecified site 220
    pseudomucinous (M8471/0)
        borderline malignancy (M8471/1)
            specified site — *see* Neoplasm, by site, uncertain behavior
            unspecified site 236.2
        specified site — *see* Neoplasm, by site, benign
        unspecified site 220
    serous (M8460/0)
        borderline malignancy (M8460/1)
            specified site — *see* Neoplasm, by site, uncertain behavior
            unspecified site 236.2
        specified site — *see* Neoplasm, by site, benign
        unspecified site 220
    specified site — *see* Neoplasm, by site, benign
    unspecified site 220
pseudomucinous (M8470/0)
    borderline malignancy (M8470/1)
        specified site — *see* Neoplasm, by site, uncertain behavior
        unspecified site 236.2
    papillary (M8471/0)
        borderline malignancy (M8471/1)
            specified site — *see* Neoplasm, by site, uncertain behavior
            unspecified site 236.2
        specified site — *see* Neoplasm, by site, benign
        unspecified site 220
    specified site — *see* Neoplasm, by site, benign
    unspecified site 220
serous (M8441/0)
    borderline malignancy (M8441/1)
        specified site — *see* Neoplasm, by site, uncertain behavior
        unspecified site 236.2
    papillary (M8460/0)
        borderline malignancy (M8460/1)
            specified site — *see* Neoplasm, by site, uncertain behavior
            unspecified site 236.2
        specified site — *see* Neoplasm, by site, benign
        unspecified site 220
    specified site — *see* Neoplasm, by site, benign
    unspecified site 220
thyroid 226
Cystathioninemia 270.4
Cystathioninuria 270.4
Cystic — *see also* condition
breast, chronic 610.1
corpora lutea 620.1
degeneration, congenital
    brain 742.4

Cystic — *see also* condition — *continued*

degeneration, congenital — *continued*

kidney (*see also* Cystic, disease, kidney) 753.10

disease

breast, chronic 610.1

kidney, congenital 753.10

medullary 753.16

multiple 753.19

polycystic — *see* Polycystic, kidney

single 753.11

specified NEC 753.19

liver, congenital 751.62

lung 518.89

congenital 748.4

pancreas, congenital 751.7

semilunar cartilage 717.5

duct — *see* condition

eyeball, congenital 743.03

fibrosis (pancreas) 277.00

with

manifestations

gastrointestinal 277.03

pulmonary 277.02

specified NEC 277.09

meconium ileus 277.01

pulmonary exacerbation 277.02

hygroma (M9173/0) 228.1

kidney, congenital 753.10

medullary 753.16

multiple 753.19

polycystic — *see* Polycystic, kidney

single 753.11

specified NEC 753.19

liver, congenital 751.62

lung 518.89

congenital 748.4

mass — *see* Cyst

mastitis, chronic 610.1

ovary 620.2

pancreas, congenital 751.7

Cysticerciasis 123.1

Cysticercosis (mammary) (subretinal) 123.1

Cysticercus 123.1

cellulosae infestation 123.1

Cystinosis (malignant) 270.0

Cystinuria 270.0

Cystitis (bacillary) (colli) (diffuse) (exudative) (hemorrhagic) (purulent) (recurrent) (septic) (suppurative) (ulcerative) 595.9

with

abortion — *see* Abortion, by type, with urinary tract infection

ectopic pregnancy (*see also* categories 633.0–633.9) 639.8

fibrosis 595.1

leukoplakia 595.1

malakoplakia 595.1

metaplasia 595.1

molar pregnancy (*see also* categories 630–632) 639.8

actinomycotic 039.8 [595.4]

acute 595.0

of trigone 595.3

allergic 595.89

amebic 006.8 [595.4]

bilharzial 120.9 [595.4]

blennorrhagic (acute) 098.11

chronic or duration of 2 months or more 098.31

bullous 595.89

calculous 594.1

chlamydial 099.53

chronic 595.2

interstitial 595.1

of trigone 595.3

complicating pregnancy, childbirth, or puerperium 646.6 ☑

affecting fetus or newborn 760.1

cystic(a) 595.81

diphtheritic 032.84

echinococcal

granulosus 122.3 [595.4]

multilocularis 122.6 [595.4]

emphysematous 595.89

encysted 595.81

follicular 595.3

following

abortion 639.8

Cystitis — *continued*

following — *continued*

ectopic or molar pregnancy 639.8

gangrenous 595.89

glandularis 595.89

gonococcal (acute) 098.11

chronic or duration of 2 months or more 098.31

incrusted 595.89

interstitial 595.1

irradiation 595.82

irritation 595.89

malignant 595.89

monilial 112.2

of trigone 595.3

panmural 595.1

polyposa 595.89

prostatic 601.3

radiation 595.82

Reiter's (abacterial) 099.3

specified NEC 595.89

subacute 595.2

submucous 595.1

syphilitic 095.8

trichomoniasis 131.09

tuberculous (*see also* Tuberculosis) 016.1 ☑

ulcerative 595.1

Cystocele (-rectocele)

female (without uterine prolapse) 618.01

with uterine prolapse 618.4

complete 618.3

incomplete 618.2

lateral 618.02

midline 618.01

paravaginal 618.02

in pregnancy or childbirth 654.4 ☑

affecting fetus or newborn 763.89

causing obstructed labor 660.2 ☑

affecting fetus or newborn 763.1

male 596.8

Cystoid

cicatrix limbus 372.64

degeneration macula 362.53

Cystolithiasis 594.1

Cystoma (M8440/0) — *see also* Neoplasm, by site, benign

endometrial, ovary 617.1

mucinous (M8470/0)

specified site — *see* Neoplasm, by site, benign

unspecified site 220

serous (M8441/0)

specified site — *see* Neoplasm, by site, benign

unspecified site 220

simple (ovary) 620.2

Cystoplegia 596.53

Cystoptosis 596.8

Cystopyelitis — *see also* Pyelitis 590.80

Cystorrhagia 596.8

Cystosarcoma phyllodes (M9020/1) 238.3

benign (M9020/0) 217

malignant (M9020/3) — *see* Neoplasm, breast, malignant

Cystostomy status V44.50

with complication 997.5

appendico-vesicostomy V44.52

cutaneous-vesicostomy V44.51

specified type NEC V44.59

Cystourethritis — *see also* Urethritis 597.89

Cystourethrocele — *see also* Cystocele

female (without uterine prolapse) 618.09

with uterine prolapse 618.4

complete 618.3

incomplete 618.2

male 596.8

Cytomegalic inclusion disease 078.5

congenital 771.1

Cytomycosis, reticuloendothelial — *see also* Histoplasmosis, American 115.00

Cytopenia 289.9

refractory ●

with

multilineage dysplasia (RCMD) ●

238.72

and ringed sideroblasts ●

(RCMD-RS) 238.72 ●

D

Daae (-Finsen) disease (epidemic pleurodynia) 074.1
Dabney's grip 074.1
Da Costa's syndrome (neurocirculatory asthenia) 306.2
Dacryoadenitis, dacryadenitis 375.00
  acute 375.01
  chronic 375.02
Dacryocystitis 375.30
  acute 375.32
  chronic 375.42
  neonatal 771.6
  phlegmonous 375.33
  syphilitic 095.8
    congenital 090.0
  trachomatous, active 076.1
    late effect 139.1
  tuberculous (see also Tuberculosis) 017.3 ☑
Dacryocystoblenorrhea 375.42
Dacryocystocele 375.43
Dacryolith, dacryolithiasis 375.57
Dacryoma 375.43
Dacryopericystitis (acute) (subacute) 375.32
  chronic 375.42
Dacryops 375.11
Dacryosialadenopathy, atrophic 710.2
Dacryostenosis 375.56
  congenital 743.65
Dactylitis
  bone (see also Osteomyelitis) 730.2 ☑
  sickle-cell 282.62 ▲
    Hb-C 282.64 ●
    Hb-SS 282.62 ●
    specified NEC 282.69 ●
  syphilitic 095.5
  tuberculous (see also Tuberculosis) 015.5 ☑
Dactylolysis spontanea 136.0
Dactylosymphysis — see also Syndactylism 755.10
Damage
  arteriosclerotic — see Arteriosclerosis
  brain 348.9
    anoxic, hypoxic 348.1
      during or resulting from a procedure 997.01
      ischemic, in newborn 768.7 ●
    child NEC 343.9
    due to birth injury 767.0
    minimal (child) (see also Hyperkinesia) 314.9
    newborn 767.0
  cardiac (see also Disease, heart)
  cardiorenal (vascular) (see also Hypertension, cardiorenal) 404.90
  central nervous system — see Damage, brain
  cerebral NEC — see Damage, brain
  coccyx, complicating delivery 665.6 ☑
  coronary (see also Ischemia, heart) 414.9
  eye, birth injury 767.8
  heart (see also Disease, heart)
    valve — see Endocarditis
  hypothalamus NEC 348.9
  liver 571.9
    alcoholic 571.3
  myocardium (see also Degeneration, myocardial) 429.1
  pelvic
    joint or ligament, during delivery 665.6 ☑
    organ NEC
      with
        abortion — see Abortion, by type, with damage to pelvic organs
        ectopic pregnancy (see also categories 633.0–633.9) 639.2

Damage — continued
  pelvic — continued
    organ — continued
      with — continued
        molar pregnancy (see also categories 630–632) 639.2
      during delivery 665.5 ☑
      following
        abortion 639.2
        ectopic or molar pregnancy 639.2
  renal (see also Disease, renal) 593.9
  skin, solar 692.79
    acute 692.72
    chronic 692.74
  subendocardium, subendocardial (see also Degeneration, myocardial) 429.1
  vascular 459.9
Dameshek's syndrome (erythroblastic anemia) 282.49
Dana-Putnam syndrome (subacute combined sclerosis with pernicious anemia) 281.0 [336.2]
Danbolt (-Closs) syndrome (acrodermatitis enteropathica) 686.8
Dandruff 690.18
Dandy fever 061
Dandy-Walker deformity or syndrome (atresia, foramen of Magendie) 742.3
  with spina bifida (see also Spina bifida) 741.0 ☑
Dangle foot 736.79 ▲
Danielssen's disease (anesthetic leprosy) 030.1 ●
Danlos' syndrome 756.83
Darier's disease (congenital) (keratosis follicularis) 757.39
  due to vitamin A deficiency 264.8
  meaning erythema annulare centrifugum 695.0
Darier-Roussy sarcoid 135
Darling's
  disease (see also Histoplasmosis, American) 115.00
  histoplasmosis (see also Histoplasmosis, American) 115.00
Dartre 054.9
Darwin's tubercle 744.29
Davidson's anemia (refractory) 284.9
Davies-Colley syndrome (slipping rib) 733.99
Davies' disease 425.0
Dawson's encephalitis 046.2
Day blindness — see also Blindness, day 368.60
Dead
  fetus
    retained (in utero) 656.4 ☑
      early pregnancy (death before 22 completed weeks gestation) 632
      late (death after 22 completed weeks gestation) 656.4 ☑
    syndrome 641.3 ☑
  labyrinth 386.50
  ovum, retained 631
Deaf and dumb NEC 389.7
Deaf mutism (acquired) (congenital) NEC 389.7
  endemic 243
  hysterical 300.11
  syphilitic, congenital 090.0
Deafness (acquired) (complete) (congenital) (hereditary) (middle ear) (partial) 389.9
  with blue sclera and fragility of bone 756.51
  auditory fatigue 389.9
  aviation 993.0
    nerve injury 951.5
  boilermakers' 951.5
  central, ►bilateral◄ 389.14
    with conductive hearing loss 389.2

Deafness — continued
  conductive (air) 389.00
    with sensorineural hearing loss 389.2
    combined types 389.08
    external ear 389.01
    inner ear 389.04
    middle ear 389.03
    multiple types 389.08
    tympanic membrane 389.02
  emotional (complete) 300.11
  functional (complete) 300.11
  high frequency 389.8
  hysterical (complete) 300.11
  injury 951.5
  low frequency 389.8
  mental 784.69
  mixed conductive and sensorineural 389.2
  nerve, ►bilateral◄ 389.12
    with conductive hearing loss 389.2
  neural, ►bilateral◄ 389.12
    with conductive hearing loss 389.2
  noise-induced 388.12
    nerve injury 951.5
  nonspeaking 389.7
  perceptive 389.10
    with conductive hearing loss 389.2
    central, ►bilateral◄ 389.14
    combined types, ►bilateral◄ 389.18
    multiple types, ►bilateral◄ 389.18
    neural, ►bilateral◄ 389.12
    sensorineural 389.10 ●
      asymmetrical 389.16 ●
      bilateral 389.18 ●
      unilateral 389.15 ●
    sensory, ►bilateral◄ 389.11 ●
  psychogenic (complete) 306.7
  sensorineural (see also Deafness, perceptive) 389.10
    asymmetrical 389.16 ●
    bilateral 389.18 ●
    unilateral 389.15 ●
  sensory, ►bilateral◄ 389.11
    with conductive hearing loss 389.2
  specified type NEC 389.8
  sudden NEC 388.2
  syphilitic 094.89
  transient ischemic 388.02
  transmission — see Deafness, conductive
  traumatic 951.5
  word (secondary to organic lesion) 784.69
    developmental 315.31
Death
  after delivery (cause not stated) (sudden) 674.9 ☑
  anesthetic
    due to
      correct substance properly administered 995.4
      overdose or wrong substance given 968.4
      specified anesthetic — see Table of Drugs and Chemicals
    during delivery 668.9 ☑
  brain 348.8
  cardiac — see Disease, heart
  cause unknown 798.2
  cot (infant) 798.0
  crib (infant) 798.0
  fetus, fetal (cause not stated) (intrauterine) 779.9
    early, with retention (before 22 completed weeks gestation) 632
    from asphyxia or anoxia (before labor) 768.0
      during labor 768.1
    late, affecting management of pregnancy (after 22 completed weeks gestation) 656.4 ☑
  from pregnancy NEC 646.9 ☑

Death — continued
  instantaneous 798.1
  intrauterine (see also Death, fetus) 779.9
    complicating pregnancy 656.4 ☑
  maternal, affecting fetus or newborn 761.6
  neonatal NEC 779.9
  sudden (cause unknown) 798.1
    during delivery 669.9 ☑
      under anesthesia NEC 668.9 ☑
    infant, syndrome (SIDS) 798.0
    puerperal, during puerperium 674.9 ☑
  unattended (cause unknown) 798.9
  under anesthesia NEC
    due to
      correct substance properly administered 995.4
      overdose or wrong substance given 968.4
      specified anesthetic — see Table of Drugs and Chemicals
    during delivery 668.9 ☑
  violent 798.1
de Beurmann-Gougerot disease (sporotrichosis) 117.1
Debility (general) (infantile) (postinfectional) 799.3
  with nutritional difficulty 269.9
  congenital or neonatal NEC 779.9
  nervous 300.5
  old age 797
  senile 797
Débove's disease (splenomegaly) 789.2
Decalcification
  bone (see also Osteoporosis) 733.00
  teeth 521.89 ▲
Decapitation 874.9
  fetal (to facilitate delivery) 763.89
Decapsulation, kidney 593.89
Decay
  dental 521.00
  senile 797
  tooth, teeth 521.00
Decensus, uterus — see Prolapse, uterus
Deciduitis (acute)
  with
    abortion — see Abortion, by type, with sepsis
    ectopic pregnancy (see also categories 633.0–633.9) 639.0
    molar pregnancy (see also categories 630–632) 639.0
  affecting fetus or newborn 760.8
  following
    abortion 639.0
    ectopic or molar pregnancy 639.0
  in pregnancy 646.6 ☑
  puerperal, postpartum 670.0 ☑
Deciduoma malignum (M9100/3) 181
Deciduous tooth (retained) 520.6
Decline (general) — see also Debility 799.3
Decompensation
  cardiac (acute) (chronic) (see also Disease, heart) 429.9
    failure — see Failure, heart
  cardiorenal (see also Hypertension, cardiorenal) 404.90
  cardiovascular (see also Disease, cardiovascular) 429.2
  heart (see also Disease, heart) 429.9
    failure — see Failure, heart
  hepatic 572.2
  myocardial (acute) (chronic) (see also Disease, heart) 429.9
    failure — see Failure, heart
  respiratory 519.9
Decompression sickness 993.3
Decrease, decreased
  blood
    platelets (see also Thrombocytopenia) 287.5
    pressure 796.3

☑ Additional Digit Required — Refer to the Tabular List for Digit Selection   ▼ Subterms under main terms may continue to next column or page

2007 ICD-9-CM   ►◄ Revised Text   ● New Line   ▲ Revised Code   **October 2006 · Volume 2 — 65**

Index

Decrease, decreased — Deficiency, deficient

Decrease, decreased — *continued*
- blood — *continued*
  - pressure — *continued*
    - due to shock following
      - injury 958.4
      - operation 998.0
  - white cell count 288.50 ●
    - specified NEC 288.59 ●
- cardiac reserve — *see* Disease, heart
- estrogen 256.39
  - postablative 256.2
- fetal movements 655.7 ☑
- fragility of erythrocytes 289.89
- function
  - adrenal (cortex) 255.4
    - medulla 255.5
  - ovary in hypopituitarism 253.4
  - parenchyma of pancreas 577.8
  - pituitary (gland) (lobe) (anterior) 253.2
    - posterior (lobe) 253.8
- functional activity 780.99
- glucose 790.29
- haptoglobin (serum) NEC 273.8
- leukocytes 288.50 ●
- libido 799.81
- lymphocytes 288.51 ●
- platelets (*see also* Thrombocytopenia) 287.5
- pulse pressure 785.9
- respiration due to shock following injury 958.4
- sexual desire 799.81
- tear secretion NEC 375.15
- tolerance
  - fat 579.8
  - salt and water 276.9
- vision NEC 369.9
- white blood cell count 288.50 ●

Decubital gangrene 707.00 *[785.4]*
Decubiti — *see also* Decubitus 707.00
Decubitus (ulcer) 707.00
- with gangrene 707.00 *[785.4]*
- ankle 707.06
- back
  - lower 707.03
  - upper 707.02
- buttock 707.05
- elbow 707.01
- head 707.09
- heel 707.07
- hip 707.04
- other site 707.09
- sacrum 707.03
- shoulder blades 707.02

Deepening acetabulum 718.85
Defect, defective 759.9
- 3-beta-hydroxysteroid dehydrogenase 255.2
- 11-hydroxylase 255.2
- 21-hydroxylase 255.2
- abdominal wall, congenital 756.70
- aorticopulmonary septum 745.0
- aortic septal 745.0
- atrial septal (ostium secundum type) 745.5
  - acquired 429.71
  - ostium primum type 745.61
  - sinus venosus 745.8
- atrioventricular
  - canal 745.69
  - septum 745.4
    - acquired 429.71
- atrium secundum 745.5
  - acquired 429.71
- auricular septal 745.5
  - acquired 429.71
- bilirubin excretion 277.4
- biosynthesis, testicular androgen 257.2
- bridge 525.60 ●
- bulbar septum 745.0
- butanol-insoluble iodide 246.1
- chromosome — *see* Anomaly, chromosome
- circulation (acquired) 459.9

Defect, defective — *continued*
- circulation — *continued*
  - congenital 747.9
  - newborn 747.9
- clotting NEC (*see also* Defect, coagulation) 286.9
- coagulation (factor) (*see also* Deficiency, coagulation factor) 286.9
  - with
    - abortion — *see* Abortion, by type, with hemorrhage
    - ectopic pregnancy (*see also* categories 634–638) 639.1
    - molar pregnancy (*see also* categories 630–632) 639.1
  - acquired (any) 286.7
  - antepartum or intrapartum 641.3 ☑
    - affecting fetus or newborn 762.1
  - causing hemorrhage of pregnancy or delivery 641.3 ☑
  - complicating pregnancy, childbirth, or puerperium 649.3 ☑ ●
  - due to
    - liver disease 286.7
    - vitamin K deficiency 286.7
  - newborn, transient 776.3
  - postpartum 666.3 ☑
  - specified type NEC 286.3
- conduction (heart) 426.9
  - bone (*see also* Deafness, conductive) 389.00
- congenital, organ or site NEC (*see also* Anomaly)
  - circulation 747.9
  - Descemet's membrane 743.9
    - specified type NEC 743.49
  - diaphragm 756.6
  - ectodermal 757.9
  - esophagus 750.9
  - pulmonic cusps — *see* Anomaly, heart valve
  - respiratory system 748.9
    - specified type NEC 748.8
- crown 525.60 ●
- cushion endocardial 745.60
- dental restoration 525.60 ●
- dentin (hereditary) 520.5
- Descemet's membrane (congenital) 743.9
  - acquired 371.30
  - specific type NEC 743.49
- deutan 368.52
- developmental (*see also* Anomaly, by site)
  - cauda equina 742.59
  - left ventricle 746.9
    - with atresia or hypoplasia of aortic orifice or valve, with hypoplasia of ascending aorta 746.7
    - in hypoplastic left heart syndrome 746.7
  - testis 752.9
  - vessel 747.9
- diaphragm
  - with elevation, eventration, or hernia — *see* Hernia, diaphragm
  - congenital 756.6
    - with elevation, eventration, or hernia 756.6
    - gross (with elevation, eventration, or hernia) 756.6
- ectodermal, congenital 757.9
- Eisenmenger's (ventricular septal defect) 745.4
- endocardial cushion 745.60
  - specified type NEC 745.69
- esophagus, congenital 750.9
- extensor retinaculum 728.9
- fibrin polymerization (*see also* Defect, coagulation) 286.3
- filling
  - biliary tract 793.3
  - bladder 793.5

Defect, defective — *continued*
- filling — *continued*
  - dental 525.60 ●
  - gallbladder 793.3
  - kidney 793.5
  - stomach 793.4
  - ureter 793.5
- fossa ovalis 745.5
- gene, carrier (suspected) of V83.89
- Gerbode 745.4
- glaucomatous, without elevated tension 365.89
- Hageman (factor) (*see also* Defect, coagulation) 286.3
- hearing (*see also* Deafness) 389.9
- high grade 317
- homogentisic acid 270.2
- interatrial septal 745.5
  - acquired 429.71
- interauricular septal 745.5
  - acquired 429.71
- interventricular septal 745.4
  - with pulmonary stenosis or atresia, dextraposition of aorta, and hypertrophy of right ventricle 745.2
  - acquired 429.71
  - in tetralogy of Fallot 745.2
- iodide trapping 246.1
- iodotyrosine dehalogenase 246.1
- kynureninase 270.2
- learning, specific 315.2
- major osseous 731.3 ●
- mental (*see also* Retardation, mental) 319
- osseous, major 731.3 ●
- osteochondral NEC 738.8
- ostium
  - primum 745.61
  - secundum 745.5
- pericardium 746.89
- peroxidase-binding 246.1
- placental blood supply — *see* Placenta, insufficiency
- platelet (qualitative) 287.1
  - constitutional 286.4
- postural, spine 737.9
- protan 368.51
- pulmonic cusps, congenital 746.00
- renal pelvis 753.9
  - obstructive 753.29
  - specified type NEC 753.3
- respiratory system, congenital 748.9
  - specified type NEC 748.8
- retina, retinal 361.30
  - with detachment (*see also* Detachment, retina, with retinal defect) 361.00
  - multiple 361.33
    - with detachment 361.02
  - nerve fiber bundle 362.85
  - single 361.30
    - with detachment 361.01
- septal (closure) (heart) NEC 745.9
  - acquired 429.71
  - atrial 745.5
  - specified type NEC 745.8
- speech NEC 784.5
  - developmental 315.39
  - secondary to organic lesion 784.5
- Taussig-Bing (transposition, aorta and overriding pulmonary artery) 745.11
- teeth, wedge 521.20
- thyroid hormone synthesis 246.1
- tritan 368.53
- ureter 753.9
  - obstructive 753.29
- vascular (acquired) (local) 459.9
  - congenital (peripheral) NEC 747.60
    - gastrointestinal 747.61
    - lower limb 747.64
    - renal 747.62
    - specified NEC 747.69
    - spinal 747.82
    - upper limb 747.63

Defect, defective — *continued*
- ventricular septal 745.4
  - with pulmonary stenosis or atresia, dextraposition of aorta, and hypertrophy of right ventricle 745.2
  - acquired 429.71
  - atrioventricular canal type 745.69
  - between infundibulum and anterior portion 745.4
  - in tetralogy of Fallot 745.2
  - isolated anterior 745.4
- vision NEC 369.9
- visual field 368.40
  - arcuate 368.43
  - heteronymous, bilateral 368.47
  - homonymous, bilateral 368.46
  - localized NEC 368.44
  - nasal step 368.44
  - peripheral 368.44
  - sector 368.43
- voice 784.40
- wedge, teeth (abrasion) 521.20

Defeminization syndrome 255.2
Deferentitis 608.4
- gonorrheal (acute) 098.14
  - chronic or duration of 2 months or over 098.34

Defibrination syndrome — *see also* Fibrinolysis 286.6
Deficiency, deficient
- 3-beta-hydroxysteroid dehydrogenase 255.2
- 6-phosphogluconic dehydrogenase (anemia) 282.2
- 11-beta-hydroxylase 255.2
- 17-alpha-hydroxylase 255.2
- 18-hydroxysteroid dehydrogenase 255.2
- 20-alpha-hydroxylase 255.2
- 21-hydroxylase 255.2
- AAT (alpha-1 antitrypsin) 273.4
- abdominal muscle syndrome 756.79
- accelerator globulin (ac G) (blood) (*see also* Defect, coagulation) 286.3
- AC globulin (congenital) (*see also* Defect, coagulation) 286.3
  - acquired 286.7
- activating factor (blood) (*see also* Defect, coagulation) 286.3
- adenohypophyseal 253.2
- adenosine deaminase 277.2
- aldolase (hereditary) 271.2
- alpha-1-antitrypsin 273.4
- alpha-1-trypsin inhibitor 273.4
- alpha-fucosidase 271.8
- alpha-lipoprotein 272.5
- alpha-mannosidase 271.8
- amino acid 270.9
- anemia — *see* Anemia, deficiency
- aneurin 265.1
  - with beriberi 265.0
- antibody NEC 279.00
- antidiuretic hormone 253.5
- antihemophilic
  - factor (A) 286.0
    - B 286.1
    - C 286.2
  - globulin (AHG) NEC 286.0
- antithrombin III 289.81
- antitrypsin 273.4
- argininosuccinate synthetase or lyase 270.6
- ascorbic acid (with scurvy) 267
- autoprothrombin
  - I (*see also* Defect, coagulation) 286.3
  - II 286.1
  - C (*see also* Defect, coagulation) 286.3
- bile salt 579.8
- biotin 266.2
- biotinidase 277.6
- bradykinase-1 277.6
- brancher enzyme (amylopectinosis) 271.0

☑ Additional Digit Required — Refer to the Tabular List for Digit Selection   ⍟ Subterms under main terms may continue to next column or page

66 — Volume 2 • October 2006   ►◄ Revised Text   ● New Line   ▲ Revised Code   **2007 ICD-9-CM**

Deficiency, deficient — *continued*
calciferol 268.9
  with
    osteomalacia 268.2
    rickets (*see also* Rickets) 268.0
calcium 275.40
  dietary 269.3
calorie, severe 261
carbamyl phosphate synthetase 270.6
cardiac (*see also* Insufficiency, myocardial) 428.0
carnitine 277.81
  due to
    hemodialysis 277.83
    inborn errors of metabolism 277.82
    valproic acid therapy 277.83
  iatrogenic 277.83
  palmitoyltransferase (CPT1, CPT2) 277.85
  palmityl transferase (CPT1, CPT2) 277.85
  primary 277.81
  secondary 277.84
carotene 264.9
Carr factor (*see also* Defect, coagulation) 286.9
central nervous system 349.9
ceruloplasmin 275.1
cevitamic acid (with scurvy) 267
choline 266.2
Christmas factor 286.1
chromium 269.3
citrin 269.1
clotting (blood) (*see also* Defect, coagulation) 286.9
coagulation factor NEC 286.9
  with
    abortion — *see* Abortion, by type, with hemorrhage
    ectopic pregnancy (*see also* categories 634–638) 639.1
    molar pregnancy (*see also* categories 630–632) 639.1
  acquired (any) 286.7
  antepartum or intrapartum 641.3 ☑
    affecting fetus or newborn 762.1
  complicating pregnancy, childbirth, or puerperium 649.3 ☑ ●
  due to
    liver disease 286.7
    vitamin K deficiency 286.7
  newborn, transient 776.3
  postpartum 666.3 ☑
  specified type NEC 286.3
color vision (congenital) 368.59
  acquired 368.55
combined, two or more coagulation factors (*see also* Defect, coagulation) 286.9
complement factor NEC 279.8
contact factor (*see also* Defect, coagulation) 286.3
copper NEC 275.1
corticoadrenal 255.4
craniofacial axis 756.0
cyanocobalamin (vitamin B_{12}) 266.2
debrancher enzyme (limit dextrinosis) 271.0
desmolase 255.2
diet 269.9
dihydrofolate reductase 281.2
dihydropteridine reductase 270.1
disaccharidase (intestinal) 271.3
disease NEC 269.9
ear(s) V48.8
edema 262
endocrine 259.9
enzymes, circulating NEC (*see also* Deficiency, by specific enzyme) 277.6
ergosterol 268.9
  with
    osteomalacia 268.2

Deficiency, deficient — *continued*
ergosterol — *continued*
  with — *continued*
    rickets (*see also* Rickets) 268.0
erythrocytic glutathione (anemia) 282.2
eyelid(s) V48.8
factor (*see also* Defect, coagulation) 286.9
  I (congenital) (fibrinogen) 286.3
    antepartum or intrapartum 641.3 ☑
      affecting fetus or newborn 762.1
    newborn, transient 776.3
    postpartum 666.3 ☑
  II (congenital) (prothrombin) 286.3
  V (congenital) (labile) 286.3
  VII (congenital) (stable) 286.3
  VIII (congenital) (functional) 286.0
    with
      functional defect 286.0
      vascular defect 286.4
  IX (Christmas) (congenital) (functional) 286.1
  X (congenital) (Stuart-Prower) 286.3
  XI (congenital) (plasma thromboplastin antecedent) 286.2
  XII (congenital) (Hageman) 286.3
  XIII (congenital) (fibrin stabilizing) 286.3
  Hageman 286.3
  multiple (congenital) 286.9
    acquired 286.7
fibrinase (*see also* Defect, coagulation) 286.3
fibrinogen (congenital) (*see also* Defect, coagulation) 286.3
  acquired 286.6
fibrin-stabilizing factor (congenital) (*see also* Defect, coagulation) 286.3
finger — *see* Absence, finger
fletcher factor (*see also* Defect, coagulation) 286.9
fluorine 269.3
folate, anemia 281.2
folic acid (vitamin B_c) 266.2
  anemia 281.2
follicle-stimulating hormone (FSH) 253.4
fructokinase 271.2
fructose-1, 6-diphosphate 271.2
fructose-1-phosphate aldolase 271.2
FSH (follicle-stimulating hormone) 253.4
fucosidase 271.8
galactokinase 271.1
galactose-1-phosphate uridyl transferase 271.1
gamma globulin in blood 279.00
glass factor (*see also* Defect, coagulation) 286.3
glucocorticoid 255.4
glucose-6-phosphatase 271.0
glucose-6-phosphate dehydrogenase anemia 282.2
glucuronyl transferase 277.4
glutathione-reductase (anemia) 282.2
glycogen synthetase 271.0
growth hormone 253.3
Hageman factor (congenital) (*see also* Defect, coagulation) 286.3
head V48.0
hemoglobin (*see also* Anemia) 285.9
hepatophosphorylase 271.0
hexose monophosphate (HMP) shunt 282.2
HGH (human growth hormone) 253.3
HG-PRT 277.2
homogentisic acid oxidase 270.2
hormone (*see also* Deficiency, by specific hormone)
  anterior pituitary (isolated) (partial) NEC 253.4

Deficiency, deficient — *continued*
hormone (*see also* Deficiency, by specific hormone) — *continued*
  anterior pituitary — *continued*
    growth (human) 253.3
    follicle-stimulating 253.4
    growth (human) (isolated) 253.3
    human growth 253.3
    interstitial cell-stimulating 253.4
    luteinizing 253.4
    melanocyte-stimulating 253.4
    testicular 257.2
  human growth hormone 253.3
humoral 279.00
  with
    hyper-IgM 279.05
      autosomal recessive 279.05
      X-linked 279.05
    increased IgM 279.05
    congenital hypogammaglobulinemia 279.04
    non-sex-linked 279.06
    selective immunoglobulin NEC 279.03
      IgA 279.01
      IgG 279.03
      IgM 279.02
        increased 279.05
    specified NEC 279.09
hydroxylase 255.2
hypoxanthine-guanine phosphoribosyltransferase (HG-PRT) 277.2
ICSH (interstitial cell-stimulating hormone) 253.4
immunity NEC 279.3
  cell-mediated 279.10
    with
      hyperimmunoglobulinemia 279.2
      thrombocytopenia and eczema 279.12
    specified NEC 279.19
  combined (severe) 279.2
    syndrome 279.2
  common variable 279.06
  humoral NEC 279.00
  IgA (secretory) 279.01
  IgG 279.03
  IgM 279.02
  immunoglobulin, selective NEC 279.03
    IgA 279.01
    IgG 279.03
    IgM 279.02
inositol (B complex) 266.2
interferon 279.4
internal organ V47.0
interstitial cell-stimulating hormone (ICSH) 253.4
intrinsic factor (Castle's) (congenital) 281.0
intrinsic (urethral) sphincter (ISD) 599.82
invertase 271.3
iodine 269.3
iron, anemia 280.9
labile factor (congenital) (*see also* Defect, coagulation) 286.3
  acquired 286.7
lacrimal fluid (acquired) 375.15
  congenital 743.64
lactase 271.3
Laki-Lorand factor (*see also* Defect, coagulation) 286.3
lecithin-cholesterol acyltranferase 272.5
LH (luteinizing hormone) 253.4
limb V49.0
  lower V49.0
    congenital (*see also* Deficiency, lower limb, congenital) 755.30
  upper V49.0
    congenital (*see also* Deficiency, upper limb, congenital) 755.20

Deficiency, deficient — *continued*
lipocaic 577.8
lipoid (high-density) 272.5
lipoprotein (familial) (high density) 272.5
liver phosphorylase 271.0
long chain 3-hydroxyacyl CoA dehydrogenase (LCHAD) 277.85
long chain/very long chain acyl CoA dehydrogenase (LCAD, VLCAD) 277.85
lower limb V49.0
  congenital 755.30
    with complete absence of distal elements 755.31
    longitudinal (complete) (partial) (with distal deficiencies, incomplete) 755.32
      with complete absence of distal elements 755.31
      combined femoral, tibial, fibular (incomplete) 755.33
      femoral 755.34
      fibular 755.37
      metatarsal(s) 755.38
      phalange(s) 755.39
        meaning all digits 755.31
      tarsal(s) 755.38
      tibia 755.36
      tibiofibular 755.35
    transverse 755.31
luteinizing hormone (LH) 253.4
lysosomal alpha-1, 4 glucosidase 271.0
magnesium 275.2
mannosidase 271.8
medium chain acyl CoA dehydrogenase (MCAD) 277.85
melanocyte-stimulating hormone (MSH) 253.4
menadione (vitamin K) 269.0
  newborn 776.0
mental (familial) (hereditary) (*see also* Retardation, mental) 319
mineral NEC 269.3
molybdenum 269.3
moral 301.7
multiple, syndrome 260
myocardial (*see also* Insufficiency, myocardial) 428.0
myophosphorylase 271.0
NADH-diaphorase or reductase (congenital) 289.7
NADH (DPNH)-methemoglobin-reductase (congenital) 289.7
neck V48.1
niacin (amide) (-tryptophan) 265.2
nicotinamide 265.2
nicotinic acid (amide) 265.2
nose V48.8
number of teeth (*see also* Anodontia) 520.0
nutrition, nutritional 269.9
  specified NEC 269.8
ornithine transcarbamylase 270.6
ovarian 256.39
oxygen (*see also* Anoxia) 799.02
pantothenic acid 266.2
parathyroid (gland) 252.1
phenylalanine hydroxylase 270.1
phosphoenolpyruvate carboxykinase 271.8
phosphofructokinase 271.2
phosphoglucomutase 271.0
phosphohexosisomerase 271.0
phosphomannomutase 271.8
phosphomannose isomerase 271.8
phosphomannosyl mutase 271.8
phosphorylase kinase, liver 271.0
pituitary (anterior) 253.2
  posterior 253.5
placenta — *see* Placenta, insufficiency
plasma
  cell 279.00

☑ Additional Digit Required — Refer to the Tabular List for Digit Selection   ᵂ Subterms under main terms may continue to next column or page

2007 ICD-9-CM   ▶◀ Revised Text   ● New Line   ▲ Revised Code   October 2006 · Volume 2 — 67

Deficiency, deficient — *continued*
  plasma — *continued*
    protein (paraproteinemia) (pyroglob-
      ulinemia) 273.8
      gamma globulin 279.00
    thromboplastin
      antecedent (PTA) 286.2
      component (PTC) 286.1
  platelet NEC 287.1
    constitutional 286.4
  polyglandular 258.9
  potassium (K) 276.8
  proaccelerin (congenital) (*see also* De-
    fect, congenital) 286.3
    acquired 286.7
  proconvertin factor (congenital) (*see
    also* Defect, coagulation) 286.3
    acquired 286.7
  prolactin 253.4
  protein 260
    anemia 281.4
    C 289.81
    plasma — *see* Deficiency, plasma,
      protein
    S 289.81
  prothrombin (congenital) (*see also*
    Defect, coagulation) 286.3
    acquired 286.7
  Prower factor (*see also* Defect, coagu-
    lation) 286.3
  PRT 277.2
  pseudocholinesterase 289.89
  psychobiological 301.6
  PTA 286.2
  PTC 286.1
  purine nucleoside phosphorylase
    277.2
  pyracin (alpha) (beta) 266.1
  pyridoxal 266.1
  pyridoxamine 266.1
  pyridoxine (derivatives) 266.1
  pyruvate carboxylase 271.8
  pyruvate dehydrogenase 271.8
  pyruvate kinase (PK) 282.3
  riboflavin (vitamin B_2) 266.0
  saccadic eye movements 379.57
  salivation 527.7
  salt 276.1
  secretion
    ovary 256.39
    salivary gland (any) 527.7
    urine 788.5
  selenium 269.3
  serum
    antitrypsin, familial 273.4
    protein (congenital) 273.8
  short chain acyl CoA dehydrogenase
    (SCAD) 277.85
  smooth pursuit movements (eye)
    379.58
  sodium (Na) 276.1
  SPCA (*see also* Defect, coagulation)
    286.3
  specified NEC 269.8
  stable factor (congenital) (*see also*
    Defect, coagulation) 286.3
    acquired 286.7
  Stuart (-Prower) factor (*see also* De-
    fect, coagulation) 286.3
  sucrase 271.3
  sucrase-isomaltase 271.3
  sulfite oxidase 270.0
  syndrome, multiple 260
  thiamine, thiaminic (chloride) 265.1
  thrombokinase (*see also* Defect, coag-
    ulation) 286.3
    newborn 776.0
  thrombopoieten 287.39
  thymolymphatic 279.2
  thyroid (gland) 244.9
  tocopherol 269.1
  toe — *see* Absence, toe
  tooth bud (*see also* Anodontia) 520.0
  trunk V48.1
  UDPG-glycogen transferase 271.0
  upper limb V49.0

Deficiency, deficient — *continued*
  upper limb — *continued*
    congenital 755.20
      with complete absence of distal
        elements 755.21
        longitudinal (complete) (partial)
          (with distal deficiencies,
          incomplete) 755.22
        carpal(s) 755.28
        combined humeral, radial,
          ulnar (incomplete)
          755.23
        humeral 755.24
        metacarpal(s) 755.28
        phalange(s) 755.29
          meaning all digits 755.21
        radial 755.26
        radioulnar 755.25
        ulnar 755.27
      transverse (complete) (partial)
        755.21
  vascular 459.9
  vasopressin 253.5
  viosterol (*see also* Deficiency, calcifer-
    ol) 268.9
  vitamin (multiple) NEC 269.2
    A 264.9
      with
        Bitôt's spot 264.1
          corneal 264.2
            with corneal ulceration
              264.3
        keratomalacia 264.4
        keratosis, follicular 264.8
        night blindness 264.5
        scar of cornea, xeroph-
          thalmic 264.6
        specified manifestation NEC
          264.8
        ocular 264.7
        xeroderma 264.8
        xerophthalmia 264.7
        xerosis
          conjunctival 264.0
            with Bitôt's spot 264.1
          corneal 264.2
            with corneal ulceration
              264.3
    B (complex) NEC 266.9
      with
        beriberi 265.0
        pellagra 265.2
      specified type NEC 266.2
    B_1 NEC 265.1
      beriberi 265.0
    B_2 266.0
    B_6 266.1
    B_{12} 266.2
    B_c (folic acid) 266.2
    C (ascorbic acid) (with scurvy) 267
    D (calciferol) (ergosterol) 268.9
      with
        osteomalacia 268.2
        rickets (*see also* Rickets)
          268.0
    E 269.1
    folic acid 266.2
    G 266.0
    H 266.2
    K 269.0
      of newborn 776.0
    nicotinic acid 265.2
    P 269.1
    PP 265.2
    specified NEC 269.1
    zinc 269.3
Deficient — *see also* Deficiency
  blink reflex 374.45
  craniofacial axis 756.0
  number of teeth (*see also* Anodontia)
    520.0
  secretion of urine 788.5
Deficit
  neurologic NEC 781.99

Deficit — *continued*
  neurologic — *continued*
    due to
      cerebrovascular lesion (*see also*
        Disease, cerebrovascular,
        acute) 436
        late effect — *see* Late effect(s)
          (of) cerebrovascular
          disease
      transient ischemic attack 435.9
  oxygen 799.02
Deflection
  radius 736.09
  septum (acquired) (nasal) (nose) 470
  spine — *see* Curvature, spine
  turbinate (nose) 470
Defluvium
  capillorum (*see also* Alopecia) 704.00
  ciliorum 374.55
  unguium 703.8
Deformity 738.9
  abdomen, congenital 759.9
  abdominal wall
    acquired 738.8
    congenital 756.70
    muscle deficiency syndrome 756.79
  acquired (unspecified site) 738.9
    specified site NEC 738.8
  adrenal gland (congenital) 759.1
  alimentary tract, congenital 751.9
    lower 751.5
    specified type NEC 751.8
    upper (any part, except tongue)
      750.9
      specified type NEC 750.8
      tongue 750.10
        specified type NEC 750.19
  ankle (joint) (acquired) 736.70
    abduction 718.47
    congenital 755.69
    contraction 718.47
    specified NEC 736.79
  anus (congenital) 751.5
    acquired 569.49
  aorta (congenital) 747.20
    acquired 447.8
    arch 747.21
      acquired 447.8
    coarctation 747.10
  aortic
    arch 747.21
      acquired 447.8
    cusp or valve (congenital) 746.9
      acquired (*see also* Endocarditis,
        aortic) 424.1
    ring 747.21
  appendix 751.5
  arm (acquired) 736.89
    congenital 755.50
  arteriovenous (congenital) (peripheral)
    NEC 747.60
    gastrointestinal 747.61
    lower limb 747.64
    renal 747.62
    specified NEC 747.69
    spinal 747.82
    upper limb 747.63
  artery (congenital) (peripheral) NEC
    (*see also* Deformity, vascular)
    747.60
    acquired 447.8
    cerebral 747.81
    coronary (congenital) 746.85
      acquired (*see also* Ischemia,
        heart) 414.9
    retinal 743.9
    umbilical 747.5
  atrial septal (congenital) (heart) 745.5
  auditory canal (congenital) (external)
    (*see also* Deformity, ear) 744.3
    acquired 380.50
  auricle
    ear (congenital) (*see also* Deformity,
      ear) 744.3
      acquired 380.32
  heart (congenital) 746.9

Deformity — *continued*
  back (acquired) — *see* Deformity,
    spine
  Bartholin's duct (congenital) 750.9
  bile duct (congenital) 751.60
    acquired 576.8
      with calculus, choledocholithia-
        sis, or stones — *see*
        Choledocholithiasis
  biliary duct or passage (congenital)
    751.60
    acquired 576.8
      with calculus, choledocholithia-
        sis, or stones — *see*
        Choledocholithiasis
  bladder (neck) (sphincter) (trigone)
    (acquired) 596.8
    congenital 753.9
  bone (acquired) NEC 738.9
    congenital 756.9
    turbinate 738.0
  boutonniere (finger) 736.21
  brain (congenital) 742.9
    acquired 348.8
    multiple 742.4
    reduction 742.2
    vessel (congenital) 747.81
  breast (acquired) 611.8
    congenital 757.9
  bronchus (congenital) 748.3
    acquired 519.19   ▲
  bursa, congenital 756.9
  canal of Nuck 752.9
  canthus (congenital) 743.9
    acquired 374.89
  capillary (acquired) 448.9
    congenital NEC (*see also* Deformity,
      vascular) 747.60
  cardiac — *see* Deformity, heart
  cardiovascular system (congenital)
    746.9
  caruncle, lacrimal (congenital) 743.9
    acquired 375.69
  cascade, stomach 537.6
  cecum (congenital) 751.5
    acquired 569.89
  cerebral (congenital) 742.9
    acquired 348.8
  cervix (acquired) (uterus) 622.8
    congenital 752.40
  cheek (acquired) 738.19
    congenital 744.9
  chest (wall) (acquired) 738.3
    congenital 754.89
    late effect of rickets 268.1
  chin (acquired) 738.19
    congenital 744.9
  choroid (congenital) 743.9
    acquired 363.8
    plexus (congenital) 742.9
      acquired 349.2
  cicatricial — *see* Cicatrix
  cilia (congenital) 743.9
    acquired 374.89
  circulatory system (congenital) 747.9
  clavicle (acquired) 738.8
    congenital 755.51
  clitoris (congenital) 752.40
    acquired 624.8
  clubfoot — *see* Clubfoot
  coccyx (acquired) 738.6
    congenital 756.10
  colon (congenital) 751.5
    acquired 569.89
  concha (ear) (congenital) (*see also* De-
    formity, ear) 744.3
    acquired 380.32
  congenital, organ or site not listed (*see
    also* Anomaly) 759.9
  cornea (congenital) 743.9
    acquired 371.70
  coronary artery (congenital) 746.85
    acquired (*see also* Ischemia, heart)
      414.9
  cranium (acquired) 738.19

☑ Additional Digit Required — Refer to the Tabular List for Digit Selection   ▧ Subterms under main terms may continue to next column or page

68 — Volume 2 • October 2006   ▶◀ Revised Text   ● New Line   ▲ Revised Code   **2007 ICD-9-CM**

Deformity — *continued*
cranium — *continued*
congenital (*see also* Deformity, skull, congenital) 756.0
cricoid cartilage (congenital) 748.3
acquired 478.79
cystic duct (congenital) 751.60
acquired 575.8
Dandy-Walker 742.3
with spina bifida (*see also* Spina bifida) 741.0 ☑
diaphragm (congenital) 756.6
acquired 738.8
digestive organ(s) or system (congenital) NEC 751.9
specified type NEC 751.8
ductus arteriosus 747.0
duodenal bulb 537.89
duodenum (congenital) 751.5
acquired 537.89
dura (congenital) 742.9
brain 742.4
acquired 349.2
spinal 742.59
acquired 349.2
ear (congenital) 744.3
acquired 380.32
auricle 744.3
causing impairment of hearing 744.02
causing impairment of hearing 744.00
external 744.3
causing impairment of hearing 744.02
internal 744.05
lobule 744.3
middle 744.03
ossicles 744.04
ossicles 744.04
ectodermal (congenital) NEC 757.9
specified type NEC 757.8
ejaculatory duct (congenital) 752.9
acquired 608.89
elbow (joint) (acquired) 736.00
congenital 755.50
contraction 718.42
endocrine gland NEC 759.2
epididymis (congenital) 752.9
acquired 608.89
torsion 608.24 ▲
epiglottis (congenital) 748.3
acquired 478.79
esophagus (congenital) 750.9
acquired 530.89
Eustachian tube (congenital) NEC 744.3
specified type NEC 744.24
extremity (acquired) 736.9
congenital, except reduction deformity 755.9
lower 755.60
upper 755.50
reduction — *see* Deformity, reduction
eye (congenital) 743.9
acquired 379.8
muscle 743.9
eyebrow (congenital) 744.89
eyelid (congenital) 743.9
acquired 374.89
specified type NEC 743.62
face (acquired) 738.19
congenital (any part) 744.9
due to intrauterine malposition and pressure 754.0
fallopian tube (congenital) 752.10
acquired 620.8
femur (acquired) 736.89
congenital 755.60
fetal
with fetopelvic disproportion 653.7 ☑
affecting fetus or newborn 763.1
causing obstructed labor 660.1 ☑
affecting fetus or newborn 763.1

Deformity — *continued*
fetal — *continued*
known or suspected, affecting management of pregnancy 655.9 ☑
finger (acquired) 736.20
boutonniere type 736.21
congenital 755.50
flexion contracture 718.44
swan neck 736.22
flexion (joint) (acquired) 736.9
congenital NEC 755.9
hip or thigh (acquired) 736.39
congenital (*see also* Subluxation, congenital, hip) 754.32
foot (acquired) 736.70
cavovarus 736.75
congenital 754.59
congenital NEC 754.70
specified type NEC 754.79
valgus (acquired) 736.79
congenital 754.60
specified type NEC 754.69
varus (acquired) 736.79
congenital 754.50
specified type NEC 754.59
forearm (acquired) 736.00
congenital 755.50
forehead (acquired) 738.19
congenital (*see also* Deformity, skull, congenital) 756.0
frontal bone (acquired) 738.19
congenital (*see also* Deformity, skull, congenital) 756.0
gallbladder (congenital) 751.60
acquired 575.8
gastrointestinal tract (congenital) NEC 751.9
acquired 569.89
specified type NEC 751.8
genitalia, genital organ(s) or system NEC
congenital 752.9
female (congenital) 752.9
acquired 629.89 ▲
external 752.40
internal 752.9
male (congenital) 752.9
acquired 608.89
globe (eye) (congenital) 743.9
acquired 360.89
gum (congenital) 750.9
acquired 523.9
gunstock 736.02
hand (acquired) 736.00
claw 736.06
congenital 755.50
minus (and plus) (intrinsic) 736.09
pill roller (intrinsic) 736.09
plus (and minus) (intrinsic) 736.09
swan neck (intrinsic) 736.09
head (acquired) 738.10
congenital (*see also* Deformity, skull congenital) 756.0
specified NEC 738.19
heart (congenital) 746.9
auricle (congenital) 746.9
septum 745.9
auricular 745.5
specified type NEC 745.8
ventricular 745.4
valve (congenital) NEC 746.9
acquired — *see* Endocarditis
pulmonary (congenital) 746.00
specified type NEC 746.89
ventricle (congenital) 746.9
heel (acquired) 736.76
congenital 755.67
hepatic duct (congenital) 751.60
acquired 576.8
with calculus, choledocholithiasis, or stones — *see* Choledocholithiasis
hip (joint) (acquired) 736.30
congenital NEC 755.63

Deformity — *continued*
hip — *continued*
flexion 718.45
congenital (*see also* Subluxation, congenital, hip) 754.32
hourglass — *see* Contraction, hourglass
humerus (acquired) 736.89
congenital 755.50
hymen (congenital) 752.40
hypophyseal (congenital) 759.2
ileocecal (coil) (valve) (congenital) 751.5
acquired 569.89
ileum (intestine) (congenital) 751.5
acquired 569.89
ilium (acquired) 738.6
congenital 755.60
integument (congenital) 757.9
intervertebral cartilage or disc (acquired) (*see also* Displacement, intervertebral disc)
congenital 756.10
intestine (large) (small) (congenital) 751.5
acquired 569.89
iris (acquired) 364.75
congenital 743.9
prolapse 364.8
ischium (acquired) 738.6
congenital 755.60
jaw (acquired) (congenital) NEC 524.9
due to intrauterine malposition and pressure 754.0
joint (acquired) NEC 738.8
congenital 755.9
contraction (abduction) (adduction) (extension) (flexion) — *see* Contraction, joint
kidney(s) (calyx) (pelvis) (congenital) 753.9
acquired 593.89
vessel 747.62
acquired 459.9
Klippel-Feil (brevicollis) 756.16
knee (acquired) NEC 736.6
congenital 755.64
labium (majus) (minus) (congenital) 752.40
acquired 624.8
lacrimal apparatus or duct (congenital) 743.9
acquired 375.69
larynx (muscle) (congenital) 748.3
acquired 478.79
web (glottic) (subglottic) 748.2
leg (lower) (upper) (acquired) NEC 736.89
congenital 755.60
reduction — *see* Deformity, reduction, lower limb
lens (congenital) 743.9
acquired 379.39
lid (fold) (congenital) 743.9
acquired 374.89
ligament (acquired) 728.9
congenital 756.9
limb (acquired) 736.9
congenital, except reduction deformity 755.9
lower 755.60
reduction (*see also* Deformity, reduction, lower limb) 755.30
upper 755.50
reduction (*see also* Deformity, reduction, upper limb) 755.20
specified NEC 736.89
lip (congenital) NEC 750.9
acquired 528.5
specified type NEC 750.26
liver (congenital) 751.60
acquired 573.8
duct (congenital) 751.60

Deformity — *continued*
liver — *continued*
duct — *continued*
acquired 576.8
with calculus, choledocholithiasis, or stones — *see* Choledocholithiasis
lower extremity — *see* Deformity, leg
lumbosacral (joint) (region) (congenital) 756.10
acquired 738.5
lung (congenital) 748.60
acquired 518.89
specified type NEC 748.69
lymphatic system, congenital 759.9
Madelung's (radius) 755.54
maxilla (acquired) (congenital) 524.9
meninges or membrane (congenital) 742.9
brain 742.4
acquired 349.2
spinal (cord) 742.59
acquired 349.2
mesentery (congenital) 751.9
acquired 568.89
metacarpus (acquired) 736.00
congenital 755.50
metatarsus (acquired) 736.70
congenital 754.70
middle ear, except ossicles (congenital) 744.03
ossicles 744.04
mitral (leaflets) (valve) (congenital) 746.9
acquired — *see* Endocarditis, mitral
Ebstein's 746.89
parachute 746.5
specified type NEC 746.89
stenosis, congenital 746.5
mouth (acquired) 528.9
congenital NEC 750.9
specified type NEC 750.26
multiple, congenital NEC 759.7
specified type NEC 759.89
muscle (acquired) 728.9
congenital 756.9
specified type NEC 756.89
sternocleidomastoid (due to intrauterine malposition and pressure) 754.1
musculoskeletal system, congenital NEC 756.9
specified type NEC 756.9
nail (acquired) 703.9
congenital 757.9
nasal — *see* Deformity, nose
neck (acquired) NEC 738.2
congenital (any part) 744.9
sternocleidomastoid 754.1
nervous system (congenital) 742.9
nipple (congenital) 757.9
acquired 611.8
nose, nasal (cartilage) (acquired) 738.0
bone (turbinate) 738.0
congenital 748.1
bent 754.0
squashed 754.0
saddle 738.0
syphilitic 090.5
septum 470
congenital 748.1
sinus (wall) (congenital) 748.1
acquired 738.0
syphilitic (congenital) 090.5
late 095.8
ocular muscle (congenital) 743.9
acquired 378.60
opticociliary vessels (congenital) 743.9
orbit (congenital) (eye) 743.9
acquired NEC 376.40
associated with craniofacial deformities 376.44
due to
bone disease 376.43

☑ Additional Digit Required — Refer to the Tabular List for Digit Selection

▽ Subterms under main terms may continue to next column or page

Deformity — *continued*
orbit — *continued*
  acquired — *continued*
    due to — *continued*
      surgery 376.47
      trauma 376.47
organ of Corti (congenital) 744.05
ovary (congenital) 752.0
  acquired 620.8
oviduct (congenital) 752.10
  acquired 620.8
palate (congenital) 750.9
  acquired 526.89
  cleft (congenital) (*see also* Cleft, palate) 749.00
  hard, acquired 526.89
  soft, acquired 528.9
pancreas (congenital) 751.7
  acquired 577.8
parachute, mitral valve 746.5
parathyroid (gland) 759.2
parotid (gland) (congenital) 750.9
  acquired 527.8
patella (acquired) 736.6
  congenital 755.64
pelvis, pelvic (acquired) (bony) 738.6
  with disproportion (fetopelvic) 653.0 ☑
    affecting fetus or newborn 763.1
    causing obstructed labor 660.1 ☑
      affecting fetus or newborn 763.1
  congenital 755.60
  rachitic (late effect) 268.1
penis (glans) (congenital) 752.9
  acquired 607.89
pericardium (congenital) 746.9
  acquired — *see* Pericarditis
pharynx (congenital) 750.9
  acquired 478.29
Pierre Robin (congenital) 756.0
pinna (acquired) 380.32
  congenital 744.3
pituitary (congenital) 759.2
pleural folds (congenital) 748.8
portal vein (congenital) 747.40
posture — *see* Curvature, spine
prepuce (congenital) 752.9
  acquired 607.89
prostate (congenital) 752.9
  acquired 602.8
pulmonary valve — *see* Endocarditis, pulmonary
pupil (congenital) 743.9
  acquired 364.75
pylorus (congenital) 750.9
  acquired 537.89
rachitic (acquired), healed or old 268.1
radius (acquired) 736.00
  congenital 755.50
  reduction — *see* Deformity, reduction, upper limb
rectovaginal septum (congenital) 752.40
  acquired 623.8
rectum (congenital) 751.5
  acquired 569.49
reduction (extremity) (limb) 755.4
  brain 742.2
  lower limb 755.30
    with complete absence of distal elements 755.31
    longitudinal (complete) (partial) (with distal deficiencies, incomplete) 755.32
      with complete absence of distal elements 755.31
      combined femoral, tibial, fibular (incomplete) 755.33
      femoral 755.34
      fibular 755.37
      metatarsal(s) 755.38
      phalange(s) 755.39
        meaning all digits 755.31

Deformity — *continued*
reduction — *continued*
  lower limb — *continued*
    longitudinal — *continued*
      tarsal(s) 755.38
      tibia 755.36
      tibiofibular 755.35
      transverse 755.31
  upper limb 755.20
    with complete absence of distal elements 755.21
    longitudinal (complete) (partial) (with distal deficiencies, incomplete) 755.22
      with complete absence of distal elements 755.21
      carpal(s) 755.28
      combined humeral, radial, ulnar (incomplete) 755.23
      humeral 755.24
      metacarpal(s) 755.28
      phalange(s) 755.29
        meaning all digits 755.21
      radial 755.26
      radioulnar 755.25
      ulnar 755.27
      transverse (complete) (partial) 755.21
renal — *see* Deformity, kidney
respiratory system (congenital) 748.9
  specified type NEC 748.8
rib (acquired) 738.3
  congenital 756.3
    cervical 756.2
rotation (joint) (acquired) 736.9
  congenital 755.9
  hip or thigh 736.39
    congenital (*see also* Subluxation, congenital, hip) 754.32
sacroiliac joint (congenital) 755.69
  acquired 738.5
sacrum (acquired) 738.5
  congenital 756.10
saddle
  back 737.8
  nose 738.0
    syphilitic 090.5
salivary gland or duct (congenital) 750.9
  acquired 527.8
scapula (acquired) 736.89
  congenital 755.50
scrotum (congenital) 752.9
  acquired 608.89
sebaceous gland, acquired 706.8
seminal tract or duct (congenital) 752.9
  acquired 608.89
septum (nasal) (acquired) 470
  congenital 748.1
shoulder (joint) (acquired) 736.89
  congenital 755.50
    specified type NEC 755.59
  contraction 718.41
sigmoid (flexure) (congenital) 751.5
  acquired 569.89
sinus of Valsalva 747.29
skin (congenital) 757.9
  acquired NEC 709.8
skull (acquired) 738.19
  congenital 756.0
    with
      anencephalus 740.0
      encephalocele 742.0
      hydrocephalus 742.3
        with spina bifida (*see also* Spina bifida) 741.0 ☑
      microcephalus 742.1
    due to intrauterine malposition and pressure 754.0
soft parts, organs or tissues (of pelvis)
  in pregnancy or childbirth NEC 654.9 ☑

Deformity — *continued*
soft parts, organs or tissues — *continued*
  in pregnancy or childbirth — *continued*
    affecting fetus or newborn 763.89
    causing obstructed labor 660.2 ☑
      affecting fetus or newborn 763.1
spermatic cord (congenital) 752.9
  acquired 608.89
    torsion 608.22 ▲
      extravaginal 608.21 ●
      intravaginal 608.22 ●
spinal
  column — *see* Deformity, spine
  cord (congenital) 742.9
    acquired 336.8
    vessel (congenital) 747.82
  nerve root (congenital) 742.9
    acquired 724.9
spine (acquired) NEC 738.5
  congenital 756.10
    due to intrauterine malposition and pressure 754.2
  kyphoscoliotic (*see also* Kyphoscoliosis) 737.30
  kyphotic (*see also* Kyphosis) 737.10
  lordotic (*see also* Lordosis) 737.20
  rachitic 268.1
  scoliotic (*see also* Scoliosis) 737.30
spleen
  acquired 289.59
  congenital 759.0
Sprengel's (congenital) 755.52
sternum (acquired) 738.3
  congenital 756.3
stomach (congenital) 750.9
  acquired 537.89
submaxillary gland (congenital) 750.9
  acquired 527.8
swan neck (acquired)
  finger 736.22
  hand 736.09
talipes — *see* Talipes
teeth, tooth NEC 520.9
testis (congenital) 752.9
  acquired 608.89
    torsion 608.20 ▲
thigh (acquired) 736.89
  congenital 755.60
thorax (acquired) (wall) 738.3
  congenital 754.89
  late effect of rickets 268.1
thumb (acquired) 736.20
  congenital 755.50
thymus (tissue) (congenital) 759.2
thyroid (gland) (congenital) 759.2
  cartilage 748.3
    acquired 478.79
tibia (acquired) 736.89
  congenital 755.60
  saber 090.5
toe (acquired) 735.9
  congenital 755.66
  specified NEC 735.8
tongue (congenital) 750.10
  acquired 529.8
tooth, teeth NEC 520.9
trachea (rings) (congenital) 748.3
  acquired 519.19 ▲
transverse aortic arch (congenital) 747.21
tricuspid (leaflets) (valve) (congenital) 746.9
  acquired — *see* Endocarditis, tricuspid
  atresia or stenosis 746.1
  specified type NEC 746.89
trunk (acquired) 738.3
  congenital 759.9
ulna (acquired) 736.00
  congenital 755.50

Deformity — *continued*
upper extremity — *see* Deformity, arm
urachus (congenital) 753.7
ureter (opening) (congenital) 753.9
  acquired 593.89
urethra (valve) (congenital) 753.9
  acquired 599.84
urinary tract or system (congenital) 753.9
  urachus 753.7
uterus (congenital) 752.3
  acquired 621.8
uvula (congenital) 750.9
  acquired 528.9
vagina (congenital) 752.40
  acquired 623.8
valve, valvular (heart) (congenital) 746.9
  acquired — *see* Endocarditis
  pulmonary 746.00
  specified type NEC 746.89
vascular (congenital) (peripheral) NEC 747.60
  acquired 459.9
  gastrointestinal 747.61
  lower limb 747.64
  renal 747.62
  specified site NEC 747.69
  spinal 747.82
  upper limb 747.63
vas deferens (congenital) 752.9
  acquired 608.89
vein (congenital) NEC (*see also* Deformity, vascular) 747.60
  brain 747.81
  coronary 746.9
  great 747.40
vena cava (inferior) (superior) (congenital) 747.40
vertebra — *see* Deformity, spine
vesicourethral orifice (acquired) 596.8
  congenital NEC 753.9
    specified type NEC 753.8
vessels of optic papilla (congenital) 743.9
visual field (contraction) 368.45
vitreous humor (congenital) 743.9
  acquired 379.29
vulva (congenital) 752.40
  acquired 624.8
wrist (joint) (acquired) 736.00
  congenital 755.50
  contraction 718.43
  valgus 736.03
    congenital 755.59
  varus 736.04
    congenital 755.59

Degeneration, degenerative
adrenal (capsule) (gland) 255.8
  with hypofunction 255.4
  fatty 255.8
  hyaline 255.8
  infectional 255.8
  lardaceous 277.39 ▲
amyloid (any site) (general) 277.39 ▲
anterior cornua, spinal cord 336.8
aorta, aortic 440.0
  fatty 447.8
  valve (heart) (*see also* Endocarditis, aortic) 424.1
arteriovascular — *see* Arteriosclerosis
artery, arterial (atheromatous) (calcareous) (*see also* Arteriosclerosis)
  amyloid 277.39 ▲
  lardaceous 277.39 ▲
  medial NEC (*see also* Arteriosclerosis, extremities) 440.20
articular cartilage NEC (*see also* Disorder, cartilage, articular) 718.0 ☑
  elbow 718.02
  knee 717.5
  patella 717.7
  shoulder 718.01
  spine (*see also* Spondylosis) 721.90

☑ Additional Digit Required — Refer to the Tabular List for Digit Selection   ⏪ Subterms under main terms may continue to next column or page

70 — Volume 2 · October 2006   ▶◀ Revised Text   ● New Line   ▲ Revised Code   *2007 ICD-9-CM*

Degeneration, degenerative —
continued
atheromatous — *see* Arteriosclerosis
bacony (any site) 277.39 ▲
basal nuclei or ganglia NEC 333.0
bone 733.90
brachial plexus 353.0
brain (cortical) (progressive) 331.9
　arteriosclerotic 437.0
　childhood 330.9
　　specified type NEC 330.8
　congenital 742.4
　cystic 348.0
　　congenital 742.4
　familial NEC 331.89
　grey matter 330.8
　heredofamilial NEC 331.89
　in
　　alcoholism 303.9 ☑ *[331.7]*
　　beriberi 265.0 *[331.7]*
　　cerebrovascular disease
　　　437.9 *[331.7]*
　　congenital hydrocephalus
　　　742.3 *[331.7]*
　　　with spina bifida (*see also*
　　　　Spina bifida)
　　　　741.0 ☑ *[331.7]*
　　Fabry's disease 272.7 *[330.2]*
　　Gaucher's disease 272.7 *[330.2]*
　　Hunter's disease or syndrome
　　　277.5 *[330.3]*
　　lipidosis
　　　cerebral 330.1
　　　generalized 272.7 *[330.2]*
　　mucopolysaccharidosis
　　　277.5 *[330.3]*
　　myxedema (*see also* Myxedema)
　　　244.9 *[331.7]*
　　neoplastic disease NEC
　　　(M8000/1) 239.9 *[331.7]*
　　Niemann-Pick disease
　　　272.7 *[330.2]*
　　sphingolipidosis 272.7 *[330.2]*
　　vitamin B$_{12}$ deficiency
　　　266.2 *[331.7]*
　motor centers 331.89
　senile 331.2
　specified type NEC 331.89
breast — *see* Disease, breast
Bruch's membrane 363.40
bundle of His 426.50
　left 426.3
　right 426.4
calcareous NEC 275.49
capillaries 448.9
　amyloid 277.39 ▲
　fatty 448.9
　lardaceous 277.39 ▲
cardiac (brown) (calcareous) (fatty) (fi-
　brous) (hyaline) (mural) (muscu-
　lar) (pigmentary) (senile) (with
　arteriosclerosis) (*see also* Degen-
　eration, myocardial) 429.1
　valve, valvular — *see* Endocarditis
cardiorenal (*see also* Hypertension,
　cardiorenal) 404.90
cardiovascular (*see also* Disease, car-
　diovascular) 429.2
　renal (*see also* Hypertension, car-
　diorenal) 404.90
cartilage (joint) — *see* Derangement,
　joint
cerebellar NEC 334.9
　primary (hereditary) (sporadic)
　　334.2
cerebral — *see* Degeneration, brain
cerebromacular 330.1
cerebrovascular 437.1
　due to hypertension 437.2
　late effect — *see* Late effect(s) (of)
　　cerebrovascular disease
cervical plexus 353.2
cervix 622.8
　due to radiation (intended effect)
　　622.8

Degeneration, degenerative —
continued
cervix — *continued*
　due to radiation — *continued*
　　adverse effect or misadventure
　　　622.8
changes, spine or vertebra (*see also*
　Spondylosis) 721.90
chitinous 277.39 ▲
chorioretinal 363.40
　congenital 743.53
　hereditary 363.50
choroid (colloid) (drusen) 363.40
　hereditary 363.50
　senile 363.41
　　diffuse secondary 363.42
cochlear 386.8
collateral ligament (knee) (medial)
　717.82
　lateral 717.81
combined (spinal cord) (subacute)
　266.2 *[336.2]*
　with anemia (pernicious)
　　281.0 *[336.2]*
　due to dietary deficiency
　　281.1 *[336.2]*
　due to vitamin B$_{12}$ deficiency ane-
　　mia (dietary) 281.1 *[336.2]*
conjunctiva 372.50
　amyloid 277.39 *[372.50]* ▲
cornea 371.40
　calcerous 371.44
　familial (hereditary) (*see also* Dys-
　　trophy, cornea) 371.50
　　macular 371.55
　　reticular 371.54
　hyaline (of old scars) 371.41
　marginal (Terrien's) 371.48
　mosaic (shagreen) 371.41
　nodular 371.46
　peripheral 371.48
　senile 371.41
cortical (cerebellar) (parenchymatous)
　334.2
　alcoholic 303.9 ☑ *[334.4]*
　diffuse, due to arteriopathy 437.0
corticostriatal-spinal 334.8
cretinoid 243
cruciate ligament (knee) (posterior)
　717.84
　anterior 717.83
cutis 709.3
　amyloid 277.39 ▲
dental pulp 522.2
disc disease — *see* Degeneration, in-
　tervertebral disc
dorsolateral (spinal cord) — *see* Degen-
　eration, combined
endocardial 424.90
extrapyramidal NEC 333.90
eye NEC 360.40
　macular (*see also* Degeneration,
　　macula) 362.50
　　congenital 362.75
　　hereditary 362.76
fatty (diffuse) (general) 272.8
　liver 571.8
　　alcoholic 571.0
　localized site — *see* Degeneration,
　　by site, fatty
　placenta — *see* Placenta, abnormal
globe (eye) NEC 360.40
　macular — *see* Degeneration,
　　macula
grey matter 330.8
heart (brown) (calcareous) (fatty) (fi-
　brous) (hyaline) (mural) (muscu-
　lar) (pigmentary) (senile) (with
　arteriosclerosis) (*see also* Degen-
　eration, myocardial) 429.1
　amyloid 277.39 *[425.7]* ▲
　atheromatous — *see* Arterioscle-
　　rosis, coronary
　gouty 274.82
　hypertensive (*see also* Hyperten-
　　sion, heart) 402.90

Degeneration, degenerative —
continued
heart (*see also* Degeneration, myocar-
　dial) — *continued*
　ischemic 414.9
　valve, valvular — *see* Endocarditis
hepatolenticular (Wilson's) 275.1
hepatorenal 572.4
heredofamilial
　brain NEC 331.89
　spinal cord NEC 336.8
hyaline (diffuse) (generalized) 728.9
　localized (*see also* Degeneration,
　　by site)
　　cornea 371.41
　　keratitis 371.41
hypertensive vascular — *see* Hyperten-
　sion
infrapatellar fat pad 729.31
internal semilunar cartilage 717.3
intervertebral disc 722.6
　with myelopathy 722.70
　cervical, cervicothoracic 722.4
　　with myelopathy 722.71
　lumbar, lumbosacral 722.52
　　with myelopathy 722.73
　thoracic, thoracolumbar 722.51
　　with myelopathy 722.72
intestine 569.89
　amyloid 277.39 ▲
　lardaceous 277.39 ▲
iris (generalized) (*see also* Atrophy,
　iris) 364.59
　pigmentary 364.53
　pupillary margin 364.54
ischemic — *see* Ischemia
joint disease (*see also* Osteoarthrosis)
　715.9 ☑
　multiple sites 715.09
　spine (*see also* Spondylosis) 721.90
kidney (*see also* Sclerosis, renal) 587
　amyloid 277.39 *[583.81]* ▲
　cyst, cystic (multiple) (solitary)
　　593.2
　　congenital (*see also* Cystic, dis-
　　　ease, kidney) 753.10
　fatty 593.89
　fibrocystic (congenital) 753.19
　lardaceous 277.39 *[583.81]* ▲
　polycystic (congenital) 753.12
　　adult type (APKD) 753.13
　　autosomal dominant 753.13
　　autosomal recessive 753.14
　　childhood type (CPKD) 753.14
　　infantile type 753.14
　waxy 277.39 *[583.81]* ▲
Kuhnt-Junius (retina) 362.52
labyrinth, osseous 386.8
lacrimal passages, cystic 375.12
lardaceous (any site) 277.39 ▲
lateral column (posterior), spinal cord
　(*see also* Degeneration, com-
　bined) 266.2 *[336.2]*
lattice 362.63
lens 366.9
　infantile, juvenile, or presenile
　　366.00
　senile 366.10
lenticular (familial) (progressive) (Wil-
　son's) (with cirrhosis of liver)
　275.1
　striate artery 437.0
lethal ball, prosthetic heart valve
　996.02
ligament
　collateral (knee) (medial) 717.82
　　lateral 717.81
　cruciate (knee) (posterior) 717.84
　　anterior 717.83
liver (diffuse) 572.8
　amyloid 277.39 ▲
　congenital (cystic) 751.62
　cystic 572.8
　　congenital 751.62
　fatty 571.8
　　alcoholic 571.0

Degeneration, degenerative —
continued
liver — *continued*
　hypertrophic 572.8
　lardaceous 277.39 ▲
　parenchymatous, acute or suba-
　　cute (*see also* Necrosis, liver)
　　570
　pigmentary 572.8
　toxic (acute) 573.8
　waxy 277.39 ▲
lung 518.89
lymph gland 289.3
　hyaline 289.3
　lardaceous 277.39 ▲
macula (acquired) (senile) 362.50
　atrophic 362.51
　Best's 362.76
　congenital 362.75
　cystic 362.54
　cystoid 362.53
　disciform 362.52
　dry 362.51
　exudative 362.52
　familial pseudoinflammatory
　　362.77
　hereditary 362.76
　hole 362.54
　juvenile (Stargardt's) 362.75
　nonexudative 362.51
　pseudohole 362.54
　wet 362.52
medullary — *see* Degeneration, brain
membranous labyrinth, congenital
　(causing impairment of hearing)
　744.05
meniscus — *see* Derangement, joint
microcystoid 362.62
mitral — *see* Insufficiency, mitral
Mönckeberg's (*see also* Arterioscle-
　sis, extremities) 440.20
moral 301.7
motor centers, senile 331.2
mural (*see also* Degeneration, myocar-
　dial) 429.1
　heart, cardiac (*see also* Degenera-
　　tion, myocardial) 429.1
　myocardium, myocardial (*see also*
　　Degeneration, myocardial)
　　429.1
muscle 728.9
　fatty 728.9
　fibrous 728.9
　heart (*see also* Degeneration, my-
　　ocardial) 429.1
　hyaline 728.9
muscular progressive 728.2
myelin, central nervous system NEC
　341.9
myocardium, myocardial (brown)
　(calcareous) (fatty) (fibrous)
　(hyaline) (mural) (muscular)
　(pigmentary) (senile) (with arte-
　riosclerosis) 429.1
　with rheumatic fever (conditions
　　classifiable to 390) 398.0
　　active, acute, or subacute 391.2
　　　with chorea 392.0
　　inactive or quiescent (with
　　　chorea) 398.0
　amyloid 277.39 *[425.7]* ▲
　congenital 746.89
　fetus or newborn 779.89
　gouty 274.82
　hypertensive (*see also* Hyperten-
　　sion, heart) 402.90
　ischemic 414.8
　rheumatic (*see also* Degeneration,
　　myocardium, with rheumatic
　　fever) 398.0
　syphilitic 093.82
nasal sinus (mucosa) (*see also* Sinusi-
　tis) 473.9
　frontal 473.1
　maxillary 473.0
nerve — *see* Disorder, nerve

☑ Additional Digit Required — Refer to the Tabular List for Digit Selection　　　　　　　　　　　　　　ᵂ Subterms under main terms may continue to next column or page
2007 ICD-9-CM　　　　▶◀ Revised Text　　　　● New Line　　　　▲ Revised Code　　　　October 2006 · Volume 2 — 71

Degeneration, degenerative — Degeneration, degenerative

Degeneration, degenerative — *continued*

nervous system 349.89
  amyloid 277.39 *[357.4]* ▲
  autonomic (*see also* Neuropathy, peripheral, autonomic) 337.9
  fatty 349.89
  peripheral autonomic NEC (*see also* Neuropathy, peripheral, autonomic) 337.9
nipple 611.9
nose 478.19 ▲
oculoacousticocerebral, congenital (progressive) 743.8
olivopontocerebellar (familial) (hereditary) 333.0
osseous labyrinth 386.8
ovary 620.8
  cystic 620.2
  microcystic 620.2
pallidal, pigmentary (progressive) 333.0
pancreas 577.8
  tuberculous (*see also* Tuberculosis) 017.9 ☑
papillary muscle 429.81
paving stone 362.61
penis 607.89
peritoneum 568.89
pigmentary (diffuse) (general)
  localized — *see* Degeneration, by site
  pallidal (progressive) 333.0
  secondary 362.65
pineal gland 259.8
pituitary (gland) 253.8
placenta (fatty) (fibrinoid) (fibroid) — *see* Placenta, abnormal
popliteal fat pad 729.31
posterolateral (spinal cord) (*see also* Degeneration, combined) 266.2 *[336.2]*
pulmonary valve (heart) (*see also* Endocarditis, pulmonary) 424.3
pulp (tooth) 522.2
pupillary margin 364.54
renal (*see also* Sclerosis, renal) 587
  fibrocystic 753.19
  polycystic 753.12
    adult type (APKD) 753.13
    autosomal dominant 753.13
    autosomal recessive 753.14
    childhood type (CPKD) 753.14
    infantile type 753.14
reticuloendothelial system 289.89
retina (peripheral) 362.60
  with retinal defect (*see also* Detachment, retina, with retinal defect) 361.00
  cystic (senile) 362.50
  cystoid 362.53
  hereditary (*see also* Dystrophy, retina) 362.70
    cerebroretinal 362.71
    congenital 362.75
    juvenile (Stargardt's) 362.75
    macula 362.76
  Kuhnt-Junius 362.52
  lattice 362.63
  macular (*see also* Degeneration, macula) 362.50
  microcystoid 362.62
  palisade 362.63
  paving stone 362.61
  pigmentary (primary) 362.74
    secondary 362.65
  posterior pole (*see also* Degeneration, macula) 362.50
  secondary 362.66
  senile 362.60
    cystic 362.53
    reticular 362.64
saccule, congenital (causing impairment of hearing) 744.05
sacculocochlear 386.8
senile 797

Degeneration, degenerative — *continued*

senile — *continued*
  brain 331.2
  cardiac, heart, or myocardium (*see also* Degeneration, myocardial) 429.1
  motor centers 331.2
  reticule 362.64
  retina, cystic 362.50
  vascular — *see* Arteriosclerosis
silicone rubber poppet (prosthetic valve) 996.02
sinus (cystic) (*see also* Sinusitis) 473.9
  polypoid 471.1
skin 709.3
  amyloid 277.39 ▲
  colloid 709.3
spinal (cord) 336.8
  amyloid 277.39 ▲
  column 733.90
  combined (subacute) (*see also* Degeneration, combined) 266.2 *[336.2]*
    with anemia (pernicious) 281.0 *[336.2]*
  dorsolateral (*see also* Degeneration, combined) 266.2 *[336.2]*
  familial NEC 336.8
  fatty 336.8
  funicular (*see also* Degeneration, combined) 266.2 *[336.2]*
  heredofamilial NEC 336.8
  posterolateral (*see also* Degeneration, combined) 266.2 *[336.2]*
  subacute combined — *see* Degeneration, combined
  tuberculous (*see also* Tuberculosis) 013.8 ☑
spine 733.90
spleen 289.59
  amyloid 277.39 ▲
  lardaceous 277.39 ▲
stomach 537.89
  lardaceous 277.39 ▲
strionigral 333.0
sudoriparous (cystic) 705.89
suprarenal (capsule) (gland) 255.8
  with hypofunction 255.4
sweat gland 705.89
synovial membrane (pulpy) 727.9
tapetoretinal 362.74
  adult or presenile form 362.50
testis (postinfectional) 608.89
thymus (gland) 254.8
  fatty 254.8
  lardaceous 277.39 ▲
thyroid (gland) 246.8
tricuspid (heart) (valve) — *see* Endocarditis, tricuspid
tuberculous NEC (*see also* Tuberculosis) 011.9 ☑
turbinate 733.90
uterus 621.8
  cystic 621.8
vascular (senile) (*see also* Arteriosclerosis)
  hypertensive — *see* Hypertension
vitreoretinal (primary) 362.73
  secondary 362.66
vitreous humor (with infiltration) 379.21
wallerian NEC — *see* Disorder, nerve
waxy (any site) 277.39 ▲
Wilson's hepatolenticular 275.1
Deglutition
  paralysis 784.99 ▲
    hysterical 300.11
  pneumonia 507.0
Degos' disease or syndrome 447.8
Degradation disorder, branched-chain amino acid 270.3
Dehiscence
  anastomosis — *see* Complications, anastomosis
  cesarean wound 674.1 ☑

Dehiscence — *continued*
  episiotomy 674.2 ☑
  operation wound 998.32
    internal 998.31
  perineal wound (postpartum) 674.2 ☑
  postoperative 998.32
    abdomen 998.32
      internal 998.31
    internal 998.31
  uterine wound 674.1 ☑
Dehydration (cachexia) 276.51
  with
    hypernatremia 276.0
    hyponatremia 276.1
  newborn 775.5
Deiters' nucleus syndrome 386.19
Déjérine's disease 356.0 ▲
Déjérine-Klumpke paralysis 767.6
Déjérine-Roussy syndrome 338.0 ▲
Déjérine-Sottas disease or neuropathy (hypertrophic) 356.0
Déjérine-Thomas atrophy or syndrome 333.0
de Lange's syndrome (Amsterdam dwarf, mental retardation, and brachycephaly) 759.89
Delay, delayed
  adaptation, cones or rods 368.63
  any plane in pelvis
    affecting fetus or newborn 763.1
    complicating delivery 660.1 ☑
  birth or delivery NEC 662.1 ☑
    affecting fetus or newborn 763.89
    second twin, triplet, or multiple mate 662.3 ☑
  closure (*see also* Fistula)
    cranial suture 756.0
    fontanel 756.0
  coagulation NEC 790.92
  conduction (cardiac) (ventricular) 426.9
  delivery NEC 662.1 ☑
    second twin, triplet, etc. 662.3 ☑
      affecting fetus or newborn 763.89
  development
    in childhood 783.40
      physiological 783.40
    intellectual NEC 315.9
    learning NEC 315.2
    reading 315.00
    sexual 259.0
    speech 315.39
      associated with hyperkinesis 314.1
    spelling 315.09
  gastric emptying 536.8
  menarche 256.39
  milestone in childhood 783.42
  motility — *see* Hypomotility
  passage of meconium (newborn) 777.1
  primary respiration 768.9
  puberty 259.0
  separation of umbilical cord 779.83
  sexual maturation, female 259.0
Del Castillo's syndrome (germinal aplasia) 606.0
Déleage's disease 359.89
Deletion syndrome
  5p 758.31
  22q11.2 758.32
  autosomal NEC 758.39
  constitutional 5q deletion 758.39 ●
Delhi (boil) (button) (sore) 085.1
Delinquency (juvenile) 312.9
  group (*see also* Disturbance, conduct) 312.2 ☑
  neurotic 312.4
Delirium, delirious 780.09
  acute (psychotic) 293.0
  alcoholic 291.0
    acute 291.0
    chronic 291.1

Delirium, delirious — *continued*
  alcoholicum 291.0
  chronic (*see also* Psychosis) 293.89
  due to or associated with physical condition — *see* Psychosis, organic
  drug-induced 292.81
  due to conditions classified elsewhere 293.0
  eclamptic (*see also* Eclampsia) 780.39
  exhaustion (*see also* Reaction, stress, acute) 308.9
  hysterical 300.11
  in
    presenile dementia 290.11
    senile dementia 290.3
  induced by drug 292.81
  manic, maniacal (acute) (*see also* Psychosis, affective) 296.0 ☑
    recurrent episode 296.1 ☑
    single episode 296.0 ☑
  puerperal 293.9
  senile 290.3
  subacute (psychotic) 293.1
  thyroid (*see also* Thyrotoxicosis) 242.9 ☑
  traumatic (*see also* Injury, intracranial)
    with
      lesion, spinal cord — *see* Injury, spinal, by site
      shock, spinal — *see* Injury, spinal, by site
  tremens (impending) 291.0
  uremic — *see* Uremia
  withdrawal
    alcoholic (acute) 291.0
      chronic 291.1
    drug 292.0

Delivery

Note — Use the following fifth-digit subclassification with categories 640–648, 651–676:

0 unspecified as to episode of care

1 delivered, with or without mention of antepartum condition

2 delivered, with mention of postpartum complication

3 antepartum condition or complication

4 postpartum condition or complication

breech (assisted) (buttocks) (complete) (frank) (spontaneous) 652.2 ☑
  affecting fetus or newborn 763.0
  extraction NEC 669.6 ☑
cesarean (for) 669.7 ☑
  abnormal
    cervix 654.6 ☑
    pelvic organs or tissues 654.9 ☑
    pelvis (bony) (major) NEC 653.0 ☑
    presentation or position 652.9 ☑
      in multiple gestation 652.6 ☑
    size, fetus 653.5 ☑
    soft parts (of pelvis) 654.9 ☑
    uterus, congenital 654.0 ☑
    vagina 654.7 ☑
    vulva 654.8 ☑
  abruptio placentae 641.2 ☑
  acromion presentation 652.8 ☑
  affecting fetus or newborn 763.4
  anteversion, cervix or uterus 654.4 ☑
  atony, uterus, ►with hemorrhage◄ 666.1 ☑
  bicornis or bicornuate uterus 654.0 ☑
  breech presentation (buttocks) (complete) (frank) 652.2 ☑
  brow presentation 652.4 ☑

Delivery — *continued*
  cesarean — *continued*
    cephalopelvic disproportion (nor-
      mally formed fetus) 653.4 ☑
    chin presentation 652.4 ☑
    cicatrix of cervix 654.6 ☑
    contracted pelvis (general) 653.1 ☑
      inlet 653.2 ☑
      outlet 653.3 ☑
    cord presentation or prolapse
      663.0 ☑
    cystocele 654.4 ☑
    deformity (acquired) (congenital)
      pelvic organs or tissues NEC
        654.9 ☑
      pelvis (bony) NEC 653.0 ☑
    displacement, uterus NEC 654.4 ☑
    disproportion NEC 653.9 ☑
    distress
      fetal 656.8 ☑
      maternal 669.0 ☑
    eclampsia 642.6 ☑
    face presentation 652.4 ☑
    failed
      forceps 660.7 ☑
      trial of labor NEC 660.6 ☑
      vacuum extraction 660.7 ☑
      ventouse 660.7 ☑
    fetal deformity 653.7 ☑
    fetal-maternal hemorrhage 656.0 ☑
    fetus, fetal
      distress 656.8 ☑
      prematurity 656.8 ☑
    fibroid (tumor) (uterus) 654.1 ☑
    footling 652.8 ☑
      with successful version 652.1 ☑
    hemorrhage (antepartum) (intra-
      partum) NEC 641.9 ☑
    hydrocephalic fetus 653.6 ☑
    incarceration of uterus 654.3 ☑
    incoordinate uterine action
      661.4 ☑
    inertia, uterus 661.2 ☑
      primary 661.0 ☑
      secondary 661.1 ☑
    lateroversion, uterus or cervix
      654.4 ☑
    mal lie 652.9 ☑
    malposition
      fetus 652.9 ☑
        in multiple gestation 652.6 ☑
      pelvic organs or tissues NEC
        654.9 ☑
      uterus NEC or cervix 654.4 ☑
    malpresentation NEC 652.9 ☑
      in multiple gestation 652.6 ☑
    maternal
      diabetes mellitus 648.0 ☑
      heart disease NEC 648.6 ☑
    meconium in liquor 656.8 ☑
      staining only 792.3
    oblique presentation 652.3 ☑
    oversize fetus 653.5 ☑
    pelvic tumor NEC 654.9 ☑
    placental insufficiency 656.5 ☑
    placenta previa 641.0 ☑
      with hemorrhage 641.1 ☑
    poor dilation, cervix 661.0 ☑
    pre-eclampsia 642.4 ☑
      severe 642.5 ☑
    previous
      cesarean delivery, section
        654.2 ☑
      surgery (to)
        cervix 654.6 ☑
        gynecological NEC 654.9 ☑
        rectum 654.8 ☑
        uterus NEC 654.9 ☑
          previous cesarean deliv-
            ery, section
            654.2 ☑
        vagina 654.7 ☑
    prolapse
      arm or hand 652.7 ☑

Delivery — *continued*
  cesarean — *continued*
    prolapse — *continued*
      uterus 654.4 ☑
    prolonged labor 662.1 ☑
    rectocele 654.4 ☑
    retroversion, uterus or cervix
      654.3 ☑
    rigid
      cervix 654.6 ☑
      pelvic floor 654.4 ☑
      perineum 654.8 ☑
      vagina 654.7 ☑
      vulva 654.8 ☑
    sacculation, pregnant uterus
      654.4 ☑
    scar(s)
      cervix 654.6 ☑
      cesarean delivery, section
        654.2 ☑
      uterus NEC 654.9 ☑
        due to previous cesarean de-
          livery, section 654.2 ☑
    Shirodkar suture in situ 654.5 ☑
    shoulder presentation 652.8 ☑
    stenosis or stricture, cervix
      654.6 ☑
    transverse presentation or lie
      652.3 ☑
    tumor, pelvic organs or tissues
      NEC 654.4 ☑
    umbilical cord presentation or
      prolapse 663.0 ☑
  completely normal case — *see* catego-
    ry 650
  complicated (by) NEC 669.9 ☑
    abdominal tumor, fetal 653.7 ☑
      causing obstructed labor
        660.1 ☑
    abnormal, abnormality of
      cervix 654.6 ☑
        causing obstructed labor
          660.2 ☑
      forces of labor 661.9 ☑
      formation of uterus 654.0 ☑
      pelvic organs or tissues 654.9 ☑
        causing obstructed labor
          660.2 ☑
      pelvis (bony) (major) NEC
        653.0 ☑
        causing obstructed labor
          660.1 ☑
      presentation or position NEC
        652.9 ☑
        causing obstructed labor
          660.0 ☑
      size, fetus 653.5 ☑
        causing obstructed labor
          660.1 ☑
      soft parts (of pelvis) 654.9 ☑
        causing obstructed labor
          660.2 ☑
      uterine contractions NEC
        661.9 ☑
      uterus (formation) 654.0 ☑
        causing obstructed labor
          660.2 ☑
      vagina 654.7 ☑
        causing obstructed labor
          660.2 ☑
    abnormally formed uterus (any
      type) (congenital) 654.0 ☑
      causing obstructed labor
        660.2 ☑
    acromion presentation 652.8 ☑
      causing obstructed labor
        660.0 ☑
    adherent placenta 667.0 ☑
      with hemorrhage 666.0 ☑
    adhesions, uterus (to abdominal
      wall) 654.4 ☑
    advanced maternal age NEC
      659.6 ☑
      multigravida 659.6 ☑
      primigravida 659.5 ☑

Delivery — *continued*
  complicated — *continued*
    air embolism 673.0 ☑
    amnionitis 658.4 ☑
    amniotic fluid embolism 673.1 ☑
    anesthetic death 668.9 ☑
    annular detachment, cervix
      665.3 ☑
    antepartum hemorrhage — *see*
      Delivery, complicated, hemor-
      rhage
    anteversion, cervix or uterus
      654.4 ☑
      causing obstructed labor
        660.2 ☑
    apoplexy 674.0 ☑
      placenta 641.2 ☑
    arrested active phase 661.1 ☑
    asymmetrical pelvis bone 653.0 ☑
      causing obstructed labor
        660.1 ☑
    atony, uterus ▶with hemorrhage◄
      (hypotonic) (inertia) 666.1 ☑
      hypertonic 661.4 ☑
    Bandl's ring 661.4 ☑
    battledore placenta — *see* Placenta,
      abnormal
    bicornis or bicornuate uterus
      654.0 ☑
      causing obstructed labor
        660.2 ☑
    birth injury to mother NEC
      665.9 ☑
    bleeding (*see also* Delivery, compli-
      cated, hemorrhage) 641.9 ☑
    breech presentation (assisted)
      (buttocks) (complete) (frank)
      (spontaneous) 652.2 ☑
      with successful version 652.1 ☑
    brow presentation 652.4 ☑
    cephalopelvic disproportion (nor-
      mally formed fetus) 653.4 ☑
      causing obstructed labor
        660.1 ☑
    cerebral hemorrhage 674.0 ☑
    cervical dystocia 661.0 ☑
    chin presentation 652.4 ☑
      causing obstructed labor
        660.0 ☑
    cicatrix
      cervix 654.6 ☑
        causing obstructed labor
          660.2 ☑
      vagina 654.7 ☑
        causing obstructed labor
          660.2 ☑
    coagulation defect 649.3 ☑ ●
    colporrhexis 665.4 ☑
      with perineal laceration 664.0 ☑
    compound presentation 652.8 ☑
      causing obstructed labor
        660.0 ☑
    compression of cord (umbilical)
      663.2 ☑
      around neck 663.1 ☑
      cord prolapsed 663.0 ☑
    contraction, contracted pelvis
      653.1 ☑
      causing obstructed labor
        660.1 ☑
      general 653.1 ☑
        causing obstructed labor
          660.1 ☑
      inlet 653.2 ☑
        causing obstructed labor
          660.1 ☑
      midpelvic 653.8 ☑
        causing obstructed labor
          660.1 ☑
      midplane 653.8 ☑
        causing obstructed labor
          660.1 ☑
      outlet 653.3 ☑
        causing obstructed labor
          660.1 ☑

Delivery — *continued*
  complicated — *continued*
    contraction ring 661.4 ☑
    cord (umbilical) 663.9 ☑
      around neck, tightly or with
        compression 663.1 ☑
        without compression
          663.3 ☑
      bruising 663.6 ☑
      complication NEC 663.9 ☑
        specified type NEC 663.8 ☑
      compression NEC 663.2 ☑
      entanglement NEC 663.3 ☑
        with compression 663.2 ☑
      forelying 663.0 ☑
      hematoma 663.6 ☑
      marginal attachment 663.8 ☑
      presentation 663.0 ☑
      prolapse (complete) (occult)
        (partial) 663.0 ☑
      short 663.4 ☑
      specified complication NEC
        663.8 ☑
      thrombosis (vessels) 663.6 ☑
      vascular lesion 663.6 ☑
      velamentous insertion 663.8 ☑
    Couvelaire uterus 641.2 ☑
    cretin pelvis (dwarf type) (male
      type) 653.1 ☑
      causing obstructed labor
        660.1 ☑
    crossbirth 652.3 ☑
      with successful version 652.1 ☑
      causing obstructed labor
        660 ☑
    cyst (Gartner's duct) 654.7 ☑
    cystocele 654.4 ☑
      causing obstructed labor
        660.2 ☑
    death of fetus (near term) 656.4 ☑
      early (before 22 completed
        weeks gestation) 632
    deformity (acquired) (congenital)
      fetus 653.7 ☑
        causing obstructed labor
          660.1 ☑
      pelvic organs or tissues NEC
        654.9 ☑
        causing obstructed labor
          660.2 ☑
      pelvis (bony) NEC 653.0 ☑
        causing obstructed labor
          660.1 ☑
    delay, delayed
      delivery in multiple pregnancy
        662.3 ☑
        due to locked mates 660.5 ☑
      following rupture of membranes
        (spontaneous) 658.2 ☑
        artificial 658.3 ☑
    depressed fetal heart tones
      659.7 ☑
    diastasis recti 665.8 ☑
    dilatation
      bladder 654.4 ☑
        causing obstructed labor
          660.2 ☑
      cervix, incomplete, poor or slow
        661.0 ☑
    diseased placenta 656.7 ☑
    displacement uterus NEC 654.4 ☑
      causing obstructed labor
        660.2 ☑
    disproportion NEC 653.9 ☑
      causing obstructed labor
        660.1 ☑
    disruptio uteri — *see* Delivery,
      complicated, rupture, uterus
    distress
      fetal 656.8 ☑
      maternal 669.0 ☑
    double uterus (congenital) 654.0 ☑
      causing obstructed labor
        660.2 ☑
    dropsy amnion 657.0 ☑

☑ Additional Digit Required — Refer to the Tabular List for Digit Selection   ▽ Subterms under main terms may continue to next column or page

74 — Volume 2   ▶◀ Revised Text   ● New Line   ▲ Revised Code   *2007 ICD-9-CM*

Delivery — *continued*
  complicated — *continued*
    placenta, placental — *continued*
      adherent (without hemorrhage)
          667.0 ☑
        with hemorrhage 666.0 ☑
      apoplexy 641.2 ☑
      battledore placenta — *see* Placenta, abnormal
      detachment (premature)
          641.2 ☑
      disease 656.7 ☑
      hemorrhage NEC 641.9 ☑
      increta (without hemorrhage)
          667.0 ☑
        with hemorrhage 666.0 ☑
      low (implantation) 641.1 ☑
        without hemorrhage 641.0 ☑
      malformation 656.7 ☑
        with hemorrhage 641.2 ☑
      malposition 641.1 ☑
        without hemorrhage 641.0 ☑
      marginal sinus rupture 641.2 ☑
      percreta 667.0 ☑
        with hemorrhage 666.0 ☑
      premature separation 641.2 ☑
      previa (central) (lateral)
          (marginal) (partial)
          641.1 ☑
        without hemorrhage 641.0 ☑
      retained (with hemorrhage)
          666.0 ☑
        without hemorrhage 667.0 ☑
      rupture of marginal sinus
          641.2 ☑
      separation (premature) 641.2 ☑
      trapped 666.0 ☑
        without hemorrhage 667.0 ☑
      vicious insertion 641.1 ☑
    polyhydramnios 657.0 ☑
    polyp, cervix 654.6 ☑
      causing obstructed labor
          660.2 ☑
    precipitate labor 661.3 ☑
    premature
      labor (before 37 completed
          weeks gestation) 644.2 ☑
      rupture, membranes 658.1 ☑
        delayed delivery following
          658.2 ☑
    presenting umbilical cord 663.0 ☑
    previous
      cesarean delivery, section
          654.2 ☑
      surgery
        cervix 654.6 ☑
          causing obstructed labor
            660.2 ☑
        gynecological NEC 654.9 ☑
          causing obstructed labor
            660.2 ☑
        perineum 654.8 ☑
        rectum 654.8 ☑
        uterus NEC 654.9 ☑
          due to previous cesarean
            delivery, section
            654.2 ☑
        vagina 654.7 ☑
          causing obstructed labor
            660.2 ☑
        vulva 654.8 ☑
    primary uterine inertia 661.0 ☑
    primipara, elderly or old 659.5 ☑
    prolapse
      arm or hand 652.7 ☑
        causing obstructed labor
            660.0 ☑
      cord (umbilical) 663.0 ☑
      fetal extremity 652.8 ☑
      foot or leg 652.8 ☑
        causing obstructed labor
            660.0 ☑
      umbilical cord (complete) (occult) (partial) 663.0 ☑
      uterus 654.4 ☑

Delivery — *continued*
  complicated — *continued*
    prolapse — *continued*
      uterus — *continued*
        causing obstructed labor
            660.2 ☑
    prolonged labor 662.1 ☑
      first stage 662.0 ☑
      second stage 662.2 ☑
      active phase 661.2 ☑
      due to
        cervical dystocia 661.0 ☑
        contraction ring 661.4 ☑
        tetanic uterus 661.4 ☑
        uterine inertia 661.2 ☑
          primary 661.0 ☑
          secondary 661.1 ☑
      latent phase 661.0 ☑
    pyrexia during labor 659.2 ☑
    rachitic pelvis 653.2 ☑
      causing obstructed labor
            660.1 ☑
    rectocele 654.4 ☑
      causing obstructed labor
            660.2 ☑
    retained membranes or portions of
          placenta 666.2 ☑
      without hemorrhage 667.1 ☑
    retarded (prolonged) birth 662.1 ☑
    retention secundines (with hemorrhage) 666.2 ☑
      without hemorrhage 667.1 ☑
    retroversion, uterus or cervix
          654.3 ☑
      causing obstructed labor
            660.2 ☑
    rigid
      cervix 654.6 ☑
        causing obstructed labor
            660.2 ☑
      pelvic floor 654.4 ☑
        causing obstructed labor
            660.2 ☑
      perineum or vulva 654.8 ☑
        causing obstructed labor
            660.2 ☑
      vagina 654.7 ☑
        causing obstructed labor
            660.2 ☑
    Robert's pelvis 653.0 ☑
      causing obstructed labor
            660.1 ☑
    rupture (*see also* Delivery, complicated, laceration)
      bladder (urinary) 665.5 ☑
      cervix 665.3 ☑
      marginal sinus 641.2 ☑
      membranes, premature 658.1 ☑
      pelvic organ NEC 665.5 ☑
      perineum (without mention of
          other laceration) — *see*
          Delivery, complicated,
          laceration, perineum
      peritoneum 665.5 ☑
      urethra 665.5 ☑
      uterus (during labor) 665.1 ☑
        before labor 665.0 ☑
    sacculation, pregnant uterus
          654.4 ☑
    sacral teratomas, fetal 653.7 ☑
      causing obstructed labor
            660.1 ☑
    scar(s)
      cervix 654.6 ☑
        causing obstructed labor
            660.2 ☑
      cesarean delivery, section
          654.2 ☑
        causing obstructed labor
            660.2 ☑
      perineum 654.8 ☑
        causing obstructed labor
            660.2 ☑
      uterus NEC 654.9 ☑

Delivery — *continued*
  complicated — *continued*
    scar(s) — *continued*
      uterus — *continued*
        causing obstructed labor
            660.2 ☑
        due to previous cesarean delivery, section 654.2 ☑
      vagina 654.7 ☑
        causing obstructed labor
            660.2 ☑
      vulva 654.8 ☑
        causing obstructed labor
            660.2 ☑
    scoliotic pelvis 653.0 ☑
      causing obstructed labor
            660.1 ☑
    secondary uterine inertia 661.1 ☑
    secundines, retained — *see* Delivery, complicated, placenta, retained
    separation
      placenta (premature) 641.2 ☑
      pubic bone 665.6 ☑
      symphysis pubis 665.6 ☑
    septate vagina 654.7 ☑
      causing obstructed labor
            660.2 ☑
    shock (birth) (obstetric) (puerperal)
          669.1 ☑
    short cord syndrome 663.4 ☑
    shoulder
      girdle dystocia 660.4 ☑
      presentation 652.8 ☑
        causing obstructed labor
            660.0 ☑
    Siamese twins 653.7 ☑
      causing obstructed labor
            660.1 ☑
    slow slope active phase 661.2 ☑
    spasm
      cervix 661.4 ☑
      uterus 661.4 ☑
    spondylolisthesis, pelvis 653.3 ☑
      causing obstructed labor
            660.1 ☑
    spondylolysis (lumbosacral)
          653.3 ☑
      causing obstructed labor
            660.1 ☑
    spondylosis 653.0 ☑
      causing obstructed labor
            660.1 ☑
    stenosis or stricture
      cervix 654.6 ☑
        causing obstructed labor
            660.2 ☑
      vagina 654.7 ☑
        causing obstructed labor
            660.2 ☑
    sudden death, unknown cause
          669.9 ☑
    tear (pelvic organ) (*see also* Delivery, complicated, laceration)
          664.9 ☑
    teratomas, sacral, fetal 653.7 ☑
      causing obstructed labor
            660.1 ☑
    tetanic uterus 661.4 ☑
    tipping pelvis 653.0 ☑
      causing obstructed labor
            660.1 ☑
    transverse
      arrest (deep) 660.3 ☑
      presentation or lie 652.3 ☑
        with successful version
            652.1 ☑
        causing obstructed labor
            660.0 ☑
    trauma (obstetrical) NEC 665.9 ☑
    tumor
      abdominal, fetal 653.7 ☑
        causing obstructed labor
            660.1 ☑

Delivery — *continued*
  complicated — *continued*
    tumor — *continued*
      pelvic organs or tissues NEC
          654.9 ☑
        causing obstructed labor
            660.2 ☑
    umbilical cord (*see also* Delivery, complicated, cord) 663.9 ☑
      around neck tightly, or with
          compression 663.1 ☑
      entanglement NEC 663.3 ☑
        with compression 663.2 ☑
      prolapse (complete) (occult)
          (partial) 663.0 ☑
    unstable lie 652.0 ☑
      causing obstructed labor
            660.0 ☑
    uterine
      inertia (*see also* Delivery, complicated, inertia, uterus)
          661.2 ☑
      spasm 661.4 ☑
    vasa previa 663.5 ☑
    velamentous insertion of cord
          663.8 ☑
    young maternal age 659.8 ☑
  delayed NEC 662.1 ☑
    following rupture of membranes
        (spontaneous) 658.2 ☑
      artificial 658.3 ☑
    second twin, triplet, etc. 662.3 ☑
  difficult NEC 669.9 ☑
    previous, affecting management of
        pregnancy or childbirth
        V23.49
    specified type NEC 669.8 ☑
  early onset (spontaneous) 644.2 ☑
  footling 652.8 ☑
    with successful version 652.1 ☑
  forceps NEC 669.5 ☑
    affecting fetus or newborn 763.2
  missed (at or near term) 656.4 ☑
  multiple gestation NEC 651.9 ☑
    with fetal loss and retention of one
        or more fetus(es) 651.6 ☑
    following (elective) fetal reduction
        651.7 ☑
    specified type NEC 651.8 ☑
      with fetal loss and retention of
          one or more fetus(es)
          651.6 ☑
      following (elective) fetal reduction 651.7 ☑
  nonviable infant 656.4 ☑
  normal — *see* category 650
  precipitate 661.3 ☑
    affecting fetus or newborn 763.6
  premature NEC (before 37 completed
        weeks gestation) 644.2 ☑
    previous, affecting management of
        pregnancy V23.41
  quadruplet NEC 651.2 ☑
    with fetal loss and retention of one
        or more fetus(es) 651.5 ☑
    following (elective) fetal reduction
        651.7 ☑
  quintuplet NEC 651.8 ☑
    with fetal loss and retention of one
        or more fetus(es) 651.6 ☑
    following (elective) fetal reduction
        651.7 ☑
  sextuplet NEC 651.8 ☑
    with fetal loss and retention of one
        or more fetus(es) 651.6 ☑
    following (elective) fetal reduction
        651.7 ☑
  specified complication NEC 669.8 ☑
  stillbirth (near term) NEC 656.4 ☑
    early (before 22 completed weeks
        gestation) 632
  term pregnancy (live birth) NEC — *see*
        category 650
    stillbirth NEC 656.4 ☑
  threatened premature 644.2 ☑

☑ Additional Digit Required — Refer to the Tabular List for Digit Selection   ᵂ Subterms under main terms may continue to next column or page

Delivery — *continued*
  triplets NEC 651.1 ☑
    with fetal loss and retention of one or more fetus(es) 651.4 ☑
    delayed delivery (one or more mates) 662.3 ☑
    following (elective) fetal reduction 651.7 ☑
    locked mates 660.5 ☑
  twins NEC 651.0 ☑
    with fetal loss and retention of one fetus 651.3 ☑
    delayed delivery (one or more mates) 662.3 ☑
    following (elective) fetal reduction 651.7 ☑
    locked mates 660.5 ☑
  uncomplicated — *see* category 650
  vacuum extractor NEC 669.5 ☑
    affecting fetus or newborn 763.3
  ventouse NEC 669.5 ☑
    affecting fetus or newborn 763.3
Dellen, cornea 371.41
Delusions (paranoid) 297.9
  grandiose 297.1
  parasitosis 300.29
  systematized 297.1
Dementia 294.8
  alcohol-induced persisting (*see also* Psychosis, alcoholic) 291.2
  Alzheimer's — *see* Alzheimer's, dementia
  arteriosclerotic (simple type) (uncomplicated) 290.40
    with
      acute confusional state 290.41
      delirium 290.41
      delusions 290.42
      depressed mood 290.43
    depressed type 290.43
    paranoid type 290.42
  Binswanger's 290.12
  catatonic (acute) (*see also* Schizophrenia) 295.2 ☑
  congenital (*see also* Retardation, mental) 319
  degenerative 290.9
    presenile-onset — *see* Dementia, presenile
    senile-onset — *see* Dementia, senile
  developmental (*see also* Schizophrenia) 295.9 ☑
  dialysis 294.8
    transient 293.9
  drug-induced persisting (*see also* Psychosis, drug) 292.82
  due to or associated with condition(s) classified elsewhere
    Alzheimer's
      with behavioral disturbance 331.0 [294.11]
      without behavioral disturbance 331.0 [294.10]
    cerebral lipidoses
      with behavioral disturbance 330.1 [294.11]
      without behavioral disturbance 330.1 [294.10]
    epilepsy
      with behavioral disturbance 345.9 ☑ [294.11]
      without behavioral disturbance 345.9 ☑ [294.10]
    hepatolenticular degeneration
      with behavioral disturbance 275.1 [294.11]
      without behavioral disturbance 275.1 [294.10]
    HIV
      with behavioral disturbance 042 [294.11]
      without behavioral disturbance 042 [294.10]

Dementia — *continued*
  due to or associated with condition(s) classified elsewhere — *continued*
    Huntington's chorea
      with behavioral disturbance 333.4 [294.11]
      without behavioral disturbance 333.4 [294.10]
    Jakob-Creutzfeldt disease (new variant)
      with behavioral disturbance 046.1 [294.11]
      without behavioral disturbance 046.1 [294.10]
    Lewy bodies
      with behavioral disturbance 331.82 [294.11]
      without behavioral disturbance 331.82 [294.10]
    multiple sclerosis
      with behavioral disturbance 340 [294.11]
      without behavioral disturbance 340 [294.10]
    neurosyphilis
      with behavioral disturbance 094.9 [294.11]
      without behavioral disturbance 094.9 [294.10]
    Parkinsonism
      with behavioral disturbance 331.82 [294.11]
      without behavioral disturbance 331.82 [294.10]
    Pelizaeus-Merzbacher disease
      with behavioral disturbance 333.0 [294.11]
      without behavioral disturbance 333.0 [294.10]
    Pick's disease
      with behavioral disturbance 331.11 [294.11]
      without behavioral disturbance 331.11 [294.10]
    polyarteritis nodosa
      with behavioral disturbance 446.0 [294.11]
      without behavioral disturbance 446.0 [294.10]
    syphilis
      with behavioral disturbance 094.1 [294.11]
      without behavioral disturbance 094.1 [294.10]
    Wilson's disease
      with behavioral disturbance 275.1 [294.11]
      without behavioral disturbance 275.1 [294.10]
  frontal 331.19
    with behavioral disturbance 331.19 [294.11]
    without behavioral disturbance 331.19 [294.10]
  frontotemporal 331.19
    with behavioral disturbance 331.19 [294.11]
    without behavioral disturbance 331.19 [294.10]
  hebephrenic (acute) 295.1 ☑
  Heller's (infantile psychosis) (*see also* Psychosis, childhood) 299.1 ☑
  idiopathic 290.9
    presenile-onset — *see* Dementia, presenile
    senile-onset — *see* Dementia, senile
  in
    arteriosclerotic brain disease 290.40
    senility 290.0
  induced by drug 292.82
  infantile, infantilia (*see also* Psychosis, childhood) 299.0 ☑
  Lewy body 331.82

Dementia — *continued*
  Lewy body — *continued*
    with behavioral disturbance 331.82 [294.11]
    without behavioral disturbance 331.82 [294.10]
  multi-infarct (cerebrovascular) (*see also* Dementia, arteriosclerotic) 290.40
  old age 290.0
  paralytica, paralytic 094.1
    juvenilis 090.40
    syphilitic 094.1
      congenital 090.40
    tabetic form 094.1
  paranoid (*see also* Schizophrenia) 295.3 ☑
  paraphrenic (*see also* Schizophrenia) 295.3 ☑
  paretic 094.1
  praecox (*see also* Schizophrenia) 295.9 ☑
  presenile 290.10
    with
      acute confusional state 290.11
      delirium 290.11
      delusional features 290.12
      depressive features 290.13
    depressed type 290.13
    paranoid type 290.12
    simple type 290.10
    uncomplicated 290.10
  primary (acute) (*see also* Schizophrenia) 295.0 ☑
  progressive, syphilitic 094.1
  puerperal — *see* Psychosis, puerperal
  schizophrenic (*see also* Schizophrenia) 295.9 ☑
  senile 290.0
    with
      acute confusional state 290.3
      delirium 290.3
      delusional features 290.20
      depressive features 290.21
    depressed type 290.21
    exhaustion 290.0
    paranoid type 290.20
    simple type (acute) (*see also* Schizophrenia) 295.0 ☑
  simplex (acute) (*see also* Schizophrenia) 295.0 ☑
  syphilitic 094.1
  uremic — *see* Uremia
  vascular 290.40
    with
      delirium 290.41
      delusions 290.42
      depressed mood 290.43
Demerol dependence — *see also* Dependence 304.0 ☑
Demineralization, ankle — *see also* Osteoporosis 733.00
Demodex folliculorum (infestation) 133.8
de Morgan's spots (senile angiomas) 448.1
Demyelinating
  polyneuritis, chronic inflammatory 357.81
Demyelination, demyelinization
  central nervous system 341.9
    specified NEC 341.8
  corpus callosum (central) 341.8
  global 340
Dengue (fever) 061
  sandfly 061
  vaccination, prophylactic (against) V05.1
  virus hemorrhagic fever 065.4
Dens
  evaginatus 520.2
  in dente 520.2
  invaginatus 520.2
Density
  increased, bone (disseminated) (generalized) (spotted) 733.99

Density — *continued*
  lung (nodular) 518.89
Dental — *see also* condition
  examination only V72.2
Dentia praecox 520.6
Denticles (in pulp) 522.2
Dentigerous cyst 526.0
Dentin
  irregular (in pulp) 522.3
  opalescent 520.5
  secondary (in pulp) 522.3
  sensitive 521.89 ▲
Dentinogenesis imperfecta 520.5
Dentinoma (M9271/0) 213.1
  upper jaw (bone) 213.0
Dentition 520.7
  abnormal 520.6
  anomaly 520.6
  delayed 520.6
  difficult 520.7
  disorder of 520.6
  precocious 520.6
  retarded 520.6
Denture sore (mouth) 528.9
Dependence

> *Note — Use the following fifth-digit subclassification with category 304:*
>
> 0 *unspecified*
> 1 *continuous*
> 2 *episodic*
> 3 *in remission*

  with
    withdrawal symptoms
      alcohol 291.81
      drug 292.0
  14-hydroxy-dihydromorphinone 304.0 ☑
  absinthe 304.6 ☑
  acemorphan 304.0 ☑
  acetanilid(e) 304.6 ☑
  acetophenetidin 304.6 ☑
  acetorphine 304.0 ☑
  acetyldihydrocodeine 304.0 ☑
  acetyldihydrocodeinone 304.0 ☑
  Adalin 304.1 ☑
  Afghanistan black 304.3 ☑
  agrypnal 304.1 ☑
  alcohol, alcoholic (ethyl) (methyl) (wood) 303.9 ☑
    maternal, with suspected fetal damage affecting management of pregnancy 655.4 ☑
  allobarbitone 304.1 ☑
  allonal 304.1 ☑
  allylisopropylacetylurea 304.1 ☑
  alphaprodine (hydrochloride) 304.0 ☑
  Alurate 304.1 ☑
  Alvodine 304.0 ☑
  amethocaine 304.6 ☑
  amidone 304.0 ☑
  amidopyrine 304.6 ☑
  aminopyrine 304.6 ☑
  amobarbital 304.1 ☑
  amphetamine(s) (type) (drugs classifiable to 969.7) 304.4 ☑
  amylene hydrate 304.6 ☑
  amylobarbitone 304.1 ☑
  amylocaine 304.6 ☑
  Amytal (sodium) 304.1 ☑
  analgesic (drug) NEC 304.6 ☑
    synthetic with morphine-like effect 304.0 ☑
  anesthetic (agent) (drug) (gas) (general) (local) NEC 304.6 ☑
  Angel dust 304.6 ☑
  anileridine 304.0 ☑
  antipyrine 304.6 ☑
  anxiolytic 304.1 ☑
  aprobarbital 304.1 ☑
  aprobarbitone 304.1 ☑
  atropine 304.6 ☑
  Avertin (bromide) 304.6 ☑

☑ Additional Digit Required — Refer to the Tabular List for Digit Selection
▽ Subterms under main terms may continue to next column or page

Dependence — *continued*
- barbenyl 304.1 ☑
- barbital(s) 304.1 ☑
- barbitone 304.1 ☑
- barbiturate(s) (compounds) (drugs classifiable to 967.0) 304.1 ☑
- barbituric acid (and compounds) 304.1 ☑
- benzedrine 304.4 ☑
- benzylmorphine 304.0 ☑
- Beta-chlor 304.1 ☑
- bhang 304.3 ☑
- blue velvet 304.0 ☑
- Brevital 304.1 ☑
- bromal (hydrate) 304.1 ☑
- bromide(s) NEC 304.1 ☑
- bromine compounds NEC 304.1 ☑
- bromisovalum 304.1 ☑
- bromoform 304.1 ☑
- Bromo-seltzer 304.1 ☑
- bromural 304.1 ☑
- butabarbital (sodium) 304.1 ☑
- butabarpal 304.1 ☑
- butallylonal 304.1 ☑
- butethal 304.1 ☑
- buthalitone (sodium) 304.1 ☑
- Butisol 304.1 ☑
- butobarbitone 304.1 ☑
- butyl chloral (hydrate) 304.1 ☑
- caffeine 304.4 ☑
- cannabis (indica) (sativa) (resin) (derivatives) (type) 304.3 ☑
- carbamazepine 304.6 ☑
- Carbrital 304.1 ☑
- carbromal 304.1 ☑
- carisoprodol 304.6 ☑
- Catha (edulis) 304.4 ☑
- chloral (betaine) (hydrate) 304.1 ☑
- chloralamide 304.1 ☑
- chloralformamide 304.1 ☑
- chloralose 304.1 ☑
- chlordiazepoxide 304.1 ☑
- Chloretone 304.1 ☑
- chlorobutanol 304.1 ☑
- chlorodyne 304.1 ☑
- chloroform 304.6 ☑
- Cliradon 304.0 ☑
- coca (leaf) and derivatives 304.2 ☑
- cocaine 304.2 ☑
  - hydrochloride 304.2 ☑
  - salt (any) 304.2 ☑
- codeine 304.0 ☑
- combination of drugs (excluding morphine or opioid type drug) NEC 304.8 ☑
  - morphine or opioid type drug with any other drug 304.7 ☑
- croton-chloral 304.1 ☑
- cyclobarbital 304.1 ☑
- cyclobarbitone 304.1 ☑
- dagga 304.3 ☑
- Delvinal 304.1 ☑
- Demerol 304.0 ☑
- desocodeine 304.0 ☑
- desomorphine 304.0 ☑
- desoxyephedrine 304.4 ☑
- DET 304.5 ☑
- dexamphetamine 304.4 ☑
- dexedrine 304.4 ☑
- dextromethorphan 304.0 ☑
- dextromoramide 304.0 ☑
- dextronorpseudoephedrine 304.4 ☑
- dextrorphan 304.0 ☑
- diacetylmorphine 304.0 ☑
- Dial 304.1 ☑
- diallylbarbituric acid 304.1 ☑
- diamorphine 304.0 ☑
- diazepam 304.1 ☑
- dibucaine 304.6 ☑
- dichloroethane 304.6 ☑
- diethyl barbituric acid 304.1 ☑
- diethylsulfone-diethylmethane 304.1 ☑
- difencloxazine 304.0 ☑

Dependence — *continued*
- dihydrocodeine 304.0 ☑
- dihydrocodeinone 304.0 ☑
- dihydrohydroxycodeinone 304.0 ☑
- dihydroisocodeine 304.0 ☑
- dihydromorphine 304.0 ☑
- dihydromorphinone 304.0 ☑
- dihydroxcodeinone 304.0 ☑
- Dilaudid 304.0 ☑
- dimenhydrinate 304.6 ☑
- dimethylmeperidine 304.0 ☑
- dimethyltriptamine 304.5 ☑
- Dionin 304.0 ☑
- diphenoxylate 304.6 ☑
- dipipanone 304.0 ☑
- d-lysergic acid diethylamide 304.5 ☑
- DMT 304.5 ☑
- Dolophine 304.0 ☑
- DOM 304.5 ☑
- Doriden 304.1 ☑
- dormiral 304.1 ☑
- Dormison 304.1 ☑
- Dromoran 304.0 ☑
- drug NEC 304.9 ☑
  - analgesic NEC 304.6 ☑
  - combination (excluding morphine or opioid type drug) NEC 304.8 ☑
    - morphine or opioid type drug with any other drug 304.7 ☑
  - complicating pregnancy, childbirth, or puerperium 648.3 ☑
    - affecting fetus or newborn 779.5
  - hallucinogenic 304.5 ☑
  - hypnotic NEC 304.1 ☑
  - narcotic NEC 304.9 ☑
  - psychostimulant NEC 304.4 ☑
  - sedative 304.1 ☑
  - soporific NEC 304.1 ☑
  - specified type NEC 304.6 ☑
  - suspected damage to fetus affecting management of pregnancy 655.5 ☑
  - synthetic, with morphine-like effect 304.0 ☑
  - tranquilizing 304.1 ☑
- duboisine 304.1 ☑
- ectylurea 304.1 ☑
- Endocaine 304.6 ☑
- Equanil 304.1 ☑
- Eskabarb 304.1 ☑
- ethchlorvynol 304.1 ☑
- ether (ethyl) (liquid) (vapor) (vinyl) 304.6 ☑
- ethidene 304.6 ☑
- ethinamate 304.1 ☑
- ethoheptazine 304.6 ☑
- ethyl
  - alcohol 303.9 ☑
  - bromide 304.6 ☑
  - carbamate 304.6 ☑
  - chloride 304.6 ☑
  - morphine 304.0 ☑
- ethylene (gas) 304.6 ☑
  - dichloride 304.6 ☑
- ethylidene chloride 304.6 ☑
- etilfen 304.1 ☑
- etorphine 304.0 ☑
- etoval 304.1 ☑
- eucodal 304.0 ☑
- euneryl 304.1 ☑
- Evipal 304.1 ☑
- Evipan 304.1 ☑
- fentanyl 304.0 ☑
- ganja 304.3 ☑
- gardenal 304.1 ☑
- gardenpanyl 304.1 ☑
- gelsemine 304.6 ☑
- Gelsemium 304.6 ☑
- Gemonil 304.1 ☑
- glucochloral 304.1 ☑
- glue (airplane) (sniffing) 304.6 ☑
- glutethimide 304.1 ☑

Dependence — *continued*
- hallucinogenics 304.5 ☑
- hashish 304.3 ☑
- headache powder NEC 304.6 ☑
- Heavenly Blue 304.5 ☑
- hedonal 304.1 ☑
- hemp 304.3 ☑
- heptabarbital 304.1 ☑
- Heptalgin 304.0 ☑
- heptobarbitone 304.1 ☑
- heroin 304.0 ☑
  - salt (any) 304.0 ☑
- hexethal (sodium) 304.1 ☑
- hexobarbital 304.1 ☑
- Hycodan 304.0 ☑
- hydrocodone 304.0 ☑
- hydromorphinol 304.0 ☑
- hydromorphinone 304.0 ☑
- hydromorphone 304.0 ☑
- hydroxycodeine 304.0 ☑
- hypnotic NEC 304.1 ☑
- Indian hemp 304.3 ☑
- inhalant 304.6 ☑
- intranarcon 304.1 ☑
- Kemithal 304.1 ☑
- ketobemidone 304.0 ☑
- khat 304.4 ☑
- kif 304.3 ☑
- Lactuca (virosa) extract 304.1 ☑
- lactucarium 304.1 ☑
- laudanum 304.0 ☑
- Lebanese red 304.3 ☑
- Leritine 304.0 ☑
- lettuce opium 304.1 ☑
- Levanil 304.1 ☑
- Levo-Dromoran 304.0 ☑
- levo-iso-methadone 304.0 ☑
- levorphanol 304.0 ☑
- Librium 304.1 ☑
- Lomotil 304.1 ☑
- Lotusate 304.1 ☑
- LSD (-25) (and derivatives) 304.5 ☑
- Luminal 304.1 ☑
- lysergic acid 304.5 ☑
  - amide 304.5 ☑
- maconha 304.3 ☑
- magic mushroom 304.5 ☑
- marihuana 304.3 ☑
- MDA (methylene dioxyamphetamine) 304.4 ☑
- Mebaral 304.1 ☑
- Medinal 304.1 ☑
- Medomin 304.1 ☑
- megahallucinogenics 304.5 ☑
- meperidine 304.0 ☑
- mephobarbital 304.1 ☑
- meprobamate 304.1 ☑
- mescaline 304.5 ☑
- methadone 304.0 ☑
- methamphetamine(s) 304.4 ☑
- methaqualone 304.1 ☑
- metharbital 304.1 ☑
- methitural 304.1 ☑
- methobarbitone 304.1 ☑
- methohexital 304.1 ☑
- methopholine 304.6 ☑
- methyl
  - alcohol 303.9 ☑
  - bromide 304.6 ☑
  - morphine 304.0 ☑
  - sulfonal 304.1 ☑
- methylaparafynol 304.1 ☑
- methylated spirit 303.9 ☑
- methylbutinol 304.6 ☑
- methyldihydromorphinone 304.0 ☑
- methylene
  - chloride 304.6 ☑
  - dichloride 304.6 ☑
  - dioxyamphetamine (MDA) 304.4 ☑
- methylphenidate 304.4 ☑
- methyprylone 304.1 ☑
- metopon 304.0 ☑
- Miltown 304.1 ☑
- morning glory seeds 304.5 ☑

Dependence — *continued*
- morphinan(s) 304.0 ☑
- morphine (sulfate) (sulfite) (type) (drugs classifiable to 965.00–965.09) 304.0 ☑
- morphine or opioid type drug (drugs classifiable to 965.00–965.09) with any other drug 304.7 ☑
- morphinol(s) 304.0 ☑
- morphinon 304.0 ☑
- morpholinylethylmorphine 304.0 ☑
- mylomide 304.1 ☑
- myristicin 304.5 ☑
- narcotic (drug) NEC 304.9 ☑
- nealbarbital 304.1 ☑
- nealbarbitone 304.1 ☑
- Nembutal 304.1 ☑
- Neonal 304.1 ☑
- Neraval 304.1 ☑
- Neravan 304.1 ☑
- neurobarb 304.1 ☑
- nicotine 305.1
- Nisentil 304.0 ☑
- nitrous oxide 304.6 ☑
- Noctec 304.1 ☑
- Noludar 304.1 ☑
- nonbarbiturate sedatives and tranquilizers with similar effect 304.1 ☑
- noptil 304.1 ☑
- normorphine 304.0 ☑
- noscapine 304.0 ☑
- Novocaine 304.6 ☑
- Numorphan 304.0 ☑
- nunol 304.1 ☑
- Nupercaine 304.6 ☑
- Oblivon 304.1 ☑
- on
  - aspirator V46.0
  - hemodialysis V45.1
  - hyperbaric chamber V46.8
  - iron lung V46.11
  - machine (enabling) V46.9
    - specified type NEC V46.8
  - peritoneal dialysis V45.1
  - Possum (Patient-Operated-Selector-Mechanism) V46.8
  - renal dialysis machine V45.1
  - respirator [ventilator] V46.11
    - encounter
      - during
        - mechanical failure V46.14
        - power failure V46.12
      - for weaning V46.13
  - supplemental oxygen V46.2
- opiate 304.0 ☑
- opioids 304.0 ☑
- opioid type drug 304.0 ☑
  - with any other drug 304.7 ☑
- opium (alkaloids) (derivatives) (tincture) 304.0 ☑
- ortal 304.1 ☑
- Oxazepam 304.1 ☑
- oxycodone 304.0 ☑
- oxymorphone 304.0 ☑
- Palfium 304.0 ☑
- Panadol 304.6 ☑
- pantopium 304.0 ☑
- pantopon 304.0 ☑
- papaverine 304.0 ☑
- paracetamol 304.6 ☑
- paracodin 304.0 ☑
- paraldehyde 304.1 ☑
- paregoric 304.0 ☑
- Parzone 304.0 ☑
- PCP (phencyclidine) 304.6 ☑
- Pearly Gates 304.5 ☑
- pentazocine 304.0 ☑
- pentobarbital 304.1 ☑
- pentobarbitone (sodium) 304.1 ☑
- Pentothal 304.1 ☑
- Percaine 304.6 ☑
- Percodan 304.0 ☑
- Perichlor 304.1 ☑
- Pernocton 304.1 ☑

☑ Additional Digit Required — Refer to the Tabular List for Digit Selection   ▽ Subterms under main terms may continue to next column or page

2007 ICD-9-CM   ▶◀ Revised Text   ● New Line   ▲ Revised Code   **Volume 2 — 77**

Dependence — *continued*
Pernoston 304.1 ✓
peronine 304.0 ✓
pethidine (hydrochloride) 304.0 ✓
petrichloral 304.1 ✓
peyote 304.5 ✓
Phanodron 304.1 ✓
phenacetin 304.6 ✓
phenadoxone 304.0 ✓
phenaglycodol 304.1 ✓
phenazocine 304.0 ✓
phencyclidine 304.6 ✓
phenmetrazine 304.4 ✓
phenobal 304.1 ✓
phenobarbital 304.1 ✓
phenobarbitone 304.1 ✓
phenomorphan 304.0 ✓
phenonyl 304.1 ✓
phenoperidine 304.0 ✓
pholcodine 304.0 ✓
piminodine 304.0 ✓
Pipadone 304.0 ✓
Pitkin's solution 304.6 ✓
Placidyl 304.1 ✓
polysubstance 304.8 ✓
Pontocaine 304.6 ✓
pot 304.3 ✓
potassium bromide 304.1 ✓
Preludin 304.4 ✓
Prinadol 304.0 ✓
probarbital 304.1 ✓
procaine 304.6 ✓
propanal 304.1 ✓
propoxyphene 304.6 ✓
psilocibin 304.5 ✓
psilocin 304.5 ✓
psilocybin 304.5 ✓
psilocyline 304.5 ✓
psilocyn 304.5 ✓
psychedelic agents 304.5 ✓
psychostimulant NEC 304.4 ✓
psychotomimetic agents 304.5 ✓
pyrahexyl 304.3 ✓
Pyramidon 304.6 ✓
quinalbarbitone 304.1 ✓
racemoramide 304.0 ✓
racemorphan 304.0 ✓
Rela 304.6 ✓
scopolamine 304.6 ✓
secobarbital 304.1 ✓
Seconal 304.1 ✓
sedative NEC 304.1 ✓
    nonbarbiturate with barbiturate
        effect 304.1 ✓
Sedormid 304.1 ✓
sernyl 304.1 ✓
sodium bromide 304.1 ✓
Soma 304.6 ✓
Somnal 304.1 ✓
Somnos 304.1 ✓
Soneryl 304.1 ✓
soporific (drug) NEC 304.1 ✓
specified drug NEC 304.6 ✓
speed 304.4 ✓
spinocaine 304.6 ✓
Stovaine 304.6 ✓
STP 304.5 ✓
stramonium 304.6 ✓
Sulfonal 304.1 ✓
sulfonethylmethane 304.1 ✓
sulfonmethane 304.1 ✓
Surital 304.1 ✓
synthetic drug with morphine-like ef-
    fect 304.0 ✓
talbutal 304.1 ✓
tetracaine 304.6 ✓
tetrahydrocannabinol 304.3 ✓
tetronal 304.1 ✓
THC 304.3 ✓
thebacon 304.0 ✓
thebaine 304.0 ✓
thiamil 304.1 ✓
thiamylal 304.1 ✓
thiopental 304.1 ✓

Dependence — *continued*
tobacco 305.1
toluene, toluol 304.6 ✓
tranquilizer NEC 304.1 ✓
    nonbarbiturate with barbiturate
        effect 304.1 ✓
tribromacetaldehyde 304.6 ✓
tribromethanol 304.6 ✓
tribromomethane 304.6 ✓
trichloroethanol 304.6 ✓
trichoroethyl phosphate 304.1 ✓
triclofos 304.1 ✓
Trional 304.1 ✓
Tuinal 304.1 ✓
Turkish Green 304.3 ✓
urethan(e) 304.6 ✓
Valium 304.1 ✓
Valmid 304.1 ✓
veganin 304.0 ✓
veramon 304.1 ✓
Veronal 304.1 ✓
versidyne 304.6 ✓
vinbarbital 304.1 ✓
vinbarbitone 304.1 ✓
vinyl bitone 304.1 ✓
vitamin B_6 266.1
wine 303.9 ✓
Zactane 304.6 ✓
Dependency
passive 301.6
reactions 301.6
Depersonalization (episode, in neurotic
    state) (neurotic) (syndrome) 300.6
Depletion
carbohydrates 271.9
complement factor 279.8
extracellular fluid 276.52
    plasma 276.52
potassium 276.8
    nephropathy 588.89
salt or sodium 276.1
    causing heat exhaustion or prostra-
        tion 992.4
    nephropathy 593.9
volume 276.50
    extracellular fluid 276.52
    plasma 276.52
Deposit
argentous, cornea 371.16
bone, in Boeck's sarcoid 135
calcareous, calcium — *see* Calcifica-
    tion
cholesterol
    retina 362.82
    skin 709.3
    vitreous (humor) 379.22
conjunctival 372.56
cornea, corneal NEC 371.10
    argentous 371.16
    in
        cystinosis 270.0 *[371.15]*
        mucopolysaccharidosis
            277.5 *[371.15]*
crystalline, vitreous (humor) 379.22
hemosiderin, in old scars of cornea
    371.11
metallic, in lens 366.45
skin 709.3
teeth, tooth (betel) (black) (green)
    (materia alba) (orange) (soft) (to-
    bacco) 523.6
urate, in kidney (*see also* Disease, re-
    nal) 593.9
Depraved appetite 307.52
Depression 311
acute (*see also* Psychosis, affective)
    296.2 ✓
    recurrent episode 296.3 ✓
    single episode 296.2 ✓
agitated (*see also* Psychosis, affective)
    296.2 ✓
    recurrent episode 296.3 ✓
    single episode 296.2 ✓
anaclitic 309.21
anxiety 300.4

Depression — *continued*
arches 734
    congenital 754.61
autogenous (*see also* Psychosis, affec-
    tive) 296.2 ✓
    recurrent episode 296.3 ✓
    single episode 296.2 ✓
basal metabolic rate (BMR) 794.7
bone marrow 289.9
central nervous system 799.1
    newborn 779.2
cerebral 331.9
    newborn 779.2
cerebrovascular 437.8
    newborn 779.2
chest wall 738.3
endogenous (*see also* Psychosis, affec-
    tive) 296.2 ✓
    recurrent episode 296.3 ✓
    single episode 296.2 ✓
functional activity 780.99
hysterical 300.11
involutional, climacteric, or
    menopausal (*see also* Psychosis,
    affective) 296.2 ✓
    recurrent episode 296.3 ✓
    single episode 296.2 ✓
manic (*see also* Psychosis, affective)
    296.80
medullary 348.8
    newborn 779.2
mental 300.4
metatarsal heads — *see* Depression,
    arches
metatarsus — *see* Depression, arches
monopolar (*see also* Psychosis, affec-
    tive) 296.2 ✓
    recurrent episode 296.3 ✓
    single episode 296.2 ✓
nervous 300.4
neurotic 300.4
nose 738.0
postpartum 648.4 ✓
psychogenic 300.4
    reactive 298.0
psychoneurotic 300.4
psychotic (*see also* Psychosis, affec-
    tive) 296.2 ✓
    reactive 298.0
    recurrent episode 296.3 ✓
    single episode 296.2 ✓
reactive 300.4
    neurotic 300.4
    psychogenic 298.0
    psychoneurotic 300.4
    psychotic 298.0
recurrent 296.3 ✓
respiratory center 348.8
    newborn 770.89
scapula 736.89
senile 290.21
situational (acute) (brief) 309.0
    prolonged 309.1
skull 754.0
sternum 738.3
visual field 368.40
Depressive reaction — *see also* Reac-
    tion, depressive
acute (transient) 309.0
    with anxiety 309.28
prolonged 309.1
situational (acute) 309.0
    prolonged 309.1
Deprivation
cultural V62.4
emotional V62.89
    affecting
        adult 995.82
        infant or child 995.51
food 994.2
    specific substance NEC 269.8
protein (familial) (kwashiorkor) 260
sleep V69.4
social V62.4
    affecting
        adult 995.82

Deprivation — *continued*
social — *continued*
    affecting — *continued*
        infant or child 995.51
symptoms, syndrome
    alcohol 291.81
    drug 292.0
    vitamins (*see also* Deficiency, vitamin)
        269.2
    water 994.3
de Quervain's
disease (tendon sheath) 727.04
thyroiditis (subacute granulomatous
    thyroiditis) 245.1
Derangement
ankle (internal) 718.97
    current injury (*see also* Disloca-
        tion, ankle) 837.0
    recurrent 718.37
cartilage (articular) NEC (*see also*
    Disorder, cartilage, articular)
    718.0 ✓
    knee 717.9
        recurrent 718.36
    recurrent 718.3 ✓
collateral ligament (knee) (medial)
    (tibial) 717.82
    current injury 844.1
    lateral (fibular) 844.0
    lateral (fibular) 717.81
        current injury 844.0
cruciate ligament (knee) (posterior)
    717.84
    anterior 717.83
        current injury 844.2
    current injury 844.2
elbow (internal) 718.92
    current injury (*see also* Disloca-
        tion, elbow) 832.00
    recurrent 718.32
gastrointestinal 536.9
heart — *see* Disease, heart
hip (joint) (internal) (old) 718.95
    current injury (*see also* Disloca-
        tion, hip) 835.00
    recurrent 718.35
intervertebral disc — *see* Displace-
    ment, intervertebral disc
joint (internal) 718.90
    ankle 718.97
        current injury (*see also* Disloca-
            tion, by site)
            knee, meniscus or cartilage (*see
                also* Tear, meniscus)
                836.2
    elbow 718.92
    foot 718.97
    hand 718.94
    hip 718.95
    knee 717.9
    multiple sites 718.99
    pelvic region 718.95
    recurrent 718.30
        ankle 718.37
        elbow 718.32
        foot 718.37
        hand 718.34
        hip 718.35
        knee 718.36
        multiple sites 718.39
        pelvic region 718.35
        shoulder (region) 718.31
        specified site NEC 718.38
        temporomandibular (old) 524.69
        wrist 718.33
    shoulder (region) 718.91
    specified site NEC 718.98
    spine NEC 724.9
    temporomandibular 524.69
    wrist 718.93
knee (cartilage) (internal) 717.9
    current injury (*see also* Tear,
        meniscus) 836.2
    ligament 717.89
        capsular 717.85

Derangement — continued
knee — continued
  ligament — continued
    collateral — see Derangement,
      collateral ligament
    cruciate — see Derangement,
      cruciate ligament
    specified NEC 717.85
    recurrent 718.36
  low back NEC 724.9
  meniscus NEC (knee) 717.5
    current injury (see also Tear,
      meniscus) 836.2
    lateral 717.40
      anterior horn 717.42
      posterior horn 717.43
      specified NEC 717.49
    medial 717.3
      anterior horn 717.1
      posterior horn 717.2
    recurrent 718.3 ☑
    site other than knee — see Disor-
      der, cartilage, articular
  mental (see also Psychosis) 298.9
  rotator cuff (recurrent) (tear) 726.10
    current 840.4
  sacroiliac (old) 724.6
    current — see Dislocation, sacroil-
      iac
  semilunar cartilage (knee) 717.5
    current injury 836.2
      lateral 836.1
      medial 836.0
    recurrent 718.3 ☑
  shoulder (internal) 718.91
    current injury (see also Disloca-
      tion, shoulder) 831.00
    recurrent 718.31
  spine (recurrent) NEC 724.9
    current — see Dislocation, spine
  temporomandibular (internal) (joint)
    (old) 524.69
    current — see Dislocation, jaw

Dercum's disease or syndrome (adiposis
  dolorosa) 272.8

Derealization (neurotic) 300.6

Dermal — see condition

Dermaphytid — see Dermatophytosis

Dermatergosis — see Dermatitis

Dermatitis (allergic) (contact) (occupational) (venenata) 692.9
  ab igne 692.82
  acneiform 692.9
  actinic (due to sun) 692.70
    acute 692.72
    chronic NEC 692.74
    other than from sun NEC 692.82
  ambustionis
    due to
      burn or scald — see Burn, by
        site
      sunburn (see also Sunburn)
        692.71
  amebic 006.6
  ammonia 691.0
  anaphylactoid NEC 692.9
  arsenical 692.4
  artefacta 698.4
    psychogenic 316 [698.4]
  asthmatic 691.8
  atopic (allergic) (intrinsic) 691.8
    psychogenic 316 [691.8]
  atrophicans 701.8
    diffusa 701.8
    maculosa 701.3
  berlock, berloque 692.72
  blastomycetic 116.0
  blister beetle 692.89
  Brucella NEC 023.9
  bullosa 694.9
    striata pratensis 692.6
  bullous 694.9
    mucosynechial, atrophic 694.60
      with ocular involvement 694.61
    seasonal 694.8

Dermatitis — continued
calorica
  due to
    burn or scald — see Burn, by
      site
    cold 692.89
    sunburn (see also Sunburn)
      692.71
  caterpillar 692.89
  cercarial 120.3
  combustionis
    due to
      burn or scald — see Burn, by
        site
      sunburn (see also Sunburn)
        692.71
  congelationis 991.5
  contusiformis 695.2
  diabetic 250.8 ☑
  diaper 691.0
  diphtheritica 032.85
  due to
    acetone 692.2
    acids 692.4
    adhesive plaster 692.4
    alcohol (skin contact) (substances
      classifiable to 980.0–980.9)
      692.4
      taken internally 693.8
    alkalis 692.4
    allergy NEC 692.9
    ammonia (household) (liquid) 692.4
    animal
      dander (cat) (dog) 692.84
      hair (cat) (dog) 692.84
    arnica 692.3
    arsenic 692.4
      taken internally 693.8
    blister beetle 692.89
    cantharides 692.3
    carbon disulphide 692.2
    caterpillar 692.89
    caustics 692.4
    cereal (ingested) 693.1
      contact with skin 692.5
    chemical(s) NEC 692.4
      internal 693.8
      irritant NEC 692.4
      taken internally 693.8
    chlorocompounds 692.2
    coffee (ingested) 693.1
      contact with skin 692.5
    cold weather 692.89
    cosmetics 692.81
    cyclohexanes 692.2
    dander, animal (cat) (dog) 692.84
    deodorant 692.81
    detergents 692.0
    dichromate 692.4
    drugs and medicinals (correct
      substance properly adminis-
      tered) (internal use) 693.0
      external (in contact with skin)
        692.3
      wrong substance given or
        taken 976.9
        specified substance — see
          Table of Drugs and
          Chemicals
      wrong substance given or taken
        977.9
        specified substance — see
          Table of Drugs and
          Chemicals
    dyes 692.89
      hair 692.89
    epidermophytosis — see Dermato-
      phytosis
    esters 692.2
    external irritant NEC 692.9
      specified agent NEC 692.89
    eye shadow 692.81
    fish (ingested) 693.1
      contact with skin 692.5
    flour (ingested) 693.1
      contact with skin 692.5

Dermatitis — continued
due to — continued
  food (ingested) 693.1
    in contact with skin 692.5
  fruit (ingested) 693.1
    contact with skin 692.5
  fungicides 692.3
  furs 692.84
  glycols 692.2
  greases NEC 692.1
  hair, animal (cat) (dog) 692.84
  hair dyes 692.89
  hot
    objects and materials — see
      Burn, by site
    weather or places 692.89
  hydrocarbons 692.2
  infrared rays, except from sun
    692.82
    solar NEC (see also Dermatitis,
      due to, sun) 692.70
  ingested substance 693.9
    drugs and medicinals (see also
      Dermatitis, due to, drugs
      and medicinals) 693.0
    food 693.1
    specified substance NEC 693.8
  ingestion or injection of chemical
    693.8
    drug (correct substance properly
      administered) 693.0
      wrong substance given or taken
        977.7
        specified substance — see
          Table of Drugs and
          Chemicals
  insecticides 692.4
  internal agent 693.9
    drugs and medicinals (see also
      Dermatitis, due to, drugs
      and medicinals) 693.0
    food (ingested) 693.1
      in contact with skin 692.5
    specified agent NEC 693.8
  iodine 692.3
  iodoform 692.3
  irradiation 692.82
  jewelry 692.83
  keratolytics 692.3
  ketones 692.2
  lacquer tree (Rhus verniciflua)
    692.6
  light (sun) NEC (see also Dermati-
    tis, due to, sun) 692.70
    other 692.82
  low temperature 692.89
  mascara 692.81
  meat (ingested) 693.1
    contact with skin 692.5
  mercury, mercurials 692.3
  metals 692.83
  milk (ingested) 693.1
    contact with skin 692.5
  Neomycin 692.3
  nylon 692.4
  oils NEC 692.1
  paint solvent 692.2
  pediculocides 692.3
  petroleum products (substances
    classifiable to 981) 692.4
  phenol 692.3
  photosensitiveness, photosensitivi-
    ty (sun) 692.72
    other light 692.82
  plants NEC 692.6
  plasters, medicated (any) 692.3
  plastic 692.4
  poison
    ivy (Rhus toxicodendron) 692.6
    oak (Rhus diversiloba) 692.6
    plant or vine 692.6
    sumac (Rhus venenata) 692.6
    vine (Rhus radicans) 692.6
  preservatives 692.89
  primrose (primula) 692.6
  primula 692.6

Dermatitis — continued
due to — continued
  radiation 692.82
    sun NEC (see also Dermatitis,
      due to, sun) 692.70
    tanning bed 692.82
  radioactive substance 692.82
  radium 692.82
  ragweed (Senecio jacobae) 692.6
  Rhus (diversiloba) (radicans) (toxi-
    codendron) (venenata) (verni-
    ciflua) 692.6
  rubber 692.4
  scabicides 692.3
  Senecio jacobae 692.6
  solar radiation — see Dermatitis,
    due to, sun
  solvents (any) (substances classifi-
    able to 982.0–982.8) 692.2
    chlorocompound group 692.2
    cyclohexane group 692.2
    ester group 692.2
    glycol group 692.2
    hydrocarbon group 692.2
    ketone group 692.2
    paint 692.2
  specified agent NEC 692.89
  sun 692.70
    acute 692.72
    chronic NEC 692.74
    specified NEC 692.79
  sunburn (see also Sunburn)
    692.71
  sunshine NEC (see also Dermatitis,
    due to, sun) 692.70
  tanning bed 692.82
  tetrachlorethylene 692.2
  toluene 692.2
  topical medications 692.3
  turpentine 692.2
  ultraviolet rays, except from sun
    692.82
    sun NEC (see also Dermatitis,
      due to, sun) 692.70
  vaccine or vaccination (correct
    substance properly adminis-
    tered) 693.0
    wrong substance given or taken
      bacterial vaccine 978.8
        specified — see Table of
          Drugs and Chemi-
          cals
      other vaccines NEC 979.9
        specified — see Table of
          Drugs and Chemi-
          cals
  varicose veins (see also Varicose,
    vein, inflamed or infected)
    454.1
  x-rays 692.82
  dyshydrotic 705.81
  dysmenorrheica 625.8
  eczematoid NEC 692.9
    infectious 690.8
  eczematous NEC 692.9
  epidemica 695.89
  erysipelatosa 695.81
  escharotica — see Burn, by site
  exfoliativa, exfoliative 695.89
    generalized 695.89
    infantum 695.81
    neonatorum 695.81
  eyelid 373.31
    allergic 373.32
    contact 373.32
    eczematous 373.31
    herpes (zoster) 053.20
      simplex 054.41
    infective 373.5
      due to
        actinomycosis 039.3 [373.5]
        herpes
          simplex 054.41
          zoster 053.20
        impetigo 684 [373.5]

☑ Additional Digit Required — Refer to the Tabular List for Digit Selection   ▽ Subterms under main terms may continue to next column or page

2007 ICD-9-CM   ▶◀ Revised Text   ● New Line   ▲ Revised Code   **Volume 2 — 79**

Derangement — Dermatitis

Dermatitis — Development

Dermatitis — continued
eyelid — continued
  infective — continued
    due to — continued
      leprosy (see also Leprosy)
        030.0 [373.4]
      lupus vulgaris (tuberculous)
        (see also Tuberculosis)
        017.0 ☑ [373.4]
      mycotic dermatitis (see also
        Dermatomycosis)
        111.9 [373.5]
      vaccinia 051.0 [373.5]
        postvaccination
          999.0 [373.5]
      yaws (see also Yaws)
        102.9 [373.4]
  facta, factitia 698.4
    psychogenic 316 [698.4]
  ficta 698.4
    psychogenic 316 [698.4]
  flexural 691.8
  follicularis 704.8
  friction 709.8
  fungus 111.9
    specified type NEC 111.8
  gangrenosa, gangrenous (infantum)
    (see also Gangrene) 785.4
  gestationis 646.8 ☑
  gonococcal 098.89
  gouty 274.89
  harvest mite 133.8
  heat 692.89
  herpetiformis (bullous) (erythematous)
    (pustular) (vesicular) 694.0
    juvenile 694.2
    senile 694.5
  hiemalis 692.89
  hypostatic, hypostatica 454.1
    with ulcer 454.2
  impetiginous 684
  infantile (acute) (chronic) (intertriginous)
    (intrinsic) (seborrheic)
    690.12
  infectiosa eczematoides 690.8
  infective (staphylococcal) (streptococcal)
    686.9
    eczematoid 690.8
  infective eczematoid 690.8
  Jacquet's (diaper dermatitis) 691.0
  leptus 133.8
  lichenified NEC 692.9
  lichenoid, chronic 701.0
  lichenoides purpurica pigmentosa
    709.1
  meadow 692.6
  medicamentosa (correct substance
    properly administered) (internal
    use) (see also Dermatitis, due
    to, drugs or medicinals) 693.0
    due to contact with skin 692.3
  mite 133.8
  multiformis 694.0
    juvenile 694.2
    senile 694.5
  napkin 691.0
  neuro 698.3
  neurotica 694.0
  nummular NEC 692.9
  osteatosis, osteatotic 706.8
  papillaris capillitii 706.1
  pellagrous 265.2
  perioral 695.3
  perstans 696.1
  photosensitivity (sun) 692.72
    other light 692.82
  pigmented purpuric lichenoid 709.1
  polymorpha dolorosa 694.0
  primary irritant 692.9
  pruriginosa 694.0
  pruritic NEC 692.9
  psoriasiform nodularis 696.2
  psychogenic 316
  purulent 686.00
  pustular contagious 051.2
  pyococcal 686.00

Dermatitis — continued
  pyocyaneus 686.09
  pyogenica 686.09
  radiation 692.82
  repens 696.1
  Ritter's (exfoliativa) 695.81
  Schamberg's (progressive pigmentary
    dermatosis) 709.09
  schistosome 120.3
  seasonal bullous 694.8
  seborrheic 690.10
    infantile 690.12
  sensitization NEC 692.9
  septic (see also Septicemia) 686.00
    gonococcal 098.89
  solar, solare NEC (see also Dermatitis,
    due to, sun) 692.70
  stasis 459.81
    due to
      postphlebitic syndrome 459.12
        with ulcer 459.13
      varicose veins — see Varicose
        ulcerated or with ulcer (varicose)
        454.2
  sunburn (see also Sunburn) 692.71
  suppurative 686.00
  traumatic NEC 709.8
  trophoneurotica 694.0
  ultraviolet, except from sun 692.82
    due to sun NEC (see also Dermatitis, due to, sun) 692.82
  varicose 454.1
    with ulcer 454.2
  vegetans 686.8
  verrucosa 117.2
  xerotic 706.8
Dermatoarthritis, lipoid 272.8 [713.0]
Dermatochalasia, dermatochalasis
  374.87
Dermatofibroma (lenticulare) (M8832/0)
  — see also Neoplasm, skin, benign
    protuberans (M8832/1) — see Neoplasm, skin, uncertain behavior
Dermatofibrosarcoma (protuberans)
  (M8832/3) — see Neoplasm, skin,
  malignant
Dermatographia 708.3
Dermatolysis (congenital) (exfoliativa)
  757.39
  acquired 701.8
  eyelids 374.34
  palpebrarum 374.34
  senile 701.8
Dermatomegaly NEC 701.8
Dermatomucomyositis 710.3
Dermatomycosis 111.9
  furfuracea 111.0
  specified type NEC 111.8
Dermatomyositis (acute) (chronic) 710.3
Dermatoneuritis of children 985.0
Dermatophiliasis 134.1
Dermatophytide — see Dermatophytosis
Dermatophytosis (Epidermophyton) (infection) (microsporum) (tinea) (Trichophyton) 110.9
  beard 110.0
  body 110.5
  deep seated 110.6
  fingernails 110.1
  foot 110.4
  groin 110.3
  hand 110.2
  nail 110.1
  perianal (area) 110.3
  scalp 110.0
  scrotal 110.8
  specified site NEC 110.8
  toenails 110.1
  vulva 110.8
Dermatopolyneuritis 985.0
Dermatorrhexis 756.83
  acquired 701.8
Dermatosclerosis — see also Scleroderma 710.1
  localized 701.0
Dermatosis 709.9

Dermatosis — continued
  Andrews' 686.8
  atopic 691.8
  Bowen's (M8081/2) — see Neoplasm,
    skin, in situ
  bullous 694.9
    specified type NEC 694.8
  erythematosquamous 690.8
  exfoliativa 695.89
  factitial 698.4
  gonococcal 098.89
  herpetiformis 694.0
    juvenile 694.2
    senile 694.5
  hysterical 300.11
  linear IgA 694.8
  menstrual NEC 709.8
  neutrophilic, acute febrile 695.89
  occupational (see also Dermatitis)
    692.9
  papulosa nigra 709.8
  pigmentary NEC 709.00
    progressive 709.09
    Schamberg's 709.09
    Siemens-Bloch 757.33
  progressive pigmentary 709.09
  psychogenic 316
  pustular subcorneal 694.1
  Schamberg's (progressive pigmentary)
    709.09
  senile NEC 709.3
  specified NEC 702.8
  Unna's (seborrheic dermatitis) 690.10
Dermographia 708.3
Dermographism 708.3
Dermoid (cyst) (M9084/0) — see also
  Neoplasm, by site, benign
    with malignant transformation
      (M9084/3) 183.0
Dermopathy
  infiltrative, with thyrotoxicosis
    242.0 ☑
  senile NEC 709.3
Dermophytosis — see Dermatophytosis
Descemet's membrane — see condition
Descemetocele 371.72
Descending — see condition
Descensus uteri (complete) (incomplete)
  (partial) (without vaginal wall prolapse) 618.1
    with mention of vaginal wall prolapse
      — see Prolapse, uterovaginal
Desensitization to allergens V07.1
Desert
  rheumatism 114.0
  sore (see also Ulcer, skin) 707.9
Desertion (child) (newborn) 995.52
  adult 995.84
Desmoid (extra-abdominal) (tumor)
  (M8821/1) — see also Neoplasm,
  connective tissue, uncertain behavior
    abdominal (M8822/1) — see Neoplasm, connective tissue, uncertain behavior
Despondency 300.4
Desquamative dermatitis NEC 695.89
Destruction
  articular facet (see also Derangement,
    joint) 718.9 ☑
    vertebra 724.9
  bone 733.90
    syphilitic 095.5
  joint (see also Derangement, joint)
    718.9 ☑
    sacroiliac 724.6
  kidney 593.89
  live fetus to facilitate birth NEC
    763.89
  ossicles (ear) 385.24
  rectal sphincter 569.49
  septum (nasal) 478.19   ▲
  tuberculous NEC (see also Tuberculosis) 011.9 ☑
  tympanic membrane 384.82
  tympanum 385.89

Destruction — continued
  vertebral disc — see Degeneration,
    intervertebral disc
Destructiveness — see also Disturbance,
  conduct 312.9
    adjustment reaction 309.3
Detachment
  cartilage (see also Sprain, by site)
    knee — see Tear, meniscus
  cervix, annular 622.8
    complicating delivery 665.3 ☑
  choroid (old) (postinfectional) (simple)
    (spontaneous) 363.70
      hemorrhagic 363.72
      serous 363.71
  knee, medial meniscus (old) 717.3
    current injury 836.0
  ligament — see Sprain, by site
  placenta (premature) — see Placenta,
    separation
  retina (recent) 361.9
    with retinal defect (rhegmatogenous) 361.00
      giant tear 361.03
      multiple 361.02
      partial
        with
          giant tear 361.03
          multiple defects 361.02
          retinal dialysis (juvenile)
            361.04
          single defect 361.01
        retinal dialysis (juvenile) 361.04
        single 361.01
        subtotal 361.05
        total 361.05
    delimited (old) (partial) 361.06
    old
      delimited 361.06
      partial 361.06
      total or subtotal 361.07
    pigment epithelium (RPE) (serous)
      362.42
      exudative 362.42
      hemorrhagic 362.43
    rhegmatogenous (see also Detachment, retina, with retinal defect) 361.00
    serous (without retinal defect)
      361.2
    specified type NEC 361.89
    traction (with vitreoretinal organization) 361.81
  vitreous humor 379.21
Detergent asthma 507.8
Deterioration
  epileptic
    with behavioral disturbance
      345.9 ☑ [294.11]
    without behavioral disturbance
      345.9 ☑ [294.10]
  heart, cardiac (see also Degeneration,
    myocardial) 429.1
  mental (see also Psychosis) 298.9
  myocardium, myocardial (see also
    Degeneration, myocardial) 429.1
  senile (simple) 797
  transplanted organ — see Complications, transplant, organ, by site
de Toni-Fanconi syndrome (cystinosis)
  270.0
Deuteranomaly 368.52
Deuteranopia (anomalous trichromat)
  (complete) (incomplete) 368.52
Deutschländer's disease — see Fracture, foot
Development
  abnormal, bone 756.9
  arrested 783.40
    bone 733.91
    child 783.40
    due to malnutrition (protein-calorie) 263.2
    fetus or newborn 764.9 ☑
    tracheal rings (congenital) 748.3

Development — *continued*
defective, congenital (*see also* Anomaly)
  cauda equina 742.59
  left ventricle 746.9
    with atresia or hypoplasia of aortic orifice or valve with hypoplasia of ascending aorta 746.7
    in hypoplastic left heart syndrome 746.7
delayed (*see also* Delay, development) 783.40
  arithmetical skills 315.1
  language (skills) 315.31
    expressive 315.31
    mixed receptive-expressive 315.32
  learning skill, specified NEC 315.2
  mixed skills 315.5
  motor coordination 315.4
  reading 315.00
  specified
    learning skill NEC 315.2
    type NEC, except learning 315.8
  speech 315.39
    associated with hyperkinesia 314.1
    phonological 315.39
  spelling 315.09
  written expression 315.2
imperfect, congenital (*see also* Anomaly)
  heart 746.9
  lungs 748.60
improper (fetus or newborn) 764.9 ☑
incomplete (fetus or newborn) 764.9 ☑
  affecting management of pregnancy 656.5 ☑
  bronchial tree 748.3
  organ or site not listed — *see* Hypoplasia
  respiratory system 748.9
sexual, precocious NEC 259.1
tardy, mental (*see also* Retardation, mental) 319

Developmental — *see* condition
Devergie's disease (pityriasis rubra pilaris) 696.4
Deviation
conjugate (eye) 378.87
  palsy 378.81
  spasm, spastic 378.82
esophagus 530.89
eye, skew 378.87
mandible, opening and closing 524.53
midline (jaw) (teeth) 524.29
  specified site NEC — *see* Malposition
occlusal plane 524.76
organ or site, congenital NEC — *see* Malposition, congenital
septum (acquired) (nasal) 470
  congenital 754.0
sexual 302.9
  bestiality 302.1
  coprophilia 302.89
  ego-dystonic
    homosexuality 302.0
    lesbianism 302.0
  erotomania 302.89
    Clérambault's 297.8
  exhibitionism (sexual) 302.4
  fetishism 302.81
    transvestic 302.3
  frotteurism 302.89
  homosexuality, ego-dystonic 302.0
    pedophilic 302.2
  lesbianism, ego-dystonic 302.0
  masochism 302.83
  narcissism 302.89
  necrophilia 302.89
  nymphomania 302.89
  pederosis 302.2
  pedophilia 302.2
  sadism 302.84

Deviation — *continued*
sexual — *continued*
  sadomasochism 302.84
  satyriasis 302.89
  specified type NEC 302.89
  transvestic fetishism 302.3
  transvestism 302.3
  voyeurism 302.82
  zoophilia (erotica) 302.1
teeth, midline 524.29
trachea 519.19
ureter (congenital) 753.4   ▲
Devic's disease 341.0
Device
cerebral ventricle (communicating) in situ V45.2
contraceptive — *see* Contraceptive, device
drainage, cerebrospinal fluid V45.2
Devil's
grip 074.1
pinches (purpura simplex) 287.2
Devitalized tooth 522.9
Devonshire colic 984.9
  specified type of lead — *see* Table of Drugs and Chemicals
Dextraposition, aorta 747.21
  with ventricular septal defect, pulmonary stenosis or atresia, and hypertrophy of right ventricle 745.2
  in tetralogy of Fallot 745.2
Dextratransposition, aorta 745.11
Dextrinosis, limit (debrancher enzyme deficiency) 271.0
Dextrocardia (corrected) (false) (isolated) (secondary) (true) 746.87
  with
    complete transposition of viscera 759.3
    situs inversus 759.3
Dextroversion, kidney (left) 753.3
Dhobie itch 110.3
Diabetes, diabetic (brittle) (congenital) (familial) (mellitus) (poorly controlled) (severe) (slight) (without complication) 250.0 ☑

Note — *Use the following fifth-digit subclassification with category 250:*

0   *type II or unspecified type, not stated as uncontrolled*

Fifth-digit 0 is for use for type II patients, even if the patient requires insulin

1   *type I [juvenile type], not stated as uncontrolled*

2   *type II or unspecified type, uncontrolled*

Fifth-digit 2 is for use for type II patients, even if the patient requires insulin

3   *type I [juvenile type], uncontrolled*

---

with
  coma (with ketoacidosis) 250.3 ☑
    hyperosmolar (nonketotic) 250.2 ☑
  complication NEC 250.9 ☑
    specified NEC 250.8 ☑
  gangrene 250.7 ☑ *[785.4]*
  hyperosmolarity 250.2 ☑
  ketosis, ketoacidosis 250.1 ☑
  osteomyelitis 250.8 ☑ *[731.8]*
  specified manisfestations NEC 250.8 ☑
acetonemia 250.1 ☑
acidosis 250.1 ☑
amyotrophy 250.6 ☑ *[358.1]*
angiopathy, peripheral 250.7 ☑ *[443.81]*
asymptomatic 790.29
autonomic neuropathy (peripheral) 250.6 ☑ *[337.1]*

Diabetes, diabetic — *continued*
bone change 250.8 ☑ *[731.8]*
bronze, bronzed 275.0
cataract 250.5 ☑ *[366.41]*
chemical 790.29
  complicating pregnancy, childbirth, or puerperium 648.8 ☑
coma (with ketoacidosis) 250.3 ☑
  hyperglycemic 250.3 ☑
  hyperosmolar (nonketotic) 250.2 ☑
  hypoglycemic 250.3 ☑
  insulin 250.3 ☑
complicating pregnancy, childbirth, or puerperium (maternal) 648.0 ☑
  affecting fetus or newborn 775.0
complication NEC 250.9 ☑
  specified NEC 250.8 ☑
dorsal sclerosis 250.6 ☑ *[340]*
dwarfism-obesity syndrome 258.1
gangrene 250.7 ☑ *[785.4]*
gastroparesis 250.6 ☑ *[536.3]*
gestational 648.8 ☑
  complicating pregnancy, childbirth, or puerperium 648.8 ☑
glaucoma 250.5 ☑ *[365.44]*
glomerulosclerosis (intercapillary) 250.4 ☑ *[581.81]*
glycogenosis, secondary 250.8 ☑ *[259.8]*
hemochromatosis 275.0
hyperosmolar coma 250.2 ☑
hyperosmolarity 250.2 ☑
hypertension-nephrosis syndrome 250.4 ☑ *[581.81]*
hypoglycemia 250.8 ☑
hypoglycemic shock 250.8 ☑
insipidus 253.5
  nephrogenic 588.1
  pituitary 253.5
  vasopressin-resistant 588.1
intercapillary glomerulosclerosis 250.4 ☑ *[581.81]*
iritis 250.5 ☑ *[364.42]*
ketosis, ketoacidosis 250.1 ☑
Kimmelstiel (-Wilson) disease or syndrome (intercapillary glomerulosclerosis) 250.4 ☑ *[581.81]*
Lancereaux's (diabetes mellitus with marked emaciation) 250.8 ☑ *[261]*
latent (chemical) 790.29
  complicating pregnancy, childbirth, or puerperium 648.8 ☑
lipoidosis 250.8 ☑ *[272.7]*
macular edema 250.5 ☑ *[362.07]*
maternal
  with manifest disease in the infant 775.1
  affecting fetus or newborn 775.0
microaneurysms, retinal 250.5 ☑ *[362.01]*
mononeuropathy 250.6 ☑ *[355.9]*
neonatal, transient 775.1
nephropathy 250.4 ☑ *[583.81]*
nephrosis (syndrome) 250.4 ☑ *[581.81]*
neuralgia 250.6 ☑ *[357.2]*
neuritis 250.6 ☑ *[357.2]*
neurogenic arthropathy 250.6 ☑ *[713.5]*
neuropathy 250.6 ☑ *[357.2]*
nonclinical 790.29
osteomyelitis 250.8 ☑ *[731.8]*
peripheral autonomic neuropathy 250.6 ☑ *[337.1]*
phosphate 275.3
polyneuropathy 250.6 ☑ *[357.2]*
renal (true) 271.4
retinal
  edema 250.5 ☑ *[362.07]*
  hemorrhage 250.5 ☑ *[362.01]*
  microaneurysms 250.5 ☑ *[362.01]*
retinitis 250.5 ☑ *[362.01]*
retinopathy 250.5 ☑ *[362.01]*

Diabetes, diabetic — *continued*
retinopathy — *continued*
  background 250.5 ☑ *[362.01]*
  nonproliverative 250.5 ☑ *[362.03]*
    mild 250.5 ☑ *[362.04]*
    moderate 250.5 ☑ *[362.05]*
    severe 250.5 ☑ *[362.06]*
  proliferative 250.5 ☑ *[362.02]*
steroid induced
  correct substance properly administered 251.8
  overdose or wrong substance given or taken 962.0
stress 790.29
subclinical 790.29
subliminal 790.29
sugar 250.0 ☑
ulcer (skin) 250.8 ☑ *[707.9]*
  lower extremity 250.8 ☑ *[707.10]*
    ankle 250.8 ☑ *[707.13]*
    calf 250.8 ☑ *[707.12]*
    foot 250.8 ☑ *[707.15]*
    heel 250.8 ☑ *[707.14]*
    knee 250.8 ☑ *[707.19]*
    specified site NEC 250.8 ☑ *[707.19]*
    thigh 250.8 ☑ *[707.11]*
    toes 250.8 ☑ *[707.15]*
  specified site NEC 250.8 ☑ *[707.8]*
xanthoma 250.8 ☑ *[272.2]*
Diacyclothrombopathia 287.1
Diagnosis deferred 799.9
Dialysis (intermittent) (treatment)
anterior retinal (juvenile) (with detachment) 361.04
extracorporeal V56.0
hemodialysis V56.0
  status only V45.1
peritoneal V56.8
  status only V45.1
renal V56.0
  status only V45.1
specified type NEC V56.8
Diamond-Blackfan anemia or syndrome (congenital hypoplastic anemia) 284.01   ▲
Diamond-Gardener syndrome (autoerythrocyte sensitization) 287.2
Diaper rash 691.0
Diaphoresis (excessive) NEC — *see also* Hyperhidrosis) 780.8
Diaphragm — *see* condition
Diaphragmalgia 786.52
Diaphragmitis 519.4
Diaphyseal aclasis 756.4
Diaphysitis 733.99
Diarrhea, diarrheal (acute) (autumn) (bilious) (bloody) (catarrhal) (choleraic) (chronic) (gravis) (green) (infantile) (lienteric) (noninfectious) (presumed noninfectious) (putrefactive) (secondary) (sporadic) (summer) (symptomatic) (thermic) 787.91
achlorhydric 536.0
allergic 558.3
amebic (*see also* Amebiasis) 006.9
  with abscess — *see* Abscess, amebic
  acute 006.0
  chronic 006.1
  nondysenteric 006.2
bacillary — *see* Dysentery, bacillary
bacterial NEC 008.5
balantidial 007.0
bile salt-induced 579.8
cachectic NEC 787.91
chilomastix 007.8
choleriformis 001.1
coccidial 007.2
Cochin-China 579.1
  anguilluliasis 127.2
  psilosis 579.1
Dientamoeba 007.8
dietetic 787.91

☑ Additional Digit Required — Refer to the Tabular List for Digit Selection   ▽ Subterms under main terms may continue to next column or page

▶◀ Revised Text   ● New Line   ▲ Revised Code

Diarrhea, diarrheal — *continued*
due to
achylia gastrica 536.8
Aerobacter aerogenes 008.2
Bacillus coli — *see* Enteritis, E. coli
bacteria NEC 008.5
bile salts 579.8
Capillaria
hepatica 128.8
philippinensis 127.5
Clostridium perfringens (C) (F) 008.46
Enterobacter aerogenes 008.2
enterococci 008.49
Escherichia coli — *see* Enteritis, E. coli
Giardia lamblia 007.1
Heterophyes heterophyes 121.6
irritating foods 787.91
Metagonimus yokogawai 121.5
Necator americanus 126.1
Paracolobactrum arizonae 008.1
Paracolon bacillus NEC 008.47
Arizona 008.1
Proteus (bacillus) (mirabilis) (Morganii) 008.3
Pseudomonas aeruginosa 008.42
S. japonicum 120.2
specified organism NEC 008.8
bacterial 008.49
viral NEC 008.69
Staphylococcus 008.41
Streptococcus 008.49
anaerobic 008.46
Strongyloides stercoralis 127.2
Trichuris trichiuria 127.3
virus NEC (*see also* Enteritis, viral) 008.69
dysenteric 009.2
due to specified organism NEC 008.8
dyspeptic 787.91
endemic 009.3
due to specified organism NEC 008.8
epidemic 009.2
due to specified organism NEC 008.8
fermentative 787.91
flagellate 007.9
Flexner's (ulcerative) 004.1
functional 564.5
following gastrointestinal surgery 564.4
psychogenic 306.4
giardial 007.1
Giardia lamblia 007.1
hill 579.1
hyperperistalsis (nervous) 306.4
infectious 009.2
due to specified organism NEC 008.8
presumed 009.3
inflammatory 787.91
due to specified organism NEC 008.8
malarial (*see also* Malaria) 084.6
mite 133.8
mycotic 117.9
nervous 306.4
neurogenic 564.5
parenteral NEC 009.2
postgastrectomy 564.4
postvagotomy 564.4
prostaglandin induced 579.8
protozoal NEC 007.9
psychogenic 306.4
septic 009.2
due to specified organism NEC 008.8
specified organism NEC 008.8
bacterial 008.49
viral NEC 008.69
Staphylococcus 008.41
Streptococcus 008.49
anaerobic 008.46

Diarrhea, diarrheal — *continued*
toxic 558.2
travelers' 009.2
due to specified organism NEC 008.8
trichomonal 007.3
tropical 579.1
tuberculous 014.8 ☑
ulcerative (chronic) (*see also* Colitis, ulcerative) 556.9
viral (*see also* Enteritis, viral) 008.8
zymotic NEC 009.2
Diastasis
cranial bones 733.99
congenital 756.0
joint (traumatic) — *see* Dislocation, by site
muscle 728.84
congenital 756.89
recti (abdomen) 728.84
complicating delivery 665.8 ☑
congenital 756.79
Diastema, teeth, tooth 524.30
Diastematomyelia 742.51
Diataxia, cerebral, infantile 343.0
Diathesis
allergic V15.09
bleeding (familial) 287.9
cystine (familial) 270.0
gouty 274.9
hemorrhagic (familial) 287.9
newborn NEC 776.0
oxalic 271.8
scrofulous (*see also* Tuberculosis) 017.2 ☑
spasmophilic (*see also* Tetany) 781.7
ulcer 569.9
uric acid 274.9
Diaz's disease or osteochondrosis 732.5
Dibothriocephaliasis 123.4
larval 123.5
Dibothriocephalus (infection) (infestation) (latus) 123.4
larval 123.5
Dicephalus 759.4
Dichotomy, teeth 520.2
Dichromat, dichromata (congenital) 368.59
Dichromatopsia (congenital) 368.59
Dichuchwa 104.0
Dicroceliasis 121.8
Didelphys, didelphic — *see also* Double uterus 752.2
Didymitis — *see also* Epididymitis 604.90
Died — *see also* Death
without
medical attention (cause unknown) 798.9
sign of disease 798.2
Dientamoeba diarrhea 007.8
Dietary
inadequacy or deficiency 269.9
surveillance and counseling V65.3
Dietl's crisis 593.4
Dieulafoy lesion (hemorrhagic)
of
duodenum 537.84
esophagus 530.82 ●
intestine 569.86
stomach 537.84
Difficult
birth, affecting fetus or newborn 763.9
delivery NEC 669.9 ☑
Difficulty
feeding 783.3
adult 783.3
breast 676.8 ☑
child 783.3
elderly 783.3
infant 783.3
newborn 779.3
nonorganic (infant) NEC 307.59
mechanical, gastroduodenal stoma 537.89

Difficulty — *continued*
reading 315.00
specific, spelling 315.09
swallowing (*see also* Dysphagia) 787.2
walking 719.7
Diffuse — *see* condition
Diffused ganglion 727.42
Di George's syndrome (thymic hypoplasia) 279.11
Digestive — *see* condition
Di Guglielmo's disease or syndrome (M9841/3) 207.0 ☑
Diktyoma (M9051/3) — *see* Neoplasm, by site, malignant
Dilaceration, tooth 520.4
Dilatation
anus 564.89
venule — *see* Hemorrhoids
aorta (focal) (general) (*see also* Aneurysm, aorta) 441.9
congenital 747.29
infectional 093.0
ruptured 441.5
syphilitic 093.0
appendix (cystic) 543.9
artery 447.8
bile duct (common) (cystic) (congenital) 751.69
acquired 576.8
bladder (sphincter) 596.8
congenital 753.8
in pregnancy or childbirth 654.4 ☑
causing obstructed labor 660.2 ☑
affecting fetus or newborn 763.1
blood vessel 459.89
bronchus, bronchi 494.0
with acute exacerbation 494.1
calyx (due to obstruction) 593.89
capillaries 448.9
cardiac (acute) (chronic) (*see also* Hypertrophy, cardiac) 429.3
congenital 746.89
valve NEC 746.89
pulmonary 746.09
hypertensive (*see also* Hypertension, heart) 402.90
cavum septi pellucidi 742.4
cecum 564.89
psychogenic 306.4
cervix (uteri) (*see also* Incompetency, cervix)
incomplete, poor, slow
affecting fetus or newborn 763.7
complicating delivery 661.0 ☑
affecting fetus or newborn 763.7
colon 564.7
congenital 751.3
due to mechanical obstruction 560.89
psychogenic 306.4
common bile duct (congenital) 751.69
acquired 576.8
with calculus, choledocholithiasis, or stones — *see* Choledocholithiasis
cystic duct 751.69
acquired (any bile duct) 575.8
duct, mammary 610.4
duodenum 564.89
esophagus 530.89
congenital 750.4
due to
achalasia 530.0
cardiospasm 530.0
Eustachian tube, congenital 744.24
fontanel 756.0
gallbladder 575.8
congenital 751.69
gastric 536.8
acute 536.1
psychogenic 306.4
heart (acute) (chronic) (*see also* Hypertrophy, cardiac) 429.3

Dilatation — *continued*
heart (*see also* Hypertrophy, cardiac) — *continued*
congenital 746.89
hypertensive (*see also* Hypertension, heart) 402.90
valve (*see also* Endocarditis)
congenital 746.89
ileum 564.89
psychogenic 306.4
inguinal rings — *see* Hernia, inguinal
jejunum 564.89
psychogenic 306.4
kidney (calyx) (collecting structures) (cystic) (parenchyma) (pelvis) 593.89
lacrimal passages 375.69
lymphatic vessel 457.1
mammary duct 610.4
Meckel's diverticulum (congenital) 751.0
meningeal vessels, congenital 742.8
myocardium (acute) (chronic) (*see also* Hypertrophy, cardiac) 429.3
organ or site, congenital NEC — *see* Distortion
pancreatic duct 577.8
pelvis, kidney 593.89
pericardium — *see* Pericarditis
pharynx 478.29
prostate 602.8
pulmonary
artery (idiopathic) 417.8
congenital 747.3
valve, congenital 746.09
pupil 379.43
rectum 564.89
renal 593.89
saccule vestibularis, congenital 744.05
salivary gland (duct) 527.8
sphincter ani 564.89
stomach 536.8
acute 536.1
psychogenic 306.4
submaxillary duct 527.8
trachea, congenital 748.3
ureter (idiopathic) 593.89
congenital 753.20
due to obstruction 593.5
urethra (acquired) 599.84
vasomotor 443.9
vein 459.89
ventricular, ventricle (acute) (chronic) (*see also* Hypertrophy, cardiac) 429.3
cerebral, congenital 742.4
hypertensive (*see also* Hypertension, heart) 402.90
venule 459.89
anus — *see* Hemorrhoids
vesical orifice 596.8
Dilated, dilation — *see* Dilatation
Diminished
hearing (acuity) (*see also* Deafness) 389.9
pulse pressure 785.9
vision NEC 369.9
vital capacity 794.2
Diminuta taenia 123.6
Diminution, sense or sensation (cold) (heat) (tactile) (vibratory) — *see also* Disturbance, sensation 782.0
Dimitri-Sturge-Weber disease (encephalocutaneous angiomatosis) 759.6
Dimple
parasacral 685.1
with abscess 685.0
pilonidal 685.1
with abscess 685.0
postanal 685.1
with abscess 685.0
Dioctophyma renale (infection) (infestation) 128.8
Dipetalonemiasis 125.4

☑ Additional Digit Required — Refer to the Tabular List for Digit Selection   ▽ Subterms under main terms may continue to next column or page

2007 ICD-9-CM   ►◄ Revised Text   ● New Line   ▲ Revised Code   **October 2006 · Volume 2 — 83**

Disease, diseased — Disease, diseased

Disease, diseased — *see also* Syndrome
— *continued*

Bird's (oxaluria) 271.8
bird fanciers' 495.2
black lung 500
bladder 596.9
    specified NEC 596.8
bleeder's 286.0
Bloch-Sulzberger (incontinentia pigmenti) 757.33
Blocq's (astasia-abasia) 307.9
blood (-forming organs) 289.9
    specified NEC 289.89
    vessel 459.9
Bloodgood's 610.1
Blount's (tibia vara) 732.4
blue 746.9
Bodechtel-Guttmann (subacute sclerosing panencephalitis) 046.2
Boeck's (sarcoidosis) 135
bone 733.90
    fibrocystic NEC 733.29
        jaw 526.2
    marrow 289.9
    Paget's (osteitis deformans) 731.0
    specified type NEC 733.99
    von Recklinghausen's (osteitis fibrosa cystica) 252.01
Bonfils' — *see* Disease, Hodgkin's
Borna 062.9
Bornholm (epidemic pleurodynia) 074.1
Bostock's (*see also* Fever, hay) 477.9
Bouchard's (myopathic dilatation of the stomach) 536.1
Bouillaud's (rheumatic heart disease) 391.9
Bourneville (-Brissaud) (tuberous sclerosis) 759.5
Bouveret (-Hoffmann) (paroxysmal tachycardia) 427.2
bowel 569.9
    functional 564.9
        psychogenic 306.4
Bowen's (M8081/2) — *see* Neoplasm, skin, in situ
Bozzolo's (multiple myeloma) (M9730/3) 203.0 ☑
Bradley's (epidemic vomiting) 078.82
Brailsford's 732.3
    radius, head 732.3
    tarsal, scaphoid 732.5
Brailsford-Morquio (mucopolysaccharidosis IV) 277.5
brain 348.9
    Alzheimer's 331.0
        with dementia — *see* Alzheimer's, dementia
    arterial, artery 437.9
    arteriosclerotic 437.0
    congenital 742.9
    degenerative — *see* Degeneration, brain
    inflammatory (*see also* Encephalitis)
        late effect — *see* category 326
    organic 348.9
        arteriosclerotic 437.0
    parasitic NEC 123.9
    Pick's 331.11
        with dementia
            with behavioral disturbance 331.11 [294.11]
            without behavioral disturbance 331.11 [294.10]
    senile 331.2
    braziers' 985.8
breast 611.9
    cystic (chronic) 610.1
    fibrocystic 610.1
    inflammatory 611.0
    Paget's (M8540/3) 174.0
    puerperal, postpartum NEC 676.3 ☑
    specified NEC 611.8
Breda's (*see also* Yaws) 102.9

Disease, diseased — *see also* Syndrome
— *continued*

Breisky's (kraurosis vulvae) 624.0
Bretonneau's (diphtheritic malignant angina) 032.0
Bright's (*see also* Nephritis) 583.9
    arteriosclerotic (*see also* Hypertension, kidney) 403.90
Brill's (recrudescent typhus) 081.1
    flea-borne 081.0
    louse-borne 081.1
Brill-Symmers (follicular lymphoma) (M9690/3) 202.0 ☑
Brill-Zinsser (recrudescent typhus) 081.1
Brinton's (leather bottle stomach) (M8142/3) 151.9
Brion-Kayser (*see also* Fever, paratyphoid) 002.9
broad
    beta 272.2
    ligament, noninflammatory 620.9
        specified NEC 620.8
Brocq's 691.8
    meaning
        atopic (diffuse) neurodermatitis 691.8
        dermatitis herpetiformis 694.0
        lichen simplex chronicus 698.3
        parapsoriasis 696.2
        prurigo 698.2
Brocq-Duhring (dermatitis herpetiformis) 694.0
Brodie's (joint) (*see also* Osteomyelitis) 730.1 ☑
bronchi 519.19 ▲
bronchopulmonary 519.19 ▲
bronze (Addison's) 255.4
    tuberculous (*see also* Tuberculosis) 017.6 ☑
Brown-Séquard 344.89
Bruck's 733.99
Bruck-de Lange (Amsterdam dwarf, mental retardation and brachycephaly) 759.89
Bruhl's (splenic anemia with fever) 285.8
Bruton's (X-linked agammaglobulinemia) 279.04
buccal cavity 528.9
Buchanan's (juvenile osteochondrosis, iliac crest) 732.1
Buchman's (osteochondrosis juvenile) 732.1
Budgerigar-Fanciers' 495.2
Büdinger-Ludloff-Läwen 717.89
Buerger's (thromboangiitis obliterans) 443.1
Bürger-Grütz (essential familial hyperlipemia) 272.3
Burns' (lower ulna) 732.3
bursa 727.9
Bury's (erythema elevatum diutinum) 695.89
Buschke's 710.1
Busquet's (*see also* Osteomyelitis) 730.1 ☑
Busse-Buschke (cryptococcosis) 117.5
C₂ (*see also* Alcoholism) 303.9 ☑
Caffey's (infantile cortical hyperostosis) 756.59
caisson 993.3
calculous 592.9
California 114.0
Calvé (-Perthes) (osteochondrosis, femoral capital) 732.1
Camurati-Engelmann (diaphyseal sclerosis) 756.59
Canavan's 330.0
capillaries 448.9
Carapata 087.1
cardiac — *see* Disease, heart
cardiopulmonary, chronic 416.9

Disease, diseased — *see also* Syndrome
— *continued*

cardiorenal (arteriosclerotic) (hepatic) (hypertensive) (vascular) (*see also* Hypertension, cardiorenal) 404.90
cardiovascular (arteriosclerotic) 429.2
    congenital 746.9
    hypertensive (*see also* Hypertension, heart) 402.90
        benign 402.10
        malignant 402.00
    renal (*see also* Hypertension, cardiorenal) 404.90
    syphilitic (asymptomatic) 093.9
carotid gland 259.8
Carrión's (Bartonellosis) 088.0
cartilage NEC 733.90
    specified NEC 733.99
Castellani's 104.8
cat-scratch 078.3
Cavare's (familial periodic paralysis) 359.3
Cazenave's (pemphigus) 694.4
cecum 569.9
celiac (adult) 579.0
    infantile 579.0
cellular tissue NEC 709.9
central core 359.0
cerebellar, cerebellum — *see* Disease, brain
cerebral (*see also* Disease, brain) 348.9
    arterial, artery 437.9
    degenerative — *see* Degeneration, brain
cerebrospinal 349.9
cerebrovascular NEC 437.9
    acute 436
        embolic — *see* Embolism, brain
        late effect — *see* Late effect(s) (of) cerebrovascular disease
        puerperal, postpartum, childbirth 674.0 ☑
        thrombotic — *see* Thrombosis, brain
    arteriosclerotic 437.0
    embolic — *see* Embolism, brain
    ischemic, generalized NEC 437.1
    late effect — *see* Late effect(s) (of) cerebrovascular disease
    occlusive 437.1
    puerperal, postpartum, childbirth 674.0 ☑
    specified type NEC 437.8
    thrombotic — *see* Thrombosis, brain
ceroid storage 272.7
cervix (uteri)
    inflammatory 616.9
        specified NEC 616.89 ▲
    noninflammatory 622.9
        specified NEC 622.8
Chabert's 022.9
Chagas' (*see also* Trypanosomiasis, American) 086.2
Chandler's (osteochondritis dissecans, hip) 732.7
Charcôt-Marie-Tooth 356.1
Charcôt's (joint) 094.0 [713.5]
    spinal cord 094.0
Charlouis' (*see also* Yaws) 102.9
Cheadle (-Möller) (-Barlow) (infantile scurvy) 267
Chédiak-Steinbrinck (-Higashi) (congenital gigantism of peroxidase granules) 288.2
cheek, inner 528.9
chest 519.9
Chiari's (hepatic vein thrombosis) 453.0
Chicago (North American blastomycosis) 116.0
chignon (white piedra) 111.2
chigoe, chigo (jigger) 134.1

Disease, diseased — *see also* Syndrome
— *continued*

childhood granulomatous 288.1
Chinese liver fluke 121.1
chlamydial NEC 078.88
cholecystic (*see also* Disease, gallbladder) 575.9
choroid 363.9
    degenerative (*see also* Degeneration, choroid) 363.40
    hereditary (*see also* Dystrophy, choroid) 363.50
    specified type NEC 363.8
Christian's (chronic histiocytosis X) 277.89
Christian-Weber (nodular nonsuppurative panniculitis) 729.30
Christmas 286.1
ciliary body 364.9
circulatory (system) NEC 459.9
    chronic, maternal, affecting fetus or newborn 760.3
    specified NEC 459.89
    syphilitic 093.9
        congenital 090.5
Civatte's (poikiloderma) 709.09
climacteric 627.2
    male 608.89
coagulation factor deficiency (congenital) (*see also* Defect, coagulation) 286.9
Coats' 362.12
coccidioidal pulmonary 114.5
    acute 114.0
    chronic 114.4
    primary 114.0
    residual 114.4
Cockayne's (microcephaly and dwarfism) 759.89
Cogan's 370.52
cold
    agglutinin 283.0
        or hemoglobinuria 283.0
        paroxysmal (cold) (nocturnal) 283.2
    hemagglutinin (chronic) 283.0
collagen NEC 710.9
    nonvascular 710.9
    specified NEC 710.8
    vascular (allergic) (*see also* Angiitis, hypersensitivity) 446.20
colon 569.9
    functional 564.9
        congenital 751.3
    ischemic 557.0
combined system (of spinal cord) 266.2 [336.2]
    with anemia (pernicious) 281.0 [336.2]
compressed air 993.3
Concato's (pericardial polyserositis) 423.2
    peritoneal 568.82
    pleural — *see* Pleurisy
congenital NEC 799.89
conjunctiva 372.9
    chlamydial 077.98
        specified NEC 077.8
    viral 077.99
        specified NEC 077.8
connective tissue, diffuse (*see also* Disease, collagen) 710.9
Conor and Bruch's (boutonneuse fever) 082.1
Conradi (-Hünermann) 756.59
Cooley's (erythroblastic anemia) 282.49
Cooper's 610.1
Corbus' 607.1
cork-handlers' 495.3
cornea (*see also* Keratopathy) 371.9
coronary (*see also* Ischemia, heart) 414.9
    congenital 746.85
    ostial, syphilitic 093.20

☑ Additional Digit Required — Refer to the Tabular List for Digit Selection
▽ Subterms under main terms may continue to next column or page

84 — Volume 2 • October 2006   ▶◀ Revised Text   ● New Line   ▲ Revised Code   *2007 ICD-9-CM*

Disease, diseased — *see also* Syndrome
— *continued*

coronary (*see also* Ischemia, heart) —
continued
ostial, syphilitic — *continued*
aortic 093.22
mitral 093.21
pulmonary 093.24
tricuspid 093.23
Corrigan's — *see* Insufficiency, aortic
Cotugno's 724.3
Coxsackie (virus) NEC 074.8
cranial nerve NEC 352.9
Creutzfeldt-Jakob (new variant) 046.1
with dementia
with behavioral disturbance
046.1 *[294.11]*
without behavioral disturbance
046.1 *[294.10]*
Crigler-Najjar (congenital hyperbilirubinemia) 277.4
Crocq's (acrocyanosis) 443.89
Crohn's (intestine) (*see also* Enteritis,
regional) 555.9
Crouzon's (craniofacial dysostosis)
756.0
Cruchet's (encephalitis lethargica)
049.8
Cruveilhier's 335.21
Cruz-Chagas (*see also* Trypanosomiasis, American) 086.2
crystal deposition (*see also* Arthritis,
due to, crystals) 712.9 ☑
Csillag's (lichen sclerosus et atrophicus) 701.0
Curschmann's 359.2
Cushing's (pituitary basophilism)
255.0
cystic
breast (chronic) 610.1
kidney, congenital (*see also* Cystic,
disease, kidney) 753.10
liver, congenital 751.62
lung 518.89
congenital 748.4
pancreas 577.2
congenital 751.7
renal, congenital (*see also* Cystic,
disease, kidney) 753.10
semilunar cartilage 717.5
cysticercus 123.1
cystine storage (with renal sclerosis)
270.0
cytomegalic inclusion (generalized)
078.5
with
pneumonia 078.5 *[484.1]*
congenital 771.1
Daae (-Finsen) (epidemic pleurodynia)
074.1
dancing 297.8
Danielssen's (anesthetic leprosy)
030.1
Darier's (congenital) (keratosis follicularis) 757.39
erythema annulare centrifugum
695.0
vitamin A deficiency 264.8
Darling's (histoplasmosis) (*see also*
Histoplasmosis, American)
115.00
Davies' 425.0
de Beurmann-Gougerot (sporotrichosis) 117.1
Débove's (splenomegaly) 789.2
deer fly (*see also* Tularemia) 021.9
deficiency 269.9
degenerative (*see also* Degeneration)
disc — *see* Degeneration, intervertebral disc
Degos' 447.8
Déjérine (-Sottas) 356.0
Déleage's 359.89
demyelinating, demyelinizing (brain
stem) (central nervous system)
341.9

Disease, diseased — *see also* Syndrome
— *continued*

demyelinating, demyelinizing —
continued
multiple sclerosis 340
specified NEC 341.8
de Quervain's (tendon sheath) 727.04
thyroid (subacute granulomatous
thyroiditis) 245.1
Dercum's (adiposis dolorosa) 272.8
Deutschländer's — *see* Fracture, foot
Devergie's (pityriasis rubra pilaris)
696.4
Devic's 341.0
diaphorase deficiency 289.7
diaphragm 519.4
diarrheal, infectious 009.2
diatomaceous earth 502
Diaz's (osteochondrosis astragalus)
732.5
digestive system 569.9
Di Guglielmo's (erythemic myelosis)
(M9841/3) 207.0 ☑
Dimitri-Sturge-Weber (encephalocutaneous angiomatosis) 759.6
disc, degenerative — *see* Degeneration, intervertebral disc
discogenic (*see also* Disease, intervertebral disc) 722.90
diverticular — *see* Diverticula
Down's (mongolism) 758.0
Dubini's (electric chorea) 049.8
Dubois' (thymus gland) 090.5
Duchenne's 094.0
locomotor ataxia 094.0
muscular dystrophy 359.1
paralysis 335.22
pseudohypertrophy, muscles 359.1
Duchenne-Griesinger 359.1
ductless glands 259.9
Duhring's (dermatitis herpetiformis)
694.0
Dukes (-Filatov) 057.8
duodenum NEC 537.9
specified NEC 537.89
Duplay's 726.2
Dupré's (meningism) 781.6
Dupuytren's (muscle contracture)
728.6
Durand-Nicolas-Favre (climatic bubo)
099.1
Duroziez's (congenital mitral stenosis)
746.5
Dutton's (trypanosomiasis) 086.9
Eales' 362.18
ear (chronic) (inner) NEC 388.9
middle 385.9
adhesive (*see also* Adhesions,
middle ear) 385.10
specified NEC 385.89
Eberth's (typhoid fever) 002.0
Ebstein's
heart 746.2
meaning diabetes 250.4 ☑ *[581.81]*
Echinococcus (*see also* Echinococcus)
122.9
ECHO virus NEC 078.89
Economo's (encephalitis lethargica)
049.8
Eddowes' (brittle bones and blue
sclera) 756.51
Edsall's 992.2
Eichstedt's (pityriasis versicolor) 111.0
Ellis-van Creveld (chondroectodermal
dysplasia) 756.55
endocardium — *see* Endocarditis
endocrine glands or system NEC
259.9
specified NEC 259.8
endomyocardial, idiopathic mural
425.2
Engelmann's (diaphyseal sclerosis)
756.59
Engel-von Recklinghausen (osteitis fibrosa cystica) 252.01
English (rickets) 268.0

Disease, diseased — *see also* Syndrome
— *continued*

Engman's (infectious eczematoid dermatitis) 690.8
enteroviral, enterovirus NEC 078.89
central nervous system NEC 048
epidemic NEC 136.9
epididymis 608.9
epigastric, functional 536.9
psychogenic 306.4
Erb (-Landouzy) 359.1
Erb-Goldflam 358.00
Erichsen's (railway spine) 300.16
esophagus 530.9
functional 530.5
psychogenic 306.4
Eulenburg's (congenital paramyotonia)
359.2
Eustachian tube 381.9
Evans' (thrombocytopenic purpura)
287.32
external auditory canal 380.9
extrapyramidal NEC 333.90
eye 379.90
anterior chamber 364.9
inflammatory NEC 364.3
muscle 378.9
eyeball 360.9
eyelid 374.9
eyeworm of Africa 125.2
Fabry's (angiokeratoma corporis diffusum) 272.7
facial nerve (seventh) 351.9
newborn 767.5
Fahr-Volhard (malignant nephrosclerosis) 403.00
fallopian tube, noninflammatory 620.9
specified NEC 620.8
familial periodic 277.31   ▲
paralysis 359.3
Fanconi's (congenital pancytopenia)
284.09   ▲
Farber's (disseminated lipogranulomatosis) 272.8
fascia 728.9
inflammatory 728.9
Fauchard's (periodontitis) 523.40   ▲
Favre-Durand-Nicolas (climatic bubo)
099.1
Favre-Racouchot (elastoidosis cutanea
nodularis) 701.8
Fede's 529.0
Feer's 985.0
Felix's (juvenile osteochondrosis, hip)
732.1
Fenwick's (gastric atrophy) 537.89
Fernels' (aortic aneurysm) 441.9
fibrocaseous, of lung (*see also* Tuberculosis, pulmonary) 011.9 ☑
fibrocystic (*see also* Fibrocystic, disease)
newborn 277.01
Fiedler's (leptospiral jaundice) 100.0
fifth 057.0
Filatoff's (infectious mononucleosis)
075
Filatov's (infectious mononucleosis)
075
file-cutters' 984.9
specified type of lead — *see* Table
of Drugs and Chemicals
filterable virus NEC 078.89
fish skin 757.1
acquired 701.1
Flajani (-Basedow) (exophthalmic goiter) 242.0 ☑
Flatau-Schilder 341.1
flax-dressers' 504
Fleischner's 732.3
flint 502
fluke — *see* Infestation, fluke
Følling's (phenylketonuria) 270.1
foot and mouth 078.4
foot process 581.3
Forbes' (glycogenosis III) 271.0

Disease, diseased — *see also* Syndrome
— *continued*

Fordyce's (ectopic sebaceous glands)
(mouth) 750.26
Fordyce-Fox (apocrine miliaria) 705.82
Fothergill's
meaning scarlatina anginosa 034.1
neuralgia (*see also* Neuralgia,
trigeminal) 350.1
Fournier's 608.83
fourth 057.8
Fox (-Fordyce) (apocrine miliaria)
705.82
Francis' (*see also* Tularemia) 021.9
Franklin's (heavy chain) 273.2
Frei's (climatic bubo) 099.1
Freiberg's (flattening metatarsal) 732.5
Friedländer's (endarteritis obliterans)
— *see* Arteriosclerosis
Friedreich's
combined systemic or ataxia 334.0
facial hemihypertrophy 756.0
myoclonia 333.2
Fröhlich's (adiposogenital dystrophy)
253.8
Frommel's 676.6 ☑
frontal sinus (chronic) 473.1
acute 461.1
Fuller's earth 502
fungus, fungous NEC 117.9
Gaisböck's (polycythemia hypertonica)
289.0
gallbladder 575.9
congenital 751.60
Gamna's (siderotic splenomegaly)
289.51
Gamstorp's (adynamia episodica
hereditaria) 359.3
Gandy-Nanta (siderotic splenomegaly)
289.51
Gannister (occupational) 502
Garré's (*see also* Osteomyelitis)
730.1 ☑
gastric (*see also* Disease, stomach)
537.9
gastrointestinal (tract) 569.9
amyloid 277.39   ▲
functional 536.9
psychogenic 306.4
Gaucher's (adult) (cerebroside lipidosis) (infantile) 272.7
Gayet's (superior hemorrhagic polioencephalitis) 265.1
Gee (-Herter) (-Heubner) (-Thaysen)
(nontropical sprue) 579.0
generalized neoplastic (M8000/6)
199.0
genital organs NEC
female 629.9
specified NEC 629.89   ▲
male 608.9
Gerhardt's (erythromelalgia) 443.82
Gerlier's (epidemic vertigo) 078.81
Gibert's (pityriasis rosea) 696.3
Gibney's (perispondylitis) 720.9
Gierke's (glycogenosis I) 271.0
Gilbert's (familial nonhemolytic jaundice) 277.4
Gilchrist's (North American blastomycosis) 116.0
Gilford (-Hutchinson) (progeria) 259.8
Gilles de la Tourette's (motor-verbal
tic) 307.23
Giovannini's 117.9
gland (lymph) 289.9
Glanzmann's (hereditary hemorrhagic
thrombasthenia) 287.1
glassblowers' 527.1
Glénard's (enteroptosis) 569.89
Glisson's (*see also* Rickets) 268.0
glomerular
membranous, idiopathic 581.1
minimal change 581.3

☑ Additional Digit Required — Refer to the Tabular List for Digit Selection   ▽ Subterms under main terms may continue to next column or page

2007 ICD-9-CM   ▶◀ Revised Text   ● New Line   ▲ Revised Code   **October 2006 · Volume 2 — 85**

Disease, diseased — Disease, diseased

Disease, diseased — *see also* Syndrome
— *continued*
  glycogen storage (Andersen's) (Cori
    types 1-7) (Forbes') (McArdle-
    Schmid-Pearson) (Pompe's)
    (types I-VII) 271.0
    cardiac 271.0 *[425.7]*
    generalized 271.0
    glucose–6–phosphatase deficiency
     271.0
    heart 271.0 *[425.7]*
    hepatorenal 271.0
    liver and kidneys 271.0
    myocardium 271.0 *[425.7]*
    von Gierke's (glycogenosis I) 271.0
  Goldflam-Erb 358.00
  Goldscheider's (epidermolysis bullosa)
   757.39
  Goldstein's (familial hemorrhagic
   telangiectasia) 448.0
  gonococcal NEC 098.0
  Goodall's (epidemic vomiting) 078.82
  Gordon's (exudative enteropathy)
   579.8
  Gougerot's (trisymptomatic) 709.1
  Gougerot-Carteaud (confluent reticulate papillomatosis) 701.8
  Gougerot-Hailey-Hailey (benign familial chronic pemphigus) 757.39
  graft-versus-host (bone marrow)
   996.85
    due to organ transplant NEC — *see*
     Complications, transplant,
     organ
  grain-handlers' 495.8
  Grancher's (splenopneumonia) — *see*
   Pneumonia
  granulomatous (childhood) (chronic)
   288.1
  graphite lung 503
  Graves' (exophthalmic goiter) 242.0 ☑
  Greenfield's 330.0
  green monkey 078.89
  Griesinger's (*see also* Ancylostomiasis)
   126.9
  grinders' 502
  Grisel's 723.5
  Gruby's (tinea tonsurans) 110.0
  Guertin's (electric chorea) 049.8
  Guillain-Barré 357.0
  Guinon's (motor-verbal tic) 307.23
  Gull's (thyroid atrophy with myxede-
   ma) 244.8
  Gull and Sutton's — *see* Hyperten-
   sion, kidney
  gum NEC 523.9
  Günther's (congenital erythropoietic
   porphyria) 277.1
  gynecological 629.9
   specified NEC 629.89   ▲
  H 270.0
  Haas' 732.3
  Habermann's (acute parapsoriasis
   varioliformis) 696.2
  Haff 985.1
  Hageman (congenital factor XII defi-
   ciency) (*see also* Defect, congenital) 286.3
  Haglund's (osteochondrosis os tibiale
   externum) 732.5
  Hagner's (hypertrophic pulmonary
   osteoarthropathy) 731.2
  Hailey-Hailey (benign familial chronic
   pemphigus) 757.39
  hair (follicles) NEC 704.9
   specified type NEC 704.8
  Hallervorden-Spatz 333.0
  Hallopeau's (lichen sclerosus et atroph-
   icus) 701.0
  Hamman's (spontaneous mediastinal
   emphysema) 518.1
  hand, foot, and mouth 074.3
  Hand-Schüller-Christian (chronic
   histiocytosis X) 277.89
  Hanot's — *see* Cirrhosis, biliary
  Hansen's (leprosy) 030.9

Disease, diseased — *see also* Syndrome
— *continued*
  Hansen's — *continued*
   benign form 030.1
   malignant form 030.0
  Harada's 363.22
  Harley's (intermittent hemoglobinuria)
   283.2
  Hartnup (pellagra-cerebellar ataxia-
   renal aminoaciduria) 270.0
  Hart's (pellagra-cerebellar ataxia-renal
   aminoaciduria) 270.0
  Hashimoto's (struma lymphomatosa)
   245.2
  Hb — *see* Disease, hemoglobin
  heart (organic) 429.9
   with
    acute pulmonary edema (*see*
     also Failure, ventricular,
     left) 428.1
    hypertensive 402.91
     with renal failure 404.93
     benign 402.11
      with renal failure
       404.13
     malignant 402.01
      with renal failure
       404.03
    kidney disease — *see* Hyperten-
     sion, cardiorenal
    rheumatic fever (conditions
     classifiable to 390)
     active 391.9
      with chorea 392.0
     inactive or quiescent (with
      chorea) 398.90
   amyloid 277.39 *[425.7]*   ▲
   aortic (valve) (*see also* Endocardi-
    tis, aortic) 424.1
   arteriosclerotic or sclerotic (mini-
    mal) (senile) — *see* Arte-
    riosclerosis, coronary
   artery, arterial — *see* Arteriosclero-
    sis, coronary
   atherosclerotic — *see* Arteriosclero-
    sis, coronary
   beer drinkers' 425.5
   beriberi 265.0 *[425.7]*
   black 416.0
   congenital NEC 746.9
    cyanotic 746.9
    maternal, affecting fetus or
     newborn 760.3
    specified type NEC 746.89
   congestive (*see also* Failure, heart)
    428.0
   coronary 414.9
   cryptogenic 429.9
   due to
    amyloidosis 277.39 *[425.7]*   ▲
    beriberi 265.0 *[425.7]*
    cardiac glycogenosis
     271.0 *[425.7]*
    Friedreich's ataxia 334.0 *[425.8]*
    gout 274.82
    mucopolysaccharidosis
     277.5 *[425.7]*
    myotonia atrophica
     359.2 *[425.8]*
    progressive muscular dystrophy
     359.1 *[425.8]*
    sarcoidosis 135 *[425.8]*
   fetal 746.9
    inflammatory 746.89
   fibroid (*see also* Myocarditis) 429.0
   functional 427.9
    postoperative 997.1
    psychogenic 306.2
   glycogen storage 271.0 *[425.7]*
   gonococcal NEC 098.85
   gouty 274.82
   hypertensive (*see also* Hyperten-
    sion, heart) 402.90
    benign 402.10
    malignant 402.00

Disease, diseased — *see also* Syndrome
— *continued*
  heart — *continued*
   hyperthyroid (*see also* Hyperthy-
    roidism) 242.9 ☑ *[425.7]*
   incompletely diagnosed — *see* Dis-
    ease, heart
   ischemic (chronic) (*see also* Is-
    chemia, heart) 414.9
    acute (*see also* Infarct, myocardi-
     um) 410.9 ☑
     without myocardial infarction
      411.89
      with coronary (artery) oc-
       clusion 411.81
    asymptomatic 412
    diagnosed on ECG or other spe-
     cial investigation but cur-
     rently presenting no
     symptoms 412
   kyphoscoliotic 416.1
   mitral (*see also* Endocarditis, mi-
    tral) 394.9
   muscular (*see also* Degeneration,
    myocardial) 429.1
   postpartum 674.8 ☑
   psychogenic (functional) 306.2
   pulmonary (chronic) 416.9
    acute 415.0
    specified NEC 416.8
   rheumatic (chronic) (inactive) (old)
    (quiescent) (with chorea)
    398.90
    active or acute 391.9
     with chorea (active)
      (rheumatic) (Syden-
      ham's) 392.0
    specified type NEC 391.8
   maternal, affecting fetus or
    newborn 760.3
   rheumatoid — *see* Arthritis,
    rheumatoid
   sclerotic — *see* Arteriosclerosis,
    coronary
   senile (*see also* Myocarditis) 429.0
   specified type NEC 429.89
   syphilitic 093.89
    aortic 093.1
     aneurysm 093.0
    asymptomatic 093.89
    congenital 090.5
   thyroid (gland) (*see also* Hyper-
    thyroidism) 242.9 ☑ *[425.7]*
   thyrotoxic (*see also* Thyrotoxicosis)
    242.9 ☑ *[425.7]*
   tuberculous (*see also* Tuberculosis)
    017.9 ☑ *[425.8]*
   valve, valvular (obstructive) (regur-
    gitant) (*see also* Endocarditis)
    congenital NEC (*see also*
     Anomaly, heart, valve)
     746.9
    pulmonary 746.00
    specified type NEC 746.89
   vascular — *see* Disease, cardiovas-
    cular
  heavy-chain (gamma G) 273.2
  Heberden's 715.04
  Hebra's
   dermatitis exfoliativa 695.89
   erythema multiforme exudativum
    695.1
   pityriasis
    maculata et circinata 696.3
    rubra 695.89
    pilaris 696.4
   prurigo 698.2
  Heerfordt's (uveoparotitis) 135
  Heidenhain's 290.10
   with dementia 290.10
  Heilmeyer-Schöner (M9842/3)
   207.1 ☑
  Heine-Medin (*see also* Poliomyelitis)
   045.9 ☑
  Heller's (*see also* Psychosis, childhood)
   299.1 ☑

Disease, diseased — *see also* Syndrome
— *continued*
  Heller-Döhle (syphilitic aortitis) 093.1
  hematopoietic organs 289.9
  hemoglobin (Hb) 282.7
   with thalassemia 282.49
   abnormal (mixed) NEC 282.7
    with thalassemia 282.49
   AS genotype 282.5
   Bart's 282.49
   C (Hb-C) 282.7
    with other abnormal hemoglobin
     NEC 282.7
    elliptocytosis 282.7
    Hb-S (without crisis) 282.63
     with
      crisis 282.64
      vaso-occlusive pain
       282.64
    sickle-cell (without crisis)
     282.63
     with
      crisis 282.64
      vaso-occlusive pain
       282.64
    thalassemia 282.49
   constant spring 282.7
   D (Hb-D) 282.7
    with other abnormal hemoglobin
     NEC 282.7
    Hb-S (without crisis) 282.68
     with crisis 282.69
    sickle-cell (without crisis)
     282.68
     with crisis 282.69
    thalassemia 282.49
   E (Hb-E) 282.7
    with other abnormal hemoglobin
     NEC 282.7
    Hb-S (without crisis) 282.68
     with crisis 282.69
    sickle-cell (without crisis)
     282.68
     with crisis 282.69
    thalassemia 282.49
   elliptocytosis 282.7
   F (Hb-F) 282.7
   G (Hb-G) 282.7
   H (Hb-H) 282.49
   hereditary persistence, fetal (HPFH)
    ("Swiss variety") 282.7
   high fetal gene 282.7
   I thalassemia 282.49
   M 289.7
   S (*see also* Disease, sickle-cell, Hb-
    S)
    thalassemia (without crisis)
     282.41
     with
      crisis 282.42
      vaso-occlusive pain
       282.42
   spherocytosis 282.7
   unstable, hemolytic 282.7
   Zurich (Hb-Zurich) 282.7
  hemolytic (fetus) (newborn) 773.2
   autoimmune (cold type) (warm
    type) 283.0
   due to or with
    incompatibility
     ABO (blood group) 773.1
     blood (group) (Duffy) (Kell)
      (Kidd) (Lewis) (M) (S)
      NEC 773.2
     Rh (blood group) (factor)
      773.0
     Rh negative mother 773.0
   unstable hemoglobin 282.7
  hemorrhagic 287.9
   newborn 776.0
  Henoch (-Schönlein) (purpura nervosa)
   287.0
  hepatic — *see* Disease, liver
  hepatolenticular 275.1
  heredodegenerative NEC
   brain 331.89

☑ Additional Digit Required — Refer to the Tabular List for Digit Selection   ▽ Subterms under main terms may continue to next column or page

86 — Volume 2 • October 2006   ▶◀ Revised Text   ● New Line   ▲ Revised Code   *2007 ICD-9-CM*

Disease, diseased — *see also* Syndrome — *continued*

heredodegenerative — *continued*
  spinal cord 336.8
Hers' (glycogenosis VI) 271.0
Herter (-Gee) (-Heubner) (nontropical sprue) 579.0
Herxheimer's (diffuse idiopathic cutaneous atrophy) 701.8
Heubner's 094.89
Heubner-Herter (nontropical sprue) 579.0
high fetal gene or hemoglobin thalassemia 282.49
Hildenbrand's (typhus) 081.9
hip (joint) NEC 719.95
  congenital 755.63
  suppurative 711.05
  tuberculous (*see also* Tuberculosis) 015.1 ☑ *[730.85]*
Hippel's (retinocerebral angiomatosis) 759.6
Hirschfeld's (acute diabetes mellitus) (*see also* Diabetes) 250.0 ☑
Hirschsprung's (congenital megacolon) 751.3
His (-Werner) (trench fever) 083.1
HIV 042
Hodgkin's (M9650/3) 201.9 ☑

Note — *Use the following fifth-digit subclassification with category 201:*

0   *unspecified site*
1   *lymph nodes of head, face, and neck*
2   *intrathoracic lymph nodes*
3   *intra-abdominal lymph nodes*
4   *lymph nodes of axilla and upper limb*
5   *lymph nodes of inguinal region and lower limb*
6   *intrapelvic lymph nodes*
7   *spleen*
8   *lymph nodes of multiple sites*

  lymphocytic
    depletion (M9653/3) 201.7 ☑
    diffuse fibrosis (M9654/3) 201.7 ☑
    reticular type (M9655/3) 201.7 ☑
    predominance (M9651/3) 201.4 ☑
  lymphocytic-histiocytic predominance (M9651/3) 201.4 ☑
  mixed cellularity (M9652/3) 201.6 ☑
  nodular sclerosis (M9656/3) 201.5 ☑
    cellular phase (M9657/3) 201.5 ☑
Hodgson's 441.9
  ruptured 441.5
Hoffa (-Kastert) (liposynovitis prepatellaris) 272.8
Holla (*see also* Spherocytosis) 282.0
homozygous-Hb-S 282.61
hoof and mouth 078.4
hookworm (*see also* Ancylostomiasis) 126.9
Horton's (temporal arteritis) 446.5
host-versus-graft (immune or nonimmune cause) 996.80
  bone marrow 996.85
  heart 996.83
  intestines 996.87
  kidney 996.81
  liver 996.82
  lung 996.84
  pancreas 996.86
  specified NEC 996.89

Disease, diseased — *see also* Syndrome — *continued*

HPFH (hereditary persistence of fetal hemoglobin) ("Swiss variety") 282.7
Huchard's disease (continued arterial hypertension) 401.9
Huguier's (uterine fibroma) 218.9
human immunodeficiency (virus) 042
hunger 251.1
Hunt's
  dyssynergia cerebellaris myoclonica 334.2
  herpetic geniculate ganglionitis 053.11
Huntington's 333.4
Huppert's (multiple myeloma) (M9730/3) 203.0 ☑
Hurler's (mucopolysaccharidosis I) 277.5
Hutchinson-Boeck (sarcoidosis) 135
Hutchinson-Gilford (progeria) 259.8
Hutchinson's, meaning
  angioma serpiginosum 709.1
  cheiropompholyx 705.81
  prurigo estivalis 692.72
hyaline (diffuse) (generalized) 728.9
  membrane (lung) (newborn) 769
hydatid (*see also* Echinococcus) 122.9
Hyde's (prurigo nodularis) 698.3
hyperkinetic (*see also* Hyperkinesia) 314.9
  heart 429.82
hypertensive (*see also* Hypertension) 401.9
hypophysis 253.9
  hyperfunction 253.1
  hypofunction 253.2
Iceland (epidemic neuromyasthenia) 049.8
I cell 272.7
ill-defined 799.89
immunologic NEC 279.9
immunoproliferative 203.8 ☑
inclusion 078.5
  salivary gland 078.5
infancy, early NEC 779.9
infective NEC 136.9
inguinal gland 289.9
internal semilunar cartilage, cystic 717.5
intervertebral disc 722.90
  with myelopathy 722.70
  cervical, cervicothoracic 722.91
    with myelopathy 722.71
  lumbar, lumbosacral 722.93
    with myelopathy 722.73
  thoracic, thoracolumbar 722.92
    with myelopathy 722.72
intestine 569.9
  functional 564.9
    congenital 751.3
    psychogenic 306.4
  lardaceous 277.39 ▲
  organic 569.9
  protozoal NEC 007.9
iris 364.9
iron
  metabolism 275.0
  storage 275.0
Isambert's (*see also* Tuberculosis, larynx) 012.3 ☑
Iselin's (osteochondrosis, fifth metatarsal) 732.5
island (scrub typhus) 081.2
itai-itai 985.5
Jadassohn's (maculopapular erythroderma) 696.2
Jadassohn-Pellizari's (anetoderma) 701.3
Jakob-Creutzfeldt (new variant) 046.1
  with dementia
    with behavioral disturbance 046.1 *[294.11]*
    without behavioral disturbance 046.1 *[294.10]*

Disease, diseased — *see also* Syndrome — *continued*

Jaksch (-Luzet) (pseudoleukemia infantum) 285.8
Janet's 300.89
Jansky-Bielschowsky 330.1
jaw NEC 526.9
  fibrocystic 526.2
Jensen's 363.05
Jeune's (asphyxiating thoracic dystrophy) 756.4
jigger 134.1
Johnson-Stevens (erythema multiforme exudativum) 695.1
joint NEC 719.9 ☑
  ankle 719.97
  Charcôt 094.0 *[713.5]*
  degenerative (*see also* Osteoarthrosis) 715.9 ☑
    multiple 715.09
    spine (*see also* Spondylosis) 721.90
  elbow 719.92
  foot 719.97
  hand 719.94
  hip 719.95
  hypertrophic (chronic) (degenerative) (*see also* Osteoarthrosis) 715.9 ☑
    spine (*see also* Spondylosis) 721.90
  knee 719.96
  Luschka 721.90
  multiple sites 719.99
  pelvic region 719.95
  sacroiliac 724.6
  shoulder (region) 719.91
  specified site NEC 719.98
  spine NEC 724.9
    pseudarthrosis following fusion 733.82
    sacroiliac 724.6
  wrist 719.93
Jourdain's (acute gingivitis) 523.00 ▲
Jüngling's (sarcoidosis) 135
Kahler (-Bozzolo) (multiple myeloma) (M9730/3) 203.0 ☑
Kalischer's 759.6
Kaposi's 757.33
  lichen ruber 697.8
    acuminatus 696.4
    moniliformis 697.8
  xeroderma pigmentosum 757.33
Kaschin-Beck (endemic polyarthritis) 716.00
  ankle 716.07
  arm 716.02
    lower (and wrist) 716.03
    upper (and elbow) 716.02
  foot (and ankle) 716.07
  forearm (and wrist) 716.03
  hand 716.04
  leg 716.06
    lower 716.06
    upper 716.05
  multiple sites 716.09
  pelvic region (hip) (thigh) 716.05
  shoulder region 716.01
  specified site NEC 716.08
Katayama 120.2
Kawasaki 446.1
Kedani (scrub typhus) 081.2
kidney (functional) (pelvis) (*see also* Disease, renal) 593.9
  chronic
    requiring chronic dialysis 585.6 ●
    stage
      I 585.1
      II (mild) 585.2
      III (moderate) 585.3
      IV (severe) 585.4
      V 585.5
  cystic (congenital) 753.10
    multiple 753.19

Disease, diseased — *see also* Syndrome — *continued*

kidney (*see also* Disease, renal) — *continued*
  cystic — *continued*
    single 753.11
    specified NEC 753.19
  fibrocystic (congenital) 753.19
  in gout 274.10
  polycystic (congenital) 753.12
    adult type (APKD) 753.13
    autosomal dominant 753.13
    autosomal recessive 753.14
    childhood type (CPKD) 753.14
    infantile type 753.14
Kienböck's (carpal lunate) (wrist) 732.3
Kimmelstiel (-Wilson) (intercapillary glomerulosclerosis) 250.4 ☑ *[581.81]*
Kinnier Wilson's (hepatolenticular degeneration) 275.1
kissing 075
Kleb's (*see also* Nephritis) 583.9
Klinger's 446.4
Klippel's 723.8
Klippel-Feil (brevicollis) 756.16
knight's 911.1
Köbner's (epidermolysis bullosa) 757.39
Koenig-Wichmann (pemphigus) 694.4
Köhler's
  first (osteoarthrosis juvenilis) 732.5
  second (Freiberg's infraction, metatarsal head) 732.5
  patellar 732.4
  tarsal navicular (bone) (osteoarthrosis juvenilis) 732.5
Köhler-Freiberg (infraction, metatarsal head) 732.5
Köhler-Mouchet (osteoarthrosis juvenilis) 732.5
Köhler-Pellegrini-Stieda (calcification, knee joint) 726.62
Kok 759.89
König's (osteochondritis dissecans) 732.7
Korsakoff's (nonalcoholic) 294.0
  alcoholic 291.1
Kostmann's (infantile genetic agranulocytosis) 288.01 ▲
Krabbe's 330.0
Kraepelin-Morel (*see also* Schizophrenia) 295.9 ☑
Kraft-Weber-Dimitri 759.6
Kufs' 330.1
Kugelberg-Welander 335.11
Kuhnt-Junius 362.52
Kümmell's (-Verneuil) (spondylitis) 721.7
Kundrat's (lymphosarcoma) 200.1 ☑
kuru 046.0
Kussmaul (-Meier) (polyarteritis nodosa) 446.0
Kyasanur Forest 065.2
Kyrle's (hyperkeratosis follicularis in cutem penetrans) 701.1
labia
  inflammatory 616.9
    specified NEC 616.89 ▲
  noninflammatory 624.9
    specified NEC 624.8
labyrinth, ear 386.8
lacrimal system (apparatus) (passages) 375.9
  gland 375.00
  specified NEC 375.89
Lafora's 333.2
Lagleyze-von Hippel (retinocerebral angiomatosis) 759.6
Lancereaux-Mathieu (leptospiral jaundice) 100.0
Landry's 357.0
Lane's 569.89
lardaceous (any site) 277.39 ▲

☑ Additional Digit Required — Refer to the Tabular List for Digit Selection   ▽ Subterms under main terms may continue to next column or page

2007 ICD-9-CM   ▶◀ Revised Text   ● New Line   ▲ Revised Code   October 2006 · Volume 2 — 87

Disease, diseased — *see also* Syndrome
— *continued*

Larrey-Weil (leptospiral jaundice) 100.0
Larsen (-Johansson) (juvenile osteopathia patellae) 732.4
larynx 478.70
Lasègue's (persecution mania) 297.9
Leber's 377.16
Lederer's (acquired infectious hemolytic anemia) 283.19
Legg's (capital femoral osteochondrosis) 732.1
Legg-Calvé-Perthes (capital femoral osteochondrosis) 732.1
Legg-Calvé-Waldenström (femoral capital osteochondrosis) 732.1
Legg-Perthes (femoral capital osteochondrosis) 732.1
Legionnaires' 482.84
Leigh's 330.8
Leiner's (exfoliative dermatitis) 695.89
Leloir's (lupus erythematosus) 695.4
Lenegre's 426.0
lens (eye) 379.39
Leriche's (osteoporosis, posttraumatic) 733.7
Letterer-Siwe (acute histiocytosis X) (M9722/3) 202.5 ☑
Lev's (acquired complete heart block) 426.0
Lewandowski's (*see also* Tuberculosis) 017.0 ☑
Lewandowski-Lutz (epidermodysplasia verruciformis) 078.19
Lewy body 331.82
  with dementia
    with behavioral disturbance 331.82 [294.11]
    without behavioral disturbance 331.82 [294.10]
Leyden's (periodic vomiting) 536.2
Libman-Sacks (verrucous endocarditis) 710.0 [424.91]
Lichtheim's (subacute combined sclerosis with pernicious anemia) 281.0 [336.2]
ligament 728.9
light chain 203.0 ☑
Lightwood's (renal tubular acidosis) 588.89
Lignac's (cystinosis) 270.0
Lindau's (retinocerebral angiomatosis) 759.6
Lindau-von Hippel (angiomatosis retinocerebellosa) 759.6
lip NEC 528.5
lipidosis 272.7
lipoid storage NEC 272.7
Lipschütz's 616.50
Little's — *see* Palsy, cerebral
liver 573.9
  alcoholic 571.3
    acute 571.1
    chronic 571.3
  chronic 571.9
    alcoholic 571.3
  cystic, congenital 751.62
  drug-induced 573.3
  due to
    chemicals 573.3
    fluorinated agents 573.3
    hypersensitivity drugs 573.3
    isoniazids 573.3
  fibrocystic (congenital) 751.62
  glycogen storage 271.0
  organic 573.9
  polycystic (congenital) 751.62
Lobo's (keloid blastomycosis) 116.2
Lobstein's (brittle bones and blue sclera) 756.51
locomotor system 334.9
Lorain's (pituitary dwarfism) 253.3
Lou Gehrig's 335.20
Lucas-Championnière (fibrinous bronchitis) 466.0

Disease, diseased — *see also* Syndrome
— *continued*

Ludwig's (submaxillary cellulitis) 528.3
luetic — *see* Syphilis
lumbosacral region 724.6
lung NEC 518.89
  black 500
  congenital 748.60
  cystic 518.89
    congenital 748.4
  fibroid (chronic) (*see also* Fibrosis, lung) 515
  fluke 121.2
    oriental 121.2
  in
    amyloidosis 277.39 [517.8] ▲
    polymyositis 710.4 [517.8]
    sarcoidosis 135 [517.8]
    Sjögren's syndrome 710.2 [517.8]
    syphilis 095.1
    systemic lupus erythematosus 710.0 [517.8]
    systemic sclerosis 710.1 [517.2]
  interstitial (chronic) 515
    acute 136.3
  nonspecific, chronic 496
  obstructive (chronic) (COPD) 496
    with
      acute
        bronchitis 491.22
        exacerbation NEC 491.21
      alveolitis, allergic (*see also* Alveolitis, allergic) 495.9
      asthma (chronic) (obstructive) 493.2 ☑
      bronchiectasis 494.0
        with acute exacerbation 494.1
      bronchitis (chronic) 491.20
        with
          acute bronchitis 491.22
          exacerbation (acute) 491.21
      decompensated 491.21 ●
        with exacerbation 491.21 ●
      emphysema NEC 492.8
      diffuse (with fibrosis) 496
    polycystic 518.89
      asthma (chronic) (obstructive) 493.2 ☑
      congenital 748.4
    purulent (cavitary) 513.0
    restrictive 518.89
    rheumatoid 714.81
      diffuse interstitial 714.81
    specified NEC 518.89
Lutembacher's (atrial septal defect with mitral stenosis) 745.5
Lutz-Miescher (elastosis perforans serpiginosa) 701.1
Lutz-Splendore-de Almeida (Brazilian blastomycosis) 116.1
Lyell's (toxic epidermal necrolysis) 695.1
  due to drug
    correct substance properly administered 695.1
    overdose or wrong substance given or taken 977.9
    specific drug — *see* Table of Drugs and Chemicals
Lyme 088.81
lymphatic (gland) (system) 289.9
  channel (noninfective) 457.9
  vessel (noninfective) 457.9
    specified NEC 457.8
lymphoproliferative (chronic) (M9970/1) 238.79 ▲
Machado-Joseph 334.8
Madelung's (lipomatosis) 272.8
Madura (actinomycotic) 039.9

Disease, diseased — *see also* Syndrome
— *continued*

Madura — *continued*
  mycotic 117.4
Magitot's 526.4
Majocchi's (purpura annularis telangiectodes) 709.1
malarial (*see also* Malaria) 084.6
Malassez's (cystic) 608.89
Malibu 919.8
  infected 919.9
malignant (M8000/3) (*see also* Neoplasm, by site, malignant)
  previous, affecting management of pregnancy V23.89
Manson's 120.1
maple bark 495.6
maple syrup (urine) 270.3
Marburg (virus) 078.89
Marchiafava (-Bignami) 341.8
Marfan's 090.49
  congenital syphilis 090.49
  meaning Marfan's syndrome 759.82
Marie-Bamberger (hypertrophic pulmonary osteoarthropathy) (secondary) 731.2
  primary or idiopathic (acropachyderma) 757.39
  pulmonary (hypertrophic osteoarthropathy) 731.2
Marie-Strümpell (ankylosing spondylitis) 720.0
Marion's (bladder neck obstruction) 596.0
Marsh's (exophthalmic goiter) 242.0 ☑
Martin's 715.27
mast cell 757.33
  systemic (M9741/3) 202.6 ☑
mastoid (*see also* Mastoiditis) 383.9
  process 385.9
maternal, unrelated to pregnancy NEC, affecting fetus or newborn 760.9
Mathieu's (leptospiral jaundice) 100.0
Mauclaire's 732.3
Mauriac's (erythema nodosum syphiliticum) 091.3
Maxcy's 081.0
McArdle (-Schmid-Pearson) (glycogenosis V) 271.0
mediastinum NEC 519.3
Medin's (*see also* Poliomyelitis) 045.9 ☑
Mediterranean (with hemoglobinopathy) 282.49
medullary center (idiopathic) (respiratory) 348.8
Meige's (chronic hereditary edema) 757.0
Meleda 757.39
Ménétrier's (hypertrophic gastritis) 535.2 ☑
Ménière's (active) 386.00
  cochlear 386.02
  cochleovestibular 386.01
  inactive 386.04
  in remission 386.04
  vestibular 386.03
meningeal — *see* Meningitis
mental (*see also* Psychosis) 298.9
Merzbacher-Pelizaeus 330.0
mesenchymal 710.9
mesenteric embolic 557.0
metabolic NEC 277.9
metal polishers' 502
metastatic — *see* Metastasis
Mibelli's 757.39
microdrepanocytic 282.49
microvascular — code to condition
Miescher's 709.3
Mikulicz's (dryness of mouth, absent or decreased lacrimation) 527.1
Milkman (-Looser) (osteomalacia with pseudofractures) 268.2
Miller's (osteomalacia) 268.2

Disease, diseased — *see also* Syndrome
— *continued*

Mills' 335.29
Milroy's (chronic hereditary edema) 757.0
Minamata 985.0
Minor's 336.1
Minot's (hemorrhagic disease, newborn) 776.0
Minot-von Willebrand-Jürgens (angiohemophilia) 286.4
Mitchell's (erythromelalgia) 443.82
mitral — *see* Endocarditis, mitral
Mljet (mal de Meleda) 757.39
Möbius', Moebius' 346.8 ☑
Moeller's 267
Möller (-Barlow) (infantile scurvy) 267
Mönckeberg's (*see also* Arteriosclerosis, extremities) 440.20
Mondor's (thrombophlebitis of breast) 451.89
Monge's 993.2
Morel-Kraepelin (*see also* Schizophrenia) 295.9 ☑
Morgagni's (syndrome) (hyperostosis frontalis interna) 733.3
Morgagni-Adams-Stokes (syncope with heart block) 426.9
Morquio (-Brailsford) (-Ullrich) (mucopolysaccharidosis IV) 277.5
Morton's (with metatarsalgia) 355.6
Morvan's 336.0
motor neuron (bulbar) (mixed type) 335.20
Mouchet's (juvenile osteochondrosis, foot) 732.5
mouth 528.9
Moyamoya 437.5
Mucha's (acute parapsoriasis varioliformis) 696.2
mu-chain 273.2
mucolipidosis (I) (II) (III) 272.7
Münchmeyer's (exostosis luxurians) 728.11
Murri's (intermittent hemoglobinuria) 283.2
muscle 359.9
  inflammatory 728.9
  ocular 378.9
musculoskeletal system 729.9
mushroom workers' 495.5
Myà's (congenital dilation, colon) 751.3
mycotic 117.9
myeloproliferative (chronic) (M9960/1) 238.79 ▲
myocardium, myocardial (*see also* Degeneration, myocardial) 429.1
  hypertensive (*see also* Hypertension, heart) 402.90
  primary (idiopathic) 425.4
myoneural 358.9
Naegeli's 287.1
nail 703.9
  specified type NEC 703.8
Nairobi sheep 066.1
nasal 478.19 ▲
  cavity NEC 478.19 ▲
  sinus (chronic) — *see* Sinusitis
navel (newborn) NEC 779.89
  delayed separation of umbilical cord 779.83
nemaline body 359.0
neoplastic, generalized (M8000/6) 199.0
nerve — *see* Disorder, nerve
nervous system (central) 349.9
  autonomic, peripheral (*see also* Neuropathy, peripheral, autonomic) 337.9
  congenital 742.9
  inflammatory — *see* Encephalitis
  parasympathetic (*see also* Neuropathy, peripheral, autonomic) 337.9
  peripheral NEC 355.9

Disease, diseased — see also Syndrome — continued

nervous system — continued
  specified NEC 349.89
  sympathetic (see also Neuropathy, peripheral, autonomic) 337.9
  vegetative (see also Neuropathy, peripheral, autonomic) 337.9
Nettleship's (urticaria pigmentosa) 757.33
Neumann's (pemphigus vegetans) 694.4
neurologic (central) NEC (see also Disease, nervous system) 349.9
  peripheral NEC 355.9
neuromuscular system NEC 358.9
Newcastle 077.8
Nicolas (-Durand) — Favre (climatic bubo) 099.1
Niemann-Pick (lipid histiocytosis) 272.7
nipple 611.9
  Paget's (M8540/3) 174.0
Nishimoto (-Takeuchi) 437.5
nonarthropod-borne NEC 078.89
  central nervous system NEC 049.9
  enterovirus NEC 078.89
nonautoimmune hemolytic NEC 283.10
Nonne-Milroy-Meige (chronic hereditary edema) 757.0
Norrie's (congenital progressive oculoacousticocerebral degeneration) 743.8
nose 478.19 ▲
nucleus pulposus — see Disease, intervertebral disc
nutritional 269.9
  maternal, affecting fetus or newborn 760.4
oasthouse, urine 270.2
obliterative vascular 447.1
Odelberg's (juvenile osteochondrosis) 732.1
Oguchi's (retina) 368.61
Ohara's (see also Tularemia) 021.9
Ollier's (chondrodysplasia) 756.4
Opitz's (congestive splenomegaly) 289.51
Oppenheim's 358.8
Oppenheim-Urbach (necrobiosis lipoidica diabeticorum) 250.8 ☑ [709.3]
optic nerve NEC 377.49
orbit 376.9
  specified NEC 376.89
Oriental liver fluke 121.1
Oriental lung fluke 121.2
Ormond's 593.4
Osgood-Schlatter 732.4
Osgood's tibia (tubercle) 732.4
Osler (-Vaquez) (polycythemia vera) (M9950/1) 238.4
Osler-Rendu (familial hemorrhagic telangiectasia) 448.0
osteofibrocystic 252.01
Otto's 715.35
outer ear 380.9
ovary (noninflammatory) NEC 620.9
  cystic 620.2
  polycystic 256.4
  specified NEC 620.8
Owren's (congenital) (see also Defect, coagulation) 286.3
Paas' 756.59
Paget's (osteitis deformans) 731.0
  with infiltrating duct carcinoma of the breast (M8541/3) — see Neoplasm, breast, malignant
  bone 731.0
    osteosarcoma in (M9184/3) — see Neoplasm, bone, malignant
  breast (M8540/3) 174.0
  extramammary (M8542/3) (see also Neoplasm, skin, malignant)

Disease, diseased — see also Syndrome — continued

Paget's — continued
  extramammary (see also Neoplasm, skin, malignant) — continued
    anus 154.3
    skin 173.5
  malignant (M8540/3)
    breast 174.0
    specified site NEC (M8542/3) — see Neoplasm, skin, malignant
    unspecified site 174.0
  mammary (M8540/3) 174.0
  nipple (M8540/3) 174.0
palate (soft) 528.9
Paltauf-Sternberg 201.9 ☑
pancreas 577.9
  cystic 577.2
    congenital 751.7
  fibrocystic 277.00
Panner's 732.3
  capitellum humeri 732.3
  head of humerus 732.3
  tarsal navicular (bone) (osteochondrosis) 732.5
panvalvular — see Endocarditis, mitral
parametrium 629.9
parasitic NEC 136.9
  cerebral NEC 123.9
  intestinal NEC 129
  mouth 112.0
  skin NEC 134.9
  specified type — see Infestation
  tongue 112.0
parathyroid (gland) 252.9
  specified NEC 252.8
Parkinson's 332.0
parodontal 523.9
Parrot's (syphilitic osteochondritis) 090.0
Parry's (exophthalmic goiter) 242.0 ☑
Parson's (exophthalmic goiter) 242.0 ☑
Pavy's 593.6
Paxton's (white piedra) 111.2
Payr's (splenic flexure syndrome) 569.89
pearl-workers' (chronic osteomyelitis) (see also Osteomyelitis) 730.1 ☑
Pel-Ebstein — see Disease, Hodgkin's
Pelizaeus-Merzbacher 330.0
  with dementia
    with behavioral disturbance 330.0 [294.11]
    without behavioral disturbance 330.0 [294.10]
Pellegrini-Stieda (calcification, knee joint) 726.62
pelvis, pelvic
  female NEC 629.9
    specified NEC 629.89 ▲
  gonococcal (acute) 098.19
    chronic or duration of 2 months or over 098.39
  infection (see also Disease, pelvis, inflammatory) 614.9
  inflammatory (female) (PID) 614.9
    with
      abortion — see Abortion, by type, with sepsis
      ectopic pregnancy (see also categories 633.0–633.9) 639.0
      molar pregnancy (see also categories 630–632) 639.0
    acute 614.3
    chronic 614.4
    complicating pregnancy 646.6 ☑
      affecting fetus or newborn 760.8

Disease, diseased — see also Syndrome — continued

pelvis, pelvic — continued
  inflammatory — continued
    following
      abortion 639.0
      ectopic or molar pregnancy 639.0
    peritonitis (acute) 614.5
      chronic NEC 614.7
    puerperal, postpartum, childbirth 670.0 ☑
    specified NEC 614.8
    organ, female NEC 629.9
      specified NEC 629.89 ▲
    peritoneum, female NEC 629.9
      specified NEC 629.89 ▲
penis 607.9
  inflammatory 607.2
peptic NEC 536.9
  acid 536.8
periapical tissues NEC 522.9
pericardium 423.9
  specified type NEC 423.8
perineum
  female
    inflammatory 616.9
      specified NEC 616.89 ▲
    noninflammatory 624.9
      specified NEC 624.8
  male (inflammatory) 682.2
periodic (familial) (Reimann's) NEC 277.31 ▲
  paralysis 359.3
periodontal NEC 523.9
  specified NEC 523.8
periosteum 733.90
peripheral
  arterial 443.9
  autonomic nervous system (see also Neuropathy, autonomic) 337.9
  nerve NEC (see also Neuropathy) 356.9
    multiple — see Polyneuropathy
  vascular 443.9
    specified type NEC 443.89
peritoneum 568.9
  pelvic, female 629.9
    specified NEC 629.89 ▲
Perrin-Ferraton (snapping hip) 719.65
persistent mucosal (middle ear) (with posterior or superior marginal perforation of ear drum) 382.2
Perthes' (capital femoral osteochondrosis) 732.1
Petit's (see also Hernia, lumbar) 553.8
Peutz-Jeghers 759.6
Peyronie's 607.85
Pfeiffer's (infectious mononucleosis) 075
pharynx 478.20
Phocas' 610.1
photochromogenic (acid-fast bacilli) (pulmonary) 031.0
  nonpulmonary 031.9
Pick's
  brain 331.11
    with dementia
      with behavioral disturbance 331.11 [294.11]
      without behavioral disturbance 331.11 [294.10]
  cerebral atrophy 331.11
    with dementia
      with behavioral disturbance 331.11 [294.11]
      without behavioral disturbance 331.11 [294.10]
  lipid histiocytosis 272.7
  liver (pericardial pseudocirrhosis of liver) 423.2
  pericardium (pericardial pseudocirrhosis of liver) 423.2
  polyserositis (pericardial pseudocirrhosis of liver) 423.2

Disease, diseased — see also Syndrome — continued

Pierson's (osteochondrosis) 732.1
pigeon fanciers' or breeders' 495.2
pineal gland 259.8
pink 985.0
Pinkus' (lichen nitidus) 697.1
pinworm 127.4
pituitary (gland) 253.9
  hyperfunction 253.1
  hypofunction 253.2
pituitary snuff-takers' 495.8
placenta
  affecting fetus or newborn 762.2
  complicating pregnancy or childbirth 656.7 ☑
pleura (cavity) (see also Pleurisy) 511.0
Plummer's (toxic nodular goiter) 242.3 ☑
pneumatic
  drill 994.9
  hammer 994.9
policeman's 729.2
Pollitzer's (hidradenitis suppurativa) 705.83
polycystic (congenital) 759.89
  congenital 748.4
  kidney or renal 753.12
    adult type (APKD) 753.13
    autosomal dominant 753.13
    autosomal recessive 753.14
    childhood type (CPKD) 753.14
    infantile type 753.14
  liver or hepatic 751.62
  lung or pulmonary 518.89
  ovary, ovaries 256.4
  spleen 759.0
Pompe's (glycogenosis II) 271.0
Poncet's (tuberculous rheumatism) (see also Tuberculosis) 015.9 ☑
Posada-Wernicke 114.9
Potain's (pulmonary edema) 514
Pott's (see also Tuberculosis) 015.0 ☑ [730.88]
  osteomyelitis 015.0 ☑ [730.88]
  paraplegia 015.0 ☑ [730.88]
  spinal curvature 015.0 ☑ [737.43]
  spondylitis 015.0 ☑ [720.81]
Potter's 753.0
Poulet's 714.2
pregnancy NEC (see also Pregnancy) 646.9 ☑
Preiser's (osteoporosis) 733.09
Pringle's (tuberous sclerosis) 759.5
Profichet's 729.9
prostate 602.9
  specified type NEC 602.8
protozoal NEC 136.8
  intestine, intestinal NEC 007.9
pseudo-Hurler's (mucolipidosis III) 272.7
psychiatric (see also Psychosis) 298.9
psychotic (see also Psychosis) 298.9
Puente's (simple glandular cheilitis) 528.5
puerperal NEC (see also Puerperal) 674.9 ☑
pulmonary (see also Disease, lung)
  amyloid 277.39 [517.8] ▲
  artery 417.9
  circulation, circulatory 417.9
    specified NEC 417.8
  diffuse obstructive (chronic) 496
    with
      acute bronchitis 491.22
      asthma (chronic) (obstructive) 493.2 ☑
      exacerbation NEC (acute) 491.21
  heart (chronic) 416.9
    specified NEC 416.8
  hypertensive (vascular) 416.0
    cardiovascular 416.0
  obstructive diffuse (chronic) 496

☑ Additional Digit Required — Refer to the Tabular List for Digit Selection   ▽ Subterms under main terms may continue to next column or page

2007 ICD-9-CM   ▶◀ Revised Text   ● New Line   ▲ Revised Code   **October 2006 · Volume 2 — 89**

Disease, diseased — *see also* Syndrome
— *continued*
pulmonary (*see also* Disease, lung) —
continued
obstructive diffuse — *continued*
with
acute bronchitis 491.22
asthma (chronic) (obstructive) 493.2 ☑
bronchitis (chronic) 491.20
with
exacerbation (acute)
491.21
acute 491.22
exacerbation NEC (acute)
491.21
decompensated 491.21 ●
with exacerbation 491.21 ●
valve (*see also* Endocarditis, pulmonary) 424.3
pulp (dental) NEC 522.9
pulseless 446.7
Putnam's (subacute combined sclerosis with pernicious anemia)
281.0 [336.2]
Pyle (-Cohn) (craniometaphyseal dysplasia) 756.89
pyramidal tract 333.90
Quervain's
tendon sheath 727.04
thyroid (subacute granulomatous
thyroiditis) 245.1
Quincke's — *see* Edema, angioneurotic
Quinquaud (acne decalvans) 704.09
rag sorters' 022.1
Raynaud's (paroxysmal digital
cyanosis) 443.0
reactive airway — *see* Asthma
Recklinghausen's (M9540/1) 237.71
bone (osteitis fibrosa cystica)
252.01
Recklinghausen-Applebaum
(hemochromatosis) 275.0
Reclus' (cystic) 610.1
rectum NEC 569.49
Refsum's (heredopathia atactica
polyneuritiformis) 356.3
Reichmann's (gastrosuccorrhea) 536.8
Reimann's (periodic) 277.31 ▲
Reiter's 099.3
renal (functional) (pelvis) (*see also*
Disease, kidney) 593.9
with
edema (*see also* Nephrosis)
581.9
exudative nephritis 583.89
lesion of interstitial nephritis
583.89
stated generalized cause — *see*
Nephritis
acute 593.9
basement membrane NEC 583.89
with
pulmonary hemorrhage
(Goodpasture's syn-
drome) 446.21 [583.81]
chronic (*see also* Disease, kidney,
chronic) 593.9
complicating pregnancy or puerperium NEC 646.2 ☑
with hypertension — *see* Toxemia, of pregnancy
affecting fetus or newborn 760.1
cystic, congenital (*see also* Cystic,
disease, kidney) 753.10
diabetic 250.4 ☑ [583.81]
due to
amyloidosis
277.39 [583.81] ▲
diabetes mellitus
250.4 ☑ [583.81]
systemic lupus erythematosis
710.0 [583.81]
end-stage 585.6
exudative 583.89

Disease, diseased — *see also* Syndrome
— *continued*
renal (*see also* Disease, kidney) —
continued
fibrocystic (congenital) 753.19
gonococcal 098.19 [583.81]
gouty 274.10
hypertensive (*see also* Hypertension, kidney) 403.90
immune complex NEC 583.89
interstitial (diffuse) (focal) 583.89
lupus 710.0 [583.81]
maternal, affecting fetus or newborn 760.1
hypertensive 760.0
phosphate-losing (tubular) 588.0
polycystic (congenital) 753.12
adult type (APKD) 753.13
autosomal dominant 753.13
autosomal recessive 753.14
childhood type (CPKD) 753.14
infantile type 753.14
specified lesion or cause NEC (*see
also* Glomerulonephritis)
583.89
subacute 581.9
syphilitic 095.4
tuberculous (*see also* Tuberculosis)
016.0 ☑ [583.81]
tubular (*see also* Nephrosis, tubular) 584.5
Rendu-Osler-Weber (familial hemorrhagic telangiectasia) 448.0
renovascular (arteriosclerotic) (*see also* Hypertension, kidney) 403.90
respiratory (tract) 519.9
acute or subacute (upper) NEC
465.9
due to fumes or vapors 506.3
multiple sites NEC 465.8
noninfectious 478.9
streptococcal 034.0
chronic 519.9
arising in the perinatal period
770.7
due to fumes or vapors 506.4
due to
aspiration of liquids or solids
508.9
external agents NEC 508.9
specified NEC 508.8
fumes or vapors 506.9
acute or subacute NEC 506.3
chronic 506.4
fetus or newborn NEC 770.9
obstructive 496
specified type NEC 519.8
upper (acute) (infectious) NEC
465.9
multiple sites NEC 465.8
noninfectious NEC 478.9
streptococcal 034.0
retina, retinal NEC 362.9
Batten's or Batten-Mayou
330.1 [362.71]
degeneration 362.89
vascular lesion 362.17
rheumatic (*see also* Arthritis) 716.8 ☑
heart — *see* Disease, heart,
rheumatic
rheumatoid (heart) — *see* Arthritis,
rheumatoid
rickettsial NEC 083.9
specified type NEC 083.8
Riedel's (ligneous thyroiditis) 245.3
Riga (-Fede) (cachectic aphthae) 529.0
Riggs' (compound periodontitis)
523.40 ▲
Ritter's 695.81
Rivalta's (cervicofacial actinomycosis)
039.3
Robles' (onchocerciasis) 125.3 [360.13]
Roger's (congenital interventricular
septal defect) 745.4
Rokitansky's (*see also* Necrosis, liver)
570

Disease, diseased — *see also* Syndrome
— *continued*
Romberg's 349.89
Rosenthal's (factor XI deficiency) 286.2
Rossbach's (hyperchlorhydria) 536.8
psychogenic 306.4
Roth (-Bernhardt) 355.1
Runeberg's (progressive pernicious
anemia) 281.0
Rust's (tuberculous spondylitis) (*see
also* Tuberculosis)
015.0 ☑ [720.81]
Rustitskii's (multiple myeloma)
(M9730/3) 203.0 ☑
Ruysch's (Hirschsprung's disease)
751.3
Sachs (-Tay) 330.1
sacroiliac NEC 724.6
salivary gland or duct NEC 527.9
inclusion 078.5
streptococcal 034.0
virus 078.5
Sander's (paranoia) 297.1
Sandhoff's 330.1
sandworm 126.9
Savill's (epidemic exfoliative dermati-
tis) 695.89
Schamberg's (progressive pigmentary
dermatosis) 709.09
Schaumann's (sarcoidosis) 135
Schenck's (sporotrichosis) 117.1
Scheuermann's (osteochondrosis)
732.0
Schilder (-Flatau) 341.1
Schimmelbusch's 610.1
Schlatter-Osgood 732.4
Schlatter's tibia (tubercle) 732.4
Schmorl's 722.30
cervical 722.39
lumbar, lumbosacral 722.32
specified region NEC 722.39
thoracic, thoracolumbar 722.31
Scholz's 330.0
Schönlein (-Henoch) (purpura
rheumatica) 287.0
Schottmüller's (*see also* Fever,
paratyphoid) 002.9
Schüller-Christian (chronic histiocytosis X) 277.89
Schultz's (agranulocytosis)
288.09 ▲
Schwalbe-Ziehen-Oppenheimer 333.6
Schweninger-Buzzi (macular atrophy)
701.3
sclera 379.19
scrofulous (*see also* Tuberculosis)
017.2 ☑
scrotum 608.9
sebaceous glands NEC 706.9
Secretan's (posttraumatic edema)
782.3
semilunar cartilage, cystic 717.5
seminal vesicle 608.9
Senear-Usher (pemphigus erythematosus) 694.4
serum NEC 999.5
Sever's (osteochondrosis calcaneum)
732.5
Sézary's (reticulosis) (M9701/3)
202.2 ☑
Shaver's (bauxite pneumoconiosis)
503
Sheehan's (postpartum pituitary
necrosis) 253.2
shimamushi (scrub typhus) 081.2
shipyard 077.1
sickle cell 282.60
with
crisis 282.62
Hb-S disease 282.61
other abnormal hemoglobin (Hb-
D) (Hb-E) (Hb-G) (Hb-J)
(Hb-K) (Hb-O) (Hb-P) (high
fetal gene) (without crisis)
282.68
with crisis 282.69

Disease, diseased — *see also* Syndrome
— *continued*
sickle cell — *continued*
elliptocytosis 282.60
Hb-C (without crisis) 282.63
with
crisis 282.64
vaso-occlusive pain 282.64
Hb-S 282.61
with
crisis 282.62
Hb-C (without crisis) 282.63
with
crisis 282.64
vaso-occlusive pain
282.64
other abnormal hemoglobin
(Hb-D) (Hb-E) (Hb-G)
(Hb-J) (Hb-K) (Hb-O)
(Hb-P) (high fetal gene)
(without crisis) 282.68
with crisis 282.69
spherocytosis 282.60
thalassemia (without crisis) 282.41
with
crisis 282.42
vaso-occlusive pain 282.42
Siegal-Cattan-Mamou (periodic)
277.31 ▲
silo fillers' 506.9
Simian B 054.3
Simmonds' (pituitary cachexia) 253.2
Simons' (progressive lipodystrophy)
272.6
Sinding-Larsen (juvenile osteopathia
patellae) 732.4
sinus (*see also* Sinusitis)
brain 437.9
specified NEC 478.19 ▲
Sirkari's 085.0
sixth 057.8
Sjögren (-Gougerot) 710.2
with lung involvement
710.2 [517.8]
Skevas-Zerfus 989.5
skin NEC 709.9
due to metabolic disorder 277.9
specified type NEC 709.8
sleeping (*see also* Narcolepsy) 347.00
meaning sleeping sickness (*see also* Trypanosomiasis) 086.5
small vessel 443.9
Smith-Strang (oasthouse urine) 270.2
Sneddon-Wilkinson (subcorneal pustular dermatosis) 694.1
South African creeping 133.8
Spencer's (epidemic vomiting) 078.82
Spielmeyer-Stock 330.1
Spielmeyer-Vogt 330.1
spine, spinal 733.90
combined system (*see also* Degeneration, combined)
266.2 [336.2]
with pernicious anemia
281.0 [336.2]
cord NEC 336.9
congenital 742.9
demyelinating NEC 341.8
joint (*see also* Disease, joint, spine)
724.9
tuberculous 015.0 ☑ [730.8] ☑
spinocerebellar 334.9
specified NEC 334.8
spleen (organic) (postinfectional)
289.50
amyloid 277.39 ▲
lardaceous 277.39 ▲
polycystic 759.0
specified NEC 289.59
sponge divers' 989.5
Stanton's (melioidosis) 025
Stargardt's 362.75
Startle 759.89
Steinert's 359.2
Sternberg's — *see* Disease, Hodgkin's

Disease, diseased — *see also* Syndrome — *continued*

Stevens-Johnson (erythema multiforme exudativum) 695.1
Sticker's (erythema infectiosum) 057.0
Stieda's (calcification, knee joint) 726.62
Still's (juvenile rheumatoid arthritis) 714.30
Stiller's (asthenia) 780.79
Stokes' (exophthalmic goiter) 242.0 ☑
Stokes-Adams (syncope with heart block) 426.9
Stokvis (-Talma) (enterogenous cyanosis) 289.7
stomach NEC (organic) 537.9
    functional 536.9
        psychogenic 306.4
    lardaceous 277.39 ▲
stonemasons' 502
storage
    glycogen (*see also* Disease, glycogen storage) 271.0
    lipid 272.7
    mucopolysaccharide 277.5
striatopallidal system 333.90
    specified NEC 333.89
Strümpell-Marie (ankylosing spondylitis) 720.0
Stuart's (congenital factor X deficiency) (*see also* Defect, coagulation) 286.3
Stuart-Prower (congenital factor X deficiency) (*see also* Defect, coagulation) 286.3
Sturge (-Weber) (-Dimitri) (encephalocutaneous angiomatosis) 759.6
Stuttgart 100.89
Sudeck's 733.7
supporting structures of teeth NEC 525.9
suprarenal (gland) (capsule) 255.9
    hyperfunction 255.3
    hypofunction 255.4
Sutton's 709.09
Sutton and Gull's — *see* Hypertension, kidney
sweat glands NEC 705.9
    specified type NEC 705.89
sweating 078.2
Sweeley-Klionsky 272.4
Swift (-Feer) 985.0
swimming pool (bacillus) 031.1
swineherd's 100.89
Sylvest's (epidemic pleurodynia) 074.1
Symmers (follicular lymphoma) (M9690/3) 202.0 ☑
sympathetic nervous system (*see also* Neuropathy, peripheral, autonomic) 337.9
synovium 727.9
syphilitic — *see* Syphilis
systemic tissue mast cell (M9741/3) 202.6 ☑
Taenzer's 757.4
Takayasu's (pulseless) 446.7
Talma's 728.85
Tangier (familial high-density lipoprotein deficiency) 272.5
Tarral-Besnier (pityriasis rubra pilaris) 696.4
Taylor's 701.8
Tay-Sachs 330.1
tear duct 375.69
teeth, tooth 525.9
    hard tissues 521.9
        specified NEC 521.89 ●
    pulp NEC 522.9
tendon 727.9
    inflammatory NEC 727.9
terminal vessel 443.9
testis 608.9
Thaysen-Gee (nontropical sprue) 579.0
Thomsen's 359.2

Disease, diseased — *see also* Syndrome — *continued*

Thomson's (congenital poikiloderma) 757.33
Thornwaldt's, Tornwaldt's (pharyngeal bursitis) 478.29
throat 478.20
    septic 034.0
thromboembolic (*see also* Embolism) 444.9
thymus (gland) 254.9
    specified NEC 254.8
thyroid (gland) NEC 246.9
    heart (*see also* Hyperthyroidism) 242.9 ☑ [425.7]
    lardaceous 277.39 ▲
    specified NEC 246.8
Tietze's 733.6
Tommaselli's
    correct substance properly administered 599.7
    overdose or wrong substance given or taken 961.4
tongue 529.9
tonsils, tonsillar (and adenoids) (chronic) 474.9
    specified NEC 474.8
tooth, teeth 525.9
    hard tissues 521.9
        specified NEC 521.89 ●
    pulp NEC 522.9
Tornwaldt's (pharyngeal bursitis) 478.29
Tourette's 307.23
trachea 519.19 ▲
tricuspid — *see* Endocarditis, tricuspid
triglyceride-storage, type I, II, III 272.7
triple vessel (coronary arteries) — *see* Arteriosclerosis, coronary
trisymptomatic, Gourgerot's 709.1
trophoblastic (*see also* Hydatidiform mole) 630
    previous, affecting management of pregnancy V23.1
tsutsugamushi (scrub typhus) 081.2
tube (fallopian), noninflammatory 620.9
    specified NEC 620.8
tuberculous NEC (*see also* Tuberculosis) 011.9 ☑
tubo-ovarian
    inflammatory (*see also* Salpingo-oophoritis) 614.2
    noninflammatory 620.9
        specified NEC 620.8
tubotympanic, chronic (with anterior perforation of ear drum) 382.1
tympanum 385.9
Uhl's 746.84
umbilicus (newborn) NEC 779.89
    delayed separation 779.83
Underwood's (sclerema neonatorum) 778.1
undiagnosed 799.9
Unna's (seborrheic dermatitis) 690.18
unstable hemoglobin hemolytic 282.7
Unverricht (-Lundborg) 333.2
Urbach-Oppenheim (necrobiosis lipoidica diabeticorum) 250.8 ☑ [709.3]
Urbach-Wiethe (lipoid proteinosis) 272.8
ureter 593.9
urethra 599.9
    specified type NEC 599.84
urinary (tract) 599.9
    bladder 596.9
        specified NEC 596.8
    maternal, affecting fetus or newborn 760.1
Usher-Senear (pemphigus erythematosus) 694.4
uterus (organic) 621.9
    infective (*see also* Endometritis) 615.9

Disease, diseased — *see also* Syndrome — *continued*

uterus — *continued*
    inflammatory (*see also* Endometritis) 615.9
    noninflammatory 621.9
        specified NEC 621.8
uveal tract
    anterior 364.9
    posterior 363.9
vagabonds' 132.1
vagina, vaginal
    inflammatory 616.9
        specified NEC 616.89 ▲
    noninflammatory 623.9
        specified NEC 623.8
Valsuani's (progressive pernicious anemia, puerperal) 648.2 ☑
    complicating pregnancy or puerperium 648.2 ☑
valve, valvular — *see* Endocarditis
van Bogaert-Nijssen (-Peiffer) 330.0
van Creveld-von Gierke (glycogenosis I) 271.0
van den Bergh's (enterogenous cyanosis) 289.7
van Neck's (juvenile osteochondrosis) 732.1
Vaquez (-Osler) (polycythemia vera) (M9950/1) 238.4
vascular 459.9
    arteriosclerotic — *see* Arteriosclerosis
    hypertensive — *see* Hypertension
    obliterative 447.1
        peripheral 443.9
    occlusive 459.9
    peripheral (occlusive) 443.9
        in diabetes mellitus 250.7 ☑ [443.81]
        specified type NEC 443.89
vas deferens 608.9
vasomotor 443.9
vasospastic 443.9
vein 459.9
venereal 099.9
    chlamydial NEC 099.50
        anus 099.52
        bladder 099.53
        cervix 099.53
        epididymis 099.54
        genitourinary NEC 099.55
            lower 099.53
            specified NEC 099.54
        pelvic inflammatory disease 099.54
        perihepatic 099.56
        peritoneum 099.56
        pharynx 099.51
        rectum 099.52
        specified site NEC 099.59
        testis 099.54
        vagina 099.53
        vulva 099.53
    complicating pregnancy, childbirth, or puerperium 647.2 ☑
    fifth 099.1
    sixth 099.1
    specified nature or type NEC 099.8
        chlamydial — *see* Disease, venereal, chlamydial
Verneuil's (syphilitic bursitis) 095.7
Verse's (calcinosis intervertebralis) 275.49 [722.90]
vertebra, vertebral NEC 733.90
    disc — *see* Disease, Intervertebral disc
vibration NEC 994.9
Vidal's (lichen simplex chronicus) 698.3
Vincent's (trench mouth) 101
Virchow's 733.99
virus (filterable) NEC 078.89
    arbovirus NEC 066.9
    arthropod-borne NEC 066.9
    central nervous system NEC 049.9

Disease, diseased — *see also* Syndrome — *continued*

virus — *continued*
    central nervous system — *continued*
        specified type NEC 049.8
    complicating pregnancy, childbirth, or puerperium 647.6 ☑
    contact (with) V01.79
        varicella V01.71
    exposure to V01.79
        varicella V01.71
    Marburg 078.89
    maternal
        with fetal damage affecting management of pregnancy 655.3 ☑
    nonarthropod-borne NEC 078.89
        central nervous system NEC 049.9
            specified NEC 049.8
    vaccination, prophylactic (against) V04.89
vitreous 379.29
vocal cords NEC 478.5
Vogt's (Cecile) 333.71 ▲
Vogt-Spielmeyer 330.1
Volhard-Fahr (malignant nephrosclerosis) 403.00
Volkmann's
    acquired 958.6
von Bechterew's (ankylosing spondylitis) 720.0
von Economo's (encephalitis lethargica) 049.8
von Eulenburg's (congenital paramyotonia) 359.2
von Gierke's (glycogenosis I) 271.0
von Graefe's 378.72
von Hippel's (retinocerebral angiomatosis) 759.6
von Hippel-Lindau (angiomatosis retinocerebellosa) 759.6
von Jaksch's (pseudoleukemia infantum) 285.8
von Recklinghausen's (M9540/1) 237.71
    bone (osteitis fibrosa cystica) 252.01
von Recklinghausen-Applebaum (hemochromatosis) 275.0
von Willebrand (-Jürgens) (angiohemophilia) 286.4
von Zambusch's (lichen sclerosus et atrophicus) 701.0
Voorhoeve's (dyschondroplasia) 756.4
Vrolik's (osteogenesis imperfecta) 756.51
vulva
    inflammatory 616.9 ●
        specified NEC 616.89 ●
    noninflammatory 624.9
        specified NEC 624.8
Wagner's (colloid milium) 709.3
Waldenström's (osteochondrosis capital femoral) 732.1
Wallgren's (obstruction of splenic vein with collateral circulation) 459.89
Wardrop's (with lymphangitis) 681.9
    finger 681.02
    toe 681.11
Wassilieff's (leptospiral jaundice) 100.0
wasting NEC 799.4
    due to malnutrition 261
    paralysis 335.21
Waterhouse-Friderichsen 036.3
waxy (any site) 277.39 ▲
Weber-Christian (nodular nonsuppurative panniculitis) 729.30
Wegner's (syphilitic osteochondritis) 090.0
Weil's (leptospiral jaundice) 100.0
    of lung 100.0

☑ Additional Digit Required — Refer to the Tabular List for Digit Selection   � Subterms under main terms may continue to next column or page

2007 ICD-9-CM   ►◄ Revised Text   ● New Line   ▲ Revised Code   October 2006 · Volume 2 — 91

Disease, diseased — *see also* Syndrome
— *continued*
Weir Mitchell's (erythromelalgia) 443.82
Werdnig-Hoffmann 335.0
Werlhof's (*see also* Purpura, thrombocytopenic) 287.39
Wermer's 258.0
Werner's (progeria adultorum) 259.8
Werner-His (trench fever) 083.1
Werner-Schultz (agranulocytosis) 288.09 ▲
Wernicke's (superior hemorrhagic polioencephalitis) 265.1
Wernicke-Posadas 114.9
Whipple's (intestinal lipodystrophy) 040.2
whipworm 127.3
White's (congenital) (keratosis follicularis) 757.39
white
  blood cell 288.9
    specified NEC 288.8
  spot 701.0
Whitmore's (melioidosis) 025
Widal-Abrami (acquired hemolytic jaundice) 283.9
Wilkie's 557.1
Wilkinson-Sneddon (subcorneal pustular dermatosis) 694.1
Willis' (diabetes mellitus) (*see also* Diabetes) 250.0 ☑
Wilson's (hepatolenticular degeneration) 275.1
Wilson-Brocq (dermatitis exfoliativa) 695.89
winter vomiting 078.82
Wise's 696.2
Wohlfart-Kugelberg-Welander 335.11
Woillez's (acute idiopathic pulmonary congestion) 518.5
Wolman's (primary familial xanthomatosis) 272.7
wool-sorters' 022.1
Zagari's (xerostomia) 527.7
Zahorsky's (exanthem subitum) 057.8
Ziehen-Oppenheim 333.6
zoonotic, bacterial NEC 027.9
  specified type NEC 027.8
Disfigurement (due to scar) 709.2
  head V48.6
  limb V49.4
  neck V48.7
  trunk V48.7
Disgerminoma — *see* Dysgerminoma
Disinsertion, retina 361.04
Disintegration, complete, of the body 799.89
  traumatic 869.1
Disk kidney 753.3
Dislocatable hip, congenital — *see also* Dislocation, hip, congenital 754.30
Dislocation (articulation) (closed) (displacement) (simple) (subluxation) 839.8

Note — "Closed" includes simple, complete, partial, uncomplicated, and unspecified dislocation.

"Open" includes dislocation specified as infected or compound and dislocation with foreign body.

"Chronic," "habitual," "old," or "recurrent" dislocations should be coded as indicated under the entry "Dislocation, recurrent," and "pathological" as indicated under the entry "Dislocation, pathological."

For late effect of dislocation see Late, effect, dislocation.

---

  with fracture — *see* Fracture, by site
  acromioclavicular (joint) (closed) 831.04
    open 831.14

Dislocation — *continued*
  anatomical site (closed)
    specified NEC 839.69
      open 839.79
    unspecified or ill-defined 839.8
      open 839.9
  ankle (scaphoid bone) (closed) 837.0
    open 837.1
  arm (closed) 839.8
    open 839.9
  astragalus (closed) 837.0
    open 837.1
  atlanto-axial (closed) 839.01
    open 839.11
  atlas (closed) 839.01
    open 839.11
  axis (closed) 839.02
    open 839.12
  back (closed) 839.8
    open 839.9
  Bell-Daly 723.8
  breast bone (closed) 839.61
    open 839.71
  capsule, joint — *see* Dislocation, by site
  carpal (bone) — *see* Dislocation, wrist
  carpometacarpal (joint) (closed) 833.04
    open 833.14
  cartilage (joint) (*see also* Dislocation, by site)
    knee — *see* Tear, meniscus
  cervical, cervicodorsal, or cervicothoracic (spine) (vertebra) — *see* Dislocation, vertebra, cervical
  chiropractic (*see also* Lesion, nonallopathic) 739.9
  chondrocostal — *see* Dislocation, costochondral
  chronic — *see* Dislocation, recurrent
  clavicle (closed) 831.04
    open 831.14
  coccyx (closed) 839.41
    open 839.51
  collar bone (closed) 831.04
    open 831.14
  compound (open) NEC 839.9
  congenital NEC 755.8
    hip (*see also* Dislocation, hip, congenital) 754.30
    lens 743.37
    rib 756.3
    sacroiliac 755.69
    spine NEC 756.19
    vertebra 756.19
  coracoid (closed) 831.09
    open 831.19
  costal cartilage (closed) 839.69
    open 839.79
  costochondral (closed) 839.69
    open 839.79
  cricoarytenoid articulation (closed) 839.69
    open 839.79
  cricothyroid (cartilage) articulation (closed) 839.69
    open 839.79
  dorsal vertebrae (closed) 839.21
    open 839.31
  ear ossicle 385.23
  elbow (closed) 832.00
    anterior (closed) 832.01
      open 832.11
    congenital 754.89
    divergent (closed) 832.09
      open 832.19
    lateral (closed) 832.04
      open 832.14
    medial (closed) 832.03
      open 832.10
    posterior (closed) 832.02
      open 832.12
    recurrent 718.32
    specified type NEC 832.09
      open 832.19
  eye 360.81

Dislocation — *continued*
  eye — *continued*
    lateral 376.36
  eyeball 360.81
    lateral 376.36
  femur
    distal end (closed) 836.50
      anterior 836.52
        open 836.62
      lateral 836.53
        open 836.63
      medial 836.54
        open 836.64
      open 836.60
      posterior 836.51
        open 836.61
    proximal end (closed) 835.00
      anterior (pubic) 835.03
        open 835.13
      obturator 835.02
        open 835.12
      open 835.10
      posterior 835.01
        open 835.11
  fibula
    distal end (closed) 837.0
      open 837.1
    proximal end (closed) 836.59
      open 836.69
  finger(s) (phalanx) (thumb) (closed) 834.00
    interphalangeal (joint) 834.02
      open 834.12
    metacarpal (bone), distal end 834.01
      open 834.11
    metacarpophalangeal (joint) 834.01
      open 834.11
    open 834.10
    recurrent 718.34
  foot (closed) 838.00
    open 838.10
    recurrent 718.37
  forearm (closed) 839.8
    open 839.9
  fracture — *see* Fracture, by site
  glenoid (closed) 831.09
    open 831.19
  habitual — *see* Dislocation, recurrent
  hand (closed) 839.8
    open 839.9
  hip (closed) 835.00
    anterior 835.03
      obturator 835.02
        open 835.12
      open 835.13
    congenital (unilateral) 754.30
      with subluxation of other hip 754.35
      bilateral 754.31
    developmental 718.75
    open 835.10
    posterior 835.01
      open 835.11
    recurrent 718.35
  humerus (closed) 831.00
    distal end (*see also* Dislocation, elbow) 832.00
    open 831.10
    proximal end (closed) 831.00
      anterior (subclavicular) (subcoracoid) (subglenoid) (closed) 831.01
        open 831.11
      inferior (closed) 831.03
        open 831.13
      open 831.10
      posterior (closed) 831.02
        open 831.12
  implant — *see* Complications, mechanical
  incus 385.23
  infracoracoid (closed) 831.01
    open 831.11
  innominate (pubic junction) (sacral junction) (closed) 839.69

Dislocation — *continued*
  innominate — *continued*
    acetabulum (*see also* Dislocation, hip) 835.00
    open 839.79
  interphalangeal (joint)
    finger or hand (closed) 834.02
      open 834.12
    foot or toe (closed) 838.06
      open 838.16
  jaw (cartilage) (meniscus) (closed) 830.0
    open 830.1
    recurrent 524.69
  joint NEC (closed) 839.8
    developmental 718.7 ☑
    open 839.9
    pathological — *see* Dislocation, pathological
    recurrent — *see* Dislocation, recurrent
  knee (closed) 836.50
    anterior 836.51
      open 836.61
    congenital (with genu recurvatum) 754.41
    habitual 718.36
    lateral 836.54
      open 836.64
    medial 836.53
      open 836.63
    old 718.36
    open 836.60
    posterior 836.52
      open 836.62
    recurrent 718.36
    rotatory 836.59
      open 836.69
  lacrimal gland 375.16
  leg (closed) 839.8
    open 839.9
  lens (crystalline) (complete) (partial) 379.32
    anterior 379.33
    congenital 743.37
    ocular implant 996.53
    posterior 379.34
    traumatic 921.3
  ligament — *see* Dislocation, by site
  lumbar (vertebrae) (closed) 839.20
    open 839.30
  lumbosacral (vertebrae) (closed) 839.20
    congenital 756.19
    open 839.30
  mandible (closed) 830.0
    open 830.1
  maxilla (inferior) (closed) 830.0
    open 830.1
  meniscus (knee) (*see also* Tear, meniscus)
    other sites — *see* Dislocation, by site
  metacarpal (bone)
    distal end (closed) 834.01
      open 834.11
    proximal end (closed) 833.05
      open 833.15
  metacarpophalangeal (joint) (closed) 834.01
    open 834.11
  metatarsal (bone) (closed) 838.04
    open 838.14
  metatarsophalangeal (joint) (closed) 838.05
    open 838.15
  midcarpal (joint) (closed) 833.03
    open 833.13
  midtarsal (joint) (closed) 838.02
    open 838.12
  Monteggia's — *see* Dislocation, hip
  multiple locations (except fingers only or toes only) (closed) 839.8
    open 839.9
  navicular (bone) foot (closed) 837.0
    open 837.1

☑ Additional Digit Required — Refer to the Tabular List for Digit Selection   ▽ Subterms under main terms may continue to next column or page

92 — Volume 2 · October 2006   ▶◀ Revised Text   ● New Line   ▲ Revised Code   *2007 ICD-9-CM*

Dislocation — continued
neck (see also Dislocation, vertebra, cervical) 839.00
Nélaton's — see Dislocation, ankle
nontraumatic (joint) — see Dislocation, pathological
nose (closed) 839.69
open 839.79
not recurrent, not current injury — see Dislocation, pathological
occiput from atlas (closed) 839.01
open 839.11
old — see Dislocation, recurrent
open (compound) NEC 839.9
ossicle, ear 385.23
paralytic (flaccid) (spastic) — see Dislocation, pathological
patella (closed) 836.3
congenital 755.64
open 836.4
pathological NEC 718.20
ankle 718.27
elbow 718.22
foot 718.27
hand 718.24
hip 718.25
knee 718.26
lumbosacral joint 724.6
multiple sites 718.29
pelvic region 718.25
sacroiliac 724.6
shoulder (region) 718.21
specified site NEC 718.28
spine 724.8
sacroiliac 724.6
wrist 718.23
pelvis (closed) 839.69
acetabulum (see also Dislocation, hip) 835.00
open 839.79
phalanx
foot or toe (closed) 838.09
open 838.19
hand or finger (see also Dislocation, finger) 834.00
postpoliomyelitic — see Dislocation, pathological
prosthesis, internal — see Complications, mechanical
radiocarpal (joint) (closed) 833.02
open 833.12
radioulnar (joint)
distal end (closed) 833.01
open 833.11
proximal end (see also Dislocation, elbow) 832.00
radius
distal end (closed) 833.00
open 833.10
proximal end (closed) 832.01
open 832.11
recurrent (see also Derangement, joint, recurrent) 718.3 ☑
elbow 718.32
hip 718.35
joint NEC 718.38
knee 718.36
lumbosacral (joint) 724.6
patella 718.36
sacroiliac 724.6
shoulder 718.31
temporomandibular 524.69
rib (cartilage) (closed) 839.69
congenital 756.3
open 839.79
sacrococcygeal (closed) 839.42
open 839.52
sacroiliac (joint) (ligament) (closed) 839.42
congenital 755.69
open 839.52
recurrent 724.6
sacrum (closed) 839.42
open 839.52
scaphoid (bone)
ankle or foot (closed) 837.0

Dislocation — continued
scaphoid — continued
ankle or foot — continued
open 837.1
wrist (closed) (see also Dislocation, wrist) 833.00
open 833.10
scapula (closed) 831.09
open 831.19
semilunar cartilage, knee — see Tear, meniscus
septal cartilage (nose) (closed) 839.69
open 839.79
septum (nasal) (old) 470
sesamoid bone — see Dislocation, by site
shoulder (blade) (ligament) (closed) 831.00
anterior (subclavicular) (subcoracoid) (subglenoid) (closed) 831.01
open 831.11
chronic 718.31
inferior 831.03
open 831.13
open 831.10
posterior (closed) 831.02
open 831.12
recurrent 718.31
skull — see Injury, intracranial
Smith's — see Dislocation, foot
spine (articular process) (see also Dislocation, vertebra) (closed) 839.40
atlanto-axial (closed) 839.01
open 839.11
recurrent 723.8
cervical, cervicodorsal, cervicothoracic (closed) (see also Dislocation, vertebrae, cervical) 839.00
open 839.10
recurrent 723.8
coccyx 839.41
open 839.51
congenital 756.19
due to birth trauma 767.4
open 839.50
recurrent 724.9
sacroiliac 839.42
recurrent 724.6
sacrum (sacrococcygeal) (sacroiliac) 839.42
open 839.52
spontaneous — see Dislocation, pathological
sternoclavicular (joint) (closed) 839.61
open 839.71
sternum (closed) 839.61
open 839.71
subastragalar — see Dislocation, foot
subglenoid (closed) 831.01
open 831.11
symphysis
jaw (closed) 830.0
open 830.1
mandibular (closed) 830.0
open 830.1
pubis (closed) 839.69
open 839.79
tarsal (bone) (joint) 838.01
open 838.11
tarsometatarsal (joint) 838.03
open 838.13
temporomandibular (joint) (closed) 830.0
open 830.1
recurrent 524.69
thigh
distal end (see also Dislocation, femur, distal end) 836.50
proximal end (see also Dislocation, hip) 835.00
thoracic (vertebrae) (closed) 839.21
open 839.31

Dislocation — continued
thumb(s) (see also Dislocation, finger) 834.00
thyroid cartilage (closed) 839.69
open 839.79
tibia
distal end (closed) 837.0
open 837.1
proximal end (closed) 836.50
anterior 836.51
open 836.61
lateral 836.54
open 836.64
medial 836.53
open 836.63
open 836.60
posterior 836.52
open 836.62
rotatory 836.59
open 836.69
tibiofibular
distal (closed) 837.0
open 837.1
superior (closed) 836.59
open 836.69
toe(s) (closed) 838.09
open 838.19
trachea (closed) 839.69
open 839.79
ulna
distal end (closed) 833.09
open 833.19
proximal end — see Dislocation, elbow
vertebra (articular process) (body) (closed) ▶(traumatic)◀ 839.40
cervical, cervicodorsal or cervicothoracic (closed) 839.00
first (atlas) 839.01
open 839.11
second (axis) 839.02
open 839.12
third 839.03
open 839.13
fourth 839.04
open 839.14
fifth 839.05
open 839.15
sixth 839.06
open 839.16
seventh 839.07
open 839.17
congenital 756.19
multiple sites 839.08
open 839.18
open 839.10
congenital 756.19
dorsal 839.21
open 839.31
recurrent 724.9
lumbar, lumbosacral 839.20
open 839.30
non-traumatic — see Displacement, intervertebral disc ●
open NEC 839.50
recurrent 724.9
specified region NEC 839.49
open 839.59
thoracic 839.21
open 839.31
wrist (carpal bone) (scaphoid) (semilunar) (closed) 833.00
carpometacarpal (joint) 833.04
open 833.14
metacarpal bone, proximal end 833.05
open 833.15
midcarpal (joint) 833.03
open 833.13
open 833.10
radiocarpal (joint) 833.02
open 833.12
radioulnar (joint) 833.01
open 833.11
recurrent 718.33
specified site NEC 833.09

Dislocation — continued
wrist — continued
specified site — continued
open 833.19
xiphoid cartilage (closed) 839.61
open 839.71
Dislodgement
artificial skin graft 996.55
decellularized allodermis graft 996.55
Disobedience, hostile (covert) (overt) — see also Disturbance, conduct 312.0 ☑
Disorder — see also Disease
academic underachievement, childhood and adolescence 313.83
accommodation 367.51
drug-induced 367.89
toxic 367.89
adjustment (see also Reaction, adjustment) 309.9
with
anxiety 309.24
anxiety and depressed mood 309.28
depressed mood 309.0
disturbance of conduct 309.3
disturbance of emotions and conduct 309.4
adrenal (capsule) (cortex) (gland) 255.9
specified type NEC 255.8
adrenogenital 255.2
affective (see also Psychosis, affective) 296.90
atypical 296.81
aggressive, unsocialized (see also Disturbance, conduct) 312.0 ☑
alcohol, alcoholic (see also Alcohol) 291.9
allergic — see Allergy
amino acid (metabolic) (see also Disturbance, metabolism, amino acid) 270.9
albinism 270.2
alkaptonuria 270.2
argininosuccinicaciduria 270.6
beta-amino-isobutyricaciduria 277.2
cystathioninuria 270.4
cystinosis 270.0
cystinuria 270.0
glycinuria 270.0
homocystinuria 270.4
imidazole 270.5
maple syrup (urine) disease 270.3
neonatal, transitory 775.89 ▲
oasthouse urine disease 270.2
ochronosis 270.2
phenylketonuria 270.1
phenylpyruvic oligophrenia 270.1
purine NEC 277.2
pyrimidine NEC 277.2
renal transport NEC 270.0
specified type NEC 270.8
transport NEC 270.0
renal 270.0
xanthinuria 277.2
amnestic (see also Amnestic syndrome) 294.8
alcohol-induced persisting 291.1
drug-induced persisting 292.83
in conditions classified elsewhere 294.0
anaerobic glycolysis with anemia 282.3
anxiety (see also Anxiety) 300.00
due to or associated with physical condition 293.84
arteriole 447.9
specified type NEC 447.8
artery 447.9
specified type NEC 447.8
articulation — see Disorder, joint
Asperger's 299.8 ☑
attachment of infancy or early childhood 313.89
attention deficit 314.00

☑ Additional Digit Required — Refer to the Tabular List for Digit Selection   ▽ Subterms under main terms may continue to next column or page

2007 ICD-9-CM   ▶◀ Revised Text   ● New Line   ▲ Revised Code   October 2006 · Volume 2 — 93

Index

Disorder — Disorder

Disorder — *see also* Disease —
  continued
  attention deficit — *continued*
    with hyperactivity 314.01
    predominantly
      combined hyperactive/inatten-
        tive 314.01
      hyperactive/impulsive 314.01
      inattentive 314.00
    residual type 314.8
  autistic 299.0 ☑
  autoimmune NEC 279.4
    hemolytic (cold type) (warm type)
      283.0
    parathyroid 252.1
    thyroid 245.2
  avoidant, childhood or adolescence
    313.21
  balance
    acid-base 276.9
      mixed (with hypercapnia) 276.4
    electrolyte 276.9
    fluid 276.9
  behavior NEC (*see also* Disturbance,
    conduct) 312.9
    disruptive 312.9
  bilirubin excretion 277.4
  bipolar (affective) (alternating) 296.80

Note — Use the following fifth-digit
subclassification with categories
296.0–296.6:

0 *unspecifed*

1 *mild*

2 *moderate*

3 *severe, without mention of psy-*
   chotic behavior

4 *severe, specified as with psychot-*
   ic behavior

5 *in partial or unspecified remission*

6 *in full remission*

    atypical 296.7
    currently
      depressed 296.5 ☑
      hypomanic 296.4 ☑
      manic 296.4 ☑
    mixed 296.6 ☑
    specified type NEC 296.89
    type I 296.7
      most recent episode (or current)
        depressed 296.5 ☑
        hypomanic 296.4 ☑
        manic 296.4 ☑
        mixed 296.6 ☑
        unspecified 296.7
      single manic episode 296.0 ☑
    type II (recurrent major depressive
      episodes with hypomania)
      296.89
  bladder 596.9
    functional NEC 596.59
    specified NEC 596.8
  bone NEC 733.90
    specified NEC 733.99
  brachial plexus 353.0
  branched-chain amino-acid degrada-
    tion 270.3
  breast 611.9
    puerperal, postpartum 676.3 ☑
    specified NEC 611.8
  Briquet's 300.81
  bursa 727.9
    shoulder region 726.10
  carbohydrate metabolism, congenital
    271.9
  cardiac, functional 427.9
    postoperative 997.1
    psychogenic 306.2
  cardiovascular, psychogenic 306.2
  cartilage NEC 733.90
    articular 718.00
      ankle 718.07
      elbow 718.02

Disorder — *see also* Disease —
  continued
  cartilage — *continued*
    articular — *continued*
      foot 718.07
      hand 718.04
      hip 718.05
      knee 717.9
      multiple sites 718.09
      pelvic region 718.05
      shoulder region 718.01
      specified
        site NEC 718.08
        type NEC 733.99
      wrist 718.03
  catatonic — *see* Catatonia
  central auitory processing 315.32
  cervical region NEC 723.9
  cervical root (nerve) NEC 353.2
  character NEC (*see also* Disorder,
    personality) 301.9
  coagulation (factor) (*see also* Defect,
    coagulation) 286.9
    factor VIII (congenital) (functional)
      286.0
    factor IX (congenital) (functional)
      286.1
    neonatal, transitory 776.3
  coccyx 724.70
    specified NEC 724.79
  cognitive 294.9
  colon 569.9
    functional 564.9
      congenital 751.3
  communication 307.9
  conduct (*see also* Disturbance, con-
    duct) 312.9
    adjustment reaction 309.3
    adolescent onset type 312.82
    childhood onset type 312.81
    compulsive 312.30
      specified type NEC 312.39
    hyperkinetic 314.2
    onset unspecified 312.89
    socialized (type) 312.20
      aggressive 312.23
      unaggressive 312.21
    specified NEC 312.89
  conduction, heart 426.9
    specified NEC 426.89
  conflict
    sexual orientation 302.0
  congenital
    glycosylation (CDG) 271.8
  convulsive (secondary) (*see also* Con-
    vulsions) 780.39
    due to injury at birth 767.0
    idiopathic 780.39
  coordination 781.3
  cornea NEC 371.89
    due to contact lens 371.82
  corticosteroid metabolism NEC 255.2
  cranial nerve — *see* Disorder, nerve,
    cranial
  cyclothymic 301.13
  degradation, branched-chain amino
    acid 270.3
  delusional 297.1
  dentition 520.6
  depersonalization 300.6
  depressive NEC 311
    atypical 296.82
    major (*see also* Psychosis, affective)
      296.2 ☑
      recurrent episode 296.3 ☑
      single episode 296.2 ☑
  development, specific 315.9
    associated with hyperkinesia 314.1
    coordination 315.4
    language 315.31
    learning 315.2
      arithmetical 315.1
      reading 315.00
    mixed 315.5
    motor coordination 315.4
    specified type NEC 315.8

Disorder — *see also* Disease —
  continued
  development, specific — *continued*
    speech 315.39
  diaphragm 519.4
  digestive 536.9
    fetus or newborn 777.9
      specified NEC 777.8
    psychogenic 306.4
  disintegrative, childhood 299.1 ☑
  dissociative 300.15
    identity 300.14
    nocturnal 307.47
  drug-related 292.9
  dysmorphic body 300.7
  dysthymic 300.4
  ear 388.9
    degenerative NEC 388.00
    external 380.9
      specified 380.89
    pinna 380.30
    specified type NEC 388.8
    vascular NEC 388.00
  eating NEC 307.50
  electrolyte NEC 276.9
    with
      abortion — *see* Abortion, by
        type, with metabolic disor-
        der
      ectopic pregnancy (*see also* cat-
        egories 633.0–633.9)
        639.4
      molar pregnancy (*see also* cate-
        gories 630–632) 639.4
    acidosis 276.2
      metabolic 276.2
      respiratory 276.2
    alkalosis 276.3
      metabolic 276.3
      respiratory 276.3
    following
      abortion 639.4
      ectopic or molar pregnancy
        639.4
    neonatal, transitory NEC 775.5
  emancipation as adjustment reaction
    309.22
  emotional (*see also* Disorder, mental,
    nonpsychotic) V40.9
  endocrine 259.9
    specified type NEC 259.8
  esophagus 530.9
    functional 530.5
    psychogenic 306.4
  explosive
    intermittent 312.34
    isolated 312.35
  expressive language 315.31
  eye 379.90
    globe — *see* Disorder, globe
    ill-defined NEC 379.99
    limited duction NEC 378.63
    specified NEC 379.8
  eyelid 374.9
    degenerative 374.50
    sensory 374.44
    specified type NEC 374.89
    vascular 374.85
  factitious (with combined psychologi-
    cal and physical signs and
    symptoms) (with predominantly
    physical signs and symptoms)
    300.19
    with predominantly psychological
      signs and symptoms 300.16
  factor, coagulation (*see also* Defect,
    coagulation) 286.9
    IX (congenital) (funcitonal) 286.1
    VIII (congenital) (functional) 286.0
  fascia 728.9
  fatty acid oxidation 277.85
  feeding — *see* Feeding
  female sexual arousal 302.72
  fluid NEC 276.9
  gastric (functional) 536.9
    motility 536.8

Disorder — *see also* Disease —
  continued
  gastric — *continued*
    psychogenic 306.4
    secretion 536.8
  gastrointestinal (functional) NEC
    536.9
    newborn (neonatal) 777.9
      specified NEC 777.8
    psychogenic 306.4
  gender (child) 302.6
    adult 302.85
  gender identity (childhood) 302.6
    adolescents 302.85
    adults (-life) 302.85
  genitourinary system, psychogenic
    306.50
  globe 360.9
    degenerative 360.20
      specified NEC 360.29
    specified type NEC 360.89
  hearing (*see also* Deafness)
    conductive type (air) (*see also*
      Deafness, conductive) 389.00
    mixed conductive and sensorineu-
      ral 389.2
    nerve, ▶bilateral◀ 389.12
    perceptive (*see also* Deafness, per-
      ceptive) 389.10
    sensorineural type NEC (*see also*
      Deafness, ▶sensorineural◀)
      389.10
  heart action 427.9
    postoperative 997.1
  hematological, transient neonatal
    776.9
    specified type NEC 776.8
  hematopoietic organs 289.9
  hemorrhagic NEC 287.9
    due to intrinsic circulating antico-
      agulants 286.5
    specified type NEC 287.8
  hemostasis (*see also* Defect, coagula-
    tion) 286.9
  homosexual conflict 302.0
  hypomanic (chronic) 301.11
  identity
    childhood and adolescence 313.82
    gender 302.6
  immune mechanism (immunity) 279.9
    single complement (C1-C9) 279.8
    specified type NEC 279.8
  impulse control (*see also* Disturbance,
    conduct, compulsive) 312.30
  infant sialic acid storage 271.8
  integument, fetus or newborn 778.9
    specified type NEC 778.8
  interactional psychotic (childhood)
    (*see also* Psychosis, childhood)
    299.1 ☑
  intermittent explosive 312.34
  intervertebral disc 722.90
    cervical, cervicothoracic 722.91
    lumbar, lumbosacral 722.93
    thoracic, thoracolumbar 722.92
  intestinal 569.9
    functional NEC 564.9
      congenital 751.3
      postoperative 564.4
    psychogenic 306.4
  introverted, of childhood and adoles-
    cence 313.22
  iron, metabolism 275.0
  isolated explosive 312.35
  joint NEC 719.90
    ankle 719.97
    elbow 719.92
    foot 719.97
    hand 719.94
    hip 719.95
    knee 719.96
    multiple sites 719.99
    pelvic region 719.95
    psychogenic 306.0
    shoulder (region) 719.91
    specified site NEC 719.98

☑ Additional Digit Required — Refer to the Tabular List for Digit Selection   ▽ Subterms under main terms may continue to next column or page

94 — Volume 2 • October 2006   ▶◀ Revised Text   ● New Line   ▲ Revised Code   *2007 ICD-9-CM*

Disorder — *see also* Disease — *continued*
joint — *continued*
  temporomandibular 524.60
    sounds on opening or closing 524.64
    specified NEC 524.69
  wrist 719.93
kidney 593.9
  functional 588.9
    specified NEC 588.89
labyrinth, labyrinthine 386.9
  specified type NEC 386.8
lactation 676.9 ☑
language (developmental) (expressive) 315.31
  mixed receptive-expressive 315.32
learning 315.9
ligament 728.9
ligamentous attachments, peripheral (*see also* Enthesopathy)
  spine 720.1
limb NEC 729.9
  psychogenic 306.0
lipid
  metabolism, congenital 272.9
  storage 272.7
lipoprotein deficiency (familial) 272.5
low back NEC 724.9
  psychogenic 306.0
lumbosacral
  plexus 353.1
  root (nerve) NEC 353.4
lymphoproliferative (chronic) NEC (M9970/1) 238.79 ▲
major depressive (*see also* Psychosis, affective) 296.2 ☑
  recurrent episode 296.3 ☑
  single episode 296.2 ☑
male erectile 607.84
  nonorganic origin 302.72
manic (*see also* Psychosis, affective) 296.0 ☑
  atypical 296.81
mathematics 315.1
meniscus NEC (*see also* Disorder, cartilage, articular) 718.0 ☑
menopausal 627.9
  specified NEC 627.8
menstrual 626.9
  psychogenic 306.52
  specified NEC 626.8
mental (nonpsychotic) 300.9
  affecting management of pregnancy, childbirth, or puerperium 648.4 ☑
  drug-induced 292.9
    hallucinogen persisting perception 292.89
    specified type NEC 292.89
  due to or associated with
    alcoholism 291.9
    drug consumption NEC 292.9
     specified type NEC 292.89
    physical condition NEC 293.9
  induced by drug 292.9
    specified type NEC 292.89
  neurotic (*see also* Neurosis) 300.9
  of infancy, childhood or adolescence 313.9
  persistent
    other
     due to conditions classified elsewhere 294.8
    unspecified
     due to conditions classified elsewhere 294.9
  presenile 310.1
    psychotic NEC 290.10
  previous, affecting management of pregnancy V23.89
  psychoneurotic (*see also* Neurosis) 300.9
  psychotic (*see also* Psychosis) 298.9
    brief 298.8

Disorder — *see also* Disease — *continued*
mental — *continued*
  psychotic (*see also* Psychosis) — *continued*
    senile 290.20
  specific, following organic brain damage 310.9
    cognitive or personality change of other type 310.1
    frontal lobe syndrome 310.0
    postconcussional syndrome 310.2
    specified type NEC 310.8
  transient
    in conditions classified elsewhere 293.9
metabolism NEC 277.9
  with
    abortion — *see* Abortion, by type, with metabolic disorder
    ectopic pregnancy (*see also* categories 633.0–633.9) 639.4
    molar pregnancy (*see also* categories 630–632) 639.4
  alkaptonuria 270.2
  amino acid (*see also* Disorder, amino acid) 270.9
    specified type NEC 270.8
  ammonia 270.6
  arginine 270.6
  argininosuccinic acid 270.6
  basal 794.7
  bilirubin 277.4
  calcium 275.40
  carbohydrate 271.9
    specified type NEC 271.8
  cholesterol 272.9
  citrulline 270.6
  copper 275.1
  corticosteroid 255.2
  cystine storage 270.0
  cystinuria 270.0
  fat 272.9
  fatty acid oxidation 277.85
  following
    abortion 639.4
    ectopic or molar pregnancy 639.4
  fructosemia 271.2
  fructosuria 271.2
  fucosidosis 271.8
  galactose-1-phosphate uridyl transferase 271.1
  glutamine 270.7
  glycine 270.7
  glycogen storage NEC 271.0
    hepatorenal 271.0
  hemochromatosis 275.0
  in labor and delivery 669.0 ☑
  iron 275.0
  lactose 271.3
  lipid 272.9
    specified type NEC 272.8
    storage 272.7
  lipoprotein (*see also* Hyperlipemia deficiency (familial)) 272.5
  lysine 270.7
  magnesium 275.2
  mannosidosis 271.8
  mineral 275.9
    specified type NEC 275.8
  mitochondrial 277.87
  mucopolysaccharide 277.5
  nitrogen 270.9
  ornithine 270.6
  oxalosis 271.8
  pentosuria 271.8
  phenylketonuria 270.1
  phosphate 275.3
  phosphorous 275.3
  plasma protein 273.9
    specified type NEC 273.8
  porphyrin 277.1

Disorder — *see also* Disease — *continued*
metabolism — *continued*
  purine 277.2
  pyrimidine 277.2
  serine 270.7
  sodium 276.9
  specified type NEC 277.89
  steroid 255.2
  threonine 270.7
  urea cycle 270.6
  xylose 271.8
micturition NEC 788.69
  psychogenic 306.53
misery and unhappiness, of childhood and adolescence 313.1
mitochondrial metabolism 277.87
mitral valve 424.0
mood (*see also* Disorder, bipolar) 296.90
  episodic 296.90
    specified NEC 296.99
  in conditions classified elsewhere 293.83
motor tic 307.20
  chronic 307.22
  transient (childhood) 307.21
movement NEC 333.90
  hysterical 300.11
  medication-induced 333.90
  periodic limb 327.51
  sleep related, unspecified 780.58
    other organic 327.59
  specified type NEC 333.99
  stereotypic 307.3
mucopolysaccharide 277.5
muscle 728.9
  psychogenic 306.0
  specified type NEC 728.3
muscular attachments, peripheral (*see also* Enthesopathy)
  spine 720.1
musculoskeletal system NEC 729.9
  psychogenic 306.0
myeloproliferative (chronic) NEC (M9960/1) 238.79 ▲
myoneural 358.9
  due to lead 358.2
  specified type NEC 358.8
  toxic 358.2
myotonic 359.2
neck region NEC 723.9
nerve 349.9
  abducens NEC 378.54
  accessory 352.4
  acoustic 388.5
  auditory 388.5
  auriculotemporal 350.8
  axillary 353.0
  cerebral — *see* Disorder, nerve, cranial
  cranial 352.9
    first 352.0
    second 377.49
    third
     partial 378.51
     total 378.52
    fourth 378.53
    fifth 350.9
    sixth 378.54
    seventh NEC 351.9
    eighth 388.5
    ninth 352.2
    tenth 352.3
    eleventh 352.4
    twelfth 352.5
    multiple 352.6
  entrapment — *see* Neuropathy, entrapment
  facial 351.9
    specified NEC 351.8
  femoral 355.2
  glossopharyngeal NEC 352.2
  hypoglossal 352.5
  iliohypogastric 355.79
  ilioinguinal 355.79

Disorder — *see also* Disease — *continued*
nerve — *continued*
  intercostal 353.8
  lateral
    cutaneous of thigh 355.1
    popliteal 355.3
  lower limb NEC 355.8
  medial, popliteal 355.4
  median NEC 354.1
  obturator 355.79
  oculomotor
    partial 378.51
    total 378.52
  olfactory 352.0
  optic 377.49
    hypoplasia 377.43 ●
    ischemic 377.41
    nutritional 377.33
    toxic 377.34
  peroneal 355.3
  phrenic 354.8
  plantar 355.6
  pneumogastric 352.3
  posterior tibial 355.5
  radial 354.3
  recurrent laryngeal 352.3
  root 353.9
    specified NEC 353.8
  saphenous 355.79
  sciatic NEC 355.0
  specified NEC 355.9
    lower limb 355.79
    upper limb 354.8
  spinal 355.9
  sympathetic NEC 337.9
  trigeminal 350.9
    specified NEC 350.8
  trochlear 378.53
  ulnar 354.2
  upper limb NEC 354.9
  vagus 352.3
nervous system NEC 349.9
  autonomic (peripheral) (*see also* Neuropathy, peripheral, autonomic) 337.9
  cranial 352.9
  parasympathetic (*see also* Neuropathy, peripheral, autonomic) 337.9
  specified type NEC 349.89
  sympathetic (*see also* Neuropathy, peripheral, autonomic) 337.9
  vegetative (*see also* Neuropathy, peripheral, autonomic) 337.9
neurohypophysis NEC 253.6
neurological NEC 781.99
  peripheral NEC 355.9
neuromuscular NEC 358.9
  hereditary NEC 359.1
  specified NEC 358.8
  toxic 358.2
neurotic 300.9
  specified type NEC 300.89
neutrophil, polymorphonuclear (functional) 288.1
nightmare 307.47
night terror 307.46
obsessive-compulsive 300.3
oppositional defiant, childhood and adolescence 313.81
optic
  chiasm 377.54
    associated with
     inflammatory disorders 377.54
     neoplasm NEC 377.52
      pituitary 377.51
     pituitary disorders 377.51
     vascular disorders 377.53
  nerve 377.49
  radiations 377.63
  tracts 377.63
orbit 376.9
  specified NEC 376.89

☑ Additional Digit Required — Refer to the Tabular List for Digit Selection   ▽ Subterms under main terms may continue to next column or page

2007 ICD-9-CM   ▶◀ Revised Text   ● New Line   ▲ Revised Code   October 2006 · Volume 2 — 95

Disorder — *see also* Disease — *continued*

orgasmic
  female 302.73
  male 302.74
overanxious, of childhood and adolescence 313.0
oxidation, fatty acid 277.85
pancreas, internal secretion (other than diabetes mellitus) 251.9
  specified type NEC 251.8
panic 300.01
  with agoraphobia 300.21
papillary muscle NEC 429.81
paranoid 297.9
  induced 297.3
  shared 297.3
parathyroid 252.9
  specified type NEC 252.8
paroxysmal, mixed 780.39
pentose phosphate pathway with anemia 282.2
periodic limb movement 327.51
peroxisomal 277.86
personality 301.9
  affective 301.10
  aggressive 301.3
  amoral 301.7
  anancastic, anankastic 301.4
  antisocial 301.7
  asocial 301.7
  asthenic 301.6
  avoidant 301.82
  borderline 301.83
  compulsive 301.4
  cyclothymic 301.13
  dependent-passive 301.6
  dyssocial 301.7
  emotional instability 301.59
  epileptoid 301.3
  explosive 301.3
  following organic brain damage 310.1
  histrionic 301.50
  hyperthymic 301.11
  hypomanic (chronic) 301.11
  hypothymic 301.12
  hysterical 301.50
  immature 301.89
  inadequate 301.6
  introverted 301.21
  labile 301.59
  moral deficiency 301.7
  narcissistic 301.81
  obsessional 301.4
  obsessive-compulsive 301.4
  overconscientious 301.4
  paranoid 301.0
  passive (-dependent) 301.6
  passive-aggressive 301.84
  pathological NEC 301.9
  pseudosocial 301.7
  psychopathic 301.9
  schizoid 301.20
    introverted 301.21
    schizotypal 301.22
  schizotypal 301.22
  seductive 301.59
  type A 301.4
  unstable 301.59
pervasive developmental 299.9 ☑
  childhood-onset 299.8 ☑
  specified NEC 299.8 ☑
phonological 315.39
pigmentation, choroid (congenital) 743.53
pinna 380.30
  specified type NEC 380.39
pituitary, thalamic 253.9
  anterior NEC 253.4
  iatrogenic 253.7
  postablative 253.7
  specified NEC 253.8
pityriasis-like NEC 696.8
platelets (blood) 287.1

Disorder — *see also* Disease — *continued*

polymorphonuclear neutrophils (functional) 288.1
porphyrin metabolism 277.1
postmenopausal 627.9
  specified type NEC 627.8
posttraumatic stress 309.81
post-traumatic stress (PTSD) 309.81 ●
  acute 309.81
  brief 309.81
  chronic 309.81
premenstrual dysphoric (PMDD) 625.4
psoriatic-like NEC 696.8
psychic, with diseases classified elsewhere 316
psychogenic NEC (*see also* condition) 300.9
  allergic NEC
    respiratory 306.1
  anxiety 300.00
    atypical 300.00
    generalized 300.02
  appetite 307.59
  articulation, joint 306.0
  asthenic 300.5
  blood 306.8
  cardiovascular (system) 306.2
  compulsive 300.3
  cutaneous 306.3
  depressive 300.4
  digestive (system) 306.4
  dysmenorrheic 306.52
  dyspneic 306.1
  eczematous 306.3
  endocrine (system) 306.6
  eye 306.7
  feeding 307.59
  functional NEC 306.9
  gastric 306.4
  gastrointestinal (system) 306.4
  genitourinary (system) 306.50
  heart (function) (rhythm) 306.2
  hemic 306.8
  hyperventilatory 306.1
  hypochondriacal 300.7
  hysterical 300.10
  intestinal 306.4
  joint 306.0
  learning 315.2
  limb 306.0
  lymphatic (system) 306.8
  menstrual 306.52
  micturition 306.53
  monoplegic NEC 306.0
  motor 307.9
  muscle 306.0
  musculoskeletal 306.0
  neurocirculatory 306.2
  obsessive 300.3
  occupational 300.89
  organ or part of body NEC 306.9
  organs of special sense 306.7
  paralytic NEC 306.0
  phobic 300.20
  physical NEC 306.9
  pruritic 306.3
  rectal 306.4
  respiratory (system) 306.1
  rheumatic 306.0
  sexual (function) 302.70
    specified type NEC 302.79
  sexual orientation conflict 302.0
  skin (allergic) (eczematous) (pruritic) 306.3
  sleep 307.40
    initiation or maintenance 307.41
      persistent 307.42
      transient 307.41
    movement 780.58
    sleep terror 307.46
    specified type NEC 307.49
  specified part of body NEC 306.8
  stomach 306.4
psychomotor NEC 307.9

Disorder — *see also* Disease — *continued*

psychomotor — *continued*
  hysterical 300.11
psychoneurotic (*see also* Neurosis) 300.9
  mixed NEC 300.89
psychophysiologic (*see also* Disorder, psychosomatic) 306.9
psychosexual identity (childhood) 302.6
  adult-life 302.85
psychosomatic NEC 306.9
  allergic NEC
    respiratory 306.1
  articulation, joint 306.0
  cardiovascular (system) 306.2
  cutaneous 306.3
  digestive (system) 306.4
  dysmenorrheic 306.52
  dyspneic 306.1
  endocrine (system) 306.6
  eye 306.7
  gastric 306.4
  gastrointestinal (system) 306.4
  genitourinary (system) 306.50
  heart (functional) (rhythm) 306.2
  hyperventilatory 306.1
  intestinal 306.4
  joint 306.0
  limb 306.0
  lymphatic (system) 306.8
  menstrual 306.52
  micturition 306.53
  monoplegic NEC 306.0
  muscle 306.0
  musculoskeletal 306.0
  neurocirculatory 306.2
  organs of special sense 306.7
  paralytic NEC 306.0
  pruritic 306.3
  rectal 306.4
  respiratory (system) 306.1
  rheumatic 306.0
  sexual (function) 302.70
  skin 306.3
  specified part of body NEC 306.8
  specified type NEC 302.79
  stomach 306.4
psychotic (*see also* Psychosis) 298.9
  brief 298.8
purine metabolism NEC 277.2
pyrimidine metabolism NEC 277.2
reactive attachment of infancy or early childhood 313.89
reading, developmental 315.00
reflex 796.1
REM sleep behavior 327.42
renal function, impaired 588.9
  specified type NEC 588.89
renal transport NEC 588.89
respiration, respiratory NEC 519.9
  due to
    aspiration of liquids or solids 508.9
    inhalation of fumes or vapors 506.9
  psychogenic 306.1
retina 362.9
  specified type NEC 362.89
rumination 307.53
sacroiliac joint NEC 724.6
sacrum 724.6
schizo-affective (*see also* Schizophrenia) 295.7 ☑
schizoid, childhood or adolescence 313.22
schizophreniform 295.4 ☑
schizotypal personality 301.22
secretion, thyrocalcitonin 246.0
seizure 345.9 ☑   ▲
  recurrent 345.9 ☑   ▲
  epileptic — *see* Epilepsy
sense of smell 781.1
  psychogenic 306.7
separation anxiety 309.21

Disorder — *see also* Disease — *continued*

sexual (*see also* Deviation, sexual) 302.9
  aversion 302.79
  desire, hypoactive 302.71
  function, psychogenic 302.70
shyness, of childhood and adolescence 313.21
single complement (C1-C9) 279.8
skin NEC 709.9
  fetus or newborn 778.9
    specified type 778.8
  psychogenic (allergic) (eczematous) (pruritic) 306.3
  specified type NEC 709.8
  vascular 709.1
sleep 780.50
  with apnea — *see* Apnea, sleep
  alcohol induced 291.82
  arousal 307.46
    confusional 327.41
  circadian rhythm 327.30
    advanced sleep phase type 327.32
    alcohol induced 291.82
    delayed sleep phase type 327.31
    drug induced 292.85
    free running type 327.34
    in conditions classified elsewhere 327.37
    irregular sleep-wake type 327.33
    jet lag type 327.35
    other 327.39
    shift work type 327.36
  drug induced 292.85
  initiation or maintenance (*see also* Insomnia) 780.52
    nonorganic origin (transient) 307.41
    persistent 307.42
  nonorganic origin 307.40
    specified type NEC 307.49
  organic specified type NEC 327.8
  periodic limb movement 327.51
  specified NEC 780.59
  wake
    cycle — *see* Disorder, sleep, circadian rhythm
    schedule — *see* Disorer, sleep, circadian rhythm
social, of childhood and adolescence 313.22
soft tissue 729.9
somatization 300.81
somatoform (atypical) (undifferentiated) 300.82
  severe 300.81
  specified type NEC 300.89
speech NEC 784.5
  nonorganic origin 307.9
spine NEC 724.9
  ligamentous or muscular attachments, peripheral 720.1
steroid metabolism NEC 255.2
stomach (functional) (*see also* Disorder, gastric) 536.9
  psychogenic 306.4
storage, iron 275.0
stress (*see also* Reaction, stress, acute) 308.3
  posttraumatic
    acute 309.81
    brief 309.81
    chronic 309.81
substitution 300.11
suspected — *see* Observation
synovium 727.9
temperature regulation, fetus or newborn 778.4
temporomandibular joint NEC 524.60
  sounds on opening or closing 524.64
  specified NEC 524.69
tendon 727.9

Disorder — see also Disease —
  continued
  tendon — continued
    shoulder region 726.10
  thoracic root (nerve) NEC 353.3
  thyrocalcitonin secretion 246.0
  thyroid (gland) NEC 246.9
    specified type NEC 246.8
  tic 307.20
    chronic (motor or vocal) 307.22
    motor-verbal 307.23
    organic origin 333.1
    transient (of childhood) 307.21
  tooth NEC 525.9
    development NEC 520.9
      specified type NEC 520.8
    eruption 520.6
    specified type NEC 525.8
  Tourette's 307.23
  transport, carbohydrate 271.9
    specified type NEC 271.8
  tubular, phosphate-losing 588.0
  tympanic membrane 384.9
  unaggressive, unsocialized (see also
    Disturbance, conduct) 312.1 ☑
  undersocialized, unsocialized (see also
    Disturbance, conduct)
    aggressive (type) 312.0 ☑
    unaggressive (type) 312.1 ☑
  vision, visual NEC 368.9
    binocular NEC 368.30
    cortex 377.73
      associated with
        inflammatory disorders
          377.73
        neoplasms 377.71
        vascular disorders 377.72
    pathway NEC 377.63
      associated with
        inflammatory disorders
          377.63
        neoplasms 377.61
        vascular disorders 377.62
  vocal tic
    chronic 307.22
  wakefulness (see also Hypersomnia)
    780.54
    nonorganic origin (transient)
      307.43
    persistent 307.44
  written expression 315.2
Disorganized globe 360.29
Displacement, displaced

> Note — For acquired displacement of
> bones, cartilage, joints, tendons, due to
> injury, see also Dislocation.
>
> Displacements at ages under one year
> should be considered congenital, provid-
> ed there is no indication the condition
> was acquired after birth.

  acquired traumatic of bone, cartilage,
    joint, tendon NEC (without
    fracture) (see also Dislocation)
    839.8
    with fracture — see Fracture, by
      site
  adrenal gland (congenital) 759.1
  alveolus and teeth, vertical 524.75
  appendix, retrocecal (congenital) 751.5
  auricle (congenital) 744.29
  bladder (acquired) 596.8
    congenital 753.8
  brachial plexus (congenital) 742.8
  brain stem, caudal 742.4
  canaliculus lacrimalis 743.65
  cardia, through esophageal hiatus
    750.6
  cerebellum, caudal 742.4
  cervix ▶— see Displacement, uterus◀
  colon (congenital) 751.4
  device, implant, or graft — see Compli-
    cations, mechanical
  epithelium
    columnar of cervix 622.10

Displacement, displaced —
  continued
  epithelium — continued
    cuboidal, beyond limits of external
      os (uterus) 752.49
  esophageal mucosa into cardia of
    stomach, congenital 750.4
  esophagus (acquired) 530.89
    congenital 750.4
  eyeball (acquired) (old) 376.36
    congenital 743.8
    current injury 871.3
    lateral 376.36
  fallopian tube (acquired) 620.4
    congenital 752.19
    opening (congenital) 752.19
  gallbladder (congenital) 751.69
  gastric mucosa 750.7
    into
      duodenum 750.7
      esophagus 750.7
      Meckel's diverticulum, congeni-
        tal 750.7
  globe (acquired) (lateral) (old) 376.36
    current injury 871.3
  graft
    artificial skin graft 996.55
    decellularized allodermis graft
      996.55
  heart (congenital) 746.87
    acquired 429.89
  hymen (congenital) (upward) 752.49
  internal prosthesis NEC — see Com-
    plications, mechanical
  intervertebral disc (with neuritis,
    radiculitis, sciatica, or other
    pain) 722.2
    with myelopathy 722.70
    cervical, cervicodorsal, cervicotho-
      racic 722.0
      with myelopathy 722.71
      due to major trauma — see
        Dislocation, vertebra, cer-
        vical
    due to trauma — see Dislocation,
      vertebra
    lumbar, lumbosacral 722.10
      with myelopathy 722.73
      due to major trauma — see
        Dislocation, vertebra,
        lumbar
    thoracic, thoracolumbar 722.11
      with myelopathy 722.72
      due to major trauma — see
        Dislocation, vertebra, tho-
        racic
  intrauterine device 996.32
  kidney (acquired) 593.0
    congenital 753.3
  lacrimal apparatus or duct (congeni-
    tal) 743.65
  macula (congenital) 743.55
  Meckel's diverticulum (congenital)
    751.0
  nail (congenital) 757.5
    acquired 703.8
  opening of Wharton's duct in mouth
    750.26
  organ or site, congenital NEC — see
    Malposition, congenital
  ovary (acquired) 620.4
    congenital 752.0
    free in peritoneal cavity (congenital)
      752.0
    into hernial sac 620.4
  oviduct (acquired) 620.4
    congenital 752.19
  parathyroid (gland) 252.8
  parotid gland (congenital) 750.26
  punctum lacrimale (congenital) 743.65
  sacroiliac (congenital) (joint) 755.69
    current injury — see Dislocation,
      sacroiliac
    old 724.6
  spine (congenital) 756.19
  spleen, congenital 759.0

Displacement, displaced —
  continued
  stomach (congenital) 750.7
    acquired 537.89
  subglenoid (closed) 831.01
  sublingual duct (congenital) 750.26
  teeth, tooth 524.30
    horizontal 524.33
    vertical 524.34
  tongue (congenital) (downward) 750.19
  trachea (congenital) 748.3
  ureter or ureteric opening or orifice
    (congenital) 753.4
  uterine opening of oviducts or fallopi-
    an tubes 752.19
  uterus, uterine (see also Malposition,
    uterus) 621.6
    congenital 752.3
  ventricular septum 746.89
    with rudimentary ventricle 746.89
  xyphoid bone (process) 738.3
Disproportion 653.9 ☑
  affecting fetus or newborn 763.1
  caused by
    conjoined twins 653.7 ☑
    contraction, pelvis (general)
      653.1 ☑
      inlet 653.2 ☑
      midpelvic 653.8 ☑
      midplane 653.8 ☑
      outlet 653.3 ☑
    fetal
      ascites 653.7 ☑
      hydrocephalus 653.6 ☑
      hydrops 653.7 ☑
      meningomyelocele 653.7 ☑
      sacral teratoma 653.7 ☑
      tumor 653.7 ☑
    hydrocephalic fetus 653.6 ☑
    pelvis, pelvic, abnormality (bony)
      NEC 653.0 ☑
    unusually large fetus 653.5 ☑
  causing obstructed labor 660.1 ☑
  cephalopelvic, normally formed fetus
    653.4 ☑
    causing obstructed labor 660.1 ☑
  fetal NEC 653.5 ☑
    causing obstructed labor 660.1 ☑
  fetopelvic, normally formed fetus
    653.4 ☑
    causing obstructed labor 660.1 ☑
  mixed maternal and fetal origin, nor-
    mally formed fetus 653.4 ☑
  pelvis, pelvic (bony) NEC 653.1 ☑
    causing obstructed labor 660.1 ☑
  specified type NEC 653.8 ☑
Disruption
  cesarean wound 674.1 ☑
  family V61.0
  gastrointestinal anastomosis 997.4
  ligament(s) (see also Sprain)
    knee
      current injury — see Disloca-
        tion, knee
      old 717.89
        capsular 717.85
        collateral (medial) 717.82
          lateral 717.81
        cruciate (posterior) 717.84
          anterior 717.83
        specified site NEC 717.85
  marital V61.10
    involving divorce or estrangement
      V61.0
  operation wound (external) 998.32
    internal 998.31
  organ transplant, anastomosis site —
    see Complications, transplant,
    organ, by site
  ossicles, ossicular chain 385.23
    traumatic — see Fracture, skull,
      base
  parenchyma
    liver (hepatic) — see Laceration,
      liver, major

Disruption — continued
  parenchyma — continued
    spleen — see Laceration, spleen,
      parenchyma, massive
  phase-shift, of 24-hour sleep-wake
    cycle, unspecified 780.55
    nonorganic origin 307.45
  sleep-wake cycle (24-hour), unspeci-
    fied 780.55
    circadian rhythm 327.33
    nonorganic origin 307.45
  suture line (external) 998.32
    internal 998.31
  wound
    cesarean operation 674.1 ☑
    episiotomy 674.2 ☑
    operation 998.32
      cesarean 674.1 ☑
      internal 998.31
    perineal (obstetric) 674.2 ☑
    uterine 674.1 ☑
Disruptio uteri — see also Rupture,
  uterus
  complicating delivery — see Delivery,
    complicated, rupture, uterus
Dissatisfaction with
  employment V62.2
  school environment V62.3
Dissecting — see condition
Dissection
  aorta 441.00
    abdominal 441.02
    thoracic 441.01
    thoracoabdominal 441.03
  artery, arterial
    carotid 443.21
    coronary 414.12
    iliac 443.22
    renal 443.23
    specified NEC 443.29
    vertebral 443.24
  vascular 459.9
  wound — see Wound, open, by site
Disseminated — see condition
Dissociated personality NEC 300.15
Dissociation
  auriculoventricular or atrioventricular
    (any degree) (AV) 426.89
    with heart block 426.0
  interference 426.89
  isorhythmic 426.89
  rhythm
    atrioventricular (AV) 426.89
    interference 426.89
Dissociative
  identity disorder 300.14
  reaction NEC 300.15
Dissolution, vertebra — see also Osteoporosis 733.00
Distention
  abdomen (gaseous) 787.3
  bladder 596.8
  cecum 569.89
  colon 569.89
  gallbladder 575.8
  gaseous (abdomen) 787.3
  intestine 569.89
  kidney 593.89
  liver 573.9
  seminal vesicle 608.89
  stomach 536.8
    acute 536.1
    psychogenic 306.4
  ureter 593.5
  uterus 621.8
Distichia, distichiasis (eyelid) 743.63
Distoma hepaticum infestation 121.3
Distomiasis 121.9
  bile passages 121.3
    due to Clonorchis sinensis 121.1
  hemic 120.9
  hepatic (liver) 121.3
    due to Clonorchis sinensis
      (clonorchiasis) 121.1
  intestinal 121.4
  liver 121.3

☑ Additional Digit Required — Refer to the Tabular List for Digit Selection

𝄞 Subterms under main terms may continue to next column or page

2007 ICD-9-CM

▶◀ Revised Text   ● New Line   ▲ Revised Code

October 2006 · Volume 2 — 97

Disorder — Distomiasis

Distomiasis — *continued*
  liver — *continued*
    due to Clonorchis sinensis 121.1
  lung 121.2
  pulmonary 121.2
Distomolar (fourth molar) 520.1
  causing crowding 524.31
Disto-occlusion (division I) (division II) 524.22
Distortion (congenital)
  adrenal (gland) 759.1
  ankle (joint) 755.69
  anus 751.5
  aorta 747.29
  appendix 751.5
  arm 755.59
  artery (peripheral) NEC (*see also* Distortion, peripheral vascular system) 747.60
    cerebral 747.81
    coronary 746.85
    pulmonary 747.3
    retinal 743.58
    umbilical 747.5
  auditory canal 744.29
    causing impairment of hearing 744.02
  bile duct or passage 751.69
  bladder 753.8
  brain 742.4
  bronchus 748.3
  cecum 751.5
  cervix (uteri) 752.49
  chest (wall) 756.3
  clavicle 755.51
  clitoris 752.49
  coccyx 756.19
  colon 751.5
  common duct 751.69
  cornea 743.41
  cricoid cartilage 748.3
  cystic duct 751.69
  duodenum 751.5
  ear 744.29
    auricle 744.29
      causing impairment of hearing 744.02
    causing impairment of hearing 744.09
    external 744.29
      causing impairment of hearing 744.02
    inner 744.05
    middle, except ossicles 744.03
      ossicles 744.04
    ossicles 744.04
  endocrine (gland) NEC 759.2
  epiglottis 748.3
  Eustachian tube 744.24
  eye 743.8
    adnexa 743.69
  face bone(s) 756.0
  fallopian tube 752.19
  femur 755.69
  fibula 755.69
  finger(s) 755.59
  foot 755.67
  gallbladder 751.69
  genitalia, genital organ(s)
    female 752.89
      external 752.49
      internal NEC 752.89
    male 752.89
      penis 752.69
  glottis 748.3
  gyri 742.4
  hand bone(s) 755.59
  heart (auricle) (ventricle) 746.89
    valve (cusp) 746.89
  hepatic duct 751.69
  humerus 755.59
  hymen 752.49
  ileum 751.5
  intestine (large) (small) 751.5
    with anomalous adhesions, fixation or malrotation 751.4

Distortion — *continued*
  jaw NEC 524.89
  jejunum 751.5
  kidney 753.3
  knee (joint) 755.64
  labium (majus) (minus) 752.49
  larynx 748.3
  leg 755.69
  lens 743.36
  liver 751.69
  lumbar spine 756.19
    with disproportion (fetopelvic) 653.0 ☑
      affecting fetus or newborn 763.1
      causing obstructed labor 660.1 ☑
  lumbosacral (joint) (region) 756.19
  lung (fissures) (lobe) 748.69
  nerve 742.8
  nose 748.1
  organ
    of Corti 744.05
    of site not listed — *see* Anomaly, specified type NEC
  ossicles, ear 744.04
  ovary 752.0
  oviduct 752.19
  pancreas 751.7
  parathyroid (gland) 759.2
  patella 755.64
  peripheral vascular system NEC 747.60
    gastrointestinal 747.61
    lower limb 747.64
    renal 747.62
    spinal 747.82
    upper limb 747.63
  pituitary (gland) 759.2
  radius 755.59
  rectum 751.5
  rib 756.3
  sacroiliac joint 755.69
  sacrum 756.19
  scapula 755.59
  shoulder girdle 755.59
  site not listed — *see* Anomaly, specified type NEC
  skull bone(s) 756.0
    with
      anencephalus 740.0
      encephalocele 742.0
      hydrocephalus 742.3
        with spina bifida (*see also* Spina bifida) 741.0 ☑
      microcephalus 742.1
  spinal cord 742.59
  spine 756.19
  spleen 759.0
  sternum 756.3
  thorax (wall) 756.3
  thymus (gland) 759.2
  thyroid (gland) 759.2
    cartilage 748.3
  tibia 755.69
  toe(s) 755.66
  tongue 750.19
  trachea (cartilage) 748.3
  ulna 755.59
  ureter 753.4
    causing obstruction 753.20
  urethra 753.8
    causing obstruction 753.6
  uterus 752.3
  vagina 752.49
  vein (peripheral) NEC (*see also* Distortion, peripheral vascular system) 747.60
    great 747.49
    portal 747.49
    pulmonary 747.49
  vena cava (inferior) (superior) 747.49
  vertebra 756.19
  visual NEC 368.15
    shape or size 368.14
  vulva 752.49
  wrist (bones) (joint) 755.59

Distress
  abdomen 789.0 ☑
  colon 564.9
  emotional V40.9
  epigastric 789.0 ☑
  fetal (syndrome) 768.4
    affecting management of pregnancy or childbirth 656.8 ☑
    liveborn infant 768.4
    first noted
      before onset of labor 768.2
      during labor ▶and◀ delivery 768.3
    stillborn infant (death before onset of labor) 768.0
      death during labor 768.1
  gastrointestinal (functional) 536.9
    psychogenic 306.4
  intestinal (functional) NEC 564.9
    psychogenic 306.4
  intrauterine — *see* Distress, fetal
  leg 729.5
  maternal 669.0 ☑
  mental V40.9
  respiratory 786.09
    acute (adult) 518.82
    adult syndrome (following shock, surgery, or trauma) 518.5
      specified NEC 518.82
    fetus or newborn 770.89
    syndrome (idiopathic) (newborn) 769
  stomach 536.9
    psychogenic 306.4
Distribution vessel, atypical NEC 747.60
  coronary artery 746.85
  spinal 747.82
Districhiasis 704.2
Disturbance — *see also* Disease
  absorption NEC 579.9
    calcium 269.3
    carbohydrate 579.8
    fat 579.8
    protein 579.8
    specified type NEC 579.8
    vitamin (*see also* Deficiency, vitamin) 269.2
  acid-base equilibrium 276.9
  activity and attention, simple, with hyperkinesis 314.01
  amino acid (metabolic) (*see also* Disorder, amino acid) 270.9
    imidazole 270.5
    maple syrup (urine) disease 270.3
    transport 270.0
  assimilation, food 579.9
  attention, simple 314.00
    with hyperactivity 314.01
  auditory, nerve, except deafness 388.5
  behavior (*see also* Disturbance, conduct) 312.9
  blood clotting (hypoproteinemia) (mechanism) (*see also* Defect, coagulation) 286.9
  central nervous system NEC 349.9
  cerebral nerve NEC 352.9
  circulatory 459.9
  conduct 312.9

> *Note* — Use the following fifth-digit subclassification with categories 312.0–312.2:
>
> *0* unspecified
>
> *1* mild
>
> *2* moderate
>
> *3* severe

    adjustment reaction 309.3
    adolescent onset type 312.82
    childhood onset type 312.81
    compulsive 312.30
      intermittent explosive disorder 312.34
      isolated explosive disorder 312.35

Disturbance — *see also* Disease — *continued*
  conduct — *continued*
    compulsive — *continued*
      kleptomania 312.32
      pathological gambling 312.31
      pyromania 312.33
    hyperkinetic 314.2
    intermittent explosive 312.34
    isolated explosive 312.35
    mixed with emotions 312.4
    socialized (type) 312.20
      aggressive 312.23
      unaggressive 312.21
    specified type NEC 312.89
    undersocialized, unsocialized
      aggressive (type) 312.0 ☑
      unaggressive (type) 312.1 ☑
  coordination 781.3
  cranial nerve NEC 352.9
  deep sensibility — *see* Disturbance, sensation
  digestive 536.9
    psychogenic 306.4
  electrolyte — *see* Imbalance, electrolyte
  emotions specific to childhood or adolescence 313.9
    with
      academic underachievement 313.83
      anxiety and fearfulness 313.0
      elective mutism 313.23
      identity disorder 313.82
      jealousy 313.3
      misery and unhappiness 313.1
      oppositional defiant disorder 313.81
      overanxiousness 313.0
      sensitivity 313.21
      shyness 313.21
      social withdrawal 313.22
      withdrawal reaction 313.22
      involving relationship problems 313.3
    mixed 313.89
    specified type NEC 313.89
  endocrine (gland) 259.9
    neonatal, transitory 775.9
      specified NEC 775.89 ▲
  equilibrium 780.4
  feeding (elderly) (infant) 783.3
    newborn 779.3
    nonorganic origin NEC 307.59
    psychogenic NEC 307.59
  fructose metabolism 271.2
  gait 781.2
    hysterical 300.11
  gastric (functional) 536.9
    motility 536.8
    psychogenic 306.4
    secretion 536.8
  gastrointestinal (functional) 536.9
    psychogenic 306.4
  habit, child 307.9
  hearing, except deafness 388.40
  heart, functional (conditions classifiable to 426, 427, 428)
    due to presence of (cardiac) prosthesis 429.4
    postoperative (immediate) 997.1
      long-term effect of cardiac surgery 429.4
    psychogenic 306.2
  hormone 259.9
  innervation uterus, sympathetic, parasympathetic 621.8
  keratinization NEC
    gingiva 523.10 ▲
    lip 528.5
    oral (mucosa) (soft tissue) 528.79
      residual ridge mucosa
        excessive 528.72
        minimal 528.71
    tongue 528.79

Disturbance — *see also* Disease — *continued*
labyrinth, labyrinthine (vestibule) 386.9
learning, specific NEC 315.2
memory (*see also* Amnesia) 780.93
  mild, following organic brain damage 310.8
mental (*see also* Disorder, mental) 300.9
  associated with diseases classified elsewhere 316
metabolism (acquired) (congenital) (*see also* Disorder, metabolism) 277.9
  with
    abortion — *see* Abortion, by type, with metabolic disorder
    ectopic pregnancy (*see also* categories 633.0–633.9) 639.4
    molar pregnancy (*see also* categories 630–632) 639.4
  amino acid (*see also* Disorder, amino acid) 270.9
    aromatic NEC 270.2
    branched-chain 270.3
    specified type NEC 270.8
    straight-chain NEC 270.7
    sulfur-bearing 270.4
    transport 270.0
  ammonia 270.6
  arginine 270.6
  argininosuccinic acid 270.6
  carbohydrate NEC 271.9
  cholesterol 272.9
  citrulline 270.6
  cystathionine 270.4
  fat 272.9
  following
    abortion 639.4
    ectopic or molar pregnancy 639.4
  general 277.9
    carbohydrate 271.9
    iron 275.0
    phosphate 275.3
    sodium 276.9
  glutamine 270.7
  glycine 270.7
  histidine 270.5
  homocystine 270.4
  in labor or delivery 669.0 ☑
  iron 275.0
  isoleucine 270.3
  leucine 270.3
  lipoid 272.9
    specified type NEC 272.8
  lysine 270.7
  methionine 270.4
  neonatal, transitory 775.9
    specified type NEC 775.89 ▲
  nitrogen 788.9
  ornithine 270.6
  phosphate 275.3
  phosphatides 272.7
  serine 270.7
  sodium NEC 276.9
  threonine 270.7
  tryptophan 270.2
  tyrosine 270.2
  urea cycle 270.6
  valine 270.3
motor 796.1
nervous functional 799.2
neuromuscular mechanism (eye) due to syphilis 094.84
nutritional 269.9
  nail 703.8
ocular motion 378.87
  psychogenic 306.7
oculogyric 378.87
  psychogenic 306.7
oculomotor NEC 378.87
  psychogenic 306.7

Disturbance — *see also* Disease — *continued*
olfactory nerve 781.1
optic nerve NEC 377.49
oral epithelium, including tongue 528.79
  residual ridge mucosa
    excessive 528.72
    minimal 528.71
personality (pattern) (trait) (*see also* Disorder, personality) 301.9
  following organic brain damage 310.1
polyglandular 258.9
psychomotor 307.9
pupillary 379.49
reflex 796.1
rhythm, heart 427.9
  postoperative (immediate) 997.1
    long-term effect of cardiac surgery 429.4
  psychogenic 306.2
salivary secretion 527.7
sensation (cold) (heat) (localization) (tactile discrimination localization) (texture) (vibratory) NEC 782.0
  hysterical 300.11
  skin 782.0
  smell 781.1
  taste 781.1
sensory (*see also* Disturbance, sensation) 782.0
  innervation 782.0
situational (transient) (*see also* Reaction, adjustment) 309.9
  acute 308.3
sleep 780.50
  with apnea — *see* Apnea, sleep
  initiation or maintenance (*see also* Insomnia) 780.52
    nonorganic origin 307.41
    nonorganic origin 307.40
      specified type NEC 307.49
    specified NEC 780.59
      nonorganic origin 307.49
    wakefulness (*see also* Hypersomnia) 780.54
      nonorganic origin 307.43
sociopathic 301.7
speech NEC 784.5
  developmental 315.39
    associated with hyperkinesis 314.1
  secondary to organic lesion 784.5
stomach (functional) (*see also* Disturbance, gastric) 536.9
sympathetic (nerve) (*see also* Neuropathy, peripheral, autonomic) 337.9
temperature sense 782.0
  hysterical 300.11
tooth
  eruption 520.6
  formation 520.4
  structure, hereditary NEC 520.5
touch (*see also* Disturbance, sensation) 782.0
vascular 459.9
  arteriosclerotic — *see* Arteriosclerosis
  vasomotor 443.9
  vasospastic 443.9
vestibular labyrinth 386.9
vision, visual NEC 368.9
  psychophysical 368.16
  specified NEC 368.8
  subjective 368.10
voice 784.40
wakefulness (initiation or maintenance) (*see also* Hypersomnia) 780.54
  nonorganic origin 307.43
Disulfiduria, beta-mercaptolactate-cysteine 270.0
Disuse atrophy, bone 733.7

Ditthomska syndrome 307.81
Diuresis 788.42
Divers'
  palsy or paralysis 993.3
  squeeze 993.3
Diverticula, diverticulosis, diverticulum (acute) (multiple) (perforated) (ruptured) 562.10
with diverticulitis 562.11
aorta (Kommerell's) 747.21
appendix (noninflammatory) 543.9
bladder (acquired) (sphincter) 596.3
  congenital 753.8
broad ligament 620.8
bronchus (congenital) 748.3
  acquired 494.0
    with acute exacerbation 494.1
calyx, calyceal (kidney) 593.89
cardia (stomach) 537.1
cecum 562.10
  with
    diverticulitis 562.11
      with hemorrhage 562.13
    hemorrhage 562.12
  congenital 751.5
colon (acquired) 562.10
  with
    diverticulitis 562.11
      with hemorrhage 562.13
    hemorrhage 562.12
  congenital 751.5
duodenum 562.00
  with
    diverticulitis 562.01
      with hemorrhage 562.03
    hemorrhage 562.02
  congenital 751.5
epiphrenic (esophagus) 530.6
esophagus (congenital) 750.4
  acquired 530.6
  epiphrenic 530.6
  pulsion 530.6
  traction 530.6
  Zenker's 530.6
Eustachian tube 381.89
fallopian tube 620.8
gallbladder (congenital) 751.69
gastric 537.1
heart (congenital) 746.89
ileum 562.00
  with
    diverticulitis 562.01
      with hemorrhage 562.03
    hemorrhage 562.02
intestine (large) 562.10
  with
    diverticulitis 562.11
      with hemorrhage 562.13
    hemorrhage 562.12
  congenital 751.5
  small 562.00
    with
      diverticulitis 562.01
        with hemorrhage 562.03
      hemorrhage 562.02
    congenital 751.5
jejunum 562.00
  with
    diverticulitis 562.01
      with hemorrhage 562.03
    hemorrhage 562.02
kidney (calyx) (pelvis) 593.89
  with calculus 592.0
Kommerell's 747.21
laryngeal ventricle (congenital) 748.3
Meckel's (displaced) (hypertrophic) 751.0
midthoracic 530.6
organ or site, congenital NEC — *see* Distortion
pericardium (congenital) (cyst) 746.89
  acquired (true) 423.8
pharyngoesophageal (pulsion) 530.6
pharynx (congenital) 750.27
pulsion (esophagus) 530.6
rectosigmoid 562.10

Diverticula, diverticulosis, diverticulum — *continued*
rectosigmoid — *continued*
  with
    diverticulitis 562.11
      with hemorrhage 562.13
    hemorrhage 562.12
  congenital 751.5
rectum 562.10
  with
    diverticulitis 562.11
      with hemorrhage 562.13
    hemorrhage 562.12
renal (calyces) (pelvis) 593.89
  with calculus 592.0
Rokitansky's 530.6
seminal vesicle 608.0
sigmoid 562.10
  with
    diverticulitis 562.11
      with hemorrhage 562.13
    hemorrhage 562.12
  congenital 751.5
small intestine 562.00
  with
    diverticulitis 562.01
      with hemorrhage 562.03
    hemorrhage 562.02
stomach (cardia) (juxtacardia) (juxtapyloric) (acquired) 537.1
  congenital 750.7
subdiaphragmatic 530.6
trachea (congenital) 748.3
  acquired 519.19
traction (esophagus) 530.6
ureter (acquired) 593.89
  congenital 753.4
ureterovesical orifice 593.89
urethra (acquired) 599.2
  congenital 753.8
ventricle, left (congenital) 746.89
vesical (urinary) 596.3
  congenital 753.8
Zenker's (esophagus) 530.6
Diverticulitis (acute) — *see also* Diverticula 562.11
with hemorrhage 562.13
bladder (urinary) 596.3
cecum (perforated) 562.11
  with hemorrhage 562.13
colon (perforated) 562.11
  with hemorrhage 562.13
duodenum 562.01
  with hemorrhage 562.03
esophagus 530.6
ileum (perforated) 562.01
  with hemorrhage 562.03
intestine (large) (perforated) 562.11
  with hemorrhage 562.13
  small 562.01
    with hemorrhage 562.03
jejunum (perforated) 562.01
  with hemorrhage 562.03
Meckel's (perforated) 751.0
pharyngoesophageal 530.6
rectosigmoid (perforated) 562.11
  with hemorrhage 562.13
rectum 562.11
  with hemorrhage 562.13
sigmoid (old) (perforated) 562.11
  with hemorrhage 562.13
small intestine (perforated) 562.01
  with hemorrhage 562.03
vesical (urinary) 596.3
Diverticulosis — *see* Diverticula
Division
cervix uteri 622.8
  external os into two openings by frenum 752.49
external (cervical) into two openings by frenum 752.49
glans penis 752.69
hymen 752.49
labia minora (congenital) 752.49
ligament (partial or complete) (current) (*see also* Sprain, by site)

☑ Additional Digit Required — Refer to the Tabular List for Digit Selection   ▽ Subterms under main terms may continue to next column or page

2007 ICD-9-CM   ▶◀ Revised Text   ● New Line   ▲ Revised Code   October 2006 · Volume 2 — 99

Division — *continued*
　ligament (*see also* Sprain, by site) — *continued*
　　with open wound — *see* Wound, open, by site
　muscle (partial or complete) (current) (*see also* Sprain, by site)
　　with open wound — *see* Wound, open, by site
　nerve — *see* Injury, nerve, by site
　penis glans 752.69
　spinal cord — *see* Injury, spinal, by site
　vein 459.9
　　traumatic — *see* Injury, vascular, by site
Divorce V61.0
Dix-Hallpike neurolabyrinthitis 386.12
Dizziness 780.4
　hysterical 300.11
　psychogenic 306.9
Doan-Wiseman syndrome (primary splenic neutropenia) 289.53 ▲
Dog bite — *see* Wound, open, by site
Döhle body-panmyelopathic syndrome 288.2
Döhle-Heller aortitis 093.1
Dolichocephaly, dolichocephalus 754.0
Dolichocolon 751.5
Dolichostenomelia 759.82
Donohue's syndrome (leprechaunism) 259.8
Donor
　blood V59.01
　　other blood components V59.09
　　stem cells V59.02
　　whole blood V59.01
　bone V59.2
　　marrow V59.3
　cornea V59.5
　egg (oocyte) (ovum) V59.70
　　over age 35 V59.73
　　　anonymous recipient V59.73
　　　designated recipient V59.74
　　under age 35 V59.71
　　　anonymous recipient V59.71
　　　designated recipient V59.72
　heart V59.8
　kidney V59.4
　liver V59.6
　lung V59.8
　lymphocyte V59.8
　organ V59.9
　　specified NEC V59.8
　potential, examination of V70.8
　skin V59.1
　specified organ or tissue NEC V59.8
　sperm V59.8
　stem cells V59.02
　tissue V59.9
　　specified type NEC V59.8
Donovanosis (granuloma venereum) 099.2
DOPS (diffuse obstructive pulmonary syndrome) 496
Double
　albumin 273.8
　aortic arch 747.21
　auditory canal 744.29
　auricle (heart) 746.82
　bladder 753.8
　external (cervical) os 752.49
　kidney with double pelvis (renal) 753.3
　larynx 748.3
　meatus urinarius 753.8
　organ or site NEC — *see* Accessory
　orifice
　　heart valve NEC 746.89
　　　pulmonary 746.09
　outlet, right ventricle 745.11
　pelvis (renal) with double ureter 753.4
　penis 752.69
　tongue 750.13
　ureter (one or both sides) 753.4
　　with double pelvis (renal) 753.4
　urethra 753.8

Double — *continued*
　urinary meatus 753.8
　uterus (any degree) 752.2
　　with doubling of cervix and vagina 752.2
　　in pregnancy or childbirth 654.0 ☑
　　　affecting fetus or newborn 763.89
　vagina 752.49
　　with doubling of cervix and uterus 752.2
　vision 368.2
　vocal cords 748.3
　vulva 752.49
　whammy (syndrome) 360.81
Douglas' pouch, cul-de-sac — *see* condition
Down's disease or syndrome (mongolism) 758.0
Down-growth, epithelial (anterior chamber) 364.61
Dracontiasis 125.7
Dracunculiasis 125.7
Dracunculosis 125.7
Drainage
　abscess (spontaneous) — *see* Abscess
　anomalous pulmonary veins to hepatic veins or right atrium 747.41
　stump (amputation) (surgical) 997.62
　suprapubic, bladder 596.8
Dream state, hysterical 300.13
Drepanocytic anemia — *see also* Disease, sickle cell 282.60
Dresbach's syndrome (elliptocytosis) 282.1
Dreschlera (infection) 118
　hawaiiensis 117.8
Dressler's syndrome (postmyocardial infarction) 411.0
Dribbling (post-void) 788.35
Drift, ulnar 736.09
Drinking (alcohol) — *see also* Alcoholism
　excessive, to excess NEC (*see also* Abuse, drugs, nondependent) 305.0 ☑
　　bouts, periodic 305.0 ☑
　　continual 303.9 ☑
　　episodic 305.0 ☑
　　habitual 303.9 ☑
　　periodic 305.0 ☑
Drip, postnasal (chronic) 784.91 ▲
　due to ●
　　allergic rhinitis — *see* Rhinitis, allergic ●
　　common cold 460 ●
　　gastroesophageal reflux — *see* Reflux, gastroesophageal ●
　　nasopharyngitis — *see* Nasopharyngitis ●
　　other known condition — code to condition ●
　　sinusitis — *see* Sinusitis ●
Drivers' license examination V70.3
Droop
　Cooper's 611.8
　facial 781.94
Drop
　finger 736.29
　foot 736.79
　hematocrit (precipitous) 790.01
　toe 735.8
　wrist 736.05
Dropped
　dead 798.1
　heart beats 426.6
Dropsy, dropsical — *see also* Edema 782.3
　abdomen 789.5
　amnion (*see also* Hydramnios) 657.0 ☑
　brain — *see* Hydrocephalus
　cardiac (*see also* Failure, heart) 428.0
　cardiorenal (*see also* Hypertension, cardiorenal) 404.90
　chest 511.9

Dropsy, dropsical — *see also* Edema — *continued*
　fetus or newborn 778.0
　　due to isoimmunization 773.3
　gangrenous (*see also* Gangrene) 785.4
　heart (*see also* Failure, heart) 428.0
　hepatic — *see* Cirrhosis, liver
　infantile — *see* Hydrops, fetalis
　kidney (*see also* Nephrosis) 581.9
　liver — *see* Cirrhosis, liver
　lung 514
　malarial (*see also* Malaria) 084.9
　neonatorum — *see* Hydrops, fetalis
　nephritic 581.9
　newborn — *see* Hydrops, fetalis
　nutritional 269.9
　ovary 620.8
　pericardium (*see also* Pericarditis) 423.9
　renal (*see also* Nephrosis) 581.9
　uremic — *see* Uremia
Drowned, drowning 994.1
　lung 518.5
Drowsiness 780.09
Drug — *see also* condition
　addiction (*see also* listing under Dependence) 304.9 ☑
　adverse effect NEC, correct substance properly administered 995.20 ▲
　allergy 995.27
　dependence (*see also* listing under Dependence) 304.9 ☑
　habit (*see also* listing under Dependence) 304.9 ☑
　hypersensitivity 995.27 ●
　induced
　　circadian rhythm sleep disorder 292.85
　　hypersomnia 292.85
　　insomnia 292.85
　　mental disorder 292.9
　　　anxiety 292.89
　　　mood 292.84
　　　sexual 292.89
　　　sleep 292.85
　　　specified type 292.89
　　parasomnia 292.85
　　persisting
　　　amnestic disorder 292.83
　　　dementia 292.82
　　psychotic disorder
　　　with
　　　　delusions 292.11
　　　　hallucinations 292.12
　　sleep disorder 292.85
　intoxication 292.89
　overdose — *see* Table of Drugs and Chemicals
　poisoning — *see* Table of Drugs and Chemicals
　therapy (maintenance) status NEC
　　chemotherapy, antineoplastic V58.11
　　immunotherapy, antineoplastic V58.12
　　long-term (current) use V58.69
　　　antibiotics V58.62
　　　anticoagulants V58.61
　　　anti-inflammatories, nonsteroidal (NSAID) V58.64
　　　antiplatelets V58.63
　　　antithrombotics V58.63
　　　aspirin V58.66
　　　insulin V58.67
　　　steroids V58.65
　wrong substance given or taken in error — *see* Table of Drugs and Chemicals
Drunkenness — *see also* Abuse, drugs, nondependent 305.0 ☑
　acute in alcoholism (*see also* Alcoholism) 303.0 ☑
　chronic (*see also* Alcoholism) 303.9 ☑
　pathologic 291.4
　simple (acute) 305.0 ☑

Drunkenness — *see also* Abuse, drugs, nondependent — *continued*
　simple — *continued*
　　in alcoholism 303.0 ☑
　sleep 307.47
Drusen
　optic disc or papilla 377.21
　retina (colloid) (hyaloid degeneration) 362.57
　　hereditary 362.77
Drusenfieber 075
Dry, dryness — *see also* condition
　eye 375.15
　　syndrome 375.15
　larynx 478.79
　mouth 527.7
　nose 478.19 ▲
　skin syndrome 701.1
　socket (teeth) 526.5
　throat 478.29
DSAP (disseminated superficial actinic porokeratosis) 692.75
Duane's retraction syndrome 378.71
Duane-Stilling-Türk syndrome (ocular retraction syndrome) 378.71
Dubini's disease (electric chorea) 049.8
Dubin-Johnson disease or syndrome 277.4
Dubois' abscess or disease 090.5
Duchenne's
　disease 094.0
　　locomotor ataxia 094.0
　　muscular dystrophy 359.1
　　pseudohypertrophy, muscles 359.1
　paralysis 335.22
　syndrome 335.22
Duchenne-Aran myelopathic, muscular atrophy (nonprogressive) (progressive) 335.21
Duchenne-Griesinger disease 359.1
Ducrey's
　bacillus 099.0
　chancre 099.0
　disease (chancroid) 099.0
Duct, ductus — *see* condition
Duengero 061
Duhring's disease (dermatitis herpetiformis) 694.0
Dukes (-Filatov) disease 057.8
Dullness
　cardiac (decreased) (increased) 785.3
Dumb ague — *see also* Malaria 084.6
Dumbness — *see also* Aphasia 784.3
Dumdum fever 085.0
Dumping syndrome (postgastrectomy) 564.2
　nonsurgical 536.8
Duodenitis (nonspecific) (peptic) 535.60
　with hemorrhage 535.61
　due to
　　Strongyloides stercoralis 127.2
Duodenocholangitis 575.8
Duodenum, duodenal — *see* condition
Duplay's disease, periarthritis, or syndrome 726.2
Duplex — *see also* Accessory
　kidney 753.3
　placenta — *see* Placenta, abnormal
　uterus 752.2
Duplication — *see also* Accessory
　anus 751.5
　aortic arch 747.21
　appendix 751.5
　biliary duct (any) 751.69
　bladder 753.8
　cecum 751.5
　　and appendix 751.5
　clitoris 752.49
　cystic duct 751.69
　digestive organs 751.8
　duodenum 751.5
　esophagus 750.4
　fallopian tube 752.19
　frontonasal process 756.0
　gallbladder 751.69
　ileum 751.5

Duplication — *see also* Accessory — *continued*
  intestine (large) (small) 751.5
  jejunum 751.5
  kidney 753.3
  liver 751.69
  nose 748.1
  pancreas 751.7
  penis 752.69
  respiratory organs NEC 748.9
  salivary duct 750.22
  spinal cord (incomplete) 742.51
  stomach 750.7
  ureter 753.4
  vagina 752.49
  vas deferens 752.89
  vocal cords 748.3
Dupré's disease or syndrome
  (meningism) 781.6
Dupuytren's
  contraction 728.6
  disease (muscle contracture) 728.6
  fracture (closed) 824.4
    ankle (closed) 824.4
      open 824.5
    fibula (closed) 824.4
      open 824.5
    open 824.5
    radius (closed) 813.42
      open 813.52
  muscle contracture 728.6
Durand-Nicolas-Favre disease (climatic bubo) 099.1
Duroziez's disease (congenital mitral stenosis) 746.5
Dust
  conjunctivitis 372.05
  reticulation (occupational) 504
Dutton's
  disease (trypanosomiasis) 086.9
  relapsing fever (West African) 087.1
Dwarf, dwarfism 259.4
  with infantilism (hypophyseal) 253.3
  achondroplastic 756.4
  Amsterdam 759.89
  bird-headed 759.89
  congenital 259.4
  constitutional 259.4
  hypophyseal 253.3
  infantile 259.4
  Levi type 253.3
  Lorain-Levi (pituitary) 253.3
  Lorain type (pituitary) 253.3
  metatropic 756.4
  nephrotic-glycosuric, with hypophosphatemic rickets 270.0
  nutritional 263.2
  ovarian 758.6
  pancreatic 577.8
  pituitary 253.3
  polydystrophic 277.5
  primordial 253.3
  psychosocial 259.4
  renal 588.0
    with hypertension — *see* Hypertension, kidney
  Russell's (uterine dwarfism and craniofacial dysostosis) 759.89
Dyke-Young anemia or syndrome (acquired macrocytic hemolytic anemia) (secondary) (symptomatic) 283.9
Dynia abnormality — *see also* Defect, coagulation 286.9
Dysacousis 388.40
Dysadrenocortism 255.9
  hyperfunction 255.3
  hypofunction 255.4
Dysarthria 784.5
Dysautonomia — *see also* Neuropathy, peripheral, autonomic 337.9
  familial 742.8
Dysbarism 993.3
Dysbasia 719.7
  angiosclerotica intermittens 443.9
    due to atherosclerosis 440.21

Dysbasia — *continued*
  hysterical 300.11
  lordotica (progressiva) 333.6
  nonorganic origin 307.9
  psychogenic 307.9
Dysbetalipoproteinemia (familial) 272.2
Dyscalculia 315.1
Dyschezia — *see also* Constipation 564.00
Dyschondroplasia (with hemangiomata) 756.4
  Voorhoeve's 756.4
Dyschondrosteosis 756.59
Dyschromia 709.00
Dyscollagenosis 710.9
Dyscoria 743.41
Dyscraniopyophalangy 759.89
Dyscrasia
  blood 289.9
    with antepartum hemorrhage 641.3 ☑
    fetus or newborn NEC 776.9
    hemorrhage, subungual 287.8
    puerperal, postpartum 666.3 ☑
  ovary 256.8
  plasma cell 273.9
  pluriglandular 258.9
  polyglandular 258.9
Dysdiadochokinesia 781.3
Dysectasia, vesical neck 596.8
Dysendocrinism 259.9
Dysentery, dysenteric (bilious) (catarrhal) (diarrhea) (epidemic) (gangrenous) (hemorrhagic) (infectious) (sporadic) (tropical) (ulcerative) 009.0
  abscess, liver (*see also* Abscess, amebic) 006.3
  amebic (*see also* Amebiasis) 006.9
    with abscess — *see* Abscess, amebic
    acute 006.0
    carrier (suspected) of V02.2
    chronic 006.1
  arthritis (*see also* Arthritis, due to, dysentery) 009.0 [711.3] ☑
    bacillary 004.9 [711.3] ☑
  asylum 004.9
  bacillary 004.9
    arthritis 004.9 [711.3] ☑
    Boyd 004.2
    Flexner 004.1
    Schmitz (-Stutzer) 004.0
    Shiga 004.0
    Shigella 004.9
      group A 004.0
      group B 004.1
      group C 004.2
      group D 004.3
      specified type NEC 004.8
    Sonne 004.3
    specified type NEC 004.8
  bacterium 004.9
  balantidial 007.0
  Balantidium coli 007.0
  Boyd's 004.2
  Chilomastix 007.8
  Chinese 004.9
  choleriform 001.1
  coccidial 007.2
  Dientamoeba fragilis 007.8
  due to specified organism NEC — *see* Enteritis, due to, by organism
  Embadomonas 007.8
  Endolimax nana — *see* Dysentery, amebic
  Entamoba, entamebic — *see* Dysentery, amebic
  Flexner's 004.1
  Flexner-Boyd 004.2
  giardial 007.1
  Giardia lamblia 007.1
  Hiss-Russell 004.1
  lamblia 007.1
  leishmanial 085.0
  malarial (*see also* Malaria) 084.6

Dysentery, dysenteric — *continued*
  metazoal 127.9
  Monilia 112.89
  protozoal NEC 007.9
  Russell's 004.8
  salmonella 003.0
  schistosomal 120.1
  Schmitz (-Stutzer) 004.0
  Shiga 004.0
  Shigella NEC (*see also* Dysentery, bacillary) 004.9
    boydii 004.2
    dysenteriae 004.0
      Schmitz 004.0
      Shiga 004.0
    flexneri 004.1
    group A 004.0
    group B 004.1
    group C 004.2
    group D 004.3
    Schmitz 004.0
    Shiga 004.0
    Sonnei 004.3
  Sonne 004.3
  strongyloidiasis 127.2
  trichomonal 007.3
  tuberculous (*see also* Tuberculosis) 014.8 ☑
  viral (*see also* Enteritis, viral) 008.8
Dysequilibrium 780.4
Dysesthesia 782.0
  hysterical 300.11
Dysfibrinogenemia (congenital) — *see also* Defect, coagulation 286.3
Dysfunction
  adrenal (cortical) 255.9
    hyperfunction 255.3
    hypofunction 255.4
  associated with sleep stages or arousal from sleep 780.56
    nonorganic origin 307.47
  bladder NEC 596.59
  bleeding, uterus 626.8
  brain, minimal (*see also* Hyperkinesia) 314.9
  cerebral 348.30
  colon 564.9
    psychogenic 306.4
  colostomy or enterostomy 569.62
  cystic duct 575.8
  diastolic 429.9
    with heart failure — *see* Failure, heart
    due to
      cardiomyopathy — *see* Cardiomyopathy
      hypertension — *see* Hypertension, heart
  endocrine NEC 259.9
  endometrium 621.8
  enteric stoma 569.62
  enterostomy 569.62
  erectile 607.84
    nonorganic origin 302.72
  esophagostomy 530.87
  Eustachian tube 381.81
  gallbladder 575.8
  gastrointestinal 536.9
  gland, glandular NEC 259.9
  heart 427.9
    postoperative (immediate) 997.1
      long-term effect of cardiac surgery 429.4
  hemoglobin 289.89   ▲
  hepatic 573.9
  hepatocellular NEC 573.9
  hypophysis 253.9
    hyperfunction 253.1
    hypofunction 253.2
    posterior lobe 253.6
      hypofunction 253.5
  kidney (*see also* Disease, renal) 593.9
  labyrinthine 386.50
    specified NEC 386.58
  liver 573.9
    constitutional 277.4

Dysfunction — *continued*
  minimal brain (child) (*see also* Hyperkinesia) 314.9
  ovary, ovarian 256.9
    hyperfunction 256.1
      estrogen 256.0
    hypofunction 256.39
      postablative 256.2
    postablative 256.2
    specified NEC 256.8
  papillary muscle 429.81
    with myocardial infarction 410.8 ☑
  parathyroid 252.8
    hyperfunction 252.00
    hypofunction 252.1
  pineal gland 259.8
  pituitary (gland) 253.9
    hyperfunction 253.1
    hypofunction 253.2
    posterior 253.6
      hypofunction 253.5
  placental — *see* Placenta, insufficiency
  platelets (blood) 287.1
  polyglandular 258.9
    specified NEC 258.8
  psychosexual 302.70
    with
      dyspareunia (functional) (psychogenic) 302.76
      frigidity 302.72
      impotence 302.72
      inhibition
        orgasm
          female 302.73
          male 302.74
        sexual
          desire 302.71
          excitement 302.72
      premature ejaculation 302.75
      sexual aversion 302.79
      specified disorder NEC 302.79
      vaginismus 306.51
  pylorus 537.9
  rectum 564.9
    psychogenic 306.4
  segmental (*see also* Dysfunction, somatic) 739.9
  senile 797
  sexual 302.70
  sinoatrial node 427.81
  somatic 739.9
    abdomen 739.9
    acromioclavicular 739.7
    cervical 739.1
    cervicothoracic 739.1
    costochondral 739.8
    costovertebral 739.8
    extremities
      lower 739.6
      upper 739.7
    head 739.0
    hip 739.5
    lumbar, lumbosacral 739.3
    occipitocervical 739.0
    pelvic 739.5
    pubic 739.5
    rib cage 739.8
    sacral 739.4
    sacrococcygeal 739.4
    sacroiliac 739.4
    specified site NEC 739.9
    sternochondral 739.8
    sternoclavicular 739.7
    temporomandibular 739.0
    thoracic, thoracolumbar 739.2
  stomach 536.9
    psychogenic 306.4
  suprarenal 255.9
    hyperfunction 255.3
    hypofunction 255.4
  symbolic NEC 784.60
    specified type NEC 784.69
  systolic 429.9
    with heart failure — *see* Failure, heart

☑ Additional Digit Required — Refer to the Tabular List for Digit Selection   ▽ Subterms under main terms may continue to next column or page

2007 ICD-9-CM   ▶◀ Revised Text   ● New Line   ▲ Revised Code   October 2006 · Volume 2 — 101

Dysfunction — continued
  temporomandibular (joint) (joint-pain-syndrome) NEC 524.60
    sounds on opening or closing 524.64
    specified NEC 524.69
  testicular 257.9
    hyperfunction 257.0
    hypofunction 257.2
    specified type NEC 257.8
  thymus 254.9
  thyroid 246.9
    complicating pregnancy, childbirth, or puerperium 648.1 ☑
    hyperfunction — see Hyperthyroidism
    hypofunction — see Hypothyroidism
  uterus, complicating delivery 661.9 ☑
    affecting fetus or newborn 763.7
    hypertonic 661.4 ☑
    hypotonic 661.2 ☑
      primary 661.0 ☑
      secondary 661.1 ☑
  velopharyngeal (acquired) 528.9
    congenital 750.29
  ventricular 429.9
    with congestive heart failure (see also Failure, heart) 428.0
    due to
      cardiomyopathy — see Cardiomyopathy
      hypertension — see Hypertension, heart
    left, reversible following sudden ● emotional stress 429.83 ●
  vesicourethral NEC 596.59
  vestibular 386.50
    specified type NEC 386.58
Dysgammaglobulinemia 279.06
Dysgenesis
  gonadal (due to chromosomal anomaly) 758.6
    pure 752.7
  kidney(s) 753.0
  ovarian 758.6
  renal 753.0
  reticular 279.2
  seminiferous tubules 758.6
  tidal platelet 287.31
Dysgerminoma (M9060/3)
  specified site — see Neoplasm, by site, malignant
  unspecified site
    female 183.0
    male 186.9
Dysgeusia 781.1
Dysgraphia 781.3
Dyshidrosis 705.81
Dysidrosis 705.81
Dysinsulinism 251.8
Dyskaryotic cervical smear 795.09
Dyskeratosis — see also Keratosis 701.1
  bullosa hereditaria 757.39
  cervix 622.10
  congenital 757.39
  follicularis 757.39
    vitamin A deficiency 264.8
  gingiva 523.8
  oral soft tissue NEC 528.79
  tongue 528.79
  uterus NEC 621.8
Dyskinesia 781.3
  biliary 575.8
  esophagus 530.5
  hysterical 300.11
  intestinal 564.89
  neuroleptic-induced tardive 333.85 ▲
  nonorganic origin 307.9
  orofacial 333.82
    due to drugs 333.85 ●
  psychogenic 307.9
  subacute, due to drugs 333.85 ●
  tardive (oral) 333.85 ▲
Dyslalia 784.5

Dyslalia — continued
  developmental 315.39
Dyslexia 784.61
  developmental 315.02
  secondary to organic lesion 784.61
Dyslipidemia 272.4
Dysmaturity — see also Immaturity 765.1 ☑
  lung 770.4
  pulmonary 770.4
Dysmenorrhea (essential) (exfoliative) (functional) (intrinsic) (membranous) (primary) (secondary) 625.3
  psychogenic 306.52
Dysmetabolic syndrome X 277.7
Dysmetria 781.3
Dysmorodystrophia mesodermalis congenita 759.82
Dysnomia 784.3
Dysorexia 783.0
  hysterical 300.11
Dysostosis
  cleidocranial, cleidocranialis 755.59
  craniofacial 756.0
  Fairbank's (idiopathic familial generalized osteophytosis) 756.50
  mandibularis 756.0
  mandibulofacial, incomplete 756.0
  multiplex 277.5
  orodigitofacial 759.89
Dyspareunia (female) 625.0
  male 608.89
  psychogenic 302.76
Dyspepsia (allergic) (congenital) (fermentative) (flatulent) (functional) (gastric) (gastrointestinal) (neurogenic) (occupational) (reflex) 536.8
  acid 536.8
  atonic 536.3
    psychogenic 306.4
  diarrhea 787.91
    psychogenic 306.4
  intestinal 564.89
    psychogenic 306.4
  nervous 306.4
  neurotic 306.4
  psychogenic 306.4
Dysphagia 787.2
  functional 300.11
  hysterical 300.11
  nervous 300.11
  psychogenic 306.4
  sideropenic 280.8
  spastica 530.5
Dysphagocytosis, congenital 288.1
Dysphasia 784.5
Dysphonia 784.49
  clericorum 784.49
  functional 300.11
  hysterical 300.11
  psychogenic 306.1
  spastica 478.79
Dyspigmentation — see also Pigmentation
  eyelid (acquired) 374.52
Dyspituitarism 253.9
  hyperfunction 253.1
  hypofunction 253.2
  posterior lobe 253.6
Dysplasia — see also Anomaly
  artery
    fibromuscular NEC 447.8
      carotid 447.8
      renal 447.3
  bladder 596.8
  bone (fibrous) NEC 733.29
    diaphyseal, progressive 756.59
    jaw 526.89
    monostotic 733.29
    polyostotic 756.54
    solitary 733.29
  brain 742.9
  bronchopulmonary, fetus or newborn 770.7
  cervix (uteri) 622.10

Dysplasia — see also Anomaly — continued
  cervix — continued
    cervical intraepithelial neoplasia I [CIN I] 622.11
    cervical intraepithelial neoplasia II [CIN II] 622.12
    cervical intraepithelial neoplasia III [CIN III] 233.1
    CIN I 622.11
    CIN II 622.12
    CIN III 233.1
    mild 622.11
    moderate 622.12
    severe 233.1
  chondroectodermal 756.55
  chondromatose 756.4
  colon 211.3
  craniocarpotarsal 759.89
  craniometaphyseal 756.89
  dentinal 520.5
  diaphyseal, progressive 756.59
  ectodermal (anhidrotic) (Bason) (Clouston's) (congenital) (Feinmesser) (hereditary) (hidrotic) (Marshall) (Robinson's) 757.31
  epiphysealis 756.9
    multiplex 756.56
    punctata 756.59
  epiphysis 756.9
    multiple 756.56
  epithelial
    epiglottis 478.79
    uterine cervix 622.10
  erythroid NEC 289.89
  eye (see also Microphthalmos) 743.10
  familial metaphyseal 756.89
  fibromuscular, artery NEC 447.8
    carotid 447.8
    renal 447.3
  fibrous
    bone NEC 733.29
    diaphyseal, progressive 756.59
    jaw 526.89
    monostotic 733.29
    polyostotic 756.54
    solitary 733.29
  high-grade, focal — see Neoplasm, by site, benign
  hip (congenital) 755.63
    with dislocation (see also Dislocation, hip, congenital) 754.30
  hypohidrotic ectodermal 757.31
  joint 755.8
  kidney 753.15
  leg 755.69
  linguofacialis 759.89
  lung 748.5
  macular 743.55
  mammary (benign) (gland) 610.9
    cystic 610.1
    specified type NEC 610.8
  metaphyseal 756.9
    familial 756.89
  monostotic fibrous 733.29
  muscle 756.89
  myeloid NEC 289.89
  nervous system (general) 742.9
  neuroectodermal 759.6
  oculoauriculovertebral 756.0
  oculodentodigital 759.89
  olfactogenital 253.4
  osteo-onycho-arthro (hereditary) 756.89
  periosteum 733.99
  polyostotic fibrous 756.54
  progressive diaphyseal 756.59
  prostate 602.3
    intraepithelial neoplasia I [PIN I] 602.3
    intraepithelial neoplasia II [PIN II] 602.3
    intraepithelial neoplasia III [PIN III] 233.4
  renal 753.15
  renofacialis 753.0

Dysplasia — see also Anomaly — continued
  retinal NEC 743.56
  retrolental 362.21
  spinal cord 742.9
  thymic, with immunodeficiency 279.2
  vagina 623.0
  vocal cord 478.5
  vulva 624.8
    intraepithelial neoplasia I [VIN I] 624.0 ▲
    intraepithelial neoplasia II [VIN II] 624.0 ▲
    intraepithelial neoplasia III [VIN III] 233.3
    VIN I 624.0 ▲
    VIN II 624.0 ▲
    VIN III 233.3
Dyspnea (nocturnal) (paroxysmal) 786.09
  asthmatic (bronchial) (see also Asthma) 493.9 ☑
    with bronchitis (see also Asthma) 493.9 ☑
      chronic 493.2 ☑
  cardiac (see also Failure, ventricular, left) 428.1
  cardiac (see also Failure, ventricular, left) 428.1
  functional 300.11
  hyperventilation 786.01
  hysterical 300.11
  Monday morning 504
  newborn 770.89
  psychogenic 306.1
  uremic — see Uremia
Dyspraxia 781.3
  syndrome 315.4
Dysproteinemia 273.8
  transient with copper deficiency 281.4
Dysprothrombinemia (constitutional) — see also Defect, coagulation 286.3
Dysreflexia, autonomic 337.3
Dysrhythmia
  cardiac 427.9
    postoperative (immediate) 997.1
      long-term effect of cardiac surgery 429.4
    specified type NEC 427.89
  cerebral or cortical 348.30
Dyssecretosis, mucoserous 710.2
Dyssocial reaction, without manifest psychiatric disorder
  adolescent V71.02
  adult V71.01
  child V71.02
Dyssomnia NEC 780.56
  nonorganic origin 307.47
Dyssplenism 289.4
Dyssynergia
  biliary (see also Disease, biliary) 576.8
  cerebellaris myoclonica 334.2
  detrusor sphincter (bladder) 596.55
  ventricular 429.89
Dystasia, hereditary areflexic 334.3
Dysthymia 300.4
Dysthymic disorder 300.4
Dysthyroidism 246.9
Dystocia 660.9 ☑
  affecting fetus or newborn 763.1
  cervical 661.0 ☑
    affecting fetus or newborn 763.7
  contraction ring 661.4 ☑
    affecting fetus or newborn 763.7
  fetal 660.9 ☑
    abnormal size 653.5 ☑
      affecting fetus or newborn 763.1
    deformity 653.7 ☑
  maternal 660.9 ☑
    affecting fetus or newborn 763.1
  positional 660.0 ☑
    affecting fetus or newborn 763.1
  shoulder (girdle) 660.4 ☑
    affecting fetus or newborn 763.1
  uterine NEC 661.4 ☑
    affecting fetus or newborn 763.7

☑ Additional Digit Required — Refer to the Tabular List for Digit Selection   ᴺᴱᶜ Subterms under main terms may continue to next column or page

102 — Volume 2 · October 2006   ▶◀ Revised Text   ● New Line   ▲ Revised Code   *2007 ICD-9-CM*

Dystonia
  acute   ●
    due to drugs 333.72   ●
    neuroleptic-induced acute 333.72 ●
  deformans progressiva 333.6
  lenticularis 333.6
  musculorum deformans 333.6
  torsion (idiopathic) 333.6
    acquired 333.79   ●
    fragments (of) 333.89
    genetic 333.6   ●
    symptomatic 333.79   ▲
Dystonic
  movements 781.0
Dystopia kidney 753.3
Dystrophia myotonica 359.2
Dystrophy, dystrophia 783.9
  adiposogenital 253.8
  asphyxiating thoracic 756.4
  Becker's type 359.1
  brevicollis 756.16
  Bruch's membrane 362.77
  cervical (sympathetic) NEC 337.0
  chondro-osseus with punctate epiphy-
      seal dysplasia 756.59
  choroid (hereditary) 363.50
    central (areolar) (partial) 363.53
      total (gyrate) 363.54
    circinate 363.53
    circumpapillary (partial) 363.51
      total 363.52
    diffuse
      partial 363.56
      total 363.57
    generalized
      partial 363.56
      total 363.57
    gyrate
      central 363.54
      generalized 363.57
    helicoid 363.52
    peripapillary — see Dystrophy,
        choroid, circumpapillary
    serpiginous 363.54
  cornea (hereditary) 371.50
    anterior NEC 371.52
    Cogan's 371.52
    combined 371.57
    crystalline 371.56
    endothelial (Fuchs') 371.57
    epithelial 371.50
      juvenile 371.51
        microscopic cystic 371.52
    granular 371.53
    lattice 371.54
    macular 371.55
    marginal (Terrien's) 371.48
    Meesman's 371.51
    microscopic cystic (epithelial)
        371.52
    nodular, Salzmann's 371.46
    polymorphous 371.58
    posterior NEC 371.58
    ring-like 371.52
    Salzmann's nodular 371.46
    stromal NEC 371.56
  dermatochondrocorneal 371.50
  Duchenne's 359.1
  due to malnutrition 263.9
  Erb's 359.1
  familial
    hyperplastic periosteal 756.59
    osseous 277.5
  foveal 362.77
  Fuchs', cornea 371.57
  Gowers' muscular 359.1
  hair 704.2
  hereditary, progressive muscular
      359.1
  hypogenital, with diabetic tendency
      759.81
  Landouzy-Déjérine 359.1
  Leyden-Möbius 359.1
  mesodermalis congenita 759.82
  muscular 359.1
    congenital (hereditary) 359.0

Dystrophy, dystrophia — *continued*
  muscular — *continued*
    congenital — *continued*
      myotonic 359.2
    distal 359.1
    Duchenne's 359.1
    Erb's 359.1
    fascioscapulohumeral 359.1
    Gowers' 359.1   ●
    hereditary (progressive) 359.1
    Landouzy-Déjérine 359.1
    limb-girdle 359.1
    myotonic 359.2
    progressive (hereditary) 359.1
        Charcôt-Marie-Tooth 356.1
    pseudohypertrophic (infantile)
        359.1
  myocardium, myocardial (see also
      Degeneration, myocardial) 429.1
  myotonic 359.2
  myotonica 359.2
  nail 703.8
    congenital 757.5
  neurovascular (traumatic) (see also
      Neuropathy, peripheral, auto-
      nomic) 337.9
  nutritional 263.9
  ocular 359.1
  oculocerebrorenal 270.8
  oculopharyngeal 359.1
  ovarian 620.8
  papillary (and pigmentary) 701.1
  pelvicrural atrophic 359.1
  pigmentary (see also Acanthosis)
      701.2
  pituitary (gland) 253.8
  polyglandular 258.8
  posttraumatic sympathetic — see
      Dystrophy, sympathetic
  progressive ophthalmoplegic 359.1
  retina, retinal (hereditary) 362.70
    albipunctate 362.74
    Bruch's membrane 362.77
    cone, progressive 362.75
    hyaline 362.77
    in
      Bassen-Kornzweig syndrome
          272.5 [362.72]
      cerebroretinal lipidosis
          330.1 [362.71]
      Refsum's disease 356.3 [362.72]
      systemic lipidosis 272.7 [362.71]
    juvenile (Stargardt's) 362.75
    pigmentary 362.74
    pigment epithelium 362.76
    progressive cone (-rod) 362.75
    pseudoinflammatory foveal 362.77
    rod, progressive 362.75
    sensory 362.75
    vitelliform 362.76
  Salzmann's nodular 371.46
  scapuloperoneal 359.1
  skin NEC 709.9
  sympathetic (posttraumatic) (reflex)
      337.20
    lower limb 337.22
    specified site NEC 337.29
    upper limb 337.21
  tapetoretinal NEC 362.74
  thoracic asphyxiating 756.4
  unguium 703.8
    congenital 757.5
  vitreoretinal (primary) 362.73
    secondary 362.66
  vulva 624.0
Dysuria 788.1
  psychogenic 306.53

E

Eagle-Barrett syndrome 756.71
Eales' disease (syndrome) 362.18
Ear — *see also* condition
  ache 388.70
    otogenic 388.71
    referred 388.72
  lop 744.29

Ear — *see also* condition — *continued*
  piercing V50.3
  swimmers' acute 380.12
  tank 380.12
  tropical 111.8 [380.15]
  wax 380.4
Earache 388.70
  otogenic 388.71
  referred 388.72
Early satiety 780.94
Eaton-Lambert syndrome — *see also*
    Neoplasm, by site, malignant
    199.1 [358.1]
Eberth's disease (typhoid fever) 002.0
Ebstein's
  anomaly or syndrome (downward dis-
      placement, tricuspid valve into
      right ventricle) 746.2
  disease (diabetes) 250.4 ☑ [581.81]
Eccentro-osteochondrodysplasia 277.5
Ecchondroma (M9210/0) — *see* Neo-
    plasm, bone, benign
Ecchondrosis (M9210/1) 238.0
Ecchordosis physaliphora 756.0
Ecchymosis (multiple) 459.89
  conjunctiva 372.72
  eye (traumatic) 921.0
  eyelids (traumatic) 921.1
  newborn 772.6
  spontaneous 782.7
  traumatic — *see* Contusion
Echinococciasis — *see* Echinococcus
Echinococcosis — *see* Echinococcus
Echinococcus (infection) 122.9
  granulosus 122.4
    liver 122.0
    lung 122.1
    orbit 122.3 [376.13]
    specified site NEC 122.3
    thyroid 122.2
  liver NEC 122.8
    granulosus 122.0
    multilocularis 122.5
  lung NEC 122.9
    granulosus 122.1
    multilocularis 122.6
  multilocularis 122.7
    liver 122.5
    specified site NEC 122.6
  orbit 122.9 [376.13]
    granulosus 122.3 [376.13]
    multilocularis 122.6 [376.13]
  specified site NEC 122.9
    granulosus 122.3
    multilocularis 122.6 [376.13]
  thyroid NEC 122.9
    granulosus 122.2
    multilocularis 122.6
Echinorhynchiasis 127.7
Echinostomiasis 121.8
Echolalia 784.69
ECHO virus infection NEC 079.1
Eclampsia, eclamptic (coma) (convul-
    sions) (delirium) 780.39
  female, child-bearing age NEC — *see*
      Eclampsia, pregnancy
  gravidarum — *see* Eclampsia, pregnan-
      cy
  male 780.39
  not associated with pregnancy or
      childbirth 780.39
  pregnancy, childbirth, or puerperium
      642.6 ☑
    with pre-existing hypertension
        642.7 ☑
    affecting fetus or newborn 760.0
  uremic 586
Eclipse blindness (total) 363.31
Economic circumstance affecting care
    V60.9
  specified type NEC V60.8
Economo's disease (encephalitis lethar-
    gica) 049.8
Ectasia, ectasis
  aorta (see also Aneurysm, aorta) 441.9
    ruptured 441.5

Ectasia, ectasis — *continued*
  breast 610.4
  capillary 448.9
  cornea (marginal) (postinfectional)
      371.71
  duct (mammary) 610.4
  kidney 593.89
  mammary duct (gland) 610.4
  papillary 448.9
  renal 593.89
  salivary gland (duct) 527.8
  scar, cornea 371.71
  sclera 379.11
Ecthyma 686.8
  contagiosum 051.2
  gangrenosum 686.09
  infectiosum 051.2
Ectocardia 746.87
Ectodermal dysplasia, congenital
    757.31
Ectodermosis erosiva pluriorificialis
    695.1
Ectopic, ectopia (congenital) 759.89
  abdominal viscera 751.8
    due to defect in anterior abdominal
        wall 756.79
  ACTH syndrome 255.0
  adrenal gland 759.1
  anus 751.5
  auricular beats 427.61
  beats 427.60
  bladder 753.5
  bone and cartilage in lung 748.69
  brain 742.4
  breast tissue 757.6
  cardiac 746.87
  cerebral 742.4
  cordis 746.87
  endometrium 617.9
  gallbladder 751.69
  gastric mucosa 750.7
  gestation — *see* Pregnancy, ectopic
  heart 746.87
  hormone secretion NEC 259.3
  hyperparathyroidism 259.3
  kidney (crossed) (intrathoracic) (pelvis)
      753.3
    in pregnancy or childbirth 654.4 ☑
      causing obstructed labor
          660.2 ☑
  lens 743.37
  lentis 743.37
  mole — *see* Pregnancy, ectopic
  organ or site NEC — *see* Malposition,
      congenital
  ovary 752.0
  pancreas, pancreatic tissue 751.7
  pregnancy — *see* Pregnancy, ectopic
  pupil 364.75
  renal 753.3
  sebaceous glands of mouth 750.26
  secretion
    ACTH 255.0
    adrenal hormone 259.3
    adrenalin 259.3
    adrenocorticotropin 255.0
    antidiuretic hormone (ADH) 259.3
    epinephrine 259.3
    hormone NEC 259.3
    norepinephrine 259.3
    pituitary (posterior) 259.3
  spleen 759.0
  testis 752.51
  thyroid 759.2
  ureter 753.4
  ventricular beats 427.69
  vesicae 753.5
Ectrodactyly 755.4
  finger (see also Absence, finger, con-
      genital) 755.29
  toe (see also Absence, toe, congenital)
      755.39
Ectromelia 755.4
  lower limb 755.30
  upper limb 755.20
Ectropion 374.10

☑ Additional Digit Required — Refer to the Tabular List for Digit Selection   ▽ Subterms under main terms may continue to next column or page

2007 ICD-9-CM   ▶◀ Revised Text   ● New Line   ▲ Revised Code   October 2006 • Volume 2 — **103**

Ectropion — continued
anus 569.49
cervix 622.0
  with mention of cervicitis 616.0
cicatricial 374.14
congenital 743.62
eyelid 374.10
  cicatricial 374.14
  congenital 743.62
  mechanical 374.12
  paralytic 374.12
  senile 374.11
  spastic 374.13
iris (pigment epithelium) 364.54
lip (congenital) 750.26
  acquired 528.5
mechanical 374.12
paralytic 374.12
rectum 569.49
senile 374.11
spastic 374.13
urethra 599.84
uvea 364.54
Eczema (acute) (allergic) (chronic) (erythematous) (fissum) (occupational) (rubrum) (squamous) 692.9
asteatotic 706.8
atopic 691.8
contact NEC 692.9
dermatitis NEC 692.9
due to specified cause — see Dermatitis, due to
dyshidrotic 705.81
external ear 380.22
flexural 691.8
gouty 274.89
herpeticum 054.0
hypertrophicum 701.8
hypostatic — see Varicose, vein
impetiginous 684
infantile (acute) (chronic) (due to any substance) (intertriginous) (seborrheic) 690.12
intertriginous NEC 692.9
  infantile 690.12
intrinsic 691.8
lichenified NEC 692.9
marginatum 110.3
nummular 692.9
pustular 686.8
seborrheic 690.18
  infantile 690.12
solare 692.72
stasis (lower extremity) 454.1
  ulcerated 454.2
vaccination, vaccinatum 999.0
varicose (lower extremity) — see Varicose, vein
verrucosum callosum 698.3
Eczematoid, exudative 691.8
Eddowes' syndrome (brittle bones and blue sclera) 756.51
Edema, edematous 782.3
with nephritis (see also Nephrosis) 581.9
allergic 995.1
angioneurotic (allergic) (any site) (with urticaria) 995.1
  hereditary 277.6
angiospastic 443.9
Berlin's (traumatic) 921.3
brain 348.5
  due to birth injury 767.8
  fetus or newborn 767.8
cardiac (see also Failure, heart) 428.0
cardiovascular (see also Failure, heart) 428.0
cerebral — see Edema, brain
cerebrospinal vessel — see Edema, brain
cervix (acute) (uteri) 622.8
  puerperal, postpartum 674.8 ☑
chronic hereditary 757.0
circumscribed, acute 995.1
  hereditary 277.6

Edema, edematous — continued
complicating pregnancy (gestational) 646.1 ☑
  with hypertension — see Toxemia, of pregnancy
conjunctiva 372.73
connective tissue 782.3
cornea 371.20
  due to contact lenses 371.24
  idiopathic 371.21
  secondary 371.22
cystoid macular 362.53
due to
  lymphatic obstruction — see Edema, lymphatic
  salt retention 276.0
epiglottis — see Edema, glottis
essential, acute 995.1
  hereditary 277.6
extremities, lower — see Edema, legs
eyelid NEC 374.82
familial, hereditary (legs) 757.0
famine 262
fetus or newborn 778.5
genital organs
  female 629.89   ▲
  male 608.86
gestational 646.1 ☑
  with hypertension — see Toxemia, of pregnancy
glottis, glottic, glottides (obstructive) (passive) 478.6
  allergic 995.1
    hereditary 277.6
  due to external agent — see Condition, respiratory, acute, due to specified agent
heart (see also Failure, heart) 428.0
  newborn 779.89
heat 992.7
hereditary (legs) 757.0
inanition 262
infectious 782.3
intracranial 348.5
  due to injury at birth 767.8
iris 364.8
joint (see also Effusion, joint) 719.0 ☑
larynx (see also Edema, glottis) 478.6
legs 782.3
  due to venous obstruction 459.2
  hereditary 757.0
localized 782.3
  due to venous obstruction 459.2
    lower extremity 459.2
lower extremities — see Edema, legs
lung 514
  acute 518.4
    with heart disease or failure (see also Failure, ventricular, left) 428.1
    congestive 428.0
  chemical (due to fumes or vapors) 506.1
  due to
    external agent(s) NEC 508.9
      specified NEC 508.8
    fumes and vapors (chemical) (inhalation) 506.1
    radiation 508.0
  chemical (acute) 506.1
    chronic 506.4
  chronic 514
    chemical (due to fumes or vapors) 506.4
    due to
      external agent(s) NEC 508.9
        specified NEC 508.8
      fumes or vapors (chemical) (inhalation) 506.4
      radiation 508.1
    due to
      external agent 508.9
        specified NEC 508.8
      high altitude 993.2
      near drowning 994.1
    postoperative 518.4

Edema, edematous — continued
lung — continued
  terminal 514
  lymphatic 457.1
    due to mastectomy operation 457.0
  macula 362.83
    cystoid 362.53
    diabetic 250.5 ☑ [362.07]
  malignant (see also Gangrene, gas) 040.0
  Milroy's 757.0
  nasopharynx 478.25
  neonatorum 778.5
  nutritional (newborn) 262
    with dyspigmentation, skin and hair 260
  optic disc or nerve — see Papilledema
  orbit 376.33
    circulatory 459.89
  palate (soft) (hard) 528.9
  pancreas 577.8
  penis 607.83
  periodic 995.1
    hereditary 277.6
  pharynx 478.25
  pitting 782.3
  pulmonary — see Edema, lung
  Quincke's 995.1
    hereditary 277.6
  renal (see also Nephrosis) 581.9
  retina (localized) (macular) (peripheral) 362.83
    cystoid 362.53
    diabetic 250.5 ☑ [362.07]
  salt 276.0
  scrotum 608.86
  seminal vesicle 608.86
  spermatic cord 608.86
  spinal cord 336.1
  starvation 262
  stasis (see also Hypertension, venous) 459.30
  subconjunctival 372.73
  subglottic (see also Edema, glottis) 478.6
  supraglottic (see also Edema, glottis) 478.6
  testis 608.86
  toxic NEC 782.3
  traumatic NEC 782.3
  tunica vaginalis 608.86
  vas deferens 608.86
  vocal cord — see Edema, glottis
  vulva (acute) 624.8
Edentia (complete) (partial) — see also Absence, tooth 520.0
  acquired (see also Edentulism) 525.40
    due to
      caries 525.13
      extraction 525.10
      periodontal disease 525.12
      specified NEC 525.19
      trauma 525.11
    causing malocclusion 524.30
  congenital (deficiency of tooth buds) 520.0
Edentulism 525.40
  complete 525.40
    class I 525.41
    class II 525.42
    class III 525.43
    class IV 525.44
  partial 525.50
    class I 525.51
    class II 525.52
    class III 525.53
    class IV 525.54
Edsall's disease 992.2
Educational handicap V62.3
Edwards' syndrome 758.2
Effect, adverse NEC
  abnormal gravitational (G) forces or states 994.9
  air pressure — see Effect, adverse, atmospheric pressure

Effect, adverse — continued
altitude (high) — see Effect, adverse, high altitude
anesthetic
  in labor and delivery NEC 668.9 ☑
  affecting fetus or newborn 763.5
antitoxin — see Complications, vaccination
atmospheric pressure 993.9
  due to explosion 993.4
  high 993.3
  low — see Effect, adverse, high altitude
  specified effect NEC 993.8
biological, correct substance properly administered (see also Effect, adverse, drug) 995.20   ▲
blood (derivatives) (serum) (transfusion) — see Complications, transfusion
chemical substance NEC 989.9
  specified — see Table of Drugs and Chemicals
cobalt, radioactive (see also Effect, adverse, radioactive substance) 990
cold (temperature) (weather) 991.9
  chilblains 991.5
  frostbite — see Frostbite
  specified effect NEC 991.8
drugs and medicinals 995.20   ▲
  correct substance properly administered 995.20   ▲
  overdose or wrong substance given or taken 977.9
  specified drug — see Table of Drugs and Chemicals
electric current (shock) 994.8
  burn — see Burn, by site
electricity (electrocution) (shock) 994.8
  burn — see Burn, by site
exertion (excessive) 994.5
exposure 994.9
  exhaustion 994.4
external cause NEC 994.9
fallout (radioactive) NEC 990
fluoroscopy NEC 990
foodstuffs
  allergic reaction (see also Allergy, food) 693.1
  anaphylactic shock due to food NEC 995.60
  noxious 988.9
    specified type NEC (see also Poisoning, by name of noxious foodstuff) 988.8
gases, fumes, or vapors — see Table of Drugs and Chemicals
glue (airplane) sniffing 304.6 ☑
heat — see Heat
high altitude NEC 993.2
  anoxia 993.2
  on
    ears 993.0
    sinuses 993.1
  polycythemia 289.0
hot weather — see Heat
hunger 994.2
immersion, foot 991.4
immunization — see Complications, vaccination
immunological agents — see Complications, vaccination
implantation (removable) of isotope or radium NEC 990
infrared (radiation) (rays) NEC 990
  burn — see Burn, by site
  dermatitis or eczema 692.82
infusion — see Complications, infusion
ingestion or injection of isotope (therapeutic) NEC 990
irradiation NEC (see also Effect, adverse, radiation) 990
isotope (radioactive) NEC 990

Effect, adverse — *continued*
  lack of care (child) (infant) (newborn)
      995.52
    adult 995.84
  lightning 994.0
  burn — *see* Burn, by site
  Lirugin — *see* Complications, vaccination
  medicinal substance, correct, properly
      administered (*see also* Effect,
      adverse, drugs) 995.20 ▲
  mesothorium NEC 990
  motion 994.6
  noise, inner ear 388.10
  other drug, medicinal and biological●
      substance 995.29   ●
  overheated places — *see* Heat
  polonium NEC 990
  psychosocial, of work environment
      V62.1
  radiation (diagnostic) (fallout) (in-
      frared) (natural source) (thera-
      peutic) (tracer) (ultraviolet) (x-
      ray) NEC 990
    with pulmonary manifestations
      acute 508.0
      chronic 508.1
    dermatitis or eczema 692.82
      due to sun NEC (*see also* Der-
          matitis, due to, sun)
          692.70
    fibrosis of lungs 508.1
    maternal with suspected damage
        to fetus affecting manage-
        ment of pregnancy 655.6 ☑
    pneumonitis 508.0
  radioactive substance NEC 990
    dermatitis or eczema 692.82
  radioactivity NEC 990
  radiotherapy NEC 990
    dermatitis or eczema 692.82
  radium NEC 990
  reduced temperature 991.9
    frostbite — *see* Frostbite
    immersion, foot (hand) 991.4
    specified effect NEC 991.8
  roentgenography NEC 990
  roentgenoscopy NEC 990
  roentgen rays NEC 990
  serum (prophylactic) (therapeutic)
      NEC 999.5
  specified NEC 995.89
    external cause NEC 994.9
  strangulation 994.7
  submersion 994.1
  teletherapy NEC 990
  thirst 994.3
  transfusion — *see* Complications,
      transfusion
  ultraviolet (radiation) (rays) NEC 990
    burn (*see also* Burn, by site)
      from sun (*see also* Sunburn)
          692.71
    dermatitis or eczema 692.82
      due to sun NEC (*see also* Der-
          matitis, due to, sun)
          692.70
  uranium NEC 990
  vaccine (any) — *see* Complications,
      vaccination
  weightlessness 994.9
  whole blood (*see also* Complications,
      transfusion)
    overdose or wrong substance given
        (*see also* Table of Drugs and
        Chemicals) 964.7
  working environment V62.1
  x-rays NEC 990
    dermatitis or eczema 692.82
Effect, remote
  of cancer — *see* condition
Effects, late — *see* Late, effect (of)
Effluvium, telogen 704.02
Effort
  intolerance 306.2

Effort — *continued*
  syndrome (aviators) (psychogenic)
      306.2
Effusion
  amniotic fluid (*see also* Rupture,
      membranes, premature)
      658.1 ☑
  brain (serous) 348.5
  bronchial (*see also* Bronchitis) 490
  cerebral 348.5
  cerebrospinal (*see also* Meningitis)
      322.9
    vessel 348.5
  chest — *see* Effusion, pleura
  intracranial 348.5
  joint 719.00
    ankle 719.07
    elbow 719.02
    foot 719.07
    hand 719.04
    hip 719.05
    knee 719.06
    multiple sites 719.09
    pelvic region 719.05
    shoulder (region) 719.01
    specified site NEC 719.08
    wrist 719.03
  meninges (*see also* Meningitis) 322.9
  pericardium, pericardial (*see also*
      Pericarditis) 423.9
    acute 420.90
  peritoneal (chronic) 568.82
  pleura, pleurisy, pleuritic, pleuroperi-
      cardial 511.9
    bacterial, nontuberculous 511.1
    fetus or newborn 511.9
    malignant 197.2
    nontuberculous 511.9
      bacterial 511.1
    pneumococcal 511.1
    staphylococcal 511.1
    streptococcal 511.1
    traumatic 862.29
      with open wound 862.39
    tuberculous (*see also* Tuberculosis,
        pleura) 012.0 ☑
      primary progressive 010.1 ☑
  pulmonary — *see* Effusion, pleura
  spinal (*see also* Meningitis) 322.9
  thorax, thoracic — *see* Effusion,
      pleura
Egg (oocyte) (ovum)
  donor V59.70
    over age 35 V59.73
      anonymous recipient V59.73
      designated recipient V59.74
    under age 35 V59.71
      anonymous recipient V59.71
      designated recipient V59.72
Eggshell nails 703.8
  congenital 757.5
Ego-dystonic
  homosexuality 302.0
  lesbianism 302.0
  sexual orientation 302.0
Egyptian splenomegaly 120.1
Ehlers-Danlos syndrome 756.83
Ehrlichiosis 082.40
  chaffeensis 082.41
  specified type NEC 082.49
Eichstedt's disease (pityriasis versicolor)
  111.0
Eisenmenger's complex or syndrome
  (ventricular septal defect) 745.4
Ejaculation, semen
  painful 608.89
    psychogenic 306.59
  premature 302.75
  retrograde 608.87
Ekbom syndrome (restless legs)
  333.94   ▲
Ekman's syndrome (brittle bones and
  blue sclera) 756.51
Elastic skin 756.83
  acquired 701.8

Elastofibroma (M8820/0) — *see* Neoplasm, connective tissue, benign
Elastoidosis
  cutanea nodularis 701.8
  cutis cystica et comedonica 701.8
Elastoma 757.39
  juvenile 757.39
  Miescher's (elastosis perforans serpig-
      inosa) 701.1
Elastomyofibrosis 425.3
Elastosis 701.8
  atrophicans 701.8
  perforans serpiginosa 701.1
  reactive perforating 701.1
  senilis 701.8
  solar (actinic) 692.74
Elbow — *see* condition
Electric
  current, electricity, effects (concus-
      sion) (fatal) (nonfatal) (shock)
      994.8
    burn — *see* Burn, by site
  feet (foot) syndrome 266.2
Electrocution 994.8
Electrolyte imbalance 276.9
  with
    abortion — *see* Abortion, by type,
        with metabolic disorder
    ectopic pregnancy (*see also* cate-
        gories 633.0–633.9) 639.4
    hyperemesis gravidarum (before 22
        completed weeks gestation)
        643.1 ☑
    molar pregnancy (*see also* cate-
        gories 630–632) 639.4
  following
    abortion 639.4
    ectopic or molar pregnancy 639.4
Elephantiasis (nonfilarial) 457.1
  arabicum (*see also* Infestation, filarial)
      125.9
  congenita hereditaria 757.0
  congenital (any site) 757.0
  due to
    Brugia (malayi) 125.1
    mastectomy operation 457.0
    Wuchereria (bancrofti) 125.0
      malayi 125.1
  eyelid 374.83
  filarial (*see also* Infestation, filarial)
      125.9
  filariensis (*see also* Infestation, filarial)
      125.9
  gingival 523.8
  glandular 457.1
  graecorum 030.9
  lymphangiectatic 457.1
  lymphatic vessel 457.1
    due to mastectomy operation 457.0
  neuromatosa 237.71
  postmastectomy 457.0
  scrotum 457.1
  streptococcal 457.1
  surgical 997.99
    postmastectomy 457.0
  telangiectodes 457.1
  vulva (nonfilarial) 624.8
Elephant man syndrome 237.71
Elevated — *see* Elevation
Elevation
  17-ketosteroids 791.9
  acid phosphatase 790.5
  alkaline phosphatase 790.5
  amylase 790.5
  antibody titers 795.79
  basal metabolic rate (BMR) 794.7
  blood pressure (*see also* Hypertension)
      401.9
    reading (incidental) (isolated) (non-
        specific), no diagnosis of hy-
        pertension 796.2
  body temperature (of unknown origin)
      (*see also* Pyrexia) 780.6
  cancer antigen 125 [CA 125] 795.82●
  carcinoembryonic antigen [CEA]   ●
      795.81   ●

Elevation — *continued*
  conjugate, eye 378.81
  C-reactive protein (CRP) 790.95
  CRP (C-reactive protein) 790.95
  diaphragm, congenital 756.6
  glucose
    fasting 790.21
    tolerance test 790.22
  immunoglobulin level 795.79
  indolacetic acid 791.9
  lactic acid dehydrogenase (LDH) level
      790.4
  leukocytes 288.60   ●
  lipase 790.5
  lipoprotein a level 272.8
  liver function test (LFT) 790.6
    alkaline phosphatase 790.5   ●
    aminotransferase 790.4   ●
    bilirubin 782.4   ●
    hepatic enzyme NEC 790.5   ●
    lactate dehydrogenase 790.4   ●
  lymphocytes 288.61   ●
  prostate specific antigen (PSA) 790.93
  renin 790.99
    in hypertension (*see also* Hyperten-
        sion, renovascular) 405.91
  Rh titer 999.7
  scapula, congenital 755.52
  sedimentation rate 790.1
  SGOT 790.4
  SGPT 790.4
  transaminase 790.4
  vanillylmandelic acid 791.9
  venous pressure 459.89
  VMA 791.9
  white blood cell count 288.60   ●
    specified NEC 288.69   ●
Elliptocytosis (congenital) (hereditary)
  282.1
  Hb-C (disease) 282.7
  hemoglobin disease 282.7
  sickle-cell (disease) 282.60
    trait 282.5
Ellison-Zollinger syndrome (gastric hypersecretion with pancreatic islet
  cell tumor) 251.5
Ellis-van Creveld disease or syndrome
  (chondroectodermal dysplasia)
  756.55
Elongation, elongated (congenital) —
  see also Distortion
  bone 756.9
  cervix (uteri) 752.49
    acquired 622.6
    hypertrophic 622.6
  colon 751.5
  common bile duct 751.69
  cystic duct 751.69
  frenulum, penis 752.69
  labia minora, acquired 624.8
  ligamentum patellae 756.89
  petiolus (epiglottidis) 748.3
  styloid bone (process) 733.99
  tooth, teeth 520.2
  uvula 750.26
    acquired 528.9
Elschnig bodies or pearls 366.51
El Tor cholera 001.1
Emaciation (due to malnutrition) 261
Emancipation disorder 309.22
Embadomoniasis 007.8
Embarrassment heart, cardiac — *see*
  Disease, heart
Embedded tooth, teeth 520.6
  root only 525.3
Embolic — *see* condition
Embolism 444.9
  with
    abortion — *see* Abortion, by type,
        with embolism
    ectopic pregnancy (*see also* cate-
        gories 633.0–633.9) 639.6
    molar pregnancy (*see also* cate-
        gories 630–632) 639.6
  air (any site) 958.0

☑ Additional Digit Required — Refer to the Tabular List for Digit Selection   ▽ Subterms under main terms may continue to next column or page

2007 ICD-9-CM   ▶◀ Revised Text   ● New Line   ▲ Revised Code   **October 2006 • Volume 2 — 105**

Index

Embolism — Embolism

Embolism — *continued*
- air — *continued*
  - with
    - abortion — *see* Abortion, by type, with embolism
    - ectopic pregnancy (*see also* categories 633.0–633.9) 639.6
    - molar pregnancy (*see also* categories 630–632) 639.6
    - due to implanted device — *see* Complications, due to (presence of) any device, implant, or graft classified to 996.0–996.5 NEC
  - following
    - abortion 639.6
    - ectopic or molar pregnancy 639.6
  - infusion, perfusion, or transfusion 999.1
  - in pregnancy, childbirth, or puerperium 673.0 ☑
  - traumatic 958.0
- amniotic fluid (pulmonary) 673.1 ☑
  - with
    - abortion — *see* Abortion, by type, with embolism
    - ectopic pregnancy (*see also* categories 633.0–633.9) 639.6
    - molar pregnancy (*see also* categories 630–632) 639.6
  - following
    - abortion 639.6
    - ectopic or molar pregnancy 639.6
- aorta, aortic 444.1
  - abdominal 444.0
  - bifurcation 444.0
  - saddle 444.0
  - thoracic 444.1
- artery 444.9
  - auditory, internal 433.8 ☑
  - basilar (*see also* Occlusion, artery, basilar) 433.0 ☑
  - bladder 444.89
  - carotid (common) (internal) (*see also* Occlusion, artery, carotid) 433.1 ☑
  - cerebellar (anterior inferior) (posterior inferior) (superior) 433.8 ☑
  - cerebral (*see also* Embolism, brain) 434.1 ☑
  - choroidal (anterior) 433.8 ☑
  - communicating posterior 433.8 ☑
  - coronary (*see also* Infarct, myocardium) 410.9 ☑
    - without myocardial infarction 411.81
  - extremity 444.22
    - lower 444.22
    - upper 444.21
  - hypophyseal 433.8 ☑
  - mesenteric (with gangrene) 557.0
  - ophthalmic (*see also* Occlusion, retina) 362.30
  - peripheral 444.22
  - pontine 433.8 ☑
  - precerebral NEC — *see* Occlusion, artery, precerebral
  - pulmonary — *see* Embolism, pulmonary
  - renal 593.81
  - retinal (*see also* Occlusion, retina) 362.30
  - specified site NEC 444.89
  - vertebral (*see also* Occlusion, artery, vertebral) 433.2 ☑
- auditory, internal 433.8 ☑
- basilar (artery) (*see also* Occlusion, artery, basilar) 433.0 ☑
- birth, mother — *see* Embolism, obstetrical

Embolism — *continued*
- blood-clot
  - with
    - abortion — *see* Abortion, by type, with embolism
    - ectopic pregnancy (*see also* categories 633.0–633.9) 639.6
    - molar pregnancy (*see also* categories 630–632) 639.6
  - following
    - abortion 639.6
    - ectopic or molar pregnancy 639.6
  - in pregnancy, childbirth, or puerperium 673.2 ☑
- brain 434.1 ☑
  - with
    - abortion — *see* Abortion, by type, with embolism
    - ectopic pregnancy (*see also* categories 633.0–633.9) 639.6
    - molar pregnancy (*see also* categories 630–632) 639.6
  - following
    - abortion 639.6
    - ectopic or molar pregnancy 639.6
  - late effect — *see* Late effect(s) (of) cerebrovascular disease
  - puerperal, postpartum, childbirth 674.0 ☑
- capillary 448.9
- cardiac (*see also* Infarct, myocardium) 410.9 ☑
- carotid (artery) (common) (internal) (*see also* Occlusion, artery, carotid) 433.1 ☑
- cavernous sinus (venous) — *see* Embolism, intracranial venous sinus
- cerebral (*see also* Embolism, brain) 434.1 ☑
- cholesterol — *see* Atheroembolism
- choroidal (anterior) (artery) 433.8 ☑
- coronary (artery or vein) (systemic) (*see also* Infarct, myocardium) 410.9 ☑
  - without myocardial infarction 411.81
- due to (presence of) any device, implant, or graft classifiable to 996.0–996.5 — *see* Complications, due to (presence of) any device, implant, or graft classified to 996.0–996.5 NEC
- encephalomalacia (*see also* Embolism, brain) 434.1 ☑
- extremities 444.22
  - lower 444.22
  - upper 444.21
- eye 362.30
- fat (cerebral) (pulmonary) (systemic) 958.1
  - with
    - abortion — *see* Abortion, by type, with embolism
    - ectopic pregnancy (*see also* categories 633.0–633.9) 639.6
    - molar pregnancy (*see also* categories 630–632) 639.6
  - complicating delivery or puerperium 673.8 ☑
  - following
    - abortion 639.6
    - ectopic or molar pregnancy 639.6
  - in pregnancy, childbirth, or the puerperium 673.8 ☑
- femoral (artery) 444.22
  - vein 453.8
    - deep 453.41
  - following
    - abortion 639.6

Embolism — *continued*
- following — *continued*
  - ectopic or molar pregnancy 639.6
  - infusion, perfusion, or transfusion
    - air 999.1
    - thrombus 999.2
- heart (fatty) (*see also* Infarct, myocardium) 410.9 ☑
- hepatic (vein) 453.0
- iliac (artery) 444.81
- iliofemoral 444.81
- in pregnancy, childbirth, or puerperium (pulmonary) — *see* Embolism, obstetrical
- intestine (artery) (vein) (with gangrene) 557.0
- intracranial (*see also* Embolism, brain) 434.1 ☑
  - venous sinus (any) 325
    - late effect — *see* category 326
    - nonpyogenic 437.6
      - in pregnancy or puerperium 671.5 ☑
- kidney (artery) 593.81
- lateral sinus (venous) — *see* Embolism, intracranial venous sinus
- longitudinal sinus (venous) — *see* Embolism, intracranial venous sinus
- lower extremity 444.22
- lung (massive) — *see* Embolism, pulmonary
- meninges (*see also* Embolism, brain) 434.1 ☑
- mesenteric (artery) (with gangrene) 557.0
- multiple NEC 444.9
- obstetrical (pulmonary) 673.2 ☑
  - air 673.0 ☑
  - amniotic fluid (pulmonary) 673.1 ☑
  - blood-clot 673.2 ☑
  - cardiac 674.8 ☑
  - fat 673.8 ☑
  - heart 674.8 ☑
  - pyemic 673.3 ☑
  - septic 673.3 ☑
  - specified NEC 674.8 ☑
- ophthalmic (*see also* Occlusion, retina) 362.30
- paradoxical NEC 444.9
- penis 607.82
- peripheral arteries NEC 444.22
  - lower 444.22
  - upper 444.21
- pituitary 253.8
- popliteal (artery) 444.22
- portal (vein) 452
- postoperative NEC 997.2
  - cerebral 997.02
  - mesenteric artery 997.71
  - other vessels 997.79
  - peripheral vascular 997.2
  - pulmonary 415.11
  - renal artery 997.72
- precerebral artery (*see also* Occlusion, artery, precerebral) 433.9 ☑
- puerperal — *see* Embolism, obstetrical
- pulmonary (artery) (vein) 415.19
  - with
    - abortion — *see* Abortion, by type, with embolism
    - ectopic pregnancy (*see also* categories 633.0–633.9) 639.6
    - molar pregnancy (*see also* categories 630–632) 639.6
  - following
    - abortion 639.6
    - ectopic or molar pregnancy 639.6
  - iatrogenic 415.11
  - in pregnancy, childbirth, or puerperium — *see* Embolism, obstetrical
  - postoperative 415.11

Embolism — *continued*
- pyemic (multiple) 038.9
  - with
    - abortion — *see* Abortion, by type, with embolism
    - ectopic pregnancy (*see also* categories 633.0–633.9) 639.6
    - molar pregnancy (*see also* categories 630–632) 639.6
  - Aerobacter aerogenes 038.49
  - enteric gram-negative bacilli 038.40
  - Enterobacter aerogenes 038.49
  - Escherichia coli 038.42
  - following
    - abortion 639.6
    - ectopic or molar pregnancy 639.6
  - Hemophilus influenzae 038.41
  - pneumococcal 038.2
  - Proteus vulgaris 038.49
  - Pseudomonas (aeruginosa) 038.43
  - puerperal, postpartum, childbirth (any organism) 673.3 ☑
  - Serratia 038.44
  - specified organism NEC 038.8
  - staphylococcal 038.10
    - aureus 038.11
    - specified organism NEC 038.19
  - streptococcal 038.0
- renal (artery) 593.81
  - vein 453.3
- retina, retinal (*see also* Occlusion, retina) 362.30
- saddle (aorta) 444.0
- septicemic — *see* Embolism, pyemic
- sinus — *see* Embolism, intracranial venous sinus
- soap
  - with
    - abortion — *see* Abortion, by type, with embolism
    - ectopic pregnancy (*see also* categories 633.0–633.9) 639.6
    - molar pregnancy (*see also* categories 630–632) 639.6
  - following
    - abortion 639.6
    - ectopic or molar pregnancy 639.6
- spinal cord (nonpyogenic) 336.1
  - in pregnancy or puerperium 671.5 ☑
  - pyogenic origin 324.1
  - late effect — *see* category 326
- spleen, splenic (artery) 444.89
- thrombus (thromboembolism) following infusion, perfusion, or transfusion 999.2
- upper extremity 444.21
- vein 453.9
  - with inflammation or phlebitis — *see* Thrombophlebitis
  - cerebral (*see also* Embolism, brain) 434.1 ☑
  - coronary (*see also* Infarct, myocardium) 410.9 ☑
    - without myocardial infarction 411.81
  - hepatic 453.0
  - lower extremity 453.8
    - deep 453.40
      - calf 453.42
      - distal (lower leg) 453.42
      - femoral 453.41
      - iliac 453.41
      - lower leg 453.42
      - peroneal 453.42
      - popliteal 453.41
      - proximal (upper leg) 453.41
      - thigh 453.41
      - tibial 453.42
  - mesenteric (with gangrene) 557.0
  - portal 452

☑ Additional Digit Required — Refer to the Tabular List for Digit Selection   ▽ Subterms under main terms may continue to next column or page

Embolism — *continued*
  vein — *continued*
    pulmonary — *see* Embolism, pulmonary
    renal 453.3
    specified NEC 453.8
      with inflammation or phlebitis — *see* Thrombophlebitis
    vena cava (inferior) (superior) 453.2
    vessels of brain (*see also* Embolism, brain) 434.1 ☑
Embolization — *see* **Embolism**
Embolus — *see* Embolism
Embryoma (M9080/1) — *see also* Neoplasm, by site, uncertain behavior
  benign (M9080/0) — *see* Neoplasm, by site, benign
  kidney (M8960/3) 189.0
  liver (M8970/3) 155.0
  malignant (M9080/3) (*see also* Neoplasm, by site, malignant)
    kidney (M8960/3) 189.0
    liver (M8970/3) 155.0
    testis (M9070/3) 186.9
      undescended 186.0
  testis (M9070/3) 186.9
    undescended 186.0
Embryonic
  circulation 747.9
  heart 747.9
  vas deferens 752.89
Embryopathia NEC 759.9
Embryotomy, fetal 763.89
Embryotoxon 743.43
  interfering with vision 743.42
Emesis — *see also* Vomiting
  gravidarum — *see* Hyperemesis, gravidarum
Emissions, nocturnal (semen) 608.89
Emotional
  crisis — *see* Crisis, emotional
  disorder (*see also* Disorder, mental) 300.9
  instability (excessive) 301.3
  overlay — *see* Reaction, adjustment
  upset 300.9
Emotionality, pathological 301.3
Emotogenic disease — *see also* Disorder, psychogenic 306.9
Emphysema (atrophic) (centriacinar) (centrilobular) (chronic) (diffuse) (essential) (hypertrophic) (interlobular) (lung) (obstructive) (panlobular) (paracatricial) (paracinar) (postural) (pulmonary) (senile) (subpleural) (traction) (unilateral) (unilobular) (vesicular) 492.8
  with bronchitis
    chronic 491.20
      with
        acute bronchitis 491.22
        exacerbation (acute) 491.21
  bullous (giant) 492.0
  cellular tissue 958.7
    surgical 998.81
  compensatory 518.2
  congenital 770.2
  conjunctiva 372.89
  connective tissue 958.7
    surgical 998.81
  due to fumes or vapors 506.4
  eye 376.89
  eyelid 374.85
    surgical 998.81
    traumatic 958.7
  fetus or newborn (interstitial) (mediastinal) (unilobular) 770.2
  heart 416.9
  interstitial 518.1
    congenital 770.2
    fetus or newborn 770.2
  laminated tissue 958.7
    surgical 998.81
  mediastinal 518.1
    fetus or newborn 770.2

Emphysema — *continued*
  newborn (interstitial) (mediastinal) (unilobular) 770.2
  obstructive diffuse with fibrosis 492.8
  orbit 376.89
  subcutaneous 958.7
    due to trauma 958.7
    nontraumatic 518.1
    surgical 998.81
  surgical 998.81
  thymus (gland) (congenital) 254.8
  traumatic 958.7
  tuberculous (*see also* Tuberculosis, pulmonary) 011.9 ☑
Employment examination (certification) V70.5
Empty sella (turcica) syndrome 253.8
Empyema (chest) (diaphragmatic) (double) (encapsulated) (general) (interlobar) (lung) (medial) (necessitatis) (perforating chest wall) (pleura) (pneumococcal) (residual) (sacculated) (streptococcal) (supradiaphragmatic) 510.9
  with fistula 510.0
  accessory sinus (chronic) (*see also* Sinusitis) 473.9
  acute 510.9
    with fistula 510.0
  antrum (chronic) (*see also* Sinusitis, maxillary) 473.0
  brain (any part) (*see also* Abscess, brain) 324.0
  ethmoidal (sinus) (chronic) (*see also* Sinusitis, ethmoidal) 473.2
  extradural (*see also* Abscess, extradural) 324.9
  frontal (sinus) (chronic) (*see also* Sinusitis, frontal) 473.1
  gallbladder (*see also* Cholecystitis, acute) 575.0
  mastoid (process) (acute) (*see also* Mastoiditis, acute) 383.00
  maxilla, maxillary 526.4
    sinus (chronic) (*see also* Sinusitis, maxillary) 473.0
  nasal sinus (chronic) (*see also* Sinusitis) 473.9
  sinus (accessory) (nasal) (*see also* Sinusitis) 473.9
  sphenoidal (chronic) (sinus) (*see also* Sinusitis, sphenoidal) 473.3
  subarachnoid (*see also* Abscess, extradural) 324.9
  subdural (*see also* Abscess, extradural) 324.9
  tuberculous (*see also* Tuberculosis, pleura) 012.0 ☑
  ureter (*see also* Ureteritis) 593.89
  ventricular (*see also* Abscess, brain) 324.0
Enameloma 520.2
Encephalitis (bacterial) (chronic) (hemorrhagic) (idiopathic) (nonepidemic) (spurious) (subacute) 323.9
  acute (*see also* Encephalitis, viral)
    disseminated (postinfectious) NEC 136.9 *[323.61]* ▲
      postimmunization or postvaccination 323.51 ▲
    inclusional 049.8
    inclusion body 049.8
    necrotizing 049.8
  arboviral, arbovirus NEC 064
  arthropod-borne (*see also* Encephalitis, viral, arthropod-borne) 064
  Australian X 062.4
  Bwamba fever 066.3
  California (virus) 062.5
  Central European 063.2
  Czechoslovakian 063.2
  Dawson's (inclusion body) 046.2
  diffuse sclerosing 046.2
  due to
    actinomycosis 039.8 *[323.41]* ▲

Encephalitis — *continued*
  due to — *continued*
    cat-scratch disease 078.3 *[323.01]* ▲
    infection classified elsewhere 136.9 *[323.41]* ●
    infectious mononucleosis 075 *[323.01]* ▲
    malaria (*see also* Malaria) 084.6 *[323.2]*
    Negishi virus 064
    ornithosis 073.7 *[323.01]* ▲
    prophylactic inoculation against smallpox 323.51
    rickettsiosis (*see also* Rickettsiosis) 083.9 *[323.1]*
    rubella 056.01
    toxoplasmosis (acquired) 130.0
      congenital (active) 771.2 *[323.41]* ▲
    typhus (fever) (*see also* Typhus) 081.9 *[323.1]*
    vaccination (smallpox) 323.51 ▲
  Eastern equine 062.2
  endemic 049.8
  epidemic 049.8
  equine (acute) (infectious) (viral) 062.9
    Eastern 062.2
    Venezuelan 066.2
    Western 062.1
  Far Eastern 063.0
  following vaccination or other immunization procedure 323.51 ▲
  herpes 054.3
  Ilheus (virus) 062.8
  inclusion body 046.2
  infectious (acute) (virus) NEC 049.8
  influenzal 487.8 *[323.41]* ▲
    lethargic 049.8
  Japanese (B type) 062.0
  La Crosse 062.5
  Langat 063.8
  late effect — *see* Late, effect, encephalitis
  lead 984.9 *[323.71]* ▲
  lethargic (acute) (infectious) (influenzal) 049.8
  lethargica 049.8
  louping ill 063.1
  lupus 710.0 *[323.81]* ▲
  lymphatica 049.0
  Mengo 049.8
  meningococcal 036.1
  mumps 072.2
  Murray Valley 062.4
  myoclonic 049.8
  Negishi virus 064
  otitic NEC 382.4 *[323.41]* ▲
  parasitic NEC 123.9 *[323.41]* ▲
  periaxialis (concentrica) (diffusa) 341.1
  postchickenpox 052.0
  postexanthematous NEC 057.9 *[323.62]* ▲
  postimmunization 323.51 ▲
  postinfectious NEC 136.9 *[323.62]* ▲
  postmeasles 055.0
  posttraumatic 323.81
  postvaccinal (smallpox) 323.51 ▲
  postvaricella 052.0
  postviral NEC 079.99 *[323.62]* ▲
    postexanthematous 057.9 *[323.62]* ▲
    specified NEC 057.8 *[323.62]* ▲
  Powassan 063.8
  progressive subcortical (Binswanger's) 290.12
  Rasmussen 323.81 ●
  Rio Bravo 049.8
  rubella 056.01
  Russian
    autumnal 062.0
    spring-summer type (taiga) 063.0
  saturnine 984.9 *[323.71]* ▲
  Semliki Forest 062.8

Encephalitis — *continued*
  serous 048
  slow-acting virus NEC 046.8
  specified cause NEC 323.81 ▲
  St. Louis type 062.3
  subacute sclerosing 046.2
  subcorticalis chronica 290.12
  summer 062.0
  suppurative 324.0
  syphilitic 094.81
    congenital 090.41
  tick-borne 063.9
  torula, torular 117.5 *[323.41]* ▲
  toxic NEC 989.9 *[323.71]* ▲
  toxoplasmic (acquired) 130.0
    congenital (active) 771.2 *[323.41]* ▲
  trichinosis 124 *[323.41]* ▲
  Trypanosomiasis (*see also* Trypanosomiasis) 086.9 *[323.2]*
  tuberculous (*see also* Tuberculosis) 013.6 ☑
  type B (Japanese) 062.0
  type C 062.3
  van Bogaert's 046.2
  Venezuelan 066.2
  Vienna type 049.8
  viral, virus 049.9
    arthropod-borne NEC 064
      mosquito-borne 062.9
        Australian X disease 062.4
        California virus 062.5
        Eastern equine 062.2
        Ilheus virus 062.8
        Japanese (B type) 062.0
        Murray Valley 062.4
        specified type NEC 062.8
        St. Louis 062.3
        type B 062.0
        type C 062.3
        Western equine 062.1
      tick-borne 063.9
        biundulant 063.2
        Central European 063.2
        Czechoslovakian 063.2
        diphasic meningoencephalitis 063.2
        Far Eastern 063.0
        Langat 063.8
        louping ill 063.1
        Powassan 063.8
        Russian spring-summer (taiga) 063.0
        specified type NEC 063.8
        vector unknown 064
        Western equine 062.1
    slow acting NEC 046.8
    specified type NEC 049.8
    vaccination, prophylactic (against) V05.0
  von Economo's 049.8
  Western equine 062.1
  West Nile type 066.41
Encephalocele 742.0 ▲
  orbit 376.81
Encephalocystocele 742.0 ▲
Encephalomalacia (brain) (cerebellar) (cerebral) (cerebrospinal) — *see also* Softening, brain 434.9 ☑
  due to
    hemorrhage (*see also* Hemorrhage, brain) 431
    recurrent spasm of artery 435.9
  embolic (cerebral) (*see also* Embolism, brain) 434.1 ☑
  subcorticalis chronicus arteriosclerotica 290.12
  thrombotic (*see also* Thrombosis, brain) 434.0 ☑
Encephalomeningitis — *see* Meningoencephalitis
Encephalomeningocele 742.0 ▲
Encephalomeningomyelitis — *see* Meningoencephalitis
Encephalomeningopathy — *see also* Meningoencephalitis 349.9

☑ Additional Digit Required — Refer to the Tabular List for Digit Selection   ▽ Subterms under main terms may continue to next column or page

2007 ICD-9-CM   ▶◀ Revised Text   ● New Line   ▲ Revised Code   **October 2006 · Volume 2 — 107**

Encephalomyelitis (chronic) (granulomatous) (hemorrhagic necrotizing, acute) (myalgic, benign) — *see also* Encephalitis 323.9
abortive disseminated 049.8
acute disseminated (ADEM) (postinfectious) 136.9 *[323.61]* ▲
  infectious 136.9 *[323.61]* ▲
  noninfectious 323.81 ▲
  postimmunization 323.51 ▲
due to
  cat-scratch disease 078.3 *[323.01]* ●
  infectious mononucleosis 075 *[323.01]* ●
  ornithosis 073.7 *[323.01]* ●
  vaccination (any) 323.51 ●
equine (acute) (infectious) 062.9
  Eastern 062.2
  Venezuelan 066.2
  Western 062.1
funicularis infectiosa 049.8
late effect — *see* Late, effect, encephalitis
Munch-Peterson's 049.8
postchickenpox 052.0
postimmunization 323.51 ▲
postmeasles 055.0
postvaccinal (smallpox) 323.51 ▲
rubella 056.01
specified cause NEC 323.81 ▲
syphilitic 094.81
West Nile 066.41
Encephalomyelocele 742.0
Encephalomyelomeningitis — *see* Meningoencephalitis
Encephalomyeloneuropathy 349.9
Encephalomyelopathy 349.9
  subacute necrotizing (infantile) 330.8
Encephalomyeloradiculitis (acute) 357.0
Encephalomyeloradiculoneuritis (acute) 357.0
Encephalomyeloradiculopathy 349.9
Encephalomyocarditis 074.23
Encephalopathia hyperbilirubinemica, newborn 774.7
  due to isoimmunization (conditions classifiable to 773.0–773.2) 773.4
Encephalopathy (acute) 348.30
alcoholic 291.2
anoxic — *see* Damage, brain, anoxic
arteriosclerotic 437.0
  late effect — *see* Late effect(s) (of) cerebrovascular disease
bilirubin, newborn 774.7
  due to isoimmunization 773.4
congenital 742.9
demyelinating (callosal) 341.8
due to
  birth injury (intracranial) 767.8
  dialysis 294.8
    transient 293.9
  hyperinsulinism — *see* Hyperinsulinism
  influenza (virus) 487.8
  lack of vitamin (*see also* Deficiency, vitamin) 269.2
  nicotinic acid deficiency 291.2
  serum (nontherapeutic) (therapeutic) 999.5
  syphilis 094.81
  trauma (postconcussional) 310.2
    current (*see also* Concussion, brain) 850.9
      with skull fracture — *see* Fracture, skull, by site, with intracranial injury
  vaccination 323.51 ▲
hepatic 572.2
hyperbilirubinemic, newborn 774.7
  due to isoimmunization (conditions classifiable to 773.0–773.2) 773.4
hypertensive 437.2

Encephalopathy — *continued*
hypoglycemic 251.2
hypoxic (*see* ▶*also*◀ Damage, brain, anoxic)
  ischemic (HIE) 768.7 ●
infantile cystic necrotizing (congenital) 341.8
lead 984.9 *[323.71]* ▲
leukopolio 330.0
metabolic (*see also* Delirium) 348.31
  toxic 349.82
necrotizing
  hemorrhagic 323.61 ●
  subacute 330.8 ●
other specified type NEC 348.39
pellagrous 265.2
portal-systemic 572.2
postcontusional 310.2
posttraumatic 310.2
saturnine 984.9 *[323.71]* ▲
septic 348.31
spongiform, subacute (viral) 046.1
subacute
  necrotizing 330.8
  spongioform 046.1
  viral, spongioform 046.1
subcortical progressive (Schilder) 341.1
  chronic (Binswanger's) 290.12
toxic 349.82
  metabolic 349.82 ▲
traumatic (postconcussional) 310.2
  current (*see also* Concussion, brain) 850.9
    with skull fracture — *see* Fracture, skull, by site, with intracranial injury
vitamin B deficiency NEC 266.9
Wernicke's (superior hemorrhagic polioencephalitis) 265.1
Encephalorrhagia — *see also* Hemorrhage, brain 432.9
healed or old V12.59
late effect — *see* Late effect(s) (of) cerebrovascular disease
Encephalosis, posttraumatic 310.2
Enchondroma (M9220/0) — *see also* Neoplasm, bone, benign
multiple, congenital 756.4
Enchondromatosis (cartilaginous) (congenital) (multiple) 756.4
Enchondroses, multiple (cartilaginous) (congenital) 756.4
Encopresis — *see also* Incontinence, feces 787.6
nonorganic origin 307.7
Encounter for — *see also* Admission for
administrative purpose only V68.9
  referral of patient without examination or treatment V68.81
  specified purpose NEC V68.89
chemotherapy, antineoplastic V58.11
dialysis
  extracorporeal (renal) V56.0
  peritoneal V56.8
end-of-life care V66.7
hospice care V66.7
immunotherapy, antineoplastic V58.12
palliative care V66.7
paternity testing V70.4
radiotherapy V58.0
respirator [ventilator] dependence
  during
    mechanical failure V46.14
    power failure V46.12
  for weaning V46.13
screening mammogram NEC V76.12
  for high-risk patient V76.11
terminal care V66.7
weaning from respirator [ventilator] V46.13
Encystment — *see* Cyst
Endamebiasis — *see* Amebiasis
Endamoeba — *see* Amebiasis

Endarteritis (bacterial, subacute) (infective) (septic) 447.6
brain, cerebral or cerebrospinal 437.4
  late effect — *see* Late effect(s) (of) cerebrovascular disease
coronary (artery) — *see* Arteriosclerosis, coronary
deformans — *see* Arteriosclerosis
embolic (*see also* Embolism) 444.9
obliterans (*see also* Arteriosclerosis)
  pulmonary 417.8
pulmonary 417.8
retina 362.18
senile — *see* Arteriosclerosis
syphilitic 093.89
  brain or cerebral 094.89
  congenital 090.5
  spinal 094.89
tuberculous (*see also* Tuberculosis) 017.9 ☑
Endemic — *see* condition
Endocarditis (chronic) (indeterminate) (interstitial) (marantis) (nonbacterial thrombotic) (residual) (sclerotic) (sclerous) (senile) (valvular) 424.90
with
  rheumatic fever (conditions classifiable to 390)
    active — *see* Endocarditis, acute, rheumatic
    inactive or quiescent (with chorea) 397.9
acute or subacute 421.9
  rheumatic (aortic) (mitral) (pulmonary) (tricuspid) 391.1
    with chorea (acute) (rheumatic) (Sydenham's) 392.0
aortic (heart) (nonrheumatic) (valve) 424.1
with
  mitral (valve) disease 396.9
    active or acute 391.1
      with chorea (acute) (rheumatic) (Sydenham's) 392.0
    bacterial 421.0
  rheumatic fever (conditions classifiable to 390)
    active — *see* Endocarditis, acute, rheumatic
    inactive or quiescent (with chorea) 395.9
      with mitral disease 396.9
  acute or subacute 421.9
  arteriosclerotic 424.1
  congenital 746.89
  hypertensive 424.1
  rheumatic (chronic) (inactive) 395.9
    with mitral (valve) disease 396.9
      active or acute 391.1
        with chorea (acute) (rheumatic) (Sydenham's) 392.0
    active or acute 391.1
      with chorea (acute) (rheumatic) (Sydenham's) 392.0
  specified cause, except rheumatic 424.1
  syphilitic 093.22
arteriosclerotic or due to arteriosclerosis 424.99
atypical verrucous (Libman-Sacks) 710.0 *[424.91]*
bacterial (acute) (any valve) (chronic) (subacute) 421.0
blastomycotic 116.0 *[421.1]*
candidal 112.81
congenital 425.3
constrictive 421.0
Coxsackie 074.22
due to
  blastomycosis 116.0 *[421.1]*
  candidiasis 112.81
  Coxsackie (virus) 074.22

Endocarditis — *continued*
due to — *continued*
  disseminated lupus erythematosus 710.0 *[424.91]*
  histoplasmosis (*see also* Histoplasmosis) 115.94
  hypertension (benign) 424.99
  moniliasis 112.81
  prosthetic cardiac valve 996.61
  Q fever 083.0 *[421.1]*
  serratia marcescens 421.0
  typhoid (fever) 002.0 *[421.1]*
fetal 425.3
gonococcal 098.84
hypertensive 424.99
infectious or infective (acute) (any valve) (chronic) (subacute) 421.0
lenta (acute) (any valve) (chronic) (subacute) 421.0
Libman-Sacks 710.0 *[424.91]*
Loeffler's (parietal fibroplastic) 421.0
malignant (acute) (any valve) (chronic) (subacute) 421.0
meningococcal 036.42
mitral (chronic) (double) (fibroid) (heart) (inactive) (valve) (with chorea) 394.9
with
  aortic (valve) disease 396.9
    active or acute 391.1
      with chorea (acute) (rheumatic) (Sydenham's) 392.0
    rheumatic fever (conditions classifiable to 390)
      active — *see* Endocarditis, acute, rheumatic
      inactive or quiescent (with chorea) 394.9
        with aortic valve disease 396.9
  active or acute 391.1
    with chorea (acute) (rheumatic) (Sydenham's) 392.0
  bacterial 421.0
  arteriosclerotic 424.0
  congenital 746.89
  hypertensive 424.0
  nonrheumatic 424.0
    acute or subacute 421.9
  syphilitic 093.21
monilial 112.81
mycotic (acute) (any valve) (chronic) (subacute) 421.0
pneumococcic (acute) (any valve) (chronic) (subacute) 421.0
pulmonary (chronic) (heart) (valve) 424.3
with
  rheumatic fever (conditions classifiable to 390)
    active — *see* Endocarditis, acute, rheumatic
    inactive or quiescent (with chorea) 397.1
  acute or subacute 421.9
  rheumatic 391.1
    with chorea (acute) (rheumatic) (Sydenham's) 392.0
  arteriosclerotic or due to arteriosclerosis 424.3
  congenital 746.09
  hypertensive or due to hypertension (benign) 424.3
  rheumatic (chronic) (inactive) (with chorea) 397.1
    active or acute 391.1
      with chorea (acute) (rheumatic) (Sydenham's) 392.0
  syphilitic 093.24
purulent (acute) (any valve) (chronic) (subacute) 421.0
rheumatic (chronic) (inactive) (with chorea) 397.9

Endocarditis — *continued*
  rheumatic — *continued*
    active or acute (aortic) (mitral) (pulmonary) (tricuspid) 391.1
      with chorea (acute) (rheumatic) (Sydenham's) 392.0
    septic (acute) (any valve) (chronic) (subacute) 421.0
    specified cause, except rheumatic 424.99
    streptococcal (acute) (any valve) (chronic) (subacute) 421.0
    subacute — *see* Endocarditis, acute
    suppurative (any valve) (acute) (chronic) (subacute) 421.0
    syphilitic NEC 093.20
    toxic (*see also* Endocarditis, acute) 421.9
    tricuspid (chronic) (heart) (inactive) (rheumatic) (valve) (with chorea) 397.0
    with
      rheumatic fever (conditions classifiable to 390)
        active — *see* Endocarditis, acute, rheumatic
        inactive or quiescent (with chorea) 397.0
    active or acute 391.1
      with chorea (acute) (rheumatic) (Sydenham's) 392.0
    arteriosclerotic 424.2
    congenital 746.89
    hypertensive 424.2
    nonrheumatic 424.2
      acute or subacute 421.9
    specified cause, except rheumatic 424.2
    syphilitic 093.23
    tuberculous (*see also* Tuberculosis) 017.9 ☑ *[424.91]*
    typhoid 002.0 *[421.1]*
    ulcerative (acute) (any valve) (chronic) (subacute) 421.0
    vegetative (acute) (any valve) (chronic) (subacute) 421.0
    verrucous (acute) (any valve) (chronic) (subacute) NEC 710.0 *[424.91]*
      nonbacterial 710.0 *[424.91]*
      nonrheumatic 710.0 *[424.91]*

Endocardium, endocardial — *see also* condition
  cushion defect 745.60
  specified type NEC 745.69

Endocervicitis — *see also* Cervicitis 616.0
  due to
    intrauterine (contraceptive) device 996.65
  gonorrheal (acute) 098.15
    chronic or duration of 2 months or over 098.35
  hyperplastic 616.0
  syphilitic 095.8
  trichomonal 131.09
  tuberculous (*see also* Tuberculosis) 016.7 ☑

Endocrine — *see* condition
Endocrinopathy, pluriglandular 258.9
Endodontitis 522.0
End-of-life care V66.7
Endomastoiditis — *see also* Mastoiditis 383.9
Endometrioma 617.9
Endometriosis 617.9
  appendix 617.5
  bladder 617.8
  bowel 617.5
  broad ligament 617.3
  cervix 617.0
  colon 617.5
  cul-de-sac (Douglas') 617.3
  exocervix 617.0
  fallopian tube 617.2
  female genital organ NEC 617.8
  gallbladder 617.8

Endometriosis — *continued*
  in scar of skin 617.6
  internal 617.0
  intestine 617.5
  lung 617.8
  myometrium 617.0
  ovary 617.1
  parametrium 617.3
  pelvic peritoneum 617.3
  peritoneal (pelvic) 617.3
  rectovaginal septum 617.4
  rectum 617.5
  round ligament 617.3
  skin 617.6
  specified site NEC 617.8
  stromal (M8931/1) 236.0
  umbilicus 617.8
  uterus 617.0
    internal 617.0
  vagina 617.4
  vulva 617.8

Endometritis (nonspecific) (purulent) (septic) (suppurative) 615.9
  with
    abortion — *see* Abortion, by type, with sepsis
    ectopic pregnancy (*see also* categories 633.0–633.9) 639.0
    molar pregnancy (*see also* categories 630–632) 639.0
  acute 615.0
  blennorrhagic 098.16
    acute 098.16
    chronic or duration of 2 months or over 098.36
  cervix, cervical (*see also* Cervicitis) 616.0
    hyperplastic 616.0
  chronic 615.1
  complicating pregnancy 646.6 ☑
    affecting fetus or newborn 760.8
  decidual 615.9
  following
    abortion 639.0
    ectopic or molar pregnancy 639.0
  gonorrheal (acute) 098.16
    chronic or duration of 2 months or over 098.36
  hyperplastic (*see also* Hyperplasia, endometrium) 621.30
    cervix 616.0
  polypoid — *see* Endometritis, hyperplastic
  puerperal, postpartum, childbirth 670.0 ☑
  senile (atrophic) 615.9
  subacute 615.0
  tuberculous (*see also* Tuberculosis) 016.7 ☑

Endometrium — *see* condition
Endomyocardiopathy, South African 425.2
Endomyocarditis — *see* Endocarditis
Endomyofibrosis 425.0
Endomyometritis — *see also* Endometritis 615.9
Endopericarditis — *see* Endocarditis
Endoperineuritis — *see* Disorder, nerve
Endophlebitis — *see also* Phlebitis 451.9
  leg 451.2
    deep (vessels) 451.19
    superficial (vessels) 451.0
  portal (vein) 572.1
  retina 362.18
  specified site NEC 451.89
  syphilitic 093.89
Endophthalmia — *see also* Endophthalmitis 360.00
  gonorrheal 098.42
Endophthalmitis (globe) (infective) (metastatic) (purulent) (subacute) 360.00
  acute 360.01
  bleb associated 379.63 ●
  chronic 360.03
  parasitic 360.13

Endophthalmitis — *continued*
  phacoanaphylactic 360.19
  specified type NEC 360.19
  sympathetic 360.11
Endosalpingioma (M9111/1) 236.2
Endosteitis — *see* Osteomyelitis
Endothelioma, bone (M9260/3) — *see* Neoplasm, bone, malignant
Endotheliosis 287.8
  hemorrhagic infectional 287.8
Endotoxemia — code to condition ●
Endotoxic shock 785.52
Endotrachelitis — *see also* Cervicitis 616.0
Enema rash 692.89
Engelmann's disease (diaphyseal sclerosis) 756.9
Engel-von Recklinghausen disease or syndrome (osteitis fibrosa cystica) 252.01
English disease — *see also* Rickets 268.0
Engman's disease (infectious eczematoid dermatitis) 690.8
Engorgement
  breast 611.79
    newborn 778.7
    puerperal, postpartum 676.2 ☑
  liver 573.9
  lung 514
  pulmonary 514
  retina, venous 362.37
  stomach 536.8
  venous, retina 362.37
Enlargement, enlarged — *see also* Hypertrophy
  abdomen 789.3 ☑
  adenoids 474.12
    and tonsils 474.10
  alveolar process or ridge 525.8
  apertures of diaphragm (congenital) 756.6
  blind spot, visual field 368.42
  gingival 523.8
  heart, cardiac (*see also* Hypertrophy, cardiac) 429.3
  lacrimal gland, chronic 375.03
  liver (*see also* Hypertrophy, liver) 789.1
  lymph gland or node 785.6
  orbit 376.46
  organ or site, congenital NEC — *see* Anomaly, specified type NEC
  parathyroid (gland) 252.01
  pituitary fossa 793.0
  prostate (simple) (soft) 600.00
    with
      other lower urinary tract symptoms (LUTS) ●
      600.01 ●
      urinary ●
        obstruction 600.01 ●
        retention 600.01 ●
  sella turcica 793.0
  spleen (*see also* Splenomegaly) 789.2
    congenital 759.0
  thymus (congenital) (gland) 254.0
  thyroid (gland) (*see also* Goiter) 240.9
  tongue 529.8
  tonsils 474.11
    and adenoids 474.10
  uterus 621.2
Enophthalmos 376.50
  due to
    atrophy of orbital tissue 376.51
    surgery 376.52
    trauma 376.52
Enostosis 526.89
Entamebiasis — *see* Amebiasis
Entamebic — *see* Amebiasis
Entanglement, umbilical cord(s) 663.3 ☑
  with compression 663.2 ☑
  affecting fetus or newborn 762.5
  around neck with compression 663.1 ☑

Entanglement, umbilical cord(s) — *continued*
  twins in monoamniotic sac 663.2 ☑
Enteralgia 789.0 ☑
Enteric — *see* condition
Enteritis (acute) (catarrhal) (choleraic) (chronic) (congestive) (diarrheal) (exudative) (follicular) (hemorrhagic) (infantile) (lienteric) (noninfectious) (perforative) (phlegmonous) (presumed noninfectious) (pseudomembranous) 558.9
  adaptive 564.9
  aertrycke infection 003.0
  allergic 558.3
  amebic (*see also* Amebiasis) 006.9
    with abscess — *see* Abscess, amebic
    acute 006.0
      with abscess — *see* Abscess, amebic
      nondysenteric 006.2
    chronic 006.1
      with abscess — *see* Abscess, amebic
      nondysenteric 006.2
    nondysenteric 006.2
  anaerobic (cocci) (gram-negative) (gram-positive) (mixed) NEC 008.46
  bacillary NEC 004.9
  bacterial NEC 008.5
    specified NEC 008.49
  Bacteroides (fragilis) (melaninogenicus) (oralis) 008.46
  Butyrivibrio (fibriosolvens) 008.46
  Campylobacter 008.43
  Candida 112.85
  Chilomastix 007.8
  choleriformis 001.1
  chronic 558.9
    ulcerative (*see also* Colitis, ulcerative) 556.9
  cicatrizing (chronic) 555.0
  Clostridium
    botulinum 005.1
    difficile 008.45
    haemolyticum 008.46
    novyi 008.46
    perfringens (C) (F) 008.46
    specified type NEC 008.46
  coccidial 007.2
  dietetic 558.9
  due to
    achylia gastrica 536.8
    adenovirus 008.62
    Aerobacter aerogenes 008.2
    anaerobes (*see also* Enteritis, anaerobic) 008.46
    Arizona (bacillus) 008.1
    astrovirus 008.66
    Bacillus coli — *see* Enteritis, E. coli
    bacteria NEC 008.5
      specified NEC 008.49
    Bacteroides (*see also* Enteritis, Bacteroides) 008.46
    Butyrivibrio (fibriosolvens) 008.46
    Calcivirus 008.65
    Camplyobacter 008.43
    Clostridium — *see* Enteritis, Clostridium
    Cockle agent 008.64
    Coxsackie (virus) 008.67
    Ditchling agent 008.64
    ECHO virus 008.67
    Enterobacter aerogenes 008.2
    enterococci 008.49
    enterovirus NEC 008.67
    Escherichia coli — *see* Enteritis, E. coli
    Eubacterium 008.46
    Fusobacterium (nucleatum) 008.46
    gram-negative bacteria NEC 008.47
      anaerobic NEC 008.46
    Hawaii agent 008.63
    irritating foods 558.9

Enteritis — continued
 due to — continued
  Klebsiella aerogenes 008.47
  Marin County agent 008.66
  Montgomery County agent 008.63
  Norwalk-like agent 008.63
  Norwalk virus 008.63
  Otofuke agent 008.63
  Paracolobactrum arizonae 008.1
  paracolon bacillus NEC 008.47
   Arizona 008.1
  Paramatta agent 008.64
  Peptococcus 008.46
  Peptostreptococcus 008.46
  Proprionibacterium 008.46
  Proteus (bacillus) (mirabilis) (morganii) 008.3
  Pseudomonas aeruginosa 008.42
  Rotavirus 008.61
  Sapporo agent 008.63
  small round virus (SRV) NEC 008.64
   featureless NEC 008.63
   structured NEC 008.63
  Snow Mountain (SM) agent 008.63
  specified
   bacteria NEC 008.49
   organism, nonbacterial NEC 008.8
   virus NEC 008.69
  Staphylococcus 008.41
  Streptococcus 008.49
   anaerobic 008.46
  Taunton agent 008.63
  Torovirus 008.69
  Treponema 008.46
  Veillonella 008.46
  virus 008.8
   specified type NEC 008.69
  Wollan (W) agent 008.64
  Yersinia enterocolitica 008.44
 dysentery — see Dysentery
 E. coli 008.00
  enterohemorrhagic 008.04
  enteroinvasive 008.03
  enteropathogenic 008.01
  enterotoxigenic 008.02
  specified type NEC 008.09
 el tor 001.1
 embadomonial 007.8
 epidemic 009.0
 Eubacterium 008.46
 fermentative 558.9
 fulminant 557.0
 Fusobacterium (nucleatum) 008.46
 gangrenous (see also Enteritis, due to, by organism) 009.0
 giardial 007.1
 gram-negative bacteria NEC 008.47
  anaerobic NEC 008.46
 infectious NEC (see also Enteritis, due to, by organism) 009.0
  presumed 009.1
 influenzal 487.8
 ischemic 557.9
  acute 557.0
  chronic 557.1
  due to mesenteric artery insufficiency 557.1
 membranous 564.9
 mucous 564.9
 myxomembranous 564.9
 necrotic (see also Enteritis, due to, by organism) 009.0
 necroticans 005.2
 necrotizing of fetus or newborn 777.5
 neurogenic 564.9
 newborn 777.8
  necrotizing 777.5
 parasitic NEC 129
 paratyphoid (fever) (see also Fever, paratyphoid) 002.9
 Peptococcus 008.46
 Peptostreptococcus 008.46
 Proprionibacterium 008.46
 protozoal NEC 007.9

Enteritis — continued
 radiation 558.1
 regional (of) 555.9
  intestine
   large (bowel, colon, or rectum) 555.1
    with small intestine 555.2
   small (duodenum, ileum, or jejunum) 555.0
    with large intestine 555.2
 Salmonella infection 003.0
 salmonellosis 003.0
 segmental (see also Enteritis, regional) 555.9
 septic (see also Enteritis, due to, by organism) 009.0
 Shigella 004.9
 simple 558.9
 spasmodic 564.9
 spastic 564.9
 staphylococcal 008.41
  due to food 005.0
 streptococcal 008.49
  anaerobic 008.46
 toxic 558.2
 Treponema (denticola) (macrodentium) 008.46
 trichomonal 007.3
 tuberculous (see also Tuberculosis) 014.8 ☑
 typhosa 002.0
 ulcerative (chronic) (see also Colitis, ulcerative) 556.9
 Veillonella 008.46
 viral 008.8
  adenovirus 008.62
  enterovirus 008.67
  specified virus NEC 008.69
 Yersinia enterocolitica 008.44
 zymotic 009.0
Enteroarticular syndrome 099.3
Enterobiasis 127.4
Enterobius vermicularis 127.4
Enterocele — see also Hernia 553.9
 pelvis, pelvic (acquired) (congenital) 618.6
 vagina, vaginal (acquired) (congenital) 618.6
Enterocolitis — see also Enteritis
 fetus or newborn 777.8
  necrotizing 777.5
 fulminant 557.0
 granulomatous 555.2
 hemorrhagic (acute) 557.0
  chronic 557.1
 necrotizing (acute) (membranous) 557.0
 primary necrotizing 777.5
 pseudomembranous 008.45
 radiation 558.1
  newborn 777.5
 ulcerative 556.0
Enterocystoma 751.5
Enterogastritis — see Enteritis
Enterogenous cyanosis 289.7
Enterolith, enterolithiasis (impaction) 560.39
 with hernia (see also Hernia, by site, with obstruction)
  gangrenous — see Hernia, by site, with gangrene
Enteropathy 569.9
 exudative (of Gordon) 579.8
 gluten 579.0
 hemorrhagic, terminal 557.0
 protein-losing 579.8
Enteroperitonitis — see also Peritonitis 567.9
Enteroptosis 569.89
Enterorrhagia 578.9
Enterospasm 564.9
 psychogenic 306.4
Enterostenosis — see also Obstruction, intestine 560.9
Enterostomy status V44.4
 with complication 569.60

Enthesopathy 726.90
 ankle and tarsus 726.70
 elbow region 726.30
  specified NEC 726.39
 hip 726.5
 knee 726.60
 peripheral NEC 726.8
 shoulder region 726.10
  adhesive 726.0
 spinal 720.1
 wrist and carpus 726.4
Entrance, air into vein — see Embolism, air
Entrapment, nerve — see Neuropathy, entrapment
Entropion (eyelid) 374.00
 cicatricial 374.04
 congenital 743.62
 late effect of trachoma (healed) 139.1
 mechanical 374.02
 paralytic 374.02
 senile 374.01
 spastic 374.03
Enucleation of eye (current) (traumatic) 871.3
Enuresis 788.30
 habit disturbance 307.6
 nocturnal 788.36
  psychogenic 307.6
 nonorganic origin 307.6
 psychogenic 307.6
Enzymopathy 277.9
Eosinopenia 288.59 ▲
Eosinophilia 288.3
 allergic 288.3
 hereditary 288.3
 idiopathic 288.3
 infiltrative 518.3
 Loeffler's 518.3
 myalgia syndrome 710.5
 pulmonary (tropical) 518.3
 secondary 288.3
 tropical 518.3
Eosinophilic — see also condition
 fasciitis 728.89
 granuloma (bone) 277.89
 infiltration lung 518.3
Ependymitis (acute) (cerebral) (chronic) (granular) — see also Meningitis 322.9
Ependymoblastoma (M9392/3)
 specified site — see Neoplasm, by site, malignant
 unspecified site 191.9
Ependymoma (epithelial) (malignant) (M9391/3)
 anaplastic type (M9392/3)
  specified site — see Neoplasm, by site, malignant
  unspecified site 191.9
 benign (M9391/0)
  specified site — see Neoplasm, by site, benign
  unspecified site 225.0
 myxopapillary (M9394/1) 237.5
 papillary (M9393/1) 237.5
 specified site — see Neoplasm, by site, malignant
 unspecified site 191.9
Ependymopathy 349.2
 spinal cord 349.2
Ephelides, ephelis 709.09
Ephemeral fever — see also Pyrexia 780.6
Epiblepharon (congenital) 743.62
Epicanthus, epicanthic fold (congenital) (eyelid) 743.63
Epicondylitis (elbow) (lateral) 726.32
 medial 726.31
Epicystitis — see also Cystitis 595.9
Epidemic — see condition
Epidermidalization, cervix — see condition
Epidermidization, cervix — see condition
Epidermis, epidermal — see condition

Epidermization, cervix — see condition
Epidermodysplasia verruciformis 078.19
Epidermoid
 cholesteatoma — see Cholesteatoma
 inclusion (see also Cyst, skin) 706.2
Epidermolysis
 acuta (combustiformis) (toxica) 695.1
 bullosa 757.39
 necroticans combustiformis 695.1
  due to drug
   correct substance properly administered 695.1
   overdose or wrong substance given or taken 977.9
   specified drug — see Table of Drugs and Chemicals
Epidermophytid — see Dermatophytosis
Epidermophytosis (infected) — see Dermatophytosis
Epidermosis, ear (middle) — see also Cholesteatoma 385.30
Epididymis — see condition
Epididymitis (nonvenereal) 604.90
 with abscess 604.0
 acute 604.99
 blennorrhagic (acute) 098.0
  chronic or duration of 2 months or over 098.2
 caseous (see also Tuberculosis) 016.4 ☑
 chlamydial 099.54
 diphtheritic 032.89 [604.91]
 filarial 125.9 [604.91]
 gonococcal (acute) 098.0
  chronic or duration of 2 months or over 098.2
 recurrent 604.99
 residual 604.99
 syphilitic 095.8 [604.91]
 tuberculous (see also Tuberculosis) 016.4 ☑
Epididymo-orchitis — see also Epididymitis 604.90
 with abscess 604.0
 chlamydial 099.54
 gonococcal (acute) 098.13
  chronic or duration of 2 months or over 098.33
Epidural — see condition
Epigastritis — see also Gastritis 535.5 ☑
Epigastrium, epigastric — see condition
Epigastrocele — see also Hernia, epigastric 553.29
Epiglottiditis (acute) 464.30
 with obstruction 464.31
 chronic 476.1
 viral 464.30
  with obstruction 464.31
Epiglottis — see condition
Epiglottitis (acute) 464.30
 with obstruction 464.31
 chronic 476.1
 viral 464.30
  with obstruction 464.31
Epignathus 759.4
Epilepsia
 partialis continua (see also Epilepsy) 345.7 ☑
 procursiva (see also Epilepsy) 345.8 ☑
Epilepsy, epileptic (idiopathic) 345.9 ☑

Note — use the following fifth-digit subclassification with categories 345.0, 345.1, 345.4–345.9:

0 without mention of intractable epilepsy

1 with intractable epilepsy

 abdominal 345.5 ☑
 absence (attack) 345.0 ☑
 akinetic 345.0 ☑
  psychomotor 345.4 ☑
 automatism 345.4 ☑
 autonomic diencephalic 345.5 ☑

☑ Additional Digit Required — Refer to the Tabular List for Digit Selection

110 — Volume 2 • October 2006   ▶◀ Revised Text   ● New Line   ▲ Revised Code   🐾 Subterms under main terms may continue to next column or page

2007 ICD-9-CM

Epilepsy, epileptic — *continued*
brain 345.9 ☑
Bravais-Jacksonian 345.5 ☑
cerebral 345.9 ☑
climacteric 345.9 ☑
clonic 345.1 ☑
clouded state 345.9 ☑
coma 345.3
communicating 345.4 ☑
complicating pregnancy, childbirth, ●
or the puerperium 649.4 ☑ ●
congenital 345.9 ☑
convulsions 345.9 ☑
cortical (focal) (motor) 345.5 ☑
cursive (running) 345.8 ☑
cysticercosis 123.1
deterioration
with behavioral disturbance
345.9 ☑ *[294.11]*
without behavioral disturbance
345.9 ☑ *[294.10]*
due to syphilis 094.89
equivalent 345.5 ☑
fit 345.9 ☑
focal (motor) 345.5 ☑
gelastic 345.8 ☑
generalized 345.9 ☑
convulsive 345.1 ☑
flexion 345.1 ☑
nonconvulsive 345.0 ☑
grand mal (idiopathic) 345.1 ☑
Jacksonian (motor) (sensory) 345.5 ☑
Kojevnikoff's, Kojevnikov's, Kojewnikoff's 345.7 ☑
laryngeal 786.2
limbic system 345.4 ☑
localization related (focal) (partial) ●
and epileptic syndromes ●
with ●
complex partial seizures ●
345.4 ☑ ●
simple partial seizures ●
345.5 ☑ ●
major (motor) 345.1 ☑
minor 345.0 ☑
mixed (type) 345.9 ☑
motor partial 345.5 ☑
musicogenic 345.1 ☑
myoclonus, myoclonic 345.1 ☑
progressive (familial) 333.2
nonconvulsive, generalized 345.0 ☑
parasitic NEC 123.9
partial (focalized) 345.5 ☑
with
impairment of consciousness
345.4 ☑
memory and ideational disturbances 345.4 ☑
without impairment of conscious- ●
ness 345.5 ☑ ●
abdominal type 345.5 ☑
motor type 345.5 ☑
psychomotor type 345.4 ☑
psychosensory type 345.4 ☑
secondarily generalized 345.4 ☑
sensory type 345.5 ☑
somatomotor type 345.5 ☑
somatosensory type 345.5 ☑
temporal lobe type 345.4 ☑
visceral type 345.5 ☑
visual type 345.5 ☑
peripheral 345.9 ☑
petit mal 345.0 ☑
photokinetic 345.8 ☑
progressive myoclonic (familial) 333.2
psychic equivalent 345.5 ☑
psychomotor 345.4 ☑
psychosensory 345.4 ☑
reflex 345.1 ☑
seizure 345.9 ☑
senile 345.9 ☑
sensory-induced 345.5 ☑
sleep (*see also* Narcolepsy) 347.00
somatomotor type 345.5 ☑

Epilepsy, epileptic — *continued*
somatosensory 345.5 ☑
specified type NEC 345.8 ☑
status (grand mal) 345.3
focal motor 345.7 ☑
petit mal 345.2
psychomotor 345.7 ☑
temporal lobe 345.7 ☑
symptomatic 345.9 ☑
temporal lobe 345.4 ☑
tonic (-clonic) 345.1 ☑
traumatic (injury unspecified) 907.0
injury specified — *see* Late, effect
(of) specified injury
twilight 293.0
uncinate (gyrus) 345.4 ☑
Unverricht (-Lundborg) (familial myoclonic) 333.2
visceral 345.5 ☑
visual 345.5 ☑
Epileptiform
convulsions 780.39
seizure 780.39
Epiloia 759.5
Epimenorrhea 626.2
Epipharyngitis — *see also* Nasopharyngitis 460
Epiphora 375.20
due to
excess lacrimation 375.21
insufficient drainage 375.22
Epiphyseal arrest 733.91
femoral head 732.2
Epiphyseolysis, epiphysiolysis — *see*
also Osteochondrosis 732.9
Epiphysitis — *see also* Osteochondrosis
732.9
juvenile 732.6
marginal (Scheuermann's) 732.0
os calcis 732.5
syphilitic (congenital) 090.0
vertebral (Scheuermann's) 732.0
Epiplocele — *see also* Hernia 553.9
Epiploitis — *see also* Peritonitis 567.9
Epiplosarcomphalocele — *see also*
Hernia, umbilicus 553.1
Episcleritis 379.00
gouty 274.89 *[379.09]*
nodular 379.02
periodica fugax 379.01
angioneurotic — *see* Edema, angioneurotic
specified NEC 379.09
staphylococcal 379.00
suppurative 379.00
syphilitic 095.0
tuberculous (*see also* Tuberculosis)
017.3 ☑ *[379.09]*
Episode
brain (*see also* Disease, cerebrovascular, acute) 436
cerebral (*see also* Disease, cerebrovascular, acute) 436
depersonalization (in neurotic state)
300.6
hyporesponsive 780.09
psychotic (*see also* Psychosis) 298.9
organic, transient 293.9
schizophrenic (acute) NEC (*see also*
Schizophrenia) 295.4 ☑
Epispadias
female 753.8
male 752.62
Episplenitis 289.59
Epistaxis (multiple) 784.7
hereditary 448.0
vicarious menstruation 625.8
Epithelioma (malignant) (M8011/3) —
see also Neoplasm, by site, malignant
adenoides cysticum (M8100/0) — *see*
Neoplasm, skin, benign
basal cell (M8090/3) — *see* Neoplasm,
skin, malignant
benign (M8011/0) — *see* Neoplasm,
by site, benign

Epithelioma — *see also* Neoplasm, by
site, malignant — *continued*
Bowen's (M8081/2) — *see* Neoplasm,
skin, in situ
calcifying (benign) (Malherbe's)
(M8110/0) — *see* Neoplasm,
skin, benign
external site — *see* Neoplasm, skin,
malignant
intraepidermal, Jadassohn (M8096/0)
— *see* Neoplasm, skin, benign
squamous cell (M8070/3) — *see* Neoplasm, by site, malignant
Epitheliopathy
pigment, retina 363.15
posterior multifocal placoid (acute)
363.15
Epithelium, epithelial — *see* condition
Epituberculosis (allergic) (with atelectasis) — *see also* Tuberculosis
010.8 ☑
Eponychia 757.5
Epstein's
nephrosis or syndrome (*see also*
Nephrosis) 581.9
pearl (mouth) 528.4
Epstein-Barr infection (viral) 075
chronic 780.79 *[139.8]*
Epulis (giant cell) (gingiva) 523.8
Equinia 024
Equinovarus (congenital) 754.51
acquired 736.71
Equivalent
convulsive (abdominal) (*see also*
Epilepsy) 345.5 ☑
epileptic (psychic) (*see also* Epilepsy)
345.5 ☑
Erb's
disease 359.1
palsy, paralysis (birth) (brachial)
(newborn) 767.6
spinal (spastic) syphilitic 094.89
pseudohypertrophic muscular dystrophy 359.1
Erb-Goldflam disease or syndrome
358.00
Erb (-Duchenne) paralysis (birth injury)
(newborn) 767.6
Erdheim's syndrome (acromegalic
macrospondylitis) 253.0
Erection, painful (persistent) 607.3
Ergosterol deficiency (vitamin D) 268.9
with
osteomalacia 268.2
rickets (*see also* Rickets) 268.0
Ergotism (ergotized grain) 988.2
from ergot used as drug (migraine
therapy)
correct substance properly administered 349.82
overdose or wrong substance given
or taken 975.0
Erichsen's disease (railway spine)
300.16
Erlacher-Blount syndrome (tibia vara)
732.4
Erosio interdigitalis blastomycetica
112.3
Erosion
arteriosclerotic plaque — *see* Arteriosclerosis, by site
artery NEC 447.2
without rupture 447.8
bone 733.99
bronchus 519.19 ▲
cartilage (joint) 733.99
cervix (uteri) (acquired) (chronic)
(congenital) 622.0
with mention of cervicitis 616.0
cornea (recurrent) (*see also* Keratitis)
371.42
traumatic 918.1
dental (idiopathic) (occupational)
521.30
extending into
dentine 521.32

Erosion — *continued*
dental — *continued*
extending into — *continued*
pulp 521.33
generalized 521.35
limited to enamel 521.31
localized 521.34
duodenum, postpyloric — *see* Ulcer,
duodenum
esophagus 530.89
gastric 535.4 ☑
intestine 569.89
lymphatic vessel 457.8
pylorus, pyloric (ulcer) 535.4 ☑
sclera 379.16
spine, aneurysmal 094.89
spleen 289.59
stomach 535.4 ☑
teeth (idiopathic) (occupational) (*see*
also Erosion, dental) 521.30
due to
medicine 521.30
persistent vomiting 521.30
urethra 599.84
uterus 621.8
vertebra 733.99
Erotomania 302.89
Clérambault's 297.8
Error
in diet 269.9
refractive 367.9
astigmatism (*see also* Astigmatism)
367.20
drug-induced 367.89
hypermetropia 367.0
hyperopia 367.0
myopia 367.1
presbyopia 367.4
toxic 367.89
Eructation 787.3
nervous 306.4
psychogenic 306.4
Eruption
creeping 126.9
drug — *see* Dermatitis, due to, drug
Hutchinson, summer 692.72
Kaposi's varicelliform 054.0
napkin (psoriasiform) 691.0
polymorphous
light (sun) 692.72
other source 692.82
psoriasiform, napkin 691.0
recalcitrant pustular 694.8
ringed 695.89
skin (*see also* Dermatitis) 782.1
creeping (meaning hookworm)
126.9
due to
chemical(s) NEC 692.4
internal use 693.8
drug — *see* Dermatitis, due to,
drug
prophylactic inoculation or vaccination against disease
— *see* Dermatitis, due to,
vaccine
smallpox vaccination NEC —
see Dermatitis, due to,
vaccine
erysipeloid 027.1
feigned 698.4
Hutchinson, summer 692.72
Kaposi's, varicelliform 054.0
vaccinia 999.0
lichenoid, axilla 698.3
polymorphous, due to light 692.72
toxic NEC 695.0
vesicular 709.8
teeth, tooth
accelerated 520.6
delayed 520.6
difficult 520.6
disturbance of 520.6
in abnormal sequence 520.6
incomplete 520.6
late 520.6

Eruption — continued
teeth, tooth — continued
natal 520.6
neonatal 520.6
obstructed 520.6
partial 520.6
persistent primary 520.6
premature 520.6
prenatal 520.6 ●
vesicular 709.8
Erysipelas (gangrenous) (infantile) (newborn) (phlegmonous) (suppurative) 035
external ear 035 [380.13]
puerperal, postpartum, childbirth 670.0 ☑
Erysipelatoid (Rosenbach's) 027.1
Erysipeloid (Rosenbach's) 027.1
Erythema, erythematous (generalized) 695.9
ab igne — see Burn, by site, first degree
annulare (centrifugum) (rheumaticum) 695.0
arthriticum epidemicum 026.1
brucellum (see also Brucellosis) 023.9
bullosum 695.1
caloricum — see Burn, by site, first degree
chronicum migrans 088.81
circinatum 695.1
diaper 691.0
due to
chemical (contact) NEC 692.4
internal 693.8
drug (internal use) 693.0
contact 692.3
elevatum diutinum 695.89
endemic 265.2
epidemic, arthritic 026.1
figuratum perstans 695.0
gluteal 691.0
gyratum (perstans) (repens) 695.1
heat — see Burn, by site, first degree
ichthyosiforme congenitum 757.1
induratum (primary) (scrofulosorum) (see also Tuberculosis) 017.1 ☑
nontuberculous 695.2
infantum febrile 057.8
infectional NEC 695.9
infectiosum 057.0
inflammation NEC 695.9
intertrigo 695.89
iris 695.1
lupus (discoid) (localized) (see also Lupus, erythematosus) 695.4
marginatum 695.0
rheumaticum — see Fever, rheumatic
medicamentosum — see Dermatitis, due to, drug
migrans 529.1
chronicum 088.81
multiforme 695.1
bullosum 695.1
conjunctiva 695.1
exudativum (Hebra) 695.1
pemphigoides 694.5
napkin 691.0
neonatorum 778.8
nodosum 695.2
tuberculous (see also Tuberculosis) 017.1 ☑
nummular, nummulare 695.1
palmar 695.0
palmaris hereditarium 695.0
pernio 991.5
perstans solare 692.72
rash, newborn 778.8
scarlatiniform (exfoliative) (recurrent) 695.0
simplex marginatum 057.8
solare (see also Sunburn) 692.71
streptogenes 696.5
toxic, toxicum NEC 695.0
newborn 778.8

Erythema, erythematous — continued
tuberculous (primary) (see also Tuberculosis) 017.0 ☑
venenatum 695.0
Erythematosus — see condition
Erythematous — see condition
Erythermalgia (primary) 443.82
Erythralgia 443.82
Erythrasma 039.0
Erythredema 985.0
polyneuritica 985.0
polyneuropathy 985.0
Erythremia (acute) (M9841/3) 207.0 ☑
chronic (M9842/3) 207.1 ☑
secondary 289.0
Erythroblastopenia (acquired) 284.8
congenital 284.01 ▲
Erythroblastophthisis 284.01 ▲
Erythroblastosis (fetalis) (newborn) 773.2
due to
ABO
antibodies 773.1
incompatibility, maternal/fetal 773.1
isoimmunization 773.1
Rh
antibodies 773.0
incompatibility, maternal/fetal 773.0
isoimmunization 773.0
Erythrocyanosis (crurum) 443.89
Erythrocythemia — see Erythremia
Erythrocytopenia 285.9
Erythrocytosis (megalosplenic) familial 289.6
oval, hereditary (see also Elliptocytosis) 282.1
secondary 289.0
stress 289.0
Erythroderma — see also Erythema 695.9
desquamativa (in infants) 695.89
exfoliative 695.89
ichthyosiform, congenital 757.1
infantum 695.89
maculopapular 696.2
neonatorum 778.8
psoriaticum 696.1
secondary 695.9
Erythrogenesis imperfecta 284.09 ▲
Erythroleukemia (M9840/3) 207.0 ☑
Erythromelalgia 443.82
Erythromelia 701.8
Erythropenia 285.9
Erythrophagocytosis 289.9
Erythrophobia 300.23
Erythroplakia
oral mucosa 528.79
tongue 528.79
Erythroplasia (Queyrat) (M8080/2)
specified site — see Neoplasm, skin, in situ
unspecified site 233.5
Erythropoiesis, idiopathic ineffective 285.0
Escaped beats, heart 427.60
postoperative 997.1
Esoenteritis — see Enteritis
Esophagalgia 530.89
Esophagectasis 530.89
due to cardiospasm 530.0
Esophagismus 530.5
Esophagitis (alkaline) (chemical) (chronic) (infectional) (necrotic) (peptic) (postoperative) (regurgitant) 530.10
acute 530.12
candidal 112.84
reflux 530.11
specified NEC 530.19
tuberculous (see also Tuberculosis) 017.8 ☑
ulcerative 530.19
Esophagocele 530.6
Esophagodynia 530.89

Esophagomalacia 530.89
Esophagoptosis 530.89
Esophagospasm 530.5
Esophagostenosis 530.3
Esophagostomiasis 127.7
Esophagostomy
complication 530.87
infection 530.86
malfunctioning 530.87
mechanical 530.87
Esophagotracheal — see condition
Esophagus — see condition
Esophoria 378.41
convergence, excess 378.84
divergence, insufficiency 378.85
Esotropia (nonaccommodative) 378.00
accommodative 378.35
alternating 378.05
with
A pattern 378.06
specified noncomitancy NEC 378.08
V pattern 378.07
X pattern 378.08
Y pattern 378.08
intermittent 378.22
intermittent 378.20
alternating 378.22
monocular 378.21
monocular 378.01
with
A pattern 378.02
specified noncomitancy NEC 378.04
V pattern 378.03
X pattern 378.04
Y pattern 378.04
intermittent 378.21
Espundia 085.5
Essential — see condition
Esterapenia 289.89
Esthesioneuroblastoma (M9522/3) 160.0
Esthesioneurocytoma (M9521/3) 160.0
Esthesioneuroepithelioma (M9523/3) 160.0
Esthiomene 099.1
Estivo-autumnal
fever 084.0
malaria 084.0
Estrangement V61.0
Estriasis 134.0
Ethanolaminuria 270.8
Ethanolism — see also Alcoholism 303.9 ☑
Ether dependence, dependency — see also Dependence 304.6 ☑
Etherism — see also Dependence 304.6 ☑
Ethmoid, ethmoidal — see condition
Ethmoiditis (chronic) (nonpurulent) (purulent) — see also Sinusitis, ethmoidal 473.2
influenzal 487.1
Woakes' 471.1
Ethylism — see also Alcoholism 303.9 ☑
Eulenburg's disease (congenital paramyotonia) 359.2
Eunuchism 257.2
Eunuchoidism 257.2
hypogonadotropic 257.2
European blastomycosis 117.5
Eustachian — see condition
Euthyroidism 244.9
Euthyroid sick syndrome 790.94
Evaluation
fetal lung maturity 659.8 ☑
for suspected condition (see also Observation) V71.9
abuse V71.81
exposure
anthrax V71.82
biologic agent NEC V71.83
SARS V71.83
neglect V71.81

Evaluation — continued
for suspected condition (see also Observation) — continued
newborn — see Observation, suspected, condition, newborn
specified condition NEC V71.89
mental health V70.2
requested by authority V70.1
nursing care V63.8
social service V63.8
Evans' syndrome (thrombocytopenic purpura) 287.32
Eventration
colon into chest — see Hernia, diaphragm
diaphragm (congenital) 756.6
Eversion
bladder 596.8
cervix (uteri) 622.0
with mention of cervicitis 616.0
foot NEC 736.79
congenital 755.67
lacrimal punctum 375.51
punctum lacrimale (postinfectional) (senile) 375.51
ureter (meatus) 593.89
urethra (meatus) 599.84
uterus 618.1
complicating delivery 665.2 ☑
affecting fetus or newborn 763.89
puerperal, postpartum 674.8 ☑
Evidence
of malignancy
cytologic
without histologic confirmation 795.06 ▲
Evisceration
birth injury 767.8
bowel (congenital) — see Hernia, ventral
congenital (see also Hernia, ventral) 553.29
operative wound 998.32
traumatic NEC 869.1
eye 871.3
Evulsion — see Avulsion
Ewing's
angioendothelioma (M9260/3) — see Neoplasm, bone, malignant
sarcoma (M9260/3) — see Neoplasm, bone, malignant
tumor (M9260/3) — see Neoplasm, bone, malignant
Exaggerated lumbosacral angle (with impinging spine) 756.12
Examination (general) (routine) (of) (for) V70.9
allergy V72.7
annual V70.0
cardiovascular preoperative V72.81
cervical Papanicolaou smear V76.2
as a part of routine gynecological examination V72.31
to confirm findings of recent normal smear following initial abnormal smear V72.32
child care (routine) V20.2
clinical research investigation (normal control patient) (participant) V70.7
dental V72.2
developmental testing (child) (infant) V20.2
donor (potential) V70.8
ear V72.19 ▲
eye V72.0
following
accident (motor vehicle) V71.4
alleged rape or seduction (victim or culprit) V71.5
inflicted injury (victim or culprit) NEC V71.6
rape or seduction, alleged (victim or culprit) V71.5
treatment (for) V67.9

☑ Additional Digit Required — Refer to the Tabular List for Digit Selection

112 — Volume 2 · October 2006

▶◀ Revised Text

● New Line

▲ Revised Code

🦉 Subterms under main terms may continue to next column or page

2007 ICD-9-CM

Examination — *continued*
  following — *continued*
    treatment — *continued*
      combined V67.6
      fracture V67.4
      involving high-risk medication
        NEC V67.51
      mental disorder V67.3
      specified condition NEC V67.59
  follow-up (routine) (following) V67.9
    cancer chemotherapy V67.2
    chemotherapy V67.2
    disease NEC V67.59
    high-risk medication NEC V67.51
    injury NEC V67.59
    population survey V70.6
    postpartum V24.2
    psychiatric V67.3
    psychotherapy V67.3
    radiotherapy V67.1
    specified surgery NEC V67.09
    surgery V67.00
      vaginal pap smear V67.01
  gynecological V72.31
    for contraceptive maintenance
      V25.40
      intrauterine device V25.42
      pill V25.41
      specified method NEC V25.49
  health (of)
    armed forces personnel V70.5
    checkup V70.0
    child, routine V20.2
    defined subpopulation NEC V70.5
    inhabitants of institutions V70.5
    occupational V70.5
    pre-employment screening V70.5
    preschool children V70.5
      for admission to school V70.3
    prisoners V70.5
      for entrance into prison V70.3
    prostitutes V70.5
    refugees V70.5
    school children V70.5
    students V70.5
  hearing V72.19 ▲
    following failed hearing screening ●
      V72.11
  infant V20.2
  laboratory V72.6
  lactating mother V24.1
  medical (for) (of) V70.9
    administrative purpose NEC V70.3
    admission to
      old age home V70.3
      prison V70.3
      school V70.3
    adoption V70.3
    armed forces personnel V70.5
    at health care facility V70.0
    camp V70.3
    child, routine V20.2
    clinical research (control) (normal
      comparison) (participant)
      V70.7
    defined subpopulation NEC V70.5
    donor (potential) V70.8
    driving license V70.3
    general V70.9
      routine V70.0
      specified reason NEC V70.8
    immigration V70.3
    inhabitants of institutions V70.5
    insurance certification V70.3
    marriage V70.3
    medicolegal reasons V70.4
    naturalization V70.3
    occupational V70.5
    population survey V70.6
    pre-employment V70.5
    preschool children V70.5
      for admission to school V70.3
    prison V70.3
    prisoners V70.5
      for entrance into prison V70.3
    prostitutes V70.5

Examination — *continued*
  medical — *continued*
    refugees V70.5
    school children V70.5
    specified reason NEC V70.8
    sport competition V70.3
    students V70.5
  medicolegal reason V70.4
  pelvic (annual) (periodic) V72.31
  periodic (annual) (routine) V70.0
  postpartum
    immediately after delivery V24.0
    routine follow-up V24.2
  pregnancy (unconfirmed) (possible)
    V72.40
    negative result V72.41
    positive result V72.42
  prenatal V22.1
    first pregnancy V22.0
    high-risk pregnancy V23.9
      specified problem NEC V23.89
  preoperative V72.84
    cardiovascular V72.81
    respiratory V72.82
    specified NEC V72.83
  preprocedural V72.84
    cardiovascular V72.81
    general physical V72.83
    respiratory V72.82
    specified NEC V72.83
  psychiatric V70.2
    follow-up not needing further care
      V67.3
    requested by authority V70.1
  radiological NEC V72.5
  respiratory preoperative V72.82
  screening — *see* Screening
  sensitization V72.7
  skin V72.7
    hypersensitivity V72.7
  special V72.9
  specified type or reason NEC V72.85
    preoperative V72.83
      specified NEC V72.83
  teeth V72.2
  vaginal Papanicolaou smear V76.47
    following hysterectomy for malig-
      nant condition V67.01
  victim or culprit following
    alleged rape or seduction V71.5
    inflicted injury NEC V71.6
  vision V72.0
  well baby V20.2

Exanthem, exanthema — *see also* Rash
  782.1
  Boston 048
  epidemic, with meningitis 048
  lichenoid psoriasiform 696.2
  subitum 057.8
  viral, virus NEC 057.9
    specified type NEC 057.8

Excess, excessive, excessively
  alcohol level in blood 790.3
  carbohydrate tissue, localized 278.1
  carotene (dietary) 278.3
  cold 991.9
    specified effect NEC 991.8
  convergence 378.84
  crying 780.95
    of
      adolescent 780.95 ●
      adult 780.95 ●
      baby 780.92 ●
      child 780.95 ●
      infant (baby) 780.92 ●
      newborn 780.92 ●
  development, breast 611.1
  diaphoresis (*see also* Hyperhidrosis)
    780.8
  distance, interarch 524.28
  divergence 378.85
  drinking (alcohol) NEC (*see also*
    Abuse, drugs, nondependent)
    305.0 ☑
    continual (*see also* Alcoholism)
      303.9 ☑

Excess, excessive, excessively —
  continued
  drinking (*see also* Abuse, drugs, non-
    dependent) — *continued*
    habitual (*see also* Alcoholism)
      303.9 ☑
  eating 783.6
  eyelid fold (congenital) 743.62
  fat 278.02
    in heart (*see also* Degeneration,
      myocardial) 429.1
    tissue, localized 278.1
  foreskin 605
  gas 787.3
  gastrin 251.5
  glucagon 251.4
  heat (*see also* Heat) 992.9
  horizontal
    overjet 524.26 ●
    overlap 524.26 ●
  interarch distance 524.28
  intermaxillary vertical dimension ●
    524.37
  interocclusal distance of teeth 524.37 ●
  large
    colon 564.7
      congenital 751.3
    fetus or infant 766.0
      with obstructed labor 660.1 ☑
        affecting management of preg-
          nancy 656.6 ☑
      causing disproportion 653.5 ☑
    newborn (weight of 4500 grams or
      more) 766.0
    organ or site, congenital NEC —
      see Anomaly, specified type
      NEC
  lid fold (congenital) 743.62
  long
    colon 751.5
    organ or site, congenital NEC —
      see Anomaly, specified type
      NEC
    umbilical cord (entangled)
      affecting fetus or newborn 762.5
      in pregnancy or childbirth
        663.3 ☑
        with compression 663.2 ☑
  menstruation 626.2
  number of teeth 520.1
    causing crowding 524.31
  nutrients (dietary) NEC 783.6
  potassium (K) 276.7
  salivation (*see also* Ptyalism) 527.7
  secretion (*see also* Hypersecretion)
    milk 676.6 ☑
    sputum 786.4
    sweat (*see also* Hyperhidrosis)
      780.8
  short
    organ or site, congenital NEC —
      see Anomaly, specified type
      NEC
    umbilical cord
      affecting fetus or newborn 762.6
      in pregnancy or childbirth
        663.4 ☑
  skin NEC 701.9
    eyelid 743.62
      acquired 374.30
  sodium (Na) 276.0
  spacing of teeth 524.32
  sputum 786.4
  sweating (*see also* Hyperhidrosis)
    780.8
  tearing (ducts) (eye) (*see also* Epipho-
    ra) 375.20
  thirst 783.5
    due to deprivation of water 994.3
  tuberosity 524.07
  vitamin
    A (dietary) 278.2
      administered as drug (chronic)
        (prolonged excessive in-
        take) 278.2

Excess, excessive, excessively —
  continued
  vitamin — *continued*
    A — *continued*
      administered as drug — *contin-
        ued*
        reaction to sudden overdose
          963.5
    D (dietary) 278.4
      administered as drug (chronic)
        (prolonged excessive in-
        take) 278.4
        reaction to sudden overdose
          963.5
  weight 278.02
    gain 783.1
      of pregnancy 646.1 ☑
    loss 783.21

Excitability, abnormal, under minor ●
  stress 309.29
Excitation
  catatonic (*see also* Schizophrenia)
    295.2 ☑
  psychogenic 298.1
  reactive (from emotional stress, psy-
    chological trauma) 298.1
Excitement
  manic (*see also* Psychosis, affective)
    296.0 ☑
    recurrent episode 296.1 ☑
    single episode 296.0 ☑
  mental, reactive (from emotional
    stress, psychological trauma)
    298.1
  state, reactive (from emotional stress,
    psychological trauma) 298.1
Excluded pupils 364.76
Excoriation (traumatic) — *see also* Injury, superficial, by site 919.8
  neurotic 698.4
Excyclophoria 378.44
Excyclotropia 378.33
Exencephalus, exencephaly 742.0
Exercise
  breathing V57.0
  remedial NEC V57.1
  therapeutic NEC V57.1
Exfoliation, teeth due to systemic
  causes 525.0
Exfoliative — *see also* condition
  dermatitis 695.89
Exhaustion, exhaustive (physical NEC)
  780.79
  battle (*see also* Reaction, stress,
    acute) 308.9
  cardiac (*see also* Failure, heart) 428.9
  delirium (*see also* Reaction, stress,
    acute) 308.9
  due to
    cold 991.8
    excessive exertion 994.5
    exposure 994.4
  fetus or newborn 779.89
  heart (*see also* Failure, heart) 428.9
  heat 992.5
    due to
      salt depletion 992.4
      water depletion 992.3
  manic (*see also* Psychosis, affective)
    296.0 ☑
    recurrent episode 296.1 ☑
    single episode 296.0 ☑
  maternal, complicating delivery
    669.8 ☑
    affecting fetus or newborn 763.89
  mental 300.5
  myocardium, myocardial (*see also*
    Failure, heart) 428.9
  nervous 300.5
  old age 797
  postinfectional NEC 780.79
  psychogenic 300.5
  psychosis (*see also* Reaction, stress,
    acute) 308.9
  senile 797
    dementia 290.0

Exhibitionism (sexual) 302.4
Exomphalos 756.79
Exophoria 378.42
  convergence, insufficiency 378.83
  divergence, excess 378.85
Exophthalmic
  cachexia 242.0 ☑
  goiter 242.0 ☑
  ophthalmoplegia 242.0 ☑ [376.22]
Exophthalmos 376.30
  congenital 743.66
  constant 376.31
  endocrine NEC 259.9 [376.22]
  hyperthyroidism 242.0 ☑ [376.21]
  intermittent NEC 376.34
  malignant 242.0 ☑ [376.21]
  pulsating 376.35
    endocrine NEC 259.9 [376.22]
  thyrotoxic 242.0 ☑ [376.21]
Exostosis 726.91
  cartilaginous (M9210/0) — see Neoplasm, bone, benign
  congenital 756.4
  ear canal, external 380.81
  gonococcal 098.89
  hip 726.5
  intracranial 733.3
  jaw (bone) 526.81
  luxurians 728.11
  multiple (cancellous) (congenital) (hereditary) 756.4
  nasal bones 726.91
  orbit, orbital 376.42
  osteocartilaginous (M9210/0) — see Neoplasm, bone, benign
  spine 721.8
    with spondylosis — see Spondylosis
  syphilitic 095.5
  wrist 726.4
Exotropia 378.10
  alternating 378.15
    with
      A pattern 378.16
      specified noncomitancy NEC 378.18
      V pattern 378.17
      X pattern 378.18
      Y pattern 378.18
    intermittent 378.24
  intermittent 378.20
    alternating 378.24
    monocular 378.23
  monocular 378.11
    with
      A pattern 378.12
      specified noncomitancy NEC 378.14
      V pattern 378.13
      X pattern 378.14
      Y pattern 378.14
    intermittent 378.23
Explanation of
  investigation finding V65.4 ☑
  medication V65.4 ☑
Exposure 994.9
  cold 991.9
    specified effect NEC 991.8
  effects of 994.9
  exhaustion due to 994.4
  to
    AIDS virus V01.79
    anthrax V01.81
    asbestos V15.84
    body fluids (hazardous) V15.85
    cholera V01.0
    communicable disease V01.9
      specified type NEC V01.89
    Escherichia coli (E. coli) V01.83
    German measles V01.4
    gonorrhea V01.6
    hazardous body fluids V15.85
    HIV V01.79
    human immunodeficiency virus V01.79
    lead V15.86

Exposure — continued
  to — continued
    meningococcus V01.84
    parasitic disease V01.89
    poliomyelitis V01.2
    potentially hazardous body fluids V15.85
    rabies V01.5
    rubella V01.4
    SARS-associated coronavirus V01.82
    smallpox V01.3
    syphilis V01.6
    tuberculosis V01.1
    varicella V01.71
    venereal disease V01.6
    viral disease NEC V01.79
      varicella V01.71
Exsanguination, fetal 772.0
Exstrophy
  abdominal content 751.8
  bladder (urinary) 753.5
Extensive — see condition
Extra — see also Accessory
  rib 756.3
    cervical 756.2
Extraction
  with hook 763.89
  breech NEC 669.6 ☑
    affecting fetus or newborn 763.0
  cataract postsurgical V45.61
  manual NEC 669.8 ☑
    affecting fetus or newborn 763.89
Extrasystole 427.60
  atrial 427.61
  postoperative 997.1
  ventricular 427.69
Extrauterine gestation or pregnancy — see Pregnancy, ectopic
Extravasation
  blood 459.0
    lower extremity 459.0
  chyle into mesentery 457.8
  pelvicalyceal 593.4
  pyelosinus 593.4
  urine 788.8
    from ureter 788.8
Extremity — see condition
Extrophy — see Exstrophy
Extroversion
  bladder 753.5
  uterus 618.1
    complicating delivery 665.2 ☑
      affecting fetus or newborn 763.89
    postpartal (old) 618.1
Extruded tooth 524.34 ●
Extrusion
  alveolus and teeth 524.75
  breast implant (prosthetic) 996.54
  device, implant, or graft — see Complications, mechanical
  eye implant (ball) (globe) 996.59
  intervertebral disc — see Displacement, intervertebral disc
  lacrimal gland 375.43
  mesh (reinforcing) 996.59
  ocular lens implant 996.53
  prosthetic device NEC — see Complications, mechanical
  vitreous 379.26
Exudate, pleura — see Effusion, pleura
Exudates, retina 362.82
Exudative — see condition
Eye, eyeball, eyelid — see condition
Eyestrain 368.13
Eyeworm disease of Africa 125.2

F

Faber's anemia or syndrome (achlorhydric anemia) 280.9
Fabry's disease (angiokeratoma corporis diffusum) 272.7
Face, facial — see condition
Facet of cornea 371.44

Faciocephalalgia, autonomic — see also Neuropathy, peripheral, autonomic 337.9
Facioscapulohumeral myopathy 359.1
Factitious disorder, illness — see Illness, factitious
Factor
  deficiency — see Deficiency, factor
  psychic, associated with diseases classified elsewhere 316
  risk — see Problem
Fahr-Volhard disease (malignant nephrosclerosis) 403.00
Failure, failed
  adenohypophyseal 253.2
  attempted abortion (legal) (see also Abortion, failed) 638.9
  bone marrow (anemia) 284.9
    acquired (secondary) 284.8
    congenital 284.09 ▲
    idiopathic 284.9
  cardiac (see also Failure, heart) 428.9
    newborn 779.89
  cardiorenal (chronic) 428.9
    hypertensive (see also Hypertension, cardiorenal) 404.93
  cardiorespiratory 799.1
    specified during or due to a procedure 997.1
      long-term effect of cardiac surgery 429.4
  cardiovascular (chronic) 428.9
  cerebrovascular 437.8
  cervical dilatation in labor 661.0 ☑
    affecting fetus or newborn 763.7
  circulation, circulatory 799.89
    fetus or newborn 779.89
    peripheral 785.50
  compensation — see Disease, heart
  congestive (see also Failure, heart) 428.0
  coronary (see also Insufficiency, coronary) 411.89
  dental restoration ●
    marginal integrity 525.61 ●
    periodontal anatomical integrity 525.65 ●
  descent of head (at term) 652.5 ☑
    affecting fetus or newborn 763.1
    in labor 660.0 ☑
      affecting fetus or newborn 763.1
  device, implant, or graft — see Complications, mechanical
  engagement of head NEC 652.5 ☑
    in labor 660.0 ☑
  extrarenal 788.9
  fetal head to enter pelvic brim 652.5 ☑
    affecting fetus or newborn 763.1
    in labor 660.0 ☑
      affecting fetus or newborn 763.1
  forceps NEC 660.7 ☑
    affecting fetus or newborn 763.1
  fusion (joint) (spinal) 996.49
  growth in childhood 783.43
  heart (acute) (sudden) 428.9
    with
      abortion — see Abortion, by type, with specified complication NEC
      acute pulmonary edema (see also Failure, ventricular, left) 428.1
        with congestion (see also Failure, heart) 428.0
      decompensation (see also Failure, heart) 428.0
      dilation — see Disease, heart
      ectopic pregnancy (see also categories 633.0–633.9) 639.8
      molar pregnancy (see also categories 630–632) 639.8
    arteriosclerotic 440.9
    combined left-right sided 428.0

Failure, failed — continued
  heart — continued
    combined systolic and diastolic 428.40
      acute 428.41
      acute on chronic 428.43
      chronic 428.42
    compensated (see also Failure, heart) 428.0
    complicating
      abortion — see Abortion, by type, with specified complication NEC
      delivery (cesarean) (instrumental) 669.4 ☑
      ectopic pregnancy (see also categories 633.0–633.9) 639.8
      molar pregnancy (see also categories 630–632) 639.8
      obstetric anesthesia or sedation 668.1 ☑
      surgery 997.1
    congestive (compensated) (decompensated) (see also Failure, heart) 428.0
      with rheumatic fever (conditions classifiable to 390)
        active 391.8
        inactive or quiescent (with chorea) 398.91
      fetus or newborn 779.89
      hypertensive (see also Hypertension, heart) 402.91
        with renal disease (see also Hypertension, cardiorenal) 404.91
          with renal failure 404.93
        benign 402.11
        malignant 402.01
      rheumatic (chronic) (inactive) (with chorea) 398.91
        active or acute 391.8
          with chorea (Sydenham's) 392.0
    decompensated (see also Failure, heart) 428.0
    degenerative (see also Degeneration, myocardial) 429.1
    diastolic 428.30
      acute 428.31
      acute on chronic 428.33
      chronic 428.32
    due to presence of (cardiac) prosthesis 429.4
    fetus or newborn 779.89
    following
      abortion 639.8
      cardiac surgery 429.4
      ectopic or molar pregnancy 639.8
    high output NEC 428.9
    hypertensive (see also Hypertension, heart) 402.91
      with renal disease (see also Hypertension, cardiorenal) 404.91
        with renal failure 404.93
      benign 402.11
      malignant 402.01
    left (ventricular) (see also Failure, ventricular, left) 428.1
      with right-sided failure (see also Failure, heart) 428.0
    low output (syndrome) NEC 428.9
    organic — see Disease, heart
    postoperative (immediate) 997.1
      long term effect of cardiac surgery 429.4
    rheumatic (chronic) (congestive) (inactive) 398.91
    right (secondary to left heart failure, conditions classifiable to 428.1) (ventricular) (see also Failure, heart) 428.0
    senile 797

Failure, failed — *continued*
  heart — *continued*
    specified during or due to a procedure 997.1
      long-term effect of cardiac surgery 429.4
    systolic 428.20
      acute 428.21
      acute on chronic 428.23
      chronic 428.22
    thyrotoxic (*see also* Thyrotoxicosis) 242.9 ☑ *[425.7]*
    valvular — *see* Endocarditis
  hepatic 572.8
    acute 570
    due to a procedure 997.4
  hepatorenal 572.4
  hypertensive heart (*see also* Hypertension, heart) 402.91
    benign 402.11
    malignant 402.01
  induction (of labor) 659.1 ☑
    abortion (legal) (*see also* Abortion, failed) 638.9
    affecting fetus or newborn 763.89
    by oxytocic drugs 659.1 ☑
    instrumental 659.0 ☑
    mechanical 659.0 ☑
    medical 659.1 ☑
    surgical 659.0 ☑
  initial alveolar expansion, newborn 770.4
  involution, thymus (gland) 254.8
  kidney — *see* Failure, renal
  lactation 676.4 ☑
  Leydig's cell, adult 257.2
  liver 572.8
    acute 570
  medullary 799.89
  mitral — *see* Endocarditis, mitral
  myocardium, myocardial (*see also* Failure, heart) 428.9
    chronic (*see also* Failure, heart) 428.0
    congestive (*see also* Failure, heart) 428.0
  ovarian (primary) 256.39
    iatrogenic 256.2
    postablative 256.2
    postirradiation 256.2
    postsurgical 256.2
  ovulation 628.0
  prerenal 788.9
  renal 586
    with
      abortion — *see* Abortion, by type, with renal failure
      ectopic pregnancy (*see also* categories 633.0–633.9) 639.3
      edema (*see also* Nephrosis) 581.9
      hypertension (*see also* Hypertension, kidney) 403.91
      hypertensive heart disease (conditions classifiable to 402) 404.92
        with heart failure 404.93
        benign 404.12
          with heart failure 404.13
        malignant 404.02
          with heart failure 404.03
      molar pregnancy (*see also* categories 630–632) 639.3
      tubular necrosis (acute) 584.5
    acute 584.9
      with lesion of necrosis
        cortical (renal) 584.6
        medullary (renal) (papillary) 584.7
        tubular 584.5
        specified pathology NEC 584.8
    chronic 585.9

Failure, failed — *continued*
  renal — *continued*
    chronic — *continued*
      hypertensive or with hypertension (*see also* Hypertension, kidney) 403.91
    due to a procedure 997.5
    following
      abortion 639.3
      crushing 958.5
      ectopic or molar pregnancy 639.3
      labor and delivery (acute) 669.3 ☑
    hypertensive (*see also* Hypertension, kidney) 403.91
    puerperal, postpartum 669.3 ☑
  respiration, respiratory 518.81
    acute 518.81
    acute and chronic 518.84
    center 348.8
      newborn 770.84
    chronic 518.83
    due to trauma, surgery or shock 518.5
    newborn 770.84
  rotation
    cecum 751.4
    colon 751.4
    intestine 751.4
    kidney 753.3
  segmentation (*see also* Fusion)
    fingers (*see also* Syndactylism, fingers) 755.11
    toes (*see also* Syndactylism, toes) 755.13
  seminiferous tubule, adult 257.2
  senile (general) 797
    with psychosis 290.20
  testis, primary (seminal) 257.2
  to progress 661.2 ☑
  to thrive
    adult 783.7
    child 783.41
  transplant 996.80
    bone marrow 996.85
    organ (immune or nonimmune cause) 996.80
      bone marrow 996.85
      heart 996.83
      intestines 996.87
      kidney 996.81
      liver 996.82
      lung 996.84
      pancreas 996.86
      specified NEC 996.89
    skin 996.52
      artificial 996.55
      decellularized allodermis 996.55
      temporary allograft or pigskin graft — omit code
  trial of labor NEC 660.6 ☑
    affecting fetus or newborn 763.1
  tubal ligation 998.89
  urinary 586
  vacuum extraction
    abortion — *see* Abortion, failed
    delivery NEC 660.7 ☑
      affecting fetus or newborn 763.1
  vasectomy 998.89
  ventouse NEC 660.7 ☑
    affecting fetus or newborn 763.1
  ventricular (*see also* Failure, heart) 428.9
    left 428.1
      with rheumatic fever (conditions classifiable to 390)
        active 391.8
          with chorea 392.0
        inactive or quiescent (with chorea) 398.91
      hypertensive (*see also* Hypertension, heart) 402.91
        benign 402.11
        malignant 402.01

Failure, failed — *continued*
  ventricular (*see also* Failure, heart) — *continued*
    left — *continued*
      rheumatic (chronic) (inactive) (with chorea) 398.91
        active or acute 391.8
          with chorea 392.0
      right (*see also* Failure, heart) 428.0
  vital centers, fetus or newborn 779.89
  weight gain in childhood 783.41
Fainting (fit) (spell) 780.2
Falciform hymen 752.49
Fallen arches 734
Falling, any organ or part — *see* Prolapse
Fall, maternal, affecting fetus or newborn 760.5
Fallopian
  insufflation
    fertility testing V26.21
    following sterilization reversal V26.22
  tube — *see* condition
Fallot's
  pentalogy 745.2
  tetrad or tetralogy 745.2
  triad or trilogy 746.09
Fallout, radioactive (adverse effect) NEC 990
False — *see also* condition
  bundle branch block 426.50
  bursa 727.89
  croup 478.75
  joint 733.82
  labor (pains) 644.1 ☑
  opening, urinary, male 752.69
  passage, urethra (prostatic) 599.4
  positive
    serological test for syphilis 795.6
    Wassermann reaction 795.6
  pregnancy 300.11
Family, familial — *see also* condition
  disruption V61.0
  hemophagocytic ●
    lymphohistiocytosis 288.4 ●
    reticulosis 288.4 ●
  Li-Fraumeni (syndrome) V84.01
  planning advice V25.09
  problem V61.9
    specified circumstance NEC V61.8
  retinoblastoma (syndrome) 190.5
Famine 994.2
  edema 262
Fanconi's anemia (congenital pancytopenia) 284.09 ▲
Fanconi (-de Toni) (-Debré) syndrome (cystinosis) 270.0
Farber (-Uzman) syndrome or disease (disseminated lipogranulomatosis) 272.8
Farcin 024
Farcy 024
Farmers'
  lung 495.0
  skin 692.74
Farsightedness 367.0
Fascia — *see* condition
Fasciculation 781.0
Fasciculitis optica 377.32
Fasciitis 729.4
  eosinophilic 728.89
  necrotizing 728.86
  nodular 728.79
  perirenal 593.4
  plantar 728.71
  pseudosarcomatous 728.79
  traumatic (old) NEC 728.79
    current — *see* Sprain, by site
Fasciola hepatica infestation 121.3
Fascioliasis 121.3
Fasciolopsiasis (small intestine) 121.4
Fasciolopsis (small intestine) 121.4
Fast pulse 785.0

Fat
  embolism (cerebral) (pulmonary) (systemic) 958.1
    with
      abortion — *see* Abortion, by type, with embolism
      ectopic pregnancy (*see also* categories 633.0–633.9) 639.6
      molar pregnancy (*see also* categories 630–632) 639.6
    complicating delivery or puerperium 673.8 ☑
    following
      abortion 639.6
      ectopic or molar pregnancy 639.6
    in pregnancy, childbirth, or the puerperium 673.8 ☑
  excessive 278.02
    in heart (*see also* Degeneration, myocardial) 429.1
  general 278.02
  hernia, herniation 729.30
    eyelid 374.34
    knee 729.31
    orbit 374.34
    retro-orbital 374.34
    retropatellar 729.31
    specified site NEC 729.39
  indigestion 579.8
  in stool 792.1
  localized (pad) 278.1
    heart (*see also* Degeneration, myocardial) 429.1
    knee 729.31
    retropatellar 729.31
  necrosis (*see also* Fatty, degeneration)
    breast (aseptic) (segmental) 611.3
    mesentery 567.82
    omentum 567.82
    peritoneum 567.82
  pad 278.1
Fatal syncope 798.1
Fatigue 780.79
  auditory deafness (*see also* Deafness) 389.9
  chronic, syndrome 780.71
  combat (*see also* Reaction, stress, acute) 308.9
  during pregnancy 646.8 ☑
  general 780.79
    psychogenic 300.5
  heat (transient) 992.6
  muscle 729.89
  myocardium (*see also* Failure, heart) 428.9
  nervous 300.5
  neurosis 300.5
  operational 300.89
  postural 729.89
  posture 729.89
  psychogenic (general) 300.5
  senile 797
  syndrome NEC 300.5
    chronic 780.71
  undue 780.79
  voice 784.49
Fatness 278.02
Fatty — *see also* condition
  apron 278.1
  degeneration (diffuse) (general) NEC 272.8
    localized — *see* Degeneration, by site, fatty
    placenta — *see* Placenta, abnormal
  heart (enlarged) (*see also* Degeneration, myocardial) 429.1
  infiltration (diffuse) (general) (*see also* Degeneration, by site, fatty) 272.8
    heart (enlarged) (*see also* Degeneration, myocardial) 429.1
  liver 571.8
    alcoholic 571.0
  necrosis — *see* Degeneration, fatty

☑ Additional Digit Required — Refer to the Tabular List for Digit Selection   ▽ Subterms under main terms may continue to next column or page

2007 *ICD-9-CM*   ▶◀ Revised Text   ● New Line   ▲ Revised Code   October 2006 • Volume 2 — 115

Failure, failed — Fatty

Fever — *continued*
Omsk hemorrhagic 065.1
O'nyong-nyong (viral) 066.3
Oropouche (viral) 066.3
Oroya 088.0
paludal (*see also* Malaria) 084.6
Panama 084.0
pappataci 066.0
paratyphoid 002.9
    A 002.1
    B (Schottmüller's) 002.2
    C (Hirschfeld) 002.3
parrot 073.9
periodic 277.31 ▲
pernicious, acute 084.0
persistent (of unknown origin) (*see also* Pyrexia) 780.6
petechial 036.0
pharyngoconjunctival 077.2
    adenoviral type 3 077.2
Philippine hemorrhagic 065.4
phlebotomus 066.0
Piry 066.8
Pixuna (viral) 066.3
Plasmodium ovale 084.3
pleural (*see also* Pleurisy) 511.0
pneumonic — *see* Pneumonia
polymer fume 987.8
postoperative 998.89
    due to infection 998.59
pretibial 100.89
puerperal, postpartum 672.0 ☑
putrid — *see* Septicemia
pyemic — *see* Septicemia
Q 083.0
    with pneumonia 083.0 [484.8]
quadrilateral 083.0
quartan (malaria) 084.2
Queensland (coastal) 083.0
    seven-day 100.89
Quintan (A) 083.1
quotidian 084.0
rabbit (*see also* Tularemia) 021.9
rat-bite 026.9
    due to
        Spirillum minor or minus 026.0
        Spirochaeta morsus muris 026.0
        Streptobacillus moniliformis 026.1
recurrent — *see* Fever, relapsing
relapsing 087.9
    Carter's (Asiatic) 087.0
    Dutton's (West African) 087.1
    Koch's 087.9
    louse-borne (epidemic) 087.0
    Novy's (American) 087.1
    Obermeyer's (European) 087.0
    spirillum NEC 087.9
    tick-borne (endemic) 087.1
remittent (bilious) (congestive) (gastric) (*see also* Malaria) 084.6
rheumatic (active) (acute) (chronic) (subacute) 390
    with heart involvement 391.9
        carditis 391.9
        endocarditis (aortic) (mitral) (pulmonary) (tricuspid) 391.1
        multiple sites 391.8
        myocarditis 391.2
        pancarditis, acute 391.8
        pericarditis 391.0
        specified type NEC 391.8
        valvulitis 391.1
    cardiac hypertrophy 398.99
    inactive or quiescent
        with cardiac hypertrophy 398.99
        carditis 398.90
        endocarditis 397.9
            aortic (valve) 395.9
                with mitral (valve) disease 396.9
            mitral (valve) 394.9

Fever — *continued*
    rheumatic — *continued*
        inactive or quiescent — *continued*
            endocarditis — *continued*
                mitral — *continued*
                    with aortic (valve) disease 396.9
                pulmonary (valve) 397.1
                tricuspid (valve) 397.0
            heart conditions (classifiable to 429.3, 429.6, 429.9) 398.99
            failure (congestive) (conditions classifiable to 428.0, 428.9) 398.91
            left ventricular failure (conditions classifiable to 428.1) 398.91
            myocardial degeneration (conditions classifiable to 429.1) 398.0
            myocarditis (conditions classifiable to 429.0) 398.0
            pancarditis 398.99
            pericarditis 393
    Rift Valley (viral) 066.3
    Rocky Mountain spotted 082.0
    rose 477.0
    Ross river (viral) 066.3
    Russian hemorrhagic 078.6
    sandfly 066.0
    San Joaquin (valley) 114.0
    São Paulo 082.0
    scarlet 034.1
    septic — *see* Septicemia
    seven-day 061
        Japan 100.89
        Queensland 100.89
    shin bone 083.1
    Singapore hemorrhagic 065.4
    solar 061
    sore 054.9
    South African tick-bite 087.1
    Southeast Asia hemorrhagic 065.4
    spinal — *see* Meningitis
    spirillary 026.0
    splenic (*see also* Anthrax) 022.9
    spotted (Rocky Mountain) 082.0
        American 082.0
        Brazilian 082.0
        Colombian 082.0
        meaning
            cerebrospinal meningitis 036.0
            typhus 082.9
    spring 309.23
    steroid
        correct substance properly administered 780.6
        overdose or wrong substance given or taken 962.0
    streptobacillary 026.1
    subtertian 084.0
    Sumatran mite 081.2
    sun 061
    swamp 100.89
    sweating 078.2
    swine 003.8
    sylvatic yellow 060.0
    Tahyna 062.5
    tertian — *see* Malaria, tertian
    Thailand hemorrhagic 065.4
    thermic 992.0
    three day 066.0
        with Coxsackie exanthem 074.8
    tick
        American mountain 066.1
        Colorado 066.1
        Kemerovo 066.1
        Mediterranean 082.1
        mountain 066.1
        nonexanthematous 066.1
        Quaranfil 066.1
    tick-bite NEC 066.1
    tick-borne NEC 066.1
        hemorrhagic NEC 065.3

Fever — *continued*
    transitory of newborn 778.4
    trench 083.1
    tsutsugamushi 081.2
    typhogastric 002.0
    typhoid (abortive) (ambulant) (any site) (hemorrhagic) (infection) (intermittent) (malignant) (rheumatic) 002.0
    typhomalarial (*see also* Malaria) 084.6
    typhus — *see* Typhus
    undulant (*see also* Brucellosis) 023.9
    unknown origin (*see also* Pyrexia) 780.6
    uremic — *see* Uremia
    uveoparotid 135
    valley (Coccidioidomycosis) 114.0
    Venezuelan equine 066.2
    Volhynian 083.1
    Wesselsbron (viral) 066.3
    West
        African 084.8
        Nile (viral) 066.40
            with
                cranial nerve disorders 066.42
                encephalitis 066.41
                optic neuritis 066.42
                other complications 066.49
                other neurologic manifestations 066.42
                polyradiculitis 066.42
    Whitmore's 025
    Wolhynian 083.1
    worm 128.9
    Yaroslav hemorrhagic 078.6
    yellow 060.9
        jungle 060.0
        sylvatic 060.0
        urban 060.1
        vaccination, prophylactic (against) V04.4
    Zika (viral) 066.3
Fibrillation
    atrial (established) (paroxysmal) 427.31
    auricular (atrial) (established) 427.31
    cardiac (ventricular) 427.41
    coronary (*see also* Infarct, myocardium) 410.9 ☑
    heart (ventricular) 427.41
    muscular 728.9
    postoperative 997.1
    ventricular 427.41
Fibrin
    ball or bodies, pleural (sac) 511.0
    chamber, anterior (eye) (gelatinous exudate) 364.04
Fibrinogenolysis (hemorrhagic) — *see* Fibrinolysis
Fibrinogenopenia (congenital) (hereditary) — *see also* Defect, coagulation 286.3
    acquired 286.6
Fibrinolysis (acquired) (hemorrhagic) (pathologic) 286.6
    with
        abortion — *see* Abortion, by type, with hemorrhage, delayed or excessive
        ectopic pregnancy (*see also* categories 633.0–633.9) 639.1
        molar pregnancy (*see also* categories 630–632) 639.1
        antepartum or intrapartum 641.3 ☑
            affecting fetus or newborn 762.1
        following
            abortion 639.1
            ectopic or molar pregnancy 639.1
        newborn, transient 776.2
        postpartum 666.3 ☑
Fibrinopenia (hereditary) — *see also* Defect, coagulation 286.3
    acquired 286.6
Fibrinopurulent — *see* condition
Fibrinous — *see* condition

Fibroadenoma (M9010/0)
    cellular intracanalicular (M9020/0) 217
    giant (intracanalicular) (M9020/0) 217
    intracanalicular (M9011/0)
        cellular (M9020/0) 217
        giant (M9020/0) 217
        specified site — *see* Neoplasm, by site, benign
        unspecified site 217
    juvenile (M9030/0) 217
    pericanalicular (M9012/0)
        specified site — *see* Neoplasm, by site, benign
        unspecified site 217
    phyllodes (M9020/0) 217
    prostate 600.20
        with
            other lower urinary tract •
                symptoms (LUTS) •
                600.21 •
            urinary •
                obstruction 600.21 •
                retention 600.21 •
    specified site — *see* Neoplasm, by site, benign
    unspecified site 217
Fibroadenosis, breast (chronic) (cystic) (diffuse) (periodic) (segmental) 610.2
Fibroangioma (M9160/0) — *see also* Neoplasm, by site, benign
    juvenile (M9160/0)
        specified site — *see* Neoplasm, by site, benign
        unspecified site 210.7
Fibrocellulitis progressiva ossificans 728.11
Fibrochondrosarcoma (M9220/3) — *see* Neoplasm, cartilage, malignant
Fibrocystic
    disease 277.00
        bone NEC 733.29
        breast 610.1
        jaw 526.2
        kidney (congenital) 753.19
        liver 751.62
        lung 518.89
            congenital 748.4
        pancreas 277.00
    kidney (congenital) 753.19
Fibrodysplasia ossificans multiplex (progressiva) 728.11
Fibroelastosis (cordis) (endocardial) (endomyocardial) 425.3
Fibroid (tumor) (M8890/0) — *see also* Neoplasm, connective tissue, benign
    disease, lung (chronic) (*see also* Fibrosis, lung) 515
    heart (disease) (*see also* Myocarditis) 429.0
    induration, lung (chronic) (*see also* Fibrosis, lung) 515
    in pregnancy or childbirth 654.1 ☑
        affecting fetus or newborn 763.89
        causing obstructed labor 660.2 ☑
            affecting fetus or newborn 763.1
    liver — *see* Cirrhosis, liver
    lung (*see also* Fibrosis, lung) 515
    pneumonia (chronic) (*see also* Fibrosis, lung) 515
    uterus (M8890/0) (*see also* Leiomyoma, uterus) 218.9
Fibrolipoma (M8851/0) — *see also* Lipoma, by site 214.9
Fibroliposarcoma (M8850/3) — *see* Neoplasm, connective tissue, malignant
Fibroma (M8810/0) — *see also* Neoplasm, connective tissue, benign
    ameloblastic (M9330/0) 213.1
        upper jaw (bone) 213.0
    bone (nonossifying) 733.99
        ossifying (M9262/0) — *see* Neoplasm, bone, benign

Fibroma — *see also* Neoplasm, connective tissue, benign — *continued*
  cementifying (M9274/0) — *see* Neoplasm, bone, benign
  chondromyxoid (M9241/0) — *see* Neoplasm, bone, benign
  desmoplastic (M8823/1) — *see* Neoplasm, connective tissue, uncertain behavior
  facial (M8813/0) — *see* Neoplasm, connective tissue, benign
  invasive (M8821/1) — *see* Neoplasm, connective tissue, uncertain behavior
  molle (M8851/0) (*see also* Lipoma, by site) 214.9
  myxoid (M8811/0) — *see* Neoplasm, connective tissue, benign
  nasopharynx, nasopharyngeal (juvenile) (M9160/0) 210.7
  nonosteogenic (nonossifying) — *see* Dysplasia, fibrous
  odontogenic (M9321/0) 213.1
    upper jaw (bone) 213.0
  ossifying (M9262/0) — *see* Neoplasm, bone, benign
  periosteal (M8812/0) — *see* Neoplasm, bone, benign
  prostate 600.20
    with
      other lower urinary tract symptoms (LUTS) 600.21 •
      urinary •
        obstruction 600.21 •
        retention 600.21 •
  soft (M8851/0) (*see also* Lipoma, by site) 214.9

Fibromatosis 728.79 ▲
  abdominal (M8822/1) — *see* Neoplasm, connective tissue, uncertain behavior
  aggressive (M8821/1) — *see* Neoplasm, connective tissue, uncertain behavior
  congenital generalized (CGF) 759.89 •
  Dupuytren's 728.6
  gingival 523.8
  plantar fascia 728.71
  proliferative 728.79
  pseudosarcomatous (proliferative) (subcutaneous) 728.79
  subcutaneous pseudosarcomatous (proliferative) 728.79

Fibromyalgia 729.1

Fibromyoma (M8890/0) — *see also* Neoplasm, connective tissue, benign
  uterus (corpus) (*see also* Leiomyoma, uterus) 218.9
    in pregnancy or childbirth 654.1 ☑
      affecting fetus or newborn 763.89
      causing obstructed labor 660.2 ☑
        affecting fetus or newborn 763.1

Fibromyositis — *see also* Myositis 729.1
  scapulohumeral 726.2

Fibromyxolipoma (M8852/0) — *see also* Lipoma, by site 214.9

Fibromyxoma (M8811/0) — *see* Neoplasm, connective tissue, benign

Fibromyxosarcoma (M8811/3) — *see* Neoplasm, connective tissue, malignant

Fibro-odontoma, ameloblastic (M9290/0) 213.1
  upper jaw (bone) 213.0

Fibro-osteoma (M9262/0) — *see* Neoplasm, bone, benign

Fibroplasia, retrolental 362.21

Fibropurulent — *see* condition

Fibrosarcoma (M8810/3) — *see also* Neoplasm, connective tissue, malignant
  ameloblastic (M9330/3) 170.1
    upper jaw (bone) 170.0
  congenital (M8814/3) — *see* Neoplasm, connective tissue, malignant
  fascial (M8813/3) — *see* Neoplasm, connective tissue, malignant
  infantile (M8814/3) — *see* Neoplasm, connective tissue, malignant
  odontogenic (M9330/3) 170.1
    upper jaw (bone) 170.0
  periosteal (M8812/3) — *see* Neoplasm, bone, malignant

Fibrosclerosis
  breast 610.3
  corpora cavernosa (penis) 607.89
  familial multifocal NEC 710.8
  multifocal (idiopathic) NEC 710.8
  penis (corpora cavernosa) 607.89

Fibrosis, fibrotic
  adrenal (gland) 255.8
  alveolar (diffuse) 516.3
  amnion 658.8 ☑
  anal papillae 569.49
  anus 569.49
  appendix, appendiceal, noninflammatory 543.9
  arteriocapillary — *see* Arteriosclerosis
  bauxite (of lung) 503
  biliary 576.8
    due to Clonorchis sinensis 121.1
  bladder 596.8
    interstitial 595.1
    localized submucosal 595.1
    panmural 595.1
  bone, diffuse 756.59
  breast 610.3
  capillary (*see also* Arteriosclerosis)
    lung (chronic) (*see also* Fibrosis, lung) 515
  cardiac (*see also* Myocarditis) 429.0
  cervix 622.8
  chorion 658.8 ☑
  corpus cavernosum 607.89
  cystic (of pancreas) 277.00
    with
      manifestations
        gastrointestinal 277.03
        pulmonary 277.02
        specified NEC 277.09
      meconium ileus 277.01
      pulmonary exacerbation 277.02
  due to (presence of) any device, implant, or graft — *see* Complications, due to (presence of) any device, implant, or graft classified to 996.0–996.5 NEC
  ejaculatory duct 608.89
  endocardium (*see also* Endocarditis) 424.90
  endomyocardial (African) 425.0
  epididymis 608.89
  eye muscle 378.62
  graphite (of lung) 503
  heart (*see also* Myocarditis) 429.0
  hepatic (*see also* Cirrhosis, liver)
    due to Clonorchis sinensis 121.1
  hepatolienal — *see* Cirrhosis, liver
  hepatosplenic — *see* Cirrhosis, liver
  infrapatellar fat pad 729.31
  interstitial pulmonary, newborn 770.7
  intrascrotal 608.89
  kidney (*see also* Sclerosis, renal) 587
  liver — *see* Cirrhosis, liver
  lung (atrophic) (capillary) (chronic) (confluent) (massive) (perialveolar) (peribronchial) 515
    with
      anthracosilicosis (occupational) 500
      anthracosis (occupational) 500
      asbestosis (occupational) 501
      bagassosis (occupational) 495.1

Fibrosis, fibrotic — *continued*
  lung — *continued*
    with — *continued*
      bauxite 503
      berylliosis (occupational) 503
      byssinosis (occupational) 504
      calcicosis (occupational) 502
      chalicosis (occupational) 502
      dust reticulation (occupational) 504
      farmers' lung 495.0
      gannister disease (occupational) 502
      graphite 503
      pneumonoconiosis (occupational) 505
      pneumosiderosis (occupational) 503
      siderosis (occupational) 503
      silicosis (occupational) 502
      tuberculosis (*see also* Tuberculosis) 011.4 ☑
  diffuse (idiopathic) (interstitial) 516.3
  due to
    bauxite 503
    fumes or vapors (chemical) (inhalation) 506.4
    graphite 503
  following radiation 508.1
  postinflammatory 515
  silicotic (massive) (occupational) 502
  tuberculous (*see also* Tuberculosis) 011.4 ☑
  lymphatic gland 289.3
  median bar 600.90
    with
      other lower urinary tract symptoms (LUTS) 600.91 •
      urinary •
        obstruction 600.91 •
        retention 600.91 •
  mediastinum (idiopathic) 519.3
  meninges 349.2
  muscle NEC 728.2
    iatrogenic (from injection) 999.9
  myocardium, myocardial (*see also* Myocarditis) 429.0
  oral submucous 528.8
  ovary 620.8
  oviduct 620.8
  pancreas 577.8
    cystic 277.00
      with
        manifestations
          gastrointestinal 277.03
          pulmonary 277.02
          specified NEC 277.09
        meconium ileus 277.01
        pulmonary exacerbation 277.02
  penis 607.89
  periappendiceal 543.9
  periarticular (*see also* Ankylosis) 718.5 ☑
  pericardium 423.1
  perineum, in pregnancy or childbirth 654.8 ☑
    affecting fetus or newborn 763.89
    causing obstructed labor 660.2 ☑
      affecting fetus or newborn 763.1
  perineural NEC 355.9
    foot 355.6
  periureteral 593.89
  placenta — *see* Placenta, abnormal
  pleura 511.0
  popliteal fat pad 729.31
  preretinal 362.56
  prostate (chronic) 600.90
    with
      other lower urinary tract symptoms (LUTS) 600.91 •

Fibrosis, fibrotic — *continued*
  prostate — *continued*
    with — *continued*
      urinary •
        obstruction 600.91 •
        retention 600.91 •
  pulmonary (chronic) (*see also* Fibrosis, lung) 515
    alveolar capillary block 516.3
    interstitial
      diffuse (idiopathic) 516.3
      newborn 770.7
  radiation — *see* Effect, adverse, radiation
  rectal sphincter 569.49
  retroperitoneal, idiopathic 593.4
  sclerosing mesenteric (idiopathic) 567.82
  scrotum 608.89
  seminal vesicle 608.89
  senile 797
  skin NEC 709.2
  spermatic cord 608.89
  spleen 289.59
    bilharzial (*see also* Schistosomiasis) 120.9
  subepidermal nodular (M8832/0) — *see* Neoplasm, skin, benign
  submucous NEC 709.2
    oral 528.8
    tongue 528.8
  syncytium — *see* Placenta, abnormal
  testis 608.89
    chronic, due to syphilis 095.8
  thymus (gland) 254.8
  tunica vaginalis 608.89
  ureter 593.89
  urethra 599.84
  uterus (nonneoplastic) 621.8
    bilharzial (*see also* Schistosomiasis) 120.9
    neoplastic (*see also* Leiomyoma, uterus) 218.9
  vagina 623.8
  valve, heart (*see also* Endocarditis) 424.90
  vas deferens 608.89
  vein 459.89
    lower extremities 459.89
  vesical 595.1

Fibrositis (periarticular) (rheumatoid) 729.0
  humeroscapular region 726.2
  nodular, chronic
    Jaccoud's 714.4
    rheumatoid 714.4
  ossificans 728.11
  scapulohumeral 726.2

Fibrothorax 511.0

Fibrotic — *see* Fibrosis

Fibrous — *see* condition

Fibroxanthoma (M8831/0) — *see also* Neoplasm, connective tissue, benign
  atypical (M8831/1) — *see* Neoplasm, connective tissue, uncertain behavior
  malignant (M8831/3) — *see* Neoplasm, connective tissue, malignant

Fibroxanthosarcoma (M8831/3) — *see* Neoplasm, connective tissue, malignant

Fiedler's
  disease (leptospiral jaundice) 100.0
  myocarditis or syndrome (acute isolated myocarditis) 422.91

Fiessinger-Leroy (-Reiter) syndrome 099.3

Fiessinger-Rendu syndrome (erythema muliforme exudativum) 695.1

Fifth disease (eruptive) 057.0
  venereal 099.1

Filaria, filarial — *see* Infestation, filarial

Filariasis — *see also* Infestation, filarial 125.9

☑ Additional Digit Required — Refer to the Tabular List for Digit Selection   ⩔ Subterms under main terms may continue to next column or page

118 — Volume 2 · October 2006   ▶◀ Revised Text   ● New Line   ▲ Revised Code   *2007 ICD-9-CM*

Filariasis — *see also* Infestation, filarial
— *continued*
  bancroftian 125.0
  Brug's 125.1
  due to
    bancrofti 125.0
    Brugia (Wuchereria) (malayi) 125.1
    Loa loa 125.2
    malayi 125.1
    organism NEC 125.6
    Wuchereria (bancrofti) 125.0
      malayi 125.1
  Malayan 125.1
  ozzardi 125.5
  specified type NEC 125.6
Filatoff's, Filatov's, Filatow's disease
  (infectious mononucleosis) 075
File-cutters' disease 984.9
  specified type of lead — *see* Table of
    Drugs and Chemicals
Filling defect
  biliary tract 793.3
  bladder 793.5
  duodenum 793.4
  gallbladder 793.3
  gastrointestinal tract 793.4
  intestine 793.4
  kidney 793.5
  stomach 793.4
  ureter 793.5
Filtering bleb, eye (postglaucoma) (status) V45.69
  with complication or rupture 997.99
  postcataract extraction (complication) 997.99
Fimbrial cyst (congenital) 752.11
Fimbriated hymen 752.49
Financial problem affecting care V60.2
Findings, abnormal, without diagnosis
  (examination) (laboratory test) 796.4
  17-ketosteroids, elevated 791.9
  acetonuria 791.6
  acid phosphatase 790.5
  albumin-globulin ratio 790.99
  albuminuria 791.0
  alcohol in blood 790.3
  alkaline phosphatase 790.5
  amniotic fluid 792.3
  amylase 790.5
  anisocytosis 790.09
  antenatal screening 796.5
  anthrax, positive 795.31
  antibody titers, elevated 795.79
  anticardiolipin antibody 795.79
  antigen-antibody reaction 795.79
  antiphospholipid antibody 795.79
  bacteriuria 791.9
  ballistocardiogram 794.39
  bicarbonate 276.9
  bile in urine 791.4
  bilirubin 277.4
  bleeding time (prolonged) 790.92
  blood culture, positive 790.7
  blood gas level (arterial) 790.91
  blood sugar level 790.29
    high 790.29
      fasting glucose 790.21
      glucose tolerance test 790.22
    low 251.2
  calcium 275.40
  cancer antigen 125 [CA 125] 795.82 ●
  carbonate 276.9
  carcinoembryonic antigen [CEA] ●
    795.81 ●
  casts, urine 791.7
  catecholamines 791.9
  cells, urine 791.7
  cerebrospinal fluid (color) (content) (pressure) 792.0
  cervical
    high risk human papillomavirus (HPV) DNA test positive 795.05

Findings, abnormal, without diagnosis
— *continued*
  cervical — *continued*
    low risk human papillomavirus (HPV) DNA test positive 795.09
  chloride 276.9
  cholesterol 272.9
  chromosome analysis 795.2
  chyluria 791.1
  circulation time 794.39
  cloudy dialysis effluent 792.5
  cloudy urine 791.9
  coagulation study 790.92
  cobalt, blood 790.6
  color of urine (unusual) NEC 791.9
  copper, blood 790.6
  C-reactive protein (CRP) 790.95
  crystals, urine 791.9
  culture, positive NEC 795.39
    blood 790.7
    HIV V08
    human immunodeficiency virus V08
    nose 795.39
    skin lesion NEC 795.39
    spinal fluid 792.0
    sputum 795.39
    stool 792.1
    throat 795.39
    urine 791.9
    viral
      human immunodeficiency V08
    wound 795.39
  echocardiogram 793.2
  echoencephalogram 794.01
  echogram NEC — *see* Findings, abnormal, structure
  electrocardiogram (ECG) (EKG) 794.31
  electroencephalogram (EEG) 794.02
  electrolyte level, urinary 791.9
  electromyogram (EMG) 794.17
    ocular 794.14
  electro-oculogram (EOG) 794.12
  electroretinogram (ERG) 794.11
  enzymes, serum NEC 790.5
  fibrinogen titer coagulation study 790.92
  filling defect — *see* Filling defect
  function study NEC 794.9
    auditory 794.15
    bladder 794.9
    brain 794.00
    cardiac 794.30
    endocrine NEC 794.6
      thyroid 794.5
    kidney 794.4
    liver 794.8
    nervous system
      central 794.00
      peripheral 794.19
    oculomotor 794.14
    pancreas 794.9
    placenta 794.9
    pulmonary 794.2
    retina 794.11
    special senses 794.19
    spleen 794.9
    vestibular 794.16
  gallbladder, nonvisualization 793.3
  glucose 790.29
    elevated
      fasting 790.21
      tolerance test 790.22
  glycosuria 791.5
  heart
    shadow 793.2
    sounds 785.3
  hematinuria 791.2
  hematocrit
    drop (precipitous) 790.01
    elevated 282.7
    low 285.9
  hematologic NEC 790.99
  hematuria 599.7

Findings, abnormal, without diagnosis
— *continued*
  hemoglobin
    elevated 282.7
    low 285.9
  hemoglobinuria 791.2
  histological NEC 795.4
  hormones 259.9
  immunoglobulins, elevated 795.79
  indolacetic acid, elevated 791.9
  iron 790.6
  karyotype 795.2
  ketonuria 791.6
  lactic acid dehydrogenase (LDH) 790.4
  lead 790.6 ●
  lipase 790.5
  lipids NEC 272.9
  lithium, blood 790.6
  liver function test 790.6
  lung field (coin lesion) (shadow) 793.1
  magnesium, blood 790.6
  mammogram 793.80
    calcification 793.89 ●
    calculus 793.89 ●
    microcalcification 793.81
  mediastinal shift 793.2
  melanin, urine 791.9
  microbiologic NEC 795.39
  mineral, blood NEC 790.6
  myoglobinuria 791.3
  nasal swab, anthrax 795.31
  neonatal screening 796.6
  nitrogen derivatives, blood 790.6
  nonvisualization of gallbladder 793.3
  nose culture, positive 795.39
  odor of urine (unusual) NEC 791.9
  oxygen saturation 790.91
  Papanicolaou (smear) 795.1
    cervix 795.00
    with
      atypical squamous cells
        cannot exclude high grade squamous intraepithelial lesion (ASC-H) 795.02
        of undetermined significance (ASC-US) 795.01
      cytologic evidence of malig- ●
        nancy 795.06 ●
      high grade squamous intraepithelial lesion (HGSIL) 795.04
      low grade squamous intraepithelial lesion (LGSIL) 795.03
      dyskaryotic 795.09
      nonspecific finding NEC 795.09
    other site 795.1
  peritoneal fluid 792.9
  phonocardiogram 794.39
  phosphorus 275.3
  pleural fluid 792.9
  pneumoencephalogram 793.0
  PO_2-oxygen ratio 790.91
  poikilocytosis 790.09
  potassium
    deficiency 276.8
    excess 276.7
  PPD 795.5
  prostate specific antigen (PSA) 790.93
  protein, serum NEC 790.99
  proteinuria 791.0
  prothrombin time (partial) (prolonged) (PT) (PTT) 790.92
  pyuria 791.9
  radiologic (x-ray) 793.99 ▲
    abdomen 793.6
    biliary tract 793.3
    breast 793.89
      abnormal mammogram NOS 793.80
      mammographic
        calcification 793.89 ●
        calculus 793.89 ●
        microcalcification 793.81 ●

Findings, abnormal, without diagnosis
— *continued*
  radiologic — *continued*
    gastrointestinal tract 793.4
    genitourinary organs 793.5
    head 793.0
    image test inconclusive due to ●
      excess body fat 793.91 ●
    intrathoracic organs NEC 793.2
    lung 793.1
    musculoskeletal 793.7
    placenta 793.99 ▲
    retroperitoneum 793.6
    skin 793.99 ▲
    skull 793.0
    subcutaneous tissue 793.99 ▲
  red blood cell 790.09
    count 790.09
    morphology 790.09
    sickling 790.09
    volume 790.09
  saliva 792.4
  scan NEC 794.9
    bladder 794.9
    bone 794.9
    brain 794.09
    kidney 794.4
    liver 794.8
    lung 794.2
    pancreas 794.9
    placental 794.9
    spleen 794.9
    thyroid 794.5
  sedimentation rate, elevated 790.1
  semen 792.2
  serological (for)
    human immunodeficiency virus (HIV)
      inconclusive 795.71
      positive V08
    syphilis — *see* Findings, serology for syphilis
  serology for syphilis
    false positive 795.6
    positive 097.1
      false 795.6
      follow-up of latent syphilis — *see* Syphilis, latent
      only finding — *see* Syphilis, latent
  serum 790.99
    blood NEC 790.99
    enzymes NEC 790.5
    proteins 790.99
  SGOT 790.4
  SGPT 790.4
  sickling of red blood cells 790.09
  skin test, positive 795.79
    tuberculin (without active tuberculosis) 795.5
  sodium 790.6
    deficiency 276.1
    excess 276.0
  spermatozoa 792.2
  spinal fluid 792.0
    culture, positive 792.0
  sputum culture, positive 795.39
    for acid-fast bacilli 795.39
  stool NEC 792.1
    bloody 578.1
      occult 792.1
    color 792.1
    culture, positive 792.1
    occult blood 792.1
  stress test 794.39
  structure, body (echogram) (thermogram) (ultrasound) (x-ray) NEC 793.99 ▲
    abdomen 793.6
    breast 793.89
      abnormal mammogram 793.80
      mammographic
        calcification 793.89 ●
        calculus 793.89 ●
        microcalcification 793.81 ●
    gastrointestinal tract 793.4

☑ Additional Digit Required — Refer to the Tabular List for Digit Selection
▽ Subterms under main terms may continue to next column or page
2007 ICD-9-CM
▶◀ Revised Text
● New Line
▲ Revised Code
October 2006 · Volume 2 — 119

☑ Additional Digit Required — Refer to the Tabular List for Digit Selection   ▽ Subterms under main terms may continue to next column or page

120 — Volume 2 • October 2006   ▶◀ Revised Text   ● New Line   ▲ Revised Code   *2007 ICD-9-CM*

Fistula — *continued*
  joint — *continued*
    elbow 719.82
    foot 719.87
    hand 719.84
    hip 719.85
    knee 719.86
    multiple sites 719.89
    pelvic region 719.85
    shoulder (region) 719.81
    specified site NEC 719.88
    tuberculous — *see* Tuberculosis, joint
    wrist 719.83
  kidney 593.89
  labium (majus) (minus) 619.8
  labyrinth, labyrinthine NEC 386.40
    combined sites 386.48
    multiple sites 386.48
    oval window 386.42
    round window 386.41
    semicircular canal 386.43
  lacrimal, lachrymal (duct) (gland) (sac) 375.61
  lacrimonasal duct 375.61
  laryngotracheal 748.3
  larynx 478.79
  lip 528.5
    congenital 750.25
  lumbar, tuberculous (*see also* Tuberculosis) 015.0 ☑ *[730.8]* ☑
  lung 510.0
  lymphatic (node) (vessel) 457.8
  mamillary 611.0
  mammary (gland) 611.0
    puerperal, postpartum 675.1 ☑
  mastoid (process) (region) 383.1
  maxillary (*see also* Sinusitis, maxillary) 473.0
  mediastinal 510.0
  mediastinobronchial 510.0
  mediastinocutaneous 510.0
  middle ear 385.89
  mouth 528.3
  nasal 478.19 ▲
    sinus (*see also* Sinusitis) 473.9
  nasopharynx 478.29
  nipple — *see* Fistula, breast
  nose 478.19 ▲
  oral (cutaneous) 528.3
    maxillary (*see also* Sinusitis, maxillary) 473.0
    nasal (with cleft palate) (*see also* Cleft, palate) 749.00
  orbit, orbital 376.10
  oro-antral (*see also* Sinusitis, maxillary) 473.0
  oval window (internal ear) 386.42
  oviduct (external) 619.2
  palate (hard) 526.89
    soft 528.9
  pancreatic 577.8
  pancreaticoduodenal 577.8
  parotid (gland) 527.4
    region 528.3
  pelvoabdominointestinal 569.81
  penis 607.89
  perianal 565.1
  pericardium (pleura) (sac) (*see also* Pericarditis) 423.8
  pericecal 569.81
  perineal — *see* Fistula, perineum
  perineorectal 569.81
  perineosigmoidal 569.81
  perineo-urethroscrotal 608.89
  perineum, perineal (with urethral involvement) NEC 599.1
    tuberculous (*see also* Tuberculosis) 017.9 ☑
    ureter 593.82
  perirectal 565.1
    tuberculous (*see also* Tuberculosis) 014.8 ☑
  peritoneum (*see also* Peritonitis) 567.22
  periurethral 599.1

Fistula — *continued*
  pharyngo-esophageal 478.29
  pharynx 478.29
    branchial cleft (congenital) 744.41
  pilonidal (infected) (rectum) 685.1
    with abscess 685.0
  pleura, pleural, pleurocutaneous, pleuroperitoneal 510.0
    stomach 510.0
    tuberculous (*see also* Tuberculosis) 012.0 ☑
  pleuropericardial 423.8
  postauricular 383.81
  postoperative, persistent 998.6
  preauricular (congenital) 744.46
  prostate 602.8
  pulmonary 510.0
    arteriovenous 417.0
      congenital 747.3
    tuberculous (*see also* Tuberculosis, pulmonary) 011.9 ☑
  pulmonoperitoneal 510.0
  rectolabial 619.1
  rectosigmoid (intercommunicating) 569.81
  rectoureteral 593.82
  rectourethral 599.1
    congenital 753.8
  rectouterine 619.1
    congenital 752.3
  rectovaginal 619.1
    congenital 752.49
    old, postpartal 619.1
    tuberculous (*see also* Tuberculosis) 014.8 ☑
  rectovesical 596.1
    congenital 753.8
  rectovesicovaginal 619.1
  rectovulvar 619.1
    congenital 752.49
  rectum (to skin) 565.1
    tuberculous (*see also* Tuberculosis) 014.8 ☑
  renal 593.89
  retroauricular 383.81
  round window (internal ear) 386.41
  salivary duct or gland 527.4
    congenital 750.24
  sclera 360.32
  scrotum (urinary) 608.89
    tuberculous (*see also* Tuberculosis) 016.5 ☑
  semicircular canals (internal ear) 386.43
  sigmoid 569.81
    vesicoabdominal 596.1
  sigmoidovaginal 619.1
    congenital 752.49
  skin 686.9
    ureter 593.82
    vagina 619.2
  sphenoidal sinus (*see also* Sinusitis, sphenoidal) 473.3
  splenocolic 289.59
  stercoral 569.81
  stomach 537.4
  sublingual gland 527.4
    congenital 750.24
  submaxillary
    gland 527.4
      congenital 750.24
    region 528.3
  thoracic 510.0
    duct 457.8
  thoracicoabdominal 510.0
  thoracicogastric 510.0
  thoracicointestinal 510.0
  thoracoabdominal 510.0
  thoracogastric 510.0
  thorax 510.0
  thyroglossal duct 759.2
  thyroid 246.8
  trachea (congenital) (external) (internal) 748.3
  tracheoesophageal 530.84
    congenital 750.3

Fistula — *continued*
  tracheoesophageal — *continued*
    following tracheostomy 519.09
  traumatic
    arteriovenous (*see also* Injury, blood vessel, by site) 904.9
      brain — *see* Injury, intracranial
  tuberculous — *see* Tuberculosis, by site
  typhoid 002.0
  umbilical 759.89
  umbilico-urinary 753.8
  urachal, urachus 753.7
  ureter (persistent) 593.82
  ureteroabdominal 593.82
  ureterocervical 593.82
  ureterorectal 593.82
  ureterosigmoido-abdominal 593.82
  ureterovaginal 619.0
  ureterovesical 596.2
  urethra 599.1
    congenital 753.8
    tuberculous (*see also* Tuberculosis) 016.3 ☑
  urethroperineal 599.1
  urethroperineovesical 596.2
  urethrorectal 599.1
    congenital 753.8
  urethroscrotal 608.89
  urethrovaginal 619.0
  urethrovesical 596.2
  urethrovesicovaginal 619.0
  urinary (persistent) (recurrent) 599.1
  uteroabdominal (anterior wall) 619.2
    congenital 752.3
  uteroenteric 619.1
  uterofecal 619.1
  uterointestinal 619.1
    congenital 752.3
  uterorectal 619.1
    congenital 752.3
  uteroureteric 619.0
  uterovaginal 619.8
  uterovesical 619.0
    congenital 752.3
  uterus 619.8
  vagina (wall) 619.8
    postpartal, old 619.8
  vaginocutaneous (postpartal) 619.2
  vaginoileal (acquired) 619.1
  vaginoperineal 619.2
  vesical NEC 596.2
  vesicoabdominal 596.2
  vesicocervicovaginal 619.0
  vesicocolic 596.1
  vesicocutaneous 596.2
  vesicoenteric 596.1
  vesicointestinal 596.1
  vesicometrorectal 619.1
  vesicoperineal 596.2
  vesicorectal 596.1
    congenital 753.8
  vesicosigmoidal 596.1
  vesicosigmoidovaginal 619.1
  vesicoureteral 596.2
  vesicoureterovaginal 619.0
  vesicourethral 596.2
  vesicourethrorectal 596.1
  vesicouterine 619.0
    congenital 752.3
  vesicovaginal 619.0
  vulvorectal 619.1
    congenital 752.49
Fit 780.39
  apoplectic (*see also* Disease, cerebrovascular, acute) 436
    late effect — *see* Late effect(s) (of) cerebrovascular disease
  epileptic (*see also* Epilepsy) 345.9 ☑
  fainting 780.2
  hysterical 300.11
  newborn 779.0
Fitting (of)
  artificial
    arm (complete) (partial) V52.0
    breast V52.4

Fitting — *continued*
  artificial — *continued*
    eye(s) V52.2
    leg(s) (complete) (partial) V52.1
  brain neuropacemaker V53.02
  cardiac pacemaker V53.31
  carotid sinus pacemaker V53.39
  cerebral ventricle (communicating) shunt V53.01
  colostomy belt V53.5
  contact lenses V53.1
  cystostomy device V53.6
  defibrillator, automatic implantable cardiac V53.32
  dentures V52.3
  device, unspecified type V53.90
    abdominal V53.5
    cardiac
      defibrillator, automatic implantable V53.32
      pacemaker V53.31
      specified NEC V53.39
    cerebral ventricle (communicating) shunt V53.01
    insulin pump V53.91
    intrauterine contraceptive V25.1
    nervous system V53.09
    orthodontic V53.4
    orthoptic V53.1
    other device V53.99
    prosthetic V52.9
      breast V52.4
      dental V52.3
      eye V52.2
      specified type NEC V52.8
    special senses V53.09
    substitution
      auditory V53.09
      nervous system V53.09
      visual V53.09
    urinary V53.6
  diaphragm (contraceptive) V25.02
  glasses (reading) V53.1
  growth rod V54.02
  hearing aid V53.2
  ileostomy device V53.5
  intestinal appliance or device NEC V53.5
  intrauterine contraceptive device V25.1
  neuropacemaker (brain) (peripheral nerve) (spinal cord) V53.02
  orthodontic device V53.4
  orthopedic (device) V53.7
    brace V53.7
    cast V53.7
    corset V53.7
    shoes V53.7
  pacemaker (cardiac) V53.31
    brain V53.02
    carotid sinus V53.39
    peripheral nerve V53.02
    spinal cord V53.02
  prosthesis V52.9
    arm (complete) (partial) V52.0
    breast V52.4
    dental V52.3
    eye V52.2
    leg (complete) (partial) V52.1
    specified type NEC V52.8
  spectacles V53.1
  wheelchair V53.8
Fitz-Hugh and Curtis syndrome 098.86
  due to
    Chlamydia trachomatis 099.56
    Neisseria gonorrhoeae (gonococcal peritonitis) 098.86
Fitz's syndrome (acute hemorrhagic pancreatitis) 577.0
Fixation
  joint — *see* Ankylosis
  larynx 478.79
  pupil 364.76
  stapes 385.22
    deafness (*see also* Deafness, conductive) 389.04

☑ Additional Digit Required — Refer to the Tabular List for Digit Selection   ▼ Subterms under main terms may continue to next column or page

Fixation — *continued*
  uterus (acquired) — *see* Malposition,
    uterus
  vocal cord 478.5
Flaccid — *see also* condition
  foot 736.79
  forearm 736.09
  palate, congenital 750.26
Flail
  chest 807.4
    newborn 767.3
  joint (paralytic) 718.80
    ankle 718.87
    elbow 718.82
    foot 718.87
    hand 718.84
    hip 718.85
    knee 718.86
    multiple sites 718.89
    pelvic region 718.85
    shoulder (region) 718.81
    specified site NEC 718.88
    wrist 718.83
Flajani (-Basedow) syndrome or disease
  (exophthalmic goiter) 242.0 ☑
Flap, liver 572.8
Flare, anterior chamber (aqueous) (eye)
  364.04
Flashback phenomena (drug) (hallucinogenic) 292.89
Flat
  chamber (anterior) (eye) 360.34
  chest, congenital 754.89
  electroencephalogram (EEG) 348.8
  foot (acquired) (fixed type) (painful)
    (postural) (spastic) 734
    congenital 754.61
      rocker bottom 754.61
      vertical talus 754.61
    rachitic 268.1
    rocker bottom (congenital) 754.61
    vertical talus, congenital 754.61
  organ or site, congenital NEC — *see*
    Anomaly, specified type NEC
  pelvis 738.6
    with disproportion (fetopelvic)
      653.2 ☑
      affecting fetus or newborn 763.1
      causing obstructed labor
        660.1 ☑
        affecting fetus or newborn
          763.1
    congenital 755.69
Flatau-Schilder disease 341.1
Flattening
  head, femur 736.39
  hip 736.39
  lip (congenital) 744.89
  nose (congenital) 754.0
    acquired 738.0
Flatulence 787.3
Flatus 787.3
  vaginalis 629.89 ▲
Flax dressers' disease 504
Flea bite — *see* Injury, superficial, by
  site
Fleischer (-Kayser) ring (corneal pigmentation) 275.1 *[371.14]*
Fleischner's disease 732.3
Fleshy mole 631
Flexibilitas cerea — *see also* Catalepsy
  300.11
Flexion
  cervix ▶— *see* Flexion, uterus◀
  contracture, joint (*see also* Contraction, joint) 718.4 ☑
  deformity, joint (*see also* Contraction, joint) 736.9 ▲
  hip, congenital (*see also* Subluxation, congenital, hip) 754.32
  uterus (*see also* Malposition, uterus)
    621.6
Flexner's
  bacillus 004.1
  diarrhea (ulcerative) 004.1
  dysentery 004.1

Flexner-Boyd dysentery 004.2
Flexure — *see* condition
Floater, vitreous 379.24
Floating
  cartilage (joint) (*see also* Disorder,
    cartilage, articular) 718.0 ☑
    knee 717.6
  gallbladder (congenital) 751.69
  kidney 593.0
    congenital 753.3
  liver (congenital) 751.69
  rib 756.3
  spleen 289.59
Flooding 626.2
Floor — *see* condition
Floppy
  infant NEC 781.99
  valve syndrome (mitral) 424.0
Flu — *see also* Influenza
  gastric NEC 008.8
Fluctuating blood pressure 796.4
Fluid
  abdomen 789.5
  chest (*see also* Pleurisy, with effusion)
    511.9
  heart (*see also* Failure, heart) 428.0
  joint (*see also* Effusion, joint) 719.0 ☑
  loss (acute) 276.50
    with
      hypernatremia 276.0
      hyponatremia 276.1
  lung (*see also* Edema, lung)
    encysted 511.8
  peritoneal cavity 789.5
  pleural cavity (*see also* Pleurisy, with
    effusion) 511.9
  retention 276.6
Flukes NEC — *see also* Infestation, fluke
  121.9
  blood NEC (*see also* Infestation,
    Schistosoma) 120.9
  liver 121.3
Fluor (albus) (vaginalis) 623.5
  trichomonal (Trichomonas vaginalis)
    131.00
Fluorosis (dental) (chronic) 520.3
Flushing 782.62
  menopausal 627.2
Flush syndrome 259.2
Flutter
  atrial or auricular 427.32
  heart (ventricular) 427.42
    atrial 427.32
  impure 427.32
  postoperative 997.1
  ventricular 427.42
Flux (bloody) (serosanguineous) 009.0
Focal — *see* condition
Fochier's abscess — *see* Abscess, by site
Focus, Assmann's — *see also* Tuberculosis 011.0 ☑
Fogo selvagem 694.4
Foix-Alajouanine syndrome 336.1 ▲
Folds, anomalous — *see also* Anomaly,
  specified type NEC
  Bowman's membrane 371.31
  Descemet's membrane 371.32
  epicanthic 743.63
  heart 746.89
  posterior segment of eye, congenital
    743.54
Folie à deux 297.3
Follicle
  cervix (nabothian) (ruptured) 616.0
  graafian, ruptured, with hemorrhage
    620.0
  nabothian 616.0
Folliclis (primary) — *see also* Tuberculosis 017.0 ☑
Follicular — *see also* condition
  cyst (atretic) 620.0
Folliculitis 704.8
  abscedens et suffodiens 704.8
  decalvans 704.09
  gonorrheal (acute) 098.0

Folliculitis — *continued*
  gonorrheal — *continued*
    chronic or duration of 2 months or
      more 098.2
  keloid, keloidalis 706.1
  pustular 704.8
  ulerythematosa reticulata 701.8
Folliculosis, conjunctival 372.02
Følling's disease (phenylketonuria)
  270.1
Follow-up (examination) (routine) (following) V67.9
  cancer chemotherapy V67.2
  chemotherapy V67.2
  fracture V67.4
  high-risk medication V67.51
  injury NEC V67.59
  postpartum
    immediately after delivery V24.0
    routine V24.2
  psychiatric V67.3
  psychotherapy V67.3
  radiotherapy V67.1
  specified condition NEC V67.59
  specified surgery NEC V67.09
  surgery V67.00
    vaginal pap smear V67.01
  treatment V67.9
    combined NEC V67.6
    fracture V67.4
    involving high-risk medication NEC
      V67.51
    mental disorder V67.3
    specified NEC V67.59
Fong's syndrome (hereditary osteoonychodysplasia) 756.89
Food
  allergy 693.1
  anaphylactic shock — *see* Anaphylactic shock, due to, food
  asphyxia (from aspiration or inhalation) (*see also* Asphyxia, food)
    933.1
  choked on (*see also* Asphyxia, food)
    933.1
  deprivation 994.2
    specified kind of food NEC 269.8
  intoxication (*see also* Poisoning, food)
    005.9
  lack of 994.2
  poisoning (*see also* Poisoning, food)
    005.9
  refusal or rejection NEC 307.59
  strangulation or suffocation (*see also*
    Asphyxia, food) 933.1
  toxemia (*see also* Poisoning, food)
    005.9
Foot — *see also* condition
  and mouth disease 078.4
  process disease 581.3
Foramen ovale (nonclosure) (patent)
  (persistent) 745.5
Forbes-Albright syndrome (nonpuerperal amenorrhea and lactation associated with pituitary tumor) 253.1
Forbes'(glycogen storage) disease
  271.0
Forced birth or delivery NEC 669.8 ☑
  affecting fetus or newborn NEC
    763.89
Forceps
  delivery NEC 669.5 ☑
    affecting fetus or newborn 763.2
Fordyce's disease (ectopic sebaceous
  glands) (mouth) 750.26
Fordyce-Fox disease (apocrine miliaria)
  705.82
Forearm — *see* condition
Foreign body

> *Note — For foreign body with open
> wound, or other injury, see Wound,
> open, or the type of injury specified.*

  accidentally left during a procedure
    998.4
  anterior chamber (eye) 871.6
    magnetic 871.5

Foreign body — *continued*
  anterior chamber — *continued*
    magnetic — *continued*
      retained or old 360.51
      retained or old 360.61
  ciliary body (eye) 871.6
    magnetic 871.5
      retained or old 360.52
      retained or old 360.62
  entering through orifice (current) (old)
    accessory sinus 932
    air passage (upper) 933.0
      lower 934.8
    alimentary canal 938
    alveolar process 935.0
    antrum (Highmore) 932
    anus 937
    appendix 936
    asphyxia due to (*see also* Asphyxia,
      food) 933.1
    auditory canal 931
    auricle 931
    bladder 939.0
    bronchioles 934.8
    bronchus (main) 934.1
    buccal cavity 935.0
    canthus (inner) 930.1
    cecum 936
    cervix (canal) uterine 939.1
    coil, ileocecal 936
    colon 936
    conjunctiva 930.1
    conjunctival sac 930.1
    cornea 930.0
    digestive organ or tract NEC 938
    duodenum 936
    ear (external) 931
    esophagus 935.1
    eye (external) 930.9
      combined sites 930.8
      intraocular — *see* Foreign body,
        by site
      specified site NEC 930.8
    eyeball 930.8
      intraocular — *see* Foreign body,
        intraocular
    eyelid 930.1
      retained or old 374.86
    frontal sinus 932
    gastrointestinal tract 938
    genitourinary tract 939.9
    globe 930.8
      penetrating 871.6
        magnetic 871.5
          retained or old 360.50
          retained or old 360.60
    gum 935.0
    Highmore's antrum 932
    hypopharynx 933.0
    ileocecal coil 936
    ileum 936
    inspiration (of) 933.1
    intestine (large) (small) 936
    lacrimal apparatus, duct, gland, or
      sac 930.2
    larynx 933.1
    lung 934.8
    maxillary sinus 932
    mouth 935.0
    nasal sinus 932
    nasopharynx 933.0
    nose (passage) 932
    nostril 932
    oral cavity 935.0
    palate 935.0
    penis 939.3
    pharynx 933.0
    pyriform sinus 933.0
    rectosigmoid 937
      junction 937
    rectum 937
    respiratory tract 934.9
      specified part NEC 934.8
    sclera 930.1
    sinus 932
      accessory 932

☑ Additional Digit Required — Refer to the Tabular List for Digit Selection   ▽ Subterms under main terms may continue to next column or page

122 — Volume 2 • October 2006   ▶◀ Revised Text   ● New Line   ▲ Revised Code   *2007 ICD-9-CM*

Foreign body — *continued*
  entering through orifice — *contin-ued*
    sinus — *continued*
      frontal 932
      maxillary 932
      nasal 932
      pyriform 933.0
    small intestine 936
    stomach (hairball) 935.2
    suffocation by (*see also* Asphyxia, food) 933.1
    swallowed 938
      tongue 933.0
    tear ducts or glands 930.2
    throat 933.0
    tongue 935.0
      swallowed 933.0
    tonsil, tonsillar 933.0
      fossa 933.0
    trachea 934.0
    ureter 939.0
    urethra 939.0
    uterus (any part) 939.1
    vagina 939.2
    vulva 939.2
    wind pipe 934.0
  granuloma (old) 728.82
    bone 733.99
    in operative wound (inadvertently left) 998.4
      due to surgical material inten-tionally left — *see* Compli-cations, due to (presence of) any device, implant, or graft classified to 996.0–996.5 NEC
    muscle 728.82
    skin 709.4
    soft tissue 709.4
    subcutaneous tissue 709.4
  in
    bone (residual) 733.99
    open wound — *see* Wound, open, by site complicated
    soft tissue (residual) 729.6
  inadvertently left in operation wound (causing adhesions, obstruction, or perforation) 998.4
  ingestion, ingested NEC 938
  inhalation or inspiration (*see also* As-phyxia, food) 933.1
  internal organ, not entering through an orifice — *see* Injury, internal, by site, with open wound
  intraocular (nonmagnetic) 871.6
    combined sites 871.6
      magnetic 871.5
        retained or old 360.59
      retained or old 360.69
    magnetic 871.5
      retained or old 360.50
    retained or old 360.60
    specified site NEC 871.6
      magnetic 871.5
        retained or old 360.59
      retained or old 360.69
    iris (nonmagnetic) 871.6
      magnetic 871.5
        retained or old 360.52
      retained or old 360.62
    lens (nonmagnetic) 871.6
      magnetic 871.5
        retained or old 360.53
      retained or old 360.63
  lid, eye 930.1
  ocular muscle 870.4
    retained or old 376.6
  old or residual
    bone 733.99
    eyelid 374.86
    middle ear 385.83
    muscle 729.6
      ocular 376.6
    retrobulbar 376.6
    skin 729.6

Foreign body — *continued*
  old or residual — *continued*
    skin — *continued*
      with granuloma 709.4
    soft tissue 729.6
      with granuloma 709.4
    subcutaneous tissue 729.6
      with granuloma 709.4
  operation wound, left accidentally 998.4
  orbit 870.4
    retained or old 376.6
  posterior wall, eye 871.6
    magnetic 871.5
      retained or old 360.55
    retained or old 360.65
  respiratory tree 934.9
    specified site NEC 934.8
  retained (old) (nonmagnetic) (in)
    anterior chamber (eye) 360.61
      magnetic 360.51
    ciliary body 360.62
      magnetic 360.52
    eyelid 374.86
    globe 360.60
      magnetic 360.50
    intraocular 360.60
      magnetic 360.50
      specified site NEC 360.69
        magnetic 360.59
    iris 360.62
      magnetic 360.52
    lens 360.63
      magnetic 360.53
    muscle 729.6
    orbit 376.6
    posterior wall of globe 360.65
      magnetic 360.55
    retina 360.65
      magnetic 360.55
    retrobulbar 376.6
    skin 729.6
      with granuloma 709.4
    soft tissue 729.6
      with granuloma 709.4
    subcutaneous tissue 729.6
      with granuloma 709.4
    vitreous 360.64
      magnetic 360.54
  retina 871.6
    magnetic 871.5
      retained or old 360.55
    retained or old 360.65
  superficial, without major open wound (*see also* Injury, superficial, by site) 919.6
  swallowed NEC 938
  vitreous (humor) 871.6
    magnetic 871.5
      retained or old 360.54
    retained or old 360.64

Forking, aqueduct of Sylvius 742.3
  with spina bifida (*see also* Spina bifi-da) 741.0 ☑
Formation
  bone in scar tissue (skin) 709.3
  connective tissue in vitreous 379.25
  Elschnig pearls (postcataract extrac-tion) 366.51
  hyaline in cornea 371.49
  sequestrum in bone (due to infection) (*see also* Osteomyelitis) 730.1 ☑
  valve
    colon, congenital 751.5
    ureter (congenital) 753.29
Formication 782.0
Fort Bragg fever 100.89
Fossa — *see also* condition
  pyriform — *see* condition
Foster-Kennedy syndrome 377.04
Fothergill's
  disease, meaning scarlatina anginosa 034.1
  neuralgia (*see also* Neuralgia, trigemi-nal) 350.1
Foul breath 784.99 ▲

Found dead (cause unknown) 798.9
Foundling V20.0
Fournier's disease (idiopathic gangrene) 608.83
Fourth
  cranial nerve — *see* condition
  disease 057.8
  molar 520.1
Foville's syndrome 344.89
Fox's
  disease (apocrine miliaria) 705.82
  impetigo (contagiosa) 684
Fox-Fordyce disease (apocrine miliaria) 705.82
Fracture (abduction) (adduction) (avul-sion) (compression) (crush) (disloca-tion) (oblique) (separation) (closed) 829.0

> *Note* — *For fracture of any of the follow-ing sites with fracture of other bones — see Fracture, multiple.*
>
> *"Closed" includes the following descrip-tions of fractures, with or without de-layed healing, unless they are specified as open or compound:*
>
> | | |
> |---|---|
> | comminuted | linear |
> | depressed | simple |
> | elevated | slipped epiph-ysis |
> | fissured | spiral |
> | greenstick | unspecified |
> | impacted | |
>
> *"Open" includes the following descrip-tions of fractures, with or without de-layed healing:*
>
> | | |
> |---|---|
> | compound | puncture |
> | infected | with foreign body |
> | missile | |
>
> *For late effect of fracture, see Late, ef-fect, fracture, by site.*

  with
    internal injuries in same region (conditions classifiable to 860–869) (*see also* Injury, internal, by site)
    pelvic region — *see* Fracture, pelvis
  acetabulum (with visceral injury) (closed) 808.0
    open 808.1
  acromion (process) (closed) 811.01
    open 811.11
  alveolus (closed) 802.8
    open 802.9
  ankle (malleolus) (closed) 824.8
    bimalleolar (Dupuytren's) (Pott's) 824.4
      open 824.5
    bone 825.21
      open 825.31
    lateral malleolus only (fibular) 824.2
      open 824.3
    medial malleolus only (tibial) 824.0
      open 824.1
    open 824.9
    pathologic 733.16
    talus 825.21
      open 825.31
    trimalleolar 824.6
      open 824.7
  antrum — *see* Fracture, skull, base
  arm (closed) 818.0
    and leg(s) (any bones) 828.0
      open 828.1
    both (any bones) (with rib(s)) (with sternum) 819.0
      open 819.1
    lower 813.80
      open 813.90

Fracture — *continued*
  arm — *continued*
    open 818.1
    upper — *see* Fracture, humerus
  astragalus (closed) 825.21
    open 825.31
  atlas — *see* Fracture, vertebra, cervi-cal, first
  axis — *see* Fracture, vertebra, cervi-cal, second
  back — *see* Fracture, vertebra, by site
  Barton's — *see* Fracture, radius, lower end
  basal (skull) — *see* Fracture, skull, base
  Bennett's (closed) 815.01
    open 815.11
  bimalleolar (closed) 824.4
    open 824.5
  bone (closed) NEC 829.0
    birth injury NEC 767.3
    open 829.1
    pathologic NEC (*see also* Fracture, pathologic) 733.10
    stress NEC (*see also* Fracture, stress) 733.95
  boot top — *see* Fracture, fibula
  boxers' — *see* Fracture, metacarpal bone(s)
  breast bone — *see* Fracture, sternum
  bucket handle (semilunar cartilage) — *see* Tear, meniscus
  bursting — *see* Fracture, phalanx, hand, distal
  calcaneus (closed) 825.0
    open 825.1
  capitate (bone) (closed) 814.07
    open 814.17
  capitellum (humerus) (closed) 812.49
    open 812.59
  carpal bone(s) (wrist NEC) (closed) 814.00
    open 814.10
    specified site NEC 814.09
      open 814.19
  cartilage, knee (semilunar) — *see* Tear, meniscus
  cervical — *see* Fracture, vertebra, cervical
  chauffeur's — *see* Fracture, ulna, lower end
  chisel — *see* Fracture, radius, upper end
  clavicle (interligamentous part) (closed) 810.00
    acromial end 810.03
      open 810.13
    due to birth trauma 767.2
    open 810.10
    shaft (middle third) 810.02
      open 810.12
    sternal end 810.01
      open 810.11
  clayshovelers' — *see* Fracture, verte-bra, cervical
  coccyx (*see also* Fracture, vertebra, coccyx)
    complicating delivery 665.6 ☑
  collar bone — *see* Fracture, clavicle
  Colles' (reversed) (closed) 813.41
    open 813.51
  comminuted — *see* Fracture, by site
  compression (*see also* Fracture, by site)
    nontraumatic — *see* Fracture, pathologic
  congenital 756.9
  coracoid process (closed) 811.02
    open 811.12
  coronoid process (ulna) (closed) 813.02
    mandible (closed) 802.23
      open 802.33
    open 813.12
  corpus cavernosum penis 959.13

☑ Additional Digit Required — Refer to the Tabular List for Digit Selection   ▽ Subterms under main terms may continue to next column or page

2007 ICD-9-CM   ▶◀ Revised Text   ● New Line   ▲ Revised Code   October 2006 • Volume 2 — 123

Fracture — continued

costochondral junction — see Fracture, rib

costosternal junction — see Fracture, rib

cranium — see Fracture, skull, by site

cricoid cartilage (closed) 807.5
  open 807.6

cuboid (ankle) (closed) 825.23
  open 825.33

cuneiform
  foot (closed) 825.24
    open 825.34
  wrist (closed) 814.03
    open 814.13

dental restorative material ●
  with loss of material 525.64 ●
  without loss of material 525.63 ●

due to
  birth injury — see Birth injury, fracture
  gunshot — see Fracture, by site, open
  neoplasm — see Fracture, pathologic
  osteoporosis — see Fracture, pathologic

Dupuytren's (ankle) (fibula) (closed) 824.4
  open 824.5
  radius 813.42
    open 813.52

Duverney's — see Fracture, ilium

elbow (see also Fracture, humerus, lower end)
  olecranon (process) (closed) 813.01
    open 813.11
  supracondylar (closed) 812.41
    open 812.51

ethmoid (bone) (sinus) — see Fracture, skull, base

face bone(s) (closed) NEC 802.8
  with
    other bone(s) — see Fracture, multiple, skull
    skull (see also Fracture, skull)
      involving other bones — see Fracture, multiple, skull
  open 802.9

fatigue — see Fracture, march

femur, femoral (closed) 821.00
  cervicotrochanteric 820.03
    open 820.13
  condyles, epicondyles 821.21
    open 821.31
  distal end — see Fracture, femur, lower end
  epiphysis (separation)
    capital 820.01
      open 820.11
    head 820.01
      open 820.11
    lower 821.22
      open 821.32
    trochanteric 820.01
      open 820.11
    upper 820.01
      open 820.11
  head 820.09
    open 820.19
  lower end or extremity (distal end) (closed) 821.20
    condyles, epicondyles 821.21
      open 821.31
    epiphysis (separation) 821.22
      open 821.32
    multiple sites 821.29
      open 821.39
    open 821.30
    specified site NEC 821.29
      open 821.39
    supracondylar 821.23
      open 821.33
    T-shaped 821.21
      open 821.31

Fracture — continued

femur, femoral — continued
  neck (closed) 820.8
    base (cervicotrochanteric) 820.03
      open 820.13
    extracapsular 820.20
      open 820.30
    intertrochanteric (section) 820.21
      open 820.31
    intracapsular 820.00
      open 820.10
    intratrochanteric 820.21
      open 820.31
    midcervical 820.02
      open 820.12
    open 820.9
    pathologic 733.14
      specified part NEC 733.15
    specified site NEC 820.09
      open 820.19
    transcervical 820.02
      open 820.12
    transtrochanteric 820.20
      open 820.30
  open 821.10
  pathologic 733.14
    specified part NEC 733.15
  peritrochanteric (section) 820.20
    open 820.30
  shaft (lower third) (middle third) (upper third) 821.01
    open 821.11
  subcapital 820.09
    open 820.19
  subtrochanteric (region) (section) 820.22
    open 820.32
  supracondylar 821.23
    open 821.33
  transepiphyseal 820.01
    open 820.11
  trochanter (greater) (lesser) (see also Fracture, femur, neck, by site) 820.20
    open 820.30
  T-shaped, into knee joint 821.21
    open 821.31
  upper end 820.8
    open 820.9

fibula (closed) 823.81
  with tibia 823.82
    open 823.92
  distal end 824.8
    open 824.9
  epiphysis
    lower 824.8
      open 824.9
    upper — see Fracture, fibula, upper end
  head — see Fracture, fibula, upper end
  involving ankle 824.2
    open 824.3
  lower end or extremity 824.8
    open 824.9
  malleolus (external) (lateral) 824.2
    open 824.3
  open NEC 823.91
  pathologic 733.16
  proximal end — see Fracture, fibula, upper end
  shaft 823.21
    with tibia 823.22
      open 823.32
    open 823.31
  stress 733.93
  torus 823.41
    with tibia 823.42
  upper end or extremity (epiphysis) (head) (proximal end) (styloid) 823.01
    with tibia 823.02
      open 823.12
    open 823.11

Fracture — continued

finger(s), of one hand (closed) (see also Fracture, phalanx, hand) 816.00
  with
    metacarpal bone(s), of same hand 817.0
      open 817.1
    thumb of same hand 816.03
      open 816.13
  open 816.10

foot, except toe(s) alone (closed) 825.20
  open 825.30

forearm (closed) NEC 813.80
  lower end (distal end) (lower epiphysis) 813.40
    open 813.50
  open 813.90
  shaft 813.20
    open 813.30
  upper end (proximal end) (upper epiphysis) 813.00
    open 813.10

fossa, anterior, middle, or posterior — see Fracture, skull, base

Fracture (abduction) (adduction) (avulsion) (compression) (crush) (dislocation) (oblique) (separation) (closed) 829.0

frontal (bone) (see also Fracture, skull, vault)
  sinus — see Fracture, skull, base

Galeazzi's — see Fracture, radius, lower end

glenoid (cavity) (fossa) (scapula) (closed) 811.03
  open 811.13

Gosselin's — see Fracture, ankle

greenstick — see Fracture, by site

grenade-throwers' — see Fracture, humerus, shaft

gutter — see Fracture, skull, vault

hamate (closed) 814.08
  open 814.18

hand, one (closed) 815.00
  carpals 814.00
    open 814.10
    specified site NEC 814.09
      open 814.19
  metacarpals 815.00
    open 815.10
  multiple, bones of one hand 817.0
    open 817.1
  open 815.10
  phalanges (see also Fracture, phalanx, hand) 816.00
    open 816.10

healing
  aftercare (see also Aftercare, fracture) V54.89
  change of cast V54.89
  complications — see condition
  convalescence V66.4
  removal of
    cast V54.89
    fixation device
      external V54.89
      internal V54.01

heel bone (closed) 825.0
  open 825.1

hip (closed) (see also Fracture, femur, neck) 820.8
  open 820.9
  pathologic 733.14

humerus (closed) 812.20
  anatomical neck 812.02
    open 812.12
  articular process (see also Fracture humerus, condyle(s)) 812.44
    open 812.54
  capitellum 812.49
    open 812.59
  condyle(s) 812.44
    lateral (external) 812.42
      open 812.52

Fracture — continued

humerus — continued
  condyle(s) — continued
    medial (internal epicondyle) 812.43
      open 812.53
      open 812.54
  distal end — see Fracture, humerus, lower end
  epiphysis
    lower (see also Fracture, humerus, condyle(s)) 812.44
      open 812.54
    upper 812.09
      open 812.19
  external condyle 812.42
    open 812.52
  great tuberosity 812.03
    open 812.13
  head 812.09
    open 812.19
  internal epicondyle 812.43
    open 812.53
  lesser tuberosity 812.09
    open 812.19
  lower end or extremity (distal end) (see also Fracture, humerus, by site) 812.40
    multiple sites NEC 812.49
      open 812.59
    open 812.50
    specified site NEC 812.49
      open 812.59
  neck 812.01
    open 812.11
    open 812.30
  pathologic 733.11
  proximal end — see Fracture, humerus, upper end
  shaft 812.21
    open 812.31
  supracondylar 812.41
    open 812.51
  surgical neck 812.01
    open 812.11
  trochlea 812.49
    open 812.59
  T-shaped 812.44
    open 812.54
  tuberosity — see Fracture, humerus, upper end
  upper end or extremity (proximal end) (see also Fracture, humerus, by site) 812.00
    open 812.10
    specified site NEC 812.09
      open 812.19

hyoid bone (closed) 807.5
  open 807.6

hyperextension — see Fracture, radius, lower end

ilium (with visceral injury) (closed) 808.41
  open 808.51

impaction, impacted — see Fracture, by site

incus — see Fracture, skull, base

innominate bone (with visceral injury) (closed) 808.49
  open 808.59

instep, of one foot (closed) 825.20
  with toe(s) of same foot 827.0
    open 827.1
  open 825.30

internal
  ear — see Fracture, skull, base
  semilunar cartilage, knee — see Tear, meniscus, medial

intertrochanteric — see Fracture, femur, neck, intertrochanteric

ischium (with visceral injury) (closed) 808.42
  open 808.52

jaw (bone) (lower) (closed) (see also Fracture, mandible) 802.20

Fracture — *continued*
jaw (*see also* Fracture, mandible) — *continued*
  angle 802.25
    open 802.35
    open 802.30
  upper — *see* Fracture, maxilla
knee
  cap (closed) 822.0
    open 822.1
  cartilage (semilunar) — *see* Tear, meniscus
  labyrinth (osseous) — *see* Fracture, skull, base
  larynx (closed) 807.5
    open 807.6
late effect — *see* Late, effects (of), fracture
Le Fort's — *see* Fracture, maxilla
leg (closed) 827.0
  with rib(s) or sternum 828.0
    open 828.1
  both (any bones) 828.0
    open 828.1
  lower — *see* Fracture, tibia
    open 827.1
  upper — *see* Fracture, femur
limb
  lower (multiple) (closed) NEC 827.0
    open 827.1
  upper (multiple) (closed) NEC 818.0
    open 818.1
long bones, due to birth trauma — *see* Birth injury, fracture
lower end or extremity (anterior lip) (posterior) 824.8
  open 824.9
lumbar — *see* Fracture, vertebra, lumbar
lunate bone (closed) 814.02
  open 814.12
malar bone (closed) 802.4
  open 802.5
Malgaigne's (closed) 808.43
  open 808.53
malleolus (closed) 824.8
  bimalleolar 824.4
    open 824.5
  lateral 824.2
    and medial (*see also* Fracture, malleolus, bimalleolar)
      with lip of tibia — *see* Fracture, malleolus, trimalleolar
      open 824.3
  medial (closed) 824.0
    and lateral (*see also* Fracture, malleolus, bimalleolar)
      with lip of tibia — *see* Fracture, malleolus, trimalleolar
      open 824.1
    open 824.9
  trimalleolar (closed) 824.6
    open 824.7
malleus — *see* Fracture, skull, base
malunion 733.81
mandible (closed) 802.20
  angle 802.25
    open 802.35
  body 802.28
    alveolar border 802.27
      open 802.37
    open 802.38
    symphysis 802.26
      open 802.36
  condylar process 802.21
    open 802.31
  coronoid process 802.23
    open 802.33
  multiple sites 802.29
    open 802.39
  open 802.30
  ramus NEC 802.24
    open 802.34
  subcondylar 802.22

Fracture — *continued*
mandible — *continued*
  subcondylar — *continued*
    open 802.32
manubrium — *see* Fracture, sternum
march 733.95
  fibula 733.93
  metatarsals 733.94
  tibia 733.93
maxilla, maxillary (superior) (upper jaw) (closed) 802.4
  inferior — *see* Fracture, mandible
  open 802.5
meniscus, knee — *see* Tear, meniscus
metacarpus, metacarpal (bone(s)), of one hand (closed) 815.00
  with phalanx, phalanges, hand (finger(s)) (thumb) of same hand 817.0
    open 817.1
  base 815.02
    first metacarpal 815.01
      open 815.11
      open 815.12
    thumb 815.01
      open 815.11
  multiple sites 815.09
    open 815.19
  neck 815.04
    open 815.14
  open 815.10
  shaft 815.03
    open 815.13
metatarsus, metatarsal (bone(s)), of one foot (closed) 825.25
  with tarsal bone(s) 825.29
    open 825.39
  open 825.35
Monteggia's (closed) 813.03
  open 813.13
Moore's — *see* Fracture, radius, lower end
multangular bone (closed)
  larger 814.05
    open 814.15
  smaller 814.06
    open 814.16
multiple (closed) 829.0

Note — Multiple fractures of sites classifiable to the same three- or four-digit category are coded to that category, except for sites classifiable to 810–818 or 820–827 in different limbs.

Multiple fractures of sites classifiable to different fourth-digit subdivisions within the same three-digit category should be dealt with according to coding rules.

Multiple fractures of sites classifiable to different three-digit categories (identifiable from the listing under "Fracture"), and of sites classifiable to 810–818 or 820–827 in different limbs should be coded according to the following list, which should be referred to in the following priority order: skull or face bones, pelvis or vertebral column, legs, arms.

arm (multiple bones in same arm except in hand alone) (sites classifiable to 810–817 with sites classifiable to a different three-digit category in 810–817 in same arm) (closed) 818.0
  open 818.1
arms, both or arm(s) with rib(s) or sternum (sites classifiable to 810–818 with sites classifiable to same range of categories in other limb or to 807) (closed) 819.0
  open 819.1
bones of trunk NEC (closed) 809.0
  open 809.1

Fracture — *continued*
multiple — *continued*
  hand, metacarpal bone(s) with phalanx or phalanges of same hand (sites classifiable to 815 with sites classifiable to 816 in same hand) (closed) 817.0
    open 817.1
  leg (multiple bones in same leg) (sites classifiable to 820–826 with sites classifiable to a different three-digit category in that range in same leg) (closed) 827.0
    open 827.1
  legs, both or leg(s) with arm(s), rib(s), or sternum (sites classifiable to 820–827 with sites classifiable to same range of categories in other leg or to 807 or 810–819) (closed) 828.0
    open 828.1
  open 829.1
  pelvis with other bones except skull or face bones (sites classifiable to 808 with sites classifiable to 805–807 or 810–829) (closed) 809.0
    open 809.1
  skull, specified or unspecified bones, or face bone(s) with any other bone(s) (sites classifiable to 800–803 with sites classifiable to 805–829) (closed) 804.0 ☑

Note — Use the following fifth-digit subclassification with categories 800, 801, 803, and 804:

0   unspecified state of consciousness

1   with no loss of consciousness

2   with brief [less than one hour] loss of consciousness

3   with moderate [1–24 hours] loss of consciousness

4   with prolonged [more than 24 hours] loss of consciousness and return to pre-existing conscious level

5   with prolonged [more than 24 hours] loss of consciousness, without return to pre-existing conscious level

Use fifth-digit 5 to designate when a patient is unconscious and dies before regaining consciousness, regardless of the duration of the loss of consciousness

6   with loss of consciousness of unspecified duration

9   with concussion, unspecified

with
  contusion, cerebral 804.1 ☑
  epidural hemorrhage 804.2 ☑
  extradural hemorrhage 804.2 ☑
  hemorrhage (intracranial) NEC 804.3 ☑
  intracranial injury NEC 804.4 ☑
  laceration, cerebral 804.1 ☑
  subarachnoid hemorrhage 804.2 ☑
  subdural hemorrhage 804.2 ☑
open 804.5 ☑
  with
    contusion, cerebral 804.6 ☑

Fracture — *continued*
multiple — *continued*
  skull, specified or unspecified bones, or face bone(s) with any other bone(s) — *continued*
    open — *continued*
      with — *continued*
        epidural hemorrhage 804.7 ☑
        extradural hemorrhage 804.7 ☑
        hemorrhage (intracranial) NEC 804.8 ☑
        intracranial injury NEC 804.9 ☑
        laceration, cerebral 804.6 ☑
        subarachnoid hemorrhage 804.7 ☑
        subdural hemorrhage 804.7 ☑
  vertebral column with other bones, except skull or face bones (sites classifiable to 805 or 806 with sites classifiable to 807–808 or 810–829) (closed) 809.0
    open 809.1
nasal (bone(s)) (closed) 802.0
  open 802.1
  sinus — *see* Fracture, skull, base
navicular
  carpal (wrist) (closed) 814.01
    open 814.11
  tarsal (ankle) (closed) 825.22
    open 825.32
neck — *see* Fracture, vertebra, cervical
neural arch — *see* Fracture, vertebra, by site
nonunion 733.82
nose, nasal, (bone) (septum) (closed) 802.0
  open 802.1
occiput — *see* Fracture, skull, base
odontoid process — *see* Fracture, vertebra, cervical
olecranon (process) (ulna) (closed) 813.01
  open 813.11
open 829.1
orbit, orbital (bone) (region) (closed) 802.8
  floor (blow-out) 802.6
    open 802.7
  open 802.9
  roof — *see* Fracture, skull, base
  specified part NEC 802.8
    open 802.9
os
  calcis (closed) 825.0
    open 825.1
  magnum (closed) 814.07
    open 814.17
  pubis (with visceral injury) (closed) 808.2
    open 808.3
  triquetrum (closed) 814.03
    open 814.13
osseous
  auditory meatus — *see* Fracture, skull, base
  labyrinth — *see* Fracture, skull, base
ossicles, auditory (incus) (malleus) (stapes) — *see* Fracture, skull, base
osteoporotic — *see* Fracture, pathologic
palate (closed) 802.8
  open 802.9
paratrooper — *see* Fracture, tibia, lower end
parietal bone — *see* Fracture, skull, vault

Fracture — Fracture

Fracture — *continued*
parry — *see* Fracture, Monteggia's
patella (closed) 822.0
  open 822.1
pathologic (cause unknown) 733.10
  ankle 733.16
  femur (neck) 733.14
    specified NEC 733.15
  fibula 733.16
  hip 733.14
  humerus 733.11
  radius (distal) 733.12
  specified site NEC 733.19
  tibia 733.16
  ulna 733.12
  vertebrae (collapse) 733.13
  wrist 733.12
pedicle (of vertebral arch) — *see*
    Fracture, vertebra, by site
pelvis, pelvic (bone(s)) (with visceral
    injury) (closed) 808.8
  multiple (with disruption of pelvic
    circle) 808.43
    open 808.53
  open 808.9
  rim (closed) 808.49
    open 808.59
peritrochanteric (closed) 820.20
  open 820.30
phalanx, phalanges, of one
  foot (closed) 826.0
    with bone(s) of same lower limb
      827.0
      open 827.1
    open 826.1
  hand (closed) 816.00
    with metacarpal bone(s) of same
      hand 817.0
      open 817.1
    distal 816.02
      open 816.12
    middle 816.01
      open 816.11
    multiple sites NEC 816.03
      open 816.13
    open 816.10
    proximal 816.01
      open 816.11
pisiform (closed) 814.04
  open 814.14
pond — *see* Fracture, skull, vault
Pott's (closed) 824.4
  open 824.5
prosthetic device, internal — *see*
    Complications, mechanical
pubis (with visceral injury) (closed)
    808.2
  open 808.3
Quervain's (closed) 814.01
  open 814.11
radius (alone) (closed) 813.81
  with ulna NEC 813.83
    open 813.93
  distal end — *see* Fracture, radius,
    lower end
  epiphysis
    lower — *see* Fracture, radius,
      lower end
    upper — *see* Fracture, radius,
      upper end
  head — *see* Fracture, radius, upper
    end
  lower end or extremity (distal end)
    (lower epiphysis) 813.42
    with ulna (lower end) 813.44
      open 813.54
    open 813.52
    torus 813.45
  neck — *see* Fracture, radius, upper
    end
  open NEC 813.91
  pathologic 733.12
  proximal end — *see* Fracture, ra-
    dius, upper end
  shaft (closed) 813.21
    with ulna (shaft) 813.23

Fracture — *continued*
radius — *continued*
  shaft — *continued*
    with ulna — *continued*
      open 813.33
    open 813.31
  upper end 813.07
    with ulna (upper end) 813.08
      open 813.18
    epiphysis 813.05
      open 813.15
    head 813.05
      open 813.15
    multiple sites 813.07
      open 813.17
    neck 813.06
      open 813.16
    open 813.17
    specified site NEC 813.07
      open 813.17
  ramus
    inferior or superior (with visceral
      injury) (closed) 808.2
      open 808.3
    ischium — *see* Fracture, ischium
    mandible 802.24
      open 802.34
  rib(s) (closed) 807.0 ☑

*Note — Use the following fifth-digit
subclassification with categories
807.0–807.1:*

0   rib(s), unspecified

1   one rib

2   two ribs

3   three ribs

4   four ribs

5   five ribs

6   six ribs

7   seven ribs

8   eight or more ribs

9   multiple ribs, unspecified

    with flail chest (open) 807.4
    open 807.1 ☑
  root, tooth 873.63
    complicated 873.73
  sacrum — *see* Fracture, vertebra,
    sacrum
  scaphoid
    ankle (closed) 825.22
      open 825.32
    wrist (closed) 814.01
      open 814.11
  scapula (closed) 811.00
    acromial, acromion (process)
      811.01
      open 811.11
    body 811.09
      open 811.19
    coracoid process 811.02
      open 811.12
    glenoid (cavity) (fossa) 811.03
      open 811.13
    neck 811.03
      open 811.13
    open 811.10
  semilunar
    bone, wrist (closed) 814.02
      open 814.12
    cartilage (interior) (knee) — *see*
      Tear, meniscus
  sesamoid bone — *see* Fracture, by site
  Shepherd's (closed) 825.21
    open 825.31
  shoulder (*see also* Fracture, humerus,
    upper end)
    blade — *see* Fracture, scapula
  silverfork — *see* Fracture, radius,
    lower end
  sinus (ethmoid) (frontal) (maxillary)
    (nasal) (sphenoidal) — *see*
    Fracture, skull, base

Fracture — *continued*
Skillern's — *see* Fracture, radius,
    shaft
skull (multiple NEC) (with face bones)
    (closed) 803.0 ☑

*Note — Use the following fifth-digit
subclassification with categories 800,
801, 803, and 804:*

*0   unspecified state of conscious-
     ness*

1   with no loss of consciousness

*2   with brief [less than one hour]
     loss of consciousness*

*3   with moderate [1-24 hours] loss
     of consciousness*

*4   with prolonged [more than 24
     hours] loss of consciousness and
     return to pre-existing conscious
     level*

*5   with prolonged [more than 24
     hours] loss of consciousness,
     without return to pre-existing
     conscious level*

*Use fifth-digit 5 to designate when a
patient is unconscious and dies before
regaining consciousness, regardless of
the duration of the loss of consciousness*

*6   with loss of consciousness of un-
     specified duration*

9   with concussion, unspecified

    with
      contusion, cerebral 803.1 ☑
      epidural hemorrhage
        803.2 ☑
      extradural hemorrhage
        803.2 ☑
      hemorrhage (intracranial)
        NEC 803.3 ☑
      intracranial injury NEC
        803.4 ☑
      laceration, cerebral 803.1 ☑
      other bones — *see* Fracture,
        multiple, skull
      subarachnoid hemorrhage
        803.2 ☑
      subdural hemorrhage
        803.2 ☑
    base (antrum) (ethmoid bone) (fos-
      sa) (internal ear) (nasal si-
      nus) (occiput) (sphenoid)
      (temporal bone) (closed)
      801.0 ☑
      with
        contusion, cerebral
          801.1 ☑
        epidural hemorrhage
          801.2 ☑
        extradural hemorrhage
          801.2 ☑
        hemorrhage (intracranial)
          NEC 801.3 ☑
        intracranial injury NEC
          801.4 ☑
        laceration, cerebral
          801.1 ☑
        subarachnoid hemorrhage
          801.2 ☑
        subdural hemorrhage
          801.2 ☑
      open 801.5 ☑
        with
          contusion, cerebral
            801.6 ☑
          epidural hemorrhage
            801.7 ☑
          extradural hemorrhage
            801.7 ☑
          hemorrhage (intracra-
            nial) NEC
            801.8 ☑

Fracture — *continued*
skull — *continued*
  base — *continued*
    open — *continued*
      with — *continued*
        intracranial injury NEC
          801.9 ☑
        laceration, cerebral
          801.6 ☑
        subarachnoid hemor-
          rhage 801.7 ☑
        subdural hemorrhage
          801.7 ☑
    birth injury 767.3
    face bones — *see* Fracture, face
      bones
    open 803.5 ☑
      with
        contusion, cerebral
          803.6 ☑
        epidural hemorrhage
          803.7 ☑
        extradural hemorrhage
          803.7 ☑
        hemorrhage (intracranial)
          NEC 803.8 ☑
        intracranial injury NEC
          803.9 ☑
        laceration, cerebral
          803.6 ☑
        subarachnoid hemorrhage
          803.7 ☑
        subdural hemorrhage
          803.7 ☑
  vault (frontal bone) (parietal bone)
    (vertex) (closed) 800.0 ☑
    with
      contusion, cerebral
        800.1 ☑
      epidural hemorrhage
        800.2 ☑
      extradural hemorrhage
        800.2 ☑
      hemorrhage (intracranial)
        NEC 800.3 ☑
      intracranial injury NEC
        800.4 ☑
      laceration, cerebral
        800.1 ☑
      subarachnoid hemorrhage
        800.2 ☑
      subdural hemorrhage
        800.2 ☑
    open 800.5 ☑
      with
        contusion, cerebral
          800.6 ☑
        epidural hemorrhage
          800.7 ☑
        extradural hemorrhage
          800.7 ☑
        hemorrhage (intracra-
          nial) NEC
          800.8 ☑
        intracranial injury NEC
          800.9 ☑
        laceration, cerebral
          800.6 ☑
        subarachnoid hemor-
          rhage 800.7 ☑
        subdural hemorrhage
          800.7 ☑
  Smith's 813.41
    open 813.51
  sphenoid (bone) (sinus) — *see* Frac-
    ture, skull, base
  spine (*see also* Fracture, vertebra, by
    site due to birth trauma) 767.4
  spinous process — *see* Fracture, ver-
    tebra, by site
  spontaneous — *see* Fracture, patho-
    logic
  sprinters' — *see* Fracture, ilium
  stapes — *see* Fracture, skull, base

☑ Additional Digit Required — Refer to the Tabular List for Digit Selection   ▽ Subterms under main terms may continue to next column or page

126 — Volume 2   ▶◀ Revised Text   ● New Line   ▲ Revised Code   *2007 ICD-9-CM*

Fracture — *continued*
  stave (*see also* Fracture, metacarpus, metacarpal bone(s))
    spine — *see* Fracture, tibia, upper end
  sternum (closed) 807.2
    with flail chest (open) 807.4
    open 807.3
  Stieda's — *see* Fracture, femur, lower end
  stress 733.95
    fibula 733.93
    metatarsals 733.94
    specified site NEC 733.95
    tibia 733.93
  styloid process
    metacarpal (closed) 815.02
      open 815.12
    radius — *see* Fracture, radius, lower end
    temporal bone — *see* Fracture, skull, base
    ulna — *see* Fracture, ulna, lower end
  supracondylar, elbow 812.41
    open 812.51
  symphysis pubis (with visceral injury) (closed) 808.2
    open 808.3
  talus (ankle bone) (closed) 825.21
    open 825.31
  tarsus, tarsal bone(s) (with metatarsus) of one foot (closed) NEC 825.29
    open 825.39
  temporal bone (styloid) — *see* Fracture, skull, base
  tendon — *see* Sprain, by site
  thigh — *see* Fracture, femur, shaft
  thumb (and finger(s)) of one hand (closed) (*see also* Fracture, phalanx, hand) 816.00
    with metacarpal bone(s) of same hand 817.0
      open 817.1
    metacarpal(s) — *see* Fracture, metacarpus
    open 816.10
  thyroid cartilage (closed) 807.5
    open 807.6
  tibia (closed) 823.80
    with fibula 823.82
      open 823.92
    condyles — *see* Fracture, tibia, upper end
    distal end 824.8
      open 824.9
    epiphysis
      lower 824.8
        open 824.9
      upper — *see* Fracture, tibia, upper end
    head (involving knee joint) — *see* Fracture, tibia, upper end
    intercondyloid eminence — *see* Fracture, tibia, upper end
    involving ankle 824.0
      open 824.9
    lower end or extremity (anterior lip) (posterior lip) 824.8
      open 824.9
    malleolus (internal) (medial) 824.0
      open 824.1
    open NEC 823.90
    pathologic 733.16
    proximal end — *see* Fracture, tibia, upper end
    shaft 823.20
      with fibula 823.22
        open 823.32
      open 823.30
    spine — *see* Fracture, tibia, upper end
    stress 733.93
    torus 823.40
      with fibula 823.42

Fracture — *continued*
  tibia — *continued*
    tuberosity — *see* Fracture, tibia, upper end
    upper end or extremity (condyle) (epiphysis) (head) (spine) (proximal end) (tuberosity) 823.00
      with fibula 823.02
        open 823.12
      open 823.10
  toe(s), of one foot (closed) 826.0
    with bone(s) of same lower limb 827.0
      open 827.1
    open 826.1
  tooth (root) 873.63
    complicated 873.73
  torus
    fibula 823.41
      with tibia 823.42
    radius 813.45
    tibia 823.40
      with fibula 823.42
  trachea (closed) 807.5
    open 807.6
  transverse process — *see* Fracture, vertebra, by site
  trapezium (closed) 814.05
    open 814.15
  trapezoid bone (closed) 814.06
    open 814.16
  trimalleolar (closed) 824.6
    open 824.7
  triquetral (bone) (closed) 814.03
    open 814.13
  trochanter (greater) (lesser) (closed) (*see also* Fracture, femur, neck, by site) 820.20
    open 820.30
  trunk (bones) (closed) 809.0
    open 809.1
  tuberosity (external) — *see* Fracture, by site
  ulna (alone) (closed) 813.82
    with radius NEC 813.83
      open 813.93
    coronoid process (closed) 813.02
      open 813.12
    distal end — *see* Fracture, ulna, lower end
    epiphysis
      lower — *see* Fracture, ulna, lower end
      upper — *see* Fracture, ulna, upper end
    head — *see* Fracture, ulna, lower end
    lower end (distal end) (head) (lower epiphysis) (styloid process) 813.43
      with radius (lower end) 813.44
        open 813.54
      open 813.53
    olecranon process (closed) 813.01
      open 813.11
    open NEC 813.92
    pathologic 733.12
    proximal end — *see* Fracture, ulna, upper end
    shaft 813.22
      with radius (shaft) 813.23
        open 813.33
      open 813.32
    styloid process — *see* Fracture, ulna, lower end
    transverse — *see* Fracture, ulna, by site
    upper end (epiphysis) 813.04
      with radius (upper end) 813.08
        open 813.18
      multiple sites 813.04
        open 813.14
      open 813.14
      specified site NEC 813.04
        open 813.14

Fracture — *continued*
  unciform (closed) 814.08
    open 814.18
  vertebra, vertebral (back) (body) (column) (neural arch) (pedicle) (spine) (spinous process) (transverse process) (closed) 805.8
    with
      hematomyelia — *see* Fracture, vertebra, by site, with spinal cord injury
      injury to
        cauda equina — *see* Fracture, vertebra, sacrum, with spinal cord injury
        nerve — *see* Fracture, vertebra, by site, with spinal cord injury
      paralysis — *see* Fracture, vertebra, by site, with spinal cord injury
      paraplegia — *see* Fracture, vertebra, by site, with spinal cord injury
      quadriplegia — *see* Fracture, vertebra, by site, with spinal cord injury
      spinal concussion — *see* Fracture, vertebra, by site, with spinal cord injury
      spinal cord injury (closed) NEC 806.8

Note — Use the following fifth-digit subclassification with categories 806.0–806.3:

C_1–C_4 *or unspecified level and* D_1–D_6 (T_1–T_6) *or unspecified level with*

  0   *unspecified spinal cord injury*
  1   *complete lesion of cord*
  2   *anterior cord syndrome*
  3   *central cord syndrome*
  4   *specified injury NEC*

C_5–C_7 *level and* D_7–D_{12} *level with:*

  5   *unspecified spinal cord injury*
  6   *complete lesion of cord*
  7   *anterior cord syndrome*
  8   *central cord syndrome*
  9   *specified injury NEC*

---

        cervical 806.0 ☑
          open 806.1 ☑
        dorsal, dorsolumbar 806.2 ☑
          open 806.3 ☑
          open 806.9
        thoracic, thoracolumbar 806.2 ☑
          open 806.3 ☑
    atlanto-axial — *see* Fracture, vertebra, cervical
    cervical (hangman) (teardrop) (closed) 805.00
      with spinal cord injury — *see* Fracture, vertebra, with spinal cord injury, cervical
      first (atlas) 805.01
        open 805.11
      second (axis) 805.02
        open 805.12
      third 805.03
        open 805.13
      fourth 805.04
        open 805.14
      fifth 805.05
        open 805.15
      sixth 805.06
        open 805.16
      seventh 805.07
        open 805.17
      multiple sites 805.08

Fracture — *continued*
  vertebra, vertebral — *continued*
    cervical — *continued*
      multiple sites — *continued*
        open 805.18
      open 805.10
    coccyx (closed) 805.6
      with spinal cord injury (closed) 806.60
        cauda equina injury 806.62
        complete lesion 806.61
          open 806.71
        open 806.72
        open 806.70
        specified type NEC 806.69
          open 806.79
      open 805.7
    collapsed 733.13
    compression, not due to trauma 733.13
    dorsal (closed) 805.2
      with spinal cord injury — *see* Fracture, vertebra, with spinal cord injury, dorsal
      open 805.3
    dorsolumbar (closed) 805.2
      with spinal cord injury — *see* Fracture, vertebra, with spinal cord injury, dorsal
      open 805.3
    due to osteoporosis 733.13
    fetus or newborn 767.4
    lumbar (closed) 805.4
      with spinal cord injury (closed) 806.4
        open 806.5
      open 805.5
    nontraumatic 733.13
    open NEC 805.9
    pathologic (any site) 733.13
    sacrum (closed) 805.6
      with spinal cord injury 806.60
        cauda equina injury 806.62
        complete lesion 806.61
          open 806.71
        open 806.72
        open 806.70
        specified type NEC 806.69
          open 806.79
      open 805.7
    site unspecified (closed) 805.8
      with spinal cord injury (closed) 806.8
        open 806.9
      open 805.9
    stress (any site) 733.95
    thoracic (closed) 805.2
      with spinal cord injury — *see* Fracture, vertebra, with spinal cord injury, thoracic
      open 805.3
    vertex — *see* Fracture, skull, vault
    vomer (bone) 802.0
      open 802.1
  Wagstaffe's — *see* Fracture, ankle
  wrist (closed) 814.00
    open 814.10
    pathologic 733.12
  xiphoid (process) — *see* Fracture, sternum
  zygoma (zygomatic arch) (closed) 802.4
    open 802.5
Fragile X syndrome 759.83
Fragilitas
  crinium 704.2
  hair 704.2
  ossium 756.51
    with blue sclera 756.51
  unguium 703.8
    congenital 757.5
Fragility
  bone 756.51
    with deafness and blue sclera 756.51
  capillary (hereditary) 287.8

Fracture — Fragility

☑ Additional Digit Required — Refer to the Tabular List for Digit Selection   ▽ Subterms under main terms may continue to next column or page

2007 ICD-9-CM   ▶◀ Revised Text   ● New Line   ▲ Revised Code   **Volume 2 — 127**

Fragility — *continued*
  hair 704.2
  nails 703.8
Fragmentation — *see* Fracture, by site
Frambesia, frambesial (tropica) — *see also* Yaws 102.9
  initial lesion or ulcer 102.0
  primary 102.0
Frambeside
  gummatous 102.4
  of early yaws 102.2
Frambesioma 102.1
Franceschetti's syndrome (mandibulo-facial dysostosis) 756.0
Francis' disease — *see also* Tularemia 021.9
Franklin's disease (heavy chain) 273.2
Frank's essential thrombocytopenia — *see also* Purpura, thrombocytopenic 287.39
Fraser's syndrome 759.89
Freckle 709.09
  malignant melanoma in (M8742/3) — *see* Melanoma
  melanotic (of Hutchinson) (M8742/2) — *see* Neoplasm, skin, in situ
Freeman-Sheldon syndrome 759.89
Freezing 991.9
  specified effect NEC 991.8
Freiberg's
  disease (osteochondrosis, second metatarsal) 732.5
  infraction of metatarsal head 732.5
  osteochondrosis 732.5
Frei's disease (climatic bubo) 099.1
Fremitus, friction, cardiac 785.3
Frenulum linguae 750.0
Frenum
  external os 752.49
  tongue 750.0
Frequency (urinary) NEC 788.41
  micturition 788.41
  nocturnal 788.43
  polyuria 788.42
  psychogenic 306.53
Frey's syndrome (auriculotemporal syndrome) 705.22
Friction
  burn (*see also* Injury, superficial, by site) 919.0
  fremitus, cardiac 785.3
  precordial 785.3
  sounds, chest 786.7
Friderichsen-Waterhouse syndrome or disease 036.3
Friedländer's
  B (bacillus) NEC (*see also* condition) 041.3
   sepsis or septicemia 038.49
  disease (endarteritis obliterans) — *see* Arteriosclerosis
Friedreich's
  ataxia 334.0
  combined systemic disease 334.0
  disease 333.2
   combined systemic 334.0
  myoclonia 333.2
  sclerosis (spinal cord) 334.0
Friedrich-Erb-Arnold syndrome (acropachyderma) 757.39
Frigidity 302.72
  psychic or psychogenic 302.72
Fröhlich's disease or syndrome (adiposogenital dystrophy) 253.8
Froin's syndrome 336.8

Frommel-Chiari syndrome 676.6 ☑
Frommel's disease 676.6 ☑
Frontal — *see also* condition
  lobe syndrome 310.0
Frostbite 991.3
  face 991.0
  foot 991.2
  hand 991.1
  specified site NEC 991.3
Frotteurism 302.89
Frozen 991.9
  pelvis 620.8
  shoulder 726.0
Fructosemia 271.2
Fructosuria (benign) (essential) 271.2
Fuchs'
  black spot (myopic) 360.21
  corneal dystrophy (endothelial) 371.57
  heterochromic cyclitis 364.21
Fucosidosis 271.8
Fugue 780.99
  dissociative 300.13
  hysterical (dissociative) 300.13
  reaction to exceptional stress (transient) 308.1
Fukuhara syndrome 277.87
Fuller Albright's syndrome (osteitis fibrosa disseminata) 756.59
Fuller's earth disease 502
Fulminant, fulminating — *see* condition
Functional — *see* condition
Functioning
  borderline intellectual V62.89
Fundus — *see also* condition
  flavimaculatus 362.76
Fungemia 117.9
Fungus, fungous
  cerebral 348.8
  disease NEC 117.9
  infection — *see* Infection, fungus
  testis (*see also* Tuberculosis) 016.5 ☑ [608.81]
Funiculitis (acute) 608.4
  chronic 608.4
  endemic 608.4
  gonococcal (acute) 098.14
   chronic or duration of 2 months or over 098.34
  tuberculous (*see also* Tuberculosis) 016.5 ☑
Funnel
  breast (acquired) 738.3
   congenital 754.81
   late effect of rickets 268.1
  chest (acquired) 738.3
   congenital 754.81
   late effect of rickets 268.1
  pelvis (acquired) 738.6
   with disproportion (fetopelvic) 653.3 ☑
    affecting fetus or newborn 763.1
    causing obstructed labor 660.1 ☑
     affecting fetus or newborn 763.1
   congenital 755.69
   tuberculous (*see also* Tuberculosis) 016.9 ☑
FUO — *see also* Pyrexia 780.6
Furfur 690.18
  microsporon 111.0
Furor, paroxysmal (idiopathic) — *see also* Epilepsy 345.8 ☑
Furriers' lung 495.8

Furrowed tongue 529.5
  congenital 750.13
Furrowing nail(s) (transverse) 703.8
  congenital 757.5
Furuncle 680.9
  abdominal wall 680.2
  ankle 680.6
  anus 680.5
  arm (any part, above wrist) 680.3
  auditory canal, external 680.0
  axilla 680.3
  back (any part) 680.2
  breast 680.2
  buttock 680.5
  chest wall 680.2
  corpus cavernosum 607.2
  ear (any part) 680.0
  eyelid 373.13
  face (any part, except eye) 680.0
  finger (any) 680.4
  flank 680.2
  foot (any part) 680.7
  forearm 680.3
  gluteal (region) 680.5
  groin 680.2
  hand (any part) 680.4
  head (any part, except face) 680.8
  heel 680.7
  hip 680.6
  kidney (*see also* Abscess, kidney) 590.2
  knee 680.6
  labium (majus) (minus) 616.4
  lacrimal
   gland (*see also* Dacryoadenitis) 375.00
   passages (duct) (sac) (*see also* Dacryocystitis) 375.30
  leg, any part except foot 680.6
  malignant 022.0
  multiple sites 680.9
  neck 680.1
  nose (external) (septum) 680.0
  orbit 376.01
  partes posteriores 680.5
  pectoral region 680.2
  penis 607.2
  perineum 680.2
  pinna 680.0
  scalp (any part) 680.8
  scrotum 608.4
  seminal vesicle 608.0
  shoulder 680.3
  skin NEC 680.9
  specified site NEC 680.8
  spermatic cord 608.4
  temple (region) 680.0
  testis 604.90
  thigh 680.6
  thumb 680.4
  toe (any) 680.7
  trunk 680.2
  tunica vaginalis 608.4
  umbilicus 680.2
  upper arm 680.3
  vas deferens 608.4
  vulva 616.4
  wrist 680.4
Furunculosis — *see also* Furuncle 680.9
  external auditory meatus 680.0 [380.13]
Fusarium (infection) 118
Fusion, fused (congenital)
  anal (with urogenital canal) 751.5
  aorta and pulmonary artery 745.0

Fusion, fused — *continued*
  astragaloscaphoid 755.67
  atria 745.5
  atrium and ventricle 745.69
  auditory canal 744.02
  auricles, heart 745.5
  binocular, with defective stereopsis 368.33
  bone 756.9
  cervical spine — *see* Fusion, spine
  choanal 748.0
  commissure, mitral valve 746.5
  cranial sutures, premature 756.0
  cusps, heart valve NEC 746.89
   mitral 746.5
   tricuspid 746.89
  ear ossicles 744.04
  fingers (*see also* Syndactylism, fingers) 755.11
  hymen 752.42
  hymeno-urethral 599.89
   causing obstructed labor 660.1 ☑
    affecting fetus or newborn 763.1
  joint (acquired) (*see also* Ankylosis)
   congenital 755.8
  kidneys (incomplete) 753.3
  labium (majus) (minus) 752.49
  larynx and trachea 748.3
  limb 755.8
   lower 755.69
   upper 755.59
  lobe, lung 748.5
  lumbosacral (acquired) 724.6
   congenital 756.15
   surgical V45.4
  nares (anterior) (posterior) 748.0
  nose, nasal 748.0
  nostril(s) 748.0
  organ or site NEC — *see* Anomaly, specified type NEC
  ossicles 756.9
   auditory 744.04
  pulmonary valve segment 746.02
  pulmonic cusps 746.02
  ribs 756.3
  sacroiliac (acquired) (joint) 724.6
   congenital 755.69
   surgical V45.4
  skull, imperfect 756.0
  spine (acquired) 724.9
   arthrodesis status V45.4
   congenital (vertebra) 756.15
   postoperative status V45.4
  sublingual duct with submaxillary duct at opening in mouth 750.26
  talonavicular (bar) 755.67
  teeth, tooth 520.2
  testes 752.89
  toes (*see also* Syndactylism, toes) 755.13
  trachea and esophagus 750.3
  twins 759.4
  urethral-hymenal 599.89
  vagina 752.49
  valve cusps — *see* Fusion, cusps, heart valve
  ventricles, heart 745.4
  vertebra (arch) — *see* Fusion, spine
  vulva 752.49
Fusospirillosis (mouth) (tongue) (tonsil) 101
Fussy infant (baby) 780.91

G

Gafsa boil 085.1
Gain, weight (abnormal) (excessive) —
    see also Weight, gain 783.1
Gaisböck's disease or syndrome (poly-
    cythemia hypertonica) 289.0
Gait
    abnormality 781.2
        hysterical 300.11
    ataxic 781.2
        hysterical 300.11
    disturbance 781.2
        hysterical 300.11
    paralytic 781.2
    scissor 781.2
    spastic 781.2
    staggering 781.2
        hysterical 300.11
Galactocele (breast) (infected) 611.5
    puerperal, postpartum 676.8 ☑
Galactophoritis 611.0
    puerperal, postpartum 675.2 ☑
Galactorrhea 676.6 ☑
    not associated with childbirth 611.6
Galactosemia (classic) (congenital) 271.1
Galactosuria 271.1
Galacturia 791.1
    bilharziasis 120.0
Galen's vein — see condition
Gallbladder — see also condition
    acute (see also Disease, gallbladder)
        575.0
Gall duct — see condition
Gallop rhythm 427.89
Gallstone (cholemic) (colic) (impacted) —
    see also Cholelithiasis
    causing intestinal obstruction 560.31
Gambling, pathological 312.31
Gammaloidosis 277.39   ▲
Gammopathy 273.9
    macroglobulinemia 273.3
    monoclonal (benign) (essential) (idio-
        pathic) (with lymphoplasmacytic
        dyscrasia) 273.1
Gamna's disease (siderotic
    splenomegaly) 289.51
Gampsodactylia (congenital) 754.71
Gamstorp's disease (adynamia episodica
    hereditaria) 359.3
Gandy-Nanta disease (siderotic
    splenomegaly) 289.51
Gang activity, without manifest psychi-
    atric disorder V71.09
    adolescent V71.02
    adult V71.01
    child V71.02
Gangliocytoma (M9490/0) — see Neo-
    plasm, connective tissue, benign
Ganglioglioma (M9505/1) — see Neo-
    plasm, by site, uncertain behavior
Ganglion 727.43
    joint 727.41
    of yaws (early) (late) 102.6
    periosteal (see also Periostitis)
        730.3 ☑
    tendon sheath (compound) (diffuse)
        727.42
    tuberculous (see also Tuberculosis)
        015.9 ☑
Ganglioneuroblastoma (M9490/3) —
    see Neoplasm, connective tissue,
    malignant
Ganglioneuroma (M9490/0) — see also
    Neoplasm, connective tissue, be-
    nign
    malignant (M9490/3) — see Neo-
        plasm, connective tissue, malig-
        nant
Ganglioneuromatosis (M9491/0) — see
    Neoplasm, connective tissue, be-
    nign
Ganglionitis
    fifth nerve (see also Neuralgia,
        trigeminal) 350.1
    gasserian 350.1

Ganglionitis — continued
    geniculate 351.1
        herpetic 053.11
        newborn 767.5
    herpes zoster 053.11
    herpetic geniculate (Hunt's syndrome)
        053.11
Gangliosidosis 330.1
Gangosa 102.5
Gangrene, gangrenous (anemia) (artery)
    (cellulitis) (dermatitis) (dry) (infec-
    tive) (moist) (pemphigus) (septic)
    (skin) (stasis) (ulcer) 785.4
    with
        arteriosclerosis (native artery)
            440.24
            bypass graft 440.30
                autologous vein 440.31
                nonautologous biological
                    440.32
        diabetes (mellitus) 250.7 ☑ [785.4]
    abdomen (wall) 785.4
    adenitis 683
    alveolar 526.5
    angina 462
        diphtheritic 032.0
    anus 569.49
    appendices epiploicae — see Gan-
        grene, mesentery
    appendix — see Appendicitis, acute
    arteriosclerotic — see Arteriosclerosis,
        with, gangrene
    auricle 785.4
    Bacillus welchii (see also Gangrene,
        gas) 040.0
    bile duct (see also Cholangitis) 576.8
    bladder 595.89
    bowel — see Gangrene, intestine
    cecum — see Gangrene, intestine
    Clostridium perfringens or welchii (see
        also Gangrene, gas) 040.0
    colon — see Gangrene, intestine
    connective tissue 785.4
    cornea 371.40
    corpora cavernosa (infective) 607.2
        noninfective 607.89
    cutaneous, spreading 785.4
    decubital (see also Decubitus)
        707.00 [785.4]
    diabetic (any site) 250.7 ☑ [785.4]
    dropsical 785.4
    emphysematous (see also Gangrene,
        gas) 040.0
    epidemic (ergotized grain) 988.2
    epididymis (infectional) (see also Epi-
        didymitis) 604.99
    erysipelas (see also Erysipelas) 035
    extremity (lower) (upper) 785.4
    gallbladder or duct (see also Cholecys-
        titis, acute) 575.0
    gas (bacillus) 040.0
        with
            abortion — see Abortion, by
                type, with sepsis
            ectopic pregnancy (see also cat-
                egories 633.0–633.9)
                639.0
            molar pregnancy (see also cate-
                gories 630–632) 639.0
        following
            abortion 639.0
            ectopic or molar pregnancy
                639.0
        puerperal, postpartum, childbirth
            670.0 ☑
    glossitis 529.0
    gum 523.8
    hernia — see Hernia, by site, with
        gangrene
    hospital noma 528.1
    intestine, intestinal (acute) (hemor-
        rhagic) (massive) 557.0
        with
            hernia — see Hernia, by site,
                with gangrene

Gangrene, gangrenous — continued
    intestine, intestinal — continued
        with — continued
            mesenteric embolism or infarc-
                tion 557.0
            obstruction (see also Obstruc-
                tion, intestine) 560.9
    laryngitis 464.00
        with obstruction 464.01
    liver 573.8
    lung 513.0
        spirochetal 104.8
    lymphangitis 457.2
    Meleney's (cutaneous) 686.09
    mesentery 557.0
        with
            embolism or infarction 557.0
            intestinal obstruction (see also
                Obstruction, intestine)
                560.9
    mouth 528.1
    noma 528.1
    orchitis 604.90
    ovary (see also Salpingo-oophoritis)
        614.2
    pancreas 577.0
    penis (infectional) 607.2
        noninfective 607.89
    perineum 785.4
    pharynx 462
    pneumonia 513.0
    Pott's 440.24
    presenile 443.1
    pulmonary 513.0
    pulp, tooth 522.1
    quinsy 475
    Raynaud's (symmetric gangrene)
        443.0 [785.4]
    rectum 569.49
    retropharyngeal 478.24
    rupture — see Hernia, by site, with
        gangrene
    scrotum 608.4
        noninfective 608.83
    senile 440.24
    septic 034.0
    septic 034.0
    sore throat 462
    spermatic cord 608.4
        noninfective 608.89
    spine 785.4
    spirochetal NEC 104.8
    spreading cutaneous 785.4
    stomach 537.89
    stomatitis 528.1
    symmetrical 443.0 [785.4]
    testis (infectional) (see also Orchitis)
        604.99
        noninfective 608.89
    throat 462
        diphtheritic 032.0
    thyroid (gland) 246.8
    tonsillitis (acute) 463
    tooth (pulp) 522.1
    tuberculous NEC (see also Tuberculo-
        sis) 011.9 ☑
    tunica vaginalis 608.4
        noninfective 608.89
    umbilicus 785.4
    uterus (see also Endometritis) 615.9
    uvulitis 528.3
    vas deferens 608.4
        noninfective 608.89
    vulva (see also Vulvitis) 616.10
Gannister disease (occupational) 502
    with tuberculosis — see Tuberculosis,
        pulmonary
Ganser's syndrome, hysterical 300.16
Gardner-Diamond syndrome (autoery-
    throcyte sensitization) 287.2
Gargoylism 277.5
Garré's
    disease (see also Osteomyelitis)
        730.1 ☑
    osteitis (sclerosing) (see also Os-
        teomyelitis) 730.1 ☑

Garré's — continued
    osteomyelitis (see also Osteomyelitis)
        730.1 ☑
Garrod's pads, knuckle 728.79
Gartner's duct
    cyst 752.41
    persistent 752.41
Gas
    asphyxia, asphyxiation, inhalation,
        poisoning, suffocation NEC
        987.9
        specified gas — see Table of Drugs
            and Chemicals
    bacillus gangrene or infection — see
        Gas, gangrene
    cyst, mesentery 568.89
    excessive 787.3
    gangrene 040.0
        with
            abortion — see Abortion, by
                type, with sepsis
            ectopic pregnancy (see also cat-
                egories 633.0–633.9)
                639.0
            molar pregnancy (see also cate-
                gories 630–632) 639.0
        following
            abortion 639.0
            ectopic or molar pregnancy
                639.0
        puerperal, postpartum, childbirth
            670.0 ☑
    on stomach 787.3
    pains 787.3
Gastradenitis 535.0 ☑
Gastralgia 536.8
    psychogenic 307.89
Gastrectasis, gastrectasia 536.1
    psychogenic 306.4
Gastric — see condition
Gastrinoma (M8153/1)
    malignant (M8153/3)
        pancreas 157.4
        specified site NEC — see Neoplasm,
            by site, malignant
        unspecified site 157.4
    specified site — see Neoplasm, by site,
        uncertain behavior
    unspecified site 235.5
Gastritis 535.5 ☑

> *Note — Use the following fifth-digit
> subclassification for category 535:*
>
> 0   *without mention of hemorrhage*
>
> 1   *with hemorrhage*

    acute 535.0 ☑
    alcoholic 535.3 ☑
    allergic 535.4 ☑
    antral 535.4 ☑
    atrophic 535.1 ☑
    atrophic-hyperplastic 535.1 ☑
    bile-induced 535.4 ☑
    catarrhal 535.0 ☑
    chronic (atrophic) 535.1 ☑
    cirrhotic 535.4 ☑
    corrosive (acute) 535.4 ☑
    dietetic 535.4 ☑
    due to diet deficiency 269.9 [535.4] ☑
    eosinophilic 535.4 ☑
    erosive 535.4 ☑
    follicular 535.4 ☑
        chronic 535.1 ☑
    giant hypertrophic 535.2 ☑
    glandular 535.4 ☑
        chronic 535.1 ☑
    hypertrophic (mucosa) 535.2 ☑
        chronic giant 211.1
    irritant 535.4 ☑
    nervous 306.4
    phlegmonous 535.0 ☑
    psychogenic 306.4
    sclerotic 535.4 ☑
    spastic 536.8
    subacute 535.0 ☑
    superficial 535.4 ☑

☑ Additional Digit Required — Refer to the Tabular List for Digit Selection   ▽ Subterms under main terms may continue to next column or page

Gastritis — *continued*
  suppurative 535.0 ☑
  toxic 535.4 ☑
  tuberculous (*see also* Tuberculosis)
    017.9 ☑
Gastrocarcinoma (M8010/3) 151.9
Gastrocolic — *see* condition
Gastrocolitis — *see* Enteritis
Gastrodisciasis 121.8
Gastroduodenitis — *see also* Gastritis
  535.5 ☑
  catarrhal 535.0 ☑
  infectional 535.0 ☑
  virus, viral 008.8
    specified type NEC 008.69
Gastrodynia 536.8
Gastroenteritis (acute) (catarrhal) (congestive) (hemorrhagic) (noninfectious) — *see also* Enteritis 558.9
  aertrycke infection 003.0
  allergic 558.3
  chronic 558.9
    ulcerative (*see also* Colitis, ulcerative) 556.9
  dietetic 558.9
  due to
    food poisoning (*see also* Poisoning, food) 005.9
    radiation 558.1
  epidemic 009.0
  functional 558.9
  infectious (*see also* Enteritis, due to, by organism) 009.0
    presumed 009.1
  salmonella 003.0
  septic (*see also* Enteritis, due to, by organism) 009.0
  toxic 558.2
  tuberculous (*see also* Tuberculosis) 014.8 ☑
  ulcerative (*see also* Colitis, ulcerative) 556.9
  viral NEC 008.8
    specified type NEC 008.69
  zymotic 009.0
Gastroenterocolitis — *see* Enteritis
Gastroenteropathy, protein-losing 579.8
Gastroenteroptosis 569.89
Gastroesophageal laceration-hemorrhage syndrome 530.7
Gastroesophagitis 530.19
Gastrohepatitis — *see also* Gastritis 535.5 ☑
Gastrointestinal — *see* condition
Gastrojejunal — *see* condition
Gastrojejunitis — *see also* Gastritis 535.5 ☑
Gastrojejunocolic — *see* condition
Gastroliths 537.89
Gastromalacia 537.89
Gastroparalysis 536.3
  diabetic 250.6 ☑ [536.3]
Gastroparesis 536.3
  diabetic 250.6 ☑ [536.3]
Gastropathy 537.9
  erythematous 535.5 ☑   ●
  exudative 579.8
Gastroptosis 537.5
Gastrorrhagia 578.0
Gastrorrhea 536.8
  psychogenic 306.4
Gastroschisis (congenital) 756.79
  acquired 569.89
Gastrospasm (neurogenic) (reflex) 536.8
  neurotic 306.4
  psychogenic 306.4
Gastrostaxis 578.0
Gastrostenosis 537.89
Gastrostomy
  attention to V55.1
  complication 536.40
    specified type 536.49
  infection 536.41
  malfunctioning 536.42
  status V44.1

Gastrosuccorrhea (continuous) (intermittent) 536.8
  neurotic 306.4
  psychogenic 306.4
Gaucher's
  disease (adult) (cerebroside lipidosis) (infantile) 272.7
  hepatomegaly 272.7
  splenomegaly (cerebroside lipidosis) 272.7
Gayet's disease (superior hemorrhagic polioencephalitis) 265.1
Gayet-Wernicke's syndrome (superior hemorrhagic polioencephalitis) 265.1
Gee (-Herter) (-Heubner) (-Thaysen) disease or syndrome (nontropical sprue) 579.0
Gélineau's syndrome — *see also* Narcolepsy 347.00
Gemination, teeth 520.2
Gemistocytoma (M9411/3)
  specified site — *see* Neoplasm, by site, malignant
  unspecified site 191.9
General, generalized — *see* condtion
Genetic
  susceptibility to
    neoplasm
      malignant, of
        breast V84.01
        endometrium V84.04
        other V84.09
        ovary V84.02
        prostate V84.03
      other disease V84.8
Genital — *see* condition
  warts 078.19
Genito-anorectal syndrome 099.1
Genitourinary system — *see* condition
Genu
  congenital 755.64
  extrorsum (acquired) 736.42
    congenital 755.64
    late effects of rickets 268.1
  introrsum (acquired) 736.41
    congenital 755.64
    late effects of rickets 268.1
  rachitic (old) 268.1
  recurvatum (acquired) 736.5
    congenital 754.40
      with dislocation of knee 754.41
    late effects of rickets 268.1
  valgum (acquired) (knock-knee) 736.41
    congenital 755.64
    late effects of rickets 268.1
  varum (acquired) (bowleg) 736.42
    congenital 755.64
    late effect of rickets 268.1
Geographic tongue 529.1
Geophagia 307.52
Geotrichosis 117.9
  intestine 117.9
  lung 117.9
  mouth 117.9
Gephyrophobia 300.29
Gerbode defect 745.4
Gerhardt's
  disease (erythromelalgia) 443.82
  syndrome (vocal cord paralysis) 478.30
Gerlier's disease (epidemic vertigo) 078.81
German measles 056.9
  exposure to V01.4
Germinoblastoma (diffuse) (M9614/3) 202.8 ☑
  follicular (M9692/3) 202.0 ☑
Germinoma (M9064/3) — *see* Neoplasm, by site, malignant
Gerontoxon 371.41
Gerstmann's syndrome (finger agnosia) 784.69
Gestation (period) — *see also* Pregnancy

Gestation — *see also* Pregnancy — *continued*
  ectopic NEC (*see also* Pregnancy, ectopic) 633.90
    with intrauterine pregnancy 633.91
Gestational proteinuria 646.2 ☑
  with hypertension — *see* Toxemia, of pregnancy
Ghon tubercle primary infection — *see also* Tuberculosis 010.0 ☑
Ghost
  teeth 520.4
  vessels, cornea 370.64
Ghoul hand 102.3
Gianotti Crosti syndrome 057.8
  due to known virus — *see* Infection, virus
  due to unknown virus 057.8
Giant
  cell
    epulis 523.8
    peripheral (gingiva) 523.8
    tumor, tendon sheath 727.02
  colon (congenital) 751.3
  esophagus (congenital) 750.4
  kidney 753.3
  urticaria 995.1
    hereditary 277.6
Giardia lamblia infestation 007.1
Giardiasis 007.1
Gibert's disease (pityriasis rosea) 696.3
Gibraltar fever — *see* Brucellosis
Giddiness 780.4
  hysterical 300.11
  psychogenic 306.9
Gierke's disease (glycogenosis I) 271.0
Gigantism (cerebral) (hypophyseal) (pituitary) 253.0
Gilbert's disease or cholemia (familial nonhemolytic jaundice) 277.4
Gilchrist's disease (North American blastomycosis) 116.0
Gilford (-Hutchinson) disease or syndrome (progeria) 259.8
Gilles de la Tourette's disease (motor-verbal tic) 307.23
Gillespie's syndrome (dysplasia oculo-dentodigitalis) 759.89
Gingivitis 523.10   ▲
  acute 523.00   ▲
    necrotizing 101
    non-plaque induced 523.01   ●
    plaque induced 523.00   ●
  catarrhal 523.00   ▲
  chronic 523.10   ▲
    non-plaque induced 523.11   ●
  desquamative 523.10   ▲
  expulsiva 523.40   ▲
  hyperplastic 523.10   ▲
  marginal, simple 523.10   ▲
  necrotizing, acute 101
  non-plaque induced 523.11   ●
  pellagrous 265.2
  plaque induced 523.10   ●
  ulcerative 523.10   ▲
    acute necrotizing 101
  Vincent's 101
Gingivoglossitis 529.0
Gingivopericementitis 523.40   ▲
Gingivosis 523.10   ▲
Gingivostomatitis 523.10   ▲
  herpetic 054.2
Giovannini's disease 117.9
GISA (glycopeptide intermediate staphylococcus aureus) V09.8 ☑
Glanders 024
Gland, glandular — *see* condition
Glanzmann (-Naegeli) disease or thrombasthenia 287.1
Glassblowers' disease 527.1
Glaucoma (capsular) (inflammatory) (noninflammatory) (primary) 365.9
  with increased episcleral venous pressure 365.82
  absolute 360.42
  acute 365.22

Glaucoma — *continued*
  acute — *continued*
    narrow angle 365.22
    secondary 365.60
  angle closure 365.20
    acute 365.22
    chronic 365.23
    intermittent 365.21
    interval 365.21
    residual stage 365.24
    subacute 365.21
  borderline 365.00
  chronic 365.11
    noncongestive 365.11
    open angle 365.11
    simple 365.11
  closed angle — *see* Glaucoma, angle closure
  congenital 743.20
    associated with other eye anomalies 743.22
    simple 743.21
  congestive — *see* Glaucoma, narrow angle
  corticosteroid-induced (glaucomatous stage) 365.31
    residual stage 365.32
  hemorrhagic 365.60
  hypersecretion 365.81
  infantile 365.14
    congenital 743.20
      associated with other eye anomalies 743.22
      simple 743.21
  in or with
    aniridia 743.45 [365.42]
    Axenfeld's anomaly 743.44 [365.41]
    concussion of globe 921.3 [365.65]
    congenital syndromes NEC 759.89 [365.44]
    dislocation of lens
      anterior 379.33 [365.59]
      posterior 379.34 [365.59]
    disorder of lens NEC 365.59
    epithelial down-growth 364.61 [365.64]
    glaucomatocyclitic crisis 364.22 [365.62]
    hypermature cataract 366.18 [365.51]
    hyphema 364.41 [365.63]
    inflammation, ocular 365.62
    iridocyclitis 364.3 [365.62]
    iris
      anomalies NEC 743.46 [365.42]
      atrophy, essential 364.51 [365.42]
      bombé 364.74 [365.61]
      rubeosis 364.42 [365.63]
    microcornea 743.41 [365.43]
    neurofibromatosis 237.71 [365.44]
    ocular
      cysts NEC 365.64
      disorders NEC 365.60
      trauma 365.65
      tumors NEC 365.64
    postdislocation of lens
      anterior 379.33 [365.59]
      posterior 379.34 [365.59]
    pseudoexfoliation of capsule 366.11 [365.52]
    pupillary block or seclusion 364.74 [365.61]
    recession of chamber angle 364.77 [365.65]
    retinal vein occlusion 362.35 [365.63]
    Rieger's anomaly or syndrome 743.44 [365.41]
    rubeosis of iris 364.42 [365.63]
    seclusion of pupil 364.74 [365.61]
    spherophakia 743.36 [365.59]
    Sturge-Weber (-Dimitri) syndrome 759.6 [365.44]
    systemic syndrome NEC 365.44
    tumor of globe 365.64

Glaucoma — *continued*
  in or with — *continued*
    vascular disorders NEC 365.63
  juvenile 365.14
  low tension 365.12
  malignant 365.83
  narrow angle (primary) 365.20
    acute 365.22
    chronic 365.23
    intermittent 365.21
    interval 365.21
    residual stage 365.24
    subacute 365.21
  newborn 743.20
    associated with other eye anomalies 743.22
    simple 743.21
  noncongestive (chronic) 365.11
  nonobstructive (chronic) 365.11
  obstructive 365.60
    due to lens changes 365.59
  open angle 365.10
    with
      borderline intraocular pressure 365.01
      cupping of optic discs 365.01
    primary 365.11
    residual stage 365.15
  phacolytic 365.51
    with hypermature cataract 366.18 *[365.51]*
  pigmentary 365.13
  postinfectious 365.60
  pseudoexfoliation 365.52
    with pseudoexfoliation of capsule 366.11 *[365.52]*
  secondary NEC 365.60
  simple (chronic) 365.11
  simplex 365.11
  steroid responders 365.03
  suspect 365.00
  syphilitic 095.8
  traumatic NEC 365.65
    newborn 767.8
  tuberculous (*see also* Tuberculosis) 017.3 ☑ *[365.62]*
  wide angle (*see also* Glaucoma, open angle) 365.10
Glaucomatous flecks (subcapsular) 366.31
Glazed tongue 529.4
Gleet 098.2
Glénard's disease or syndrome (enteroptosis) 569.89
Glinski-Simmonds syndrome (pituitary cachexia) 253.2
Glioblastoma (multiforme) (M9440/3)
  with sarcomatous component (M9442/3)
    specified site — *see* Neoplasm, by site, malignant
    unspecified site 191.9
  giant cell (M9441/3)
    specified site — *see* Neoplasm, by site, malignant
    unspecified site 191.9
  specified site — *see* Neoplasm, by site, malignant
  unspecified site 191.9
Glioma (malignant) (M9380/3)
  astrocytic (M9400/3)
    specified site — *see* Neoplasm, by site, malignant
    unspecified site 191.9
  mixed (M9382/3)
    specified site — *see* Neoplasm, by site, malignant
    unspecified site 191.9
  nose 748.1
  specified site NEC — *see* Neoplasm, by site, malignant
  subependymal (M9383/1) 237.5
  unspecified site 191.9
Gliomatosis cerebri (M9381/3) 191.0
Glioneuroma (M9505/1) — *see* Neoplasm, by site, uncertain behavior

Gliosarcoma (M9380/3)
  specified site — *see* Neoplasm, by site, malignant
  unspecified site 191.9
Gliosis (cerebral) 349.89
  spinal 336.0
Glisson's
  cirrhosis — *see* Cirrhosis, portal
  disease (*see also* Rickets) 268.0
Glissonitis 573.3
Globinuria 791.2
Globus 306.4
  hystericus 300.11
Glomangioma (M8712/0) — *see also* Hemangioma 228.00
Glomangiosarcoma (M8710/3) — *see* Neoplasm, connective tissue, malignant
Glomerular nephritis — *see also* Nephritis 583.9
Glomerulitis — *see also* Nephritis 583.9
Glomerulonephritis — *see also* Nephritis 583.9
  with
    edema (*see also* Nephrosis) 581.9
    lesion of
      exudative nephritis 583.89
      interstitial nephritis (diffuse) (focal) 583.89
      necrotizing glomerulitis 583.4
        acute 580.4
        chronic 582.4
      renal necrosis 583.9
        cortical 583.6
        medullary 583.7
      specified pathology NEC 583.89
        acute 580.89
        chronic 582.89
    necrosis, renal 583.9
      cortical 583.6
      medullary (papillary) 583.7
    specified pathology or lesion NEC 583.89
  acute 580.9
    with
      exudative nephritis 580.89
      interstitial nephritis (diffuse) (focal) 580.89
      necrotizing glomerulitis 580.4
      extracapillary with epithelial crescents 580.4
    poststreptococcal 580.0
    proliferative (diffuse) 580.0
    rapidly progressive 580.4
    specified pathology NEC 580.89
  arteriolar (*see also* Hypertension, kidney) 403.90
  arteriosclerotic (*see also* Hypertension, kidney) 403.90
  ascending (*see also* Pyelitis) 590.80
  basement membrane NEC 583.89
    with
      pulmonary hemorrhage (Goodpasture's syndrome) 446.21 *[583.81]*
  chronic 582.9
    with
      exudative nephritis 582.89
      interstitial nephritis (diffuse) (focal) 582.89
      necrotizing glomerulitis 582.4
      specified pathology or lesion NEC 582.89
    endothelial 582.2
    extracapillary with epithelial crescents 582.4
    hypocomplementemic persistent 582.2
    lobular 582.2
    membranoproliferative 582.2
    membranous 582.1
      and proliferative (mixed) 582.2
      sclerosing 582.1
    mesangiocapillary 582.2
    mixed membranous and proliferative 582.2

Glomerulonephritis — *see also* Nephritis — *continued*
  chronic — *continued*
    proliferative (diffuse) 582.0
    rapidly progressive 582.4
    sclerosing 582.1
  cirrhotic — *see* Sclerosis, renal
  desquamative — *see* Nephrosis
  due to or associated with
    amyloidosis 277.39 *[583.81]* ▲
      with nephrotic syndrome 277.39 *[581.81]* ▲
      chronic 277.39 *[582.81]* ▲
    diabetes mellitus 250.4 ☑ *[583.81]*
      with nephrotic syndrome 250.4 ☑ *[581.81]*
    diphtheria 032.89 *[580.81]*
    gonococcal infection (acute) 098.19 *[583.81]*
      chronic or duration of 2 months or over 098.39 *[583.81]*
    infectious hepatitis 070.9 *[580.81]*
    malaria (with nephrotic syndrome) 084.9 *[581.81]*
    mumps 072.79 *[580.81]*
    polyarteritis (nodosa) (with nephrotic syndrome) 446.0 *[581.81]*
    specified pathology NEC 583.89
      acute 580.89
      chronic 582.89
    streptotrichosis 039.8 *[583.81]*
    subacute bacterial endocarditis 421.0 *[580.81]*
    syphilis (late) 095.4
      congenital 090.5 *[583.81]*
      early 091.69 *[583.81]*
    systemic lupus erythematosus 710.0 *[583.81]*
      with nephrotic syndrome 710.0 *[581.81]*
      chronic 710.0 *[582.81]*
    tuberculosis (*see also* Tuberculosis) 016.0 *[583.81]*
    typhoid fever 002.0 *[580.81]*
  extracapillary with epithelial crescents 583.4
    acute 580.4
    chronic 582.4
  exudative 583.89
    acute 580.89
    chronic 582.89
  focal (*see also* Nephritis) 583.9
    embolic 580.4
  granular 582.89
  granulomatous 582.89
  hydremic (*see also* Nephrosis) 581.9
  hypocomplementemic persistent 583.2
    with nephrotic syndrome 581.2
    chronic 582.2
  immune complex NEC 583.89
  infective (*see also* Pyelitis) 590.80
  interstitial (diffuse) (focal) 583.89
    with nephrotic syndrome 581.89
    acute 580.89
    chronic 582.89
  latent or quiescent 582.9
  lobular 583.2
    with nephrotic syndrome 581.2
    chronic 582.2
  membranoproliferative 583.2
    with nephrotic syndrome 581.2
    chronic 582.2
  membranous 583.1
    with nephrotic syndrome 581.1
    and proliferative (mixed) 583.2
      with nephrotic syndrome 581.2
      chronic 582.2
    chronic 582.1
    sclerosing 582.1
      with nephrotic syndrome 581.1
  mesangiocapillary 583.2
    with nephrotic syndrome 581.2
    chronic 582.2
  minimal change 581.3

Glomerulonephritis — *see also* Nephritis — *continued*
  mixed membranous and proliferative 583.2
    with nephrotic syndrome 581.2
    chronic 582.2
  necrotizing 583.4
    acute 580.4
    chronic 582.4
  nephrotic (*see also* Nephrosis) 581.9
  old — *see* Glomerulonephritis, chronic
  parenchymatous 581.89
  poststreptococcal 580.0
  proliferative (diffuse) 583.0
    with nephrotic syndrome 581.0
    acute 580.0
    chronic 582.0
  purulent (*see also* Pyelitis) 590.80
  quiescent — *see* Nephritis, chronic
  rapidly progressive 583.4
    acute 580.4
    chronic 582.4
  sclerosing membranous (chronic) 582.1
    with nephrotic syndrome 581.1
  septic (*see also* Pyelitis) 590.80
  specified pathology or lesion NEC 583.89
    with nephrotic syndrome 581.89
    acute 580.89
    chronic 582.89
  suppurative (acute) (disseminated) (*see also* Pyelitis) 590.80
  toxic — *see* Nephritis, acute
  tubal, tubular — *see* Nephrosis, tubular
  type II (Ellis) — *see* Nephrosis
  vascular — *see* Hypertension, kidney
Glomerulosclerosis — *see also* Sclerosis, renal 587
  focal 582.1
    with nephrotic syndrome 581.1
  intercapillary (nodular) (with diabetes) 250.4 ☑ *[581.81]*
Glossagra 529.6
Glossalgia 529.6
Glossitis 529.0
  areata exfoliativa 529.1
  atrophic 529.4
  benign migratory 529.1
  gangrenous 529.0
  Hunter's 529.4
  median rhomboid 529.2
  Moeller's 529.4
  pellagrous 265.2
Glossocele 529.8
Glossodynia 529.6
  exfoliativa 529.4
Glossoncus 529.8
Glossophytia 529.3
Glossoplegia 529.8
Glossoptosis 529.8
Glossopyrosis 529.6
Glossotrichia 529.3
Glossy skin 701.9
Glottis — *see* condition
Glottitis — *see* Glossitis
Glucagonoma (M8152/0)
  malignant (M8152/3)
    pancreas 157.4
    specified site NEC — *see* Neoplasm, by site, malignant
    unspecified site 157.4
  pancreas 211.7
  specified site NEC — *see* Neoplasm, by site, benign
  unspecified site 211.7
Glucoglycinuria 270.7
Glue ear syndrome 381.20
Glue sniffing (airplane glue) — *see also* Dependence 304.6 ☑
Glycinemia (with methylmalonic acidemia) 270.7
Glycinuria (renal) (with ketosis) 270.0

☑ Additional Digit Required — Refer to the Tabular List for Digit Selection   ▽ Subterms under main terms may continue to next column or page

2007 ICD-9-CM   ▶◀ Revised Text   ● New Line   ▲ Revised Code   **October 2006 • Volume 2 — 131**

Glycogen
infiltration (*see also* Disease, glycogen storage) 271.0
storage disease (*see also* Disease, glycogen storage) 271.0
Glycogenosis — *see also* Disease, glycogen storage 271.0
cardiac 271.0 *[425.7]*
Cori, types I-VII 271.0
diabetic, secondary 250.8 ☑ *[259.8]*
diffuse (with hepatic cirrhosis) 271.0
generalized 271.0
glucose-6-phosphatase deficiency 271.0
hepatophosphorylase deficiency 271.0
hepatorenal 271.0
myophosphorylase deficiency 271.0
Glycopenia 251.2
Glycopeptide
intermediate staphylococcus aureus (GISA) V09.8 ☑
resistant
enterococcus V09.8 ☑
staphylococcus aureus (GRSA) V09.8 ☑
Glycoprolinuria 270.8
Glycosuria 791.5
renal 271.4
Gnathostoma (spinigerum) (infection) (infestation) 128.1
wandering swellings from 128.1
Gnathostomiasis 128.1
Goiter (adolescent) (colloid) (diffuse) (dipping) (due to iodine deficiency) (endemic) (euthyroid) (heart) (hyperplastic) (internal) (intrathoracic) (juvenile) (mixed type) (nonendemic) (parenchymatous) (plunging) (sporadic) (subclavicular) (substernal) 240.9
with
hyperthyroidism (recurrent) (*see also* Goiter, toxic) 242.0 ☑
thyrotoxicosis (*see also* Goiter, toxic) 242.0 ☑
adenomatous (*see also* Goiter, nodular) 241.9
cancerous (M8000/3) 193
complicating pregnancy, childbirth, or puerperium 648.1 ☑
congenital 246.1
cystic (*see also* Goiter, nodular) 241.9
due to enzyme defect in synthesis of thyroid hormone (butane-insoluble iodine) (coupling) (deiodinase) (iodide trapping or organification) (iodotyrosine dehalogenase) (peroxidase) 246.1
dyshormonogenic 246.1
exophthalmic (*see also* Goiter, toxic) 242.0 ☑
familial (with deaf-mutism) 243
fibrous 245.3
lingual 759.2
lymphadenoid 245.2
malignant (M8000/3) 193
multinodular (nontoxic) 241.1
toxic or with hyperthyroidism (*see also* Goiter, toxic) 242.2 ☑
nodular (nontoxic) 241.9
with
hyperthyroidism (*see also* Goiter, toxic) 242.3 ☑
thyrotoxicosis (*see also* Goiter, toxic) 242.3 ☑
endemic 241.9
exophthalmic (diffuse) (*see also* Goiter, toxic) 242.0 ☑
multinodular (nontoxic) 241.1
sporadic 241.9
toxic (*see also* Goiter, toxic) 242.3 ☑
uninodular (nontoxic) 241.0
nontoxic (nodular) 241.9
multinodular 241.1
uninodular 241.0

Goiter — *continued*
pulsating (*see also* Goiter, toxic) 242.0 ☑
simple 240.0
toxic 242.0 ☑

Note — Use the following fifth-digit subclassification with category 242:

0 without mention of thyrotoxic crisis or storm
1 with mention of thyrotoxic crisis or storm

adenomatous 242.3 ☑
multinodular 242.2 ☑
uninodular 242.1 ☑
multinodular 242.2 ☑
nodular 242.3 ☑
multinodular 242.2 ☑
uninodular 242.1 ☑
uninodular 242.1 ☑
uninodular (nontoxic) 241.0
toxic or with hyperthyroidism (*see also* Goiter, toxic) 242.1 ☑
Goldberg (-Maxwell) (-Morris) syndrome (testicular feminization) 259.5
Goldblatt's
hypertension 440.1
kidney 440.1
Goldenhar's syndrome (oculoauriculovertebral dysplasia) 756.0
Goldflam-Erb disease or syndrome 358.00
Goldscheider's disease (epidermolysis bullosa) 757.39
Goldstein's disease (familial hemorrhagic telangiectasia) 448.0
Golfer's elbow 726.32
Goltz-Gorlin syndrome (dermal hypoplasia) 757.39
Gonadoblastoma (M9073/1)
specified site — *see* Neoplasm, by site, uncertain behavior
unspecified site
female 236.2
male 236.4
Gonecystitis — *see also* Vesiculitis 608.0
Gongylonemiasis 125.6
mouth 125.6
Gonococcemia 098.89
Gonococcus, gonococcal (disease) (infection) — *see also* condition 098.0
anus 098.7
bursa 098.52
chronic NEC 098.2
complicating pregnancy, childbirth, or puerperium 647.1 ☑
affecting fetus or newborn 760.2
conjunctiva, conjunctivitis (neonatorum) 098.40
dermatosis 098.89
endocardium 098.84
epididymo-orchitis 098.13
chronic or duration of 2 months or over 098.33
eye (newborn) 098.40
fallopian tube (chronic) 098.37
acute 098.17
genitourinary (acute) (organ) (system) (tract) (*see also* Gonorrhea) 098.0
lower 098.0
chronic 098.2
upper 098.10
chronic 098.30
heart NEC 098.85
joint 098.50
keratoderma 098.81
keratosis (blennorrhagica) 098.81
lymphatic (gland) (node) 098.89
meninges 098.82
orchitis (acute) 098.13
chronic or duration of 2 months or over 098.33

Gonococcus, gonococcal — *see also* condition — *continued*
pelvis (acute) 098.19
chronic or duration of 2 months or over 098.39
pericarditis 098.83
peritonitis 098.86
pharyngitis 098.6
pharynx 098.6
proctitis 098.7
pyosalpinx (chronic) 098.37
acute 098.17
rectum 098.7
septicemia 098.89
skin 098.89
specified site NEC 098.89
synovitis 098.51
tendon sheath 098.51
throat 098.6
urethra (acute) 098.0
chronic or duration of 2 months or over 098.2
vulva (acute) 098.0
chronic or duration of 2 months or over 098.2
Gonocytoma (M9073/1)
specified site — *see* Neoplasm, by site, uncertain behavior
unspecified site
female 236.2
male 236.4
Gonorrhea 098.0
acute 098.0
Bartholin's gland (acute) 098.0
chronic or duration of 2 months or over 098.2
bladder (acute) 098.11
chronic or duration of 2 months or over 098.31
carrier (suspected of) V02.7
cervix (acute) 098.15
chronic or duration of 2 months or over 098.35
chronic 098.2
complicating pregnancy, childbirth, or puerperium 647.1 ☑
affecting fetus or newborn 760.2
conjunctiva, conjunctivitis (neonatorum) 098.40
contact V01.6
Cowper's gland (acute) 098.0
chronic or duration of 2 months or over 098.2
duration of two months or over 098.2
exposure to V01.6
fallopian tube (chronic) 098.37
acute 098.17
genitourinary (acute) (organ) (system) (tract) 098.0
chronic 098.2
duration of two months or over 098.2
kidney (acute) 098.19
chronic or duration of 2 months or over 098.39
ovary (acute) 098.19
chronic or duration of 2 months or over 098.39
pelvis (acute) 098.19
chronic or duration of 2 months or over 098.39
penis (acute) 098.0
chronic or duration of 2 months or over 098.2
prostate (acute) 098.12
chronic or duration of 2 months or over 098.32
seminal vesicle (acute) 098.14
chronic or duration of 2 months or over 098.34
specified site NEC — *see* Gonococcus
spermatic cord (acute) 098.14
chronic or duration of 2 months or over 098.34
urethra (acute) 098.0

Gonorrhea — *continued*
urethra — *continued*
chronic or duration of 2 months or over 098.2
vagina (acute) 098.0
chronic or duration of 2 months or over 098.2
vas deferens (acute) 098.14
chronic or duration of 2 months or over 098.34
vulva (acute) 098.0
chronic or duration of 2 months or over 098.2
Goodpasture's syndrome (pneumorenal) 446.21
Good's syndrome 279.06
Gopalan's syndrome (burning feet) 266.2
Gordon's disease (exudative enteropathy) 579.8
Gorlin-Chaudhry-Moss syndrome 759.89
Gougerot-Blum syndrome (pigmented purpuric lichenoid dermatitis) 709.1
Gougerot-Carteaud disease or syndrome (confluent reticulate papillomatosis) 701.8
Gougerot-Hailey-Hailey disease (benign familial chronic pemphigus) 757.39
Gougerot (-Houwer) -Sjögren syndrome (keratoconjunctivitis sicca) 710.2
Gougerot's syndrome (trisymptomatic) 709.1
Gouley's syndrome (constrictive pericarditis) 423.2
Goundou 102.6
Gout, gouty 274.9
with specified manifestations NEC 274.89
arthritis (acute) 274.0
arthropathy 274.0
degeneration, heart 274.82
diathesis 274.9
eczema 274.89
episcleritis 274.89 *[379.09]*
external ear (tophus) 274.81
glomerulonephritis 274.10
iritis 274.89 *[364.11]*
joint 274.0
kidney 274.10
lead 984.9
specified type of lead — *see* Table of Drugs and Chemicals
nephritis 274.10
neuritis 274.89 *[357.4]*
phlebitis 274.89 *[451.9]*
rheumatic 714.0
saturnine 984.9
specified type of lead — *see* Table of Drugs and Chemicals
spondylitis 274.0
synovitis 274.0
syphilitic 095.8
tophi 274.0
ear 274.81
heart 274.82
specified site NEC 274.82
Gowers'
muscular dystrophy 359.1
syndrome (vasovagal attack) 780.2
Gowers-Paton-Kennedy syndrome 377.04
Gradenigo's syndrome 383.02
Graft-versus-host disease (bone marrow) 996.85
due to organ transplant NEC — *see* Complications, transplant, organ
Graham Steell's murmur (pulmonic regurgitation) — *see also* Endocarditis, pulmonary 424.3
Grain-handlers' disease or lung 495.8
Grain mite (itch) 133.8
Grand
mal (idiopathic) (*see also* Epilepsy) 345.1 ☑

☑ Additional Digit Required — Refer to the Tabular List for Digit Selection   Subterms under main terms may continue to next column or page

132 — Volume 2   ▶◀ Revised Text   ● New Line   ▲ Revised Code   *2007 ICD-9-CM*

Grand — *continued*
- mal (*see also* Epilepsy) — *continued*
  - hysteria of Charcôt 300.11
  - nonrecurrent or isolated 780.39
  - multipara
    - affecting management of labor and delivery 659.4 ☑
    - status only (not pregnant) V61.5

Granite workers' lung 502

Granular — *see also* condition
- inflammation, pharynx 472.1
- kidney (contracting) (*see also* Sclerosis, renal) 587
- liver — *see* Cirrhosis, liver
- nephritis — *see* Nephritis

Granulation tissue, abnormal — *see also* Granuloma
- abnormal or excessive 701.5
- postmastoidectomy cavity 383.33
- postoperative 701.5
- skin 701.5

Granulocytopenia, granulocytopenic
- (primary) 288.00 ▲
- malignant 288.09 ▲

Granuloma NEC 686.1
- abdomen (wall) 568.89
  - skin (pyogenicum) 686.1
    - from residual foreign body 709.4
- annulare 695.89
- anus 569.49
- apical 522.6
- appendix 543.9
- aural 380.23
- beryllium (skin) 709.4
  - lung 503
- bone (*see also* Osteomyelitis) 730.1 ☑
  - eosinophilic 277.89
  - from residual foreign body 733.99
- canaliculus lacrimalis 375.81
- cerebral 348.8
- cholesterin, middle ear 385.82
- coccidioidal (progressive) 114.3
  - lung 114.4
  - meninges 114.2
  - primary (lung) 114.0
- colon 569.89
- conjunctiva 372.61
- dental 522.6
- ear, middle (cholesterin) 385.82
  - with otitis media — *see* Otitis media
- eosinophilic 277.89
  - bone 277.89
  - lung 277.89
  - oral mucosa 528.9
- exuberant 701.5
- eyelid 374.89
- facial
  - lethal midline 446.3
  - malignant 446.3
- faciale 701.8
- fissuratum (gum) 523.8
- foot NEC 686.1
- foreign body (in soft tissue) NEC 728.82
  - bone 733.99
  - in operative wound 998.4
  - muscle 728.82
  - skin 709.4
  - subcutaneous tissue 709.4
- fungoides 202.1 ☑
- gangraenescens 446.3
- giant cell (central) (jaw) (reparative) 526.3
  - gingiva 523.8
  - peripheral (gingiva) 523.8
- gland (lymph) 289.3
- Hodgkin's (M9661/3) 201.1 ☑
- ileum 569.89
- infectious NEC 136.9
- inguinale (Donovan) 099.2
  - venereal 099.2
- intestine 569.89
- iridocyclitis 364.10
- jaw (bone) 526.3

Granuloma — *continued*
- jaw — *continued*
  - reparative giant cell 526.3
- kidney (*see also* Infection, kidney) 590.9
- lacrimal sac 375.81
- larynx 478.79
- lethal midline 446.3
- lipid 277.89
- lipoid 277.89
- liver 572.8
- lung (infectious) (*see also* Fibrosis, lung) 515
  - coccidioidal 114.4
  - eosinophilic 277.89
- lymph gland 289.3
- Majocchi's 110.6
- malignant, face 446.3
- mandible 526.3
- mediastinum 519.3
- midline 446.3
- monilial 112.3
- muscle 728.82
  - from residual foreign body 728.82
- nasal sinus (*see also* Sinusitis) 473.9
- operation wound 998.59
  - foreign body 998.4
  - stitch (external) 998.89
    - internal wound 998.89
  - talc 998.7
- oral mucosa, eosinophilic or pyogenic 528.9
- orbit, orbital 376.11
- paracoccidioidal 116.1
- penis, venereal 099.2
- periapical 522.6
- peritoneum 568.89
  - due to ova of helminths NEC (*see also* Helminthiasis) 128.9
- postmastoidectomy cavity 383.33
- postoperative — *see* Granuloma, operation wound
- prostate 601.8
- pudendi (ulcerating) 099.2
- pudendorum (ulcerative) 099.2
- pulp, internal (tooth) 521.49
- pyogenic, pyogenicum (skin) 686.1
  - maxillary alveolar ridge 522.6
  - oral mucosa 528.9
- rectum 569.49
- reticulohistiocytic 277.89
- rubrum nasi 705.89
- sarcoid 135
- Schistosoma 120.9
- septic (skin) 686.1
- silica (skin) 709.4
- sinus (accessory) (infectional) (nasal) (*see also* Sinusitis) 473.9
- skin (pyogenicum) 686.1
  - from foreign body or material 709.4
- sperm 608.89
- spine
  - syphilitic (epidural) 094.89
  - tuberculous (*see also* Tuberculosis) 015.0 ☑ [730.88]
- stitch (postoperative) 998.89
  - internal wound 998.89
- suppurative (skin) 686.1
- suture (postoperative) 998.89
  - internal wound 998.89
- swimming pool 031.1
- talc 728.82
  - in operation wound 998.7
- telangiectaticum (skin) 686.1
- tracheostomy 519.09 ●
- trichophyticum 110.6
- tropicum 102.4
- umbilicus 686.1
  - newborn 771.4
- urethra 599.84
- uveitis 364.10
- vagina 099.2
- venereum 099.2
- vocal cords 478.5
- Wegener's (necrotizing respiratory granulomatosis) 446.4

Granulomatosis NEC 686.1
- disciformis chronica et progressiva 709.3
- infantiseptica 771.2
- lipoid 277.89
- lipophagic, intestinal 040.2
- miliary 027.0
- necrotizing, respiratory 446.4
- progressive, septic 288.1
- Wegener's (necrotizing respiratory) 446.4

Granulomatous tissue — *see* Granuloma

Granulosis rubra nasi 705.89

Graphite fibrosis (of lung) 503

Graphospasm 300.89
- organic 333.84

Grating scapula 733.99

Gravel (urinary) — *see also* Calculus 592.9

Graves' disease (exophthalmic goiter) — *see also* Goiter, toxic 242.0 ☑

Gravis — *see* condition

Grawitz's tumor (hypernephroma) (M8312/3) 189.0

Grayness, hair (premature) 704.3
- congenital 757.4

Gray or grey syndrome (chloramphenicol) (newborn) 779.4

Greenfield's disease 330.0

Green sickness 280.9

Greenstick fracture — *see* Fracture, by site

Greig's syndrome (hypertelorism) 756.0

Griesinger's disease — *see also* Ancylostomiasis 126.9

Grinders'
- asthma 502
- lung 502
- phthisis (*see also* Tuberculosis) 011.4 ☑

Grinding, teeth 306.8

Grip
- Dabney's 074.1
- devil's 074.1

Grippe, grippal — *see also* Influenza
- Balkan 083.0
- intestinal 487.8
- summer 074.8

Grippy cold 487.1

Grisel's disease 723.5

Groin — *see* condition

Grooved
- nails (transverse) 703.8
- tongue 529.5
  - congenital 750.13

Ground itch 126.9

Growing pains, children 781.99

Growth (fungoid) (neoplastic) (new) (M8000/1) — *see also* Neoplasm, by site, unspecified nature
- adenoid (vegetative) 474.12
- benign (M8000/0) — *see* Neoplasm, by site, benign
- fetal, poor 764.9 ☑
  - affecting management of pregnancy 656.5 ☑
- malignant (M8000/3) — *see* Neoplasm, by site, malignant
- rapid, childhood V21.0
- secondary (M8000/6) — *see* Neoplasm, by site, malignant, secondary

GRSA (glycopeptide resistant staphylococcus aureus) V09.8 ☑

Gruber's hernia — *see* Hernia, Gruber's

Gruby's disease (tinea tonsurans) 110.0

G-trisomy 758.0

Guama fever 066.3

Gubler (-Millard) paralysis or syndrome 344.89

Guérin-Stern syndrome (arthrogryposis multiplex congenita) 754.89

Guertin's disease (electric chorea) 049.8

Guillain-Barré disease or syndrome 357.0

Guinea worms (infection) (infestation) 125.7

Guinon's disease (motor-verbal tic) 307.23

Gull and Sutton's disease — *see* Hypertension, kidney

Gull's disease (thyroid atrophy with myxedema) 244.8

Gum — *see* condition

Gumboil 522.7

Gumma (syphilitic) 095.9
- artery 093.89
  - cerebral or spinal 094.89
- bone 095.5
  - of yaws (late) 102.6
- brain 094.89
- cauda equina 094.89
- central nervous system NEC 094.9
- ciliary body 095.8 [364.11]
- congenital 090.5
  - testis 090.5
- eyelid 095.8 [373.5]
- heart 093.89
- intracranial 094.89
- iris 095.8 [364.11]
- kidney 095.4
- larynx 095.8
- leptomeninges 094.2
- liver 095.3
- meninges 094.2
- myocardium 093.82
- nasopharynx 095.8
- neurosyphilitic 094.9
- nose 095.8
- orbit 095.8
- palate (soft) 095.8
- penis 095.8
- pericardium 093.81
- pharynx 095.8
- pituitary 095.8
- scrofulous (see also Tuberculosis) 017.0 ☑
- skin 095.8
- specified site NEC 095.8
- spinal cord 094.89
- tongue 095.8
- tonsil 095.8
- trachea 095.8
- tuberculous (*see also* Tuberculosis) 017.0 ☑
- ulcerative due to yaws 102.4
- ureter 095.8
- yaws 102.4
  - bone 102.6

Gunn's syndrome (jaw-winking syndrome) 742.8

Gunshot wound — *see also* Wound, open, by site
- fracture — *see* Fracture, by site, open
- internal organs (abdomen, chest, or pelvis) — *see* Injury, internal, by site, with open wound
- intracranial — *see* Laceration, brain, with open intracranial wound

Günther's disease or syndrome (congenital erythropoietic porphyria) 277.1

Gustatory hallucination 780.1

Gynandrism 752.7

Gynandroblastoma (M8632/1)
- specified site — *see* Neoplasm, by site, uncertain behavior
- unspecified site
  - female 236.2
  - male 236.4

Gynandromorphism 752.7

Gynatresia (congenital) 752.49

Gynecoid pelvis, male 738.6

Gynecological examination V72.31
- for contraceptive maintenance V25.40

Gynecomastia 611.1

Gynephobia 300.29

Gyrate scalp 757.39

H

Haas' disease (osteochondrosis head of humerus) 732.3

☑ Additional Digit Required — Refer to the Tabular List for Digit Selection   ▽ Subterms under main terms may continue to next column or page

2007 ICD-9-CM   ▶◀ Revised Text   ● New Line   ▲ Revised Code   October 2006 · Volume 2 — 133

Habermann's disease (acute parapsoriasis varioliformis) 696.2
Habit, habituation
  chorea 307.22
  disturbance, child 307.9
  drug (*see also* Dependence) 304.9 ☑
  laxative (*see also* Abuse, drugs, non-dependent) 305.9 ☑
  spasm 307.20
    chronic 307.22
    transient (of childhood) 307.21
  tic 307.20
    chronic 307.22
    transient (of childhood) 307.21
  use of
    nonprescribed drugs (*see also* Abuse, drugs, nondependent) 305.9 ☑
    patent medicines (*see also* Abuse, drugs, nondependent) 305.9 ☑
  vomiting 536.2
Hadfield-Clarke syndrome (pancreatic infantilism) 577.8
Haff disease 985.1
Hageman factor defect, deficiency, or disease — *see also* Defect, coagulation 286.3
Haglund's disease (osteochondrosis os tibiale externum) 732.5
Haglund-Läwen-Fründ syndrome 717.89
Hagner's disease (hypertrophic pulmonary osteoarthropathy) 731.2
Hag teeth, tooth 524.39
Hailey-Hailey disease (benign familial chronic pemphigus) 757.39
Hair — *see also* condition
  plucking 307.9
Hairball in stomach 935.2
Hairy black tongue 529.3
Half vertebra 756.14
Halitosis 784.99 ▲
Hallermann-Streiff syndrome 756.0
Hallervorden-Spatz disease or syndrome 333.0
Hallopeau's
  acrodermatitis (continua) 696.1
  disease (lichen sclerosis et atrophicus) 701.0
Hallucination (auditory) (gustatory) (olfactory) (tactile) 780.1
  alcohol induced 291.3
  drug-induced 292.12
  visual 368.16
Hallucinosis 298.9
  alcohol-induced (acute) 291.3
  drug-induced 292.12
Hallus — *see* Hallux
Hallux 735.9
  malleus (acquired) 735.3
  rigidus (acquired) 735.2
    congenital 755.66
    late effects of rickets 268.1
  valgus (acquired) 735.0
    congenital 755.66
  varus (acquired) 735.1
    congenital 755.66
Halo, visual 368.15
Hamartoblastoma 759.6
Hamartoma 759.6
  epithelial (gingival), odontogenic, central, or peripheral (M9321/0) 213.1
    upper jaw (bone) 213.0
  vascular 757.32
Hamartosis, hamartoses NEC 759.6
Hamman's disease or syndrome (spontaneous mediastinal emphysema) 518.1
Hamman-Rich syndrome (diffuse interstitial pulmonary fibrosis) 516.3
Hammer toe (acquired) 735.4
  congenital 755.66
  late effects of rickets 268.1
Hand — *see* condition

Hand-foot syndrome 282.61
Hand-Schüller-Christian disease or syndrome (chronic histiocytosis x) 277.89
Hanging (asphyxia) (strangulation) (suffocation) 994.7
Hangnail (finger) (with lymphangitis) 681.02
Hangover (alcohol) — *see also* Abuse, drugs, nondependent 305.0 ☑
Hanot-Chauffard (-Troisier) syndrome (bronze diabetes) 275.0
Hanot's cirrhosis or disease — *see* Cirrhosis, biliary
Hansen's disease (leprosy) 030.9
  benign form 030.1
  malignant form 030.0
Harada's disease or syndrome 363.22
Hard chancre 091.0
Hardening
  artery — *see* Arteriosclerosis
  brain 348.8
  liver 571.8
Hard firm prostate 600.10
  with
    urinary   ●
      obstruction 600.11   ●
      retention 600.11   ●
Harelip — *see also* Cleft, lip 749.10
Hare's syndrome (M8010/3) (carcinoma, pulmonary apex) 162.3
Harkavy's syndrome 446.0
Harlequin (fetus) 757.1
  color change syndrome 779.89
Harley's disease (intermittent hemoglobinuria) 283.2
Harris'
  lines 733.91
  syndrome (organic hyperinsulinism) 251.1
Hart's disease or syndrome (pellagra-cerebellar ataxia-renal aminoaciduria) 270.0
Hartmann's pouch (abnormal sacculation of gallbladder neck) 575.8
  of intestine V44.3
    attention to V55.3
Hartnup disease (pellagra-cerebellar ataxia-renal aminoaciduria) 270.0
Harvester lung 495.0
Hashimoto's disease or struma (struma lymphomatosa) 245.2
Hassall-Henle bodies (corneal warts) 371.41
Haut mal — *see also* Epilepsy 345.1 ☑
Haverhill fever 026.1
Hawaiian wood rose dependence 304.5 ☑
Hawkins' keloid 701.4
Hay
  asthma (*see also* Asthma) 493.0 ☑
  fever (allergic) (with rhinitis) 477.9
    with asthma (bronchial) (*see also* Asthma) 493.0 ☑
    allergic, due to grass, pollen, ragweed, or tree 477.0
    conjunctivitis 372.05
    due to
      dander, animal (cat) (dog) 477.2
      dust 477.8
      fowl 477.8
      hair, animal (cat) (dog) 477.2
      pollen 477.0
      specified allergen other than pollen 477.8
Hayem-Faber syndrome (achlorhydric anemia) 280.9
Hayem-Widal syndrome (acquired hemolytic jaundice) 283.9
Haygarth's nodosities 715.04
Hazard-Crile tumor (M8350/3) 193
Hb (abnormal)
  disease — *see* Disease, hemoglobin
  trait — *see* Trait
H disease 270.0
Head — *see also* condition

Head — *see also* condition —
  continued
  banging 307.3
Headache 784.0
  allergic 346.2 ☑
  cluster 346.2 ☑
  due to
    loss, spinal fluid 349.0
    lumbar puncture 349.0
    saddle block 349.0
  emotional 307.81
  histamine 346.2 ☑
  lumbar puncture 349.0
  menopausal 627.2
  migraine 346.9 ☑
  nonorganic origin 307.81
  postspinal 349.0
  psychogenic 307.81
  psychophysiologic 307.81
  sick 346.1 ☑
  spinal 349.0
    complicating labor and delivery 668.8 ☑
    postpartum 668.8 ☑
  spinal fluid loss 349.0
  tension 307.81
  vascular 784.0
    migraine type 346.9 ☑
  vasomotor 346.9 ☑
Health
  advice V65.4 ☑
  audit V70.0
  checkup V70.0
  education V65.4 ☑
  hazard (*see also* History of) V15.9
    falling V15.88
    specified cause NEC V15.89
  instruction V65.4 ☑
  services provided because (of)
    boarding school residence V60.6
    holiday relief for person providing home care V60.5
    inadequate
      housing V60.1
      resources V60.2
    lack of housing V60.0
    no care available in home V60.4
    person living alone V60.3
    poverty V60.3
    residence in institution V60.6
    specified cause NEC V60.8
    vacation relief for person providing home care V60.5
Healthy
  donor (*see also* Donor) V59.9
  infant or child
    accompanying sick mother V65.0
    receiving care V20.1
  person
    accompanying sick relative V65.0
    admitted for sterilization V25.2
    receiving prophylactic inoculation or vaccination (*see also* Vaccination, prophylactic) V05.9
Hearing examination V72.19   ▲
  following failed hearing screening   ●
    V72.11   ●
Heart — *see* condition
Heartburn 787.1
  psychogenic 306.4
Heat (effects) 992.9
  apoplexy 992.0
  burn (*see also* Burn, by site)
    from sun (*see also* Sunburn) 692.71
  collapse 992.1
  cramps 992.2
  dermatitis or eczema 692.89
  edema 992.7
  erythema — *see* Burn, by site
  excessive 992.9
    specified effect NEC 992.8
  exhaustion 992.5
    anhydrotic 992.3
    due to
      salt (and water) depletion 992.4
Head — *see also* condition

Heat — *continued*
  exhaustion — *continued*
    due to — *continued*
      water depletion 992.3
    fatigue (transient) 992.6
    fever 992.0
    hyperpyrexia 992.0
    prickly 705.1
    prostration — *see* Heat, exhaustion
    pyrexia 992.0
    rash 705.1
    specified effect NEC 992.8
    stroke 992.0
    sunburn (*see also* Sunburn) 692.71
    syncope 992.1
Heavy-chain disease 273.2
Heavy-for-dates (fetus or infant) 766.1
  4500 grams or more 766.0
  exceptionally 766.0
Hebephrenia, hebephrenic (acute) — *see also* Schizophrenia 295.1 ☑
  dementia (praecox) (*see also* Schizophrenia) 295.1 ☑
  schizophrenia (*see also* Schizophrenia) 295.1 ☑
Heberden's
  disease or nodes 715.04
  syndrome (angina pectoris) 413.9
Hebra's disease
  dermatitis exfoliativa 695.89
  erythema multiforme exudativum 695.1
  pityriasis 695.89
    maculata et circinata 696.3
    rubra 695.89
    pilaris 696.4
  prurigo 698.2
Hebra, nose 040.1
Hedinger's syndrome (malignant carcinoid) 259.2
Heel — *see* condition
Heerfordt's disease or syndrome (uveoparotitis) 135
Hegglin's anomaly or syndrome 288.2
Heidenhain's disease 290.10
  with dementia 290.10
Heilmeyer-Schöner disease (M9842/3) 207.1 ☑
Heine-Medin disease — *see also* Poliomyelitis 045.9 ☑
Heinz-body anemia, congenital 282.7
Heller's disease or syndrome (infantile psychosis) — *see also* Psychosis, childhood 299.1 ☑
H.E.L.L.P 642.5 ☑
Helminthiasis — *see also* Infestation, by specific parasite 128.9
  Ancylostoma (*see also* Ancylostoma) 126.9
  intestinal 127.9
    mixed types (types classifiable to more than one of the categories 120.0–127.7) 127.8
    specified type 127.7
  mixed types (intestinal) (types classifiable to more than one of the categories 120.0–127.7) 127.8
  Necator americanus 126.1
  specified type NEC 128.8
  Trichinella 124
Heloma 700
Hemangioblastoma (M9161/1) — *see also* Neoplasm, connective tissue, uncertain behavior
  malignant (M9161/3) — *see* Neoplasm, connective tissue, malignant
Hemangioblastomatosis, cerebelloretinal 759.6
Hemangioendothelioma (M9130/1) — *see also* Neoplasm, by site, uncertain behavior
  benign (M9130/0) 228.00
  bone (diffuse) (M9130/3) — *see* Neoplasm, bone, malignant

☑ Additional Digit Required — Refer to the Tabular List for Digit Selection   ⟲ Subterms under main terms may continue to next column or page

134 — Volume 2 · October 2006   ▶◀ Revised Text   ● New Line   ▲ Revised Code   **2007 ICD-9-CM**

Hemangioendothelioma — *see also*
Neoplasm, by site, uncertain
behavior — *continued*
malignant (M9130/3) — *see* Neoplasm, connective tissue, malignant
nervous system (M9130/0) 228.09
Hemangioendotheliosarcoma
(M9130/3) — *see* Neoplasm, connective tissue, malignant
Hemangiofibroma (M9160/0) — *see*
Neoplasm, by site, benign
Hemangiolipoma (M8861/0) — *see*
Lipoma
Hemangioma (M9120/0) 228.00
arteriovenous (M9123/0) — *see* Hemangioma, by site
brain 228.02
capillary (M9131/0) — *see* Hemangioma, by site
cavernous (M9121/0) — *see* Hemangioma, by site
central nervous system NEC 228.09
choroid 228.09
heart 228.09
infantile (M9131/0) — *see* Hemangioma, by site
intra-abdominal structures 228.04
intracranial structures 228.02
intramuscular (M9132/0) — *see* Hemangioma, by site
iris 228.09
juvenile (M9131/0) — *see* Hemangioma, by site
malignant (M9120/3) — *see* Neoplasm, connective tissue, malignant
meninges 228.09
brain 228.02
spinal cord 228.09
peritoneum 228.04
placenta — *see* Placenta, abnormal
plexiform (M9131/0) — *see* Hemangioma, by site
racemose (M9123/0) — *see* Hemangioma, by site
retina 228.03
retroperitoneal tissue 228.04
sclerosing (M8832/0) — *see* Neoplasm, skin, benign
simplex (M9131/0) — *see* Hemangioma, by site
skin and subcutaneous tissue 228.01
specified site NEC 228.09
spinal cord 228.09
venous (M9122/0) — *see* Hemangioma, by site
verrucous keratotic (M9142/0) — *see*
Hemangioma, by site
Hemangiomatosis (systemic) 757.32
involving single site — *see* Hemangioma
Hemangiopericytoma (M9150/1) — *see*
also Neoplasm, connective tissue,
uncertain behavior
benign (M9150/0) — *see* Neoplasm,
connective tissue, benign
malignant (M9150/3) — *see* Neoplasm, connective tissue, malignant
Hemangiosarcoma (M9120/3) — *see*
Neoplasm, connective tissue, malignant
Hemarthrosis (nontraumatic) 719.10
ankle 719.17
elbow 719.12
foot 719.17
hand 719.14
hip 719.15
knee 719.16
multiple sites 719.19
pelvic region 719.15
shoulder (region) 719.11
specified site NEC 719.18
traumatic — *see* Sprain, by site
wrist 719.13

Hematemesis 578.0
with ulcer — *see* Ulcer, by site, with
hemorrhage
due to S. japonicum 120.2
Goldstein's (familial hemorrhagic
telangiectasia) 448.0
newborn 772.4
due to swallowed maternal blood
777.3
Hematidrosis 705.89
Hematinuria — *see also* Hemoglobinuria
791.2
malarial 084.8
paroxysmal 283.2
Hematite miners' lung 503
Hematobilia 576.8
Hematocele (congenital) (diffuse) (idiopathic) 608.83
broad ligament 620.7
canal of Nuck 629.0
cord, male 608.83
fallopian tube 620.8
female NEC 629.0
ischiorectal 569.89
male NEC 608.83
ovary 629.0
pelvis, pelvic
female 629.0
with ectopic pregnancy (*see also*
Pregnancy, ectopic)
633.90
with intrauterine pregnancy
633.91
male 608.83
periuterine 629.0
retrouterine 629.0
scrotum 608.83
spermatic cord (diffuse) 608.83
testis 608.84
traumatic — *see* Injury, internal,
pelvis
tunica vaginalis 608.83
uterine ligament 629.0
uterus 621.4
vagina 623.6
vulva 624.5
Hematocephalus 742.4
Hematochezia — *see also* Melena 578.1
Hematochyluria — *see also* Infestation,
filarial 125.9
Hematocolpos 626.8
Hematocornea 371.12
Hematogenous — *see* condition
Hematoma (skin surface intact) (traumatic) — *see also* Contusion

> *Note — Hematomas are coded according
> to origin and the nature and site of the
> hematoma or the accompanying injury.
> Hematomas of unspecified origin are
> coded as injuries of the sites involved,
> except:*
>
> (a) *hematomas of genital organs
>   which are coded as diseases of
>   the organ involved unless they
>   complicate pregnancy or delivery*
>
> (b) *hematomas of the eye which are
>   coded as diseases of the eye.*
>
> *For late effect of hematoma classifiable
> to 920–924 see Late, effect, contusion*

with
crush injury — *see* Crush
fracture — *see* Fracture, by site
injury of internal organs (*see also*
Injury, internal, by site)
kidney — *see* Hematoma, kidney traumatic
liver — *see* Hematoma, liver,
traumatic
spleen — *see* Hematoma, spleen
nerve injury — *see* Injury, nerve
open wound — *see* Wound, open,
by site
skin surface intact — *see* Contusion

Hematoma — *see also* Contusion —
continued
abdomen (wall) — *see* Contusion, abdomen
amnion 658.8 ☑
aorta, dissecting 441.00
abdominal 441.02
thoracic 441.01
thoracoabdominal 441.03
arterial (complicating trauma) 904.9
specified site — *see* Injury, blood
vessel, by site
auricle (ear) 380.31
birth injury 767.8
skull 767.19
brain (traumatic) 853.0 ☑

> *Note — Use the following fifth-digit
> subclassification with categories
> 851–854:*
>
> 0 *unspecified state of conscious-
>   ness*
>
> 1 *with no loss of consciousness*
>
> 2 *with brief [less than one hour]
>   loss of consciousness*
>
> 3 *with moderate [1–24 hours] loss
>   of consciousness*
>
> 4 *with prolonged [more than 24
>   hours] loss of consciousness and
>   return to pre–existing conscious
>   level*
>
> 5 *with prolonged [more than 24
>   hours] loss of consciousness,
>   without return to pre–existing
>   conscious level*
>
> *Use fifth-digit 5 to designate when a
> patient is unconscious and dies before
> regaining consciousness, regardless of
> the duration of the loss of consciousness*
>
> 6 *with loss of consciousness of un-
>   specified duration*
>
> 9 *with concussion, unspecified*

with
cerebral
contusion — *see* Contusion,
brain
laceration — *see* Laceration,
brain
open intracranial wound
853.1 ☑
skull fracture — *see* Fracture,
skull, by site
extradural or epidural 852.4 ☑
with open intracranial wound
852.5 ☑
fetus or newborn 767.0
nontraumatic 432.0
fetus or newborn NEC 767.0
nontraumatic (*see also* Hemorrhage, brain) 431
epidural or extradural 432.0
newborn NEC 772.8
subarachnoid, arachnoid, or
meningeal (*see also* Hemorrhage, subarachnoid)
430
subdural (*see also* Hemorrhage,
subdural) 432.1
subarachnoid, arachnoid, or
meningeal 852.0 ☑
with open intracranial wound
852.1 ☑
fetus or newborn 772.2
nontraumatic (*see also* Hemorrhage, subarachnoid) 430
subdural 852.2 ☑
with open intracranial wound
852.3 ☑
fetus or newborn (localized)
767.0
nontraumatic (*see also* Hemorrhage, subdural) 432.1

Hematoma — *see also* Contusion —
continued
breast (nontraumatic) 611.8
broad ligament (nontraumatic) 620.7
complicating delivery 665.7 ☑
traumatic — *see* Injury, internal,
broad ligament
calcified NEC 959.9
capitis 920
due to birth injury 767.19
newborn 767.19
cerebral — *see* Hematoma, brain
cesarean section wound 674.3 ☑
chorion — *see* Placenta, abnormal
complicating delivery (perineum) (vulva) 664.5 ☑
pelvic 665.7 ☑
vagina 665.7 ☑
corpus
cavernosum (nontraumatic) 607.82
luteum (nontraumatic) (ruptured)
620.1
dura (mater) — *see* Hematoma, brain,
subdural
epididymis (nontraumatic) 608.83
epidural (traumatic) (*see also*
Hematoma, brain, extradural)
spinal — *see* Injury, spinal, by site
episiotomy 674.3 ☑
external ear 380.31
extradural (*see also* Hematoma, brain,
extradural)
fetus or newborn 767.0
nontraumatic 432.0
fetus or newborn 767.0
fallopian tube 620.8
genital organ (nontraumatic)
female NEC 629.89   ▲
male NEC 608.83
traumatic (external site) 922.4
internal — *see* Injury, internal,
genital organ
graafian follicle (ruptured) 620.0
internal organs (abdomen, chest, or
pelvis) (*see also* Injury, internal,
by site)
kidney — *see* Hematoma, kidney,
traumatic
liver — *see* Hematoma, liver, traumatic
spleen — *see* Hematoma, spleen
intracranial — *see* Hematoma, brain
kidney, cystic 593.81
traumatic 866.01
with open wound into cavity
866.11
labia (nontraumatic) 624.5
lingual (and other parts of neck, scalp,
or face, except eye) 920
liver (subcapsular) 573.8
birth injury 767.8
fetus or newborn 767.8
traumatic NEC 864.01
with
laceration — *see* Laceration,
liver
open wound into cavity
864.11
mediastinum — *see* Injury, internal,
mediastinum
meninges, meningeal (brain) (*see also*
Hematoma, brain, subarach-
noid)
spinal — *see* Injury, spinal, by site
mesosalpinx (nontraumatic) 620.8
traumatic — *see* Injury, internal,
pelvis
muscle (traumatic) — *see* Contusion,
by site
nasal (septum) (and other part(s) of
neck, scalp, or face, except eye)
920
obstetrical surgical wound 674.3 ☑
orbit, orbital (nontraumatic) 376.32
traumatic 921.2

☑ Additional Digit Required — Refer to the Tabular List for Digit Selection   ▽ Subterms under main terms may continue to next column or page

2007 ICD-9-CM   ▶◀ Revised Text   ● New Line   ▲ Revised Code   October 2006 • Volume 2 — 135

Hematoma — see also Contusion — continued
ovary (corpus luteum) (nontraumatic) 620.1
traumatic — see Injury, internal, ovary
pelvis (female) (nontraumatic) 629.89
complicating delivery 665.7 ☑ ▲
male 608.83
traumatic (see also Injury, internal, pelvis)
specified organ NEC (see also Injury, internal, pelvis) 867.6
penis (nontraumatic) 607.82
pericranial (and neck, or face any part, except eye) 920
due to injury at birth 767.19
perineal wound (obstetrical) 674.3 ☑
complicating delivery 664.5 ☑
perirenal, cystic 593.81
pinna 380.31
placenta — see Placenta, abnormal
postoperative 998.12
retroperitoneal (nontraumatic) 568.81
traumatic — see Injury, internal, retroperitoneum
retropubic, male 568.81
scalp (and neck, or face any part, except eye) 920
fetus or newborn 767.19
scrotum (nontraumatic) 608.83
traumatic 922.4
seminal vesicle (nontraumatic) 608.83
traumatic — see Injury, internal, seminal, vesicle
spermatic cord (see also Injury, internal, spermatic cord)
nontraumatic 608.83
spinal (cord) (meninges) (see also Injury, spinal, by site)
fetus or newborn 767.4
nontraumatic 336.1
spleen 865.01
with
laceration — see Laceration, spleen
open wound into cavity 865.11
sternocleidomastoid, birth injury 767.8
sternomastoid, birth injury 767.8
subarachnoid (see also Hematoma, brain, subarachnoid)
fetus or newborn 772.2
nontraumatic (see also Hemorrhage, subarachnoid) 430
newborn 772.2
subdural (see also Hematoma, brain, subdural)
fetus or newborn (localized) 767.0
nontraumatic (see also Hemorrhage, subdural) 432.1
subperiosteal (syndrome) 267
traumatic — see Hematoma, by site
superficial, fetus or newborn 772.6
syncytium — see Placenta, abnormal
testis (nontraumatic) 608.83
birth injury 767.8
traumatic 922.4
tunica vaginalis (nontraumatic) 608.83
umbilical cord 663.6 ☑
affecting fetus or newborn 762.6
uterine ligament (nontraumatic) 620.7
traumatic — see Injury, internal, pelvis
uterus 621.4
traumatic — see Injury, internal, pelvis
vagina (nontraumatic) (ruptured) 623.6
complicating delivery 665.7 ☑
traumatic 922.4
vas deferens (nontraumatic) 608.83

Hematoma — see also Contusion — continued
vas deferens — continued
traumatic — see Injury, internal, vas deferens
vitreous 379.23
vocal cord 920
vulva (nontraumatic) 624.5
complicating delivery 664.5 ☑
fetus or newborn 767.8
traumatic 922.4
Hematometra 621.4
Hematomyelia 336.1
with fracture of vertebra (see also Fracture, vertebra, by site, with spinal cord injury) 806.8
fetus or newborn 767.4
Hematomyelitis 323.9
late effect — see category 326
Hematoperitoneum — see also Hemoperitoneum 568.81
Hematopneumothorax — see also Hemothorax 511.8
Hematopoiesis, cyclic 288.02 ●
Hematoporphyria (acquired) (congenital) 277.1
Hematoporphyrinuria (acquired) (congenital) 277.1
Hematorachis, hematorrhachis 336.1
fetus or newborn 767.4
Hematosalpinx 620.8
with
ectopic pregnancy (see also categories 633.0–633.9) 639.2
infectional (see also Salpingo-oophoritis) 614.2
molar pregnancy (see also categories 630–632) 639.2
Hematospermia 608.82
Hematothorax — see also Hemothorax 511.8
Hematotympanum 381.03
Hematuria (benign) (essential) (idiopathic) 599.7
due to S. hematobium 120.0
endemic 120.0
intermittent 599.7
malarial 084.8
paroxysmal 599.7
sulfonamide
correct substance properly administered 599.7
overdose or wrong substance given or taken 961.0
tropical (bilharziasis) 120.0
tuberculous (see also Tuberculosis) 016.9 ☑
Hematuric bilious fever 084.8
Hemeralopia 368.10
Hemiabiotrophy 799.89
Hemi-akinesia 781.8
Hemianalgesia — see also Disturbance, sensation 782.0
Hemianencephaly 740.0
Hemianesthesia — see also Disturbance, sensation 782.0
Hemianopia, hemianopsia (altitudinal) (homonymous) 368.46
binasal 368.47
bitemporal 368.47
heteronymous 368.47
syphilitic 095.8
Hemiasomatognosia 307.9
Hemiathetosis 781.0
Hemiatrophy 799.89
cerebellar 334.8
face 349.89
progressive 349.89
fascia 728.9
leg 728.2
tongue 529.8
Hemiballism (us) 333.5
Hemiblock (cardiac) (heart) (left) 426.2
Hemicardia 746.89
Hemicephalus, hemicephaly 740.0
Hemichorea 333.5

Hemicrania 346.9 ☑
congenital malformation 740.0
Hemidystrophy — see Hemiatrophy
Hemiectromelia 755.4
Hemihypalgesia — see also Disturbance, sensation 782.0
Hemihypertrophy (congenital) 759.89
cranial 756.0
Hemihypesthesia — see also Disturbance, sensation 782.0
Hemi-inattention 781.8
Hemimelia 755.4
lower limb 755.30
paraxial (complete) (incomplete) (intercalary) (terminal) 755.32
fibula 755.37
tibia 755.36
transverse (complete) (partial) 755.31
upper limb 755.20
paraxial (complete) (incomplete) (intercalary) (terminal) 755.22
radial 755.26
ulnar 755.27
transverse (complete) (partial) 755.21
Hemiparalysis — see also Hemiplegia 342.9 ☑
Hemiparesis — see also Hemiplegia 342.9 ☑
Hemiparesthesia — see also Disturbance, sensation 782.0
Hemiplegia 342.9 ☑
acute (see also Disease, cerebrovascular, acute) 436
alternans facialis 344.89
apoplectic (see also Disease, cerebrovascular, acute) 436
late effect or residual
affecting
dominant side 438.21
nondominant side 438.22
unspecified side 438.20
arteriosclerotic 437.0
late effect or residual
affecting
dominant side 438.21
nondominant side 438.22
unspecified side 438.20
ascending (spinal) NEC 344.89
attack (see also Disease, cerebrovascular, acute) 436
brain, cerebral (current episode) 437.8
congenital 343.1
cerebral — see Hemiplegia, brain
congenital (cerebral) (spastic) (spinal) 343.1
conversion neurosis (hysterical) 300.11
cortical — see Hemiplegia, brain
due to
arteriosclerosis 437.0
late effect or residual
affecting
dominant side 438.21
nondominant side 438.22
unspecified side 438.20
cerebrovascular lesion (see also Disease, cerebrovascular, acute) 436
late effect
affecting
dominant side 438.21
nondominant side 438.22
unspecified side 438.20
embolic (current) (see also Embolism, brain) 434.1 ☑
late effect
affecting
dominant side 438.21
nondominant side 438.22
unspecified side 438.20
flaccid 342.0 ☑
hypertensive (current episode) 437.8

Hemiplegia — continued
infantile (postnatal) 343.4
late effect
birth injury, intracranial or spinal 343.4
cerebrovascular lesion — see Late effect(s) (of) cerebrovascular disease
viral encephalitis 139.0
middle alternating NEC 344.89
newborn NEC 767.0
seizure (current episode) (see also Disease, cerebrovascular, acute) 436
spastic 342.1 ☑
congenital or infantile 343.1
specified NEC 342.8 ☑
thrombotic (current) (see also Thrombosis, brain) 434.0 ☑
late effect — see Late effect(s) (of) cerebrovascular disease
Hemisection, spinal cord — see Fracture, vertebra, by site, with spinal cord injury
Hemispasm 781.0
facial 781.0
Hemispatial neglect 781.8
Hemisporosis 117.9
Hemitremor 781.0
Hemivertebra 756.14
Hemobilia 576.8
Hemocholecyst 575.8
Hemochromatosis (acquired) (diabetic) (hereditary) (liver) (myocardium) (primary idiopathic) (secondary) 275.0
with refractory anemia 238.72 ▲
Hemodialysis V56.0
Hemoglobin — see also condition
abnormal (disease) — see Disease, hemoglobin
AS genotype 282.5
fetal, hereditary persistence 282.7
high-oxygen-affinity 289.0
low NEC 285.9
S (Hb-S), heterozygous 282.5
Hemoglobinemia 283.2
due to blood transfusion NEC 999.8
bone marrow 996.85
paroxysmal 283.2
Hemoglobinopathy (mixed) — see also Disease, hemoglobin 282.7
with thalassemia 282.49
sickle-cell 282.60
with thalassemia (without crisis) 282.41
with
crisis 282.42
vaso-occlusive pain 282.42
Hemoglobinuria, hemoglobinuric 791.2
with anemia, hemolytic, acquired (chronic) NEC 283.2
cold (agglutinin) (paroxysmal) (with Raynaud's syndrome) 283.2
due to
exertion 283.2
hemolysis (from external causes) NEC 283.2
exercise 283.2
fever (malaria) 084.8
infantile 791.2
intermittent 283.2
malarial 084.8
march 283.2
nocturnal (paroxysmal) 283.2
paroxysmal (cold) (nocturnal) 283.2
Hemolymphangioma (M9175/0) 228.1
Hemolysis
fetal — see Jaundice, fetus or newborn
intravascular (disseminated) NEC 286.6
with
abortion — see Abortion, by type, with hemorrhage, delayed or excessive

☑ Additional Digit Required — Refer to the Tabular List for Digit Selection
Subterms under main terms may continue to next column or page

136 — Volume 2 · October 2006 ▶◀ Revised Text ● New Line ▲ Revised Code 2007 ICD-9-CM

Hemolysis — continued
  intravascular — continued
    with — continued
      ectopic pregnancy (see also categories 633.0–633.9) 639.1
      hemorrhage of pregnancy 641.3 ☑
        affecting fetus or newborn 762.1
      molar pregnancy (see also categories 630–632) 639.1
    acute 283.2
    following
      abortion 639.1
      ectopic or molar pregnancy 639.1
    neonatal — see Jaundice, fetus or newborn
    transfusion NEC 999.8
      bone marrow 996.85
Hemolytic — see also condition
  anemia — see Anemia, hemolytic
  uremic syndrome 283.11
Hemometra 621.4
Hemopericardium (with effusion) 423.0
  newborn 772.8
  traumatic (see also Hemothorax, traumatic) 860.2
    with open wound into thorax 860.3
Hemoperitoneum 568.81
  infectional (see also Peritonitis) 567.29
  traumatic — see Injury, internal, peritoneum
Hemophagocytic syndrome 288.4 ●
  infection-associated 288.4 ●
Hemophilia (familial) (hereditary) 286.0
  A 286.0
    carrier (asymptomatic) V83.01
      symptomatic V83.02
  acquired 286.5
  B (Leyden) 286.1
  C 286.2
  calcipriva (see also Fibrinolysis) 286.7
  classical 286.0
  nonfamilial 286.7
  secondary 286.5
  vascular 286.4
Hemophilus influenzae NEC 041.5
  arachnoiditis (basic) (brain) (spinal) 320.0
    late effect — see category 326
  bronchopneumonia 482.2
  cerebral ventriculitis 320.0
    late effect — see category 326
  cerebrospinal inflammation 320.0
    late effect — see category 326
  infection NEC 041.5
  leptomeningitis 320.0
    late effect — see category 326
  meningitis (cerebral) (cerebrospinal) (spinal) 320.0
    late effect — see category 326
  meningomyelitis 320.0
    late effect — see category 326
  pachymeningitis (adhesive) (fibrous) (hemorrhagic) (hypertrophic) (spinal) 320.0
    late effect — see category 326
  pneumonia (broncho-) 482.2
Hemophthalmos 360.43
Hemopneumothorax — see also Hemothorax 511.8
  traumatic 860.4
    with open wound into thorax 860.5
Hemoptysis 786.3
  due to Paragonimus (westermani) 121.2
  newborn 770.3
  tuberculous (see also Tuberculosis, pulmonary) 011.9 ☑
Hemorrhage, hemorrhagic (nontraumatic) 459.0
  abdomen 459.0
  accidental (antepartum) 641.2 ☑
    affecting fetus or newborn 762.1

Hemorrhage, hemorrhagic — continued
  adenoid 474.8
  adrenal (capsule) (gland) (medulla) 255.4
    newborn 772.5
  after labor — see Hemorrhage, postpartum
  alveolar
    lung, newborn 770.3
    process 525.8
  alveolus 525.8
  amputation stump (surgical) 998.11
    secondary, delayed 997.69
  anemia (chronic) 280.0
    acute 285.1
  antepartum — see Hemorrhage, pregnancy
  anus (sphincter) 569.3
  apoplexy (stroke) 432.9
  arachnoid — see Hemorrhage, subarachnoid
  artery NEC 459.0
    brain (see also Hemorrhage, brain) 431
    middle meningeal — see Hemorrhage, subarachnoid
  basilar (ganglion) (see also Hemorrhage, brain) 431
  bladder 596.8
  blood dyscrasia 289.9
  bowel 578.9
    newborn 772.4
  brain (miliary) (nontraumatic) 431
    with
      birth injury 767.0
      arachnoid — see Hemorrhage, subarachnoid
    due to
      birth injury 767.0
      rupture of aneurysm (congenital) (see also Hemorrhage, subarachnoid) 430
        mycotic 431
      syphilis 094.89
    epidural or extradural — see Hemorrhage, extradural
    fetus or newborn (anoxic) (hypoxic) (due to birth trauma) (nontraumatic) 767.0
      intraventricular 772.10
        grade I 772.11
        grade II 772.12
        grade III 772.13
        grade IV 772.14
    iatrogenic 997.02
    postoperative 997.02
    puerperal, postpartum, childbirth 674.0 ☑
    stem 431
    subarachnoid, arachnoid, or meningeal — see Hemorrhage, subarachnoid
    subdural — see Hemorrhage, subdural

Hemorrhage, hemorrhagic — continued
  brain — continued
    traumatic NEC 853.0 ☑

> *Note — Use the following fifth-digit subclassification with categories 851–854:*
>
> 0 *unspecified state of consciousness*
>
> 1 *with no loss of consciousness*
>
> 2 *with brief [less than one hour] loss of consciousness*
>
> 3 *with moderate [1–24 hours] loss of consciousness*
>
> 4 *with prolonged [more than 24 hours] loss of consciousness and return to pre-existing conscious level*
>
> 5 *with prolonged [more than 24 hours] loss of consciousness, without return to pre-existing conscious level*
>
> *Use fifth-digit 5 to designate when a patient is unconscious and dies before regaining consciousness, regardless of the duration of the loss of consciousness*
>
> 6 *with loss of consciousness of unspecified duration*
>
> 9 *with concussion, unspecified*

      with
        cerebral
          contusion — see Contusion, brain
          laceration — see Laceration, brain
        open intracranial wound 853.1 ☑
        skull fracture — see Fracture, skull, by site
      extradural or epidural 852.4 ☑
        with open intracranial wound 852.5 ☑
      subarachnoid 852.0 ☑
        with open intracranial wound 852.1 ☑
      subdural 852.2 ☑
        with open intracranial wound 852.3 ☑
  breast 611.79
  bronchial tube — see Hemorrhage, lung
  bronchopulmonary — see Hemorrhage, lung
  bronchus (cause unknown) (see also Hemorrhage, lung) 786.3
  bulbar (see also Hemorrhage, brain) 431
  bursa 727.89
  capillary 448.9
    primary 287.8
  capsular — see Hemorrhage, brain
  cardiovascular 429.89
  cecum 578.9
  cephalic (see also Hemorrhage, brain) 431
  cerebellar (see also Hemorrhage, brain) 431
  cerebellum (see also Hemorrhage, brain) 431
  cerebral (see also Hemorrhage, brain) 431
    fetus or newborn (anoxic) (traumatic) 767.0
  cerebromeningeal (see also Hemorrhage, brain) 431
  cerebrospinal (see also Hemorrhage, brain) 431
  cerebrovascular accident — see Hemorrhage, brain
  cerebrum (see also Hemorrhage, brain) 431

Hemorrhage, hemorrhagic — continued
  cervix (stump) (uteri) 622.8
  cesarean section wound 674.3 ☑
  chamber, anterior (eye) 364.41
  childbirth — see Hemorrhage, complicating, delivery
  choroid 363.61
    expulsive 363.62
  ciliary body 364.41
  cochlea 386.8
  colon — see Hemorrhage, intestine
  complicating
    delivery 641.9 ☑
      affecting fetus or newborn 762.1
      associated with
        afibrinogenemia 641.3 ☑
          affecting fetus or newborn 763.89
        coagulation defect 641.3 ☑
          affecting fetus or newborn 763.89
        hyperfibrinolysis 641.3 ☑
          affecting fetus or newborn 763.89
        hypofibrinogenemia 641.3 ☑
          affecting fetus or newborn 763.89
      due to
        low-lying placenta 641.1 ☑
          affecting fetus or newborn 762.0
        placenta previa 641.1 ☑
          affecting fetus or newborn 762.0
        premature separation of placenta 641.2 ☑
          affecting fetus or newborn 762.1
      retained
        placenta 666.0 ☑
        secundines 666.2 ☑
      trauma 641.8 ☑
        affecting fetus or newborn 763.89
      uterine leiomyoma 641.8 ☑
        affecting fetus or newborn 763.89
    surgical procedure 998.11
  concealed NEC 459.0
  congenital 772.9
  conjunctiva 372.72
    newborn 772.8
  cord, newborn 772.0
    slipped ligature 772.3
    stump 772.3
  corpus luteum (ruptured) 620.1
  cortical (see also Hemorrhage, brain) 431
  cranial 432.9
  cutaneous 782.7
    newborn 772.6
  cystitis — see Cystitis
  cyst, pancreas 577.2
  delayed
    with
      abortion — see Abortion, by type, with hemorrhage, delayed or excessive
      ectopic pregnancy (see also categories 633.0–633.9) 639.1
      molar pregnancy (see also categories 630–632) 639.1
    following
      abortion 639.1
      ectopic or molar pregnancy 639.1
    postpartum 666.2 ☑
  diathesis (familial) 287.9
    newborn 776.0
  disease 287.9
    newborn 776.0
    specified type NEC 287.8
  disorder 287.9

Hemorrhage, hemorrhagic —
continued
  disorder — *continued*
    due to intrinsic circulating antico-
        agulants 286.5
      specified type NEC 287.8
    due to
      any device, implant or graft (pres-
          ence of) classifiable to
          996.0–996.5 — *see* Complica-
          tions, due to (presence of)
          any device, implant, or graft
          classified to 996.0–996.5NEC
        intrinsic circulating anticoagulant
          286.5
  duodenum, duodenal 537.89
    ulcer — *see* Ulcer, duodenum, with
        hemorrhage
  dura mater — *see* Hemorrhage, sub-
      dural
  endotracheal — *see* Hemorrhage, lung
  epicranial subaponeurotic (massive)
      767.11
  epidural — *see* Hemorrhage, extradu-
      ral
  episiotomy 674.3 ☑
  esophagus 530.82
    varix (*see also* Varix, esophagus,
        bleeding) 456.0
  excessive
    with
      abortion — *see* Abortion, by
          type, with hemorrhage,
          delayed or excessive
        ectopic pregnancy (*see also* cat-
            egories 633.0–633.9)
            639.1
        molar pregnancy (*see also* cate-
            gories 630–632) 639.1
    following
      abortion 639.1
      ectopic or molar pregnancy
          639.1
  external 459.0
  extradural (traumatic) (*see also* Hem-
      orrhage, brain, traumatic, ex-
      tradural)
    birth injury 767.0
    fetus or newborn (anoxic) (traumat-
        ic) 767.0
    nontraumatic 432.0
  eye 360.43
    chamber (anterior) (aqueous)
        364.41
    fundus 362.81
  eyelid 374.81
  fallopian tube 620.8
  fetomaternal 772.0
    affecting management of pregnancy
        or puerperium 656.0 ☑
  fetus, fetal 772.0
    from
      cut end of co-twin's cord 772.0
      placenta 772.0
      ruptured cord 772.0
      vasa previa 772.0
    into
      co-twin 772.0
      mother's circulation 772.0
        affecting management of
            pregnancy or puerperi-
            um 656.0 ☑
  fever (*see also* Fever, hemorrhagic)
      065.9
    with renal syndrome 078.6
    arthropod-borne NEC 065.9
    Bangkok 065.4
    Crimean 065.0
    dengue virus 065.4
    epidemic 078.6
    Junin virus 078.7
    Korean 078.6
    Machupo virus 078.7
    mite-borne 065.8
    mosquito-borne 065.4
    Philippine 065.4

Hemorrhage, hemorrhagic —
continued
  fever (*see also* Fever, hemorrhagic) —
      continued
    Russian (Yaroslav) 078.6
    Singapore 065.4
    southeast Asia 065.4
    Thailand 065.4
    tick-borne NEC 065.3
  fibrinogenolysis (*see also* Fibrinolysis)
      286.6
  fibrinolytic (acquired) (*see also* Fibri-
      nolysis) 286.6
  fontanel 767.19
  from tracheostomy stoma 519.09
  fundus, eye 362.81
  funis
    affecting fetus or newborn 772.0
    complicating delivery 663.8 ☑
  gastric (*see also* Hemorrhage, stom-
      ach) 578.9
  gastroenteric 578.9
    newborn 772.4
  gastrointestinal (tract) 578.9
    newborn 772.4
  genitourinary (tract) NEC 599.89
  gingiva 523.8
  globe 360.43
  gravidarum — *see* Hemorrhage, preg-
      nancy
  gum 523.8
  heart 429.89
  hypopharyngeal (throat) 784.8
  intermenstrual 626.6
    irregular 626.6
    regular 626.5
  internal (organs) 459.0
    capsule (*see also* Hemorrhage,
        brain) 431
    ear 386.8
    newborn 772.8
  intestine 578.9
    congenital 772.4
    newborn 772.4
  into
    bladder wall 596.7
    bursa 727.89
    corpus luysii (*see also* Hemorrhage,
        brain) 431
  intra-abdominal 459.0
    during or following surgery 998.11
  intra-alveolar, newborn (lung) 770.3
  intracerebral (*see also* Hemorrhage,
      brain) 431
  intracranial NEC 432.9
    puerperal, postpartum, childbirth
        674.0 ☑
    traumatic — *see* Hemorrhage,
        brain, traumatic
  intramedullary NEC 336.1
  intraocular 360.43
  intraoperative 998.11
  intrapartum — *see* Hemorrhage,
      complicating, delivery
  intrapelvic
    female 629.89   ▲
    male 459.0
  intraperitoneal 459.0
  intrapontine (*see also* Hemorrhage,
      brain) 431
  intrauterine 621.4
    complicating delivery — *see* Hemor-
        rhage, complicating, delivery
    in pregnancy or childbirth — *see*
        Hemorrhage, pregnancy
    postpartum (*see also* Hemorrhage,
        postpartum) 666.1 ☑
  intraventricular (*see also* Hemorrhage,
      brain) 431
    fetus or newborn (anoxic) (traumat-
        ic) 772.10
      grade I 772.11
      grade II 772.12
      grade III 772.13
      grade IV 772.14
  intravesical 596.7

Hemorrhage, hemorrhagic —
continued
  iris (postinfectional) (postinflammato-
      ry) (toxic) 364.41
  joint (nontraumatic) 719.10
    ankle 719.17
    elbow 719.12
    foot 719.17
    forearm 719.13
    hand 719.14
    hip 719.15
    knee 719.16
    lower leg 719.16
    multiple sites 719.19
    pelvic region 719.15
    shoulder (region) 719.11
    specified site NEC 719.18
    thigh 719.15
    upper arm 719.12
    wrist 719.13
  kidney 593.81
  knee (joint) 719.16
  labyrinth 386.8
  leg NEC 459.0
  lenticular striate artery (*see also*
      Hemorrhage, brain) 431
  ligature, vessel 998.11
  liver 573.8
  lower extremity NEC 459.0
  lung 786.3
    newborn 770.3
    tuberculous (*see also* Tuberculosis,
        pulmonary) 011.9 ☑
  malaria 084.8
  marginal sinus 641.2 ☑
  massive subaponeurotic, birth injury
      767.11
  maternal, affecting fetus or newborn
      762.1
  mediastinum 786.3
  medulla (*see also* Hemorrhage, brain)
      431
  membrane (brain) (*see also* Hemor-
      rhage, subarachnoid) 430
    spinal cord — *see* Hemorrhage,
        spinal cord
  meninges, meningeal (brain) (middle)
      (*see also* Hemorrhage, subarach-
      noid) 430
    spinal cord — *see* Hemorrhage,
        spinal cord
  mesentery 568.81
  metritis 626.8
  midbrain (*see also* Hemorrhage, brain)
      431
  mole 631
  mouth 528.9
  mucous membrane NEC 459.0
    newborn 772.8
  muscle 728.89
  nail (subungual) 703.8
  nasal turbinate 784.7
    newborn 772.8
  nasopharynx 478.29
  navel, newborn 772.3
  newborn 772.9
    adrenal 772.5
    alveolar (lung) 770.3
    brain (anoxic) (hypoxic) (due to
        birth trauma) 767.0
    cerebral (anoxic) (hypoxic) (due to
        birth trauma) 767.0
    conjunctiva 772.8
    cutaneous 772.6
    diathesis 776.0
    due to vitamin K deficiency 776.0
    epicranial subaponeurotic (mas-
        sive) 767.11
    gastrointestinal 772.4
    internal (organs) 772.8
    intestines 772.4
    intra-alveolar (lung) 770.3
    intracranial (from any perinatal
        cause) 767.0
    intraventricular (from any perinatal
        cause) 772.10

Hemorrhage, hemorrhagic —
continued
  newborn — *continued*
    intraventricular — *continued*
      grade I 772.11
      grade II 772.12
      grade III 772.13
      grade IV 772.14
    lung 770.3
    pulmonary (massive) 770.3
    spinal cord, traumatic 767.4
    stomach 772.4
    subaponeurotic (massive) 767.11
    subarachnoid (from any perinatal
        cause) 772.2
    subconjunctival 772.8
    subgaleal 767.11
    umbilicus 772.0
      slipped ligature 772.3
      vasa previa 772.0
  nipple 611.79
  nose 784.7
    newborn 772.8
  obstetrical surgical wound 674.3 ☑
  omentum 568.89
    newborn 772.4
  optic nerve (sheath) 377.42
  orbit 376.32
  ovary 620.1
  oviduct 620.8
  pancreas 577.8
  parathyroid (gland) (spontaneous)
      252.8
  parturition — *see* Hemorrhage, com-
      plicating, delivery
  penis 607.82
  pericardium, pericarditis 423.0
  perineal wound (obstetrical) 674.3 ☑
  peritoneum, peritoneal 459.0
  peritonsillar tissue 474.8
    after operation on tonsils 998.11
    due to infection 475
  petechial 782.7
  pituitary (gland) 253.8
  placenta NEC 641.9 ☑
    affecting fetus or newborn 762.1
    from surgical or instrumental
        damage 641.8 ☑
      affecting fetus or newborn 762.1
    previa 641.1 ☑
      affecting fetus or newborn 762.0
  pleura — *see* Hemorrhage, lung
  polioencephalitis, superior 265.1
  polymyositis — *see* Polymyositis
  pons (*see also* Hemorrhage, brain) 431
  pontine (*see also* Hemorrhage, brain)
      431
  popliteal 459.0
  postcoital 626.7
  postextraction (dental) 998.11
  postmenopausal 627.1
  postnasal 784.7
  postoperative 998.11
  postpartum (atonic) (following delivery
      of placenta) 666.1 ☑
    delayed or secondary (after 24
        hours) 666.2 ☑
    retained placenta 666.0 ☑
    third stage 666.0 ☑
  pregnancy (concealed) 641.9 ☑
    accidental 641.2 ☑
      affecting fetus or newborn 762.1
    before 22 completed weeks gesta-
        tion 640.9 ☑
      affecting fetus or newborn 762.1
    due to
      abruptio placenta 641.2 ☑
        affecting fetus or newborn
            762.1
      afibrinogenemia or other coagu-
          lation defect (conditions
          classifiable to
          286.0–286.9) 641.3 ☑
        affecting fetus or newborn
            762.1

☑ Additional Digit Required — Refer to the Tabular List for Digit Selection   ▽ Subterms under main terms may continue to next column or page

138 — Volume 2 · October 2006   ▶◀ Revised Text   ● New Line   ▲ Revised Code   *2007 ICD-9-CM*

Hemorrhage, hemorrhagic — *continued*
pregnancy — *continued*
  due to — *continued*
    coagulation defect 641.3 ☑
      affecting fetus or newborn 762.1
    hyperfibrinolysis 641.3 ☑
      affecting fetus or newborn 762.1
    hypofibrinogenemia 641.3 ☑
      affecting fetus or newborn 762.1
    leiomyoma, uterus 641.8 ☑
      affecting fetus or newborn 762.1
    low-lying placenta 641.1 ☑
      affecting fetus or newborn 762.1
    marginal sinus (rupture) 641.2 ☑
      affecting fetus or newborn 762.1
    placenta previa 641.1 ☑
      affecting fetus or newborn 762.0
    premature separation of placenta (normally implanted) 641.2 ☑
      affecting fetus or newborn 762.1
    threatened abortion 640.0 ☑
      affecting fetus or newborn 762.1
    trauma 641.8 ☑
      affecting fetus or newborn 762.1
  early (before 22 completed weeks gestation) 640.9 ☑
    affecting fetus or newborn 762.1
  previous, affecting management of pregnancy or childbirth V23.49
  unavoidable — *see* Hemorrhage, pregnancy, due to placenta previa
prepartum (mother) — *see* Hemorrhage, pregnancy
preretinal, cause unspecified 362.81
prostate 602.1
puerperal (*see also* Hemorrhage, postpartum) 666.1 ☑
pulmonary (*see also* Hemorrhage, lung)
  newborn (massive) 770.3
  renal syndrome 446.21
purpura (primary) (*see also* Purpura, thrombocytopenic) 287.39
rectum (sphincter) 569.3
recurring, following initial hemorrhage at time of injury 958.2
renal 593.81
  pulmonary syndrome 446.21
respiratory tract (*see also* Hemorrhage, lung) 786.3
retina, retinal (deep) (superficial) (vessels) 362.81
  diabetic 250.5 ☑ *[362.01]*
  due to birth injury 772.8
retrobulbar 376.89
retroperitoneal 459.0
retroplacental (*see also* Placenta, separation) 641.2 ☑
scalp 459.0
  due to injury at birth 767.19
scrotum 608.83
secondary (nontraumatic) 459.0
  following initial hemorrhage at time of injury 958.2
seminal vesicle 608.83
skin 782.7
  newborn 772.6
spermatic cord 608.83
spinal (cord) 336.1
  aneurysm (ruptured) 336.1
  syphilitic 094.89

Hemorrhage, hemorrhagic — *continued*
spinal — *continued*
  due to birth injury 767.4
  fetus or newborn 767.4
spleen 289.59
spontaneous NEC 459.0
  petechial 782.7
stomach 578.9
  newborn 772.4
  ulcer — *see* Ulcer, stomach, with hemorrhage
subaponeurotic, newborn 767.11
  massive (birth injury) 767.11
subarachnoid (nontraumatic) 430
  fetus or newborn (anoxic) (traumatic) 772.2
  puerperal, postpartum, childbirth 674.0 ☑
  traumatic — *see* Hemorrhage, brain, traumatic, subarachnoid
subconjunctival 372.72
  due to birth injury 772.8
  newborn 772.8
subcortical (*see also* Hemorrhage, brain) 431
subcutaneous 782.7
subdiaphragmatic 459.0
subdural (nontraumatic) 432.1
  due to birth injury 767.0
  fetus or newborn (anoxic) (hypoxic) (due to birth trauma) 767.0
  puerperal, postpartum, childbirth 674.0 ☑
  spinal 336.1
  traumatic — *see* Hemorrhage, brain, traumatic, subdural
subgaleal 767.11
subhyaloid 362.81
subperiosteal 733.99
subretinal 362.81
subtentorial (*see also* Hemorrhage, subdural) 432.1
subungual 703.8
  due to blood dyscrasia 287.8
suprarenal (capsule) (gland) 255.4
  fetus or newborn 772.5
tentorium (traumatic) (*see also* Hemorrhage, brain, traumatic)
  fetus or newborn 767.0
  nontraumatic — *see* Hemorrhage, subdural
testis 608.83
thigh 459.0
third stage 666.0 ☑
thorax — *see* Hemorrhage, lung
throat 784.8
thrombocythemia 238.71   ▲
thymus (gland) 254.8
thyroid (gland) 246.3
  cyst 246.3
tongue 529.8
tonsil 474.8
  postoperative 998.11
tooth socket (postextraction) 998.11
trachea — *see* Hemorrhage, lung
traumatic (*see also* nature of injury)
  brain — *see* Hemorrhage, brain, traumatic
  recurring or secondary (following initial hemorrhage at time of injury) 958.2
  tuberculous NEC (*see also* Tuberculosis, pulmonary) 011.9 ☑
tunica vaginalis 608.83
ulcer — *see* Ulcer, by site, with hemorrhage
umbilicus, umbilical cord 772.0
  after birth, newborn 772.3
  complicating delivery 663.8 ☑
    affecting fetus or newborn 772.0
  slipped ligature 772.3
  stump 772.3
unavoidable (due to placenta previa) 641.1 ☑

Hemorrhage, hemorrhagic — *continued*
unavoidable — *continued*
  affecting fetus or newborn 762.0
upper extremity 459.0
urethra (idiopathic) 599.84
uterus, uterine (abnormal) 626.9
  climacteric 627.0
  complicating delivery — *see* Hemorrhage, complicating, delivery
  due to
    intrauterine contraceptive device 996.76
      perforating uterus 996.32
  functional or dysfunctional 626.8
  in pregnancy — *see* Hemorrhage, pregnancy
  intermenstrual 626.6
    irregular 626.6
    regular 626.5
  postmenopausal 627.1
  postpartum (*see also* Hemorrhage, postpartum) 666.1 ☑
  prepubertal 626.8
  pubertal 626.3
  puerperal (immediate) 666.1 ☑
vagina 623.8
vasa previa 663.5 ☑
  affecting fetus or newborn 772.0
vas deferens 608.83
ventricular (*see also* Hemorrhage, brain) 431
vesical 596.8
viscera 459.0
  newborn 772.8
vitreous (humor) (intraocular) 379.23
vocal cord 478.5
vulva 624.8
Hemorrhoids (anus) (rectum) (without complication) 455.6
bleeding, prolapsed, strangulated, or ulcerated NEC 455.8
external 455.5
internal 455.2
complicated NEC 455.8
complicating pregnancy and puerperium 671.8 ☑
external 455.3
  with complication NEC 455.5
  bleeding, prolapsed, strangulated, or ulcerated 455.5
  thrombosed 455.4
internal 455.0
  with complication NEC 455.2
  bleeding, prolapsed, strangulated, or ulcerated 455.2
  thrombosed 455.1
residual skin tag 455.9
sentinel pile 455.9
thrombosed NEC 455.7
  external 455.4
  internal 455.1
Hemosalpinx 620.8
Hemosiderosis 275.0
dietary 275.0
pulmonary (idiopathic) 275.0 *[516.1]*
transfusion NEC 999.8
  bone marrow 996.85
Hemospermia 608.82
Hemothorax 511.8
bacterial, nontuberculous 511.1
newborn 772.8
nontuberculous 511.8
  bacterial 511.1
pneumococcal 511.1
postoperative 998.11
staphylococcal 511.1
streptococcal 511.1
traumatic 860.2
  with
    open wound into thorax 860.3
    pneumothorax 860.4
      with open wound into thorax 860.5
tuberculous (*see also* Tuberculosis, pleura) 012.0 ☑

Hemotympanum 385.89
Hench-Rosenberg syndrome (palindromic arthritis) — *see also* Rheumatism, palindromic 719.3 ☑
Henle's warts 371.41
Henoch (-Schönlein)
disease or syndrome (allergic purpura) 287.0
purpura (allergic) 287.0
Henpue, henpuye 102.6
Heparitinuria 277.5
Hepar lobatum 095.3
Hepatalgia 573.8
Hepatic — *see also* condition
flexure syndrome 569.89
Hepatitis 573.3
acute (*see also* Necrosis, liver) 570
  alcoholic 571.1
  infective 070.1
    with hepatic coma 070.0
alcoholic 571.1
amebic — *see* Abscess, liver, amebic
anicteric (acute) — *see* Hepatitis, viral
antigen-associated (HAA) — *see* Hepatitis, viral, type B
Australian antigen (positive) — *see* Hepatitis, viral, type B
autoimmune 571.49   ●
catarrhal (acute) 070.1
  with hepatic coma 070.0
  chronic 571.40
  newborn 070.1
    with hepatic coma 070.0
chemical 573.3
cholangiolitic 573.8
cholestatic 573.8
chronic 571.40
  active 571.49
    viral — *see* Hepatitis, viral
  aggressive 571.49
  persistent 571.41
  viral — *see* Hepatitis, viral
cytomegalic inclusion virus 078.5 *[573.1]*
diffuse 573.3
"dirty needle" — *see* Hepatitis, viral
drug-induced 573.3
due to
  Coxsackie 074.8 *[573.1]*
  cytomegalic inclusion virus 078.5 *[573.1]*
  infectious mononucleosis 075 *[573.1]*
  malaria 084.9 *[573.2]*
  mumps 072.71
  secondary syphilis 091.62
  toxoplasmosis (acquired) 130.5
    congenital (active) 771.2
epidemic — *see* Hepatitis, viral, type A
fetus or newborn 774.4
fibrous (chronic) 571.49
  acute 570
from injection, inoculation, or transfusion (blood) (other substance) (plasma) (serum) (onset within 8 months after administration) — *see* Hepatitis, viral
fulminant (viral) (*see also* Hepatitis, viral) 070.9
  with hepatic coma 070.6
  type A 070.1
    with hepatic coma 070.0
  type B — *see* Hepatitis, viral, type B
giant cell (neonatal) 774.4
hemorrhagic 573.8
history of
  B V12.09
  C V12.09
homologous serum — *see* Hepatitis, viral
hypertrophic (chronic) 571.49
  acute 570
infectious, infective (acute) (chronic) (subacute) 070.1

Hepatitis — *continued*
infectious, infective — *continued*
  with hepatic coma 070.0
inoculation — *see* Hepatitis, viral
interstitial (chronic) 571.49
  acute 570
lupoid 571.49
malarial 084.9 *[573.2]*
malignant (*see also* Necrosis, liver) 570
neonatal (toxic) 774.4
newborn 774.4
parenchymatous (acute) (*see also* Necrosis, liver) 570
peliosis 573.3
persistent, chronic 571.41
plasma cell 571.49
postimmunization — *see* Hepatitis, viral
postnecrotic 571.49
posttransfusion — *see* Hepatitis, viral
recurrent 571.49
septic 573.3
serum — *see* Hepatitis, viral
  carrier (suspected of) V02.61
subacute (*see also* Necrosis, liver) 570
suppurative (diffuse) 572.0
syphilitic (late) 095.3
  congenital (early) 090.0 *[573.2]*
    late 090.5 *[573.2]*
  secondary 091.62
toxic (noninfectious) 573.3
  fetus or newborn 774.4
tuberculous (*see also* Tuberculosis) 017.9 ☑
viral (acute) (anicteric) (cholangiolitic) (cholestatic) (chronic) (subacute) 070.9
  with hepatic coma 070.6
  AU-SH type virus — *see* Hepatitis, viral, type B
  Australian antigen — *see* Hepatitis, viral, type B
  B-antigen — *see* Hepatitis, viral, type B
  Coxsackie 074.8 *[573.1]*
  cytomegalic inclusion 078.5 *[573.1]*
  IH (virus) — *see* Hepatitis, viral, type A
  infectious hepatitis virus — *see* Hepatitis, viral, type A
  serum hepatitis virus — *see* Hepatitis, viral, type B
  SH — *see* Hepatitis, viral, type B
  specified type NEC 070.59
    with hepatic coma 070.49
  type A 070.1
    with hepatic coma 070.0
  type B (acute) 070.30
    with
      hepatic coma 070.20
        with hepatitis delta 070.21
      hepatitis delta 070.31
        with hepatic coma 070.21
    carrier status V02.61
    chronic 070.32
      with
        hepatic coma 070.22
          with hepatitis delta 070.23
        hepatitis delta 070.33
          with hepatic coma 070.23
  type C
    acute 070.51
      with hepatic coma 070.41
    carrier status V02.62
    chronic 070.54
      with hepatic coma 070.44
    in remission 070.54 ●
    unspecified 070.70
      with hepatic coma 070.71
  type delta (with hepatitis B carrier state) 070.52

Hepatitis — *continued*
viral — *continued*
  type delta — *continued*
    with
      active hepatitis B disease — *see* Hepatitis, viral, type B
      hepatic coma 070.42
  type E 070.53
    with hepatic coma 070.43
  vaccination and inoculation (prophylactic) V05.3
  Waldenström's (lupoid hepatitis) 571.49
Hepatization, lung (acute) — *see also* Pneumonia, lobar
  chronic (*see also* Fibrosis, lung) 515
Hepatoblastoma (M8970/3) 155.0
Hepatocarcinoma (M8170/3) 155.0
Hepatocholangiocarcinoma (M8180/3) 155.0
Hepatocholangioma, benign (M8180/0) 211.5
Hepatocholangitis 573.8
Hepatocystitis — *see also* Cholecystitis 575.10
Hepatodystrophy 570
Hepatolenticular degeneration 275.1
Hepatolithiasis — *see* Choledocholithiasis
Hepatoma (malignant) (M8170/3) 155.0
  benign (M8170/0) 211.5
  congenital (M8970/3) 155.0
  embryonal (M8970/3) 155.0
Hepatomegalia glycogenica diffusa 271.0
Hepatomegaly — *see also* Hypertrophy, liver 789.1
  congenital 751.69
    syphilitic 090.0
  due to Clonorchis sinensis 121.1
  Gaucher's 272.7
  syphilitic (congenital) 090.0
Hepatoptosis 573.8
Hepatorrhexis 573.8
Hepatosis, toxic 573.8
Hepatosplenomegaly 571.8
  due to S. japonicum 120.2
  hyperlipemic (Bürger-Grutz type) 272.3
Herald patch 696.3
Hereditary — *see* condition
Heredodegeneration 330.9
  macular 362.70
Heredopathia atactica polyneuritiformis 356.3
Heredosyphilis — *see also* Syphilis, congenital 090.9
Hermaphroditism (true) 752.7
  with specified chromosomal anomaly — *see* Anomaly, chromosomes, sex
Hernia, hernial (acquired) (recurrent) 553.9
  with
    gangrene (obstructed) NEC 551.9
    obstruction NEC 552.9
      and gangrene 551.9
  abdomen (wall) — *see* Hernia, ventral
  abdominal, specified site NEC 553.8
    with
      gangrene (obstructed) 551.8
      obstruction 552.8
        and gangrene 551.8
  appendix 553.8
    with
      gangrene (obstructed) 551.8
      obstruction 552.8
        and gangrene 551.8
  bilateral (inguinal) — *see* Hernia, inguinal
  bladder (sphincter)
    congenital (female) (male) 756.71
    female (*see also* Cystocele, female) 618.01
    male 596.8

Hernia, hernial — *continued*
brain 348.4
  congenital 742.0
broad ligament 553.8
cartilage, vertebral — *see* Displacement, intervertebral disc
cerebral 348.4
  congenital 742.0
  endaural 742.0
ciliary body 364.8
  traumatic 871.1
colic 553.9
  with
    gangrene (obstructed) 551.9
    obstruction 552.9
      and gangrene 551.9
colon 553.9
  with
    gangrene (obstructed) 551.9
    obstruction 552.9
      and gangrene 551.9
colostomy (stoma) 569.69
Cooper's (retroperitoneal) 553.8
  with
    gangrene (obstructed) 551.8
    obstruction 552.8
      and gangrene 551.8
crural — *see* Hernia, femoral
diaphragm, diaphragmatic 553.3
  with
    gangrene (obstructed) 551.3
    obstruction 552.3
      and gangrene 551.3
  congenital 756.6
  due to gross defect of diaphragm 756.6
  traumatic 862.0
    with open wound into cavity 862.1
direct (inguinal) — *see* Hernia, inguinal
disc, intervertebral — *see* Displacement, intervertebral disc
diverticulum, intestine 553.9
  with
    gangrene (obstructed) 551.9
    obstruction 552.9
      and gangrene 551.9
double (inguinal) — *see* Hernia, inguinal
due to adhesion with obstruction 560.81
duodenojejunal 553.8
  with
    gangrene (obstructed) 551.8
    obstruction 552.8
      and gangrene 551.8
en glissade — *see* Hernia, inguinal
enterostomy (stoma) 569.69
epigastric 553.29
  with
    gangrene (obstruction) 551.29
    obstruction 552.29
      and gangrene 551.29
  recurrent 553.21
    with
      gangrene (obstructed) 551.21
      obstruction 552.21
        and gangrene 551.21
esophageal hiatus (sliding) 553.3
  with
    gangrene (obstructed) 551.3
    obstruction 552.3
      and gangrene 551.3
  congenital 750.6
external (inguinal) — *see* Hernia, inguinal
fallopian tube 620.4
fascia 728.89
fat 729.30
  eyelid 374.34
  orbital 374.34
  pad 729.30
    eye, eyelid 374.34
    knee 729.31
    orbit 374.34

Hernia, hernial — *continued*
fat — *continued*
  pad — *continued*
    popliteal (space) 729.31
    specified site NEC 729.39
femoral (unilateral) 553.00
  with
    gangrene (obstructed) 551.00
    obstruction 552.00
      with gangrene 551.00
  bilateral 553.02
    gangrenous (obstructed) 551.02
    obstructed 552.02
      with gangrene 551.02
    recurrent 553.03
      gangrenous (obstructed) 551.03
      obstructed 552.03
        with gangrene 551.03
  recurrent (unilateral) 553.01
    bilateral 553.03
      gangrenous (obstructed) 551.03
      obstructed 552.03
        with gangrene 551.01
    gangrenous (obstructed) 551.01
    obstructed 552.01
      with gangrene 551.01
foramen
  Bochdalek 553.3
    with
      gangrene (obstructed) 551.3
      obstruction 552.3
        and gangrene 551.3
    congenital 756.6
  magnum 348.4
  Morgagni, Morgagnian 553.3
    with
      gangrene 551.3
      obstruction 552.3
        and gangrene 551.3
    congenital 756.6
funicular (umbilical) 553.1
  with
    gangrene (obstructed) 551.1
    obstruction 552.1
      and gangrene 551.1
  spermatic cord — *see* Hernia, inguinal
gangrenous — *see* Hernia, by site, with gangrene
gastrointestinal tract 553.9
  with
    gangrene (obstructed) 551.9
    obstruction 552.9
      and gangrene 551.9
gluteal — *see* Hernia, femoral
Gruber's (internal mesogastric) 553.8
  with
    gangrene (obstructed) 551.8
    obstruction 552.8
      and gangrene 551.8
Hesselbach's 553.8
  with
    gangrene (obstructed) 551.8
    obstruction 552.8
      and gangrene 551.8
hiatal (esophageal) (sliding) 553.3
  with
    gangrene (obstructed) 551.3
    obstruction 552.3
      and gangrene 551.3
  congenital 750.6
incarcerated (*see also* Hernia, by site, with obstruction) 552.9
  gangrenous (*see also* Hernia, by site, with gangrene) 551.9
incisional 553.21
  with
    gangrene (obstructed) 551.21
    obstruction 552.21
      and gangrene 551.21
  lumbar — *see* Hernia, lumbar
  recurrent 553.21
    with
      gangrene (obstructed) 551.21

Hernia, hernial — *continued*
incisional — *continued*
  recurrent — *continued*
    with — *continued*
      obstruction 552.21
        and gangrene 551.21
indirect (inguinal) — *see* Hernia, inguinal
infantile — *see* Hernia, inguinal
infrapatellar fat pad 729.31
inguinal (direct) (double) (encysted) (external) (funicular) (indirect) (infantile) (internal) (interstitial) (oblique) (scrotal) (sliding) 550.9 ☑

> *Note* — *Use the following fifth-digit subclassification with category 550:*
>
> 0   *unilateral or unspecified (not specified as recurrent)*
>
> 1   *unilateral or unspecified, recurrent*
>
> 2   *bilateral (not specified as recurrent)*
>
> 3   *bilateral, recurrent*

  with
    gangrene (obstructed) 550.0 ☑
    obstruction 550.1 ☑
      and gangrene 550.0 ☑
internal 553.8
  with
    gangrene (obstructed) 551.8
    obstruction 552.8
      and gangrene 551.8
  inguinal — *see* Hernia, inguinal
interstitial 553.9
  with
    gangrene (obstructed) 551.9
    obstruction 552.9
      and gangrene 551.9
  inguinal — *see* Hernia, inguinal
intervertebral cartilage or disc — *see* Displacement, intervertebral disc
intestine, intestinal 553.9
  with
    gangrene (obstructed) 551.9
    obstruction 552.9
      and gangrene 551.9
intra-abdominal 553.9
  with
    gangrene (obstructed) 551.9
    obstruction 552.9
      and gangrene 551.9
intraparietal 553.9
  with
    gangrene (obstructed) 551.9
    obstruction 552.9
      and gangrene 551.9
iris 364.8
  traumatic 871.1
irreducible (*see also* Hernia, by site, with obstruction) 552.9
  gangrenous (with obstruction) (*see also* Hernia, by site, with gangrene) 551.9
ischiatic 553.8
  with
    gangrene (obstructed) 551.8
    obstruction 552.8
      and gangrene 551.8
ischiorectal 553.8
  with
    gangrene (obstructed) 551.8
    obstruction 552.8
      and gangrene 551.8
lens 379.32
  traumatic 871.1
linea
  alba — *see* Hernia, epigastric
  semilunaris — *see* Hernia, spigelian
Littre's (diverticular) 553.9
  with
    gangrene (obstructed) 551.9

Hernia, hernial — *continued*
Littre's — *continued*
  with — *continued*
    obstruction 552.9
      and gangrene 551.9
lumbar 553.8
  with
    gangrene (obstructed) 551.8
    obstruction 552.8
      and gangrene 551.8
  intervertebral disc 722.10
lung (subcutaneous) 518.89
  congenital 748.69
mediastinum 519.3
mesenteric (internal) 553.8
  with
    gangrene (obstructed) 551.8
    obstruction 552.8
      and gangrene 551.8
mesocolon 553.8
  with
    gangrene (obstructed) 551.8
    obstruction 552.8
      and gangrene 551.8
muscle (sheath) 728.89
nucleus pulposus — *see* Displacement, intervertebral disc
oblique (inguinal) — *see* Hernia, inguinal
obstructive (*see also* Hernia, by site, with obstruction) 552.9
  gangrenous (with obstruction) (*see also* Hernia, by site, with gangrene) 551.9
obturator 553.8
  with
    gangrene (obstructed) 551.8
    obstruction 552.8
      and gangrene 551.8
omental 553.8
  with
    gangrene (obstructed) 551.8
    obstruction 552.8
      and gangrene 551.8
orbital fat (pad) 374.34
ovary 620.4
oviduct 620.4
paracolostomy (stoma) 569.69
paraduodenal 553.8
  with
    gangrene (obstructed) 551.8
    obstruction 552.8
      and gangrene 551.8
paraesophageal 553.3
  with
    gangrene (obstructed) 551.3
    obstruction 552.3
      and gangrene 551.3
  congenital 750.6
parahiatal 553.3
  with
    gangrene (obstructed) 551.3
    obstruction 552.3
      and gangrene 551.3
paraumbilical 553.1
  with
    gangrene (obstructed) 551.1
    obstruction 552.1
      and gangrene 551.1
parietal 553.9
  with
    gangrene (obstructed) 551.9
    obstruction 552.9
      and gangrene 551.9
perineal 553.8
  with
    gangrene (obstructed) 551.8
    obstruction 552.8
      and gangrene 551.8
peritoneal sac, lesser 553.8
  with
    gangrene (obstructed) 551.8
    obstruction 552.8
      and gangrene 551.8
popliteal fat pad 729.31
postoperative 553.21

Hernia, hernial — *continued*
postoperative — *continued*
  with
    gangrene (obstructed) 551.21
    obstruction 552.21
      and gangrene 551.21
pregnant uterus 654.4 ☑
prevesical 596.8
properitoneal 553.8
  with
    gangrene (obstructed) 551.8
    obstruction 552.8
      and gangrene 551.8
pudendal 553.8
  with
    gangrene (obstructed) 551.8
    obstruction 552.8
      and gangrene 551.8
rectovaginal 618.6
retroperitoneal 553.8
  with
    gangrene (obstructed) 551.8
    obstruction 552.8
      and gangrene 551.8
Richter's (parietal) 553.9
  with
    gangrene (obstructed) 551.9
    obstruction 552.9
      and gangrene 551.9
Rieux's, Riex's (retrocecal) 553.8
  with
    gangrene (obstructed) 551.8
    obstruction 552.8
      and gangrene 551.8
sciatic 553.8
  with
    gangrene (obstructed) 551.8
    obstruction 552.8
      and gangrene 551.8
scrotum, scrotal — *see* Hernia, inguinal
sliding (inguinal) (*see also* Hernia, inguinal)
  hiatus — *see* Hernia, hiatal
spigelian 553.29
  with
    gangrene (obstructed) 551.29
    obstruction 552.29
      and gangrene 551.29
spinal (*see also* Spina bifida) 741.9 ☑
  with hydrocephalus 741.0 ☑
strangulated (*see also* Hernia, by site, with obstruction) 552.9
  gangrenous (with obstruction) (*see also* Hernia, by site, with gangrene) 551.9
supraumbilicus (linea alba) — *see* Hernia, epigastric
tendon 727.9
testis (nontraumatic) 550.9 ☑
  meaning
    scrotal hernia 550.9 ☑
    symptomatic late syphilis 095.8
Treitz's (fossa) 553.8
  with
    gangrene (obstructed) 551.8
    obstruction 552.8
      and gangrene 551.8
tunica
  albuginea 608.89
  vaginalis 752.89
umbilicus, umbilical 553.1
  with
    gangrene (obstructed) 551.1
    obstruction 552.1
      and gangrene 551.1
ureter 593.89
  with obstruction 593.4
uterus 621.8
  pregnant 654.4 ☑
vaginal (posterior) 618.6
Velpeau's (femoral) (*see also* Hernia, femoral) 553.00
ventral 553.20
  with
    gangrene (obstructed) 551.20

Hernia, hernial — *continued*
ventral — *continued*
  with — *continued*
    obstruction 552.20
      and gangrene 551.20
  incisional 553.21
  recurrent 553.21
    with
      gangrene (obstructed) 551.21
      obstruction 552.21
        and gangrene 551.21
vesical
  congenital (female) (male) 756.71
  female (*see also* Cystocele, female) 618.01
  male 596.8
vitreous (into anterior chamber) 379.21
  traumatic 871.1
Herniation — *see also* Hernia
brain (stem) 348.4
cerebral 348.4
gastric mucosa (into duodenal bulb) 537.89
mediastinum 519.3
nucleus pulposus — *see* Displacement, intervertebral disc
Herpangina 074.0
Herpes, herpetic 054.9
auricularis (zoster) 053.71
  simplex 054.73
blepharitis (zoster) 053.20
  simplex 054.41
circinate 110.5
circinatus 110.5
  bullous 694.5
conjunctiva (simplex) 054.43
  zoster 053.21
cornea (simplex) 054.43
  disciform (simplex) 054.43
  zoster 053.21
encephalitis 054.3
eye (zoster) 053.29
  simplex 054.40
eyelid (zoster) 053.20
  simplex 054.41
febrilis 054.9
fever 054.9
geniculate ganglionitis 053.11
genital, genitalis 054.10
  specified site NEC 054.19
gestationis 646.8 ☑
gingivostomatitis 054.2
iridocyclitis (simplex) 054.44
  zoster 053.22
iris (any site) 695.1
iritis (simplex) 054.44
keratitis (simplex) 054.43
  dendritic 054.42
  disciform 054.43
  interstitial 054.43
    zoster 053.21
keratoconjunctivitis (simplex) 054.43
  zoster 053.21
labialis 054.9
  meningococcal 036.89
lip 054.9
meningitis (simplex) 054.72
  zoster 053.0
ophthalmicus (zoster) 053.20
  simplex 054.40
otitis externa (zoster) 053.71
  simplex 054.73
penis 054.13
perianal 054.10
pharyngitis 054.79
progenitalis 054.10
scrotum 054.19
septicemia 054.5
simplex 054.9
  complicated 054.8
    ophthalmic 054.40
      specified NEC 054.49
    specified NEC 054.79
  congenital 771.2
  external ear 054.73

☑ Additional Digit Required — Refer to the Tabular List for Digit Selection   ⏃ Subterms under main terms may continue to next column or page

2007 ICD-9-CM   ▶◀ Revised Text   ● New Line   ▲ Revised Code   **Volume 2 — 141**

Hernia, hernial — Herpes, herpetic

Herpes, herpetic — *continued*
  simplex — *continued*
    keratitis 054.43
      dendritic 054.42
    meningitis 054.72
    myelitis 054.74 ●
    neuritis 054.79
    specified complication NEC 054.79
      ophthalmic 054.49
    visceral 054.71
  stomatitis 054.2
  tonsurans 110.0
    maculosus (of Hebra) 696.3
  visceral 054.71
  vulva 054.12
  vulvovaginitis 054.11
  whitlow 054.6
  zoster 053.9
    auricularis 053.71
    complicated 053.8
      specified NEC 053.79
    conjunctiva 053.21
    cornea 053.21
    ear 053.71
    eye 053.29
    geniculate 053.11
    keratitis 053.21
      interstitial 053.21
    myelitis 053.14 ●
    neuritis 053.10
    ophthalmicus(a) 053.20
    oticus 053.71
    otitis externa 053.71
    specified complication NEC 053.79
    specified site NEC 053.9
  zosteriform, intermediate type 053.9
Herrick's
  anemia (hemoglobin S disease) 282.61
  syndrome (hemoglobin S disease)
    282.61
Hers' disease (glycogenosis VI) 271.0
Herter (-Gee) disease or syndrome
  (nontropical sprue) 579.0
Herter's infantilism (nontropical sprue)
  579.0
Herxheimer's disease (diffuse idiopathic
  cutaneous atrophy) 701.8
Herxheimer's reaction 995.0
Hesitancy, urinary 788.64 ●
Hesselbach's hernia — *see* Hernia,
  Hesselbach's
Heterochromia (congenital) 743.46
  acquired 364.53
  cataract 366.33
  cyclitis 364.21
  hair 704.3
  iritis 364.21
  retained metallic foreign body 360.62
    magnetic 360.52
  uveitis 364.21
Heterophoria 378.40
  alternating 378.45
  vertical 378.43
Heterophyes, small intestine 121.6
Heterophyiasis 121.6
Heteropsia 368.8
Heterotopia, heterotopic — *see also*
  Malposition, congenital
  cerebralis 742.4
  pancreas, pancreatic 751.7
  spinalis 742.59
Heterotropia 378.30
  intermittent 378.20
    vertical 378.31
  vertical (constant) (intermittent)
    378.31
Heubner's disease 094.89
Heubner-Herter disease or syndrome
  (nontropical sprue) 579.0
Hexadactylism 755.0 ☑
Heyd's syndrome (hepatorenal) 572.4
HGSIL (high grade squamous intraepithe-
  lial lesion) 795.04
Hibernoma (M8880/0) — *see* Lipoma
Hiccough 786.8
  epidemic 078.89

Hiccough — *continued*
  psychogenic 306.1
Hiccup — *see also* Hiccough 786.8
Hicks (-Braxton) contractures 644.1 ☑
Hidden penis 752.65
Hidradenitis (axillaris) (suppurative)
  705.83
Hidradenoma (nodular) (M8400/0) —
  see also Neoplasm, skin, benign
  clear cell (M8402/0) — *see* Neoplasm,
    skin, benign
  papillary (M8405/0) — *see* Neoplasm,
    skin, benign
Hidrocystoma (M8404/0) — *see* Neoplasm, skin, benign
HIE (hypoxic-ischemic encephalopathy) ●
  768.7 ●
High
  A₂ anemia 282.49
  altitude effects 993.2
    anoxia 993.2
    on
      ears 993.0
      sinuses 993.1
    polycythemia 289.0
  arch
    foot 755.67
    palate 750.26
  artery (arterial) tension (*see also* Hy-
    pertension) 401.9
    without diagnosis of hypertension
      796.2
  basal metabolic rate (BMR) 794.7
  blood pressure (*see also* Hypertension)
    401.9
    incidental reading (isolated) (non-
      specific), no diagnosis of hy-
      pertension 796.2
  compliance bladder 596.4
  diaphragm (congenital) 756.6
  frequency deafness (congenital) (region-
    al) 389.8
  head at term 652.5 ☑
    affecting fetus or newborn 763.1
  output failure (cardiac) (*see also* Fail-
    ure, heart) 428.9
  oxygen-affinity hemoglobin 289.0
  palate 750.26
  risk
    behavior — *see* Problem
    cervical, human papillomavirus
      (HPV) DNA test positive
      795.05
    family situation V61.9
      specified circumstance NEC
        V61.8
    individual NEC V62.89
    infant NEC V20.1
    patient taking drugs (prescribed)
      V67.51
      nonprescribed (*see also* Abuse,
        drugs, nondependent)
        305.9 ☑
    pregnancy V23.89
      inadequate prenatal care V23.7
      specified problem NEC V23.89
  temperature (of unknown origin) (*see*
    also Pyrexia) 780.6
  thoracic rib 756.3
Hildenbrand's disease (typhus) 081.9
Hilger's syndrome 337.0
Hill diarrhea 579.1
Hilliard's lupus — *see also* Tuberculosis
  017.0 ☑
Hilum — *see* condition
Hip — *see* condition
Hippel's disease (retinocerebral an-
  giomatosis) 759.6
Hippus 379.49
Hirschfeld's disease (acute diabetes
  mellitus) — *see also* Diabetes
  250.0 ☑
Hirschsprung's disease or megacolon
  (congenital) 751.3
Hirsuties — *see also* Hypertrichosis
  704.1

Hirsutism — *see also* Hypertrichosis
  704.1
Hirudiniasis (external) (internal) 134.2
Hiss-Russell dysentery 004.1
Histamine cephalgia 346.2 ☑
Histidinemia 270.5
Histidinuria 270.5
Histiocytic syndromes 288.4 ●
Histiocytoma (M8832/0) — *see also*
  Neoplasm, skin, benign
  fibrous (M8830/0) (*see also* Neoplasm,
    skin, benign)
    atypical (M8830/1) — *see* Neo-
      plasm, connective tissue,
      uncertain behavior
    malignant (M8830/3) — *see* Neo-
      plasm, connective tissue,
      malignant
Histiocytosis (acute) (chronic) (subacute)
  277.89
  acute differentiated progressive
    (M9722/3) 202.5 ☑
  cholesterol 277.89
  essential 277.89
  lipid, lipoid (essential) 272.7
  lipochrome (familial) 288.1
  malignant (M9720/3) 202.3 ☑
  X (chronic) 277.89
    acute (progressive) (M9722/3)
      202.5 ☑
Histoplasmosis 115.90
  with
    endocarditis 115.94
    meningitis 115.91
    pericarditis 115.93
    pneumonia 115.95
    retinitis 115.92
    specified manifestation NEC
      115.99
  African (due to Histoplasma duboisii)
    115.10
    with
      endocarditis 115.14
      meningitis 115.11
      pericarditis 115.13
      pneumonia 115.15
      retinitis 115.12
      specified manifestation NEC
        115.19
  American (due to Histoplasma capsu-
    latum) 115.00
    with
      endocarditis 115.04
      meningitis 115.01
      pericarditis 115.03
      pneumonia 115.05
      retinitis 115.02
      specified manifestation NEC
        115.09
  Darling's — *see* Histoplasmosis,
    American
  large form (*see also* Histoplasmosis,
    African) 115.10
  lung 115.05
  small form (*see also* Histoplasmosis,
    American) 115.00
History (personal) of
  abuse
    emotional V15.42
    neglect V15.42
    physical V15.41
    sexual V15.41
  affective psychosis V11.1
  alcoholism V11.3
    specified as drinking problem (*see*
      also Abuse, drugs, nondepen-
      dent) 305.0 ☑
  allergy to
    analgesic agent NEC V14.6
    anesthetic NEC V14.4
    antibiotic agent NEC V14.1
      penicillin V14.0
    anti-infective agent NEC V14.3
    diathesis V15.09
    drug V14.9
      specified type NEC V14.8

History of — *continued*
  allergy to — *continued*
    eggs V15.03
    food additives V15.05
    insect bite V15.06
    latex V15.07
    medicinal agents V14.9
      specified type NEC V14.8
    milk products V15.02
    narcotic agent NEC V14.5
    nuts V15.05
      peanuts V15.01
    penicillin V14.0
    radiographic dye V15.08
    seafood V15.04
    serum V14.7
    specified food NEC V15.05
    specified nonmedicinal agents NEC
      V15.09
    spider bite V15.06
    sulfa V14.2
    sulfonamides V14.2
    therapeutic agent NEC V15.09
    vaccine V14.7
  anemia V12.3
  arthritis V13.4
  benign neoplasm of brain V12.41
  blood disease V12.3
  calculi, urinary V13.01
  cardiovascular disease V12.50
    myocardial infarction 412
  child abuse V15.41
  cigarette smoking V15.82
  circulatory system disease V12.50
    myocardial infarction 412
  congenital malformation V13.69
  contraception V15.7
  diathesis, allergic V15.09
  digestive system disease V12.70
    peptic ulcer V12.71
    polyps, colonic V12.72
    specified NEC V12.79
  disease (of) V13.9
    blood V12.3
    blood-forming organs V12.3
    cardiovascular system V12.50
    circulatory system V12.50
    digestive system V12.70
      peptic ulcer V12.71
      polyps, colonic V12.72
      specified NEC V12.79
    infectious V12.00
      malaria V12.03
      poliomyelitis V12.02
      specified NEC V12.09
      tuberculosis V12.01
    parasitic V12.00
      specified NEC V12.09
    respiratory system V12.60
      pneumonia V12.61
      specified NEC V12.69
    skin V13.3
    specified site NEC V13.8
    subcutaneous tissue V13.3
    trophoblastic V13.1
      affecting management of preg-
        nancy V23.1
  disorder (of) V13.9
    endocrine V12.2
    genital system V13.29
    hematological V12.3
    immunity V12.2
    mental V11.9
      affective type V11.1
      manic-depressive V11.1
      neurosis V11.2
      schizophrenia V11.0
      specified type NEC V11.8
    metabolic V12.2
    musculoskeletal NEC V13.5
    nervous system V12.40
      specified type NEC V12.49
    obstetric V13.29
      affecting management of current
        pregnancy V23.49
      pre-term labor V23.41

☑ Additional Digit Required — Refer to the Tabular List for Digit Selection

▼ Subterms under main terms may continue to next column or page

History of — *continued*
  disorder — *continued*
    obstetric — *continued*
      pre-term labor V13.21
    sense organs V12.40
      specified type NEC V12.49
    specified site NEC V13.8
    urinary system V13.00
      calculi V13.01
      infection V13.02
      nephrotic syndrome V13.03
      specified NEC V13.09
  drug use
    nonprescribed (*see also* Abuse,
      drugs, nondependent)
      305.9 ☑
    patent (*see also* Abuse, drugs, non-
      dependent) 305.9 ☑
  effect NEC of external cause V15.89
  embolism (pulmonary) V12.51
  emotional abuse V15.42
  encephalitis V12.42
  endocrine disorder V12.2
  extracorporeal membrane oxygenation
    (ECMO) V15.87
  falling V15.88
  family
    allergy V19.6
    anemia V18.2
    arteriosclerosis V17.4
    arthritis V17.7
    asthma V17.5
    blindness V19.0
    blood disorder NEC V18.3
    cardiovascular disease V17.4
    carrier, genetic disease V18.9
    cerebrovascular disease V17.1
    chronic respiratory condition NEC
      V17.6
    colonic polyps V18.51   ●
    congenital anomalies V19.5
    consanguinity V19.7
    coronary artery disease V17.3
    cystic fibrosis V18.1
    deafness V19.2
    diabetes mellitus V18.0
    digestive disorders V18.59   ▲
    disease or disorder (of)
      allergic V19.6
      blood NEC V18.3
      cardiovascular NEC V17.4
      cerebrovascular V17.1
      colonic polyps V18.51   ●
      coronary artery V17.3
      digestive V18.59   ▲
      ear NEC V19.3
      endocrine V18.1
      eye NEC V19.1
      genitourinary NEC V18.7
      hypertensive V17.4
      infectious V18.8
      ischemic heart V17.3
      kidney V18.69
        polycystic V18.61
      mental V17.0
      metabolic V18.1
      musculoskeletal NEC V17.89
        osteoporosis V17.81
      neurological NEC V17.2
      parasitic V18.8
      psychiatric condition V17.0
      skin condition V19.4
    ear disorder NEC V19.3
    endocrine disease V18.1
    epilepsy V17.2
    eye disorder NEC V19.1
    genetic disease carrier V18.9
    genitourinary disease NEC V18.7
    glomerulonephritis V18.69
    gout V18.1
    hay fever V17.6
    hearing loss V19.2
    hematopoietic neoplasia V16.7
    Hodgkin's disease V16.7
    Huntington's chorea V17.2
    hydrocephalus V19.5

History of — *continued*
  family — *continued*
    hypertension V17.4
    hypospadias V13.61
    infectious disease V18.8
    ischemic heart disease V17.3
    kidney disease V18.69
      polycystic V18.61
    leukemia V16.6
    lymphatic malignant neoplasia
      NEC V16.7
    malignant neoplasm (of) NEC V16.9
      anorectal V16.0
      anus V16.0
      appendix V16.0
      bladder V16.59
      bone V16.8
      brain V16.8
      breast V16.3
        male V16.8
      bronchus V16.1
      cecum V16.0
      cervix V16.49
      colon V16.0
      duodenum V16.0
      esophagus V16.0
      eye V16.8
      gallbladder V16.0
      gastrointestinal tract V16.0
      genital organs V16.40
      hemopoietic NEC V16.7
      ileum V16.0
      ilium V16.8
      intestine V16.0
      intrathoracic organs NEC V16.2
      kidney V16.51
      larynx V16.2
      liver V16.0
      lung V16.1
      lymphatic NEC V16.7
      ovary V16.41
      oviduct V16.41
      pancreas V16.0
      penis V16.49
      prostate V16.42
      rectum V16.0
      respiratory organs NEC V16.2
      skin V16.8
      specified site NEC V16.8
      stomach V16.0
      testis V16.43
      trachea V16.1
      ureter V16.59
      urethra V16.59
      urinary organs V16.59
      uterus V16.49
      vagina V16.49
      vulva V16.49
    mental retardation V18.4
    metabolic disease NEC V18.1
    mongolism V19.5
    multiple myeloma V16.7
    musculoskeletal disease NEC
      V17.89
      osteoporosis V17.81
    nephritis V18.69
    nephrosis V18.69
    osteoporosis V17.81
    parasitic disease V18.8
    polycystic kidney disease V18.61
    psychiatric disorder V17.0
    psychosis V17.0
    retardation, mental V18.4
    retinitis pigmentosa V19.1
    schizophrenia V17.0
    skin conditions V19.4
    specified condition NEC V19.8
    stroke (cerebrovascular) V17.1
    visual loss V19.0
  genital system disorder V13.29
    pre-term labor V13.21
  health hazard V15.9
    falling V15.88
    specified cause NEC V15.89
  hepatitis
    B V12.09

History of — *continued*
  hepatitis — *continued*
    C V12.09
  Hodgkin's disease V10.72
  immunity disorder V12.2
  infection
    central nervous system
    urinary (tract)
  infectious disease V12.00
    malaria V12.03
    poliomyelitis V12.02
    specified NEC V12.09
    tuberculosis V12.01
  injury NEC V15.5
  insufficient prenatal care V23.7
  irradiation V15.3
  leukemia V10.60
    lymphoid V10.61
    monocytic V10.63
    myeloid V10.62
    specified type NEC V10.69
  little or no prenatal care V23.7
  low birth weight (*see also* Status, low
    birth weight) V21.30
  lymphosarcoma V10.71
  malaria V12.03
  malignant neoplasm (of) V10.9
    accessory sinus V10.22
    adrenal V10.88
    anus V10.06
    bile duct V10.09
    bladder V10.51
    bone V10.81
    brain V10.85
    breast V10.3
    bronchus V10.11
    cervix uteri V10.41
    colon V10.05
    connective tissue NEC V10.89
    corpus uteri V10.42
    digestive system V10.00
      specified part NEC V10.09
    duodenum V10.09
    endocrine gland NEC V10.88
    epididymis V10.48
    esophagus V10.03
    eye V10.84
    fallopian tube V10.44
    female genital organ V10.40
      specified site NEC V10.44
    gallbladder V10.09
    gastrointestinal tract V10.00
    gum V10.02
    hematopoietic NEC V10.79
    hypopharynx V10.02
    ileum V10.09
    intrathoracic organs NEC V10.20
    jejunum V10.09
    kidney V10.52
    large intestine V10.05
    larynx V10.21
    lip V10.02
    liver V10.07
    lung V10.11
    lymphatic NEC V10.79
    lymph glands or nodes NEC V10.79
    male genital organ V10.45
      specified site NEC V10.49
    mediastinum V10.29
    melanoma (of skin) V10.82
    middle ear V10.22
    mouth V10.02
      specified part NEC V10.02
    nasal cavities V10.22
    nasopharynx V10.02
    nervous system NEC V10.86
    nose V10.22
    oropharynx V10.02
    ovary V10.43
    pancreas V10.09
    parathyroid V10.88
    penis V10.49
    pharynx V10.02
    pineal V10.88
    pituitary V10.88
    placenta V10.44

History of — *continued*
  malignant neoplasm — *continued*
    pleura V10.29
    prostate V10.46
    rectosigmoid junction V10.06
    rectum V10.06
    renal pelvis V10.53
    respiratory organs NEC V10.20
    salivary gland V10.02
    skin V10.83
      melanoma V10.82
    small intestine NEC V10.09
    soft tissue NEC V10.89
    specified site NEC V10.89
    stomach V10.04
    testis V10.47
    thymus V10.29
    thyroid V10.87
    tongue V10.01
    trachea V10.12
    ureter V10.59
    urethra V10.59
    urinary organ V10.50
    uterine adnexa V10.44
    uterus V10.42
    vagina V10.44
    vulva V10.44
  manic-depressive psychosis V11.1
  meningitis V12.42
  mental disorder V11.9
    affective type V11.1
    manic-depressive V11.1
    neurosis V11.2
    schizophrenia V11.0
    specified type NEC V11.8
  metabolic disorder V12.2
  musculoskeletal disorder NEC V13.5
  myocardial infarction 412
  neglect (emotional) V15.42
  nephrotic syndrome V13.03
  nervous system disorder V12.40
    specified type NEC V12.49
  neurosis V11.2
  noncompliance with medical treat-
    ment V15.81
  nutritional deficiency V12.1
  obstetric disorder V13.29
    affecting management of current
      pregnancy V23.49
      pre-term labor V23.41
    pre-term labor V13.21
  parasitic disease V12.00
    specified NEC V12.09
  perinatal problems V13.7
    low birth weight (*see also* Status,
      low birth weight) V21.30
  physical abuse V15.41
  poisoning V15.6
  poliomyelitis V12.02
  polyps, colonic V12.72
  poor obstetric V13.29
    affecting management of current
      pregnancy V23.49
      pre-term labor V23.41
    pre-term labor V13.21
  psychiatric disorder V11.9
    affective type V11.1
    manic-depressive V11.1
    neurosis V11.2
    schizophrenia V11.0
    specified type NEC V11.8
  psychological trauma V15.49
    emotional abuse V15.42
    neglect V15.42
    physical abuse V15.41
    rape V15.41
  psychoneurosis V11.2
  radiation therapy V15.3
  rape V15.41
  respiratory system disease V12.60
    pneumonia V12.61
    specified NEC V12.69
  reticulosarcoma V10.71
  schizophrenia V11.0
  skin disease V13.3
  smoking (tobacco) V15.82

☑ Additional Digit Required — Refer to the Tabular List for Digit Selection   ᵂᵁᴸ Subterms under main terms may continue to next column or page

2007 ICD-9-CM   ▶◀ Revised Text   ● New Line   ▲ Revised Code   **October 2006 · Volume 2 — 143**

History of — *continued*
subcutaneous tissue disease V13.3
surgery (major) to
   great vessels V15.1
   heart V15.1
   major organs NEC V15.2
syndrome, nephrotic V13.03
thrombophlebitis V12.52
thrombosis V12.51
tobacco use V15.82
trophoblastic disease V13.1
   affecting management of pregnancy V23.1
tuberculosis V12.01
ulcer, peptic V12.71
urinary system disorder V13.00
   calculi V13.01
   infection V13.02
   nephrotic syndrome V13.03
   specified NEC V13.09
His-Werner disease (trench fever) 083.1
Hives (bold) — *see also* Urticaria 708.9
HIV infection (disease) (illness) — *see* Human immunodeficiency virus (disease) (illness) (infection)
Hoarseness 784.49
Hobnail liver — *see* Cirrhosis, portal
Hobo, hoboism V60.0
Hodgkin's
disease (M9650/3) 201.9 ☑
   lymphocytic
      depletion (M9653/3) 201.7 ☑
         diffuse fibrosis (M9654/3) 201.7 ☑
         reticular type (M9655/3) 201.7 ☑
         predominance (M9651/3) 201.4 ☑
      lymphocytic-histiocytic predominance (M9651/3) 201.4 ☑
   mixed cellularity (M9652/3) 201.6 ☑
   nodular sclerosis (M9656/3) 201.5 ☑
      cellular phase (M9657/3) 201.5 ☑
granuloma (M9661/3) 201.1 ☑
lymphogranulomatosis (M9650/3) 201.9 ☑
lymphoma (M9650/3) 201.9 ☑
lymphosarcoma (M9650/3) 201.9 ☑
paragranuloma (M9660/3) 201.0 ☑
sarcoma (M9662/3) 201.2 ☑
Hodgson's disease (aneurysmal dilatation of aorta) 441.9
ruptured 441.5
Hodi-potsy 111.0
Hoffa (-Kastert) disease or syndrome (liposynovitis prepatellaris) 272.8
Hoffmann-Bouveret syndrome (paroxysmal tachycardia) 427.2
Hoffman's syndrome 244.9 [359.5]
Hole
macula 362.54
optic disc, crater-like 377.22
retina (macula) 362.54
   round 361.31
      with detachment 361.01
Holla disease — *see also* Spherocytosis 282.0
Holländer-Simons syndrome (progressive lipodystrophy) 272.6
Hollow foot (congenital) 754.71
acquired 736.73
Holmes' syndrome (visual disorientation) 368.16
Holoprosencephaly 742.2
due to
   trisomy 13 758.1
   trisomy 18 758.2
Holthouse's hernia — *see* Hernia, inguinal
Homesickness 309.89
Homocystinemia 270.4
Homocystinuria 270.4

Homologous serum jaundice (prophylactic) (therapeutic) — *see* Hepatitis, viral
Homosexuality — omit code
ego-dystonic 302.0
pedophilic 302.2
problems with 302.0
Homozygous Hb-S disease 282.61
Honeycomb lung 518.89
congenital 748.4
Hong Kong ear 117.3
HOOD (hereditary osteo-onychodysplasia) 756.89
Hooded
clitoris 752.49
penis 752.69
Hookworm (anemia) (disease) (infestation) — *see* Ancylostomiasis
Hoppe-Goldflam syndrome 358.00
Hordeolum (external) (eyelid) 373.11
internal 373.12
Horn
cutaneous 702.8
   cheek 702.8
   eyelid 702.8
   penis 702.8
iliac 756.89
nail 703.8
   congenital 757.5
papillary 700
Horner's
syndrome (*see also* Neuropathy, peripheral, autonomic) 337.9
   traumatic 954.0
teeth 520.4
Horseshoe kidney (congenital) 753.3
Horton's
disease (temporal arteritis) 446.5
headache or neuralgia 346.2 ☑
Hospice care V66.7
Hospitalism (in children) NEC 309.83
Hourglass contraction, contracture
bladder 596.8
gallbladder 575.2
   congenital 751.69
stomach 536.8
   congenital 750.7
   psychogenic 306.4
uterus 661.4 ☑
   affecting fetus or newborn 763.7
Household circumstance affecting care V60.9
specified type NEC V60.8
Housemaid's knee 727.2
Housing circumstance affecting care V60.9
specified type NEC V60.8
HTLV-I infection 079.51
HTLV-II infection 079.52
HTLV-III/LAV (disease) (illness) (infection) — *see* Human immunodeficiency virus (disease) (illness) (infection)
HTLV-III (disease) (illness) (infection) — *see* Human immunodeficiency virus (disease) (illness) (infection)
Huchard's disease (continued arterial hypertension) 401.9
Hudson-Stähli lines 371.11
Huguier's disease (uterine fibroma) 218.9
Human bite (open wound) — see also Wound, open, by site
intact skin surface — *see* Contusion
Human immunodeficiency virus (disease) (illness) 042
infection V08
   with symptoms, symptomatic 042
Human immunodeficiency virus-2 infection 079.53
Human immunovirus (disease) (illness) (infection) — *see* Human immunodeficiency virus (disease) (illness) (infection)
Human papillomavirus 079.4

Human papillomavirus — *continued*
cervical
   high risk, DNA test positive 795.05
   low risk, DNA test positive 795.09
Human T-cell lymphotrophic virus-I infection 079.51
Human T-cell lymphotrophic virus-II infection 079.52
Human T-cell lymphotrophic virus-III (disease) (illness) (infection) — *see* Human immunodeficiency virus (disease) (illness) (infection)
Humpback (acquired) 737.9
congenital 756.19
Hum, venous — omit code
Hunchback (acquired) 737.9
congenital 756.19
Hunger 994.2
air, psychogenic 306.1
disease 251.1
Hunner's ulcer — *see also* Cystitis 595.1
Hunt's
neuralgia 053.11
syndrome (herpetic geniculate ganglionitis) 053.11
   dyssynergia cerebellaris myoclonica 334.2
Hunter's glossitis 529.4
Hunterian chancre 091.0
Hunter (-Hurler) syndrome (mucopolysaccharidosis II) 277.5
Huntington's
chorea 333.4
disease 333.4
Huppert's disease (multiple myeloma) (M9730/3) 203.0 ☑
Hurler (-Hunter) disease or syndrome (mucopolysaccharidosis II) 277.5
Hürthle cell
adenocarcinoma (M8290/3) 193
adenoma (M8290/0) 226
carcinoma (M8290/3) 193
tumor (M8290/0) 226
Hutchinson's
disease meaning
   angioma serpiginosum 709.1
   cheiropompholyx 705.81
   prurigo estivalis 692.72
   summer eruption, or summer prurigo 692.72
incisors 090.5
melanotic freckle (M8742/2) (*see also* Neoplasm, skin, in situ)
   malignant melanoma in (M8742/3) — *see* Melanoma
teeth or incisors (congenital syphilis) 090.5
Hutchinson-Boeck disease or syndrome (sarcoidosis) 135
Hutchinson-Gilford disease or syndrome (progeria) 259.8
Hyaline
degeneration (diffuse) (generalized) 728.9
   localized — *see* Degeneration, by site
membrane (disease) (lung) (newborn) 769
Hyalinosis cutis et mucosae 272.8
Hyalin plaque, sclera, senile 379.16
Hyalitis (asteroid) 379.22
syphilitic 095.8
Hydatid
cyst or tumor (*see also* Echinococcus)
   fallopian tube 752.11
mole — *see* Hydatidiform mole
Morgagni (congenital) 752.89
   fallopian tube 752.11
Hydatidiform mole (benign) (complicating pregnancy) (delivered) (undelivered) 630
invasive (M9100/1) 236.1
malignant (M9100/1) 236.1
previous, affecting management of pregnancy V23.1
Hydatidosis — *see* Echinococcus

Hyde's disease (prurigo nodularis) 698.3
Hydradenitis 705.83
Hydradenoma (M8400/0) — *see* Hidradenoma
Hydralazine lupus or syndrome
correct substance properly administered 695.4
overdose or wrong substance given or taken 972.6
Hydramnios 657.0 ☑
affecting fetus or newborn 761.3
Hydrancephaly 742.3
with spina bifida (*see also* Spina bifida) 741.0 ☑
Hydranencephaly 742.3
with spina bifida (*see also* Spina bifida) 741.0 ☑
Hydrargyrism NEC 985.0
Hydrarthrosis — *see also* Effusion, joint 719.0 ☑
gonococcal 098.50
intermittent (*see also* Rheumatism, palindromic) 719.3 ☑
of yaws (early) (late) 102.6
syphilitic 095.8
   congenital 090.5
Hydremia 285.9
Hydrencephalocele (congenital) 742.0
Hydrencephalomeningocele (congenital) 742.0
Hydroa 694.0
aestivale 692.72
gestationis 646.8 ☑
herpetiformis 694.0
pruriginosa 694.0
vacciniforme 692.72
Hydroadenitis 705.83
Hydrocalycosis — *see also* Hydronephrosis 591
congenital 753.29
Hydrocalyx — *see also* Hydronephrosis 591
Hydrocele (calcified) (chylous) (idiopathic) (infantile) (inguinal canal) (recurrent) (senile) (spermatic cord) (testis) (tunica vaginalis) 603.9
canal of Nuck (female) 629.1
   male 603.9
congenital 778.6
encysted 603.0
   congenital 778.6
female NEC 629.89 ▲
infected 603.1
round ligament 629.89 ▲
specified type NEC 603.8
   congenital 778.6
spinalis (*see also* Spina bifida) 741.9 ☑
vulva 624.8
Hydrocephalic fetus
affecting management or pregnancy 655.0 ☑
causing disproportion 653.6 ☑
   with obstructed labor 660.1 ☑
      affecting fetus or newborn 763.1
Hydrocephalus (acquired) (external) (internal) (malignant) (noncommunicating) (obstructive) (recurrent) 331.4
aqueduct of Sylvius stricture 742.3
   with spina bifida (*see also* Spina bifida) 741.0 ☑
chronic 742.3
   with spina bifida (*see also* Spina bifida) 741.0 ☑
communicating 331.3
congenital (external) (internal) 742.3
   with spina bifida (*see also* Spina bifida) 741.0 ☑
due to
   stricture of aqueduct of Sylvius 742.3
      with spina bifida (*see also* Spina bifida) 741.0 ☑
toxoplasmosis (congenital) 771.2

☑ Additional Digit Required — Refer to the Tabular List for Digit Selection   Subterms under main terms may continue to next column or page

144 — Volume 2 • October 2006   ▶◀ Revised Text   ● New Line   ▲ Revised Code   **2007 ICD-9-CM**

Hydrocephalus — *continued*
fetal affecting management of pregnancy 655.0 ☑
foramen Magendie block (acquired) 331.3
congenital 742.3
with spina bifida (*see also* Spina bifida) 741.0 ☑
newborn 742.3
with spina bifida (*see also* Spina bifida) 741.0 ☑
otitic 348.2
syphilitic, congenital 090.49
tuberculous (*see also* Tuberculosis) 013.8 ☑
Hydrocolpos (congenital) 623.8
Hydrocystoma (M8404/0) — *see* Neoplasm, skin, benign
Hydroencephalocele (congenital) 742.0
Hydroencephalomeningocele (congenital) 742.0
Hydrohematopneumothorax — *see also* Hemothorax 511.8
Hydromeningitis — *see* Meningitis
Hydromeningocele (spinal) — *see also* Spina bifida 741.9 ☑
cranial 742.0
Hydrometra 621.8
Hydrometrocolpos 623.8
Hydromicrocephaly 742.1
Hydromphalus (congenital) (since birth) 757.39
Hydromyelia 742.53
Hydromyelocele — *see also* Spina bifida 741.9 ☑
Hydronephrosis 591
atrophic 591
congenital 753.29
due to S. hematobium 120.0
early 591
functionless (infected) 591
infected 591
intermittent 591
primary 591
secondary 591
tuberculous (*see also* Tuberculosis) 016.0 ☑
Hydropericarditis — *see also* Pericarditis 423.9
Hydropericardium — *see also* Pericarditis 423.9
Hydroperitoneum 789.5
Hydrophobia 071
Hydrophthalmos — *see also* Buphthalmia 743.20
Hydropneumohemothorax — *see also* Hemothorax 511.8
Hydropneumopericarditis — *see also* Pericarditis 423.9
Hydropneumopericardium — *see also* Pericarditis 423.9
Hydropneumothorax 511.8
nontuberculous 511.8
bacterial 511.1
pneumococcal 511.1
staphylococcal 511.1
streptococcal 511.1
traumatic 860.0
with open wound into thorax 860.1
tuberculous (*see also* Tuberculosis, pleura) 012.0 ☑
Hydrops 782.3
abdominis 789.5
amnii (complicating pregnancy) (*see also* Hydramnios) 657.0 ☑
articulorum intermittens (*see also* Rheumatism, palindromic) 719.3 ☑
cardiac (*see also* Failure, heart) 428.0
congenital — *see* Hydrops, fetalis
endolymphatic (*see also* Disease, Ménière's) 386.00
fetal(is) or newborn 778.0
due to isoimmunization 773.3
not due to isoimmunization 778.0
gallbladder 575.3

Hydrops — *continued*
idiopathic (fetus or newborn) 778.0
joint (see also Effusion, joint) 719.0 ☑
labyrinth (*see also* Disease, Ménière's) 386.00
meningeal NEC 331.4
nutritional 262
pericardium — *see* Pericarditis
pleura (*see also* Hydrothorax) 511.8
renal (*see also* Nephrosis) 581.9
spermatic cord (*see also* Hydrocele) 603.9
Hydropyonephrosis — *see also* Pyelitis 590.80
chronic 590.00
Hydrorachis 742.53
Hydrorrhea (nasal) 478.19 ▲
gravidarum 658.1 ☑
pregnancy 658.1 ☑
Hydrosadenitis 705.83
Hydrosalpinx (fallopian tube) (follicularis) 614.1
Hydrothorax (double) (pleural) 511.8
chylous (nonfilarial) 457.8
filaria (*see also* Infestation, filarial) 125.9
nontuberculous 511.8
bacterial 511.1
pneumococcal 511.1
staphylococcal 511.1
streptococcal 511.1
traumatic 862.29
with open wound into thorax 862.39
tuberculous (*see also* Tuberculosis, pleura) 012.0 ☑
Hydroureter 593.5
congenital 753.22
Hydroureteronephrosis — *see also* Hydronephrosis 591
Hydrourethra 599.84
Hydroxykynureninuria 270.2
Hydroxyprolinemia 270.8
Hydroxyprolinuria 270.8
Hygroma (congenital) (cystic) (M9173/0) 228.1
prepatellar 727.3
subdural — *see* Hematoma, subdural
Hymen — *see* condition
Hymenolepiasis (diminuta) (infection) (infestation) (nana) 123.6
Hymenolepsis (diminuta) (infection) (infestation) (nana) 123.6
Hypalgesia — *see also* Disturbance, sensation 782.0
Hyperabduction syndrome 447.8
Hyperacidity, gastric 536.8
psychogenic 306.4
Hyperactive, hyperactivity
basal cell, uterine cervix 622.10
bladder 596.51
bowel (syndrome) 564.9
sounds 787.5
cervix epithelial (basal) 622.10
child 314.01
colon 564.9
gastrointestinal 536.8
psychogenic 306.4
intestine 564.9
labyrinth (unilateral) 386.51
with loss of labyrinthine reactivity 386.58
bilateral 386.52
nasal mucous membrane 478.19 ▲
stomach 536.8
thyroid (gland) (*see also* Thyrotoxicosis) 242.9 ☑
Hyperacusis 388.42
Hyperadrenalism (cortical) 255.3
medullary 255.6
Hyperadrenocorticism 255.3
congenital 255.2
iatrogenic
correct substance properly administered 255.3

Hyperadrenocorticism — *continued*
iatrogenic — *continued*
overdose or wrong substance given or taken 962.0
Hyperaffectivity 301.11
Hyperaldosteronism (atypical) (hyperplastic) (normoaldosteronal) (normotensive) (primary) 255.10
secondary 255.14
Hyperalgesia — *see also* Disturbance, sensation 782.0
Hyperalimentation 783.6
carotene 278.3
specified NEC 278.8
vitamin A 278.2
vitamin D 278.4
Hyperaminoaciduria 270.9
arginine 270.6
citrulline 270.6
cystine 270.0
glycine 270.0
lysine 270.7
ornithine 270.6
renal (types I, II, III) 270.0
Hyperammonemia (congenital) 270.6
Hyperamnesia 780.99
Hyperamylasemia 790.5
Hyperaphia 782.0
Hyperazotemia 791.9
Hyperbetalipoproteinemia (acquired) (essential) (familial) (hereditary) (primary) (secondary) 272.0
with prebetalipoproteinemia 272.2
Hyperbilirubinemia 782.4
congenital 277.4
constitutional 277.4
neonatal (transient) (*see also* Jaundice, fetus or newborn) 774.6
of prematurity 774.2
Hyperbilirubinemica encephalopathia, newborn 774.7
due to isoimmunization 773.4
Hypercalcemia, hypercalcemic (idiopathic) 275.42
nephropathy 588.89
Hypercalcinuria 275.40
Hypercapnia 786.09
with mixed acid-based disorder 276.4
fetal, affecting newborn 770.89
Hypercarotinemia 278.3
Hypercementosis 521.5
Hyperchloremia 276.9
Hyperchlorhydria 536.8
neurotic 306.4
psychogenic 306.4
Hypercholesterinemia — *see* Hypercholesterolemia
Hypercholesterolemia 272.0
with hyperglyceridemia, endogenous 272.2
essential 272.0
familial 272.0
hereditary 272.0
primary 272.0
pure 272.0
Hypercholesterolosis 272.0
Hyperchylia gastrica 536.8
psychogenic 306.4
Hyperchylomicronemia (familial) (with hyperbetalipoproteinemia) 272.3
Hypercoagulation syndrome (primary) 289.81
secondary 289.82
Hypercorticosteronism
correct substance properly administered 255.3
overdose or wrong substance given or taken 962.0
Hypercortisonism
correct substance properly administered 255.3
overdose or wrong substance given or taken 962.0
Hyperdynamic beta-adrenergic state or syndrome (circulatory) 429.82
Hyperekplexia 759.89

Hyperelectrolytemia 276.9
Hyperemesis 536.2
arising during pregnancy — *see* Hyperemesis, gravidarum
gravidarum (mild) (before 22 completed weeks gestation) 643.0 ☑
with
carbohydrate depletion 643.1 ☑
dehydration 643.1 ☑
electrolyte imbalance 643.1 ☑
metabolic disturbance 643.1 ☑
affecting fetus or newborn 761.8
severe (with metabolic disturbance) 643.1 ☑
psychogenic 306.4
Hyperemia (acute) 780.99
anal mucosa 569.49
bladder 596.7
cerebral 437.8
conjunctiva 372.71
ear, internal, acute 386.30
enteric 564.89
eye 372.71
eyelid (active) (passive) 374.82
intestine 564.89
iris 364.41
kidney 593.81
labyrinth 386.30
liver (active) (passive) 573.8
lung 514
ovary 620.8
passive 780.99
pulmonary 514
renal 593.81
retina 362.89
spleen 289.59
stomach 537.89
Hyperesthesia (body surface) — *see also* Disturbance, sensation 782.0
larynx (reflex) 478.79
hysterical 300.11
pharynx (reflex) 478.29
Hyperestrinism 256.0
Hyperestrogenism 256.0
Hyperestrogenosis 256.0
Hyperexplexia 759.89
Hyperextension, joint 718.80
ankle 718.87
elbow 718.82
foot 718.87
hand 718.84
hip 718.85
knee 718.86
multiple sites 718.89
pelvic region 718.85
shoulder (region) 718.81
specified site NEC 718.88
wrist 718.83
Hyperfibrinolysis — *see* Fibrinolysis
Hyperfolliculinism 256.0
Hyperfructosemia 271.2
Hyperfunction
adrenal (cortex) 255.3
androgenic, acquired benign 255.3
medulla 255.6
virilism 255.2
corticoadrenal NEC 255.3
labyrinth — *see* Hyperactive, labyrinth
medulloadrenal 255.6
ovary 256.1
estrogen 256.0
pancreas 577.8
parathyroid (gland) 252.00
pituitary (anterior) (gland) (lobe) 253.1
testicular 257.0
Hypergammaglobulinemia 289.89
monoclonal, benign (BMH) 273.1
polyclonal 273.0
Waldenström's 273.0
Hyperglobulinemia 273.8
Hyperglycemia 790.29 ▲
maternal
affecting fetus or newborn 775.0
manifest diabetes in infant 775.1
postpancreatectomy (complete) (partial) 251.3

☑ Additional Digit Required — Refer to the Tabular List for Digit Selection   ▽ Subterms under main terms may continue to next column or page

2007 ICD-9-CM   ▶◀ Revised Text   ● New Line   ▲ Revised Code   **October 2006 · Volume 2 — 145**

Hyperglyceridemia 272.1
  endogenous 272.1
  essential 272.1
  familial 272.1
  hereditary 272.1
  mixed 272.3
  pure 272.1
Hyperglycinemia 270.7
Hypergonadism
  ovarian 256.1
  testicular (infantile) (primary) 257.0
Hyperheparinemia — *see also* Circulating anticoagulants 286.5
Hyperhidrosis, hyperidrosis 705.21
  axilla 705.21
  face 705.21
  focal (localized) 705.21
    primary 705.21
      axilla 705.21
      face 705.21
      palms 705.21
      soles 705.21
    secondary 705.22
      axilla 705.22
      face 705.22
      palms 705.22
      soles 705.22
  generalized 780.8
  palms 705.21
  psychogenic 306.3
  secondary 780.8
  soles 705.21
Hyperhistidinemia 270.5
Hyperinsulinism (ectopic) (functional) (organic) NEC 251.1
  iatrogenic 251.0
  reactive 251.2
  spontaneous 251.2
  therapeutic misadventure (from administration of insulin) 962.3
Hyperiodemia 276.9
Hyperirritability (cerebral), in newborn 779.1
Hyperkalemia 276.7
Hyperkeratosis — *see also* Keratosis 701.1
  cervix 622.2
  congenital 757.39
  cornea 371.89
  due to yaws (early) (late) (palmar or plantar) 102.3
  eccentrica 757.39
  figurata centrifuga atrophica 757.39
  follicularis 757.39
    in cutem penetrans 701.1
  limbic (cornea) 371.89
  palmoplantaris climacterica 701.1
  pinta (carate) 103.1
  senile (with pruritus) 702.0
  tongue 528.79
  universalis congenita 757.1
  vagina 623.1
  vocal cord 478.5
  vulva 624.0
Hyperkinesia, hyperkinetic (disease) (reaction) (syndrome) 314.9
  with
    attention deficit — *see* Disorder, attention deficit
    conduct disorder 314.2
    developmental delay 314.1
    simple disturbance of activity and attention 314.01
    specified manifestation NEC 314.8
  heart (disease) 429.82
  of childhood or adolescence NEC 314.9
Hyperlacrimation — *see also* Epiphora 375.20
Hyperlipemia — *see also* Hyperlipidemia 272.4
Hyperlipidemia 272.4
  carbohydrate-induced 272.1
  combined 272.4
  endogenous 272.1
  exogenous 272.3

Hyperlipidemia — *continued*
  fat-induced 272.3
  group
    A 272.0
    B 272.1
    C 272.2
    D 272.3
  mixed 272.2
  specified type NEC 272.4
Hyperlipidosis 272.7
  hereditary 272.7
Hyperlipoproteinemia (acquired) (essential) (familial) (hereditary) (primary) (secondary) 272.4
  Fredrickson type
    I 272.3
    IIa 272.0
    IIb 272.2
    III 272.2
    IV 272.1
    V 272.3
  low-density-lipoid-type (LDL) 272.0
  very-low-density-lipoid-type (VLDL) 272.1
Hyperlucent lung, unilateral 492.8
Hyperluteinization 256.1
Hyperlysinemia 270.7
Hypermagnesemia 275.2
  neonatal 775.5
Hypermaturity (fetus or newborn)
  post-term infant 766.21
  prolonged gestation infant 766.22
Hypermenorrhea 626.2
Hypermetabolism 794.7
Hypermethioninemia 270.4
Hypermetropia (congenital) 367.0
Hypermobility
  cecum 564.9
  coccyx 724.71
  colon 564.9
    psychogenic 306.4
  ileum 564.89
  joint (acquired) 718.80
    ankle 718.87
    elbow 718.82
    foot 718.87
    hand 718.84
    hip 718.85
    knee 718.86
    multiple sites 718.89
    pelvic region 718.85
    shoulder (region) 718.81
    specified site NEC 718.88
    wrist 718.83
  kidney, congenital 753.3
  meniscus (knee) 717.5
  scapula 718.81
  stomach 536.8
    psychogenic 306.4
  syndrome 728.5
  testis, congenital 752.52
  urethral 599.81
Hypermotility
  gastrointestinal 536.8
  intestine 564.9
    psychogenic 306.4
  stomach 536.8
Hypernasality 784.49
Hypernatremia 276.0
  with water depletion 276.0
Hypernephroma (M8312/3) 189.0
Hyperopia 367.0
Hyperorexia 783.6
Hyperornithinemia 270.6
Hyperosmia — *see also* Disturbance, sensation 781.1
Hyperosmolality 276.0
Hyperosteogenesis 733.99
Hyperostosis 733.99
  calvarial 733.3
  cortical 733.3
    infantile 756.59
  frontal, internal of skull 733.3
  interna frontalis 733.3
  monomelic 733.99
  skull 733.3

Hyperostosis — *continued*
  skull — *continued*
    congenital 756.0
  vertebral 721.8
    with spondylosis — *see* Spondylosis
    ankylosing 721.6
Hyperovarianism 256.1
Hyperovarism, hyperovaria 256.1
Hyperoxaluria (primary) 271.8
Hyperoxia 987.8
Hyperparathyroidism 252.00
  ectopic 259.3
  other 252.08
  primary 252.01
  secondary (of renal origin) 588.81
    non-renal 252.02
  tertiary 252.08
Hyperpathia — *see also* Disturbance, sensation 782.0
  psychogenic 307.80
Hyperperistalsis 787.4
  psychogenic 306.4
Hyperpermeability, capillary 448.9
Hyperphagia 783.6
Hyperphenylalaninemia 270.1
Hyperphoria 378.40
  alternating 378.45
Hyperphosphatemia 275.3
Hyperpiesia — *see also* Hypertension 401.9
Hyperpiesis — *see also* Hypertension 401.9
Hyperpigmentation — *see* Pigmentation
Hyperpinealism 259.8
Hyperpipecolatemia 270.7
Hyperpituitarism 253.1
Hyperplasia, hyperplastic
  adenoids (lymphoid tissue) 474.12
    and tonsils 474.10
  adrenal (capsule) (cortex) (gland) 255.8
    with
      sexual precocity (male) 255.2
      virilism, adrenal 255.2
      virilization (female) 255.2
    congenital 255.2
    due to excess ACTH (ectopic) (pituitary) 255.0
    medulla 255.8
  alpha cells (pancreatic)
    with
      gastrin excess 251.5
      glucagon excess 251.4
  appendix (lymphoid) 543.0
  artery, fibromuscular NEC 447.8
    carotid 447.8
    renal 447.3
  bone 733.99
    marrow 289.9
  breast (*see also* Hypertrophy, breast) 611.1
  carotid artery 447.8
  cementation, cementum (teeth) (tooth) 521.5
  cervical gland 785.6
  cervix (uteri) 622.10
    basal cell 622.10
    congenital 752.49
    endometrium 622.10
    polypoid 622.10
  chin 524.05
  clitoris, congenital 752.49
  dentin 521.5
  endocervicitis 616.0
  endometrium, endometrial (adenomatous) (atypical) (cystic) (glandular) (polypoid) (uterus) 621.30
    with atypia 621.33
    without atypia
      complex 621.32
      simple 621.31
    cervix 622.10
  epithelial 709.8
    focal, oral, including tongue 528.79
    mouth (focal) 528.79
    nipple 611.8

Hyperplasia, hyperplastic — *continued*
  epithelial — *continued*
    skin 709.8
    tongue (focal) 528.79
    vaginal wall 623.0
  erythroid 289.9
  fascialis ossificans (progressiva) 728.11
  fibromuscular, artery NEC 447.8
    carotid 447.8
    renal 447.3
  genital
    female 629.89   ▲
    male 608.89
  gingiva 523.8
  glandularis
    cystica uteri 621.30
    endometrium (uterus) 621.30
    interstitialis uteri 621.30
  granulocytic 288.69   ▲
  gum 523.8
  hymen, congenital 752.49
  islands of Langerhans 251.1
  islet cell (pancreatic) 251.9
    alpha cells
      with excess
        gastrin 251.5
        glucagon 251.4
    beta cells 251.1
  juxtaglomerular (complex) (kidney) 593.89
  kidney (congenital) 753.3
  liver (congenital) 751.69
  lymph node (gland) 785.6
  lymphoid (diffuse) (nodular) 785.6
    appendix 543.0
    intestine 569.89
  mandibular 524.02
    alveolar 524.72
    unilateral condylar 526.89
  Marchand multiple nodular (liver) — *see* Cirrhosis, postnecrotic
  maxillary 524.01
    alveolar 524.71
  medulla, adrenal 255.8
  myometrium, myometrial 621.2
  nose (lymphoid) (polypoid) 478.19   ▲
  oral soft tissue (inflammatory) (irritative) (mucosa) NEC 528.9
    gingiva 523.8
    tongue 529.8
  organ or site, congenital NEC — *see* Anomaly, specified type NEC
  ovary 620.8
  palate, papillary 528.9
  pancreatic islet cells 251.9
    alpha
      with excess
        gastrin 251.5
        glucagon 251.4
    beta 251.1
  parathyroid (gland) 252.01
  persistent, vitreous (primary) 743.51
  pharynx (lymphoid) 478.29
  prostate 600.90
    with
      other lower urinary tract symptoms (LUTS) 600.91   ●
      urinary
        obstruction 600.91   ●
        retention 600.91   ●
    adenofibromatous 600.20
      with
        other lower urinary tract symptoms (LUTS) 600.21   ●
        urinary
          obstruction 600.21   ●
          retention 600.21   ●
    nodular 600.10
      with
        urinary
          obstruction 600.11   ●

☑ Additional Digit Required — Refer to the Tabular List for Digit Selection   ▽ Subterms under main terms may continue to next column or page

146 — Volume 2 • October 2006   ▶◀ Revised Text   ● New Line   ▲ Revised Code   *2007 ICD-9-CM*

Hyperplasia, hyperplastic —
  continued
  prostate — *continued*
    nodular — *continued*
      with — *continued*
        urinary — *continued*
          retention 600.11 ●
  renal artery (fibromuscular) 447.3
  reticuloendothelial (cell) 289.9
  salivary gland (any) 527.1
  Schimmelbusch's 610.1
  suprarenal (capsule) (gland) 255.8
  thymus (gland) (persistent) 254.0
  thyroid (*see also* Goiter) 240.9
    primary 242.0 ☑
    secondary 242.2 ☑
  tonsil (lymphoid tissue) 474.11
    and adenoids 474.10
  urethrovaginal 599.89
  uterus, uterine (myometrium) 621.2
    endometrium (*see also* Hyperplasia, endometrium) 621.30
  vitreous (humor), primary persistent 743.51
  vulva 624.3
  zygoma 738.11
Hyperpnea — *see also* Hyperventilation 786.01
Hyperpotassemia 276.7
Hyperprebetalipoproteinemia 272.1
  with chylomicronemia 272.3
  familial 272.1
Hyperprolactinemia 253.1
Hyperprolinemia 270.8
Hyperproteinemia 273.8
Hyperprothrombinemia 289.89

Hyperpselaphesia 782.0
Hyperpyrexia 780.6
  heat (effects of) 992.0
  malarial (*see also* Malaria) 084.6
  malignant, due to anesthetic 995.86
  rheumatic — *see* Fever, rheumatic
  unknown origin (*see also* Pyrexia) 780.6
Hyperreactor, vascular 780.2
Hyperreflexia 796.1
  bladder, autonomic 596.54
    with cauda equina 344.61
  detrusor 344.61
Hypersalivation — *see also* Ptyalism 527.7
Hypersarcosinemia 270.8
Hypersecretion
  ACTH 255.3
  androgens (ovarian) 256.1
  calcitonin 246.0
  corticoadrenal 255.3
  cortisol 255.0
  estrogen 256.0
  gastric 536.8
    psychogenic 306.4
  gastrin 251.5
  glucagon 251.4
  hormone
    ACTH 255.3
    anterior pituitary 253.1
    growth NEC 253.0
    ovarian androgen 256.1
    testicular 257.0
    thyroid stimulating 242.8 ☑
  insulin — *see* Hyperinsulinism

Hypersecretion — *continued*
  lacrimal glands (*see also* Epiphora) 375.20
  medulloadrenal 255.6
  milk 676.6 ☑
  ovarian androgens 256.1
  pituitary (anterior) 253.1
  salivary gland (any) 527.7
  testicular hormones 257.0
  thyrocalcitonin 246.0
  upper respiratory 478.9
Hypersegmentation, hereditary 288.2
  eosinophils 288.2
  neutrophil nuclei 288.2
Hypersensitive, hypersensitiveness, hypersensitivity — *see also* Allergy
  angiitis 446.20
    specified NEC 446.29
  carotid sinus 337.0
  colon 564.9
    psychogenic 306.4
  DNA (deoxyribonucleic acid) NEC 287.2
  drug (*see also* Allergy, drug) 995.27 ▲
  esophagus 530.89
  insect bites — *see* Injury, superficial, by site
  labyrinth 386.58
  pain (*see also* Disturbance, sensation) 782.0
  pneumonitis NEC 495.9
  reaction (*see also* Allergy) 995.3
    upper respiratory tract NEC 478.8
  stomach (allergic) (nonallergic) 536.8

Hypersensitive, hypersensitiveness, hypersensitivity — *see also* Allergy
  — *continued*
  stomach — *continued*
    psychogenic 306.4
Hypersomatotropism (classic) 253.0
Hypersomnia, unspecified 780.54
  with sleep apnea, unspecified 780.53
  alcohol induced 291.82
  drug induced 292.85
  due to
    medical condition classified elsewhere 327.14
    mental disorder 327.15
  idiopathic
    with long sleep time 327.11
    without long sleep time 327.12
  menstrual related 327.13
  nonorganic origin 307.43
    persistent (primary) 307.44
    transient 307.43
  organic 327.10
    other 327.19
  primary 307.44
  recurrent 327.13
Hypersplenia 289.4
Hypersplenism 289.4
Hypersteatosis 706.3
Hyperstimulation, ovarian 256.1
Hypersuprarenalism 255.3
Hypersusceptibility — *see* Allergy
Hyper-TBG-nemia 246.8
Hypertelorism 756.0
  orbit, orbital 376.41

☑ Additional Digit Required — Refer to the Tabular List for Digit Selection   ▽ Subterms under main terms may continue to next column or page

2007 ICD-9-CM   ▶◀ Revised Text   ● New Line   ▲ Revised Code   October 2006 · Volume 2 — 147

	Malignant	Benign	Unspecified
Hypertension, hypertensive (arterial) (arteriolar) (crisis) (degeneration) (disease) (essential) (fluctuating) (idiopathic) (intermittent) (labile) (low renin) (orthostatic) (paroxysmal) (primary) (systemic) (uncontrolled) (vascular)	401.0	401.1	401.9
with			
chronic kidney disease			
stage I through stage IV, or unspecified ●	403.00	403.10	403.90
stage V or end stage renal disese ●	403.01	403.11	403.91
heart involvement (conditions classifiable to 429.0–429.3, 429.8, 429.9 due to hypertension) (see also Hypertension, heart)	402.00	402.10	402.90
with kidney involvement — see Hypertension, cardiorenal			
renal involvement (only conditions classifiable to 585, 586, 587) (excludes conditions classifiable to 584) (see also Hypertension, kidney)	403.00	403.10	403.90
with heart involvement — see Hypertension, cardiorenal			
failure (and sclerosis) (see also Hypertension, kidney)	403.01	403.11	403.91
sclerosis without failure (see also Hypertension, kidney)	403.00	403.10	403.90
accelerated (see also Hypertension, by type, malignant))	401.0	—	—
antepartum — see Hypertension, complicating pregnancy, childbirth, or the puerperium			
cardiorenal (disease)	404.00	404.10	404.90
with			
chronic kidney disease			
stage I through stage IV, or unspecified ●	404.00	404.10	404.90
and heart failure ●	404.01	404.11	404.91
stage V or end stage renal disease ●	404.02	404.12	404.92
and heart failure ●	404.03	404.13	404.93
heart failure	404.01	404.11	404.91
and chronic kidney disease	404.02	404.12	404.92
stage I through stage IV or unspecified ●	404.02	404.12	404.92
stave V or end stage renal disease ●	404.03	404.13	404.93
cardiovascular disease (arteriosclerotic) (sclerotic)	402.00	402.10	402.90
with			
heart failure	402.01	402.11	402.91
renal involvement (conditions classifiable to 403) (see also Hypertension, cardiorenal)	404.00	404.10	404.90
cardiovascular renal (disease) (sclerosis) (see also Hypertension, cardiorenal)	404.00	404.10	404.90
cerebrovascular disease NEC	437.2	437.2	437.2
complicating pregnancy, childbirth, or the puerperium	642.2 ☑	642.0 ☑	642.9 ☑
with			
albuminuria (and edema) (mild)	—	—	642.4 ☑
severe	—	—	642.5 ☑
chronic kidney disesae ●	642.2 ☑	642.2 ☑	642.2 ☑
and heart disease ●	642.2 ☑	642.2 ☑	642.2 ☑
edema (mild)	—	—	642.4 ☑
severe	—	—	642.5 ☑
heart disease	642.2 ☑	642.2 ☑	642.2 ☑
and ►chronic kidney◄ disease	642.2 ☑	642.2 ☑	642.2 ☑
renal disease	642.2 ☑	642.2 ☑	642.2 ☑
and heart disease	642.2 ☑	642.2 ☑	642.2 ☑
chronic	642.2 ☑	642.0 ☑	642.0 ☑
with pre-eclampsia or eclampsia	642.7 ☑	642.7 ☑	642.7 ☑
fetus or newborn	760.0	760.0	760.0
essential	—	642.0 ☑	642.0 ☑
with pre-eclampsia or eclampsia	—	642.7 ☑	642.7 ☑
fetus or newborn	760.0	760.0	760.0
fetus or newborn	760.0	760.0	760.0
gestational	—	—	642.3 ☑
pre-existing	642.2 ☑	642.0 ☑	642.0 ☑
with pre-eclampsia or eclampsia	642.7 ☑	642.7 ☑	642.7 ☑
fetus or newborn	760.0	760.0	760.0
secondary to renal disease	642.1 ☑	642.1 ☑	642.1 ☑
with pre-eclampsia or eclampsia	642.7 ☑	642.7 ☑	642.7 ☑
fetus or newborn	760.0	760.0	760.0
transient	—	—	642.3 ☑
due to			
aldosteronism, primary	405.09	405.19	405.99
brain tumor	405.09	405.19	405.99
bulbar poliomyelitis	405.09	405.19	405.99
calculus			
kidney	405.09	405.19	405.99
ureter	405.09	405.19	405.99
coarctation, aorta	405.09	405.19	405.99
Cushing's disease	405.09	405.19	405.99
glomerulosclerosis (see also Hypertension, kidney)	403.00	403.10	403.90
periarteritis nodosa	405.09	405.19	405.99
pheochromocytoma	405.09	405.19	405.99
polycystic kidney(s)	405.09	405.19	405.99
polycythemia	405.09	405.19	405.99
porphyria	405.09	405.19	405.99
pyelonephritis	405.09	405.19	405.99
Hypertension, hypertensive — continued			
due to — continued			
renal (artery)			
aneurysm	405.01	405.11	405.91
anomaly	405.01	405.11	405.91
embolism	405.01	405.11	405.91
fibromuscular hyperplasia	405.01	405.11	405.91
occlusion	405.01	405.11	405.91
stenosis	405.01	405.11	405.91
thrombosis	405.01	405.11	405.91
encephalopathy	437.2	437.2	437.2
gestational (transient) NEC	—	—	642.3 ☑
Goldblatt's	440.1	440.1	440.1
heart (disease) (conditions classifiable to 429.0–429.3, 429.8, 429.9			
due to hypertension)	402.00	402.10	402.90
with heart failure	402.01	402.11	402.91
hypertensive kidney disease (conditions classifiable to 403) (see also Hypertension, cardiorenal)	404.00	404.10	404.90
renal sclerosis (see also Hypertension, cardiorenal)	404.00	404.10	404.90
intracranial, benign	—	348.2	—
intraocular	—	—	365.04
kidney	403.00	403.10	403.90
with			
chronic kidney disease			
stage I through stage IV, or unspecified ●	403.00	403.10	403.90
stage V or end stage renal disese ●	403.01	403.11	403.91
heart involvement (conditions classifiable to 429.0–429.3, 429.8, 429.9 due to hypertension) (see also Hypertension, cardiorenal)	404.00	404.10	404.90
hypertensive heart (disease) (conditions classifiable to 402) (see also Hypertension, cardiorenal)	404.00	404.10	404.90
lesser circulation	—	—	416.0
necrotizing	401.0	—	—
ocular	—	—	365.04
portal (due to chronic liver disease)	—	—	572.3
postoperative	—	—	997.91
psychogenic	—	—	306.2
puerperal, postpartum — see Hypertension, complicating pregnancy, childbirth, or the puerperium			
pulmonary (artery)	—	—	416.8
with cor pulmonale (chronic)	—	—	416.8
acute	—	—	415.0
idiopathic	—	—	416.0
primary	—	—	416.0
of newborn	—	—	747.83
secondary	—	—	416.8
renal (disease) (see also Hypertension, kidney)	403.00	403.10	403.90
renovascular NEC	405.01	405.11	405.91
secondary NEC	405.09	405.19	405.99
due to			
aldosteronism, primary	405.09	405.19	405.99
brain tumor	405.09	405.19	405.99
bulbar poliomyelitis	405.09	405.19	405.99
calculus			
kidney	405.09	405.19	405.99
ureter	405.09	405.19	405.99
coarctation, aorta	405.09	405.19	405.99
Cushing's disease	405.09	405.19	405.99
glomerulosclerosis (see also Hypertension, kidney)	403.00	403.10	403.90
periarteritis nodosa	405.09	405.19	405.99
pheochromocytoma	405.09	405.19	405.99
polycystic kidney(s)	405.09	405.19	405.99
polycythemia	405.09	405.19	405.99
porphyria	405.09	405.19	405.99
pyelonephritis	405.09	405.19	405.99
renal (artery)			
aneurysm	405.01	405.11	405.91
anomaly	405.01	405.11	405.91
embolism	405.01	405.11	405.91
fibromuscular hyperplasia	405.01	405.11	405.91
occlusion	405.01	405.11	405.91
stenosis	405.01	405.11	405.91
thrombosis	405.01	405.11	405.91
transient	—	—	796.2
of pregnancy	—	—	642.3 ☑
vascular degeneration	401.0	401.1	401.9
venous, chronic (asymptomatic) (idiopathic)	—	—	459.30
with			
complication, NEC	—	—	459.39
inflammation	—	—	459.32
with ulcer	—	—	459.33
ulcer	—	—	459.31
with inflammation	—	—	459.33
due to			
deep vein thrombosis (see also Syndrome, postphlebetic)	—	—	459.10

☑ Additional Digit Required — Refer to the Tabular List for Digit Selection   ▽ Subterms under main terms may continue to next column or page

2007 ICD-9-CM   ►◄ Revised Text   ● New Line   ▲ Revised Code   **October 2006 · Volume 2 — 149**

Index

Hyperthecosis, ovary — Hypertrophy, hypertrophic

Hyperthecosis, ovary 256.8
Hyperthermia (of unknown origin) — *see also* Pyrexia 780.6
  malignant (due to anesthesia) 995.86
  newborn 778.4
Hyperthymergasia — *see also* Psychosis, affective 296.0 ☑
  reactive (from emotional stress, psychological trauma) 298.1
  recurrent episode 296.1 ☑
  single episode 296.0 ☑
Hyperthymism 254.8
Hyperthyroid (recurrent) — *see* Hyperthyroidism
Hyperthyroidism (latent) (preadult) (recurrent) (without goiter) 242.9 ☑

Note — *Use the following fifth-digit subclassification with category 242:*

  0 *without mention of thyrotoxic crisis or storm*
  1 *with mention of thyrotoxic crisis or storm*

  with
    goiter (diffuse) 242.0 ☑
      adenomatous 242.3 ☑
        multinodular 242.2 ☑
        uninodular 242.1 ☑
      nodular 242.3 ☑
        multinodular 242.2 ☑
        uninodular 242.1 ☑
    thyroid nodule 242.1 ☑
  complicating pregnancy, childbirth, or puerperium 648.1 ☑
  neonatal (transient) 775.3
Hypertonia — *see* Hypertonicity
Hypertonicity
  bladder 596.51
  fetus or newborn 779.89
  gastrointestinal (tract) 536.8
  infancy 779.89
    due to electrolyte imbalance 779.89
  muscle 728.85
  stomach 536.8
    psychogenic 306.4
  uterus, uterine (contractions) 661.4 ☑
    affecting fetus or newborn 763.7
Hypertony — *see* Hypertonicity
Hypertransaminemia 790.4
Hypertrichosis 704.1
  congenital 757.4
  eyelid 374.54
  lanuginosa 757.4
    acquired 704.1
Hypertriglyceridemia, essential 272.1
Hypertrophy, hypertrophic
  adenoids (infectional) 474.12
    and tonsils (faucial) (infective) (lingual) (lymphoid) 474.10
  adrenal 255.8
  alveolar process or ridge 525.8
  anal papillae 569.49
  apocrine gland 705.82
  artery NEC 447.8
    carotid 447.8
    congenital (peripheral) NEC 747.60
      gastrointestinal 747.61
      lower limb 747.64
      renal 747.62
      specified NEC 747.69
      spinal 747.82
      upper limb 747.63
    renal 447.3
  arthritis (chronic) (*see also* Osteoarthrosis) 715.9 ☑
    spine (*see also* Spondylosis) 721.90
  arytenoid 478.79
  asymmetrical (heart) 429.9
  auricular — *see* Hypertrophy, cardiac
  Bartholin's gland 624.8
  bile duct 576.8
  bladder (sphincter) (trigone) 596.8
  blind spot, visual field 368.42
  bone 733.99
  brain 348.8

Hypertrophy, hypertrophic — *continued*
  breast 611.1
    cystic 610.1
    fetus or newborn 778.7
    fibrocystic 610.1
    massive pubertal 611.1
    puerperal, postpartum 676.3 ☑
    senile (parenchymatous) 611.1
  cardiac (chronic) (idiopathic) 429.3
    with
      rheumatic fever (conditions classifiable to 390)
        active 391.8
          with chorea 392.0
        inactive or quiescent (with chorea) 398.99
    congenital NEC 746.89
    fatty (*see also* Degeneration, myocardial) 429.1
    hypertensive (*see also* Hypertension, heart) 402.90
    rheumatic (with chorea) 398.99
      active or acute 391.8
        with chorea 392.0
    valve (*see also* Endocarditis) 424.90
      congenital NEC 746.89
  cartilage 733.99
  cecum 569.89
  cervix (uteri) 622.6
    congenital 752.49
    elongation 622.6
  clitoris (cirrhotic) 624.2
    congenital 752.49
  colon 569.89
    congenital 751.3
  conjunctiva, lymphoid 372.73
  cornea 371.89
  corpora cavernosa 607.89
  duodenum 537.89
  endometrium (uterus) (*see also* Hyperplasia, endometrium) 621.30
    cervix 622.6
  epididymis 608.89
  esophageal hiatus (congenital) 756.6
    with hernia — *see* Hernia, diaphragm
  eyelid 374.30
  falx, skull 733.99
  fat pad 729.30
    infrapatellar 729.31
    knee 729.31
    orbital 374.34
    popliteal 729.31
    prepatellar 729.31
    retropatellar 729.31
    specified site NEC 729.39
  foot (congenital) 755.67
  frenum, frenulum (tongue) 529.8
    linguae 529.8
    lip 528.5
  gallbladder or cystic duct 575.8
  gastric mucosa 535.2 ☑
  gingiva 523.8
  gland, glandular (general) NEC 785.6
  gum (mucous membrane) 523.8
  heart (idiopathic) (*see also* Hypertrophy, cardiac)
    valve (*see also* Endocarditis)
      congenital NEC 746.89
  hemifacial 754.0
  hepatic — *see* Hypertrophy, liver
  hiatus (esophageal) 756.6
  hilus gland 785.6
  hymen, congenital 752.49
  ileum 569.89
  infrapatellar fat pad 729.31
  intestine 569.89
  jejunum 569.89
  kidney (compensatory) 593.1
    congenital 753.3
  labial frenulum 528.5
  labium (majus) (minus) 624.3
  lacrimal gland, chronic 375.03
  ligament 728.9

Hypertrophy, hypertrophic — *continued*
  ligament — *continued*
    spinal 724.8
  linguae frenulum 529.8
  lingual tonsil (infectional) 474.11
  lip (frenum) 528.5
    congenital 744.81
  liver 789.1
    acute 573.8
    cirrhotic — *see* Cirrhosis, liver
    congenital 751.69
    fatty — *see* Fatty, liver
  lymph gland 785.6
    tuberculous — *see* Tuberculosis, lymph gland
  mammary gland — *see* Hypertrophy, breast
  maxillary frenulum 528.5
  Meckel's diverticulum (congenital) 751.0
  medial meniscus, acquired 717.3
  median bar 600.90
    with
      other lower urinary tract symptoms (LUTS) 600.91 ●
      urinary
        obstruction 600.91 ●
        retention 600.91 ●
  mediastinum 519.3
  meibomian gland 373.2
  meniscus, knee, congenital 755.64
  metatarsal head 733.99
  metatarsus 733.99
  mouth 528.9
  mucous membrane
    alveolar process 523.8
    nose 478.19 ▲
    turbinate (nasal) 478.0
  muscle 728.9
  muscular coat, artery NEC 447.8
    carotid 447.8
    renal 447.3
  myocardium (*see also* Hypertrophy, cardiac) 429.3
    idiopathic 425.4
  myometrium 621.2
  nail 703.8
    congenital 757.5
  nasal 478.19 ▲
    alae 478.19 ▲
    bone 738.0
    cartilage 478.19 ▲
      mucous membrane (septum) 478.19 ▲
    sinus (*see also* Sinusitis) 473.9
    turbinate 478.0
  nasopharynx, lymphoid (infectional) (tissue) (wall) 478.29
  neck, uterus 622.6
  nipple 611.1
  normal aperture diaphragm (congenital) 756.6
  nose (*see also* Hypertrophy, nasal) 478.19 ▲
  orbit 376.46
  organ or site, congenital NEC — *see* Anomaly, specified type NEC
  osteoarthropathy (pulmonary) 731.2
  ovary 620.8
  palate (hard) 526.89
    soft 528.9
  pancreas (congenital) 751.7
  papillae
    anal 569.49
    tongue 529.3
  parathyroid (gland) 252.01
  parotid gland 527.1
  penis 607.89
  phallus 607.89
    female (clitoris) 624.2
  pharyngeal tonsil 474.12
  pharyngitis 472.1
  pharynx 478.29

Hypertrophy, hypertrophic — *continued*
  pharynx — *continued*
    lymphoid (infectional) (tissue) (wall) 478.29
  pituitary (fossa) (gland) 253.8
  popliteal fat pad 729.31
  preauricular (lymph) gland (Hampstead) 785.6
  prepuce (congenital) 605
    female 624.2
  prostate (asymptomatic) (early) (recurrent) 600.90
    with
      other lower urinary tract symptlms (LUTS) 600.91 ●
      urinary
        obstruction 600.91 ●
        retention 600.91 ●
    adenofibromatous 600.20
      with
        other lower urinary tract symptoms (LUTS) 600.21 ●
        urinary
          obstruction 600.21 ●
          retention 600.21 ●
    benign 600.00
      with
        other lower urinary tract symptoms (LUTS) 600.01 ●
        urinary
          obstruction 600.01 ●
          retention 600.01 ●
    congenital 752.89
  pseudoedematous hypodermal 757.0
  pseudomuscular 359.1
  pylorus (muscle) (sphincter) 537.0
    congenital 750.5
    infantile 750.5
  rectal sphincter 569.49
  rectum 569.49
  renal 593.1
  rhinitis (turbinate) 472.0
  salivary duct or gland 527.1
    congenital 750.26
  scaphoid (tarsal) 733.99
  scar 701.4
  scrotum 608.89
  sella turcica 253.8
  seminal vesicle 608.89
  sigmoid 569.89
  skin condition NEC 701.9
  spermatic cord 608.89
  spinal ligament 724.8
  spleen — *see* Splenomegaly
  spondylitis (spine) (*see also* Spondylosis) 721.90
  stomach 537.89
  subaortic stenosis (idiopathic) 425.1
  sublingual gland 527.1
    congenital 750.26
  submaxillary gland 527.1
  suprarenal (gland) 255.8
  tendon 727.9
  testis 608.89
    congenital 752.89
  thymic, thymus (congenital) (gland) 254.0
  thyroid (gland) (*see also* Goiter) 240.9
    primary 242.0 ☑
    secondary 242.2 ☑
  toe (congenital) 755.65
    acquired 735.8
  tongue 529.8
    congenital 750.15
    frenum 529.8
    papillae (foliate) 529.3
  tonsil (faucial) (infective) (lingual) (lymphoid) 474.11
    with
      adenoiditis 474.01
      tonsillitis 474.00
        and adenoiditis 474.02
    and adenoids 474.10

☑ Additional Digit Required — Refer to the Tabular List for Digit Selection   ▽ Subterms under main terms may continue to next column or page

150 — Volume 2 • October 2006   ▶◀ Revised Text   ● New Line   ▲ Revised Code   *2007 ICD-9-CM*

Hypertrophy, hypertrophic —
continued
tunica vaginalis 608.89
turbinate (mucous membrane) 478.0
ureter 593.89
urethra 599.84
uterus 621.2
puerperal, postpartum 674.8 ☑
uvula 528.9
vagina 623.8
vas deferens 608.89
vein 459.89
ventricle, ventricular (heart) (left)
(right) (see also Hypertrophy,
cardiac)
congenital 746.89
due to hypertension (left) (right)
(see also Hypertension,
heart) 402.90
benign 402.10
malignant 402.00
right with ventricular septal defect,
pulmonary stenosis or atre-
sia, and dextraposition of
aorta 745.2
verumontanum 599.89
vesical 596.8
vocal cord 478.5
vulva 624.3
stasis (nonfilarial) 624.3
Hypertropia (intermittent) (periodic)
378.31
Hypertyrosinemia 270.2
Hyperuricemia 790.6
Hypervalinemia 270.3
Hyperventilation (tetany) 786.01
hysterical 300.11
psychogenic 306.1
syndrome 306.1
Hyperviscidosis 277.00
Hyperviscosity (of serum) (syndrome)
NEC 273.3
polycythemic 289.0
sclerocythemic 282.8
Hypervitaminosis (dietary) NEC 278.8
A (dietary) 278.2
D (dietary) 278.4
from excessive administration or use
of vitamin preparations (chronic)
278.8
reaction to sudden overdose 963.5
vitamin A 278.2
reaction to sudden overdose
963.5
vitamin D 278.4
reaction to sudden overdose
963.5
vitamin K
correct substance properly administered 278.8
overdose or wrong substance
given or taken 964.3
Hypervolemia 276.6
Hypesthesia — see also Disturbance,
sensation 782.0
cornea 371.81
Hyphema (anterior chamber) (ciliary
body) (iris) 364.41
traumatic 921.3
Hyphemia — see Hyphema
Hypoacidity, gastric 536.8
psychogenic 306.4
Hypoactive labyrinth (function) — see
Hypofunction, labyrinth
Hypoadrenalism 255.4
tuberculous (see also Tuberculosis)
017.6 ☑
Hypoadrenocorticism 255.4
pituitary 253.4
Hypoalbuminemia 273.8
Hypoaldosteronism 255.4   ●
Hypoalphalipoproteinemia 272.5
Hypobarism 993.2
Hypobaropathy 993.2
Hypobetalipoproteinemia (familial)
272.5

Hypocalcemia 275.41
cow's milk 775.4
dietary 269.3
neonatal 775.4
phosphate-loading 775.4
Hypocalcification, teeth 520.4
Hypochloremia 276.9
Hypochlorhydria 536.8
neurotic 306.4
psychogenic 306.4
Hypocholesteremia 272.5
Hypochondria (reaction) 300.7
Hypochondriac 300.7
Hypochondriasis 300.7
Hypochromasia blood cells 280.9
Hypochromic anemia 280.9
due to blood loss (chronic) 280.0
acute 285.1
microcytic 280.9
Hypocoagulability — see also Defect,
coagulation 286.9
Hypocomplementemia 279.8
Hypocythemia (progressive) 284.9
Hypodontia — see also Anodontia 520.0
Hypoeosinophilia 288.59   ▲
Hypoesthesia — see Disturbance,
sensation 782.0
cornea 371.81
tactile 782.0
Hypoestrinism 256.39
Hypoestrogenism 256.39
Hypoferremia 280.9
due to blood loss (chronic) 280.0
Hypofertility
female 628.9
male 606.1
Hypofibrinogenemia 286.3
acquired 286.6
congenital 286.3
Hypofunction
adrenal (gland) 255.4
cortex 255.4
medulla 255.5
specified NEC 255.5
cerebral 331.9
corticoadrenal NEC 255.4
intestinal 564.89
labyrinth (unilateral) 386.53
with loss of labyrinthine reactivity
386.55
bilateral 386.54
with loss of labyrinthine reactivity 386.56
Leydig cell 257.2
ovary 256.39
postablative 256.2
pituitary (anterior) (gland) (lobe) 253.2
posterior 253.5
testicular 257.2
iatrogenic 257.1
postablative 257.1
postirradiation 257.1
postsurgical 257.1
Hypogammaglobulinemia 279.00
acquired primary 279.06
non-sex-linked, congenital 279.06
sporadic 279.06
transient of infancy 279.09
Hypogenitalism (congenital) (female)
(male) 752.89
penis 752.69
Hypoglycemia (spontaneous) 251.2
coma 251.0
diabetic 250.3 ☑
diabetic 250.8 ☑
due to insulin 251.0
therapeutic misadventure 962.3
familial (idiopathic) 251.2
following gastrointestinal surgery
579.3
infantile (idiopathic) 251.2
in infant of diabetic mother 775.0
leucine-induced 270.3
neonatal 775.6
reactive 251.2
specified NEC 251.1

Hypoglycemic shock 251.0
diabetic 250.8 ☑
due to insulin 251.0
functional (syndrome) 251.1
Hypogonadism
female 256.39
gonadotrophic (isolated) 253.4
hypogonadotropic (isolated) (with
anosmia) 253.4
isolated 253.4
male 257.2
hereditary familial (Reifenstein's
syndrome) 259.5
ovarian (primary) 256.39
pituitary (secondary) 253.4
testicular (primary) (secondary) 257.2
Hypohidrosis 705.0
Hypohidrotic ectodermal dysplasia
757.31
Hypoidrosis 705.0
Hypoinsulinemia, postsurgical 251.3
postpancreatectomy (complete) (partial) 251.3
Hypokalemia 276.8
Hypokinesia 780.99
Hypoleukia splenica 289.4
Hypoleukocytosis 288.50   ▲
Hypolipidemia 272.5
Hypolipoproteinemia 272.5
Hypomagnesemia 275.2
neonatal 775.4
Hypomania, hypomanic reaction — see
also Psychosis, affective 296.0 ☑
recurrent episode 296.1 ☑
single episode 296.0 ☑
Hypomastia (congenital) 757.6
Hypomenorrhea 626.1
Hypometabolism 783.9
Hypomotility
gastrointestinal tract 536.8
psychogenic 306.4
intestine 564.89
psychogenic 306.4
stomach 536.8
psychogenic 306.4
Hyponasality 784.49
Hyponatremia 276.1
Hypo-ovarianism 256.39
Hypo-ovarism 256.39
Hypoparathyroidism (idiopathic) (surgically induced) 252.1
neonatal 775.4
Hypopharyngitis 462
Hypophoria 378.40
Hypophosphatasia 275.3
Hypophosphatemia (acquired) (congenital) (familial) 275.3
renal 275.3
Hypophyseal, hypophysis — see also
condition
dwarfism 253.3
gigantism 253.0
syndrome 253.8
Hypophyseothalamic syndrome 253.8
Hypopiesis — see Hypotension
Hypopigmentation 709.00
eyelid 374.53
Hypopinealism 259.8
Hypopituitarism (juvenile) (syndrome)
253.2
due to
hormone therapy 253.7
hypophysectomy 253.7
radiotherapy 253.7
postablative 253.7
postpartum hemorrhage 253.2
Hypoplasia, hypoplasis 759.89
adrenal (gland) 759.1
alimentary tract 751.8
lower 751.2
upper 750.8
anus, anal (canal) 751.2
aorta 747.22
aortic
arch (tubular) 747.10

Hypoplasia, hypoplasis — continued
aortic — continued
orifice or valve with hypoplasia of
ascending aorta and defective
development of left ventricle
(with mitral valve atresia)
746.7
appendix 751.2
areola 757.6
arm (see also Absence, arm, congenital) 755.20
artery (congenital) (peripheral) 747.60
brain 747.81
cerebral 747.81
coronary 746.85
gastrointestinal 747.61
lower limb 747.64
pulmonary 747.3
renal 747.62
retinal 743.58
specified NEC 747.69
spinal 747.82
umbilical 747.5
upper limb 747.63
auditory canal 744.29
causing impairment of hearing
744.02
biliary duct (common) or passage
751.61
bladder 753.8
bone NEC 756.9
face 756.0
malar 756.0
mandible 524.04
alveolar 524.74
marrow 284.9
acquired (secondary) 284.8
congenital 284.09   ▲
idiopathic 284.9
maxilla 524.03
alveolar 524.73
skull (see also Hypoplasia, skull)
756.0
brain 742.1
gyri 742.2
specified part 742.2
breast (areola) 757.6
bronchus (tree) 748.3
cardiac 746.89
valve — see Hypoplasia, heart,
valve
vein 746.89
carpus (see also Absence, carpal,
congenital) 755.28
cartilaginous 756.9
cecum 751.2
cementum 520.4
hereditary 520.5
cephalic 742.1
cerebellum 742.2
cervix (uteri) 752.49
chin 524.06
clavicle 755.51
coccyx 756.19
colon 751.2
corpus callosum 742.2
cricoid cartilage 748.3
dermal, focal (Goltz) 757.39
digestive organ(s) or tract NEC 751.8
lower 751.2
upper 750.8
ear 744.29
auricle 744.23
lobe 744.29
middle, except ossicles 744.03
ossicles 744.04
ossicles 744.04
enamel of teeth (neonatal) (postnatal)
(prenatal) 520.4
hereditary 520.5
endocrine (gland) NEC 759.2
endometrium 621.8
epididymis 752.89
epiglottis 748.3
erythroid, congenital 284.01   ▲
erythropoietic, chronic acquired 284.8

☑ Additional Digit Required — Refer to the Tabular List for Digit Selection   ▽ Subterms under main terms may continue to next column or page

2007 ICD-9-CM   ▶◀ Revised Text   ● New Line   ▲ Revised Code   October 2006 · Volume 2 — 151

Index

Hypoplasia, hypoplasis — Hysterotomy, affecting fetus or newborn

Hypoplasia, hypoplasis — continued
  esophagus 750.3
  Eustachian tube 744.24
  eye (see also Microphthalmos) 743.10
    lid 743.62
  face 744.89
    bone(s) 756.0
  fallopian tube 752.19
  femur (see also Absence, femur, congenital) 755.34
  fibula (see also Absence, fibula, congenital) 755.37
  finger (see also Absence, finger, congenital) 755.29
  focal dermal 757.39
  foot 755.31
  gallbladder 751.69
  genitalia, genital organ(s)
    female 752.89
      external 752.49
      internal NEC 752.89
    in adiposogenital dystrophy 253.8
    male 752.89
      penis 752.69
  glottis 748.3
  hair 757.4
  hand 755.21
  heart 746.89
    left (complex) (syndrome) 746.7
    valve NEC 746.89
      pulmonary 746.01
  humerus (see also Absence, humerus, congenital) 755.24
  hymen 752.49
  intestine (small) 751.1
    large 751.2
  iris 743.46
  jaw 524.09
  kidney(s) 753.0
  labium (majus) (minus) 752.49
  labyrinth, membranous 744.05
  lacrimal duct (apparatus) 743.65
  larynx 748.3
  leg (see also Absence, limb, congenital, lower) 755.30
  limb 755.4
    lower (see also Absence, limb, congenital, lower) 755.30
    upper (see also Absence, limb, congenital, upper) 755.20
  liver 751.69
  lung (lobe) 748.5
  mammary (areolar) 757.6
  mandibular 524.04
    alveolar 524.74
    unilateral condylar 526.89
  maxillary 524.03
    alveolar 524.73
  medullary 284.9
  megakaryocytic 287.30
  metacarpus (see also Absence, metacarpal, congenital) 755.28
  metatarsus (see also Absence, metatarsal, congenital) 755.38
  muscle 756.89
    eye 743.69
  myocardium (congenital) (Uhl's anomaly) 746.84
  nail(s) 757.5
  nasolacrimal duct 743.65
  nervous system NEC 742.8
  neural 742.8
  nose, nasal 748.1
  ophthalmic (see also Microphthalmos) 743.10
  optic nerve 377.43   ●
  organ
    of Corti 744.05
    or site NEC — see Anomaly, by site
  osseous meatus (ear) 744.03
  ovary 752.0
  oviduct 752.19
  pancreas 751.7

Hypoplasia, hypoplasis — continued
  parathyroid (gland) 759.2
  parotid gland 750.26
  patella 755.64
  pelvis, pelvic girdle 755.69
  penis 752.69
  peripheral vascular system (congenital) NEC 747.60
    gastrointestinal 747.61
    lower limb 747.64
    renal 747.62
    specified NEC 747.69
    spinal 747.82
    upper limb 747.63
  pituitary (gland) 759.2
  pulmonary 748.5
    arteriovenous 747.3
    artery 747.3
    valve 746.01
  punctum lacrimale 743.65
  radioulnar (see also Absence, radius, congenital, with ulna) 755.25
  radius (see also Absence, radius, congenital) 755.26
  rectum 751.2
  respiratory system NEC 748.9
  rib 756.3
  sacrum 756.19
  scapula 755.59
  shoulder girdle 755.59
  skin 757.39
  skull (bone) 756.0
    with
      anencephalus 740.0
      encephalocele 742.0
      hydrocephalus 742.3
        with spina bifida (see also Spina bifida) 741.0 ☑
      microcephalus 742.1
  spinal (cord) (ventral horn cell) 742.59
    vessel 747.82
  spine 756.19
  spleen 759.0
  sternum 756.3
  tarsus (see also Absence, tarsal, congenital) 755.38
  testis, testicle 752.89
  thymus (gland) 279.11
  thyroid (gland) 243
    cartilage 748.3
  tibiofibular (see also Absence, tibia, congenital, with fibula) 755.35
  toe (see also Absence, toe, congenital) 755.39
  tongue 750.16
  trachea (cartilage) (rings) 748.3
  Turner's (tooth) 520.4
  ulna (see also Absence, ulna, congenital) 755.27
  umbilical artery 747.5
  ureter 753.29
  uterus 752.3
  vagina 752.49
  vascular (peripheral) NEC (see also Hypoplasia, peripheral vascular system) 747.60
    brain 747.81
  vein(s) (peripheral) NEC (see also Hypoplasia, peripheral vascular system) 747.60
    brain 747.81
    cardiac 746.89
    great 747.49
    portal 747.49
    pulmonary 747.49
  vena cava (inferior) (superior) 747.49
  vertebra 756.19
  vulva 752.49
  zonule (ciliary) 743.39
  zygoma 738.12
Hypopotassemia 276.8
Hypoproaccelerinemia — see also Defect, coagulation 286.3

Hypoproconvertinemia (congenital) — see also Defect, coagulation 286.3
Hypoproteinemia (essential) (hypermetabolic) (idiopathic) 273.8
Hypoproteinosis 260
Hypoprothrombinemia (congenital) (hereditary) (idiopathic) — see also Defect, coagulation 286.3
  acquired 286.7
  newborn 776.3
Hypopselaphesia 782.0
Hypopyon (anterior chamber) (eye) 364.05
  iritis 364.05
  ulcer (cornea) 370.04
Hypopyrexia 780.99
Hyporeflex 796.1
Hyporeninemia, extreme 790.99
  in primary aldosteronism 255.10
Hyporesponsive episode 780.09
Hyposecretion
  ACTH 253.4
  ovary 256.39
    postablative 256.2
  salivary gland (any) 527.7
Hyposegmentation of neutrophils, hereditary 288.2
Hyposiderinemia 280.9
Hyposmolality 276.1
  syndrome 276.1
Hyposomatotropism 253.3
Hyposomnia, unspecified — see also Insomnia 780.52
  with sleep apnea, unspecified 780.51   ▲
Hypospadias (male) 752.61
  female 753.8
Hypospermatogenesis 606.1
Hyposphagma 372.72
Hyposplenism 289.59
Hypostasis, pulmonary 514
Hypostatic — see condition
Hyposthenuria 593.89
Hyposuprarenalism 255.4
Hypo-TBG-nemia 246.8
Hypotension (arterial) (constitutional) 458.9
  chronic 458.1
  iatrogenic 458.29
  maternal, syndrome (following labor and delivery) 669.2 ☑
  of hemodialysis 458.21
  orthostatic (chronic) 458.0
    dysautonomic-dyskinetic syndrome 333.0
  permanent idiopathic 458.1
  postoperative 458.29
  postural 458.0
  specified type NEC 458.8
  transient 796.3
Hypothermia (accidental) 991.6
  anesthetic 995.89
  newborn NEC 778.3
  not associated with low environmental temperature 780.99
Hypothymergasia — see also Psychosis, affective 296.2 ☑
  recurrent episode 296.3 ☑
  single episode 296.2 ☑
Hypothyroidism (acquired) 244.9
  complicating pregnancy, childbirth, or puerperium 648.1 ☑
  congenital 243
  due to
    ablation 244.1
      radioactive iodine 244.1
      surgical 244.0
    iodine (administration) (ingestion) 244.2
      radioactive 244.1
    irradiation therapy 244.1
    p-aminosalicylic acid (PAS) 244.3
    phenylbutazone 244.3

Hypothyroidism — continued
  due to — continued
    resorcinol 244.3
    specified cause NEC 244.8
    surgery 244.0
  goitrous (sporadic) 246.1
  iatrogenic NEC 244.3
  iodine 244.2
  pituitary 244.8
  postablative NEC 244.1
  postsurgical 244.0
  primary 244.9
  secondary NEC 244.8
  specified cause NEC 244.8
  sporadic goitrous 246.1
Hypotonia, hypotonicity, hypotony 781.3
  benign congenital 358.8
  bladder 596.4
  congenital 779.89
    benign 358.8
  eye 360.30
    due to
      fistula 360.32
      ocular disorder NEC 360.33
    following loss of aqueous or vitreous 360.33
    primary 360.31
  infantile muscular (benign) 359.0
  muscle 728.9
  uterus, uterine (contractions) — see Inertia, uterus
Hypotrichosis 704.09
  congenital 757.4
  lid (congenital) 757.4
    acquired 374.55
  postinfectional NEC 704.09
Hypotropia 378.32
Hypoventilation 786.09
  congenital central alveolar syndrome 327.25
  idiopathic sleep related nonobstructive alveolar 327.24
  sleep related, in conditions classifiable elsewhere 327.26
Hypovitaminosis — see also Deficiency, vitamin 269.2
Hypovolemia 276.52
  surgical shock 998.0
  traumatic (shock) 958.4
Hypoxemia — see also Anoxia 799.02
  sleep related, in conditions classifiable elsewhere 327.26
Hypoxia — see also Anoxia 799.02
  cerebral 348.1
    during or resulting from a procedure 997.01
    newborn 770.88   ▲
      mild or moderate 768.6
      severe 768.5
  fetal, affecting newborn 770.88   ▲
  intrauterine — see Distress, fetal
  myocardial (see also Insufficiency, coronary) 411.89
    arteriosclerotic — see Arteriosclerosis, coronary
  newborn 770.88   ▲
  sleep related 327.24
Hypoxic-ischemic encephalopathy ● (HIE) 768.7   ●
Hypsarrhythmia — see also Epilepsy 345.6 ☑
Hysteralgia, pregnant uterus 646.8 ☑
Hysteria, hysterical 300.10
  anxiety 300.20
  Charcôt's gland 300.11
  conversion (any manifestation) 300.11
  dissociative type NEC 300.15
  psychosis, acute 298.1
Hysteroepilepsy 300.11
Hysterotomy, affecting fetus or newborn 763.89

☑ Additional Digit Required — Refer to the Tabular List for Digit Selection   ▽ Subterms under main terms may continue to next column or page

152 — Volume 2 · October 2006   ▶◀ Revised Text   ● New Line   ▲ Revised Code   *2007 ICD-9-CM*

I

Iatrogenic syndrome of excess cortisol
255.0
Iceland disease (epidemic neuromyasthenia) 049.8
Ichthyosis (congenita) 757.1
  acquired 701.1
  fetalis gravior 757.1
  follicularis 757.1
  hystrix 757.39
  lamellar 757.1
  lingual 528.6
  palmaris and plantaris 757.39
  simplex 757.1
  vera 757.1
  vulgaris 757.1
Ichthyotoxism 988.0
  bacterial (see also Poisoning, food) 005.9
Icteroanemia, hemolytic (acquired) 283.9
  congenital (see also Spherocytosis) 282.0
Icterus — see also Jaundice 782.4
  catarrhal — see Icterus, infectious
  conjunctiva 782.4
    newborn 774.6
  epidemic — see Icterus, infectious
  febrilis — see Icterus, infectious
  fetus or newborn — see Jaundice, fetus or newborn
  gravis (see also Necrosis, liver) 570
    complicating pregnancy 646.7 ☑
      affecting fetus or newborn 760.8
    fetus or newborn NEC 773.0
    obstetrical 646.7 ☑
      affecting fetus or newborn 760.8
  hematogenous (acquired) 283.9
  hemolytic (acquired) 283.9
    congenital (see also Spherocytosis) 282.0
  hemorrhagic (acute) 100.0
    leptospiral 100.0
    newborn 776.0
    spirochetal 100.0
  infectious 070.1
    with hepatic coma 070.0
    leptospiral 100.0
    spirochetal 100.0
  intermittens juvenilis 277.4
  malignant (see also Necrosis, liver) 570
  neonatorum (see also Jaundice, fetus or newborn) 774.6
  pernicious (see also Necrosis, liver) 570
  spirochetal 100.0
Ictus solaris, solis 992.0
Ideation
  suicidal V62.84
Identity disorder 313.82
  dissociative 300.14
  gender role (child) 302.6
    adult 302.85
  psychosexual (child) 302.6
    adult 302.85
Idioglossia 307.9
Idiopathic — see condition
Idiosyncrasy — see also Allergy 995.3
  drug, medicinal substance, and biological — see Allergy, drug
Idiot, idiocy (congenital) 318.2
  amaurotic (Bielschowsky) (-Jansky) (family) (infantile (late)) (juvenile (late)) (Vogt-Spielmeyer) 330.1
  microcephalic 742.1
  Mongolian 758.0
  oxycephalic 756.0
Id reaction (due to bacteria) 692.89
IgE asthma 493.0 ☑
Ileitis (chronic) — see also Enteritis 558.9
  infectious 009.0
  noninfectious 558.9
  regional (ulcerative) 555.0
    with large intestine 555.2

Ileitis — see also Enteritis — continued
  segmental 555.0
    with large intestine 555.2
  terminal (ulcerative) 555.0
    with large intestine 555.2
Ileocolitis — see also Enteritis 558.9
  infectious 009.0
  regional 555.2
  ulcerative 556.1
Ileostomy status V44.2
  with complication 569.60
Ileotyphus 002.0
Ileum — see condition
Ileus (adynamic) (bowel) (colon) (inhibitory) (intestine) (neurogenic) (paralytic) 560.1
  arteriomesenteric duodenal 537.2
  due to gallstone (in intestine) 560.31
  duodenal, chronic 537.2
  following gastrointestinal surgery 997.4
  gallstone 560.31
  mechanical (see also Obstruction, intestine) 560.9
  meconium 777.1
    due to cystic fibrosis 277.01
  myxedema 564.89
  postoperative 997.4
  transitory, newborn 777.4
Iliac — see condition
Iliotibial band friction syndrome 728.89
Illegitimacy V61.6
Ill, louping 063.1
Illness — see also Disease
  factitious 300.19
    with
      combined psychological and physical signs and symptoms 300.19
      predominantly
        physical signs and symptoms 300.19
        psychological symptoms 300.16
    chronic (with physical symptoms) 301.51
  heart — see Disease, heart
  manic-depressive (see also Psychosis, affective) 296.80
  mental (see also Disorder, mental) 300.9
Imbalance 781.2
  autonomic (see also Neuropathy, peripheral, autonomic) 337.9
  electrolyte 276.9
    with
      abortion — see Abortion, by type, with metabolic disorder
      ectopic pregnancy (see also categories 633.0–633.9) 639.4
      hyperemesis gravidarum (before 22 completed weeks gestation) 643.1 ☑
      molar pregnancy (see also categories 630–632) 639.4
    following
      abortion 639.4
      ectopic or molar pregnancy 639.4
    neonatal, transitory NEC 775.5
  endocrine 259.9
  eye muscle NEC 378.9
    heterophoria — see Heterophoria
  glomerulotubular NEC 593.89
  hormone 259.9
  hysterical (see also Hysteria) 300.10
  labyrinth NEC 386.50
  posture 729.9
  sympathetic (see also Neuropathy, peripheral, autonomic) 337.9
Imbecile, imbecility 318.0
  moral 301.7

Imbecile, imbecility — continued
  old age 290.9
  senile 290.9
  specified IQ — see IQ
  unspecified IQ 318.0
Imbedding, intrauterine device 996.32
Imbibition, cholesterol (gallbladder) 575.6
Imerslund (-Gräsbeck) syndrome (anemia due to familial selective vitamin B_{12} malabsorption) 281.1
Iminoacidopathy 270.8
Iminoglycinuria, familial 270.8
Immature — see also Immaturity
  personality 301.89
Immaturity 765.1 ☑
  extreme 765.0 ☑
  fetus or infant light-for-dates — see Light-for-dates
  lung, fetus or newborn 770.4
  organ or site NEC — see Hypoplasia
  pulmonary, fetus or newborn 770.4
  reaction 301.89
  sexual (female) (male) 259.0
Immersion 994.1
  foot 991.4
  hand 991.4
Immobile, immobility
  intestine 564.89
  joint — see Ankylosis
  syndrome (paraplegic) 728.3
Immunization
  ABO
    affecting management of pregnancy 656.2 ☑
      fetus or newborn 773.1
  complication — see Complications, vaccination
  Rh factor
    affecting management of pregnancy 656.1 ☑
      fetus or newborn 773.0
    from transfusion 999.7
Immunodeficiency 279.3
  with
    adenosine-deaminase deficiency 279.2
    defect, predominant
      B-cell 279.00
      T-cell 279.10
    hyperimmunoglobulinemia 279.2
    lymphopenia, hereditary 279.2
    thrombocytopenia and eczema 279.12
    thymic
      aplasia 279.2
      dysplasia 279.2
  autosomal recessive, Swiss-type 279.2
  common variable 279.06
  severe combined (SCID) 279.2
  to Rh factor
    affecting management of pregnancy 656.1 ☑
      fetus or newborn 773.0
  X-linked, with increased IgM 279.05
Immunotherapy, prophylactic V07.2
  antineoplastic V58.12
Impaction, impacted
  bowel, colon, rectum 560.30
    with hernia (see also Hernia, by site, with obstruction)
      gangrenous — see Hernia, by site, with gangrene
    by
      calculus 560.39
      gallstone 560.31
    fecal 560.39
    specified type NEC 560.39
  calculus — see Calculus
  cerumen (ear) (external) 380.4
  cuspid 520.6
  dental 520.6
  fecal, feces 560.39
    with hernia (see also Hernia, by site, with obstruction)

Impaction, impacted — continued
  fecal, feces — continued
    with hernia (see also Hernia, by site, with obstruction) — continued
      gangrenous — see Hernia, by site, with gangrene
  fracture — see Fracture, by site
  gallbladder — see Cholelithiasis
  gallstone(s) — see Cholelithiasis
    in intestine (any part) 560.31
  intestine(s) 560.30
    with hernia (see also Hernia, by site, with obstruction)
      gangrenous — see Hernia, by site, with gangrene
    by
      calculus 560.39
      gallstone 560.31
    fecal 560.39
    specified type NEC 560.39
  intrauterine device (IUD) 996.32
  molar 520.6
  shoulder 660.4 ☑
    affecting fetus or newborn 763.1
  tooth, teeth 520.6
  turbinate 733.99
Impaired, impairment (function)
  arm V49.1
    movement, involving
      musculoskeletal system V49.1
      nervous system V49.2
  auditory discrimination 388.43
  back V48.3
  body (entire) V49.89
  cognitive, mild, so stated 331.83 ●
  glucose
    fasting 790.21
    tolerance test (oral) 790.22
  hearing (see also Deafness) 389.9
  heart — see Disease, heart
  kidney (see also Disease, renal) 593.9
    disorder resulting from 588.9
      specified NEC 588.89
  leg V49.1
    movement, involving
      musculoskeletal system V49.1
      nervous system V49.2
  limb V49.1
    movement, involving
      musculoskeletal system V49.1
      nervous system V49.2
  liver 573.8
  mastication 524.9
  mild cognitive, so stated 331.83 ●
  mobility
    ear ossicles NEC 385.22
    incostapedial joint 385.22
    malleus 385.21
  myocardium, myocardial (see also Insufficiency, myocardial) 428.0
  neuromusculoskeletal NEC V49.89
    back V48.3
    head V48.2
    limb V49.2
    neck V48.3
    spine V48.3
    trunk V48.3
  rectal sphincter 787.99
  renal (see also Disease, renal) 593.9
    disorder resulting from 588.9
      specified NEC 588.89
  spine V48.3
  vision NEC 369.9
    both eyes NEC 369.3
    moderate 369.74
      both eyes 369.25
        with impairment of lesser eye (specified as)
          blind, not further specified 369.15
          low vision, not further specified 369.23
        near-total 369.17
        profound 369.18
        severe 369.24

☑ Additional Digit Required — Refer to the Tabular List for Digit Selection   ▼ Subterms under main terms may continue to next column or page

2007 ICD-9-CM   ▶◀ Revised Text   ● New Line   ▲ Revised Code   **October 2006 · Volume 2 — 153**

Impaired, impairment — *continued*
vision — *continued*
moderate — *continued*
both eyes — *continued*
with impairment of lesser eye
— *continued*
total 369.16
one eye 369.74
with vision of other eye
(specified as)
near-normal 369.75
normal 369.76
near-total 369.64
both eyes 369.04
with impairment of lesser eye
(specified as)
blind, not further speci-
fied 369.02
total 369.03
one eye 369.64
with vision of other eye
(specified as)
near normal 369.65
normal 369.66
one eye 369.60
with low vision of other eye
369.10
profound 369.67
both eyes 369.08
with impairment of lesser eye
(specified as)
blind, not further speci-
fied 369.05
near-total 369.07
total 369.06
one eye 369.67
with vision of other eye
(specified as)
near-normal 369.68
normal 369.69
severe 369.71
both eyes 369.22
with impairment of lesser eye
(specified as)
blind, not further speci-
fied 369.11
low vision, not further
specified 369.21
near-total 369.13
profound 369.14
total 369.12
one eye 369.71
with vision of other eye
(specified as)
near-normal 369.72
normal 369.73
total
both eyes 369.01
one eye 369.61
with vision of other eye
(specified as)
near-normal 369.62
normal 369.63
Impaludism — *see* Malaria
Impediment, speech NEC 784.5
psychogenic 307.9
secondary to organic lesion 784.5
Impending
cerebrovascular accident or attack
435.9
coronary syndrome 411.1
delirium tremens 291.0
myocardial infarction 411.1
Imperception, auditory (acquired)
(congenital) 389.9
Imperfect
aeration, lung (newborn) 770.5
closure (congenital)
alimentary tract NEC 751.8
lower 751.5
upper 750.8
atrioventricular ostium 745.69
atrium (secundum) 745.5
primum 745.61
branchial cleft or sinus 744.41
choroid 743.59

Imperfect — *continued*
closure — *continued*
cricoid cartilage 748.3
cusps, heart valve NEC 746.89
pulmonary 746.09
ductus
arteriosus 747.0
Botalli 747.0
ear drum 744.29
causing impairment of hearing
744.03
endocardial cushion 745.60
epiglottis 748.3
esophagus with communication to
bronchus or trachea 750.3
Eustachian valve 746.89
eyelid 743.62
face, facial (*see also* Cleft, lip)
749.10
foramen
Botalli 745.5
ovale 745.5
genitalia, genital organ(s) or system
female 752.89
external 752.49
internal NEC 752.89
uterus 752.3
male 752.89
penis 752.69
glottis 748.3
heart valve (cusps) NEC 746.89
interatrial ostium or septum 745.5
interauricular ostium or septum
745.5
interventricular ostium or septum
745.4
iris 743.46
kidney 753.3
larynx 748.3
lens 743.36
lip (*see also* Cleft, lip) 749.10
nasal septum or sinus 748.1
nose 748.1
omphalomesenteric duct 751.0
optic nerve entry 743.57
organ or site NEC — *see* Anomaly,
specified type, by site
ostium
interatrial 745.5
interauricular 745.5
interventricular 745.4
palate (*see also* Cleft, palate)
749.00
preauricular sinus 744.46
retina 743.56
roof of orbit 742.0
sclera 743.47
septum
aortic 745.0
aorticopulmonary 745.0
atrial (secundum) 745.5
primum 745.61
between aorta and pulmonary
artery 745.0
heart 745.9
interatrial (secundum) 745.5
primum 745.61
interauricular (secundum) 745.5
primum 745.61
interventricular 745.4
with pulmonary stenosis or
atresia, dextraposition
of aorta, and hypertro-
phy of right ventricle
745.2
in tetralogy of Fallot 745.2
nasal 748.1
ventricular 745.4
with pulmonary stenosis or
atresia, dextraposition
of aorta, and hypertro-
phy of right ventricle
745.2
in tetralogy of Fallot 745.2
skull 756.0

Imperfect — *continued*
closure — *continued*
skull — *continued*
with
anencephalus 740.0
encephalocele 742.0
hydrocephalus 742.3
with spina bifida (*see also*
Spina bifida)
741.0 ☑
microcephalus 742.1
spine (with meningocele) (*see also*
Spina bifida) 741.90
thyroid cartilage 748.3
trachea 748.3
tympanic membrane 744.29
causing impairment of hearing
744.03
uterus (with communication to
bladder, intestine, or rectum)
752.3
uvula 749.02
with cleft lip (*see also* Cleft,
palate, with cleft lip)
749.20
vitelline duct 751.0
development — *see* Anomaly, by site
erection 607.84
fusion — *see* Imperfect, closure
inflation lung (newborn) 770.5
intestinal canal 751.5
poise 729.9
rotation — *see* Malrotation
septum, ventricular 745.4
Imperfectly descended testis 752.51
Imperforate (congenital) — *see also*
Atresia
anus 751.2
bile duct 751.61
cervix (uteri) 752.49
esophagus 750.3
hymen 752.42
intestine (small) 751.1
large 751.2
jejunum 751.1
pharynx 750.29
rectum 751.2
salivary duct 750.23
urethra 753.6
urinary meatus 753.6
vagina 752.49
Impervious (congenital) — *see also*
Atresia
anus 751.2
bile duct 751.61
esophagus 750.3
intestine (small) 751.1
large 751.5
rectum 751.2
urethra 753.6
Impetiginization of other dermatoses
684
Impetigo (any organism) (any site) (bullous) (circinate) (contagiosa)
(neonatorum) (simplex) 684
Bockhart's (superficial folliculitis)
704.8
external ear 684 *[380.13]*
eyelid 684 *[373.5]*
Fox's (contagiosa) 684
furfuracea 696.5
herpetiformis 694.3
nonobstetrical 694.3
staphylococcal infection 684
ulcerative 686.8
vulgaris 684
Impingement, soft tissue between
teeth 524.89
anterior 524.81
posterior 524.82
Implantation
anomalous (*see also* Anomaly, specified type, by site)
ureter 753.4

Implantation — *continued*
cyst
external area or site (skin) NEC
709.8
iris 364.61
vagina 623.8
vulva 624.8
dermoid (cyst)
external area or site (skin) NEC
709.8
iris 364.61
vagina 623.8
vulva 624.8
placenta, low or marginal — *see* Placenta previa
Implant, endometrial 617.9
Impotence (sexual) 607.84
organic origin NEC 607.84
psychogenic 302.72
Impoverished blood 285.9
Impression, basilar 756.0
Imprisonment V62.5
Improper
development, infant 764.9 ☑
Improperly tied umbilical cord (causing
hemorrhage) 772.3
Impulses, obsessional 300.3
Impulsive neurosis 300.3
Inaction, kidney — *see also* Disease,
renal 593.9
Inactive — *see* condition
Inadequate, inadequacy
aesthetics of dental resoration ●
525.67 ●
biologic 301.6
cardiac and renal — *see* Hypertension,
cardiorenal
constitutional 301.6
development
child 783.40
fetus 764.9 ☑
affecting management of pregnancy 656.5 ☑
genitalia
after puberty NEC 259.0
congenital — *see* Hypoplasia,
genitalia
lungs 748.5
organ or site NEC — *see* Hypoplasia, by site
dietary 269.9
distance, interarch 524.28
education V62.3
environment
economic problem V60.2
household condition NEC V60.1
poverty V60.2
unemployment V62.0
functional 301.6
household care, due to
family member
handicapped or ill V60.4
temporarily away from home
V60.4
on vacation V60.5
technical defects in home V60.1
temporary absence from home of
person rendering care V60.4
housing (heating) (space) V60.1
interarch distance 524.28
material resources V60.2
mental (*see also* Retardation, mental)
319
nervous system 799.2
personality 301.6
prenatal care in current pregnancy
V23.7
pulmonary
function 786.09
newborn 770.89
ventilation, newborn 770.89
respiration 786.09
newborn 770.89
sample, Papanicolaou smear 795.08
social 301.6
Inanition 263.9

☑ Additional Digit Required — Refer to the Tabular List for Digit Selection   ▽ Subterms under main terms may continue to next column or page

154 — Volume 2 · October 2006   ▶◀ Revised Text   ● New Line   ▲ Revised Code   *2007 ICD-9-CM*

Inanition — *continued*
  with edema 262
  due to
    deprivation of food 994.2
    malnutrition 263.9
  fever 780.6
Inappropriate secretion
  ACTH 255.0
  antidiuretic hormone (ADH) (excessive) 253.6
    deficiency 253.5
  ectopic hormone NEC 259.3
  pituitary (posterior) 253.6
Inattention after or at birth 995.52
Inborn errors of metabolism — *see* Disorder, metabolism
Incarceration, incarcerated
  bubonocele (*see also* Hernia, inguinal, with obstruction)
    gangrenous — *see* Hernia, inguinal, with gangrene
  colon (by hernia) (*see also* Hernia, by site with obstruction)
    gangrenous — *see* Hernia, by site, with gangrene
  enterocele 552.9
    gangrenous 551.9
  epigastrocele 552.29
    gangrenous 551.29
  epiplocele 552.9
    gangrenous 551.9
  exomphalos 552.1
    gangrenous 551.1
  fallopian tube 620.8
  hernia (*see also* Hernia, by site, with obstruction)
    gangrenous — *see* Hernia, by site, with gangrene
  iris, in wound 871.1
  lens, in wound 871.1
  merocele (*see also* Hernia, femoral, with obstruction) 552.00
  omentum (by hernia) (*see also* Hernia, by site, with obstruction)
    gangrenous — *see* Hernia, by site, with gangrene
  omphalocele 756.79
  rupture (meaning hernia) (*see also* Hernia, by site, with obstruction) 552.9
    gangrenous (*see also* Hernia, by site, with gangrene) 551.9
  sarcoepiplocele 552.9
    gangrenous 551.9
  sarcoepiplomphalocele 552.1
    with gangrene 551.1
  uterus 621.8
    gravid 654.3 ☑
      causing obstructed labor 660.2 ☑
        affecting fetus or newborn 763.1
Incident, cerebrovascular — *see also* Disease, cerebrovascular, acute 436
Incineration (entire body) (from fire, conflagration, electricity, or lightning) — *see* Burn, multiple, specified sites
Incised wound
  external — *see* Wound, open, by site
  internal organs (abdomen, chest, or pelvis) — *see* Injury, internal, by site, with open wound
Incision, incisional
  hernia — *see* Hernia, incisional
  surgical, complication — *see* Complications, surgical procedures
  traumatic
    external — *see* Wound, open, by site
    internal organs (abdomen, chest, or pelvis) — *see* Injury, internal, by site, with open wound
Inclusion
  azurophilic leukocytic 288.2

Inclusion — *continued*
  blennorrhea (neonatal) (newborn) 771.6
  cyst — *see* Cyst, skin
  gallbladder in liver (congenital) 751.69
Incompatibility
  ABO
    affecting management of pregnancy 656.2 ☑
    fetus or newborn 773.1
    infusion or transfusion reaction 999.6
  blood (group) (Duffy) (E) (K(ell)) (Kidd) (Lewis) (M) (N) (P) (S) NEC
    affecting management of pregnancy 656.2 ☑
    fetus or newborn 773.2
    infusion or transfusion reaction 999.6
  contour of existing restoration of tooth ●
    with oral health 525.65 ●
  marital V61.10
    involving divorce or estrangement V61.0
  Rh (blood group) (factor)
    affecting management of pregnancy 656.1 ☑
    fetus or newborn 773.0
    infusion or transfusion reaction 999.7
  Rhesus — *see* Incompatibility, Rh
Incompetency, incompetence, incompetent
  annular
    aortic (valve) (*see also* Insufficiency, aortic) 424.1
    mitral (valve) (*see also* Insufficiency, mitral) 424.0
    pulmonary valve (heart) (*see also* Endocarditis, pulmonary) 424.3
  aortic (valve) (*see also* Insufficiency, aortic) 424.1
    syphilitic 093.22
  cardiac (orifice) 530.0
    valve — *see* Endocarditis
  cervix, cervical (os) 622.5
    in pregnancy 654.5 ☑
      affecting fetus or newborn 761.0
  esophagogastric (junction) (sphincter) 530.0
  heart valve, congenital 746.89
  mitral (valve) — *see* Insufficiency, mitral
  papillary muscle (heart) 429.81
  pelvic fundus
    pubocervical tissue 618.81
    rectovaginal tissue 618.82
  pulmonary valve (heart) (*see also* Endocarditis, pulmonary) 424.3
    congenital 746.09
  tricuspid (annular) (rheumatic) (valve) (*see also* Endocarditis, tricuspid) 397.0
  valvular — *see* Endocarditis
  vein, venous (saphenous) (varicose) (*see also* Varicose, vein) 454.9
  velopharyngeal (closure)
    acquired 528.9
    congenital 750.29
Incomplete — *see also* condition
  bladder emptying 788.21
  expansion lungs (newborn) 770.5
  gestation (liveborn) — *see* Immaturity
  rotation — *see* Malrotation
Incontinence 788.30
  without sensory awareness 788.34
  anal sphincter 787.6
  continuous leakage 788.37
  feces 787.6
    due to hysteria 300.11
    nonorganic origin 307.7
  hysterical 300.11
  mixed (male) (female) (urge and stress) 788.33

Incontinence — *continued*
  overflow 788.38
  paradoxical 788.39
  rectal 787.6
  specified NEC 788.39
  stress (female) 625.6
    male NEC 788.32
  urethral sphincter 599.84
  urge 788.31
    and stress (male) (female) 788.33
  urine 788.30
    active 788.30
    male 788.30
      stress 788.32
        and urge 788.33
    neurogenic 788.39
    nonorganic origin 307.6
    stress (female) 625.6
      male NEC 788.32
    urge 788.31
      and stress 788.33
Incontinentia pigmenti 757.33
Incoordinate
  uterus (action) (contractions) 661.4 ☑
    affecting fetus or newborn 763.7
Incoordination
  esophageal-pharyngeal (newborn) 787.2
  muscular 781.3
  papillary muscle 429.81
Increase, increased
  abnormal, in development 783.9
  androgens (ovarian) 256.1
  anticoagulants (antithrombin) (anti-VIIIa) (anti-IXa) (anti-Xa) (anti-XIa) 286.5
    postpartum 666.3 ☑
  cold sense (*see also* Disturbance, sensation) 782.0
  estrogen 256.0
  function
    adrenal (cortex) 255.3
      medulla 255.6
    pituitary (anterior) (gland) (lobe) 253.1
      posterior 253.6
  heat sense (*see also* Disturbance, sensation) 782.0
  intracranial pressure 781.99
    injury at birth 767.8
  light reflex of retina 362.13
  permeability, capillary 448.9
  pressure
    intracranial 781.99
      injury at birth 767.8
    intraocular 365.00
  pulsations 785.9
  pulse pressure 785.9
  sphericity, lens 743.36
  splenic activity 289.4
  venous pressure 459.89
    portal 572.3
Incrustation, cornea, lead or zinc 930.0
Incyclophoria 378.44
Incyclotropia 378.33
Indeterminate sex 752.7
India rubber skin 756.83
Indicanuria 270.2
Indigestion (bilious) (functional) 536.8
  acid 536.8
  catarrhal 536.8
  due to decomposed food NEC 005.9
  fat 579.8
  nervous 306.4
  psychogenic 306.4
Indirect — *see* condition
Indolent bubo NEC 099.8
Induced
  abortion — *see* Abortion, induced
  birth, affecting fetus or newborn 763.89
  delivery — *see* Delivery
  labor — *see* Delivery
Induration, indurated
  brain 348.8
  breast (fibrous) 611.79

Induration, indurated — *continued*
  breast — *continued*
    puerperal, postpartum 676.3 ☑
  broad ligament 620.8
  chancre 091.0
    anus 091.1
    congenital 090.0
    extragenital NEC 091.2
  corpora cavernosa (penis) (plastic) 607.89
  liver (chronic) 573.8
    acute 573.8
  lung (black) (brown) (chronic) (fibroid) (*see also* Fibrosis, lung) 515
    essential brown 275.0 [516.1]
  penile 607.89
  phlebitic — *see* Phlebitis
  skin 782.8
  stomach 537.89
Induratio penis plastica 607.89
Industrial — *see* condition
Inebriety — *see also* Abuse, drugs, nondependent 305.0 ☑
Inefficiency
  kidney (*see also* Disease, renal) 593.9
  thyroid (acquired) (gland) 244.9
Inelasticity, skin 782.8
Inequality, leg (acquired) (length) 736.81
  congenital 755.30
Inertia
  bladder 596.4
    neurogenic 596.54
      with cauda equina syndrome 344.61
  stomach 536.8
    psychogenic 306.4
  uterus, uterine 661.2 ☑
    affecting fetus or newborn 763.7
    primary 661.0 ☑
    secondary 661.1 ☑
  vesical 596.4
    neurogenic 596.54
      with cauda equina 344.61
Infant — *see also* condition
  excessive crying of 780.92
  fussy (baby) 780.91
  held for adoption V68.89
  newborn — *see* Newborn
  post-term (gestation period over 40 completed weeks to 42 completed weeks) 766.21
  prolonged gestation of (period over 42 completed weeks) 766.22
  syndrome of diabetic mother 775.0
"Infant Hercules" syndrome 255.2
Infantile — *see also* condition
  genitalia, genitals 259.0
    in pregnancy or childbirth NEC 654.4 ☑
      affecting fetus or newborn 763.89
      causing obstructed labor 660.2 ☑
        affecting fetus or newborn 763.1
  heart 746.9
  kidney 753.3
  lack of care 995.52
  macula degeneration 362.75
  melanodontia 521.05
  os, uterus (*see also* Infantile, genitalia) 259.0
  pelvis 738.6
    with disproportion (fetopelvic) 653.1 ☑
      affecting fetus or newborn 763.1
      causing obstructed labor 660.1 ☑
        affecting fetus or newborn 763.1
  penis 259.0
  testis 257.2
  uterus (*see also* Infantile, genitalia) 259.0
  vulva 752.49
Infantilism 259.9

☑ Additional Digit Required — Refer to the Tabular List for Digit Selection   ▽ Subterms under main terms may continue to next column or page

2007 ICD-9-CM   ▶◀ Revised Text   ● New Line   ▲ Revised Code   October 2006 · Volume 2 — 155

Infantilism — *continued*
  with dwarfism (hypophyseal) 253.3
  Brissaud's (infantile myxedema) 244.9
  celiac 579.0
  Herter's (nontropical sprue) 579.0
  hypophyseal 253.3
  hypothalamic (with obesity) 253.8
  idiopathic 259.9
  intestinal 579.0
  pancreatic 577.8
  pituitary 253.3
  renal 588.0
  sexual (with obesity) 259.0
Infants, healthy liveborn — *see* Newborn
Infarct, infarction
  adrenal (capsule) (gland) 255.4
  amnion 658.8 ☑
  anterior (with contiguous portion of intraventricular septum) NEC (*see also* Infarct, myocardium) 410.1 ☑
  appendices epiploicae 557.0
  bowel 557.0
  brain (stem) 434.91
    embolic (*see also* Embolism, brain) 434.11
    healed or old without residuals V12.59
    iatrogenic 997.02
    lacunar 434.91
    late effect — *see* Late effect(s) (of) cerebrovascular disease
    postoperative 997.02
    puerperal, postpartum, childbirth 674.0 ☑
    thrombotic (*see also* Thrombosis, brain) 434.01
  breast 611.8
  Brewer's (kidney) 593.81
  cardiac (*see also* Infarct, myocardium) 410.9 ☑
  cerebellar (*see also* Infarct, brain) 434.91
    embolic (*see also* Embolism, brain) 434.11
  cerebral (*see also* Infarct, brain) 434.91
    embolic (*see also* Embolism, brain) 434.11
    thrombotic (*see also* Infarct, brain) 434.01
  chorion 658.8 ☑
  colon (acute) (agnogenic) (embolic) (hemorrhagic) (nonocclusive) (nonthrombotic) (occlusive) (segmental) (thrombotic) (with gangrene) 557.0
  coronary artery (*see also* Infarct, myocardium) 410.9 ☑
  cortical 434.91
  embolic (*see also* Embolism) 444.9
  fallopian tube 620.8
  gallbladder 575.8
  heart (*see also* Infarct, myocardium) 410.9 ☑
  hepatic 573.4
  hypophysis (anterior lobe) 253.8
  impending (myocardium) 411.1
  intestine (acute) (agnogenic) (embolic) (hemorrhagic) (nonocclusive) (nonthrombotic) (occlusive) (thrombotic) (with gangrene) 557.0
  kidney 593.81
  lacunar 434.91
  liver 573.4
  lung (embolic) (thrombotic) 415.19
    with
      abortion — *see* Abortion, by type, with, embolism
      ectopic pregnancy (*see also* categories 633.0–633.9) 639.6
      molar pregnancy (*see also* categories 630–632) 639.6

Infarct, infarction — *continued*
  lung — *continued*
    following
      abortion 639.6
      ectopic or molar pregnancy 639.6
    iatrogenic 415.11
    in pregnancy, childbirth, or puerperium — *see* Embolism, obstetrical
    postoperative 415.11
  lymph node or vessel 457.8
  medullary (brain) — *see* Infarct, brain
  meibomian gland (eyelid) 374.85
  mesentery, mesenteric (embolic) (thrombotic) (with gangrene) 557.0
  midbrain — *see* Infarct, brain
  myocardium, myocardial (acute or with a stated duration of 8 weeks or less) (with hypertension) 410.9 ☑

Note — Use the following fifth-digit subclassification with category 410:

0   *episode unspecified*

1   *initial episode*

2   *subsequent episode without recurrence*

---

    with symptoms after 8 weeks from date of infarction 414.8
    anterior (wall) (with contiguous portion of intraventricular septum) NEC 410.1 ☑
    anteroapical (with contiguous portion of intraventricular septum) 410.1 ☑
    anterolateral (wall) 410.0 ☑
    anteroseptal (with contiguous portion of intraventricular septum) 410.1 ☑
    apical-lateral 410.5 ☑
    atrial 410.8 ☑
    basal-lateral 410.5 ☑
    chronic (with symptoms after 8 weeks from date of infarction) 414.8
    diagnosed on ECG, but presenting no symptoms 412
    diaphragmatic wall (with contiguous portion of intraventricular septum) 410.4 ☑
    healed or old, currently presenting no symptoms 412
    high lateral 410.5 ☑
    impending 411.1
    inferior (wall) (with contiguous portion of intraventricular septum) 410.4 ☑
    inferolateral (wall) 410.2 ☑
    inferoposterior wall 410.3 ☑
    lateral wall 410.5 ☑
    non-ST elevation (NSTEMI) nontransmural 410.7 ☑
    papillary muscle 410.8 ☑
    past (diagnosed on ECG or other special investigation, but currently presenting no symptoms) 412
      with symptoms NEC 414.8
    posterior (strictly) (true) (wall) 410.6 ☑
    posterobasal 410.6 ☑
    posteroinferior 410.3 ☑
    posterolateral 410.5 ☑
    previous, currently presenting no symptoms 412
    septal 410.8 ☑
    specified site NEC 410.8 ☑
    ST elevation (STEMI) 410.9 ☑
      anterior (wall) 410.1 ☑
      anterolateral (wall) 410.0 ☑
      inferior (wall) 410.4 ☑
      inferolateral (wall) 410.2 ☑

Infarct, infarction — *continued*
  myocardium, myocardial — *continued*
    ST elevation — *continued*
      inferoposterior wall 410.3 ☑
      lateral wall 410.5 ☑
      posterior (strictly) (true) (wall) 410.6 ☑
      specified site NEC 410.8 ☑
    subendocardial 410.7 ☑
    syphilitic 093.82
    non-ST elevation myocardial infarction (NSTEMI) 410.7 ☑
    nontransmural 410.7 ☑
  omentum 557.0
  ovary 620.8
  pancreas 577.8
  papillary muscle (*see also* Infarct, myocardium) 410.8 ☑
  parathyroid gland 252.8
  pituitary (gland) 253.8
  placenta (complicating pregnancy) 656.7 ☑
    affecting fetus or newborn 762.2
  pontine — *see* Infarct, brain
  posterior NEC (*see also* Infarct, myocardium) 410.6 ☑
  prostate 602.8
  pulmonary (artery) (hemorrhagic) (vein) 415.19
    with
      abortion — *see* Abortion, by type, with embolism
      ectopic pregnancy (*see also* categories 633.0–633.9) 639.6
      molar pregnancy (*see also* categories 630–632) 639.6
    following
      abortion 639.6
      ectopic or molar pregnancy 639.6
    iatrogenic 415.11
    in pregnancy, childbirth, or puerperium — *see* Embolism, obstetrical
    postoperative 415.11
  renal 593.81
    embolic or thrombotic 593.81
  retina, retinal 362.84
    with occlusion — *see* Occlusion, retina
  spinal (acute) (cord) (embolic) (nonembolic) 336.1
  spleen 289.59
    embolic or thrombotic 444.89
  subchorionic — *see* Infarct, placenta
  subendocardial (*see also* Infarct, myocardium) 410.7 ☑
  suprarenal (capsule) (gland) 255.4
  syncytium — *see* Infarct, placenta
  testis 608.83
  thrombotic (*see also* Thrombosis) 453.9
    artery, arterial — *see* Embolism
  thyroid (gland) 246.3
  ventricle (heart) (*see also* Infarct, myocardium) 410.9 ☑
Infecting — *see* condition
Infection, infected, infective (opportunistic) 136.9
  with lymphangitis — *see* Lymphangitis
  abortion — *see* Abortion, by type, with, sepsis
  abscess (skin) — *see* Abscess, by site
  Absidia 117.7
  Acanthocheilonema (perstans) 125.4
    streptocerca 125.6
  accessory sinus (chronic) (*see also* Sinusitis) 473.9
  Achorion — *see* Dermatophytosis
  Acremonium falciforme 117.4
  acromioclavicular (joint) 711.91
  actinobacillus
    lignieresii 027.8
    mallei 024

Infection, infected, infective — *continued*
  actinobacillus — *continued*
    muris 026.1
  actinomadura — *see* Actinomycosis
  Actinomyces (israelii) (*see also* Actinomycosis)
    muris-ratti 026.1
  Actinomycetales (actinomadura) (Actinomyces) (Nocardia) (Streptomyces) — *see* Actinomycosis
  actinomycotic NEC (*see also* Actinomycosis) 039.9
  adenoid (chronic) 474.01
    acute 463
    and tonsil (chronic) 474.02
    acute or subacute 463
  adenovirus NEC 079.0
    in diseases classified elsewhere — *see* category 079
    unspecified nature or site 079.0
  Aerobacter aerogenes NEC 041.85
    enteritis 008.2
  aerogenes capsulatus (*see also* Gangrene, gas) 040.0
  aertrycke (*see also* Infection, Salmonella) 003.9
  ajellomyces dermatitidis 116.0
  alimentary canal NEC (*see also* Enteritis, due to, by organism) 009.0
  Allescheria boydii 117.6
  Alternaria 118
  alveolus, alveolar (process) (pulpal origin) 522.4
  ameba, amebic (histolytica) (*see also* Amebiasis) 006.9
    acute 006.0
    chronic 006.1
    free-living 136.2
    hartmanni 007.8
    specified
      site NEC 006.8
      type NEC 007.8
  amniotic fluid or cavity 658.4 ☑
    affecting fetus or newborn 762.7
  anaerobes (cocci) (gram-negative) (gram-positive) (mixed) NEC 041.84
  anal canal 569.49
  Ancylostoma braziliense 126.2
  Angiostrongylus cantonensis 128.8
  anisakiasis 127.1
  Anisakis larva 127.1
  anthrax (*see also* Anthrax) 022.9
  antrum (chronic) (*see also* Sinusitis, maxillary) 473.0
  anus (papillae) (sphincter) 569.49
  arbor virus NEC 066.9
  arbovirus NEC 066.9
  argentophil-rod 027.0
  Ascaris lumbricoides 127.0
  ascomycetes 117.4
  Aspergillus (flavus) (fumigatus) (terreus) 117.3
  atypical
    acid-fast (bacilli) (*see also* Mycobacterium, atypical) 031.9
    mycobacteria (*see also* Mycobacterium, atypical) 031.9
  auditory meatus (circumscribed) (diffuse) (external) (*see also* Otitis, externa) 380.10
  auricle (ear) (*see also* Otitis, externa) 380.10
  axillary gland 683
  Babesiasis 088.82
  Babesiosis 088.82
  Bacillus NEC 041.89
    abortus 023.1
    anthracis (*see also* Anthrax) 022.9
    cereus (food poisoning) 005.89
    coli — *see* Infection, Escherichia coli
    coliform NEC 041.85
    Ducrey's (any location) 099.0
    Flexner's 004.1

☑ Additional Digit Required — Refer to the Tabular List for Digit Selection   ▽ Subterms under main terms may continue to next column or page

156 — Volume 2   ▶◀ Revised Text   ● New Line   ▲ Revised Code   *2007 ICD-9-CM*

Infection, infected, infective — *continued*
Bacillus — *continued*
   Friedländer's NEC 041.3
   fusiformis 101
   gas (gangrene) (*see also* Gangrene, gas) 040.0
   mallei 024
   melitensis 023.0
   paratyphoid, paratyphosus 002.9
      A 002.1
      B 002.2
      C 002.3
   Schmorl's 040.3
   Shiga 004.0
   suipestifer (*see also* Infection, Salmonella) 003.9
   swimming pool 031.1
   typhosa 002.0
   welchii (*see also* Gangrene, gas) 040.0
   Whitmore's 025
  bacterial NEC 041.9
   specified NEC 041.89
      anaerobic NEC 041.84
      gram-negative NEC 041.85
         anaerobic NEC 041.84
  Bacterium
   paratyphosum 002.9
      A 002.1
      B 002.2
      C 002.3
   typhosum 002.0
  Bacteroides (fragilis) (melaninogenicus) (oralis) NEC 041.82
  balantidium coli 007.0
  Bartholin's gland 616.89 ▲
  Basidiobolus 117.7
  Bedsonia 079.98
   specified NEC 079.88
  bile duct 576.1
  bladder (*see also* Cystitis) 595.9
  Blastomyces, blastomycotic 116.0
   brasiliensis 116.1
   dermatitidis 116.0
   European 117.5
   loboi 116.2
   North American 116.0
   South American 116.1
  bleb ●
   postprocedural 379.60 ●
      stage 1 379.61 ●
      stage 2 379.62 ●
      stage 3 379.63 ●
  blood stream — *see* Septicemia
  bone 730.9 ☑
   specified — *see* Osteomyelitis
  Bordetella 033.9
   bronchiseptica 033.8
   parapertussis 033.1
   pertussis 033.0
  Borrelia
   bergdorfi 088.81
   vincentii (mouth) (pharynx) (tonsil) 101
  brain (*see also* Encephalitis) 323.9
   late effect — *see* category 326
   membranes (*see also* Meningitis) 322.9
   septic 324.0
      late effect — *see* category 326
   meninges (*see also* Meningitis) 320.9
  branchial cyst 744.42
  breast 611.0
   puerperal, postpartum 675.2 ☑
      with nipple 675.9 ☑
         specified type NEC 675.8 ☑
      nonpurulent 675.2 ☑
      purulent 675.1 ☑
  bronchus (*see also* Bronchitis) 490
   fungus NEC 117.9
  Brucella 023.9
   abortus 023.1
   canis 023.3
   melitensis 023.0

Infection, infected, infective — *continued*
Brucella — *continued*
   mixed 023.8
   suis 023.2
  Brugia (Wuchereria) malayi 125.1
  bursa — *see* Bursitis
  buttocks (skin) 686.9
  Candida (albicans) (tropicalis) (*see also* Candidiasis) 112.9
   congenital 771.7
  Candiru 136.8
  Capillaria
   hepatica 128.8
   philippinensis 127.5
  cartilage 733.99
  cat liver fluke 121.0
  cellulitis — *see* Cellulitis, by site
  Cephalosporum falciforme 117.4
  Cercomonas hominis (intestinal) 007.3
  cerebrospinal (*see also* Meningitis) 322.9
   late effect — *see* category 326
  cervical gland 683
  cervix (*see also* Cervicitis) 616.0
  cesarean section wound 674.3 ☑
  Chilomastix (intestinal) 007.8
  Chlamydia 079.98
   specified NEC 079.88
  cholera (*see also* Cholera) 001.9
  chorionic plate 658.8 ☑
  Cladosporium
   bantianum 117.8
   carrionii 117.2
   mansoni 111.1
   trichoides 117.8
   werneckii 111.1
  Clonorchis (sinensis) (liver) 121.1
  Clostridium (haemolyticum) (novyi) NEC 041.84
   botulinum 005.1
   histolyticum (*see also* Gangrene, gas) 040.0
   oedematiens (*see also* Gangrene, gas) 040.0
   perfringens 041.83
      due to food 005.2
   septicum (*see also* Gangrene, gas) 040.0
   sordellii (*see also* Gangrene, gas) 040.0
   welchii (*see also* Gangrene, gas) 040.0
      due to food 005.2
  Coccidioides (immitis) (*see also* Coccidioidomycosis) 114.9
  coccus NEC 041.89
  colon (*see also* Enteritis, due to, by organism) 009.0
   bacillus — *see* Infection, Escherichia coli
  colostomy or enterostomy 569.61
  common duct 576.1
  complicating pregnancy, childbirth, or puerperium NEC 647.9 ☑
   affecting fetus or newborn 760.2
  Condiobolus 117.7
  congenital NEC 771.89
   Candida albicans 771.7
   chronic 771.2
   cytomegalovirus 771.1
   hepatitis, viral 771.2
   herpes simplex 771.2
   listeriosis 771.2
   malaria 771.2
   poliomyelitis 771.2
   rubella 771.0
   toxoplasmosis 771.2
   tuberculosis 771.2
   urinary (tract) 771.82
   vaccinia 771.2
  coronavirus 079.89
   SARS-associated 079.82
  corpus luteum (*see also* Salpingo-oophoritis) 614.2

Infection, infected, infective — *continued*
Corynebacterium diphtheriae — *see* Diphtheria
Coxsackie (*see also* Coxsackie) 079.2
   endocardium 074.22
   heart NEC 074.20
   in diseases classified elsewhere — *see* category 079 ☑
   meninges 047.0
   myocardium 074.23
   pericardium 074.21
   pharynx 074.0
   specified disease NEC 074.8
   unspecified nature or site 079.2
  Cryptococcus neoformans 117.5
  Cryptosporidia 007.4
  Cunninghamella 117.7
  cyst — *see* Cyst
  Cysticercus cellulosae 123.1
  cytomegalovirus 078.5
   congenital 771.1
  dental (pulpal origin) 522.4
  deuteromycetes 117.4
  Dicrocoelium dendriticum 121.8
  Dipetalonema (perstans) 125.4
   streptocerca 125.6
  diphtherial — *see* Diphtheria
  Diphyllobothrium (adult) (latum) (pacificum) 123.4
   larval 123.5
  Diplogonoporus (grandis) 123.8
  Dipylidium (caninum) 123.8
  Dirofilaria 125.6
  dog tapeworm 123.8
  Dracunculus medinensis 125.7
  Dreschlera 118
   hawaiiensis 117.8
  Ducrey's bacillus (any site) 099.0
  due to or resulting from
   device, implant, or graft (any) (presence of) — *see* Complications, infection and inflammation, due to (presence of) any device, implant, or graft classified to 996.0–996.5 NEC
   injection, inoculation, infusion, transfusion, or vaccination (prophylactic) (therapeutic) 999.3
   injury NEC — *see* Wound, open, by site, complicated
   surgery 998.59
  duodenum 535.6 ☑
  ear (*see also* Otitis)
   external (*see also* Otitis, externa) 380.10
   inner (*see also* Labyrinthitis) 386.30
   middle — *see* Otitis, media
  Eaton's agent NEC 041.81
  Eberthella typhosa 002.0
  Ebola 078.89
  echinococcosis 122.9
  Echinococcus (*see also* Echinococcus) 122.9
  Echinostoma 121.8
  ECHO virus 079.1
   in diseases classified elsewhere — *see* category 079 ☑
   unspecified nature or site 079.1
  Ehrlichiosis 082.40
   chaffeensis 082.41
   specified type NEC 082.49
  Endamoeba — *see* Infection, ameba
  endocardium (*see also* Endocarditis) 421.0
  endocervix (*see also* Cervicitis) 616.0
  Entamoeba — *see* Infection, ameba
  enteric (*see also* Enteritis, due to, by organism) 009.0
  Enterobacter aerogenes NEC 041.85
  Enterobacter sakazakii 041.85
  Enterobius vermicularis 127.4
  enterococcus NEC 041.04

Infection, infected, infective — *continued*
enterovirus NEC 079.89
   central nervous system NEC 048
   enteritis 008.67
   meningitis 047.9
Entomophthora 117.7
Epidermophyton — *see* Dermatophytosis
epidermophytosis — *see* Dermatophytosis
episiotomy 674.3 ☑
Epstein-Barr virus 075
   chronic 780.79 [139.8]
erysipeloid 027.1
Erysipelothrix (insidiosa) (rhusiopathiae) 027.1
erythema infectiosum 057.0
Escherichia coli NEC 041.4
   enteritis — *see* Enteritis, E. coli
   generalized 038.42
   intestinal — *see* Enteritis, E. coli
esophagostomy 530.86
ethmoidal (chronic) (sinus) (*see also* Sinusitis, ethmoidal) 473.2
Eubacterium 041.84
Eustachian tube (ear) 381.50
   acute 381.51
   chronic 381.52
exanthema subitum 057.8
external auditory canal (meatus) (*see also* Otitis, externa) 380.10
eye NEC 360.00
eyelid 373.9
   specified NEC 373.8
fallopian tube (*see also* Salpingo-oophoritis) 614.2
fascia 728.89
Fasciola
   gigantica 121.3
   hepatica 121.3
Fasciolopsis (buski) 121.4
fetus (intra-amniotic) — *see* Infection, congenital
filarial — *see* Infestation, filarial
finger (skin) 686.9
   abscess (with lymphangitis) 681.00
      pulp 681.01
   cellulitis (with lymphangitis) 681.00
   distal closed space (with lymphangitis) 681.00
   nail 681.02
      fungus 110.1
fish tapeworm 123.4
   larval 123.5
flagellate, intestinal 007.9
fluke — *see* Infestation, fluke
focal
   teeth (pulpal origin) 522.4
   tonsils 474.00
      and adenoids 474.02
Fonsecaea
   compactum 117.2
   pedrosoi 117.2
food (*see also* Poisoning, food) 005.9
foot (skin) 686.9
   fungus 110.4
Francisella tularensis (*see also* Tularemia) 021.9
frontal sinus (chronic) (*see also* Sinusitis, frontal) 473.1
fungus NEC 117.9
   beard 110.0
   body 110.5
   dermatiacious NEC 117.8
   foot 110.4
   groin 110.3
   hand 110.2
   nail 110.1
   pathogenic to compromised host only 118
   perianal (area) 110.3
   scalp 110.0
   scrotum 110.8
   skin 111.9

☑ Additional Digit Required — Refer to the Tabular List for Digit Selection   ▽ Subterms under main terms may continue to next column or page

2007 ICD-9-CM   ▶◀ Revised Text   ● New Line   ▲ Revised Code   **October 2006 · Volume 2 — 157**

Infection, infected, infective —
continued
fungus — *continued*
  skin — *continued*
    foot 110.4
    hand 110.2
    toenails 110.1
    trachea 117.9
  Fusarium 118
  Fusobacterium 041.84
  gallbladder (*see also* Cholecystitis, acute) 575.0
  Gardnerella vaginalis 041.89
  gas bacillus (*see also* Gas, gangrene) 040.0
  gastric (*see also* Gastritis) 535.5 ☑
  Gastrodiscoides hominis 121.8
  gastroenteric (*see also* Enteritis, due to, by organism) 009.0
  gastrointestinal (*see also* Enteritis, due to, by organism) 009.0
  gastrostomy 536.41
  generalized NEC (*see also* Septicemia) 038.9
  genital organ or tract NEC
    female 614.9
      with
        abortion — *see* Abortion, by type, with sepsis
        ectopic pregnancy (*see also* categories 633.0–633.9) 639.0
        molar pregnancy (*see also* categories 630–632) 639.0
      complicating pregnancy 646.6 ☑
        affecting fetus or newborn 760.8
      following
        abortion 639.0
        ectopic or molar pregnancy 639.0
      puerperal, postpartum, childbirth 670.0 ☑
      minor or localized 646.6 ☑
        affecting fetus or newborn 760.8
    male 608.4
  genitourinary tract NEC 599.0
  Ghon tubercle, primary (*see also* Tuberculosis) 010.0 ☑
  Giardia lamblia 007.1
  gingival (chronic) 523.10 ▲
    acute 523.00 ▲
    Vincent's 101
  glanders 024
  Glenosporopsis amazonica 116.2
  Gnathostoma spinigerum 128.1
  Gongylonema 125.6
  gonococcal NEC (*see also* Gonococcus) 098.0
  gram-negative bacilli NEC 041.85
    anaerobic 041.84
  guinea worm 125.7
  gum (*see also* Infection, gingival) 523.10 ▲
  Hantavirus 079.81
  heart 429.89
  Helicobacter pylori (H. pylori) 041.86
  helminths NEC 128.9
    intestinal 127.9
      mixed (types classifiable to more than one category in 120.0–127.7) 127.8
      specified type NEC 127.7
    specified type NEC 128.8
  Hemophilus influenzae NEC 041.5
    generalized 038.41
  herpes (simplex) (*see also* Herpes, simplex) 054.9
    congenital 771.2
    zoster (*see also* Herpes, zoster) 053.9
      eye NEC 053.29
  Heterophyes heterophyes 121.6

Infection, infected, infective —
continued
Histoplasma (*see also* Histoplasmosis) 115.90
  capsulatum (*see also* Histoplasmosis, American) 115.00
  duboisii (*see also* Histoplasmosis, African) 115.10
HIV V08
  with symptoms, symptomatic 042
hookworm (*see also* Ancylostomiasis) 126.9
human immunodeficiency virus V08
  with symptoms, symptomatic 042
human papillomavirus 079.4
hydrocele 603.1
hydronephrosis 591
Hymenolepis 123.6
hypopharynx 478.29
inguinal glands 683
  due to soft chancre 099.0
intestine, intestinal (*see also* Enteritis, due to, by organism) 009.0
intrauterine (*see also* Endometritis) 615.9
  complicating delivery 646.6 ☑
isospora belli or hominis 007.2
Japanese B encephalitis 062.0
jaw (bone) (acute) (chronic) (lower) (subacute) (upper) 526.4
joint — *see* Arthritis, infectious or infective
kidney (cortex) (hematogenous) 590.9
  with
    abortion — *see* Abortion, by type, with urinary tract infection
    calculus 592.0
    ectopic pregnancy (*see also* categories 633.0–633.9) 639.8
    molar pregnancy (*see also* categories 630–632) 639.8
    complicating pregnancy or puerperium 646.6 ☑
      affecting fetus or newborn 760.1
    following
      abortion 639.8
      ectopic or molar pregnancy 639.8
    pelvis and ureter 590.3
Klebsiella pneumoniae NEC 041.3
knee (skin) NEC 686.9
  joint — *see* Arthritis, infectious
Koch's (*see also* Tuberculosis, pulmonary) 011.9 ☑
labia (majora) (minora) (*see also* Vulvitis) 616.10
lacrimal
  gland (*see also* Dacryoadenitis) 375.00
  passages (duct) (sac) (*see also* Dacryocystitis) 375.30
larynx NEC 478.79
leg (skin) NEC 686.9
Leishmania (*see also* Leishmaniasis) 085.9
  braziliensis 085.5
  donovani 085.0
  ethiopica 085.3
  furunculosa 085.1
  infantum 085.0
  mexicana 085.4
  tropica (minor) 085.1
    major 085.2
Leptosphaeria senegalensis 117.4
leptospira (*see also* Leptospirosis) 100.9
  Australis 100.89
  Bataviae 100.89
  pyrogenes 100.89
  specified type NEC 100.89
leptospirochetal NEC (*see also* Leptospirosis) 100.9
Leptothrix — *see* Actinomycosis

Infection, infected, infective —
continued
Listeria monocytogenes (listeriosis) 027.0
  congenital 771.2
liver fluke — *see* Infestation, fluke, liver
Loa loa 125.2
  eyelid 125.2 *[373.6]*
Loboa loboi 116.2
local, skin (staphylococcal) (streptococcal) NEC 686.9
  abscess — *see* Abscess, by site
  cellulitis — *see* Cellulitis, by site
  ulcer (*see also* Ulcer, skin) 707.9
Loefflerella
  mallei 024
  whitmori 025
lung 518.89
  atypical Mycobacterium 031.0
    tuberculous (*see also* Tuberculosis, pulmonary) 011.9 ☑
  basilar 518.89
  chronic 518.89
  fungus NEC 117.9
  spirochetal 104.8
  virus — *see* Pneumonia, virus
lymph gland (axillary) (cervical) (inguinal) 683
  mesenteric 289.2
lymphoid tissue, base of tongue or posterior pharynx, NEC 474.00
madurella
  grisea 117.4
  mycetomii 117.4
major
  with
    abortion — *see* Abortion, by type, with sepsis
    ectopic pregnancy (*see also* categories 633.0–633.9) 639.0
    molar pregnancy (*see also* categories 630–632) 639.0
  following
    abortion 639.0
    ectopic or molar pregnancy 639.0
  puerperal, postpartum, childbirth 670.0 ☑
Malassezia furfur 111.0
Malleomyces
  mallei 024
  pseudomallei 025
mammary gland 611.0
  puerperal, postpartum 675.2 ☑
Mansonella (ozzardi) 125.5
mastoid (suppurative) — *see* Mastoiditis
maxilla, maxillary 526.4
  sinus (chronic) (*see also* Sinusitis, maxillary) 473.0
mediastinum 519.2
medina 125.7
meibomian
  cyst 373.12
  gland 373.12
melioidosis 025
meninges (*see also* Meningitis) 320.9
meningococcal (*see also* condition) 036.9
  brain 036.1
  cerebrospinal 036.0
  endocardium 036.42
  generalized 036.2
  meninges 036.0
  meningococcemia 036.2
  specified site NEC 036.89
mesenteric lymph nodes or glands NEC 289.2
Metagonimus 121.5
metatarsophalangeal 711.97
microorganism resistant to drugs — *see* Resistance (to), drugs by microorganisms
Microsporidia 136.8

Infection, infected, infective —
continued
microsporum, microsporic — *see* Dermatophytosis
Mima polymorpha NEC 041.85
mixed flora NEC 041.89
Monilia (*see also* Candidiasis) 112.9
  neonatal 771.7
monkeypox 057.8
Monosporium apiospermum 117.6
mouth (focus) NEC 528.9
  parasitic 136.9
Mucor 117.7
muscle NEC 728.89
mycelium NEC 117.9
mycetoma
  actinomycotic NEC (*see also* Actinomycosis) 039.9
  mycotic NEC 117.4
Mycobacterium, mycobacterial (*see also* Mycobacterium) 031.9
Mycoplasma NEC 041.81
mycotic NEC 117.9
  pathogenic to compromised host only 118
  skin NEC 111.9
  systemic 117.9
myocardium NEC 422.90
nail (chronic) (with lymphangitis) 681.9
  finger 681.02
    fungus 110.1
  ingrowing 703.0
  toe 681.11
    fungus 110.1
nasal sinus (chronic) (*see also* Sinusitis) 473.9
nasopharynx (chronic) 478.29
  acute 460
navel 686.9
  newborn 771.4
Neisserian — *see* Gonococcus
Neotestudina rosatii 117.4
newborn, generalized 771.89
nipple 611.0
  puerperal, postpartum 675.0 ☑
    with breast 675.9 ☑
      specified type NEC 675.8 ☑
Nocardia — *see* Actinomycosis
nose 478.19 ▲
nostril 478.19 ▲
obstetrical surgical wound 674.3 ☑
Oesophagostomum (apiostomum) 127.7
Oestrus ovis 134.0
Oidium albicans (*see also* Candidiasis) 112.9
Onchocerca (volvulus) 125.3
  eye 125.3 *[360.13]*
  eyelid 125.3 *[373.6]*
operation wound 998.59
Opisthorchis (felineus) (tenuicollis) (viverrini) 121.0
orbit 376.00
  chronic 376.10
ovary (*see also* Salpingo-oophoritis) 614.2
Oxyuris vermicularis 127.4
pancreas 577.0
Paracoccidioides brasiliensis 116.1
Paragonimus (westermani) 121.2
parainfluenza virus 079.89
parameningococcus NEC 036.9
  with meningitis 036.0
parasitic NEC 136.9
paratyphoid 002.9
  type A 002.1
  type B 002.2
  type C 002.3
paraurethral ducts 597.89
parotid gland 527.2
Pasteurella NEC 027.2
  multocida (cat-bite) (dog-bite) 027.2
  pestis (*see also* Plague) 020.9
  pseudotuberculosis 027.2
  septica (cat-bite) (dog-bite) 027.2

☑ Additional Digit Required — Refer to the Tabular List for Digit Selection   ▽ Subterms under main terms may continue to next column or page

158 — Volume 2 · October 2006   ▶◀ Revised Text   ● New Line   ▲ Revised Code   *2007 ICD-9-CM*

Infection, infected, infective — *continued*
- Pasteurella — *continued*
  - tularensis (*see also* Tularemia) 021.9
- pelvic, female (*see also* Disease, pelvis, inflammatory) 614.9
- penis (glans) (retention) NEC 607.2
  - herpetic 054.13
- Peptococcus 041.84
- Peptostreptococcus 041.84
- periapical (pulpal origin) 522.4
- peridental 523.30 ▲
- perineal wound (obstetrical) 674.3 ☑
- periodontal 523.31 ▲
- periorbital 376.00
  - chronic 376.10
- perirectal 569.49
- perirenal (*see also* Infection, kidney) 590.9
- peritoneal (*see also* Peritonitis) 567.9
- periureteral 593.89
- periurethral 597.89
- Petriellidium boydii 117.6
- pharynx 478.29
  - Coxsackie virus 074.0
  - phlegmonous 462
  - posterior, lymphoid 474.00
- Phialophora
  - gougerotii 117.8
  - jeanselmei 117.8
  - verrucosa 117.2
- Piedraia hortai 111.3
- pinna, acute 380.11
- pinta 103.9
  - intermediate 103.1
  - late 103.2
  - mixed 103.3
  - primary 103.0
- pinworm 127.4
- pityrosporum furfur 111.0
- pleuropneumonia-like organisms NEC (PPLO) 041.81
- pneumococcal NEC 041.2
  - generalized (purulent) 038.2
- Pneumococcus NEC 041.2
- postoperative wound 998.59
- posttraumatic NEC 958.3
- postvaccinal 999.3
- prepuce NEC 607.1
- Proprionibacterium 041.84
- prostate (capsule) (*see also* Prostatitis) 601.9
- Proteus (mirabilis) (morganii) (vulgaris) NEC 041.6
  - enteritis 008.3
- protozoal NEC 136.8
  - intestinal NEC 007.9
- Pseudomonas NEC 041.7
  - mallei 024
  - pneumonia 482.1
  - pseudomallei 025
- psittacosis 073.9
- puerperal, postpartum (major) 670.0 ☑
  - minor 646.6 ☑
- pulmonary — *see* Infection, lung
- purulent — *see* Abscess
- putrid, generalized — *see* Septicemia
- pyemic — *see* Septicemia
- Pyrenochaeta romeroi 117.4
- Q fever 083.0
- rabies 071
- rectum (sphincter) 569.49
- renal (*see also* Infection, kidney) 590.9
  - pelvis and ureter 590.3
- resistant to drugs — *see* Resistance (to), drugs by microorganisms
- respiratory 519.8
  - chronic 519.8
  - influenzal (acute) (upper) 487.1
  - lung 518.89
  - rhinovirus 460
  - syncytial virus 079.6
  - upper (acute) (infectious) NEC 465.9

Infection, infected, infective — *continued*
- respiratory — *continued*
  - upper — *continued*
    - with flu, grippe, or influenza 487.1
    - influenzal 487.1
    - multiple sites NEC 465.8
    - streptococcal 034.0
    - viral NEC 465.9
- respiratory syncytial virus (RSV) 079.6
- resulting from presence of shunt or other internal prosthetic device — *see* Complications, infection and inflammation, due to (presence of) any device, implant, or graft classified to 996.0–996.5 NEC
- retroperitoneal 567.39
- retrovirus 079.50
  - human immunodeficiency virus type 2 [HIV2] 079.53
  - human T-cell lymphotrophic virus type I [HTLV-I] 079.51
  - human T-cell lymphotrophic virus type II [HTLV-II] 079.52
  - specified NEC 079.59
- Rhinocladium 117.1
- Rhinosporidium — *see* beri 117.0
- rhinovirus
  - in diseases classified elsewhere — *see* category 079 ☑
  - unspecified nature or site 079.3
- Rhizopus 117.7
- rickettsial 083.9
- rickettsialpox 083.2
- rubella (*see also* Rubella) 056.9
  - congenital 771.0
- Saccharomyces (*see also* Candidiasis) 112.9
- Saksenaea 117.7
- salivary duct or gland (any) 527.2
- Salmonella (aertrycke) (callinarum) (choleraesuis) (enteritidis) (suipestifer) (typhimurium) 003.9
  - with
    - arthritis 003.23
    - gastroenteritis 003.0
    - localized infection 003.20
      - specified type NEC 003.29
    - meningitis 003.21
    - osteomyelitis 003.24
    - pneumonia 003.22
    - septicemia 003.1
    - specified manifestation NEC 003.8
  - due to food (poisoning) (any serotype) (*see also* Poisoning, food, due to, Salmonella)
  - hirschfeldii 002.3
  - localized 003.20
    - specified type NEC 003.29
  - paratyphi 002.9
    - A 002.1
    - B 002.2
    - C 002.3
  - schottmuelleri 002.2
  - specified type NEC 003.8
  - typhi 002.0
  - typhosa 002.0
- saprophytic 136.8
- Sarcocystis, lindemanni 136.5
- SARS-associated coronavirus 079.82
- scabies 133.0
- Schistosoma — *see* Infestation, Schistosoma
- Schmorl's bacillus 040.3
- scratch or other superficial injury — *see* Injury, superficial, by site
- scrotum (acute) NEC 608.4
- secondary, burn or open wound (dislocation) (fracture) 958.3
- seminal vesicle (*see also* Vesiculitis) 608.0

Infection, infected, infective — *continued*
- septic
  - generalized — *see* Septicemia
  - localized, skin (*see also* Abscess) 682.9
- septicemic — *see* Septicemia
- seroma 998.51
- Serratia (marcescens) 041.85
  - generalized 038.44
- sheep liver fluke 121.3
- Shigella 004.9
  - boydii 004.2
  - dysenteriae 004.0
  - flexneri 004.1
  - group
    - A 004.0
    - B 004.1
    - C 004.2
    - D 004.3
  - Schmitz (-Stutzer) 004.0
  - schmitzii 004.0
  - Shiga 004.0
  - sonnei 004.3
  - specified type NEC 004.8
- Sin Nombre virus 079.81
- sinus (*see also* Sinusitis) 473.9
  - pilonidal 685.1
    - with abscess 685.0
  - skin NEC 686.9
- Skene's duct or gland (*see also* Urethritis) 597.89
- skin (local) (staphylococcal) (streptococcal) NEC 686.9
  - abscess — *see* Abscess, by site
  - cellulitis — *see* Cellulitis, by site
  - due to fungus 111.9
    - specified type NEC 111.8
  - mycotic 111.9
    - specified type NEC 111.8
  - ulcer (*see also* Ulcer, skin) 707.9
- slow virus 046.9
  - specified condition NEC 046.8
- Sparganum (mansoni) (proliferum) 123.5
- spermatic cord NEC 608.4
- sphenoidal (chronic) (sinus) (*see also* Sinusitis, sphenoidal) 473.3
- Spherophorus necrophorus 040.3
- spinal cord NEC (*see also* Encephalitis) 323.9
  - abscess 324.1
    - late effect — *see* category 326
  - late effect — *see* category 326
  - meninges — *see* Meningitis
  - streptococcal 320.2
- Spirillum
  - minus or minor 026.0
  - morsus muris 026.0
  - obermeieri 087.0
- spirochetal NEC 104.9
  - lung 104.8
  - specified nature or site NEC 104.8
- spleen 289.59
- Sporothrix schenckii 117.1
- Sporotrichum (schenckii) 117.1
- Sporozoa 136.8
- staphylococcal NEC 041.10
  - aureus 041.11
  - food poisoning 005.0
  - generalized (purulent) 038.10
    - aureus 038.11
    - specified organism NEC 038.19
  - pneumonia 482.40
    - aureus 482.41
    - specified type NEC 482.49
  - septicemia 038.10
    - aureus 038.11
    - specified organism NEC 038.19
  - specified NEC 041.19
- steatoma 706.2
- Stellantchasmus falcatus 121.6
- Streptobacillus moniliformis 026.1
- streptococcal NEC 041.00
  - generalized (purulent) 038.0

Infection, infected, infective — *continued*
- streptococcal — *continued*
  - Group
    - A 041.01
    - B 041.02
    - C 041.03
    - D [enterococcus] 041.04
    - G 041.05
  - pneumonia — *see* Pneumonia, streptococcal
  - septicemia 038.0
  - sore throat 034.0
  - specified NEC 041.09
- Streptomyces — *see* Actinomycosis
- streptotrichosis — *see* Actinomycosis
- Strongyloides (stercoralis) 127.2
- stump (amputation) (posttraumatic) (surgical) 997.62
  - traumatic — *see* Amputation, traumatic, by site, complicated
- subcutaneous tissue, local NEC 686.9
- submaxillary region 528.9
- suipestifer (*see also* Infection, Salmonella) 003.9
- swimming pool bacillus 031.1
- syphilitic — *see* Syphilis
- systemic — *see* Septicemia
- Taenia — *see* Infestation, Taenia
- Taeniarhynchus saginatus 123.2
- tapeworm — *see* Infestation, tapeworm
- tendon (sheath) 727.89
- Ternidens diminutus 127.7
- testis (*see also* Orchitis) 604.90
- thigh (skin) 686.9
- threadworm 127.4
- throat 478.29
  - pneumococcal 462
  - staphylococcal 462
  - streptococcal 034.0
  - viral NEC (*see also* Pharyngitis) 462
- thumb (skin) 686.9
  - abscess (with lymphangitis) 681.00
    - pulp 681.01
  - cellulitis (with lymphangitis) 681.00
  - nail 681.02
- thyroglossal duct 529.8
- toe (skin) 686.9
  - abscess (with lymphangitis) 681.10
  - cellulitis (with lymphangitis) 681.10
  - nail 681.11
    - fungus 110.1
- tongue NEC 529.0
  - parasitic 112.0
- tonsil (faucial) (lingual) (pharyngeal) 474.00
  - acute or subacute 463
  - and adenoid 474.02
  - tag 474.00
- tooth, teeth 522.4
  - periapical (pulpal origin) 522.4
  - peridental 523.30 ▲
  - periodontal 523.31 ▲
  - pulp 522.0
  - socket 526.5
- Torula histolytica 117.5
- Toxocara (cani) (cati) (felis) 128.0
- Toxoplasma gondii (*see also* Toxoplasmosis) 130.9
- trachea, chronic 491.8
  - fungus 117.9
- traumatic NEC 958.3
- trematode NEC 121.9
- trench fever 083.1
- Treponema
  - denticola 041.84
  - macrodenticum 041.84
  - pallidum (*see also* Syphilis) 097.9
- Trichinella (spiralis) 124
- Trichomonas 131.9
  - bladder 131.09

☑ Additional Digit Required — Refer to the Tabular List for Digit Selection   ▽ Subterms under main terms may continue to next column or page

2007 ICD-9-CM   ▶◀ Revised Text   ● New Line   ▲ Revised Code   **October 2006 · Volume 2 — 159**

Infection, infected, infective —
continued
  Trichomonas — *continued*
    cervix 131.09
    hominis 007.3
    intestine 007.3
    prostate 131.03
    specified site NEC 131.8
    urethra 131.02
    urogenitalis 131.00
    vagina 131.01
    vulva 131.01
  Trichophyton, trichophytid — *see*
    Dermatophytosis
  Trichosporon (beigelii) cutaneum
    111.2
  Trichostrongylus 127.6
  Trichuris (trichiuria) 127.3
  Trombicula (irritans) 133.8
  Trypanosoma (*see also* Trypanosomia-
    sis) 086.9
    cruzi 086.2
  tubal (*see also* Salpingo-oophoritis)
    614.2
  tuberculous NEC (*see also* Tuberculo-
    sis) 011.9 ☑
  tubo-ovarian (*see also* Salpingo-
    oophoritis) 614.2
  tunica vaginalis 608.4
  tympanic membrane — *see* Myringitis
  typhoid (abortive) (ambulant) (bacillus)
    002.0
  typhus 081.9
    flea-borne (endemic) 081.0
    louse-borne (epidemic) 080
    mite-borne 081.2
    recrudescent 081.1
    tick-borne 082.9
      African 082.1
      North Asian 082.2
  umbilicus (septic) 686.9
    newborn NEC 771.4
  ureter 593.89
  urethra (*see also* Urethritis) 597.80
  urinary (tract) NEC 599.0
    with
      abortion — *see* Abortion, by
        type, with urinary tract
        infection
      ectopic pregnancy (*see also* cat-
        egories 633.0–633.9)
        639.8
      molar pregnancy (*see also* cate-
        gories 630–632) 639.8
    candidal 112.2
    complicating pregnancy, childbirth,
      or puerperium 646.6 ☑
      affecting fetus or newborn 760.1
    asymptomatic 646.5 ☑
      affecting fetus or newborn
        760.1
    diplococcal (acute) 098.0
      chronic 098.2
    due to Trichomonas (vaginalis)
      131.00
    following
      abortion 639.8
      ectopic or molar pregnancy
        639.8
    gonococcal (acute) 098.0
      chronic or duration of 2
        months or over 098.2
    newborn 771.82
    trichomonal 131.00
    tuberculous (*see also* Tuberculosis)
      016.3 ☑
    uterus, uterine (*see also* Endometri-
      tis) 615.9
    utriculus masculinus NEC 597.89
    vaccination 999.3
    vagina (granulation tissue) (wall)
      (*see also* Vaginitis) 616.10
    varicella 052.9
    varicose veins — *see* Varicose,
      veins
    variola 050.9

Infection, infected, infective —
continued
  urinary — *continued*
    variola — *continued*
      major 050.0
      minor 050.1
    vas deferens NEC 608.4
    Veillonella 041.84
    verumontanum 597.89
    vesical (*see also* Cystitis) 595.9
    Vibrio
      cholerae 001.0
        El Tor 001.1
      parahaemolyticus (food poison-
        ing) 005.4
      vulnificus 041.85
    Vincent's (gums) (mouth) (tonsil)
      101
    virus, viral 079.99
      adenovirus
        in diseases classified elsewhere
          — *see* category 079 ☑
        unspecified nature or site 079.0
      central nervous system NEC 049.9
        enterovirus 048
          meningitis 047.9
            specified type NEC 047.8
        slow virus 046.9
        specified condition NEC 046.8
      chest 519.8
      conjunctivitis 077.99
        specified type NEC 077.8
      coronavirus 079.89
        SARS-associated 079.82
      Coxsackie (*see also* Infection, Cox-
        sackie) 079.2
      Ebola 065.8
      ECHO
        in diseases classified elsewhere
          — *see* category 079 ☑
        unspecified nature or site 079.1
      encephalitis 049.9
        arthropod-borne NEC 064
        tick-borne 063.9
          specified type NEC 063.8
      enteritis NEC (*see also* Enteritis,
        viral) 008.8
      exanthem NEC 057.9
      Hantavirus 079.81
      human papilloma 079.4
      in diseases classified elsewhere —
        see category 079 ☑
      intestine (*see also* Enteritis, viral)
        008.8
      lung — *see* Pneumonia, viral
      respiratory syncytial (RSV) 079.6
      retrovirus 079.50
      rhinovirus
        in diseases classified elsewhere
          — *see* category 079 ☑
        unspecified nature or site 079.3
      salivary gland disease 078.5
      slow 046.9
        specified condition NEC 046.8
      specified type NEC 079.89
        in diseases classified elsewhere
          — *see* category 079 ☑
      unspecified nature or site 079.99
    warts NEC 078.10
    vulva (*see also* Vulvitis) 616.10
    whipworm 127.3
    Whitmore's bacillus 025
    wound (local) (posttraumatic) NEC
      958.3
      with
        dislocation — *see* Dislocation,
          by site, open
        fracture — *see* Fracture, by site,
          open
        open wound — *see* Wound,
          open, by site, complicated
      postoperative 998.59
      surgical 998.59
    Wuchereria 125.0
      bancrofti 125.0
      malayi 125.1

Infection, infected, infective —
continued
  yaws — *see* Yaws
  yeast (*see also* Candidiasis) 112.9
  yellow fever (*see also* Fever, yellow)
    060.9
  Yersinia pestis (*see also* Plague) 020.9
  Zeis' gland 373.12
  zoonotic bacterial NEC 027.9
  Zopfia senegalensis 117.4
Infective, infectious — *see* condition
Inferiority complex 301.9
  constitutional psychopathic 301.9
Infertility
  female 628.9
    age related 628.8
    associated with
      adhesions, peritubal
        614.6 [628.2]
      anomaly
        cervical mucus 628.4
        congenital
          cervix 628.4
          fallopian tube 628.2
          uterus 628.3
          vagina 628.4
      anovulation 628.0
      dysmucorrhea 628.4
      endometritis, tuberculous (*see
        also* Tuberculosis)
        016.7 ☑ [628.3]
      Stein-Leventhal syndrome
        256.4 [628.0]
    due to
      adiposogenital dystrophy
        253.8 [628.1]
      anterior pituitary disorder NEC
        253.4 [628.1]
        hyperfunction 253.1 [628.1]
      cervical anomaly 628.4
      fallopian tube anomaly 628.2
      ovarian failure 256.39 [628.0]
      Stein-Leventhal syndrome
        256.4 [628.0]
      uterine anomaly 628.3
      vaginal anomaly 628.4
    nonimplantation 628.3
    origin
      cervical 628.4
      pituitary-hypothalamus NEC
        253.8 [628.1]
        anterior pituitary NEC
          253.4 [628.1]
          hyperfunction NEC
            253.1 [628.1]
        dwarfism 253.3 [628.1]
        panhypopituitarism
          253.2 [628.1]
      specified NEC 628.8
      tubal (block) (occlusion) (steno-
        sis) 628.2
        adhesions 614.6 [628.2]
      uterine 628.3
      vaginal 628.4
    previous, requiring supervision of
      pregnancy V23.0
  male 606.9
    absolute 606.0
    due to
      azoospermia 606.0
      drug therapy 606.8
      extratesticular cause NEC 606.8
      germinal cell
        aplasia 606.0
        desquamation 606.1
      hypospermatogenesis 606.1
      infection 606.8
      obstruction, afferent ducts
        606.8
      oligospermia 606.1
      radiation 606.8
      spermatogenic arrest (complete)
        606.0
        incomplete 606.1
      systemic disease 606.8
Infestation 134.9

Infestation — *continued*
  Acanthocheilonema (perstans) 125.4
    streptocerca 125.6
  Acariasis 133.9
    demodex folliculorum 133.8
    Sarcoptes scabiei 133.0
    trombiculae 133.8
  Agamofilaria streptocerca 125.6
  Ancylostoma, Ankylostoma 126.9
    americanum 126.1
    braziliense 126.2
    canium 126.8
    ceylanicum 126.3
    duodenale 126.0
    new world 126.1
    old world 126.0
  Angiostrongylus cantonensis 128.8
  anisakiasis 127.1
  Anisakis larva 127.1
  arthropod NEC 134.1
  Ascaris lumbricoides 127.0
  Bacillus fusiformis 101
  Balantidium coli 007.0
  beef tapeworm 123.2
  Bothriocephalus (latus) 123.4
    larval 123.5
  broad tapeworm 123.4
    larval 123.5
  Brugia malayi 125.1
  Candiru 136.8
  Capillaria
    hepatica 128.8
    philippinensis 127.5
  cat liver fluke 121.0
  Cercomonas hominis (intestinal) 007.3
  cestodes 123.9
    specified type NEC 123.8
  chigger 133.8
  chigoe 134.1
  Chilomastix 007.8
  Clonorchis (sinensis) (liver) 121.1
  coccidia 007.2
  complicating pregnancy, childbirth,
    or puerperium 647.9 ☑
    affecting fetus or newborn 760.8
  Cysticercus cellulosae 123.1
  Demodex folliculorum 133.8
  Dermatobia (hominis) 134.0
  Dibothriocephalus (latus) 123.4
    larval 123.5
  Dicrocoelium dendriticum 121.8
  Diphyllobothrium (adult) (intestinal)
    (latum) (pacificum) 123.4
    larval 123.5
  Diplogonoporus (grandis) 123.8
  Dipylidium (caninum) 123.8
  Distoma hepaticum 121.3
  dog tapeworm 123.8
  Dracunculus medinensis 125.7
  dragon worm 125.7
  dwarf tapeworm 123.6
  Echinococcus (*see also* Echinococcus)
    122.9
  Echinostoma ilocanum 121.8
  Embadomonas 007.8
  Endamoeba (histolytica) — *see* Infec-
    tion, ameba
  Entamoeba (histolytica) — *see* Infec-
    tion, ameba
  Enterobius vermicularis 127.4
  Epidermophyton — *see* Dermatophy-
    tosis
  eyeworm 125.2
  Fasciola
    gigantica 121.3
    hepatica 121.3
  Fasciolopsis (buski) (small intestine)
    121.4
    blood NEC (*see also* Schistosomia-
      sis) 120.9
    cat liver 121.0
    filarial 125.9
      due to
        Acanthocheilonema (per-
          stans) 125.4
          streptocerca 125.6

☑ Additional Digit Required — Refer to the Tabular List for Digit Selection   ▽ Subterms under main terms may continue to next column or page

160 — Volume 2   ▶◀ Revised Text   ● New Line   ▲ Revised Code   *2007 ICD-9-CM*

Infestation — *continued*
Fasciolopsis — *continued*
  filarial — *continued*
    due to — *continued*
      Brugia (Wuchereria) malayi 125.1
      Dracunculus medinensis 125.7
      guinea worms 125.7
      Mansonella (ozzardi) 125.5
      Onchocerca volvulus 125.3
        eye 125.3 *[360.13]*
        eyelid 125.3 *[373.6]*
      Wuchereria (bancrofti) 125.0
        malayi 125.1
      specified type NEC 125.6
  fish tapeworm 123.4
    larval 123.5
  fluke 121.9
    intestinal (giant) 121.4
    liver (sheep) 121.3
      cat 121.0
      Chinese 121.1
      clonorchiasis 121.1
      fascioliasis 121.3
      Oriental 121.1
    lung (oriental) 121.2
    sheep liver 121.3
  fly larva 134.0
  Gasterophilus (intestinalis) 134.0
  Gastrodiscoides hominis 121.8
  Giardia lamblia 007.1
  Gnathostoma (spinigerum) 128.1
  Gongylonema 125.6
  guinea worm 125.7
  helminth NEC 128.9
    intestinal 127.9
      mixed (types classifiable to more than one category in 120.0–127.7) 127.8
      specified type NEC 127.7
    specified type NEC 128.8
  Heterophyes heterophyes (small intestine) 121.6
  hookworm (*see also* Infestation, ancylostoma) 126.9
  Hymenolepis (diminuta) (nana) 123.6
  intestinal NEC 129
  leeches (aquatic) (land) 134.2
  Leishmania — *see* Leishmaniasis
  lice (*see also* Infestation, pediculus) 132.9
  Linguatulidae, linguatula (pentastoma) (serrata) 134.1
  Loa loa 125.2
    eyelid 125.2 *[373.6]*
  louse (*see also* Infestation, pediculus) 132.9
    body 132.1
    head 132.0
    pubic 132.2
  maggots 134.0
  Mansonella (ozzardi) 125.5
  medina 125.7
  Metagonimus yokogawai (small intestine) 121.5
  Microfilaria streptocerca 125.3
    eye 125.3 *[360.13]*
    eyelid 125.3 *[373.6]*
  Microsporon furfur 111.0
  microsporum — *see* Dermatophytosis
  mites 133.9
    scabic 133.0
    specified type NEC 133.8
  monilia (albicans) (*see also* Candidiasis) 112.9
    vagina 112.1
    vulva 112.1
  mouth 112.0
  Necator americanus 126.1
  nematode (intestinal) 127.9
    Ancylostoma (*see also* Ancylostoma) 126.9
    Ascaris lumbricoides 127.0
    conjunctiva NEC 128.9
    Dioctophyma 128.8

Infestation — *continued*
nematode — *continued*
  Enterobius vermicularis 127.4
  Gnathostoma spinigerum 128.1
  Oesophagostomum (apiostomum) 127.7
  Physaloptera 127.4
  specified type NEC 127.7
  Strongyloides stercoralis 127.2
  Ternidens diminutus 127.7
  Trichinella spiralis 124
  Trichostrongylus 127.6
  Trichuris (trichiuria) 127.3
Oesophagostomum (apiostomum) 127.7
Oestrus ovis 134.0
Onchocerca (volvulus) 125.3
  eye 125.3 *[360.13]*
  eyelid 125.3 *[373.6]*
Opisthorchis (felineus) (tenuicollis) (viverrini) 121.0
Oxyuris vermicularis 127.4
Paragonimus (westermani) 121.2
parasite, parasitic NEC 136.9
  eyelid 134.9 *[373.6]*
  intestinal 129
  mouth 112.0
  orbit 376.13
  skin 134.9
  tongue 112.0
pediculus 132.9
  capitis (humanus) (any site) 132.0
  corporis (humanus) (any site) 132.1
  eyelid 132.0 *[373.6]*
  mixed (classifiable to more than one category in 132.0–132.2) 132.3
  pubis (any site) 132.2
phthirus (pubis) (any site) 132.2
  with any infestation classifiable to 132.0, 132.1 and 132.3
pinworm 127.4
pork tapeworm (adult) 123.0
protozoal NEC 136.8
pubic louse 132.2
rat tapeworm 123.6
red bug 133.8
roundworm (large) NEC 127.0
sand flea 134.1
saprophytic NEC 136.8
Sarcoptes scabiei 133.0
scabies 133.0
Schistosoma 120.9
  bovis 120.8
  cercariae 120.3
  hematobium 120.0
  intercalatum 120.8
  japonicum 120.2
  mansoni 120.1
  mattheii 120.8
  specified
    site — *see* Schistosomiasis
    type NEC 120.8
  spindale 120.8
screw worms 134.0
skin NEC 134.9
Sparganum (mansoni) (proliferum) 123.5
  larval 123.5
specified type NEC 134.8
Spirometra larvae 123.5
Sporozoa NEC 136.8
Stellantchasmus falcatus 121.6
Strongyloides 127.2
Strongylus (gibsoni) 127.7
Taenia 123.3
  diminuta 123.6
  Echinococcus (*see also* Echinococcus) 122.9
  mediocanellata 123.2
  nana 123.6
  saginata (mediocanellata) 123.2
  solium (intestinal form) 123.0
    larval form 123.1
Taeniarhynchus saginatus 123.2
tapeworm 123.9

Infestation — *continued*
tapeworm — *continued*
  beef 123.2
  broad 123.4
    larval 123.5
  dog 123.8
  dwarf 123.6
  fish 123.4
    larval 123.5
  pork 123.0
  rat 123.6
Ternidens diminutus 127.7
Tetranychus molestissimus 133.8
threadworm 127.4
tongue 112.0
Toxocara (cani) (cati) (felis) 128.0
trematode(s) NEC 121.9
Trichina spiralis 124
Trichinella spiralis 124
Trichocephalus 127.3
Trichomonas 131.9
  bladder 131.09
  cervix 131.09
  intestine 007.3
  prostate 131.03
  specified site NEC 131.8
  urethra (female) (male) 131.02
  urogenital 131.00
  vagina 131.01
  vulva 131.01
Trichophyton — *see* Dermatophytosis
Trichostrongylus instabilis 127.6
Trichuris (trichiuria) 127.3
Trombicula (irritans) 133.8
Trypanosoma — *see* Trypanosomiasis
Tunga penetrans 134.1
Uncinaria americana 126.1
whipworm 127.3
worms NEC 128.9
  intestinal 127.9
Wuchereria 125.0
  bancrofti 125.0
  malayi 125.1

Infiltrate, infiltration
with an iron compound 275.0
amyloid (any site) (generalized) 277.39 ▲
calcareous (muscle) NEC 275.49
  localized — *see* Degeneration, by site
calcium salt (muscle) 275.49
corneal (*see also* Edema, cornea) 371.20
eyelid 373.9
fatty (diffuse) (generalized) 272.8
  localized — *see* Degeneration, by site, fatty
glycogen, glycogenic (*see also* Disease, glycogen storage) 271.0
heart, cardiac
  fatty (*see also* Degeneration, myocardial) 429.1
  glycogenic 271.0 *[425.7]*
inflammatory in vitreous 379.29
kidney (*see also* Disease, renal) 593.9
leukemic (M9800/3) — *see* Leukemia
liver 573.8
  fatty — *see* Fatty, liver
  glycogen (*see also* Disease, glycogen storage) 271.0
lung (*see also* Infiltrate, pulmonary) 518.3
  eosinophilic 518.3
  x-ray finding only 793.1
lymphatic (*see also* Leukemia, lymphatic) 204.9 ✓
  gland, pigmentary 289.3
muscle, fatty 728.9
myelogenous (*see also* Leukemia, myeloid) 205.9 ✓
myocardium, myocardial
  fatty (*see also* Degeneration, myocardial) 429.1
  glycogenic 271.0 *[425.7]*
pulmonary 518.3

Infiltrate, infiltration — *continued*
pulmonary — *continued*
  with
    eosinophilia 518.3
    pneumonia — *see* Pneumonia, by type
  x-ray finding only 793.1
Ranke's primary (*see also* Tuberculosis) 010.0 ✓
skin, lymphocytic (benign) 709.8
thymus (gland) (fatty) 254.8
urine 788.8
vitreous humor 379.29
Infirmity 799.89
senile 797
Inflammation, inflamed, inflammatory (with exudation)
abducens (nerve) 378.54
accessory sinus (chronic) (*see also* Sinusitis) 473.9
adrenal (gland) 255.8
alimentary canal — *see* Enteritis
alveoli (teeth) 526.5
  scorbutic 267
amnion — *see* Amnionitis
anal canal 569.49
antrum (chronic) (*see also* Sinusitis, maxillary) 473.0
anus 569.49
appendix (*see also* Appendicitis) 541
arachnoid — *see* Meningitis
areola 611.0
  puerperal, postpartum 675.0 ✓
areolar tissue NEC 686.9
artery — *see* Arteritis
auditory meatus (external) (*see also* Otitis, externa) 380.10
Bartholin's gland 616.89 ▲
bile duct or passage 576.1
bladder (*see also* Cystitis) 595.9
bleb ●
  postprocedural 379.60 ●
    stage 1 379.61 ●
    stage 2 379.62 ●
    stage 3 379.63 ●
bone — *see* Osteomyelitis
bowel (*see also* Enteritis) 558.9
brain (*see also* Encephalitis) 323.9
  late effect — *see* category 326
  membrane — *see* Meningitis
breast 611.0
  puerperal, postpartum 675.2 ✓
broad ligament (*see also* Disease, pelvis, inflammatory) 614.4
  acute 614.3
bronchus — *see* Bronchitis
bursa — *see* Bursitis
capsule
  liver 573.3
  spleen 289.59
catarrhal (*see also* Catarrh) 460
  vagina 616.10
cecum (*see also* Appendicitis) 541
cerebral (*see also* Encephalitis) 323.9
  late effect — *see* category 326
  membrane — *see* Meningitis
cerebrospinal (*see also* Meningitis) 322.9
  late effect — *see* category 326
  meningococcal 036.0
  tuberculous (*see also* Tuberculosis) 013.6 ✓
cervix (uteri) (*see also* Cervicitis) 616.0
chest 519.9
choroid NEC (*see also* Choroiditis) 363.20
cicatrix (tissue) — *see* Cicatrix
colon (*see also* Enteritis) 558.9
  granulomatous 555.1
  newborn 558.9
connective tissue (diffuse) NEC 728.9
cornea (*see also* Keratitis) 370.9
  with ulcer (*see also* Ulcer, cornea) 370.00
corpora cavernosa (penis) 607.2

Index

Inflammation, inflamed, inflammatory — Inhalation

Inflammation, inflamed, inflammatory
— *continued*
cranial nerve — *see* Disorder, nerve, cranial
diarrhea — *see* Diarrhea
disc (intervertebral) (space) 722.90
  cervical, cervicothoracic 722.91
  lumbar, lumbosacral 722.93
  thoracic, thoracolumbar 722.92
Douglas' cul-de-sac or pouch (chronic) (*see also* Disease, pelvis, inflammatory) 614.4
  acute 614.3
due to (presence of) any device, implant, or graft classifiable to 996.0–996.5 — *see* Complications, infection and inflammation, due to (presence of) any device, implant, or graft classified to 996.0–996.5 NEC
duodenum 535.6 ☑
dura mater — *see* Meningitis
ear (*see also* Otitis)
  external (*see also* Otitis, externa) 380.10
  inner (*see also* Labyrinthitis) 386.30
  middle — *see* Otitis media
esophagus 530.10
ethmoidal (chronic) (sinus) (*see also* Sinusitis, ethmoidal) 473.2
Eustachian tube (catarrhal) 381.50
  acute 381.51
  chronic 381.52
extrarectal 569.49
eye 379.99
eyelid 373.9
  specified NEC 373.8
fallopian tube (*see also* Salpingo-oophoritis) 614.2
fascia 728.9
fetal membranes (acute) 658.4 ☑
  affecting fetus or newborn 762.7
follicular, pharynx 472.1
frontal (chronic) (sinus) (*see also* Sinusitis, frontal) 473.1
gallbladder (*see also* Cholecystitis, acute) 575.0
gall duct (*see also* Cholecystitis) 575.10
gastrointestinal (*see also* Enteritis) 558.9
genital organ (diffuse) (internal)
  female 614.9
    with
      abortion — *see* Abortion, by type, with sepsis
      ectopic pregnancy (*see also* categories 633.0–633.9) 639.0
      molar pregnancy (*see also* categories 630–632) 639.0
      complicating pregnancy, childbirth, or puerperium 646.6 ☑
        affecting fetus or newborn 760.8
      following
        abortion 639.0
        ectopic or molar pregnancy 639.0
  male 608.4
gland (lymph) (*see also* Lymphadenitis) 289.3
glottis (*see also* Laryngitis) 464.00
  with obstruction 464.01
granular, pharynx 472.1
gum 523.10 ▲
heart (*see also* Carditis) 429.89
hepatic duct 576.8
hernial sac — *see* Hernia, by site
ileum (*see also* Enteritis) 558.9
  terminal or regional 555.0
    with large intestine 555.2
intervertebral disc 722.90

Inflammation, inflamed, inflammatory
intervertebral disc — *continued*
  cervical, cervicothoracic 722.91
  lumbar, lumbosacral 722.93
  thoracic, thoracolumbar 722.92
intestine (*see also* Enteritis) 558.9
jaw (acute) (bone) (chronic) (lower) (suppurative) (upper) 526.4
jejunum — *see* Enteritis
joint NEC (*see also* Arthritis) 716.9 ☑
  sacroiliac 720.2
kidney (*see also* Nephritis) 583.9
knee (joint) 716.66
  tuberculous (active) (*see also* Tuberculosis) 015.2 ☑
labium (majus) (minus) (*see also* Vulvitis) 616.10
lacrimal
  gland (*see also* Dacryoadenitis) 375.00
  passages (duct) (sac) (*see also* Dacryocystitis) 375.30
larynx (*see also* Laryngitis) 464.00
  with obstruction 464.01
  diphtheritic 032.3
leg NEC 686.9
lip 528.5
liver (capsule) (*see also* Hepatitis) 573.3
  acute 570
  chronic 571.40
  suppurative 572.0
lung (acute) (*see also* Pneumonia) 486
  chronic (interstitial) 518.89
lymphatic vessel (*see also* Lymphangitis) 457.2
lymph node or gland (*see also* Lymphadenitis) 289.3
mammary gland 611.0
  puerperal, postpartum 675.2 ☑
maxilla, maxillary 526.4
  sinus (chronic) (*see also* Sinusitis, maxillary) 473.0
membranes of brain or spinal cord — *see* Meningitis
meninges — *see* Meningitis
mouth 528.00 ▲
muscle 728.9
myocardium (*see also* Myocarditis) 429.0
nasal sinus (chronic) (*see also* Sinusitis) 473.9
nasopharynx — *see* Nasopharyngitis
navel 686.9
  newborn NEC 771.4
nerve NEC 729.2
nipple 611.0
  puerperal, postpartum 675.0 ☑
nose 478.19 ▲
  suppurative 472.0
oculomotor nerve 378.51
optic nerve 377.30
orbit (chronic) 376.10
  acute 376.00
  chronic 376.10
ovary (*see also* Salpingo-oophoritis) 614.2
oviduct (*see also* Salpingo-oophoritis) 614.2
pancreas — *see* Pancreatitis
parametrium (chronic) (*see also* Disease, pelvis, inflammatory) 614.4
  acute 614.3
parotid region 686.9
  gland 527.2
pelvis, female (*see also* Disease, pelvis, inflammatory) 614.9
penis (corpora cavernosa) 607.2
perianal 569.49
pericardium (*see also* Pericarditis) 423.9
perineum (female) (male) 686.9
perirectal 569.49
peritoneum (*see also* Peritonitis) 567.9

Inflammation, inflamed, inflammatory
— *continued*
periuterine (*see also* Disease, pelvis, inflammatory) 614.9
perivesical (*see also* Cystitis) 595.9
petrous bone (*see also* Petrositis) 383.20
pharynx (*see also* Pharyngitis) 462
  follicular 472.1
  granular 472.1
pia mater — *see* Meningitis
pleura — *see* Pleurisy
postmastoidectomy cavity 383.30
  chronic 383.33
prostate (*see also* Prostatitis) 601.9
rectosigmoid — *see* Rectosigmoiditis
rectum (*see also* Proctitis) 569.49
respiratory, upper (*see also* Infection, respiratory, upper) 465.9
  chronic, due to external agent — *see* Condition, respiratory, chronic, due to, external agent
  due to
    fumes or vapors (chemical) (inhalation) 506.2
    radiation 508.1
retina (*see also* Retinitis) 363.20
retrocecal (*see also* Appendicitis) 541
retroperitoneal (*see also* Peritonitis) 567.9
salivary duct or gland (any) (suppurative) 527.2
scorbutic, alveoli, teeth 267
scrotum 608.4
sigmoid — *see* Enteritis
sinus (*see also* Sinusitis) 473.9
Skene's duct or gland (*see also* Urethritis) 597.89
skin 686.9
spermatic cord 608.4
sphenoidal (sinus) (*see also* Sinusitis, sphenoidal) 473.3
spinal
  cord (*see also* Encephalitis) 323.9
    late effect — *see* category 326
  membrane — *see* Meningitis
  nerve — *see* Disorder, nerve
spine (*see also* Spondylitis) 720.9
spleen (capsule) 289.59
stomach — *see* Gastritis
stricture, rectum 569.49
subcutaneous tissue NEC 686.9
suprarenal (gland) 255.8
synovial (fringe) (membrane) — *see* Bursitis
tendon (sheath) NEC 726.90
testis (*see also* Orchitis) 604.90
thigh 686.9
throat (*see also* Sore throat) 462
thymus (gland) 254.8
thyroid (gland) (*see also* Thyroiditis) 245.9
tongue 529.0
tonsil — *see* Tonsillitis
trachea — *see* Tracheitis
trochlear nerve 378.53
tubal (*see also* Salpingo-oophoritis) 614.2
tuberculous NEC (*see also* Tuberculosis) 011.9 ☑
tubo-ovarian (*see also* Salpingo-oophoritis) 614.2
tunica vaginalis 608.4
tympanic membrane — *see* Myringitis
umbilicus, umbilical 686.9
  newborn NEC 771.4
uterine ligament (*see also* Disease, pelvis, inflammatory) 614.4
  acute 614.3
uterus (catarrhal) (*see also* Endometritis) 615.9
uveal tract (anterior) (*see also* Iridocyclitis) 364.3
  posterior — *see* Chorioretinitis
  sympathetic 360.11

Inflammation, inflamed, inflammatory
— *continued*
vagina (*see also* Vaginitis) 616.10
vas deferens 608.4
vein (*see also* Phlebitis) 451.9
  thrombotic 451.9
    cerebral (*see also* Thrombosis, brain) 434.0 ☑
    leg 451.2
      deep (vessels) NEC 451.19
      superficial (vessels) 451.0
    lower extremity 451.2
      deep (vessels) NEC 451.19
      superficial (vessels) 451.0
vocal cord 478.5
vulva (*see also* Vulvitis) 616.10
Inflation, lung imperfect (newborn) 770.5
Influenza, influenzal 487.1
  with
    bronchitis 487.1
    bronchopneumonia 487.0
    cold (any type) 487.1
    digestive manifestations 487.8
    hemoptysis 487.1
    involvement of
      gastrointestinal tract 487.8
      nervous system 487.8
    laryngitis 487.1
    manifestations NEC 487.8
      respiratory 487.1
        pneumonia 487.0
    pharyngitis 487.1
    pneumonia (any form classifiable to 480–483, 485–486) 487.0
    respiratory manifestations NEC 487.1
    sinusitis 487.1
    sore throat 487.1
    tonsillitis 487.1
    tracheitis 487.1
    upper respiratory infection (acute) 487.1
  abdominal 487.8
  Asian 487.1
  bronchial 487.1
  bronchopneumonia 487.0
  catarrhal 487.1
  epidemic 487.1
  gastric 487.8
  intestinal 487.8
  laryngitis 487.1
  maternal affecting fetus or newborn 760.2
    manifest influenza in infant 771.2
  pharyngitis 487.1
  pneumonia (any form) 487.0
  respiratory (upper) 487.1
  stomach 487.8
  vaccination, prophylactic (against) V04.81
Influenza-like disease 487.1
Infraction, Freiberg's (metatarsal head) 732.5
Infraeruption, teeth 524.34
Infusion complication, misadventure, or reaction — *see* Complication, infusion
Ingestion
  chemical — *see* Table of Drugs and Chemicals
  drug or medicinal substance
    overdose or wrong substance given or taken 977.9
    specified drug — *see* Table of Drugs and Chemicals
  foreign body NEC (*see also* Foreign body) 938
Ingrowing
  hair 704.8
  nail (finger) (toe) (infected) 703.0
Inguinal — *see also* condition
  testis 752.51
Inhalation
  carbon monoxide 986

Inhalation — *continued*
- flame
  - lung 947.1
  - mouth 947.0
- food or foreign body (*see also* Asphyxia, food or foreign body) 933.1
- gas, fumes, or vapor (noxious) 987.9
  - specified agent — *see* Table of Drugs and Chemicals
- liquid or vomitus (*see also* Asphyxia, food or foreign body) 933.1
- lower respiratory tract NEC 934.9
- meconium (fetus or newborn) 770.11
  - with respiratory symptoms 770.12
- mucus (*see also* Asphyxia, mucus) 933.1
- oil (causing suffocation) (*see also* Asphyxia, food or foreign body) 933.1
- pneumonia — *see* Pneumonia, aspiration
- smoke 987.9
- steam 987.9
- stomach contents or secretions (*see also* Asphyxia, food or foreign body) 933.1
  - in labor and delivery 668.0 ☑

Inhibition, inhibited
- academic as adjustment reaction 309.23
- orgasm
  - female 302.73
  - male 302.74
- sexual
  - desire 302.71
  - excitement 302.72
- work as adjustment reaction 309.23

Inhibitor, systemic lupus erythematosus (presence of) 286.5

Iniencephalus, iniencephaly 740.2

Injected eye 372.74

Injury 959.9

> *Note* — For abrasion, insect bite (nonvenomous), blister, or scratch, see Injury, superficial.
>
> For laceration, traumatic rupture, tear, or penetrating wound of internal organs, such as heart, lung, liver, kidney, pelvic organs, whether or not accompanied by open wound in the same region, see Injury, internal.
>
> For nerve injury, see Injury, nerve.
>
> For late effect of injuries classifiable to 850–854, 860–869, 900–919, 950–959, see Late, effect, injury, by type.

- abdomen, abdominal (viscera) (*see also* Injury, internal, abdomen)
  - muscle or wall 959.12
- acoustic, resulting in deafness 951.5
- adenoid 959.09
- adrenal (gland) — *see* Injury, internal, adrenal
- alveolar (process) 959.09
- ankle (and foot) (and knee) (and leg, except thigh) 959.7
- anterior chamber, eye 921.3
- anus 959.19
- aorta (thoracic) 901.0
  - abdominal 902.0
- appendix — *see* Injury, internal, appendix
- arm, upper (and shoulder) 959.2
- artery (complicating trauma) (*see also* Injury, blood vessel, by site) 904.9
  - cerebral or meningeal (*see also* Hemorrhage, brain, traumatic, subarachnoid) 852.0 ☑
- auditory canal (external) (meatus) 959.09
- auricle, auris, ear 959.09
- axilla 959.2
- back 959.19

Injury — *continued*
- bile duct — *see* Injury, internal, bile duct
- birth (*see also* Birth, injury)
  - canal NEC, complicating delivery 665.9 ☑
- bladder (sphincter) — *see* Injury, internal, bladder
- blast (air) (hydraulic) (immersion) (underwater) NEC 869.0
  - with open wound into cavity NEC 869.1
  - abdomen or thorax — *see* Injury, internal, by site
  - brain — *see* Concussion, brain
  - ear (acoustic nerve trauma) 951.5
    - with perforation of tympanic membrane — *see* Wound, open, ear, drum
- blood vessel NEC 904.9
  - abdomen 902.9
    - multiple 902.87
    - specified NEC 902.89
  - aorta (thoracic) 901.0
    - abdominal 902.0
  - arm NEC 903.9
  - axillary 903.00
    - artery 903.01
    - vein 903.02
  - azygos vein 901.89
  - basilic vein 903.1
  - brachial (artery) (vein) 903.1
  - bronchial 901.89
  - carotid artery 900.00
    - common 900.01
    - external 900.02
    - internal 900.03
  - celiac artery 902.20
    - specified branch NEC 902.24
  - cephalic vein (arm) 903.1
  - colica dextra 902.26
  - cystic
    - artery 902.24
    - vein 902.39
  - deep plantar 904.6
  - digital (artery) (vein) 903.5
  - due to accidental puncture or laceration during procedure 998.2
  - extremity
    - lower 904.8
      - multiple 904.7
      - specified NEC 904.7
    - upper 903.9
      - multiple 903.8
      - specified NEC 903.8
  - femoral
    - artery (superficial) 904.1
      - above profunda origin 904.0
      - common 904.0
    - vein 904.2
  - gastric
    - artery 902.21
    - vein 902.39
  - head 900.9
    - intracranial — *see* Injury, intracranial
    - multiple 900.82
    - specified NEC 900.89
  - hemiazygos vein 901.89
  - hepatic
    - artery 902.22
    - vein 902.11
  - hypogastric 902.59
    - artery 902.51
    - vein 902.52
  - ileocolic
    - artery 902.26
    - vein 902.31
  - iliac 902.50
    - artery 902.53
    - specified branch NEC 902.59
    - vein 902.54
  - innominate
    - artery 901.1
    - vein 901.3

Injury — *continued*
- blood vessel — *continued*
  - intercostal (artery) (vein) 901.81
  - jugular vein (external) 900.81
    - internal 900.1
  - leg NEC 904.8
  - mammary (artery) (vein) 901.82
  - mesenteric
    - artery 902.20
      - inferior 902.27
        - specified branch NEC 902.29
      - superior (trunk) 902.25
        - branches, primary 902.26
    - vein 902.39
      - inferior 902.32
      - superior (and primary subdivisions) 902.31
  - neck 900.9
    - multiple 900.82
    - specified NEC 900.89
  - ovarian 902.89
    - artery 902.81
    - vein 902.82
  - palmar artery 903.4
  - pelvis 902.9
    - multiple 902.87
    - specified NEC 902.89
  - plantar (deep) (artery) (vein) 904.6
  - popliteal 904.40
    - artery 904.41
    - vein 904.42
  - portal 902.33
  - pulmonary 901.40
    - artery 901.41
    - vein 901.42
  - radial (artery) (vein) 903.2
  - renal 902.40
    - artery 902.41
    - specified NEC 902.49
    - vein 902.42
  - saphenous
    - artery 904.7
    - vein (greater) (lesser) 904.3
  - splenic
    - artery 902.23
    - vein 902.34
  - subclavian
    - artery 901.1
    - vein 901.3
  - suprarenal 902.49
  - thoracic 901.9
    - multiple 901.83
    - specified NEC 901.89
  - tibial 904.50
    - artery 904.50
      - anterior 904.51
      - posterior 904.53
    - vein 904.50
      - anterior 904.52
      - posterior 904.54
  - ulnar (artery) (vein) 903.3
  - uterine 902.59
    - artery 902.55
    - vein 902.56
  - vena cava
    - inferior 902.10
      - specified branches NEC 902.19
    - superior 901.2
- brachial plexus 953.4
  - newborn 767.6
- brain NEC (*see also* Injury, intracranial) 854.0 ☑
- breast 959.19
- broad ligament — *see* Injury, internal, broad ligament
- bronchus, bronchi — *see* Injury, internal, bronchus
- brow 959.09
- buttock 959.19
- canthus, eye 921.1
- cathode ray 990
- cauda equina 952.4
  - with fracture, vertebra — *see* Fracture, vertebra, sacrum

Injury — *continued*
- cavernous sinus (*see also* Injury, intracranial) 854.0 ☑
- cecum — *see* Injury, internal, cecum
- celiac ganglion or plexus 954.1
- cerebellum (*see also* Injury, intracranial) 854.0 ☑
- cervix (uteri) — *see* Injury, internal, cervix
- cheek 959.09
- chest (*see also* Injury, internal, chest) wall 959.11
- childbirth (*see also* Birth, injury)
  - maternal NEC 665.9 ☑
- chin 959.09
- choroid (eye) 921.3
- clitoris 959.14
- coccyx 959.19
  - complicating delivery 665.6 ☑
- colon — *see* Injury, internal, colon
- common duct — *see* Injury, internal, common duct
- conjunctiva 921.1
  - superficial 918.2
- cord
  - spermatic — *see* Injury, internal, spermatic cord
  - spinal — *see* Injury, spinal, by site
- cornea 921.3
  - abrasion 918.1
  - due to contact lens 371.82
  - penetrating — *see* Injury, eyeball, penetrating
  - superficial 918.1
    - due to contact lens 371.82
- cortex (cerebral) (*see also* Injury, intracranial) 854.0 ☑
  - visual 950.3
- costal region 959.11
- costochondral 959.11
- cranial
  - bones — *see* Fracture, skull, by site
  - cavity (*see also* Injury, intracranial) 854.0 ☑
  - nerve — *see* Injury, nerve, cranial
- crushing — *see* Crush
- cutaneous sensory nerve
  - lower limb 956.4
  - upper limb 955.5
- delivery (*see also* Birth, injury)
  - maternal NEC 665.9 ☑
- Descemet's membrane — *see* Injury, eyeball, penetrating
- diaphragm — *see* Injury, internal, diaphragm
- diffuse axonal — *see* Injury, intracranial
- duodenum — *see* Injury, internal, duodenum
- ear (auricle) (canal) (drum) (external) 959.09
- elbow (and forearm) (and wrist) 959.3
- epididymis 959.14
- epigastric region 959.12
- epiglottis 959.09
- epiphyseal, current — *see* Fracture, by site
- esophagus — *see* Injury, internal, esophagus
- Eustachian tube 959.09
- extremity (lower) (upper) NEC 959.8
- eye 921.9
  - penetrating eyeball — *see* Injury, eyeball, penetrating
  - superficial 918.9
- eyeball 921.3
  - penetrating 871.7
    - with
      - partial loss (of intraocular tissue) 871.2
      - prolapse or exposure (of intraocular tissue) 871.1
    - without prolapse 871.0
  - foreign body (nonmagnetic) 871.6

☑ Additional Digit Required — Refer to the Tabular List for Digit Selection   🔄 Subterms under main terms may continue to next column or page

2007 ICD-9-CM   ▶◀ Revised Text   ● New Line   ▲ Revised Code   **Volume 2 — 163**

Inhalation — Injury

Injury — *continued*
eyeball — *continued*
  penetrating — *continued*
    foreign body — *continued*
      magnetic 871.5
    superficial 918.9
eyebrow 959.09
eyelid(s) 921.1
  laceration — *see* Laceration, eyelid
  superficial 918.0
face (and neck) 959.09
fallopian tube — *see* Injury, internal, fallopian tube
finger(s) (nail) 959.5
flank 959.19
foot (and ankle) (and knee) (and leg, except thigh) 959.7
forceps NEC 767.9
  scalp 767.19
forearm (and elbow) (and wrist) 959.3
forehead 959.09
gallbladder — *see* Injury, internal, gallbladder
gasserian ganglion 951.2
gastrointestinal tract — *see* Injury, internal, gastrointestinal tract
genital organ(s)
  with
    abortion — *see* Abortion, by type, with, damage to pelvic organs
    ectopic pregnancy (*see also* categories 633.0–633.9) 639.2
    molar pregnancy (*see also* categories 630–632) 639.2
  external 959.14
    fracture of corpus cavernosum penis 959.13
  following
    abortion 639.2
    ectopic or molar pregnancy 639.2
  internal — *see* Injury, internal, genital organs
  obstetrical trauma NEC 665.9 ☑
    affecting fetus or newborn 763.89
gland
  lacrimal 921.1
    laceration 870.8
  parathyroid 959.09
  salivary 959.09
  thyroid 959.09
globe (eye) (*see also* Injury, eyeball) 921.3
grease gun — *see* Wound, open, by site, complicated
groin 959.19
gum 959.09
hand(s) (except fingers) 959.4
head NEC 959.01
  with
    loss of consciousness 850.5
    skull fracture — *see* Fracture, skull, by site
heart — *see* Injury, internal, heart
heel 959.7
hip (and thigh) 959.6
hymen 959.14
hyperextension (cervical) (vertebra) 847.0
ileum — *see* Injury, internal, ileum
iliac region 959.19
infrared rays NEC 990
instrumental (during surgery) 998.2
  birth injury — *see* Birth, injury
  nonsurgical (*see also* Injury, by site) 959.9
  obstetrical 665.9 ☑
    affecting fetus or newborn 763.89
    bladder 665.5 ☑
    cervix 665.3 ☑
    high vaginal 665.4 ☑
    perineal NEC 664.9 ☑

Injury — *continued*
instrumental — *continued*
  obstetrical — *continued*
    urethra 665.5 ☑
    uterus 665.5 ☑
internal 869.0

Note — For injury of internal organ(s) by foreign body entering through a natural orifice (e.g., inhaled, ingested, or swallowed) — *see* Foreign body, entering through orifice.

For internal injury of any of the following sites with internal injury of any other of the sites — *see* Injury, internal, multiple.

  with
    fracture
      pelvis — *see* Fracture, pelvis
      specified site, except pelvis — *see* Injury, internal, by site
    open wound into cavity 869.1
  abdomen, abdominal (viscera) NEC 868.00
    with
      fracture, pelvis — *see* Fracture, pelvis
      open wound into cavity 868.10
    specified site NEC 868.09
      with open wound into cavity 868.19
  adrenal (gland) 868.01
    with open wound into cavity 868.11
  aorta (thoracic) 901.0
    abdominal 902.0
  appendix 863.85
    with open wound into cavity 863.95
  bile duct 868.02
    with open wound into cavity 868.12
  bladder (sphincter) 867.0
    with
      abortion — *see* Abortion, by type, with damage to pelvic organs
      ectopic pregnancy (*see also* categories 633.0–633.9) 639.2
      molar pregnancy (*see also* categories 630–632) 639.2
      open wound into cavity 867.1
    following
      abortion 639.2
      ectopic or molar pregnancy 639.2
    obstetrical trauma 665.5 ☑
      affecting fetus or newborn 763.89
  blood vessel — *see* Injury, blood vessel, by site
  broad ligament 867.6
    with open wound into cavity 867.7
  bronchus, bronchi 862.21
    with open wound into cavity 862.31
  cecum 863.89
    with open wound into cavity 863.99
  cervix (uteri) 867.4
    with
      abortion — *see* Abortion, by type, with damage to pelvic organs
      ectopic pregnancy (*see also* categories 633.0–633.9) 639.2
      molar pregnancy (*see also* categories 630–632) 639.2
      open wound into cavity 867.5

Injury — *continued*
internal — *continued*
  cervix — *continued*
    following
      abortion 639.2
      ectopic or molar pregnancy 639.2
    obstetrical trauma 665.3 ☑
      affecting fetus or newborn 763.89
  chest (*see also* Injury, internal, intrathoracic organs) 862.8
    with open wound into cavity 862.9
  colon 863.40
    with
      open wound into cavity 863.50
      rectum 863.46
        with open wound into cavity 863.56
    ascending (right) 863.41
      with open wound into cavity 863.51
    descending (left) 863.43
      with open wound into cavity 863.53
    multiple sites 863.46
      with open wound into cavity 863.56
    sigmoid 863.44
      with open wound into cavity 863.54
    specified site NEC 863.49
      with open wound into cavity 863.59
    transverse 863.42
      with open wound into cavity 863.52
  common duct 868.02
    with open wound into cavity 868.12
  complicating delivery 665.9 ☑
    affecting fetus or newborn 763.89
  diaphragm 862.0
    with open wound into cavity 862.1
  duodenum 863.21
    with open wound into cavity 863.31
  esophagus (intrathoracic) 862.22
    with open wound into cavity 862.32
    cervical region 874.4
      complicated 874.5
  fallopian tube 867.6
    with open wound into cavity 867.7
  gallbladder 868.02
    with open wound into cavity 868.12
  gastrointestinal tract NEC 863.80
    with open wound into cavity 863.90
  genital organ NEC 867.6
    with open wound into cavity 867.7
  heart 861.00
    with open wound into thorax 861.10
  ileum 863.29
    with open wound into cavity 863.39
  intestine NEC 863.89
    with open wound into cavity 863.99
    large NEC 863.40
      with open wound into cavity 863.50
    small NEC 863.20
      with open wound into cavity 863.30
  intra-abdominal (organ) 868.00
    with open wound into cavity 868.10

Injury — *continued*
internal — *continued*
  intra-abdominal — *continued*
    multiple sites 868.09
      with open wound into cavity 868.19
    specified site NEC 868.09
      with open wound into cavity 868.19
  intrathoracic organs (multiple) 862.8
    with open wound into cavity 862.9
    diaphragm (only) — *see* Injury, internal, diaphragm
    heart (only) — *see* Injury, internal, heart
    lung (only) — *see* Injury, internal, lung
    specified site NEC 862.29
      with open wound into cavity 862.39
  intrauterine (*see also* Injury, internal, uterus) 867.4
    with open wound into cavity 867.5
  jejunum 863.29
    with open wound into cavity 863.39
  kidney (subcapsular) 866.00
    with
      disruption of parenchyma (complete) 866.03
        with open wound into cavity 866.13
      hematoma (without rupture of capsule) 866.01
        with open wound into cavity 866.11
      laceration 866.02
        with open wound into cavity 866.12
      open wound into cavity 866.10
  liver 864.00
    with
      contusion 864.01
        with open wound into cavity 864.11
      hematoma 864.01
        with open wound into cavity 864.11
      laceration 864.05
        with open wound into cavity 864.15
      major (disruption of hepatic parenchyma) 864.04
        with open wound into cavity 864.14
      minor (capsule only) 864.02
        with open wound into cavity 864.12
      moderate (involving parenchyma) 864.03
        with open wound into cavity 864.13
      multiple 864.04
      stellate 864.04
        with open wound into cavity 864.14
      open wound into cavity 864.10
  lung 861.20
    with open wound into thorax 861.30
    hemopneumothorax — *see* Hemopneumothorax, traumatic
    hemothorax — *see* Hemothorax, traumatic
    pneumohemothorax — *see* Pneumohemothorax, traumatic

Injury — *continued*
  internal — *continued*
    lung — *continued*
      pneumothorax — *see* Pneumoth-
        orax, traumatic
      transfusion related, acute ●
        (TRALI) 518.7 ●
    mediastinum 862.29
      with open wound into cavity
        862.39
    mesentery 863.89
      with open wound into cavity
        863.99
    mesosalpinx 867.6
      with open wound into cavity
        867.7
    multiple 869.0

> *Note* — *Multiple internal injuries of sites classifiable to the same three- or four-digit category should be classified to that category.*
>
> *Multiple injuries classifiable to different fourth-digit subdivisions of 861 (heart and lung injuries) should be dealt with according to coding rules.*

    internal
      with open wound into cavity
        869.1
    intra–abdominal organ (sites
      classifiable to 863–868)
      with
        intrathoracic organ(s)
          (sites classifiable to
          861–862) 869.0
          with open wound into
            cavity 869.1
        other intra–abdominal or-
          gan(s) (sites classifi-
          able to 863–868,
          except where classi-
          fiable to the same
          three–digit category)
          868.09
          with open wound into
            cavity 868.19
    intrathoracic organ (sites classi-
      fiable to 861–862)
      with
        intra–abdominal organ(s)
          (sites classifiable to
          863–868) 869.0
          with open wound into
            cavity 869.1
        other intrathoracic or-
          gan(s) (sites classifi-
          able to 861–862,
          except where classi-
          fiable to the same
          three–digit category)
          862.8
          with open wound into
            cavity 862.9
    myocardium — *see* Injury, internal,
      heart
    ovary 867.6
      with open wound into cavity
        867.7
    pancreas (multiple sites) 863.84
      with open wound into cavity
        863.94
      body 863.82
        with open wound into cavity
          863.92
      head 863.81
        with open wound into cavity
          863.91
      tail 863.83
        with open wound into cavity
          863.93
    pelvis, pelvic (organs) (viscera)
      867.8
      with
        fracture, pelvis — *see* Frac-
          ture, pelvis
        open wound into cavity 867.9

Injury — *continued*
  internal — *continued*
    pelvis, pelvic — *continued*
      specified site NEC 867.6
        with open wound into cavity
          867.7
    peritoneum 868.03
      with open wound into cavity
        868.13
    pleura 862.29
      with open wound into cavity
        862.39
    prostate 867.6
      with open wound into cavity
        867.7
    rectum 863.45
      with
        colon 863.46
          with open wound into
           cavity 863.56
        open wound into cavity
          863.55
    retroperitoneum 868.04
      with open wound into cavity
        868.14
    round ligament 867.6
      with open wound into cavity
        867.7
    seminal vesicle 867.6
      with open wound into cavity
        867.7
    spermatic cord 867.6
      with open wound into cavity
        867.7
      scrotal — *see* Wound, open,
        spermatic cord
    spleen 865.00
      with
        disruption of parenchyma
          (massive) 865.04
          with open wound into
           cavity 865.14
        hematoma (without rupture
          of capsule) 865.01
          with open wound into
           cavity 865.11
        open wound into cavity
          865.10
        tear, capsular 865.02
          with open wound into
           cavity 865.12
          extending into parenchy-
           ma 865.03
           with open wound into
            cavity 865.13
    stomach 863.0
      with open wound into cavity
        863.1
    suprarenal gland (multiple) 868.01
      with open wound into cavity
        868.11
    thorax, thoracic (cavity) (organs)
      (multiple) (*see also* Injury,
      internal, intrathoracic or-
      gans) 862.8
      with open wound into cavity
        862.9
    thymus (gland) 862.29
      with open wound into cavity
        862.39
    trachea (intrathoracic) 862.29
      with open wound into cavity
        862.39
      cervical region (*see also* Wound,
        open, trachea) 874.02
    ureter 867.2
      with open wound into cavity
        867.3
    urethra (sphincter) 867.0
      with
        abortion — *see* Abortion, by
          type, with damage to
          pelvic organs
        ectopic pregnancy (*see also*
          categories
          633.0–633.9) 639.2

Injury — *continued*
  internal — *continued*
    urethra — *continued*
      with — *continued*
        molar pregnancy (*see also*
          categories 630–632)
          639.2
        open wound into cavity 867.1
      following
        abortion 639.2
        ectopic or molar pregnancy
          639.2
      obstetrical trauma 665.5 ☑
        affecting fetus or newborn
          763.89
    uterus 867.4
      with
        abortion — *see* Abortion, by
          type, with damage to
          pelvic organs
        ectopic pregnancy (*see also*
          categories
          633.0–633.9) 639.2
        molar pregnancy (*see also*
          categories 630–632)
          639.2
        open wound into cavity 867.5
      following
        abortion 639.2
        ectopic or molar pregnancy
          639.2
      obstetrical trauma NEC 665.5 ☑
        affecting fetus or newborn
          763.89
    vas deferens 867.6
      with open wound into cavity
        867.7
    vesical (sphincter) 867.0
      with open wound into cavity
        867.1
    viscera (abdominal) (*see also* In-
      jury, internal, multiple)
      868.00
      with
        fracture, pelvis — *see* Frac-
          ture, pelvis
        open wound into cavity
          868.10
        thoracic NEC (*see also* Injury,
          internal, intrathoracic or-
          gans) 862.8
          with open wound into cavity
           862.9
  interscapular region 959.19
  intervertebral disc 959.19
  intestine — *see* Injury, internal, intes-
    tine
  intra–abdominal (organs) NEC — *see*
    Injury, internal, intra-abdominal

Injury — *continued*
  intracranial 854.0 ☑

> *Note* — *Use the following fifth-digit subclassification with categories 851–854:*
>
> 0   *unspecified state of conscious-ness*
>
> 1   *with no loss of consciousness*
>
> 2   *with brief [less than one hour] loss of consciousness*
>
> 3   *with moderate [1–24 hours] loss of consciousness*
>
> 4   *with prolonged [more than 24 hours] loss of consciousness and return to pre–existing conscious level*
>
> 5   *with prolonged [more than 24 hours] loss of consciousness, without return to pre–existing conscious level*
>
> *Use fifth-digit 5 to designate when a patient is unconscious and dies before regaining consciousness, regardless of the duration of the loss of consciousness*
>
> 6   *with loss of consciousness of un-specified duration*
>
> 9   *with concussion, unspecified*

    with
      open intracranial wound
        854.1 ☑
      skull fracture — *see* Fracture,
        skull, by site
    contusion 851.8 ☑
      with open intracranial wound
        851.9 ☑
      brain stem 851.4 ☑
        with open intracranial wound
          851.5 ☑
      cerebellum 851.4 ☑
        with open intracranial wound
          851.5 ☑
      cortex (cerebral) 851.0 ☑
        with open intracranial wound
          851.2 ☑
    hematoma — *see* Injury, intracra-
      nial, hemorrhage
    hemorrhage 853.0 ☑
      with
        laceration — *see* Injury, in-
          tracranial, laceration
        open intracranial wound
          853.1 ☑
      extradural 852.4 ☑
        with open intracranial wound
          852.5 ☑
      subarachnoid 852.0 ☑
        with open intracranial wound
          852.1 ☑
      subdural 852.2 ☑
        with open intracranial wound
          852.3 ☑
    laceration 851.8 ☑
      with open intracranial wound
        851.9 ☑
      brain stem 851.6 ☑
        with open intracranial wound
          851.7 ☑
      cerebellum 851.6 ☑
        with open intracranial wound
          851.7 ☑
      cortex (cerebral) 851.2 ☑
        with open intracranial wound
          851.3 ☑
    intraocular — *see* Injury, eyeball,
      penetrating
    intrathoracic organs (multiple) — *see*
      Injury, internal, intrathoracic
      organs
    intrauterine — *see* Injury, internal,
      intrauterine

☑ Additional Digit Required — Refer to the Tabular List for Digit Selection   ▽ Subterms under main terms may continue to next column or page

2007 ICD-9-CM   ▶◀ Revised Text   ● New Line   ▲ Revised Code   October 2006 · Volume 2 — 165

Injury — *continued*
iris 921.3
  penetrating — *see* Injury, eyeball, penetrating
jaw 959.09
jejunum — *see* Injury, internal, jejunum
joint NEC 959.9
  old or residual 718.80
    ankle 718.87
    elbow 718.82
    foot 718.87
    hand 718.84
    hip 718.85
    knee 718.86
    multiple sites 718.89
    pelvic region 718.85
    shoulder (region) 718.81
    specified site NEC 718.88
    wrist 718.83
kidney — *see* Injury, internal, kidney
knee (and ankle) (and foot) (and leg, except thigh) 959.7
labium (majus) (minus) 959.14
labyrinth, ear 959.09
lacrimal apparatus, gland, or sac 921.1
  laceration 870.8
larynx 959.09
late effect — *see* Late, effects (of), injury
leg, except thigh (and ankle) (and foot) (and knee) 959.7
  upper or thigh 959.6
lens, eye 921.3
  penetrating — *see* Injury, eyeball, penetrating
lid, eye — *see* Injury, eyelid
lip 959.09
liver — *see* Injury, internal, liver
lobe, parietal — *see* Injury, intracranial
lumbar (region) 959.19
  plexus 953.5
lumbosacral (region) 959.19
  plexus 953.5
lung — *see* Injury, internal, lung
malar region 959.09
mastoid region 959.09
maternal, during pregnancy, affecting fetus or newborn 760.5
maxilla 959.09
mediastinum — *see* Injury, internal, mediastinum
membrane
  brain (*see also* Injury, intracranial) 854.0 ☑
  tympanic 959.09
meningeal artery — *see* Hemorrhage, brain, traumatic, subarachnoid
meninges (cerebral) — *see* Injury, intracranial
mesenteric
  artery — *see* Injury, blood vessel, mesenteric, artery
  plexus, inferior 954.1
  vein — *see* Injury, blood vessel, mesenteric, vein
mesentery — *see* Injury, internal, mesentery
mesosalpinx — *see* Injury, internal, mesosalpinx
middle ear 959.09
midthoracic region 959.11
mouth 959.09
multiple (sites not classifiable to the same four–digit category in 959.0–959.7) 959.8
  internal 869.0
    with open wound into cavity 869.1
musculocutaneous nerve 955.4
nail
  finger 959.5
  toe 959.7
nasal (septum) (sinus) 959.09

Injury — *continued*
nasopharynx 959.09
neck (and face) 959.09
nerve 957.9
  abducens 951.3
  abducent 951.3
  accessory 951.6
  acoustic 951.5
  ankle and foot 956.9
  anterior crural, femoral 956.1
  arm (*see also* Injury, nerve, upper limb) 955.9
  auditory 951.5
  axillary 955.0
  brachial plexus 953.4
  cervical sympathetic 954.0
  cranial 951.9
    first or olfactory 951.8
    second or optic 950.0
    third or oculomotor 951.0
    fourth or trochlear 951.1
    fifth or trigeminal 951.2
    sixth or abducens 951.3
    seventh or facial 951.4
    eighth, acoustic, or auditory 951.5
    ninth or glossopharyngeal 951.8
    tenth, pneumogastric, or vagus 951.8
    eleventh or accessory 951.6
    twelfth or hypoglossal 951.7
    newborn 767.7
  cutaneous sensory
    lower limb 956.4
    upper limb 955.5
  digital (finger) 955.6
    toe 956.5
  facial 951.4
    newborn 767.5
  femoral 956.1
  finger 955.9
  foot and ankle 956.9
  forearm 955.9
  glossopharyngeal 951.8
  hand and wrist 955.9
  head and neck, superficial 957.0
  hypoglossal 951.7
  involving several parts of body 957.8
  leg (*see also* Injury, nerve, lower limb) 956.9
  lower limb 956.9
    multiple 956.9
    specified site NEC 956.5
  lumbar plexus 953.5
  lumbosacral plexus 953.5
  median 955.1
    forearm 955.1
    wrist and hand 955.1
  multiple (in several parts of body) (sites not classifiable to the same three-digit category) 957.8
  musculocutaneous 955.4
  musculospiral 955.3
    upper arm 955.3
  oculomotor 951.0
  olfactory 951.8
  optic 950.0
  pelvic girdle 956.9
    multiple sites 956.8
    specified site NEC 956.5
  peripheral 957.9
    multiple (in several regions) (sites not classifiable to the same three-digit category) 957.8
    specified site NEC 957.1
  peroneal 956.3
    ankle and foot 956.3
    lower leg 956.3
  plantar 956.5
  plexus 957.9
    celiac 954.1
    mesenteric, inferior 954.1
    spinal 953.9

Injury — *continued*
nerve — *continued*
  plexus — *continued*
    spinal — *continued*
      brachial 953.4
      lumbosacral 953.5
      multiple sites 953.8
      sympathetic NEC 954.1
  pneumogastric 951.8
  radial 955.3
    wrist and hand 955.3
  sacral plexus 953.5
  sciatic 956.0
    thigh 956.0
  shoulder girdle 955.9
    multiple 955.8
    specified site NEC 955.7
  specified site NEC 957.1
  spinal 953.9
    plexus — *see* Injury, nerve, plexus, spinal
    root 953.9
      cervical 953.0
      dorsal 953.1
      lumbar 953.2
      multiple sites 953.8
      sacral 953.3
    splanchnic 954.1
    sympathetic NEC 954.1
      cervical 954.0
  thigh 956.9
  tibial 956.5
    ankle and foot 956.2
    lower leg 956.5
    posterior 956.2
  toe 956.9
  trigeminal 951.2
  trochlear 951.1
  trunk, excluding shoulder and pelvic girdles 954.9
    specified site NEC 954.8
    sympathetic NEC 954.1
  ulnar 955.2
    forearm 955.2
    wrist (and hand) 955.2
  upper limb 955.9
    multiple 955.8
    specified site NEC 955.7
  vagus 951.8
  wrist and hand 955.9
nervous system, diffuse 957.8
nose (septum) 959.09
obstetrical NEC 665.9 ☑
  affecting fetus or newborn 763.89
occipital (region) (scalp) 959.09
  lobe (*see also* Injury, intracranial) 854.0 ☑
optic 950.9
  chiasm 950.1
  cortex 950.3
  nerve 950.0
  pathways 950.2
orbit, orbital (region) 921.2
  penetrating 870.3
    with foreign body 870.4
ovary — *see* Injury, internal, ovary
paint-gun — *see* Wound, open, by site, complicated
palate (soft) 959.09
pancreas — *see* Injury, internal, pancreas
parathyroid (gland) 959.09
parietal (region) (scalp) 959.09
  lobe — *see* Injury, intracranial
pelvic
  floor 959.19
    complicating delivery 664.1 ☑
      affecting fetus or newborn 763.89
    joint or ligament, complicating delivery 665.6 ☑
      affecting fetus or newborn 763.89
  organs (*see also* Injury, internal, pelvis)

Injury — *continued*
pelvic — *continued*
  organs (*see also* Injury, internal, pelvis) — *continued*
    with
      abortion — *see* Abortion, by type, with damage to pelvic organs
      ectopic pregnancy (*see also* categories 633.0–633.9) 639.2
      molar pregnancy (*see also* categories 633.0–633.9) 639.2
    following
      abortion 639.2
      ectopic or molar pregnancy 639.2
    obstetrical trauma 665.5 ☑
      affecting fetus or newborn 763.89
pelvis 959.19
penis 959.14
  fracture of corpus cavernosum 959.13
perineum 959.14
peritoneum — *see* Injury, internal, peritoneum
periurethral tissue
  with
    abortion — *see* Abortion, by type, with damage to pelvic organs
    ectopic pregnancy (*see also* categories 633.0–633.9) 639.2
    molar pregnancy (*see also* categories 630–632) 639.2
  complicating delivery 665.5 ☑
    affecting fetus or newborn 763.89
  following
    abortion 639.2
    ectopic or molar pregnancy 639.2
phalanges
  foot 959.7
  hand 959.5
pharynx 959.09
pleura — *see* Injury, internal, pleura
popliteal space 959.7
post-cardiac surgery (syndrome) 429.4
prepuce 959.14
prostate — *see* Injury, internal, prostate
pubic region 959.19
pudenda 959.14
radiation NEC 990
radioactive substance or radium NEC 990
rectovaginal septum 959.14
rectum — *see* Injury, internal, rectum
retina 921.3
  penetrating — *see* Injury, eyeball, penetrating
retroperitoneal — *see* Injury, internal, retroperitoneum
roentgen rays NEC 990
round ligament — *see* Injury, internal, round ligament
sacral (region) 959.19
  plexus 953.5
sacroiliac ligament NEC 959.19
sacrum 959.19
salivary ducts or glands 959.09
scalp 959.09
  due to birth trauma 767.19
  fetus or newborn 767.19
scapular region 959.2
sclera 921.3
  penetrating — *see* Injury, eyeball, penetrating
  superficial 918.2
scrotum 959.14

☑ Additional Digit Required — Refer to the Tabular List for Digit Selection   ▽ Subterms under main terms may continue to next column or page

166 — Volume 2 · October 2006   ▶◀ Revised Text   ● New Line   ▲ Revised Code   *2007 ICD-9-CM*

Injury — continued

seminal vesicle — see Injury, internal, seminal vesicle

shoulder (and upper arm) 959.2

sinus

  cavernous (see also Injury, intracranial) 854.0 ☑

  nasal 959.09

skeleton NEC, birth injury 767.3

skin NEC 959.9

skull — see Fracture, skull, by site

soft tissue (of external sites) (severe) — see Wound, open, by site

specified site NEC 959.8

spermatic cord — see Injury, internal, spermatic cord

spinal (cord) 952.9

  with fracture, vertebra — see Fracture, vertebra, by site, with spinal cord injury

  cervical (C$_1$-C$_4$) 952.00

    with

      anterior cord syndrome 952.02

      central cord syndrome 952.03

      complete lesion of cord 952.01

      incomplete lesion NEC 952.04

      posterior cord syndrome 952.04

    C$_5$-C$_7$ level 952.05

      with

        anterior cord syndrome 952.07

        central cord syndrome 952.08

        complete lesion of cord 952.06

        incomplete lesion NEC 952.09

        posterior cord syndrome 952.09

    specified type NEC 952.09

    specified type NEC 952.04

  dorsal (D$_1$-D$_6$) (T$_1$-T$_6$) (thoracic) 952.10

    with

      anterior cord syndrome 952.12

      central cord syndrome 952.13

      complete lesion of cord 952.11

      incomplete lesion NEC 952.14

      posterior cord syndrome 952.14

  D$_7$-D$_{12}$ level (T$_7$-T$_{12}$) 952.15

    with

      anterior cord syndrome 952.17

      central cord syndrome 952.18

      complete lesion of cord 952.16

      incomplete lesion NEC 952.19

      posterior cord syndrome 952.19

    specified type NEC 952.19

    specified type NEC 952.14

  lumbar 952.2

  multiple sites 952.8

  nerve (root) NEC — see Injury, nerve, spinal, root

  plexus 953.9

    brachial 953.4

    lumbosacral 953.5

    multiple sites 953.8

  sacral 952.3

  thoracic (see also Injury, spinal, dorsal) 952.10

spleen — see Injury, internal, spleen

Injury — continued

stellate ganglion 954.1

sternal region 959.11

stomach — see Injury, internal, stomach

subconjunctival 921.1

subcutaneous 959.9

subdural — see Injury, intracranial

submaxillary region 959.09

submental region 959.09

subungual

  fingers 959.5

  toes 959.7

superficial 919 ☑

> Note — Use the following fourth-digit subdivisions with categories 910–919:
>
> 0   Abrasion or friction burn without mention of infection
>
> 1   Abrasion or friction burn, infected
>
> 2   Blister without mention of infection
>
> 3   Blister, infected
>
> 4   Insect bite, nonvenomous, without mention of infection
>
> 5   Insect bite, nonvenomous, infected
>
> 6   Superficial foreign body (splinter) without major open wound and without mention of infection
>
> 7   Superficial foreign body (splinter) without major open wound, infected
>
> 8   Other and unspecified superficial injury without mention of infection
>
> 9   Other and unspecified superficial injury, infected
>
> For late effects of superficial injury, see category 906.2.

  abdomen, abdominal (muscle) (wall) (and other part(s) of trunk) 911 ☑

  ankle (and hip, knee, leg, or thigh) 916 ☑

  anus (and other part(s) of trunk) 911 ☑

  arm 913 ☑

    upper (and shoulder) 912 ☑

  auditory canal (external) (meatus) (and other part(s) of face, neck, or scalp, except eye) 910 ☑

  axilla (and upper arm) 912 ☑

  back (and other part(s) of trunk) 911 ☑

  breast (and other part(s) of trunk) 911 ☑

  brow (and other part(s) of face, neck, or scalp, except eye) 910 ☑

  buttock (and other part(s) of trunk) 911 ☑

  canthus, eye 918.0

  cheek(s) (and other part(s) of face, neck, or scalp, except eye) 910 ☑

  chest wall (and other part(s) of trunk) 911 ☑

  chin (and other part(s) of face, neck, or scalp, except eye) 910 ☑

  clitoris (and other part(s) of trunk) 911 ☑

  conjunctiva 918.2

  cornea 918.1

    due to contact lens 371.82

  costal region (and other part(s) of trunk) 911 ☑

Injury — continued

superficial — continued

  ear(s) (auricle) (canal) (drum) (external) (and other part(s) of face, neck, or scalp, except eye) 910 ☑

  elbow (and forearm) (and wrist) 913 ☑

  epididymis (and other part(s) of trunk) 911 ☑

  epigastric region (and other part(s) of trunk) 911 ☑

  epiglottis (and other part(s) of face, neck, or scalp, except eye) 910 ☑

  eye(s) (and adnexa) NEC 918.9

  eyelid(s) (and periocular area) 918.0

  face (any part(s), except eye) (and neck or scalp) 910 ☑

  finger(s) (nail) (any) 915 ☑

  flank (and other part(s) of trunk) 911 ☑

  foot (phalanges) (and toe(s)) 917 ☑

  forearm (and elbow) (and wrist) 913 ☑

  forehead (and other part(s) of face, neck, or scalp, except eye) 910 ☑

  globe (eye) 918.9

  groin (and other part(s) of trunk) 911 ☑

  gum(s) (and other part(s) of face, neck, or scalp, except eye) 910 ☑

  hand(s) (except fingers alone) 914 ☑

  head (and other part(s) of face, neck, or scalp, except eye) 910 ☑

  heel (and foot or toe) 917 ☑

  hip (and ankle, knee, leg, or thigh) 916 ☑

  iliac region (and other part(s) of trunk) 911 ☑

  interscapular region (and other part(s) of trunk) 911 ☑

  iris 918.9

  knee (and ankle, hip, leg, or thigh) 916 ☑

  labium (majus) (minus) (and other part(s) of trunk) 911 ☑

  lacrimal (apparatus) (gland) (sac) 918.0

  leg (lower) (upper) (and ankle, hip, knee, or thigh) 916 ☑

  lip(s) (and other part(s) of face, neck, or scalp, except eye) 910 ☑

  lower extremity (except foot) 916 ☑

  lumbar region (and other part(s) of trunk) 911 ☑

  malar region (and other part(s) of face, neck, or scalp, except eye) 910 ☑

  mastoid region (and other part(s) of face, neck, or scalp, except eye) 910 ☑

  midthoracic region (and other part(s) of trunk) 911 ☑

  mouth (and other part(s) of face, neck, or scalp, except eye) 910 ☑

  multiple sites (not classifiable to the same three-digit category) 919 ☑

  nasal (septum) (and other part(s) of face, neck, or scalp, except eye) 910 ☑

  neck (and face or scalp, any part(s), except eye) 910 ☑

  nose (septum) (and other part(s) of face, neck, or scalp, except eye) 910 ☑

Injury — continued

superficial — continued

  occipital region (and other part(s) of face, neck, or scalp, except eye) 910 ☑

  orbital region 918.0

  palate (soft) (and other part(s) of face, neck, or scalp, except eye) 910 ☑

  parietal region (and other part(s) of face, neck, or scalp, except eye) 910 ☑

  penis (and other part(s) of trunk) 911 ☑

  perineum (and other part(s) of trunk) 911 ☑

  periocular area 918.0

  pharynx (and other part(s) of face, neck, or scalp, except eye) 910 ☑

  popliteal space (and ankle, hip, leg, or thigh) 916 ☑

  prepuce (and other part(s) of trunk) 911 ☑

  pubic region (and other part(s) of trunk) 911 ☑

  pudenda (and other part(s) of trunk) 911 ☑

  sacral region (and other part(s) of trunk) 911 ☑

  salivary (ducts) (glands) (and other part(s) of face, neck, or scalp, except eye) 910 ☑

  scalp (and other part(s) of face or neck, except eye) 910 ☑

  scapular region (and upper arm) 912 ☑

  sclera 918.2

  scrotum (and other part(s) of trunk) 911 ☑

  shoulder (and upper arm) 912 ☑

  skin NEC 919 ☑

  specified site(s) NEC 919 ☑

  sternal region (and other part(s) of trunk) 911 ☑

  subconjunctival 918.2

  subcutaneous NEC 919 ☑

  submaxillary region (and other part(s) of face, neck, or scalp, except eye) 910 ☑

  submental region (and other part(s) of face, neck, or scalp, except eye) 910 ☑

  supraclavicular fossa (and other part(s) of face, neck, or scalp, except eye) 910 ☑

  supraorbital 918.0

  temple (and other part(s) of face, neck, or scalp, except eye) 910 ☑

  temporal region (and other part(s) of face, neck, or scalp, except eye) 910 ☑

  testis (and other part(s) of trunk) 911 ☑

  thigh (and ankle, hip, knee, or leg) 916 ☑

  thorax, thoracic (external) (and other part(s) of trunk) 911 ☑

  throat (and other part(s) of face, neck, or scalp, except eye) 910 ☑

  thumb(s) (nail) 915 ☑

  toe(s) (nail) (subungual) (and foot) 917 ☑

  tongue (and other part(s) of face, neck, or scalp, except eye) 910 ☑

  tooth, teeth (see also Abrasion, dental) 521.20

  trunk (any part(s)) 911 ☑

  tunica vaginalis 959.14

☑ Additional Digit Required — Refer to the Tabular List for Digit Selection   ▽ Subterms under main terms may continue to next column or page

2007 ICD-9-CM   ▶◀ Revised Text   ● New Line   ▲ Revised Code   **Volume 2 — 167**

Injury — *continued*
  superficial — *continued*
    tympanum, tympanic membrane (and other part(s) of face, neck, or scalp, except eye) 910 ☑
      upper extremity NEC 913 ☑
    uvula (and other part(s) of face, neck, or scalp, except eye) 910 ☑
    vagina (and other part(s) of trunk) 911 ☑
    vulva (and other part(s) of trunk) 911 ☑
    wrist (and elbow) (and forearm) 913 ☑
  supraclavicular fossa 959.19
  supraorbital 959.09
  surgical complication (external or internal site) 998.2
  symphysis pubis 959.19
    complicating delivery 665.6 ☑
      affecting fetus or newborn 763.89
  temple 959.09
  temporal region 959.09
  testis 959.14
  thigh (and hip) 959.6
  thorax, thoracic (external) 959.11
    cavity — *see* Injury, internal, thorax
    internal — *see* Injury, internal, intrathoracic organs
  throat 959.09
  thumb(s) (nail) 959.5
  thymus — *see* Injury, internal, thymus
  thyroid (gland) 959.09
  toe (nail) (any) 959.7
  tongue 959.09
  tonsil 959.09
  tooth NEC 873.63
    complicated 873.73
  trachea — *see* Injury, internal, trachea
  trunk 959.19
  tunica vaginalis 959.14
  tympanum, tympanic membrane 959.09
  ultraviolet rays NEC 990
  ureter — *see* Injury, internal, ureter
  urethra (sphincter) — *see* Injury, internal, urethra
  uterus — *see* Injury, internal, uterus
  uvula 959.09
  vagina 959.14
  vascular — *see* Injury, blood vessel
  vas deferens — *see* Injury, internal, vas deferens
  vein (*see also* Injury, blood vessel, by site) 904.9
  vena cava
    inferior 902.10
    superior 901.2
  vesical (sphincter) — *see* Injury, internal, vesical
  viscera (abdominal) — *see* Injury, internal, viscera
    with fracture, pelvis — *see* Fracture, pelvis
  visual 950.9
    cortex 950.3
  vitreous (humor) 871.2
  vulva 959.14
  whiplash (cervical spine) 847.0
  wringer — *see* Crush, by site
  wrist (and elbow) (and forearm) 959.3
  x-ray NEC 990
Inoculation — *see also* Vaccination
  complication or reaction — *see* Complication, vaccination
Insanity, insane — *see also* Psychosis 298.9
  adolescent (*see also* Schizophrenia) 295.9 ☑

Insanity, insane — *see also* Psychosis — *continued*
  alternating (*see also* Psychosis, affective, circular) 296.7
  confusional 298.9
    acute 293.0
    subacute 293.1
  delusional 298.9
  paralysis, general 094.1
    progressive 094.1
  paresis, general 094.1
  senile 290.20
Insect
  bite — *see* Injury, superficial, by site
  venomous, poisoning by 989.5
Insemination, artificial V26.1
Insensitivity
  androgen 259.5
    partial 259.5
Insertion
  cord (umbilical) lateral or velamentous 663.8 ☑
    affecting fetus or newborn 762.6
  intrauterine contraceptive device V25.1
  placenta, vicious — *see* Placenta, previa
  subdermal implantable contraceptive V25.5
  velamentous, umbilical cord 663.8 ☑
    affecting fetus or newborn 762.6
Insolation 992.0
  meaning sunstroke 992.0
Insomnia, unspecified 780.52
  with sleep apnea, unspecified 780.51
  adjustment 307.41
  alcohol induced 291.82
  behavioral, of childhood V69.5
  drug induced 292.85
  due to
    medical condition classified elsewhere 327.01
    mental disorder 327.02
  idiopathic 307.42
  nonorganic origin 307.41
    persistent (primary) 307.42
    transient 307.41
  organic 327.00
    other 327.09
  paradoxical 307.42
  primary 307.42
  psychophysiological 307.42
  subjective complaint 307.49
Inspiration
  food or foreign body (*see also* Asphyxia, food or foreign body) 933.1
  mucus (*see also* Asphyxia, mucus) 933.1
Inspissated bile syndrome, newborn 774.4
Instability
  detrusor 596.59
  emotional (excessive) 301.3
  joint (posttraumatic) 718.80
    ankle 718.87
    elbow 718.82
    foot 718.87
    hand 718.84
    hip 718.85
    knee 718.86
    lumbosacral 724.6
    multiple sites 718.89
    pelvic region 718.85
    sacroiliac 724.6
    shoulder (region) 718.81
    specified site NEC 718.88
    wrist 718.83
  lumbosacral 724.6
  nervous 301.89
  personality (emotional) 301.59
  thyroid, paroxysmal 242.9 ☑
  urethral 599.83
  vasomotor 780.2
Insufficiency, insufficient
  accommodation 367.4
  adrenal (gland) (acute) (chronic) 255.4

Insufficiency, insufficient — *continued*
  adrenal — *continued*
    medulla 255.5
    primary 255.4
    specified site NEC 255.5
  adrenocortical 255.4
  anterior ▶(occlusal)◀ guidance 524.54
  anus 569.49
  aortic (valve) 424.1
    with
      mitral (valve) disease 396.1
        insufficiency, incompetence, or regurgitation 396.3
        stenosis or obstruction 396.1
      stenosis or obstruction 424.1
        with mitral (valve) disease 396.8
    congenital 746.4
    rheumatic 395.1
      with
        mitral (valve) disease 396.1
          insufficiency, incompetence, or regurgitation 396.3
          stenosis or obstruction 396.1
        stenosis or obstruction 395.2
          with mitral (valve) disease 396.8
    specified cause NEC 424.1
    syphilitic 093.22
  arterial 447.1
    basilar artery 435.0
    carotid artery 435.8
    cerebral 437.1
    coronary (acute or subacute) 411.89
    mesenteric 557.1
    peripheral 443.9
    precerebral 435.9
    vertebral artery 435.1
    vertebrobasilar 435.3
  arteriovenous 459.9
  basilar artery 435.0
  biliary 575.8
  cardiac (*see also* Insufficiency, myocardial) 428.0
    complicating surgery 997.1
    due to presence of (cardiac) prosthesis 429.4
    postoperative 997.1
      long-term effect of cardiac surgery 429.4
    specified during or due to a procedure 997.1
      long-term effect of cardiac surgery 429.4
  cardiorenal (*see also* Hypertension, cardiorenal) 404.90
  cardiovascular (*see also* Disease, cardiovascular) 429.2
    renal (*see also* Hypertension, cardiorenal) 404.90
  carotid artery 435.8
  cerebral (vascular) 437.9
  cerebrovascular 437.9
    with transient focal neurological signs and symptoms 435.9
    acute 437.1
      with transient focal neurological signs and symptoms 435.9
  circulatory NEC 459.9
    fetus or newborn 779.89
  convergence 378.83
  coronary (acute or subacute) 411.89
    chronic or with a stated duration of over 8 weeks 414.8
  corticoadrenal 255.4
  dietary 269.9
  divergence 378.85
  food 994.2
  gastroesophageal 530.89
  gonadal
    ovary 256.39

Insufficiency, insufficient — *continued*
  gonadal — *continued*
    testis 257.2
  gonadotropic hormone secretion 253.4
  heart (*see also* Insufficiency, myocardial)
    fetus or newborn 779.89
    valve (*see also* Endocarditis) 424.90
      congenital NEC 746.89
  hepatic 573.8
  idiopathic autonomic 333.0
  interocclusal distance of teeth (ridge) 524.36
  kidney
    acute 593.9
    chronic 585.9
  labyrinth, labyrinthine (function) 386.53
    bilateral 386.54
    unilateral 386.53
  lacrimal 375.15
  liver 573.8
  lung (acute) (*see also* Insufficiency, pulmonary) 518.82
    following trauma, surgery, or shock 518.5
    newborn 770.89
  mental (congenital) (*see also* Retardation, mental) 319
  mesenteric 557.1
  mitral (valve) 424.0
    with
      aortic (valve) disease 396.3
        insufficiency, incompetence, or regurgitation 396.3
        stenosis or obstruction 396.2
      obstruction or stenosis 394.2
        with aortic valve disease 396.8
    congenital 746.6
    rheumatic 394.1
      with
        aortic (valve) disease 396.3
          insufficiency, incompetence, or regurgitation 396.3
          stenosis or obstruction 396.2
        obstruction or stenosis 394.2
          with aortic valve disease 396.8
        active or acute 391.1
          with chorea, rheumatic (Sydenham's) 392.0
    specified cause, except rheumatic 424.0
  muscle
    heart — *see* Insufficiency, myocardial
    ocular (*see also* Strabismus) 378.9
  myocardial, myocardium (with arteriosclerosis) 428.0
    with rheumatic fever (conditions classifiable to 390)
      active, acute, or subacute 391.2
        with chorea 392.0
      inactive or quiescent (with chorea) 398.0
    congenital 746.89
    due to presence of (cardiac) prosthesis 429.4
    fetus or newborn 779.89
    following cardiac surgery 429.4
    hypertensive (*see also* Hypertension, heart) 402.91
      benign 402.11
      malignant 402.01
    postoperative 997.1
      long-term effect of cardiac surgery 429.4
    rheumatic 398.0
      active, acute, or subacute 391.2
        with chorea (Sydenham's) 392.0

Insufficiency, insufficient — continued
  myocardial, myocardium — continued
    syphilitic 093.82
  nourishment 994.2
  organic 799.89
  ovary 256.39
    postablative 256.2
  pancreatic 577.8
  parathyroid (gland) 252.1
  peripheral vascular (arterial) 443.9
  pituitary (anterior) 253.2
    posterior 253.5
  placental — see Placenta, insufficiency
  platelets 287.5
  prenatal care in current pregnancy
    V23.7
  progressive pluriglandular 258.9
  pseudocholinesterase 289.89
  pulmonary (acute) 518.82
    following
      shock 518.5
      surgery 518.5
      trauma 518.5
    newborn 770.89
    valve (see also Endocarditis, pulmonary) 424.3
      congenital 746.09
  pyloric 537.0
  renal 593.9   ▲
    acute 593.9
    chronic 585.9
    due to a procedure 997.5
  respiratory 786.09
    acute 518.82
      following shock, surgery, or trauma 518.5
    newborn 770.89
  rotation — see Malrotation
  suprarenal 255.4
    medulla 255.5
  tarso-orbital fascia, congenital 743.66
  tear film 375.15
  testis 257.2
  thyroid (gland) (acquired) (see also Hypothyroidism)
    congenital 243
  tricuspid (see also Endocarditis, tricuspid) 397.0
    congenital 746.89
    syphilitic 093.23
  urethral sphincter 599.84
  valve, valvular (heart) (see also Endocarditis) 424.90
  vascular 459.9
    intestine NEC 557.9
    mesenteric 557.1
    peripheral 443.9
    renal (see also Hypertension, kidney) 403.90
  velopharyngeal
    acquired 528.9
    congenital 750.29
  venous (peripheral) 459.81
  ventricular — see Insufficiency, myocardial
  vertebral artery 435.1
  vertebrobasilar artery 435.3
  weight gain during pregnancy 646.8 ☑
  zinc 269.3
Insufflation
  fallopian
    fertility testing V26.21
    following sterilization reversal V26.22
  meconium 770.11
    with respiratory symptoms 770.12
Insular — see condition
Insulinoma (M8151/0)
  malignant (M8151/3)
    pancreas 157.4
    specified site — see Neoplasm, by site, malignant
    unspecified site 157.4
  pancreas 211.7

Insulinoma — continued
  specified site — see Neoplasm, by site, benign
  unspecified site 211.7
Insuloma — see Insulinoma
Insult
  brain 437.9
    acute 436
  cerebral 437.9
    acute 436
  cerebrovascular 437.9
    acute 436
  vascular NEC 437.9
    acute 436
Insurance examination (certification) V70.3
Intemperance — see also Alcoholism 303.9 ☑
Interception of pregnancy (menstrual extraction) V25.3
Interference   ●
  balancing side 524.56   ●
  non-working side 524.56   ●
Intermenstrual
  bleeding 626.6
    irregular 626.6
    regular 626.5
  hemorrhage 626.6
    irregular 626.6
    regular 626.5
  pain(s) 625.2
Intermittent — see condition
Internal — see condition
Interproximal wear 521.10
Interruption
  aortic arch 747.11
  bundle of His 426.50
  fallopian tube (for sterilization) V25.2
  phase-shift, sleep cycle 307.45
  repeated REM-sleep 307.48
  sleep
    due to perceived environmental disturbances 307.48
    phase-shift, of 24-hour sleep-wake cycle 307.45
    repeated REM-sleep type 307.48
  vas deferens (for sterilization) V25.2
Intersexuality 752.7
Interstitial — see condition
Intertrigo 695.89
  labialis 528.5
Intervertebral disc — see condition
Intestine, intestinal — see also condition
  flu 487.8
Intolerance
  carbohydrate NEC 579.8
  cardiovascular exercise, with pain (at rest) (with less than ordinary activity) (with ordinary activity) V47.2
  cold 780.99
  dissacharide (hereditary) 271.3
  drug
    correct substance properly administered 995.27   ▲
    wrong substance given or taken in error 977.9
    specified drug — see Table of Drugs and Chemicals
  effort 306.2
  fat NEC 579.8
  foods NEC 579.8
  fructose (hereditary) 271.2
  glucose (-galactose) (congenital) 271.3
  gluten 579.0
  lactose (hereditary) (infantile) 271.3
  lysine (congenital) 270.7
  milk NEC 579.8
  protein (familial) 270.7
  starch NEC 579.8
  sucrose (-isomaltose) (congenital) 271.3
Intoxicated NEC — see also Alcoholism 305.0 ☑

Intoxication
  acid 276.2
  acute
    alcoholic 305.0 ☑
      with alcoholism 303.0 ☑
      hangover effects 305.0 ☑
    caffeine 305.9 ☑
    hallucinogenic (see also Abuse, drugs, nondependent) 305.3 ☑
  alcohol (acute) 305.0 ☑
    with alcoholism 303.0 ☑
    hangover effects 305.0 ☑
    idiosyncratic 291.4
    pathological 291.4
  alimentary canal 558.2
  ammonia (hepatic) 572.2
  caffeine 305.9 ☑
  chemical (see also Table of Drugs and Chemicals)
    via placenta or breast milk 760.70
      alcohol 760.71
      anticonvulsants
      antifungals
      anti-infective agents 760.74
      antimetabolics
      cocaine 760.75
      "crack" 760.75
      hallucinogenic agents NEC 760.73
      medicinal agents NEC 760.79
      narcotics 760.72
      obstetric anesthetic or analgesic drug 763.5
      specified agent NEC 760.79
      suspected, affecting management of pregnancy 655.5 ☑
  cocaine, through placenta or breast milk 760.75
  delirium
    alcohol 291.0
    drug 292.81
  drug 292.89
    with delirium 292.81
    correct substance properly administered (see also Allergy, drug) 995.27   ▲
    newborn 779.4
    obstetric anesthetic or sedation 668.9 ☑
      affecting fetus or newborn 763.5
    overdose or wrong substance given or taken — see Table of Drugs and Chemicals
    pathologic 292.2
    specific to newborn 779.4
    via placenta or breast milk 760.70
      alcohol 760.71
      anticonvulsants 760.77
      antifungals 760.74
      anti-infective agents 760.74
      antimetabolics 760.78
      cocaine 760.75
      "crack" 760.75
      hallucinogenic agents 760.73
      medicinal agents NEC 760.79
      narcotics 760.72
      obstetric anesthetic or analgesic drug 763.5
      specified agent NEC 760.79
      suspected, affecting management of pregnancy 655.5 ☑
  enteric — see Intoxication, intestinal
  fetus or newborn, via placenta or breast milk 760.70
    alcohol 760.71
    anticonvulsants 760.77
    antifungals 760.74
    anti-infective agents 760.74
    antimetabolics 760.78
    cocaine 760.75
    "crack" 760.75
    hallucinogenic agents 760.73
    medicinal agents NEC 760.79

Intoxication — continued
  fetus or newborn, via placenta or breast milk — continued
    narcotics 760.72
    obstetric anesthetic or analgesic drug 763.5
    specified agent NEC 760.79
    suspected, affecting management of pregnancy 655.5 ☑
  food — see Poisoning, food
  gastrointestinal 558.2
  hallucinogenic (acute) 305.3 ☑
  hepatocerebral 572.2
  idiosyncratic alcohol 291.4
  intestinal 569.89
    due to putrefaction of food 005.9
  methyl alcohol (see also Alcoholism) 305.0 ☑
    with alcoholism 303.0 ☑
  pathologic 291.4
    drug 292.2
  potassium (K) 276.7
  septic
    with
      abortion — see Abortion, by type, with sepsis
      ectopic pregnancy (see also categories 633.0–633.9) 639.0
      molar pregnancy (see also categories 630–632) 639.0
    during labor 659.3 ☑
    following
      abortion 639.0
      ectopic or molar pregnancy 639.0
    generalized — see Septicemia
    puerperal, postpartum, childbirth 670.0 ☑
  serum (prophylactic) (therapeutic) 999.5
  uremic — see Uremia
  water 276.6
Intracranial — see condition
Intrahepatic gallbladder 751.69
Intraligamentous — see condition
  pregnancy — see Pregnancy, cornual
Intraocular — see also condition
  sepsis 360.00
Intrathoracic — see also condition
  kidney 753.3
  stomach — see Hernia, diaphragm
Intrauterine contraceptive device
  checking V25.42
  insertion V25.1
  in situ V45.51
  management V25.42
  prescription V25.02
  repeat V25.42
  reinsertion V25.42
  removal V25.42
Intraventricular — see condition
Intrinsic deformity — see Deformity
Intruded tooth 524.34   ●
Intrusion, repetitive, of sleep (due to environmental disturbances) (with atypical polysomnographic features) 307.48
Intumescent, lens (eye) NEC 366.9
  senile 366.12
Intussusception (colon) (enteric) (intestine) (rectum) 560.0
  appendix 543.9
  congenital 751.5
  fallopian tube 620.8
  ileocecal 560.0
  ileocolic 560.0
  ureter (with obstruction) 593.4
Invagination
  basilar 756.0
  colon or intestine 560.0
Invalid (since birth) 799.89
Invalidism (chronic) 799.89
Inversion
  albumin-globulin (A-G) ratio 273.8
  bladder 596.8

☑ Additional Digit Required — Refer to the Tabular List for Digit Selection   ▽ Subterms under main terms may continue to next column or page

2007 ICD-9-CM   ►◄ Revised Text   ● New Line   ▲ Revised Code   October 2006 · Volume 2 — 169

Inversion — *continued*
- cecum (*see also* Intussusception) 560.0
- cervix 622.8
- nipple 611.79
  - congenital 757.6
  - puerperal, postpartum 676.3 ☑
- optic papilla 743.57
- organ or site, congenital NEC — *see* Anomaly, specified type NEC
- sleep rhythm 327.39
  - nonorganic origin 307.45
- testis (congenital) 752.51
- uterus (postinfectional) (postpartal, old) 621.7
  - chronic 621.7
  - complicating delivery 665.2 ☑
    - affecting fetus or newborn 763.89
- vagina — *see* Prolapse, vagina

Investigation
- allergens V72.7
- clinical research (control) (normal comparison) (participant) V70.7

Inviability — *see* Immaturity

Involuntary movement, abnormal 781.0

Involution, involutional — *see also* condition
- breast, cystic or fibrocystic 610.1
- depression (*see also* Psychosis, affective) 296.2 ☑
  - recurrent episode 296.3 ☑
  - single episode 296.2 ☑
- melancholia (*see also* Psychosis, affective) 296.2 ☑
  - recurrent episode 296.3 ☑
  - single episode 296.2 ☑
- ovary, senile 620.3
- paranoid state (reaction) 297.2
- paraphrenia (climacteric) (menopause) 297.2
- psychosis 298.8
- thymus failure 254.8

IQ
- under 20 318.2
- 20-34 318.1
- 35-49 318.0
- 50-70 317

IRDS 769
Irideremia 743.45
Iridis rubeosis 364.42
- diabetic 250.5 ☑ *[364.42]*
Iridochoroiditis (panuveitis) 360.12
Iridocyclitis NEC 364.3
- acute 364.00
  - primary 364.01
  - recurrent 364.02
- chronic 364.10
  - in
    - lepromatous leprosy 030.0 *[364.11]*
    - sarcoidosis 135 *[364.11]*
    - tuberculosis (*see also* Tuberculosis) 017.3 ☑ *[364.11]*
- due to allergy 364.04
- endogenous 364.01
- gonococcal 098.41
- granulomatous 364.10
- herpetic (simplex) 054.44
  - zoster 053.22
- hypopyon 364.05
- lens induced 364.23
- nongranulomatous 364.00
- primary 364.01
- recurrent 364.02
- rheumatic 364.10
- secondary 364.04
  - infectious 364.03
  - noninfectious 364.04
- subacute 364.00
  - primary 364.01
  - recurrent 364.02
- sympathetic 360.11
- syphilitic (secondary) 091.52

Iridocyclitis — *continued*
- tuberculous (chronic) (*see also* Tuberculosis) 017.3 ☑ *[364.11]*
Iridocyclochoroiditis (panuveitis) 360.12
Iridodialysis 364.76
Iridodonesis 364.8
Iridoplegia (complete) (partial) (reflex) 379.49
Iridoschisis 364.52
Iris — *see* condition
Iritis 364.3
- acute 364.00
  - primary 364.01
  - recurrent 364.02
- chronic 364.10
  - in
    - sarcoidosis 135 *[364.11]*
    - tuberculosis (*see also* Tuberculosis) 017.3 ☑ *[364.11]*
- diabetic 250.5 ☑ *[364.42]*
- due to
  - allergy 364.04
  - herpes simplex 054.44
  - leprosy 030.0 *[364.11]*
- endogenous 364.01
- gonococcal 098.41
- gouty 274.89 *[364.11]*
- granulomatous 364.10
- hypopyon 364.05
- lens induced 364.23
- nongranulomatous 364.00
- papulosa 095.8 *[364.11]*
- primary 364.01
- recurrent 364.02
- rheumatic 364.10
- secondary 364.04
  - infectious 364.03
  - noninfectious 364.04
- subacute 364.00
  - primary 364.01
  - recurrent 364.02
- sympathetic 360.11
- syphilitic (secondary) 091.52
  - congenital 090.0 *[364.11]*
  - late 095.8 *[364.11]*
- tuberculous (*see also* Tuberculosis) 017.3 ☑ *[364.11]*
- uratic 274.89 *[364.11]*
Iron
- deficiency anemia 280.9
- metabolism disease 275.0
- storage disease 275.0
Iron-miners' lung 503
Irradiated enamel (tooth, teeth) 521.89 ▲
Irradiation
- burn — *see* Burn, by site
- effects, adverse 990
Irreducible, irreducibility — *see* condition
Irregular, irregularity
- action, heart 427.9
- alveolar process 525.8
- bleeding NEC 626.4
- breathing 786.09
- colon 569.89
- contour of cornea 743.41
  - acquired 371.70
- dentin in pulp 522.3
- eye movements NEC 379.59
- menstruation (cause unknown) 626.4
- periods 626.4
- prostate 602.9
- pupil 364.75
- respiratory 786.09
- septum (nasal) 470
- shape, organ or site, congenital NEC — *see* Distortion
- sleep-wake rhythm (non-24-hour) 327.39
  - nonorganic origin 307.45
- vertebra 733.99
Irritability (nervous) 799.2
- bladder 596.8
  - neurogenic 596.54

Irritability — *continued*
- bladder — *continued*
  - neurogenic — *continued*
    - with cauda equina syndrome 344.61
- bowel (syndrome) 564.1
- bronchial (*see also* Bronchitis) 490
- cerebral, newborn 779.1
- colon 564.1
  - psychogenic 306.4
- duodenum 564.89
- heart (psychogenic) 306.2
- ileum 564.89
- jejunum 564.89
- myocardium 306.2
- rectum 564.89
- stomach 536.9
  - psychogenic 306.4
- sympathetic (nervous system) (*see also* Neuropathy, peripheral, autonomic) 337.9
- urethra 599.84
- ventricular (heart) (psychogenic) 306.2
Irritable — *see* Irritability
Irritation
- anus 569.49
- axillary nerve 353.0
- bladder 596.8
- brachial plexus 353.0
- brain (traumatic) (*see also* Injury, intracranial) 854.0 ☑
  - nontraumatic — *see* Encephalitis
- bronchial (*see also* Bronchitis) 490
- cerebral (traumatic) (*see also* Injury, intracranial) 854.0 ☑
  - nontraumatic — *see* Encephalitis
- cervical plexus 353.2
- cervix (*see also* Cervicitis) 616.0
- choroid, sympathetic 360.11
- cranial nerve — *see* Disorder, nerve, cranial
- digestive tract 536.9
  - psychogenic 306.4
- gastric 536.9
  - psychogenic 306.4
- gastrointestinal (tract) 536.9
  - functional 536.9
  - psychogenic 306.4
- globe, sympathetic 360.11
- intestinal (bowel) 564.9
- labyrinth 386.50
- lumbosacral plexus 353.1
- meninges (traumatic) (*see also* Injury, intracranial) 854.0 ☑
  - nontraumatic — *see* Meningitis
- myocardium 306.2
- nerve — *see* Disorder, nerve
- nervous 799.2
- nose 478.19 ▲
- penis 607.89
- perineum 709.9
- peripheral
  - autonomic nervous system (*see also* Neuropathy, peripheral, autonomic) 337.9
  - nerve — *see* Disorder, nerve
- peritoneum (*see also* Peritonitis) 567.9
- pharynx 478.29
- plantar nerve 355.6
- spinal (cord) (traumatic) (*see also* Injury, spinal, by site)
  - nerve (*see also* Disorder, nerve)
    - root NEC 724.9
      - traumatic — *see* Injury, nerve, spinal
    - nontraumatic — *see* Myelitis
- stomach 536.9
  - psychogenic 306.4
- sympathetic nerve NEC (*see also* Neuropathy, peripheral, autonomic) 337.9
- ulnar nerve 354.2
- vagina 623.9
Isambert's disease 012.3 ☑
Ischemia, ischemic 459.9

Ischemia, ischemic — *continued*
- basilar artery (with transient neurologic deficit) 435.0
- bone NEC 733.40
- bowel (transient) 557.9
  - acute 557.0
  - chronic 557.1
  - due to mesenteric artery insufficiency 557.1
- brain (*see also* Ischemia, cerebral)
  - recurrent focal 435.9
- cardiac (*see also* Ischemia, heart) 414.9
- cardiomyopathy 414.8
- carotid artery (with transient neurologic deficit) 435.8
- cerebral (chronic) (generalized) 437.1
  - arteriosclerotic 437.0
  - intermittent (with transient neurologic deficit) 435.9
  - newborn 779.2 •
  - puerperal, postpartum, childbirth 674.0 ☑
  - recurrent focal (with transient neurologic deficit) 435.9
  - transient (with transient neurologic deficit) 435.9
- colon 557.9
  - acute 557.0
  - chronic 557.1
  - due to mesenteric artery insufficiency 557.1
- coronary (chronic) (*see also* Ischemia, heart) 414.9
- heart (chronic or with a stated duration of over 8 weeks) 414.9
  - acute or with a stated duration of 8 weeks or less (*see also* Infarct, myocardium) 410.9 ☑
    - without myocardial infarction 411.89
    - with coronary (artery) occlusion 411.81
  - subacute 411.89
- intestine (transient) 557.9
  - acute 557.0
  - chronic 557.1
  - due to mesenteric artery insufficiency 557.1
- kidney 593.81
- labyrinth 386.50
- muscles, leg 728.89
- myocardium, myocardial (chronic or with a stated duration of over 8 weeks) 414.8
  - acute (*see also* Infarct, myocardium) 410.9 ☑
    - without myocardial infarction 411.89
    - with coronary (artery) occlusion 411.81
- renal 593.81
- retina, retinal 362.84
- small bowel 557.9
  - acute 557.0
  - chronic 557.1
  - due to mesenteric artery insufficiency 557.1
- spinal cord 336.1
- subendocardial (*see also* Insufficiency, coronary) 411.89
- vertebral artery (with transient neurologic deficit) 435.1
Ischialgia — *see also* Sciatica 724.3
Ischiopagus 759.4
Ischium, ischial — *see* condition
Ischomenia 626.8
Ischuria 788.5
Iselin's disease or osteochondrosis 732.5
Islands of
- parotid tissue in
  - lymph nodes 750.26
  - neck structures 750.26
- submaxillary glands in
  - fascia 750.26

☑ Additional Digit Required — Refer to the Tabular List for Digit Selection ▽ Subterms under main terms may continue to next column or page

170 — Volume 2 · October 2006   ▶◀ Revised Text   ● New Line   ▲ Revised Code   *2007 ICD-9-CM*

Islands of — *continued*
  submaxillary glands in — *continued*
    lymph nodes 750.26
    neck muscles 750.26
Islet cell tumor, pancreas (M8150/0)
    211.7
Isoimmunization NEC — *see also* Incom-
    patibility 656.2 ☑
  fetus or newborn 773.2
    ABO blood groups 773.1
    Rhesus (Rh) factor 773.0
Isolation V07.0
  social V62.4
Isosporosis 007.2
Issue
  medical certificate NEC V68.0
    cause of death V68.0
    fitness V68.0

Issue — *continued*
  medical certificate — *continued*
    incapacity V68.0
  repeat prescription NEC V68.1
    appliance V68.1
    contraceptive V25.40
      device NEC V25.49
        intrauterine V25.42
        specified type NEC V25.49
      pill V25.41
    glasses V68.1
    medicinal substance V68.1
Itch — *see also* Pruritus 698.9
  bakers' 692.89
  barbers' 110.0
  bricklayers' 692.89
  cheese 133.8
  clam diggers' 120.3
  coolie 126.9

Itch — *see also* Pruritus — *continued*
  copra 133.8
  Cuban 050.1
  dew 126.9
  dhobie 110.3
  eye 379.99
  filarial (*see also* Infestation, filarial)
    125.9
  grain 133.8
  grocers' 133.8
  ground 126.9
  harvest 133.8
  jock 110.3
  Malabar 110.9
    beard 110.0
    foot 110.4
    scalp 110.0
  meaning scabies 133.0
  Norwegian 133.0

Itch — *see also* Pruritus — *continued*
  perianal 698.0
  poultrymen's 133.8
  sarcoptic 133.0
  scrub 134.1
  seven year V61.10
    meaning scabies 133.0
  straw 133.8
  swimmers' 120.3
  washerwoman's 692.4
  water 120.3
  winter 698.8
Itsenko-Cushing syndrome (pituitary
    basophilism) 255.0
Ivemark's syndrome (asplenia with
    congenital heart disease) 759.0
Ivory bones 756.52
Ixodes 134.8
Ixodiasis 134.8

☑ Additional Digit Required — Refer to the Tabular List for Digit Selection   ▽ Subterms under main terms may continue to next column or page

2007 ICD-9-CM   ▶◀ Revised Text   ● New Line   ▲ Revised Code   **Volume 2 — 171**

J

Jaccoud's nodular fibrositis, chronic
(Jaccoud's syndrome) 714.4
Jackson's
membrane 751.4
paralysis or syndrome 344.89
veil 751.4
Jacksonian
epilepsy (see also Epilepsy) 345.5 ☑
seizures (focal) (see also Epilepsy)
345.5 ☑
Jacob's ulcer (M8090/3) — see Neoplasm, skin, malignant, by site
Jacquet's dermatitis (diaper dermatitis)
691.0
Jadassohn's
blue nevus (M8780/0) — see Neoplasm, skin, benign
disease (maculopapular erythroderma)
696.2
intraepidermal epithelioma (M8096/0)
— see Neoplasm, skin, benign
Jadassohn-Lewandowski syndrome
(pachyonychia congenita) 757.5
Jadassohn-Pellizari's disease (anetoderma) 701.3
Jadassohn-Tièche nevus (M8780/0) —
see Neoplasm, skin, benign
Jaffe-Lichtenstein (-Uehlinger) syndrome 252.01
Jahnke's syndrome (encephalocutaneous angiomatosis) 759.6
Jakob-Creutzfeldt disease (syndrome)
(new variant) 046.1
with dementia
with behavioral disturbance
046.1 [294.11]
without behavioral disturbance
046.1 [294.10]
Jaksch (-Luzet) disease or syndrome
(pseudoleukemia infantum) 285.8
Jamaican
neuropathy 349.82
paraplegic tropical ataxic-spastic
syndrome 349.82
Janet's disease (psychasthenia) 300.89
Janiceps 759.4
Jansky-Bielschowsky amaurotic familial idiocy 330.1
Japanese
B type encephalitis 062.0
river fever 081.2
seven-day fever 100.89
Jaundice (yellow) 782.4
acholuric (familial) (splenomegalic)
(see also Spherocytosis) 282.0
acquired 283.9
breast milk 774.39
catarrhal (acute) 070.1
with hepatic coma 070.0
chronic 571.9
epidemic — see Jaundice, epidemic
cholestatic (benign) 782.4
chronic idiopathic 277.4
epidemic (catarrhal) 070.1
with hepatic coma 070.0
leptospiral 100.0
spirochetal 100.0
febrile (acute) 070.1
with hepatic coma 070.0
leptospiral 100.0
spirochetal 100.0
fetus or newborn 774.6
due to or associated with
ABO
absence or deficiency of enzyme
system for bilirubin conjugation (congenital) 774.39
antibodies 773.1
blood group incompatibility NEC
773.2
breast milk inhibitors to conjugation 774.39
associated with preterm delivery 774.2
bruising 774.1

Jaundice — continued
fetus or newborn — continued
due to or associated with — continued
Crigler-Najjar syndrome
277.4 [774.31]
delayed conjugation 774.30
associated with preterm delivery 774.2
development 774.39
drugs or toxins transmitted
from mother 774.1
G-6-PD deficiency 282.2 [774.0]
galactosemia 271.1 [774.5]
Gilbert's syndrome
277.4 [774.31]
hepatocellular damage 774.4
hereditary hemolytic anemia
(see also Anemia,
hemolytic) 282.9 [774.0]
hypothyroidism, congenital
243 [774.31]
incompatibility, maternal/fetal
NEC 773.2
incompatibility, maternal/fetal
773.1
infection 774.1
inspissated bile syndrome 774.4
isoimmunization NEC 773.2
isoimmunization 773.1
mucoviscidosis 277.01 [774.5]
obliteration of bile duct, congenital 751.61 [774.5]
polycythemia 774.1
preterm delivery 774.2
red cell defect 282.9 [774.0]
Rh
antibodies 773.0
incompatibility, maternal/fetal 773.0
isoimmunization 773.0
spherocytosis (congenital)
282.0 [774.0]
swallowed maternal blood 774.1
physiological NEC 774.6
from injection, inoculation, infusion,
or transfusion (blood) (plasma)
(serum) (other substance) (onset
within 8 months after administration) — see Hepatitis, viral
Gilbert's (familial nonhemolytic) 277.4
hematogenous 283.9
hemolytic (acquired) 283.9
congenital (see also Spherocytosis)
282.0
hemorrhagic (acute) 100.0
leptospiral 100.0
newborn 776.0
spirochetal 100.0
hepatocellular 573.8
homologous (serum) — see Hepatitis,
viral
idiopathic, chronic 277.4
infectious (acute) (subacute) 070.1
with hepatic coma 070.0
leptospiral 100.0
spirochetal 100.0
leptospiral 100.0
malignant (see also Necrosis, liver)
570
newborn (physiological) (see also
Jaundice, fetus or newborn)
774.6
nonhemolytic, congenital familial
(Gilbert's) 277.4
nuclear, newborn (see also Kernicterus of newborn) 774.7
obstructive NEC (see also Obstruction,
biliary) 576.8
postimmunization — see Hepatitis,
viral
posttransfusion — see Hepatitis, viral
regurgitation (see also Obstruction,
biliary) 576.8

Jaundice — continued
serum (homologous) (prophylactic)
(therapeutic) — see Hepatitis,
viral
spirochetal (hemorrhagic) 100.0
symptomatic 782.4
newborn 774.6
Jaw — see condition
Jaw-blinking 374.43
congenital 742.8
Jaw-winking phenomenon or syndrome
742.8
Jealousy
alcoholic 291.5
childhood 313.3
sibling 313.3
Jejunitis — see also Enteritis 558.9
Jejunostomy status V44.4
Jejunum, jejunal — see condition
Jensen's disease 363.05
Jericho boil 085.1
Jerks, myoclonic 333.2
Jervell-Lange-Nielsen syndrome 426.82
Jeune's disease or syndrome (asphyxiating thoracic dystrophy) 756.4
Jigger disease 134.1
Job's syndrome (chronic granulomatous
disease) 288.1
Jod-Basedow phenomenon 242.8 ☑
Johnson-Stevens disease (erythema
multiforme exudativum) 695.1
Joint — see also condition
Charcôt's 094.0 [713.5]
false 733.82
flail — see Flail, joint
mice — see Loose, body, joint, by site
sinus to bone 730.9 ☑
von Gies' 095.8
Jordan's anomaly or syndrome 288.2
Josephs-Diamond-Blackfan anemia
(congenital hypoplastic)
284.01 ▲
Joubert syndrome 759.89
Jumpers' knee 727.2
Jungle yellow fever 060.0
Jüngling's disease (sarcoidosis) 135
Junin virus hemorrhagic fever 078.7
Juvenile — see also condition
delinquent 312.9
group (see also Disturbance, conduct) 312.2 ☑
neurotic 312.4

K

Kabuki syndrome 759.89
Kahler (-Bozzolo) disease (multiple
myeloma) (M9730/3) 203.0 ☑
Kakergasia 300.9
Kakke 265.0
Kala-azar (Indian) (infantile) (Mediterranean) (Sudanese) 085.0
Kalischer's syndrome (encephalocutaneous angiomatosis) 759.6
Kallmann's syndrome (hypogonadotropic hypogonadism with anosmia)
253.4
Kanner's syndrome (autism) — see also
Psychosis, childhood 299.0 ☑
Kaolinosis 502
Kaposi's
disease 757.33
lichen ruber 696.4
acuminatus 696.4
moniliformis 697.8
xeroderma pigmentosum 757.33
sarcoma (M9140/3) 176.9
adipose tissue 176.1
aponeurosis 176.1
artery 176.1
blood vessel 176.1
bursa 176.1
connective tissue 176.1
external genitalia 176.8
fascia 176.1
fatty tissue 176.1
fibrous tissue 176.1

Kaposi's — continued
sarcoma — continued
gastrointestinal tract NEC 176.3
ligament 176.1
lung 176.4
lymph
gland(s) 176.5
node(s) 176.5
lymphatic(s) NEC 176.1
muscle (skeletal) 176.1
oral cavity NEC 176.8
palate 176.2
scrotum 176.8
skin 176.0
soft tissue 176.1
specified site NEC 176.8
subcutaneous tissue 176.1
synovia 176.1
tendon (sheath) 176.1
vein 176.1
vessel 176.1
viscera NEC 176.9
vulva 176.8
varicelliform eruption 054.0
vaccinia 999.0
Kartagener's syndrome or triad (sinusitis, bronchiectasis, situs inversus)
759.3
Kasabach-Merritt syndrome (capillary
hemangioma associated with
thrombocytopenic purpura) 287.39
Kaschin-Beck disease (endemic polyarthritis) — see Disease, Kaschin-Beck
Kast's syndrome (dyschondroplasia with
hemangiomas) 756.4
Katatonia — see Catatonia
Katayama disease or fever 120.2
Kathisophobia 781.0
Kawasaki disease 446.1
Kayser-Fleischer ring (cornea) (pseudosclerosis) 275.1 [371.14]
Kaznelson's syndrome (congenital hypoplastic anemia) 284.01 ▲
Kearns-Sayre syndrome 277.87
Kedani fever 081.2
Kelis 701.4
Kelly (-Patterson) syndrome
(sideropenic dysphagia) 280.8
Keloid, cheloid 701.4
Addison's (morphea) 701.0
cornea 371.00
Hawkins' 701.4
scar 701.4
Keloma 701.4
Kenya fever 082.1
Keratectasia 371.71
congenital 743.41
Keratinization NEC ●
alveolar ridge mucosa ●
excessive 528.72 ●
minimal 528.71 ●
Keratitis (nodular) (nonulcerative) (simple) (zonular) NEC 370.9
with ulceration (see also Ulcer, cornea)
370.00
actinic 370.24
arborescens 054.42
areolar 370.22
bullosa 370.8
deep — see Keratitis, interstitial
dendritic(a) 054.42
desiccation 370.34
diffuse interstitial 370.52
disciform(is) 054.43
varicella 052.7 [370.44]
epithelialis vernalis 372.13 [370.32]
exposure 370.34
filamentary 370.23
gonococcal (congenital) (prenatal)
098.43
herpes, herpetic (simplex) NEC 054.43
zoster 053.21
hypopyon 370.04
in
chickenpox 052.7 [370.44]

☑ Additional Digit Required — Refer to the Tabular List for Digit Selection   ▽ Subterms under main terms may continue to next column or page

2007 ICD-9-CM   ▶◀ Revised Text   ● New Line   ▲ Revised Code   October 2006 · Volume 2 — 173

Keratitis — *continued*
  in — *continued*
    exanthema (*see also* Exanthem)
      057.9 *[370.44]*
    paravaccinia (*see also* Paravac-
      cinia) 051.9 *[370.44]*
    smallpox (*see also* Smallpox)
      050.9 *[370.44]*
    vernal conjunctivitis
      372.13 *[370.32]*
  interstitial (nonsyphilitic) 370.50
    with ulcer (*see also* Ulcer, cornea)
      370.00
    diffuse 370.52
    herpes, herpetic (simplex) 054.43
      zoster 053.21
    syphilitic (congenital) (hereditary)
      090.3
    tuberculous (*see also* Tuberculosis)
      017.3 ☑ *[370.59]*
  lagophthalmic 370.34
  macular 370.22
  neuroparalytic 370.35
  neurotrophic 370.35
  nummular 370.22
  oyster-shuckers' 370.8
  parenchymatous — *see* Keratitis, in-
    terstitial
  petrificans 370.8
  phlyctenular 370.31
  postmeasles 055.71
  punctata, punctate 370.21
    leprosa 030.0 *[370.21]*
    profunda 090.3
    superficial (Thygeson's) 370.21
  purulent 370.8
  pustuliformis profunda 090.3
  rosacea 695.3 *[370.49]*
  sclerosing 370.54
  specified type NEC 370.8
  stellate 370.22
  striate 370.22
  superficial 370.20
    with conjunctivitis (*see also* Kerato-
      conjunctivitis) 370.40
    punctate (Thygeson's) 370.21
  suppurative 370.8
  syphilitic (congenital) (prenatal) 090.3
  trachomatous 076.1
    late effect 139.1
  tuberculous (phlyctenular) (see also
    Tuberculosis) 017.3 ☑ *[370.31]*
  ulcerated (*see also* Ulcer, cornea)
    370.00
  vesicular 370.8
  welders' 370.24
  xerotic (*see also* Keratomalacia)
    371.45
    vitamin A deficiency 264.4
Keratoacanthoma 238.2
Keratocele 371.72
Keratoconjunctivitis — *see also* Keratitis 370.40
  adenovirus type 8 077.1
  epidemic 077.1
  exposure 370.34
  gonococcal 098.43
  herpetic (simplex) 054.43
    zoster 053.21
  in
    chickenpox 052.7 *[370.44]*
    exanthema (*see also* Exanthem)
      057.9 *[370.44]*
    paravaccinia (*see also* Paravac-
      cinia) 051.9 *[370.44]*
    smallpox (*see also* Smallpox)
      050.9 *[370.44]*
  infectious 077.1
  neurotrophic 370.35
  phlyctenular 370.31
  postmeasles 055.71
  shipyard 077.1
  sicca (Sjögren's syndrome) 710.2
    not in Sjögren's syndrome 370.33
  specified type NEC 370.49

Keratoconjunctivitis — *see also*
  Keratitis — *continued*
    tuberculous (phlyctenular) (*see also*
      Tuberculosis) 017.3 ☑ *[370.31]*
Keratoconus 371.60
  acute hydrops 371.62
  congenital 743.41
  stable 371.61
Keratocyst (dental) 526.0
Keratoderma, keratodermia (congenital)
    (palmaris et plantaris) (symmetri-
    cal) 757.39
  acquired 701.1
  blennorrhagica 701.1
    gonococcal 098.81
  climacterium 701.1
  eccentrica 757.39
  gonorrheal 098.81
  punctata 701.1
  tylodes, progressive 701.1
Keratodermatocele 371.72
Keratoglobus 371.70
  congenital 743.41
    associated with buphthalmos
      743.22
Keratohemia 371.12
Keratoiritis — *see also* Iridocyclitis
    364.3
  syphilitic 090.3
  tuberculous (*see also* Tuberculosis)
    017.3 ☑ *[364.11]*
Keratolysis exfoliativa (congenital)
    757.39
  acquired 695.89
  neonatorum 757.39
Keratoma 701.1
  congenital 757.39
  malignum congenitale 757.1
  palmaris et plantaris hereditarium
    757.39
  senile 702.0
Keratomalacia 371.45
  vitamin A deficiency 264.4
Keratomegaly 743.41
Keratomycosis 111.1
  nigricans (palmaris) 111.1
Keratopathy 371.40
  band (*see also* Keratitis) 371.43
  bullous (*see also* Keratitis) 371.23
  degenerative (*see also* Degeneration,
    cornea) 371.40
    hereditary (*see also* Dystrophy,
      cornea) 371.50
  discrete colliquative 371.49
Keratoscleritis, tuberculous — *see also*
    Tuberculosis 017.3 ☑ *[370.31]*
Keratosis 701.1
  actinic 702.0
  arsenical 692.4
  blennorrhagica 701.1
    gonococcal 098.81
  congenital (any type) 757.39
  ear (middle) (*see also* Cholesteatoma)
    385.30
  female genital (external) 629.89 ▲
  follicularis 757.39
    acquired 701.1
    congenital (acneiformis) (Siemens')
      757.39
    spinulosa (decalvans) 757.39
    vitamin A deficiency 264.8
  follicular, vitamin A deficiency 264.8
  gonococcal 098.81
  larynx, laryngeal 478.79
  male genital (external) 608.89
  middle ear (*see also* Cholesteatoma)
    385.30
  nigricans 701.2
    congenital 757.39
  obturans 380.21
  oral epithelium
    residual ridge mucosa
      excessive 528.72
      minimal 528.71
  palmaris et plantaris (symmetrical)
    757.39

Keratosis — *continued*
  penile 607.89
  pharyngeus 478.29
  pilaris 757.39
    acquired 701.1
  punctata (palmaris et plantaris) 701.1
  scrotal 608.89
  seborrheic 702.19
    inflamed 702.11
  senilis 702.0
  solar 702.0
  suprafollicularis 757.39
  tonsillaris 478.29
  vagina 623.1
  vegetans 757.39
  vitamin A deficiency 264.8
Kerato-uveitis — *see also* Iridocyclitis
    364.3
Keraunoparalysis 994.0
Kerion (celsi) 110.0
Kernicterus of newborn (not due to
    isoimmunization) 774.7
  due to isoimmunization (conditions
    classifiable to 773.0–773.2)
    773.4
Ketoacidosis 276.2
  diabetic 250.1 ☑
Ketonuria 791.6
  branched-chain, intermittent 270.3
Ketosis 276.2
  diabetic 250.1 ☑
Kidney — *see* condition
Kienböck's
  disease 732.3
    adult 732.8
    osteochondrosis 732.3
**Kimmelstiel (-Wilson) disease or syn-
  drome** (intercapillary glomerulosclerosis) 250.4 ☑ *[581.81]*
Kink, kinking
  appendix 543.9
  artery 447.1
  cystic duct, congenital 751.61
  hair (acquired) 704.2
  ileum or intestine (*see also* Obstruc-
    tion, intestine) 560.9
  Lane's (*see also* Obstruction, intestine)
    560.9
  organ or site, congenital NEC — *see*
    Anomaly, specified type NEC,
    by site
  ureter (pelvic junction) 593.3
    congenital 753.20
  vein(s) 459.2
    caval 459.2
    peripheral 459.2
Kinnier Wilson's disease (hepatolentic-
    ular degeneration) 275.1
Kissing
  osteophytes 721.5
  spine 721.5
  vertebra 721.5
Klauder's syndrome (erythema multi-
    forme, exudativum) 695.1
Klebs' disease — *see also* Nephritis
    583.9
Kleine-Levin syndrome 327.13
Klein-Waardenburg syndrome (ptosisepi-
    canthus) 270.2
Kleptomania 312.32
Klinefelter's syndrome 758.7
Klinger's disease 446.4
Klippel's disease 723.8
Klippel-Feil disease or syndrome (bre-
    vicollis) 756.16
Klippel-Trenaunay syndrome 759.89
Klumpke (-Déjérine) palsy, paralysis
    (birth) (newborn) 767.6
Klüver-Bucy (-Terzian) syndrome 310.0
Knee — *see* condition
Knifegrinders' rot — *see also* Tubercu-
    losis 011.4 ☑
Knock-knee (acquired) 736.41
  congenital 755.64
Knot
  intestinal, syndrome (volvulus) 560.2

Knot — *continued*
  umbilical cord (true) 663.2 ☑
    affecting fetus or newborn 762.5
Knots, surfer 919.8
  infected 919.9
Knotting (of)
  hair 704.2
  intestine 560.2
Knuckle pads (Garrod's) 728.79
Köbner's disease (epidermolysis bullosa)
    757.39
Koch's
  infection (*see also* Tuberculosis, pul-
    monary) 011.9 ☑
  relapsing fever 087.9
Koch-Weeks conjunctivitis 372.03
Koenig-Wichman disease (pemphigus)
    694.4
Köhler's disease (osteochondrosis) 732.5
  first (osteochondrosis juvenilis) 732.5
  second (Freiburg's infarction,
    metatarsal head) 732.5
  patellar 732.4
  tarsal navicular (bone) (osteoarthrosis
    juvenilis) 732.5
Köhler-Mouchet disease (osteoarthrosis
    juvenilis) 732.5
**Köhler-Pellegrini-Stieda disease or
  syndrome** (calcification, knee joint)
    726.62
Koilonychia 703.8
  congenital 757.5
Kojevnikov's, Kojewnikoff's epilepsy
    — *see also* Epilepsy 345.7 ☑
König's
  disease (osteochondritis dissecans)
    732.7
  syndrome 564.89
Koniophthisis — *see also* Tuberculosis
    011.4 ☑
Koplik's spots 055.9
Kopp's asthma 254.8
Korean hemorrhagic fever 078.6
**Korsakoff (-Wernicke) disease, psy-
  chosis, or syndrome** (nonalco-
  holic) 294.0
  alcoholic 291.1
Korsakov's disease — *see* Korsakoff's
  disease
Korsakow's disease — *see* Korsakoff's
  disease
Kostmann's disease or syndrome (infan-
  tile genetic agranulocytosis)
    288.01 ▲
Krabbe's
  disease (leukodystrophy) 330.0
  syndrome
    congenital muscle hypoplasia
      756.89
    cutaneocerebral angioma 759.6
Kraepelin-Morel disease — *see also*
    Schizophrenia 295.9 ☑
Kraft-Weber-Dimitri disease 759.6
Kraurosis
  ani 569.49
  penis 607.0
  vagina 623.8
  vulva 624.0
Kreotoxism 005.9
Krukenberg's
  spindle 371.13
  tumor (M8490/6) 198.6
Kufs' disease 330.1
Kugelberg-Welander disease 335.11
Kuhnt-Junius degeneration or disease
    362.52
Kulchitsky's cell carcinoma (carcinoid
    tumor of intestine) 259.2
Kümmell's disease or spondylitis 721.7
Kundrat's disease (lymphosarcoma)
    200.1 ☑
Kunekune — *see* Dermatophytosis
Kunkel syndrome (lupoid hepatitis)
    571.49
Kupffer cell sarcoma (M9124/3) 155.0
Kuru 046.0

Kussmaul's
coma (diabetic) 250.3 ☑
disease (polyarteritis nodosa) 446.0
respiration (air hunger) 786.09
Kwashiorkor (marasmus type) 260
Kyasanur Forest disease 065.2
Kyphoscoliosis, kyphoscoliotic (acquired) — see also Scoliosis 737.30
congenital 756.19
due to radiation 737.33
heart (disease) 416.1
idiopathic 737.30
infantile
progressive 737.32
resolving 737.31
late effect of rickets 268.1 [737.43]
specified NEC 737.39
thoracogenic 737.34
tuberculous (see also Tuberculosis)
015.0 ☑ [737.43]
Kyphosis, kyphotic (acquired) (postural) 737.10
adolescent postural 737.0
congenital 756.19
dorsalis juvenilis 732.0
due to or associated with
Charcôt-Marie-Tooth disease
356.1 [737.41]
mucopolysaccharidosis
277.5 [737.41]
neurofibromatosis 237.71 [737.41]
osteitis
deformans 731.0 [737.41]
fibrosa cystica 252.01 [737.41]
osteoporosis (see also Osteoporosis)
733.0 ☑ [737.41]
poliomyelitis (see also Poliomyelitis)
138 [737.41]
radiation 737.11
tuberculosis (see also Tuberculosis)
015.0 ☑ [737.41]
Kümmell's 721.7
late effect of rickets 268.1 [737.41]
Morquio-Brailsford type (spinal)
277.5 [737.41]
pelvis 738.6
postlaminectomy 737.12
specified cause NEC 737.19
syphilitic, congenital 090.5 [737.41]
tuberculous (see also Tuberculosis)
015.0 ☑ [737.41]
Kyrle's disease (hyperkeratosis follicularis in cutem penetrans) 701.1

L

Labia, labium — see condition
Labiated hymen 752.49
Labile
blood pressure 796.2
emotions, emotionality 301.3
vasomotor system 443.9
Labioglossal paralysis 335.22
Labium leporinum — see also Cleft, lip
749.10
Labor — see also Delivery
with complications — see Delivery,
complicated
abnormal NEC 661.9 ☑
affecting fetus or newborn 763.7
arrested active phase 661.1 ☑
affecting fetus or newborn 763.7
desultory 661.2 ☑
affecting fetus or newborn 763.7
dyscoordinate 661.4 ☑
affecting fetus or newborn 763.7
early onset (22-36 weeks gestation)
644.2 ☑
failed
induction 659.1 ☑
mechanical 659.0 ☑
medical 659.1 ☑
surgical 659.0 ☑
trial (vaginal delivery) 660.6 ☑
false 644.1 ☑

Labor — see also Delivery —
continued
forced or induced, affecting fetus or
newborn 763.89
hypertonic 661.4 ☑
affecting fetus or newborn 763.7
hypotonic 661.2 ☑
affecting fetus or newborn 763.7
primary 661.0 ☑
affecting fetus or newborn 763.7
secondary 661.1 ☑
affecting fetus or newborn 763.7
incoordinate 661.4 ☑
affecting fetus or newborn 763.7
irregular 661.2 ☑
affecting fetus or newborn 763.7
long — see Labor, prolonged
missed (at or near term) 656.4 ☑
obstructed NEC 660.9 ☑
affecting fetus or newborn 763.1
due to female genital mutilation
660.8 ☑
specified cause NEC 660.8 ☑
affecting fetus or newborn 763.1
pains, spurious 644.1 ☑
precipitate 661.3 ☑
affecting fetus or newborn 763.6
premature 644.2 ☑
threatened 644.0 ☑
prolonged or protracted 662.1 ☑
first stage 662.0 ☑
affecting fetus or newborn
763.89
second stage 662.2 ☑
affecting fetus or newborn
763.89
affecting fetus or newborn 763.89
threatened NEC 644.1 ☑
undelivered 644.1 ☑
Labored breathing — see also Hyperventilation 786.09
Labyrinthitis (inner ear) (destructive)
(latent) 386.30
circumscribed 386.32
diffuse 386.31
focal 386.32
purulent 386.33
serous 386.31
suppurative 386.33
syphilitic 095.8
toxic 386.34
viral 386.35
Laceration — see also Wound, open, by
site
accidental, complicating surgery 998.2
Achilles tendon 845.09
with open wound 892.2
anus (sphincter) 879.6
with
abortion — see Abortion, by
type, with damage to
pelvic organs
ectopic pregnancy (see also categories 633.0–633.9)
639.2
molar pregnancy (see also categories 630–632) 639.2
complicated 879.7
complicating delivery 664.2 ☑
with laceration of anal or rectal
mucosa 664.3 ☑
following
abortion 639.2
ectopic or molar pregnancy
639.2
nontraumatic, nonpuerperal 565.0
bladder (urinary)
with
abortion — see Abortion, by
type, with damage to
pelvic organs
ectopic pregnancy (see also categories 633.0–633.9)
639.2
molar pregnancy (see also categories 630–632) 639.2

Laceration — see also Wound, open, by
site — continued
bladder — continued
following
abortion 639.2
ectopic or molar pregnancy
639.2
obstetrical trauma 665.5 ☑
blood vessel — see Injury, blood vessel, by site
bowel
with
abortion — see Abortion, by
type, with damage to
pelvic organs
ectopic pregnancy (see also categories 633.0–633.9)
639.2
molar pregnancy (see also categories 630–632) 639.2
following
abortion 639.2
ectopic or molar pregnancy
639.2
obstetrical trauma 665.5 ☑
brain (cerebral) (membrane) (with
hemorrhage) 851.8 ☑

> Note — Use the following fifth-digit
> subclassification with categories
> 851–854:
>
> 0   unspecified state of consciousness
>
> 1   with no loss of consciousness
>
> 2   with brief [less than one hour]
> loss of consciousness
>
> 3   with moderate [1–24 hours] loss
> of consciousness
>
> 4   with prolonged [more than 24
> hours] loss of consciousness and
> return to pre–existing conscious
> level
>
> 5   with prolonged [more than 24
> hours] loss of consciousness,
> without return to pre–existing
> conscious level
>
> Use fifth-digit 5 to designate when a
> patient is unconscious and dies before
> regaining consciousness, regardless of
> the duration of the loss of consciousness
>
> 6   with loss of consciousness of unspecified duration
>
> 9   with concussion, unspecified

with
open intracranial wound
851.9 ☑
skull fracture — see Fracture,
skull, by site
cerebellum 851.6 ☑
with open intracranial wound
851.7 ☑
cortex 851.2 ☑
with open intracranial wound
851.3 ☑
during birth 767.0
stem 851.6 ☑
with open intracranial wound
851.7 ☑
broad ligament
with
abortion — see Abortion, by
type, with damage to
pelvic organs
ectopic pregnancy (see also categories 633.0–633.9)
639.2
molar pregnancy (see also categories 630–632) 639.2
following
abortion 639.2
ectopic or molar pregnancy
639.2

Laceration — see also Wound, open, by
site — continued
broad ligament — continued
nontraumatic 620.6
obstetrical trauma 665.6 ☑
syndrome (nontraumatic) 620.6
capsule, joint — see Sprain, by site
cardiac — see Laceration, heart
causing eversion of cervix uteri (old)
622.0
central, complicating delivery 664.4 ☑
cerebellum — see Laceration, brain,
cerebellum
cerebral (see also Laceration, brain)
during birth 767.0
cervix (uteri)
with
abortion — see Abortion, by
type, with damage to
pelvic organs
ectopic pregnancy (see also categories 633.0–633.9)
639.2
molar pregnancy (see also categories 630–632) 639.2
following
abortion 639.2
ectopic or molar pregnancy
639.2
nonpuerperal, nontraumatic 622.3
obstetrical trauma (current)
665.3 ☑
old (postpartal) 622.3
traumatic — see Injury, internal,
cervix
chordae heart 429.5
complicated 879.9
cornea — see Laceration, eyeball
superficial 918.1
cortex (cerebral) — see Laceration,
brain, cortex
esophagus 530.89
eye(s) — see Laceration, ocular
eyeball NEC 871.4
with prolapse or exposure of intraocular tissue 871.1
penetrating — see Penetrating
wound, eyeball
specified as without prolapse of intraocular tissue 871.0
eyelid NEC 870.8
full thickness 870.1
involving lacrimal passages
870.2
skin (and periocular area) 870.0
penetrating — see Penetrating
wound, orbit
fourchette
with
abortion — see Abortion, by
type, with damage to
pelvic organs
ectopic pregnancy (see also categories 633.0–633.9)
639.2
molar pregnancy (see also categories 630–632) 639.2
complicating delivery 664.0 ☑
following
abortion 639.2
ectopic or molar pregnancy
639.2
heart (without penetration of heart
chambers) 861.02
with
open wound into thorax 861.12
penetration of heart chambers
861.03
with open wound into thorax
861.13
hernial sac — see Hernia, by site
internal organ (abdomen) (chest)
(pelvis) NEC — see Injury, internal, by site
NEC — see Injury, internal, by site
kidney (parenchyma) 866.02

Kussmaul's — Laceration

Laceration — see also Wound, open, by site — continued
kidney — continued
  with
    complete disruption of parenchyma (rupture) 866.03
      with open wound into cavity 866.13
    open wound into cavity 866.12
labia
  complicating delivery 664.0 ☑
ligament (see also Sprain, by site)
  with open wound — see Wound, open, by site
liver 864.05
  with open wound into cavity 864.15
  major (disruption of hepatic parenchyma) 864.04
    with open wound into cavity 864.14
  minor (capsule only) 864.02
    with open wound into cavity 864.12
  moderate (involving parenchyma without major disruption) 864.03
    with open wound into cavity 864.13
  multiple 864.04
    with open wound into cavity 864.14
  stellate 864.04
    with open wound into cavity 864.14
lung 861.22
  with open wound into thorax 861.32
meninges — see Laceration, brain
meniscus (knee) (see also Tear, meniscus) 836.2
  old 717.5
  site other than knee (see also Sprain, by site)
    old NEC (see also Disorder, cartilage, articular) 718.0 ☑
muscle (see also Sprain, by site)
  with open wound — see Wound, open, by site
myocardium — see Laceration, heart
nerve — see Injury, nerve, by site
ocular NEC (see also Laceration, eyeball) 871.4
  adnexa NEC 870.8
    penetrating 870.3
      with foreign body 870.4
orbit (eye) 870.8
  penetrating 870.3
    with foreign body 870.4
pelvic
  floor (muscles)
    with
      abortion — see Abortion, by type, with damage to pelvic organs
      ectopic pregnancy (see also categories 633.0–633.9) 639.2
      molar pregnancy (see also categories 630–632) 639.2
    complicating delivery 664.1 ☑
    following
      abortion 639.2
      ectopic or molar pregnancy 639.2
    nonpuerperal 618.7
    old (postpartal) 618.7
  organ NEC
    with
      abortion — see Abortion, by type, with damage to pelvic organs

Laceration — see also Wound, open, by site — continued
pelvic — continued
  organ — continued
    with — continued
      ectopic pregnancy (see also categories 633.0–633.9) 639.2
      molar pregnancy (see also categories 630–632) 639.2
    complicating delivery 665.5 ☑
      affecting fetus or newborn 763.89
    following
      abortion 639.2
      ectopic or molar pregnancy 639.2
    obstetrical trauma 665.5 ☑
perineum, perineal (old) (postpartal) 618.7
  with
    abortion — see Abortion, by type, with damage to pelvic floor
    ectopic pregnancy (see also categories 633.0–633.9) 639.2
    molar pregnancy (see also categories 630–632) 639.2
  complicating delivery 664.4 ☑
    first degree 664.0 ☑
    second degree 664.1 ☑
    third degree 664.2 ☑
    fourth degree 664.3 ☑
    central 664.4 ☑
    involving
      anal sphincter 664.2 ☑
      fourchette 664.0 ☑
      hymen 664.0 ☑
      labia 664.0 ☑
      pelvic floor 664.1 ☑
      perineal muscles 664.1 ☑
      rectovaginal septum 664.2 ☑
        with anal mucosa 664.3 ☑
      skin 664.0 ☑
      sphincter (anal) 664.2 ☑
        with anal mucosa 664.3 ☑
      vagina 664.0 ☑
      vaginal muscles 664.1 ☑
      vulva 664.0 ☑
    secondary 674.2 ☑
  following
    abortion 639.2
    ectopic or molar pregnancy 639.2
  male 879.6
    complicated 879.7
  muscles, complicating delivery 664.1 ☑
  nonpuerperal, current injury 879.6
    complicated 879.7
  secondary (postpartal) 674.2 ☑
peritoneum
  with
    abortion — see Abortion, by type, with damage to pelvic organs
    ectopic pregnancy (see also categories 633.0–633.9) 639.2
    molar pregnancy (see also categories 630–632) 639.2
  following
    abortion 639.2
    ectopic or molar pregnancy 639.2
  obstetrical trauma 665.5 ☑
periurethral tissue
  with
    abortion — see Abortion, by type, with damage to pelvic organs

Laceration — see also Wound, open, by site — continued
periurethral tissue — continued
  with — continued
    ectopic pregnancy (see also categories 633.0–633.9) 639.2
    molar pregnancy (see also categories 630–632) 639.2
  following
    abortion 639.2
    ectopic or molar pregnancy 639.2
  obstetrical trauma 665.5 ☑
rectovaginal (septum)
  with
    abortion — see Abortion, by type, with damage to pelvic organs
    ectopic pregnancy (see also categories 633.0–633.9) 639.2
    molar pregnancy (see also categories 630–632) 639.2
  complicating delivery 665.4 ☑
    with perineum 664.2 ☑
      involving anal or rectal mucosa 664.3 ☑
  following
    abortion 639.2
    ectopic or molar pregnancy 639.2
  nonpuerperal 623.4
  old (postpartal) 623.4
spinal cord (meninges) (see also Injury, spinal, by site)
  due to injury at birth 767.4
  fetus or newborn 767.4
spleen 865.09
  with
    disruption of parenchyma (massive) 865.04
      with open wound into cavity 865.14
    open wound into cavity 865.19
  capsule (without disruption of parenchyma) 865.02
    with open wound into cavity 865.12
  parenchyma 865.03
    with open wound into cavity 865.13
    massive disruption (rupture) 865.04
      with open wound into cavity 865.14
tendon 848.9
  with open wound — see Wound, open, by site
  Achilles 845.09
    with open wound 892.2
  lower limb NEC 844.9
    with open wound NEC 894.2
  upper limb NEC 840.9
    with open wound NEC 884.2
tentorium cerebelli — see Laceration, brain, cerebellum
tongue 873.64
  complicated 873.74
urethra
  with
    abortion — see Abortion, by type, with damage to pelvic organs
    ectopic pregnancy (see also categories 633.0–633.9) 639.2
    molar pregnancy (see also categories 630–632) 639.2
  following
    abortion 639.2
    ectopic or molar pregnancy 639.2
  nonpuerperal, nontraumatic 599.84
  obstetrical trauma 665.5 ☑

Laceration — see also Wound, open, by site — continued
uterus
  with
    abortion — see Abortion, by type, with damage to pelvic organs
    ectopic pregnancy (see also categories 633.0–633.9) 639.2
    molar pregnancy (see also categories 630–632) 639.2
  following
    abortion 639.2
    ectopic or molar pregnancy 639.2
  nonpuerperal, nontraumatic 621.8
  obstetrical trauma NEC 665.5 ☑
  old (postpartal) 621.8
vagina
  with
    abortion — see Abortion, by type, with damage to pelvic organs
    ectopic pregnancy (see also categories 633.0–633.9) 639.2
    molar pregnancy (see also categories 630–632) 639.2
    perineal involvement, complicating delivery 664.0 ☑
  complicating delivery 665.4 ☑
    first degree 664.0 ☑
    second degree 664.1 ☑
    third degree 664.2 ☑
    fourth degree 664.3 ☑
    high 665.4 ☑
    muscles 664.1 ☑
    sulcus 665.4 ☑
    wall 665.4 ☑
  following
    abortion 639.2
    ectopic or molar pregnancy 639.2
  nonpuerperal, nontraumatic 623.4
  old (postpartal) 623.4
valve, heart — see Endocarditis
vulva
  with
    abortion — see Abortion, by type, with damage to pelvic organs
    ectopic pregnancy (see also categories 633.0–633.9) 639.2
    molar pregnancy (see also categories 630–632) 639.2
  complicating delivery 664.0 ☑
  following
    abortion 639.2
    ectopic or molar pregnancy 639.2
  nonpuerperal, nontraumatic 624.4
  old (postpartal) 624.4
Lachrymal — see condition
Lachrymonasal duct — see condition
Lack of
  adequate intermaxillary vertical dimension 524.36 ●
  appetite (see also Anorexia) 783.0
  care
    in home V60.4
    of adult 995.84
    of infant (at or after birth) 995.52
  coordination 781.3
  development (see also Hypoplasia)
    physiological in childhood 783.40
  education V62.3
  energy 780.79
  financial resources V60.2
  food 994.2
    in environment V60.8
  growth in childhood 783.43
  heating V60.1
  housing (permanent) (temporary) V60.0

Lack of — *continued*
  housing — *continued*
    adequate V60.1
  material resources V60.2
  medical attention 799.89
  memory (*see also* Amnesia) 780.93
    mild, following organic brain damage 310.1
  ovulation 628.0
  person able to render necessary care V60.4
  physical exercise V69.0
  physiologic development in childhood 783.40
  posterior occlusal support 524.57
  prenatal care in current pregnancy V23.7
  shelter V60.0
  sleep V69.4
  water 994.3
Lacrimal — *see* condition
Lacrimation, abnormal — *see also* Epiphora 375.20
Lacrimonasal duct — *see* condition
Lactation, lactating (breast) (puerperal) (postpartum)
  defective 676.4 ☑
  disorder 676.9 ☑
    specified type NEC 676.8 ☑
  excessive 676.6 ☑
  failed 676.4 ☑
  mastitis NEC 675.2 ☑
  mother (care and/or examination) V24.1
  nonpuerperal 611.6
  suppressed 676.5 ☑
Lacticemia 271.3
  excessive 276.2
Lactosuria 271.3
Lacunar skull 756.0
Laennec's cirrhosis (alcoholic) 571.2
  nonalcoholic 571.5
Lafora's disease 333.2
Lagleyze-von Hippel disease (retinocerebral angiomatosis) 759.6
Lag, lid (nervous) 374.41
Lagophthalmos (eyelid) (nervous) 374.20
  cicatricial 374.23
  keratitis (*see also* Keratitis) 370.34
  mechanical 374.22
  paralytic 374.21
La grippe — *see* Influenza
Lahore sore 085.1
Lakes, venous (cerebral) 437.8
Laki-Lorand factor deficiency — *see also* Defect, coagulation 286.3
Lalling 307.9
Lambliasis 007.1
Lame back 724.5
Lancereaux's diabetes (diabetes mellitus with marked emaciation) 250.8 ☑ *[261]*
Landouzy-Déjérine dystrophy (fascioscapulohumeral atrophy) 359.1
Landry's disease or paralysis 357.0
Landry-Guillain-Barré syndrome 357.0
Lane's
  band 751.4
  disease 569.89
  kink (*see also* Obstruction, intestine) 560.9
Langdon Down's syndrome (mongolism) 758.0
Language abolition 784.69
Lanugo (persistent) 757.4
Laparoscopic surgical procedure converted to open procedure V64.41
Lardaceous
  degeneration (any site) 277.39 ▲
  disease 277.39 ▲
  kidney 277.39 *[583.81]* ▲
  liver 277.39 ▲
Large
  baby (regardless of gestational age) 766.1

Large — *continued*
  baby — *continued*
    exceptionally (weight of 4500 grams or more) 766.0
    of diabetic mother 775.0
  ear 744.22
  fetus (*see also* Oversize, fetus)
    causing disproportion 653.5 ☑
      with obstructed labor 660.1 ☑
    for dates
      fetus or newborn (regardless of gestational age) 766.1
      affecting management of pregnancy 656.6 ☑
    exceptionally (weight of 4500 grams or more) 766.0
  physiological cup 743.57
  stature 783.9
  waxy liver 277.39 ▲
  white kidney — *see* Nephrosis
Larsen-Johansson disease (juvenile osteopathia patellae) 732.4
Larsen's syndrome (flattened facies and multiple congenital dislocations) 755.8
Larva migrans
  cutaneous NEC 126.9
    ancylostoma 126.9
  of Diptera in vitreous 128.0
  visceral NEC 128.0
Laryngeal — *see also* condition 786.2
  syncope 786.2
Laryngismus (acute) (infectious) (stridulous) 478.75
  congenital 748.3
  diphtheritic 032.3
Laryngitis (acute) (edematous) (fibrinous) (gangrenous) (infective) (infiltrative) (malignant) (membranous) (phlegmonous) (pneumococcal) (pseudomembranous) (septic) (subglottic) (suppurative) (ulcerative) (viral) 464.00
  with
    influenza, flu, or grippe 487.1
    obstruction 464.01
    tracheitis (*see also* Laryngotracheitis) 464.20
      with obstruction 464.21
      acute 464.20
        with obstruction 464.21
      chronic 476.1
  atrophic 476.0
  Borrelia vincentii 101
  catarrhal 476.0
  chronic 476.0
    with tracheitis (chronic) 476.1
    due to external agent — *see* Condition, respiratory, chronic, due to
  diphtheritic (membranous) 032.3
  due to external agent — *see* Inflammation, respiratory, upper, due to
  Hemophilus influenzae 464.00
    with obstruction 464.01
  H. influenzae 464.00
    with obstruction 464.01
  hypertrophic 476.0
  influenzal 487.1
  pachydermic 478.79
  sicca 476.0
  spasmodic 478.75
    acute 464.00
      with obstruction 464.01
  streptococcal 034.0
  stridulous 478.75
  syphilitic 095.8
    congenital 090.5
  tuberculous (*see also* Tuberculosis, larynx) 012.3 ☑
  Vincent's 101
Laryngocele (congenital) (ventricular) 748.3
Laryngofissure 478.79
  congenital 748.3
Laryngomalacia (congenital) 748.3

Laryngopharyngitis (acute) 465.0
  chronic 478.9
  due to external agent — *see* Condition, respiratory, chronic, due to
  due to external agent — *see* Inflammation, respiratory, upper, due to
  septic 034.0
Laryngoplegia — *see also* Paralysis, vocal cord 478.30
Laryngoptosis 478.79
Laryngospasm 478.75
  due to external agent — *see* Condition, respiratory, acute, due to
Laryngostenosis 478.74
  congenital 748.3
Laryngotracheitis (acute) (infectional) (viral) — *see also* Laryngitis 464.20
  with obstruction 464.21
  atrophic 476.1
  Borrelia vincenti 101
  catarrhal 476.1
  chronic 476.1
    due to external agent — *see* Condition, respiratory, chronic, due to
  diphtheritic (membranous) 032.3
  due to external agent — *see* Inflammation, respiratory, upper, due to
  H. influenzae 464.20
    with obstruction 464.21
  hypertrophic 476.1
  influenzal 487.1
  pachydermic 478.75
  sicca 476.1
  spasmodic 478.75
    acute 464.20
      with obstruction 464.21
  streptococcal 034.0
  stridulous 478.75
  syphilitic 095.8
    congenital 090.5
  tuberculous (*see also* Tuberculosis, larynx) 012.3 ☑
  Vincent's 101
Laryngotracheobronchitis — *see also* Bronchitis 490
  acute 466.0
  chronic 491.8
  viral 466.0
Laryngotracheobronchopneumonitis — *see* Pneumonia, broncho-
Larynx, laryngeal — *see* condition
Lasègue's disease (persecution mania) 297.9
Lassa fever 078.89
Lassitude — *see also* Weakness 780.79
Late — *see also* condition
  effect(s) (of) (*see also* condition)
    abscess
      intracranial or intraspinal (conditions classifiable to 324) — *see* category 326
    adverse effect of drug, medicinal or biological substance 909.5
    allergic reaction 909.9
    amputation
      postoperative (late) 997.60
      traumatic (injury classifiable to 885–887 and 895–897) 905.9
    burn (injury classifiable to 948–949) 906.9
      extremities NEC (injury classifiable to 943 or 945) 906.7
      hand or wrist (injury classifiable to 944) 906.6
      eye (injury classifiable to 940) 906.5
      face, head, and neck (injury classifiable to 941) 906.5
      specified site NEC (injury classifiable to 942 and 946–947) 906.8

Late — *see also* condition — *continued*
  effect(s) (*see also* condition) — *continued*
    cerebrovascular disease (conditions classifiable to 430–437) 438.9
    with
      alterations of sensations 438.6
      aphasia 438.11
      apraxia 438.81
      ataxia 438.84
      cognitive deficits 438.0
      disturbances of vision 438.7
      dysphagia 438.82
      dysphasia 438.12
      facial droop 438.83
      facial weakness 438.83
      hemiplegia/hemiparesis affecting
        dominant side 438.21
        nondominant side 438.22
        unspecified side 438.20
      monoplegia of lower limb affecting
        dominant side 438.41
        nondominant side 438.42
        unspecified side 438.40
      monoplegia of upper limb affecting
        dominant side 438.31
        nondominant side 438.32
        unspecified side 438.30
      paralytic syndrome NEC affecting
        bilateral 438.53
        dominant side 438.51
        nondominant side 438.52
        unspecified side 438.50
      specified type NEC 438.19
      speech and language deficit 438.10
      vertigo 438.85
    specified type NEC 438.89
    childbirth complication(s) 677
    complication(s) of
      childbirth 677
      delivery 677
      pregnancy 677
      puerperium 677
      surgical and medical care (conditions classifiable to 996–999) 909.3
      trauma (conditions classifiable to 958) 908.6
    contusion (injury classifiable to 920–924) 906.3
    crushing (injury classifiable to 925–929) 906.4
    delivery complication(s) 677
    dislocation (injury classifiable to 830–839) 905.6
    encephalitis or encephalomyelitis (conditions classifiable to 323) — *see* category 326
      in infectious diseases 139.8
        viral (conditions classifiable to 049.8, 049.9, 062–064) 139.0
    external cause NEC (conditions classifiable to 995) 909.9
      certain conditions classifiable to categories 991-994 909.4
    foreign body in orifice (injury classifiable to 930–939) 908.5

☑ Additional Digit Required — Refer to the Tabular List for Digit Selection   ⩒ Subterms under main terms may continue to next column or page

2007 ICD-9-CM   ▶◀ Revised Text   ● New Line   ▲ Revised Code   October 2006 · Volume 2 — 177

Late — *see also* condition — *continued*
  effect(s) (*see also* condition) — *continued*
    fracture (multiple) (injury classifiable to 828–829) 905.5
    extremity
      lower (injury classifiable to 821–827) 905.4
      neck of femur (injury classifiable to 820) 905.3
      upper (injury classifiable to 810–819) 905.2
    face and skull (injury classifiable to 800–804) 905.0
    skull and face (injury classifiable to 800–804) 905.0
    spine and trunk (injury classifiable to 805 and 807–809) 905.1
      with spinal cord lesion (injury classifiable to 806) 907.2
  infection
    pyogenic, intracranial — *see* category 326
  infectious diseases (conditions classifiable to 001–136) NEC 139.8
  injury (injury classifiable to 959) 908.9
    blood vessel 908.3
      abdomen and pelvis (injury classifiable to 902) 908.4
      extremity (injury classifiable to 903–904) 908.3
      head and neck (injury classifiable to 900) 908.3
      intracranial (injury classifiable to 850–854) 907.0
        with skull fracture 905.0
      thorax (injury classifiable to 901) 908.4
    internal organ NEC (injury classifiable to 867 and 869) 908.2
      abdomen (injury classifiable to 863–866 and 868) 908.1
      thorax (injury classifiable to 860–862) 908.0
    intracranial (injury classifiable to 850–854) 907.0
      with skull fracture (injury classifiable to 800–801 and 803–804) 905.0
    nerve NEC (injury classifiable to 957) 907.9
      cranial (injury classifiable to 950–951) 907.1
      peripheral NEC (injury classifiable to 957) 907.9
      lower limb and pelvic girdle (injury classifiable to 956) 907.5
      upper limb and shoulder girdle (injury classifiable to 955) 907.4
      roots and plexus(es), spinal (injury classifiable to 953) 907.3
      trunk (injury classifiable to 954) 907.3
    spinal
      cord (injury classifiable to 806 and 952) 907.2
      nerve root(s) and plexus(es) (injury classifiable to 953) 907.3
    superficial (injury classifiable to 910–919) 906.2

Late — *see also* condition — *continued*
  effect(s) (*see also* condition) — *continued*
    injury — *continued*
      tendon (tendon injury classifiable to 840–848, 880–884 with .2, and 890–894 with .2) 905.8
    meningitis
      bacterial (conditions classifiable to 320) — *see* category 326
      unspecified cause (conditions classifiable to 322) — *see* category 326
    myelitis (*see also* Late, effect(s) (of), encephalitis) — *see* category 326
    parasitic diseases (conditions classifiable to 001–136 NEC) 139.8
    phlebitis or thrombophlebitis of intracranial venous sinuses (conditions classifiable to 325) — *see* category 326
    poisoning due to drug, medicinal or biological substance (conditions classifiable to 960–979) 909.0
    poliomyelitis, acute (conditions classifiable to 045) 138
    pregnancy complication(s) 677
    puerperal complication(s) 677
    radiation (conditions classifiable to 990) 909.2
    rickets 268.1
    sprain and strain without mention of tendon injury (injury classifiable to 840–848, except tendon injury) 905.7
      tendon involvement 905.8
  toxic effect of
    drug, medicinal or biological substance (conditions classifiable to 960–979) 909.0
    nonmedical substance (conditions classifiable to 980–989) 909.1
    trachoma (conditions classifiable to 076) 139.1
  tuberculosis 137.0
    bones and joints (conditions classifiable to 015) 137.3
    central nervous system (conditions classifiable to 013) 137.1
    genitourinary (conditions classifiable to 016) 137.2
    pulmonary (conditions classifiable to 010–012) 137.0
    specified organs NEC (conditions classifiable to 014, 017–018) 137.4
  viral encephalitis (conditions classifiable to 049.8, 049.9, 062–064) 139.0
  wound, open
    extremity (injury classifiable to 880–884 and 890–894, except .2) 906.1
      tendon (injury classifiable to 880–884 with .2 and 890–894 with .2) 905.8
    head, neck, and trunk (injury classifiable to 870–879) 906.0
  infant
    post-term (gestation period over 40 completed weeks to 42 completed weeks) 766.21
    prolonged gestation (period over 42 completed weeks) 766.22
Latent — *see* condition
Lateral — *see* condition

Laterocession — *see* Lateroversion
Lateroflexion — *see* Lateroversion
Lateroversion
  cervix — *see* Lateroversion, uterus
  uterus, uterine (cervix) (postinfectional) (postpartal, old) 621.6
    congenital 752.3
    in pregnancy or childbirth 654.4 ☑
      affecting fetus or newborn 763.89
Lathyrism 988.2
Launois-Bensaude's lipomatosis 272.8
Launois-Cléret syndrome (adiposogenital dystrophy) 253.8
Launois' syndrome (pituitary gigantism) 253.0
Laurence-Moon-Biedl syndrome (obesity, polydactyly, and mental retardation) 759.89
LAV (disease) (illness) (infection) — *see* Human immunodeficiency virus (disease) (illness) (infection)
LAV/HTLV-III (disease) (illness) (infection) — *see* Human immunodeficiency virus (disease) (illness) (infection)
Lawford's syndrome (encephalocutaneous angiomatosis) 759.6
Laxative habit — *see also* Abuse, drugs, nondependent 305.9 ☑
Lax, laxity — *see also* Relaxation
  ligament 728.4
  skin (acquired) 701.8
    congenital 756.83
Lazy leukocyte syndrome 288.09 ▲
LCAD (long chain/very long chain acyl CoA dehydrogenase deficiency, VLCAD) 277.85
LCHAD (long chain 3-hydroxyacyl CoA dehydrogenase deficiency) 277.85
Lead — *see also* condition
  exposure to V15.86
  incrustation of cornea 371.15
  poisoning 984.9
    specified type of lead — *see* Table of Drugs and Chemicals
Lead miners' lung 503
Leakage
  amniotic fluid 658.1 ☑
    with delayed delivery 658.2 ☑
    affecting fetus or newborn 761.1
  bile from drainage tube (T tube) 997.4
  blood (microscopic), fetal, into maternal circulation 656.0 ☑
    affecting management of pregnancy or puerperium 656.0 ☑
  device, implant, or graft — *see* Complications, mechanical
  spinal fluid at lumbar puncture site 997.09
  urine, continuous 788.37
Leaky heart — *see* Endocarditis
Learning defect, specific NEC (strephosymbolia) 315.2
Leather bottle stomach (M8142/3) 151.9
Leber's
  congenital amaurosis 362.76
  optic atrophy (hereditary) 377.16
Lederer's anemia or disease (acquired infectious hemolytic anemia) 283.19
Lederer-Brill syndrome (acquired infectious hemolytic anemia) 283.19
Leeches (aquatic) (land) 134.2
Left-sided neglect 781.8
Leg — *see* condition
Legal investigation V62.5
Legg (-Calvé) -Perthes disease or syndrome (osteochondrosis, femoral capital) 732.1
Legionnaires' disease 482.84
Leigh's disease 330.8
Leiner's disease (exfoliative dermatitis) 695.89

Leiofibromyoma (M8890/0) — *see also* Leiomyoma
  uterus (cervix) (corpus) (*see also* Leiomyoma, uterus) 218.9
Leiomyoblastoma (M8891/1) — *see* Neoplasm, connective tissue, uncertain behavior
Leiomyofibroma (M8890/0) — *see also* Neoplasm, connective tissue, benign
  uterus (cervix) (corpus) (*see also* Leiomyoma, uterus) 218.9
Leiomyoma (M8890/0) — *see also* Neoplasm, connective tissue, benign
  bizarre (M8893/0) — *see* Neoplasm, connective tissue, benign
  cellular (M8892/1) — *see* Neoplasm, connective tissue, uncertain behavior
  epithelioid (M8891/1) — *see* Neoplasm, connective tissue, uncertain behavior
  prostate (polypoid) 600.20
    with
      other lower urinary tract symptoms (LUTS) 600.21 ●
      urinary ●
        obstruction 600.21 ●
        retention 600.21 ●
  uterus (cervix) (corpus) 218.9
    interstitial 218.1
    intramural 218.1
    submucous 218.0
    subperitoneal 218.2
    subserous 218.2
  vascular (M8894/0) — *see* Neoplasm, connective tissue, benign
Leiomyomatosis (intravascular) (M8890/1) — *see* Neoplasm, connective tissue, uncertain behavior
Leiomyosarcoma (M8890/3) — *see also* Neoplasm, connective tissue, malignant
  epithelioid (M8891/3) — *see* Neoplasm, connective tissue, malignant
Leishmaniasis 085.9
  American 085.5
    cutaneous 085.4
    mucocutaneous 085.5
  Asian desert 085.2
  Brazilian 085.5
  cutaneous 085.9
    acute necrotizing 085.2
    American 085.4
    Asian desert 085.2
    diffuse 085.3
    dry form 085.1
    Ethiopian 085.3
    eyelid 085.5 [373.6]
    late 085.1
    lepromatous 085.3
    recurrent 085.1
    rural 085.2
    ulcerating 085.1
    urban 085.1
    wet form 085.2
    zoonotic form 085.2
  dermal (*see also* Leishmaniasis, cutaneous)
    post kala-azar 085.0
  eyelid 085.5 [373.6]
  infantile 085.0
  Mediterranean 085.0
  mucocutaneous (American) 085.5
  naso-oral 085.5
  nasopharyngeal 085.5
  Old World 085.1
  tegumentaria diffusa 085.4
  vaccination, prophylactic (against) V05.2
  visceral (Indian) 085.0
Leishmanoid, dermal — *see also* Leishmaniasis, cutaneous
  post kala-azar 085.0

Leloir's disease 695.4
Lemiere syndrome 451.89
Lenegre's disease 426.0
Lengthening, leg 736.81
Lennox-Gastaut syndrome 345.0 ☑
  with tonic seizures 345.1 ☑
Lennox's syndrome — *see also* Epilepsy
  345.0 ☑
Lens — *see* condition
Lenticonus (anterior) (posterior) (congenital) 743.36
Lenticular degeneration, progressive 275.1
Lentiglobus (posterior) (congenital) 743.36
Lentigo (congenital) 709.09
  juvenile 709.09
  Maligna (M8742/2) (*see also* Neoplasm, skin, in situ)
    melanoma (M8742/3) — *see* Melanoma
  senile 709.09
Leonine leprosy 030.0
Leontiasis
  ossium 733.3
  syphilitic 095.8
    congenital 090.5
Léopold-Lévi's syndrome (paroxysmal thyroid instability) 242.9 ☑
Lepore hemoglobin syndrome 282.49
Lepothrix 039.0
Lepra 030.9
  Willan's 696.1
Leprechaunism 259.8
Lepromatous leprosy 030.0
Leprosy 030.9
  anesthetic 030.1
  beriberi 030.1
  borderline (group B) (infiltrated) (neuritic) 030.3
  cornea (*see also* Leprosy, by type) 030.9 [371.89]
  dimorphous (group B) (infiltrated) (lepromatous) (neuritic) (tuberculoid) 030.3
  eyelid 030.0 [373.4]
  indeterminate (group I) (macular) (neuritic) (uncharacteristic) 030.2
  leonine 030.0
  lepromatous (diffuse) (infiltrated) (macular) (neuritic) (nodular) (type L) 030.0
  macular (early) (neuritic) (simple) 030.2
  maculoanesthetic 030.1
  mixed 030.0
  neuro 030.1
  nodular 030.0
  primary neuritic 030.3
  specified type or group NEC 030.8
  tubercular 030.1
  tuberculoid (macular) (maculoanesthetic) (major) (minor) (neuritic) (type T) 030.1
Leptocytosis, hereditary 282.49
Leptomeningitis (chronic) (circumscribed) (hemorrhagic) (nonsuppurative) — *see also* Meningitis 322.9
  aseptic 047.9
    adenovirus 049.1
    Coxsackie virus 047.0
    ECHO virus 047.1
    enterovirus 047.9
    lymphocytic choriomeningitis 049.0
  epidemic 036.0
  late effect — *see* category 326
  meningococcal 036.0
  pneumococcal 320.1
  syphilitic 094.2
  tuberculous (*see also* Tuberculosis, meninges) 013.0 ☑
Leptomeningopathy — *see also* Meningitis 322.9
Leptospiral — *see* condition
Leptospirochetal — *see* condition

Leptospirosis 100.9
  autumnalis 100.89
  canicula 100.89
  grippotyphosa 100.89
  hebdomidis 100.89
  icterohemorrhagica 100.0
  nanukayami 100.89
  pomona 100.89
  Weil's disease 100.0
Leptothricosis — *see* Actinomycosis
Leptothrix infestation — *see* Actinomycosis
Leptotricosis — *see* Actinomycosis
Leptus dermatitis 133.8
Leriche's syndrome (aortic bifurcation occlusion) 444.0
Léris pleonosteosis 756.89
Léri-Weill syndrome 756.59
Lermoyez's syndrome — *see also* Disease, Ménière's 386.00
Lesbianism — *omit code*
  ego-dystonic 302.0
  problems with 302.0
Lesch-Nyhan syndrome (hypoxanthineguanine-phosphoribosyltransferase deficiency) 277.2
Lesion▶(s)◀
  abducens nerve 378.54
  alveolar process 525.8
  anorectal 569.49
  aortic (valve) — *see* Endocarditis, aortic
  auditory nerve 388.5
  basal ganglion 333.90
  bile duct (*see also* Disease, biliary) 576.8
  bladder 596.9
  bone 733.90
  brachial plexus 353.0
  brain 348.8
    congenital 742.9
    vascular (*see also* Lesion, cerebrovascular) 437.9
      degenerative 437.1
      healed or old without residuals V12.59
      hypertensive 437.2
      late effect — *see* Late effect(s) (of) cerebrovascular disease
  buccal 528.9
  calcified — *see* Calcification
  canthus 373.9
  carate — *see* Pinta, lesions
  cardia 537.89
  cardiac — *see also* Disease, heart
    congenital 746.9
    valvular — *see* Endocarditis
  cauda equina 344.60
    with neurogenic bladder 344.61
  cecum 569.89
  cerebral — *see* Lesion, brain
  cerebrovascular (*see also* Disease, cerebrovascular NEC) 437.9
    degenerative 437.1
      healed or old without residuals V12.59
    hypertensive 437.2
    specified type NEC 437.8
  cervical root (nerve) NEC 353.2
  chiasmal 377.54
    associated with
      inflammatory disorders 377.54
      neoplasm NEC 377.52
        pituitary 377.51
      pituitary disorders 377.51
      vascular disorders 377.53
  chorda tympani 351.8
  coin, lung 793.1
  colon 569.89
  congenital — *see* Anomaly
  conjunctiva 372.9
  coronary artery (*see also* Ischemia, heart) 414.9
  cranial nerve 352.9
    first 352.0

Lesion▶(s)◀ — *continued*
  cranial nerve — *continued*
    second 377.49
    third
      partial 378.51
      total 378.52
    fourth 378.53
    fifth 350.9
    sixth 378.54
    seventh 351.9
    eighth 388.5
    ninth 352.2
    tenth 352.3
    eleventh 352.4
    twelfth 352.5
  cystic — *see* Cyst
  degenerative — *see* Degeneration
  dermal (skin) 709.9
  Dieulafoy (hemorrhagic)
    of
      duodenum 537.84
      intestine 569.86
      stomach 537.84
  duodenum 537.89
    with obstruction 537.3
  eyelid 373.9
  gasserian ganglion 350.8
  gastric 537.89
  gastroduodenal 537.89
  gastrointestinal 569.89
  glossopharyngeal nerve 352.2
  heart (organic) (*see also* Disease, heart)
    vascular — *see* Disease, cardiovascular
  helix (ear) 709.9
  high grade myelodysplastic syndrome 238.73 ●
  hyperchromic, due to pinta (carate) 103.1
  hyperkeratotic (*see also* Hyperkeratosis) 701.1
  hypoglossal nerve 352.5
  hypopharynx 478.29
  hypothalamic 253.9
  ileocecal coil 569.89
  ileum 569.89
  iliohypogastric nerve 355.79
  ilioinguinal nerve 355.79
  in continuity — *see* Injury, nerve, by site
  inflammatory — *see* Inflammation
    intestine 569.89
  intracerebral — *see* Lesion, brain
  intrachiasmal (optic) (*see also* Lesion, chiasmal) 377.54
  intracranial, space-occupying NEC 784.2
  joint 719.90
    ankle 719.97
    elbow 719.92
    foot 719.97
    hand 719.94
    hip 719.95
    knee 719.96
    multiple sites 719.99
    pelvic region 719.95
    sacroiliac (old) 724.6
    shoulder (region) 719.91
    specified site NEC 719.98
    wrist 719.93
  keratotic (*see also* Keratosis) 701.1
  kidney (*see also* Disease, renal) 593.9
  laryngeal nerve (recurrent) 352.3
  leonine 030.0
  lip 528.5
  liver 573.8
  low grade myelodysplastic syndrome 238.72 ●
  lumbosacral
    plexus 353.1
    root (nerve) NEC 353.4
  lung 518.89
    coin 793.1
  maxillary sinus 473.0
  mitral — *see* Endocarditis, mitral

Lesion▶(s)◀ — *continued*
  motor cortex 348.8
  nerve (*see also* Disorder, nerve) 355.9
  nervous system 349.9
    congenital 742.9
  nonallopathic NEC 739.9
    in region (of)
      abdomen 739.9
      acromioclavicular 739.7
      cervical, cervicothoracic 739.1
      costochondral 739.8
      costovertebral 739.8
      extremity
        lower 739.6
        upper 739.7
      head 739.0
      hip 739.5
      lower extremity 739.6
      lumbar, lumbosacral 739.3
      occipitocervical 739.0
      pelvic 739.5
      pubic 739.5
      rib cage 739.8
      sacral, sacrococcygeal, sacroiliac 739.4
      sternochondral 739.8
      sternoclavicular 739.7
      thoracic, thoracolumbar 739.2
      upper extremity 739.7
  nose (internal) 478.19   ▲
  obstructive — *see* Obstruction
  obturator nerve 355.79
  occlusive
    artery — *see* Embolism, artery
  organ or site NEC — *see* Disease, by site
  osteolytic 733.90
  paramacular, of retina 363.32
  peptic 537.89
  periodontal, due to traumatic occlusion 523.8
  perirectal 569.49
  peritoneum (granulomatous) 568.89
  pigmented (skin) 709.00
  pinta — *see* Pinta, lesions
  polypoid — *see* Polyp
  prechiasmal (optic) (*see also* Lesion, chiasmal) 377.54
  primary (*see also* Syphilis, primary)
    carate 103.0
    pinta 103.0
    yaws 102.0
  pulmonary 518.89
    valve (*see also* Endocarditis, pulmonary) 424.3
  pylorus 537.89
  radiation NEC 990
  radium NEC 990
  rectosigmoid 569.89
  retina, retinal (*see also* Retinopathy)
    vascular 362.17
  retroperitoneal 568.89
  romanus 720.1
  sacroiliac (joint) 724.6
  salivary gland 527.8
    benign lymphoepithelial 527.8
  saphenous nerve 355.79
  secondary — *see* Syphilis, secondary
  sigmoid 569.89
  sinus (accessory) (nasal) (*see also* Sinusitis) 473.9
  skin 709.9
    suppurative 686.00
  SLAP (superior glenoid labrum) 840.7
  space-occupying, intracranial NEC 784.2
  spinal cord 336.9
    congenital 742.9
    traumatic (complete) (incomplete) (transverse) (*see also* Injury, spinal, by site)
      with
        broken
          back — *see* Fracture, vertebra, by site, with spinal cord injury

Index

Leloir's disease — Lesion(s)

☑ Additional Digit Required — Refer to the Tabular List for Digit Selection   ▽ Subterms under main terms may continue to next column or page

2007 ICD-9-CM   ▶◀ Revised Text   ● New Line   ▲ Revised Code   **October 2006 · Volume 2 — 179**

Lesion▶(s)◀ — *continued*
spinal cord — *continued*
traumatic (*see also* Injury, spinal, by site) — *continued*
with — *continued*
broken — *continued*
neck — *see* Fracture, vertebra, cervical, with spinal cord injury
fracture, vertebra — *see* Fracture, vertebra, by site, with spinal cord injury
spleen 289.50
stomach 537.89
superior glenoid labrum (SLAP) 840.7
syphilitic — *see* Syphilis
tertiary — *see* Syphilis, tertiary
thoracic root (nerve) 353.3
tonsillar fossa 474.9
tooth, teeth 525.8
white spot 521.01
traumatic NEC (*see also* nature and site of injury) 959.9
tricuspid (valve) — *see* Endocarditis, tricuspid
trigeminal nerve 350.9
ulcerated or ulcerative — *see* Ulcer
uterus NEC 621.9
vagina 623.8
vagus nerve 352.3
valvular — *see* Endocarditis
vascular 459.9
affecting central nervous system (*see also* Lesion, cerebrovascular) 437.9
following trauma (*see also* Injury, blood vessel, by site) 904.9
retina 362.17
traumatic — *see* Injury, blood vessel, by site
umbilical cord 663.6 ☑
affecting fetus or newborn 762.6
visual
cortex NEC (*see also* Disorder, visual, cortex) 377.73
pathway NEC (*see also* Disorder, visual, pathway) 377.63
warty — *see* Verruca
white spot, on teeth 521.01
x-ray NEC 990
Lethargic — *see* condition
Lethargy 780.79
Letterer-Siwe disease (acute histiocytosis X) (M9722/3) 202.5 ☑
Leucinosis 270.3
Leucocoria 360.44
Leucosarcoma (M9850/3) 207.8 ☑
Leukasmus 270.2
Leukemia, leukemic (congenital) (M9800/3) 208.9 ☑

Note — *Use the following fifth-digit subclassification for categories 203–208:*

0   without mention of remission

1   with remission

acute NEC (M9801/3) 208.0 ☑
aleukemic NEC (M9804/3) 208.8 ☑
granulocytic (M9864/3) 205.8 ☑
basophilic (M9870/3) 205.1 ☑
blast (cell) (M9801/3) 208.0 ☑
blastic (M9801/3) 208.0 ☑
granulocytic (M9861/3) 205.0 ☑
chronic NEC (M9803/3) 208.1 ☑
compound (M9810/3) 207.8 ☑
eosinophilic (M9880/3) 205.1 ☑
giant cell (M9910/3) 207.2 ☑
granulocytic (M9860/3) 205.9 ☑
acute (M9861/3) 205.0 ☑
aleukemic (M9864/3) 205.8 ☑
blastic (M9861/3) 205.0 ☑
chronic (M9863/3) 205.1 ☑
subacute (M9862/3) 205.2 ☑
subleukemic (M9864/3) 205.8 ☑

Leukemia, leukemic — *continued*
hairy cell (M9940/3) 202.4 ☑
hemoblastic (M9801/3) 208.0
histiocytic (M9890/3) 206.9 ☑
lymphatic (M9820/3) 204.9 ☑
acute (M9821/3) 204.0 ☑
aleukemic (M9824/3) 204.8 ☑
chronic (M9823/3) 204.1 ☑
subacute (M9822/3) 204.2 ☑
subleukemic (M9824/3) 204.8 ☑
lymphoblastic (M9821/3) 204.0 ☑
lymphocytic (M9820/3) 204.9 ☑
acute (M9821/3) 204.0 ☑
aleukemic (M9824/3) 204.8 ☑
chronic (M9823/3) 204.1 ☑
subacute (M9822/3) 204.2 ☑
subleukemic (M9824/3) 204.8 ☑
lymphogenous (M9820/3) — *see* Leukemia, lymphoid
lymphoid (M9820/3) 204.9 ☑
acute (M9821/3) 204.0 ☑
aleukemic (M9824/3) 204.8 ☑
blastic (M9821/3) 204.0 ☑
chronic (M9823/3) 204.1 ☑
subacute (M9822/3) 204.2 ☑
subleukemic (M9824/3) 204.8 ☑
lymphosarcoma cell (M9850/3) 207.8 ☑
mast cell (M9900/3) 207.8 ☑
megakaryocytic (M9910/3) 207.2 ☑
megakaryocytoid (M9910/3) 207.2 ☑
mixed (cell) (M9810/3) 207.8 ☑
monoblastic (M9891/3) 206.0 ☑
monocytic (Schilling-type) (M9890/3) 206.9 ☑
acute (M9891/3) 206.0 ☑
aleukemic (M9894/3) 206.8 ☑
chronic (M9893/3) 206.1 ☑
Naegeli-type (M9863/3) 205.1 ☑
subacute (M9892/3) 206.2 ☑
subleukemic (M9894/3) 206.8 ☑
monocytoid (M9890/3) 206.9 ☑
acute (M9891/3) 206.0 ☑
aleukemic (M9894/3) 206.8 ☑
chronic (M9893/3) 206.1 ☑
myelogenous (M9863/3) 205.1 ☑
subacute (M9892/3) 206.2 ☑
subleukemic (M9894/3) 206.8 ☑
monomyelocytic (M9860/3) — *see* Leukemia, myelomonocytic
myeloblastic (M9861/3) 205.0 ☑
myelocytic (M9863/3) 205.1 ☑
acute (M9861/3) 205.0 ☑
myelogenous (M9860/3) 205.9 ☑
acute (M9861/3) 205.0 ☑
aleukemic (M9864/3) 205.8 ☑
chronic (M9863/3) 205.1 ☑
monocytoid (M9863/3) 205.1 ☑
subacute (M9862/3) 205.2 ☑
subleukemic (M9864) 205.8 ☑
myeloid (M9860/3) 205.9 ☑
acute (M9861/3) 205.0 ☑
aleukemic (M9864/3) 205.8 ☑
chronic (M9863/3) 205.1 ☑
subacute (M9862/3) 205.2 ☑
subleukemic (M9864/3) 205.8 ☑
myelomonocytic (M9860/3) 205.9 ☑
acute (M9861/3) 205.0 ☑
chronic (M9863/3) 205.1 ☑
Naegeli-type monocytic (M9863/3) 205.1 ☑
neutrophilic (M9865/3) 205.1 ☑
plasma cell (M9830/3) 203.1 ☑
plasmacytic (M9830/3) 203.1 ☑
prolymphocytic (M9825/3) — *see* Leukemia, lymphoid
promyelocytic, acute (M9866/3) 205.0 ☑
Schilling-type monocytic (M9890/3) — *see* Leukemia, monocytic
stem cell (M9801/3) 208.0 ☑
subacute NEC (M9802/3) 208.2 ☑
subleukemic NEC (M9804/3) 208.8 ☑
thrombocytic (M9910/3) 207.2 ☑

Leukemia, leukemic — *continued*
undifferentiated (M9801/3) 208.0 ☑
Leukemoid reaction ▶(basophilic)◀ (lymphocytic) (monocytic) (myelocytic) ▶(neutrophilic)◀ 288.62 ▲
Leukoclastic vasculitis 446.29
Leukocoria 360.44
Leukocythemia — *see* Leukemia
Leukocytopenia 288.50 ●
Leukocytosis 288.60 ▲
basophilic 288.8
eosinophilic 288.3
lymphocytic 288.8
monocytic 288.8
neutrophilic 288.8
Leukoderma 709.09
syphilitic 091.3
late 095.8
Leukodermia — *see also* Leukoderma 709.09
Leukodystrophy (cerebral) (globoid cell) (metachromatic) (progressive) (sudanophilic) 330.0
Leukoedema, mouth or tongue 528.79
Leukoencephalitis
acute hemorrhagic (postinfectious) NEC 136.9 *[323.61]* ▲
postimmunization or postvaccinal 323.51 ▲
subacute sclerosing 046.2
van Bogaert's 046.2
van Bogaert's (sclerosing) 046.2
Leukoencephalopathy — *see also* Encephalitis 323.9
acute necrotizing hemorrhagic (postinfection) 136.9 *[323.61]* ▲
postimmunization or postvaccinal 323.51 ▲
metachromatic 330.0
multifocal (progressive) 046.3
progressive multifocal 046.3
Leukoerythroblastosis 289.9 ▲
Leukoerythrosis 289.0
Leukokeratosis — *see also* Leukoplakia 702.8
mouth 528.6
nicotina palati 528.79
tongue 528.6
Leukokoria 360.44
Leukokraurosis vulva, vulvae 624.0
Leukolymphosarcoma (M9850/3) 207.8 ☑
Leukoma (cornea) (interfering with central vision) 371.03
adherent 371.04
Leukomalacia, periventricular 779.7
Leukomelanopathy, hereditary 288.2
Leukonychia (punctata) (striata) 703.8
congenital 757.5
Leukopathia
unguium 703.8
congenital 757.5
Leukopenia 288.50 ▲
basophilic 288.59 ●
cyclic 288.02 ▲
eosinophilic 288.59 ●
familial 288.59 ▲
malignant ▶(*see also* Agranulocytosis)◀ 288.09 ▲
periodic 288.02 ▲
transitory neonatal 776.7
Leukopenic — *see* condition
Leukoplakia 702.8
anus 569.49
bladder (postinfectional) 596.8
buccal 528.6
cervix (uteri) 622.2
esophagus 530.83
gingiva 528.6
kidney (pelvis) 593.89
larynx 478.79
lip 528.6
mouth 528.6
oral soft tissue (including tongue) (mucosa) 528.6

Leukoplakia — *continued*
palate 528.6
pelvis (kidney) 593.89
penis (infectional) 607.0
rectum 569.49
syphilitic 095.8
tongue 528.6
tonsil 478.29
ureter (postinfectional) 593.89
urethra (postinfectional) 599.84
uterus 621.8
vagina 623.1
vesical 596.8
vocal cords 478.5
vulva 624.0
Leukopolioencephalopathy 330.0
Leukorrhea (vagina) 623.5
due to trichomonas (vaginalis) 131.00
trichomonal (Trichomonas vaginalis) 131.00
Leukosarcoma (M9850/3) 207.8 ☑
Leukosis (M9800/3) — *see* Leukemia
Lev's disease or syndrome (acquired complete heart block) 426.0
Levi's syndrome (pituitary dwarfism) 253.3
Levocardia (isolated) 746.87
with situs inversus 759.3
Levulosuria 271.2
Lewandowski's disease (primary) — *see also* Tuberculosis 017.0 ☑
Lewandowski-Lutz disease (epidermodysplasia verruciformis) 078.19
Lewy body dementia 331.82
Lewy body disease 331.82
Leyden's disease (periodic vomiting) 536.2
Leyden-Möbius dystrophy 359.1
Leydig cell
carcinoma (M8650/3)
specified site — *see* Neoplasm, by site, malignant
unspecified site
female 183.0
male 186.9
tumor (M8650/1)
benign (M8650/0)
specified site — *see* Neoplasm, by site, benign
unspecified site
female 220
male 222.0
malignant (M8650/3)
specified site — *see* Neoplasm, by site, malignant
unspecified site
female 183.0
male 186.9
specified site — *see* Neoplasm, by site, uncertain behavior
unspecified site
female 236.2
male 236.4
Leydig-Sertoli cell tumor (M8631/0)
specified site — *see* Neoplasm, by site, benign
unspecified site
female 220
male 222.0
LGSIL (low grade squamous intraepithelial lesion) 795.03
Liar, pathologic 301.7
Libman-Sacks disease or syndrome 710.0 *[424.91]*
Lice (infestation) 132.9
body (pediculus corporis) 132.1
crab 132.2
head (pediculus capitis) 132.0
mixed (classifiable to more than one of the categories 132.0–132.2) 132.3
pubic (pediculus pubis) 132.2
Lichen 697.9
albus 701.0
annularis 695.89
atrophicus 701.0

☑ Additional Digit Required — Refer to the Tabular List for Digit Selection
▽ Subterms under main terms may continue to next column or page
180 — Volume 2 · October 2006
▶◀ Revised Text   ● New Line   ▲ Revised Code
2007 ICD-9-CM

Lichen — continued
  corneus obtusus 698.3
  myxedematous 701.8
  nitidus 697.1
  pilaris 757.39
    acquired 701.1
  planopilaris 697.0
  planus (acute) (chronicus) (hyper-
    trophic) (verrucous) 697.0
    morphoeicus 701.0
    sclerosus (et atrophicus) 701.0
  ruber 696.4
    acuminatus 696.4
    moniliformis 697.8
    obtusus corneus 698.3
    of Wilson 697.0
    planus 697.0
  sclerosus (et atrophicus) 701.0
  scrofulosus (primary) (see also Tuber-
    culosis) 017.0 ☑
  simplex (Vidal's) 698.3
    chronicus 698.3
    circumscriptus 698.3
  spinulosus 757.39
    mycotic 117.9
  striata 697.8
  urticatus 698.2
Lichenification 698.3
  nodular 698.3
Lichenoides tuberculosis (primary) —
  see also Tuberculosis 017.0 ☑
Lichtheim's disease or syndrome
  (subacute combined sclerosis with
  pernicious anemia) 281.0 [336.2]
Lien migrans 289.59
Lientery — see also Diarrhea 787.91
  infectious 009.2
Life circumstance problem NEC V62.89
Li-Fraumeni cancer syndrome V84.01
Ligament — see condition
Light-for-dates (infant) 764.0 ☑
  with signs of fetal malnutrition
    764.1 ☑
  affecting management of pregnancy
    656.5 ☑
Light-headedness 780.4
Lightning (effects) (shock) (stroke)
  (struck by) 994.0
  burn — see Burn, by site
  foot 266.2
Lightwood's disease or syndrome (renal
  tubular acidosis) 588.89
Lignac's disease (cystinosis) 270.0
Lignac (-Fanconi) syndrome (cystinosis)
  270.0
**Lignac (-de Toni) (-Fanconi) (-Debré)
  syndrome** (cystinosis) 270.0
Ligneous thyroiditis 245.3
Likoff's syndrome (angina in
  menopausal women) 413.9
Limb — see condition
Limitation of joint motion — see also
  Stiffness, joint 719.5 ☑
  sacroiliac 724.6
Limit dextrinosis 271.0
Limited
  cardiac reserve — see Disease, heart
  duction, eye NEC 378.63
  mandibular range of motion 524.52
Lindau's disease (retinocerebral an-
  giomatosis) 759.6
Lindau (-von Hippel) disease (angiomato-
  sis retinocerebellosa) 759.6
Linea corneae senilis 371.41
Lines
  Beau's (transverse furrows on finger-
    nails) 703.8
  Harris' 733.91
  Hudson-Stähli 371.11
  Stähli's 371.11
Lingua
  geographical 529.1
  nigra (villosa) 529.3
  plicata 529.5
    congenital 750.13
  tylosis 528.6

Lingual (tongue) — see also condition
  thyroid 759.2
Linitis (gastric) 535.4 ☑
  plastica (M8142/3) 151.9
Lioderma essentialis (cum melanosis et
  telangiectasia) 757.33
Lip — see also condition
  biting 528.9
Lipalgia 272.8
Lipedema — see Edema
Lipemia — see also Hyperlipidemia 272.4
  retina, retinalis 272.3
Lipidosis 272.7
  cephalin 272.7
  cerebral (infantile) (juvenile) (late)
    330.1
  cerebroretinal 330.1 [362.71]
  cerebroside 272.7
  cerebrospinal 272.7
  chemically-induced 272.7
  cholesterol 272.7
  diabetic 250.8 ☑ [272.7]
  dystopic (hereditary) 272.7
  glycolipid 272.7
  hepatosplenomegalic 272.3
  hereditary, dystopic 272.7
  sulfatide 330.0
Lipoadenoma (M8324/0) — see Neoplasm, by site, benign
Lipoblastoma (M8881/0) — see Lipoma,
  by site
Lipoblastomatosis (M8881/0) — see
  Lipoma, by site
Lipochondrodystrophy 277.5
Lipochrome histiocytosis (familial)
  288.1
Lipodystrophia progressiva 272.6
Lipodystrophy (progressive) 272.6
  insulin 272.6
  intestinal 040.2
  mesenteric 567.82
Lipofibroma (M8851/0) — see Lipoma,
  by site
Lipoglycoproteinosis 272.8
Lipogranuloma, sclerosing 709.8
Lipogranulomatosis (disseminated)
  272.8
  kidney 272.8
Lipoid — see also condition
  histiocytosis 272.7
    essential 272.7
  nephrosis (see also Nephrosis) 581.3
  proteinosis of Urbach 272.8
Lipoidemia — see also Hyperlipidemia
  272.4
Lipoidosis — see also Lipidosis 272.7
Lipoma (M8850/0) 214.9
  breast (skin) 214.1
  face 214.0
  fetal (M8881/0) (see also Lipoma, by
    site)
  fat cell (M8880/0) — see Lipoma,
    by site
  infiltrating (M8856/0) — see Lipoma,
    by site
  intra-abdominal 214.3
  intramuscular (M8856/0) — see
    Lipoma, by site
  intrathoracic 214.2
  kidney 214.3
  mediastinum 214.2
  muscle 214.8
  peritoneum 214.3
  retroperitoneum 214.3
  skin 214.1
    face 214.0
  spermatic cord 214.4
  spindle cell (M8857/0) — see Lipoma,
    by site
  stomach 214.3
  subcutaneous tissue 214.1
    face 214.0
  thymus 214.2
  thyroid gland 214.2
Lipomatosis (dolorosa) 272.8
  epidural 214.8

Lipomatosis — continued
  fetal (M8881/0) — see Lipoma, by site
  Launois-Bensaude's 272.8
Lipomyohemangioma (M8860/0)
  specified site — see Neoplasm, connec-
    tive tissue, benign
  unspecified site 223.0
Lipomyoma (M8860/0)
  specified site — see Neoplasm, connec-
    tive tissue, benign
  unspecified site 223.0
Lipomyxoma (M8852/0) — see Lipoma,
  by site
Lipomyxosarcoma (M8852/3) — see
  Neoplasm, connective tissue, malignant
Lipophagocytosis 289.89
Lipoproteinemia (alpha) 272.4
  broad-beta 272.2
  floating-beta 272.2
  hyper-pre-beta 272.1
Lipoproteinosis (Rössle-Urbach-Wiethe)
  272.8
Liposarcoma (M8850/3) — see also
  Neoplasm, connective tissue, malignant
  differentiated type (M8851/3) — see
    Neoplasm, connective tissue,
    malignant
  embryonal (M8852/3) — see Neo-
    plasm, connective tissue, malig-
    nant
  mixed type (M8855/3) — see Neo-
    plasm, connective tissue, malig-
    nant
  myxoid (M8852/3) — see Neoplasm,
    connective tissue, malignant
  pleomorphic (M8854/3) — see Neo-
    plasm, connective tissue, malig-
    nant
  round cell (M8853/3) — see Neo-
    plasm, connective tissue, malig-
    nant
  well differentiated type (M8851/3) —
    see Neoplasm, connective tis-
    sue, malignant
Liposynovitis prepatellaris 272.8
Lipping
  cervix 622.0
  spine (see also Spondylosis) 721.90
  vertebra (see also Spondylosis) 721.90
Lip pits (mucus), congenital 750.25
Lipschütz disease or ulcer 616.50
Lipuria 791.1
  bilharziasis 120.0
Liquefaction, vitreous humor 379.21
Lisping 307.9
Lissauer's paralysis 094.1
Lissencephalia, lissencephaly 742.2
Listerellose 027.0
Listeriose 027.0
Listeriosis 027.0
  congenital 771.2
  fetal 771.2
  suspected fetal damage affecting
    management of pregnancy
    655.4 ☑
Listlessness 780.79
Lithemia 790.6
Lithiasis — see also Calculus
  hepatic (duct) — see Choledocholithi-
    asis
  urinary 592.9
Lithopedion 779.9
  affecting management of pregnancy
    656.8 ☑
Lithosis (occupational) 502
  with tuberculosis — see Tuberculosis,
    pulmonary
Lithuria 791.9
Litigation V62.5
Little
  league elbow 718.82
  stroke syndrome 435.9
Little's disease — see Palsy, cerebral

Littre's
  gland — see condition
  hernia — see Hernia, Littre's
Littritis — see also Urethritis 597.89
Livedo 782.61
  annularis 782.61
  racemose 782.61
  reticularis 782.61
Live flesh 781.0
Liver — see also condition
  donor V59.6
Livida, asphyxia
  newborn 768.6
Living
  alone V60.3
  with handicapped person V60.4
Lloyd's syndrome 258.1
Loa loa 125.2
Loasis 125.2
Lobe, lobar — see condition
Lobo's disease or blastomycosis 116.2
Lobomycosis 116.2
Lobotomy syndrome 310.0
Lobstein's disease (brittle bones and
  blue sclera) 756.51
Lobster-claw hand 755.58
Lobulation (congenital) — see also
  Anomaly, specified type NEC, by
  site
  kidney, fetal 753.3
  liver, abnormal 751.69
  spleen 759.0
Lobule, lobular — see condition
Local, localized — see condition
Locked bowel or intestine — see also
  Obstruction, intestine 560.9
Locked-in state 344.81
Locked twins 660.5 ☑
  affecting fetus or newborn 763.1
Locking
  joint (see also Derangement, joint)
    718.90
  knee 717.9
Lockjaw — see also Tetanus 037
Locomotor ataxia (progressive) 094.0
Löffler's
  endocarditis 421.0
  eosinophilia or syndrome 518.3
  pneumonia 518.3
  syndrome (eosinophilic pneumonitis)
    518.3
Löfgren's syndrome (sarcoidosis) 135
Loiasis 125.2
  eyelid 125.2 [373.6]
Loneliness V62.89
Lone star fever 082.8
Longitudinal stripes or grooves, nails
  703.8
  congenital 757.5
Long labor 662.1 ☑
  affecting fetus or newborn 763.89
  first stage 662.0 ☑
  second stage 662.2 ☑
Long-term (current) **drug use** V58.69
  antibiotics V58.62
  anticoagulants V58.61
  anti-inflammatories, non-steroidal
    (NSAID) V58.64
  antiplatelets/antithrombotics V58.63
  aspirin V58.66
  insulin V58.67
  steroids V58.65
Loop
  intestine (see also Volvulus) 560.2
  intrascleral nerve 379.29
  vascular on papilla (optic) 743.57
Loose — see also condition
  body
    in tendon sheath 727.82
    joint 718.10
      ankle 718.17
      elbow 718.12
      foot 718.17
      hand 718.14
      hip 718.15
      knee 717.6

☑ Additional Digit Required — Refer to the Tabular List for Digit Selection   ▽ Subterms under main terms may continue to next column or page

2007 ICD-9-CM   ▶◀ Revised Text   ● New Line   ▲ Revised Code   **Volume 2 — 181**

Loose — see also condition — continued
- body — continued
  - joint — continued
    - multiple sites 718.19
    - pelvic region 718.15
    - prosthetic implant — see Complications, mechanical
    - shoulder (region) 718.11
    - specified site NEC 718.18
    - wrist 718.13
  - cartilage (joint) (see also Loose, body, joint) 718.1 ☑
    - knee 717.6
  - facet (vertebral) 724.9
  - prosthetic implant — see Complications, mechanical
  - sesamoid, joint (see also Loose, body, joint) 718.1 ☑
  - tooth, teeth 525.8
Loosening epiphysis 732.9
Looser (-Debray) -Milkman syndrome (osteomalacia with pseudofractures) 268.2
Lop ear (deformity) 744.29
Lorain's disease or syndrome (pituitary dwarfism) 253.3
Lorain-Levi syndrome (pituitary dwarfism) 253.3
Lordosis (acquired) (postural) 737.20
- congenital 754.2
- due to or associated with
  - Charcôt-Marie-Tooth disease 356.1 [737.42]
  - mucopolysaccharidosis 277.5 [737.42]
  - neurofibromatosis 237.71 [737.42]
  - osteitis
    - deformans 731.0 [737.42]
    - fibrosa cystica 252.01 [737.42]
  - osteoporosis (see also Osteoporosis) 733.00 [737.42]
  - poliomyelitis (see also Poliomyelitis) 138 [737.42]
  - tuberculosis (see also Tuberculosis) 015.0 ☑ [737.42]
- late effect of rickets 268.1 [737.42]
- postlaminectomy 737.21
- postsurgical NEC 737.22
- rachitic 268.1 [737.42]
- specified NEC 737.29
- tuberculous (see also Tuberculosis) 015.0 ☑ [737.42]

Loss
- appetite 783.0
  - hysterical 300.11
  - nonorganic origin 307.59
  - psychogenic 307.59
- blood — see Hemorrhage
- central vision 368.41
- consciousness 780.09
  - transient 780.2
- control, sphincter, rectum 787.6
  - nonorganic origin 307.7
- ear ossicle, partial 385.24
- elasticity, skin 782.8
- extremity or member, traumatic, current — see Amputation, traumatic
- fluid (acute) 276.50
  - with
    - hypernatremia 276.0
    - hyponatremia 276.1
  - fetus or newborn 775.5
- hair 704.00
- hearing (see also Deafness)
  - central, ▶bilateral◀ 389.14
  - conductive (air) 389.00
    - with sensorineural hearing loss 389.2
    - combined types 389.08
    - external ear 389.01
    - inner ear 389.04
    - middle ear 389.03
    - multiple types 389.08
    - tympanic membrane 389.02

Loss — continued
- hearing (see also Deafness) — continued
  - mixed type 389.2
  - nerve, ▶bilateral◀ 389.12
  - neural, ▶bilateral◀ 389.12
  - noise-induced 388.12
  - perceptive NEC (see also Loss, hearing, sensorineural) 389.10
  - sensorineural 389.10
    - with conductive hearing loss 389.2
    - asymmetrical 389.16 ●
    - central, ▶bilateral◀ 389.14
    - combined types, ▶bilateral◀ 389.18
    - multiple types, ▶bilateral◀ 389.18
    - neural, ▶bilateral◀ 389.12
    - sensory, ▶bilateral◀ 389.11
    - unilateral 389.15 ●
  - sensory, ▶bilateral◀ 389.11
  - specified type NEC 389.8
  - sudden NEC 388.2
- height 781.91
- labyrinthine reactivity (unilateral) 386.55
  - bilateral 386.56
- memory (see also Amnesia) 780.93
  - mild, following organic brain damage 310.1
- mind (see also Psychosis) 298.9
- occlusal vertical dimension 524.37
- organ or part — see Absence, by site, acquired
- sensation 782.0
- sense of
  - smell (see also Disturbance, sensation) 781.1
  - taste (see also Disturbance, sensation) 781.1
  - touch (see also Disturbance, sensation) 781.1
- sight (acquired) (complete) (congenital) — see Blindness
- spinal fluid
  - headache 349.0
- substance of
  - bone (see also Osteoporosis) 733.00
  - cartilage 733.99
    - ear 380.32
  - vitreous (humor) 379.26
- tooth, teeth
  - acquired 525.10
    - due to
      - caries 525.13
      - extraction 525.10
      - periodontal disease 525.12
      - specified NEC 525.19
      - trauma 525.11
- vision, visual (see also Blindness) 369.9
  - both eyes (see also Blindness, both eyes) 369.3
  - complete (see also Blindness, both eyes) 369.00
  - one eye 369.8
  - sudden 368.11
  - transient 368.12
- vitreous 379.26
- voice (see also Aphonia) 784.41
- weight (cause unknown) 783.21
Lou Gehrig's disease 335.20
Louis-Bar syndrome (ataxia-telangiectasia) 334.8
Louping ill 063.1
Lousiness — see Lice
Low
- back syndrome 724.2
- basal metabolic rate (BMR) 794.7
- birthweight 765.1 ☑
  - extreme (less than 1000 grams) 765.0 ☑
  - for gestational age 764.0 ☑

Low — continued
- birthweight — continued
  - status (see also Status, low birth weight) V21.30
- bladder compliance 596.52
- blood pressure (see also Hypotension) 458.9
  - reading (incidental) (isolated) (nonspecific) 796.3
- cardiac reserve — see Disease, heart
- compliance bladder 596.52
- frequency deafness — see Disorder, hearing
- function (see also Hypofunction)
  - kidney (see also Disease, renal) 593.9
  - liver 573.9
- hemoglobin 285.9
- implantation, placenta — see Placenta, previa
- insertion, placenta — see Placenta, previa
- lying
  - kidney 593.0
  - organ or site, congenital — see Malposition, congenital
  - placenta — see Placenta, previa
- output syndrome (cardiac) (see also Failure, heart) 428.9
- platelets (blood) (see also Thrombocytopenia) 287.5
- reserve, kidney (see also Disease, renal) 593.9
- risk
  - cervical, human papillomavirus (HPV) DNA test positive 795.09
- salt syndrome 593.9
- tension glaucoma 365.12
- vision 369.9
  - both eyes 369.20
  - one eye 369.70
Lower extremity — see condition
Lowe (-Terrey-MacLachlan) syndrome (oculocerebrorenal dystrophy) 270.8
Lown (-Ganong) -Levine syndrome (short P-R interval, normal QRS complex, and paroxysmal supraventricular tachycardia) 426.81
LSD reaction — see also Abuse, drugs, nondependent 305.3 ☑
L-shaped kidney 753.3
Lucas-Championnière disease (fibrinous bronchitis) 466.0
Lucey-Driscoll syndrome (jaundice due to delayed conjugation) 774.30
Ludwig's
- angina 528.3
- disease (submaxillary cellulitis) 528.3
Lues (venerea), **luetic** — see Syphilis
Luetscher's syndrome (dehydration) 276.51
Lumbago 724.2
- due to displacement, intervertebral disc 722.10
Lumbalgia 724.2
- due to displacement, intervertebral disc 722.10
Lumbar — see condition
Lumbarization, vertebra 756.15
Lumbermen's itch 133.8
Lump — see also Mass
- abdominal 789.3 ☑
- breast 611.72
- chest 786.6
- epigastric 789.3 ☑
- head 784.2
- kidney 753.3
- liver 789.1
- lung 786.6
- mediastinal 786.6
- neck 784.2
- nose or sinus 784.2
- pelvic 789.3 ☑

Lump — see also Mass — continued
- skin 782.2
- substernal 786.6
- throat 784.2
- umbilicus 789.3 ☑
Lunacy — see also Psychosis 298.9
Lunatomalacia 732.3
Lung — see also condition
- donor V59.8
- drug addict's 417.8
- mainliners' 417.8
- vanishing 492.0
Lupoid (miliary) **of Boeck** 135
Lupus 710.0
- anticoagulant 289.81
- Cazenave's (erythematosus) 695.4
- discoid (local) 695.4
- disseminated 710.0
- erythematodes (discoid) (local) 695.4
- erythematosus (discoid) (local) 695.4
  - disseminated 710.0
  - eyelid 373.34
  - systemic 710.0
    - with
      - encephalitis 710.0 [323.81] ▲
      - lung involvement 710.0 [517.8]
  - inhibitor (presence of) 286.5
- exedens 017.0 ☑
- eyelid (see also Tuberculosis) 017.0 ☑ [373.4]
- Hilliard's 017.0 ☑
- hydralazine
  - correct substance properly administered 695.4
  - overdose or wrong substance given or taken 972.6
- miliaris disseminatus faciei 017.0 ☑
- nephritis 710.0 [583.81]
  - acute 710.0 [580.81]
  - chronic 710.0 [582.81]
- nontuberculous, not disseminated 695.4
- pernio (Besnier) 135
- tuberculous (see also Tuberculosis) 017.0 ☑
  - eyelid (see also Tuberculosis) 017.0 ☑ [373.4]
- vulgaris 017.0 ☑
Luschka's joint disease 721.90
Luteinoma (M8610/0) 220
Lutembacher's disease or syndrome (atrial septal defect with mitral stenosis) 745.5
Luteoma (M8610/0) 220
Lutz-Miescher disease (elastosis perforans serpiginosa) 701.1
Lutz-Splendore-de Almeida disease (Brazilian blastomycosis) 116.1
Luxatio
- bulbi due to birth injury 767.8
- coxae congenita (see also Dislocation, hip, congenital) 754.30
- erecta — see Dislocation, shoulder
- imperfecta — see Sprain, by site
- perinealis — see Dislocation, hip
Luxation — see also Dislocation, by site
- eyeball 360.81
  - due to birth injury 767.8
  - lateral 376.36
- genital organs (external) NEC — see Wound, open, genital organs
- globe (eye) 360.81
  - lateral 376.36
- lacrimal gland (postinfectional) 375.16
- lens (old) (partial) 379.32
  - congenital 743.37
    - syphilitic 090.49 [379.32]
  - Marfan's disease 090.49
  - spontaneous 379.32
- penis — see Wound, open, penis
- scrotum — see Wound, open, scrotum
- testis — see Wound, open, testis
L-xyloketosuria 271.8
Lycanthropy — see also Psychosis 298.9

Lyell's disease or syndrome (toxic epidermal necrolysis) 695.1
  due to drug
    correct substance properly administered 695.1
    overdose or wrong substance given or taken 977.9
    specified drug — see Table of Drugs and Chemicals
Lyme disease 088.81
Lymph
  gland or node — see condition
  scrotum (see also Infestation, filarial) 125.9
Lymphadenitis 289.3
  with
    abortion — see Abortion, by type, with sepsis
    ectopic pregnancy (see also categories 633.0–633.9) 639.0
    molar pregnancy (see also categories 630–632) 639.0
  acute 683
    mesenteric 289.2
  any site, except mesenteric 289.3
    acute 683
    chronic 289.1
    mesenteric (acute) (chronic) (non-specific) (subacute) 289.2
    subacute 289.1
      mesenteric 289.2
  breast, puerperal, postpartum 675.2
  chancroidal (congenital) 099.0
  chronic 289.1
    mesenteric 289.2
  dermatopathic 695.89
  due to
    anthracosis (occupational) 500
    Brugia (Wuchereria) malayi 125.1
    diphtheria (toxin) 032.89
    lymphogranuloma venereum 099.1
    Wuchereria bancrofti 125.0
  following
    abortion 639.0
    ectopic or molar pregnancy 639.0
  generalized 289.3
  gonorrheal 098.89
  granulomatous 289.1
  infectional 683
  mesenteric (acute) (chronic) (nonspecific) (subacute) 289.2
    due to Bacillus typhi 002.0
    tuberculous (see also Tuberculosis) 014.8 ☑
  mycobacterial 031.8
  purulent 683
  pyogenic 683
  regional 078.3
  septic 683
  streptococcal 683
  subacute, unspecified site 289.1
  suppurative 683
  syphilitic (early) (secondary) 091.4
    late 095.8
  tuberculous — see Tuberculosis, lymph gland
  venereal 099.1
Lymphadenoid goiter 245.2
Lymphadenopathy (general) 785.6
  due to toxoplasmosis (acquired) 130.7
    congenital (active) 771.2
Lymphadenopathy-associated virus (disease) (illness) (infection) — see Human immunodeficiency virus (disease) (illness) (infection)
Lymphadenosis 785.6
  acute 075
Lymphangiectasis 457.1
  conjunctiva 372.89
  postinfectional 457.1
  scrotum 457.1
Lymphangiectatic elephantiasis, non-filarial 457.1
Lymphangioendothelioma (M9170/0) 228.1

Lymphangioendothelioma — continued
  malignant (M9170/3) — see Neoplasm, connective tissue, malignant
Lymphangioma (M9170/0) 228.1
  capillary (M9171/0) 228.1
  cavernous (M9172/0) 228.1
  cystic (M9173/0) 228.1
  malignant (M9170/3) — see Neoplasm, connective tissue, malignant
Lymphangiomyoma (M9174/0) 228.1
Lymphangiomyomatosis (M9174/1) — see Neoplasm, connective tissue, uncertain behavior
Lymphangiosarcoma (M9170/3) — see Neoplasm, connective tissue, malignant
Lymphangitis 457.2
  with
    abortion — see Abortion, by type, with sepsis
    abscess — see Abscess, by site
    cellulitis — see Abscess, by site
    ectopic pregnancy (see also categories 633.0–633.9) 639.0
    molar pregnancy (see also categories 630–632) 639.0
  acute (with abscess or cellulitis) 682.9
    specified site — see Abscess, by site
  breast, puerperal, postpartum 675.2 ☑
  chancroidal 099.0
  chronic (any site) 457.2
  due to
    Brugia (Wuchereria) malayi 125.1
    Wuchereria bancrofti 125.0
  following
    abortion 639.0
    ectopic or molar pregnancy 639.0
  gangrenous 457.2
  penis
    acute 607.2
    gonococcal (acute) 098.0
      chronic or duration of 2 months or more 098.2
  puerperal, postpartum, childbirth 670.0 ☑
  strumous, tuberculous (see also Tuberculosis) 017.2 ☑
  subacute (any site) 457.2
  tuberculous — see Tuberculosis, lymph gland
Lymphatic (vessel) — see condition
Lymphatism 254.8
  scrofulous (see also Tuberculosis) 017.2 ☑
Lymphectasia 457.1
Lymphedema — see also Elephantiasis 457.1
  acquired (chronic) 457.1
  chronic hereditary 757.0
  congenital 757.0
  idiopathic hereditary 757.0
  praecox 457.1
  secondary 457.1
  surgical NEC 997.99
    postmastectomy (syndrome) 457.0
Lymph-hemangioma (M9120/0) — see Hemangioma, by site
Lymphoblastic — see condition
Lymphoblastoma (diffuse) (M9630/3) 200.1 ☑
  giant follicular (M9690/3) 202.0 ☑
  macrofollicular (M9690/3) 202.0 ☑
Lymphoblastosis, acute benign 075
Lymphocele 457.8
Lymphocythemia 288.51 ▲
Lymphocytic — see also condition
  chorioencephalitis (acute) (serous) 049.0
  choriomeningitis (acute) (serous) 049.0

Lymphocytoma (diffuse) (malignant) (M9620/3) 200.1 ☑
Lymphocytomatosis (M9620/3) 200.1 ☑
Lymphocytopenia 288.51 ▲
Lymphocytosis (symptomatic) 288.61 ▲
  infectious (acute) 078.89
Lymphoepithelioma (M8082/3) — see Neoplasm, by site, malignant
Lymphogranuloma (malignant) (M9650/3) 201.9 ☑
  inguinale 099.1
  venereal (any site) 099.1
    with stricture of rectum 099.1
  venereum 099.1
Lymphogranulomatosis (malignant) (M9650/3) 201.9 ☑
  benign (Boeck's sarcoid) (Schaumann's) 135
  Hodgkin's (M9650/3) 201.9 ☑
Lymphohistiocytosis, familial hemophagocytic 288.4 ●
Lymphoid — see condition
Lympholeukoblastoma (M9850/3) 207.8 ☑
Lympholeukosarcoma (M9850/3) 207.8 ☑
Lymphoma (malignant) (M9590/3) 202.8 ☑

> Note — Use the following fifth-digit subclassification with categories 200–202:
>
> 0 unspecified site, extranodal and solid organ sites
>
> 1 lymph nodes of head, face, and neck
>
> 2 intrathoracic lymph nodes
>
> 3 intra–abdominal lymph nodes
>
> 4 lymph nodes of axilla and upper limb
>
> 5 lymph nodes of inguinal region and lower limb
>
> 6 intrapelvic lymph nodes
>
> 7 spleen
>
> 8 lymph nodes of multiple sites

  benign (M9590/0) — see Neoplasm, by site, benign
  Burkitt's type (lymphoblastic) (undifferentiated) (M9750/3) 200.2 ☑
  Castleman's (mediastinal lymph node hyperplasia) 785.6
  centroblastic-centrocytic
    diffuse (M9614/3) 202.8 ☑
    follicular (M9692/3) 202.0 ☑
  centroblastic type (diffuse) (M9632/3) 202.8 ☑
    follicular (M9697/3) 202.0 ☑
  centrocytic (M9622/3) 202.8 ☑
  compound (M9613/3) 200.8 ☑
  convoluted cell type (lymphoblastic) (M9602/3) 202.8 ☑
  diffuse NEC (M9590/3) 202.8 ☑
  follicular (giant) (M9690/3) 202.0 ☑
    center cell (diffuse) (M9615/3) 202.8 ☑
    cleaved (diffuse) (M9623/3) 202.8 ☑
      follicular (M9695/3) 202.0 ☑
    non-cleaved (diffuse) (M9633/3) 202.8 ☑
      follicular (M9698/3) 202.0 ☑
    centroblastic-centrocytic (M9692/3) 202.0 ☑
    centroblastic type (M9697/3) 202.0 ☑
    lymphocytic
      intermediate differentiation (M9694/3) 202.0 ☑
      poorly differentiated (M9696/3) 202.0 ☑

Lymphoma — continued
  follicular — continued
    mixed (cell type) (lymphocytic-histiocytic) (small cell and large cell) (M9691/3) 202.0 ☑
  germinocytic (M9622/3) 202.8 ☑
  giant, follicular or follicle (M9690/3) 202.0 ☑
  histiocytic (diffuse) (M9640/3) 200.0 ☑
    nodular (M9642/3) 200.0 ☑
    pleomorphic cell type (M9641/3) 200.0 ☑
  Hodgkin's (M9650/3) (see also Disease, Hodgkin's) 201.9 ☑
  immunoblastic (type) (M9612/3) 200.8 ☑
  large cell (M9640/3) 200.0 ☑
    nodular (M9642/3) 200.0 ☑
    pleomorphic cell type (M9641/3) 200.0 ☑
  lymphoblastic (diffuse) (M9630/3) 200.1 ☑
    Burkitt's type (M9750/3) 200.2 ☑
    convoluted cell type (M9602/3) 202.8 ☑
  lymphocytic (cell type) (diffuse) (M9620/3) 200.1 ☑
    with plasmacytoid differentiation, diffuse (M9611/3) 200.8 ☑
    intermediate differentiation (diffuse) (M9621/3) 200.1 ☑
      follicular (M9694/3) 202.0 ☑
      nodular (M9694/3) 202.0 ☑
    nodular (M9690/3) 202.0 ☑
    poorly differentiated (diffuse) (M9630/3) 200.1 ☑
      follicular (M9696/3) 202.0 ☑
      nodular (M9696/3) 202.0 ☑
    well differentiated (diffuse) (M9620/3) 200.1 ☑
      follicular (M9693/3) 202.0 ☑
      nodular (M9693/3) 202.0 ☑
  lymphocytic-histiocytic, mixed (diffuse) (M9613/3) 200.8 ☑
    follicular (M9691/3) 202.0 ☑
    nodular (M9691/3) 202.0 ☑
  lymphoplasmacytoid type (M9611/3) 200.8 ☑
  lymphosarcoma type (M9610/3) 200.1 ☑
  macrofollicular (M9690/3) 202.0 ☑
  mixed cell type (diffuse) (M9613/3) 200.8 ☑
    follicular (M9691/3) 202.0 ☑
    nodular (M9691/3) 202.0 ☑
  nodular (M9690/3) 202.0 ☑
    histiocytic (M9642/3) 200.0 ☑
    lymphocytic (M9690/3) 202.0 ☑
      intermediate differentiation (M9694/3) 202.0 ☑
      poorly differentiated (M9696/3) 202.0 ☑
    mixed (cell type) (lymphocytic-histiocytic) (small cell and large cell) (M9691/3) 202.0 ☑
  non-Hodgkin's type NEC (M9591/3) 202.8 ☑
  reticulum cell (type) (M9640/3) 200.0 ☑
  small cell and large cell, mixed (diffuse) (M9613/3) 200.8 ☑
    follicular (M9691/3) 202.0 ☑
    nodular (9691/3) 202.0 ☑
  stem cell (type) (M9601/3) 202.8 ☑
  T-cell 202.1 ☑
  undifferentiated (cell type) (non-Burkitt's) (M9600/3) 202.8 ☑
    Burkitt's type (M9750/3) 200.2 ☑
Lymphomatosis (M9590/3) — see also Lymphoma
  granulomatous 099.1
Lymphopathia
  venereum 099.1
  veneris 099.1

☑ Additional Digit Required — Refer to the Tabular List for Digit Selection   ▽ Subterms under main terms may continue to next column or page

2007 ICD-9-CM   ▶◀ Revised Text   ● New Line   ▲ Revised Code   **October 2006 · Volume 2 — 183**

Lymphopenia 288.51 ▲
  familial 279.2
Lymphoreticulosis, benign (of inoculation) 078.3
Lymphorrhea 457.8
Lymphosarcoma (M9610/3) 200.1 ☑
  diffuse (M9610/3) 200.1 ☑
    with plasmacytoid differentiation (M9611/3) 200.8 ☑
    lymphoplasmacytic (M9611/3) 200.8 ☑
  follicular (giant) (M9690/3) 202.0 ☑
    lymphoblastic (M9696/3) 202.0 ☑
    lymphocytic, intermediate differentiation (M9694/3) 202.0 ☑
    mixed cell type (M9691/3) 202.0 ☑
  giant follicular (M9690/3) 202.0 ☑
  Hodgkin's (M9650/3) 201.9 ☑
  immunoblastic (M9612/3) 200.8 ☑
  lymphoblastic (diffuse) (M9630/3) 200.1 ☑
    follicular (M9696/3) 202.0 ☑
    nodular (M9696/3) 202.0 ☑
  lymphocytic (diffuse) (M9620/3) 200.1 ☑
    intermediate differentiation (diffuse) (M9621/3) 200.1 ☑
      follicular (M9694/3) 202.0 ☑
      nodular (M9694/3) 202.0 ☑
    mixed cell type (diffuse) (M9613/3) 200.8 ☑
      follicular (M9691/3) 202.0 ☑
      nodular (M9691/3) 202.0 ☑
  nodular (M9690/3) 202.0 ☑
    lymphoblastic (M9696/3) 202.0 ☑
    lymphocytic, intermediate differentiation (M9694/3) 202.0 ☑
    mixed cell type (M9691/3) 202.0 ☑
  prolymphocytic (M9631/3) 200.1 ☑
  reticulum cell (M9640/3) 200.0 ☑
Lymphostasis 457.8
Lypemania — *see also* Melancholia 296.2 ☑
Lyssa 071

M

Macacus ear 744.29
Maceration
  fetus (cause not stated) 779.9
  wet feet, tropical (syndrome) 991.4
Machado-Joseph disease 334.8
Machupo virus hemorrhagic fever 078.7
Macleod's syndrome (abnormal transradiancy, one lung) 492.8
Macrocephalia, macrocephaly 756.0
Macrocheilia (congenital) 744.81
Macrochilia (congenital) 744.81
Macrocolon (congenital) 751.3
Macrocornea 743.41
  associated with buphthalmos 743.22
Macrocytic — *see* condition
Macrocytosis 289.89
Macrodactylia, macrodactylism (fingers) (thumbs) 755.57
  toes 755.65
Macrodontia 520.2
Macroencephaly 742.4
Macrogenia 524.05
Macrogenitosomia (female) (male) (praecox) 255.2
Macrogingivae 523.8
Macroglobulinemia (essential) (idiopathic) (monoclonal) (primary) (syndrome) (Waldenström's) 273.3
Macroglossia (congenital) 750.15
  acquired 529.8
Macrognathia, macrognathism (congenital) 524.00
  mandibular 524.02
    alveolar 524.72
  maxillary 524.01
    alveolar 524.71
Macrogyria (congenital) 742.4

Macrohydrocephalus — *see also* Hydrocephalus 331.4
Macromastia — *see also* Hypertrophy, breast 611.1
Macrophage activation syndrome ● 288.4 ●
Macropsia 368.14
Macrosigmoid 564.7
  congenital 751.3
Macrospondylitis, acromegalic 253.0
Macrostomia (congenital) 744.83
Macrotia (external ear) (congenital) 744.22
Macula
  cornea, corneal
    congenital 743.43
      interfering with vision 743.42
      interfering with central vision 371.03
      not interfering with central vision 371.02
  degeneration (*see also* Degeneration, macula) 362.50
    hereditary (*see also* Dystrophy, retina) 362.70
  edema, cystoid 362.53
Maculae ceruleae 132.1
Macules and papules 709.8
Maculopathy, toxic 362.55
Madarosis 374.55
Madelung's
  deformity (radius) 755.54
  disease (lipomatosis) 272.8
  lipomatosis 272.8
Madness — *see also* Psychosis 298.9
  myxedema (acute) 293.0
    subacute 293.1
Madura
  disease (actinomycotic) 039.9
    mycotic 117.4
  foot (actinomycotic) 039.4
    mycotic 117.4
Maduromycosis (actinomycotic) 039.9
  mycotic 117.4
Maffucci's syndrome (dyschondroplasia with hemangiomas) 756.4
Magenblase syndrome 306.4
Main en griffe (acquired) 736.06
  congenital 755.59
Maintenance
  chemotherapy regimen or treatment V58.11
  dialysis regimen or treatment
    extracorporeal (renal) V56.0
    peritoneal V56.8
    renal V56.0
  drug therapy or regimen
    chemotherapy, antineoplastic V58.11
    immunotherapy, antineoplastic V58.12
  external fixation NEC V54.89
  radiotherapy V58.0
  traction NEC V54.89
Majocchi's
  disease (purpura annularis telangiectodes) 709.1
  granuloma 110.6
Major — *see* condition
Mal
  cerebral (idiopathic) (*see also* Epilepsy) 345.9 ☑
  comital (*see also* Epilepsy) 345.9 ☑
  de los pintos (*see also* Pinta) 103.9
  de Meleda 757.39
  de mer 994.6
  lie — *see* Presentation, fetal
  perforant (*see also* Ulcer, lower extremity) 707.15
Malabar itch 110.9
  beard 110.0
  foot 110.4
  scalp 110.0
Malabsorption 579.9
  calcium 579.8
  carbohydrate 579.8

Malabsorption — *continued*
  disaccharide 271.3
  drug-induced 579.8
  due to bacterial overgrowth 579.8
  fat 579.8
  folate, congenital 281.2
  galactose 271.1
  glucose-galactose (congenital) 271.3
  intestinal 579.9
  isomaltose 271.3
  lactose (hereditary) 271.3
  methionine 270.4
  monosaccharide 271.8
  postgastrectomy 579.3
  postsurgical 579.3
  protein 579.8
  sucrose (-isomaltose) (congenital) 271.3
  syndrome 579.9
    postgastrectomy 579.3
    postsurgical 579.3
Malacia, bone 268.2
  juvenile (*see also* Rickets) 268.0
  Kienböck's (juvenile) (lunate) (wrist) 732.3
    adult 732.8
Malacoplakia
  bladder 596.8
  colon 569.89
  pelvis (kidney) 593.89
  ureter 593.89
  urethra 599.84
Malacosteon 268.2
  juvenile (*see also* Rickets) 268.0
Maladaptation — *see* Maladjustment
Maladie de Roger 745.4
Maladjustment
  conjugal V61.10
    involving divorce or estrangement V61.0
  educational V62.3
  family V61.9
    specified circumstance NEC V61.8
  marital V61.10
    involving divorce or estrangement V61.0
  occupational V62.2
  simple, adult (*see also* Reaction, adjustment) 309.9
  situational acute (*see also* Reaction, adjustment) 309.9
  social V62.4
Malaise 780.79
Malakoplakia — *see* Malacoplakia
Malaria, malarial (fever) 084.6
  algid 084.9
  any type, with
    algid malaria 084.9
    blackwater fever 084.8
    fever
      blackwater 084.8
      hemoglobinuric (bilious) 084.8
    hemoglobinuria, malarial 084.8
    hepatitis 084.9 *[573.2]*
    nephrosis 084.9 *[581.81]*
    pernicious complication NEC 084.9
      cardiac 084.9
      cerebral 084.9
  cardiac 084.9
  carrier (suspected) of V02.9
  cerebral 084.9
  complicating pregnancy, childbirth, or puerperium 647.4 ☑
  congenital 771.2
  congestion, congestive 084.6
    brain 084.9
  continued 084.0
  estivo-autumnal 084.0
  falciparum (malignant tertian) 084.0
  hematinuria 084.8
  hematuria 084.8
  hemoglobinuria 084.8
  hemorrhagic 084.6
  induced (therapeutically) 084.7
    accidental — *see* Malaria, by type
  liver 084.9 *[573.2]*

Malaria, malarial — *continued*
  malariae (quartan) 084.2
  malignant (tertian) 084.0
  mixed infections 084.5
  monkey 084.4
  ovale 084.3
  pernicious, acute 084.0
  Plasmodium, P.
    falciparum 084.0
    malariae 084.2
    ovale 084.3
    vivax 084.1
  quartan 084.2
  quotidian 084.0
  recurrent 084.6
    induced (therapeutically) 084.7
      accidental — *see* Malaria, by type
  remittent 084.6
  specified types NEC 084.4
  spleen 084.6
  subtertian 084.0
  tertian (benign) 084.1
    malignant 084.0
  tropical 084.0
  typhoid 084.6
  vivax (benign tertian) 084.1
Malassez's disease (testicular cyst) 608.89
Malassimilation 579.9
Maldescent, testis 752.51
Maldevelopment — *see also* Anomaly, by site
  brain 742.9
  colon 751.5
  hip (joint) 755.63
    congenital dislocation (*see also* Dislocation, hip, congenital) 754.30
  mastoid process 756.0
  middle ear, except ossicles 744.03
    ossicles 744.04
  newborn (not malformation) 764.9 ☑
  ossicles, ear 744.04
  spine 756.10
  toe 755.66
Male type pelvis 755.69
  with disproportion (fetopelvic) 653.2 ☑
    affecting fetus or newborn 763.1
    causing obstructed labor 660.1 ☑
      affecting fetus or newborn 763.1
Malformation (congenital) — *see also* Anomaly
  bone 756.9
  bursa 756.9
  Chiari
    type I 348.4
    type II (*see also* Spina bifida) 741.0 ☑
    type III 742.0
    type IV 742.2
  circulatory system NEC 747.9
    specified type NEC 747.89
  cochlea 744.05
  digestive system NEC 751.9
    lower 751.5
      specified type NEC 751.8
    upper 750.9
  eye 743.9
  gum 750.9
  heart 746.9
    specified type NEC 746.89
    valve 746.9
  internal ear 744.05
  joint NEC 755.9
    specified type NEC 755.8
  Mondini's (congenital) (malformation, cochlea) 744.05
  muscle 756.9
  nervous system (central) 742.9
  pelvic organs or tissues
    in pregnancy or childbirth 654.9 ☑
      affecting fetus or newborn 763.89
      causing obstructed labor 660.2 ☑

☑ Additional Digit Required — Refer to the Tabular List for Digit Selection   ▽ Subterms under main terms may continue to next column or page

184 — Volume 2 · October 2006   ▶◀ Revised Text   ● New Line   ▲ Revised Code   **2007 ICD-9-CM**

Malformation — *see also* Anomaly — *continued*
  pelvic organs or tissues — *continued*
    in pregnancy or childbirth — *continued*
      causing obstructed labor — *continued*
        affecting fetus or newborn 763.1
  placenta (*see also* Placenta, abnormal) 656.7 ☑
  respiratory organs 748.9
    specified type NEC 748.8
  Rieger's 743.44
  sense organs NEC 742.9
    specified type NEC 742.8
  skin 757.9
    specified type NEC 757.8
  spinal cord 742.9
  teeth, tooth NEC 520.9
  tendon 756.9
  throat 750.9
  umbilical cord (complicating delivery) 663.9 ☑
    affecting fetus or newborn 762.6
  umbilicus 759.9
  urinary system NEC 753.9
    specified type NEC 753.8
Malfunction — *see also* Dysfunction
  arterial graft 996.1
  cardiac pacemaker 996.01
  catheter device — *see* Complications, mechanical, catheter
  colostomy 569.62
    valve 569.62 ●
  cystostomy 997.5
  device, implant, or graft NEC — *see* Complications, mechanical
  enteric stoma 569.62
  enterostomy 569.62
  esophagostomy 530.87
  gastroenteric 536.8
  gastrostomy 536.42
  ileostomy ●
    valve 569.62 ●
  nephrostomy 997.5
  pacemaker — *see* Complications, mechanical, pacemaker
  prosthetic device, internal — *see* Complications, mechanical
  tracheostomy 519.02
  valve ●
    colostomy 569.62 ●
    ileostomy 569.62 ●
  vascular graft or shunt 996.1
Malgaigne's fracture (closed) 808.43
  open 808.53
Malherbe's
  calcifying epithelioma (M8110/0) — *see* Neoplasm, skin, benign
  tumor (M8110/0) — *see* Neoplasm, skin, benign
Malibu disease 919.8
  infected 919.9
Malignancy (M8000/3) — *see* Neoplasm, by site, malignant
Malignant — *see* condition
Malingerer, malingering V65.2
Mallet, finger (acquired) 736.1
  congenital 755.59
  late effect of rickets 268.1
Malleus 024
Mallory's bodies 034.1
Mallory-Weiss syndrome 530.7
Malnutrition (calorie) 263.9
  complicating pregnancy 648.9 ☑
  degree
    first 263.1
    second 263.0
    third 262
    mild 263.1
    moderate 263.0
    severe 261
      protein-calorie 262
  fetus 764.2 ☑

Malnutrition — *continued*
  fetus — *continued*
    "light-for-dates" 764.1 ☑
  following gastrointestinal surgery 579.3
  intrauterine or fetal 764.2 ☑
    fetus or infant "light-for-dates" 764.1 ☑
  lack of care, or neglect (child) (infant) 995.52
    adult 995.84
  malignant 260
  mild 263.1
  moderate 263.0
  protein 260
  protein-calorie 263.9
    severe 262
    specified type NEC 263.8
  severe 261
    protein-calorie NEC 262
Malocclusion (teeth) 524.4
  angle's class I 524.21 ●
  angle's class II 524.22 ●
  angle's class III 524.23 ●
  due to
    abnormal swallowing 524.59
    accessory teeth (causing crowding) 524.31
    dentofacial abnormality NEC 524.89
    impacted teeth (causing crowding) 520.6
    missing teeth 524.30
    mouth breathing 524.59
    sleep postures 524.59
    supernumerary teeth (causing crowding) 524.31
    thumb sucking 524.59
    tongue, lip, or finger habits 524.59
  temporomandibular (joint) 524.69
Malposition
  cardiac apex (congenital) 746.87
  cervix — *see* Malposition, uterus
  congenital
    adrenal (gland) 759.1
    alimentary tract 751.8
      lower 751.5
      upper 750.8
    aorta 747.21
    appendix 751.5
    arterial trunk 747.29
    artery (peripheral) NEC (*see also* Malposition, congenital, peripheral vascular system) 747.60
      coronary 746.85
      pulmonary 747.3
    auditory canal 744.29
      causing impairment of hearing 744.02
    auricle (ear) 744.29
      causing impairment of hearing 744.02
    cervical 744.43
    biliary duct or passage 751.69
    bladder (mucosa) 753.8
      exteriorized or extroverted 753.5
    brachial plexus 742.8
    brain tissue 742.4
    breast 757.6
    bronchus 748.3
    cardiac apex 746.87
    cecum 751.5
    clavicle 755.51
    colon 751.5
    digestive organ or tract NEC 751.8
      lower 751.5
      upper 750.8
    ear (auricle) (external) 744.29
      ossicles 744.04
    endocrine (gland) NEC 759.2
    epiglottis 748.3
    Eustachian tube 744.24
    eye 743.8
    facial features 744.89
    fallopian tube 752.19

Malposition — *continued*
  congenital — *continued*
    finger(s) 755.59
      supernumerary 755.01
    foot 755.67
    gallbladder 751.69
    gastrointestinal tract 751.8
    genitalia, genital organ(s) or tract
      female 752.89
        external 752.49
        internal NEC 752.89
      male 752.89
        penis 752.69
        scrotal transposition 752.81
    glottis 748.3
    hand 755.59
    heart 746.87
      dextrocardia 746.87
        with complete transposition of viscera 759.3
    hepatic duct 751.69
    hip (joint) (*see also* Dislocation, hip, congenital) 754.30
    intestine (large) (small) 751.5
      with anomalous adhesions, fixation, or malrotation 751.4
    joint NEC 755.8
    kidney 753.3
    larynx 748.3
    limb 755.8
      lower 755.69
      upper 755.59
    liver 751.69
    lung (lobe) 748.69
    nail(s) 757.5
    nerve 742.8
    nervous system NEC 742.8
    nose, nasal (septum) 748.1
    organ or site NEC — *see* Anomaly, specified type NEC, by site
    ovary 752.0
    pancreas 751.7
    parathyroid (gland) 759.2
    patella 755.64
    peripheral vascular system 747.60
      gastrointestinal 747.61
      lower limb 747.64
      renal 747.62
      specified NEC 747.69
      spinal 747.82
      upper limb 747.63
    pituitary (gland) 759.2
    respiratory organ or system NEC 748.9
    rib (cage) 756.3
      supernumerary in cervical region 756.2
    scapula 755.59
    shoulder 755.59
    spinal cord 742.59
    spine 756.19
    spleen 759.0
    sternum 756.3
    stomach 750.7
    symphysis pubis 755.69
    testis (undescended) 752.51
    thymus (gland) 759.2
    thyroid (gland) (tissue) 759.2
      cartilage 748.3
    toe(s) 755.66
      supernumerary 755.02
    tongue 750.19
    trachea 748.3
    uterus 752.3
    vein(s) (peripheral) NEC (*see also* Malposition, congenital, peripheral vascular system) 747.60
      great 747.49
      portal 747.49
      pulmonary 747.49
      vena cava (inferior) (superior) 747.49
  device, implant, or graft — *see* Complications, mechanical

Malposition — *continued*
  fetus NEC (*see also* Presentation, fetal) 652.9 ☑
    with successful version 652.1 ☑
    affecting fetus or newborn 763.1
    before labor, affecting fetus or newborn 761.7
    causing obstructed labor 660.0 ☑
    in multiple gestation (one fetus or more) 652.6 ☑
      with locking 660.5 ☑
      causing obstructed labor 660.0 ☑
  gallbladder (*see also* Disease, gallbladder) 575.8
  gastrointestinal tract 569.89
    congenital 751.8
  heart (*see also* Malposition, congenital, heart) 746.87
  intestine 569.89
    congenital 751.5
  pelvic organs or tissues
    in pregnancy or childbirth 654.4 ☑
      affecting fetus or newborn 763.89
      causing obstructed labor 660.2 ☑
        affecting fetus or newborn 763.1
  placenta — *see* Placenta, previa
  stomach 537.89
    congenital 750.7
  tooth, teeth 524.30
    with impaction 520.6
  uterus (acquired) (acute) (adherent) (any degree) (asymptomatic) (postinfectional) (postpartal, old) 621.6
    anteflexion or anteversion (*see also* Anteversion, uterus) 621.6
    congenital 752.3
    flexion 621.6
      lateral (*see also* Lateroversion, uterus) 621.6
    in pregnancy or childbirth 654.4 ☑
      affecting fetus or newborn 763.89
      causing obstructed labor 660.2 ☑
        affecting fetus or newborn 763.1
    inversion 621.6
    lateral (flexion) (version) (*see also* Lateroversion, uterus) 621.6
    lateroflexion (*see also* Lateroversion, uterus) 621.6
    lateroversion (*see also* Lateroversion, uterus) 621.6
    retroflexion or retroversion (*see also* Retroversion, uterus) 621.6
Malposture 729.9
Malpresentation, fetus — *see also* Presentation, fetal 652.9 ☑
Malrotation
  cecum 751.4
  colon 751.4
  intestine 751.4
  kidney 753.3
Malta fever — *see also* Brucellosis 023.9
Maltosuria 271.3
Maltreatment (of)
  adult 995.80
    emotional 995.82
    multiple forms 995.85
    neglect (nutritional) 995.84
    physical 995.81
    psychological 995.82
    sexual 995.83
  child 995.50
    emotional 995.51
    multiple forms 995.59
    neglect (nutritional) 995.52
    physical 995.54
      shaken infant syndrome 995.55
    psychological 995.51

☑ Additional Digit Required — Refer to the Tabular List for Digit Selection   Subterms under main terms may continue to next column or page

2007 ICD-9-CM   ▶◀ Revised Text   ● New Line   ▲ Revised Code   October 2006 · Volume 2 — 185

Maltreatment — *continued*
  child — *continued*
    sexual 995.53
  spouse (*see also* Maltreatment, adult) 995.80
Malt workers' lung 495.4
Malum coxae senilis 715.25
Malunion, fracture 733.81
Mammillitis — *see also* Mastitis 611.0
  puerperal, postpartum 675.2 ☑
Mammitis — *see also* Mastitis 611.0
  puerperal, postpartum 675.2 ☑
Mammographic
  calcification 793.89 ●
  calculus 793.89 ●
  microcalcification 793.81 ●
Mammoplasia 611.1
Management
  contraceptive V25.9
    specified type NEC V25.8
  procreative V26.9
    specified type NEC V26.8
Mangled NEC — *see also* nature and site of injury 959.9
Mania (monopolar) — *see also* Psychosis, affective 296.0 ☑
  alcoholic (acute) (chronic) 291.9
  Bell's — *see* Mania, chronic
  chronic 296.0 ☑
    recurrent episode 296.1 ☑
    single episode 296.0 ☑
  compulsive 300.3
  delirious (acute) 296.0 ☑
    recurrent episode 296.1 ☑
    single episode 296.0 ☑
  epileptic (*see also* Epilepsy) 345.4 ☑
  hysterical 300.10
  inhibited 296.89
  puerperal (after delivery) 296.0 ☑
    recurrent episode 296.1 ☑
    single episode 296.0 ☑
  recurrent episode 296.1 ☑
  senile 290.8
  single episode 296.0 ☑
  stupor 296.89
  stuporous 296.89
  unproductive 296.89
Manic-depressive insanity, psychosis, reaction, or syndrome — *see also* Psychosis, affective 296.80
  circular (alternating) 296.7
    currently
      depressed 296.5 ☑
      episode unspecified 296.7
      hypomanic, previously depressed 296.4 ☑
      manic 296.4 ☑
      mixed 296.6 ☑
  depressed (type), depressive 296.2 ☑
    atypical 296.82
    recurrent episode 296.3 ☑
    single episode 296.2 ☑
  hypomanic 296.0 ☑
    recurrent episode 296.1 ☑
    single episode 296.0 ☑
  manic 296.0 ☑
    atypical 296.81
    recurrent episode 296.1 ☑
    single episode 296.0 ☑
  mixed NEC 296.89
  perplexed 296.89
  stuporous 296.89
Manifestations, rheumatoid
  lungs 714.81
  pannus — *see* Arthritis, rheumatoid
  subcutaneous nodules — *see* Arthritis, rheumatoid
Mankowsky's syndrome (familial dysplastic osteopathy) 731.2
Mannoheptulosuria 271.8
Mannosidosis 271.8
Manson's
  disease (schistosomiasis) 120.1
  pyosis (pemphigus contagiosus) 684
  schistosomiasis 120.1
Mansonellosis 125.5

Manual — *see* condition
Maple bark disease 495.6
Maple bark-strippers' lung 495.6
Maple syrup (urine) disease or syndrome 270.3
Marable's syndrome (celiac artery compression) 447.4
Marasmus 261
  brain 331.9
  due to malnutrition 261
  intestinal 569.89
  nutritional 261
  senile 797
  tuberculous NEC (*see also* Tuberculosis) 011.9 ☑
Marble
  bones 756.52
  skin 782.61
Marburg disease (virus) 078.89
March
  foot 733.94
  hemoglobinuria 283.2
Marchand multiple nodular hyperplasia (liver) 571.5
Marchesani (-Weill) syndrome (brachymorphism and ectopia lentis) 759.89
Marchiafava (-Bignami) disease or syndrome 341.8
Marchiafava-Micheli syndrome (paroxysmal nocturnal hemoglobinuria) 283.2
Marcus Gunn's syndrome (jaw-winking syndrome) 742.8
Marfan's
  congenital syphilis 090.49
  disease 090.49
  syndrome (arachnodactyly) 759.82
    meaning congenital syphilis 090.49
    with luxation of lens 090.49 [379.32]
Marginal
  implantation, placenta — *see* Placenta, previa
  placenta — *see* Placenta, previa
  sinus (hemorrhage) (rupture) 641.2 ☑
    affecting fetus or newborn 762.1
Marie's
  cerebellar ataxia 334.2
  syndrome (acromegaly) 253.0
Marie-Bamberger disease or syndrome (hypertrophic) (pulmonary) (secondary) 731.2
  idiopathic (acropachyderma) 757.39
  primary (acropachyderma) 757.39
Marie-Charcôt-Tooth neuropathic atrophy, muscle 356.1
Marie-Strümpell arthritis or disease (ankylosing spondylitis) 720.0
Marihuana, marijuana
  abuse (*see also* Abuse, drugs, nondependent) 305.2 ☑
  dependence (*see also* Dependence) 304.3 ☑
Marion's disease (bladder neck obstruction) 596.0
Marital conflict V61.10
Mark
  port wine 757.32
  raspberry 757.32
  strawberry 757.32
  stretch 701.3
  tattoo 709.09
Maroteaux-Lamy syndrome (mucopolysaccharidosis VI) 277.5
Marriage license examination V70.3
Marrow (bone)
  arrest 284.9
  megakaryocytic 287.30
  poor function 289.9
Marseilles fever 082.1
Marshall's (hidrotic) **ectodermal dysplasia** 757.31
Marsh's disease (exophthalmic goiter) 242.0 ☑
Marsh fever — *see also* Malaria 084.6

Martin-Albright syndrome (pseudohypoparathyroidism) 275.49
Martin's disease 715.27
Martorell-Fabre syndrome (pulseless disease) 446.7
Masculinization, female, with adrenal hyperplasia 255.2
Masculinovoblastoma (M8670/0) 220
Masochism 302.83
Masons' lung 502
Mass
  abdominal 789.3 ☑
  anus 787.99
  bone 733.90
  breast 611.72
  cheek 784.2
  chest 786.6
  cystic — *see* Cyst
  ear 388.8
  epigastric 789.3 ☑
  eye 379.92
  female genital organ 625.8
  gum 784.2
  head 784.2
  intracranial 784.2
  joint 719.60
    ankle 719.67
    elbow 719.62
    foot 719.67
    hand 719.64
    hip 719.65
    knee 719.66
    multiple sites 719.69
    pelvic region 719.65
    shoulder (region) 719.61
    specified site NEC 719.68
    wrist 719.63
  kidney (*see also* Disease, kidney) 593.9
  lung 786.6
  lymph node 785.6
  malignant (M8000/3) — *see* Neoplasm, by site, malignant
  mediastinal 786.6
  mouth 784.2
  muscle (limb) 729.89
  neck 784.2
  nose or sinus 784.2
  palate 784.2
  pelvis, pelvic 789.3 ☑
  penis 607.89
  perineum 625.8
  rectum 787.99
  scrotum 608.89
  skin 782.2
  specified organ NEC — *see* Disease of specified organ or site
  splenic 789.2
  substernal 786.6
    thyroid (*see also* Goiter) 240.9
  superficial (localized) 782.2
  testes 608.89
  throat 784.2
  tongue 784.2
  umbilicus 789.3 ☑
  uterus 625.8
  vagina 625.8
  vulva 625.8
Massive — *see* condition
Mastalgia 611.71
  psychogenic 307.89
Mast cell
  disease 757.33
    systemic (M9741/3) 202.6 ☑
  leukemia (M9900/3) 207.8 ☑
  sarcoma (M9742/3) 202.6 ☑
  tumor (M9740/1) 238.5
    malignant (M9740/3) 202.6 ☑
Masters-Allen syndrome 620.6
Mastitis (acute) (adolescent) (diffuse) (interstitial) (lobular) (nonpuerperal) (nonsuppurative) (parenchymatous) (phlegmonous) (simple) (subacute) (suppurative) 611.0
  chronic (cystic) (fibrocystic) 610.1
  cystic 610.1

Mastitis — *continued*
  cystic — *continued*
    Schimmelbusch's type 610.1
  fibrocystic 610.1
  infective 611.0
  lactational 675.2 ☑
  lymphangitis 611.0
  neonatal (noninfective) 778.7
    infective 771.5
  periductal 610.4
  plasma cell 610.4
  puerperalis 675.2 ☑
  puerperal, postpartum, (interstitial) (nonpurulent) (parenchymatous) 675.2 ☑
    purulent 675.1 ☑
    stagnation 676.2 ☑
  retromammary 611.0
    puerperal, postpartum 675.1 ☑
  submammary 611.0
    puerperal, postpartum 675.1 ☑
Mastocytoma (M9740/1) 238.5
  malignant (M9740/3) 202.6 ☑
Mastocytosis 757.33
  malignant (M9741/3) 202.6 ☑
  systemic (M9741/3) 202.6 ☑
Mastodynia 611.71
  psychogenic 307.89
Mastoid — *see* condition
Mastoidalgia — *see also* Otalgia 388.70
Mastoiditis (coalescent) (hemorrhagic) (pneumococcal) (streptococcal) (suppurative) 383.9
  acute or subacute 383.00
    with
      Gradenigo's syndrome 383.02
      petrositis 383.02
      specified complication NEC 383.02
      subperiosteal abscess 383.01
  chronic (necrotic) (recurrent) 383.1
  tuberculous (*see also* Tuberculosis) 015.6 ☑
Mastopathy, mastopathia 611.9
  chronica cystica 610.1
  diffuse cystic 610.1
  estrogenic 611.8
  ovarian origin 611.8
Mastoplasia 611.1
Masturbation 307.9
Maternal condition, affecting fetus or newborn
  acute yellow atrophy of liver 760.8
  albuminuria 760.1
  anesthesia or analgesia 763.5
  blood loss 762.1
  chorioamnionitis 762.7
  circulatory disease, chronic (conditions classifiable to 390–459, 745–747) 760.3
  congenital heart disease (conditions classifiable to 745–746) 760.3
  cortical necrosis of kidney 760.1
  death 761.6
  diabetes mellitus 775.0
    manifest diabetes in the infant 775.1
  disease NEC 760.9
    circulatory system, chronic (conditions classifiable to 390–459, 745–747) 760.3
    genitourinary system (conditions classifiable to 580–599) 760.1
    respiratory (conditions classifiable to 490–519, 748) 760.3
  eclampsia 760.0
  hemorrhage NEC 762.1
  hepatitis acute, malignant, or subacute 760.8
  hyperemesis (gravidarum) 761.8
  hypertension (arising during pregnancy) (conditions classifiable to 642) 760.0

Maternal condition, affecting fetus or newborn — continued

infection

  disease classifiable to 001-136 ☑, 760.2

  genital tract NEC 760.8

  urinary tract 760.1

influenza 760.2

  manifest influenza in the infant 771.2

injury (conditions classifiable to 800–996) 760.5

malaria 760.2

  manifest malaria in infant or fetus 771.2

malnutrition 760.4

necrosis of liver 760.8

nephritis (conditions classifiable to 580–583) 760.1

nephrosis (conditions classifiable to 581) 760.1

noxious substance transmitted via breast milk or placenta 760.70

  alcohol 760.71

  anticonvulsants 760.77

  antifungals 760.74

  anti-infective agents 760.74

  antimetabolics 760.78

  cocaine 760.75

  "crack" 760.75

  diethylstilbestrol [DES] 760.76

  hallucinogenic agents 760.73

  medicinal agents NEC 760.79

  narcotics 760.72

  obstetric anesthetic or analgesic drug 760.72

  specified agent NEC 760.79

nutritional disorder (conditions classifiable to 260–269) 760.4

operation unrelated to current delivery 760.6

pre-eclampsia 760.0

pyelitis or pyelonephritis, arising during pregnancy (conditions classifiable to 590) 760.1

renal disease or failure 760.1

respiratory disease, chronic (conditions classifiable to 490–519, 748) 760.3

rheumatic heart disease (chronic) (conditions classifiable to 393–398) 760.3

rubella (conditions classifiable to 056) 760.2

  manifest rubella in the infant or fetus 771.0

surgery unrelated to current delivery 760.6

  to uterus or pelvic organs 763.89

syphilis (conditions classifiable to 090–097) 760.2

  manifest syphilis in the infant or fetus 090.0

thrombophlebitis 760.3

toxemia (of pregnancy) 760.0

  pre-eclamptic 760.0

toxoplasmosis (conditions classifiable to 130) 760.2

  manifest toxoplasmosis in the infant or fetus 771.2

transmission of chemical substance through the placenta 760.70

  alcohol 760.71

  anticonvulsants 760.77

  antifungals 760.74

  anti-infective 760.74

  antimetabolics 760.78

  cocaine 760.75

  "crack" 760.75

  diethylstilbestrol [DES] 760.76

  hallucinogenic agents 760.73

  narcotics 760.72

  specified substance NEC 760.79

uremia 760.1

urinary tract conditions (conditions classifiable to 580–599) 760.1

Maternal condition, affecting fetus or newborn — continued

vomiting (pernicious) (persistent) (vicious) 761.8

Maternity — see Delivery

Matheiu's disease (leptospiral jaundice) 100.0

Mauclaire's disease or osteochondrosis 732.3

Maxcy's disease 081.0

Maxilla, maxillary — see condition

May (-Hegglin) anomaly or syndrome 288.2

Mayaro fever 066.3

Mazoplasia 610.8

MBD (minimal brain dysfunction), child — see also Hyperkinesia 314.9

MCAD (medium chain acyl CoA dehydrogenase deficiency) 277.85

McArdle (-Schmid-Pearson) disease or syndrome (glycogenosis V) 271.0

McCune-Albright syndrome (osteitis fibrosa disseminata) 756.59

MCLS (mucocutaneous lymph node syndrome) 446.1

McQuarrie's syndrome (idiopathic familial hypoglycemia) 251.2

Measles (black) (hemorrhagic) (suppressed) 055.9

with

  encephalitis 055.0

  keratitis 055.71

  keratoconjunctivitis 055.71

  otitis media 055.2

  pneumonia 055.1

complication 055.8

  specified type NEC 055.79

encephalitis 055.0

French 056.9

German 056.9

keratitis 055.71

keratoconjunctivitis 055.71

liberty 056.9

otitis media 055.2

pneumonia 055.1

specified complications NEC 055.79

vaccination, prophylactic (against) V04.2

Meatitis, urethral — see also Urethritis 597.89

Meat poisoning — see Poisoning, food

Meatus, meatal — see condition

Meat-wrappers' asthma 506.9

Meckel's

diverticulitis 751.0

diverticulum (displaced) (hypertrophic) 751.0

Meconium

aspiration 770.11

  with

    pneumonia 770.12

    pneumonitis 770.12

    respiratory symptoms 770.12

  below vocal cords 770.11

    with respiratory symptoms 770.12

  syndrome 770.12

delayed passage in newborn 777.1

ileus 777.1

  due to cystic fibrosis 277.01

in liquor 792.3

  noted during delivery 656.8 ☑

insufflation 770.11

  with respiratory symptoms 770.12

obstruction

  fetus or newborn 777.1

    in mucoviscidosis 277.01

passage of 792.3

  noted during delivery 763.84

peritonitis 777.6

plug syndrome (newborn) NEC 777.1

staining 779.84

Median — see also condition

arcuate ligament syndrome 447.4

bar (prostate) 600.90

Median — see also condition — continued

bar — continued

  with

    other lower urinary tract symptoms (LUTS) 600.91 ●

    urinary ●

      obstruction 600.91 ●

      retention 600.91 ●

rhomboid glossitis 529.2

vesical orifice 600.90

  with

    other lower urinary tract symptoms (LUTS) 600.91 ●

    urinary ●

      obstruction 600.91 ●

      retention 600.91 ●

Mediastinal shift 793.2

Mediastinitis (acute) (chronic) 519.2

actinomycotic 039.8

syphilitic 095.8

tuberculous (see also Tuberculosis) 012.8 ☑

Mediastinopericarditis — see also Pericarditis 423.9

acute 420.90

chronic 423.8

  rheumatic 393

rheumatic, chronic 393

Mediastinum, mediastinal — see condition

Medical services provided for — see Health, services provided because (of)

Medicine poisoning (by overdose) (wrong substance given or taken in error) 977.9

specified drug or substance — see Table of Drugs and Chemicals

Medin's disease (poliomyelitis) 045.9 ☑

Mediterranean

anemia (with other hemoglobinopathy) 282.49

disease or syndrome (hemipathic) 282.49

fever (see also Brucellosis) 023.9

  familial 277.31 ▲

kala-azar 085.0

leishmaniasis 085.0

tick fever 082.1

Medulla — see condition

Medullary

cystic kidney 753.16

sponge kidney 753.17

Medullated fibers

optic (nerve) 743.57

retina 362.85

Medulloblastoma (M9470/3) 191.6

desmoplastic (M9471/3) 191.6

specified site — see Neoplasm, by site, malignant

unspecified site 191.6

Medulloepithelioma (M9501/3) — see also Neoplasm, by site, malignant

teratoid (M9502/3) — see Neoplasm, by site, malignant

Medullomyoblastoma (M9472/3)

specified site — see Neoplasm, by site, malignant

unspecified site 191.6

Meekeren-Ehlers-Danlos syndrome 756.83

Megacaryocytic — see condition

Megacolon (acquired) (functional) (not Hirschsprung's disease) 564.7

aganglionic 751.3

congenital, congenitum 751.3

Hirschsprung's (disease) 751.3

psychogenic 306.4

toxic (see also Colitis, ulcerative) 556.9

Megaduodenum 537.3

Megaesophagus (functional) 530.0

congenital 750.4

Megakaryocytic — see condition

Megalencephaly 742.4

Megalerythema (epidermicum) (infectiosum) 057.0

Megalia, cutis et ossium 757.39

Megaloappendix 751.5

Megalocephalus, megalocephaly NEC 756.0

Megalocornea 743.41

associated with buphthalmos 743.22

Megalocytic anemia 281.9

Megalodactylia (fingers) (thumbs) 755.57

toes 755.65

Megaloduodenum 751.5

Megaloesophagus (functional) 530.0

congenital 750.4

Megalogastria (congenital) 750.7

Megalomania 307.9

Megalophthalmos 743.8

Megalopsia 368.14

Megalosplenia — see also Splenomegaly 789.2

Megaloureter 593.89

congenital 753.22

Megarectum 569.49

Megasigmoid 564.7

congenital 751.3

Megaureter 593.89

congenital 753.22

Megrim 346.9 ☑

Meibomian

cyst 373.2

  infected 373.12

gland — see condition

infarct (eyelid) 374.85

stye 373.11

Meibomitis 373.12

Meige

-Milroy disease (chronic hereditary edema) 757.

syndrome (blepharospasm-oro-mandibular dystonia) 333.82

Melalgia, nutritional 266.2

Melancholia — see also Psychosis, affective 296.90

climacteric 296.2 ☑

  recurrent episode 296.3 ☑

  single episode 296.2 ☑

hypochondriac 300.7

intermittent 296.2 ☑

  recurrent episode 296.3 ☑

  single episode 296.2 ☑

involutional 296.2 ☑

  recurrent episode 296.3 ☑

  single episode 296.2 ☑

menopausal 296.2 ☑

  recurrent episode 296.3 ☑

  single episode 296.2 ☑

puerperal 296.2 ☑

reactive (from emotional stress, psychological trauma) 298.0

recurrent 296.3 ☑

senile 290.21

stuporous 296.2 ☑

  recurrent episode 296.3 ☑

  single episode 296.2 ☑

Melanemia 275.0

Melanoameloblastoma (M9363/0) — see Neoplasm, bone, benign

Melanoblastoma (M8720/3) — see Melanoma

Melanoblastosis

Block-Sulzberger 757.33

cutis linearis sive systematisata 757.33

Melanocarcinoma (M8720/3) — see Melanoma

Melanocytoma, eyeball (M8726/0) 224.0

Melanoderma, melanodermia 709.09

Addison's (primary adrenal insufficiency) 255.4

Melanodontia, infantile 521.05

Melanodontoclasia 521.05

Melanoepithelioma (M8720/3) — see Melanoma

Index

Melanoma — Meningitis

Melanoma (malignant) (M8720/3) 172.9

Note — Except where otherwise indicated, the morphological varieties of melanoma in the list below should be coded by site as for "Melanoma (malignant)". Internal sites should be coded to malignant neoplasm of those sites.

abdominal wall 172.5
ala nasi 172.3
amelanotic (M8730/3) — *see*
 Melanoma, by site
ankle 172.7
anus, anal 154.3
 canal 154.2
arm 172.6
auditory canal (external) 172.2
auricle (ear) 172.2
auricular canal (external) 172.2
axilla 172.5
axillary fold 172.5
back 172.5
balloon cell (M8722/3) — *see*
 Melanoma, by site
benign (M8720/0) — *see* Neoplasm,
 skin, benign
breast (female) (male) 172.5
brow 172.3
buttock 172.5
canthus (eye) 172.1
cheek (external) 172.3
chest wall 172.5
chin 172.3
choroid 190.6
conjunctiva 190.3
ear (external) 172.2
epithelioid cell (M8771/3) (*see also*
 Melanoma, by site)
 and spindle cell, mixed (M8775/3)
  — *see* Melanoma, by site
external meatus (ear) 172.2
eye 190.9
eyebrow 172.3
eyelid (lower) (upper) 172.1
face NEC 172.3
female genital organ (external) NEC
 184.4
finger 172.6
flank 172.5
foot 172.7
forearm 172.6
forehead 172.3
foreskin 187.1
gluteal region 172.5
groin 172.5
hand 172.6
heel 172.7
helix 172.2
hip 172.7
in
 giant pigmented nevus (M8761/3)
  — *see* Melanoma, by site
 Hutchinson's melanotic freckle
  (M8742/3) — *see* Melanoma,
  by site
 junctional nevus (M8740/3) — *see*
  Melanoma, by site
 precancerous melanosis (M8741/3)
  — *see* Melanoma, by site
interscapular region 172.5
iris 190.0
jaw 172.3
juvenile (M8770/0) — *see* Neoplasm,
 skin, benign
knee 172.7
labium
 majus 184.1
 minus 184.2
lacrimal gland 190.2
leg 172.7
lip (lower) (upper) 172.0
liver 197.7
lower limb NEC 172.7
male genital organ (external) NEC
 187.9
meatus, acoustic (external) 172.2
meibomian gland 172.1

Melanoma — *continued*
metastatic
 of or from specified site — *see*
  Melanoma, by site
 site not of skin — *see* Neoplasm,
  by site, malignant, secondary
 to specified site — *see* Neoplasm,
  by site, malignant, secondary
 unspecified site 172.9
nail 172.9
 finger 172.6
 toe 172.7
neck 172.4
nodular (M8721/3) — *see* Melanoma,
 by site
nose, external 172.3
orbit 190.1
penis 187.4
perianal skin 172.5
perineum 172.5
pinna 172.2
popliteal (fossa) (space) 172.7
prepuce 187.1
pubes 172.5
pudendum 184.4
retina 190.5
scalp 172.4
scrotum 187.7
septum nasal (skin) 172.3
shoulder 172.6
skin NEC 172.8
spindle cell (M8772/3) (*see also*
 Melanoma, by site)
 type A (M8773/3) 190.0
 type B (M8774/3) 190.0
submammary fold 172.5
superficial spreading (M8743/3) —
 see Melanoma, by site
temple 172.3
thigh 172.7
toe 172.7
trunk NEC 172.5
umbilicus 172.5
upper limb NEC 172.6
vagina vault 184.0
vulva 184.4
Melanoplakia 528.9
Melanosarcoma (M8720/3) — *see also*
 Melanoma
 epithelioid cell (M8771/3) — *see*
  Melanoma
Melanosis 709.09
 addisonian (primary adrenal insufficiency) 255.4
  tuberculous (*see also* Tuberculosis)
   017.6 ☑
 adrenal 255.4
 colon 569.89
 conjunctiva 372.55
  congenital 743.49
 corii degenerativa 757.33
 cornea (presenile) (senile) 371.12
  congenital 743.43
   interfering with vision 743.42
 eye 372.55
  congenital 743.49
 jute spinners' 709.09
 lenticularis progressiva 757.33
 liver 573.8
 precancerous (M8741/2) (*see also*
  Neoplasm, skin, in situ)
  malignant melanoma in (M8741/3)
   — *see* Melanoma
 prenatal 743.43
  interfering with vision 743.42
 Riehl's 709.09
 sclera 379.19
  congenital 743.47
 suprarenal 255.4
 tar 709.09
 toxic 709.09
Melanuria 791.9
Melasma 709.09
 adrenal (gland) 255.4
 suprarenal (gland) 255.4

MELAS syndrome (mitochondrial encephalopathy, lactic acidosis and
 stroke-like episodes) 277.87
Melena 578.1
 due to
  swallowed maternal blood 777.3
  ulcer — *see* Ulcer, by site, with
   hemorrhage
 newborn 772.4
  due to swallowed maternal blood
   777.3
Meleney's
 gangrene (cutaneous) 686.09
 ulcer (chronic undermining) 686.09
Melioidosis 025
Melitensis, febris 023.0
Melitococcosis 023.0
Melkersson (-Rosenthal) syndrome
 351.8
Mellitus, diabetes — *see* Diabetes
Melorheostosis (bone) (leri) 733.99
Meloschisis 744.83
Melotia 744.29
Membrana
 capsularis lentis posterior 743.39
 epipapillaris 743.57
Membranacea placenta — *see* Placenta,
 abnormal
Membranaceous uterus 621.8
Membrane, membranous — *see also*
 condition
 folds, congenital — *see* Web
 Jackson's 751.4
 over face (causing asphyxia), fetus or
  newborn 768.9
 premature rupture — *see* Rupture,
  membranes, premature
 pupillary 364.74
  persistent 743.46
 retained (complicating delivery) (with
  hemorrhage) 666.2 ☑
  without hemorrhage 667.1 ☑
 secondary (eye) 366.50
 unruptured (causing asphyxia) 768.9
 vitreous humor 379.25
Membranitis, fetal 658.4 ☑
 affecting fetus or newborn 762.7
Memory disturbance, loss or lack —
 see also Amnesia 780.93
 mild, following organic brain damage
  310.1
Menadione (vitamin K) **deficiency** 269.0
Menarche, precocious 259.1
Mendacity, pathologic 301.7
Mendelson's syndrome (resulting from
 a procedure) 997.3
 obstetric 668.0 ☑
Mende's syndrome (ptosis-epicanthus)
 270.2
Ménétrier's disease or syndrome (hypertrophic gastritis) 535.2 ☑
**Ménière's disease, syndrome, or verti-
 go** 386.00
 cochlear 386.02
 cochleovestibular 386.01
 inactive 386.04
 in remission 386.04
 vestibular 386.03
Meninges, meningeal — *see* condition
Meningioma (M9530/0) — *see also*
 Neoplasm, meninges, benign
 angioblastic (M9535/0) — *see* Neoplasm, meninges, benign
 angiomatous (M9534/0) — *see* Neoplasm, meninges, benign
 endotheliomatous (M9531/0) — *see*
  Neoplasm, meninges, benign
 fibroblastic (M9532/0) — *see* Neoplasm, meninges, benign
 fibrous (M9532/0) — *see* Neoplasm,
  meninges, benign
 hemangioblastic (M9535/0) — *see*
  Neoplasm, meninges, benign
 hemangiopericytic (M9536/0) — *see*
  Neoplasm, meninges, benign

Meningioma — *see also* Neoplasm,
 meninges, benign — *continued*
 malignant (M9530/3) — *see* Neoplasm, meninges, malignant
 meningiothelial (M9531/0) — *see*
  Neoplasm, meninges, benign
 meningotheliomatous (M9531/0) —
  see Neoplasm, meninges, benign
 mixed (M9537/0) — *see* Neoplasm,
  meninges, benign
 multiple (M9530/1) 237.6
 papillary (M9538/1) 237.6
 psammomatous (M9533/0) — *see*
  Neoplasm, meninges, benign
 syncytial (M9531/0) — *see* Neoplasm,
  meninges, benign
 transitional (M9537/0) — *see* Neoplasm, meninges, benign
Meningiomatosis (diffuse) (M9530/1)
 237.6
Meningism — *see also* Meningismus
 781.6
Meningismus (infectional) (pneumococcal) 781.6
 due to serum or vaccine
  997.09 *[321.8]*
 influenzal NEC 487.8
Meningitis (basal) (basic) (basilar) (brain)
 (cerebral) (cervical) (congestive)
 (diffuse) (hemorrhagic) (infantile)
 (membranous) (metastatic) (nonspecific) (pontine) (progressive) (simple)
 (spinal) (subacute) (sympathetica)
 (toxic) 322.9
 abacterial NEC (*see also* Meningitis,
  aseptic) 047.9
 actinomycotic 039.8 *[320.7]*
 adenoviral 049.1
 Aerobacter aerogenes 320.82
 anaerobes (cocci) (gram-negative)
  (gram-positive) (mixed) (NEC)
  320.81
 arbovirus NEC 066.9 *[321.2]*
  specified type NEC 066.8 *[321.2]*
 aseptic (acute) NEC 047.9
  adenovirus 049.1
  Coxsackie virus 047.0
  due to
   adenovirus 049.1
   Coxsackie virus 047.0
   ECHO virus 047.1
   enterovirus 047.9
   mumps 072.1
   poliovirus (*see also* Poliomyeli-
    tis) 045.2 ☑ *[321.2]*
  ECHO virus 047.1
  herpes (simplex) virus 054.72
   zoster 053.0
  leptospiral 100.81
  lymphocytic choriomeningitis 049.0
  noninfective 322.0
 Bacillus pyocyaneus 320.89
 bacterial NEC 320.9
  anaerobic 320.81
  gram-negative 320.82
   anaerobic 320.81
 Bacteroides (fragilis) (oralis)
  (melaninogenicus) 320.81
 cancerous (M8000/6) 198.4
 candidal 112.83
 carcinomatous (M8010/6) 198.4
 caseous (*see also* Tuberculosis,
  meninges) 013.0 ☑
 cerebrospinal (acute) (chronic) (diplococcal) (endemic) (epidemic)
  (fulminant) (infectious) (malignant) (meningococcal) (sporadic)
  036.0
  carrier (suspected) of V02.59
 chronic NEC 322.2
 clear cerebrospinal fluid NEC 322.0
 Clostridium (haemolyticum) (novyi)
  NEC 320.81
 coccidioidomycosis 114.2
 Coxsackie virus 047.0
 cryptococcal 117.5 *[321.0]*

☑ Additional Digit Required — Refer to the Tabular List for Digit Selection ▼ Subterms under main terms may continue to next column or page

188 — Volume 2   ▶◀ Revised Text   ● New Line   ▲ Revised Code   *2007 ICD-9-CM*

Meningitis — continued
diplococcal 036.0
  gram-negative 036.0
  gram-positive 320.1
Diplococcus pneumoniae 320.1
due to
  actinomycosis 039.8 [320.7]
  adenovirus 049.1
  coccidiomycosis 114.2
  enterovirus 047.9
    specified NEC 047.8
  histoplasmosis (see also Histoplasmosis) 115.91
  Listerosis 027.0 [320.7]
  Lyme disease 088.81 [320.7]
  moniliasis 112.83
  mumps 072.1
  neurosyphilis 094.2
  nonbacterial organisms NEC 321.8
  oidiomycosis 112.83
  poliovirus (see also Poliomyelitis) 045.2 ☑ [321.2]
  preventive immunization, inoculation, or vaccination 997.09 [321.8]
  sarcoidosis 135 [321.4]
  sporotrichosis 117.1 [321.1]
  syphilis 094.2
    acute 091.81
    congenital 090.42
    secondary 091.81
  trypanosomiasis (see also Trypanosomiasis) 086.9 [321.3]
  whooping cough 033.9 [320.7]
ECHO virus 047.1
E. coli 320.82
endothelial-leukocytic, benign, recurrent 047.9
Enterobacter aerogenes 320.82
enteroviral 047.9
  specified type NEC 047.8
enterovirus 047.9
  specified NEC 047.8
eosinophilic 322.1
epidemic NEC 036.0
Escherichia coli (E. coli) 320.82
Eubacterium 320.81
fibrinopurulent NEC 320.9
  specified type NEC 320.89
Friedländer (bacillus) 320.82
fungal NEC 117.9 [321.1]
Fusobacterium 320.81
gonococcal 098.82
gram-negative bacteria NEC 320.82
  anaerobic 320.81
  cocci 036.0
    specified NEC 320.82
gram-negative cocci NEC 036.0
  specified NEC 320.82
gram-positive cocci NEC 320.9
herpes (simplex) virus 054.72
  zoster 053.0
H. influenzae 320.0
infectious NEC 320.9
influenzal 320.0
Klebsiella pneumoniae 320.82
late effect — see Late, effect, meningitis
leptospiral (aseptic) 100.81
Listerella (monocytogenes) 027.0 [320.7]
Listeria monocytogenes 027.0 [320.7]
lymphocytic (acute) (benign) (serous) 049.0
  choriomeningitis virus 049.0
meningococcal (chronic) 036.0
Mima polymorpha 320.82
Mollaret's 047.9
monilial 112.83
mumps (virus) 072.1
mycotic NEC 117.9 [321.1]
Neisseria 036.0
neurosyphilis 094.2
nonbacterial NEC (see also Meningitis, aseptic) 047.9
nonpyogenic NEC 322.0

Meningitis — continued
oidiomycosis 112.83
ossificans 349.2
Peptococcus 320.81
Peptostreptococcus 320.81
pneumococcal 320.1
poliovirus (see also Poliomyelitis) 045.2 ☑ [321.2]
Proprionibacterium 320.81
Proteus morganii 320.82
Pseudomonas (aeruginosa) (pyocyaneus) 320.82
purulent NEC 320.9
  specified organism NEC 320.89
pyogenic NEC 320.9
  specified organism NEC 320.89
Salmonella 003.21
septic NEC 320.9
  specified organism NEC 320.89
serosa circumscripta NEC 322.0
serous NEC (see also Meningitis, aseptic) 047.9
  lymphocytic 049.0
  syndrome 348.2
Serratia (marcescens) 320.82
specified organism NEC 320.89
sporadic cerebrospinal 036.0
sporotrichosis 117.1 [321.1]
staphylococcal 320.3
sterile 997.09
streptococcal (acute) 320.2
suppurative 320.9
  specified organism NEC 320.89
syphilitic 094.2
  acute 091.81
  congenital 090.42
  secondary 091.81
torula 117.5 [321.0]
traumatic (complication of injury) 958.8
Treponema (denticola) (macrodenticum) 320.81
trypanosomiasis 086.1 [321.3]
tuberculous (see also Tuberculosis, meninges) 013.0 ☑
typhoid 002.0 [320.7]
Veillonella 320.81
Vibrio vulnificus 320.82
viral, virus NEC (see also Meningitis, aseptic) 047.9
Wallgren's (see also Meningitis, aseptic) 047.9
Meningocele (congenital) (spinal) — see also Spina bifida 741.9 ☑
acquired (traumatic) 349.2
cerebral 742.0
cranial 742.0
Meningocerebritis — see Meningoencephalitis
Meningococcemia (acute) (chronic) 036.2
Meningococcus, meningococcal — see also condition 036.9
adrenalitis, hemorrhagic 036.3
carditis 036.40
carrier (suspected) of V02.59
cerebrospinal fever 036.0
encephalitis 036.1
endocarditis 036.42
exposure to V01.84
infection NEC 036.9
meningitis (cerebrospinal) 036.0
myocarditis 036.43
optic neuritis 036.81
pericarditis 036.41
septicemia (chronic) 036.2
Meningoencephalitis — see also Encephalitis 323.9
acute NEC 048
bacterial, purulent, pyogenic, or septic — see Meningitis
chronic NEC 094.1
diffuse NEC 094.1
diphasic 063.2
due to
  actinomycosis 039.8 [320.7]

Meningoencephalitis — see also Encephalitis — continued
due to — continued
  blastomycosis NEC (see also Blastomycosis) 116.0 [323.41] ▲
  free-living amebae 136.2
  Listeria monocytogenes 027.0 [320.7]
  Lyme disease 088.81 [320.7]
  mumps 072.2
  Naegleria (amebae) (gruberi) (organisms) 136.2
  rubella 056.01
  sporotrichosis 117.1 [321.1]
  toxoplasmosis (acquired) 130.0
  congenital (active) 771.2 [323.41] ▲
  Trypanosoma 086.1 [323.2]
epidemic 036.0
herpes 054.3
herpetic 054.3
H. influenzae 320.0
infectious (acute) 048
influenzal 320.0
late effect — see category 326
Listeria monocytogenes 027.0 [320.7]
lymphocytic (serous) 049.0
mumps 072.2
parasitic NEC 123.9 [323.41] ▲
pneumococcal 320.1
primary amebic 136.2
rubella 056.01
serous 048
  lymphocytic 049.0
specific 094.2
staphylococcal 320.3
streptococcal 320.2
syphilitic 094.2
toxic NEC 989.9 [323.71] ▲
due to
  carbon tetrachloride 987.8 [323.71] ▲
  hydroxyquinoline derivatives poisoning 961.3 [323.71] ▲
  lead 984.9 [323.71] ▲
  mercury 985.0 [323.71] ▲
  thallium 985.8 [323.71] ▲
toxoplasmosis (acquired) 130.0
trypanosomic 086.1 [323.2]
tuberculous (see also Tuberculosis, meninges) 013.0 ☑
virus NEC 048
Meningoencephalocele 742.0
syphilitic 094.89
congenital 090.49
Meningoencephalomyelitis — see also Meningoencephalitis 323.9
acute NEC 048
  disseminated (postinfectious) 136.9 [323.61]
  postimmunization or postvaccination 323.51 ▲
due to
  actinomycosis 039.8 [320.7]
  torula 117.5 [323.41] ▲
  toxoplasma or toxoplasmosis (acquired) 130.0
  congenital (active) 771.2 [323.41] ▲
late effect — see category 326
Meningoencephalomyelopathy — see also Meningoencephalomyelitis 349.9
Meningoencephalopathy — see also Meningoencephalitis 348.39
Meningoencephalopoliomyelitis — see also Poliomyelitis, bulbar 045.0 ☑
late effect 138
Meningomyelitis — see also Meningoencephalitis 323.9
blastomycotic NEC (see also Blastomycosis) 116.0 [323.41] ▲
due to
  actinomycosis 039.8 [320.7]

Meningomyelitis — see also Meningoencephalitis — continued
due to — continued
  blastomycosis (see also Blastomycosis) 116.0 [323.41] ▲
  Meningococcus 036.0
  sporotrichosis 117.1 [323.41] ▲
  torula 117.5 [323.41] ▲
late effect — see category 326
lethargic 049.8
meningococcal 036.0
syphilitic 094.2
tuberculous (see also Tuberculosis, meninges) 013.0 ☑
Meningomyelocele — see also Spina bifida 741.9 ☑
syphilitic 094.89
Meningomyeloneuritis — see Meningoencephalitis
Meningoradiculitis — see Meningitis
Meningovascular — see condition
Meniscocytosis 282.60
Menkes' syndrome — see Syndrome, Menkes'
Menolipsis 626.0
Menometrorrhagia 626.2
Menopause, menopausal (symptoms) (syndrome) 627.2
arthritis (any site) NEC 716.3 ☑
artificial 627.4
bleeding 627.0
crisis 627.2
depression (see also Psychosis, affective) 296.2 ☑
  agitated 296.2 ☑
    recurrent episode 296.3 ☑
    single episode 296.2 ☑
  psychotic 296.2 ☑
    recurrent episode 296.3 ☑
    single episode 296.2 ☑
  recurrent episode 296.3 ☑
  single episode 296.2 ☑
melancholia (see also Psychosis, affective) 296.2 ☑
  recurrent episode 296.3 ☑
  single episode 296.2 ☑
paranoid state 297.2
paraphrenia 297.2
postsurgical 627.4
premature 256.31
  postirradiation 256.2
  postsurgical 256.2
psychoneurosis 627.2
psychosis NEC 298.8
surgical 627.4
toxic polyarthritis NEC 716.39
Menorrhagia (primary) 626.2
climacteric 627.0
menopausal 627.0
postclimacteric 627.1
postmenopausal 627.1
preclimacteric 627.0
premenopausal 627.0
puberty (menses retained) 626.3
Menorrhalgia 625.3
Menoschesis 626.8
Menostaxis 626.2
Menses, retention 626.8
Menstrual — see also Menstruation
cycle, irregular 626.4
disorders NEC 626.9
extraction V25.3
fluid, retained 626.8
molimen 625.4
period, normal V65.5
regulation V25.3
Menstruation
absent 626.0
anovulatory 628.0
delayed 626.8
difficult 625.3
disorder 626.9
  psychogenic 306.52
  specified NEC 626.8
during pregnancy 640.8 ☑

☑ Additional Digit Required — Refer to the Tabular List for Digit Selection   ▽ Subterms under main terms may continue to next column or page

2007 ICD-9-CM   ▶◀ Revised Text   ● New Line   ▲ Revised Code   October 2006 · Volume 2 — 189

Menstruation — *continued*
excessive 626.2
frequent 626.2
infrequent 626.1
irregular 626.4
latent 626.8
membranous 626.8
painful (primary) (secondary) 625.3
   psychogenic 306.52
passage of clots 626.2
precocious 626.8
protracted 626.8
retained 626.8
retrograde 626.8
scanty 626.1
suppression 626.8
vicarious (nasal) 625.8
Mentagra — *see also* Sycosis 704.8
Mental — *see also* condition
deficiency (*see also* Retardation, mental) 319
deterioration (*see also* Psychosis) 298.9
disorder (*see also* Disorder, mental) 300.9
exhaustion 300.5
insufficiency (congenital) (*see also* Retardation, mental) 319
observation without need for further medical care NEC V71.09
retardation (*see also* Retardation, mental) 319
subnormality (*see also* Retardation, mental) 319
   mild 317
   moderate 318.0
   profound 318.2
   severe 318.1
   upset (*see also* Disorder, mental) 300.9
Meralgia paresthetica 355.1
Mercurial — *see* condition
Mercurialism NEC 985.0
Merergasia 300.9
Merkel cell tumor — *see* Neoplasm, by site, malignant
Merocele — *see also* Hernia, femoral 553.00
Meromelia 755.4
lower limb 755.30
   intercalary 755.32
      femur 755.34
         tibiofibular (complete) (incomplete) 755.33
      fibula 755.37
      metatarsal(s) 755.38
      tarsal(s) 755.38
      tibia 755.36
      tibiofibular 755.35
   terminal (complete) (partial) (transverse) 755.31
   longitudinal 755.32
      metatarsal(s) 755.38
      phalange(s) 755.39
      tarsal(s) 755.38
   transverse 755.31
upper limb 755.20
   intercalary 755.22
      carpal(s) 755.28
      humeral 755.24
         radioulnar (complete) (incomplete) 755.23
      metacarpal(s) 755.28
      phalange(s) 755.29
      radial 755.26
      radioulnar 755.25
      ulnar 755.27
   terminal (complete) (partial) (transverse) 755.21
   longitudinal 755.22
      carpal(s) 755.28
      metacarpal(s) 755.28
      phalange(s) 755.29
   transverse 755.21
Merosmia 781.1

MERRF syndrome (myoclonus with epilepsy and with ragged red fibers) 277.87
Merycism — *see also* Vomiting psychogenic 307.53
Merzbacher-Pelizaeus disease 330.0
Mesaortitis — *see* Aortitis
Mesarteritis — *see* Arteritis
Mesencephalitis — *see also* Encephalitis 323.9
late effect — *see* category 326
Mesenchymoma (M8990/1) — *see also* Neoplasm, connective tissue, uncertain behavior
benign (M8990/0) — *see* Neoplasm, connective tissue, benign
malignant (M8990/3) — *see* Neoplasm, connective tissue, malignant
Mesenteritis
retractile 567.82
sclerosing 567.82
Mesentery, mesenteric — *see* condition
Mesiodens, mesiodentes 520.1
causing crowding 524.31
Mesio-occlusion 524.23
Mesocardia (with asplenia) 746.87
Mesocolon — *see* condition
Mesonephroma (malignant) (M9110/3) — *see also* Neoplasm, by site, malignant
benign (M9110/0) — *see* Neoplasm, by site, benign
Mesophlebitis — *see* Phlebitis
Mesostromal dysgenesis 743.51
Mesothelioma (malignant) (M9050/3) — *see also* Neoplasm, by site, malignant
benign (M9050/0) — *see* Neoplasm, by site, benign
biphasic type (M9053/3) (*see also* Neoplasm, by site, malignant)
   benign (M9053/0) — *see* Neoplasm, by site, benign
epithelioid (M9052/3) (*see also* Neoplasm, by site, malignant)
   benign (M9052/0) — *see* Neoplasm, by site, benign
fibrous (M9051/3) (*see also* Neoplasm, by site, malignant)
   benign (M9051/0) — *see* Neoplasm, by site, benign
Metabolic syndrome 277.7
Metabolism disorder 277.9
specified type NEC 277.89
Metagonimiasis 121.5
Metagonimus infestation (small intestine) 121.5
Metal
pigmentation (skin) 709.00
polishers' disease 502
Metalliferous miners' lung 503
Metamorphopsia 368.14
Metaplasia
bone, in skin 709.3
breast 611.8
cervix — *omit code*
endometrium (squamous) 621.8
esophagus 530.85
intestinal, of gastric mucosa 537.89
kidney (pelvis) (squamous) (*see also* Disease, renal) 593.89
myelogenous 289.89
myeloid 289.89
   agnogenic 238.76 ●
   megakaryocytic 238.76 ●
spleen 289.59
squamous cell
   amnion 658.8 ☑
   bladder 596.8
   cervix — *see* condition
   trachea 519.19 ●
   tracheobronchial tree 519.19 ▲
uterus 621.8
   cervix — *see* condition

Metastasis, metastatic
abscess — *see* Abscess
calcification 275.40
cancer, neoplasm, or disease
   from specified site (M8000/3) — *see* Neoplasm, by site, malignant
   to specified site (M8000/6) — *see* Neoplasm, by site, secondary
deposits (in) (M8000/6) — *see* Neoplasm, by site, secondary
pneumonia 038.8 [484.8]
spread (to) (M8000/6) — *see* Neoplasm, by site, secondary
Metatarsalgia 726.70
anterior 355.6
due to Freiberg's disease 732.5
Morton's 355.6
Metatarsus, metatarsal — *see also* condition
abductus valgus (congenital) 754.60
adductus varus (congenital) 754.53
primus varus 754.52
valgus (adductus) (congenital) 754.60
varus (abductus) (congenital) 754.53
   primus 754.52
Methemoglobinemia 289.7
acquired (with sulfhemoglobinemia) 289.7
congenital 289.7
enzymatic 289.7
Hb-M disease 289.7
hereditary 289.7
toxic 289.7
Methemoglobinuria — *see also* Hemoglobinuria 791.2
Methicillin-resistant staphylococcus aureus (MRSA) V09.0
Methioninemia 270.4
Metritis (catarrhal) (septic) (suppurative) — *see also* Endometritis 615.9
blennorrhagic 098.16
   chronic or duration of 2 months or over 098.36
cervical (*see also* Cervicitis) 616.0
gonococcal 098.16
   chronic or duration of 2 months or over 098.36
hemorrhagic 626.8
puerperal, postpartum, childbirth 670.0 ☑
tuberculous (*see also* Tuberculosis) 016.7 ☑
Metropathia hemorrhagica 626.8
Metroperitonitis — *see also* Peritonitis, pelvic, female 614.5
Metrorrhagia 626.6
arising during pregnancy — *see* Hemorrhage, pregnancy
postpartum NEC 666.2 ☑
primary 626.6
psychogenic 306.59
puerperal 666.2 ☑
Metrorrhexis — *see* Rupture, uterus
Metrosalpingitis — *see also* Salpingo-oophoritis 614.2
Metrostaxis 626.6
Metrovaginitis — *see also* Endometritis 615.9
gonococcal (acute) 098.16
   chronic or duration of 2 months or over 098.36
Mexican fever — *see* Typhus, Mexican
Meyenburg-Altherr-Uehlinger syndrome 733.99
Meyer-Schwickerath and Weyers syndrome (dysplasia oculodentodigitalis) 759.89
Meynert's amentia (nonalcoholic) 294.0
alcoholic 291.1
Mibelli's disease 757.39
Mice, joint — *see also* Loose, body, joint 718.1 ☑
knee 717.6
Micheli-Rietti syndrome (thalassemia minor) 282.49

Michotte's syndrome 721.5
Micrencephalon, micrencephaly 742.1
Microalbuminuria 791.0
Microaneurysm, retina 362.14
diabetic 250.5 ☑ [362.01]
Microangiopathy 443.9
diabetic (peripheral) 250.7 ☑ [443.81]
   retinal 250.5 ☑ [362.01]
peripheral 443.9
   diabetic 250.7 ☑ [443.81]
retinal 362.18
   diabetic 250.5 ☑ [362.01]
thrombotic 446.6
   Moschcowitz's (thrombotic thrombocytopenic purpura) 446.6
Microcalcification, mammographic 793.81
Microcephalus, microcephalic, microcephaly 742.1
due to toxoplasmosis (congenital) 771.2
Microcheilia 744.82
Microcolon (congenital) 751.5
Microcornea (congenital) 743.41
Microcytic — *see* condition
Microdeletions NEC 758.33
Microdontia 520.2
Microdrepanocytosis (thalassemia-Hb-S disease) 282.49
Microembolism
atherothrombotic — *see* Atheroembolism
retina 362.33
Microencephalon 742.1
Microfilaria streptocerca infestation 125.3
Microgastria (congenital) 750.7
Microgenia 524.06
Microgenitalia (congenital) 752.89
penis 752.64
Microglioma (M9710/3)
specified site — *see* Neoplasm, by site, malignant
unspecified site 191.9
Microglossia (congenital) 750.16
Micrognathia, micrognathism (congenital) 524.00
mandibular 524.04
   alveolar 524.74
maxillary 524.03
   alveolar 524.73
Microgyria (congenital) 742.2
Microinfarct, heart — *see also* Insufficiency, coronary 411.89
Microlithiasis, alveolar, pulmonary 516.2
Micromyelia (congenital) 742.59
Micropenis 752.64
Microphakia (congenital) 743.36
Microphthalmia (congenital) — *see also* Microphthalmos 743.10
Microphthalmos (congenital) 743.10
associated with eye and adnexal anomalies NEC 743.12
due to toxoplasmosis (congenital) 771.2
isolated 743.11
simple 743.11
syndrome 759.89
Micropsia 368.14
Microsporidiosis 136.8
Microsporon furfur infestation 111.0
Microsporosis — *see also* Dermatophytosis 110.9
nigra 111.1
Microstomia (congenital) 744.84
Microthelia 757.6
Microthromboembolism — *see* Embolism
Microtia (congenital) (external ear) 744.23
Microtropia 378.34
Micturition
disorder NEC 788.69
   psychogenic 306.53
frequency 788.41

☑ Additional Digit Required — Refer to the Tabular List for Digit Selection   ▽ Subterms under main terms may continue to next column or page

190 — Volume 2 • October 2006   ▶◀ Revised Text   ● New Line   ▲ Revised Code   *2007 ICD-9-CM*

Micturition — *continued*
  frequency — *continued*
    psychogenic 306.53
  nocturnal 788.43
  painful 788.1
    psychogenic 306.53
Middle
  ear — *see* condition
  lobe (right) syndrome 518.0
Midplane — *see* condition
Miescher's disease 709.3
  cheilitis 351.8
  granulomatosis disciformis 709.3
Miescher-Leder syndrome or granulomatosis 709.3
Mieten's syndrome 759.89
Migraine (idiopathic) 346.9 ☑
  with aura 346.0 ☑
  abdominal (syndrome) 346.2 ☑
  allergic (histamine) 346.2 ☑
  atypical 346.1 ☑
  basilar 346.2 ☑
  classical 346.0 ☑
  common 346.1 ☑
  hemiplegic 346.8 ☑
  lower-half 346.2 ☑
  menstrual 625.4
  ophthalmic 346.8 ☑
  ophthalmoplegic 346.8 ☑
  retinal 346.2 ☑
  variant 346.2 ☑
Migrant, social V60.0
Migratory, migrating — *see also* condition
  person V60.0
  testis, congenital 752.52
Mikulicz's disease or syndrome (dryness of mouth, absent or decreased lacrimation) 527.1
Milian atrophia blanche 701.3
Miliaria (crystallina) (rubra) (tropicalis) 705.1
  apocrine 705.82
Miliary — *see* condition
Milium — *see also* Cyst, sebaceous 706.2
  colloid 709.3
  eyelid 374.84
Milk
  crust 690.11
  excess secretion 676.6 ☑
  fever, female 672.0 ☑
  poisoning 988.8
  retention 676.2 ☑
  sickness 988.8
  spots 423.1
Milkers' nodes 051.1
Milk-leg (deep vessels) 671.4 ☑
  complicating pregnancy 671.3 ☑
  nonpuerperal 451.19
  puerperal, postpartum, childbirth 671.4 ☑
Milkman (-Looser) disease or syndrome (osteomalacia with pseudofractures) 268.2
Milky urine — *see also* Chyluria 791.1
Millar's asthma (laryngismus stridulus) 478.75
Millard-Gubler-Foville paralysis 344.89
Millard-Gubler paralysis or syndrome 344.89
Miller-Dieker syndrome 758.33
Miller's disease (osteomalacia) 268.2
Miller Fisher's syndrome 357.0
Milles' syndrome (encephalocutaneous angiomatosis) 759.6
Mills' disease 335.29
Millstone makers' asthma or lung 502
Milroy's disease (chronic hereditary edema) 757.0
Miners' — *see also* condition
  asthma 500
  elbow 727.2
  knee 727.2
  lung 500
  nystagmus 300.89

Miners' — *see also* condition — *continued*
  phthisis (see also Tuberculosis) 011.4 ☑
  tuberculosis (see also Tuberculosis) 011.4 ☑
Minkowski-Chauffard syndrome — *see also* Spherocytosis 282.0
Minor — *see* condition
Minor's disease 336.1
Minot's disease (hemorrhagic disease, newborn) 776.0
Minot-von Willebrand (-Jürgens) disease or syndrome (angiohemophilia) 286.4
Minus (and plus) hand (intrinsic) 736.09
Miosis (persistent) (pupil) 379.42
Mirizzi's syndrome (hepatic duct stenosis) — *see also* Obstruction, biliary 576.2
  with calculus, cholelithiasis, or stones — *see* Choledocholithiasis
Mirror writing 315.09
  secondary to organic lesion 784.69
Misadventure (prophylactic) (therapeutic) — *see also* Complications 999.9
  administration of insulin 962.3
  infusion — *see* Complications, infusion
  local applications (of fomentations, plasters, etc.) 999.9
    burn or scald — *see* Burn, by site
  medical care (early) (late) NEC 999.9
    adverse effect of drugs or chemicals — *see* Table of Drugs and Chemicals
    burn or scald — *see* Burn, by site
  radiation NEC 990
  radiotherapy NEC 990
  surgical procedure (early) (late) — *see* Complications, surgical procedure
  transfusion — *see* Complications, transfusion
  vaccination or other immunological procedure — *see* Complications, vaccination
Misanthropy 301.7
Miscarriage — *see* Abortion, spontaneous
Mischief, malicious, child — *see also* Disturbance, conduct 312.0 ☑
Misdirection
  aqueous 365.83
Mismanagement, feeding 783.3
Misplaced, misplacement
  kidney (see also Disease, renal) 593.0
    congenital 753.3
  organ or site, congenital NEC — *see* Malposition, congenital
Missed
  abortion 632
  delivery (at or near term) 656.4 ☑
  labor (at or near term) 656.4 ☑
Missing — *see also* Absence
  teeth (acquired) 525.10
    congenital (see also Anodontia) 520.0
    due to
      caries 525.13
      extraction 525.10
      periodontal disease 525.12
      specified NEC 525.19
      trauma 525.11
  vertebrae (congenital) 756.13
Misuse of drugs NEC — *see also* Abuse, drug, nondependent 305.9 ☑
Mitchell's disease (erythromelalgia) 443.82
Mite(s)
  diarrhea 133.8
  grain (itch) 133.8
  hair follicle (itch) 133.8
  in sputum 133.8

Mitochondrial encephalopathy, lactic acidosis and stroke-like episodes (MELAS syndrome) 277.87
Mitochondrial neurogastrointestinal encephalopathy syndrome (MNGIE) 277.87
Mitral — *see* condition
Mittelschmerz 625.2
Mixed — *see* condition
Mljet disease (mal de Meleda) 757.39
Mobile, mobility
  cecum 751.4
  coccyx 733.99
  excessive — *see* Hypermobility
  gallbladder 751.69
  kidney 593.0
    congenital 753.3
  organ or site, congenital NEC — *see* Malposition, congenital
  spleen 289.59
Mobitz heart block (atrioventricular) 426.10
  type I (Wenckebach's) 426.13
  type II 426.12
Möbius'
  disease 346.8 ☑
  syndrome
    congenital oculofacial paralysis 352.6
    ophthalmoplegic migraine 346.8 ☑
Moeller (-Barlow) disease (infantile scurvy) 267
  glossitis 529.4
Mohr's syndrome (types I and II) 759.89
Mola destruens (M9100/1) 236.1
Molarization, premolars 520.2
Molar pregnancy 631
  hydatidiform (delivered) (undelivered) 630
Molding, head (during birth) — *omit code*
Mold(s) in vitreous 117.9
Mole (pigmented) (M8720/0) — *see also* Neoplasm, skin, benign
  blood 631
  Breus' 631
  cancerous (M8720/3) — *see* Melanoma
  carneous 631
  destructive (M9100/1) 236.1
  ectopic — *see* Pregnancy, ectopic
  fleshy 631
  hemorrhagic 631
  hydatid, hydatidiform (benign) (complicating pregnancy) (delivered) (undelivered) (see also Hydatidiform mole) 630
    invasive (M9100/1) 236.1
    malignant (M9100/1) 236.1
    previous, affecting management of pregnancy V23.1
  invasive (hydatidiform) (M9100/1) 236.1
  malignant
    meaning
      malignant hydatidiform mole (M9100/1) 236.1
      melanoma (M8720/3) — *see* Melanoma
  nonpigmented (M8730/0) — *see* Neoplasm, skin, benign
  pregnancy NEC 631
  skin (M8720/0) — *see* Neoplasm, skin, benign
  tubal — *see* Pregnancy, tubal
  vesicular (see also Hydatidiform mole) 630
Molimen, molimina (menstrual) 625.4
Mollaret's meningitis 047.9
Mollities (cerebellar) (cerebral) 437.8
  ossium 268.2
Molluscum
  contagiosum 078.0
  epitheliale 078.0
  fibrosum (M8851/0) — *see* Lipoma, by site

Molluscum — *continued*
  pendulum (M8851/0) — *see* Lipoma, by site
Mönckeberg's arteriosclerosis, degeneration, disease, or sclerosis — *see also* Arteriosclerosis, extremities 440.20
Monday fever 504
Monday morning dyspnea or asthma 504
Mondini's malformation (cochlea) 744.05
Mondor's disease (thrombophlebitis of breast) 451.89
Mongolian, mongolianism, mongolism, mongoloid 758.0
  spot 757.33
Monilethrix (congenital) 757.4
Monilia infestation — *see* Candidiasis
Moniliasis — *see also* Candidiasis
  neonatal 771.7
  vulvovaginitis 112.1
Monkeypox 057.8
Monoarthritis 716.60
  ankle 716.67
  arm 716.62
    lower (and wrist) 716.63
    upper (and elbow) 716.62
  foot (and ankle) 716.67
  forearm (and wrist) 716.63
  hand 716.64
  leg 716.66
    lower 716.66
    upper 716.65
  pelvic region (hip) (thigh) 716.65
  shoulder (region) 716.61
  specified site NEC 716.68
Monoblastic — *see* condition
Monochromatism (cone) (rod) 368.54
Monocytic — *see* condition
Monocytopenia 288.59 ●
Monocytosis (symptomatic) 288.63 ▲
Monofixation syndrome 378.34
Monomania — *see also* Psychosis 298.9
Mononeuritis 355.9
  cranial nerve — *see* Disorder, nerve, cranial
  femoral nerve 355.2
  lateral
    cutaneous nerve of thigh 355.1
    popliteal nerve 355.3
  lower limb 355.8
    specified nerve NEC 355.79
  medial popliteal nerve 355.4
  median nerve 354.1
  multiplex 354.5
  plantar nerve 355.6
  posterior tibial nerve 355.5
  radial nerve 354.3
  sciatic nerve 355.0
  ulnar nerve 354.2
  upper limb 354.9
    specified nerve NEC 354.8
  vestibular 388.5
Mononeuropathy — *see also* Mononeuritis 355.9
  diabetic NEC 250.6 ☑ [355.9]
    lower limb 250.6 ☑ [355.8]
    upper limb 250.6 ☑ [354.9]
  iliohypogastric nerve 355.79
  ilioinguinal nerve 355.79
  obturator nerve 355.79
  saphenous nerve 355.79
Mononucleosis, infectious 075
  with hepatitis 075 [573.1]
Monoplegia 344.5
  brain (current episode) (see also Paralysis, brain) 437.8
    fetus or newborn 767.8
  cerebral (current episode) (see also Paralysis, brain) 437.8
  congenital or infantile (cerebral) (spastic) (spinal) 343.3
  embolic (current) (see also Embolism, brain) 434.1 ☑

☑ Additional Digit Required — Refer to the Tabular List for Digit Selection
▽ Subterms under main terms may continue to next column or page
2007 ICD-9-CM
▶◀ Revised Text   ● New Line   ▲ Revised Code
October 2006 · Volume 2 — 191

Monoplegia — continued
- embolic (see also Embolism, brain) — continued
  - late effect — see Late effect(s) (of) cerebrovascular disease
  - infantile (cerebral) (spastic) (spinal) 343.3
  - lower limb 344.30
    - affecting
      - dominant side 344.31
      - nondominant side 344.32
    - due to late effect of cerebrovascular accident — see Late effect(s) (of) cerebrovascular accident
  - newborn 767.8
  - psychogenic 306.0
    - specified as conversion reaction 300.11
  - thrombotic (current) (see also Thrombosis, brain) 434.0 ☑
    - late effect — see Late effect(s) (of) cerebrovascular disease
  - transient 781.4
  - upper limb 344.40
    - affecting
      - dominant side 344.41
      - nondominant side 344.42
    - due to late effect of cerebrovascular accident — see Late effect(s) (of) cerebrovascular accident

Monorchism, monorchidism 752.89
Monteggia's fracture (closed) 813.03
- open 813.13

Mood swings
- brief compensatory 296.99
- rebound 296.99

Mooren's ulcer (cornea) 370.07
Moore's syndrome — see also Epilepsy 345.5 ☑
Mooser bodies 081.0
Mooser-Neill reaction 081.0
Moral
- deficiency 301.7
- imbecility 301.7

Morax-Axenfeld conjunctivitis 372.03
Morbilli — see also Measles 055.9
Morbus
- anglicus, anglorum 268.0
- Beigel 111.2
- caducus (see also Epilepsy) 345.9 ☑
- caeruleus 746.89
- celiacus 579.0
- comitialis (see also Epilepsy) 345.9 ☑
- cordis (see also Disease, heart)
  - valvulorum — see Endocarditis
- coxae 719.95
  - tuberculous (see also Tuberculosis) 015.1 ☑
- hemorrhagicus neonatorum 776.0
- maculosus neonatorum 772.6
- renum 593.0
- senilis (see also Osteoarthrosis) 715.9 ☑

Morel-Kraepelin disease — see also Schizophrenia 295.9 ☑
Morel-Moore syndrome (hyperostosis frontalis interna) 733.3
Morel-Morgagni syndrome (hyperostosis frontalis interna) 733.3
Morgagni
- cyst, organ, hydatid, or appendage 752.89
  - fallopian tube 752.11
- disease or syndrome (hyperostosis frontalis interna) 733.3

Morgagni-Adams-Stokes syndrome (syncope with heart block) 426.9
Morgagni-Stewart-Morel syndrome (hyperostosis frontalis interna) 733.3
Moria — see also Psychosis 298.9
Morning sickness 643.0 ☑
Moron 317
Morphea (guttate) (linear) 701.0
Morphine dependence — see also Dependence 304.0 ☑

Morphinism — see also Dependence 304.0 ☑
Morphinomania — see also Dependence 304.0 ☑
Morphoea 701.0
Morquio (-Brailsford) (-Ullrich) disease or syndrome (mucopolysaccharidosis IV) 277.5
- kyphosis 277.5

Morris syndrome (testicular feminization) 259.5
Morsus humanus (open wound) — see also Wound, open, by site
- skin surface intact — see Contusion

Mortification (dry) (moist) — see also Gangrene 785.4
Morton's
- disease 355.6
- foot 355.6
- metatarsalgia (syndrome) 355.6
- neuralgia 355.6
- neuroma 355.6
- syndrome (metatarsalgia) (neuralgia) 355.6
- toe 355.6

Morvan's disease 336.0
Mosaicism, mosaic (chromosomal) 758.9
- autosomal 758.5
- sex 758.81

Moschcowitz's syndrome (thrombotic thrombocytopenic purpura) 446.6
Mother yaw 102.0
Motion sickness (from travel, any vehicle) (from roundabouts or swings) 994.6
Mottled teeth (enamel) (endemic) (nonendemic) 520.3
Mottling enamel (endemic) (nonendemic) (teeth) 520.3
Mouchet's disease 732.5
Mould(s) (in vitreous) 117.9
Moulders'
- bronchitis 502
- tuberculosis (see also Tuberculosis) 011.4 ☑

Mounier-Kuhn syndrome 748.3
- with
  - acute exacerbation 494.1
  - bronchiectasis 494.0
    - with (acute) exacerbation 494.1
- acquired 519.19 ▲
  - with bronchiectasis 494.0
    - with (acute) exacerbation 494.1

Mountain
- fever — see Fever, mountain
- sickness 993.2
  - with polycythemia, acquired 289.0
  - acute 289.0
- tick fever 066.1

Mouse, joint — see also Loose, body, joint 718.1 ☑
- knee 717.6

Mouth — see condition
Movable
- coccyx 724.71
- kidney (see also Disease, renal) 593.0
  - congenital 753.3
- organ or site, congenital NEC — see Malposition, congenital
- spleen 289.59

Movement
- abnormal (dystonic) (involuntary) 781.0
- decreased fetal 655.7 ☑
- paradoxical facial 374.43

Moya Moya disease 437.5
Mozart's ear 744.29
MRSA (methicillin-resistant staphylococcus aureus) V09.0
Mucha's disease (acute parapsoriasis varioliformis) 696.2
Mucha-Haberman syndrome (acute parapsoriasis varioliformis) 696.2
Mu-chain disease 273.2
Mucinosis (cutaneous) (papular) 701.8

Mucocele
- appendix 543.9
- buccal cavity 528.9
- gallbladder (see also Disease, gallbladder) 575.3
- lacrimal sac 375.43
- orbit (eye) 376.81
- salivary gland (any) 527.6
- sinus (accessory) (nasal) 478.19 ▲
- turbinate (bone) (middle) (nasal) 478.19 ▲
- uterus 621.8

Mucocutaneous lymph node syndrome (acute) (febrile) (infantile) 446.1
Mucoenteritis 564.9
Mucolipidosis I, II, III 272.7
Mucopolysaccharidosis (types 1-6) 277.5
- cardiopathy 277.5 [425.7]
Mucormycosis (lung) 117.7
Mucositis — see also Inflammation, by site 528.00 ▲
- cervix (ulcerative) 616.81 ●
- due to
  - antineoplastic therapy (ulcerative) ● 528.01
  - other drugs (ulcerative) 528.02 ●
  - specified NEC 528.09 ●
- gastrointestinal (ulcerative) 538 ●
- nasal (ulcerative) 478.11 ●
- necroticans agranulocytica ▶(see also Agranulocytosis)◀ 288.09 ▲
- ulcerative 528.00 ●
- vagina (ulcerative) 616.81 ●
- vulva (ulcerative) 616.81 ●

Mucous — see also condition
- patches (syphilitic) 091.3
  - congenital 090.0

Mucoviscidosis 277.00
- with meconium obstruction 277.01

Mucus
- asphyxia or suffocation (see also Asphyxia, mucus) 933.1
  - newborn 770.18
- in stool 792.1
- plug (see also Asphyxia, mucus) 933.1
  - aspiration, of newborn 770.17
  - tracheobronchial 519.19 ▲
    - newborn 770.18

Muguet 112.0
Mulberry molars 090.5
Mullerian mixed tumor (M8950/3) — see Neoplasm, by site, malignant
Multicystic kidney 753.19
Multilobed placenta — see Placenta, abnormal
Multinodular prostate 600.10
- with
  - urinary ●
    - obstruction 600.11 ●
    - retention 600.11 ●

Multiparity V61.5
- affecting
  - fetus or newborn 763.89
  - management of
    - labor and delivery 659.4 ☑
    - pregnancy V23.3
  - requiring contraceptive management (see also Contraception) V25.9

Multipartita placenta — see Placenta, abnormal
Multiple, multiplex — see also condition
- birth
  - affecting fetus or newborn 761.5
  - healthy liveborn — see Newborn, multiple
- digits (congenital) 755.00
  - fingers 755.01
  - toes 755.02
- organ or site NEC — see Accessory
- personality 300.14
- renal arteries 747.62

Mumps 072.9
- with complication 072.8
  - specified type NEC 072.79
- encephalitis 072.2

Mumps — continued
- hepatitis 072.71
- meningitis (aseptic) 072.1
- meningoencephalitis 072.2
- oophoritis 072.79
- orchitis 072.0
- pancreatitis 072.3
- polyneuropathy 072.72
- vaccination, prophylactic (against) V04.6

Mumu — see also Infestation, filarial 125.9
Münchausen syndrome 301.51
Münchmeyer's disease or syndrome (exostosis luxurians) 728.11
Mural — see condition
Murmur (cardiac) (heart) (nonorganic) (organic) 785.2
- abdominal 787.5
- aortic (valve) (see also Endocarditis, aortic) 424.1
- benign — omit code
- cardiorespiratory 785.2
- diastolic — see condition
- Flint (see also Endocarditis, aortic) 424.1
- functional — omit code
- Graham Steell (pulmonic regurgitation) (see also Endocarditis, pulmonary) 424.3
- innocent — omit code
- insignificant — omit code
- midsystolic 785.2
- mitral (valve) — see Stenosis, mitral
- physiologic — see condition
- presystolic, mitral — see Insufficiency, mitral
- pulmonic (valve) (see also Endocarditis, pulmonary) 424.3
- Still's (vibratory) — omit code
- systolic (valvular) — see condition
- tricuspid (valve) — see Endocarditis, tricuspid
- undiagnosed 785.2
- valvular — see condition
- vibratory — omit code

Murri's disease (intermittent hemoglobinuria) 283.2
Muscae volitantes 379.24
Muscle, muscular — see condition
Musculoneuralgia 729.1
Mushrooming hip 718.95
Mushroom workers' (pickers') lung 495.5
Mutation
- factor V leiden 289.81
- prothrombin gene 289.81

Mutism — see also Aphasia 784.3
- akinetic 784.3
- deaf (acquired) (congenital) 389.7
- hysterical 300.11
- selective (elective) 313.23
  - adjustment reaction 309.83

Myà's disease (congenital dilation, colon) 751.3
Myalgia (intercostal) 729.1
- eosinophilia syndrome 710.5
- epidemic 074.1
  - cervical 078.89
- psychogenic 307.89
- traumatic NEC 959.9

Myasthenia 358.00
- cordis — see Failure, heart
- gravis 358.00
  - with exacerbation (acute) 358.01
    - in crisis 358.01
  - neonatal 775.2
  - pseudoparalytica 358.00
- stomach 536.8
  - psychogenic 306.4
- syndrome
  - in
    - botulism 005.1 [358.1]
    - diabetes mellitus 250.6 ☑ [358.1]

☑ Additional Digit Required — Refer to the Tabular List for Digit Selection
▽ Subterms under main terms may continue to next column or page
192 — Volume 2 · October 2006
▶◀ Revised Text
● New Line
▲ Revised Code
2007 ICD-9-CM

Myasthenia — continued
　syndrome — continued
　　in — continued
　　　hypothyroidism (see also Hypothyroidism)
　　　　244.9 [358.1]
　　　malignant neoplasm NEC
　　　　199.1 [358.1]
　　　pernicious anemia 281.0 [358.1]
　　　thyrotoxicosis (see also Thyrotoxicosis) 242.9 ☑ [358.1]
Myasthenic 728.87
Mycelium infection NEC 117.9
Mycetismus 988.1
Mycetoma (actinomycotic) 039.9
　bone 039.8
　　mycotic 117.4
　foot 039.4
　　mycotic 117.4
　madurae 039.9
　　mycotic 117.4
　maduromycotic 039.9
　　mycotic 117.4
　mycotic 117.4
　nocardial 039.9
Mycobacteriosis — see Mycobacterium
Mycobacterium, mycobacterial (infection) 031.9
　acid-fast (bacilli) 031.9
　anonymous (see also Mycobacterium, atypical) 031.9
　atypical (acid-fast bacilli) 031.9
　　cutaneous 031.1
　　pulmonary 031.0
　　　tuberculous (see also Tuberculosis, pulmonary) 011.9 ☑
　　specified site NEC 031.8
　avium 031.0
　　intracellulare complex bacteremia (MAC) 031.2
　balnei 031.1
　Battey 031.0
　cutaneous 031.1
　disseminated 031.2
　　avium-intracellulare complex (DMAC) 031.2
　fortuitum 031.0
　intracellulare (battey bacillus) 031.0
　kakerifu 031.8
　kansasii 031.0
　kasongo 031.8
　leprae — see Leprosy
　luciflavum 031.0
　marinum 031.1
　pulmonary 031.0
　　tuberculous (see also Tuberculosis, pulmonary) 011.9 ☑
　scrofulaceum 031.1
　tuberculosis (human, bovine) (see also Tuberculosis)
　　avian type 031.0
　ulcerans 031.1
　xenopi 031.0
Mycosis, mycotic 117.9
　cutaneous NEC 111.9
　ear 111.8 [380.15]
　fungoides (M9700/3) 202.1 ☑
　mouth 112.0
　pharynx 117.9
　skin NEC 111.9
　stomatitis 112.0
　systemic NEC 117.9
　tonsil 117.9
　vagina, vaginitis 112.1
Mydriasis (persistent) (pupil) 379.43
Myelatelia 742.59
Myelinoclasis, perivascular, acute (postinfectious) NEC
　136.9 [323.61]
　postimmunization or postvaccinal
　　323.51 ▲
Myelinosis, central pontine 341.8

Myelitis (ascending) (cerebellar) (childhood) (chronic) (descending) (diffuse) (disseminated) (pressure) (progressive) (spinal cord) (subacute) — see also Encephalitis 323.9
　acute (transverse) 341.20 ●
　　idiopathic 341.22 ●
　　in conditions classified elsewhere ●
　　　341.21
　due to
　　infection classified elsewhere ●
　　　136.9 [323.42]
　　specified cause NEC 323.82 ●
　　vaccination (any) 323.52 ●
　　viral diseases classified elsewhere ●
　　　323.02
　herpes simplex 054.74 ●
　herpes zoster 053.14 ●
　late effect — see category 326
　optic neuritis in 341.0
　postchickenpox 052.2 ▲
　postimmunization 323.52 ●
　postinfectious 136.9 [323.63] ●
　postvaccinal 323.52 ▲
　postvaricella 052.2 ●
　syphilitic (transverse) 094.89
　toxic 989.9 [323.72] ●
　transverse 323.82
　　acute 341.20 ●
　　　idiopathic 341.22 ●
　　　in conditions classified else- ●
　　　　where 341.21 ●
　　idiopathic 341.22 ●
　tuberculous (see also Tuberculosis)
　　013.6 ☑
　virus 049.9
Myeloblastic — see condition
Myelocele — see also Spina bifida
　741.9 ☑
　with hydrocephalus 741.0 ☑
Myelocystocele — see also Spina bifida
　741.9 ☑
Myelocytic — see condition
Myelocytoma 205.1 ☑
Myelodysplasia (spinal cord) 742.59
　meaning myelodysplastic syndrome — see Syndrome, myelodysplastic
Myeloencephalitis — see Encephalitis
Myelofibrosis 289.83 ▲
　with myeloid metaplasia 238.76 ●
　idiopathic (chronic) 238.76 ●
　megakaryocytic 238.79 ●
　primary 238.76 ●
　secondary 289.83 ●
Myelogenous — see condition
Myeloid — see condition
Myelokathexis 288.09 ▲
Myeloleukodystrophy 330.0
Myelolipoma (M8870/0) — see Neoplasm, by site, benign
Myeloma (multiple) (plasma cell) (plasmacytic) (M9730/3) 203.0 ☑
　monostotic (M9731/1) 238.6
　solitary (M9731/1) 238.6
Myelomalacia 336.8
Myelomata, multiple (M9730/3)
　203.0 ☑
Myelomatosis (M9730/3) 203.0 ☑
Myelomeningitis — see Meningoencephalitis
Myelomeningocele (spinal cord) — see also Spina bifida 741.9 ☑
　fetal, causing fetopelvic disproportion
　　653.7 ☑
Myelo-osteo-musculodysplasia hereditaria 756.89
Myelopathic — see condition
Myelopathy (spinal cord) 336.9
　cervical 721.1
　diabetic 250.6 ☑ [336.3]
　drug-induced 336.8
　due to or with
　　carbon tetrachloride
　　　987.8 [323.72] ▲

Myelopathy — continued
　due to or with — continued
　　degeneration or displacement, intervertebral disc 722.70
　　　cervical, cervicothoracic 722.71
　　　lumbar, lumbosacral 722.73
　　　thoracic, thoracolumbar 722.72
　　hydroxyquinoline derivatives
　　　961.3 [323.72] ▲
　　infection — see Encephalitis
　　intervertebral disc disorder 722.70
　　　cervical, cervicothoracic 722.71
　　　lumbar, lumbosacral 722.73
　　　thoracic, thoracolumbar 722.72
　　lead 984.9 [323.72] ▲
　　mercury 985.0 [323.72] ▲
　　neoplastic disease (see also Neoplasm, by site) 239.9 [336.3]
　　pernicious anemia 281.0 [336.3]
　　spondylosis 721.91
　　　cervical 721.1
　　　lumbar, lumbosacral 721.42
　　　thoracic 721.41
　　thallium 985.8 [323.72] ▲
　lumbar, lumbosacral 721.42
　necrotic (subacute) 336.1
　radiation-induced 336.8
　spondylogenic NEC 721.91
　　cervical 721.1
　　lumbar, lumbosacral 721.42
　　thoracic 721.41
　thoracic 721.41
　toxic NEC 989.9 [323.72] ▲
　transverse (see also ▶Myelitis◀)
　　323.82 ▲
　vascular 336.1
Myelophthisis 284.2 ●
Myeloproliferative disease (M9960/1)
　238.79 ▲
Myeloradiculitis — see also Polyneuropathy 357.0
Myeloradiculodysplasia (spinal) 742.59
Myelosarcoma (M9930/3) 205.3 ☑
Myelosclerosis 289.89
　with myeloid metaplasia (M9961/1)
　　238.76 ▲
　disseminated, of nervous system 340
　megakaryocytic (M9961/1)
　　238.79 ▲
Myelosis (M9860/3) — see also
　Leukemia, myeloid 205.9 ☑
　acute (M9861/3) 205.0 ☑
　aleukemic (M9864/3) 205.8 ☑
　chronic (M9863/3) 205.1 ☑
　erythremic (M9840/3) 207.0 ☑
　　acute (M9841/3) 207.0 ☑
　megakaryocytic (M9920/3) 207.2 ☑
　nonleukemic (chronic) 288.8
　subacute (M9862/3) 205.2 ☑
Myesthenia — see Myasthenia
Myiasis (cavernous) 134.0
　orbit 134.0 [376.13]
Myoadenoma, prostate 600.20
　with
　　other lower urinary tract symp- ●
　　　toms (LUTS) 600.21 ●
　　urinary ●
　　　obstruction 600.21 ●
　　　retention 600.21 ●
Myoblastoma
　granular cell (M9580/0) (see also Neoplasm, connective tissue, benign)
　　malignant (M9580/3) — see Neoplasm, connective tissue, malignant
　tongue (M9580/0) 210.1
Myocardial — see condition
Myocardiopathy (congestive) (constrictive) (familial) (hypertrophic nonobstructive) (idiopathic) (infiltrative) (obstructive) (primary) (restrictive) (sporadic) 425.4
　alcoholic 425.5
　amyloid 277.39 [425.7] ▲
　beriberi 265.0 [425.7]

Myocardiopathy — continued
　cobalt-beer 425.5
　due to
　　amyloidosis 277.39 [425.7] ▲
　　beriberi 265.0 [425.7]
　　cardiac glycogenosis 271.0 [425.7]
　　Chagas' disease 086.0
　　Friedreich's ataxia 334.0 [425.8]
　　influenza 487.8 [425.8]
　　mucopolysaccharidosis
　　　277.5 [425.7]
　　myotonia atrophica 359.2 [425.8]
　　progressive muscular dystrophy
　　　359.1 [425.8]
　　sarcoidosis 135 [425.8]
　glycogen storage 271.0 [425.7]
　hypertrophic obstructive 425.1
　metabolic NEC 277.9 [425.7]
　nutritional 269.9 [425.7]
　obscure (African) 425.2
　peripartum 674.5 ☑
　postpartum 674.5 ☑
　secondary 425.9
　thyrotoxic (see also Thyrotoxicosis)
　　242.9 ☑ [425.7]
　toxic NEC 425.9
Myocarditis (fibroid) (interstitial) (old) (progressive) (senile) (with arteriosclerosis) 429.0
　with
　　rheumatic fever (conditions classifiable to 390) 398.0
　　　active (see also Myocarditis, acute, rheumatic) 391.2
　　　inactive or quiescent (with chorea) 398.0
　active (nonrheumatic) 422.90
　　rheumatic 391.2
　　　with chorea (acute) (rheumatic) (Sydenham's) 392.0
　acute or subacute (interstitial) 422.90
　　due to Streptococcus (beta-hemolytic) 391.2
　　idiopathic 422.91
　　rheumatic 391.2
　　　with chorea (acute) (rheumatic) (Sydenham's) 392.0
　　specified type NEC 422.99
　aseptic of newborn 074.23
　bacterial (acute) 422.92
　chagasic 086.0
　chronic (interstitial) 429.0
　congenital 746.89
　constrictive 425.4
　Coxsackie (virus) 074.23
　diphtheritic 032.82
　due to or in
　　Coxsackie (virus) 074.23
　　diphtheria 032.82
　　epidemic louse-borne typhus
　　　080 [422.0]
　　influenza 487.8 [422.0]
　　Lyme disease 088.81 [422.0]
　　scarlet fever 034.1 [422.0]
　　toxoplasmosis (acquired) 130.3
　　tuberculosis (see also Tuberculosis)
　　　017.9 ☑ [422.0]
　　typhoid 002.0 [422.0]
　　typhus NEC 081.9 [422.0]
　eosinophilic 422.91
　epidemic of newborn 074.23
　Fiedler's (acute) (isolated) (subacute)
　　422.91
　giant cell (acute) (subacute) 422.91
　gonococcal 098.85
　granulomatous (idiopathic) (isolated) (nonspecific) 422.91
　hypertensive (see also Hypertension, heart) 402.90
　idiopathic 422.91
　　granulomatous 422.91
　infective 422.92
　influenzal 487.8 [422.0]
　isolated (diffuse) (granulomatous)
　　422.91
　malignant 422.99

☑ Additional Digit Required — Refer to the Tabular List for Digit Selection
▼ Subterms under main terms may continue to next column or page
2007 ICD-9-CM
▶◀ Revised Text　　●New Line　　▲ Revised Code
October 2006 · Volume 2 — 193

Index

Myocarditis — Narrowing

Myocarditis — continued
meningococcal 036.43
nonrheumatic, active 422.90
parenchymatous 422.90
pneumococcal (acute) (subacute) 422.92
rheumatic (chronic) (inactive) (with chorea) 398.0
active or acute 391.2
with chorea (acute) (rheumatic) (Sydenham's) 392.0
septic 422.92
specific (giant cell) (productive) 422.91
staphylococcal (acute) (subacute) 422.92
suppurative 422.92
syphilitic (chronic) 093.82
toxic 422.93
rheumatic (see also Myocarditis, acute rheumatic) 391.2
tuberculous (see also Tuberculosis) 017.9 ☑ [422.0]
typhoid 002.0 [422.0]
valvular — see Endocarditis
viral, except Coxsackie 422.91
Coxsackie 074.23
of newborn (Coxsackie) 074.23
Myocardium, myocardial — see condition
Myocardosis — see also Cardiomyopathy 425.4
Myoclonia (essential) 333.2
epileptica 333.2
Friedrich's 333.2
massive 333.2
Myoclonic
epilepsy, familial (progressive) 333.2
jerks 333.2
Myoclonus (familial essential) (multifocal) (simplex) 333.2
with epilepsy and with ragged red fibers (MERRF syndrome) 277.87
facial 351.8
massive (infantile) 333.2
pharyngeal 478.29
Myodiastasis 728.84
Myoendocarditis — see also Endocarditis
acute or subacute 421.9
Myoepithelioma (M8982/0) — see Neoplasm, by site, benign
Myofascitis (acute) 729.1
low back 724.2
Myofibroma (M8890/0) — see also Neoplasm, connective tissue, benign
uterus (cervix) (corpus) (see also Leiomyoma) 218.9
Myofibromatosis ●
infantile 759.89 ●
Myofibrosis 728.2
heart (see also Myocarditis) 429.0
humeroscapular region 726.2
scapulohumeral 726.2
Myofibrositis — see also Myositis 729.1
scapulohumeral 726.2
Myogelosis (occupational) 728.89
Myoglobinuria 791.3
Myoglobulinuria, primary 791.3
Myokymia — see also Myoclonus
facial 351.8
Myolipoma (M8860/0)
specified site — see Neoplasm, connective tissue, benign
unspecified site 223.0
Myoma (M8895/0) — see also Neoplasm, connective tissue, benign
cervix (stump) (uterus) (see also Leiomyoma) 218.9
malignant (M8895/3) — see Neoplasm, connective tissue, malignant
prostate 600.20

Myoma — see also Neoplasm, connective tissue, benign — continued
prostate — continued
with
other lower urinary tract ●
symptoms (LUTS) ●
600.21 ●
urinary ●
obstruction 600.21 ●
retention 600.21 ●
uterus (cervix) (corpus) (see also Leiomyoma) 218.9
in pregnancy or childbirth 654.1 ☑
affecting fetus or newborn 763.89
causing obstructed labor 660.2 ☑
affecting fetus or newborn 763.1
Myomalacia 728.9
cordis, heart (see also Degeneration, myocardial) 429.1
Myometritis — see also Endometritis 615.9
Myometrium — see condition
Myonecrosis, clostridial 040.0
Myopathy 359.9
alcoholic 359.4
amyloid 277.39 [359.6] ▲
benign, congenital 359.0
central core 359.0
centronuclear 359.0
congenital (benign) 359.0
critical illness 359.81
distal 359.1
due to drugs 359.4
endocrine 259.9 [359.5]
specified type NEC 259.8 [359.5]
extraocular muscles 376.82
facioscapulohumeral 359.1
in
Addison's disease 255.4 [359.5]
amyloidosis 277.39 [359.6] ▲
cretinism 243 [359.5]
Cushing's syndrome 255.0 [359.5]
disseminated lupus erythematosus 710.0 [359.6]
giant cell arteritis 446.5 [359.6]
hyperadrenocorticism NEC 255.3 [359.5]
hyperparathyroidism 252.01 [359.5]
hypopituitarism 253.2 [359.5]
hypothyroidism (see also Hypothyroidism) 244.9 [359.5]
malignant neoplasm NEC (M8000/3) 199.1 [359.6]
myxedema (see also Myxedema) 244.9 [359.5]
polyarteritis nodosa 446.0 [359.6]
rheumatoid arthritis 714.0 [359.6]
sarcoidosis 135 [359.6]
scleroderma 710.1 [359.6]
Sjögren's disease 710.2 [359.6]
thyrotoxicosis (see also Thyrotoxicosis) 242.9 ☑ [359.5]
inflammatory 359.89
intensive care (ICU) 359.81
limb-girdle 359.1
myotubular 359.0
necrotizing, acute 359.81
nemaline 359.0
ocular 359.1
oculopharyngeal 359.1
of critical illness 359.81
primary 359.89
progressive NEC 359.89
quadriplegic, acute 359.81
rod body 359.0
scapulohumeral 359.1
specified type NEC 359.89
toxic 359.4
Myopericarditis — see also Pericarditis 423.9

Myopia (axial) (congenital) (increased curvature or refraction, nucleus of lens) 367.1
degenerative, malignant 360.21
malignant 360.21
progressive high (degenerative) 360.21
Myosarcoma (M8895/3) — see Neoplasm, connective tissue, malignant
Myosis (persistent) 379.42
stromal (endolymphatic) (M8931/1) 236.0
Myositis 729.1
clostridial 040.0
due to posture 729.1
epidemic 074.1
fibrosa or fibrous (chronic) 728.2
Volkmann's (complicating trauma) 958.6
infective 728.0
interstitial 728.81
multiple — see Polymyositis
occupational 729.1
orbital, chronic 376.12
ossificans 728.12
circumscribed 728.12
progressive 728.11
traumatic 728.12
progressive fibrosing 728.11
purulent 728.0
rheumatic 729.1
rheumatoid 729.1
suppurative 728.0
syphilitic 095.6
traumatic (old) 729.1
Myospasia impulsiva 307.23
Myotonia (acquisita) (intermittens) 728.85
atrophica 359.2
congenita 359.2
dystrophica 359.2
Myotonic pupil 379.46
Myriapodiasis 134.1
Myringitis
with otitis media — see Otitis media
acute 384.00
specified type NEC 384.09
bullosa hemorrhagica 384.01
bullous 384.01
chronic 384.1
Mysophobia 300.29
Mytilotoxism 988.0
Myxadenitis labialis 528.5
Myxedema (adult) (idiocy) (infantile) (juvenile) (thyroid gland) — see also Hypothyroidism 244.9
circumscribed 242.9 ☑
congenital 243
cutis 701.8
localized (pretibial) 242.9 ☑
madness (acute) 293.0
subacute 293.1
papular 701.8
pituitary 244.8
postpartum 674.8 ☑
pretibial 242.9 ☑
primary 244.9
Myxochondrosarcoma (M9220/3) — see Neoplasm, cartilage, malignant
Myxofibroma (M8811/0) — see also Neoplasm, connective tissue, benign
odontogenic (M9320/0) 213.1
upper jaw (bone) 213.0
Myxofibrosarcoma (M8811/3) — see Neoplasm, connective tissue, malignant
Myxolipoma (M8852/0) — see also Lipoma, by site 214.9
Myxoliposarcoma (M8852/3) — see Neoplasm, connective tissue, malignant
Myxoma (M8840/0) — see also Neoplasm, connective tissue, benign
odontogenic (M9320/0) 213.1
upper jaw (bone) 213.0

Myxosarcoma (M8840/3) — see Neoplasm, connective tissue, malignant

N

Naegeli's
disease (hereditary hemorrhagic thrombasthenia) 287.1
leukemia, monocytic (M9863/3) 205.1 ☑
syndrome (incontinentia pigmenti) 757.33
Naffziger's syndrome 353.0
Naga sore — see also Ulcer, skin 707.9
Nägele's pelvis 738.6
with disproportion (fetopelvic) 653.0 ☑
affecting fetus or newborn 763.1
causing obstructed labor 660.1 ☑
affecting fetus or newborn 763.1
Nager-de Reynier syndrome (dysostosis mandibularis) 756.0
Nail — see also condition
biting 307.9
patella syndrome (hereditary osteoonychodysplasia) 756.89
Nanism, nanosomia — see also Dwarfism 259.4
hypophyseal 253.3
pituitary 253.3
renis, renalis 588.0
Nanukayami 100.89
Napkin rash 691.0
Narcissism 301.81
Narcolepsy 347.00
with cataplexy 347.01
in conditions classified elsewhere 347.10
with cataplexy 347.11
Narcosis
carbon dioxide (respiratory) 786.09
due to drug
correct substance properly administered 780.09
overdose or wrong substance given or taken 977.9
specified drug — see Table of Drugs and Chemicals
Narcotism (chronic) — see also Dependence 304.9 ☑
acute
correct substance properly administered 349.82
overdose or wrong substance given or taken 967.8
specified drug — see Table of Drugs and Chemicals
NARP (ataxia and retinitis pigmentosa) 277.87
Narrow
anterior chamber angle 365.02
pelvis (inlet) (outlet) — see Contraction, pelvis
Narrowing
artery NEC 447.1
auditory, internal 433.8 ☑
basilar 433.0 ☑
with other precerebral artery 433.3 ☑
bilateral 433.3 ☑
carotid 433.1 ☑
with other precerebral artery 433.3 ☑
bilateral 433.3 ☑
cerebellar 433.8 ☑
choroidal 433.8 ☑
communicating posterior 433.8 ☑
coronary (see also Arteriosclerosis, coronary)
congenital 746.85
due to syphilis 090.5
hypophyseal 433.8 ☑
pontine 433.8 ☑
precerebral NEC 433.9 ☑
multiple or bilateral 433.3 ☑
specified NEC 433.8 ☑

Narrowing — continued
  artery — continued
    vertebral 433.2 ☑
      with other precerebral artery 433.3 ☑
      bilateral 433.3 ☑
  auditory canal (external) (see also Stricture, ear canal, acquired) 380.50
  cerebral arteries 437.0
  cicatricial — see Cicatrix
  congenital — see Anomaly, congenital
  coronary artery — see Narrowing, artery, coronary
  ear, middle 385.22
  Eustachian tube (see also Obstruction, Eustachian tube) 381.60
  eyelid 374.46
    congenital 743.62
  intervertebral disc or space NEC — see Degeneration, intervertebral disc
  joint space, hip 719.85
  larynx 478.74
  lids 374.46
    congenital 743.62
  mesenteric artery (with gangrene) 557.0
  palate 524.89
  palpebral fissure 374.46
  retinal artery 362.13
  ureter 593.3
  urethra (see also Stricture, urethra) 598.9
Narrowness, abnormal, eyelid 743.62
Nasal — see condition
Nasolacrimal — see condition
Nasopharyngeal — see also condition
  bursa 478.29
  pituitary gland 759.2
  torticollis 723.5
Nasopharyngitis (acute) (infective) (subacute) 460
  chronic 472.2
    due to external agent — see Condition, respiratory, chronic, due to
  due to external agent — see Condition, respiratory, due to
  septic 034.0
  streptococcal 034.0
  suppurative (chronic) 472.2
  ulcerative (chronic) 472.2
Nasopharynx, nasopharyngeal — see condition
Natal tooth, teeth 520.6
Nausea — see also Vomiting 787.02
  with vomiting 787.01
  epidemic 078.82
  gravidarum — see Hyperemesis, gravidarum
  marina 994.6
Navel — see condition
Neapolitan fever — see also Brucellosis 023.9
Nearsightedness 367.1
Near-syncope 780.2
Nebécourt's syndrome 253.3
Nebula, cornea (eye) 371.01
  congenital 743.43
  interfering with vision 743.42
Necator americanus infestation 126.1
Necatoriasis 126.1
Neck — see condition
Necrencephalus — see also Softening, brain 437.8
Necrobacillosis 040.3
Necrobiosis 799.89
  brain or cerebral (see also Softening, brain) 437.8
  lipoidica 709.3
    diabeticorum 250.8 ☑ [709.3]
Necrodermolysis 695.1
Necrolysis, toxic epidermal 695.1

Necrolysis, toxic epidermal — continued
  due to drug
    correct substance properly administered 695.1
    overdose or wrong substance given or taken 977.9
    specified drug — see Table of Drugs and Chemicals
Necrophilia 302.89
Necrosis, necrotic
  adrenal (capsule) (gland) 255.8
  antrum, nasal sinus 478.19 ▲
  aorta (hyaline) (see also Aneurysm, aorta) 441.9
    cystic medial 441.00
      abdominal 441.02
      thoracic 441.01
      thoracoabdominal 441.03
    ruptured 441.5
  arteritis 446.0
  artery 447.5
  aseptic, bone 733.40
    femur (head) (neck) 733.42
      medial condyle 733.43
    humoral head 733.41
    medial femoral condyle 733.43
    specific site NEC 733.49
    talus 733.44
  avascular, bone NEC (see also Necrosis, aseptic, bone) 733.40
  bladder (aseptic) (sphincter) 596.8
  bone (see also Osteomyelitis) 730.1 ☑
    acute 730.0 ☑
    aseptic or avascular 733.40
      femur (head) (neck) 733.42
        medial condyle 733.43
      humoral head 733.41
      medial femoral condyle 733.43
      specified site NEC 733.49
      talus 733.44
    ethmoid 478.19 ▲
    ischemic 733.40
    jaw 526.4
    marrow 289.89
    Paget's (osteitis deformans) 731.0
    tuberculous — see Tuberculosis, bone
  brain (softening) (see also Softening, brain) 437.8
  breast (aseptic) (fat) (segmental) 611.3
  bronchus, bronchi 519.19 ▲
  central nervous system NEC (see also Softening, brain) 437.8
  cerebellar (see also Softening, brain) 437.8
  cerebral (softening) (see also Softening, brain) 437.8
  cerebrospinal (softening) (see also Softening, brain) 437.8
  cornea (see also Keratitis) 371.40
  cortical, kidney 583.6
  cystic medial (aorta) 441.00
    abdominal 441.02
    thoracic 441.01
    thoracoabdominal 441.03
  dental 521.09
    pulp 522.1
  due to swallowing corrosive substance — see Burn, by site
  ear (ossicle) 385.24
  esophagus 530.89
  ethmoid (bone) 478.19 ▲
  eyelid 374.50
  fat, fatty (generalized) (see also Degeneration, fatty) 272.8
    abdominal wall 567.82
    breast (aseptic) (segmental) 611.3
    intestine 569.89
    localized — see Degeneration, by site, fatty
    mesentery 567.82
    omentum 567.82
    pancreas 577.8
    peritoneum 567.82
    skin (subcutaneous) 709.3

Necrosis, necrotic — continued
  fat, fatty (see also Degeneration, fatty) — continued
    skin — continued
      newborn 778.1
  femur (aseptic) (avascular) 733.42
    head 733.42
    medial condyle 733.43
    neck 733.42
  gallbladder (see also Cholecystitis, acute) 575.0
  gangrenous 785.4
  gastric 537.89
  glottis 478.79
  heart (myocardium) — see Infarct, myocardium
  hepatic (see also Necrosis, liver) 570
  hip (aseptic) (avascular) 733.42
  intestine (acute) (hemorrhagic) (massive) 557.0
  ischemic 785.4
  jaw 526.4
  kidney (bilateral) 583.9
    acute 584.9
    cortical 583.6
      acute 584.6
        with
          abortion — see Abortion, by type, with renal failure
          ectopic pregnancy (see also categories 633.0–633.9) 639.3
          molar pregnancy (see also categories 630–632) 639.3
        complicating pregnancy 646.2 ☑
        affecting fetus or newborn 760.1
        following labor and delivery 669.3 ☑
    medullary (papillary) (see also Pyelitis) 590.80
      in
        acute renal failure 584.7
        nephritis, nephropathy 583.7
    papillary (see also Pyelitis) 590.80
      in
        acute renal failure 584.7
        nephritis, nephropathy 583.7
    tubular 584.5
      with
        abortion — see Abortion, by type, with renal failure
        ectopic pregnancy (see also categories 633.0–633.9) 639.3
        molar pregnancy (see also categories 630–632) 639.3
      complicating
        abortion 639.3
        ectopic or molar pregnancy 639.3
        pregnancy 646.2 ☑
          affecting fetus or newborn 760.1
      following labor and delivery 669.3 ☑
      traumatic 958.5
  larynx 478.79
  liver (acute) (congenital) (diffuse) (massive) (subacute) 570
    with
      abortion — see Abortion, by type, with specified complication NEC
      ectopic pregnancy (see also categories 633.0–633.9) 639.8
      molar pregnancy (see also categories 630–632) 639.8
    complicating pregnancy 646.7 ☑
      affecting fetus or newborn 760.8

Necrosis, necrotic — continued
  liver — continued
    following
      abortion 639.8
      ectopic or molar pregnancy 639.8
      obstetrical 646.7 ☑
      postabortal 639.8
      puerperal, postpartum 674.8 ☑
      toxic 573.3
  lung 513.0
  lymphatic gland 683
  mammary gland 611.3
  mastoid (chronic) 383.1
  mesentery 557.0
    fat 567.82
  mitral valve — see Insufficiency, mitral
  myocardium, myocardial — see Infarct, myocardium
  nose (septum) 478.19 ▲
  omentum 557.0
    with mesenteric infarction 557.0
    fat 567.82
  orbit, orbital 376.10
  ossicles, ear (aseptic) 385.24
  ovary (see also Salpingo-oophoritis) 614.2
  pancreas (aseptic) (duct) (fat) 577.8
    acute 577.0
    infective 577.0
  papillary, kidney (see also Pyelitis) 590.80
  perineum 624.8 ●
  peritoneum 557.0
    with mesenteric infarction 557.0
    fat 567.82
  pharynx 462
    in granulocytopenia 288.09 ▲
  phosphorus 983.9
  pituitary (gland) (postpartum) (Sheehan) 253.2
  placenta (see also Placenta, abnormal) 656.7 ☑
  pneumonia 513.0
  pulmonary 513.0
  pulp (dental) 522.1
  pylorus 537.89
  radiation — see Necrosis, by site
  radium — see Necrosis, by site
  renal — see Necrosis, kidney
  sclera 379.19
  scrotum 608.89
  skin or subcutaneous tissue 709.8
    due to burn — see Burn, by site
    gangrenous 785.4
  spine, spinal (column) 730.18
    acute 730.18
    cord 336.1
  spleen 289.59
  stomach 537.89
  stomatitis 528.1
  subcutaneous fat 709.3
    fetus or newborn 778.1
  subendocardial — see Infarct, myocardium
  suprarenal (capsule) (gland) 255.8
  teeth, tooth 521.09
  testis 608.89
  thymus (gland) 254.8
  tonsil 474.8
  trachea 519.19 ▲
  tuberculous NEC — see Tuberculosis
  tubular (acute) (anoxic) (toxic) 584.5
    due to a procedure 997.5
  umbilical cord, affecting fetus or newborn 762.6
  vagina 623.8
  vertebra (lumbar) 730.18
    acute 730.18
    tuberculous (see also Tuberculosis) 015.0 ☑ [730.8] ☑
  vesical (aseptic) (bladder) 596.8
  vulva 624.8 ●
  x-ray — see Necrosis, by site
Necrospermia 606.0

☑ Additional Digit Required — Refer to the Tabular List for Digit Selection   ▽ Subterms under main terms may continue to next column or page

2007 ICD-9-CM   ►◄ Revised Text   ● New Line   ▲ Revised Code   October 2006 · Volume 2 — **195**

Necrotizing angiitis 446.0
Negativism 301.7
Neglect (child) (newborn) NEC 995.52
    adult 995.84
    after or at birth 995.52
    hemispatial 781.8
    left-sided 781.8

Neglect — *continued*
    sensory 781.8
    visuospatial 781.8
Negri bodies 071
Neill-Dingwall syndrome (microcephaly
    and dwarfism) 759.89

Neisserian infection NEC — *see* Gono-
    coccus
Nematodiasis NEC — *see also* Infesta-
    tion, Nematode 127.9
    ancylostoma (*see also* Ancylostomia-
        sis) 126.9

Neoformans cryptococcus infection
    117.5
Neonatal — *see also* condition
    adrenoleukodystrophy 277.86
    teeth, tooth 520.6
Neonatorum — *see* condition

	Malignant				Uncertain Behavior	Unspecified
	Primary	Secondary	Ca in situ	Benign		
Neoplasm, neoplastic	199.1	199.1	234.9	229.9	238.9	239.9

Notes — 1. The list below gives the code numbers for neoplasms by anatomical site. For each site there are six possible code numbers according to whether the neoplasm in question is malignant, benign, in situ, of uncertain behavior, or of unspecified nature. The description of the neoplasm will often indicate which of the six columns is appropriate; e.g., malignant melanoma of skin, benign fibroadenoma of breast, carcinoma in situ of cervix uteri.

Where such descriptors are not present, the remainder of the Index should be consulted where guidance is given to the appropriate column for each morphological (histological) variety listed; e.g., Mesonephroma — see Neoplasm, malignant; Embryoma — see also Neoplasm, uncertain behavior; Disease, Bowen's — see Neoplasm, skin, in situ. However, the guidance in the Index can be overridden if one of the descriptors mentioned above is present; e.g., malignant adenoma of colon is coded to 153.9 and not to 211.3 as the adjective "malignant" overrides the Index entry "Adenoma — see also Neoplasm, benign."

*2. Sites marked with the sign * (e.g., face NEC*) should be classified to malignant neoplasm of skin of these sites if the variety of neoplasm is a squamous cell carcinoma or an epidermoid carcinoma, and to benign neoplasm of skin of these sites if the variety of neoplasm is a papilloma (any type).*

Site	Primary	Secondary	Ca in situ	Benign	Uncertain Behavior	Unspecified
abdomen, abdominal	195.2	198.89	234.8	229.8	238.8	239.8
cavity	195.2	198.89	234.8	229.8	238.8	239.8
organ	195.2	198.89	234.8	229.8	238.8	239.8
viscera	195.2	198.89	234.8	229.8	238.8	239.8
wall	173.5	198.2	232.5	216.5	238.2	239.2
connective tissue	171.5	198.89	—	215.5	238.1	239.2
abdominopelvic	195.8	198.89	234.8	229.8	238.8	239.8
accessory sinus — see Neoplasm, sinus						
acoustic nerve	192.0	198.4	—	225.1	237.9	239.7
acromion (process)	170.4	198.5	—	213.4	238.0	239.2
adenoid (pharynx) (tissue)	147.1	198.89	230.0	210.7	235.1	239.0
adipose tissue (see also Neoplasm, connective tissue)	171.9	198.89	—	215.9	238.1	239.2
adnexa (uterine)	183.9	198.82	233.3	221.8	236.3	239.5
adrenal (cortex) (gland) (medulla)	194.0	198.7	234.8	227.0	237.2	239.7
ala nasi (external)	173.3	198.2	232.3	216.3	238.2	239.2
alimentary canal or tract NEC	159.9	197.8	230.9	211.9	235.5	239.0
alveolar	143.9	198.89	230.0	210.4	235.1	239.0
mucosa	143.9	198.89	230.0	210.4	235.1	239.0
lower	143.1	198.89	230.0	210.4	235.1	239.0
upper	143.0	198.89	230.0	210.4	235.1	239.0
ridge or process	170.1	198.5	—	213.1	238.0	239.2
carcinoma	143.9	—	—	—	—	—
lower	143.1	—	—	—	—	—
upper	143.0	—	—	—	—	—
lower	170.1	198.5	—	213.1	238.0	239.2
mucosa	143.9	198.89	230.0	210.4	235.1	239.0
lower	143.1	198.89	230.0	210.4	235.1	239.0
upper	143.0	198.89	230.0	210.4	235.1	239.0
upper	170.0	198.5	—	213.0	238.0	239.2
sulcus	145.1	198.89	230.0	210.4	235.1	239.0
alveolus	143.9	198.89	230.0	210.4	235.1	239.0
lower	143.1	198.89	230.0	210.4	235.1	239.0
upper	143.0	198.89	230.0	210.4	235.1	239.0
ampulla of Vater	156.2	197.8	230.8	211.5	235.3	239.0
ankle NEC*	195.5	198.89	232.7	229.8	238.8	239.8
anorectum, anorectal (junction)	154.8	197.5	230.7	211.4	235.2	239.0
antecubital fossa or space*	195.4	198.89	232.6	229.8	238.8	239.8
antrum (Highmore) (maxillary)	160.2	197.3	231.8	212.0	235.9	239.1
pyloric	151.2	197.8	230.2	211.1	235.2	239.0
tympanicum	160.1	197.3	231.8	212.0	235.9	239.1
anus, anal	154.3	197.5	230.6	211.4	235.5	239.0
canal	154.2	197.5	230.5	211.4	235.5	239.0
contiguous sites with rectosigmoid junction or rectum	154.8	—	—	—	—	—
margin	173.5	198.2	232.5	216.5	238.2	239.2
skin	173.5	198.2	232.5	216.5	238.2	239.2
sphincter	154.2	197.5	230.5	211.4	235.5	239.0
aorta (thoracic)	171.4	198.89	—	215.4	238.1	239.2
Neoplasm, neoplastic — *continued*						
aorta — *continued*						
abdominal	171.5	198.89	—	215.5	238.1	239.2
aortic body	194.6	198.89	—	227.6	237.3	239.7
aponeurosis	171.9	198.89	—	215.9	238.1	239.2
palmar	171.2	198.89	—	215.2	238.1	239.2
plantar	171.3	198.89	—	215.3	238.1	239.2
appendix	153.5	197.5	230.3	211.3	235.2	239.0
arachnoid (cerebral)	192.1	198.4	—	225.2	237.6	239.7
spinal	192.3	198.4	—	225.4	237.6	239.7
areola (female)	174.0	198.81	233.0	217	238.3	239.3
male	175.0	198.81	233.0	217	238.3	239.3
arm NEC*	195.4	198.89	232.6	229.8	238.8	239.8
artery — see Neoplasm, connective tissue						
aryepiglottic fold	148.2	198.89	230.0	210.8	235.1	239.0
hypopharyngeal aspect	148.2	198.89	230.0	210.8	235.1	239.0
laryngeal aspect	161.1	197.3	231.0	212.1	235.6	239.1
marginal zone	148.2	198.89	230.0	210.8	235.1	239.0
arytenoid (cartilage)	161.3	197.3	231.0	212.1	235.6	239.1
fold — see Neoplasm, aryepiglottic						
atlas	170.2	198.5	—	213.2	238.0	239.2
atrium, cardiac	164.1	198.89	—	212.7	238.8	239.8
auditory						
canal (external) (skin)	173.2	198.2	232.2	216.2	238.2	239.2
internal	160.1	197.3	231.8	212.0	235.9	239.1
nerve	192.0	198.4	—	225.1	237.9	239.7
tube	160.1	197.3	231.8	212.0	235.9	239.1
Eustachian	160.1	197.3	231.8	212.0	235.9	239.1
opening	147.2	198.89	230.0	210.7	235.1	239.0
auricle, ear	173.2	198.2	232.2	216.2	238.2	239.2
cartilage	171.0	198.89	—	215.0	238.1	239.2
auricular canal (external)	173.2	198.2	232.2	216.2	238.2	239.2
internal	160.1	197.3	231.8	212.0	235.9	239.1
autonomic nerve or nervous system NEC	171.9	198.89	—	215.9	238.1	239.2
axilla, axillary	195.1	198.89	234.8	229.8	238.8	239.8
fold	173.5	198.2	232.5	216.5	238.2	239.2
back NEC*	195.8	198.89	232.5	229.8	238.8	239.8
Bartholin's gland	184.1	198.82	233.3	221.2	236.3	239.5
basal ganglia	191.0	198.3	—	225.0	237.5	239.6
basis pedunculi	191.7	198.3	—	225.0	237.5	239.6
bile or biliary (tract)	156.9	197.8	230.8	211.5	235.3	239.0
canaliculi (biliferi) (intrahepatic)	155.1	197.8	230.8	211.5	235.3	239.0
canals, interlobular	155.1	197.8	230.8	211.5	235.3	239.0
contiguous sites	156.8	—	—	—	—	—
duct or passage (common) (cystic) (extrahepatic)	156.1	197.8	230.8	211.5	235.3	239.0
contiguous sites with gallbladder	156.8	—	—	—	—	—
interlobular	155.1	197.8	230.8	211.5	235.3	239.0
intrahepatic and	155.1	197.8	230.8	211.5	235.3	239.0
extrahepatic	156.9	197.8	230.8	211.5	235.3	239.0
bladder (urinary)	188.9	198.1	233.7	223.3	236.7	239.4
contiguous sites	188.8	—	—	—	—	—
dome	188.1	198.1	233.7	223.3	236.7	239.4
neck	188.5	198.1	233.7	223.3	236.7	239.4
orifice	188.9	198.1	233.7	223.3	236.7	239.4
ureteric	188.6	198.1	233.7	223.3	236.7	239.4
urethral	188.5	198.1	233.7	223.3	236.7	239.4
sphincter	188.8	198.1	233.7	223.3	236.7	239.4
trigone	188.0	198.1	233.7	223.3	236.7	239.4
urachus	188.7	—	233.7	223.3	236.7	239.4
wall	188.9	198.1	233.7	223.3	236.7	239.4
anterior	188.3	198.1	233.7	223.3	236.7	239.4
lateral	188.2	198.1	233.7	223.3	236.7	239.4
posterior	188.4	198.1	233.7	223.3	236.7	239.4
blood vessel — see Neoplasm, connective tissue						

☑ Additional Digit Required — Refer to the Tabular List for Digit Selection

▽ Subterms under main terms may continue to next column or page

	Malignant			Benign	Uncertain Behavior	Unspecified
	Primary	Secondary	Ca in situ			

Neoplasm, neoplastic —
continued

bone (periosteum)	170.9	198.5	—	213.9	238.0	239.2

Note — Carcinomas and adenocarcinomas, of any type other than intraosseous or odontogenic, of the sites listed under "Neoplasm, bone" should be considered as constituting metastatic spread from an unspecified primary site and coded to 198.5 for morbidity coding and to 199.1 for underlying cause of death coding.

	Primary	Secondary	Ca in situ	Benign	Uncertain Behavior	Unspecified
acetabulum	170.6	198.5	—	213.6	238.0	239.2
acromion (process)	170.4	198.5	—	213.4	238.0	239.2
ankle	170.8	198.5	—	213.8	238.0	239.2
arm NEC	170.4	198.5	—	213.4	238.0	239.2
astragalus	170.8	198.5	—	213.8	238.0	239.2
atlas	170.2	198.5	—	213.2	238.0	239.2
axis	170.2	198.5	—	213.2	238.0	239.2
back NEC	170.2	198.5	—	213.2	238.0	239.2
calcaneus	170.8	198.5	—	213.8	238.0	239.2
calvarium	170.0	198.5	—	213.0	238.0	239.2
carpus (any)	170.5	198.5	—	213.5	238.0	239.2
cartilage NEC	170.9	198.5	—	213.9	238.0	239.2
clavicle	170.3	198.5	—	213.3	238.0	239.2
clivus	170.0	198.5	—	213.0	238.0	239.2
coccygeal vertebra	170.6	198.5	—	213.6	238.0	239.2
coccyx	170.6	198.5	—	213.6	238.0	239.2
costal cartilage	170.3	198.5	—	213.3	238.0	239.2
costovertebral joint	170.3	198.5	—	213.3	238.0	239.2
cranial	170.0	198.5	—	213.0	238.0	239.2
cuboid	170.8	198.5	—	213.8	238.0	239.2
cuneiform	170.9	198.5	—	213.9	238.0	239.2
ankle	170.8	198.5	—	213.8	238.0	239.2
wrist	170.5	198.5	—	213.5	238.0	239.2
digital	170.9	198.5	—	213.9	238.0	239.2
finger	170.5	198.5	—	213.5	238.0	239.2
toe	170.8	198.5	—	213.8	238.0	239.2
elbow	170.4	198.5	—	213.4	238.0	239.2
ethmoid (labyrinth)	170.0	198.5	—	213.0	238.0	239.2
face	170.0	198.5	—	213.0	238.0	239.2
lower jaw	170.1	198.5	—	213.1	238.0	239.2
femur (any part)	170.7	198.5	—	213.7	238.0	239.2
fibula (any part)	170.7	198.5	—	213.7	238.0	239.2
finger (any)	170.5	198.5	—	213.5	238.0	239.2
foot	170.8	198.5	—	213.8	238.0	239.2
forearm	170.4	198.5	—	213.4	238.0	239.2
frontal	170.0	198.5	—	213.0	238.0	239.2
hand	170.5	198.5	—	213.5	238.0	239.2
heel	170.8	198.5	—	213.8	238.0	239.2
hip	170.6	198.5	—	213.6	238.0	239.2
humerus (any part)	170.4	198.5	—	213.4	238.0	239.2
hyoid	170.0	198.5	—	213.0	238.0	239.2
ilium	170.6	198.5	—	213.6	238.0	239.2
innominate	170.6	198.5	—	213.6	238.0	239.2
intervertebral cartilage or disc	170.2	198.5	—	213.2	238.0	239.2
ischium	170.6	198.5	—	213.6	238.0	239.2
jaw (lower)	170.1	198.5	—	213.1	238.0	239.2
upper	170.0	198.5	—	213.0	238.0	239.2
knee	170.7	198.5	—	213.7	238.0	239.2
leg NEC	170.7	198.5	—	213.7	238.0	239.2
limb NEC	170.9	198.5	—	213.9	238.0	239.2
lower (long bones)	170.7	198.5	—	213.7	238.0	239.2
short bones	170.8	198.5	—	213.8	238.0	239.2
upper (long bones)	170.4	198.5	—	213.4	238.0	239.2
short bones	170.5	198.5	—	213.5	238.0	239.2
long	170.9	198.5	—	213.9	238.0	239.2
lower limbs NEC	170.7	198.5	—	213.7	238.0	239.2
upper limbs NEC	170.4	198.5	—	213.4	238.0	239.2
malar	170.0	198.5	—	213.0	238.0	239.2
mandible	170.1	198.5	—	213.1	238.0	239.2
marrow NEC	202.9 ☑	198.5	—	—	—	238.79 ▲
mastoid	170.0	198.5	—	213.0	238.0	239.2
maxilla, maxillary (superior)	170.0	198.5	—	213.0	238.0	239.2
inferior	170.1	198.5	—	213.1	238.0	239.2
metacarpus (any)	170.5	198.5	—	213.5	238.0	239.2
metatarsus (any)	170.8	198.5	—	213.8	238.0	239.2
navicular (ankle)	170.8	198.5	—	213.8	238.0	239.2
hand	170.5	198.5	—	213.5	238.0	239.2

Neoplasm, neoplastic —
continued

bone — *continued*

	Primary	Secondary	Ca in situ	Benign	Uncertain Behavior	Unspecified
nose, nasal	170.0	198.5	—	213.0	238.0	239.2
occipital	170.0	198.5	—	213.0	238.0	239.2
orbit	170.0	198.5	—	213.0	238.0	239.2
parietal	170.0	198.5	—	213.0	238.0	239.2
patella	170.8	198.5	—	213.8	238.0	239.2
pelvic	170.6	198.5	—	213.6	238.0	239.2
phalanges	170.9	198.5	—	213.9	238.0	239.2
foot	170.8	198.5	—	213.8	238.0	239.2
hand	170.5	198.5	—	213.5	238.0	239.2
pubic	170.6	198.5	—	213.6	238.0	239.2
radius (any part)	170.4	198.5	—	213.4	238.0	239.2
rib	170.3	198.5	—	213.3	238.0	239.2
sacral vertebra	170.6	198.5	—	213.6	238.0	239.2
sacrum	170.6	198.5	—	213.6	238.0	239.2
scaphoid (of hand)	170.5	198.5	—	213.5	238.0	239.2
of ankle	170.8	198.5	—	213.8	238.0	239.2
scapula (any part)	170.4	198.5	—	213.4	238.0	239.2
sella turcica	170.0	198.5	—	213.0	238.0	239.2
short	170.9	198.5	—	213.9	238.0	239.2
lower limb	170.8	198.5	—	213.8	238.0	239.2
upper limb	170.5	198.5	—	213.5	238.0	239.2
shoulder	170.4	198.5	—	213.4	238.0	239.2
skeleton, skeletal NEC	170.9	198.5	—	213.9	238.0	239.2
skull	170.0	198.5	—	213.0	238.0	239.2
sphenoid	170.0	198.5	—	213.0	238.0	239.2
spine, spinal (column)	170.2	198.5	—	213.2	238.0	239.2
coccyx	170.6	198.5	—	213.6	238.0	239.2
sacrum	170.6	198.5	—	213.6	238.0	239.2
sternum	170.3	198.5	—	213.3	238.0	239.2
tarsus (any)	170.8	198.5	—	213.8	238.0	239.2
temporal	170.0	198.5	—	213.0	238.0	239.2
thumb	170.5	198.5	—	213.5	238.0	239.2
tibia (any part)	170.7	198.5	—	213.7	238.0	239.2
toe (any)	170.8	198.5	—	213.8	238.0	239.2
trapezium	170.5	198.5	—	213.5	238.0	239.2
trapezoid	170.5	198.5	—	213.5	238.0	239.2
turbinate	170.0	198.5	—	213.0	238.0	239.2
ulna (any part)	170.4	198.5	—	213.4	238.0	239.2
unciform	170.5	198.5	—	213.5	238.0	239.2
vertebra (column)	170.2	198.5	—	213.2	238.0	239.2
coccyx	170.6	198.5	—	213.6	238.0	239.2
sacrum	170.6	198.5	—	213.6	238.0	239.2
vomer	170.0	198.5	—	213.0	238.0	239.2
wrist	170.5	198.5	—	213.5	238.0	239.2
xiphoid process	170.3	198.5	—	213.3	238.0	239.2
zygomatic	170.0	198.5	—	213.0	238.0	239.2
book-leaf (mouth)	145.8	198.89	230.0	210.4	235.1	239.0
bowel — *see* Neoplasm, intestine						
brachial plexus	171.2	198.89	—	215.2	238.1	239.2
brain NEC	191.9	198.3	—	225.0	237.5	239.6
basal ganglia	191.0	198.3	—	225.0	237.5	239.6
cerebellopontine angle	191.6	198.3	—	225.0	237.5	239.6
cerebellum NOS	191.6	198.3	—	225.0	237.5	239.6
cerebrum	191.0	198.3	—	225.0	237.5	239.6
choroid plexus	191.5	198.3	—	225.0	237.5	239.6
contiguous sites	191.8	—	—	—	—	—
corpus callosum	191.8	198.3	—	225.0	237.5	239.6
corpus striatum	191.0	198.3	—	225.0	237.5	239.6
cortex (cerebral)	191.0	198.3	—	225.0	237.5	239.6
frontal lobe	191.1	198.3	—	225.0	237.5	239.6
globus pallidus	191.0	198.3	—	225.0	237.5	239.6
hippocampus	191.2	198.3	—	225.0	237.5	239.6
hypothalamus	191.0	198.3	—	225.0	237.5	239.6
internal capsule	191.0	198.3	—	225.0	237.5	239.6
medulla oblongata	191.7	198.3	—	225.0	237.5	239.6
meninges	192.1	198.4	—	225.2	237.6	239.7
midbrain	191.7	198.3	—	225.0	237.5	239.6
occipital lobe	191.4	198.3	—	225.0	237.5	239.6
parietal lobe	191.3	198.3	—	225.0	237.5	239.6
peduncle	191.7	198.3	—	225.0	237.5	239.6
pons	191.7	198.3	—	225.0	237.5	239.6
stem	191.7	198.3	—	225.0	237.5	239.6

☑ Additional Digit Required — Refer to the Tabular List for Digit Selection
Ⓥ Subterms under main terms may continue to next column or page

198 — Volume 2 • October 2006   ▶◀ Revised Text   ● New Line   ▲ Revised Code   2007 ICD-9-CM

Neoplasm, neoplastic — continued	Malignant Primary	Malignant Secondary	Malignant Ca in situ	Benign	Uncertain Behavior	Unspecified
brain — continued						
tapetum	191.8	198.3	—	225.0	237.5	239.6
temporal lobe	191.2	198.3	—	225.0	237.5	239.6
thalamus	191.0	198.3	—	225.0	237.5	239.6
uncus	191.2	198.3	—	225.0	237.5	239.6
ventricle (floor)	191.5	198.3	—	225.0	237.5	239.6
branchial (cleft) (vestiges)	146.8	198.89	230.0	210.6	235.1	239.0
breast (connective tissue) (female) (glandular tissue) (soft parts)	174.9	198.81	233.0	217	238.3	239.3
areola	174.0	198.81	233.0	217	238.3	239.3
male	175.0	198.81	233.0	217	238.3	239.3
axillary tail	174.6	198.81	233.0	217	238.3	239.3
central portion	174.1	198.81	233.0	217	238.3	239.3
contiguous sites	174.8	—	—	—	—	—
ectopic sites	174.8	198.81	233.0	217	238.3	239.3
inner	174.8	198.81	233.0	217	238.3	239.3
lower	174.8	198.81	233.0	217	238.3	239.3
lower-inner quadrant	174.3	198.81	233.0	217	238.3	239.3
lower-outer quadrant	174.5	198.81	233.0	217	238.3	239.3
male	175.9	198.81	233.0	217	238.3	239.3
areola	175.0	198.81	233.0	217	238.3	239.3
ectopic tissue	175.9	198.81	233.0	217	238.3	239.3
nipple	175.0	198.81	233.0	217	238.3	239.3
mastectomy site (skin)	173.5	198.2	—	—	—	—
specified as breast tissue	174.8	198.81	—	—	—	—
midline	174.8	198.81	233.0	217	238.3	239.3
nipple	174.0	198.81	233.0	217	238.3	239.3
male	175.0	198.81	233.0	217	238.3	239.3
outer	174.8	198.81	233.0	217	238.3	239.3
skin	173.5	198.2	232.5	216.5	238.2	239.2
tail (axillary)	174.6	198.81	233.0	217	238.3	239.3
upper	174.8	198.81	233.0	217	238.3	239.3
upper-inner quadrant	174.2	198.81	233.0	217	238.3	239.3
upper-outer quadrant	174.4	198.81	233.0	217	238.3	239.3
broad ligament	183.3	198.82	233.3	221.0	236.3	239.5
bronchiogenic, bronchogenic (lung)	162.9	197.0	231.2	212.3	235.7	239.1
bronchiole	162.9	197.0	231.2	212.3	235.7	239.1
bronchus	162.9	197.0	231.2	212.3	235.7	239.1
carina	162.2	197.0	231.2	212.3	235.7	239.1
contiguous sites with lung or trachea	162.8	—	—	—	—	—
lower lobe of lung	162.5	197.0	231.2	212.3	235.7	239.1
main	162.2	197.0	231.2	212.3	235.7	239.1
middle lobe of lung	162.4	197.0	231.2	212.3	235.7	239.1
upper lobe of lung	162.3	197.0	231.2	212.3	235.7	239.1
brow	173.3	198.2	232.3	216.3	238.2	239.2
buccal (cavity)	145.9	198.89	230.0	210.4	235.1	239.0
commissure	145.0	198.89	230.0	210.4	235.1	239.0
groove (lower) (upper)	145.1	198.89	230.0	210.4	235.1	239.0
mucosa	145.0	198.89	230.0	210.4	235.1	239.0
sulcus (lower) (upper)	145.1	198.89	230.0	210.4	235.1	239.0
bulbourethral gland	189.3	198.1	233.9	223.81	236.99	239.5
bursa — see Neoplasm, connective tissue						
buttock NEC*	195.3	198.89	232.5	229.8	238.8	239.8
calf*	195.5	198.89	232.7	229.8	238.8	239.8
calvarium	170.0	198.5	—	213.0	238.0	239.2
calyx, renal	189.1	198.0	233.9	223.1	236.91	239.5
canal						
anal	154.2	197.5	230.5	211.4	235.5	239.0
auditory (external)	173.2	198.2	232.2	216.2	238.2	239.2
auricular (external)	173.2	198.2	232.2	216.2	238.2	239.2
canaliculi, biliary (biliferi) (intrahepatic)	155.1	197.8	230.8	211.5	235.3	239.0

Neoplasm, neoplastic — continued	Malignant Primary	Malignant Secondary	Malignant Ca in situ	Benign	Uncertain Behavior	Unspecified
canthus (eye) (inner) (outer)	173.1	198.2	232.1	216.1	238.2	239.2
capillary — see Neoplasm, connective tissue						
caput coli	153.4	197.5	230.3	211.3	235.2	239.0
cardia (gastric)	151.0	197.8	230.2	211.1	235.2	239.0
cardiac orifice (stomach)	151.0	197.8	230.2	211.1	235.2	239.0
cardio-esophageal junction	151.0	197.8	230.2	211.1	235.2	239.0
cardio-esophagus	151.0	197.8	230.2	211.1	235.2	239.0
carina (bronchus)	162.2	197.0	231.2	212.3	235.7	239.1
carotid (artery)	171.0	198.89	—	215.0	238.1	239.2
body	194.5	198.89	—	227.5	237.3	239.7
carpus (any bone)	170.5	198.5	—	213.5	238.0	239.2
cartilage (articular) (joint) NEC (see also Neoplasm, bone)	170.9	198.5	—	213.9	238.0	239.2
arytenoid	161.3	197.3	231.0	212.1	235.6	239.1
auricular	171.0	198.89	—	215.0	238.1	239.2
bronchi	162.2	197.3	—	212.3	235.7	239.1
connective tissue — see Neoplasm, connective tissue						
costal	170.3	198.5	—	213.3	238.0	239.2
cricoid	161.3	197.3	231.0	212.1	235.6	239.1
cuneiform	161.3	197.3	231.0	212.1	235.6	239.1
ear (external)	171.0	198.89	—	215.0	238.1	239.2
ensiform	170.3	198.5	—	213.3	238.0	239.2
epiglottis	161.1	197.3	231.0	212.1	235.6	239.1
anterior surface	146.4	198.89	230.0	210.6	235.1	239.0
eyelid	171.0	198.89	—	215.0	238.1	239.2
intervertebral	170.2	198.5	—	213.2	238.0	239.2
larynx, laryngeal	161.3	197.3	231.0	212.1	235.6	239.1
nose, nasal	160.0	197.3	231.8	212.0	235.9	239.1
pinna	171.0	198.89	—	215.0	238.1	239.2
rib	170.3	198.5	—	213.3	238.0	239.2
semilunar (knee)	170.7	198.5	—	213.7	238.0	239.2
thyroid	161.3	197.3	231.0	212.1	235.6	239.1
trachea	162.0	197.3	231.1	212.2	235.7	239.1
cauda equina	192.2	198.3	—	225.3	237.5	239.7
cavity						
buccal	145.9	198.89	230.0	210.4	235.1	239.0
nasal	160.0	197.3	231.8	212.0	235.9	239.1
oral	145.9	198.89	230.0	210.4	235.1	239.0
peritoneal	158.9	197.6	—	211.8	235.4	239.0
tympanic	160.1	197.3	231.8	212.0	235.9	239.1
cecum	153.4	197.5	230.3	211.3	235.2	239.0
central						
nervous system — see Neoplasm, nervous system						
white matter	191.0	198.3	—	225.0	237.5	239.6
cerebellopontine (angle)	191.6	198.3	—	225.0	237.5	239.6
cerebellum, cerebellar	191.6	198.3	—	225.0	237.5	239.6
cerebrum, cerebral (cortex) (hemisphere) (white matter)	191.0	198.3	—	225.0	237.5	239.6
meninges	192.1	198.4	—	225.2	237.6	239.7
peduncle	191.7	198.3	—	225.0	237.5	239.6
ventricle (any)	191.5	198.3	—	225.0	237.5	239.6
cervical region	195.0	198.89	234.8	229.8	238.8	239.8
cervix (cervical) (uteri) (uterus)	180.9	198.82	233.1	219.0	236.0	239.5
canal	180.0	198.82	233.1	219.0	236.0	239.5
contiguous sites	180.8	—	—	—	—	—
endocervix (canal) (gland)	180.0	198.82	233.1	219.0	236.0	239.5
exocervix	180.1	198.82	233.1	219.0	236.0	239.5
external os	180.1	198.82	233.1	219.0	236.0	239.5
internal os	180.0	198.82	233.1	219.0	236.0	239.5
nabothian gland	180.0	198.82	233.1	219.0	236.0	239.5
squamocolumnar junction	180.8	198.82	233.1	219.0	236.0	239.5
stump	180.8	198.82	233.1	219.0	236.0	239.5

☑ Additional Digit Required — Refer to the Tabular List for Digit Selection   ▽ Subterms under main terms may continue to next column or page

2007 ICD-9-CM   ▶◀ Revised Text   ● New Line   ▲ Revised Code   Volume 2 — 199

Neoplasm, neoplastic —	Primary	Secondary	Ca in situ	Benign	Uncertain Behavior	Unspecified
continued						
cheek	195.0	198.89	234.8	229.8	238.8	239.8
external	173.3	198.2	232.3	216.3	238.2	239.2
inner aspect	145.0	198.89	230.0	210.4	235.1	239.0
internal	145.0	198.89	230.0	210.4	235.1	239.0
mucosa	145.0	198.89	230.0	210.4	235.1	239.0
chest (wall) NEC	195.1	198.89	234.8	229.8	238.8	239.8
chiasma opticum	192.0	198.4	—	225.1	237.9	239.7
chin	173.3	198.2	232.3	216.3	238.2	239.2
choana	147.3	198.89	230.0	210.7	235.1	239.0
cholangiole	155.1	197.8	230.8	211.5	235.3	239.0
choledochal duct	156.1	197.8	230.8	211.5	235.3	239.0
choroid	190.6	198.4	234.0	224.6	238.8	239.8
plexus	191.5	198.3	—	225.0	237.5	239.6
ciliary body	190.0	198.4	234.0	224.0	238.8	239.8
clavicle	170.3	198.5	—	213.3	238.0	239.2
clitoris	184.3	198.82	233.3	221.2	236.3	239.5
clivus	170.0	198.5	—	213.0	238.0	239.2
cloacogenic zone	154.8	197.5	230.7	211.4	235.5	239.0
coccygeal						
body or glomus	194.6	198.89	—	227.6	237.3	239.7
vertebra	170.6	198.5	—	213.6	238.0	239.2
coccyx	170.6	198.5	—	213.6	238.0	239.2
colon (*see also* Neoplasm, intestine, large)						
and rectum	154.0	197.5	230.4	211.4	235.2	239.0
columnella	173.3	198.2	232.3	216.3	238.2	239.2
column, spinal — *see* Neoplasm, spine						
commissure						
labial, lip	140.6	198.89	230.0	210.4	235.1	239.0
laryngeal	161.0	197.3	231.0	212.1	235.6	239.1
common (bile) duct	156.1	197.8	230.8	211.5	235.3	239.0
concha	173.2	198.2	232.2	216.2	238.2	239.2
nose	160.0	197.3	231.8	212.0	235.9	239.1
conjunctiva	190.3	198.4	234.0	224.3	238.8	239.8
connective tissue						
NEC	171.9	198.89	—	215.9	238.1	239.2

Note — For neoplasms of connective tissue (blood vessel, bursa, fascia, ligament, muscle, peripheral nerves, sympathetic and parasympathetic nerves and ganglia, synovia, tendon, etc.) or of morphological types that indicate connective tissue, code according to the list under "Neoplasm, connective tissue"; for sites that do not appear in this list, code to neoplasm of that site; e.g.,

liposarcoma, shoulder 171.2

leiomyosarcoma, stomach 151.9

neurofibroma, chest wall 215.4

Morphological types that indicate connective tissue appear in the proper place in the alphabetic index with the instruction "see Neoplasm, connective tissue..."

	Primary	Secondary	Ca in situ	Benign	Uncertain Behavior	Unspecified
abdomen	171.5	198.89	—	215.5	238.1	239.2
abdominal wall	171.5	198.89	—	215.5	238.1	239.2
ankle	171.3	198.89	—	215.3	238.1	239.2
antecubital fossa or space	171.2	198.89	—	215.2	238.1	239.2
arm	171.2	198.89	—	215.2	238.1	239.2
auricle (ear)	171.0	198.89	—	215.0	238.1	239.2
axilla	171.4	198.89	—	215.4	238.1	239.2
back	171.7	198.89	—	215.7	238.1	239.2
breast (female) (*see also* Neoplasm, breast)	174.9	198.81	233.0	217	238.3	239.3
male	175.9	198.81	233.0	217	238.3	239.3
buttock	171.6	198.89	—	215.6	238.1	239.2
calf	171.3	198.89	—	215.3	238.1	239.2
cervical region	171.0	198.89	—	215.0	238.1	239.2
cheek	171.0	198.89	—	215.0	238.1	239.2
chest (wall)	171.4	198.89	—	215.4	238.1	239.2
chin	171.0	198.89	—	215.0	238.1	239.2
contiguous sites	171.8	—	—	—	—	—
diaphragm	171.4	198.89	—	215.4	238.1	239.2
ear (external)	171.0	198.89	—	215.0	238.1	239.2
elbow	171.2	198.89	—	215.2	238.1	239.2
extrarectal	171.6	198.89	—	215.6	238.1	239.2
extremity	171.8	198.89	—	215.8	238.1	239.2
lower	171.3	198.89	—	215.3	238.1	239.2
upper	171.2	198.89	—	215.2	238.1	239.2

Neoplasm, neoplastic —	Primary	Secondary	Ca in situ	Benign	Uncertain Behavior	Unspecified
continued						
connective tissue — *continued*						
eyelid	171.0	198.89	—	215.0	238.1	239.2
face	171.0	198.89	—	215.0	238.1	239.2
finger	171.2	198.89	—	215.2	238.1	239.2
flank	171.7	198.89	—	215.7	238.1	239.2
foot	171.3	198.89	—	215.3	238.1	239.2
forearm	171.2	198.89	—	215.2	238.1	239.2
forehead	171.0	198.89	—	215.0	238.1	239.2
gastric	171.5	198.89	—	215.5	238.1	—
gastrointestinal	171.5	198.89	—	215.5	238.1	—
gluteal region	171.6	198.89	—	215.6	238.1	239.2
great vessels NEC	171.4	198.89	—	215.4	238.1	239.2
groin	171.6	198.89	—	215.6	238.1	239.2
hand	171.2	198.89	—	215.2	238.1	239.2
head	171.0	198.89	—	215.0	238.1	239.2
heel	171.3	198.89	—	215.3	238.1	239.2
hip	171.3	198.89	—	215.3	238.1	239.2
hypochondrium	171.5	198.89	—	215.5	238.1	239.2
iliopsoas muscle	171.6	198.89	—	215.5	238.1	239.2
infraclavicular region	171.4	198.89	—	215.4	238.1	239.2
inguinal (canal) (region)	171.6	198.89	—	215.6	238.1	239.2
intestine	171.5	198.89	—	215.5	238.1	—
intrathoracic	171.4	198.89	—	215.4	238.1	239.2
ischorectal fossa	171.6	198.89	—	215.6	238.1	239.2
jaw	143.9	198.89	230.0	210.4	235.1	239.0
knee	171.3	198.89	—	215.3	238.1	239.2
leg	171.3	198.89	—	215.3	238.1	239.2
limb NEC	171.9	198.89	—	215.8	238.1	239.2
lower	171.3	198.89	—	215.3	238.1	239.2
upper	171.2	198.89	—	215.2	238.1	239.2
nates	171.6	198.89	—	215.6	238.1	239.2
neck	171.0	198.89	—	215.0	238.1	239.2
orbit	190.1	198.4	234.0	224.1	238.8	239.8
pararectal	171.6	198.89	—	215.6	238.1	239.2
para-urethral	171.6	198.89	—	215.6	238.1	239.2
paravaginal	171.6	198.89	—	215.6	238.1	239.2
pelvis (floor)	171.6	198.89	—	215.6	238.1	239.2
pelvo-abdominal	171.8	198.89	—	215.8	238.1	239.2
perineum	171.6	198.89	—	215.6	238.1	239.2
perirectal (tissue)	171.6	198.89	—	215.6	238.1	239.2
periurethral (tissue)	171.6	198.89	—	215.6	238.1	239.2
popliteal fossa or space	171.3	198.89	—	215.3	238.1	239.2
presacral	171.6	198.89	—	215.6	238.1	239.2
psoas muscle	171.5	198.89	—	215.5	238.1	239.2
pterygoid fossa	171.0	198.89	—	215.0	238.1	239.2
rectovaginal septum or wall	171.6	198.89	—	215.6	238.1	239.2
rectovesical	171.6	198.89	—	215.6	238.1	239.2
retroperitoneum	158.0	197.6	—	211.8	235.4	239.0
sacrococcygeal region	171.6	198.89	—	215.6	238.1	239.2
scalp	171.0	198.89	—	215.0	238.1	239.2
scapular region	171.4	198.89	—	215.4	238.1	239.2
shoulder	171.2	198.89	—	215.2	238.1	239.2
skin (dermis) NEC	173.9	198.2	232.9	216.9	238.2	239.2
stomach	171.5	198.89	—	215.5	238.1	—
submental	171.0	198.89	—	215.0	238.1	239.2
supraclavicular region	171.0	198.89	—	215.0	238.1	239.2
temple	171.0	198.89	—	215.0	238.1	239.2
temporal region	171.0	198.89	—	215.0	238.1	239.2
thigh	171.3	198.89	—	215.3	238.1	239.2
thoracic (duct) (wall)	171.4	198.89	—	215.4	238.1	239.2
thorax	171.4	198.89	—	215.4	238.1	239.2
thumb	171.2	198.89	—	215.2	238.1	239.2
toe	171.3	198.89	—	215.3	238.1	239.2
trunk	171.7	198.89	—	215.7	238.1	239.2
umbilicus	171.5	198.89	—	215.5	238.1	239.2
vesicorectal	171.6	198.89	—	215.6	238.1	239.2
wrist	171.2	198.89	—	215.2	238.1	239.2
conus medullaris	192.2	198.3	—	225.3	237.5	239.7
cord (true) (vocal)	161.0	197.3	231.0	212.1	235.6	239.1

	Malignant					
	Primary	Secondary	Ca in situ	Benign	Uncertain Behavior	Unspecified
Neoplasm, neoplastic —						
continued						
cord — *continued*						
false	161.1	197.3	231.0	212.1	235.6	239.1
spermatic	187.6	198.82	233.6	222.8	236.6	239.5
spinal (cervical) (lumbar)						
(thoracic)	192.2	198.3	—	225.3	237.5	239.7
cornea (limbus)	190.4	198.4	234.0	224.4	238.8	239.8
corpus						
albicans	183.0	198.6	233.3	220	236.2	239.5
callosum, brain	191.8	198.3	—	225.0	237.5	239.6
cavernosum	187.3	198.82	233.5	222.1	236.6	239.5
gastric	151.4	197.8	230.2	211.1	235.2	239.0
penis	187.3	198.82	233.5	222.1	236.6	239.5
striatum, cerebrum	191.0	198.3	—	225.0	237.5	239.6
uteri	182.0	198.82	233.2	219.1	236.0	239.5
isthmus	182.1	198.82	233.2	219.1	236.0	239.5
cortex						
adrenal	194.0	198.7	234.8	227.0	237.2	239.7
cerebral	191.0	198.3	—	225.0	237.5	239.6
costal cartilage	170.3	198.5	—	213.3	238.0	239.2
costovertebral joint	170.3	198.5	—	213.3	238.0	239.2
Cowper's gland	189.3	198.1	233.9	223.81	236.99	239.5
cranial (fossa, any)	191.9	198.3	—	225.0	237.5	239.6
meninges	192.1	198.4	—	225.2	237.6	239.7
nerve (any)	192.0	198.4	—	225.1	237.9	239.7
craniobuccal pouch	194.3	198.89	234.8	227.3	237.0	239.7
craniopharyngeal (duct)						
(pouch)	194.3	198.89	234.8	227.3	237.0	239.7
cricoid	148.0	198.89	230.0	210.8	235.1	239.0
cartilage	161.3	197.3	231.0	212.1	235.6	239.1
cricopharynx	148.0	198.89	230.0	210.8	235.1	239.0
crypt of Morgagni	154.8	197.5	230.7	211.4	235.2	239.0
crystalline lens	190.0	198.4	234.0	224.0	238.8	239.8
cul-de-sac (Douglas')	158.8	197.6	—	211.8	235.4	239.0
cuneiform cartilage	161.3	197.3	231.0	212.1	235.6	239.1
cutaneous — *see*						
Neoplasm, skin						
cutis — *see* Neoplasm,						
skin						
cystic (bile) duct						
(common)	156.1	197.8	230.8	211.5	235.3	239.0
dermis — *see* Neoplasm,						
skin						
diaphragm	171.4	198.89	—	215.4	238.1	239.2
digestive organs, system,						
tube, or tract						
NEC	159.9	197.8	230.9	211.9	235.5	239.0
contiguous sites with						
peritoneum	159.8	—	—	—	—	—
disc, intervertebral	170.2	198.5	—	213.2	238.0	239.2
disease, generalized	199.0	199.0	234.9	229.9	238.9	199.0
disseminated	199.0	199.0	234.9	229.9	238.9	199.0
Douglas' cul-de-sac or						
pouch	158.8	197.6	—	211.8	235.4	239.0
duodenojejunal						
junction	152.8	197.4	230.7	211.2	235.2	239.0
duodenum	152.0	197.4	230.7	211.2	235.2	239.0
dura (cranial) (mater)	192.1	198.4	—	225.2	237.6	239.7
cerebral	192.1	198.4	—	225.2	237.6	239.7
spinal	192.3	198.4	—	225.4	237.6	239.7
ear (external)	173.2	198.2	232.2	216.2	238.2	239.2
auricle or auris	173.2	198.2	232.2	216.2	238.2	239.2
canal, external	173.2	198.2	232.2	216.2	238.2	239.2
cartilage	171.0	198.89	—	215.0	238.1	239.2
external meatus	173.2	198.2	232.2	216.2	238.2	239.2
inner	160.1	197.3	231.8	212.0	235.9	239.8
lobule	173.2	198.2	232.2	216.2	238.2	239.2
middle	160.1	197.3	231.8	212.0	235.9	239.8
contiguous sites with						
accessory sinuses						
or nasal						
cavities	160.8	—	—	—	—	—
skin	173.2	198.2	232.2	216.2	238.2	239.2
earlobe	173.2	198.2	232.2	216.2	238.2	239.2
ejaculatory duct	187.8	198.82	233.6	222.8	236.6	239.5
elbow NEC*	195.4	198.89	232.6	229.8	238.8	239.8
endocardium	164.1	198.89	—	212.7	238.8	239.8

	Malignant					
	Primary	Secondary	Ca in situ	Benign	Uncertain Behavior	Unspecified
Neoplasm, neoplastic —						
continued						
endocervix (canal)						
(gland)	180.0	198.82	233.1	219.0	236.0	239.5
endocrine gland NEC	194.9	198.89	—	227.9	237.4	239.7
pluriglandular NEC	194.8	198.89	234.8	227.8	237.4	239.7
endometrium (gland)						
(stroma)	182.0	198.82	233.2	219.1	236.0	239.5
ensiform cartilage	170.3	198.5	—	213.3	238.0	239.2
enteric — *see* Neoplasm,						
intestine						
ependyma (brain)	191.5	198.3	—	225.0	237.5	239.6
epicardium	164.1	198.89	—	212.7	238.8	239.8
epididymis	187.5	198.82	233.6	222.3	236.6	239.5
epidural	192.9	198.4	—	225.9	237.9	239.7
epiglottis	161.1	197.3	231.0	212.1	235.6	239.1
anterior aspect or						
surface	146.4	198.89	230.0	210.6	235.1	239.0
cartilage	161.3	197.3	231.0	212.1	235.6	239.1
free border (margin)	146.4	198.89	230.0	210.6	235.1	239.0
junctional region	146.5	198.89	230.0	210.6	235.1	239.0
posterior (laryngeal)						
surface	161.1	197.3	231.0	212.1	235.6	239.1
suprahyoid portion	161.1	197.3	231.0	212.1	235.6	239.1
esophagogastric						
junction	151.0	197.8	230.2	211.1	235.2	239.0
esophagus	150.9	197.8	230.1	211.0	235.5	239.0
abdominal	150.2	197.8	230.1	211.0	235.5	239.0
cervical	150.0	197.8	230.1	211.0	235.5	239.0
contiguous sites	150.8	—	—	—	—	—
distal (third)	150.5	197.8	230.1	211.0	235.5	239.0
lower (third)	150.5	197.8	230.1	211.0	235.5	239.0
middle (third)	150.4	197.8	230.1	211.0	235.5	239.0
proximal (third)	150.3	197.8	230.1	211.0	235.5	239.0
specified part NEC	150.8	197.8	230.1	211.0	235.5	239.0
thoracic	150.1	197.8	230.1	211.0	235.5	239.0
upper (third)	150.3	197.8	230.1	211.0	235.5	239.0
ethmoid (sinus)	160.3	197.3	231.8	212.0	235.9	239.1
bone or labyrinth	170.0	198.5	—	213.0	238.0	239.2
Eustachian tube	160.1	197.3	231.8	212.0	235.9	239.1
exocervix	180.1	198.82	233.1	219.0	236.0	239.5
external						
meatus (ear)	173.2	198.2	232.2	216.2	238.2	239.2
os, cervix uteri	180.1	198.82	233.1	219.0	236.0	239.5
extradural	192.9	198.4	—	225.9	237.9	239.7
extrahepatic (bile)						
duct	156.1	197.8	230.8	211.5	235.3	239.0
contiguous sites with						
gallbladder	156.8	—	—	—	—	—
extraocular muscle	190.1	198.4	234.0	224.1	238.8	239.8
extrarectal	195.3	198.89	234.8	229.8	238.8	239.8
extremity*	195.8	198.89	232.8	229.8	238.8	239.8
lower*	195.5	198.89	232.7	229.8	238.8	239.8
upper*	195.4	198.89	232.6	229.8	238.8	239.8
eye NEC	190.9	198.4	234.0	224.9	238.8	239.8
contiguous sites	190.8	—	—	—	—	—
specified sites NEC	190.8	198.4	234.0	224.8	238.8	239.8
eyeball	190.0	198.4	234.0	224.0	238.8	239.8
eyebrow	173.3	198.2	232.3	216.3	238.2	239.2
eyelid (lower) (skin)						
(upper)	173.1	198.2	232.1	216.1	238.2	239.2
cartilage	171.0	198.89	—	215.0	238.1	239.2
face NEC*	195.0	198.89	232.3	229.8	238.8	239.8
fallopian tube						
(accessory)	183.2	198.82	233.3	221.0	236.3	239.5
falx (cerebelli)						
(cerebri)	192.1	198.4	—	225.2	237.6	239.7
fascia (*see also* Neoplasm,						
connective tissue)						
palmar	171.2	198.89	—	215.2	238.1	239.2
plantar	171.3	198.89	—	215.3	238.1	239.2
fatty tissue — *see*						
Neoplasm, connective						
tissue						
fauces, faucial NEC	146.9	198.89	230.0	210.6	235.1	239.0
pillars	146.2	198.89	230.0	210.6	235.1	239.0
tonsil	146.0	198.89	230.0	210.5	235.1	239.0
femur (any part)	170.7	198.5	—	213.7	238.0	239.2
fetal membrane	181	198.82	233.2	219.8	236.1	239.5

☑ Additional Digit Required — Refer to the Tabular List for Digit Selection ▽ Subterms under main terms may continue to next column or page

Neoplasm, neoplastic — *continued*

	Malignant					
	Primary	Secondary	Ca in situ	Benign	Uncertain Behavior	Unspecified
fibrous tissue — *see* Neoplasm, connective tissue						
fibula (any part)	170.7	198.5	—	213.7	238.0	239.2
filum terminale	192.2	198.3	—	225.3	237.5	239.7
finger NEC*	195.4	198.89	232.6	229.8	238.8	239.8
flank NEC*	195.8	198.89	232.5	229.8	238.8	239.8
follicle, nabothian	180.0	198.82	233.1	219.0	236.0	239.5
foot NEC*	195.5	198.89	232.7	229.8	238.8	239.8
forearm NEC*	195.4	198.89	232.6	229.8	238.8	239.8
forehead (skin)	173.3	198.2	232.3	216.3	238.2	239.2
foreskin	187.1	198.82	233.5	222.1	236.6	239.5
fornix						
pharyngeal	147.3	198.89	230.0	210.7	235.1	239.0
vagina	184.0	198.82	233.3	221.1	236.3	239.5
fossa (of)						
anterior (cranial)	191.9	198.3	—	225.0	237.5	239.6
cranial	191.9	198.3	—	225.0	237.5	239.6
ischiorectal	195.3	198.89	234.8	229.8	238.8	239.8
middle (cranial)	191.9	198.3	—	225.0	237.5	239.6
pituitary	194.3	198.89	234.8	227.3	237.0	239.7
posterior (cranial)	191.9	198.3	—	225.0	237.5	239.6
pterygoid	171.0	198.89	—	215.0	238.1	239.2
pyriform	148.1	198.89	230.0	210.8	235.1	239.0
Rosenmüller	147.2	198.89	230.0	210.7	235.1	239.0
tonsillar	146.1	198.89	230.0	210.6	235.1	239.0
fourchette	184.4	198.82	233.3	221.2	236.3	239.5
frenulum						
labii — *see* Neoplasm, lip, internal						
linguae	141.3	198.89	230.0	210.1	235.1	239.0
frontal						
bone	170.0	198.5	—	213.0	238.0	239.2
lobe, brain	191.1	198.3	—	225.0	237.5	239.6
meninges	192.1	198.4	—	225.2	237.6	239.7
pole	191.1	198.3	—	225.0	237.5	239.6
sinus	160.4	197.3	231.8	212.0	235.9	239.1
fundus						
stomach	151.3	197.8	230.2	211.1	235.2	239.0
uterus	182.0	198.82	233.2	219.1	236.0	239.5
gallbladder	156.0	197.8	230.8	211.5	235.3	239.0
contiguous sites with extrahepatic bile ducts	156.8	—	—	—	—	—
gall duct						
(extrahepatic)	156.1	197.8	230.8	211.5	235.3	239.0
intrahepatic	155.1	197.8	230.8	211.5	235.3	239.0
ganglia (*see also* Neoplasm, connective tissue)	171.9	198.89	—	215.9	238.1	239.2
basal	191.0	198.3	—	225.0	237.5	239.6
ganglion (*see also* Neoplasm, connective tissue)	171.9	198.89	—	215.9	238.1	239.2
cranial nerve	192.0	198.4	—	225.1	237.9	239.7
Gartner's duct	184.0	198.82	233.3	221.1	236.3	239.5
gastric — *see* Neoplasm, stomach						
gastrocolic	159.8	197.8	230.9	211.9	235.5	239.0
gastroesophageal junction	151.0	197.8	230.2	211.1	235.2	239.0
gastrointestinal (tract) NEC	159.9	197.8	230.9	211.9	235.5	239.0
generalized	199.0	199.0	234.9	229.9	238.9	199.0
genital organ or tract						
female NEC	184.9	198.82	233.3	221.9	236.3	239.5
contiguous sites	184.8	—	—	—	—	—
specified site NEC	184.8	198.82	233.3	221.8	236.3	239.5
male NEC	187.9	198.82	233.6	222.9	236.6	239.5
contiguous sites	187.8	—	—	—	—	—
specified site NEC	187.8	198.82	233.6	222.8	236.6	239.5
genitourinary tract						
female	184.9	198.82	233.3	221.9	236.3	239.5
male	187.9	198.82	233.6	222.9	236.6	239.5

Neoplasm, neoplastic — *continued*

	Malignant					
	Primary	Secondary	Ca in situ	Benign	Uncertain Behavior	Unspecified
gingiva (alveolar) (marginal)	143.9	198.89	230.0	210.4	235.1	239.0
lower	143.1	198.89	230.0	210.4	235.1	239.0
mandibular	143.1	198.89	230.0	210.4	235.1	239.0
maxillary	143.0	198.89	230.0	210.4	235.1	239.0
upper	143.0	198.89	230.0	210.4	235.1	239.0
gland, glandular (lymphatic) (system) (*see also* Neoplasm, lymph gland)						
endocrine NEC	194.9	198.89	—	227.9	237.4	239.7
salivary — *see* Neoplasm, salivary, gland						
glans penis	187.2	198.82	233.5	222.1	236.6	239.5
globus pallidus	191.0	198.3	—	225.0	237.5	239.6
glomus						
coccygeal	194.6	198.89	—	227.6	237.3	239.7
jugularis	194.6	198.89	—	227.6	237.3	239.7
glosso-epiglottic fold(s)	146.4	198.89	230.0	210.6	235.1	239.0
glossopalatine fold	146.2	198.89	230.0	210.6	235.1	239.0
glossopharyngeal sulcus	146.1	198.89	230.0	210.6	235.1	239.0
glottis	161.0	197.3	231.0	212.1	235.6	239.1
gluteal region*	195.3	198.89	232.5	229.8	238.8	239.8
great vessels NEC	171.4	198.89	—	215.4	238.1	239.2
groin NEC	195.3	198.89	232.5	229.8	238.8	239.8
gum	143.9	198.89	230.0	210.4	235.1	239.0
contiguous sites	143.8	—	—	—	—	—
lower	143.1	198.89	230.0	210.4	235.1	239.0
upper	143.0	198.89	230.0	210.4	235.1	239.0
hand NEC*	195.4	198.89	232.6	229.8	238.8	239.8
head NEC*	195.0	198.89	232.4	229.8	238.8	239.8
heart	164.1	198.89	—	212.7	238.8	239.8
contiguous sites with mediastinum or thymus	164.8	—	—	—	—	—
heel NEC*	195.5	198.89	232.7	229.8	238.8	239.8
helix	173.2	198.2	232.2	216.2	238.2	239.2
hematopoietic, hemopoietic tissue NEC	202.8 ☑	198.89	—	—	—	238.79 ▲
hemisphere, cerebral	191.0	198.3	—	225.0	237.5	239.6
hemorrhoidal zone	154.2	197.5	230.5	211.4	235.5	239.0
hepatic	155.2	197.7	230.8	211.5	235.3	239.0
duct (bile)	156.1	197.8	230.8	211.5	235.3	239.0
flexure (colon)	153.0	197.5	230.3	211.3	235.2	239.0
primary	155.0	—	—	—	—	—
hilus of lung	162.2	197.0	231.2	212.3	235.7	239.1
hip NEC*	195.5	198.89	232.7	229.8	238.8	239.8
hippocampus, brain	191.2	198.3	—	225.0	237.5	239.6
humerus (any part)	170.4	198.5	—	213.4	238.0	239.2
hymen	184.0	198.82	233.3	221.1	236.3	239.5
hypopharynx, hypopharyngeal NEC	148.9	198.89	230.0	210.8	235.1	239.0
contiguous sites	148.8	—	—	—	—	—
postcricoid region	148.0	198.89	230.0	210.8	235.1	239.0
posterior wall	148.3	198.89	230.0	210.8	235.1	239.0
pyriform fossa (sinus)	148.1	198.89	230.0	210.8	235.1	239.0
specified site NEC	148.8	198.89	230.0	210.8	235.1	239.0
wall	148.9	198.89	230.0	210.8	235.1	239.0
posterior	148.3	198.89	230.0	210.8	235.1	239.0
hypophysis	194.3	198.89	234.8	227.3	237.0	239.7
hypothalamus	191.0	198.3	—	225.0	237.5	239.6
ileocecum, ileocecal (coil) (junction) (valve)	153.4	197.5	230.3	211.3	235.2	239.0
ileum	152.2	197.4	230.7	211.2	235.2	239.0
ilium	170.6	198.5	—	213.6	238.0	239.2
immunoproliferative NEC	203.8 ☑	—	—	—	—	—
infraclavicular (region)*	195.1	198.89	232.5	229.8	238.8	239.8
inguinal (region)*	195.3	198.89	232.5	229.8	238.8	239.8
insula	191.0	198.3	—	225.0	237.5	239.6

☑ Additional Digit Required — Refer to the Tabular List for Digit Selection

▽ Subterms under main terms may continue to next column or page

▶◀ Revised Text   ● New Line   ▲ Revised Code

Neoplasm, neoplastic — continued	Primary	Secondary	Ca in situ	Benign	Uncertain Behavior	Unspecified
insular tissue						
(pancreas)	157.4	197.8	230.9	211.7	235.5	239.0
brain	191.0	198.3	—	225.0	237.5	239.6
interarytenoid fold	148.2	198.89	230.0	210.8	235.1	239.0
hypopharyngeal aspect	148.2	198.89	230.0	210.8	235.1	239.0
laryngeal aspect	161.1	197.3	231.0	212.1	235.6	239.1
marginal zone	148.2	198.89	230.0	210.8	235.1	239.0
interdental papillae	143.9	198.89	230.0	210.4	235.1	239.0
lower	143.1	198.89	230.0	210.4	235.1	239.0
upper	143.0	198.89	230.0	210.4	235.1	239.0
internal						
capsule	191.0	198.3	—	225.0	237.5	239.6
os (cervix)	180.0	198.82	233.1	219.0	236.0	239.5
intervertebral cartilage or disc	170.2	198.5	—	213.2	238.0	239.2
intestine, intestinal	159.0	197.8	230.7	211.9	235.2	239.0
large	153.9	197.5	230.3	211.3	235.2	239.0
appendix	153.5	197.5	230.3	211.3	235.2	239.0
caput coli	153.4	197.5	230.3	211.3	235.2	239.0
cecum	153.4	197.5	230.3	211.3	235.2	239.0
colon	153.9	197.5	230.3	211.3	235.2	239.0
and rectum	154.0	197.5	230.4	211.4	235.2	239.0
ascending	153.6	197.5	230.3	211.3	235.2	239.0
caput	153.4	197.5	230.3	211.3	235.2	239.0
contiguous sites	153.8	—	—	—	—	—
descending	153.2	197.5	230.3	211.3	235.2	239.0
distal	153.2	197.5	230.3	211.3	235.2	239.0
left	153.2	197.5	230.3	211.3	235.2	239.0
pelvic	153.3	197.5	230.3	211.3	235.2	239.0
right	153.6	197.5	230.3	211.3	235.2	239.0
sigmoid (flexure)	153.3	197.5	230.3	211.3	235.2	239.0
transverse	153.1	197.5	230.3	211.3	235.2	239.0
contiguous sites	153.8	—	—	—	—	—
hepatic flexure	153.0	197.5	230.3	211.3	235.2	239.0
ileocecum, ileocecal (coil) (valve)	153.4	197.5	230.3	211.3	235.2	239.0
sigmoid flexure (lower) (upper)	153.3	197.5	230.3	211.3	235.2	239.0
splenic flexure	153.7	197.5	230.3	211.3	235.2	239.0
small	152.9	197.4	230.7	211.2	235.2	239.0
contiguous sites	152.8	—	—	—	—	—
duodenum	152.0	197.4	230.7	211.2	235.2	239.0
ileum	152.2	197.4	230.7	211.2	235.2	239.0
jejunum	152.1	197.4	230.7	211.2	235.2	239.0
tract NEC	159.0	197.8	230.7	211.9	235.2	239.0
intra-abdominal	195.2	198.89	234.8	229.8	238.8	239.8
intracranial NEC	191.9	198.3	—	225.0	237.5	239.6
intrahepatic (bile)						
duct	155.1	197.8	230.8	211.5	235.3	239.0
intraocular	190.0	198.4	234.0	224.0	238.8	239.8
intraorbital	190.1	198.4	234.0	224.1	238.8	239.8
intrasellar	194.3	198.89	234.8	227.3	237.0	239.7
intrathoracic (cavity) (organs NEC)	195.1	198.89	234.8	229.8	238.8	239.8
contiguous sites with respiratory organs	165.8	—	—	—	—	—
iris	190.0	198.4	234.0	224.0	238.8	239.8
ischiorectal (fossa)	195.3	198.89	234.8	229.8	238.8	239.8
ischium	170.6	198.5	—	213.6	238.0	239.2
island of Reil	191.0	198.3	—	225.0	237.5	239.6
islands or islets of Langerhans	157.4	197.8	230.9	211.7	235.5	239.0
isthmus uteri	182.1	198.82	233.2	219.1	236.0	239.5
jaw	195.0	198.89	234.8	229.8	238.8	239.8
bone	170.1	198.5	—	213.1	238.0	239.2
carcinoma	143.9	—	—	—	—	—
lower	143.1	—	—	—	—	—
upper	143.0	—	—	—	—	—
lower	170.1	198.5	—	213.1	238.0	239.2
upper	170.0	198.5	—	213.0	238.0	239.2
carcinoma (any type) (lower)(upper)	195.0	—	—	—	—	—
skin	173.3	198.2	232.3	216.3	238.2	239.2

Neoplasm, neoplastic — continued	Primary	Secondary	Ca in situ	Benign	Uncertain Behavior	Unspecified
jaw — continued						
soft tissues	143.9	198.89	230.0	210.4	235.1	239.0
lower	143.1	198.89	230.0	210.4	235.1	239.0
upper	143.0	198.89	230.0	210.4	235.1	239.0
jejunum	152.1	197.4	230.7	211.2	235.2	239.0
joint NEC (see also Neoplasm, bone)	170.9	198.5	—	213.9	238.0	239.2
acromioclavicular	170.4	198.5	—	213.4	238.0	239.2
bursa or synovial membrane — see Neoplasm, connective tissue						
costovertebral	170.3	198.5	—	213.3	238.0	239.2
sternocostal	170.3	198.5	—	213.3	238.0	239.2
temporomandibular	170.1	198.5	—	213.1	238.0	239.2
junction						
anorectal	154.8	197.5	230.7	211.4	235.5	239.0
cardioesophageal	151.0	197.8	230.2	211.1	235.2	239.0
esophagogastric	151.0	197.8	230.2	211.1	235.2	239.0
gastroesophageal	151.0	197.8	230.2	211.1	235.2	239.0
hard and soft palate	145.5	198.89	230.0	210.4	235.1	239.0
ileocecal	153.4	197.5	230.3	211.3	235.2	239.0
pelvirectal	154.0	197.5	230.4	211.4	235.2	239.0
pelviureteric	189.1	198.0	233.9	223.1	236.91	239.5
rectosigmoid	154.0	197.5	230.4	211.4	235.2	239.0
squamocolumnar, of cervix	180.8	198.82	233.1	219.0	236.0	239.5
kidney (parenchyma)	189.0	198.0	233.9	223.0	236.91	239.5
calyx	189.1	198.0	233.9	223.1	236.91	239.5
hilus	189.1	198.0	233.9	223.1	236.91	239.5
pelvis	189.1	198.0	233.9	223.1	236.91	239.5
knee NEC*	195.5	198.89	232.7	229.8	238.8	239.8
labia (skin)	184.4	198.82	233.3	221.2	236.3	239.5
majora	184.1	198.82	233.3	221.2	236.3	239.5
minora	184.2	198.82	233.3	221.2	236.3	239.5
labial (see also Neoplasm, lip)						
sulcus (lower) (upper)	145.1	198.89	230.0	210.4	235.1	239.0
labium (skin)	184.4	198.82	233.3	221.2	236.3	239.5
majus	184.1	198.82	233.3	221.2	236.3	239.5
minus	184.2	198.82	233.3	221.2	236.3	239.5
lacrimal						
canaliculi	190.7	198.4	234.0	224.7	238.8	239.8
duct (nasal)	190.7	198.4	234.0	224.7	238.8	239.8
gland	190.2	198.4	234.0	224.2	238.8	239.8
punctum	190.7	198.4	234.0	224.7	238.8	239.8
sac	190.7	198.4	234.0	224.7	238.8	239.8
Langerhans, islands or islets	157.4	197.8	230.9	211.7	235.5	239.0
laryngopharynx	148.9	198.89	230.0	210.8	235.1	239.0
larynx, laryngeal NEC	161.9	197.3	231.0	212.1	235.6	239.1
aryepiglottic fold	161.1	197.3	231.0	212.1	235.6	239.1
cartilage (arytenoid) (cricoid) (cuneiform) (thyroid)	161.3	197.3	231.0	212.1	235.6	239.1
commissure (anterior) (posterior)	161.0	197.3	231.0	212.1	235.6	239.1
contiguous sites	161.8	—	—	—	—	—
extrinsic NEC	161.1	197.3	231.0	212.1	235.6	239.1
meaning hypopharynx	148.9	198.89	230.0	210.8	235.1	239.0
interarytenoid fold	161.1	197.3	231.0	212.1	235.6	239.1
intrinsic	161.0	197.3	231.0	212.1	235.6	239.1
ventricular band	161.1	197.3	231.0	212.1	235.6	239.1
leg NEC*	195.5	198.89	232.7	229.8	238.8	239.8
lens, crystalline	190.0	198.4	234.0	224.0	238.8	239.8
lid (lower) (upper)	173.1	198.2	232.1	216.1	238.2	239.2
ligament (see also Neoplasm, connective tissue)						
broad	183.3	198.82	233.3	221.0	236.3	239.5
Mackenrodt's	183.8	198.82	233.3	221.8	236.3	239.5
non-uterine — see Neoplasm, connective tissue						

Neoplasm, neoplastic — *continued*

	Malignant					
	Primary	Secondary	Ca in situ	Benign	Uncertain Behavior	Unspecified
ligament (*see also* Neoplasm, connective tissue) — *continued*						
round	183.5	198.82	—	221.0	236.3	239.5
sacro-uterine	183.4	198.82	—	221.0	236.3	239.5
uterine	183.4	198.82	—	221.0	236.3	239.5
utero-ovarian	183.8	198.82	233.3	221.8	236.3	239.5
uterosacral	183.4	198.82	—	221.0	236.3	239.5
limb*	195.8	198.89	232.8	229.8	238.8	239.8
lower*	195.5	198.89	232.7	229.8	238.8	239.8
upper*	195.4	198.89	232.6	229.8	238.8	239.8
limbus of cornea	190.4	198.4	234.0	224.4	238.8	239.8
lingual NEC (*see also* Neoplasm, tongue)	141.9	198.89	230.0	210.1	235.1	239.0
lingula, lung	162.3	197.0	231.2	212.3	235.7	239.1
lip (external) (lipstick area) (vermillion border)	140.9	198.89	230.0	210.0	235.1	239.0
buccal aspect — *see* Neoplasm, lip, internal						
commissure	140.6	198.89	230.0	210.4	235.1	239.0
contiguous sites	140.8	—	—	—	—	—
with oral cavity or pharynx	149.8	—	—	—	—	—
frenulum — *see* Neoplasm, lip, internal						
inner aspect — *see* Neoplasm, lip, internal						
internal (buccal) (frenulum) (mucosa) (oral)	140.5	198.89	230.0	210.0	235.1	239.0
lower	140.4	198.89	230.0	210.0	235.1	239.0
upper	140.3	198.89	230.0	210.0	235.1	239.0
lower	140.1	198.89	230.0	210.0	235.1	239.0
internal (buccal) (frenulum) (mucosa) (oral)	140.4	198.89	230.0	210.0	235.1	239.0
mucosa — *see* Neoplasm, lip, internal						
oral aspect — *see* Neoplasm, lip, internal						
skin (commissure) (lower) (upper)	173.0	198.2	232.0	216.0	238.2	239.2
upper	140.0	198.89	230.0	210.0	235.1	239.0
internal (buccal) (frenulum) (mucosa) (oral)	140.3	198.89	230.0	210.0	235.1	239.0
liver	155.2	197.7	230.8	211.5	235.3	239.0
primary	155.0	—	—	—	—	—
lobe						
azygos	162.3	197.0	231.2	212.3	235.7	239.1
frontal	191.1	198.3	—	225.0	237.5	239.6
lower	162.5	197.0	231.2	212.3	235.7	239.1
middle	162.4	197.0	231.2	212.3	235.7	239.1
occipital	191.4	198.3	—	225.0	237.5	239.6
parietal	191.3	198.3	—	225.0	237.5	239.6
temporal	191.2	198.3	—	225.0	237.5	239.6
upper	162.3	197.0	231.2	212.3	235.7	239.1
lumbosacral plexus	171.6	198.4	—	215.6	238.1	239.2
lung	162.9	197.0	231.2	212.3	235.7	239.1
azygos lobe	162.3	197.0	231.2	212.3	235.7	239.1
carina	162.2	197.0	231.2	212.3	235.7	239.1
contiguous sites with bronchus or trachea	162.8	—	—	—	—	—
hilus	162.2	197.0	231.2	212.3	235.7	239.1
lingula	162.3	197.0	231.2	212.3	235.7	239.1
lobe NEC	162.9	197.0	231.2	212.3	235.7	239.1
lower lobe	162.5	197.0	231.2	212.3	235.7	239.1

Neoplasm, neoplastic — *continued*

	Malignant					
	Primary	Secondary	Ca in situ	Benign	Uncertain Behavior	Unspecified
lung — *continued*						
main bronchus	162.2	197.0	231.2	212.3	235.7	239.1
middle lobe	162.4	197.0	231.2	212.3	235.7	239.1
upper lobe	162.3	197.0	231.2	212.3	235.7	239.1
lymph, lymphatic						
channel NEC (*see also* Neoplasm, connective tissue)	171.9	198.89	—	215.9	238.1	239.2
gland (secondary)	—	196.9	—	229.0	238.8	239.8
abdominal	—	196.2	—	229.0	238.8	239.8
aortic	—	196.2	—	229.0	238.8	239.8
arm	—	196.3	—	229.0	238.8	239.8
auricular (anterior) (posterior)	—	196.0	—	229.0	238.8	239.8
axilla, axillary	—	196.3	—	229.0	238.8	239.8
brachial	—	196.3	—	229.0	238.8	239.8
bronchial	—	196.1	—	229.0	238.8	239.8
bronchopulmonary	—	196.1	—	229.0	238.8	239.8
celiac	—	196.2	—	229.0	238.8	239.8
cervical	—	196.0	—	229.0	238.8	239.8
cervicofacial	—	196.0	—	229.0	238.8	239.8
Cloquet	—	196.5	—	229.0	238.8	239.8
colic	—	196.2	—	229.0	238.8	239.8
common duct	—	196.2	—	229.0	238.8	239.8
cubital	—	196.3	—	229.0	238.8	239.8
diaphragmatic	—	196.1	—	229.0	238.8	239.8
epigastric, inferior	—	196.6	—	229.0	238.8	239.8
epitrochlear	—	196.3	—	229.0	238.8	239.8
esophageal	—	196.1	—	229.0	238.8	239.8
face	—	196.0	—	229.0	238.8	239.8
femoral	—	196.5	—	229.0	238.8	239.8
gastric	—	196.2	—	229.0	238.8	239.8
groin	—	196.5	—	229.0	238.8	239.8
head	—	196.0	—	229.0	238.8	239.8
hepatic	—	196.2	—	229.0	238.8	239.8
hilar (pulmonary)	—	196.1	—	229.0	238.8	239.8
splenic	—	196.2	—	229.0	238.8	239.8
hypogastric	—	196.6	—	229.0	238.8	239.8
ileocolic	—	196.2	—	229.0	238.8	239.8
iliac	—	196.6	—	229.0	238.8	239.8
infraclavicular	—	196.3	—	229.0	238.8	239.8
inguina, inguinal	—	196.5	—	229.0	238.8	239.8
innominate	—	196.1	—	229.0	238.8	239.8
intercostal	—	196.1	—	229.0	238.8	239.8
intestinal	—	196.2	—	229.0	238.8	239.8
intra-abdominal	—	196.2	—	229.0	238.8	239.8
intrapelvic	—	196.6	—	229.0	238.8	239.8
intrathoracic	—	196.1	—	229.0	238.8	239.9
jugular	—	196.0	—	229.0	238.8	239.8
leg	—	196.5	—	229.0	238.8	239.8
limb						
lower	—	196.5	—	229.0	238.8	239.8
upper	—	196.3	—	229.0	238.8	239.8
lower limb	—	196.5	—	229.0	238.8	238.9
lumbar	—	196.2	—	229.0	238.8	239.8
mandibular	—	196.0	—	229.0	238.8	239.8
mediastinal	—	196.1	—	229.0	238.8	239.8
mesenteric (inferior) (superior)	—	196.2	—	229.0	238.8	239.8
midcolic	—	196.2	—	229.0	238.8	239.8
multiple sites in categories 196.0–196.6	—	196.8	—	229.0	238.8	239.8
neck	—	196.0	—	229.0	238.8	239.8
obturator	—	196.6	—	229.0	238.8	239.8
occipital	—	196.0	—	229.0	238.8	239.8
pancreatic	—	196.2	—	229.0	238.8	239.8
para-aortic	—	196.2	—	229.0	238.8	239.8
paracervical	—	196.6	—	229.0	238.8	239.8
parametrial	—	196.6	—	229.0	238.8	239.8
parasternal	—	196.1	—	229.0	238.8	239.8
parotid	—	196.0	—	229.0	238.8	239.8
pectoral	—	196.3	—	229.0	238.8	239.8
pelvic	—	196.6	—	229.0	238.8	239.8
peri-aortic	—	196.2	—	229.0	238.8	239.8

	Malignant					
	Primary	Secondary	Ca in situ	Benign	Uncertain Behavior	Unspecified
Neoplasm, neoplastic — *continued*						
lymph, lymphatic — *continued*						
gland — *continued*						
peripancreatic	—	196.2	—	229.0	238.8	239.8
popliteal	—	196.5	—	229.0	238.8	239.8
porta hepatis	—	196.2	—	229.0	238.8	239.8
portal	—	196.2	—	229.0	238.8	239.8
preauricular	—	196.0	—	229.0	238.8	239.8
prelaryngeal	—	196.0	—	229.0	238.8	239.8
presymphysial	—	196.6	—	229.0	238.8	239.8
pretracheal	—	196.0	—	229.0	238.8	239.8
primary (any site) NEC	202.9 ☑	—	—	—	—	—
pulmonary (hiler)	—	196.1	—	229.0	238.8	239.8
pyloric	—	196.2	—	229.0	238.8	239.8
retroperitoneal	—	196.2	—	229.0	238.8	239.8
retropharyngeal	—	196.0	—	229.0	238.8	239.8
Rosenmüller's	—	196.5	—	229.0	238.8	239.8
sacral	—	196.6	—	229.0	238.8	239.8
scalene	—	196.0	—	229.0	238.8	239.8
site NEC	—	196.9	—	229.0	238.8	239.8
splenic (hilar)	—	196.2	—	229.0	238.8	239.8
subclavicular	—	196.3	—	229.0	238.8	239.8
subinguinal	—	196.5	—	229.0	238.8	239.8
sublingual	—	196.0	—	229.0	238.8	239.8
submandibular	—	196.0	—	229.0	238.8	239.8
submaxillary	—	196.0	—	229.0	238.8	239.8
submental	—	196.0	—	229.0	238.8	239.8
subscapular	—	196.3	—	229.0	238.8	239.8
supraclavicular	—	196.0	—	229.0	238.8	239.8
thoracic	—	196.1	—	229.0	238.8	239.8
tibial	—	196.5	—	229.0	238.8	239.8
tracheal	—	196.1	—	229.0	238.8	239.8
tracheobronchial	—	196.1	—	229.0	238.8	239.8
upper limb	—	196.3	—	229.0	238.8	239.8
Virchow's	—	196.0	—	229.0	238.8	239.8
node (*see also* Neoplasm, lymph gland)						
primary NEC	202.9 ☑	—	—	—	—	—
vessel (*see also* Neoplasm, connective tissue)	171.9	198.89	—	215.9	238.1	239.2
malar	170.0	198.5	—	213.0	238.0	239.2
region — *see* Neoplasm, cheek						
mammary gland — *see* Neoplasm, breast						
mandible	170.1	198.5	—	213.1	238.0	239.2
alveolar						
mucose	143.1	198.89	230.0	210.4	235.1	239.0
ridge or process	170.1	198.5	—	213.1	238.0	239.2
carcinoma	143.1	—	—	—	—	—
carcinoma	143.1	—	—	—	—	—
marrow (bone) NEC	202.9 ☑	198.5	—	—	—	238.79 ▲
mastectomy site (skin)	173.5	198.2	—	—	—	—
specified as breast tissue	174.8	198.81	—	—	—	—
mastoid (air cells) (antrum) (cavity)	160.1	197.3	231.8	212.0	235.9	239.1
bone or process	170.0	198.5	—	213.0	238.0	239.2
maxilla, maxillary (superior)	170.0	198.5	—	213.0	238.0	239.2
alveolar						
mucosa	143.0	198.89	230.0	210.4	235.1	239.0
ridge or process	170.0	198.5	—	213.0	238.0	239.2
carcinoma	143.0	—	—	—	—	—
antrum	160.2	197.3	231.8	212.0	235.9	239.1
carcinoma	143.0	—	—	—	—	—
inferior — *see* Neoplasm, mandible						
sinus	160.2	197.3	231.8	212.0	235.9	239.1
meatus						
external (ear)	173.2	198.2	232.2	216.2	238.2	239.2
Meckel's diverticulum	152.3	197.4	230.7	211.2	235.2	239.0

	Malignant					
	Primary	Secondary	Ca in situ	Benign	Uncertain Behavior	Unspecified
Neoplasm, neoplastic — *continued*						
mediastinum, mediastinal	164.9	197.1	—	212.5	235.8	239.8
anterior	164.2	197.1	—	212.5	235.8	239.8
contiguous sites with heart and thymus	164.8	—	—	—	—	—
posterior	164.3	197.1	—	212.5	235.8	239.8
medulla						
adrenal	194.0	198.7	234.8	227.0	237.2	239.7
oblongata	191.7	198.3	—	225.0	237.5	239.6
meibomian gland	173.1	198.2	232.1	216.1	238.2	239.2
meninges (brain) (cerebral) (cranial) (intracranial)	192.1	198.4	—	225.2	237.6	239.7
spinal (cord)	192.3	198.4	—	225.4	237.6	239.7
meniscus, knee joint (lateral) (medial)	170.7	198.5	—	213.7	238.0	239.2
mesentery, mesenteric	158.8	197.6	—	211.8	235.4	239.0
mesoappendix	158.8	197.6	—	211.8	235.4	239.0
mesocolon	158.8	197.6	—	211.8	235.4	239.0
mesopharynx — *see* Neoplasm, oropharynx						
mesosalpinx	183.3	198.82	233.3	221.0	236.3	239.5
mesovarium	183.3	198.82	233.3	221.0	236.3	239.5
metacarpus (any bone)	170.5	198.5	—	213.5	238.0	239.2
metastatic NEC (*see also* Neoplasm, by site, secondary)	—	199.1	—	—	—	—
metatarsus (any bone)	170.8	198.5	—	213.8	238.0	239.2
midbrain	191.7	198.3	—	225.0	237.5	239.6
milk duct — *see* Neoplasm, breast						
mons						
pubis	184.4	198.82	233.3	221.2	236.3	239.5
veneris	184.4	198.82	233.3	221.2	236.3	239.5
motor tract	192.9	198.4	—	225.9	237.9	239.7
brain	191.9	198.3	—	225.0	237.5	239.6
spinal	192.2	198.3	—	225.3	237.5	239.7
mouth	145.9	198.89	230.0	210.4	235.1	239.0
contiguous sites	145.8	—	—	—	—	—
floor	144.9	198.89	230.0	210.3	235.1	239.0
anterior portion	144.0	198.89	230.0	210.3	235.1	239.0
contiguous sites	144.8	—	—	—	—	—
lateral portion	144.1	198.89	230.0	210.3	235.1	239.0
roof	145.5	198.89	230.0	210.4	235.1	239.0
specified part NEC	145.8	198.89	230.0	210.4	235.1	239.0
vestibule	145.1	198.89	230.0	210.4	235.1	239.0
mucosa						
alveolar (ridge or process)	143.9	198.89	230.0	210.4	235.1	239.0
lower	143.1	198.89	230.0	210.4	235.1	239.0
upper	143.0	198.89	230.0	210.4	235.1	239.0
buccal	145.0	198.89	230.0	210.4	235.1	239.0
cheek	145.0	198.89	230.0	210.4	235.1	239.0
lip — *see* Neoplasm, lip, internal						
nasal	160.0	197.3	231.8	212.0	235.9	239.1
oral	145.0	198.89	230.0	210.4	235.1	239.0
Müllerian duct						
female	184.8	198.82	233.3	221.8	236.3	239.5
male	187.8	198.82	233.6	222.8	236.6	239.5
multiple sites NEC	199.0	199.0	234.9	229.9	238.9	199.0
muscle (*see also* Neoplasm, connective tissue)						
extraocular	190.1	198.4	234.0	224.1	238.8	239.8
myocardium	164.1	198.89	—	212.7	238.8	239.8
myometrium	182.0	198.82	233.2	219.1	236.0	239.5
myopericardium	164.1	198.89	—	212.7	238.8	239.8
nabothian gland (follicle)	180.0	198.82	233.1	219.0	236.0	239.5
Nackenrodt's ligament	183.8	198.82	233.3	221.8	236.3	239.5
nail	173.9	198.2	232.9	216.9	238.2	239.2
finger	173.6	198.2	232.6	216.6	238.2	239.2
toe	173.7	198.2	232.7	216.7	238.2	239.2

☑ Additional Digit Required — Refer to the Tabular List for Digit Selection

▽ Subterms under main terms may continue to next column or page

Neoplasm, neoplastic — continued	Malignant Primary	Malignant Secondary	Malignant Ca in situ	Benign	Uncertain Behavior	Unspecified
nares, naris (anterior) (posterior)	160.0	197.3	231.8	212.0	235.9	239.1
nasal — see Neoplasm, nose						
nasolabial groove	173.3	198.2	232.3	216.3	238.2	239.2
nasolacrimal duct	190.7	198.4	234.0	224.7	238.8	239.8
nasopharynx, nasopharyngeal	147.9	198.89	230.0	210.7	235.1	239.0
contiguous sites	147.8	—	—	—	—	—
floor	147.3	198.89	230.0	210.7	235.1	239.0
roof	147.0	198.89	230.0	210.7	235.1	239.0
specified site NEC	147.8	198.89	230.0	210.7	235.1	239.0
wall	147.9	198.89	230.0	210.7	235.1	239.0
anterior	147.3	198.89	230.0	210.7	235.1	239.0
lateral	147.2	198.89	230.0	210.7	235.1	239.0
posterior	147.1	198.89	230.0	210.7	235.1	239.0
superior	147.0	198.89	230.0	210.7	235.1	239.0
nates	173.5	198.2	232.5	216.5	238.2	239.2
neck NEC*	195.0	198.89	234.8	229.8	238.8	239.8
nerve (autonomic) (ganglion) (parasympathetic) (peripheral) (sympathetic) (see also Neoplasm, connective tissue)						
abducens	192.0	198.4	—	225.1	237.9	239.7
accessory (spinal)	192.0	198.4	—	225.1	237.9	239.7
acoustic	192.0	198.4	—	225.1	237.9	239.7
auditory	192.0	198.4	—	225.1	237.9	239.7
brachial	171.2	198.89	—	215.2	238.1	239.2
cranial (any)	192.0	198.4	—	225.1	237.9	239.7
facial	192.0	198.4	—	225.1	237.9	239.7
femoral	171.3	198.89	—	215.3	238.1	239.2
glossopharyngeal	192.0	198.4	—	225.1	237.9	239.7
hypoglossal	192.0	198.4	—	225.1	237.9	239.7
intercostal	171.4	198.89	—	215.4	238.1	239.2
lumbar	171.7	198.89	—	215.7	238.1	239.2
median	171.2	198.89	—	215.2	238.1	239.2
obturator	171.3	198.89	—	215.3	238.1	239.2
oculomotor	192.0	198.4	—	225.1	237.9	239.7
olfactory	192.0	198.4	—	225.1	237.9	239.7
optic	192.0	198.4	—	225.1	237.9	239.7
peripheral NEC	171.9	198.89	—	215.9	238.1	239.2
radial	171.2	198.89	—	215.2	238.1	239.2
sacral	171.6	198.89	—	215.6	238.1	239.2
sciatic	171.3	198.89	—	215.3	238.1	239.2
spinal NEC	171.9	198.89	—	215.9	238.1	239.2
trigeminal	192.0	198.4	—	225.1	237.9	239.7
trochlear	192.0	198.4	—	225.1	237.9	239.7
ulnar	171.2	198.89	—	215.2	238.1	239.2
vagus	192.0	198.4	—	225.1	237.9	239.7
nervous system (central) NEC	192.9	198.4	—	225.9	237.9	239.7
autonomic NEC	171.9	198.89	—	215.9	238.1	239.2
brain (see also Neoplasm, brain)						
membrane or meninges	192.1	198.4	—	225.2	237.6	239.7
contiguous sites	192.8	—	—	—	—	—
parasympathetic NEC	171.9	198.89	—	215.9	238.1	239.2
sympathetic NEC	171.9	198.89	—	215.9	238.1	239.2
nipple (female)	174.0	198.81	233.0	217	238.3	239.3
male	175.0	198.81	233.0	217	238.3	239.3
nose, nasal	195.0	198.89	234.8	229.8	238.8	239.8
ala (external)	173.3	198.2	232.3	216.3	238.2	239.2
bone	170.0	198.5	—	213.0	238.0	239.2
cartilage	160.0	197.3	231.8	212.0	235.9	239.1
cavity	160.0	197.3	231.8	212.0	235.9	239.1
contiguous sites with accessory sinuses or middle ear	160.8	—	—	—	—	—
choana	147.3	198.89	230.0	210.7	235.1	239.0
external (skin)	173.3	198.2	232.3	216.3	238.2	239.2
fossa	160.0	197.3	231.8	212.0	235.9	239.1
internal	160.0	197.3	231.8	212.0	235.9	239.1

Neoplasm, neoplastic — continued	Malignant Primary	Malignant Secondary	Malignant Ca in situ	Benign	Uncertain Behavior	Unspecified
nose, nasal — continued						
mucosa	160.0	197.3	231.8	212.0	235.9	239.1
septum	160.0	197.3	231.8	212.0	235.9	239.1
posterior margin	147.3	198.89	230.0	210.7	235.1	239.0
sinus — see Neoplasm, sinus						
skin	173.3	198.2	232.3	216.3	238.2	239.2
turbinate (mucosa)	160.0	197.3	231.8	212.0	235.9	239.1
bone	170.0	198.5	—	213.0	238.0	239.2
vestibule	160.0	197.3	231.8	212.0	235.9	239.1
nostril	160.0	197.3	231.8	212.0	235.9	239.1
nucleus pulposus	170.2	198.5	—	213.2	238.0	239.2
occipital						
bone	170.0	198.5	—	213.0	238.0	239.2
lobe or pole, brain	191.4	198.3	—	225.0	237.5	239.6
odontogenic — see Neoplasm, jaw bone						
oesophagus — see Neoplasm, esophagus						
olfactory nerve or bulb	192.0	198.4	—	225.1	237.9	239.7
olive (brain)	191.7	198.3	—	225.0	237.5	239.6
omentum	158.8	197.6	—	211.8	235.4	239.0
operculum (brain)	191.0	198.3	—	225.0	237.5	239.6
optic nerve, chiasm, or tract	192.0	198.4	—	225.1	237.9	239.7
oral (cavity)	145.9	198.89	230.0	210.4	235.1	239.0
contiguous sites with lip or pharynx	149.8	—	—	—	—	—
ill-defined	149.9	198.89	230.0	210.4	235.1	239.0
mucosa	145.9	198.89	230.0	210.4	235.1	239.0
orbit	190.1	198.4	234.0	224.1	238.8	239.8
bone	170.0	198.5	—	213.0	238.0	239.2
eye	190.1	198.4	234.0	224.1	238.8	239.8
soft parts	190.1	198.4	234.0	224.1	238.8	239.8
organ of Zuckerkandl	194.6	198.89	—	227.6	237.3	239.7
oropharynx	146.9	198.89	230.0	210.6	235.1	239.0
branchial cleft (vestige)	146.8	198.89	230.0	210.6	235.1	239.0
contiguous sites	146.8	—	—	—	—	—
junctional region	146.5	198.89	230.0	210.6	235.1	239.0
lateral wall	146.6	198.89	230.0	210.6	235.1	239.0
pillars of fauces	146.2	198.89	230.0	210.6	235.1	239.0
posterior wall	146.7	198.89	230.0	210.6	235.1	239.0
specified part NEC	146.8	198.89	230.0	210.6	235.1	239.0
vallecula	146.3	198.89	230.0	210.6	235.1	239.0
os						
external	180.1	198.82	233.1	219.0	236.0	239.5
internal	180.0	198.82	233.1	219.0	236.0	239.5
ovary	183.0	198.6	233.3	220	236.2	239.5
oviduct	183.2	198.82	233.3	221.0	236.3	239.5
palate	145.5	198.89	230.0	210.4	235.1	239.0
hard	145.2	198.89	230.0	210.4	235.1	239.0
junction of hard and soft palate	145.5	198.89	230.0	210.4	235.1	239.0
soft	145.3	198.89	230.0	210.4	235.1	239.0
nasopharyngeal surface	147.3	198.89	230.0	210.7	235.1	239.0
posterior surface	147.3	198.89	230.0	210.7	235.1	239.0
superior surface	147.3	198.89	230.0	210.7	235.1	239.0
palatoglossal arch	146.2	198.89	230.0	210.6	235.1	239.0
palatopharyngeal arch	146.2	198.89	230.0	210.6	235.1	239.0
pallium	191.0	198.3	—	225.0	237.5	239.6
palpebra	173.1	198.2	232.1	216.1	238.2	239.2
pancreas	157.9	197.8	230.9	211.6	235.5	239.0
body	157.1	197.8	230.9	211.6	235.5	239.0
contiguous sites	157.8	—	—	—	—	—
duct (of Santorini) (of Wirsung)	157.3	197.8	230.9	211.6	235.5	239.0
ectopic tissue	157.8	197.8	230.9	211.6	235.5	239.0
head	157.0	197.8	230.9	211.6	235.5	239.0
islet cells	157.4	197.8	230.9	211.7	235.5	239.0
neck	157.8	197.8	230.9	211.6	235.5	239.0
tail	157.2	197.8	230.9	211.6	235.5	239.0
para-aortic body	194.6	198.89	—	227.6	237.3	239.7
paraganglion NEC	194.6	198.89	—	227.6	237.3	239.7

☑ Additional Digit Required — Refer to the Tabular List for Digit Selection

▽ Subterms under main terms may continue to next column or page

▶◀ Revised Text   ● New Line   ▲ Revised Code   2007 ICD-9-CM

Index

Neoplasm, neoplastic — continued

	Malignant					
	Primary	Secondary	Ca in situ	Benign	Uncertain Behavior	Unspecified
parametrium	183.4	198.82	—	221.0	236.3	239.5
paranephric	158.0	197.6	—	211.8	235.4	239.0
pararectal	195.3	198.89	—	229.8	238.8	239.8
parasagittal (region)	195.0	198.89	234.8	229.8	238.8	239.8
parasellar	192.9	198.4	—	225.9	237.9	239.7
parathyroid (gland)	194.1	198.89	234.8	227.1	237.4	239.7
paraurethral	195.3	198.89	—	229.8	238.8	239.8
gland	189.4	198.1	233.9	223.89	236.99	239.5
paravaginal	195.3	198.89	—	229.8	238.8	239.8
parenchyma, kidney	189.0	198.0	233.9	223.0	236.91	239.5
parietal						
bone	170.0	198.5	—	213.0	238.0	239.2
lobe, brain	191.3	198.3	—	225.0	237.5	239.6
paroophoron	183.3	198.82	233.3	221.0	236.3	239.5
parotid (duct) (gland)	142.0	198.89	230.0	210.2	235.0	239.0
parovarium	183.3	198.82	233.3	221.0	236.3	239.5
patella	170.8	198.5	—	213.8	238.0	239.2
peduncle, cerebral	191.7	198.3	—	225.0	237.5	239.6
pelvirectal junction	154.0	197.5	230.4	211.4	235.2	239.0
pelvis, pelvic	195.3	198.89	234.8	229.8	238.8	239.8
bone	170.6	198.5	—	213.6	238.0	239.2
floor	195.3	198.89	234.8	229.8	238.8	239.8
renal	189.1	198.0	233.9	223.1	236.91	239.5
viscera	195.3	198.89	234.8	229.8	238.8	239.8
wall	195.3	198.89	234.8	229.8	238.8	239.8
pelvo-abdominal	195.8	198.89	234.8	229.8	238.8	239.8
penis	187.4	198.82	233.5	222.1	236.6	239.5
body	187.3	198.82	233.5	222.1	236.6	239.5
corpus (cavernosum)	187.3	198.82	233.5	222.1	236.6	239.5
glans	187.2	198.82	233.5	222.1	236.6	239.5
skin NEC	187.4	198.82	233.5	222.1	236.6	239.5
periadrenal (tissue)	158.0	197.6	—	211.8	235.4	239.0
perianal (skin)	173.5	198.2	232.5	216.5	238.2	239.2
pericardium	164.1	198.89	—	212.7	238.8	239.8
perinephric	158.0	197.6	—	211.8	235.4	239.0
perineum	195.3	198.89	234.8	229.8	238.8	239.8
periodontal tissue NEC	143.9	198.89	230.0	210.4	235.1	239.0
periosteum — see Neoplasm, bone						
peripancreatic	158.0	197.6	—	211.8	235.4	239.0
peripheral nerve NEC	171.9	198.89	—	215.9	238.1	239.2
perirectal (tissue)	195.3	198.89	—	229.8	238.8	239.8
perirenal (tissue)	158.0	197.6	—	211.8	235.4	239.0
peritoneum, peritoneal (cavity)	158.9	197.6	—	211.8	235.4	239.0
contiguous sites	158.8	—	—	—	—	—
with digestive organs	159.8	—	—	—	—	—
parietal	158.8	197.6	—	211.8	235.4	239.0
pelvic	158.8	197.6	—	211.8	235.4	239.0
specified part NEC	158.8	197.6	—	211.8	235.4	239.0
peritonsillar (tissue)	195.0	198.89	234.8	229.8	238.8	239.8
periurethral tissue	195.3	198.89	—	229.8	238.8	239.8
phalanges	170.9	198.5	—	213.9	238.0	239.2
foot	170.8	198.5	—	213.8	238.0	239.2
hand	170.5	198.5	—	213.5	238.0	239.2
pharynx, pharyngeal	149.0	198.89	230.0	210.9	235.1	239.0
bursa	147.1	198.89	230.0	210.7	235.1	239.0
fornix	147.3	198.89	230.0	210.7	235.1	239.0
recess	147.2	198.89	230.0	210.7	235.1	239.0
region	149.0	198.89	230.0	210.9	235.1	239.0
tonsil	147.1	198.89	230.0	210.7	235.1	239.0
wall (lateral) (posterior)	149.0	198.89	230.0	210.9	235.1	239.0
pia mater (cerebral) (cranial)	192.1	198.4	—	225.2	237.6	239.7
spinal	192.3	198.4	—	225.4	237.6	239.7
pillars of fauces	146.2	198.89	230.0	210.6	235.1	239.0
pineal (body) (gland)	194.4	198.89	234.8	227.4	237.1	239.7
pinna (ear) NEC	173.2	198.2	232.2	216.2	238.2	239.2
cartilage	171.0	198.89	—	215.0	238.1	239.2
piriform fossa or sinus	148.1	198.89	230.0	210.8	235.1	239.0
pituitary (body) (fossa) (gland) (lobe)	194.3	198.89	234.8	227.3	237.0	239.7

Neoplasm, neoplastic — continued

	Malignant					
	Primary	Secondary	Ca in situ	Benign	Uncertain Behavior	Unspecified
placenta	181	198.82	233.2	219.8	236.1	239.5
pleura, pleural (cavity)	163.9	197.2	—	212.4	235.8	239.1
contiguous sites	163.8	—	—	—	—	—
parietal	163.0	197.2	—	212.4	235.8	239.1
visceral	163.1	197.2	—	212.4	235.8	239.1
plexus						
brachial	171.2	198.89	—	215.2	238.1	239.2
cervical	171.0	198.89	—	215.0	238.1	239.2
choroid	191.5	198.3	—	225.0	237.5	239.6
lumbosacral	171.6	198.89	—	215.6	238.1	239.2
sacral	171.6	198.89	—	215.6	238.1	239.2
pluri-endocrine	194.8	198.89	234.8	227.8	237.4	239.7
pole						
frontal	191.1	198.3	—	225.0	237.5	239.6
occipital	191.4	198.3	—	225.0	237.5	239.6
pons (varolii)	191.7	198.3	—	225.0	237.5	239.6
popliteal fossa or space*	195.5	198.89	234.8	229.8	238.8	239.8
postcricoid (region)	148.0	198.89	230.0	210.8	235.1	239.0
posterior fossa (cranial)	191.9	198.3	—	225.0	237.5	239.6
postnasal space	147.9	198.89	230.0	210.7	235.1	239.0
prepuce	187.1	198.82	233.5	222.1	236.6	239.5
prepylorus	151.1	197.8	230.2	211.1	235.2	239.0
presacral (region)	195.3	198.89	—	229.8	238.8	239.8
prostate (gland)	185	198.82	233.4	222.2	236.5	239.5
utricle	189.3	198.1	233.9	223.81	236.99	239.5
pterygoid fossa	171.0	198.89	—	215.0	238.1	239.2
pubic bone	170.6	198.5	—	213.6	238.0	239.2
pudenda, pudendum (female)	184.4	198.82	233.3	221.2	236.3	239.5
pulmonary	162.9	197.0	231.2	212.3	235.7	239.1
putamen	191.0	198.3	—	225.0	237.5	239.6
pyloric						
antrum	151.2	197.8	230.2	211.1	235.2	239.0
canal	151.1	197.8	230.2	211.1	235.2	239.0
pylorus	151.1	197.8	230.2	211.1	235.2	239.0
pyramid (brain)	191.7	198.3	—	225.0	237.5	239.6
pyriform fossa or sinus	148.1	198.89	230.0	210.8	235.1	239.0
radius (any part)	170.4	198.5	—	213.4	238.0	239.2
Rathke's pouch	194.3	198.89	234.8	227.3	237.0	239.7
rectosigmoid (colon) (junction)	154.0	197.5	230.4	211.4	235.2	239.0
contiguous sites with anus or rectum	154.8	—	—	—	—	—
rectouterine pouch	158.8	197.6	—	211.8	235.4	239.0
rectovaginal septum or wall	195.3	198.89	234.8	229.8	238.8	239.8
rectovesical septum	195.3	198.89	234.8	229.8	238.8	239.8
rectum (ampulla)	154.1	197.5	230.4	211.4	235.2	239.0
and colon	154.0	197.5	230.4	211.4	235.2	239.0
contiguous sites with anus or rectosigmoid junction	154.8	—	—	—	—	—
renal	189.0	198.0	233.9	223.0	236.91	239.5
calyx	189.1	198.0	233.9	223.1	236.91	239.5
hilus	189.1	198.0	233.9	223.1	236.91	239.5
parenchyma	189.0	198.0	233.9	223.0	236.91	239.5
pelvis	189.1	198.0	233.9	223.1	236.91	239.5
respiratory						
organs or system NEC	165.9	197.3	231.9	212.9	235.9	239.1
contiguous sites with intrathoracic organs	165.8	—	—	—	—	—
specified sites NEC	165.8	197.3	231.8	212.8	235.9	239.1
tract NEC	165.9	197.3	231.9	212.9	235.9	239.1
upper	165.0	197.3	231.9	212.9	235.9	239.1
retina	190.5	198.4	234.0	224.5	238.8	239.8
retrobulbar	190.1	198.4	—	224.1	238.8	239.8
retrocecal	158.0	197.6	—	211.8	235.4	239.0
retromolar (area) (triangle) (trigone)	145.6	198.89	230.0	210.4	235.1	239.0
retro-orbital	195.0	198.89	234.8	229.8	238.8	239.8

Neoplasm, parametrium — Neoplasm, retro-orbital

Neoplasm, neoplastic — *continued*	Malignant					
	Primary	Secondary	Ca in situ	Benign	Uncertain Behavior	Unspecified
retroperitoneal (space)						
(tissue)	158.0	197.6	—	211.8	235.4	239.0
contiguous sites	158.8	—	—	—	—	—
retroperitoneum	158.0	197.6	—	211.8	235.4	239.0
contiguous sites	158.8	—	—	—	—	—
retropharyngeal	149.0	198.89	230.0	210.9	235.1	239.0
retrovesical (septum)	195.3	198.89	234.8	229.8	238.8	239.8
rhinencephalon	191.0	198.3	—	225.0	237.5	239.6
rib	170.3	198.5	—	213.3	238.0	239.2
Rosenmüller's fossa	147.2	198.89	230.0	210.7	235.1	239.0
round ligament	183.5	198.82	—	221.0	236.3	239.5
sacrococcyx,						
sacrococcygeal	170.6	198.5	—	213.6	238.0	239.2
region	195.3	198.89	234.8	229.8	238.8	239.8
sacrouterine ligament	183.4	198.82	—	221.0	236.3	239.5
sacrum, sacral						
(vertebra)	170.6	198.5	—	213.6	238.0	239.2
salivary gland or duct						
(major)	142.9	198.89	230.0	210.2	235.0	239.0
contiguous sites	142.8	—	—	—	—	—
minor NEC	145.9	198.89	230.0	210.4	235.1	239.0
parotid	142.0	198.89	230.0	210.2	235.0	239.0
pluriglandular	142.8	198.89	—	210.2	235.0	239.0
sublingual	142.2	198.89	230.0	210.2	235.0	239.0
submandibular	142.1	198.89	230.0	210.2	235.0	239.0
submaxillary	142.1	198.89	230.0	210.2	235.0	239.0
salpinx (uterine)	183.2	198.82	233.3	221.0	236.3	239.5
Santorini's duct	157.3	197.8	230.9	211.6	235.5	239.0
scalp	173.4	198.2	232.4	216.4	238.2	239.2
scapula (any part)	170.4	198.5	—	213.4	238.0	239.2
scapular region	195.1	198.89	234.8	229.8	238.8	239.8
scar NEC (*see also*						
Neoplasm, skin)	173.9	198.2	232.9	216.9	238.2	239.2
sciatic nerve	171.3	198.89	—	215.3	238.1	239.2
sclera	190.0	198.4	234.0	224.0	238.8	239.8
scrotum (skin)	187.7	198.82	—	222.4	236.6	239.5
sebaceous gland — *see*						
Neoplasm, skin						
sella turcica	194.3	198.89	234.8	227.3	237.0	239.7
bone	170.0	198.5	—	213.0	238.0	239.2
semilunar cartilage						
(knee)	170.7	198.5	—	213.7	238.0	239.2
seminal vesicle	187.8	198.82	233.6	222.8	236.6	239.5
septum						
nasal	160.0	197.3	231.8	212.0	235.9	239.1
posterior margin	147.3	198.89	230.0	210.7	235.1	239.0
rectovaginal	195.3	198.89	234.8	229.8	238.8	239.8
rectovesical	195.3	198.89	234.8	229.8	238.8	239.8
urethrovaginal	184.9	198.82	233.3	221.9	236.3	239.5
vesicovaginal	184.9	198.82	233.3	221.9	236.3	239.5
shoulder NEC*	195.4	198.89	232.6	229.8	238.8	239.8
sigmoid flexure (lower)						
(upper)	153.3	197.5	230.3	211.3	235.2	239.0
sinus (accessory)	160.9	197.3	231.8	212.0	235.9	239.1
bone (any)	170.0	198.5	—	213.0	238.0	239.2
contiguous sites with						
middle ear or nasal						
cavities	160.8	—	—	—	—	—
ethmoidal	160.3	197.3	231.8	212.0	235.9	239.1
frontal	160.4	197.3	231.8	212.0	235.9	239.1
maxillary	160.2	197.3	231.8	212.0	235.9	239.1
nasal, paranasal						
NEC	160.9	197.3	231.8	212.0	235.9	239.1
pyriform	148.1	198.89	230.0	210.8	235.1	239.0
sphenoidal	160.5	197.3	231.8	212.0	235.9	239.1
skeleton, skeletal						
NEC	170.9	198.5	—	213.9	238.0	239.2
Skene's gland	189.4	198.1	233.9	223.89	236.99	239.5
skin NEC	173.9	198.2	232.9	216.9	238.2	239.2
abdominal wall	173.5	198.2	232.5	216.5	238.2	239.2
ala nasi	173.3	198.2	232.3	216.3	238.2	239.2
ankle	173.7	198.2	232.7	216.7	238.2	239.2
antecubital space	173.6	198.2	232.6	216.6	238.2	239.2
anus	173.5	198.2	232.5	216.5	238.2	239.2
arm	173.6	198.2	232.6	216.6	238.2	239.2
auditory canal						
(external)	173.2	198.2	232.2	216.2	238.2	239.2

Neoplasm, neoplastic — *continued* skin — *continued*	Malignant					
	Primary	Secondary	Ca in situ	Benign	Uncertain Behavior	Unspecified
auricle (ear)	173.2	198.2	232.2	216.2	238.2	239.2
auricular canal						
(external)	173.2	198.2	232.2	216.2	238.2	239.2
axilla, axillary fold	173.5	198.2	232.5	216.5	238.2	239.2
back	173.5	198.2	232.5	216.5	238.2	239.2
breast	173.5	198.2	232.5	216.5	238.2	239.2
brow	173.3	198.2	232.3	216.3	238.2	239.2
buttock	173.5	198.2	232.5	216.5	238.2	239.2
calf	173.7	198.2	232.7	216.7	238.2	239.2
canthus (eye) (inner)						
(outer)	173.1	198.2	232.1	216.1	238.2	239.2
cervical region	173.4	198.2	232.4	216.4	238.2	239.2
cheek (external)	173.3	198.2	232.3	216.3	238.2	239.2
chest (wall)	173.5	198.2	232.5	216.5	238.2	239.2
chin	173.3	198.2	232.3	216.3	238.2	239.2
clavicular area	173.5	198.2	232.5	216.5	238.2	239.2
clitoris	—	198.82	233.3	221.2	236.3	239.5
columnella	173.3	198.2	232.3	216.3	238.2	239.2
concha	173.2	198.2	232.2	216.2	238.2	239.2
contiguous sites	173.8	—	—	—	—	—
ear (external)	173.2	198.2	232.2	216.2	238.2	239.2
elbow	173.6	198.2	232.6	216.6	238.2	239.2
eyebrow	173.3	198.2	232.3	216.3	—	239.2
eyelid	173.1	198.2	232.1	—	238.2	239.2
face NEC	173.3	198.2	232.3	216.3	238.2	239.2
female genital organs						
(external)	184.4	198.82	233.3	221.2	236.3	239.5
clitoris	184.3	198.82	233.3	221.2	236.3	239.5
labium NEC	184.4	198.82	233.3	221.2	236.3	239.5
majus	184.1	198.82	233.3	221.2	236.3	239.5
minus	184.2	198.82	233.3	221.2	236.3	239.5
pudendum	184.4	198.82	233.3	221.2	236.3	239.5
vulva	184.4	198.82	233.3	221.2	236.3	239.5
finger	173.6	198.2	232.6	216.6	238.2	239.2
flank	173.5	198.2	232.5	216.5	238.2	239.2
foot	173.7	198.2	232.7	216.7	238.2	239.2
forearm	173.6	198.2	232.6	216.6	238.2	239.2
forehead	173.3	198.2	232.3	216.3	238.2	239.2
glabella	173.3	198.2	232.3	216.3	238.2	239.2
gluteal region	173.5	198.2	232.5	216.5	238.2	239.2
groin	173.5	198.2	232.5	216.5	238.2	239.2
hand	173.6	198.2	232.6	216.6	238.2	239.2
head NEC	173.4	198.2	232.4	216.4	238.2	239.2
heel	173.7	198.2	232.7	216.7	238.2	239.2
helix	173.2	198.2	—	216.2	238.2	239.2
hip	173.7	198.2	232.7	216.7	238.2	239.2
infraclavicular						
region	173.5	198.2	232.5	216.5	238.2	239.2
inguinal region	173.5	198.2	232.5	216.5	238.2	239.2
jaw	173.3	198.2	232.3	216.3	238.2	239.2
knee	173.7	198.2	232.7	216.7	238.2	239.2
labia						
majora	184.1	198.82	233.3	221.2	236.3	239.5
minora	184.2	198.82	233.3	221.2	236.3	239.5
leg	173.7	198.2	232.7	216.7	238.2	239.2
lid (lower) (upper)	—	198.2	232.1	216.1	238.2	239.2
limb NEC	173.9	198.2	232.9	216.9	238.2	239.5
lower	173.7	198.2	232.7	216.7	238.2	239.2
upper	173.6	198.2	232.6	216.6	238.2	239.2
lip (lower) (upper)	173.0	198.2	232.0	216.0	238.2	239.2
male genital organs	187.9	198.82	233.6	222.9	236.6	239.5
penis	187.4	198.82	233.5	222.1	236.6	239.5
prepuce	187.1	198.82	233.5	222.1	236.6	239.5
scrotum	187.7	198.82	233.6	222.4	236.6	239.5
mastectomy site	173.5	198.2	—	—	—	—
specified as breast						
tissue	174.8	198.81	—	—	—	—
meatus, acoustic						
(external)	173.2	198.2	232.2	216.2	238.2	239.2
nates	173.5	198.2	232.5	216.5	238.2	239.0
neck	173.4	198.2	232.4	216.4	238.2	239.2
nose (external)	173.3	198.2	232.3	216.3	238.2	239.2
palm	173.6	198.2	232.6	216.6	238.2	239.2
palpebra	173.1	198.2	232.1	216.1	238.2	239.2
penis NEC	187.4	198.82	233.5	222.1	236.6	239.5
perianal	173.5	198.2	232.5	216.5	238.2	239.2

Neoplasm, neoplastic —	Malignant					
	Primary	Secondary	Ca in situ	Benign	Uncertain Behavior	Unspecified
continued						
skin — *continued*						
perineum	173.5	198.2	232.5	216.5	238.2	239.2
pinna	173.2	198.2	232.2	216.2	238.2	239.2
plantar	173.7	198.2	232.7	216.7	238.2	239.2
popliteal fossa or space	173.7	198.2	232.7	216.7	238.2	239.2
prepuce	187.1	198.82	233.5	222.1	236.6	239.5
pubes	173.5	198.2	232.5	216.5	238.2	239.2
sacrococcygeal region	173.5	198.2	232.5	216.5	238.2	239.2
scalp	173.4	198.2	232.4	216.4	238.2	239.2
scapular region	173.5	198.2	232.5	216.5	238.2	239.2
scrotum	187.7	198.82	233.6	222.4	236.6	239.5
shoulder	173.6	198.2	232.6	216.6	238.2	239.2
sole (foot)	173.7	198.2	232.7	216.7	238.2	239.2
specified sites NEC	173.8	198.2	232.8	216.8	232.8	239.2
submammary fold	173.5	198.2	232.5	216.5	238.2	239.2
supraclavicular region	173.4	198.2	232.4	216.4	238.2	239.2
temple	173.3	198.2	232.3	216.3	238.2	239.2
thigh	173.7	198.2	232.7	216.7	238.2	239.2
thoracic wall	173.5	198.2	232.5	216.5	238.2	239.2
thumb	173.6	198.2	232.6	216.6	238.2	239.2
toe	173.7	198.2	232.7	216.7	238.2	239.2
tragus	173.2	198.2	232.2	216.2	238.2	239.2
trunk	173.5	198.2	232.5	216.5	238.2	239.2
umbilicus	173.5	198.2	232.5	216.5	238.2	239.2
vulva	184.4	198.82	233.3	221.2	236.3	239.5
wrist	173.6	198.2	232.6	216.6	238.2	239.2
skull	170.0	198.5	—	213.0	238.0	239.2
soft parts or tissues — *see* Neoplasm, connective tissue						
specified site NEC	195.8	198.89	234.8	229.8	238.8	239.8
specified site — *see* Neoplasm, skin						
spermatic cord	187.6	198.82	233.6	222.8	236.6	239.5
sphenoid	160.5	197.3	231.8	212.0	235.9	239.1
bone	170.0	198.5	—	213.0	238.0	239.2
sinus	160.5	197.3	231.8	212.0	235.9	239.1
sphincter						
anal	154.2	197.5	230.5	211.4	235.5	239.0
of Oddi	156.1	197.8	230.8	211.5	235.3	239.0
spine, spinal (column)	170.2	198.5	—	213.2	238.0	239.2
bulb	191.7	198.3	—	225.0	237.5	239.6
coccyx	170.6	198.5	—	213.6	238.0	239.2
cord (cervical) (lumbar) (sacral) (thoracic)	192.2	198.3	—	225.3	237.5	239.7
dura mater	192.3	198.4	—	225.4	237.6	239.7
lumbosacral	170.2	198.5	—	213.2	238.0	239.2
membrane	192.3	198.4	—	225.4	237.6	239.7
meninges	192.3	198.4	—	225.4	237.6	239.7
nerve (root)	171.9	198.89	—	215.9	238.1	239.2
pia mater	192.3	198.4	—	225.4	237.6	239.7
root	171.9	198.89	—	215.9	238.1	239.2
sacrum	170.6	198.5	—	213.6	238.0	239.2
spleen, splenic NEC	159.1	197.8	230.9	211.9	235.5	239.0
flexure (colon)	153.7	197.5	230.3	211.3	235.2	239.0
stem, brain	191.7	198.3	—	225.0	237.5	239.6
Stensen's duct	142.0	198.89	230.0	210.2	235.0	239.0
sternum	170.3	198.5	—	213.3	238.0	239.2
stomach	151.9	197.8	230.2	211.1	235.2	239.0
antrum (pyloric)	151.2	197.8	230.2	211.1	235.2	239.0
body	151.4	197.8	230.2	211.1	235.2	239.0
cardia	151.0	197.8	230.2	211.1	235.2	239.0
cardiac orifice	151.0	197.8	230.2	211.1	235.2	239.0
contiguous sites	151.8	—	—	—	—	—
corpus	151.4	197.8	230.2	211.1	235.2	239.0
fundus	151.3	197.8	230.2	211.1	235.2	239.0
greater curvature NEC	151.6	197.8	230.2	211.1	235.2	239.0
lesser curvature NEC	151.5	197.8	230.2	211.1	235.2	239.0
prepylorus	151.1	197.8	230.2	211.1	235.2	239.0
pylorus	151.1	197.8	230.2	211.1	235.2	239.0
wall NEC	151.9	197.8	230.2	211.1	235.2	239.0

Neoplasm, neoplastic —	Malignant					
	Primary	Secondary	Ca in situ	Benign	Uncertain Behavior	Unspecified
continued						
stomach — *continued*						
wall — *continued*						
anterior NEC	151.8	197.8	230.2	211.1	235.2	239.0
posterior NEC	151.8	197.8	230.2	211.1	235.2	239.0
stroma, endometrial	182.0	198.82	233.2	219.1	236.0	239.5
stump, cervical	180.8	198.82	233.1	219.0	236.0	239.5
subcutaneous (nodule) (tissue) NEC — *see* Neoplasm, connective tissue						
subdural	192.1	198.4	—	225.2	237.6	239.7
subglottis, subglottic	161.2	197.3	231.0	212.1	235.6	239.1
sublingual	144.9	198.89	230.0	210.3	235.1	239.0
gland or duct	142.2	198.89	230.0	210.2	235.0	239.0
submandibular gland	142.1	198.89	230.0	210.2	235.0	239.0
submaxillary gland or duct	142.1	198.89	230.0	210.2	235.0	239.0
submental	195.0	198.89	234.8	229.8	238.8	239.8
subpleural	162.9	197.0	—	212.3	235.7	239.1
substernal	164.2	197.1	—	212.5	235.8	239.8
sudoriferous, sudoriparous gland, site unspecified	173.9	198.2	232.9	216.9	238.2	239.2
specified site — *see* Neoplasm, skin						
supraclavicular region	195.0	198.89	234.8	229.8	238.8	239.8
supraglottis	161.1	197.3	231.0	212.1	235.6	239.1
suprarenal (capsule) (cortex) (gland) (medulla)	194.0	198.7	234.8	227.0	237.2	239.7
suprasellar (region)	191.9	198.3	—	225.0	237.5	239.6
sweat gland (apocrine) (eccrine), site unspecified	173.9	198.2	232.9	216.9	238.2	239.2
sympathetic nerve or nervous system NEC	171.9	198.89	—	215.9	238.1	239.2
symphysis pubis	170.6	198.5	—	213.6	238.0	239.2
synovial membrane — *see* Neoplasm, connective tissue						
tapetum, brain	191.8	198.3	—	225.0	237.5	239.6
tarsus (any bone)	170.8	198.5	—	213.8	238.0	239.2
temple (skin)	173.3	198.2	232.3	216.3	238.2	239.2
temporal						
bone	170.0	198.5	—	213.0	238.0	239.2
lobe or pole	191.2	198.3	—	225.0	237.5	239.6
region	195.0	198.89	234.8	229.8	238.8	239.8
skin	173.3	198.2	232.3	216.3	238.2	239.2
tendon (sheath) — *see* Neoplasm, connective tissue						
tentorium (cerebelli)	192.1	198.4	—	225.2	237.6	239.7
testis, testes (descended) (scrotal)	186.9	198.82	233.6	222.0	236.4	239.5
ectopic	186.0	198.82	233.6	222.0	236.4	239.5
retained	186.0	198.82	233.6	222.0	236.4	239.5
undescended	186.0	198.82	233.6	222.0	236.4	239.5
thalamus	191.0	198.3	—	225.0	237.5	239.6
thigh NEC*	195.5	198.89	234.8	229.8	238.8	239.8
thorax, thoracic (cavity) (organs NEC)	195.1	198.89	234.8	229.8	238.8	239.8
duct	171.4	198.89	—	215.4	238.1	239.2
wall NEC	195.1	198.89	234.8	229.8	238.8	239.8
throat	149.0	198.89	230.0	210.9	235.1	239.0
thumb NEC*	195.4	198.89	232.6	229.8	238.8	239.8
thymus (gland)	164.0	198.89	—	212.6	235.8	239.8
contiguous sites with heart and mediastinum	164.8	—	—	—	—	—
thyroglossal duct	193	198.89	234.8	226	237.4	239.7
thyroid (gland)	193	198.89	234.8	226	237.4	239.7
cartilage	161.3	197.3	231.0	212.1	235.6	239.1
tibia (any part)	170.7	198.5	—	213.7	238.0	239.2
toe NEC*	195.5	198.89	232.7	229.8	238.8	239.8
tongue	141.9	198.89	230.0	210.1	235.1	239.0
anterior (two-thirds) NEC	141.4	198.89	230.0	210.1	235.1	239.0

☑ Additional Digit Required — Refer to the Tabular List for Digit Selection

▽ Subterms under main terms may continue to next column or page

2007 ICD-9-CM   ▶◀ Revised Text   ● New Line   ▲ Revised Code   **Volume 2 — 209**

Neoplasm, tongue — Neoplasm — Neoplasm, Wharton's duct

	Malignant					
	Primary	Secondary	Ca in situ	Benign	Uncertain Behavior	Unspecified
Neoplasm, neoplastic — continued						
tongue — continued						
anterior — continued						
dorsal surface	141.1	198.89	230.0	210.1	235.1	239.0
ventral surface	141.3	198.89	230.0	210.1	235.1	239.0
base (dorsal surface)	141.0	198.89	230.0	210.1	235.1	239.0
border (lateral)	141.2	198.89	230.0	210.1	235.1	239.0
contiguous sites	141.8	—	—	—	—	—
dorsal surface NEC	141.1	198.89	230.0	210.1	235.1	239.0
fixed part NEC	141.0	198.89	230.0	210.1	235.1	239.0
foreamen cecum	141.1	198.89	230.0	210.1	235.1	239.0
frenulum linguae	141.3	198.89	230.0	210.1	235.1	239.0
junctional zone	141.5	198.89	230.0	210.1	235.1	239.0
margin (lateral)	141.2	198.89	230.0	210.1	235.1	239.0
midline NEC	141.1	198.89	230.0	210.1	235.1	239.0
mobile part NEC	141.4	198.89	230.0	210.1	235.1	239.0
posterior (third)	141.0	198.89	230.0	210.1	235.1	239.0
root	141.0	198.89	230.0	210.1	235.1	239.0
surface (dorsal)	141.1	198.89	230.0	210.1	235.1	239.0
base	141.0	198.89	230.0	210.1	235.1	239.0
ventral	141.3	198.89	230.0	210.1	235.1	239.0
tip	141.2	198.89	230.0	210.1	235.1	239.0
tonsil	141.6	198.89	230.0	210.1	235.1	239.0
tonsil	146.0	198.89	230.0	210.5	235.1	239.0
fauces, faucial	146.0	198.89	230.0	210.5	235.1	239.0
lingual	141.6	198.89	230.0	210.1	235.1	239.0
palatine	146.0	198.89	230.0	210.5	235.1	239.0
pharyngeal	147.1	198.89	230.0	210.7	235.1	239.0
pillar (anterior) (posterior)	146.2	198.89	230.0	210.6	235.1	239.0
tonsillar fossa	146.1	198.89	230.0	210.6	235.1	239.0
tooth socket NEC	143.9	198.89	230.0	210.4	235.1	239.0
trachea (cartilage) (mucosa)	162.0	197.3	231.1	212.2	235.7	239.1
contiguous sites with bronchus or lung	162.8	—	—	—	—	—
tracheobronchial	162.8	197.3	231.1	212.2	235.7	239.1
contiguous sites with lung	162.8	—	—	—	—	—
tragus	173.2	198.2	232.2	216.2	238.2	239.2
trunk NEC*	195.8	198.89	232.5	229.8	238.8	239.8
tubo-ovarian	183.8	198.82	233.3	221.8	236.3	239.5
tunica vaginalis	187.8	198.82	233.6	222.8	236.6	239.5
turbinate (bone)	170.0	198.5	—	213.0	238.0	239.2
nasal	160.0	197.3	231.8	212.0	235.9	239.1
tympanic cavity	160.1	197.3	231.8	212.0	235.9	239.1
ulna (any part)	170.4	198.5	—	213.4	238.0	239.2
umbilicus, umbilical	173.5	198.2	232.5	216.5	238.2	239.2
uncus, brain	191.2	198.3	—	225.0	237.5	239.6
unknown site or unspecified	199.1	199.1	234.9	229.9	238.9	239.9
urachus	188.7	198.1	233.7	223.3	236.7	239.4
ureter-bladder (junction)	188.6	198.1	233.7	223.3	236.7	239.4
ureter, ureteral	189.2	198.1	233.9	223.2	236.91	239.5
orifice (bladder)	188.6	198.1	233.7	223.3	236.7	239.4
urethra, urethral (gland)	189.3	198.1	233.9	223.81	236.99	239.5
orifice, internal	188.5	198.1	233.7	223.3	236.7	239.4
urethrovaginal (septum)	184.9	198.82	233.3	221.9	236.3	239.5
urinary organ or system NEC	189.9	198.1	233.9	223.9	236.99	239.5
bladder — see Neoplasm, bladder						
contiguous sites	189.8	—	—	—	—	—
specified sites NEC	189.8	198.1	233.9	223.89	236.99	239.5
utero-ovarian	183.8	198.82	233.3	221.8	236.3	239.5
ligament	183.3	198.82	—	221.0	236.3	239.5
uterosacral ligament	183.4	198.82	—	221.0	236.3	239.5
uterus, uteri, uterine	179	198.82	233.2	219.9	236.0	239.5
adnexa NEC	183.9	198.82	233.3	221.8	236.3	239.5
contiguous sites	183.8	—	—	—	—	—
body	182.0	198.82	233.2	219.1	236.0	239.5
contiguous sites	182.8	—	—	—	—	—
cervix	180.9	198.82	233.1	219.0	236.0	239.5
Neoplasm, neoplastic — continued						
uterus, uteri, uterine — continued						
cornu	182.0	198.82	233.2	219.1	236.0	239.5
corpus	182.0	198.82	233.2	219.1	236.0	239.5
endocervix (canal) (gland)	180.0	198.82	233.1	219.0	236.0	239.5
endometrium	182.0	198.82	233.2	219.1	236.0	239.5
exocervix	180.1	198.82	233.1	219.0	236.0	239.5
external os	180.1	198.82	233.1	219.0	236.0	239.5
fundus	182.0	198.82	233.2	219.1	236.0	239.5
internal os	180.0	198.82	233.1	219.0	236.0	239.5
isthmus	182.1	198.82	233.2	219.1	236.0	239.5
ligament	183.4	198.82	—	221.0	236.3	239.5
broad	183.3	198.82	233.3	221.0	236.3	239.5
round	183.5	198.82	—	221.0	236.3	239.5
lower segment	182.1	198.82	233.2	219.1	236.0	239.5
myometrium	182.0	198.82	233.2	219.1	236.0	239.5
squamocolumnar junction	180.8	198.82	233.1	219.0	236.0	239.5
tube	183.2	198.82	233.3	221.0	236.3	239.5
utricle, prostatic	189.3	198.1	233.9	223.81	236.99	239.5
uveal tract	190.0	198.4	234.0	224.0	238.8	239.8
uvula	145.4	198.89	230.0	210.4	235.1	239.0
vagina, vaginal (fornix) (vault) (wall)	184.0	198.82	233.3	221.1	236.3	239.5
vaginovesical	184.9	198.82	233.3	221.9	236.3	239.5
septum	194.9	198.82	233.3	221.9	236.3	239.5
vallecula (epiglottis)	146.3	198.89	230.0	210.6	235.1	239.0
vascular — see Neoplasm, connective tissue						
vas deferens	187.6	198.82	233.6	222.8	236.6	239.5
Vater's ampulla	156.2	197.8	230.8	211.5	235.3	239.0
vein, venous — see Neoplasm, connective tissue						
vena cava (abdominal) (inferior)	171.5	198.89	—	215.5	238.1	239.2
superior	171.4	198.89	—	215.4	238.1	239.2
ventricle (cerebral) (floor) (fourth) (lateral) (third)	191.5	198.3	—	225.0	237.5	239.6
cardiac (left) (right)	164.1	198.89	—	212.7	238.8	239.8
ventricular band of larynx	161.1	197.3	231.0	212.1	235.6	239.1
ventriculus — see Neoplasm, stomach						
vermillion border — see Neoplasm, lip						
vermis, cerebellum	191.6	198.3	—	225.0	237.5	239.6
vertebra (column)	170.2	198.5	—	213.2	238.0	239.2
coccyx	170.6	198.5	—	213.6	238.0	239.2
sacrum	170.6	198.5	—	213.6	238.0	239.2
vesical — see Neoplasm, bladder						
vesicle, seminal	187.8	198.82	233.6	222.8	236.6	239.5
vesicocervical tissue	184.9	198.82	233.3	221.9	236.3	239.5
vesicorectal	195.3	198.89	234.8	229.8	238.8	239.8
vesicovaginal	184.9	198.82	233.3	221.9	236.3	239.5
septum	184.9	198.82	233.3	221.9	236.3	239.5
vessel (blood) — see Neoplasm, connective tissue						
vestibular gland, greater	184.1	198.82	233.3	221.2	236.3	239.5
vestibule						
mouth	145.1	198.89	230.0	210.4	235.1	239.0
nose	160.0	197.3	231.8	212.0	235.9	239.1
Virchow's gland	—	196.0	—	229.0	238.8	239.8
viscera NEC	195.8	198.89	234.8	229.8	238.8	239.8
vocal cords (true)	161.0	197.3	231.0	212.1	235.6	239.1
false	161.1	197.3	231.0	212.1	235.6	239.1
vomer	170.0	198.5	—	213.0	238.0	239.2
vulva	184.4	198.82	233.3	221.2	236.3	239.5
vulvovaginal gland	184.4	198.82	233.3	221.2	236.3	239.5
Waldeyer's ring	149.1	198.89	230.0	210.9	235.1	239.0
Wharton's duct	142.1	198.89	230.0	210.2	235.0	239.0

☑ Additional Digit Required — Refer to the Tabular List for Digit Selection   ▽ Subterms under main terms may continue to next column or page

210 — Volume 2   ▶◀ Revised Text   ● New Line   ▲ Revised Code   2007 ICD-9-CM

	Malignant					
	Primary	Secondary	Ca in situ	Benign	Uncertain Behavior	Unspecified
Neoplasm, neoplastic — *continued*						
white matter (central) (cerebral)	191.0	198.3	—	225.0	237.5	239.6
windpipe	162.0	197.3	231.1	212.2	235.7	239.1
Wirsung's duct	157.3	197.8	230.9	211.6	235.5	239.0
wolffian (body) (duct)						
female	184.8	198.82	233.3	221.8	236.3	239.5
male	187.8	198.82	233.6	222.8	236.6	239.5
womb — *see* Neoplasm, uterus						
wrist NEC*	195.4	198.89	232.6	229.8	238.8	239.8
xiphoid process	170.3	198.5	—	213.3	238.0	239.2
Zuckerkandl's organ	194.6	198.89	—	227.6	237.3	239.7

☑ Additional Digit Required — Refer to the Tabular List for Digit Selection   ▽ Subterms under main terms may continue to next column or page

2007 ICD-9-CM   ▶◀ Revised Text   ● New Line   ▲ Revised Code   **Volume 2 — 211**

Neovascularization
- choroid 362.16
- ciliary body 364.42
- cornea 370.60
  - deep 370.63
  - localized 370.61
- iris 364.42
- retina 362.16
- subretinal 362.16

Nephralgia 788.0

Nephritis, nephritic (albuminuric) (azotemic) (congenital) (degenerative) (diffuse) (disseminated) (epithelial) (familial) (focal) (granulomatous) (hemorrhagic) (infantile) (nonsuppurative, excretory) (uremic) 583.9
- with
  - edema — see Nephrosis
  - lesion of
    - glomerulonephritis
      - hypocomplementemic persistent 583.2
        - with nephrotic syndrome 581.2
        - chronic 582.2
      - lobular 583.2
        - with nephrotic syndrome 581.2
        - chronic 582.2
      - membranoproliferative 583.2
        - with nephrotic syndrome 581.2
        - chronic 582.2
      - membranous 583.1
        - with nephrotic syndrome 581.1
        - chronic 582.1
      - mesangiocapillary 583.2
        - with nephrotic syndrome 581.2
        - chronic 582.2
      - mixed membranous and proliferative 583.2
        - with nephrotic syndrome 581.2
        - chronic 582.2
      - proliferative (diffuse) 583.0
        - with nephrotic syndrome 581.0
        - acute 580.0
        - chronic 582.0
        - rapidly progressive 583.4
          - acute 580.4
          - chronic 582.4
      - interstitial nephritis (diffuse) (focal) 583.89
        - with nephrotic syndrome 581.89
        - acute 580.89
        - chronic 582.89
      - necrotizing glomerulitis 583.4
        - acute 580.4
        - chronic 582.4
      - renal necrosis 583.9
        - cortical 583.6
        - medullary 583.7
      - specified pathology NEC 583.89
        - with nephrotic syndrome 581.89
        - acute 580.89
        - chronic 582.89
    - necrosis, renal 583.9
      - cortical 583.6
      - medullary (papillary) 583.7
    - nephrotic syndrome (see also Nephrosis) 581.9
    - papillary necrosis 583.7
    - specified pathology NEC 583.89
- acute 580.9
  - extracapillary with epithelial crescents 580.4
  - hypertensive (see also Hypertension, kidney) 403.90
  - necrotizing 580.4
  - poststreptococcal 580.0

Nephritis, nephritic — continued
- acute — continued
  - proliferative (diffuse) 580.0
  - rapidly progressive 580.4
  - specified pathology NEC 580.89
- amyloid 277.39 [583.81] ▲
  - chronic 277.39 [582.81] ▲
- arteriolar (see also Hypertension, kidney) 403.90
- arteriosclerotic (see also Hypertension, kidney) 403.90
- ascending (see also Pyelitis) 590.80
- atrophic 582.9
- basement membrane NEC 583.89
  - with
    - pulmonary hemorrhage (Goodpasture's syndrome) 446.21 [583.81]
- calculous, calculus 592.0
- cardiac (see also Hypertension, kidney) 403.90
- cardiovascular (see also Hypertension, kidney) 403.90
- chronic 582.9
  - arteriosclerotic (see also Hypertension, kidney) 403.90
  - hypertensive (see also Hypertension, kidney) 403.90
- cirrhotic (see also Sclerosis, renal) 587
- complicating pregnancy, childbirth, or puerperium 646.2 ☑
  - with hypertension 642.1 ☑
    - affecting fetus or newborn 760.0
  - affecting fetus or newborn 760.1
- croupous 580.9
- desquamative — see Nephrosis
- due to
  - amyloidosis 277.39 [583.81] ▲
    - chronic 277.39 [582.81] ▲
  - arteriosclerosis (see also Hypertension, kidney) 403.90
  - diabetes mellitus 250.4 ☑ [583.81]
    - with nephrotic syndrome 250.4 ☑ [581.81]
  - diphtheria 032.89 [580.81]
  - gonococcal infection (acute) 098.19 [583.81]
    - chronic or duration of 2 months or over 098.39 [583.81]
  - gout 274.10
  - infectious hepatitis 070.9 [580.81]
  - mumps 072.79 [580.81]
  - specified kidney pathology NEC 583.89
    - acute 580.89
    - chronic 582.89
  - streptotrichosis 039.8 [583.81]
  - subacute bacterial endocarditis 421.0 [580.81]
  - systemic lupus erythematosus 710.0 [583.81]
    - chronic 710.0 [582.81]
  - typhoid fever 002.0 [580.81]
- endothelial 582.2
- end stage (chronic) (terminal) NEC 585.6
- epimembranous 581.1
- exudative 583.89
  - with nephrotic syndrome 581.89
  - acute 580.89
  - chronic 582.89
- gonococcal (acute) 098.19 [583.81]
  - chronic or duration of 2 months or over 098.39 [583.81]
- gouty 274.10
- hereditary (Alport's syndrome) 759.89
- hydremic — see Nephrosis
- hypertensive (see also Hypertension, kidney) 403.90
- hypocomplementemic persistent 583.2
  - with nephrotic syndrome 581.2
  - chronic 582.2
- immune complex NEC 583.89
- infective (see also Pyelitis) 590.80
- interstitial (diffuse) (focal) 583.89
  - with nephrotic syndrome 581.89

Nephritis, nephritic — continued
- interstitial — continued
  - acute 580.89
  - chronic 582.89
- latent or quiescent — see Nephritis, chronic
- lead 984.9
  - specified type of lead — see Table of Drugs and Chemicals
- lobular 583.2
  - with nephrotic syndrome 581.2
  - chronic 582.2
- lupus 710.0 [583.81]
  - acute 710.0 [580.81]
  - chronic 710.0 [582.81]
- membranoproliferative 583.2
  - with nephrotic syndrome 581.2
  - chronic 582.2
- membranous 583.1
  - with nephrotic syndrome 581.1
  - chronic 582.1
- mesangiocapillary 583.2
  - with nephrotic syndrome 581.2
  - chronic 582.2
- minimal change 581.3
- mixed membranous and proliferative 583.2
  - with nephrotic syndrome 581.2
  - chronic 582.2
- necrotic, necrotizing 583.4
  - acute 580.4
  - chronic 582.4
- nephrotic — see Nephrosis
- old — see Nephritis, chronic
- parenchymatous 581.89
- polycystic 753.12
  - adult type (APKD) 753.13
  - autosomal dominant 753.13
  - autosomal recessive 753.14
  - childhood type (CPKD) 753.14
  - infantile type 753.14
- poststreptococcal 580.0
- pregnancy — see Nephritis, complicating pregnancy
- proliferative 583.0
  - with nephrotic syndrome 581.0
  - acute 580.0
  - chronic 582.0
- purulent (see also Pyelitis) 590.80
- rapidly progressive 583.4
  - acute 580.4
  - chronic 582.4
- salt-losing or salt-wasting (see also Disease, renal) 593.9
- saturnine 984.9
  - specified type of lead — see Table of Drugs and Chemicals
- septic (see also Pyelitis) 590.80
- specified pathology NEC 583.89
  - acute 580.89
  - chronic 582.89
- staphylococcal (see also Pyelitis) 590.80
- streptotrichosis 039.8 [583.81]
- subacute (see also Nephrosis) 581.9
- suppurative (see also Pyelitis) 590.80
- syphilitic (late) 095.4
  - congenital 090.5 [583.81]
  - early 091.69 [583.81]
- terminal (chronic) (end-stage) NEC 585.6
- toxic — see Nephritis, acute
- tubal, tubular — see Nephrosis, tubular
- tuberculous (see also Tuberculosis) 016.0 ☑ [583.81]
- type II (Ellis) — see Nephrosis
- vascular — see Hypertension, kidney
- war 580.9

Nephroblastoma (M8960/3) 189.0
- epithelial (M8961/3) 189.0
- mesenchymal (M8962/3) 189.0

Nephrocalcinosis 275.49

Nephrocystitis, pustular — see also Pyelitis 590.80

Nephrolithiasis (congenital) (pelvis) (recurrent) 592.0
- uric acid 274.11

Nephroma (M8960/3) 189.0
- mesoblastic (M8960/1) 236.9 ☑

Nephronephritis — see also Nephrosis 581.9

Nephronopthisis 753.16

Nephropathy — see also Nephritis 583.9
- with
  - exudative nephritis 583.89
  - interstitial nephritis (diffuse) (focal) 583.89
  - medullary necrosis 583.7
  - necrosis 583.9
    - cortical 583.6
    - medullary or papillary 583.7
  - papillary necrosis 583.7
  - specified lesion or cause NEC 583.89
- analgesic 583.89
  - with medullary necrosis, acute 584.7
- arteriolar (see also Hypertension, kidney) 403.90
- arteriosclerotic (see also Hypertension, kidney) 403.90
- complicating pregnancy 646.2 ☑
- diabetic 250.4 ☑ [583.81]
- gouty 274.10
  - specified type NEC 274.19
- hereditary amyloid 277.31 ●
- hypercalcemic 588.89
- hypertensive (see also Hypertension, kidney) 403.90
- hypokalemic (vacuolar) 588.89
- IgA 583.9
- obstructive 593.89
  - congenital 753.20
- phenacetin 584.7
- phosphate-losing 588.0
- potassium depletion 588.89
- proliferative (see also Nephritis, proliferative) 583.0
- protein-losing 588.89
- salt-losing or salt-wasting (see also Disease, renal) 593.9
- sickle-cell (see also Disease, sickle-cell) 282.60 [583.81]
- toxic 584.5
- vasomotor 584.5
- water-losing 588.89

Nephroptosis — see also Disease, renal 593.0
- congenital (displaced) 753.3

Nephropyosis — see also Abscess, kidney 590.2

Nephrorrhagia 593.81

Nephrosclerosis (arteriolar) (arteriosclerotic) (chronic) (hyaline) — see also Hypertension, kidney 403.90
- gouty 274.10
- hyperplastic (arteriolar) (see also Hypertension, kidney) 403.90
- senile (see also Sclerosis, renal) 587

Nephrosis, nephrotic (Epstein's) (syndrome) 581.9
- with
  - lesion of
    - focal glomerulosclerosis 581.1
    - glomerulonephritis
      - endothelial 581.2
      - hypocomplementemic persistent 581.2
      - lobular 581.2
      - membranoproliferative 581.2
      - membranous 581.1
      - mesangiocapillary 581.2
      - minimal change 581.3
      - mixed membranous and proliferative 581.2
      - proliferative 581.0
      - segmental hyalinosis 581.1
    - specified pathology NEC 581.89
- acute — see Nephrosis, tubular
- anoxic — see Nephrosis, tubular

☑ Additional Digit Required — Refer to the Tabular List for Digit Selection   ▽ Subterms under main terms may continue to next column or page

212 — Volume 2 • October 2006   ►◄ Revised Text   ● New Line   ▲ Revised Code   *2007 ICD-9-CM*

Nephrosis, nephrotic — *continued*
  arteriosclerotic (*see also* Hypertension, kidney) 403.90
  chemical — *see* Nephrosis, tubular
  cholemic 572.4
  complicating pregnancy, childbirth, or puerperium — *see* Nephritis, complicating pregnancy
  diabetic 250.4 ☑ *[581.81]*
  hemoglobinuric — *see* Nephrosis, tubular
  in
    amyloidosis 277.39 *[581.81]* ▲
    diabetes mellitus 250.4 ☑ *[581.81]*
    epidemic hemorrhagic fever 078.6
    malaria 084.9 *[581.81]*
    polyarteritis 446.0 *[581.81]*
    systemic lupus erythematosus 710.0 *[581.81]*
  ischemic — *see* Nephrosis, tubular
  lipoid 581.3
  lower nephron — *see* Nephrosis, tubular
  lupoid 710.0 *[581.81]*
  lupus 710.0 *[581.81]*
  malarial 084.9 *[581.81]*
  minimal change 581.3
  necrotizing — *see* Nephrosis, tubular
  osmotic (sucrose) 588.89
  polyarteritic 446.0 *[581.81]*
  radiation 581.9
  specified lesion or cause NEC 581.89
  syphilitic 095.4
  toxic — *see* Nephrosis, tubular
  tubular (acute) 584.5
    due to a procedure 997.5
    radiation 581.9
Nephrosonephritis hemorrhagic (endemic) 078.6
Nephrostomy status V44.6
  with complication 997.5
Nerve — *see* condition
Nerves 799.2
Nervous — *see also* condition 799.2
  breakdown 300.9
  heart 306.2
  stomach 306.4
  tension 799.2
Nervousness 799.2
Nesidioblastoma (M8150/0)
  pancreas 211.7
  specified site NEC — *see* Neoplasm, by site, benign
  unspecified site 211.7
Netherton's syndrome (ichthyosiform erythroderma) 757.1
Nettle rash 708.8
Nettleship's disease (urticaria pigmentosa) 757.33
Neumann's disease (pemphigus vegetans) 694.4
Neuralgia, neuralgic (acute) — *see also* Neuritis 729.2
  accessory (nerve) 352.4
  acoustic (nerve) 388.5
  ankle 355.8
  anterior crural 355.8
  anus 787.99
  arm 723.4
  auditory (nerve) 388.5
  axilla 353.0
  bladder 788.1
  brachial 723.4
  brain — *see* Disorder, nerve, cranial
  broad ligament 625.9
  cerebral — *see* Disorder, nerve, cranial
  ciliary 346.2 ☑
  cranial nerve (*see also* Disorder, nerve, cranial)
    fifth or trigeminal (*see also* Neuralgia, trigeminal) 350.1
  ear 388.71
    middle 352.1
  facial 351.8
  finger 354.9

Neuralgia, neuralgic — *see also* Neuritis — *continued*
  flank 355.8
  foot 355.8
  forearm 354.9
  Fothergill's (*see also* Neuralgia, trigeminal) 350.1
    postherpetic 053.12
  glossopharyngeal (nerve) 352.1
  groin 355.8
  hand 354.9
  heel 355.8
  Horton's 346.2 ☑
  Hunt's 053.11
  hypoglossal (nerve) 352.5
  iliac region 355.8
  infraorbital (*see also* Neuralgia, trigeminal) 350.1
  inguinal 355.8
  intercostal (nerve) 353.8
    postherpetic 053.19
  jaw 352.1
  kidney 788.0
  knee 355.8
  loin 355.8
  malarial (*see also* Malaria) 084.6
  mastoid 385.89
  maxilla 352.1
  median thenar 354.1
  metatarsal 355.6
  middle ear 352.1
  migrainous 346.2 ☑
  Morton's 355.6
  nerve, cranial — *see* Disorder, nerve, cranial
  nose 352.0
  occipital 723.8
  olfactory (nerve) 352.0
  ophthalmic 377.30
    postherpetic 053.19
  optic (nerve) 377.30
  penis 607.9
  perineum 355.8
  pleura 511.0
  postherpetic NEC 053.19
    geniculate ganglion 053.11
    ophthalmic 053.19
    trifacial 053.12
    trigeminal 053.12
  pubic region 355.8
  radial (nerve) 723.4
  rectum 787.99
  sacroiliac joint 724.3
  sciatic (nerve) 724.3
  scrotum 608.9
  seminal vesicle 608.9
  shoulder 354.9
  Sluder's 337.0
  specified nerve NEC — *see* Disorder, nerve
  spermatic cord 608.9
  sphenopalatine (ganglion) 337.0
  subscapular (nerve) 723.4
  suprascapular (nerve) 723.4
  testis 608.89
  thenar (median) 354.1
  thigh 355.8
  tongue 352.5
  trifacial (nerve) (*see also* Neuralgia, trigeminal) 350.1
  trigeminal (nerve) 350.1
    postherpetic 053.12
  tympanic plexus 388.71
  ulnar (nerve) 723.4
  vagus (nerve) 352.3
  wrist 354.9
  writers' 300.89
    organic 333.84
Neurapraxia — *see* Injury, nerve, by site
Neurasthenia 300.5
  cardiac 306.2
  gastric 306.4
  heart 306.2
  postfebrile 780.79
  postviral 780.79

Neurilemmoma (M9560/0) — *see also* Neoplasm, connective tissue, benign
  acoustic (nerve) 225.1
  malignant (M9560/3) (*see also* Neoplasm, connective tissue, malignant)
    acoustic (nerve) 192.0
Neurilemmosarcoma (M9560/3) — *see* Neoplasm, connective tissue, malignant
Neurilemoma — *see* Neurilemmoma
Neurinoma (M9560/0) — *see* Neurilemmoma
Neurinomatosis (M9560/1) — *see also* Neoplasm, connective tissue, uncertain behavior
  centralis 759.5
Neuritis — *see also* Neuralgia 729.2
  abducens (nerve) 378.54
  accessory (nerve) 352.4
  acoustic (nerve) 388.5
    syphilitic 094.86
  alcoholic 357.5
    with psychosis 291.1
  amyloid, any site 277.39 *[357.4]* ▲
  anterior crural 355.8
  arising during pregnancy 646.4 ☑
  arm 723.4
  ascending 355.2
  auditory (nerve) 388.5
  brachial NEC 723.4
    due to displacement, intervertebral disc 722.0
  cervical 723.4
  chest (wall) 353.8
  costal region 353.8
  cranial nerve (*see also* Disorder, nerve, cranial)
    first or olfactory 352.0
    second or optic 377.30
    third or oculomotor 378.52
    fourth or trochlear 378.53
    fifth or trigeminal (*see also* Neuralgia, trigeminal) 350.1
    sixth or abducens 378.54
    seventh or facial 351.8
      newborn 767.5
    eighth or acoustic 388.5
    ninth or glossopharyngeal 352.1
    tenth or vagus 352.3
    eleventh or accessory 352.4
    twelfth or hypoglossal 352.5
  Déjérine-Sottas 356.0
  diabetic 250.6 ☑ *[357.2]*
  diphtheritic 032.89 *[357.4]*
  due to
    beriberi 265.0 *[357.4]*
    displacement, prolapse, protrusion, or rupture of intervertebral disc 722.2
      cervical 722.0
      lumbar, lumbosacral 722.10
      thoracic, thoracolumbar 722.11
    herniation, nucleus pulposus 722.2
      cervical 722.0
      lumbar, lumbosacral 722.10
      thoracic, thoracolumbar 722.11
  endemic 265.0 *[357.4]*
  facial (nerve) 351.8
    newborn 767.5
  general — *see* Polyneuropathy
  geniculate ganglion 351.1
    due to herpes 053.11
  glossopharyngeal (nerve) 352.1
  gouty 274.89 *[357.4]*
  hypoglossal (nerve) 352.5
  ilioinguinal (nerve) 355.8
  in diseases classified elsewhere — *see* Polyneuropathy, in
  infectious (multiple) 357.0
  intercostal (nerve) 353.8
  interstitial hypertrophic progressive NEC 356.9
  leg 355.8

Neuritis — *see also* Neuralgia — *continued*
  lumbosacral NEC 724.4
  median (nerve) 354.1
    thenar 354.1
  multiple (acute) (infective) 356.9
    endemic 265.0 *[357.4]*
  multiplex endemica 265.0 *[357.4]*
  nerve root (*see also* Radiculitis) 729.2
  oculomotor (nerve) 378.52
  olfactory (nerve) 352.0
  optic (nerve) 377.30
    in myelitis 341.0
    meningococcal 036.81
  pelvic 355.8
  peripheral (nerve) (*see also* Neuropathy, peripheral)
    complicating pregnancy or puerperium 646.4 ☑
    specified nerve NEC — *see* Mononeuritis
  pneumogastric (nerve) 352.3
  postchickenpox 052.7
  postherpetic 053.19
  progressive hypertrophic interstitial NEC 356.9
  puerperal, postpartum 646.4 ☑
  radial (nerve) 723.4
  retrobulbar 377.32
    syphilitic 094.85
  rheumatic (chronic) 729.2
  sacral region 355.8
  sciatic (nerve) 724.3
    due to displacement of intervertebral disc 722.10
  serum 999.5
  specified nerve NEC — *see* Disorder, nerve
  spinal (nerve) 355.9
    root (*see also* Radiculitis) 729.2
  subscapular (nerve) 723.4
  suprascapular (nerve) 723.4
  syphilitic 095.8
  thenar (median) 354.1
  thoracic NEC 724.4
  toxic NEC 357.7
  trochlear (nerve) 378.53
  ulnar (nerve) 723.4
  vagus (nerve) 352.3
Neuroangiomatosis, encephalofacial 759.6
Neuroastrocytoma (M9505/1) — *see* Neoplasm, by site, uncertain behavior
Neuro-avitaminosis 269.2
Neuroblastoma (M9500/3)
  olfactory (M9522/3) 160.0
  specified site — *see* Neoplasm, by site, malignant
  unspecified site 194.0
Neurochorioretinitis — *see also* Chorioretinitis 363.20
Neurocirculatory asthenia 306.2
Neurocytoma (M9506/0) — *see* Neoplasm, by site, benign
Neurodermatitis (circumscribed) (circumscripta) (local) 698.3
  atopic 691.8
  diffuse (Brocq) 691.8
  disseminated 691.8
  nodulosa 698.3
Neuroencephalomyelopathy, optic 341.0
Neuroepithelioma (M9503/3) — *see also* Neoplasm, by site, malignant
  olfactory (M9521/3) 160.0
Neurofibroma (M9540/0) — *see also* Neoplasm, connective tissue, benign
  melanotic (M9541/0) — *see* Neoplasm, connective tissue, benign
  multiple (M9540/1) 237.70
    type 1 237.71
    type 2 237.72
  plexiform (M9550/0) — *see* Neoplasm, connective tissue, benign

☑ Additional Digit Required — Refer to the Tabular List for Digit Selection   ▽ Subterms under main terms may continue to next column or page

2007 ICD-9-CM   ▶◀ Revised Text   ● New Line   ▲ Revised Code   October 2006 · Volume 2 — 213

Neurofibromatosis (multiple) (M9540/1) 237.70
 acoustic 237.72
 malignant (M9540/3) — see Neoplasm, connective tissue, malignant
 type 1 237.71
 type 2 237.72
 von Recklinghausen's 237.71
Neurofibrosarcoma (M9540/3) — see Neoplasm, connective tissue, malignant
Neurogenic — see also condition
 bladder (atonic) (automatic) (autonomic) (flaccid) (hypertonic) (hypotonic) (inertia) (infranuclear) (irritable) (motor) (nonreflex) (nuclear) (paralysis) (reflex) (sensory) (spastic) (supranuclear) (uninhibited) 596.54
 with cauda equina syndrome 344.61
 bowel 564.81
 heart 306.2
Neuroglioma (M9505/1) — see Neoplasm, by site, uncertain behavior
Neurolabyrinthitis (of Dix and Hallpike) 386.12
Neurolathyrism 988.2
Neuroleprosy 030.1
Neuroleptic malignant syndrome 333.92
Neurolipomatosis 272.8
Neuroma (M9570/0) — see also Neoplasm, connective tissue, benign
 acoustic (nerve) (M9560/0) 225.1
 amputation (traumatic) (see also Injury, nerve, by site)
 surgical complication (late) 997.61
 appendix 211.3
 auditory nerve 225.1
 digital 355.6
 toe 355.6
 interdigital (toe) 355.6
 intermetatarsal 355.6
 Morton's 355.6
 multiple 237.70
 type 1 237.71
 type 2 237.72
 nonneoplastic 355.9
 arm NEC 354.9
 leg NEC 355.8
 lower extremity NEC 355.8
 specified site NEC — see Mononeuritis, by site
 upper extremity NEC 354.9
 optic (nerve) 225.1
 plantar 355.6
 plexiform (M9550/0) — see Neoplasm, connective tissue, benign
 surgical (nonneoplastic) 355.9
 arm NEC 354.9
 leg NEC 355.8
 lower extremity NEC 355.8
 upper extremity NEC 354.9
 traumatic (see also Injury, nerve, by site)
 old — see Neuroma, nonneoplastic
Neuromyalgia 729.1
Neuromyasthenia (epidemic) 049.8
Neuromyelitis 341.8
 ascending 357.0
 optica 341.0
Neuromyopathy NEC 358.9
Neuromyositis 729.1
Neuronevus (M8725/0) — see Neoplasm, skin, benign
Neuronitis 357.0
 ascending (acute) 355.2
 vestibular 386.12
Neuroparalytic — see condition
Neuropathy, neuropathic — see also Disorder, nerve 355.9
 acute motor 357.82
 alcoholic 357.5
 with psychosis 291.1

Neuropathy, neuropathic — see also Disorder, nerve — continued
 arm NEC 354.9
 ataxia and retinitis pigmentosa (NARP syndrome) 277.87
 autonomic (peripheral) — see Neuropathy, peripheral, autonomic
 axillary nerve 353.0
 brachial plexus 353.0
 cervical plexus 353.2
 chronic
 progressive segmentally demyelinating 357.89
 relapsing demyelinating 357.89
 congenital sensory 356.2
 Déjérine-Sottas 356.0
 diabetic 250.6 ☑ [357.2]
 entrapment 355.9
 iliohypogastric nerve 355.79
 ilioinguinal nerve 355.79
 lateral cutaneous nerve of thigh 355.1
 median nerve 354.0
 obturator nerve 355.79
 peroneal nerve 355.3
 posterior tibial nerve 355.5
 saphenous nerve 355.79
 ulnar nerve 354.2
 facial nerve 351.9
 hereditary 356.9
 peripheral 356.0
 sensory (radicular) 356.2
 hypertrophic
 Charcôt-Marie-Tooth 356.1
 Déjérine-Sottas 356.0
 interstitial 356.9
 Refsum 356.3
 intercostal nerve 354.8
 ischemic — see Disorder, nerve
 Jamaican (ginger) 357.7
 leg NEC 355.8
 lower extremity NEC 355.8
 lumbar plexus 353.1
 median nerve 354.1
 motor
 acute 357.82
 multiple (acute) (chronic) (see also Polyneuropathy) 356.9
 optic 377.39
 ischemic 377.41
 nutritional 377.33
 toxic 377.34
 peripheral (nerve) (see also Polyneuropathy) 356.9
 arm NEC 354.9
 autonomic 337.9
 amyloid 277.39 [337.1] ▲
 idiopathic 337.0
 in
 amyloidosis 277.39 [337.1] ▲
 diabetes (mellitus) 250.6 ☑ [337.1]
 diseases classified elsewhere 337.1
 gout 274.89 [337.1]
 hyperthyroidism 242.9 ☑ [337.1]
 due to
 antitetanus serum 357.6
 arsenic 357.7
 drugs 357.6
 lead 357.7
 organophosphate compounds 357.7
 toxic agent NEC 357.7
 hereditary 356.0
 idiopathic 356.9
 progressive 356.4
 specified type NEC 356.8
 in diseases classified elsewhere — see Polyneuropathy, in
 leg NEC 355.8
 lower extremity NEC 355.8
 upper extremity NEC 354.9
 plantar nerves 355.6

Neuropathy, neuropathic — see also Disorder, nerve — continued
 progressive hypertrophic interstitial 356.9
 radicular NEC 729.2
 brachial 723.4
 cervical NEC 723.4
 hereditary sensory 356.2
 lumbar 724.4
 lumbosacral 724.4
 thoracic NEC 724.4
 sacral plexus 353.1
 sciatic 355.0
 spinal nerve NEC 355.9
 root (see also Radiculitis) 729.2
 toxic 357.7
 trigeminal sensory 350.8
 ulnar nerve 354.2
 upper extremity NEC 354.9
 uremic 585.9 [357.4]
 vitamin B$_{12}$ 266.2 [357.4]
 with anemia (pernicious) 281.0 [357.4]
 due to dietary deficiency 281.1 [357.4]
Neurophthisis — see also Disorder, nerve
 diabetic 250.6 ☑ [357.2]
 peripheral 356.9
Neuropraxia — see Injury, nerve
Neuroretinitis 363.05
 syphilitic 094.85
Neurosarcoma (M9540/3) — see Neoplasm, connective tissue, malignant
Neurosclerosis — see Disorder, nerve
Neurosis, neurotic 300.9
 accident 300.16
 anancastic, anankastic 300.3
 anxiety (state) 300.00
 generalized 300.02
 panic type 300.01
 asthenic 300.5
 bladder 306.53
 cardiac (reflex) 306.2
 cardiovascular 306.2
 climacteric, unspecified type 627.2
 colon 306.4
 compensation 300.16
 compulsive, compulsion 300.3
 conversion 300.11
 craft 300.89
 cutaneous 306.3
 depersonalization 300.6
 depressive (reaction) (type) 300.4
 endocrine 306.6
 environmental 300.89
 fatigue 300.5
 functional (see also Disorder, psychosomatic) 306.9
 gastric 306.4
 gastrointestinal 306.4
 genitourinary 306.50
 heart 306.2
 hypochondriacal 300.7
 hysterical 300.10
 conversion type 300.11
 dissociative type 300.15
 impulsive 300.3
 incoordination 306.0
 larynx 306.1
 vocal cord 306.1
 intestine 306.4
 larynx 306.1
 hysterical 300.11
 sensory 306.1
 menopause, unspecified type 627.2
 mixed NEC 300.89
 musculoskeletal 306.0
 obsessional 300.3
 phobia 300.3
 obsessive-compulsive 300.3
 occupational 300.89
 ocular 306.7
 oral 307.0

Neurosis, neurotic — continued
 organ (see also Disorder, psychosomatic) 306.9
 pharynx 306.1
 phobic 300.20
 posttraumatic (acute) (situational) 309.81
 chronic 309.81
 psychasthenic (type) 300.89
 railroad 300.16
 rectum 306.4
 respiratory 306.1
 rumination 306.4
 senile 300.89
 sexual 302.70
 situational 300.89
 specified type NEC 300.89
 state 300.9
 with depersonalization episode 300.6
 stomach 306.4
 vasomotor 306.2
 visceral 306.4
 war 300.16
Neurospongioblastosis diffusa 759.5
Neurosyphilis (arrested) (early) (inactive) (late) (latent) (recurrent) 094.9
 with ataxia (cerebellar) (locomotor) (spastic) (spinal) 094.0
 acute meningitis 094.2
 aneurysm 094.89
 arachnoid (adhesive) 094.2
 arteritis (any artery) 094.89
 asymptomatic 094.3
 congenital 090.40
 dura (mater) 094.89
 general paresis 094.1
 gumma 094.9
 hemorrhagic 094.9
 juvenile (asymptomatic) (meningeal) 090.40
 leptomeninges (aseptic) 094.2
 meningeal 094.2
 meninges (adhesive) 094.2
 meningovascular (diffuse) 094.2
 optic atrophy 094.84
 parenchymatous (degenerative) 094.1
 paresis (see also Paresis, general) 094.1
 paretic (see also Paresis, general) 094.1
 relapse 094.9
 remission in (sustained) 094.9
 serological 094.3
 specified nature or site NEC 094.89
 tabes (dorsalis) 094.0
 juvenile 090.40
 tabetic 094.0
 juvenile 090.40
 taboparesis 094.1
 juvenile 090.40
 thrombosis 094.89
 vascular 094.89
Neurotic — see also Neurosis 300.9
 excoriation 698.4
 psychogenic 306.3
Neurotmesis — see Injury, nerve, by site
Neurotoxemia — see Toxemia
Neuro-occlusion 524.21
Neutropenia, neutropenic (idiopathic) (pernicious) (primary) 288.00 ▲
 chronic 288.09 ▲
 hypoplastic 288.09 ●
 congenital (nontransient) 288.01 ▲
 cyclic 288.02 ●
 drug induced 288.03 ●
 due to infection 288.04 ●
 fever 288.00 ▲
 genetic 288.01 ●
 immune 288.09 ●
 infantile 288.01 ●
 malignant 288.09 ●
 neonatal, transitory (isoimmune) (maternal transfer) 776.7
 periodic 288.02 ●
 splenic 289.53 ●

Neutropenia, neutropenic —
continued
  splenomegaly 289.53 ●
  toxic 288.09 ●
Neutrophilia, hereditary giant 288.2
Nevocarcinoma (M8720/3) — *see*
  Melanoma
Nevus (M8720/0) — *see also* Neoplasm,
  skin, benign

Note — *Except where otherwise indicated, varieties of nevus in the list below that are followed by a morphology code number (M----/0) should be coded by site as for "Neoplasm, skin, benign."*

  acanthotic 702.8
  achromic (M8730/0)
  amelanotic (M8730/0)
  anemic, anemicus 709.09
  angiomatous (M9120/0) (*see also* Hemangioma) 228.00
  araneus 448.1
  avasculosus 709.09
  balloon cell (M8722/0)
  bathing trunk (M8761/1) 238.2
  blue (M8780/0)
    cellular (M8790/0)
    giant (M8790/0)
    Jadassohn's (M8780/0)
    malignant (M8780/3) — *see*
      Melanoma
  capillary (M9131/0) (*see also* Hemangioma) 228.00
  cavernous (M9121/0) (*see also* Hemangioma) 228.00
  cellular (M8720/0)
    blue (M8790/0)
  comedonicus 757.33
  compound (M8760/0)
  conjunctiva (M8720/0) 224.3
  dermal (M8750/0)
    and epidermal (M8760/0)
  epithelioid cell (and spindle cell) (M8770/0)
  flammeus 757.32
    osteohypertrophic 759.89
  hairy (M8720/0)
  halo (M8723/0)
  hemangiomatous (M9120/0) (*see also* Hemangioma) 228.00
  intradermal (M8750/0)
  intraepidermal (M8740/0)
  involuting (M8724/0)
  Jadassohn's (blue) (M8780/0)
  junction, junctional (M8740/0)
    malignant melanoma in (M8740/3) — *see* Melanoma
  juvenile (M8770/0)
  lymphatic (M9170/0) 228.1
  magnocellular (M8726/0)
    specified site — *see* Neoplasm, by site, benign
    unspecified site 224.0
  malignant (M8720/3) — *see* Melanoma
  meaning hemangioma (M9120/0) (*see also* Hemangioma) 228.00
  melanotic (pigmented) (M8720/0)
  multiplex 759.5
  nonneoplastic 448.1
  nonpigmented (M8730/0)
  nonvascular (M8720/0)
  oral mucosa, white sponge 750.26
  osteohypertrophic, flammeus 759.89
  papillaris (M8720/0)
  papillomatosus (M8720/0)
  pigmented (M8720/0)
    giant (M8761/1) (*see also* Neoplasm, skin, uncertain behavior)
    malignant melanoma in (M8761/3) — *see* Melanoma
    systematicus 757.33
  pilosus (M8720/0)
  port wine 757.32
  sanguineous 757.32

Nevus — *see also* Neoplasm, skin, benign — *continued*
  sebaceous (senile) 702.8
  senile 448.1
  spider 448.1
  spindle cell (and epithelioid cell) (M8770/0)
  stellar 448.1
  strawberry 757.32
  syringocystadenomatous papilliferous (M8406/0)
  unius lateris 757.33
  Unna's 757.32
  vascular 757.32
  verrucous 757.33
  white sponge (oral mucosa) 750.26
Newborn (infant) (liveborn)
  affected by maternal abuse of drugs (gestational) (via placenta) (via breast milk) (*see also* Noxious, substances transmitted through placenta or breast milk affecting fetus or newborn) 760.70
  apnea 770.81
    obstructive 770.82
    specified NEC 770.82
  cardiomyopathy 425.4
    congenital 425.3
  convulsion 779.0
  electrolyte imbalance NEC (transitory) 775.5
  gestation
    24 completed weeks 765.22
    25-26 completed weeks 765.23
    27-28 completed weeks 765.24
    29-30 completed weeks 765.25
    31-32 completed weeks 765.26
    33-34 completed weeks 765.27
    35-36 completed weeks 765.28
    37 or more completed weeks 765.29
    less than 24 completed weeks 765.21
    unspecified completed weeks 765.20
  infection 771.89
    candida 771.7
    mastitis 771.5
    specified NEC 771.89
    urinary tract 771.82
  mastitis 771.5
  multiple NEC
    born in hospital (without mention of cesarean delivery or section) V37.00
      with cesarean delivery or section V37.01
    born outside hospital
      hospitalized V37.1
      not hospitalized V37.2
    mates all liveborn
      born in hospital (without mention of cesarean delivery or section) V34.00
        with cesarean delivery or section V34.01
      born outside hospital
        hospitalized V34.1
        not hospitalized V34.2
    mates all stillborn
      born in hospital (without mention of cesarean delivery or section) V35.00
        with cesarean delivery or section V35.01
      born outside hospital
        hospitalized V35.1
        not hospitalized V35.2
    mates liveborn and stillborn
      born in hospital (without mention of cesarean delivery or section) V36.00
        with cesarean delivery or section V36.01
      born outside hospital
        hospitalized V36.1

Newborn — *continued*
  multiple — *continued*
    mates liveborn and stillborn — *continued*
      born outside hospital — *continued*
        not hospitalized V36.2
  omphalitis 771.4
  seizure 779.0
  sepsis 771.81
  single
    born in hospital (without mention of cesarean delivery or section) V30.00
      with cesarean delivery or section V30.01
    born outside hospital
      hospitalized V30.1
      not hospitalized V30.2
  specified condition NEC 779.89
  twin NEC
    born in hospital (without mention of cesarean delivery or section) V33.00
      with cesarean delivery or section V33.01
    born outside hospital
      hospitalized V33.1
      not hospitalized V33.2
    mate liveborn
      born in hospital V31.0 ☑
      born outside hospital
        hospitalized V31.1
        not hospitalized V31.2
    mate stillborn
      born in hospital V32.0 ☑
      born outside hospital
        hospitalized V32.1
        not hospitalized V32.2
  unspecified as to single or multiple birth
    born in hospital (without mention of cesarean delivery or section) V39.00
      with cesarean delivery or section V39.01
    born outside hospital
      hospitalized V39.1
      not hospitalized V39.2
Newcastle's conjunctivitis or disease 077.8
Nezelof's syndrome (pure alymphocytosis) 279.13
Niacin (amide) **deficiency** 265.2
Nicolas-Durand-Favre disease (climatic bubo) 099.1
Nicolas-Favre disease (climatic bubo) 099.1
Nicotinic acid (amide) **deficiency** 265.2
Niemann-Pick disease (lipid histiocytosis) (splenomegaly) 272.7
Night
  blindness (*see also* Blindness, night) 368.60
    congenital 368.61
    vitamin A deficiency 264.5
  cramps 729.82
  sweats 780.8
  terrors, child 307.46
Nightmare 307.47
  REM-sleep type 307.47
Nipple — *see* condition
Nisbet's chancre 099.0
Nishimoto (-Takeuchi) disease 437.5
Nitritoid crisis or reaction — *see* Crisis, nitritoid
Nitrogen retention, extrarenal 788.9
Nitrosohemoglobinemia 289.89
Njovera 104.0
No
  diagnosis 799.9
  disease (found) V71.9
  room at the inn V65.0
Nocardiasis — *see* Nocardiosis
Nocardiosis 039.9
  with pneumonia 039.1

Nocardiosis — *continued*
  lung 039.1
  specified type NEC 039.8
Nocturia 788.43
  psychogenic 306.53
Nocturnal — *see also* condition
  dyspnea (paroxysmal) 786.09
  emissions 608.89
  enuresis 788.36
    psychogenic 307.6
  frequency (micturition) 788.43
    psychogenic 306.53
Nodal rhythm disorder 427.89
Nodding of head 781.0
Node(s) — *see also* Nodule(s)
  Heberden's 715.04
  larynx 478.79
  lymph — *see* condition
  milkers' 051.1
  Osler's 421.0
  rheumatic 729.89
  Schmorl's 722.30
    lumbar, lumbosacral 722.32
    specified region NEC 722.39
    thoracic, thoracolumbar 722.31
  singers' 478.5
  skin NEC 782.2
  tuberculous — *see* Tuberculosis, lymph gland
  vocal cords 478.5
Nodosities, Haygarth's 715.04
Nodule(s), nodular
  actinomycotic (*see also* Actinomycosis) 039.9
  arthritic — *see* Arthritis, nodosa
  cutaneous 782.2
  Haygarth's 715.04
  inflammatory — *see* Inflammation
  juxta-articular 102.7
    syphilitic 095.7
    yaws 102.7
  larynx 478.79
  lung, solitary 518.89
    emphysematous 492.8
  milkers' 051.1
  prostate 600.10
    with
      urinary
        obstruction 600.11 ●
        retention 600.11 ●
  rheumatic 729.89
  rheumatoid — *see* Arthritis, rheumatoid
  scrotum (inflammatory) 608.4
  singers' 478.5
  skin NEC 782.2
  solitary, lung 518.89
    emphysematous 492.8
  subcutaneous 782.2
  thyroid (gland) (nontoxic) (uninodular) 241.0
    with
      hyperthyroidism 242.1 ☑
      thyrotoxicosis 242.1 ☑
    toxic or with hyperthyroidism 242.1 ☑
  vocal cords 478.5
Noma (gangrenous) (hospital) (infective) 528.1
  auricle (*see also* Gangrene) 785.4
  mouth 528.1
  pudendi (*see also* Vulvitis) 616.10
  vulvae (*see also* Vulvitis) 616.10
Nomadism V60.0
Non-adherence
  artificial skin graft 996.55
  decellularized allodermis graft 996.55
Non-autoimmune hemolytic anemia NEC 283.10
Nonclosure — *see also* Imperfect, closure
  ductus
    arteriosus 747.0
    Botalli 747.0
  Eustachian valve 746.89
  foramen
    Botalli 745.5

Neutropenia, neutropenic — Nonclosure

Nonclosure — *see also* Imperfect, closure
— *continued*
foramen — *continued*
ovale 745.5
Noncompliance with medical treat-ment V15.81
Nondescent (congenital) — *see also* Malposition, congenital
cecum 751.4
colon 751.4
testis 752.51
Nondevelopment
brain 742.1
specified part 742.2
heart 746.89
organ or site, congenital NEC — *see* Hypoplasia
Nonengagement
head NEC 652.5 ☑
in labor 660.1 ☑
affecting fetus or newborn 763.1
Nonexanthematous tick fever 066.1
Nonexpansion, lung (newborn) NEC 770.4
Nonfunctioning
cystic duct (*see also* Disease, gallbladder) 575.8
gallbladder (*see also* Disease, gallbladder) 575.8
kidney (*see also* Disease, renal) 593.9
labyrinth 386.58
Nonhealing
stump (surgical) 997.69
wound, surgical 998.83
Nonimplantation of ovum, causing in-fertility 628.3
Noninsufflation, fallopian tube 628.2
Nonne-Milroy-Meige syndrome (chronic hereditary edema) 757.0
Nonovulation 628.0
Nonpatent fallopian tube 628.2
Nonpneumatization, lung NEC 770.4
Nonreflex bladder 596.54
with cauda equina 344.61
Nonretention of food — *see* Vomiting
Nonrotation — *see* Malrotation
Nonsecretion, urine — *see also* Anuria 788.5

Nonsecretion, urine — *see also* Anuria
— *continued*
newborn 753.3
Nonunion
fracture 733.82
organ or site, congenital NEC — *see* Imperfect, closure
symphysis pubis, congenital 755.69
top sacrum, congenital 756.19
Nonviability 765.0 ☑
Nonvisualization, gallbladder 793.3
Nonvitalized tooth 522.9
Non-working side interference 524.56
Normal
delivery — *see* category 650
menses V65.5
state (feared complaint unfounded) V65.5
Normoblastosis 289.89
Normocytic anemia (infectional) 285.9
due to blood loss (chronic) 280.0
acute 285.1
Norrie's disease (congenital) (progressive oculoacousticocerebral degeneration) 743.8
North American blastomycosis 116.0
Norwegian itch 133.0
Nosebleed 784.7
Nose, nasal — *see* condition
Nosomania 298.9
Nosophobia 300.29
Nostalgia 309.89
Notched lip, congenital — *see also* Cleft, lip 749.10
Notching nose, congenital (tip) 748.1
Notch of iris 743.46
Nothnagel's
syndrome 378.52
vasomotor acroparesthesia 443.89
Novy's relapsing fever (American) 087.1
Noxious
foodstuffs, poisoning by
fish 988.0
fungi 988.1
mushrooms 988.1
plants (food) 988.2
shellfish 988.0
specified type NEC 988.8

Noxious — *continued*
foodstuffs, poisoning by — *continued*
toadstool 988.1
substances transmitted through pla-centa or breast milk (affecting fetus or newborn) 760.70
acetretin 760.78
alcohol 760.71
aminopterin 760.78
antiandrogens 760.79
anticonvulsant 760.77
antifungal 760.74
anti-infective agents 760.74
antimetabolic 760.78
atorvastatin 760.78
carbamazepine 760.77
cocaine 760.75
"crack" 760.75
diethylstilbestrol (DES) 760.76
divalproex sodium 760.77
endocrine disrupting chemicals 760.79
estrogens 760.79
etretinate 760.78
fluconazole 760.74
fluvastatin 760.78
hallucinogenic agents NEC 760.73
hormones 760.79
lithium 760.79
lovastatin 760.78
medicinal agents NEC 760.79
methotrexate 760.78
misoprostil 760.79
narcotics 760.72
obstetric anesthetic or analgesic 763.5
phenobarbital 760.77
phenytoin 760.77
pravastatin 760.78
progestins 760.79
retinoic acid 760.78
simvastatin 760.78
solvents 760.79
specified agent NEC 760.79
statins 760.78
suspected, affecting management of pregnancy 655.5 ☑

Noxious — *continued*
substances transmitted through pla-centa or breast milk — *contin-ued*
tetracycline 760.74
thalidomide 760.79
trimethadione 760.77
valproate 760.77
valproic acid 760.77
vitamin A 760.78
Nuchal hitch (arm) 652.8 ☑
Nucleus pulposus — *see* condition
Numbness 782.0
Nuns' knee 727.2
Nursemaid's
elbow 832.0 ☑
shoulder 831.0 ☑
Nutmeg liver 573.8
Nutrition, deficient or insufficient (particular kind of food) 269.9
due to
insufficient food 994.2
lack of
care (child) (infant) 995.52
adult 995.84
food 994.2
Nyctalopia — *see also* Blindness, night 368.60
vitamin A deficiency 264.5
Nycturia 788.43
psychogenic 306.53
Nymphomania 302.89
Nystagmus 379.50
associated with vestibular system disorders 379.54
benign paroxysmal positional 386.11
central positional 386.2
congenital 379.51
deprivation 379.53
dissociated 379.55
latent 379.52
miners' 300.89
positional
benign paroxysmal 386.11
central 386.2
specified NEC 379.56
vestibular 379.54
visual deprivation 379.53

☑ Additional Digit Required — Refer to the Tabular List for Digit Selection   ▽ Subterms under main terms may continue to next column or page

216 — Volume 2   ▶◀ Revised Text   ● New Line   ▲ Revised Code   *2007 ICD-9-CM*

O

Oasthouse urine disease 270.2
Obermeyer's relapsing fever (European) 087.0
Obesity (constitutional) (exogenous) (familial) (nutritional) (simple) 278.00
  adrenal 255.8
  complicating pregnancy, childbirth, ●
    or puerperium 649.1 ☑   ●
  due to hyperalimentation 278.00
  endocrine NEC 259.9
  endogenous 259.9
  Fröhlich's (adiposogenital dystrophy) 253.8
  glandular NEC 259.9
  hypothyroid (see also Hypothyroidism) 244.9
  morbid 278.01
  of pregnancy 649.1 ☑   ▲
  pituitary 253.8
  severe 278.01
  thyroid (see also Hypothyroidism) 244.9
Oblique — see also condition
  lie before labor, affecting fetus or newborn 761.7
Obliquity, pelvis 738.6
Obliteration
  abdominal aorta 446.7
  appendix (lumen) 543.9
  artery 447.1
  ascending aorta 446.7
  bile ducts 576.8
    with calculus, choledocholithiasis, or stones — see Choledocholithiasis
    congenital 751.61
      jaundice from 751.61 [774.5]
  common duct 576.8
    with calculus, choledocholithiasis, or stones — see Choledocholithiasis
    congenital 751.61
  cystic duct 575.8
    with calculus, choledocholithiasis, or stones — see Choledocholithiasis
  disease, arteriolar 447.1
  endometrium 621.8
  eye, anterior chamber 360.34
  fallopian tube 628.2
  lymphatic vessel 457.1
    postmastectomy 457.0
  organ or site, congenital NEC — see Atresia
  placental blood vessels — see Placenta, abnormal
  supra-aortic branches 446.7
  ureter 593.89
  urethra 599.84
  vein 459.9
  vestibule (oral) 525.8
Observation (for) V71.9
  without need for further medical care V71.9
  accident NEC V71.4
    at work V71.3
  criminal assault V71.6
  deleterious agent ingestion V71.89
  disease V71.9
    cardiovascular V71.7
    heart V71.7
    mental V71.09
    specified condition NEC V71.89
  foreign body ingestion V71.89
  growth and development variations V21.8
  injuries (accidental) V71.4
    inflicted NEC V71.6
      during alleged rape or seduction V71.5
  malignant neoplasm, suspected V71.1
  postpartum
    immediately after delivery V24.0
    routine follow-up V24.2

Observation — continued
  pregnancy
    high-risk V23.9
      specified problem NEC V23.89
    normal (without complication) V22.1
      with nonobstetric complication V22.2
    first V22.0
  rape or seduction, alleged V71.5
    injury during V71.5
  suicide attempt, alleged V71.89
  suspected (undiagnosed) (unproven)
    abuse V71.81
    cardiovascular disease V71.7
    child or wife battering victim V71.6
    concussion (cerebral) V71.6
    condition NEC V71.89
      infant — see Observation, suspected, condition, newborn
      newborn V29.9
        cardiovascular disease V29.8
        congenital anomaly V29.8
        genetic V29.3
        infectious V29.0
        ingestion foreign object V29.8
        injury V29.8
        metabolic V29.3
        neoplasm V29.8
        neurological V29.1
        poison, poisoning V29.8
        respiratory V29.2
        specified NEC V29.8
    exposure
      anthrax V71.82
      biologic agent NEC V71.83
      SARS V71.83
    infectious disease not requiring isolation V71.89
    malignant neoplasm V71.1
    mental disorder V71.09
    neglect V71.81
    neoplasm
      benign V71.89
      malignant V71.1
    specified condition NEC V71.89
    tuberculosis V71.2
  tuberculosis, suspected V71.2
Obsession, obsessional 300.3
  ideas and mental images 300.3
  impulses 300.3
  neurosis 300.3
  phobia 300.3
  psychasthenia 300.3
  ruminations 300.3
  state 300.3
  syndrome 300.3
Obsessive-compulsive 300.3
  neurosis 300.3
  personality 301.4
  reaction 300.3
Obstetrical trauma NEC (complicating delivery) 665.9 ☑
  with
    abortion — see Abortion, by type, with damage to pelvic organs
    ectopic pregnancy (see also categories 633.0–633.9) 639.2
    molar pregnancy (see also categories 630–632) 639.2
  affecting fetus or newborn 763.89
  following
    abortion 639.2
    ectopic or molar pregnancy 639.2
Obstipation — see also Constipation 564.00
  psychogenic 306.4
Obstruction, obstructed, obstructive
  airway NEC 519.8
    with
      allergic alveolitis NEC 495.9
      asthma NEC (see also Asthma) 493.9 ☑
      bronchiectasis 494.0

Obstruction, obstructed, obstructive
— continued
  airway — continued
    with — continued
      bronchiectasis — continued
        with acute exacerbation 494.1
      bronchitis (chronic) (see also Bronchitis, with, obstruction) 491.20
      emphysema NEC 492.8
      chronic 496
        with
          allergic alveolitis NEC 495.5
          asthma NEC (see also Asthma) 493.2 ☑
          bronchiectasis 494.0
            with acute exacerbation 494.1
          bronchitis (chronic) (see also Bronchitis, with, obstruction) 491.20
          emphysema NEC 492.8
      due to
        bronchospasm 519.11   ▲
        foreign body 934.9
        inhalation of fumes or vapors 506.9
        laryngospasm 478.75
  alimentary canal (see also Obstruction, intestine) 560.9
  ampulla of Vater 576.2
    with calculus, cholelithiasis, or stones — see Choledocholithiasis
  aortic (heart) (valve) (see also Stenosis, aortic) 424.1
    rheumatic (see also Stenosis, aortic, rheumatic) 395.0
  aortoiliac 444.0
  aqueduct of Sylvius 331.4
    congenital 742.3
      with spina bifida (see also Spina bifida) 741.0 ☑
  Arnold-Chiari (see also Spina bifida) 741.0 ☑
  artery (see also Embolism, artery) 444.9
    basilar (complete) (partial) (see also Occlusion, artery, basilar) 433.0 ☑
    carotid (complete) (partial) (see also Occlusion, artery, carotid) 433.1 ☑
    precerebral — see Occlusion, artery, precerebral NEC
    retinal (central) (see also Occlusion, retina) 362.30
    vertebral (complete) (partial) (see also Occlusion, artery, vertebral) 433.2 ☑
  asthma (chronic) (with obstructive pulmonary disease) 493.2 ☑
  band (intestinal) 560.81
  bile duct or passage (see also Obstruction, biliary) 576.2
    congenital 751.61
      jaundice from 751.61 [774.5]
  biliary (duct) (tract) 576.2
    with calculus 574.51
      with cholecystitis (chronic) 574.41
        acute 574.31
    congenital 751.61
      jaundice from 751.61 [774.5]
    gallbladder 575.2
      with calculus 574.21
        with cholecystitis (chronic) 574.11
          acute 574.01
  bladder neck (acquired) 596.0
    congenital 753.6
  bowel (see also Obstruction, intestine) 560.9
  bronchus 519.19   ▲

Obstruction, obstructed, obstructive
— continued
  canal, ear (see also Stricture, ear canal, acquired) 380.50
  cardia 537.89
  caval veins (inferior) (superior) 459.2
  cecum (see also Obstruction, intestine) 560.9
  circulatory 459.9
  colon (see also Obstruction, intestine) 560.9
    sympathicotonic 560.89
  common duct (see also Obstruction, biliary) 576.2
    congenital 751.61
  coronary (artery) (heart) (see also Arteriosclerosis, coronary)
    acute (see also Infarct, myocardium) 410.9 ☑
      without myocardial infarction 411.81
  cystic duct (see also Obstruction, gallbladder) 575.2
    congenital 751.61
  device, implant, or graft — see Complications, due to (presence of) any device, implant, or graft classified to 996.0–996.5 NEC
  due to foreign body accidentally left in operation wound 998.4
  duodenum 537.3
    congenital 751.1
    due to
      compression NEC 537.3
      cyst 537.3
      intrinsic lesion or disease NEC 537.3
      scarring 537.3
      torsion 537.3
      ulcer 532.91
      volvulus 537.3
  ejaculatory duct 608.89
  endocardium 424.90
    arteriosclerotic 424.99
    specified cause, except rheumatic 424.99
  esophagus 530.3
  eustachian tube (complete) (partial) 381.60
    cartilaginous
      extrinsic 381.63
      intrinsic 381.62
    due to
      cholesteatoma 381.61
      osseous lesion NEC 381.61
      polyp 381.61
    osseous 381.61
  fallopian tube (bilateral) 628.2
  fecal 560.39
    with hernia (see also Hernia, by site, with obstruction)
      gangrenous — see Hernia, by site, with gangrene
  foramen of Monro (congenital) 742.3
    with spina bifida (see also Spina bifida) 741.0 ☑
  foreign body — see Foreign body
  gallbladder 575.2
    with calculus, cholelithiasis, or stones 574.21
      with cholecystitis (chronic) 574.11
        acute 574.01
    congenital 751.69
      jaundice from 751.69 [774.5]
  gastric outlet 537.0
  gastrointestinal (see also Obstruction, intestine) 560.9
  glottis 478.79
  hepatic 573.8
    duct (see also Obstruction, biliary) 576.2
      congenital 751.61
    icterus (see also Obstruction, biliary) 576.8
      congenital 751.61

☑ Additional Digit Required — Refer to the Tabular List for Digit Selection   ▼ Subterms under main terms may continue to next column or page

2007 ICD-9-CM   ▶◀ Revised Text   ● New Line   ▲ Revised Code   **October 2006 · Volume 2 — 217**

Obstruction, obstructed, obstructive
— *continued*
ileocecal coil (*see also* Obstruction, intestine) 560.9
ileum (*see also* Obstruction, intestine) 560.9
iliofemoral (artery) 444.81
internal anastomosis — *see* Complications, mechanical, graft
intestine (mechanical) (neurogenic) (paroxysmal) (postinfectional) (reflex) 560.9
  with
    adhesions (intestinal) (peritoneal) 560.81
    hernia (*see also* Hernia, by site, with obstruction)
      gangrenous — *see* Hernia, by site, with gangrene
  adynamic (*see also* Ileus) 560.1
  by gallstone 560.31
  congenital or infantile (small) 751.1
    large 751.2
  due to
    Ascaris lumbricoides 127.0
    mural thickening 560.89
    procedure 997.4
      involving urinary tract 997.5
  impaction 560.39
  infantile — *see* Obstruction, intestine, congenital
  newborn
    due to
      fecaliths 777.1
      inspissated milk 777.2
      meconium (plug) 777.1
        in mucoviscidosis 277.01
      transitory 777.4
    specified cause NEC 560.89
    transitory, newborn 777.4
  volvulus 560.2
intracardiac ball valve prosthesis 996.02
jaundice (*see also* Obstruction, biliary) 576.8
  congenital 751.61
jejunum (*see also* Obstruction, intestine) 560.9
kidney 593.89
labor 660.9 ☑
  affecting fetus or newborn 763.1
  by
    bony pelvis (conditions classifiable to 653.0–653.9) 660.1 ☑
    deep transverse arrest 660.3 ☑
    impacted shoulder 660.4 ☑
    locked twins 660.5 ☑
    malposition (fetus) (conditions classifiable to 652.0–652.9) 660.0 ☑
      head during labor 660.3 ☑
      persistent occipitoposterior position 660.3 ☑
    soft tissue, pelvic (conditions classifiable to 654.0–654.9) 660.2 ☑
lacrimal
  canaliculi 375.53
    congenital 743.65
    punctum 375.52
    sac 375.54
lacrimonasal duct 375.56
  congenital 743.65
  neonatal 375.55
lacteal, with steatorrhea 579.2
laryngitis (*see also* Laryngitis) 464.01
larynx 478.79
  congenital 748.3
liver 573.8
  cirrhotic (*see also* Cirrhosis, liver) 571.5
lung 518.89
  with
    asthma — *see* Asthma
    bronchitis (chronic) 491.20

Obstruction, obstructed, obstructive
— *continued*
lung — *continued*
  with — *continued*
    emphysema NEC 492.8
  airway, chronic 496
  chronic NEC 496
    with
      asthma (chronic) (obstructive) 493.2 ☑
  disease, chronic 496
    with
      asthma (chronic) (obstructive) 493.2 ☑
  emphysematous 492.8
lymphatic 457.1
meconium
  fetus or newborn 777.1
    in mucoviscidosis 277.01
  newborn due to fecaliths 777.1
mediastinum 519.3
mitral (rheumatic) — *see* Stenosis, mitral
nasal 478.19   ▲
  duct 375.56
    neonatal 375.55
  sinus — *see* Sinusitis
nasolacrimal duct 375.56
  congenital 743.65
  neonatal 375.55
nasopharynx 478.29
nose 478.19   ▲
organ or site, congenital NEC — *see* Atresia
pancreatic duct 577.8
parotid gland 527.8
pelviureteral junction (*see also* Obstruction, ureter) 593.4
pharynx 478.29
portal (circulation) (vein) 452
prostate 600.90
  with
    other lower urinary tract   ●
      symptoms (LUTS)   ●
      600.91   ●
    urinary   ●
      obstruction 600.91   ●
      retention 600.91   ●
  valve (urinary) 596.0
pulmonary
  valve (heart) (*see also* Endocarditis, pulmonary) 424.3
  vein, isolated 747.49
pyemic — *see* Septicemia
pylorus (acquired) 537.0
  congenital 750.5
  infantile 750.5
rectosigmoid (*see also* Obstruction, intestine) 560.9
rectum 569.49
renal 593.89
respiratory 519.8
  chronic 496
retinal (artery) (vein) (central) (*see also* Occlusion, retina) 362.30
salivary duct (any) 527.8
  with calculus 527.5
sigmoid (*see also* Obstruction, intestine) 560.9
sinus (accessory) (nasal) (*see also* Sinusitis) 473.9
Stensen's duct 527.8
stomach 537.89
  acute 536.1
  congenital 750.7
submaxillary gland 527.8
  with calculus 527.5
thoracic duct 457.1
thrombotic — *see* Thrombosis
tooth eruption 520.6
trachea 519.19   ▲
tracheostomy airway 519.09
tricuspid — *see* Endocarditis, tricuspid
upper respiratory, congenital 748.8
ureter (functional) 593.4

Obstruction, obstructed, obstructive
— *continued*
ureter — *continued*
  congenital 753.20
  due to calculus 592.1
  ureteropelvic junction, congenital 753.21
  ureterovesical junction, congenital 753.22
urethra 599.60
  congenital 753.6
urinary (moderate) 599.60
  organ or tract (lower) 599.60
    due to
      benign prostatic hypertrophy (BPH) - see category 600
    specified NEC 599.69
      due to
        benign prostatic hypertrophy (BPH) — see category 600
  prostatic valve 596.0
uropathy 599.60
uterus 621.8
vagina 623.2
valvular — *see* Endocarditis
vascular graft or shunt 996.1
  atherosclerosis — *see* Arteriosclerosis, coronary
  embolism 996.74
  occlusion NEC 996.74
  thrombus 996.74
vein, venous 459.2
  caval (inferior) (superior) 459.2
  thrombotic — *see* Thrombosis
vena cava (inferior) (superior) 459.2
ventricular shunt 996.2
vesical 596.0
vesicourethral orifice 596.0
vessel NEC 459.9
Obturator — *see* condition
Occlusal
  plane deviation 524.76
  wear, teeth 521.10
Occlusion
anus 569.49
  congenital 751.2
  infantile 751.2
aortoiliac (chronic) 444.0
aqueduct of Sylvius 331.4
  congenital 742.3
    with spina bifida (*see also* Spina bifida) 741.0 ☑
arteries of extremities, lower 444.22
  without thrombus or embolus (*see also* Arteriosclerosis, extremities) 440.20
  due to stricture or stenosis 447.1
  upper 444.21
    without thrombus or embolus (*see also* Arteriosclerosis, extremities) 440.20
    due to stricture or stenosis 447.1
artery NEC (*see also* Embolism, artery) 444.9
  auditory, internal 433.8 ☑
  basilar 433.0 ☑
    with other precerebral artery 433.3 ☑
    bilateral 433.3 ☑
  brain or cerebral (*see also* Infarct, brain) 434.9 ☑
  carotid 433.1 ☑
    with other precerebral artery 433.3 ☑
    bilateral 433.3 ☑
  cerebellar (anterior inferior) (posterior inferior) (superior) 433.8 ☑
  cerebral (*see also* Infarct, brain) 434.9 ☑
  choroidal (anterior) 433.8 ☑
  communicating posterior 433.8 ☑

Occlusion — *continued*
artery (*see also* Embolism, artery) — *continued*
  coronary (thrombotic) (*see also* Infarct, myocardium) 410.9 ☑
    acute 410.9 ☑
      without myocardial infarction 411.81
    healed or old 412
  hypophyseal 433.8 ☑
  iliac (artery) 444.81
  mesenteric (embolic) (thrombotic) (with gangrene) 557.0
  pontine 433.8 ☑
  precerebral NEC 433.9 ☑
    late effect — *see* Late effect(s) (of) cerebrovascular disease
    multiple or bilateral 433.3 ☑
    puerperal, postpartum, childbirth 674.0 ☑
    specified NEC 433.8 ☑
  renal 593.81
  retinal — *see* Occlusion, retina, artery
  spinal 433.8 ☑
  vertebral 433.2 ☑
    with other precerebral artery 433.3 ☑
    bilateral 433.3 ☑
basilar (artery) — *see* Occlusion, artery, basilar
bile duct (any) (*see also* Obstruction, biliary) 576.2
bowel (*see also* Obstruction, intestine) 560.9
brain (artery) (vascular) (*see also* Infarct, brain) 434.9 ☑
breast (duct) 611.8
carotid (artery) (common) (internal) — *see* Occlusion, artery, carotid
cerebellar (anterior inferior) (artery) (posterior inferior) (superior) 433.8 ☑
cerebral (artery) (*see also* Infarct, brain) 434.9 ☑
cerebrovascular (*see also* Infarct, brain) 434.9 ☑
  diffuse 437.0
cervical canal (*see also* Stricture, cervix) 622.4
  by falciparum malaria 084.0
cervix (uteri) (*see also* Stricture, cervix) 622.4
choanal 748.0
choroidal (artery) 433.8 ☑
colon (*see also* Obstruction, intestine) 560.9
communicating posterior artery 433.8 ☑
coronary (artery) (thrombotic) (*see also* Infarct, myocardium) 410.9 ☑
  without myocardial infarction 411.81
  acute 410.9 ☑
    without myocardial infarction 411.81
  healed or old 412
cystic duct (*see also* Obstruction, gallbladder) 575.2
  congenital 751.69
disto
  division I 524.22
  division II 524.22
embolic — *see* Embolism
fallopian tube 628.2
  congenital 752.19
gallbladder (*see also* Obstruction, gallbladder) 575.2
  congenital 751.69
    jaundice from 751.69 [774.5]
gingiva, traumatic 523.8
hymen 623.3
  congenital 752.42
hypophyseal (artery) 433.8 ☑
iliac artery 444.81

☑ Additional Digit Required — Refer to the Tabular List for Digit Selection   ▽ Subterms under main terms may continue to next column or page

218 — Volume 2 • October 2006   ▶◀ Revised Text   ● New Line   ▲ Revised Code   **2007 ICD-9-CM**

Occlusion — *continued*
  intestine (*see also* Obstruction, intestine) 560.9
  kidney 593.89
  lacrimal apparatus — *see* Stenosis, lacrimal
  lung 518.89
  lymph or lymphatic channel 457.1
  mammary duct 611.8
  mesenteric artery (embolic) (thrombotic) (with gangrene) 557.0
  nose 478.1 ☑
    congenital 748.0
  organ or site, congenital NEC — *see* Atresia
  oviduct 628.2
    congenital 752.19
  periodontal, traumatic 523.8
  peripheral arteries (lower extremity) 444.22
    without thrombus or embolus (*see also* Arteriosclerosis, extremities) 440.20
    due to stricture or stenosis 447.1
    upper extremity 444.21
      without thrombus or embolus (*see also* Arteriosclerosis, extremities) 440.20
      due to stricture or stenosis 447.1
  pontine (artery) 433.8 ☑
  posterior lingual, of mandibular teeth 524.29
  precerebral artery — *see* Occlusion, artery, precerebral NEC
  puncta lacrimalia 375.52
  pupil 364.74
  pylorus (*see also* Stricture, pylorus) 537.0
  renal artery 593.81
  retina, retinal (vascular) 362.30
    artery, arterial 362.30
      branch 362.32
      central (total) 362.31
      partial 362.33
      transient 362.34
      tributary 362.32
    vein 362.30
      branch 362.36
      central (total) 362.35
      incipient 362.37
      partial 362.37
      tributary 362.36
  spinal artery 433.8 ☑
  stent
    coronary 996.72
  teeth (mandibular) (posterior lingual) 524.29
  thoracic duct 457.1
  tubal 628.2
  ureter (complete) (partial) 593.4
    congenital 753.29
  urethra (*see also* Stricture, urethra) 598.9
    congenital 753.6
  uterus 621.8
  vagina 623.2
  vascular NEC 459.9
  vein — *see* Thrombosis
  vena cava (inferior) (superior) 453.2
  ventricle (brain) NEC 331.4
  vertebral (artery) — *see* Occlusion, artery, vertebral
  vessel (blood) NEC 459.9
  vulva 624.8
Occlusio pupillae 364.74
Occupational
  problems NEC V62.2
  therapy V57.21
Ochlophobia 300.29
Ochronosis (alkaptonuric) (congenital) (endogenous) 270.2
  with chloasma of eyelid 270.2
Ocular muscle — *see also* condition
  myopathy 359.1
  torticollis 781.93

Oculoauriculovertebral dysplasia 756.0
Oculogyric
  crisis or disturbance 378.87
    psychogenic 306.7
Oculomotor syndrome 378.81
Oddi's sphincter spasm 576.5
Odelberg's disease (juvenile osteochondrosis) 732.1
Odontalgia 525.9
Odontoameloblastoma (M9311/0) 213.1
  upper jaw (bone) 213.0
Odontoclasia 521.05
Odontoclasis 873.63
  complicated 873.73
Odontodysplasia, regional 520.4
Odontogenesis imperfecta 520.5
Odontoma (M9280/0) 213.1
  ameloblastic (M9311/0) 213.1
    upper jaw (bone) 213.0
  calcified (M9280/0) 213.1
    upper jaw (bone) 213.0
  complex (M9282/0) 213.1
    upper jaw (bone) 213.0
  compound (M9281/0) 213.1
    upper jaw (bone) 213.0
  fibroameloblastic (M9290/0) 213.1
    upper jaw (bone) 213.0
  follicular 526.0
    upper jaw (bone) 213.0
Odontomyelitis (closed) (open) 522.0
Odontonecrosis 521.09
Odontorrhagia 525.8
Odontosarcoma, ameloblastic (M9290/3) 170.1
  upper jaw (bone) 170.0
Odynophagia 787.2
Oesophagostomiasis 127.7
Oesophagostomum infestation 127.7
Oestriasis 134.0
Ogilvie's syndrome (sympathicotonic colon obstruction) 560.89
Oguchi's disease (retina) 368.61
Ohara's disease — *see also* Tularemia 021.9
Oidiomycosis — *see also* Candidiasis 112.9
Oidiomycotic meningitis 112.83
Oidium albicans infection — *see also* Candidiasis 112.9
Old age 797
  dementia (of) 290.0
Olfactory — *see* condition
Oligemia 285.9
Oligergasia — *see also* Retardation, mental 319
Oligoamnios 658.0 ☑
  affecting fetus or newborn 761.2
Oligoastrocytoma, mixed (M9382/3)
  specified site — *see* Neoplasm, by site, malignant
  unspecified site 191.9
Oligocythemia 285.9
Oligodendroblastoma (M9460/3)
  specified site — *see* Neoplasm, by site, malignant
  unspecified site 191.9
Oligodendroglioma (M9450/3)
  anaplastic type (M9451/3)
    specified site — *see* Neoplasm, by site, malignant
    unspecified site 191.9
  specified site — *see* Neoplasm, by site, malignant
  unspecified site 191.9
Oligodendroma — *see* Oligodendroglioma
Oligodontia — *see also* Anodontia 520.0
Oligoencephalon 742.1
Oligohydramnios 658.0 ☑
  affecting fetus or newborn 761.2
  due to premature rupture of membranes 658.1 ☑
    affecting fetus or newborn 761.2
Oligohydrosis 705.0
Oligomenorrhea 626.1

Oligophrenia — *see also* Retardation, mental 319
  phenylpyruvic 270.1
Oligospermia 606.1
Oligotrichia 704.09
  congenita 757.4
Oliguria 788.5
  with
    abortion — *see* Abortion, by type, with renal failure
    ectopic pregnancy (*see also* categories 633.0–633.9) 639.3
    molar pregnancy (*see also* categories 630–632) 639.3
  complicating
    abortion 639.3
    ectopic or molar pregnancy 639.3
    pregnancy 646.2 ☑
      with hypertension — *see* Toxemia, of pregnancy
  due to a procedure 997.5
  following labor and delivery 669.3 ☑
  heart or cardiac — *see* Failure, heart
  puerperal, postpartum 669.3 ☑
  specified due to a procedure 997.5
Ollier's disease (chondrodysplasia) 756.4
Omentitis — *see also* Peritonitis 567.9
Omentocele — *see also* Hernia, omental 553.8
Omentum, omental — *see* condition
Omphalitis (congenital) (newborn) 771.4
  not of newborn 686.9
  tetanus 771.3
Omphalocele 756.79
Omphalomesenteric duct, persistent 751.0
Omphalorrhagia, newborn 772.3
Omsk hemorrhagic fever 065.1
Onanism 307.9
Onchocerciasis 125.3
  eye 125.3 [360.13]
Onchocercosis 125.3
Oncocytoma (M8290/0) — *see* Neoplasm, by site, benign
Ondine's curse 348.8
Oneirophrenia — *see also* Schizophrenia 295.4 ☑
Onychauxis 703.8
  congenital 757.5
Onychia (with lymphangitis) 681.9
  dermatophytic 110.1
  finger 681.02
  toe 681.11
Onychitis (with lymphangitis) 681.9
  finger 681.02
  toe 681.11
Onychocryptosis 703.0
Onychodystrophy 703.8
  congenital 757.5
Onychogryphosis 703.8
Onychogryposis 703.8
Onycholysis 703.8
Onychomadesis 703.8
Onychomalacia 703.8
Onychomycosis 110.1
  finger 110.1
  toe 110.1
Onycho-osteodysplasia 756.89
Onychophagy 307.9
Onychoptosis 703.8
Onychorrhexis 703.8
  congenital 757.5
Onychoschizia 703.8
Onychotrophia — *see also* Atrophy, nail 703.8
O'nyong-nyong fever 066.3
Onyxis (finger) (toe) 703.0
Onyxitis (with lymphangitis) 681.9
  finger 681.02
  toe 681.11
Oocyte (egg) (ovum)
  donor V59.70
    over age 35 V59.73
      anonymous recipient V59.73
      designated recipient V59.74
    under age 35 V59.71

Oocyte — *continued*
  donor — *continued*
    under age 35 — *continued*
      anonymous recipient V59.71
      designated recipient V59.72
Oophoritis (cystic) (infectional) (interstitial) — *see also* Salpingo-oophoritis 614.2
  complicating pregnancy 646.6 ☑
  fetal (acute) 752.0
  gonococcal (acute) 098.19
    chronic or duration of 2 months or over 098.39
  tuberculous (*see also* Tuberculosis) 016.6 ☑
Opacity, opacities
  cornea 371.00
    central 371.03
    congenital 743.43
      interfering with vision 743.42
    degenerative (*see also* Degeneration, cornea) 371.40
    hereditary (*see also* Dystrophy, cornea) 371.50
    inflammatory (*see also* Keratitis) 370.9
    late effect of trachoma (healed) 139.1
    minor 371.01
    peripheral 371.02
  enamel (fluoride) (nonfluoride) (teeth) 520.3
  lens (*see also* Cataract) 366.9
  snowball 379.22
  vitreous (humor) 379.24
    congenital 743.51
Opalescent dentin (hereditary) 520.5
Open, opening
  abnormal, organ or site, congenital — *see* Imperfect, closure
  angle with
    borderline intraocular pressure 365.01
    cupping of discs 365.01
  bite (anterior) (posterior) 524.29
  false — *see* Imperfect, closure
  margin on tooth restoration 525.61 ●
  restoration margins 525.61   ●
  wound — *see* Wound, open, by site
Operation
  causing mutilation of fetus 763.89
  destructive, on live fetus, to facilitate birth 763.89
  for delivery, fetus or newborn 763.89
  maternal, unrelated to current delivery, affecting fetus or newborn 760.6
Operational fatigue 300.89
Operative — *see* condition
Operculitis (chronic) 523.40   ▲
  acute 523.30   ▲
Operculum, retina 361.32
  with detachment 361.01
Ophiasis 704.01
Ophthalmia — *see also* Conjunctivitis 372.30
  actinic rays 370.24
  allergic (acute) 372.05
    chronic 372.14
  blennorrhagic (neonatorum) 098.40
  catarrhal 372.03
  diphtheritic 032.81
  Egyptian 076.1
  electric, electrica 370.24
  gonococcal (neonatorum) 098.40
  metastatic 360.11
  migraine 346.8 ☑
  neonatorum, newborn 771.6
    gonococcal 098.40
  nodosa 360.14
  phlyctenular 370.31
    with ulcer (*see also* Ulcer, cornea) 370.00
  sympathetic 360.11
Ophthalmitis — *see* Ophthalmia
Ophthalmocele (congenital) 743.66

☑ Additional Digit Required — Refer to the Tabular List for Digit Selection   ▽ Subterms under main terms may continue to next column or page

2007 ICD-9-CM   ▶◀ Revised Text   ● New Line   ▲ Revised Code   **October 2006 · Volume 2 — 219**

Ophthalmoneuromyelitis 341.0
Ophthalmopathy, infiltrative with thyrotoxicosis 242.0 ☑
Ophthalmoplegia — *see also* Strabismus 378.9
anterior internuclear 378.86
ataxia-areflexia syndrome 357.0
bilateral 378.9
diabetic 250.5 ☑ *[378.86]*
exophthalmic 242.0 ☑ *[376.22]*
external 378.55
progressive 378.72
total 378.56
internal (complete) (total) 367.52
internuclear 378.86
migraine 346.8 ☑
painful 378.55
Parinaud's 378.81
progressive external 378.72
supranuclear, progressive 333.0
total (external) 378.56
internal 367.52
unilateral 378.9
Opisthognathism 524.00
Opisthorchiasis (felineus) (tenuicollis) (viverrini) 121.0
Opisthotonos, opisthotonus 781.0
Opitz's disease (congestive splenomegaly) 289.51
Opiumism — *see also* Dependence 304.0 ☑
Oppenheim's disease 358.8
Oppenheim-Urbach disease or syndrome (necrobiosis lipoidica diabeticorum) 250.8 ☑ *[709.3]*
Opsoclonia 379.59
Optic nerve — *see* condition
Orbit — *see* condition
Orchioblastoma (M9071/3) 186.9
Orchitis (nonspecific) (septic) 604.90
with abscess 604.0
blennorrhagic (acute) 098.13
chronic or duration of 2 months or over 098.33
diphtheritic 032.89 *[604.91]*
filarial 125.9 *[604.91]*
gangrenous 604.99
gonococcal (acute) 098.13
chronic or duration of 2 months or over 098.33
mumps 072.0
parotidea 072.0
suppurative 604.99
syphilitic 095.8 *[604.91]*
tuberculous (*see also* Tuberculosis) 016.5 ☑ *[608.81]*
Orf 051.2
Organic — *see also* condition
heart — *see* Disease, heart
insufficiency 799.89
Oriental
bilharziasis 120.2
schistosomiasis 120.2
sore 085.1
Orientation
ego-dystonic sexual 302.0
Orifice — *see* condition
Origin, both great vessels from right ventricle 745.11
Ormond's disease or syndrome 593.4
Ornithosis 073.9
with
complication 073.8
specified NEC 073.7
pneumonia 073.0
pneumonitis (lobular) 073.0
Orodigitofacial dysostosis 759.89
Oropouche fever 066.3
Orotaciduria, oroticaciduria (congenital) (hereditary) (pyrimidine deficiency) 281.4
Oroya fever 088.0
Orthodontics V58.5
adjustment V53.4
aftercare V58.5
fitting V53.4

Orthopnea 786.02
Orthoptic training V57.4
Osgood-Schlatter
disease 732.4
osteochondrosis 732.4
Osler's
disease (M9950/1) (polycythemia vera) 238.4
nodes 421.0
Osler-Rendu disease (familial hemorrhagic telangiectasia) 448.0
Osler-Vaquez disease (M9950/1) (polycythemia vera) 238.4
Osler-Weber-Rendu syndrome (familial hemorrhagic telangiectasia) 448.0
Osmidrosis 705.89
Osseous — *see* condition
Ossification
artery — *see* Arteriosclerosis
auricle (ear) 380.39
bronchus 519.19 ▲
cardiac (*see also* Degeneration, myocardial) 429.1
cartilage (senile) 733.99
coronary (artery) — *see* Arteriosclerosis, coronary
diaphragm 728.10
ear 380.39
middle (*see also* Otosclerosis) 387.9
falx cerebri 349.2
fascia 728.10
fontanel
defective or delayed 756.0
premature 756.0
heart (*see also* Degeneration, myocardial) 429.1
valve — *see* Endocarditis
larynx 478.79
ligament
posterior longitudinal 724.8
cervical 723.7
meninges (cerebral) 349.2
spinal 336.8
multiple, eccentric centers 733.99
muscle 728.10
heterotopic, postoperative 728.13
myocardium, myocardial (*see also* Degeneration, myocardial) 429.1
penis 607.81
periarticular 728.89
sclera 379.16
tendon 727.82
trachea 519.19 ▲
tympanic membrane (*see also* Tympanosclerosis) 385.00
vitreous (humor) 360.44
Osteitis (*see also* Osteomyelitis 730.2 ☑
acute 730.0 ☑
alveolar 526.5
chronic 730.1 ☑
condensans (ilii) 733.5
deformans (Paget's) 731.0
due to or associated with malignant neoplasm (*see also* Neoplasm, bone, malignant) 170.9 *[731.1]*
due to yaws 102.6
fibrosa NEC 733.29
cystica (generalisata) 252.01
disseminata 756.59
osteoplastica 252.01
fragilitans 756.51
Garré's (sclerosing) 730.1 ☑
infectious (acute) (subacute) 730.0 ☑
chronic or old 730.1 ☑
jaw (acute) (chronic) (lower) (neonatal) (suppurative) (upper) 526.4
parathyroid 252.01
petrous bone (*see also* Petrositis) 383.20
pubis 733.5
sclerotic, nonsuppurative 730.1 ☑
syphilitic 095.5
tuberculosa
cystica (of Jüngling) 135

Osteitis — *see also* Osteomyelitis — *continued*
tuberculosa — *continued*
multiplex cystoides 135
Osteoarthritica spondylitis (spine) — *see also* Spondylosis 721.90
Osteoarthritis — *see also* Osteoarthrosis 715.9 ☑
distal interphalangeal 715.9 ☑
hyperplastic 731.2
interspinalis (*see also* Spondylosis) 721.90
spine, spinal NEC (*see also* Spondylosis) 721.90
Osteoarthropathy — *see also* Osteoarthrosis 715.9 ☑
chronic idiopathic hypertrophic 757.39
familial idiopathic 757.39
hypertrophic pulmonary 731.2
secondary 731.2
idiopathic hypertrophic 757.39
primary hypertrophic 731.2
pulmonary hypertrophic 731.2
secondary hypertrophic 731.2
Osteoarthrosis (degenerative) (hypertrophic) (rheumatoid) 715.9 ☑

> *Note* — *Use the following fifth-digit subclassification with category 715:*
>
> 0 *site unspecified*
>
> 1 *shoulder region*
>
> 2 *upper arm*
>
> 3 *forearm*
>
> 4 *hand*
>
> 5 *pelvic region and thigh*
>
> 6 *lower leg*
>
> 7 *ankle and foot*
>
> 8 *other specified sites except spine*
>
> 9 *multiple sites*

Deformans alkaptonurica 270.2
generalized 715.09
juvenilis (Köhler's) 732.5
localized 715.3 ☑
idiopathic 715.1 ☑
primary 715.1 ☑
secondary 715.2 ☑
multiple sites, not specified as generalized 715.89
polyarticular 715.09
spine (*see also* Spondylosis) 721.90
temporomandibular joint 524.69
Osteoblastoma (M9200/0) — *see* Neoplasm, bone, benign
Osteochondritis — *see also* Osteochondrosis 732.9
dissecans 732.7
hip 732.7
ischiopubica 732.1
multiple 756.59
syphilitic (congenital) 090.0
Osteochondrodermodysplasia 756.59
Osteochondrodystrophy 277.5
deformans 277.5
familial 277.5
fetalis 756.4
Osteochondrolysis 732.7
Osteochondroma (M9210/0) — *see also* Neoplasm, bone, benign
multiple, congenital 756.4
Osteochondromatosis (M9210/1) 238.0
synovial 727.82
Osteochondromyxosarcoma (M9180/3) — *see* Neoplasm, bone, malignant
Osteochondropathy NEC 732.9
Osteochondrosarcoma (M9180/3) — *see* Neoplasm, bone, malignant
Osteochondrosis 732.9
acetabulum 732.1
adult spine 732.8
astragalus 732.5
Blount's 732.4

Osteochondrosis — *continued*
Buchanan's (juvenile osteochondrosis of iliac crest) 732.1
Buchman's (juvenile osteochondrosis) 732.1
Burns' 732.3
calcaneus 732.5
capitular epiphysis (femur) 732.1
carpal
lunate (wrist) 732.3
scaphoid 732.3
coxae juvenilis 732.1
deformans juvenilis (coxae) (hip) 732.1
Scheuermann's 732.0
spine 732.0
tibia 732.4
vertebra 732.0
Diaz's (astragalus) 732.5
dissecans (knee) (shoulder) 732.7
femoral capital epiphysis 732.1
femur (head) (juvenile) 732.1
foot (juvenile) 732.5
Freiberg's (disease) (second metatarsal) 732.5
Haas' 732.3
Haglund's (os tibiale externum) 732.5
hand (juvenile) 732.3
head of
femur 732.1
humerus (juvenile) 732.3
hip (juvenile) 732.1
humerus (juvenile) 732.3
iliac crest (juvenile) 732.1
ilium (juvenile) 732.1
ischiopubic synchondrosis 732.1
Iselin's (osteochondrosis fifth metatarsal) 732.5
juvenile, juvenilis 732.6
arm 732.3
capital femoral epiphysis 732.1
capitellum humeri 732.3
capitular epiphysis 732.1
carpal scaphoid 732.3
clavicle, sternal epiphysis 732.6
coxae 732.1
deformans 732.1
foot 732.5
hand 732.3
hip and pelvis 732.1
lower extremity, except foot 732.4
lunate, wrist 732.3
medial cuneiform bone 732.5
metatarsal (head) 732.5
metatarsophalangeal 732.5
navicular, ankle 732.5
patella 732.4
primary patellar center (of Köhler) 732.4
specified site NEC 732.6
spine 732.0
tarsal scaphoid 732.5
tibia (epiphysis) (tuberosity) 732.4
upper extremity 732.3
vertebra (body) (Calvé) 732.0
epiphyseal plates (of Scheuermann) 732.0
Kienböck's (disease) 732.3
Köhler's (disease) (navicular, ankle) 732.5
patellar 732.4
tarsal navicular 732.5
Legg-Calvé-Perthes (disease) 732.1
lower extremity (juvenile) 732.4
lunate bone 732.3
Mauclaire's 732.3
metacarpal heads (of Mauclaire) 732.3
metatarsal (fifth) (head) (second) 732.5
navicular, ankle 732.5
os calcis 732.5
Osgood-Schlatter 732.4
os tibiale externum 732.5
Panner's 732.3
patella (juvenile) 732.4
patellar center
primary (of Köhler) 732.4

Osteochondrosis — *continued*
  patellar center — *continued*
    secondary (of Sinding-Larsen) 732.4
  pelvis (juvenile) 732.1
  Pierson's 732.1
  radial head (juvenile) 732.3
  Scheuermann's 732.0
  Sever's (calcaneum) 732.5
  Sinding-Larsen (secondary patellar center) 732.4
  spine (juvenile) 732.0
    adult 732.8
  symphysis pubis (of Pierson) (juvenile) 732.1
  syphilitic (congenital) 090.0
  tarsal (navicular) (scaphoid) 732.5
  tibia (proximal) (tubercle) 732.4
  tuberculous — *see* Tuberculosis, bone
  ulna 732.3
  upper extremity (juvenile) 732.3
  van Neck's (juvenile osteochondrosis) 732.1
  vertebral (juvenile) 732.0
    adult 732.8
Osteoclastoma (M9250/1) 238.0
  malignant (M9250/3) — *see* Neoplasm, bone, malignant
Osteocopic pain 733.90
Osteodynia 733.90
Osteodystrophy
  azotemic 588.0
  chronica deformans hypertrophica 731.0
  congenital 756.50
    specified type NEC 756.59
  deformans 731.0
  fibrosa localisata 731.0
  parathyroid 252.01
  renal 588.0
Osteofibroma (M9262/0) — *see* Neoplasm, bone, benign
Osteofibrosarcoma (M9182/3) — *see* Neoplasm, bone, malignant
Osteogenesis imperfecta 756.51
Osteogenic — *see* condition
Osteoma (M9180/0) — *see also* Neoplasm, bone, benign
  osteoid (M9191/0) (*see also* Neoplasm, bone, benign)
  giant (M9200/0) — *see* Neoplasm, bone, benign
Osteomalacia 268.2
  chronica deformans hypertrophica 731.0
  due to vitamin D deficiency 268.2
  infantile (*see also* Rickets) 268.0
  juvenile (*see also* Rickets) 268.0
  pelvis 268.2
  vitamin D-resistant 275.3
Osteomalacic bone 268.2
Osteomalacosis 268.2
Osteomyelitis (general) (infective) (localized) (neonatal) (purulent) (pyogenic) (septic) (staphylococcal) (streptococcal) (suppurative) (with periostitis) 730.2 ✓

Note — Use the following fifth-digit subclassification with category 730:

0	site unspecified
1	shoulder region
2	upper arm
3	forearm
4	hand
5	pelvic region and thigh
6	lower leg
7	ankle and foot
8	other specified sites
9	multiple sites

  acute or subacute 730.0 ✓
  chronic or old 730.1 ✓

Osteomyelitis — *continued*
  due to or associated with
    diabetes mellitus 250.8 ✓ *[731.8]* ✓
    tuberculosis (*see also* Tuberculosis, bone) 015.9 ✓ *[730.8]* ✓
      limb bones 015.5 ✓ *[730.8]* ✓
      specified bones NEC 015.7 ✓ *[730.8]* ✓
      spine 015.0 ✓ *[730.8]* ✓
    typhoid 002.0 *[730.8]* ✓
  Garré's 730.1 ✓
  jaw (acute) (chronic) (lower) (neonatal) (suppurative) (upper) 526.4
  nonsuppurating 730.1 ✓
  orbital 376.03
  petrous bone (*see also* Petrositis) 383.20
  Salmonella 003.24
  sclerosing, nonsuppurative 730.1 ✓
  sicca 730.1 ✓
  syphilitic 095.5
    congenital 090.0 *[730.8]* ✓
  tuberculous — *see* Tuberculosis, bone
  typhoid 002.0 *[730.8]* ✓
Osteomyelofibrosis 289.89
Osteomyelosclerosis 289.89
Osteonecrosis 733.40
  meaning osteomyelitis 730.1 ✓
Osteo-onycho-arthro dysplasia 756.89
Osteo-onychodysplasia, hereditary 756.89
Osteopathia
  condensans disseminata 756.53
  hyperostotica multiplex infantilis 756.59
  hypertrophica toxica 731.2
  striata 756.4
Osteopathy resulting from poliomyelitis — *see also* Poliomyelitis 045.9 ✓ *[730.7]* ✓
  familial dysplastic 731.2
Osteopecilia 756.53
Osteopenia 733.90
Osteoperiostitis — *see also* Osteomyelitis 730.2 ✓
  ossificans toxica 731.2
  toxica ossificans 731.2
Osteopetrosis (familial) 756.52
Osteophyte — *see* Exostosis
Osteophytosis — *see* Exostosis
Osteopoikilosis 756.53
Osteoporosis (generalized) 733.00
  circumscripta 731.0
  disuse 733.03
  drug-induced 733.09
  idiopathic 733.02
  postmenopausal 733.01
  posttraumatic 733.7
  screening V82.81
  senile 733.01
  specified type NEC 733.09
Osteoporosis-osteomalacia syndrome 268.2
Osteopsathyrosis 756.51
Osteoradionecrosis, jaw 526.89
Osteosarcoma (M9180/3) — *see also* Neoplasm, bone, malignant
  chondroblastic (M9181/3) — *see* Neoplasm, bone, malignant
  fibroblastic (M9182/3) — *see* Neoplasm, bone, malignant
  in Paget's disease of bone (M9184/3) — *see* Neoplasm, bone, malignant
  juxtacortical (M9190/3) — *see* Neoplasm, bone, malignant
  parosteal (M9190/3) — *see* Neoplasm, bone, malignant
  telangiectatic (M9183/3) — *see* Neoplasm, bone, malignant
Osteosclerosis 756.52
  fragilis (generalisata) 756.52
Osteosclerotic anemia 289.89
Osteosis
  acromegaloid 757.39
  cutis 709.3

Osteosis — *continued*
  parathyroid 252.01
  renal fibrocystic 588.0
Österreicher-Turner syndrome 756.89
Ostium
  atrioventriculare commune 745.69
  primum (arteriosum) (defect) (persistent) 745.61
  secundum (arteriosum) (defect) (patent) (persistent) 745.5
Ostrum-Furst syndrome 756.59
Os, uterus — *see* condition
Otalgia 388.70
  otogenic 388.71
  referred 388.72
Othematoma 380.31
Otitic hydrocephalus 348.2
Otitis 382.9
  with effusion 381.4
    purulent 382.4
    secretory 381.4
    serous 381.4
    suppurative 382.4
  acute 382.9
  adhesive (*see also* Adhesions, middle ear) 385.10
  chronic 382.9
    with effusion 381.3
    mucoid, mucous (simple) 381.20
    purulent 382.3
    secretory 381.3
    serous 381.10
    suppurative 382.3
  diffuse parasitic 136.8
  externa (acute) (diffuse) (hemorrhagica) 380.10
    actinic 380.22
    candidal 112.82
    chemical 380.22
    chronic 380.23
      mycotic — *see* Otitis, externa, mycotic
      specified type NEC 380.23
    circumscribed 380.10
    contact 380.22
    due to
      erysipelas 035 *[380.13]*
      impetigo 684 *[380.13]*
      seborrheic dermatitis 690.10 *[380.13]*
    eczematoid 380.22
    furuncular 680.0 *[380.13]*
    infective 380.10
      chronic 380.16
    malignant 380.14
    mycotic (chronic) 380.15
      due to
        aspergillosis 117.3 *[380.15]*
        moniliasis 112.82
        otomycosis 111.8 *[380.15]*
    reactive 380.22
    specified type NEC 380.22
    tropical 111.8 *[380.15]*
  insidiosa (*see also* Otosclerosis) 387.9
  interna (*see also* Labyrinthitis) 386.30
  media (hemorrhagic) (staphylococcal) (streptococcal) 382.9
    acute 382.9
      with effusion 381.00
      allergic 381.04
        mucoid 381.05
        sanguineous 381.06
        serous 381.04
      catarrhal 381.00
      exudative 381.00
      mucoid 381.02
        allergic 381.05
      necrotizing 382.00
        with spontaneous rupture of ear drum 382.01
      in
        influenza 487.8 *[382.02]*
        measles 055.2
        scarlet fever 034.1 *[382.02]*
      nonsuppurative 381.00

Otitis — *continued*
  media — *continued*
    acute — *continued*
      purulent 382.00
        with spontaneous rupture of ear drum 382.01
      sanguineous 381.03
        allergic 381.06
      secretory 381.01
      seromucinous 381.02
      serous 381.01
        allergic 381.04
      suppurative 382.00
        with spontaneous rupture of ear drum 382.01
        due to
          influenza 487.8 *[382.02]*
          scarlet fever 034.1 *[382.02]*
      transudative 381.00
    adhesive (*see also* Adhesions, middle ear) 385.10
    allergic 381.4
      acute 381.04
        mucoid 381.05
        sanguineous 381.06
        serous 381.04
      chronic 381.3
    catarrhal 381.4
      acute 381.00
      chronic (simple) 381.10
    chronic 382.9
      with effusion 381.3
      adhesive (*see also* Adhesions, middle ear) 385.10
      allergic 381.3
      atticoantral, suppurative (with posterior or superior marginal perforation of ear drum) 382.2
      benign suppurative (with anterior or perforation of ear drum) 382.1
      catarrhal 381.10
      exudative 381.3
      mucinous 381.20
      mucoid, mucous (simple) 381.20
      mucosanguineous 381.29
      nonsuppurative 381.3
      purulent 382.3
      secretory 381.3
      seromucinous 381.3
      serosanguineous 381.19
      serous (simple) 381.10
      suppurative 382.3
        atticoantral (with posterior or superior marginal perforation of ear drum) 382.2
        benign (with anterior perforation of ear drum) 382.1
        tuberculous (*see also* Tuberculosis) 017.4 ✓
      tubotympanic 382.1
      transudative 381.3
    exudative 381.4
      acute 381.00
      chronic 381.3
    fibrotic (*see also* Adhesions, middle ear) 385.10
    mucoid, mucous 381.4
      acute 381.02
      chronic (simple) 381.20
    mucosanguineous, chronic 381.29
    nonsuppurative 381.4
      acute 381.00
      chronic 381.3
    postmeasles 055.2
    purulent 382.4
      acute 382.00
        with spontaneous rupture of ear drum 382.01
      chronic 382.3
    sanguineous, acute 381.03
      allergic 381.06

✓ Additional Digit Required — Refer to the Tabular List for Digit Selection   ▽ Subterms under main terms may continue to next column or page

2007 ICD-9-CM   ►◄ Revised Text   ● New Line   ▲ Revised Code   **Volume 2 — 221**

Osteochondrosis — Otitis

Index

Otitis — Pain(s)

Otitis — *continued*
  media — *continued*
    secretory 381.4
      acute or subacute 381.01
      chronic 381.3
    seromucinous 381.4
      acute or subacute 381.02
      chronic 381.3
    serosanguineous, chronic 381.19
    serous 381.4
      acute or subacute 381.01
      chronic (simple) 381.10
    subacute — *see* Otitis, media,
        acute
    suppurative 382.4
      acute 382.00
        with spontaneous rupture of
            ear drum 382.01
      chronic 382.3
        atticoantral 382.2
        benign 382.1
        tuberculous (*see also* Tuber-
            culosis) 017.4 ☑
        tubotympanic 382.1
    transudative 381.4
      acute 381.00
      chronic 381.3
    tuberculous (*see also* Tuberculosis)
        017.4 ☑
  postmeasles 055.2
Otoconia 386.8
Otolith syndrome 386.19
Otomycosis 111.8 *[380.15]*
  in
    aspergillosis 117.3 *[380.15]*
    moniliasis 112.82
Otopathy 388.9
Otoporosis — *see also* Otosclerosis 387.9
Otorrhagia 388.69
  traumatic — *see* nature of injury
Otorrhea 388.60
  blood 388.69
  cerebrospinal (fluid) 388.61
Otosclerosis (general) 387.9
  cochlear (endosteal) 387.2
  involving
    otic capsule 387.2
    oval window
      nonobliterative 387.0
      obliterative 387.1
    round window 387.2
  nonobliterative 387.0
  obliterative 387.1
  specified type NEC 387.8
Otospongiosis — *see also* Otosclerosis
    387.9
Otto's disease or pelvis 715.35
Outburst, aggressive — *see also* Distur-
    bance, conduct 312.0 ☑
  in children or adolescents 313.9
Outcome of delivery
  multiple birth NEC V27.9
    all liveborn V27.5
    all stillborn V27.7
    some liveborn V27.6
    unspecified V27.9
  single V27.9
    liveborn V27.0
    stillborn V27.1
  twins V27.9
    both liveborn V27.2
    both stillborn V27.4
    one liveborn, one stillborn V27.3
Outlet — *see also* condition
  syndrome (thoracic) 353.0
Outstanding ears (bilateral) 744.29
Ovalocytosis (congenital) (hereditary) —
    see also Elliptocytosis 282.1
Ovarian — *see also* condition
  pregnancy — *see* Pregnancy, ovarian
  remnant syndrome 620.8
  vein syndrome 593.4
Ovaritis (cystic) — *see also* Salpingo-
    oophoritis 614.2
Ovary, ovarian — *see* condition
Overactive — *see also* Hyperfunction

Overactive — *see also* Hyperfunction —
    continued
  bladder 596.51
  eye muscle (*see also* Strabismus)
      378.9
  hypothalamus 253.8
  thyroid (*see also* Thyrotoxicosis)
      242.9 ☑
Overactivity, child 314.01
Overbite (deep) (excessive) (horizontal)
    (vertical) 524.29
Overbreathing — *see also* Hyperventila-
    tion 786.01
Overconscientious personality 301.4
Overdevelopment — *see also* Hypertro-
    phy
  breast (female) (male) 611.1
  nasal bones 738.0
  prostate, congenital 752.89
Overdistention — *see* Distention
Overdose overdosage (drug) 977.9
  specified drug or substance — *see*
      Table of Drugs and Chemicals
Overeating 783.6
  nonorganic origin 307.51
Overexertion (effects) (exhaustion) 994.5
Overexposure (effects) 994.9
  exhaustion 994.4
Overfeeding — *see also* Overeating 783.6
Overfill, endodontic 526.62   ●
Overgrowth, bone NEC 733.99
Overhanging   ●
  tooth restoration 525.62
  unrepairable, dental restorative ma-
      terials 525.62   ●
Overheated (effects) (places) — *see* Heat
Overinhibited child 313.0
Overjet 524.29
  excessive horizontal 524.26   ●
Overlaid, overlying (suffocation) 994.7
Overlap
  excessive horizontal 524.26
Overlapping toe (acquired) 735.8
  congenital (fifth toe) 755.66
Overload
  fluid 276.6
  potassium (K) 276.7
  sodium (Na) 276.0
Overnutrition — *see also* Hyperalimen-
    tation 783.6
Overproduction — *see also* Hypersecre-
    tion
  ACTH 255.3
  cortisol 255.0
  growth hormone 253.0
  thyroid-stimulating hormone (TSH)
      242.8 ☑
Overriding
  aorta 747.21
  finger (acquired) 736.29
    congenital 755.59
  toe (acquired) 735.8
    congenital 755.66
Oversize
  fetus (weight of 4500 grams or more)
      766.0
    affecting management of pregnancy
        656.6 ☑
    causing disproportion 653.5 ☑
      with obstructed labor 660.1 ☑
        affecting fetus or newborn 763.1
Overstimulation, ovarian 256.1
Overstrained 780.79
  heart — *see* Hypertrophy, cardiac
Overweight — *see also* Obesity 278.00
Overwork 780.79
Oviduct — *see* condition
Ovotestis 752.7
Ovulation (cycle)
  failure or lack of 628.0
  pain 625.2
Ovum
  blighted 631
  donor V59.70
    over age 35 V59.73
      anonymous recipient V59.73

Ovum — *continued*
  donor — *continued*
    over age 35 — *continued*
      designated recipient V59.74
    under age 35 V59.71
      anonymous recipient V59.71
      designated recipient V59.72
  dropsical 631
  pathologic 631
Owren's disease or syndrome (parahe-
    mophilia) — *see also* Defect, coagu-
    lation 286.3
Oxalosis 271.8
Oxaluria 271.8
Ox heart — *see* Hypertrophy, cardiac
OX syndrome 758.6
Oxycephaly, oxycephalic 756.0
  syphilitic, congenital 090.0
Oxyuriasis 127.4
Oxyuris vermicularis (infestation) 127.4
Ozena 472.0

P

Pacemaker syndrome 429.4
Pachyderma, pachydermia 701.8
  laryngis 478.5
  laryngitis 478.79
  larynx (verrucosa) 478.79
Pachydermatitis 701.8
Pachydermatocele (congenital) 757.39
  acquired 701.8
Pachydermatosis 701.8
Pachydermoperiostitis
  secondary 731.2
Pachydermoperiostosis
  primary idiopathic 757.39
  secondary 731.2
Pachymeningitis (adhesive) (basal)
    (brain) (cerebral) (cervical) (chronic)
    (circumscribed) (external) (fibrous)
    (hemorrhagic) (hypertrophic) (inter-
    nal) (purulent) (spinal) (suppura-
    tive) — *see also* Meningitis 322.9
  gonococcal 098.82
Pachyonychia (congenital) 757.5
  acquired 703.8
Pachyperiosteodermia
  primary or idiopathic 757.39
  secondary 731.2
Pachyperiostosis
  primary or idiopathic 757.39
  secondary 731.2
Pacinian tumor (M9507/0) — *see* Neo-
    plasm, skin, benign
Pads, knuckle or Garrod's 728.79
Paget's disease (osteitis deformans)
    731.0
  with infiltrating duct carcinoma of the
      breast (M8541/3) — *see* Neo-
      plasm, breast, malignant
  bone 731.0
    osteosarcoma in (M9184/3) — *see*
        Neoplasm, bone, malignant
  breast (M8540/3) 174.0
  extramammary (M8542/3) (*see also*
      Neoplasm, skin, malignant)
    anus 154.3
    skin 173.5
  malignant (M8540/3)
    breast 174.0
    specified site NEC (M8542/3) —
        see Neoplasm, skin, malig-
        nant
    unspecified site 174.0
  mammary (M8540/3) 174.0
  necrosis of bone 731.0
  nipple (M8540/3) 174.0
  osteitis deformans 731.0
Paget-Schroetter syndrome (intermit-
    tent venous claudication) 453.8
Pain(s) 780.96   ▲
  abdominal 789.0 ☑
  acute 338.19   ●
    due to trauma 338.11   ●
    postoperative 338.18   ●
      post-thoracotomy 338.12   ●

Pain(s) — *continued*
  adnexa (uteri) 625.9
  alimentary, due to vascular insufficien-
      cy 557.9
  anginoid (*see also* Pain, precordial)
      786.51
  anus 569.42
  arch 729.5
  arm 729.5
  axillary 729.5   ●
  back (postural) 724.5
    low 724.2
    psychogenic 307.89
  bile duct 576.9
  bladder 788.9
  bone 733.90
  breast 611.71
    psychogenic 307.89
  broad ligament 625.9
  cancer associated 338.3   ●
  cartilage NEC 733.90
  cecum 789.0 ☑
  cervicobrachial 723.3
  chest (central) 786.50
    atypical 786.59
    midsternal 786.51
    musculoskeletal 786.59
    noncardiac 786.59
    substernal 786.51
    wall (anterior) 786.52
  chronic 338.29   ●
    associated with significant psy-   ●
        chosocial dysfunction
        338.4   ●
    due to trauma 338.21   ●
    postoperative 338.28   ●
      post-thoracotomy 338.22   ●
    syndrome 338.4   ●
  coccyx 724.79
  colon 789.0 ☑
  common duct 576.9
  coronary — *see* Angina
  costochondral 786.52
  diaphragm 786.52
  due to (presence of) any device, im-
      plant, or graft classifiable to
      996.0–996.5 — *see* Complica-
      tions, due to (presence of) any
      device, implant, or graft classi-
      fied to 996.0–996.5 NEC
    malignancy (primary) (secondary)●
        338.3   ●
  ear (*see also* Otalgia) 388.70
  epigastric, epigastrium 789.06
  extremity (lower) (upper) 729.5
  eye 379.91
  face, facial 784.0
    atypical 350.2
    nerve 351.8
  false (labor) 644.1 ☑
  female genital organ NEC 625.9
    psychogenic 307.89
  finger 729.5
  flank 789.0 ☑
  foot 729.5
  gallbladder 575.9
  gas (intestinal) 787.3
  gastric 536.8
  generalized 780.96   ▲
  genital organ
    female 625.9
    male 608.9
    psychogenic 307.89
  groin 789.0 ☑
  growing 781.99
  hand 729.5
  head (*see also* Headache) 784.0
  heart (see also Pain, precordial)
      786.51
  infraorbital (*see also* Neuralgia,
      trigeminal) 350.1
  intermenstrual 625.2
  jaw 526.9
  joint 719.40
    ankle 719.47
    elbow 719.42

☑ Additional Digit Required — Refer to the Tabular List for Digit Selection   Ⱳ Subterms under main terms may continue to next column or page

222 — Volume 2 • October 2006   ▶◀ Revised Text   ● New Line   ▲ Revised Code   *2007 ICD-9-CM*

Pain(s) — continued
joint — continued
  foot 719.47
  hand 719.44
  hip 719.45
  knee 719.46
  multiple sites 719.49
  pelvic region 719.45
  psychogenic 307.89
  shoulder (region) 719.41
  specified site NEC 719.48
  wrist 719.43
kidney 788.0
labor, false or spurious 644.1 ☑
laryngeal 784.1
leg 729.5
limb 729.5
low back 724.2
lumbar region 724.2
mastoid (see also Otalgia) 388.70
maxilla 526.9
metacarpophalangeal (joint) 719.44
metatarsophalangeal (joint) 719.47
mouth 528.9
muscle 729.1
  intercostal 786.59
musculoskeletal (see also Pain, by ●
  site) 729.1 ●
nasal 478.19 ▲
nasopharynx 478.29
neck NEC 723.1
  psychogenic 307.89
neoplasm related (acute) (chronic) ●
  338.3 ●
nerve NEC 729.2
neuromuscular 729.1
nose 478.19 ▲
ocular 379.91
ophthalmic 379.91
orbital region 379.91
osteocopic 733.90
ovary 625.9
  psychogenic 307.89
over heart (see also Pain, precordial)
  786.51
ovulation 625.2
pelvic (female) 625.9
  male NEC 789.0 ☑
    psychogenic 307.89
  psychogenic 307.89
penis 607.9
  psychogenic 307.89
pericardial (see also Pain, precordial)
  786.51
perineum
  female 625.9
  male 608.9
pharynx 478.29
pleura, pleural, pleuritic 786.52
postoperative 338.18
  acute 338.18
  chronic 338.28
post-thoracotomy 338.12
  acute 338.12
  chronic 338.22
preauricular 388.70
precordial (region) 786.51
  psychogenic 307.89
psychogenic 307.80
  cardiovascular system 307.89
  gastrointestinal system 307.89
  genitourinary system 307.89
  heart 307.89
  musculoskeletal system 307.89
  respiratory system 307.89
  skin 306.3
radicular (spinal) (see also Radiculitis)
  729.2
rectum 569.42
respiration 786.52
retrosternal 786.51
rheumatic NEC 729.0
  muscular 729.1
rib 786.50
root (spinal) (see also Radiculitis)
  729.2

Pain(s) — continued
round ligament (stretch) 625.9
sacroiliac 724.6
sciatic 724.3
scrotum 608.9
  psychogenic 307.89
seminal vesicle 608.9
sinus 478.19 ▲
skin 782.0
spermatic cord 608.9
spinal root (see also Radiculitis) 729.2
stomach 536.8
  psychogenic 307.89
substernal 786.51
temporomandibular (joint) 524.62
temporomaxillary joint 524.62
testis 608.9
  psychogenic 307.89
thoracic spine 724.1
  with radicular and visceral pain
    724.4
throat 784.1
tibia 733.90
toe 729.5
tongue 529.6
tooth 525.9
trigeminal (see also Neuralgia,
  trigeminal) 350.1
tumor associated 338.3 ●
umbilicus 789.05
ureter 788.0
urinary (organ) (system) 788.0
uterus 625.9
  psychogenic 307.89
vagina 625.9
vertebrogenic (syndrome) 724.5
vesical 788.9
vulva 625.9
xiphoid 733.90
Painful — see also Pain
arc syndrome 726.19
coitus
  female 625.0
  male 608.89
    psychogenic 302.76
ejaculation (semen) 608.89
  psychogenic 302.79
erection 607.3
feet syndrome 266.2
menstruation 625.3
  psychogenic 306.52
micturition 788.1
ophthalmoplegia 378.55
respiration 786.52
scar NEC 709.2
urination 788.1
wire sutures 998.89
Painters' colic 984.9
specified type of lead — see Table of
  Drugs and Chemicals
● **Palate** — see condition
● **Palatoplegia** 528.9
● **Palatoschisis** — see also Cleft, palate
  749.00
● **Palilalia** 784.69
Palindromic arthritis — see also
  Rheumatism, palindromic 719.3 ☑
Palliative care V66.7
Pallor 782.61
  temporal, optic disc 377.15
Palmar — see also condition
  fascia — see condition
Palpable
cecum 569.89
kidney 593.89
liver 573.9
lymph nodes 785.6
ovary 620.8
prostate 602.9
spleen (see also Splenomegaly) 789.2
uterus 625.8
Palpitation (heart) 785.1
  psychogenic 306.2
Palsy — see also Paralysis 344.9
atrophic diffuse 335.20
Bell's 351.0

Palsy — see also Paralysis —
  continued
Bell's — continued
  newborn 767.5
birth 767.7
brachial plexus 353.0
  fetus or newborn 767.6
brain (see also Palsy, cerebral)
  noncongenital or noninfantile
    344.89
    late effect — see Late effect(s)
      (of) cerebrovascular dis-
      ease
  syphilitic 094.89
    congenital 090.49
bulbar (chronic) (progressive) 335.22
  pseudo NEC 335.23
  supranuclear NEC 344.8 ☑
cerebral (congenital) (infantile) (spastic) 343.9
  athetoid 333.71 ▲
  diplegic 343.0
    late effect — see Late effect(s)
      (of) cerebrovascular dis-
      ease
  hemiplegic 343.1
  monoplegic 343.3
  noncongenital or noninfantile
    437.8
    late effect — see Late effect(s)
      (of) cerebrovascular dis-
      ease
  paraplegic 343.0
  quadriplegic 343.2
  spastic, not congenital or infantile
    344.89
  syphilitic 094.89
    congenital 090.49
  tetraplegic 343.2
cranial nerve (see also Disorder,
  nerve, cranial)
  multiple 352.6
creeping 335.21
divers' 993.3
Erb's (birth injury) 767.6
facial 351.0
  newborn 767.5
glossopharyngeal 352.2
Klumpke (-Déjérine) 767.6
lead 984.9
  specified type of lead — see Table
    of Drugs and Chemicals
median nerve (tardy) 354.0
peroneal nerve (acute) (tardy) 355.3
progressive supranuclear 333.0
pseudobulbar NEC 335.23
radial nerve (acute) 354.3
seventh nerve 351.0
  newborn 767.5
shaking (see also Parkinsonism) 332.0
spastic (cerebral) (spinal) 343.9
  hemiplegic 343.1
specified nerve NEC — see Disorder,
  nerve
supranuclear NEC 356.8
  progressive 333.0
ulnar nerve (tardy) 354.2
wasting 335.21
Paltauf-Sternberg disease 201.9 ☑
Paludism — see Malaria
Panama fever 084.0
Panaris (with lymphangitis) 681.9
finger 681.02
toe 681.11
Panaritium (with lymphangitis) 681.9
finger 681.02
toe 681.11
Panarteritis (nodosa) 446.0
brain or cerebral 437.4
Pancake heart 793.2
with cor pulmonale (chronic) 416.9
Pancarditis (acute) (chronic) 429.89
with
  rheumatic
    fever (active) (acute) (chronic)
      (subacute) 391.8

Pancarditis — continued
with — continued
  rheumatic — continued
    fever — continued
      inactive or quiescent 398.99
  rheumatic, acute 391.8
    chronic or inactive 398.99
Pancoast's syndrome or tumor (carcinoma, pulmonary apex) (M8010/3)
  162.3
Pancoast-Tobias syndrome (M8010/3)
  (carcinoma, pulmonary apex) 162.3
Pancolitis 556.6
Pancreas, pancreatic — see condition
Pancreatitis 577.0
acute (edematous) (hemorrhagic) (recurrent) 577.0
annular 577.0
apoplectic 577.0
calcerceous 577.0
chronic (infectious) 577.1
  recurrent 577.1
cystic 577.2
fibrous 577.8
gangrenous 577.0
hemorrhagic (acute) 577.0
interstitial (chronic) 577.1
  acute 577.0
malignant 577.0
mumps 072.3
painless 577.1
recurrent 577.1
relapsing 577.1
subacute 577.0
suppurative 577.0
syphilitic 095.8
Pancreatolithiasis 577.8
Pancytolysis 289.9
Pancytopenia (acquired) 284.1 ▲
with malformations 284.09 ▲
congenital 284.09 ▲
Panencephalitis — see also Encephalitis
subacute, sclerosing 046.2
Panhematopenia 284.8
congenital 284.09 ▲
constitutional 284.09 ▲
splenic, primary 289.4
Panhemocytopenia 284.8
congenital 284.09 ▲
constitutional 284.09 ▲
Panhypogonadism 257.2
Panhypopituitarism 253.2
prepubertal 253.3
Panic (attack) (state) 300.01
reaction to exceptional stress (transient) 308.0
Panmyelopathy, familial constitutional
  284.09 ▲
Panmyelophthisis 284.2 ▲
acquired (secondary) 284.8
congenital 284.2 ▲
idiopathic 284.9
Panmyelosis (acute) (M9951/1)
  238.79 ▲
Panner's disease 732.3
capitellum humeri 732.3
head of humerus 732.3
tarsal navicular (bone) (osteochondrosis) 732.5
Panneuritis endemica 265.0 [357.4]
Panniculitis 729.30
back 724.8
knee 729.31
mesenteric 567.82
neck 723.6
nodular, nonsuppurative 729.30
sacral 724.8
specified site NEC 729.39
Panniculus adiposus (abdominal) 278.1
Pannus ▶(corneal)◀ 370.62
abdominal (symptomatic) 278.1 ●
allergic eczematous 370.62
degenerativus 370.62
keratic 370.62
rheumatoid — see Arthritis, rheumatoid

☑ Additional Digit Required — Refer to the Tabular List for Digit Selection   ▽ Subterms under main terms may continue to next column or page

2007 ICD-9-CM   ▶◀ Revised Text   ● New Line   ▲ Revised Code   **October 2006 · Volume 2 — 223**

Pannus — *continued*
trachomatosus, trachomatous (active)
076.1 *[370.62]*
late effect 139.1
Panophthalmitis 360.02
Panotitis — *see* Otitis media
Pansinusitis (chronic) (hyperplastic)
(nonpurulent) (purulent) 473.8
acute 461.8
due to fungus NEC 117.9
tuberculous (*see also* Tuberculosis)
012.8 ☑
Panuveitis 360.12
sympathetic 360.11
Panvalvular disease — *see* Endocarditis,
mitral
Papageienkrankheit 073.9
Papanicolaou smear
cervix (screening test) V76.2
as part of gynecological examination V72.31
for suspected malignant neoplasm
V76.2
no disease found V71.1
inadequate sample 795.08
nonspecific abnormal finding
795.00
with
atypical squamous cells
cannot exclude high grade
squamous intraep-
ithelial lesion (ASC-
H) 795.02
of undetermined signifi-
cance (ASC-US)
795.01
cytologic evidence of malig-●
nancy 795.06   ●
high grade squamous intraepithelial lesion (HGSIL)
795.04
low grade squamous intraepithelial lesion (LGSIL)
795.03
nonspecific finding NEC 795.09
to confirm findings of recent
normal smear following
initial abnormal smear
V72.32
unsatisfactory 795.08
other specified site (*see also* Screening, malignant neoplasm)
for suspected malignant neoplasm
(*see also* Screening, malignant neoplasm)
no disease found V71.1
nonspecific abnormal finding 795.1
vagina V76.47
following hysterectomy for malignant condition V67.01
Papilledema 377.00
associated with
decreased ocular pressure 377.02
increased intracranial pressure
377.01
retinal disorder 377.03
choked disc 377.00
infectional 377.00
Papillitis 377.31
anus 569.49
chronic lingual 529.4
necrotizing, kidney 584.7
optic 377.31
rectum 569.49
renal, necrotizing 584.7
tongue 529.0
Papilloma (M8050/0) — *see also* Neoplasm, by site, benign

Note — *Except where otherwise indicated, the morphological varieties of papilloma in the list below should be coded
by site as for "Neoplasm, benign."*

acuminatum (female) (male) 078.11
bladder (urinary) (transitional cell)
(M8120/1) 236.7
benign (M8120/0) 223.3

Papilloma — *see also* Neoplasm, by site,
benign — *continued*
choroid plexus (M9390/0) 225.0
anaplastic type (M9390/3) 191.5
malignant (M9390/3) 191.5
ductal (M8503/0)
dyskeratotic (M8052/0)
epidermoid (M8052/0)
hyperkeratotic (M8052/0)
intracystic (M8504/0)
intraductal (M8503/0)
inverted (M8053/0)
keratotic (M8052/0)
parakeratotic (M8052/0)
pinta (primary) 103.0
renal pelvis (transitional cell)
(M8120/1) 236.99
benign (M8120/0) 223.1
Schneiderian (M8121/0)
specified site — *see* Neoplasm, by
site, benign
unspecified site 212.0
serous surface (M8461/0)
borderline malignancy (M8461/1)
specified site — *see* Neoplasm,
by site, uncertain behav-
ior
unspecified site 236.2
specified site — *see* Neoplasm, by
site, benign
unspecified site 220
squamous (cell) (M8052/0)
transitional (cell) (M8120/0)
bladder (urinary) (M8120/1) 236.7
inverted type (M8121/1) — *see*
Neoplasm, by site, uncertain
behavior
renal pelvis (M8120/1) 236.91
ureter (M8120/1) 236.91
ureter (transitional cell) (M8120/1)
236.91
benign (M8120/0) 223.2
urothelial (M8120/1) — *see* Neoplasm,
by site, uncertain behavior
verrucous (M8051/0)
villous (M8261/1) — *see* Neoplasm,
by site, uncertain behavior
yaws, plantar or palmar 102.1
Papillomata, multiple, of yaws 102.1
Papillomatosis (M8060/0) — *see also*
Neoplasm, by site, benign
confluent and reticulate 701.8
cutaneous 701.8
ductal, breast 610.1
Gougerot-Carteaud (confluent reticulate) 701.8
intraductal (diffuse) (M8505/0) — *see*
Neoplasm, by site, benign
subareolar duct (M8506/0) 217
Papillon-Léage and Psaume syndrome
(orodigitofacial dysostosis) 759.89
Papule 709.8
carate (primary) 103.0
fibrous, of nose (M8724/0) 216.3
pinta (primary) 103.0
Papulosis, malignant 447.8
Papyraceous fetus 779.89
complicating pregnancy 646.0 ☑
Paracephalus 759.7
Parachute mitral valve 746.5
Paracoccidioidomycosis 116.1
mucocutaneous-lymphangitic 116.1
pulmonary 116.1
visceral 116.1
Paracoccidiomycosis — *see* Paracoccidioidomycosis
Paracusis 388.40
Paradentosis 523.5
Paradoxical facial movements 374.43
Paraffinoma 999.9
Paraganglioma (M8680/1)
adrenal (M8700/0) 227.0
malignant (M8700/3) 194.0
aortic body (M8691/1) 237.3
malignant (M8691/3) 194.6
carotid body (M8692/1) 237.3

Paraganglioma — *continued*
carotid body — *continued*
malignant (M8692/3) 194.5
chromaffin (M8700/0) (*see also* Neoplasm, by site, benign)
malignant (M8700/3) — *see* Neoplasm, by site, malignant
extra-adrenal (M8693/1)
malignant (M8693/3)
specified site — *see* Neoplasm,
by site, malignant
unspecified site 194.6
specified site — *see* Neoplasm, by
site, uncertain behavior
unspecified site 237.3
glomus jugulare (M8690/1) 237.3
malignant (M8690/3) 194.6
jugular (M8690/1) 237.3
malignant (M8680/3)
specified site — *see* Neoplasm,
by site, malignant
unspecified site 194.6
nonchromaffin (M8693/1)
malignant (M8693/3)
specified site — *see* Neoplasm,
by site, malignant
unspecified site 194.6
specified site — *see* Neoplasm, by
site, uncertain behavior
unspecified site 237.3
parasympathetic (M8682/1)
specified site — *see* Neoplasm, by
site, uncertain behavior
unspecified site 237.3
specified site — *see* Neoplasm, by site,
uncertain behavior
sympathetic (M8681/1)
specified site — *see* Neoplasm, by
site, uncertain behavior
unspecified site 237.3
unspecified site 237.3
Parageusia 781.1
psychogenic 306.7
Paragonimiasis 121.2
Paragranuloma, Hodgkin's (M9660/3)
201.0 ☑
Parahemophilia — *see also* Defect, coagulation 286.3
Parakeratosis 690.8
psoriasiformis 696.2
variegata 696.2
Paralysis, paralytic (complete) (incomplete) 344.9
with
broken
back — *see* Fracture, vertebra,
by site, with spinal cord
injury
neck — *see* Fracture, vertebra,
cervical, with spinal cord
injury
fracture, vertebra — *see* Fracture,
vertebra, by site, with spinal
cord injury
syphilis 094.89
abdomen and back muscles 355.9
abdominal muscles 355.9
abducens (nerve) 378.54
abductor 355.9
lower extremity 355.8
upper extremity 354.9
accessory nerve 352.4
accommodation 367.51
hysterical 300.11
acoustic nerve 388.5
agitans 332.0
arteriosclerotic 332.0
alternating 344.89
oculomotor 344.89
amyotrophic 335.20
ankle 355.8
anterior serratus 355.9
anus (sphincter) 569.49
apoplectic (current episode) (*see also*
Disease, cerebrovascular, acute)
436

Paralysis, paralytic — *continued*
apoplectic (*see also* Disease, cerebrovascular, acute) — *continued*
late effect — *see* Late effect(s) (of)
cerebrovascular disease
arm 344.40
affecting
dominant side 344.41
nondominant side 344.42
both 344.2
hysterical 300.11
late effect — *see* Late effect(s) (of)
cerebrovascular disease
psychogenic 306.0
transient 781.4
traumatic NEC (*see also* Injury,
nerve, upper limb) 955.9
arteriosclerotic (current episode) 437.0
late effect — *see* Late effect(s) (of)
cerebrovascular disease
ascending (spinal), acute 357.0
associated, nuclear 344.89
asthenic bulbar 358.00
ataxic NEC 334.9
general 094.1
athetoid 333.71   ▲
atrophic 356.9
infantile, acute (*see also* Poliomyelitis, with paralysis) 045.1 ☑
muscle NEC 355.9
progressive 335.21
spinal (acute) (*see also* Poliomyelitis, with paralysis) 045.1 ☑
attack (*see also* Disease, cerebrovascular, acute) 436
axillary 353.0
Babinski-Nageotte's 344.89
Bell's 351.0
newborn 767.5
Benedikt's 344.89
birth (injury) 767.7
brain 767.0
intracranial 767.0
spinal cord 767.4
bladder (sphincter) 596.53
neurogenic 596.54
with cauda equina syndrome
344.61
puerperal, postpartum, childbirth
665.5 ☑
sensory 596.54
with cauda equina 344.61
spastic 596.54
with cauda equina 344.61
bowel, colon, or intestine (*see also*
Ileus) 560.1
brachial plexus 353.0
due to birth injury 767.6
newborn 767.6
brain
congenital — *see* Palsy, cerebral
current episode 437.8
diplegia 344.2
hemiplegia 342.9 ☑
late effect — *see* Late effect(s)
(of) cerebrovascular dis-
ease
infantile — *see* Palsy, cerebral
late effect — *see* Late effect(s) (of)
cerebrovascular disease
monoplegia (*see also* Monoplegia)
late effect — *see* Late effect(s)
(of) cerebrovascular dis-
ease
paraplegia 344.1
quadriplegia — *see* Quadriplegia
syphilitic, congenital 090.49
triplegia 344.89
bronchi 519.19   ▲
Brown-Séquard's 344.89
bulbar (chronic) (progressive) 335.22
infantile (*see also* Poliomyelitis,
bulbar) 045.0 ☑
poliomyelitic (*see also* Poliomyelitis,
bulbar) 045.0 ☑

Paralysis, paralytic — *continued*
  bulbar — *continued*
    pseudo 335.23
    supranuclear 344.89
  bulbospinal 358.00
  cardiac (*see also* Failure, heart) 428.9
  cerebral
    current episode 437.8
    spastic, infantile — *see* Palsy, cerebral
  cerebrocerebellar 437.8
    diplegic infantile 343.0
  cervical
    plexus 353.2
    sympathetic NEC 337.0
  Céstan-Chenais 344.89
  Charcôt-Marie-Tooth type 356.1
  childhood — *see* Palsy, cerebral
  Clark's 343.9
  colon (*see also* Ileus) 560.1
  compressed air 993.3
  compression
    arm NEC 354.9
    cerebral — *see* Paralysis, brain
    leg NEC 355.8
    lower extremity NEC 355.8
    upper extremity NEC 354.9
  congenital (cerebral) (spastic) (spinal) — *see* Palsy, cerebral
  conjugate movement (of eye) 378.81
    cortical (nuclear) (supranuclear) 378.81
  convergence 378.83
  cordis (*see also* Failure, heart) 428.9
  cortical (*see also* Paralysis, brain) 437.8
  cranial or cerebral nerve (*see also* Disorder, nerve, cranial) 352.9
  creeping 335.21
  crossed leg 344.89
  crutch 953.4
  deglutition 784.99 ▲
    hysterical 300.11
  dementia 094.1
  descending (spinal) NEC 335.9
  diaphragm (flaccid) 519.4
    due to accidental section of phrenic nerve during procedure 998.2
  digestive organs NEC 564.89
  diplegic — *see* Diplegia
  divergence (nuclear) 378.85
  divers' 993.3
  Duchenne's 335.22
  due to intracranial or spinal birth injury — *see* Palsy, cerebral
  embolic (current episode) (*see also* Embolism, brain) 434.1 ☑
    late effect — *see* Late effect(s) (of) cerebrovascular disease
  enteric (*see also* Ileus) 560.1
    with hernia — *see* Hernia, by site, with obstruction
  Erb (-Duchenne) (birth) (newborn) 767.6
  Erb's syphilitic spastic spinal 094.89
  esophagus 530.89
  essential, infancy (*see also* Poliomyelitis) 045.9 ☑
  extremity
    lower — *see* Paralysis, leg
    spastic (hereditary) 343.3
      noncongenital or noninfantile 344.1
      transient (cause unknown) 781.4
    upper — *see* Paralysis, arm
  eye muscle (extrinsic) 378.55
    intrinsic 367.51
  facial (nerve) 351.0
    birth injury 767.5
    congenital 767.5
    following operation NEC 998.2
    newborn 767.5
  familial 359.3
    periodic 359.3
    spastic 334.1

Paralysis, paralytic — *continued*
  fauces 478.29
  finger NEC 354.9
  foot NEC 355.8
  gait 781.2
  gastric nerve 352.3
  gaze 378.81
  general 094.1
    ataxic 094.1
    insane 094.1
    juvenile 090.40
    progressive 094.1
    tabetic 094.1
  glossopharyngeal (nerve) 352.2
  glottis (*see also* Paralysis, vocal cord) 478.30
  gluteal 353.4
  Gubler (-Millard) 344.89
  hand 354.9
    hysterical 300.11
    psychogenic 306.0
  heart (*see also* Failure, heart) 428.9
  hemifacial, progressive 349.89
  hemiplegic — *see* Hemiplegia
  hyperkalemic periodic (familial) 359.3
  hypertensive (current episode) 437.8
  hypoglossal (nerve) 352.5
  hypokalemic periodic 359.3
  Hyrtl's sphincter (rectum) 569.49
  hysterical 300.11
  ileus (*see also* Ileus) 560.1
  infantile (*see also* Poliomyelitis) 045.9 ☑
    atrophic acute 045.1 ☑
    bulbar 045.0 ☑
    cerebral — *see* Palsy, cerebral
    paralytic 045.1 ☑
    progressive acute 045.9 ☑
    spastic — *see* Palsy, cerebral
    spinal 045.9 ☑
  infective (*see also* Poliomyelitis) 045.9 ☑
  inferior nuclear 344.9
  insane, general or progressive 094.1
  internuclear 378.86
  interosseous 355.9
  intestine (*see also* Ileus) 560.1
  intracranial (current episode) (*see also* Paralysis, brain) 437.8
    due to birth injury 767.0
  iris 379.49
    due to diphtheria (toxin) 032.81 [379.49]
  ischemic, Volkmann's (complicating trauma) 958.6
  isolated sleep, recurrent
  Jackson's 344.89
  jake 357.7
  Jamaica ginger (jake) 357.7
  juvenile general 090.40
  Klumpke (-Déjérine) (birth) (newborn) 767.6
  labioglossal (laryngeal) (pharyngeal) 335.22
  Landry's 357.0
  laryngeal nerve (recurrent) (superior) (*see also* Paralysis, vocal cord) 478.30
  larynx (*see also* Paralysis, vocal cord) 478.30
    due to diphtheria (toxin) 032.3
  late effect
    due to
      birth injury, brain or spinal (cord) — *see* Palsy, cerebral
      edema, brain or cerebral — *see* Paralysis, brain
      lesion
        late effect — *see* Late effect(s) (of) cerebrovascular disease
      spinal (cord) — *see* Paralysis, spinal
  lateral 335.24
  lead 984.9

Paralysis, paralytic — *continued*
  lead — *continued*
    specified type of lead — *see* Table of Drugs and Chemicals
  left side — *see* Hemiplegia
  leg 344.30
    affecting
      dominant side 344.31
      nondominant side 344.32
    both (*see also* Paraplegia) 344.1
    crossed 344.89
    hysterical 300.11
    psychogenic 306.0
    transient or transitory 781.4
      traumatic NEC (*see also* Injury, nerve, lower limb) 956.9
  levator palpebrae superioris 374.31
  limb NEC 344.5
    all four — *see* Quadriplegia
    quadriplegia — *see* Quadriplegia
  lip 528.5
  Lissauer's 094.1
  local 355.9
  lower limb (*see also* Paralysis, leg)
    both (*see also* Paraplegia) 344.1
  lung 518.89
    newborn 770.89
  median nerve 354.1
  medullary (tegmental) 344.89
  mesencephalic NEC 344.89
    tegmental 344.89
  middle alternating 344.89
  Millard-Gubler-Foville 344.89
  monoplegic — *see* Monoplegia
  motor NEC 344.9
    cerebral — *see* Paralysis, brain
    spinal — *see* Paralysis, spinal
  multiple
    cerebral — *see* Paralysis, brain
    spinal — *see* Paralysis, spinal
  muscle (flaccid) 359.9
    due to nerve lesion NEC 355.9
    eye (extrinsic) 378.55
      intrinsic 367.51
      oblique 378.51
    iris sphincter 364.8
    ischemic (complicating trauma) (Volkmann's) 958.6
    pseudohypertrophic 359.1
  muscular (atrophic) 359.9
    progressive 335.21
  musculocutaneous nerve 354.9
  musculospiral 354.9
  nerve (*see also* Disorder, nerve)
    third or oculomotor (partial) 378.51
      total 378.52
    fourth or trochlear 378.53
    sixth or abducens 378.54
    seventh or facial 351.0
      birth injury 767.5
      due to
        injection NEC 999.9
        operation NEC 997.09
      newborn 767.5
    accessory 352.4
    auditory 388.5
    birth injury 767.7
    cranial or cerebral (*see also* Disorder, nerve, cranial) 352.9
    facial 351.0
      birth injury 767.5
      newborn 767.5
    laryngeal (*see also* Paralysis, vocal cord) 478.30
    newborn 767.7
    phrenic 354.8
      newborn 767.7
    radial 354.3
      birth injury 767.6
      newborn 767.6
    syphilitic 094.89
    traumatic NEC (*see also* Injury, nerve, by site) 957.9
    trigeminal 350.9
    ulnar 354.2
  newborn NEC 767.0

Paralysis, paralytic — *continued*
  normokalemic periodic 359.3
  obstetrical, newborn 767.7
  ocular 378.9
  oculofacial, congenital 352.6
  oculomotor (nerve) (partial) 378.51
    alternating 344.89
    external bilateral 378.55
    total 378.52
  olfactory nerve 352.0
  palate 528.9
  palatopharyngolaryngeal 352.6
  paratrigeminal 350.9
  periodic (familial) (hyperkalemic) (hypokalemic) (normokalemic) (secondary) 359.3
  peripheral
    autonomic nervous system — *see* Neuropathy, peripheral, autonomic
    nerve NEC 355.9
  peroneal (nerve) 355.3
  pharynx 478.29
  phrenic nerve 354.8
  plantar nerves 355.6
  pneumogastric nerve 352.3
  poliomyelitis (current) (*see also* Poliomyelitis, with paralysis) 045.1 ☑
    bulbar 045.0 ☑
  popliteal nerve 355.3
  pressure (*see also* Neuropathy, entrapment) 355.9
  progressive 335.21
    atrophic 335.21
    bulbar 335.22
    general 094.1
    hemifacial 349.89
    infantile, acute (*see also* Poliomyelitis) 045.9 ☑
    multiple 335.20
  pseudobulbar 335.23
  pseudohypertrophic 359.1
    muscle 359.1
  psychogenic 306.0
  pupil, pupillary 379.49
  quadriceps 355.8
  quadriplegic (*see also* Quadriplegia) 344.0 ☑
  radial nerve 354.3
    birth injury 767.6
  rectum (sphincter) 569.49
  rectus muscle (eye) 378.55
  recurrent
    isolated sleep 327.43
    laryngeal nerve (*see also* Paralysis, vocal cord) 478.30
  respiratory (muscle) (system) (tract) 786.09
    center NEC 344.89
      fetus or newborn 770.87 ▲
    congenital 768.9
    newborn 768.9
  right side — *see* Hemiplegia
  Saturday night 354.3
  saturnine 984.9
    specified type of lead — *see* Table of Drugs and Chemicals
  sciatic nerve 355.0
  secondary — *see* Paralysis, late effect
  seizure (cerebral) (current episode) (*see also* Disease, cerebrovascular, acute) 436
    late effect — *see* Late effect(s) (of) cerebrovascular disease
  senile NEC 344.9
  serratus magnus 355.9
  shaking (*see also* Parkinsonism) 332.0
  shock (*see also* Disease, cerebrovascular, acute) 436
    late effect — *see* Late effect(s) (of) cerebrovascular disease
  shoulder 354.9
  soft palate 528.9
  spasmodic — *see* Paralysis, spastic
  spastic 344.9

☑ Additional Digit Required — Refer to the Tabular List for Digit Selection
▽ Subterms under main terms may continue to next column or page

2007 ICD-9-CM   ►◄ Revised Text   ● New Line   ▲ Revised Code   **October 2006 · Volume 2 — 225**

Paralysis, paralytic — *continued*
  spastic — *continued*
    cerebral infantile — *see* Palsy, cerebral
    congenital (cerebral) — *see* Palsy, cerebral
    familial 334.1
    hereditary 334.1
    infantile 343.9
    noncongenital or noninfantile, cerebral 344.9
    syphilitic 094.0
      spinal 094.89
  sphincter, bladder (*see also* Paralysis, bladder) 596.53
  spinal (cord) NEC 344.1
    accessory nerve 352.4
    acute (*see also* Poliomyelitis) 045.9 ☑
    ascending acute 357.0
    atrophic (acute) (*see also* Poliomyelitis, with paralysis) 045.1 ☑
      spastic, syphilitic 094.89
    congenital NEC 343.9
    hemiplegic — *see* Hemiplegia
    hereditary 336.8
    infantile (*see also* Poliomyelitis) 045.9 ☑
    late effect NEC 344.89
    monoplegic — *see* Monoplegia
    nerve 355.9
    progressive 335.10
    quadriplegic — *see* Quadriplegia
    spastic NEC 343.9
    traumatic — *see* Injury, spinal, by site
  sternomastoid 352.4
  stomach 536.3
    diabetic 250.6 ☑ *[536.3]*
    nerve (nondiabetic) 352.3
  stroke (current episode) — *see* Infarct, brain
    late effect — *see* Late effect(s) (of) cerebrovascular disease
  subscapularis 354.8
  superior nuclear NEC 334.9
  supranuclear 356.8
  sympathetic
    cervical NEC 337.0
    nerve NEC (*see also* Neuropathy, peripheral, autonomic) 337.9
    nervous system — *see* Neuropathy, peripheral, autonomic
  syndrome 344.9
    specified NEC 344.89
  syphilitic spastic spinal (Erb's) 094.89
  tabetic general 094.1
  thigh 355.8
  throat 478.29
    diphtheritic 032.0
    muscle 478.29
  thrombotic (current episode) (*see also* Thrombosis, brain) 434.0 ☑
    late effect — *see* Late effect(s) (of) cerebrovascular disease
  thumb NEC 354.9
  tick (-bite) 989.5
  Todd's (postepileptic transitory paralysis) 344.89
  toe 355.6
  tongue 529.8
  transient
    arm or leg NEC 781.4
    traumatic NEC (*see also* Injury, nerve, by site) 957.9
  trapezius 352.4
  traumatic, transient NEC (*see also* Injury, nerve, by site) 957.9
  trembling (*see also* Parkinsonism) 332.0
  triceps brachii 354.9
  trigeminal nerve 350.9
  trochlear nerve 378.53
  ulnar nerve 354.2
  upper limb (*see also* Paralysis, arm)
    both (*see also* Diplegia) 344.2

Paralysis, paralytic — *continued*
  uremic — *see* Uremia
  uveoparotitic 135
  uvula 528.9
    hysterical 300.11
    postdiphtheritic 032.0
  vagus nerve 352.3
  vasomotor NEC 337.9
  velum palati 528.9
  vesical (*see also* Paralysis, bladder) 596.53
  vestibular nerve 388.5
  visual field, psychic 368.16
  vocal cord 478.30
    bilateral (partial) 478.33
      complete 478.34
    complete (bilateral) 478.34
    unilateral (partial) 478.31
      complete 478.32
  Volkmann's (complicating trauma) 958.6
  wasting 335.21
  Weber's 344.89
  wrist NEC 354.9
Paramedial orifice, urethrovesical 753.8
Paramenia 626.9
Parametritis (chronic) — *see also* Disease, pelvis, inflammatory 614.4
  acute 614.3
  puerperal, postpartum, childbirth 670.0 ☑
Parametrium, parametric — *see* condition
Paramnesia — *see also* Amnesia 780.93
Paramolar 520.1
  causing crowding 524.31
Paramyloidosis 277.30   ▲
Paramyoclonus multiplex 333.2
Paramyotonia 359.2
  congenita 359.2
Paraneoplastic syndrome — *see* condition
Parangi — *see also* Yaws 102.9
Paranoia 297.1
  alcoholic 291.5
  querulans 297.8
  senile 290.20
Paranoid
  dementia (*see also* Schizophrenia) 295.3 ☑
    praecox (acute) 295.3 ☑
    senile 290.20
  personality 301.0
  psychosis 297.9
    alcoholic 291.5
    climacteric 297.2
    drug-induced 292.11
    involutional 297.2
    menopausal 297.2
    protracted reactive 298.4
    psychogenic 298.4
      acute 298.3
    senile 290.20
  reaction (chronic) 297.9
    acute 298.3
  schizophrenia (acute) (*see also* Schizophrenia) 295.3 ☑
  state 297.9
    alcohol-induced 291.5
    climacteric 297.2
    drug-induced 292.11
    due to or associated with
      arteriosclerosis (cerebrovascular) 290.42
      presenile brain disease 290.12
      senile brain disease 290.20
    involutional 297.2
    menopausal 297.2
    senile 290.20
    simple 297.0
    specified type NEC 297.8
  tendencies 301.0
  traits 301.0
  trends 301.0
  type, psychopathic personality 301.0

Paraparesis — *see also* Paralysis 344.9
Paraphasia 784.3
Paraphilia — *see also* Deviation, sexual 302.9
Paraphimosis (congenital) 605
  chancroidal 099.0
Paraphrenia, paraphrenic (late) 297.2
  climacteric 297.2
  dementia (*see also* Schizophrenia) 295.3 ☑
  involutional 297.2
  menopausal 297.2
  schizophrenia (acute) (*see also* Schizophrenia) 295.3 ☑
Paraplegia 344.1
  with
    broken back — *see* Fracture, vertebra, by site, with spinal cord injury
    fracture, vertebra — *see* Fracture, vertebra, by site, with spinal cord injury
  ataxic — *see* Degeneration, combined, spinal cord
  brain (current episode) (*see also* Paralysis, brain) 437.8
  cerebral (current episode) (*see also* Paralysis, brain) 437.8
  congenital or infantile (cerebral) (spastic) (spinal) 343.0
  cortical — *see* Paralysis, brain
  familial spastic 334.1
  functional (hysterical) 300.11
  hysterical 300.11
  infantile 343.0
  late effect 344.1
  Pott's (*see also* Tuberculosis) 015.0 ☑ *[730.88]*
  psychogenic 306.0
  spastic
    Erb's spinal 094.89
    hereditary 334.1
    not infantile or congenital 344.1
  spinal (cord)
    traumatic NEC — *see* Injury, spinal, by site
  syphilitic (spastic) 094.89
  traumatic NEC — *see* Injury, spinal, by site
Paraproteinemia 273.2
  benign (familial) 273.1
  monoclonal 273.1
  secondary to malignant or inflammatory disease 273.1
Parapsoriasis 696.2
  en plaques 696.2
  guttata 696.2
  lichenoides chronica 696.2
  retiformis 696.2
  varioliformis (acuta) 696.2
Parascarlatina 057.8
Parasitic — *see also* condition
  disease NEC (*see also* Infestation, parasitic) 136.9
    contact V01.89
    exposure to V01.89
    intestinal NEC 129
    skin NEC 134.9
  stomatitis 112.0
  sycosis 110.0
    beard 110.0
    scalp 110.0
  twin 759.4
Parasitism NEC 136.9
  intestinal NEC 129
  skin NEC 134.9
  specified — *see* Infestation
Parasitophobia 300.29
Parasomnia 307.47
  alcohol induced 291.82
  drug induced 292.85
  nonorganic origin 307.47
  organic 327.40
    in conditions classified elsewhere 327.44
    other 327.49

Paraspadias 752.69
Paraspasm facialis 351.8
Parathyroid gland — *see* condition
Parathyroiditis (autoimmune) 252.1
Parathyroprival tetany 252.1
Paratrachoma 077.0
Paratyphilitis — *see also* Appendicitis 541
Paratyphoid (fever) — *see* Fever, paratyphoid
Paratyphus — *see* Fever, paratyphoid
Paraurethral duct 753.8
Para-urethritis 597.89
  gonococcal (acute) 098.0
    chronic or duration of 2 months or over 098.2
Paravaccinia NEC 051.9
  milkers' node 051.1
Paravaginitis — *see also* Vaginitis 616.10
Parencephalitis — *see also* Encephalitis 323.9
  late effect — *see* category 326
Parergasia 298.9
Paresis — *see also* Paralysis 344.9
  accommodation 367.51
  bladder (spastic) (sphincter) (*see also* Paralysis, bladder) 596.53
    tabetic 094.0
  bowel, colon, or intestine (*see also* Ileus) 560.1
  brain or cerebral — *see* Paralysis, brain
  extrinsic muscle, eye 378.55
  general 094.1
    arrested 094.1
    brain 094.1
    cerebral 094.1
    insane 094.1
    juvenile 090.40
      remission 090.49
    progressive 094.1
    remission (sustained) 094.1
    tabetic 094.1
  heart (*see also* Failure, heart) 428.9
  infantile (*see also* Poliomyelitis) 045.9 ☑
  insane 094.1
  juvenile 090.40
  late effect — *see* Paralysis, late effect
  luetic (general) 094.1
  peripheral progressive 356.9
  pseudohypertrophic 359.1
  senile NEC 344.9
  stomach 536.3
    diabetic 250.6 ☑ *[536.3]*
  syphilitic (general) 094.1
    congenital 090.40
  transient, limb 781.4
  vesical (sphincter) NEC 596.53
Paresthesia — *see also* Disturbance, sensation 782.0
  Berger's (paresthesia of lower limb) 782.0
  Bernhardt 355.1
  Magnan's 782.0
Paretic — *see* condition
Parinaud's
  conjunctivitis 372.02
  oculoglandular syndrome 372.02
  ophthalmoplegia 378.81
  syndrome (paralysis of conjugate upward gaze) 378.81
Parkes Weber and Dimitri syndrome (encephalocutaneous angiomatosis) 759.6
Parkinson's disease, syndrome, or tremor — *see* Parkinsonism
Parkinsonism (arteriosclerotic) (idiopathic) (primary) 332.0
  associated with orthostatic hypotension (idiopathic) (symptomatic) 333.0
  due to drugs 332.1
  neuroleptic-induced 332.1
  secondary 332.1

☑ Additional Digit Required — Refer to the Tabular List for Digit Selection
▽ Subterms under main terms may continue to next column or page

226 — Volume 2 • October 2006
▶◀ Revised Text
● New Line
▲ Revised Code
2007 ICD-9-CM

Index — Paralysis, paralytic — Parkinsonism

Parkinsonism — *continued*
　syphilitic 094.82
Parodontitis 523.40　　　　　　　▲
Parodontosis 523.5
Paronychia (with lymphangitis) 681.9
　candidal (chronic) 112.3
　chronic 681.9
　　candidal 112.3
　　finger 681.02
　　toe 681.11
　finger 681.02
　toe 681.11
　tuberculous (primary) (*see also* Tuberculosis) 017.0 ☑
Parorexia NEC 307.52
　hysterical 300.11
Parosmia 781.1
　psychogenic 306.7
Parotid gland — *see* condition
Parotiditis — *see also* Parotitis 527.2
　epidemic 072.9
　infectious 072.9
Parotitis 527.2
　allergic 527.2
　chronic 527.2
　epidemic (*see also* Mumps) 072.9
　infectious (*see also* Mumps) 072.9
　noninfectious 527.2
　nonspecific toxic 527.2
　not mumps 527.2
　postoperative 527.2
　purulent 527.2
　septic 527.2
　suppurative (acute) 527.2
　surgical 527.2
　toxic 527.2
Paroxysmal — *see also* condition
　dyspnea (nocturnal) 786.09
Parrot's disease (syphilitic osteochondritis) 090.0
Parrot fever 073.9
Parry's disease or syndrome (exophthalmic goiter) 242.0 ☑
Parry-Romberg syndrome 349.89
Parsonage-Aldren-Turner syndrome 353.5
Parsonage-Turner syndrome 353.5
Parson's disease (exophthalmic goiter) 242.0 ☑
Pars planitis 363.21
Particolored infant 757.39
Parturition — *see* Delivery
Passage
　false, urethra 599.4
　meconium noted during delivery 763.84
　of sounds or bougies (*see also* Attention to artificial opening) V55.9
Passive — *see* condition
Pasteurella septica 027.2
Pasteurellosis — *see also* Infection, Pasteurella 027.2
PAT (paroxysmal atrial tachycardia) 427.0
Patau's syndrome (trisomy D1) 758.1
Patch
　herald 696.3
Patches
　mucous (syphilitic) 091.3
　　congenital 090.0
　smokers' (mouth) 528.6
Patellar — *see* condition
Patellofemoral syndrome 719.46
Patent — *see also* Imperfect closure
　atrioventricular ostium 745.69
　canal of Nuck 752.41
　cervix 622.5
　　complicating pregnancy 654.5 ☑
　　　affecting fetus or newborn 761.0
　ductus arteriosus or Botalli 747.0
　Eustachian
　　tube 381.7
　　valve 746.89
　foramen
　　Botalli 745.5
　　ovale 745.5

Patent — *see also* Imperfect closure — *continued*
　interauricular septum 745.5
　interventricular septum 745.4
　omphalomesenteric duct 751.0
　os (uteri) — *see* Patent, cervix
　ostium secundum 745.5
　urachus 753.7
　vitelline duct 751.0
Paternity testing V70.4
Paterson-Kelly syndrome or web (sideropenic dysphagia) 280.8
Paterson (-Brown) (-Kelly) syndrome (sideropenic dysphagia) 280.8
Paterson's syndrome (sideropenic dysphagia) 280.8
Pathologic, pathological — *see also* condition
　asphyxia 799.01
　drunkenness 291.4
　emotionality 301.3
　fracture — *see* Fracture, pathologic
　liar 301.7
　personality 301.9
　resorption, tooth 521.40
　　external 521.42
　　internal 521.41
　　specified NEC 521.49
　sexuality (*see also* Deviation, sexual) 302.9
Pathology (of) — *see* ▶*also*◀ Disease
　periradicular, associated with previ- ●
　　ous endodontic treatment ●
　　526.69 ●
Patterned motor discharge, idiopathic — *see also* Epilepsy 345.5 ☑
Patulous — *see also* Patent
　anus 569.49
　Eustachian tube 381.7
Pause, sinoatrial 427.81
Pavor nocturnus 307.46
Pavy's disease 593.6
Paxton's disease (white piedra) 111.2
Payr's disease or syndrome (splenic flexure syndrome) 569.89
PBA (pseudobulbar affect) 310.8
Pearls
　Elschnig 366.51
　enamel 520.2
Pearl-workers' disease (chronic osteomyelitis) — *see also* Osteomyelitis 730.1 ☑
Pectenitis 569.49
Pectenosis 569.49
Pectoral — *see* condition
Pectus
　carinatum (congenital) 754.82
　　acquired 738.3
　　rachitic (*see also* Rickets) 268.0
　excavatum (congenital) 754.81
　　acquired 738.3
　　rachitic (*see also* Rickets) 268.0
　recurvatum (congenital) 754.81
　　acquired 738.3
Pedatrophia 261
Pederosis 302.2
Pediculosis (infestation) 132.9
　capitis (head louse) (any site) 132.0
　corporis (body louse) (any site) 132.1
　eyelid 132.0 [373.6]
　mixed (classifiable to more than one category in 132.0–132.2) 132.3
　pubis (pubic louse) (any site) 132.2
　vestimenti 132.1
　vulvae 132.2
Pediculus (infestation) — *see* Pediculosis
Pedophilia 302.2
Peg-shaped teeth 520.2
Pelade 704.01
Pel's crisis 094.0
Pel-Ebstein disease — *see* Disease, Hodgkin's
Pelger-Huët anomaly or syndrome (hereditary hyposegmentation) 288.2
Peliosis (rheumatica) 287.0

Pelizaeus-Merzbacher
　disease 330.0
　sclerosis, diffuse cerebral 330.0
Pellagra (alcoholic or with alcoholism) 265.2
　with polyneuropathy 265.2 [357.4]
Pellagra-cerebellar-ataxia-renal aminoaciduria syndrome 270.0
Pellegrini's disease (calcification, knee joint) 726.62
Pellegrini (-Stieda) disease or syndrome (calcification, knee joint) 726.62
Pellizzi's syndrome (pineal) 259.8
Pelvic — *see also* condition
　congestion-fibrosis syndrome 625.5
　kidney 753.3
Pelvioectasis 591
Pelviolithiasis 592.0
Pelviperitonitis
　female (*see also* Peritonitis, pelvic, female) 614.5
　male (*see also* Peritonitis) 567.21
Pelvis, pelvic — *see also* condition or type
　infantile 738.6
　Nägele's 738.6
　obliquity 738.6
　Robert's 755.69
Pemphigoid 694.5
　benign, mucous membrane 694.60
　　with ocular involvement 694.61
　bullous 694.5
　cicatricial 694.60
　　with ocular involvement 694.61
　juvenile 694.2
Pemphigus 694.4
　benign 694.5
　　chronic familial 757.39
　Brazilian 694.4
　circinatus 694.0
　congenital, traumatic 757.39
　conjunctiva 694.61
　contagiosus 684
　erythematodes 694.4
　erythematosus 694.4
　foliaceus 694.4
　frambesiodes 694.4
　gangrenous (*see also* Gangrene) 785.4
　malignant 694.4
　neonatorum, newborn 684
　ocular 694.61
　papillaris 694.4
　seborrheic 694.4
　South American 694.4
　syphilitic (congenital) 090.0
　vegetans 694.4
　vulgaris 694.4
　wildfire 694.4
Pendred's syndrome (familial goiter with deaf-mutism) 243
Pendulous
　abdomen 701.9
　　in pregnancy or childbirth 654.4 ☑
　　　affecting fetus or newborn 763.89
　breast 611.8
Penetrating wound — *see also* Wound, open, by site
　with internal injury — *see* Injury, internal, by site, with open wound
　eyeball 871.7
　　with foreign body (nonmagnetic) 871.6
　　　magnetic 871.5
　ocular (*see also* Penetrating wound, eyeball) 871.7
　　adnexa 870.3
　　　with foreign body 870.4
　　orbit 870.3
　　　with foreign body 870.4
Penetration, pregnant uterus by instrument
　with
　　abortion — *see* Abortion, by type, with damage to pelvic organs

Penetration, pregnant uterus by instrument — *continued*
　with — *continued*
　　ectopic pregnancy (*see also* categories 633.0–633.9) 639.2
　　molar pregnancy (*see also* categories 630–632) 639.2
　complication of delivery 665.1 ☑
　　affecting fetus or newborn 763.89
　following
　　abortion 639.2
　　ectopic or molar pregnancy 639.2
Penfield's syndrome — *see also* Epilepsy 345.5 ☑
Penicilliosis of lung 117.3
Penis — *see* condition
Penitis 607.2
Pentalogy (of Fallot) 745.2
Penta X syndrome 758.81
Pentosuria (benign) (essential) 271.8
Peptic acid disease 536.8
Peregrinating patient V65.2
Perforated — *see* Perforation
Perforation, perforative (nontraumatic)
　antrum (*see also* Sinusitis, maxillary) 473.0
　appendix 540.0
　　with peritoneal abscess 540.1
　atrial septum, multiple 745.5
　attic, ear 384.22
　　healed 384.81
　bile duct, except cystic (*see also* Disease, biliary) 576.3
　　cystic 575.4
　bladder (urinary) 596.6
　　with
　　　abortion — *see* Abortion, by type, with damage to pelvic organs
　　　ectopic pregnancy (*see also* categories 633.0–633.9) 639.2
　　　molar pregnancy (*see also* categories 630–632) 639.2
　　following
　　　abortion 639.2
　　　ectopic or molar pregnancy 639.2
　　obstetrical trauma 665.5 ☑
　bowel 569.83
　　with
　　　abortion — *see* Abortion, by type, with damage to pelvic organs
　　　ectopic pregnancy (*see also* categories 633.0–633.9) 639.2
　　　molar pregnancy (*see also* categories 630–632) 639.2
　　fetus or newborn 777.6
　　following
　　　abortion 639.2
　　　ectopic or molar pregnancy 639.2
　　obstetrical trauma 665.5 ☑
　broad ligament
　　with
　　　abortion — *see* Abortion, by type, with damage to pelvic organs
　　　ectopic pregnancy (*see also* categories 633.0–633.9) 639.2
　　　molar pregnancy (*see also* categories 630–632) 639.2
　　following
　　　abortion 639.2
　　　ectopic or molar pregnancy 639.2
　　obstetrical trauma 665.6 ☑
　by
　　device, implant, or graft — *see* Complications, mechanical
　　foreign body left accidentally in operation wound 998.4

☑ Additional Digit Required — Refer to the Tabular List for Digit Selection　　　　　　　▽ Subterms under main terms may continue to next column or page

2007 ICD-9-CM　　　　　　▶◀ Revised Text　　　● New Line　　　▲ Revised Code　　　**October 2006 • Volume 2 — 227**

Perforation, perforative — *continued*
by — *continued*
  instrument (any) during a procedure, accidental 998.2
cecum 540.0
  with peritoneal abscess 540.1
cervix (uteri) (*see also* Injury, internal, cervix)
  with
    abortion — *see* Abortion, by type, with damage to pelvic organs
    ectopic pregnancy (*see also* categories 633.0–633.9) 639.2
    molar pregnancy (*see also* categories 630–632) 639.2
  following
    abortion 639.2
    ectopic or molar pregnancy 639.2
  obstetrical trauma 665.3 ☑
colon 569.83
common duct (bile) 576.3
cornea (*see also* Ulcer, cornea) 370.00
  due to ulceration 370.06
cystic duct 575.4
diverticulum (*see also* Diverticula) 562.10
  small intestine 562.00
duodenum, duodenal (ulcer) — *see* Ulcer, duodenum, with perforation
ear drum — *see* Perforation, tympanum
enteritis — *see* Enteritis
esophagus 530.4
ethmoidal sinus (*see also* Sinusitis, ethmoidal) 473.2
foreign body (external site) (*see also* Wound, open, by site, complicated)
  internal site, by ingested object — *see* Foreign body
frontal sinus (*see also* Sinusitis, frontal) 473.1
gallbladder or duct (*see also* Disease, gallbladder) 575.4
gastric (ulcer) — *see* Ulcer, stomach, with perforation
heart valve — *see* Endocarditis
ileum (*see also* Perforation, intestine) 569.83
instrumental
  external — *see* Wound, open, by site
  pregnant uterus, complicating delivery 665.9 ☑
  surgical (accidental) (blood vessel) (nerve) (organ) 998.2
intestine 569.83
  with
    abortion — *see* Abortion, by type, with damage to pelvic organs
    ectopic pregnancy (*see also* categories 633.0–633.9) 639.2
    molar pregnancy (*see also* categories 630–632) 639.2
  fetus or newborn 777.6
  obstetrical trauma 665.5 ☑
  ulcerative NEC 569.83
jejunum, jejunal 569.83
  ulcer — *see* Ulcer, gastrojejunal, with perforation
mastoid (antrum) (cell) 383.89
maxillary sinus (*see also* Sinusitis, maxillary) 473.0
membrana tympani — *see* Perforation, tympanum
nasal
  septum 478.19 ▲
    congenital 748.1
    syphilitic 095.8
  sinus (*see also* Sinusitis) 473.9

Perforation, perforative — *continued*
nasal — *continued*
  sinus (*see also* Sinusitis) — *continued*
    congenital 748.1
palate (hard) 526.89
  soft 528.9
    syphilitic 095.8
      syphilitic 095.8
palatine vault 526.89
  syphilitic 095.8
    congenital 090.5
pelvic
  floor
    with
      abortion — *see* Abortion, by type, with damage to pelvic organs
      ectopic pregnancy (*see also* categories 633.0–633.9) 639.2
      molar pregnancy (*see also* categories 630–632) 639.2
    obstetrical trauma 664.1 ☑
  organ
    with
      abortion — *see* Abortion, by type, with damage to pelvic organs
      ectopic pregnancy (*see also* categories 633.0–633.9) 639.2
      molar pregnancy (*see also* categories 630–632) 639.2
    following
      abortion 639.2
      ectopic or molar pregnancy 639.2
    obstetrical trauma 665.5 ☑
perineum — *see* Laceration, perineum
periurethral tissue
  with
    abortion — *see* Abortion, by type, with damage to pelvic organs
    ectopic pregnancy (*see also* categories 630–632) 639.2
    molar pregnancy (*see also* categories 630–632) 639.2
pharynx 478.29
pylorus, pyloric (ulcer) — *see* Ulcer, stomach, with perforation
rectum 569.49
root canal space 526.61 ●
sigmoid 569.83
sinus (accessory) (chronic) (nasal) (*see also* Sinusitis) 473.9
sphenoidal sinus (*see also* Sinusitis, sphenoidal) 473.3
stomach (due to ulcer) — *see* Ulcer, stomach, with perforation
surgical (accidental) (by instrument) (blood vessel) (nerve) (organ) 998.2
traumatic
  external — *see* Wound, open, by site
  eye (*see also* Penetrating wound, ocular) 871.7
  internal organ — *see* Injury, internal, by site
  tympanum (membrane) (persistent posttraumatic) (postinflammatory) 384.20
  with
    otitis media — *see* Otitis media
  attic 384.22
  central 384.21
  healed 384.81
  marginal NEC 384.23
  multiple 384.24
  pars flaccida 384.22
  total 384.25

Perforation, perforative — *continued*
tympanum — *continued*
  traumatic — *see* Wound, open, ear, drum
typhoid, gastrointestinal 002.0
ulcer — *see* Ulcer, by site, with perforation
ureter 593.89
urethra
  with
    abortion — *see* Abortion, by type, with damage to pelvic organs
    ectopic pregnancy (*see also* categories 633.0–633.9) 639.2
    molar pregnancy (*see also* categories 630–632) 639.2
  following
    abortion 639.2
    ectopic or molar pregnancy 639.2
  obstetrical trauma 665.5 ☑
uterus (*see also* Injury, internal, uterus)
  with
    abortion — *see* Abortion, by type, with damage to pelvic organs
    ectopic pregnancy (*see also* categories 633.0–633.9) 639.2
    molar pregnancy (*see also* categories 630–632) 639.2
  by intrauterine contraceptive device 996.32
  following
    abortion 639.2
    ectopic or molar pregnancy 639.2
  obstetrical trauma — *see* Injury, internal, uterus, obstetrical trauma
uvula 528.9
  syphilitic 095.8
vagina — *see* Laceration, vagina
viscus NEC 799.89
  traumatic 868.00
    with open wound into cavity 868.10
Periadenitis mucosa necrotica recurrens 528.2
Periangiitis 446.0
Periantritis 535.4 ☑
Periappendicitis (acute) — *see also* Appendicitis 541
Periarteritis (disseminated) (infectious) (necrotizing) (nodosa) 446.0
Periarthritis (joint) 726.90
  Duplay's 726.2
  gonococcal 098.50
  humeroscapularis 726.2
  scapulohumeral 726.2
  shoulder 726.2
  wrist 726.4
Periarthrosis (angioneural) — *see* Periarthritis
Peribronchitis 491.9
  tuberculous (*see also* Tuberculosis) 011.3 ☑
Pericapsulitis, adhesive (shoulder) 726.0
Pericarditis (granular) (with decompensation) (with effusion) 423.9
  with
    rheumatic fever (conditions classifiable to 390)
      active (*see also* Pericarditis, rheumatic) 391.0
      inactive or quiescent 393
  actinomycotic 039.8 *[420.0]*
  acute (nonrheumatic) 420.90
    with chorea (acute) (rheumatic) (Sydenham's) 392.0
    bacterial 420.99
    benign 420.91

Pericarditis — *continued*
acute — *continued*
  hemorrhagic 420.90
  idiopathic 420.91
  infective 420.90
  nonspecific 420.91
  rheumatic 391.0
    with chorea (acute) (rheumatic) (Sydenham's) 392.0
  sicca 420.90
  viral 420.91
adhesive or adherent (external) (internal) 423.1
  acute — *see* Pericarditis, acute
  rheumatic (external) (internal) 393
amebic 006.8 *[420.0]*
bacterial (acute) (subacute) (with serous or seropurulent effusion) 420.99
calcareous 423.2
cholesterol (chronic) 423.8
  acute 420.90
chronic (nonrheumatic) 423.8
  rheumatic 393
constrictive 423.2
Coxsackie 074.21
due to
  actinomycosis 039.8 *[420.0]*
  amebiasis 006.8 *[420.0]*
  Coxsackie (virus) 074.21
  histoplasmosis (*see also* Histoplasmosis) 115.93
  nocardiosis 039.8 *[420.0]*
  tuberculosis (*see also* Tuberculosis) 017.9 ☑ *[420.0]*
fibrinocaseous (*see also* Tuberculosis) 017.9 ☑ *[420.0]*
fibrinopurulent 420.99
fibrinous — *see* Pericarditis, rheumatic
fibropurulent 420.99
fibrous 423.1
gonococcal 098.83
hemorrhagic 423.0
idiopathic (acute) 420.91
infective (acute) 420.90
meningococcal 036.41
neoplastic (chronic) 423.8
  acute 420.90
nonspecific 420.91
obliterans, obliterating 423.1
plastic 423.1
pneumococcal (acute) 420.99
postinfarction 411.0
purulent (acute) 420.99
rheumatic (active) (acute) (with effusion) (with pneumonia) 391.0
  with chorea (acute) (rheumatic) (Sydenham's) 392.0
  chronic or inactive (with chorea) 393
septic (acute) 420.99
serofibrinous — *see* Pericarditis, rheumatic
staphylococcal (acute) 420.99
streptococcal (acute) 420.99
suppurative (acute) 420.99
syphilitic 093.81
tuberculous (acute) (chronic) (*see also* Tuberculosis) 017.9 ☑ *[420.0]*
uremic 585.9 *[420.0]*
viral (acute) 420.91
Pericardium, pericardial — *see* condition
Pericellulitis — *see also* Cellulitis 682.9
Pericementitis 523.40 ▲
  acute 523.30 ▲
  chronic (suppurative) 523.40 ▲
Pericholecystitis — *see also* Cholecystitis 575.10
Perichondritis
  auricle 380.00
    acute 380.01
    chronic 380.02
  bronchus 491.9
  ear (external) 380.00

☑ Additional Digit Required — Refer to the Tabular List for Digit Selection   ▽ Subterms under main terms may continue to next column or page

228 — Volume 2 · October 2006   ►◄ Revised Text   ● New Line   ▲ Revised Code   *2007 ICD-9-CM*

Perichondritis — *continued*
  ear — *continued*
    acute 380.01
    chronic 380.02
  larynx 478.71
    syphilitic 095.8
    typhoid 002.0 *[478.71]*
  nose 478.19
  pinna 380.00
    acute 380.01
    chronic 380.02
  trachea 478.9
Periclasia 523.5
Pericolitis 569.89
Pericoronitis (chronic) 523.40 ▲
  acute 523.30 ▲
Pericystitis — *see also* Cystitis 595.9
Pericytoma (M9150/1) — *see also* Neoplasm, connective tissue, uncertain behavior
  benign (M9150/0) — *see* Neoplasm, connective tissue, benign
  malignant (M9150/3) — *see* Neoplasm, connective tissue, malignant
Peridacryocystitis, acute 375.32
Peridiverticulitis — *see also* Diverticulitis 562.11
Periduodenitis 535.6 ☑
Periendocarditis — *see also* Endocarditis 424.90
  acute or subacute 421.9
Periepididymitis — *see also* Epididymitis 604.90
Perifolliculitis (abscedens) 704.8
  capitis, abscedens et suffodiens 704.8
  dissecting, scalp 704.8
  scalp 704.8
  superficial pustular 704.8
Perigastritis (acute) 535.0 ☑
Perigastrojejunitis (acute) 535.0 ☑
Perihepatitis (acute) 573.3
  chlamydial 099.56
  gonococcal 098.86
Peri-ileitis (subacute) 569.89
Perilabyrinthitis (acute) — *see* Labyrinthitis
Perimeningitis — *see* Meningitis
Perimetritis — *see also* Endometritis 615.9
Perimetrosalpingitis — *see also* Salpingo-oophoritis 614.2
Perineocele 618.05
Perinephric — *see* condition
Perinephritic — *see* condition
Perinephritis — *see also* Infection, kidney 590.9
  purulent (*see also* Abscess, kidney) 590.2
Perineum, perineal — *see* condition
Perineuritis NEC 729.2
Periodic — *see also* condition
  disease (familial) 277.31 ▲
  edema 995.1
    hereditary 277.6
  fever 277.31
  limb movement disorder 327.51
  paralysis (familial) 359.3
  peritonitis 277.31 ▲
  polyserositis 277.31 ▲
  somnolence (*see also* Narcolepsy) 347.00
Periodontal
  cyst 522.8
  pocket 523.8
Periodontitis (chronic) (complex) (compound) (simplex) 523.40 ▲
  acute 523.33 ●
  aggressive 523.30 ●
    generalized 523.32 ●
    localized 523.31 ●
  apical 522.6
    acute (pulpal origin) 522.4
  generalized 523.42 ●
  localized 523.41 ●
Periodontoclasia 523.5

Periodontosis 523.5
Periods — *see also* Menstruation
  heavy 626.2
  irregular 626.4
Perionychia (with lymphangitis) 681.9
  finger 681.02
  toe 681.11
Perioophoritis — *see also* Salpingo-oophoritis 614.2 ▲
Periorchitis — *see also* Orchitis 604.90
Periosteum, periosteal — *see* condition
Periostitis (circumscribed) (diffuse) (infective) 730.3 ☑

Note — *Use the following fifth-digit subclassification with category 730:*

  0   *site unspecified*
  1   *shoulder region*
  2   *upper arm*
  3   *forearm*
  4   *hand*
  5   *pelvic region and thigh*
  6   *lower leg*
  7   *ankle and foot*
  8   *other specified sites*
  9   *multiple sites*

---

  with osteomyelitis (*see also* Osteomyelitis) 730.2 ☑
    acute or subacute 730.0 ☑
    chronic or old 730.1 ☑
  albuminosa, albuminosus 730.3 ☑
  alveolar 526.5
  alveolodental 526.5
  dental 526.5
  gonorrheal 098.89
  hyperplastica, generalized 731.2
  jaw (lower) (upper) 526.4
  monomelic 733.99
  orbital 376.02
  syphilitic 095.5
    congenital 090.0 *[730.8]* ☑
    secondary 091.61
  tuberculous (*see also* Tuberculosis, bone) 015.9 ☑ *[730.8]* ☑
  yaws (early) (hypertrophic) (late) 102.6
Periostosis — *see also* Periostitis 730.3 ☑
  with osteomyelitis (*see also* Osteomyelitis) 730.2 ☑
    acute or subacute 730.0 ☑
    chronic or old 730.1 ☑
  hyperplastic 756.59
Peripartum cardiomyopathy 674.5 ☑
Periphlebitis — *see also* Phlebitis 451.9
  lower extremity 451.2
    deep (vessels) 451.19
    superficial (vessels) 451.0
  portal 572.1
  retina 362.18
  superficial (vessels) 451.0
  tuberculous (*see also* Tuberculosis) 017.9 ☑
    retina 017.3 ☑ *[362.18]*
Peripneumonia — *see* Pneumonia
Periproctitis 569.49 ●
Periprostatitis — *see also* Prostatitis 601.9
Perirectal — *see* condition
Perirenal — *see* condition
Perisalpingitis — *see also* Salpingo-oophoritis 614.2
Perisigmoiditis 569.89 ●
Perisplenitis (infectional) 289.59 ●
Perispondylitis — *see* Spondylitis ●
Peristalsis reversed or visible 787.4 ●
Peritendinitis — *see also* Tenosynovitis 726.90
  adhesive (shoulder) 726.0
Perithelioma (M9150/1) — *see* Pericytoma ●
Peritoneum, peritoneal — *see also* condition

Peritoneum, peritoneal — *see also* condition — *continued*
  equilibration test V56.32
Peritonitis (acute) (adhesive) (fibrinous) (hemorrhagic) (idiopathic) (localized) (perforative) (primary) (with adhesions) (with effusion) 567.9
  with or following
    abortion — *see* Abortion, by type, with sepsis
    abscess 567.21
    appendicitis 540.0
      with peritoneal abscess 540.1
    ectopic pregnancy (*see also* categories 633.0–633.9) 639.0
    molar pregnancy (*see also* categories 630–632) 639.0
  aseptic 998.7
  bacterial 567.29
    spontaneous 567.23
  bile, biliary 567.81
  chemical 998.7
  chlamydial 099.56
  chronic proliferative 567.89
  congenital NEC 777.6
  diaphragmatic 567.22
  diffuse NEC 567.29
  diphtheritic 032.83
  disseminated NEC 567.29
  due to
    bile 567.81
    foreign
      body or object accidentally left during a procedure (instrument) (sponge) (swab) 998.4
      substance accidentally left during a procedure (chemical) (powder) (talc) 998.7
    talc 998.7
    urine 567.89
  fibrinopurulent 567.29
  fibrinous 567.29
  fibrocaseous (*see also* Tuberculosis) 014.0 ☑
  fibropurulent 567.29
  general, generalized (acute) 567.21
  gonococcal 098.86
  in infective disease NEC 136.9 *[567.0]*
  meconium (newborn) 777.6
  pancreatic 577.8
  paroxysmal, benign 277.31 ▲
  pelvic
    female (acute) 614.5
      chronic NEC 614.7
        with adhesions 614.6
      puerperal, postpartum, childbirth 670.0 ☑
    male (acute) 567.21
  periodic (familial) 277.31 ▲
  phlegmonous 567.29
  pneumococcal 567.1
  postabortal 639.0
  proliferative, chronic 567.89
  puerperal, postpartum, childbirth 670.0 ☑
  purulent 567.29
  septic 567.29
  spontaneous bacterial 567.23
  staphylococcal 567.29
  streptococcal 567.29
  subdiaphragmatic 567.29
  subphrenic 567.29
  suppurative 567.29
  syphilitic 095.2
    congenital 090.0 *[567.0]*
  talc 998.7
  tuberculous (*see also* Tuberculosis) 014.0 ☑
  urine 567.89
Peritonsillar — *see* condition
Peritonsillitis 475
Perityphlitis — *see also* Appendicitis 541
Periureteritis 593.89
Periurethral — *see* condition

Periurethritis (gangrenous) 597.89
Periuterine — *see* condition
Perivaginitis — *see also* Vaginitis 616.10
Perivasculitis, retinal 362.18
Perivasitis (chronic) 608.4
Periventricular leukomalacia 779.7
Perivesiculitis (seminal) — *see also* Vesiculitis 608.0
Perlèche 686.8
  due to
    moniliasis 112.0
    riboflavin deficiency 266.0
Pernicious — *see* condition
Pernio, perniosis 991.5
Persecution
  delusion 297.9
  social V62.4
Perseveration (tonic) 784.69
Persistence, persistent (congenital) 759.89
  anal membrane 751.2
  arteria stapedia 744.04
  atrioventricular canal 745.69
  bloody ejaculate 792.2
  branchial cleft 744.41
  bulbus cordis in left ventricle 745.8
  canal of Cloquet 743.51
  capsule (opaque) 743.51
  cilioretinal artery or vein 743.51
  cloaca 751.5
  communication — *see* Fistula, congenital
  convolutions
    aortic arch 747.21
    fallopian tube 752.19
    oviduct 752.19
    uterine tube 752.19
  double aortic arch 747.21
  ductus
    arteriosus 747.0
    Botalli 747.0
  fetal
    circulation 747.83
    form of cervix (uteri) 752.49
    hemoglobin (hereditary) ("Swiss variety") 282.7
    pulmonary hypertension 747.83
  foramen
    Botalli 745.5
    ovale 745.5
  Gartner's duct 752.41
  hemoglobin, fetal (hereditary) (HPFH) 282.7
  hyaloid
    artery (generally incomplete) 743.51
    system 743.51
  hymen (tag)
    in pregnancy or childbirth 654.8 ☑
      causing obstructed labor 660.2 ☑
  lanugo 757.4
  left
    posterior cardinal vein 747.49
    root with right arch of aorta 747.21
    superior vena cava 747.49
  Meckel's diverticulum 751.0
  mesonephric duct 752.89
    fallopian tube 752.11
  mucosal disease (middle ear) (with posterior or superior marginal perforation of ear drum) 382.2
  nail(s), anomalous 757.5
  occiput, anterior or posterior 660.3 ☑
    fetus or newborn 763.1
  omphalomesenteric duct 751.0
  organ or site NEC — *see* Anomaly, specified type NEC
  ostium
    atrioventriculare commune 745.69
    primum 745.61
    secundum 745.5
  ovarian rests in fallopian tube 752.19
  pancreatic tissue in intestinal tract 751.5

☑ Additional Digit Required — Refer to the Tabular List for Digit Selection   ▽ Subterms under main terms may continue to next column or page

2007 ICD-9-CM   ▶◀ Revised Text   ● New Line   ▲ Revised Code   **October 2006 · Volume 2 — 229**

Persistence, persistent — *continued*
  primary (deciduous)
    teeth 520.6
      vitreous hyperplasia 743.51
  pulmonary hypertension 747.83
  pupillary membrane 743.46
    iris 743.46
  Rhesus (Rh) titer 999.7
  right aortic arch 747.21
  sinus
    urogenitalis 752.89
    venosus with imperfect incorporation in right auricle 747.49
  thymus (gland) 254.8
    hyperplasia 254.0
  thyroglossal duct 759.2
  thyrolingual duct 759.2
  truncus arteriosus or communis 745.0
  tunica vasculosa lentis 743.39
  umbilical sinus 753.7
  urachus 753.7
  vegetative state 780.03
  vitelline duct 751.0
  wolffian duct 752.89
Person (with)
  admitted for clinical research, as participant or control subject V70.7
  awaiting admission to adequate facility elsewhere V63.2
    undergoing social agency investigation V63.8
  concern (normal) about sick person in family V61.49
  consulting on behalf of another V65.19
    pediatric pre-birth visit for expectant mother V65.11
  feared
    complaint in whom no diagnosis was made V65.5
    condition not demonstrated V65.5
  feigning illness V65.2
  healthy, accompanying sick person V65.0
  living (in)
    without
      adequate
        financial resources V60.2
        housing (heating) (space) V60.1
      housing (permanent) (temporary) V60.0
      material resources V60.2
      person able to render necessary care V60.4
      shelter V60.0
    alone V60.3
    boarding school V60.6
    residence remote from hospital or medical care facility V63.0
    residential institution V60.6
  medical services in home not available V63.1
  on waiting list V63.2
    undergoing social agency investigation V63.8
  sick or handicapped in family V61.49
  "worried well" V65.5
Personality
  affective 301.10
  aggressive 301.3
  amoral 301.7
  anancastic, anankastic 301.4
  antisocial 301.7
  asocial 301.7
  asthenic 301.6
  avoidant 301.82
  borderline 301.83
  change 310.1
  compulsive 301.4
  cycloid 301.13
  cyclothymic 301.13
  dependent 301.6
  depressive (chronic) 301.12
  disorder, disturbance NEC 301.9

Personality — *continued*
  disorder, disturbance — *continued*
    with
      antisocial disturbance 301.7
      pattern disturbance NEC 301.9
      sociopathic disturbance 301.7
      trait disturbance 301.9
    dual 300.14
    dyssocial 301.7
    eccentric 301.89
      "haltlose" type 301.89
    emotionally unstable 301.59
    epileptoid 301.3
    explosive 301.3
    fanatic 301.0
    histrionic 301.50
    hyperthymic 301.11
    hypomanic 301.11
    hypothymic 301.12
    hysterical 301.50
    immature 301.89
    inadequate 301.6
    labile 301.59
    masochistic 301.89
    morally defective 301.7
    multiple 300.14
    narcissistic 301.81
    obsessional 301.4
    obsessive-compulsive 301.4
    overconscientious 301.4
    paranoid 301.0
    passive (-dependent) 301.6
    passive-aggressive 301.84
    pathologic NEC 301.9
    pattern defect or disturbance 301.9
    pseudosocial 301.7
    psychoinfantile 301.59
    psychoneurotic NEC 301.89
    psychopathic 301.9
      with
        amoral trend 301.7
        antisocial trend 301.7
        asocial trend 301.7
        pathologic sexuality (*see also* Deviation, sexual) 302.9
      mixed types 301.9
    schizoid 301.20
      with sexual deviation (*see also* Deviation, sexual) 302.9
      antisocial 301.7
      dyssocial 301.7
      introverted 301.21
      schizotypal 301.22
    type A 301.4
    unstable (emotional) 301.59
Perthes' disease (capital femoral osteochondrosis) 732.1
Pertussis — *see also* Whooping cough 033.9
  vaccination, prophylactic (against) V03.6
Peruvian wart 088.0
Perversion, perverted
  appetite 307.52
    hysterical 300.11
  function
    pineal gland 259.8
    pituitary gland 253.9
      anterior lobe
        deficient 253.2
        excessive 253.1
      posterior lobe 253.6
    placenta — *see* Placenta, abnormal
  sense of smell or taste 781.1
    psychogenic 306.7
  sexual (*see also* Deviation, sexual) 302.9
Pervious, congenital — *see also* Imperfect, closure
  ductus arteriosus 747.0
Pes (congenital) — *see also* Talipes 754.70
  abductus (congenital) 754.60
    acquired 736.79
  acquired NEC 736.79
    planus 734

Pes — *see also* Talipes — *continued*
  adductus (congenital) 754.79
    acquired 736.79
  cavus 754.71
    acquired 736.73
  planovalgus (congenital) 754.69
    acquired 736.79
  planus (acquired) (any degree) 734
    congenital 754.61
    rachitic 268.1
  valgus (congenital) 754.61
    acquired 736.79
  varus (congenital) 754.50
    acquired 736.79
Pest — *see also* Plague 020.9
Pestis — *see also* Plague 020.9
  bubonica 020.0
  fulminans 020.0
  minor 020.8
  pneumonica — *see* Plague, pneumonic
Petechial
  fever 036.0
  typhus 081.9
Petechia, petechiae 782.7
  fetus or newborn 772.6
Petges-Cléjat or Petges-Clégat syndrome (poikilodermatomyositis) 710.3
Petit's
  disease (*see also* Hernia, lumbar) 553.8
Petit mal (idiopathic) — *see also* Epilepsy 345.0 ☑
  status 345.2
Petrellidosis 117.6
Petrositis 383.20
  acute 383.21
  chronic 383.22
Peutz-Jeghers disease or syndrome 759.6
Peyronie's disease 607.85
Pfeiffer's disease 075
Phacentocele 379.32
  traumatic 921.3
Phacoanaphylaxis 360.19
Phacocele (old) 379.32
  traumatic 921.3
Phaehyphomycosis 117.8
Phagedena (dry) (moist) — *see also* Gangrene 785.4
  arteriosclerotic 440.24
  geometric 686.09
  penis 607.89
  senile 440.2 ☑ [785.4]
  sloughing 785.4
  tropical (*see also* Ulcer, skin) 707.9
  vulva 616.50
Phagedenic — *see also* condition
  abscess (*see also* Abscess)
    chancroid 099.0
  bubo NEC 099.8
  chancre 099.0
  ulcer (tropical) (*see also* Ulcer, skin) 707.9
Phagomania 307.52
Phakoma 362.89
Phantom limb (syndrome) 353.6
Pharyngeal — *see also* condition
  arch remnant 744.41
  pouch syndrome 279.11
Pharyngitis (acute) (catarrhal) (gangrenous) (infective) (malignant) (membranous) (phlegmonous) (pneumococcal) (pseudomembranous) (simple) (staphylococcal) (subacute) (suppurative) (ulcerative) (viral) 462
  with influenza, flu, or grippe 487.1
  aphthous 074.0
  atrophic 472.1
  chlamydial 099.51
  chronic 472.1
  Coxsackie virus 074.0
  diphtheritic (membranous) 032.0
  follicular 472.1
  fusospirochetal 101

Pharyngitis — *continued*
  gonococcal 098.6
  granular (chronic) 472.1
  herpetic 054.79
  hypertrophic 472.1
  infectional, chronic 472.1
  influenzal 487.1
  lymphonodular, acute 074.8
  septic 034.0
  streptococcal 034.0
  tuberculous (*see also* Tuberculosis) 012.8 ☑
  vesicular 074.0
Pharyngoconjunctival fever 077.2
Pharyngoconjunctivitis, viral 077.2
Pharyngolaryngitis (acute) 465.0
  chronic 478.9
  septic 034.0
Pharyngoplegia 478.29
Pharyngotonsillitis 465.8
  tuberculous 012.8 ☑
Pharyngotracheitis (acute) 465.8
  chronic 478.9
Pharynx, pharyngeal — *see* condition
Phase of life problem NEC V62.89
Phenomenon
  Arthus' 995.21   ▲
  flashback (drug) 292.89
  jaw-winking 742.8
  Jod-Basedow 242.8 ☑
  L. E. cell 710.0
  lupus erythematosus cell 710.0
  Pelger-Huët (hereditary hyposegmentation) 288.2
  Raynaud's (paroxysmal digital cyanosis) (secondary) 443.0
  Reilly's (*see also* Neuropathy, peripheral, autonomic) 337.9
  vasomotor 780.2
  vasospastic 443.9
  vasovagal 780.2
  Wenckebach's, heart block (second degree) 426.13
Phenylketonuria (PKU) 270.1
Phenylpyruvicaciduria 270.1
Pheochromoblastoma (M8700/3)
  specified site — *see* Neoplasm, by site, malignant
  unspecified site 194.0
Pheochromocytoma (M8700/0)
  malignant (M8700/3)
    specified site — *see* Neoplasm, by site, malignant
    unspecified site 194.0
  specified site — *see* Neoplasm, by site, benign
  unspecified site 227.0
Phimosis (congenital) 605
  chancroidal 099.0
  due to infection 605
Phlebectasia — *see also* Varicose, vein 454.9
  congenital NEC 747.60
  esophagus (*see also* Varix, esophagus) 456.1
    with hemorrhage (*see also* Varix, esophagus, bleeding) 456.0
Phlebitis (infective) (pyemic) (septic) (suppurative) 451.9
  antecubital vein 451.82
  arm NEC 451.84
    axillary vein 451.89
    basilic vein 451.82
    deep 451.83
    superficial 451.82
  axillary vein 451.89
  basilic vein 451.82
  blue 451.9
  brachial vein 451.83
  breast, superficial 451.89
  cavernous (venous) sinus — *see* Phlebitis, intracranial sinus
  cephalic vein 451.82
  cerebral (venous) sinus — *see* Phlebitis, intracranial sinus
  chest wall, superficial 451.89

Phlebitis — *continued*
complicating pregnancy or puerperium 671.9 ☑
  affecting fetus or newborn 760.3
cranial (venous) sinus — *see* Phlebitis, intracranial sinus
deep (vessels) 451.19
  femoral vein 451.11
  specified vessel NEC 451.19
due to implanted device — *see* Complications, due to (presence of) any device, implant, or graft classified to 996.0–996.5 NEC
during or resulting from a procedure 997.2
femoral vein (deep) (superficial) 451.11
femoropopliteal 451.19
following infusion, perfusion, or transfusion 999.2
gouty 274.89 *[451.9]*
hepatic veins 451.89
iliac vein 451.81
iliofemoral 451.11
intracranial sinus (any) (venous) 325
  late effect — *see* category 326
  nonpyogenic 437.6
    in pregnancy or puerperium 671.5 ☑
jugular vein 451.89
lateral (venous) sinus — *see* Phlebitis, intracranial sinus
leg 451.2
  deep (vessels) 451.19
    femoral vein 451.11
    specified vessel NEC 451.19
  superficial (vessels) 451.0
    femoral vein 451.11
longitudinal sinus — *see* Phlebitis, intracranial sinus
lower extremity 451.2
  deep (vessels) 451.19
    femoral vein 451.11
    specified vessel NEC 451.19
  migrans, migrating (superficial) 453.1
  superficial (vessels) 451.0
    femoral vein 451.11
pelvic
  with
    abortion — *see* Abortion, by type, with sepsis
    ectopic pregnancy (*see also* categories 633.0–633.9) 639.0
    molar pregnancy (*see also* categories 630–632) 639.0
  following
    abortion 639.0
    ectopic or molar pregnancy 639.0
  puerperal, postpartum 671.4 ☑
popliteal vein 451.19
portal (vein) 572.1
postoperative 997.2
pregnancy 671.9 ☑
  deep 671.3 ☑
  specified type NEC 671.5 ☑
  superficial 671.2 ☑
puerperal, postpartum, childbirth 671.9 ☑
  deep 671.4 ☑
  lower extremities 671.2 ☑
  pelvis 671.4 ☑
  specified site NEC 671.5 ☑
  superficial 671.2 ☑
radial vein 451.83
retina 362.18
saphenous (great) (long) 451.0
  accessory or small 451.0
sinus (meninges) — *see* Phlebitis, intracranial sinus
specified site NEC 451.89
subclavian vein 451.89
syphilitic 093.89
tibial vein 451.19
ulcer, ulcerative 451.9

Phlebitis — *continued*
ulcer, ulcerative — *continued*
  leg 451.2
    deep (vessels) 451.19
      femoral vein 451.11
      specified vessel NEC 451.19
    superficial (vessels) 451.0
      femoral vein 451.11
    lower extremity 451.2
      deep (vessels) 451.19
        femoral vein 451.11
        specified vessel NEC 451.19
      superficial (vessels) 451.0
  ulnar vein 451.83
  umbilicus 451.89
  upper extremity (*see also* Phlebitis, arm)
    deep (veins) 451.83
      brachial vein 451.83
      radial vein 451.83
      ulnar vein 451.83
    superficial (veins) 451.82
      antecubital vein 451.82
      basilica vein 451.82
      cephalic vein 451.82
  uterus (septic) (*see also* Endometritis) 615.9
  varicose (leg) (lower extremity) (*see also* Varicose, vein) 454.1
Phlebofibrosis 459.89
Phleboliths 459.89
Phlebosclerosis 459.89
Phlebothrombosis — *see* Thrombosis
Phlebotomus fever 066.0
Phlegmasia
alba dolens (deep vessels) 451.19
  complicating pregnancy 671.3 ☑
  nonpuerperal 451.19
  puerperal, postpartum, childbirth 671.4 ☑
cerulea dolens 451.19
Phlegm, choked on 933.1
Phlegmon — *see also* Abscess 682.9
erysipelatous (*see also* Erysipelas) 035
iliac 682.2
  fossa 540.1
throat 478.29
Phlegmonous — *see* condition
Phlyctenulosis (allergic) (keratoconjunctivitis) (nontuberculous) 370.31
cornea 370.31
  with ulcer (*see also* Ulcer, cornea) 370.00
tuberculous (*see also* Tuberculosis) 017.3 ☑ *[370.31]*
Phobia, phobic (reaction) 300.20
animal 300.29
  isolated NEC 300.29
obsessional 300.3
simple NEC 300.29
social 300.23
specified NEC 300.29
state 300.20
Phocas' disease 610.1
Phocomelia 755.4
lower limb 755.32
  complete 755.33
  distal 755.35
  proximal 755.34
upper limb 755.22
  complete 755.23
  distal 755.25
  proximal 755.24
Phoria — *see also* Heterophoria 378.40
Phosphate-losing tubular disorder 588.0
Phosphatemia 275.3
Phosphaturia 275.3
Photoallergic response 692.72
Photocoproporphyria 277.1
Photodermatitis (sun) 692.72
light other than sun 692.82
Photokeratitis 370.24
Photo-ophthalmia 370.24
Photophobia 368.13
Photopsia 368.15

Photoretinitis 363.31
Photoretinopathy 363.31
Photosensitiveness (sun) 692.72
light other than sun 692.82
Photosensitization (skin) (sun) 692.72
light other than sun 692.82
Phototoxic response 692.72
Phrenitis 323.9
Phrynoderma 264.8
Phthiriasis (pubis) (any site) 132.2
with any infestation classifiable to 132.0, 132.1, 132.3
Phthirus infestation — *see* Phthiriasis
Phthisis — *see also* Tuberculosis 011.9 ☑
bulbi (infectional) 360.41
colliers' 011.4 ☑
cornea 371.05
eyeball (due to infection) 360.41
millstone makers' 011.4 ☑
miners' 011.4 ☑
potters' 011.4 ☑
sandblasters' 011.4 ☑
stonemasons' 011.4 ☑
Phycomycosis 117.7
Physalopteriasis 127.7
Physical therapy NEC V57.1
breathing exercises V57.0
Physiological cup, optic papilla
borderline, glaucoma suspect 365.00
enlarged 377.14
glaucomatous 377.14
Phytobezoar 938
intestine 936
stomach 935.2
Pian — *see also* Yaws 102.9
Pianoma 102.1
Piarhemia, piarrhemia — *see also* Hyperlipemia 272.4
bilharziasis 120.9
Pica 307.52
hysterical 300.11
Pick's
cerebral atrophy 331.11
  with dementia
    with behavioral disturbance 331.11 *[294.11]*
    without behavioral disturbance 331.11 *[294.10]*
disease
  brain 331.11
    dementia in
      with behavioral disturbance 331.11 *[294.11]*
      without behavioral disturbance 331.11 *[294.10]*
  lipid histiocytosis 272.7
  liver (pericardial pseudocirrhosis of liver) 423.2
  pericardium (pericardial pseudocirrhosis of liver) 423.2
  polyserositis (pericardial pseudocirrhosis of liver) 423.2
syndrome
  heart (pericardial pseudocirrhosis of liver) 423.2
  liver (pericardial pseudocirrhosis of liver) 423.2
tubular adenoma (M8640/0)
  specified site — *see* Neoplasm, by site, benign
  unspecified site
    female 220
    male 222.0
Pick-Herxheimer syndrome (diffuse idiopathic cutaneous atrophy) 701.8
Pick-Niemann disease (lipid histiocytosis) 272.7
Pickwickian syndrome (cardiopulmonary obesity) 278.8
Piebaldism, classic 709.09
Piedra 111.2
beard 111.2
  black 111.3
  white 111.2
black 111.3

Piedra — *continued*
scalp 111.3
  black 111.3
  white 111.3
white 111.2
Pierre Marie-Bamberger syndrome (hypertrophic pulmonary osteoarthropathy) 731.2
Pierre Marie's syndrome (pulmonary hypertrophic osteoarthropathy) 731.2
Pierre Mauriac's syndrome (diabetes-dwarfism-obesity) 258.1
Pierre Robin deformity or syndrome (congenital) 756.0
Pierson's disease or osteochondrosis 732.1
Pigeon
breast or chest (acquired) 738.3
  congenital 754.82
  rachitic (*see also* Rickets) 268.0
breeders' disease or lung 495.2
fanciers' disease or lung 495.2
toe 735.8
Pigmentation (abnormal) 709.00
anomaly 709.00
  congenital 757.33
  specified NEC 709.09
conjunctiva 372.55
cornea 371.10
  anterior 371.11
  posterior 371.13
  stromal 371.12
lids (congenital) 757.33
  acquired 374.52
limbus corneae 371.10
metals 709.00
optic papilla, congenital 743.57
retina (congenital) (grouped) (nevoid) 743.53
  acquired 362.74
scrotum, congenital 757.33
Piles — *see* Hemorrhoids
Pili
annulati or torti (congenital) 757.4
incarnati 704.8
Pill roller hand (intrinsic) 736.09
Pilomatrixoma (M8110/0) — *see* Neoplasm, skin, benign
Pilonidal — *see* condition
Pimple 709.8
PIN I (prostatic intraepithelial neoplasia I) 602.3
PIN II (prostatic intraepithelial neoplasia II) 602.3
PIN III (prostatic intraepithelial neoplasia III) 233.4
Pinched nerve — *see* Neuropathy, entrapment
Pineal body or gland — *see* condition
Pinealoblastoma (M9362/3) 194.4
Pinealoma (M9360/1) 237.1
  malignant (M9360/3) 194.4
Pineoblastoma (M9362/3) 194.4
Pineocytoma (M9361/1) 237.1
Pinguecula 372.51
Pinhole meatus — *see also* Stricture, urethra 598.9
Pink
disease 985.0
eye 372.03
puffer 492.8
Pinkus' disease (lichen nitidus) 697.1
Pinpoint
meatus (*see also* Stricture, urethra) 598.9
os uteri (*see also* Stricture, cervix) 622.4
Pinselhaare (congenital) 757.4
Pinta 103.9
cardiovascular lesions 103.2
chancre (primary) 103.0
erythematous plaques 103.1
hyperchromic lesions 103.1
hyperkeratosis 103.1
lesions 103.9

Pinta — *continued*
lesions — *continued*
cardiovascular 103.2
hyperchromic 103.1
intermediate 103.1
late 103.2
mixed 103.3
primary 103.0
skin (achromic) (cicatricial)
(dyschromic) 103.2
hyperchromic 103.1
mixed (achromic and hyperchromic) 103.3
papule (primary) 103.0
skin lesions (achromic) (cicatricial)
(dyschromic) 103.2
hyperchromic 103.1
mixed (achromic and hyperchromic) 103.3
vitiligo 103.2
Pintid 103.0
Pinworms (disease) (infection) (infestation) 127.4
Piry fever 066.8
Pistol wound — *see* Gunshot wound
Pitchers' elbow 718.82
Pithecoid pelvis 755.69
with disproportion (fetopelvic) 653.2 ☑
affecting fetus or newborn 763.1
causing obstructed labor 660.1 ☑
Pithiatism 300.11
Pit, lip (mucus), **congenital** 750.25
Pitted — *see also* Pitting
teeth 520.4
Pitting (edema) — *see also* Edema 782.3
lip 782.3
nail 703.8
congenital 757.5
Pituitary gland — *see* condition
Pituitary snuff-takers' disease 495.8
Pityriasis 696.5
alba 696.5
capitis 690.11
circinata (et maculata) 696.3
Hebra's (exfoliative dermatitis) 695.89
lichenoides et varioliformis 696.2
maculata (et circinata) 696.3
nigra 111.1
pilaris 757.39
acquired 701.1
Hebra's 696.4
rosea 696.3
rotunda 696.3
rubra (Hebra) 695.89
pilaris 696.4
sicca 690.18
simplex 690.18
specified type NEC 696.5
streptogenes 696.5
versicolor 111.0
scrotal 111.0
Placenta, placental
ablatio 641.2 ☑
affecting fetus or newborn 762.1
abnormal, abnormality 656.7 ☑
with hemorrhage 641.8 ☑
affecting fetus or newborn 762.1
affecting fetus or newborn 762.2
abruptio 641.2 ☑
affecting fetus or newborn 762.1
accessory lobe — *see* Placenta, abnormal
accreta (without hemorrhage) 667.0 ☑
with hemorrhage 666.0 ☑
adherent (without hemorrhage)
667.0 ☑
with hemorrhage 666.0 ☑
apoplexy — *see* Placenta, separation
battledore — *see* Placenta, abnormal
bilobate — *see* Placenta, abnormal
bipartita — *see* Placenta, abnormal
carneous mole 631
centralis — *see* Placenta, previa
circumvallata — *see* Placenta, abnormal

Placenta, placental — *continued*
cyst (amniotic) — *see* Placenta, abnormal
deficiency — *see* Placenta, insufficiency
degeneration — *see* Placenta, insufficiency
detachment (partial) (premature) (with
hemorrhage) 641.2 ☑
affecting fetus or newborn 762.1
dimidiata — *see* Placenta, abnormal
disease 656.7 ☑
affecting fetus or newborn 762.2
duplex — *see* Placenta, abnormal
dysfunction — *see* Placenta, insufficiency
fenestrata — *see* Placenta, abnormal
fibrosis — *see* Placenta, abnormal
fleshy mole 631
hematoma — *see* Placenta, abnormal
hemorrhage NEC — *see* Placenta,
separation
hormone disturbance or malfunction
— *see* Placenta, abnormal
hyperplasia — *see* Placenta, abnormal
increta (without hemorrhage) 667.0 ☑
with hemorrhage 666.0 ☑
infarction 656.7 ☑
affecting fetus or newborn 762.2
insertion, vicious — *see* Placenta,
previa
insufficiency
affecting
fetus or newborn 762.2
management of pregnancy
656.5 ☑
lateral — *see* Placenta, previa
low implantation or insertion — *see*
Placenta, previa
low-lying — *see* Placenta, previa
malformation — *see* Placenta, abnormal
malposition — *see* Placenta, previa
marginalis, marginata — *see* Placenta,
previa
marginal sinus (hemorrhage) (rupture)
641.2 ☑
affecting fetus or newborn 762.1
membranacea — *see* Placenta, abnormal
multilobed — *see* Placenta, abnormal
multipartita — *see* Placenta, abnormal
necrosis — *see* Placenta, abnormal
percreta (without hemorrhage)
667.0 ☑
with hemorrhage 666.0 ☑
polyp 674.4 ☑
previa (central) (centralis) (complete)
(lateral) (marginal) (marginalis)
(partial) (partialis) (total) (with
hemorrhage) 641.1 ☑
without hemorrhage (before labor
and delivery) (during pregnancy) 641.0 ☑
affecting fetus or newborn 762.0
noted
before labor, without hemorrhage (with cesarean delivery) 641.0 ☑
during pregnancy (without
hemorrhage) 641.0 ☑
retention (with hemorrhage) 666.0 ☑
without hemorrhage 667.0 ☑
fragments, complicating puerperium (delayed hemorrhage)
666.2 ☑
without hemorrhage 667.1 ☑
postpartum, puerperal 666.2 ☑
separation (normally implanted) (partial) (premature) (with hemorrhage) 641.2 ☑
affecting fetus or newborn 762.1
septuplex — *see* Placenta, abnormal
small — *see* Placenta, insufficiency
softening (premature) — *see* Placenta,
abnormal

Placenta, placental — *continued*
spuria — *see* Placenta, abnormal
succenturiata — *see* Placenta, abnormal
syphilitic 095.8
transfusion syndromes 762.3
transmission of chemical substance
— *see* Absorption, chemical,
through placenta
trapped (with hemorrhage) 666.0 ☑
without hemorrhage 667.0 ☑
trilobate — *see* Placenta, abnormal
tripartita — *see* Placenta, abnormal
triplex — *see* Placenta, abnormal
varicose vessel — *see* Placenta, abnormal
vicious insertion — *see* Placenta, previa
Placentitis
affecting fetus or newborn 762.7
complicating pregnancy 658.4 ☑
Plagiocephaly (skull) 754.0
Plague 020.9
abortive 020.8
ambulatory 020.8
bubonic 020.0
cellulocutaneous 020.1
lymphatic gland 020.0
pneumonic 020.5
primary 020.3
secondary 020.4
pulmonary — *see* Plague, pneumonic
pulmonic — *see* Plague, pneumonic
septicemic 020.2
tonsillar 020.9
septicemic 020.2
vaccination, prophylactic (against)
V03.3
Planning, family V25.09
contraception V25.9
procreation V26.4
Plaque
artery, arterial — *see* Arteriosclerosis
calcareous — *see* Calcification
Hollenhorst's (retinal) 362.33
tongue 528.6
Plasma cell myeloma 203.0 ☑
Plasmacytoma, plasmocytoma (solitary)
(M9731/1) 238.6
benign (M9731/0) — *see* Neoplasm,
by site, benign
malignant (M9731/3) 203.8 ☑
Plasmacytopenia 288.59 ●
Plasmacytosis 288.64 ▲
Plaster ulcer — *see also* Decubitus
707.00
Platybasia 756.0
Platyonychia (congenital) 757.5
acquired 703.8
Platypelloid pelvis 738.6
with disproportion (fetopelvic) 653.2 ☑
affecting fetus or newborn 763.1
causing obstructed labor 660.1 ☑
affecting fetus or newborn 763.1
congenital 755.69
Platyspondylia 756.19
Plethora 782.62
newborn 776.4
Pleuralgia 786.52
Pleura, pleural — *see* condition
Pleurisy (acute) (adhesive) (chronic)
(costal) (diaphragmatic) (double)
(dry) (fetid) (fibrinous) (fibrous) (interlobar) (latent) (lung) (old) (plastic)
(primary) (residual) (sicca) (sterile)
(subacute) (unresolved) (with adherent pleura) 511.0
with
effusion (without mention of cause)
511.9
bacterial, nontuberculous 511.1
nontuberculous NEC 511.9
bacterial 511.1
pneumococcal 511.1
specified type NEC 511.8
staphylococcal 511.1

Pleurisy — *continued*
with — *continued*
effusion — *continued*
streptococcal 511.1
tuberculous (*see also* Tuberculosis, pleura) 012.0 ☑
primary, progressive 010.1 ☑
influenza, flu, or grippe 487.1
tuberculosis — *see* Pleurisy, tuberculous
encysted 511.8
exudative (*see also* Pleurisy, with effusion) 511.9
bacterial, nontuberculous 511.1
fibrinopurulent 510.9
with fistula 510.0
fibropurulent 510.9
with fistula 510.0
hemorrhagic 511.8
influenzal 487.1
pneumococcal 511.0
with effusion 511.1
purulent 510.9
with fistula 510.0
septic 510.9
with fistula 510.0
serofibrinous (*see also* Pleurisy, with
effusion) 511.9
bacterial, nontuberculous 511.1
seropurulent 510.9
with fistula 510.0
serous (*see also* Pleurisy, with effusion) 511.9
bacterial, nontuberculous 511.1
staphylococcal 511.0
with effusion 511.1
streptococcal 511.0
with effusion 511.1
suppurative 510.9
with fistula 510.0
traumatic (post) (current) 862.29
with open wound into cavity
862.39
tuberculous (with effusion) (*see also*
Tuberculosis, pleura) 012.0 ☑
primary, progressive 010.1 ☑
Pleuritis sicca — *see* Pleurisy
Pleurobronchopneumonia — *see also*
Pneumonia, broncho- 485
Pleurodynia 786.52
epidemic 074.1
viral 074.1
Pleurohepatitis 573.8
Pleuropericarditis — *see also* Pericarditis 423.9
acute 420.90
Pleuropneumonia (acute) (bilateral)
(double) (septic) — *see also* Pneumonia 486
chronic (*see also* Fibrosis, lung) 515
Pleurorrhea — *see also* Hydrothorax
511.8
Plexitis, brachial 353.0
Plica
knee 727.83
polonica 132.0
syndrome 727.83
tonsil 474.8
Plicae dysphonia ventricularis 784.49
Plicated tongue 529.5
congenital 750.13
Plug
bronchus NEC 519.19 ▲
meconium (newborn) NEC 777.1
mucus — *see* Mucus, plug
Plumbism 984.9
specified type of lead — *see* Table of
Drugs and Chemicals
Plummer's disease (toxic nodular goiter)
242.3 ☑
Plummer-Vinson syndrome (sideropenic
dysphagia) 280.8
Pluricarential syndrome of infancy 260
Plurideficiency syndrome of infancy
260

☑ Additional Digit Required — Refer to the Tabular List for Digit Selection
▷◁ Revised Text   ● New Line   ▲ Revised Code
232 — Volume 2 • October 2006
▽ Subterms under main terms may continue to next column or page
2007 ICD-9-CM

Plus (and minus) hand (intrinsic)
736.09
PMDD (premenstrual dysphoric disorder)
625.4
PMS 625.4
**Pneumathemia — see Air, embolism,
by type**
Pneumatic drill or hammer disease
994.9
Pneumatocele (lung) 518.89
intracranial 348.8
tension 492.0
Pneumatosis
cystoides intestinalis 569.89
peritonei 568.89
pulmonum 492.8
Pneumaturia 599.84
Pneumoblastoma (M8981/3) — see
Neoplasm, lung, malignant
Pneumocephalus 348.8
Pneumococcemia 038.2
Pneumococcus, pneumococcal — see
condition
Pneumoconiosis (due to) (inhalation of)
505
aluminum 503
asbestos 501
bagasse 495.1
bauxite 503
beryllium 503
carbon electrode makers' 503
coal
miners' (simple) 500
workers' (simple) 500
cotton dust 504
diatomite fibrosis 502
dust NEC 504
inorganic 503
lime 502
marble 502
organic NEC 504
fumes or vapors (from silo) 506.9
graphite 503
hard metal 503
mica 502
moldy hay 495.0
rheumatoid 714.81
silica NEC 502
and carbon 500
silicate NEC 502
talc 502
Pneumocystis carinii pneumonia 136.3
Pneumocystis jiroveci pneumonia ●
136.3 ●
Pneumocystosis 136.3
with pneumonia 136.3
Pneumoenteritis 025
Pneumohemopericardium — see also
Pericarditis 423.9
Pneumohemothorax — see also
Hemothorax 511.8
traumatic 860.4
with open wound into thorax 860.5
Pneumohydropericardium — see also
Pericarditis 423.9
Pneumohydrothorax — see also Hydrothorax 511.8
Pneumomediastinum 518.1
congenital 770.2
fetus or newborn 770.2
Pneumomycosis 117.9
Pneumonia (acute) (Alpenstich) (benign)
(bilateral) (brain) (cerebral) (circumscribed) (congestive) (creeping) (delayed resolution) (double) (epidemic) (fever) (flash) (fulminant) (fungoid) (granulomatous) (hemorrhagic) (incipient) (infantile) (infectious)
(infiltration) (insular) (intermittent)
(latent) (lobe) (migratory) (newborn)
(organized) (overwhelming) (primary) (progressive) (pseudolobar) (purulent) (resolved) (secondary) (senile) (septic) (suppurative) (terminal) (true) (unresolved) (vesicular)
486

Pneumonia — continued
with influenza, flu, or grippe 487.0
adenoviral 480.0
adynamic 514
alba 090.0
allergic 518.3
alveolar — see Pneumonia, lobar
anaerobes 482.81
anthrax 022.1 [484.5]
apex, apical — see Pneumonia, lobar
ascaris 127.0 [484.8]
aspiration 507.0
due to
aspiration of microorganisms
bacterial 482.9
specified type NEC 482.89
specified organism NEC
483.8
bacterial NEC 482.89
viral 480.9
specified type NEC 480.8
food (regurgitated) 507.0
gastric secretions 507.0
milk 507.0
oils, essences 507.1
solids, liquids NEC 507.8
vomitus 507.0
fetal 770.18
due to
blood 770.16
clear amniotic fluid 770.14
meconium 770.12
postnatal stomach contents
770.86
newborn 770.18
due to
blood 770.16
clear amniotic fluid 770.14
meconium 770.12
postnatal stomach contents
770.86
asthenic 514
atypical (disseminated) (focal) (primary) 486
with influenza 487.0
bacillus 482.9
specified type NEC 482.89
bacterial 482.9
specified type NEC 482.89
Bacteroides (fragilis) (oralis)
(melaninogenicus) 482.81
basal, basic, basilar — see Pneumonia, lobar
broncho-, bronchial (confluent)
(croupous) (diffuse) (disseminated) (hemorrhagic) (involving
lobes) (lobar) (terminal) 485
with influenza 487.0
allergic 518.3
aspiration (see also Pneumonia,
aspiration) 507.0
bacterial 482.9
specified type NEC 482.89
capillary 466.19
with bronchospasm or obstruction 466.19
chronic (see also Fibrosis, lung)
515
congenital (infective) 770.0
diplococcal 481
Eaton's agent 483.0
Escherichia coli (E. coli) 482.82
Friedländer's bacillus 482.0
Hemophilus influenzae 482.2
hiberno-vernal 083.0 [484.8]
hypostatic 514
influenzal 487.0
inhalation (see also Pneumonia,
aspiration) 507.0
due to fumes or vapors (chemical) 506.0
Klebsiella 482.0
lipid 507.1
endogenous 516.8
Mycoplasma (pneumoniae) 483.0
ornithosis 073.0

Pneumonia — continued
broncho-, bronchial — continued
pleuropneumonia-like organisms
(PPLO) 483.0
pneumococcal 481
Proteus 482.83
Pseudomonas 482.1
specified organism NEC 483.8
bacterial NEC 482.89
staphylococcal 482.40
aureus 482.41
specified type NEC 482.49
streptococcal — see Pneumonia,
streptococcal
typhoid 002.0 [484.8]
viral, virus (see also Pneumonia,
viral) 480.9
Butyrivibrio (fibriosolvens) 482.81
Candida 112.4
capillary 466.19
with bronchospasm or obstruction
466.19
caseous (see also Tuberculosis)
011.6 ☑
catarrhal — see Pneumonia, broncho-
central — see Pneumonia, lobar
Chlamydia, chlamydial 483.1
pneumoniae 483.1
psittaci 073.0
specified type NEC 483.1
trachomatis 483.1
cholesterol 516.8
chronic (see also Fibrosis, lung) 515
cirrhotic (chronic) (see also Fibrosis,
lung) 515
Clostridium (haemolyticum) (novyi)
NEC 482.81
confluent — see Pneumonia, broncho-
congenital (infective) 770.0
aspiration 770.18
croupous — see Pneumonia, lobar
cytomegalic inclusion 078.5 [484.1]
deglutition (see also Pneumonia, aspiration) 507.0
desquamative interstitial 516.8
diffuse — see Pneumonia, broncho-
diplococcal, diplococcus (broncho-)
(lobar) 481
disseminated (focal) — see Pneumonia, broncho-
due to
adenovirus 480.0
anaerobes 482.81
Bacterium anitratum 482.83
Chlamydia, chlamydial 483.1
pneumoniae 483.1
psittaci 073.0
specified type NEC 483.1
trachomatis 483.1
coccidioidomycosis 114.0
Diplococcus (pneumoniae) 481
Eaton's agent 483.0
Escherichia coli (E. coli) 482.82
Friedländer's bacillus 482.0
fumes or vapors (chemical) (inhalation) 506.0
fungus NEC 117.9 [484.7]
coccidioidomycosis 114.0
Hemophilus influenzae (H. influenzae) 482.2
Herellea 482.83
influenza 487.0
Klebsiella pneumoniae 482.0
Mycoplasma (pneumoniae) 483.0
parainfluenza virus 480.2
pleuropneumonia-like organism
(PPLO) 483.0
Pneumococcus 481
Pneumocystis carinii 136.3
Pneumocystis jiroveci 136.3 ●
Proteus 482.83
Pseudomonas 482.1
respiratory syncytial virus 480.1
rickettsia 083.9 [484.8]
SARS-associated coronavirus 480.3

Pneumonia — continued
due to — continued
specified
bacteria NEC 482.89
organism NEC 483.8
virus NEC 480.8
Staphylococcus 482.40
aureus 482.41
specified type NEC 482.49
Streptococcus (see also Pneumonia, streptococcal)
pneumoniae 481
virus (see also Pneumonia, viral)
480.9
SARS-associated coronavirus
480.3
Eaton's agent 483.0
embolic, embolism — (see Embolism,
pulmonary)
eosinophilic 518.3
Escherichia coli (E. coli) 482.82
Eubacterium 482.81
fibrinous — see Pneumonia, lobar
fibroid (chronic) (see also Fibrosis,
lung) 515
fibrous (see also Fibrosis, lung) 515
Friedländer's bacillus 482.0
Fusobacterium (nucleatum) 482.81
gangrenous 513.0
giant cell (see also Pneumonia, viral)
480.9
gram-negative bacteria NEC 482.83
anaerobic 482.81
grippal 487.0
Hemophilus influenzae (bronchial)
(lobar) 482.2
hypostatic (broncho-) (lobar) 514
in
actinomycosis 039.1
anthrax 022.1 [484.5]
aspergillosis 117.3 [484.6]
candidiasis 112.4
coccidioidomycosis 114.0
cytomegalic inclusion disease
078.5 [484.1]
histoplasmosis (see also Histoplasmosis) 115.95
infectious disease NEC
136.9 [484.8]
measles 055.1
mycosis, systemic NEC
117.9 [484.7]
nocardiasis, nocardiosis 039.1
ornithosis 073.0
pneumocystosis 136.3
psittacosis 073.0
Q fever 083.0 [484.8]
salmonellosis 003.22
toxoplasmosis 130.4
tularemia 021.2
typhoid (fever) 002.0 [484.8]
varicella 052.1
whooping cough (see also Whooping cough) 033.9 [484.3]
infective, acquired prenatally 770.0
influenzal (broncho) (lobar) (virus)
487.0
inhalation (see also Pneumonia, aspiration) 507.0
fumes or vapors (chemical) 506.0
interstitial 516.8
with influenzal 487.0
acute 136.3
chronic (see also Fibrosis, lung)
515
desquamative 516.8
hypostatic 514
lipid 507.1
lymphoid 516.8
plasma cell 136.3
Pseudomonas 482.1
intrauterine (infective) 770.0
aspiration 770.18
blood 770.16
clear amniotic fluid 770.14
meconium 770.12

☑ Additional Digit Required — Refer to the Tabular List for Digit Selection
⬛ Subterms under main terms may continue to next column or page
2007 ICD-9-CM   ▶◀ Revised Text   ● New Line   ▲ Revised Code   **October 2006 · Volume 2 — 233**

Plus — Pneumonia

Pneumonia — continued
  intrauterine — continued
    aspiration — continued
      postnatal stomach contents 770.86
    Klebsiella pneumoniae 482.0
    Legionnaires' 482.84
    lipid, lipoid (exogenous) (interstitial) 507.1
      endogenous 516.8
    lobar (diplococcal) (disseminated) (double) (interstitial) (pneumococcal, any type) 481
      with influenza 487.0
      bacterial 482.9
        specified type NEC 482.89
      chronic (see also Fibrosis, lung) 515
      Escherichia coli (E. coli) 482.82
      Friedländer's bacillus 482.0
      Hemophilus influenzae (H. influenzae) 482.2
    hypostatic 514
    influenzal 487.0
    Klebsiella 482.0
    ornithosis 073.0
    Proteus 482.83
    Pseudomonas 482.1
    psittacosis 073.0
    specified organism NEC 483.8
      bacterial NEC 482.89
    staphylococcal 482.40
      aureus 482.41
      specified type NEC 482.49
    streptococcal — see Pneumonia, streptococcal
    viral, virus (see also Pneumonia, viral) 480.9
  lobular (confluent) — see Pneumonia, broncho-
  Löffler's 518.3
  massive — see Pneumonia, lobar
  meconium aspiration 770.12
  metastatic NEC 038.8 [484.8]
  Mycoplasma (pneumoniae) 483.0
  necrotic 513.0
  nitrogen dioxide 506.9
  orthostatic 514
  parainfluenza virus 480.2
  parenchymatous (see also Fibrosis, lung) 515
  passive 514
  patchy — see Pneumonia, broncho-
  Peptococcus 482.81
  Peptostreptococcus 482.81
  plasma cell 136.3
  pleurolobar — see Pneumonia, lobar
  pleuropneumonia-like organism (PPLO) 483.0
  pneumococcal (broncho) (lobar) 481
  Pneumocystis (carinii) ▶(jiroveci)◀ 136.3
  postinfectional NEC 136.9 [484.8]
  postmeasles 055.1
  postoperative 997.3
  primary atypical 486
  Proprionibacterium 482.81
  Proteus 482.83
  Pseudomonas 482.1
  psittacosis 073.0
  radiation 508.0
  respiratory syncytial virus 480.1
  resulting from a procedure 997.3
  rheumatic 390 [517.1]
  Salmonella 003.22
  SARS-associated coronavirus 480.3
  segmented, segmental — see Pneumonia, broncho-
  Serratia (marcescens) 482.83
  specified
    bacteria NEC 482.89
    organism NEC 483.8
    virus NEC 480.8
  spirochetal 104.8 [484.8]
  staphylococcal (broncho) (lobar) 482.40

Pneumonia — continued
  staphylococcal — continued
    aureus 482.41
    specified type NEC 482.49
  static, stasis 514
  streptococcal (broncho) (lobar) NEC 482.30
    Group
      A 482.31
      B 482.32
      specified NEC 482.39
    pneumoniae 481
    specified type NEC 482.39
    Streptococcus pneumoniae 481
  traumatic (complication) (early) (secondary) 958.8
  tuberculous (any) (see also Tuberculosis) 011.6 ✓
  tularemic 021.2
  TWAR agent 483.1
  varicella 052.1
  Veillonella 482.81
  viral, virus (broncho) (interstitial) (lobar) 480.9
    with influenza, flu, or grippe 487.0
    adenoviral 480.0
    parainfluenza 480.2
    respiratory syncytial 480.1
    SARS-associated coronavirus 480.3
    specified type NEC 480.8
  white (congenital) 090.0
Pneumonic — see condition
Pneumonitis (acute) (primary) — see also Pneumonia 486
  allergic 495.9
    specified type NEC 495.8
  aspiration 507.0
    due to fumes or gases 506.0
    fetal 770.18
      due to
        blood 770.16
        clear amniotic fluid 770.14
        meconium 770.12
        postnatal stomach contents 770.86
    newborn 770.18
      due to
        blood 770.16
        clear amniotic fluid 770.14
        meconium 770.12
        postnatal stomach contents 770.86
    obstetric 668.0 ✓
  chemical 506.0
    due to fumes or gases 506.0
  cholesterol 516.8
  chronic (see also Fibrosis, lung) 515
  congenital rubella 771.0
  crack 506.0
  due to
    crack (cocaine) 506.0
    fumes or vapors 506.0
    inhalation
      food (regurgitated), milk, vomitus 507.0
      oils, essences 507.1
      saliva 507.0
      solids, liquids NEC 507.8
    toxoplasmosis (acquired) 130.4
      congenital (active) 771.2 [484.8]
  eosinophilic 518.3
  fetal aspiration 770.18
    due to
      blood 770.16
      clear amniotic fluid 770.14
      meconium 770.12
      postnatal stomach contents 770.86
  hypersensitivity 495.9
  interstitial (chronic) (see also Fibrosis, lung) 515
    lymphoid 516.8
  lymphoid, interstitial 516.8
  meconium aspiration 770.12

Pneumonitis — see also Pneumonia — continued
  postanesthetic
    correct substance properly administered 507.0
    obstetric 668.0 ✓
    overdose or wrong substance given 968.4
      specified anesthetic — see Table of Drugs and Chemicals
  postoperative 997.3
    obstetric 668.0 ✓
  radiation 508.0
  rubella, congenital 771.0
  "ventilation" 495.7
  wood-dust 495.8
Pneumoconiosis — see Pneumoconiosis
Pneumoparotid 527.8
Pneumopathy NEC 518.89
  alveolar 516.9
    specified NEC 516.8
  due to dust NEC 504
  parietoalveolar 516.9
    specified condition NEC 516.8
Pneumopericarditis — see also Pericarditis 423.9
  acute 420.90
Pneumopericardium — see also Pericarditis
  congenital 770.2
  fetus or newborn 770.2
  traumatic (post) (see also Pneumothorax, traumatic) 860.0
    with open wound into thorax 860.1
Pneumoperitoneum 568.89
  fetus or newborn 770.2
Pneumophagia (psychogenic) 306.4
Pneumopleurisy, pneumopleuritis — see also Pneumonia 486
Pneumopyopericardium 420.99
Pneumopyothorax — see also Pyopneumothorax 510.9
  with fistula 510.0
Pneumorrhagia 786.3
  newborn 770.3
  tuberculous (see also Tuberculosis, pulmonary) 011.9 ✓
Pneumosiderosis (occupational) 503
Pneumothorax (acute) (chronic) 512.8
  congenital 770.2
  due to operative injury of chest wall or lung 512.1
    accidental puncture or laceration 512.1
  fetus or newborn 770.2
  iatrogenic 512.1
  postoperative 512.1
  spontaneous 512.8
    fetus or newborn 770.2
    tension 512.0
  sucking 512.8
    iatrogenic 512.1
    postoperative 512.1
  tense valvular, infectional 512.0
  tension 512.0
    iatrogenic 512.1
    postoperative 512.1
    spontaneous 512.0
  traumatic 860.0
    with
      hemothorax 860.4
        with open wound into thorax 860.5
      open wound into thorax 860.1
  tuberculous (see also Tuberculosis) 011.7 ✓
Pocket(s)
  endocardial (see also Endocarditis) 424.90
  periodontal 523.8
Podagra 274.9
Podencephalus 759.89
Poikilocytosis 790.09
Poikiloderma 709.09
  Civatte's 709.09

Poikiloderma — continued
  congenital 757.33
  vasculare atrophicans 696.2
Poikilodermatomyositis 710.3
Pointed ear 744.29
Poise imperfect 729.9
Poisoned — see Poisoning
Poisoning (acute) — see also Table of Drugs and Chemicals
  Bacillus, B.
    aertrycke (see also Infection, Salmonella) 003.9
    botulinus 005.1
    cholerae (suis) (see also Infection, Salmonella) 003.9
    paratyphosus (see also Infection, Salmonella) 003.9
    suipestifer (see also Infection, Salmonella) 003.9
  bacterial toxins NEC 005.9
  berries, noxious 988.2
  blood (general) — see Septicemia
  botulism 005.1
  bread, moldy, mouldy — see Poisoning, food
  damaged meat — see Poisoning, food
  death-cap (Amanita phalloides) (Amanita verna) 988.1
  decomposed food — see Poisoning, food
  diseased food — see Poisoning, food
  drug — see Table of Drugs and Chemicals
  epidemic, fish, meat, or other food — see Poisoning, food
  fava bean 282.2
  fish (bacterial) (see also Poisoning, food)
    noxious 988.0
  food (acute) (bacterial) (diseased) (infected) NEC 005.9
    due to
      bacillus
        aertrycke (see also Poisoning, food, due to Salmonella) 003.9
        botulinus 005.1
        cereus 005.89
        choleraesuis (see also Poisoning, food, due to Salmonella) 003.9
        paratyphosus (see also Poisoning, food, due to Salmonella) 003.9
        suipestifer (see also Poisoning, food, due to Salmonella) 003.9
      Clostridium 005.3
        botulinum 005.1
        perfringens 005.2
        welchii 005.2
      Salmonella (aertrycke) (callinarum) (choleraesuis) (enteritidis) (paratyphi) (suipestifer) 003.9
        with
          gastroenteritis 003.0
          localized infection(s) (see also Infection, Salmonella) 003.20
          septicemia 003.1
          specified manifestation NEC 003.8
        specified bacterium NEC 005.89
      Staphylococcus 005.0
      Streptococcus 005.89
      Vibrio parahaemolyticus 005.4
      Vibrio vulnificus 005.81
    noxious or naturally toxic 988.0
      berries 988.2
      fish 988.0
      mushroom 988.1
      plants NEC 988.2
  ice cream — see Poisoning, food
  ichthyotoxism (bacterial) 005.9
  kreotoxism, food 005.9

✓ Additional Digit Required — Refer to the Tabular List for Digit Selection

▽ Subterms under main terms may continue to next column or page

Poisoning — *see also* Table of Drugs and Chemicals — *continued*
  malarial — *see* Malaria
  meat — *see* Poisoning, food
  mushroom (noxious) 988.1
  mussel (*see also* Poisoning, food) noxious 988.0
  noxious foodstuffs (*see also* Poisoning, food, noxious) 988.9
    specified type NEC 988.8
  plants, noxious 988.2
  pork (*see also* Poisoning, food)
    specified NEC 988.8
    Trichinosis 124
  ptomaine — *see* Poisoning, food
  putrefaction, food — *see* Poisoning, food
  radiation 508.0
  Salmonella (*see also* Infection, Salmonella) 003.9
  sausage (*see also* Poisoning, food)
    Trichinosis 124
  saxitoxin 988.0
  shellfish (*see also* Poisoning, food) noxious 988.0
  Staphylococcus, food 005.0
  toxic, from disease NEC 799.89
  truffles — *see* Poisoning, food
  uremic — *see* Uremia
  uric acid 274.9
Poison ivy, oak, sumac or other plant dermatitis 692.6
Poker spine 720.0
Policeman's disease 729.2
Polioencephalitis (acute) (bulbar) — *see also* Poliomyelitis, bulbar 045.0 ✓
  inferior 335.22
  influenzal 487.8
  superior hemorrhagic (acute) (Wernicke's) 265.1
  Wernicke's (superior hemorrhagic) 265.1
Polioencephalomyelitis (acute) (anterior) (bulbar) — *see also* Polioencephalitis 045.0 ✓
Polioencephalopathy, superior hemorrhagic 265.1
  with
    beriberi 265.0
    pellagra 265.2
Poliomeningoencephalitis — *see* Meningoencephalitis
Poliomyelitis (acute) (anterior) (epidemic) 045.9 ✓

Note — Use the following fifth-digit subclassification with category 045:

  0 poliovirus, unspecified type
  1 poliovirus, type I
  2 poliovirus, type II
  3 poliovirus, type III

  with
    paralysis 045.1 ✓
      bulbar 045.0 ✓
  abortive 045.2 ✓
  ascending 045.9 ✓
    progressive 045.9 ✓
  bulbar 045.0 ✓
  cerebral 045.0 ✓
  chronic 335.21
  congenital 771.2
  contact V01.2
  deformities 138
  exposure to V01.2
  late effect 138
  nonepidemic 045.9 ✓
  nonparalytic 045.2 ✓
  old with deformity 138
  posterior, acute 053.19
  residual 138
  sequelae 138
  spinal, acute 045.9 ✓
  syphilitic (chronic) 094.89

Poliomyelitis — *continued*
  vaccination, prophylactic (against) V04.0
Poliosis (eyebrow) (eyelashes) 704.3
  circumscripta (congenital) 757.4
    acquired 704.3
  congenital 757.4
Pollakiuria 788.41
  psychogenic 306.53
Pollinosis 477.0
Pollitzer's disease (hidradenitis suppurativa) 705.83
Polyadenitis — *see also* Adenitis 289.3
  malignant 020.0
Polyalgia 729.9
Polyangiitis (essential) 446.0
Polyarteritis (nodosa) (renal) 446.0
Polyarthralgia 719.49
  psychogenic 306.0
Polyarthritis, polyarthropathy NEC 716.59
  due to or associated with other specified conditions — *see* Arthritis, due to or associated with
  endemic (*see also* Disease, Kaschin-Beck) 716.0 ✓
  inflammatory 714.9
    specified type NEC 714.89
  juvenile (chronic) 714.30
    acute 714.31
  migratory — *see* Fever, rheumatic
  rheumatic 714.0
    fever (acute) — *see* Fever, rheumatic
Polycarential syndrome of infancy 260
Polychondritis (atrophic) (chronic) (relapsing) 733.99
Polycoria 743.46
Polycystic (congenital) (disease) 759.89
  degeneration, kidney — *see* Polycystic, kidney
  kidney (congenital) 753.12
    adult type (APKD) 753.13
    autosomal dominant 753.13
    autosomal recessive 753.14
    childhood type (CPKD) 753.14
    infantile type 753.14
  liver 751.62
  lung 518.89
    congenital 748.4
  ovary, ovaries 256.4
  spleen 759.0
Polycythemia (primary) (rubra) (vera) (M9950/1) 238.4
  acquired 289.0
  benign 289.0
    familial 289.6
  due to
    donor twin 776.4
    fall in plasma volume 289.0
    high altitude 289.0
    maternal-fetal transfusion 776.4
    stress 289.0
  emotional 289.0
  erythropoietin 289.0
  familial (benign) 289.6
  Gaisböck's (hypertonica) 289.0
  high altitude 289.0
  hypertonica 289.0
  hypoxemic 289.0
  neonatorum 776.4
  nephrogenous 289.0
  relative 289.0
  secondary 289.0
  spurious 289.0
  stress 289.0
Polycytosis cryptogenica 289.0
Polydactylism, polydactyly 755.00
  fingers 755.01
  toes 755.02
Polydipsia 783.5
Polydystrophic oligophrenia 277.5
Polyembryoma (M9072/3) — *see* Neoplasm, by site, malignant
Polygalactia 676.6 ✓

Polyglandular
  deficiency 258.9
  dyscrasia 258.9
  dysfunction 258.9
  syndrome 258.8
Polyhydramnios — *see also* Hydramnios 657.0 ✓
Polymastia 757.6
Polymenorrhea 626.2
Polymicrogyria 742.2
Polymyalgia 725
  arteritica 446.5
  rheumatica 725
Polymyositis (acute) (chronic) (hemorrhagic) 710.4
  with involvement of
    lung 710.4 *[517.8]*
    skin 710.3
  ossificans (generalisata) (progressiva) 728.19
  Wagner's (dermatomyositis) 710.3
Polyneuritis, polyneuritic — *see also* Polyneuropathy 356.9
  alcoholic 357.5
    with psychosis 291.1
  cranialis 352.6
  demyelinating, chronic inflammatory 357.81
  diabetic 250.6 ✓ *[357.2]*
  due to lack of vitamin NEC 269.2 *[357.4]*
  endemic 265.0 *[357.4]*
  erythredema 985.0
  febrile 357.0
  hereditary ataxic 356.3
  idiopathic, acute 357.0
  infective (acute) 357.0
  nutritional 269.9 *[357.4]*
  postinfectious 357.0
Polyneuropathy (peripheral) 356.9
  alcoholic 357.5
  amyloid 277.39 *[357.4]* ▲
  arsenical 357.7
  critical illness 357.82
  diabetic 250.6 ✓ *[357.2]*
  due to
    antitetanus serum 357.6
    arsenic 357.7
    drug or medicinal substance 357.6
      correct substance properly administered 357.6
      overdose or wrong substance given or taken 977.9
      specified drug — *see* Table of Drugs and Chemicals
    lack of vitamin NEC 269.2 *[357.4]*
    lead 357.7
    organophosphate compounds 357.7
    pellagra 265.2 *[357.4]*
    porphyria 277.1 *[357.4]*
    serum 357.6
    toxic agent NEC 357.7
  hereditary 356.0
  idiopathic 356.9
    progressive 356.4
  in
    amyloidosis 277.39 *[357.4]* ▲
    avitaminosis 269.2 *[357.4]*
      specified NEC 269.1 *[357.4]*
    beriberi 265.0 *[357.4]*
    collagen vascular disease NEC 710.9 *[357.1]*
    deficiency
      B-complex NEC 266.2 *[357.4]*
      vitamin B 266.1 *[357.4]*
      vitamin B6 266.9 *[357.4]*
    diabetes 250.6 ✓ *[357.2]*
    diphtheria (*see also* Diphtheria) 032.89 *[357.4]*
    disseminated lupus erythematosus 710.0 *[357.1]*
    herpes zoster 053.13
    hypoglycemia 251.2 *[357.4]*

Polyneuropathy — *continued*
  in — *continued*
    malignant neoplasm (M8000/3) NEC 199.1 *[357.3]*
    mumps 072.72
    pellagra 265.2 *[357.4]*
    polyarteritis nodosa 446.0 *[357.1]*
    porphyria 277.1 *[357.4]*
    rheumatoid arthritis 714.0 *[357.1]*
    sarcoidosis 135 *[357.4]*
    uremia 585.9 *[357.4]*
  lead 357.7
  nutritional 269.9 *[357.4]*
    specified NEC 269.8 *[357.4]*
  postherpetic 053.13
  progressive 356.4
  sensory (hereditary) 356.2
Polyonychia 757.5
Polyopia 368.2
  refractive 368.15
Polyorchism, polyorchidism (three testes) 752.89
Polyorrhymenitis (peritoneal) — *see also* Polyserositis 568.82
  pericardial 423.2
Polyostotic fibrous dysplasia 756.54
Polyotia 744.1
Polyphagia 783.6
Polypoid — *see* condition
Polyposis — *see also* Polyp
  coli (adenomatous) (M8220/0) 211.3
    adenocarcinoma in (M8220/3) 153.9
    carcinoma in (M8220/3) 153.9
  familial (M8220/0) 211.3
  intestinal (adenomatous) (M8220/0) 211.3
  multiple (M8221/0) — *see* Neoplasm, by site, benign

Polyp, polypus

Note — Polyps of organs or sites that do not appear in the list below should be coded to the residual category for diseases of the organ or site concerned.

  accessory sinus 471.8
  adenoid tissue 471.0
  adenomatous (M8210/0) (*see also* Neoplasm, by site, benign)
    adenocarcinoma in (M8210/3) — *see* Neoplasm, by site, malignant
    carcinoma in (M8210/3) — *see* Neoplasm, by site, malignant
    multiple (M8221/0) — *see* Neoplasm, by site, benign
  antrum 471.8
  anus, anal (canal) (nonadenomatous) 569.0
    adenomatous 211.4
  Bartholin's gland 624.6
  bladder (M8120/1) 236.7
  broad ligament 620.8
  cervix (uteri) 622.7
    adenomatous 219.0
    in pregnancy or childbirth 654.6 ✓
      affecting fetus or newborn 763.89
      causing obstructed labor 660.2 ✓
    mucous 622.7
    nonneoplastic 622.7
  choanal 471.0
  cholesterol 575.6
  clitoris 624.6
  colon (M8210/0) (*see also* Polyp, adenomatous) 211.3
  corpus uteri 621.0
  dental 522.0
  ear (middle) 385.30
  endometrium 621.0
  ethmoidal (sinus) 471.8
  fallopian tube 620.8
  female genital organs NEC 624.8
  frontal (sinus) 471.8
  gallbladder 575.6
  gingiva 523.8

✓ Additional Digit Required — Refer to the Tabular List for Digit Selection   ⟲ Subterms under main terms may continue to next column or page

2007 ICD-9-CM   ▶◀ Revised Text   ● New Line   ▲ Revised Code   **October 2006 · Volume 2 — 235**

Poisoning — Polyp, polypus

Polyp, polypus — *continued*
gum 523.8
labia 624.6
larynx (mucous) 478.4
malignant (M8000/3) — *see* Neoplasm, by site, malignant
maxillary (sinus) 471.8
middle ear 385.30
myometrium 621.0
nares
anterior 471.9
posterior 471.0
nasal (mucous) 471.9
cavity 471.0
septum 471.9
nasopharyngeal 471.0
neoplastic (M8210/0) — *see* Neoplasm, by site, benign
nose (mucous) 471.9
oviduct 620.8
paratubal 620.8
pharynx 478.29
congenital 750.29
placenta, placental 674.4 ☑
prostate 600.20
with
other lower urinary tract symptoms (LUTS) 600.21 ●
urinary ●
obstruction 600.21 ●
retention 600.21 ●
pudenda 624.6
pulp (dental) 522.0
rectosigmoid 211.4
rectum (nonadenomatous) 569.0
adenomatous 211.4
septum (nasal) 471.9
sinus (accessory) (ethmoidal) (frontal) (maxillary) (sphenoidal) 471.8
sphenoidal (sinus) 471.8
stomach (M8210/0) 211.1
tube, fallopian 620.8
turbinate, mucous membrane 471.8
ureter 593.89
urethra 599.3
uterine
ligament 620.8
tube 620.8
uterus (body) (corpus) (mucous) 621.0
in pregnancy or childbirth 654.1 ☑
affecting fetus or newborn 763.89
causing obstructed labor 660.2 ☑
vagina 623.7
vocal cord (mucous) 478.4
vulva 624.6
Polyradiculitis (acute) 357.0
Polyradiculoneuropathy (acute) (segmentally demyelinating) 357.0
Polysarcia 278.00
Polyserositis (peritoneal) 568.82
due to pericarditis 423.2
paroxysmal (familial) 277.31 ▲
pericardial 423.2
periodic ▶(familial)◀ 277.31 ▲
pleural — *see* Pleurisy
recurrent 277.31 ▲
tuberculous (*see also* Tuberculosis, polyserositis) 018.9 ☑
Polysialia 527.7
Polysplenia syndrome 759.0
Polythelia 757.6
Polytrichia — *see also* Hypertrichosis 704.1
Polyunguia (congenital) 757.5
acquired 703.8
Polyuria 788.42
Pompe's disease (glycogenosis II) 271.0
Pompholyx 705.81
Poncet's disease (tuberculous rheumatism) — *see also* Tuberculosis 015.9 ☑
Pond fracture — *see* Fracture, skull, vault

Ponos 085.0
Pons, pontine — *see* condition
Poor
aesthetics of existing restoration of tooth 525.67 ●
contractions, labor 661.2 ☑
affecting fetus or newborn 763.7
fetal growth NEC 764.9 ☑
affecting management of pregnancy 656.5 ☑
incorporation
artificial skin graft 996.55
decellularized allodermis graft 996.55
obstetrical history V13.29
affecting management of current pregnancy V23.49
pre-term labor V23.41
pre-term labor V13.21
sucking reflex (newborn) 796.1
vision NEC 369.9
Poradenitis, nostras 099.1
Porencephaly (congenital) (developmental) (true) 742.4
acquired 348.0
nondevelopmental 348.0
traumatic (post) 310.2
Porocephaliasis 134.1
Porokeratosis 757.39
disseminated superficial actinic (DSAP) 692.75
Poroma, eccrine (M8402/0) — *see* Neoplasm, skin, benign
Porphyria (acute) (congenital) (constitutional) (erythropoietic) (familial) (hepatica) (idiopathic) (idiosyncratic) (intermittent) (latent) (mixed hepatic) (photosensitive) (South African genetic) (Swedish) 277.1
acquired 277.1
cutaneatarda
hereditaria 277.1
symptomatica 277.1
due to drugs
correct substance properly administered 277.1
overdose or wrong substance given or taken 977.9
specified drug — *see* Table of Drugs and Chemicals
secondary 277.1
toxic NEC 277.1
variegata 277.1
Porphyrinuria (acquired) (congenital) (secondary) 277.1
Porphyruria (acquired) (congenital) 277.1
Portal — *see* condition
Port wine nevus or mark 757.32
Posadas-Wernicke disease 114.9
Position
fetus, abnormal (*see also* Presentation, fetal) 652.9 ☑
teeth, faulty (*see also* Anomaly, position tooth) 524.30
Positive
culture (nonspecific) 795.39
AIDS virus V08
blood 790.7
HIV V08
human immunodeficiency virus V08
nose 795.39
skin lesion NEC 795.39
spinal fluid 792.0
sputum 795.39
stool 792.1
throat 795.39
urine 791.9
wound 795.39
findings, anthrax 795.31
HIV V08
human immunodeficiency virus (HIV) V08
PPD 795.5
serology
AIDS virus V08

Positive — *continued*
serology — *continued*
AIDS virus — *continued*
inconclusive 795.71
HIV V08
inconclusive 795.71
human immunodeficiency virus (HIV) V08
inconclusive 795.71
syphilis 097.1
with signs or symptoms — *see* Syphilis, by site and stage
false 795.6
skin test 795.7 ☑
tuberculin (without active tuberculosis) 795.5
VDRL 097.1
with signs or symptoms — *see* Syphilis, by site and stage
false 795.6
Wassermann reaction 097.1
false 795.6
Postcardiotomy syndrome 429.4
Postcaval ureter 753.4
Postcholecystectomy syndrome 576.0
Postclimacteric bleeding 627.1
Postcommissurotomy syndrome 429.4
Postconcussional syndrome 310.2
Postcontusional syndrome 310.2
Postcricoid region — *see* condition
Post-dates (pregnancy) — *see* Pregnancy
Postencephalitic — *see also* condition
syndrome 310.8
Posterior — *see* condition
Posterolateral sclerosis (spinal cord) — *see* Degeneration, combined
Postexanthematous — *see* condition
Postfebrile — *see* condition
Postgastrectomy dumping syndrome 564.2
Posthemiplegic chorea 344.89
Posthemorrhagic anemia (chronic) 280.0
acute 285.1
newborn 776.5
Posthepatitis syndrome 780.79
Postherpetic neuralgia (intercostal) (syndrome) (zoster) 053.19
geniculate ganglion 053.11
ophthalmica 053.19
trigeminal 053.12
Posthitis 607.1
Postimmunization complication or reaction — *see* Complications, vaccination
Postinfectious — *see* condition
Postinfluenzal syndrome 780.79
Postlaminectomy syndrome 722.80
cervical, cervicothoracic 722.81
kyphosis 737.12
lumbar, lumbosacral 722.83
thoracic, thoracolumbar 722.82
Postleukotomy syndrome 310.0
Postlobectomy syndrome 310.0
Postmastectomy lymphedema (syndrome) 457.0
Postmaturity, postmature (fetus or newborn) (gestation period over 42 completed weeks) 766.22
affecting management of pregnancy
post-term pregnancy 645.1 ☑
prolonged pregnancy 645.2 ☑
syndrome 766.22
Postmeasles — *see also* condition
complication 055.8
specified NEC 055.79
Postmenopausal
endometrium (atrophic) 627.8
suppurative (*see also* Endometritis) 615.9
hormone replacement therapy V07.4
status (age related) (natural) V49.81
Postnasal drip 784.91 ▲
Postnatal — *see* condition
Postoperative — *see also* condition
confusion state 293.9

Postoperative — *see also* condition — *continued*
psychosis 293.9
status NEC (*see also* Status (post)) V45.89
Postpancreatectomy hyperglycemia 251.3
Postpartum — *see also* condition
anemia 648.2 ☑
cardiomyopathy 674.5 ☑
observation
immediately after delivery V24.0
routine follow-up V24.2
Postperfusion syndrome NEC 999.8
bone marrow 996.85
Postpoliomyelitic — *see* condition
Postsurgery status NEC — *see also* Status (post V45.89
Post-term (pregnancy) 645.1 ☑
infant (gestation period over 40 completed weeks to 42 completed weeks) 766.21
Posttraumatic — *see* condition
Posttraumatic brain syndrome, nonpsychotic 310.2
Post-traumatic stress disorder (PTSD) ●
309.81 ●
Post-typhoid abscess 002.0
Postures, hysterical 300.11
Postvaccinal reaction or complication — *see* Complications, vaccination
Postvagotomy syndrome 564.2
Postvalvulotomy syndrome 429.4
Postvasectomy sperm count V25.8
Potain's disease (pulmonary edema) 514
Potain's syndrome (gastrectasis with dyspepsia) 536.1
Pott's
curvature (spinal) (*see also* Tuberculosis) 015.0 ☑ [737.43]
disease or paraplegia (*see also* Tuberculosis) 015.0 ☑ [730.88]
fracture (closed) 824.4
open 824.5
gangrene 440.24
osteomyelitis (*see also* Tuberculosis) 015.0 ☑ [730.88]
spinal curvature (*see also* Tuberculosis) 015.0 ☑ [737.43]
tumor, puffy (*see also* Osteomyelitis) 730.2 ☑
Potter's
asthma 502
disease 753.0
facies 754.0
lung 502
syndrome (with renal agenesis) 753.0
Pouch
bronchus 748.3
Douglas' — *see* condition
esophagus, esophageal (congenital) 750.4
acquired 530.6
gastric 537.1
Hartmann's (abnormal sacculation of gallbladder neck) 575.8
of intestine V44.3
attention to V55.3
pharynx, pharyngeal (congenital) 750.27
Poulet's disease 714.2
Poultrymen's itch 133.8
Poverty V60.2
Prader-Labhart-Willi-Fanconi syndrome (hypogenital dystrophy with diabetic tendency) 759.81
Prader-Willi syndrome (hypogenital dystrophy with diabetic tendency) 759.81
Preachers' voice 784.49
Pre-AIDS — *see* Human immunodeficiency virus (disease) (illness) (infection)
Preauricular appendage 744.1
Prebetalipoproteinemia (acquired) (essential) (familial) (hereditary) (primary) (secondary) 272.1

☑ Additional Digit Required — Refer to the Tabular List for Digit Selection   ▽ Subterms under main terms may continue to next column or page

236 — Volume 2 · October 2006   ▶◀ Revised Text   ● New Line   ▲ Revised Code   *2007 ICD-9-CM*

Prebetalipoproteinemia — *continued*
  with chylomicronemia 272.3
Precipitate labor 661.3 ☑
  affecting fetus or newborn 763.6
Preclimacteric bleeding 627.0
  menorrhagia 627.0
Precocious
  adrenarche 259.1
  menarche 259.1
  menstruation 626.8
  pubarche 259.1
  puberty NEC 259.1
  sexual development NEC 259.1
  thelarche 259.1
Precocity, sexual (constitutional) (cryptogenic) (female) (idiopathic) (male)
  NEC 259.1
  with adrenal hyperplasia 255.2
Precordial pain 786.51
  psychogenic 307.89
Predeciduous teeth 520.2
Prediabetes, prediabetic 790.29
  complicating pregnancy, childbirth,
    or puerperium 648.8 ☑
    fetus or newborn 775.89 ▲
Predislocation status of hip, at birth
  — *see also* Subluxation, congenital,
    hip 754.32
Preeclampsia (mild) 642.4 ☑
  with pre-existing hypertension
    642.7 ☑
  affecting fetus or newborn 760.0
  severe 642.5 ☑
  superimposed on pre-existing hyper-
    tensive disease 642.7 ☑
Preeruptive color change, teeth, tooth
  520.8
Preexcitation 426.7
  atrioventricular conduction 426.7
  ventricular 426.7
Preglaucoma 365.00
Pregnancy (single) (uterine) (without
  sickness) V22.2

> *Note* — *Use the following fifth-digit*
> *subclassification with categories*
> *640–648, 651–676:*
>
> 0   *unspecified as to episode of care*
>
> 1   *delivered, with or without mention*
>   *of antepartum condition*
>
> 2   *delivered, with mention of postpar-*
>   *tum complication*
>
> 3   *antepartum condition or complica-*
>   *tion*
>
> 4   *postpartum condition or complica-*
>   *tion*

  abdominal (ectopic) 633.00
    with intrauterine pregnancy 633.01
    affecting fetus or newborn 761.4
  abnormal NEC 646.9 ☑
  ampullar — *see* Pregnancy, tubal
  broad ligament — *see* Pregnancy,
    cornual
  cervical — *see* Pregnancy, cornual
  combined (extrauterine and intrauter-
    ine) — *see* Pregnancy, cornual
  complicated (by)
    abnormal, abnormality NEC
      646.9 ☑
      cervix 654.6 ☑
      cord (umbilical) 663.9 ☑
      glucose tolerance (conditions
        classifiable to
        790.21–790.29) 648.8 ☑
      pelvic organs or tissues NEC
        654.9 ☑
      pelvis (bony) 653.0 ☑
      perineum or vulva 654.8 ☑
      placenta, placental (vessel)
        656.7 ☑
      position
        cervix 654.4 ☑
        placenta 641.1 ☑

Pregnancy — *continued*
  complicated — *continued*
    abnormal, abnormality — *contin-*
      ued
      position — *continued*
        placenta — *continued*
          without hemorrhage
            641.0 ☑
        uterus 654.4 ☑
      size, fetus 653.5 ☑
      uterus (congenital) 654.0 ☑
    abscess or cellulitis
      bladder 646.6 ☑
      genitourinary tract (conditions
        classifiable to 590, 595,
        597, 599.0, 614.0–614.5,
        614.7–614.9, 615)
        646.6 ☑
      kidney 646.6 ☑
      urinary tract NEC 646.6 ☑
    adhesion, pelvic peritoneal 648.9 ☑
    air embolism 673.0 ☑
    albuminuria 646.2 ☑
      with hypertension — *see* Toxe-
        emia, of pregnancy
    amnionitis 658.4 ☑
    amniotic fluid embolism 673.1 ☑
    anemia (conditions classifiable to
      280–285) 648.2 ☑
    appendicitis 648.9 ☑   ●
    atrophy, yellow (acute) (liver) (sub-
      acute) 646.7 ☑
    bacilluria, asymptomatic 646.5 ☑
    bacteriuria, asymptomatic 646.5 ☑
    bariatric surgery status 649.2 ☑●
    bicornis or bicornuate uterus
      654.0 ☑
    biliary problems 646.8 ☑
    bone and joint disorders (condi-
      tions classifiable to 720–724
      or conditions affecting lower
      limbs classifiable to 711–719,
      725–738) 648.7 ☑
    breech presentation (buttocks)
      (complete) (frank) 652.2 ☑
      with successful version 652.1 ☑
    cardiovascular disease (conditions
      classifiable to 390–398,
      410–429) 648.6 ☑
      congenital (conditions classifi-
        able to 745–747) 648.5 ☑
      cerebrovascular disorders (condi-
        tions classifiable to 430–434,
        436–437) 674.0 ☑
    cervicitis (conditions classifiable to
      616.0) 646.6 ☑
    chloasma (gravidarum) 646.8 ☑
    cholelithiasis 646.8 ☑
    chorea (gravidarum) — *see*
      Eclampsia, pregnancy
    coagulation defect 649.3 ☑   ●
    contraction, pelvis (general)
      653.1 ☑
      inlet 653.2 ☑
      outlet 653.3 ☑
    convulsions (eclamptic) (uremic)
      642.6 ☑
      with pre-existing hypertension
        642.7 ☑
    current disease or condition
      (nonobstetric)
      abnormal glucose tolerance
        648.8 ☑
      anemia 648.2 ☑
      bone and joint (lower limb)
        648.7 ☑
      cardiovascular 648.6 ☑
        congenital 648.5 ☑
      cerebrovascular 674.0 ☑
      diabetic 648.0 ☑
      drug dependence 648.3 ☑
      female genital mutilation
        648.9 ☑
      genital organ or tract 646.6 ☑
      gonorrheal 647.1 ☑

Pregnancy — *continued*
  complicated — *continued*
    current disease or condition —
      continued
      hypertensive 642.2 ☑
        chronic kidney 642.2 ☑   ●
        renal 642.1 ☑
      infectious 647.9 ☑
        specified type NEC 647.8 ☑
      liver 646.7 ☑
      malarial 647.4 ☑
      nutritional deficiency 648.9 ☑
      parasitic NEC 647.8 ☑
      periodontal disease 648.9 ☑
      renal 646.2 ☑
        hypertensive 642.1 ☑
      rubella 647.5 ☑
      specified condition NEC
        648.9 ☑
      syphilitic 647.0 ☑
      thyroid 648.1 ☑
      tuberculous 647.3 ☑
      urinary 646.6 ☑
      venereal 647.2 ☑
      viral NEC 647.6 ☑
    cystitis 646.6 ☑
    cystocele 654.4 ☑
    death of fetus (near term) 656.4 ☑
      early pregnancy (before 22
        completed weeks gesta-
        tion) 632
    deciduitis 646.6 ☑
    decreased fetal movements
      655.7 ☑
    diabetes (mellitus) (conditions
      classifiable to 250) 648.0 ☑
    disorders of liver 646.7 ☑
    displacement, uterus NEC 654.4 ☑
    disproportion — *see* Disproportion
    double uterus 654.0 ☑
    drug dependence (conditions clas-
      sifiable to 304) 648.3 ☑
    dysplasia, cervix 654.6 ☑
    early onset of delivery (sponta-
      neous) 644.2 ☑
    eclampsia, eclamptic (coma) (con-
      vulsions) (delirium) (nephri-
      tis) (uremia) 642.6 ☑
      with pre-existing hypertension
        642.7 ☑
    edema 646.1 ☑
      with hypertension — *see* Tox-
        emia, of pregnancy
    effusion, amniotic fluid 658.1 ☑
      delayed delivery following
        658.2 ☑
    embolism
      air 673.0 ☑
      amniotic fluid 673.1 ☑
      blood-clot 673.2 ☑
      cerebral 674.0 ☑
      pulmonary NEC 673.2 ☑
      pyemic 673.3 ☑
      septic 673.3 ☑
    emesis (gravidarum) — *see* Pregnan-
      cy, complicated, vomiting
    endometritis (conditions classifi-
      able to 615.0–615.9) 646.6 ☑
      decidual 646.6 ☑
    epilepsy 649.4 ☑   ●
    excessive weight gain NEC 646.1 ☑
    face presentation 652.4 ☑
    failure, fetal head to enter pelvic
      brim 652.5 ☑
    false labor (pains) 644.1 ☑
    fatigue 646.8 ☑
    fatty metamorphosis of liver
      646.7 ☑
    female genital mutilation 648.9 ☑
    fetal
      death (near term) 656.4 ☑
        early (before 22 completed
          weeks gestation) 632
      deformity 653.7 ☑
      distress 656.8 ☑

Pregnancy — *continued*
  complicated — *continued*
    fetal — *continued*
      reduction of multiple fetuses
        reduced to single fetus
        651.7 ☑
    fibroid (tumor) (uterus) 654.1 ☑
    footling presentation 652.8 ☑
      with successful version 652.1 ☑
    gallbladder disease 646.8 ☑
    gastric banding status 649.2 ☑ ●
    gastric bypass status for obesity ●
    goiter 648.1 ☑
    gonococcal infection (conditions
      classifiable to 098) 647.1 ☑
    gonorrhea (conditions classifiable
      to 098) 647.1 ☑
    hemorrhage 641.9 ☑
      accidental 641.2 ☑
      before 22 completed weeks ges-
        tation NEC 640.9 ☑
      cerebrovascular 674.0 ☑
      due to
        afibrinogenemia or other co-
          agulation defect (condi-
          tions classifiable to
          286.0–286.9) 641.3 ☑
        leiomyoma, uterine 641.8 ☑
        marginal sinus (rupture)
          641.2 ☑
        premature separation, placen-
          ta 641.2 ☑
        trauma 641.8 ☑
      early (before 22 completed
        weeks gestation) 640.9 ☑
      threatened abortion 640.0 ☑
      unavoidable 641.1 ☑
    hepatitis (acute) (malignant) (suba-
      cute) 646.7 ☑
      viral 647.6 ☑
    herniation of uterus 654.4 ☑
    high head at term 652.5 ☑
    hydatidiform mole (delivered) (un-
      delivered) 630
    hydramnios 657.0 ☑
    hydrocephalic fetus 653.6 ☑
    hydrops amnii 657.0 ☑
    hydrorrhea 658.1 ☑
    hyperemesis (gravidarum) — *see*
      Hyperemesis, gravidarum
    hypertension — *see* Hypertension,
      complicating pregnancy
    hypertensive
      chronic kidney disease   ●
        642.2 ☑   ●
      heart and chronic kidney dis-●
        ease 642.2 ☑   ●
      heart and renal disease 642.2 ☑
      heart disease 642.2 ☑
      renal disease 642.2 ☑
    hypertensive heart and chronic ●
      kidney disease 642.2 ☑ ●
    hyperthyroidism 648.1 ☑
    hypothyroidism 648.1 ☑
    hysteralgia 646.8 ☑
    icterus gravis 646.7 ☑
    incarceration, uterus 654.3 ☑
    incompetent cervix (os) 654.5 ☑
    infection 647.9 ☑
      amniotic fluid 658.4 ☑
      bladder 646.6 ☑
      genital organ (conditions classi-
        fiable to 614.0–614.5,
        614.7–614.9, 615)
        646.6 ☑
      kidney (conditions classifiable
        to 590.0–590.9) 646.6 ☑
      urinary (tract) 646.6 ☑
        asymptomatic 646.5 ☑
    infective and parasitic diseases
      NEC 647.8 ☑
    inflammation
      bladder 646.6 ☑

☑ Additional Digit Required — Refer to the Tabular List for Digit Selection   ▽ Subterms under main terms may continue to next column or page

2007 ICD-9-CM   ▶◀ Revised Text   ● New Line   ▲ Revised Code   **October 2006 · Volume 2 — 237**

Pregnancy — *continued*
  complicated — *continued*
    inflammation — *continued*
      genital organ (conditions classifiable to 614.0–614.5, 614.7–614.9, 615) 646.6 ☑
      urinary tract NEC 646.6 ☑
    insufficient weight gain 646.8 ☑
    intrauterine fetal death (near term) NEC 656.4 ☑
      early (before 22 completed weeks' gestation) 632
    malaria (conditions classifiable to 084) 647.4 ☑
    malformation, uterus (congenital) 654.0 ☑
    malnutrition (conditions classifiable to 260–269) 648.9 ☑
    malposition
      fetus — *see* Pregnancy, complicated, malpresentation
      uterus or cervix 654.4 ☑
    malpresentation 652.9 ☑
      with successful version 652.1 ☑
      in multiple gestation 652.6 ☑
      specified type NEC 652.8 ☑
    marginal sinus hemorrhage or rupture 641.2 ☑
    maternal obesity syndrome 646.1 ☑
    menstruation 640.8 ☑
    mental disorders (conditions classifiable to 290–303, ▶305.0, 305.2-305.9, 306–316,◀ 317–319) 648.4 ☑
    mentum presentation 652.4 ☑
    missed
      abortion 632
      delivery (at or near term) 656.4 ☑
      labor (at or near term) 656.4 ☑
    necrosis
      genital organ or tract (conditions classifiable to 614.0–614.5, 614.7–614.9, 615) 646.6 ☑
      liver (conditions classifiable to 570) 646.7 ☑
      renal, cortical 646.2 ☑
    nephritis or nephrosis (conditions classifiable to 580–589) 646.2 ☑
      with hypertension 642.1 ☑
    nephropathy NEC 646.2 ☑
    neuritis (peripheral) 646.4 ☑
    nutritional deficiency (conditions classifiable to 260–269) 648.9 ☑
    obesity 649.1 ☑ ●
      surgery status 649.2 ☑ ●
    oblique lie or presentation 652.3 ☑
      with successful version 652.1 ☑
    obstetrical trauma NEC 665.9 ☑
    oligohydramnios NEC 658.0 ☑
    onset of contractions before 37 weeks 644.0 ☑
    oversize fetus 653.5 ☑
    papyraceous fetus 646.0 ☑
    patent cervix 654.5 ☑
    pelvic inflammatory disease (conditions classifiable to 614.0–614.5, 614.7–614.9, 615) 646.6 ☑
    pelvic peritoneal adhesion 648.9 ☑
    placenta, placental
      abnormality 656.7 ☑
      abruptio or ablatio 641.2 ☑
      detachment 641.2 ☑
      disease 656.7 ☑
      infarct 656.7 ☑
      low implantation 641.1 ☑
        without hemorrhage 641.0 ☑
      malformation 656.7 ☑

Pregnancy — *continued*
  complicated — *continued*
    placenta, placental — *continued*
      malposition 641.1 ☑
        without hemorrhage 641.0 ☑
      marginal sinus hemorrhage 641.2 ☑
      previa 641.1 ☑
        without hemorrhage 641.0 ☑
      separation (premature) (undelivered) 641.2 ☑
    placentitis 658.4 ☑
    polyhydramnios 657.0 ☑
    postmaturity
      post-term 645.1 ☑
      prolonged 645.2 ☑
    prediabetes 648.8 ☑
    pre-eclampsia (mild) 642.4 ☑
      severe 642.5 ☑
      superimposed on pre-existing hypertensive disease 642.7 ☑
    premature rupture of membranes 658.1 ☑
      with delayed delivery 658.2 ☑
    previous
      infertility V23.0
      nonobstetric condition V23.89
      poor obstetrical history V23.49
      premature delivery V23.41
      trophoblastic disease (conditions classifiable to 630) V23.1
    prolapse, uterus 654.4 ☑
    proteinuria (gestational) 646.2 ☑
      with hypertension — *see* Toxemia, of pregnancy
    pruritus (neurogenic) 646.8 ☑
    psychosis or psychoneurosis 648.4 ☑
    ptyalism 646.8 ☑
    pyelitis (conditions classifiable to 590.0–590.9) 646.6 ☑
    renal disease or failure NEC 646.2 ☑
      with secondary hypertension 642.1 ☑
      hypertensive 642.2 ☑
    retention, retained dead ovum 631
    retroversion, uterus 654.3 ☑
    Rh immunization, incompatibility, or sensitization 656.1 ☑
    rubella (conditions classifiable to 056) 647.5 ☑
    rupture
      amnion (premature) 658.1 ☑
        with delayed delivery 658.2 ☑
      marginal sinus (hemorrhage) 641.2 ☑
      membranes (premature) 658.1 ☑
        with delayed delivery 658.2 ☑
      uterus (before onset of labor) 665.0 ☑
    salivation (excessive) 646.8 ☑
    salpingo-oophoritis (conditions classifiable to 614.0–614.2) 646.6 ☑
    septicemia (conditions classifiable to 038.0–038.9) 647.8 ☑
      postpartum 670.0 ☑
      puerperal 670.0 ☑
    smoking 649.0 ☑ ●
    spasms, uterus (abnormal) 646.8 ☑
    specified condition NEC 646.8 ☑
    spotting 649.5 ☑ ●
    spurious labor pains 644.1 ☑
    status post ●
      bariatric surgery 649.2 ☑ ●
      gastric banding 649.2 ☑ ●
      gastric bypass for obesity 649.2 ☑ ●

Pregnancy — *continued*
  complicated — *continued*
    status post — *continued*
      obesity surgery 649.2 ☑ ●
    superfecundation 651.9 ☑
    superfetation 651.9 ☑
    syphilis (conditions classifiable to 090–097) 647.0 ☑
    threatened
      abortion 640.0 ☑
      premature delivery 644.2 ☑
      premature labor 644.0 ☑
    thrombophlebitis (superficial) 671.2 ☑
      deep 671.3 ☑
    thrombosis 671.9 ☑
      venous (superficial) 671.2 ☑
        deep 671.3 ☑
    thyroid dysfunction (conditions classifiable to 240–246) 648.1 ☑
    thyroiditis 648.1 ☑
    thyrotoxicosis 648.1 ☑
    tobacco use disorder 649.0 ☑ ●
    torsion of uterus 654.4 ☑
    toxemia — *see* Toxemia, of pregnancy
    transverse lie or presentation 652.3 ☑
      with successful version 652.1 ☑
    trauma 648.9 ☑
      obstetrical 665.9 ☑
    tuberculosis (conditions classifiable to 010–018) 647.3 ☑
    tumor
      cervix 654.6 ☑
      ovary 654.4 ☑
      pelvic organs or tissue NEC 654.4 ☑
      uterus (body) 654.1 ☑
        cervix 654.6 ☑
      vagina 654.7 ☑
      vulva 654.8 ☑
    unstable lie 652.0 ☑
    uremia — *see* Pregnancy, complicated, renal disease
    urethritis 646.6 ☑
    vaginitis or vulvitis (conditions classifiable to 616.1) 646.6 ☑
    varicose
      placental vessels 656.7 ☑
      veins (legs) 671.0 ☑
        perineum 671.1 ☑
        vulva 671.1 ☑
    varicosity, labia or vulva 671.1 ☑
    venereal disease NEC (conditions classifiable to 099) 647.2 ☑
    viral disease NEC (conditions classifiable to 042, 050–055, 057–079) 647.6 ☑
    vomiting (incoercible) (pernicious) (persistent) (uncontrollable) (vicious) 643.9 ☑
      due to organic disease or other cause 643.8 ☑
      early — *see* Hyperemesis, gravidarum
      late (after 22 completed weeks gestation) 643.2 ☑
    young maternal age 659.8 ☑
  complications NEC 646.9 ☑
  cornual 633.80
    with intrauterine pregnancy 633.81
    affecting fetus or newborn 761.4
  death, maternal NEC 646.9 ☑
  delivered — *see* Delivery
  ectopic (ruptured) NEC 633.90
    with intrauterine pregnancy 633.91
    abdominal — *see* Pregnancy, abdominal
    affecting fetus or newborn 761.4
    combined (extrauterine and intrauterine) — *see* Pregnancy, cornual
    ovarian — *see* Pregnancy, ovarian

Pregnancy — *continued*
  ectopic — *continued*
    specified type NEC 633.80
      with intrauterine pregnancy 633.81
      affecting fetus or newborn 761.4
    tubal — *see* Pregnancy, tubal
  examination, pregnancy
    negative result V72.41
    not confirmed V72.40
    positive result V72.42
  extrauterine — *see* Pregnancy, ectopic
  fallopian — *see* Pregnancy, tubal
  false 300.11
    labor (pains) 644.1 ☑
  fatigue 646.8 ☑
  illegitimate V61.6
  incidental finding V22.2
  in double uterus 654.0 ☑
  interstitial — *see* Pregnancy, cornual
  intraligamentous — *see* Pregnancy, cornual
  intramural — *see* Pregnancy, cornual
  intraperitoneal — *see* Pregnancy, abdominal
  isthmian — *see* Pregnancy, tubal
  management affected by
    abnormal, abnormality
      fetus (suspected) 655.9 ☑
        specified NEC 655.8 ☑
      placenta 656.7 ☑
    advanced maternal age NEC 659.6 ☑
      multigravida 659.6 ☑
      primigravida 659.5 ☑
    antibodies (maternal)
      anti-c 656.1 ☑
      anti-d 656.1 ☑
      anti-e 656.1 ☑
      blood group (ABO) 656.2 ☑
        Rh(esus) 656.1 ☑
    appendicitis 648.9 ☑ ●
    bariatric surgery status 649.2 ☑ ●●
    coagulation defect 649.3 ☑ ●
    elderly multigravida 659.6 ☑
    elderly primigravida 659.5 ☑
    epilepsy 649.4 ☑ ●
    fetal (suspected)
      abnormality 655.9 ☑
        acid-base balance 656.8 ☑
        heart rate or rhythm 659.7 ☑
        specified NEC 655.8 ☑
      acidemia 656.3 ☑
      anencephaly 655.0 ☑
      bradycardia 659.7 ☑
      central nervous system malformation 655.0 ☑
      chromosomal abnormalities (conditions classifiable to 758.0–758.9) 655.1 ☑
      damage from
        drugs 655.5 ☑
          obstetric, anesthetic, or sedative 655.5 ☑
        environmental toxins 655.8 ☑
        intrauterine contraceptive device 655.8 ☑
        maternal
          alcohol addiction 655.4 ☑
          disease NEC 655.4 ☑
          drug use 655.5 ☑
          listeriosis 655.4 ☑
          rubella 655.3 ☑
          toxoplasmosis 655.4 ☑
          viral infection 655.3 ☑
        radiation 655.6 ☑
      death (near term) 656.4 ☑
        early (before 22 completed weeks' gestation) 632
      distress 656.8 ☑
      excessive growth 656.6 ☑
      fetal-maternal hemorrhage 656.0 ☑
      growth retardation 656.5 ☑

☑ Additional Digit Required — Refer to the Tabular List for Digit Selection   ▼ Subterms under main terms may continue to next column or page

238 — Volume 2 • October 2006   ►◄ Revised Text   ● New Line   ▲ Revised Code   *2007 ICD-9-CM*

Pregnancy — *continued*
　management affected by — *continued*
　　fetal — *continued*
　　　hereditary disease 655.2 ☑
　　　hereditary disease in family
　　　　(possibly) affecting fetus
　　　　655.2 ☑
　　　hydrocephalus 655.0 ☑
　　　incompatibility, blood groups
　　　　(ABO) 656.2 ☑
　　　intrauterine death 656.4 ☑
　　　poor growth 656.5 ☑
　　　Rh(esus) 656.1 ☑
　　　spina bifida (with
　　　　myelomeningocele)
　　　　655.0 ☑
　　gastric banding status 649.2 ☑ ●
　　gastric bypass status for obesity ●
　　　649.2 ☑　　　　　　　　　　　●
　　insufficient prenatal care V23.7
　　intrauterine death 656.4 ☑
　　isoimmunization (ABO) 656.2 ☑
　　　Rh(esus) 656.1 ☑
　　large-for-dates fetus 656.6 ☑
　　light-for-dates fetus 656.5 ☑
　　meconium in liquor 656.8 ☑
　　mental disorder (conditions classi-
　　　fiable to 290–303, ▶305.0,
　　　305.2–305.9, 306–316,◀
　　　317–319) 648.4 ☑
　　multiparity (grand) 659.4 ☑
　　obesity 649.1 ☑　　　　　　　　●
　　　surgery status 649.2 ☑　　　●
　　poor obstetric history V23.49
　　　pre-term labor V23.41
　　postmaturity
　　　post-term 645.1 ☑
　　　prolonged 645.2 ☑
　　post-term pregnancy 645.1 ☑
　　previous
　　　abortion V23.2
　　　　habitual 646.3 ☑
　　　cesarean delivery 654.2 ☑
　　　difficult delivery V23.49
　　　forceps delivery V23.49
　　　habitual abortions 646.3 ☑
　　　hemorrhage, antepartum or
　　　　postpartum V23.49
　　　hydatidiform mole V23.1
　　　infertility V23.0
　　　malignancy NEC V23.89
　　　nonobstetrical conditions
　　　　V23.8 ☑
　　　premature delivery V23.41
　　　trophoblastic disease (condi-
　　　　tions in 630) V23.1
　　　vesicular mole V23.1
　　prolonged pregnancy 645.2 ☑
　　small-for-dates fetus 656.5 ☑
　　smoking 649.0 ☑　　　　　　　●
　　spotting 649.5 ☑　　　　　　　●
　　tobacco use disorder 649.0 ☑　●
　　young maternal age 659.8 ☑
　maternal death NEC 646.9 ☑
　mesometric (mural) — *see* Pregnancy,
　　cornual
　molar 631
　　hydatidiform (*see also* Hydatidiform
　　　mole) 630
　　previous, affecting management
　　　of pregnancy V23.1
　　previous, affecting management of
　　　pregnancy V23.49
　multiple NEC 651.9 ☑
　　with fetal loss and retention of one
　　　or more fetus(es) 651.6 ☑
　　affecting fetus or newborn 761.5
　　following (elective) fetal reduction
　　　651.7 ☑
　　specified type NEC 651.8 ☑
　　　with fetal loss and retention of
　　　　one or more fetus(es)
　　　　651.6 ☑

Pregnancy — *continued*
　multiple — *continued*
　　specified type — *continued*
　　　following (elective) fetal reduc-
　　　　tion 651.7 ☑
　mural — *see* Pregnancy, cornual
　observation NEC V22.1
　　first pregnancy V22.0
　　high-risk V23.9
　　　specified problem NEC V23.89
　ovarian 633.20
　　with intrauterine pregnancy 633.21
　　affecting fetus or newborn 761.4
　possible, not (yet) confirmed V72.40
　postmature
　　post-term 645.1 ☑
　　prolonged 645.2 ☑
　post-term 645.1 ☑
　prenatal care only V22.1
　　first pregnancy V22.0
　　high-risk V23.9
　　　specified problem NEC V23.89
　prolonged 645.2 ☑
　quadruplet NEC 651.2 ☑
　　with fetal loss and retention of one
　　　or more fetus(es) 651.5 ☑
　　affecting fetus or newborn 761.5
　　following (elective) fetal reduction
　　　651.7 ☑
　quintuplet NEC 651.8 ☑
　　with fetal loss and retention of one
　　　or more fetus(es) 651.6 ☑
　　affecting fetus or newborn 761.5
　　following (elective) fetal reduction
　　　651.7 ☑
　sextuplet NEC 651.8 ☑
　　with fetal loss and retention of one
　　　or more fetus(es) 651.6 ☑
　　affecting fetus or newborn 761.5
　　following (elective) fetal reduction
　　　651.7 ☑
　spurious 300.11
　superfecundation NEC 651.9 ☑
　　with fetal loss and retention of one
　　　or more fetus(es) 651.6 ☑
　　following (elective) fetal reduction
　　　651.7 ☑
　superfetation NEC 651.9 ☑
　　with fetal loss and retention of one
　　　or more fetus(es) 651.6 ☑
　　following (elective) fetal reduction
　　　651.7 ☑
　supervision (of) (for) (*see also* Pregnan-
　　cy, management affected by)
　　elderly
　　　multigravida V23.82
　　　primigravida V23.81
　　high-risk V23.9
　　　insufficient prenatal care V23.7
　　　specified problem NEC V23.89
　　multiparity V23.3
　　normal NEC V22.1
　　　first V22.0
　　poor
　　　obstetric history V23.49
　　　　pre-term labor V23.41
　　　reproductive history V23.5
　　previous
　　　abortion V23.2
　　　hydatidiform mole V23.1
　　　infertility V23.0
　　　neonatal death V23.5
　　　stillbirth V23.5
　　　trophoblastic disease V23.1
　　　vesicular mole V23.1
　　specified problem NEC V23.89
　　young
　　　multigravida V23.84
　　　primigravida V23.83
　triplet NEC 651.1 ☑
　　with fetal loss and retention of one
　　　or more fetus(es) 651.4 ☑
　　affecting fetus or newborn 761.5
　　following (elective) fetal reduction
　　　651.7 ☑
　tubal (with rupture) 633.10

Pregnancy — *continued*
　tubal — *continued*
　　with intrauterine pregnancy 633.11
　　affecting fetus or newborn 761.4
　twin NEC 651.0 ☑
　　with fetal loss and retention of one
　　　fetus 651.3 ☑
　　affecting fetus or newborn 761.5
　　following (elective) fetal reduction
　　　651.7 ☑
　unconfirmed V72.40
　undelivered (no other diagnosis) V22.2
　　with false labor 644.1 ☑
　　high-risk V23.9
　　　specified problem NEC V23.89
　unwanted NEC V61.7
Pregnant uterus — *see* condition
Preiser's disease (osteoporosis) 733.09
Prekwashiorkor 260
Preleukemia 238.75　　　　　　　　　▲
Preluxation of hip, congenital — *see
　also* Subluxation, congenital, hip
　754.32
Premature — *see also* condition
　beats (nodal) 427.60
　　atrial 427.61
　　auricular 427.61
　　postoperative 997.1
　　specified type NEC 427.69
　　supraventricular 427.61
　　ventricular 427.69
　birth NEC 765.1 ☑
　closure
　　cranial suture 756.0
　　fontanel 756.0
　　foramen ovale 745.8
　contractions 427.60
　　atrial 427.61
　　auricular 427.61
　　auriculoventricular 427.61
　　heart (extrasystole) 427.60
　　junctional 427.60
　　nodal 427.60
　　postoperative 997.1
　　ventricular 427.69
　ejaculation 302.75
　infant NEC 765.1 ☑
　　excessive 765.0 ☑
　　light-for-dates — *see* Light-for-
　　　dates
　labor 644.2 ☑
　　threatened 644.0 ☑
　lungs 770.4
　menopause 256.31
　puberty 259.1
　rupture of membranes or amnion
　　658.1 ☑
　　affecting fetus or newborn 761.1
　　delayed delivery following 658.2 ☑
　senility (syndrome) 259.8
　separation, placenta (partial) — *see*
　　Placenta, separation
　ventricular systole 427.69
Prematurity NEC 765.1 ☑
　extreme 765.0 ☑
Premenstrual syndrome 625.4
Premenstrual tension 625.4
Premolarization, cuspids 520.2
Premyeloma 273.1
Prenatal
　care, normal pregnancy V22.1
　　first V22.0
　death, cause unknown — *see* Death,
　　fetus
　screening — *see* Antenatal, screening
　teeth 520.6　　　　　　　　　　　●
Prepartum — *see* condition
**Preponderance, left or right ventricu-
　lar** 429.3
Prepuce — *see* condition
PRES (posterior reversible encephalopa- ●
　thy syndrome) 348.39　　　　　　　●
Presbycardia 797
　hypertensive (*see also* Hypertension,
　　heart) 402.90
Presbycusis 388.01

Presbyesophagus 530.89
Presbyophrenia 310.1
Presbyopia 367.4
Prescription of contraceptives NEC
　V25.02
　diaphragm V25.02
　oral (pill) V25.01
　　emergency V25.03
　　postcoital V25.03
　　repeat V25.41
　repeat V25.40
　　oral (pill) V25.41
Presenile — *see also* condition
　aging 259.8
　dementia (*see also* Dementia, prese-
　　nile) 290.10
Presenility 259.8
Presentation, fetal
　abnormal 652.9 ☑
　　with successful version 652.1 ☑
　　before labor, affecting fetus or
　　　newborn 761.7
　　causing obstructed labor 660.0 ☑
　　　affecting fetus or newborn, any,
　　　　except breech 763.1
　　in multiple gestation (one or more)
　　　652.6 ☑
　　specified NEC 652.8 ☑
　arm 652.7 ☑
　　causing obstructed labor 660.0 ☑
　breech (buttocks) (complete) (frank)
　　652.2 ☑
　　with successful version 652.1 ☑
　　before labor, affecting fetus or
　　　newborn 761.7
　　before labor, affecting fetus or
　　　newborn 761.7
　brow 652.4 ☑
　　causing obstructed labor 660.0 ☑
　buttocks 652.2 ☑
　chin 652.4 ☑
　complete 652.2 ☑
　compound 652.8 ☑
　cord 663.0 ☑
　extended head 652.4 ☑
　face 652.4 ☑
　　to pubes 652.8 ☑
　footling 652.8 ☑
　frank 652.2 ☑
　hand, leg, or foot NEC 652.8 ☑
　incomplete 652.8 ☑
　mentum 652.4 ☑
　multiple gestation (one fetus or more)
　　652.6 ☑
　oblique 652.3 ☑
　　with successful version 652.1 ☑
　shoulder 652.8 ☑
　　affecting fetus or newborn 763.1
　transverse 652.3 ☑
　　with successful version 652.1 ☑
　umbilical cord 663.0 ☑
　unstable 652.0 ☑
Prespondylolisthesis (congenital) (lum-
　bosacral) 756.11
Pressure
　area, skin ulcer (*see also* Decubitus)
　　707.00
　atrophy, spine 733.99
　birth, fetus or newborn NEC 767.9
　brachial plexus 353.0
　brain 348.4
　　injury at birth 767.0
　　cerebral — *see* Pressure, brain
　chest 786.59
　cone, tentorial 348.4
　　injury at birth 767.0
　funis — *see* Compression, umbilical
　　cord
　hyposystolic (*see also* Hypotension)
　　458.9
　increased
　　intracranial 781.99
　　　due to
　　　　benign intracranial hyperten-
　　　　　sion 348.2

☑ Additional Digit Required — Refer to the Tabular List for Digit Selection　　　　　　　　　▽ Subterms under main terms may continue to next column or page

Pressure — continued
  increased — continued
    intracranial — continued
      due to — continued
        hydrocephalus — see hydrocephalus
        injury at birth 767.8
    intraocular 365.00
    lumbosacral plexus 353.1
    mediastinum 519.3
    necrosis (chronic) (skin) (see also Decubitus) 707.00
    nerve — see Compression, nerve
    paralysis (see also Neuropathy, entrapment) 355.9
    sore (chronic) (see also Decubitus) 707.00
    spinal cord 336.9
    ulcer (chronic) (see also Decubitus) 707.00
    umbilical cord — see Compression, umbilical cord
    venous, increased 459.89
Pre-syncope 780.2
Preterm infant NEC 765.1 ☑
  extreme 765.0 ☑
Priapism (penis) 607.3
Prickling sensation — see also Disturbance, sensation 782.0
Prickly heat 705.1
Primary — see condition
Primigravida, elderly
  affecting
    fetus or newborn 763.89
    management of pregnancy, labor, and delivery 659.5 ☑
Primipara, old
  affecting
    fetus or newborn 763.89
    management of pregnancy, labor, and delivery 659.5 ☑
Primula dermatitis 692.6
Primus varus (bilateral) (metatarsus) 754.52
P.R.I.N.D. 436
Pringle's disease (tuberous sclerosis) 759.5
Prinzmetal's angina 413.1
Prinzmetal-Massumi syndrome (anterior or chest wall) 786.52
Prizefighter ear 738.7
Problem (with) V49.9
  academic V62.3
  acculturation V62.4
  adopted child V61.29
  aged
    in-law V61.3
    parent V61.3
    person NEC V61.8
  alcoholism in family V61.41
  anger reaction (see also Disturbance, conduct) 312.0 ☑
  behavioral V40.9
    specified NEC V40.3
  behavior, child 312.9
  betting V69.3
  cardiorespiratory NEC V47.2
  career choice V62.2
  care of sick or handicapped person in family or household V61.49
  communication V40.1
  conscience regarding medical care V62.6
  delinquency (juvenile) 312.9
  diet, inappropriate V69.1
  digestive NEC V47.3
  ear NEC V41.3
  eating habits, inappropriate V69.1
  economic V60.2
    affecting care V60.9
      specified type NEC V60.8
  educational V62.3
  enuresis, child 307.6
  exercise, lack of V69.0
  eye NEC V41.1
  family V61.9

Problem — continued
  family — continued
    specified circumstance NEC V61.8
  fear reaction, child 313.0
  feeding (elderly) (infant) 783.3
    newborn 779.3
    nonorganic 307.59
  fetal, affecting management of pregnancy 656.9 ☑
    specified type NEC 656.8 ☑
  financial V60.2
  foster child V61.29
    specified NEC V41.8
  functional V41.9
    specified type NEC V41.8
  gambling V69.3
  genital NEC V47.5
  head V48.9
    deficiency V48.0
    disfigurement V48.6
    mechanical V48.2
    motor V48.2
    movement of V48.2
    sensory V48.4
    specified condition NEC V48.8
  hearing V41.2
  high-risk sexual behavior V69.2
  identity 313.82
  influencing health status NEC V49.89
  internal organ NEC V47.9
    deficiency V47.0
    mechanical or motor V47.1
  interpersonal NEC V62.81
  jealousy, child 313.3
  learning V40.0
  legal V62.5
  life circumstance NEC V62.89
  lifestyle V69.9
    specified NEC V69.8
  limb V49.9
    deficiency V49.0
    disfigurement V49.4
    mechanical V49.1
    motor V49.2
    movement, involving
      musculoskeletal system V49.1
      nervous system V49.2
    sensory V49.3
    specified condition NEC V49.5
  litigation V62.5
  living alone V60.3
  loneliness NEC V62.89
  marital V61.10
    involving
      divorce V61.0
      estrangement V61.0
      psychosexual disorder 302.9
      sexual function V41.7
    relationship V61.10
  mastication V41.6
  medical care, within family V61.49
  mental V40.9
    specified NEC V40.2
  mental hygiene, adult V40.9
  multiparity V61.5
  nail biting, child 307.9
  neck V48.9
    deficiency V48.1
    disfigurement V48.7
    mechanical V48.3
    motor V48.3
    movement V48.3
    sensory V48.5
    specified condition NEC V48.8
  neurological NEC 781.99
  none (feared complaint unfounded) V65.5
  occupational V62.2
  parent-child V61.20
    relationship V61.20
  partner V61.10
    relationship V61.10
  personal NEC V62.89
    interpersonal conflict NEC V62.81
  personality (see also Disorder, personality) 301.9

Problem — continued
  phase of life V62.89
  placenta, affecting management of pregnancy 656.9 ☑
    specified type NEC 656.8 ☑
  poverty V60.2
  presence of sick or handicapped person in family or household V61.49
  psychiatric 300.9
  psychosocial V62.9
    specified type NEC V62.89
  relational NEC V62.81
  relationship, childhood 313.3
  religious or spiritual belief
    other than medical care V62.89
    regarding medical care V62.6
  self-damaging behavior V69.8
  sexual
    behavior, high-risk V69.2
    function NEC V41.7
  sibling
    relational V61.8
    relationship V61.8
  sight V41.0
  sleep disorder, child 307.40
  sleep, lack of V69.4
  smell V41.5
  speech V40.1
  spite reaction, child (see also Disturbance, conduct) 312.0 ☑
  spoiled child reaction (see also Disturbance, conduct) 312.1 ☑
  swallowing V41.6
  tantrum, child (see also Disturbance, conduct) 312.1 ☑
  taste V41.5
  thumb sucking, child 307.9
  tic (child) 307.21
  trunk V48.9
    deficiency V48.1
    disfigurement V48.7
    mechanical V48.3
    motor V48.3
    movement V48.3
    sensory V48.5
    specified condition NEC V48.8
  unemployment V62.0
  urinary NEC V47.4
  voice production V41.4
Procedure (surgical) **not done** NEC V64.3
  because of
    contraindication V64.1
    patient's decision V64.2
      for reasons of conscience or religion V62.6
    specified reason NEC V64.3
Procidentia
  anus (sphincter) 569.1
  rectum (sphincter) 569.1
  stomach 537.89
  uteri 618.1
Proctalgia 569.42
  fugax 564.6
  spasmodic 564.6
    psychogenic 307.89
Proctitis 569.49
  amebic 006.8
  chlamydial 099.52
  gonococcal 098.7
  granulomatous 555.1
  idiopathic 556.2
    with ulcerative sigmoiditis 556.3
  tuberculous (see also Tuberculosis) 014.8 ☑
  ulcerative (chronic) (nonspecific) 556.2
    with ulcerative sigmoiditis 556.3
Proctocele
  female (without uterine prolapse) 618.04
    with uterine prolapse 618.4
      complete 618.3
      incomplete 618.2
  male 569.49
Proctocolitis, idiopathic 556.2

Proctocolitis, idiopathic — continued
    with ulcerative sigmoiditis 556.3
Proctoptosis 569.1
Proctosigmoiditis 569.89
  ulcerative (chronic) 556.3
Proctospasm 564.6
  psychogenic 306.4
Prodromal-AIDS — see Human immunodeficiency virus (disease) (illness) (infection)
Profichet's disease or syndrome 729.9
Progeria (adultorum) (syndrome) 259.8
Prognathism (mandibular) (maxillary) 524.00
Progonoma (melanotic) (M9363/0) — see Neoplasm, by site, benign
Progressive — see condition
Prolapse, prolapsed
  anus, anal (canal) (sphincter) 569.1
  arm or hand, complicating delivery 652.7 ☑
    causing obstructed labor 660.0 ☑
      affecting fetus or newborn 763.1
    fetus or newborn 763.1
  bladder (acquired) (mucosa) (sphincter)
    congenital (female) (male) 756.71
    female (see also Cystocele, female) 618.01
    male 596.8
  breast implant (prosthetic) 996.54
  cecostomy 569.69
  cecum 569.89
  cervix, cervical (hypertrophied) 618.1
    anterior lip, obstructing labor 660.2 ☑
      affecting fetus or newborn 763.1
    congenital 752.49
    postpartal (old) 618.1
    stump 618.84   ●
  ciliary body 871.1
  colon (pedunculated) 569.89
  colostomy 569.69
  conjunctiva 372.73
  cord — see Prolapse, umbilical cord
  disc (intervertebral) — see Displacement, intervertebral disc
  duodenum 537.89
  eye implant (orbital) 996.59
    lens (ocular) 996.53
  fallopian tube 620.4
  fetal extremity, complicating delivery 652.8 ☑
    causing obstructed labor 660.0 ☑
    fetus or newborn 763.1
  funis — see Prolapse, umbilical cord
  gastric (mucosa) 537.89
  genital, female 618.9
    specified NEC 618.89
  globe 360.81
  ileostomy bud 569.69
  intervertebral disc — see Displacement, intervertebral disc
  intestine (small) 569.89
  iris 364.8
    traumatic 871.1
  kidney (see also Disease, renal) 593.0
    congenital 753.3
  laryngeal muscles or ventricle 478.79
  leg, complicating delivery 652.8 ☑
    causing obstructed labor 660.0 ☑
    fetus or newborn 763.1
  liver 573.8
  meatus urinarius 599.5
  mitral valve 424.0
  ocular lens implant 996.53
  organ or site, congenital NEC — see Malposition, congenital
  ovary 620.4
  pelvic (floor), female 618.89
  perineum, female 618.89
  pregnant uterus 654.4 ☑
  rectum (mucosa) (sphincter) 569.1
    due to Trichuris trichiuria 127.3
  spleen 289.59

☑ Additional Digit Required — Refer to the Tabular List for Digit Selection   ▽ Subterms under main terms may continue to next column or page

240 — Volume 2 • October 2006   ▶◀ Revised Text   ● New Line   ▲ Revised Code   *2007 ICD-9-CM*

Prolapse, prolapsed — *continued*
  stomach 537.89
  umbilical cord
    affecting fetus or newborn 762.4
    complicating delivery 663.0 ☑
  ureter 593.89
    with obstruction 593.4
  ureterovesical orifice 593.89
  urethra (acquired) (infected) (mucosa)
    599.5
    congenital 753.8
  uterovaginal 618.4
    complete 618.3
    incomplete 618.2
    specified NEC 618.89
  uterus (first degree) (second degree)
    (third degree) (complete) (with-
    out vaginal wall prolapse) 618.1
    with mention of vaginal wall pro-
      lapse — *see* Prolapse,
      uterovaginal
    congenital 752.3
    in pregnancy or childbirth 654.4 ☑
      affecting fetus or newborn 763.1
      causing obstructed labor
        660.2 ☑
        affecting fetus or newborn
          763.1
    postpartal (old) 618.1
  uveal 871.1
  vagina (anterior) (posterior) (vault)
    (wall) (without uterine prolapse)
    618.00
    with uterine prolapse 618.4
      complete 618.3
      incomplete 618.2
    paravaginal 618.02
    posthysterectomy 618.5
    specified NEC 618.09
  vitreous (humor) 379.26
    traumatic 871.1
  womb — *see* Prolapse, uterus
Prolapsus, female 618.9
Proliferative — *see* condition
Prolinemia 270.8
Prolinuria 270.8
Prolonged, prolongation
  bleeding time (*see also* Defect, coagu-
    lation) 790.92
    "idiopathic" (in von Willebrand's
      disease) 286.4
  coagulation time (*see also* Defect, co-
    agulation) 790.92
  gestation syndrome 766.22
  labor 662.1 ☑
    affecting fetus or newborn 763.89
    first stage 662.0 ☑
    second stage 662.2 ☑
  pregnancy 645.2 ☑
  PR interval 426.11
  prothrombin time (*see also* Defect,
    coagulation) 790.92
  QT interval 794.31
    syndrome 426.82
  rupture of membranes (24 hours or
    more prior to onset of labor)
    658.2 ☑
  uterine contractions in labor 661.4 ☑
    affecting fetus or newborn 763.7
Prominauris 744.29
Prominence
  auricle (ear) (congenital) 744.29
    acquired 380.32
  ischial spine or sacral promontory
    with disproportion (fetopelvic)
    653.3 ☑
    affecting fetus or newborn 763.1
    causing obstructed labor
      660.1 ☑
      affecting fetus or newborn
        763.1
  nose (congenital) 748.1
    acquired 738.0
Pronation
  ankle 736.79
  foot 736.79

Pronation — *continued*
  foot — *continued*
    congenital 755.67
Prophylactic
  administration of
    antibiotics V07.39
    antitoxin, any V07.2
    antivenin V07.2
    chemotherapeutic agent NEC
      V07.39
      fluoride V07.31
    diphtheria antitoxin V07.2
    gamma globulin V07.2
    immune sera (gamma globulin)
      V07.2
    RhoGAM V07.2
    tetanus antitoxin V07.2
  chemotherapy NEC V07.39
    fluoride V07.31
  hormone replacement (post-
    menopausal) V07.4
  immunotherapy V07.2
  measure V07.9
    specified type NEC V07.8
  postmenopausal hormone replace-
    ment V07.4
  sterilization V25.2
Proptosis (ocular) — *see also* Exophthalmos 376.30
  thyroid 242.0 ☑
Propulsion
  eyeball 360.81
Prosecution, anxiety concerning V62.5
Prostate, prostatic — *see* condition
Prostatism 600.90
  with
    other lower urinary tract symp- ●
      toms (LUTS) 600.91 ●
    urinary ●
      obstruction 600.91 ●
      retention 600.91 ●
Prostatitis (congestive) (suppurative)
  601.9
  acute 601.0
  cavitary 601.8
  chlamydial 099.54
  chronic 601.1
  diverticular 601.8
  due to Trichomonas (vaginalis) 131.03
  fibrous 600.90
    with
      other lower urinary tract ●
        symptoms (LUTS) ●
        600.91 ●
      urinary ●
        obstruction 600.91 ●
        retention 600.91 ●
  gonococcal (acute) 098.12
    chronic or duration of 2 months or
      over 098.32
  granulomatous 601.8
  hypertrophic 600.00
    with
      other lower urinary tract ●
        symptoms (LUTS) ●
        600.01 ●
      urinary ●
        obstruction 600.01 ●
        retention 600.01 ●
  specified type NEC 601.8
  subacute 601.1
  trichomonal 131.03
  tuberculous (*see also* Tuberculosis)
    016.5 ☑ *[601.4]*
Prostatocystitis 601.3
Prostatorrhea 602.8
Prostatoseminovesiculitis, trichomonal
  131.03
Prostration 780.79
  heat 992.5
    anhydrotic 992.3
    due to
      salt (and water) depletion 992.4
      water depletion 992.3
  nervous 300.5
  newborn 779.89

Prostration — *continued*
  senile 797
Protanomaly 368.51
Protanopia (anomalous trichromat)
  (complete) (incomplete) 368.51
Protein
  deficiency 260
  malnutrition 260
  sickness (prophylactic) (therapeutic)
    999.5
Proteinemia 790.99
Proteinosis
  alveolar, lung or pulmonary 516.0
  lipid 272.8
  lipoid (of Urbach) 272.8
Proteinuria — *see also* Albuminuria
  791.0
  Bence-Jones NEC 791.0
  gestational 646.2 ☑
    with hypertension — *see* Toxemia,
      of pregnancy
  orthostatic 593.6
  postural 593.6
Proteolysis, pathologic 286.6
Protocoproporphyria 277.1
Protoporphyria (erythrohepatic) (erythropoietic) 277.1
Protrusio acetabuli 718.65
Protrusion
  acetabulum (into pelvis) 718.65
  device, implant, or graft — *see* Compli-
    cations, mechanical
  ear, congenital 744.29
  intervertebral disc — *see* Displace-
    ment, intervertebral disc
  nucleus pulposus — *see* Displace-
    ment, intervertebral disc
Proud flesh 701.5
Prune belly (syndrome) 756.71
Prurigo (ferox) (gravis) (Hebra's) (hebrae)
  (mitis) (simplex) 698.2
  agria 698.3
  asthma syndrome 691.8
  Besnier's (atopic dermatitis) (infantile
    eczema) 691.8
  eczematodes allergicum 691.8
  estivalis (Hutchinson's) 692.72
  Hutchinson's 692.72
  nodularis 698.3
  psychogenic 306.3
Pruritus, pruritic 698.9
  ani 698.0
    psychogenic 306.3
  conditions NEC 698.9
    psychogenic 306.3
  due to Onchocerca volvulus 125.3
  ear 698.9
  essential 698.9
  genital organ(s) 698.1
    psychogenic 306.3
  gravidarum 646.8 ☑
  hiemalis 698.8
  neurogenic (any site) 306.3
  perianal 698.0
  psychogenic (any site) 306.3
  scrotum 698.1
    psychogenic 306.3
  senile, senilis 698.8
  Trichomonas 131.9
  vulva, vulvae 698.1
    psychogenic 306.3
Psammocarcinoma (M8140/3) — *see*
  Neoplasm, by site, malignant
Pseudarthrosis, pseudoarthrosis (bone)
  733.82
  joint following fusion V45.4
Pseudoacanthosis
  nigricans 701.8
Pseudoaneurysm — *see* Aneurysm
Pseudoangina (pectoris) — *see* Angina
Pseudoangioma 452
Pseudo-Argyll-Robertson pupil 379.45
Pseudoarteriosus 747.89
Pseudoarthrosis — *see* Pseudarthrosis
Pseudoataxia 799.89
Pseudobulbar affect (PBA) 310.8

Pseudobursa 727.89
Pseudocholera 025
Pseudochromidrosis 705.89
Pseudocirrhosis, liver, pericardial
  423.2
Pseudocoarctation 747.21
Pseudocowpox 051.1
Pseudocoxalgia 732.1
Pseudocroup 478.75
Pseudocyesis 300.11
Pseudocyst
  lung 518.89
  pancreas 577.2
  retina 361.19
Pseudodementia 300.16
Pseudoelephantiasis neuroarthritica
  757.0
Pseudoemphysema 518.89
Pseudoencephalitis
  superior (acute) hemorrhagic 265.1
Pseudoerosion cervix, congenital
  752.49
Pseudoexfoliation, lens capsule 366.11
Pseudofracture (idiopathic) (multiple)
  (spontaneous) (symmetrical) 268.2
Pseudoglanders 025
Pseudoglioma 360.44
Pseudogout — *see* Chondrocalcinosis
Pseudohallucination 780.1
Pseudohemianesthesia 782.0
Pseudohemophilia (Bernuth's) (heredi-
  tary) (typeB) 286.4
  type A 287.8
  vascular 287.8
Pseudohermaphroditism 752.7
  with chromosomal anomaly — *see*
    Anomaly, chromosomal
  adrenal 255.2
  female (without adrenocortical disor-
    der) 752.7
    with adrenocortical disorder 255.2
    adrenal 255.2
  male (without gonadal disorder) 752.7
    with
      adrenocortical disorder 255.2
      cleft scrotum 752.7
      feminizing testis 259.5
      gonadal disorder 257.9
      adrenal 255.2
Pseudohole, macula 362.54
Pseudo-Hurler's disease (mucolipidosis
  III) 272.7
Pseudohydrocephalus 348.2
**Pseudohypertrophic muscular dystro-
  phy** (Erb's) 359.1
Pseudohypertrophy, muscle 359.1
Pseudohypoparathyroidism 275.49
Pseudoinfluenza 487.1
Pseudoinsomnia 307.49
Pseudoleukemia 288.8
  infantile 285.8
Pseudomembranous — *see* condition
Pseudomeningocele (cerebral) (infective)
  349.2
  postprocedural 997.01
  spinal 349.2
Pseudomenstruation 626.8
Pseudomucinous
  cyst (ovary) (M8470/0) 220
  peritoneum 568.89
Pseudomyeloma 273.1
Pseudomyxoma peritonei (M8480/6)
  197.6
Pseudoneuritis optic (nerve) 377.24
  papilla 377.24
    congenital 743.57
Pseudoneuroma — *see* Injury, nerve, by
  site
Pseudo-obstruction
  intestine (chronic) (idiopathic) (inter-
    mittent secondary) (primary)
    564.89
    acute 560.89
Pseudopapilledema 377.24
Pseudoparalysis
  arm or leg 781.4

☑ Additional Digit Required — Refer to the Tabular List for Digit Selection   ▽ Subterms under main terms may continue to next column or page

2007 ICD-9-CM   ▶◀ Revised Text   ● New Line   ▲ Revised Code   October 2006 • Volume 2 — 241

Pseudoparalysis — *continued*
atonic, congenital 358.8
Pseudopelade 704.09
Pseudophakia V43.1
Pseudopolycythemia 289.0
Pseudopolyposis, colon 556.4
Pseudoporencephaly 348.0
Pseudopseudohypoparathyroidism
275.49
Pseudopsychosis 300.16
Pseudopterygium 372.52
Pseudoptosis (eyelid) 374.34
Pseudorabies 078.89
Pseudoretinitis, pigmentosa 362.65
Pseudorickets 588.0
senile (Pozzi's) 731.0
Pseudorubella 057.8
Pseudoscarlatina 057.8
Pseudoscelrema 778.1
Pseudosclerosis (brain)
Jakob's 046.1
of Westphal (-Strümpell) (hepatolenticular degeneration) 275.1
spastic 046.1
with dementia
with behavioral disturbance
046.1 [294.11]
without behavioral disturbance
046.1 [294.10]
Pseudoseizure 780.39
non-psychiatric 780.39
psychiatric 300.11
Pseudotabes 799.89
diabetic 250.6 ☑ [337.1]
Pseudotetanus — *see also* Convulsions
780.39
Pseudotetany 781.7
hysterical 300.11
Pseudothalassemia 285.0
Pseudotrichinosis 710.3
Pseudotruncus arteriosus 747.29
Pseudotuberculosis, pasteurella (infection) 027.2
Pseudotumor
cerebri 348.2
orbit (inflammatory) 376.11
Pseudo-Turner's syndrome 759.89
Pseudoxanthoma elasticum 757.39
Psilosis (sprue) (tropical) 579.1
Monilia 112.89
nontropical 579.0
not sprue 704.00
Psittacosis 073.9
Psoitis 728.89
Psora NEC 696.1
Psoriasis 696.1
any type, except arthropathic 696.1
arthritic, arthropathic 696.0
buccal 528.6
flexural 696.1
follicularis 696.1
guttate 696.1
inverse 696.1
mouth 528.6
nummularis 696.1
psychogenic 316 [696.1]
punctata 696.1
pustular 696.1
rupioides 696.1
vulgaris 696.1
Psorospermiasis 136.4
Psorospermosis 136.4
follicularis (vegetans) 757.39
Psychalgia 307.80
Psychasthenia 300.89
compulsive 300.3
mixed compulsive states 300.3
obsession 300.3
Psychiatric disorder or problem NEC
300.9
Psychogenic — *see also* condition
factors associated with physical conditions 316
Psychoneurosis, psychoneurotic — *see also* Neurosis 300.9
anxiety (state) 300.00

Psychoneurosis, psychoneurotic — *see also* Neurosis — *continued*
climacteric 627.2
compensation 300.16
compulsion 300.3
conversion hysteria 300.11
depersonalization 300.6
depressive type 300.4
dissociative hysteria 300.15
hypochondriacal 300.7
hysteria 300.10
conversion type 300.11
dissociative type 300.15
mixed NEC 300.89
neurasthenic 300.5
obsessional 300.3
obsessive-compulsive 300.3
occupational 300.89
personality NEC 301.89
phobia 300.20
senile NEC 300.89
Psychopathic — *see also* condition
constitution, posttraumatic 310.2
with psychosis 293.9
personality 301.9
amoral trends 301.7
antisocial trends 301.7
asocial trends 301.7
mixed types 301.7
state 301.9
Psychopathy, sexual — *see also* Deviation, sexual 302.9
Psychophysiologic, psychophysiological condition — *see* Reaction, psychophysiologic
Psychose passionelle 297.8
Psychosexual identity disorder 302.6
adult-life 302.85
childhood 302.6
Psychosis 298.9
acute hysterical 298.1
affecting management of pregnancy, childbirth, or puerperium 648.4 ☑
affective (*see also* Disorder, mood) 296.90

Note — Use the following fifth-digit subclassification with categories 296.0–296.6:

0   unspecified
1   mild
2   moderate
3   severe, without mention of psychotic behavior
4   severe, specified as with psychotic behavior
5   in partial or unspecified remission
6   in full remission

drug-induced 292.84
due to or associated with physical condition 293.83
involutional 293.83
recurrent episode 296.3 ☑
single episode 296.2 ☑
manic-depressive 296.80
circular (alternating) 296.7
currently depressed 296.5 ☑
currently manic 296.4 ☑
depressed type 296.2 ☑
atypical 296.82
recurrent episode 296.3 ☑
single episode 296.2 ☑
manic 296.0 ☑
atypical 296.81
recurrent episode 296.1 ☑
single episode 296.0 ☑
mixed type NEC 296.89
specified type NEC 296.89
senile 290.21
specified type NEC 296.99
alcoholic 291.9

Psychosis — *continued*
alcoholic — *continued*
with
anxiety 291.89
delirium tremens 291.0
delusions 291.5
dementia 291.2
hallucinosis 291.3
jealousy 291.5
mood disturbance 291.89
paranoia 291.5
persisting amnesia 291.1
sexual dysfunction 291.89
sleep disturbance 291.89
amnestic confabulatory 291.1
delirium tremens 291.0
hallucinosis 291.3
Korsakoff's, Korsakov's, Korsakow's 291.1
paranoid type 291.5
pathological intoxication 291.4
polyneuritic 291.1
specified type NEC 291.89
alternating (*see also* Psychosis, manic-depressive, circular) 296.7
anergastic (*see also* Psychosis, organic) 294.9
arteriosclerotic 290.40
with
acute confusional state 290.41
delirium 290.41
delusions 290.42
depressed mood 290.43
depressed type 290.43
paranoid type 290.42
simple type 290.40
uncomplicated 290.40
atypical 298.9
depressive 296.82
manic 296.81
borderline (schizophrenia) (*see also* Schizophrenia) 295.5 ☑
of childhood (*see also* Psychosis, childhood) 299.8 ☑
prepubertal 299.8 ☑
brief reactive 298.8
childhood, with origin specific to 299.9 ☑

Note — Use the following fifth-digit subclassification with category 299:

0   current or active state
1   residual state

atypical 299.8 ☑
specified type NEC 299.8 ☑
circular (*see also* Psychosis, manic-depressive, circular) 296.7
climacteric (*see also* Psychosis, involutional) 298.8
confusional 298.9
acute 293.0
reactive 298.2
subacute 293.1
depressive (*see also* Psychosis, affective) 296.2 ☑
atypical 296.82
involutional 296.2 ☑
with hypomania (bipolar II) 296.89
recurrent episode 296.3 ☑
single episode 296.2 ☑
psychogenic 298.0
reactive (emotional stress) (psychological trauma) 298.0
recurrent episode 296.3 ☑
with hypomania (bipolar II) 296.89
single episode 296.2 ☑
disintegrative, childhood (*see also* Psychosis, childhood) 299.1 ☑
drug 292.9
with
affective syndrome 292.84
amnestic syndrome 292.83
anxiety 292.89

Psychosis — *continued*
drug — *continued*
with — *continued*
delirium 292.81
withdrawal 292.0
delusions 292.11
dementia 292.82
depressive state 292.84
hallucinations 292.12
hallucinosis 292.12
mood disorder 292.84
mood disturbance 292.84
organic personality syndrome NEC 292.89
sexual dysfunction 292.89
sleep disturbance 292.89
withdrawal syndrome (and delirium) 292.0
affective syndrome 292.84
delusions 292.11
hallucinatory state 292.12
hallucinosis 292.12
paranoid state 292.11
specified type NEC 292.89
withdrawal syndrome (and delirium) 292.0
due to or associated with physical condition (*see also* Psychosis, organic) 293.9
epileptic NEC 294.8
excitation (psychogenic) (reactive) 298.1
exhaustive (*see also* Reaction, stress, acute) 308.9
hypomanic (*see also* Psychosis, affective) 296.0 ☑
recurrent episode 296.1 ☑
single episode 296.0 ☑
hysterical 298.8
acute 298.1
in
conditions classified elsewhere with
delusions 293.81
hallucinations 293.82
pregnancy, childbirth, or puerperium 648.4 ☑
incipient 298.8
schizophrenic (*see also* Schizophrenia) 295.5 ☑
induced 297.3
infantile (*see also* Psychosis, childhood) 299.0 ☑
infective 293.9
acute 293.0
subacute 293.1
interactional (childhood) (*see also* Psychosis, childhood) 299.1 ☑
involutional 298.8
depressive (*see also* Psychosis, affective) 296.2 ☑
recurrent episode 296.3 ☑
single episode 296.2 ☑
melancholic 296.2 ☑
recurrent episode 296.3 ☑
single episode 296.2 ☑
paranoid state 297.2
paraphrenia 297.2
Korsakoff's, Korakov's, Korsakow's (nonalcoholic) 294.0
alcoholic 291.1
mania (phase) (*see also* Psychosis, affective) 296.0 ☑
recurrent episode 296.1 ☑
single episode 296.0 ☑
manic (*see also* Psychosis, affective) 296.0 ☑
atypical 296.81
recurrent episode 296.1 ☑
single episode 296.0 ☑
manic-depressive 296.80
circular 296.7
currently
depressed 296.5 ☑
manic 296.4 ☑
mixed 296.6 ☑

☑ Additional Digit Required — Refer to the Tabular List for Digit Selection
▽ Subterms under main terms may continue to next column or page
242 — Volume 2   ▶◀ Revised Text   ● New Line   ▲ Revised Code   *2007 ICD-9-CM*

Psychosis — *continued*
  manic-depressive — *continued*
    depressive 296.2 ☑
      recurrent episode 296.3 ☑
        with hypomania (bipolar II) 296.89
      single episode 296.2 ☑
    hypomanic 296.0 ☑
      recurrent episode 296.1 ☑
      single episode 296.0 ☑
    manic 296.0 ☑
      atypical 296.81
      recurrent episode 296.1 ☑
      single episode 296.0 ☑
    mixed NEC 296.89
    perplexed 296.89
    stuporous 296.89
  menopausal (*see also* Psychosis, involutional) 298.8
  mixed schizophrenic and affective (*see also* Schizophrenia) 295.7 ☑
  multi-infarct (cerebrovascular) (*see also* Psychosis, arteriosclerotic) 290.40
  organic NEC 294.9
    due to or associated with
      addiction
        alcohol (*see also* Psychosis, alcoholic) 291.9
        drug (*see also* Psychosis, drug) 292.9
      alcohol intoxication, acute (*see also* Psychosis, alcoholic) 291.9
      alcoholism (*see also* Psychosis, alcoholic) 291.9
      arteriosclerosis (cerebral) (*see also* Psychosis, arteriosclerotic) 290.40
      cerebrovascular disease
        acute (psychosis) 293.0
        arteriosclerotic (*see also* Psychosis, arteriosclerotic) 290.40
      childbirth — *see* Psychosis, puerperal
      dependence
        alcohol (*see also* Psychosis, alcoholic) 291.9
        drug 292.9
      disease
        alcoholic liver (*see also* Psychosis, alcoholic) 291.9
        brain
          arteriosclerotic (*see also* Psychosis, arteriosclerotic) 290.40
          cerebrovascular
            acute (psychosis) 293.0
            arteriosclerotic (*see also* Psychosis, arteriosclerotic) 290.40
        endocrine or metabolic 293.9
          acute (psychosis) 293.0
          subacute (psychosis) 293.1
        Jakob-Creutzfeldt (new variant)
          with behavioral disturbance 046.1 [294.11]
          without behavioral disturbance 046.1 [294.10]
        liver, alcoholic (*see also* Psychosis, alcoholic) 291.9
      disorder
        cerebrovascular
          acute (psychosis) 293.0
        endocrine or metabolic 293.9
          acute (psychosis) 293.0
          subacute (psychosis) 293.1
      epilepsy
        with behavioral disturbance 345.9 ☑ [294.11]

Psychosis — *continued*
  organic — *continued*
    due to or associated with — *continued*
      epilepsy — *continued*
        without behavioral disturbance 345.9 ☑ [294.10]
        transient (acute) 293.0
      Huntington's chorea
        with behavioral disturbance 333.4 [294.11]
        without behavioral disturbance 333.4 [294.10]
      infection
        brain 293.9
          acute (psychosis) 293.0
          chronic 294.8
          subacute (psychosis) 293.1
        intracranial NEC 293.9
          acute (psychosis) 293.0
          chronic 294.8
          subacute (psychosis) 293.1
      intoxication
        alcoholic (acute) (*see also* Psychosis, alcoholic) 291.9
          pathological 291.4
        drug (*see also* Psychosis, drug) 292.2
      ischemia
        cerebrovascular (generalized) (*see also* Psychosis, arteriosclerotic) 290.40
      Jakob-Creutzfeldt disease (syndrome) (new variant)
        with behavioral disturbance 046.1 [294.11]
        without behavioral disturbance 046.1 [294.10]
      multiple sclerosis
        with behavioral disturbance 340 [294.11]
        without behavioral disturbance 340 [294.10]
      physical condition NEC 293.9
        with
          delusions 293.81
          hallucinations 293.82
      presenility 290.10
      puerperium — *see* Psychosis, puerperal
      sclerosis, multiple
        with behavioral disturbance 340 [294.11]
        without behavioral disturbance 340 [294.10]
      senility 290.20
      status epilepticus
        with behavioral disturbance 345.3 [294.11]
        without behavioral disturbance 345.3 [294.10]
      trauma
        brain (birth) (from electrical current) (surgical) 293.9
          acute (psychosis) 293.0
          chronic 294.8
          subacute (psychosis) 293.1
        unspecified physical condition 293.9
          with
            delusion 293.81
            hallucinations 293.82
    infective 293.9
      acute (psychosis) 293.0
      subacute 293.1
    posttraumatic 293.9
      acute 293.0
      subacute 293.1
    specified type NEC 294.8

Psychosis — *continued*
  organic — *continued*
    transient 293.9
      with
        anxiety 293.84
        delusions 293.81
        depression 293.83
        hallucinations 293.82
      depressive type 293.83
      hallucinatory type 293.82
      paranoid type 293.81
      specified type NEC 293.89
  paranoic 297.1
  paranoid (chronic) 297.9
    alcoholic 291.5
    chronic 297.1
    climacteric 297.2
    involutional 297.2
    menopausal 297.2
    protracted reactive 298.4
    psychogenic 298.4
      acute 298.3
    schizophrenic (*see also* Schizophrenia) 295.3 ☑
    senile 290.20
  paroxysmal 298.9
    senile 290.20
  polyneuritic, alcoholic 291.1
  postoperative 293.9
  postpartum — *see* Psychosis, puerperal
  prepsychotic (*see also* Schizophrenia) 295.5 ☑
  presbyophrenic (type) 290.8
  presenile (*see also* Dementia, presenile) 290.10
  prison 300.16
  psychogenic 298.8
    depressive 298.0
    paranoid 298.4
      acute 298.3
  puerperal
    specified type — *see* categories 295-298 ☑
    unspecified type 293.89
      acute 293.0
      chronic 293.89
      subacute 293.1
  reactive (emotional stress) (psychological trauma) 298.8
    brief 298.8
    confusion 298.2
    depressive 298.0
    excitation 298.1
  schizo-affective (depressed) (excited) (*see also* Schizophrenia) 295.7 ☑
  schizophrenia, schizophrenic (*see also* Schizophrenia) 295.9 ☑
    borderline type 295.5 ☑
    of childhood (*see also* Psychosis, childhood) 299.8 ☑
    catatonic (excited) (withdrawn) 295.2 ☑
    childhood type (*see also* Psychosis, childhood) 299.9 ☑
    hebephrenic 295.1 ☑
    incipient 295.5 ☑
    latent 295.5 ☑
    paranoid 295.3 ☑
    prepsychotic 295.5 ☑
    prodromal 295.5 ☑
    pseudoneurotic 295.5 ☑
    pseudopsychopathic 295.5 ☑
    schizophreniform 295.4 ☑
    simple 295.0 ☑
    undifferentiated type 295.9 ☑
  schizophreniform 295.4 ☑
  senile NEC 290.20
    with
      delusional features 290.20
      depressive features 290.21
    depressed type 290.21
    paranoid type 290.20
    simple deterioration 290.20

Psychosis — *continued*
  senile — *continued*
    specified type — *see* categories 295-298 ☑
  shared 297.3
  situational (reactive) 298.8
  symbiotic (childhood) (*see also* Psychosis, childhood) 299.1 ☑
  toxic (acute) 293.9
Psychotic — *see also* condition 298.9
  episode 298.9
    due to or associated with physical conditions (*see also* Psychosis, organic) 293.9
Pterygium (eye) 372.40
  central 372.43
  colli 744.5
  double 372.44
  peripheral (stationary) 372.41
    progressive 372.42
  recurrent 372.45
Ptilosis 374.55
Ptomaine (poisoning) — *see also* Poisoning, food 005.9
Ptosis (adiposa) 374.30
  breast 611.8
  cecum 569.89
  colon 569.89
  congenital (eyelid) 743.61
    specified site NEC — *see* Anomaly, specified type NEC
  epicanthus syndrome 270.2
  eyelid 374.30
    congenital 743.61
    mechanical 374.33
    myogenic 374.32
    paralytic 374.31
  gastric 537.5
  intestine 569.89
  kidney (*see also* Disease, renal) 593.0
    congenital 753.3
  liver 573.8
  renal (*see also* Disease, renal) 593.0
    congenital 753.3
  splanchnic 569.89
  spleen 289.59
  stomach 537.5
  viscera 569.89
PTSD (Post-traumatic stress disorder) ● 309.81 ●
Ptyalism 527.7
  hysterical 300.11
  periodic 527.2
  pregnancy 646.8 ☑
  psychogenic 306.4
Ptyalolithiasis 527.5
Pubalgia 848.8
Pubarche, precocious 259.1
Pubertas praecox 259.1
Puberty V21.1
  abnormal 259.9
  bleeding 626.3
  delayed 259.0
  precocious (constitutional) (cryptogenic) (idiopathic) NEC 259.1
    due to
      adrenal
        cortical hyperfunction 255.2
        hyperplasia 255.2
      cortical hyperfunction 255.2
      ovarian hyperfunction 256.1
        estrogen 256.0
      pineal tumor 259.8
      testicular hyperfunction 257.0
  premature 259.1
    due to
      adrenal cortical hyperfunction 255.2
      pineal tumor 259.8
      pituitary (anterior) hyperfunction 253.1
Puckering, macula 362.56
Pudenda, pudendum — *see* condition
Puente's disease (simple glandular cheilitis) 528.5

☑ Additional Digit Required — Refer to the Tabular List for Digit Selection   ▽ Subterms under main terms may continue to next column or page

2007 ICD-9-CM   ▶◀ Revised Text   ● New Line   ▲ Revised Code   October 2006 · Volume 2 — 243

Puerperal
- abscess
  - areola 675.1 ☑
  - Bartholin's gland 646.6 ☑
  - breast 675.1 ☑
  - cervix (uteri) 670.0 ☑
  - fallopian tube 670.0 ☑
  - genital organ 670.0 ☑
  - kidney 646.6 ☑
  - mammary 675.1 ☑
  - mesosalpinx 670.0 ☑
  - nabothian 646.6 ☑
  - nipple 675.0 ☑
  - ovary, ovarian 670.0 ☑
  - oviduct 670.0 ☑
  - parametric 670.0 ☑
  - para-uterine 670.0 ☑
  - pelvic 670.0 ☑
  - perimetric 670.0 ☑
  - periuterine 670.0 ☑
  - retro-uterine 670.0 ☑
  - subareolar 675.1 ☑
  - suprapelvic 670.0 ☑
  - tubal (ruptured) 670.0 ☑
  - tubo-ovarian 670.0 ☑
  - urinary tract NEC 646.6 ☑
  - uterine, uterus 670.0 ☑
  - vagina (wall) 646.6 ☑
  - vaginorectal 646.6 ☑
  - vulvovaginal gland 646.6 ☑
- accident 674.9 ☑
- adnexitis 670.0 ☑
- afibrinogenemia, or other coagulation defect 666.3 ☑
- albuminuria (acute) (subacute) 646.2 ☑
  - pre-eclamptic 642.4 ☑
- anemia (conditions classifiable to 280–285) 648.2 ☑
- anuria 669.3 ☑
- apoplexy 674.0 ☑
- asymptomatic bacteriuria 646.5 ☑
- atrophy, breast 676.3 ☑
- blood dyscrasia 666.3 ☑
- caked breast 676.2 ☑
- cardiomyopathy 674.5 ☑
- cellulitis — see Puerperal, abscess
- cerebrovascular disorder (conditions classifiable to 430–434, 436–437) 674.0 ☑
- cervicitis (conditions classifiable to 616.0) 646.6 ☑
- coagulopathy (any) 666.3 ☑
- complications 674.9 ☑
  - specified type NEC 674.8 ☑
- convulsions (eclamptic) (uremic) 642.6 ☑
  - with pre-existing hypertension 642.7 ☑
- cracked nipple 676.1 ☑
- cystitis 646.6 ☑
- cystopyelitis 646.6 ☑
- deciduitis (acute) 670.0 ☑
- delirium NEC 293.9
- diabetes (mellitus) (conditions classifiable to 250) 648.0 ☑
- disease 674.9 ☑
  - breast NEC 676.3 ☑
  - cerebrovascular (acute) 674.0 ☑
  - nonobstetric NEC (see also Pregnancy, complicated, current disease or condition) 648.9 ☑
  - pelvis inflammatory 670.0 ☑
  - renal NEC 646.2 ☑
  - tubo-ovarian 670.0 ☑
  - Valsuani's (progressive pernicious anemia) 648.2 ☑
- disorder
  - lactation 676.9 ☑
    - specified type NEC 676.8 ☑
  - nonobstetric NEC (see also Pregnancy, complicated, current disease or condition) 648.9 ☑

Puerperal — continued
- disruption
  - cesarean wound 674.1 ☑
  - episiotomy wound 674.2 ☑
  - perineal laceration wound 674.2 ☑
- drug dependence (conditions classifiable to 304) 648.3 ☑
- eclampsia 642.6 ☑
  - with pre-existing hypertension 642.7 ☑
- embolism (pulmonary) 673.2 ☑
  - air 673.0 ☑
  - amniotic fluid 673.1 ☑
  - blood-clot 673.2 ☑
  - brain or cerebral 674.0 ☑
  - cardiac 674.8 ☑
  - fat 673.8 ☑
  - intracranial sinus (venous) 671.5 ☑
  - pyemic 673.3 ☑
  - septic 673.3 ☑
  - spinal cord 671.5 ☑
- endometritis (conditions classifiable to 615.0–615.9) 670.0 ☑
- endophlebitis — see Puerperal, phlebitis
- endotrachelitis 646.6 ☑
- engorgement, breasts 676.2 ☑
- erysipelas 670.0 ☑
- failure
  - lactation 676.4 ☑
  - renal, acute 669.3 ☑
- fever 670.0 ☑
  - meaning pyrexia (of unknown origin) 672.0 ☑
  - meaning sepsis 670.0 ☑
- fissure, nipple 676.1 ☑
- fistula
  - breast 675.1 ☑
  - mammary gland 675.1 ☑
  - nipple 675.0 ☑
- galactophoritis 675.2 ☑
- galactorrhea 676.6 ☑
- gangrene
  - gas 670.0 ☑
  - uterus 670.0 ☑
- gonorrhea (conditions classifiable to 098) 647.1 ☑
- hematoma, subdural 674.0 ☑
- hematosalpinx, infectional 670.0 ☑
- hemiplegia, cerebral 674.0 ☑
- hemorrhage 666.1 ☑
  - brain 674.0 ☑
  - bulbar 674.0 ☑
  - cerebellar 674.0 ☑
  - cerebral 674.0 ☑
  - cortical 674.0 ☑
  - delayed (after 24 hours) (uterine) 666.2 ☑
  - extradural 674.0 ☑
  - internal capsule 674.0 ☑
  - intracranial 674.0 ☑
  - intrapontine 674.0 ☑
  - meningeal 674.0 ☑
  - pontine 674.0 ☑
  - subarachnoid 674.0 ☑
  - subcortical 674.0 ☑
  - subdural 674.0 ☑
  - uterine, delayed 666.2 ☑
  - ventricular 674.0 ☑
- hemorrhoids 671.8 ☑
- hepatorenal syndrome 674.8 ☑
- hypertrophy
  - breast 676.3 ☑
  - mammary gland 676.3 ☑
- induration breast (fibrous) 676.3 ☑
- infarction
  - lung — see Puerperal, embolism
  - pulmonary — see Puerperal, embolism
- infection
  - Bartholin's gland 646.6 ☑
  - breast 675.2 ☑
    - with nipple 675.9 ☑

Puerperal — continued
- infection — continued
  - breast — continued
    - with nipple — continued
      - specified type NEC 675.8 ☑
  - cervix 646.6 ☑
  - endocervix 646.6 ☑
  - fallopian tube 670.0 ☑
  - generalized 670.0 ☑
  - genital tract (major) 670.0 ☑
    - minor or localized 646.6 ☑
  - kidney (bacillus coli) 646.6 ☑
  - mammary gland 675.2 ☑
    - with nipple 675.9 ☑
      - specified type NEC 675.8 ☑
  - nipple 675.0 ☑
    - with breast 675.9 ☑
      - specified type NEC 675.8 ☑
  - ovary 670.0 ☑
  - pelvic 670.0 ☑
  - peritoneum 670.0 ☑
  - renal 646.6 ☑
  - tubo-ovarian 670.0 ☑
  - urinary (tract) NEC 646.6 ☑
    - asymptomatic 646.5 ☑
  - uterus, uterine 670.0 ☑
  - vagina 646.6 ☑
- inflammation (see also Puerperal, infection)
  - areola 675.1 ☑
  - Bartholin's gland 646.6 ☑
  - breast 675.2 ☑
  - broad ligament 670.0 ☑
  - cervix (uteri) 646.6 ☑
  - fallopian tube 670.0 ☑
  - genital organs 670.0 ☑
    - localized 646.6 ☑
  - mammary gland 675.2 ☑
  - nipple 675.0 ☑
  - ovary 670.0 ☑
  - oviduct 670.0 ☑
  - pelvis 670.0 ☑
  - periuterine 670.0 ☑
  - tubal 670.0 ☑
  - vagina 646.6 ☑
  - vein — see Puerperal, phlebitis
- inversion, nipple 676.3 ☑
- ischemia, cerebral 674.0 ☑
- lymphangitis 670.0 ☑
  - breast 675.2 ☑
- malaria (conditions classifiable to 084) 647.4 ☑
- malnutrition 648.9 ☑
- mammillitis 675.0 ☑
- mammitis 675.2 ☑
- mania 296.0 ☑
  - recurrent episode 296.1 ☑
  - single episode 296.0 ☑
- mastitis 675.2 ☑
  - purulent 675.1 ☑
  - retromammary 675.1 ☑
  - submammary 675.1 ☑
- melancholia 296.2 ☑
  - recurrent episode 296.3 ☑
  - single episode 296.2 ☑
- mental disorder (conditions classifiable to 290–303, ▶305.0, 305.2–305.9, 306–316◀, 317–319) 648.4 ☑
- metritis (septic) (suppurative) 670.0 ☑
- metroperitonitis 670.0 ☑
- metrorrhagia 666.2 ☑
- metrosalpingitis 670.0 ☑
- metrovaginitis 670.0 ☑
- milk leg 671.4 ☑
- monoplegia, cerebral 674.0 ☑
- necrosis
  - kidney, tubular 669.3 ☑
  - liver (acute) (subacute) (conditions classifiable to 570) 674.8 ☑
  - ovary 670.0 ☑
  - renal cortex 669.3 ☑
- nephritis or nephrosis (conditions classifiable to 580–589) 646.2 ☑

Puerperal — continued
- nephritis or nephrosis — continued
  - with hypertension 642.1 ☑
- nutritional deficiency (conditions classifiable to 260–269) 648.9 ☑
- occlusion, precerebral artery 674.0 ☑
- oliguria 669.3 ☑
- oophoritis 670.0 ☑
- ovaritis 670.0 ☑
- paralysis
  - bladder (sphincter) 665.5 ☑
  - cerebral 674.0 ☑
- paralytic stroke 674.0 ☑
- parametritis 670.0 ☑
- paravaginitis 646.6 ☑
- pelviperitonitis 670.0 ☑
- perimetritis 670.0 ☑
- perimetrosalpingitis 670.0 ☑
- perinephritis 646.6 ☑
- perioophoritis 670.0 ☑
- periphlebitis — see Puerperal, phlebitis
- perisalpingitis 670.0 ☑
- peritoneal infection 670.0 ☑
- peritonitis (pelvic) 670.0 ☑
- perivaginitis 646.6 ☑
- phlebitis 671.9 ☑
  - deep 671.4 ☑
  - intracranial sinus (venous) 671.5 ☑
  - pelvic 671.4 ☑
  - specified site NEC 671.5 ☑
  - superficial 671.2 ☑
- phlegmasia alba dolens 671.4 ☑
- placental polyp 674.4 ☑
- pneumonia, embolic — see Puerperal, embolism
- prediabetes 648.8 ☑
- pre-eclampsia (mild) 642.4 ☑
  - with pre-existing hypertension 642.7 ☑
  - severe 642.5 ☑
- psychosis, unspecified (see also Psychosis, puerperal) 293.89
- pyelitis 646.6 ☑
- pyelocystitis 646.6 ☑
- pyelohydronephrosis 646.6 ☑
- pyelonephritis 646.6 ☑
- pyelonephrosis 646.6 ☑
- pyemia 670.0 ☑
- pyocystitis 646.6 ☑
- pyohemia 670.0 ☑
- pyometra 670.0 ☑
- pyonephritis 646.6 ☑
- pyonephrosis 646.6 ☑
- pyo-oophoritis 670.0 ☑
- pyosalpingitis 670.0 ☑
- pyosalpinx 670.0 ☑
- pyrexia (of unknown origin) 672.0 ☑
- renal
  - disease NEC 646.2 ☑
  - failure, acute 669.3 ☑
- retention
  - decidua (fragments) (with delayed hemorrhage) 666.2 ☑
    - without hemorrhage 667.1 ☑
  - placenta (fragments) (with delayed hemorrhage) 666.2 ☑
    - without hemorrhage 667.1 ☑
  - secundines (fragments) (with delayed hemorrhage) 666.2 ☑
    - without hemorrhage 667.1 ☑
- retracted nipple 676.0 ☑
- rubella (conditions classifiable to 056) 647.5 ☑
- salpingitis 670.0 ☑
- salpingo-oophoritis 670.0 ☑
- salpingo-ovaritis 670.0 ☑
- salpingoperitonitis 670.0 ☑
- sapremia 670.0 ☑
- secondary perineal tear 674.2 ☑
- sepsis (pelvic) 670.0 ☑
- septicemia 670.0 ☑
- subinvolution (uterus) 674.8 ☑

☑ Additional Digit Required — Refer to the Tabular List for Digit Selection   ᵂ Subterms under main terms may continue to next column or page

244 — Volume 2 · October 2006   ▶◀ Revised Text   ● New Line   ▲ Revised Code   **2007 ICD-9-CM**

Puerperal — *continued*
  sudden death (cause unknown) 674.9 ☑
  suppuration — *see* Puerperal, abscess
  syphilis (conditions classifiable to 090–097) 647.0 ☑
  tetanus 670.0 ☑
  thelitis 675.0 ☑
  thrombocytopenia 666.3 ☑
  thrombophlebitis (superficial) 671.2 ☑
    deep 671.4 ☑
    pelvic 671.4 ☑
    specified site NEC 671.5 ☑
  thrombosis (venous) — *see* Thrombosis, puerperal
  thyroid dysfunction (conditions classifiable to 240–246) 648.1 ☑
  toxemia (*see also* Toxemia, of pregnancy) 642.4 ☑
    eclamptic 642.6 ☑
      with pre-existing hypertension 642.7 ☑
    pre-eclamptic (mild) 642.4 ☑
      with
        convulsions 642.6 ☑
        pre-existing hypertension 642.7 ☑
      severe 642.5 ☑
  tuberculosis (conditions classifiable to 010–018) 647.3 ☑
  uremia 669.3 ☑
  vaginitis (conditions classifiable to 616.1) 646.6 ☑
  varicose veins (legs) 671.0 ☑
    vulva or perineum 671.1 ☑
  vulvitis (conditions classifiable to 616.1) 646.6 ☑
  vulvovaginitis (conditions classifiable to 616.1) 646.6 ☑
  white leg 671.4 ☑
Pulled muscle — *see* Sprain, by site
Pulmolithiasis 518.89
Pulmonary — *see* condition
Pulmonitis (unknown etiology) 486
Pulpitis (acute) (anachoretic) (chronic) (hyperplastic) (putrescent) (suppurative) (ulcerative) 522.0
Pulpless tooth 522.9
Pulse
  alternating 427.89
    psychogenic 306.2
  bigeminal 427.89
  fast 785.0
  feeble, rapid, due to shock following injury 958.4
  rapid 785.0
  slow 427.89
  strong 785.9
  trigeminal 427.89
  water-hammer (*see also* Insufficiency, aortic) 424.1
  weak 785.9
Pulseless disease 446.7
Pulsus
  alternans or trigeminy 427.89
    psychogenic 306.2
Punch drunk 310.2
Puncta lacrimalia occlusion 375.52
Punctiform hymen 752.49
Puncture (traumatic) — *see also* Wound, open, by site
  accidental, complicating surgery 998.2
  bladder, nontraumatic 596.6
  by
    device, implant, or graft — *see* Complications, mechanical
    foreign body
      internal organs (*see also* Injury, internal, by site)
      by ingested object — *see* Foreign body
    left accidentally in operation wound 998.4
    instrument (any) during a procedure, accidental 998.2

Puncture — *see also* Wound, open, by site — *continued*
  internal organs, abdomen, chest, or pelvis — *see* Injury, internal, by site
  kidney, nontraumatic 593.89
Pupil — *see* condition
Pupillary membrane 364.74
  persistent 743.46
Pupillotonia 379.46
  pseudotabetic 379.46
Purpura 287.2
  abdominal 287.0
  allergic 287.0
  anaphylactoid 287.0
  annularis telangiectodes 709.1
  arthritic 287.0
  autoerythrocyte sensitization 287.2
  autoimmune 287.0
  bacterial 287.0
  Bateman's (senile) 287.2
  capillary fragility (hereditary) (idiopathic) 287.8
  cryoglobulinemic 273.2
  devil's pinches 287.2
  fibrinolytic (*see also* Fibrinolysis) 286.6
  fulminans, fulminous 286.6
  gangrenous 287.0
  hemorrhagic (*see also* Purpura, thrombocytopenic) 287.39
    nodular 272.7
    nonthrombocytopenic 287.0
    thrombocytopenic 287.39
  Henoch's (purpura nervosa) 287.0
  Henoch-Schönlein (allergic) 287.0
  hypergammaglobulinemic (benign primary) (Waldenström's) 273.0
  idiopathic 287.31
    nonthrombocytopenic 287.0
    thrombocytopenic 287.31
  immune thrombocytopenic 287.31
  infectious 287.0
  malignant 287.0
  neonatorum 772.6
  nervosa 287.0
  newborn NEC 772.6
  nonthrombocytopenic 287.2
    hemorrhagic 287.0
    idiopathic 287.0
  nonthrombopenic 287.2
  peliosis rheumatica 287.0
  pigmentaria, progressiva 709.09
  posttransfusion 287.4
  primary 287.0
  primitive 287.0
  red cell membrane sensitivity 287.2
  rheumatica 287.0
  Schönlein (-Henoch) (allergic) 287.0
  scorbutic 267
  senile 287.2
  simplex 287.2
  symptomatica 287.0
  telangiectasia annularis 709.1
  thrombocytopenic (*see also* Thrombocytopenia) 287.30
    congenital 287.33
    essential 287.30
    hereditary 287.31
    idiopathic 287.31
    immune 287.31
    neonatal, transitory (*see also* Thrombocytopenia, neonatal transitory) 776.1
    primary 287.30
    puerperal, postpartum 666.3 ☑
    thrombotic 446.6
  thrombohemolytic (*see also* Fibrinolysis) 286.6
  thrombopenic (*see also* Thrombocytopenia) 287.30
    congenital 287.33
    essential 287.30
    thrombotic 446.6
      thrombocytic 446.6
      thrombocytopenic 446.6

Purpura — *continued*
  toxic 287.0
  variolosa 050.0
  vascular 287.0
  visceral symptoms 287.0
  Werlhof's (*see also* Purpura, thrombocytopenic) 287.39
Purpuric spots 782.7
Purulent — *see* condition
Pus
  absorption, general — *see* Septicemia
  in
    stool 792.1
    urine 791.9
  tube (rupture) (*see also* Salpingo-oophoritis) 614.2
Pustular rash 782.1
Pustule 686.9
  malignant 022.0
  nonmalignant 686.9
Putnam-Dana syndrome (subacute combined sclerosis with pernicious anemia) 281.0 [336.2]
Putnam's disease (subacute combined sclerosis with pernicious anemia) 281.0 [336.2]
Putrefaction, intestinal 569.89
Putrescent pulp (dental) 522.1
Pyarthritis — *see* Pyarthrosis
Pyarthrosis — *see also* Arthritis, pyogenic 711.0 ☑
  tuberculous — *see* Tuberculosis, joint
Pycnoepilepsy, pycnolepsy (idiopathic) — *see also* Epilepsy 345.0 ☑
Pyelectasia 593.89
Pyelectasis 593.89
Pyelitis (congenital) (uremic) 590.80
  with
    abortion — *see* Abortion, by type, with specified complication NEC
    contracted kidney 590.00
    ectopic pregnancy (*see also* categories 633.0–633.9) 639.8
    molar pregnancy (*see also* categories 630–632) 639.8
  acute 590.10
    with renal medullary necrosis 590.11
  chronic 590.00
    with
      renal medullary necrosis 590.01
  complicating pregnancy, childbirth, or puerperium 646.6 ☑
    affecting fetus or newborn 760.1
  cystica 590.3
    following
      abortion 639.8
      ectopic or molar pregnancy 639.8
  gonococcal 098.19
    chronic or duration of 2 months or over 098.39
  tuberculous (*see also* Tuberculosis) 016.0 ☑ [590.81]
Pyelocaliectasis 593.89
Pyelocystitis — *see also* Pyelitis 590.80
Pyelohydronephrosis 591
Pyelonephritis — *see also* Pyelitis 590.80
  acute 590.10
    with renal medullary necrosis 590.11
  chronic 590.00
  syphilitic (late) 095.4
  tuberculous (*see also* Tuberculosis) 016.0 ☑ [590.81]
Pyelonephrosis — *see also* Pyelitis 590.80
  chronic 590.00
Pyelophlebitis 451.89
Pyelo-ureteritis cystica 590.3
Pyemia, pyemic (purulent) — *see also* Septicemia 038.9
  abscess — *see* Abscess

Pyemia, pyemic — *see also* Septicemia — *continued*
  arthritis (*see also* Arthritis, pyogenic) 711.0 ☑
  Bacillus coli 038.42
  embolism — *see* Embolism, pyemic
  fever 038.9
  infection 038.9
  joint (*see also* Arthritis, pyogenic) 711.0 ☑
  liver 572.1
  meningococcal 036.2
  newborn 771.81
  phlebitis — *see* Phlebitis
  pneumococcal 038.2
  portal 572.1
  postvaccinal 999.3
  specified organism NEC 038.8
  staphylococcal 038.10
    aureus 038.11
    specified organism NEC 038.19
  streptococcal 038.0
  tuberculous — *see* Tuberculosis, miliary
Pygopagus 759.4
Pykno-epilepsy, pyknolepsy (idiopathic) — *see also* Epilepsy 345.0 ☑
Pyle (-Cohn) disease (craniometaphyseal dysplasia) 756.89
Pylephlebitis (suppurative) 572.1
Pylethrombophlebitis 572.1
Pylethrombosis 572.1
Pyloritis — *see also* Gastritis 535.5 ☑
Pylorospasm (reflex) 537.81
  congenital or infantile 750.5
  neurotic 306.4
  newborn 750.5
  psychogenic 306.4
Pylorus, pyloric — *see* condition
Pyoarthrosis — *see* Pyarthrosis
Pyocele
  mastoid 383.00
  sinus (accessory) (nasal) (*see also* Sinusitis) 473.9
  turbinate (bone) 473.9
  urethra (*see also* Urethritis) 597.0
Pyococcal dermatitis 686.00
Pyococcide, skin 686.00
Pyocolpos — *see also* Vaginitis 616.10
Pyocyaneus dermatitis 686.09
Pyocystitis — *see also* Cystitis 595.9
Pyoderma, pyodermia 686.00
  gangrenosum 686.01
  specified type NEC 686.09
  vegetans 686.8
Pyodermatitis 686.00
  vegetans 686.8
Pyogenic — *see* condition
Pyohemia — *see* Septicemia
Pyohydronephrosis — *see also* Pyelitis 590.80
Pyometra 615.9
Pyometritis — *see also* Endometritis 615.9
Pyometrium — *see also* Endometritis 615.9
Pyomyositis 728.0
  ossificans 728.19
  tropical (bungpagga) 040.81
Pyonephritis — *see also* Pyelitis 590.80
  chronic 590.00
Pyonephrosis (congenital) — *see also* Pyelitis 590.80
  acute 590.10
Pyo-oophoritis — *see also* Salpingo-oophoritis 614.2
Pyo-ovarium — *see also* Salpingo-oophoritis 614.2
Pyopericarditis 420.99
Pyopericardium 420.99
Pyophlebitis — *see* Phlebitis
Pyopneumopericardium 420.99
Pyopneumothorax (infectional) 510.9
  with fistula 510.0
  subdiaphragmatic (*see also* Peritonitis) 567.29

☑ Additional Digit Required — Refer to the Tabular List for Digit Selection   ▽ Subterms under main terms may continue to next column or page

2007 ICD-9-CM   ▶◀ Revised Text   ● New Line   ▲ Revised Code   **Volume 2 — 245**

Pyopneumothorax — *continued*
  subphrenic (*see also* Peritonitis) 567.29
  tuberculous (*see also* Tuberculosis, pleura) 012.0 ☑
Pyorrhea (alveolar) (alveolaris) 523.40
  degenerative 523.5
Pyosalpingitis — *see also* Salpingo-oophoritis 614.2
Pyosalpinx — *see also* Salpingo-oophoritis 614.2
Pyosepticemia — *see* Septicemia
Pyosis
  Corlett's (impetigo) 684
  Manson's (pemphigus contagiosus) 684
Pyothorax 510.9
  with fistula 510.0
  tuberculous (*see also* Tuberculosis, pleura) 012.0 ☑
Pyoureter 593.89
  tuberculous (*see also* Tuberculosis) 016.2 ☑
Pyramidopallidonigral syndrome 332.0
Pyrexia (of unknown origin) (P.U.O.) 780.6
  atmospheric 992.0
  during labor 659.2 ☑
  environmentally-induced newborn 778.4
  heat 992.0
  newborn, environmentally-induced 778.4
  puerperal 672.0 ☑
Pyroglobulinemia 273.8
Pyromania 312.33
Pyrosis 787.1
Pyrroloporphyria 277.1
Pyuria (bacterial) 791.9

Q

Q fever 083.0
  with pneumonia 083.0 [484.8]
Quadricuspid aortic valve 746.89
Quadrilateral fever 083.0
Quadriparesis — *see* Quadriplegia
  meaning muscle weakness 728.87
Quadriplegia 344.00
  with fracture, vertebra (process) — *see* Fracture, vertebra, cervical, with spinal cord injury
  brain (current episode) 437.8
  C1-C4
    complete 344.01
    incomplete 344.02
  C5-C7
    complete 344.03
    incomplete 344.04
  cerebral (current episode) 437.8
  congenital or infantile (cerebral) (spastic) (spinal) 343.2
  cortical 437.8
  embolic (current episode) (*see also* Embolism, brain) 434.1 ☑
  infantile (cerebral) (spastic) (spinal) 343.2
  newborn NEC 767.0
  specified NEC 344.09
  thrombotic (current episode) (*see also* Thrombosis, brain) 434.0 ☑
  traumatic — *see* Injury, spinal, cervical
Quadruplet
  affected by maternal complications of pregnancy 761.5
  healthy liveborn — *see* Newborn, multiple
  pregnancy (complicating delivery) NEC 651.8 ☑
    with fetal loss and retention of one or more fetus(es) 651.5 ☑
    following (elective) fetal reduction 651.7 ☑
Quarrelsomeness 301.3

Quartan
  fever 084.2
  malaria (fever) 084.2
Queensland fever 083.0
  coastal 083.0
  seven-day 100.89
Quervain's disease 727.04
  thyroid (subacute granulomatous thyroiditis) 245.1
Queyrat's erythroplasia (M8080/2)
  specified site — *see* Neoplasm, skin, in situ
  unspecified site 233.5
Quincke's disease or edema — *see* Edema, angioneurotic
Quinquaud's disease (acne decalvans) 704.09
Quinsy (gangrenous) 475
Quintan fever 083.1
Quintuplet
  affected by maternal complications of pregnancy 761.5
  healthy liveborn — *see* Newborn, multiple
  pregnancy (complicating delivery) NEC 651.2 ☑
    with fetal loss and retention of one or more fetus(es) 651.6 ☑
    following (elective) fetal reduction 651.7 ☑
Quotidian
  fever 084.0
  malaria (fever) 084.0

R

Rabbia 071
Rabbit fever — *see also* Tularemia 021.9
Rabies 071
  contact V01.5
  exposure to V01.5
  inoculation V04.5
    reaction — *see* Complications, vaccination
  vaccination, prophylactic (against) V04.5
Rachischisis — *see also* Spina bifida 741.9 ☑
Rachitic — *see also* condition
  deformities of spine 268.1
  pelvis 268.1
    with disproportion (fetopelvic) 653.2 ☑
      affecting fetus or newborn 763.1
      causing obstructed labor 660.1 ☑
        affecting fetus or newborn 763.1
Rachitis, rachitism — *see also* Rickets
  acute 268.0
  fetalis 756.4
  renalis 588.0
  tarda 268.0
Racket nail 757.5
Radial nerve — *see* condition
Radiation effects or sickness — *see also* Effect, adverse, radiation
  cataract 366.46
  dermatitis 692.82
    sunburn (*see also* Sunburn) 692.71
Radiculitis (pressure) (vertebrogenic) 729.2
  accessory nerve 723.4
  anterior crural 724.4
  arm 723.4
  brachial 723.4
  cervical NEC 723.4
  due to displacement of intervertebral disc — *see* Neuritis, due to, displacement intervertebral disc
  leg 724.4
  lumbar NEC 724.4
  lumbosacral 724.4
  rheumatic 729.2
  syphilitic 094.89
  thoracic (with visceral pain) 724.4

Radiculomyelitis 357.0
  toxic, due to
    Clostridium tetani 037
    Corynebacterium diphtheriae 032.89
Radiculopathy — *see also* Radiculitis 729.2
Radioactive substances, adverse effect — *see* Effect, adverse, radioactive substance
Radiodermal burns (acute) (chronic) (occupational) — *see* Burn, by site
Radiodermatitis 692.82
Radionecrosis — *see* Effect, adverse, radiation
Radiotherapy session V58.0
Radium, adverse effect — *see* Effect, adverse, radioactive substance
Raeder-Harbitz syndrome (pulseless disease) 446.7
Rage — *see also* Disturbance, conduct 312.0 ☑
  meaning rabies 071
Rag sorters' disease 022.1
Raillietiniasis 123.8
Railroad neurosis 300.16
Railway spine 300.16
Raised — *see* Elevation
Raiva 071
Rake teeth, tooth 524.39
Rales 786.7
Ramifying renal pelvis 753.3
Ramsay Hunt syndrome (herpetic geniculate ganglionitis) 053.11
  meaning dyssynergia cerebellaris myoclonica 334.2
Ranke's primary infiltration — *see also* Tuberculosis 010.0 ☑
Ranula 527.6
  congenital 750.26
Rape
  adult 995.83
  alleged, observation or examination V71.5
  child 995.53
Rapid
  feeble pulse, due to shock, following injury 958.4
  heart (beat) 785.0
    psychogenic 306.2
  respiration 786.06
    psychogenic 306.1
  second stage (delivery) 661.3 ☑
    affecting fetus or newborn 763.6
  time-zone change syndrome 327.35
Rarefaction, bone 733.99
Rash 782.1
  canker 034.1
  diaper 691.0
  drug (internal use) 693.0
    contact 692.3
  ECHO 9 virus 078.89
  enema 692.89
  food (*see also* Allergy, food) 693.1
  heat 705.1
  napkin 691.0
  nettle 708.8
  pustular 782.1
  rose 782.1
    epidemic 056.9
    of infants 057.8
  scarlet 034.1
  serum (prophylactic) (therapeutic) 999.5
  toxic 782.1
  wandering tongue 529.1
Rasmussen's aneurysm — *see also* Tuberculosis 011.2 ☑
Rat-bite fever 026.9
  due to Streptobacillus moniliformis 026.1
  spirochetal (morsus muris) 026.0
Rathke's pouch tumor (M9350/1) 237.0
Raymond (-Céstan) syndrome 433.8 ☑

Raynaud's
  disease or syndrome (paroxysmal digital cyanosis) 443.0
  gangrene (symmetric) 443.0 [785.4]
  phenomenon (paroxysmal digital cyanosis) (secondary) 443.0
RDS 769
Reaction
  acute situational maladjustment (*see also* Reaction, adjustment) 309.9
  adaptation (*see also* Reaction, adjustment) 309.9
  adjustment 309.9
    with
      anxious mood 309.24
        with depressed mood 309.28
      conduct disturbance 309.3
        combined with disturbance of emotions 309.4
      depressed mood 309.0
        brief 309.0
          with anxious mood 309.28
        prolonged 309.1
      elective mutism 309.83
      mixed emotions and conduct 309.4
      mutism, elective 309.83
      physical symptoms 309.82
      predominant disturbance (of)
        conduct 309.3
        emotions NEC 309.29
          mixed 309.28
        mixed, emotions and conduct 309.4
        specified type NEC 309.89
      specific academic or work inhibition 309.23
      withdrawal 309.83
    depressive 309.0
      with conduct disturbance 309.4
      brief 309.0
      prolonged 309.1
    specified type NEC 309.89
  adverse food NEC 995.7
  affective (*see also* Psychosis, affective) 296.90
    specified type NEC 296.99
  aggressive 301.3
    unsocialized (*see also* Disturbance, conduct) 312.0 ☑
  allergic (*see also* Allergy) 995.3
    drug, medicinal substance, and biological — *see* Allergy, drug
    food — *see* Allergy, food
    serum 999.5
  anaphylactic — *see* Shock, anaphylactic
  anesthesia — *see* Anesthesia, complication
  anger 312.0 ☑
  antisocial 301.7
  antitoxin (prophylactic) (therapeutic) — *see* Complications, vaccination
  anxiety 300.00
  Arthus 995.21
  asthenic 300.5
  compulsive 300.3
  conversion (anesthetic) (autonomic) (hyperkinetic) (mixed paralytic) (paresthetic) 300.11
  deoxyribonuclease (DNA) (DNase) hypersensitivity NEC 287.2
  depressive 300.4
    acute 309.0
    affective (*see also* Psychosis, affective) 296.2 ☑
      recurrent episode 296.3 ☑
      single episode 296.2 ☑
    brief 309.0
    manic (*see also* Psychosis, affective) 296.80
    neurotic 300.4
    psychoneurotic 300.4

Reaction — *continued*
  depressive — *continued*
    psychotic 298.0
    dissociative 300.15
  drug NEC (*see also* Table of Drugs and Chemicals) 995.20 ▲
    allergic (*see* ►*also*◄ Allergy, drug) 995.27 ▲
    correct substance properly administered 995.20 ▲
    obstetric anesthetic or analgesic NEC 668.9 ☑
      affecting fetus or newborn 763.5
      specified drug — *see* Table of Drugs and Chemicals
    overdose or poisoning 977.9
      specified drug — *see* Table of Drugs and Chemicals
    specific to newborn 779.4
    transmitted via placenta or breast milk — *see* Absorption, drug, through placenta
    withdrawal NEC 292.0
      infant of dependent mother 779.5
    wrong substance given or taken in error 977.9
      specified drug — *see* Table of Drugs and Chemicals
  dyssocial 301.7
  dystonic, acute, due to drugs 333.72●
  erysipeloid 027.1
  fear 300.20
    child 313.0
  fluid loss, cerebrospinal 349.0
  food (*see also* Allergy, food)
    adverse NEC 995.7
    anaphylactic shock — *see* Anaphylactic shock, due to, food
  foreign
    body NEC 728.82
      in operative wound (inadvertently left) 998.4
        due to surgical material intentionally left — *see* Complications, due to (presence of) any device, implant, or graft classified to 996.0–996.5 NEC
      substance accidentally left during a procedure (chemical) (powder) (talc) 998.7
      body or object (instrument) (sponge) (swab) 998.4
  graft-versus-host (GVH) 996.85
  grief (acute) (brief) 309.0
    prolonged 309.1
  gross stress (*see also* Reaction, stress, acute) 308.9
  group delinquent (*see also* Disturbance, conduct) 312.2 ☑
  Herxheimer's 995.0
  hyperkinetic (*see also* Hyperkinesia) 314.9
  hypochondriacal 300.7
  hypoglycemic, due to insulin 251.0
    therapeutic misadventure 962.3
  hypomanic (*see also* Psychosis, affective) 296.0 ☑
    recurrent episode 296.1 ☑
    single episode 296.0 ☑
  hysterical 300.10
    conversion type 300.11
    dissociative 300.15
  id (bacterial cause) 692.89
  immature NEC 301.89
    aggressive 301.3
    emotional instability 301.59
  immunization — *see* Complications, vaccination
  incompatibility
    blood group (ABO) (infusion) (transfusion) 999.6
    Rh (factor) (infusion) (transfusion) 999.7

Reaction — *continued*
  inflammatory — *see* Infection
  infusion — *see* Complications, infusion
  inoculation (immune serum) — *see* Complications, vaccination
  insulin 995.23 ▲
  involutional
    paranoid 297.2
    psychotic (*see also* Psychosis, affective, depressive) 296.2 ☑
  leukemoid ►(basophilic)◄ (lymphocytic) (monocytic) (myelocytic) ►(neutrophilic)◄ 288.62 ▲
  LSD (*see also* Abuse, drugs, nondependent) 305.3 ☑
  lumbar puncture 349.0
  manic-depressive (*see also* Psychosis, affective) 296.80
    depressed 296.2 ☑
      recurrent episode 296.3 ☑
      single episode 296.2 ☑
    hypomanic 296.0 ☑
  neurasthenic 300.5
  neurogenic (*see also* Neurosis) 300.9
  neurotic NEC 300.9
  neurotic-depressive 300.4
  nitritoid — *see* Crisis, nitritoid
  obsessive compulsive 300.3
  organic 293.9
    acute 293.0
    subacute 293.1
  overanxious, child or adolescent 313.0
  paranoid (chronic) 297.9
    acute 298.3
    climacteric 297.2
    involutional 297.2
    menopausal 297.2
    senile 290.20
    simple 297.0
  passive
    aggressive 301.84
    dependency 301.6
  personality (*see also* Disorder, personality) 301.9
  phobic 300.20
  postradiation — *see* Effect, adverse, radiation
  psychogenic NEC 300.9
  psychoneurotic (*see also* Neurosis) 300.9
    anxiety 300.00
    compulsive 300.3
    conversion 300.11
    depersonalization 300.6
    depressive 300.4
    dissociative 300.15
    hypochondriacal 300.7
    hysterical 300.10
      conversion type 300.11
      dissociative type 300.15
    neurasthenic 300.5
    obsessive 300.3
    obsessive-compulsive 300.3
    phobic 300.20
    tension state 300.9
  psychophysiologic NEC (*see also* Disorder, psychosomatic) 306.9
    cardiovascular 306.2
    digestive 306.4
    endocrine 306.6
    gastrointestinal 306.4
    genitourinary 306.50
    heart 306.2
    hemic 306.8
    intestinal (large) (small) 306.4
    laryngeal 306.1
    lymphatic 306.8
    musculoskeletal 306.0
    pharyngeal 306.1
    respiratory 306.1
    skin 306.3
    special sense organs 306.7
  psychosomatic (*see also* Disorder, psychosomatic) 306.9
  psychotic (*see also* Psychosis) 298.9

Reaction — *continued*
  psychotic (*see also* Psychosis) — *continued*
    depressive 298.0
    due to or associated with physical condition (*see also* Psychosis, organic) 293.9
    involutional (*see also* Psychosis, affective) 296.2 ☑
      recurrent episode 296.3 ☑
      single episode 296.2 ☑
  pupillary (myotonic) (tonic) 379.46
  radiation — *see* Effect, adverse, radiation
  runaway (*see also* Disturbance, conduct)
    socialized 312.2 ☑
    undersocialized, unsocialized 312.1 ☑
  scarlet fever toxin — *see* Complications, vaccination
  schizophrenic (*see also* Schizophrenia) 295.9 ☑
    latent 295.5 ☑
  serological for syphilis — *see* Serology for syphilis
  serum (prophylactic) (therapeutic) 999.5
    immediate 999.4
  situational (*see also* Reaction, adjustment) 309.9
    acute, to stress 308.3
    adjustment (*see also* Reaction, adjustment) 309.9
  somatization (*see also* Disorder, psychosomatic) 306.9
  spinal puncture 349.0
  spite, child (*see also* Disturbance, conduct) 312.0 ☑
  stress, acute 308.9
    with predominant disturbance (of)
      consciousness 308.1
      emotions 308.0
      mixed 308.4
      psychomotor 308.2
      specified type NEC 308.3
    bone or cartilage — *see* Fracture, stress
  surgical procedure — *see* Complications, surgical procedure
  tetanus antitoxin — *see* Complications, vaccination
  toxin-antitoxin — *see* Complications, vaccination
  transfusion (blood) (bone marrow) (lymphocytes) (allergic) — *see* Complications, transfusion
  tuberculin skin test, nonspecific (without active tuberculosis) 795.5
    positive (without active tuberculosis) 795.5
  ultraviolet — *see* Effect, adverse, ultraviolet
  undersocialized, unsocialized (*see also* Disturbance, conduct)
    aggressive (type) 312.0 ☑
    unaggressive (type) 312.1 ☑
  vaccination (any) — *see* Complications, vaccination
  white graft (skin) 996.52
  withdrawing, child or adolescent 313.22
  x-ray — *see* Effect, adverse, x-rays
Reactive depression — *see also* Reaction, depressive 300.4
  neurotic 300.4
  psychoneurotic 300.4
  psychotic 298.0
Rebound tenderness 789.6 ☑
Recalcitrant patient V15.81
Recanalization, thrombus — *see* Thrombosis
Recession, receding
  chamber angle (eye) 364.77
  chin 524.06

Recession, receding — *continued*
  gingival (postinfective) (postoperative) 523.20
    generalized 523.25
    localized 523.24
    minimal 523.21
    moderate 523.22
    severe 523.23
Recklinghausen-Applebaum disease (hemochromatosis) 275.0
Recklinghausen's disease (M9540/1) 237.71
  bones (osteitis fibrosa cystica) 252.01
Reclus' disease (cystic) 610.1
Recrudescent typhus (fever) 081.1
Recruitment, auditory 388.44
Rectalgia 569.42
Rectitis 569.49
Rectocele
  female (without uterine prolapse) 618.04
    with uterine prolapse 618.4
      complete 618.3
      incomplete 618.2
    in pregnancy or childbirth 654.4 ☑
      causing obstructed labor 660.2 ☑
        affecting fetus or newborn 763.1
  male 569.49
  vagina, vaginal (outlet) 618.04
Rectosigmoiditis 569.89
  ulcerative (chronic) 556.3
Rectosigmoid junction — *see* condition
Rectourethral — *see* condition
Rectovaginal — *see* condition
Rectovesical — *see* condition
Rectum, rectal — *see* condition
Recurrent — *see* condition
Red bugs 133.8
Red cedar asthma 495.8
Redness
  conjunctiva 379.93
  eye 379.93
  nose 478.19 ▲
Reduced ventilatory or vital capacity 794.2
Reduction
  function
    kidney (*see also* Disease, renal) 593.9
    liver 573.8
  ventilatory capacity 794.2
  vital capacity 794.2
Redundant, redundancy
  abdomen 701.9
  anus 751.5
  cardia 537.89
  clitoris 624.2
  colon (congenital) 751.5
  foreskin (congenital) 605
  intestine 751.5
  labia 624.3
  organ or site, congenital NEC — *see* Accessory
  panniculus (abdominal) 278.1
  prepuce (congenital) 605
  pylorus 537.89
  rectum 751.5
  scrotum 608.89
  sigmoid 751.5
  skin (of face) 701.9
    eyelids 374.30
  stomach 537.89
  uvula 528.9
  vagina 623.8
Reduplication — *see* Duplication
Referral
  adoption (agency) V68.89
  nursing care V63.8
  patient without examination or treatment V68.81
  social services V63.8
Reflex — *see also* condition
  blink, deficient 374.45
  hyperactive gag 478.29
  neurogenic bladder NEC 596.54
    atonic 596.54

☑ Additional Digit Required — Refer to the Tabular List for Digit Selection   ▽ Subterms under main terms may continue to next column or page

2007 ICD-9-CM   ►◄ Revised Text   ● New Line   ▲ Revised Code   **October 2006 · Volume 2 — 247**

Reflex — *see also* condition — *continued*
- neurogenic bladder — *continued*
  - atonic — *continued*
    - with cauda equina syndrome 344.61
  - vasoconstriction 443.9
  - vasovagal 780.2

Reflux
- esophageal 530.81
  - with esophagitis 530.11
- esophagitis 530.11
- gastroesophageal 530.81
- mitral — *see* Insufficiency, mitral
- ureteral — *see* Reflux, vesicoureteral
- vesicoureteral 593.70
  - with
    - reflux nephropathy 593.73
      - bilateral 593.72
      - unilateral 593.71

Reformed gallbladder 576.0
Reforming, artificial openings — *see also* Attention to, artificial, opening V55.9
Refractive error — *see also* Error, refractive 367.9
Refsum's disease or syndrome (heredopathia atactica polyneuritiformis) 356.3
Refusal of
- food 307.59
  - hysterical 300.11
- treatment because of, due to
  - patient's decision NEC V64.2
  - reason of conscience or religion V62.6

Regaud
- tumor (M8082/3) — *see* Neoplasm, nasopharynx, malignant
- type carcinoma (M8082/3) — *see* Neoplasm, nasopharynx, malignant

Regional — *see* condition
Regulation feeding (elderly) (infant) 783.3
- newborn 779.3
Regurgitated
- food, choked on 933.1
- stomach contents, choked on 933.1
Regurgitation
- aortic (valve) (*see also* Insufficiency, aortic) 424.1
  - congenital 746.4
  - syphilitic 093.22
- food (*see also* Vomiting)
  - with reswallowing — *see* Rumination
  - newborn 779.3
- gastric contents — *see* Vomiting
- heart — *see* Endocarditis
- mitral (valve) (*see also* Insufficiency, mitral)
  - congenital 746.6
- myocardial — *see* Endocarditis
- pulmonary (heart) (valve) (*see also* Endocarditis, pulmonary) 424.3
- stomach — *see* Vomiting
- tricuspid — *see* Endocarditis, tricuspid
- valve, valvular — *see* Endocarditis
- vesicoureteral — *see* Reflux, vesicoureteral

Rehabilitation V57.9
- multiple types V57.89
- occupational V57.21
- specified type NEC V57.89
- speech V57.3
- vocational V57.22
Reichmann's disease or syndrome (gastrosuccorrhea) 536.8
Reifenstein's syndrome (hereditary familial hypogonadism, male) 259.5
Reilly's syndrome or phenomenon — *see also* Neuropathy, peripheral, autonomic 337.9

Reimann's periodic disease 277.31 ▲
Reinsertion, contraceptive device V25.42
Reiter's disease, syndrome, or urethritis 099.3 *[711.1]* ☑
Rejection
- food, hysterical 300.11
- transplant 996.80
  - bone marrow 996.85
  - corneal 996.51
  - organ (immune or nonimmune cause) 996.80
    - bone marrow 996.85
    - heart 996.83
    - intestines 996.87
    - kidney 996.81
    - liver 996.82
    - lung 996.84
    - pancreas 996.86
    - specified NEC 996.89
  - skin 996.52
    - artificial 996.55
    - decellularized allodermis 996.55
Relapsing fever 087.9
- Carter's (Asiatic) 087.0
- Dutton's (West African) 087.1
- Koch's 087.9
- louse-borne (epidemic) 087.0
- Novy's (American) 087.1
- Obermeyer's (European) 087.0
- Spirillum 087.9
- tick-borne (endemic) 087.1
Relaxation
- anus (sphincter) 569.49
  - due to hysteria 300.11
- arch (foot) 734
  - congenital 754.61
- back ligaments 728.4
- bladder (sphincter) 596.59
- cardio-esophageal 530.89
- cervix (*see also* Incompetency, cervix) 622.5
- diaphragm 519.4
- inguinal rings — *see* Hernia, inguinal
- joint (capsule) (ligament) (paralytic) (*see also* Derangement, joint) 718.90
  - congenital 755.8
- lumbosacral joint 724.6
- pelvic floor 618.89
- pelvis 618.89
- perineum 618.89
- posture 729.9
- rectum (sphincter) 569.49
- sacroiliac (joint) 724.6
- scrotum 608.89
- urethra (sphincter) 599.84
- uterus (outlet) 618.89
- vagina (outlet) 618.89
- vesical 596.59
Remains
- canal of Cloquet 743.51
- capsule (opaque) 743.51
Remittent fever (malarial) 084.6
Remnant
- canal of Cloquet 743.51
- capsule (opaque) 743.51
- cervix, cervical stump (acquired) (postoperative) 622.8
- cystic duct, postcholecystectomy 576.0
- fingernail 703.8
  - congenital 757.5
- meniscus, knee 717.5
- thyroglossal duct 759.2
- tonsil 474.8
  - infected 474.00
- urachus 753.7
Remote effect of cancer — *see* condition
Removal (of)
- catheter (urinary) (indwelling) V53.6
  - from artificial opening — *see* Attention to, artificial, opening
  - non-vascular V58.82

Removal — *continued*
- catheter — *continued*
  - vascular V58.81
- cerebral ventricle (communicating) shunt V53.01
- device (*see also* Fitting (of))
  - contraceptive V25.42
  - fixation
    - external V54.89
    - internal V54.01
  - traction V54.89
- drains V58.49 ●
- dressing
  - wound V58.30 ●
    - nonsurgical V58.30 ●
    - surgical V58.31 ●
- ileostomy V55.2
- Kirschner wire V54.89
- nonvascular catheter V58.82
- pin V54.01
- plaster cast V54.89
- plate (fracture) V54.01
- rod V54.01
- screw V54.01
- splint, external V54.89
- staples V58.32 ●
- subdermal implantable contraceptive V25.43
- ►sutures◄ V58.32 ▲
- traction device, external V54.89
- vascular catheter V58.81
- wound packing V58.30 ●
  - nonsurgical V58.30 ●
  - surgical V58.31 ●
Ren
- arcuatus 753.3
- mobile, mobilis (*see also* Disease, renal) 593.0
  - congenital 753.3
- unguliformis 753.3
Renal — *see also* condition
- glomerulohyalinosis-diabetic syndrome 250.4 ☑ *[581.81]*
Rendu-Osler-Weber disease or syndrome (familial hemorrhagic telangiectasia) 448.0
Reninoma (M8361/1) 236.91
Rénon-Delille syndrome 253.8
Repair
- pelvic floor, previous, in pregnancy or childbirth 654.4 ☑
  - affecting fetus or newborn 763.89
- scarred tissue V51
Replacement by artificial or mechanical device or prosthesis of — *see also* Fitting (of
- artificial skin V43.83
- bladder V43.5
- blood vessel V43.4
- breast V43.82
- eye globe V43.0
- heart
  - with
    - assist device V43.21
    - fully implantable artificial heart V43.22
  - valve V43.3
- intestine V43.89
- joint V43.60
  - ankle V43.66
  - elbow V43.62
  - finger V43.69
  - hip (partial) (total) V43.64
  - knee V43.65
  - shoulder V43.61
  - specified NEC V43.69
  - wrist V43.63
- kidney V43.89
- larynx V43.81
- lens V43.1
- limb(s) V43.7
- liver V43.89
- lung V43.89
- organ NEC V43.89
- pancreas V43.89
- skin (artificial) V43.83

Replacement by artificial or mechanical device or prosthesis of — *see also* Fitting (of — *continued*
- tissue NEC V43.89
Reprogramming
- cardiac pacemaker V53.31
Request for expert evidence V68.2
Reserve, decreased or low
- cardiac — *see* Disease, heart
- kidney (*see also* Disease, renal) 593.9
Residual — *see also* condition
- bladder 596.8
- foreign body — *see* Retention, foreign body
- state, schizophrenic (*see also* Schizophrenia) 295.6 ☑
- urine 788.69
Resistance, resistant (to)
- activated protein C 289.81

Note — use the following subclassification for categories V09.5, V09.7, V09.8, V09.9:

0	*without mention of resistance to multiple drugs*
1	*with resistance to multiple drugs*

    V09.5 quinolones and fluoroquinolones

    V09.7 antimycobacterial agents

    V09.8 specified drugs NEC

    V09.9 unspecified drugs

- drugs by microorganisms V09.9 ☑
- Amikacin V09.4
- aminoglycosides V09.4
- Amodiaquine V09.5 ☑
- Amoxicillin V09.0
- Ampicillin V09.0
- antimycobacterial agents V09.7 ☑
- Azithromycin V09.2
- Azlocillin V09.0
- Aztreonam V09.1
- Bacampicillin V09.0
- Bacitracin V09.8 ☑
- Benznidazole V09.8 ☑
- B-lactam antibiotics V09.1
- Capreomycin V09.7 ☑
- Carbenicillin V09.0
- Cefaclor V09.1
- Cefadroxil V09.1
- Cefamandole V09.1
- Cefatetan V09.1
- Cefazolin V09.1
- Cefixime V09.1
- Cefonicid V09.1
- Cefoperazone V09.1
- Ceforanide V09.1
- Cefotaxime V09.1
- Cefoxitin V09.1
- Ceftazidime V09.1
- Ceftizoxime V09.1
- Ceftriaxone V09.1
- Cefuroxime V09.1
- Cephalexin V09.1
- Cephaloglycin V09.1
- Cephaloridine V09.1
- Cephalosporins V09.1
- Cephalothin V09.1
- Cephapirin V09.1
- Cephradine V09.1
- Chloramphenicol V09.8 ☑
- Chloraquine V09.5 ☑
- Chlorguanide V09.8 ☑
- Chlorproguanil V09.8 ☑
- Chlortetracycline V09.3
- Cinoxacin V09.5 ☑
- Ciprofloxacin V09.5 ☑
- Clarithromycin V09.2
- Clindamycin V09.8 ☑
- Clioquinol V09.5 ☑
- Clofazimine V09.7 ☑
- Cloxacillin V09.0

☑ Additional Digit Required — Refer to the Tabular List for Digit Selection   ᵂ Subterms under main terms may continue to next column or page

248 — Volume 2 · October 2006   ►◄ Revised Text   ● New Line   ▲ Revised Code   *2007 ICD-9-CM*

Resistance, resistant — *continued*
  drugs by microorganisms — *continued*
    Cyclacillin V09.0
    Cycloserine V09.7 ✓
    Dapsone [DZ] V09.7 ✓
    Demeclocycline V09.3
    Dicloxacillin V09.0
    Doxycycline V09.3
    Enoxacin V09.5 ✓
    Erythromycin V09.2
    Ethambutol [EMB] V09.7 ✓
    Ethionamide [ETA] V09.7 ✓
    fluoroquinolones V09.5 ✓
    Gentamicin V09.4
    Halofantrine V09.8 ✓
    Imipenem V09.1
    Iodoquinol V09.5 ✓
    Isoniazid [INH] V09.7 ✓
    Kanamycin V09.4
    macrolides V09.2
    Mafenide V09.6
    MDRO (multiple drug resistant organisms) NOS V09.91
    Mefloquine V09.8 ✓
    Melasoprol V09.8 ✓
    Methacycline V09.3
    Methenamine V09.8 ✓
    Methicillin V09.0
    Metronidazole V09.8 ✓
    Mezlocillin V09.0
    Minocycline V09.3
    multiple drug resistant organisms NOS V09.91
    Nafcillin V09.0
    Nalidixic acid V09.5 ✓
    Natamycin V09.2
    Neomycin V09.4
    Netilmicin V09.4
    Nimorazole V09.8 ✓
    Nitrofurantoin V09.8 ✓
    Nitrofurtimox V09.8 ✓
    Norfloxacin V09.5 ✓
    Nystatin V09.2
    Ofloxacin V09.5 ✓
    Oleandomycin V09.2
    Oxacillin V09.0
    Oxytetracycline V09.3
    Para-amino salicylic acid [PAS] V09.7 ✓
    Paromomycin V09.4
    Penicillin (G) (V) (VK) V09.0
    penicillins V09.0
    Pentamidine V09.8 ✓
    Piperacillin V09.0
    Primaquine V09.5 ✓
    Proguanil V09.8 ✓
    Pyrazinamide [PZA] V09.7 ✓
    Pyrimethamine/Sulfalene V09.8 ✓
    Pyrimethamine/Sulfodoxine V09.8 ✓
    Quinacrine V09.5 ✓
    Quinidine V09.8 ✓
    Quinine V09.8 ✓
    quinolones V09.5 ✓
    Rifabutin V09.7 ✓
    Rifampin [RIF] V09.7 ✓
    Rifamycin V09.7 ✓
    Rolitetracycline V09.3
    specified drugs NEC V09.8 ✓
    Spectinomycin V09.8 ✓
    Spiramycin V09.2
    Streptomycin [SM] V09.4
    Sulfacetamide V09.6
    Sulfacytine V09.6
    Sulfadiazine V09.6
    Sulfadoxine V09.6
    Sulfamethoxazole V09.6
    Sulfapyridine V09.6
    Sulfasalizine V09.6
    Sulfasoxazole V09.6
    sulfonamides V09.6
    Sulfoxone V09.7 ✓
    tetracycline V09.3
    tetracyclines V09.3

Resistance, resistant — *continued*
  drugs by microorganisms — *continued*
    Thiamphenicol V09.8 ✓
    Ticarcillin V09.0
    Tinidazole V09.8 ✓
    Tobramycin V09.4
    Triamphenicol V09.8 ✓
    Trimethoprim V09.8 ✓
    Vancomycin V09.8 ✓
  insulin 277.7
  thyroid hormone 246.8 ●

Resorption
  biliary 576.8
    purulent or putrid (*see also* Cholecystitis) 576.8
  dental (roots) 521.40
    alveoli 525.8
    pathological
      external 521.42
      internal 521.41
      specified NEC 521.49
  septic — *see* Septicemia
  teeth (roots) 521.40
    pathological
      external 521.42
      internal 521.41
      specified NEC 521.49

Respiration
  asymmetrical 786.09
  bronchial 786.09
  Cheyne-Stokes (periodic respiration) 786.04
  decreased, due to shock following injury 958.4
  disorder of 786.00
    psychogenic 306.1
    specified NEC 786.09
  failure 518.81
    acute 518.81
    acute and chronic 518.84
    chronic 518.83
    newborn 770.84
  insufficiency 786.09
    acute 518.82
    newborn NEC 770.89
  Kussmaul (air hunger) 786.09
  painful 786.52
  periodic 786.09
    high altitude 327.22
  poor 786.09
    newborn NEC 770.89
  sighing 786.7
    psychogenic 306.1
  wheezing 786.07

Respiratory — *see also* condition
  distress 786.09
    acute 518.82
    fetus or newborn NEC 770.89
    syndrome (newborn) 769
      adult (following shock, surgery, or trauma) 518.5
      specified NEC 518.82
  failure 518.81
    acute 518.81
    acute and chronic 518.84
    chronic 518.83

Respiratory syncytial virus (RSV) 079.6
  bronchiolitis 466.11
  pneumonia 480.1
  vaccination, prophylactic (against) V04.82

Response
  photoallergic 692.72
  phototoxic 692.72

Restless legs syndrome ▶(RLS)◀ 333.94 ▲

Restlessness 799.2

Restoration of organ continuity from previous sterilization (tuboplasty) (vasoplasty) V26.0

Rest, rests
  mesonephric duct 752.89
    fallopian tube 752.11
  ovarian, in fallopian tubes 752.19
  wolffian duct 752.89

Restriction of housing space V60.1

Restzustand, schizophrenic — *see also* Schizophrenia 295.6 ✓

Retained — *see* Retention

Retardation
  development, developmental, specific (*see also* Disorder, development, specific) 315.9
    learning, specific 315.2
      arithmetical 315.1
      language (skills) 315.31
        expressive 315.31
        mixed receptive-expressive 315.32
      mathematics 315.1
      reading 315.00
        phonological 315.39
      written expression 315.2
    motor 315.4
  endochondral bone growth 733.91
  growth (physical) in childhood 783.43
    due to malnutrition 263.2
    fetal (intrauterine) 764.9 ✓
      affecting management of pregnancy 656.5 ✓
  intrauterine growth 764.9 ✓
    affecting management of pregnancy 656.5 ✓
  mental 319
    borderline V62.89
    mild, IQ 50-70 317
    moderate, IQ 35-49 318.0
    profound, IQ under 20 318.2
    severe, IQ 20-34 318.1
  motor, specific 315.4
  physical 783.43
    child 783.43
    due to malnutrition 263.2
    fetus (intrauterine) 764.9 ✓
      affecting management of pregnancy 656.5 ✓
  psychomotor NEC 307.9
  reading 315.00

Retching — *see* Vomiting

Retention, retained
  bladder (*see also* Retention, urine) 788.20
    psychogenic 306.53
  carbon dioxide 276.2
  cyst — *see* Cyst
  dead
    fetus (after 22 completed weeks gestation) 656.4 ✓
      early fetal death (before 22 completed weeks gestation) 632
    ovum 631
  decidua (following delivery) (fragments) (with hemorrhage) 666.2 ✓
    without hemorrhage 667.1 ✓
  deciduous tooth 520.6
  dental root 525.3
  fecal (*see also* Constipation) 564.00
  fluid 276.6
  foreign body (*see also* Foreign body, retained)
    bone 733.99
    current trauma — *see* Foreign body, by site or type
    middle ear 385.83
    muscle 729.6
    soft tissue NEC 729.6
  gastric 536.8
  membranes (following delivery) (with hemorrhage) 666.2 ✓
    with abortion — *see* Abortion, by type
    without hemorrhage 667.1 ✓
  menses 626.8
  milk (puerperal) 676.2 ✓
  nitrogen, extrarenal 788.9
  placenta (total) (with hemorrhage) 666.0 ✓
    with abortion — *see* Abortion, by type
    without hemorrhage 667.0 ✓

Retention, retained — *continued*
  placenta — *continued*
    portions or fragments 666.2 ✓
    without hemorrhage 667.1 ✓
  products of conception
    early pregnancy (fetal death before 22 completed weeks gestation) 632
    following
      abortion — *see* Abortion, by type
      delivery 666.2 ✓
        with hemorrhage 666.2 ✓
        without hemorrhage 667.1 ✓
    secundines (following delivery) (with hemorrhage) 666.2 ✓
    with abortion — *see* Abortion, by type
    without hemorrhage 667.1 ✓
    complicating puerperium (delayed hemorrhage) 666.2 ✓
  smegma, clitoris 624.8
  urine NEC 788.20
    bladder, incomplete emptying 788.21
    due to
      benign prostatic hypertrophy (BPH) — *see* category 600
    due to
      benign prostatic hypertrophy (BPH) — *see* category 600
    psychogenic 306.53
    specified NEC 788.29
  water (in tissue) (*see also* Edema) 782.3

Reticulation, dust (occupational) 504

Reticulocytosis NEC 790.99

Reticuloendotheliosis
  acute infantile (M9722/3) 202.5 ✓
  leukemic (M9940/3) 202.4 ✓
  malignant (M9720/3) 202.3 ✓
  nonlipid (M9722/3) 202.5 ✓

Reticulohistiocytoma (giant cell) 277.89

Reticulohistiocytosis, multicentric 272.8

Reticulolymphosarcoma (diffuse) (M9613/3) 200.8 ✓
  follicular (M9691/3) 202.0 ✓
  nodular (M9691/3) 202.0 ✓

Reticulosarcoma (M9640/3) 200.0 ✓
  nodular (M9642/3) 200.0 ✓
  pleomorphic cell type (M9641/3) 200.0 ✓

Reticulosis (skin)
  acute of infancy (M9722/3) 202.5 ✓
  familial hemophagocytic 288.4 ●
  histiocytic medullary (M9721/3) 202.3 ✓
  lipomelanotic 695.89
  malignant (M9720/3) 202.3 ✓
  Sézary's (M9701/3) 202.2 ✓

Retina, retinal — *see* condition

Retinitis — *see also* Chorioretinitis 363.20
  albuminurica 585.9 [363.10]
  arteriosclerotic 440.8 [362.13]
  central angiospastic 362.41
  Coat's 362.12
  diabetic 250.5 ✓ [362.01]
  disciformis 362.52
  disseminated 363.10
    metastatic 363.14
    neurosyphilitic 094.83
    pigment epitheliopathy 363.15
  exudative 362.12
  focal 363.00
    in histoplasmosis 115.92
      capsulatum 115.02
      duboisii 115.12
    juxtapapillary 363.05
    macular 363.06
    paramacular 363.06
    peripheral 363.08
    posterior pole NEC 363.07
  gravidarum 646.8 ✓

✓ Additional Digit Required — Refer to the Tabular List for Digit Selection   ⓦ Subterms under main terms may continue to next column or page

2007 ICD-9-CM   ▶◀ Revised Text   ● New Line   ▲ Revised Code   **October 2006 • Volume 2 — 249**

Rhinorrhea 478.19 ▲
  cerebrospinal (fluid) 349.81
  paroxysmal (*see also* Fever, hay) 477.9
  spasmodic (*see also* Fever, hay) 477.9
Rhinosalpingitis 381.50
  acute 381.51
  chronic 381.52
Rhinoscleroma 040.1
Rhinosporidiosis 117.0
Rhinovirus infection 079.3
Rhizomelic chrondrodysplasia puncta-ta 277.86
Rhizomelique, pseudopolyarthritic 446.5
Rhoads and Bomford anemia (refracto-ry) 238.72 ▲
Rhus
  diversiloba dermatitis 692.6
  radicans dermatitis 692.6
  toxicodendron dermatitis 692.6
  venenata dermatitis 692.6
  verniciflua dermatitis 692.6
Rhythm
  atrioventricular nodal 427.89
  disorder 427.9
    coronary sinus 427.89
    ectopic 427.89
    nodal 427.89
    escape 427.89
    heart, abnormal 427.9
      fetus or newborn — *see* Abnormal, heart rate
    idioventricular 426.89
      accelerated 427.89
    nodal 427.89
    sleep, inversion 327.39
      nonorganic origin 307.45
Rhytidosis facialis 701.8
Rib — *see also* condition
  cervical 756.2
Riboflavin deficiency 266.0
Rice bodies — *see also* Loose, body, joint 718.1 ✓
  knee 717.6
Richter's hernia — *see* Hernia, Richter's
Ricinism 988.2
Rickets (active) (acute) (adolescent) (adult) (chest wall) (congenital) (current) (infantile) (intestinal) 268.0
  celiac 579.0
  fetal 756.4
  hemorrhagic 267
  hypophosphatemic with nephrotic-glycosuric dwarfism 270.0
  kidney 588.0
  late effect 268.1
  renal 588.0
  scurvy 267
  vitamin D-resistant 275.3
Rickettsial disease 083.9
  specified type NEC 083.8
Rickettsialpox 083.2
Rickettsiosis NEC 083.9
  specified type NEC 083.8
  tick-borne 082.9
    specified type NEC 082.8
  vesicular 083.2
Ricord's chancre 091.0
Riddoch's syndrome (visual disorienta-tion) 368.16
Rider's
  bone 733.99
  chancre 091.0
Ridge, alveolus — *see also* condition
  edentulous
    atrophy 525.20
      mandible 525.20
        minimal 525.21
        moderate 525.22
        severe 525.23
      maxilla 525.20
        minimal 525.24
        moderate 525.25
        severe 525.26
    flabby 525.20

Ridged ear 744.29
Riedel's
  disease (ligneous thyroiditis) 245.3
  lobe, liver 751.69
  struma (ligneous thyroiditis) 245.3
  thyroiditis (ligneous) 245.3
Rieger's anomaly or syndrome (meso-dermal dysgenesis, anterior ocular segment) 743.44
Riehl's melanosis 709.09
Rietti-Greppi-Micheli anemia or syn-drome 282.49
Rieux's hernia — *see* Hernia, Rieux's
Rift Valley fever 066.3
Riga's disease (cachectic aphthae) 529.0
Riga-Fede disease (cachectic aphthae) 529.0
Riggs' disease (compound periodontitis) 523.40 ▲
Right middle lobe syndrome 518.0
Rigid, rigidity — *see also* condition
  abdominal 789.4 ✓
  articular, multiple congenital 754.89
  back 724.8
  cervix uteri
    in pregnancy or childbirth 654.6 ✓
      affecting fetus or newborn 763.89
      causing obstructed labor 660.2 ✓
        affecting fetus or newborn 763.1
  hymen (acquired) (congenital) 623.3
  nuchal 781.6
  pelvic floor
    in pregnancy or childbirth 654.4 ✓
      affecting fetus or newborn 763.89
      causing obstructed labor 660.2 ✓
        affecting fetus or newborn 763.1
  perineum or vulva
    in pregnancy or childbirth 654.8 ✓
      affecting fetus or newborn 763.89
      causing obstructed labor 660.2 ✓
        affecting fetus or newborn 763.1
  spine 724.8
  vagina
    in pregnancy or childbirth 654.7 ✓
      affecting fetus or newborn 763.89
      causing obstructed labor 660.2 ✓
        affecting fetus or newborn 763.1
Rigors 780.99
Riley-Day syndrome (familial dysautono-mia) 742.8
Ring(s)
  aorta 747.21
  Bandl's, complicating delivery 661.4 ✓
    affecting fetus or newborn 763.7
  contraction, complicating delivery 661.4 ✓
    affecting fetus or newborn 763.7
  esophageal (congenital) 750.3
  Fleischer (-Kayser) (cornea) 275.1 [371.14]
  hymenal, tight (acquired) (congenital) 623.3
  Kayser-Fleischer (cornea) 275.1 [371.14]
  retraction, uterus, pathological 661.4 ✓
    affecting fetus or newborn 763.7
  Schatzki's (esophagus) (congenital) (lower) 750.3
    acquired 530.3
  Soemmering's 366.51
  trachea, abnormal 748.3
  vascular (congenital) 747.21
  Vossius' 921.3

Ring(s) — *continued*
  Vossius' — *continued*
    late effect 366.21
Ringed hair (congenital) 757.4
Ringing in the ear — *see also* Tinnitus 388.30
Ringworm 110.9
  beard 110.0
  body 110.5
  Burmese 110.9
  corporeal 110.5
  foot 110.4
  groin 110.3
  hand 110.2
  honeycomb 110.0
  nails 110.1
  perianal (area) 110.3
  scalp 110.0
  specified site NEC 110.8
  Tokelau 110.5
Rise, venous pressure 459.89
Risk
  factor — *see* Problem
  falling
  suicidal 300.9
Ritter's disease (dermatitis exfoliativa neonatorum) 695.81
Rivalry, sibling 313.3
Rivalta's disease (cervicofacial actinomy-cosis) 039.3
River blindness 125.3 [360.13]
Robert's pelvis 755.69
  with disproportion (fetopelvic) 653.0 ✓
    affecting fetus or newborn 763.1
    causing obstructed labor 660.1 ✓
      affecting fetus or newborn 763.1
Robinson's (hidrotic) **ectodermal dyspla-sia** 757.31
Robin's syndrome 756.0
Robles' disease (onchocerciasis) 125.3 [360.13]
Rochalimea — *see* Rickettsial disease
Rocky Mountain fever (spotted) 082.0
Rodent ulcer (M8090/3) — *see also* Neoplasm, skin, malignant
  cornea 370.07
Roentgen ray, adverse effect — *see* Ef-fect, adverse, x-ray
Roetheln 056.9
Roger's disease (congenital interventric-ular septal defect) 745.4
Rokitansky's
  disease (*see also* Necrosis, liver) 570
  tumor 620.2
Rokitansky-Aschoff sinuses (mucosal outpouching of gallbladder) — *see also* Disease, gallbladder 575.8
Rokitansky-Kuster-Hauser syndrome (congenital absence vagina) 752.49
Rollet's chancre (syphilitic) 091.0
Rolling of head 781.0
Romano-Ward syndrome (prolonged QT interval syndrome) 426.82
Romanus lesion 720.1
Romberg's disease or syndrome 349.89
Roof, mouth — *see* condition
Rosacea 695.3
  acne 695.3
  keratitis 695.3 [370.49]
Rosary, rachitic 268.0
Rose
  cold 477.0
  fever 477.0
  rash 782.1
    epidemic 056.9
    of infants 057.8
Rosenbach's erysipelatoid or erysipeloid 027.1
Rosen-Castleman-Liebow syndrome (pulmonary proteinosis) 516.0
Rosenthal's disease (factor XI deficiency) 286.2
Roseola 057.8
  infantum, infantilis 057.8
Rossbach's disease (hyperchlorhydria) 536.8

Rossbach's disease — *continued*
  psychogenic 306.4
Rössle-Urbach-Wiethe lipoproteinosis 272.8
Ross river fever 066.3
Rostan's asthma (cardiac) — *see also* Failure, ventricular, left 428.1
Rot
  Barcoo (*see also* Ulcer, skin) 707.9
  knife-grinders' (*see also* Tuberculosis) 011.4 ✓
Rotation
  anomalous, incomplete or insufficient — *see* Malrotation
  cecum (congenital) 751.4
  colon (congenital) 751.4
  manual, affecting fetus or newborn 763.89
  spine, incomplete or insufficient 737.8
  tooth, teeth 524.35
  vertebra, incomplete or insufficient 737.8
Rot-Bernhardt disease 355.1
Röteln 056.9
Roth-Bernhardt disease or syndrome 355.1
Roth's disease or meralgia 355.1
Rothmund (-Thomson) syndrome 757.33
Rotor's disease or syndrome (idiopathic hyperbilirubinemia) 277.4
Rotundum ulcus — *see* Ulcer, stomach
Round
  back (with wedging of vertebrae) 737.10
    late effect of rickets 268.1
  hole, retina 361.31
    with detachment 361.01
  ulcer (stomach) — *see* Ulcer, stomach
  worms (infestation) (large) NEC 127.0
Roussy-Lévy syndrome 334.3
Routine postpartum follow-up V24.2
Roy (-Jutras) syndrome (acropachyder-ma) 757.39
Rubella (German measles) 056.9
  complicating pregnancy, childbirth, or puerperium 647.5 ✓
  complication 056.8
    neurological 056.00
      encephalomyelitis 056.01
      specified type NEC 056.09
    specified type NEC 056.79
  congenital 771.0
  contact V01.4
  exposure to V01.4
  maternal
    with suspected fetal damage affect-ing management of pregnan-cy 655.3 ✓
      affecting fetus or newborn 760.2
        manifest rubella in infant 771.0
  specified complications NEC 056.79
  vaccination, prophylactic (against) V04.3
Rubeola (measles) — *see also* Measles 055.9
  complicated 055.8
  meaning rubella (*see also* Rubella) 056.9
  scarlatinosis 057.8
Rubeosis iridis 364.42
  diabetica 250.5 ✓ [364.42]
Rubinstein-Taybi's syndrome (brachy-dactylia, short stature and mental retardation) 759.89
Rudimentary (congenital) — *see also* Agenesis
  arm 755.22
  bone 756.9
  cervix uteri 752.49
  eye (*see also* Microphthalmos) 743.10
  fallopian tube 752.19
  leg 755.32
  lobule of ear 744.21
  patella 755.64

Rudimentary — *see also* Agenesis —
  continued
  respiratory organs in thoracopagus
    759.4
  tracheal bronchus 748.3
  uterine horn 752.3
  uterus 752.3
    in male 752.7
    solid or with cavity 752.3
  vagina 752.49
Rud's syndrome (mental deficiency,
  epilepsy, and infantilism) 759.89
Ruiter-Pompen (-Wyers) syndrome
  (angiokeratoma corporis diffusum)
  272.7
Ruled out condition — *see also* Observation, suspected V71.9
Rumination — *see also* Vomiting
  disorder 307.53
  neurotic 300.3
  obsessional 300.3
  psychogenic 307.53
Runaway reaction — *see also* Disturbance, conduct
  socialized 312.2 ☑
  undersocialized, unsocialized 312.1 ☑
Runeberg's disease (progressive pernicious anemia) 281.0
Runge's syndrome (postmaturity)
  766.22
Rupia 091.3
  congenital 090.0
  tertiary 095.9
Rupture, ruptured 553.9
  abdominal viscera NEC 799.89
    obstetrical trauma 665.5 ☑
  abscess (spontaneous) — *see* Abscess,
    by site
  amnion — *see* Rupture, membranes
  aneurysm — *see* Aneurysm
  anus (sphincter) — *see* Laceration,
    anus
  aorta, aortic 441.5
    abdominal 441.3
    arch 441.1
    ascending 441.1
    descending 441.5
      abdominal 441.3
      thoracic 441.1
    syphilitic 093.0
    thoracoabdominal 441.6
    thorax, thoracic 441.1
    transverse 441.1
    traumatic (thoracic) 901.0
      abdominal 902.0
    valve or cusp (*see also* Endocardi-
      tis, aortic) 424.1
  appendix (with peritonitis) 540.0
    with peritoneal abscess 540.1
    traumatic — *see* Injury, internal,
      gastrointestinal tract
  arteriovenous fistula, brain (congeni-
    tal) 430
  artery 447.2
    brain (*see also* Hemorrhage, brain)
      431
    coronary (*see also* Infarct, my-
      ocardium) 410.9 ☑
    heart (*see also* Infarct, myocardi-
      um) 410.9 ☑
    pulmonary 417.8
    traumatic (complication) (*see also*
      Injury, blood vessel, by site)
      904.9
  bile duct, except cystic (*see also* Dis-
    ease, biliary) 576.3
    cystic 575.4
    traumatic — *see* Injury, internal,
      intra-abdominal
  bladder (sphincter) 596.6
    with
      abortion — *see* Abortion, by
        type, with damage to
        pelvic organs

Rupture, ruptured — *continued*
  bladder — *continued*
    with — *continued*
      ectopic pregnancy (*see also* cat-
        egories 633.0–633.9)
        639.2
      molar pregnancy (*see also* cate-
        gories 630–632) 639.2
    following
      abortion 639.2
      ectopic or molar pregnancy
        639.2
    nontraumatic 596.6
    obstetrical trauma 665.5 ☑
    spontaneous 596.6
    traumatic — *see* Injury, internal,
      bladder
  blood vessel (*see also* Hemorrhage)
    459.0
    brain (*see also* Hemorrhage, brain)
      431
    heart (*see also* Infarct, myocardi-
      um) 410.9 ☑
    traumatic (complication) (*see also*
      Injury, blood vessel, by site)
      904.9
  bone — *see* Fracture, by site
  bowel 569.89
    traumatic — *see* Injury, internal,
      intestine
  Bowman's membrane 371.31
  brain
    aneurysm (congenital) (*see also*
      Hemorrhage, subarachnoid)
      430
      late effect — *see* Late effect(s)
        (of) cerebrovascular dis-
        ease
      syphilitic 094.87
    hemorrhagic (*see also* Hemorrhage,
      brain) 431
    injury at birth 767.0
    syphilitic 094.89
  capillaries 448.9
  cardiac (*see also* Infarct, myocardium)
    410.9 ☑
  cartilage (articular) (current) (*see also*
    Sprain, by site)
    knee — *see* Tear, meniscus
    semilunar — *see* Tear, meniscus
  cecum (with peritonitis) 540.0
    with peritoneal abscess 540.1
    traumatic 863.89
      with open wound into cavity
        863.99
  cerebral aneurysm (congenital) (*see*
    also Hemorrhage, subarachnoid)
    430
    late effect — *see* Late effect(s) (of)
      cerebrovascular disease
  cervix (uteri)
    with
      abortion — *see* Abortion, by
        type, with damage to
        pelvic organs
      ectopic pregnancy (*see also* cat-
        egories 633.0–633.9)
        639.2
      molar pregnancy (*see also* cate-
        gories 630–632) 639.2
    following
      abortion 639.2
      ectopic or molar pregnancy
        639.2
    obstetrical trauma 665.3 ☑
    traumatic — *see* Injury, internal,
      cervix
  chordae tendineae 429.5
  choroid (direct) (indirect) (traumatic)
    363.63
  circle of Willis (*see also* Hemorrhage,
    subarachnoid) 430
    late effect — *see* Late effect(s) (of)
      cerebrovascular disease
  colon 569.89

Rupture, ruptured — *continued*
  colon — *continued*
    traumatic — *see* Injury, internal,
      colon
  cornea (traumatic) (*see also* Rupture,
    eye)
    due to ulcer 370.00
  coronary (artery) (thrombotic) (*see also*
    Infarct, myocardium) 410.9 ☑
  corpus luteum (infected) (ovary) 620.1
  cyst — *see* Cyst
  cystic duct (*see also* Disease, gallblad-
    der) 575.4
  Descemet's membrane 371.33
    traumatic — *see* Rupture, eye
  diaphragm (*see also* Hernia, di-
    aphragm)
    traumatic — *see* Injury, internal,
      diaphragm
  diverticulum
    bladder 596.3
    intestine (large) (*see also* Diverticu-
      la) 562.10
      small 562.00
  duodenal stump 537.89
  duodenum (ulcer) — *see* Ulcer, duode-
    num, with perforation
  ear drum (*see also* Perforation, tympa-
    num) 384.20
    with otitis media — *see* Otitis me-
      dia
    traumatic — *see* Wound, open, ear
  esophagus 530.4
    traumatic 862.22
      with open wound into cavity
        862.32
      cervical region — *see* Wound,
        open, esophagus
  eye (without prolapse of intraocular
    tissue) 871.0
    with
      exposure of intraocular tissue
        871.1
      partial loss of intraocular tissue
        871.2
      prolapse of intraocular tissue
        871.1
    due to burn 940.5
  fallopian tube 620.8
    due to pregnancy — *see* Pregnancy,
      tubal
    traumatic — *see* Injury, internal,
      fallopian tube
  fontanel 767.3
  free wall (ventricle) (*see also* Infarct,
    myocardium) 410.9 ☑
  gallbladder or duct (*see also* Disease,
    gallbladder) 575.4
    traumatic — *see* Injury, internal,
      gallbladder
  gastric (*see also* Rupture, stomach)
    537.89
    vessel 459.0
  globe (eye) (traumatic) — *see* Rupture,
    eye
  graafian follicle (hematoma) 620.0
  heart (auricle) (ventricle) (*see also* In-
    farct, myocardium) 410.9 ☑
    infectional 422.90
    traumatic — *see* Rupture, my-
      ocardium, traumatic
  hymen 623.8
  internal
    organ, traumatic (*see also* Injury,
      internal, by site)
      heart — *see* Rupture, myocardi-
        um, traumatic
      kidney — *see* Rupture, kidney
      liver — *see* Rupture, liver
      spleen — *see* Rupture, spleen,
        traumatic
    semilunar cartilage — *see* Tear,
      meniscus
  intervertebral disc — *see* Displace-
    ment, intervertebral disc

Rupture, ruptured — *continued*
  intervertebral disc — *see* Displace-
    ment, intervertebral disc — *con-*
    tinued
    traumatic (current) — *see* Disloca-
      tion, vertebra
  intestine 569.89
    traumatic — *see* Injury, internal,
      intestine
  intracranial, birth injury 767.0
  iris 364.76
    traumatic — *see* Rupture, eye
  joint capsule — *see* Sprain, by site
  kidney (traumatic) 866.03
    with open wound into cavity
      866.13
    due to birth injury 767.8
    nontraumatic 593.89
  lacrimal apparatus (traumatic) 870.2
  lens (traumatic) 366.20
  ligament (*see also* Sprain, by site)
    with open wound — *see* Wound,
      open, by site
    old (*see also* Disorder, cartilage,
      articular) 718.0 ☑
  liver (traumatic) 864.04
    with open wound into cavity
      864.14
    due to birth injury 767.8
    nontraumatic 573.8
  lymphatic (node) (vessel) 457.8
  marginal sinus (placental) (with hem-
    orrhage) 641.2 ☑
    affecting fetus or newborn 762.1
  meaning hernia — *see* Hernia
  membrana tympani (*see also* Perfora-
    tion, tympanum) 384.20
    with otitis media — *see* Otitis me-
      dia
    traumatic — *see* Wound, open, ear
  membranes (spontaneous)
    artificial
      delayed delivery following
        658.3 ☑
        affecting fetus or newborn
          761.1
      fetus or newborn 761.1
    delayed delivery following 658.2 ☑
      affecting fetus or newborn 761.1
    premature (less than 24 hours pri-
      or to onset of labor) 658.1 ☑
      affecting fetus or newborn 761.1
      delayed delivery following
        658.2 ☑
        affecting fetus or newborn
          761.1
  meningeal artery (*see also* Hemor-
    rhage, subarachnoid) 430
    late effect — *see* Late effect(s) (of)
      cerebrovascular disease
  meniscus (knee) (*see also* Tear,
    meniscus)
    old (*see also* Derangement, menis-
      cus) 717.5
      site other than knee — *see* Dis-
        order, cartilage, articular
    site other than knee — *see* Sprain,
      by site
  mesentery 568.89
    traumatic — *see* Injury, internal,
      mesentery
  mitral — *see* Insufficiency, mitral
  muscle (traumatic) NEC (*see also*
    Sprain, by site)
    with open wound — *see* Wound,
      open, by site
    nontraumatic 728.83
  musculotendinous cuff (nontraumatic)
    (shoulder) 840.4
  mycotic aneurysm, causing cerebral
    hemorrhage (*see also* Hemor-
    rhage, subarachnoid) 430
    late effect — *see* Late effect(s) (of)
      cerebrovascular disease
  myocardium, myocardial (*see also* In-
    farct, myocardium) 410.9 ☑

☑ Additional Digit Required — Refer to the Tabular List for Digit Selection   ▽ Subterms under main terms may continue to next column or page

252 — Volume 2   ▶◀ Revised Text   ● New Line   ▲ Revised Code   *2007 ICD-9-CM*

Rupture, ruptured — *continued*

myocardium, myocardial (*see also* Infarct, myocardium) — *continued*
traumatic 861.03
with open wound into thorax 861.13
nontraumatic (meaning hernia) (*see also* Hernia, by site) 553.9
obstructed (*see also* Hernia, by site, with obstruction) 552.9
gangrenous (*see also* Hernia, by site, with gangrene) 551.9
operation wound 998.32
internal 998.31
ovary, ovarian 620.8
corpus luteum 620.1
follicle (graafian) 620.0
oviduct 620.8
due to pregnancy — *see* Pregnancy, tubal
pancreas 577.8
traumatic — *see* Injury, internal, pancreas
papillary muscle (ventricular) 429.6
pelvic
floor, complicating delivery 664.1 ☑
organ NEC — *see* Injury, pelvic, organs
penis (traumatic) — *see* Wound, open, penis
perineum 624.8
during delivery (*see also* Laceration, perineum, complicating delivery) 664.4 ☑
pharynx (nontraumatic) (spontaneous) 478.29
pregnant uterus (before onset of labor) 665.0 ☑
prostate (traumatic) — *see* Injury, internal, prostate
pulmonary
artery 417.8
valve (heart) (*see also* Endocarditis, pulmonary) 424.3
vein 417.8
vessel 417.8
pupil, sphincter 364.75
pus tube (*see also* Salpingo-oophoritis) 614.2
pyosalpinx (*see also* Salpingo-oophoritis) 614.2
rectum 569.49
traumatic — *see* Injury, internal, rectum
retina, retinal (traumatic) (without detachment) 361.30
with detachment (*see also* Detachment, retina, with retinal defect) 361.00
rotator cuff (capsule) (traumatic) 840.4
nontraumatic, complete 727.61
sclera 871.0
semilunar cartilage, knee (*see also* Tear, meniscus) 836.2

Rupture, ruptured — *continued*

semilunar cartilage, knee (*see also* Tear, meniscus) — *continued*
old (*see also* Derangement, meniscus) 717.5
septum (cardiac) 410.8 ☑
sigmoid 569.89
traumatic — *see* Injury, internal, colon, sigmoid
sinus of Valsalva 747.29
spinal cord (*see also* Injury, spinal, by site)
due to injury at birth 767.4
fetus or newborn 767.4
syphilitic 094.89
traumatic (*see also* Injury, spinal, by site)
with fracture — *see* Fracture, vertebra, by site, with spinal cord injury
spleen 289.59
congenital 767.8
due to injury at birth 767.8
malarial 084.9
nontraumatic 289.59
spontaneous 289.59
traumatic 865.04
with open wound into cavity 865.14
splenic vein 459.0
stomach 537.89
due to injury at birth 767.8
traumatic — *see* Injury, internal, stomach
ulcer — *see* Ulcer, stomach, with perforation
synovium 727.50
specified site NEC 727.59
tendon (traumatic) (*see also* Sprain, by site)
with open wound — *see* Wound, open, by site
Achilles 845.09
nontraumatic 727.67
ankle 845.09
nontraumatic 727.68
biceps (long head) 840.8
nontraumatic 727.62
foot 845.10
interphalangeal (joint) 845.13
metatarsophalangeal (joint) 845.12
nontraumatic 727.68
specified site NEC 845.19
tarsometatarsal (joint) 845.11
hand 842.10
carpometacarpal (joint) 842.11
interphalangeal (joint) 842.13
metacarpophalangeal (joint) 842.12
nontraumatic 727.63
extensors 727.63
flexors 727.64
specified site NEC 842.19
nontraumatic 727.60
specified site NEC 727.69
patellar 844.8

Rupture, ruptured — *continued*

tendon (*see also* Sprain, by site) — *continued*
patellar — *continued*
nontraumatic 727.66
quadriceps 844.8
nontraumatic 727.65
rotator cuff (capsule) 840.4
nontraumatic, complete 727.61
wrist 842.00
carpal (joint) 842.01
nontraumatic 727.63
extensors 727.63
flexors 727.64
radiocarpal (joint) (ligament) 842.02
radioulnar (joint), distal 842.09
specified site NEC 842.09
testis (traumatic) 878.2
complicated 878.3
due to syphilis 095.8
thoracic duct 457.8
tonsil 474.8
traumatic
with open wound — *see* Wound, open, by site
aorta — *see* Rupture, aorta, traumatic
ear drum — *see* Wound, open, ear, drum
external site — *see* Wound, open, by site
eye 871.2
globe (eye) — *see* Wound, open, eyeball
internal organ (abdomen, chest, or pelvis) (*see also* Injury, internal, by site)
heart — *see* Rupture, myocardium, traumatic
kidney — *see* Rupture, kidney
liver — *see* Rupture, liver
spleen — *see* Rupture, spleen, traumatic
ligament, muscle, or tendon (*see also* Sprain, by site)
with open wound — *see* Wound, open, by site
meaning hernia — *see* Hernia
tricuspid (heart) (valve) — *see* Endocarditis, tricuspid
tube, tubal 620.8
abscess (*see also* Salpingo-oophoritis) 614.2
due to pregnancy — *see* Pregnancy, tubal
tympanum, tympanic (membrane) (*see also* Perforation, tympanum) 384.20
with otitis media — *see* Otitis media
traumatic — *see* Wound, open, ear, drum
umbilical cord 663.8 ☑
fetus or newborn 772.0
ureter (traumatic) (*see also* Injury, internal, ureter) 867.2

Rupture, ruptured — *continued*

ureter (*see also* Injury, internal, ureter) — *continued*
nontraumatic 593.89
urethra 599.84
with
abortion — *see* Abortion, by type, with damage to pelvic organs
ectopic pregnancy (*see also* categories 633.0–633.9) 639.2
molar pregnancy (*see also* categories 630–632) 639.2
following
abortion 639.2
ectopic or molar pregnancy 639.2
obstetrical trauma 665.5 ☑
traumatic — *see* Injury, internal urethra
uterosacral ligament 620.8
uterus (traumatic) (*see also* Injury, internal uterus)
affecting fetus or newborn 763.89
during labor 665.1 ☑
nonpuerperal, nontraumatic 621.8
nontraumatic 621.8
pregnant (during labor) 665.1 ☑
before labor 665.0 ☑
vagina 878.6
complicated 878.7
complicating delivery — *see* Laceration, vagina, complicating delivery
valve, valvular (heart) — *see* Endocarditis
varicose vein — *see* Varicose, vein
varix — *see* Varix
vena cava 459.0
ventricle (free wall) (left) (*see also* Infarct, myocardium) 410.9 ☑
vesical (urinary) 596.6
traumatic — *see* Injury, internal, bladder
vessel (blood) 459.0
pulmonary 417.8
viscus 799.89
vulva 878.4
complicated 878.5
complicating delivery 664.0 ☑
Russell's dwarf (uterine dwarfism and craniofacial dysostosis) 759.89
Russell's dysentery 004.8
Russell (-Silver) syndrome (congenital hemihypertrophy and short stature) 759.89
Russian spring-summer type encephalitis 063.0
Rust's disease (tuberculous spondylitis) 015.0 ☑ *[720.81]*
Rustitskii's disease (multiple myeloma) (M9730/3) 203.0 ☑
Ruysch's disease (Hirschsprung's disease) 751.3
Rytand-Lipsitch syndrome (complete atrioventricular block) 426.0

S

Saber
shin 090.5
tibia 090.5
Saccharomyces infection — *see also*
Candidiasis 112.9
Saccharopinuria 270.7
Saccular — *see* condition
Sacculation
aorta (nonsyphilitic) (*see also*
Aneurysm, aorta) 441.9
ruptured 441.5
syphilitic 093.0
bladder 596.3
colon 569.89
intralaryngeal (congenital) (ventricular) 748.3
larynx (congenital) (ventricular) 748.3
organ or site, congenital — *see* Distortion
pregnant uterus, complicating delivery 654.4 ☑
affecting fetus or newborn 763.1
causing obstructed labor 660.2 ☑
affecting fetus or newborn 763.1
rectosigmoid 569.89
sigmoid 569.89
ureter 593.89
urethra 599.2
vesical 596.3
Sachs (-Tay) disease (amaurotic familial idiocy) 330.1
Sacks-Libman disease 710.0 [424.91]
Sac, lacrimal — *see* condition
Sacralgia 724.6
Sacralization
fifth lumbar vertebra 756.15
incomplete (vertebra) 756.15
Sacrodynia 724.6
Sacroiliac joint — *see* condition
Sacroiliitis NEC 720.2
Sacrum — *see* condition
Saddle
back 737.8
embolus, aorta 444.0
nose 738.0
congenital 754.0
due to syphilis 090.5
Sadism (sexual) 302.84
Saemisch's ulcer 370.04
Saenger's syndrome 379.46
Sago spleen 277.39
Sailors' skin 692.74
Saint
Anthony's fire (*see also* Erysipelas) 035
Guy's dance — *see* Chorea
Louis-type encephalitis 062.3
triad (*see also* Hernia, diaphragm) 553.3
Vitus' dance — *see* Chorea
Salicylism
correct substance properly administered 535.4 ☑
overdose or wrong substance given or taken 965.1
Salivary duct or gland — *see also* condition
virus disease 078.5
Salivation (excessive) — *see also* Ptyalism 527.7
Salmonella (aertrycke) (choleraesuis) (enteritidis) (gallinarum) (suipestifer) (typhimurium) — *see also* Infection, Salmonella 003.9
arthritis 003.23
carrier (suspected) of V02.3
meningitis 003.21
osteomyelitis 003.24
pneumonia 003.22
septicemia 003.1
typhosa 002.0
carrier (suspected) of V02.1

Salmonellosis 003.0
with pneumonia 003.22
Salpingitis (catarrhal) (fallopian tube) (nodular) (pseudofollicular) (purulent) (septic) — *see also* Salpingo-oophoritis 614.2
ear 381.50
acute 381.51
chronic 381.52
Eustachian (tube) 381.50
acute 381.51
chronic 381.52
follicularis 614.1
gonococcal (chronic) 098.37
acute 098.17
interstitial, chronic 614.1
isthmica nodosa 614.1
old — *see* Salpingo-oophoritis, chronic
puerperal, postpartum, childbirth 670.0 ☑
specific (chronic) 098.37
acute 098.17
tuberculous (acute) (chronic) (*see also* Tuberculosis) 016.6 ☑
venereal (chronic) 098.37
acute 098.17
Salpingocele 620.4
Salpingo-oophoritis (catarrhal) (purulent) (ruptured) (septic) (suppurative) 614.2
acute 614.0
with
abortion — *see* Abortion, by type, with sepsis
ectopic pregnancy (*see also* categories 633.0–633.9) 639.0
molar pregnancy (*see also* categories 630–632) 639.0
following
abortion 639.0
ectopic or molar pregnancy 639.0
gonococcal 098.17
puerperal, postpartum, childbirth 670.0 ☑
tuberculous (*see also* Tuberculosis) 016.6 ☑
chronic 614.1
gonococcal 098.37
tuberculous (see also Tuberculosis) 016.6 ☑
complicating pregnancy 646.6 ☑
affecting fetus or newborn 760.8
gonococcal (chronic) 098.37
acute 098.17
old — *see* Salpingo-oophoritis, chronic
puerperal 670.0 ☑
specific — *see* Salpingo-oophoritis, gonococcal
subacute (*see also* Salpingo-oophoritis, acute) 614.0
tuberculous (acute) (chronic) (*see also* Tuberculosis) 016.6 ☑
venereal — *see* Salpingo-oophoritis, gonococcal
Salpingo-ovaritis — *see also* Salpingo-oophoritis 614.2
Salpingoperitonitis — *see also* Salpingo-oophoritis 614.2
Salt-losing
nephritis (*see also* Disease, renal) 593.9
syndrome (*see also* Disease, renal) 593.9
Salt-rheum — *see also* Eczema 692.9
Salzmann's nodular dystrophy 371.46
Sampson's cyst or tumor 617.1
Sandblasters'
asthma 502
lung 502
Sander's disease (paranoia) 297.1
Sandfly fever 066.0
Sandhoff's disease 330.1
Sanfilippo's syndrome (mucopolysaccharidosis III) 277.5

Salmonellosis 003.0
Sanger-Brown's ataxia 334.2
San Joaquin Valley fever 114.0
Sao Paulo fever or typhus 082.0
Saponification, mesenteric 567.89
Sapremia — *see* Septicemia
Sarcocele (benign)
syphilitic 095.8
congenital 090.5
Sarcoepiplocele — *see also* Hernia 553.9
Sarcoepiplomphalocele — *see also* Hernia, umbilicus 553.1
Sarcoid (any site) 135
with lung involvement 135 [517.8]
Boeck's 135
Darier-Roussy 135
Spiegler-Fendt 686.8
Sarcoidosis 135
cardiac 135 [425.8]
lung 135 [517.8]
Sarcoma (M8800/3) — *see also* Neoplasm, connective tissue, malignant
alveolar soft part (M9581/3) — *see* Neoplasm, connective tissue, malignant
ameloblastic (M9330/3) 170.1
upper jaw (bone) 170.0
botryoid (M8910/3) — *see* Neoplasm, connective tissue, malignant
botryoides (M8910/3) — *see* Neoplasm, connective tissue, malignant
cerebellar (M9480/3) 191.6
circumscribed (arachnoidal) (M9471/3) 191.6
circumscribed (arachnoidal) cerebellar (M9471/3) 191.6
clear cell, of tendons and aponeuroses (M9044/3) — *see* Neoplasm, connective tissue, malignant
embryonal (M8991/3) — *see* Neoplasm, connective tissue, malignant
endometrial (stromal) (M8930/3) 182.0
isthmus 182.1
endothelial (M9130/3) (*see also* Neoplasm, connective tissue, malignant)
bone (M9260/3) — *see* Neoplasm, bone, malignant
epithelioid cell (M8804/3) — *see* Neoplasm, connective tissue, malignant
Ewing's (M9260/3) — *see* Neoplasm, bone, malignant
follicular dendritic cell 202.9 ☑
germinoblastic (diffuse) (M9632/3) 202.8 ☑
follicular (M9697/3) 202.0 ☑
giant cell (M8802/3) (*see also* Neoplasm, connective tissue, malignant)
bone (M9250/3) — *see* Neoplasm, bone, malignant
glomoid (M8710/3) — *see* Neoplasm, connective tissue, malignant
granulocytic (M9930/3) 205.3 ☑
hemangioendothelial (M9130/3) — *see* Neoplasm, connective tissue, malignant
hemorrhagic, multiple (M9140/3) — *see* Kaposi's, sarcoma
Hodgkin's (M9662/3) 201.2 ☑
immunoblastic (M9612/3) 200.8 ☑
interdigitating dendritic cell 202.9 ☑
Kaposi's (M9140/3) — *see* Kaposi's, sarcoma
Kupffer cell (M9124/3) 155.0
Langerhans cell 202.9 ☑
leptomeningeal (M9530/3) — *see* Neoplasm, meninges, malignant
lymphangioendothelial (M9170/3) — *see* Neoplasm, connective tissue, malignant

Sarcoma — *see also* Neoplasm, connective tissue, malignant — *continued*
lymphoblastic (M9630/3) 200.1 ☑
lymphocytic (M9620/3) 200.1 ☑
mast cell (M9740/3) 202.6 ☑
melanotic (M8720/3) — *see* Melanoma
meningeal (M9530/3) — *see* Neoplasm, meninges, malignant
meningothelial (M9530/3) — *see* Neoplasm, meninges, malignant
mesenchymal (M8800/3) (*see also* Neoplasm, connective tissue, malignant)
mixed (M8990/3) — *see* Neoplasm, connective tissue, malignant
mesothelial (M9050/3) — *see* Neoplasm, by site, malignant
monstrocellular (M9481/3)
specified site — *see* Neoplasm, by site, malignant
unspecified site 191.9
myeloid (M9930/3) 205.3 ☑
neurogenic (M9540/3) — *see* Neoplasm, connective tissue, malignant
odontogenic (M9270/3) 170.1
upper jaw (bone) 170.0
osteoblastic (M9180/3) — *see* Neoplasm, bone, malignant
osteogenic (M9180/3) (*see also* Neoplasm, bone, malignant)
juxtacortical (M9190/3) — *see* Neoplasm, bone, malignant
periosteal (M9190/3) — *see* Neoplasm, bone, malignant
periosteal (M8812/3) (*see also* Neoplasm, bone, malignant)
osteogenic (M9190/3) — *see* Neoplasm, bone, malignant
plasma cell (M9731/3) 203.8 ☑
pleomorphic cell (M8802/3) — *see* Neoplasm, connective tissue, malignant
reticuloendothelial (M9720/3) 202.3 ☑
reticulum cell (M9640/3) 200.0 ☑
nodular (M9642/3) 200.0 ☑
pleomorphic cell type (M9641/3) 200.0 ☑
round cell (M8803/3) — *see* Neoplasm, connective tissue, malignant
small cell (M8803/3) — *see* Neoplasm, connective tissue, malignant
spindle cell (M8801/3) — *see* Neoplasm, connective tissue, malignant
stromal (endometrial) (M8930/3) 182.0
isthmus 182.1
synovial (M9040/3) (*see also* Neoplasm, connective tissue, malignant)
biphasic type (M9043/3) — *see* Neoplasm, connective tissue, malignant
epithelioid cell type (M9042/3) — *see* Neoplasm, connective tissue, malignant
spindle cell type (M9041/3) — *see* Neoplasm, connective tissue, malignant
Sarcomatosis
meningeal (M9539/3) — *see* Neoplasm, meninges, malignant
specified site NEC (M8800/3) — *see* Neoplasm, connective tissue, malignant
unspecified site (M8800/6) 171.9
Sarcosinemia 270.8
Sarcosporidiosis 136.5
Satiety, early 780.94
Saturnine — *see* condition
Saturnism 984.9

☑ Additional Digit Required — Refer to the Tabular List for Digit Selection   ▽ Subterms under main terms may continue to next column or page

2007 ICD-9-CM   ▶◀ Revised Text   ● New Line   ▲ Revised Code   **October 2006 · Volume 2 — 255**

Saturnism — *continued*
specified type of lead — *see* Table of
Drugs and Chemicals
Satyriasis 302.89
Sauriasis — *see* Ichthyosis
Sauriderma 757.39
Sauriosis — *see* Ichthyosis
Savill's disease (epidemic exfoliative
dermatitis) 695.89
SBE (subacute bacterial endocarditis)
421.0
Scabies (any site) 133.0
Scabs 782.8
Scaglietti-Dagnini syndrome (acrome-
galic macrospondylitis) 253.0
Scald, scalded — *see also* Burn, by site
skin syndrome 695.1
Scalenus anticus (anterior) syndrome
353.0
Scales 782.8
Scalp — *see* condition
Scaphocephaly 756.0
Scaphoiditis, tarsal 732.5
Scapulalgia 733.90
Scapulohumeral myopathy 359.1
Scarabiasis 134.1
Scarlatina 034.1
anginosa 034.1
maligna 034.1
myocarditis, acute 034.1 *[422.0]*
old (*see also* Myocarditis) 429.0
otitis media 034.1 *[382.02]*
ulcerosa 034.1
Scarlatinella 057.8
Scarlet fever (albuminuria) (angina)
(convulsions) (lesions of lid) (rash)
034.1
Scar, scarring — *see also* Cicatrix 709.2
adherent 709.2
atrophic 709.2
cervix
in pregnancy or childbirth 654.6 ☑
affecting fetus or newborn
763.89
causing obstructed labor
660.2 ☑
affecting fetus or newborn
763.1
cheloid 701.4
chorioretinal 363.30
disseminated 363.35
macular 363.32
peripheral 363.34
posterior pole NEC 363.33
choroid (*see also* Scar, chorioretinal)
363.30
compression, pericardial 423.9
congenital 757.39
conjunctiva 372.64
cornea 371.00
xerophthalmic 264.6
due to previous cesarean delivery,
complicating pregnancy or
childbirth 654.2 ☑
affecting fetus or newborn 763.89
duodenal (bulb) (cap) 537.3
hypertrophic 701.4
keloid 701.4
labia 624.4
lung (base) 518.89
macula 363.32
disseminated 363.35
peripheral 363.34
muscle 728.89
myocardium, myocardial 412
painful 709.2
papillary muscle 429.81
posterior pole NEC 363.33
macular — *see* Scar, macula
postnecrotic (hepatic) (liver) 571.9
psychic V15.49
retina (*see also* Scar, chorioretinal)
363.30
trachea 478.9
uterus 621.8

Scar, scarring — *see also* Cicatrix —
continued
uterus — *continued*
in pregnancy or childbirth NEC
654.9 ☑
affecting fetus or newborn
763.89
due to previous cesarean delivery 654.2 ☑
vulva 624.4
**Schamberg's disease, dermatitis, or
dermatosis** (progressive pigmentary dermatosis) 709.09
Schatzki's ring (esophagus) (lower)
(congenital) 750.3
acquired 530.3
Schaufenster krankheit 413.9
Schaumann's
benign lymphogranulomatosis 135
disease (sarcoidosis) 135
syndrome (sarcoidosis) 135
Scheie's syndrome (mucopolysaccharidosis IS) 277.5
Schenck's disease (sporotrichosis) 117.1
**Scheuermann's disease or osteochon-
drosis** 732.0
Scheuthauer-Marie-Sainton syndrome
(cleidocranialis dysostosis) 755.59
Schilder (-Flatau) disease 341.1
Schilling-type monocytic leukemia
(M9890/3) 206.9 ☑
**Schimmelbusch's disease, cystic mas-
titis, or hyperplasia** 610.1
Schirmer's syndrome (encephalocuta-
neous angiomatosis) 759.6
Schistocelia 756.79
Schistoglossia 750.13
Schistosoma infestation — *see* Infesta-
tion, Schistosoma
Schistosomiasis 120.9
Asiatic 120.2
bladder 120.0
chestermani 120.8
colon 120.1
cutaneous 120.3
due to
S. hematobium 120.0
S. japonicum 120.2
S. mansoni 120.1
S. mattheii 120.8
eastern 120.2
genitourinary tract 120.0
intestinal 120.1
lung 120.2
Manson's (intestinal) 120.1
Oriental 120.2
pulmonary 120.2
specified type NEC 120.8
vesical 120.0
Schizencephaly 742.4
Schizo-affective psychosis — *see also*
Schizophrenia 295.7 ☑
Schizodontia 520.2
Schizoid personality 301.20
introverted 301.21
schizotypal 301.22
Schizophrenia, schizophrenic (reaction)
295.9 ☑

Note — *Use the following fifth-digit
subclassification with category 295:*

0   *unspecified*

1   *subchronic*

2   *chronic*

3   *subchronic with acute exacerbation*

4   *chronic with acute exacerbation*

5   *in remission*

acute (attack) NEC 295.8 ☑
episode 295.4 ☑
atypical form 295.8 ☑
borderline 295.5 ☑
catalepsy 295.2 ☑

Schizophrenia, schizophrenic —
continued
catatonic (type) (acute) (excited)
(withdrawn) 295.2 ☑
childhood (type) (*see also* Psychosis,
childhood) 299.9 ☑
chronic NEC 295.6 ☑
coenesthesiopathic 295.8 ☑
cyclic (type) 295.7 ☑
disorganized (type) 295.1 ☑
flexibilitas cerea 295.2 ☑
hebephrenic (type) (acute) 295.1 ☑
incipient 295.5 ☑
latent 295.5 ☑
paranoid (type) (acute) 295.3 ☑
paraphrenic (acute) 295.3 ☑
prepsychotic 295.5 ☑
primary (acute) 295.0 ☑
prodromal 295.5 ☑
pseudoneurotic 295.5 ☑
pseudopsychopathic 295.5 ☑
reaction 295.9 ☑
residual type (state) 295.6 ☑
restzustand 295.6 ☑
schizo-affective (type) (depressed) (excited) 295.7 ☑
schizophreniform type 295.4 ☑
simple (type) (acute) 295.0 ☑
simplex (acute) 295.0 ☑
specified type NEC 295.8 ☑
syndrome of childhood NEC (*see also*
Psychosis, childhood) 299.9 ☑
undifferentiated type 295.9 ☑
acute 295.8 ☑
chronic 295.6 ☑
Schizothymia 301.20
introverted 301.21
schizotypal 301.22
Schlafkrankheit 086.5
Schlatter-Osgood disease (osteochondrosis, tibial tubercle) 732.4
Schlatter's tibia (osteochondrosis) 732.4
Schloffer's tumor — *see also* Peritonitis
567.29
Schmidt's syndrome
sphallo-pharyngo-laryngeal hemiplegia
352.6
thyroid-adrenocortical insufficiency
258.1
vagoaccessory 352.6
Schmincke
carcinoma (M8082/3) — *see* Neoplasm, nasopharynx, malignant
tumor (M8082/3) — *see* Neoplasm,
nasopharynx, malignant
Schmitz (-Stutzer) dysentery 004.0
Schmorl's disease or nodes 722.30
lumbar, lumbosacral 722.32
specified region NEC 722.39
thoracic, thoracolumbar 722.31
Schneiderian
carcinoma (M8121/3)
specified site — *see* Neoplasm, by
site, malignant
unspecified site 160.0
papilloma (M8121/0)
specified site — *see* Neoplasm, by
site, benign
unspecified site 212.0
Schneider's syndrome 047.9
Schnitzler syndrome 273.1
Schoffer's tumor — *see also* Peritonitis
567.29
Scholte's syndrome (malignant carcinoid) 259.2
Scholz's disease 330.0
**Scholz (-Bielschowsky-Henneberg)
syndrome** 330.0
Schönlein (-Henoch) disease (primary)
(purpura) (rheumatic) 287.0
School examination V70.3
Schottmüller's disease — *see also*
Fever, paratyphoid 002.9
Schroeder's syndrome (endocrine-hyper-
tensive) 255.3

Schüller-Christian disease or syndrome
(chronic histiocytosis X) 277.89
Schultz's disease or syndrome (agranulocytosis) 288.09   ▲
Schultze's acroparesthesia, simple
443.89
Schwalbe-Ziehen-Oppenheimer disease
333.6
Schwannoma (M9560/0) — *see also*
Neoplasm, connective tissue, benign
malignant (M9560/3) — *see* Neoplasm, connective tissue, malignant
Schwartz-Bartter syndrome (inappropriate secretion of antidiuretic hormone) 253.6
Schwartz (-Jampel) syndrome 756.89
Schweninger-Buzzi disease (macular
atrophy) 701.3
Sciatic — *see* condition
Sciatica (infectional) 724.3
due to
displacement of intervertebral disc
722.10
herniation, nucleus pulposus
722.10
wallet 724.3
Scimitar syndrome (anomalous venous
drainage, right lung to inferior vena
cava) 747.49
Sclera — *see* condition
Sclerectasia 379.11
Scleredema
adultorum 710.1
Buschke's 710.1
newborn 778.1
Sclerema
adiposum (newborn) 778.1
adultorum 710.1
edematosum (newborn) 778.1
neonatorum 778.1
newborn 778.1
Scleriasis — *see* Scleroderma
Scleritis 379.00
with corneal involvement 379.05
anterior (annular) (localized) 379.03
brawny 379.06
granulomatous 379.09
posterior 379.07
specified NEC 379.09
suppurative 379.09
syphilitic 095.0
tuberculous (nodular) (*see also* Tuberculosis) 017.3 ☑ *[379.09]*
Sclerochoroiditis — *see also* Scleritis
379.00
Scleroconjunctivitis — *see also* Scleritis
379.00
Sclerocystic ovary (syndrome) 256.4
Sclerodactylia 701.0
Scleroderma, sclerodermia (acrosclerot-
ic) (diffuse) (generalized) (progressive) (pulmonary) 710.1
circumscribed 701.0
linear 701.0
localized (linear) 701.0
newborn 778.1
Sclerokeratitis 379.05
meaning sclerosing keratitis 370.54
tuberculous (*see also* Tuberculosis)
017.3 ☑ *[379.09]*
Scleromalacia
multiple 731.0
perforans 379.04
Scleroma, trachea 040.1
Scleromyxedema 701.8
Scleroperikeratitis 379.05
Sclerose en plaques 340
Sclerosis, sclerotic
adrenal (gland) 255.8
Alzheimer's 331.0
with dementia — *see* Alzheimer's,
dementia
amyotrophic (lateral) 335.20

Sclerosis, sclerotic — *continued*
  annularis fibrosi
    aortic 424.1
    mitral 424.0
  aorta, aortic 440.0
    valve (*see also* Endocarditis, aortic)
        424.1
  artery, arterial, arteriolar, arteriovas-
      cular — *see* Arteriosclerosis
  ascending multiple 340
  Baló's (concentric) 341.1
  basilar — *see* Sclerosis, brain
  bone (localized) NEC 733.99
  brain (general) (lobular) 341.9
    Alzheimer's — *see* Alzheimer's, de-
        mentia
    artery, arterial 437.0
    atrophic lobar 331.0
      with dementia
        with behavioral disturbance
            331.0 [294.11]
        without behavioral distur-
            bance 331.0 [294.10]
    diffuse 341.1
      familial (chronic) (infantile)
          330.0
      infantile (chronic) (familial)
          330.0
      Pelizaeus-Merzbacher type
          330.0
    disseminated 340
    hereditary 334.2
    infantile (degenerative) (diffuse)
        330.0
    insular 340
    Krabbe's 330.0
    miliary 340
    multiple 340
    Pelizaeus-Merzbacher 330.0
    progressive familial 330.0
    senile 437.0
    tuberous 759.5
  bulbar, progressive 340
  bundle of His 426.50
    left 426.3
    right 426.4
  cardiac — *see* Arteriosclerosis, coro-
      nary
  cardiorenal (*see also* Hypertension,
      cardiorenal) 404.90
  cardiovascular (*see also* Disease, car-
      diovascular) 429.2
    renal (*see also* Hypertension, car-
        diorenal) 404.90
  centrolobar, familial 330.0
  cerebellar — *see* Sclerosis, brain
  cerebral — *see* Sclerosis, brain
  cerebrospinal 340
    disseminated 340
    multiple 340
  cerebrovascular 437.0
  choroid 363.40
    diffuse 363.56
  combined (spinal cord) (*see also* De-
      generation, combined)
    multiple 340
  concentric, Baló's 341.1
  cornea 370.54
  coronary (artery) — *see* Arteriosclero-
      sis, coronary
  corpus cavernosum
    female 624.8
    male 607.89
  Dewitzky's
    aortic 424.1
    mitral 424.0
  diffuse NEC 341.1
  disease, heart — *see* Arteriosclerosis,
      coronary
  disseminated 340
  dorsal 340
  dorsolateral (spinal cord) — *see* Degen-
      eration, combined
  endometrium 621.8
  extrapyramidal 333.90
  eye, nuclear (senile) 366.16

Sclerosis, sclerotic — *continued*
  Friedreich's (spinal cord) 334.0
  funicular (spermatic cord) 608.89
  gastritis 535.4 ☑
  general (vascular) — *see* Arteriosclero-
      sis
  gland (lymphatic) 457.8
  hepatic 571.9
  hereditary
    cerebellar 334.2
    spinal 334.0
  idiopathic cortical (Garré's) (*see also*
      Osteomyelitis) 730.1 ☑
  ilium, piriform 733.5
  insular 340
    pancreas 251.8
  Islands of Langerhans 251.8
  kidney — *see* Sclerosis, renal
  larynx 478.79
  lateral 335.24
    amyotrophic 335.20
    descending 335.24
    primary 335.24
    spinal 335.24
  liver 571.9
  lobar, atrophic (of brain) 331.0
    with dementia
      with behavioral disturbance
          331.0 [294.11]
      without behavioral disturbance
          331.0 [294.10]
  lung (*see also* Fibrosis, lung) 515
  mastoid 383.1
  mitral — *see* Endocarditis, mitral
  Mönckeberg's (medial) (*see also* Arte-
      riosclerosis, extremities) 440.20
  multiple (brain stem) (cerebral) (gener-
      alized) (spinal cord) 340
  myocardium, myocardial — *see* Arte-
      riosclerosis, coronary
  nuclear (senile), eye 366.16
  ovary 620.8
  pancreas 577.8
  penis 607.89
  peripheral arteries (*see also* Arte-
      riosclerosis, extremities) 440.20
  plaques 340
  pluriglandular 258.8
  polyglandular 258.8
  posterior (spinal cord) (syphilitic)
      094.0
  posterolateral (spinal cord) — *see* De-
      generation, combined
  prepuce 607.89
  primary lateral 335.24
  progressive systemic 710.1
  pulmonary (*see also* Fibrosis, lung)
      515
    artery 416.0
    valve (heart) (*see also* Endocarditis,
        pulmonary) 424.3
  renal 587
    with
      cystine storage disease 270.0
      hypertension (*see also* Hyperten-
          sion, kidney) 403.90
      hypertensive heart disease
          (conditions classifiable to
          402) (*see also* Hyperten-
          sion, cardiorenal) 404.90
      arteriolar (hyaline) (*see also* Hyper-
          tension, kidney) 403.90
      hyperplastic (*see also* Hyperten-
          sion, kidney) 403.90
  retina (senile) (vascular) 362.17
  rheumatic
    aortic valve 395.9
    mitral valve 394.9
  Schilder's 341.1
  senile — *see* Arteriosclerosis
  spinal (cord) (general) (progressive)
      (transverse) 336.8
    ascending 357.0
    combined (*see also* Degeneration,
        combined)
      multiple 340

Sclerosis, sclerotic — *continued*
  spinal — *continued*
    combined (*see also* Degeneration,
        combined) — *continued*
      syphilitic 094.89
    disseminated 340
    dorsolateral — *see* Degeneration,
        combined
    hereditary (Friedreich's) (mixed
        form) 334.0
    lateral (amyotrophic) 335.24
    multiple 340
    posterior (syphilitic) 094.0
  stomach 537.89
  subendocardial, congenital 425.3
  systemic (progressive) 710.1
    with lung involvement
        710.1 [517.2]
  tricuspid (heart) (valve) — *see* Endo-
      carditis, tricuspid
  tuberous (brain) 759.5
  tympanic membrane (*see also* Tym-
      panosclerosis) 385.00
  valve, valvular (heart) — *see* Endo-
      carditis
  vascular — *see* Arteriosclerosis
  vein 459.89
Sclerotenonitis 379.07
Sclerotitis — *see also* Scleritis 379.00
  syphilitic 095.0
  tuberculous (*see also* Tuberculosis)
      017.3 ☑ [379.09]
Scoliosis (acquired) (postural) 737.30
  congenital 754.2
  due to or associated with
    Charcôt-Marie-Tooth disease
        356.1 [737.43]
    mucopolysaccharidosis
        277.5 [737.43]
    neurofibromatosis 237.71 [737.43]
    osteitis
      deformans 731.0 [737.43]
      fibrosa cystica 252.01 [737.43]
    osteoporosis (*see also* Osteoporosis)
        733.00 [737.43]
    poliomyelitis 138 [737.43]
    radiation 737.33
    tuberculosis (*see also* Tuberculosis)
        015.0 ☑ [737.43]
  idiopathic 737.30
    infantile
      progressive 737.32
      resolving 737.31
  paralytic 737.39
  rachitic 268.1
  sciatic 724.3
  specified NEC 737.39
  thoracogenic 737.34
  tuberculous (*see also* Tuberculosis)
      015.0 ☑ [737.43]
Scoliotic pelvis 738.6
  with disproportion (fetopelvic) 653.0 ☑
    affecting fetus or newborn 763.1
    causing obstructed labor 660.1 ☑
      affecting fetus or newborn 763.1
Scorbutus, scorbutic 267
  anemia 281.8
Scotoma (ring) 368.44
  arcuate 368.43
  Bjerrum 368.43
  blind spot area 368.42
  central 368.41
  centrocecal 368.41
  paracecal 368.42
  paracentral 368.41
  scintillating 368.12
  Seidel 368.43
Scratch — *see* Injury, superficial, by site
Screening (for) V82.9
  alcoholism V79.1
  anemia, deficiency NEC V78.1
    iron V78.0
  anomaly, congenital V82.89
  antenatal, ▶of mother◀ V28.9
    alphafetoprotein levels, raised
        V28.1

Screening — *continued*
  antenatal, ▶of mother◀ — *contin-
      ued*
    based on amniocentesis V28.2
      chromosomal anomalies V28.0
      raised alphafetoprotein levels
          V28.1
    fetal growth retardation using ultra-
        sonics V28.4
    ultrasonics V28.4
    isoimmunization V28.5
    malformations using ultrasonics
        V28.3
    raised alphafetoprotein levels V28.1
    specified condition NEC V28.8
    Streptococcus B V28.6
  arterial hypertension V81.1
  arthropod-borne viral disease NEC
      V73.5
  asymptomatic bacteriuria V81.5
  bacterial
    conjunctivitis V74.4
    disease V74.9
      specified condition NEC V74.8
  bacteriuria, asymptomatic V81.5
  blood disorder NEC V78.9
    specified type NEC V78.8
  bronchitis, chronic V81.3
  brucellosis V74.8
  cancer — *see* Screening, malignant
      neoplasm
  cardiovascular disease NEC V81.2
  cataract V80.2
  Chagas' disease V75.3
  chemical poisoning V82.5
  cholera V74.0
  cholesterol level V77.91
  chromosomal
    anomalies
      by amniocentesis, antenatal
          V28.0
      maternal postnatal V82.4
    athletes V70.3
  condition
    cardiovascular NEC V81.2
    eye NEC V80.2
    genitourinary NEC V81.6
    neurological V80.0
    respiratory NEC V81.4
    skin V82.0
    specified NEC V82.89
  congenital
    anomaly V82.89
      eye V80.2
    dislocation of hip V82.3
    eye condition or disease V80.2
  conjunctivitis, bacterial V74.4
  contamination NEC (*see also* Poison-
      ing) V82.5
  coronary artery disease V81.0
  cystic fibrosis V77.6
  deficiency anemia NEC V78.1
    iron V78.0
  dengue fever V73.5
  depression V79.0
  developmental handicap V79.9
    in early childhood V79.3
    specified type NEC V79.8
  diabetes mellitus V77.1
  diphtheria V74.3
  disease or disorder V82.9
    bacterial V74.9
      specified NEC V74.8
    blood V78.9
      specified type NEC V78.8
    blood-forming organ V78.9
      specified type NEC V78.8
    cardiovascular NEC V81.2
      hypertensive V81.1
      ischemic V81.0
    Chagas' V75.3
    chlamydial V73.98
      specified NEC V73.88
    ear NEC V80.3
    endocrine NEC V77.99
    eye NEC V80.2

☑ Additional Digit Required — Refer to the Tabular List for Digit Selection   ᵛᵉᵗ Subterms under main terms may continue to next column or page

Screening — *continued*
  disease or disorder — *continued*
    genitourinary NEC V81.6
    heart NEC V81.2
      hypertensive V81.1
      ischemic V81.0
    immunity NEC V77.99
    infectious NEC V75.9
    lipoid NEC V77.91
    mental V79.9
      specified type NEC V79.8
    metabolic NEC V77.99
      inborn NEC V77.7
    neurological V80.0
    nutritional NEC V77.99
    rheumatic NEC V82.2
    rickettsial V75.0
    sickle-cell V78.2
      trait V78.2
    specified type NEC V82.89
    thyroid V77.0
    vascular NEC V81.2
      ischemic V81.0
    venereal V74.5
    viral V73.99
      arthropod-borne NEC V73.5
      specified type NEC V73.89
  dislocation of hip, congenital V82.3
  drugs in athletes V70.3
  emphysema (chronic) V81.3
  encephalitis, viral (mosquito or tick borne) V73.5
  endocrine disorder NEC V77.99
  eye disorder NEC V80.2
    congenital V80.2
  fever
    dengue V73.5
    hemorrhagic V73.5
    yellow V73.4
  filariasis V75.6
  galactosemia V77.4
  genetic V82.79 •
    disease carrier status V82.71 •
  genitourinary condition NEC V81.6
  glaucoma V80.1
  gonorrhea V74.5
  gout V77.5
  Hansen's disease V74.2
  heart disease NEC V81.2
    hypertensive V81.1
    ischemic V81.0
  heavy metal poisoning V82.5
  helminthiasis, intestinal V75.7
  hematopoietic malignancy V76.89
  hemoglobinopathies NEC V78.3
  hemorrhagic fever V73.5
  Hodgkin's disease V76.89
  hormones in athletes V70.3
  hypercholesterolemia V77.91
  hyperlipdemia V77.91
  hypertension V81.1
  immunity disorder NEC V77.99
  inborn errors of metabolism NEC V77.7
  infection
    bacterial V74.9
      specified type NEC V74.8
    mycotic V75.4
    parasitic NEC V75.8
  infectious disease V75.9
    specified type NEC V75.8
  ingestion of radioactive substance V82.5
  intestinal helminthiasis V75.7
  iron deficiency anemia V78.0
  ischemic heart disease V81.0
  lead poisoning V82.5
  leishmaniasis V75.2
  leprosy V74.2
  leptospirosis V74.8
  leukemia V76.89
  lipoid disorder NEC V77.91
  lymphoma V76.89
  malaria V75.1
  malignant neoplasm (of) V76.9
    bladder V76.3

Screening — *continued*
  malignant neoplasm — *continued*
    blood V76.89
    breast V76.10
      mammogram NEC V76.12
        for high-risk patient V76.11
      specified type NEC V76.19
    cervix V76.2
    colon V76.51
    colorectal V76.51
    hematopoietic system V76.89
    intestine V76.50
      colon V76.51
      small V76.52
    lung V76.0
    lymph (glands) V76.89
    nervous system V76.81
    oral cavity V76.42
    other specified neoplasm NEC V76.89
    ovary V76.46
    prostate V76.44
    rectum V76.41
    respiratory organs V76.0
    skin V76.43
    specified sites NEC V76.49
    testis V76.45
    vagina V76.47
      following hysterectomy for malignant condition V67.01
  malnutrition V77.2
  mammogram NEC V76.12
    for high-risk patient V76.11
  maternal postnatal chromosomal anomalies V82.4
  measles V73.2
  mental
    disorder V79.9
      specified type NEC V79.8
    retardation V79.2
  metabolic disorder NEC V77.99
  metabolic errors, inborn V77.7
  mucoviscidosis V77.6
  multiphasic V82.6
  mycosis V75.4
  mycotic infection V75.4
  nephropathy V81.5
  neurological condition V80.0
  nutritional disorder V77.99
  obesity V77.8
  osteoporosis V82.81
  parasitic infection NEC V75.8
  phenylketonuria V77.3
  plague V74.8
  poisoning
    chemical NEC V82.5
    contaminated water supply V82.5
    heavy metal V82.5
  poliomyelitis V73.0
  postnatal chromosomal anomalies, maternal V82.4
  prenatal — *see* Screening, antenatal
  pulmonary tuberculosis V74.1
  radiation exposure V82.5
  renal disease V81.5
  respiratory condition NEC V81.4
  rheumatic disorder NEC V82.2
  rheumatoid arthritis V82.1
  rickettsial disease V75.0
  rubella V73.3
  schistosomiasis V75.5
  senile macular lesions of eye V80.2
  sickle-cell anemia, disease, or trait V78.2
  skin condition V82.0
  sleeping sickness V75.3
  smallpox V73.1
  special V82.9
    specified condition NEC V82.89
  specified type NEC V82.89
  spirochetal disease V74.9
    specified type NEC V74.8
  stimulants in athletes V70.3
  syphilis V74.5
  tetanus V74.8
  thyroid disorder V77.0

Screening — *continued*
  trachoma V73.6
  trypanosomiasis V75.3
  tuberculosis, pulmonary V74.1
  venereal disease V74.5
  viral encephalitis
    mosquito-borne V73.5
    tick-borne V73.5
  whooping cough V74.8
  worms, intestinal V75.7
  yaws V74.6
  yellow fever V73.4
Scrofula — *see also* Tuberculosis 017.2 ☑
Scrofulide (primary) — *see also* Tuberculosis 017.0 ☑
Scrofuloderma, scrofulodermia (any site) (primary) — *see also* Tuberculosis 017.0 ☑
Scrofulosis (universal) — *see also* Tuberculosis 017.2 ☑
Scrofulosis lichen (primary) — *see also* Tuberculosis 017.0 ☑
Scrofulous — *see* condition
Scrotal tongue 529.5
  congenital 750.13
Scrotum — *see* condition
Scurvy (gum) (infantile) (rickets) (scorbutic) 267
Sea-blue histiocyte syndrome 272.7
Seabright-Bantam syndrome (pseudohypoparathyroidism) 275.49
Seasickness 994.6
Seatworm 127.4
Sebaceous
  cyst (*see also* Cyst, sebaceous) 706.2
  gland disease NEC 706.9
Sebocystomatosis 706.2
Seborrhea, seborrheic 706.3
  adiposa 706.3
  capitis 690.11
  congestiva 695.4
  corporis 706.3
  dermatitis 690.10
    infantile 690.12
  diathesis in infants 695.89
  eczema 690.18
    infantile 690.12
  keratosis 702.19
    inflamed 702.11
  nigricans 705.89
  sicca 690.18
  wart 702.19
    inflamed 702.11
Seckel's syndrome 759.89
Seclusion pupil 364.74
Seclusiveness, child 313.22
Secondary — *see also* condition
  neoplasm — *see* Neoplasm, by site, malignant, secondary
Secretan's disease or syndrome (post-traumatic edema) 782.3
Secretion
  antidiuretic hormone, inappropriate (syndrome) 253.6
  catecholamine, by pheochromocytoma 255.6
  hormone
    antidiuretic, inappropriate (syndrome) 253.6
    by
      carcinoid tumor 259.2
      pheochromocytoma 255.6
    ectopic NEC 259.3
  urinary
    excessive 788.42
    suppression 788.5
Section
  cesarean
    affecting fetus or newborn 763.4
    post mortem, affecting fetus or newborn 761.6
    previous, in pregnancy or childbirth 654.2 ☑
      affecting fetus or newborn 763.89

Section — *continued*
  nerve, traumatic — *see* Injury, nerve, by site
Seeligmann's syndrome (ichthyosis congenita) 757.1
Segmentation, incomplete (congenital) — *see also* Fusion
  bone NEC 756.9
  lumbosacral (joint) 756.15
  vertebra 756.15
    lumbosacral 756.15
Seizure 780.39
  akinetic (idiopathic) (*see also* Epilepsy) 345.0 ☑
    psychomotor 345.4 ☑
  apoplexy, apoplectic (*see also* Disease, cerebrovascular, acute) 436
  atonic (*see also* Epilepsy) 345.0 ☑
  autonomic 300.11
  brain or cerebral (*see also* Disease, cerebrovascular, acute) 436
  convulsive (*see also* Convulsions) 780.39
  cortical (focal) (motor) (*see also* Epilepsy) 345.5 ☑
  epilepsy, epileptic (cryptogenic) (*see also* Epilepsy) 345.9 ☑
  epileptiform, epileptoid 780.39
    focal (*see also* Epilepsy) 345.5 ☑
  febrile ▶(simple)◀ 780.31
    with status epilepticus 345.3
    atypical 780.32 •
    complex 780.32 •
    complicated 780.32 •
  heart — *see* Disease, heart
  hysterical 300.11
  Jacksonian (focal) (*see also* Epilepsy) 345.5 ☑
    motor type 345.5 ☑
    sensory type 345.5 ☑
  newborn 779.0
  paralysis (*see also* Disease, cerebrovascular, acute) 436
  recurrent 345.9 ☑ ▲
    epileptic — *see* Epilepsy
  repetitive 780.39
    epileptic — *see* Epilepsy
  salaam (*see also* Epilepsy) 345.6 ☑
  uncinate (*see also* Epilepsy) 345.4 ☑
Self-mutilation 300.9
Semicoma 780.09
Semiconsciousness 780.09
Seminal
  vesicle — *see* condition
  vesiculitis (*see also* Vesiculitis) 608.0
Seminoma (M9061/3)
  anaplastic type (M9062/3)
    specified site — *see* Neoplasm, by site, malignant
    unspecified site 186.9
  specified site — *see* Neoplasm, by site, malignant
  spermatocytic (M9063/3)
    specified site — *see* Neoplasm, by site, malignant
    unspecified site 186.9
  unspecified site 186.9
Semliki Forest encephalitis 062.8
Senear-Usher disease or syndrome (pemphigus erythematosus) 694.4
Senecio jacobae dermatitis 692.6
Senectus 797
Senescence 797
Senile — *see also* condition 797
  cervix (atrophic) 622.8
  degenerative atrophy, skin 701.3
  endometrium (atrophic) 621.8
  fallopian tube (atrophic) 620.3
  heart (failure) 797
  lung 492.8
  ovary (atrophic) 620.3
  syndrome 259.8
  vagina, vaginitis (atrophic) 627.3
  wart 702.0
Senility 797

☑ Additional Digit Required — Refer to the Tabular List for Digit Selection   ▽ Subterms under main terms may continue to next column or page

258 — Volume 2 · October 2006   ▶◀ Revised Text   ● New Line   ▲ Revised Code   2007 ICD-9-CM

Senility — *continued*
with
 acute confusional state 290.3
 delirium 290.3
 mental changes 290.9
 psychosis NEC (*see also* Psychosis, senile) 290.20
 premature (syndrome) 259.8
Sensation
 burning (*see also* Disturbance, sensation) 782.0
  tongue 529.6
 choking 784.99 ▲
 loss of (*see also* Disturbance, sensation) 782.0
 prickling (*see also* Disturbance, sensation) 782.0
 tingling (*see also* Disturbance, sensation) 782.0
Sense loss (touch) — *see also* Disturbance, sensation 782.0
 smell 781.1
 taste 781.1
Sensibility disturbance NEC (cortical) (deep) (vibratory) — *see also* Disturbance, sensation 782.0
Sensitive dentine 521.89 ▲
Sensitiver Beziehungswahn 297.8
Sensitivity, sensitization — *see also* Allergy
 autoerythrocyte 287.2
 carotid sinus 337.0
 child (excessive) 313.21
 cold, autoimmune 283.0
 methemoglobin 289.7
 suxamethonium 289.89
 tuberculin, without clinical or radiological symptoms 795.5
Sensory
 extinction 781.8
 neglect 781.8
Separation
 acromioclavicular — *see* Dislocation, acromioclavicular
 anxiety, abnormal 309.21
 apophysis, traumatic — *see* Fracture, by site
 choroid 363.70
  hemorrhagic 363.72
  serous 363.71
 costochondral (simple) (traumatic) — *see* Dislocation, costochondral
 delayed
  umbilical cord 779.83
 epiphysis, epiphyseal
  nontraumatic 732.9
   upper femoral 732.2
  traumatic — *see* Fracture, by site
 fracture — *see* Fracture, by site
 infundibulum cardiac from right ventricle by a partition 746.83
 joint (current) (traumatic) — *see* Dislocation, by site
 placenta (normally implanted) — *see* Placenta, separation
 pubic bone, obstetrical trauma 665.6 ☑
 retina, retinal (*see also* Detachment, retina) 361.9
  layers 362.40
   sensory (*see also* Retinoschisis) 361.10
   pigment epithelium (exudative) 362.42
    hemorrhagic 362.43
 sternoclavicular (traumatic) — *see* Dislocation, sternoclavicular
 symphysis pubis, obstetrical trauma 665.6 ☑
 tracheal ring, incomplete (congenital) 748.3
Sepsis (generalized) 995.91
 with
  abortion — *see* Abortion, by type, with sepsis
  acute organ dysfunction 995.92 ●

Sepsis — *continued*
 with — *continued*
  ectopic pregnancy (*see also* categories 633.0–633.9) 639.0
  molar pregnancy (*see also* categories 630–632) 639.0
  multiple organ dysfunction (MOD) ● 995.92 ●
 buccal 528.3
 complicating labor 659.3 ☑
 dental (pulpal origin) 522.4
 female genital organ NEC 614.9
 fetus (intrauterine) 771.81
 following
  abortion 639.0
  ectopic or molar pregnancy 639.0
  infusion, perfusion, or transfusion 999.3
 Friedländer's 038.49
 intraocular 360.00
 localized
  in operation wound 998.59
  skin (*see also* Abscess) 682.9
 malleus 024
 nadir 038.9
 newborn (organism unspecified) NEC 771.81
 oral 528.3
 puerperal, postpartum, childbirth (pelvic) 670.0 ☑
 resulting from infusion, injection, transfusion, or vaccination 999.3
 severe 995.92
 skin, localized (*see also* Abscess) 682.9
 umbilical (newborn) (organism unspecified) 771.89
  tetanus 771.3
 urinary 599.0
  meaning sepsis 995.91
  meaning urinary tract infection 599.0
Septate — *see also* Septum
Septic — *see also* condition
 adenoids 474.01
  and tonsils 474.02
 arm (with lymphangitis) 682.3
 embolus — *see* Embolism
 finger (with lymphangitis) 681.00
 foot (with lymphangitis) 682.7
 gallbladder (*see also* Cholecystitis) 575.8
 hand (with lymphangitis) 682.4
 joint (*see also* Arthritis, septic) 711.0 ☑
 kidney (*see also* Infection, kidney) 590.9
 leg (with lymphangitis) 682.6
 mouth 528.3
 nail 681.9
  finger 681.02
  toe 681.11
 shock (endotoxic) 785.52
 sore (*see also* Abscess) 682.9
  throat 034.0
   milk-borne 034.0
   streptococcal 034.0
 spleen (acute) 289.59
 teeth (pulpal origin) 522.4
 throat 034.0
 thrombus — *see* Thrombosis
 toe (with lymphangitis) 681.10
 tonsils 474.00
  and adenoids 474.02
 umbilical cord (newborn) (organism unspecified) 771.89
 uterus (*see also* Endometritis) 615.9
Septicemia, septicemic (generalized) (suppurative) 038.9
 with
  abortion — *see* Abortion, by type, with sepsis
  ectopic pregnancy (*see also* categories 633.0–633.9) 639.0

Septicemia, septicemic — *continued*
 with — *continued*
  molar pregnancy (*see also* categories 630–632) 639.0
 Aerobacter aerogenes 038.49
 anaerobic 038.3
 anthrax 022.3
 Bacillus coli 038.42
 Bacteroides 038.3
 Clostridium 038.3
 complicating labor 659.3 ☑
 cryptogenic 038.9
 enteric gram-negative bacilli 038.40
 Enterobacter aerogenes 038.49
 Erysipelothrix (insidiosa) (rhusiopathiae) 027.1
 Escherichia coli 038.42
 following
  abortion 639.0
  ectopic or molar pregnancy 639.0
  infusion, injection, transfusion, or vaccination 999.3
 Friedländer's (bacillus) 038.49
 gangrenous 038.9
 gonococcal 098.89
 gram-negative (organism) 038.40
  anaerobic 038.3
 Hemophilus influenzae 038.41
 herpes (simplex) 054.5
 herpetic 054.5
 Listeria monocytogenes 027.0
 meningeal — *see* Meningitis
 meningococcal (chronic) (fulminating) 036.2
 navel, newborn (organism unspecified) 771.89
 newborn (organism unspecified) 771.81
 plague 020.2
 pneumococcal 038.2
 postabortal 639.0
 postoperative 998.59
 Proteus vulgaris 038.49
 Pseudomonas (aeruginosa) 038.43
 puerperal, postpartum 670.0 ☑
 Salmonella (aertrycke) (callinarum) (choleraesuis) (enteritidis) (suipestifer) 003.1
 Serratia 038.44
 Shigella (*see also* Dysentery, bacillary) 004.9
 specified organism NEC 038.8
 staphylococcal 038.10
  aureus 038.11
  specified organism NEC 038.19
 streptococcal (anaerobic) 038.0
 Streptococcus pneumoniae 038.2
 suipestifer 003.1
 umbilicus, newborn (organism unspecified) 771.89
 viral 079.99
 Yersinia enterocolitica 038.49
Septum, septate (congenital) — *see also* Anomaly, specified type NEC
 anal 751.2
 aqueduct of Sylvius 742.3
  with spina bifida (*see also* Spina bifida) 741.0 ☑
 hymen 752.49
 uterus (*see also* Double, uterus) 752.2
 vagina 752.49
  in pregnancy or childbirth 654.7 ☑
   affecting fetus or newborn 763.89
   causing obstructed labor 660.2 ☑
    affecting fetus or newborn 763.1
Sequestration
 lung (congenital) (extralobar) (intralobar) 748.5
 orbit 376.10
 pulmonary artery (congenital) 747.3
 splenic 289.52
Sequestrum
 bone (*see also* Osteomyelitis) 730.1 ☑

Sequestrum — *continued*
 bone (*see also* Osteomyelitis) — *continued*
  jaw 526.4
   dental 525.8
  jaw bone 526.4
  sinus (accessory) (nasal) (*see also* Sinusitis) 473.9
   maxillary 473.0
Sequoiosis asthma 495.8
Serology for syphilis
 doubtful
  with signs or symptoms — *see* Syphilis, by site and stage
  follow-up of latent syphilis — *see* Syphilis, latent
 false positive 795.6
 negative, with signs or symptoms — *see* Syphilis, by site and stage
 positive 097.1
  with signs or symptoms — *see* Syphilis, by site and stage
  false 795.6
  follow-up of latent syphilis — *see* Syphilis, latent
  only finding — *see* Syphilis, latent
 reactivated 097.1
Seroma (postoperative) (non-infected) 998.13
 infected 998.51
Seropurulent — *see* condition
Serositis, multiple 569.89
 pericardial 423.2
 peritoneal 568.82
 pleural — *see* Pleurisy
Serotonin syndrome 333.99
Serous — *see* condition
Sertoli cell
 adenoma (M8640/0)
  specified site — *see* Neoplasm, by site, benign
  unspecified site
   female 220
   male 222.0
 carcinoma (M8640/3)
  specified site — *see* Neoplasm, by site, malignant
  unspecified site 186.9
 syndrome (germinal aplasia) 606.0
 tumor (M8640/0)
  with lipid storage (M8641/0)
   specified site — *see* Neoplasm, by site, benign
   unspecified site
    female 220
    male 222.0
  specified site — *see* Neoplasm, by site, benign
  unspecified site
   female 220
   male 222.0
Sertoli-Leydig cell tumor (M8631/0)
 specified site — *see* Neoplasm, by site, benign
 unspecified site
  female 220
  male 222.0
Serum
 allergy, allergic reaction 999.5
  shock 999.4
 arthritis 999.5 [713.6]
 complication or reaction NEC 999.5
 disease NEC 999.5
 hepatitis 070.3 ☑
 intoxication 999.5
 jaundice (homologous) — *see* Hepatitis, viral, type B
 neuritis 999.5
 poisoning NEC 999.5
 rash NEC 999.5
 reaction NEC 999.5
 sickness NEC 999.5
Sesamoiditis 733.99
Seven-day fever 061
 of
  Japan 100.89

☑ Additional Digit Required — Refer to the Tabular List for Digit Selection   ▽ Subterms under main terms may continue to next column or page

2007 ICD-9-CM ▶◀ Revised Text ● New Line ▲ Revised Code **October 2006 · Volume 2 — 259**

Seven-day fever — *continued*
  of — *continued*
    Queensland 100.89
Sever's disease or osteochondrosis
  (calcaneum) 732.5
Sex chromosome mosaics 758.81
Sextuplet
  affected by maternal complications of
    pregnancy 761.5
  healthy liveborn — *see* Newborn,
    multiple
  pregnancy (complicating delivery) NEC
    651.8 ☑
    with fetal loss and retention of one
      or more fetus(es) 651.6 ☑
    following (elective) fetal reduction
      651.7 ☑
Sexual
  anesthesia 302.72
  deviation (*see also* Deviation, sexual)
    302.9
  disorder (*see also* Deviation, sexual)
    302.9
  frigidity (female) 302.72
  function, disorder of (psychogenic)
    302.70
    specified type NEC 302.79
  immaturity (female) (male) 259.0
  impotence 607.84
    organic origin NEC 607.84
    psychogenic 302.72
  precocity (constitutional) (cryptogenic)
    (female) (idiopathic) (male) NEC
    259.1
    with adrenal hyperplasia 255.2
  sadism 302.84
Sexuality, pathological — *see also* Deviation, sexual 302.9
Sézary's disease, reticulosis, or syndrome (M9701/3) 202.2 ☑
Shadow, lung 793.1
Shaken infant syndrome 995.55
Shaking
  head (tremor) 781.0
  palsy or paralysis (*see also* Parkinsonism) 332.0
Shallowness, acetabulum 736.39
Shaver's disease or syndrome (bauxite pneumoconiosis) 503
Shearing
  artificial skin graft 996.55
  decellularized allodermis graft 996.55
Sheath (tendon) — *see* condition
Shedding
  nail 703.8
  teeth, premature, primary (deciduous)
    520.6
Sheehan's disease or syndrome (postpartum pituitary necrosis) 253.2
Shelf, rectal 569.49
Shell
  shock (current) (*see also* Reaction,
    stress, acute) 308.9
    lasting state 300.16
  teeth 520.5
Shield kidney 753.3
Shifting
  pacemaker 427.89
  sleep-work schedule (affecting sleep)
    327.36
Shift, mediastinal 793.2
Shiga's
  bacillus 004.0
  dysentery 004.0
Shigella (dysentery) — *see also* Dysentery, bacillary 004.9
  carrier (suspected) of V02.3
Shigellosis — *see also* Dysentery, bacillary 004.9
Shingles — *see also* Herpes, zoster 053.9
  eye NEC 053.29
Shin splints 844.9
Shipyard eye or disease 077.1
Shirodkar suture, in pregnancy
  654.5 ☑
Shock 785.50

Shock — *continued*
  with
    abortion — *see* Abortion, by type,
      with shock
    ectopic pregnancy (*see also* categories 633.0–633.9) 639.5
    molar pregnancy (*see also* categories 630–632) 639.5
  allergic — *see* Shock, anaphylactic
  anaclitic 309.21
  anaphylactic 995.0
    chemical — *see* Table of Drugs and Chemicals
    correct medicinal substance properly administered 995.0
    drug or medicinal substance
      correct substance properly administered 995.0
      overdose or wrong substance given or taken 977.9
      specified drug — *see* Table of Drugs and Chemicals
    following sting(s) 989.5
    food — *see* Anaphylactic shock, due to, food
    immunization 999.4
    serum 999.4
  anaphylactoid — *see* Shock, anaphylactic
  anesthetic
    correct substance properly administered 995.4
    overdose or wrong substance given 968.4
    specified anesthetic — *see* Table of Drugs and Chemicals
  birth, fetus or newborn NEC 779.89
  cardiogenic 785.51
  chemical substance — *see* Table of Drugs and Chemicals
  circulatory 785.59
  complicating
    abortion — *see* Abortion, by type, with shock
    ectopic pregnancy (*see also* categories 633.0–633.9) 639.5
    labor and delivery 669.1 ☑
    molar pregnancy (*see also* categories 630–632) 639.5
  culture 309.29
  due to
    drug 995.0
      correct substance properly administered 995.0
      overdose or wrong substance given or taken 977.9
      specified drug — *see* Table of Drugs and Chemicals
    food — *see* Anaphylactic shock, due to, food
  during labor and delivery 669.1 ☑
  electric 994.8
  endotoxic 785.52
    due to surgical procedure 998.0
  following
    abortion 639.5
    ectopic or molar pregnancy 639.5
    injury (immediate) (delayed) 958.4
    labor and delivery 669.1 ☑
  gram-negative 785.52
  hematogenic 785.59
  hemorrhagic
    due to
      disease 785.59
      surgery (intraoperative) (postoperative) 998.0
      trauma 958.4
  hypovolemic NEC 785.59
    surgical 998.0
    traumatic 958.4
  insulin 251.0
    therapeutic misadventure 962.3
  kidney 584.5

Shock — *continued*
  kidney — *continued*
    traumatic (following crushing)
      958.5
  lightning 994.0
  lung 518.5
  nervous (*see also* Reaction, stress, acute) 308.9
  obstetric 669.1 ☑
    with
      abortion — *see* Abortion, by type, with shock
      ectopic pregnancy (*see also* categories 633.0–633.9) 639.5
      molar pregnancy (*see also* categories 630–632) 639.5
    following
      abortion 639.5
      ectopic or molar pregnancy 639.5
  paralysis, paralytic (*see also* Disease, cerebrovascular, acute) 436
    late effect — *see* Late effect(s) (of) cerebrovascular disease
  pleural (surgical) 998.0
    due to trauma 958.4
  postoperative 998.0
    with
      abortion — *see* Abortion, by type, with shock
      ectopic pregnancy (*see also* categories 633.0–633.9) 639.5
      molar pregnancy (*see also* categories 630–632) 639.5
    following
      abortion 639.5
      ectopic or molar pregnancy 639.5
  psychic (*see also* Reaction, stress, acute) 308.9
    past history (of) V15.49
  psychogenic (*see also* Reaction, stress, acute) 308.9
  septic 785.52
    with
      abortion — *see* Abortion, by type, with shock
      ectopic pregnancy (*see also* categories 633.0–633.9) 639.5
      molar pregnancy (*see also* categories 630–632) 639.5
    due to
      surgical procedure 998.0
      transfusion NEC 999.8
        bone marrow 996.85
    following
      abortion 639.5
      ectopic or molar pregnancy 639.5
      surgical procedure 998.0
      transfusion NEC 999.8
        bone marrow 996.85
  spinal (*see also* Injury, spinal, by site)
    with spinal bone injury — *see* Fracture, vertebra, by site, with spinal cord injury
  surgical 998.0
  therapeutic misadventure NEC (*see also* Complications) 998.89
  thyroxin 962.7
  toxic 040.82
  transfusion — *see* Complications, transfusion
  traumatic (immediate) (delayed) 958.4
Shoemakers' chest 738.3
Short, shortening, shortness
  Achilles tendon (acquired) 727.81
  arm 736.89
    congenital 755.20
  back 737.9
  bowel syndrome 579.3
  breath 786.05

Short, shortening, shortness — *continued*
  chain acyl CoA dehydrogenase deficiency (SCAD) 277.85
  common bile duct, congenital 751.69
  cord (umbilical) 663.4 ☑
    affecting fetus or newborn 762.6
  cystic duct, congenital 751.69
  esophagus (congenital) 750.4
  femur (acquired) 736.81
    congenital 755.34
  frenulum linguae 750.0
  frenum, lingual 750.0
  hamstrings 727.81
  hip (acquired) 736.39
    congenital 755.63
  leg (acquired) 736.81
    congenital 755.30
  metatarsus (congenital) 754.79
    acquired 736.79
  organ or site, congenital NEC — *see* Distortion
  palate (congenital) 750.26
  P-R interval syndrome 426.81
  radius (acquired) 736.09
    congenital 755.26
  round ligament 629.89   ▲
  sleeper 307.49
  stature, constitutional (hereditary) 783.43
  tendon 727.81
    Achilles (acquired) 727.81
      congenital 754.79
    congenital 756.89
  thigh (acquired) 736.81
    congenital 755.34
  tibialis anticus 727.81
  umbilical cord 663.4 ☑
    affecting fetus or newborn 762.6
  urethra 599.84
  uvula (congenital) 750.26
  vagina 623.8
Shortsightedness 367.1
Shoshin (acute fulminating beriberi) 265.0
Shoulder — *see* condition
Shovel-shaped incisors 520.2
Shower, thromboembolic — *see* Embolism
Shunt (status)
  aortocoronary bypass V45.81
  arterial-venous (dialysis) V45.1
  arteriovenous, pulmonary (acquired) 417.0
    congenital 747.3
    traumatic (complication) 901.40
  cerebral ventricle (communicating) in situ V45.2
  coronary artery bypass V45.81
  surgical, prosthetic, with complications — *see* Complications, shunt
  vascular NEC V45.89
Shutdown
  renal 586
    with
      abortion — *see* Abortion, by type, with renal failure
      ectopic pregnancy (*see also* categories 633.0–633.9) 639.3
      molar pregnancy (*see also* categories 630–632) 639.3
    complicating
      abortion 639.3
      ectopic or molar pregnancy 639.3
    following labor and delivery 669.3 ☑
Shwachman's syndrome 288.02   ▲
Shy-Drager syndrome (orthostatic hypotension with multisystem degeneration) 333.0
Sialadenitis (any gland) (chronic) (suppurative) 527.2
  epidemic — *see* Mumps

☑ Additional Digit Required — Refer to the Tabular List for Digit Selection   ▽ Subterms under main terms may continue to next column or page

260 — Volume 2 · October 2006   ▶◀ Revised Text   ● New Line   ▲ Revised Code   **2007 ICD-9-CM**

Small, smallness — *continued*
for dates
fetus or newborn 764.0 ✓
with malnutrition 764.1 ✓
affecting management of pregnancy 656.5 ✓
infant, term 764.0 ✓
with malnutrition 764.1 ✓
affecting management of pregnancy 656.5 ✓
introitus, vagina 623.3
kidney, unknown cause 589.9
bilateral 589.1
unilateral 589.0
ovary 620.8
pelvis
with disproportion (fetopelvic) 653.1 ✓
affecting fetus or newborn 763.1
causing obstructed labor 660.1 ✓
affecting fetus or newborn 763.1
placenta — *see* Placenta, insufficiency
uterus 621.8
white kidney 582.9
Smith's fracture (separation) (closed) 813.41
open 813.51
Smith-Lemli Opitz syndrome (cerebrohepatorenal syndrome) 759.89
Smith-Magenis syndrome 758.33
Smith-Strang disease (oasthouse urine) 270.2
Smokers'
bronchitis 491.0
cough 491.0
syndrome (*see also* Abuse, drugs, nondependent) 305.1
throat 472.1
tongue 528.6
Smoking complicating pregnancy, childbirth, or the puerperium 649.0 ●
Smothering spells 786.09
Snaggle teeth, tooth 524.39
Snapping
finger 727.05
hip 719.65
jaw 524.69
temporomandibular joint sounds on opening or closing 524.64
knee 717.9
thumb 727.05
Sneddon-Wilkinson disease or syndrome (subcorneal pustular dermatosis) 694.1
Sneezing 784.99 ▲
intractable 478.19 ▲
Sniffing
cocaine (*see also* Dependence) 304.2 ✓
ether (*see also* Dependence) 304.6 ✓
glue (airplane) (*see also* Dependence) 304.6 ✓
Snoring 786.09
Snow blindness 370.24
Snuffles (nonsyphilitic) 460
syphilitic (infant) 090.0
Social migrant V60.0
Sodoku 026.0
Soemmering's ring 366.51
Soft — *see also* condition
enlarged prostate 600.00
with
other lower urinary tract symptoms (LUTS) 600.01 ●
urinary
obstruction 600.01 ●
retention 600.01 ●
nails 703.8
Softening
bone 268.2
brain (necrotic) (progressive) 434.9 ✓
arteriosclerotic 437.0
congenital 742.4

Softening — *continued*
brain — *continued*
embolic (*see also* Embolism, brain) 434.1 ✓
hemorrhagic (*see also* Hemorrhage, brain) 431
occlusive 434.9 ✓
thrombotic (*see also* Thrombosis, brain) 434.0 ✓
cartilage 733.92
cerebellar — *see* Softening, brain
cerebral — *see* Softening, brain
cerebrospinal — *see* Softening, brain
myocardial, heart (*see also* Degeneration, myocardial) 429.1
nails 703.8
spinal cord 336.8
stomach 537.89
Solar fever 061
Soldier's
heart 306.2
patches 423.1
Solitary
cyst
bone 733.21
kidney 593.2
kidney (congenital) 753.0
tubercle, brain (*see also* Tuberculosis, brain) 013.2 ✓
ulcer, bladder 596.8
Somatization reaction, somatic reaction — *see also* Disorder, psychosomatic 306.9
disorder 300.81
Somatoform disorder 300.82
atypical 300.82
severe 300.81
undifferentiated 300.82
Somnambulism 307.46
hysterical 300.13
Somnolence 780.09
nonorganic origin 307.43
periodic 349.89
Sonne dysentery 004.3
Soor 112.0
Sore
Delhi 085.1
desert (*see also* Ulcer, skin) 707.9
eye 379.99
Lahore 085.1
mouth 528.9
canker 528.2
due to dentures 528.9
muscle 729.1
Naga (*see also* Ulcer, skin) 707.9
oriental 085.1
pressure (*see also* Decubitus) 707.00
with gangrene (*see also* Decubitus) 707.00 [785.4]
skin NEC 709.9
soft 099.0
throat 462
with influenza, flu, or grippe 487.1
acute 462
chronic 472.1
clergyman's 784.49
coxsackie (virus) 074.0
diphtheritic 032.0
epidemic 034.0
gangrenous 462
herpetic 054.79
influenzal 487.1
malignant 462
purulent 462
putrid 462
septic 034.0
streptococcal (ulcerative) 034.0
ulcerated 462
viral NEC 462
Coxsackie 074.0
tropical (*see also* Ulcer, skin) 707.9
veldt (*see also* Ulcer, skin) 707.9
Sotos' syndrome (cerebral gigantism) 253.0
Sounds
friction, pleural 786.7

Sounds — *continued*
succussion, chest 786.7
temporomandibular joint on opening or closing 524.64
South African cardiomyopathy syndrome 425.2
South American
blastomycosis 116.1
trypanosomiasis — *see* Trypanosomiasis
Southeast Asian hemorrhagic fever 065.4
Spacing, teeth, abnormal 524.30
excessive 524.32
Spade-like hand (congenital) 754.89
Spading nail 703.8
congenital 757.5
Spanemia 285.9
Spanish collar 605
Sparganosis 123.5
Spasmodic — *see* condition
Spasmophilia — *see also* Tetany 781.7
Spasm, spastic, spasticity — *see also* condition 781.0
accommodation 367.53
ampulla of Vater (*see also* Disease, gallbladder) 576.8
anus, ani (sphincter) (reflex) 564.6
psychogenic 306.4
artery NEC 443.9
basilar 435.0
carotid 435.8
cerebral 435.9
specified artery NEC 435.8
retinal (*see also* Occlusion, retinal, artery) 362.30
vertebral 435.1
vertebrobasilar 435.3
Bell's 351.0
bladder (sphincter, external or internal) 596.8
bowel 564.9
psychogenic 306.4
bronchus, bronchiole 519.11 ▲
cardia 530.0
cardiac — *see* Angina
carpopedal (*see also* Tetany) 781.7
cecum 564.9
psychogenic 306.4
cerebral (arteries) (vascular) 435.9
specified artery NEC 435.8
cerebrovascular 435.9
cervix, complicating delivery 661.4 ✓
affecting fetus or newborn 763.7
ciliary body (of accommodation) 367.53
colon 564.1
psychogenic 306.4
common duct (*see also* Disease, biliary) 576.8
compulsive 307.22
conjugate 378.82
convergence 378.84
coronary (artery) — *see* Angina
diaphragm (reflex) 786.8
psychogenic 306.1
duodenum, duodenal (bulb) 564.89
esophagus (diffuse) 530.5
psychogenic 306.4
facial 351.8
fallopian tube 620.8
gait 781.2
gastrointestinal (tract) 536.8
psychogenic 306.4
glottis 478.75
hysterical 300.11
psychogenic 306.1
specified as conversion reaction 300.11
reflex through recurrent laryngeal nerve 478.75
habit 307.20
chronic 307.22
transient (of childhood) 307.21
heart — *see* Angina

Spasm, spastic, spasticity — *see also* condition — *continued*
hourglass — *see* Contraction, hourglass
hysterical 300.11
infantile (*see also* Epilepsy) 345.6 ✓
internal oblique, eye 378.51
intestinal 564.9
psychogenic 306.4
larynx, laryngeal 478.75
hysterical 300.11
psychogenic 306.1
specified as conversion reaction 300.11
levator palpebrae superioris 333.81
lightning (*see also* Epilepsy) 345.6 ✓
mobile 781.0
muscle 728.85
back 724.8
psychogenic 306.0
nerve, trigeminal 350.1
nervous 306.0
nodding 307.3
infantile (*see also* Epilepsy) 345.6 ✓
occupational 300.89
oculogyric 378.87
ophthalmic artery 362.30
orbicularis 781.0
perineal 625.8
peroneo-extensor (*see also* Flat, foot) 734
pharynx (reflex) 478.29
hysterical 300.11
psychogenic 306.1
specified as conversion reaction 300.11
pregnant uterus, complicating delivery 661.4 ✓
psychogenic 306.0
pylorus 537.81
adult hypertrophic 537.0
congenital or infantile 750.5
psychogenic 306.4
rectum (sphincter) 564.6
psychogenic 306.4
retinal artery NEC (*see also* Occlusion, retina, artery) 362.30
sacroiliac 724.6
salaam (infantile) (*see also* Epilepsy) 345.6 ✓
saltatory 781.0
sigmoid 564.9
psychogenic 306.4
sphincter of Oddi (*see also* Disease, gallbladder) 576.5
stomach 536.8
neurotic 306.4
throat 478.29
hysterical 300.11
psychogenic 306.1
specified as conversion reaction 300.11
tic 307.20
chronic 307.22
transient (of childhood) 307.21
tongue 529.8
torsion 333.6
trigeminal nerve 350.1
postherpetic 053.12
ureter 593.89
urethra (sphincter) 599.84
uterus 625.8
complicating labor 661.4 ✓
affecting fetus or newborn 763.7
vagina 625.1
psychogenic 306.51
vascular NEC 443.9
vasomotor NEC 443.9
vein NEC 459.89
vesical (sphincter, external or internal) 596.8
viscera 789.0 ✓
Spasmus nutans 307.3
Spastic — *see also* Spasm
child 343.9

✓ Additional Digit Required — Refer to the Tabular List for Digit Selection   ▽ Subterms under main terms may continue to next column or page

Spasticity — see also Spasm
  cerebral, child 343.9
Speakers' throat 784.49
Specific, specified — see condition
Speech
  defect, disorder, disturbance, impediment NEC 784.5
    psychogenic 307.9
  therapy V57.3
Spells 780.39
  breath-holding 786.9
Spencer's disease (epidemic vomiting) 078.82
Spens' syndrome (syncope with heart block) 426.9
Spermatic cord — see condition
Spermatocele 608.1
  congenital 752.89
Spermatocystitis 608.4
Spermatocytoma (M9063/3)
  specified site — see Neoplasm, by site, malignant
  unspecified site 186.9
Spermatorrhea 608.89
Sperm counts
  fertility testing V26.21
  following sterilization reversal V26.22
  postvasectomy V25.8
Sphacelus — see also Gangrene 785.4
Sphenoidal — see condition
Sphenoiditis (chronic) — see also Sinusitis, sphenoidal 473.3
Sphenopalatine ganglion neuralgia 337.0
Sphericity, increased, lens 743.36
Spherocytosis (congenital) (familial) (hereditary) 282.0
  hemoglobin disease 282.7
  sickle-cell (disease) 282.60
Spherophakia 743.36
Sphincter — see condition
Sphincteritis, sphincter of Oddi — see also Cholecystitis 576.8
Sphingolipidosis 272.7
Sphingolipodystrophy 272.7
Sphingomyelinosis 272.7
Spicule tooth 520.2
Spider
  finger 755.59
  nevus 448.1
  vascular 448.1
Spiegler-Fendt sarcoid 686.8
Spielmeyer-Stock disease 330.1
Spielmeyer-Vogt disease 330.1
Spina bifida (aperta) 741.9 ☑

> Note — Use the following fifth-digit subclassification with category 741:
>
> 0   unspecified region
> 1   cervical region
> 2   dorsal [thoracic} region
> 3   lumbar region

  with hydrocephalus 741.0 ☑
    fetal (suspected), affecting management of pregnancy 655.0 ☑
  occulta 756.17
Spindle, Krukenberg's 371.13
Spine, spinal — see condition
Spiradenoma (eccrine) (M8403/0) — see Neoplasm, skin, benign
Spirillosis NEC — see also Fever, relapsing 087.9
Spirillum minus 026.0
Spirillum obermeieri infection 087.0
Spirochetal — see condition
Spirochetosis 104.9
  arthritic, arthritica 104.9 *[711.8]* ☑
  bronchopulmonary 104.8
  icterohemorrhagica 100.0
  lung 104.8
Spitting blood — see also Hemoptysis 786.3
Splanchnomegaly 569.89
Splanchnoptosis 569.89
Spleen, splenic — see also condition

Spleen, splenic — see also condition — continued
  agenesis 759.0
  flexure syndrome 569.89
  neutropenia syndrome 289.53 ▲
  sequestration syndrome 289.52
Splenectasis — see also Splenomegaly 789.2
Splenitis (interstitial) (malignant) (nonspecific) 289.59
  malarial (see also Malaria) 084.6
  tuberculous (see also Tuberculosis) 017.7 ☑
Splenocele 289.59
Splenomegalia — see Splenomegaly
Splenomegalic — see condition
Splenomegaly 789.2
  Bengal 789.2
  cirrhotic 289.51
  congenital 759.0
  congestive, chronic 289.51
  cryptogenic 789.2
  Egyptian 120.1
  Gaucher's (cerebroside lipidosis) 272.7
  idiopathic 789.2
  malarial (see also Malaria) 084.6
  neutropenic 289.53 ▲
  Niemann-Pick (lipid histiocytosis) 272.7
  siderotic 289.51
  syphilitic 095.8
    congenital 090.0
  tropical (Bengal) (idiopathic) 789.2
Splenopathy 289.50
Splenopneumonia — see Pneumonia
Splenoptosis 289.59
Splinter — see Injury, superficial, by site
Split, splitting
  heart sounds 427.89
  lip, congenital (see also Cleft, lip) 749.10
  nails 703.8
  urinary stream 788.61
Spoiled child reaction — see also Disturbance, conduct 312.1 ☑
Spondylarthritis — see also Spondylosis 721.90
Spondylarthrosis — see also Spondylosis 721.90
Spondylitis 720.9
  ankylopoietica 720.0
  ankylosing (chronic) 720.0
  atrophic 720.9
    ligamentosa 720.9
  chronic (traumatic) (see also Spondylosis) 721.90
  deformans (chronic) (see also Spondylosis) 721.90
  gonococcal 098.53
  gouty 274.0
  hypertrophic (see also Spondylosis) 721.90
  infectious NEC 720.9
  juvenile (adolescent) 720.0
  Kümmell's 721.7
  Marie-Strümpell (ankylosing) 720.0
  muscularis 720.9
  ossificans ligamentosa 721.6
  osteoarthritica (see also Spondylosis) 721.90
  posttraumatic 721.7
  proliferative 720.0
  rheumatoid 720.0
  rhizomelica 720.0
  sacroiliac NEC 720.2
  senescent (see also Spondylosis) 721.90
  senile (see also Spondylosis) 721.90
  static (see also Spondylosis) 721.90
  traumatic (chronic) (see also Spondylosis) 721.90
  tuberculous (see also Tuberculosis) 015.0 ☑ *[720.81]*
  typhosa 002.0 *[720.81]*
Spondyloarthrosis — see also Spondylosis 721.90

Spondylolisthesis (congenital) (lumbosacral) 756.12
  with disproportion (fetopelvic) 653.3 ☑
    affecting fetus or newborn 763.1
    causing obstructed labor 660.1 ☑
      affecting fetus or newborn 763.1
  acquired 738.4
    degenerative 738.4
    traumatic 738.4
      acute (lumbar) — see Fracture, vertebra, lumbar
      site other than lumbosacral — see Fracture, vertebra, by site
Spondylolysis (congenital) 756.11
  acquired 738.4
  cervical 756.19
  lumbosacral region 756.11
    with disproportion (fetopelvic) 653.3 ☑
      affecting fetus or newborn 763.1
      causing obstructed labor 660.1 ☑
        affecting fetus or newborn 763.1
Spondylopathy
  inflammatory 720.9
    specified type NEC 720.89
  traumatic 721.7
Spondylose rhizomelique 720.0
Spondylosis 721.90
  with
    disproportion 653.3 ☑
      affecting fetus or newborn 763.1
      causing obstructed labor 660.1 ☑
        affecting fetus or newborn 763.1
    myelopathy NEC 721.91
  cervical, cervicodorsal 721.0
    with myelopathy 721.1
  inflammatory 720.9
  lumbar, lumbosacral 721.3
    with myelopathy 721.42
  sacral 721.3
    with myelopathy 721.42
  thoracic 721.2
    with myelopathy 721.41
  traumatic 721.7
Sponge
  divers' disease 989.5
  inadvertently left in operation wound 998.4
  kidney (medullary) 753.17
Spongioblastoma (M9422/3)
  multiforme (M9440/3)
    specified site — see Neoplasm, by site, malignant
    unspecified site 191.9
  polare (M9423/3)
    specified site — see Neoplasm, by site, malignant
    unspecified site 191.9
  primitive polar (M9443/3)
    specified site — see Neoplasm, by site, malignant
    unspecified site 191.9
  specified site — see Neoplasm, by site, malignant
  unspecified site 191.9
Spongiocytoma (M9400/3)
  specified site — see Neoplasm, by site, malignant
  unspecified site 191.9
Spongioneuroblastoma (M9504/3) — see Neoplasm, by site, malignant
Spontaneous — see also condition
  fracture — see Fracture, pathologic
Spoon nail 703.8
  congenital 757.5
Sporadic — see condition
Sporotrichosis (bones) (cutaneous) (disseminated) (epidermal) (lymphatic) (lymphocutaneous) (mucous membranes) (pulmonary) (skeletal) (visceral) 117.1

Sporotrichum schenckii infection 117.1
Spots, spotting
  atrophic (skin) 701.3
  Bitôt's (in the young child) 264.1
  café au lait 709.09
  cayenne pepper 448.1
  complicating pregnancy 649.5 ☑ ●
  cotton wool (retina) 362.83
  de Morgan's (senile angiomas) 448.1
  Fúchs' black (myopic) 360.21
  intermenstrual
    irregular 626.6
    regular 626.5
  interpalpebral 372.53
  Koplik's 055.9
  liver 709.09
  Mongolian (pigmented) 757.33
  of pregnancy 641.9 ☑
  purpuric 782.7
  ruby 448.1
Spotted fever — see Fever, spotted
Sprain, strain (joint) (ligament) (muscle) (tendon) 848.9
  abdominal wall (muscle) 848.8
  Achilles tendon 845.09
  acromioclavicular 840.0
  ankle 845.00
    and foot 845.00
  anterior longitudinal, cervical 847.0
  arm 840.9
    upper 840.9
    and shoulder 840.9
  astragalus 845.00
  atlanto-axial 847.0
  atlanto-occipital 847.0
  atlas 847.0
  axis 847.0
  back (see also Sprain, spine) 847.9
  breast bone 848.40
  broad ligament — see Injury, internal, broad ligament
  calcaneofibular 845.02
  carpal 842.01
  carpometacarpal 842.11
  cartilage
    costal, without mention of injury to sternum 848.3
      involving sternum 848.42
    ear 848.8
    knee 844.9
      with current tear (see also Tear, meniscus) 836.2
    semilunar (knee) 844.8
      with current tear (see also Tear, meniscus) 836.2
    septal, nose 848.0
    thyroid region 848.2
    xiphoid 848.49
  cervical, cervicodorsal, cervicothoracic 847.0
  chondrocostal, without mention of injury to sternum 848.3
    involving sternum 848.42
  chondrosternal 848.42
  chronic (joint) — see Derangement, joint
  clavicle 840.9
  coccyx 847.4
  collar bone 840.9
  collateral, knee (medial) (tibial) 844.1
    lateral (fibular) 844.0
    recurrent or old 717.89
      lateral 717.81
      medial 717.82
  coracoacromial 840.8
  coracoclavicular 840.1
  coracohumeral 840.2
  coracoid (process) 840.9
  coronary, knee 844.8
  costal cartilage, without mention of injury to sternum 848.3
    involving sternum 848.42
  cricoarytenoid articulation 848.2
  cricothyroid articulation 848.2

☑ Additional Digit Required — Refer to the Tabular List for Digit Selection   ▽ Subterms under main terms may continue to next column or page

2007 ICD-9-CM   ▶◀ Revised Text   ● New Line   ▲ Revised Code   **October 2006 · Volume 2 — 263**

Sprain, strain — *continued*
- cruciate
  - knee 844.2
  - old 717.89
    - anterior 717.83
    - posterior 717.84
- deltoid
  - ankle 845.01
  - shoulder 840.8
- dorsal (spine) 847.1
- ear cartilage 848.8
- elbow 841.9
  - and forearm 841.9
  - specified site NEC 841.8
- femur (proximal end) 843.9
  - distal end 844.9
- fibula (proximal end) 844.9
  - distal end 845.00
- fibulocalcaneal 845.02
- finger(s) 842.10
- foot 845.10
  - and ankle 845.00
- forearm 841.9
  - and elbow 841.9
  - specified site NEC 841.8
- glenoid (shoulder) (*see also* SLAP lesion) 840.8
- hand 842.10
- hip 843.9
  - and thigh 843.9
- humerus (proximal end) 840.9
  - distal end 841.9
- iliofemoral 843.0
- infraspinatus 840.3
- innominate
  - acetabulum 843.9
  - pubic junction 848.5
  - sacral junction 846.1
- internal
  - collateral, ankle 845.01
  - semilunar cartilage 844.8
    - with current tear (*see also* Tear, meniscus) 836.2
    - old 717.5
- interphalangeal
  - finger 842.13
  - toe 845.13
- ischiocapsular 843.1
- jaw (cartilage) (meniscus) 848.1
  - old 524.69
- knee 844.9
  - and leg 844.9
  - old 717.5
    - collateral
      - lateral 717.81
      - medial 717.82
    - cruciate
      - anterior 717.83
      - posterior 717.84
- late effect — *see* Late, effects (of), sprain
- lateral collateral, knee 844.0
  - old 717.81
- leg 844.9
  - and knee 844.9
- ligamentum teres femoris 843.8
- low back 846.9
- lumbar (spine) 847.2
- lumbosacral 846.0
  - chronic or old 724.6
- mandible 848.1
  - old 524.69
- maxilla 848.1
- medial collateral, knee 844.1
  - old 717.82
- meniscus
  - jaw 848.1
    - old 524.69
  - knee 844.8
    - with current tear (*see also* Tear, meniscus) 836.2
    - old 717.5
  - mandible 848.1
    - old 524.69
  - specified site NEC 848.8
- metacarpal 842.10

Sprain, strain — *continued*
- metacarpal — *continued*
  - distal 842.12
  - proximal 842.11
- metacarpophalangeal 842.12
- metatarsal 845.10
- metatarsophalangeal 845.12
- midcarpal 842.19
- midtarsal 845.19
- multiple sites, except fingers alone or toes alone 848.8
- neck 847.0
- nose (septal cartilage) 848.0
- occiput from atlas 847.0
- old — *see* Derangement, joint
- orbicular, hip 843.8
- patella(r) 844.8
  - old 717.89
- pelvis 848.5
- phalanx
  - finger 842.10
  - toe 845.10
- radiocarpal 842.02
- radiohumeral 841.2
- radioulnar 841.9
  - distal 842.09
- radius, radial (proximal end) 841.9
  - and ulna 841.9
    - distal 842.09
  - collateral 841.0
  - distal end 842.00
- recurrent — *see* Sprain, by site
- rib (cage), without mention of injury to sternum 848.3
  - involving sternum 848.42
- rotator cuff (capsule) 840.4
- round ligament (*see also* Injury, internal, round ligament)
  - femur 843.8
- sacral (spine) 847.3
- sacrococcygeal 847.3
- sacroiliac (region) 846.9
  - chronic or old 724.6
  - ligament 846.1
  - specified site NEC 846.8
- sacrospinatus 846.2
- sacrospinous 846.2
- sacrotuberous 846.3
- scaphoid bone, ankle 845.00
- scapula(r) 840.9
- semilunar cartilage (knee) 844.8
  - with current tear (*see also* Tear, meniscus) 836.2
  - old 717.5
- septal cartilage (nose) 848.0
- shoulder 840.9
  - and arm, upper 840.9
  - blade 840.9
- specified site NEC 848.8
- spine 847.9
  - cervical 847.0
  - coccyx 847.4
  - dorsal 847.1
  - lumbar 847.2
  - lumbosacral 846.0
    - chronic or old 724.6
  - sacral 847.3
  - sacroiliac (*see also* Sprain, sacroiliac) 846.9
    - chronic or old 724.6
  - thoracic 847.1
- sternoclavicular 848.41
- sternum 848.40
- subglenoid (*see also* SLAP lesion) 840.8
- subscapularis 840.5
- supraspinatus 840.6
- symphysis
  - jaw 848.1
    - old 524.69
  - mandibular 848.1
    - old 524.69
  - pubis 848.5
- talofibular 845.09
- tarsal 845.10
- tarsometatarsal 845.11

Sprain, strain — *continued*
- temporomandibular 848.1
  - old 524.69
- teres
  - ligamentum femoris 843.8
  - major or minor 840.8
- thigh (proximal end) 843.9
  - and hip 843.9
  - distal end 844.9
- thoracic (spine) 847.1
- thorax 848.8
- thumb 842.10
- thyroid cartilage or region 848.2
- tibia (proximal end) 844.9
  - distal end 845.00
- tibiofibular
  - distal 845.03
  - superior 844.3
- toe(s) 845.10
- trachea 848.8
- trapezoid 840.8
- ulna, ulnar (proximal end) 841.9
  - collateral 841.1
  - distal end 842.00
- ulnohumeral 841.3
- vertebrae (*see also* Sprain, spine) 847.9
  - cervical, cervicodorsal, cervicothoracic 847.0
- wrist (cuneiform) (scaphoid) (semilunar) 842.00
- xiphoid cartilage 848.49

Sprengel's deformity (congenital) 755.52
Spring fever 309.23
Sprue 579.1
- celiac 579.0
- idiopathic 579.0
- meaning thrush 112.0
- nontropical 579.0
- tropical 579.1
Spur — *see also* Exostosis
- bone 726.91
  - calcaneal 726.73
- calcaneal 726.73
- iliac crest 726.5
- nose (septum) 478.19   ▲
  - bone 726.91
- septal 478.19   ▲
Spuria placenta — *see* Placenta, abnormal
Spurway's syndrome (brittle bones and blue sclera) 756.51
Sputum, abnormal (amount) (color) (excessive) (odor) (purulent) 786.4
- bloody 786.3
Squamous — *see also* condition
- cell metaplasia
  - bladder 596.8
  - cervix — *see* condition
- epithelium in
  - cervical canal (congenital) 752.49
  - uterine mucosa (congenital) 752.3
- metaplasia
  - bladder 596.8
  - cervix — *see* condition
Squashed nose 738.0
- congenital 754.0
Squeeze, divers' 993.3
Squint — *see also* Strabismus 378.9
- accommodative (*see also* Esotropia) 378.00
- concomitant (*see also* Heterotropia) 378.30
Stab — *see also* Wound, open, by site
- internal organs — *see* Injury, internal, by site, with open wound
Staggering gait 781.2
- hysterical 300.11
Staghorn calculus 592.0
Stain, staining
- meconium 779.84
- port wine 757.32
- tooth, teeth (hard tissues) 521.7
  - due to
    - accretions 523.6

Stain, staining — *continued*
- tooth, teeth — *continued*
  - due to — *continued*
    - deposits (betel) (black) (green) (materia alba) (orange) (tobacco) 523.6
    - metals (copper) (silver) 521.7
    - nicotine 523.6
    - pulpal bleeding 521.7
    - tobacco 523.6
Stälh's
- ear 744.29
- pigment line (cornea) 371.11
Stälhi's pigment lines (cornea) 371.11
Stammering 307.0
Standstill
- atrial 426.6
- auricular 426.6
- cardiac (*see also* Arrest, cardiac) 427.5
- sinoatrial 426.6
- sinus 426.6
- ventricular (*see also* Arrest, cardiac) 427.5
Stannosis 503
Stanton's disease (melioidosis) 025
Staphylitis (acute) (catarrhal) (chronic) (gangrenous) (membranous) (suppurative) (ulcerative) 528.3
Staphylococcemia 038.10
- aureus 038.11
- specified organism NEC 038.19
Staphylococcus, staphylococcal — *see* condition
Staphyloderma (skin) 686.00
Staphyloma 379.11
- anterior, localized 379.14
- ciliary 379.11
- cornea 371.73
- equatorial 379.13
- posterior 379.12
- posticum 379.12
- ring 379.15
- sclera NEC 379.11
Starch eating 307.52
Stargardt's disease 362.75
Starvation (inanition) (due to lack of food) 994.2
- edema 262
- voluntary NEC 307.1
Stasis
- bile (duct) (*see also* Disease, biliary) 576.8
- bronchus (*see also* Bronchitis) 490
- cardiac (*see also* Failure, heart) 428.0
- cecum 564.89
- colon 564.89
- dermatitis (*see also* Varix, with stasis dermatitis) 454.1
- duodenal 536.8
- eczema (*see also* Varix, with stasis dermatitis) 454.1
- edema (*see also* Hypertension, venous) 459.30
- foot 991.4
- gastric 536.3
- ileocecal coil 564.89
- ileum 564.89
- intestinal 564.89
- jejunum 564.89
- kidney 586
- liver 571.9
  - cirrhotic — *see* Cirrhosis, liver
- lymphatic 457.8
- pneumonia 514
- portal 571.9
- pulmonary 514
- rectal 564.89
- renal 586
  - tubular 584.5
- stomach 536.3
- ulcer
  - with varicose veins 454.0
  - without varicose veins 459.81
- urine NEC (*see also* Retention, urine) 788.20
- venous 459.81

State
  affective and paranoid, mixed, organic
    psychotic 294.8
  agitated 307.9
    acute reaction to stress 308.2
  anxiety (neurotic) (see also Anxiety)
    300.00
    specified type NEC 300.09
  apprehension (see also Anxiety)
    300.00
    specified type NEC 300.09
  climacteric, female 627.2
    following induced menopause
      627.4
  clouded
    epileptic (see also Epilepsy)
      345.9 ☑
    paroxysmal (idiopathic) (see also
      Epilepsy) 345.9 ☑
  compulsive (mixed) (with obsession)
    300.3
  confusional 298.9
    acute 293.0
      with
        arteriosclerotic dementia
          290.41
        presenile brain disease
          290.11
        senility 290.3
      alcoholic 291.0
      drug-induced 292.81
    epileptic 293.0
    postoperative 293.9
    reactive (emotional stress) (psycho-
      logical trauma) 298.2
    subacute 293.1
  constitutional psychopathic 301.9
  convulsive (see also Convulsions)
    780.39
  depressive NEC 311
    induced by drug 292.84
    neurotic 300.4
  dissociative 300.15
  hallucinatory 780.1
    induced by drug 292.12
  hypercoagulable (primary) 289.81
    secondary 289.82
  hyperdynamic beta-adrenergic circu-
    latory 429.82
  locked-in 344.81
  menopausal 627.2
    artificial 627.4
    following induced menopause
      627.4
  neurotic NEC 300.9
    with depersonalization episode
      300.6
  obsessional 300.3
  oneiroid (see also Schizophrenia)
    295.4 ☑
  panic 300.01
  paranoid 297.9
    alcohol-induced 291.5
    arteriosclerotic 290.42
    climacteric 297.2
    drug-induced 292.11
    in
      presenile brain disease 290.12
      senile brain disease 290.20
    involutional 297.2
    menopausal 297.2
    senile 290.20
    simple 297.0
  postleukotomy 310.0
  pregnant (see also Pregnancy) V22.2
  psychogenic, twilight 298.2
  psychotic, organic (see also Psychosis,
    organic) 294.9
    mixed paranoid and affective 294.8
    senile or presenile NEC 290.9
    transient NEC 293.9
      with
        anxiety 293.84
        delusions 293.81
        depression 293.83
        hallucinations 293.82

State — continued
  residual schizophrenic (see also
    Schizophrenia) 295.6 ☑
  tension (see also Anxiety) 300.9
  transient organic psychotic 293.9
    anxiety type 293.84
    depressive type 293.83
    hallucinatory type 293.83
    paranoid type 293.81
    specified type NEC 293.89
  twilight
    epileptic 293.0
    psychogenic 298.2
  vegetative (persistent) 780.03
Status (post)
  absence
    epileptic (see also Epilepsy) 345.2
    of organ, acquired (postsurgical) —
      see Absence, by site, ac-
      quired
  anastomosis of intestine (for bypass)
    V45.3
  anginosus 413.9
  angioplasty, percutaneous translumi-
    nal coronary V45.82
  ankle prosthesis V43.66
  aortocoronary bypass or shunt V45.81
  arthrodesis V45.4
  artificially induced condition NEC
    V45.89
  artificial opening (of) V44.9
    gastrointestinal tract NEC V44.4
    specified site NEC V44.8
    urinary tract NEC V44.6
    vagina V44.7
  aspirator V46.0
  asthmaticus (see also Asthma)
    493.9 ☑
  awaiting organ transplant V49.83
  bariatric surgery V45.86 ●
    complicating pregnancy, child- ●
      birth, or the puerperium ●
      649.2 ☑ ●
  bed confinement V49.84
  breast implant removal V45.83
  cardiac
    device (in situ) V45.00
      carotid sinus V45.09
        fitting or adjustment V53.39
      defibrillator, automatic im-
        plantable V45.02
      pacemaker V45.01
        fitting or adjustment V53.31
  carotid sinus stimulator V45.09
  cataract extraction V45.61
  chemotherapy V66.2
    current V58.69
  circumcision, female 629.20
  clitorectomy (female genital mutilation
    type I) 629.21
    with excision of labia minora (fe-
      male genital mutilation type
      II) 629.22
  colostomy V44.3
  contraceptive device V45.59
    intrauterine V45.51
    subdermal V45.52
  convulsivus idiopathicus (see also
    Epilepsy) 345.3
  coronary artery bypass or shunt
    V45.81
  cutting ●
    female genital 629.20 ●
      specified NEC 629.29 ●
      type I 629.21 ●
      type II 629.22 ●
      type III 629.23 ●
      type IV 629.29 ●
  cystostomy V44.50
    appendico-vesicostomy V44.52
    cutaneous-vesicostomy V44.51
    specified type NEC V44.59
  defibrillator, automatic implantable
    cardiac V45.02
  dental crowns V45.84
  dental fillings V45.84

Status — continued
  dental restoration V45.84
  dental sealant V49.82
  dialysis (hemo) (peritoneal) V45.1
  donor V59.9
  drug therapy or regimen V67.59
    high-risk medication NEC V67.51
  elbow prosthesis V43.62
  enterostomy V44.4
  epileptic, epilepticus (absence) (grand
    mal) (see also Epilepsy) 345.3
    focal motor 345.7 ☑
    partial 345.7 ☑
    petit mal 345.2
    psychomotor 345.7 ☑
    temporal lobe 345.7 ☑
  estrogen receptor ●
    negative [ER-] V86.1 ●
    positive [ER+] V86.0 ●
  eye (adnexa) surgery V45.69
  female genital
    cutting 629.20 ●
      specified NEC 629.29 ●
      type I 629.21 ●
      type II 629.22 ●
      type III 629.23 ●
      type IV 629.29 ●
    mutilation 629.20 ●
      type I 629.21 ●
      type II 629.22 ●
      type III 629.23 ●
      type IV 629.29 ●
  filtering bleb (eye) (postglaucoma)
    V45.69
    with rupture or complication
      997.99
    postcataract extraction (complica-
      tion) 997.99
  finger joint prosthesis V43.69
  gastric ●
    banding V45.86 ●
      complicating pregnancy, ●
        childbirth, or the puer- ●
        perium 649.2 ☑ ●
    bypass for obesity V45.86 ●
      complicating pregnancy, ●
        childbirth, or the puer- ●
        perium 649.2 ☑ ●
  gastrostomy V44.1
  grand mal 345.3
  heart valve prosthesis V43.3
  hemodialysis V45.1
  hip prosthesis (joint) (partial) (total)
    V43.64
  ileostomy V44.2
  infibulation (female genital mutilation
    type III) 629.23
  insulin pump V45.85
  intestinal bypass V45.3
  intrauterine contraceptive device
    V45.51
  jejunostomy V44.4
  knee joint prosthesis V43.65
  lacunaris 437.8
  lacunosis 437.8
  low birth weight V21.30
    less than 500 grams V21.31
    1000–1499 grams V21.33
    1500–1999 grams V21.34
    2000–2500 grams V21.35
    500–999 grams V21.32
  lymphaticus 254.8
  malignant neoplasm, ablated or ex-
    cised — see History, malignant
    neoplasm
  marmoratus 333.79 ▲
  mutilation, female 629.20
    type I 629.21
    type II 629.22
    type III 629.23
    type IV 629.29 ●
  nephrostomy V44.6
  neuropacemaker NEC V45.89
    brain V45.89
    carotid sinus V45.09
    neurologic NEC V45.89

Status — continued
  obesity surgery V45.86 ●
    compliating pregnancy, child- ●
      birth, or the puerperium ●
      649.2 ☑ ●
  organ replacement
    by artificial or mechanical device
      or prosthesis of
      artery V43.4
      artificial skin V43.83
      bladder V43.5
      blood vessel V43.4
      breast V43.82
      eye globe V43.0
      heart
        assist device V43.21
        fully implantable artificial
          heart V43.22
        valve V43.3
      intestine V43.89
      joint V43.60
        ankle V43.66
        elbow V43.62
        finger V43.69
        hip (partial) (total) V43.64
        knee V43.65
        shoulder V43.61
        specified NEC V43.69
        wrist V43.63
      kidney V43.89
      larynx V43.81
      lens V43.1
      limb(s) V43.7
      liver V43.89
      lung V43.89
      organ NEC V43.89
      pancreas V43.89
      skin (artificial) V43.83
      tissue NEC V43.89
      vein V43.4
    by organ transplant (heterologous)
      (homologous) — see Status,
      transplant
  pacemaker
    brain V45.89
    cardiac V45.01
    carotid sinus V45.09
    neurologic NEC V45.89
    specified site NEC V45.89
  percutaneous transluminal coronary
    angioplasty V45.82
  peritoneal dialysis V45.1
  petit mal 345.2
  postcommotio cerebri 310.2
  postmenopausal (age related) (natural)
    V49.81
  postoperative NEC V45.89
  postpartum NEC V24.2
    care immediately following delivery
      V24.0
    routine follow-up V24.2
  postsurgical NEC V45.89
  renal dialysis V45.1
  respirator [ventilator] V46.11
    encounter
      during
        mechanical failure V46.14
        power failure V46.12
      for weaning V46.13
  reversed jejunal transposition (for by-
    pass) V45.3
  shoulder prosthesis V43.61
  shunt
    aortocoronary bypass V45.81
    arteriovenous (for dialysis) V45.1
    cerebrospinal fluid V45.2
    vascular NEC V45.89
      aortocoronary (bypass) V45.81
    ventricular (communicating) (for
      drainage) V45.2
  sterilization
    tubal ligation V26.51
    vasectomy V26.52
  subdermal contraceptive device
    V45.52
  thymicolymphaticus 254.8

☑ Additional Digit Required — Refer to the Tabular List for Digit Selection   ▽ Subterms under main terms may continue to next column or page

2007 ICD-9-CM   ►◄ Revised Text   ● New Line   ▲ Revised Code   **October 2006 · Volume 2 — 265**

Status — continued
  thymicus 254.8
  thymolymphaticus 254.8
  tooth extraction 525.10
  tracheostomy V44.0
  transplant
    blood vessel V42.89
    bone V42.4
      marrow V42.81
    cornea V42.5
    heart V42.1
      valve V42.2
    intestine V42.84
    kidney V42.0
    liver V42.7
    lung V42.6
    organ V42.9
      specified site NEC V42.89
    pancreas V42.83
    peripheral stem cells V42.82
    skin V42.3
    stem cells, peripheral V42.82
    tissue V42.9
      specified type NEC V42.89
    vessel, blood V42.89
  tubal ligation V26.51
  ureterostomy V44.6
  urethrostomy V44.6
  vagina, artificial V44.7
  vascular shunt NEC V45.89
    aortocoronary (bypass) V45.81
  vasectomy V26.52
  ventilator [respirator] V46.11
    encounter
      during
        mechanical failure V46.14
        power failure V46.12
      for weaning V46.13
  wrist prosthesis V43.63
Stave fracture — see Fracture,
  metacarpus, metacarpal bone(s)
Steal
  subclavian artery 435.2
  vertebral artery 435.1
Stealing, solitary, child problem — see
  also Disturbance, conduct 312.1 ☑
Steam burn — see Burn, by site
Steatocystoma multiplex 706.2
Steatoma (infected) 706.2
  eyelid (cystic) 374.84
    infected 373.13
Steatorrhea (chronic) 579.8
  with lacteal obstruction 579.2
  idiopathic 579.0
    adult 579.0
    infantile 579.0
  pancreatic 579.4
  primary 579.0
  secondary 579.8
  specified cause NEC 579.8
  tropical 579.1
Steatosis 272.8
  heart (see also Degeneration, myocar-
    dial) 429.1
  kidney 593.89
  liver 571.8
**Steele-Richardson (-Olszewski) Syn-
drome** 333.0
Steinbrocker's syndrome — see also
  Neuropathy, peripheral, autonomic
  337.9
Steinert's disease 359.2
Stein-Leventhal syndrome (polycystic
  ovary) 256.4
Stein's syndrome (polycystic ovary)
  256.4
STEMI (ST elevation myocardial infarc- ●
  tion — see also — Infarct, my-   ●
  ocardium, ST elevation 410.9 ☑ ●
Stenocardia — see also Angina 413.9
Stenocephaly 756.0
Stenosis (cicatricial) — see also Stricture
  ampulla of Vater 576.2
    with calculus, cholelithiasis, or
      stones — see Choledocholithi-
      asis

Stenosis — see also Stricture —
  continued
  anus, anal (canal) (sphincter) 569.2
    congenital 751.2
  aorta (ascending) 747.22
    arch 747.10
    arteriosclerotic 440.0
    calcified 440.0
  aortic (valve) 424.1
    with
      mitral (valve)
        insufficiency or incompe-
          tence 396.2
        stenosis or obstruction 396.0
    atypical 396.0
    congenital 746.3
    rheumatic 395.0
      with
        insufficiency, incompetency
          or regurgitation 395.2
          with mitral (valve) disease
            396.8
        mitral (valve)
          disease (stenosis) 396.0
          insufficiency or incompe-
            tence 396.2
          stenosis or obstruction
            396.0
    specified cause, except rheumatic
      424.1
    syphilitic 093.22
  aqueduct of Sylvius (congenital) 742.3
    with spina bifida (see also Spina
      bifida) 741.0 ☑
    acquired 331.4
  artery NEC 447.1
    basilar — see Narrowing, artery,
      basilar
    carotid (common) (internal) — see
      Narrowing, artery, carotid
    celiac 447.4
    cerebral 437.0
      due to
        embolism (see also Em-
          bolism, brain) 434.1 ☑
        thrombus (see also Thrombo-
          sis, brain) 434.0 ☑
    precerebral — see Narrowing,
      artery, precerebral
    pulmonary (congenital) 747.3
      acquired 417.8
    renal 440.1
    vertebral — see Narrowing, artery,
      vertebral
  bile duct or biliary passage (see also
    Obstruction, biliary) 576.2
    congenital 751.61
  bladder neck (acquired) 596.0
    congenital 753.6
  brain 348.8
  bronchus 519.19   ▲
    syphilitic 095.8
  cardia (stomach) 537.89
    congenital 750.7
  cardiovascular (see also Disease, car-
    diovascular) 429.2
  carotid artery — see Narrowing,
    artery, carotid
  cervix, cervical (canal) 622.4
    congenital 752.49
    in pregnancy or childbirth 654.6 ☑
      affecting fetus or newborn
        763.89
      causing obstructed labor
        660.2 ☑
        affecting fetus or newborn
          763.1
  colon (see also Obstruction, intestine)
    560.9
    congenital 751.2
  colostomy 569.62
  common bile duct (see also Obstruc-
    tion, biliary) 576.2
    congenital 751.61
  coronary (artery) — see Arterioscle-
    sis, coronary

Stenosis — see also Stricture —
  continued
  cystic duct (see also Obstruction,
    gallbladder) 575.2
    congenital 751.61
  due to (presence of) any device, im-
    plant, or graft classifiable to
    996.0–996.5 — see Complica-
    tions, due to (presence of) any
    device, implant, or graft classi-
    fied to 996.0–996.5 NEC
  duodenum 537.3
    congenital 751.1
  ejaculatory duct NEC 608.89
  endocervical os — see Stenosis, cervix
  enterostomy 569.62
  esophagostomy 530.87
  esophagus 530.3
    congenital 750.3
    syphilitic 095.8
      congenital 090.5
  external ear canal 380.50
    secondary to
      inflammation 380.53
      surgery 380.52
      trauma 380.51
  gallbladder (see also Obstruction,
    gallbladder) 575.2
  glottis 478.74
  heart valve (acquired) (see also Endo-
    carditis)
    congenital NEC 746.89
      aortic 746.3
      mitral 746.5
      pulmonary 746.02
      tricuspid 746.1
  hepatic duct (see also Obstruction,
    biliary) 576.2
  hymen 623.3
  hypertrophic subaortic (idiopathic)
    425.1
  infundibulum cardiac 746.83
  intestine (see also Obstruction, intes-
    tine) 560.9
    congenital (small) 751.1
      large 751.2
  lacrimal
    canaliculi 375.53
    duct 375.56
      congenital 743.65
    punctum 375.52
      congenital 743.65
    sac 375.54
      congenital 743.65
  lacrimonasal duct 375.56
    congenital 743.65
    neonatal 375.55
  larynx 478.74
    congenital 748.3
    syphilitic 095.8
      congenital 090.5
  mitral (valve) (chronic) (inactive) 394.0
    with
      aortic (valve)
        disease (insufficiency) 396.1
        insufficiency or incompe-
          tence 396.1
        stenosis or obstruction 396.0
      incompetency, insufficiency or
        regurgitation 394.2
        with aortic valve disease
          396.8
    active or acute 391.1
      with chorea (acute) (rheumatic)
        (Sydenham's) 392.0
    congenital 746.5
    specified cause, except rheumatic
      424.0
    syphilitic 093.21
  myocardium, myocardial (see also
    Degeneration, myocardial) 429.1
    hypertrophic subaortic (idiopathic)
      425.1
  nares (anterior) (posterior)
    478.19   ▲
    congenital 748.0

Stenosis — see also Stricture —
  continued
  nasal duct 375.56
    congenital 743.65
  nasolacrimal duct 375.56
    congenital 743.65
    neonatal 375.55
  organ or site, congenital NEC — see
    Atresia
  papilla of Vater 576.2
    with calculus, cholelithiasis, or
      stones — see Choledocholithi-
      asis
  pulmonary (artery) (congenital) 747.3
    with ventricular septal defect, dex-
      traposition of aorta and hy-
      pertrophy of right ventricle
      745.2
    acquired 417.8
    infundibular 746.83
    in tetralogy of Fallot 745.2
    subvalvular 746.83
    valve (see also Endocarditis, pul-
      monary) 424.3
      congenital 746.02
    vein 747.49
      acquired 417.8
    vessel NEC 417.8
  pulmonic (congenital) 746.02
    infundibular 746.83
    subvalvular 746.83
  pylorus (hypertrophic) 537.0
    adult 537.0
    congenital 750.5
    infantile 750.5
  rectum (sphincter) (see also Stricture,
    rectum) 569.2
  renal artery 440.1
  salivary duct (any) 527.8
  sphincter of Oddi (see also Obstruc-
    tion, biliary) 576.2
  spinal 724.00
    cervical 723.0
    lumbar, lumbosacral 724.02
    nerve (root) NEC 724.9
    specified region NEC 724.09
    thoracic, thoracolumbar 724.01
  stomach, hourglass 537.6
  subaortic 746.81
    hypertrophic (idiopathic) 425.1
  supra (valvular)-aortic 747.22
  trachea 519.19   ▲
    congenital 748.3
    syphilitic 095.8
    tuberculous (see also Tuberculosis)
      012.8 ☑
  tracheostomy 519.02
  tricuspid (valve) (see also Endocardi-
    tis, tricuspid) 397.0
    congenital 746.1
    nonrheumatic 424.2
  tubal 628.2
  ureter (see also Stricture, ureter)
    593.3
    congenital 753.29
  urethra (see also Stricture, urethra)
    598.9
  vagina 623.2
    congenital 752.49
    in pregnancy or childbirth 654.7 ☑
      affecting fetus or newborn
        763.89
      causing obstructed labor
        660.2 ☑
        affecting fetus or newborn
          763.1
  valve (cardiac) (heart) (see also Endo-
    carditis) 424.90
    congenital NEC 746.89
      aortic 746.3
      mitral 746.5
      pulmonary 746.02
      tricuspid 746.1
      urethra 753.6
  valvular (see also Endocarditis)
    424.90

☑ Additional Digit Required — Refer to the Tabular List for Digit Selection   ▽ Subterms under main terms may continue to next column or page

266 — Volume 2 · October 2006   ►◄ Revised Text   ● New Line   ▲ Revised Code   2007 ICD-9-CM

Stenosis — see also Stricture —
    continued
  valvular (see also Endocarditis) —
    continued
    congenital NEC 746.89
     urethra 753.6
  vascular graft or shunt 996.1
    atherosclerosis — see Arteriosclero-
     sis, extremities
    embolism 996.74
    occlusion NEC 996.74
    thrombus 996.74
  vena cava (inferior) (superior) 459.2
    congenital 747.49
  ventricular shunt 996.2
  vulva 624.8
Stercolith — see also Fecalith 560.39
  appendix 543.9
Stercoraceous, stercoral ulcer 569.82
  anus or rectum 569.41
Stereopsis, defective
  with fusion 368.33
  without fusion 368.32
Stereotypes NEC 307.3
Sterility
  female — see Infertility, female
  male (see also Infertility, male) 606.9
Sterilization, admission for V25.2
  status
    tubal ligation V26.51
    vasectomy V26.52
Sternalgia — see also Angina 413.9
Sternopagus 759.4
Sternum bifidum 756.3
Sternutation 784.99 ▲
Steroid
  effects (adverse) (iatrogenic)
    cushingoid
     correct substance properly ad-
      ministered 255.0
     overdose or wrong substance
      given or taken 962.0
    diabetes
     correct substance properly ad-
      ministered 251.8
     overdose or wrong substance
      given or taken 962.0
    due to
     correct substance properly ad-
      ministered 255.8
     overdose or wrong substance
      given or taken 962.0
    fever
     correct substance properly ad-
      ministered 780.6
     overdose or wrong substance
      given or taken 962.0
    withdrawal
     correct substance properly ad-
      ministered 255.4
     overdose or wrong substance
      given or taken 962.0
  responder 365.03
Stevens-Johnson disease or syndrome
  (erythema multiforme exudativum)
  695.1
Stewart-Morel syndrome (hyperostosis
  frontalis interna) 733.3
Sticker's disease (erythema infectiosum)
  057.0
Stickler syndrome 759.89
Sticky eye 372.03
Stieda's disease (calcification, knee joint)
  726.62
Stiff
  back 724.8
  neck (see also Torticollis) 723.5
Stiff-baby 759.89
Stiff-man syndrome 333.91
Stiffness, joint NEC 719.50
  ankle 719.57
  back 724.8
  elbow 719.52
  finger 719.54
  hip 719.55
  knee 719.56

Stiffness, joint — continued
  multiple sites 719.59
  sacroiliac 724.6
  shoulder 719.51
  specified site NEC 719.58
  spine 724.9
  surgical fusion V45.4
  wrist 719.53
Stigmata, congenital syphilis 090.5
Stillbirth, stillborn NEC 779.9
Still's disease or syndrome 714.30
Stiller's disease (asthenia) 780.79
Still-Felty syndrome (rheumatoid
  arthritis with splenomegaly and
  leukopenia) 714.1
Stilling-Türk-Duane syndrome (ocular
  retraction syndrome) 378.71
Stimulation, ovary 256.1
Sting (animal) (bee) (fish) (insect) (jellyfish) (Portuguese man-o-war)
  (wasp) (venomous) 989.5
  anaphylactic shock or reaction 989.5
  plant 692.6
Stippled epiphyses 756.59
Stitch
  abscess 998.59
  burst (in external operation wound)
    998.32
    internal 998.31
  in back 724.5
Stojano's (subcostal) **syndrome** 098.86
Stokes-Adams syndrome (syncope with
  heart block) 426.9
Stokes' disease (exophthalmic goiter)
  242.0 ☑
Stokvis' (-Talma) disease (enterogenous
  cyanosis) 289.7
Stomach — see condition
Stoma malfunction
  colostomy 569.62
  cystostomy 997.5
  enterostomy 569.62
  esophagostomy 530.87
  gastrostomy 536.42
  ileostomy 569.62
  nephrostomy 997.5
  tracheostomy 519.02
  ureterostomy 997.5
Stomatitis 528.00 ▲
  angular 528.5
    due to dietary or vitamin deficiency
     266.0
  aphthous 528.2
  candidal 112.0
  catarrhal 528.00 ▲
  denture 528.9
  diphtheritic (membranous) 032.0
  due to
    dietary deficiency 266.0
    thrush 112.0
    vitamin deficiency 266.0
  epidemic 078.4
  epizootic 078.4
  follicular 528.00 ▲
  gangrenous 528.1
  herpetic 054.2
  herpetiformis 528.2
  malignant 528.00 ▲
  membranous acute 528.00 ▲
  monilial 112.0
  mycotic 112.0
  necrotic 528.1
    ulcerative 101
  necrotizing ulcerative 101
  parasitic 112.0
  septic 528.00 ▲
  specified NEC 528.09 ●
  spirochetal 101
  suppurative (acute) 528.00 ▲
  ulcerative 528.00 ▲
    necrotizing 101
  ulceromembranous 101
  vesicular 528.00 ▲
    with exanthem 074.3
  Vincent's 101
Stomatocytosis 282.8

Stomatomycosis 112.0
Stomatorrhagia 528.9
Stone(s) — see also Calculus
  bladder 594.1
    diverticulum 594.0
  cystine 270.0
  heart syndrome (see also Failure,
    ventricular, left) 428.1
  kidney 592.0
  prostate 602.0
  pulp (dental) 522.2
  renal 592.0
  salivary duct or gland (any) 527.5
  ureter 592.1
  urethra (impacted) 594.2
  urinary (duct) (impacted) (passage)
    592.9
    bladder 594.1
     diverticulum 594.0
    lower tract NEC 594.9
    specified site 594.8
  xanthine 277.2
Stonecutters' lung 502
  tuberculous (see also Tuberculosis)
    011.4 ☑
Stonemasons'
  asthma, disease, or lung 502
    tuberculous (see also Tuberculosis)
     011.4 ☑
  phthisis (see also Tuberculosis)
    011.4 ☑
Stoppage
  bowel (see also Obstruction, intestine)
    560.9
  heart (see also Arrest, cardiac) 427.5
  intestine (see also Obstruction, intes-
    tine) 560.9
  urine NEC (see also Retention, urine)
    788.20
Storm, thyroid (apathetic) — see also
  Thyrotoxicosis 242.9 ☑
Strabismus (alternating) (congenital)
  (nonparalytic) 378.9
  concomitant (see also Heterotropia)
    378.30
  convergent (see also Esotropia)
    378.00
  divergent (see also Exotropia)
    378.10
  convergent (see also Esotropia) 378.00
  divergent (see also Exotropia) 378.10
  due to adhesions, scars — see Strabis-
    mus, mechanical
  in neuromuscular disorder NEC
    378.73
  intermittent 378.20
    vertical 378.31
  latent 378.40
    convergent (esophoria) 378.41
    divergent (exophoria) 378.42
    vertical 378.43
  mechanical 378.60
    due to
     Brown's tendon sheath syn-
      drome 378.61
     specified musculofascial disor-
      der NEC 378.62
  paralytic 378.50
    third or oculomotor nerve (partial)
     378.51
     total 378.52
    fourth or trochlear nerve 378.53
    sixth or abducens nerve 378.54
    specified type NEC 378.73
    vertical (hypertropia) 378.31
Strain — see also Sprain, by site ▲
  eye NEC 368.13
  heart — see Disease, heart
  meaning gonorrhea — see Gonorrhea
  on urination 788.65 ●
  physical NEC V62.89
  postural 729.9
  psychological NEC V62.89
Strands
  conjunctiva 372.62
  vitreous humor 379.25

Strangulation, strangulated 994.7
  appendix 543.9
  asphyxiation or suffocation by 994.7
  bladder neck 596.0
  bowel — see Strangulation, intestine
  colon — see Strangulation, intestine
  cord (umbilical) — see Compression,
    umbilical cord
  due to birth injury 767.8
  food or foreign body (see also Asphyx-
    ia, food) 933.1
  hemorrhoids 455.8
    external 455.5
    internal 455.2
  hernia (see also Hernia, by site, with
    obstruction)
    gangrenous — see Hernia, by site,
     with gangrene
  intestine (large) (small) 560.2
    with hernia (see also Hernia, by
     site, with obstruction)
     gangrenous — see Hernia, by
      site, with gangrene
    congenital (small) 751.1
     large 751.2
  mesentery 560.2
  mucus (see also Asphyxia, mucus)
    933.1
    newborn 770.18
  omentum 560.2
  organ or site, congenital NEC — see
    Atresia
  ovary 620.8
    due to hernia 620.4
  penis 607.89
    foreign body 939.3
  rupture (see also Hernia, by site, with
    obstruction) 552.9
    gangrenous (see also Hernia, by
     site, with gangrene) 551.9
  stomach, due to hernia (see also Her-
    nia, by site, with obstruction)
    552.9
    with gangrene (see also Hernia, by
     site, with gangrene) 551.9
  umbilical cord — see Compression,
    umbilical cord
  vesicourethral orifice 596.0
Strangury 788.1
Strawberry
  gallbladder (see also Disease, gallblad-
    der) 575.6
  mark 757.32
  tongue (red) (white) 529.3
Straw itch 133.8
Streak, ovarian 752.0
Strephosymbolia 315.01
  secondary to organic lesion 784.69
Streptobacillary fever 026.1
Streptobacillus moniliformis 026.1
Streptococcemia 038.0
Streptococcicosis — see Infection,
  streptococcal
Streptococcus, streptococcal — see
  condition
Streptoderma 686.00
Streptomycosis — see Actinomycosis
Streptothricosis — see Actinomycosis
Streptothrix — see Actinomycosis
Streptotrichosis — see Actinomycosis
Stress
  fracture — see Fracture, stress
  polycythemia 289.0
  reaction (gross) (see also Reaction,
    stress, acute) 308.9
Stretching, nerve — see Injury, nerve,
  by site
Striae (albicantes) (atrophicae) (cutis
  distensae) (distensae) 701.3
Striations of nails 703.8
Stricture — see also Stenosis 799.89
  ampulla of Vater 576.2
    with calculus, cholelithiasis, or
     stones — see Choledocholithi-
     asis
  anus (sphincter) 569.2

☑ Additional Digit Required — Refer to the Tabular List for Digit Selection   🔄 Subterms under main terms may continue to next column or page

2007 ICD-9-CM   ▶◀ Revised Text   ● New Line   ▲ Revised Code   October 2006 • Volume 2 — **267**

Stricture — *see also* Stenosis — *continued*
anus — *continued*
   congenital 751.2
   infantile 751.2
aorta (ascending) 747.22
  arch 747.10
  arteriosclerotic 440.0
  calcified 440.0
aortic (valve) (*see also* Stenosis, aortic) 424.1
  congenital 746.3
aqueduct of Sylvius (congenital) 742.3
  with spina bifida (*see also* Spina bifida) 741.0 ☑
  acquired 331.4
artery 447.1
  basilar — *see* Narrowing, artery, basilar
  carotid (common) (internal) — *see* Narrowing, artery, carotid
  celiac 447.4
  cerebral 437.0
   congenital 747.81
   due to
    embolism (*see also* Embolism, brain) 434.1 ☑
    thrombus (*see also* Thrombosis, brain) 434.0 ☑
  congenital (peripheral) 747.60
   cerebral 747.81
   coronary 746.85
   gastrointestinal 747.61
   lower limb 747.64
   renal 747.62
   retinal 743.58
   specified NEC 747.69
   spinal 747.82
   umbilical 747.5
   upper limb 747.63
  coronary — *see* Arteriosclerosis, coronary
   congenital 746.85
  precerebral — *see* Narrowing, artery, precerebral NEC
  pulmonary (congenital) 747.3
   acquired 417.8
  renal 440.1
  vertebral — *see* Narrowing, artery, vertebral
auditory canal (congenital) (external) 744.02
  acquired (*see also* Stricture, ear canal, acquired) 380.50
bile duct or passage (any) (postoperative) (*see also* Obstruction, biliary) 576.2
  congenital 751.61
bladder 596.8
  congenital 753.6
  neck 596.0
   congenital 753.6
bowel (*see also* Obstruction, intestine) 560.9
brain 348.8
bronchus 519.19   ▲
  syphilitic 095.8
cardia (stomach) 537.89
  congenital 750.7
cardiac (*see also* Disease, heart)
  orifice (stomach) 537.89
cardiovascular (*see also* Disease, cardiovascular) 429.2
carotid artery — *see* Narrowing, artery, carotid
cecum (*see also* Obstruction, intestine) 560.9
cervix, cervical (canal) 622.4
  congenital 752.49
  in pregnancy or childbirth 654.6 ☑
   affecting fetus or newborn 763.89
   causing obstructed labor 660.2 ☑
    affecting fetus or newborn 763.1

Stricture — *see also* Stenosis — *continued*
colon (*see also* Obstruction, intestine) 560.9
  congenital 751.2
colostomy 569.62
common bile duct (*see also* Obstruction, biliary) 576.2
  congenital 751.61
coronary (artery) — *see* Arteriosclerosis, coronary
  congenital 746.85
cystic duct (*see also* Obstruction, gallbladder) 575.2
  congenital 751.61
cystostomy 997.5
digestive organs NEC, congenital 751.8
duodenum 537.3
  congenital 751.1
ear canal (external) (congenital) 744.02
  acquired 380.50
   secondary to
    inflammation 380.53
    surgery 380.52
    trauma 380.51
ejaculatory duct 608.85
enterostomy 569.62
esophagostomy 530.87
esophagus (corrosive) (peptic) 530.3
  congenital 750.3
  syphilitic 095.8
   congenital 090.5
eustachian tube (*see also* Obstruction, Eustachian tube) 381.60
  congenital 744.24
fallopian tube 628.2
  gonococcal (chronic) 098.37
   acute 098.17
  tuberculous (*see also* Tuberculosis) 016.6 ☑
gallbladder (*see also* Obstruction, gallbladder) 575.2
  congenital 751.69
glottis 478.74
heart (*see also* Disease, heart)
  congenital NEC 746.89
  valve (*see also* Endocarditis)
   congenital NEC 746.89
    aortic 746.3
    mitral 746.5
    pulmonary 746.02
    tricuspid 746.1
hepatic duct (*see also* Obstruction, biliary) 576.2
hourglass, of stomach 537.6
hymen 623.3
hypopharynx 478.29
intestine (*see also* Obstruction, intestine) 560.9
  congenital (small) 751.1
   large 751.2
  ischemic 557.1
lacrimal
  canaliculi 375.53
   congenital 743.65
  punctum 375.52
   congenital 743.65
  sac 375.54
   congenital 743.65
lacrimonasal duct 375.56
  congenital 743.65
  neonatal 375.55
larynx 478.79
  congenital 748.3
  syphilitic 095.8
   congenital 090.5
lung 518.89
meatus
  ear (congenital) 744.02
   acquired (*see also* Stricture, ear canal, acquired) 380.50
  osseous (congenital) (ear) 744.03
   acquired (*see also* Stricture, ear canal, acquired) 380.50

Stricture — *see also* Stenosis — *continued*
meatus — *continued*
  urinarius (*see also* Stricture, urethra) 598.9
   congenital 753.6
mitral (valve) (*see also* Stenosis, mitral) 394.0
  congenital 746.5
  specified cause, except rheumatic 424.0
myocardium, myocardial (*see also* Degeneration, myocardial) 429.1
  hypertrophic subaortic (idiopathic) 425.1
nares (anterior) (posterior) 478.19   ▲
  congenital 748.0
nasal duct 375.56
  congenital 743.65
  neonatal 375.55
nasolacrimal duct 375.56
  congenital 743.65
  neonatal 375.55
nasopharynx 478.29
  syphilitic 095.8
nephrostomy 997.5
nose 478.19   ▲
  congenital 748.0
nostril (anterior) (posterior) 478.19   ▲
  congenital 748.0
organ or site, congenital NEC — *see* Atresia
osseous meatus (congenital) (ear) 744.03
  acquired (*see also* Stricture, ear canal, acquired) 380.50
os uteri (*see also* Stricture, cervix) 622.4
oviduct — *see* Stricture, fallopian tube
pelviureteric junction 593.3
pharynx (dilation) 478.29
prostate 602.8
pulmonary, pulmonic
  artery (congenital) 747.3
   acquired 417.8
   noncongenital 417.8
  infundibulum (congenital) 746.83
  valve (*see also* Endocarditis, pulmonary) 424.3
   congenital 746.02
  vein (congenital) 747.49
   acquired 417.8
  vessel NEC 417.8
punctum lacrimale 375.52
  congenital 743.65
pylorus (hypertrophic) 537.0
  adult 537.0
  congenital 750.5
  infantile 750.5
rectosigmoid 569.89
rectum (sphincter) 569.2
  congenital 751.2
  due to
   chemical burn 947.3
   irradiation 569.2
   lymphogranuloma venereum 099.1
  gonococcal 098.7
  inflammatory 099.1
  syphilitic 095.8
  tuberculous (*see also* Tuberculosis) 014.8 ☑
renal artery 440.1
salivary duct or gland (any) 527.8
sigmoid (flexure) (*see also* Obstruction, intestine) 560.9
spermatic cord 608.85
stoma (following) (of)
  colostomy 569.62
  cystostomy 997.5
  enterostomy 569.62
  esophagostomy 530.87
  gastrostomy 536.42
  ileostomy 569.62

Stricture — *see also* Stenosis — *continued*
stoma — *continued*
  nephrostomy 997.5
  tracheostomy 519.02
  ureterostomy 997.5
stomach 537.89
  congenital 750.7
  hourglass 537.6
subaortic 746.81
  hypertrophic (acquired) (idiopathic) 425.1
subglottic 478.74
syphilitic NEC 095.8
tendon (sheath) 727.81
trachea 519.19   ▲
  congenital 748.3
  syphilitic 095.8
  tuberculous (*see also* Tuberculosis) 012.8 ☑
tracheostomy 519.02
tricuspid (valve) (*see also* Endocarditis, tricuspid) 397.0
  congenital 746.1
  nonrheumatic 424.2
tunica vaginalis 608.85
ureter (postoperative) 593.3
  congenital 753.29
  tuberculous (*see also* Tuberculosis) 016.2 ☑
ureteropelvic junction 593.3
  congenital 753.21
ureterovesical orifice 593.3
  congenital 753.22
urethra (anterior) (meatal) (organic) (posterior) (spasmodic) 598.9
  associated with schistosomiasis (*see also* Schistosomiasis) 120.9 [598.01]
  congenital (valvular) 753.6
  due to
   infection 598.00
    syphilis 095.8 [598.01]
   trauma 598.1
  gonococcal 098.2 [598.01]
  gonorrheal 098.2 [598.01]
  infective 598.00
  late effect of injury 598.1
  postcatheterization 598.2
  postobstetric 598.1
  postoperative 598.2
  specified cause NEC 598.8
  syphilitic 095.8 [598.01]
  traumatic 598.1
  valvular, congenital 753.6
urinary meatus (*see also* Stricture, urethra) 598.9
  congenital 753.6
uterus, uterine 621.5
  os (external) (internal) — *see* Stricture, cervix
vagina (outlet) 623.2
  congenital 752.49
valve (cardiac) (heart) (*see also* Endocarditis) 424.90
  congenital (cardiac) (heart) NEC 746.89
   aortic 746.3
   mitral 746.5
   pulmonary 746.02
   tricuspid 746.1
   urethra 753.6
valvular (*see also* Endocarditis) 424.90
vascular graft or shunt 996.1
  atherosclerosis — *see* Arteriosclerosis, extremities
  embolism 996.74
  occlusion NEC 996.74
  thrombus 996.74
vas deferens 608.85
  congenital 752.89
vein 459.2
vena cava (inferior) (superior) NEC 459.2
  congenital 747.49

☑ Additional Digit Required — Refer to the Tabular List for Digit Selection
         � Subterms under main terms may continue to next column or page

268 — Volume 2 · October 2006   ►◄ Revised Text   ● New Line   ▲ Revised Code   **2007 ICD-9-CM**

Stricture — *see also* Stenosis — *continued*
  ventricular shunt 996.2
  vesicourethral orifice 596.0
    congenital 753.6
  vulva (acquired) 624.8
Stridor 786.1
  congenital (larynx) 748.3
Stridulous — *see* condition
Strippling of nails 703.8
Stroke 434.91
  apoplectic (*see also* Disease, cerebrovascular, acute) 436
  brain — *see* Infarct, brain
  embolic 434.11
  epileptic — *see* Epilepsy
  healed or old V12.59
  heart — *see* Disease, heart
  heat 992.0
  hemorrhage — *see* Hemorrhage, brain
  iatrogenic 997.02
  in evolution 435.9
  ischemic 434.91
  late effect — *see* Late effect(s) (of) cerebrovascular disease
  lightning 994.0
  paralytic — *see* Infarct, brain
  postoperative 997.02
  progressive 435.9
  thrombotic 434.01
Stromatosis, endometrial (M8931/1) 236.0
Strong pulse 785.9
Strongyloides stercoralis infestation 127.2
Strongyloidiasis 127.2
Strongyloidosis 127.2
Strongylus (gibsoni) infestation 127.7
Strophulus (newborn) 779.89
  pruriginosus 698.2
Struck by lightning 994.0
Struma — *see also* Goiter 240.9
  fibrosa 245.3
  Hashimoto (struma lymphomatosa) 245.2
  lymphomatosa 245.2
  nodosa (simplex) 241.9
    endemic 241.9
    multinodular 241.1
    sporadic 241.9
    toxic or with hyperthyroidism 242.3 ☑
      multinodular 242.2 ☑
      uninodular 242.1 ☑
    toxicosa 242.3 ☑
      multinodular 242.2 ☑
      uninodular 242.1 ☑
    uninodular 241.0
  ovarii (M9090/0) 220
    and carcinoid (M9091/1) 236.2
    malignant (M9090/3) 183.0
  Riedel's (ligneous thyroiditis) 245.3
  scrofulous (*see also* Tuberculosis) 017.2 ☑
  tuberculous (*see also* Tuberculosis) 017.2 ☑
    abscess 017.2 ☑
    adenitis 017.2 ☑
    lymphangitis 017.2 ☑
    ulcer 017.2 ☑
Strumipriva cachexia — *see also* Hypothyroidism 244.9
Strümpell-Marie disease or spine (ankylosing spondylitis) 720.0
Strümpell-Westphal pseudosclerosis (hepatolenticular degeneration) 275.1
Stuart's disease (congenital factor X deficiency) — *see also* Defect, coagulation 286.3
Stuart-Prower factor deficiency (congenital factor X deficiency) — *see also* Defect, coagulation 286.3
Students' elbow 727.2
Stuffy nose 478.19 ▲
Stump — *see also* Amputation

Stump — *see also* Amputation — *continued*
  cervix, cervical (healed) 622.8
Stupor 780.09
  catatonic (*see also* Schizophrenia) 295.2 ☑
  circular (*see also* Psychosis, manic-depressive, circular) 296.7
  manic 296.89
  manic-depressive (*see also* Psychosis, affective) 296.89
  mental (anergic) (delusional) 298.9
  psychogenic 298.8
  reaction to exceptional stress (transient) 308.2
  traumatic NEC (*see also* Injury, intracranial)
    with spinal (cord)
      lesion — *see* Injury, spinal, by site
      shock — *see* Injury, spinal, by site
Sturge (-Weber) (-Dimitri) disease or syndrome (encephalocutaneous angiomatosis) 759.6
Sturge-Kalischer-Weber syndrome (encephalocutaneous angiomatosis) 759.6
Stuttering 307.0
Sty, stye 373.11
  external 373.11
  internal 373.12
  meibomian 373.12
Subacidity, gastric 536.8
  psychogenic 306.4
Subacute — *see* condition
Subarachnoid — *see* condition
Subclavian steal syndrome 435.2
Subcortical — *see* condition
Subcostal syndrome 098.86
  nerve compression 354.8
Subcutaneous, subcuticular — *see* condition
Subdelirium 293.1
Subdural — *see* condition
Subendocardium — *see* condition
Subependymoma (M9383/1) 237.5
Suberosis 495.3
Subglossitis — *see* Glossitis
Subhemophilia 286.0
Subinvolution (uterus) 621.1
  breast (postlactational) (postpartum) 611.8
  chronic 621.1
  puerperal, postpartum 674.8 ☑
Sublingual — *see* condition
Sublinguitis 527.2
Subluxation — *see also* Dislocation, by site
  congenital NEC (*see also* Malposition, congenital)
    hip (unilateral) 754.32
      with dislocation of other hip 754.35
      bilateral 754.33
    joint
      lower limb 755.69
      shoulder 755.59
      upper limb 755.59
    lower limb (joint) 755.69
    shoulder (joint) 755.59
    upper limb (joint) 755.59
  lens 379.32
    anterior 379.33
    posterior 379.34
  rotary, cervical region of spine — *see* Fracture, vertebra, cervical
Submaxillary — *see* condition
Submersion (fatal) (nonfatal) 994.1
Submissiveness (undue), in child 313.0
Submucous — *see* condition
Subnormal, subnormality
  accommodation (*see also* Disorder, accommodation) 367.9
  mental (*see also* Retardation, mental) 319

Subnormal, subnormality — *continued*
  mental (*see also* Retardation, mental) — *continued*
    mild 317
    moderate 318.0
    profound 318.2
    severe 318.1
  temperature (accidental) 991.6
    not associated with low environmental temperature 780.99
Subphrenic — *see* condition
Subscapular nerve — *see* condition
Subseptus uterus 752.3
Subsiding appendicitis 542
Substernal thyroid — *see also* Goiter 240.9
  congenital 759.2
Substitution disorder 300.11
Subtentorial — *see* condition
Subtertian
  fever 084.0
  malaria (fever) 084.0
Subthyroidism (acquired) — *see also* Hypothyroidism 244.9
  congenital 243
Succenturiata placenta — *see* Placenta, abnormal
Succussion sounds, chest 786.7
Sucking thumb, child 307.9
Sudamen 705.1
Sudamina 705.1
Sudanese kala-azar 085.0
Sudden
  death, cause unknown (less than 24 hours) 798.1
    during childbirth 669.9 ☑
    infant 798.0
    puerperal, postpartum 674.9 ☑
  hearing loss NEC 388.2
  heart failure (*see also* Failure, heart) 428.9
  infant death syndrome 798.0
Sudeck's atrophy, disease, or syndrome 733.7
SUDS (sudden unexplained death) 798.2
Suffocation — *see also* Asphyxia 799.01
  by
    bed clothes 994.7
    bunny bag 994.7
    cave-in 994.7
    constriction 994.7
    drowning 994.1
    inhalation
      food or foreign body (*see also* Asphyxia, food or foreign body) 933.1
      oil or gasoline (*see also* Asphyxia, food or foreign body) 933.1
    overlying 994.7
    plastic bag 994.7
    pressure 994.7
    strangulation 994.7
  during birth 768.1
  mechanical 994.7
Sugar
  blood
    high 790.29
    low 251.2
  in urine 791.5
Suicide, suicidal (attempted)
  by poisoning — *see* Table of Drugs and Chemicals
  ideation V62.84
  risk 300.9
  tendencies 300.9
  trauma NEC (*see also* nature and site of injury) 959.9
Suipestifer infection — *see also* Infection, Salmonella 003.9
Sulfatidosis 330.0
Sulfhemoglobinemia, sulphemoglobinemia (acquired) (congenital) 289.7
Sumatran mite fever 081.2
Summer — *see* condition

Sunburn 692.71
  first degree 692.71
  second degree 692.76
  third degree 692.77
  dermatitis 692.71
  due to
    other ultraviolet radiation 692.82
    tanning bed 692.82
Sunken
  acetabulum 718.85
  fontanels 756.0
Sunstroke 992.0
Superfecundation 651.9 ☑
  with fetal loss and retention of one or more fetus(es) 651.6 ☑
  following (elective) fetal reduction 651.7 ☑
Superfetation 651.9 ☑
  with fetal loss and retention of one or more fetus(es) 651.6 ☑
  following (elective) fetal reduction 651.7 ☑
Superinvolution uterus 621.8
Supernumerary (congenital)
  aortic cusps 746.89
  auditory ossicles 744.04
  bone 756.9
  breast 757.6
  carpal bones 755.56
  cusps, heart valve NEC 746.89
    mitral 746.5
    pulmonary 746.09
  digit(s) 755.00
    finger 755.01
    toe 755.02
  ear (lobule) 744.1
  fallopian tube 752.19
  finger 755.01
  hymen 752.49
  kidney 753.3
  lacrimal glands 743.64
  lacrimonasal duct 743.65
  lobule (ear) 744.1
  mitral cusps 746.5
  muscle 756.82
  nipples 757.6
  organ or site NEC — *see* Accessory
  ossicles, auditory 744.04
  ovary 752.0
  oviduct 752.19
  pulmonic cusps 746.09
  rib 756.3
    cervical or first 756.2
    syndrome 756.2
  roots (of teeth) 520.2
  spinal vertebra 756.19
  spleen 759.0
  tarsal bones 755.67
  teeth 520.1
    causing crowding 524.31
  testis 752.89
  thumb 755.01
  toe 755.02
  uterus 752.2
  vagina 752.49
  vertebra 756.19
Supervision (of)
  contraceptive method previously prescribed V25.40
    intrauterine device V25.42
    oral contraceptive (pill) V25.41
    specified type NEC V25.49
    subdermal implantable contraceptive V25.43
  dietary (for) V65.3
    allergy (food) V65.3
    colitis V65.3
    diabetes mellitus V65.3
    food allergy intolerance V65.3
    gastritis V65.3
    hypercholesterolemia V65.3
    hypoglycemia V65.3
    intolerance (food) V65.3
    obesity V65.3
    specified NEC V65.3
  lactation V24.1

☑ Additional Digit Required — Refer to the Tabular List for Digit Selection   ▽ Subterms under main terms may continue to next column or page

2007 ICD-9-CM   ▶◀ Revised Text   ● New Line   ▲ Revised Code   **October 2006 · Volume 2 — 269**

Supervision — continued
  pregnancy — see Pregnancy, supervision of
Supplemental teeth 520.1
  causing crowding 524.31
Suppression
  binocular vision 368.31
  lactation 676.5 ☑
  menstruation 626.8
  ovarian secretion 256.39
  renal 586
  urinary secretion 788.5
  urine 788.5
Suppuration, suppurative — see also condition
  accessory sinus (chronic) (see also Sinusitis) 473.9
  adrenal gland 255.8
  antrum (chronic) (see also Sinusitis, maxillary) 473.0
  bladder (see also Cystitis) 595.89
  bowel 569.89
  brain 324.0
    late effect 326
  breast 611.0
    puerperal, postpartum 675.1 ☑
  dental periosteum 526.5
  diffuse (skin) 686.00
  ear (middle) (see also Otitis media) 382.4
    external (see also Otitis, externa) 380.10
    internal 386.33
  ethmoidal (sinus) (chronic) (see also Sinusitis, ethmoidal) 473.2
  fallopian tube (see also Salpingo-oophoritis) 614.2
  frontal (sinus) (chronic) (see also Sinusitis, frontal) 473.1
  gallbladder (see also Cholecystitis, acute) 575.0
  gum 523.30   ▲
  hernial sac — see Hernia, by site
  intestine 569.89
  joint (see also Arthritis, suppurative) 711.0 ☑
  labyrinthine 386.33
  lung 513.0
  mammary gland 611.0
    puerperal, postpartum 675.1 ☑
  maxilla, maxillary 526.4
    sinus (chronic) (see also Sinusitis, maxillary) 473.0
  muscle 728.0
  nasal sinus (chronic) (see also Sinusitis) 473.9
  pancreas 577.0
  parotid gland 527.2
  pelvis, pelvic
    female (see also Disease, pelvis, inflammatory) 614.4
      acute 614.3
    male (see also Peritonitis) 567.21
  pericranial (see also Osteomyelitis) 730.2 ☑
  salivary duct or gland (any) 527.2
  sinus (nasal) (see also Sinusitis) 473.9
  sphenoidal (sinus) (chronic) (see also Sinusitis, sphenoidal) 473.3
  thymus (gland) 254.1
  thyroid (gland) 245.0
  tonsil 474.8
  uterus (see also Endometritis) 615.9
  vagina 616.10
  wound (see also Wound, open, by site, complicated)
    dislocation — see Dislocation, by site, compound
    fracture — see Fracture, by site, open
    scratch or other superficial injury — see Injury, superficial, by site
Supraeruption, teeth 524.34
Supraglottitis 464.50
  with obstruction 464.51

Suprapubic drainage 596.8
Suprarenal (gland) — see condition
Suprascapular nerve — see condition
Suprasellar — see condition
Supraspinatus syndrome 726.10
Surfer knots 919.8
  infected 919.9
Surgery
  cosmetic NEC V50.1
    following healed injury or operation V51
    hair transplant V50.0
  elective V50.9
    breast augmentation or reduction V50.1
    circumcision, ritual or routine (in absence of medical indication) V50.2
    cosmetic NEC V50.1
    ear piercing V50.3
    face-lift V50.1
    following healed injury or operation V51
    hair transplant V50.0
  not done because of
    contraindication V64.1
    patient's decision V64.2
    specified reason NEC V64.3
  plastic
    breast augmentation or reduction V50.1
    cosmetic V50.1
    face-lift V50.1
    following healed injury or operation V51
    repair of scarred tissue (following healed injury or operation) V51
    specified type NEC V50.8
  previous, in pregnancy or childbirth
    cervix 654.6 ☑
      affecting fetus or newborn 763.89
      causing obstructed labor 660.2 ☑
        affecting fetus or newborn 763.1
    pelvic soft tissues NEC 654.9 ☑
      affecting fetus or newborn 763.89
      causing obstructed labor 660.2 ☑
        affecting fetus or newborn 763.1
    perineum or vulva 654.8 ☑
    uterus NEC 654.9 ☑
      affecting fetus or newborn 763.89
      causing obstructed labor 660.2 ☑
        affecting fetus or newborn 763.1
      due to previous cesarean delivery 654.2 ☑
    vagina 654.7 ☑
Surgical
  abortion — see Abortion, legal
  emphysema 998.81
  kidney (see also Pyelitis) 590.80
  operation NEC 799.9
  procedures, complication or misadventure — see Complications, surgical procedure
  shock 998.0
Susceptibility
  genetic
    to
      neoplasm
        malignant, of
          breast V84.01
          endometrium V84.04
          other V84.09
          ovary V84.02
          prostate V84.03
        other disease V84.8

Suspected condition, ruled out — see also Observation, suspected V71.9
  specified condition NEC V71.89
Suspended uterus, in pregnancy or childbirth 654.4 ☑
  affecting fetus or newborn 763.89
  causing obstructed labor 660.2 ☑
    affecting fetus or newborn 763.1
Sutton and Gull's disease (arteriolar nephrosclerosis) — see also Hypertension, kidney 403.90
Sutton's disease 709.09
Suture
  burst (in external operation wound) 998.32
    internal 998.31
  inadvertently left in operation wound 998.4
  removal V58.32   ▲
  Shirodkar, in pregnancy (with or without cervical incompetence) 654.5 ☑
Swab inadvertently left in operation wound 998.4
Swallowed, swallowing
  difficulty (see also Dysphagia) 787.2
  foreign body NEC (see also Foreign body) 938
Swamp fever 100.89
Swan neck hand (intrinsic) 736.09
Sweat(s), sweating
  disease or sickness 078.2
  excessive (see also Hyperhidrosis) 780.8
  fetid 705.89
  fever 078.2
  gland disease 705.9
    specified type NEC 705.89
  miliary 078.2
  night 780.8
Sweeley-Klionsky disease (angiokeratoma corporis diffusum) 272.7
Sweet's syndrome (acute febrile neutrophilic dermatosis) 695.89
Swelling
  abdominal (not referable to specific organ) 789.3 ☑
  adrenal gland, cloudy 255.8
  ankle 719.07
  anus 787.99
  arm 729.81
  breast 611.72
  Calabar 125.2
  cervical gland 785.6
  cheek 784.2
  chest 786.6
  ear 388.8
  epigastric 789.3 ☑
  extremity (lower) (upper) 729.81
  eye 379.92
  female genital organ 625.8
  finger 729.81
  foot 729.81
  glands 785.6
  gum 784.2
  hand 729.81
  head 784.2
  inflammatory — see Inflammation
  joint (see also Effusion, joint) 719.0 ☑
    tuberculous — see Tuberculosis, joint
  kidney, cloudy 593.89
  leg 729.81
  limb 729.81
  liver 573.8
  lung 786.6
  lymph nodes 785.6
  mediastinal 786.6
  mouth 784.2
  muscle (limb) 729.81
  neck 784.2
  nose or sinus 784.2
  palate 784.2
  pelvis 789.3 ☑
  penis 607.83
  perineum 625.8

Swelling — continued
  rectum 787.99
  scrotum 608.86
  skin 782.2
  splenic (see also Splenomegaly) 789.2
  substernal 786.6
  superficial, localized (skin) 782.2
  testicle 608.86
  throat 784.2
  toe 729.81
  tongue 784.2
  tubular (see also Disease, renal) 593.9
  umbilicus 789.3 ☑
  uterus 625.8
  vagina 625.8
  vulva 625.8
  wandering, due to Gnathostoma (spinigerum) 128.1
  white — see Tuberculosis, arthritis
Swift's disease 985.0
Swimmers'
  ear (acute) 380.12
  itch 120.3
Swimming in the head 780.4
Swollen — see also Swelling
  glands 785.6
Swyer-James syndrome (unilateral hyperlucent lung) 492.8
Swyer's syndrome (XY pure gonadal dysgenesis) 752.7
Sycosis 704.8
  barbae (not parasitic) 704.8
  contagiosa 110.0
  lupoid 704.8
  mycotic 110.0
  parasitic 110.0
  vulgaris 704.8
Sydenham's chorea — see Chorea, Sydenham's
Sylvatic yellow fever 060.0
Sylvest's disease (epidemic pleurodynia) 074.1
Symblepharon 372.63
  congenital 743.62
Symonds' syndrome 348.2
Sympathetic — see condition
Sympatheticotonia — see also Neuropathy, peripheral, autonomic 337.9
Sympathicoblastoma (M9500/3)
  specified site — see Neoplasm, by site, malignant
  unspecified site 194.0
Sympathicogonioma (M9500/3) — see Sympathicoblastoma
Sympathoblastoma (M9500/3) — see Sympathicoblastoma
Sympathogonioma (M9500/3) — see Sympathicoblastoma
Symphalangy — see also Syndactylism 755.10
Symptoms, specified (general) NEC 780.99
  abdomen NEC 789.9
  bone NEC 733.90
  breast NEC 611.79
  cardiac NEC 785.9
  cardiovascular NEC 785.9
  chest NEC 786.9
  development NEC 783.9
  digestive system NEC 787.99
  eye NEC 379.99
  gastrointestinal tract NEC 787.99
  genital organs NEC
    female 625.9
    male 608.9
  head and neck NEC 784.99   ▲
  heart NEC 785.9
  joint NEC 719.60
    ankle 719.67
    elbow 719.62
    foot 719.67
    hand 719.64
    hip 719.65
    knee 719.66
    multiple sites 719.69
    pelvic region 719.65

☑ Additional Digit Required — Refer to the Tabular List for Digit Selection
🔄 Subterms under main terms may continue to next column or page

270 — Volume 2 · October 2006
▶◀ Revised Text   ● New Line   ▲ Revised Code
2007 ICD-9-CM

Symptoms, specified — *continued*
  joint — *continued*
    shoulder (region) 719.61
    specified site NEC 719.68
    wrist 719.63
  larynx NEC 784.99   ▲
  limbs NEC 729.89
  lymphatic system NEC 785.9
  menopausal 627.2
  metabolism NEC 783.9
  mouth NEC 528.9
  muscle NEC 728.9
  musculoskeletal NEC 781.99
    limbs NEC 729.89
  nervous system NEC 781.99
  neurotic NEC 300.9
  nutrition, metabolism, and development NEC 783.9
  pelvis NEC 789.9
    female 625.9
  peritoneum NEC 789.9
  respiratory system NEC 786.9
  skin and integument NEC 782.9
  subcutaneous tissue NEC 782.9
  throat NEC 784.99   ▲
  tonsil NEC 784.99   ▲
  urinary system NEC 788.9
  vascular NEC 785.9
Sympus 759.89
Synarthrosis 719.80
  ankle 719.87
  elbow 719.82
  foot 719.87
  hand 719.84
  hip 719.85
  knee 719.86
  multiple sites 719.89
  pelvic region 719.85
  shoulder (region) 719.81
  specified site NEC 719.88
  wrist 719.83
Syncephalus 759.4
Synchondrosis 756.9
  abnormal (congenital) 756.9
  ischiopubic (van Neck's) 732.1
Synchysis (senile) (vitreous humor) 379.21
  scintillans 379.22
Syncope (near) (pre-) 780.2
  anginosa 413.9
  bradycardia 427.89
  cardiac 780.2
  carotid sinus 337.0
  complicating delivery 669.2 ☑
  due to lumbar puncture 349.0
  fatal 798.1
  heart 780.2
  heat 992.1
  laryngeal 786.2
  tussive 786.2
  vasoconstriction 780.2
  vasodepressor 780.2
  vasomotor 780.2
  vasovagal 780.2
Syncytial infarct — *see* Placenta, abnormal
Syndactylism, syndactyly (multiple sites) 755.10
  fingers (without fusion of bone) 755.11
    with fusion of bone 755.12
  toes (without fusion of bone) 755.13
    with fusion of bone 755.14
Syndrome — *see also* Disease
  with 5q deletion 238.74   ●
  5q minus 238.74   ●
  abdominal
    acute 789.0 ☑
    migraine 346.2 ☑
    muscle deficiency 756.79
  Abercrombie's (amyloid degeneration) 277.39   ▲
  abnormal innervation 374.43
  abstinence
    alcohol 291.81
    drug 292.0

Syndrome — *see also* Disease — *continued*
  Abt-Letterer-Siwe (acute histiocytosis X) (M9722/3) 202.5 ☑
  Achard-Thiers (adrenogenital) 255.2
  acid pulmonary aspiration 997.3
    obstetric (Mendelson's) 668.0 ☑
  acquired immune deficiency 042
  acquired immunodeficiency 042
  acrocephalosyndactylism 755.55
  acute abdominal 789.0 ☑
  acute chest 517.3
  acute coronary 411.1
  Adair-Dighton (brittle bones and blue sclera, deafness) 756.51
  Adams-Stokes (-Morgagni) (syncope with heart block) 426.9
  addisonian 255.4
  Adie (-Holmes) (pupil) 379.46
  adiposogenital 253.8
  adrenal
    hemorrhage 036.3
    meningococcic 036.3
  adrenocortical 255.3
  adrenogenital (acquired) (congenital) 255.2
    feminizing 255.2
    iatrogenic 760.79
    virilism (acquired) (congenital) 255.2
  affective organic NEC 293.89
    drug-induced 292.84
  afferent loop NEC 537.89
  African macroglobulinemia 273.3
  Ahumada-Del Castillo (nonpuerperal galactorrhea and amenorrhea) 253.1
  air blast concussion — *see* Injury, internal, by site
  Alagille 759.89
  Albright (-Martin) (pseudohypoparathyroidism) 275.49
  Albright-McCune-Sternberg (osteitis fibrosa disseminata) 756.59
  alcohol withdrawal 291.81
  Alder's (leukocyte granulation anomaly) 288.2
  Aldrich (-Wiskott) (eczema-thrombocytopenia) 279.12
  Alibert-Bazin (mycosis fungoides) (M9700/3) 202.1 ☑
  Alice in Wonderland 293.89
  Allen-Masters 620.6
  Alligator baby (ichthyosis congenita) 757.1
  Alport's (hereditary hematuria-nephropathy-deafness) 759.89
  Alvarez (transient cerebral ischemia) 435.9
  alveolar capillary block 516.3
  Alzheimer's 331.0
    with dementia — *see* Alzheimer's, dementia
  amnestic (confabulatory) 294.0
    alcohol-induced persisting 291.1
    drug-induced 292.83
    posttraumatic 294.0
  amotivational 292.89
  amyostatic 275.1
  amyotrophic lateral sclerosis 335.20
  androgen insensitivity 259.5
  Angelman 759.89
  angina (*see also* Angina) 413.9
  ankyloglossia superior 750.0
  anterior
    chest wall 786.52
    compartment (tibial) 958.8
    spinal artery 433.8 ☑
      compression 721.1
    tibial (compartment) 958.8
  antibody deficiency 279.00
    agammaglobulinemic 279.00
    congenital 279.04
    hypogammaglobulinemic 279.00
  anticardiolipin antibody 795.79
  antimongolism 758.39

Syndrome — *see also* Disease — *continued*
  antiphospholipid antibody 795.79
  Anton (-Babinski) (hemiasomatognosia) 307.9
  anxiety (*see also* Anxiety) 300.00
    organic 293.84
  aortic
    arch 446.7
    bifurcation (occlusion) 444.0
    ring 747.21
  Apert's (acrocephalosyndactyly) 755.55
  Apert-Gallais (adrenogenital) 255.2
  aphasia-apraxia-alexia 784.69
  apical ballooning 429.83   ▲
  "approximate answers" 300.16
  arcuate ligament (-celiac axis) 447.4
  arcus aortae 446.7
  arc welders' 370.24
  argentaffin, argintaffinoma 259.2
  Argonz-Del Castillo (nonpuerperal galactorrhea and amenorrhea) 253.1
  Argyll Robertson's (syphilitic) 094.89
    nonsyphilitic 379.45
  Armenian 277.31   ●
  arm-shoulder (*see also* Neuropathy, peripheral, autonomic) 337.9
  Arnold-Chiari (*see also* Spina bifida) 741.0 ☑
    type I 348.4
    type II 741.0 ☑
    type III 742.0
    type IV 742.2
  Arrillaga-Ayerza (pulmonary artery sclerosis with pulmonary hypertension) 416.0
  arteriomesenteric duodenum occlusion 537.89
  arteriovenous steal 996.73
  arteritis, young female (obliterative brachiocephalic) 446.7
  aseptic meningitis — *see* Meningitis, aseptic
  Asherman's 621.5
  Asperger's 299.8 ☑
  asphyctic (*see also* Anxiety) 300.00
  aspiration, of newborn (massive) 770.18
    meconium 770.12
  ataxia-telangiectasia 334.8
  Audry's (acropachyderma) 757.39
  auriculotemporal 350.8
  autosomal (*see also* Abnormal, autosomes NEC)
    deletion 758.39
      5p 758.31
      22q11.2 758.32
  Avellis' 344.89
  Axenfeld's 743.44
  Ayerza (-Arrillaga) (pulmonary artery sclerosis with pulmonary hypertension) 416.0
  Baader's (erythema multiforme exudativum) 695.1
  Baastrup's 721.5
  Babinski (-Vaquez) (cardiovascular syphilis) 093.89
  Babinski-Fröhlich (adiposogenital dystrophy) 253.8
  Babinski-Nageotte 344.89
  Bagratuni's (temporal arteritis) 446.5
  Bakwin-Krida (craniometaphyseal dysplasia) 756.89
  Balint's (psychic paralysis of visual disorientation) 368.16
  Ballantyne (-Runge) (postmaturity) 766.22
  ballooning posterior leaflet 424.0
  Banti's — *see* Cirrhosis, liver
  Bardet-Biedl (obesity, polydactyly, and mental retardation) 759.89
  Bard-Pic's (carcinoma, head of pancreas) 157.0
  Barlow's (mitral valve prolapse) 424.0

Syndrome — *see also* Disease — *continued*
  Barlow (-Möller) (infantile scurvy) 267
  Baron Munchausen's 301.51
  Barré-Guillain 357.0
  Barré-Liéou (posterior cervical sympathetic) 723.2
  Barrett's (chronic peptic ulcer of esophagus) 530.85
  Bársony-Polgár (corkscrew esophagus) 530.5
  Bársony-Teschendorf (corkscrew esophagus) 530.5
  Barth 759.89
  Bartter's (secondary hyperaldosteronism with juxtaglomerular hyperplasia) 255.13
  Basedow's (exophthalmic goiter) 242.0 ☑
  basilar artery 435.0
  basofrontal 377.04
  Bassen-Kornzweig (abetalipoproteinemia) 272.5
  Batten-Steinert 359.2
  battered
    adult 995.81
    baby or child 995.54
    spouse 995.81
  Baumgarten-Cruveilhier (cirrhosis of liver) 571.5
  Beals 759.82
  Bearn-Kunkel (-Slater) (lupoid hepatitis) 571.49
  Beau's (*see also* Degeneration, myocardial) 429.1
  Bechterew-Strümpell-Marie (ankylosing spondylitis) 720.0
  Beck's (anterior spinal artery occlusion) 433.8 ☑
  Beckwith (-Wiedemann) 759.89
  Behçet's 136.1
  Bekhterev-Strümpell-Marie (ankylosing spondylitis) 720.0
  Benedikt's 344.89
  Béquez César (-Steinbrinck-Chédiak-Higashi) (congenital gigantism of peroxidase granules) 288.2
  Bernard-Horner (*see also* Neuropathy, peripheral, autonomic) 337.9
  Bernard-Sergent (acute adrenocortical insufficiency) 255.4
  Bernhardt-Roth 355.1
  Bernheim's (*see also* Failure, heart) 428.0
  Bertolotti's (sacralization of fifth lumbar vertebra) 756.15
  Besnier-Boeck-Schaumann (sarcoidosis) 135
  Bianchi's (aphasia-apraxia-alexia syndrome) 784.69
  Biedl-Bardet (obesity, polydactyly, and mental retardation) 759.89
  Biemond's (obesity, polydactyly, and mental retardation) 759.89
  big spleen 289.4
  bilateral polycystic ovarian 256.4
  Bing-Horton's 346.2 ☑
  Biörck (-Thorson) (malignant carcinoid) 259.2
  Blackfan-Diamond (congenital hypoplastic anemia) 284.01   ▲
  black lung 500
  black widow spider bite 989.5
  bladder neck (*see also* Incontinence, urine) 788.30
  blast (concussion) — *see* Blast, injury
  blind loop (postoperative) 579.2
  Bloch-Siemens (incontinentia pigmenti) 757.33
  Bloch-Sulzberger (incontinentia pigmenti) 757.33
  Bloom (-Machacek) (-Torre) 757.39
  Blount-Barber (tibia vara) 732.4
  blue
    bloater 491.20

☑ Additional Digit Required — Refer to the Tabular List for Digit Selection   ▽ Subterms under main terms may continue to next column or page

2007 ICD-9-CM   ▶◀ Revised Text   ● New Line   ▲ Revised Code   **October 2006 · Volume 2 — 271**

Symptoms, specified — Syndrome

Syndrome — *see also* Disease — *continued*
  blue — *continued*
    bloater — *continued*
      with
        acute bronchitis 491.22
        exacerbation (acute) 491.21
      diaper 270.0
      drum 381.02
      sclera 756.51
      toe 445.02
  Boder-Sedgwick (ataxia-telangiectasia) 334.8
  Boerhaave's (spontaneous esophageal rupture) 530.4
  Bonnevie-Ullrich 758.6
  Bonnier's 386.19
  Borjeson-Forssman-Lehmann 759.89 ●
  Bouillaud's (rheumatic heart disease) 391.9
  Bourneville (-Pringle) (tuberous sclerosis) 759.5
  Bouveret (-Hoffmann) (paroxysmal tachycardia) 427.2
  brachial plexus 353.0
  Brachman-de Lange (Amsterdam dwarf, mental retardation, and brachycephaly) 759.89
  bradycardia-tachycardia 427.81
  Brailsford-Morquio (dystrophy) (mucopolysaccharidosis IV) 277.5
  brain (acute) (chronic) (nonpsychotic) (organic) (with behavioral reaction) (with neurotic reaction) 310.9
    with
      presenile brain disease (*see also* Dementia, presenile) 290.10
      psychosis, psychotic reaction (*see also* Psychosis, organic) 294.9
    chronic alcoholic 291.2
    congenital (*see also* Retardation, mental) 319
    postcontusional 310.2
    posttraumatic
      nonpsychotic 310.2
      psychotic 293.9
        acute 293.0
        chronic (*see also* Psychosis, organic) 294.8
        subacute 293.1
    psycho-organic (*see also* Syndrome, psycho-organic) 310.9
    psychotic (*see also* Psychosis, organic) 294.9
    senile (*see also* Dementia, senile) 290.0
  branchial arch 744.41
  Brandt's (acrodermatitis enteropathica) 686.8
  Brennemann's 289.2
  Briquet's 300.81
  Brissaud-Meige (infantile myxedema) 244.9
  broad ligament laceration 620.6
  Brock's (atelectasis due to enlarged lymph nodes) 518.0
  broken heart 429.83 ●
  Brown-Séquard 344.89
  brown spot 756.59
  Brown's tendon sheath 378.61
  Brugada 746.89
  Brugsch's (acropachyderma) 757.39
  bubbly lung 770.7
  Buchem's (hyperostosis corticalis) 733.3
  Budd-Chiari (hepatic vein thrombosis) 453.0
  Büdinger-Ludloff-Läwen 717.89
  bulbar 335.22
    lateral (*see also* Disease, cerebrovascular, acute) 436

Syndrome — *see also* Disease — *continued*
  Bullis fever 082.8
  bundle of Kent (anomalous atrioventricular excitation) 426.7
  Bürger-Grütz (essential familial hyperlipemia) 272.3
  Burke's (pancreatic insufficiency and chronic neutropenia) 577.8
  Burnett's (milk-alkali) 275.42
  Burnier's (hypophyseal dwarfism) 253.3
  burning feet 266.2
  Bywaters' 958.5
  Caffey's (infantile cortical hyperostosis) 756.59
  Calvé-Legg-Perthes (osteochrondrosis, femoral capital) 732.1
  Caplan (-Colinet) syndrome 714.81
  capsular thrombosis (*see also* Thrombosis, brain) 434.0 ☑
  carbohydrate-deficient glycoprotein (CDGS) 271.8
  carcinogenic thrombophlebitis 453.1
  carcinoid 259.2
  cardiac asthma (*see also* Failure, ventricular, left) 428.1
  cardiacos negros 416.0
  cardiopulmonary obesity 278.8
  cardiorenal (*see also* Hypertension, cardiorenal) 404.90
  cardiorespiratory distress (idiopathic), newborn 769
  cardiovascular renal (*see also* Hypertension, cardiorenal) 404.90
  cardiovasorenal 272.7
  Carini's (ichthyosis congenita) 757.1
  carotid
    artery (internal) 435.8
    body or sinus 337.0
  carpal tunnel 354.0
  Carpenter's 759.89
  Cassidy (-Scholte) (malignant carcinoid) 259.2
  cat-cry 758.31
  cauda equina 344.60
  causalgia 355.9
    lower limb 355.71
    upper limb 354.4
  cavernous sinus 437.6
  celiac 579.0
    artery compression 447.4
    axis 447.4
  central pain 338.0 ●
  cerebellomedullary malformation (*see also* Spina bifida) 741.0 ☑
  cerebral gigantism 253.0
  cerebrohepatorenal 759.89
  cervical (root) (spine) NEC 723.8
    disc 722.71
    posterior, sympathetic 723.2
    rib 353.0
    sympathetic paralysis 337.0
    traumatic (acute) NEC 847.0
  cervicobrachial (diffuse) 723.3
  cervicocranial 723.2
  cervicodorsal outlet 353.2
  Céstan's 344.89
  Céstan (-Raymond) 433.8 ☑
  Céstan-Chenais 344.89
  chancriform 114.1
  Charcôt's (intermittent claudication) 443.9
    angina cruris 443.9
    due to atherosclerosis 440.21
  Charcôt-Marie-Tooth 356.1
  Charcôt-Weiss-Baker 337.0
  CHARGE association 759.89
  Cheadle (-Möller) (-Barlow) (infantile scurvy) 267
  Chédiak-Higashi (-Steinbrinck) (congenital gigantism of peroxidase granules) 288.2
  chest wall 786.52
  Chiari's (hepatic vein thrombosis) 453.0

Syndrome — *see also* Disease — *continued*
  Chiari-Frommel 676.6 ☑
  chiasmatic 368.41
  Chilaiditi's (subphrenic displacement, colon) 751.4
  chondroectodermal dysplasia 756.55
  chorea-athetosis-agitans 275.1
  Christian's (chronic histiocytosis X) 277.89
  chromosome 4 short arm deletion 758.39
  chronic pain 338.4 ●
  Churg-Strauss 446.4
  Clarke-Hadfield (pancreatic infantilism) 577.8
  Claude's 352.6
  Claude Bernard-Horner (*see also* Neuropathy, peripheral, autonomic) 337.9
  Clérambault's
    automatism 348.8
    erotomania 297.8
  Clifford's (postmaturity) 766.22
  climacteric 627.2
  Clouston's (hidrotic ectodermal dysplasia) 757.31
  clumsiness 315.4
  Cockayne's (microencephaly and dwarfism) 759.89
  Cockayne-Weber (epidermolysis bullosa) 757.39
  Coffin-Lowry 759.89
  Cogan's (nonsyphilitic interstitial keratitis) 370.52
  cold injury (newborn) 778.2
  Collet (-Sicard) 352.6
  combined immunity deficiency 279.2
  compartment(al) (anterior) (deep) (posterior) 958.8
    nontraumatic
      abdomen 729.73 ●
      arm 729.71 ●
      buttock 729.72 ●
      fingers 729.71 ●
      foot 729.72 ●
      forearm 729.71 ●
      hand 729.71 ●
      hip 729.72 ●
      leg 729.72 ●
      lower extremity 729.72 ●
      shoulder 729.71 ●
      specified site NEC 729.79 ●
      thigh 729.72 ●
      toes 729.72 ●
      upper extremity 729.71 ●
      wrist 729.71 ●
    traumatic 958.90
      adomen 958.93 ●
      arm 958.91 ●
      buttock 958.92 ●
      fingers 958.91 ●
      foot 958.92 ●
      forearm 958.91 ●
      hand 958.91 ●
      hip 958.92 ●
      leg 958.92 ●
      lower extremity 958.92 ●
      shoulder 958.91 ●
      specified site NEC 958.99 ●
      thigh 958.92 ●
      tibial 958.92 ●
      toes 958.92 ●
      upper extremity 958.91 ●
      wrist 958.91 ●
  compression 958.5
    cauda equina 344.60
      with neurogenic bladder 344.61
  concussion 310.2
  congenital
    affecting more than one system 759.7
      specified type NEC 759.89
    congenital central alveolar hypoventilation 327.25
    facial diplegia 352.6

Syndrome — *see also* Disease — *continued*
  congenital — *continued*
    muscular hypertrophy-cerebral 759.89
    congestion-fibrosis (pelvic) 625.5
    conjunctivourethrosynovial 099.3
    Conn (-Louis) (primary aldosteronism) 255.12
    Conradi (-Hünermann) (chondrodysplasia calcificans congenita) 756.59
    conus medullaris 336.8
    Cooke-Apert-Gallais (adrenogenital) 255.2
    Cornelia de Lange's (Amsterdam dwarf, mental retardation, and brachycephaly) 759.8 ☑
    coronary insufficiency or intermediate 411.1
    cor pulmonale 416.9
    corticosexual 255.2
    Costen's (complex) 524.60
    costochondral junction 733.6
    costoclavicular 353.0
    costovertebral 253.0
    Cotard's (paranoia) 297.1
    Cowden 759.6
    craniovertebral 723.2
    Creutzfeldt-Jakob (new variant) 046.1
      with dementia
        with behavioral disturbance 046.1 [294.11]
        without behavioral disturbance 046.1 [294.10]
    crib death 798.0
    cricopharyngeal 787.2
    cri-du-chat 758.31
    Crigler-Najjar (congenital hyperbilirubinemia) 277.4
    crocodile tears 351.8
    Cronkhite-Canada 211.3
    croup 464.4
    CRST (cutaneous systemic sclerosis) 710.1
    crush 958.5
    crushed lung (*see also* Injury, internal, lung) 861.20
    Cruveilhier-Baumgarten (cirrhosis of liver) 571.5
    cubital tunnel 354.2
    Cuiffini-Pancoast (M8010/3) (carcinoma, pulmonary apex) 162.3
    Curschmann (-Batten) (-Steinert) 359.2
    Cushing's (iatrogenic) (idiopathic) (pituitary basophilism) (pituitary-dependent) 255.0
      overdose or wrong substance given or taken 962.0
    Cyriax's (slipping rib) 733.99
    cystic duct stump 576.0
    Da Costa's (neurocirculatory asthenia) 306.2
    Dameshek's (erythroblastic anemia) 282.49
    Dana-Putnam (subacute combined sclerosis with pernicious anemia) 281.0 [336.2]
    Danbolt (-Closs) (acrodermatitis enteropathica) 686.8
    Dandy-Walker (atresia, foramen of Magendie) 742.3
      with spina bifida (*see also* Spina bifida) 741.0 ☑
    Danlos' 756.83
    Davies-Colley (slipping rib) 733.99
    dead fetus 641.3 ☑
    defeminization 255.2
    defibrination (*see also* Fibrinolysis) 286.6
    Degos' 447.8
    Deiters' nucleus 386.19
    Déjérine-Roussy 338.0 ▲
    Déjérine-Thomas 333.0

Syndrome — *see also* Disease — *continued*

de Lange's (Amsterdam dwarf, mental retardation, and brachycephaly) (Cornelia) 759.89
Del Castillo's (germinal aplasia) 606.0
deletion chromosomes 758.39
delusional
  induced by drug 292.11
dementia-aphonia, of childhood (*see also* Psychosis, childhood) 299.1 ☑
demyelinating NEC 341.9
denial visual hallucination 307.9
depersonalization 300.6
Dercum's (adiposis dolorosa) 272.8
de Toni-Fanconi (-Debré) (cystinosis) 270.0
diabetes-dwarfism-obesity (juvenile) 258.1
diabetes mellitus-hypertension-nephrosis 250.4 ☑ [581.81]
diabetes mellitus in newborn infant 775.1
diabetes-nephrosis 250.4 ☑ [581.81]
diabetic amyotrophy 250.6 ☑ [358.1]
Diamond-Blackfan (congenital hypoplastic anemia) 284.01
Diamond-Gardener (autoerythrocyte sensitization) 287.2
DIC (diffuse or disseminated intravascular coagulopathy) (*see also* Fibrinolysis) 286.6
diencephalohypophyseal NEC 253.8
diffuse cervicobrachial 723.3
diffuse obstructive pulmonary 496
DiGeorge's (thymic hypoplasia) 279.11
Dighton's 756.51
Di Guglielmo's (erythremic myelosis) (M9841/3) 207.0 ☑
disequilibrium 276.9
disseminated platelet thrombosis 446.6
Ditthomska 307.81
Doan-Wiseman (primary splenic neutropenia) 288.0 ☑
Doan-Wisemann (primary splenic neutropenia) 289.53 ●
Döhle body-panmyelopathic 288.2
Donohue's (leprechaunism) 259.8
dorsolateral medullary (*see also* Disease, cerebrovascular, acute) 436
double athetosis 333.71 ●
double whammy 360.81
Down's (mongolism) 758.0
Dresbach's (elliptocytosis) 282.1
Dressler's (postmyocardial infarction) 411.0
  hemoglobinuria 283.2
  postcardiotomy 429.4 ●
drug withdrawal, infant, of dependent mother 779.5
dry skin 701.1
  eye 375.15
DSAP (disseminated superficial actinic porokeratosis) 692.75
Duane's (retraction) 378.71
Duane-Stilling-Türk (ocular retraction syndrome) 378.71
Dubin-Johnson (constitutional hyperbilirubinemia) 277.4
Dubin-Sprinz (constitutional hyperbilirubinemia) 277.4
Duchenne's 335.22
due to abnormality
  autosomal NEC (*see also* Abnormal, autosomes NEC) 758.5
    13 758.1
    18 758.2
    21 or 22 758.0
    D1 758.1
    E3 758.2
    G 758.0
  chromosomal 758.89
  sex 758.81

Syndrome — *see also* Disease — *continued*

dumping 564.2
  nonsurgical 536.8
Duplay's 726.2
Dupré's (meningism) 781.6
Dyke-Young (acquired macrocytic hemolytic anemia) 283.9
dyspraxia 315.4
dystocia, dystrophia 654.9 ☑
Eagle-Barret 756.71
Eales' 362.18
Eaton-Lambert (*see also* Neoplasm, by site, malignant) 199.1 [358.1]
Ebstein's (downward displacement, tricuspid valve into right ventricle) 746.2
ectopic ACTH secretion 255.0
eczema-thrombocytopenia 279.12
Eddowes' (brittle bones and blue sclera) 756.51
Edwards' 758.2
efferent loop 537.89
effort (aviators') (psychogenic) 306.2
Ehlers-Danlos 756.83
Eisenmenger's (ventricular septal defect) 745.4
Ekbom's (restless legs) 333.94 ▲
Ekman's (brittle bones and blue sclera) 756.51
electric feet 266.2
Elephant man 237.71
Ellison-Zollinger (gastric hypersecretion with pancreatic islet cell tumor) 251.5
Ellis-van Creveld (chondroectodermal dysplasia) 756.55
embryonic fixation 270.2
empty sella (turcica) 253.8
endocrine-hypertensive 255.3
Engel-von Recklinghausen (osteitis fibrosa cystica) 252.01
enteroarticular 099.3
entrapment — *see* Neuropathy, entrapment
eosinophilia myalgia 710.5
epidemic vomiting 078.82
Epstein's — *see* Nephrosis
Erb (-Oppenheim)-Goldflam 358.00
Erdheim's (acromegalic macrospondylitis) 253.0
Erlacher-Blount (tibia vara) 732.4
erythrocyte fragmentation 283.19
euthyroid sick 790.94
Evans' (thrombocytopenic purpura) 287.32
excess cortisol, iatrogenic 255.0
exhaustion 300.5
extrapyramidal 333.90
eyelid-malar-mandible 756.0
eye retraction 378.71
Faber's (achlorhydric anemia) 280.9
Fabry (-Anderson) (angiokeratoma corporis diffusum) 272.7
facet 724.8
Fallot's 745.2
falx (*see also* Hemorrhage, brain) 431
familial eczema-thrombocytopenia 279.12
Fanconi (-de Toni) (-Debré) (cystinosis) 270.0
Fanconi's (anemia) (congenital pancytopenia) 284.09 ▲
Farber (-Uzman) (disseminated lipogranulomatosis) 272.8
fatigue NEC 300.5
  chronic 780.71
faulty bowel habit (idiopathic megacolon) 564.7
FDH (focal dermal hypoplasia) 757.39
fecal reservoir 560.39
Feil-Klippel (brevicollis) 756.16
Felty's (rheumatoid arthritis with splenomegaly and leukopenia) 714.1
fertile eunuch 257.2

Syndrome — *see also* Disease — *continued*

fetal alcohol 760.71
  late effect 760.71
fibrillation-flutter 427.32
fibrositis (periarticular) 729.0
Fiedler's (acute isolated myocarditis) 422.91
Fiessinger-Leroy (-Reiter) 099.3
Fiessinger-Rendu (erythema multiforme exudativum) 695.1
first arch 756.0
Fisher's 357.0
fish odor 270.8 ●
Fitz's (acute hemorrhagic pancreatitis) 577.0
Fitz-Hugh and Curtis 098.86
  due to
    Chlamydia trachomatis 099.56
    Neisseria gonorrhoeae (gonococcal peritonitis) 098.86
Flajani (-Basedow) (exophthalmic goiter) 242.0 ☑
floppy
  infant 781.99
  valve (mitral) 424.0
flush 259.2
Foix-Alajouanine 336.1
Fong's (hereditary osteo-onychodysplasia) 756.89
foramen magnum 348.4
Forbes-Albright (nonpuerperal amenorrhea and lactation associated with pituitary tumor) 253.1
Foster-Kennedy 377.04
Foville's (peduncular) 344.89
fragile X 759.83
Franceschetti's (mandibulofacial dysostosis) 756.0
Fraser's 759.89
Freeman-Sheldon 759.89
Frey's (auriculotemporal) 705.22
Friderichsen-Waterhouse 036.3
Friedrich-Erb-Arnold (acropachyderma) 757.39
Fröhlich's (adiposogenital dystrophy) 253.8
Froin's 336.8
Frommel-Chiari 676.6 ☑
frontal lobe 310.0
Fukuhara 277.87
Fuller Albright's (osteitis fibrosa disseminata) 756.59
functional
  bowel 564.9
  prepubertal castrate 752.89
Gaisböck's (polycythemia hypertonica) 289.0
ganglion (basal, brain) 333.90
geniculi 351.1
Ganser's, hysterical 300.16
Gardner-Diamond (autoerythrocyte sensitization) 287.2
gastroesophageal junction 530.0
gastroesophageal laceration-hemorrhage 530.7
gastrojejunal loop obstruction 537.89
Gayet-Wernicke's (superior hemorrhagic polioencephalitis) 265.1
Gee-Herter-Heubner (nontropical sprue) 579.0
Gélineau's (*see also* Narcolepsy) 347.00
genito-anorectal 099.1
Gerhardt's (vocal cord paralysis) 478.30
Gerstmann's (finger agnosia) 784.69
Gianotti Crosti 057.8
  due to known virus — *see* Infection, virus
  due to unknown virus 057.8
Gilbert's 277.4
Gilford (-Hutchinson) (progeria) 259.8
Gilles de la Tourette's 307.23
Gillespie's (dysplasia oculodentodigitalis) 759.89

Syndrome — *see also* Disease — *continued*

Glénard's (enteroptosis) 569.89
Glinski-Simmonds (pituitary cachexia) 253.2
glucuronyl transferase 277.4
glue ear 381.20
Goldberg (-Maxwell) (-Morris) (testicular feminization) 259.5
Goldenhar's (oculoauriculovertebral dysplasia) 756.0
Goldflam-Erb 358.00
Goltz-Gorlin (dermal hypoplasia) 757.39
Good's 279.06
Goodpasture's (pneumorenal) 446.21
Gopalan's (burning feet) 266.2
Gorlin-Chaudhry-Moss 759.89
Gougerot-Blum (pigmented purpuric lichenoid dermatitis) 709.1
Gougerot-Carteaud (confluent reticulate papillomatosis) 701.8
Gougerot (-Houwer)-Sjögren (keratoconjunctivitis sicca) 710.2
Gouley's (constrictive pericarditis) 423.2
Gowers' (vasovagal attack) 780.2
Gowers-Paton-Kennedy 377.04
Gradenigo's 383.02
gray or grey (chloramphenicol) (newborn) 779.4
Greig's (hypertelorism) 756.0
Gubler-Millard 344.89
Guérin-Stern (arthrogryposis multiplex congenita) 754.89
Guillain-Barré (-Strohl) 357.0
Gunn's (jaw-winking syndrome) 742.8
Günther's (congenital erythropoietic porphyria) 277.1
gustatory sweating 350.8
H3O 759.81
Hadfield-Clarke (pancreatic infantilism) 577.8
Haglund-Läwen-Fründ 717.89
hairless women 257.8
hair tourniquet (*see also* Injury, superficial, by site)
  finger 915.8
    infected 915.9
  penis 911.8
    infected 911.9
  toe 917.8
    infected 917.9
Hallermann-Streiff 756.0
Hallervorden-Spatz 333.0
Hamman's (spontaneous mediastinal emphysema) 518.1
Hamman-Rich (diffuse interstitial pulmonary fibrosis) 516.3
hand-foot 282.61
Hand-Schüller-Christian (chronic histiocytosis X) 277.89
Hanot-Chauffard (-Troisier) (bronze diabetes) 275.0
Harada's 363.22
Hare's (M8010/3) (carcinoma, pulmonary apex) 162.3
Harkavy's 446.0
harlequin color change 779.89
Harris' (organic hyperinsulinism) 251.1
Hart's (pellagra-cerebellar ataxia-renal aminoaciduria) 270.0
Hayem-Faber (achlorhydric anemia) 280.9
Hayem-Widal (acquired hemolytic jaundice) 283.9
Heberden's (angina pectoris) 413.9
Hedinger's (malignant carcinoid) 259.2
Hegglin's 288.2
Heller's (infantile psychosis) (*see also* Psychosis, childhood) 299.1 ☑
H.E.L.L.P 642.5 ☑
hemolytic-uremic (adult) (child) 283.11
hemophagocytic 288.4   ●

☑ Additional Digit Required — Refer to the Tabular List for Digit Selection   ▽ Subterms under main terms may continue to next column or page

2007 ICD-9-CM   ►◄ Revised Text   ● New Line   ▲ Revised Code   **October 2006 • Volume 2 — 273**

Syndrome — *see also* Disease — *continued*
  hemophagocytic — *continued*
    infection-associated 288.4 ●
  Hench-Rosenberg (palindromic arthritis) (*see also* Rheumatism, palindromic) 719.3 ☑
  Henoch-Schönlein (allergic purpura) 287.0
  hepatic flexure 569.89
  hepatorenal 572.4
    due to a procedure 997.4
    following delivery 674.8 ☑
  hepatourologic 572.4
  Herrick's (hemoglobin S disease) 282.61
  Herter (-Gee) (nontropical sprue) 579.0
  Heubner-Herter (nontropical sprue) 579.0
  Heyd's (hepatorenal) 572.4
  HHHO 759.81
  high grade myelodysplastic 238.73 ●
    with 5q deletion 238.73 ●
  Hilger's 337.0
  histiocytic 288.4 ●
  Hoffa (-Kastert) (liposynovitis prepatellaris) 272.8
  Hoffmann's 244.9 *[359.5]*
  Hoffmann-Bouveret (paroxysmal tachycardia) 427.2
  Hoffmann-Werdnig 335.0
  Holländer-Simons (progressive lipodystrophy) 272.6
  Holmes' (visual disorientation) 368.16
  Holmes-Adie 379.46
  Hoppe-Goldflam 358.00
  Horner's (*see also* Neuropathy, peripheral, autonomic) 337.9
    traumatic — *see* Injury, nerve, cervical sympathetic
  hospital addiction 301.51
  Hunt's (herpetic geniculate ganglionitis) 053.11
    dyssynergia cerebellaris myoclonica 334.2
  Hunter (-Hurler) (mucopolysaccharidosis II) 277.5
  hunterian glossitis 529.4
  Hurler (-Hunter) (mucopolysaccharidosis II) 277.5
  Hutchinson-Boeck (sarcoidosis) 135
  Hutchinson-Gilford (progeria) 259.8
  Hutchinson's incisors or teeth 090.5
  hydralazine
    correct substance properly administered 695.4
    overdose or wrong substance given or taken 972.6
  hydraulic concussion (abdomen) (*see also* Injury, internal, abdomen) 868.00
  hyperabduction 447.8
  hyperactive bowel 564.9
  hyperaldosteronism with hypokalemic alkalosis (Bartter's) 255.13
  hypercalcemic 275.42
  hypercoagulation NEC 289.89
  hypereosinophilic (idiopathic) 288.3
  hyperkalemic 276.7
  hyperkinetic (*see also* Hyperkinesia) heart 429.82
  hyperlipemia-hemolytic anemia-icterus 571.1
  hypermobility 728.5
  hypernatremia 276.0
  hyperosmolarity 276.0
  hypersomnia-bulimia 349.89
  hypersplenic 289.4
  hypersympathetic (*see also* Neuropathy, peripheral, autonomic) 337.9
  hypertransfusion, newborn 776.4
  hyperventilation, psychogenic 306.1
  hyperviscosity (of serum) NEC 273.3
    polycythemic 289.0
    sclerothymic 282.8

Syndrome — *see also* Disease — *continued*
  hypoglycemic (familial) (neonatal) 251.2
    functional 251.1
  hypokalemic 276.8
  hypophyseal 253.8
  hypophyseothalamic 253.8
  hypopituitarism 253.2
  hypoplastic left heart 746.7
  hypopotassemia 276.8
  hyposmolality 276.1
  hypotension, maternal 669.2 ☑
  hypotonia-hypomentia-hypogonadism-obesity 759.81
  ICF (intravascular coagulation-fibrinolysis) (*see also* Fibrinolysis) 286.6
  idiopathic cardiorespiratory distress, newborn 769
  idiopathic nephrotic (infantile) 581.9
  iliotibial band 728.89
  Imerslund (-Gräsbeck) (anemia due to familial selective vitamin B_{12} malabsorption) 281.1
  immobility (paraplegic) 728.3
  immunity deficiency, combined 279.2
  impending coronary 411.1
  impingement
    shoulder 726.2
    vertebral bodies 724.4
  inappropriate secretion of antidiuretic hormone (ADH) 253.6
  incomplete
    mandibulofacial 756.0
  infant
    death, sudden (SIDS) 798.0
    Hercules 255.2
    of diabetic mother 775.0
    shaken 995.55
  infantilism 253.3
  inferior vena cava 459.2
  influenza-like 487.1
  inspissated bile, newborn 774.4
  insufficient sleep 307.44
  intermediate coronary (artery) 411.1
  internal carotid artery (*see also* Occlusion, artery, carotid) 433.1 ☑
  interspinous ligament 724.8
  intestinal
    carcinoid 259.2
    gas 787.3
    knot 560.2
  intravascular
    coagulation-fibrinolysis (ICF) (*see also* Fibrinolysis) 286.6
    coagulopathy (*see also* Fibrinolysis) 286.6
  inverted Marfan's 759.89
  IRDS (idiopathic respiratory distress, newborn) 769
  irritable
    bowel 564.1
    heart 306.2
    weakness 300.5
  ischemic bowel (transient) 557.9
    chronic 557.1
    due to mesenteric artery insufficiency 557.1
  Itsenko-Cushing (pituitary basophilism) 255.0
  IVC (intravascular coagulopathy) (*see also* Fibrinolysis) 286.6
  Ivemark's (asplenia with congenital heart disease) 759.0
  Jaccoud's 714.4
  Jackson's 344.89
  Jadassohn-Lewandowski (pachyonchia congenita) 757.5
  Jaffe-Lichtenstein (-Uehlinger) 252.01
  Jahnke's (encephalocutaneous angiomatosis) 759.6
  Jakob-Creutzfeldt (new variant) 046.1
    with dementia
      with behavioral disturbance 046.1 *[294.11]*

Syndrome — *see also* Disease — *continued*
  Jakob-Creutzfeldt — *continued*
    with dementia — *continued*
      without behavioral disturbance 046.1 *[294.10]*
  Jaksch's (pseudoleukemia infantum) 285.8
  Jaksch-Hayem (-Luzet) (pseudoleukemia infantum) 285.8
  jaw-winking 742.8
  jejunal 564.2
  Jervell-Lange-Nielsen 426.82
  jet lag 327.35
  Jeune's (asphyxiating thoracic dystrophy of newborn) 756.4
  Job's (chronic granulomatous disease) 288.1
  Jordan's 288.2
  Joseph-Diamond-Blackfan (congenital hypoplastic anemia) 284.01 ▲
  Joubert 759.89
  jugular foramen 352.6
  Kabuki 759.89
  Kahler's (multiple myeloma) (M9730/3) 203.0 ☑
  Kalischer's (encephalocutaneous angiomatosis) 759.6
  Kallmann's (hypogonadotropic hypogonadism with anosmia) 253.4
  Kanner's (autism) (*see also* Psychosis, childhood) 299.0 ☑
  Kartagener's (sinusitis, bronchiectasis, situs inversus) 759.3
  Kasabach-Merritt (capillary hemangioma associated with thrombocytopenic purpura) 287.39
  Kast's (dyschondroplasia with hemangiomas) 756.4
  Kaznelson's (congenital hypoplastic anemia) 284.01 ▲
  Kearns-Sayre 277.87
  Kelly's (sideropenic dysphagia) 280.8
  Kimmelstiel-Wilson (intercapillary glomerulosclerosis) 250.4 ☑ *[581.81]*
  Klauder's (erythema multiforme exudativum) 695.1
  Kleine-Levin 327.13
  Klein-Waardenburg (ptosis-epicanthus) 270.2
  Klippel-Feil (brevicollis) 756.16
  Klippel-Trenaunay 759.89
  Klumpke (-Déjérine) (injury to brachial plexus at birth) 767.6
  Klüver-Bucy (-Terzian) 310.0
  Köhler-Pellegrini-Stieda (calcification, knee joint) 726.62
  König's 564.89
  Korsakoff's (nonalcoholic) 294.0
  Korsakoff (-Wernicke) (nonalcoholic) 294.0
    alcoholic 291.1
  Korsakoff's
    alcoholic 291.1
  Kostmann's (infantile genetic agranulocytosis) 288.01 ▲
  Krabbe's
    congenital muscle hypoplasia 756.89
    cutaneocerebral angioma 759.6
  Kunkel (lupoid hepatitis) 571.49
  labyrinthine 386.50
  laceration, broad ligament 620.6
  Langdon Down (mongolism) 758.0
  Larsen's (flattened facies and multiple congenital dislocations) 755.8
  lateral
    cutaneous nerve of thigh 355.1
    medullary (*see also* Disease, cerebrovascular acute) 436
  Launois' (pituitary gigantism) 253.0
  Launois-Cléret (adiposogenital dystrophy) 253.8

Syndrome — *see also* Disease — *continued*
  Laurence-Moon (-Bardet)-Biedl (obesity, polydactyly, and mental retardation) 759.89
  Lawford's (encephalocutaneous angiomatosis) 759.6
  lazy
    leukocyte 288.09 ▲
    posture 728.3
  Lederer-Brill (acquired infectious hemolytic anemia) 283.19
  Legg-Calvé-Perthes (osteochondrosis capital femoral) 732.1
  Lemiere 451.89
  Lennox's (*see also* Epilepsy) 345.0 ☑
  Lennox-Gastaut syndrome 345.0 ☑
    with tonic seizures 345.1 ☑
  lenticular 275.1
  Léopold-Lévi's (paroxysmal thyroid instability) 242.9 ☑
  Lepore hemoglobin 282.49
  Leriche's (aortic bifurcation occlusion) 444.0
  Léri-Weill 756.59
  Lermoyez's (*see also* Disease, Ménière's) 386.00
  Lesch-Nyhan (hypoxanthine-guanine-phosphoribosyltransferase deficiency) 277.2
  Lev's (acquired complete heart block) 426.0
  Levi's (pituitary dwarfism) 253.3
  Lévy-Roussy 334.3
  Lichtheim's (subacute combined sclerosis with pernicious anemia) 281.0 *[336.2]*
  Li-Fraumeni V84.01
  Lightwood's (renal tubular acidosis) 588.89
  Lignac (-de Toni) (-Fanconi) (-Debré) (cystinosis) 270.0
  Likoff's (angina in menopausal women) 413.9
  liver-kidney 572.4
  Lloyd's 258.1
  lobotomy 310.0
  Löffler's (eosinophilic pneumonitis) 518.3
  Löfgren's (sarcoidosis) 135
  long arm 18 or 21 deletion 758.39
  Looser (-Debray)-Milkman (osteomalacia with pseudofractures) 268.2
  Lorain-Levi (pituitary dwarfism) 253.3
  Louis-Bar (ataxia-telangiectasia) 334.8
  low
    atmospheric pressure 993.2
    back 724.2
      psychogenic 306.0
    output (cardiac) (*see also* Failure, heart) 428.9
  Lowe's (oculocerebrorenal dystrophy) 270.8
  lower radicular, newborn 767.4
  Lowe-Terrey-MacLachlan (oculocerebrorenal dystrophy) 270.8
  Lown (-Ganong)-Levine (short P-R interval, normal QRS complex, and supraventricular tachycardia) 426.81
  Lucey-Driscoll (jaundice due to delayed conjugation) 774.30
  Luetscher's (dehydration) 276.51
  lumbar vertebral 724.4
  Lutembacher's (atrial septal defect with mitral stenosis) 745.5
  Lyell's (toxic epidermal necrolysis) 695.1
    due to drug
      correct substance properly administered 695.1
      overdose or wrong substance given or taken 977.9
      specified drug — *see* Table of Drugs and Chemicals

☑ Additional Digit Required — Refer to the Tabular List for Digit Selection   ⬚ Subterms under main terms may continue to next column or page

2007 ICD-9-CM   ▶◀ Revised Text   ● New Line   ▲ Revised Code   October 2006 • Volume 2 — 275

Syndrome — *see also* Disease — *continued*

pellagra-cerebellar ataxia-renal aminoaciduria 270.0
pellagroid 265.2
Pellegrini-Stieda 726.62
Pellizzi's (pineal) 259.8
pelvic congestion (-fibrosis) 625.5
Pendred's (familial goiter with deaf-mutism) 243
Penfield's (*see also* Epilepsy) 345.5 ☑
Penta X 758.81
peptic ulcer — *see* Ulcer, peptic 533.9 ☑
perabduction 447.8
periodic 277.31 ▲
periurethral fibrosis 593.4
persistent fetal circulation 747.83
Petges-Cléjat (poikilodermatomyositis) 710.3
Peutz-Jeghers 759.6
Pfeiffer (acrocephalosyndactyly) 755.55
phantom limb 353.6
pharyngeal pouch 279.11
Pick's (pericardial pseudocirrhosis of liver) 423.2
  heart 423.2
  liver 423.2
Pick-Herxheimer (diffuse idiopathic cutaneous atrophy) 701.8
Pickwickian (cardiopulmonary obesity) 278.8
PIE (pulmonary infiltration with eosinophilia) 518.3
Pierre Marie-Bamberger (hypertrophic pulmonary osteoarthropathy) 731.2
Pierre Mauriac's (diabetes-dwarfism-obesity) 258.1
Pierre Robin 756.0
pigment dispersion, iris 364.53
pineal 259.8
pink puffer 492.8
pituitary 253.0
placental
  dysfunction 762.2
  insufficiency 762.2
  transfusion 762.3
plantar fascia 728.71
plica knee 727.83
Plummer-Vinson (sideropenic dysphagia) 280.8
pluricarential of infancy 260
plurideficiency of infancy 260
pluriglandular (compensatory) 258.8
polycarential of infancy 260
polyglandular 258.8
polysplenia 759.0
pontine 433.8 ☑
popliteal
  artery entrapment 447.8
  web 756.89
postartificial menopause 627.4
postcardiac injury ●
  postcardiotomy 429.4 ●
  postmyocardial infarction 411.0 ●
postcardiotomy 429.4
postcholecystectomy 576.0
postcommissurotomy 429.4
postconcussional 310.2
postcontusional 310.2
postencephalitic 310.8
posterior
  cervical sympathetic 723.2
  fossa compression 348.4
  inferior cerebellar artery (*see also* Disease, cerebrovascular, acute) 436
  reversible encephalopathy (PRES) ●
    348.39 ●
postgastrectomy (dumping) 564.2
post-gastric surgery 564.2
posthepatitis 780.79
postherpetic (neuralgia) (zoster) 053.19

Syndrome — *see also* Disease — *continued*

postherpetic — *continued*
  geniculate ganglion 053.11
  ophthalmica 053.19
postimmunization — *see* Complications, vaccination
postinfarction 411.0
postinfluenza (asthenia) 780.79
postirradiation 990
postlaminectomy 722.80
  cervical, cervicothoracic 722.81
  lumbar, lumbosacral 722.83
  thoracic, thoracolumbar 722.82
postleukotomy 310.0
postlobotomy 310.0
postmastectomy lymphedema 457.0
postmature (of newborn) 766.22
postmyocardial infarction 411.0
postoperative NEC 998.9
  blind loop 579.2
postpartum panhypopituitary 253.2
postperfusion NEC 999.8
  bone marrow 996.85
postpericardiotomy 429.4
postphlebitic (asymptomatic) 459.10
  with
    complications NEC 459.19
    inflammation 459.12
      and ulcer 459.13
    stasis dermatitis 459.12
      with ulcer 459.13
    ulcer 459.11
      with inflammation 459.13
postpolio (myelitis) 138
postvagotomy 564.2
postvalvulotomy 429.4
postviral (asthenia) NEC 780.79
Potain's (gastrectasis with dyspepsia) 536.1
potassium intoxication 276.7
Potter's 753.0
Prader (-Labhart) -Willi (-Fanconi) 759.81
preinfarction 411.1
preleukemic 238.75 ▲
premature senility 259.8
premenstrual 625.4
premenstrual tension 625.4
pre ulcer 536.9
Prinzmetal-Massumi (anterior chest wall syndrome) 786.52
Profichet's 729.9
progeria 259.8
progressive pallidal degeneration 333.0
prolonged gestation 766.22
Proteus (dermal hypoplasia) 757.39
prune belly 756.71
prurigo-asthma 691.8
pseudocarpal tunnel (sublimis) 354.0
pseudohermaphroditism-virilism-hirsutism 255.2
pseudoparalytica 358.00
pseudo-Turner's 759.89
psycho-organic 293.9
  acute 293.0
  anxiety type 293.84
  depressive type 293.83
  hallucinatory type 293.82
  nonpsychotic severity 310.1
    specified focal (partial) NEC 310.8
  paranoid type 293.81
  specified type NEC 293.89
  subacute 293.1
pterygolymphangiectasia 758.6
ptosis-epicanthus 270.2
pulmonary
  arteriosclerosis 416.0
  hypoperfusion (idiopathic) 769
  renal (hemorrhagic) 446.21
pulseless 446.7
Putnam-Dana (subacute combined sclerosis with pernicious anemia) 281.0 *[336.2]*

Syndrome — *see also* Disease — *continued*

pyloroduodenal 537.89
pyramidopallidonigral 332.0
pyriformis 355.0
QT interval prolongation 426.82
radicular NEC 729.2
  lower limbs 724.4
  upper limbs 723.4
    newborn 767.4
Raeder-Harbitz (pulseless disease) 446.7
Ramsay Hunt's
  dyssynergia cerebellaris myoclonica 334.2
  herpetic geniculate ganglionitis 053.11
rapid time-zone change 327.35
Raymond (-Céstan) 433.8 ☑
Raynaud's (paroxysmal digital cyanosis) 443.0
RDS (respiratory distress syndrome, newborn) 769
Refsum's (heredopathia atactica polyneuritiformis) 356.3
Reichmann's (gastrosuccorrhea) 536.8
Reifenstein's (hereditary familial hypogonadism, male) 259.5
Reilly's (*see also* Neuropathy, peripheral, autonomic) 337.9
Reiter's 099.3
renal glomerulohyalinosis-diabetic 250.4 ☑ *[581.81]*
Rendu-Osler-Weber (familial hemorrhagic telangiectasia) 448.0
renofacial (congenital biliary fibroangiomatosis) 753.0
Rénon-Delille 253.8
respiratory distress (idiopathic) (newborn) 769
  adult (following shock, surgery, or trauma) 518.5
    specified NEC 518.82
    type II 770.6 ●
restless legs ▶(RLS)◀ 333.94 ▲
retinoblastoma (familial) 190.5
retraction (Duane's) 378.71
retroperitoneal fibrosis 593.4
retroviral seroconversion (acute) V08 ●
Rett's 330.8
Reye's 331.81
Reye-Sheehan (postpartum pituitary necrosis) 253.2
Riddoch's (visual disorientation) 368.16
Ridley's (*see also* Failure, ventricular, left) 428.1
Rieger's (mesodermal dysgenesis, anterior ocular segment) 743.44
Rietti-Greppi-Micheli (thalassemia minor) 282.49
right ventricular obstruction — *see* Failure, heart
Riley-Day (familial dysautonomia) 742.8
Robin's 756.0
Rokitansky-Kuster-Hauser (congenital absence, vagina) 752.49
Romano-Ward (prolonged QT interval syndrome) 426.82
Romberg's 349.89
Rosen-Castleman-Liebow (pulmonary proteinosis) 516.0
rotator cuff, shoulder 726.10
Roth's 355.1
Rothmund's (congenital poikiloderma) 757.33
Rotor's (idiopathic hyperbilirubinemia) 277.4
Roussy-Lévy 334.3
Roy (-Jutras) (acropachyderma) 757.39
rubella (congenital) 771.0
Rubinstein-Taybi's (brachydactylia, short stature, and mental retardation) 759.89

Syndrome — *see also* Disease — *continued*

Rud's (mental deficiency, epilepsy, and infantilism) 759.89
Ruiter-Pompen (-Wyers) (angiokeratoma corporis diffusum) 272.7
Runge's (postmaturity) 766.22
Russell (-Silver) (congenital hemihypertrophy and short stature) 759.89
Rytand-Lipsitch (complete atrioventricular block) 426.0
sacralization-scoliosis-sciatica 756.15
sacroiliac 724.6
Saenger's 379.46
salt
  depletion (*see also* Disease, renal) 593.9
  due to heat NEC 992.8
    causing heat exhaustion or prostration 992.4
  low (*see also* Disease, renal) 593.9
salt-losing (*see also* Disease, renal) 593.9
Sanfilippo's (mucopolysaccharidosis III) 277.5
Scaglietti-Dagnini (acromegalic macrospondylitis) 253.0
scalded skin 695.1
scalenus anticus (anterior) 353.0
scapulocostal 354.8
scapuloperoneal 359.1
scapulovertebral 723.4
Schaumann's (sarcoidosis) 135
Scheie's (mucopolysaccharidosis IS) 277.5
Scheuthauer-Marie-Sainton (cleidocranialis dysostosis) 755.59
Schirmer's (encephalocutaneous angiomatosis) 759.6
schizophrenic, of childhood NEC (*see also* Psychosis, childhood) 299.9 ☑
Schmidt's
  sphallo-pharyngo-laryngeal hemiplegia 352.6
  thyroid-adrenocortical insufficiency 258.1
  vagoaccessory 352.6
Schneider's 047.9
Schnitzler 273.1
Scholte's (malignant carcinoid) 259.2
Scholz (-Bielschowsky-Henneberg) 330.0
Schroeder's (endocrine-hypertensive) 255.3
Schüller-Christian (chronic histiocytosis X) 277.89
Schultz's (agranulocytosis) 288.09 ▲
Schwartz (-Jampel) 756.89
Schwartz-Bartter (inappropriate secretion of antidiuretic hormone) 253.6
Scimitar (anomalous venous drainage, right lung to inferior vena cava) 747.49
sclerocystic ovary 256.4
sea-blue histiocyte 272.7
Seabright-Bantam (pseudohypoparathyroidism) 275.49
Seckel's 759.89
Secretan's (posttraumatic edema) 782.3
secretoinhibitor (keratoconjunctivitis sicca) 710.2
Seeligmann's (ichthyosis congenita) 757.1
Senear-Usher (pemphigus erythematosus) 694.4
senilism 259.8
seroconversion, retroviral (acute) ●
  V08
serotonin 333.99
serous meningitis 348.2
Sertoli cell (germinal aplasia) 606.0

☑ Additional Digit Required — Refer to the Tabular List for Digit Selection

⍓ Subterms under main terms may continue to next column or page

Syndrome — *see also* Disease — *continued*

sex chromosome mosaic 758.81
Sézary's (reticulosis) (M9701/3) 202.2 ☑
shaken infant 995.55
Shaver's (bauxite pneumoconiosis) 503
Sheehan's (postpartum pituitary necrosis) 253.2
shock (traumatic) 958.4
  kidney 584.5
    following crush injury 958.5
  lung 518.5
  neurogenic 308.9
  psychic 308.9
short
  bowel 579.3
  P-R interval 426.81
shoulder-arm (*see also* Neuropathy, peripheral, autonomic) 337.9
shoulder-girdle 723.4
shoulder-hand (*see also* Neuropathy, peripheral, autonomic) 337.9
Shwachman's 288.02 ▲
Shy-Drager (orthostatic hypotension with multisystem degeneration) 333.0
Sicard's 352.6
sicca (keratoconjunctivitis) 710.2
sick
  cell 276.1
  cilia 759.89
  sinus 427.81
sideropenic 280.8
Siemens'
  ectodermal dysplasia 757.31
  keratosis follicularis spinulosa (decalvans) 757.39
Silfverskiöld's (osteochondrodystrophy, extremities) 756.50
Silver's (congenital hemihypertrophy and short stature) 759.89
Silvestroni-Bianco (thalassemia minima) 282.49
Simons' (progressive lipodystrophy) 272.6
sinusitis-bronchiectasis-situs inversus 759.3
sinus tarsi 726.79
Sipple's (medullary thyroid carcinoma-pheochromocytoma) 193
Sjögren (-Gougerot) (keratoconjunctivitis sicca) 710.2
  with lung involvement 710.2 [517.8]
Sjögren-Larsson (ichthyosis congenita) 757.1
Slocumb's 255.3
Sluder's 337.0
Smith-Lemli-Opitz (cerebrohepatorenal syndrome) 759.89
Smith-Magenis 758.33
smokers' 305.1
Sneddon-Wilkinson (subcorneal pustular dermatosis) 694.1
Sotos' (cerebral gigantism) 253.0
South African cardiomyopathy 425.2
spasmodic
  upward movement, eye(s) 378.82
  winking 307.20
specified NEC 528.09 ●
Spens' (syncope with heart block) 426.9
spherophakia-brachymorphia 759.89
spinal cord injury (*see also* Injury, spinal, by site)
  with fracture, vertebra — *see* Fracture, vertebra, by site, with spinal cord injury
  cervical — *see* Injury, spinal, cervical
  fluid malabsorption (acquired) 331.3
splenic
  agenesis 759.0

Syndrome — *see also* Disease — *continued*

splenic — *continued*
  flexure 569.89
  neutropenia 289.53 ▲
  sequestration 289.52
Spurway's (brittle bones and blue sclera) 756.51
staphylococcal scalded skin 695.1
Stein's (polycystic ovary) 256.4
Steinbrocker's (*see also* Neuropathy, peripheral, autonomic) 337.9
Stein-Leventhal (polycystic ovary) 256.4
Stevens-Johnson (erythema multiforme exudativum) 695.1
Stewart-Morel (hyperostosis frontalis interna) 733.3
Stickler 759.89
stiff-baby 759.89
stiff-man 333.91
Still's (juvenile rheumatoid arthritis) 714.30
Still-Felty (rheumatoid arthritis with splenomegaly and leukopenia) 714.1
Stilling-Türk-Duane (ocular retraction syndrome) 378.71
Stojano's (subcostal) 098.86
Stokes (-Adams) (syncope with heart block) 426.9
Stokvis-Talma (enterogenous cyanosis) 289.7
stone heart (*see also* Failure, ventricular, left) 428.1
straight-back 756.19
stroke (*see also* Disease, cerebrovascular, acute) 436
  little 435.9
Sturge-Kalischer-Weber (encephalotrigeminal angiomatosis) 759.6
Sturge-Weber (-Dimitri) (encephalocutaneous angiomatosis) 759.6
subclavian-carotid obstruction (chronic) 446.7
subclavian steal 435.2
subcoracoid-pectoralis minor 447.8
subcostal 098.86
  nerve compression 354.8
subperiosteal hematoma 267
subphrenic interposition 751.4
Sudden infant death (SIDS) 798.0
Sudeck's 733.7
Sudeck-Leriche 733.7
superior
  cerebellar artery (*see also* Disease, cerebrovascular, acute) 436
  mesenteric artery 557.1
  pulmonary sulcus (tumor) (M8010/3) 162.3
  vena cava 459.2
suprarenal cortical 255.3
supraspinatus 726.10
swallowed blood 777.3
sweat retention 705.1
Sweet's (acute febrile neutrophilic dermatosis) 695.89
Swyer's (XY pure gonadal dysgenesis) 752.7
Swyer-James (unilateral hyperlucent lung) 492.8
Symonds' 348.2
sympathetic
  cervical paralysis 337.0
  pelvic 625.5
syndactylic oxycephaly 755.55
syphilitic-cardiovascular 093.89
systemic
  fibrosclerosing 710.8
  inflammatory response (SIRS) 995.90
    due to
      infectious process 995.91
        with ▶acute◀ organ dysfunction 995.92

Syndrome — *see also* Disease — *continued*

systemic — *continued*
  inflammatory response — *continued*
    due to — *continued*
      non-infectious process 995.93
        with ▶acute◀ organ dysfunction 995.94
systolic click (-murmur) 785.2
Tabagism 305.1
tachycardia-bradycardia 427.81
Takayasu (-Onishi) (pulseless disease) 446.7
Takotsubo 429.83 ●
Tapia's 352.6
tarsal tunnel 355.5
Taussig-Bing (transposition, aorta and overriding pulmonary artery) 745.11
Taybi's (otopalatodigital) 759.89
Taylor's 625.5
teething 520.7
tegmental 344.89
telangiectasis-pigmentation-cataract 757.33
temporal 383.02
  lobectomy behavior 310.0
temporomandibular joint-pain-dysfunction [TMJ] NEC 524.60
  specified NEC 524.69
Terry's 362.21
testicular feminization 259.5
testis, nonvirilizing 257.8
tethered (spinal) cord 742.59
thalamic 338.0 ▲
Thibierge-Weissenbach (cutaneous systemic sclerosis) 710.1
Thiele 724.6
thoracic outlet (compression) 353.0
thoracogenous rheumatic (hypertrophic pulmonary osteoarthropathy) 731.2
Thorn's (*see also* Disease, renal) 593.9
Thorson-Biörck (malignant carcinoid) 259.2
thrombopenia-hemangioma 287.39
thyroid-adrenocortical insufficiency 258.1
Tietze's 733.6
time-zone (rapid) 327.35
Tobias' (carcinoma, pulmonary apex) (M8010/3) 162.3
toilet seat 926.0
Tolosa-Hunt 378.55
Toni-Fanconi (cystinosis) 270.0
Touraine's (hereditary osteo-onychodysplasia) 756.89
Touraine-Solente-Golé (acropachyderma) 757.39
toxic
  oil 710.5
  shock 040.82
transfusion
  fetal-maternal 772.0
  twin
    donor (infant) 772.0
    recipient (infant) 776.4
transient left ventricular apical ballooning 429.83 ●
Treacher Collins' (incomplete mandibulofacial dysostosis) 756.0
trigeminal plate 259.8
triple X female 758.81
trisomy NEC 758.5
  13 or D_1 758.1
  16-18 or E 758.2
  18 or E_3 758.2
  20 758.5
  21 or G (mongolism) 758.0
  22 or G (mongolism) 758.0
  G 758.0
Troisier-Hanot-Chauffard (bronze diabetes) 275.0

Syndrome — *see also* Disease — *continued*

tropical wet feet 991.4
Trousseau's (thrombophlebitis migrans visceral cancer) 453.1
Türk's (ocular retraction syndrome) 378.71
Turner's 758.6
Turner-Varny 758.6
twin-to-twin transfusion 762.3
  recipient twin 776.4
Uehlinger's (acropachyderma) 757.39
Ullrich (-Bonnevie) (-Turner) 758.6
Ullrich-Feichtiger 759.89
underwater blast injury (abdominal) (*see also* Injury, internal, abdomen) 868.00
universal joint, cervix 620.6
Unverricht (-Lundborg) 333.2
Unverricht-Wagner (dermatomyositis) 710.3
upward gaze 378.81
Urbach-Oppenheim (necrobiosis lipoidica diabeticorum) 250.8 ☑ [709.3]
Urbach-Wiethe (lipoid proteinosis) 272.8
uremia, chronic 585.9
urethral 597.81
urethro-oculoarticular 099.3
urethro-oculosynovial 099.3
urohepatic 572.4
uveocutaneous 364.24
uveomeningeal, uveomeningitis 363.22
vagohypoglossal 352.6
vagovagal 780.2
van Buchem's (hyperostosis corticalis) 733.3
van der Hoeve's (brittle bones and blue sclera, deafness) 756.51
van der Hoeve-Halbertsma-Waardenburg (ptosis-epicanthus) 270.2
van der Hoeve-Waardenburg-Gualdi (ptosis-epicanthus) 270.2
vanishing twin 651.33
van Neck-Odelberg (juvenile osteochondrosis) 732.1
vascular splanchnic 557.0
vasomotor 443.9
vasovagal 780.2
VATER 759.89
Velo-cardio-facial 758.32
vena cava (inferior) (superior) (obstruction) 459.2
Verbiest's (claudicatio intermittens spinalis) 435.1
Vernet's 352.6
vertebral
  artery 435.1
    compression 721.1
  lumbar 724.4
  steal 435.1
vertebrogenic (pain) 724.5
vertiginous NEC 386.9
video display tube 723.8
Villaret's 352.6
Vinson-Plummer (sideropenic dysphagia) 280.8
virilizing adrenocortical hyperplasia, congenital 255.2
virus, viral 079.99
visceral larval migrans 128.0
visual disorientation 368.16
vitamin B_6 deficiency 266.1
vitreous touch 997.99
Vogt's (corpus striatum) 333.71 ▲
Vogt-Koyanagi 364.24
Volkmann's 958.6
von Bechterew-Strümpell (ankylosing spondylitis) 720.0
von Graefe's 378.72
von Hippel-Lindau (angiomatosis retinocerebellosa) 759.6
von Schroetter's (intermittent venous claudication) 453.8

☑ Additional Digit Required — Refer to the Tabular List for Digit Selection   ⁿᵉʷ Subterms under main terms may continue to next column or page

2007 ICD-9-CM   ▶◀ Revised Text   ● New Line   ▲ Revised Code   October 2006 • Volume 2 — 277

Index

Syndrome — Syphilis, syphilitic

☞ Subterms under main terms may continue to next column or page

Syndrome — see also Disease — continued

von Willebrand (-Jürgens) (angiohemophilia) 286.4
Waardenburg-Klein (ptosis epicanthus) 270.2
Wagner (-Unverricht) (dermatomyositis) 710.3
Waldenström's (macroglobulinemia) 273.3
Waldenström-Kjellberg (sideropenic dysphagia) 280.8
Wallenberg's (posterior inferior cerebellar artery) (see also Disease, cerebrovascular, acute) 436
Waterhouse (-Friderichsen) 036.3
water retention 276.6
Weber's 344.89
Weber-Christian (nodular nonsuppurative panniculitis) 729.30
Weber-Cockayne (epidermolysis bullosa) 757.39
Weber-Dimitri (encephalocutaneous angiomatosis) 759.6
Weber-Gubler 344.89
Weber-Leyden 344.89
Weber-Osler (familial hemorrhagic telangiectasia) 448.0
Wegener's (necrotizing respiratory granulomatosis) 446.4
Weill-Marchesani (brachymorphism and ectopia lentis) 759.89
Weingarten's (tropical eosinophilia) 518.3
Weiss-Baker (carotid sinus syncope) 337.0
Weissenbach-Thibierge (cutaneous systemic sclerosis) 710.1
Werdnig-Hoffmann 335.0
Werlhof-Wichmann (see also Purpura, thrombocytopenic) 287.39
Wermer's (polyendocrine adenomatosis) 258.0
Werner's (progeria adultorum) 259.8
Wernicke's (nonalcoholic) (superior hemorrhagic polioencephalitis) 265.1
Wernicke-Korsakoff (nonalcoholic) 294.0
alcoholic 291.1
Westphal-Strümpell (hepatolenticular degeneration) 275.1
wet
brain (alcoholic) 303.9 ☑
feet (maceration) (tropical) 991.4
lung
adult 518.5
newborn 770.6
whiplash 847.0
Whipple's (intestinal lipodystrophy) 040.2
"whistling face" (craniocarpotarsal dystrophy) 759.89
Widal (-Abrami) (acquired hemolytic jaundice) 283.9
Wilkie's 557.1
Wilkinson-Sneddon (subcorneal pustular dermatosis) 694.1
Willan-Plumbe (psoriasis) 696.1
Willebrand (-Jürgens) (angiohemophilia) 286.4
Willi-Prader (hypogenital dystrophy with diabetic tendency) 759.81
Wilson's (hepatolenticular degeneration) 275.1
Wilson-Mikity 770.7
Wiskott-Aldrich (eczema-thrombocytopenia) 279.12
withdrawal
alcohol 291.81
drug 292.0
infant of dependent mother 779.5
Woakes' (ethmoiditis) 471.1

Syndrome — see also Disease — continued

Wolff-Parkinson-White (anomalous atrioventricular excitation) 426.7
Wright's (hyperabduction) 447.8
X
cardiac 413.9
dysmetabolic 277.7
xiphoidalgia 733.99
XO 758.6
XXX 758.81
XXXXY 758.81
XXY 758.7
yellow vernix (placental dysfunction) 762.2
Zahorsky's 074.0
Zellweger 277.86
Zieve's (jaundice, hyperlipemia and hemolytic anemia) 571.1
Zollinger-Ellison (gastric hypersecretion with pancreatic islet cell tumor) 251.5
Zuelzer-Ogden (nutritional megaloblastic anemia) 281.2
Synechia (iris) (pupil) 364.70
anterior 364.72
peripheral 364.73
intrauterine (traumatic) 621.5
posterior 364.71
vulvae, congenital 752.49
Synesthesia — see also Disturbance, sensation 782.0
Synodontia 520.2
Synophthalmus 759.89
Synorchidism 752.89
Synorchism 752.89
Synostosis (congenital) 756.59
astragaloscaphoid 755.67
radioulnar 755.53
talonavicular (bar) 755.67
tarsal 755.67
Synovial — see condition
Synovioma (M9040/3) — see also Neoplasm, connective tissue, malignant
benign (M9040/0) — see Neoplasm, connective tissue, benign
Synoviosarcoma (M9040/3) — see Neoplasm, connective tissue, malignant
Synovitis 727.00
chronic crepitant, wrist 727.2
due to crystals — see Arthritis, due to crystals
gonococcal 098.51
gouty 274.0
syphilitic 095.7
congenital 090.0
traumatic, current — see Sprain, by site
tuberculous — see Tuberculosis, synovitis
villonodular 719.20
ankle 719.27
elbow 719.22
foot 719.27
hand 719.24
hip 719.25
knee 719.26
multiple sites 719.29
pelvic region 719.25
shoulder (region) 719.21
specified site NEC 719.28
wrist 719.23
Syphilide 091.3
congenital 090.0
newborn 090.0
tubercular 095.8
congenital 090.0
Syphilis, syphilitic (acquired) 097.9
with lung involvement 095.1
abdomen (late) 095.2
acoustic nerve 094.86
adenopathy (secondary) 091.4
adrenal (gland) 095.8

Syphilis, syphilitic — continued
adrenal — continued
with cortical hypofunction 095.8
age under 2 years NEC (see also Syphilis, congenital) 090.9
acquired 097.9
alopecia (secondary) 091.82
anemia 095.8
aneurysm (artery) (ruptured) 093.89
aorta 093.0
central nervous system 094.89
congenital 090.5
anus 095.8
primary 091.1
secondary 091.3
aorta, aortic (arch) (abdominal) (insufficiency) (pulmonary) (regurgitation) (stenosis) (thoracic) 093.89
aneurysm 093.0
arachnoid (adhesive) 094.2
artery 093.89
cerebral 094.89
spinal 094.89
arthropathy (neurogenic) (tabetic) 094.0 [713.5]
asymptomatic — see Syphilis, latent
ataxia, locomotor (progressive) 094.0
atrophoderma maculatum 091.3
auricular fibrillation 093.89
Bell's palsy 094.89
bladder 095.8
bone 095.5
secondary 091.61
brain 094.89
breast 095.8
bronchus 095.8
bubo 091.0
bulbar palsy 094.89
bursa (late) 095.7
cardiac decompensation 093.89
cardiovascular (early) (late) (primary) (secondary) (tertiary) 093.9
specified type and site NEC 093.89
causing death under 2 years of age (see also Syphilis, congenital) 090.9
stated to be acquired NEC 097.9
central nervous system (any site) (early) (late) (latent) (primary) (recurrent) (relapse) (secondary) (tertiary) 094.9
with
ataxia 094.0
paralysis, general 094.1
juvenile 090.40
paresis (general) 094.1
juvenile 090.40
tabes (dorsalis) 094.0
juvenile 090.40
taboparesis 094.1
juvenile 090.40
aneurysm (ruptured) 094.87
congenital 090.40
juvenile 090.40
remission in (sustained) 094.9
serology doubtful, negative, or positive 094.9
specified nature or site NEC 094.89
vascular 094.89
cerebral 094.89
meningovascular 094.2
nerves 094.89
sclerosis 094.89
thrombosis 094.89
cerebrospinal 094.89
tabetic 094.0
cerebrovascular 094.89
cervix 095.8
chancre (multiple) 091.0
extragenital 091.2
Rollet's 091.2
Charcôt's joint 094.0 [713.5]
choked disc 094.89 [377.00]
chorioretinitis 091.51
congenital 090.0 [363.13]
late 094.83

Syphilis, syphilitic — continued
choroiditis 091.51
congenital 090.0 [363.13]
late 094.83
prenatal 090.0 [363.13]
choroidoretinitis (secondary) 091.51
congenital 090.0 [363.13]
late 094.83
ciliary body (secondary) 091.52
late 095.8 [364.11]
colon (late) 095.8
combined sclerosis 094.89
complicating pregnancy, childbirth or puerperium 647.0 ☑
affecting fetus or newborn 760.2
condyloma (latum) 091.3
congenital 090.9
with
encephalitis 090.41
paresis (general) 090.40
tabes (dorsalis) 090.40
taboparesis 090.40
chorioretinitis, choroiditis 090.0 [363.13]
early or less than 2 years after birth NEC 090.2
with manifestations 090.0
latent (without manifestations) 090.1
negative spinal fluid test 090.1
serology, positive 090.1
symptomatic 090.0
interstitial keratitis 090.3
juvenile neurosyphilis 090.40
late or 2 years or more after birth NEC 090.7
chorioretinitis, choroiditis 090.5 [363.13]
interstitial keratitis 090.3
juvenile neurosyphilis NEC 090.40
latent (without manifestations) 090.6
negative spinal fluid test 090.6
serology, positive 090.6
symptomatic or with manifestations NEC 090.5
interstitial keratitis 090.3
conjugal 097.9
tabes 094.0
conjunctiva 095.8 [372.10]
contact V01.6
cord, bladder 094.0
cornea, late 095.8 [370.59]
coronary (artery) 093.89
sclerosis 093.89
coryza 095.8
congenital 090.0
cranial nerve 094.89
cutaneous — see Syphilis, skin
dacryocystitis 095.8
degeneration, spinal cord 094.89
d'emblée 095.8
dementia 094.1
paralytica 094.1
juvenilis 090.40
destruction of bone 095.5
dilatation, aorta 093.0
due to blood transfusion 097.9
dura mater 094.89
ear 095.8
inner 095.8
nerve (eighth) 094.86
neurorecurrence 094.86
early NEC 091.0
cardiovascular 093.9
central nervous system 094.9
paresis 094.1
tabes 094.0
latent (without manifestations) (less than 2 years after infection) 092.9
negative spinal fluid test 092.9

Syphilis, syphilitic — continued

early — continued
  latent — continued
    serological relapse following treatment 092.0
    serology positive 092.9
  paresis 094.1
  relapse (treated, untreated) 091.7
  skin 091.3
  symptomatic NEC 091.89
    extragenital chancre 091.2
    primary, except extragenital chancre 091.0
    secondary (see also Syphilis, secondary) 091.3
      relapse (treated, untreated) 091.7
  tabes 094.0
  ulcer 091.3
eighth nerve 094.86
endemic, nonvenereal 104.0
endocarditis 093.20
  aortic 093.22
  mitral 093.21
  pulmonary 093.24
  tricuspid 093.23
epididymis (late) 095.8
epiglottis 095.8
epiphysitis (congenital) 090.0
esophagus 095.8
Eustachian tube 095.8
exposure to V01.6
eye 095.8 [363.13]
  neuromuscular mechanism 094.85
eyelid 095.8 [373.5]
  with gumma 095.8 [373.5]
  ptosis 094.89
fallopian tube 095.8
fracture 095.5
gallbladder (late) 095.8
gastric 095.8
  crisis 094.0
  polyposis 095.8
general 097.9
  paralysis 094.1
    juvenile 090.40
genital (primary) 091.0
glaucoma 095.8
gumma (late) NEC 095.9
  cardiovascular system 093.9
  central nervous system 094.9
  congenital 090.5
  heart or artery 093.89
heart 093.89
  block 093.89
  decompensation 093.89
  disease 093.89
  failure 093.89
  valve (see also Syphilis, endocarditis) 093.20
hemianesthesia 094.89
hemianopsia 095.8
hemiparesis 094.89
hemiplegia 094.89
hepatic artery 093.89
hepatitis 095.3
hepatomegaly 095.3
  congenital 090.0
hereditaria tarda (see also Syphilis, congenital, late) 090.7
hereditary (see also Syphilis, congenital) 090.9
  interstitial keratitis 090.3
Hutchinson's teeth 090.5
hyalitis 095.8
inactive — see Syphilis, latent
infantum NEC (see also Syphilis, congenital) 090.9
inherited — see Syphilis, congenital
internal ear 095.8
intestine (late) 095.8
iris, iritis (secondary) 091.52
  late 095.8 [364.11]
joint (late) 095.8

Syphilis, syphilitic — continued

keratitis (congenital) (early) (interstitial) (late) (parenchymatous) (punctata profunda) 090.3
kidney 095.4
lacrimal apparatus 095.8
laryngeal paralysis 095.8
larynx 095.8
late 097.0
  cardiovascular 093.9
  central nervous system 094.9
  latent or 2 years or more after infection (without manifestations) 096
    negative spinal fluid test 096
    serology positive 096
  paresis 094.1
  specified site NEC 095.8
  symptomatic or with symptoms 095.9
  tabes 094.0
latent 097.1
  central nervous system 094.9
  date of infection unspecified 097.1
  early or less than 2 years after infection 092.9
  late or 2 years or more after infection 096
  serology
    doubtful
      follow-up of latent syphilis 097.1
      central nervous system 094.9
      date of infection unspecified 097.1
      early or less than 2 years after infection 092.9
      late or 2 years or more after infection 096
    positive, only finding 097.1
      date of infection unspecified 097.1
      early or less than 2 years after infection 097.1
      late or 2 years or more after infection 097.1
lens 095.8
leukoderma 091.3
  late 095.8
lienis 095.8
lip 091.3
  chancre 091.2
  late 095.8
  primary 091.2
Lissauer's paralysis 094.1
liver 095.3
  secondary 091.62
locomotor ataxia 094.0
lung 091.3
lymphadenitis (secondary) 091.4
lymph gland (early) (secondary) 091.4
  late 095.8
macular atrophy of skin 091.3
  striated 095.8
maternal, affecting fetus or newborn 760.2
  manifest syphilis in newborn — see Syphilis, congenital
mediastinum (late) 095.8
meninges (adhesive) (basilar) (brain) (spinal cord) 094.2
meningitis 094.2
  acute 091.81
  congenital 090.42
meningoencephalitis 094.2
meningovascular 094.2
  congenital 090.49
mesarteritis 093.89
  brain 094.89
  spine 094.89
middle ear 095.8
mitral stenosis 093.21
monoplegia 094.89
mouth (secondary) 091.3
  late 095.8

Syphilis, syphilitic — continued

mucocutaneous 091.3
  late 095.8
mucous
  membrane 091.3
    late 095.8
  patches 091.3
    congenital 090.0
mulberry molars 090.5
muscle 095.6
myocardium 093.82
myositis 095.6
nasal sinus 095.8
neonatorum NEC (see also Syphilis, congenital) 090.9
nerve palsy (any cranial nerve) 094.89
nervous system, central 094.9
neuritis 095.8
  acoustic nerve 094.86
neurorecidive of retina 094.83
neuroretinitis 094.85
newborn (see also Syphilis, congenital) 090.9
nodular superficial 095.8
nonvenereal, endemic 104.0
nose 095.8
  saddle back deformity 090.5
  septum 095.8
    perforated 095.8
occlusive arterial disease 093.89
ophthalmic 095.8 [363.13]
ophthalmoplegia 094.89
optic nerve (atrophy) (neuritis) (papilla) 094.84
orbit (late) 095.8
orchitis 095.8
organic 097.9
osseous (late) 095.5
osteochondritis (congenital) 090.0
osteoporosis 095.5
ovary 095.8
oviduct 095.8
palate 095.8
  gumma 095.8
  perforated 090.5
pancreas (late) 095.8
pancreatitis 095.8
paralysis 094.89
  general 094.1
  juvenile 090.40
paraplegia 094.89
paresis (general) 094.1
  juvenile 090.40
paresthesia 094.89
Parkinson's disease or syndrome 094.82
paroxysmal tachycardia 093.89
pemphigus (congenital) 090.0
penis 091.0
  chancre 091.0
  late 095.8
pericardium 093.81
perichondritis, larynx 095.8
periosteum 095.5
  congenital 090.0
  early 091.61
  secondary 091.61
peripheral nerve 095.8
petrous bone (late) 095.5
pharynx 095.8
  secondary 091.3
pituitary (gland) 095.8
placenta 095.8
pleura (late) 095.8
pneumonia, white 090.0
pontine (lesion) 094.89
portal vein 093.89
primary NEC 091.2
  anal 091.1
  and secondary (see also Syphilis, secondary) 091.9
  cardiovascular 093.9
  central nervous system 094.9
  extragenital chancre NEC 091.2
  fingers 091.2
  genital 091.0

Syphilis, syphilitic — continued

primary — continued
  lip 091.2
  specified site NEC 091.2
  tonsils 091.2
prostate 095.8
psychosis (intracranial gumma) 094.89
ptosis (eyelid) 094.89
pulmonary (late) 095.1
  artery 093.89
pulmonum 095.1
pyelonephritis 095.4
recently acquired, symptomatic NEC 091.89
rectum 095.8
respiratory tract 095.8
retina
  late 094.83
  neurorecidive 094.83
retrobulbar neuritis 094.85
salpingitis 095.8
sclera (late) 095.0
sclerosis
  cerebral 094.89
  coronary 093.89
  multiple 094.89
  subacute 094.89
scotoma (central) 095.8
scrotum 095.8
secondary (and primary) 091.9
  adenopathy 091.4
  anus 091.3
  bone 091.61
  cardiovascular 093.9
  central nervous system 094.9
  chorioretinitis, choroiditis 091.51
  hepatitis 091.62
  liver 091.62
  lymphadenitis 091.4
  meningitis, acute 091.81
  mouth 091.3
  mucous membranes 091.3
  periosteum 091.61
  periostitis 091.61
  pharynx 091.3
  relapse (treated) (untreated) 091.7
  skin 091.3
  specified form NEC 091.89
  tonsil 091.3
  ulcer 091.3
  viscera 091.69
  vulva 091.3
seminal vesicle (late) 095.8
seronegative
  with signs or symptoms — see Syphilis, by site or stage
seropositive
  with signs or symptoms — see Syphilis, by site and stage
  follow-up of latent syphilis — see Syphilis, latent
  only finding — see Syphilis, latent
seventh nerve (paralysis) 094.89
sinus 095.8
sinusitis 095.8
skeletal system 095.5
skin (early) (secondary) (with ulceration) 091.3
  late or tertiary 095.8
small intestine 095.8
spastic spinal paralysis 094.0
spermatic cord (late) 095.8
spinal (cord) 094.89
  with
    paresis 094.1
    tabes 094.0
spleen 095.8
splenomegaly 095.8
spondylitis 095.5
staphyloma 095.8
stigmata (congenital) 090.5
stomach 095.8
synovium (late) 095.7
tabes dorsalis (early) (late) 094.0
  juvenile 090.40

Syphilis, syphilitic — *continued*
  tabetic type 094.0
    juvenile 090.40
  taboparesis 094.1
    juvenile 090.40
  tachycardia 093.89
  tendon (late) 095.7
  tertiary 097.0
    with symptoms 095.8
    cardiovascular 093.9
    central nervous system 094.9
    multiple NEC 095.8
    specified site NEC 095.8
  testis 095.8
  thorax 095.8
  throat 095.8
  thymus (gland) 095.8
  thyroid (late) 095.8
  tongue 095.8
  tonsil (lingual) 095.8
    primary 091.2
    secondary 091.3
  trachea 095.8
  tricuspid valve 093.23
  tumor, brain 094.89
  tunica vaginalis (late) 095.8
  ulcer (any site) (early) (secondary) 091.3
    late 095.9
    perforating 095.9
      foot 094.0
  urethra (stricture) 095.8
  urogenital 095.8
  uterus 095.8
  uveal tract (secondary) 091.50
    late 095.8 [363.13]
  uveitis (secondary) 091.50
    late 095.8 [363.13]
  uvula (late) 095.8
    perforated 095.8
  vagina 091.0
    late 095.8
  valvulitis NEC 093.20
  vascular 093.89
    brain or cerebral 094.89
  vein 093.89
    cerebral 094.89
  ventriculi 095.8
  vesicae urinariae 095.8
  viscera (abdominal) 095.2
    secondary 091.69
  vitreous (hemorrhage) (opacities) 095.8
  vulva 091.0
    late 095.8
    secondary 091.3
Syphiloma 095.9
  cardiovascular system 093.9
  central nervous system 094.9
  circulatory system 093.9
  congenital 090.5
Syphilophobia 300.29
Syringadenoma (M8400/0) — *see also* Neoplasm, skin, benign
  papillary (M8406/0) — *see* Neoplasm, skin, benign
Syringobulbia 336.0
Syringocarcinoma (M8400/3) — *see* Neoplasm, skin, malignant
Syringocystadenoma (M8400/0) — *see also* Neoplasm, skin, benign
  papillary (M8406/0) — *see* Neoplasm, skin, benign
Syringocystoma (M8407/0) — *see* Neoplasm, skin, benign
Syringoma (M8407/0) — *see also* Neoplasm, skin, benign
  chondroid (M8940/0) — *see* Neoplasm, by site, benign
Syringomyelia 336.0
Syringomyelitis 323.9
  late effect — *see* category 326
Syringomyelocele — *see also* Spina bifida 741.9 ☑
Syringopontia 336.0

Syringopontia — *continued*
  disease, combined — *see* Degeneration, combined
  fibrosclerosing syndrome 710.8
  inflammatory response syndrome (SIRS) 995.90
    due to
      infectious process 995.91
        with organ dysfunction 995.92
      non-infectious process 995.93
        with organ dysfunction 995.94
  lupus erythematosus 710.0
    inhibitor 286.5
System, systemic — *see also* condition
  disease, combined — *see* Degeneration, combined
  fibrosclerosing syndrome 710.8
  inflammatory response syndrome (SIRS) 995.90
    due to
      infectious process 995.91
        with ▶acute◀ organ dysfunction 995.92
      non-infectious process 995.93
        with ▶acute◀ organ dysfunction 995.94
  lupus erythematosus 710.0
    inhibitor 286.5

T

Tab — *see* Tag
Tabacism 989.84
Tabacosis 989.84
Tabardillo 080
  flea-borne 081.0
  louse-borne 080
Tabes, tabetic
  with
    central nervous system syphilis 094.0
    Charcôt's joint 094.0 [713.5]
    cord bladder 094.0
    crisis, viscera (any) 094.0
    paralysis, general 094.1
    paresis (general) 094.1
    perforating ulcer 094.0
  arthropathy 094.0 [713.5]
  bladder 094.0
  bone 094.0
  cerebrospinal 094.0
  congenital 090.40
  conjugal 094.0
  dorsalis 094.0
    neurosyphilis 094.0
  early 094.0
  juvenile 090.40
  latent 094.0
  mesenterica (*see also* Tuberculosis) 014.8 ☑
  paralysis insane, general 094.1
  peripheral (nonsyphilitic) 799.89
  spasmodic 094.0
    not dorsal or dorsalis 343.9
  syphilis (cerebrospinal) 094.0
Taboparalysis 094.1
Taboparesis (remission) 094.1
  with
    Charcôt's joint 094.1 [713.5]
    cord bladder 094.1
    perforating ulcer 094.1
  juvenile 090.40
Tache noir 923.20
Tachyalimentation 579.3
Tachyarrhythmia, tachyrhythmia — *see also* Tachycardia
  paroxysmal with sinus bradycardia 427.81
Tachycardia 785.0
  atrial 427.89
  auricular 427.89
  AV nodal re-entry (re-entrant) 427.89
  newborn 779.82
  nodal 427.89

Tachycardia — *continued*
  nodal — *continued*
    nonparoxysmal atrioventricular 426.89
    nonparoxysmal atrioventricular (nodal) 426.89
  paroxysmal 427.2
    with sinus bradycardia 427.81
    atrial (PAT) 427.0
      psychogenic 316 [427.0]
    atrioventricular (AV) 427.0
      psychogenic 316 [427.0]
    essential 427.2
    junctional 427.0
    nodal 427.0
    psychogenic 316 [427.2]
      atrial 316 [427.0]
      supraventricular 316 [427.0]
      ventricular 316 [427.1]
    supraventricular 427.0
      psychogenic 316 [427.0]
    ventricular 427.1
      psychogenic 316 [427.1]
  postoperative 997.1
  psychogenic 306.2
  sick sinus 427.81
  sinoauricular 427.89
  sinus 427.89
  supraventricular 427.89
  ventricular (paroxysmal) 427.1
    psychogenic 316 [427.1]
Tachygastria 536.8 ●
Tachypnea 786.06
  hysterical 300.11
  newborn (idiopathic) (transitory) 770.6
  psychogenic 306.1
  transitory, of newborn 770.6
Taenia (infection) (infestation) — *see also* Infestation, taenia 123.3
  diminuta 123.6
  echinococcal infestation (*see also* Echinococcus) 122.9
  nana 123.6
  saginata infestation 123.2
  solium (intestinal form) 123.0
    larval form 123.1
Taeniasis (intestine) — *see also* Infestation, taenia 123.3
  saginata 123.2
  solium 123.0
Taenzer's disease 757.4
Tag (hypertrophied skin) (infected) 701.9
  adenoid 474.8
  anus 455.9
  endocardial (*see also* Endocarditis) 424.90
  hemorrhoidal 455.9
  hymen 623.8
  perineal 624.8
  preauricular 744.1
  rectum 455.9
  sentinel 455.9
  skin 701.9
    accessory 757.39
    anus 455.9
    congenital 757.39
    preauricular 744.1
    rectum 455.9
  tonsil 474.8
  urethra, urethral 599.84
  vulva 624.8
Tahyna fever 062.5
Takayasu (-Onishi) disease or syndrome (pulseless disease) 446.7
Takotsubo syndrome 429.83 ●
Talc granuloma 728.82
  in operation wound 998.7
Talcosis 502
Talipes (congenital) 754.70
  acquired NEC 736.79
    planus 734
  asymmetric 754.79
    acquired 736.79
  calcaneovalgus 754.62
    acquired 736.76
  calcaneovarus 754.59

Talipes — *continued*
  calcaneovarus — *continued*
    acquired 736.76
  calcaneus 754.79
    acquired 736.76
  cavovarus 754.59
    acquired 736.75
  cavus 754.71
    acquired 736.73
  equinovalgus 754.69
    acquired 736.72
  equinovarus 754.51
    acquired 736.71
  equinus 754.79
    acquired, NEC 736.72
  percavus 754.71
    acquired 736.73
  planovalgus 754.69
    acquired 736.79
  planus (acquired) (any degree) 734
    congenital 754.61
    due to rickets 268.1
  valgus 754.60
    acquired 736.79
  varus 754.50
    acquired 736.79
Talma's disease 728.85
Talon noir 924.20 ●
  hand 923.20 ●
  heel 924.20 ●
  toe 924.3 ●
Tamponade heart (Rose's) — *see also* Pericarditis 423.9
Tanapox 078.89
Tangier disease (familial high-density lipoprotein deficiency) 272.5
Tank ear 380.12
Tantrum (childhood) — *see also* Disturbance, conduct 312.1 ☑
Tapeworm (infection) (infestation) — *see also* Infestation, tapeworm 123.9
Tapia's syndrome 352.6
Tarantism 297.8
Target-oval cell anemia 282.49
Tarlov's cyst 355.9
Tarral-Besnier disease (pityriasis rubra pilaris) 696.4
Tarsalgia 729.2
Tarsal tunnel syndrome 355.5
Tarsitis (eyelid) 373.00
  syphilitic 095.8 [373.00]
  tuberculous (*see also* Tuberculosis) 017.0 ☑ [373.4]
Tartar (teeth) 523.6
Tattoo (mark) 709.09
Taurodontism 520.2
Taussig-Bing defect, heart, or syndrome (transposition, aorta and overriding pulmonary artery) 745.11
Taybi's syndrome (otopalatodigital) 759.89
Tay's choroiditis 363.41
Taylor's
  disease (diffuse idiopathic cutaneous atrophy) 701.8
  syndrome 625.5
Tay-Sachs
  amaurotic familial idiocy 330.1
  disease 330.1
Tear stone 375.57
Tear, torn (traumatic) — *see also* Wound, open, by site
  anus, anal (sphincter) 863.89
    with open wound in cavity 863.99
    complicating delivery 664.2 ☑
      with mucosa 664.3 ☑
    nontraumatic, nonpuerperal 565.0
  articular cartilage, old (*see also* Disorder, cartilage, articular) 718.0 ☑
  bladder
    with
      abortion — *see* Abortion, by type, with damage to pelvic organs

☑ Additional Digit Required — Refer to the Tabular List for Digit Selection   ⑨ Subterms under main terms may continue to next column or page

280 — Volume 2 • October 2006   ▶◀ Revised Text   ● New Line   ▲ Revised Code   *2007 ICD-9-CM*

Tear, torn — *see also* Wound, open, by site — *continued*
  bladder — *continued*
    with — *continued*
      ectopic pregnancy (*see also* categories 633.0–633.9) 639.2
      molar pregnancy (*see also* categories 630–632) 639.2
    following
      abortion 639.2
      ectopic or molar pregnancy 639.2
    obstetrical trauma 665.5 ☑
  bowel
    with
      abortion — *see* Abortion, by type, with damage to pelvic organs
      ectopic pregnancy (*see also* categories 633.0–633.9) 639.2
      molar pregnancy (*see also* categories 630–632) 639.2
    following
      abortion 639.2
      ectopic or molar pregnancy 639.2
    obstetrical trauma 665.5 ☑
  broad ligament
    with
      abortion — *see* Abortion, by type, with damage to pelvic organs
      ectopic pregnancy (*see also* categories 633.0–633.9) 639.2
      molar pregnancy (*see also* categories 630–632) 639.2
    following
      abortion 639.2
      ectopic or molar pregnancy 639.2
    obstetrical trauma 665.6 ☑
  bucket handle (knee) (meniscus) — *see* Tear, meniscus
  capsule
    joint — *see* Sprain, by site
    spleen — *see* Laceration, spleen, capsule
  cartilage (*see also* Sprain, by site)
    articular, old (*see also* Disorder, cartilage, articular) 718.0 ☑
    knee — *see* Tear, meniscus
    semilunar (knee) (current injury) — *see* Tear, meniscus
  cervix
    with
      abortion — *see* Abortion, by type, with damage to pelvic organs
      ectopic pregnancy (*see also* categories 633.0–633.9) 639.2
      molar pregnancy (*see also* categories 630–632) 639.2
    following
      abortion 639.2
      ectopic or molar pregnancy 639.2
    obstetrical trauma (current) 665.3 ☑
    old 622.3
  internal organ (abdomen, chest, or pelvis) — *see* Injury, internal, by site
  ligament (*see also* Sprain, by site)
    with open wound — *see* Wound, open by site
  meniscus (knee) (current injury) 836.2
    bucket handle 836.0
      old 717.0
    lateral 836.1
      anterior horn 836.1
        old 717.42
      bucket handle 836.1

Tear, torn — *see also* Wound, open, by site — *continued*
  meniscus — *continued*
    lateral — *continued*
      bucket handle — *continued*
        old 717.41
      old 717.40
      posterior horn 836.1
        old 717.43
      specified site NEC 836.1
        old 717.49
    medial 836.0
      anterior horn 836.0
        old 717.1
      bucket handle 836.0
        old 717.0
        old 717.3
      posterior horn 836.0
        old 717.2
    old NEC 717.5
    site other than knee — *see* Sprain, by site
  muscle (*see also* Sprain, by site)
    with open wound — *see* Wound, open by site
  pelvic
    floor, complicating delivery 664.1 ☑
    organ NEC
      with
        abortion — *see* Abortion, by type, with damage to pelvic organs
        ectopic pregnancy (*see also* categories 633.0–633.9) 639.2
        molar pregnancy (*see also* categories 630–632) 639.2
      following
        abortion 639.2
        ectopic or molar pregnancy 639.2
      obstetrical trauma 665.5 ☑
  perineum (*see also* Laceration, perineum)
    obstetrical trauma 665.5 ☑
  periurethral tissue
    with
      abortion — *see* Abortion, by type, with damage to pelvic organs
      ectopic pregnancy (*see also* categories 633.0–633.9) 639.2
      molar pregnancy (*see also* categories 630–632) 639.2
    following
      abortion 639.2
      ectopic or molar pregnancy 639.2
    obstetrical trauma 665.5 ☑
  rectovaginal septum — *see* Laceration, rectovaginal septum
  retina, retinal (recent) (with detachment) 361.00
    without detachment 361.30
    dialysis (juvenile) (with detachment) 361.04
    giant (with detachment) 361.03
    horseshoe (without detachment) 361.32
    multiple (with detachment) 361.02
      without detachment 361.33
    old
      delimited (partial) 361.06
      partial 361.06
      total or subtotal 361.07
    partial (without detachment)
      giant 361.03
      multiple defects 361.02
      old (delimited) 361.06
      single defect 361.01
    round hole (without detachment) 361.31

Tear, torn — *see also* Wound, open, by site — *continued*
  retina, retinal — *continued*
    single defect (with detachment) 361.01
    total or subtotal (recent) 361.05
      old 361.07
  rotator cuff (traumatic) 840.4
    current injury 840.4
    degenerative 726.10
    nontraumatic 727.61
  semilunar cartilage, knee (*see also* Tear, meniscus) 836.2
    old 717.5
  tendon (*see also* Sprain, by site)
    with open wound — *see* Wound, open by site
  tentorial, at birth 767.0
  umbilical cord
    affecting fetus or newborn 772.0
    complicating delivery 663.8 ☑
  urethra
    with
      abortion — *see* Abortion, by type, with damage to pelvic organs
      ectopic pregnancy (*see also* categories 633.0–633.9) 639.2
      molar pregnancy (*see also* categories 630–632) 639.2
    following
      abortion 639.2
      ectopic or molar pregnancy 639.2
    obstetrical trauma 665.5 ☑
  uterus — *see* Injury, internal, uterus
  vagina — *see* Laceration, vagina
  vessel, from catheter 998.2
  vulva, complicating delivery 664.0 ☑
Teething 520.7
  syndrome 520.7
Teeth, tooth — *see also* condition
  grinding 306.8
  prenatal 520.6
Tegmental syndrome 344.89
Telangiectasia, telangiectasis (verrucous) 448.9
  ataxic (cerebellar) 334.8
  familial 448.0
  hemorrhagic, hereditary (congenital) (senile) 448.0
  hereditary hemorrhagic 448.0
  retina 362.15
  spider 448.1
Telecanthus (congenital) 743.63
Telescoped bowel or intestine — *see also* Intussusception 560.0
Teletherapy, adverse effect NEC 990
Telogen effluvium 704.02
Temperature
  body, high (of unknown origin) (*see also* Pyrexia) 780.6
  cold, trauma from 991.9
    newborn 778.2
    specified effect NEC 991.8
  high
    body (of unknown origin) (*see also* Pyrexia) 780.6
    trauma from — *see* Heat
Temper tantrum (childhood) — *see also* Disturbance, conduct 312.1 ☑
Temple — *see* condition
Temporal — *see also* condition
  lobe syndrome 310.0
Temporomandibular joint-pain-dysfunction syndrome 524.60
Temporosphenoidal — *see* condition
Tendency
  bleeding (*see also* Defect, coagulation) 286.9
  homosexual, ego-dystonic 302.0
  paranoid 301.0
  suicide 300.9

Tenderness
  abdominal (generalized) (localized) 789.6 ☑
  rebound 789.6 ☑
  skin 782.0
Tendinitis, tendonitis — *see also* Tenosynovitis 726.90
  Achilles 726.71
  adhesive 726.90
    shoulder 726.0
  calcific 727.82
    shoulder 726.11
  gluteal 726.5
  patellar 726.64
  peroneal 726.79
  pes anserinus 726.61
  psoas 726.5
  tibialis (anterior) (posterior) 726.72
  trochanteric 726.5
Tendon — *see* condition
Tendosynovitis — *see* Tenosynovitis
Tendovaginitis — *see* Tenosynovitis
Tenesmus 787.99
  rectal 787.99
  vesical 788.9
Tenia — *see* Taenia
Teniasis — *see* Taeniasis
Tennis elbow 726.32
Tenonitis — *see also* Tenosynovitis
  eye (capsule) 376.04
Tenontosynovitis — *see* Tenosynovitis
Tenontothecitis — *see* Tenosynovitis
Tenophyte 727.9
Tenosynovitis 727.00
  adhesive 726.90
    shoulder 726.0
  ankle 727.06
  bicipital (calcifying) 726.12
  buttock 727.09
  due to crystals — *see* Arthritis, due to crystals
  elbow 727.09
  finger 727.05
  foot 727.06
  gonococcal 098.51
  hand 727.05
  hip 727.09
  knee 727.09
  radial styloid 727.04
  shoulder 726.10
    adhesive 726.0
  spine 720.1
  supraspinatus 726.10
  toe 727.06
  tuberculous — *see* Tuberculosis, tenosynovitis
  wrist 727.05
Tenovaginitis — *see* Tenosynovitis
Tension
  arterial, high (*see also* Hypertension) 401.9
    without diagnosis of hypertension 796.2
  headache 307.81
  intraocular (elevated) 365.00
  nervous 799.2
  ocular (elevated) 365.00
  pneumothorax 512.0
    iatrogenic 512.1
    postoperative 512.1
    spontaneous 512.0
  premenstrual 625.4
  state 300.9
Tentorium — *see* condition
Teratencephalus 759.89
Teratism 759.7
Teratoblastoma (malignant) (M9080/3) — *see* Neoplasm, by site, malignant
Teratocarcinoma (M9081/3) — *see also* Neoplasm, by site, malignant
  liver 155.0
Teratoma (solid) (M9080/1) — *see also* Neoplasm, by site, uncertain behavior
  adult (cystic) (M9080/0) — *see* Neoplasm, by site, benign

☑ Additional Digit Required — Refer to the Tabular List for Digit Selection   ▽ Subterms under main terms may continue to next column or page

2007 ICD-9-CM   ▶◀ Revised Text   ● New Line   ▲ Revised Code   October 2006 • Volume 2 — 281

Teratoma — see also Neoplasm, by site,
uncertain behavior — continued
and embryonal carcinoma, mixed
(M9081/3) — see Neoplasm, by
site, malignant
benign (M9080/0) — see Neoplasm,
by site, benign
combined with choriocarcinoma
(M9101/3) — see Neoplasm, by
site, malignant
cystic (adult) (M9080/0) — see Neoplasm, by site, benign
differentiated type (M9080/0) — see
Neoplasm, by site, benign
embryonal (M9080/3) (see also Neoplasm, by site, malignant)
liver 155.0
fetal
sacral, causing fetopelvic disproportion 653.7 ☑
immature (M9080/3) — see Neoplasm,
by site, malignant
liver (M9080/3) 155.0
adult, benign, cystic, differentiated
type or mature (M9080/0)
211.5
malignant (M9080/3) (see also Neoplasm, by site, malignant)
anaplastic type (M9082/3) — see
Neoplasm, by site, malignant
intermediate type (M9083/3) — see
Neoplasm, by site, malignant
liver (M9080/3) 155.0
trophoblastic (M9102/3)
specified site — see Neoplasm,
by site, malignant
unspecified site 186.9
undifferentiated type (M9082/3) —
see Neoplasm, by site, malignant
mature (M9080/0) — see Neoplasm,
by site, benign
ovary (M9080/0) 220
embryonal, immature, or malignant
(M9080/3) 183.0
suprasellar (M9080/3) — see Neoplasm, by site, malignant
testis (M9080/3) 186.9
adult, benign, cystic, differentiated
type or mature (M9080/0)
222.0
undescended 186.0
Terminal care V66.7
Termination
anomalous (see also Malposition,
congenital)
portal vein 747.49
right pulmonary vein 747.42
pregnancy (legal) (therapeutic) — see
Abortion, legal 635.9 ☑
fetus NEC 779.6
illegal (see also Abortion, illegal)
636.9 ☑
Ternidens diminutus infestation 127.7
Terrors, night (child) 307.46
Terry's syndrome 362.21
Tertiary — see condition
Tessellated fundus, retina (tigroid)
362.89
Test(s)
adequacy
hemodialysis V56.31
peritoneal dialysis V56.32
AIDS virus V72.6
allergen V72.7
bacterial disease NEC (see also
Screening, by name of disease)
V74.9
basal metabolic rate V72.6
blood-alcohol V70.4
blood-drug V70.4
for therapeutic drug monitoring
V58.83
blood typing V72.86
Rh typing V72.86 ●
developmental, infant or child V20.2

Test(s) — continued
Dick V74.8
fertility V26.21
genetic
female V26.32 ●
for genetic disease carrier status
female V26.31 ●
male V26.34 ●
male V26.39 ●
hearing V72.19 ▲
following failed hearing screening ●
V72.11 ●
HIV V72.6
human immunodeficiency virus V72.6
Kveim V82.89
laboratory V72.6
for medicolegal reason V70.4
male partner of habitual aborter ●
V26.35 ●
Mantoux (for tuberculosis) V74.1
mycotic organism V75.4
parasitic agent NEC V75.8
paternity V70.4
peritoneal equilibration V56.32
pregnancy
negative result V72.41
positive result V72.42
first pregnancy V72.42
unconfirmed V72.40
preoperative V72.84
cardiovascular V72.81
respiratory V72.82
specified NEC V72.83
procreative management NEC V26.29
genetic disease carrier status ●
female V26.31 ●
male V26.34 ●
Rh typing V72.86 ●
sarcoidosis V82.89
Schick V74.3
Schultz-Charlton V74.8
skin, diagnostic
allergy V72.7
bacterial agent NEC (see also
Screening, by name of disease) V74.9
Dick V74.8
hypersensitivity V72.7
Kveim V82.89
Mantoux V74.1
mycotic organism V75.4
parasitic agent NEC V75.8
sarcoidosis V82.89
Schick V74.3
Schultz-Charlton V74.8
tuberculin V74.1
specified type NEC V72.85
tuberculin V74.1
vision V72.0
Wassermann
positive (see also Serology for
syphilis, positive) 097.1
false 795.6
Testicle, testicular, testis — see also
condition
feminization (syndrome) 259.5
Tetanus, tetanic (cephalic) (convulsions)
037
with
abortion — see Abortion, by type,
with sepsis
ectopic pregnancy (see also categories 633.0–633.9) 639.0
molar pregnancy — see categories
630–632 639.0
following
abortion 639.0
ectopic or molar pregnancy 639.0
inoculation V03.7
reaction (due to serum) — see
Complications, vaccination
neonatorum 771.3
puerperal, postpartum, childbirth
670.0
Tetany, tetanic 781.7
alkalosis 276.3

Tetany, tetanic — continued
associated with rickets 268.0
convulsions 781.7
hysterical 300.11
functional (hysterical) 300.11
hyperkinetic 781.7
hysterical 300.11
hyperpnea 786.01
hysterical 300.11
psychogenic 306.1
hyperventilation 786.01
hysterical 300.11
psychogenic 306.1
hypocalcemic, neonatal 775.4
hysterical 300.11
neonatal 775.4
parathyroid (gland) 252.1
parathyroprival 252.1
postoperative 252.1
postthyroidectomy 252.1
pseudotetany 781.7
hysterical 300.11
psychogenic 306.1
specified as conversion reaction
300.11
Tetralogy of Fallot 745.2
Tetraplegia — see Quadriplegia
Thailand hemorrhagic fever 065.4
Thalassanemia 282.49
Thalassemia (alpha) (beta) (disease) (Hb-
C) (Hb-D) (Hb-E) (Hb-H) (Hb-I) (high
fetal gene) (high fetal hemoglobin)
(intermedia) (major) (minima) (minor) (mixed) (trait) (with other
hemoglobinopathy) 282.49
Hb-S (without crisis) 282.41
with
crisis 282.42
vaso-occlusive pain 282.42
sickle-cell (without crisis) 282.41
with
crisis 282.42
vaso-occlusive pain 282.42
Thalassemic variants 282.49
Thaysen-Gee disease (nontropical sprue)
579.0
Thecoma (M8600/0) 220
malignant (M8600/3) 183.0
Thelarche, precocious 259.1
Thelitis 611.0
puerperal, postpartum 675.0 ☑
Therapeutic — see condition
Therapy V57.9
blood transfusion, without reported
diagnosis V58.2
breathing V57.0
chemotherapy, antineoplastic V58.11
fluoride V07.31
prophylactic NEC V07.39
dialysis (intermittent) (treatment)
extracorporeal V56.0
peritoneal V56.8
renal V56.0
specified type NEC V56.8
exercise NEC V57.1
breathing V57.0
extracorporeal dialysis (renal) V56.0
fluoride prophylaxis V07.31
hemodialysis V56.0
hormone replacement (postmenopausal) V07.4
immunotherapy antineoplastic V58.12
long term oxygen therapy V46.2
occupational V57.21
orthoptic V57.4
orthotic V57.81
peritoneal dialysis V56.8
physical NEC V57.1
postmenopausal hormone replacement V07.4
radiation V58.0
speech V57.3
vocational V57.22
Thermalgesia 782.0
Thermalgia 782.0
Thermanalgesia 782.0

Thermanesthesia 782.0
Thermic — see condition
Thermography (abnormal) 793.99 ▲
breast 793.89
Thermoplegia 992.0
Thesaurismosis
amyloid 277.39 ▲
bilirubin 277.4
calcium 275.40
cystine 270.0
glycogen (see also Disease, glycogen
storage) 271.0
kerasin 272.7
lipoid 272.7
melanin 255.4
phosphatide 272.7
urate 274.9
Thiaminic deficiency 265.1
with beriberi 265.0
Thibierge-Weissenbach syndrome (cutaneous systemic sclerosis) 710.1
Thickened endometrium 793.5
Thickening
bone 733.99
extremity 733.99
breast 611.79
hymen 623.3
larynx 478.79
nail 703.8
congenital 757.5
periosteal 733.99
pleura (see also Pleurisy) 511.0
skin 782.8
subepiglottic 478.79
tongue 529.8
valve, heart — see Endocarditis
Thiele syndrome 724.6
Thigh — see condition
Thinning vertebra — see also Osteoporosis 733.00
Thirst, excessive 783.5
due to deprivation of water 994.3
Thomsen's disease 359.2
Thomson's disease (congenital poikiloderma) 757.33
Thoracic — see also condition
kidney 753.3
outlet syndrome 353.0
stomach — see Hernia, diaphragm
Thoracogastroschisis (congenital)
759.89
Thoracopagus 759.4
Thoracoschisis 756.3
**Thoracoscopic surgical procedure
converted to open procedure**
V64.42
Thorax — see condition
Thorn's syndrome — see also Disease,
renal 593.9
Thornwaldt's, Tornwaldt's
bursitis (pharyngeal) 478.29
cyst 478.26
disease (pharyngeal bursitis) 478.29
Thorson-Biörck syndrome (malignant
carcinoid) 259.2
Threadworm (infection) (infestation)
127.4
Threatened
abortion or miscarriage 640.0 ☑
with subsequent abortion (see also
Abortion, spontaneous)
634.9 ☑
affecting fetus 762.1
labor 644.1 ☑
affecting fetus or newborn 761.8
premature 644.0 ☑
miscarriage 640.0 ☑
affecting fetus 762.1
premature
delivery 644.2 ☑
affecting fetus or newborn 761.8
labor 644.0 ☑
before 22 completed weeks gestation 640.0 ☑
Three-day fever 066.0
Threshers' lung 495.0

☑ Additional Digit Required — Refer to the Tabular List for Digit Selection   ▽ Subterms under main terms may continue to next column or page

282 — Volume 2 • October 2006   ▶◀ Revised Text   ● New Line   ▲ Revised Code   *2007 ICD-9-CM*

Thrix annulata (congenital) 757.4
Throat — *see* condition
Thrombasthenia (Glanzmann's) (hemorrhagic) (hereditary) 287.1
Thromboangitis 443.1
  obliterans (general) 443.1
    cerebral 437.1
    vessels
      brain 437.1
      spinal cord 437.1
Thromboarteritis — *see* Arteritis
Thromboasthenia (Glanzmann's) (hemorrhagic) (hereditary) 287.1
Thrombocytasthenia (Glanzmann's) 287.1
Thrombocythemia (primary) (M9962/1) 238.71 ▲
  essential 238.71 ●
  hemorrhagic 238.71 ●
  idiopathic ▶(hemorrhagic)◀ (M9962/1) 238.71 ▲
Thrombocytopathy (dystrophic) (granulopenic) 287.1
Thrombocytopenia, thrombocytopenic 287.5
  with
    absent radii (TAR) syndrome
    giant hemangioma
  amegakaryocytic, congenital 287.33
  congenital 287.33
  cyclic 287.39
  dilutional 287.4
  due to
    drugs 287.4
    extracorporeal circulation of blood 287.4
    massive blood transfusion 287.4
    platelet alloimmunization 287.4
  essential 287.30
  hereditary 287.33
  Kasabach-Merritt 287.39
  neonatal, transitory 776.1
    due to
      exchange transfusion 776.1
      idiopathic maternal thrombocytopenia 776.1
      isoimmunization 776.1
  primary 287.30
  puerperal, postpartum 666.3 ☑
  purpura (*see also* Purpura, thrombocytopenic) 287.30
    thrombotic 446.6
  secondary 287.4
  sex-linked 287.39
Thrombocytosis 238.71 ▲
  essential 238.71 ●
  primary 238.71 ●
Thromboembolism — *see* Embolism
Thrombopathy (Bernard-Soulier) 287.1
  constitutional 286.4
  Willebrand-Jürgens (angiohemophilia) 286.4
Thrombopenia — *see also* Thrombocytopenia 287.5
Thrombophlebitis 451.9
  antecubital vein 451.82
  antepartum (superficial) 671.2 ☑
    affecting fetus or newborn 760.3
    deep 671.3 ☑
  arm 451.89
    deep 451.83
    superficial 451.82
  breast, superficial 451.89
  cavernous (venous) sinus — *see* Thrombophlebitis, intracranial venous sinus
  cephalic vein 451.82
  cerebral (sinus) (vein) 325
    late effect — *see* category 326
    nonpyogenic 437.6
      in pregnancy or puerperium 671.5 ☑
    late effect — *see* Late effect(s) (of) cerebrovascular disease

Thrombophlebitis — *continued*
  due to implanted device — *see* Complications, due to (presence of) any device, implant or graft classified to 996.0–996.5 NEC
  during or resulting from a procedure NEC 997.2
  femoral 451.11
  femoropopliteal 451.19
  following infusion, perfusion, or transfusion 999.2
  hepatic (vein) 451.89
  idiopathic, recurrent 453.1
  iliac vein 451.81
  iliofemoral 451.11
  intracranial venous sinus (any) 325
    late effect — *see* category 326
    nonpyogenic 437.6
      in pregnancy or puerperium 671.5 ☑
    late effect — *see* Late effect(s) (of) cerebrovascular disease
  jugular vein 451.89
  lateral (venous) sinus — *see* Thrombophlebitis, intracranial venous sinus
  leg 451.2
    deep (vessels) 451.19
      femoral vein 451.11
      specified vessel NEC 451.19
    superficial (vessels) 451.0
      femoral vein 451.11
  longitudinal (venous) sinus — *see* Thrombophlebitis, intracranial venous sinus
  lower extremity 451.2
    deep (vessels) 451.19
      femoral vein 451.11
      specified vessel NEC 451.19
    superficial (vessels) 451.0
  migrans, migrating 453.1
  pelvic
    with
      abortion — *see* Abortion, by type, with sepsis
      ectopic pregnancy (*see also* categories 633.0–633.9) 639.0
      molar pregnancy (*see also* categories 630–632) 639.0
    following
      abortion 639.0
      ectopic or molar pregnancy 639.0
    puerperal 671.4 ☑
  popliteal vein 451.19
  portal (vein) 572.1
  postoperative 997.2
  pregnancy (superficial) 671.2 ☑
    affecting fetus or newborn 760.3
    deep 671.3 ☑
  puerperal, postpartum, childbirth (extremities) (superficial) 671.2 ☑
    deep 671.4 ☑
    pelvic 671.4 ☑
    specified site NEC 671.5 ☑
  radial vein 451.83
  saphenous (greater) (lesser) 451.0
  sinus (intracranial) — *see* Thrombophlebitis, intracranial venous sinus
  specified site NEC 451.89
  tibial vein 451.19
Thrombosis, thrombotic (marantic) (multiple) (progressive) (septic) (vein) (vessel) 453.9
  with childbirth or during the puerperium — *see* Thrombosis, puerperal, postpartum
  antepartum — *see* Thrombosis, pregnancy
  aorta, aortic 444.1
    abdominal 444.0
    bifurcation 444.0

Thrombosis, thrombotic — *continued*
  aorta, aortic — *continued*
    saddle 444.0
    terminal 444.0
    thoracic 444.1
    valve — *see* Endocarditis, aortic
  apoplexy (*see also* Thrombosis, brain) 434.0
    late effect — *see* Late effect(s) (of) cerebrovascular disease
  appendix, septic — *see* Appendicitis, acute
  arteriolar-capillary platelet, disseminated 446.6
  artery, arteries (postinfectional) 444.9
    auditory, internal 433.8 ☑
    basilar (*see also* Occlusion, artery, basilar) 433.0 ☑
    carotid (common) (internal) (*see also* Occlusion, artery, carotid) 433.1 ☑
      with other precerebral artery 433.3 ☑
    cerebellar (anterior inferior) (posterior inferior) (superior) 433.8 ☑
    cerebral (*see also* Thrombosis, brain) 434.0 ☑
    choroidal (anterior) 433.8 ☑
    communicating posterior 433.8 ☑
    coronary (*see also* Infarct, myocardium) 410.9 ☑
      without myocardial infarction 411.81
      due to syphilis 093.89
      healed or specified as old 412
    extremities 444.22
      lower 444.22
      upper 444.21
    femoral 444.22
    hepatic 444.89
    hypophyseal 433.8 ☑
    meningeal, anterior or posterior 433.8 ☑
    mesenteric (with gangrene) 557.0
    ophthalmic (*see also* Occlusion, retina) 362.30
    pontine 433.8 ☑
    popliteal 444.22
    precerebral — *see* Occlusion, artery, precerebral NEC
    pulmonary 415.19
      iatrogenic 415.11
      postoperative 415.11
    renal 593.81
    retinal (*see also* Occlusion, retina) 362.30
    specified site NEC 444.89
    spinal, anterior or posterior 433.8 ☑
    traumatic (complication) (early) (*see also* Injury, blood vessel, by site) 904.9
    vertebral (*see also* Occlusion, artery, vertebral) 433.2 ☑
      with other precerebral artery 433.3 ☑
  atrial (endocardial) 424.90
    without endocarditis 429.89 ●
    due to syphilis 093.89
  auricular (*see also* Infarct, myocardium) 410.9 ☑
  axillary (vein) 453.8
  basilar (artery) (*see also* Occlusion, artery, basilar) 433.0 ☑
  bland NEC 453.9
  brain (artery) (stem) 434.0 ☑
    due to syphilis 094.89
    iatrogenic 997.02
    late effect — *see* Late effect(s) (of) cerebrovascular disease
    postoperative 997.02
    puerperal, postpartum, childbirth 674.0 ☑

Thrombosis, thrombotic — *continued*
  brain — *continued*
    sinus (*see also* Thrombosis, intracranial venous sinus) 325
  capillary 448.9
    arteriolar, generalized 446.6
  cardiac (*see also* Infarct, myocardium) 410.9 ☑
    due to syphilis 093.89
    healed or specified as old 412
    valve — *see* Endocarditis
  carotid (artery) (common) (internal) (*see also* Occlusion, artery, carotid) 433.1 ☑
    with other precerebral artery 433.3 ☑
  cavernous sinus (venous) — *see* Thrombosis, intracranial venous sinus
  cerebellar artery (anterior inferior) (posterior inferior) (superior) 433.8 ☑
    late effect — *see* Late effect(s) (of) cerebrovascular disease
  cerebral (arteries) (*see also* Thrombosis, brain) 434.0 ☑
    late effect — *see* Late effect(s) (of) cerebrovascular disese
  coronary (artery) (*see also* Infarct, myocardium) 410.9 ☑
    without myocardial infarction 411.81
    due to syphilis 093.89
    healed or specified as old 412
  corpus cavernosum 607.82
  cortical (*see also* Thrombosis, brain) 434.0 ☑
  due to (presence of) any device, implant, or graft classifiable to 996.0–996.5 — *see* Complications, due to (presence of) any device, implant, or graft classified to 996.0–996.5 NEC
  effort 453.8
  endocardial — *see* Infarct, myocardium
  eye (*see also* Occlusion, retina) 362.30
  femoral (vein) 453.8
    with inflammation or phlebitis 451.11
    artery 444.22
    deep 453.41
  genital organ, male 608.83
  heart (chamber) (*see also* Infarct, myocardium) 410.9 ☑
  hepatic (vein) 453.0
    artery 444.89
    infectional or septic 572.1
  iliac (vein) 453.8
    with inflammation or phlebitis 451.81
    artery (common) (external) (internal) 444.81
  inflammation, vein — *see* Thrombophlebitis
  internal carotid artery (*see also* Occlusion, artery, carotid) 433.1 ☑
    with other precerebral artery 433.3 ☑
  intestine (with gangrene) 557.0
  intracranial (*see also* Thrombosis, brain) 434.0 ☑
    venous sinus (any) 325
      nonpyogenic origin 437.6
        in pregnancy or puerperium 671.5 ☑
  intramural (*see also* Infarct, myocardium) 410.9 ☑
    without
      cardiac condition 429.89
      coronary artery disease 429.89
      myocardial infarction 429.89
    healed or specified as old 412
  jugular (bulb) 453.8
  kidney 593.81

Thrombosis, thrombotic —
continued
kidney — *continued*
  artery 593.81
lateral sinus (venous) — *see* Thrombosis, intracranial venous sinus
leg 453.8
  with inflammation or phlebitis —
    see Thrombophlebitis
  deep (vessels) 453.40
    lower (distal) 453.42
    upper (proximal) 453.41
  superficial (vessels) 453.8
liver (venous) 453.0
  artery 444.89
  infectional or septic 572.1
  portal vein 452
longitudinal sinus (venous) — *see*
  Thrombosis, intracranial venous
  sinus
lower extremity 453.8
  deep vessels 453.40
    calf 453.42
    distal (lower leg) 453.42
    femoral 453.41
    iliac 453.41
    lower leg 453.42
    peroneal 453.42
    popliteal 453.41
    proximal (upper leg) 453.41
    thigh 453.41
    tibial 453.42
lung 415.19
  iatrogenic 415.11
  postoperative 415.11
marantic, dural sinus 437.6
meninges (brain) (*see also* Thrombosis, brain) 434.0 ☑
mesenteric (artery) (with gangrene) 557.0
  vein (inferior) (superior) 557.0
mitral — *see* Insufficiency, mitral
mural (heart chamber) (*see also* Infarct, myocardium) 410.9 ☑
  without
    cardiac condition 429.89
    coronary artery disease 429.89
    myocardial infarction 429.89
  due to syphilis 093.89
  following myocardial infarction 429.79
  healed or specified as old 412
omentum (with gangrene) 557.0
ophthalmic (artery) (*see also* Occlusion, retina) 362.30
pampiniform plexus (male) 608.83
  female 620.8
parietal (*see also* Infarct, myocardium) 410.9 ☑
penis, penile 607.82
peripheral arteries 444.22
  lower 444.22
  upper 444.21
platelet 446.6
portal 452
  due to syphilis 093.89
  infectional or septic 572.1
precerebral artery (*see also* Occlusion, artery, precerebral NEC)
pregnancy 671.9 ☑
  deep (vein) 671.3 ☑
  superficial (vein) 671.2 ☑
  puerperal, postpartum, childbirth 671.9 ☑
    brain (artery) 674.0 ☑
      venous 671.5 ☑
    cardiac 674.8 ☑
    cerebral (artery) 674.0 ☑
      venous 671.5 ☑
    deep (vein) 671.4 ☑
    intracranial sinus (nonpyogenic) (venous) 671.5 ☑
    pelvic 671.4 ☑
    pulmonary (artery) 673.2 ☑
    specified site NEC 671.5 ☑
    superficial 671.2 ☑

Thrombosis, thrombotic —
continued
pulmonary (artery) (vein) 415.19
  iatrogenic 415.11
  postoperative 415.11
renal (artery) 593.81
  vein 453.3
resulting from presence of shunt or other internal prosthetic device — *see* Complications, due to (presence of) any device, implant, or graft classified to 996.0–996.5 NEC
retina, retinal (artery) 362.30
  arterial branch 362.32
  central 362.31
  partial 362.33
  vein
    central 362.35
    tributary (branch) 362.36
scrotum 608.83
seminal vesicle 608.83
sigmoid (venous) sinus — *see* Thrombosis, intracranial venous sinus 325
silent NEC 453.9
sinus, intracranial (venous) (any) (*see also* Thrombosis, intracranial venous sinus) 325
softening, brain (*see also* Thrombosis, brain) 434.0 ☑
specified site NEC 453.8
spermatic cord 608.83
spinal cord 336.1
  due to syphilis 094.89
  in pregnancy or puerperium 671.5 ☑
  pyogenic origin 324.1
    late effect — *see* category 326
spleen, splenic 289.59
  artery 444.89
testis 608.83
traumatic (complication) (early) (*see also* Injury, blood vessel, by site) 904.9
tricuspid — *see* Endocarditis, tricuspid
tumor — *see* Neoplasm, by site
tunica vaginalis 608.83
umbilical cord (vessels) 663.6 ☑
  affecting fetus or newborn 762.6
vas deferens 608.83
vein
  deep 453.40
  lower extremity — *see* Thrombosis, lower extremity
vena cava (inferior) (superior) 453.2
Thrombus — *see* Thrombosis
Thrush 112.0
  newborn 771.7
Thumb — *see also* condition
  gamekeeper's 842.12
  sucking (child problem) 307.9
Thygeson's superficial punctate keratitis 370.21
Thymergasia — *see also* Psychosis, affective 296.80
Thymitis 254.8
Thymoma (benign) (M8580/0) 212.6
  malignant (M8580/3) 164.0
Thymus, thymic (gland) — *see* condition
Thyrocele — *see also* Goiter 240.9
Thyroglossal — *see also* condition
  cyst 759.2
  duct, persistent 759.2
Thyroid (body) (gland) — *see also* condition
  hormone resistance 246.8 ●
  lingual 759.2
Thyroiditis 245.9
  acute (pyogenic) (suppurative) 245.0
    nonsuppurative 245.0
  autoimmune 245.2
  chronic (nonspecific) (sclerosing) 245.8
    fibrous 245.3
    lymphadenoid 245.2

Thyroiditis — *continued*
chronic — *continued*
  lymphocytic 245.2
  lymphoid 245.2
complicating pregnancy, childbirth, or puerperium 648.1 ☑
de Quervain's (subacute granulomatous) 245.1
fibrous (chronic) 245.3
giant (cell) (follicular) 245.1
granulomatous (de Quervain's) (subacute) 245.1
Hashimoto's (struma lymphomatosa) 245.2
iatrogenic 245.4
invasive (fibrous) 245.3
ligneous 245.3
lymphocytic (chronic) 245.2
lymphoid 245.2
lymphomatous 245.2
pseudotuberculous 245.1
pyogenic 245.0
radiation 245.4
Riedel's (ligneous) 245.3
subacute 245.1
suppurative 245.0
tuberculous (*see also* Tuberculosis) 017.5 ☑
viral 245.1
woody 245.3
Thyrolingual duct, persistent 759.2
Thyromegaly 240.9
Thyrotoxic
  crisis or storm (*see also* Thyrotoxicosis) 242.9 ☑
  heart failure (*see also* Thyrotoxicosis) 242.9 ☑ *[425.7]*
Thyrotoxicosis 242.9 ☑

Note — Use the following fifth-digit subclassification with category 242:

0   without mention of thyrotoxic crisis or storm

1   with mention of thyrotoxic crisis or storm

with
  goiter (diffuse) 242.0 ☑
    adenomatous 242.3 ☑
      multinodular 242.2 ☑
      uninodular 242.1 ☑
    nodular 242.3 ☑
      multinodular 242.2 ☑
      uninodular 242.1 ☑
  infiltrative
    dermopathy 242.0 ☑
    ophthalmopathy 242.0 ☑
  thyroid acropachy 242.0 ☑
complicating pregnancy, childbirth, or puerperium 648.1 ☑
due to
  ectopic thyroid nodule 242.4 ☑
  ingestion of (excessive) thyroid material 242.8 ☑
  specified cause NEC 242.8 ☑
factitia 242.8 ☑
heart 242.9 ☑ *[425.7]*
neonatal (transient) 775.3
TIA (transient ischemic attack) 435.9
  with transient neurologic deficit 435.9
  late effect — *see* Late effect(s) (of) cerebrovascular disease
Tibia vara 732.4
Tic 307.20
  breathing 307.20
  child problem 307.21
  compulsive 307.22
  convulsive 307.20
  degenerative (generalized) (localized) 333.3
    facial 351.8
  douloureux (*see also* Neuralgia, trigeminal) 350.1
    atypical 350.2
  habit 307.20
    chronic (motor or vocal) 307.22 *

Tic — *continued*
habit — *continued*
  transient (of childhood) 307.21
lid 307.20
  transient (of childhood) 307.21
motor-verbal 307.23
occupational 300.89
orbicularis 307.20
  transient (of childhood) 307.21
organic origin 333.3
postchoreic — *see* Chorea
psychogenic 307.20
  compulsive 307.22
salaam 781.0
spasm 307.20
  chronic (motor or vocal) 307.22
  transient (of childhood) 307.21
Tick-bite fever NEC 066.1
  African 087.1
  Colorado (virus) 066.1
  Rocky Mountain 082.0
Tick (-borne) fever NEC 066.1
  American mountain 066.1
  Colorado 066.1
  hemorrhagic NEC 065.3
    Crimean 065.0
    Kyasanur Forest 065.2
    Omsk 065.1
  mountain 066.1
  nonexanthematous 066.1
Tick paralysis 989.5
Tics and spasms, compulsive 307.22
Tietze's disease or syndrome 733.6
Tight, tightness
  anus 564.89
  chest 786.59
  fascia (lata) 728.9
  foreskin (congenital) 605
  hymen 623.3
  introitus (acquired) (congenital) 623.3
  rectal sphincter 564.89
  tendon 727.81
    Achilles (heel) 727.81
  urethral sphincter 598.9
Tilting vertebra 737.9
Timidity, child 313.21
Tinea (intersecta) (tarsi) 110.9
  amiantacea 110.0
  asbestina 110.0
  barbae 110.0
  beard 110.0
  black dot 110.0
  blanca 111.2
  capitis 110.0
  corporis 110.5
  cruris 110.3
  decalvans 704.09
  flava 111.0
  foot 110.4
  furfuracea 111.0
  imbricata (Tokelau) 110.5
  lepothrix 039.0
  manuum 110.2
  microsporic (*see also* Dermatophytosis) 110.9
  nigra 111.1
  nodosa 111.2
  pedis 110.4
  scalp 110.0
  specified site NEC 110.8
  sycosis 110.0
  tonsurans 110.0
  trichophytic (*see also* Dermatophytosis) 110.9
  unguium 110.1
  versicolor 111.0
Tingling sensation — *see also* Disturbance, sensation 782.0
Tin-miners' lung 503
Tinnitus (aurium) 388.30
  audible 388.32
  objective 388.32
  subjective 388.31
Tipped, teeth 524.33 ●
Tipping
  pelvis 738.6

☑ Additional Digit Required — Refer to the Tabular List for Digit Selection   ▽ Subterms under main terms may continue to next column or page

284 — Volume 2 · October 2006   ▶◀ Revised Text   ● New Line   ▲ Revised Code   *2007 ICD-9-CM*

Tipping — *continued*
  pelvis — *continued*
    with disproportion (fetopelvic) 653.0 ☑
      affecting fetus or newborn 763.1
      causing obstructed labor 660.1 ☑
        affecting fetus or newborn 763.1
  teeth 524.33
Tiredness 780.79
Tissue — *see* condition
Tobacco
  abuse (affecting health) NEC (*see also* Abuse, drugs, nondependent) 305.1
  heart 989.84
  use disorder complicating pregnan●cy, childbirth, or the puerperi●um 649.0 ☑
Tobias' syndrome (carcinoma, pulmonary apex) (M8010/3) 162.3
Tocopherol deficiency 269.1
Todd's
  cirrhosis — *see* Cirrhosis, biliary
  paralysis (postepileptic transitory paralysis) 344.89
Toe — *see* condition
Toilet, artificial opening — *see also* Attention to, artificial, opening V55.9
Tokelau ringworm 110.5
Tollwut 071
Tolosa-Hunt syndrome 378.55
Tommaselli's disease
  correct substance properly administered 599.7
  overdose or wrong substance given or taken 961.4
Tongue — *see also* condition
  worms 134.1
Tongue tie 750.0
Tonic pupil 379.46
Toni-Fanconi syndrome (cystinosis) 270.0
Tonsil — *see* condition
Tonsillitis (acute) (catarrhal) (croupous) (follicular) (gangrenous) (infective) (lacunar) (lingual) (malignant) (membranous) (phlegmonous) (pneumococcal) (pseudomembranous) (purulent) (septic) (staphylococcal) (subacute) (suppurative) (toxic) (ulcerative) (vesicular) (viral) 463
  with influenza, flu, or grippe 487.1
  chronic 474.00
  diphtheritic (membranous) 032.0
  hypertrophic 474.00
  influenzal 487.1
  parenchymatous 475
  streptococcal 034.0
  tuberculous (*see also* Tuberculosis) 012.8 ☑
  Vincent's 101
Tonsillopharyngitis 465.8
Toothache 525.9
Tooth, teeth — *see* condition
Topagnosis 782.0
Tophi (gouty) 274.0
  ear 274.81
  heart 274.82
  specified site NEC 274.82
Torn — *see* Tear, torn
Tornwaldt's bursitis (disease) (pharyngeal bursitis) 478.29
  cyst 478.26
Torpid liver 573.9
Torsion
  accessory tube 620.5
  adnexa (female) 620.5
  aorta (congenital) 747.29
    acquired 447.1
  appendix
    epididymis 608.24 ●
    testis 608.23 ●

Torsion — *continued*
  bile duct 576.8
    with calculus, choledocholithiasis or stones — *see* Choledocholithiasis
    congenital 751.69
  bowel, colon, or intestine 560.2
  cervix ▶— *see* Malposition, uterus◀
  duodenum 537.3
  dystonia — *see* Dystonia, torsion
  epididymis 608.24 ▲
    appendix 608.24 ▲
  fallopian tube 620.5
  gallbladder (*see also* Disease, gallbladder) 575.8
    congenital 751.69
  gastric 537.89
  hydatid of Morgagni (female) 620.5
  kidney (pedicle) 593.89
  Meckel's diverticulum (congenital) 751.0
  mesentery 560.2
  omentum 560.2
  organ or site, congenital NEC — *see* Anomaly, specified type NEC
  ovary (pedicle) 620.5
    congenital 752.0
  oviduct 620.5
  penis 607.89
    congenital 752.69
  renal 593.89
  spasm — *see* Dystonia, torsion
  spermatic cord 608.22 ▲
    extravaginal 608.21 ●
    intravaginal 608.22 ●
  spleen 289.59
  testicle, testis 608.20 ▲
    appendix 608.23 ●
  tibia 736.89
  umbilical cord — *see* Compression, umbilical cord
  uterus (*see also* Malposition, uterus) 621.6
Torticollis (intermittent) (spastic) 723.5
  congenital 754.1
    sternomastoid 754.1
  due to birth injury 767.8
  hysterical 300.11
  ocular 781.93
  psychogenic 306.0
    specified as conversion reaction 300.11
  rheumatic 723.5
  rheumatoid 714.0
  spasmodic 333.83
  traumatic, current NEC 847.0
Tortuous
  artery 447.1
  fallopian tube 752.19
  organ or site, congenital NEC — *see* Distortion
  renal vessel (congenital) 747.62
  retina vessel (congenital) 743.58
    acquired 362.17
  ureter 593.4
  urethra 599.84
  vein — *see* Varicose, vein
Torula, torular (infection) 117.5
  histolytica 117.5
  lung 117.5
Torulosis 117.5
Torus
  fracture
    fibula 823.41
      with tibia 823.42
    radius 813.45
    tibia 823.40
      with fibula 823.42
  mandibularis 526.81
  palatinus 526.81
Touch, vitreous 997.99
Touraine-Solente-Golé syndrome (acropachyderma) 757.39
Touraine's syndrome (hereditary osteo-onychodysplasia) 756.89

Tourette's disease (motor-verbal tic) 307.23
Tower skull 756.0
  with exophthalmos 756.0
Toxemia 799.89
  with
    abortion — *see* Abortion, by type, with toxemia
  bacterial — *see* Septicemia
  biliary (*see also* Disease, biliary) 576.8
  burn — *see* Burn, by site
  congenital NEC 779.89
  eclamptic 642.6 ☑
    with pre-existing hypertension 642.7 ☑
  erysipelatous (*see also* Erysipelas) 035
  fatigue 799.89
  fetus or newborn NEC 779.89
  food (*see also* Poisoning, food) 005.9
  gastric 537.89
  gastrointestinal 558.2
  intestinal 558.2
  kidney (*see also* Disease, renal) 593.9
  lung 518.89
  malarial NEC (*see also* Malaria) 084.6
  maternal (of pregnancy), affecting fetus or newborn 760.0
  myocardial — *see* Myocarditis, toxic
  of pregnancy (mild) (pre-eclamptic) 642.4 ☑
    with
      convulsions 642.6 ☑
      pre-existing hypertension 642.7 ☑
    affecting fetus or newborn 760.0
    severe 642.5 ☑
  pre-eclamptic — *see* Toxemia, of pregnancy
  puerperal, postpartum — *see* Toxemia, of pregnancy
  pulmonary 518.89
  renal (*see also* Disease, renal) 593.9
  septic (*see also* Septicemia) 038.9
  small intestine 558.2
  staphylococcal 038.10
    aureus 038.11
    due to food 005.0
    specified organism NEC 038.19
  stasis 799.89
  stomach 537.89
  uremic (*see also* Uremia) 586
  urinary 586
Toxemica cerebropathia psychica (nonalcoholic) 294.0
  alcoholic 291.1
Toxic (poisoning) — *see also* condition
  from drug or poison — *see* Table of Drugs and Chemicals
  oil syndrome 710.5
  shock syndrome 040.82
  thyroid (gland) (*see also* Thyrotoxicosis) 242.9 ☑
Toxicemia — *see* Toxemia
Toxicity
  dilantin
    asymptomatic 796.0
    symptomatic — *see* Table of Drugs and Chemicals
  drug
    asymptomatic 796.0
    symptomatic — *see* Table of Drugs and Chemicals
  fava bean 282.2
  from drug or poison
    asymptomatic 796.0
    symptomatic — *see* Table of Drugs and Chemicals
Toxicosis — *see also* Toxemia 799.89
  capillary, hemorrhagic 287.0
Toxinfection 799.89
  gastrointestinal 558.2
Toxocariasis 128.0
Toxoplasma infection, generalized 130.9
Toxoplasmosis (acquired) 130.9
  with pneumonia 130.4

Toxoplasmosis — *continued*
  congenital, active 771.2
  disseminated (multisystemic) 130.8
  maternal
    with suspected damage to fetus affecting management of pregnancy 655.4 ☑
    affecting fetus or newborn 760.2
    manifest toxoplasmosis in fetus or newborn 771.2
  multiple sites 130.8
  multisystemic disseminated 130.8
  specified site NEC 130.7
Trabeculation, bladder 596.8
Trachea — *see* condition
Tracheitis (acute) (catarrhal) (infantile) (membranous) (plastic) (pneumococcal) (septic) (suppurative) (viral) 464.10
  with
    bronchitis 490
      acute or subacute 466.0
      chronic 491.8
      tuberculosis — *see* Tuberculosis, pulmonary
    laryngitis (acute) 464.20
      with obstruction 464.21
      chronic 476.1
      tuberculous (*see also* Tuberculosis, larynx) 012.3 ☑
    obstruction 464.11
  chronic 491.8
    with
      bronchitis (chronic) 491.8
      laryngitis (chronic) 476.1
    due to external agent — *see* Condition, respiratory, chronic, due to
  diphtheritic (membranous) 032.3
    due to external agent — *see* Inflammation, respiratory, upper, due to
  edematous 464.11
  influenzal 487.1
  streptococcal 034.0
  syphilitic 095.8
  tuberculous (*see also* Tuberculosis) 012.8 ☑
Trachelitis (nonvenereal) — *see also* Cervicitis 616.0
  trichomonal 131.09
Tracheobronchial — *see* condition
Tracheobronchitis — *see also* Bronchitis 490
  acute or subacute 466.0
    with bronchospasm or obstruction 466.0
  chronic 491.8
  influenzal 487.1
  senile 491.8
Tracheobronchomegaly (congenital) 748.3
  with bronchiectasis 494.0
    with (acute) exacerbation 494.1
  acquired 519.19 ▲
    with bronchiectasis 494.0
      with (acute) exacerbation 494.1
Tracheobronchopneumonitis — *see* Pneumonia, broncho
Tracheocele (external) (internal) 519.19 ▲
  congenital 748.3
Tracheomalacia 519.19 ▲
  congenital 748.3
Tracheopharyngitis (acute) 465.8
  chronic 478.9
    due to external agent — *see* Condition, respiratory, chronic, due to
  due to external agent — *see* Inflammation, respiratory, upper, due to
Tracheostenosis 519.19 ▲
  congenital 748.3
Tracheostomy
  attention to V55.0
  complication 519.00

Tracheostomy — *continued*
- granuloma 519.09 ●
- hemorrhage 519.09
- infection 519.01
- malfunctioning 519.02
- obstruction 519.09
- sepsis 519.01
- status V44.0
- stenosis 519.02

Trachoma, trachomatous 076.9
- active (stage) 076.1
- contraction of conjunctiva 076.1
- dubium 076.0
- healed or late effect 139.1
- initial (stage) 076.0
- Türck's (chronic catarrhal laryngitis) 476.0

Trachyphonia 784.49

Training
- insulin pump V65.46
- orthoptic V57.4
- orthotic V57.81

Train sickness 994.6

Trait
- hemoglobin
  - abnormal NEC 282.7
    - with thalassemia 282.49
  - C (*see also* Disease, hemoglobin, C) 282.7
    - with elliptocytosis 282.7
  - S (Hb-S) 282.5
  - Lepore 282.49
    - with other abnormal hemoglobin NEC 282.49
- paranoid 301.0
- sickle-cell 282.5
  - with
    - elliptocytosis 282.5
    - spherocytosis 282.5

Traits, paranoid 301.0

Tramp V60.0

Trance 780.09
- hysterical 300.13

Transaminasemia 790.4

Transfusion, blood
- without reported diagnosis V58.2
- donor V59.01
  - stem cells V59.02
- incompatible 999.6
- reaction or complication — *see* Complications, transfusion
- related acute lung injury (TRALI) ●
  - 518.7 ●
- syndrome
  - fetomaternal 772.0
  - twin-to-twin
    - blood loss (donor twin) 772.0
    - recipient twin 776.4

Transient — *see also* condition
- alteration of awareness 780.02
- blindness 368.12
- deafness (ischemic) 388.02
- global amnesia 437.7
- person (homeless) NEC V60.0

Transitional, lumbosacral joint of vertebra 756.19

Translocation
- autosomes NEC 758.5
  - 13-15 758.1
  - 16-18 758.2
  - 21 or 22 758.0
  - balanced in normal individual 758.4
  - D₁ 758.1
  - E₃ 758.2
  - G 758.0
  - balanced autosomal in normal individual 758.4
- chromosomes NEC 758.89
- Down's syndrome 758.0

Translucency, iris 364.53

Transmission of chemical substances through the placenta (affecting fetus or newborn) 760.70
- alcohol 760.71
- anticonvulsants 760.77

Transmission of chemical substances through the placenta — *continued*
- antifungals 760.74
- anti-infective agents 760.74
- antimetabolics 760.78
- cocaine 760.75
- "crack" 760.75
- diethylstilbestrol [DES] 760.76
- hallucinogenic agents 760.73
- medicinal agents NEC 760.79
- narcotics 760.72
- obstetric anesthetic or analgesic drug 763.5
- specified agent NEC 760.79
- suspected, affecting management of pregnancy 655.5 ☑

Transplant(ed)
- bone V42.4
  - marrow V42.81
- complication (*see also* Complications, due to (presence of) any device, implant, or graft classified to 996.0–996.5 NEC)
  - bone marrow 996.85
  - corneal graft NEC 996.79
    - infection or inflammation 996.69
    - reaction 996.51
    - rejection 996.51
  - organ (failure) (immune or nonimmune cause) (infection) (rejection) 996.80
    - bone marrow 996.85
    - heart 996.83
    - intestines 996.87
    - kidney 996.81
    - liver 996.82
    - lung 996.84
    - pancreas 996.86
    - specified NEC 996.89
  - skin NEC 996.79
    - infection or inflammation 996.69
    - rejection 996.52
      - artificial 996.55
      - decellularized allodermis 996.55
- cornea V42.5
- hair V50.0
- heart V42.1
  - valve V42.2
- intestine V42.84
- kidney V42.0
- liver V42.7
- lung V42.6
- organ V42.9
  - specified NEC V42.89
- pancreas V42.83
- peripheral stem cells V42.82
- skin V42.3
- stem cells, peripheral V42.82
- tissue V42.9
  - specified NEC V42.89

Transplants, ovarian, endometrial 617.1

Transposed — *see* Transposition

Transposition (congenital) — *see also* Malposition, congenital
- abdominal viscera 759.3
- aorta (dextra) 745.11
- appendix 751.5
- arterial trunk 745.10
- colon 751.5
- great vessels (complete) 745.10
  - both originating from right ventricle 745.11
  - corrected 745.12
  - double outlet right ventricle 745.11
  - incomplete 745.11
  - partial 745.11
  - specified type NEC 745.19
- heart 746.87
  - with complete transposition of viscera 759.3
- intestine (large) (small) 751.5

Transposition — *see also* Malposition, congenital — *continued*
- pulmonary veins 747.49
- reversed jejunal (for bypass) (status) V45.3
- scrotal 752.81
- stomach 750.7
  - with general transposition of viscera 759.3
- teeth, tooth 524.30
- vessels (complete) 745.10
  - partial 745.11
- viscera (abdominal) (thoracic) 759.3

Trans-sexualism 302.50
- with
  - asexual history 302.51
  - heterosexual history 302.53
  - homosexual history 302.52

Transverse — *see also* condition
- arrest (deep), in labor 660.3 ☑
  - affecting fetus or newborn 763.1
- lie 652.3 ☑
  - before labor, affecting fetus or newborn 761.7
  - causing obstructed labor 660.0 ☑
    - affecting fetus or newborn 763.1
  - during labor, affecting fetus or newborn 763.1

Transvestism, transvestitism (transvestic fetishism) 302.3

Trapped placenta (with hemorrhage) 666.0 ☑
- without hemorrhage 667.0 ☑

Traumatic — *see* condition

Trauma, traumatism — *see also* Injury, by site 959.9
- birth — *see* Birth, injury NEC
- causing hemorrhage of pregnancy or delivery 641.8 ☑
- complicating
  - abortion — *see* Abortion, by type, with damage to pelvic organs
  - ectopic pregnancy (*see also* categories 633.0–633.9) 639.2
  - molar pregnancy (*see also* categories 630–632) 639.2
- during delivery NEC 665.9 ☑
- following
  - abortion 639.2
  - ectopic or molar pregnancy 639.2
- maternal, during pregnancy, affecting fetus or newborn 760.5
- neuroma — *see* Injury, nerve, by site
- previous major, affecting management of pregnancy, childbirth, or puerperium V23.89
- psychic (current) (*see also* Reaction, adjustment)
  - previous (history) V15.49
- psychologic, previous (affecting health) V15.49
- transient paralysis — *see* Injury, nerve, by site

Treacher Collins' syndrome (incomplete facial dysostosis) 756.0

Treitz's hernia — *see* Hernia, Treitz's

Trematode infestation NEC 121.9

Trematodiasis NEC 121.9

Trembles 988.8

Trembling paralysis — *see also* Parkinsonism 332.0

Tremor 781.0
- essential (benign) 333.1
- familial 333.1
- flapping (liver) 572.8
- hereditary 333.1
- hysterical 300.11
- intention 333.1
- medication-induced postural 333.1
- mercurial 985.0
- muscle 728.85
- Parkinson's (*see also* Parkinsonism) 332.0
- psychogenic 306.0
  - specified as conversion reaction 300.11

Tremor — *continued*
- senilis 797
- specified type NEC 333.1

Trench
- fever 083.1
- foot 991.4
- mouth 101
- nephritis — *see* Nephritis, acute

Treponema pallidum infection — *see also* Syphilis 097.9

Treponematosis 102.9
- due to
  - T. pallidum — *see* Syphilis
  - T. pertenue (yaws) (*see also* Yaws) 102.9

Triad
- Kartagener's 759.3
- Reiter's (complete) (incomplete) 099.3
- Saint's (*see also* Hernia, diaphragm) 553.3

Trichiasis 704.2
- cicatricial 704.2
- eyelid 374.05
  - with entropion (*see also* Entropion) 374.00

Trichinella spiralis (infection) (infestation) 124

Trichinelliasis 124

Trichinellosis 124

Trichiniasis 124

Trichinosis 124

Trichobezoar 938
- intestine 936
- stomach 935.2

Trichocephaliasis 127.3

Trichocephalosis 127.3

Trichocephalus infestation 127.3

Trichoclasis 704.2

Trichoepithelioma (M8100/0) — *see also* Neoplasm, skin, benign
- breast 217
- genital organ NEC — *see* Neoplasm, by site, benign
- malignant (M8100/3) — *see* Neoplasm, skin, malignant

Trichofolliculoma (M8101/0) — *see* Neoplasm, skin, benign

Tricholemmoma (M8102/0) — *see* Neoplasm, skin, benign

Trichomatosis 704.2

Trichomoniasis 131.9
- bladder 131.09
- cervix 131.09
- intestinal 007.3
- prostate 131.03
- seminal vesicle 131.09
- specified site NEC 131.8
- urethra 131.02
- urogenitalis 131.00
- vagina 131.01
- vulva 131.01
- vulvovaginal 131.01

Trichomycosis 039.0
- axillaris 039.0
- nodosa 111.2
- nodularis 111.2
- rubra 039.0

Trichonocardiosis (axillaris) (palmellina) 039.0

Trichonodosis 704.2

Trichophytide — *see* Dermatophytosis

Trichophytid, trichophyton infection — *see also* Dermatophytosis 110.9

Trichophytobezoar 938
- intestine 936
- stomach 935.2

Trichophytosis — *see* Dermatophytosis

Trichoptilosis 704.2

Trichorrhexis (nodosa) 704.2

Trichosporosis nodosa 111.2

Trichostasis spinulosa (congenital) 757.4

Trichostrongyliasis (small intestine) 127.6

Trichostrongylosis 127.6

Trichostrongylus (instabilis) infection 127.6
Trichotillomania 312.39
Trichromat, anomalous (congenital) 368.59
Trichromatopsia, anomalous (congenital) 368.59
Trichuriasis 127.3
Trichuris trichiuria (any site) (infection) (infestation) 127.3
Tricuspid (valve) — *see* condition
Trifid — *see also* Accessory
   kidney (pelvis) 753.3
   tongue 750.13
Trigeminal neuralgia — *see* Neuralgia, trigeminal 350.1
Trigeminoencephaloangiomatosis 759.6
Trigeminy 427.89
   postoperative 997.1
Trigger finger (acquired) 727.03
   congenital 756.89
Trigonitis (bladder) (chronic) (pseudomembranous) 595.3
   tuberculous (*see also* Tuberculosis) 016.1 ☑
Trigonocephaly 756.0
Trihexosidosis 272.7
Trilobate placenta — *see* Placenta, abnormal
Trilocular heart 745.8
Trimethylaminuria 270.8 ●
Tripartita placenta — *see* Placenta, abnormal
Triple — *see also* Accessory
   kidneys 753.3
   uteri 752.2
   X female 758.81
Triplegia 344.89
   congenital or infantile 343.8
Triplet
   affected by maternal complications of pregnancy 761.5
   healthy liveborn — *see* Newborn, multiple
   pregnancy (complicating delivery) NEC 651.1 ☑
     with fetal loss and retention of one or more fetus(es) 651.4 ☑
     following (elective) fetal reduction 651.7 ☑
Triplex placenta — *see* Placenta, abnormal
Triplication — *see* Accessory
Trismus 781.0
   neonatorum 771.3
   newborn 771.3
Trisomy (syndrome) NEC 758.5
   13 (partial) 758.1
   16-18 758.2
   18 (partial) 758.2
   21 (partial) 758.0
   22 758.0
   autosomes NEC 758.5
   D_1 758.1
   E_3 758.2
   G (group) 758.0
   group D_1 758.1
   group E 758.2
   group G 758.0
Tritanomaly 368.53
Tritanopia 368.53
Troisier-Hanot-Chauffard syndrome (bronze diabetes) 275.0
Trombidiosis 133.8
Trophedema (hereditary) 757.0
   congenital 757.0
Trophoblastic disease — *see also* Hydatidiform mole 630
   previous, affecting management of pregnancy V23.1
Tropholymphedema 757.0
Trophoneurosis NEC 356.9
   arm NEC 354.9
   disseminated 710.1
   facial 349.89

Trophoneurosis — *continued*
   leg NEC 355.8
   lower extremity NEC 355.8
   upper extremity NEC 354.9
Tropical — *see also* condition
   maceration feet (syndrome) 991.4
   wet foot (syndrome) 991.4
Trouble — *see also* Disease
   bowel 569.9
   heart — *see* Disease, heart
   intestine 569.9
   kidney (*see also* Disease, renal) 593.9
   nervous 799.2
   sinus (*see also* Sinusitis) 473.9
Trousseau's syndrome (thrombophlebitis migrans) 453.1
Truancy, childhood — *see also* Disturbance, conduct
   socialized 312.2 ☑
   undersocialized, unsocialized 312.1 ☑
Truncus
   arteriosus (persistent) 745.0
   common 745.0
   communis 745.0
Trunk — *see* condition
Trychophytide — *see* Dermatophytosis
Trypanosoma infestation — *see* Trypanosomiasis
Trypanosomiasis 086.9
   with meningoencephalitis 086.9 [323.2]
   African 086.5
     due to Trypanosoma 086.5
       gambiense 086.3
       rhodesiense 086.4
   American 086.2
     with
       heart involvement 086.0
       other organ involvement 086.1
     without mention of organ involvement 086.2
   Brazilian — *see* Trypanosomiasis, American
   Chagas' — *see* Trypanosomiasis, American
   due to Trypanosoma
     cruzi — *see* Trypanosomiasis, American
     gambiense 086.3
     rhodesiense 086.4
   gambiensis, Gambian 086.3
   North American — *see* Trypanosomiasis, American
   rhodesiensis, Rhodesian 086.4
   South American — *see* Trypanosomiasis, American
T-shaped incisors 520.2
Tsutsugamushi fever 081.2
Tubercle — *see also* Tuberculosis
   brain, solitary 013.2 ☑
   Darwin's 744.29
   epithelioid noncaseating 135
   Ghon, primary infection 010.0 ☑
Tuberculid, tuberculide (indurating) (lichenoid) (miliary) (papulonecrotic) (primary) (skin) (subcutaneous) — *see also* Tuberculosis 017.0 ☑
Tuberculoma — *see also* Tuberculosis
   brain (any part) 013.2 ☑
   meninges (cerebral) (spinal) 013.1 ☑
   spinal cord 013.4 ☑

Tuberculosis, tubercular, tuberculous (calcification) (calcified) (caseous) (chromogenic acid-fast bacilli) (congenital) (degeneration) (disease) (fibrocaseous) (fistula) (gangrene) (interstitial) (isolated circumscribed lesions) (necrosis) (parenchymatous) (ulcerative) 011.9 ☑

Note — Use the following fifth-digit subclassification with categories 010-018:

0   *unspecified*

1   *bacteriological or histological examination not done*

2   *bacteriological or histological examination unknown (at present)*

3   *tubercle bacilli found (in sputum) by microscopy*

4   *tubercle bacilli not found (in sputum) by microscopy, but found by bacterial culture*

5   *tubercle bacilli not found by bacteriological exam–ination, but tuberculosis confirmed histologically*

6   *tubercle bacilli not found by bacteriological or histological examination, but tuberculosis confirmed by other methods [inoculation of animals]*

For tuberculous conditions specified as late effects or sequelae, see category 137.

   abdomen 014.8 ☑
     lymph gland 014.8 ☑
   abscess 011.9 ☑
     arm 017.9 ☑
     bone (*see also* Osteomyelitis, due to, tuberculosis) 015.9 ☑ [730.8]
       hip 015.1 ☑ [730.85]
       knee 015.2 ☑ [730.86]
       sacrum 015.0 ☑ [730.88]
       specified site NEC 015.7 ☑ [730.88]
       spinal 015.0 ☑ [730.88]
       vertebra 015.0 ☑ [730.88]
     brain 013.3 ☑
     breast 017.9 ☑
     Cowper's gland 016.5 ☑
     dura (mater) 013.8 ☑
       brain 013.3 ☑
       spinal cord 013.5 ☑
     epidural 013.8 ☑
       brain 013.3 ☑
       spinal cord 013.5 ☑
     frontal sinus — *see* Tuberculosis, sinus
     genital organs NEC 016.9 ☑
       female 016.7 ☑
       male 016.5 ☑
     genitourinary NEC 016.9 ☑
     gland (lymphatic) — *see* Tuberculosis, lymph gland
     hip 015.1 ☑
     iliopsoas 015.0 ☑ [730.88]
     intestine 014.8 ☑
     ischiorectal 014.8 ☑
     joint 015.9 ☑
       hip 015.1 ☑
       knee 015.2 ☑
       specified joint NEC 015.8 ☑
       vertebral 015.0 ☑ [730.88]
     kidney 016.0 ☑ [590.81]
     knee 015.2 ☑
     lumbar 015.0 ☑ [730.88]
     lung 011.2 ☑
       primary, progressive 010.8 ☑
     meninges (cerebral) (spinal) 013.0 ☑
     pelvic 016.9 ☑

Tuberculosis, tubercular, tuberculous — *continued*
   abscess — *continued*
     pelvic — *continued*
       female 016.7 ☑
       male 016.5 ☑
     perianal 014.8 ☑
       fistula 014.8 ☑
     perinephritic 016.0 ☑ [590.81]
     perineum 017.9 ☑
     perirectal 014.8 ☑
     psoas 015.0 ☑ [730.88]
     rectum 014.8 ☑
     retropharyngeal 012.8 ☑
     sacrum 015.0 ☑ [730.88]
     scrofulous 017.2 ☑
     scrotum 016.5 ☑
     skin 017.0 ☑
       primary 017.0 ☑
     spinal cord 013.5 ☑
     spine or vertebra (column) 015.0 ☑ [730.88]
     strumous 017.2 ☑
     subdiaphragmatic 014.8 ☑
     testis 016.5 ☑
     thigh 017.9 ☑
     urinary 016.3 ☑
       kidney 016.0 ☑ [590.81]
     uterus 016.7 ☑
   accessory sinus — *see* Tuberculosis, sinus
   Addison's disease 017.6 ☑
   adenitis (*see also* Tuberculosis, lymph gland) 017.2 ☑
   adenoids 012.8 ☑
   adenopathy (*see also* Tuberculosis, lymph gland) 017.2 ☑
     tracheobronchial 012.1 ☑
       primary progressive 010.8 ☑
   adherent pericardium 017.9 ☑ [420.0]
   adnexa (uteri) 016.7 ☑
   adrenal (capsule) (gland) 017.6 ☑
   air passage NEC 012.8 ☑
   alimentary canal 014.8 ☑
   anemia 017.9 ☑
   ankle (joint) 015.8 ☑
     bone 015.5 ☑ [730.87]
   anus 014.8 ☑
   apex (*see also* Tuberculosis, pulmonary) 011.9 ☑
   apical (*see also* Tuberculosis, pulmonary) 011.9 ☑
   appendicitis 014.8 ☑
   appendix 014.8 ☑
   arachnoid 013.0 ☑
   artery 017.9 ☑
   arthritis (chronic) (synovial) 015.9 ☑ [711.40]
     ankle 015.8 ☑ [730.87]
     hip 015.1 ☑ [711.45]
     knee 015.2 ☑ [711.46]
     specified site NEC 015.8 ☑ [711.48]
     spine or vertebra (column) 015.0 ☑ [720.81]
     wrist 015.8 ☑ [730.83]
   articular — *see* Tuberculosis, joint
   ascites 014.0 ☑
   asthma (*see also* Tuberculosis, pulmonary) 011.9 ☑
   axilla, axillary 017.2 ☑
     gland 017.2 ☑
   bilateral (*see also* Tuberculosis, pulmonary) 011.9 ☑
   bladder 016.1 ☑
   bone (*see also* Osteomyelitis, due to, tuberculosis) 015.9 ☑ [730.8]
     hip 015.1 ☑ [730.85]
     knee 015.2 ☑ [730.86]
     limb NEC 015.5 ☑ [730.88]
     sacrum 015.0 ☑ [730.88]
     specified site NEC 015.7 ☑ [730.88]
     spinal or vertebral column 015.0 ☑ [730.88]
   bowel 014.8 ☑

☑ Additional Digit Required — Refer to the Tabular List for Digit Selection   ▽ Subterms under main terms may continue to next column or page

2007 ICD-9-CM   ►◄ Revised Text   ● New Line   ▲ Revised Code   October 2006 · Volume 2 — 287

Tuberculosis, tubercular, tuberculous
— *continued*
- bowel — *continued*
  - miliary 018.9 ☑
- brain 013.2 ☑
- breast 017.9 ☑
- broad ligament 016.7 ☑
- bronchi, bronchial, bronchus 011.3 ☑
  - ectasia, ectasis 011.5 ☑
  - fistula 011.3 ☑
    - primary, progressive 010.8 ☑
  - gland 012.1 ☑
    - primary, progressive 010.8 ☑
  - isolated 012.2 ☑
  - lymph gland or node 012.1 ☑
    - primary, progressive 010.8 ☑
- bronchiectasis 011.5 ☑
- bronchitis 011.3 ☑
- bronchopleural 012.0 ☑
- bronchopneumonia, bronchopneumonic 011.6 ☑
- bronchorrhagia 011.3 ☑
- bronchotracheal 011.3 ☑
  - isolated 012.2 ☑
- bronchus — *see* Tuberculosis, bronchi
- bronze disease (Addison's) 017.6 ☑
- buccal cavity 017.9 ☑
- bulbourethral gland 016.5 ☑
- bursa (*see also* Tuberculosis, joint) 015.9 ☑
- cachexia NEC (*see also* Tuberculosis, pulmonary) 011.9 ☑
- cardiomyopathy 017.9 ☑ *[425.8]*
- caries (*see also* Tuberculosis, bone) 015.9 ☑ *[730.8]*
- cartilage (*see also* Tuberculosis, bone) 015.9 ☑ *[730.8]*
  - intervertebral 015.0 ☑ *[730.88]*
- catarrhal (*see also* Tuberculosis, pulmonary) 011.9 ☑
- cecum 014.8 ☑
- cellular tissue (primary) 017.0 ☑
- cellulitis (primary) 017.0 ☑
- central nervous system 013.9 ☑
  - specified site NEC 013.8 ☑
- cerebellum (current) 013.2 ☑
- cerebral (current) 013.2 ☑
  - meninges 013.0 ☑
- cerebrospinal 013.6 ☑
  - meninges 013.0 ☑
- cerebrum (current) 013.2 ☑
- cervical 017.2 ☑
  - gland 017.2 ☑
  - lymph nodes 017.2 ☑
- cervicitis (uteri) 016.7 ☑
- cervix 016.7 ☑
- chest (*see also* Tuberculosis, pulmonary) 011.9 ☑
- childhood type or first infection 010.0 ☑
- choroid 017.3 ☑ *[363.13]*
- choroiditis 017.3 ☑ *[363.13]*
- ciliary body 017.3 ☑ *[364.11]*
- colitis 014.8 ☑
- colliers' 011.4 ☑
- colliquativa (primary) 017.0 ☑
- colon 014.8 ☑
  - ulceration 014.8 ☑
- complex, primary 010.0 ☑
- complicating pregnancy, childbirth, or puerperium 647.3 ☑
  - affecting fetus or newborn 760.2
- congenital 771.2
- conjunctiva 017.3 ☑ *[370.31]*
- connective tissue 017.9 ☑
  - bone — *see* Tuberculosis, bone
- contact V01.1
- converter (tuberculin skin test) (without disease) 795.5
- cornea (ulcer) 017.3 ☑ *[370.31]*
- Cowper's gland 016.5 ☑
- coxae 015.1 ☑ *[730.85]*
- coxalgia 015.1 ☑ *[730.85]*
- cul-de-sac of Douglas 014.8 ☑

Tuberculosis, tubercular, tuberculous
— *continued*
- curvature, spine 015.0 ☑ *[737.40]*
- cutis (colliquativa) (primary) 017.0 ☑
- cystitis 016.1 ☑
- cyst, ovary 016.6 ☑
- dacryocystitis 017.3 ☑ *[375.32]*
- dactylitis 015.5 ☑
- diarrhea 014.8 ☑
- diffuse (*see also* Tuberculosis, miliary) 018.9 ☑
  - lung — *see* Tuberculosis, pulmonary
  - meninges 013.0 ☑
- digestive tract 014.8 ☑
- disseminated (*see also* Tuberculosis, miliary) 018.9 ☑
  - meninges 013.0 ☑
- duodenum 014.8 ☑
- dura (mater) 013.9 ☑
  - abscess 013.8 ☑
    - cerebral 013.3 ☑
    - spinal 013.5 ☑
- dysentery 014.8 ☑
- ear (inner) (middle) 017.4 ☑
  - bone 015.6 ☑
  - external (primary) 017.0 ☑
  - skin (primary) 017.0 ☑
- elbow 015.8 ☑
- emphysema — *see* Tuberculosis, pulmonary
- empyema 012.0 ☑
- encephalitis 013.6 ☑
- endarteritis 017.9 ☑
- endocarditis (any valve) 017.9 ☑ *[424.91]*
- endocardium (any valve) 017.9 ☑ *[424.91]*
- endocrine glands NEC 017.9 ☑
- endometrium 016.7 ☑
- enteric, enterica 014.8 ☑
- enteritis 014.8 ☑
- enterocolitis 014.8 ☑
- epididymis 016.4 ☑
- epididymitis 016.4 ☑
- epidural abscess 013.8 ☑
  - brain 013.3 ☑
  - spinal cord 013.5 ☑
- epiglottis 012.3 ☑
- episcleritis 017.3 ☑ *[379.00]*
- erythema (induratum) (nodosum) (primary) 017.1 ☑
- esophagus 017.8 ☑
- Eustachian tube 017.4 ☑
- exposure to V01.1
- exudative 012.0 ☑
  - primary, progressive 010.1 ☑
- eye 017.3 ☑
  - glaucoma 017.3 ☑ *[365.62]*
- eyelid (primary) 017.0 ☑
  - lupus 017.0 ☑ *[373.4]*
- fallopian tube 016.6 ☑
- fascia 017.9 ☑
- fauces 012.8 ☑
- finger 017.9 ☑
- first infection 010.0 ☑
- fistula, perirectal 014.8 ☑
- Florida 011.6 ☑
- foot 017.9 ☑
- funnel pelvis 137.3
- gallbladder 017.9 ☑
- galloping (*see also* Tuberculosis, pulmonary) 011.9 ☑
- ganglionic 015.9 ☑
- gastritis 017.9 ☑
- gastrocolic fistula 014.8 ☑
- gastroenteritis 014.8 ☑
- gastrointestinal tract 014.8 ☑
- general, generalized 018.9 ☑
  - acute 018.0 ☑
  - chronic 018.8 ☑
- genital organs NEC 016.9 ☑
  - female 016.7 ☑
  - male 016.5 ☑

Tuberculosis, tubercular, tuberculous
— *continued*
- genitourinary NEC 016.9 ☑
- genu 015.2 ☑
- glandulae suprarenalis 017.6 ☑
- glandular, general 017.2 ☑
- glottis 012.3 ☑
- grinders' 011.4 ☑
- groin 017.2 ☑
- gum 017.9 ☑
- hand 017.9 ☑
- heart 017.9 ☑ *[425.8]*
- hematogenous — *see* Tuberculosis, miliary
- hemoptysis (*see also* Tuberculosis, pulmonary) 011.9 ☑
- hemorrhage NEC (*see also* Tuberculosis, pulmonary) 011.9 ☑
- hemothorax 012.0 ☑
- hepatitis 017.9 ☑
- hilar lymph nodes 012.1 ☑
  - primary, progressive 010.8 ☑
- hip (disease) (joint) 015.1 ☑
  - bone 015.1 ☑ *[730.85]*
- hydrocephalus 013.8 ☑
- hydropneumothorax 012.0 ☑
- hydrothorax 012.0 ☑
- hypoadrenalism 017.6 ☑
- hypopharynx 012.8 ☑
- ileocecal (hyperplastic) 014.8 ☑
- ileocolitis 014.8 ☑
- ileum 014.8 ☑
- iliac spine (superior) 015.0 ☑ *[730.88]*
- incipient NEC (*see also* Tuberculosis, pulmonary) 011.9 ☑
- indurativa (primary) 017.1 ☑
- infantile 010.0 ☑
- infection NEC 011.9 ☑
  - without clinical manifestation 010.0 ☑
- infraclavicular gland 017.2 ☑
- inguinal gland 017.2 ☑
- inguinalis 017.2 ☑
- intestine (any part) 014.8 ☑
- iris 017.3 ☑ *[364.11]*
- iritis 017.3 ☑ *[364.11]*
- ischiorectal 014.8 ☑
- jaw 015.7 ☑ *[730.88]*
- jejunum 014.8 ☑
- joint 015.9 ☑
  - hip 015.1 ☑
  - knee 015.2 ☑
  - specified site NEC 015.8 ☑
  - vertebral 015.0 ☑ *[730.88]*
- keratitis 017.3 ☑ *[370.31]*
  - interstitial 017.3 ☑ *[370.59]*
- keratoconjunctivitis 017.3 ☑ *[370.31]*
- kidney 016.0 ☑
- knee (joint) 015.2 ☑
- kyphoscoliosis 015.0 ☑ *[737.43]*
- kyphosis 015.0 ☑ *[737.41]*
- lacrimal apparatus, gland 017.3 ☑
- laryngitis 012.3 ☑
- larynx 012.3 ☑
- leptomeninges, leptomeningitis (cerebral) (spinal) 013.0 ☑
- lichenoides (primary) 017.0 ☑
- linguae 017.9 ☑
- lip 017.9 ☑
- liver 017.9 ☑
- lordosis 015.0 ☑ *[737.42]*
- lung — *see* Tuberculosis, pulmonary
- luposa 017.0 ☑
  - eyelid 017.0 ☑ *[373.4]*
- lymphadenitis — *see* Tuberculosis, lymph gland
- lymphangitis — *see* Tuberculosis, lymph gland
- lymphatic (gland) (vessel) — *see* Tuberculosis, lymph gland
- lymph gland or node (peripheral) 017.2 ☑
  - abdomen 014.8 ☑
  - bronchial 012.1 ☑

Tuberculosis, tubercular, tuberculous
— *continued*
- lymph gland or node — *continued*
  - bronchial — *continued*
    - primary, progressive 010.8 ☑
  - cervical 017.2 ☑
  - hilar 012.1 ☑
    - primary, progressive 010.8 ☑
  - intrathoracic 012.1 ☑
    - primary, progressive 010.8 ☑
  - mediastinal 012.1 ☑
    - primary, progressive 010.8 ☑
  - mesenteric 014.8 ☑
  - peripheral 017.2 ☑
  - retroperitoneal 014.8 ☑
  - tracheobronchial 012.1 ☑
    - primary, progressive 010.8 ☑
- malignant NEC (*see also* Tuberculosis, pulmonary) 011.9 ☑
- mammary gland 017.9 ☑
- marasmus NEC (*see also* Tuberculosis, pulmonary) 011.9 ☑
- mastoiditis 015.6 ☑
- maternal, affecting fetus or newborn 760.2
- mediastinal (lymph) gland or node 012.1 ☑
  - primary, progressive 010.8 ☑
- mediastinitis 012.8 ☑
  - primary, progressive 010.8 ☑
- mediastinopericarditis 017.9 ☑ *[420.0]*
- mediastinum 012.8 ☑
  - primary, progressive 010.8 ☑
- medulla 013.9 ☑
  - brain 013.2 ☑
  - spinal cord 013.4 ☑
- melanosis, Addisonian 017.6 ☑
- membrane, brain 013.0 ☑
- meninges (cerebral) (spinal) 013.0 ☑
- meningitis (basilar) (brain) (cerebral) (cerebrospinal) (spinal) 013.0 ☑
- meningoencephalitis 013.0 ☑
- mesentery, mesenteric 014.8 ☑
  - lymph gland or node 014.8 ☑
- miliary (any site) 018.9 ☑
  - acute 018.0 ☑
  - chronic 018.8 ☑
  - specified type NEC 018.8 ☑
- millstone makers' 011.4 ☑
- miners' 011.4 ☑
- moulders' 011.4 ☑
- mouth 017.9 ☑
- multiple 018.9 ☑
  - acute 018.0 ☑
  - chronic 018.8 ☑
- muscle 017.9 ☑
- myelitis 013.6 ☑
- myocarditis 017.9 ☑ *[422.0]*
- myocardium 017.9 ☑ *[422.0]*
- nasal (passage) (sinus) 012.8 ☑
- nasopharynx 012.8 ☑
- neck gland 017.2 ☑
- nephritis 016.0 ☑ *[583.81]*
- nerve 017.9 ☑
- nose (septum) 012.8 ☑
- ocular 017.3 ☑
- old NEC 137.0
  - without residuals V12.01
- omentum 014.8 ☑
- oophoritis (acute) (chronic) 016.6 ☑
- optic 017.3 ☑ *[377.39]*
  - nerve trunk 017.3 ☑ *[377.39]*
  - papilla, papillae 017.3 ☑ *[377.39]*
- orbit 017.3 ☑
- orchitis 016.5 ☑ *[608.81]*
- organ, specified NEC 017.9 ☑
- orificialis (primary) 017.0 ☑
- osseous (*see also* Tuberculosis, bone) 015.9 ☑ *[730.8]*
- osteitis (*see also* Tuberculosis, bone) 015.9 ☑ *[730.8]*
- osteomyelitis (*see also* Tuberculosis, bone) 015.9 ☑ *[730.8]*
- otitis (media) 017.4 ☑

☑ Additional Digit Required — Refer to the Tabular List for Digit Selection

Subterms under main terms may continue to next column or page

▶◀ Revised Text   ● New Line   ▲ Revised Code

Tuberculosis, tubercular, tuberculous — *continued*
ovaritis (acute) (chronic) 016.6 ☑
ovary (acute) (chronic) 016.6 ☑
oviducts (acute) (chronic) 016.6 ☑
pachymeningitis 013.0 ☑
palate (soft) 017.9 ☑
pancreas 017.9 ☑
papulonecrotic (primary) 017.0 ☑
parathyroid glands 017.9 ☑
paronychia (primary) 017.0 ☑
parotid gland or region 017.9 ☑
perineum 017.9 ☑
pelvic organ NEC 016.9 ☑
    female 016.7 ☑
    male 016.5 ☑
pelvis (bony) 015.7 ☑ *[730.85]*
penis 016.5 ☑
peribronchitis 011.3 ☑
pericarditis 017.9 ☑ *[420.0]*
pericardium 017.9 ☑ *[420.0]*
perichondritis, larynx 012.3 ☑
perineum 017.9 ☑
periostitis (*see also* Tuberculosis, bone) 015.9 ☑ *[730.8]* ☑
periphlebitis 017.9 ☑
    eye vessel 017.3 ☑ *[362.18]*
    retina 017.3 ☑ *[362.18]*
perirectal fistula 014.8 ☑
peritoneal gland 014.8 ☑
peritoneum 014.0 ☑
peritonitis 014.0 ☑
pernicious NEC (*see also* Tuberculosis, pulmonary) 011.9 ☑
pharyngitis 012.8 ☑
pharynx 012.8 ☑
phlyctenulosis (conjunctiva) 017.3 ☑ *[370.31]*
phthisis NEC (*see also* Tuberculosis, pulmonary) 011.9 ☑
pituitary gland 017.9 ☑
placenta 016.7 ☑
pleura, pleural, pleurisy, pleuritis (fibrinous) (obliterative) (purulent) (simple plastic) (with effusion) 012.0 ☑
    primary, progressive 010.1 ☑
pneumonia, pneumonic 011.6 ☑
pneumothorax 011.7 ☑
polyserositis 018.9 ☑
    acute 018.0 ☑
    chronic 018.8 ☑
potters' 011.4 ☑
prepuce 016.5 ☑
primary 010.9 ☑
    complex 010.0 ☑
    complicated 010.8 ☑
       with pleurisy or effusion 010.1 ☑
    progressive 010.8 ☑
       with pleurisy or effusion 010.1 ☑
    skin 017.0 ☑
proctitis 014.8 ☑
prostate 016.5 ☑ *[601.4]*
prostatitis 016.5 ☑ *[601.4]*
pulmonaris (*see also* Tuberculosis, pulmonary) 011.9 ☑
pulmonary (artery) (incipient) (malignant) (multiple round foci) (pernicious) (reinfection stage) 011.9 ☑
    cavitated or with cavitation 011.2 ☑
       primary, progressive 010.8 ☑
    childhood type or first infection 010.0 ☑
    chromogenic acid-fast bacilli 795.39
    fibrosis or fibrotic 011.4 ☑
    infiltrative 011.0 ☑
       primary, progressive 010.9 ☑
    nodular 011.1 ☑
    specified NEC 011.8 ☑
    sputum positive only 795.39

Tuberculosis, tubercular, tuberculous — *continued*
pulmonary — *continued*
    status following surgical collapse of lung NEC 011.9 ☑
pyelitis 016.0 ☑ *[590.81]*
pyelonephritis 016.0 ☑ *[590.81]*
pyemia — *see* Tuberculosis, miliary
pyonephrosis 016.0 ☑
pyopneumothorax 012.0 ☑
pyothorax 012.0 ☑
rectum (with abscess) 014.8 ☑
    fistula 014.8 ☑
reinfection stage (*see also* Tuberculosis, pulmonary) 011.9 ☑
renal 016.0 ☑
renis 016.0 ☑
reproductive organ 016.7 ☑
respiratory NEC (*see also* Tuberculosis, pulmonary) 011.9 ☑
    specified site NEC 012.8 ☑
retina 017.3 ☑ *[363.13]*
retroperitoneal (lymph gland or node) 014.8 ☑
    gland 014.8 ☑
retropharyngeal abscess 012.8 ☑
rheumatism 015.9 ☑
rhinitis 012.8 ☑
sacroiliac (joint) 015.8 ☑
sacrum 015.0 ☑ *[730.88]*
salivary gland 017.9 ☑
salpingitis (acute) (chronic) 016.6 ☑
sandblasters' 011.4 ☑
sclera 017.3 ☑ *[379.09]*
scoliosis 015.0 ☑ *[737.43]*
scrofulous 017.2 ☑
scrotum 016.5 ☑
seminal tract or vesicle 016.5 ☑ *[608.81]*
senile NEC (*see also* Tuberculosis, pulmonary) 011.9 ☑
septic NEC (*see also* Tuberculosis, miliary) 018.9 ☑
shoulder 015.8 ☑
    blade 015.7 ☑ *[730.8]* ☑
sigmoid 014.8 ☑
sinus (accessory) (nasal) 012.8 ☑
    bone 015.7 ☑ *[730.88]*
    epididymis 016.4 ☑
skeletal NEC (*see also* Osteomyelitis, due to tuberculosis) 015.9 ☑ *[730.8]* ☑
skin (any site) (primary) 017.0 ☑
small intestine 014.8 ☑
soft palate 017.9 ☑
spermatic cord 016.5 ☑
spinal
    column 015.0 ☑ *[730.88]*
    cord 013.4 ☑
    disease 015.0 ☑ *[730.88]*
    medulla 013.4 ☑
    membrane 013.0 ☑
    meninges 013.0 ☑
spine 015.0 ☑ *[730.88]*
spleen 017.7 ☑
splenitis 017.7 ☑
spondylitis 015.0 ☑ *[720.81]*
spontaneous pneumothorax — *see* Tuberculosis, pulmonary
sternoclavicular joint 015.8 ☑
stomach 017.9 ☑
stonemasons' 011.4 ☑
struma 017.2 ☑
subcutaneous tissue (cellular) (primary) 017.0 ☑
subcutis (primary) 017.0 ☑
subdeltoid bursa 017.9 ☑
submaxillary 017.9 ☑
    region 017.9 ☑
supraclavicular gland 017.2 ☑
suprarenal (capsule) (gland) 017.6 ☑
swelling, joint (*see also* Tuberculosis, joint) 015.9 ☑
symphysis pubis 015.7 ☑ *[730.88]*

Tuberculosis, tubercular, tuberculous — *continued*
synovitis 015.9 ☑ *[727.01]*
    hip 015.1 ☑ *[727.01]*
    knee 015.2 ☑ *[727.01]*
    specified site NEC 015.8 ☑ *[727.01]*
    spine or vertebra 015.0 ☑ *[727.01]*
systemic — *see* Tuberculosis, miliary
tarsitis (eyelid) 017.0 ☑ *[373.4]*
    ankle (bone) 015.5 ☑ *[730.87]*
tendon (sheath) — *see* Tuberculosis, tenosynovitis
tenosynovitis 015.9 ☑ *[727.01]*
    hip 015.1 ☑ *[727.01]*
    knee 015.2 ☑ *[727.01]*
    specified site NEC 015.8 ☑ *[727.01]*
    spine or vertebra 015.0 ☑ *[727.01]*
testis 016.5 ☑ *[608.81]*
throat 012.8 ☑
thymus gland 017.9 ☑
thyroid gland 017.5 ☑
toe 017.9 ☑
tongue 017.9 ☑
tonsil (lingual) 012.8 ☑
tonsillitis 012.8 ☑
trachea, tracheal 012.8 ☑
    gland 012.1 ☑
       primary, progressive 010.8 ☑
    isolated 012.2 ☑
tracheobronchial 011.3 ☑
    glandular 012.1 ☑
       primary, progressive 010.8 ☑
    isolated 012.2 ☑
    lymph gland or node 012.1 ☑
       primary, progressive 010.8 ☑
tubal 016.6 ☑
tunica vaginalis 016.5 ☑
typhlitis 014.8 ☑
ulcer (primary) (skin) 017.0 ☑
    bowel or intestine 014.8 ☑
    specified site NEC — *see* Tuberculosis, by site
unspecified site — *see* Tuberculosis, pulmonary
ureter 016.2 ☑
urethra, urethral 016.3 ☑
urinary organ or tract 016.3 ☑
    kidney 016.0 ☑
uterus 016.7 ☑
uveal tract 017.3 ☑ *[363.13]*
uvula 017.9 ☑
vaccination, prophylactic (against) V03.2
vagina 016.7 ☑
vas deferens 016.5 ☑
vein 017.9 ☑
verruca (primary) 017.0 ☑
verrucosa (cutis) (primary) 017.0 ☑
vertebra (column) 015.0 ☑ *[730.88]*
vesiculitis 016.5 ☑ *[608.81]*
viscera NEC 014.8 ☑
vulva 016.7 ☑ *[616.51]*
wrist (joint) 015.8 ☑
    bone 015.5 ☑ *[730.83]*

Tuberculum
auriculae 744.29
occlusal 520.2
paramolare 520.2
Tuberosity
jaw, excessive 524.07   ●
maxillary, entire 524.07   ●
Tuberous sclerosis (brain) 759.5
Tube, tubal, tubular — *see also* condition
ligation, admission for V25.2
Tubo-ovarian — *see* condition
Tuboplasty, after previous sterilization V26.0
Tubotympanitis 381.10
Tularemia 021.9
with
    conjunctivitis 021.3
    pneumonia 021.2
bronchopneumonic 021.2
conjunctivitis 021.3

Tularemia — *continued*
cryptogenic 021.1
disseminated 021.8
enteric 021.1
generalized 021.8
glandular 021.8
intestinal 021.1
oculoglandular 021.3
ophthalmic 021.3
pneumonia 021.2
pulmonary 021.2
specified NEC 021.8
typhoidal 021.1
ulceroglandular 021.0
vaccination, prophylactic (against) V03.4
Tularensis conjunctivitis 021.3
Tumefaction — *see also* Swelling
liver (*see also* Hypertrophy, liver) 789.1
Tumor (M8000/1) — *see also* Neoplasm, by site, unspecified nature
Abrikossov's (M9580/0) (*see also* Neoplasm, connective tissue, benign)
    malignant (M9580/3) — *see* Neoplasm, connective tissue, malignant
acinar cell (M8550/1) — *see* Neoplasm, by site, uncertain behavior
acinic cell (M8550/1) — *see* Neoplasm, by site, uncertain behavior
adenomatoid (M9054/0) (*see also* Neoplasm, by site, benign)
    odontogenic (M9300/0) 213.1
       upper jaw (bone) 213.0
adnexal (skin) (M8390/0) — *see* Neoplasm, skin, benign
adrenal
    cortical (benign) (M8370/0) 227.0
       malignant (M8370/3) 194.0
    rest (M8671/0) — *see* Neoplasm, by site, benign
alpha cell (M8152/0)
    malignant (M8152/3)
       pancreas 157.4
       specified site NEC — *see* Neoplasm, by site, malignant
       unspecified site 157.4
    pancreas 211.7
    specified site NEC — *see* Neoplasm, by site, benign
    unspecified site 211.7
aneurysmal (*see also* Aneurysm) 442.9
aortic body (M8691/1) 237.3
    malignant (M8691/3) 194.6
argentaffin (M8241/1) — *see* Neoplasm, by site, uncertain behavior
basal cell (M8090/1) (*see also* Neoplasm, skin, uncertain behavior)
benign (M8000/0) — *see* Neoplasm, by site, benign
beta cell (M8151/0)
    malignant (M8151/3)
       pancreas 157.4
       specified site — *see* Neoplasm, by site, malignant
       unspecified site 157.4
    pancreas 211.7
    specified site NEC — *see* Neoplasm, by site, benign
    unspecified site 211.7
blood — *see* Hematoma
Brenner (M9000/0) 220
    borderline malignancy (M9000/1) 236.2
    malignant (M9000/3) 183.0
    proliferating (M9000/1) 236.2
Brooke's (M8100/0) — *see* Neoplasm, skin, benign
brown fat (M8880/0) — *see* Lipoma, by site
Burkitt's (M9750/3) 200.2 ☑

☑ Additional Digit Required — Refer to the Tabular List for Digit Selection   ▽ Subterms under main terms may continue to next column or page

2007 ICD-9-CM   ►◄ Revised Text   ● New Line   ▲ Revised Code   **October 2006 · Volume 2 — 289**

Tumor — *see also* Neoplasm, by site, unspecified nature — *continued*
calcifying epithelial odontogenic (M9340/0) 213.1
upper jaw (bone) 213.0
carcinoid (M8240/1) — *see* Carcinoid
carotid body (M8692/1) 237.3
malignant (M8692/3) 194.5
Castleman's (mediastinal lymph node hyperplasia) 785.6
cells (M8001/1) (*see also* Neoplasm, by site, unspecified nature)
benign (M8001/0) — *see* Neoplasm, by site, benign
malignant (M8001/3) — *see* Neoplasm, by site, malignant
uncertain whether benign or malignant (M8001/1) — *see* Neoplasm, by site, uncertain nature
cervix
in pregnancy or childbirth 654.6 ☑
affecting fetus or newborn 763.89
causing obstructed labor 660.2 ☑
affecting fetus or newborn 763.1
chondromatous giant cell (M9230/0) — *see* Neoplasm, bone, benign
chromaffin (M8700/0) (*see also* Neoplasm, by site, benign)
malignant (M8700/3) — *see* Neoplasm, by site, malignant
Cock's peculiar 706.2
Codman's (benign chondroblastoma) (M9230/0) — *see* Neoplasm, bone, benign
dentigerous, mixed (M9282/0) 213.1
upper jaw (bone) 213.0
dermoid (M9084/0) — *see* Neoplasm, by site, benign
with malignant transformation (M9084/3) 183.0
desmoid (extra-abdominal) (M8821/1) (*see also* Neoplasm, connective tissue, uncertain behavior)
abdominal (M8822/1) — *see* Neoplasm, connective tissue, uncertain behavior
embryonal (mixed) (M9080/1) (*see also* Neoplasm, by site, uncertain behavior)
liver (M9080/3) 155.0
endodermal sinus (M9071/3)
specified site — *see* Neoplasm, by site, malignant
unspecified site
female 183.0
male 186.9
epithelial
benign (M8010/0) — *see* Neoplasm, by site, benign
malignant (M8010/3) — *see* Neoplasm, by site, malignant
Ewing's (M9260/3) — *see* Neoplasm, bone, malignant
fatty — *see* Lipoma
fetal, causing disproportion 653.7 ☑
causing obstructed labor 660.1 ☑
fibroid (M8890/0) — *see* Leiomyoma
G cell (M8153/1)
malignant (M8153/3)
pancreas 157.4
specified site NEC — *see* Neoplasm, by site, malignant
unspecified site 157.4
specified site — *see* Neoplasm, by site, uncertain behavior
unspecified site 235.5
giant cell (type) (M8003/1) (*see also* Neoplasm, by site, unspecified nature)
bone (M9250/1) 238.0

Tumor — *see also* Neoplasm, by site, unspecified nature — *continued*
giant cell (*see also* Neoplasm, by site, unspecified nature) — *continued*
bone — *continued*
malignant (M9250/3) — *see* Neoplasm, bone, malignant
chondromatous (M9230/0) — *see* Neoplasm, bone, benign
malignant (M8003/3) — *see* Neoplasm, by site, malignant
peripheral (gingiva) 523.8
soft parts (M9251/1) (*see also* Neoplasm, connective tissue, uncertain behavior)
malignant (M9251/3) — *see* Neoplasm, connective tissue, malignant
tendon sheath 727.02
glomus (M8711/0) (*see also* Hemangioma, by site)
jugulare (M8690/1) 237.3
malignant (M8690/3) 194.6
gonadal stromal (M8590/1) — *see* Neoplasm, by site, uncertain behavior
granular cell (M9580/0) (*see also* Neoplasm, connective tissue, benign)
malignant (M9580/3) — *see* Neoplasm, connective tissue, malignant
granulosa cell (M8620/1) 236.2
malignant (M8620/3) 183.0
granulosa cell-theca cell (M8621/1) 236.2
malignant (M8621/3) 183.0
Grawitz's (hypernephroma) (M8312/3) 189.0
hazard-crile (M8350/3) 193
hemorrhoidal — *see* Hemorrhoids
hilar cell (M8660/0) 220
Hürthle cell (benign) (M8290/0) 226
malignant (M8290/3) 193
hydatid (*see also* Echinococcus) 122.9
hypernephroid (M8311/1) (*see also* Neoplasm, by site, uncertain behavior)
interstitial cell (M8650/1) (*see also* Neoplasm, by site, uncertain behavior)
benign (M8650/0) — *see* Neoplasm, by site, benign
malignant (M8650/3) — *see* Neoplasm, by site, malignant
islet cell (M8150/0)
malignant (M8150/3)
pancreas 157.4
specified site — *see* Neoplasm, by site, malignant
unspecified site 157.4
pancreas 211.7
specified site NEC — *see* Neoplasm, by site, benign
unspecified site 211.7
juxtaglomerular (M8361/1) 236.91
Krukenberg's (M8490/6) 198.6
Leydig cell (M8650/1)
benign (M8650/0)
specified site — *see* Neoplasm, by site, benign
unspecified site
female 220
male 222.0
malignant (M8650/3)
specified site — *see* Neoplasm, by site, malignant
unspecified site
female 183.0
male 186.9
specified site — *see* Neoplasm, by site, uncertain behavior
unspecified site
female 236.2

Tumor — *see also* Neoplasm, by site, unspecified nature — *continued*
Leydig cell — *continued*
unspecified site — *continued*
male 236.4
lipid cell, ovary (M8670/0) 220
lipoid cell, ovary (M8670/0) 220
lymphomatous, benign (M9590/0) (*see also* Neoplasm, by site, benign)
Malherbe's (M8110/0) — *see* Neoplasm, skin, benign
malignant (M8000/3) (*see also* Neoplasm, by site, malignant)
fusiform cell (type) (M8004/3) — *see* Neoplasm, by site, malignant
giant cell (type) (M8003/3) — *see* Neoplasm, by site, malignant
mixed NEC (M8940/3) — *see* Neoplasm, by site, malignant
small cell (type) (M8002/3) — *see* Neoplasm, by site, malignant
spindle cell (type) (M8004/3) — *see* Neoplasm, by site, malignant
mast cell (M9740/1) 238.5
malignant (M9740/3) 202.6 ☑
melanotic, neuroectodermal (M9363/0) — *see* Neoplasm, by site, benign
Merkel cell — *see* Neoplasm, by site, malignant
mesenchymal
malignant (M8800/3) — *see* Neoplasm, connective tissue, malignant
mixed (M8990/1) — *see* Neoplasm, connective tissue, uncertain behavior
mesodermal, mixed (M8951/3) (*see also* Neoplasm, by site, malignant)
liver 155.0
mesonephric (M9110/1) (*see also* Neoplasm, by site, uncertain behavior)
malignant (M9110/3) — *see* Neoplasm, by site, malignant
metastatic
from specified site (M8000/3) — *see* Neoplasm, by site, malignant
to specified site (M8000/6) — *see* Neoplasm, by site, malignant, secondary
mixed NEC (M8940/0) (*see also* Neoplasm, by site, benign)
malignant (M8940/3) — *see* Neoplasm, by site, malignant
mucocarcinoid, malignant (M8243/3) — *see* Neoplasm, by site, malignant
mucoepidermoid (M8430/1) — *see* Neoplasm, by site, uncertain behavior
Mullerian, mixed (M8950/3) — *see* Neoplasm, by site, malignant
myoepithelial (M8982/0) — *see* Neoplasm, by site, benign
neurogenic olfactory (M9520/3) 160.0
nonencapsulated sclerosing (M8350/3) 193
odontogenic (M9270/1) 238.0
adenomatoid (M9300/0) 213.1
upper jaw (bone) 213.0
benign (M9270/0) 213.1
upper jaw (bone) 213.0
calcifying epithelial (M9340/0) 213.1
upper jaw (bone) 213.0
malignant (M9270/3) 170.1
upper jaw (bone) 170.0
squamous (M9312/0) 213.1
upper jaw (bone) 213.0
ovarian stromal (M8590/1) 236.2
ovary
in pregnancy or childbirth 654.4 ☑

Tumor — *see also* Neoplasm, by site, unspecified nature — *continued*
ovary — *continued*
in pregnancy or childbirth — *continued*
affecting fetus or newborn 763.89
causing obstructed labor 660.2 ☑
affecting fetus or newborn 763.1
pacinian (M9507/0) — *see* Neoplasm, skin, benign
Pancoast's (M8010/3) 162.3
papillary — *see* Papilloma
pelvic, in pregnancy or childbirth 654.9 ☑
affecting fetus or newborn 763.89
causing obstructed labor 660.2 ☑
affecting fetus or newborn 763.1
phantom 300.11
plasma cell (M9731/1) 238.6
benign (M9731/0) — *see* Neoplasm, by site, benign
malignant (M9731/3) 203.8 ☑
polyvesicular vitelline (M9071/3)
specified site — *see* Neoplasm, by site, malignant
unspecified site
female 183.0
male 186.9
Pott's puffy (*see also* Osteomyelitis) 730.2 ☑
Rathke's pouch (M9350/1) 237.0
regaud's (M8082/3) — *see* Neoplasm, nasopharynx, malignant
rete cell (M8140/0) 222.0
retinal anlage (M9363/0) — *see* Neoplasm, by site, benign
Rokitansky's 620.2
salivary gland type, mixed (M8940/0) (*see also* Neoplasm, by site, benign)
malignant (M8940/3) — *see* Neoplasm, by site, malignant
Sampson's 617.1
Schloffer's (*see also* Peritonitis) 567.29
Schmincke (M8082/3) — *see* Neoplasm, nasopharynx, malignant
sebaceous (*see also* Cyst, sebaceous) 706.2
secondary (M8000/6) — *see* Neoplasm, by site, secondary
Sertoli cell (M8640/0)
with lipid storage (M8641/0)
specified site — *see* Neoplasm, by site, benign
unspecified site
female 220
male 222.0
specified site — *see* Neoplasm, by site, benign
unspecified site
female 220
male 222.0
Sertoli-Leydig cell (M8631/0)
specified site, — *see* Neoplasm, by site, benign
unspecified site
female 220
male 222.0
sex cord (-stromal) (M8590/1) — *see* Neoplasm, by site, uncertain behavior
skin appendage (M8390/0) — *see* Neoplasm, skin, benign
soft tissue
benign (M8800/0) — *see* Neoplasm, connective tissue, benign
malignant (M8800/3) — *see* Neoplasm, connective tissue, malignant
sternomastoid 754.1

☑ Additional Digit Required — Refer to the Tabular List for Digit Selection ▽ Subterms under main terms may continue to next column or page

290 — Volume 2 ▶◀ Revised Text ● New Line ▲ Revised Code 2007 ICD-9-CM

Tumor — *see also* Neoplasm, by site, unspecified nature — *continued*
  stromal
    abdomen
      benign 215.5 ●
      malignant 171.5 ●
      uncertain behavior 238.1 ●
    digestive system 238.1 ●
      benign 215.5 ●
      malignant 171.5 ●
      uncertain behavior 238.1 ●
    gastric 238.1
      benign 215.5
      malignant 171.5
      uncertain behavior 238.1
    gastrointestinal 238.1
      benign 215.5
      malignant 171.5
      uncertain behavior 238.1
    intestine ▶(small) (large)◀ 238.1
      benign 215.5 ●
      malignant 171.5 ●
      uncertain behavior 238.1 ●
    stomach 238.1
      benign 215.5
      malignant 171.5
      uncertain behavior 238.1
  superior sulcus (lung) (pulmonary) (syndrome) (M8010/3) 162.3
  suprasulcus (M8010/3) 162.3
  sweat gland (M8400/1) (*see also* Neoplasm, skin, uncertain behavior)
    benign (M8400/0) — *see* Neoplasm, skin, benign
    malignant (M8400/3) — *see* Neoplasm, skin, malignant
  syphilitic brain 094.89
    congenital 090.49
  testicular stromal (M8590/1) 236.4
  theca cell (M8600/0) 220
  theca cell-granulosa cell (M8621/1) 236.2
  theca-lutein (M8610/0) 220
  turban (M8200/0) 216.4
  uterus
    in pregnancy or childbirth 654.1 ☑
      affecting fetus or newborn 763.89
      causing obstructed labor 660.2 ☑
        affecting fetus or newborn 763.1
  vagina
    in pregnancy or childbirth 654.7 ☑
      affecting fetus or newborn 763.89
      causing obstructed labor 660.2 ☑
        affecting fetus or newborn 763.1
  varicose (*see also* Varicose, vein) 454.9
  von Recklinghausen's (M9540/1) 237.71
  vulva
    in pregnancy or childbirth 654.8 ☑
      affecting fetus or newborn 763.89
      causing obstructed labor 660.2 ☑
        affecting fetus or newborn 763.1
  Warthin's (salivary gland) (M8561/0) 210.2
  white (*see also* Tuberculosis, arthritis)
  White-Darier 757.39
  Wilms' (nephroblastoma) (M8960/3) 189.0
  yolk sac (M9071/3)
    specified site — *see* Neoplasm, by site, malignant
    unspecified site
      female 183.0
      male 186.9
Tumorlet (M8040/1) — *see* Neoplasm, by site, uncertain behavior
Tungiasis 134.1

Tunica vasculosa lentis 743.39
Tunnel vision 368.45
Turban tumor (M8200/0) 216.4
Türck's trachoma (chronic catarrhal laryngitis) 476.0
Türk's syndrome (ocular retraction syndrome) 378.71
Turner's
  hypoplasia (tooth) 520.4
  syndrome 758.6
  tooth 520.4
Turner-Kieser syndrome (hereditary osteo-onychodysplasia) 756.89
Turner-Varny syndrome 758.6
Turricephaly 756.0
Tussis convulsiva — *see also* Whooping cough 033.9
Twin
  affected by maternal complications of pregnancy 761.5
  conjoined 759.4
  healthy liveborn — *see* Newborn, twin
  pregnancy (complicating delivery) NEC 651.0 ☑
    with fetal loss and retention of one fetus 651.3 ☑
    following (elective) fetal reduction
Twinning, teeth 520.2
Twist, twisted
  bowel, colon, or intestine 560.2
  hair (congenital) 757.4
  mesentery 560.2
  omentum 560.2
  organ or site, congenital NEC — *see* Anomaly, specified type NEC
  ovarian pedicle 620.5
    congenital 752.0
  umbilical cord — *see* Compression, umbilical cord
Twitch 781.0
Tylosis 700
  buccalis 528.6
  gingiva 523.8
  linguae 528.6
  palmaris et plantaris 757.39
Tympanism 787.3
Tympanites (abdominal) (intestine) 787.3
Tympanitis — *see* Myringitis
Tympanosclerosis 385.00
  involving
    combined sites NEC 385.09
      with tympanic membrane 385.03
    tympanic membrane 385.01
      with ossicles 385.02
        and middle ear 385.03
Tympanum — *see* condition
Tympany
  abdomen 787.3
  chest 786.7
Typhlitis — *see also* Appendicitis 541
Typhoenteritis 002.0
Typhogastric fever 002.0
Typhoid (abortive) (ambulant) (any site) (fever) (hemorrhagic) (infection) (intermittent) (malignant) (rheumatic) 002.0
  with pneumonia 002.0 *[484.8]*
  abdominal 002.0
  carrier (suspected) of V02.1
  cholecystitis (current) 002.0
  clinical (Widal and blood test negative) 002.0
  endocarditis 002.0 *[421.1]*
  inoculation reaction — *see* Complications, vaccination
  meningitis 002.0 *[320.7]*
  mesenteric lymph nodes 002.0
  myocarditis 002.0 *[422.0]*
  osteomyelitis (*see also* Osteomyelitis, due to, typhoid) 002.0 *[730.8]* ☑
  perichondritis, larynx 002.0 *[478.71]*
  pneumonia 002.0 *[484.8]*
  spine 002.0 *[720.81]*
  ulcer (perforating) 002.0

Typhoid — *continued*
  vaccination, prophylactic (against) V03.1
  Widal negative 002.0
Typhomalaria (fever) — *see also* Malaria 084.6
Typhomania 002.0
Typhoperitonitis 002.0
Typhus (fever) 081.9
  abdominal, abdominalis 002.0
  African tick 082.1
  amarillic (*see also* Fever, Yellow) 060.9
  brain 081.9
  cerebral 081.9
  classical 080
  endemic (flea-borne) 081.0
  epidemic (louse-borne) 080
  exanthematic NEC 080
  exanthematicus SAI 080
    brillii SAI 081.1
    Mexicanus SAI 081.0
    pediculo vestimenti causa 080
    typhus murinus 081.0
  flea-borne 081.0
  Indian tick 082.1
  Kenya tick 082.1
  louse-borne 080
  Mexican 081.0
    flea-borne 081.0
    louse-borne 080
    tabardillo 080
  mite-borne 081.2
  murine 081.0
  North Asian tick-borne 082.2
  petechial 081.9
  Queensland tick 082.3
  rat 081.0
  recrudescent 081.1
  recurrent (*see also* Fever, relapsing) 087.9
  São Paulo 082.0
  scrub (China) (India) (Malaya) (New Guinea) 081.2
  shop (of Malaya) 081.0
  Siberian tick 082.2
  tick-borne NEC 082.9
  tropical 081.2
  vaccination, prophylactic (against) V05.8
Tyrosinemia 270.2
  neonatal 775.89 ▲
Tyrosinosis (Medes) (Sakai) 270.2
Tyrosinuria 270.2
Tyrosyluria 270.2

U

Uehlinger's syndrome (acropachyderma) 757.39
Uhl's anomaly or disease (hypoplasia of myocardium, right ventricle) 746.84
Ulcerosa scarlatina 034.1
Ulcer, ulcerated, ulcerating, ulceration, ulcerative 707.9
  with gangrene 707.9 *[785.4]*
  abdomen (wall) (*see also* Ulcer, skin) 707.8
  ala, nose 478.19 ▲
  alveolar process 526.5
  amebic (intestine) 006.9
    skin 006.6
  anastomotic — *see* Ulcer, gastrojejunal
  anorectal 569.41
  antral — *see* Ulcer, stomach
  anus (sphincter) (solitary) 569.41
    varicose — *see* Varicose, ulcer, anus
  aorta — *see* Aneuysm ●
  aphthous (oral) (recurrent) 528.2
    genital organ(s)
      female 616.89 ▲
      male 608.89
    mouth 528.2
  arm (*see also* Ulcer, skin) 707.8

Ulcer, ulcerated, ulcerating, ulceration, ulcerative — *continued*
  arteriosclerotic plaque — *see* Arteriosclerosis, by site
  artery NEC 447.2
    without rupture 447.8
  atrophic NEC — *see* Ulcer, skin
  Barrett's (chronic peptic ulcer of esophagus) 530.85
  bile duct 576.8
  bladder (solitary) (sphincter) 596.8
    bilharzial (*see also* Schistosomiasis) 120.9 *[595.4]*
    submucosal (*see also* Cystitis) 595.1
    tuberculous (*see also* Tuberculosis) 016.1 ☑
  bleeding NEC — *see* Ulcer, peptic, with hemorrhage
  bone 730.9 ☑
  bowel (*see also* Ulcer, intestine) 569.82
  breast 611.0
  bronchitis 491.8
  bronchus 519.19 ▲
  buccal (cavity) (traumatic) 528.9
  burn (acute) — *see* Ulcer, duodenum
  Buruli 031.1
  buttock (*see also* Ulcer, skin) 707.8
  decubitus (*see also* Ulcer, decubitus) 707.00
  cancerous (M8000/3) — *see* Neoplasm, by site, malignant
  cardia — *see* Ulcer, stomach
  cardio-esophageal (peptic) 530.20
    with bleeding 530.21
  cecum (*see also* Ulcer, intestine) 569.82
  cervix (uteri) (trophic) 622.0
    with mention of cervicitis 616.0
  chancroidal 099.0
  chest (wall) (*see also* Ulcer, skin) 707.8
  Chiclero 085.4
  chin (pyogenic) (*see also* Ulcer, skin) 707.8
  chronic (cause unknown) (*see also* Ulcer, skin)
    penis 607.89
  Cochin-China 085.1
  colitis — *see* Colitis, ulcerative
  colon (*see also* Ulcer, intestine) 569.82
  conjunctiva (acute) (postinfectional) 372.00
  cornea (infectional) 370.00
    with perforation 370.06
    annular 370.02
    catarrhal 370.01
    central 370.03
    dendritic 054.42
    marginal 370.01
    mycotic 370.05
    phlyctenular, tuberculous (*see also* Tuberculosis) 017.3 ☑ *[370.31]*
    ring 370.02
    rodent 370.07
    serpent, serpiginous 370.04
    superficial marginal 370.01
    tuberculous (*see also* Tuberculosis) 017.3 ☑ *[370.31]*
  corpus cavernosum (chronic) 607.89
  crural — *see* Ulcer, lower extremity
  Curling's — *see* Ulcer, duodenum
  Cushing's — *see* Ulcer, peptic
  cystitis (interstitial) 595.1
  decubitus (unspecified site) 707.00
    with gangrene 707.00 *[785.4]*
    ankle 707.06
    back
      lower 707.03
      upper 707.02
    buttock 707.05
    elbow 707.01
    head 707.09
    heel 707.07

Ulcer, ulcerated, ulcerating, ulceration, ulcerative — *continued*

decubitus — *continued*
- hip 707.04
- other site 707.09
- sacrum 707.03
- shoulder blades 707.02

dendritic 054.42

diabetes, diabetic (mellitus) 250.8 ☑ *[707.9]*
- lower limb 250.8 ☑ *[707.10]*
  - ankle 250.8 ☑ *[707.13]*
  - calf 250.8 ☑ *[707.12]*
  - foot 250.8 ☑ *[707.15]*
  - heel 250.8 ☑ *[707.14]*
  - knee 250.8 ☑ *[707.19]*
  - specified site NEC 250.8 ☑ *[707.19]*
  - thigh 250.8 ☑ *[707.11]*
  - toes 250.8 ☑ *[707.15]*
- specified site NEC 250.8 ☑ *[707.8]*

Dieulafoy — *see* Lesion, Dieulafoy

due to
- infection NEC — *see* Ulcer, skin
- radiation, radium — *see* Ulcer, by site
- trophic disturbance (any region) — *see* Ulcer, skin
- x-ray — *see* Ulcer, by site

duodenum, duodenal (eroded) (peptic) 532.9 ☑

Note — *Use the following fifth-digit subclassification with categories 531–534:*

0   *without mention of obstruction*

1   *with obstruction*

with
- hemorrhage (chronic) 532.4 ☑
  - and perforation 532.6 ☑
- perforation (chronic) 532.5 ☑
  - and hemorrhage 532.6 ☑
- acute 532.3 ☑
  - with
    - hemorrhage 532.0 ☑
      - and perforation 532.2 ☑
    - perforation 532.1 ☑
      - and hemorrhage 532.2 ☑
- bleeding (recurrent) — *see* Ulcer, duodenum, with hemorrhage
- chronic 532.7 ☑
  - with
    - hemorrhage 532.4 ☑
      - and perforation 532.6 ☑
    - perforation 532.5 ☑
      - and hemorrhage 532.6 ☑
- penetrating — *see* Ulcer, duodenum, with perforation
- perforating — *see* Ulcer, duodenum, with perforation

dysenteric NEC 009.0

elusive 595.1

endocarditis (any valve) (acute) (chronic) (subacute) 421.0

enteritis — *see* Colitis, ulcerative

enterocolitis 556.0

epiglottis 478.79

esophagus (peptic) 530.20
- with bleeding 530.21
- due to ingestion
  - aspirin 530.20
  - chemicals 530.20
  - medicinal agents 530.20
- fungal 530.20
- infectional 530.20
- varicose (*see also* Varix, esophagus) 456.1
  - bleeding (*see also* Varix, esophagus, bleeding) 456.0

eye NEC 360.00
- dendritic 054.42

eyelid (region) 373.01

face (*see also* Ulcer, skin) 707.8

fauces 478.29

Ulcer, ulcerated, ulcerating, ulceration, ulcerative — *continued*

Fenwick (-Hunner) (solitary) (*see also* Cystitis) 595.1

fistulous NEC — *see* Ulcer, skin

foot (indolent) (*see also* Ulcer, lower extremity) 707.15
- perforating 707.15
  - leprous 030.1
  - syphilitic 094.0
- trophic 707.15
- varicose 454.0
  - inflamed or infected 454.2

frambesial, initial or primary 102.0

gallbladder or duct 575.8

gall duct 576.8

gangrenous (*see also* Gangrene) 785.4

gastric — *see* Ulcer, stomach

gastrocolic — *see* Ulcer, gastrojejunal

gastroduodenal — *see* Ulcer, peptic

gastroesophageal — *see* Ulcer, stomach

gastrohepatic — *see* Ulcer, stomach

gastrointestinal — *see* Ulcer, gastrojejunal

gastrojejunal (eroded) (peptic) 534.9 ☑

Note — *Use the following fifth-digit subclassification with categories 531–534:*

0   *without mention of obstruction*

1   *with obstruction*

with
- hemorrhage (chronic) 534.4 ☑
  - and perforation 534.6 ☑
- perforation 534.5 ☑
  - and hemorrhage 534.6 ☑
- acute 534.3 ☑
  - with
    - hemorrhage 534.0 ☑
      - and perforation 534.2 ☑
    - perforation 534.1 ☑
      - and hemorrhage 534.2 ☑
- bleeding (recurrent) — *see* Ulcer, gastrojejunal, with hemorrhage
- chronic 534.7 ☑
  - with
    - hemorrhage 534.4 ☑
      - and perforation 534.6 ☑
    - perforation 534.5 ☑
      - and hemorrhage 534.6 ☑
- penetrating — *see* Ulcer, gastrojejunal, with perforation
- perforating — *see* Ulcer, gastrojejunal, with perforation

gastrojejunocolic — *see* Ulcer, gastrojejunal

genital organ
- female 629.89 ▲
- male 608.89

gingiva 523.8

gingivitis 523.10 ▲

glottis 478.79

granuloma of pudenda 099.2

groin (*see also* Ulcer, skin) 707.8

gum 523.8

gumma, due to yaws 102.4

hand (*see also* Ulcer, skin) 707.8

hard palate 528.9

heel (*see also* Ulcer, lower extremity) 707.14
- decubitus (*see also* Ulcer, decubitus) 707.07

hemorrhoids 455.8
- external 455.5
- internal 455.2

hip (*see also* Ulcer, skin) 707.8
- decubitus (*see also* Ulcer, decubitus) 707.04

Hunner's 595.1

hypopharynx 478.29

hypopyon (chronic) (subacute) 370.04

hypostaticum — *see* Ulcer, varicose

ileocolitis 556.1

Ulcer, ulcerated, ulcerating, ulceration, ulcerative — *continued*

ileum (*see also* Ulcer, intestine) 569.82

intestine, intestinal 569.82
- with perforation 569.83
- amebic 006.9
- duodenal — *see* Ulcer, duodenum
- granulocytopenic (with hemorrhage) 288.09 ▲
- marginal 569.82
- perforating 569.83
- small, primary 569.82
- stercoraceous 569.82
- stercoral 569.82
- tuberculous (*see also* Tuberculosis) 014.8 ☑
- typhoid (fever) 002.0
- varicose 456.8

ischemic 707.9
- lower extremity (*see also* Ulcer, lower extremity) 707.10
  - ankle 707.13
  - calf 707.12
  - foot 707.15
  - heel 707.14
  - knee 707.19
  - specified site NEC 707.19
  - thigh 707.11
  - toes 707.15

jejunum, jejunal — *see* Ulcer, gastrojejunal

keratitis (*see also* Ulcer, cornea) 370.00

knee — *see* Ulcer, lower extremity

labium (majus) (minus) 616.50

laryngitis (*see also* Laryngitis) 464.00
- with obstruction 464.01

larynx (aphthous) (contact) 478.79
- diphtheritic 032.3

leg — *see* Ulcer, lower extremity

lip 528.5

Lipschütz's 616.50

lower extremity (atrophic) (chronic) (neurogenic) (perforating) (pyogenic) (trophic) (tropical) 707.10
- with gangrene (*see also* Ulcer, lower extremity) 707.10 *[785.4]*
  - arteriosclerotic 440.24
- ankle 707.13
- arteriosclerotic 440.23
  - with gangrene 440.24
- calf 707.12
- decubitus 707.00
  - with gangrene 707.00 *[785.4]*
  - ankle 707.06
  - buttock 707.05
  - heel 707.07
  - hip 707.04
- foot 707.15
- heel 707.14
- knee 707.19
- specified site NEC 707.19
- thigh 707.11
- toes 707.15
- varicose 454.0
  - inflamed or infected 454.2

luetic — *see* Ulcer, syphilitic

lung 518.89
- tuberculous (*see also* Tuberculosis) 011.2 ☑

malignant (M8000/3) — *see* Neoplasm, by site, malignant

marginal NEC — *see* Ulcer, gastrojejunal

meatus (urinarius) 597.89

Meckel's diverticulum 751.0

Meleney's (chronic undermining) 686.09

Mooren's (cornea) 370.07

mouth (traumatic) 528.9

mycobacterial (skin) 031.1

nasopharynx 478.29

navel cord (newborn) 771.4

neck (*see also* Ulcer, skin) 707.8
- uterus 622.0

Ulcer, ulcerated, ulcerating, ulceration, ulcerative — *continued*

neurogenic NEC — *see* Ulcer, skin

nose, nasal (infectional) (passage) 478.19 ▲
- septum 478.19 ▲
- varicose 456.8

skin — *see* Ulcer, skin

spirochetal NEC 104.8

oral mucosa (traumatic) 528.9

palate (soft) 528.9

penetrating NEC — *see* Ulcer, peptic, with perforation

penis (chronic) 607.89

peptic (site unspecified) 533.9 ☑

Note — *Use the following fifth-digit subclassification with categories 531–534:*

0   *without mention of obstruction*

1   *with obstruction*

with
- hemorrhage 533.4 ☑
  - and perforation 533.6 ☑
- perforation (chronic) 533.5 ☑
  - and hemorrhage 533.6 ☑
- acute 533.3 ☑
  - with
    - hemorrhage 533.0 ☑
      - and perforation 533.2 ☑
    - perforation 533.1 ☑
      - and hemorrhage 533.2 ☑
- bleeding (recurrent) — *see* Ulcer, peptic, with hemorrhage
- chronic 533.7 ☑
  - with
    - hemorrhage 533.4 ☑
      - and perforation 533.6 ☑
    - perforation 533.5 ☑
      - and hemorrhage 533.6 ☑
- penetrating — *see* Ulcer, peptic, with perforation
- perforating NEC (*see also* Ulcer, peptic, with perforation) 533.5 ☑

skin 707.9

perineum (*see also* Ulcer, skin) 707.8

peritonsillar 474.8

phagedenic (tropical) NEC — *see* Ulcer, skin

pharynx 478.29

phlebitis — *see* Phlebitis

plaster (*see also* Ulcer, decubitus) 707.00

popliteal space — *see* Ulcer, lower extremity

postpyloric — *see* Ulcer, duodenum

prepuce 607.89

prepyloric — *see* Ulcer, stomach

pressure (*see also* Ulcer, decubitus) 707.00

primary of intestine 569.82
- with perforation 569.83

proctitis 556.2
- with ulcerative sigmoiditis 556.3

prostate 601.8

pseudopeptic — *see* Ulcer, peptic

pyloric — *see* Ulcer, stomach

rectosigmoid 569.82
- with perforation 569.83

rectum (sphincter) (solitary) 569.41
- stercoraceous, stercoral 569.41
- varicose — *see* Varicose, ulcer, anus

retina (*see also* Chorioretinitis) 363.20

rodent (M8090/3) (*see also* Neoplasm, skin, malignant)
- cornea 370.07

round — *see* Ulcer, stomach

sacrum (region) (*see also* Ulcer, skin) 707.8

Saemisch's 370.04

scalp (*see also* Ulcer, skin) 707.8

sclera 379.09

scrofulous (*see also* Tuberculosis) 017.2 ☑

☑ Additional Digit Required — Refer to the Tabular List for Digit Selection   ▽ Subterms under main terms may continue to next column or page

292 — Volume 2 • October 2006   ►◄ Revised Text   ● New Line   ▲ Revised Code   **2007 ICD-9-CM**

Ulcer, ulcerated, ulcerating, ulceration, ulcerative — *continued*
- scrotum 608.89
  - tuberculous (*see also* Tuberculosis) 016.5 ☑
  - varicose 456.4
- seminal vesicle 608.89
- sigmoid 569.82
  - with perforation 569.83
- skin (atrophic) (chronic) (neurogenic) (non-healing) (perforating) (pyogenic) (trophic) 707.9
  - with gangrene 707.9 [785.4]
  - amebic 006.6
  - decubitus (*see also* Ulcer, decubitus) 707.00
    - with gangrene 707.00 [785.4]
  - in granulocytopenia 288.09 ▲
  - lower extremity (*see also* Ulcer, lower extremity) 707.10
    - with gangrene 707.10 [785.4]
      - arteriosclerotic 440.24
    - ankle 707.13
    - arteriosclerotic 440.23
      - with gangrene 440.24
    - calf 707.12
    - foot 707.15
    - heel 707.14
    - knee 707.19
    - specified site NEC 707.19
    - thigh 707.11
    - toes 707.15
  - mycobacterial 031.1
  - syphilitic (early) (secondary) 091.3
  - tuberculous (primary) (*see also* Tuberculosis) 017.0 ☑
  - varicose — *see* Ulcer, varicose
- sloughing NEC — *see* Ulcer, skin
- soft palate 528.9
- solitary, anus or rectum (sphincter) 569.41
- sore throat 462
  - streptococcal 034.0
- spermatic cord 608.89
- spine (tuberculous) 015.0 ☑ [730.88]
- stasis (leg) (venous) 454.0
  - with varicose veins 454.0
  - without varicose veins 459.81
  - inflamed or infected 454.2
- stercoral, stercoraceous 569.82
  - with perforation 569.83
  - anus or rectum 569.41
- stomach (eroded) (peptic) (round) 531.9 ☑

Note — Use the following fifth-digit subclassification with categories 531–534:

0	*without mention of obstruction*
1	*with obstruction*

  - with
    - hemorrhage 531.4 ☑
      - and perforation 531.6 ☑
    - perforation (chronic) 531.5 ☑
      - and hemorrhage 531.6 ☑
  - acute 531.3 ☑
    - with
      - hemorrhage 531.0 ☑
        - and perforation 531.2 ☑
      - perforation 531.1 ☑
        - and hemorrhage 531.2 ☑
  - bleeding (recurrent) — *see* Ulcer, stomach, with hemorrhage
  - chronic 531.7 ☑
    - with
      - hemorrhage 531.4 ☑
        - and perforation 531.6 ☑
      - perforation 531.5 ☑
        - and hemorrhage 531.6 ☑
  - penetrating — *see* Ulcer, stomach, with perforation
  - perforating — *see* Ulcer, stomach, with perforation
- stoma, stomal — *see* Ulcer, gastrojejunal

Ulcer, ulcerated, ulcerating, ulceration, ulcerative — *continued*
- stomatitis 528.00 ▲
- stress — *see* Ulcer, peptic
- strumous (tuberculous) (*see also* Tuberculosis) 017.2 ☑
- submental (*see also* Ulcer, skin) 707.8
- submucosal, bladder 595.1
- syphilitic (any site) (early) (secondary) 091.3
  - late 095.9
  - perforating 095.9
    - foot 094.0
- testis 608.89
- thigh — *see* Ulcer, lower extremity
- throat 478.29
  - diphtheritic 032.0
- toe — *see* Ulcer, lower extremity
- tongue (traumatic) 529.0
- tonsil 474.8
  - diphtheritic 032.0
- trachea 519.19 ▲
- trophic — *see* Ulcer, skin
- tropical NEC (*see also* Ulcer, skin) 707.9
- tuberculous — *see* Tuberculosis, ulcer
- tunica vaginalis 608.89
- turbinate 730.9 ☑
- typhoid (fever) 002.0
  - perforating 002.0
- umbilicus (newborn) 771.4
- unspecified site NEC — *see* Ulcer, skin
- urethra (meatus) (*see also* Urethritis) 597.89
- uterus 621.8
  - cervix 622.0
    - with mention of cervicitis 616.0
  - neck 622.0
    - with mention of cervicitis 616.0
- vagina 616.89 ▲
- valve, heart 421.0
- varicose (lower extremity, any part) 454.0
  - anus — *see* Varicose, ulcer, anus
  - broad ligament 456.5
  - esophagus (*see also* Varix, esophagus) 456.1
    - bleeding (*see also* Varix, esophagus, bleeding) 456.0
  - inflamed or infected 454.2
  - nasal septum 456.8
  - perineum 456.6
  - rectum — *see* Varicose, ulcer, anus
  - scrotum 456.4
  - specified site NEC 456.8
  - sublingual 456.3
  - vulva 456.6
- vas deferens 608.89
- vesical (*see also* Ulcer, bladder) 596.8
- vulva (acute) (infectional) 616.50
  - Behçet's syndrome 136.1 [616.51]
  - herpetic 054.12
  - tuberculous 016.7 ☑ [616.51]
- vulvobuccal, recurring 616.50
- x-ray — *see* Ulcer, by site
- yaws 102.4

Ulcus — *see also* Ulcer
- cutis tuberculosum (*see also* Tuberculosis) 017.0 ☑
- duodeni — *see* Ulcer, duodenum
- durum 091.9
  - extragenital 091.2
- gastrojejunale — *see* Ulcer, gastrojejunal
- hypostaticum — *see* Ulcer, varicose
- molle (cutis) (skin) 099.0
- serpens corneae (pneumococcal) 370.04
- ventriculi — *see* Ulcer, stomach

Ulegyria 742.4
Ulerythema
- acneiforma 701.8
- centrifugum 695.4
- ophryogenes 757.4

Ullrich-Feichtiger syndrome 759.89

Ullrich (-Bonnevie) (-Turner) syndrome 758.6
Ulnar — *see* condition
Ulorrhagia 523.8
Ulorrhea 523.8
Umbilicus, umbilical — *see also* condition
- cord necrosis, affecting fetus or newborn 762.6
Unacceptable ●
- existing dental restoration ●
  - contours 525.65 ●
  - morphology 525.65 ●
Unavailability of medical facilities (at) V63.9
- due to
  - investigation by social service agency V63.8
  - lack of services at home V63.1
  - remoteness from facility V63.0
  - waiting list V63.2
- home V63.1
- outpatient clinic V63.0
- specified reason NEC V63.8
Uncinaria americana infestation 126.1
Uncinariasis — *see also* Ancylostomiasis 126.9
Unconscious, unconsciousness 780.09
Underdevelopment — *see also* Undeveloped
- sexual 259.0
Underfill, endodontic 526.63 ●
Undernourishment 269.9
Undernutrition 269.9
Under observation — *see* Observation
Underweight 783.22
- for gestational age — *see* Light-for-dates
Underwood's disease (sclerema neonatorum) 778.1
Undescended — *see also* Malposition, congenital
- cecum 751.4
- colon 751.4
- testis 752.51
Undetermined diagnosis or cause 799.9
Undeveloped, undevelopment — *see also* Hypoplasia
- brain (congenital) 742.1
- cerebral (congenital) 742.1
- fetus or newborn 764.9 ☑
- heart 746.89
- lung 748.5
- testis 259.0
- uterus 259.0
Undiagnosed (disease) 799.9
Undulant fever — *see also* Brucellosis 023.9
Unemployment, anxiety concerning V62.0
Unequal leg (acquired) (length) 736.81
- congenital 755.30
Unerupted teeth, tooth 520.6
Unextracted dental root 525.3
Unguis incarnatus 703.0
Unicornis uterus 752.3
Unicorporeus uterus 752.3
Uniformis uterus 752.3
Unilateral — *see also* condition
- development, breast 611.8
- organ or site, congenital NEC — *see* Agenesis
- vagina 752.49
Unilateralis uterus 752.3
Unilocular heart 745.8
Uninhibited bladder 596.54
- with cauda equina syndrome 344.61
- neurogenic — *see also* Neurogenic, bladder 596.54
Union, abnormal — *see also* Fusion
- divided tendon 727.89
- larynx and trachea 748.3
Universal
- joint, cervix 620.6
- mesentery 751.4

Unknown
- cause of death 799.9
- diagnosis 799.9
Unna's disease (seborrheic dermatitis) 690.10
Unresponsiveness, adrenocorticotropin (ACTH) 255.4
Unsatisfactory ●
- restoration, tooth (existing) 525.60 ●
  - specified NEC 525.69 ●
- smear 795.08 ●
Unsoundness of mind — *see also* Psychosis 298.9
Unspecified cause of death 799.9
Unstable
- back NEC 724.9
- colon 569.89
- joint — *see* Instability, joint
- lie 652.0 ☑
  - affecting fetus or newborn (before labor) 761.7
  - causing obstructed labor 660.0 ☑
    - affecting fetus or newborn 763.1
- lumbosacral joint (congenital) 756.19
  - acquired 724.6
- sacroiliac 724.6
- spine NEC 724.9
Untruthfulness, child problem — *see also* Disturbance, conduct 312.0 ☑
Unverricht (-Lundborg) disease, syndrome, or epilepsy 333.2
Unverricht-Wagner syndrome (dermatomyositis) 710.3
Upper respiratory — *see* condition
Upset
- gastric 536.8
  - psychogenic 306.4
- gastrointestinal 536.8
  - psychogenic 306.4
  - virus (*see also* Enteritis, viral) 008.8
- intestinal (large) (small) 564.9
  - psychogenic 306.4
- menstruation 626.9
- mental 300.9
- stomach 536.8
  - psychogenic 306.4
Urachus — *see also* condition
- patent 753.7
- persistent 753.7
Uratic arthritis 274.0
Urbach's lipoid proteinosis 272.8
Urbach-Oppenheim disease or syndrome (necrobiosis lipoidica diabeticorum) 250.8 ☑ [709.3]
Urbach-Wiethe disease or syndrome (lipoid proteinosis) 272.8
Urban yellow fever 060.1
Urea, blood, high — *see* Uremia
Uremia, uremic (absorption) (amaurosis) (amblyopia) (aphasia) (apoplexy) (coma) (delirium) (dementia) (dropsy) (dyspnea) (fever) (intoxication) (mania) (paralysis) (poisoning) (toxemia) (vomiting) 586
- with
  - abortion — *see* Abortion, by type, with renal failure
  - ectopic pregnancy (*see also* categories 633.0–633.9) 639.3
  - hypertension (*see also* Hypertension, kidney) 403.91
  - molar pregnancy (*see also* categories 630–632) 639.3
- chronic 585.9
- complicating
  - abortion 639.3
  - ectopic or molar pregnancy 639.3
  - hypertension (*see also* Hypertension, kidney) 403.91
  - labor and delivery 669.3 ☑
- congenital 779.89
- extrarenal 788.9
- hypertensive (chronic) (*see also* Hypertension, kidney) 403.91

Uremia, uremic — *continued*
  maternal NEC, affecting fetus or new-born 760.1
  neuropathy 585.9 *[357.4]*
  pericarditis 585.9 *[420.0]*
  prerenal 788.9
  pyelitic (*see also* Pyelitis) 590.80
Ureteralgia 788.0
Ureterectasis 593.89
Ureteritis 593.89
  cystica 590.3
  due to calculus 592.1
  gonococcal (acute) 098.19
    chronic or duration of 2 months or over 098.39
  nonspecific 593.89
Ureterocele (acquired) 593.89
  congenital 753.23
Ureterolith 592.1
Ureterolithiasis 592.1
Ureterostomy status V44.6
  with complication 997.5
Ureter, ureteral — *see condition*
Urethralgia 788.9
Urethra, urethral — *see condition*
Urethritis (abacterial) (acute) (allergic) (anterior) (chronic) (nonvenereal) (posterior) (recurrent) (simple) (subacute) (ulcerative) (undifferentiated) 597.80
  diplococcal (acute) 098.0
    chronic or duration of 2 months or over 098.2
  due to Trichomonas (vaginalis) 131.02
  gonococcal (acute) 098.0
    chronic or duration of 2 months or over 098.2
  nongonococcal (sexually transmitted) 099.40
    Chlamydia trachomatis 099.41
    Reiter's 099.3
    specified organism NEC 099.49
  nonspecific (sexually transmitted) (*see also* Urethritis, nongonococcal) 099.40
  not sexually transmitted 597.80
  Reiter's 099.3
  trichomonal or due to Trichomonas (vaginalis) 131.02
  tuberculous (*see also* Tuberculosis) 016.3 ☑
  venereal NEC (*see also* Urethritis, nongonococcal) 099.40
Urethrocele
  female 618.03
    with uterine prolapse 618.4
      complete 618.3
      incomplete 618.2
  male 599.5
Urethrolithiasis 594.2

Urethro-oculoarticular syndrome 099.3
Urethro-oculosynovial syndrome 099.3
Urethrorectal — *see condition*
Urethrorrhagia 599.84
Urethrorrhea 788.7
Urethrostomy status V44.6
  with complication 997.5
Urethrotrigonitis 595.3
Urethrovaginal — *see condition*
Urhidrosis, uridrosis 705.89
Uric acid
  diathesis 274.9
  in blood 790.6
Uricacidemia 790.6
Uricemia 790.6
Uricosuria 791.9
Urination
  frequent 788.41
  painful 788.1
  urgency 788.63
Urinemia — *see* Uremia
Urine, urinary — *see also* condition
  abnormality NEC 788.69
  blood in (*see also* Hematuria) 599.7
  discharge, excessive 788.42
  enuresis 788.30
    nonorganic origin 307.6
  extravasation 788.8
  frequency 788.41
  hesitancy 788.64   ●
  incontinence 788.30
    active 788.30
    female 788.30
      stress 625.6
        and urge 788.33
    male 788.30
      stress 788.32
        and urge 788.33
    mixed (stress and urge) 788.33
    neurogenic 788.39
    nonorganic origin 307.6
    overflow 788.38
    stress (female) 625.6
      male NEC 788.32
  intermittent stream 788.61
  pus in 791.9
  retention or stasis NEC 788.20
    bladder, incomplete emptying 788.21
    psychogenic 306.53
    specified NEC 788.29
  secretion
    deficient 788.5
    excessive 788.42
    frequency 788.41
  strain 788.65   ●
  stream
    intermittent 788.61
    slowing 788.62
    splitting 788.61

Urine, urinary — *see also* condition — *continued*
  stream — *continued*
    weak 788.62
  urgency 788.63
Urinoma NEC 599.9
  bladder 596.8
  kidney 593.89
  renal 593.89
  ureter 593.89
  urethra 599.84
Uroarthritis, infectious 099.3
Urodialysis 788.5
Urolithiasis 592.9
Uronephrosis 593.89
Uropathy 599.9
  obstructive 599.60
Urosepsis 599.0
  meaning sepsis 995.91
  meaning urinary tract infection 599.0
Urticaria 708.9
  with angioneurotic edema 995.1
    hereditary 277.6
  allergic 708.0
  cholinergic 708.5
  chronic 708.8
  cold, familial 708.2
  dermatographic 708.3
  due to
    cold or heat 708.2
    drugs 708.0
    food 708.0
    inhalants 708.0
    plants 708.8
    serum 999.5
  factitial 708.3
  giant 995.1
    hereditary 277.6
  gigantea 995.1
    hereditary 277.6
  idiopathic 708.1
  larynx 995.1
    hereditary 277.6
  neonatorum 778.8
  nonallergic 708.1
  papulosa (Hebra) 698.2
  perstans hemorrhagica 757.39
  pigmentosa 757.33
  recurrent periodic 708.8
  serum 999.5
  solare 692.72
  specified type NEC 708.8
  thermal (cold) (heat) 708.2
  vibratory 708.4
Urticarioides acarodermatitis 133.9
Use of   ●
  nonprescribed drugs (*see also* Abuse, drugs, nondependent) 305.9 ☑
  patent medicines (*see also* Abuse, drugs, nondependent) 305.9 ☑

Usher-Senear disease (pemphigus erythematosus) 694.4
Uta 085.5
Uterine size-date discrepancy 649.6 ☑   ▲
Uteromegaly 621.2
Uterovaginal — *see condition*
Uterovesical — *see condition*
Uterus — *see condition*
Utriculitis (utriculus prostaticus) 597.89
Uveal — *see condition*
Uveitis (anterior) — *see also* Iridocyclitis 364.3
  acute or subacute 364.00
    due to or associated with
      gonococcal infection 098.41
      herpes (simplex) 054.44
        zoster 053.22
    primary 364.01
    recurrent 364.02
    secondary (noninfectious) 364.04
      infectious 364.03
  allergic 360.11
  chronic 364.10
    due to or associated with
      sarcoidosis 135 *[364.11]*
      tuberculosis (*see also* Tuberculosis) 017.3 ☑ *[364.11]*
  due to
    operation 360.11
    toxoplasmosis (acquired) 130.2
      congenital (active) 771.2
  granulomatous 364.10
  heterochromic 364.21
  lens-induced 364.23
  nongranulomatous 364.00
  posterior 363.20
    disseminated — *see* Chorioretinitis, disseminated
    focal — *see* Chorioretinitis, focal
  recurrent 364.02
  sympathetic 360.11
  syphilitic (secondary) 091.50
    congenital 090.0 *[363.13]*
    late 095.8 *[363.13]*
  tuberculous (*see also* Tuberculosis) 017.3 ☑ *[364.11]*
Uveoencephalitis 363.22
Uveokeratitis — *see also* Iridocyclitis 364.3
Uveoparotid fever 135
Uveoparotitis 135
Uvula — *see condition*
Uvulitis (acute) (catarrhal) (chronic) (gangrenous) (membranous) (suppurative) (ulcerative) 528.3

☑ Additional Digit Required — Refer to the Tabular List for Digit Selection   ▽ Subterms under main terms may continue to next column or page

294 — Volume 2 • October 2006   ▶◀ Revised Text   ● New Line   ▲ Revised Code   *2007 ICD-9-CM*

V

Vaccination
complication or reaction — *see* Complications, vaccination
not carried out V64.00
because of
acute illness V64.01
allergy to vaccine or component V64.04
caregiver refusal V64.05
chronic illness V64.02
immune compromised state V64.03
patient had disease being vaccinated against V64.08
patient refusal V64.06
reason NEC V64.09
religious reasons V64.07
prophylactic (against) V05.9
arthropod-borne viral
disease NEC V05.1
encephalitis V05.0
chickenpox V05.4
cholera (alone) V03.0
with typhoid-paratyphoid (cholera + TAB) V06.0
common cold V04.7
diphtheria (alone) V03.5
with
poliomyelitis (DTP+ polio) V06.3
tetanus V06.5
pertussis combined (DTP) (DTaP) V06.1
typhoid-paratyphoid (DTP + TAB) V06.2
disease (single) NEC V05.9
bacterial NEC V03.9
specified type NEC V03.89
combination NEC V06.9
specified type NEC V06.8
specified type NEC V05.8
encephalitis, viral, arthropod-borne V05.0
Hemophilus influenzae, type B [Hib] V03.81
hepatitis, viral V05.3
influenza V04.81
with
Streptococcus pneumoniae [pneumococcus] V06.6
leishmaniasis V05.2
measles (alone) V04.2
with mumps-rubella (MMR) V06.4
mumps (alone) V04.6
with measles and rubella (MMR) V06.4
pertussis alone V03.6
plague V03.3
poliomyelitis V04.0
with diphtheria-tetanus-pertussis (DTP + polio) V06.3
rabies V04.5
respiratory syncytial virus (RSV) V04.82
rubella (alone) V04.3
with measles and mumps (MMR) V06.4
smallpox V04.1
Streptococcus pneumoniae [pneumococcus] V03.82
with
influenza V06.6
tetanus toxoid (alone) V03.7
with diphtheria [Td] [DT] V06.5
with
pertussis (DTP) (DTaP) V06.1
with poliomyelitis (DTP+polio) V06.3
tuberculosis (BCG) V03.2
tularemia V03.4
typhoid-paratyphoid (TAB) (alone) V03.1

Vaccination — *continued*
prophylactic — *continued*
typhoid-paratyphoid — *continued*
with diphtheria-tetanus-pertussis (TAB + DTP) V06.2
varicella V05.4
viral
disease NEC V04.89
encephalitis, arthropod-borne V05.0
hepatitis V05.3
yellow fever V04.4
Vaccinia (generalized) 999.0
without vaccination 051.0
congenital 771.2
conjunctiva 999.3
eyelids 999.0 *[373.5]*
localized 999.3
nose 999.3
not from vaccination 051.0
eyelid 051.0 *[373.5]*
sine vaccinatione 051.0
Vacuum
extraction of fetus or newborn 763.3
in sinus (accessory) (nasal) (*see also* Sinusitis) 473.9
Vagabond V60.0
Vagabondage V60.0
Vagabonds' disease 132.1
Vaginalitis (tunica) 608.4
Vagina, vaginal — *see* condition
Vaginismus (reflex) 625.1
functional 306.51
hysterical 300.11
psychogenic 306.51
Vaginitis (acute) (chronic) (circumscribed) (diffuse) (emphysematous) (Hemophilus vaginalis) (nonspecific) (nonvenereal) (ulcerative) 616.10
with
abortion — *see* Abortion, by type, with sepsis
ectopic pregnancy (*see also* categories 633.0–633.9) 639.0
molar pregnancy (*see also* categories 630–632) 639.0
adhesive, congenital 752.49
atrophic, postmenopausal 627.3
bacterial 616.10
blennorrhagic (acute) 098.0
chronic or duration of 2 months or over 098.2
candidal 112.1
chlamydial 099.53
complicating pregnancy or puerperium 646.6 ☑
affecting fetus or newborn 760.8
congenital (adhesive) 752.49
due to
C. albicans 112.1
Trichomonas (vaginalis) 131.01
following
abortion 639.0
ectopic or molar pregnancy 639.0
gonococcal (acute) 098.0
chronic or duration of 2 months or over 098.2
granuloma 099.2
Monilia 112.1
mycotic 112.1
pinworm 127.4 *[616.11]*
postirradiation 616.10
postmenopausal atrophic 627.3
senile (atrophic) 627.3
syphilitic (early) 091.0
late 095.8
trichomonal 131.01
tuberculous (*see also* Tuberculosis) 016.7 ☑
venereal NEC 099.8
Vaginosis — *see* Vaginitis
Vagotonia 352.3
Vagrancy V60.0
Vallecula — *see* condition
Valley fever 114.0

Valsuani's disease (progressive pernicious anemia, puerperal) 648.2 ☑
Valve, valvular (formation) — *see also* condition
cerebral ventricle (communicating) in situ V45.2
cervix, internal os 752.49
colon 751.5
congenital NEC — *see* Atresia
formation, congenital NEC — *see* Atresia
heart defect — *see* Anomaly, heart, valve
ureter 753.29
pelvic junction 753.21
vesical orifice 753.22
urethra 753.6
Valvulitis (chronic) — *see also* Endocarditis 424.90
rheumatic (chronic) (inactive) (with chorea) 397.9
active or acute (aortic) (mitral) (pulmonary) (tricuspid) 391.1
syphilitic NEC 093.20
aortic 093.22
mitral 093.21
pulmonary 093.24
tricuspid 093.23
Valvulopathy — *see* Endocarditis
van Bogaert-Nijssen (-Peiffer) disease 330.0
van Bogaert's leukoencephalitis (sclerosing) (subacute) 046.2
van Buchem's syndrome (hyperostosis corticalis) 733.3
Vancomycin (glycopeptide)
intermediate staphylococcus aureus (VISA/GISA) V09.8 ☑
resistant
enterococcus (VRE) V09.8 ☑
staphylococcus aureus (VRSA/GRSA) V09.8 ☑
van Creveld-von Gierke disease (glycogenosis I) 271.0
van den Bergh's disease (enterogenous cyanosis) 289.7
van der Hoeve-Halbertsma-Waardenburg syndrome (ptosis-epicanthus) 270.2
van der Hoeve-Waardenburg-Gualdi syndrome (ptosis epicanthus) 270.2
van der Hoeve's syndrome (brittle bones and blue sclera, deafness) 756.51
Vanillism 692.89
Vanishing lung 492.0
Vanishing twin 651.33
van Neck (-Odelberg) disease or syndrome (juvenile osteochondrosis) 732.1
Vapor asphyxia or suffocation NEC 987.9
specified agent — *see* Table of Drugs and Chemicals
Vaquez's disease (M9950/1) 238.4
Vaquez-Osler disease (polycythemia vera) (M9950/1) 238.4
Variance, lethal ball, prosthetic heart valve 996.02
Variants, thalassemic 282.49
Variations in hair color 704.3
Varicella 052.9
with
complication 052.8
specified NEC 052.7
pneumonia 052.1
vaccination and inoculation (prophylactic) V05.4
exposure to V01.71
vaccination and inoculation (against) (prophylactic) V05.4
Varices — *see* Varix
Varicocele (scrotum) (thrombosed) 456.4
ovary 456.5
perineum 456.6
spermatic cord (ulcerated) 456.4

Varicose
aneurysm (ruptured) (*see also* Aneurysm) 442.9
dermatitis (lower extremity) — *see* Varicose, vein, inflamed or infected
eczema — *see* Varicose, vein
phlebitis — *see* Varicose, vein, inflamed or infected
placental vessel — *see* Placenta, abnormal
tumor — *see* Varicose, vein
ulcer (lower extremity, any part) 454.0
anus 455.8
external 455.5
internal 455.2
esophagus (*see also* Varix, esophagus) 456.1
bleeding (*see also* Varix, esophagus, bleeding) 456.0
inflamed or infected 454.2
nasal septum 456.8
perineum 456.6
rectum — *see* Varicose, ulcer, anus
scrotum 456.4
specified site NEC 456.8
vein (lower extremity) (ruptured) (*see also* Varix) 454.9
with
complications NEC 454.8
edema 454.8
inflammation or infection 454.1
ulcerated 454.2
pain 454.8
stasis dermatitis 454.1
with ulcer 454.2
swelling 454.8
ulcer 454.0
inflamed or infected 454.2
anus — *see* Hemorrhoids
broad ligament 456.5
congenital (peripheral) 747.60
gastrointestinal 747.61
lower limb 747.64
renal 747.62
specified NEC 747.69
upper limb 747.63
esophagus (ulcerated) (*see also* Varix, esophagus) 456.1
bleeding (*see also* Varix, esophagus, bleeding) 456.0
inflamed or infected 454.1
with ulcer 454.2
in pregnancy or puerperium 671.0 ☑
vulva or perineum 671.1 ☑
nasal septum (with ulcer) 456.8
pelvis 456.5
perineum 456.6
in pregnancy, childbirth, or puerperium 671.1 ☑
rectum — *see* Hemorrhoids
scrotum (ulcerated) 456.4
specified site NEC 456.8
sublingual 456.3
ulcerated 454.0
inflamed or infected 454.2
umbilical cord, affecting fetus or newborn 762.6
urethra 456.8
vulva 456.6
in pregnancy, childbirth, or puerperium 671.1 ☑
vessel (*see also* Varix)
placenta — *see* Placenta, abnormal
Varicosis, varicosities, varicosity — *see also* Varix 454.9
Variola 050.9
hemorrhagic (pustular) 050.0
major 050.0
minor 050.1
modified 050.2
Varioloid 050.2
Variolosa, purpura 050.0
Varix (lower extremity) (ruptured) 454.9

☑ Additional Digit Required — Refer to the Tabular List for Digit Selection
Subterms under main terms may continue to next column or page
2007 ICD-9-CM
▶◀ Revised Text ● New Line ▲ Revised Code
Volume 2 — 295

Varix — *continued*
with
complications NEC 454.8
edema 454.8
inflammation or infection 454.1
with ulcer 454.2
pain 454.8
stasis dermatitis 454.1
with ulcer 454.2
swelling 454.8
ulcer 454.0
with inflammation or infection 454.2
aneurysmal (*see also* Aneurysm) 442.9
anus — *see* Hemorrhoids
arteriovenous (congenital) (peripheral) NEC 747.60
gastrointestinal 747.61
lower limb 747.64
renal 747.62
specified NEC 747.69
spinal 747.82
upper limb 747.63
bladder 456.5
broad ligament 456.5
congenital (peripheral) 747.60
esophagus (ulcerated) 456.1
bleeding 456.0
in
cirrhosis of liver 571.5 *[456.20]*
portal hypertension 572.3 *[456.20]*
congenital 747.69
in
cirrhosis of liver 571.5 *[456.21]*
with bleeding 571.5 *[456.20]*
portal hypertension 572.3 *[456.21]*
with bleeding 572.3 *[456.20]*
gastric 456.8
inflamed or infected 454.1
ulcerated 454.2
in pregnancy or puerperium 671.0 ☑
perineum 671.1 ☑
vulva 671.1 ☑
labia (majora) 456.6
orbit 456.8
congenital 747.69
ovary 456.5
papillary 448.1
pelvis 456.5
perineum 456.6
in pregnancy or puerperium 671.1 ☑
pharynx 456.8
placenta — *see* Placenta, abnormal
prostate 456.8
rectum — *see* Hemorrhoids
renal papilla 456.8
retina 362.17
scrotum (ulcerated) 456.4
sigmoid colon 456.8
specified site NEC 456.8
spinal (cord) (vessels) 456.8
spleen, splenic (vein) (with phlebolith) 456.8
sublingual 456.3
ulcerated 454.0
inflamed or infected 454.2
umbilical cord, affecting fetus or newborn 762.6
uterine ligament 456.5
vocal cord 456.8
vulva 456.6
in pregnancy, childbirth, or puerperium 671.1 ☑
Vasa previa 663.5 ☑
affecting fetus or newborn 762.6
hemorrhage from, affecting fetus or newborn 772.0
Vascular — *see also* condition
loop on papilla (optic) 743.57

Vascular — *see also* condition — *continued*
sheathing, retina 362.13
spasm 443.9
spider 448.1
Vascularity, pulmonary, congenital 747.3
Vascularization
choroid 362.16
cornea 370.60
deep 370.63
localized 370.61
retina 362.16
subretinal 362.16
Vasculitis 447.6
allergic 287.0
cryoglobulinemic 273.2
disseminated 447.6
kidney 447.8
leukocytoclastic 446.29
nodular 695.2
retinal 362.18
rheumatic — *see* Fever, rheumatic
Vasculopathy
cardiac allograft 996.83
Vas deferens — *see* condition
Vas deferentitis 608.4
Vasectomy, admission for V25.2
Vasitis 608.4
nodosa 608.4
scrotum 608.4
spermatic cord 608.4
testis 608.4
tuberculous (*see also* Tuberculosis) 016.5 ☑
tunica vaginalis 608.4
vas deferens 608.4
Vasodilation 443.9
Vasomotor — *see* condition
Vasoplasty, after previous sterilization V26.0
Vasoplegia, splanchnic — *see also* Neuropathy, peripheral, autonomic 337.9
Vasospasm 443.9
cerebral (artery) 435.9
with transient neurologic deficit 435.9
coronary 413.1 ●
nerve
arm NEC 354.9
autonomic 337.9
brachial plexus 353.0
cervical plexus 353.2
leg NEC 355.8
lower extremity NEC 355.8
peripheral NEC 355.9
spinal NEC 355.9
sympathetic 337.9
upper extremity NEC 354.9
peripheral NEC 443.9
retina (artery) (*see also* Occlusion, retinal, artery) 362.30
Vasospastic — *see* condition
Vasovagal attack (paroxysmal) 780.2
psychogenic 306.2
Vater's ampulla — *see* condition
VATER syndrome 759.89
Vegetation, vegetative
adenoid (nasal fossa) 474.2
consciousness (persistent) 780.03
endocarditis (acute) (any valve) (chronic) (subacute) 421.0
heart (mycotic) (valve) 421.0
state (persistent) 780.03
Veil
Jackson's 751.4
over face (causing asphyxia) 768.9
Vein, venous — *see* condition
Veldt sore — *see also* Ulcer, skin 707.9
Velo-cardio-facial syndrome 758.32
Velpeau's hernia — *see* Hernia, femoral
Venereal
balanitis NEC 099.8
bubo 099.1
disease 099.9

Venereal — *continued*
disease — *continued*
specified nature or type NEC 099.8
granuloma inguinale 099.2
lymphogranuloma (Durand-Nicolas-Favre), any site 099.1
salpingitis 098.37
urethritis (*see also* Urethritis, non-gonococcal) 099.40
vaginitis NEC 099.8
warts 078.19
Vengefulness, in child — *see also* Disturbance, conduct 312.0 ☑
Venofibrosis 459.89
Venom, venomous
bite or sting (animal or insect) 989.5
poisoning 989.5
Venous — *see* condition
Ventouse delivery NEC 669.5 ☑
affecting fetus or newborn 763.3
Ventral — *see* condition
Ventricle, ventricular — *see also* condition
escape 427.69
standstill (*see also* Arrest, cardiac) 427.5
Ventriculitis, cerebral — *see also* Meningitis 322.9
Ventriculostomy status V45.2
Verbiest's syndrome (claudicatio intermittens spinalis) 435.1
Vernet's syndrome 352.6
Verneuil's disease (syphilitic bursitis) 095.7
Verruca (filiformis) 078.10
acuminata (any site) 078.11
necrogenica (primary) (*see also* Tuberculosis) 017.0 ☑
peruana 088.0
peruviana 088.0
plana (juvenilis) 078.19
plantaris 078.19
seborrheica 702.19
inflamed 702.11
senilis 702.0
tuberculosa (primary) (*see also* Tuberculosis) 017.0 ☑
venereal 078.19
viral NEC 078.10
Verrucosities — *see also* Verruca 078.10
Verrucous endocarditis (acute) (any valve) (chronic) (subacute) 710.0 *[424.91]*
nonbacterial 710.0 *[424.91]*
Verruga
peruana 088.0
peruviana 088.0
Verse's disease (calcinosis intervertebralis) 275.49 *[722.90]*
Version
before labor, affecting fetus or newborn 761.7
cephalic (correcting previous malposition) 652.1 ☑
affecting fetus or newborn 763.1
cervix ▶ — *see* Version, ◀ uterus
uterus (postinfectional) (postpartal, old) (*see also* Malposition, uterus) 621.6
forward — *see* Anteversion, uterus
lateral — *see* Lateroversion, uterus
Vertebra, vertebral — *see* condition
Vertigo 780.4
auditory 386.19
aural 386.19
benign paroxysmal positional 386.11
central origin 386.2
cerebral 386.2
Dix and Hallpike (epidemic) 386.12
endemic paralytic 078.81
epidemic 078.81
Dix and Hallpike 386.12
Gerlier's 078.81
Pedersen's 386.12
vestibular neuronitis 386.12
epileptic — *see* Epilepsy

Vertigo — *continued*
Gerlier's (epidemic) 078.81
hysterical 300.11
labyrinthine 386.10
laryngeal 786.2
malignant positional 386.2
Ménière's (*see also* Disease, Ménière's) 386.00
menopausal 627.2
otogenic 386.19
paralytic 078.81
paroxysmal positional, benign 386.11
Pedersen's (epidemic) 386.12
peripheral 386.10
specified type NEC 386.19
positional
benign paroxysmal 386.11
malignant 386.2
Verumontanitis (chronic) — *see also* Urethritis 597.89
Vesania — *see also* Psychosis 298.9
Vesical — *see* condition
Vesicle
cutaneous 709.8
seminal — *see* condition
skin 709.8
Vesicocolic — *see* condition
Vesicoperineal — *see* condition
Vesicorectal — *see* condition
Vesicourethrorectal — *see* condition
Vesicovaginal — *see* condition
Vesicular — *see* condition
Vesiculitis (seminal) 608.0
amebic 006.8
gonorrheal (acute) 098.14
chronic or duration of 2 months or over 098.34
trichomonal 131.09
tuberculous (*see also* Tuberculosis) 016.5 ☑ *[608.81]*
Vestibulitis (ear) — *see also* Labyrinthitis 386.30
nose (external) 478.19 ▲
vulvar 616.10
Vestibulopathy, acute peripheral (recurrent) 386.12
Vestige, vestigial — *see also* Persistence
branchial 744.41
structures in vitreous 743.51
Vibriosis NEC 027.9
Vidal's disease (lichen simplex chronicus) 698.3
Video display tube syndrome 723.8
Vienna-type encephalitis 049.8
Villaret's syndrome 352.6
Villous — *see* condition
VIN I (vulvar intraepithelial neoplasia I) 624.0 ▲
VIN II (vulvar intraepithelial neoplasia II) 624.0 ▲
VIN III (vulvar intraepithelial neoplasia III) 233.3
Vincent's
angina 101
bronchitis 101
disease 101
gingivitis 101
infection (any site) 101
laryngitis 101
stomatitis 101
tonsillitis 101
Vinson-Plummer syndrome (sideropenic dysphagia) 280.8
Viosterol deficiency — *see also* Deficiency, calciferol 268.9
Virchow's disease 733.99
Viremia 790.8
Virilism (adrenal) (female) NEC 255.2
with
3-beta-hydroxysteroid dehydrogenase defect 255.2
11-hydroxylase defect 255.2
21-hydroxylase defect 255.2
adrenal
hyperplasia 255.2
insufficiency (congenital) 255.2

Virilism — *continued*
with — *continued*
cortical hyperfunction 255.2
Virilization (female) (suprarenal) — *see also* Virilism 255.2
isosexual 256.4
Virulent bubo 099.0
Virus, viral — *see also* condition
infection NEC (*see also* Infection, viral) 079.99
septicemia 079.99
VISA (vancomycin intermediate staphylococcus aureus) V09.8 ☑
Viscera, visceral — *see* condition
Visceroptosis 569.89
Visible peristalsis 787.4
Vision, visual
binocular, suppression 368.31
blurred, blurring 368.8
hysterical 300.11
defect, defective (*see also* Impaired, vision) 369.9
disorientation (syndrome) 368.16
disturbance NEC (*see also* Disturbance, vision) 368.9
hysterical 300.11
examination V72.0
field, limitation 368.40
fusion, with defective steropsis 368.33
hallucinations 368.16
halos 368.16
loss 369.9
both eyes (*see also* Blindness, both eyes) 369.3
complete (*see also* Blindness, both eyes) 369.00
one eye 369.8
sudden 368.16
low (both eyes) 369.20
one eye (other eye normal) (*see also* Impaired, vision) 369.70
blindness, other eye 369.10
perception, simultaneous without fusion 368.32
tunnel 368.45
Vitality, lack or want of 780.79
newborn 779.89
Vitamin deficiency NEC — *see also* Deficiency, vitamin 269.2
Vitelline duct, persistent 751.0
Vitiligo 709.01
due to pinta (carate) 103.2
eyelid 374.53
vulva 624.8
Vitium cordis — *see* Disease, heart
Vitreous — *see also* condition
touch syndrome 997.99
VLCAD (long chain/very long chain acyl CoA dehydrogenase deficiency, LCAD) 277.85
Vocal cord — *see* condition
Vocational rehabilitation V57.22
Vogt's (Cecile) disease or syndrome 333.7 ☑
Vogt-Koyanagi syndrome 364.24
Vogt-Spielmeyer disease (amaurotic familial idiocy) 330.1
Voice
change (*see also* Dysphonia) 784.49
loss (*see also* Aphonia) 784.41
Volhard-Fahr disease (malignant nephrosclerosis) 403.00
Volhynian fever 083.1
Volkmann's ischemic contracture or paralysis (complicating trauma) 958.6
Voluntary starvation 307.1
Volvulus (bowel) (colon) (intestine) 560.2
with
hernia (*see also* Hernia, by site, with obstruction)
gangrenous — *see* Hernia, by site, with gangrene
perforation 560.2
congenital 751.5
duodenum 537.3

Volvulus — *continued*
fallopian tube 620.5
oviduct 620.5
stomach (due to absence of gastrocolic ligament) 537.89
Vomiting 787.03
with nausea 787.01
allergic 535.4 ☑
asphyxia 933.1
bilious (cause unknown) 787.0 ☑
following gastrointestinal surgery 564.3
blood (*see also* Hematemesis) 578.0
causing asphyxia, choking, or suffocation (*see also* Asphyxia, food) 933.1
cyclical 536.2
psychogenic 306.4
epidemic 078.82
fecal matter 569.89
following gastrointestinal surgery 564.3
functional 536.8
psychogenic 306.4
habit 536.2
hysterical 300.11
nervous 306.4
neurotic 306.4
newborn 779.3
of or complicating pregnancy 643.9 ☑
due to
organic disease 643.8 ☑
specific cause NEC 643.8 ☑
early — *see* Hyperemesis, gravidarum
late (after 22 completed weeks of gestation) 643.2 ☑
pernicious or persistent 536.2
complicating pregnancy — *see* Hyperemesis, gravidarum
psychogenic 306.4
physiological 787.0 ☑
psychic 306.4
psychogenic 307.54
stercoral 569.89
uncontrollable 536.2
psychogenic 306.4
uremic — *see* Uremia
winter 078.82
von Bechterew (-Strumpell) disease or syndrome (ankylosing spondylitis) 720.0
von Bezold's abscess 383.01
von Economo's disease (encephalitis lethargica) 049.8
von Eulenburg's disease (congenital paramyotonia) 359.2
von Gierke's disease (glycogenosis I) 271.0
von Gies' joint 095.8
von Graefe's disease or syndrome 378.72
von Hippel (-Lindau) disease or syndrome (retinocerebral angiomatosis) 759.6
von Jaksch's anemia or disease (pseudoleukemia infantum) 285.8
von Recklinghausen-Applebaum disease (hemochromatosis) 275.0
von Recklinghausen's
disease or syndrome (nerves) (skin) (M9540/1) 237.71
bones (osteitis fibrosa cystica) 252.01
tumor (M9540/1) 237.71
von Schroetter's syndrome (intermittent venous claudication) 453.8
von Willebrand (-Jürgens) (-Minot) disease or syndrome (angiohemophilia) 286.4
von Zambusch's disease (lichen sclerosus et atrophicus) 701.0
Voorhoeve's disease or dyschondroplasia 756.4
Vossius' ring 921.3
late effect 366.21

Voyeurism 302.82
VRE (vancomycin resistant enterococcus) V09.8 ☑
Vrolik's disease (osteogenesis imperfecta) 756.51
VRSA (vancomycin resistant staphylococcus aureus) V09.8 ☑
Vulva — *see* condition
Vulvismus 625.1
Vulvitis (acute) (allergic) (aphthous) (chronic) (gangrenous) (hypertrophic) (intertriginous) 616.10
with
abortion — *see* Abortion, by type, with sepsis
ectopic pregnancy (*see also* categories 633.0–633.9) 639.0
molar pregnancy (*see also* categories 630–632) 639.0
adhesive, congenital 752.49
blennorrhagic (acute) 098.0
chronic or duration of 2 months or over 098.2
chlamydial 099.53
complicating pregnancy or puerperium 646.6 ☑
due to Ducrey's bacillus 099.0
following
abortion 639.0
ectopic or molar pregnancy 639.0
gonococcal (acute) 098.0
chronic or duration of 2 months or over 098.2
herpetic 054.11
leukoplakic 624.0
monilial 112.1
puerperal, postpartum, childbirth 646.6 ☑
syphilitic (early) 091.0
late 095.8
trichomonal 131.01
Vulvodynia 625.9
Vulvorectal — *see* condition
Vulvovaginitis — *see also* Vulvitis 616.10
amebic 006.8
chlamydial 099.53
gonococcal (acute) 098.0
chronic or duration of 2 months or over 098.2
herpetic 054.11
monilial 112.1
trichomonal (Trichomonas vaginalis) 131.01

W

Waardenburg-Klein syndrome (ptosis-epicanthus) 270.2
Waardenburg's syndrome 756.89
meaning ptosis-epicanthus 270.2
Wagner's disease (colloid milium) 709.3
Wagner (-Unverricht) syndrome (dermatomyositis) 710.3
Waiting list, person on V63.2
undergoing social agency investigation V63.8
Wakefulness disorder — *see also* Hypersomnia 780.54
nonorganic origin 307.43
Waldenström's
disease (osteochondrosis, capital femoral) 732.1
hepatitis (lupoid hepatitis) 571.49
hypergammaglobulinemia 273.0
macroglobulinemia 273.3
purpura, hypergammaglobulinemic 273.0
syndrome (macroglobulinemia) 273.3
Waldenström-Kjellberg syndrome (sideropenic dysphagia) 280.8
Walking
difficulty 719.7
psychogenic 307.9
sleep 307.46
hysterical 300.13
Wall, abdominal — *see* condition

Wallenberg's syndrome (posterior inferior cerebellar artery) — *see also* Disease, cerebrovascular, acute 436
Wallgren's
disease (obstruction of splenic vein with collateral circulation) 459.89
meningitis (*see also* Meningitis, aseptic) 047.9
Wandering
acetabulum 736.39
gallbladder 751.69
kidney, congenital 753.3
organ or site, congenital NEC — *see* Malposition, congenital
pacemaker (atrial) (heart) 427.89
spleen 289.59
Wardrop's disease (with lymphangitis) 681.9
finger 681.02
toe 681.11
War neurosis 300.16
Wart (common) (digitate) (filiform) (infectious) (viral) 078.10
external genital organs (venereal) 078.19
fig 078.19
Hassall-Henle's (of cornea) 371.41
Henle's (of cornea) 371.41
juvenile 078.19
moist 078.10
Peruvian 088.0
plantar 078.19
prosector (*see also* Tuberculosis) 017.0 ☑
seborrheic 702.19
inflamed 702.11
senile 702.0
specified NEC 078.19
syphilitic 091.3
tuberculous (*see also* Tuberculosis) 017.0 ☑
venereal (female) (male) 078.19
Warthin's tumor (salivary gland) (M8561/0) 210.2
Washerwoman's itch 692.4
Wassilieff's disease (leptospiral jaundice) 100.0
Wasting
disease 799.4
due to malnutrition 261
extreme (due to malnutrition) 261
muscular NEC 728.2
palsy, paralysis 335.21
pelvic muscle 618.83
Water
clefts 366.12
deprivation of 994.3
in joint (*see also* Effusion, joint) 719.0 ☑
intoxication 276.6
itch 120.3
lack of 994.3
loading 276.6
on
brain — *see* Hydrocephalus
chest 511.8
poisoning 276.6
Waterbrash 787.1
Water-hammer pulse — *see also* Insufficiency, aortic 424.1
Waterhouse (-Friderichsen) disease or syndrome 036.3
Water-losing nephritis 588.89
Wax in ear 380.4
Waxy
degeneration, any site 277.39 ▲
disease 277.39 ▲
kidney 277.39 *[583.81]* ▲
liver (large) 277.39 ▲
spleen 277.39 ▲
Weak, weakness (generalized) 780.79
arches (acquired) 734
congenital 754.61
bladder sphincter 596.59

☑ Additional Digit Required — Refer to the Tabular List for Digit Selection   ꟿ Subterms under main terms may continue to next column or page

2007 ICD-9-CM   ▶◀ Revised Text   ● New Line   ▲ Revised Code   October 2006 · Volume 2 — **297**

Weak, weakness — *continued*
congenital 779.89
eye muscle — *see* Strabismus
facial 781.94
foot (double) — *see* Weak, arches
heart, cardiac (*see also* Failure, heart) 428.9
congenital 746.9
mind 317
muscle (generalized) 728.87
myocardium (*see also* Failure, heart) 428.9
newborn 779.89
pelvic fundus
pubocervical tissue 618.81
rectovaginal tissue 618.82
pulse 785.9
senile 797
urinary stream 788.62
valvular — *see* Endocarditis
Wear, worn, tooth, teeth (approximal) (hard tissues) (interproximal) (occlusal) — *see also* Attrition, teeth 521.10
Weather, weathered
effects of
cold NEC 991.9
specified effect NEC 991.8
hot (*see also* Heat) 992.9
skin 692.74
Weber-Christian disease or syndrome (nodular nonsuppurative panniculitis) 729.30
Weber-Cockayne syndrome (epidermolysis bullosa) 757.39
Weber-Dimitri syndrome 759.6
Weber-Gubler syndrome 344.89
Weber-Leyden syndrome 344.89
Weber-Osler syndrome (familial hemorrhagic telangiectasia) 448.0
Weber's paralysis or syndrome 344.89
Web, webbed (congenital) — *see also* Anomaly, specified type NEC
canthus 743.63
digits (*see also* Syndactylism) 755.10
duodenal 751.5
esophagus 750.3
fingers (*see also* Syndactylism, fingers) 755.11
larynx (glottic) (subglottic) 748.2
neck (pterygium colli) 744.5
Paterson-Kelly (sideropenic dysphagia) 280.8
popliteal syndrome 756.89
toes (*see also* Syndactylism, toes) 755.13
Wedge-shaped or wedging vertebra — *see also* Osteoporosis 733.00
Wegener's granulomatosis or syndrome 446.4
Wegner's disease (syphilitic osteochondritis) 090.0
Weight
gain (abnormal) (excessive) 783.1
during pregnancy 646.1 ☑
insufficient 646.8 ☑
less than 1000 grams at birth 765.0 ☑
loss (cause unknown) 783.21
Weightlessness 994.9
Weil's disease (leptospiral jaundice) 100.0
Weill-Marchesani syndrome (brachymorphism and ectopia lentis) 759.89
Weingarten's syndrome (tropical eosinophilia) 518.3
Weir Mitchell's disease (erythromelalgia) 443.82
Weiss-Baker syndrome (carotid sinus syncope) 337.0
Weissenbach-Thibierge syndrome (cutaneous systemic sclerosis) 710.1
Wen — *see also* Cyst, sebaceous 706.2
Wenckebach's phenomenon, heart block (second degree) 426.13
Werdnig-Hoffmann syndrome (muscular atrophy) 335.0

Werlhof-Wichmann syndrome — *see also* Purpura, thrombocytopenic 287.39
Werlhof's disease — *see also* Purpura, thrombocytopenic 287.39
Wermer's syndrome or disease (polyendocrine adenomatosis) 258.0
Werner's disease or syndrome (progeria adultorum) 259.8
Werner-His disease (trench fever) 083.1
Werner-Schultz disease (agranulocytosis) 288.09 ▲
Wernicke's encephalopathy, disease, or syndrome (superior hemorrhagic polioencephalitis) 265.1
Wernicke-Korsakoff syndrome or psychosis (nonalcoholic) 294.0
alcoholic 291.1
Wernicke-Posadas disease — *see also* Coccidioidomycosis 114.9
Wesselsbron fever 066.3
West African fever 084.8
West Nile
encephalitis 066.41
encephalomyelitis 066.41
fever 066.40
with
cranial nerve disorders 066.42
encephalitis 066.41
optic neuritis 066.42
other complications 066.49
other neurologic manifestations 066.42
polyradiculitis 066.42
virus 066.40
Westphal-Strümpell syndrome (hepatolenticular degeneration) 275.1
Wet
brain (alcoholic) (*see also* Alcoholism) 303.9 ☑
feet, tropical (syndrome) (maceration) 991.4
lung (syndrome)
adult 518.5
Wharton's duct — *see* condition
Wheal 709.8
Wheezing 786.07
Whiplash injury or syndrome 847.0
Whipple's disease or syndrome (intestinal lipodystrophy) 040.2
Whipworm 127.3
"Whistling face" syndrome (craniocarpotarsal dystrophy) 759.89
White — *see also* condition
kidney
large — *see* Nephrosis
small 582.9
leg, puerperal, postpartum, childbirth 671.4 ☑
nonpuerperal 451.19
mouth 112.0
patches of mouth 528.6
sponge nevus of oral mucosa 750.26
spot lesions, teeth 521.01
White's disease (congenital) (keratosis follicularis) 757.39
Whitehead 706.2
Whitlow (with lymphangitis) 681.01
herpetic 054.6
Whitmore's disease or fever (melioidosis) 025
Whooping cough 033.9
with pneumonia 033.9 [484.3]
due to
Bordetella
bronchoseptica 033.8
with pneumonia 033.8 [484.3]
parapertussis 033.1
with pneumonia 033.1 [484.3]
pertussis 033.0
with pneumonia 033.0 [484.3]

Whooping cough — *continued*
due to — *continued*
specified organism NEC 033.8
with pneumonia 033.8 [484.3]
vaccination, prophylactic (against) V03.6
Wichmann's asthma (laryngismus stridulus) 478.75
Widal (-Abrami) syndrome (acquired hemolytic jaundice) 283.9
Widening aorta — *see also* Aneurysm, aorta 441.9
ruptured 441.5
Wilkie's disease or syndrome 557.1
Wilkinson-Sneddon disease or syndrome (subcorneal pustular dermatosis) 694.1
Willan's lepra 696.1
Willan-Plumbe syndrome (psoriasis) 696.1
Willebrand (-Jürgens) syndrome or thrombopathy (angiohemophilia) 286.4
Willi-Prader syndrome (hypogenital dystrophy with diabetic tendency) 759.81
Willis' disease (diabetes mellitus) — *see also* Diabetes 250.0 ☑
Wilms' tumor or neoplasm (nephroblastoma) (M8960/3) 189.0
Wilson's
disease or syndrome (hepatolenticular degeneration) 275.1
hepatolenticular degeneration 275.1
lichen ruber 697.0
Wilson-Brocq disease (dermatitis exfoliativa) 695.89
Wilson-Mikity syndrome 770.7
Window — *see also* Imperfect, closure
aorticopulmonary 745.0
Winged scapula 736.89
Winter — *see also* condition
vomiting disease 078.82
Wise's disease 696.2
Wiskott-Aldrich syndrome (eczema-thrombocytopenia) 279.12
Withdrawal symptoms, syndrome
alcohol 291.81
delirium (acute) 291.0
chronic 291.1
newborn 760.71
drug or narcotic 292.0
newborn, infant of dependent mother 779.5
steroid NEC
correct substance properly administered 255.4
overdose or wrong substance given or taken 962.0
Withdrawing reaction, child or adolescent 313.22
Witts' anemia (achlorhydric anemia) 280.9
Witzelsucht 301.9
Woakes' syndrome (ethmoiditis) 471.1
Wohlfart-Kugelberg-Welander disease 335.11
Woillez's disease (acute idiopathic pulmonary congestion) 518.5
Wolff-Parkinson-White syndrome (anomalous atrioventricular excitation) 426.7
Wolhynian fever 083.1
Wolman's disease (primary familial xanthomatosis) 272.7
Wood asthma 495.8
Woolly, wooly hair (congenital) (nevus) 757.4
Wool-sorters' disease 022.1
Word
blindness (congenital) (developmental) 315.01
secondary to organic lesion 784.61
deafness (secondary to organic lesion) 784.69
developmental 315.31

Worm(s) (colic) (fever) (infection) (infestation) — *see also* Infestation 128.9
guinea 125.7
in intestine NEC 127.9
Worm-eaten soles 102.3
Worn out — *see also* Exhaustion 780.79
"Worried well" V65.5
Wound, open (by cutting or piercing instrument) (by firearms) (cut) (dissection) (incised) (laceration) (penetration) (perforating) (puncture) (with initial hemorrhage, not internal) 879.8

Note — *For fracture with open wound, see Fracture.*

For laceration, traumatic rupture, tear or penetrating wound of internal organs, such as heart, lung, liver, kidney, pelvic organs, etc., whether or not accompanied by open wound or fracture in the same region, see Injury, internal.

For contused wound, see Contusion. For crush injury, see Crush. For abrasion, insect bite (nonvenomous), blister, or scratch, see Injury, superficial.

Complicated includes wounds with:
delayed healing
delayed treatment
foreign body
primary infection

For late effect of open wound, see Late, effect, wound, open, by site.

abdomen, abdominal (external) (muscle) 879.2
complicated 879.3
wall (anterior) 879.2
complicated 879.3
lateral 879.4
complicated 879.5
alveolar (process) 873.62
complicated 873.72
ankle 891.0
with tendon involvement 891.2
complicated 891.1
anterior chamber, eye (*see also* Wound, open, intraocular) 871.9
anus 879.6
complicated 879.7
arm 884.0
with tendon involvement 884.2
complicated 884.1
forearm 881.00
with tendon involvement 881.20
complicated 881.10
multiple sites — *see* Wound, open, multiple, upper limb
upper 880.03
with tendon involvement 880.23
complicated 880.13
multiple sites (with axillary or shoulder regions) 880.09
with tendon involvement 880.29
complicated 880.19
artery — *see* Injury, blood vessel, by site
auditory
canal (external) (meatus) 872.02
complicated 872.12
ossicles (incus) (malleus) (stapes) 872.62
complicated 872.72
auricle, ear 872.01
complicated 872.11
axilla 880.02
with tendon involvement 880.22
complicated 880.12
with tendon involvement 880.29
involving other sites of upper arm 880.09
complicated 880.19
back 876.0

Wound, open — *continued*
  back — *continued*
    complicated 876.1
  bladder — *see* Injury, internal, bladder
  blood vessel — *see* Injury, blood vessel, by site
  brain — *see* Injury, intracranial, with open intracranial wound
  breast 879.0
    complicated 879.1
  brow 873.42
    complicated 873.52
  buccal mucosa 873.61
    complicated 873.71
  buttock 877.0
    complicated 877.1
  calf 891.0
    with tendon involvement 891.2
    complicated 891.1
  canaliculus lacrimalis 870.8
    with laceration of eyelid 870.2
  canthus, eye 870.8
    laceration — *see* Laceration, eyelid
  cavernous sinus — *see* Injury, intracranial
  cerebellum — *see* Injury, intracranial
  cervical esophagus 874.4
    complicated 874.5
  cervix — *see* Injury, internal, cervix
  cheek(s) (external) 873.41
    complicated 873.51
    internal 873.61
      complicated 873.71
  chest (wall) (external) 875.0
    complicated 875.1
  chin 873.44
    complicated 873.54
  choroid 363.63
  ciliary body (eye) (*see also* Wound, open, intraocular) 871.9
  clitoris 878.8
    complicated 878.9
  cochlea 872.64
    complicated 872.74
  complicated 879.9
  conjunctiva — *see* Wound, open, intraocular
  cornea (nonpenetrating) (*see also* Wound, open, intraocular) 871.9
  costal region 875.0
    complicated 875.1
  Descemet's membrane (*see also* Wound, open, intraocular) 871.9
  digit(s)
    foot 893.0
      with tendon involvement 893.2
      complicated 893.1
    hand 883.0
      with tendon involvement 883.2
      complicated 883.1
  drumhead, ear 872.61
    complicated 872.71
  ear 872.8
    canal 872.02
      complicated 872.12
    complicated 872.9
    drum 872.61
      complicated 872.71
    external 872.00
      complicated 872.10
    multiple sites 872.69
      complicated 872.79
    ossicles (incus) (malleus) (stapes) 872.62
      complicated 872.72
    specified part NEC 872.69
      complicated 872.79
  elbow 881.01
    with tendon involvement 881.21
    complicated 881.11
  epididymis 878.2
    complicated 878.3
  epigastric region 879.2
    complicated 879.3
  epiglottis 874.01

Wound, open — *continued*
  epiglottis — *continued*
    complicated 874.11
  esophagus (cervical) 874.4
    complicated 874.5
    thoracic — *see* Injury, internal, esophagus
  Eustachian tube 872.63
    complicated 872.73
  extremity
    lower (multiple) NEC 894.0
      with tendon involvement 894.2
      complicated 894.1
    upper (multiple) NEC 884.0
      with tendon involvement 884.2
      complicated 884.1
  eye(s) (globe) — *see* Wound, open, intraocular
  eyeball NEC 871.9
    laceration (*see also* Laceration, eyeball) 871.4
    penetrating (*see also* Penetrating wound, eyeball) 871.7
  eyebrow 873.42
    complicated 873.52
  eyelid NEC 870.8
    laceration — *see* Laceration, eyelid
  face 873.40
    complicated 873.50
    multiple sites 873.49
      complicated 873.59
    specified part NEC 873.49
      complicated 873.59
  fallopian tube — *see* Injury, internal, fallopian tube
  finger(s) (nail) (subungual) 883.0
    with tendon involvement 883.2
    complicated 883.1
  flank 879.4
    complicated 879.5
  foot (any part except toe(s) alone) 892.0
    with tendon involvement 892.2
    complicated 892.1
  forearm 881.00
    with tendon involvement 881.20
    complicated 881.10
  forehead 873.42
    complicated 873.52
  genital organs (external) NEC 878.8
    complicated 878.9
    internal — *see* Injury, internal, by site
  globe (eye) (*see also* Wound, open, eyeball) 871.9
  groin 879.4
    complicated 879.5
  gum(s) 873.62
    complicated 873.72
  hand (except finger(s) alone) 882.0
    with tendon involvement 882.2
    complicated 882.1
  head NEC 873.8
    with intracranial injury — *see* Injury, intracranial
    due to or associated with skull fracture — *see* Fracture, skull
    complicated 873.9
    scalp — *see* Wound, open, scalp
  heel 892.0
    with tendon involvement 892.2
    complicated 892.1
  high-velocity (grease gun) — *see* Wound, open, complicated, by site
  hip 890.0
    with tendon involvement 890.2
    complicated 890.1
  hymen 878.6
    complicated 878.7
  hypochondrium 879.4
    complicated 879.5
  hypogastric region 879.2
    complicated 879.3
  iliac (region) 879.4

Wound, open — *continued*
  iliac — *continued*
    complicated 879.5
  incidental to
    dislocation — *see* Dislocation, open, by site
    fracture — *see* Fracture, open, by site
    intracranial injury — *see* Injury, intracranial, with open intracranial wound
    nerve injury — *see* Injury, nerve, by site
  inguinal region 879.4
    complicated 879.5
  instep 892.0
    with tendon involvement 892.2
    complicated 892.1
  interscapular region 876.0
    complicated 876.1
  intracranial — *see* Injury, intracranial, with open intracranial wound
  intraocular 871.9
    with
      partial loss (of intraocular tissue) 871.2
      prolapse or exposure (of intraocular tissue) 871.1
      without prolapse (of intraocular tissue) 871.0
    laceration (*see also* Laceration, eyeball) 871.4
    penetrating 871.7
      with foreign body (nonmagnetic) 871.6
        magnetic 871.5
  iris (*see also* Wound, open, eyeball) 871.9
  jaw (fracture not involved) 873.44
    with fracture — *see* Fracture, jaw
    complicated 873.54
  knee 891.0
    with tendon involvement 891.2
    complicated 891.1
  labium (majus) (minus) 878.4
    complicated 878.5
  lacrimal apparatus, gland, or sac 870.8
    with laceration of eyelid 870.2
  larynx 874.01
    with trachea 874.00
      complicated 874.10
    complicated 874.11
  leg (multiple) 891.0
    with tendon involvement 891.2
    complicated 891.1
    lower 891.0
      with tendon involvement 891.2
      complicated 891.1
    thigh 890.0
      with tendon involvement 890.2
      complicated 890.1
    upper 890.0
      with tendon involvement 890.2
      complicated 890.1
  lens (eye) (alone) (*see also* Cataract, traumatic) 366.20
    with involvement of other eye structures — *see* Wound, open, eyeball
  limb
    lower (multiple) NEC 894.0
      with tendon involvement 894.2
      complicated 894.1
    upper (multiple) NEC 884.0
      with tendon involvement 884.2
      complicated 884.1
  lip 873.43
    complicated 873.53
  loin 876.0
    complicated 876.1
  lumbar region 876.0
    complicated 876.1
  malar region 873.41
    complicated 873.51
  mastoid region 873.49

Wound, open — *continued*
  mastoid region — *continued*
    complicated 873.59
  mediastinum — *see* Injury, internal, mediastinum
  midthoracic region 875.0
    complicated 875.1
  mouth 873.60
    complicated 873.70
    floor 873.64
      complicated 873.74
    multiple sites 873.69
      complicated 873.79
    specified site NEC 873.69
      complicated 873.79
  multiple, unspecified site(s) 879.8

> Note — Multiple open wounds of sites classifiable to the same four-digit category should be classified to that category unless they are in different limbs.
>
> Multiple open wounds of sites classifiable to different four-digit categories, or to different limbs, should be coded separately.

    complicated 879.9
    lower limb(s) (one or both) (sites classifiable to more than one three-digit category in 890 to 893) 894.0
      with tendon involvement 894.2
      complicated 894.1
    upper limb(s) (one or both) (sites classifiable to more than one three-digit category in 880 to 883) 884.0
      with tendon involvement 884.2
      complicated 884.1
  muscle — *see* Sprain, by site
  nail
    finger(s) 883.0
      complicated 883.1
    thumb 883.0
      complicated 883.1
    toe(s) 893.0
      complicated 893.1
  nape (neck) 874.8
    complicated 874.9
    specified part NEC 874.8
      complicated 874.9
  nasal (*see also* Wound, open, nose)
    cavity 873.22
      complicated 873.32
    septum 873.21
      complicated 873.31
    sinuses 873.23
      complicated 873.33
  nasopharynx 873.22
    complicated 873.32
  neck 874.8
    complicated 874.9
    nape 874.8
      complicated 874.9
    specified part NEC 874.8
      complicated 874.9
  nerve — *see* Injury, nerve, by site
  non-healing surgical 998.83
  nose 873.20
    complicated 873.30
    multiple sites 873.29
      complicated 873.39
    septum 873.21
      complicated 873.31
    sinuses 873.23
      complicated 873.33
  occipital region — *see* Wound, open, scalp
  ocular NEC 871.9
    adnexa 870.9
      specified region NEC 870.8
    laceration (*see also* Laceration, ocular) 871.4
    muscle (extraocular) 870.3
      with foreign body 870.4
      eyelid 870.1

☑ Additional Digit Required — Refer to the Tabular List for Digit Selection   ⬝ Subterms under main terms may continue to next column or page

2007 ICD-9-CM   ▶◀ Revised Text   ● New Line   ▲ Revised Code   **Volume 2 — 299**

Zollinger-Ellison syndrome (gastric hypersecretion with pancreatic islet cell tumor) 251.5
Zona — *see also* Herpes, zoster 053.9

Zoophilia (erotica) 302.1
Zoophobia 300.29
Zoster (herpes) — *see also* Herpes, zoster 053.9

Zuelzer **(-Ogden) anemia or syndrome** (nutritional megaloblastic anemia) 281.2

Zygodactyly — *see also* Syndactylism 755.10
Zygomycosis 117.7
Zymotic — *see* condition

SECTION 2

Alphabetic Index to Poisoning and External Causes of Adverse Effects of Drugs and Other Chemical Substances

TABLE OF DRUGS AND CHEMICALS

This table contains a classification of drugs and other chemical substances to identify poisoning states and external causes of adverse effects.

Each of the listed substances in the table is assigned a code according to the poisoning classification (960-989). These codes are used when there is a statement of poisoning, overdose, wrong substance given or taken, or intoxication.

The table also contains a listing of external causes of adverse effects. An adverse effect is a pathologic manifestation due to ingestion or exposure to drugs or other chemical substances (e.g., dermatitis, hypersensitivity reaction, aspirin gastritis). The adverse effect is to be identified by the appropriate code found in Section 1, Index to Diseases and Injuries. An external cause code can then be used to identify the circumstances involved. The table headings pertaining to external causes are defined below:

Accidental poisoning (E850-E869) — accidental overdose of drug, wrong substance given or taken, drug taken inadvertently, accidents in the usage of drugs and biologicals in medical and surgical procedures, and to show external causes of poisonings classifiable to 980-989.

Therapeutic use (E930-E949) — a correct substance properly administered in therapeutic or prophylactic dosage as the external cause of adverse effects.

Suicide attempt (E950-E952) — instances in which self-inflicted injuries or poisonings are involved.

Assault (E961-E962) — injury or poisoning inflicted by another person with the intent to injure or kill.

Undetermined (E980-E982) — to be used when the intent of the poisoning or injury cannot be determined whether it was intentional or accidental.

The American Hospital Formulary Service list numbers are included in the table to help classify new drugs not identified in the table by name. The AHFS list numbers are keyed to the continually revised American Hospital Formulary Service (AHFS).* These listings are found in the table under the main term **Drug**.

Excluded from the table are radium and other radioactive substances. The classification of adverse effects and complications pertaining to these substances will be found in Section 1, Index to Diseases and Injuries, and Section 3, Index to External Causes of Injuries.

Although certain substances are indexed with one or more subentries, the majority are listed according to one use or state. It is recognized that many substances may be used in various ways, in medicine and in industry, and may cause adverse effects whatever the state of the agent (solid, liquid, or fumes arising from a liquid). In cases in which the reported data indicates a use or state not in the table, or which is clearly different from the one listed, an attempt should be made to classify the substance in the form which most nearly expresses the reported facts.

*American Hospital Formulary Service, 2 vol. (Washington, D.C.: American Society of Hospital Pharmacists, 1959-)

	Poisoning	Accident	Therapeutic Use	Suicide Attempt	Assault	Undetermined
External Cause (E-Code)						
1-propanol	980.3	E860.4	—	E950.9	E962.1	E980.9
2-propanol	980.2	E860.3	—	E950.9	E962.1	E980.9
2, 4-D (dichlorophenoxyacetic acid)	989.4	E863.5	—	E950.6	E962.1	E980.7
2, 4-toluene diisocyanate	983.0	E864.0	—	E950.7	E962.1	E980.6
2, 4, 5-T (trichlorophenoxyacetic acid)	989.2	E863.5	—	E950.6	E962.1	E980.7
14-hydroxydihydromorphinone	965.09	E850.2	E935.2	E950.0	E962.0	E980.0
ABOB	961.7	E857	E931.7	E950.4	E962.0	E980.4
Abrus (seed)	988.2	E865.3	—	E950.9	E962.1	E980.9
Absinthe	980.0	E860.1	—	E950.9	E962.1	E980.9
beverage	980.0	E860.0	—	E950.9	E962.1	E980.9
Acenocoumarin, acenocoumarol	964.2	E858.2	E934.2	E950.4	E962.0	E980.4
Acepromazine	969.1	E853.0	E939.1	E950.3	E962.0	E980.3
Acetal	982.8	E862.4	—	E950.9	E962.1	E980.9
Acetaldehyde (vapor)	987.8	E869.8	—	E952.8	E962.2	E982.8
liquid	989.89	E866.8	—	E950.9	E962.1	E980.9
Acetaminophen	965.4	E850.4	E935.4	E950.0	E962.0	E980.0
Acetaminosalol	965.1	E850.3	E935.3	E950.0	E962.0	E980.0
Acetanilid(e)	965.4	E850.4	E935.4	E950.0	E962.0	E980.0
Acetarsol, acetarsone	961.1	E857	E931.1	E950.4	E962.0	E980.4
Acetazolamide	974.2	E858.5	E944.2	E950.4	E962.0	E980.4
Acetic						
acid	983.1	E864.1	—	E950.7	E962.1	E980.6
with sodium acetate (ointment)	976.3	E858.7	E946.3	E950.4	E962.0	E980.4
irrigating solution	974.5	E858.5	E944.5	E950.4	E962.0	E980.4
lotion	976.2	E858.7	E946.2	E950.4	E962.0	E980.4
anhydride	983.1	E864.1	—	E950.7	E962.1	E980.6
ether (vapor)	982.8	E862.4	—	E950.9	E962.1	E980.9
Acetohexamide	962.3	E858.0	E932.3	E950.4	E962.0	E980.4
Acetomenaphthone	964.3	E858.2	E934.3	E950.4	E962.0	E980.4
Acetomorphine	965.01	E850.0	E935.0	E950.0	E962.0	E980.0
Acetone (oils) (vapor)	982.8	E862.4	—	E950.9	E962.1	E980.9
Acetophenazine (maleate)	969.1	E853.0	E939.1	E950.3	E962.0	E980.3
Acetophenetidin	965.4	E850.4	E935.4	E950.0	E962.0	E980.0
Acetophenone	982.0	E862.4	—	E950.9	E962.1	E980.9
Acetorphine	965.09	E850.2	E935.2	E950.0	E962.0	E980.0
Acetosulfone (sodium)	961.8	E857	E931.8	E950.4	E962.0	E980.4
Acetrizoate (sodium)	977.8	E858.8	E947.8	E950.4	E962.0	E980.4
Acetylcarbromal	967.3	E852.2	E937.3	E950.2	E962.0	E980.2
Acetylcholine (chloride)	971.0	E855.3	E941.0	E950.4	E962.0	E980.4
Acetylcysteine	975.5	E858.6	E945.5	E950.4	E962.0	E980.4
Acetyldigitoxin	972.1	E858.3	E942.1	E950.4	E962.0	E980.4
Acetyldihydrocodeine	965.09	E850.2	E935.2	E950.0	E962.0	E980.0
Acetyldihydrocodeinone	965.09	E850.2	E935.2	E950.0	E962.0	E980.0
Acetylene (gas) (industrial)	987.1	E868.1	—	E951.8	E962.2	E981.8
incomplete combustion of — see Carbon monoxide, fuel, utility						
tetrachloride (vapor)	982.3	E862.4	—	E950.9	E962.1	E980.9
Acetyliodosalicylic acid	965.1	E850.3	E935.3	E950.0	E962.0	E980.0
Acetylphenylhydrazine	965.8	E850.8	E935.8	E950.0	E962.0	E980.0
Acetylsalicylic acid	965.1	E850.3	E935.3	E950.0	E962.0	E980.0
Achromycin	960.4	E856	E930.4	E950.4	E962.0	E980.4
ophthalmic preparation	976.5	E858.7	E946.5	E950.4	E962.0	E980.4
topical NEC	976.0	E858.7	E946.0	E950.4	E962.0	E980.4
Acidifying agents	963.2	E858.1	E933.2	E950.4	E962.0	E980.4
Acids (corrosive) NEC	983.1	E864.1	—	E950.7	E962.1	E980.6
Aconite (wild)	988.2	E865.4	—	E950.9	E962.1	E980.9
Aconitine (liniment)	976.8	E858.7	E946.8	E950.4	E962.0	E980.4
Aconitum ferox	988.2	E865.4	—	E950.9	E962.1	E980.9
Acridine	983.0	E864.0	—	E950.7	E962.1	E980.6
vapor	987.8	E869.8	—	E952.8	E962.2	E982.8
Acriflavine	961.9	E857	E931.9	E950.4	E962.0	E980.4
Acrisorcin	976.0	E858.7	E946.0	E950.4	E962.0	E980.4
Acrolein (gas)	987.8	E869.8	—	E952.8	E962.2	E982.8
liquid	989.89	E866.8	—	E950.9	E962.1	E980.9
Actaea spicata	988.2	E865.4	—	E950.9	E962.1	E980.9
Acterol	961.5	E857	E931.5	E950.4	E962.0	E980.4
ACTH	962.4	E858.0	E932.4	E950.4	E962.0	E980.4
Acthar	962.4	E858.0	E932.4	E950.4	E962.0	E980.4
Actinomycin (C) (D)	960.7	E856	E930.7	E950.4	E962.0	E980.4
Adalin (acetyl)	967.3	E852.2	E937.3	E950.2	E962.0	E980.2
Adenosine (phosphate)	977.8	E858.8	E947.8	E950.4	E962.0	E980.4
ADH	962.5	E858.0	E932.5	E950.4	E962.0	E980.4
Adhesives	989.89	E866.6	—	E950.9	E962.1	E980.9
Adicillin	960.0	E856	E930.0	E950.4	E962.0	E980.4
Adiphenine	975.1	E855.6	E945.1	E950.4	E962.0	E980.4
Adjunct, pharmaceutical	977.4	E858.8	E947.4	E950.4	E962.0	E980.4

	Poisoning	Accident	Therapeutic Use	Suicide Attempt	Assault	Undetermined
External Cause (E-Code)						
Adrenal (extract, cortex or medulla) (glucocorticoids) (hormones) (mineralocorticoids)	962.0	E858.0	E932.0	E950.4	E962.0	E980.4
ENT agent	976.6	E858.7	E946.6	E950.4	E962.0	E980.4
ophthalmic preparation	976.5	E858.7	E946.5	E950.4	E962.0	E980.4
topical NEC	976.0	E858.7	E946.0	E950.4	E962.0	E980.4
Adrenalin	971.2	E855.5	E941.2	E950.4	E962.0	E980.4
Adrenergic blocking agents	971.3	E855.6	E941.3	E950.4	E962.0	E980.4
Adrenergics	971.2	E855.5	E941.2	E950.4	E962.0	E980.4
Adrenochrome (derivatives)	972.8	E858.3	E942.8	E950.4	E962.0	E980.4
Adrenocorticotropic hormone	962.4	E858.0	E932.4	E950.4	E962.0	E980.4
Adrenocorticotropin	962.4	E858.0	E932.4	E950.4	E962.0	E980.4
Adriamycin	960.7	E856	E930.7	E950.4	E962.0	E980.4
Aerosol spray — see Sprays						
Aerosporin	960.8	E856	E930.8	E950.4	E962.0	E980.4
ENT agent	976.6	E858.7	E946.6	E950.4	E962.0	E980.4
ophthalmic preparation	976.5	E858.7	E946.5	E950.4	E962.0	E980.4
topical NEC	976.0	E858.7	E946.0	E950.4	E962.0	E980.4
Aethusa cynapium	988.2	E865.4	—	E950.9	E962.1	E980.9
Afghanistan black	969.6	E854.1	E939.6	E950.3	E962.0	E980.3
Aflatoxin	989.7	E865.9	—	E950.9	E962.1	E980.9
African boxwood	988.2	E865.4	—	E950.9	E962.1	E980.9
Agar (-agar)	973.3	E858.4	E943.3	E950.4	E962.0	E980.4
Agricultural agent NEC	989.89	E863.9	—	E950.6	E962.1	E980.7
Agrypnol	967.0	E851	E937.0	E950.1	E962.0	—
Air contaminant(s), source or type not specified	987.9	E869.9	—	E952.9	E962.2	E982.9
specified type — see specific substance						
Akee	988.2	E865.4	—	E950.9	E962.1	E980.9
Akrinol	976.0	E858.7	E946.0	E950.4	E962.0	E980.4
Alantolactone	961.6	E857	E931.6	E950.4	E962.0	E980.4
Albamycin	960.8	E856	E930.8	E950.4	E962.0	E980.4
Albumin (normal human serum)	964.7	E858.2	E934.7	E950.4	E962.0	E980.4
Albuterol	975.7	E858.6	E945.7	E950.4	E962.0	E980.4
Alcohol	980.9	E860.9	—	E950.9	E962.1	E980.9
absolute	980.0	E860.1	—	E950.9	E962.1	E980.9
beverage	980.0	E860.0	E947.8	E950.9	E962.1	E980.9
amyl	980.3	E860.4	—	E950.9	E962.1	E980.9
antifreeze	980.1	E860.2	—	E950.9	E962.1	E980.9
butyl	980.3	E860.4	—	E950.9	E962.1	E980.9
dehydrated	980.0	E860.1	—	E950.9	E962.1	E980.9
beverage	980.0	E860.0	E947.8	E950.9	E962.1	E980.9
denatured	980.0	E860.1	—	E950.9	E962.1	E980.9
deterrents	977.3	E858.8	E947.3	E950.4	E962.0	E980.4
diagnostic (gastric function)	977.8	E858.8	E947.8	E950.4	E962.0	E980.4
ethyl	980.0	E860.1	—	E950.9	E962.1	E980.9
beverage	980.0	E860.0	E947.8	E950.9	E962.1	E980.9
grain	980.0	E860.1	—	E950.9	E962.1	E980.9
beverage	980.0	E860.0	E947.8	E950.9	E962.1	E980.9
industrial	980.9	E860.9	—	E950.9	E962.1	E980.9
isopropyl	980.2	E860.3	—	E950.9	E962.1	E980.9
methyl	980.1	E860.2	—	E950.9	E962.1	E980.9
preparation for consumption	980.0	E860.0	E947.8	E950.9	E962.1	E980.9
propyl	980.3	E860.4	—	E950.9	E962.1	E980.9
secondary	980.2	E860.3	—	E950.9	E962.1	E980.9
radiator	980.1	E860.2	—	E950.9	E962.1	E980.9
rubbing	980.2	E860.3	—	E950.9	E962.1	E980.9
specified type NEC	980.8	E860.8	—	E950.9	E962.1	E980.9
surgical	980.9	E860.9	—	E950.9	E962.1	E980.9
vapor (from any type of alcohol)	987.8	E869.8	—	E952.8	E962.2	E982.8
wood	980.1	E860.2	—	E950.9	E962.1	E980.9
Alcuronium chloride	975.2	E858.6	E945.2	E950.4	E962.0	E980.4
Aldactone	974.4	E858.5	E944.4	E950.4	E962.0	E980.4
Aldicarb	989.3	E863.2	—	E950.6	E962.1	E980.7
Aldomet	972.6	E858.3	E942.6	E950.4	E962.0	E980.4
Aldosterone	962.0	E858.0	E932.0	E950.4	E962.0	E980.4
Aldrin (dust)	989.2	E863.0	—	E950.6	E962.1	E980.7
Algeldrate	973.0	E858.4	E943.0	E950.4	E962.0	E980.4
Alidase	963.4	E858.1	E933.4	E950.4	E962.0	E980.4
Aliphatic thiocyanates	989.0	E866.8	—	E950.9	E962.1	E980.9
Alkaline antiseptic solution (aromatic)	976.6	E858.7	E946.6	E950.4	E962.0	E980.4

☑ Additional Digit Required — Refer to the Tabular List for Digit Selection   ▽ Subterms under main terms may continue to next column or page

304 — Volume 2   ▶◀ Revised Text   ● New Line   ▲ Revised Code   2007 ICD-9-CM

	Poisoning	Accident	Therapeutic Use	Suicide Attempt	Assault	Undetermined
Alkalinizing agents						
(medicinal)	963.3	E858.1	E933.3	E950.4	E962.0	E980.4
Alkalis, caustic	983.2	E864.2	—	E950.7	E962.1	E980.6
Alkalizing agents						
(medicinal)	963.3	E858.1	E933.3	E950.4	E962.0	E980.4
Alka-seltzer	965.1	E850.3	E935.3	E950.0	E962.0	E980.0
Alkavervir	972.6	E858.3	E942.6	E950.4	E962.0	E980.4
Allegron	969.0	E854.0	E939.0	E950.3	E962.0	E980.3
Alleve — Naproxen						
Allobarbital,						
allobarbitone	967.0	E851	E937.0	E950.1	E962.0	E980.1
Allopurinol	974.7	E858.5	E944.7	E950.4	E962.0	E980.4
Allylestrenol	962.2	E858.0	E932.2	E950.4	E962.0	E980.4
Allylisopropylacetylurea	967.8	E852.8	E937.8	E950.2	E962.0	E980.2
Allylisopropylmalonylurea	967.0	E851	E937.0	E950.1	E962.0	E980.1
Allyltribromide	967.3	E852.2	E937.3	E950.2	E962.0	E980.2
Aloe, aloes, aloin	973.1	E858.4	E943.1	E950.4	E962.0	E980.4
Alosetron	973.8	E858.4	E943.8	E950.4	E962.0	E980.4
Aloxidone	966.0	E855.0	E936.0	E950.4	E962.0	E980.4
Aloxiprin	965.1	E850.3	E935.3	E950.0	E962.0	E980.0
Alpha amylase	963.4	E858.1	E933.4	E950.4	E962.0	E980.4
Alphaprodine						
(hydrochloride)	965.09	E850.2	E935.2	E950.0	E962.0	E980.0
Alpha tocopherol	963.5	E858.1	E933.5	E950.4	E962.0	E980.4
Alseroxylon	972.6	E858.3	E942.6	E950.4	E962.0	E980.4
Alum (ammonium)						
(potassium)	983.2	E864.2	—	E950.7	E962.1	E980.6
medicinal (astringent) NEC	976.2	E858.7	E946.2	E950.4	E962.0	E980.4
Aluminium, aluminum (gel)						
(hydroxide)	973.0	E858.4	E943.0	E950.4	E962.0	E980.4
acetate solution	976.2	E858.7	E946.2	E950.4	E962.0	E980.4
aspirin	965.1	E850.3	E935.3	E950.0	E962.0	E980.0
carbonate	973.0	E858.4	E943.0	E950.4	E962.0	E980.4
glycinate	973.0	E858.4	E943.0	E950.4	E962.0	E980.4
nicotinate	972.2	E858.3	E942.2	E950.4	E962.0	E980.4
ointment (surgical) (topical)	976.3	E858.7	E946.3	E950.4	E962.0	E980.4
phosphate	973.0	E858.4	E943.0	E950.4	E962.0	E980.4
subacetate	976.2	E858.7	E946.2	E950.4	E962.0	E980.4
topical NEC	976.3	E858.7	E946.3	E950.4	E962.0	E980.4
Alurate	967.0	E851	E937.0	E950.1	E962.0	E980.1
Alverine (citrate)	975.1	E858.6	E945.1	E950.4	E962.0	E980.4
Alvodine	965.09	E850.2	E935.2	E950.0	E962.0	E980.0
Amanita phalloides	988.1	E865.5	—	E950.9	E962.1	E980.9
Amantadine (hydrochloride)	966.4	E855.0	E936.4	E950.4	E962.0	E980.4
Ambazone	961.9	E857	E931.9	E950.4	E962.0	E980.4
Ambenonium	971.0	E855.3	E941.0	E950.4	E962.0	E980.4
Ambutonium bromide	971.1	E855.4	E941.1	E950.4	E962.0	E980.4
Ametazole	977.8	E858.8	E947.8	E950.4	E962.0	E980.4
Amethocaine (infiltration)						
(topical)	968.5	E855.2	E938.5	E950.4	E962.0	E980.4
nerve block (peripheral)						
(plexus)	968.6	E855.2	E938.6	E950.4	E962.0	E980.4
spinal	968.7	E855.2	E938.7	E950.4	E962.0	E980.4
Amethopterin	963.1	E858.1	E933.1	E950.4	E962.0	E980.4
Amfepramone	977.0	E858.8	E947.0	E950.4	E962.0	E980.4
Amidon	965.02	E850.1	E935.1	E950.0	E962.0	E980.0
Amidopyrine	965.5	E850.5	E935.5	E950.0	E962.0	E980.0
Aminacrine	976.0	E858.7	E946.0	E950.4	E962.0	E980.4
Aminitrozole	961.5	E857	E931.5	E950.4	E962.0	E980.4
Aminoacetic acid	974.5	E858.5	E944.5	E950.4	E962.0	E980.4
Amino acids	974.5	E858.5	E944.5	E950.4	E962.0	E980.4
Aminocaproic acid	964.4	E858.2	E934.4	E950.4	E962.0	E980.4
Aminoethylisothiourium	963.8	E858.1	E933.8	E950.4	E962.0	E980.4
Aminoglutethimide	966.3	E855.0	E936.3	E950.4	E962.0	E980.4
Aminometradine	974.3	E858.5	E944.3	E950.4	E962.0	E980.4
Aminopentamide	971.1	E855.4	E941.1	E950.4	E962.0	E980.4
Aminophenazone	965.5	E850.5	E935.5	E950.0	E962.0	E980.0
Aminophenol	983.0	E864.0	—	E950.7	E962.1	E980.6
Aminophenylpyridone	969.5	E853.8	E939.5	E950.3	E962.0	E980.3
Aminophyllin	975.7	E858.6	E945.7	E950.4	E962.0	E980.4
Aminopterin	963.1	E858.1	E933.1	E950.4	E962.0	E980.4
Aminopyrine	965.5	E850.5	E935.5	E950.0	E962.0	E980.0
Aminosalicylic acid	961.8	E857	E931.8	E950.4	E962.0	E980.4
Amiphenazole	970.1	E854.3	E940.1	E950.4	E962.0	E980.4
Amiquinsin	972.6	E858.3	E942.6	E950.4	E962.0	E980.4
Amisometradine	974.3	E858.5	E944.3	E950.4	E962.0	E980.4
Amitriptyline	969.0	E854.0	E939.0	E950.3	E962.0	E980.3
Ammonia (fumes) (gas)						
(vapor)	987.8	E869.8	—	E952.8	E962.2	E982.8
liquid (household) NEC	983.2	E861.4	—	E950.7	E962.1	E980.6
spirit, aromatic	970.8	E854.3	E940.8	E950.4	E962.0	E980.4

	Poisoning	Accident	Therapeutic Use	Suicide Attempt	Assault	Undetermined
Ammoniated mercury	976.0	E858.7	E946.0	E950.4	E962.0	E980.4
Ammonium						
carbonate	983.2	E864.2	—	E950.7	E962.1	E980.6
chloride (acidifying agent)	963.2	E858.1	E933.2	E950.4	E962.0	E980.4
expectorant	975.5	E858.6	E945.5	E950.4	E962.0	E980.4
compounds (household)						
NEC	983.2	E861.4	—	E950.7	E962.1	E980.6
fumes (any usage)	987.8	E869.8	—	E952.8	E962.2	E982.8
industrial	983.2	E864.2	—	E950.7	E962.1	E980.6
ichthyosulfonate	976.4	E858.7	E946.4	E950.4	E962.0	E980.4
mandelate	961.9	E857	E931.9	E950.4	E962.0	E980.4
Amobarbital	967.0	E851	E937.0	E950.1	E962.0	E980.1
Amodiaquin(e)	961.4	E857	E931.4	E950.4	E962.0	E980.4
Amopyroquin(e)	961.4	E857	E931.4	E950.4	E962.0	E980.4
Amphenidone	969.5	E853.8	E939.5	E950.3	E962.0	E980.3
Amphetamine	969.7	E854.2	E939.7	E950.3	E962.0	E980.3
Amphomycin	960.8	E856	E930.8	E950.4	E962.0	E980.4
Amphotericin B	960.1	E856	E930.1	E950.4	E962.0	E980.4
topical	976.0	E858.7	E946.0	E950.4	E962.0	E980.4
Ampicillin	960.0	E856	E930.0	E950.4	E962.0	E980.4
Amprotropine	971.1	E855.4	E941.1	E950.4	E962.0	E980.4
Amygdalin	977.8	E858.8	E947.8	E950.4	E962.0	E980.4
Amyl						
acetate (vapor)	982.8	E862.4	—	E950.9	E962.1	E980.9
alcohol	980.3	E860.4	—	E950.9	E962.1	E980.9
nitrite (medicinal)	972.4	E858.3	E942.4	E950.4	E962.0	E980.4
Amylase (alpha)	963.4	E858.1	E933.4	E950.4	E962.0	E980.4
Amylene hydrate	980.8	E860.8	—	E950.9	E962.1	E980.9
Amylobarbitone	967.0	E851	E937.0	E950.1	E962.0	E980.1
Amylocaine	968.9	E855.2	E938.9	E950.4	E962.0	E980.4
infiltration (subcutaneous)	968.5	E855.2	E938.5	E950.4	E962.0	E980.4
nerve block (peripheral)						
(plexus)	968.6	E855.2	E938.6	E950.4	E962.0	E980.4
spinal	968.7	E855.2	E938.7	E950.4	E962.0	E980.4
topical (surface)	968.5	E855.2	E938.5	E950.4	E962.0	E980.4
Amytal (sodium)	967.0	E851	E937.0	E950.1	E962.0	E980.1
Analeptics	970.0	E854.3	E940.0	E950.4	E962.0	E980.4
Analgesics	965.9	E850.9	E935.9	E950.0	E962.0	E980.0
aromatic NEC	965.4	E850.4	E935.4	E950.0	E962.0	E980.0
non-narcotic NEC	965.7	E850.7	E935.7	E950.0	E962.0	E980.0
specified NEC	965.8	E850.8	E935.8	E950.0	E962.0	E980.0
Anamirta cocculus	988.2	E865.3	—	E950.9	E962.1	E980.9
Ancillin	960.0	E856	E930.0	E950.4	E962.0	E980.4
Androgens (anabolic						
congeners)	962.1	E858.0	E932.1	E950.4	E962.0	E980.4
Androstalone	962.1	E858.0	E932.1	E950.4	E962.0	E980.4
Androsterone	962.1	E858.0	E932.1	E950.4	E962.0	E980.4
Anemone pulsatilla	988.2	E865.4	—	E950.9	E962.1	E980.9
Anesthesia, anesthetic (general)						
NEC	968.4	E855.1	E938.4	E950.4	E962.0	E980.4
block (nerve) (plexus)	968.6	E855.2	E938.6	E950.4	E962.0	E980.4
gaseous NEC	968.2	E855.1	E938.2	E950.4	E962.0	E980.4
halogenated hydrocarbon						
derivatives NEC	968.2	E855.1	E938.2	E950.4	E962.0	E980.4
infiltration (intradermal)						
(subcutaneous)						
(submucosal)	968.5	E855.2	E938.5	E950.4	E962.0	E980.4
intravenous	968.3	E855.1	E938.3	E950.4	E962.0	E980.4
local NEC	968.9	E855.2	E938.9	E950.4	E962.0	E980.4
nerve blocking (peripheral)						
(plexus)	968.6	E855.2	E938.6	E950.4	E962.0	E980.4
rectal NEC	968.3	E855.1	E938.3	E950.4	E962.0	E980.4
spinal	968.7	E855.2	E938.7	E950.4	E962.0	E980.4
surface	968.5	E855.2	E938.5	E950.4	E962.0	E980.4
topical	968.5	E855.2	E938.5	E950.4	E962.0	E980.4
Aneurine	963.5	E858.1	E933.5	E950.4	E962.0	E980.4
Anginine — see Glyceryl						
trinitrate						
Angio-Conray	977.8	E858.8	E947.8	E950.4	E962.0	E980.4
Angiotensin	971.2	E855.5	E941.2	E950.4	E962.0	E980.4
Anhydrohydroxyprogesterone	962.2	E858.0	E932.2	E950.4	E962.0	E980.4
Anhydron	974.3	E858.5	E944.3	E950.4	E962.0	E980.4
Anileridine	965.09	E850.2	E935.2	E950.0	E962.0	E980.0
Aniline (dye) (liquid)	983.0	E864.0	—	E950.7	E962.1	E980.6
analgesic	965.4	E850.4	E935.4	E950.0	E962.0	E980.0
derivatives, therapeutic						
NEC	965.4	E850.4	E935.4	E950.0	E962.0	E980.0
vapor	987.8	E869.8	—	E952.8	E962.2	E982.8
Aniscoropine	971.1	E855.4	E941.1	E950.4	E962.0	E980.4
Anisindione	964.2	E858.2	E934.2	E950.4	E962.0	E980.4
Anorexic agents	977.0	E858.8	E947.0	E950.4	E962.0	E980.4

		External Cause (E-Code)				
	Poisoning	Accident	Therapeutic Use	Suicide Attempt	Assault	Undetermined
Ant (bite) (sting)	—	E905.5	—	E950.9	E962.1	E980.9
Antabuse	977.3	E858.8	E947.3	E950.4	E962.0	E980.4
Antacids	973.0	E858.4	E943.0	E950.4	E962.0	E980.4
Antazoline	963.0	E858.1	E933.0	E950.4	E962.0	E980.4
Anthralin	976.4	E858.7	E946.4	E950.4	E962.0	E980.4
Anthramycin	960.7	E856	E930.7	E950.4	E962.0	E980.4
Antiadrenergics	971.3	E855.6	E941.3	E950.4	E962.0	E980.4
Antiallergic agents	963.0	E858.1	E933.0	E950.4	E962.0	E980.4
Antianemic agents NEC	964.1	E858.2	E934.1	E950.4	E962.0	E980.4
Antiaris toxicaria	988.2	E865.4	—	E950.9	E962.1	E980.9
Antiarteriosclerotic agents	972.2	E858.3	E942.2	E950.4	E962.0	E980.4
Antiasthmatics	975.7	E858.6	E945.7	E950.4	E962.0	E980.4
Antibiotics	960.9	E856	E930.9	E950.4	E962.0	E980.4
antifungal	960.1	E856	E930.1	E950.4	E962.0	E980.4
antimycobacterial	960.6	E856	E930.6	E950.4	E962.0	E980.4
antineoplastic	960.7	E856	E930.7	E950.4	E962.0	E980.4
cephalosporin (group)	960.5	E856	E930.5	E950.4	E962.0	E980.4
chloramphenicol (group)	960.2	E856	E930.2	E950.4	E962.0	E980.4
macrolides	960.3	E856	E930.3	E950.4	E962.0	E980.4
specified NEC	960.8	E856	E930.8	E950.4	E962.0	E980.4
tetracycline (group)	960.4	E856	E930.4	E950.4	E962.0	E980.4
Anticancer agents NEC	963.1	E858.1	E933.1	E950.4	E962.0	E980.4
antibiotics	960.7	E856	E930.7	E950.4	E962.0	E980.4
Anticholinergics	971.1	E855.4	E941.1	E950.4	E962.0	E980.4
Anticholinesterase (organophosphorus) (reversible)	971.0	E855.3	E941.0	E950.4	E962.0	E980.4
Anticoagulants	964.2	E858.2	E934.2	E950.4	E962.0	E980.4
antagonists	964.5	E858.2	E934.5	E950.4	E962.0	E980.4
Anti-common cold agents NEC	975.6	E858.6	E945.6	E950.4	E962.0	E980.4
Anticonvulsants NEC	966.3	E855.0	E936.3	E950.4	E962.0	E980.4
Antidepressants	969.0	E854.0	E939.0	E950.3	E962.0	E980.3
Antidiabetic agents	962.3	E858.0	E932.3	E950.4	E962.0	E980.4
Antidiarrheal agents	973.5	E858.4	E943.5	E950.4	E962.0	E980.4
Antidiuretic hormone	962.5	E858.0	E932.5	E950.4	E962.0	E980.4
Antidotes NEC	977.2	E858.8	E947.2	E950.4	E962.0	E980.4
Antiemetic agents	963.0	E858.1	E933.0	E950.4	E962.0	E980.4
Antiepilepsy agent NEC	966.3	E855.0	E936.3	E950.4	E962.0	E980.4
Antifertility pills	962.2	E858.0	E932.2	E950.4	E962.0	E980.4
Antiflatulents	973.8	E858.4	E943.8	E950.4	E962.0	E980.4
Antifreeze	989.89	E866.8	—	E950.9	E962.1	E980.9
alcohol	980.1	E860.2	—	E950.9	E962.1	E980.9
ethylene glycol	982.8	E862.4	—	E950.9	E962.1	E980.9
Antifungals (nonmedicinal) (sprays)	989.4	E863.6	—	E950.6	E962.1	E980.7
medicinal NEC	961.9	E857	E931.9	E950.4	E962.0	E980.4
antibiotic	960.1	E856	E930.1	E950.4	E962.0	E980.4
topical	976.0	E858.7	E946.0	E950.4	E962.0	E980.4
Antigastric secretion agents	973.0	E858.4	E943.0	E950.4	E962.0	E980.4
Antihelmintics	961.6	E857	E931.6	E950.4	E962.0	E980.4
Antihemophilic factor (human)	964.7	E858.2	E934.7	E950.4	E962.0	E980.4
Antihistamine	963.0	E858.1	E933.0	E950.4	E962.0	E980.4
Antihypertensive agents NEC	972.6	E858.3	E942.6	E950.4	E962.0	E980.4
Anti-infectives NEC	961.9	E857	E931.9	E950.4	E962.0	E980.4
antibiotics	960.9	E856	E930.9	E950.4	E962.0	E980.4
specified NEC	960.8	E856	E930.8	E950.4	E962.0	E980.4
antihelmintic	961.6	E857	E931.6	E950.4	E962.0	E980.4
antimalarial	961.4	E857	E931.4	E950.4	E962.0	E980.4
antimycobacterial NEC	961.8	E857	E931.8	E950.4	E962.0	E980.4
antibiotics	960.6	E856	E930.6	E950.4	E962.0	E980.4
antiprotozoal NEC	961.5	E857	E931.5	E950.4	E962.0	—
blood	961.4	E857	E931.4	E950.4	E962.0	E980.4
antiviral	961.7	E857	E931.7	E950.4	E962.0	E980.4
arsenical	961.1	E857	E931.1	E950.4	E962.0	E980.4
ENT agents	976.6	E858.7	E946.6	E950.4	E962.0	E980.4
heavy metals NEC	961.2	E857	E931.2	E950.4	E962.0	E980.4
local	976.0	E858.7	E946.0	E950.4	E962.0	E980.4
ophthalmic preparation	976.5	E858.7	E946.5	E950.4	E962.0	E980.4
topical NEC	976.0	E858.7	E946.0	E950.4	E962.0	E980.4
Anti-inflammatory agents (topical)	976.0	E858.7	E946.0	E950.4	E962.0	E980.4
Antiknock (tetraethyl lead)	984.1	E862.1	—	E950.9	—	E980.9
Antilipemics	972.2	E858.3	E942.2	E950.4	E962.0	E980.4
Antimalarials	961.4	E857	E931.4	E950.4	E962.0	E980.4
Antimony (compounds) (vapor) NEC	985.4	E866.2	—	E950.9	E962.1	E980.9

		External Cause (E-Code)				
	Poisoning	Accident	Therapeutic Use	Suicide Attempt	Assault	Undetermined
Antimony (compounds) (vapor) — continued						
anti-infectives	961.2	E857	E931.2	E950.4	E962.0	E980.4
pesticides (vapor)	985.4	E863.4	—	E950.6	E962.2	E980.7
potassium tartrate	961.2	E857	E931.2	E950.4	E962.0	E980.4
tartrated	961.2	E857	E931.2	E950.4	E962.0	E980.4
Antimuscarinic agents	971.1	E855.4	E941.1	E950.4	E962.0	E980.4
Antimycobacterials NEC	961.8	E857	E931.8	E950.4	E962.0	E980.4
antibiotics	960.6	E856	E930.6	E950.4	E962.0	E980.4
Antineoplastic agents	963.1	E858.1	E933.1	E950.4	E962.0	E980.4
antibiotics	960.7	E856	E930.7	E950.4	E962.0	E980.4
Anti-Parkinsonism agents	966.4	E855.0	E936.4	E950.4	E962.0	E980.4
Antiphlogistics	965.69	E850.6	E935.6	E950.0	E962.0	E980.0
Antiprotozoals NEC	961.5	E857	E931.5	E950.4	E962.0	E980.4
blood	961.4	E857	E931.4	E950.4	E962.0	E980.4
Antipruritics (local)	976.1	E858.7	E946.1	E950.4	E962.0	E980.4
Antipsychotic agents NEC	969.3	E853.8	E939.3	E950.3	E962.0	E980.3
Antipyretics	965.9	E850.9	E935.9	E950.0	E962.0	E980.0
specified NEC	965.8	E850.8	E935.8	E950.0	E962.0	E980.0
Antipyrine	965.5	E850.5	E935.5	E950.0	E962.0	E980.0
Antirabies serum (equine)	979.9	E858.8	E949.9	E950.4	E962.0	E980.4
Antirheumatics	965.69	E850.6	E935.6	E950.0	E962.0	E980.0
Antiseborrheics	976.4	E858.7	E946.4	E950.4	E962.0	E980.4
Antiseptics (external) (medicinal)	976.0	E858.7	E946.0	E950.4	E962.0	E980.4
Antistine	963.0	E858.1	E933.0	E950.4	E962.0	E980.4
Antithyroid agents	962.8	E858.0	E932.8	E950.4	E962.0	E980.4
Antitoxin, any	979.9	E858.8	E949.9	E950.4	E962.0	E980.4
Antituberculars	961.8	E857	E931.8	E950.4	E962.0	E980.4
antibiotics	960.6	E856	E930.6	E950.4	E962.0	E980.4
Antitussives	975.4	E858.6	E945.4	E950.4	E962.0	E980.4
Antivaricose agents (sclerosing)	972.7	E858.3	E942.7	E950.4	E962.0	E980.4
Antivenin (crotaline) (spider-bite)	979.9	E858.8	E949.9	E950.4	E962.0	E980.4
Antivert	963.0	E858.1	E933.0	E950.4	E962.0	E980.4
Antivirals NEC	961.7	E857	E931.7	E950.4	E962.0	E980.4
Ant poisons — see Pesticides						
Antrol	989.4	E863.4	—	E950.6	E962.1	E980.7
fungicide	989.4	E863.6	—	E950.6	E962.1	E980.7
Apomorphine hydrochloride (emetic)	973.6	E858.4	E943.6	E950.4	E962.0	E980.4
Appetite depressants, central	977.0	E858.8	E947.0	E950.4	E962.0	E980.4
Apresoline	972.6	E858.3	E942.6	E950.4	E962.0	E980.4
Aprobarbital, aprobarbitone	967.0	E851	E937.0	E950.1	E962.0	E980.1
Apronalide	967.8	E852.8	E937.8	E950.2	E962.0	E980.2
Aqua fortis	983.1	E864.1	—	E950.7	E962.1	E980.6
Arachis oil (topical)	976.3	E858.7	E946.3	E950.4	E962.0	E980.4
cathartic	973.2	E858.4	E943.2	E950.4	E962.0	E980.4
Aralen	961.4	E857	E931.4	E950.4	E962.0	E980.4
Arginine salts	974.5	E858.5	E944.5	E950.4	E962.0	E980.4
Argyrol	976.0	E858.7	E946.0	E950.4	E962.0	E980.4
ENT agent	976.6	E858.7	E946.6	E950.4	E962.0	E980.4
ophthalmic preparation	976.5	E858.7	E946.5	E950.4	E962.0	E980.4
Aristocort	962.0	E858.0	E932.0	E950.4	E962.0	E980.4
ENT agent	976.6	E858.7	E946.6	E950.4	E962.0	E980.4
ophthalmic preparation	976.5	E858.7	E946.5	E950.4	E962.0	E980.4
topical NEC	976.0	E858.7	E946.0	E950.4	E962.0	E980.4
Aromatics, corrosive	983.0	E864.0	—	E950.7	E962.1	E980.6
disinfectants	983.0	E861.4	—	E950.7	E962.1	E980.6
Arsenate of lead (insecticide)	985.1	E863.4	—	E950.8	E962.1	E980.8
herbicide	985.1	E863.5	—	E950.8	E962.1	E980.8
Arsenic, arsenicals (compounds) (dust) (fumes) (vapor) NEC	985.1	E866.3	—	E950.8	E962.1	E980.8
anti-infectives	961.1	E857	E931.1	E950.4	E962.0	E980.4
pesticide (dust) (fumes)	985.1	E863.4	—	E950.8	E962.1	E980.8
Arsine (gas)	985.1	E866.3	—	E950.8	E962.1	E980.8
Arsphenamine (silver)	961.1	E857	E931.1	E950.4	E962.0	E980.4
Arsthinol	961.1	E857	E931.1	E950.4	E962.0	E980.4
Artane	971.1	E855.4	E941.1	E950.4	E962.0	E980.4
Arthropod (venomous) NEC	989.5	E905.5	—	E950.9	E962.1	E980.9
Asbestos	989.81	E866.8	—	E950.9	E962.1	E980.9
Ascaridole	961.6	E857	E931.6	E950.4	E962.0	E980.4
Ascorbic acid	963.5	E858.1	E933.5	E950.4	E962.0	E980.4
Asiaticoside	976.0	E858.7	E946.0	E950.4	E962.0	E980.4
Aspidium (oleoresin)	961.6	E857	E931.6	E950.4	E962.0	E980.4

☑ Additional Digit Required — Refer to the Tabular List for Digit Selection   ▽ Subterms under main terms may continue to next column or page

	Poisoning	Accident	Therapeutic Use	Suicide Attempt	Assault	Undeter-mined
Aspirin	965.1	E850.3	E935.3	E950.0	E962.0	E980.0
Astringents (local)	976.2	E858.7	E946.2	E950.4	E962.0	E980.4
Atabrine	961.3	E857	E931.3	E950.4	E962.0	E980.4
Ataractics	969.5	E853.8	E939.5	E950.3	E962.0	E980.3
Atonia drug, intestinal	973.3	E858.4	E943.3	E950.4	E962.0	E980.4
Atophan	974.7	E858.5	E944.7	E950.4	E962.0	E980.4
Atropine	971.1	E855.4	E941.1	E950.4	E962.0	E980.4
Attapulgite	973.5	E858.4	E943.5	E950.4	E962.0	E980.4
Attenuvax	979.4	E858.8	E949.4	E950.4	E962.0	E980.4
Aureomycin	960.4	E856	E930.4	E950.4	E962.0	E980.4
ophthalmic preparation	976.5	E858.7	E946.5	E950.4	E962.0	E980.4
topical NEC	976.0	E858.7	E946.0	E950.4	E962.0	E980.4
Aurothioglucose	965.69	E850.6	E935.6	E950.0	E962.0	E980.0
Aurothioglycanide	965.69	E850.6	E935.6	E950.0	E962.0	E980.0
Aurothiomalate	965.69	E850.6	E935.6	E950.0	E962.0	E980.0
Automobile fuel	981	E862.1	—	E950.9	E962.1	E980.9
Autonomic nervous system agents NEC	971.9	E855.9	E941.9	E950.4	E962.0	E980.4
Avlosulfon	961.8	E857	E931.8	E950.4	E962.0	E980.4
Avomine	967.8	E852.8	E937.8	E950.2	E962.0	E980.2
Azacyclonol	969.5	E853.8	E939.5	E950.3	E962.0	E980.3
Azapetine	971.3	E855.6	E941.3	E950.4	E962.0	E980.4
Azaribine	963.1	E858.1	E933.1	E950.4	E962.0	E980.4
Azaserine	960.7	E856	E930.7	E950.4	E962.0	E980.4
Azathioprine	963.1	E858.1	E933.1	E950.4	E962.0	E980.4
Azosulfamide	961.0	E857	E931.0	E950.4	E962.0	E980.4
Azulfidine	961.0	E857	E931.0	E950.4	E962.0	E980.4
Azuresin	977.8	E858.8	E947.8	E950.4	E962.0	E980.4
Bacimycin	976.0	E858.7	E946.0	E950.4	E962.0	E980.4
ophthalmic preparation	976.5	E858.7	E946.5	E950.4	E962.0	E980.4
Bacitracin	960.8	E856	E930.8	E950.4	E962.0	E980.4
ENT agent	976.6	E858.7	E946.6	E950.4	E962.0	E980.4
ophthalmic preparation	976.5	E858.7	E946.5	E950.4	E962.0	E980.4
topical NEC	976.0	E858.7	E946.0	E950.4	E962.0	E980.4
Baking soda	963.3	E858.1	E933.3	E950.4	E962.0	E980.4
BAL	963.8	E858.1	E933.8	E950.4	E962.0	E980.4
Bamethan (sulfate)	972.5	E858.3	E942.5	E950.4	E962.0	E980.4
Bamipine	963.0	E858.1	E933.0	E950.4	E962.0	E980.4
Baneberry	988.2	E865.4	—	E950.9	E962.1	E980.9
Banewort	988.2	E865.4	—	E950.9	E962.1	E980.9
Barbenyl	967.0	E851	E937.0	E950.1	E962.0	E980.1
Barbital, barbitone	967.0	E851	E937.0	E950.1	E962.0	E980.1
Barbiturates, barbituric acid	967.0	E851	E937.0	E950.1	E962.0	E980.1
anesthetic (intravenous)	968.3	E855.1	E938.3	E950.4	E962.0	E980.4
Barium (carbonate) (chloride) (sulfate)	985.8	E866.4	—	E950.9	E962.1	E980.9
diagnostic agent	977.8	E858.8	E947.8	E950.4	E962.0	E980.4
pesticide	985.8	E863.4	—	E950.6	E962.1	E980.7
rodenticide	985.8	E863.7	—	E950.6	E962.1	E980.7
Barrier cream	976.3	E858.7	E946.3	E950.4	E962.0	E980.4
Battery acid or fluid	983.1	E864.1	—	E950.7	E962.1	E980.6
Bay rum	980.8	E860.8	—	E950.9	E962.1	E980.9
BCG vaccine	978.0	E858.8	E948.0	E950.4	E962.0	E980.4
Bearsfoot	988.2	E865.4	—	E950.9	E962.1	E980.9
Beclamide	966.3	E855.0	E936.3	E950.4	E962.0	E980.4
Bee (sting) (venom)	989.5	E905.3	—	E950.9	E962.1	E980.9
Belladonna (alkaloids)	971.1	E855.4	E941.1	E950.4	E962.0	E980.4
Bemegride	970.0	E854.3	E940.0	E950.4	E962.0	E980.4
Benactyzine	969.8	E855.8	E939.8	E950.3	E962.0	E980.3
Benadryl	963.0	E858.1	E933.0	E950.4	E962.0	E980.4
Bendrofluazide	974.3	E858.5	E944.3	E950.4	E962.0	E980.4
Bendroflumethiazide	974.3	E858.5	E944.3	E950.4	E962.0	E980.4
Benemid	974.7	E858.5	E944.7	E950.4	E962.0	E980.4
Benethamine penicillin G	960.0	E856	E930.0	E950.4	E962.0	E980.4
Benisone	976.0	E858.7	E946.0	E950.4	E962.0	E980.4
Benoquin	976.8	E858.7	E946.8	E950.4	E962.0	E980.4
Benoxinate	968.5	E855.2	E938.5	E950.4	E962.0	E980.4
Bentonite	976.3	E858.7	E946.3	E950.4	E962.0	E980.4
Benzalkonium (chloride)	976.0	E858.7	E946.0	E950.4	E962.0	E980.4
ophthalmic preparation	976.5	E858.7	E946.5	E950.4	E962.0	E980.4
Benzamidosalicylate (calcium)	961.8	E857	E931.8	E950.4	E962.0	E980.4
Benzathine penicillin	960.0	E856	E930.0	E950.4	E962.0	E980.4
Benzcarbimine	963.1	E858.1	E933.1	E950.4	E962.0	E980.4
Benzedrex	971.2	E855.5	E941.2	E950.4	E962.0	E980.4
Benzedrine (amphetamine)	969.7	E854.2	E939.7	E950.3	E962.0	E980.3
Benzene (acetyl) (dimethyl) (methyl) (solvent) (vapor)	982.0	E862.4	—	E950.9	E962.1	E980.9
hexachloride (gamma) (insecticide) (vapor)	989.2	E863.0	—	E950.6	E962.1	E980.7
Benzethonium	976.0	E858.7	E946.0	E950.4	E962.0	E980.4
Benzhexol (chloride)	966.4	E855.0	E936.4	E950.4	E962.0	E980.4
Benzilonium	971.1	E855.4	E941.1	E950.4	E962.0	E980.4
Benzin(e) — see Ligroin						
Benziodarone	972.4	E858.3	E942.4	E950.4	E962.0	E980.4
Benzocaine	968.5	E855.2	E938.5	E950.4	E962.0	E980.4
Benzodiapin	969.4	E853.2	E939.4	E950.3	E962.0	E980.3
Benzodiazepines (tranquilizers) NEC	969.4	E853.2	E939.4	E950.3	E962.0	E980.3
Benzoic acid (with salicylic acid) (anti-infective)	976.0	E858.7	E946.0	E950.4	E962.0	E980.4
Benzoin	976.3	E858.7	E946.3	E950.4	E962.0	E980.4
Benzol (vapor)	982.0	E862.4	—	E950.9	E962.1	E980.9
Benzomorphan	965.09	E850.2	E935.2	E950.0	E962.0	E980.0
Benzonatate	975.4	E858.6	E945.4	E950.4	E962.0	E980.4
Benzothiadiazides	974.3	E858.5	E944.3	E950.4	E962.0	E980.4
Benzoylpas	961.8	E857	E931.8	E950.4	E962.0	E980.4
Benzperidol	969.5	E853.8	E939.5	E950.3	E962.0	E980.3
Benzphetamine	977.0	E858.8	E947.0	E950.4	E962.0	E980.4
Benzpyrinium	971.0	E855.3	E941.0	E950.4	E962.0	E980.4
Benzquinamide	963.0	E858.1	E933.0	E950.4	E962.0	E980.4
Benzthiazide	974.3	E858.5	E944.3	E950.4	E962.0	E980.4
Benztropine	971.1	E855.4	E941.1	E950.4	E962.0	E980.4
Benzyl						
acetate	982.8	E862.4	—	E950.9	E962.1	E980.9
benzoate (anti-infective)	976.0	E858.7	E946.0	E950.4	E962.0	E980.4
morphine	965.09	E850.2	E935.2	E950.0	E962.0	E980.0
penicillin	960.0	E856	E930.0	E950.4	E962.0	E980.4
Bephenium hydroxynapthoate	961.6	E857	E931.6	E950.4	E962.0	E980.4
Bergamot oil	989.89	E866.8	—	E950.9	E962.1	E980.9
Berries, poisonous	988.2	E865.3	—	E950.9	E962.1	E980.9
Beryllium (compounds) (fumes)	985.3	E866.4	—	E950.9	E962.1	E980.9
Beta-carotene	976.3	E858.7	E946.3	E950.4	E962.0	E980.4
Beta-Chlor	967.1	E852.0	E937.1	E950.2	E962.0	E980.2
Betamethasone	962.0	E858.0	E932.0	E950.4	E962.0	E980.4
topical	976.0	E858.7	E946.0	E950.4	E962.0	E980.4
Betazole	977.8	E858.8	E947.8	E950.4	E962.0	E980.4
Bethanechol	971.0	E855.3	E941.0	E950.4	E962.0	E980.4
Bethanidine	972.6	E858.3	E942.6	E950.4	E962.0	E980.4
Betula oil	976.3	E858.7	E946.3	E950.4	E962.0	E980.4
Bhang	969.6	E854.1	E939.6	E950.3	E962.0	E980.3
Bialamicol	961.5	E857	E931.5	E950.4	E962.0	E980.4
Bichloride of mercury — see Mercury, chloride						
Bichromates (calcium) (crystals) (potassium) (sodium)	983.9	E864.3	—	E950.7	E962.1	E980.6
fumes	987.8	E869.8	—	E952.8	E962.2	E982.8
Biguanide derivatives, oral	962.3	E858.0	E932.3	E950.4	E962.0	E980.4
Biligrafin	977.8	E858.8	E947.8	E950.4	E962.0	E980.4
Bilopaque	977.8	E858.8	E947.8	E950.4	E962.0	E980.4
Bioflavonoids	972.8	E858.3	E942.8	E950.4	E962.0	E980.4
Biological substance NEC	979.9	E858.8	E949.9	E950.4	E962.0	E980.4
Biperiden	966.4	E855.0	E936.4	E950.4	E962.0	E980.4
Bisacodyl	973.1	E858.4	E943.1	E950.4	E962.0	E980.4
Bishydroxycoumarin	964.2	E858.2	E934.2	E950.4	E962.0	E980.4
Bismarsen	961.1	E857	E931.1	E950.4	E962.0	E980.4
Bismuth (compounds) NEC	985.8	E866.4	—	E950.9	E962.1	E980.9
anti-infectives	961.2	E857	E931.2	E950.4	E962.0	E980.4
subcarbonate	973.5	E858.4	E943.5	E950.4	E962.0	E980.4
sulfarsphenamine	961.1	E857	E931.1	E950.4	E962.0	E980.4
Bithionol	961.6	E857	E931.6	E950.4	E962.0	E980.4
Bitter almond oil	989.0	E866.8	—	E950.9	E962.1	E980.9
Bittersweet	988.2	E865.4	—	E950.9	E962.1	E930.9
Black						
flag	989.4	E863.4	—	E950.6	E962.1	E980.7
henbane	988.2	E865.4	—	E950.9	E962.1	E980.9
leaf (40)	989.4	E863.4	—	E950.6	E962.1	E980.7
widow spider (bite)	989.5	E905.1	—	E950.9	E962.1	E980.9
antivenin	979.9	E858.8	E949.9	E950.4	E962.0	E980.4
Blast furnace gas (carbon monoxide from)	986	E868.8	—	E952.1	E962.2	E982.1
Bleach NEC	983.9	E864.3	—	E950.7	E962.1	E980.6
Bleaching solutions	983.9	E864.3	—	E950.7	E962.1	E980.6
Bleomycin (sulfate)	960.7	E856	E930.7	E950.4	E962.0	E980.4
Blockain	968.9	E855.2	E938.9	E950.4	E962.0	E980.4
infiltration (subcutaneous)	968.5	E855.2	E938.5	E950.4	E962.0	E980.4

	External Cause (E-Code)					
	Poisoning	Accident	Therapeutic Use	Suicide Attempt	Assault	Undeter-mined
Blockain — *continued*						
nerve block (peripheral)						
(plexus)	968.6	E855.2	E938.6	E950.4	E962.0	E980.4
topical (surface)	968.5	E855.2	E938.5	E950.4	E962.0	E980.4
Blood (derivatives) (natural)						
(plasma) (whole)	964.7	E858.2	E934.7	E950.4	E962.0	E980.4
affecting agent	964.9	E858.2	E934.9	E950.4	E962.0	E980.4
specified NEC	964.8	E858.2	E934.8	E950.4	E962.0	E980.4
substitute						
(macromolecular)	964.8	E858.2	E934.8	E950.4	E962.0	E980.4
Blue velvet	965.09	E850.2	E935.2	E950.0	E962.0	E980.0
Bone meal	989.89	E866.5	—	E950.9	E962.1	E980.9
Bonine	963.0	E858.1	E933.0	E950.4	E962.0	E980.4
Boracic acid	976.0	E858.7	E946.0	E950.4	E962.0	E980.4
ENT agent	976.6	E858.7	E946.6	E950.4	E962.0	E980.4
ophthalmic preparation	976.5	E858.7	E946.5	E950.4	E962.0	E980.4
Borate (cleanser) (sodium)	989.6	E861.3	—	E950.9	E962.1	E980.9
Borax (cleanser)	989.6	E861.3	—	E950.9	E962.1	E980.9
Boric acid	976.0	E858.7	E946.0	E950.4	E962.0	E980.4
ENT agent	976.6	E858.7	E946.6	E950.4	E962.0	E980.4
ophthalmic preparation	976.5	E858.7	E946.5	E950.4	E962.0	E980.4
Boron hydride NEC	989.89	E866.8	—	E950.9	E962.1	E980.9
fumes or gas	987.8	E869.8	—	E952.8	E962.2	E982.8
Botox	975.3	E858.6	E945.3	E950.4	E962.0	E980.4
Brake fluid vapor	987.8	E869.8	—	E952.8	E962.2	E982.8
Brass (compounds) (fumes)	985.8	E866.4	—	E950.9	E962.1	E980.9
Brasso	981	E861.3	—	E950.9	E962.1	E980.9
Bretylium (tosylate)	972.6	E858.3	E942.6	E950.4	E962.0	E980.4
Brevital (sodium)	968.3	E855.1	E938.3	E950.4	E962.0	E980.4
British antilewisite	963.8	E858.1	E933.8	E950.4	E962.0	E980.4
Bromal (hydrate)	967.3	E852.2	E937.3	E950.2	E962.0	E980.2
Bromelains	963.4	E858.1	E933.4	E950.4	E962.0	E980.4
Bromides NEC	967.3	E852.2	E937.3	E950.2	E962.0	E980.2
Bromine (vapor)	987.8	E869.8	—	E952.8	E962.2	E982.8
compounds (medicinal)	967.3	E852.2	E937.3	E950.2	E962.0	E980.2
Bromisovalum	967.3	E852.2	E937.3	E950.2	E962.0	E980.2
Bromobenzyl cyanide	987.5	E869.3	—	E952.8	E962.2	E982.8
Bromodiphenhydramine	963.0	E858.1	E933.0	E950.4	E962.0	E980.4
Bromoform	967.3	E852.2	E937.3	E950.2	E962.0	E980.2
Bromophenol blue						
reagent	977.8	E858.8	E947.8	E950.4	E962.0	E980.4
Bromosalicylhydroxamic						
acid	961.8	E857	E931.8	E950.4	E962.0	E980.4
Bromo-seltzer	965.4	E850.4	E935.4	E950.0	E962.0	E980.0
Brompheniramine	963.0	E858.1	E933.0	E950.4	E962.0	E980.4
Bromural	967.3	E852.2	E937.3	E950.2	E962.0	E980.2
Brown spider (bite) (venom)	989.5	E905.1	—	E950.9	E962.1	E980.9
Brucia	988.2	E865.3	—	E950.9	E962.1	E980.9
Brucine	989.1	E863.7	—	E950.6	E962.1	E980.7
Brunswick green — *see* Copper						
Bruten — *see* Ibuprofen						
Bryonia (alba) (dioica)	988.2	E865.4	—	E950.9	E962.1	E980.9
Buclizine	969.5	E853.8	E939.5	E950.3	E962.0	E980.3
Bufferin	965.1	E850.3	E935.3	E950.0	E962.0	E980.0
Bufotenine	969.6	E854.1	E939.6	E950.3	E962.0	E980.3
Buphenine	971.2	E855.5	E941.2	E950.4	E962.0	E980.4
Bupivacaine	968.9	E855.2	E938.9	E950.4	E962.0	E980.4
infiltration (subcutaneous)	968.5	E855.2	E938.5	E950.4	E962.0	E980.4
nerve block (peripheral)						
(plexus)	968.6	E855.2	E938.6	E950.4	E962.0	E980.4
Busulfan	963.1	E858.1	E933.1	E950.4	E962.0	E980.4
Butabarbital (sodium)	967.0	E851	E937.0	E950.1	E962.0	E980.1
Butabarbitone	967.0	E851	E937.0	E950.1	E962.0	E980.1
Butabarpal	967.0	E851	E937.0	E950.1	E962.0	E980.1
Butacaine	968.5	E855.2	E938.5	E950.4	E962.0	E980.4
Butallylonal	967.0	E851	E937.0	E950.1	E962.0	E980.1
Butane (distributed in mobile						
container)	987.0	E868.0	—	E951.1	E962.2	E981.1
distributed through pipes	987.0	E867	—	E951.0	E962.2	E981.0
incomplete combustion of — *see*						
Carbon monoxide, butane						
Butanol	980.3	E860.4	—	E950.9	E962.1	E980.9
Butanone	982.8	E862.4	—	E950.9	E962.1	E980.9
Butaperazine	969.1	E853.0	E939.1	E950.3	E962.0	E980.3
Butazolidin	965.5	E850.5	E935.5	E950.0	E962.0	E980.0
Butethal	967.0	E851	E937.0	E950.1	E962.0	E980.1
Butethamate	971.1	E855.4	E941.1	E950.4	E962.0	E980.4
Buthalitone (sodium)	968.3	E855.1	E938.3	E950.4	E962.0	E980.4
Butisol (sodium)	967.0	E851	E937.0	E950.1	E962.0	E980.1
Butobarbital,						
butobarbitone	967.0	E851	E937.0	E950.1	E962.0	E980.1
Butriptyline	969.0	E854.0	E939.0	E950.3	E962.0	E980.3
Buttercups	988.2	E865.4	—	E950.9	E962.1	E980.9
Butter of antimony — *see*						
Antimony						
Butyl						
acetate (secondary)	982.8	E862.4	—	E950.9	E962.1	E980.9
alcohol	980.3	E860.4	—	E950.9	E962.1	E980.9
carbinol	980.8	E860.8	—	E950.9	E962.1	E980.9
carbitol	982.8	E862.4	—	E950.9	E962.1	E980.9
cellosolve	982.8	E862.4	—	E950.9	E962.1	E980.9
chloral (hydrate)	967.1	E852.0	E937.1	E950.2	E962.0	E980.2
formate	982.8	E862.4	—	E950.9	E962.1	E980.9
scopolammonium bromide	971.1	E855.4	E941.1	E950.4	E962.0	E980.4
Butyn	968.5	E855.2	E938.5	E950.4	E962.0	E980.4
Butyrophenone (-based						
tranquilizers)	969.2	E853.1	E939.2	E950.3	E962.0	E980.3
Cacodyl, cacodylic acid — *see*						
Arsenic						
Cactinomycin	960.7	E856	E930.7	E950.4	E962.0	E980.4
Cade oil (chloride) (compounds)	976.4	E858.7	E946.4	E950.4	E962.0	E980.4
Cadmium (chloride) (compounds)						
(dust) (fumes) (oxide)	985.5	E866.4	—	E950.9	E962.1	E980.9
sulfide (medicinal) NEC	976.4	E858.7	E946.4	E950.4	E962.0	E980.4
Caffeine	969.7	E854.2	E939.7	E950.3	E962.0	E980.3
Calabar bean	988.2	E865.4	—	E950.9	E962.1	E980.9
Caladium seguinium	988.2	E865.4	—	E950.9	E962.1	E980.9
Calamine (liniment) (lotion)	976.3	E858.7	E946.3	E950.4	E962.0	E980.4
Calciferol	963.5	E858.1	E933.5	E950.4	E962.0	E980.4
Calcium (salts) NEC	974.5	E858.5	E944.5	E950.4	E962.0	E980.4
acetylsalicylate	965.1	E850.3	E935.3	E950.0	E962.0	E980.0
benzamidosalicylate	961.8	E857	E931.8	E950.4	E962.0	E980.4
carbaspirin	965.1	E850.3	E935.3	E950.0	E962.0	E980.0
carbimide (citrated)	977.3	E858.8	E947.3	E950.4	E962.0	E980.4
carbonate (antacid)	973.0	E858.4	E943.0	E950.4	E962.0	E980.4
cyanide (citrated)	977.3	E858.8	E947.3	E950.4	E962.0	E980.4
dioctyl sulfosuccinate	973.2	E858.4	E943.2	E950.4	E962.0	E980.4
disodium edathamil	963.8	E858.1	E933.8	E950.4	E962.0	E980.4
disodium edetate	963.8	E858.1	E933.8	E950.4	E962.0	E980.4
EDTA	963.8	E858.1	E933.8	E950.4	E962.0	E980.4
hydrate, hydroxide	983.2	E864.2	—	E950.7	E962.1	E980.6
mandelate	961.9	E857	E931.9	E950.4	E962.0	E980.4
oxide	983.2	E864.2	—	E950.7	E962.1	E980.6
Calomel — *see* Mercury, chloride						
Caloric agents NEC	974.5	E858.5	E944.5	E950.4	E962.0	E980.4
Calusterone	963.1	E858.1	E933.1	E950.4	E962.0	E980.4
Camoquin	961.4	E857	E931.4	E950.4	E962.0	E980.4
Camphor (oil)	976.1	E858.7	E946.1	E950.4	E962.0	E980.4
Candeptin	976.0	E858.7	E946.0	E950.4	E962.0	E980.4
Candicidin	976.0	E858.7	E946.0	E950.4	E962.0	E980.4
Cannabinols	969.6	E854.1	E939.6	E950.3	E962.0	E980.3
Cannabis (derivatives) (indica)						
(sativa)	969.6	E854.1	E939.6	E950.3	E962.0	E980.3
Canned heat	980.1	E860.2	—	E950.9	E962.1	E980.9
Cantharides, cantharidin,						
cantharis	976.8	E858.7	E946.8	E950.4	E962.0	E980.4
Capillary agents	972.8	E858.3	E942.8	E950.4	E962.0	E980.4
Capreomycin	960.6	E856	E930.6	E950.4	E962.0	E980.4
Captodiame,						
captodiamine	969.5	E853.8	E939.5	E950.3	E962.0	E980.3
Caramiphen (hydrochloride)	971.1	E855.4	E941.1	E950.4	E962.0	E980.4
Carbachol	971.0	E855.3	E941.0	E950.4	E962.0	E980.4
Carbacrylamine resins	974.5	E858.5	E944.5	E950.4	E962.0	E980.4
Carbamate (sedative)	967.8	E852.8	E937.8	E950.2	E962.0	E980.2
herbicide	989.3	E863.5	—	E950.6	E962.1	E980.7
insecticide	989.3	E863.2	—	E950.6	E962.1	E980.7
Carbamazepine	966.3	E855.0	E936.3	E950.4	E962.0	E980.4
Carbamic esters	967.8	E852.8	E937.8	E950.2	E962.0	E980.2
Carbamide	974.4	E858.5	E944.4	E950.4	E962.0	E980.4
topical	976.8	E858.7	E946.8	E950.4	E962.0	E980.4
Carbamylcholine chloride	971.0	E855.3	E941.0	E950.4	E962.0	E980.4
Carbarsone	961.1	E857	E931.1	E950.4	E962.0	E980.4
Carbaryl	989.3	E863.2	—	E950.6	E962.1	E980.7
Carbaspirin	965.1	E850.3	E935.3	E950.0	E962.0	E980.0
Carbazochrome	972.8	E858.3	E942.8	E950.4	E962.0	E980.4
Carbenicillin	960.0	E856	E930.0	E950.4	E962.0	E980.4
Carbenoxolone	973.8	E858.4	E943.8	E950.4	E962.0	E980.4
Carbetapentane	975.4	E858.6	E945.4	E950.4	E962.0	E980.4
Carbimazole	962.8	E858.0	E932.8	E950.4	E962.0	E980.4
Carbinol	980.1	E860.2	—	E950.9	E962.1	E980.9
Carbinoxamine	963.0	E858.1	E933.0	E950.4	E962.0	E980.4
Carbitol	982.8	E862.4	—	E950.9	E962.1	E980.9

☑ Additional Digit Required — Refer to the Tabular List for Digit Selection

Subterms under main terms may continue to next column or page

	Poisoning	Accident	Therapeutic Use	Suicide Attempt	Assault	Undetermined
Carbocaine	968.9	E855.2	E938.9	E950.4	E962.0	E980.4
infiltration (subcutaneous)	968.5	E855.2	E938.5	E950.4	E962.0	E980.4
nerve block (peripheral) (plexus)	968.6	E855.2	E938.6	E950.4	E962.0	E980.4
topical (surface)	968.5	E855.2	E938.5	E950.4	E962.0	E980.4
Carbol-fuchsin solution	976.0	E858.7	E946.0	E950.4	E962.0	E980.4
Carbolic acid — see also Phenol)	983.0	E864.0	—	E950.7	E962.1	E980.6
Carbomycin	960.8	E856	E930.8	E950.4	E962.0	E980.4
Carbon						
bisulfide (liquid) (vapor)	982.2	E862.4	—	E950.9	E962.1	E980.9
dioxide (gas)	987.8	E869.8	—	E952.8	E962.2	E982.8
disulfide (liquid) (vapor)	982.2	E862.4	—	E950.9	E962.1	E980.9
monoxide (from incomplete combustion of) (in) NEC	986	E868.9	—	E952.1	E962.2	E982.1
blast furnace gas	986	E868.8	—	E952.1	E962.2	E982.1
butane (distributed in mobile container)	986	E868.0	—	E951.1	E962.2	E981.1
distributed through pipes	986	E867	—	E951.0	E962.2	E981.0
charcoal fumes	986	E868.3	—	E952.1	E962.2	E982.1
coal						
gas (piped)	986	E867	—	E951.0	E962.2	E981.0
solid (in domestic stoves, fireplaces)	986	E868.3	—	E952.1	E962.2	E982.1
coke (in domestic stoves, fireplaces)	986	E868.3	—	E952.1	E962.2	E982.1
exhaust gas (motor) not in transit	986	E868.2	—	E952.0	E962.2	E982.0
combustion engine, any not in watercraft	986	E868.2	—	E952.0	E962.2	E982.0
farm tractor, not in transit	986	E868.2	—	E952.0	E962.2	E982.0
gas engine	986	E868.2	—	E952.0	E962.2	E982.0
motor pump	986	E868.2	—	E952.0	E962.2	E982.0
motor vehicle, not in transit	986	E868.2	—	E952.0	E962.2	E982.0
fuel (in domestic use)	986	E868.3	—	E952.1	E962.2	E982.1
gas (piped)	986	E867	—	E951.0	E962.2	E981.0
in mobile container	986	E868.0	—	E951.1	E962.2	E981.1
utility	986	E868.1	—	E951.8	E962.2	E981.8
in mobile container	986	E868.0	—	E951.1	E962.2	E981.1
piped (natural)	986	E867	—	E951.0	E962.2	E981.0
illuminating gas	986	E868.1	—	E951.8	E962.2	E981.8
industrial fuels or gases, any	986	E868.8	—	E952.1	E962.2	E982.1
kerosene (in domestic stoves, fireplaces)	986	E868.3	—	E952.1	E962.2	E982.1
kiln gas or vapor	986	E868.8	—	E952.1	E962.2	E982.1
motor exhaust gas, not in transit	986	E868.2	—	E952.0	E962.2	E982.0
piped gas (manufactured) (natural)	986	E867	—	E951.0	E962.2	E981.0
producer gas	986	E868.8	—	E952.1	E962.2	E982.1
propane (distributed in mobile container)	986	E868.0	—	E951.1	E962.2	E981.1
distributed through pipes	986	E867	—	E951.0	E962.2	E981.0
specified source NEC	986	E868.8	—	E952.1	E962.2	E982.1
stove gas	986	E868.1	—	E951.8	E962.2	E981.8
piped	986	E867	—	E951.0	E962.2	E981.0
utility gas	986	E868.1	—	E951.8	E962.2	E981.8
piped	986	E867	—	E951.0	E962.2	E981.0
water gas	986	E868.1	—	E951.8	E962.2	E981.8
wood (in domestic stoves, fireplaces)	986	E868.3	—	E952.1	E962.2	E982.1
tetrachloride (vapor) NEC	987.8	E869.8	—	E952.8	E962.2	E982.8
liquid (cleansing agent) NEC	982.1	E861.3	—	E950.9	E962.1	E980.9
solvent	982.1	E862.4	—	E950.9	E962.1	E980.9
Carbonic acid (gas)	987.8	E869.8	—	E952.8	E962.2	E982.8
anhydrase inhibitors	974.2	E858.5	E944.2	E950.4	E962.0	E980.4
Carbowax	976.3	E858.7	E946.3	E950.4	E962.0	E980.4
Carbrital	967.0	E851	E937.0	E950.1	E962.0	E980.1
Carbromal (derivatives)	967.3	E852.2	E937.3	E950.2	E962.0	E980.2
Cardiac						
depressants	972.0	E858.3	E942.0	E950.4	E962.0	E980.4
rhythm regulators	972.0	E858.3	E942.0	E950.4	E962.0	E980.4
Cardiografin	977.8	E858.8	E947.8	E950.4	E962.0	E980.4
Cardio-green	977.8	E858.8	E947.8	E950.4	E962.0	E980.4
Cardiotonic glycosides	972.1	E858.3	E942.1	E950.4	E962.0	E980.4

	Poisoning	Accident	Therapeutic Use	Suicide Attempt	Assault	Undetermined
Cardiovascular agents NEC	972.9	E858.3	E942.9	E950.4	E962.0	E980.4
Cardrase	974.2	E858.5	E944.2	E950.4	E962.0	E980.4
Carfusin	976.0	E858.7	E946.0	E950.4	E962.0	E980.4
Carisoprodol	968.0	E855.1	E938.0	E950.4	E962.0	E980.4
Carmustine	963.1	E858.1	E933.1	E950.4	E962.0	E980.4
Carotene	963.5	E858.1	E933.5	E950.4	E962.0	E980.4
Carphenazine (maleate)	969.1	E853.0	E939.1	E950.3	E962.0	E980.3
Carter's Little Pills	973.1	E858.4	E943.1	E950.4	E962.0	E980.4
Cascara (sagrada)	973.1	E858.4	E943.1	E950.4	E962.0	E980.4
Cassava	988.2	E865.4	—	E950.9	E962.1	E980.9
Castellani's paint	976.0	E858.7	E946.0	E950.4	E962.0	E980.4
Castor						
bean	988.2	E865.3	—	E950.9	E962.1	E980.9
oil	973.1	E858.4	E943.1	E950.4	E962.0	E980.4
Caterpillar (sting)	989.5	E905.5	—	E950.9	E962.1	E980.9
Catha (edulis)	970.8	E854.3	E940.8	E950.4	E962.0	E980.4
Cathartics NEC	973.3	E858.4	E943.3	E950.4	E962.0	E980.4
contact	973.1	E858.4	E943.1	E950.4	E962.0	E980.4
emollient	973.2	E858.4	E943.2	E950.4	E962.0	E980.4
intestinal irritants	973.1	E858.4	E943.1	E950.4	E962.0	E980.4
saline	973.3	E858.4	E943.3	E950.4	E962.0	E980.4
Cathomycin	960.8	E856	E930.8	E950.4	E962.0	E980.4
Caustic(s)	983.9	E864.4	—	E950.7	E962.1	E980.6
alkali	983.2	E864.2	—	E950.7	E962.1	E980.6
hydroxide	983.2	E864.2	—	E950.7	E962.1	E980.6
potash	983.2	E864.2	—	E950.7	E962.1	E980.6
soda	983.2	E864.2	—	E950.7	E962.1	E980.6
specified NEC	983.9	E864.3	—	E950.7	E962.1	E980.6
Ceepryn	976.0	E858.7	E946.0	E950.4	E962.0	E980.4
ENT agent	976.6	E858.7	E946.6	E950.4	E962.0	E980.4
lozenges	976.6	E858.7	E946.6	E950.4	E962.0	E980.4
Celestone	962.0	E858.0	E932.0	E950.4	E962.0	E980.4
topical	976.0	E858.7	E946.0	E950.4	E962.0	E980.4
Cellosolve	982.8	E862.4	—	E950.9	E962.1	E980.9
Cell stimulants and proliferants	976.8	E858.7	E946.8	E950.4	E962.0	E980.4
Cellulose derivatives, cathartic	973.3	E858.4	E943.3	E950.4	E962.0	E980.4
nitrates (topical)	976.3	E858.7	E946.3	E950.4	E962.0	E980.4
Centipede (bite)	989.5	E905.4	—	E950.9	E962.1	E980.9
Central nervous system						
depressants	968.4	E855.1	E938.4	E950.4	E962.0	E980.4
anesthetic (general) NEC	968.4	E855.1	E938.4	E950.4	E962.0	E980.4
gases NEC	968.2	E855.1	E938.2	E950.4	E962.0	E980.4
intravenous	968.3	E855.1	E938.3	E950.4	E962.0	E980.4
barbiturates	967.0	E851	E937.0	E950.1	E962.0	E980.1
bromides	967.3	E852.2	E937.3	E950.2	E962.0	E980.2
cannabis sativa	969.6	E854.1	E939.6	E950.3	E962.0	E980.3
chloral hydrate	967.1	E852.0	E937.1	E950.2	E962.0	E980.2
hallucinogenics	969.6	E854.1	E939.6	E950.3	E962.0	E980.3
hypnotics	967.9	E852.9	E937.9	E950.2	E962.0	E980.2
specified NEC	967.8	E852.8	E937.8	E950.2	E962.0	E980.2
muscle relaxants	968.0	E855.1	E938.0	E950.4	E962.0	E980.4
paraldehyde	967.2	E852.1	E937.2	E950.2	E962.0	E980.2
sedatives	967.9	E852.9	E937.9	E950.2	E962.0	E980.2
mixed NEC	967.6	E852.5	E937.6	E950.2	E962.0	E980.2
specified NEC	967.8	E852.8	E937.8	E950.2	E962.0	E980.2
muscle-tone depressants	—	—	—	—	—	E980.4
stimulants	970.9	E854.3	E940.9	E950.4	E962.0	E980.4
amphetamines	969.7	E854.2	E939.7	E950.3	E962.0	E980.3
analeptics	970.0	E854.3	E940.0	E950.4	E962.0	E980.4
antidepressants	969.0	E854.0	E939.0	E950.3	E962.0	E980.3
opiate antagonists	970.1	E854.3	E940.1	E950.4	E962.0	E980.4
specified NEC	970.8	E854.3	E940.8	E950.4	E962.0	E980.4
Cephalexin	960.5	E856	E930.5	E950.4	E962.0	E980.4
Cephaloglycin	960.5	E856	E930.5	E950.4	E962.0	E980.4
Cephaloridine	960.5	E856	E930.5	E950.4	E962.0	E980.4
Cephalosporins NEC	960.5	E856	E930.5	E950.4	E962.0	E980.4
N (adicillin)	960.0	E856	E930.0	E950.4	E962.0	E980.4
Cephalothin (sodium)	960.5	E856	E930.5	E950.4	E962.0	E980.4
Cerbera (odallam)	988.2	E865.4	—	E950.9	E962.1	E980.9
Cerberin	972.1	E858.3	E942.1	E950.4	E962.0	E980.4
Cerebral stimulants	970.9	E854.3	E940.9	E950.4	E962.0	E980.4
psychotherapeutic	969.7	E854.2	E939.7	E950.3	E962.0	E980.3
specified NEC	970.8	E854.3	E940.8	E950.4	E962.0	E980.4
Cetalkonium (chloride)	976.0	E858.7	E946.0	E950.4	E962.0	E980.4
Cetoxime	963.0	E858.1	E933.0	E950.4	E962.0	E980.4
Cetrimide	976.2	E858.7	E946.2	E950.4	E962.0	E980.4
Cetylpyridinium	976.0	E858.7	E946.0	E950.4	E962.0	E980.4
ENT agent	976.6	E858.7	E946.6	E950.4	E962.0	E980.4

☑ Additional Digit Required — Refer to the Tabular List for Digit Selection

Subterms under main terms may continue to next column or page

	Poisoning	Accident	Therapeutic Use	Suicide Attempt	Assault	Undetermined
Cetylpyridinium — *continued*						
lozenges	976.6	E858.7	E946.6	E950.4	E962.0	E980.4
Cevadilla — *see Sabadilla*						
Cevitamic acid	963.5	E858.1	E933.5	E950.4	E962.0	E980.4
Chalk, precipitated	973.0	E858.4	E943.0	E950.4	E962.0	E980.4
Charcoal						
fumes (carbon monoxide)	986	E868.3	—	E952.1	E962.2	E982.1
industrial	986	E868.8	—	E952.1	E962.2	E982.1
medicinal (activated)	973.0	E858.4	E943.0	E950.4	E962.0	E980.4
Chelating agents NEC	977.2	E858.8	E947.2	E950.4	E962.0	E980.4
Chelidonium majus	988.2	E865.4	—	E950.9	E962.1	E980.9
Chemical substance	989.9	E866.9	—	E950.9	E962.1	E980.9
specified NEC	989.89	E866.8	—	E950.9	E962.1	E980.9
Chemotherapy, antineoplastic	963.1	E858.1	E933.1	E950.4	E962.0	E980.4
Chenopodium (oil)	961.6	E857	E931.6	E950.4	E962.0	E980.4
Cherry laurel	988.2	E865.4	—	E950.9	E962.1	E980.9
Chiniofon	961.3	E857	E931.3	E950.4	E962.0	E980.4
Chlophedianol	975.4	E858.6	E945.4	E950.4	E962.0	E980.4
Chloral (betaine) (formamide) (hydrate)	967.1	E852.0	E937.1	E950.2	E962.0	E980.2
Chloralamide	967.1	E852.0	E937.1	E950.2	E962.0	E980.2
Chlorambucil	963.1	E858.1	E933.1	E950.4	E962.0	E980.4
Chloramphenicol	960.2	E856	E930.2	E950.4	E962.0	E980.4
ENT agent	976.6	E858.7	E946.6	E950.4	E962.0	E980.4
ophthalmic preparation	976.5	E858.7	E946.5	E950.4	E962.0	E980.4
topical NEC	976.0	E858.7	E946.0	E950.4	E962.0	E980.4
Chlorate(s) (potassium) (sodium)						
NEC	983.9	E864.3	—	E950.7	E962.1	E980.6
herbicides	989.4	E863.5	—	E950.6	E962.1	E980.7
Chlorcyclizine	963.0	E858.1	E933.0	E950.4	E962.0	E980.4
Chlordan(e) (dust)	989.2	E863.0	—	E950.6	E962.1	E980.7
Chlordantoin	976.0	E858.7	E946.0	E950.4	E962.0	E980.4
Chlordiazepoxide	969.4	E853.2	E939.4	E950.3	E962.0	E980.3
Chloresium	976.8	E858.7	E946.8	E950.4	E962.0	E980.4
Chlorethiazol	967.1	E852.0	E937.1	E950.2	E962.0	E980.2
Chlorethyl — *see Ethyl, chloride*						
Chloretone	967.1	E852.0	E937.1	E950.2	E962.0	E980.2
Chlorex	982.3	E862.4	—	E950.9	E962.1	E980.9
Chlorhexadol	967.1	E852.0	E937.1	E950.2	E962.0	E980.2
Chlorhexidine (hydrochloride)	976.0	E858.7	E946.0	E950.4	E962.0	E980.4
Chlorhydroxyquinolin	976.0	E858.7	E946.0	E950.4	E962.0	E980.4
Chloride of lime (bleach)	983.9	E864.3	—	E950.7	E962.1	E980.6
Chlorinated						
camphene	989.2	E863.0	—	E950.6	E962.1	E980.7
diphenyl	989.89	E866.8	—	E950.9	E962.1	E980.9
hydrocarbons NEC	989.2	E863.0	—	E950.6	E962.1	E980.7
solvent	982.3	E862.4	—	E950.9	E962.1	E980.9
lime (bleach)	983.9	E864.3	—	E950.7	E962.1	E980.6
naphthalene — see Naphthalene						
pesticides NEC	989.2	E863.0	—	E950.6	E962.1	E980.7
soda — see Sodium, hypochlorite						
Chlorine (fumes) (gas)	987.6	E869.8	—	E952.8	E962.2	E982.8
bleach	983.9	E864.3	—	E950.7	E962.1	E980.6
compounds NEC	983.9	E864.3	—	E950.7	E962.1	E980.6
disinfectant	983.9	E861.4	—	E950.7	E962.1	E980.6
releasing agents NEC	983.9	E864.3	—	E950.7	E962.1	E980.6
Chlorisondamine	972.3	E858.3	E942.3	E950.4	E962.0	E980.4
Chlormadinone	962.2	E858.0	E932.2	E950.4	E962.0	E980.4
Chlormerodrin	974.0	E858.5	E944.0	E950.4	E962.0	E980.4
Chlormethiazole	967.1	E852.0	E937.1	E950.2	E962.0	E980.2
Chlormethylenecycline	960.4	E856	E930.4	E950.4	E962.0	E980.4
Chlormezanone	969.5	E853.8	E939.5	E950.3	E962.0	E980.3
Chloroacetophenone	987.5	E869.3	—	E952.8	E962.2	E982.8
Chloroaniline	983.0	E864.0	—	E950.7	E962.1	E980.6
Chlorobenzene, chlorobenzol	982.0	E862.4	—	E950.9	E962.1	E980.9
Chlorobutanol	967.1	E852.0	E937.1	E950.2	E962.0	E980.2
Chlorodinitrobenzene	983.0	E864.0	—	E950.7	E962.1	E980.6
dust or vapor	987.8	E869.8	—	E952.8	E962.2	E982.8
Chloroethane — *see Ethyl, chloride*						
Chloroform (fumes) (vapor)	987.8	E869.8	—	E952.8	E962.2	E982.8
anesthetic (gas)	968.2	E855.1	E938.2	E950.4	E962.0	E980.4
liquid NEC	968.4	E855.1	E938.4	E950.4	E962.0	E980.4
solvent	982.3	E862.4	—	E950.9	E962.1	E980.9
Chloroguanide	961.4	E857	E931.4	E950.4	E962.0	E980.4
Chloromycetin	960.2	E856	E930.2	E950.4	E962.0	E980.4

	Poisoning	Accident	Therapeutic Use	Suicide Attempt	Assault	Undetermined
Chloromycetin — *continued*						
ENT agent	976.6	E858.7	E946.6	E950.4	E962.0	E980.4
ophthalmic preparation	976.5	E858.7	E946.5	E950.4	E962.0	E980.4
otic solution	976.6	E858.7	E946.6	E950.4	E962.0	E980.4
topical NEC	976.0	E858.7	E946.0	E950.4	E962.0	E980.4
Chloronitrobenzene	983.0	E864.0	—	E950.7	E962.1	E980.6
dust or vapor	987.8	E869.8	—	E952.8	E962.2	E982.8
Chlorophenol	983.0	E864.0	—	E950.7	E962.1	E980.6
Chlorophenothane	989.2	E863.0	—	E950.6	E962.1	E980.7
Chlorophyll (derivatives)	976.8	E858.7	E946.8	E950.4	E962.0	E980.4
Chloropicrin (fumes)	987.8	E869.8	—	E952.8	E962.2	E982.8
fumigant	989.4	E863.8	—	E950.6	E962.1	E980.7
fungicide	989.4	E863.6	—	E950.6	E962.1	E980.7
pesticide (fumes)	989.4	E863.4	—	E950.6	E962.1	E980.7
Chloroprocaine	968.9	E855.2	E938.9	E950.4	E962.0	E980.4
infiltration (subcutaneous)	968.5	E855.2	E938.5	E950.4	E962.0	E980.4
nerve block (peripheral) (plexus)	968.6	E855.2	E938.6	E950.4	E962.0	E980.4
Chloroptic	976.5	E858.7	E946.5	E950.4	E962.0	E980.4
Chloropurine	963.1	E858.1	E933.1	E950.4	E962.0	E980.4
Chloroquine (hydrochloride) (phosphate)	961.4	E857	E931.4	E950.4	E962.0	E980.4
Chlorothen	963.0	E858.1	E933.0	E950.4	E962.0	E980.4
Chlorothiazide	974.3	E858.5	E944.3	E950.4	E962.0	E980.4
Chlorotrianisene	962.2	E858.0	E932.2	E950.4	E962.0	E980.4
Chlorovinyldichloroarsine	985.1	E866.3	—	E950.8	E962.1	E980.8
Chloroxylenol	976.0	E858.7	E946.0	E950.4	E962.0	E980.4
Chlorphenesin (carbamate)	968.0	E855.1	E938.0	E950.4	E962.0	E980.4
topical (antifungal)	976.0	E858.7	E946.0	E950.4	E962.0	E980.4
Chlorpheniramine	963.0	E858.1	E933.0	E950.4	E962.0	E980.4
Chlorphenoxamine	966.4	E855.0	E936.4	E950.4	E962.0	E980.4
Chlorphentermine	977.0	E858.8	E947.0	E950.4	E962.0	E980.4
Chlorproguanil	961.4	E857	E931.4	E950.4	E962.0	E980.4
Chlorpromazine	969.1	E853.0	E939.1	E950.3	E962.0	E980.3
Chlorpropamide	962.3	E858.0	E932.3	E950.4	E962.0	E980.4
Chlorprothixene	969.3	E853.8	E939.3	E950.3	E962.0	E980.3
Chlorquinaldol	976.0	E858.7	E946.0	E950.4	E962.0	E980.4
Chlortetracycline	960.4	E856	E930.4	E950.4	E962.0	E980.4
Chlorthalidone	974.4	E858.5	E944.4	E950.4	E962.0	E980.4
Chlortrianisene	962.2	E858.0	E932.2	E950.4	E962.0	E980.4
Chlor-Trimeton	963.0	E858.1	E933.0	E950.4	E962.0	E980.4
Chlorzoxazone	968.0	E855.1	E938.0	E950.4	E962.0	E980.4
Choke damp	987.8	E869.8	—	E952.8	E962.2	E982.8
Cholebrine	977.8	E858.8	E947.8	E950.4	E962.0	E980.4
Cholera vaccine	978.2	E858.8	E948.2	E950.4	E962.0	E980.4
Cholesterol-lowering agents	972.2	E858.3	E942.2	E950.4	E962.0	E980.4
Cholestyramine (resin)	972.2	E858.3	E942.2	E950.4	E962.0	E980.4
Cholic acid	973.4	E858.4	E943.4	E950.4	E962.0	E980.4
Choline						
dihydrogen citrate	977.1	E858.8	E947.1	E950.4	E962.0	E980.4
salicylate	965.1	E850.3	E935.3	E950.0	E962.0	E980.0
theophyllinate	974.1	E858.5	E944.1	E950.4	E962.0	E980.4
Cholinergics	971.0	E855.3	E941.0	E950.4	E962.0	E980.4
Cholografin	977.8	E858.8	E947.8	E950.4	E962.0	E980.4
Chorionic gonadotropin	962.4	E858.0	E932.4	E950.4	E962.0	E980.4
Chromates	983.9	E864.3	—	E950.7	E962.1	E980.6
dust or mist	987.8	E869.8	—	E952.8	E962.2	E982.8
lead	984.0	E866.0	—	E950.9	E962.1	E980.9
paint	984.0	E861.5	—	E950.9	E962.1	E980.9
Chromic acid	983.9	E864.3	—	E950.7	E962.1	E980.6
dust or mist	987.8	E869.8	—	E952.8	E962.2	E982.8
Chromium	985.6	E866.4	—	E950.9	E962.1	E980.9
compounds — see Chromates						
Chromonar	972.4	E858.3	E942.4	E950.4	E962.0	E980.4
Chromyl chloride	983.9	E864.3	—	E950.7	E962.1	E980.6
Chrysarobin (ointment)	976.4	E858.7	E946.4	E950.4	E962.0	E980.4
Chrysazin	973.1	E858.4	E943.1	E950.4	E962.0	E980.4
Chymar	963.4	E858.1	E933.4	E950.4	E962.0	E980.4
ophthalmic preparation	976.5	E858.7	E946.5	E950.4	E962.0	E980.4
Chymotrypsin	963.4	E858.1	E933.4	E950.4	E962.0	E980.4
ophthalmic preparation	976.5	E858.7	E946.5	E950.4	E962.0	E980.4
Cicuta maculata or virosa	988.2	E865.4	—	E950.9	E962.1	E980.9
Cigarette lighter fluid	981	E862.1	—	E950.9	E962.1	E980.9
Cinchocaine (spinal)	968.7	E855.2	E938.7	E950.4	E962.0	E980.4
topical (surface)	968.5	E855.2	E938.5	E950.4	E962.0	E980.4
Cinchona	961.4	E857	E931.4	E950.4	E962.0	E980.4
Cinchonine alkaloids	961.4	E857	E931.4	E950.4	E962.0	E980.4
Cinchophen	974.7	E858.5	E944.7	E950.4	E962.0	E980.4
Cinnarizine	963.0	E858.1	E933.0	E950.4	E962.0	E980.4
Citanest	968.9	E855.2	E938.9	E950.4	E962.0	E980.4

☑ Additional Digit Required — Refer to the Tabular List for Digit Selection   Subterms under main terms may continue to next column or page

310 — Volume 2   ▶◀ Revised Text   ● New Line   ▲ Revised Code   *2007 ICD-9-CM*

	Poisoning	Accident	Therapeutic Use	Suicide Attempt	Assault	Undetermined
External Cause (E-Code)						
Citanest — *continued*						
infiltration (subcutaneous)	968.5	E855.2	E938.5	E950.4	E962.0	E980.4
nerve block (peripheral) (plexus)	968.6	E855.2	E938.6	E950.4	E962.0	E980.4
Citric acid	989.89	E866.8	—	E950.9	E962.1	E980.9
Citrovorum factor	964.1	E858.2	E934.1	E950.4	E962.0	E980.4
Claviceps purpurea	988.2	E865.4	—	E950.9	E962.1	E980.9
Cleaner, cleansing agent						
NEC	989.89	E861.3	—	E950.9	E962.1	E980.9
of paint or varnish	982.8	E862.9	—	E950.9	E962.1	E980.9
Clematis vitalba	988.2	E865.4	—	E950.9	E962.1	E980.9
Clemizole	963.0	E858.1	E933.0	E950.4	E962.0	E980.4
penicillin	960.0	E856	E930.0	E950.4	E962.0	E980.4
Clidinium	971.1	E855.4	E941.1	E950.4	E962.0	E980.4
Clindamycin	960.8	E856	E930.8	E950.4	E962.0	E980.4
Cliradon	965.09	E850.2	E935.2	E950.0	E962.0	E980.0
Clocortolone	962.0	E858.0	E932.0	E950.4	E962.0	E980.4
Clofedanol	975.4	E858.6	E945.4	E950.4	E962.0	E980.4
Clofibrate	972.2	E858.3	E942.2	E950.4	E962.0	E980.4
Clomethiazole	967.1	E852.0	E937.1	E950.2	E962.0	E980.2
Clomiphene	977.8	E858.8	E947.8	E950.4	E962.0	E980.4
Clonazepam	969.4	E853.2	E939.4	E950.3	E962.0	E980.3
Clonidine	972.6	E858.3	E942.6	E950.4	E962.0	E980.4
Clopamide	974.3	E858.5	E944.3	E950.4	E962.0	E980.4
Clorazepate	969.4	E853.2	E939.4	E950.3	E962.0	E980.3
Clorexolone	974.4	E858.5	E944.4	E950.4	E962.0	E980.4
Clorox (bleach)	983.9	E864.3	—	E950.7	E962.1	E980.6
Clortermine	977.0	E858.8	E947.0	E950.4	E962.0	E980.4
Clotrimazole	976.0	E858.7	E946.0	E950.4	E962.0	E980.4
Cloxacillin	960.0	E856	E930.0	E950.4	E962.0	E980.4
Coagulants NEC	964.5	E858.2	E934.5	E950.4	E962.0	E980.4
Coal (carbon monoxide from) — *see also* Carbon, monoxide, coal						
oil — *see* Kerosene						
tar NEC	983.0	E864.0	—	E950.7	E962.1	E980.6
fumes	987.8	E869.8	—	E952.8	E962.2	E982.8
medicinal (ointment)	976.4	E858.7	E946.4	E950.4	E962.0	E980.4
analgesics NEC	965.5	E850.5	E935.5	E950.0	E962.0	E980.0
naphtha (solvent)	981	E862.0	—	E950.9	E962.1	E980.9
Cobalt (fumes) (industrial)	985.8	E866.4	—	E950.9	E962.1	E980.9
Cobra (venom)	989.5	E905.0	—	E950.9	E962.1	E980.9
Coca (leaf)	970.8	E854.3	E940.8	E950.4	E962.0	E980.4
Cocaine (hydrochloride) (salt)	970.8	E854.3	E940.8	E950.4	E962.0	E980.4
topical anesthetic	968.5	E855.2	E938.5	E950.4	E962.0	E980.4
Coccidioidin	977.8	E858.8	E947.8	E950.4	E962.0	E980.4
Cocculus indicus	988.2	E865.3	—	E950.9	E962.1	E980.9
Cochineal	989.89	E866.8	—	E950.9	E962.1	E980.9
medicinal products	977.4	E858.8	E947.4	E950.4	E962.0	E980.4
Codeine	965.09	E850.2	E935.2	E950.0	E962.0	E980.0
Coffee	989.89	E866.8	—	E950.9	E962.1	E980.9
Cogentin	971.1	E855.4	E941.1	E950.4	E962.0	E980.4
Coke fumes or gas (carbon monoxide)	986	E868.3	—	E952.1	E962.2	E982.1
industrial use	986	E868.8	—	E952.1	E962.2	E982.1
Colace	973.2	E858.4	E943.2	E950.4	E962.0	E980.4
Colchicine	974.7	E858.5	E944.7	E950.4	E962.0	E980.4
Colchicum	988.2	E865.3	—	E950.9	E962.1	E980.9
Cold cream	976.3	E858.7	E946.3	E950.4	E962.0	E980.4
Colestipol	972.2	E858.3	E942.2	E950.4	E962.0	E980.4
Colistimethate	960.8	E856	E930.8	E950.4	E962.0	E980.4
Colistin	960.8	E856	E930.8	E950.4	E962.0	E980.4
Collagen	977.8	E866.8	E947.8	E950.9	E962.1	E980.9
Collagenase	976.8	E858.7	E946.8	E950.4	E962.0	E980.4
Collodion (flexible)	976.3	E858.7	E946.3	E950.4	E962.0	E980.4
Colocynth	973.1	E858.4	E943.1	E950.4	E962.0	E980.4
Coloring matter — *see* Dye(s)						
Combustion gas — *see* Carbon, monoxide						
Compazine	969.1	E853.0	E939.1	E950.3	E962.0	E980.3
Compound						
42 (warfarin)	989.4	E863.7	—	E950.6	E962.1	E980.7
269 (endrin)	989.2	E863.0	—	E950.6	E962.1	E980.7
497 (dieldrin)	989.2	E863.0	—	E950.6	E962.1	E980.7
1080 (sodium fluoroacetate)	989.4	E863.7	—	E950.6	E962.1	E980.7
3422 (parathion)	989.3	E863.1	—	E950.6	E962.1	E980.7
3911 (phorate)	989.3	E863.1	—	E950.6	E962.1	E980.7
3956 (toxaphene)	989.2	E863.0	—	E950.6	E962.1	E980.7
4049 (malathion)	989.3	E863.1	—	E950.6	E962.1	E980.7
Compound — *continued*						
4124 (dicapthon)	989.4	E863.4	—	E950.6	E962.1	E980.7
E (cortisone)	962.0	E858.0	E932.0	E950.4	E962.0	E980.4
F (hydrocortisone)	962.0	E858.0	E932.0	E950.4	E962.0	E980.4
Congo red	977.8	E858.8	E947.8	E950.4	E962.0	E980.4
Coniine, conine	965.7	E850.7	E935.7	E950.0	E962.0	E980.0
Conium (maculatum)	988.2	E865.4	—	E950.9	E962.1	E980.9
Conjugated estrogens (equine)	962.2	E858.0	E932.2	E950.4	E962.0	E980.4
Contac	975.6	E858.6	E945.6	E950.4	E962.0	E980.4
Contact lens solution	976.5	E858.7	E946.5	E950.4	E962.0	E980.4
Contraceptives (oral)	962.2	E858.0	E932.2	E950.4	E962.0	E980.4
vaginal	976.8	E858.7	E946.8	E950.4	E962.0	E980.4
Contrast media (roentgenographic)	977.8	E858.8	E947.8	E950.4	E962.0	E980.4
Convallaria majalis	988.2	E865.4	—	E950.9	E962.1	E980.9
Copper (dust) (fumes) (salts)						
NEC	985.8	E866.4	—	E950.9	E962.1	E980.9
arsenate, arsenite	985.1	E866.3	—	E950.8	E962.1	E980.8
insecticide	985.1	E863.4	—	E950.8	E962.1	E980.8
emetic	973.6	E858.4	E943.6	E950.4	E962.0	E980.4
fungicide	985.8	E863.6	—	E950.6	E962.1	E980.7
insecticide	985.8	E863.4	—	E950.6	E962.1	E980.7
oleate	976.0	E858.7	E946.0	E950.4	E962.0	E980.4
sulfate	983.9	E864.3	—	E950.7	E962.1	E980.6
cupric	973.6	E858.4	E943.6	E950.4	E962.0	E980.4
cuprous	983.9	E864.3	—	E950.7	E962.1	E980.6
fungicide	983.9	E863.6	—	E950.7	E962.1	E980.6
Copperhead snake (bite) (venom)	989.5	E905.0	—	E950.9	E962.1	E980.9
Coral (sting)	989.5	E905.6	—	E950.9	E962.1	E980.9
snake (bite) (venom)	989.5	E905.0	—	E950.9	E962.1	E980.9
Cordran	976.0	E858.7	E946.0	E950.4	E962.0	E980.4
Corn cures	976.4	E858.7	E946.4	E950.4	E962.0	E980.4
Cornhusker's lotion	976.3	E858.7	E946.3	E950.4	E962.0	E980.4
Corn starch	976.3	E858.7	E946.3	E950.4	E962.0	E980.4
Corrosive	983.9	E864.4	—	E950.7	E962.1	E980.6
acids NEC	983.1	E864.1	—	E950.7	E962.1	E980.6
aromatics	983.0	E864.0	—	E950.7	E962.1	E980.6
disinfectant	983.0	E861.4	—	E950.7	E962.1	E980.6
fumes NEC	987.9	E869.9	—	E952.9	E962.2	E982.9
specified NEC	983.9	E864.3	—	E950.7	E962.1	E980.6
sublimate — *see* Mercury, chloride						
Cortate	962.0	E858.0	E932.0	E950.4	E962.0	E980.4
Cort-Dome	962.0	E858.0	E932.0	E950.4	E962.0	E980.4
ENT agent	976.6	E858.7	E946.6	E950.4	E962.0	E980.4
ophthalmic preparation	976.5	E858.7	E946.5	E950.4	E962.0	E980.4
topical NEC	976.0	E858.7	E946.0	E950.4	E962.0	E980.4
Cortef	962.0	E858.0	E932.0	E950.4	E962.0	E980.4
ENT agent	976.6	E858.7	E946.6	E950.4	E962.0	E980.4
ophthalmic preparation	976.5	E858.7	E946.5	E950.4	E962.0	E980.4
topical NEC	976.0	E858.7	E946.0	E950.4	E962.0	E980.4
Corticosteroids (fluorinated)	962.0	E858.0	E932.0	E950.4	E962.0	E980.4
ENT agent	976.6	E858.7	E946.6	E950.4	E962.0	E980.4
ophthalmic preparation	976.5	E858.7	E946.5	E950.4	E962.0	E980.4
topical NEC	976.0	E858.7	E946.0	E950.4	E962.0	E980.4
Corticotropin	962.4	E858.0	E932.4	E950.4	E962.0	E980.4
Cortisol	962.0	E858.0	E932.0	E950.4	E962.0	E980.4
ENT agent	976.6	E858.7	E946.6	E950.4	E962.0	E980.4
ophthalmic preparation	976.5	E858.7	E946.5	E950.4	E962.0	E980.4
topical NEC	976.0	E858.7	E946.0	E950.4	E962.0	E980.4
Cortisone derivatives (acetate)	962.0	E858.0	E932.0	E950.4	E962.0	E980.4
ENT agent	976.6	E858.7	E946.6	E950.4	E962.0	E980.4
ophthalmic preparation	976.5	E858.7	E946.5	E950.4	E962.0	E980.4
topical NEC	976.0	E858.7	E946.0	E950.4	E962.0	E980.4
Cortogen	962.0	E858.0	E932.0	E950.4	E962.0	E980.4
ENT agent	976.6	E858.7	E946.6	E950.4	E962.0	E980.4
ophthalmic preparation	976.5	E858.7	E946.5	E950.4	E962.0	E980.4
Cortone	962.0	E858.0	E932.0	E950.4	E962.0	E980.4
ENT agent	976.6	E858.7	E946.6	E950.4	E962.0	E980.4
ophthalmic preparation	976.5	E858.7	E946.5	E950.4	E962.0	E980.4
Cortril	962.0	E858.0	E932.0	E950.4	E962.0	E980.4
ENT agent	976.6	E858.7	E946.6	E950.4	E962.0	E980.4
ophthalmic preparation	976.5	E858.7	E946.5	E950.4	E962.0	E980.4
topical NEC	976.0	E858.7	E946.0	E950.4	E962.0	E980.4
Cosmetics	989.89	E866.7	—	E950.9	E962.1	E980.9
Cosyntropin	977.8	E858.8	E947.8	E950.4	E962.0	E980.4
Cotarnine	964.5	E858.2	E934.5	E950.4	E962.0	E980.4

☑ Additional Digit Required — Refer to the Tabular List for Digit Selection

Subterms under main terms may continue to next column or page

2007 ICD-9-CM

►◄ Revised Text

● New Line

▲ Revised Code

Volume 2 — 311

		External Cause (E-Code)				
	Poisoning	Accident	Therapeutic Use	Suicide Attempt	Assault	Undetermined
Cottonseed oil	976.3	E858.7	E946.3	E950.4	E962.0	E980.4
Cough mixtures						
(antitussives)	975.4	E858.6	E945.4	E950.4	E962.0	E980.4
containing opiates	965.09	E850.2	E935.2	E950.0	E962.0	E980.0
expectorants	975.5	E858.6	E945.5	E950.4	E962.0	E980.4
Coumadin	964.2	E858.2	E934.2	E950.4	E962.0	E980.4
rodenticide	989.4	E863.7	—	E950.6	E962.1	E980.7
Coumarin	964.2	E858.2	E934.2	E950.4	E962.0	E980.4
Coumetarol	964.2	E858.2	E934.2	E950.4	E962.0	E980.4
Cowbane	988.2	E865.4	—	E950.9	E962.1	E980.9
Cozyme	963.5	E858.1	E933.5	E950.4	E962.0	E980.4
Crack	970.8	E854.3	E940.8	E950.4	E962.0	E980.4
Creolin	983.0	E864.0	—	E950.7	E962.1	E980.6
disinfectant	983.0	E861.4	—	E950.7	E962.1	E980.6
Creosol (compound)	983.0	E864.0	—	E950.7	E962.1	E980.6
Creosote (beechwood) (coal						
tar)	983.0	E864.0	—	E950.7	E962.1	E980.6
medicinal (expectorant)	975.5	E858.6	E945.5	E950.4	E962.0	E980.4
syrup	975.5	E858.6	E945.5	E950.4	E962.0	E980.4
Cresol	983.0	E864.0	—	E950.7	E962.1	E980.6
disinfectant	983.0	E861.4	—	E950.7	E962.1	E980.6
Cresylic acid	983.0	E864.0	—	E950.7	E962.1	E980.6
Cropropamide	965.7	E850.7	E935.7	E950.0	E962.0	E980.0
with crotethamide	970.0	E854.3	E940.0	E950.4	E962.0	E980.4
Crotamiton	976.0	E858.7	E946.0	E950.4	E962.0	E980.4
Crotethamide	965.7	E850.7	E935.7	E950.0	E962.0	E980.0
with cropropamide	970.0	E854.3	E940.0	E950.4	E962.0	E980.4
Croton (oil)	973.1	E858.4	E943.1	E950.4	E962.0	E980.4
chloral	967.1	E852.0	E937.1	E950.2	E962.0	E980.2
Crude oil	981	E862.1	—	E950.9	E962.1	E980.9
Cryogenine	965.8	E850.8	E935.8	E950.0	E962.0	E980.0
Cryolite (pesticide)	989.4	E863.4	—	E950.6	E962.1	E980.7
Cryptenamine	972.6	E858.3	E942.6	E950.4	E962.0	E980.4
Crystal violet	976.0	E858.7	E946.0	E950.4	E962.0	E980.4
Cuckoopint	988.2	E865.4	—	E950.9	E962.1	E980.9
Cumetharol	964.2	E858.2	E934.2	E950.4	E962.0	E980.4
Cupric sulfate	973.6	E858.4	E943.6	E950.4	E962.0	E980.4
Cuprous sulfate	983.9	E864.3	—	E950.7	E962.1	E980.6
Curare, curarine	975.2	E858.6	E945.2	E950.4	E962.0	E980.4
Cyanic acid — see Cyanide(s)						
Cyanide(s) (compounds)						
(hydrogen) (potassium)						
(sodium) NEC	989.0	E866.8	—	E950.9	E962.1	E980.9
dust or gas (inhalation)						
NEC	987.7	E869.8	—	E952.8	E962.2	E982.8
fumigant	989.0	E863.8	—	E950.6	E962.1	E980.7
mercuric — see Mercury						
pesticide (dust) (fumes)	989.0	E863.4	—	E950.6	E962.1	E980.7
Cyanocobalamin	964.1	E858.2	E934.1	E950.4	E962.0	E980.4
Cyanogen (chloride) (gas)						
NEC	987.8	E869.8	—	E952.8	E962.2	E982.8
Cyclaine	968.5	E855.2	E938.5	E950.4	E962.0	E980.4
Cyclamen europaeum	988.2	E865.4	—	E950.9	E962.1	E980.9
Cyclandelate	972.5	E858.3	E942.5	E950.4	E962.0	E980.4
Cyclazocine	965.09	E850.2	E935.2	E950.0	E962.0	E980.0
Cyclizine	963.0	E858.1	E933.0	E950.4	E962.0	E980.4
Cyclobarbital,						
cyclobarbitone	967.0	E851	E937.0	E950.1	E962.0	E980.1
Cycloguanil	961.4	E857	E931.4	E950.4	E962.0	E980.4
Cyclohexane	982.0	E862.4	—	E950.9	E962.1	E980.9
Cyclohexanol	980.8	E860.8	—	E950.9	E962.1	E980.9
Cyclohexanone	982.8	E862.4	—	E950.9	E962.1	E980.9
Cyclomethycaine	968.5	E855.2	E938.5	E950.4	E962.0	E980.4
Cyclopentamine	971.2	E855.5	E941.2	E950.4	E962.0	E980.4
Cyclopenthiazide	974.3	E858.5	E944.3	E950.4	E962.0	E980.4
Cyclopentolate	971.1	E855.4	E941.1	E950.4	E962.0	E980.4
Cyclophosphamide	963.1	E858.1	E933.1	E950.4	E962.0	E980.4
Cyclopropane	968.2	E855.1	E938.2	E950.4	E962.0	E980.4
Cycloserine	960.6	E856	E930.6	E950.4	E962.0	E980.4
Cyclothiazide	974.3	E858.5	E944.3	E950.4	E962.0	E980.4
Cycrimine	966.4	E855.0	E936.4	E950.4	E962.0	E980.4
Cymarin	972.1	E858.3	E942.1	E950.4	E962.0	E980.4
Cyproheptadine	963.0	E858.1	E933.0	E950.4	E962.0	E980.4
Cyprolidol	969.0	E854.0	E939.0	E950.3	E962.0	E980.3
Cytarabine	963.1	E858.1	E933.1	E950.4	E962.0	E980.4
Cytisus						
laburnum	988.2	E865.4	—	E950.9	E962.1	E980.9
scoparius	988.2	E865.4	—	E950.9	E962.1	E980.9
Cytomel	962.7	E858.0	E932.7	E950.4	E962.0	E980.4
Cytosine (antineoplastic)	963.1	E858.1	E933.1	E950.4	E962.0	E980.4
Cytoxan	963.1	E858.1	E933.1	E950.4	E962.0	E980.4
Dacarbazine	963.1	E858.1	E933.1	E950.4	E962.0	E980.4
Dactinomycin	960.7	E856	E930.7	E950.4	E962.0	E980.4
DADPS	961.8	E857	E931.8	E950.4	E962.0	E980.4
Dakin's solution (external)	976.0	E858.7	E946.0	E950.4	E962.0	E980.4
Dalmane	969.4	E853.2	E939.4	E950.3	E962.0	E980.3
DAM	977.2	E858.8	E947.2	E950.4	E962.0	E980.4
Danilone	964.2	E858.2	E934.2	E950.4	E962.0	E980.4
Danthron	973.1	E858.4	E943.1	E950.4	E962.0	E980.4
Dantrolene	975.2	E858.6	E945.2	E950.4	E962.0	E980.4
Daphne (gnidium)						
(mezereum)	988.2	E865.4	—	E950.9	E962.1	E980.9
berry	988.2	E865.3	—	E950.9	E962.1	E980.9
Dapsone	961.8	E857	E931.8	E950.4	E962.0	E980.4
Daraprim	961.4	E857	E931.4	E950.4	E962.0	E980.4
Darnel	988.2	E865.3	—	E950.9	E962.1	E980.9
Darvon	965.8	E850.8	E935.8	E950.0	E962.0	E980.0
Daunorubicin	960.7	E856	E930.7	E950.4	E962.0	E980.4
DBI	962.3	E858.0	E932.3	E950.4	E962.0	E980.4
D-Con (rodenticide)	989.4	E863.7	—	E950.6	E962.1	E980.7
DDS	961.8	E857	E931.8	E950.4	E962.0	E980.4
DDT	989.2	E863.0	—	E950.6	E962.1	E980.7
Deadly nightshade	988.2	E865.4	—	E950.9	E962.1	E980.9
berry	988.2	E865.3	—	E950.9	E962.1	E980.9
Deanol	969.7	E854.2	E939.7	E950.3	E962.0	E980.3
Debrisoquine	972.6	E858.3	E942.6	E950.4	E962.0	E980.4
Decaborane	989.89	E866.8	—	E950.9	E962.1	E980.9
fumes	987.8	E869.8	—	E952.8	E962.2	E982.8
Decadron	962.0	E858.0	E932.0	E950.4	E962.0	E980.4
ENT agent	976.6	E858.7	E946.6	E950.4	E962.0	E980.4
ophthalmic preparation	976.5	E858.7	E946.5	E950.4	E962.0	E980.4
topical NEC	976.0	E858.7	E946.0	E950.4	E962.0	E980.4
Decahydronaphthalene	982.0	E862.4	—	E950.9	E962.1	E980.9
Decalin	982.0	E862.4	—	E950.9	E962.1	E980.9
Decamethonium	975.2	E858.6	E945.2	E950.4	E962.0	E980.4
Decholin	973.4	E858.4	E943.4	E950.4	E962.0	E980.4
sodium (diagnostic)	977.8	E858.8	E947.8	E950.4	E962.0	E980.4
Declomycin	960.4	E856	E930.4	E950.4	E962.0	E980.4
Deferoxamine	963.8	E858.1	E933.8	E950.4	E962.0	E980.4
Dehydrocholic acid	973.4	E858.4	E943.4	E950.4	E962.0	E980.4
DeKalin	982.0	E862.4	—	E950.9	E962.1	E980.9
Delalutin	962.2	E858.0	E932.2	E950.4	E962.0	E980.4
Delphinium	988.2	E865.3	—	E950.9	E962.1	E980.9
Deltasone	962.0	E858.0	E932.0	E950.4	E962.0	E980.4
Deltra	962.0	E858.0	E932.0	E950.4	E962.0	E980.4
Delvinal	967.0	E851	E937.0	E950.1	E962.0	E980.1
Demecarium (bromide)	971.0	E855.3	E941.0	E950.4	E962.0	E980.4
Demeclocycline	960.4	E856	E930.4	E950.4	E962.0	E980.4
Demecolcine	963.1	E858.1	E933.1	E950.4	E962.0	E980.4
Demelanizing agents	976.8	E858.7	E946.8	E950.4	E962.0	E980.4
Demerol	965.09	E850.2	E935.2	E950.0	E962.0	E980.0
Demethylchlortetracycline	960.4	E856	E930.4	E950.4	E962.0	E980.4
Demethyltetracycline	960.4	E856	E930.4	E950.4	E962.0	E980.4
Demeton	989.3	E863.1	—	E950.6	E962.1	E980.7
Demulcents	976.3	E858.7	E946.3	E950.4	E962.0	E980.4
Demulen	962.2	E858.0	E932.2	E950.4	E962.0	E980.4
Denatured alcohol	980.0	E860.1	—	E950.9	E962.1	E980.9
Dendrid	976.5	E858.7	E946.5	E950.4	E962.0	E980.4
Dental agents, topical	976.7	E858.7	E946.7	E950.4	E962.0	E980.4
Deodorant spray (feminine						
hygiene)	976.8	E858.7	E946.8	E950.4	E962.0	E980.4
Deoxyribonuclease	963.4	E858.1	E933.4	E950.4	E962.0	E980.4
Depressants						
appetite, central	977.0	E858.8	E947.0	E950.4	E962.0	E980.4
cardiac	972.0	E858.3	E942.0	E950.4	E962.0	E980.4
central nervous system						
(anesthetic)	968.4	E855.1	E938.4	E950.4	E962.0	E980.4
psychotherapeutic	969.5	E853.9	E939.5	E950.3	E962.0	E980.3
Dequalinium	976.0	E858.7	E946.0	E950.4	E962.0	E980.4
Dermolate	976.2	E858.7	E946.2	E950.4	E962.0	E980.4
DES	962.2	E858.0	E932.2	E950.4	E962.0	E980.4
Desenex	976.0	E858.7	E946.0	E950.4	E962.0	E980.4
Deserpidine	972.6	E858.3	E942.6	E950.4	E962.0	E980.4
Desipramine	969.0	E854.0	E939.0	E950.3	E962.0	E980.3
Deslanoside	972.1	E858.3	E942.1	E950.4	E962.0	E980.4
Desocodeine	965.09	E850.2	E935.2	E950.0	E962.0	E980.0
Desomorphine	965.09	E850.2	E935.2	E950.0	E962.0	E980.0
Desonide	976.0	E858.7	E946.0	E950.4	E962.0	E980.4
Desoxycorticosterone						
derivatives	962.0	E858.0	E932.0	E950.4	E962.0	E980.4
Desoxyephedrine	969.7	E854.2	E939.7	E950.3	E962.0	E980.3
DET	969.6	E854.1	E939.6	E950.3	E962.0	E980.3

☑ Additional Digit Required — Refer to the Tabular List for Digit Selection

Subterms under main terms may continue to next column or page

	Poisoning	External Cause (E-Code)				
		Accident	Therapeutic Use	Suicide Attempt	Assault	Undetermined
Detergents (ingested)						
(synthetic)	989.6	E861.0	—	E950.9	E962.1	E980.9
ENT agent	976.6	E858.7	E946.6	E950.4	E962.0	E980.4
external medication	976.2	E858.7	E946.2	E950.4	E962.0	E980.4
ophthalmic preparation	976.5	E858.7	E946.5	E950.4	E962.0	E980.4
topical NEC	976.0	E858.7	E946.0	E950.4	E962.0	E980.4
Deterrent, alcohol	977.3	E858.8	E947.3	E950.4	E962.0	E980.4
Detrothyronine	962.7	E858.0	E932.7	E950.4	E962.0	E980.4
Dettol (external medication)	976.0	E858.7	E946.0	E950.4	E962.0	E980.4
Dexamethasone	962.0	E858.0	E932.0	E950.4	E962.0	E980.4
Dexamphetamine	969.7	E854.2	E939.7	E950.3	E962.0	E980.3
Dexedrine	969.7	E854.2	E939.7	E950.3	E962.0	E980.3
Dexpanthenol	963.5	E858.1	E933.5	E950.4	E962.0	E980.4
Dextran	964.8	E858.2	E934.8	E950.4	E962.0	E980.4
Dextriferron	964.0	E858.2	E934.0	E950.4	E962.0	E980.4
Dextroamphetamine	969.7	E854.2	E939.7	E950.3	E962.0	E980.3
Dextro calcium						
pantothenate	963.5	E858.1	E933.5	E950.4	E962.0	E980.4
Dextromethorphan	975.4	E858.6	E945.4	E950.4	E962.0	E980.4
Dextromoramide	965.09	E850.2	E935.2	E950.0	E962.0	E980.0
Dextro pantothenyl						
alcohol	963.5	E858.1	E933.5	E950.4	E962.0	E980.4
topical	976.8	E858.7	E946.8	E950.4	E962.0	E980.4
Dextropropoxyphene						
(hydrochloride)	965.8	E850.8	E935.8	E950.0	E962.0	E980.0
Dextrorphan	965.09	E850.2	E935.2	E950.0	E962.0	E980.0
Dextrose NEC	974.5	E858.5	E944.5	E950.4	E962.0	E980.4
Dextrothyroxin	962.7	E858.0	E932.7	E950.4	E962.0	E980.4
DFP	971.0	E855.3	E941.0	E950.4	E962.0	E980.4
DHE-45	972.9	E858.3	E942.9	E950.4	E962.0	E980.4
Diabinese	962.3	E858.0	E932.3	E950.4	E962.0	E980.4
Diacetyl monoxime	977.2	E858.8	E947.2	E950.4	E962.0	E980.4
Diacetylmorphine	965.01	E850.0	E935.0	E950.0	E962.0	E980.0
Diagnostic agents	977.8	E858.8	E947.8	E950.4	E962.0	E980.4
Dial (soap)	976.2	E858.7	E946.2	E950.4	E962.0	E980.4
sedative	967.0	E851	E937.0	E950.1	E962.0	E980.1
Diallylbarbituric acid	967.0	E851	E937.0	E950.1	E962.0	E980.1
Diaminodiphenylsulfone	961.8	E857	E931.8	E950.4	E962.0	E980.4
Diamorphine	965.01	E850.0	E935.0	E950.0	E962.0	E980.0
Diamox	974.2	E858.5	E944.2	E950.4	E962.0	E980.4
Diamthazole	976.0	E858.7	E946.0	E950.4	E962.0	E980.4
Diaphenylsulfone	961.8	E857	E931.8	E950.4	E962.0	E980.4
Diasone (sodium)	961.8	E857	E931.8	E950.4	E962.0	E980.4
Diazepam	969.4	E853.2	E939.4	E950.3	E962.0	E980.3
Diazinon	989.3	E863.1	—	E950.6	E962.1	E980.7
Diazomethane (gas)	987.8	E869.8	—	E952.8	E962.2	E982.8
Diazoxide	972.5	E858.3	E942.5	E950.4	E962.0	E980.4
Dibenamine	971.3	E855.6	E941.3	E950.4	E962.0	E980.4
Dibenzheptropine	963.0	E858.1	E933.0	E950.4	E962.0	E980.4
Dibenzyline	971.3	E855.6	E941.3	E950.4	E962.0	E980.4
Diborane (gas)	987.8	E869.8	—	E952.8	E962.2	E982.8
Dibromomannitol	963.1	E858.1	E933.1	E950.4	E962.0	E980.4
Dibucaine (spinal)	968.7	E855.2	E938.7	E950.4	E962.0	E980.4
topical (surface)	968.5	E855.2	E938.5	E950.4	E962.0	E980.4
Dibunate sodium	975.4	E858.6	E945.4	E950.4	E962.0	E980.4
Dibutoline	971.1	E855.4	E941.1	E950.4	E962.0	E980.4
Dicapthon	989.4	E863.4	—	E950.6	E962.1	E980.7
Dichloralphenazone	967.1	E852.0	E937.1	E950.2	E962.0	E980.2
Dichlorodifluoromethane	987.4	E869.2	—	E952.8	E962.2	E982.8
Dichloroethane	982.3	E862.4	—	E950.9	E962.1	E980.9
Dichloroethylene	982.3	E862.4	—	E950.9	E962.1	E980.9
Dichloroethyl sulfide	987.8	E869.8	—	E952.8	E962.2	E982.8
Dichlorohydrin	982.3	E862.4	—	E950.9	E962.1	E980.9
Dichloromethane (solvent)						
(vapor)	982.3	E862.4	—	E950.9	E962.1	E980.9
Dichlorophen(e)	961.6	E857	E931.6	E950.4	E962.0	E980.4
Dichlorphenamide	974.2	E858.5	E944.2	E950.4	E962.0	E980.4
Dichlorvos	989.3	E863.1	—	E950.6	E962.1	E980.7
Diclofenac sodium	965.69	E850.6	E935.6	E950.0	E962.0	E980.0
Dicoumarin, dicumarol	964.2	E858.2	E934.2	E950.4	E962.0	E980.4
Dicyanogen (gas)	987.8	E869.8	—	E952.8	E962.2	E982.8
Dicyclomine	971.1	E855.4	E941.1	E950.4	E962.0	E980.4
Dieldrin (vapor)	989.2	E863.0	—	E950.6	E962.1	E980.7
Dienestrol	962.2	E858.0	E932.2	E950.4	E962.0	E980.4
Dietetics	977.0	E858.8	E947.0	E950.4	E962.0	E980.4
Diethazine	966.4	E855.0	E936.4	E950.4	E962.0	E980.4
Diethyl						
barbituric acid	967.0	E851	E937.0	E950.1	E962.0	E980.1
carbamazine	961.6	E857	E931.6	E950.4	E962.0	E980.4
carbinol	980.8	E860.8	—	E950.9	E962.1	E980.9
carbonate	982.8	E862.4	—	E950.9	E962.1	E980.9

	Poisoning	External Cause (E-Code)				
		Accident	Therapeutic Use	Suicide Attempt	Assault	Undetermined
Diethyl — *continued*						
dioxide	982.8	E862.4	—	E950.9	E962.1	E980.9
ether (vapor) — see ther(s)						
glycol (monoacetate) (monoethyl						
ether)	982.8	E862.4	—	E950.9	E962.1	E980.9
propion	977.0	E858.8	E947.0	E950.4	E962.0	E980.4
stilbestrol	962.2	E858.0	E932.2	E950.4	E962.0	E980.4
Diethylene						
Diethylsulfone-diethylmethane	967.8	E852.8	E937.8	E950.2	E962.0	E980.2
Difencloxazine	965.09	E850.2	E935.2	E950.0	E962.0	E980.0
Diffusin	963.4	E858.1	E933.4	E950.4	E962.0	E980.4
Diflos	971.0	E855.3	E941.0	E950.4	E962.0	E980.4
Digestants	973.4	E858.4	E943.4	E950.4	E962.0	E980.4
Digitalin(e)	972.1	E858.3	E942.1	E950.4	E962.0	E980.4
Digitalis glycosides	972.1	E858.3	E942.1	E950.4	E962.0	E980.4
Digitoxin	972.1	E858.3	E942.1	E950.4	E962.0	E980.4
Digoxin	972.1	E858.3	E942.1	E950.4	E962.0	E980.4
Dihydrocodeine	965.09	E850.2	E935.2	E950.0	E962.0	E980.0
Dihydrocodeinone	965.09	E850.2	E935.2	E950.0	E962.0	E980.0
Dihydroergocristine	972.9	E858.3	E942.9	E950.4	E962.0	E980.4
Dihydroergotamine	972.9	E858.3	E942.9	E950.4	E962.0	E980.4
Dihydroergotoxine	972.9	E858.3	E942.9	E950.4	E962.0	E980.4
Dihydrohydroxycodeinone	965.09	E850.2	E935.2	E950.0	E962.0	E980.0
Dihydrohydroxymorphinone	965.09	E850.2	E935.2	E950.0	E962.0	E980.0
Dihydroisocodeine	965.09	E850.2	E935.2	E950.0	E962.0	E980.0
Dihydromorphine	965.09	E850.2	E935.2	E950.0	E962.0	E980.0
Dihydromorphinone	965.09	E850.2	E935.2	E950.0	E962.0	E980.0
Dihydrostreptomycin	960.6	E856	E930.6	E950.4	E962.0	E980.4
Dihydrotachysterol	962.6	E858.0	E932.6	E950.4	E962.0	E980.4
Dihydroxyanthraquinone	973.1	E858.4	E943.1	E950.4	E962.0	E980.4
Dihydroxycodeinone	965.09	E850.2	E935.2	E950.0	E962.0	E980.0
Diiodohydroxyquin	961.3	E857	E931.3	E950.4	E962.0	E980.4
topical	976.0	E858.7	E946.0	E950.4	E962.0	E980.4
Diiodohydroxyquinoline	961.3	E857	E931.3	E950.4	E962.0	E980.4
Dilantin	966.1	E855.0	E936.1	E950.4	E962.0	E980.4
Dilaudid	965.09	E850.2	E935.2	E950.0	E962.0	E980.0
Diloxanide	961.5	E857	E931.5	E950.4	E962.0	E980.4
Dimefline	970.0	E854.3	E940.0	E950.4	E962.0	E980.4
Dimenhydrinate	963.0	E858.1	E933.0	E950.4	E962.0	E980.4
Dimercaprol	963.8	E858.1	E933.8	E950.4	E962.0	E980.4
Dimercaptopropanol	963.8	E858.1	E933.8	E950.4	E962.0	E980.4
Dimetane	963.0	E858.1	E933.0	E950.4	E962.0	E980.4
Dimethicone	976.3	E858.7	E946.3	E950.4	E962.0	E980.4
Dimethindene	963.0	E858.1	E933.0	E950.4	E962.0	E980.4
Dimethisoquin	968.5	E855.2	E938.5	E950.4	E962.0	E980.4
Dimethisterone	962.2	E858.0	E932.2	E950.4	E962.0	E980.4
Dimethoxanate	975.4	E858.6	E945.4	E950.4	E962.0	E980.4
Dimethyl						
arsine, arsinic acid — see						
Arsenic						
carbinol	980.2	E860.3	—	E950.9	E962.1	E980.9
diguanide	962.3	E858.0	E932.3	E950.4	E962.0	E980.4
ketone	982.8	E862.4	—	E950.9	E962.1	E980.9
vapor	987.8	E869.8	—	E952.8	E962.2	E982.8
meperidine	965.09	E850.2	E935.2	E950.0	E962.0	E980.0
parathion	989.3	E863.1	—	E950.6	E962.1	E980.7
polysiloxane	973.8	E858.4	E943.8	E950.4	E962.0	E980.4
sulfate (fumes)	987.8	E869.8	—	E952.8	E962.2	E982.8
liquid	983.9	E864.3	—	E950.7	E962.1	E980.6
sulfoxide NEC	982.8	E862.4	—	E950.9	E962.1	E980.9
medicinal	976.4	E858.7	E946.4	E950.4	E962.0	E980.4
triptamine	969.6	E854.1	E939.6	E950.3	E962.0	E980.3
tubocurarine	975.2	E858.6	E945.2	E950.4	E962.0	E980.4
Dindevan	964.2	E858.2	E934.2	E950.4	E962.0	E980.4
Dinitrobenzene	983.0	E864.0	—	E950.7	E962.1	E980.6
vapor	987.8	E869.8	—	E952.8	E962.2	E982.8
Dinitro (-ortho-) cresol						
(herbicide) (spray)	989.4	E863.5	—	E950.6	E962.1	E980.7
insecticide	989.4	E863.4	—	E950.6	E962.1	E980.7
Dinitro-orthocresol						
(herbicide)	989.4	E863.5	—	E950.6	E962.1	E980.7
insecticide	989.4	E863.4	—	E950.6	E962.1	E980.7
Dinitrophenol (herbicide)						
(spray)	989.4	E863.5	—	E950.6	E962.1	E980.7
insecticide	989.4	E863.4	—	E950.6	E962.1	E980.7
Dinoprost	975.0	E858.6	E945.0	E950.4	E962.0	E980.4
Dioctyl sulfosuccinate (calcium)						
(sodium)	973.2	E858.4	E943.2	E950.4	E962.0	E980.4
Diodoquin	961.3	E857	E931.3	E950.4	E962.0	E980.4
Dione derivatives NEC	966.3	E855.0	E936.3	E950.4	E962.0	E980.4
Dionin	965.09	E850.2	E935.2	E950.0	E962.0	E980.0

	Poisoning	External Cause (E-Code)				
		Accident	Therapeutic Use	Suicide Attempt	Assault	Undetermined
Dioxane	982.8	E862.4	—	E950.9	E962.1	E980.9
Dioxin — see Herbicide						
Dioxyline	972.5	E858.3	E942.5	E950.4	E962.0	E980.4
Dipentene	982.8	E862.4	—	E950.9	E962.1	E980.9
Diphemanil	971.1	E855.4	E941.1	E950.4	E962.0	E980.4
Diphenadione	964.2	E858.2	E934.2	E950.4	E962.0	E980.4
Diphenhydramine	963.0	E858.1	E933.0	E950.4	E962.0	E980.4
Diphenidol	963.0	E858.1	E933.0	E950.4	E962.0	E980.4
Diphenoxylate	973.5	E858.4	E943.5	E950.4	E962.0	E980.4
Diphenylchloroarsine	985.1	E866.3	—	E950.8	E962.1	E980.8
Diphenylhydantoin						
(sodium)	966.1	E855.0	E936.1	E950.4	E962.0	E980.4
Diphenylpyraline	963.0	E858.1	E933.0	E950.4	E962.0	E980.4
Diphtheria						
antitoxin	979.9	E858.8	E949.9	E950.4	E962.0	E980.4
toxoid	978.5	E858.8	E948.5	E950.4	E962.0	E980.4
with tetanus toxoid	978.9	E858.8	E948.9	E950.4	E962.0	E980.4
with pertussis						
component	978.6	E858.8	E948.6	E950.4	E962.0	E980.4
vaccine	978.5	E858.8	E948.5	E950.4	E962.0	E980.4
Dipipanone	965.09	E850.2	E935.2	E950.0	E962.0	E980.0
Diplovax	979.5	E858.8	E949.5	E950.4	E962.0	E980.4
Diprophylline	975.1	E858.6	E945.1	E950.4	E962.0	E980.4
Dipyridamole	972.4	E858.3	E942.4	E950.4	E962.0	E980.4
Dipyrone	965.5	E850.5	E935.5	E950.0	E962.0	E980.0
Diquat	989.4	E863.5	—	E950.6	E962.1	E980.7
Disinfectant NEC	983.9	E861.4	—	E950.7	E962.1	E980.6
alkaline	983.2	E861.4	—	E950.7	E962.1	E980.6
aromatic	983.0	E861.4	—	E950.7	E962.1	E980.6
Disipal	966.4	E855.0	E936.4	E950.4	E962.0	E980.4
Disodium edetate	963.8	E858.1	E933.8	E950.4	E962.0	E980.4
Disulfamide	974.4	E858.5	E944.4	E950.4	E962.0	E980.4
Disulfanilamide	961.0	E857	E931.0	E950.4	E962.0	E980.4
Disulfiram	977.3	E858.8	E947.3	E950.4	E962.0	E980.4
Dithiazanine	961.6	E857	E931.6	E950.4	E962.0	E980.4
Dithioglycerol	963.8	E858.1	E933.8	E950.4	E962.0	E980.4
Dithranol	976.4	E858.7	E946.4	E950.4	E962.0	E980.4
Diucardin	974.3	E858.5	E944.3	E950.4	E962.0	E980.4
Diupres	974.3	E858.5	E944.3	E950.4	E962.0	E980.4
Diuretics NEC	974.4	E858.5	E944.4	E950.4	E962.0	E980.4
carbonic acid anhydrase						
inhibitors	974.2	E858.5	E944.2	E950.4	E962.0	E980.4
mercurial	974.0	E858.5	E944.0	E950.4	E962.0	E980.4
osmotic	974.4	E858.5	E944.4	E950.4	E962.0	E980.4
purine derivatives	974.1	E858.5	E944.1	E950.4	E962.0	E980.4
saluretic	974.3	E858.5	E944.3	E950.4	E962.0	E980.4
Diuril	974.3	E858.5	E944.3	E950.4	E962.0	E980.4
Divinyl ether	968.2	E855.1	E938.2	E950.4	E962.0	E980.4
D-lysergic acid						
diethylamide	969.6	E854.1	E939.6	E950.3	E962.0	E980.3
DMCT	960.4	E856	E930.4	E950.4	E962.0	E980.4
DMSO	982.8	E862.4	—	E950.9	E962.1	E980.9
DMT	969.6	E854.1	E939.6	E950.3	E962.0	E980.3
DNOC	989.4	E863.5	—	E950.6	E962.1	E980.7
DOCA	962.0	E858.0	E932.0	E950.4	E962.0	E980.4
Dolophine	965.02	E850.1	E935.1	E950.0	E962.0	E980.0
Doloxene	965.8	E850.8	E935.8	E950.0	E962.0	E980.0
DOM	969.6	E854.1	E939.6	E950.3	E962.0	E980.3
Domestic gas — see Gas, utility						
Domiphen (bromide)						
(lozenges)	976.6	E858.7	E946.6	E950.4	E962.0	E980.4
Dopa (levo)	966.4	E855.0	E936.4	E950.4	E962.0	E980.4
Dopamine	971.2	E855.5	E941.2	E950.4	E962.0	E980.4
Doriden	967.5	E852.4	E937.5	E950.2	E962.0	E980.2
Dormiral	967.0	E851	E937.0	E950.1	E962.0	E980.1
Dormison	967.8	E852.8	E937.8	E950.2	E962.0	E980.2
Dornase	963.4	E858.1	E933.4	E950.4	E962.0	E980.4
Dorsacaine	968.5	E855.2	E938.5	E950.4	E962.0	E980.4
Dothiepin hydrochloride	969.0	E854.0	E939.0	E950.3	E962.0	E980.3
Doxapram	970.0	E854.3	E940.0	E950.4	E962.0	E980.4
Doxepin	969.0	E854.0	E939.0	E950.3	E962.0	E980.3
Doxorubicin	960.7	E856	E930.7	E950.4	E962.0	E980.4
Doxycycline	960.4	E856	E930.4	E950.4	E962.0	E980.4
Doxylamine	963.0	E858.1	E933.0	E950.4	E962.0	E980.4
Dramamine	963.0	E858.1	E933.0	E950.4	E962.0	E980.4
Drano (drain cleaner)	983.2	E864.2	—	E950.7	E962.1	E980.6
Dromoran	965.09	E850.2	E935.2	E950.0	E962.0	E980.0
Dromostanolone	962.1	E858.0	E932.1	E950.4	E962.0	E980.4
Droperidol	969.2	E853.1	E939.2	E950.3	E962.0	E980.3
Drotrecogin alfa	964.2	E858.2	E934.2	E950.4	E962.0	E980.4
Drug	977.9	E858.9	E947.9	E950.5	E962.0	E980.5

	Poisoning	External Cause (E-Code)				
		Accident	Therapeutic Use	Suicide Attempt	Assault	Undetermined
Drug — continued						
AHFS List						
4:00 antihistamine drugs	963.0	E858.1	E933.0	E950.4	E962.0	E980.4
8:04 amebacides	961.5	E857	E931.5	E950.4	E962.0	E980.4
arsenical anti-infectives	961.1	E857	E931.1	E950.4	E962.0	E980.4
quinoline derivatives	961.3	E857	E931.3	E950.4	E962.0	E980.4
8:08 anthelmintics	961.6	E857	E931.6	E950.4	E962.0	E980.4
quinoline derivatives	961.3	E857	E931.3	E950.4	E962.0	E980.4
8:12.04 antifungal						
antibiotics	960.1	E856	E930.1	E950.4	E962.0	E980.4
8:12.06 cephalosporins	960.5	E856	E930.5	E950.4	E962.0	E980.4
8:12.08 chloramphenicol	960.2	E856	E930.2	E950.4	E962.0	E980.4
8:12.12 erythromycins	960.3	E856	E930.3	E950.4	E962.0	E980.4
8:12.16 penicillins	960.0	E856	E930.0	E950.4	E962.0	E980.4
8:12.20 streptomycins	960.6	E856	E930.6	E950.4	E962.0	E980.4
8:12.24 tetracyclines	960.4	E856	E930.4	E950.4	E962.0	E980.4
8:12.28 other antibiotics	960.8	E856	E930.8	E950.4	E962.0	E980.4
antimycobacterial	960.6	E856	E930.6	E950.4	E962.0	E980.4
macrolides	960.3	E856	E930.3	E950.4	E962.0	E980.4
8:16 antituberculars	961.8	E857	E931.8	E950.4	E962.0	E980.4
antibiotics	960.6	E856	E930.6	E950.4	E962.0	E980.4
8:18 antivirals	961.7	E857	E931.7	E950.4	E962.0	E980.4
8:20 plasmodicides						
(antimalarials)	961.4	E857	E931.4	E950.4	E962.0	E980.4
8:24 sulfonamides	961.0	E857	E931.0	E950.4	E962.0	E980.4
8:26 sulfones	961.8	E857	E931.8	E950.4	E962.0	E980.4
8:28 treponemicides	961.2	E857	E931.2	E950.4	E962.0	E980.4
8:32 trichomonacides	961.5	E857	E931.5	E950.4	E962.0	E980.4
nitrofuran derivatives	961.9	E857	E931.9	E950.4	E962.0	E980.4
quinoline derivatives	961.3	E857	E931.3	E950.4	E962.0	E980.4
8:36 urinary germicides	961.9	E857	E931.9	E950.4	E962.0	E980.4
quinoline derivatives	961.3	E857	E931.3	E950.4	E962.0	E980.4
8:40 other anti-infectives	961.9	E857	E931.9	E950.4	E962.0	E980.4
10:00 antineoplastic						
agents	963.1	E858.1	E933.1	E950.4	E962.0	E980.4
antibiotics	960.7	E856	E930.7	E950.4	E962.0	E980.4
progestogens	962.2	E858.0	E932.2	E950.4	E962.0	E980.4
12:04 parasympathomimetic						
(cholinergic) agents	971.0	E855.3	E941.0	E950.4	E962.0	E980.4
12:08 parasympatholytic						
(cholinergic-blocking)						
agents	971.1	E855.4	E941.1	E950.4	E962.0	E980.4
12:12 Sympathomimetic						
(adrenergic) agents	971.2	E855.5	E941.2	E950.4	E962.0	E980.4
12:16 sympatholytic						
(adrenergic-blocking)						
agents	971.3	E855.6	E941.3	E950.4	E962.0	E980.4
12:20 skeletal muscle relaxants						
central nervous system						
muscle-tone						
depressants	968.0	E855.1	E938.0	E950.4	E962.0	E980.4
myoneural blocking						
agents	975.2	E858.6	E945.2	E950.4	E962.0	E980.4
16:00 blood derivatives	964.7	E858.2	E934.7	E950.4	E962.0	E980.4
20:04.04 iron preparations	964.0	E858.2	E934.0	E950.4	E962.0	E980.4
20:04.08 liver and stomach						
preparations	964.1	E858.2	E934.1	E950.4	E962.0	E980.4
20:04 antianemia drugs	964.1	E858.2	E934.1	E950.4	E962.0	E980.4
20:12.04 anticoagulants	964.2	E858.2	E934.2	E950.4	E962.0	E980.4
20:12.08 antiheparin						
agents	964.5	E858.2	E934.5	E950.4	E962.0	E980.4
20:12.12 coagulants	964.5	E858.2	E934.5	E950.4	E962.0	E980.4
20:12.16 hemostatics NEC	964.5	E858.2	E934.5	E950.4	E962.0	E980.4
capillary active drugs	972.8	E858.3	E942.8	E950.4	E962.0	E980.4
24:04 cardiac drugs	972.9	E858.3	E942.9	E950.4	E962.0	E980.4
cardiotonic agents	972.1	E858.3	E942.1	E950.4	E962.0	E980.4
rhythm regulators	972.0	E858.3	E942.0	E950.4	E962.0	E980.4
24:06 antilipemic agents	972.2	E858.3	E942.2	E950.4	E962.0	E980.4
thyroid derivatives	962.7	E858.0	E932.7	E950.4	E962.0	E980.4
24:08 hypotensive agents	972.6	E858.3	E942.6	E950.4	E962.0	E980.4
adrenergic blocking						
agents	971.3	E855.6	E941.3	E950.4	E962.0	E980.4
ganglion blocking agents	972.3	E858.3	E942.3	E950.4	E962.0	E980.4
vasodilators	972.5	E858.3	E942.5	E950.4	E962.0	E980.4
24:12 vasodilating agents						
NEC	972.5	E858.3	E942.5	E950.4	E962.0	E980.4
coronary	972.4	E858.3	E942.4	E950.4	E962.0	E980.4
nicotinic acid derivatives	972.2	E858.3	E942.2	E950.4	E962.0	E980.4
24:16 sclerosing agents	972.7	E858.3	E942.7	E950.4	E962.0	E980.4
28:04 general anesthetics	968.4	E855.1	E938.4	E950.4	E962.0	E980.4
gaseous anesthetics	968.2	E855.1	E938.2	E950.4	E962.0	E980.4
halothane	968.1	E855.1	E938.1	E950.4	E962.0	E980.4

☑ Additional Digit Required — Refer to the Tabular List for Digit Selection

▽ Subterms under main terms may continue to next column or page

Drug	Poisoning	Accident	Therapeutic Use	Suicide Attempt	Assault	Undetermined
Drug — *continued*						
28:04 general anesthetics — *continued*						
intravenous anesthetics	968.3	E855.1	E938.3	E950.4	E962.0	E980.4
28:08 analgesics and						
antipyretics	965.9	E850.9	E935.9	E950.0	E962.0	E980.0
antirheumatics	965.69	E850.6	E935.6	E950.0	E962.0	E980.0
aromatic analgesics	965.4	E850.4	E935.4	E950.0	E962.0	E980.0
non-narcotic NEC	965.7	E850.7	E935.7	E950.0	E962.0	E980.0
opium alkaloids	965.00	E850.2	E935.2	E950.0	E962.0	E980.0
heroin	965.01	E850.0	E935.0	E950.0	E962.0	E980.0
methadone	965.02	E850.1	E935.1	E950.0	E962.0	E980.0
specified type NEC	965.09	E850.2	E935.2	E950.0	E962.0	E980.0
pyrazole derivatives	965.5	E850.5	E935.5	E950.0	E962.0	E980.0
salicylates	965.1	E850.3	E935.3	E950.0	E962.0	E980.0
specified NEC	965.8	E850.8	E935.8	E950.0	E962.0	E980.0
28:10 narcotic antagonists	970.1	E854.3	E940.1	E950.4	E962.0	E980.4
28:12 anticonvulsants	966.3	E855.0	E936.3	E950.4	E962.0	E980.4
barbiturates	967.0	E851	E937.0	E950.1	E962.0	E980.1
benzodiazepine-based tranquilizers	969.4	E853.2	E939.4	E950.3	E962.0	E980.3
bromides	967.3	E852.2	E937.3	E950.2	E962.0	E980.2
hydantoin derivatives	966.1	E855.0	E936.1	E950.4	E962.0	E980.4
oxazolidine (derivatives)	966.0	E855.0	E936.0	E950.4	E962.0	E980.4
succinimides	966.2	E855.0	E936.2	E950.4	E962.0	E980.4
28:16.04 antidepressants	969.0	E854.0	E939.0	E950.3	E962.0	E980.3
28:16.08 tranquilizers	969.5	E853.9	E939.5	E950.3	E962.0	E980.3
benzodiazepine-based	969.4	E853.2	E939.4	E950.3	E962.0	E980.3
butyrophenone-based	969.2	E853.1	E939.2	E950.3	E962.0	E980.3
major NEC	969.3	E853.8	E939.3	E950.3	E962.0	E980.3
phenothiazine-based	969.1	E853.0	E939.1	E950.3	E962.0	E980.3
28:16.12 other psychotherapeutic agents	969.8	E855.8	E939.8	E950.3	E962.0	E980.3
28:20 respiratory and cerebral stimulants	970.9	E854.3	E940.9	E950.4	E962.0	E980.4
analeptics	970.0	E854.3	E940.0	E950.4	E962.0	E980.4
anorexigenic agents	977.0	E858.8	E947.0	E950.4	E962.0	E980.4
psychostimulants	969.7	E854.2	E939.7	E950.3	E962.0	E980.3
specified NEC	970.8	E854.3	E940.8	E950.4	E962.0	E980.4
28:24 sedatives and hypnotics	967.9	E852.9	E937.9	E950.2	E962.0	E980.2
barbiturates	967.0	E851	E937.0	E950.1	E962.0	E980.1
benzodiazepine-based tranquilizers	969.4	E853.2	E939.4	E950.3	E962.0	E980.3
chloral hydrate (group)	967.1	E852.0	E937.1	E950.2	E962.0	E980.2
glutethamide group	967.5	E852.4	E937.5	E950.2	E962.0	E980.2
intravenous anesthetics	968.3	E855.1	E938.3	E950.4	E962.0	E980.4
methaqualone (compounds)	967.4	E852.3	E937.4	E950.2	E962.0	E980.2
paraldehyde	967.2	E852.1	E937.2	E950.2	E962.0	E980.2
phenothiazine-based tranquilizers	969.1	E853.0	E939.1	E950.3	E962.0	E980.3
specified NEC	967.8	E852.8	E937.8	E950.2	E962.0	E980.2
thiobarbiturates	968.3	E855.1	E938.3	E950.4	E962.0	E980.4
tranquilizer NEC	969.5	E853.9	E939.5	E950.3	E962.0	E980.3
36:04 to 36:88 diagnostic agents	977.8	E858.8	E947.8	E950.4	E962.0	E980.4
40:00 electrolyte, caloric, and water balance agents NEC	974.5	E858.5	E944.5	E950.4	E962.0	E980.4
40:04 acidifying agents	963.2	E858.1	E933.2	E950.4	E962.0	E980.4
40:08 alkalinizing agents	963.3	E858.1	E933.3	E950.4	E962.0	E980.4
40:10 ammonia detoxicants	974.5	E858.5	E944.5	E950.4	E962.0	E980.4
40:12 replacement solutions	974.5	E858.5	E944.5	E950.4	E962.0	E980.4
plasma expanders	964.8	E858.2	E934.8	E950.4	E962.0	E980.4
40:16 sodium-removing resins	974.5	E858.5	E944.5	E950.4	E962.0	E980.4
40:18 potassium-removing resins	974.5	E858.5	E944.5	E950.4	E962.0	E980.4
40:20 caloric agents	974.5	E858.5	E944.5	E950.4	E962.0	E980.4
40:24 salt and sugar substitutes	974.5	E858.5	E944.5	E950.4	E962.0	E980.4
40:28 diuretics NEC	974.4	E858.5	E944.4	E950.4	E962.0	E980.4
carbonic acid anhydrase inhibitors	974.2	E858.5	E944.2	E950.4	E962.0	E980.4
mercurials	974.0	E858.5	E944.0	E950.4	E962.0	E980.4
purine derivatives	974.1	E858.5	E944.1	E950.4	E962.0	E980.4
saluretics	974.3	E858.5	E944.3	E950.4	E962.0	E980.4
thiazides	974.3	E858.5	E944.3	E950.4	E962.0	E980.4
40:36 irrigating solutions	974.5	E858.5	E944.5	E950.4	E962.0	E980.4

Drug	Poisoning	Accident	Therapeutic Use	Suicide Attempt	Assault	Undetermined
Drug — *continued*						
40:40 uricosuric agents	974.7	E858.5	E944.7	E950.4	E962.0	E980.4
44:00 enzymes	963.4	E858.1	E933.4	E950.4	E962.0	E980.4
fibrinolysis-affecting agents	964.4	E858.2	E934.4	E950.4	E962.0	E980.4
gastric agents	973.4	E858.4	E943.4	E950.4	E962.0	E980.4
48:00 expectorants and cough preparations						
antihistamine agents	963.0	E858.1	E933.0	E950.4	E962.0	E980.4
antitussives	975.4	E858.6	E945.4	E950.4	E962.0	E980.4
codeine derivatives	965.09	E850.2	E935.2	E950.0	E962.0	E980.0
expectorants	975.5	E858.6	E945.5	E950.4	E962.0	E980.4
narcotic agents NEC	965.09	E850.2	E935.2	E950.0	E962.0	E980.0
52:04.04 antibiotics (EENT)						
ENT agent	976.6	E858.7	E946.6	E950.4	E962.0	E980.4
ophthalmic preparation	976.5	E858.7	E946.5	E950.4	E962.0	E980.4
52:04.06 antivirals (EENT)						
ENT agent	976.6	E858.7	E946.6	E950.4	E962.0	E980.4
ophthalmic preparation	976.5	E858.7	E946.5	E950.4	E962.0	E980.4
52:04.08 sulfonamides (EENT)						
ENT agent	976.6	E858.7	E946.6	E950.4	E962.0	E980.4
ophthalmic preparation	976.5	E858.7	E946.5	E950.4	E962.0	E980.4
52:04.12 miscellaneous anti-infectives (EENT)						
ENT agent	976.6	E858.7	E946.6	E950.4	E962.0	E980.4
ophthalmic preparation	976.5	E858.7	E946.5	E950.4	E962.0	E980.4
52:04 anti-infectives (EENT)						
ENT agent	976.6	E858.7	E946.6	E950.4	E962.0	E980.4
ophthalmic preparation	976.5	E858.7	E946.5	E950.4	E962.0	E980.4
52:08 anti-inflammatory agents (EENT)						
ENT agent	976.6	E858.7	E946.6	E950.4	E962.0	E980.4
ophthalmic preparation	976.5	E858.7	E946.5	E950.4	E962.0	E980.4
52:10 carbonic anhydrase inhibitors	974.2	E858.5	E944.2	E950.4	E962.0	E980.4
52:12 contact lens solutions	976.5	E858.7	E946.5	E950.4	E962.0	E980.4
52:16 local anesthetics (EENT)	968.5	E855.2	E938.5	E950.4	E962.0	E980.4
52:20 miotics	971.0	E855.3	E941.0	E950.4	E962.0	E980.4
52:24 mydriatics						
adrenergics	971.2	E855.5	E941.2	E950.4	E962.0	E980.4
anticholinergics	971.1	E855.4	E941.1	E950.4	E962.0	E980.4
antimuscarinics	971.1	E855.4	E941.1	E950.4	E962.0	E980.4
parasympatholytics	971.1	E855.4	E941.1	E950.4	E962.0	E980.4
spasmolytics	971.1	E855.4	E941.1	E950.4	E962.0	E980.4
sympathomimetics	971.2	E855.5	E941.2	E950.4	E962.0	E980.4
52:28 mouth washes and gargles	976.6	E858.7	E946.6	E950.4	E962.0	E980.4
52:32 vasoconstrictors (EENT)	971.2	E855.5	E941.2	E950.4	E962.0	E980.4
52:36 unclassified agents (EENT)						
ENT agent	976.6	E858.7	E946.6	E950.4	E962.0	E980.4
ophthalmic preparation	976.5	E858.7	E946.5	E950.4	E962.0	E980.4
56:04 antacids and adsorbents	973.0	E858.4	E943.0	E950.4	E962.0	E980.4
56:08 antidiarrhea agents	973.5	E858.4	E943.5	E950.4	E962.0	E980.4
56:10 antiflatulents	973.8	E858.4	E943.8	E950.4	E962.0	E980.4
56:12 cathartics NEC	973.3	E858.4	E943.3	E950.4	E962.0	E980.4
emollients	973.2	E858.4	E943.2	E950.4	E962.0	E980.4
irritants	973.1	E858.4	E943.1	E950.4	E962.0	E980.4
56:16 digestants	973.4	E858.4	E943.4	E950.4	E962.0	E980.4
56:20 emetics and antiemetics						
antiemetics	963.0	E858.1	E933.0	E950.4	E962.0	E980.4
emetics	973.6	E858.4	E943.6	E950.4	E962.0	E980.4
56:24 lipotropic agents	977.1	E858.8	E947.1	E950.4	E962.0	E980.4
56:40 miscellaneous G.I. drugs	973.8	E858.4	E943.8	E950.4	E962.0	E980.4
60:00 gold compounds	965.69	E850.6	E935.6	E950.0	E962.0	E980.0
64:00 heavy metal antagonists	963.8	E858.1	E933.8	E950.4	E962.0	E980.4
68:04 adrenals	962.0	E858.0	E932.0	E950.4	E962.0	E980.4
68:08 androgens	962.1	E858.0	E932.1	E950.4	E962.0	E980.4
68:12 contraceptives, oral	962.2	E858.0	E932.2	E950.4	E962.0	E980.4
68:16 estrogens	962.2	E858.0	E932.2	E950.4	E962.0	E980.4
68:18 gonadotropins	962.4	E858.0	E932.4	E950.4	E962.0	E980.4
68:20.08 insulins	962.3	E858.0	E932.3	E950.4	E962.0	E980.4
68:20 insulins and antidiabetic agents	962.3	E858.0	E932.3	E950.4	E962.0	E980.4
68:24 parathyroid	962.6	E858.0	E932.6	E950.4	E962.0	E980.4
68:28 pituitary (posterior)	962.5	E858.0	E932.5	E950.4	E962.0	E980.4
anterior	962.4	E858.0	E932.4	E950.4	E962.0	E980.4

☑ Additional Digit Required — Refer to the Tabular List for Digit Selection   ▼ Subterms under main terms may continue to next column or page

2007 ICD-9-CM   ▶◀ Revised Text   ● New Line   ▲ Revised Code   **Volume 2 — 315**

Drug — continued	Poisoning	Accident	Therapeutic Use	Suicide Attempt	Assault	Undetermined
68:32 progestogens	962.2	E858.0	E932.2	E950.4	E962.0	E980.4
68:34 other corpus luteum hormones NEC	962.2	E858.0	E932.2	E950.4	E962.0	E980.4
68:36 thyroid and antithyroid						
antithyroid	962.8	E858.0	E932.8	E950.4	E962.0	E980.4
thyroid (derivatives)	962.7	E858.0	E932.7	E950.4	E962.0	E980.4
72:00 local anesthetics						
NEC	968.9	E855.2	E938.9	E950.4	E962.0	E980.4
infiltration (intradermal) (subcutaneous) (submucosal)	968.5	E855.2	E938.5	E950.4	E962.0	E980.4
nerve blocking (peripheral) (plexus) (regional)	968.6	E855.2	E938.6	E950.4	E962.0	E980.4
spinal	968.7	E855.2	E938.7	E950.4	E962.0	E980.4
topical (surface)	968.5	E855.2	E938.5	E950.4	E962.0	E980.4
76:00 oxytocics	975.0	E858.6	E945.0	E950.4	E962.0	E980.4
78:00 radioactive agents	990	—	—	—	—	—
80:04 serums NEC	979.9	E858.8	E949.9	E950.4	E962.0	E980.4
immune gamma globulin (human)	964.6	E858.2	E934.6	E950.4	E962.0	E980.4
80:08 toxoids NEC	978.8	E858.8	E948.8	E950.4	E962.0	E980.4
diphtheria	978.5	E858.8	E948.5	E950.4	E962.0	E980.4
and diphtheria	978.9	E858.8	E948.9	E950.4	E962.0	E980.4
with pertussis component	978.6	E858.8	E948.6	E950.4	E962.0	E980.4
and tetanus	978.9	E858.8	E948.9	E950.4	E962.0	E980.4
with pertussis component	978.6	E858.8	E948.6	E950.4	E962.0	E980.4
tetanus	978.4	E858.8	E948.4	E950.4	E962.0	E980.4
80:12 vaccines	979.9	E858.8	E949.9	E950.4	E962.0	E980.4
bacterial NEC	978.8	E858.8	E948.8	E950.4	E962.0	E980.4
with other bacterial components	978.9	E858.8	E948.9	E950.4	E962.0	E980.4
pertussis component	978.6	E858.8	E948.6	E950.4	E962.0	E980.4
viral and rickettsial components	979.7	E858.8	E949.7	E950.4	E962.0	E980.4
rickettsial NEC	979.6	E858.8	E949.6	E950.4	E962.0	E980.4
with bacterial component	979.7	E858.8	E949.7	E950.4	E962.0	E980.4
pertussis component	978.6	E858.8	E948.6	E950.4	E962.0	E980.4
viral component	979.7	E858.8	E949.7	E950.4	E962.0	E980.4
viral NEC	979.6	E858.8	E949.6	E950.4	E962.0	E980.4
with bacterial component	979.7	E858.8	E949.7	E950.4	E962.0	E980.4
pertussis component	978.6	E858.8	E948.6	E950.4	E962.0	E980.4
rickettsial component	979.7	E858.8	E949.7	E950.4	E962.0	E980.4
84:04.04 antibiotics (skin and mucous membrane)	976.0	E858.7	E946.0	E950.4	E962.0	E980.4
84:04.08 fungicides (skin and mucous membrane)	976.0	E858.7	E946.0	E950.4	E962.0	E980.4
84:04.12 scabicides and pediculicides (skin and mucous membrane)	976.0	E858.7	E946.0	E950.4	E962.0	E980.4
84:04.16 miscellaneous local anti-infectives (skin and mucous membrane)	976.0	E858.7	E946.0	E950.4	E962.0	E980.4
84:06 anti-inflammatory agents (skin and mucous membrane)	976.0	E858.7	E946.0	E950.4	E962.0	E980.4
84:08 antipruritics and local anesthetics						
antipruritics	976.1	E858.7	E946.1	E950.4	E962.0	E980.4
local anesthetics	968.5	E855.2	E938.5	E950.4	E962.0	E980.4
84:12 astringents	976.2	E858.7	E946.2	E950.4	E962.0	E980.4
84:16 cell stimulants and proliferants	976.8	E858.7	E946.8	E950.4	E962.0	E980.4
84:20 detergents	976.2	E858.7	E946.2	E950.4	E962.0	E980.4
84:24 emollients, demulcents, and protectants	976.3	E858.7	E946.3	E950.4	E962.0	E980.4
84:28 keratolytic agents	976.4	E858.7	E946.4	E950.4	E962.0	E980.4
84:32 keratoplastic agents	976.4	E858.7	E946.4	E950.4	E962.0	E980.4
84:36 miscellaneous agents (skin and mucous membrane)	976.8	E858.7	E946.8	E950.4	E962.0	E980.4

Drug — continued	Poisoning	Accident	Therapeutic Use	Suicide Attempt	Assault	Undetermined
86:00 spasmolytic agents	975.1	E858.6	E945.1	E950.4	E962.0	E980.4
antiasthmatics	975.7	E858.6	E945.7	E950.4	E962.0	E980.4
papaverine	972.5	E858.3	E942.5	E950.4	E962.0	E980.4
theophylline	974.1	E858.5	E944.1	E950.4	E962.0	E980.4
88:04 vitamin A	963.5	E858.1	E933.5	E950.4	E962.0	E980.4
88:08 vitamin B complex	963.5	E858.1	E933.5	E950.4	E962.0	E980.4
hematopoietic vitamin	964.1	E858.2	E934.1	E950.4	E962.0	E980.4
nicotinic acid derivatives	972.2	E858.3	E942.2	E950.4	E962.0	E980.4
88:12 vitamin C	963.5	E858.1	E933.5	E950.4	E962.0	E980.4
88:16 vitamin D	963.5	E858.1	E933.5	E950.4	E962.0	E980.4
88:20 vitamin E	963.5	E858.1	E933.5	E950.4	E962.0	E980.4
88:24 vitamin K activity	964.3	E858.2	E934.3	E950.4	E962.0	E980.4
88:28 multivitamin preparations	963.5	E858.1	E933.5	E950.4	E962.0	E980.4
92:00 unclassified therapeutic agents	977.8	E858.8	E947.8	E950.4	E962.0	E980.4
specified NEC	977.8	E858.8	E947.8	E950.4	E962.0	E980.4
Duboisine	971.1	E855.4	E941.1	E950.4	E962.0	E980.4
Dulcolax	973.1	E858.4	E943.1	E950.4	E962.0	E980.4
Duponol (C) (EP)	976.2	E858.7	E946.2	E950.4	E962.0	E980.4
Durabolin	962.1	E858.0	E932.1	E950.4	E962.0	E980.4
Dyclone	968.5	E855.2	E938.5	E950.4	E962.0	E980.4
Dyclonine	968.5	E855.2	E938.5	E950.4	E962.0	E980.4
Dydrogesterone	962.2	E858.0	E932.2	E950.4	E962.0	E980.4
Dyes NEC	989.89	E866.8	—	E950.9	E962.1	E980.9
diagnostic agents	977.8	E858.8	E947.8	E950.4	E962.0	E980.4
pharmaceutical NEC	977.4	E858.8	E947.4	E950.4	E962.0	E980.4
Dyfols	971.0	E855.3	E941.0	E950.4	E962.0	E980.4
Dymelor	962.3	E858.0	E932.3	E950.4	E962.0	E980.4
Dynamite	989.89	E866.8	—	E950.9	E962.1	E980.9
fumes	987.8	E869.8	—	E952.8	E962.2	E982.8
Dyphylline	975.1	E858.6	E945.1	E950.4	E962.0	E980.4
Ear preparations	976.6	E858.7	E946.6	E950.4	E962.0	E980.4
Echothiophate, ecothiopate	971.0	E855.3	E941.0	E950.4	E962.0	E980.4
Ecstasy	969.7	E854.2	E939.7	E950.3	E962.0	E980.3
Ectylurea	967.8	E852.8	E937.8	E950.2	E962.0	E980.2
Edathamil disodium	963.8	E858.1	E933.8	E950.4	E962.0	E980.4
Edecrin	974.4	E858.5	E944.4	E950.4	E962.0	E980.4
Edetate, disodium (calcium)	963.8	E858.1	E933.8	E950.4	E962.0	E980.4
Edrophonium	971.0	E855.3	E941.0	E950.4	E962.0	E980.4
Elase	976.8	E858.7	E946.8	E950.4	E962.0	E980.4
Elaterium	973.1	E858.4	E943.1	E950.4	E962.0	E980.4
Elder	988.2	E865.4	—	E950.9	E962.1	E980.9
berry (unripe)	988.2	E865.3	—	E950.9	E962.1	E980.9
Electrolytes NEC	974.5	E858.5	E944.5	E950.4	E962.0	E980.4
Electrolytic agent NEC	974.5	E858.5	E944.5	E950.4	E962.0	E980.4
Embramine	963.0	E858.1	E933.0	E950.4	E962.0	E980.4
Emetics	973.6	E858.4	E943.6	E950.4	E962.0	E980.4
Emetine (hydrochloride)	961.5	E857	E931.5	E950.4	E962.0	E980.4
Emollients	976.3	E858.7	E946.3	E950.4	E962.0	E980.4
Emylcamate	969.5	E853.8	E939.5	E950.3	E962.0	E980.3
Encainide	972.0	E858.3	E942.0	E950.4	E962.0	E980.4
Encyprate	969.0	E854.0	E939.0	E950.3	E962.0	E980.3
Endocaine	968.5	E855.2	E938.5	E950.4	E962.0	E980.4
Endrin	989.2	E863.0	—	E950.6	E962.1	E980.7
Enflurane	968.2	E855.1	E938.2	E950.4	E962.0	E980.4
Enovid	962.2	E858.0	E932.2	E950.4	E962.0	E980.4
ENT preparations (anti-infectives)	976.6	E858.7	E946.6	E950.4	E962.0	E980.4
Enzodase	963.4	E858.1	E933.4	E950.4	E962.0	E980.4
Enzymes NEC	963.4	E858.1	E933.4	E950.4	E962.0	E980.4
Epanutin	966.1	E855.0	E936.1	E950.4	E962.0	E980.4
Ephedra (tincture)	971.2	E855.5	E941.2	E950.4	E962.0	E980.4
Ephedrine	971.2	E855.5	E941.2	E950.4	E962.0	E980.4
Epiestriol	962.2	E858.0	E932.2	E950.4	E962.0	E980.4
Epilim — see Sodium valproate						
Epinephrine	971.2	E855.5	E941.2	E950.4	E962.0	E980.4
Epsom salt	973.3	E858.4	E943.3	E950.4	E962.0	E980.4
Equanil	969.5	E853.8	E939.5	E950.3	E962.0	E980.3
Equisetum (diuretic)	974.4	E858.5	E944.4	E950.4	E962.0	E980.4
Ergometrine	975.0	E858.6	E945.0	E950.4	E962.0	E980.4
Ergonovine	975.0	E858.6	E945.0	E950.4	E962.0	E980.4
Ergot NEC	988.2	E865.4	—	E950.9	E962.1	E980.9
medicinal (alkaloids)	975.0	E858.6	E945.0	E950.4	E962.0	E980.4
Ergotamine (tartrate) (for migraine) NEC	972.9	E858.3	E942.9	E950.4	E962.0	E980.4
Ergotrate	975.0	E858.6	E945.0	E950.4	E962.0	E980.4
Erythrityl tetranitrate	972.4	E858.3	E942.4	E950.4	E962.0	E980.4
Erythrol tetranitrate	972.4	E858.3	E942.4	E950.4	E962.0	E980.4
Erythromycin	960.3	E856	E930.3	E950.4	E962.0	E980.4
ophthalmic preparation	976.5	E858.7	E946.5	E950.4	E962.0	E980.4

☑ Additional Digit Required — Refer to the Tabular List for Digit Selection

Subterms under main terms may continue to next column or page

	Poisoning	External Cause (E-Code)				
		Accident	Therapeutic Use	Suicide Attempt	Assault	Undetermined
Erythromycin — *continued*						
topical NEC	976.0	E858.7	E946.0	E950.4	E962.0	E980.4
Eserine	971.0	E855.3	E941.0	E950.4	E962.0	E980.4
Eskabarb	967.0	E851	E937.0	E950.1	E962.0	E980.1
Eskalith	969.8	E855.8	E939.8	E950.3	E962.0	E980.3
Estradiol (cypionate) (dipropionate)						
(valerate)	962.2	E858.0	E932.2	E950.4	E962.0	E980.4
Estriol	962.2	E858.0	E932.2	E950.4	E962.0	E980.4
Estrogens (with						
progestogens)	962.2	E858.0	E932.2	E950.4	E962.0	E980.4
Estrone	962.2	E858.0	E932.2	E950.4	E962.0	E980.4
Etafedrine	971.2	E855.5	E941.2	E950.4	E962.0	E980.4
Ethacrynate sodium	974.4	E858.5	E944.4	E950.4	E962.0	E980.4
Ethacrynic acid	974.4	E858.5	E944.4	E950.4	E962.0	E980.4
Ethambutol	961.8	E857	E931.8	E950.4	E962.0	E980.4
Ethamide	974.2	E858.5	E944.2	E950.4	E962.0	E980.4
Ethamivan	970.0	E854.3	E940.0	E950.4	E962.0	E980.4
Ethamsylate	964.5	E858.2	E934.5	E950.4	E962.0	E980.4
Ethanol	980.0	E860.1	—	E950.9	E962.1	E980.9
beverage	980.0	E860.0	—	E950.9	E962.1	E980.9
Ethchlorvynol	967.8	E852.8	E937.8	E950.2	E962.0	E980.2
Ethebenecid	974.7	E858.5	E944.7	E950.4	E962.0	E980.4
Ether(s) (diethyl) (ethyl)						
(vapor)	987.8	E869.8	—	E952.8	E962.2	E982.8
anesthetic	968.2	E855.1	E938.2	E950.4	E962.0	E980.4
petroleum — *see* Ligroin						
solvent	982.8	E862.4	—	E950.9	E962.1	E980.9
Ethidine chloride (vapor)	987.8	E869.8	—	E952.8	E962.2	E982.8
liquid (solvent)	982.3	E862.4	—	E950.9	E962.1	E980.9
Ethinamate	967.8	E852.8	E937.8	E950.2	E962.0	E980.2
Ethinylestradiol	962.2	E858.0	E932.2	E950.4	E962.0	E980.4
Ethionamide	961.8	E857	E931.8	E950.4	E962.0	E980.4
Ethisterone	962.2	E858.0	E932.2	E950.4	E962.0	E980.4
Ethobral	967.0	E851	E937.0	E950.1	E962.0	E980.1
Ethocaine (infiltration)						
(topical)	968.5	E855.2	E938.5	E950.4	E962.0	E980.4
nerve block (peripheral)						
(plexus)	968.6	E855.2	E938.6	E950.4	E962.0	E980.4
spinal	968.7	E855.2	E938.7	E950.4	E962.0	E980.4
Ethoheptazine (citrate)	965.7	E850.7	E935.7	E950.0	E962.0	E980.0
Ethopropazine	966.4	E855.0	E936.4	E950.4	E962.0	E980.4
Ethosuximide	966.2	E855.0	E936.2	E950.4	E962.0	E980.4
Ethotoin	966.1	E855.0	E936.1	E950.4	E962.0	E980.4
Ethoxazene	961.9	E857	E931.9	E950.4	E962.0	E980.4
Ethoxzolamide	974.2	E858.5	E944.2	E950.4	E962.0	E980.4
Ethyl						
acetate (vapor)	982.8	E862.4	—	E950.9	E962.1	E980.9
alcohol	980.0	E860.1	—	E950.9	E962.1	E980.9
beverage	980.0	E860.0	—	E950.9	E962.1	E980.9
aldehyde (vapor)	987.8	E869.8	—	E952.8	E962.2	E982.8
liquid	989.89	E866.8	—	E950.9	E962.1	E980.9
aminobenzoate	968.5	E855.2	E938.5	E950.4	E962.0	E980.4
biscoumacetate	964.2	E858.2	E934.2	E950.4	E962.0	E980.4
bromide (anesthetic)	968.2	E855.1	E938.2	E950.4	E962.0	E980.4
carbamate (antineoplastic)	963.1	E858.1	E933.1	E950.4	E962.0	E980.4
carbinol	980.3	E860.4	—	E950.9	E962.1	E980.9
chaulmoograte	961.8	E857	E931.8	E950.4	E962.0	E980.4
chloride (vapor)	987.8	E869.8	—	E952.8	E962.2	E982.8
anesthetic (local)	968.5	E855.2	E938.5	E950.4	E962.0	E980.4
inhaled	968.2	E855.1	E938.2	E950.4	E962.0	E980.4
solvent	982.3	E862.4	—	E950.9	E962.1	E980.9
estranol	962.1	E858.0	E932.1	E950.4	E962.0	E980.4
ether — *see* Ether(s)						
formate (solvent) NEC	982.8	E862.4	—	E950.9	E962.1	E980.9
iodoacetate	987.5	E869.3	—	E952.8	E962.2	E982.8
lactate (solvent) NEC	982.8	E862.4	—	E950.9	E962.1	E980.9
methylcarbinol	980.8	E860.8	—	E950.9	E962.1	E980.9
morphine	965.09	E850.2	E935.2	E950.0	E962.0	E980.0
Ethylene (gas)	987.1	E869.8	—	E952.8	E962.2	E982.8
anesthetic (general)	968.2	E855.1	E938.2	E950.4	E962.0	E980.4
chlorohydrin (vapor)	982.3	E862.4	—	E950.9	E962.1	E980.9
dichloride (vapor)	982.3	E862.4	—	E950.9	E962.1	E980.9
glycol(s) (any) (vapor)	982.8	E862.4	—	E950.9	E962.1	E980.9
Ethylidene						
chloride NEC	982.3	E862.4	—	E950.9	E962.1	E980.9
diethyl ether	982.8	E862.4	—	E950.9	E962.1	E980.9
Ethynodiol	962.2	E858.0	E932.2	E950.4	E962.0	E980.4
Etidocaine	968.9	E855.2	E938.9	E950.4	E962.0	E980.4
infiltration (subcutaneous)	968.5	E855.2	E938.5	E950.4	E962.0	E980.4
nerve (peripheral) (plexus)	968.6	E855.2	E938.6	E950.4	E962.0	E980.4
Etilfen	967.0	E851	E937.0	E950.1	E962.0	E980.1

	Poisoning	External Cause (E-Code)				
		Accident	Therapeutic Use	Suicide Attempt	Assault	Undetermined
Etomide	965.7	E850.7	E935.7	E950.0	E962.0	E980.0
Etorphine	965.09	E850.2	E935.2	E950.0	E962.0	E980.0
Etoval	967.0	E851	E937.0	E950.1	E962.0	E980.1
Etryptamine	969.0	E854.0	E939.0	E950.3	E962.0	E980.3
Eucaine	968.5	E855.2	E938.5	E950.4	E962.0	E980.4
Eucalyptus (oil) NEC	975.5	E858.6	E945.5	E950.4	E962.0	E980.4
Eucatropine	971.1	E855.4	E941.1	E950.4	E962.0	E980.4
Eucodal	965.09	E850.2	E935.2	E950.0	E962.0	E980.0
Euneryl	967.0	E851	E937.0	E950.1	E962.0	E980.1
Euphthalmine	971.1	E855.4	E941.1	E950.4	E962.0	E980.4
Eurax	976.0	E858.7	E946.0	E950.4	E962.0	E980.4
Euresol	976.4	E858.7	E946.4	E950.4	E962.0	E980.4
Euthroid	962.7	E858.0	E932.7	E950.4	E962.0	E980.4
Evans blue	977.8	E858.8	E947.8	E950.4	E962.0	E980.4
Evipal	967.0	E851	E937.0	E950.1	E962.0	E980.1
sodium	968.3	E855.1	E938.3	E950.4	E962.0	E980.4
Evipan	967.0	E851	E937.0	E950.1	E962.0	E980.1
sodium	968.3	E855.1	E938.3	E950.4	E962.0	E980.4
Exalgin	965.4	E850.4	E935.4	E950.0	E962.0	E980.0
Excipients,						
pharmaceutical	977.4	E858.8	E947.4	E950.4	E962.0	E980.4
Exhaust gas — *see* Carbon, monoxide						
Ex-Lax (phenolphthalein)	973.1	E858.4	E943.1	E950.4	E962.0	E980.4
Expectorants	975.5	E858.6	E945.5	E950.4	E962.0	E980.4
External medications (skin)						
(mucous membrane)	976.9	E858.7	E946.9	E950.4	E962.0	E980.4
dental agent	976.7	E858.7	E946.7	E950.4	E962.0	E980.4
ENT agent	976.6	E858.7	E946.6	E950.4	E962.0	E980.4
ophthalmic preparation	976.5	E858.7	E946.5	E950.4	E962.0	E980.4
specified NEC	976.8	E858.7	E946.8	E950.4	E962.0	E980.4
Eye agents (anti-infective)	976.5	E858.7	E946.5	E950.4	E962.0	E980.4
Factor IX complex (human)	964.5	E858.2	E934.5	E950.4	E962.0	E980.4
Fecal softeners	973.2	E858.4	E943.2	E950.4	E962.0	E980.4
Fenbutrazate	977.0	E858.8	E947.0	E950.4	E962.0	E980.4
Fencamfamin	970.8	E854.3	E940.8	E950.4	E962.0	E980.4
Fenfluramine	977.0	E858.8	E947.0	E950.4	E962.0	E980.4
Fenoprofen	965.61	E850.6	E935.6	E950.0	E962.0	E980.0
Fentanyl	965.09	E850.2	E935.2	E950.0	E962.0	E980.0
Fentazin	969.1	E853.0	E939.1	E950.3	E962.0	E980.3
Fenticlor, fentichlor	976.0	E858.7	E946.0	E950.4	E962.0	E980.4
Fer de lance (bite) (venom)	989.5	E905.0	—	E950.9	E962.1	E980.9
Ferric — *see* Iron						
Ferrocholinate	964.0	E858.2	E934.0	E950.4	E962.0	E980.4
Ferrous fumerate, gluconate, lactate, salt NEC, sulfate						
(medicinal)	964.0	E858.2	E934.0	E950.4	E962.0	E980.4
Ferrum — *see* Iron						
Fertilizers NEC	989.89	E866.5	—	E950.9	E962.1	E980.4
with herbicide mixture	989.4	E863.5	—	E950.6	E962.1	E980.7
Fibrinogen (human)	964.7	E858.2	E934.7	E950.4	E962.0	E980.4
Fibrinolysin	964.4	E858.2	E934.4	E950.4	E962.0	E980.4
Fibrinolysis-affecting agents	964.4	E858.2	E934.4	E950.4	E962.0	E980.4
Filix mas	961.6	E857	E931.6	E950.4	E962.0	E980.4
Fiorinal	965.1	E850.3	E935.3	E950.0	E962.0	E980.0
Fire damp	987.1	E869.8	—	E952.8	E962.2	E982.8
Fish, nonbacterial or noxious	988.0	E865.2	—	E950.9	E962.1	E980.9
shell	988.0	E865.1	—	E950.9	E962.1	E980.9
Flagyl	961.5	E857	E931.5	E950.4	E962.0	E980.4
Flavoxate	975.1	E858.6	E945.1	E950.4	E962.0	E980.4
Flaxedil	975.2	E858.6	E945.2	E950.4	E962.0	E980.4
Flaxseed (medicinal)	976.3	E858.7	E946.3	E950.4	E962.0	E980.4
Florantyrone	973.4	E858.4	E943.4	E950.4	E962.0	E980.4
Floraquin	961.3	E857	E931.3	E950.4	E962.0	E980.4
Florinef	962.0	E858.0	E932.0	E950.4	E962.0	E980.4
ENT agent	976.6	E858.7	E946.6	E950.4	E962.0	E980.4
ophthalmic preparation	976.5	E858.7	E946.5	E950.4	E962.0	E980.4
topical NEC	976.0	E858.7	E946.0	E950.4	E962.0	E980.4
Flowers of sulfur	976.4	E858.7	E946.4	E950.4	E962.0	E980.4
Floxuridine	963.1	E858.1	E933.1	E950.4	E962.0	E980.4
Flucytosine	961.9	E857	E931.9	E950.4	E962.0	E980.4
Fludrocortisone	962.0	E858.0	E932.0	E950.4	E962.0	E980.4
ENT agent	976.6	E858.7	E946.6	E950.4	E962.0	E980.4
ophthalmic preparation	976.5	E858.7	E946.5	E950.4	E962.0	E980.4
topical NEC	976.0	E858.7	E946.0	E950.4	E962.0	E980.4
Flumethasone	976.0	E858.7	E946.0	E950.4	E962.0	E980.4
Flumethiazide	974.3	E858.5	E944.3	E950.4	E962.0	E980.4
Flumidin	961.7	E857	E931.7	E950.4	E962.0	E980.4
Flunitrazepam	969.4	E853.2	E939.4	E950.3	E962.0	E980.3

☑ Additional Digit Required — Refer to the Tabular List for Digit Selection

▽ Subterms under main terms may continue to next column or page

	Poisoning	Accident	Therapeutic Use	Suicide Attempt	Assault	Undetermined
Fluocinolone	976.0	E858.7	E946.0	E950.4	E962.0	E980.4
Fluocortolone	962.0	E858.0	E932.0	E950.4	E962.0	E980.4
Fluohydrocortisone	962.0	E858.0	E932.0	E950.4	E962.0	E980.4
ENT agent	976.6	E858.7	E946.6	E950.4	E962.0	E980.4
ophthalmic preparation	976.5	E858.7	E946.5	E950.4	E962.0	E980.4
topical NEC	976.0	E858.7	E946.0	E950.4	E962.0	E980.4
Fluonid	976.0	E858.7	E946.0	E950.4	E962.0	E980.4
Fluopromazine	969.1	E853.0	E939.1	E950.3	E962.0	E980.3
Fluoracetate	989.4	E863.7	—	E950.6	E962.1	E980.7
Fluorescein (sodium)	977.8	E858.8	E947.8	E950.4	E962.0	E980.4
Fluoride(s) (pesticides) (sodium) NEC	989.4	E863.4	—	E950.6	E962.1	E980.7
hydrogen — see Hydrofluoric acid						
medicinal	976.7	E858.7	E946.7	E950.4	E962.0	E980.4
not pesticide NEC	983.9	E864.4	—	E950.7	E962.1	E980.6
stannous	976.7	E858.7	E946.7	E950.4	E962.0	E980.4
Fluorinated corticosteroids	962.0	E858.0	E932.0	E950.4	E962.0	E980.4
Fluorine (compounds) (gas)	987.8	E869.8	—	E952.8	E962.2	E982.8
salt — see Fluoride(s)						
Fluoristan	976.7	E858.7	E946.7	E950.4	E962.0	E980.4
Fluoroacetate	989.4	E863.7	—	E950.6	E962.1	E980.7
Fluorodeoxyuridine	963.1	E858.1	E933.1	E950.4	E962.0	E980.4
Fluorometholone (topical) NEC	976.0	E858.7	E946.0	E950.4	E962.0	E980.4
ophthalmic preparation	976.5	E858.7	E946.5	E950.4	E962.0	E980.4
Fluorouracil	963.1	E858.1	E933.1	E950.4	E962.0	E980.4
Fluothane	968.1	E855.1	E938.1	E950.4	E962.0	E980.4
Fluoxetine hydrochloride	969.0	E854.0	E939.0	E950.3	E962.0	E980.3
Fluoxymesterone	962.1	E858.0	E932.1	E950.4	E962.0	E980.4
Fluphenazine	969.1	E853.0	E939.1	E950.3	E962.0	E980.3
Fluprednisolone	962.0	E858.0	E932.0	E950.4	E962.0	E980.4
Flurandrenolide	976.0	E858.7	E946.0	E950.4	E962.0	E980.4
Flurazepam (hydrochloride)	969.4	E853.2	E939.4	E950.3	E962.0	E980.3
Flurbiprofen	965.61	E850.6	E935.6	E950.0	E962.0	E980.0
Flurobate	976.0	E858.7	E946.0	E950.4	E962.0	E980.4
Flurothyl	969.8	E855.8	E939.8	E950.3	E962.0	E980.3
Fluroxene	968.2	E855.1	E938.2	E950.4	E962.0	E980.4
Folacin	964.1	E858.2	E934.1	E950.4	E962.0	E980.4
Folic acid	964.1	E858.2	E934.1	E950.4	E962.0	E980.4
Follicle stimulating hormone	962.4	E858.0	E932.4	E950.4	E962.0	E980.4
Food, foodstuffs, nonbacterial or noxious	988.9	E865.9	—	E950.9	E962.1	E980.9
berries, seeds	988.2	E865.3	—	E950.9	E962.1	E980.9
fish	988.0	E865.2	—	E950.9	E962.1	E980.9
mushrooms	988.1	E865.5	—	E950.9	E962.1	E980.9
plants	988.2	E865.9	—	E950.9	E962.1	E980.9
specified type NEC	988.2	E865.4	—	E950.9	E962.1	E980.9
shellfish	988.0	E865.1	—	E950.9	E962.1	E980.9
specified NEC	988.8	E865.8	—	E950.9	E962.1	E980.9
Fool's parsley	988.2	E865.4	—	E950.9	E962.1	E980.9
Formaldehyde (solution)	989.89	E861.4	—	E950.9	E962.1	E980.9
fungicide	989.4	E863.6	—	E950.6	E962.1	E980.7
gas or vapor	987.8	E869.8	—	E952.8	E962.2	E982.8
Formalin	989.89	E861.4	—	E950.9	E962.1	E980.9
fungicide	989.4	E863.6	—	E950.6	E962.1	E980.7
vapor	987.8	E869.8	—	E952.8	E962.2	E982.8
Formic acid	983.1	E864.1	—	E950.7	E962.1	E980.6
automobile	981	E862.1	—	E950.9	E962.1	E980.9
exhaust gas, not in transit	986	E868.2	—	E952.0	E962.2	E982.0
vapor NEC	987.1	E869.8	—	E952.8	E962.2	E982.8
gas (domestic use) (see also Carbon, monoxide, fuel) utility	987.1	E868.1	—	E951.8	E962.2	E981.8
incomplete combustion of — see Carbon, monoxide, fuel, utility						
in mobile container	987.0	E868.0	—	E951.1	E962.2	E981.1
piped (natural)	987.1	E867	—	E951.0	E962.2	E981.0
industrial, incomplete combustion	986	E868.3	—	E952.1	E962.2	E982.1
vapor	987.8	E869.8	—	E952.8	E962.2	E982.8
Fowler's solution	985.1	E866.3	—	E950.8	E962.1	E980.8
Foxglove	988.2	E865.4	—	E950.9	E962.1	E980.9
Fox green	977.8	E858.8	E947.8	E950.4	E962.0	E980.4
Framycetin	960.8	E856	E930.8	E950.4	E962.0	E980.4
Frangula (extract)	973.1	E858.4	E943.1	E950.4	E962.0	E980.4
Frei antigen	977.8	E858.8	E947.8	E950.4	E962.0	E980.4
Freons	987.4	E869.2	—	E952.8	E962.2	E982.8
Fructose	974.5	E858.5	E944.5	E950.4	E962.0	E980.4
Frusemide	974.4	E858.5	E944.4	E950.4	E962.0	E980.4
FSH	962.4	E858.0	E932.4	E950.4	E962.0	E980.4
Fuel						
Fugillin	960.8	E856	E930.8	E950.4	E962.0	E980.4
Fulminate of mercury	985.0	E866.1	—	E950.9	E962.1	E980.9
Fulvicin	960.1	E856	E930.1	E950.4	E962.0	E980.4
Fumadil	960.8	E856	E930.8	E950.4	E962.0	E980.4
Fumagillin	960.8	E856	E930.8	E950.4	E962.0	E980.4
Fumes (from)	987.9	E869.9	—	E952.9	E962.2	E982.9
carbon monoxide — see Carbon, monoxide						
charcoal (domestic use)	986	E868.3	—	E952.1	E962.2	E982.1
chloroform — see Chloroform						
coke (in domestic stoves, fireplaces)	986	E868.3	—	E952.1	E962.2	E982.1
corrosive NEC	987.8	E869.8	—	E952.8	E962.2	E982.8
ether — see Ether(s)						
freons	987.4	E869.2	—	E952.8	E962.2	E982.8
hydrocarbons	987.1	E869.8	—	E952.8	E962.2	E982.8
petroleum (liquefied)	987.0	E868.0	—	E951.1	E962.2	E981.1
distributed through pipes (pure or mixed with air)	987.0	E867	—	E951.0	E962.2	E981.0
lead — see Lead						
metals — see specified metal						
nitrogen dioxide	987.2	E869.0	—	E952.8	E962.2	E982.8
pesticides — see Pesticides						
petroleum (liquefied)	987.0	E868.0	—	E951.1	E962.2	E981.1
distributed through pipes (pure or mixed with air)	987.0	E867	—	E951.0	E962.2	E981.0
polyester	987.8	E869.8	—	E952.8	E962.2	E982.8
specified, source other (see also substance specified)	987.8	E869.8	—	E952.8	E962.2	E982.8
sulfur dioxide	987.3	E869.1	—	E952.8	E962.2	E982.8
Fumigants	989.4	E863.8	—	E950.6	E962.1	E980.7
Fungicides — see also Antifungals	989.4	E863.6	—	E950.6	E962.1	E980.7
Fungi, noxious, used as food	988.1	E865.5	—	E950.9	E962.1	E980.9
Fungizone	960.1	E856	E930.1	E950.4	E962.0	E980.4
topical	976.0	E858.7	E946.0	E950.4	E962.0	E980.4
Furacin	976.0	E858.7	E946.0	E950.4	E962.0	E980.4
Furadantin	961.9	E857	E931.9	E950.4	E962.0	E980.4
Furazolidone	961.9	E857	E931.9	E950.4	E962.0	E980.4
Furnace (coal burning) (domestic), gas from	986	E868.3	—	E952.1	E962.2	E982.1
industrial	986	E868.8	—	E952.1	E962.2	E982.1
Furniture polish	989.89	E861.2	—	E950.9	E962.1	E980.9
Furosemide	974.4	E858.5	E944.4	E950.4	E962.0	E980.4
Furoxone	961.9	E857	E931.9	E950.4	E962.0	E980.4
Fusel oil (amyl) (butyl) (propyl)	980.3	E860.4	—	E950.9	E962.1	E980.9
Fusidic acid	960.8	E856	E930.8	E950.4	E962.0	E980.4
Gallamine	975.2	E858.6	E945.2	E950.4	E962.0	E980.4
Gallotannic acid	976.2	E858.7	E946.2	E950.4	E962.0	E980.4
Gamboge	973.1	E858.4	E943.1	E950.4	E962.0	E980.4
Gamimune	964.6	E858.2	E934.6	E950.4	E962.0	E980.4
Gamma-benzene hexachloride (vapor)	989.2	E863.0	—	E950.6	E962.1	E980.7
Gamma globulin	964.6	E858.2	E934.6	E950.4	E962.0	E980.4
Gamma hydroxy butyrate (GHB)	968.4	E855.1	E938.4	E950.4	E962.0	E980.4
Gamulin	964.6	E858.2	E934.6	E950.4	E962.0	E980.4
Ganglionic blocking agents	972.3	E858.3	E942.3	E950.4	E962.0	E980.4
Ganja	969.6	E854.1	E939.6	E950.3	E962.0	E980.3
Garamycin	960.8	E856	E930.8	E950.4	E962.0	E980.4
ophthalmic preparation	976.5	E858.7	E946.5	E950.4	E962.0	E980.4
topical NEC	976.0	E858.7	E946.0	E950.4	E962.0	E980.4
Gardenal	967.0	E851	E937.0	E950.1	E962.0	E980.1
Gardepanyl	967.0	E851	E937.0	E950.1	E962.0	E980.1
Gas	987.9	E869.9	—	E952.9	E962.2	E982.9
acetylene	987.1	E868.1	—	E951.8	E962.2	E981.8
incomplete combustion of — see Carbon, monoxide, fuel, utility						
air contaminants, source or type not specified	987.9	E869.9	—	E952.9	E962.2	E982.9
anesthetic (general) NEC	968.2	E855.1	E938.2	E950.4	E962.0	E980.4

☑ Additional Digit Required — Refer to the Tabular List for Digit Selection

Subterms under main terms may continue to next column or page

		External Cause (E-Code)				
	Poisoning	Accident	Therapeutic Use	Suicide Attempt	Assault	Undeter-mined
Gas — *continued*						
blast furnace	986	E868.8	—	E952.1	E962.2	E982.1
butane — see Butane						
carbon monoxide — see Carbon, monoxide						
chlorine	987.6	E869.8	—	E952.8	E962.2	E982.8
coal — see Carbon, monoxide, coal						
cyanide	987.7	E869.8	—	E952.8	E962.2	E982.8
dicyanogen	987.8	E869.8	—	E952.8	E962.2	E982.8
domestic — see Gas, utility						
exhaust — see Carbon, monoxide, exhaust gas						
from wood- or coal-burning stove or fireplace	986	E868.3	—	E952.1	E962.2	E982.1
fuel (domestic use) (*see also* Carbon, monoxide, fuel)						
industrial use	986	E868.8	—	E952.1	E962.2	E982.1
utility	987.1	E868.1	—	E951.8	E962.2	E981.8
incomplete combustion of — see Carbon, monoxide, fuel, utility						
in mobile container	987.0	E868.0	—	E951.1	E962.2	E981.1
piped (natural)	987.1	E867	—	E951.0	E962.2	E981.0
garage	986	E868.2	—	E952.0	E962.2	E982.0
hydrocarbon NEC	987.1	E869.8	—	E952.8	E962.2	E982.8
incomplete combustion of — see Carbon, monoxide, fuel, utility						
liquefied (mobile container)	987.0	E868.0	—	E951.1	E962.2	E981.1
piped	987.0	E867	—	E951.0	E962.2	E981.0
hydrocyanic acid	987.7	E869.8	—	E952.8	E962.2	E982.8
illuminating — see Gas, utility						
incomplete combustion, any — see Carbon, monoxide						
kiln	986	E868.8	—	E952.1	E962.2	E982.1
lacrimogenic	987.5	E869.3	—	E952.8	E962.2	E982.8
marsh	987.1	E869.8	—	E952.8	E962.2	E982.8
motor exhaust, not in transit	986	E868.8	—	E952.1	E962.2	E982.1
mustard — see Mustard, gas						
natural	987.1	E867	—	E951.0	E962.2	E981.0
nerve (war)	987.9	E869.9	—	E952.9	E962.2	E982.9
oils	981	E862.1	—	E950.9	E962.1	E980.9
petroleum (liquefied) (distributed in mobile containers)	987.0	E868.0	—	E951.1	E962.2	E981.1
piped (pure or mixed with air)	987.0	E867	—	E951.1	E962.2	E981.1
piped (manufactured) (natural) NEC	987.1	E867	—	E951.0	E962.2	E981.0
producer	986	E868.8	—	E952.1	E962.2	E982.1
propane — see Propane						
refrigerant (freon)	987.4	E869.2	—	E952.8	E962.2	E982.8
not freon	987.9	E869.9	—	E952.9	E962.2	E982.9
sewer	987.8	E869.8	—	E952.8	E962.2	E982.8
specified source NEC (see also substance specified)	987.8	E869.8	—	E952.8	E962.2	E982.8
stove — see Gas, utility						
tear	987.5	E869.3	—	E952.8	E962.2	E982.8
utility (for cooking, heating, or lighting) (piped) NEC	987.1	E868.1	—	E951.8	E962.2	E981.8
incomplete combustion of — see Carbon, monoxide, fuel, utility						
in mobile container	987.0	E868.0	—	E951.1	E962.2	E981.1
piped (natural)	987.1	E867	—	E951.0	E962.2	E981.0
water	987.1	E868.1	—	E951.8	E962.2	E981.8
incomplete combustion of — see Carbon, monoxide, fuel, utility						
Gaseous substance — see Gas						
Gasoline, gasolene	981	E862.1	—	E950.9	E962.1	E980.9
vapor	987.1	E869.8	—	E952.8	E962.2	E982.8
Gastric enzymes	973.4	E858.4	E943.4	E950.4	E962.0	E980.4
Gastrografin	977.8	E858.8	E947.8	E950.4	E962.0	E980.4
Gastrointestinal agents	973.9	E858.4	E943.9	E950.4	E962.0	E980.4
specified NEC	973.8	E858.4	E943.8	E950.4	E962.0	E980.4
Gaultheria procumbens	988.2	E865.4	—	E950.9	E962.1	E980.9
Gelatin (intravenous)	964.8	E858.2	E934.8	E950.4	E962.0	E980.4
absorbable (sponge)	964.5	E858.2	E934.5	E950.4	E962.0	E980.4
Gelfilm	976.8	E858.7	E946.8	E950.4	E962.0	E980.4

		External Cause (E-Code)				
	Poisoning	Accident	Therapeutic Use	Suicide Attempt	Assault	Undeter-mined
Gelfoam	964.5	E858.2	E934.5	E950.4	E962.0	E980.4
Gelsemine	970.8	E854.3	E940.8	E950.4	E962.0	E980.4
Gelsemium (sempervirens)	988.2	E865.4	—	E950.9	E962.1	E980.9
Gemonil	967.0	E851	E937.0	E950.1	E962.0	E980.1
Gentamicin	960.8	E856	E930.8	E950.4	E962.0	E980.4
ophthalmic preparation	976.5	E858.7	E946.5	E950.4	E962.0	E980.4
topical NEC	976.0	E858.7	E946.0	E950.4	E962.0	E980.4
Gentian violet	976.0	E858.7	E946.0	E950.4	E962.0	E980.4
Gexane	976.0	E858.7	E946.0	E950.4	E962.0	E980.4
Gila monster (venom)	989.5	E905.0	—	E950.9	E962.1	E980.9
Ginger, Jamaica	989.89	E866.8	—	E950.9	E962.1	E980.9
Gitalin	972.1	E858.3	E942.1	E950.4	E962.0	E980.4
Gitoxin	972.1	E858.3	E942.1	E950.4	E962.0	E980.4
Glandular extract (medicinal)						
NEC	977.9	E858.9	E947.9	E950.5	E962.0	E980.5
Glaucarubin	961.5	E857	E931.5	E950.4	E962.0	E980.4
Globin zinc insulin	962.3	E858.0	E932.3	E950.4	E962.0	E980.4
Glucagon	962.3	E858.0	E932.3	E950.4	E962.0	E980.4
Glucochloral	967.1	E852.0	E937.1	E950.2	E962.0	E980.2
Glucocorticoids	962.0	E858.0	E932.0	E950.4	E962.0	E980.4
Glucose	974.5	E858.5	E944.5	E950.4	E962.0	E980.4
oxidase reagent	977.8	E858.8	E947.8	E950.4	E962.0	E980.4
Glucosulfone sodium	961.8	E857	E931.8	E950.4	E962.0	E980.4
Glue(s)	989.89	E866.6	—	E950.9	E962.1	E980.9
Glutamic acid						
(hydrochloride)	973.4	E858.4	E943.4	E950.4	E962.0	E980.4
Glutaraldehyde	989.89	E861.4	—	E950.9	E962.1	E980.9
Glutathione	963.8	E858.1	E933.8	E950.4	E962.0	E980.4
Glutethimide (group)	967.5	E852.4	E937.5	E950.2	E962.0	E980.2
Glycerin (lotion)	976.3	E858.7	E946.3	E950.4	E962.0	E980.4
Glycerol (topical)	976.3	E858.7	E946.3	E950.4	E962.0	E980.4
Glyceryl						
guaiacolate	975.5	E858.6	E945.5	E950.4	E962.0	E980.4
triacetate (topical)	976.0	E858.7	E946.0	E950.4	E962.0	E980.4
trinitrate	972.4	E858.3	E942.4	E950.4	E962.0	E980.4
Glycine	974.5	E858.5	E944.5	E950.4	E962.0	E980.4
Glycobiarsol	961.1	E857	E931.1	E950.4	E962.0	E980.4
Glycols (ether)	982.8	E862.4	—	E950.9	E962.1	E980.9
Glycopyrrolate	971.1	E855.4	E941.1	E950.4	E962.0	E980.4
Glymidine	962.3	E858.0	E932.3	E950.4	E962.0	E980.4
Gold (compounds) (salts)	965.69	E850.6	E935.6	E950.0	E962.0	E980.0
Golden sulfide of antimony	985.4	E866.2	—	E950.9	E962.1	E980.9
Goldylocks	988.2	E865.4	—	E950.9	E962.1	E980.9
Gonadal tissue extract	962.9	E858.0	E932.9	E950.4	E962.0	E980.4
beverage	980.0	E860.0	—	E950.9	E962.1	E980.9
female	962.2	E858.0	E932.2	E950.4	E962.0	E980.4
male	962.1	E858.0	E932.1	E950.4	E962.0	E980.4
Gonadotropin	962.4	E858.0	E932.4	E950.4	E962.0	E980.4
Grain alcohol	980.0	E860.1	—	E950.9	E962.1	E980.9
Gramicidin	960.8	E856	E930.8	E950.4	E962.0	E980.4
Gratiola officinalis	988.2	E865.4	—	E950.9	E962.1	E980.9
Grease	989.89	E866.8	—	E950.9	E962.1	E980.9
Green hellebore	988.2	E865.4	—	E950.9	E962.1	E980.9
Green soap	976.2	E858.7	E946.2	E950.4	E962.0	E980.4
Grifulvin	960.1	E856	E930.1	E950.4	E962.0	E980.4
Griseofulvin	960.1	E856	E930.1	E950.4	E962.0	E980.4
Growth hormone	962.4	E858.0	E932.4	E950.4	E962.0	E980.4
Guaiacol	975.5	E858.6	E945.5	E950.4	E962.0	E980.4
Guaiac reagent	977.8	E858.8	E947.8	E950.4	E962.0	E980.4
Guaifenesin	975.5	E858.6	E945.5	E950.4	E962.0	E980.4
Guaiphenesin	975.5	E858.6	E945.5	E950.4	E962.0	E980.4
Guanatol	961.4	E857	E931.4	E950.4	E962.0	E980.4
Guanethidine	972.6	E858.3	E942.6	E950.4	E962.0	E980.4
Guano	989.89	E866.5	—	E950.9	E962.1	E980.9
Guanochlor	972.6	E858.3	E942.6	E950.4	E962.0	E980.4
Guanoctine	972.6	E858.3	E942.6	E950.4	E962.0	E980.4
Guanoxan	972.6	E858.3	E942.6	E950.4	E962.0	E980.4
Hair treatment agent NEC	976.4	E858.7	E946.4	E950.4	E962.0	E980.4
Halcinonide	976.0	E858.7	E946.0	E950.4	E962.0	E980.4
Halethazole	976.0	E858.7	E946.0	E950.4	E962.0	E980.4
Hallucinogens	969.6	E854.1	E939.6	E950.3	E962.0	E980.3
Haloperidol	969.2	E853.1	E939.2	E950.3	E962.0	E980.3
Haloprogin	976.0	E858.7	E946.0	E950.4	E962.0	E980.4
Halotex	976.0	E858.7	E946.0	E950.4	E962.0	E980.4
Halothane	968.1	E855.1	E938.1	E950.4	E962.0	E980.4
Halquinols	976.0	E858.7	E946.0	E950.4	E962.0	E980.4
Harmonyl	972.6	E858.3	E942.6	E950.4	E962.0	E980.4
Hartmann's solution	974.5	E858.5	E944.5	E950.4	E962.0	E980.4
Hashish	969.6	E854.1	E939.6	E950.3	E962.0	E980.3

		External Cause (E-Code)								External Cause (E-Code)				
	Poisoning	Accident	Therapeutic Use	Suicide Attempt	Assault	Undetermined		Poisoning	Accident	Therapeutic Use	Suicide Attempt	Assault	Undetermined
Hawaiian wood rose seeds	969.6	E854.1	E939.6	E950.3	E962.0	E980.3	Hydrargaphen	976.0	E858.7	E946.0	E950.4	E962.0	E980.4
Headache cures, drugs, powders NEC	977.9	E858.9	E947.9	E950.5	E962.0	E980.9	Hydrazine	983.9	E864.3	—	E950.7	E962.1	E980.6
Heavenly Blue (morning glory)	969.6	E854.1	E939.6	E950.3	E962.0	E980.3	Hydriodic acid	975.5	E858.6	E945.5	E950.4	E962.0	E980.4
Heavy metal antagonists	963.8	E858.1	E933.8	E950.4	E962.0	E980.4	Hydrocarbon gas	987.1	E869.8	—	E952.8	E962.2	E982.8
anti-infectives	961.2	E857	E931.2	E950.4	E962.0	E980.4	incomplete combustion of — see Carbon, monoxide, fuel, utility						
Hedaquinium	976.0	E858.7	E946.0	E950.4	E962.0	E980.4	liquefied (mobile						
Hedge hyssop	988.2	E865.4	—	E950.9	E962.1	E980.9	container)	987.0	E868.0	—	E951.1	E962.2	E981.1
Heet	976.8	E858.7	E946.8	E950.4	E962.0	E980.4	piped (natural)	987.0	E867	—	E951.0	E962.2	E981.0
Helenin	961.6	E857	E931.6	E950.4	E962.0	E980.4	Hydrochloric acid (liquid)	983.1	E864.1	—	E950.7	E962.1	E980.6
Hellebore (black) (green) (white)	988.2	E865.4	—	E950.9	E962.1	E980.9	medicinal	973.4	E858.4	E943.4	E950.4	E962.0	E980.4
Hemlock	988.2	E865.4	—	E950.9	E962.1	E980.9	vapor	987.8	E869.8	—	E952.8	E962.2	E982.8
Hemostatics	964.5	E858.2	E934.5	E950.4	E962.0	E980.4	Hydrochlorothiazide	974.3	E858.5	E944.3	E950.4	E962.0	E980.4
capillary active drugs	972.8	E858.3	E942.8	E950.4	E962.0	E980.4	Hydrocodone	965.09	E850.2	E935.2	E950.0	E962.0	E980.0
Henbane	988.2	E865.4	—	E950.9	E962.1	E980.9	Hydrocortisone	962.0	E858.0	E932.0	E950.4	E962.0	E980.4
Heparin (sodium)	964.2	E858.2	E934.2	E950.4	E962.0	E980.4	ENT agent	976.6	E858.7	E946.6	E950.4	E962.0	E980.4
Heptabarbital, heptabarbitone	967.0	E851	E937.0	E950.1	E962.0	E980.1	ophthalmic preparation	976.5	E858.7	E946.5	E950.4	E962.0	E980.4
Heptachlor	989.2	E863.0	—	E950.6	E962.1	E980.7	topical NEC	976.0	E858.7	E946.0	E950.4	E962.0	E980.4
Heptalgin	965.09	E850.2	E935.2	E950.0	E962.0	E980.0	Hydrocortone	962.0	E858.0	E932.0	E950.4	E962.0	E980.4
Herbicides	989.4	E863.5	—	E950.6	E962.1	E980.7	ENT agent	976.6	E858.7	E946.6	E950.4	E962.0	E980.4
Heroin	965.01	E850.0	E935.0	E950.0	E962.0	E980.0	ophthalmic preparation	976.5	E858.7	E946.5	E950.4	E962.0	E980.4
Herplex	976.5	E858.7	E946.5	E950.4	E962.0	E980.4	topical NEC	976.0	E858.7	E946.0	E950.4	E962.0	E980.4
HES	964.8	E858.2	E934.8	E950.4	E962.0	E980.4	Hydrocyanic acid — see Cyanide(s)						
Hetastarch	964.8	E858.2	E934.8	E950.4	E962.0	E980.4	Hydroflumethiazide	974.3	E858.5	E944.3	E950.4	E962.0	E980.4
Hexachlorocyclohexane	989.2	E863.0	—	E950.6	E962.1	E980.7	Hydrofluoric acid (liquid)	983.1	E864.1	—	E950.7	E962.1	E980.6
Hexachlorophene	976.2	E858.7	E946.2	E950.4	E962.0	E980.4	vapor	987.8	E869.8	—	E952.8	E962.2	E982.8
Hexadimethrine (bromide)	964.5	E858.2	E934.5	E950.4	E962.0	E980.4	Hydrogen	987.8	E869.8	—	E952.8	E962.2	E982.8
Hexafluorenium	975.2	E858.6	E945.2	E950.4	E962.0	E980.4	arsenide	985.1	E866.3	—	E950.8	E962.1	E980.8
Hexa-germ	976.2	E858.7	E946.2	E950.4	E962.0	E980.4	arseniureted	985.1	E866.3	—	E950.8	E962.1	E980.8
Hexahydrophenol	980.8	E860.8	—	E950.9	E962.1	E980.9	cyanide (salts)	989.0	E866.8	—	E950.9	E962.1	E980.9
Hexalin	980.8	E860.8	—	E950.9	E962.1	E980.9	gas	987.7	E869.8	—	E952.8	E962.2	E982.8
Hexamethonium	972.3	E858.3	E942.3	E950.4	E962.0	E980.4	fluoride (liquid)	983.1	E864.1	—	E950.7	E962.1	E980.6
Hexamethyleneamine	961.9	E857	E931.9	E950.4	E962.0	E980.4	vapor	987.8	E869.8	—	E952.8	E962.2	E982.8
Hexamine	961.9	E857	E931.9	E950.4	E962.0	E980.4	peroxide (solution)	976.6	E858.7	E946.6	E950.4	E962.0	E980.4
Hexanone	982.8	E862.4	—	E950.9	E962.1	E980.9	phosphureted	987.8	E869.8	—	E952.8	E962.2	E982.8
Hexapropymate	967.8	E852.8	E937.8	E950.2	E962.0	E980.2	sulfide (gas)	987.8	E869.8	—	E952.8	E962.2	E982.8
Hexestrol	962.2	E858.0	E932.2	E950.4	E962.0	E980.4	arseniureted	985.1	E866.3	—	E950.8	E962.1	E980.8
Hexethal (sodium)	967.0	E851	E937.0	E950.1	E962.0	E980.1	sulfureted	987.8	E869.8	—	E952.8	E962.2	E982.8
Hexetidine	976.0	E858.7	E946.0	E950.4	E962.0	E980.4	Hydromorphinol	965.09	E850.2	E935.2	E950.0	E962.0	E980.0
Hexobarbital, hexobarbitone	967.0	E851	E937.0	E950.1	E962.0	E980.1	Hydromorphinone	965.09	E850.2	E935.2	E950.0	E962.0	E980.0
sodium (anesthetic)	968.3	E855.1	E938.3	E950.4	E962.0	E980.4	Hydromorphone	965.09	E850.2	E935.2	E950.0	E962.0	E980.0
soluble	968.3	E855.1	E938.3	E950.4	E962.0	E980.4	Hydromox	974.3	E858.5	E944.3	E950.4	E962.0	E980.4
Hexocyclium	971.1	E855.4	E941.1	E950.4	E962.0	E980.4	Hydrophilic lotion	976.3	E858.7	E946.3	E950.4	E962.0	E980.4
Hexoestrol	962.2	E858.0	E932.2	E950.4	E962.0	E980.4	Hydroquinone	983.0	E864.0	—	E950.7	E962.1	E980.6
Hexone	982.8	E862.4	—	E950.9	E962.1	E980.9	vapor	987.8	E869.8	—	E952.8	E962.2	E982.8
Hexylcaine	968.5	E855.2	E938.5	E950.4	E962.0	E980.4	Hydrosulfuric acid (gas)	987.8	E869.8	—	E952.8	E962.2	E982.8
Hexylresorcinol	961.6	E857	E931.6	E950.4	E962.0	E980.4	Hydrous wool fat (lotion)	976.3	E858.7	E946.3	E950.4	E962.0	E980.4
Hinkle's pills	973.1	E858.4	E943.1	E950.4	E962.0	E980.4	Hydroxide, caustic	983.2	E864.2	—	E950.7	E962.1	E980.6
Histalog	977.8	E858.8	E947.8	E950.4	E962.0	E980.4	Hydroxocobalamin	964.1	E858.2	E934.1	E950.4	E962.0	E980.4
Histamine (phosphate)	972.5	E858.3	E942.5	E950.4	E962.0	E980.4	Hydroxyamphetamine	971.2	E855.5	E941.2	E950.4	E962.0	E980.4
Histoplasmin	977.8	E858.8	E947.8	E950.4	E962.0	E980.4	Hydroxychloroquine	961.4	E857	E931.4	E950.4	E962.0	E980.4
Holly berries	988.2	E865.3	—	E950.9	E962.1	E980.9	Hydroxydihydrocodeinone	965.09	E850.2	E935.2	E950.0	E962.0	E980.0
Homatropine	971.1	E855.4	E941.1	E950.4	E962.0	E980.4	Hydroxyethyl starch	964.8	E858.2	E934.8	E950.4	E962.0	E980.4
Homo-tet	964.6	E858.2	E934.6	E950.4	E962.0	E980.4	Hydroxyphenamate	969.5	E853.8	E939.5	E950.3	E962.0	E980.3
Hormones (synthetic substitute)							Hydroxyphenylbutazone	965.5	E850.5	E935.5	E950.0	E962.0	E980.0
NEC	962.9	E858.0	E932.9	E950.4	E962.0	E980.4	Hydroxyprogesterone	962.2	E858.0	E932.2	E950.4	E962.0	E980.4
adrenal cortical steroids	962.0	E858.0	E932.0	E950.4	E962.0	E980.4	Hydroxyquinoline derivatives	961.3	E857	E931.3	E950.4	E962.0	E980.4
antidiabetic agents	962.3	E858.0	E932.3	E950.4	E962.0	E980.4	Hydroxystilbamidine	961.5	E857	E931.5	E950.4	E962.0	E980.4
follicle stimulating	962.4	E858.0	E932.4	E950.4	E962.0	E980.4	Hydroxyurea	963.1	E858.1	E933.1	E950.4	E962.0	E980.4
gonadotropic	962.4	E858.0	E932.4	E950.4	E962.0	E980.4	Hydroxyzine	969.5	E853.8	E939.5	E950.3	E962.0	E980.3
growth	962.4	E858.0	E932.4	E950.4	E962.0	E980.4	Hyoscine (hydrobromide)	971.1	E855.4	E941.1	E950.4	E962.0	E980.4
ovarian (substitutes)	962.2	E858.0	E932.2	E950.4	E962.0	E980.4	Hyoscyamine	971.1	E855.4	E941.1	E950.4	E962.0	E980.4
parathyroid (derivatives)	962.6	E858.0	E932.6	E950.4	E962.0	E980.4	Hyoscyamus (albus) (niger)	988.2	E865.4	—	E950.9	E962.1	E980.9
pituitary (posterior)	962.5	E858.0	E932.5	E950.4	E962.0	E980.4	Hypaque	977.8	E858.8	E947.8	E950.4	E962.0	E980.4
anterior	962.4	E858.0	E932.4	E950.4	E962.0	E980.4	Hypertussis	964.6	E858.2	E934.6	E950.4	E962.0	E980.4
thyroid (derivative)	962.7	E858.0	E932.7	E950.4	E962.0	E980.4	Hypnotics NEC	967.9	E852.9	E937.9	E950.2	E962.0	E980.2
Hornet (sting)	989.5	E905.3	—	E950.9	E962.1	E980.9	Hypochlorites — see Sodium, hypochlorite						
Horticulture agent NEC	989.4	E863.9	—	E950.6	E962.1	E980.7	Hypotensive agents NEC	972.6	E858.3	E942.6	E950.4	E962.0	E980.4
Hyaluronidase	963.4	E858.1	E933.4	E950.4	E962.0	E980.4	Ibufenac	965.69	E850.6	E935.6	E950.0	E962.0	E980.0
Hyazyme	963.4	E858.1	E933.4	E950.4	E962.0	E980.4	Ibuprofen	965.61	E850.6	E935.6	E950.0	E962.0	E980.0
Hycodan	965.09	E850.2	E935.2	E950.0	E962.0	E980.0	ICG	977.8	E858.8	E947.8	E950.4	E962.0	E980.4
Hydantoin derivatives	966.1	E855.0	E936.1	E950.4	E962.0	E980.4	Ichthammol	976.4	E858.7	E946.4	E950.4	E962.0	E980.4
Hydeltra	962.0	E858.0	E932.0	E950.4	E962.0	E980.4	Ichthyol	976.4	E858.7	E946.4	E950.4	E962.0	E980.4
Hydergine	971.3	E855.6	E941.3	E950.4	E962.0	E980.4	Idoxuridine	976.5	E858.7	E946.5	E950.4	E962.0	E980.4
Hydrabamine penicillin	960.0	E856	E930.0	E950.4	E962.0	E980.4	IDU	976.5	E858.7	E946.5	E950.4	E962.0	E980.4
Hydralazine, hydrallazine	972.6	E858.3	E942.6	E950.4	E962.0	E980.4	Iletin	962.3	E858.0	E932.3	E950.4	E962.0	E980.4
							Ilex	988.2	E865.4	—	E950.9	E962.1	E980.9

☑ Additional Digit Required — Refer to the Tabular List for Digit Selection

▽ Subterms under main terms may continue to next column or page

▶◀ Revised Text   ● New Line   ▲ Revised Code

Index

Hawaiian wood rose seeds — Ilex

	Poisoning	Accident	Therapeutic Use	Suicide Attempt	Assault	Undetermined
Illuminating gas — see Gas, utility						
Ilopan	963.5	E858.1	E933.5	E950.4	E962.0	E980.4
Ilotycin	960.3	E856	E930.3	E950.4	E962.0	E980.4
ophthalmic preparation	976.5	E858.7	E946.5	E950.4	E962.0	E980.4
topical NEC	976.0	E858.7	E946.0	E950.4	E962.0	E980.4
Imipramine	969.0	E854.0	E939.0	E950.3	E962.0	E980.3
Immu-G	964.6	E858.2	E934.6	E950.4	E962.0	E980.4
Immuglobin	964.6	E858.2	E934.6	E950.4	E962.0	E980.4
Immune serum globulin	964.6	E858.2	E934.6	E950.4	E962.0	E980.4
Immunosuppressive agents	963.1	E858.1	E933.1	E950.4	E962.0	E980.4
Immu-tetanus	964.6	E858.2	E934.6	E950.4	E962.0	E980.4
Indandione (derivatives)	964.2	E858.2	E934.2	E950.4	E962.0	E980.4
Inderal	972.0	E858.3	E942.0	E950.4	E962.0	E980.4
Indian						
hemp	969.6	E854.1	E939.6	E950.3	E962.0	E980.3
tobacco	988.2	E865.4	—	E950.9	E962.1	E980.9
Indigo carmine	977.8	E858.8	E947.8	E950.4	E962.0	E980.4
Indocin	965.69	E850.6	E935.6	E950.0	E962.0	E980.0
Indocyanine green	977.8	E858.8	E947.8	E950.4	E962.0	E980.4
Indomethacin	965.69	E850.6	E935.6	E950.0	E962.0	E980.0
Industrial						
alcohol	980.9	E860.9	—	E950.9	E962.1	E980.9
fumes	987.8	E869.8	—	E952.8	E962.2	E982.8
solvents (fumes) (vapors)	982.8	E862.9	—	E950.9	E962.1	E980.9
Influenza vaccine	979.6	E858.8	E949.6	E950.4	E962.0	E982.8
Ingested substances NEC	989.9	E866.9	—	E950.9	E962.1	E980.9
INH (isoniazid)	961.8	E857	E931.8	E950.4	E962.0	E980.4
Inhalation, gas (noxious) — see Gas						
Ink	989.89	E866.8	—	E950.9	E962.1	E980.9
Innovar	967.6	E852.5	E937.6	E950.2	E962.0	E980.2
Inositol niacinate	972.2	E858.3	E942.2	E950.4	E962.0	E980.4
Inproquone	963.1	E858.1	E933.1	E950.4	E962.0	E980.4
Insecticides — see also						
Pesticides	989.4	E863.4	—	E950.6	E962.1	E980.7
chlorinated	989.2	E863.0	—	E950.6	E962.1	E980.7
mixtures	989.4	E863.3	—	E950.6	E962.1	E980.7
organochlorine (compounds)	989.2	E863.0	—	E950.6	E962.1	E980.7
organophosphorus (compounds)	989.3	E863.1	—	E950.6	E962.1	E980.7
Insect (sting), venomous	989.5	E905.5	—	E950.9	E962.1	E980.9
Insular tissue extract	962.3	E858.0	E932.3	E950.4	E962.0	E980.4
Insulin (amorphous) (globin) (isophane) (Lente) (NPH) (protamine) (Semilente) (Ultralente) (zinc)	962.3	E858.0	E932.3	E950.4	E962.0	E980.4
Intranarcon	968.3	E855.1	E938.3	E950.4	E962.0	E980.4
Inulin	977.8	E858.8	E947.8	E950.4	E962.0	E980.4
Invert sugar	974.5	E858.5	E944.5	E950.4	E962.0	E980.4
Inza — see Naproxen						
Iodide NEC — see also						
Iodine	976.0	E858.7	E946.0	E950.4	E962.0	E980.4
mercury (ointment)	976.0	E858.7	E946.0	E950.4	E962.0	E980.4
methylate	976.0	E858.7	E946.0	E950.4	E962.0	E980.4
potassium (expectorant) NEC	975.5	E858.6	E945.5	E950.4	E962.0	E980.4
Iodinated glycerol	975.5	E858.6	E945.5	E950.4	E962.0	E980.4
Iodine (antiseptic, external) (tincture) NEC	976.0	E858.7	E946.0	E950.4	E962.0	E980.4
diagnostic	977.8	E858.8	E947.8	E950.4	E962.0	E980.4
for thyroid conditions (antithyroid)	962.8	E858.0	E932.8	E950.4	E962.0	E980.4
vapor	987.8	E869.8	—	E952.8	E962.2	E982.8
Iodized oil	977.8	E858.8	E947.8	E950.4	E962.0	E980.4
Iodobismitol	961.2	E857	E931.2	E950.4	E962.0	E980.4
Iodochlorhydroxyquin	961.3	E857	E931.3	E950.4	E962.0	E980.4
topical	976.0	E858.7	E946.0	E950.4	E962.0	E980.4
Iodoform	976.0	E858.7	E946.0	E950.4	E962.0	E980.4
Iodopanoic acid	977.8	E858.8	E947.8	E950.4	E962.0	E980.4
Iodophthalein	977.8	E858.8	E947.8	E950.4	E962.0	E980.4
Ion exchange resins	974.5	E858.5	E944.5	E950.4	E962.0	E980.4
Iopanoic acid	977.8	E858.8	E947.8	E950.4	E962.0	E980.4
Iophendylate	977.8	E858.8	E947.8	E950.4	E962.0	E980.4
Iothiouracil	962.8	E858.0	E932.8	E950.4	E962.0	E980.4
Ipecac	973.6	E858.4	E943.6	E950.4	E962.0	E980.4
Ipecacuanha	973.6	E858.4	E943.6	E950.4	E962.0	E980.4
Ipodate	977.8	E858.8	E947.8	E950.4	E962.0	E980.4
Ipral	967.0	E851	E937.0	E950.1	E962.0	E980.1

	Poisoning	Accident	Therapeutic Use	Suicide Attempt	Assault	Undetermined
Ipratropium	975.1	E858.6	E945.1	E950.4	E962.0	E980.4
Iproniazid	969.0	E854.0	E939.0	E950.3	E962.0	E980.3
Iron (compounds) (medicinal) (preparations)	964.0	E858.2	E934.0	E950.4	E962.0	E980.4
dextran	964.0	E858.2	E934.0	E950.4	E962.0	E980.4
nonmedicinal (dust) (fumes) NEC	985.8	E866.4	—	E950.9	E962.1	E980.9
Irritant drug	977.9	E858.9	E947.9	E950.5	E962.0	E980.5
Ismelin	972.6	E858.3	E942.6	E950.4	E962.0	E980.4
Isoamyl nitrite	972.4	E858.3	E942.4	E950.4	E962.0	E980.4
Isobutyl acetate	982.8	E862.4	—	E950.9	E962.1	E980.9
Isocarboxazid	969.0	E854.0	E939.0	E950.3	E962.0	E980.3
Isoephedrine	971.2	E855.5	E941.2	E950.4	E962.0	E980.4
Isoetharine	971.2	E855.5	E941.2	E950.4	E962.0	E980.4
Isofluorophate	971.0	E855.3	E941.0	E950.4	E962.0	E980.4
Isoniazid (INH)	961.8	E857	E931.8	E950.4	E962.0	E980.4
Isopentaquine	961.4	E857	E931.4	E950.4	E962.0	E980.4
Isophane insulin	962.3	E858.0	E932.3	E950.4	E962.0	E980.4
Isopregnenone	962.2	E858.0	E932.2	E950.4	E962.0	E980.4
Isoprenaline	971.2	E855.5	E941.2	E950.4	E962.0	E980.4
Isopropamide	971.1	E855.4	E941.1	E950.4	E962.0	E980.4
Isopropanol	980.2	E860.3	—	E950.9	E962.1	E980.9
topical (germicide)	976.0	E858.7	E946.0	E950.4	E962.0	E980.4
Isopropyl						
acetate	982.8	E862.4	—	E950.9	E962.1	E980.9
alcohol	980.2	E860.3	—	E950.9	E962.1	E980.9
topical (germicide)	976.0	E858.7	E946.0	E950.4	E962.0	E980.4
ether	982.8	E862.4	—	E950.9	E962.1	E980.9
Isoproterenol	971.2	E855.5	E941.2	E950.4	E962.0	E980.4
Isosorbide dinitrate	972.4	E858.3	E942.4	E950.4	E962.0	E980.4
Isothipendyl	963.0	E858.1	E933.0	E950.4	E962.0	E980.4
Isoxazolyl penicillin	960.0	E856	E930.0	E950.4	E962.0	E980.4
Isoxsuprine hydrochloride	972.5	E858.3	E942.5	E950.4	E962.0	E980.4
I-thyroxine sodium	962.7	E858.0	E932.7	E950.4	E962.0	E980.4
Jaborandi (pilocarpus) (extract)	971.0	E855.3	E941.0	E950.4	E962.0	E980.4
Jalap	973.1	E858.4	E943.1	E950.4	E962.0	E980.4
Jamaica						
dogwood (bark)	965.7	E850.7	E935.7	E950.0	E962.0	E980.0
ginger	989.89	E866.8	—	E950.9	E962.1	E980.9
Jatropha	988.2	E865.4	—	E950.9	E962.1	E980.9
curcas	988.2	E865.3	—	E950.9	E962.1	E980.9
Jectofer	964.0	E858.2	E934.0	E950.4	E962.0	E980.4
Jellyfish (sting)	989.5	E905.6	—	E950.9	E962.1	E980.9
Jequirity (bean)	988.2	E865.3	—	E950.9	E962.1	E980.9
Jimson weed	988.2	E865.4	—	E950.9	E962.1	E980.9
seeds	988.2	E865.3	—	E950.9	E962.1	E980.9
Juniper tar (oil) (ointment)	976.4	E858.7	E946.4	E950.4	E962.0	E980.4
Kallikrein	972.5	E858.3	E942.5	E950.4	E962.0	E980.4
Kanamycin	960.6	E856	E930.6	E950.4	E962.0	E980.4
Kantrex	960.6	E856	E930.6	E950.4	E962.0	E980.4
Kaolin	973.5	E858.4	E943.5	E950.4	E962.0	E980.4
Karaya (gum)	973.3	E858.4	E943.3	E950.4	E962.0	E980.4
Kemithal	968.3	E855.1	E938.3	E950.4	E962.0	E980.4
Kenacort	962.0	E858.0	E932.0	E950.4	E962.0	E980.4
Keratolytics	976.4	E858.7	E946.4	E950.4	E962.0	E980.4
Keratoplastics	976.4	E858.7	E946.4	E950.4	E962.0	E980.4
Kerosene, kerosine (fuel) (solvent) NEC	981	E862.1	—	E950.9	E962.1	E980.9
insecticide	981	E863.4	—	E950.6	E962.1	E980.7
vapor	987.1	E869.8	—	E952.8	E962.2	E982.8
Ketamine	968.3	E855.1	E938.3	E950.4	E962.0	E980.4
Ketobemidone	965.09	E850.2	E935.2	E950.0	E962.0	E980.0
Ketols	982.8	E862.4	—	E950.9	E962.1	E980.9
Ketone oils	982.8	E862.4	—	E950.9	E962.1	E980.9
Ketoprofen	965.61	E850.6	E935.6	E950.0	E962.0	E980.0
Kiln gas or vapor (carbon monoxide)	986	E868.8	—	E952.1	E962.2	E982.1
Konsyl	973.3	E858.4	E943.3	E950.4	E962.0	E980.4
Kosam seed	988.2	E865.3	—	E950.9	E962.1	E980.9
Krait (venom)	989.5	E905.0	—	E950.9	E962.1	E980.9
Kwell (insecticide)	989.2	E863.0	—	E950.6	E962.1	E980.7
anti-infective (topical)	976.0	E858.7	E946.0	E950.4	E962.0	E980.4
Laburnum (flowers) (seeds)	988.2	E865.3	—	E950.9	E962.1	E980.9
leaves	988.2	E865.4	—	E950.9	E962.1	E980.9
Lacquers	989.89	E861.6	—	E950.9	E962.1	E980.9
Lacrimogenic gas	987.5	E869.3	—	E952.8	E962.2	E982.8
Lactic acid	983.1	E864.1	—	E950.7	E962.1	E980.6
Lactobacillus acidophilus	973.5	E858.4	E943.5	E950.4	E962.0	E980.4
Lactoflavin	963.5	E858.1	E933.5	E950.4	E962.0	E980.4
Lactuca (virosa) (extract)	967.8	E852.8	E937.8	E950.2	E962.0	E980.2

☑ Additional Digit Required — Refer to the Tabular List for Digit Selection

▽ Subterms under main terms may continue to next column or page

2007 ICD-9-CM

▶◀ Revised Text   ● New Line   ▲ Revised Code

Volume 2 — 321

Illuminating gas — Lactuca

	Poisoning	Accident	Therapeutic Use	Suicide Attempt	Assault	Undeter-mined
Lactucarium	967.8	E852.8	E937.8	E950.2	E962.0	E980.2
Laevulose	974.5	E858.5	E944.5	E950.4	E962.0	E980.4
Lanatoside (C)	972.1	E858.3	E942.1	E950.4	E962.0	E980.4
Lanolin (lotion)	976.3	E858.7	E946.3	E950.4	E962.0	E980.4
Largactil	969.1	E853.0	E939.1	E950.3	E962.0	E980.3
Larkspur	988.2	E865.3	—	E950.9	E962.1	E980.9
Laroxyl	969.0	E854.0	E939.0	E950.3	E962.0	E980.3
Lasix	974.4	E858.5	E944.4	E950.4	E962.0	E980.4
Latex	989.82	E866.8	—	E950.9	E962.1	E980.9
Lathyrus (seed)	988.2	E865.3	—	E950.9	E962.1	E980.9
Laudanum	965.09	E850.2	E935.2	E950.0	E962.0	E980.0
Laudexium	975.2	E858.6	E945.2	E950.4	E962.0	E980.4
Laurel, black or cherry	988.2	E865.4	—	E950.9	E962.1	E980.9
Laurolinium	976.0	E858.7	E946.0	E950.4	E962.0	E980.4
Lauryl sulfoacetate	976.2	E858.7	E946.2	E950.4	E962.0	E980.4
Laxatives NEC	973.3	E858.4	E943.3	E950.4	E962.0	E980.4
emollient	973.2	E858.4	E943.2	E950.4	E962.0	E980.4
L-dopa	966.4	E855.0	E936.4	E950.4	E962.0	E980.4
Lead (dust) (fumes) (vapor)						
NEC	984.9	E866.0	—	E950.9	E962.1	E980.9
acetate (dust)	984.1	E866.0	—	E950.9	E962.1	E980.9
anti-infectives	961.2	E857	E931.2	E950.4	E962.0	E980.4
antiknock compound						
(tetraethyl)	984.1	E862.1	—	E950.9	E962.1	E980.9
arsenate, arsenite (dust)						
(insecticide) (vapor)	985.1	E863.4	—	E950.8	E962.1	E980.8
herbicide	985.1	E863.5	—	E950.8	E962.1	E980.8
carbonate	984.0	E866.0	—	E950.9	E962.1	E980.9
paint	984.0	E861.5	—	E950.9	E962.1	E980.9
chromate	984.0	E866.0	—	E950.9	E962.1	E980.9
paint	984.0	E861.5	—	E950.9	E962.1	E980.9
dioxide	984.0	E866.0	—	E950.9	E962.1	E980.9
inorganic (compound)	984.0	E866.0	—	E950.9	E962.1	E980.9
paint	984.0	E861.5	—	E950.9	E962.1	E980.9
iodide	984.0	E866.0	—	E950.9	E962.1	E980.9
pigment (paint)	984.0	E861.5	—	E950.9	E962.1	E980.9
monoxide (dust)	984.0	E866.0	—	E950.9	E962.1	E980.9
paint	984.0	E861.5	—	E950.9	E962.1	E980.9
organic	984.1	E866.0	—	E950.9	E962.1	E980.9
oxide	984.0	E866.0	—	E950.9	E962.1	E980.9
paint	984.0	E861.5	—	E950.9	E962.1	E980.9
paint	984.0	E861.5	—	E950.9	E962.1	E980.9
salts	984.0	E866.0	—	E950.9	E962.1	E980.9
specified compound NEC	984.8	E866.0	—	E950.9	E962.1	E980.9
tetra-ethyl	984.1	E862.1	—	E950.9	E962.1	E980.9
Lebanese red	969.6	E854.1	E939.6	E950.3	E962.0	E980.3
Lente Iletin (insulin)	962.3	E858.0	E932.3	E950.4	E962.0	E980.4
Leptazol	970.0	E854.3	E940.0	E950.4	E962.0	E980.4
Leritine	965.09	E850.2	E935.2	E950.0	E962.0	E980.0
Letter	962.7	E858.0	E932.7	E950.4	E962.0	E980.4
Lettuce opium	967.8	E852.8	E937.8	E950.2	E962.0	E980.2
Leucovorin (factor)	964.1	E858.2	E934.1	E950.4	E962.0	E980.4
Leukeran	963.1	E858.1	E933.1	E950.4	E962.0	E980.4
Levalbuterol	975.7	E858.6	E945.7	E950.4	E962.0	E980.4
Levallorphan	970.1	E854.3	E940.1	E950.4	E962.0	E980.4
Levanil	967.8	E852.8	E937.8	E950.2	E962.0	E980.2
Levarterenol	971.2	E855.5	E941.2	E950.4	E962.0	E980.4
Levodopa	966.4	E855.0	E936.4	E950.4	E962.0	E980.4
Levo-dromoran	965.09	E850.2	E935.2	E950.0	E962.0	E980.0
Levoid	962.7	E858.0	E932.7	E950.4	E962.0	E980.4
Levo-iso-methadone	965.02	E850.1	E935.1	E950.0	E962.0	E980.0
Levomepromazine	967.8	E852.8	E937.8	E950.2	E962.0	E980.2
Levoprome	967.8	E852.8	E937.8	E950.2	E962.0	E980.2
Levopropoxyphene	975.4	E858.6	E945.4	E950.4	E962.0	E980.4
Levorphan, levophanol	965.09	E850.2	E935.2	E950.0	E962.0	E980.0
Levothyroxine (sodium)	962.7	E858.0	E932.7	E950.4	E962.0	E980.4
Levsin	971.1	E855.4	E941.1	E950.4	E962.0	E980.4
Levulose	974.5	E858.5	E944.5	E950.4	E962.0	E980.4
Lewisite (gas)	985.1	E866.3	—	E950.8	E962.1	E980.8
Librium	969.4	E853.2	E939.4	E950.3	E962.0	E980.3
Lidex	976.0	E858.7	E946.0	E950.4	E962.0	E980.4
Lidocaine (infiltration)						
(topical)	968.5	E855.2	E938.5	E950.4	E962.0	E980.4
nerve block (peripheral)						
(plexus)	968.6	E855.2	E938.6	E950.4	E962.0	E980.4
spinal	968.7	E855.2	E938.7	E950.4	E962.0	E980.4
Lighter fluid	981	E862.1	—	E950.9	E962.1	E980.9
Lignocaine (infiltration)						
(topical)	968.5	E855.2	E938.5	E950.4	E962.0	E980.4
nerve block (peripheral)						
(plexus)	968.6	E855.2	E938.6	E950.4	E962.0	E980.4
Lignocaine — continued						
spinal	968.7	E855.2	E938.7	E950.4	E962.0	E980.4
Ligroin(e) (solvent)	981	E862.0	—	E950.9	E962.1	E980.9
vapor	987.1	E869.8	—	E952.8	E962.2	E982.8
Ligustrum vulgare	988.2	E865.3	—	E950.9	E962.1	E980.9
Lily of the valley	988.2	E865.4	—	E950.9	E962.1	E980.9
Lime (chloride)	983.2	E864.2	—	E950.7	E962.1	E980.6
solution, sulferated	976.4	E858.7	E946.4	E950.4	E962.0	E980.4
Limonene	982.8	E862.4	—	E950.9	E962.1	E980.9
Lincomycin	960.8	E856	E930.8	E950.4	E962.0	E980.4
Lindane (insecticide) (vapor)	989.2	E863.0	—	E950.6	E962.1	E980.7
anti-infective (topical)	976.0	E858.7	E946.0	E950.4	E962.0	E980.4
Liniments NEC	976.9	E858.7	E946.9	E950.4	E962.0	E980.4
Linoleic acid	972.2	E858.3	E942.2	E950.4	E962.0	E980.4
Liothyronine	962.7	E858.0	E932.7	E950.4	E962.0	E980.4
Liotrix	962.7	E858.0	E932.7	E950.4	E962.0	E980.4
Lipancreatin	973.4	E858.4	E943.4	E950.4	E962.0	E980.4
Lipo-Lutin	962.2	E858.0	E932.2	E950.4	E962.0	E980.4
Lipotropic agents	977.1	E858.8	E947.1	E950.4	E962.0	E980.4
Liquefied petroleum						
gases	987.0	E868.0	—	E951.1	E962.2	E981.1
piped (pure or mixed with						
air)	987.0	E867	—	E951.0	E962.2	E981.0
Liquid petrolatum	973.2	E858.4	E943.2	E950.4	E962.0	E980.4
substance	989.9	E866.9	—	E950.9	E962.1	E980.9
specified NEC	989.89	E866.8	—	E950.9	E962.1	E980.9
Lirugen	979.4	E858.8	E949.4	E950.4	E962.0	E980.4
Lithane	969.8	E855.8	E939.8	E950.3	E962.0	E980.3
Lithium	985.8	E866.4	—	E950.9	E962.1	E980.9
carbonate	969.8	E855.8	E939.8	E950.3	E962.0	E980.3
Lithonate	969.8	E855.8	E939.8	E950.3	E962.0	E980.3
Liver (extract) (injection)						
(preparations)	964.1	E858.2	E934.1	E950.4	E962.0	E980.4
Lizard (bite) (venom)	989.5	E905.0	—	E950.9	E962.1	E980.9
LMD	964.8	E858.2	E934.8	E950.4	E962.0	E980.4
Lobelia	988.2	E865.4	—	E950.9	E962.1	E980.9
Lobeline	970.0	E854.3	E940.0	E950.4	E962.0	E980.4
Locorten	976.0	E858.7	E946.0	E950.4	E962.0	E980.4
Lolium temulentum	988.2	E865.3	—	E950.9	E962.1	E980.9
Lomotil	973.5	E858.4	E943.5	E950.4	E962.0	E980.4
Lomustine	963.1	E858.1	E933.1	E950.4	E962.0	E980.4
Lophophora williamsii	969.6	E854.1	E939.6	E950.3	E962.0	E980.3
Lorazepam	969.4	E853.2	E939.4	E950.3	E962.0	E980.3
Lotions NEC	976.9	E858.7	E946.9	E950.4	E962.0	E980.4
Lotronex	973.8	E858.4	E943.8	E950.4	E962.0	E980.4
Lotusate	967.0	E851	E937.0	E950.1	E962.0	E980.1
Lowila	976.2	E858.7	E946.2	E950.4	E962.0	E980.4
Loxapine	969.3	E853.8	E939.3	E950.3	E962.0	E980.3
Lozenges (throat)	976.6	E858.7	E946.6	E950.4	E962.0	E980.4
LSD (25)	969.6	E854.1	E939.6	E950.3	E962.0	E980.3
L-Tryptophan — see amino acid						
Lubricating oil NEC	981	E862.2	—	E950.9	E962.1	E980.9
Lucanthone	961.6	E857	E931.6	E950.4	E962.0	E980.4
Luminal	967.0	E851	E937.0	E950.1	E962.0	E980.1
Lung irritant (gas) NEC	987.9	E869.9	—	E952.9	E962.2	E982.9
Lutocylol	962.2	E858.0	E932.2	E950.4	E962.0	E980.4
Lutromone	962.2	E858.0	E932.2	E950.4	E962.0	E980.4
Lututrin	975.0	E858.6	E945.0	E950.4	E962.0	E980.4
Lye (concentrated)	983.2	E864.2	—	E950.7	E962.1	E980.6
Lygranum (skin test)	977.8	E858.8	E947.8	E950.4	E962.0	E980.4
Lymecycline	960.4	E856	E930.4	E950.4	E962.0	E980.4
Lymphogranuloma venereum						
antigen	977.8	E858.8	E947.8	E950.4	E962.0	E980.4
Lynestrenol	962.2	E858.0	E932.2	E950.4	E962.0	E980.4
Lyovac Sodium Edecrin	974.4	E858.5	E944.4	E950.4	E962.0	E980.4
Lypressin	962.5	E858.0	E932.5	E950.4	E962.0	E980.4
Lysergic acid (amide)						
(diethylamide)	969.6	E854.1	E939.6	E950.3	E962.0	E980.3
Lysergide	969.6	E854.1	E939.6	E950.3	E962.0	E980.3
Lysine vasopressin	962.5	E858.0	E932.5	E950.4	E962.0	E980.4
Lysol	983.0	E864.0	—	E950.7	E962.1	E980.6
Lytta (vitatta)	976.8	E858.7	E946.8	E950.4	E962.0	E980.4
Mace	987.5	E869.3	—	E952.8	E962.2	E982.8
Macrolides (antibiotics)	960.3	E856	E930.3	E950.4	E962.0	E980.4
Mafenide	976.0	E858.7	E946.0	E950.4	E962.0	E980.4
Magaldrate	973.0	E858.4	E943.0	E950.4	E962.0	E980.4
Magic mushroom	969.6	E854.1	E939.6	E950.3	E962.0	E980.3
Magnamycin	960.8	E856	E930.8	E950.4	E962.0	E980.4
Magnesia magma	973.0	E858.4	E943.0	E950.4	E962.0	E980.4
Magnesium (compounds)						
(fumes) NEC	985.8	E866.4	—	E950.9	E962.1	E980.9

	Poisoning	Accident	Therapeutic Use	Suicide Attempt	Assault	Undetermined
Magnesium (compounds)						
(fumes) — *continued*						
antacid	973.0	E858.4	E943.0	E950.4	E962.0	E980.4
carbonate	973.0	E858.4	E943.0	E950.4	E962.0	E980.4
cathartic	973.3	E858.4	E943.3	E950.4	E962.0	E980.4
citrate	973.3	E858.4	E943.3	E950.4	E962.0	E980.4
hydroxide	973.0	E858.4	E943.0	E950.4	E962.0	E980.4
oxide	973.0	E858.4	E943.0	E950.4	E962.0	E980.4
sulfate (oral)	973.3	E858.4	E943.3	E950.4	E962.0	E980.4
intravenous	966.3	E855.0	E936.3	E950.4	E962.0	E980.4
trisilicate	973.0	E858.4	E943.0	E950.4	E962.0	E980.4
Malathion (insecticide)	989.3	E863.1	—	E950.6	E962.1	E980.7
Male fern (oleoresin)	961.6	E857	E931.6	E950.4	E962.0	E980.4
Mandelic acid	961.9	E857	E931.9	E950.4	E962.0	E980.4
Manganese compounds (fumes) NEC	985.2	E866.4	—	E950.9	E962.1	E980.9
Mannitol (diuretic) (medicinal) NEC	974.4	E858.5	E944.4	E950.4	E962.0	E980.4
hexanitrate	972.4	E858.3	E942.4	E950.4	E962.0	E980.4
mustard	963.1	E858.1	E933.1	E950.4	E962.0	E980.4
Mannomustine	963.1	E858.1	E933.1	E950.4	E962.0	E980.4
MAO inhibitors	969.0	E854.0	E939.0	E950.3	E962.0	E980.3
Mapharsen	961.1	E857	E931.1	E950.4	E962.0	E980.4
Marcaine	968.9	E855.2	E938.9	E950.4	E962.0	E980.4
infiltration (subcutaneous)	968.5	E855.2	E938.5	E950.4	E962.0	E980.4
nerve block (peripheral) (plexus)	968.6	E855.2	E938.6	E950.4	E962.0	E980.4
Marezine	963.0	E858.1	E933.0	E950.4	E962.0	E980.4
Marihuana, marijuana (derivatives)	969.6	E854.1	E939.6	E950.3	E962.0	E980.3
Marine animals or plants (sting)	989.5	E905.6	—	E950.9	E962.1	E980.9
Marplan	969.0	E854.0	E939.0	E950.3	E962.0	E980.3
Marsh gas	987.1	E869.8	—	E952.8	E962.2	E982.8
Marsilid	969.0	E854.0	E939.0	E950.3	E962.0	E980.3
Matulane	963.1	E858.1	E933.1	E950.4	E962.0	E980.4
Mazindol	977.0	E858.8	E947.0	E950.4	E962.0	E980.4
MDMA	969.7	E854.2	E939.7	E950.3	E962.0	E980.3
Meadow saffron	988.2	E865.3	—	E950.9	E962.1	E980.9
Measles vaccine	979.4	E858.8	E949.4	E950.4	E962.0	E980.4
Meat, noxious or nonbacterial	988.8	E865.0	—	E950.9	E962.1	E980.9
Mebanazine	969.0	E854.0	E939.0	E950.3	E962.0	E980.3
Mebaral	967.0	E851	E937.0	E950.1	E962.0	E980.1
Mebendazole	961.6	E857	E931.6	E950.4	E962.0	E980.4
Mebeverine	975.1	E858.6	E945.1	E950.4	E962.0	E980.4
Mebhydroline	963.0	E858.1	E933.0	E950.4	E962.0	E980.4
Mebrophenhydramine	963.0	E858.1	E933.0	E950.4	E962.0	E980.4
Mebutamate	969.5	E853.8	E939.5	E950.3	E962.0	E980.3
Mecamylamine (chloride)	972.3	E858.3	E942.3	E950.4	E962.0	E980.4
Mechlorethamine hydrochloride	963.1	E858.1	E933.1	E950.4	E962.0	E980.4
Meclizene (hydrochloride)	963.0	E858.1	E933.0	E950.4	E962.0	E980.4
Meclofenoxate	970.0	E854.3	E940.0	E950.4	E962.0	E980.4
Meclozine (hydrochloride)	963.0	E858.1	E933.0	E950.4	E962.0	E980.4
Medazepam	969.4	E853.2	E939.4	E950.3	E962.0	E980.3
Medicine, medicinal substance	977.9	E858.9	E947.9	E950.5	E962.0	E980.5
specified NEC	977.8	E858.8	E947.8	E950.4	E962.0	E980.4
Medinal	967.0	E851	E937.0	E950.1	E962.0	E980.1
Medomin	967.0	E851	E937.0	E950.1	E962.0	E980.1
Medroxyprogesterone	962.2	E858.0	E932.2	E950.4	E962.0	E980.4
Medrysone	976.5	E858.7	E946.5	E950.4	E962.0	E980.4
Mefenamic acid	965.7	E850.7	E935.7	E950.0	E962.0	E980.0
Megahallucinogen	969.6	E854.1	E939.6	E950.3	E962.0	E980.3
Megestrol	962.2	E858.0	E932.2	E950.4	E962.0	E980.4
Meglumine	977.8	E858.8	E947.8	E950.4	E962.0	E980.4
Meladinin	976.3	E858.7	E946.3	E950.4	E962.0	E980.4
Melanizing agents	976.3	E858.7	E946.3	E950.4	E962.0	E980.4
Melarsoprol	961.1	E857	E931.1	E950.4	E962.0	E980.4
Melia azedarach	988.2	E865.3	—	E950.9	E962.1	E980.9
Mellaril	969.1	E853.0	E939.1	E950.3	E962.0	E980.3
Meloxine	976.3	E858.7	E946.3	E950.4	E962.0	E980.4
Melphalan	963.1	E858.1	E933.1	E950.4	E962.0	E980.4
Menadiol sodium diphosphate	964.3	E858.2	E934.3	E950.4	E962.0	E980.4
Menadione (sodium bisulfite)	964.3	E858.2	E934.3	E950.4	E962.0	E980.4
Menaphthone	964.3	E858.2	E934.3	E950.4	E962.0	E980.4
Meningococcal vaccine	978.8	E858.8	E948.8	E950.4	E962.0	E980.4
Menningovax-C	978.8	E858.8	E948.8	E950.4	E962.0	E980.4

	Poisoning	Accident	Therapeutic Use	Suicide Attempt	Assault	Undetermined
Menotropins	962.4	E858.0	E932.4	E950.4	E962.0	E980.4
Menthol NEC	976.1	E858.7	E946.1	E950.4	E962.0	E980.4
Mepacrine	961.3	E857	E931.3	E950.4	E962.0	E980.4
Meparfynol	967.8	E852.8	E937.8	E950.2	E962.0	E980.2
Mepazine	969.1	E853.0	E939.1	E950.3	E962.0	E980.3
Mepenzolate	971.1	E855.4	E941.1	E950.4	E962.0	E980.4
Meperidine	965.09	E850.2	E935.2	E950.0	E962.0	E980.0
Mephenamin(e)	966.4	E855.0	E936.4	E950.4	E962.0	E980.4
Mephenesin (carbamate)	968.0	E855.1	E938.0	E950.4	E962.0	E980.4
Mephenoxalone	969.5	E853.8	E939.5	E950.3	E962.0	E980.3
Mephentermine	971.2	E855.5	E941.2	E950.4	E962.0	E980.4
Mephenytoin	966.1	E855.0	E936.1	E950.4	E962.0	E980.4
Mephobarbital	967.0	E851	E937.0	E950.1	E962.0	E980.1
Mepiperphenidol	971.1	E855.4	E941.1	E950.4	E962.0	E980.4
Mepivacaine	968.9	E855.2	E938.9	E950.4	E962.0	E980.4
infiltration (subcutaneous)	968.5	E855.2	E938.5	E950.4	E962.0	E980.4
nerve block (peripheral) (plexus)	968.6	E855.2	E938.6	E950.4	E962.0	E980.4
topical (surface)	968.5	E855.2	E938.5	E950.4	E962.0	E980.4
Meprednisone	962.0	E858.0	E932.0	E950.4	E962.0	E980.4
Meprobam	969.5	E853.8	E939.5	E950.3	E962.0	E980.3
Meprobamate	969.5	E853.8	E939.5	E950.3	E962.0	E980.3
Mepyramine (maleate)	963.0	E858.1	E933.0	E950.4	E962.0	E980.4
Meralluride	974.0	E858.5	E944.0	E950.4	E962.0	E980.4
Merbaphen	974.0	E858.5	E944.0	E950.4	E962.0	E980.4
Merbromin	976.0	E858.7	E946.0	E950.4	E962.0	E980.4
Mercaptomerin	974.0	E858.5	E944.0	E950.4	E962.0	E980.4
Mercaptopurine	963.1	E858.1	E933.1	E950.4	E962.0	E980.4
Mercumatilin	974.0	E858.5	E944.0	E950.4	E962.0	E980.4
Mercuramide	974.0	E858.5	E944.0	E950.4	E962.0	E980.4
Mercuranin	976.0	E858.7	E946.0	E950.4	E962.0	E980.4
Mercurochrome	976.0	E858.7	E946.0	E950.4	E962.0	E980.4
Mercury, mercuric, mercurous (compounds) (cyanide) (fumes) (nonmedicinal) (vapor) NEC	985.0	E866.1	—	E950.9	E962.1	E980.9
ammoniated	976.0	E858.7	E946.0	E950.4	E962.0	E980.4
anti-infective	961.2	E857	E931.2	E950.4	E962.0	E980.4
topical	976.0	E858.7	E946.0	E950.4	E962.0	E980.4
chloride (antiseptic) NEC	976.0	E858.7	E946.0	E950.4	E962.0	E980.4
fungicide	985.0	E863.6	—	E950.6	E962.1	E980.7
diuretic compounds	974.0	E858.5	E944.0	E950.4	E962.0	E980.4
fungicide	985.0	E863.6	—	E950.6	E962.1	E980.7
organic (fungicide)	985.0	E863.6	—	E950.6	E962.1	E980.7
Merethoxylline	974.0	E858.5	E944.0	E950.4	E962.0	E980.4
Mersalyl	974.0	E858.5	E944.0	E950.4	E962.0	E980.4
Merthiolate (topical)	976.0	E858.7	E946.0	E950.4	E962.0	E980.4
ophthalmic preparation	976.5	E858.7	E946.5	E950.4	E962.0	E980.4
Meruvax	979.4	E858.8	E949.4	E950.4	E962.0	E980.4
Mescal buttons	969.6	E854.1	E939.6	E950.3	E962.0	E980.3
Mescaline (salts)	969.6	E854.1	E939.6	E950.3	E962.0	E980.3
Mesoridazine besylate	969.1	E853.0	E939.1	E950.3	E962.0	E980.3
Mestanolone	962.1	E858.0	E932.1	E950.4	E962.0	E980.4
Mestranol	962.2	E858.0	E932.2	E950.4	E962.0	E980.4
Metacresylacetate	976.0	E858.7	E946.0	E950.4	E962.0	E980.4
Metaldehyde (snail killer) NEC	989.4	E863.4	—	E950.6	E962.1	E980.7
Metals (heavy) (nonmedicinal) NEC	985.9	E866.4	—	E950.9	E962.1	E980.9
dust, fumes, or vapor NEC	985.9	E866.4	—	E950.9	E962.1	E980.9
light NEC	985.9	E866.4	—	E950.9	E962.1	E980.9
dust, fumes, or vapor NEC	985.9	E866.4	—	E950.9	E962.1	E980.9
pesticides (dust) (vapor)	985.9	E863.4	—	E950.6	E962.1	E980.7
Metamucil	973.3	E858.4	E943.3	E950.4	E962.0	E980.4
Metaphen	976.0	E858.7	E946.0	E950.4	E962.0	E980.4
Metaproterenol	975.1	E858.6	E945.1	E950.4	E962.0	E980.4
Metaraminol	972.8	E858.3	E942.8	E950.4	E962.0	E980.4
Metaxalone	968.0	E855.1	E938.0	E950.4	E962.0	E980.4
Metformin	962.3	E858.0	E932.3	E950.4	E962.0	E980.4
Methacycline	960.4	E856	E930.4	E950.4	E962.0	E980.4
Methadone	965.02	E850.1	E935.1	E950.0	E962.0	E980.0
Methallenestril	962.2	E858.0	E932.2	E950.4	E962.0	E980.4
Methamphetamine	969.7	E854.2	E939.7	E950.3	E962.0	E980.3
Methandienone	962.1	E858.0	E932.1	E950.4	E962.0	E980.4
Methandriol	962.1	E858.0	E932.1	E950.4	E962.0	E980.4
Methandrostenolone	962.1	E858.0	E932.1	E950.4	E962.0	E980.4
Methane gas	987.1	E869.8	—	E952.8	E962.2	E982.8
Methanol	980.1	E860.2	—	E950.9	E962.1	E980.9
vapor	987.8	E869.8	—	E952.8	E962.2	E982.8
Methantheline	971.1	E855.4	E941.1	E950.4	E962.0	E980.4

	Poisoning	Accident	Therapeutic Use	Suicide Attempt	Assault	Undetermined
Methaphenilene	963.0	E858.1	E933.0	E950.4	E962.0	E980.4
Methapyrilene	963.0	E858.1	E933.0	E950.4	E962.0	E980.4
Methaqualone (compounds)	967.4	E852.3	E937.4	E950.2	E962.0	E980.2
Metharbital, metharbitone	967.0	E851	E937.0	E950.1	E962.0	E980.1
Methazolamide	974.2	E858.5	E944.2	E950.4	E962.0	E980.4
Methdilazine	963.0	E858.1	E933.0	E950.4	E962.0	E980.4
Methedrine	969.7	E854.2	E939.7	E950.3	E962.0	E980.3
Methenamine (mandelate)	961.9	E857	E931.9	E950.4	E962.0	E980.4
Methenolone	962.1	E858.0	E932.1	E950.4	E962.0	E980.4
Methergine	975.0	E858.6	E945.0	E950.4	E962.0	E980.4
Methiacil	962.8	E858.0	E932.8	E950.4	E962.0	E980.4
Methicillin (sodium)	960.0	E856	E930.0	E950.4	E962.0	E980.4
Methimazole	962.8	E858.0	E932.8	E950.4	E962.0	E980.4
Methionine	977.1	E858.8	E947.1	E950.4	E962.0	E980.4
Methisazone	961.7	E857	E931.7	E950.4	E962.0	E980.4
Methitural	967.0	E851	E937.0	E950.1	E962.0	E980.1
Methixene	971.1	E855.4	E941.1	E950.4	E962.0	E980.4
Methobarbital, methobarbitone	967.0	E851	E937.0	E950.1	E962.0	E980.1
Methocarbamol	968.0	E855.1	E938.0	E950.4	E962.0	E980.4
Methohexital, methohexitone (sodium)	968.3	E855.1	E938.3	E950.4	E962.0	E980.4
Methoin	966.1	E855.0	E936.1	E950.4	E962.0	E980.4
Methopholine	965.7	E850.7	E935.7	E950.0	E962.0	E980.0
Methorate	975.4	E858.6	E945.4	E950.4	E962.0	E980.4
Methoserpidine	972.6	E858.3	E942.6	E950.4	E962.0	E980.4
Methotrexate	963.1	E858.1	E933.1	E950.4	E962.0	E980.4
Methotrimeprazine	967.8	E852.8	E937.8	E950.2	E962.0	E980.2
Methoxa-Dome	976.3	E858.7	E946.3	E950.4	E962.0	E980.4
Methoxamine	971.2	E855.5	E941.2	E950.4	E962.0	E980.4
Methoxsalen	976.3	E858.7	E946.3	E950.4	E962.0	E980.4
Methoxybenzyl penicillin	960.0	E856	E930.0	E950.4	E962.0	E980.4
Methoxychlor	989.2	E863.0	—	E950.6	E962.1	E980.7
Methoxyflurane	968.2	E855.1	E938.2	E950.4	E962.0	E980.4
Methoxyphenamine	971.2	E855.5	E941.2	E950.4	E962.0	E980.4
Methoxypromazine	969.1	E853.0	E939.1	E950.3	E962.0	E980.3
Methoxypsoralen	976.3	E858.7	E946.3	E950.4	E962.0	E980.4
Methscopolamine (bromide)	971.1	E855.4	E941.1	E950.4	E962.0	E980.4
Methsuximide	966.2	E855.0	E936.2	E950.4	E962.0	E980.4
Methyclothiazide	974.3	E858.5	E944.3	E950.4	E962.0	E980.4
Methyl						
acetate	982.8	E862.4	—	E950.9	E962.1	E980.9
acetone	982.8	E862.4	—	E950.9	E962.1	E980.9
alcohol	980.1	E860.2	—	E950.9	E962.1	E980.9
amphetamine	969.7	E854.2	E939.7	E950.3	E962.0	E980.3
androstanolone	962.1	E858.0	E932.1	E950.4	E962.0	E980.4
atropine	971.1	E855.4	E941.1	E950.4	E962.0	E980.4
benzene	982.0	E862.4	—	E950.9	E962.1	E980.9
bromide (gas)	987.8	E869.8	—	E952.8	E962.2	E982.8
fumigant	987.8	E863.8	—	E950.6	E962.2	E980.7
butanol	980.8	E860.8	—	E950.9	E962.1	E980.9
carbinol	980.1	E860.2	—	E950.9	E962.1	E980.9
cellosolve	982.8	E862.4	—	E950.9	E962.1	E980.9
cellulose	973.3	E858.4	E943.3	E950.4	E962.0	E980.4
chloride (gas)	987.8	E869.8	—	E952.8	E962.2	E982.8
cyclohexane	982.8	E862.4	—	E950.9	E962.1	E980.9
cyclohexanone	982.8	E862.4	—	E950.9	E962.1	E980.9
dihydromorphinone	965.09	E850.2	E935.2	E950.0	E962.0	E980.0
ergometrine	975.0	E858.6	E945.0	E950.4	E962.0	E980.4
ergonovine	975.0	E858.6	E945.0	E950.4	E962.0	E980.4
ethyl ketone	982.8	E862.4	—	E950.9	E962.1	E980.9
hydrazine	983.9	E864.3	—	E950.7	E962.1	E980.6
isobutyl ketone	982.8	E862.4	—	E950.9	E962.1	E980.9
morphine NEC	965.09	E850.2	E935.2	E950.0	E962.0	E980.0
parafynol	967.8	E852.8	E937.8	E950.2	E962.0	E980.2
parathion	989.3	E863.1	—	E950.6	E962.1	E980.7
pentynol NEC	967.8	E852.8	E937.8	E950.2	E962.0	E980.2
peridol	969.2	E853.1	E939.2	E950.3	E962.0	E980.3
phenidate	969.7	E854.2	E939.7	E950.3	E962.0	E980.3
prednisolone	962.0	E858.0	E932.0	E950.4	E962.0	E980.4
ENT agent	976.6	E858.7	E946.6	E950.4	E962.0	E980.4
ophthalmic preparation	976.5	E858.7	E946.5	E950.4	E962.0	E980.4
topical NEC	976.0	E858.7	E946.0	E950.4	E962.0	E980.4
propylcarbinol	980.8	E860.8	—	E950.9	E962.1	E980.9
rosaniline NEC	976.0	E858.7	E946.0	E950.4	E962.0	E980.4
salicylate NEC	976.3	E858.7	E946.3	E950.4	E962.0	E980.4
sulfate (fumes)	987.8	E869.8	—	E952.8	E962.2	E982.8
liquid	983.9	E864.3	—	E950.7	E962.1	E980.6
sulfonal	967.8	E852.8	E937.8	E950.2	E962.0	E980.2
testosterone	962.1	E858.0	E932.1	E950.4	E962.0	E980.4
Methyl — continued						
thiouracil	962.8	E858.0	E932.8	E950.4	E962.0	E980.4
Methylated spirit	980.0	E860.1	—	E950.9	E962.1	E980.9
Methyldopa	972.6	E858.3	E942.6	E950.4	E962.0	E980.4
Methylene						
blue	961.9	E857	E931.9	E950.4	E962.0	E980.4
chloride or dichloride (solvent) NEC	982.3	E862.4	—	E950.9	E962.1	E980.9
Methylhexabital	967.0	E851	E937.0	E950.1	E962.0	E980.1
Methylparaben (ophthalmic)	976.5	E858.7	E946.5	E950.4	E962.0	E980.4
Methyprylon	967.5	E852.4	E937.5	E950.2	E962.0	E980.2
Methysergide	971.3	E855.6	E941.3	E950.4	E962.0	E980.4
Metoclopramide	963.0	E858.1	E933.0	E950.4	E962.0	E980.4
Metofoline	965.7	E850.7	E935.7	E950.0	E962.0	E980.0
Metopon	965.09	E850.2	E935.2	E950.0	E962.0	E980.0
Metronidazole	961.5	E857	E931.5	E950.4	E962.0	E980.4
Metycaine	968.9	E855.2	E938.9	E950.4	E962.0	E980.4
infiltration (subcutaneous)	968.5	E855.2	E938.5	E950.4	E962.0	E980.4
nerve block (peripheral) (plexus)	968.6	E855.2	E938.6	E950.4	E962.0	E980.4
topical (surface)	968.5	E855.2	E938.5	E950.4	E962.0	E980.4
Metyrapone	977.8	E858.8	E947.8	E950.4	E962.0	E980.4
Mevinphos	989.3	E863.1	—	E950.6	E962.1	E980.7
Mezereon (berries)	988.2	E865.3	—	E950.9	E962.1	E980.9
Micatin	976.0	E858.7	E946.0	E950.4	E962.0	E980.4
Miconazole	976.0	E858.7	E946.0	E950.4	E962.0	E980.4
Midol	965.1	E850.3	E935.3	E950.0	E962.0	E980.0
Mifepristone	962.9	E858.0	E932.9	E950.4	E962.0	E980.4
Milk of magnesia	973.0	E858.4	E943.0	E950.4	E962.0	E980.4
Millipede (tropical) (venomous)	989.5	E905.4	—	E950.9	E962.1	E980.9
Miltown	969.5	E853.8	E939.5	E950.3	E962.0	E980.3
Mineral						
oil (medicinal)	973.2	E858.4	E943.2	E950.4	E962.0	E980.4
nonmedicinal	981	E862.1	—	E950.9	E962.1	E980.9
topical	976.3	E858.7	E946.3	E950.4	E962.0	E980.4
salts NEC	974.6	E858.5	E944.6	E950.4	E962.0	E980.4
spirits	981	E862.0	—	E950.9	E962.1	E980.9
Minocycline	960.4	E856	E930.4	E950.4	E962.0	E980.4
Mithramycin (antineoplastic)	960.7	E856	E930.7	E950.4	E962.0	E980.4
Mitobronitol	963.1	E858.1	E933.1	E950.4	E962.0	E980.4
Mitomycin (antineoplastic)	960.7	E856	E930.7	E950.4	E962.0	E980.4
Mitotane	963.1	E858.1	E933.1	E950.4	E962.0	E980.4
Moderil	972.6	E858.3	E942.6	E950.4	E962.0	E980.4
Mogadon — see Nitrazepam						
Molindone	969.3	E853.8	E939.3	E950.3	E962.0	E980.3
Monistat	976.0	E858.7	E946.0	E950.4	E962.0	E980.4
Monkshood	988.2	E865.4	—	E950.9	E962.1	E980.9
Monoamine oxidase inhibitors	969.0	E854.0	E939.0	E950.3	E962.0	E980.3
Monochlorobenzene	982.0	E862.4	—	E950.9	E962.1	E980.9
Monosodium glutamate	989.89	E866.8	—	E950.9	E962.1	E980.9
Monoxide, carbon — see Carbon, monoxide						
Moperone	969.2	E853.1	E939.2	E950.3	E962.0	E980.3
Morning glory seeds	969.6	E854.1	E939.6	E950.3	E962.0	E980.3
Moroxydine (hydrochloride)	961.7	E857	E931.7	E950.4	E962.0	E980.4
Morphazinamide	961.8	E857	E931.8	E950.4	E962.0	E980.4
Morphinans	965.09	E850.2	E935.2	E950.0	E962.0	E980.0
Morphine NEC	965.09	E850.2	E935.2	E950.0	E962.0	E980.0
antagonists	970.1	E854.3	E940.1	E950.4	E962.0	E980.4
Morpholinylethylmorphine	965.09	E850.2	E935.2	E950.0	E962.0	E980.0
Morrhuate sodium	972.7	E858.3	E942.7	E950.4	E962.0	E980.4
Moth balls — see also						
Pesticides	989.4	E863.4	—	E950.6	E962.1	E980.7
naphthalene	983.0	E863.4	—	E950.7	E962.1	E980.6
Motor exhaust gas — see Carbon, monoxide, exhaust gas						
Mouth wash	976.6	E858.7	E946.6	E950.4	E962.0	E980.4
Mucolytic agent	975.5	E858.6	E945.5	E950.4	E962.0	E980.4
Mucomyst	975.5	E858.6	E945.5	E950.4	E962.0	E980.4
Mucous membrane agents (external)	976.9	E858.7	E946.9	E950.4	E962.0	E980.4
specified NEC	976.8	E858.7	E946.8	E950.4	E962.0	E980.4
Mumps						
immune globulin (human)	964.6	E858.2	E934.6	E950.4	E962.0	E980.4
skin test antigen	977.8	E858.8	E947.8	E950.4	E962.0	E980.4
vaccine	979.6	E858.8	E949.6	E950.4	E962.0	E980.4

☑ Additional Digit Required — Refer to the Tabular List for Digit Selection   ▽ Subterms under main terms may continue to next column or page

	Poisoning	Accident	Therapeutic Use	Suicide Attempt	Assault	Undetermined
Mumpsvax	979.6	E858.8	E949.6	E950.4	E962.0	E980.4
Muriatic acid — *see* Hydrochloric acid						
Muscarine	971.0	E855.3	E941.0	E950.4	E962.0	E980.4
Muscle affecting agents						
NEC	975.3	E858.6	E945.3	E950.4	E962.0	E980.4
oxytocic	975.0	E858.6	E945.0	E950.4	E962.0	E980.4
relaxants	975.3	E858.6	E945.3	E950.4	E962.0	E980.4
central nervous system	968.0	E855.1	E938.0	E950.4	E962.0	E980.4
skeletal	975.2	E858.6	E945.2	E950.4	E962.0	E980.4
smooth	975.1	E858.6	E945.1	E950.4	E962.0	E980.4
Mushrooms, noxious	988.1	E865.5	—	E950.9	E962.1	E980.9
Mussel, noxious	988.0	E865.1	—	E950.9	E962.1	E980.9
Mustard (emetic)	973.6	E858.4	E943.6	E950.4	E962.0	E980.4
gas	987.8	E869.8	—	E952.8	E962.2	E982.8
nitrogen	963.1	E858.1	E933.1	E950.4	E962.0	E980.4
Mustine	963.1	E858.1	E933.1	E950.4	E962.0	E980.4
M-vac	979.4	E858.8	E949.4	E950.4	E962.0	E980.4
Mycifradin	960.8	E856	E930.8	E950.4	E962.0	E980.4
topical	976.0	E858.7	E946.0	E950.4	E962.0	E980.4
Mycitracin	960.8	E856	E930.8	E950.4	E962.0	E980.4
ophthalmic preparation	976.5	E858.7	E946.5	E950.4	E962.0	E980.4
Mycostatin	960.1	E856	E930.1	E950.4	E962.0	E980.4
topical	976.0	E858.7	E946.0	E950.4	E962.0	E980.4
Mydriacyl	971.1	E855.4	E941.1	E950.4	E962.0	E980.4
Myelobromal	963.1	E858.1	E933.1	E950.4	E962.0	E980.4
Myleran	963.1	E858.1	E933.1	E950.4	E962.0	E980.4
Myochrysin(e)	965.69	E850.6	E935.6	E950.0	E962.0	E980.0
Myoneural blocking agents	975.2	E858.6	E945.2	E950.4	E962.0	E980.4
Myristica fragrans	988.2	E865.3	—	E950.9	E962.1	E980.9
Myristicin	988.2	E865.3	—	E950.9	E962.1	E980.9
Mysoline	966.3	E855.0	E936.3	E950.4	E962.0	E980.4
Nafcillin (sodium)	960.0	E856	E930.0	E950.4	E962.0	E980.4
Nail polish remover	982.8	E862.4	—	E950.9	E962.1	E908.9
Nalidixic acid	961.9	E857	E931.9	E950.4	E962.0	E980.4
Nalorphine	970.1	E854.3	E940.1	E950.4	E962.0	E980.4
Naloxone	970.1	E854.3	E940.1	E950.4	E962.0	E980.4
Nandrolone (decanoate) (phenproprioate)	962.1	E858.0	E932.1	E950.4	E962.0	E980.4
Naphazoline	971.2	E855.5	E941.2	E950.4	E962.0	E980.4
Naphtha (painter's) (petroleum)	981	E862.0	—	E950.9	E962.1	E980.9
solvent	981	E862.0	—	E950.9	E962.1	E980.9
vapor	987.1	E869.8	—	E952.8	E962.2	E982.8
Naphthalene (chlorinated)	983.0	E864.0	—	E950.7	E962.1	E980.6
insecticide or moth repellent	983.0	E863.4	—	E950.7	E962.1	E980.6
vapor	987.8	E869.8	—	E952.8	E962.2	E982.8
Naphthol	983.0	E864.0	—	E950.7	E962.1	E980.6
Naphthylamine	983.0	E864.0	—	E950.7	E962.1	E980.6
Naprosyn — see Naproxen						
Naproxen	965.61	E850.6	E935.6	E950.0	E962.0	E980.0
Narcotic (drug)	967.9	E852.9	E937.9	E950.2	E962.0	E980.2
analgesic NEC	965.8	E850.8	E935.8	E950.0	E962.0	E980.0
antagonist	970.1	E854.3	E940.1	E950.4	E962.0	E980.4
specified NEC	967.8	E852.8	E937.8	E950.2	E962.0	E980.2
Narcotine	975.4	E858.6	E945.4	E950.4	E962.0	E980.4
Nardil	969.0	E854.0	E939.0	E950.3	E962.0	E980.3
Natrium cyanide — see Cyanide(s)						
Natural						
blood (product)	964.7	E858.2	E934.7	E950.4	E962.0	E980.4
gas (piped)	987.1	E867	—	E951.0	E962.2	E981.0
incomplete combustion	986	E867	—	E951.0	E962.2	E981.0
Nealbarbital, nealbarbitone	967.0	E851	E937.0	E950.1	E962.0	E980.1
Nectadon	975.4	E858.6	E945.4	E950.4	E962.0	E980.4
Nematocyst (sting)	989.5	E905.6	—	E950.9	E962.1	E980.9
Nembutal	967.0	E851	E937.0	E950.1	E962.0	E980.1
Neoarsphenamine	961.1	E857	E931.1	E950.4	E962.0	E980.4
Neocinchophen	974.7	E858.5	E944.7	E950.4	E962.0	E980.4
Neomycin	960.8	E856	E930.8	E950.4	E962.0	E980.4
ENT agent	976.6	E858.7	E946.6	E950.4	E962.0	E980.4
ophthalmic preparation	976.5	E858.7	E946.5	E950.4	E962.0	E980.4
topical NEC	976.0	E858.7	E946.0	E950.4	E962.0	E980.4
Neonal	967.0	E851	E937.0	E950.1	E962.0	E980.1
Neoprontosil	961.0	E857	E931.0	E950.4	E962.0	E980.4
Neosalvarsan	961.1	E857	E931.1	E950.4	E962.0	E980.4
Neosilversalvarsan	961.1	E857	E931.1	E950.4	E962.0	E980.4
Neosporin	960.8	E856	E930.8	E950.4	E962.0	E980.4

	Poisoning	Accident	Therapeutic Use	Suicide Attempt	Assault	Undetermined
Neosporin — *continued*						
ENT agent	976.6	E858.7	E946.6	E950.4	E962.0	E980.4
opthalmic preparation	976.5	E858.7	E946.5	E950.4	E962.0	E980.4
topical NEC	976.0	E858.7	E946.0	E950.4	E962.0	E980.4
Neostigmine	971.0	E855.3	E941.0	E950.4	E962.0	E980.4
Neraval	967.0	E851	E937.0	E950.1	E962.0	E980.1
Neravan	967.0	E851	E937.0	E950.1	E962.0	E980.1
Nerium oleander	988.2	E865.4	—	E950.9	E962.1	E980.9
Nerve gases (war)	987.9	E869.9	—	E952.9	E962.2	E982.9
Nesacaine	968.9	E855.2	E938.9	E950.4	E962.0	E980.4
infiltration (subcutaneous)	968.5	E855.2	E938.5	E950.4	E962.0	E980.4
nerve block (peripheral) (plexus)	968.6	E855.2	E938.6	E950.4	E962.0	E980.4
Neurobarb	967.0	E851	E937.0	E950.1	E962.0	E980.1
Neuroleptics NEC	969.3	E853.8	E939.3	E950.3	E962.0	E980.3
Neuroprotective agent	977.8	E858.8	E947.8	E950.4	E962.0	E980.4
Neutral spirits	980.0	E860.1	—	E950.9	E962.1	E980.9
beverage	980.0	E860.0	—	E950.9	E962.1	E980.9
Niacin, niacinamide	972.2	E858.3	E942.2	E950.4	E962.0	E980.4
Nialamide	969.0	E854.0	E939.0	E950.3	E962.0	E980.3
Nickle (carbonyl) (compounds) (fumes) (tetracarbonyl) (vapor)	985.8	E866.4	—	E950.9	E962.1	E980.9
Niclosamide	961.6	E857	E931.6	E950.4	E962.0	E980.4
Nicomorphine	965.09	E850.2	E935.2	E950.0	E962.0	E980.0
Nicotinamide	972.2	E858.3	E942.2	E950.4	E962.0	E980.4
Nicotine (insecticide) (spray) (sulfate) NEC	989.4	E863.4	—	E950.6	E962.1	E980.7
not insecticide	989.89	E866.8	—	E950.9	E962.1	E980.9
Nicotinic acid (derivatives)	972.2	E858.3	E942.2	E950.4	E962.0	E980.4
Nicotinyl alcohol	972.2	E858.3	E942.2	E950.4	E962.0	E980.4
Nicoumalone	964.2	E858.2	E934.2	E950.4	E962.0	E980.4
Nifenazone	965.5	E850.5	E935.5	E950.0	E962.0	E980.0
Nifuraldezone	961.9	E857	E931.9	E950.4	E962.0	E980.4
Nightshade (deadly)	988.2	E865.4	—	E950.9	E962.1	E980.9
Nikethamide	970.0	E854.3	E940.0	E950.4	E962.0	E980.4
Nilstat	960.1	E856	E930.1	E950.4	E962.0	E980.4
topical	976.0	E858.7	E946.0	E950.4	E962.0	E980.4
Nimodipine	977.8	E858.8	E947.8	E950.4	E962.0	E980.4
Niridazole	961.6	E857	E931.6	E950.4	E962.0	E980.4
Nisentil	965.09	E850.2	E935.2	E950.0	E962.0	E980.0
Nitrates	972.4	E858.3	E942.4	E950.4	E962.0	E980.4
Nitrazepam	969.4	E853.2	E939.4	E950.3	E962.0	E980.3
Nitric						
acid (liquid)	983.1	E864.1	—	E950.7	E962.1	E980.6
vapor	987.8	E869.8	—	E952.8	E962.2	E982.8
oxide (gas)	987.2	E869.0	—	E952.8	E962.2	E982.8
Nitrite, amyl (medicinal) (vapor)	972.4	E858.3	E942.4	E950.4	E962.0	E980.4
Nitroaniline	983.0	E864.0	—	E950.7	E962.1	E980.6
vapor	987.8	E869.8	—	E952.8	E962.2	E982.8
Nitrobenzene, nitrobenzol	983.0	E864.0	—	E950.7	E962.1	E980.6
vapor	987.8	E869.8	—	E952.8	E962.2	E982.8
Nitrocellulose	976.3	E858.7	E946.3	E950.4	E962.0	E980.4
Nitrofuran derivatives	961.9	E857	E931.9	E950.4	E962.0	E980.4
Nitrofurantoin	961.9	E857	E931.9	E950.4	E962.0	E980.4
Nitrofurazone	976.0	E858.7	E946.0	E950.4	E962.0	E980.4
Nitrogen (dioxide) (gas) (oxide)	987.2	E869.0	—	E952.8	E962.2	E982.8
mustard (antineoplastic)	963.1	E858.1	E933.1	E950.4	E962.0	E980.4
nonmedicinal	989.89	E866.8	—	E950.9	E962.1	E980.9
fumes	987.8	E869.8	—	E952.8	E962.2	E982.8
Nitroglycerin, nitroglycerol (medicinal)	972.4	E858.3	E942.4	E950.4	E962.0	E980.4
Nitrohydrochloric acid	983.1	E864.1	—	E950.7	E962.1	E980.6
Nitromersol	976.0	E858.7	E946.0	E950.4	E962.0	E980.4
Nitronaphthalene	983.0	E864.0	—	E950.7	E962.2	E980.6
Nitrophenol	983.0	E864.0	—	E950.7	E962.2	E980.6
Nitrothiazol	961.6	E857	E931.6	E950.4	E962.0	E980.4
Nitrotoluene, nitrotoluol	983.0	E864.0	—	E950.7	E962.1	E980.6
vapor	987.8	E869.8	—	E952.8	E962.2	E982.8
Nitrous	968.2	E855.1	E938.2	E950.4	E962.0	E980.4
acid (liquid)	983.1	E864.1	—	E950.7	E962.1	E980.6
fumes	987.2	E869.0	—	E952.8	E962.2	E982.8
oxide (anesthetic) NEC	968.2	E855.1	E938.2	E950.4	E962.0	E980.4
Nitrozone	976.0	E858.7	E946.0	E950.4	E962.0	E980.4
Noctec	967.1	E852.0	E937.1	E950.2	E962.0	E980.2
Noludar	967.5	E852.4	E937.5	E950.2	E962.0	E980.2
Noptil	967.0	E851	E937.0	E950.1	E962.0	E980.1
Noradrenalin	971.2	E855.5	E941.2	E950.4	E962.0	E980.4
Noramidopyrine	965.5	E850.5	E935.5	E950.0	E962.0	E980.0

☑ Additional Digit Required — Refer to the Tabular List for Digit Selection

▽ Subterms under main terms may continue to next column or page

Substance	Poisoning	Accident	Therapeutic Use	Suicide Attempt	Assault	Undetermined
Norepinephrine	971.2	E855.5	E941.2	E950.4	E962.0	E980.4
Norethandrolone	962.1	E858.0	E932.1	E950.4	E962.0	E980.4
Norethindrone	962.2	E858.0	E932.2	E950.4	E962.0	E980.4
Norethisterone	962.2	E858.0	E932.2	E950.4	E962.0	E980.4
Norethynodrel	962.2	E858.0	E932.2	E950.4	E962.0	E980.4
Norlestrin	962.2	E858.0	E932.2	E950.4	E962.0	E980.4
Norlutin	962.2	E858.0	E932.2	E950.4	E962.0	E980.4
Normison — see Benzodiazepines						
Normorphine	965.09	E850.2	E935.2	E950.0	E962.0	E980.0
Nortriptyline	969.0	E854.0	E939.0	E950.3	E962.0	E980.3
Noscapine	975.4	E858.6	E945.4	E950.4	E962.0	E980.4
Nose preparations	976.6	E858.7	E946.6	E950.4	E962.0	E980.4
Novobiocin	960.8	E856	E930.8	E950.4	E962.0	E980.4
Novocain (infiltration) (topical)	968.5	E855.2	E938.5	E950.4	E962.0	E980.4
nerve block (peripheral) (plexus)	968.6	E855.2	E938.6	E950.4	E962.0	E980.4
spinal	968.7	E855.2	E938.7	E950.4	E962.0	E980.4
Noxythiolin	961.9	E857	E931.9	E950.4	E962.0	E980.4
NPH Iletin (insulin)	962.3	E858.0	E932.3	E950.4	E962.0	E980.4
Numorphan	965.09	E850.2	E935.2	E950.0	E962.0	E980.0
Nunol	967.0	E851	E937.0	E950.1	E962.0	E980.1
Nupercaine (spinal anesthetic)	968.7	E855.2	E938.7	E950.4	E962.0	E980.4
topical (surface)	968.5	E855.2	E938.5	E950.4	E962.0	E980.4
Nutmeg oil (liniment)	976.3	E858.7	E946.3	E950.4	E962.0	E980.4
Nux vomica	989.1	E863.7	—	E950.6	E962.1	E980.7
Nydrazid	961.8	E857	E931.8	E950.4	E962.0	E980.4
Nylidrin	971.2	E855.5	E941.2	E950.4	E962.0	E980.4
Nystatin	960.1	E856	E930.1	E950.4	E962.0	E980.4
topical	976.0	E858.7	E946.0	E950.4	E962.0	E980.4
Nytol	963.0	E858.1	E933.0	E950.4	E962.0	E980.4
Oblivion	967.8	E852.8	E937.8	E950.2	E962.0	E980.2
Octyl nitrite	972.4	E858.3	E942.4	E950.4	E962.0	E980.4
Oestradiol (cypionate) (dipropionate)(valerate)	962.2	E858.0	E932.2	E950.4	E962.0	E980.4
Oestriol	962.2	E858.0	E932.2	E950.4	E962.0	E980.4
Oestrone	962.2	E858.0	E932.2	E950.4	E962.0	E980.4
Oil (of) NEC	989.89	E866.8	—	E950.9	E962.1	E980.9
bitter almond	989.0	E866.8	—	E950.9	E962.1	E980.9
camphor	976.1	E858.7	E946.1	E950.4	E962.0	E980.4
colors	989.89	E861.6	—	E950.9	E962.1	E980.9
fumes	987.8	E869.8	—	E952.8	E962.2	E982.8
lubricating	981	E862.2	—	E950.9	E962.1	E980.9
specified source, other — see substance specified						
vitriol (liquid)	983.1	E864.1	—	E950.7	E962.1	E980.6
fumes	987.8	E869.8	—	E952.8	E962.2	E982.8
wintergreen (bitter) NEC	976.3	E858.7	E946.3	E950.4	E962.0	E980.4
Ointments NEC	976.9	E858.7	E946.9	E950.4	E962.0	E980.4
Oleander	988.2	E865.4	—	E950.9	E962.1	E980.9
Oleandomycin	960.3	E856	E930.3	E950.4	E962.0	E980.4
Oleovitamin A	963.5	E858.1	E933.5	E950.4	E962.0	E980.4
Oleum ricini	973.1	E858.4	E943.1	E950.4	E962.0	E980.4
Olive oil (medicinal) NEC	973.2	E858.4	E943.2	E950.4	E962.0	E980.4
OMPA	989.3	E863.1	—	E950.6	E962.1	E980.7
Oncovin	963.1	E858.1	E933.1	E950.4	E962.0	E980.4
Ophthaine	968.5	E855.2	E938.5	E950.4	E962.0	E980.4
Ophthetic	968.5	E855.2	E938.5	E950.4	E962.0	E980.4
Opiates, opioids, opium NEC	965.00	E850.2	E935.2	E950.0	E962.0	E980.0
antagonists	970.1	E854.3	E940.1	E950.4	E962.0	E980.4
Oracon	962.2	E858.0	E932.2	E950.4	E962.0	E980.4
Oragrafin	977.8	E858.8	E947.8	E950.4	E962.0	E980.4
Oral contraceptives	962.2	E858.0	E932.2	E950.4	E962.0	E980.4
Orciprenaline	975.1	E858.6	E945.1	E950.4	E962.0	E980.4
Organidin	975.5	E858.6	E945.5	E950.4	E962.0	E980.4
Organophosphates	989.3	E863.1	—	E950.6	E962.1	E980.7
Orimune	979.5	E858.8	E949.5	E950.4	E962.0	E980.4
Orinase	962.3	E858.0	E932.3	E950.4	E962.0	E980.4
Orphenadrine	966.4	E855.0	E936.4	E950.4	E962.0	E980.4
Ortal (sodium)	967.0	E851	E937.0	E950.1	E962.0	E980.1
Orthoboric acid	976.0	E858.7	E946.0	E950.4	E962.0	E980.4
ENT agent	976.6	E858.7	E946.6	E950.4	E962.0	E980.4
ophthalmic preparation	976.5	E858.7	E946.5	E950.4	E962.0	E980.4
Orthocaine	968.5	E855.2	E938.5	E950.4	E962.0	E980.4
Ortho-Novum	962.2	E858.0	E932.2	E950.4	E962.0	E980.4
Orthotolidine (reagent)	977.8	E858.8	E947.8	E950.4	E962.0	E980.4
Osmic acid (liquid)	983.1	E864.1	—	E950.7	E962.1	E980.6
fumes	987.8	E869.8	—	E952.8	E962.2	E982.8
Osmotic diuretics	974.4	E858.5	E944.4	E950.4	E962.0	E980.4
Ouabain	972.1	E858.3	E942.1	E950.4	E962.0	E980.4
Ovarian hormones (synthetic substitutes)	962.2	E858.0	E932.2	E950.4	E962.0	E980.4
Ovral	962.2	E858.0	E932.2	E950.4	E962.0	E980.4
Ovulation suppressants	962.2	E858.0	E932.2	E950.4	E962.0	E980.4
Ovulen	962.2	E858.0	E932.2	E950.4	E962.0	E980.4
Oxacillin (sodium)	960.0	E856	E930.0	E950.4	E962.0	E980.4
Oxalic acid	983.1	E864.1	—	E950.7	E962.1	E980.6
Oxanamide	969.5	E853.8	E939.5	E950.3	E962.0	E980.3
Oxandrolone	962.1	E858.0	E932.1	E950.4	E962.0	E980.4
Oxaprozin	965.61	E850.6	E935.6	E950.0	E962.0	E980.0
Oxazepam	969.4	E853.2	E939.4	E950.3	E962.0	E980.3
Oxazolidine derivatives	966.0	E855.0	E936.0	E950.4	E962.0	E980.4
Ox bile extract	973.4	E858.4	E943.4	E950.4	E962.0	E980.4
Oxedrine	971.2	E855.5	E941.2	E950.4	E962.0	E980.4
Oxeladin	975.4	E858.6	E945.4	E950.4	E962.0	E980.4
Oxethazaine NEC	968.5	E855.2	E938.5	E950.4	E962.0	E980.4
Oxidizing agents NEC	983.9	E864.3	—	E950.7	E962.1	E980.6
Oxolinic acid	961.3	E857	E931.3	E950.4	E962.0	E980.4
Oxophenarsine	961.1	E857	E931.1	E950.4	E962.0	E980.4
Oxsoralen	976.3	E858.7	E946.3	E950.4	E962.0	E980.4
Oxtriphylline	975.7	E858.6	E945.7	E950.4	E962.0	E980.4
Oxybuprocaine	968.5	E855.2	E938.5	E950.4	E962.0	E980.4
Oxybutynin	975.1	E858.6	E945.1	E950.4	E962.0	E980.4
Oxycodone	965.09	E850.2	E935.2	E950.0	E962.0	E980.0
Oxygen	987.8	E869.8	—	E952.8	E962.2	E982.8
Oxylone	976.0	E858.7	E946.0	E950.4	E962.0	E980.4
ophthalmic preparation	976.5	E858.7	E946.5	E950.4	E962.0	E980.4
Oxymesterone	962.1	E858.0	E932.1	E950.4	E962.0	E980.4
Oxymetazoline	971.2	E855.5	E941.2	E950.4	E962.0	E980.4
Oxymetholone	962.1	E858.0	E932.1	E950.4	E962.0	E980.4
Oxymorphone	965.09	E850.2	E935.2	E950.0	E962.0	E980.0
Oxypertine	969.0	E854.0	E939.0	E950.3	E962.0	E980.3
Oxyphenbutazone	965.5	E850.5	E935.5	E950.0	E962.0	E980.0
Oxyphencyclimine	971.1	E855.4	E941.1	E950.4	E962.0	E980.4
Oxyphenisatin	973.1	E858.4	E943.1	E950.4	E962.0	E980.4
Oxyphenonium	971.1	E855.4	E941.1	E950.4	E962.0	E980.4
Oxyquinoline	961.3	E857	E931.3	E950.4	E962.0	E980.4
Oxytetracycline	960.4	E856	E930.4	E950.4	E962.0	E980.4
Oxytocics	975.0	E858.6	E945.0	E950.4	E962.0	E980.4
Oxytocin	975.0	E858.6	E945.0	E950.4	E962.0	E980.4
Ozone	987.8	E869.8	—	E952.8	E962.2	E982.8
PABA	976.3	E858.7	E946.3	E950.4	E962.0	E980.4
Packed red cells	964.7	E858.2	E934.7	E950.4	E962.0	E980.4
Paint NEC	989.89	E861.6	—	E950.9	E962.1	E980.9
cleaner	982.8	E862.9	—	E950.9	E962.1	E980.9
fumes NEC	987.8	E869.8	—	E952.8	E962.1	E982.8
lead (fumes)	984.0	E861.5	—	E950.9	E962.1	E980.9
solvent NEC	982.8	E862.9	—	E950.9	E962.1	E980.9
stripper	982.8	E862.9	—	E950.9	E962.1	E980.9
Palfium	965.09	E850.2	E935.2	E950.0	E962.0	E980.0
Palivizumab	979.9	E858.8	E949.6	E950.4	E962.0	E980.4
Paludrine	961.4	E857	E931.4	E950.4	E962.0	E980.4
PAM	977.2	E855.8	E947.2	E950.4	E962.0	E980.4
Pamaquine (naphthoate)	961.4	E857	E931.4	E950.4	E962.0	E980.4
Pamprin	965.1	E850.3	E935.3	E950.0	E962.0	E980.0
Panadol	965.4	E850.4	E935.4	E950.0	E962.0	E980.0
Pancreatic dornase (mucolytic)	963.4	E858.1	E933.4	E950.4	E962.0	E980.4
Pancreatin	973.4	E858.4	E943.4	E950.4	E962.0	E980.4
Pancrelipase	973.4	E858.4	E943.4	E950.4	E962.0	E980.4
Pangamic acid	963.5	E858.1	E933.5	E950.4	E962.0	E980.4
Panthenol	963.5	E858.1	E933.5	E950.4	E962.0	E980.4
topical	976.8	E858.7	E946.8	E950.4	E962.0	E980.4
Pantopaque	977.8	E858.8	E947.8	E950.4	E962.0	E980.4
Pantopon	965.00	E850.2	E935.2	E950.0	E962.0	E980.0
Pantothenic acid	963.5	E858.1	E933.5	E950.4	E962.0	E980.4
Panwarfin	964.2	E858.2	E934.2	E950.4	E962.0	E980.4
Papain	973.4	E858.4	E943.4	E950.4	E962.0	E980.4
Papaverine	972.5	E858.3	E942.5	E950.4	E962.0	E980.4
Para-aminobenzoic acid	976.3	E858.7	E946.3	E950.4	E962.0	E980.4
Para-aminophenol derivatives	965.4	E850.4	E935.4	E950.0	E962.0	E980.0
Para-aminosalicylic acid (derivatives)	961.8	E857	E931.8	E950.4	E962.0	E980.4
Paracetaldehyde (medicinal)	967.2	E852.1	E937.2	E950.2	E962.0	E980.2
Paracetamol	965.4	E850.4	E935.4	E950.0	E962.0	E980.0
Paracodin	965.09	E850.2	E935.2	E950.0	E962.0	E980.0
Paradione	966.0	E855.0	E936.0	E950.4	E962.0	E980.4

☑ Additional Digit Required — Refer to the Tabular List for Digit Selection   Subterms under main terms may continue to next column or page

326 — Volume 2   ►◄ Revised Text   ● New Line   ▲ Revised Code   2007 ICD-9-CM

Index   Norepinephrine — Paradione

	Poisoning	Accident	Therapeutic Use	Suicide Attempt	Assault	Undeter-mined
Paraffin(s) (wax)	981	E862.3	—	E950.9	E962.1	E980.9
liquid (medicinal)	973.2	E858.4	E943.2	E950.4	E962.0	E980.4
nonmedicinal (oil)	981	E962.1	—	E950.9	E962.1	E980.9
Paraldehyde (medicinal)	967.2	E852.1	E937.2	E950.2	E962.0	E980.2
Paramethadione	966.0	E855.0	E936.0	E950.4	E962.0	E980.4
Paramethasone	962.0	E858.0	E932.0	E950.4	E962.0	E980.4
Paraquat	989.4	E863.5	—	E950.6	E962.1	E980.7
Parasympatholytics	971.1	E855.4	E941.1	E950.4	E962.0	E980.4
Parasympathomimetics	971.0	E855.3	E941.0	E950.4	E962.0	E980.4
Parathion	989.3	E863.1	—	E950.6	E962.1	E980.7
Parathormone	962.6	E858.0	E932.6	E950.4	E962.0	E980.4
Parathyroid (derivatives)	962.6	E858.0	E932.6	E950.4	E962.0	E980.4
Paratyphoid vaccine	978.1	E858.8	E948.1	E950.4	E962.0	E980.4
Paredrine	971.2	E855.5	E941.2	E950.4	E962.0	E980.4
Paregoric	965.00	E850.2	E935.2	E950.0	E962.0	E980.0
Pargyline	972.3	E858.3	E942.3	E950.4	E962.0	E980.4
Paris green	985.1	E866.3	—	E950.8	E962.1	E980.8
insecticide	985.1	E863.4	—	E950.8	E962.1	E980.8
Parnate	969.0	E854.0	E939.0	E950.3	E962.0	E980.3
Paromomycin	960.8	E856	E930.8	E950.4	E962.0	E980.4
Paroxypropione	963.1	E858.1	E933.1	E950.4	E962.0	E980.4
Parzone	965.09	E850.2	E935.2	E950.0	E962.0	E980.0
PAS	961.8	E857	E931.8	E950.4	E962.0	E980.4
PCBs	981	E862.3	—	E950.9	E962.1	E980.9
PCP (pentachlorophenol)	989.4	E863.6	—	E950.6	E962.1	E980.7
herbicide	989.4	E863.5	—	E950.6	E962.1	E980.7
insecticide	989.4	E863.4	—	E950.6	E962.1	E980.7
phencyclidine	968.3	E855.1	E938.3	E950.4	E962.0	E980.4
Peach kernel oil (emulsion)	973.2	E858.4	E943.2	E950.4	E962.0	E980.4
Peanut oil (emulsion) **NEC**	973.2	E858.4	E943.2	E950.4	E962.0	E980.4
topical	976.3	E858.7	E946.3	E950.4	E962.0	E980.4
Pearly Gates (morning glory seeds)	969.6	E854.1	E939.6	E950.3	E962.0	E980.3
Pecazine	969.1	E853.0	E939.1	E950.3	E962.0	E980.3
Pecilocin	960.1	E856	E930.1	E950.4	E962.0	E980.4
Pectin (with kaolin) **NEC**	973.5	E858.4	E943.5	E950.4	E962.0	E980.4
Pelletierine tannate	961.6	E857	E931.6	E950.4	E962.0	E980.4
Pemoline	969.7	E854.2	E939.7	E950.3	E962.0	E980.3
Pempidine	972.3	E858.3	E942.3	E950.4	E962.0	E980.4
Penamecillin	960.0	E856	E930.0	E950.4	E962.0	E980.4
Penethamate hydriodide	960.0	E856	E930.0	E950.4	E962.0	E980.4
Penicillamine	963.8	E858.1	E933.8	E950.4	E962.0	E980.4
Penicillin (any type)	960.0	E856	E930.0	E950.4	E962.0	E980.4
Penicillinase	963.4	E858.1	E933.4	E950.4	E962.0	E980.4
Pentachlorophenol (fungicide)	989.4	E863.6	—	E950.6	E962.1	E980.7
herbicide	989.4	E863.5	—	E950.6	E962.1	E980.7
insecticide	989.4	E863.4	—	E950.6	E962.1	E980.7
Pentaerythritol	972.4	E858.3	E942.4	E950.4	E962.0	E980.4
chloral	967.1	E852.0	E937.1	E950.2	E962.0	E980.2
tetranitrate NEC	972.4	E858.3	E942.4	E950.4	E962.0	E980.4
Pentagastrin	977.8	E858.8	E947.8	E950.4	E962.0	E980.4
Pentalin	982.3	E862.4	—	E950.9	E962.1	E980.9
Pentamethonium (bromide)	972.3	E858.3	E942.3	E950.4	E962.0	E980.4
Pentamidine	961.5	E857	E931.5	E950.4	E962.0	E980.4
Pentanol	980.8	E860.8	—	E950.9	E962.1	E980.9
Pentaquine	961.4	E857	E931.4	E950.4	E962.0	E980.4
Pentazocine	965.8	E850.8	E935.8	E950.0	E962.0	E980.0
Penthienate	971.1	E855.4	E941.1	E950.4	E962.0	E980.4
Pentobarbital, pentobarbitone (sodium)	967.0	E851	E937.0	E950.1	E962.0	E980.1
Pentolinium (tartrate)	972.3	E858.3	E942.3	E950.4	E962.0	E980.4
Pentothal	968.3	E855.1	E938.3	E950.4	E962.0	E980.4
Pentylenetetrazol	970.0	E854.3	E940.0	E950.4	E962.0	E980.4
Pentylsalicylamide	961.8	E857	E931.8	E950.4	E962.0	E980.4
Pepsin	973.4	E858.4	E943.4	E950.4	E962.0	E980.4
Peptavlon	977.8	E858.8	E947.8	E950.4	E962.0	E980.4
Percaine (spinal)	968.7	E855.2	E938.7	E950.4	E962.0	E980.4
topical (surface)	968.5	E855.2	E938.5	E950.4	E962.0	E980.4
Perchloroethylene (vapor)	982.3	E862.4	—	E950.9	E962.1	E980.9
medicinal	961.6	E857	E931.6	E950.4	E962.0	E980.4
Percodan	965.09	E850.2	E935.2	E950.0	E962.0	E980.0
Percogesic	965.09	E850.2	E935.2	E950.0	E962.0	E980.0
Percorten	962.0	E858.0	E932.0	E950.4	E962.0	E980.4
Pergonal	962.4	E858.0	E932.4	E950.4	E962.0	E980.4
Perhexiline	972.4	E858.3	E942.4	E950.4	E962.0	E980.4
Periactin	963.0	E858.1	E933.0	E950.4	E962.0	E980.4
Periclor	967.1	E852.0	E937.1	E950.2	E962.0	E980.2
Pericyazine	969.1	E853.0	E939.1	E950.3	E962.0	E980.3
Peritrate	972.4	E858.3	E942.4	E950.4	E962.0	E980.4
Permanganates NEC	983.9	E864.3	—	E950.7	E962.1	E980.6

	Poisoning	Accident	Therapeutic Use	Suicide Attempt	Assault	Undeter-mined
Permanganates — *continued*						
potassium (topical)	976.0	E858.7	E946.0	E950.4	E962.0	E980.4
Pernocton	967.0	E851	E937.0	E950.1	E962.0	E980.1
Pernoston	967.0	E851	E937.0	E950.1	E962.0	E980.1
Peronin(e)	965.09	E850.2	E935.2	E950.0	E962.0	E980.0
Perphenazine	969.1	E853.0	E939.1	E950.3	E962.0	E980.3
Pertofrane	969.0	E854.0	E939.0	E950.3	E962.0	E980.3
Pertussis						
immune serum (human)	964.6	E858.2	E934.6	E950.4	E962.0	E980.4
vaccine (with diphtheria toxoid) (with tetanus toxoid)	978.6	E858.8	E948.6	E950.4	E962.0	E980.4
Peruvian balsam	976.8	E858.7	E946.8	E950.4	E962.0	E980.4
Pesticides (dust) (fumes) (vapor)	989.4	E863.4	—	E950.6	E962.1	E980.7
arsenic	985.1	E863.4	—	E950.8	E962.1	E980.8
chlorinated	989.2	E863.0	—	E950.6	E962.1	E980.7
cyanide	989.0	E863.4	—	E950.6	E962.1	E980.7
kerosene	981	E863.4	—	E950.6	E962.1	E980.7
mixture (of compounds)	989.4	E863.3	—	E950.6	E962.1	E980.7
naphthalene	983.0	E863.4	—	E950.7	E962.1	E980.6
organochlorine (compounds)	989.2	E863.0	—	E950.6	E962.1	E980.7
petroleum (distillate) (products) NEC	981	E863.4	—	E950.6	E962.1	E980.7
specified ingredient NEC	989.4	E863.4	—	E950.6	E962.1	E980.7
strychnine	989.1	E863.4	—	E950.6	E962.1	E980.7
thallium	985.8	E863.7	—	E950.6	E962.1	E980.7
Pethidine (hydrochloride)	965.09	E850.2	E935.2	E950.0	E962.0	E980.0
Petrichloral	967.1	E852.0	E937.1	E950.2	E962.0	E980.2
Petrol	981	E862.1	—	E950.9	E962.1	E980.9
vapor	987.1	E869.8	—	E952.8	E962.2	E982.8
Petrolatum (jelly) (ointment)	976.3	E858.7	E946.3	E950.4	E962.0	E980.4
hydrophilic	976.3	E858.7	E946.3	E950.4	E962.0	E980.4
liquid	973.2	E858.4	E943.2	E950.4	E962.0	E980.4
topical	976.3	E858.7	E946.3	E950.4	E962.0	E980.4
nonmedicinal	981	E862.1	—	E950.9	E962.1	E980.9
Petroleum (cleaners) (fuels) (products) NEC	981	E862.1	—	E950.9	E962.1	E980.9
benzin(e) — see Ligroin						
ether — see Ligroin						
jelly — see Petrolatum						
naphtha — see Ligroin						
pesticide	981	E863.4	—	E950.6	E962.1	E980.7
solids	981	E862.3	—	E950.9	E962.1	E980.9
solvents	981	E862.0	—	E950.9	E962.1	E980.9
vapor	987.1	E869.8	—	E952.8	E962.2	E982.8
Peyote	969.6	E854.1	E939.6	E950.3	E962.0	E980.3
Phanodorm, phanodorn	967.0	E851	E937.0	E950.1	E962.0	E980.1
Phanquinone, phanquone	961.5	E857	E931.5	E950.4	E962.0	E980.4
Pharmaceutical excipient or adjunct	977.4	E858.8	E947.4	E950.4	E962.0	E980.4
Phenacemide	966.3	E855.0	E936.3	E950.4	E962.0	E980.4
Phenacetin	965.4	E850.4	E935.4	E950.0	E962.0	E980.0
Phenadoxone	965.09	E850.2	E935.2	E950.0	E962.0	E980.0
Phenaglycodol	969.5	E853.8	E939.5	E950.3	E962.0	E980.3
Phenantoin	966.1	E855.0	E936.1	E950.4	E962.0	E980.4
Phenaphthazine reagent	977.8	E858.8	E947.8	E950.4	E962.0	E980.4
Phenazocine	965.09	E850.2	E935.2	E950.0	E962.0	E980.0
Phenazone	965.5	E850.5	E935.5	E950.0	E962.0	E980.0
Phenazopyridine	976.1	E858.7	E946.1	E950.4	E962.0	E980.4
Phenbenicillin	960.0	E856	E930.0	E950.4	E962.0	E980.4
Phenbutrazate	977.0	E858.8	E947.0	E950.4	E962.0	E980.4
Phencyclidine	968.3	E855.1	E938.3	E950.4	E962.0	E980.4
Phendimetrazine	977.0	E858.8	E947.0	E950.4	E962.0	E980.4
Phenelzine	969.0	E854.0	E939.0	E950.3	E962.0	E980.3
Phenergan	967.8	E852.8	E937.8	E950.2	E962.0	E980.2
Phenethicillin (potassium)	960.0	E856	E930.0	E950.4	E962.0	E980.4
Phenetsal	965.1	E850.3	E935.3	E950.0	E962.0	E980.0
Pheneturide	966.3	E855.0	E936.3	E950.4	E962.0	E980.4
Phenformin	962.3	E858.0	E932.3	E950.4	E962.0	E980.4
Phenglutarimide	971.1	E855.4	E941.1	E950.4	E962.0	E980.4
Phenicarbazide	965.8	E850.8	E935.8	E950.0	E962.0	E980.0
Phenindamine (tartrate)	963.0	E858.1	E933.0	E950.4	E962.0	E980.4
Phenindione	964.2	E858.2	E934.2	E950.4	E962.0	E980.4
Pheniprazine	969.0	E854.0	E939.0	E950.3	E962.0	E980.3
Pheniramine (maleate)	963.0	E858.1	E933.0	E950.4	E962.0	E980.4
Phenmetrazine	977.0	E858.8	E947.0	E950.4	E962.0	E980.4
Phenobal	967.0	E851	E937.0	E950.1	E962.0	E980.1
Phenobarbital	967.0	E851	E937.0	E950.1	E962.0	E980.1
Phenobarbitone	967.0	E851	E937.0	E950.1	E962.0	E980.1
Phenoctide	976.0	E858.7	E946.0	E950.4	E962.0	E980.4

☑ Additional Digit Required — Refer to the Tabular List for Digit Selection

▽ Subterms under main terms may continue to next column or page

	Poisoning	External Cause (E-Code) Accident	Therapeutic Use	Suicide Attempt	Assault	Undetermined
Phenol (derivatives) NEC	983.0	E864.0	—	E950.7	E962.1	E980.6
disinfectant	983.0	E864.0	—	E950.7	E962.1	E980.6
pesticide	989.4	E863.4	—	E950.6	E962.1	E980.7
red	977.8	E858.8	E947.8	E950.4	E962.0	E980.4
Phenolphthalein	973.1	E858.4	E943.1	E950.4	E962.0	E980.4
Phenolsulfonphthalein	977.8	E858.8	E947.8	E950.4	E962.0	E980.4
Phenomorphan	965.09	E850.2	E935.2	E950.0	E962.0	E980.0
Phenonyl	967.0	E851	E937.0	E950.1	E962.0	E980.1
Phenoperidine	965.09	E850.2	E935.2	E950.0	E962.0	E980.0
Phenoquin	974.7	E858.5	E944.7	E950.4	E962.0	E980.4
Phenothiazines (tranquilizers) NEC	969.1	E853.0	E939.1	E950.3	E962.0	E980.3
insecticide	989.3	E863.4	—	E950.6	E962.1	E980.7
Phenoxybenzamine	971.3	E855.6	E941.3	E950.4	E962.0	E980.4
Phenoxymethyl penicillin	960.0	E856	E930.0	E950.4	E962.0	E980.4
Phenprocoumon	964.2	E858.2	E934.2	E950.4	E962.0	E980.4
Phensuximide	966.2	E855.0	E936.2	E950.4	E962.0	E980.4
Phentermine	977.0	E858.8	E947.0	E950.4	E962.0	E980.4
Phentolamine	971.3	E855.6	E941.3	E950.4	E962.0	E980.4
Phenyl						
butazone	965.5	E850.5	E935.5	E950.0	E962.0	E980.0
enediamine	983.0	E864.0	—	E950.7	E962.1	E980.6
hydrazine	983.0	E864.0	—	E950.7	E962.1	E980.6
antineoplastic	963.1	E858.1	E933.1	E950.4	E962.0	E980.4
mercuric compounds — see Mercury						
salicylate	976.3	E858.7	E946.3	E950.4	E962.0	E980.4
Phenylephrin	971.2	E855.5	E941.2	E950.4	E962.0	E980.4
Phenylethylbiguanide	962.3	E858.0	E932.3	E950.4	E962.0	E980.4
Phenylpropanolamine	971.2	E855.5	E941.2	E950.4	E962.0	E980.4
Phenylsulfthion	989.3	E863.1	—	E950.6	E962.1	E980.7
Phenyramidol, phenyramidon	965.7	E850.7	E935.7	E950.0	E962.0	E980.0
Phenytoin	966.1	E855.0	E936.1	E950.4	E962.0	E980.4
pHisoHex	976.2	E858.7	E946.2	E950.4	E962.0	E980.4
Pholcodine	965.09	E850.2	E935.2	E950.0	E962.0	E980.0
Phorate	989.3	E863.1	—	E950.6	E962.1	E980.7
Phosdrin	989.3	E863.1	—	E950.6	E962.1	E980.7
Phosgene (gas)	987.8	E869.8	—	E952.8	E962.2	E982.8
Phosphate (tricresyl)	989.89	E866.8	—	E950.9	E962.1	E980.9
organic	989.3	E863.1	—	E950.6	E962.1	E980.7
solvent	982.8	E862.4	—	E950.9	E962.1	E980.9
Phosphine	987.8	E869.8	—	E952.8	E962.2	E982.8
fumigant	987.8	E863.8	—	E950.6	E962.2	E980.7
Phospholine	971.0	E855.3	E941.0	E950.4	E962.0	E980.4
Phosphoric acid	983.1	E864.1	—	E950.7	E962.1	E980.6
Phosphorus (compounds) NEC	983.9	E864.3	—	E950.7	E962.1	E980.6
rodenticide	983.9	E863.7	—	E950.7	E962.1	E980.6
Phthalimidoglutarimide	967.8	E852.8	E937.8	E950.2	E962.0	E980.2
Phthalylsulfathiazole	961.0	E857	E931.0	E950.4	E962.0	E980.4
Phylloquinone	964.3	E858.2	E934.3	E950.4	E962.0	E980.4
Physeptone	965.02	E850.1	E935.1	E950.0	E962.0	E980.0
Physostigma venenosum	988.2	E865.4	—	E950.9	E962.1	E980.9
Physostigmine	971.0	E855.3	E941.0	E950.4	E962.0	E980.4
Phytolacca decandra	988.2	E865.4	—	E950.9	E962.1	E980.9
Phytomenadione	964.3	E858.2	E934.3	E950.4	E962.0	E980.4
Phytonadione	964.3	E858.2	E934.3	E950.4	E962.0	E980.4
Picric (acid)	983.0	E864.0	—	E950.7	E962.1	E980.6
Picrotoxin	970.0	E854.3	E940.0	E950.4	E962.0	E980.4
Pilocarpine	971.0	E855.3	E941.0	E950.4	E962.0	E980.4
Pilocarpus (jaborandi) extract	971.0	E855.3	E941.0	E950.4	E962.0	E980.4
Pimaricin	960.1	E856	E930.1	E950.4	E962.0	E980.4
Piminodine	965.09	E850.2	E935.2	E950.0	E962.0	E980.0
Pine oil, pinesol (disinfectant)	983.9	E861.4	—	E950.7	E962.1	E980.6
Pinkroot	961.6	E857	E931.6	E950.4	E962.0	E980.4
Pipadone	965.09	E850.2	E935.2	E950.0	E962.0	E980.0
Pipamazine	963.0	E858.1	E933.0	E950.4	E962.0	E980.4
Pipazethate	975.4	E858.6	E945.4	E950.4	E962.0	E980.4
Pipenzolate	971.1	E855.4	E941.1	E950.4	E962.0	E980.4
Piperacetazine	969.1	E853.0	E939.1	E950.3	E962.0	E980.3
Piperazine NEC	961.6	E857	E931.6	E950.4	E962.0	E980.4
estrone sulfate	962.2	E858.0	E932.2	E950.4	E962.0	E980.4
Piper cubeba	988.2	E865.4	—	E950.9	E962.1	E980.9
Piperidione	975.4	E858.6	E945.4	E950.4	E962.0	E980.4
Piperidolate	971.1	E855.4	E941.1	E950.4	E962.0	E980.4
Piperocaine	968.9	E855.2	E938.9	E950.4	E962.0	E980.4
infiltration (subcutaneous)	968.5	E855.2	E938.5	E950.4	E962.0	E980.4
Piperocaine — continued						
nerve block (peripheral) (plexus)	968.6	E855.2	E938.6	E950.4	E962.0	E980.4
topical (surface)	968.5	E855.2	E938.5	E950.4	E962.0	E980.4
Pipobroman	963.1	E858.1	E933.1	E950.4	E962.0	E980.4
Pipradrol	970.8	E854.3	E940.8	E950.4	E962.0	E980.4
Piscidia (bark) (erythrina)	965.7	E850.7	E935.7	E950.0	E962.0	E980.0
Pitch	983.0	E864.0	—	E950.7	E962.1	E980.6
Pitkin's solution	968.7	E855.2	E938.7	E950.4	E962.0	E980.4
Pitocin	975.0	E858.6	E945.0	E950.4	E962.0	E980.4
Pitressin (tannate)	962.5	E858.0	E932.5	E950.4	E962.0	E980.4
Pituitary extracts (posterior)	962.5	E858.0	E932.5	E950.4	E962.0	E980.4
anterior	962.4	E858.0	E932.4	E950.4	E962.0	E980.4
Pituitrin	962.5	E858.0	E932.5	E950.4	E962.0	E980.4
Placental extract	962.9	E858.0	E932.9	E950.4	E962.0	E980.4
Placidyl	967.8	E852.8	E937.8	E950.2	E962.0	E980.2
Plague vaccine	978.3	E858.8	E948.3	E950.4	E962.0	E980.4
Plant foods or fertilizers NEC	989.89	E866.5	—	E950.9	E962.1	E980.9
mixed with herbicides	989.4	E863.5	—	E950.6	E962.1	E980.7
Plants, noxious, used as food	988.2	E865.9	—	E950.9	E962.1	E980.9
berries and seeds	988.2	E865.3	—	E950.9	E962.1	E980.9
specified type NEC	988.2	E865.4	—	E950.9	E962.1	E980.9
Plasma (blood)	964.7	E858.2	E934.7	E950.4	E962.0	E980.4
expanders	964.8	E858.2	E934.8	E950.4	E962.0	E980.4
Plasmanate	964.7	E858.2	E934.7	E950.4	E962.0	E980.4
Plegicil	969.1	E853.0	E939.1	E950.3	E962.0	E980.3
Podophyllin	976.4	E858.7	E946.4	E950.4	E962.0	E980.4
Podophyllum resin	976.4	E858.7	E946.4	E950.4	E962.0	E980.4
Poison NEC	989.9	E866.9	—	E950.9	E962.1	E980.9
Poisonous berries	988.2	E865.3	—	E950.9	E962.1	E980.9
Pokeweed (any part)	988.2	E865.4	—	E950.9	E962.1	E980.9
Poldine	971.1	E855.4	E941.1	E950.4	E962.0	E980.4
Poliomyelitis vaccine	979.5	E858.8	E949.5	E950.4	E962.0	E980.4
Poliovirus vaccine	979.5	E858.8	E949.5	E950.4	E962.0	E980.4
Polish (car) (floor) (furniture) (metal) (silver)	989.89	E861.2	—	E950.9	E962.1	E980.9
abrasive	989.89	E861.3	—	E950.9	E962.1	E980.9
porcelain	989.89	E861.3	—	E950.9	E962.1	E980.9
Poloxalkol	973.2	E858.4	E943.2	E950.4	E962.0	E980.4
Polyaminostyrene resins	974.5	E858.5	E944.5	E950.4	E962.0	E980.4
Polychlorinated biphenyl — see PCBs						
Polycycline	960.4	E856	E930.4	E950.4	E962.0	E980.4
Polyester resin hardener	982.8	E862.4	—	E950.9	E962.1	E980.9
fumes	987.8	E869.8	—	E952.8	E962.2	E982.8
Polyestradiol (phosphate)	962.2	E858.0	E932.2	E950.4	E962.0	E980.4
Polyethanolamine alkyl sulfate	976.2	E858.7	E946.2	E950.4	E962.0	E980.4
Polyethylene glycol	976.3	E858.7	E946.3	E950.4	E962.0	E980.4
Polyferose	964.0	E858.2	E934.0	E950.4	E962.0	E980.4
Polymyxin B	960.8	E856	E930.8	E950.4	E962.0	E980.4
ENT agent	976.6	E858.7	E946.6	E950.4	E962.0	E980.4
ophthalmic preparation	976.5	E858.7	E946.5	E950.4	E962.0	E980.4
topical NEC	976.0	E858.7	E946.0	E950.4	E962.0	E980.4
Polynoxylin(e)	976.0	E858.7	E946.0	E950.4	E962.0	E980.4
Polyoxymethyleneurea	976.0	E858.7	E946.0	E950.4	E962.0	E980.4
Polytetrafluoroethylene (inhaled)	987.8	E869.8	—	E952.8	E962.2	E982.8
Polythiazide	974.3	E858.5	E944.3	E950.4	E962.0	E980.4
Polyvinylpyrrolidone	964.8	E858.2	E934.8	E950.4	E962.0	E980.4
Pontocaine (hydrochloride) (infiltration) (topical)	968.5	E855.2	E938.5	E950.4	E962.0	E980.4
nerve block (peripheral) (plexus)	968.6	E855.2	E938.6	E950.4	E962.0	E980.4
spinal	968.7	E855.2	E938.7	E950.4	E962.0	E980.4
Pot	969.6	E854.1	E939.6	E950.3	E962.0	E980.3
Potash (caustic)	983.2	E864.2	—	E950.7	E962.1	E980.6
Potassic saline injection (lactated)	974.5	E858.5	E944.5	E950.4	E962.0	E980.4
Potassium (salts) NEC	974.5	E858.5	E944.5	E950.4	E962.0	E980.4
aminosalicylate	961.8	E857	E931.8	E950.4	E962.0	E980.4
arsenite (solution)	985.1	E866.3	—	E950.8	E962.1	E980.8
bichromate	983.9	E864.3	—	E950.7	E962.1	E980.6
bisulfate	983.9	E864.3	—	E950.7	E962.1	E980.6
bromide (medicinal) NEC	967.3	E852.2	E937.3	E950.2	E962.0	E980.2
carbonate	983.2	E864.2	—	E950.7	E962.1	E980.6
chlorate NEC	983.9	E864.3	—	E950.7	E962.1	E980.6
cyanide — see Cyanide						

☑ Additional Digit Required — Refer to the Tabular List for Digit Selection   ▽ Subterms under main terms may continue to next column or page

	Poisoning	Accident	Therapeutic Use	Suicide Attempt	Assault	Undeter-mined
External Cause (E-Code)						
Potassium (salts) — *continued*						
hydroxide	983.2	E864.2	—	E950.7	E962.1	E980.6
iodide (expectorant) NEC	975.5	E858.6	E945.5	E950.4	E962.0	E980.4
nitrate	989.89	E866.8	—	E950.9	E962.1	E980.9
oxalate	983.9	E864.3	—	E950.7	E962.1	E980.6
perchlorate NEC	977.8	E858.8	E947.8	E950.4	E962.0	E980.4
antithyroid	962.8	E858.0	E932.8	E950.4	E962.0	E980.4
permanganate	976.0	E858.7	E946.0	E950.4	E962.0	E980.4
nonmedicinal	983.9	E864.3	—	E950.7	E962.1	E980.6
Povidone-iodine (anti-infective) NEC	976.0	E858.7	E946.0	E950.4	E962.0	E980.4
Practolol	972.0	E858.3	E942.0	E950.4	E962.0	E980.4
Pralidoxime (chloride)	977.2	E858.8	E947.2	E950.4	E962.0	E980.4
Pramoxine	968.5	E855.2	E938.5	E950.4	E962.0	E980.4
Prazosin	972.6	E858.3	E942.6	E950.4	E962.0	E980.4
Prednisolone	962.0	E858.0	E932.0	E950.4	E962.0	E980.4
ENT agent	976.6	E858.7	E946.6	E950.4	E962.0	E980.4
ophthalmic preparation	976.5	E858.7	E946.5	E950.4	E962.0	E980.4
topical NEC	976.0	E858.7	E946.0	E950.4	E962.0	E980.4
Prednisone	962.0	E858.0	E932.0	E950.4	E962.0	E980.4
Pregnanediol	962.2	E858.0	E932.2	E950.4	E962.0	E980.4
Pregneninolone	962.2	E858.0	E932.2	E950.4	E962.0	E980.4
Preludin	977.0	E858.8	E947.0	E950.4	E962.0	E980.4
Premarin	962.2	E858.0	E932.2	E950.4	E962.0	E980.4
Prenylamine	972.4	E858.3	E942.4	E950.4	E962.0	E980.4
Preparation H	976.8	E858.7	E946.8	E950.4	E962.0	E980.4
Preservatives	989.89	E866.8	—	E950.9	E962.1	E980.9
Pride of China	988.2	E865.3	—	E950.9	E962.1	E980.9
Prilocaine	968.9	E855.2	E938.9	E950.4	E962.0	E980.4
infiltration (subcutaneous)	968.5	E855.2	E938.5	E950.4	E962.0	E980.4
nerve block (peripheral) (plexus)	968.6	E855.2	E938.6	E950.4	E962.0	E980.4
Primaquine	961.4	E857	E931.4	E950.4	E962.0	E980.4
Primidone	966.3	E855.0	E936.3	E950.4	E962.0	E980.4
Primula (veris)	988.2	E865.4	—	E950.9	E962.1	E980.9
Prinadol	965.09	E850.2	E935.2	E950.0	E962.0	E980.0
Priscol, Priscoline	971.3	E855.6	E941.3	E950.4	E962.0	E980.4
Privet	988.2	E865.4	—	E950.9	E962.1	E980.9
Privine	971.2	E855.5	E941.2	E950.4	E962.0	E980.4
Pro-Banthine	971.1	E855.4	E941.1	E950.4	E962.0	E980.4
Probarbital	967.0	E851	E937.0	E950.1	E962.0	E980.1
Probenecid	974.7	E858.5	E944.7	E950.4	E962.0	E980.4
Procainamide (hydrochloride)	972.0	E858.3	E942.0	E950.4	E962.0	E980.4
Procaine (hydrochloride) (infiltration) (topical)	968.5	E855.2	E938.5	E950.4	E962.0	E980.4
nerve block (peripheral) (plexus)	968.6	E855.2	E938.6	E950.4	E962.0	E980.4
penicillin G	960.0	E856	E930.0	E950.4	E962.0	E980.4
spinal	968.7	E855.2	E938.7	E950.4	E962.0	E980.4
Procalmidol	969.5	E853.8	E939.5	E950.3	E962.0	E980.3
Procarbazine	963.1	E858.1	E933.1	E950.4	E962.0	E980.4
Prochlorperazine	969.1	E853.0	E939.1	E950.3	E962.0	E980.3
Procyclidine	966.4	E855.0	E936.4	E950.4	E962.0	E980.4
Producer gas	986	E868.8	—	E952.1	E962.2	E982.1
Profenamine	966.4	E855.0	E936.4	E950.4	E962.0	E980.4
Profenil	975.1	E858.6	E945.1	E950.4	E962.0	E980.4
Progesterones	962.2	E858.0	E932.2	E950.4	E962.0	E980.4
Progestin	962.2	E858.0	E932.2	E950.4	E962.0	E980.4
Progestogens (with estrogens)	962.2	E858.0	E932.2	E950.4	E962.0	E980.4
Progestone	962.2	E858.0	E932.2	E950.4	E962.0	E980.4
Proguanil	961.4	E857	E931.4	E950.4	E962.0	E980.4
Prolactin	962.4	E858.0	E932.4	E950.4	E962.0	E980.4
Proloid	962.7	E858.0	E932.7	E950.4	E962.0	E980.4
Proluton	962.2	E858.0	E932.2	E950.4	E962.0	E980.4
Promacetin	961.8	E857	E931.8	E950.4	E962.0	E980.4
Promazine	969.1	E853.0	E939.1	E950.3	E962.0	E980.3
Promedol	965.09	E850.2	E935.2	E950.0	E962.0	E980.0
Promethazine	967.8	E852.8	E937.8	E950.2	E962.0	E980.2
Promin	961.8	E857	E931.8	E950.4	E962.0	E980.4
Pronestyl (hydrochloride)	972.0	E858.3	E942.0	E950.4	E962.0	E980.4
Pronetalol, pronethalol	972.0	E858.3	E942.0	E950.4	E962.0	E980.4
Prontosil	961.0	E857	E931.0	E950.4	E962.0	E980.4
Propamidine isethionate	961.5	E857	E931.5	E950.4	E962.0	E980.4
Propanal (medicinal)	967.8	E852.8	E937.8	E950.2	E962.0	E980.2
Propane (gas) (distributed in mobile container)	987.0	E868.0	—	E951.1	E962.2	E981.1
distributed through pipes	987.0	E867	—	E951.0	E962.2	E981.0
incomplete combustion of — *see* Carbon monoxide, Propane						

	Poisoning	Accident	Therapeutic Use	Suicide Attempt	Assault	Undeter-mined
External Cause (E-Code)						
Propanidid	968.3	E855.1	E938.3	E950.4	E962.0	E980.4
Propanol	980.3	E860.4	—	E950.9	E962.1	E980.9
Propantheline	971.1	E855.4	E941.1	E950.4	E962.0	E980.4
Proparacaine	968.5	E855.2	E938.5	E950.4	E962.0	E980.4
Propatyl nitrate	972.4	E858.3	E942.4	E950.4	E962.0	E980.4
Propicillin	960.0	E856	E930.0	E950.4	E962.0	E980.4
Propiolactone (vapor)	987.8	E869.8	—	E952.8	E962.2	E982.8
Propiomazine	967.8	E852.8	E937.8	E950.2	E962.0	E980.2
Propionaldehyde (medicinal)	967.8	E852.8	E937.8	E950.2	E962.0	E980.2
Propionate compound	976.0	E858.7	E946.0	E950.4	E962.0	E980.4
Propion gel	976.0	E858.7	E946.0	E950.4	E962.0	E980.4
Propitocaine	968.9	E855.2	E938.9	E950.4	E962.0	E980.4
infiltration (subcutaneous)	968.5	E855.2	E938.5	E950.4	E962.0	E980.4
nerve block (peripheral) (plexus)	968.6	E855.2	E938.6	E950.4	E962.0	E980.4
Propoxur	989.3	E863.2	—	E950.6	E962.1	E980.7
Propoxycaine	968.9	E855.2	E938.9	E950.4	E962.0	E980.4
infiltration (subcutaneous)	968.5	E855.2	E938.5	E950.4	E962.0	E980.4
nerve block (peripheral) (plexus)	968.6	E855.2	E938.6	E950.4	E962.0	E980.4
topical (surface)	968.5	E855.2	E938.5	E950.4	E962.0	E980.4
Propoxyphene (hydrochloride)	965.8	E850.8	E935.8	E950.0	E962.0	E980.0
Propranolol	972.0	E858.3	E942.0	E950.4	E962.0	E980.4
Propyl						
alcohol	980.3	E860.4	—	E950.9	E962.1	E980.9
carbinol	980.3	E860.4	—	E950.9	E962.1	E980.9
hexadrine	971.2	E855.5	E941.2	E950.4	E962.0	E980.4
iodone	977.8	E858.8	E947.8	E950.4	E962.0	E980.4
thiouracil	962.8	E858.0	E932.8	E950.4	E962.0	E980.4
Propylene	987.1	E869.8	—	E952.8	E962.2	E982.8
Propylparaben (ophthalmic)	976.5	E858.7	E946.5	E950.4	E962.0	E980.4
Proscillaridin	972.1	E858.3	E942.1	E950.4	E962.0	E980.4
Prostaglandins	975.0	E858.6	E945.0	E950.4	E962.0	E980.4
Prostigmin	971.0	E855.3	E941.0	E950.4	E962.0	E980.4
Protamine (sulfate)	964.5	E858.2	E934.5	E950.4	E962.0	E980.4
zinc insulin	962.3	E858.0	E932.3	E950.4	E962.0	E980.4
Protectants (topical)	976.3	E858.7	E946.3	E950.4	E962.0	E980.4
Protein hydrolysate	974.5	E858.5	E944.5	E950.4	E962.0	E980.4
Prothiaden — *see* Dothiepin hydrochloride						
Prothionamide	961.8	E857	E931.8	E950.4	E962.0	E980.4
Prothipendyl	969.5	E853.8	E939.5	E950.3	E962.0	E980.3
Protokylol	971.2	E855.5	E941.2	E950.4	E962.0	E980.4
Protopam	977.2	E858.8	E947.2	E950.4	E962.0	E980.4
Protoveratrine(s) (A) (B)	972.6	E858.3	E942.6	E950.4	E962.0	E980.4
Protriptyline	969.0	E854.0	E939.0	E950.3	E962.0	E980.3
Provera	962.2	E858.0	E932.2	E950.4	E962.0	E980.4
Provitamin A	963.5	E858.1	E933.5	E950.4	E962.0	E980.4
Proxymetacaine	968.5	E855.2	E938.5	E950.4	E962.0	E980.4
Proxyphylline	975.1	E858.6	E945.1	E950.4	E962.0	E980.4
Prozac — *see* Fluoxetine hydrochloride						
Prunus						
laurocerasus	988.2	E865.4	—	E950.9	E962.1	E980.9
virginiana	988.2	E865.4	—	E950.9	E962.1	E980.9
Prussic acid	989.0	E866.8	—	E950.9	E962.1	E980.9
vapor	987.7	E869.8	—	E952.8	E962.2	E982.8
Pseudoephedrine	971.2	E855.5	E941.2	E950.4	E962.0	E980.4
Psilocin	969.6	E854.1	E939.6	E950.3	E962.0	E980.3
Psilocybin	969.6	E854.1	E939.6	E950.3	E962.0	E980.3
PSP	977.8	E858.8	E947.8	E950.4	E962.0	E980.4
Psychedelic agents	969.6	E854.1	E939.6	E950.3	E962.0	E980.3
Psychodysleptics	969.6	E854.1	E939.6	E950.3	E962.0	E980.3
Psychostimulants	969.7	E854.2	E939.7	E950.3	E962.0	E980.3
Psychotherapeutic agents	969.9	E855.9	E939.9	E950.3	E962.0	E980.3
antidepressants	969.0	E854.0	E939.0	E950.3	E962.0	E980.3
specified NEC	969.8	E855.8	E939.8	E950.3	E962.0	E980.3
tranquilizers NEC	969.5	E853.9	E939.5	E950.3	E962.0	E980.3
Psychotomimetic agents	969.6	E854.1	E939.6	E950.3	E962.0	E980.3
Psychotropic agents	969.9	E854.8	E939.9	E950.3	E962.0	E980.3
specified NEC	969.8	E854.8	E939.8	E950.3	E962.0	E980.3
Psyllium	973.3	E858.4	E943.3	E950.4	E962.0	E980.4
Pteroylglutamic acid	964.1	E858.2	E934.1	E950.4	E962.0	E980.4
Pteroyltriglutamate	963.1	E858.1	E933.1	E950.4	E962.0	E980.4
PTFE	987.8	E869.8	—	E952.8	E962.2	E982.8
Pulsatilla	988.2	E865.4	—	E950.9	E962.1	E980.9
Purex (bleach)	983.9	E864.3	—	E950.7	E962.1	E980.6
Purine diuretics	974.1	E858.5	E944.1	E950.4	E962.0	E980.4

☑ Additional Digit Required — Refer to the Tabular List for Digit Selection

2007 ICD-9-CM

▶◀ Revised Text

● New Line

▲ Revised Code

Ⓦ Subterms under main terms may continue to next column or page

Volume 2 — 329

	Poisoning	External Cause (E-Code)				
		Accident	Therapeutic Use	Suicide Attempt	Assault	Undetermined
Purinethol	963.1	E858.1	E933.1	E950.4	E962.0	E980.4
PVP	964.8	E858.2	E934.8	E950.4	E962.0	E980.4
Pyrabital	965.7	E850.7	E935.7	E950.0	E962.0	E980.0
Pyramidon	965.5	E850.5	E935.5	E950.0	E962.0	E980.0
Pyrantel (pamoate)	961.6	E857	E931.6	E950.4	E962.0	E980.4
Pyrathiazine	963.0	E858.1	E933.0	E950.4	E962.0	E980.4
Pyrazinamide	961.8	E857	E931.8	E950.4	E962.0	E980.4
Pyrazinoic acid (amide)	961.8	E857	E931.8	E950.4	E962.0	E980.4
Pyrazole (derivatives)	965.5	E850.5	E935.5	E950.0	E962.0	E980.0
Pyrazolone (analgesics)	965.5	E850.5	E935.5	E950.0	E962.0	E980.0
Pyrethrins, pyrethrum	989.4	E863.4	—	E950.6	E962.1	E980.7
Pyribenzamine	963.0	E858.1	E933.0	E950.4	E962.0	E980.4
Pyridine (liquid) (vapor)	982.0	E862.4	—	E950.9	E962.1	E980.9
aldoxime chloride	977.2	E858.8	E947.2	E950.4	E962.0	E980.4
Pyridium	976.1	E858.7	E946.1	E950.4	E962.0	E980.4
Pyridostigmine	971.0	E855.3	E941.0	E950.4	E962.0	E980.4
Pyridoxine	963.5	E858.1	E933.5	E950.4	E962.0	E980.4
Pyrilamine	963.0	E858.1	E933.0	E950.4	E962.0	E980.4
Pyrimethamine	961.4	E857	E931.4	E950.4	E962.0	E980.4
Pyrogallic acid	983.0	E864.0	—	E950.7	E962.1	E980.6
Pyroxylin	976.3	E858.7	E946.3	E950.4	E962.0	E980.4
Pyrrobutamine	963.0	E858.1	E933.0	E950.4	E962.0	E980.4
Pyrrocitine	968.5	E855.2	E938.5	E950.4	E962.0	E980.4
Pyrvinium (pamoate)	961.6	E857	E931.6	E950.4	E962.0	E980.4
PZI	962.3	E858.0	E932.3	E950.4	E962.0	E980.4
Quaalude	967.4	E852.3	E937.4	E950.2	E962.0	E980.2
Quaternary ammonium derivatives	971.1	E855.4	E941.1	E950.4	E962.0	E980.4
Quicklime	983.2	E864.2	—	E950.7	E962.1	E980.6
Quinacrine	961.3	E857	E931.3	E950.4	E962.0	E980.4
Quinaglute	972.0	E858.3	E942.0	E950.4	E962.0	E980.4
Quinalbarbitone	967.0	E851	E937.0	E950.1	E962.0	E980.1
Quinestradiol	962.2	E858.0	E932.2	E950.4	E962.0	E980.4
Quinethazone	974.3	E858.5	E944.3	E950.4	E962.0	E980.4
Quinidine (gluconate) (polygalacturonate) (salts) (sulfate)	972.0	E858.3	E942.0	E950.4	E962.0	E980.4
Quinine	961.4	E857	E931.4	E950.4	E962.0	E980.4
Quiniobine	961.3	E857	E931.3	E950.4	E962.0	E980.4
Quinolines	961.3	E857	E931.3	E950.4	E962.0	E980.4
Quotane	968.5	E855.2	E938.5	E950.4	E962.0	E980.4
Rabies						
immune globulin (human)	964.6	E858.2	E934.6	E950.4	E962.0	E980.4
vaccine	979.1	E858.8	E949.1	E950.4	E962.0	E980.4
Racemoramide	965.09	E850.2	E935.2	E950.0	E962.0	E980.0
Racemorphan	965.09	E850.2	E935.2	E950.0	E962.0	E980.0
Radiator alcohol	980.1	E860.2	—	E950.9	E962.1	E980.9
Radio-opaque (drugs) (materials)	977.8	E858.8	E947.8	E950.4	E962.0	E980.4
Ranunculus	988.2	E865.4	—	E950.9	E962.1	E980.9
Rat poison	989.4	E863.7	—	E950.6	E962.1	E980.7
Rattlesnake (venom)	989.5	E905.0	—	E950.9	E962.1	E980.9
Raudixin	972.6	E858.3	E942.6	E950.4	E962.0	E980.4
Rautensin	972.6	E858.3	E942.6	E950.4	E962.0	E980.4
Rautina	972.6	E858.3	E942.6	E950.4	E962.0	E980.4
Rautotal	972.6	E858.3	E942.6	E950.4	E962.0	E980.4
Rauwiloid	972.6	E858.3	E942.6	E950.4	E962.0	E980.4
Rauwoldin	972.6	E858.3	E942.6	E950.4	E962.0	E980.4
Rauwolfia (alkaloids)	972.6	E858.3	E942.6	E950.4	E962.0	E980.4
Realgar	985.1	E866.3	—	E950.8	E962.1	E980.8
Red cells, packed	964.7	E858.2	E934.7	E950.4	E962.0	E980.4
Reducing agents, industrial NEC	983.9	E864.3	—	E950.7	E962.1	E980.6
Refrigerant gas (freon)	987.4	E869.2	—	E952.8	E962.2	E982.8
central nervous system	968.0	E855.1	E938.0	E950.4	E962.0	E980.4
not freon	987.9	E869.9	—	E952.9	E962.2	E982.9
Regroton	974.4	E858.5	E944.4	E950.4	E962.0	E980.4
Rela	968.0	E855.1	E938.0	E950.4	E962.0	E980.4
Relaxants, skeletal muscle (autonomic)	975.2	E858.6	E945.2	E950.4	E962.0	E980.4
Renese	974.3	E858.5	E944.3	E950.4	E962.0	E980.4
Renografin	977.8	E858.8	E947.8	E950.4	E962.0	E980.4
Replacement solutions	974.5	E858.5	E944.5	E950.4	E962.0	E980.4
Rescinnamine	972.6	E858.3	E942.6	E950.4	E962.0	E980.4
Reserpine	972.6	E858.3	E942.6	E950.4	E962.0	E980.4
Resorcin, resorcinol	976.4	E858.7	E946.4	E950.4	E962.0	E980.4
Respaire	975.5	E858.6	E945.5	E950.4	E962.0	E980.4
Respiratory agents NEC	975.8	E858.6	E945.8	E950.4	E962.0	E980.4
Retinoic acid	976.8	E858.7	E946.8	E950.4	E962.0	E980.4
Retinol	963.5	E858.1	E933.5	E950.4	E962.0	E980.4

	Poisoning	External Cause (E-Code)				
		Accident	Therapeutic Use	Suicide Attempt	Assault	Undetermined
Rh (D) immune globulin (human)	964.6	E858.2	E934.6	E950.4	E962.0	E980.4
Rhodine	965.1	E850.3	E935.3	E950.0	E962.0	E980.0
RhoGAM	964.6	E858.2	E934.6	E950.4	E962.0	E980.4
Riboflavin	963.5	E858.1	E933.5	E950.4	E962.0	E980.4
Ricin	989.89	E866.8	—	E950.9	E962.1	E980.9
Ricinus communis	988.2	E865.3	—	E950.9	E962.1	E980.9
Rickettsial vaccine NEC	979.6	E858.8	E949.6	E950.4	E962.0	E980.4
with viral and bacterial vaccine	979.7	E858.8	E949.7	E950.4	E962.0	E980.4
Rifampin	960.6	E856	E930.6	E950.4	E962.0	E980.4
Rimifon	961.8	E857	E931.8	E950.4	E962.0	E980.4
Ringer's injection (lactated)	974.5	E858.5	E944.5	E950.4	E962.0	E980.4
Ristocetin	960.8	E856	E930.8	E950.4	E962.0	E980.4
Ritalin	969.7	E854.2	E939.7	E950.3	E962.0	E980.3
Roach killers — see Pesticides						
Rocky Mountain spotted fever vaccine	979.6	E858.8	E949.6	E950.4	E962.0	E980.4
Rodenticides	989.4	E863.7	—	E950.6	E962.1	E980.7
Rohypnol	969.4	E853.2	E939.4	E950.3	E962.0	E980.3
Rolaids	973.0	E858.4	E943.0	E950.4	E962.0	E980.4
Rolitetracycline	960.4	E856	E930.4	E950.4	E962.0	E980.4
Romilar	975.4	E858.6	E945.4	E950.4	E962.0	E980.4
Rose water ointment	976.3	E858.7	E946.3	E950.4	E962.0	E980.4
Rosuvastatin calcium	972.1	E858.3	E942.2	E950.4	E962.0	E980.4
Rotenone	989.4	E863.7	—	E950.6	E962.1	E980.7
Rotoxamine	963.0	E858.1	E933.0	E950.4	E962.0	E980.4
Rough-on-rats	989.4	E863.7	—	E950.6	E962.1	E980.7
RU486	962.9	E858.0	E932.9	E950.4	E962.0	E980.4
Rubbing alcohol	980.2	E860.3	—	E950.9	E962.1	E980.9
Rubella virus vaccine	979.4	E858.8	E949.4	E950.4	E962.0	E980.4
Rubelogen	979.4	E858.8	E949.4	E950.4	E962.0	E980.4
Rubeovax	979.4	E858.8	E949.4	E950.4	E962.0	E980.4
Rubidomycin	960.7	E856	E930.7	E950.4	E962.0	E980.4
Rue	988.2	E865.4	—	E950.9	E962.1	E980.9
Ruta	988.2	E865.4	—	E950.9	E962.1	E980.9
Sabadilla (medicinal)	976.0	E858.7	E946.0	E950.4	E962.0	E980.4
pesticide	989.4	E863.4	—	E950.6	E962.1	E980.7
Sabin oral vaccine	979.5	E858.8	E949.5	E950.4	E962.0	E980.4
Saccharated iron oxide	964.0	E858.2	E934.0	E950.4	E962.0	E980.4
Saccharin	974.5	E858.5	E944.5	E950.4	E962.0	E980.4
Safflower oil	972.2	E858.3	E942.2	E950.4	E962.0	E980.4
Salbutamol sulfate	975.7	E858.6	E945.7	E950.4	E962.0	E980.4
Salicylamide	965.1	E850.3	E935.3	E950.0	E962.0	E980.0
Salicylate(s)	965.1	E850.3	E935.3	E950.0	E962.0	E980.0
methyl	976.3	E858.7	E946.3	E950.4	E962.0	E980.4
theobromine calcium	974.1	E858.5	E944.1	E950.4	E962.0	E980.4
Salicylazosulfapyridine	961.0	E857	E931.0	E950.4	E962.0	E980.4
Salicylhydroxamic acid	976.0	E858.7	E946.0	E950.4	E962.0	E980.4
Salicylic acid (keratolytic) NEC	976.4	E858.7	E946.4	E950.4	E962.0	E980.4
congeners	965.1	E850.3	E935.3	E950.0	E962.0	E980.0
salts	965.1	E850.3	E935.3	E950.0	E962.0	E980.0
Saliniazid	961.8	E857	E931.8	E950.4	E962.0	E980.4
Salol	976.3	E858.7	E946.3	E950.4	E962.0	E980.4
Salt (substitute) NEC	974.5	E858.5	E944.5	E950.4	E962.0	E980.4
Saluretics	974.3	E858.5	E944.3	E950.4	E962.0	E980.4
Saluron	974.3	E858.5	E944.3	E950.4	E962.0	E980.4
Salvarsan 606 (neosilver) (silver)	961.1	E857	E931.1	E950.4	E962.0	E980.4
Sambucus canadensis	988.2	E865.4	—	E950.9	E962.1	E980.9
berry	988.2	E865.3	—	E950.9	E962.1	E980.9
Sandril	972.6	E858.3	E942.6	E950.4	E962.0	E980.4
Sanguinaria canadensis	988.2	E865.4	—	E950.9	E962.1	E980.9
Saniflush (cleaner)	983.9	E861.3	—	E950.7	E962.1	E980.6
Santonin	961.6	E857	E931.6	E950.4	E962.0	E980.4
Santyl	976.8	E858.7	E946.8	E950.4	E962.0	E980.4
Sarkomycin	960.7	E856	E930.7	E950.4	E962.0	E980.4
Saroten	969.0	E854.0	E939.0	E950.3	E962.0	E980.3
Saturnine — see Lead						
Savin (oil)	976.4	E858.7	E946.4	E950.4	E962.0	E980.4
Scammony	973.1	E858.4	E943.1	E950.4	E962.0	E980.4
Scarlet red	976.8	E858.7	E946.8	E950.4	E962.0	E980.4
Scheele's green	985.1	E866.3	—	E950.8	E962.1	E980.8
insecticide	985.1	E863.4	—	E950.8	E962.1	E980.8
Schradan	989.3	E863.1	—	E950.6	E962.1	E980.7
Schweinfurt(h) green	985.1	E866.3	—	E950.8	E962.1	E980.8
insecticide	985.1	E863.4	—	E950.8	E962.1	E980.8
Scilla — see Squill						
Sclerosing agents	972.7	E858.3	E942.7	E950.4	E962.0	E980.4

☑ Additional Digit Required — Refer to the Tabular List for Digit Selection ▽ Subterms under main terms may continue to next column or page

		External Cause (E-Code)			
	Poisoning	Accident	Therapeutic Use	Suicide Attempt	Assault	Undetermined

Substance	Poisoning	Accident	Therapeutic Use	Suicide Attempt	Assault	Undetermined
Scopolamine	971.1	E855.4	E941.1	E950.4	E962.0	E980.4
Scouring powder	989.89	E861.3	—	E950.9	E962.1	E980.9
Sea						
anemone (sting)	989.5	E905.6	—	E950.9	E962.1	E980.9
cucumber (sting)	989.5	E905.6	—	E950.9	E962.1	E980.9
snake (bite) (venom)	989.5	E905.0	—	E950.9	E962.1	E980.9
urchin spine (puncture)	989.5	E905.6	—	E950.9	E962.1	E980.9
Secbutabarbital	967.0	E851	E937.0	E950.1	E962.0	E980.1
Secbutabarbitone	967.0	E851	E937.0	E950.1	E962.0	E980.1
Secobarbital	967.0	E851	E937.0	E950.1	E962.0	E980.1
Seconal	967.0	E851	E937.0	E950.1	E962.0	E980.1
Secretin	977.8	E858.8	E947.8	E950.4	E962.0	E980.4
Sedatives, nonbarbiturate	967.9	E852.9	E937.9	E950.2	E962.0	E980.2
specified NEC	967.8	E852.8	E937.8	E950.2	E962.0	E980.2
Sedormid	967.8	E852.8	E937.8	E950.2	E962.0	E980.2
Seed (plant)	988.2	E865.3	—	E950.9	E962.1	E980.9
disinfectant or dressing	989.89	E866.5	—	E950.9	E962.1	E980.9
Selenium (fumes) NEC	985.8	E866.4	—	E950.9	E962.1	E980.9
disulfide or sulfide	976.4	E858.7	E946.4	E950.4	E962.0	E980.4
Selsun	976.4	E858.7	E946.4	E950.4	E962.0	E980.4
Senna	973.1	E858.4	E943.1	E950.4	E962.0	E980.4
Septisol	976.2	E858.7	E946.2	E950.4	E962.0	E980.4
Serax	969.4	E853.2	E939.4	E950.3	E962.0	E980.3
Serenesil	967.8	E852.8	E937.8	E950.2	E962.0	E980.2
Serenium (hydrochloride)	961.9	E857	E931.9	E950.4	E962.0	E980.4
Serepax — see Oxazepam						
Sernyl	968.3	E855.1	E938.3	E950.4	E962.0	E980.4
Serotonin	977.8	E858.8	E947.8	E950.4	E962.0	E980.4
Serpasil	972.6	E858.3	E942.6	E950.4	E962.0	E980.4
Sewer gas	987.8	E869.8	—	E952.8	E962.2	E982.8
Shampoo	989.6	E861.0	—	E950.9	E962.1	E980.9
Shellfish, nonbacterial or						
noxious	988.0	E865.1	—	E950.9	E962.1	E980.9
Silicones NEC	989.83	E866.8	E947.8	E950.9	E962.1	E980.9
Silvadene	976.0	E858.7	E946.0	E950.4	E962.0	E980.4
Silver (compound) (medicinal)						
NEC	976.0	E858.7	E946.0	E950.4	E962.0	E980.4
anti-infectives	976.0	E858.7	E946.0	E950.4	E962.0	E980.4
arsphenamine	961.1	E857	E931.1	E950.4	E962.0	E980.4
nitrate	976.0	E858.7	E946.0	E950.4	E962.0	E980.4
ophthalmic preparation	976.5	E858.7	E946.5	E950.4	E962.0	E980.4
toughened (keratolytic)	976.4	E858.7	E946.4	E950.4	E962.0	E980.4
nonmedicinal (dust)	985.8	E866.4	—	E950.9	E962.1	E980.9
protein (mild) (strong)	976.0	E858.7	E946.0	E950.4	E962.0	E980.4
salvarsan	961.1	E857	E931.1	E950.4	E962.0	E980.4
Simethicone	973.8	E858.4	E943.8	E950.4	E962.0	E980.4
Sinequan	969.0	E854.0	E939.0	E950.3	E962.0	E980.3
Singoserp	972.6	E858.3	E942.6	E950.4	E962.0	E980.4
Sintrom	964.2	E858.2	E934.2	E950.4	E962.0	E980.4
Sitosterols	972.2	E858.3	E942.2	E950.4	E962.0	E980.4
Skeletal muscle relaxants	975.2	E858.6	E945.2	E950.4	E962.0	E980.4
Skin						
agents (external)	976.9	E858.7	E946.9	E950.4	E962.0	E980.4
specified NEC	976.8	E858.7	E946.8	E950.4	E962.0	E980.4
test antigen	977.8	E858.8	E947.8	E950.4	E962.0	E980.4
Sleep-eze	963.0	E858.1	E933.0	E950.4	E962.0	E980.4
Sleeping draught (drug) (pill)						
(tablet)	967.9	E852.9	E937.9	E950.2	E962.0	E980.2
Smallpox vaccine	979.0	E858.8	E949.0	E950.4	E962.0	E980.4
Smelter fumes NEC	985.9	E866.4	—	E950.9	E962.1	E980.9
Smog	987.3	E869.1	—	E952.8	E962.2	E982.8
Smoke NEC	987.9	E869.9	—	E952.9	E962.2	E982.9
Smooth muscle relaxant	975.1	E858.6	E945.1	E950.4	E962.0	E980.4
Snail killer	989.4	E863.4	—	E950.6	E962.1	E980.7
Snake (bite) (venom)	989.5	E905.0	—	E950.9	E962.1	E980.9
Snuff	989.89	E866.8	—	E950.9	E962.1	E980.9
Soap (powder) (product)	989.6	E861.1	—	E950.9	E962.1	E980.9
bicarb	963.3	E858.1	E933.3	E950.4	E962.0	E980.4
chlorinated — see Sodium,						
hypochlorite						
medicinal, soft	976.2	E858.7	E946.2	E950.4	E962.0	E980.4
Soda (caustic)	983.2	E864.2	—	E950.7	E962.1	E980.6
Sodium						
acetosulfone	961.8	E857	E931.8	E950.4	E962.0	E980.4
acetrizoate	977.8	E858.8	E947.8	E950.4	E962.0	E980.4
amytal	967.0	E851	E937.0	E950.1	E962.0	E980.1
arsenate — see Arsenic						
bicarbonate	963.3	E858.1	E933.3	E950.4	E962.0	E980.4
bichromate	983.9	E864.3	—	E950.7	E962.1	E980.6
biphosphate	963.2	E858.1	E933.2	E950.4	E962.0	E980.4
bisulfate	983.9	E864.3	—	E950.7	E962.1	E980.6

Substance	Poisoning	Accident	Therapeutic Use	Suicide Attempt	Assault	Undetermined
Sodium — continued						
borate (cleanser)	989.6	E861.3	—	E950.9	E962.1	E980.9
bromide NEC	967.3	E852.2	E937.3	E950.2	E962.0	E980.2
cacodylate (nonmedicinal)						
NEC	978.8	E858.8	E948.8	E950.4	E962.0	E980.4
anti-infective	961.1	E857	E931.1	E950.4	E962.0	E980.4
herbicide	989.4	E863.5	—	E950.6	E962.1	E980.7
calcium edetate	963.8	E858.1	E933.8	E950.4	E962.0	E980.4
carbonate NEC	983.2	E864.2	—	E950.7	E962.1	E980.6
chlorate NEC	983.9	E864.3	—	E950.7	E962.1	E980.6
herbicide	983.9	E863.5	—	E950.7	E962.1	E980.6
chloride NEC	974.5	E858.5	E944.5	E950.4	E962.0	E980.4
chromate	983.9	E864.3	—	E950.7	E962.1	E980.6
citrate	963.3	E858.1	E933.3	E950.4	E962.0	E980.4
cyanide — see Cyanide(s)						
cyclamate	974.5	E858.5	E944.5	E950.4	E962.0	E980.4
diatrizoate	977.8	E858.8	E947.8	E950.4	E962.0	E980.4
dibunate	975.4	E858.6	E945.4	E950.4	E962.0	E980.4
dioctyl sulfosuccinate	973.2	E858.4	E943.2	E950.4	E962.0	E980.4
edetate	963.8	E858.1	E933.8	E950.4	E962.0	E980.4
ethacrynate	974.4	E858.5	E944.4	E950.4	E962.0	E980.4
fluoracetate (dust)						
(rodenticide)	989.4	E863.7	—	E950.6	E962.1	E980.7
fluoride — see Fluoride(s)						
free salt	974.5	E858.5	E944.5	E950.4	E962.0	E980.4
glucosulfone	961.8	E857	E931.8	E950.4	E962.0	E980.4
hydroxide	983.2	E864.2	—	E950.7	E962.1	E980.6
hypochlorite (bleach) NEC	983.9	E864.3	—	E950.7	E962.1	E980.6
disinfectant	983.9	E861.4	—	E950.7	E962.1	E980.6
medicinal (anti-infective)						
(external)	976.0	E858.7	E946.0	E950.4	E962.0	E980.4
vapor	987.8	E869.8	—	E952.8	E962.2	E982.8
hyposulfite	976.0	E858.7	E946.0	E950.4	E962.0	E980.4
indigotindisulfonate	977.8	E858.8	E947.8	E950.4	E962.0	E980.4
iodide	977.8	E858.8	E947.8	E950.4	E962.0	E980.4
iothalamate	977.8	E858.8	E947.8	E950.4	E962.0	E980.4
iron edetate	964.0	E858.2	E934.0	E950.4	E962.0	E980.4
lactate	963.3	E858.1	E933.3	E950.4	E962.0	E980.4
lauryl sulfate	976.2	E858.7	E946.2	E950.4	E962.0	E980.4
L-triiodothyronine	962.7	E858.0	E932.7	E950.4	E962.0	E980.4
metrizoate	977.8	E858.8	E947.8	E950.4	E962.0	E980.4
monofluoracetate (dust)						
(rodenticide)	989.4	E863.7	—	E950.6	E962.1	E980.7
morrhuate	972.7	E858.3	E942.7	E950.4	E962.0	E980.4
nafcillin	960.0	E856	E930.0	E950.4	E962.0	E980.4
nitrate (oxidizing agent)	983.9	E864.3	—	E950.7	E962.1	E980.6
nitrite (medicinal)	972.4	E858.3	E942.4	E950.4	E962.0	E980.4
nitroferricyanide	972.6	E858.3	E942.6	E950.4	E962.0	E980.4
nitroprusside	972.6	E858.3	E942.6	E950.4	E962.0	E980.4
para-aminohippurate	977.8	E858.8	E947.8	E950.4	E962.0	E980.4
perborate (nonmedicinal)						
NEC	989.89	E866.8	—	E950.9	E962.1	E980.9
medicinal	976.6	E858.7	E946.6	E950.4	E962.0	E980.4
soap	989.6	E861.1	—	E950.9	E962.1	E980.9
percarbonate — see Sodium,						
perborate						
phosphate	973.3	E858.4	E943.3	E950.4	E962.0	E980.4
polystyrene sulfonate	974.5	E858.5	E944.5	E950.4	E962.0	E980.4
propionate	976.0	E858.7	E946.0	E950.4	E962.0	E980.4
psylliate	972.7	E858.3	E942.7	E950.4	E962.0	E980.4
removing resins	974.5	E858.5	E944.5	E950.4	E962.0	E980.4
salicylate	965.1	E850.3	E935.3	E950.0	E962.0	E980.0
sulfate	973.3	E858.4	E943.3	E950.4	E962.0	E980.4
sulfoxone	961.8	E857	E931.8	E950.4	E962.0	E980.4
tetradecyl sulfate	972.7	E858.3	E942.7	E950.4	E962.0	E980.4
thiopental	968.3	E855.1	E938.3	E950.4	E962.0	E980.4
thiosalicylate	965.1	E850.3	E935.3	E950.0	E962.0	E980.0
thiosulfate	976.0	E858.7	E946.0	E950.4	E962.0	E980.4
tolbutamide	977.8	E858.8	E947.8	E950.4	E962.0	E980.4
tyropanoate	977.8	E858.8	E947.8	E950.4	E962.0	E980.4
valproate	966.3	E855.0	E936.3	E950.4	E962.0	E980.4
Solanine	977.8	E858.8	E947.8	E950.4	E962.0	E980.4
Solanum dulcamara	988.2	E865.4	—	E950.9	E962.1	E980.9
Solapsone	961.8	E857	E931.8	E950.4	E962.0	E980.4
Solasulfone	961.8	E857	E931.8	E950.4	E962.0	E980.4
Soldering fluid	983.1	E864.1	—	E950.7	E962.1	E980.6
Solid substance	989.9	E866.9	—	E950.9	E962.1	E980.9
specified NEC	989.9	E866.8	—	E950.9	E962.1	E980.9
Solvents, industrial	982.8	E862.9	—	E950.9	E962.1	E980.9
naphtha	981	E862.0	—	E950.9	E962.1	E980.9
petroleum	981	E862.0	—	E950.9	E962.1	E980.9
specified NEC	982.8	E862.4	—	E950.9	E962.1	E980.9

☑ Additional Digit Required — Refer to the Tabular List for Digit Selection   ▽ Subterms under main terms may continue to next column or page

2007 ICD-9-CM   ►◄ Revised Text   ● New Line   ▲ Revised Code   Volume 2 — 331

Index

Soma — Sulfur, sulfureted, sulfuric, sulfurous, sulfuryl (compounds) NEC

	Poisoning	Accident	Therapeutic Use	Suicide Attempt	Assault	Undetermined
Soma	968.0	E855.1	E938.0	E950.4	E962.0	E980.4
Somatotropin	962.4	E858.0	E932.4	E950.4	E962.0	E980.4
Sominex	963.0	E858.1	E933.0	E950.4	E962.0	E980.4
Somnos	967.1	E852.0	E937.1	E950.2	E962.0	E980.2
Somonal	967.0	E851	E937.0	E950.1	E962.0	E980.1
Soneryl	967.0	E851	E937.0	E950.1	E962.0	E980.1
Soothing syrup	977.9	E858.9	E947.9	E950.5	E962.0	E980.5
Sopor	967.4	E852.3	E937.4	E950.2	E962.0	E980.2
Soporific drug	967.9	E852.9	E937.9	E950.2	E962.0	E980.2
specified type NEC	967.8	E852.8	E937.8	E950.2	E962.0	E980.2
Sorbitol NEC	977.4	E858.8	E947.4	E950.4	E962.0	E980.4
Sotradecol	972.7	E858.3	E942.7	E950.4	E962.0	E980.4
Spacoline	975.1	E858.6	E945.1	E950.4	E962.0	E980.4
Spanish fly	976.8	E858.7	E946.8	E950.4	E962.0	E980.4
Sparine	969.1	E853.0	E939.1	E950.3	E962.0	E980.3
Sparteine	975.0	E858.6	E945.0	E950.4	E962.0	E980.4
Spasmolytics	975.1	E858.6	E945.1	E950.4	E962.0	E980.4
anticholinergics	971.1	E855.4	E941.1	E950.4	E962.0	E980.4
Spectinomycin	960.8	E856	E930.8	E950.4	E962.0	E980.4
Speed	969.7	E854.2	E939.7	E950.3	E962.0	E980.3
Spermicides	976.8	E858.7	E946.8	E950.4	E962.0	E980.4
Spider (bite) (venom)	989.5	E905.1	—	E950.9	E962.1	E980.9
antivenin	979.9	E858.8	E949.9	E950.4	E962.0	E980.4
Spigelia (root)	961.6	E857	E931.6	E950.4	E962.0	E980.4
Spiperone	969.2	E853.1	E939.2	E950.3	E962.0	E980.3
Spiramycin	960.3	E856	E930.3	E950.4	E962.0	E980.4
Spirilene	969.5	E853.8	E939.5	E950.3	E962.0	E980.3
Spirit(s) (neutral) NEC	980.0	E860.1	—	E950.9	E962.1	E980.9
beverage	980.0	E860.0	—	E950.9	E962.1	E980.9
industrial	980.9	E860.9	—	E950.9	E962.1	E980.9
mineral	981	E862.0	—	E950.9	E962.1	E980.9
of salt — see Hydrochloric acid						
surgical	980.9	E860.9	—	E950.9	E962.1	E980.9
Spironolactone	974.4	E858.5	E944.4	E950.4	E962.0	E980.4
Sponge, absorbable (gelatin)	964.5	E858.2	E934.5	E950.4	E962.0	E980.4
Sporostacin	976.0	E858.7	E946.0	E950.4	E962.0	E980.4
Sprays (aerosol)	989.89	E866.8	—	E950.9	E962.1	E980.9
cosmetic	989.89	E866.7	—	E950.9	E962.1	E980.9
medicinal NEC	977.9	E858.9	E947.9	E950.5	E962.0	E980.5
pesticides — see Pesticides						
specified content — see substance specified						
Spurge flax	988.2	E865.4	—	E950.9	E962.1	E980.9
Spurges	988.2	E865.4	—	E950.9	E962.1	E980.9
Squill (expectorant) NEC	975.5	E858.6	E945.5	E950.4	E962.0	E980.4
rat poison	989.4	E863.7	—	E950.6	E962.1	E980.7
Squirting cucumber (cathartic)	973.1	E858.4	E943.1	E950.4	E962.0	E980.4
Stains	989.89	E866.8	—	E950.9	E962.1	E980.9
Stannous — see also Tin						
fluoride	976.7	E858.7	E946.7	E950.4	E962.0	E980.4
Stanolone	962.1	E858.0	E932.1	E950.4	E962.0	E980.4
Stanozolol	962.1	E858.0	E932.1	E950.4	E962.0	E980.4
Staphisagria or stavesacre (pediculicide)	976.0	E858.7	E946.0	E950.4	E962.0	E980.4
Stelazine	969.1	E853.0	E939.1	E950.3	E962.0	E980.3
Stemetil	969.1	E853.0	E939.1	E950.3	E962.0	E980.3
Sterculia (cathartic) (gum)	973.3	E858.4	E943.3	E950.4	E962.0	E980.4
Sternutator gas	987.8	E869.8	—	E952.8	E962.2	E982.8
Steroids NEC	962.0	E858.0	E932.0	E950.4	E962.0	E980.4
ENT agent	976.6	E858.7	E946.6	E950.4	E962.0	E980.4
ophthalmic preparation	976.5	E858.7	E946.5	E950.4	E962.0	E980.4
topical NEC	976.0	E858.7	E946.0	E950.4	E962.0	E980.4
Stibine	985.8	E866.4	—	E950.9	E962.1	E980.9
Stibophen	961.2	E857	E931.2	E950.4	E962.0	E980.4
Stilbamide, stilbamidine	961.5	E857	E931.5	E950.4	E962.0	E980.4
Stilbestrol	962.2	E858.0	E932.2	E950.4	E962.0	E980.4
Stimulants (central nervous system)	970.9	E854.3	E940.9	E950.4	E962.0	E980.4
analeptics	970.0	E854.3	E940.0	E950.4	E962.0	E980.4
opiate antagonist	970.1	E854.3	E940.1	E950.4	E962.0	E980.4
psychotherapeutic NEC	969.0	E854.0	E939.0	E950.3	E962.0	E980.3
specified NEC	970.8	E854.3	E940.8	E950.4	E962.0	E980.4
Storage batteries (acid) (cells)	983.1	E864.1	—	E950.7	E962.1	E980.6
Stovaine	968.9	E855.2	E938.9	E950.4	E962.0	E980.4
infiltration (subcutaneous)	968.5	E855.2	E938.5	E950.4	E962.0	E980.4
nerve block (peripheral) (plexus)	968.6	E855.2	E938.6	E950.4	E962.0	E980.4
spinal	968.7	E855.2	E938.7	E950.4	E962.0	E980.4
Stovaine — continued						
topical (surface)	968.5	E855.2	E938.5	E950.4	E962.0	E980.4
Stovarsal	961.1	E857	E931.1	E950.4	E962.0	E980.4
Stove gas — see Gas, utility						
Stoxil	976.5	E858.7	E946.5	E950.4	E962.0	E980.4
STP	969.6	E854.1	E939.6	E950.3	E962.0	E980.3
Stramonium (medicinal) NEC	971.1	E855.4	E941.1	E950.4	E962.0	E980.4
natural state	988.2	E865.4	—	E950.9	E962.1	E980.9
Streptodornase	964.4	E858.2	E934.4	E950.4	E962.0	E980.4
Streptoduocin	960.6	E856	E930.6	E950.4	E962.0	E980.4
Streptokinase	964.4	E858.2	E934.4	E950.4	E962.0	E980.4
Streptomycin	960.6	E856	E930.6	E950.4	E962.0	E980.4
Streptozocin	960.7	E856	E930.7	E950.4	E962.0	E980.4
Stripper (paint) (solvent)	982.8	E862.9	—	E950.9	E962.1	E980.9
Strobane	989.2	E863.0	—	E950.6	E962.1	E980.7
Strophanthin	972.1	E858.3	E942.1	E950.4	E962.0	E980.4
Strophanthus hispidus or kombe	988.2	E865.4	—	E950.9	E962.1	E980.9
Strychnine (rodenticide) (salts)	989.1	E863.7	—	E950.6	E962.1	E980.7
medicinal NEC	970.8	E854.3	E940.8	E950.4	E962.0	E980.4
Strychnos (ignatii) — see Strychnine						
Styramate	968.0	E855.1	E938.0	E950.4	E962.0	E980.4
Styrene	983.0	E864.0	—	E950.7	E962.1	E980.6
Succinimide (anticonvulsant)	966.2	E855.0	E936.2	E950.4	E962.0	E980.4
mercuric — see Mercury						
Succinylcholine	975.2	E858.6	E945.2	E950.4	E962.0	E980.4
Succinylsulfathiazole	961.0	E857	E931.0	E950.4	E962.0	E980.4
Sucrose	974.5	E858.5	E944.5	E950.4	E962.0	E980.4
Sulfacetamide	961.0	E857	E931.0	E950.4	E962.0	E980.4
ophthalmic preparation	976.5	E858.7	E946.5	E950.4	E962.0	E980.4
Sulfachlorpyridazine	961.0	E857	E931.0	E950.4	E962.0	E980.4
Sulfacytine	961.0	E857	E931.0	E950.4	E962.0	E980.4
Sulfadiazine	961.0	E857	E931.0	E950.4	E962.0	E980.4
silver (topical)	976.0	E858.7	E946.0	E950.4	E962.0	E980.4
Sulfadimethoxine	961.0	E857	E931.0	E950.4	E962.0	E980.4
Sulfadimidine	961.0	E857	E931.0	E950.4	E962.0	E980.4
Sulfaethidole	961.0	E857	E931.0	E950.4	E962.0	E980.4
Sulfafurazole	961.0	E857	E931.0	E950.4	E962.0	E980.4
Sulfaguanidine	961.0	E857	E931.0	E950.4	E962.0	E980.4
Sulfamerazine	961.0	E857	E931.0	E950.4	E962.0	E980.4
Sulfameter	961.0	E857	E931.0	E950.4	E962.0	E980.4
Sulfamethizole	961.0	E857	E931.0	E950.4	E962.0	E980.4
Sulfamethoxazole	961.0	E857	E931.0	E950.4	E962.0	E980.4
Sulfamethoxydiazine	961.0	E857	E931.0	E950.4	E962.0	E980.4
Sulfamethoxypyridazine	961.0	E857	E931.0	E950.4	E962.0	E980.4
Sulfamethylthiazole	961.0	E857	E931.0	E950.4	E962.0	E980.4
Sulfamylon	976.0	E858.7	E946.0	E950.4	E962.0	E980.4
Sulfan blue (diagnostic dye)	977.8	E858.8	E947.8	E950.4	E962.0	E980.4
Sulfanilamide	961.0	E857	E931.0	E950.4	E962.0	E980.4
Sulfanilylguanidine	961.0	E857	E931.0	E950.4	E962.0	E980.4
Sulfaphenazole	961.0	E857	E931.0	E950.4	E962.0	E980.4
Sulfaphenylthiazole	961.0	E857	E931.0	E950.4	E962.0	E980.4
Sulfaproxyline	961.0	E857	E931.0	E950.4	E962.0	E980.4
Sulfapyridine	961.0	E857	E931.0	E950.4	E962.0	E980.4
Sulfapyrimidine	961.0	E857	E931.0	E950.4	E962.0	E980.4
Sulfarsphenamine	961.1	E857	E931.1	E950.4	E962.0	E980.4
Sulfasalazine	961.0	E857	E931.0	E950.4	E962.0	E980.4
Sulfasomizole	961.0	E857	E931.0	E950.4	E962.0	E980.4
Sulfasuxidine	961.0	E857	E931.0	E950.4	E962.0	E980.4
Sulfinpyrazone	974.7	E858.5	E944.7	E950.4	E962.0	E980.4
Sulfisoxazole	961.0	E857	E931.0	E950.4	E962.0	E980.4
ophthalmic preparation	976.5	E858.7	E946.5	E950.4	E962.0	E980.4
Sulfomyxin	960.8	E856	E930.8	E950.4	E962.0	E980.4
Sulfonal	967.8	E852.8	E937.8	E950.2	E962.0	E980.2
Sulfonamides (mixtures)	961.0	E857	E931.0	E950.4	E962.0	E980.4
Sulfones	961.8	E857	E931.8	E950.4	E962.0	E980.4
Sulfonethylmethane	967.8	E852.8	E937.8	E950.2	E962.0	E980.2
Sulfonmethane	967.8	E852.8	E937.8	E950.2	E962.0	E980.2
Sulfonphthal, sulfonphthol	977.8	E858.8	E947.8	E950.4	E962.0	E980.4
Sulfonylurea derivatives, oral	962.3	E858.0	E932.3	E950.4	E962.0	E980.4
Sulfoxone	961.8	E857	E931.8	E950.4	E962.0	E980.4
Sulfur, sulfureted, sulfuric, sulfurous, sulfuryl (compounds) NEC	989.89	E866.8	—	E950.9	E962.1	E980.9
acid	983.1	E864.1	—	E950.7	E962.1	E980.6
dioxide	987.3	E869.1	—	E952.8	E962.2	E982.8

☑ Additional Digit Required — Refer to the Tabular List for Digit Selection   ▽ Subterms under main terms may continue to next column or page

Substance	Poisoning	Accident	Therapeutic Use	Suicide Attempt	Assault	Undetermined
Sulfur, sulfureted, sulfuric, sulfurous, sulfuryl (compounds) — *continued*						
ether — *see* Ether(s)						
hydrogen	987.8	E869.8	—	E952.8	E962.2	E982.8
medicinal (keratolytic) (ointment)						
NEC	976.4	E858.7	E946.4	E950.4	E962.0	E980.4
pesticide (vapor)	989.4	E863.4	—	E950.6	E962.1	E980.7
vapor NEC	987.8	E869.8	—	E952.8	E962.2	E982.8
Sulkowitch's reagent	977.8	E858.8	E947.8	E950.4	E962.0	E980.4
Sulphadione	961.8	E857	E931.8	E950.4	E962.0	E980.4
Sulph — *see also* Sulf-						
Sulthiame, sultiame	966.3	E855.0	E936.3	E950.4	E962.0	E980.4
Superinone	975.5	E858.6	E945.5	E950.4	E962.0	E980.4
Suramin	961.5	E857	E931.5	E950.4	E962.0	E980.4
Surfacaine	968.5	E855.2	E938.5	E950.4	E962.0	E980.4
Surital	968.3	E855.1	E938.3	E950.4	E962.0	E980.4
Sutilains	976.8	E858.7	E946.8	E950.4	E962.0	E980.4
Suxamethonium (bromide) (chloride) (iodide)	975.2	E858.6	E945.2	E950.4	E962.0	E980.4
Suxethonium (bromide)	975.2	E858.6	E945.2	E950.4	E962.0	E980.4
Sweet oil (birch)	976.3	E858.7	E946.3	E950.4	E962.0	E980.4
Sym-dichloroethyl ether	982.3	E862.4	—	E950.9	E962.1	E980.9
Sympatholytics	971.3	E855.6	E941.3	E950.4	E962.0	E980.4
Sympathomimetics	971.2	E855.5	E941.2	E950.4	E962.0	E980.4
Synagis	979.6	E858.8	E949.6	E950.4	E962.0	E980.4
Synalar	976.0	E858.7	E946.0	E950.4	E962.0	E980.4
Synthroid	962.7	E858.0	E932.7	E950.4	E962.0	E980.4
Syntocinon	975.0	E858.6	E945.0	E950.4	E962.0	E980.4
Syrosingopine	972.6	E858.3	E942.6	E950.4	E962.0	E980.4
Systemic agents (primarily)	963.9	E858.1	E933.9	E950.4	E962.0	E980.4
specified NEC	963.8	E858.1	E933.8	E950.4	E962.0	E980.4
Tablets — *see also* specified substance	977.9	E858.9	E947.9	E950.5	E962.0	E980.5
Tace	962.2	E858.0	E932.2	E950.4	E962.0	E980.4
Tacrine	971.0	E855.3	E941.0	E950.4	E962.0	E980.4
Talbutal	967.0	E851	E937.0	E950.1	E962.0	E980.1
Talc	976.3	E858.7	E946.3	E950.4	E962.0	E980.4
Talcum	976.3	E858.7	E946.3	E950.4	E962.0	E980.4
Tandearil, tanderil	965.5	E850.5	E935.5	E950.0	E962.0	E980.0
Tannic acid	983.1	E864.1	—	E950.7	E962.1	E980.6
medicinal (astringent)	976.2	E858.7	E946.2	E950.4	E962.0	E980.4
Tannin — *see* Tannic acid						
Tansy	988.2	E865.4	—	E950.9	E962.1	E980.9
TAO	960.3	E856	E930.3	E950.4	E962.0	E980.4
Tapazole	962.8	E858.0	E932.8	E950.4	E962.0	E980.4
Tar NEC	983.0	E864.0	—	E950.7	E962.1	E980.6
camphor — *see* Naphthalene						
fumes	987.8	E869.8	—	E952.8	E962.2	E982.8
Taractan	969.3	E853.8	E939.3	E950.3	E962.0	E980.3
Tarantula (venomous)	989.5	E905.1	—	E950.9	E962.1	E980.9
Tartar emetic (anti-infective)	961.2	E857	E931.2	E950.4	E962.0	E980.4
Tartaric acid	983.1	E864.1	—	E950.7	E962.1	E980.6
Tartrated antimony (anti-infective)	961.2	E857	E931.2	E950.4	E962.0	E980.4
TCA — *see* Trichloroacetic acid						
TDI	983.0	E864.0	—	E950.7	E962.1	E980.6
vapor	987.8	E869.8	—	E952.8	E962.2	E982.8
Tear gas	987.5	E869.3	—	E952.8	E962.2	E982.8
Teclothiazide	974.3	E858.5	E944.3	E950.4	E962.0	E980.4
Tegretol	966.3	E855.0	E936.3	E950.4	E962.0	E980.4
Telepaque	977.8	E858.8	E947.8	E950.4	E962.0	E980.4
Tellurium	985.8	E866.4	—	E950.9	E962.1	E980.9
fumes	985.8	E866.4	—	E950.9	E962.1	E980.9
TEM	963.1	E858.1	E933.1	E950.4	E962.0	E980.4
Temazepan — *see* Benzodiazepines						
TEPA	963.1	E858.1	E933.1	E950.4	E962.0	E980.4
TEPP	989.3	E863.1	—	E950.6	E962.1	E980.7
Terbutaline	971.2	E855.5	E941.2	E950.4	E962.0	E980.4
Teroxalene	961.6	E857	E931.6	E950.4	E962.0	E980.4
Terpin hydrate	975.5	E858.6	E945.5	E950.4	E962.0	E980.4
Terramycin	960.4	E856	E930.4	E950.4	E962.0	E980.4
Tessalon	975.4	E858.6	E945.4	E950.4	E962.0	E980.4
Testosterone	962.1	E858.0	E932.1	E950.4	E962.0	E980.4
Tetanus (vaccine)	978.4	E858.8	E948.4	E950.4	E962.0	E980.4
antitoxin	979.9	E858.8	E949.9	E950.4	E962.0	E980.4
immune globulin (human)	964.6	E858.2	E934.6	E950.4	E962.0	E980.4
toxoid	978.4	E858.8	E948.4	E950.4	E962.0	E980.4
with diphtheria toxoid	978.9	E858.8	E948.9	E950.4	E962.0	E980.4

Substance	Poisoning	Accident	Therapeutic Use	Suicide Attempt	Assault	Undetermined
Tetanus — *continued*						
toxoid — *continued*						
with diphtheria toxoid — *continued*						
with pertussis	978.6	E858.8	E948.6	E950.4	E962.0	E980.4
Tetrabenazine	969.5	E853.8	E939.5	E950.3	E962.0	E980.3
Tetracaine (infiltration) (topical)	968.5	E855.2	E938.5	E950.4	E962.0	E980.4
nerve block (peripheral) (plexus)	968.6	E855.2	E938.6	E950.4	E962.0	E980.4
spinal	968.7	E855.2	E938.7	E950.4	E962.0	E980.4
Tetrachlorethylene — *see* Tetrachloroethylene						
Tetrachlormethiazide	974.3	E858.5	E944.3	E950.4	E962.0	E980.4
Tetrachloroethane (liquid) (vapor)	982.3	E862.4	—	E950.9	E962.1	E980.9
paint or varnish	982.3	E861.6	—	E950.9	E962.1	E980.9
Tetrachloroethylene (liquid) (vapor)	982.3	E862.4	—	E950.9	E962.1	E980.9
medicinal	961.6	E857	E931.6	E950.4	E962.0	E980.4
Tetrachloromethane — *see* Carbon, tetrachloride						
Tetracycline	960.4	E856	E930.4	E950.4	E962.0	E980.4
ophthalmic preparation	976.5	E858.7	E946.5	E950.4	E962.0	E980.4
topical NEC	976.0	E858.7	E946.0	E950.4	E962.0	E980.4
Tetraethylammonium chloride	972.3	E858.3	E942.3	E950.4	E962.0	E980.4
Tetraethyl lead (antiknock compound)	984.1	E862.1	—	E950.9	E962.1	E980.9
Tetraethyl pyrophosphate	989.3	E863.1	—	E950.6	E962.1	E980.7
Tetraethylthiuram disulfide	977.3	E858.8	E947.3	E950.4	E962.0	E980.4
Tetrahydroaminoacridine	971.0	E855.3	E941.0	E950.4	E962.0	E980.4
Tetrahydrocannabinol	969.6	E854.1	E939.6	E950.3	E962.0	E980.3
Tetrahydronaphthalene	982.0	E862.4	—	E950.9	E962.1	E980.9
Tetrahydrozoline	971.2	E855.5	E941.2	E950.4	E962.0	E980.4
Tetralin	982.0	E862.4	—	E950.9	E962.1	E980.9
Tetramethylthiuram (disulfide) NEC	989.4	E863.6	—	E950.6	E962.1	E980.7
medicinal	976.2	E858.7	E946.2	E950.4	E962.0	E980.4
Tetronal	967.8	E852.8	E937.8	E950.2	E962.0	E980.2
Tetryl	983.0	E864.0	—	E950.7	E962.1	E980.6
Thalidomide	967.8	E852.8	E937.8	E950.2	E962.0	E980.2
Thallium (compounds) (dust) NEC	985.8	E866.4	—	E950.9	E962.1	E980.9
pesticide (rodenticide)	985.8	E863.7	—	E950.6	E962.1	E980.7
THC	969.6	E854.1	E939.6	E950.3	E962.0	E980.3
Thebacon	965.09	E850.2	E935.2	E950.0	E962.0	E980.0
Thebaine	965.09	E850.2	E935.2	E950.0	E962.0	E980.0
Theobromine (calcium salicylate)	974.1	E858.5	E944.1	E950.4	E962.0	E980.4
Theophylline (diuretic)	974.1	E858.5	E944.1	E950.4	E962.0	E980.4
ethylenediamine	975.7	E858.6	E945.7	E950.4	E962.0	E980.4
Thiabendazole	961.6	E857	E931.6	E950.4	E962.0	E980.4
Thialbarbital, thialbarbitone	968.3	E855.1	E938.3	E950.4	E962.0	E980.4
Thiamine	963.5	E858.1	E933.5	E950.4	E962.0	E980.4
Thiamylal (sodium)	968.3	E855.1	E938.3	E950.4	E962.0	E980.4
Thiazesim	969.0	E854.0	E939.0	E950.3	E962.0	E980.3
Thiazides (diuretics)	974.3	E858.5	E944.3	E950.4	E962.0	E980.4
Thiethylperazine	963.0	E858.1	E933.0	E950.4	E962.0	E980.4
Thimerosal (topical)	976.0	E858.7	E946.0	E950.4	E962.0	E980.4
ophthalmic preparation	976.5	E858.7	E946.5	E950.4	E962.0	E980.4
Thioacetazone	961.8	E857	E931.8	E950.4	E962.0	E980.4
Thiobarbiturates	968.3	E855.1	E938.3	E950.4	E962.0	E980.4
Thiobismol	961.2	E857	E931.2	E950.4	E962.0	E980.4
Thiocarbamide	962.8	E858.0	E932.8	E950.4	E962.0	E980.4
Thiocarbarsone	961.1	E857	E931.1	E950.4	E962.0	E980.4
Thiocarlide	961.8	E857	E931.8	E950.4	E962.0	E980.4
Thioguanine	963.1	E858.1	E933.1	E950.4	E962.0	E980.4
Thiomercaptomerin	974.0	E858.5	E944.0	E950.4	E962.0	E980.4
Thiomerin	974.0	E858.5	E944.0	E950.4	E962.0	E980.4
Thiopental, thiopentone (sodium)	968.3	E855.1	E938.3	E950.4	E962.0	E980.4
Thiopropazate	969.1	E853.0	E939.1	E950.3	E962.0	E980.3
Thioproperazine	969.1	E853.0	E939.1	E950.3	E962.0	E980.3
Thioridazine	969.1	E853.0	E939.1	E950.3	E962.0	E980.3
Thio-TEPA, thiotepa	963.1	E858.1	E933.1	E950.4	E962.0	E980.4
Thiothixene	969.3	E853.8	E939.3	E950.3	E962.0	E980.3
Thiouracil	962.8	E858.0	E932.8	E950.4	E962.0	E980.4
Thiourea	962.8	E858.0	E932.8	E950.4	E962.0	E980.4

☑ Additional Digit Required — Refer to the Tabular List for Digit Selection

▶◀ Revised Text　　● New Line　　▲ Revised Code

▽ Subterms under main terms may continue to next column or page

Substance	Poisoning	Accident	Therapeutic Use	Suicide Attempt	Assault	Undetermined
Thiphenamil	971.1	E855.4	E941.1	E950.4	E962.0	E980.4
Thiram NEC	989.4	E863.6	—	E950.6	E962.1	E980.7
medicinal	976.2	E858.7	E946.2	E950.4	E962.0	E980.4
Thonzylamine	963.0	E858.1	E933.0	E950.4	E962.0	E980.4
Thorazine	969.1	E853.0	E939.1	E950.3	E962.0	E980.3
Thornapple	988.2	E865.4	—	E950.9	E962.1	E980.9
Throat preparation (lozenges)						
NEC	976.6	E858.7	E946.6	E950.4	E962.0	E980.4
Thrombin	964.5	E858.2	E934.5	E950.4	E962.0	E980.4
Thrombolysin	964.4	E858.2	E934.4	E950.4	E962.0	E980.4
Thymol	983.0	E864.0	—	E950.7	E962.1	E980.6
Thymus extract	962.9	E858.0	E932.9	E950.4	E962.0	E980.4
Thyroglobulin	962.7	E858.0	E932.7	E950.4	E962.0	E980.4
Thyroid (derivatives)						
(extract)	962.7	E858.0	E932.7	E950.4	E962.0	E980.4
Thyrolar	962.7	E858.0	E932.7	E950.4	E962.0	E980.4
Thyrothrophin, thyrotropin	977.8	E858.8	E947.8	E950.4	E962.0	E980.4
Thyroxin(e)	962.7	E858.0	E932.7	E950.4	E962.0	E980.4
Tigan	963.0	E858.1	E933.0	E950.4	E962.0	E980.4
Tigloidine	968.0	E855.1	E938.0	E950.4	E962.0	E980.4
Tin (chloride) (dust) (oxide)						
NEC	985.8	E866.4	—	E950.9	E962.1	E980.9
anti-infectives	961.2	E857	E931.2	E950.4	E962.0	E980.4
Tinactin	976.0	E858.7	E946.0	E950.4	E962.0	E980.4
Tincture, iodine — see Iodine						
Tindal	969.1	E853.0	E939.1	E950.3	E962.0	E980.3
Titanium (compounds)						
(vapor)	985.8	E866.4	—	E950.9	E962.1	E980.9
ointment	976.3	E858.7	E946.3	E950.4	E962.0	E980.4
Titroid	962.7	E858.0	E932.7	E950.4	E962.0	E980.4
TMTD — see Tetramethylthiuram disulfide						
TNT	989.89	E866.8	—	E950.9	E962.1	E980.9
fumes	987.8	E869.8	—	E952.8	E962.2	E982.8
Toadstool	988.1	E865.5	—	E950.9	E962.1	E980.9
Tobacco NEC	989.84	E866.8	—	E950.9	E962.1	E980.9
Indian	988.2	E865.4	—	E950.9	E962.1	E980.9
smoke, second-hand	987.8	E869.4	—	—	—	—
Tocopherol	963.5	E858.1	E933.5	E950.4	E962.0	E980.4
Tocosamine	975.0	E858.6	E945.0	E950.4	E962.0	E980.4
Tofranil	969.0	E854.0	E939.0	E950.3	E962.0	E980.3
Toilet deodorizer	989.89	E866.8	—	E950.9	E962.1	E980.9
Tolazamide	962.3	E858.0	E932.3	E950.4	E962.0	E980.4
Tolazoline	971.3	E855.6	E941.3	E950.4	E962.0	E980.4
Tolbutamide	962.3	E858.0	E932.3	E950.4	E962.0	E980.4
sodium	977.8	E858.8	E947.8	E950.4	E962.0	E980.4
Tolmetin	965.69	E850.6	E935.6	E950.0	E962.0	E980.0
Tolnaftate	976.0	E858.7	E946.0	E950.4	E962.0	E980.4
Tolpropamine	976.1	E858.7	E946.1	E950.4	E962.0	E980.4
Tolserol	968.0	E855.1	E938.0	E950.4	E962.0	E980.4
Toluene (liquid) (vapor)	982.0	E862.4	—	E950.9	E962.1	E980.9
diisocyanate	983.0	E864.0	—	E950.7	E962.1	E980.6
Toluidine	983.0	E864.0	—	E950.7	E962.1	E980.6
vapor	987.8	E869.8	—	E952.8	E962.2	E982.8
Toluol (liquid) (vapor)	982.0	E862.4	—	E950.9	E962.1	E980.9
Tolylene-2, 4-diisocyanate	983.0	E864.0	—	E950.7	E962.1	E980.6
Tonics, cardiac	972.1	E858.3	E942.1	E950.4	E962.0	E980.4
Toxaphene (dust) (spray)	989.2	E863.0	—	E950.6	E962.1	E980.7
Toxoids NEC	978.8	E858.8	E948.8	E950.4	E962.0	E980.4
Tractor fuel NEC	981	E862.1	—	E950.9	E962.1	E980.9
Tragacanth	973.3	E858.4	E943.3	E950.4	E962.0	E980.4
Tramazoline	971.2	E855.5	E941.2	E950.4	E962.0	E980.4
Tranquilizers	969.5	E853.9	E939.5	E950.3	E962.0	E980.3
benzodiazepine-based	969.4	E853.2	E939.4	E950.3	E962.0	E980.3
butyrophenone-based	969.2	E853.1	E939.2	E950.3	E962.0	E980.3
major NEC	969.3	E853.8	E939.3	E950.3	E962.0	E980.3
phenothiazine-based	969.1	E853.0	E939.1	E950.3	E962.0	E980.3
specified NEC	969.5	E853.8	E939.5	E950.3	E962.0	E980.3
Trantoin	961.9	E857	E931.9	E950.4	E962.0	E980.4
Tranxene	969.4	E853.2	E939.4	E950.3	E962.0	E980.3
Tranylcypromine (sulfate)	969.0	E854.0	E939.0	E950.3	E962.0	E980.3
Trasentine	975.1	E858.6	E945.1	E950.4	E962.0	E980.4
Travert	974.5	E858.5	E944.5	E950.4	E962.0	E980.4
Trecator	961.8	E857	E931.8	E950.4	E962.0	E980.4
Tretinoin	976.8	E858.7	E946.8	E950.4	E962.0	E980.4
Triacetin	976.0	E858.7	E946.0	E950.4	E962.0	E980.4
Triacetyloleandomycin	960.3	E856	E930.3	E950.4	E962.0	E980.4
Triamcinolone	962.0	E858.0	E932.0	E950.4	E962.0	E980.4
ENT agent	976.6	E858.7	E946.6	E950.4	E962.0	E980.4
medicinal (keratolytic)	976.4	E858.7	E946.4	E950.4	E962.0	E980.4
Triamcinolone — continued						
ophthalmic preparation	976.5	E858.7	E946.5	E950.4	E962.0	E980.4
topical NEC	976.0	E858.7	E946.0	E950.4	E962.0	E980.4
Triamterene	974.4	E858.5	E944.4	E950.4	E962.0	E980.4
Triazaquone	963.1	E858.1	E933.1	E950.4	E962.0	E980.4
Tribromacetaldehyde	967.3	E852.2	E937.3	E950.2	E962.0	E980.2
Tribromoethanol	968.2	E855.1	E938.2	E950.4	E962.0	E980.4
Tribromomethane	967.3	E852.2	E937.3	E950.2	E962.0	E980.2
Trichlorethane	982.3	E862.4	—	E950.9	E962.1	E980.9
Trichlormethiazide	974.3	E858.5	E944.3	E950.4	E962.0	E980.4
Trichloroacetic acid	983.1	E864.1	—	E950.7	E962.1	E980.6
Trichloroethanol	967.1	E852.0	E937.1	E950.2	E962.0	E980.2
Trichloroethylene (liquid)						
(vapor)	982.3	E862.4	—	E950.9	E962.1	E980.9
anesthetic (gas)	968.2	E855.1	E938.2	E950.4	E962.0	E980.4
Trichloroethyl phosphate	967.1	E852.0	E937.1	E950.2	E962.0	E980.2
Trichlorofluoromethane						
NEC	987.4	E869.2	—	E952.8	E962.2	E982.8
Trichlorotriethylamine	963.1	E858.1	E933.1	E950.4	E962.0	E980.4
Trichomonacides NEC	961.5	E857	E931.5	E950.4	E962.0	E980.4
Trichomycin	960.1	E856	E930.1	E950.4	E962.0	E980.4
Triclofos	967.1	E852.0	E937.1	E950.2	E962.0	E980.2
Tricresyl phosphate	989.89	E866.8	—	E950.9	E962.1	E980.9
solvent	982.8	E862.4	—	E950.9	E962.1	E980.9
Tricyclamol	966.4	E855.0	E936.4	E950.4	E962.0	E980.4
Tridesilon	976.0	E858.7	E946.0	E950.4	E962.0	E980.4
Tridihexethyl	971.1	E855.4	E941.1	E950.4	E962.0	E980.4
Tridione	966.0	E855.0	E936.0	E950.4	E962.0	E980.4
Triethanolamine NEC	983.2	E864.2	—	E950.7	E962.1	E980.6
detergent	983.2	E861.0	—	E950.7	E962.1	E980.6
trinitrate	972.4	E858.3	E942.4	E950.4	E962.0	E980.4
Triethanomelamine	963.1	E858.1	E933.1	E950.4	E962.0	E980.4
Triethylene melamine	963.1	E858.1	E933.1	E950.4	E962.0	E980.4
Triethylenephosphoramide	963.1	E858.1	E933.1	E950.4	E962.0	E980.4
Triethylenethiophosphoramide	963.1	E858.1	E933.1	E950.4	E962.0	E980.4
Trifluoperazine	969.1	E853.0	E939.1	E950.3	E962.0	E980.3
Trifluperidol	969.2	E853.1	E939.2	E950.3	E962.0	E980.3
Triflupromazine	969.1	E853.0	E939.1	E950.3	E962.0	E980.3
Trihexyphenidyl	971.1	E855.4	E941.1	E950.4	E962.0	E980.4
Triiodothyronine	962.7	E858.0	E932.7	E950.4	E962.0	E980.4
Trilene	968.2	E855.1	E938.2	E950.4	E962.0	E980.4
Trimeprazine	963.0	E858.1	E933.0	E950.4	E962.0	E980.4
Trimetazidine	972.4	E858.3	E942.4	E950.4	E962.0	E980.4
Trimethadione	966.0	E855.0	E936.0	E950.4	E962.0	E980.4
Trimethaphan	972.3	E858.3	E942.3	E950.4	E962.0	E980.4
Trimethidinium	972.3	E858.3	E942.3	E950.4	E962.0	E980.4
Trimethobenzamide	963.0	E858.1	E933.0	E950.4	E962.0	E980.4
Trimethylcarbinol	980.8	E860.8	—	E950.9	E962.1	E980.9
Trimethylpsoralen	976.3	E858.7	E946.3	E950.4	E962.0	E980.4
Trimeton	963.0	E858.1	E933.0	E950.4	E962.0	E980.4
Trimipramine	969.0	E854.0	E939.0	E950.3	E962.0	E980.3
Trimustine	963.1	E858.1	E933.1	E950.4	E962.0	E980.4
Trinitrin	972.4	E858.3	E942.4	E950.4	E962.0	E980.4
Trinitrophenol	983.0	E864.0	—	E950.7	E962.1	E980.6
Trinitrotoluene	989.89	E866.8	—	E950.9	E962.1	E980.9
fumes	987.8	E869.8	—	E952.8	E962.2	E982.8
Trional	967.8	E852.8	E937.8	E950.2	E962.0	E980.2
Trioxide of arsenic — see Arsenic						
Trioxsalen	976.3	E858.7	E946.3	E950.4	E962.0	E980.4
Tripelennamine	963.0	E858.1	E933.0	E950.4	E962.0	E980.4
Triperidol	969.2	E853.1	E939.2	E950.3	E962.0	E980.3
Triprolidine	963.0	E858.1	E933.0	E950.4	E962.0	E980.4
Trisoralen	976.3	E858.7	E946.3	E950.4	E962.0	E980.4
Troleandomycin	960.3	E856	E930.3	E950.4	E962.0	E980.4
Trolnitrate (phosphate)	972.4	E858.3	E942.4	E950.4	E962.0	E980.4
Trometamol	963.3	E858.1	E933.3	E950.4	E962.0	E980.4
Tromethamine	963.3	E858.1	E933.3	E950.4	E962.0	E980.4
Tronothane	968.5	E855.2	E938.5	E950.4	E962.0	E980.4
Tropicamide	971.1	E855.4	E941.1	E950.4	E962.0	E980.4
Troxidone	966.0	E855.0	E936.0	E950.4	E962.0	E980.4
Tryparsamide	961.1	E857	E931.1	E950.4	E962.0	E980.4
Trypsin	963.4	E858.1	E933.4	E950.4	E962.0	E980.4
Tryptizol	969.0	E854.0	E939.0	E950.3	E962.0	E980.3
Tuaminoheptane	971.2	E855.5	E941.2	E950.4	E962.0	E980.4
Tuberculin (old)	977.8	E858.8	E947.8	E950.4	E962.0	E980.4
Tubocurare	975.2	E858.6	E945.2	E950.4	E962.0	E980.4
Tubocurarine	975.2	E858.6	E945.2	E950.4	E962.0	E980.4
Turkish green	969.6	E854.1	E939.6	E950.3	E962.0	E980.3
Turpentine (spirits of) (liquid)						
(vapor)	982.8	E862.4	—	E950.9	E962.1	E980.9

☑ Additional Digit Required — Refer to the Tabular List for Digit Selection

▽ Subterms under main terms may continue to next column or page

	Poisoning	Accident	Therapeutic Use	Suicide Attempt	Assault	Undetermined
Tybamate	969.5	E853.8	E939.5	E950.3	E962.0	E980.3
Tyloxapol	975.5	E858.6	E945.5	E950.4	E962.0	E980.4
Tymazoline	971.2	E855.5	E941.2	E950.4	E962.0	E980.4
Typhoid vaccine	978.1	E858.8	E948.1	E950.4	E962.0	E980.4
Typhus vaccine	979.2	E858.8	E949.2	E950.4	E962.0	E980.4
Tyrothricin	976.0	E858.7	E946.0	E950.4	E962.0	E980.4
ENT agent	976.6	E858.7	E946.6	E950.4	E962.0	E980.4
ophthalmic preparation	976.5	E858.7	E946.5	E950.4	E962.0	E980.4
Undecenoic acid	976.0	E858.7	E946.0	E950.4	E962.0	E980.4
Undecylenic acid	976.0	E858.7	E946.0	E950.4	E962.0	E980.4
Unna's boot	976.3	E858.7	E946.3	E950.4	E962.0	E980.4
Uracil mustard	963.1	E858.1	E933.1	E950.4	E962.0	E980.4
Uramustine	963.1	E858.1	E933.1	E950.4	E962.0	E980.4
Urari	975.2	E858.6	E945.2	E950.4	E962.0	E980.4
Urea	974.4	E858.5	E944.4	E950.4	E962.0	E980.4
topical	976.8	E858.7	E946.8	E950.4	E962.0	E980.4
Urethan(e) (antineoplastic)	963.1	E858.1	E933.1	E950.4	E962.0	E980.4
Urginea (maritima) (scilla) — see Squill						
Uric acid metabolism agents NEC	974.7	E858.5	E944.7	E950.4	E962.0	E980.4
Urokinase	964.4	E858.2	E934.4	E950.4	E962.0	E980.4
Urokon	977.8	E858.8	E947.8	E950.4	E962.0	E980.4
Urotropin	961.9	E857	E931.9	E950.4	E962.0	E980.4
Urtica	988.2	E865.4	—	E950.9	E962.1	E980.9
Utility gas — see Gas, utility						
Vaccine NEC	979.9	E858.8	E949.9	E950.4	E962.0	E980.4
bacterial NEC	978.8	E858.8	E948.8	E950.4	E962.0	E980.4
with						
other bacterial component	978.9	E858.8	E948.9	E950.4	E962.0	E980.4
pertussis component	978.6	E858.8	E948.6	E950.4	E962.0	E980.4
viral-rickettsial component	979.7	E858.8	E949.7	E950.4	E962.0	E980.4
mixed NEC	978.9	E858.8	E948.9	E950.4	E962.0	E980.4
BCG	978.0	E858.8	E948.0	E950.4	E962.0	E980.4
cholera	978.2	E858.8	E948.2	E950.4	E962.0	E980.4
diphtheria	978.5	E858.8	E948.5	E950.4	E962.0	E980.4
influenza	979.6	E858.8	E949.6	E950.4	E962.0	E980.4
measles	979.4	E858.8	E949.4	E950.4	E962.0	E980.4
meningococcal	978.8	E858.8	E948.8	E950.4	E962.0	E980.4
mumps	979.6	E858.8	E949.6	E950.4	E962.0	E980.4
paratyphoid	978.1	E858.8	E948.1	E950.4	E962.0	E980.4
pertussis (with diphtheria toxoid) (with tetanus toxoid)	978.6	E858.8	E948.6	E950.4	E962.0	E980.4
plague	978.3	E858.8	E948.3	E950.4	E962.0	E980.4
poliomyelitis	979.5	E858.8	E949.5	E950.4	E962.0	E980.4
poliovirus	979.5	E858.8	E949.5	E950.4	E962.0	E980.4
rabies	979.1	E858.8	E949.1	E950.4	E962.0	E980.4
respiratory syncytial virus	979.6	E858.8	E949.6	E950.4	E962.0	E980.4
rickettsial NEC	979.6	E858.8	E949.6	E950.4	E962.0	E980.4
with						
bacterial component	979.7	E858.8	E949.7	E950.4	E962.0	E980.4
pertussis component	978.6	E858.8	E948.6	E950.4	E962.0	E980.4
viral component	979.7	E858.8	E949.7	E950.4	E962.0	E980.4
Rocky mountain spotted fever	979.6	E858.8	E949.6	E950.4	E962.0	E980.4
rotavirus	979.6	E858.8	E949.6	E950.4	E962.0	E980.4
rubella virus	979.4	E858.8	E949.4	E950.4	E962.0	E980.4
sabin oral	979.5	E858.8	E949.5	E950.4	E962.0	E980.4
smallpox	979.0	E858.8	E949.0	E950.4	E962.0	E980.4
tetanus	978.4	E858.8	E948.4	E950.4	E962.0	E980.4
typhoid	978.1	E858.8	E948.1	E950.4	E962.0	E980.4
typhus	979.2	E858.8	E949.2	E950.4	E962.0	E980.4
viral NEC	979.6	E858.8	E949.6	E950.4	E962.0	E980.4
with						
bacterial component	979.7	E858.8	E949.7	E950.4	E962.0	E980.4
pertussis component	978.6	E858.8	E948.6	E950.4	E962.0	E980.4
rickettsial component	979.7	E858.8	E949.7	E950.4	E962.0	E980.4
yellow fever	979.3	E858.8	E949.3	E950.4	E962.0	E980.4
Vaccinia immune globulin (human)	964.6	E858.2	E934.6	E950.4	E962.0	E980.4
Vaginal contraceptives	976.8	E858.7	E946.8	E950.4	E962.0	E980.4
Valethamate	971.1	E855.4	E941.1	E950.4	E962.0	E980.4
Valisone	976.0	E858.7	E946.0	E950.4	E962.0	E980.4
Valium	969.4	E853.2	E939.4	E950.3	E962.0	E980.3
Valmid	967.8	E852.8	E937.8	E950.2	E962.0	E980.2
Vanadium	985.8	E866.4	—	E950.9	E962.1	E980.9
Vancomycin	960.8	E856	E930.8	E950.4	E962.0	E980.4
Vapor — see also Gas	987.9	E869.9	—	E952.9	E962.2	E982.9
kiln (carbon monoxide)	986	E868.8	—	E952.1	E962.2	E982.1

	Poisoning	Accident	Therapeutic Use	Suicide Attempt	Assault	Undetermined
Vapor — see also Gas — continued						
lead — see Lead						
specified source NEC (see also specific substance)	987.8	E869.8	—	E952.8	E962.2	E982.8
Varidase	964.4	E858.2	E934.4	E950.4	E962.0	E980.4
Varnish	989.89	E861.6	—	E950.9	E962.1	E980.9
cleaner	982.8	E862.9	—	E950.9	E962.1	E980.9
Vaseline	976.3	E858.7	E946.3	E950.4	E962.0	E980.4
Vasodilan	972.5	E858.3	E942.5	E950.4	E962.0	E980.4
Vasodilators NEC	972.5	E858.3	E942.5	E950.4	E962.0	E980.4
coronary	972.4	E858.3	E942.4	E950.4	E962.0	E980.4
Vasopressin	962.5	E858.0	E932.5	E950.4	E962.0	E980.4
Vasopressor drugs	962.5	E858.0	E932.5	E950.4	E962.0	E980.4
Venom, venomous (bite) (sting)	989.5	E905.9	—	E950.9	E962.1	E980.9
arthropod NEC	989.5	E905.5	—	E950.9	E962.1	E980.9
bee	989.5	E905.3	—	E950.9	E962.1	E980.9
centipede	989.5	E905.4	—	E950.9	E962.1	E980.9
hornet	989.5	E905.3	—	E950.9	E962.1	E980.9
lizard	989.5	E905.0	—	E950.9	E962.1	E980.9
marine animals or plants	989.5	E905.6	—	E950.9	E962.1	E980.9
millipede (tropical)	989.5	E905.4	—	E950.9	E962.1	E980.9
plant NEC	989.5	E905.7	—	E950.9	E962.1	E980.9
marine	989.5	E905.6	—	E950.9	E962.1	E980.9
scorpion	989.5	E905.2	—	E950.9	E962.1	E980.9
snake	989.5	E905.0	—	E950.9	E962.1	E980.9
specified NEC	989.5	E905.8	—	E950.9	E962.1	E980.9
spider	989.5	E905.1	—	E950.9	E962.1	E980.9
wasp	989.5	E905.3	—	E950.9	E962.1	E980.9
Ventolin — see Salbutamol sulfate						
Veramon	967.0	E851	E937.0	E950.1	E962.0	E980.1
Veratrum						
album	988.2	E865.4	—	E950.9	E962.1	E980.9
alkaloids	972.6	E858.3	E942.6	E950.4	E962.0	E980.4
viride	988.2	E865.4	—	E950.9	E962.1	E980.9
Verdigris — see also Copper	985.8	E866.4	—	E950.9	E962.1	E980.9
Veronal	967.0	E851	E937.0	E950.1	E962.0	E980.1
Veroxil	961.6	E857	E931.6	E950.4	E962.0	E980.4
Versidyne	965.7	E850.7	E935.7	E950.0	E962.0	E980.0
Viagra	972.5	E858.3	E942.5	E950.4	E962.0	E980.4
Vienna						
green	985.1	E866.3	—	E950.8	E962.1	E980.8
insecticide	985.1	E863.4	—	E950.6	E962.1	E980.7
red	989.89	E866.8	—	E950.9	E962.1	E980.9
pharmaceutical dye	977.4	E858.8	E947.4	E950.4	E962.0	E980.4
Vinbarbital, vinbarbitone	967.0	E851	E937.0	E950.1	E962.0	E980.1
Vinblastine	963.1	E858.1	E933.1	E950.4	E962.0	E980.4
Vincristine	963.1	E858.1	E933.1	E950.4	E962.0	E980.4
Vinesthene, vinethene	968.2	E855.1	E938.2	E950.4	E962.0	E980.4
Vinyl						
bital	967.0	E851	E937.0	E950.1	E962.0	E980.1
ether	968.2	E855.1	E938.2	E950.4	E962.0	E980.4
Vioform	961.3	E857	E931.3	E950.4	E962.0	E980.4
topical	976.0	E858.7	E946.0	E950.4	E962.0	E980.4
Viomycin	960.6	E856	E930.6	E950.4	E962.0	E980.4
Viosterol	963.5	E858.1	E933.5	E950.4	E962.0	E980.4
Viper (venom)	989.5	E905.0	—	E950.9	E962.1	E980.9
Viprynium (embonate)	961.6	E857	E931.6	E950.4	E962.0	E980.4
Virugon	961.7	E857	E931.7	E950.4	E962.0	E980.4
Visine	976.5	E858.7	E946.5	E950.4	E962.0	E980.4
Vitamins NEC	963.5	E858.1	E933.5	E950.4	E962.0	E980.4
B$_{12}$	964.1	E858.2	E934.1	E950.4	E962.0	E980.4
hematopoietic	964.1	E858.2	E934.1	E950.4	E962.0	E980.4
K	964.3	E858.2	E934.3	E950.4	E962.0	E980.4
Vleminckx's solution	976.4	E858.7	E946.4	E950.4	E962.0	E980.4
Voltaren — see Diclofenac sodium						
Warfarin (potassium) (sodium)	964.2	E858.2	E934.2	E950.4	E962.0	E980.4
rodenticide	989.4	E863.7	—	E950.6	E962.1	E980.7
Wasp (sting)	989.5	E905.3	—	E950.9	E962.1	E980.9
Water						
balance agents NEC	974.5	E858.5	E944.5	E950.4	E962.0	E980.4
gas	987.1	E868.1	—	E951.8	E962.2	E981.8
incomplete combustion of — see Carbon, monoxide, fuel, utility						
hemlock	988.2	E865.4	—	E950.9	E962.1	E980.9

		External Cause (E-Code)				
	Poisoning	Accident	Therapeutic Use	Suicide Attempt	Assault	Undeter-mined
Water — *continued*						
moccasin (venom)	989.5	E905.0	—	E950.9	E962.1	E980.9
Wax (paraffin) (petroleum)	981	E862.3	—	E950.9	E962.1	E980.9
automobile	989.89	E861.2	—	E950.9	E962.1	E980.9
floor	981	E862.0	—	E950.9	E962.1	E980.9
Weed killers NEC	989.4	E863.5	—	E950.6	E962.1	E980.7
Welldorm	967.1	E852.0	E937.1	E950.2	E962.0	E980.2
White						
arsenic — *see* Arsenic						
hellebore	988.2	E865.4	—	E950.9	E962.1	E980.9
lotion (keratolytic)	976.4	E858.7	E946.4	E950.4	E962.0	E980.4
spirit	981	E862.0	—	E950.9	E962.1	E980.9
Whitewashes	989.89	E861.6	—	E950.9	E962.1	E980.9
Whole blood	964.7	E858.2	E934.7	E950.4	E962.0	E980.4
Wild						
black cherry	988.2	E865.4	—	E950.9	E962.1	E980.9
poisonous plants NEC	988.2	E865.4	—	E950.9	E962.1	E980.9
Window cleaning fluid	989.89	E861.3	—	E950.9	E962.1	E980.9
Wintergreen (oil)	976.3	E858.7	E946.3	E950.4	E962.0	E980.4
Witch hazel	976.2	E858.7	E946.2	E950.4	E962.0	E980.4
Wood						
alcohol	980.1	E860.2	—	E950.9	E962.1	E980.9
spirit	980.1	E860.2	—	E950.9	E962.1	E980.9
Woorali	975.2	E858.6	E945.2	E950.4	E962.0	E980.4
Wormseed, American	961.6	E857	E931.6	E950.4	E962.0	E980.4
Xanthine diuretics	974.1	E858.5	E944.1	E950.4	E962.0	E980.4
Xanthocillin	960.0	E856	E930.0	E950.4	E962.0	E980.4
Xanthotoxin	976.3	E858.7	E946.3	E950.4	E962.0	E980.4
Xigris	964.2	E858.2	E934.2	E950.4	E962.0	E980.4
Xylene (liquid) (vapor)	982.0	E862.4	—	E950.9	E962.1	E980.9
Xylocaine (infiltration)						
(topical)	968.5	E855.2	E938.5	E950.4	E962.0	E980.4
nerve block (peripheral)						
(plexus)	968.6	E855.2	E938.6	E950.4	E962.0	E980.4
spinal	968.7	E855.2	E938.7	E950.4	E962.0	E980.4
Xylol (liquid) (vapor)	982.0	E862.4	—	E950.9	E962.1	E980.9
Xylometazoline	971.2	E855.5	E941.2	E950.4	E962.0	E980.4
Yellow						
fever vaccine	979.3	E858.8	E949.3	E950.4	E962.0	E980.4
jasmine	988.2	E865.4	—	E950.9	E962.1	E980.9
Yew	988.2	E865.4	—	E950.9	E962.1	E980.9
Zactane	965.7	E850.7	E935.7	E950.0	E962.0	E980.0
Zaroxolyn	974.3	E858.5	E944.3	E950.4	E962.0	E980.4
Zephiran (topical)	976.0	E858.7	E946.0	E950.4	E962.0	E980.4
ophthalmic preparation	976.5	E858.7	E946.5	E950.4	E962.0	E980.4
Zerone	980.1	E860.2	—	E950.9	E962.1	E980.9
Zinc (compounds) (fumes) (salts)						
(vapor) NEC	985.8	E866.4	—	E950.9	E962.1	E980.9
anti-infectives	976.0	E858.7	E946.0	E950.4	E962.0	E980.4
antivaricose	972.7	E858.3	E942.7	E950.4	E962.0	E980.4
bacitracin	976.0	E858.7	E946.0	E950.4	E962.0	E980.4
chloride	976.2	E858.7	E946.2	E950.4	E962.0	E980.4
gelatin	976.3	E858.7	E946.3	E950.4	E962.0	E980.4
oxide	976.3	E858.7	E946.3	E950.4	E962.0	E980.4
peroxide	976.0	E858.7	E946.0	E950.4	E962.0	E980.4
pesticides	985.8	E863.4	—	E950.6	E962.1	E980.7
phosphide (rodenticide)	985.8	E863.7	—	E950.6	E962.1	E980.7
stearate	976.3	E858.7	E946.3	E950.4	E962.0	E980.4
sulfate (antivaricose)	972.7	E858.3	E942.7	E950.4	E962.0	E980.4
ENT agent	976.6	E858.7	E946.6	E950.4	E962.0	E980.4
ophthalmic solution	976.5	E858.7	E946.5	E950.4	E962.0	E980.4
topical NEC	976.0	E858.7	E946.0	E950.4	E962.0	E980.4
undecylenate	976.0	E858.7	E946.0	E950.4	E962.0	E980.4
Zovant	964.2	E858.2	E934.2	E950.4	E962.0	E980.4
Zoxazolamine	968.0	E855.1	E938.0	E950.4	E962.0	E980.4
Zygadenus (venenosus)	988.2	E865.4	—	E950.9	E962.1	E980.9

☑ Additional Digit Required — Refer to the Tabular List for Digit Selection ▽ Subterms under main terms may continue to next column or page

336 — Volume 2 ▶◀ Revised Text ● New Line ▲ Revised Code **2007 ICD-9-CM**

SECTION 3

Alphabetic Index to External Causes of Injury and Poisoning (E Code)

This section contains the index to the codes which classify environmental events, circumstances, and other conditions as the cause of injury and other adverse effects. Where a code from the section Supplementary Classification of External Causes of Injury and Poisoning (E800-E999) is applicable, it is intended that the E code shall be used in addition to a code from the main body of the classification, Chapters 1 to 17.

The alphabetic index to the E codes is organized by main terms which describe the accident, circumstance, event, or specific agent which caused the injury or other adverse effect.

Note — Transport accidents (E800-E848) include accidents involving:

> *aircraft and spacecraft (E840-E845)*
>
> *watercraft (E830-E838)*
>
> *motor vehicle (E810-E825)*
>
> *railway (E800-E807)*
>
> *other road vehicles (E826-E829)*

For definitions and examples related to transport accidents — see Volume 1 code categories E800-E848.

The fourth-digit subdivisions for use with categories E800-E848 to identify the injured person are found at the end of this section.

For identifying the place in which an accident or poisoning occurred (circumstances classifiable to categories E850-E869 and E880-E928) — see the listing in this section under "Accident, occurring."

See the Table of Drugs and Chemicals (Section 2 of this volume) for identifying the specific agent involved in drug overdose or a wrong substance given or taken in error, and for intoxication or poisoning by a drug or other chemical substance.

The specific adverse effect, reaction, or localized toxic effect to a correct drug or substance properly administered in therapeutic or prophylactic dosage should be classified according to the nature of the adverse effect (e.g., allergy, dermatitis, tachycardia) listed in Section 1 of this volume.

☑ Additional Digit Required — Refer to the Tabular List for Digit Selection
2007 ICD-9-CM   ▶◀ Revised Text   ● New Line   ▲ Revised Code

⊽ Subterms under main terms may continue to next column or page
Volume 2 — 337

Abandonment — Accident (to)

A

Abandonment
- causing exposure to weather conditions — *see* Exposure
- child, with intent to injure or kill E968.4
- helpless person, infant, newborn E904.0
  - with intent to injure or kill E968.4

Abortion, criminal, injury to child E968.8

Abuse (alleged) (suspected)
- adult
  - by
    - child E967.4
    - ex-partner E967.3
    - ex-spouse E967.3
    - father E967.0
    - grandchild E967.7
    - grandparent E967.6
    - mother E967.2
    - non-related caregiver E967.8
    - other relative E967.7
    - other specified person E967.1
    - partner E967.3
    - sibling E967.5
    - spouse E967.3
    - stepfather E967.0
    - stepmother E967.2
    - unspecified person E967.9
- child
  - by
    - boyfriend of parent or guardian E967.0
    - child E967.4
    - father E967.0
    - female partner of parent or guardian E967.2
    - girlfriend of parent or guardian E967.2
    - grandchild E967.7
    - grandparent E967.6
    - male partner of parent or guardian E967.0
    - mother E967.2
    - non-related caregiver E967.8
    - other relative E967.7
    - other specified person(s) E967.1
    - sibling E967.5
    - stepfather E967.0
    - stepmother E967.2
    - unspecified person E967.9

Accident (to) E928.9
- aircraft (in transit) (powered) E841 ☑
  - at landing, take-off E840 ☑
  - due to, caused by cataclysm — *see* categories E908 ☑, E909 ☑
  - late effect of E929.1
  - unpowered (*see also* Collision, aircraft, unpowered) E842 ☑
  - while alighting, boarding E843 ☑
- amphibious vehicle
  - on
    - land — *see* Accident, motor vehicle
    - water — *see* Accident, watercraft
- animal-drawn vehicle NEC E827 ☑
- animal, ridden NEC E828 ☑
- balloon (*see also* Collision, aircraft, unpowered) E842 ☑
- caused by, due to
  - abrasive wheel (metalworking) E919.3
  - animal NEC E906.9
    - being ridden (in sport or transport) E828 ☑
  - avalanche NEC E909.2
  - band saw E919.4
  - bench saw E919.4
  - bore, earth-drilling or mining (land) (seabed) E919.1
  - bulldozer E919.7

Accident (to) — *continued*
- caused by, due to — *continued*
  - cataclysmic
    - earth surface movement or eruption E909.9
    - storm E908.9
  - chain
    - hoist E919.2
      - agricultural operations E919.0
      - mining operations E919.1
    - saw E920.1
  - circular saw E919.4
  - cold (excessive) (*see also* Cold, exposure to) E901.9
  - combine E919.0
  - conflagration — *see* Conflagration
  - corrosive liquid, substance NEC E924.1
  - cotton gin E919.8
  - crane E919.2
    - agricultural operations E919.0
    - mining operations E919.1
  - cutting or piercing instrument (*see also* Cut) E920.9
  - dairy equipment E919.8
  - derrick E919.2
    - agricultural operations E919.0
    - mining operations E919.1
  - drill E920.1
    - earth (land) (seabed) E919.1
    - hand (powered) E920.1
      - not powered E920.4
    - metalworking E919.3
    - woodworking E919.4
  - earth(-)
    - drilling machine E919.1
    - moving machine E919.7
    - scraping machine E919.7
  - electric
    - current (*see also* Electric shock) E925.9
    - motor (*see also* Accident, machine, by type of machine)
      - current (of) — *see* Electric shock
  - elevator (building) (grain) E919.2
    - agricultural operations E919.0
    - mining operations E919.1
  - environmental factors NEC E928.9
  - excavating machine E919.7
  - explosive material (*see also* Explosion) E923.9
  - farm machine E919.0
  - firearm missile — *see* Shooting
  - fire, flames (*see also* Fire)
    - conflagration — *see* Conflagration
  - forging (metalworking) machine E919.3
  - forklift (truck) E919.2
    - agricultural operations E919.0
    - mining operations E919.1
  - gas turbine E919.5
  - harvester E919.0
  - hay derrick, mower, or rake E919.0
  - heat (excessive) (*see also* Heat) E900.9
  - hoist (*see also* Accident, caused by, due to, lift) E919.2
    - chain — *see* Accident, caused by, due to, chain
    - shaft E919.1
  - hot
    - liquid E924.0
      - caustic or corrosive E924.1
    - object (not producing fire or flames) E924.8
    - substance E924.9
      - caustic or corrosive E924.1
      - liquid (metal) NEC E924.0
      - specified type NEC E924.8
  - human bite E928.3
  - ignition — *see* Ignition
  - internal combustion engine E919.5
  - landslide NEC E909.2

Accident (to) — *continued*
- caused by, due to — *continued*
  - lathe (metalworking) E919.3
    - turnings E920.8
    - woodworking E919.4
  - lift, lifting (appliances) E919.2
    - agricultural operations E919.0
    - mining operations E919.1
    - shaft E919.1
  - lightning NEC E907
  - machine, machinery (*see also* Accident, machine)
    - drilling, metal E919.3
    - manufacturing, for manufacture of
      - beverages E919.8
      - clothing E919.8
      - foodstuffs E919.8
      - paper E919.8
      - textiles E919.8
    - milling, metal E919.3
    - moulding E919.4
    - power press, metal E919.3
    - printing E919.8
    - rolling mill, metal E919.3
    - sawing, metal E919.3
    - specified type NEC E919.8
    - spinning E919.8
    - weaving E919.8
  - natural factor NEC E928.9
  - overhead plane E919.4
  - plane E920.4
    - overhead E919.4
  - powered
    - hand tool NEC E920.1
    - saw E919.4
      - hand E920.1
  - printing machine E919.8
  - pulley (block) E919.2
    - agricultural operations E919.0
    - mining operations E919.1
    - transmission E919.6
  - radial saw E919.4
  - radiation — *see* Radiation
  - reaper E919.0
  - road scraper E919.7
    - when in transport under its own power — *see* categories E810-E825 ☑
  - roller coaster E919.8
  - sander E919.4
  - saw E920.4
    - band E919.4
    - bench E919.4
    - chain E920.1
    - circular E919.4
    - hand E920.4
      - powered E920.1
    - powered, except hand E919.4
    - radial E919.4
  - sawing machine, metal E919.3
  - shaft
    - hoist E919.1
    - lift E919.1
    - transmission E919.6
  - shears E920.4
    - hand E920.4
      - powered E920.1
    - mechanical E919.3
  - shovel E920.4
    - steam E919.7
  - spinning machine E919.8
  - steam (*see also* Burning, steam)
    - engine E919.5
    - shovel E919.7
  - thresher E919.0
  - thunderbolt NEC E907
  - tractor E919.0
    - when in transport under its own power — *see* categories E810-E825 ☑
  - transmission belt, cable, chain, gear, pinion, pulley, shaft E919.6
  - turbine (gas) (water driven) E919.5
  - under-cutter E919.1

Accident (to) — *continued*
- caused by, due to — *continued*
  - weaving machine E919.8
  - winch E919.2
    - agricultural operations E919.0
    - mining operations E919.1
- diving E883.0
  - with insufficient air supply E913.2
- glider (hang) (*see also* Collision, aircraft, unpowered) E842 ☑
- hovercraft
  - on
    - land — *see* Accident, motor vehicle
    - water — *see* Accident, watercraft
- ice yacht (*see also* Accident, vehicle NEC) E848
- in
  - medical, surgical procedure
    - as, or due to misadventure — *see* Misadventure
    - causing an abnormal reaction or later complication without mention of misadventure — *see* Reaction, abnormal
- kite carrying a person (*see also* Collision, involving aircraft, unpowered) E842 ☑
- land yacht (*see also* Accident, vehicle NEC) E848
- late effect of — *see* Late effect
- launching pad E845 ☑
- machine, machinery (*see also* Accident, caused by, due to, by specific type of machine) E919.9
  - agricultural including animal-powered E919.0
  - earth-drilling E919.1
  - earth moving or scraping E919.7
  - excavating E919.7
  - involving transport under own power on highway or transport vehicle — *see* categories E810-E825 ☑, E840-E845 ☑
  - lifting (appliances) E919.2
  - metalworking E919.3
  - mining E919.1
  - prime movers, except electric motors E919.5
    - electric motors — *see* Accident, machine, by specific type of machine
  - recreational E919.8
  - specified type NEC E919.8
  - transmission E919.6
  - watercraft (deck) (engine room) (galley) (laundry) (loading) E836 ☑
  - woodworking or forming E919.4
- motor vehicle (on public highway) (traffic) E819
  - due to cataclysm — *see* categories E908 ☑, E909 ☑
  - involving
    - collision (*see also* Collision, motor vehicle) E812 ☑
    - nontraffic, not on public highway — *see* categories E820-E825 ☑
    - not involving collision — *see* categories E816-E819 ☑
- nonmotor vehicle NEC E829 ☑
  - nonroad — *see* Accident, vehicle NEC
  - road, except pedal cycle, animal-drawn vehicle, or animal being ridden E829 ☑
- nonroad vehicle NEC — *see* Accident, vehicle NEC
- not elsewhere classifiable involving
  - cable car (not on rails) E847
    - on rails E829 ☑
  - coal car in mine E846

Accident (to) — *continued*
- not elsewhere classifiable involving — *continued*
  - hand truck — *see* Accident, vehicle NEC
  - logging car E846
  - sled(ge), meaning snow or ice vehicle E848
  - tram, mine or quarry E846
  - truck
    - mine or quarry E846
    - self-propelled, industrial E846
    - station baggage E846
  - tub, mine or quarry E846
  - vehicle NEC E848
    - snow and ice E848
    - used only on industrial premises E846
  - wheelbarrow E848
- occurring (at) (in)
  - apartment E849.0
  - baseball field, diamond E849.4
  - construction site, any E849.3
  - dock E849.8
    - yard E849.3
  - dormitory E849.7
  - factory (building) (premises) E849.3
  - farm E849.1
    - buildings E849.1
    - house E849.0
  - football field E849.4
  - forest E849.8
  - garage (place of work) E849.3
    - private (home) E849.0
  - gravel pit E849.2
  - gymnasium E849.4
  - highway E849.5
  - home (private) (residential) E849.0
    - institutional E849.7
  - hospital E849.7
  - hotel E849.6
  - house (private) (residential) E849.0
    - movie E849.6
    - public E849.6
  - institution, residential E849.7
  - jail E849.7
  - mine E849.2
  - motel E849.6
  - movie house E849.6
  - office (building) E849.6
  - orphanage E849.7
  - park (public) E849.4
    - mobile home E849.8
    - trailer E849.8
  - parking lot or place E849.8
  - place
    - industrial NEC E849.3
    - parking E849.8
    - public E849.8
      - specified place NEC E849.5
    - recreational NEC E849.4
    - sport NEC E849.4
  - playground (park) (school) E849.4
  - prison E849.6
  - public building NEC E849.6
  - quarry E849.2
  - railway
    - line NEC E849.8
    - yard E849.3
  - residence
    - home (private) E849.0
  - resort (beach) (lake) (mountain) (seashore) (vacation) E849.4
  - restaurant E849.6
  - sand pit E849.2
  - school (building) (private) (public) (state) E849.6
    - reform E849.7
    - riding E849.4
  - seashore E849.8
    - resort E849.4
  - shop (place of work) E849.3
    - commercial E849.6
  - skating rink E849.4
  - sports palace E849.4
  - stadium E849.4

Accident (to) — *continued*
- occurring — *continued*
  - store E849.6
  - street E849.5
  - swimming pool (public) E849.4
    - private home or garden E849.0
  - tennis court, public E849.4
  - theatre, theater E849.6
  - trailer court E849.8
  - tunnel E849.8
    - under construction E849.2
  - warehouse E849.3
  - yard
    - dock E849.3
    - industrial E849.3
    - private (home) E849.0
    - railway E849.3
  - off-road type motor vehicle (not on public highway) NEC E821 ☑
  - on public highway — *see* categories E810-E819 ☑
- pedal cycle E826 ☑
- railway E807 ☑
  - due to cataclysm — *see* categories E908 ☑, E909 ☑
  - involving
    - avalanche E909.2
    - burning by engine, locomotive, train (*see also* Explosion, railway engine) E803 ☑
    - collision (*see also* Collision, railway) E800 ☑
    - derailment (*see also* Derailment, railway) E802 ☑
    - explosion (*see also* Explosion, railway engine) E803 ☑
    - fall (*see also* Fall, from, railway rolling stock) E804 ☑
    - fire (*see also* Explosion, railway engine) E803 ☑
    - hitting by, being struck by
      - object falling in, on, from, rolling stock, train, vehicle E806 ☑
      - rolling stock, train, vehicle E805 ☑
    - overturning, railway rolling stock, train, vehicle (*see also* Derailment, railway) E802 ☑
    - running off rails, railway (*see also* Derailment, railway) E802 ☑
    - specified circumstances NEC E806 ☑
    - train or vehicle hit by
      - avalanche E909.2
      - falling object (earth, rock, tree) E806 ☑
        - due to cataclysm — *see* categories E908 ☑, E909 ☑
      - landslide E909.2
- roller skate E885.1
- scooter (nonmotorized) E885.0
- skateboard E885.2
- ski(ing) E885.3
  - jump E884.9
  - lift or tow (with chair or gondola) E847
- snowboard E885.4
- snow vehicle, motor driven (not on public highway) E820 ☑
  - on public highway — *see* categories E810-E819 ☑
- spacecraft E845 ☑
- specified cause NEC E928.8
- street car E829 ☑
- traffic NEC E819 ☑
- vehicle NEC (with pedestrian) E848
  - battery powered
    - airport passenger vehicle E846
    - truck (baggage) (mail) E846

Accident (to) — *continued*
- vehicle — *continued*
  - powered commercial or industrial (with other vehicle or object within commercial or industrial premises) E846
  - watercraft E838 ☑
    - with
      - drowning or submersion resulting from
        - accident other than to watercraft E832 ☑
        - accident to watercraft E830 ☑
      - injury, except drowning or submersion, resulting from
        - accident other than to watercraft — *see* categories E833-E838 ☑
        - accident to watercraft E831 ☑
    - due to, caused by cataclysm — *see* categories E908 ☑, E909 ☑
  - machinery E836 ☑
- **Acid throwing** E961
- **Acosta syndrome** E902.0
- **Aeroneurosis** E902.1
- **Aero-otitis media** — *see* Effects of, air pressure
- **Aerosinusitis** — *see* Effects of, air pressure
- **After-effect, late** — *see* Late effect
- **Air**
  - blast
    - in
      - terrorism E979.2
      - war operations E993
  - embolism (traumatic) NEC E928.9
    - in
      - infusion or transfusion E874.1
      - perfusion E874.2
    - sickness E903
- **Alpine sickness** E902.0
- **Altitude sickness** — *see* Effects of, air pressure
- **Anaphylactic shock, anaphylaxis** — *see also* Table of Drugs and Chemicals E947.9
  - due to bite or sting (venomous) — *see* Bite, venomous
- **Andes disease** E902.0
- **Apoplexy**
  - heat — *see* Heat
- **Arachnidism** E905.1
- **Arson** E968.0
- **Asphyxia, asphyxiation**
  - by
    - chemical
      - in
        - terrorism E979.7
        - war operations E997.2
    - explosion — *see* Explosion
    - food (bone) (regurgitated food) (seed) E911
    - foreign object, except food E912
    - fumes
      - in
        - terrorism (chemical weapons) E979.7
        - war operations E997.2
    - gas (*see also* Table of Drugs and Chemicals)
      - in
        - terrorism E979.7
        - war operations E997.2
      - legal
        - execution E978
        - intervention (tear) E972
        - tear E972
    - mechanical means (*see also* Suffocation) E913.9
  - from
    - conflagration — *see* Conflagration
    - fire (*see also* Fire) E899
      - in
        - terrorism E979.3

Asphyxia, asphyxiation — *continued*
- from — *continued*
  - fire (*see also* Fire) — *continued*
    - in — *continued*
      - war operations E990.9
  - ignition — *see* Ignition
- **Aspiration**
  - foreign body — *see* Foreign body, aspiration
  - mucus, not of newborn (with asphyxia, obstruction respiratory passage, suffocation) E912
  - phlegm (with asphyxia, obstruction respiratory passage, suffocation) E912
  - vomitus (with asphyxia, obstruction respiratory passage, suffocation) (*see also* Foreign body, aspiration, food) E911
- **Assassination** (attempt) — *see also* Assault E968.9
- **Assault** (homicidal) (by) (in) E968.9
  - acid E961
    - swallowed E962.1
  - air gun E968.6
  - BB gun E968.6
  - bite NEC E968.8
    - of human being E968.7
  - bomb ((placed in) car or house) E965.8
    - antipersonnel E965.5
    - letter E965.7
    - petrol E965.6
  - brawl (hand) (fists) (foot) E960.0
  - burning, burns (by fire) E968.0
    - acid E961
      - swallowed E962.1
    - caustic, corrosive substance E961
      - swallowed E962.1
    - chemical from swallowing caustic, corrosive substance NEC E962.1
    - hot liquid E968.3
    - scalding E968.3
    - vitriol E961
      - swallowed E962.1
  - caustic, corrosive substance E961
    - swallowed E962.1
  - cut, any part of body E966
  - dagger E966
  - drowning E964
  - explosive(s) E965.9
    - bomb (*see also* Assault, bomb) E965.8
    - dynamite E965.8
  - fight (hand) (fists) (foot) E960.0
    - with weapon E968.9
      - blunt or thrown E968.2
      - cutting or piercing E966
      - firearm — *see* Shooting, homicide
  - fire E968.0
  - firearm(s) — *see* Shooting, homicide
  - garrotting E963
  - gunshot (wound) — *see* Shooting, homicide
  - hanging E963
  - injury NEC E968.9
  - knife E966
  - late effect of E969
  - ligature E963
  - poisoning E962.9
    - drugs or medicinals E962.0
    - gas(es) or vapors, except drugs and medicinals E962.2
    - solid or liquid substances, except drugs and medicinals E962.1
  - puncture, any part of body E966
  - pushing
    - before moving object, train, vehicle E968.5
    - from high place E968.1
  - rape E960.1
  - scalding E968.3
  - shooting — *see* Shooting, homicide
  - sodomy E960.1
  - stab, any part of body E966

☑ Additional Digit Required — Refer to the Tabular List for Digit Selection   ▽ Subterms under main terms may continue to next column or page

2007 ICD-9-CM   ▶◀ Revised Text   ● New Line   ▲ Revised Code   **Volume 2 — 339**

Assault — *continued*
strangulation E963
submersion E964
suffocation E963
transport vehicle E968.5
violence NEC E968.9
vitriol E961
swallowed E962.1
weapon E968.9
blunt or thrown E968.2
cutting or piercing E966
firearm — *see* Shooting, homicide
wound E968.9
cutting E966
gunshot — *see* Shooting, homicide
knife E966
piercing E966
puncture E966
stab E966
Attack by animal NEC E906.9
Avalanche E909.2
falling on or hitting
motor vehicle (in motion) (on public highway) E909.2
railway train E909.2
Aviators' disease E902.1

B

Barotitis, barodontalgia, barosinusitis, barotrauma (otitic) (sinus) — *see* Effects of, air pressure
Battered
baby or child (syndrome) — *see* Abuse, child; category E967 ☑
person other than baby or child — *see* Assault
Bayonet wound — *see also* Cut, by bayonet E920.3
in
legal intervention E974
terrorism E979.8
war operations E995
Bean in nose E912
Bed set on fire NEC E898.0
Beheading (by guillotine)
homicide E966
legal execution E978
Bending, injury in E927
Bends E902.0
Bite
animal NEC E906.5
other specified (except arthropod) E906.3
venomous NEC E905.9
arthropod (nonvenomous) NEC E906.4
venomous — *see* Sting
black widow spider E905.1
cat E906.3
centipede E905.4
cobra E905.0
copperhead snake E905.0
coral snake E905.0
dog E906.0
fer de lance E905.0
gila monster E905.0
human being
accidental E928.3
assault E968.7
insect (nonvenomous) E906.4
venomous — *see* Sting
krait E905.0
late effect of — *see* Late effect
lizard E906.2
venomous E905.0
mamba E905.0
marine animal
nonvenomous E906.3
snake E906.2
venomous E905.6
snake E905.0
millipede E906.4
venomous E905.4
moray eel E906.3
rat E906.1
rattlesnake E905.0
rodent, except rat E906.3

Bite — *continued*
serpent — *see* Bite, snake
shark E906.3
snake (venomous) E905.0
nonvenomous E906.2
sea E905.0
spider E905.1
nonvenomous E906.4
tarantula (venomous) E905.1
venomous NEC E905.9
by specific animal — *see* category E905 ☑
viper E905.0
water moccasin E905.0
Blast (air)
from nuclear explosion E996
in
terrorism E979.2
from nuclear explosion E979.5
underwater E979.0
war operations E993
from nuclear explosion E996
underwater E992
Blizzard E908.3
Blow E928.9
by law-enforcing agent, police (on duty) E975
with blunt object (baton) (nightstick) (stave) (truncheon) E973
Blowing up — *see also* Explosion E923.9
Brawl (hand) (fists) (foot) E960.0
Breakage (accidental)
cable of cable car not on rails E847
ladder (causing fall) E881.0
part (any) of
animal-drawn vehicle E827 ☑
ladder (causing fall) E881.0
motor vehicle
in motion (on public highway) E818 ☑
not on public highway E825 ☑
nonmotor road vehicle, except animal-drawn vehicle or pedal cycle E829 ☑
off-road type motor vehicle (not on public highway) NEC E821 ☑
on public highway E818 ☑
pedal cycle E826 ☑
scaffolding (causing fall) E881.1
snow vehicle, motor-driven (not on public highway) E820 ☑
on public highway E818 ☑
vehicle NEC — *see* Accident, vehicle
Broken
glass
fall on E888.0
injury by E920.8
power line (causing electric shock) E925.1
Bumping against, into (accidentally)
object (moving) E917.9
caused by crowd E917.1
with subsequent fall E917.6
furniture E917.3
with subsequent fall E917.7
in
running water E917.2
sports E917.0
with subsequent fall E917.5
stationary E917.4
with subsequent fall E917.8
person(s) E917.9
with fall E886.9
in sports E886.0
as, or caused by, a crowd E917.1
with subsequent fall E917.6
in sports E917.0
with fall E886.0
Burning, burns (accidental) (by) (from) (on) E899
acid (any kind) E924.1
swallowed — *see* Table of Drugs and Chemicals

Burning, burns — *continued*
bedclothes (*see also* Fire, specified NEC) E898.0
blowlamp (*see also* Fire, specified NEC) E898.1
blowtorch (*see also* Fire, specified NEC) E898.1
boat, ship, watercraft — *see* categories E830 ☑, E831 ☑, E837 ☑
bonfire (controlled) E897
uncontrolled E892
candle (*see also* Fire, specified NEC) E898.1
caustic liquid, substance E924.1
swallowed — *see* Table of Drugs and Chemicals
chemical E924.1
from swallowing caustic, corrosive substance — *see* Table of Drugs and Chemicals
in
terrorism E979.7
war operations E997.2
cigar(s) or cigarette(s) (*see also* Fire, specified NEC) E898.1
clothes, clothing, nightdress — *see* Ignition, clothes
with conflagration — *see* Conflagration
conflagration — *see* Conflagration
corrosive liquid, substance E924.1
swallowed — *see* Table of Drugs and Chemicals
electric current (*see also* Electric shock) E925.9
fire, flames (*see also* Fire) E899
flare, Verey pistol E922.8
heat
from appliance (electrical) E924.8
in local application, or packing during medical or surgical procedure E873.5
homicide (attempt) (*see also* Assault, burning) E968.0
hot
liquid E924.0
caustic or corrosive E924.1
object (not producing fire or flames) E924.8
substance E924.9
caustic or corrosive E924.1
liquid (metal) NEC E924.0
specified type NEC E924.8
tap water E924.2
ignition (*see also* Ignition)
clothes, clothing, nightdress (*see also* Ignition, clothes)
with conflagration — *see* Conflagration
highly inflammable material (benzine) (fat) (gasoline) (kerosene) (paraffin) (petrol) E894
in
terrorism E979.3
from nuclear explosion E979.5
petrol bomb E979.3
war operations (from fire-producing device or conventional weapon) E990.9
from nuclear explosion E996
petrol bomb E990.0
inflicted by other person
stated as
homicidal, intentional (*see also* Assault, burning) E968.0
undetermined whether accidental or intentional (*see also* Burn, stated as undetermined whether accidental or intentional) E988.1
internal, from swallowed caustic, corrosive liquid, substance — *see* Table of Drugs and Chemicals
lamp (*see also* Fire, specified NEC) E898.1

Burning, burns — *continued*
late effect of NEC E929.4
lighter (cigar) (cigarette) (*see also* Fire, specified NEC) E898.1
lightning E907
liquid (boiling) (hot) (molten) E924.0
caustic, corrosive (external) E924.1
swallowed — *see* Table of Drugs and Chemicals
local application of externally applied substance in medical or surgical care E873.5
machinery — *see* Accident, machine
matches (*see also* Fire, specified NEC) E898.1
medicament, externally applied E873.5
metal, molten E924.0
object (hot) E924.8
producing fire or flames — *see* Fire
oven (electric) (gas) E924.8
pipe (smoking) (*see also* Fire, specified NEC) E898.1
radiation — *see* Radiation
railway engine, locomotive, train (*see also* Explosion, railway engine) E803 ☑
self-inflicted (unspecified whether accidental or intentional) E988.1
caustic or corrosive substance NEC E988.7
stated as intentional, purposeful E958.1
caustic or corrosive substance NEC E958.7
stated as undetermined whether accidental or intentional E988.1
caustic or corrosive substance NEC E988.7
steam E924.0
pipe E924.8
substance (hot) E924.9
boiling or molten E924.0
caustic, corrosive (external) E924.1
swallowed — *see* Table of Drugs and Chemicals
suicidal (attempt) NEC E958.1
caustic substance E958.7
late effect of E959
tanning bed E926.2
therapeutic misadventure
overdose of radiation E873.2
torch, welding (*see also* Fire, specified NEC) E898.1
trash fire (*see also* Burning, bonfire) E897
vapor E924.0
vitriol E924.1
x-rays E926.3
in medical, surgical procedure — *see* Misadventure, failure, in dosage, radiation
Butted by animal E906.8

C

Cachexia, lead or saturnine E866.0
from pesticide NEC (*see also* Table of Drugs and Chemicals) E863.4
Caisson disease E902.2
Capital punishment (any means) E978
Car sickness E903
Casualty (not due to war) NEC E928.9
terrorism E979.8
war (*see also* War operations) E995
Cat
bite E906.3
scratch E906.8
Cataclysmic (any injury)
earth surface movement or eruption E909.9
specified type NEC E909.8
storm or flood resulting from storm E908.9
specified type NEC E909.8
Catching fire — *see* Ignition

☑ Additional Digit Required — Refer to the Tabular List for Digit Selection   ⌐ Subterms under main terms may continue to next column or page

340 — Volume 2   ▶◀ Revised Text   ● New Line   ▲ Revised Code   *2007 ICD-9-CM*

☑ Additional Digit Required — Refer to the Tabular List for Digit Selection
▽ Subterms under main terms may continue to next column or page

2007 ICD-9-CM   ►◄ Revised Text   ● New Line   ▲ Revised Code   Volume 2 — 341

Collision — *continued*
  pedestrian(s) — *continued*
    and — *continued*
      object not falling from, fixed or
        set in motion by any vehi-
        cle classifiable to — *contin-
        ued*
        with subsequent fall E917.6
      caused by a crowd E917.1
        with subsequent fall
          E917.6
      furniture E917.3
        with subsequent fall
          E917.7
      in
        running water E917.2
          with drowning or sub-
            mersion — *see*
            Submersion
        sports E917.0
          with subsequent fall
            E917.5
        stationary E917.4
          with subsequent fall
            E917.8
      vehicle, nonmotor, nonroad
        E848
    in
      running water E917.2
        with drowning or submersion
        — *see* Submersion
      sports E917.0
        with fall E886.0
  person(s) (using pedestrian con-
    veyance) (*see also* Collision,
    pedestrian) E917.9
  railway (rolling stock) (train) (vehicle)
    (with (subsequent) derailment,
    explosion, fall or fire) E800 ☑
    with antecedent derailment
      E802 ☑
    and
      animal (carrying person) (herd-
        ed) (unattended) E801 ☑
      another railway train or vehicle
        E800 ☑
      buffers E801 ☑
      fallen tree on railway E801 ☑
      farm machinery, nonmotor (in
        transport) (stationary)
        E801 ☑
      gates E801 ☑
      nonmotor vehicle E801 ☑
      object (fallen) (fixed) (movable)
        (moving) not falling from,
        set in motion by, aircraft
        or motor vehicle NEC
        E801 ☑
      pedal cycle E801 ☑
      pedestrian (conveyance) E805 ☑
      person (using pedestrian con-
        veyance) E805 ☑
      platform E801 ☑
      rock on railway E801 ☑
      street car E801 ☑
  snow vehicle, motor-driven (not on
    public highway) E820 ☑
    and
      animal (being ridden) (-drawn
        vehicle) E820 ☑
      another off-road motor vehicle
        E820 ☑
      other motor vehicle, not on
        public highway E820 ☑
      other object or vehicle NEC,
        fixed or movable, not set
        in motion by aircraft or
        motor vehicle on highway
        E820 ☑
      pedal cycle E820 ☑
      pedestrian (conveyance) E820 ☑
      railway train E820 ☑
    on public highway — *see* Collision,
      motor vehicle
  street car(s) E829 ☑

Collision — *continued*
  street car(s) — *continued*
    and
      animal, herded, not being rid-
        den, unattended E829 ☑
      nonmotor road vehicle NEC
        E829 ☑
      object (fallen) (fixed) (movable)
        (moving) not falling from
        or set in motion by air-
        craft, animal-drawn vehi-
        cle, animal being ridden,
        motor vehicle, pedal cycle,
        or railway train E829 ☑
      pedestrian (conveyance) E829 ☑
      person (using pedestrian con-
        veyance) E829 ☑
  vehicle
    animal-drawn — *see* Collision, an-
      imal-drawn vehicle
    motor — *see* Collision, motor vehi-
      cle
    nonmotor
      nonroad E848
        and
          another nonmotor, non-
            road vehicle E848
          object (fallen) (fixed) (mov-
            able) (moving) not
            falling from or set in
            motion by aircraft,
            animal-drawn vehi-
            cle, animal being
            ridden, motor vehi-
            cle, nonmotor road
            vehicle, pedal cycle,
            railway train, or
            streetcar E848
      road, except animal being rid-
        den, animal-drawn vehi-
        cle, or pedal cycle E829 ☑
        and
          animal, herded, not being
            ridden, unattended
            E829 ☑
          another nonmotor road
            vehicle, except ani-
            mal being ridden,
            animal-drawn vehi-
            cle, or pedal cycle
            E829 ☑
          object (fallen) (fixed) (mov-
            able) (moving) not
            falling from or set in
            motion by, aircraft,
            animal-drawn vehi-
            cle, animal being
            ridden, motor vehi-
            cle, pedal cycle, or
            railway train
            E829 ☑
          pedestrian (conveyance)
            E829 ☑
          person (using pedestrian
            conveyance)
            E829 ☑
          vehicle, nonmotor, non-
            road E829 ☑
    watercraft E838 ☑
      and
        person swimming or water ski-
          ing E838 ☑
      causing
        drowning, submersion E830 ☑
        injury except drowning, submer-
          sion E831 ☑
Combustion, spontaneous — *see* Ignition
**Complication of medical or surgical
    procedure or treatment**
  as an abnormal reaction — *see* Reac-
    tion, abnormal
  delayed, without mention of misadven-
    ture — *see* Reaction, abnormal
  due to misadventure — *see* Misadven-
    ture

Compression
  divers' squeeze E902.2
  trachea by
    food E911
    foreign body, except food E912
Conflagration
  building or structure, except private
    dwelling (barn) (church) (conva-
    lescent or residential home)
    (factory) (farm outbuilding)
    (hospital) (hotel) (institution)
    (educational) (domitory) (residen-
    tial) (school) (shop) (store) (the-
    ater) E891.9
    with or causing (injury due to)
      accident or injury NEC E891.9
        specified circumstance NEC
          E891.8
      burns, burning E891.3
      carbon monoxide E891.2
      fumes E891.2
        polyvinylchloride (PVC) or
          similar material
          E891.1
      smoke E891.2
    causing explosion E891.0
    in terrorism E979.3
  not in building or structure E892
  private dwelling (apartment) (boarding
    house) (camping place) (caravan)
    (farmhouse) (home (private))
    (house) (lodging house) (private
    garage) (rooming house) (tene-
    ment) E890.9
    with or causing (injury due to)
      accident or injury NEC E890.9
        specified circumstance NEC
          E890.8
      burns, burning E890.3
      carbon monoxide E890.2
      fumes E890.2
        polyvinylchloride (PVC) or
          similar material
          E890.1
      smoke E890.2
    causing explosion E890.0
Constriction, external
  caused by
    hair E928.4
    other object E928.5
Contact with
  dry ice E901.1
  liquid air, hydrogen, nitrogen E901.1
Cramp(s)
  Heat — *see* Heat
  swimmers (*see also* category E910)
    E910.2
    not in recreation or sport E910.3
Cranking (car) (truck) (bus) (engine), injury by E917.9
Crash
  aircraft (in transit) (powered) E841 ☑
    at landing, take-off E840 ☑
    in
      terrorism E979.1
      war operations E994
    on runway NEC E840 ☑
    stated as
      homicidal E968.8
      suicidal E958.6
      undetermined whether acciden-
        tal or intentional E988.6
    unpowered E842 ☑
  glider E842 ☑
  motor vehicle (*see also* Accident, mo-
    tor vehicle)
    homicidal E968.5
    suicidal E958.5
    undetermined whether accidental
      or intentional E988.5
Crushed (accidentally) E928.9
  between
    boat(s), ship(s), watercraft (and
      dock or pier) (without acci-
      dent to watercraft) E838 ☑

Crushed — *continued*
  between — *continued*
    boat(s), ship(s), watercraft — *contin-
      ued*
      after accident to, or collision,
        watercraft E831 ☑
    objects (moving) (stationary and
      moving) E918
  by
    avalanche NEC E909.2
    boat, ship, watercraft after accident
      to, collision, watercraft
      E831 ☑
    cave-in E916
      with asphyxiation or suffocation
        (*see also* Suffocation, due
        to, cave-in) E913.3
    crowd, human stampede E917.1
    falling
      aircraft (*see also* Accident, air-
        craft) E841 ☑
      in
        terrorism E979.1
        war operations E994
    earth, material E916
      with asphyxiation or suffoca-
        tion (*see also* Suffoca-
        tion, due to, cave-in)
        E913.3
    object E916
      on ship, watercraft E838 ☑
      while loading, unloading wa-
        tercraft E838 ☑
    landslide NEC E909.2
    lifeboat after abandoning ship
      E831 ☑
    machinery — *see* Accident, ma-
      chine
    railway rolling stock, train, vehicle
      (part of) E805 ☑
    street car E829 ☑
    vehicle NEC — *see* Accident, vehi-
      cle NEC
  in
    machinery — *see* Accident, ma-
      chine
    object E918
    transport accident — *see* categories
      E800-E848 ☑
  late effect of NEC E929.9
Cut, cutting (any part of body) (accidental) E920.9
  by
    arrow E920.8
    axe E920.4
    bayonet (*see also* Bayonet wound)
      E920.3
    blender E920.2
    broken glass E920.8
      following fall E888.0
    can opener E920.4
      powered E920.2
    chisel E920.4
    circular saw E919.4
    cutting or piercing instrument (*see
      also* category) E920 ☑
      following fall E888.0
      late effect of E929.8
    dagger E920.3
    dart E920.8
    drill — *see* Accident, caused by
      drill
    edge of stiff paper E920.8
    electric
      beater E920.2
      fan E920.2
      knife E920.2
      mixer E920.2
    fork E920.4
    garden fork E920.4
    hand saw or tool (not powered)
      E920.4
      powered E920.1
    hedge clipper E920.4
      powered E920.1
    hoe E920.4

☑ Additional Digit Required — Refer to the Tabular List for Digit Selection   ▽ Subterms under main terms may continue to next column or page

342 — Volume 2   ▶◀ Revised Text   ● New Line   ▲ Revised Code   *2007 ICD-9-CM*

Cut, cutting — *continued*
  by — *continued*
    ice pick E920.4
    knife E920.3
      electric E920.2
    lathe turnings E920.8
    lawn mower E920.4
      powered E920.0
      riding E919.8
    machine — *see* Accident, machine
    meat
      grinder E919.8
      slicer E919.8
    nails E920.8
    needle E920.4
      hypodermic E920.5
    object, edged, pointed, sharp — *see* category E920 ☑
      following fall E888.0
    paper cutter E920.4
    piercing instrument (*see also* category) E920 ☑
      late effect of E929.8
    pitchfork E920.4
    powered
      can opener E920.2
      garden cultivator E920.1
        riding E919.8
      hand saw E920.1
      hand tool NEC E920.1
      hedge clipper E920.1
      household appliance or implement E920.2
      lawn mower (hand) E920.0
        riding E919.8
      rivet gun E920.1
      staple gun E920.1
    rake E920.4
    saw
      circular E919.4
      hand E920.4
    scissors E920.4
    screwdriver E920.4
    sewing machine (electric) (powered) E920.2
      not powered E920.4
    shears E920.4
    shovel E920.4
    spade E920.4
    splinters E920.8
    sword E920.3
    tin can lid E920.8
    wood slivers E920.8
  homicide (attempt) E966
  inflicted by other person
    stated as
      intentional, homicidal E966
      undetermined whether accidental or intentional E986
  late effect of NEC E929.8
  legal
    execution E978
    intervention E974
  self-inflicted (unspecified whether accidental or intentional) E986
    stated as intentional, purposeful E956
  stated as undetermined whether accidental or intentional E986
  suicidal (attempt) E956
  terrorism E979.8
  war operations E995
Cyclone E908.1

D

Death due to injury occurring one year or more previous — *see* Late effect
Decapitation (accidental circumstances) NEC E928.9
  homicidal E966
  legal execution (by guillotine) E978
Deprivation — *see also* Privation
  homicidal intent E968.4

Derailment (accidental)
  railway (rolling stock) (train) (vehicle) (with subsequent collision) E802 ☑
    with
      collision (antecedent) (*see also* Collision, railway) E800 ☑
      explosion (subsequent) (without antecedent collision) E802 ☑
        antecedent collision E803 ☑
      fall (without collision (antecedent)) E802 ☑
      fire (without collision (antecedent)) E802 ☑
  street car E829 ☑
Descent
  parachute (voluntary) (without accident to aircraft) E844 ☑
    due to accident to aircraft — *see* categories E840-E842 ☑
Desertion
  child, with intent to injure or kill E968.4
  helpless person, infant, newborn E904.0
    with intent to injure or kill E968.4
Destitution — *see* Privation
Disability, late effect or sequela of injury — *see* Late effect
Disease
  Andes E902.0
  aviators' E902.1
  caisson E902.2
  range E902.0
Divers' disease, palsy, paralysis, squeeze E902.0
Dog bite E906.0
Dragged by
  cable car (not on rails) E847
    on rails E829 ☑
  motor vehicle (on highway) E814 ☑
    not on highway, nontraffic accident E825 ☑
  street car E829 ☑
Drinking poison (accidental) — *see* Table of Drugs and Chemicals
Drowning — *see* Submersion
Dust in eye E914

E

Earth falling (on) (with asphyxia or suffocation (by pressure)) — *see also* Suffocation, due to, cave-in E913.3
  as, or due to, a cataclysm (involving any transport vehicle) — *see* categories E908 ☑, E909
  not due to cataclysmic action E913.3
    motor vehicle (in motion) (on public highway) E813 ☑
      not on public highway E825 ☑
    nonmotor road vehicle NEC E829 ☑
    pedal cycle E826 ☑
    railway rolling stock, train, vehicle E806 ☑
    street car E829 ☑
  struck or crushed by E916
    with asphyxiation or suffocation E913.3
    with injury other than asphyxia, suffocation E916
Earthquake (any injury) E909.0
Effect(s) (adverse) of
  air pressure E902.9
    at high altitude E902.9
      in aircraft E902.1
    residence or prolonged visit (causing conditions classifiable to E902.0) E902.0
    due to
      diving E902.2
      specified cause NEC E902.8
    in aircraft E902.1

Effect(s) (adverse) of — *continued*
  cold, excessive (exposure to) (*see also* Cold, exposure to) E901.9
  heat (excessive) (*see also* Heat) E900.9
  hot
    place — *see* Heat
    weather E900.0
  insulation — *see* Heat
  late — *see* Late effect of
  motion E903
  nuclear explosion or weapon
    in
      terrorism E979.5
      war operations (blast) (fireball) (heat) (radiation) (direct) (secondary) E996
  radiation — *see* Radiation
  terrorism, secondary E979.9
  travel E903
Electric shock, electrocution (accidental) (from exposed wire, faulty appliance, high voltage cable, live rail, open socket) (by) (in) E925.9
  appliance or wiring
    domestic E925.0
    factory E925.2
    farm (building) E925.8
      house E925.0
    home E925.0
    industrial (conductor) (control apparatus) (transformer) E925.2
    outdoors E925.8
    public building E925.8
    residential institution E925.8
    school E925.8
    specified place NEC E925.8
  caused by other person
    stated as
      intentional, homicidal E968.8
      undetermined whether accidental or intentional E988.4
  electric power generating plant, distribution station E925.1
  homicide (attempt) E968.8
  legal execution E978
  lightning E907
  machinery E925.9
    domestic E925.0
    factory E925.2
    farm E925.8
    home E925.0
  misadventure in medical or surgical procedure
    in electroshock therapy E873.4
  self-inflicted (undetermined whether accidental or intentional) E988.4
    stated as intentional E958.4
  stated as undetermined whether accidental or intentional E988.4
  suicidal (attempt) E958.4
  transmission line E925.1
Electrocution — *see* Electric shock
Embolism
  air (traumatic) NEC — *see* Air, embolism
Encephalitis
  lead or saturnine E866.0
    from pesticide NEC E863.4
Entanglement
  in
    bedclothes, causing suffocation E913.0
    wheel of pedal cycle E826 ☑
Entry of foreign body, material, any — *see* Foreign body
Execution, legal (any method) E978
Exhaustion
  cold — *see* Cold, exposure to
  due to excessive exertion E927
  heat — *see* Heat
Explosion (accidental) (in) (of) (on) E923.9
  acetylene E923.2
  aerosol can E921.8

Explosion — *continued*
  aircraft (in transit) (powered) E841 ☑
    at landing, take-off E840 ☑
    in
      terrorism E979.1
      war operations E994
    unpowered E842 ☑
  air tank (compressed) (in machinery) E921.1
  anesthetic gas in operating theatre E923.2
  automobile tire NEC E921.8
    causing transport accident — *see* categories E810-E825 ☑
  blasting (cap) (materials) E923.1
  boiler (machinery), not on transport vehicle E921.0
    steamship — *see* Explosion, watercraft
  bomb E923.8
    in
      terrorism E979.2
      war operations E993
        after cessation of hostilities E998
        atom, hydrogen or nuclear E996
        injury by fragments from E991.9
          antipersonnel bomb E991.3
  butane E923.2
  caused by
    other person
      stated as
        intentional, homicidal — *see* Assault, explosive
        undetermined whether accidental or homicidal E985.5
  coal gas E923.2
  detonator E923.1
  dynamite E923.1
  explosive (material) NEC E923.9
    gas(es) E923.2
    missile E923.8
      in
        terrorism E979.2
        war operations E993
          injury by fragments from E991.9
            antipersonnel bomb E991.3
    used in blasting operations E923.1
  fire-damp E923.2
  fireworks E923.0
  gas E923.2
    cylinder (in machinery) E921.1
    pressure tank (in machinery) E921.1
  gasoline (fumes) (tank) not in moving motor vehicle E923.2
  grain store (military) (munitions) E923.8
  grenade E923.8
    in
      terrorism E979.2
      war operations E993
        injury by fragments from E991.9
  homicide (attempt) — *see* Assault, explosive
  hot water heater, tank (in machinery) E921.0
  in mine (of explosive gases) NEC E923.2
  late effect of NEC E929.8
  machinery (*see also* Accident, machine)
    pressure vessel — *see* Explosion, pressure vessel
  methane E923.2
  missile E923.8
    in
      terrorism E979.2
      war operations E993

☑ Additional Digit Required — Refer to the Tabular List for Digit Selection
▽ Subterms under main terms may continue to next column or page
2007 ICD-9-CM   ▶◀ Revised Text   ● New Line   ▲ Revised Code   **Volume 2 — 343**

Cut, cutting — Explosion

Explosion — *continued*
missile — *continued*
in — *continued*
war operations — *continued*
injury by fragments from
E991.9
motor vehicle (part of)
in motion (on public highway)
E818 ☑
not on public highway E825 ☑
munitions (dump) (factory) E923.8
in
terrorism E979.2
war operations E993
of mine E923.8
in
terrorism
at sea or in harbor E979.0
land E979.2
marine E979.0
war operations
after cessation of hostilities
E998
at sea or in harbor E992
land E993
after cessation of hostilities E998
injury by fragments from
E991.9
marine E992
own weapons
in
terrorism (*see also* Suicide)
E979.2
war operations E993
injury by fragments from
E991.9
antipersonnel bomb
E991.3
pressure
cooker E921.8
gas tank (in machinery) E921.1
vessel (in machinery) E921.9
on transport vehicle — *see* categories E800-E848 ☑
specified type NEC E921.8
propane E923.2
railway engine, locomotive, train
(boiler) (with subsequent collision, derailment, fall) E803 ☑
with
collision (antecedent) (*see also*
Collision, railway) E800 ☑
derailment (antecedent) E802 ☑
fire (without antecedent collision
or derailment) E803 ☑
secondary fire resulting from — *see*
Fire
self-inflicted (unspecified whether accidental or intentional) E985.5
stated as intentional, purposeful
E955.5
shell (artillery) E923.8
in
terrorism E979.2
war operations E993
injury by fragments from
E991.9
stated as undetermined whether
caused accidentally or purposely inflicted E985.5
steam or water lines (in machinery)
E921.0
suicide (attempted) E955.5
terrorism — *see* Terrorism, explosion
torpedo E923.8
in
terrorism E979.0
war operations E992
transport accident — *see* categories
E800-E848 ☑
war operations — *see* War operations,
explosion
watercraft (boiler) E837 ☑

Explosion — *continued*
watercraft — *continued*
causing drowning, submersion (after jumping from watercraft)
E830 ☑
Exposure (weather) (conditions) (rain)
(wind) E904.3
with homicidal intent E968.4
excessive E904.3
cold (*see also* Cold, exposure to)
E901.9
self-inflicted — *see* Cold, exposure to, self-inflicted
heat (*see also* Heat) E900.9
helpless person, infant, newborn due
to abandonment or neglect
E904.0
noise E928.1
prolonged in deep-freeze unit or refrigerator E901.1
radiation — *see* Radiation
resulting from transport accident —
see categories E800-E848 ☑
smoke from, due to
fire — *see* Fire
tobacco, second-hand E869.4
vibration E928.2

F

Fallen on by
animal (horse) (not being ridden)
E906.8
being ridden (in sport or transport)
E828 ☑
Fall, falling (accidental) E888.9
building E916
burning E891.8
private E890.8
down
escalator E880.0
ladder E881.0
in boat, ship, watercraft E833 ☑
staircase E880.9
stairs, steps — *see* Fall, from,
stairs
earth (with asphyxia or suffocation (by
pressure)) (*see also* Earth,
falling) E913.3
from, off
aircraft (at landing, take-off) (in-
transit) (while alighting,
boarding) E843 ☑
resulting from accident to aircraft — *see* categories
E840-E842 ☑
animal (in sport or transport)
E828 ☑
animal-drawn vehicle E827 ☑
balcony E882
bed E884.4
bicycle E826 ☑
boat, ship, watercraft (into water)
E832 ☑
after accident to, collision, fire
on E830 ☑
and subsequently struck by
(part of) boat E831 ☑
and subsequently struck by
(part of) while alighting,
boat E831 ☑
burning, crushed, sinking
E830 ☑
and subsequently struck by
(part of) boat E831 ☑
bridge E882
building E882
burning (uncontrolled fire)
E891.8
in terrorism E979.3
private E890.8
bunk in boat, ship, watercraft
E834 ☑
due to accident to watercraft
E831 ☑
cable car (not on rails) E847

Fall, falling — *continued*
from, off — *continued*
cable car — *continued*
on rails E829 ☑
car — *see* Fall from motor vehicle
chair E884.2
cliff E884.1
commode E884.6
curb (sidewalk) E880.1
elevation aboard ship E834 ☑
due to accident to ship E831 ☑
embankment E884.9
escalator E880.0
fire escape E882
flagpole E882
furniture NEC E884.5
gangplank (into water) (*see also*
Fall, from, boat) E832 ☑
to deck, dock E834 ☑
hammock on ship E834 ☑
due to accident to watercraft
E831 ☑
haystack E884.9
high place NEC E884.9
stated as undetermined whether
accidental or intentional
— *see* Jumping, from,
high place
horse (in sport or transport)
E828 ☑
in-line skates E885.1
ladder E881.0
in boat, ship, watercraft E833 ☑
due to accident to watercraft
E831 ☑
machinery (*see also* Accident, machine)
not in operation E884.9
motor vehicle (in motion) (on public
highway) E818 ☑
not on public highway E825 ☑
stationary, except while
alighting, boarding,
entering, leaving
E884.9
while alighting, boarding,
entering, leaving
E824 ☑
stationary, except while alighting, boarding, entering,
leaving E884.9
while alighting, boarding, entering, leaving, except off-
road type motor vehicle
E817 ☑
off-road type — *see* Fall,
from, off-road type mo-
tor vehicle
nonmotor road vehicle (while
alighting, boarding) NEC
E829 ☑
stationary, except while alighting, boarding, entering,
leaving E884.9
off road type motor vehicle (not on
public highway) NEC E821 ☑
on public highway E818 ☑
while alighting, boarding,
entering, leaving
E817 ☑
snow vehicle — *see* Fall from
snow vehicle, motor-driv-
en
one
deck to another on ship E834 ☑
due to accident to ship
E831 ☑
level to another NEC E884.9
boat, ship, or watercraft
E834 ☑
due to accident to water-
craft E831 ☑
pedal cycle E826 ☑
playground equipment E884.0

Fall, falling — *continued*
from, off — *continued*
railway rolling stock, train, vehicle
(while alighting, boarding)
E804 ☑
with
collision (*see also* Collision,
railway) E800 ☑
derailment (*see also* Derailment, railway) E802 ☑
explosion (*see also* Explosion, railway engine)
E803 ☑
rigging (aboard ship) E834 ☑
due to accident to watercraft
E831 ☑
roller skates E885.1
scaffolding E881.1
scooter (nonmotorized) E885.0
sidewalk (curb) E880.1
moving E885.9
skateboard E885.2
skis E885.3
snowboard E885.4
snow vehicle, motor-driven (not on
public highway) E820 ☑
on public highway E818 ☑
while alighting, boarding,
entering, leaving
E817 ☑
stairs, steps E880.9
boat, ship, watercraft E833 ☑
due to accident to watercraft
E831 ☑
motor bus, motor vehicle — *see*
Fall, from, motor vehicle,
while alighting, boarding
street car E829 ☑
stationary vehicle NEC E884.9
stepladder E881.0
street car (while boarding, alighting) E829 ☑
stationary, except while boarding or alighting E884.9
structure NEC E882
burning (uncontrolled fire)
E891.8
in terrorism E979.3
table E884.9
toilet E884.6
tower E882
tree E884.9
turret E882
vehicle NEC (*see also* Accident, vehicle NEC)
stationary E884.9
viaduct E882
wall E882
wheelchair E884.3
window E882
in, on
aircraft (at landing, take-off) (in-
transit) E843 ☑
resulting from accident to aircraft — *see* categories
E840-E842 ☑
boat, ship, watercraft E835 ☑
due to accident to watercraft
E831 ☑
one level to another NEC
E834 ☑
on ladder, stairs E833 ☑
cutting or piercing instrument or
machine E888.0
deck (of boat, ship, watercraft)
E835 ☑
due to accident to watercraft
E831 ☑
escalator E880.0
gangplank E835 ☑
glass, broken E888.0
knife E888.0
ladder E881.0
in boat, ship, watercraft E833 ☑
due to accident to watercraft
E831 ☑

☑ Additional Digit Required — Refer to the Tabular List for Digit Selection

☑ Subterms under main terms may continue to next column or page

▶◀ Revised Text   ● New Line   ▲ Revised Code

Fall, falling — Foreign body, object or material

☑ Additional Digit Required — Refer to the Tabular List for Digit Selection   ▽ Subterms under main terms may continue to next column or page

2007 ICD-9-CM   ►◄ Revised Text   ● New Line   ▲ Revised Code   **Volume 2 — 345**

Foreign body, object or material —
continued
  vagina (causing injury or obstruction)
    E915
Found dead, injured
  from exposure (to) — *see* Exposure
  on
    public highway E819 ☑
    railway right of way E807 ☑
Fracture (circumstances unknown or
    unspecified) E887
  due to specified external means — *see*
    manner of accident
  late effect of NEC E929.3
  occurring in water transport NEC
    E835 ☑
Freezing — *see* Cold, exposure to
Frostbite E901.0
  due to manmade conditions E901.1
Frozen — *see* Cold, exposure to

G

Garrotting, homicidal (attempted) E963
Gored E906.8
Gunshot wound — *see also* Shooting
    E922.9

H

Hailstones, injury by E904.3
Hairball (stomach) (with obstruction)
    E915
Hanged himself — *see also* Hanging,
    self-inflicted E983.0
Hang gliding E842 ☑
Hanging (accidental) E913.8
  caused by other person
    in accidental circumstances
      E913.8
    stated as
      intentional, homicidal E963
      undetermined whether acciden-
        tal or intentional E983.0
  homicide (attempt) E963
  in bed or cradle E913.0
  legal execution E978
  self-inflicted (unspecified whether ac-
    cidental or intentional) E983.0
    in accidental circumstances
      E913.8
    stated as intentional, purposeful
      E953.0
    stated as undetermined whether acci-
      dental or intentional E983.0
  suicidal (attempt) E953.0
Heat (apoplexy) (collapse) (cramps) (ef-
    fects of) (excessive) (exhaustion)
    (fever) (prostration) (stroke) E900.9
  due to
    manmade conditions (as listed in
      E900.1, except boat, ship,
      watercraft) E900.1
    weather (conditions) E900.0
  from
    electric heating appartus causing
      burning E924.8
    nuclear explosion
      in
        terrorism E979.5
        war operations E996
    generated in, boiler, engine, evapora-
      tor, fire room of boat, ship, wa-
      tercraft E838 ☑
  inappropriate in local application or
    packing in medical or surgical
    procedure E873.5
  late effect of NEC E989
Hemorrhage
  delayed following medical or surgical
    treatment without mention of
    misadventure — *see* Reaction,
    abnormal
  during medical or surgical treatment
    as misadventure — *see* Misad-
    venture, cut

High
  altitude, effects E902.9
  level of radioactivity, effects — *see*
    Radiation
  pressure effects (*see also* Effects of,
    air pressure)
    from rapid descent in water (caus-
      ing caisson or divers' disease,
      palsy, or paralysis) E902.2
  temperature, effects — *see* Heat
Hit, hitting (accidental) by
  aircraft (propeller) (without accident
    to aircraft) E844 ☑
    unpowered E842 ☑
  avalanche E909.2
  being thrown against object in or part
    of
    motor vehicle (in motion) (on public
      highway) E818 ☑
      not on public highway E825 ☑
    nonmotor road vehicle NEC
      E829 ☑
    street car E829 ☑
  boat, ship, watercraft
    after fall from watercraft E838 ☑
      damaged, involved in accident
        E831 ☑
    while swimming, water skiing
      E838 ☑
  bullet (*see also* Shooting) E922.9
    from air gun E922.4
    in
      terrorism E979.4
      war operations E991.2
        rubber E991.0
  flare, Verey pistol (*see also* Shooting)
    E922.8
  hailstones E904.3
  landslide E909.2
  law-enforcing agent (on duty) E975
    with blunt object (baton) (night
      stick) (stave) (truncheon)
      E973
  machine — *see* Accident, machine
  missile
    firearm (*see also* Shooting) E922.9
    in
      terrorism — *see* Terrorism,
        missile
      war operations — *see* War oper-
        ations, missile
  motor vehicle (on public highway)
    (traffic accident) E814 ☑
    not on public highway, nontraffic
      accident E822 ☑
  nonmotor road vehicle NEC E829 ☑
  object
    falling E916
      from, in, on
        aircraft E844 ☑
          due to accident to aircraft
            — *see* categories
            E840-E842 ☑
          unpowered E842 ☑
        boat, ship, watercraft
          E838 ☑
          due to accident to water-
            craft E831 ☑
        building E916
          burning (uncontrolled fire)
            E891.8
            in terrorism E979.3
            private E890.8
        cataclysmic
          earth surface movement
            or eruption E909.9
          storm E908.9
        cave-in E916
          with asphyxiation or suffo-
            cation (*see also* Suf-
            focation, due to,
            cave-in) E913.3
        earthquake E909.0
        motor vehicle (in motion) (on
          public highway)
          E818 ☑

Hit, hitting by — *continued*
  object — *continued*
    falling — *continued*
      from, in, on — *continued*
        motor vehicle — *contin-
          ued*
          not on public highway
            E825 ☑
          stationary E916
        nonmotor road vehicle NEC
          E829 ☑
        pedal cycle E826 ☑
        railway rolling stock, train,
          vehicle E806 ☑
        street car E829 ☑
        structure, burning NEC
          E891.8
        vehicle, stationary E916
    moving NEC — *see* Striking
      against, object
    projected NEC — *see* Striking
      against, object
    set in motion by
      compressed air or gas, spring,
        striking, throwing — *see*
        Striking against, object
      explosion — *see* Explosion
    thrown into, on, or towards
      motor vehicle (in motion) (on
        public highway) E818 ☑
        not on public highway
          E825 ☑
      nonmotor road vehicle NEC
        E829 ☑
      pedal cycle E826 ☑
      street car E829 ☑
  off-road type motor vehicle (not on
    public highway) E821 ☑
    on public highway E814 ☑
  other person(s) E917.9
    with blunt or thrown object E917.9
      in sports E917.0
        with subsequent fall E917.5
      intentionally, homicidal E968.2
    as, or caused by, a crowd E917.1
      with subsequent fall E917.6
    in sports E917.0
  pedal cycle E826 ☑
  police (on duty) E975
    with blunt object (baton) (night-
      stick) (stave) (truncheon)
      E973
  railway, rolling stock, train, vehicle
    (part of) E805 ☑
  shot — *see* Shooting
  snow vehicle, motor-driven (not on
    public highway) E820 ☑
    on public highway E814 ☑
  street car E829 ☑
  vehicle NEC — *see* Accident, vehicle
    NEC
Homicide, homicidal (attempt) (justifi-
    able) — *see also* Assault E968.9
Hot
  liquid, object, substance, accident
    caused by (*see also* Accident,
    caused by, hot, by type of sub-
    stance)
    late effect of E929.8
  place, effects — *see* Heat
  weather, effects E900.0
Humidity, causing problem E904.3
Hunger E904.1
  resulting from
    abandonment or neglect E904.0
    transport accident — *see* categories
      E800-E848 ☑
Hurricane (any injury) E908.0
Hypobarism, hypobaropathy — *see*
    Effects of, air pressure
Hypothermia — *see* Cold, exposure to

I

Ictus
  caloris — *see* Heat

Ictus — *continued*
  solaris E900.0
Ignition (accidental)
  anesthetic gas in operating theatre
    E923.2
  bedclothes
    with
      conflagration — *see* Conflagra-
        tion
      ignition (of)
        clothing — *see* Ignition,
          clothes
        highly inflammable material
          (benzine) (fat) (gasoline)
          (kerosene) (paraffin)
          (petrol) E894
  benzine E894
  clothes, clothing (from controlled fire)
    (in building) E893.9
    with conflagration — *see* Conflagra-
      tion
    from
      bonfire E893.2
      highly inflammable material
        E894
      sources or material as listed in
        E893.8
      trash fire E893.2
      uncontrolled fire — *see* Confla-
        gration
    in
      private dwelling E893.0
      specified building or structure,
        except private dwelling
        E893.1
    not in building or structure E893.2
  explosive material — *see* Explosion
  fat E894
  gasoline E894
  kerosene E894
  material
    explosive — *see* Explosion
    highly inflammable E894
      with conflagration — *see* Confla-
        gration
      with explosion E923.2
  nightdress — *see* Ignition, clothes
  paraffin E894
  petrol E894
Immersion — *see* Submersion
Implantation of quills of porcupine
    E906.8
Inanition (from) E904.9
  hunger — *see* Lack of, food
  resulting from homicidal intent
    E968.4
  thirst — *see* Lack of, water
Inattention after, at birth E904.0
  homicidal, infanticidal intent E968.4
Infanticide — *see also* Assault
Ingestion
  foreign body (causing injury) (with
    obstruction) — *see* Foreign
    body, alimentary canal
  poisonous substance NEC — *see* Ta-
    ble of Drugs and Chemicals
Inhalation
  excessively cold substance, manmade
    E901.1
  foreign body — *see* Foreign body, aspi-
    ration
  liquid air, hydrogen, nitrogen E901.1
  mucus, not of newborn (with asphyx-
    ia, obstruction respiratory pas-
    sage, suffocation) E912
  phlegm (with asphyxia, obstruction
    respiratory passage, suffocation)
    E912
  poisonous gas — *see* Table of Drugs
    and Chemicals
  smoke from, due to
    fire — *see* Fire
    tobacco, second-hand E869.4
  vomitus (with asphyxia, obstruction
    respiratory passage, suffocation)
    E911

Injury, injured (accidental(ly)) NEC
E928.9
by, caused by, from
air rifle (BB gun) E922.4
animal (not being ridden) NEC
E906.9
being ridden (in sport or transport) E828 ☑
assault (see also Assault) E968.9
avalanche E909.2
bayonet (see also Bayonet wound)
E920.3
being thrown against some part of,
or object in
motor vehicle (in motion) (on
public highway) E818 ☑
not on public highway
E825 ☑
nonmotor road vehicle NEC
E829 ☑
off-road motor vehicle NEC
E821 ☑
railway train E806 ☑
snow vehicle, motor-driven
E820 ☑
street car E829 ☑
bending E927
bite, human E928.3
broken glass E920.8
bullet — see Shooting
cave-in (see also Suffocation, due
to, cave-in) E913.3
without asphyxiation or suffocation E916
earth surface movement or
eruption E909.9
storm E908.9
cloudburst E908.8
cutting or piercing instrument (see
also Cut) E920.9
cyclone E908.1
earthquake E909.0
earth surface movement or eruption E909.9
electric current (see also Electric
shock) E925.9
explosion (see also Explosion)
E923.9
fire — see Fire
flare, Verey pistol E922.8
flood E908.2
foreign body — see Foreign body
hailstones E904.3
hurricane E908.0
landslide E909.2
law-enforcing agent, police, in
course of legal intervention
— see Legal intervention
lightning E907
live rail or live wire — see Electric
shock
machinery (see also Accident, machine)
aircraft, without accident to aircraft E844 ☑
boat, ship, watercraft (deck)
(engine room) (galley)
(laundry) (loading)
E836 ☑
missile
explosive E923.8
firearm — see Shooting
in
terrorism — see Terrorism,
missile
war operations — see War
operations, missile
moving part of motor vehicle (in
motion) (on public highway)
E818 ☑
not on public highway, nontraffic accident E825 ☑
while alighting, boarding, entering, leaving — see Fall,
from, motor vehicle, while
alighting, boarding

Injury, injured — continued
by, caused by, from — continued
nail E920.8
needle (sewing) E920.4
hypodermic E920.5
noise E928.1
object
fallen on
motor vehicle (in motion) (on
public highway)
E818 ☑
not on public highway
E825 ☑
falling — see Hit by, object,
falling
paintball gun E922.5
radiation — see Radiation
railway rolling stock, train, vehicle
(part of) E805 ☑
door or window E806 ☑
rotating propeller, aircraft E844 ☑
rough landing of off-road type motor vehicle (after leaving
ground or rough terrain)
E821 ☑
snow vehicle E820 ☑
saber (see also Wound, saber)
E920.3
shot — see Shooting
sound waves E928.1
splinter or sliver, wood E920.8
straining E927
street car (door) E829 ☑
suicide (attempt) E958.9
sword E920.3
terrorism — see Terrorism
third rail — see Electric shock
thunderbolt E907
tidal wave E909.4
caused by storm E908.0
tornado E908.1
torrential rain E908.2
twisting E927
vehicle NEC — see Accident, vehicle NEC
vibration E928.2
volcanic eruption E909.1
weapon burst, in war operations
E993
weightlessness (in spacecraft, real
or simulated) E928.0
wood splinter or sliver E920.8
due to
civil insurrection — see War operations
occurring after cessation of
hostilities E998
terrorism — see Terrorism
war operations — see War operations
occurring after cessation of
hostilities E998
homicidal (see also Assault) E968.9
inflicted (by)
in course of arrest (attempted),
suppression of disturbance,
maintenance of order, by law
enforcing agents — see Legal
intervention
law-enforcing agent (on duty) —
see Legal intervention
other person
stated as
accidental E928.9
homicidal, intentional — see
Assault
undetermined whether accidental or intentional —
see Injury, stated as
undetermined
police (on duty) — see Legal intervention
in, on
civil insurrection — see War operations
fight E960.0

Injury, injured — continued
in, on — continued
parachute descent (voluntary)
(without accident to aircraft)
E844 ☑
with accident to aircraft — see
categories E840-E842 ☑
public highway E819 ☑
railway right of way E807 ☑
terrorism — see Terrorism
war operations — see War operations
late effect of E929.9
purposely (inflicted) by other person(s)
— see Assault
self-inflicted (unspecified whether accidental or intentional) E988.9
stated as
accidental E928.9
intentionally, purposely E958.9
specified cause NEC E928.8
stated as
hanging E983.0
knife E986
late effect of E989
puncture (any part of body) E986
shooting — see Shooting, stated as
undetermined whether accidental or intentional
specified means NEC E988.8
stab (any part of body) E986
strangulation — see Suffocation,
stated as undetermined
whether accidental or intentional
submersion E984
suffocation — see Suffocation,
stated as undetermined
whether accidental or intentional
undetermined whether accidentally
or purposely inflicted (by)
E988.9
cut (any part of body) E986
cutting or piercing instrument
(classifiable to E920)
E986
drowning E984
explosive(s) (missile) E985.5
falling from high place E987.9
manmade structure, except
residential E987.1
natural site E987.2
residential premises E987.0
to child due to criminal abortion
E968.8
Insufficient nourishment — see also
Lack of, food
homicidal intent E968.4
Insulation, effects — see Heat
Interruption of respiration by
food lodged in esophagus E911
foreign body, except food, in esophagus E912
Intervention, legal — see Legal intervention
Intoxication, drug or poison — see
Table of Drugs and Chemicals
Irradiation — see Radiation

J

Jammed (accidentally)
between objects (moving) (stationary
and moving) E918
in object E918
**Jumped or fell from high place, so
stated** — see Jumping, from, high
place, stated as
in undetermined circumstances
Jumping
before train, vehicle or other moving
object (unspecified whether accidental or intentional) E988.0
stated as
intentional, purposeful E958.0
suicidal (attempt) E958.0

Jumping — continued
from
aircraft
by parachute (voluntarily)
(without accident to air-
craft) E844 ☑
due to accident to aircraft — see
categories E840-E842 ☑
boat, ship, watercraft (into water)
after accident to, fire on, watercraft E830 ☑
and subsequently struck by
(part of) boat E831 ☑
burning, crushed, sinking
E830 ☑
and subsequently struck by
(part of) boat E831 ☑
voluntarily, without accident (to
boat) with injury other
than drowning or submer-
sion E883.0
building (see also Jumping, from,
high place)
burning (uncontrolled fire)
E891.8
in terrorism E979.3
private E890.8
cable car (not on rails) E847
on rails E829 ☑
high place
in accidental circumstances or
in sport — see categories
E880-E884 ☑
stated as
with intent to injure self
E957.9
man-made structures
NEC E957.1
natural sites E957.2
residential premises
E957.0
in undetermined circum-
stances E987.9
man-made structures
NEC E987.1
natural sites E987.2
residential premises
E987.0
suicidal (attempt) E957.9
man-made structures
NEC E957.1
natural sites E957.1
residential premises
E957.0
motor vehicle (in motion) (on public
highway) — see Fall, from,
motor vehicle
nonmotor road vehicle NEC
E829 ☑
street car E829 ☑
structure (see also Jumping, from,
high place)
burning NEC (uncontrolled fire)
E891.8
in terrorism E979.3
into water
with injury other than drowning or
submersion E883.0
drowning or submersion — see
Submersion
from, off, watercraft — see Jumping, from, boat
Justifiable homicide — see Assault

K

Kicked by
animal E906.8
person(s) (accidentally) E917.9
with intent to injure or kill E960.0
as, or caused by a crowd E917.1
with subsequent fall E917.6
in fight E960.0
in sports E917.0
with subsequent fall E917.5
Kicking against
object (moving) E917.9

☑ Additional Digit Required — Refer to the Tabular List for Digit Selection   ▽ Subterms under main terms may continue to next column or page

2007 ICD-9-CM   ▶◀ Revised Text   ● New Line   ▲ Revised Code   **Volume 2 — 347**

Kicking against — continued
  object — continued
    in sports E917.0
      with subsequent fall E917.5
    stationary E917.4
      with subsequent fall E917.8
  person — see Striking against, person
Killed, killing (accidentally) NEC — see
    also Injury E928.9
  in
    action — see War operations
    brawl, fight (hand) (fists) (foot)
      E960.0
      by weapon (see also Assault)
        cutting, piercing E966
        firearm — see Shooting,
          homicide
  self
    stated as
      accident E928.9
      suicide — see Suicide
    unspecified whether accidental or
      suicidal E988.9
Knocked down (accidentally) (by) NEC
    E928.9
  animal (not being ridden) E906.8
    being ridden (in sport or transport)
      E828 ☑
  blast from explosion (see also Explo-
    sion) E923.9
  crowd, human stampede E917.6
  late effect of — see Late effect
  person (accidentally) E917.9
    in brawl, fight E960.0
    in sports E917.5
  transport vehicle — see vehicle in-
    volved under Hit by
  while boxing E917.5

L

Laceration NEC E928.9
Lack of
  air (refrigerator or closed place), suffo-
    cation by E913.2
  care (helpless person) (infant) (new-
    born) E904.0
    homicidal intent E968.4
  food except as result of transport acci-
    dent E904.1
    helpless person, infant, newborn
      due to
      abandonment or neglect E904.0
  water except as result of transport
    accident E904.2
    helpless person, infant, newborn
      due to
      abandonment or neglect E904.0
Landslide E909.2
  falling on, hitting
    motor vehicle (any) (in motion) (on
      or off public highway) E909.2
    railway rolling stock, train, vehicle
      E909.2
Late effect of
  accident NEC (accident classifiable to
    E928.9) E929.9
    specified NEC (accident classifiable
      to E910–E928.8) E929.8
  assault E969
  fall, accidental (accident classifiable
    to E880–E888) E929.3
  fire, accident caused by (accident
    classifiable to E890–E899)
    E929.4
  homicide, attempt (any means) E969
  injury due to terrorism E999.1
  injury undetermined whether acciden-
    tally or purposely inflicted (in-
    jury classifiable to E980–E988)
    E989
  legal intervention (injury classifiable
    to E970–E976) E977

Late effect of — continued
  medical or surgical procedure, test or
    therapy
    as, or resulting in, or from
      abnormal or delayed reaction or
        complication — see Reac-
        tion, abnormal
      misadventure — see Misadven-
        ture
  motor vehicle accident (accident clas-
    sifiable to E810–E825) E929.0
  natural or environmental factor, acci-
    dent due to (accident classifiable
    to E900–E909) E929.5
  poisoning, accidental (accident classi-
    fiable to E850–E858,
    E860–E869) E929.2
  suicide, attempt (any means) E959
  transport accident NEC (accident
    classifiable to E800–E807,
    E826–E838, E840–E848)
    E929.1
  war operations, injury due to (injury
    classifiable to E990–E998)
    E999.9
Launching pad accident E845 ☑
Legal
  execution, any method E978
  intervention (by) (injury from) E976
    baton E973
    bayonet E974
    blow E975
    blunt object (baton) (nightstick)
      (stave) (truncheon) E973
    cutting or piercing instrument
      E974
    dynamite E971
    execution, any method E973
    explosive(s) (shell) E971
    firearm(s) E970
    gas (asphyxiation) (poisoning) (tear)
      E972
    grenade E971
    late effect of E977
    machine gun E970
    manhandling E975
    mortar bomb E971
    nightstick E973
    revolver E970
    rifle E970
    specified means NEC E975
    stabbing E974
    stave E973
    truncheon E973
Lifting, injury in E927
Lightning (shock) (stroke) (struck by)
    E907
Liquid (noncorrosive) in eye E914
  corrosive E924.1
Loss of control
  motor vehicle (on public highway)
    (without antecedent collision)
    E816 ☑
    with
      antecedent collision on public
        highway — see Collision,
        motor vehicle
      involving any object, person
        or vehicle not on public
        highway E816 ☑
      not on public highway, non-
        traffic accident E825 ☑
        with antecedent collision
          — see Collision,
          motor vehicle, not
          on public highway
      on public highway — see
        Collision, motor vehicle
    off-road type motor vehicle (not on
      public highway) E821 ☑
      on public highway — see Loss of
        control, motor vehicle
    snow vehicle, motor-driven (not on
      public highway) E820 ☑
      on public highway — see Loss of
        control, motor vehicle

Lost at sea E832 ☑
  with accident to watercraft E830 ☑
  in war operations E995
Low
  pressure, effects — see Effects of, air
    pressure
  temperature, effects — see Cold, expo-
    sure to
**Lying before train, vehicle or other
    moving object** (unspecified
    whether accidental or intentional)
    E988.0
  stated as intentional, purposeful, sui-
    cidal (attempt) E958.0
Lynching — see also Assault E968.9

M

**Malfunction, atomic power plant in
    water transport** E838 ☑
Mangled (accidentally) NEC E928.9
Manhandling (in brawl, fight) E960.0
  legal intervention E975
Manslaughter (nonaccidental) — see
    Assault
Marble in nose E912
Mauled by animal E906.8
Medical procedure, complication of
  delayed or as an abnormal reaction
    without mention of misadventure
    — see Reaction, abnormal
  due to or as a result of misadventure
    — see Misadventure
**Melting of fittings and furniture in
    burning**
  in terrorism E979.3
Minamata disease E865.2
**Misadventure(s) to patient(s) during
    surgical or medical care** E876.9
  contaminated blood, fluid, drug or bi-
    ological substance (presence of
    agents and toxins as listed in
    E875) E875.9
    administered (by) NEC E875.9
      infusion E875.0
      injection E875.1
      specified means NEC E875.2
      transfusion E875.0
      vaccination E875.1
  cut, cutting, puncture, perforation or
    hemorrhage (accidental) (inad-
    vertent) (inappropriate) (during)
    E870.9
    aspiration of fluid or tissue (by
      puncture or catheterization,
      except heart) E870.5
    biopsy E870.8
      needle (aspirating) E870.5
    blood sampling E870.5
    catheterization E870.5
      heart E870.6
    dialysis (kidney) E870.2
    endoscopic examination E870.4
    enema E870.7
    infusion E870.1
    injection E870.3
    lumbar puncture E870.5
    needle biopsy E870.5
    paracentesis, abdominal E870.5
    perfusion E870.2
    specified procedure NEC E870.8
    surgical operation E870.0
    thoracentesis E870.5
    transfusion E870.1
    vaccination E870.3
  excessive amount of blood or other
    fluid during transfusion or infu-
    sion E873.0
  failure
    in dosage E873.9
      electroshock therapy E873.4
      inappropriate temperature (too
        hot or too cold) in local
        application and packing
        E873.5

**Misadventure(s) to patient(s) during
    surgical or medical care** —
    continued
  failure — continued
    in dosage — continued
      infusion
        excessive amount of fluid
          E873.0
        incorrect dilution of fluid
          E873.1
      insulin-shock therapy E873.4
      nonadministration of necessary
        drug or medicinal E873.6
      overdose (see also Overdose)
      radiation, in therapy E873.2
    radiation
      inadvertent exposure of pa-
        tient (receiving radia-
        tion for test or therapy)
        E873.3
      not receiving radiation for
        test or therapy —
        see Radiation
    overdose E873.2
    specified procedure NEC E873.8
    transfusion
      excessive amount of blood
        E873.0
  mechanical, of instrument or appa-
    ratus (during procedure)
    E874.9
    aspiration of fluid or tissue (by
      puncture or catheteriza-
      tion, except of heart)
      E874.4
    biopsy E874.8
      needle (aspirating) E874.4
    blood sampling E874.4
    catheterization E874.4
      heart E874.5
    dialysis (kidney) E874.2
    endoscopic examination E874.3
    enema E874.8
    infusion E874.1
    injection E874.8
    lumbar puncture E874.4
    needle biopsy E874.4
    paracentesis, abdominal E874.4
    perfusion E874.2
    specified procedure NEC E874.8
    surgical operation E874.0
    thoracentesis E874.4
    transfusion E874.1
    vaccination E874.8
  sterile precautions (during proce-
    dure) E872.9
    aspiration of fluid or tissue (by
      puncture or catheteriza-
      tion, except heart) E872.5
    biopsy E872.8
      needle (aspirating) E872.5
    blood sampling E872.5
    catheterization E872.5
      heart E872.6
    dialysis (kidney) E872.2
    endoscopic examination E872.4
    enema E872.8
    infusion E872.1
    injection E872.3
    lumbar puncture E872.5
    needle biopsy E872.5
    paracentesis, abdominal E872.5
    perfusion E872.2
    removal of catheter or packing
      E872.8
    specified procedure NEC E872.8
    surgical operation E872.0
    thoracentesis E872.5
    transfusion E872.1
    vaccination E872.3
  suture or ligature during surgical
    procedure E876.2
  to introduce or to remove tube or
    instrument E876.4

☑ Additional Digit Required — Refer to the Tabular List for Digit Selection

▽ Subterms under main terms may continue to next column or page

▶◀ Revised Text   ● New Line   ▲ Revised Code

Misadventure(s) to patient(s) during surgical or medical care — *continued*
failure — *continued*
  to introduce or to remove tube or instrument — *continued*
    foreign object left in body — *see* Misadventure, foreign object
  foreign object left in body (during procedure) E871.9
  aspiration of fluid or tissue (by puncture or catheterization, except heart) E871.5
  biopsy E871.8
    needle (aspirating) E871.5
  blood sampling E871.5
  catheterization E871.5
    heart E871.6
  dialysis (kidney) E871.2
  endoscopic examination E871.4
  enema E871.8
  infusion E871.1
  injection E871.3
  lumbar puncture E871.5
  needle biopsy E871.5
  paracentesis, abdominal E871.5
  perfusion E871.2
  removal of catheter or packing E871.7
  specified procedure NEC E871.8
  surgical operation E871.0
  thoracentesis E871.5
  transfusion E871.1
  vaccination E871.3
hemorrhage — *see* Misadventure, cut
inadvertent exposure of patient to radiation (being received for test or therapy) E873.3
inappropriate
  operation performed E876.5
  temperature (too hot or too cold) in local application or packing E873.5
infusion (*see also* Misadventure, by specific type, infusion)
  excessive amount of fluid E873.0
  incorrect dilution of fluid E873.1
  wrong fluid E876.1
mismatched blood in transfusion E876.0
nonadministration of necessary drug or medicinal E873.6
overdose (*see also* Overdose)
  radiation, in therapy E873.2
perforation — *see* Misadventure, cut
performance of inappropriate operation E876.5
puncture — *see* Misadventure, cut
specified type NEC E876.8
  failure
    suture or ligature during surgical operation E876.2
    to introduce or to remove tube or instrument E876.4
      foreign object left in body E871.9
    infusion of wrong fluid E876.1
    performance of inappropriate operation E876.5
    transfusion of mismatched blood E876.0
  wrong
    fluid in infusion E876.1
    placement of endotracheal tube during anesthetic procedure E876.3
  transfusion (*see also* Misadventure, by specific type, transfusion)
    excessive amount of blood E873.0
    mismatched blood E876.0
  wrong
    drug given in error — *see* Table of Drugs and Chemicals
    fluid in infusion E876.1

Misadventure(s) to patient(s) during surgical or medical care — *continued*
wrong — *continued*
  placement of endotracheal tube during anesthetic procedure E876.3
Motion (effects) E903
  sickness E903
Mountain sickness E902.0
Mucus aspiration or inhalation, not of newborn (with asphyxia, obstruction respiratory passage, suffocation) E912
Mudslide of cataclysmic nature E909.2
Murder (attempt) — *see also* Assault E968.9

N

Nail, injury by E920.8
Needlestick (sewing needle) E920.4
  hypodermic E920.5
Neglect — *see also* Privation
  criminal E968.4
  homicidal intent E968.4
Noise (causing injury) (pollution) E928.1

O

Object
falling
  from, in, on, hitting
    aircraft E844 ☑
      due to accident to aircraft — *see* categories E840-E842 ☑
    machinery (*see also* Accident, machine)
      not in operation E916
    motor vehicle (in motion) (on public highway) E818 ☑
      not on public highway E825 ☑
      stationary E916
    nonmotor road vehicle NEC E829 ☑
    pedal cycle E826 ☑
    person E916
    railway rolling stock, train, vehicle E806 ☑
    street car E829 ☑
    watercraft E838 ☑
      due to accident to watercraft E831 ☑
set in motion by
  accidental explosion of pressure vessel — *see* category E921 ☑
  firearm — *see* category E922 ☑
  machine(ry) — *see* Accident, machine
  transport vehicle — *see* categories E800-E848 ☑
thrown from, in, on, towards
  aircraft E844 ☑
  cable car (not on rails) E847
    on rails E829 ☑
  motor vehicle (in motion) (on public highway) E818 ☑
    not on public highway E825 ☑
  nonmotor road vehicle NEC E829 ☑
  pedal cycle E826 ☑
  street car E829 ☑
  vehicle NEC — *see* Accident, vehicle NEC
Obstruction
air passages, larynx, respiratory passages
  by
    external means NEC — *see* Suffocation
    food, any type (regurgitated) (vomited) E911
    material or object, except food E912

Obstruction — *continued*
air passages, larynx, respiratory passages — *continued*
  by — *continued*
    mucus E912
    phlegm E912
    vomitus E911
digestive tract, except mouth or pharynx
  by
    food, any type E915
    foreign body (any) E915
esophagus
  without asphyxia or obstruction of respiratory passage E915
  food E911
  foreign body, except food E912
mouth or pharynx
  by
    food, any type E911
    material or object, except food E912
respiration — *see* Obstruction, air passages
Oil in eye E914
Overdose
anesthetic (drug) — *see* Table of Drugs and Chemicals
drug — *see* Table of Drugs and Chemicals
Overexertion (lifting) (pulling) (pushing) E927
Overexposure (accidental) (to)
cold (*see also* Cold, exposure to) E901.9
  due to manmade conditions E901.1
heat (*see also* Heat) E900.9
radiation — *see* Radiation
radioactivity — *see* Radiation
sun, except sunburn E900.0
weather — *see* Exposure
wind — *see* Exposure
Overheated — *see also* Heat E900.9
Overlaid E913.0
Overturning (accidental)
animal-drawn vehicle E827 ☑
boat, ship, watercraft
  causing
    drowning, submersion E830 ☑
    injury except drowning, submersion E831 ☑
machinery — *see* Accident, machine
motor vehicle (*see also* Loss of control, motor vehicle) E816 ☑
  with antecedent collision on public highway — *see* Collision, motor vehicle
  not on public highway, nontraffic accident E825 ☑
    with antecedent collision — *see* Collision, motor vehicle, not on public highway
nonmotor road vehicle NEC E829 ☑
off-road type motor vehicle — *see* Loss of control, off-road type motor vehicle
pedal cycle E826 ☑
railway rolling stock, train, vehicle (*see also* Derailment, railway) E802 ☑
street car E829 ☑
vehicle NEC — *see* Accident, vehicle NEC

P

Palsy, divers' E902.2
Parachuting (voluntary) (without accident to aircraft) E844 ☑
  due to accident to aircraft — *see* categories E840-E842 ☑
Paralysis
divers' E902.2
lead or saturnine E866.0
  from pesticide NEC E863.4
Pecked by bird E906.8

Phlegm aspiration or inhalation (with asphyxia, obstruction respiratory passage, suffocation) E912
Piercing — *see also* Cut E920.9
Pinched
  between objects (moving) (stationary and moving) E918
  in object E918
Pinned under
  machine(ry) — *see* Accident, machine
Place of occurrence of accident — *see* Accident (to), occurring (at) (in)
Plumbism E866.0
  from insecticide NEC E863.4
Poisoning (accidental) (by) — *see also* Table of Drugs and Chemicals
carbon monoxide
  generated by
    aircraft in transit E844 ☑
    motor vehicle
      in motion (on public highway) E818 ☑
      not on public highway E825 ☑
    watercraft (in transit) (not in transit) E838 ☑
caused by injection of poisons or toxins into or through skin by plant thorns, spines, or other mechanism E905.7
  marine or sea plants E905.6
fumes or smoke due to
  conflagration — *see* Conflagration
  explosion or fire — *see* Fire
  ignition — *see* Ignition
gas
  in legal intervention E972
  legal execution, by E978
    on watercraft E838
  used as anesthetic — *see* Table of Drugs and Chemicals
in
  terrorism (chemical weapons) E979.7
  war operations E997.2
    execution E978
    intervention
      by gas E972
late effect of — *see* Late effect
legal
Pressure, external, causing asphyxia, suffocation — *see also* Suffocation E913.9
Privation E904.9
food (*see also* Lack of, food) E904.1
helpless person, infant, newborn due to abandonment or neglect E904.0
late effect of NEC E929.5
resulting from transport accident — *see* categories E800-E848 ☑
water (*see also* Lack of, water) E904.2
Projected objects, striking against or struck by — *see* Striking against, object
Prolonged stay in
high altitude (causing conditions as listed in E902.0) E902.0
weightless environment E928.0
Prostration
heat — *see* Heat
Pulling, injury in E927
Puncture, puncturing — *see also* Cut E920.9
  by
    plant thorns or spines E920.8
      toxic reaction E905.7
        marine or sea plants E905.6
    sea-urchin spine E905.6
Pushing (injury in) (overexertion) E927
by other person(s) (accidental) E917.9
  with fall E886.9
    in sports E886.0
  as, or caused by, a crowd, human stampede E917.1
    with subsequent fall E917.6

Pushing — *continued*
by other person(s) — *continued*
before moving vehicle or object
stated as
intentional, homicidal E968.5
undetemined whether accidental or intentional E988.8
from
high place
in accidental circumstances — *see* categories E880-E884 ☑
stated as
intentional, homicidal E968.1
undetermined whether accidental or intentional E987.9
man-made structure, except residential E987.1
natural site E987.2
residential E987.0
motor vehicle (*see also* Fall, from, motor vehicle) E818 ☑
stated as
intentional, homicidal E968.5
undetermined whether accidental or intentional E988.8
in sports E917.0
with fall E886.0

R

Radiation (exposure to) E926.9
abnormal reaction to medical test or therapy E879.2
arc lamps E926.2
atomic power plant (malfunction) NEC E926.9
in water transport E838 ☑
electromagnetic, ionizing E926.3
gamma rays E926.3
in
terrorism (from or following nuclear explosion) (direct) (secondary) E979.5
laser E979.8
war operations (from or following nuclear explosion) (direct) (secondary) E996
laser(s) E997.0
water transport E838 ☑
inadvertent exposure of patient (receiving test or therapy) E873.3
infrared (heaters and lamps) E926.1
excessive heat E900.1
ionized, ionizing (particles, artificially accelerated) E926.8
electromagnetic E926.3
isotopes — *see* Radiation, radioactive isotopes
laser(s) E926.4
in
terrorism E979.8
war operations E997.0
misadventure in medical care — *see* Misadventure, failure, in dosage, radiation
late effect of NEC E929.8
excessive heat from — *see* Heat
light sources (visible) (ultraviolet) E926.2
misadventure in medical or surgical procedure — *see* Misadventure, failure, in dosage, radiation
overdose (in medical or surgical procedure) E873.2
radar E926.0
radioactive isotopes E926.5
atomic power plant malfunction E926.5

Radiation — *continued*
radioactive isotopes — *continued*
atomic power plant malfunction — *continued*
in water transport E838 ☑
misadventure in medical or surgical treatment — *see* Misadventure, failure, in dosage, radiation
radiobiologicals — *see* Radiation, radioactive isotopes
radiofrequency E926.0
radiopharmaceuticals — *see* Radiation, radioactive isotopes
radium NEC E926.9
sun E926.2
excessive heat from E900.0
tanning bed E926.2
welding arc or torch E926.2
excessive heat from E900.1
x-rays (hard) (soft) E926.3
misadventure in medical or surgical treatment — *see* Misadventure, failure, in dosage, radiation
Rape E960.1
Reaction, abnormal to or following
(medical or surgical procedure) E879.9
amputation (of limbs) E878.5
anastomosis (arteriovenous) (blood vessel) (gastrojejunal) (skin) (tendon) (natural, artificial material, tissue) E878.2
external stoma, creation of E878.3
aspiration (of fluid) E879.4
tissue E879.8
biopsy E879.8
blood
sampling E879.7
transfusion
procedure E879.8
bypass — *see* Reaction, abnormal, anastomosis
catheterization
cardiac E879.0
urinary E879.6
colostomy E878.3
cystostomy E878.3
dialysis (kidney) E879.1
drugs or biologicals — *see* Table of Drugs and Chemicals
duodenostomy E878.3
electroshock therapy E879.3
formation of external stoma E878.3
gastrostomy E878.3
graft — *see* Reaction, abnormal, anastomosis
hypothermia E879.8
implant, implantation (of)
artificial
internal device (cardiac pacemaker) (electrodes in brain) (heart valve prosthesis) (orthopedic) E878.1
material or tissue (for anastomosis or bypass) E878.2
with creation of external stoma E878.3
natural tissues (for anastomosis or bypass) E878.2
with creation of external stoma E878.3
as transplantion — *see* Reaction, abnormal, transplant
infusion
procedure E879.8
injection
procedure E879.8
specific type of procedure) E879.9
insertion of gastric or duodenal sound E879.5
insulin-shock therapy E879.3
lumbar puncture E879.4
perfusion E879.1

Reaction, abnormal to or following — *continued*
procedures other than surgical operation (*see also* Reaction, abnormal, by
specified procedure NEC E879.8
radiological procedure or therapy E879.2
removal of organ (partial) (total) NEC E878.6
with
anastomosis, bypass or graft E878.2
formation of external stoma E878.3
implant of artificial internal device E878.1
transplant(ation)
partial organ E878.4
whole organ E878.0
sampling
blood E879.7
fluid NEC E879.4
tissue E879.8
shock therapy E879.3
surgical operation (*see also* Reaction, abnormal, by specified type of operation) E878.9
restorative NEC E878.4
with
anastomosis, bypass or graft E878.2
fomation of external stoma E878.3
implant(ation) — *see* Reaction, abnormal, implant
transplant(ation) — *see* Reaction, abnormal, transplant
specified operation NEC E878.8
thoracentesis E879.4
transfusion
procedure E879.8
transplant, transplantation (heart) (kidney) (liver) E878.0
partial organ E878.4
ureterostomy E878.3
vaccination E879.8
Reduction in
atmospheric pressure (*see also* Effects of, air pressure)
while surfacing from
deep water diving causing caisson or divers' disease, palsy or paralysis E902.2
underground E902.8
Residual (effect) — *see* Late effect
Rock falling on or hitting (accidentally)
motor vehicle (in motion) (on public highway) E818 ☑
not on public highway E825 ☑
nonmotor road vehicle NEC E829 ☑
pedal cycle E826 ☑
person E916
railway rolling stock, train, vehicle E806 ☑
Running off, away
animal (being ridden) (in sport or transport) E828 ☑
not being ridden E906.8
animal-drawn vehicle E827 ☑
rails, railway (*see also* Derailment) E802 ☑
roadway
motor vehicle (without antecedent collision) E816 ☑
with
antecedent collision — *see* Collision motor vehicle
subsequent collision
involving any object, person or vehicle not on public highway E816 ☑

Running off, away — *continued*
roadway — *continued*
motor vehicle — *continued*
with — *continued*
subsequent collision — *continued*
on public highway E811 ☑
nontraffic accident E825 ☑
with antecedent collision — *see* Collision, motor vehicle, not on public highway
nonmotor road vehicle NEC E829 ☑
pedal cycle E826 ☑
Run over (accidentally) (by)
animal (not being ridden) E906.8
being ridden (in sport or transport) E828 ☑
animal-drawn vehicle E827 ☑
machinery — *see* Accident, machine
motor vehicle (on public highway) — *see* Hit by, motor vehicle
nonmotor road vehicle NEC E829 ☑
railway train E805 ☑
street car E829 ☑
vehicle NEC E848

S

Saturnism E866.0
from insecticide NEC E863.4
Scald, scalding (accidental) (by) (from) (in) E924.0
acid — *see* Scald, caustic
boiling tap water E924.2
caustic or corrosive liquid, substance E924.1
swallowed — *see* Table of Drugs and Chemicals
homicide (attempt) — *see* Assault, burning
inflicted by other person
stated as
intentional or homicidal E968.3
undetermined whether accidental or intentional E988.2
late effect of NEC E929.8
liquid (boiling) (hot) E924.0
local application of externally applied substance in medical or surgical care E873.5
molten metal E924.0
self-inflicted (unspecified whether accidental or intentional) E988.2
stated as intentional, purposeful E958.2
stated as undetermined whether accidental or intentional E988.2
steam E924.0
tap water (boiling) E924.2
transport accident — *see* categories E800-E848 ☑
vapor E924.0
Scratch, cat E906.8
Sea
sickness E903
Self-mutilation — *see* Suicide
Sequelae (of)
in
terrorism E999.1
war operations E999.0
Shock
anaphylactic (*see also* Table of Drugs and Chemicals) E947.9
due to
bite (venomous) — *see* Bite, venomous NEC
sting — *see* Sting
electric (*see also* Electric shock) E925.9
from electric appliance or current (*see also* Electric shock) E925.9
Shooting, shot (accidental(ly)) E922.9
air gun E922.4
BB gun E922.4

☑ Additional Digit Required — Refer to the Tabular List for Digit Selection   ▽ Subterms under main terms may continue to next column or page

350 — Volume 2   ▶◀ Revised Text   ● New Line   ▲ Revised Code   *2007 ICD-9-CM*

Shooting, shot — *continued*
  hand gun (pistol) (revolver) E922.0
  himself (*see also* Shooting, self-inflicted) E985.4
    hand gun (pistol) (revolver) E985.0
    military firearm, except hand gun E985.3
      hand gun (pistol) (revolver) E985.0
    rifle (hunting) E985.2
      military E985.3
    shotgun (automatic) E985.1
    specified firearm NEC E985.4
    Verey pistol E985.4
  homicide (attempt) E965.4
    air gun E968.6
    BB gun E968.6
    hand gun (pistol) (revolver) E965.0
    military firearm, except hand gun E965.3
      hand gun (pistol) (revolver) E965.0
    paintball gun E965.4
    rifle (hunting) E965.2
      military E965.3
    shotgun (automatic) E965.1
    specified firearm NEC E965.4
    Verey pistol E965.4
  in
    terrorism — *see* Terrorism, shooting
    war operations — *see* War operations, shooting
  inflicted by other person
    in accidental circumstances E922.9
      hand gun (pistol) (revolver) E922.0
      military firearm, except hand gun E922.3
        hand gun (pistol) (revolver) E922.0
      rifle (hunting) E922.2
        military E922.3
      shotgun (automatic) E922.1
      specified firearm NEC E922.8
      Verey pistol E922.8
    stated as
      intentional, homicidal E965.4
        hand gun (pistol) (revolver) E965.0
        military firearm, except hand gun E965.3
          hand gun (pistol) (revolver) E965.0
        paintball gun E965.4
        rifle (hunting) E965.2
          military E965.3
        shotgun (automatic) E965.1
        specified firearm E965.4
        Verey pistol E965.4
      undetermined whether accidental or intentional E985.4
        air gun E985.6
        BB gun E985.6
        hand gun (pistol) (revolver) E985.0
        military firearm, except hand gun E985.3
          hand gun (pistol) (revolver) E985.0
        paintball gun E985.7
        rifle (hunting) E985.2
        shotgun (automatic) E985.1
        specified firearm NEC E985.4
        Verey pistol E985.4
  legal
    execution E978
    intervention E970
  military firearm, except hand gun E922.3
    hand gun (pistol) (revolver) E922.0
  paintball gun E922.5
  rifle (hunting) E922.2
    military E922.3

Shooting, shot — *continued*
  self-inflicted (unspecified whether accidental or intentional) E985.4
    air gun E985.6
    BB gun E985.6
    hand gun (pistol) (revolver) E985.0
    military firearm, except hand gun E985.3
      hand gun (pistol) (revolver) E985.0
    paintball gun E985.7
    rifle (hunting) E985.2
      military E985.3
    shotgun (automatic) E985.1
    specified firearm NEC E985.4
    stated as
      accidental E922.9
        hand gun (pistol) (revolver) E922.0
        military firearm, except hand gun E922.3
          hand gun (pistol) (revolver) E922.0
        paintball gun E922.5
        rifle (hunting) E922.2
          military E922.3
        shotgun (automatic) E922.1
        specified firearm NEC E922.8
        Verey pistol E922.8
      intentional, purposeful E955.4
        hand gun (pistol) (revolver) E955.0
        military firearm, except hand gun E955.3
          hand gun (pistol) (revolver) E955.0
        paintball gun E955.7
        rifle (hunting) E955.2
          military E955.3
        shotgun (automatic) E955.1
        specified firearm NEC E955.4
        Verey pistol E955.4
    shotgun (automatic) E922.1
    specified firearm NEC E922.8
    stated as undetermined whether accidental or intentional E985.4
      hand gun (pistol) (revolver) E985.0
      military firearm, except hand gun E985.3
        hand gun (pistol) (revolver) E985.0
      paintball gun E985.7
      rifle (hunting) E985.2
        military E985.3
      shotgun (automatic) E985.1
      specified firearm NEC E985.4
      Verey pistol E985.4
    suicidal (attempt) E955.4
      air gun E955.6
      BB gun E955.6
      hand gun (pistol) (revolver) E955.0
      military firearm, except hand gun E955.3
        hand gun (pistol) (revolver) E955.0
      paintball gun E955.7
      rifle (hunting) E955.2
        military E955.3
      shotgun (automatic) E955.1
      specified firearm NEC E955.4
      Verey pistol E955.4
    Verey pistol E922.8
Shoving (accidentally) by other person — *see also* Pushing by other person E917.9
Sickness
  air E903
  alpine E902.0
  car E903
  motion E903
  mountain E902.0
  sea E903
  travel E903
Sinking (accidental)
  boat, ship, watercraft (causing drowning, submersion) E830 ☑

Sinking — *continued*
  boat, ship, watercraft — *continued*
    causing injury except drowning, submersion E831 ☑
Siriasis E900.0
Skydiving E844 ☑
Slashed wrists — *see also* Cut, self-inflicted E986
Slipping (accidental)
  on
    deck (of boat, ship, watercraft) (icy) (oily) (wet) E835 ☑
    ice E885.9
    ladder of ship E833 ☑
      due to accident to watercraft E831 ☑
    mud E885.9
    oil E885.9
    snow E885.9
    stairs of ship E833 ☑
      due to accident to watercraft E831 ☑
    surface
      slippery E885 ☑
      wet E885 ☑
Sliver, wood, injury by E920.8
Smothering, smothered — *see also* Suffocation E913.9
Smouldering building or structure in terrorism E979.3
Sodomy (assault) E960.1
Solid substance in eye (any part) or adnexa E914
Sound waves (causing injury) E928.1
Splinter, injury by E920.8
Stab, stabbing E966
  accidental — *see* Cut
Starvation E904.1
  helpless person, infant, newborn — *see* Lack of food
  homicidal intent E968.4
  late effect of NEC E929.5
  resulting from accident connected with transport — *see* categories E800-E848 ☑
Stepped on
  by
    animal (not being ridden) E906.8
      being ridden (in sport or transport) E828 ☑
    crowd E917.1
    person E917.9
      in sports E917.0
  in sports E917.0
Stepping on
  object (moving) E917.9
    in sports E917.0
      with subsequent fall E917.5
    stationary E917.4
      with subsequent fall E917.8
  person E917.9
    as, or caused by a crowd E917.1
      with subsequent fall E917.6
    in sports E917.0
Sting E905.9
  ant E905.5
  bee E905.3
  caterpillar E905.5
  coral E905.6
  hornet E905.3
  insect NEC E905.5
  jellyfish E905.6
  marine animal or plant E905.6
  nematocysts E905.6
  scorpion E905.2
  sea anemone E905.6
  sea cucumber E905.6
  wasp E905.3
  yellow jacket E905.3
Storm E908.9
  specified type NEC E908.8
Straining, injury in E927
Strangling — *see* Suffocation
Strangulation — *see* Suffocation
Strenuous movements (in recreational or other activities) E927

Striking against
  bottom (when jumping or diving into water) E883.0
  object (moving) E917.9
    caused by crowd E917.1
      with subsequent fall E917.6
    furniture E917.3
      with subsequent fall E917.7
    in
      running water E917.2
        with drowning or submersion — *see* Submersion
    sports E917.0
      with subsequent fall E917.5
    stationary E917.4
      with subsequent fall E917.8
    person(s) E917.9
      with fall E886.9
        in sports E886.0
      as, or caused by, a crowd E917.1
        with subsequent fall E917.6
      in sports E917.0
        with fall E886.0
Stroke
  heat — *see* Heat
  lightning E907
Struck by — *see also* Hit by
  bullet
    in
      terrorism E979.4
      war operations E991.2
        rubber E991.0
  lightning E907
  missile
    in terrorism — *see* Terrorism, missile
  object
    falling
      from, in, on
        building
          burning (uncontrolled fire)
            in terrorism E979.3
  thunderbolt E907
Stumbling over animal, carpet, curb, rug or (small) object (with fall) E885.9
  without fall — *see* Striking against, object
Submersion (accidental) E910.8
  boat, ship, watercraft (causing drowning, submersion) E830 ☑
    causing injury except drowning, submersion E831 ☑
  by other person
    in accidental circumstances — *see* category E910 ☑
    intentional, homicidal E964
    stated as undetermined whether accidental or intentional E984
  due to
    accident
      machinery — *see* Accident, machine
      to boat, ship, watercraft E830 ☑
      transport — *see* categories E800-E848 ☑
    avalanche E909.2
    cataclysmic
      earth surface movement or eruption E909.9
      storm E908.9
    cloudburst E908.8
    cyclone E908.1
    fall
      from
        boat, ship, watercraft (not involved in accident) E832 ☑
          burning, crushed E830 ☑
          involved in accident, collision E830 ☑
        gangplank (into water) E832 ☑
        overboard NEC E832 ☑
    flood E908.2

☑ Additional Digit Required — Refer to the Tabular List for Digit Selection   ▽ Subterms under main terms may continue to next column or page

2007 ICD-9-CM   ►◄ Revised Text   ● New Line   ▲ Revised Code   **Volume 2 — 351**

Submersion (accidental) —
continued
  due to — *continued*
    hurricane E908.0
    jumping into water E910.8
      from boat, ship, watercraft
        burning, crushed, sinking
          E830 ☑
        involved in accident, collision
          E830 ☑
        not involved in accident, for
          swim E910.2
      in recreational activity (without
        diving equipment) E910.2
        with or using diving equip-
          ment E910.1
      to rescue another person
        E910.3
  homicide (attempt) E964
  in
    bathtub E910.4
    specified activity, not sport, trans-
      port or recreational E910.3
    sport or recreational activity (with-
      out diving equipment)
      E910.2
      with or using diving equipment
        E910.1
    water skiing E910.0
    swimming pool NEC E910.8
    terrorism E979.8
    war operations E995
    water transport E832 ☑
      due to accident to boat, ship,
        watercraft E830 ☑
  landslide E909.2
    overturning boat, ship, watercraft
      E909.2
    sinking boat, ship, watercraft
      E909.2
    submersion boat, ship, watercraft
      E909.2
  tidal wave E909.4
    caused by storm E908.0
  torrential rain E908.2
  late effect of NEC E929.8
  quenching tank E910.8
  self-inflicted (unspecified whether ac-
    cidental or intentional) E984
    in accidental circumstances — see
      category E910 ☑
    stated as intentional, purposeful
      E954
  stated as undetermined whether acci-
    dental or intentional E984
  suicidal (attempted) E954
  while
    attempting rescue of another per-
      son E910.3
    engaged in
      marine salvage E910.3
      underwater construction or
        repairs E910.3
    fishing, not from boat E910.2
    hunting, not from boat E910.2
    ice skating E910.2
    pearl diving E910.3
    placing fishing nets E910.3
    playing in water E910.2
    scuba diving E910.1
      nonrecreational E910.3
    skin diving E910.1
    snorkel diving E910.2
    spear fishing underwater E910.1
    surfboarding E910.2
    swimming (swimming pool) E910.2
    wading (in water) E910.2
    water skiing E910.0
Sucked
  into
    jet (aircraft) E844 ☑
Suffocation (accidental) (by external
  means) (by pressure) (mechanical)
  E913.9

Suffocation — *continued*
  caused by other person
    in accidental circumstances — see
      category E913 ☑
    stated as
      intentional, homicidal E963
      undetermined whether acciden-
        tal or intentional E983.9
        by, in
          hanging E983.0
          plastic bag E983.1
          specified means NEC
            E983.8
  due to, by
    avalanche E909.2
    bedclothes E913.0
    bib E913.0
    blanket E913.0
    cave-in E913.3
      caused by cataclysmic earth
        surface movement or
        eruption E909.9
    conflagration — see Conflagration
    explosion — see Explosion
    falling earth, other substance
      E913.3
    fire — see Fire
    food, any type (ingestion) (inhala-
      tion) (regurgitated) (vomited)
      E911
    foreign body, except food (ingestion)
      (inhalation) E912
    ignition — see Ignition
    landslide E909.2
    machine(ry) — see Accident, ma-
      chine
    material, object except food enter-
      ing by nose or mouth, ingest-
      ed, inhaled E912
    mucus (aspiration) (inhalation), not
      of newborn E912
    phlegm (aspiration) (inhalation)
      E912
    pillow E913.0
    plastic bag — see Suffocation, in,
      plastic bag
    sheet (plastic) E913.0
    specified means NEC E913.8
    vomitus (aspiration) (inhalation)
      E911
  homicidal (attempt) E963
  in
    airtight enclosed place E913.2
    baby carriage E913.0
    bed E913.0
    closed place E913.2
    cot, cradle E913.0
    perambulator E913.0
    plastic bag (in accidental circum-
      stances) E913.1
      homicidal, purposely inflicted
        by other person E963
      self-inflicted (unspecified
        whether accidental or in-
        tentional) E983.1
        in accidental circumstances
          E913.1
        intentional, suicidal E953.1
        stated as undetermined whether
          accidentally or purposely
          inflicted E983.1
      suicidal, purposely self-inflicted
        E953.1
    refrigerator E913.2
  self-inflicted (see also Suffocation,
    stated as undetermined whether
    accidental or intentional)
    E953.9
    in accidental circumstances — see
      category E913 ☑
    stated as intentional, purposeful
      — see Suicide, suffocation
  stated as undetermined whether acci-
    dental or intentional E983.9
    by, in
      hanging E983.0

Suffocation — *continued*
  stated as undetermined whether acci-
    dental or intentional — *contin-
    ued*
    by, in — *continued*
      plastic bag E983.1
      specified means NEC E983.8
  suicidal — see Suicide, suffocation
Suicide, suicidal (attempted) (by) E958.9
  burning, burns E958.1
  caustic substance E958.7
    poisoning E950.7
    swallowed E950.7
  cold, extreme E958.3
  cut (any part of body) E956
  cutting or piercing instrument (classi-
    fiable to E920) E956
  drowning E954
  electrocution E958.4
  explosive(s) (classifiable to E923)
    E955.5
  fire E958.1
  firearm (classifiable to E922) — see
    Shooting, suicidal
  hanging E953.0
  jumping
    before moving object, train, vehicle
      E958.0
    from high place — see Jumping,
      from, high place, stated as,
      suicidal
  knife E956
  late effect of E959
  motor vehicle, crashing of E958.5
  poisoning — see Table of Drugs and
    Chemicals
  puncture (any part of body) E956
  scald E958.2
  shooting — see Shooting, suicidal
  specified means NEC E958.8
  stab (any part of body) E956
  strangulation — see Suicide, suffoca-
    tion
  submersion E954
  suffocation E953.9
    by, in
      hanging E953.0
      plastic bag E953.1
      specified means NEC E953.8
  wound NEC E958.9
Sunburn E926.2
Sunstroke E900.0
Supersonic waves (causing injury)
  E928.1
Surgical procedure, complication of
  delayed or as an abnormal reaction
    without mention of misadven-
    ture — see Reaction, abnormal
  due to or as a result of misadventure
    — see Misadventure
Swallowed, swallowing
  foreign body — see Foreign body, ali-
    mentary canal
  poison — see Table of Drugs and
    Chemicals
  substance
    caustic — see Table of Drugs and
      Chemicals
    corrosive — see Table of Drugs and
      Chemicals
    poisonous — see Table of Drugs
      and Chemicals
Swimmers cramp — see also category
  E910 E910.2
  not in recreation or sport E910.3
Syndrome, battered
  baby or child — see Abuse, child
  wife — see Assault

T

Tackle in sport E886.0
Terrorism (injury) (by) (in) E979.8
  air blast E979.2
  aircraft burned, destroyed, exploded,
    shot down E979.1
    used as a weapon E979.1

Terrorism — *continued*
  anthrax E979.6
  asphyxia from
    chemical (weapons) E979.7
    fire, conflagration (caused by fire-
      producing device) E979.3
      from nuclear explosion E979.5
    gas or fumes E979.7
  bayonet E979.8
  biological agents E979.6
  blast (air) (effects) E979.2
    from nuclear explosion E979.5
    underwater E979.0
  bomb (antipersonnel) (mortar) (explo-
    sion) (fragments) E979.2
  bullet(s) (from carbine, machine gun,
    pistol, rifle, shotgun) E979.4
  burn from
    chemical E979.7
    fire, conflagration (caused by fire-
      producing device) E979.3
      from nuclear explosion E979.5
    gas E979.7
  burning aircraft E979.1
  chemical E979.7
  cholera E979.6
  conflagration E979.3
  crushed by falling aircraft E979.1
  depth-charge E979.0
  destruction of aircraft E979.1
  disability, as sequelae one year or
    more after injury E999.1
  drowning E979.8
  effect
    of nuclear weapon (direct) (sec-
      ondary) E979.5
    secondary NEC E979.9
    sequelae E999.1
  explosion (artillery shell) (breech-
    block) (cannon block) E979.2
    aircraft E979.1
    bomb (antipersonnel) (mortar)
      E979.2
    nuclear (atom) (hydrogen)
      E979.5
    depth-charge E979.0
    grenade E979.2
    injury by fragments from E979.2
    land-mine E979.2
    marine weapon E979.0
    mine (land) E979.2
      at sea or in harbor E979.0
      marine E979.0
    missile (explosive) NEC E979.2
    munitions (dump) (factory) E979.2
    nuclear (weapon) E979.5
      other direct and secondary ef-
        fects of E979.5
    sea-based artillery shell E979.0
    torpedo E979.0
  exposure to ionizing radiation from
    nuclear explosion E979.5
  falling aircraft E979.1
  firearms E979.4
  fireball effects from nuclear explosion
    E979.5
  fire or fire-producing device E979.3
  fragments from artillery shell, bomb
    NEC, grenade, guided missile,
    land-mine, rocket, shell, shrap-
    nel E979.2
  gas or fumes E979.7
  grenade (explosion) (fragments)
    E979.2
  guided missile (explosion) (fragments)
    E979.2
    nuclear E979.5
  heat from nuclear explosion E979.5
  hot substances E979.3
  hydrogen cyanide E979.7
  land-mine (explosion) (fragments)
    E979.2
  laser(s) E979.8
  late effect of E999.1
  lewisite E979.7

☑ Additional Digit Required — Refer to the Tabular List for Digit Selection   ◄ Subterms under main terms may continue to next column or page

352 — Volume 2   ►◄ Revised Text   ● New Line   ▲ Revised Code   2007 ICD-9-CM

Terrorism — *continued*
  lung irritant (chemical) (fumes) (gas) E979.7
  marine mine E979.0
  mine E979.2
    at sea E979.0
    in harbor E979.0
    land (explosion) (fragments) E979.2
    marine E979.0
  missile (explosion) (fragments) (guided) E979.2
    marine E979.0
    nuclear weapons E979.5
  mortar bomb (explosion) (fragments) E979.2
  mustard gas E979.7
  nerve gas E979.7
  nuclear weapons E979.5
  pellets (shotgun) E979.4
  petrol bomb E979.3
  phosgene E979.7
  piercing object E979.8
  poisoning (chemical) (fumes) (gas) E979.7
  radiation, ionizing from nuclear explosion E979.5
  rocket (explosion) (fragments) E979.2
  saber, sabre E979.8
  sarin E979.7
  screening smoke E979.7
  sequelae effect (of) E999.1
  shell (aircraft) (artillery) (cannon) (land-based) (explosion) (fragments) E979.2
    sea-based E979.0
  shooting E979.4
    bullet(s) E979.4
    pellet(s) (rifle) (shotgun) E979.4
  shrapnel E979.2
  smallpox E979.7
  stabbing object(s) E979.8
  submersion E979.8
  torpedo E979.0
  underwater blast E979.0
  vesicant (chemical) (fumes) (gas) E979.7
  weapon burst E979.2
Thermic fever E900.9
Thermoplegia E900.9
Thirst — *see also* Lack of water
  resulting from accident connected with transport — *see* categories E800-E848 ☑
Thrown (accidentally)
  against object in or part of vehicle
    by motion of vehicle
      aircraft E844 ☑
      boat, ship, watercraft E838 ☑
      motor vehicle (on public highway) E818 ☑
        not on public highway E825 ☑
      off-road type (not on public highway) E821 ☑
        on public highway E818 ☑
      snow vehicle E820 ☑
        on public highway E818 ☑
      nonmotor road vehicle NEC E829 ☑
      railway rolling stock, train, vehicle E806 ☑
      street car E829 ☑
  from
    animal (being ridden) (in sport or transport) E828 ☑
    high place, homicide (attempt) E968.1
    machinery — *see* Accident, machine
    vehicle NEC — *see* Accident, vehicle NEC
  off — *see* Thrown, from

Thrown — *continued*
  overboard (by motion of boat, ship, watercraft) E832 ☑
    by accident to boat, ship, watercraft E830 ☑
Thunderbolt NEC E907
Tidal wave (any injury) E909.4
  caused by storm E908.0
Took
  overdose of drug — *see* Table of Drugs and Chemicals
  poison — *see* Table of Drugs and Chemicals
Tornado (any injury) E908.1
Torrential rain (any injury) E908.2
Traffic accident NEC E819 ☑
Trampled by animal E906.8
  being ridden (in sport or transport) E828 ☑
Trapped (accidentally)
  between
    objects (moving) (stationary and moving) E918
  by
    door of
      elevator E918
      motor vehicle (on public highway) (while alighting, boarding) — *see* Fall, from, motor vehicle, while alighting
      railway train (underground) E806 ☑
      street car E829 ☑
      subway train E806 ☑
  in object E918
Travel (effects) E903
  sickness E903
Tree
  falling on or hitting E916
    motor vehicle (in motion) (on public highway) E818 ☑
      not on public highway E825 ☑
    nonmotor road vehicle NEC E829 ☑
    pedal cycle E826 ☑
    person E916
    railway rolling stock, train, vehicle E806 ☑
    street car E829 ☑
Trench foot E901.0
Tripping over animal, carpet, curb, rug, or small object (with fall) E885 ☑
  without fall — *see* Striking against, object
Tsunami E909.4
Twisting, injury in E927

V

Violence, nonaccidental — *see also* Assault E968.9
Volcanic eruption (any injury) E909.1
Vomitus in air passages (with asphyxia, obstruction or suffocation) E911

W

War operations (during hostilities) (injury) (by) (in) E995
  after cessation of hostilities, injury due to E998
  air blast E993
  aircraft burned, destroyed, exploded, shot down E994
  asphyxia from
    chemical E997.2
    fire, conflagration (caused by fire producing device or conventional weapon) E990.9
      from nuclear explosion E996
      petrol bomb E990.0
    fumes E997.2
    gas E997.2
  battle wound NEC E995

War operations — *continued*
  bayonet E995
  biological warfare agents E997.1
  blast (air) (effects) E993
    from nuclear explosion E996
    underwater E992
  bomb (mortar) (explosion) E993
    after cessation of hostilities E998
    fragments, injury by E991.9
      antipersonnel E991.3
  bullet(s) (from carbine, machine gun, pistol, rifle, shotgun) E991.2
    rubber E991.0
  burn from
    chemical E997.2
    fire, conflagration (caused by fire-producing device or conventional weapon) E990.9
      from nuclear explosion E996
      petrol bomb E990.0
    gas E997.2
  burning aircraft E994
  chemical E997.2
  chlorine E997.2
  conventional warfare, specified form NEC E995
  crushing by falling aircraft E994
  depth charge E992
  destruction of aircraft E994
  disability as sequela one year or more after injury E999.0
  drowning E995
  effect (direct) (secondary) nuclear weapon E996
  explosion (artillery shell) (breech block) (cannon shell) E993
    after cessation of hostilities of bomb, mine placed in war E998
    aircraft E994
    bomb (mortar) E993
      atom E996
      hydrogen E996
      injury by fragments from E991.9
        antipersonnel E991.3
      nuclear E996
    depth charge E992
    injury by fragments from E991.9
      antipersonnel E991.3
    marine weapon E992
    mine
      at sea or in harbor E992
      land E993
        injury by fragments from E991.9
      marine E992
    munitions (accidental) (being used in war) (dump) (factory) E993
    nuclear (weapon) E996
    own weapons (accidental) E993
      injury by fragments from E991.9
        antipersonnel E991.3
    sea-based artillery shell E992
    torpedo E992
  exposure to ionizing radiation from nuclear explosion E996
  falling aircraft E994
  fireball effects from nuclear explosion E996
  fire or fire-producing device E990.9
    petrol bomb E990.0
  fragments from
    antipersonnel bomb E991.3
    artillery shell, bomb NEC, grenade, guided missile, land mine, rocket, shell, shrapnel E991.9
  fumes E997.2
  gas E997.2
  grenade (explosion) E993
    fragments, injury by E991.9
  guided missile (explosion) E993
    fragments, injury by E991.9

War operations — *continued*
  guided missile — *continued*
    nuclear E996
  heat from nuclear explosion E996
  injury due to, but occurring after cessation of hostilities E998
  lacrimator (gas) (chemical) E997.2
  land mine (explosion) E993
    after cessation of hostilities E998
    fragments, injury by E991.9
  laser(s) E997.0
  late effect of E999.0
  lewisite E997.2
  lung irritant (chemical) (fumes) (gas) E997.2
  marine mine E992
  mine
    after cessation of hostilities E998
    at sea E992
    in harbor E992
    land (explosion) E993
      fragments, injury by E991.9
    marine E992
  missile (guided) (explosion) E993
    fragments, injury by E991.9
    marine E992
    nuclear E996
  mortar bomb (explosion) E993
    fragments, injury by E991.9
  mustard gas E997.2
  nerve gas E997.2
  phosgene E997.2
  poisoning (chemical) (fumes) (gas) E997.2
  radiation, ionizing from nuclear explosion E996
  rocket (explosion) E993
    fragments, injury by E991.9
  saber, sabre E995
  screening smoke E997.8
  shell (aircraft) (artillery) (cannon) (land based) (explosion) E993
    fragments, injury by E991.9
    sea-based E992
  shooting E991.2
    after cessation of hostilities E998
    bullet(s) E991.2
      rubber E991.0
    pellet(s) (rifle) E991.1
    shrapnel E991.9
    submersion E995
    torpedo E992
  unconventional warfare, except by nuclear weapon E997.9
    biological (warfare) E997.1
    gas, fumes, chemicals E997.2
    laser(s) E997.0
    specified type NEC E997.8
  underwater blast E992
  vesicant (chemical) (fumes) (gas) E997.2
  weapon burst E993
Washed
  away by flood — *see* Flood
  away by tidal wave — *see* Tidal wave
  off road by storm (transport vehicle) E908.9
  overboard E832 ☑
Weather exposure — *see also* Exposure
  cold E901.0
  hot E900.0
Weightlessness (causing injury) (effects of) (in spacecraft, real or simulated) E928.0
Wound (accidental) NEC — *see also* Injury E928.9
  battle (*see also* War operations) E995
  bayonet E920.3
  in
    legal intervention E974
    war operations E995
  gunshot — *see* Shooting
  incised — *see* Cut
  saber, sabre E920.3
    in war operations E995

Railway Accidents (E800-E807)

The following fourth-digit subdivisions are for use with categories E800-E807 to identify the injured person:

.0 Railway employee
Any person who by virtue of his employment in connection with a railway, whether by the railway company or not, is at increased risk of involvement in a railway accident, such as:
  catering staff on train
  postal staff on train
  driver
  railway fireman
  guard
  shunter
  porter
  sleeping car attendant

.1 Passenger on railway
Any authorized person traveling on a train, except a railway employee
EXCLUDES intending passenger waiting at station (.8)
  unauthorized rider on railway vehicle (.8)

.2 Pedestrian See definition (r), E-Codes-2

.3 Pedal cyclist See definition (p), E-Codes-2

.8 Other specified person Intending passenger waiting at station
Unauthorized rider on railway vehicle

.9 Unspecified person

Motor Vehicle Traffic and Nontraffic Accidents (E810-E825)

The following fourth-digit subdivisions are for use with categories E810-E819 and E820-E825 to identify the injured person:

.0 Driver of motor vehicle other than motorcycle See definition (1), E-Codes-2

.1 Passenger in motor vehicle other than motorcycle See definition (1), E-Codes-2

.2 Motorcyclist See definition (1), E-Codes-2

.3 Passenger on motorcycle See definition (1), E-Codes-2

.4 Occupant of streetcar

.5 Rider of animal; occupant of animal-drawn vehicle

.6 Pedal cyclist See definition (p), E-Codes-2

.7 Pedestrian See definition (r), E-Codes-2

.8 Other specified person
Occupant of vehicle other than above
Person in railway train involved in accident
Unauthorized rider of motor vehicle

.9 Unspecified person

Other Road Vehicle Accidents (E826-E829)

(animal-drawn vehicle, streetcar, pedal cycle, and other nonmotor road vehicle accidents)

The following fourth-digit subdivisions are for use with categories E826-E829 to identify the injured person:

.0 Pedestrian See definition (r), E-Codes-2

.1 Pedal cyclist (does not apply to codes E827, E828, E829) See definition (p), E-Codes-2

.2 Rider of animal (does not apply to code E829)

.3 Occupant of animal-drawn vehicle (does not apply to codes E828, E829)

.4 Occupant of streetcar

.8 Other specified person

.9 Unspecified person

Water Transport Accidents (E830-E838)

The following fourth-digit subdivisions are for use with categories E830-E838 to identify the injured person:

.0 Occupant of small boat, unpowered

.1 Occupant of small boat, powered See definition (t), E-Codes-2
EXCLUDES water skier (.4)

.2 Occupant of other watercraft — crew
Persons:
  engaged in operation of watercraft
    providing passenger services [cabin attendants, ship's physician, catering personnel]
    working on ship during voyage in other capacity [musician in band, operators of shops and beauty parlors]

.3 Occupant of other watercraft — other than crew
Passenger
Occupant of lifeboat, other than crew, after abandoning ship

.4 Water skier

.5 Swimmer

.6 Dockers, stevedores
Longshoreman employed on the dock in loading and unloading ships

.8 Other specified person
Immigration and custom officials on board ship
Persons:
  accompanying passenger or member of crew visiting boat
Pilot (guiding ship into port)

.9 Unspecified person

Air and Space Transport Accidents (E840-E845)

The following fourth-digit subdivisions are for use with categories E840-E845 to identify the injured person:

.0 Occupant of spacecraft
  Crew
  Passenger (civilian) } in military aircraft [air force]
  (military) [army] [national guard] [navy]
  Troops

.1 Occupant of military aircraft, any
EXCLUDES occupants of aircraft operated under jurisdiction of police departments (.5) parachutist (.7)

.2 Crew of commercial aircraft (powered) in surface to surface transport

.3 Other occupant of commercial aircraft (powered) in surface to surface transport
Flight personnel:
  not part of crew
  on familiarization flight Passenger on aircraft

.4 Occupant of commercial aircraft (powered) in surface to air transport
Occupant [crew] [passenger] of aircraft (powered) engaged in activities, such as:
  air drops of emergency supplies
  air drops of parachutists, except from military craft
  crop dusting
  lowering of construction material [bridge or telephone pole]
  sky writing

.5 Occupant of other powered aircraft
Occupant [crew] [passenger] of aircraft (powered) engaged in activities, such as:
  aerial spraying (crops)(fire retardants)
  aerobatic flying
  aircraft racing
  rescue operation
  storm surveillance
  traffic suveillance
Occupant of private plane NOS

.6 Occupant of unpowered aircraft, except parachutist
Occupant of aircraft classifiable to E842

.7 Parachutist (military)(other)
Person making voluntary descent
  person making descent after accident to aircraft (.1-.6)

.8 Ground crew, airline employee
Persons employed at airfields (civil)(military) or launching pads, not occupants of aircraft

.9 Other person

1. INFECTIOUS AND PARASITIC DISEASES (001-139)

Note: Categories for "late effects" of infectious and parasitic diseases are to be found at 137-139.

INCLUDES   diseases generally recognized as communicable or transmissible as well as a few diseases of unknown but possibly infectious origin

EXCLUDES   *acute respiratory infections (460-466)*
carrier or suspected carrier of infectious organism (V02.0-V02.9)
certain localized infections
influenza (487.0-487.8)

INTESTINAL INFECTIOUS DISEASES (001-009)

EXCLUDES   *helminthiases (120.0-129)*

✓4ᵗʰ 001 Cholera

DEF: An acute infectious enteritis caused by a potent enterotoxin elaborated by *Vibrio cholerae*; the vibrio produces a toxin in the intestinal tract that changes the permeability of the mucosa leading to diarrhea and dehydration.

    001.0   Due to Vibrio cholerae
    001.1   Due to Vibrio cholerae el tor
    001.9   Cholera, unspecified

✓4ᵗʰ 002 Typhoid and paratyphoid fevers

DEF: Typhoid fever: an acute generalized illness caused by *Salmonella typhi*; notable clinical features are fever, headache, abdominal pain, cough, toxemia, leukopenia, abnormal pulse, rose spots on the skin, bacteremia, hyperplasia of intestinal lymph nodes, mesenteric lymphadenopathy, and Peyer's patches in the intestines.

DEF: Paratyphoid fever: a prolonged febrile illness, much like typhoid but usually less severe; caused by salmonella serotypes other than *S. typhi*, especially *S. enteritidis* serotypes paratyphi A and B and *S. choleraesuis*.

    002.0   Typhoid fever
       Typhoid (fever) (infection) [any site]
    002.1   Paratyphoid fever A
    002.2   Paratyphoid fever B
    002.3   Paratyphoid fever C
    002.9   Paratyphoid fever, unspecified

✓4ᵗʰ 003 Other salmonella infections

INCLUDES   infection or food poisoning by Salmonella [any serotype]

DEF: Infections caused by a genus of gram-negative, anaerobic bacteria of the family *Enterobacteriaceae*; affecting warm-blooded animals, like humans; major symptoms are enteric fevers, acute gastroenteritis and septicemia.

    003.0   Salmonella gastroenteritis
       Salmonellosis
    003.1   Salmonella septicemia   `HIV`
✓5ᵗʰ **003.2   Localized salmonella infections**
       003.20   Localized salmonella infection, unspecified   `HIV`
       003.21   Salmonella meningitis   `HIV`
       003.22   Salmonella pneumonia   `HIV`
       003.23   Salmonella arthritis   `HIV`
       003.24   Salmonella osteomyelitis   `HIV`
       003.29   Other   `HIV`
    003.8   Other specified salmonella infections   `HIV`
    003.9   Salmonella infection, unspecified   `HIV`

✓4ᵗʰ 004 Shigellosis

INCLUDES   bacillary dysentery

DEF: Acute infectious dysentery caused by the genus *Shigella*, of the family *Enterobacteriaceae*; affecting the colon causing the release of blood-stained stools with accompanying tenesmus, abdominal cramps and fever.

    004.0   Shigella dysenteriae
       Infection by group A Shigella (Schmitz) (Shiga)
    004.1   Shigella flexneri
       Infection by group B Shigella
    004.2   Shigella boydii
       Infection by group C Shigella

    004.3   Shigella sonnei
       Infection by group D Shigella
    004.8   Other specified Shigella infections
    004.9   Shigellosis, unspecified

✓4ᵗʰ 005 Other food poisoning (bacterial)

EXCLUDES   *salmonella infections (003.0-003.9)*
toxic effect of:
food contaminants (989.7)
noxious foodstuffs (988.0-988.9)

DEF: Enteritis caused by ingesting contaminated foods and characterized by diarrhea, abdominal pain, vomiting; symptoms may be mild or life threatening.

    005.0   Staphylococcal food poisoning
       Staphylococcal toxemia specified as due to food
    005.1   Botulism
       Food poisoning due to Clostridium botulinum
    005.2   Food poisoning due to Clostridium perfringens [C. welchii]
       Enteritis necroticans
    005.3   Food poisoning due to other Clostridia
    005.4   Food poisoning due to Vibrio parahaemolyticus
✓5ᵗʰ **005.8   Other bacterial food poisoning**

EXCLUDES   *salmonella food poisoning (003.0-003.9)*

       005.81   Food poisoning due to Vibrio vulnificus
       005.89   Other bacterial food poisoning
         Food poisoning due to Bacillus cereus
    005.9   Food poisoning, unspecified

✓4ᵗʰ 006 Amebiasis

INCLUDES   infection due to Entamoeba histolytica
EXCLUDES   *amebiasis due to organisms other than Entamoeba histolytica (007.8)*

DEF: Infection of the large intestine caused by *Entamoeba histolytica*; usually asymptomatic but symptoms may range from mild diarrhea to profound life-threatening dysentery. Extraintestinal complications include hepatic abscess, which may rupture into the lung, pericardium or abdomen, causing life-threatening infections.

    006.0   Acute amebic dysentery without mention of abscess
       Acute amebiasis
       DEF: Sudden, severe *Entamoeba histolytica* infection causing bloody stools.
    006.1   Chronic intestinal amebiasis without mention of abscess
       Chronic:
         amebiasis
         amebic dysentery
    006.2   Amebic nondysenteric colitis
       DEF: *Entamoeba histolytica* infection with inflamed colon but no dysentery.
    006.3   Amebic liver abscess
       Hepatic amebiasis
    006.4   Amebic lung abscess
       Amebic abscess of lung (and liver)
    006.5   Amebic brain abscess
       Amebic abscess of brain (and liver) (and lung)
    006.6   Amebic skin ulceration
       Cutaneous amebiasis
    006.8   Amebic infection of other sites
       Amebic: Ameboma
         appendicitis
         balanitis
       EXCLUDES   *specific infections by free-living amebae (136.2)*
    006.9   Amebiasis, unspecified
       Amebiasis NOS

✓4ᵗʰ / ✓5ᵗʰ Additional Digit Required   `Nonspecific PDx`   `Unacceptable PDx`   `Manifestation Code`   `MCV` Major Cardiovascular Condition   ▶◀ Revised Text   ● New Code   ▲ Revised Code Title

2007 ICD•9•CM   **Volume 1 — 1**

√4th **007 Other protozoal intestinal diseases**

INCLUDES   protozoal:
- colitis
- diarrhea
- dysentery

007.0 Balantidiasis
Infection by Balantidium coli

007.1 Giardiasis
Infection by Giardia lamblia   Lambliasis

007.2 Coccidiosis   HIV
Infection by Isospora belli and Isospora hominis
Isosporiasis

007.3 Intestinal trichomoniasis
DEF: Colitis, diarrhea, or dysentery caused by the protozoa *Trichomonas*.

007.4 Cryptosporidiosis
AHA: 4Q, '97, 30

DEF: An intestinal infection by protozoan parasites causing intractable diarrhea in patients with AIDS and other immunosuppressed individuals.

007.5 Cyclosporiasis
AHA: 4Q, '00, 38

DEF: An infection of the small intestine by the protozoal organism, *Cyclospora caytenanesis*, spread to humans though ingestion of contaminated water or food. Symptoms include watery diarrhea with frequent explosive bowel movements, loss of appetite, loss of weight, bloating, increased gas, stomach cramps, nausea, vomiting, muscle aches, low grade fever, and fatigue.

007.8 Other specified protozoal intestinal diseases
Amebiasis due to organisms other than Entamoeba histolytica

007.9 Unspecified protozoal intestinal disease
Flagellate diarrhea   Protozoal dysentery NOS

√4th **008 Intestinal infections due to other organisms**

INCLUDES   any condition classifiable to 009.0-009.3 with mention of the responsible organisms

EXCLUDES   food poisoning by these organisms (005.0-005.9)

√5th **008.0 Escherichia coli [E. coli]**
AHA: 4Q, '92, 17

   008.00 E. coli, unspecified
E. coli enteritis NOS

   008.01 Enteropathogenic E. coli
DEF: *E. coli* causing inflammation of intestines.

   008.02 Enterotoxigenic E. coli
DEF: A toxic reaction to *E. coli* of the intestinal mucosa, causing voluminous watery secretions.

   008.03 Enteroinvasive E. coli
DEF: *E. coli* infection penetrating intestinal mucosa.

   008.04 Enterohemorrhagic E. coli
DEF: *E. coli* infection penetrating the intestinal mucosa, producing microscopic ulceration and bleeding.

   008.09 Other intestinal E. coli infections

008.1 Arizona group of paracolon bacilli

008.2 Aerobacter aerogenes
Enterobacter aeogenes

008.3 Proteus (mirabilis) (morganii)

√5th **008.4 Other specified bacteria**
AHA: 4Q, '92, 18

008.41 Staphylococcus   CC
Staphylococcal enterocolitis

CC Excl: 001.1, 002.0, 002.9-003.0, 004.9-005.2, 006.0-006.2, 006.9, 007.1-009.0, 014.80-014.86, 112.85, 129, 487.8, 536.3, 536.8, 555.0-557.9, 558.2-558.9, 564.1, 775.0-775.9, 777.5, 777.8

008.42 Pseudomonas   CC
CC Excl: See code 008.41

AHA: 2Q, '89, 10

008.43 Campylobacter   CC
CC Excl: See code 008.41

008.44 Yersinia enterocolitica   CC
CC Excl: See code 008.41

008.45 Clostridium difficile   CC
Pseudomembranous colitis
CC Excl: See code 008.41

DRG 182

DEF: An overgrowth of a species of bacterium that is a part of the normal colon flora in human infants and sometimes in adults; produces a toxin that causes pseudomembranous enterocolitis.; typically is seen in patients undergoing antibiotic therapy.

008.46 Other anaerobes   CC
Anaerobic enteritis NOS
Bacteroides (fragilis)
Gram-negative anaerobes
CC Excl: See code 008.41

008.47 Other gram-negative bacteria   CC
Gram-negative enteritis NOS
EXCLUDES   gram-negative anaerobes (008.46)
CC Excl: See code 008.41

008.49 Other   CC
CC Excl: See code 008.41

AHA: 2Q, '89, 10; 1Q, '88, 6

008.5 Bacterial enteritis, unspecified

√5th **008.6 Enteritis due to specified virus**
AHA: 4Q, '92, 18

008.61 Rotavirus
008.62 Adenovirus
008.63 Norwalk virus
Norwalk-like agent
008.64 Other small round viruses [SRVs]
Small round virus NOS
008.65 Calicivirus
DEF: Enteritis due to a subgroup of *Picornaviruses*.
008.66 Astrovirus
008.67 Enterovirus NEC
Coxsackie virus   Echovirus
EXCLUDES   poliovirus (045.0-045.9)
008.69 Other viral enteritis
Torovirus
AHA: 1Q, '03, 10

008.8 Other organism, not elsewhere classified
Viral: Viral:
enteritis NOS   gastroenteritis
EXCLUDES   influenza with involvement of gastrointestinal tract (487.8)
DRG 182

N Newborn Age: 0   P Pediatric Age: 0-17   M Maternity Age: 12-55   A Adult Age: 15-124   CC CC Condition   MC Major Complication   CD Complex Dx   HIV HIV Related Dx

2 — Volume 1 • February 2006   **2007 ICD•9•CM**

✓4ᵗʰ 009 Ill-defined intestinal infections

EXCLUDES   diarrheal disease or intestinal infection due to specified organism (001.0-008.8)
diarrhea following gastrointestinal surgery (564.4)
intestinal malabsorption (579.0-579.9)
ischemic enteritis (557.0-557.9)
other noninfectious gastroenteritis and colitis (558.1-558.9)
regional enteritis (555.0-555.9)
ulcerative colitis (556)

009.0 Infectious colitis, enteritis, and gastroenteritis

Colitis
Enteritis   } septic
Gastroenteritis

Dysentery: Dysentery:
  NOS   hemorrhagic
  catarrhal

AHA: 3Q, '99, 4

DEF: Colitis: An inflammation of mucous membranes of the colon.
DEF: Enteritis: An inflammation of mucous membranes of the small intestine.
DEF: Gastroenteritis: An inflammation of mucous membranes of stomach and intestines.

009.1 Colitis, enteritis, and gastroenteritis of presumed infectious origin

EXCLUDES   colitis NOS (558.9)
enteritis NOS (558.9)
gastroenteritis NOS (558.9)

AHA: 3Q, '99, 6

009.2 Infectious diarrhea
Diarrhea:
  dysenteric
  epidemic
Infectious diarrheal disease NOS

009.3 Diarrhea of presumed infectious origin

EXCLUDES   diarrhea NOS (787.91)

AHA: N-D, '87, 7

TUBERCULOSIS (010-018)

INCLUDES   infection by Mycobacterium tuberculosis (human) (bovine)

EXCLUDES   congenital tuberculosis (771.2)
late effects of tuberculosis (137.0-137.4)

The following fifth-digit subclassification is for use with categories 010-018:

0 **unspecified**
1 **bacteriological or histological examination not done**
2 **bacteriological or histological examination unknown (at present)**
3 **tubercle bacilli found (in sputum) by microscopy**
4 **tubercle bacilli not found (in sputum) by microscopy, but found by bacterial culture**
5 **tubercle bacilli not found by bacteriological examination, but tuberculosis confirmed histologically**
6 **tubercle bacilli not found by bacteriological or histological examination but tuberculosis confirmed by other methods [inoculation of animals]**

DEF: An infection by *Mycobacterium tuberculosis* causing the formation of small, rounded nodules, called tubercles, that can disseminate throughout the body via lymph and blood vessels. Localized tuberculosis is most often seen in the lungs.

✓4ᵗʰ 010 Primary tuberculous infection

DEF: Tuberculosis of the lungs occurring when the patient is first infected.

§ ✓5ᵗʰ 010.0 Primary tuberculous infection   HIV

EXCLUDES   nonspecific reaction to tuberculin skin test without active tuberculosis (795.5)
positive PPD (795.5)
positive tuberculin skin test without active tuberculosis (795.5)

DEF: Hilar or paratracheal lymph node enlargement in pulmonary tuberculosis.

§ ✓5ᵗʰ 010.1 Tuberculous pleurisy in primary progressive tuberculosis   HIV

DEF: Inflammation and exudation in the lining of the tubercular lung.

§ ✓5ᵗʰ 010.8 Other primary progressive tuberculosis   HIV

EXCLUDES   tuberculous erythema nodosum (017.1)

§ ✓5ᵗʰ 010.9 Primary tuberculous infection, unspecified   HIV

✓4ᵗʰ 011 Pulmonary tuberculosis   HIV

Use additional code to identify any associated silicosis (502)

§ ✓5ᵗʰ 011.0 Tuberculosis of lung, infiltrative   CC HIV

CC Excl: 011.00-012.86, 017.90-018.96, 031.0, 031.2-031.9, 041.81-041.9, 137.0, 139.8, 480.0-480.2, 480.8-487.1, 494.0-508.9, 517.1, 518.89

§ ✓5ᵗʰ 011.1 Tuberculosis of lung, nodular   CC HIV

CC Excl: See code 011.0

§ ✓5ᵗʰ 011.2 Tuberculosis of lung with cavitation   CC HIV

CC Excl: See code 011.0

§ ✓5ᵗʰ 011.3 Tuberculosis of bronchus   CC HIV

EXCLUDES   isolated bronchial tuberculosis (012.2)

CC Excl: See code 011.0

§ ✓5ᵗʰ 011.4 Tuberculous fibrosis of lung   CC HIV

CC Excl: See code 011.0

§ ✓5ᵗʰ 011.5 Tuberculous bronchiectasis   CC HIV

CC Excl: See code 011.0

§ ✓5ᵗʰ 011.6 Tuberculous pneumonia [any form]   CC HIV

CC Excl: For codes 011.60-011.65: See code 011.0

CC Excl: For code 011.66: 011.66, 139.8, 480.0-480.2, 480.8-487.1, 494.0-508.9, 517.1, 518.89

DEF: Inflammatory pulmonary reaction to tuberculous cells.

§ ✓5ᵗʰ 011.7 Tuberculous pneumothorax   CC HIV

CC Excl: See code 011.0

DEF: Spontaneous rupture of damaged tuberculous pulmonary tissue.

§ ✓5ᵗʰ 011.8 Other specified pulmonary tuberculosis   CC HIV

CC Excl: See code 011.0

§ ✓5ᵗʰ 011.9 Pulmonary tuberculosis, unspecified   CC HIV
Respiratory tuberculosis NOS
Tuberculosis of lung NOS

CC Excl: See code 011.0

---

§ Requires fifth-digit. See beginning of section 010-018 for codes and definitions.

✓4ᵗʰ ✓5ᵗʰ Additional Digit Required   Nonspecific PDx   Unacceptable PDx   Manifestation Code   MCV Major Cardiovascular Condition   ▶◀ Revised Text   ● New Code   ▲ Revised Code Title

Infectious and Parasitic Diseases

012–016.3

√4ᵗʰ **012 Other respiratory tuberculosis**

> EXCLUDES   *respiratory tuberculosis, unspecified (011.9)*

§ √5ᵗʰ **012.0 Tuberculous pleurisy** CC HIV
> Tuberculosis of pleura
> Tuberculous empyema
> Tuberculous hydrothorax
> > EXCLUDES   *pleurisy with effusion without mention of cause (511.9)*
> > *tuberculous pleurisy in primary progressive tuberculosis (010.1)*
>
> **CC Excl:** See code 011.0
>
> **DEF:** Inflammation and exudation in the lining of the tubercular lung.

§ √5ᵗʰ **012.1 Tuberculosis of intrathoracic lymph nodes** CC HIV
> Tuberculosis of lymph nodes:
> > hilar
> > mediastinal
> > tracheobronchial
> Tuberculous tracheobronchial adenopathy
> > EXCLUDES   *that specified as primary (010.0-010.9)*
>
> **CC Excl:** See code 011.0

§ √5ᵗʰ **012.2 Isolated tracheal or bronchial tuberculosis** HIV

§ √5ᵗʰ **012.3 Tuberculous laryngitis** HIV
> Tuberculosis of glottis

§ √5ᵗʰ **012.8 Other specified respiratory tuberculosis** HIV
> Tuberculosis of: Tuberculosis of:
> > mediastinum   nose (septum)
> > nasopharynx   sinus [any nasal]

√4ᵗʰ **013 Tuberculosis of meninges and central nervous system**

§ √5ᵗʰ **013.0 Tuberculous meningitis** CC HIV
> Tuberculosis of meninges (cerebral) (spinal)
> Tuberculous:
> > leptomeningitis
> > meningoencephalitis
> > EXCLUDES   *tuberculoma of meninges (013.1)*
>
> **CC Excl:** 003.21, 013.00-013.16, 013.40-013.56, 013.80-013.96, 017.90-017.96, 031.2, 031.8-031.9, 036.0, 041.81-041.89, 041.9, 047.0-047.9, 049.0-049.1, 053.0, 054.72, 072.1, 090.42, 091.81, 094.2, 098.89, 100.81, 112.83, 114.2, 115.01, 115.11, 115.91, 130.0, 137.1, 139.8, 320.0-320.9, 321.0-321.8, 322.0-322.9, 349.89, 349.9, 357.0

§ √5ᵗʰ **013.1 Tuberculoma of meninges** CC HIV
> **CC Excl:** See code 013.0

§ √5ᵗʰ **013.2 Tuberculoma of brain** CC HIV
> Tuberculosis of brain (current disease)
> **CC Excl:** 013.20-013.36, 013.60-013.96, 017.90-017.96, 031.2-031.9, 041.81, 041.9, 137.1, 139.8

§ √5ᵗʰ **013.3 Tuberculous abscess of brain** CC HIV
> **CC Excl:** See code 013.2

§ √5ᵗʰ **013.4 Tuberculoma of spinal cord** CC HIV
> **CC Excl:** 013.00-013.16, 013.40-013.56, 013.80-013.96, 017.90-017.96, 031.2, 031.9, 041.81-041.89, 041.9, 137.1, 139.8

§ √5ᵗʰ **013.5 Tuberculous abscess of spinal cord** CC HIV
> **CC Excl:** See code 013.4

§ √5ᵗʰ **013.6 Tuberculous encephalitis or myelitis** CC HIV
> **CC Excl:** 013.20-013.36, 013.60-013.96, 017.90-017.96, 031.2-031.9, 041.81-041.89, 041.9, 137.1, 139.8

§ √5ᵗʰ **013.8 Other specified tuberculosis of central nervous system** CC HIV
> **CC Excl:** 013.80-013.96, 017.90-017.96, 031.2-031.9, 041.81-041.89, 041.9, 137.1, 139.8

§ √5ᵗʰ **013.9 Unspecified tuberculosis of central nervous system** CC HIV
> Tuberculosis of central nervous system NOS
> **CC Excl:** See code 013.8

√4ᵗʰ **014 Tuberculosis of intestines, peritoneum, and mesenteric glands**

§ √5ᵗʰ **014.0 Tuberculous peritonitis** CC HIV
> Tuberculous ascites
> **CC Excl:** 014.00-014.86, 017.90-017.96, 031.2-031.9, 041.81-041.9, 139.8
>
> **DEF:** Tuberculous inflammation of the membrane lining the abdomen.

§ √5ᵗʰ **014.8 Other** CC HIV
> Tuberculosis (of):
> > anus
> > intestine (large) (small)
> > mesenteric glands
> > rectum
> > retroperitoneal (lymph nodes)
> Tuberculous enteritis
> **CC Excl: For code 014.80, 014.82-014.86:** See code 014.0
>
> **CC Excl: For code 014.81:** 014.81, 139.8

√4ᵗʰ **015 Tuberculosis of bones and joints**
> Use additional code to identify manifestation, as:
> > tuberculous:
> > > arthropathy (711.4)
> > > necrosis of bone (730.8)
> > > osteitis (730.8)
> > > osteomyelitis (730.8)
> > > synovitis (727.01)
> > > tenosynovitis (727.01)

§ √5ᵗʰ **015.0 Vertebral column** HIV
> Pott's disease
> Use additional code to identify manifestation, as:
> > curvature of spine [Pott's] (737.4)
> > kyphosis (737.4)
> > spondylitis (720.81)

§ √5ᵗʰ **015.1 Hip** HIV

§ √5ᵗʰ **015.2 Knee** HIV

§ √5ᵗʰ **015.5 Limb bones** HIV
> Tuberculous dactylitis

§ √5ᵗʰ **015.6 Mastoid** HIV
> Tuberculous mastoiditis

§ √5ᵗʰ **015.7 Other specified bone** HIV

§ √5ᵗʰ **015.8 Other specified joint** HIV

§ √5ᵗʰ **015.9 Tuberculosis of unspecified bones and joints** HIV

√4ᵗʰ **016 Tuberculosis of genitourinary system**

§ √5ᵗʰ **016.0 Kidney** CC HIV
> Renal tuberculosis
> Use additional code to identify manifestation, as:
> > tuberculous:
> > > nephropathy (583.81)
> > > pyelitis (590.81)
> > > pyelonephritis (590.81)
> **CC Excl:** 016.00-016.36, 016.90-016.96, 017.90-017.96, 031.2-031.9, 041.81-041.89, 041.9, 137.2, 139.8

§ √5ᵗʰ **016.1 Bladder** CC HIV
> **CC Excl:** See code 016.0

§ √5ᵗʰ **016.2 Ureter** CC HIV
> **CC Excl:** See code 016.0

§ √5ᵗʰ **016.3 Other urinary organs** CC HIV
> **CC Excl:** See code 016.0

---

§ Requires fifth-digit. See beginning of section 010-018 for codes and definitions.

N Newborn Age: 0   P Pediatric Age: 0-17   M Maternity Age: 12-55   A Adult Age: 15-124   CC CC Condition   MC Major Complication   CD Complex Dx   HIV HIV Related Dx

§ ✓5th **016.4 Epididymis**   CC HIV ♂
CC Excl: 016.40-016.56, 016.90-016.96, 017.90-017.96, 031.2-031.9, 041.81-041.89, 041.9, 137.2, 139.8

§ ✓5th **016.5 Other male genital organs**   CC HIV ♂
Use additional code to identify manifestation, as:
tuberculosis of:
prostate (601.4)
seminal vesicle (608.81)
testis (608.81)
CC Excl: See code 016.4

§ ✓5th **016.6 Tuberculous oophoritis and salpingitis**   CC HIV ♀
CC Excl: 016.60-016.96, 017.90-017.96, 031.2-031.9, 041.81-041.9, 137.2, 139.8

§ ✓5th **016.7 Other female genital organs**   CC HIV ♀
Tuberculous:
cervicitis
endometritis
CC Excl: See code 016.6

§ ✓5th **016.9 Genitourinary tuberculosis, unspecified**   CC HIV
CC Excl: 016.90-016.96, 017.90-017.96, 031.2-031.9, 041.81-041.9, 137.2, 139.8

✓4th **017 Tuberculosis of other organs**

§ ✓5th **017.0 Skin and subcutaneous cellular tissue**   HIV

Lupus: Tuberculosis:
   exedens   cutis
   vulgaris   lichenoides
Scrofuloderma   papulonecrotica
Tuberculosis: verrucosa cutis
   colliquativa
> EXCLUDES   lupus erythematosus (695.4)
>   disseminated (710.0)
>   lupus NOS (710.0)
>   nonspecific reaction to tuberculin skin
>   test without active tuberculosis
>   (795.5)
>   positive PPD (795.5)
>   positive tuberculin skin test without
>   active tuberculosis (795.5)

§ ✓5th **017.1 Erythema nodosum with hypersensitivity reaction in tuberculosis**   HIV
Bazin's disease   Erythema:
Erythema: nodosum, tuberculous
  induratum   Tuberculosis indurativa
> EXCLUDES   erythema nodosum NOS (695.2)

DEF: Tender, inflammatory, bilateral nodules appearing on the shins and thought to be an allergic reaction to tuberculotoxin.

§ ✓5th **017.2 Peripheral lymph nodes**   CC HIV
Scrofula   Tuberculous adenitis
Scrofulous abscess
> EXCLUDES   tuberculosis of lymph nodes:
>   bronchial and mediastinal (012.1)
>   mesenteric and retroperitoneal
>   (014.8)
>   tuberculous tracheobronchial
>   adenopathy (012.1)
CC Excl: 017.20-017.26, 017.90-017.96, 031.2-031.9, 041.81-041.9, 139.8

DEF: Scrofula: Old name for tuberculous cervical lymphadenitis.

§ ✓5th **017.3 Eye**   CC HIV
Use additional code to identify manifestation, as:
tuberculous:
chorioretinitis, disseminated (363.13)
episcleritis (379.09)
interstitial keratitis (370.59)
iridocyclitis, chronic (364.11)
keratoconjunctivitis (phlyctenular) (370.31)
CC Excl: 017.30-017.36, 017.90-017.96, 031.2-031.9, 041.81-041.9, 139.8

§ ✓5th **017.4 Ear**   CC HIV
Tuberculosis of ear
Tuberculous otitis media
> EXCLUDES   tuberculous mastoiditis (015.6)
CC Excl: 017.40-017.46, 017.90-017.96, 031.2-031.9, 041.81-041.9, 139.8

§ ✓5th **017.5 Thyroid gland**   CC HIV
CC Excl: 017.50-017.56, 017.90-017.96, 031.2-031.9, 041.81-041.9, 139.8

§ ✓5th **017.6 Adrenal glands**   CC HIV
Addison's disease, tuberculous
CC Excl: 017.60-017.66, 017.90-017.96, 031.2-031.9, 041.81-041.9, 139.8

§ ✓5th **017.7 Spleen**   CC HIV
CC Excl: 017.70-017.76, 017.90-017.96, 031.2-031.9, 041.81-041.9, 139.8

§ ✓5th **017.8 Esophagus**   CC HIV
CC Excl: 017.80-017.96, 031.2-031.9, 041.81-041.9, 139.8

§ ✓5th **017.9 Other specified organs**   CC HIV
Use additional code to identify manifestation, as:
tuberculosis of:
endocardium [any valve] (424.91)
myocardium (422.0)
pericardium (420.0)
CC Excl: 017.90-017.96, 031.2-031.9, 041.81-041.9, 139.8

✓4th **018 Miliary tuberculosis**
> INCLUDES   tuberculosis:
>   disseminated
>   generalized
>   miliary, whether of a single specified site,
>   multiple sites, or unspecified site
>   polyserositis

DEF: A form of tuberculosis caused by caseous material carried through the bloodstream planting seedlike tubercles in various body organs.

§ ✓5th **018.0 Acute miliary tuberculosis**   CC HIV
CC Excl: 017.90-018.96, 031.2-031.9, 041.81-041.9, 139.8

§ ✓5th **018.8 Other specified miliary tuberculosis**   CC HIV
CC Excl: See code 018.0

§ ✓5th **018.9 Miliary tuberculosis, unspecified**   CC HIV
CC Excl: See code 018.0

ZOONOTIC BACTERIAL DISEASES (020-027)

✓4th **020 Plague**
> INCLUDES   infection by Yersinia [Pasteurella] pestis

020.0 Bubonic
DEF: Most common acute and severe form of plague characterized by lymphadenopathy (buboes), chills, fever and headache.

020.1 Cellulocutaneous
DEF: Plague characterized by inflammation and necrosis of skin.

020.2 Septicemic
DEF: Plague characterized by massive infection in the bloodstream.

020.3 Primary pneumonic
DEF: Plague characterized by massive pulmonary infection.

020.4 Secondary pneumonic
DEF: Lung infection as a secondary complication of plague.

020.5 Pneumonic, unspecified

020.8 Other specified types of plague
Abortive plague   Pestis minor
Ambulatory plague

020.9 Plague, unspecified

§ Requires fifth-digit. See beginning of section 010-018 for codes and definitions.

✓4th / ✓5th Additional Digit Required   Nonspecific PDx   Unacceptable PDx   Manifestation Code   MCV Major Cardiovascular Condition   ▶◀ Revised Text   ● New Code   ▲ Revised Code Title

2007 ICD•9•CM   **Volume 1 — 5**

✓4ᵗʰ 021 Tularemia

INCLUDES deerfly fever
infection by Francisella [Pasteurella] tularensis
rabbit fever

DEF: A febrile disease transmitted by the bites of deer flies, fleas and ticks, by inhalations of aerosolized *F. tularensis* or by ingestion of contaminated food or water; patients quickly develop fever, chills, weakness, headache, backache and malaise.

021.0　Ulceroglandular tularemia
DEF: Lesions occur at the site *Francisella tularensis* organism enters body, usually the fingers or hands.

021.1　Enteric tularemia
Tularemia:　　　　　　Tularemia:
　cryptogenic　　　　　　typhoidal
　intestinal

021.2　Pulmonary tularemia
Bronchopneumonic tularemia

021.3　Oculoglandular tularemia
DEF: Painful conjunctival infection by *Francisella tularensis* organism with possible corneal, preauricular lymph, or lacrimal involvement.

021.8　Other specified tularemia
Tularemia:　　　　　　　　　　Tularemia:
　generalized or disseminated　　glandular

021.9　Unspecified tularemia

✓4ᵗʰ 022 Anthrax
AHA: 4Q '02, 70

DEF: An infectious bacterial disease usually transmitted by contact with infected animals or their discharges or products; it is classified by primary routes of inoculation as cutaneous, gastrointestinal and by inhalation.

022.0　Cutaneous anthrax
Malignant pustule

022.1　Pulmonary anthrax
Respiratory anthrax
Wool-sorters' disease

022.2　Gastrointestinal anthrax

022.3　Anthrax septicemia

022.8　Other specified manifestations of anthrax

022.9　Anthrax, unspecified

✓4ᵗʰ 023 Brucellosis

INCLUDES fever:
　　　　　Malta
　　　　　Mediterranean
　　　　　undulant

DEF: An infectious disease caused by gram-negative, aerobic coccobacilli organisms; it is transmitted to humans through contact with infected tissue or dairy products; fever, sweating, weakness and aching are symptoms.

023.0　Brucella melitensis
DEF: Infection from direct or indirect contact with infected sheep or goats.

023.1　Brucella abortus
DEF: Infection from direct or indirect contact with infected cattle.

023.2　Brucella suis
DEF: Infection from direct or indirect contact with infected swine.

023.3　Brucella canis
DEF: Infection from direct or indirect contact with infected dogs.

023.8　Other brucellosis
Infection by more than one organism

023.9　Brucellosis, unspecified

024 Glanders
Infection by:
　Actinobacillus mallei　　　　Farcy
　Malleomyces mallei　　　　　Malleus
　Pseudomonas mallei

DEF: Equine infection causing mucosal inflammation and skin ulcers in humans.

025 Melioidosis
Infection by:　　　　　　　Infection by:
　Malleomyces pseudomallei　Pseudoglanders
　Pseudomonas pseudomallei　Whitmore's bacillus

DEF: Rare infection caused by *Pseudomonas pseudomallei*; clinical symptoms range from localized infection to fatal septicemia.

✓4ᵗʰ 026 Rat-bite fever

026.0　Spirillary fever
Rat-bite fever due to Spirillum minor [S. minus]
Sodoku

026.1　Streptobacillary fever
Epidemic arthritic erythema
Haverhill fever
Rat-bite fever due to Streptobacillus moniliformis

026.9　Unspecified rat-bite fever

✓4ᵗʰ 027 Other zoonotic bacterial diseases

027.0　Listeriosis
Infection　　}
Septicemia　} by Listeria monocytogenes

Use additional code to identify manifestation, as meningitis (320.7)
EXCLUDES congenital listeriosis (771.2)

027.1　Erysipelothrix infection
Erysipeloid (of Rosenbach)
Infection　　} by Erysipelothrix insidiosa
Septicemia　}　　[E. rhusiopathiae]

DEF: Usually associated with handling of fish, meat, or poultry; symptoms range from localized inflammation to septicemia.

027.2　Pasteurellosis
Pasteurella pseudotuberculosis infection
Mesenteric adenitis　　　　}
Septic infection (cat　　　　} by Pasteurella multocida
　bite) (dog bite)　　　　　}　　[P. septica]

EXCLUDES infection by:
　Francisella [Pasteurella] tularensis (021.0-021.9)
　Yersinia [Pasteurella] pestis (020.0-020.9)

DEF: Swelling, abscesses, or septicemia from *Pasteurella multocida*, commonly transmitted to humans by a dog or cat scratch.

027.8　Other specified zoonotic bacterial diseases

027.9　Unspecified zoonotic bacterial disease

OTHER BACTERIAL DISEASES (030-041)
EXCLUDES bacterial venereal diseases (098.0-099.9)
bartonellosis (088.0)

✓4ᵗʰ 030 Leprosy

INCLUDES Hansen's disease
infection by Mycobacterium leprae

030.0　Lepromatous [type L]
Lepromatous leprosy (macular) (diffuse) (infiltrated) (nodular) (neuritic)
DEF: Infectious, disseminated leprosy bacilli with lesions and deformities.

030.1　Tuberculoid [type T]
Tuberculoid leprosy (macular) (maculoanesthetic) (major) (minor) (neuritic)
DEF: Relatively benign, self-limiting leprosy with neuralgia and scales.

030.2　Indeterminate [group I]
Indeterminate [uncharacteristic] leprosy (macular) (neuritic)
DEF: Uncharacteristic leprosy, frequently an early manifestation.

030.3　Borderline [group B]
Borderline or dimorphous leprosy (infiltrated) (neuritic)
DEF: Transitional form of leprosy, neither lepromatous nor tuberculoid.

N Newborn Age: 0　　P Pediatric Age: 0-17　　M Maternity Age: 12-55　　A Adult Age: 15-124　　CC CC Condition　　MC Major Complication　　CD Complex Dx　　HIV HIV Related Dx

6 — Volume 1　　　　　　　　　　　　　　　　　　　　　　　　　　　　　　　　　　2007 ICD•9•CM

030.8   **Other specified leprosy**

030.9   **Leprosy, unspecified**

√4ᵗʰ **031 Diseases due to other mycobacteria**

     031.0   **Pulmonary**   `CC`

         Battey disease

         Infection by Mycobacterium:

            avium

            intracellulare [Battey bacillus]

            kansasii

         CC Excl: 011.00-012.86, 017.90-017.96, 031.0, 031.2-031.9, 041.81-041.9, 137.0, 139.8, 480.0-480.2, 480.8-487.1, 494.0-508.9, 517.1, 518.89

     031.1   **Cutaneous**

         Buruli ulcer

         Infection by Mycobacterium:

            marinum [M. balnei]

            ulcerans

     031.2   **Disseminated**   `HIV`

         Disseminated mycobacterium avium-intracellulare complex (DMAC)

         Mycobacterium avium-intracellulare complex (MAC) bacteremia

         AHA: 4Q, '97, 31

         DEF: Disseminated mycobacterium avium-intracellulare complex (DMAC): A serious systemic form of MAC commonly observed in patients in the late course of AIDS.

         DEF: Mycobacterium avium-intracellulare complex (MAC) bacterium: Human pulmonary disease, lymphadenitis in children and systemic disease in immunocompromised individuals caused by a slow growing, gram-positive, aerobic organism.

     031.8   **Other specified mycobacterial diseases**   `HIV`

     031.9   **Unspecified diseases due to mycobacteria**   `HIV`

         Atypical mycobacterium infection NOS

√4ᵗʰ **032 Diphtheria**

     `INCLUDES`   infection by Corynebacterium diphtheriae

     032.0   **Faucial diphtheria**

         Membranous angina, diphtheritic

         DEF: Diphtheria of the throat.

     032.1   **Nasopharyngeal diphtheria**

     032.2   **Anterior nasal diphtheria**

     032.3   **Laryngeal diphtheria**

         Laryngotracheitis, diphtheritic

√5ᵗʰ   **032.8**   **Other specified diphtheria**

         032.81 Conjunctival diphtheria

               Pseudomembranous diphtheritic conjunctivitis

         032.82 Diphtheritic myocarditis

         032.83 Diphtheritic peritonitis

         032.84 Diphtheritic cystitis

         032.85 Cutaneous diphtheria

         032.89 Other

     032.9   **Diphtheria, unspecified**

√4ᵗʰ **033 Whooping cough**

     `INCLUDES`   pertussis

     Use additional code to identify any associated pneumonia (484.3)

     DEF: An acute, highly contagious respiratory tract infection caused by *Bordetella pertussis* and *B. bronchiseptica*; characteristic paroxysmal cough.

     033.0   **Bordetella pertussis [B. pertussis]**

     033.1   **Bordetella parapertussis [B. parapertussis]**

     033.8   **Whooping cough due to other specified organism**

         Bordetella bronchiseptica [B. bronchiseptica]

     033.9   **Whooping cough, unspecified organism**

√4ᵗʰ **034 Streptococcal sore throat and scarlet fever**

     034.0   **Streptococcal sore throat**

         Septic: Streptococcal:

            angina   laryngitis

            sore throat   pharyngitis

         Streptococcal: tonsillitis

            angina

     034.1   **Scarlet fever**

         Scarlatina

         `EXCLUDES`   *parascarlatina (057.8)*

         DEF: Streptococcal infection and fever with red rash spreading from trunk.

035 Erysipelas

     `EXCLUDES`   *postpartum or puerperal erysipelas (670)*

     DEF: An acute superficial cellulitis involving the dermal lymphatics; it is often caused by group A streptococci.

√4ᵗʰ **036 Meningococcal infection**

     036.0   **Meningococcal meningitis**   `CC`

         Cerebrospinal fever (meningococcal)

         Meningitis:

            cerebrospinal

            epidemic

         CC Excl: 003.21, 013.00-013.16, 036.0, 036.89-036.9, 041.81-041.9, 047.0-047.9, 049.0-049.1, 053.0, 054.72, 072.1, 090.42, 091.81, 094.2, 098.89, 100.81, 112.83, 114.2, 115.01, 115.11, 115.91, 130.0, 139.8, 320.0-322.9, 349.89-349.9, 357.0

     036.1   **Meningococcal encephalitis**   `CC`

         CC Excl: 036.1, 036.89, 036.9, 041.81-041.89, 041.9, 139.8

     036.2   **Meningococcemia**   `CC`

         Meningococcal septicemia

         CC Excl: 003.1, 020.2, 036.2, 036.89-036.9, 038.0-038.9, 041.81-041.9, 054.5, 139.8, 995.90-995.94

     036.3   **Waterhouse-Friderichsen syndrome, meningococcal**   `CC`

         Meningococcal hemorrhagic adrenalitis

         Meningococcic adrenal syndrome

         Waterhouse-Friderichsen syndrome NOS

         CC Excl: 036.3, 036.89, 036.9, 041.81-041.89, 041.9, 139.8

√5ᵗʰ   **036.4**   **Meningococcal carditis**

         036.40 Meningococcal carditis, unspecified   `CC`

            CC Excl: 036.40, 036.89-036.9, 041.81-041.9, 139.8

         036.41 Meningococcal pericarditis   `CC`

            CC Excl: 036.41, 036.89-036.9, 041.81-041.9, 139.8

            DEF: Meningococcal infection of the outer membrane of the heart.

         036.42 Meningococcal endocarditis   `CC`

            CC Excl: 036.42, 036.89-036.9, 041.81-041.9, 139.8

            DEF: Meningococcal infection of the membranes lining the cavities of the heart.

         036.43 Meningococcal myocarditis   `CC`

            CC Excl: 036.43, 041.81-041.9, 139.8

            DEF: Meningococcal infection of the muscle of the heart.

√5ᵗʰ   **036.8**   **Other specified meningococcal infections**

         036.81 Meningococcal optic neuritis   `CC`

            CC Excl: 036.81, 036.89-036.9, 041.81-041.9, 139.8

         036.82 Meningococcal arthropathy   `CC`

            CC Excl: 036.82-036.9, 041.81-041.9, 139.8

         036.89 Other   `CC`

            CC Excl: 036.89-036.9, 041.81-041.9, 139.8

     036.9   **Meningococcal infection, unspecified**   `CC`

         Meningococcal infection NOS

         CC Excl: See code 036.89

Infectious and Parasitic Diseases

037–040.1

037 Tetanus   `CC`

> EXCLUDES   tetanus:
> > complicating:
> > > abortion (634-638 with .0, 639.0)
> > > ectopic or molar pregnancy (639.0)
> > neonatorum (771.3)
> > puerperal (670)

CC Excl: 037, 139.8

DEF: An acute, often fatal, infectious disease caused by the anaerobic, spore-forming bacillus *Clostridium tetani*; the bacillus most often enters the body through a contaminated wound, burns, surgical wounds, or cutaneous ulcers. Symptoms include lockjaw, spasms, seizures, and paralysis.

✓4ᵗʰ 038 Septicemia

> Use additional code for systemic inflammatory response syndrome (SIRS) (995.91-995.92)
> > EXCLUDES   bacteremia (790.7)
> > during labor (659.3)
> > following ectopic or molar pregnancy (639.0)
> > following infusion, injection, transfusion, or vaccination (999.3)
> > postpartum, puerperal (670)
> > septicemia (sepsis) of newborn (771.81)
> > that complicating abortion (634-638 with .0, 639.0)

AHA: 2Q, '04, 16; 4Q, '88, 10; 3Q, '88, 12

DEF: A systemic disease associated with the presence and persistence of pathogenic microorganisms or their toxins in the blood.

038.0 Streptococcal septicemia   `CC` `HIV`

CC Excl: 003.1, 020.2, 036.2, 038.0-038.9, 040.82-041.7, 041.81-041.9, 054.5, 139.8, 995.90-995.95, V09.0-V09.91

AHA: 4Q, '03, 79; 2Q, '96, 5

✓5ᵗʰ 038.1 Staphylococcal septicemia

AHA: 4Q, '97, 32

038.10 Staphylococcal septicemia, unspecified   `CC` `HIV`

CC Excl: See code 038.0

038.11 Staphylococcus aureus septicemia   `CC` `HIV`

CC Excl: See code 038.0

AHA: 1Q, '05, 7; 2Q, '00, 5; 4Q, '98, 42

DRG 416

038.19 Other staphylococcal septicemia   `CC` `HIV`

CC Excl: See code 038.0

AHA: 2Q, '00, 5

DRG 416

038.2 Pneumococcal septicemia [Streptococcus pneumoniae septicemia]   `CC` `HIV`

CC Excl: See code 038.0

AHA: 2Q, '96, 5; 1Q, '91, 13

038.3 Septicemia due to anaerobes   `CC` `HIV`

Septicemia due to bacteroides
> EXCLUDES   gas gangrene (040.0)
> > that due to anaerobic streptococci (038.0)

CC Excl: See code 038.0

✓5ᵗʰ 038.4 Septicemia due to other gram-negative organisms

DEF: Infection of blood by microorganisms categorized as gram-negative by Gram's method of staining for identification of bacteria.

038.40 Gram-negative organism, unspecified `CC` `HIV`

Gram-negative septicemia NOS

CC Excl: See code 038.0

038.41 Hemophilus influenzae [H. influenzae]   `CC` `HIV`

CC Excl: See code 038.0

038.42 Escherichia coli [E. coli]   `CC` `HIV`

CC Excl: See code 038.0

AHA: 4Q, '03, 73

DRG 416

038.43 Pseudomonas   `CC` `HIV`

CC Excl: See code 038.0

038.44 Serratia   `CC` `HIV`

CC Excl: See code 038.0

038.49 Other   `CC` `HIV`

CC Excl: See code 038.0

DRG 416

038.8 Other specified septicemias   `CC` `HIV`

> EXCLUDES   septicemia (due to):
> > anthrax (022.3)
> > gonococcal (098.89)
> > herpetic (054.5)
> > meningococcal (036.2)
> > septicemic plague (020.2)

CC Excl: See code 038.0

038.9 Unspecified septicemia   `CC` `HIV`

Septicemia NOS
> EXCLUDES   bacteremia NOS (790.7)

CC Excl: See code 038.0

AHA: ▶2Q, '05, 18-19;◀ 2Q, '04, 16; 4Q, '03, 79; 2Q, '00, 3; 3Q, '99, 5, 9; 1Q, '98, 5; 3Q, '96, 16; 2Q, '96, 6

DRG 416

✓4ᵗʰ 039 Actinomycotic infections

> INCLUDES   actinomycotic mycetoma
> > infection by Actinomycetales, such as species of Actinomyces, Actinomadura, Nocardia, Streptomyces
> > maduromycosis (actinomycotic)
> > schizomycetoma (actinomycotic)

DEF: Inflammatory lesions and abscesses at site of infection by *Actinomyces israelii*.

039.0 Cutaneous   `HIV`

Erythrasma   Trichomycosis axillaris

039.1 Pulmonary   `HIV`

Thoracic actinomycosis

039.2 Abdominal   `HIV`

039.3 Cervicofacial

039.4 Madura foot   `HIV`

> EXCLUDES   madura foot due to mycotic infection (117.4)

039.8 Of other specified sites   `HIV`

039.9 Of unspecified site   `HIV`

Actinomycosis NOS   Nocardiosis NOS
Maduromycosis NOS

✓4ᵗʰ 040 Other bacterial diseases

> EXCLUDES   bacteremia NOS (790.7)
> > bacterial infection NOS (041.9)

040.0 Gas gangrene   `CC`

Gas bacillus infection or gangrene
Infection by Clostridium:
> histolyticum
> oedematiens
> perfringens [welchii]
> septicum
> sordellii
Malignant edema
Myonecrosis, clostridial
Myositis, clostridial

CC Excl: 040.0, 139.8

AHA: 1Q, '95, 11

040.1 Rhinoscleroma

DEF: Growths on the nose and nasopharynx caused by *Klebsiella rhinoscleromatis*.

 Newborn Age: 0   Pediatric Age: 0-17   Maternity Age: 12-55   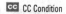 Adult Age: 15-124   `CC` CC Condition   `MC` Major Complication   `CD` Complex Dx   `HIV` HIV Related Dx

8 — Volume 1 • February 2006   *2007 ICD•9•CM*

040.2   Whipple's disease
Intestinal lipodystrophy

040.3   Necrobacillosis
DEF: Infection with *Fusobacterium necrophorum* causing abscess or necrosis.

√5th **040.8   Other specified bacterial diseases**

040.81 Tropical pyomyositis

040.82 Toxic shock syndrome   `CC`
Use additional code to identify the organism
CC Excl: 040.82, 338.0-338.4, 780.91-780.99, 785.50-785.59, 785.9, 799.81-799.89
AHA: 4Q, '02, 44
DEF: Syndrome caused by staphylococcal exotoxin that may rapidly progress to severe and intractable shock; symptoms include characteristic sunburn-like rash with peeling of skin on palms and soles, sudden onset high fever, vomiting, diarrhea, myalgia, and hypotension.

040.89 Other
AHA: N-D, '86, 7

√4th **041 Bacterial infection in conditions classified elsewhere and of unspecified site**
Note: This category is provided to be used as an additional code to identify the bacterial agent in diseases classified elsewhere. This category will also be used to classify bacterial infections of unspecified nature or site.
> EXCLUDES   bacteremia NOS (790.7)
> septicemia (038.0-038.9)
AHA: 2Q, '01, 12; J-A, '84, 19

√5th **041.0   Streptococcus**

041.00 Streptococcus, unspecified

041.01 Group A
AHA: 1Q, '02, 3

041.02 Group B

041.03 Group C

041.04 Group D [Enterococcus]

041.05 Group G

041.09 Other Streptococcus

√5th **041.1   Staphylococcus**

041.10 Staphylococcus, unspecified

041.11 Staphylococcus aureus
AHA: 4Q, '03, 104, 106; 2Q, '01, 11; 4Q, '98, 42, 54; 4Q, '97, 32

041.19 Other Staphylococcus

041.2   Pneumococcus

041.3   Friedländer's bacillus
Infection by Klebsiella pneumoniae

041.4   Escherichia coli [E. coli]

041.5   Hemophilus influenzae [H. influenzae]

041.6   Proteus (mirabilis) (morganii)

041.7   Pseudomonas
AHA: 4Q, '02, 45

√5th **041.8   Other specified bacterial infections**

041.81 Mycoplasma
Eaton's agent
Pleuropneumonia-like organisms [PPLO]

041.82 Bacteroides fragilis
DEF: Anaerobic gram-negative bacilli of the gastrointestinal tract; frequently implicated in intra-abdominal infection; commonly resistant to antibiotics.

041.83 Clostridium perfringens

041.84 Other anaerobes
Gram-negative anaerobes
> EXCLUDES   Helicobacter pylori (041.86)

041.85 Other gram-negative organisms
Aerobacter aerogenes
Gram-negative bacteria NOS
Mima polymorpha
Serratia
> EXCLUDES   gram-negative anaerobes (041.84)
AHA: 1Q, '95, 18

041.86 Helicobacter pylori [H. pylori]
AHA: 4Q, '95, 60

041.89 Other specified bacteria
AHA: 2Q, '03, 7

041.9   Bacterial infection, unspecified
AHA: 2Q, '91, 9

HUMAN IMMUNODEFICIENCY VIRUS (HIV) INFECTION (042)

042 Human immunodeficiency virus [HIV] disease   `CC`
Acquired immune deficiency syndrome
Acquired immunodeficiency syndrome
AIDS
AIDS-like syndrome
AIDS-related complex
ARC
HIV infection, symptomatic
Use additional code(s) to identify all manifestations of HIV
Use additional code to identify HIV-2 infection (079.53)
> EXCLUDES   asymptomatic HIV infection status (V08)
> exposure to HIV virus (V01.79)
> nonspecific serologic evidence of HIV (795.71)

CC Excl: 042, 139.8
AHA: 1Q, '05, 7; 2Q, '04, 11; 1Q, '04, 5; 1Q, '03, 15; 1Q, '99, 14; 4Q, '97, 30, 31; 1Q, '93, 21; 2Q, '92, 11; 3Q, '90, 17; J-A, '87, 8

POLIOMYELITIS AND OTHER NON-ARTHROPOD-BORNE VIRAL DISEASES OF CENTRAL NERVOUS SYSTEM (045-049)

√4th **045 Acute poliomyelitis**
> EXCLUDES   late effects of acute poliomyelitis (138)

The following fifth-digit subclassification is for use with category 045:
    0 poliovirus, unspecified type
    1 poliovirus type I
    2 poliovirus type II
    3 poliovirus type III

√5th **045.0   Acute paralytic poliomyelitis specified as bulbar**
Infantile paralysis (acute)   } specified as bulbar
Poliomyelitis (acute) (anterior)
Polioencephalitis (acute) (bulbar)
Polioencephalomyelitis (acute) (anterior) (bulbar)
DEF: Acute paralytic infection occurring where the brain merges with the spinal cord; affecting breathing, swallowing, and heart rate.

√5th **045.1   Acute poliomyelitis with other paralysis**
Paralysis: Paralysis:
  acute atrophic, spinal   infantile, paralytic
Poliomyelitis (acute)   } with paralysis except
  anterior   bulbar
  epidemic
DEF: Paralytic infection affecting peripheral or spinal nerves.

√5th **045.2   Acute nonparalytic poliomyelitis**
Poliomyelitis (acute)   } specified as nonparalytic
  anterior
  epidemic
DEF: Nonparalytic infection causing pain, stiffness, and paresthesias.

√5th **045.9   Acute poliomyelitis, unspecified**
Infantile paralysis   } unspecified whether
Poliomyelitis (acute)   paralytic or
  anterior   nonparalytic
  epidemic

√4th **046 Slow virus infection of central nervous system**

046.0   Kuru
DEF: A chronic, progressive, fatal nervous system disorder; clinical symptoms include cerebellar ataxia, trembling, spasticity and progressive dementia.

046.1   Jakob-Creutzfeldt disease
Subacute spongiform encephalopathy
DEF: Communicable, progressive spongiform encephalopathy thought to be caused by an infectious particle known as a "prion" (proteinaceous infection particle). This is a progressive, fatal disease manifested principally by mental deterioration.

√4th √5th **Additional Digit Required**   **Nonspecific PDx**   **Unacceptable PDx**   **Manifestation Code**   **MCV** Major Cardiovascular Condition   ►◄ Revised Text   ● New Code   ▲ Revised Code Title

2007 ICD•9•CM   **Volume 1 — 9**

046.2 Subacute sclerosing panencephalitis `CC`
Dawson's inclusion body encephalitis
Van Bogaert's sclerosing leukoencephalitis
CC Excl: 046.2, 139.8

DEF: Progressive viral infection causing cerebral dysfunction, blindness, dementia, and death (SSPE).

046.3 Progressive multifocal leukoencephalopathy `HIV`
Multifocal leukoencephalopathy NOS
DEF: Infection affecting cerebral cortex in patients with weakened immune systems.

046.8 Other specified slow virus infection of central `HIV`
nervous system

046.9 Unspecified slow virus infection of central `HIV`
nervous system

✓4ᵗʰ 047 Meningitis due to enterovirus
INCLUDES   meningitis: meningitis:
abacterial   viral
aseptic

EXCLUDES   meningitis due to:
adenovirus (049.1)
arthropod-borne virus (060.0-066.9)
leptospira (100.81)
virus of:
herpes simplex (054.72)
herpes zoster (053.0)
lymphocytic choriomeningitis (049.0)
mumps (072.1)
poliomyelitis (045.0-045.9)
any other infection specifically classified
elsewhere

AHA: J-F, '87, 6

047.0 Coxsackie virus
047.1 ECHO virus
Meningo-eruptive syndrome
047.8 Other specified viral meningitis
047.9 Unspecified viral meningitis
Viral meningitis NOS

048 Other enterovirus diseases of central nervous system
Boston exanthem

✓4ᵗʰ 049 Other non-arthropod-borne viral diseases of central nervous system
EXCLUDES   late effects of viral encephalitis (139.0)

049.0 Lymphocytic choriomeningitis
Lymphocytic:
meningitis (serous) (benign)
meningoencephalitis (serous) (benign)

049.1 Meningitis due to adenovirus
DEF: Inflammation of lining of brain caused by Arenaviruses and usually occurring in adults in fall and winter months.

049.8 Other specified non-arthropod-borne viral `HIV`
diseases of central nervous system
Encephalitis: Encephalitis:
acute: lethargica
inclusion body   Rio Bravo
necrotizing   von Economo's disease
epidemic

049.9 Unspecified non-arthropod-borne viral `HIV`
diseases of central nervous system
Viral encephalitis NOS

VIRAL DISEASES ACCOMPANIED BY EXANTHEM (050-057)
EXCLUDES   arthropod-borne viral diseases (060.0-066.9)
Boston exanthem (048)

✓4ᵗʰ 050 Smallpox
050.0 Variola major
Hemorrhagic (pustular) smallpox
Malignant smallpox
Purpura variolosa
DEF: Form of smallpox known for its high mortality; exists only in laboratories.

050.1 Alastrim
Variola minor
DEF: Mild form of smallpox known for its low mortality rate.

050.2 Modified smallpox
Varioloid
DEF: Mild form occurring in patients with history of infection or vaccination.

050.9 Smallpox, unspecified

✓4ᵗʰ 051 Cowpox and paravaccinia
051.0 Cowpox
Vaccinia not from vaccination
EXCLUDES   vaccinia (generalized) (from vaccination) (999.0)
DEF: A disease contracted by milking infected cows; vesicles usually appear on the fingers, may spread to hands and adjacent areas and usually disappear without scarring; other associated features of the disease may include local edema, lymphangitis and regional lymphadenitis with or without fever.

051.1 Pseudocowpox
Milkers' node
DEF: Hand lesions and mild fever in dairy workers caused by exposure to paravaccinia.

051.2 Contagious pustular dermatitis
Ecthyma contagiosum
Orf
DEF: Skin eruptions caused by exposure to poxvirus-infected sheep or goats.

051.9 Paravaccinia, unspecified

✓4ᵗʰ 052 Chickenpox
DEF: Contagious infection by *Varicella-zoster* virus causing rash with pustules and fever.

052.0 Postvaricella encephalitis `CC`
Postchickenpox encephalitis
CC Excl: 051.9-052.0, 052.7-052.9, 078.88-078.89, 079.81, 079.88-079.99, 139.8

052.1 Varicella (hemorrhagic) pneumonitis `CC`
CC Excl: 051.9-052.9, 078.88-078.89, 079.81, 079.88-079.99, 139.8

052.2 Postvaricella myelitis `CC`
Postchickenpox myelitis
CC Excl: 051.9-052.9, 053.14, 054.74, 078.88-078.89, 079.81, 079.88-079.99, 139.8, 323.01-323.02, 323.41-323.82, 341.20-341.22

052.7 With other specified complications `CC`
CC Excl: 051.9, 052.7-052.9, 078.88-078.89, 079.81, 079.88-079.89, 079.98-079.99, 139.8
AHA: 1Q, '02, 3

052.8 With unspecified complication `CC`
CC Excl: See code 052.7

052.9 Varicella without mention of complication `CC`
Chickenpox NOS   Varicella NOS
CC Excl: See code 052.7

✓4ᵗʰ 053 Herpes zoster
INCLUDES   shingles
zona
DEF: Self-limiting infection by *varicella-zoster* virus causing unilateral eruptions and neuralgia along affected nerves.

053.0 With meningitis `CC` `HIV`
CC Excl: 003.21, 013.00-013.16, 036.0,047.0-047.9, 049.0-049.1, 053.0-053.19, 053.79-053.9, 054.72, 054.74-054.9, 072.1, 078.88-079.99, 090.42, 091.81, 094.2, 098.89, 100.81, 112.83, 114.2, 115.01, 115.11, 115.91, 130.0, 139.8, 320.0-322.9, 349.89-349.9, 357.0
DEF: *Varicella-zoster* virus infection causing inflammation of the lining of the brain and/or spinal cord.

✓5ᵗʰ 053.1 With other nervous system complications
053.10 With unspecified nervous system `CC` `HIV`
complication
CC Excl: 053.0-053.19, 053.79-053.9, 054.72, 054.74-054.9, 078.88-078.89, 079.81, 079.88-079.99, 139.8

N Newborn Age: 0   P Pediatric Age: 0-17   M Maternity Age: 12-55   A Adult Age: 15-124   CC CC Condition   MC Major Complication   CD Complex Dx   HIV HIV Related Dx

10 — Volume 1 • October 2006   2007 ICD•9•CM

053.11 Geniculate herpes zoster `CC` `HIV`
Herpetic geniculate ganglionitis
CC Excl: See code 053.10
DEF: Unilateral eruptions and neuralgia along the facial nerve geniculum affecting face and outer and middle ear.

053.12 Postherpetic trigeminal neuralgia `CC` `HIV`
CC Excl: See code 053.10
DEF: Severe oral or nasal pain following a herpes zoster infection.

053.13 Postherpetic polyneuropathy `CC` `HIV`
CC Excl: See code 053.10
DEF: Multiple areas of pain following a herpes zoster infection.

053.14 Herpes zoster myelitis `CC` `HIV`
CC Excl: 052.2, 053.0-053.19, 053.79-053.9, 054.72, 054.74-054.9, 078.88-078.89, 079.81, 079.88-079.99, 139.8, 323.01-323.02, 323.41-323.82, 341.20-341.22

053.19 Other `CC` `HIV`
CC Excl: See code 053.10

√5th **053.2 With ophthalmic complications**
053.20 Herpes zoster dermatitis of eyelid `HIV`
Herpes zoster ophthalmicus
053.21 Herpes zoster keratoconjunctivitis `HIV`
053.22 Herpes zoster iridocyclitis `HIV`
053.29 Other `HIV`

√5th **053.7 With other specified complications**
053.71 Otitis externa due to herpes zoster `HIV`
053.79 Other `CC` `HIV`
CC Excl: 053.0-054.71, 054.73-054.9, 078.88-078.89, 079.81, 079.88-079.99, 139.8

053.8 With unspecified complication `CC` `HIV`
CC Excl: See code 053.79

053.9 Herpes zoster without mention of complication `HIV`
Herpes zoster NOS

√4th **054 Herpes simplex**
EXCLUDES congenital herpes simplex (771.2)

054.0 Eczema herpeticum `HIV`
Kaposi's varicelliform eruption
DEF: Herpes simplex virus invading site of preexisting skin inflammation.

√5th **054.1 Genital herpes**
AHA: J-F, '87, 15, 16

054.10 Genital herpes, unspecified `HIV`
Herpes progenitalis
054.11 Herpetic vulvovaginitis `HIV` ♀
054.12 Herpetic ulceration of vulva `HIV` ♀
054.13 Herpetic infection of penis `HIV` ♂
054.19 Other `HIV`

054.2 Herpetic gingivostomatitis `HIV`

054.3 Herpetic meningoencephalitis `CC` `HIV`
Herpes encephalitis   Simian B disease
CC Excl: 054.3, 054.74-054.9, 139.8
DEF: Inflammation of the brain and its lining, caused by infection of herpes simplex 1 in adults and simplex 2 in newborns.

√5th **054.4 With ophthalmic complications**
054.40 With unspecified ophthalmic complication `HIV`
054.41 Herpes simplex dermatitis of eyelid `HIV`
054.42 Dendritic keratitis `HIV`
054.43 Herpes simplex disciform keratitis `HIV`
054.44 Herpes simplex iridocyclitis `HIV`
054.49 Other `HIV`

054.5 Herpetic septicemia `CC` `HIV`
CC Excl: 003.1, 020.2, 036.2, 038.0, 038.10-038.9, 054.5, 054.74-054.9, 139.8, 995.90-995.94
AHA: 2Q, '00, 5

054.6 Herpetic whitlow `HIV`
Herpetic felon
DEF: A primary infection of the terminal segment of a finger by herpes simplex; intense itching and pain start the disease, vesicles form, and tissue ultimately is destroyed.

√5th **054.7 With other specified complications**
054.71 Visceral herpes simplex `CC` `HIV`
CC Excl: 054.71-054.72, 054.74-054.9, 139.8
054.72 Herpes simplex meningitis `CC` `HIV`
CC Excl: 003.21, 013.00-013.16, 036.0,047.0-047.9, 049.0-049.1, 053.0, 054.72, 054.74-054.9, 072.1, 090.42, 091.81, 094.2, 098.89, 100.81, 112.83, 114.2, 115.01, 115.11, 115.91, 130.0, 139.8, 320.0-322.9, 349.89-349.9, 357.0
054.73 Herpes simplex otitis externa `HIV`
054.74 Herpes simplex myelitis `CC` `HIV`
CC Excl: 052.2, 053.14, 054.74-054.9, 078.88-078.89, 079.81, 079.88-079.99, 139.8, 323.01-323.02, 323.41-323.82, 341.20-341.22
054.79 Other `CC` `HIV`
CC Excl: 054.74-054.9, 078.88-078.89, 079.81, 079.88-079.99, 139.8

054.8 With unspecified complication `CC` `HIV`
CC Excl: See code 054.79

054.9 Herpes simplex without mention of complication `HIV`

√4th **055 Measles**
INCLUDES   morbilli   rubeola

055.0 Postmeasles encephalitis `CC`
CC Excl: 055.0, 055.79-055.9, 078.88-078.89, 079.81, 079.88-079.99, 139.8

055.1 Postmeasles pneumonia `CC`
CC Excl: 055.1, 055.79-055.9, 078.88-078.89, 079.81, 079.88-079.99, 139.8

055.2 Postmeasles otitis media `CC`
CC Excl: 055.2, 055.79-055.9, 078.88-078.89, 079.81, 079.88-079.99, 139.8

√5th **055.7 With other specified complications**
055.71 Measles keratoconjunctivitis `CC`
Measles keratitis
CC Excl: 055.71-055.9, 078.88-078.89, 079.81, 079.88-079.99, 139.8
055.79 Other `CC`
CC Excl: 055.79-055.9, 078.88-078.89, 079.81, 079.88--079.99, 139.8

055.8 With unspecified complication `CC`
CC Excl: 055.79, 055.8-055.9, 056.09, 078.88-078.89, 079.81, 079.88-079.89, 079.98-079.99, 139.8

055.9 Measles without mention of complication

√4th **056 Rubella**
INCLUDES   German measles
EXCLUDES   congenital rubella (771.0)
DEF: Acute but usually benign togavirus infection causing fever, sore throat, and rash; associated with complications to fetus as a result of maternal infection.

√5th **056.0 With neurological complications**
056.00 With unspecified neurological complication `CC`
CC Excl: 056.00-056.09, 056.79-056.9, 078.88-078.89, 079.81, 079.88-079.99, 139.8
056.01 Encephalomyelitis due to rubella `CC`
Encephalitis   ⎫
Meningoencephalitis ⎬ due to rubella
         ⎭
CC Excl: See code 056.00
056.09 Other `CC`
CC Excl: See code 056.00

√4th √5th Additional Digit Required   Nonspecific PDx   Unacceptable PDx   Manifestation Code   `MCV` Major Cardiovascular Condition ◄► Revised Text   ● New Code   ▲ Revised Code Title

Infectious and Parasitic Diseases

053.11–056.09

Infectious and Parasitic Diseases

056.7–066.2

☑5ᵗʰ **056.7** **With other specified complications**
056.71 **Arthritis due to rubella** `CC`
CC Excl: 056.71-056.9, 078.88-078.89, 079.81, 079.88-079.99, 139.8

056.79 **Other** `CC`
CC Excl: See code 056.00

056.8 **With unspecified complications** `CC`
CC Excl: 056.00, 056.01, 056.79-056.9, 078.88-078.89, 079.81, 079.88-079.99, 139.8

056.9 **Rubella without mention of complication**

☑4ᵗʰ **057** **Other viral exanthemata**
DEF: Skin eruptions or rashes and fever caused by viruses, including poxviruses.

057.0 **Erythema infectiosum [fifth disease]**
DEF: A moderately contagious, benign, epidemic disease, usually seen in children, and of probable viral etiology; a red macular rash appears on the face and may spread to the limbs and trunk.

057.8 **Other specified viral exanthemata**
Dukes (-Filatow) disease
Exanthema subitum [sixth disease]
Fourth disease
Parascarlatina
Pseudoscarlatina
Roseola infantum

057.9 **Viral exanthem, unspecified**

ARTHROPOD-BORNE VIRAL DISEASES (060-066)

Use additional code to identify any associated meningitis (321.2)
EXCLUDES *late effects of viral encephalitis (139.0)*

☑4ᵗʰ **060** **Yellow fever**
DEF: Fever and jaundice from infection by mosquito-borne virus of genus *Flavivirus*.

060.0 **Sylvatic**
Yellow fever: Yellow fever:
  jungle   sylvan
DEF: Yellow fever transmitted from animal to man, via mosquito.

060.1 **Urban**
DEF: Yellow fever transmitted from man to man, via mosquito.

060.9 **Yellow fever, unspecified**

061 **Dengue**
Breakbone fever
EXCLUDES *hemorrhagic fever caused by dengue virus (065.4)*
DEF: Acute, self-limiting infection by mosquito-borne virus characterized by fever and generalized aches.

☑4ᵗʰ **062** **Mosquito-borne viral encephalitis**
062.0 **Japanese encephalitis**
Japanese B encephalitis
DEF: Flavivirus causing inflammation of the brain, with a wide range of clinical manifestations.

062.1 **Western equine encephalitis**
DEF: Alphavirus WEE infection causing inflammation of the brain, found in areas west of the Mississippi; transmitted horse to mosquito to man.

062.2 **Eastern equine encephalitis**
EXCLUDES *Venezuelan equine encephalitis (066.2)*
DEF: Alphavirus EEE causing inflammation of the brain and spinal cord, found as far north as Canada and south into South America and Mexico; transmitted horse to mosquito to man.

062.3 **St. Louis encephalitis**
DEF: Epidemic form caused by Flavivirus and transmitted by mosquito, and characterized by fever, difficulty in speech, and headache.

062.4 **Australian encephalitis**
Australian arboencephalitis Murray Valley
Australian X disease   encephalitis
DEF: Flavivirus causing inflammation of the brain, occurring in Australia and New Guinea.

062.5 **California virus encephalitis**
Encephalitis: Tahyna fever
  California
  La Crosse
DEF: Bunyamwere virus causing inflammation of the brain.

062.8 **Other specified mosquito-borne viral encephalitis**
Encephalitis by Ilheus virus
EXCLUDES *West Nile virus (066.40-066.49)*

062.9 **Mosquito-borne viral encephalitis, unspecified**

☑4ᵗʰ **063** **Tick-borne viral encephalitis**
INCLUDES diphasic meningoencephalitis

063.0 **Russian spring-summer [taiga] encephalitis**

063.1 **Louping ill**
DEF: Inflammation of brain caused by virus transmitted sheep to tick to man; incidence usually limited to British Isles.

063.2 **Central European encephalitis**
DEF: Inflammation of brain caused by virus transmitted by tick; limited to central Europe and presenting with two distinct phases.

063.8 **Other specified tick-borne viral encephalitis**
Langat encephalitis
Powassan encephalitis

063.9 **Tick-borne viral encephalitis, unspecified**

064 **Viral encephalitis transmitted by other and unspecified arthropods**
Arthropod-borne viral encephalitis, vector unknown
Negishi virus encephalitis
EXCLUDES *viral encephalitis NOS (049.9)*

☑4ᵗʰ **065** **Arthropod-borne hemorrhagic fever**
065.0 **Crimean hemorrhagic fever [CHF Congo virus]**
Central Asian hemorrhagic fever

065.1 **Omsk hemorrhagic fever**

065.2 **Kyasanur Forest disease**

065.3 **Other tick-borne hemorrhagic fever**

065.4 **Mosquito-borne hemorrhagic fever**
Chikungunya hemorrhagic fever
Dengue hemorrhagic fever
EXCLUDES *Chikungunya fever (066.3)*
dengue (061)
yellow fever (060.0-060.9)

065.8 **Other specified arthropod-borne hemorrhagic fever**
Mite-borne hemorrhagic fever

065.9 **Arthropod-borne hemorrhagic fever, unspecified**
Arbovirus hemorrhagic fever NOS

☑4ᵗʰ **066** **Other arthropod-borne viral diseases**
066.0 **Phlebotomus fever**
Changuinola fever
Sandfly fever
DEF: Sandfly-borne viral infection occurring in Asia, Mideast and South America.

066.1 **Tick-borne fever**
Nairobi sheep disease
Tick fever:
  American mountain
  Colorado
  Kemerovo
  Quaranfil

066.2 **Venezuelan equine fever**
Venezuelan equine encephalitis
DEF: Alphavirus VEE infection causing inflammation of the brain, usually limited to South America, Mexico, and Florida; transmitted horse to mosquito to man

`N` Newborn Age: 0 `P` Pediatric Age: 0-17 `M` Maternity Age: 12-55 `A` Adult Age: 15-124 `CC` CC Condition `MC` Major Complication `CD` Complex Dx `HIV` HIV Related Dx

12 — Volume 1 *2007 ICD•9•CM*

066.3   **Other mosquito-borne fever**

Fever (viral):	Fever (viral):
Bunyamwera	Oropouche
Bwamba	Pixuna
Chikungunya	Rift valley
Guama	Ross river
Mayaro	Wesselsbron
Mucambo	Zika
O'Nyong-Nyong	

> EXCLUDES   dengue (061)
> yellow fever (060.0-060.9)

√5ᵗʰ   **066.4**   **West Nile fever**

AHA: 4Q, '02, 44

DEF: Mosquito-borne fever causing fatal inflammation of the brain, the lining of the brain, or of the lining of the brain and spinal cord.

066.40   **West Nile fever, unspecified**
West Nile fever NOS
West Nile fever without complications
West Nile virus NOS

066.41   **West Nile fever with encephalitis**
West Nile encephalitis
West Nile encephalomyelitis
AHA: 4Q, '04, 51

066.42   **West Nile fever with other neurologic manifestation**
Use additional code to specify the neurologic manifestation
AHA: 4Q, '04, 51

066.49   **West Nile fever with other complications**
Use additional code to specify the other conditions

066.8   **Other specified arthropod-borne viral diseases**
Chandipura fever   Piry fever

066.9   **Arthropod-borne viral disease, unspecified**
Arbovirus infection NOS

OTHER DISEASES DUE TO VIRUSES AND CHLAMYDIAE (070-079)

√4ᵗʰ   **070 Viral hepatitis**

> INCLUDES   viral hepatitis (acute) (chronic)
> EXCLUDES   cytomegalic inclusion virus hepatitis (078.5)

The following fifth-digit subclassification is for use with categories 070.2 and 070.3:

    0   acute or unspecified, without mention of hepatitis delta
    1   acute or unspecified, with hepatitis delta
    2   chronic, without mention of hepatitis delta
    3   chronic, with hepatitis delta

DEF: Hepatitis A : HAV infection is self-limiting with flulike symptoms; transmission, fecal-oral.

DEF: Hepatitis B: HBV infection can be chronic and systemic; transmission, bodily fluids.

DEF: Hepatitis C: HCV infection can be chronic and systemic; transmission, blood transfusion and unidentified agents.

DEF: Hepatitis D (delta): HDV occurs only in the presence of hepatitis B virus.

DEF: Hepatitis E: HEV is epidemic form; transmission and nature under investigation.

070.0   **Viral hepatitis A with hepatic coma**

070.1   **Viral hepatitis A without mention of hepatic coma**
Infectious hepatitis

√5ᵗʰ   **070.2**   **Viral hepatitis B with hepatic coma**   CC
CC Excl: 070.0-070.9, 078.88-078.89, 079.81, 079.88-079.99, 139.8
AHA: 4Q, '91, 28

√5ᵗʰ   **070.3**   **Viral hepatitis B without mention of hepatic coma**   CC
Serum hepatitis
CC Excl: See code 070.2
AHA: 1Q, '93, 28; 4Q, '91, 28

√5ᵗʰ   **070.4**   **Other specified viral hepatitis with hepatic coma**
AHA: 4Q, '91, 28

070.41   **Acute hepatitis C with hepatic coma**   CC
CC Excl: See code 070.2

070.42   **Hepatitis delta without mention of active**   CC
hepatitis B disease with hepatic coma
Hepatitis delta with hepatitis B carrier state
CC Excl: See code 070.2

070.43   **Hepatitis E with hepatic coma**   CC
CC Excl: See code 070.2

070.44   **Chronic hepatitis C with hepatic coma**   CC
CC Excl: See code 070.2

070.49   **Other specified viral hepatitis with**   CC
hepatic coma
CC Excl: See code 070.2

√5ᵗʰ   **070.5**   **Other specified viral hepatitis without mention of hepatic coma**
AHA: 4Q, '91, 28

070.51   **Acute hepatitis C without mention**   CC
of hepatic coma
CC Excl: See code 070.2

070.52   **Hepatitis delta without mention of**   CC
active hepatititis B disease or hepatic coma
CC Excl: See code 070.2

070.53   **Hepatitis E without mention of**   CC
hepatic coma
CC Excl: See code 070.2

070.54   **Chronic hepatitis C without mention**   CC
of hepatic coma
CC Excl: See code 070.2

070.59   **Other specified viral hepatitis**   CC
without mention of hepatic coma
CC Excl: See code 070.2

070.6   **Unspecified viral hepatitis with hepatic coma**   CC
> EXCLUDES   unspecified viral hepatitis C with
> hepatic coma (070.71)

CC Excl: See code 070.2

√5ᵗʰ   **070.7**   **Unspecified viral hepatitis C**

070.70   **Unspecified viral hepatitis C without**   CC
hepatic coma
Unspecified viral hepatitis C NOS
CC Excl: See code 070.2
AHA: 4Q, '04, 52

070.71   **Unspecified viral hepatitis C with**   CC
hepatic coma
CC Excl: See code 070.2
AHA: 4Q, '04, 52

070.9   **Unspecified viral hepatitis without mention**   CC
of hepatic coma
Viral hepatitis NOS
> EXCLUDES   unspecified viral hepatitis C without
> hepatic coma (070.70)

CC Excl: See code 070.2

071 Rabies
Hydrophobia   Lyssa
DEF: Acute infectious disease of the CNS caused by a rhabdovirus; usually spread by virus-laden saliva from bites by infected animals; it progresses from fever, restlessness, and extreme excitability, to hydrophobia, seizures, confusion and death.

√4ᵗʰ   **072 Mumps**
DEF: Acute infectious disease caused by paramyxovirus; usually seen in children less than 15 years of age; salivary glands are typically enlarged, and other organs, such as testes, pancreas and meninges, are often involved.

072.0   **Mumps orchitis**   CC♂
CC Excl: 072.0, 072.79-072.9, 078.88-078.89, 079.81, 079.88-079.99, 139.8

072.1   **Mumps meningitis**   CC
CC Excl: 003.21, 013.00-013.16, 036.0, 047.0-049.1, 053.0, 054.72, 072.1, 072.79-072.9, 078.88-078.89, 079.81, 079.88-079.99, 090.42, 091.81, 094.2, 098.89, 100.81, 112.83, 114.2, 115.01, 115.11, 115.91, 130.0, 139.8, 320.0-322.9, 349.89-349.9, 357.0

072.2 Mumps encephalitis `CC`
Mumps meningoencephalitis
CC Excl: 072.2, 072.79-072.9, 078.88-078.89, 079.81, 079.88-079.99, 139.8

072.3 Mumps pancreatitis `CC`
CC Excl: 072.3, 072.79-072.9, 078.88-078.89, 079.81, 079.88-079.99, 139.8

√5ᵗʰ **072.7 Mumps with other specified complications**
072.71 Mumps hepatitis `CC`
CC Excl: 072.71, 072.79-072.9, 078.88-078.89, 079.81, 079.88-079.99, 139.8

072.72 Mumps polyneuropathy `CC`
CC Excl: 072.72-072.9, 078.88-078.89, 079.81, 079.88-079.99, 139.8

072.79 Other `CC`
CC Excl: 072.79-072.9, 078.88-078.89, 079.81, 079.88-079.99, 139.8

072.8 Mumps with unspecified complication `CC`
CC Excl: 072.79-072.9, 078.88-078.89, 079.81, 079.88-079.99

072.9 Mumps without mention of complication
Epidemic parotitis   Infectious parotitis

√4ᵗʰ **073 Ornithosis**
INCLUDES   parrot fever
psittacosis
DEF: *Chlamydia psittaci* infection often transmitted from birds to humans.

073.0 With pneumonia
Lobular pneumonitis due to ornithosis
073.7 With other specified complications
073.8 With unspecified complication
073.9 Ornithosis, unspecified

√4ᵗʰ **074 Specific diseases due to Coxsackie virus**
EXCLUDES   Coxsackie virus:
infection NOS (079.2)
meningitis (047.0)

074.0 Herpangina
Vesicular pharyngitis
DEF: Acute infectious coxsackie virus infection causing throat lesions, fever, and vomiting; generally affects children in summer.

074.1 Epidemic pleurodynia
Bornholm disease   Epidemic:
Devil's grip   myalgia
                      myositis
DEF: Paroxysmal pain in chest, accompanied by fever and usually limited to children and young adults; caused by coxsackie virus.

√5ᵗʰ **074.2 Coxsackie carditis**
074.20 Coxsackie carditis, unspecified
074.21 Coxsackie pericarditis
DEF: Coxsackie infection of the outer lining of the heart.
074.22 Coxsackie endocarditis
DEF: Coxsackie infection within the heart's cavities.
074.23 Coxsackie myocarditis
Aseptic myocarditis of newborn
DEF: Coxsackie infection of the muscle of the heart.

074.3 Hand, foot, and mouth disease
Vesicular stomatitis and exanthem
DEF: Mild coxsackie infection causing lesions on hands, feet and oral mucosa, most commonly seen in preschool children.

074.8 Other specified diseases due to Coxsackie virus
Acute lymphonodular pharyngitis

075 Infectious mononucleosis
Glandular fever   Pfeiffer's disease
Monocytic angina
AHA: 3Q, '01, 13; M-A, '87, 8
DEF: Acute infection by Epstein-Barr virus causing fever, sore throat, enlarged lymph glands and spleen, and fatigue; usually seen in teens and young adults.

√4ᵗʰ **076 Trachoma**
EXCLUDES   *late effect of trachoma (139.1)*
DEF: A chronic infectious disease of the cornea and conjunctiva caused by a strain of the bacteria *Chlamydia trachomatis*; the infection can cause photophobia, pain, excessive tearing and sometimes blindness.

076.0 Initial stage
Trachoma dubium
076.1 Active stage
Granular conjunctivitis (trachomatous)
Trachomatous:
follicular conjunctivitis
pannus
076.9 Trachoma, unspecified
Trachoma NOS

√4ᵗʰ **077 Other diseases of conjunctiva due to viruses and Chlamydiae**
EXCLUDES   *ophthalmic complications of viral diseases classified elsewhere*

077.0 Inclusion conjunctivitis
Paratrachoma   Swimming pool conjunctivitis
EXCLUDES   *inclusion blennorrhea (neonatal) (771.6)*
DEF: Pus in conjunctiva caused by *Chlamydiae trachomatis*.

077.1 Epidemic keratoconjunctivitis
Shipyard eye
DEF: Highly contagious corneal or conjunctival infection caused by adenovirus type 8; symptoms include inflammation and corneal infiltrates.

077.2 Pharyngoconjunctival fever
Viral pharyngoconjunctivitis
077.3 Other adenoviral conjunctivitis
Acute adenoviral follicular conjunctivitis
077.4 Epidemic hemorrhagic conjunctivitis
Apollo:
conjunctivitis
disease
Conjunctivitis due to enterovirus type 70
Hemorrhagic conjunctivitis (acute) (epidemic)
077.8 Other viral conjunctivitis
Newcastle conjunctivitis
√5ᵗʰ **077.9 Unspecified diseases of conjunctiva due to viruses and Chlamydiae**
077.98 Due to Chlamydiae
077.99 Due to viruses
Viral conjunctivitis NOS

√4ᵗʰ **078 Other diseases due to viruses and Chlamydiae**
EXCLUDES   *viral infection NOS (079.0-079.9)*
viremia NOS (790.8)

078.0 Molluscum contagiosum
DEF: Benign poxvirus infection causing small bumps on the skin or conjunctiva; transmitted by close contact.

√5ᵗʰ **078.1 Viral warts**
Viral warts due to human papilloma virus
AHA: 2Q, '97, 9; 4Q, '93, 22
DEF: A keratotic papilloma of the epidermis caused by the human papilloma virus; the superficial vegetative lesions last for varying durations and eventually regress spontaneously.

078.10 Viral warts, unspecified
Condyloma NOS   Verruca:
Verruca: Vulgaris
   NOS   Warts (infectious)
078.11 Condyloma acuminatum
DEF: Clusters of mucosa or epidermal lesions on external genitalia; viral infection is sexually transmitted.

078.19 Other specified viral warts
Genital warts NOS   Verruca:
Verruca: plantaris
plana

N Newborn Age: 0   P Pediatric Age: 0-17   M Maternity Age: 12-55   A Adult Age: 15-124   CC CC Condition   MC Major Complication   CD Complex Dx   HIV HIV Related Dx

14 — Volume 1   *2007 ICD•9•CM*

078.2 Sweating fever
  Miliary fever   Sweating disease
  DEF: A viral infection characterized by profuse sweating; various papular, vesicular and other eruptions cause the blockage of sweat glands.

078.3 Cat-scratch disease
  Benign lymphoreticulosis (of inoculation)
  Cat-scratch fever

078.4 Foot and mouth disease
  Aphthous fever   Epizootic:
  Epizootic: stomatitis
    aphthae
  DEF: Ulcers on oral mucosa, legs, and feet after exposure to infected animal.

078.5 Cytomegaloviral disease   `HIV`
  Cytomegalic inclusion disease
  Salivary gland virus disease
  Use additional code to identify manifestation, as:
    cytomegalic inclusion virus:
      hepatitis (573.1)
      pneumonia (484.1)
    EXCLUDES *congenital cytomegalovirus infection (771.1)*
  AHA: 1Q, '03, 10; 3Q, '98, 4; 2Q, '93, 11; 1Q, '89, 9

  DEF: A herpes virus inclusion associated with serious disease morbidity including fever, leukopenia, pneumonia, retinitis, hepatitis and organ transplant; often leads to syndromes such as hepatomegaly, splenomegaly and thrombocytopenia; a common post-transplant complication for organ transplant recipients.

078.6 Hemorrhagic nephrosonephritis
  Hemorrhagic fever: Hemorrhagic fever:
    epidemic   Russian
    Korean   with renal syndrome
  DEF: Viral infection causing kidney dysfunction and bleeding disorders.

078.7 Arenaviral hemorrhagic fever
  Hemorrhagic fever: Hemorrhagic fever:
    Argentine   Junin virus
    Bolivian   Machupo virus

√5th **078.8 Other specified diseases due to viruses and Chlamydiae**
    EXCLUDES *epidemic diarrhea (009.2)*
              lymphogranuloma venereum (099.1)

  078.81 Epidemic vertigo
  078.82 Epidemic vomiting syndrome
    Winter vomiting disease

  078.88 Other specified diseases due to Chlamydiae
    AHA: 4Q, '96, 22

  078.89 Other specified diseases due to viruses
    Epidemic cervical myalgia
    Marburg disease
    Tanapox

√4th **079 Viral and chlamydial infection in conditions classified elsewhere and of unspecified site**
  Note: This category is provided to be used as an additional code to identify the viral agent in diseases classifiable elsewhere. This category will also be used to classify virus infection of unspecified nature or site.

  079.0 Adenovirus
  079.1 ECHO virus
    DEF: An "orphan" enteric RNA virus, certain serotypes of which are associated with human disease, especially aseptic meningitis.

  079.2 Coxsackie virus
    DEF: A heterogenous group of viruses associated with aseptic meningitis, myocarditis, pericarditis, and acute onset juvenile diabetes.

  079.3 Rhinovirus
    DEF: Rhinoviruses affect primarily the upper respiratory tract. Over 100 distinct types infect humans.

079.4 Human papillomavirus
  AHA: 2Q, '97, 9; 4Q, '93, 22

  DEF: Viral infection caused by the genus *Papillomavirus* causing cutaneous and genital warts, including verruca vulgaris and condyloma acuminatum; certain types are associated with cervical dysplasia, cancer and other genital malignancies.

√5th **079.5 Retrovirus**
    EXCLUDES *human immunodeficiency virus, type 1 [HIV-1] (042)*
              human T-cell lymphotrophic virus, type III [HTLV-III] (042)
              lymphadenopathy-associated virus [LAV] (042)
  AHA: 4Q, '93, 22, 23

  DEF: A large group of RNA viruses that carry reverse transcriptase and include the leukoviruses and lentiviruses.

  079.50 Retrovirus, unspecified
  079.51 Human T-cell lymphotrophic virus, type I [HTLV-I]
  079.52 Human T-cell lymphotrophic virus, type II [HTLV-II]
  079.53 Human immunodeficiency virus, type 2 [HIV-2]
  079.59 Other specified retrovirus

079.6 Respiratory syncytial virus (RSV)
  AHA: 4Q, '96, 27, 28

  DEF: The major respiratory pathogen of young children, causing severe bronchitis and bronchopneumonia, and minor infection in adults.

√5th **079.8 Other specified viral and chlamydial infections**
  AHA: 1Q, '88, 12

  079.81 Hantavirus
    AHA: 4Q, '95, 60

    DEF: An infection caused by the Muerto Canyon virus whose primary rodent reservoir is the deer mouse Peromyscus maniculatus; commonly characterized by fever, myalgias, headache, cough and rapid decline.

  079.82 SARS-associated coronavirus   `CC`
    CC Excl: 011.00-012.16, 012.80-012.86, 017.90-017.96, 021.2, 031.0, 039.1, 079.82, 079.89, 115.05, 115.15, 115.95, 122.1, 130.4, 136.3, 480.0-480.2, 480.8-487.1, 494.0-508.9, 517.1, 517.8, 518.89, 519.8-519.9, 748.61

    AHA: 4Q, '03, 46

    DEF: A life-threatening respiratory disease described as severe acute respiratory syndrome (SARS); etiology coronavirus; most common presenting symptoms may range from mild to more severe forms of flu-like conditions; fever, chills, cough, headache, myalgia; diagnosis of SARS is based upon clinical, laboratory, and epidemiological criteria.

  079.88 Other specified chlamydial infection
  079.89 Other specified viral infection

√5th **079.9 Unspecified viral and chlamydial infections**
    EXCLUDES *viremia NOS (790.8)*
  AHA: 2Q, '91, 8

  079.98 Unspecified chlamydial infection
    Chlamydial infections NOS
  079.99 Unspecified viral infection
    Viral infections NOS

RICKETTSIOSES AND OTHER ARTHROPOD-BORNE DISEASES (080-088)

    EXCLUDES *arthropod-borne viral diseases (060.0-066.9)*

080 Louse-borne [epidemic] typhus
  Typhus (fever):   Typhus (fever):
    classical   exanthematic NOS
    epidemic   louse-borne
  DEF: *Rickettsia prowazekii*; causes severe headache, rash, high fever.

√4th √5th Additional Digit Required   Nonspecific PDx   Unacceptable PDx   Manifestation Code   `MCV` Major Cardiovascular Condition   ►◄ Revised Text   ● New Code   ▲ Revised Code Title

2007 ICD·9·CM   Volume 1 — 15

✓4th **081 Other typhus**

081.0 Murine [endemic] typhus
Typhus (fever):   Typhus (fever):
   endemic   flea-borne
DEF: Milder typhus caused by *Rickettsia typhi (mooseri)*; transmitted by rat flea.

081.1 Brill's disease
Brill-Zinsser disease
Recrudescent typhus (fever)

081.2 Scrub typhus
Japanese river fever   Mite-borne typhus
Kedani fever   Tsutsugamushi

081.9 Typhus, unspecified
Typhus (fever) NOS

✓4th **082 Tick-borne rickettsioses**

082.0 Spotted fevers
Rocky mountain spotted fever
Sao Paulo fever

082.1 Boutonneuse fever
African tick typhus   Marseilles fever
India tick typhus   Mediterranean tick fever
Kenya tick typhus

082.2 North Asian tick fever
Siberian tick typhus

082.3 Queensland tick typhus

✓5th **082.4 Ehrlichiosis**
AHA: 4Q, '00, 38

082.40 **Ehrlichiosis, unspecified**

082.41 **Ehrlichiosis chaffeensis [E. chaffeensis]**
DEF: A febrile illness caused by bacterial infection, also called human monocytic ehrlichiosis (HME). Causal organism is *Ehrlichia chaffeensis*, transmitted by the Lone Star tick, *Amblyomma americanum*. Symptoms include fever, chills, myalgia, nausea, vomiting, diarrhea, confusion, and severe headache occurring one week after a tick bite. Clinical findings are lymphadenopathy, rash, thrombocytopenia, leukopenia, and abnormal liver function tests.

082.49 **Other ehrlichiosis**

082.8 Other specified tick-borne rickettsioses
Lone star fever
AHA: 4Q, '99, 19

082.9 Tick-borne rickettsiosis, unspecified
Tick-borne typhus NOS

✓4th **083 Other rickettsioses**

083.0 Q fever
DEF: Infection of *Coxiella burnettii* usually acquired through airborne organisms.

083.1 Trench fever
Quintan fever   Wolhynian fever

083.2 Rickettsialpox
Vesicular rickettsiosis
DEF: Infection of *Rickettsia akari* usually acquired through a mite bite.

083.8 Other specified rickettsioses

083.9 Rickettsiosis, unspecified

✓4th **084 Malaria**
Note: Subcategories 084.0-084.6 exclude the listed conditions with mention of pernicious complications (084.8-084.9).
EXCLUDES *congenital malaria (771.2)*
DEF: Mosquito-borne disease causing high fever and prostration and cataloged by species of *Plasmodium: P. falciparum, P. malariae, P. ovale,* and *P. vivax.*

084.0 Falciparum malaria [malignant tertian]
Malaria (fever):
   by Plasmodium falciparum
   subtertian

084.1 Vivax malaria [benign tertian]
Malaria (fever) by Plasmodium vivax

084.2 Quartan malaria
Malaria (fever) by Plasmodium malariae
Malariae malaria

084.3 Ovale malaria
Malaria (fever) by Plasmodium ovale

084.4 Other malaria
Monkey malaria

084.5 Mixed malaria
Malaria (fever) by more than one parasite

084.6 Malaria, unspecified
Malaria (fever) NOS

084.7 Induced malaria
Therapeutically induced malaria
EXCLUDES *accidental infection from syringe, blood transfusion, etc. (084.0-084.6, above, according to parasite species)*
transmission from mother to child during delivery (771.2)

084.8 Blackwater fever
Hemoglobinuric: Malarial hemoglobinuria
   fever (bilious)
   malaria
DEF: Severe hemic and renal complication of *Plasmodium falciparum* infection.

084.9 Other pernicious complications of malaria
Algid malaria
Cerebral malaria
Use additional code to identify complication, as:
   malarial:
      hepatitis (573.2)
      nephrosis (581.81)

✓4th **085 Leishmaniasis**

085.0 Visceral [kala-azar]
Dumdum fever   Leishmaniasis:
Infection by Leishmania: dermal, post-kala-azar
   donovani   Mediterranean
   infantum   visceral (Indian)

085.1 Cutaneous, urban
Aleppo boil   Leishmaniasis, cutaneous:
Baghdad boil   dry form
Delhi boil   late
Infection by Leishmania recurrent
   tropica (minor)   ulcerating
              Oriental sore

085.2 Cutaneous, Asian desert
Infection by Leishmania tropica major
Leishmaniasis, cutaneous:
   acute necrotizing
   rural
   wet form
   zoonotic form

085.3 Cutaneous, Ethiopian
Infection by Leishmania ethiopica
Leishmaniasis, cutaneous:
   diffuse
   lepromatous

085.4 Cutaneous, American
Chiclero ulcer
Infection by Leishmania mexicana
Leishmaniasis tegumentaria diffusa

085.5 Mucocutaneous (American)
Espundia
Infection by Leishmania braziliensis
Uta

085.9 Leishmaniasis, unspecified

✓4th **086 Trypanosomiasis**
Use additional code to identify manifestations, as:
trypanosomiasis:
   encephalitis (323.2)
   meningitis (321.3)

N Newborn Age: 0   **P** Pediatric Age: 0-17   **M** Maternity Age: 12-55   **A** Adult Age: 15-124   **CC** CC Condition   **MC** Major Complication   **CD** Complex Dx   **HIV** HIV Related Dx

086.0 Chagas' disease with heart involvement `CC`

American trypanosomiasis } with heart
Infection by Trypanosoma cruzi } involvement

Any condition classifiable to 086.2 with heart involvement

CC Excl: 086.0, 139.8

086.1 Chagas' disease with other organ involvement

American trypanosomiasis } with involvement of
Infection by Trypanosoma } organ other
cruzi } than heart

Any condition classifiable to 086.2 with involvement of organ other than heart

086.2 Chagas' disease without mention of organ involvement

American trypanosomiasis
Infection by Trypanosoma cruzi

086.3 Gambian trypanosomiasis

Gambian sleeping sickness
Infection by Trypanosoma gambiense

086.4 Rhodesian trypanosomiasis

Infection by Trypanosoma rhodesiense
Rhodesian sleeping sickness

086.5 African trypanosomiasis, unspecified

Sleeping sickness NOS

086.9 Trypanosomiasis, unspecified

√4ᵗʰ **087 Relapsing fever**

`INCLUDES` recurrent fever

DEF: Infection of *Borrelia*; symptoms are episodic and include fever and arthralgia.

087.0 Louse-borne

087.1 Tick-borne

087.9 Relapsing fever, unspecified

√4ᵗʰ **088 Other arthropod-borne diseases**

088.0 Bartonellosis

Carrión's disease   Verruga peruana
Oroya fever

√5ᵗʰ **088.8 Other specified arthropod-borne diseases**

088.81 Lyme disease

Erythema chronicum migrans
AHA: 4Q, '91, 15; 3Q, '90, 14; 2Q, '89, 10

DEF: A recurrent multisystem disorder caused by the spirochete *Borrelia burgdorferi* with the carrier being the tick *Ixodes dammini*; the disease begins with lesions of erythema chronicum migrans; it is followed by arthritis of the large joints, myalgia, malaise, and neurological and cardiac manifestations.

088.82 Babesiosis

Babesiasis
AHA: 4Q, '93, 23

DEF: A tick-borne disease caused by infection of *Babesia*, characterized by fever, malaise, listlessness, severe anemia and hemoglobinuria.

088.89 Other

088.9 Arthropod-borne disease, unspecified

SYPHILIS AND OTHER VENEREAL DISEASES (090-099)

`EXCLUDES` nonvenereal endemic syphilis (104.0)
urogenital trichomoniasis (131.0)

√4ᵗʰ **090 Congenital syphilis**

DEF: Infection by spirochete *Treponema pallidum* acquired in utero from the infected mother.

090.0 Early congenital syphilis, symptomatic

Congenital syphilitic: Congenital syphilitic:
choroiditis   splenomegaly
coryza (chronic)   Syphilitic (congenital):
hepatomegaly   epiphysitis
mucous patches   osteochondritis
periostitis   pemphigus
Any congenital syphilitic condition specified as early or manifest less than two years after birth

090.1 Early congenital syphilis, latent

Congenital syphilis without clinical manifestations, with positive serological reaction and negative spinal fluid test, less than two years after birth

090.2 Early congenital syphilis, unspecified

Congenital syphilis NOS, less than two years after birth

090.3 Syphilitic interstitial keratitis

Syphilitic keratitis: Syphilitic keratitis:
parenchymatous   punctata profunda
`EXCLUDES` interstitial keratitis NOS (370.50)

√5ᵗʰ **090.4 Juvenile neurosyphilis**

Use additional code to identify any associated mental disorder

DEF: *Treponema pallidum* infection involving the nervous system.

090.40 Juvenile neurosyphilis, unspecified `CC`

Congenital neurosyphilis
Dementia paralytica juvenilis
Juvenile:
general paresis
tabes
taboparesis

CC Excl: 090.0-097.9, 099.40-099.9, 139.8

090.41 Congenital syphilitic encephalitis `CC`

CC Excl: See code 090.40

DEF: Congenital *Treponema pallidum* infection involving the brain.

090.42 Congenital syphilitic meningitis `CC`

CC Excl: 003.21, 013.00-013.16, 036.0, 047.0-049.1, 053.0, 054.72, 072.1, 090.0-097.9, 098.89, 099.40-099.9, 100.81, 112.83, 114.2, 115.01, 115.11, 115.91, 130.0, 139.8, 320.0-322.9, 349.89-349.9, 357.0

DEF: Congenital *Treponema pallidum* infection involving the lining of the brain and/or spinal cord.

090.49 Other `CC`

CC Excl: See code 090.40

090.5 Other late congenital syphilis, symptomatic

Gumma due to congenital syphilis
Hutchinson's teeth
Syphilitic saddle nose
Any congenital syphilitic condition specified as late or manifest two years or more after birth

090.6 Late congenital syphilis, latent

Congenital syphilis without clinical manifestations, with positive serological reaction and negative spinal fluid test, two years or more after birth

090.7 Late congenital syphilis, unspecified

Congenital syphilis NOS, two years or more after birth

090.9 Congenital syphilis, unspecified

√4ᵗʰ **091 Early syphilis, symptomatic**

`EXCLUDES` early cardiovascular syphilis (093.0-093.9)
early neurosyphilis (094.0-094.9)

091.0 Genital syphilis (primary)

Genital chancre

DEF: Genital lesion at the site of initial infection by *Treponema pallidum*.

091.1 Primary anal syphilis

DEF: Anal lesion at the site of initial infection by *Treponema pallidum*.

091.2 Other primary syphilis

Primary syphilis of: Primary syphilis of:
breast   lip
fingers   tonsils

DEF: Lesion at the site of initial infection by *Treponema pallidum*.

√4ᵗʰ √5ᵗʰ Additional Digit Required   `Nonspecific PDx`   `Unacceptable PDx`   `Manifestation Code`   `MCV` Major Cardiovascular Condition ▶◀ Revised Text ● New Code ▲ Revised Code Title

2007 ICD•9•CM   **Volume 1 — 17**

091.3 Secondary syphilis of skin or mucous membranes
Condyloma latum   Secondary syphilis of:
Secondary syphilis of: skin
    anus   tonsils
    mouth   vulva
    pharynx
DEF: Transitory or chronic lesions following initial syphilis infection.

091.4 Adenopathy due to secondary syphilis
Syphilitic adenopathy (secondary)
Syphilitic lymphadenitis (secondary)

√5th **091.5 Uveitis due to secondary syphilis**
091.50 Syphilitic uveitis, unspecified
091.51 Syphilitic chorioretinitis (secondary)
DEF: Inflammation of choroid and retina as a secondary infection.

091.52 Syphilitic iridocyclitis (secondary)
DEF: Inflammation of iris and ciliary body as a secondary infection.

√5th **091.6 Secondary syphilis of viscera and bone**
091.61 Secondary syphilitic periostitis
DEF: Inflammation of outer layers of bone as a secondary infection.

091.62 Secondary syphilitic hepatitis
Secondary syphilis of liver
091.69 Other viscera

091.7 Secondary syphilis, relapse
Secondary syphilis, relapse (treated) (untreated)
DEF: Return of symptoms of syphilis following asymptomatic period.

√5th **091.8 Other forms of secondary syphilis**
091.81 Acute syphilitic meningitis (secondary)
DEF: Sudden, severe inflammation of the lining of the brain and/or spinal cord as a secondary infection.

091.82 Syphilitic alopecia
DEF: Hair loss following initial syphillis infection.

091.89 Other
091.9 Unspecified secondary syphilis

√4th **092 Early syphilis, latent**
INCLUDES   syphilis (acquired) without clinical manifestations, with positive serological reaction and negative spinal fluid test, less than two years after infection

092.0 Early syphilis, latent, serological relapse after treatment
092.9 Early syphilis, latent, unspecified

√4th **093 Cardiovascular syphilis**
093.0 Aneurysm of aorta, specified as syphilitic   CC
Dilatation of aorta, specified as syphilitic
CC Excl: See code 090.40

093.1 Syphilitic aortitis   CC
CC Excl: See code 090.40
DEF: Inflammation of the aorta – the main artery leading from the heart.

√5th **093.2 Syphilitic endocarditis**
DEF: Inflammation of the tissues lining the cavities of the heart.
093.20 Valve, unspecified   CC
Syphilitic ostial coronary disease
CC Excl: See code 090.40

093.21 Mitral valve   CC
CC Excl: See code 090.40

093.22 Aortic valve   CC
Syphilitic aortic incompetence or stenosis
CC Excl: See code 090.40

093.23 Tricuspid valve   CC
CC Excl: See code 090.40

093.24 Pulmonary valve   CC
CC Excl: See code 090.40

√5th **093.8 Other specified cardiovascular syphilis**
093.81 Syphilitic pericarditis   CC
CC Excl: See code 090.40
DEF: Inflammation of the outer lining of the heart.

093.82 Syphilitic myocarditis   CC
CC Excl: See code 090.40
DEF: Inflammation of the muscle of the heart.

093.89 Other   CC
CC Excl: See code 090.40

093.9 Cardiovascular syphilis, unspecified   CC
CC Excl: See code 090.40

√4th **094 Neurosyphilis**
Use additional code to identify any associated mental disorder
094.0 Tabes dorsalis   CC
Locomotor ataxia (progressive)
Posterior spinal sclerosis (syphilitic)
Tabetic neurosyphilis
Use additional code to identify manifestation, as:
   neurogenic arthropathy [Charcot's joint disease] (713.5)
CC Excl: See code 090.40
DEF: Progressive degeneration of nerves associated with long-term syphilis; causing pain, wasting away, incontinence, and ataxia.

094.1 General paresis   CC
Dementia paralytica
General paralysis (of the insane) (progressive)
Paretic neurosyphilis
Taboparesis
CC Excl: See code 090.40
DEF: Degeneration of brain associated with long-term syphilis, causing loss of brain function, progressive dementia, and paralysis.

094.2 Syphilitic meningitis   CC
Meningovascular syphilis
EXCLUDES   acute syphilitic meningitis (secondary) (091.81)
CC Excl: See code 090.42
DEF: Inflammation of the lining of the brain and/or spinal cord.

094.3 Asymptomatic neurosyphilis   CC
CC Excl: See code 090.40

√5th **094.8 Other specified neurosyphilis**
094.81 Syphilitic encephalitis   CC
CC Excl: See code 090.40

094.82 Syphilitic Parkinsonism
DEF: Decreased motor function, tremors, and muscular rigidity.

094.83 Syphilitic disseminated retinochoroiditis
DEF: Inflammation of retina and choroid due to neurosyphilis.

094.84 Syphilitic optic atrophy
DEF: Degeneration of the eye and its nerves due to neurosyphilis.

N Newborn Age: 0   P Pediatric Age: 0-17   M Maternity Age: 12-55   A Adult Age: 15-124   CC CC Condition   MC Major Complication   CD Complex Dx   HIV HIV Related Dx

18 — Volume 1   2007 ICD•9•CM

094.85 Syphilitic retrobulbar neuritis
DEF: Inflammation of the posterior optic nerve to neurosyphilis.

094.86 Syphilitic acoustic neuritis
DEF: Inflammation of acoustic nerve due to neurosyphilis.

094.87 Syphilitic ruptured cerebral aneurysm `CC`
CC Excl: See code 090.40

094.89 Other `CC`
CC Excl: See code 090.40

094.9 Neurosyphilis, unspecified `CC`
Gumma (syphilitic) ⎫
Syphilis (early) (late) ⎬ of central nervous system
Syphiloma ⎭ NOS

CC Excl: See code 090.40

`√4ᵗʰ` **095 Other forms of late syphilis, with symptoms**
INCLUDES gumma (syphilitic)
syphilis, late, tertiary, or unspecified stage

095.0 Syphilitic episcleritis
095.1 Syphilis of lung
095.2 Syphilitic peritonitis
095.3 Syphilis of liver
095.4 Syphilis of kidney
095.5 Syphilis of bone
095.6 Syphilis of muscle
Syphilitic myositis
095.7 Syphilis of synovium, tendon, and bursa
Syphilitic: Syphilitic:
bursitis   synovitis
095.8 Other specified forms of late symptomatic syphilis
EXCLUDES *cardiovascular syphilis (093.0-093.9)*
neurosyphilis (094.0-094.9)
095.9 Late symptomatic syphilis, unspecified
096 Late syphilis, latent
Syphilis (acquired) without clinical manifestations, with positive serological reaction and negative spinal fluid test, two years or more after infection

`√4ᵗʰ` **097 Other and unspecified syphilis**
097.0 Late syphilis, unspecified
097.1 Latent syphilis, unspecified
Positive serological reaction for syphilis
097.9 Syphilis, unspecified
Syphilis (acquired) NOS
EXCLUDES *syphilis NOS causing death under two years of age (090.9)*

`√4ᵗʰ` **098 Gonococcal infections**
DEF: *Neisseria gonorrhoeae* infection generally acquired in utero or in sexual congress.

098.0 Acute, of lower genitourinary tract `CC`
Gonococcal: Gonorrhea (acute):
Bartholinitis (acute)   NOS
urethritis (acute)   genitourinary (tract) NOS
vulvovaginitis (acute)
CC Excl: 098.0-098.39, 098.89, 099.40-099.9, 139.8

`√5ᵗʰ` **098.1 Acute, of upper genitourinary tract**
098.10 Gonococcal infection (acute) of upper genitourinary tract, site unspecified `CC`
CC Excl: See code 098.0

098.11 Gonococcal cystitis (acute) `CC`
Gonorrhea (acute) of bladder
CC Excl: See code 098.0

098.12 Gonococcal prostatitis (acute) `CC`♂
CC Excl: See code 098.0

098.13 Gonococcal epididymo-orchitis (acute) `CC`♂
Gonococcal orchitis (acute)
CC Excl: See code 098.0

DEF: Acute inflammation of the testes.

098.14 Gonococcal seminal vesiculitis (acute) `CC`♂
Gonorrhea (acute) of seminal vesicle
CC Excl: See code 098.0

098.15 Gonococcal cervicitis (acute) `CC`♀
Gonorrhea (acute) of cervix
CC Excl: See code 098.0

098.16 Gonococcal endometritis (acute) `CC`♀
Gonorrhea (acute) of uterus
CC Excl: See code 098.0

098.17 Gonococcal salpingitis, specified as acute `CC`♀
CC Excl: See code 098.0

DEF: Acute inflammation of the fallopian tubes.

098.19 Other `CC`
CC Excl: See code 098.0

098.2 Chronic, of lower genitourinary tract
Gonococcal: ⎫
Bartholinitis ⎪ specified as chronic
urethritis ⎬ or with
vulvovaginitis ⎪ duration of
Gonorrhea: ⎪ two months
NOS ⎪ or more
genitourinary (tract) ⎭

Any condition classifiable to 098.0 specified as chronic or with duration of two months or more

`√5ᵗʰ` **098.3 Chronic, of upper genitourinary tract**
INCLUDES any condition classifiable to 098.1 stated as chronic or with a duration of two months or more

098.30 Chronic gonococcal infection of upper genitourinary tract, site unspecified
098.31 Gonococcal cystitis, chronic
Any condition classifiable to 098.11, specified as chronic
Gonorrhea of bladder, chronic
098.32 Gonococcal prostatitis, chronic ♂
Any condition classifiable to 098.12, specified as chronic
098.33 Gonococcal epididymo-orchitis, chronic ♂
Any condition classifiable to 098.13, specified as chronic
Chronic gonococcal orchitis
DEF: Chronic inflammation of the testes.
098.34 Gonococcal seminal vesiculitis, chronic ♂
Any condition classifiable to 098.14, specified as chronic
Gonorrhea of seminal vesicle, chronic
098.35 Gonococcal cervicitis, chronic ♀
Any condition classifiable to 098.15, specified as chronic
Gonorrhea of cervix, chronic
098.36 Gonococcal endometritis, chronic ♀
Any condition classifiable to 098.16, specified as chronic
DEF: Chronic inflammation of the uterus.
098.37 Gonococcal salpingitis (chronic) ♀
DEF: Chronic inflammation of the fallopian tubes.
098.39 Other

  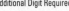

Infectious and Parasitic Diseases

098.4–100.9

√5ᵗʰ **098.4 Gonococcal infection of eye**
    098.40 Gonococcal conjunctivitis (neonatorum)
        Gonococcal ophthalmia (neonatorum)
        DEF: Infection of conjunctiva present at birth.

    098.41 Gonococcal iridocyclitis
        DEF: Inflammation and infection of iris and ciliary body.

    098.42 Gonococcal endophthalmia
        DEF: Inflammation and infection of contents of eyeball.

    098.43 Gonococcal keratitis
        DEF: Inflammation and infection of the cornea.

    098.49 Other

√5ᵗʰ **098.5 Gonococcal infection of joint**
    098.50 Gonococcal arthritis
        Gonococcal infection of joint NOS
    098.51 Gonococcal synovitis and tenosynovitis
    098.52 Gonococcal bursitis
        DEF: Inflammation of the sac-like cavities in a joint.

    098.53 Gonococcal spondylitis
    098.59 Other
        Gonococcal rheumatism
  098.6 Gonococcal infection of pharynx
  098.7 Gonococcal infection of anus and rectum
        Gonococcal proctitis

√5ᵗʰ **098.8 Gonococcal infection of other specified sites**
    098.81 Gonococcal keratosis (blennorrhagica)
        DEF: Pustular skin lesions caused by *Neisseria gonorrhoeae*.

    098.82 Gonococcal meningitis
        DEF: Inflammation of lining of brain and/or spinal cord.

    098.83 Gonococcal pericarditis
        DEF: Inflammation of the outer lining of the heart.

    098.84 Gonococcal endocarditis
        DEF: Inflammation of tissues lining the cavities of heart.

    098.85 Other gonococcal heart disease
    098.86 Gonococcal peritonitis
        DEF: Inflammation of the membrane lining the abdomen.

    098.89 Other
        Gonococcemia

√4ᵗʰ **099 Other venereal diseases**
  099.0 Chancroid
    Bubo (inguinal):   Chancre:
      chancroidal   Ducrey's
      due to Hemophilus simple
        ducreyi   soft
                   Ulcus molle (cutis) (skin)
    DEF: A sexually transmitted disease caused by *Haemophilus ducreyi*; it is identified by a painful primary ulcer at the site of inoculation (usually external genitalia) with related lymphadenitis.

  099.1 Lymphogranuloma venereum
    Climatic or tropical bubo
    (Durand-) Nicolas-Favre disease
    Esthiomene
    Lymphogranuloma inguinale
    DEF: Sexually transmitted infection of *Chlamydia trachomatis* causing skin lesions.

  099.2 Granuloma inguinale
    Donovanosis   Granuloma venereum
    Granuloma pudendi Pudendal ulcer
    (ulcerating)
    DEF: Chronic, sexually transmitted infection of *Calymmatobacterium granulomatis* causing progressive, anogenital skin ulcers.

  099.3 Reiter's disease
    Reiter's syndrome
    Use additional code for associated:
      arthropathy (711.1)
      conjunctivitis (372.33)
    DEF: A symptom complex of unknown etiology consisting of urethritis, conjunctivitis, arthritis and myocutaneous lesions. It occurs most commonly in young men and patients with HIV and may precede or follow AIDS. Also a form of reactive arthritis.

√5ᵗʰ **099.4 Other nongonococcal urethritis [NGU]**
    099.40 Unspecified
        Nonspecific urethritis
    099.41 Chlamydia trachomatis
    099.49 Other specified organism

√5ᵗʰ **099.5 Other venereal diseases due to Chlamydia trachomatis**
    EXCLUDES *Chlamydia trachomatis infection of conjunctiva (076.0-076.9, 077.0, 077.9)*
        Lymphogranuloma venereum (099.1)
    DEF: Venereal diseases caused by *Chlamydia trachomatis* at other sites besides the urethra (e.g., pharynx, anus and rectum, conjunctiva and peritoneum).

    099.50 Unspecified site
    099.51 Pharynx
    099.52 Anus and rectum
    099.53 Lower genitourinary sites
        EXCLUDES *urethra (099.41)*
        Use additional code to specify site of infection, such as:
          bladder (595.4)
          cervix (616.0)
          vagina and vulva (616.11)
    099.54 Other genitourinary sites
        Use additional code to specify site of infection, such as:
          pelvic inflammatory disease NOS (614.9)
          testis and epididymis (604.91)
    099.55 Unspecified genitourinary site
    099.56 Peritoneum
        Perihepatitis
    099.59 Other specified site
  099.8 Other specified venereal diseases
  099.9 Venereal disease, unspecified

OTHER SPIROCHETAL DISEASES (100-104)

√4ᵗʰ **100 Leptospirosis**
  DEF: An infection of any spirochete of the genus Leptospire in blood. This zoonosis is transmitted to humans most often by exposure with contaminated animal tissues or water and less often by contact with urine. Patients present with flulike symptoms, the most common being muscle aches involving the thighs and low back. Treatment is with hydration and antibiotics.

  100.0 Leptospirosis icterohemorrhagica
    Leptospiral or spirochetal jaundice (hemorrhagic)
    Weil's disease
√5ᵗʰ **100.8 Other specified leptospiral infections**
    100.81 Leptospiral meningitis (aseptic)
    100.89 Other
        Fever: Infection by Leptospira:
          Fort Bragg   australis
          pretibial   bataviae
          swamp   pyrogenes
  100.9 Leptospirosis, unspecified

N Newborn Age: 0   P Pediatric Age: 0-17   M Maternity Age: 12-55   A Adult Age: 15-124   CC CC Condition   MC Major Complication   CD Complex Dx   HIV HIV Related Dx

20 — Volume 1   *2007 ICD•9•CM*

101 Vincent's angina
Acute necrotizing ulcerative: Trench mouth
    gingivitis   Vincent's:
    stomatitis   gingivitis
Fusospirochetal pharyngitis   infection [any site]
Spirochetal stomatitis

DEF: Painful ulceration with edema and hypermic patches of the oropharyngeal and throat membranes; it is caused by spreading of acute ulcerative gingivitis.

✓4th 102 Yaws
INCLUDES   frambesia
                pian

DEF: An infectious, endemic, tropical disease caused by *Treponema pertenue*; it usually affects persons 15 years old or younger; a primary cutaneous lesion develops, then a granulomatous skin eruption, and occasionally lesions that destroy skin and bone.

102.0 Initial lesions
Chancre of yaws
Frambesia, initial or primary
Initial frambesial ulcer
Mother yaw

102.1 Multiple papillomata and wet crab yaws
Butter yaws   Plantar or palmar
Frambesioma   papilloma of yaws
Pianoma

102.2 Other early skin lesions
Cutaneous yaws, less than five years after infection
Early yaws (cutaneous) (macular) (papular)
    (maculopapular) (micropapular)
Frambeside of early yaws

102.3 Hyperkeratosis
Ghoul hand
Hyperkeratosis, palmar or plantar (early) (late) due
    to yaws
Worm-eaten soles

DEF: Overgrowth of skin of palm of bottoms of feet, due to yaws.

102.4 Gummata and ulcers
Gummatous frambeside
Nodular late yaws (ulcerated)

DEF: Rubbery lesions and areas of dead skin caused by yaws.

102.5 Gangosa
Rhinopharyngitis mutilans

DEF: Massive, mutilating lesions of the nose and oral cavity caused by yaws.

102.6 Bone and joint lesions
Goundou
Gumma, bone } of yaws (late)
Gummatous osteitis or
    periostitis

Hydrarthrosis
Osteitis } of yaws (early) (late)
Periostitis (hypertrophic)

102.7 Other manifestations
Juxta-articular nodules of yaws
Mucosal yaws

102.8 Latent yaws
Yaws without clinical manifestations, with positive
    serology

102.9 Yaws, unspecified

✓4th 103 Pinta
DEF: A chronic form of treponematosis, endemic in areas of tropical America; it is identified by the presence of red, violet, blue, coffee-colored or white spots on the skin.

103.0 Primary lesions
Chancre (primary)
Papule (primary) } of pinta [carate]
Pintid

103.1 Intermediate lesions
Erythematous plaques
Hyperchromic lesions } of pinta [carate]
Hyperkeratosis

103.2 Late lesions
Cardiovascular lesions
Skin lesions:
    achromic
    cicatricial } of pinta [carate]
    dyschromic
Vitiligo

103.3 Mixed lesions
Achromic and hyperchromic skin lesions of pinta
    [carate]

103.9 Pinta, unspecified

✓4th 104 Other spirochetal infection
104.0 Nonvenereal endemic syphilis
Bejel   Njovera

DEF: *Treponema pallidum, T. pertenue*, or *T. caroteum* infection transmitted non-sexually, causing lesions on mucosa and skin.

104.8 Other specified spirochetal infections
EXCLUDES   relapsing fever (087.0-087.9)
               syphilis (090.0-097.9)

104.9 Spirochetal infection, unspecified

MYCOSES (110-118)
Use additional code to identify manifestation as:
arthropathy (711.6)
meningitis (321.0-321.1)
otitis externa (380.15)
EXCLUDES   infection by Actinomycetales, such as species of
               Actinomyces, Actinomadura, Nocardia,
               Streptomyces (039.0-039.9)

✓4th 110 Dermatophytosis
INCLUDES   infection by species of Epidermophyton,
               Microsporum, and Trichophyton
               tinea, any type except those in 111

DEF: Superficial infection of the skin caused by a parasitic fungus.

110.0 Of scalp and beard
Kerion   Trichophytic tinea
Sycosis, mycotic   [black dot tinea], scalp

110.1 Of nail
Dermatophytic onychia   Tinea unguium
Onychomycosis

110.2 Of hand
Tinea manuum

110.3 Of groin and perianal area
Dhobie itch   Tinea cruris
Eczema marginatum

110.4 Of foot
Athlete's foot   Tinea pedis

110.5 Of the body
Herpes circinatus   Tinea imbricata [Tokelau]

110.6 Deep seated dermatophytosis
Granuloma trichophyticum
Majocchi's granuloma

110.8 Of other specified sites

110.9 Of unspecified site
Favus NOS   Ringworm NOS
Microsporic tinea NOS

✓4th 111 Dermatomycosis, other and unspecified
111.0 Pityriasis versicolor
Infection by Malassezia [Pityrosporum] furfur
Tinea flava
Tinea versicolor

✓4th ✓5th Additional Digit Required   Nonspecific PDx   Unacceptable PDx   Manifestation Code   MCV Major Cardiovascular Condition ►◄ Revised Text ● New Code ▲ Revised Code Title

Volume 1 — 21

Infectious and Parasitic Diseases

111.1–115.0

111.1   Tinea nigra
     Infection by Cladosporium species
     Keratomycosis nigricans
     Microsporosis nigra
     Pityriasis nigra
     Tinea palmaris nigra

111.2   Tinea blanca
     Infection by Trichosporon (beigelii) cutaneum
     White piedra

111.3   Black piedra
     Infection by Piedraia hortai

111.8   Other specified dermatomycoses

111.9   Dermatomycosis, unspecified

√4ᵗʰ 112 Candidiasis

     INCLUDES   infection by Candida species
                     moniliasis

     EXCLUDES   *neonatal monilial infection (771.7)*

DEF: Fungal infection caused by Candida; usually seen in mucous membranes or skin.

112.0   Of mouth   `CC` `HIV`
     Thrush (oral)
     CC Excl: 112.0-112.9, 117.9, 139.8

112.1   Of vulva and vagina   ♀
     Candidal vulvovaginitis   Monilial vulvovaginitis

112.2   Of other urogenital sites
     Candidal balanitis
     AHA: 4Q, '03, 105; 4Q, '96, 33

112.3   Of skin and nails   `HIV`
     Candidal intertrigo
     Candidal onychia
     Candidal perionyxis [paronychia]

112.4   Of lung   `CC` `HIV`
     Candidal pneumonia
     CC Excl: See code 112.0
     AHA: 2Q, '98, 7

112.5   Disseminated   `CC` `HIV`
     Systemic candidiasis
     CC Excl: See code 112.0
     AHA: 2Q, '00, 5; 2Q, '89, 10

√5ᵗʰ 112.8   Of other specified sites

     112.81   Candidal endocarditis   `CC` `HIV`
         CC Excl: See code 112.0

     112.82   Candidal otitis externa   `CC` `HIV`
            Otomycosis in moniliasis
         CC Excl: See code 112.0

     112.83   Candidal meningitis   `CC` `HIV`
         CC Excl: 003.21, 013.00-013.16, 036.0, 047.0-047.9, 049.0-049.1, 053.0, 054.72, 072.1, 090.42, 091.81, 094.2, 098.89, 100.81, 112.0-112.9, 114.2, 115.01, 115.11, 115.91, 117.9, 130.0, 139.8, 320.0-322.9, 349.89-349.9, 357.0

     112.84   Candidal esophagitis   `CC` `HIV`
         CC Excl: See code 112.0
         AHA: 4Q, '92, 19

     112.85   Candidal enteritis   `CC` `HIV`
         CC Excl: See code 112.0
         AHA: 4Q, '92, 19

     112.89   Other
         AHA: 1Q, '92, 17; 3Q, '91, 20

112.9   Of unspecified site   `HIV`

√4ᵗʰ 114 Coccidioidomycosis

     INCLUDES   infection by Coccidioides (immitis)
                     Posada-Wernicke disease

     AHA: 4Q, '93, 23

DEF: A fungal disease caused by inhalation of dust particles containing arthrospores of *Coccidiodes immitis*; a self-limited respiratory infection; the primary form is known as San Joaquin fever, desert fever or valley fever.

114.0   Primary coccidioidomycosis (pulmonary)   `CC` `HIV`
     Acute pulmonary coccidioidomycosis
     Coccidioidomycotic pneumonitis
     Desert rheumatism
     Pulmonary coccidioidomycosis
     San Joaquin Valley fever
     CC Excl: 114.0, 114.3-114.9, 117.9, 139.8

DEF: Acute, self-limiting *Coccidioides immitis* infection of the lung.

114.1   Primary extrapulmonary coccidioidomycosis   `HIV`
     Chancriform syndrome
     Primary cutaneous coccidioidomycosis

DEF: Acute, self-limiting *Coccidioides immitis* infection in nonpulmonary site.

114.2   Coccidioidal meningitis   `CC` `HIV`
     CC Excl: 003.21, 013.00-013.16, 036.0, 047.0-047.9, 049.0-049.1, 053.0, 054.72, 072.1, 090.42, 091.81, 094.2, 098.89, 100.81, 112.83, 114.2-114.9, 115.01, 115.11, 115.91, 117.9, 130.0, 139.8, 320.0-322.9, 349.89-349.9, 357.0

DEF: *Coccidioides immitis* infection of the lining of the brain and/or spinal cord.

114.3   Other forms of progressive coccidioidomycosis   `CC` `HIV`
     Coccidioidal granuloma
     Disseminated coccidioidomycosis
     CC Excl: 114.3, 114.9, 117.9, 139.8

114.4   Chronic pulmonary coccidioidomycosis   `HIV`

114.5   Pulmonary coccidioidomycosis, unspecified   `HIV`

114.9   Coccidioidomycosis, unspecified   `CC` `HIV`
     CC Excl: See code 114.3

√4ᵗʰ 115 Histoplasmosis

The following fifth-digit subclassification is for use with category 115:

   0 **without mention of manifestation**
   1 **meningitis**
   2 **retinitis**
   3 **pericarditis**
   4 **endocarditis**
   5 **pneumonia**
   9 **other**

√5ᵗʰ 115.0   Infection by Histoplasma capsulatum   `CC 0-5` `HIV`
     American histoplasmosis
     Darling's disease
     Reticuloendothelial cytomycosis
     Small form histoplasmosis

     CC Excl: For code 115.00: 115.00, 115.09, 115.90, 115.99, 117.9, 139.8; **CC Excl: For code 115.01:** 003.21, 013.00-013.16, 036.0, 047.0-049.1, 053.0, 054.72, 072.1, 090.42, 091.81, 094.2, 098.89, 100.81, 112.83, 114.2, 115.00-115.01, 115.09, 115.11, 115.90-115.91, 115.99, 117.9, 130.0, 139.8, 320.0-322.9, 349.89-349.9, 357.0; **CC Excl: For code 115.02:** 115.00, 115.02, 115.09, 115.90, 115.92, 115.99, 117.9, 139.8; **CC Excl: For code 115.03:** 115.00, 115.03, 115.09, 115.90, 115.93, 115.99, 117.9, 139.8; **CC Excl: For code 115.04:** 115.00, 115.04, 115.09, 115.90, 115.94, 115.99, 117.9, 139.8; **CC Excl: For code 115.05:** 115.00, 115.05-115.09, 115.90, 115.95-115.99, 117.9, 139.8, 480.0-480.2, 480.8-487.1, 494.0-508.9, 517.1, 518.89

`N` Newborn Age: 0   `P` Pediatric Age: 0-17   `M` Maternity Age: 12-55   `A` Adult Age: 15-124   `CC` CC Condition   `MC` Major Complication   `CD` Complex Dx   `HIV` HIV Related Dx

22 — Volume 1   *2007 ICD•9•CM*

√5th **115.1** **Infection by Histoplasma duboisii** `CC` `HIV`
African histoplasmosis
Large form histoplasmosis
CC Excl: For code 115.10: 115.10, 115.19, 115.90, 115.99, 117.9, 139.8;
CC Excl: For code 115.11: 003.21, 013.00-013.16, 036.0, 047.0-047.9,
049.0-049.1, 053.0, 054.72, 072.1, 090.42, 091.81, 094.2, 098.89, 100.81,
112.83, 114.2, 115.01, 115.10-115.11, 115.19, 115.90-115.91, 115.99,
117.9, 130.0, 139.8, 320.0-322.9, 349.89-349.9, 357.0;
CC Excl: For code 115.12: 115.10, 115.12, 115.19, 115.90, 115.92, 115.99,
117.9, 139.8; **CC Excl: For code 115.13:** 115.10, 115.13, 115.19, 115.90,
115.93, 115.99, 117.9, 139.8; **CC Excl: For code 115.14:** 115.10, 115.14,
115.19, 115.90, 115.94, 115.99, 117.9, 139.8; **CC Excl: For code 115.15:**
115.05, 115.10, 115.15-115.19, 115.90, 115.95-115.99, 117.9, 139.8, 480.0-
480.2, 480.8-487.1, 494.0-508.9, 517.1, 518.89; **CC Excl: For code 115.19:**
115.10, 115.19, 115.90, 115.99, 117.9, 139.8

√5th **115.9** **Histoplasmosis, unspecified** `CC` `HIV`
Histoplasmosis NOS
CC Excl: For code 115.90: 115.90, 115.99, 117.9, 139.8;
CC Excl: For code 115.91: 003.21, 013.00-013.16, 036.0, 047.0-047.9,
049.0-049.1, 053.0, 054.72, 072.1, 090.42, 091.81, 094.2, 098.89, 100.81,
112.83, 114.2, 115.01, 115.11, 115.91, 115.99, 117.9, 130.0, 139.8, 320.0-
322.9, 349.89-349.9, 357.0; **CC Excl: For code 115.92:** 115.92, 115.99,
117.9, 139.8; **CC Excl: For code 115.93:** 115.93, 115.99, 117.9, 139.8;
CC Excl: For code 115.94: 115.94, 115.99, 117.9, 139.8;
CC Excl: For code 115.95: 115.05, 115.15, 115.95, 115.99, 117.9, 139.8;
CC Excl: For code 115.99: 115.99, 117.9, 139.8

√4th **116 Blastomycotic infection**

116.0 **Blastomycosis** `CC`
Blastomycotic dermatitis
Chicago disease
Cutaneous blastomycosis
Disseminated blastomycosis
Gilchrist's disease
Infection by Blastomyces [Ajellomyces] dermatitidis
North American blastomycosis
Primary pulmonary blastomycosis
CC Excl: 116.0, 117.9, 139.8

116.1 **Paracoccidioidomycosis** `CC`
Brazilian blastomycosis
Infection by Paracoccidioides [Blastomyces]
brasiliensis
Lutz-Splendore-Almeida disease
Mucocutaneous-lymphangitic
paracoccidioidomycosis
Pulmonary paracoccidioidomycosis
South American blastomycosis
Visceral paracoccidioidomycosis
CC Excl: 116.1, 117.9, 139.8

116.2 **Lobomycosis**
Infections by Loboa [Blastomyces] loboi
Keloidal blastomycosis
Lobo's disease

√4th **117 Other mycoses**

117.0 **Rhinosporidiosis**
Infection by Rhinosporidium seeberi

117.1 **Sporotrichosis**
Cutaneous sporotrichosis
Disseminated sporotrichosis
Infection by Sporothrix [Sporotrichum] schenckii
Lymphocutaneous sporotrichosis
Pulmonary sporotrichosis
Sporotrichosis of the bones

117.2 **Chromoblastomycosis**
Chromomycosis
Infection by Cladosporidium carrionii, Fonsecaea
compactum, Fonsecaea pedrosoi, Phialophora
verrucosa

117.3 **Aspergillosis** `CC`
Infection by Aspergillus species, mainly A.
fumigatus, A. flavus group, A. terreus group
CC Excl: 117.3, 117.9, 139.8

AHA: 4Q, '97, 40

117.4 **Mycotic mycetomas** `CC`
Infection by various genera and species of
Ascomycetes and Deuteromycetes, such as
Acremonium [Cephalosporium] falciforme,
Neotestudina rosatii, Madurella grisea,
Madurella mycetomii, Pyrenochaeta romeroi,
Zopfia [Leptosphaeria] senegalensis
Madura foot, mycotic
Maduromycosis, mycotic
EXCLUDES *actinomycotic mycetomas (039.0-039.9)*
CC Excl: 117.4, 117.9, 139.8

117.5 **Cryptococcosis** `CC` `HIV`
Busse-Buschke's disease
European cryptococcosis
Infection by Cryptococcus neoformans
Pulmonary cryptococcosis
Systemic cryptococcosis
Torula
CC Excl: 117.5, 117.9, 139.8

117.6 **Allescheriosis [Petriellidosis]** `CC`
Infections by Allescheria [Petriellidium] boydii
[Monosporium apiospermum]
EXCLUDES *mycotic mycetoma (117.4)*
CC Excl: 117.6, 117.9, 139.8

117.7 **Zygomycosis [Phycomycosis or Mucormycosis]** `CC`
Infection by species of Absidia, Basidiobolus,
Conidiobolus, Cunninghamella,
Entomophthora, Mucor, Rhizopus, Saksenaea
CC Excl: 117.7, 117.9, 139.8

117.8 **Infection by dematiacious fungi,
[Phaehyphomycosis]**
Infection by dematiacious fungi, such as
Cladosporium trichoides [bantianum],
Dreschlera hawaiiensis, Phialophora
gougerotii, Phialophora jeanselmi

117.9 **Other and unspecified mycoses**

118 Opportunistic mycoses `CC` `HIV`
Infection of skin, subcutaneous tissues, and/or organs by a
wide variety of fungi generally considered to be
pathogenic to compromised hosts only (e.g., infection
by species of Alternaria, Dreschlera, Fusarium)
CC Excl: 117.9, 118, 139.8

HELMINTHIASES (120-129)

√4th **120 Schistosomiasis [bilharziasis]**
DEF: Infection caused by *Schistosoma*, a genus of flukes or trematode
parasites.

120.0 **Schistosoma haematobium**
Vesical schistosomiasis NOS

120.1 **Schistosoma mansoni**
Intestinal schistosomiasis NOS

120.2 **Schistosoma japonicum**
Asiatic schistosomiasis NOS
Katayama disease or fever

120.3 **Cutaneous**
Cercarial dermatitis
Infection by cercariae of Schistosoma
Schistosome dermatitis
Swimmers' itch

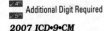
2007 ICD•9•CM

√4th √5th Additional Digit Required   `Nonspecific PDx`   `Unacceptable PDx`   `Manifestation Code`   `MCV` Major Cardiovascular Condition ▶◀ Revised Text ● New Code ▲ Revised Code Title

Volume 1 — 23

120.8   Other specified schistosomiasis
    Infection by Schistosoma:
        bovis
        intercalatum
        mattheii
        spindale
    Schistosomiasis chestermani

120.9   Schistosomiasis, unspecified
    Blood flukes NOS
    Hemic distomiasis

✓4ᵗʰ **121   Other trematode infections**

  121.0   Opisthorchiasis
    Infection by:
        cat liver fluke
        Opisthorchis (felineus) (tenuicollis) (viverrini)

  121.1   Clonorchiasis
    Biliary cirrhosis due to clonorchiasis
    Chinese liver fluke disease
    Hepatic distomiasis due to Clonorchis sinensis
    Oriental liver fluke disease

  121.2   Paragonimiasis
    Infection by Paragonimus
    Lung fluke disease (oriental)
    Pulmonary distomiasis

  121.3   Fascioliasis
    Infection by Fasciola:
        gigantica
        hepatica
    Liver flukes NOS
    Sheep liver fluke infection

  121.4   Fasciolopsiasis
    Infection by Fasciolopsis (buski)
    Intestinal distomiasis

  121.5   Metagonimiasis
    Infection by Metagonimus yokogawai

  121.6   Heterophyiasis
    Infection by:
        Heterophyes heterophyes
        Stellantchasmus falcatus

  121.8   Other specified trematode infections
    Infection by:
        Dicrocoelium dendriticum
        Echinostoma ilocanum
        Gastrodiscoides hominis

  121.9   Trematode infection, unspecified
    Distomiasis NOS
    Fluke disease NOS

✓4ᵗʰ **122   Echinococcosis**
    INCLUDES   echinococciasis
               hydatid disease
               hydatidosis

    DEF: Infection caused by larval forms of tapeworms of the genus *Echinococcus*.

  122.0   Echinococcus granulosus infection of liver
  122.1   Echinococcus granulosus infection of lung
  122.2   Echinococcus granulosus infection of thyroid
  122.3   Echinococcus granulosus infection, other
  122.4   Echinococcus granulosus infection, unspecified
  122.5   Echinococcus multilocularis infection of liver
  122.6   Echinococcus multilocularis infection, other
  122.7   Echinococcus multilocularis infection, unspecified
  122.8   Echinococcosis, unspecified, of liver
  122.9   Echinococcosis, other and unspecified

✓4ᵗʰ **123   Other cestode infection**

  123.0   Taenia solium infection, intestinal form
    Pork tapeworm (adult) (infection)

  123.1   Cysticercosis
    Cysticerciasis
    Infection by Cysticercus cellulosae [larval form of
        Taenia solium]
    AHA: 2Q, '97, 8

123.2   Taenia saginata infection
    Beef tapeworm (infection)
    Infection by Taeniarhynchus saginatus

123.3   Taeniasis, unspecified

123.4   Diphyllobothriasis, intestinal
    Diphyllobothrium (adult) (latum) (pacificum)
        infection
    Fish tapeworm (infection)

123.5   Sparganosis [larval diphyllobothriasis]
    Infection by:
        Diphyllobothrium larvae
        Sparganum (mansoni) (proliferum)
        Spirometra larvae

123.6   Hymenolepiasis
    Dwarf tapeworm (infection)
    Hymenolepis (diminuta) (nana) infection
    Rat tapeworm (infection)

123.8   Other specified cestode infection
    Diplogonoporus (grandis) ⎫
    Dipylidium (caninum)   ⎬ infection
    Dog tapeworm (infection)

123.9   Cestode infection, unspecified
    Tapeworm (infection) NOS

124   Trichinosis
    Trichinella spiralis infection   Trichiniasis
    Trichinellosis
    DEF: Infection by *Trichinella spiralis*, the smallest of the parasitic nematodes.

✓4ᵗʰ **125   Filarial infection and dracontiasis**

  125.0   Bancroftian filariasis
    Chyluria   ⎫
    Elephantiasis   ⎪
    Infection   ⎬ due to Wuchereria bancrofti
    Lymphadenitis   ⎪
    Lymphangitis   ⎭
    Wuchereriasis

  125.1   Malayan filariasis
    Brugia filariasis ⎫
    Chyluria   ⎪
    Elephantiasis   ⎪ due to Brugia
    Infection   ⎬ [Wuchereria]
    Lymphadenitis   ⎪ malayi
    Lymphangitis   ⎭

  125.2   Loiasis
    Eyeworm disease of Africa   Loa loa infection

  125.3   Onchocerciasis
    Onchocerca volvulus infection
    Onchocercosis

  125.4   Dipetalonemiasis
    Infection by:
        Acanthocheilonema perstans
        Dipetalonema perstans

  125.5   Mansonella ozzardi infection
    Filariasis ozzardi

  125.6   Other specified filariasis
    Dirofilaria infection
    Infection by:
        Acanthocheilonema streptocerca
        Dipetalonema streptocerca

  125.7   Dracontiasis
    Guinea-worm infection
    Infection by Dracunculus medinensis

  125.9   Unspecified filariasis

✓4ᵗʰ **126   Ancylostomiasis and necatoriasis**
    INCLUDES   cutaneous larva migrans due to Ancylostoma
               hookworm (disease) (infection)
               uncinariasis

  126.0   Ancylostoma duodenale
  126.1   Necator americanus
  126.2   Ancylostoma braziliense
  126.3   Ancylostoma ceylanicum

N Newborn Age: 0   P Pediatric Age: 0-17   M Maternity Age: 12-55   A Adult Age: 15-124   CC CC Condition   MC Major Complication   CD Complex Dx   HIV HIV Related Dx

126.8 **Other specified Ancylostoma**

126.9 **Ancylostomiasis and necatoriasis, unspecified**
Creeping eruption NOS
Cutaneous larva migrans NOS

✓4ᵗʰ **127 Other intestinal helminthiases**

127.0 **Ascariasis**
Ascaridiasis
Infection by Ascaris lumbricoides
Roundworm infection

127.1 **Anisakiasis**
Infection by Anisakis larva

127.2 **Strongyloidiasis**   HIV
Infection by Strongyloides stercoralis
EXCLUDES *trichostrongyliasis (127.6)*

127.3 **Trichuriasis**
Infection by Trichuris trichiura
Trichocephaliasis
Whipworm (disease) (infection)

127.4 **Enterobiasis**
Infection by Enterobius vermicularis
Oxyuriasis
Oxyuris vermicularis infection
Pinworm (disease) (infection)
Threadworm infection

127.5 **Capillariasis**
Infection by Capillaria philippinensis
EXCLUDES *infection by Capillaria hepatica (128.8)*

127.6 **Trichostrongyliasis**
Infection by Trichostrongylus species

127.7 **Other specified intestinal helminthiasis**
Infection by:
Oesophagostomum apiostomum and related
species
Ternidens diminutus
other specified intestinal helminth
Physalopteriasis

127.8 **Mixed intestinal helminthiasis**
Infection by intestinal helminths classified to more
than one of the categories 120.0-127.7
Mixed helminthiasis NOS

127.9 **Intestinal helminthiasis, unspecified**

✓4ᵗʰ **128 Other and unspecified helminthiases**

128.0 **Toxocariasis**
Larva migrans visceralis
Toxocara (canis) (cati) infection
Visceral larva migrans syndrome

128.1 **Gnathostomiasis**
Infection by Gnathostoma spinigerum and related
species

128.8 **Other specified helminthiasis**
Infection by:
Angiostrongylus cantonensis
Capillaria hepatica
other specified helminth

128.9 **Helminth infection, unspecified**
Helminthiasis NOS   Worms NOS

129 Intestinal parasitism, unspecified

OTHER INFECTIOUS AND PARASITIC DISEASES (130–136)

✓4ᵗʰ **130 Toxoplasmosis**
INCLUDES infection by toxoplasma gondii
toxoplasmosis (acquired)
EXCLUDES *congenital toxoplasmosis (771.2)*

130.0 **Meningoencephalitis due to toxoplasmosis** CC HIV
Encephalitis due to acquired toxoplasmosis
CC Excl: 130.0, 130.7-130.9, 139.8

130.1 **Conjunctivitis due to toxoplasmosis** CC HIV
CC Excl: 130.1, 130.7-130.9, 139.8

130.2 **Chorioretinitis due to toxoplasmosis** CC HIV
Focal retinochoroiditis due to acquired
toxoplasmosis
CC Excl: 130.2, 130.7-130.9, 139.8

130.3 **Myocarditis due to toxoplasmosis** CC HIV
CC Excl: 130.3, 130.7-130.9, 139.8

130.4 **Pneumonitis due to toxoplasmosis** CC HIV
CC Excl: 130.4, 130.7-130.9, 139.8, 480.0-480.2, 480.8-487.1, 494.0-508.9,
517.1, 518.89

130.5 **Hepatitis due to toxoplasmosis** CC HIV
CC Excl: 130.5-130.9, 139.8

130.7 **Toxoplasmosis of other specified sites** CC HIV
CC Excl: 130.7-130.9, 139.8

130.8 **Multisystemic disseminated toxoplasmosis** CC HIV
Toxoplasmosis of multiple sites
CC Excl: See code 130.7

130.9 **Toxoplasmosis, unspecified** HIV

✓4ᵗʰ **131 Trichomoniasis**
INCLUDES infection due to Trichomonas (vaginalis)

✓5ᵗʰ **131.0** **Urogenital trichomoniasis**

131.00 **Urogenital trichomoniasis, unspecified**
Fluor (vaginalis)   ⎫ trichomonal or due to
Leukorrhea   ⎬ Trichomonas
(vaginalis)   ⎭ (vaginalis)

DEF: *Trichomonas vaginalis* infection of reproductive
and urinary organs, transmitted through coitus.

131.01 **Trichomonal vulvovaginitis** ♀
Vaginitis, trichomonal or due to
Trichomonas (vaginalis)
DEF: *Trichomonas vaginalis* infection of vulva and
vagina; often asymptomatic, transmitted through coitus.

131.02 **Trichomonal urethritis**
DEF: *Trichomonas vaginalis* infection of the urethra.

131.03 **Trichomonal prostatitis** ♂
DEF: *Trichomonas vaginalis* infection of the prostate.

131.09 **Other**

131.8 **Other specified sites**
EXCLUDES *intestinal (007.3)*

131.9 **Trichomoniasis, unspecified**

✓4ᵗʰ **132 Pediculosis and phthirus infestation**

132.0 **Pediculus capitis [head louse]**

132.1 **Pediculus corporis [body louse]**

132.2 **Phthirus pubis [pubic louse]**
Pediculus pubis

132.3 **Mixed infestation**
Infestation classifiable to more than one of the
categories 132.0-132.2

132.9 **Pediculosis, unspecified**

✓4ᵗʰ **133 Acariasis**

133.0 **Scabies**
Infestation by Sarcoptes scabiei   Sarcoptic itch
Norwegian scabies

133.8 **Other acariasis**
Chiggers   Infestation by:
Infestation by: Trombicula
Demodex folliculorum

133.9 **Acariasis, unspecified**
Infestation by mites NOS

| ✓4ᵗʰ ✓5ᵗʰ Additional Digit Required | Nonspecific PDx | Unacceptable PDx | Manifestation Code | MCV Major Cardiovascular Condition | ►◄ Revised Text | ● New Code | ▲ Revised Code Title |

2007 ICD•9•CM   **Volume 1 — 25**

Infectious and Parasitic Diseases

126.8–133.9

√4ᵗʰ **134 Other infestation**

134.0 Myiasis

Infestation by:
  Dermatobia (hominis)
  fly larvae
  Gasterophilus (intestinalis)

Infestation by:
  maggots
  Oestrus ovis

134.1 Other arthropod infestation

Infestation by:
  chigoe
  sand flea
  Tunga penetrans

Jigger disease
Scarabiasis
Tungiasis

134.2 Hirudiniasis

Hirudiniasis (external) (internal)
Leeches (aquatic) (land)

134.8 Other specified infestations

134.9 Infestation, unspecified

Infestation (skin) NOS   Skin parasites NOS

135 Sarcoidosis `CC`

Besnier-Boeck-Schaumann disease
Lupoid (miliary) of Boeck
Lupus pernio (Besnier)
Lymphogranulomatosis, benign (Schaumann's)
Sarcoid (any site):
  NOS
  Boeck
  Darier-Roussy
Uveoparotid fever

CC Excl: 135, 139.8

DEF: A chronic, granulomatous reticulosis (abnormal increase in cells), affecting any organ or tissue; acute form has high rate of remission; chronic form is progressive.

√4ᵗʰ **136 Other and unspecified infectious and parasitic diseases**

136.0 Ainhum

Dactylolysis spontanea

DEF: A disease affecting the toes, especially the fifth digit, and sometimes the fingers, especially seen in black adult males; it is characterized by a linear constriction around the affected digit leading to spontaneous amputation of the distal part of the digit.

136.1 Behçet's syndrome

DEF: A chronic inflammatory disorder of unknown etiology involving the small blood vessels; it is characterized by recurrent aphthous ulceration of the oral and pharyngeal mucous membranes and the genitalia, skin lesions, severe uvetis, retinal vascularitis and optic atrophy.

136.2 Specific infections by free-living amebae

Meningoencephalitis due to Naegleria

136.3 Pneumocystosis `CC` `HIV`

Pneumonia due to Pneumocystis carinii
▶Pneumonia due to Pneumocystis jiroveci◀

CC Excl: 136.3, 139.8, 480.0- 480.2, 480.8-487.1, 494.0-508.9, 517.1, 518.89

AHA: 1Q, '05, 7; 1Q, '03, 15; N-D, '87, 5-6

DEF: Pneumocystis carinii fungus causing pneumonia in immunocompromised patients; a leading cause of death among AIDS patients.

136.4 Psorospermiasis

136.5 Sarcosporidiosis

Infection by Sarcocystis lindemanni

DEF: Sarcocystis infection causing muscle cysts of intestinal inflammation.

136.8 Other specified infectious and parasitic diseases `HIV`

Candiru infestation

136.9 Unspecified infectious and parasitic diseases

Infectious disease NOS   Parasitic disease NOS

AHA: 2Q, '91, 8

LATE EFFECTS OF INFECTIOUS AND PARASITIC DISEASES (137-139)

√4ᵗʰ **137 Late effects of tuberculosis**

Note: This category is to be used to indicate conditions classifiable to 010-018 as the cause of late effects, which are themselves classified elsewhere. The "late effects" include those specified as such, as sequelae, or as due to old or inactive tuberculosis, without evidence of active disease.

137.0 Late effects of respiratory or unspecified tuberculosis `CC`

CC Excl: 137.0, 139.8

137.1 Late effects of central nervous system tuberculosis `CC`

CC Excl: 137.1, 139.8

137.2 Late effects of genitourinary tuberculosis `CC`

CC Excl: 137.2, 139.8

137.3 Late effects of tuberculosis of bones and joints

137.4 Late effects of tuberculosis of other specified organs

138 Late effects of acute poliomyelitis `CC`

Note: This category is to be used to indicate conditions classifiable to 045 as the cause of late effects, which are themselves classified elsewhere. The "late effects" include conditions specified as such, or as sequelae, or as due to old or inactive poliomyelitis, without evidence of active disease.

CC Excl: 138, 139.8

√4ᵗʰ **139 Late effects of other infectious and parasitic diseases**

Note: This category is to be used to indicate conditions classifiable to categories 001-009, 020-041, 046-136 as the cause of late effects, which are themselves classified elsewhere. The "late effects" include conditions specified as such; they also include sequela of diseases classifiable to the above categories if there is evidence that the disease itself is no longer present.

139.0 Late effects of viral encephalitis

Late effects of conditions classifiable to 049.8-049.9, 062-064

139.1 Late effects of trachoma

Late effects of conditions classifiable to 076

139.8 Late effects of other and unspecified infectious and parasitic diseases

AHA: 4Q, '91, 15; 3Q, '90, 14; M-A, '87, 8

`N` Newborn Age: 0   `P` Pediatric Age: 0-17   `M` Maternity Age: 12-55   `A` Adult Age: 15-124   `CC` CC Condition   `MC` Major Complication   `CD` Complex Dx   `HIV` HIV Related Dx

26 — Volume 1 • October 2006

2007 ICD•9•CM

2. NEOPLASMS (140-239)

Notes:

1. Content

This chapter contains the following broad groups:

140-195	Malignant neoplasms, stated or presumed to be primary, of specified sites, except of lymphatic and hematopoietic tissue
196-198	Malignant neoplasms, stated or presumed to be secondary, of specified sites
199	Malignant neoplasms, without specification of site
200-208	Malignant neoplasms, stated or presumed to be primary, of lymphatic and hematopoietic tissue
210-229	Benign neoplasms
230-234	Carcinoma in situ
235-238	Neoplasms of uncertain behavior [see Note, above category 235]
239	Neoplasms of unspecified nature

2. Functional activity

All neoplasms are classified in this chapter, whether or not functionally active. An additional code from Chapter 3 may be used to identify such functional activity associated with any neoplasm, e.g.:

> catecholamine-producing malignant pheochromocytoma of adrenal:
>
> > code 194.0, additional code 255.6
>
> basophil adenoma of pituitary with Cushing's syndrome:
>
> > code 227.3, additional code 255.0

3. Morphology [Histology]

For those wishing to identify the histological type of neoplasms, a comprehensive coded nomenclature, which comprises the morphology rubrics of the ICD-Oncology, is given in Appendix A.

4. Malignant neoplasms overlapping site boundaries

Categories 140-195 are for the classification of primary malignant neoplasms according to their point of origin. A malignant neoplasm that overlaps two or more subcategories within a three-digit rubric and whose point of origin cannot be determined should be classified to the subcategory .8 "Other."

For example, "carcinoma involving tip and ventral surface of tongue" should be assigned to 141.8. On the other hand, "carcinoma of tip of tongue, extending to involve the ventral surface" should be coded to 141.2, as the point of origin, the tip, is known. Three subcategories (149.8, 159.8, 165.8) have been provided for malignant neoplasms that overlap the boundaries of three-digit rubrics within certain systems.

Overlapping malignant neoplasms that cannot be classified as indicated above should be assigned to the appropriate subdivision of category 195 (Malignant neoplasm of other and ill-defined sites).

AHA: 2Q, '90, 7

DEF: An abnormal growth, such as a tumor. Morphology determines behavior, i.e., whether it will remain intact (benign) or spread to adjacent tissue (malignant). The term mass is not synonymous with neoplasm, as it is often used to describe cysts and thickenings such as those occurring with hematoma or infection.

MALIGNANT NEOPLASM OF LIP, ORAL CAVITY, AND PHARYNX (140-149)

> **EXCLUDES** carcinoma in situ (230.0)

√4ᵗʰ 140 Malignant neoplasm of lip

> **EXCLUDES** skin of lip (173.0)

140.0 Upper lip, vermilion border

Upper lip:	Upper lip:
NOS	lipstick area
external	

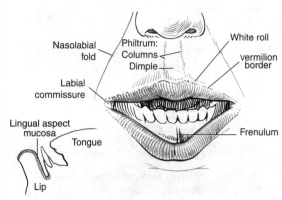

Lip

140.1 Lower lip, vermilion border

Lower lip:	Lower lip:
NOS	lipstick area
external	

140.3 Upper lip, inner aspect

Upper lip:	Upper lip:
buccal aspect	mucosa
frenulum	oral aspect

140.4 Lower lip, inner aspect

Lower lip:	Lower lip:
buccal aspect	mucosa
frenulum	oral aspect

140.5 Lip, unspecified, inner aspect

> Lip, not specified whether upper or lower:
> > buccal aspect
> > frenulum
> > mucosa
> > oral aspect

140.6 Commissure of lip

> Labial commissure

140.8 Other sites of lip

> Malignant neoplasm of contiguous or overlapping sites of lip whose point of origin cannot be determined

140.9 Lip, unspecified, vermilion border

> Lip, not specified as upper or lower:
> > NOS
> > external
> > lipstick area

√4ᵗʰ 141 Malignant neoplasm of tongue

141.0 Base of tongue

> Dorsal surface of base of tongue
> Fixed part of tongue NOS

141.1 Dorsal surface of tongue

> Anterior two-thirds of tongue, dorsal surface
> Dorsal tongue NOS
> Midline of tongue
>
> > **EXCLUDES** *dorsal surface of base of tongue (141.0)*

Tongue

√4ᵗʰ √5ᵗʰ Additional Digit Required   Nonspecific PDx   Unacceptable PDx   Manifestation Code   **MCV** Major Cardiovascular Condition   ►◄ Revised Text   ● New Code   ▲ Revised Code Title

2007 ICD•9•CM   Volume 1 — 27

Neoplasms

141.2–146.7

Main Salivary Glands

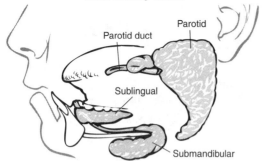

- Parotid duct
- Parotid
- Sublingual
- Submandibular

141.2   **Tip and lateral border of tongue**

141.3   **Ventral surface of tongue**
Anterior two-thirds of tongue, ventral surface
Frenulum linguae

141.4   **Anterior two-thirds of tongue, part unspecified**
Mobile part of tongue NOS

141.5   **Junctional zone**
Border of tongue at junction of fixed and mobile parts at insertion of anterior tonsillar pillar

141.6   **Lingual tonsil**

141.8   **Other sites of tongue**
Malignant neoplasm of contiguous or overlapping sites of tongue whose point of origin cannot be determined

141.9   **Tongue, unspecified**
Tongue NOS

✓4th **142 Malignant neoplasm of major salivary glands**
INCLUDES   salivary ducts
EXCLUDES   *malignant neoplasm of minor salivary glands:*
NOS (145.9)
buccal mucosa (145.0)
soft palate (145.3)
tongue (141.0-141.9)
tonsil, palatine (146.0)

142.0   **Parotid gland**

142.1   **Submandibular gland**
Submaxillary gland

142.2   **Sublingual gland**

142.8   **Other major salivary glands**
Malignant neoplasm of contiguous or overlapping sites of salivary glands and ducts whose point of origin cannot be determined

142.9   **Salivary gland, unspecified**
Salivary gland (major) NOS

✓4th **143 Malignant neoplasm of gum**
INCLUDES   alveolar (ridge) mucosa
gingiva (alveolar) (marginal)
interdental papillae
EXCLUDES   *malignant odontogenic neoplasms (170.0-170.1)*

143.0   **Upper gum**

143.1   **Lower gum**

143.8   **Other sites of gum**
Malignant neoplasm of contiguous or overlapping sites of gum whose point of origin cannot be determined

143.9   **Gum, unspecified**

✓4th **144 Malignant neoplasm of floor of mouth**

144.0   **Anterior portion**
Anterior to the premolar-canine junction

144.1   **Lateral portion**

144.8   **Other sites of floor of mouth**
Malignant neoplasm of contiguous or overlapping sites of floor of mouth whose point of origin cannot be determined

144.9   **Floor of mouth, part unspecified**

✓4th **145 Malignant neoplasm of other and unspecified parts of mouth**
EXCLUDES   *mucosa of lips (140.0-140.9)*

145.0   **Cheek mucosa**
Buccal mucosa
Cheek, inner aspect

145.1   **Vestibule of mouth**
Buccal sulcus (upper) (lower)
Labial sulcus (upper) (lower)

145.2   **Hard palate**

145.3   **Soft palate**
EXCLUDES   *nasopharyngeal [posterior] [superior] surface of soft palate (147.3)*

145.4   **Uvula**

145.5   **Palate, unspecified**
Junction of hard and soft palate   Roof of mouth

145.6   **Retromolar area**

145.8   **Other specified parts of mouth**
Malignant neoplasm of contiguous or overlapping sites of mouth whose point of origin cannot be determined

145.9   **Mouth, unspecified**
Buccal cavity NOS
Minor salivary gland, unspecified site
Oral cavity NOS

✓4th **146 Malignant neoplasm of oropharynx**

146.0   **Tonsil**
Tonsil:
NOS
faucial
palatine
EXCLUDES   *lingual tonsil (141.6)*
pharyngeal tonsil (147.1)

AHA: S-O, '87, 8

146.1   **Tonsillar fossa**

146.2   **Tonsillar pillars (anterior) (posterior)**
Faucial pillar   Palatoglossal arch
Glossopalatine fold   Palatopharyngeal arch

146.3   **Vallecula**
Anterior and medial surface of the pharyngoepiglottic fold

146.4   **Anterior aspect of epiglottis**
Epiglottis, free border [margin]
Glossoepiglottic fold(s)
EXCLUDES   *epiglottis:*
NOS (161.1)
suprahyoid portion (161.1)

146.5   **Junctional region**
Junction of the free margin of the epiglottis, the aryepiglottic fold, and the pharyngoepiglottic fold

146.6   **Lateral wall of oropharynx**

146.7   **Posterior wall of oropharynx**

Mouth

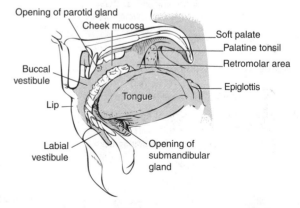

- Opening of parotid gland
- Cheek mucosa
- Soft palate
- Palatine tonsil
- Retromolar area
- Buccal vestibule
- Epiglottis
- Lip
- Tongue
- Labial vestibule
- Opening of submandibular gland

N Newborn Age: 0   P Pediatric Age: 0-17   M Maternity Age: 12-55   A Adult Age: 15-124   CC CC Condition   MC Major Complication   CD Complex Dx   HIV HIV Related Dx

28 — Volume 1   *2007 ICD•9•CM*

Oropharynx

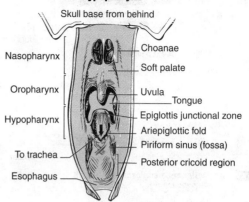

Hypopharynx

146.8   **Other specified sites of oropharynx**
Branchial cleft
Malignant neoplasm of contiguous or overlapping sites of oropharynx whose point of origin cannot be determined

146.9   **Oropharynx, unspecified**
AHA: 2Q, '02, 6

√4th **147 Malignant neoplasm of nasopharynx**

147.0   **Superior wall**
Roof of nasopharynx

147.1   **Posterior wall**
Adenoid   Pharyngeal tonsil

147.2   **Lateral wall**
Fossa of Rosenmüller   Pharyngeal recess
Opening of auditory tube

147.3   **Anterior wall**
Floor of nasopharynx
Nasopharyngeal [posterior] [superior] surface of soft palate
Posterior margin of nasal septum and choanae

147.8   **Other specified sites of nasopharynx**
Malignant neoplasm of contiguous or overlapping sites of nasopharynx whose point of origin cannot be determined

147.9   **Nasopharynx, unspecified**
Nasopharyngeal wall NOS

√4th **148 Malignant neoplasm of hypopharynx**

148.0   **Postcricoid region**

148.1   **Pyriform sinus**
Pyriform fossa

148.2   **Aryepiglottic fold, hypopharyngeal aspect**
Aryepiglottic fold or interarytenoid fold:
NOS
marginal zone
EXCLUDES   *aryepiglottic fold or interarytenoid fold, laryngeal aspect (161.1)*

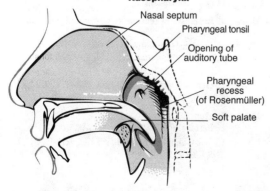

Nasopharynx

148.3   **Posterior hypopharyngeal wall**

148.8   **Other specified sites of hypopharynx**
Malignant neoplasm of contiguous or overlapping sites of hypopharynx whose point of origin cannot be determined

148.9   **Hypopharynx, unspecified**
Hypopharyngeal wall NOS
Hypopharynx NOS

√4th **149 Malignant neoplasm of other and ill-defined sites within the lip, oral cavity, and pharynx**

149.0   **Pharynx, unspecified**

149.1   **Waldeyer's ring**

149.8   **Other**
Malignant neoplasms of lip, oral cavity, and pharynx whose point of origin cannot be assigned to any one of the categories 140-148
EXCLUDES   *"book leaf" neoplasm [ventral surface of tongue and floor of mouth] (145.8)*

149.9   **Ill-defined**

MALIGNANT NEOPLASM OF DIGESTIVE ORGANS AND PERITONEUM (150-159)

EXCLUDES   *carcinoma in situ (230.1-230.9)*

√4th **150 Malignant neoplasm of esophagus**

150.0   **Cervical esophagus**   `CC`
CC Excl: 150.0-150.9, 159.0, 159.8-159.9, 176.3, 195.8, 199.0-199.1, 239.0, 239.8-239.9

150.1   **Thoracic esophagus**   `CC`
CC Excl: See code 150.0

150.2   **Abdominal esophagus**   `CC`
EXCLUDES   *adenocarcinoma (151.0)*
cardio-esophageal junction (151.0)
CC Excl: See code 150.0

150.3   **Upper third of esophagus**   `CC`
CC Excl: See code 150.0
Proximal third of esophagus

150.4   **Middle third of esophagus**   `CC`
CC Excl: See code 150.0

√4th Additional Digit Required   Nonspecific PDx   Unacceptable PDx   Manifestation Code   `MCV` Major Cardiovascular Condition   ◄ Revised Text   ● New Code   ▲ Revised Code Title
√5th

150.5 Lower third of esophagus   `cc`
Distal third of esophagus
> **EXCLUDES**   adenocarcinoma (151.0)
> cardio-esophageal junction (151.0)

CC Excl: See code 150.0

150.8 Other specified part   `cc`
Malignant neoplasm of contiguous or overlapping
sites of esophagus whose point of origin cannot
be determined

CC Excl: See code 150.0

150.9 Esophagus, unspecified   `cc`
CC Excl: See code 150.0

✓4ᵗʰ 151 Malignant neoplasm of stomach
> **EXCLUDES** ▶ malignant stromal tumor of stomach (171.5)◀

151.0 Cardia   `cc`
Cardiac orifice
Cardio-esophageal junction
> **EXCLUDES**   squamous cell carcinoma (150.2, 150.5)

CC Excl: 151.0-151.9, 159.0, 159.8-159.9, 176.3, 195.8, 199.0-199.1,
239.0, 239.8-239.9

151.1 Pylorus   `cc`
Prepylorus   Pyloric canal
CC Excl: See code 151.0

151.2 Pyloric antrum   `cc`
Antrum of stomach NOS
CC Excl: See code 151.0

151.3 Fundus of stomach   `cc`
CC Excl: See code 151.0

151.4 Body of stomach   `cc`
CC Excl: See code 151.0

151.5 Lesser curvature, unspecified   `cc`
Lesser curvature, not classifiable to 151.1-151.4
CC Excl: See code 151.0

151.6 Greater curvature, unspecified   `cc`
Greater curvature, not classifiable to 151.0-151.4
CC Excl: See code 151.0

151.8 Other specified sites of stomach   `cc`
Anterior wall, not classifiable to 151.0-151.4
Posterior wall, not classifiable to 151.0-151.4
Malignant neoplasm of contiguous or overlapping
sites of stomach whose point of origin cannot
be determined

CC Excl: See code 151.0

151.9 Stomach, unspecified   `cc`
Carcinoma ventriculi   Gastric cancer
CC Excl: See code 151.0

AHA: 2Q, '01, 17

✓4ᵗʰ 152 Malignant neoplasm of small intestine, including duodenum
> **EXCLUDES** ▶ malignant stromal tumor of small intestine
> (171.5)◀

152.0 Duodenum   `cc`
CC Excl: 152.0, 152.8-152.9, 159.0, 159.8-159.9, 176.3, 195.8,
199.0-199.1, 239.0, 239.8-239.9

152.1 Jejunum   `cc`
CC Excl: 152.1, 152.8-152.9, 159.0, 159.8-159.9, 176.3, 195.8,
199.0-199.1, 239.0, 239.8-239.9

152.2 Ileum   `cc`
> **EXCLUDES**   ileocecal valve (153.4)

CC Excl: 152.2, 152.8-152.9, 159.0, 159.8-159.9, 176.3, 195.8,
199.0-199.1, 239.0, 239.8-239.9

152.3 Meckel's diverticulum   `cc`
CC Excl: 152.3-152.9, 159.0, 159.8-159.9, 176.3, 195.8, 199.0-
199.1, 239.0, 239.8-239.9

152.8 Other specified sites of small intestine   `cc`
Duodenojejunal junction
Malignant neoplasm of contiguous or overlapping
sites of small intestine whose point of origin
cannot be determined

CC Excl: 152.8-152.9, 159.0, 159.8-159.9, 176.3, 195.8, 199.0-199.1,
239.0, 239.8-239.9

152.9 Small intestine, unspecified   `cc`
CC Excl: See code 152.8

✓4ᵗʰ 153 Malignant neoplasm of colon

153.0 Hepatic flexure   `cc`
CC Excl: 153.0, 153.8-153.9, 159.0, 159.8-159.9, 176.3, 195.8,
199.0-199.1, 239.0, 239.8-239.9

153.1 Transverse colon   `cc`
CC Excl: 153.1, 153.8-153.9, 159.0, 159.8-159.9, 176.3, 195.8,
199.0-199.1, 239.0, 239.8-239.9

153.2 Descending colon   `cc`
Left colon
CC Excl: 153.2, 153.8-153.9, 159.0, 159.8-159.9, 176.3, 195.8,
199.0-199.1, 239.0, 239.8-239.9

153.3 Sigmoid colon   `cc`
Sigmoid (flexure)
> **EXCLUDES**   rectosigmoid junction (154.0)

CC Excl: 153.3, 153.8-153.9, 159.0, 159.8-159.9, 176.3, 195.8, 199.0-199.1,
239.0, 239.8-239.9

153.4 Cecum   `cc`
Ileocecal valve
CC Excl: 153.4, 153.8-153.9, 159.0, 159.8-159.9, 176.3, 195.8,
199.0-199.1, 239.0, 239.8-239.9

153.5 Appendix   `cc`
CC Excl: 153.5, 153.8-153.9, 159.0, 159.8-159.9, 176.3, 195.8,
199.0-199.1, 239.0, 239.8-239.9

153.6 Ascending colon   `cc`
Right colon
CC Excl: 153.6, 153.8-153.9, 159.0, 159.8-159.9, 176.3, 195.8,
199.0-199.1, 239.0, 239.8-239.9

153.7 Splenic flexure   `cc`
CC Excl: 153.7-153.9, 159.0, 159.8-159.9, 176.3, 195.8, 199.0-199.1,
239.0, 239.8-239.9

153.8 Other specified sites of large intestine   `cc`
Malignant neoplasm of contiguous or overlapping
sites of colon whose point of origin cannot be
determined
> **EXCLUDES**   ileocecal valve (153.4)
> rectosigmoid junction (154.0)

CC Excl: 153.8-153.9, 159.0, 159.8-159.9, 176.3, 195.8, 199.0-199.1,
239.0, 239.8-239.9

153.9 Colon, unspecified   `cc`
Large intestine NOS
CC Excl: See code 153.8

✓4ᵗʰ 154 Malignant neoplasm of rectum, rectosigmoid junction, and anus

154.0 Rectosigmoid junction   `cc`
Colon with rectum
Rectosigmoid (colon)
CC Excl: 154.0, 154.8, 159.0, 159.8-159.9, 176.3, 195.8, 199.0-199.1,
239.0, 239.8-239.9

154.1 Rectum   `cc`
Rectal ampulla
CC Excl: 154.1, 154.8, 159.0, 159.8-159.9, 176.3, 195.8, 199.0-199.1,
239.0, 239.8-239.9

| `N` Newborn Age: 0 | `P` Pediatric Age: 0-17 | `M` Maternity Age: 12-55 | `A` Adult Age: 15-124 | `CC` CC Condition | `MC` Major Complication | `CD` Complex Dx | `HIV` HIV Related Dx |

Colon

Anatomical distribution of large bowel cancers

154.2 Anal canal `CC`
Anal sphincter
> EXCLUDES   skin of anus (172.5, 173.5)

CC Excl: 154.2-154.8, 159.0, 159.8-159.9, 176.3, 195.8, 199.0-199.1, 239.0, 239.8-239.9

AHA: 1Q, '01, 8

154.3 Anus, unspecified `CC`
> EXCLUDES   anus:
>> margin (172.5, 173.5)
>> skin (172.5, 173.5)
>> perianal skin (172.5, 173.5)

CC Excl: See code 154.2

154.8 Other `CC`
Anorectum
Cloacogenic zone
Malignant neoplasm of contiguous or overlapping sites of rectum, rectosigmoid junction, and anus whose point of origin cannot be determined

CC Excl: 154.8, 159.0, 159.8-159.9, 176.3, 195.8, 199.0-199.1, 239.0, 239.8-239.9

√4th **155 Malignant neoplasm of liver and intrahepatic bile ducts**

155.0 Liver, primary `CC`
Carcinoma:
  liver, specified as primary
  hepatocellular
  liver cell
Hepatoblastoma

CC Excl: 155.0-155.2, 159.0, 159.8-159.9, 176.3, 195.8, 199.0-199.1, 239.0, 239.8-239.9

155.1 Intrahepatic bile ducts `CC`
Canaliculi biliferi   Intrahepatic:
Interlobular: biliary passages
  bile ducts   canaliculi
  biliary canals   gall duct
> EXCLUDES   hepatic duct (156.1)

CC Excl: See code 155.0

155.2 Liver, not specified as primary or secondary `CC`
CC Excl: See code 155.0

√4th **156 Malignant neoplasm of gallbladder and extrahepatic bile ducts**

156.0 Gallbladder `CC`
CC Excl: 156.0, 156.8-156.9, 159.0, 159.8-159.9, 176.3, 195.8, 199.0-199.1, 239.0, 239.8-239.9

156.1 Extrahepatic bile ducts `CC`
Biliary duct or passage NOS
Common bile duct
Cystic duct
Hepatic duct
Sphincter of Oddi

CC Excl: 156.1, 156.8-156.9, 159.0, 159.8-159.9, 176.3, 195.8, 199.0-199.1, 239.0, 239.8-239.9

156.2 Ampulla of Vater `CC`
CC Excl: 156.2-156.9, 159.0, 159.8-159.9, 176.3, 195.8, 199.0-199.1, 239.0, 239.8-239.9

DEF: Malignant neoplasm in the area of dilation at the juncture of the common bile and pancreatic ducts near the opening into the lumen of the duodenum.

156.8 Other specified sites of gallbladder and extrahepatic bile ducts `CC`
Malignant neoplasm of contiguous or overlapping sites of gallbladder and extrahepatic bile ducts whose point of origin cannot be determined

CC Excl: 156.8-156.9, 159.0, 159.8-159.9, 176.3, 195.8, 199.0-199.1, 239.0, 239.8-239.9

156.9 Biliary tract, part unspecified `CC`
Malignant neoplasm involving both intrahepatic and extrahepatic bile ducts

CC Excl: See code 156.8

√4th **157 Malignant neoplasm of pancreas**

157.0 Head of pancreas `CC`
CC Excl: 157.0-157.9, 159.0, 159.8-159.9, 176.3, 195.8, 199.0-199.1, 239.0, 239.8-239.9

AHA: ▶2Q, '05, 9;◀ 4Q, '00, 40

157.1 Body of pancreas `CC`
CC Excl: See code 157.0

157.2 Tail of pancreas `CC`
CC Excl: See code 157.0

157.3 Pancreatic duct `CC`
Duct of:
  Santorini
  Wirsung

CC Excl: See code 157.0

157.4 Islets of Langerhans `CC`
Islets of Langerhans, any part of pancreas
Use additional code to identify any functional activity

CC Excl: See code 157.0

DEF: Malignant neoplasm within the structures of the pancreas that produce insulin, somatostatin and glucagon.

157.8 Other specified sites of pancreas `CC`
Ectopic pancreatic tissue
Malignant neoplasm of contiguous or overlapping sites of pancreas whose point of origin cannot be determined

CC Excl: See code 157.0

157.9 Pancreas, part unspecified `CC`
CC Excl: See code 157.0

AHA: 4Q, '89, 11

√4th **158 Malignant neoplasm of retroperitoneum and peritoneum**

158.0 Retroperitoneum
Periadrenal tissue   Perirenal tissue
Perinephric tissue   Retrocecal tissue

√4th Additional Digit Required   Nonspecific PDx   Unacceptable PDx   Manifestation Code   `MCV` Major Cardiovascular Condition   ▶◀ Revised Text   ● New Code   ▲ Revised Code Title

Neoplasms

158.8–162.5

Retroperitoneum and Peritoneum

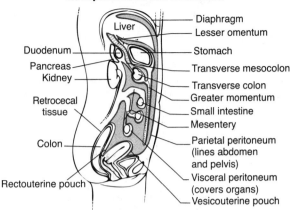

158.8 Specified parts of peritoneum
Cul-de-sac (of Douglas)
Mesentery
Mesocolon
Omentum
Peritoneum:
  parietal
  pelvic
Rectouterine pouch
Malignant neoplasm of contiguous or overlapping sites of retroperitoneum and peritoneum whose point of origin cannot be determined

158.9 Peritoneum, unspecified

√4th **159 Malignant neoplasm of other and ill-defined sites within the digestive organs and peritoneum**

159.0 Intestinal tract, part unspecified
Intestine NOS

159.1 Spleen, not elsewhere classified
Angiosarcoma } of spleen
Fibrosarcoma
  EXCLUDES Hodgkin's disease (201.0-201.9)
  lymphosarcoma (200.1)
  reticulosarcoma (200.0)

159.8 Other sites of digestive system and intra-abdominal organs
Malignant neoplasm of digestive organs and peritoneum whose point of origin cannot be assigned to any one of the categories 150-158
  EXCLUDES anus and rectum (154.8)
  cardio-esophageal junction (151.0)
  colon and rectum (154.0)

159.9 Ill-defined
Alimentary canal or tract NOS
Gastrointestinal tract NOS
  EXCLUDES abdominal NOS (195.2)
  intra-abdominal NOS (195.2)

MALIGNANT NEOPLASM OF RESPIRATORY AND INTRATHORACIC ORGANS (160-165)
  EXCLUDES carcinoma in situ (231.0-231.9)

√4th **160 Malignant neoplasm of nasal cavities, middle ear, and accessory sinuses**

160.0 Nasal cavities
Cartilage of nose   Septum of nose
Conchae, nasal   Vestibule of nose
Internal nose
  EXCLUDES nasal bone (170.0)
  nose NOS (195.0)
  olfactory bulb (192.0)
  posterior margin of septum and choanae (147.3)
  skin of nose (172.3, 173.3)
  turbinates (170.0)

160.1 Auditory tube, middle ear, and mastoid air cells
Antrum tympanicum   Tympanic cavity
Eustachian tube
  EXCLUDES auditory canal (external) (172.2, 173.2)
  bone of ear (meatus) (170.0)
  cartilage of ear (171.0)
  ear (external) (skin) (172.2, 173.2)

160.2 Maxillary sinus
Antrum (Highmore) (maxillary)

160.3 Ethmoidal sinus

160.4 Frontal sinus

160.5 Sphenoidal sinus

160.8 Other
Malignant neoplasm of contiguous or overlapping sites of nasal cavities, middle ear, and accessory sinuses whose point of origin cannot be determined

160.9 Accessory sinus, unspecified

√4th **161 Malignant neoplasm of larynx**

161.0 Glottis
Intrinsic larynx
Laryngeal commissure (anterior) (posterior)
True vocal cord
Vocal cord NOS

161.1 Supraglottis
Aryepiglottic fold or interarytenoid fold, laryngeal aspect
Epiglottis (suprahyoid portion) NOS
Extrinsic larynx
False vocal cords
Posterior (laryngeal) surface of epiglottis
Ventricular bands
  EXCLUDES anterior aspect of epiglottis (146.4)
  aryepiglottic fold or interarytenoid fold:
  NOS (148.2)
  hypopharyngeal aspect (148.2)
  marginal zone (148.2)

161.2 Subglottis

161.3 Laryngeal cartilages
Cartilage: Cartilage:
  arytenoid   cuneiform
  cricoid   thyroid

161.8 Other specified sites of larynx
Malignant neoplasm of contiguous or overlapping sites of larynx whose point of origin cannot be determined

161.9 Larynx, unspecified

√4th **162 Malignant neoplasm of trachea, bronchus, and lung**

162.0 Trachea
Cartilage } of trachea
Mucosa

162.2 Main bronchus `CC`
Carina
Hilus of lung
CC Excl: 162.2, 162.8-162.9, 165.8-165.9, 176.4, 195.8, 199.0-199.1, 239.1, 239.8-239.9

162.3 Upper lobe, bronchus or lung `CC`
CC Excl: 162.3, 162.8-162.9, 165.8-165.9, 176.4, 195.8, 199.0-199.1, 239.1, 239.8-239.9
AHA: 1Q, '04, 4

162.4 Middle lobe, bronchus or lung `CC`
CC Excl: 162.4, 162.8-162.9, 165.8-165.9, 176.4, 195.8, 199.0-199.1, 239.1, 239.8-239.9

162.5 Lower lobe, bronchus or lung `CC`
CC Excl: 162.5-162.9, 165.8-165.9, 176.4, 195.8, 199.0-199.1, 239.1, 239.8-239.9

162.8   **Other parts of bronchus or lung**   `CC`
Malignant neoplasm of contiguous or overlapping sites of bronchus or lung whose point of origin cannot be determined
CC Excl: 162.8-162.9, 165.8-165.9, 176.4, 195.8, 199.0-199.1, 239.1, 239.8-239.9

162.9   **Bronchus and lung, unspecified**   `CC`
CC Excl: See code 162.8
AHA: 2Q, '97, 3; 4Q, '96, 48

✓4ʰ 163 Malignant neoplasm of pleura

163.0   **Parietal pleura**   `CC`
CC Excl: 163.0-163.9, 165.8-165.9, 195.8, 199.0-199.1, 239.1, 239.8-239.9

163.1   **Visceral pleura**   `CC`
CC Excl: See code 163.0

163.8   **Other specified sites of pleura**   `CC`
Malignant neoplasm of contiguous or overlapping sites of pleura whose point of origin cannot be determined
CC Excl: See code 163.0

163.9   **Pleura, unspecified**   `CC`
CC Excl: See code 163.0

✓4ʰ 164 Malignant neoplasm of thymus, heart, and mediastinum

164.0   **Thymus**   `CC`
CC Excl: 164.0

164.1   **Heart**   `CC`
Endocardium   Myocardium
Epicardium   Pericardium
`EXCLUDES`   *great vessels (171.4)*
CC Excl: 164.1

164.2   **Anterior mediastinum**   `CC`
CC Excl: 164.2-164.9, 165.8-165.9, 195.8, 199.0-199.1, 239.1, 239.8-239.9

164.3   **Posterior mediastinum**   `CC`
CC Excl: See code 164.2

164.8   **Other**   `CC`
Malignant neoplasm of contiguous or overlapping sites of thymus, heart, and mediastinum whose point of origin cannot be determined
CC Excl: See code 164.2

164.9   **Mediastinum, part unspecified**   `CC`
CC Excl: See code 164.2

✓4ʰ 165 Malignant neoplasm of other and ill-defined sites within the respiratory system and intrathoracic organs

165.0   **Upper respiratory tract, part unspecified**

165.8   **Other**
Malignant neoplasm of respiratory and intrathoracic organs whose point of origin cannot be assigned to any one of the categories 160-164

165.9   **Ill-defined sites within the respiratory system**
Respiratory tract NOS
`EXCLUDES`   *intrathoracic NOS (195.1)*
thoracic NOS (195.1)

MALIGNANT NEOPLASM OF BONE, CONNECTIVE TISSUE, SKIN, AND BREAST (170-176)

`EXCLUDES`   *carcinoma in situ:*   *carcinoma in situ:*
breast (233.0)   *skin (232.0-232.9)*

✓4ʰ 170 Malignant neoplasm of bone and articular cartilage
`INCLUDES`   cartilage (articular) (joint)
periosteum
`EXCLUDES`   *bone marrow NOS (202.9)*
cartilage:
ear (171.0)
eyelid (171.0)
larynx (161.3)
nose (160.0)
synovia (171.0-171.9)

Skull

Orbital rim — Frontal — Roof — Zygoma (malar) — Ethmoid — Zygomatic arch — Lacrimal — Condylar process — Nasal — Maxilla — Palate — Coronoid process — Alveolar margins — Ramus — Mandible — Body — Angle — Symphysis

170.0   **Bones of skull and face, except mandible**

Bone:	Bone:
ethmoid	sphenoid
frontal	temporal
malar	zygomatic
nasal	Maxilla (superior)
occipital	Turbinate
orbital	Upper jaw bone
parietal	Vomer

`EXCLUDES`   *carcinoma, any type except intraosseous or odontogenic:*
maxilla, maxillary (sinus) (160.2)
upper jaw bone (143.0)
jaw bone (lower) (170.1)

170.1   **Mandible**
Inferior maxilla
Jaw bone NOS
Lower jaw bone
`EXCLUDES`   *carcinoma, any type except intraosseous or odontogenic:*
jaw bone NOS (143.9)
lower (143.1)
upper jaw bone (170.0)

170.2   **Vertebral column, excluding sacrum and coccyx**
Spinal column   Vertebra
Spine
`EXCLUDES`   *sacrum and coccyx (170.6)*

170.3   **Ribs, sternum, and clavicle**
Costal cartilage
Costovertebral joint
Xiphoid process

170.4   **Scapula and long bones of upper limb**
Acromion   Radius
Bones NOS of upper limb   Ulna
Humerus
AHA: 2Q, '99, 9

170.5   **Short bones of upper limb**
Carpal   Scaphoid (of hand)
Cuneiform, wrist   Semilunar or lunate
Metacarpal   Trapezium
Navicular, of hand   Trapezoid
Phalanges of hand   Unciform
Pisiform

170.6   **Pelvic bones, sacrum, and coccyx**
Coccygeal vertebra   Pubic bone
Ilium   Sacral vertebra
Ischium

170.7   **Long bones of lower limb**
Bones NOS of lower limb
Femur
Fibula
Tibia

✓4ʰ ✓5ʰ Additional Digit Required   Nonspecific PDx   Unacceptable PDx   Manifestation Code   `MCV` Major Cardiovascular Condition   ►◄ Revised Text   ● New Code   ▲ Revised Code Title

2007 ICD•9•CM   **Volume 1 — 33**

Neoplasms

170.8 Short bones of lower limb
  Astragalus [talus]   Navicular (of ankle)
  Calcaneus   Patella
  Cuboid   Phalanges of foot
  Cuneiform, ankle   Tarsal
  Metatarsal

170.9 Bone and articular cartilage, site unspecified

✓4th 171 Malignant neoplasm of connective and other soft tissue
  INCLUDES   blood vessel
              bursa
              fascia
              fat
              ligament, except uterine
              ►malignant stromal tumors◄
              muscle
              peripheral, sympathetic, and parasympathetic
                  nerves and ganglia
              synovia
              tendon (sheath)
  EXCLUDES   cartilage (of):
                  articular (170.0-170.9)
                  larynx (161.3)
                  nose (160.0)
              connective tissue:
                  breast (174.0-175.9)
                  internal organs ►(except stromal tumors)◄—
                      code to malignant neoplasm of the site
                      [e.g., leiomyosarcoma of stomach, 151.9]
              heart (164.1)
              uterine ligament (183.4)

171.0 Head, face, and neck
  Cartilage of: Cartilage of:
      ear   eyelid
  AHA: 2Q, '99, 6

171.2 Upper limb, including shoulder
  Arm   Forearm
  Finger   Hand

171.3 Lower limb, including hip
  Foot   Thigh
  Leg   Toe
  Popliteal space

171.4 Thorax
  Axilla   Great vessels
  Diaphragm
  EXCLUDES   heart (164.1)
              mediastinum (164.2-164.9)
              thymus (164.0)

171.5 Abdomen
  Abdominal wall   Hypochondrium
  EXCLUDES   peritoneum (158.8)
              retroperitoneum (158.0)

171.6 Pelvis
  Buttock   Inguinal region
  Groin   Perineum
  EXCLUDES   pelvic peritoneum (158.8)
              retroperitoneum (158.0)
              uterine ligament, any (183.3-183.5)

171.7 Trunk, unspecified
  Back NOS   Flank NOS

171.8 Other specified sites of connective and other soft tissue
  Malignant neoplasm of contiguous or overlapping
      sites of connective tissue whose point of origin
      cannot be determined

171.9 Connective and other soft tissue, site unspecified

✓4th 172 Malignant melanoma of skin
  INCLUDES   melanocarcinoma
              melanoma (skin) NOS
  EXCLUDES   skin of genital organs (184.0-184.9, 187.1-187.9)
              sites other than skin—code to malignant
                  neoplasm of the site
  DEF: Malignant neoplasm of melanocytes; most common in skin, may involve
  oral cavity, esophagus, anal canal, vagina, leptomeninges, or conjunctiva.

172.0 Lip
  EXCLUDES   vermilion border of lip (140.0-140.1, 140.9)

172.1 Eyelid, including canthus

172.2 Ear and external auditory canal
  Auricle (ear)
  Auricular canal, external
  External [acoustic] meatus
  Pinna

172.3 Other and unspecified parts of face
  Cheek (external)   Forehead
  Chin   Nose, external
  Eyebrow   Temple

172.4 Scalp and neck

172.5 Trunk, except scrotum
  Axilla   Perianal skin
  Breast   Perineum
  Buttock   Umbilicus
  Groin
  EXCLUDES   anal canal (154.2)
              anus NOS (154.3)
              scrotum (187.7)

172.6 Upper limb, including shoulder
  Arm   Forearm
  Finger   Hand

172.7 Lower limb, including hip
  Ankle   Leg
  Foot   Popliteal area
  Heel   Thigh
  Knee   Toe

172.8 Other specified sites of skin
  Malignant melanoma of contiguous or overlapping
      sites of skin whose point of origin cannot be
      determined

172.9 Melanoma of skin, site unspecified

✓4th 173 Other malignant neoplasm of skin
  INCLUDES   malignant neoplasm of:
                  sebaceous glands
                  sudoriferous, sudoriparous glands
                  sweat glands
  EXCLUDES   Kaposi's sarcoma (176.0-176.9)
              malignant melanoma of skin (172.0-172.9)
              skin of genital organs (184.0-184.9, 187.1-187.9)
  AHA: 1Q, '00, 18; 2Q, '96, 12

173.0 Skin of lip
  EXCLUDES   vermilion border of lip (140.0-140.1, 140.9)

173.1 Eyelid, including canthus
  EXCLUDES   cartilage of eyelid (171.0)

173.2 Skin of ear and external auditory canal
  Auricle (ear)   External meatus
  Auricular canal, external   Pinna
  EXCLUDES   cartilage of ear (171.0)

173.3 Skin of other and unspecified parts of face
  Cheek, external   Forehead
  Chin   Nose, external
  Eyebrow   Temple
  AHA: 1Q, '00, 3

173.4 Scalp and skin of neck

173.5 Skin of trunk, except scrotum
  Axillary fold   Skin of:
  Perianal skin   buttock
  Skin of: chest wall
      abdominal wall   groin
      anus   perineum
      back   Umbilicus
      breast
  EXCLUDES   anal canal (154.2)
              anus NOS (154.3)
              skin of scrotum (187.7)
  AHA: 1Q, '01, 8

N Newborn Age: 0 P Pediatric Age: 0-17 M Maternity Age: 12-55 A Adult Age: 15-124 CC CC Condition MC Major Complication CD Complex Dx HIV HIV Related Dx

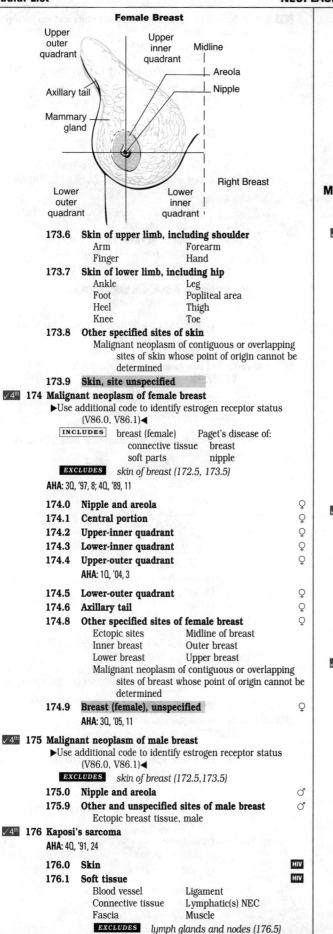

Female Breast

Upper outer quadrant

Upper inner quadrant

Midline

Areola

Nipple

Axillary tail

Mammary gland

Lower outer quadrant

Lower inner quadrant

Right Breast

173.6 Skin of upper limb, including shoulder
Arm   Forearm
Finger   Hand

173.7 Skin of lower limb, including hip
Ankle   Leg
Foot   Popliteal area
Heel   Thigh
Knee   Toe

173.8 Other specified sites of skin
Malignant neoplasm of contiguous or overlapping sites of skin whose point of origin cannot be determined

173.9 Skin, site unspecified

√4ᵗʰ 174 Malignant neoplasm of female breast
▶Use additional code to identify estrogen receptor status (V86.0, V86.1)◀

INCLUDES   breast (female)   Paget's disease of:
      connective tissue   breast
      soft parts   nipple

EXCLUDES   *skin of breast (172.5, 173.5)*

AHA: 3Q, '97, 8; 4Q, '89, 11

174.0 Nipple and areola ♀
174.1 Central portion ♀
174.2 Upper-inner quadrant ♀
174.3 Lower-inner quadrant ♀
174.4 Upper-outer quadrant ♀
AHA: 1Q, '04, 3

174.5 Lower-outer quadrant ♀
174.6 Axillary tail ♀
174.8 Other specified sites of female breast ♀
Ectopic sites   Midline of breast
Inner breast   Outer breast
Lower breast   Upper breast
Malignant neoplasm of contiguous or overlapping sites of breast whose point of origin cannot be determined

174.9 Breast (female), unspecified ♀
AHA: 3Q, '05, 11

√4ᵗʰ 175 Malignant neoplasm of male breast
▶Use additional code to identify estrogen receptor status (V86.0, V86.1)◀

EXCLUDES   *skin of breast (172.5, 173.5)*

175.0 Nipple and areola ♂
175.9 Other and unspecified sites of male breast ♂
Ectopic breast tissue, male

√4ᵗʰ 176 Kaposi's sarcoma
AHA: 4Q, '91, 24

176.0 Skin HIV
176.1 Soft tissue HIV
Blood vessel   Ligament
Connective tissue   Lymphatic(s) NEC
Fascia   Muscle
EXCLUDES   *lymph glands and nodes (176.5)*

176.2 Palate HIV
176.3 Gastrointestinal sites HIV
176.4 Lung CC HIV
CC Excl: 162.8-162.9, 165.8-165.9, 176.4, 195.8, 199.0-199.1, 239.1, 239.8-239.9

176.5 Lymph nodes CC HIV
CC Excl: 176.5, 195.8, 196.0-196.9, 199.0-199.1, 239.8-239.9

176.8 Other specified sites HIV
Oral cavity NEC

176.9 Unspecified HIV
Viscera NOS

MALIGNANT NEOPLASM OF GENITOURINARY ORGANS (179-189)

EXCLUDES   *carcinoma in situ (233.1-233.9)*

179 Malignant neoplasm of uterus, part unspecified ♀

√4ᵗʰ 180 Malignant neoplasm of cervix uteri
INCLUDES   invasive malignancy [carcinoma]
EXCLUDES   *carcinoma in situ (233.1)*

180.0 Endocervix ♀
Cervical canal NOS   Endocervical gland
Endocervical canal

180.1 Exocervix ♀
180.8 Other specified sites of cervix ♀
Cervical stump
Squamocolumnar junction of cervix
Malignant neoplasm of contiguous or overlapping sites of cervix uteri whose point of origin cannot be determined

180.9 Cervix uteri, unspecified ♀

181 Malignant neoplasm of placenta ♀
Choriocarcinoma NOS
Chorioepithelioma NOS
EXCLUDES   *chorioadenoma (destruens) (236.1)*
      hydatidiform mole (630)
        malignant (236.1)
      invasive mole (236.1)
      male choriocarcinoma NOS (186.0-186.9)

√4ᵗʰ 182 Malignant neoplasm of body of uterus
EXCLUDES   *carcinoma in situ (233.2)*

182.0 Corpus uteri, except isthmus ♀
Cornu   Fundus
Endometrium   Myometrium

182.1 Isthmus ♀
Lower uterine segment

182.8 Other specified sites of body of uterus ♀
Malignant neoplasm of contiguous or overlapping sites of body of uterus whose point of origin cannot be determined
EXCLUDES   *uterus NOS (179)*

√4ᵗʰ 183 Malignant neoplasm of ovary and other uterine adnexa
EXCLUDES   *Douglas' cul-de-sac (158.8)*

183.0 Ovary ♀
Use additional code to identify any functional activity

183.2 Fallopian tube ♀
Oviduct   Uterine tube

183.3 Broad ligament ♀
Mesovarium   Parovarian region

183.4 Parametrium ♀
Uterine ligament NOS   Uterosacral ligament

183.5 Round ligament ♀
AHA: 3Q, '99, 5

183.8 Other specified sites of uterine adnexa ♀
Tubo-ovarian
Utero-ovarian
Malignant neoplasm of contiguous or overlapping sites of ovary and other uterine adnexa whose point of origin cannot be determined

183.9 Uterine adnexa, unspecified ♀

√4ᵗʰ √5ᵗʰ Additional Digit Required   Nonspecific PDx   Unacceptable PDx   Manifestation Code   MCV Major Cardiovascular Condition   ▶◀ Revised Text   ● New Code   ▲ Revised Code Title

2007 ICD•9•CM   October 2006 • Volume 1 — 35

Neoplasms

184–191.2

✓4ᵗʰ **184 Malignant neoplasm of other and unspecified female genital organs**

> EXCLUDES   *carcinoma in situ (233.3)*

184.0 Vagina ♀
> Gartner's duct   Vaginal vault

184.1 Labia majora ♀
> Greater vestibular [Bartholin's] gland

184.2 Labia minora ♀

184.3 Clitoris ♀

184.4 Vulva, unspecified ♀
> External female genitalia NOS
> Pudendum

184.8 Other specified sites of female genital organs ♀
> Malignant neoplasm of contiguous or overlapping sites of female genital organs whose point of origin cannot be determined

184.9 Female genital organ, site unspecified ♀
> Female genitourinary tract NOS

185 Malignant neoplasm of prostate ♂
> EXCLUDES   *seminal vesicles (187.8)*

> AHA: 3Q, '03, 13; 3Q, '99, 5; 3Q, '92, 7

✓4ᵗʰ **186 Malignant neoplasm of testis**
> Use additional code to identify any functional activity

186.0 Undescended testis ♂
> Ectopic testis   Retained testis

186.9 Other and unspecified testis ♂
> Testis: Testis:
>   NOS   scrotal
>   descended

✓4ᵗʰ **187 Malignant neoplasm of penis and other male genital organs**

187.1 Prepuce ♂
> Foreskin

187.2 Glans penis ♂

187.3 Body of penis ♂
> Corpus cavernosum

187.4 Penis, part unspecified ♂
> Skin of penis NOS

187.5 Epididymis ♂

187.6 Spermatic cord ♂
> Vas deferens

187.7 Scrotum ♂
> Skin of scrotum

187.8 Other specified sites of male genital organs ♂
> Seminal vesicle
> Tunica vaginalis
> Malignant neoplasm of contiguous or overlapping sites of penis and other male genital organs whose point of origin cannot be determined

187.9 Male genital organ, site unspecified ♂
> Male genital organ or tract NOS

✓4ᵗʰ **188 Malignant neoplasm of bladder**
> EXCLUDES   *carcinoma in situ (233.7)*

188.0 Trigone of urinary bladder

188.1 Dome of urinary bladder

188.2 Lateral wall of urinary bladder

188.3 Anterior wall of urinary bladder

188.4 Posterior wall of urinary bladder

188.5 Bladder neck
> Internal urethral orifice

188.6 Ureteric orifice

188.7 Urachus

188.8 Other specified sites of bladder
> Malignant neoplasm of contiguous or overlapping sites of bladder whose point of origin cannot be determined

188.9 Bladder, part unspecified
> Bladder wall NOS
> AHA: 1Q, '00, 5

✓4ᵗʰ **189 Malignant neoplasm of kidney and other and unspecified urinary organs**

189.0 Kidney, except pelvis CC
> Kidney NOS   Kidney parenchyma
> CC Excl: 189.0-189.1, 189.8-189.9, 195.8, 199.0-199.1, 239.5, 239.8-239.9

> AHA: ▶2Q, '05, 4;◀ 2Q, '04, 4

189.1 Renal pelvis CC
> Renal calyces   Ureteropelvic junction
> CC Excl: See code 189.0

189.2 Ureter CC
> EXCLUDES   *ureteric orifice of bladder (188.6)*
> CC Excl: 189.2, 189.8-189.9, 195.8, 199.0-199.1, 239.5, 239.8-239.9

189.3 Urethra
> EXCLUDES   *urethral orifice of bladder (188.5)*

189.4 Paraurethral glands

189.8 Other specified sites of urinary organs
> Malignant neoplasm of contiguous or overlapping sites of kidney and other urinary organs whose point of origin cannot be determined

189.9 Urinary organ, site unspecified
> Urinary system NOS

MALIGNANT NEOPLASM OF OTHER AND UNSPECIFIED SITES (190-199)

> EXCLUDES   *carcinoma in situ (234.0-234.9)*

✓4ᵗʰ **190 Malignant neoplasm of eye**
> EXCLUDES   *carcinoma in situ (234.0)*
>   *eyelid (skin) (172.1, 173.1)*
>   *cartilage (171.0)*
>   *optic nerve (192.0)*
>   *orbital bone (170.0)*

190.0 Eyeball, except conjunctiva, cornea, retina, and choroid
> Ciliary body   Sclera
> Crystalline lens   Uveal tract
> Iris

190.1 Orbit
> Connective tissue of orbit
> Extraocular muscle
> Retrobulbar
> EXCLUDES   *bone of orbit (170.0)*

190.2 Lacrimal gland

190.3 Conjunctiva

190.4 Cornea

190.5 Retina

190.6 Choroid

190.7 Lacrimal duct
> Lacrimal sac   Nasolacrimal duct

190.8 Other specified sites of eye
> Malignant neoplasm of contiguous or overlapping sites of eye whose point of origin cannot be determined

190.9 Eye, part unspecified

✓4ᵗʰ **191 Malignant neoplasm of brain**
> EXCLUDES   *cranial nerves (192.0)*
>   *retrobulbar area (190.1)*

191.0 Cerebrum, except lobes and ventricles CC
> Basal ganglia   Globus pallidus
> Cerebral cortex   Hypothalamus
> Corpus striatum   Thalamus
> CC Excl: 191.0-191.9, 192.0-192.1, 192.8-192.9, 195.8, 199.0-199.1, 239.6-239.9

191.1 Frontal lobe CC
> CC Excl: See code 191.0

> AHA: ▶4Q, '05, 118◀

191.2 Temporal lobe CC
> Hippocampus   Uncus
> CC Excl: See code 191.0

N Newborn Age: 0   P Pediatric Age: 0-17   M Maternity Age: 12-55   A Adult Age: 15-124   CC CC Condition   MC Major Complication   CD Complex Dx   HIV HIV Related Dx

Neoplasms

Brain and Meninges

Fourth ventricle — Cerebrum
Corpus callosum
Thalamus
Hypothalamus
Hypophysis
Cerebellum — Pons
Medulla oblongata
Midsagittal Section (between hemispheres)

191.3   **Parietal lobe**   `CC`
      CC Excl: See code 191.0

191.4   **Occipital lobe**   `CC`
      CC Excl: See code 191.0

191.5   **Ventricles**   `CC`
      Choroid plexus   Floor of ventricle
      CC Excl: See code 191.0

191.6   **Cerebellum NOS**   `CC`
      Cerebellopontine angle
      CC Excl: See code 191.0

191.7   **Brain stem**   `CC`
      Cerebral peduncle   Midbrain
      Medulla oblongata   Pons
      CC Excl: See code 191.0

191.8   **Other parts of brain**   `CC`
      Corpus callosum
      Tapetum
      Malignant neoplasm of contiguous or overlapping sites of brain whose point of origin cannot be determined
      CC Excl: See code 191.0

191.9   **Brain, unspecified**   `CC`
      Cranial fossa NOS
      CC Excl: See code 191.0

√4ᵗʰ 192   **Malignant neoplasm of other and unspecified parts of nervous system**
      EXCLUDES   *peripheral, sympathetic, and parasympathetic nerves and ganglia (171.0-171.9)*

192.0   **Cranial nerves**   `CC`
      Olfactory bulb
      CC Excl: 192.0, 192.8-192.9, 195.8, 199.0-199.1, 239.6-239.9

192.1   **Cerebral meninges**   `CC`
      Dura (mater)   Meninges NOS
      Falx (cerebelli) (cerebri)   Tentorium
      CC Excl: 192.1, 192.8-192.9, 195.8, 199.0-199.1, 239.6-239.9

192.2   **Spinal cord**   `CC`
      Cauda equina
      CC Excl: 192.2, 192.8-192.9, 195.8, 199.0-199.1, 239.6-239.9

192.3   **Spinal meninges**   `CC`
      CC Excl: 192.3-192.9, 195.8, 199.0-199.1, 239.6-239.9

192.8   **Other specified sites of nervous system**   `CC`
      Malignant neoplasm of contiguous or overlapping sites of other parts of nervous system whose point of origin cannot be determined
      CC Excl: 191.0-191.9, 192.0-192.9, 195.8, 199.0-199.1, 239.6-239.9

192.9   **Nervous system, part unspecified**
      Nervous system (central) NOS
      EXCLUDES   *meninges NOS (192.1)*

193   **Malignant neoplasm of thyroid gland**
      Sipple's syndrome
      Thyroglossal duct
      Use additional code to identify any functional activity

√4ᵗʰ 194   **Malignant neoplasm of other endocrine glands and related structures**
      Use additional code to identify any functional activity
      EXCLUDES   *islets of Langerhans (157.4)*
                 ovary (183.0)
                 testis (186.0-186.9)
                 thymus (164.0)

194.0   **Adrenal gland**
      Adrenal cortex   Suprarenal gland
      Adrenal medulla

194.1   **Parathyroid gland**

194.3   **Pituitary gland and craniopharyngeal duct**
      Craniobuccal pouch   Rathke's pouch
      Hypophysis   Sella turcica
      AHA: J-A, '85, 9

194.4   **Pineal gland**

194.5   **Carotid body**

194.6   **Aortic body and other paraganglia**
      Coccygeal body   Para-aortic body
      Glomus jugulare

194.8   **Other**
      Pluriglandular involvement NOS
      Note: If the sites of multiple involvements are known, they should be coded separately.

194.9   **Endocrine gland, site unspecified**

√4ᵗʰ 195   **Malignant neoplasm of other and ill-defined sites**
      INCLUDES   malignant neoplasms of contiguous sites, not elsewhere classified, whose point of origin cannot be determined
      EXCLUDES   *malignant neoplasm:*
                 lymphatic and hematopoietic tissue (200.0-208.9)
                 secondary sites (196.0-198.8)
                 unspecified site (199.0-199.1)

195.0   **Head, face, and neck**
      Cheek NOS   Nose NOS
      Jaw NOS   Supraclavicular region NOS
      AHA: 4Q, '03, 107

195.1   **Thorax**
      Axilla   Intrathoracic NOS
      Chest (wall) NOS

195.2   **Abdomen**
      Intra-abdominal NOS
      AHA: 2Q, '97, 3

195.3   **Pelvis**
      Groin
      Inguinal region NOS
      Presacral region
      Sacrococcygeal region
      Sites overlapping systems within pelvis, as:
          rectovaginal (septum)
          rectovesical (septum)

195.4   **Upper limb**

195.5   **Lower limb**

195.8   **Other specified sites**
      Back NOS   Trunk NOS
      Flank NOS

√4ᵗʰ 196   **Secondary and unspecified malignant neoplasm of lymph nodes**
      EXCLUDES   *any malignant neoplasm of lymph nodes, specified as primary (200.0-202.9)*
                 Hodgkin's disease (201.0-201.9)
                 lymphosarcoma (200.1)
                 other forms of lymphoma (202.0-202.9)
                 reticulosarcoma (200.0)
      AHA: 2Q, '92, 3; M-J, '85, 3

√4ᵗʰ Additional Digit Required   **Nonspecific PDx**   Unacceptable PDx   **Manifestation Code**   **MCV** Major Cardiovascular Condition   ◄► Revised Text   ● New Code   ▲ Revised Code Title

2007 ICD•9•CM   **Volume 1 — 37**

Neoplasms

196.0–199.0

Lymph Nodes

Head, neck, and face

Left subclavian vein

Intrathoracic

Intraabdominal

Cisterna chyli

Nodes generally accompany large blood vessels

Inguinal and lower limb

Thoracic duct empties into the left subclavian vein

Axillary and upper limb

Thoracic duct (transmits lymph through diaphragm using one-way valves)

Intrapelvic

196.0 Lymph nodes of head, face, and neck `CC`
Cervical   Scalene
Cervicofacial   Supraclavicular
CC Excl: 176.5, 195.8, 196.0-196.9, 199.0-199.1, 239.8-239.9

196.1 Intrathoracic lymph nodes `CC`
Bronchopulmonary   Mediastinal
Intercostal   Tracheobronchial
CC Excl: See code 196.0

196.2 Intra-abdominal lymph nodes `CC`
Intestinal   Retroperitoneal
Mesenteric
CC Excl: See code 196.0
AHA: 4Q, '03, 111

196.3 Lymph nodes of axilla and upper limb `CC`
Brachial   Infraclavicular
Epitrochlear   Pectoral
CC Excl: See code 196.0

196.5 Lymph nodes of inguinal region and lower limb `CC`
Femoral   Popliteal
Groin   Tibial
CC Excl: See code 196.0

196.6 Intrapelvic lymph nodes `CC`
Hypogastric   Obturator
Iliac   Parametrial
CC Excl: See code 196.0

196.8 Lymph nodes of multiple sites `CC`
CC Excl: See code 196.0

196.9 Site unspecified `CC`
Lymph nodes NOS
CC Excl: See code 196.0

√4th **197 Secondary malignant neoplasm of respiratory and digestive systems**
EXCLUDES lymph node metastasis (196.0-196.9)
AHA: M-J, '85, 3

197.0 Lung `CC`
Bronchus
CC Excl: 195.8, 197.0, 197.3, 198.89-199.1, 239.8-239.9
AHA: ▶1Q, '06, 4;◄ 2Q, '99, 9

197.1 Mediastinum `CC`
CC Excl: 195.8, 197.1, 197.3, 198.89-199.1, 239.8-239.9

197.2 Pleura `CC`
CC Excl: 195.8, 197.2-197.3, 198.89-199.1, 239.8-239.9
AHA: 4Q, '03, 110; 4Q, '89, 11

197.3 Other respiratory organs `CC`
Trachea
CC Excl: 195.8, 197.0-197.3, 198.89-199.1, 239.8-239.9

197.4 Small intestine, including duodenum `CC`
CC Excl: 195.8, 197.4, 197.8, 198.89-199.1, 239.8-239.9

197.5 Large intestine and rectum `CC`
CC Excl: 195.8, 197.5, 197.8, 198.89-199.1, 239.8-239.9

197.6 Retroperitoneum and peritoneum `CC`
CC Excl: 195.8, 197.6, 197.8, 198.89-199.1, 239.8-239.9
AHA: 2Q, '04, 4; 4Q, '89, 11

197.7 Liver, specified as secondary `CC`
CC Excl: 195.8, 197.7-197.8, 198.89-199.1, 239.8-239.9
AHA: ▶1Q, '06, 4;◄ 2Q, '05, 9

197.8 Other digestive organs and spleen `CC`
CC Excl: 195.8, 197.4-197.8, 198.89-199.1, 239.8-239.9
AHA: 2Q, '97, 3; 2Q, '92, 3

√4th **198 Secondary malignant neoplasm of other specified sites**
EXCLUDES lymph node metastasis (196.0-196.9)
AHA: M-J, '85, 3

198.0 Kidney `CC`
CC Excl: 195.8, 198.0-198.1, 198.89-199.1, 239.8-239.9

198.1 Other urinary organs `CC`
CC Excl: See code 198.0

198.2 Skin `CC`
Skin of breast
CC Excl: 195.8, 198.2, 198.89-199.1, 239.8-239.9

198.3 Brain and spinal cord `CC`
CC Excl: 195.8, 198.3, 198.89-199.1, 239.8-239.9
AHA: 3Q, '99, 7

198.4 Other parts of nervous system `CC`
Meninges (cerebral) (spinal)
CC Excl: 195.8, 198.4, 198.89-199.1, 239.8-239.9
AHA: J-F, '87, 7

198.5 Bone and bone marrow `CC`
CC Excl: 195.8, 198.5, 198.89-199.1, 239.8-239.9
AHA: 4Q, '03, 110; 3Q, '99, 5; 2Q, '92, 3; 1Q, '91, 16; 4Q, '89, 10
DRG 239

198.6 Ovary `CC` ♀
CC Excl: 195.8, 198.6, 198.89-199.1, 239.8-239.9

198.7 Adrenal gland `CC`
Suprarenal gland
CC Excl: 195.8, 198.7, 198.89-199.1, 239.8-239.9

√5th **198.8 Other specified sites**
198.81 Breast `CC`
EXCLUDES skin of breast (198.2)
CC Excl: 195.8, 198.81, 198.89-199.1, 239.8-239.9

198.82 Genital organs `CC`
CC Excl: 195.8, 198.82, 198.89-199.1, 239.8-239.9

198.89 Other `CC`
EXCLUDES retroperitoneal lymph nodes (196.2)
CC Excl: 195.8, 198.89-199.1, 239.8-239.9
AHA: 2Q, '05, 4; 2Q, '97, 4

√4th **199 Malignant neoplasm without specification of site**
199.0 Disseminated `CC`
Carcinomatosis
Generalized:
   cancer   unspecified site
   malignancy   (primary)
Multiple cancer   (secondary)
CC Excl: See code 198.89
AHA: 4Q, '89, 10

Newborn Age: 0   Pediatric Age: 0-17   Maternity Age: 12-55   Adult Age: 15-124   CC CC Condition   MC Major Complication   CD Complex Dx   HIV HIV Related Dx

38 — Volume 1 • October 2006   2007 ICD•9•CM

199.1 Other

Cancer
Carcinoma } unspecified site (primary)
Malignancy } (secondary)

AHA: ▶1Q, '06, 4◀

MALIGNANT NEOPLASM OF LYMPHATIC AND HEMATOPOIETIC TISSUE (200-208)

EXCLUDES secondary neoplasm of:
bone marrow (198.5)
spleen (197.8)
secondary and unspecified neoplasm of lymph
nodes (196.0-196.9)

The following fifth-digit subclassification is for use with
categories 200-202:

0 unspecified site, extranodal and solid organ sites
1 lymph nodes of head, face, and neck
2 intrathoracic lymph nodes
3 intra-abdominal lymph nodes
4 lymph nodes of axilla and upper limb
5 lymph nodes of inguinal region and lower limb
6 intrapelvic lymph nodes
7 spleen
8 lymph nodes of multiple sites

√4ᵗʰ **200 Lymphosarcoma and reticulosarcoma**
AHA: 2Q, '92, 3; N-D, '86, 5

√5ᵗʰ **200.0 Reticulosarcoma**   CC HIV
Lymphoma (malignant):
histiocytic (diffuse):
nodular
pleomorphic cell type
reticulum cell type
Reticulum cell sarcoma:
NOS
pleomorphic cell type

CC Excl: For code 200.00: 200.00-200.08, 239.8-239.9; For code 200.01:
200.00, 200.01, 200.08, 239.8-239.9; For code 200.02: 200.00, 200.02,
200.08, 239.8-239.9; For code 200.03: 200.00, 200.03, 200.08,
239.8-239.9; For code 200.04: 200.00, 200.04, 200.08, 239.8-239.9;
For code 200.05: 200.00, 200.05, 200.08, 239.8-239.9; For code 200.06:
200.00, 200.06, 200.08, 239.8-239.9; For code 200.07: 200.00, 200.07-
200.08, 239.8-239.9; For code 200.08: 200.00-200.08, 239.8-239.9

AHA: For Code 200.03: 3Q, '01, 12

DEF: Malignant lymphoma of primarily histolytic cells; commonly
originates in reticuloendothelium of lymph nodes.

√5ᵗʰ **200.1 Lymphosarcoma**   CC
Lymphoblastoma (diffuse)   Lymphosarcoma:
Lymphoma (malignant):   NOS
lymphoblastic (diffuse)   diffuse NOS
lymphocytic (cell type)   lymphoblastic
                  (diffuse)
(diffuse)   lymphocytic (diffuse)
lymphosarcoma type   prolymphocytic

EXCLUDES lymphosarcoma:
follicular or nodular (202.0)
mixed cell type (200.8)
lymphosarcoma cell leukemia (207.8)

CC Excl: For code 200.10: 200.10-200.18, 239.8-239.9; For code 200.11:
200.10, 200.11, 200.18, 239.8-239.9; For code 200.12: 200.10, 200.12,
200.18, 239.8-239.9; For code 200.13: 200.10, 200.13, 200.18, 239.8-
239.9; For code 200.14: 200.10, 200.14, 200.18, 239.8-239.9; For code
200.15: 200.10, 200.15, 200.18, 239.8-239.9; For code 200.16: 200.10,
200.16, 200.18, 239.8-239.9; For code 200.17: 200.10, 200.17-200.18,
239.8-239.9; For code 200.18: 200.10-200.18, 239.8-239.9

DEF: Malignant lymphoma created from anaplastic lymphoid cells
resembling lymphocytes or lymphoblasts.

√5ᵗʰ **200.2 Burkitt's tumor or lymphoma**   CC HIV
Malignant lymphoma, Burkitt's type

CC Excl: For code 200.20: 200.20-200.28, 239.8-239.9; For code 200.21:
200.20, 200.21, 200.28, 239.8-239.9; For code 200.22: 200.20, 200.22,
200.28, 239.8-239.9; For code 200.23: 200.20, 200.23, 200.28, 239.8-
239.9; For code 200.24: 200.20, 200.24, 200.28, 239.8-239.9; For code
200.25: 200.20, 200.25, 200.28, 239.8-239.9; For code 200.26: 200.20,
200.26, 200.28, 239.8-239.9; For code 200.27: 200.20, 200.27-200.28,
239.8-239.9; For code 200.28: 200.20-200.28, 239.8-239.9

DEF: Large osteolytic lesion most common in jaw or as abdominal
mass; usually found in central Africa but reported elsewhere.

√5ᵗʰ **200.8 Other named variants**   CC HIV
Lymphoma (malignant):
lymphoplasmacytoid type
mixed lymphocytic-histiocytic (diffuse)
Lymphosarcoma, mixed cell type (diffuse)
Reticulolymphosarcoma (diffuse)

CC Excl: For code 200.80: 200.80-200.88, 239.8-239.9; For code 200.81:
200.80, 200.81, 200.88, 239.8-239.9; For code 200.82: 200.80, 200.82,
200.88, 239.8-239.9; For code 200.83: 200.80, 200.83, 200.88, 239.8-
239.9; For code 200.84: 200.80, 200.84, 200.88, 239.8-239.9; For code
200.85: 200.80, 200.85, 200.88, 239.8-239.9; For code 200.86: 200.80,
200.86, 200.88, 239.8-239.9; For code 200.87: 200.80, 200.87-200.88,
239.8-239.9; For code 200.88: 200.80-200.88, 239.8-239.9

√4ᵗʰ **201 Hodgkin's disease**
AHA: 2Q, '92, 3; N-D, '86, 5

DEF: Painless, progressive enlargement of lymph nodes, spleen and general
lymph tissue; symptoms include anorexia, lassitude, weight loss, fever,
pruritis, night sweats, anemia.

√5ᵗʰ **201.0 Hodgkin's paragranuloma**   CC
CC Excl: For code 201.00: 201.00-201.08, 201.90, 239.8-239.9;
For code 201.01: 201.00, 201.01, 201.08, 201.90-201.91, 239.8-239.9;
For code 201.02: 201.00, 201.02, 201.08, 201.90, 201.92, 239.8-239.9;
For code 201.03: 201.00, 201.03, 201.08, 201.90, 201.93, 239.8-239.9;
For code 201.04: 201.00, 201.04, 201.08, 201.90, 201.94, 239.8-239.9;
For code 201.05: 201.00, 201.05, 201.08, 201.90, 201.95, 239.8-239.9;
For code 201.06: 201.00, 201.06, 201.08, 201.90, 201.96, 239.8-239.9;
For code 201.07: 201.00, 201.07-201.08, 201.90, 201.97, 239.8-239.9;
For code 201.08: 201.00-201.08, 201.90, 201.98, 239.8-239.9

√5ᵗʰ **201.1 Hodgkin's granuloma**   CC
CC Excl: For code 201.10: 201.10-201.18, 201.90, 201.98, 239.8-239.9;
For code 201.11: 201.10, 201.11, 201.18, 201.90-201.91, 201.98, 239.8-
239.9; For code 201.12: 201.10, 201.12, 201.18, 201.90, 201.92, 201.98,
239.8-239.9; For code 201.13: 201.10, 201.13, 201.18, 201.90, 201.93,
201.98, 239.8-239.9; For code 201.14: 201.10, 201.14, 201.18, 201.90,
201.94, 201.98, 239.8-239.9; For code 201.15: 201.10, 201.15, 201.18,
201.90, 201.95, 201.98, 239.8-239.9; For code 201.16: 201.10, 201.16,
201.18, 201.90, 201.96, 201.98, 239.8-239.9; For code 201.17: 201.10,
201.17-201.18, 201.90, 201.97-201.98, 239.8-239.9; For code 201.18:
201.10-201.18, 201.90, 201.98, 239.8-239.9

AHA: 2Q, '99, 7

√5ᵗʰ **201.2 Hodgkin's sarcoma**   CC
CC Excl: For code 201.20: 201.20-201.28, 201.90, 201.98, 239.8-239.9;
For code 201.21: 201.20, 201.21, 201.28, 201.90-201.91, 201.98, 239.8-
239.9; For code 201.22: 201.20, 201.22, 201.28, 201.90, 201.92, 201.98,
239.8-239.9; For code 201.23: 201.20, 201.23, 201.28, 201.90, 201.93,
201.98, 239.8-239.9; For code 201.24: 201.20, 201.24, 201.28, 201.90,
201.94, 201.98, 239.8-239.9; For code 201.25: 201.20, 201.25, 201.28,
201.90, 201.95, 201.98, 239.8-239.9; For code 201.26: 201.20, 201.26,
201.28, 201.90, 201.96, 201.98, 239.8-239.9; For code 201.27: 201.20,
201.27-201.28, 201.90, 201.97-201.98, 239.8-239.9; For code 201.28:
201.20-201.28, 201.90, 201.98, 239.8-239.9

√4ᵗʰ √5ᵗʰ Additional Digit Required   Nonspecific PDx   Unacceptable PDx   Manifestation Code   MCV Major Cardiovascular Condition   ▶◀ Revised Text   ● New Code   ▲ Revised Code Title

2007 ICD•9•CM   October 2006 • Volume 1 — 39

Neoplasms

201.4–202.3

§ ✓5th **201.4 Lymphocytic-histiocytic predominance** `CC`
CC Excl: For code **201.40**: 201.40-201.48, 201.90, 201.98, 239.8-239.9; For code **201.41**: 201.40, 201.41, 201.48, 201.90-201.91, 201.98, 239.8-239.9; For code **201.42**: 201.40, 201.42, 201.48, 201.90, 201.92, 201.98, 239.8-239.9; For code **201.43**: 201.40, 201.43, 201.48, 201.90, 201.93, 201.98, 239.8-239.9; For code **201.44**: 201.40, 201.44, 201.48, 201.90, 201.94, 201.98, 239.8-239.9; For code **201.45**: 201.40, 201.45, 201.48, 201.90, 201.95, 201.98, 239.8-239.9; For code **201.46**: 201.40, 201.46, 201.48, 201.90, 201.96, 201.98, 239.8-239.9; For code **201.47**: 201.40, 201.47-201.48, 201.90, 201.97-201.98, 239.8-239.9; For code **201.48**: 201.40-201.48, 201.90, 201.98, 239.8-239.9

§ ✓5th **201.5 Nodular sclerosis** `CC`
Hodgkin's disease, nodular sclerosis:
   NOS
   cellular phase
CC Excl: For code **201.50**: 201.50-201.58, 201.90, 201.98, 239.8-239.9; For code **201.51**: 201.50, 201.51, 201.58, 201.90-201.91, 201.98, 239.8-239.9; For code **201.52**: 201.50, 201.52, 201.58, 201.90, 201.92, 201.98, 239.8-239.9; For code **201.53**: 201.50, 201.53, 201.58, 201.90, 201.93, 201.98, 239.8-239.9; For code **201.54**: 201.50, 201.54, 201.58, 201.90, 201.94, 201.98, 239.8-239.9; For code **201.55**: 201.50, 201.55, 201.58, 201.90, 201.95, 201.98, 239.8-239.9; For code **201.56**: 201.50, 201.56, 201.58, 201.90, 201.96, 201.98, 239.8-239.9; For code **201.57**: 201.50, 201.57-201.58, 201.90, 201.97-201.98, 239.8-239.9; For code **201.58**: 201.50-201.58, 201.90, 201.98, 239.8-239.9

§ ✓5th **201.6 Mixed cellularity** `CC`
CC Excl: For code **201.60**: 201.60-201.68, 201.90, 201.98, 239.8-239.9; For code **201.61**: 201.60, 201.61, 201.68, 201.90-201.91, 201.98, 239.8-239.9; For code **201.62**: 201.60, 201.62, 201.68, 201.90, 201.92, 201.98, 239.8-239.9; For code **201.63**: 201.60, 201.63, 201.68, 201.90, 201.93, 201.98, 239.8-239.9; For code **201.64**: 201.60, 201.64, 201.68, 201.90, 201.94, 201.98, 239.8-239.9; For code **201.65**: 201.60, 201.65, 201.68, 201.90, 201.95, 201.98, 239.8-239.9; For code **201.66**: 201.60, 201.66, 201.68, 201.90, 201.96, 201.98, 239.8-239.9; For code **201.67**: 201.60, 201.67-201.68, 201.90, 201.97-201.98, 239.8-239.9; For code **201.68**: 201.60-201.68, 201.90, 201.98, 239.8-239.9

§ ✓5th **201.7 Lymphocytic depletion** `CC`
Hodgkin's disease, lymphocytic depletion:
   NOS
   diffuse fibrosis
   reticular type
CC Excl: For code **201.70**: 201.70-201.78, 201.90, 201.98, 239.8-239.9; For code **201.71**: 201.70, 201.71, 201.78, 201.90, 201.91, 201.98, 239.8-239.9; For code **201.72**: 201.70, 201.72, 201.78, 201.90, 201.92, 201.98, 239.8-239.9; For code **201.73**: 201.70, 201.73, 201.78, 201.90, 201.93, 201.98, 239.8-239.9; For code **201.74**: 201.70, 201.74, 201.78, 201.90, 201.94, 201.98, 239.8-239.9; For code **201.75**: 201.70, 201.75, 201.78, 201.90, 201.95, 201.98, 239.8-239.9; For code **201.76**: 201.70, 201.76, 201.78, 201.90, 201.96, 201.98, 239.8-239.9; For code **201.77**: 201.70, 201.77-201.78, 201.90, 201.97-201.98, 239.8-239.9; For code **201.78**: 201.70-201.78, 201.98, 239.8-239.9

§ ✓5th **201.9 Hodgkin's disease, unspecified** `CC`
Hodgkin's:
   disease NOS
   lymphoma NOS
Malignant:
   lymphogranuloma
   lymphogranulomatosis
CC Excl: For code **201.90**: 201.90-201.98, 239.8-239.9; For code **201.91**: 201.90, 201.91, 201.98, 239.8-239.9; For code **201.92**: 201.90, 201.92, 201.98, 239.8-239.9; For code **201.93**: 201.90, 201.93, 201.98, 239.8-239.9; For code **201.94**: 201.90, 201.94, 201.98, 239.8-239.9; For code **201.95**: 201.90, 201.95, 201.98, 239.8-239.9; For code **201.96**: 201.90, 201.96, 201.98, 239.8-239.9; For code **201.97**: 201.90, 201.97-201.98, 239.8-239.9; For code **201.98**: 201.90-201.98, 239.8-239.9

✓4th **202 Other malignant neoplasms of lymphoid and histiocytic tissue**
AHA: 2Q, '92, 3; N-D, '86, 5

§ ✓5th **202.0 Nodular lymphoma** `CC`
Brill-Symmers disease   Lymphosarcoma:
Lymphoma: follicular (giant)
   follicular (giant)   nodular
   lymphocytic, nodular
CC Excl: For code **202.00**: 202.00-202.08, 202.80, 202.90, 239.8-239.9; For code **202.01**: 202.00, 202.01, 202.08, 202.81, 202.91, 239.8-239.9; For code **202.02**: 202.00, 202.02, 202.08, 202.82, 202.92, 239.8-239.9; For code **202.03**: 202.00, 202.03, 202.08, 202.83, 202.93, 239.8-239.9; For code **202.04**: 202.00, 202.04, 202.08, 202.84, 202.94, 239.8-239.9; For code **202.05**: 202.00, 202.05, 202.08, 202.85, 202.95, 239.8-239.9; For code **202.06**: 202.00, 202.06, 202.08, 202.86, 202.96, 239.8-239.9; For code **202.07**: 202.00, 202.07-202.08, 202.87, 202.97, 239.8-239.9; For code **202.08**: 202.00-202.08, 202.88, 202.98, 239.8-239.9

DEF: Lymphomatous cells clustered into nodules within the lymph node; usually occurs in older adults and may involve all nodes and possibly extranodal sites.

§ ✓5th **202.1 Mycosis fungoides** `CC`
CC Excl: For code **202.10**: 202.10-202.18, 202.80, 202.90, 239.8-239.9; For code **202.11**: 202.10, 202.11, 202.18, 202.81, 202.91, 239.8-239.9; For code **202.12**: 202.10, 202.12, 202.18, 202.82, 202.92, 239.8-239.9; For code **202.13**: 202.10, 202.13, 202.18, 202.83, 202.93, 239.8-239.9; For code **202.14**: 202.10, 202.14, 202.18, 202.84, 202.94, 239.8-239.9; For code **202.15**: 202.10, 202.15, 202.18, 202.85, 202.95, 239.8-239.9; For code **202.16**: 202.10, 202.16, 202.18, 202.86, 202.96, 239.8-239.9; For code **202.17**: 202.10, 202.17-202.18, 202.87, 202.97, 239.8-239.9; For code **202.18**: 202.10-202.18, 202.88, 202.98, 239.8-239.9

AHA: 2Q, '92, 4

DEF: Type of cutaneous T-cell lymphoma; may evolve into generalized lymphoma; formerly thought to be of fungoid origin.

§ ✓5th **202.2 Sézary's disease** `CC`
CC Excl: For code **202.20**: 202.20-202.28, 202.80, 202.90, 239.8-239.9; For code **202.21**: 202.20, 202.21, 202.28, 202.81, 202.91, 239.8-239.9; For code **202.22**: 202.20, 202.22, 202.28, 202.82, 202.92, 239.8-239.9; For code **202.23**: 202.20, 202.23, 202.28, 202.83, 202.93, 239.8-239.9; For code **202.24**: 202.20, 202.24, 202.28, 202.84, 202.94, 239.8-239.9; For code **202.25**: 202.20, 202.25, 202.28, 202.85, 202.95, 239.8-239.9; For code **202.26**: 202.20, 202.26, 202.28, 202.86, 202.96, 239.8-239.9; For code **202.27**: 202.20, 202.27-202.28, 202.87, 202.97, 239.8-239.9; For code **202.28**: 202.20-202.28, 202.88, 202.98, 239.8-239.9

AHA: 2Q, '99, 7

DEF: Type of cutaneous T-cell lymphoma with erythroderma, intense pruritus, peripheral lymphadenopathy, abnormal hyperchromatic mononuclear cells in skin, lymph nodes and peripheral blood.

§ ✓5th **202.3 Malignant histiocytosis** `CC`
Histiocytic medullary reticulosis
Malignant:
   reticuloendotheliosis
   reticulosis
CC Excl: For code **202.30**: 202.30-202.38, 202.80, 202.90, 239.8-239.9; For code **202.31**: 202.30, 202.31, 202.38, 202.81, 202.91, 239.8-239.9; For code **202.32**: 202.30, 202.32, 202.38, 202.82, 202.92, 239.8-239.9; For code **202.33**: 202.30, 202.33, 202.38, 202.83, 202.93, 239.8-239.9; For code **202.34**: 202.30, 202.34, 202.38, 202.84, 202.94, 239.8-239.9; For code **202.35**: 202.30, 202.35, 202.38, 202.85, 202.95, 239.8-239.9; For code **202.36**: 202.30, 202.36, 202.38, 202.86, 202.96, 239.8-239.9; For code **202.37**: 202.30, 202.37-202.38, 202.87, 202.97, 239.8-239.9; For code **202.38**: 202.30-202.38, 202.88, 202.98, 239.8-239.9

§ Requires fifth-digit. See beginning of section 200–208 for codes and definitions.

 Newborn Age: 0   P Pediatric Age: 0-17   M Maternity Age: 12-55   A Adult Age: 15-124   `CC` CC Condition   `MC` Major Complication   `CD` Complex Dx   `HIV` HIV Related Dx

§ ✓5th **202.4 Leukemic reticuloendotheliosis**   cc
Hairy-cell leukemia

CC Excl: For code 202.40: 202.40-202.48, 202.80, 202.90, 239.8-239.9;
For code 202.41: 202.40, 202.41, 202.48, 202.81, 202.91, 239.8-239.9;
For code 202.42: 202.40, 202.42, 202.48, 202.82, 202.92, 239.8-239.9;
For code 202.43: 202.40, 202.43, 202.48, 202.83, 202.93, 239.8-239.9;
For code 202.44: 202.40, 202.44, 202.48, 202.84, 202.94, 239.8-239.9;
For code 202.45: 202.40, 202.45, 202.48, 202.85, 202.95, 239.8-239.9;
For code 202.46: 202.40, 202.46, 202.48, 202.86, 202.96, 239.8-239.9;
For code 202.47: 202.40, 202.47-202.48, 202.87, 202.97, 239.8-239.9;
For code 202.48: 202.40-202.48, 202.88, 202.98, 239.8-239.9

DEF: Chronic leukemia with large, mononuclear cells with "hairy" appearance in marrow, spleen, liver, blood.

§ ✓5th **202.5 Letterer-Siwe disease**   cc
Acute:
   differentiated progressive histiocytosis
   histiocytosis X (progressive)
   infantile reticuloendotheliosis
   reticulosis of infancy
   EXCLUDES   *Hand-Schüller-Christian disease*
             (277.89)
             histiocytosis (acute) (chronic) (277.89)
             histiocytosis X (chronic) (277.89)

CC Excl: For code 202.50: 202.50-202.58, 202.80, 202.90, 239.8-239.9;
For code 202.51: 202.50, 202.51, 202.58, 202.81, 202.91, 239.8-239.9;
For code 202.52: 202.50, 202.52, 202.58, 202.82, 202.92, 239.8-239.9;
For code 202.53: 202.50, 202.53, 202.58, 202.83, 202.93, 239.8-239.9;
For code 202.54: 202.50, 202.54, 202.58, 202.84, 202.94, 239.8-239.9;
For code 202.55: 202.50, 202.55, 202.58, 202.85, 202.95, 239.8-239.9;
For code 202.56: 202.50, 202.56, 202.58, 202.86, 202.96, 239.8-239.9;
For code 202.57: 202.50, 202.57-202.58, 202.87, 202.97, 239.8-239.9;
For code 202.58: 202.50-202.58, 202.88, 202.98, 239.8-239.9

DEF: A recessive reticuloendotheliosis of early childhood, with a hemorrhagic tendency, eczema-like skin eruption, hepatosplenomegaly, including lymph node enlargement, and progressive anemia; it is often a fatal disease with no established cause.

§ ✓5th **202.6 Malignant mast cell tumors**   cc
Malignant: Mast cell sarcoma
   mastocytoma   Systemic tissue mast
   mastocytosis   cell disease
   EXCLUDES   *mast cell leukemia (207.8)*

CC Excl: For code 202.60: 202.60-202.68, 202.80, 202.90, 239.8-239.9;
For code 202.61: 202.60, 202.61, 202.68, 202.81, 202.91, 239.8-239.9;
For code 202.62: 202.60, 202.62, 202.68, 202.82, 202.92, 239.8-239.9;
For code 202.63: 202.60, 202.63, 202.68, 202.83, 202.93, 239.8-239.9;
For code 202.64: 202.60, 202.64, 202.68, 202.84, 202.94, 239.8-239.9;
For code 202.65: 202.60, 202.65, 202.68, 202.85, 202.95, 239.8-239.9;
For code 202.66: 202.60, 202.66, 202.68, 202.86, 202.96, 239.8-239.9;
For code 202.67: 202.60, 202.67-202.68, 202.87, 202.97, 239.8-239.9;
For code 202.68: 202.60-202.68, 202.88, 202.98, 239.8-239.9

§ ✓5th **202.8 Other lymphomas**   cc HIV
Lymphoma (malignant):
   NOS
   diffuse
   EXCLUDES   *benign lymphoma (229.0)*

CC Excl: For code 202.80: 202.80-202.88, 202.90, 239.8-239.9;
For code 202.81: 202.80, 202.81, 202.88, 202.91, 239.8-239.9; **For code 202.82:** 202.80, 202.82, 202.88, 202.92, 239.8-239.9; **For code 202.83:** 202.80, 202.83, 202.88, 202.93, 239.8-239.9; **For code 202.84:** 202.80, 202.84, 202.88, 202.94, 239.8-239.9; **For code 202.85:** 202.80, 202.85, 202.88, 202.95, 239.8-239.9; **For code 202.86:** 202.80, 202.86, 202.88, 202.96, 239.8-239.9; **For code 202.87:** 202.80, 202.87-202.88, 202.97, 239.8-239.9; **For code 202.88:** 202.80-202.88, 202.98, 239.8-239.9

AHA: 2Q, '92, 4

§ ✓5th **202.9 Other and unspecified malignant neoplasms of lymphoid and histiocytic tissue**   cc
Follicular dendritic cell sarcoma
Interdigitating dendritic cell sarcoma
Langerhans cell sarcoma
Malignant neoplasm of bone marrow NOS

CC Excl: For code 202.90: 202.90-202.98, 239.8-239.9; **For code 202.91:** 202.90, 202.91, 202.98, 239.8-239.9; **For code 202.92:** 202.90, 202.92, 202.98, 239.8-239.9; **For code 202.93:** 202.90, 202.93, 202.98, 239.8-239.9; **For code 202.94:** 202.90, 202.94, 202.98, 239.8-239.9; **For code 202.95:** 202.90, 202.95, 202.98, 239.8-239.9; **For code 202.96:** 202.90, 202.96, 202.98, 239.8-239.9; **For code 202.97:** 202.90, 202.97-202.98, 239.8-239.9; **For code 202.98:** 202.90-202.98, 239.8-239.9

✓4th **203 Multiple myeloma and immunoproliferative neoplasms**
AHA: 4Q, '91, 26

The following fifth-digit subclassification is for use with category 203:
   0 **without mention of remission**
   1 **in remission**

✓5th **203.0 Multiple myeloma**   cc
Kahler's disease   Myelomatosis
   EXCLUDES   *solitary myeloma (238.6)*

CC Excl: 203.00-208.91, 239.8-239.9

AHA: 1Q, '96, 16; 4Q, '89,10

✓5th **203.1 Plasma cell leukemia**   cc
Plasmacytic leukemia

CC Excl: See code 203.0

AHA: 4Q, '90, 26; S-O, '86, 12

✓5th **203.8 Other immunoproliferative neoplasms**   cc
CC Excl: See code 203.0

AHA: 4Q, '90, 26; S-O, '86, 12

✓4th **204 Lymphoid leukemia**
   INCLUDES   leukemia:
            lymphatic
            lymphoblastic
            lymphocytic
            lymphogenous
AHA: 3Q, '93, 4

The following fifth-digit subclassification is for use with category 204:
   0 **without mention of remission**
   1 **in remission**

✓5th **204.0 Acute**   cc
   EXCLUDES   *acute exacerbation of chronic lymphoid
             leukemia (204.1)*

CC Excl: See code 203.0

AHA: 3Q, '99, 6

✓5th **204.1 Chronic**   cc
CC Excl: See code 203.0

✓5th **204.2 Subacute**   cc
CC Excl: See code 203.0

✓5th **204.8 Other lymphoid leukemia**   cc
Aleukemic leukemia: Aleukemic leukemia:
   lymphatic   lymphoid
   lymphocytic
CC Excl: See code 203.0

✓5th **204.9 Unspecified lymphoid leukemia**   cc
CC Excl: See code 203.0

§ Requires fifth-digit. See beginning of section 200–208 for codes and definitions.

✓4th Additional Digit Required   Nonspecific PDx   Unacceptable PDx   Manifestation Code   MCV Major Cardiovascular Condition   ►◄ Revised Text   ● New Code   ▲ Revised Code Title

Neoplasms

√4ᵗʰ **205 Myeloid leukemia**

INCLUDES leukemia:
granulocytic myelomonocytic
myeloblastic myelosclerotic
myelocytic myelosis
myelogenous

AHA: 3Q, '93, 3; 4Q, '91, 26; 4Q, '90, 3; M-J, '85, 18

The following fifth-digit subclassification is for use with category 205:
0 without mention of remission
1 in remission

√5ᵗʰ **205.0 Acute** CC
Acute promyelocytic leukemia
EXCLUDES acute exacerbation of chronic myeloid leukemia (205.1)
CC Excl: See code 203.0

√5ᵗʰ **205.1 Chronic** CC
Eosinophilic leukemia Neutrophilic leukemia
CC Excl: See code 203.0
AHA: 1Q, '00, 6; J-A, '85, 13

√5ᵗʰ **205.2 Subacute** CC
CC Excl: See code 203.0

√5ᵗʰ **205.3 Myeloid sarcoma** CC
Chloroma Granulocytic sarcoma
CC Excl: See code 203.0

√5ᵗʰ **205.8 Other myeloid leukemia** CC
Aleukemic leukemia: Aleukemic leukemia:
granulocytic myeloid
myelogenous Aleukemic myelosis
CC Excl: See code 203.0

√5ᵗʰ **205.9 Unspecified myeloid leukemia** CC
CC Excl: See code 203.0

√4ᵗʰ **206 Monocytic leukemia**

INCLUDES leukemia:
histiocytic
monoblastic
monocytoid

The following fifth-digit subclassification is for use with category 206:
0 without mention of remission
1 in remission

√5ᵗʰ **206.0 Acute** CC
EXCLUDES acute exacerbation of chronic monocytic leukemia (206.1)
CC Excl: See code 203.0

√5ᵗʰ **206.1 Chronic** CC
CC Excl: See code 203.0

√5ᵗʰ **206.2 Subacute** CC
CC Excl: See code 203.0

√5ᵗʰ **206.8 Other monocytic leukemia** CC
Aleukemic:
monocytic leukemia
monocytoid leukemia
CC Excl: See code 203.0

√5ᵗʰ **206.9 Unspecified monocytic leukemia** CC
CC Excl: See code 203.0

√4ᵗʰ **207 Other specified leukemia**
EXCLUDES leukemic reticuloendotheliosis (202.4)
plasma cell leukemia (203.1)

The following fifth-digit subclassification is for use with category 207:
0 without mention of remission
1 in remission

√5ᵗʰ **207.0 Acute erythremia and erythroleukemia** CC
Acute erythremic myelosis
Di Guglielmo's disease
Erythremic myelosis
CC Excl: See code 203.0
DEF: Erythremia: polycythemia vera.
DEF: Erythroleukemia: a malignant blood dyscrasia (a myeloproliferative disorder).

√5ᵗʰ **207.1 Chronic erythremia** CC
Heilmeyer-Schöner disease
CC Excl: See code 203.0

√5ᵗʰ **207.2 Megakaryocytic leukemia** CC
Megakaryocytic myelosis Thrombocytic leukemia
CC Excl: See code 203.0

√5ᵗʰ **207.8 Other specified leukemia** CC
Lymphosarcoma cell leukemia
CC Excl: See code 203.0

√4ᵗʰ **208 Leukemia of unspecified cell type**

The following fifth-digit subclassification is for use with category 208:
0 without mention of remission
1 in remission

√5ᵗʰ **208.0 Acute** CC
Acute leukemia NOS Stem cell leukemia
Blast cell leukemia
EXCLUDES acute exacerbation of chronic unspecified leukemia (208.1)
CC Excl: See code 203.0

√5ᵗʰ **208.1 Chronic** CC
Chronic leukemia NOS
CC Excl: See code 203.0

√5ᵗʰ **208.2 Subacute** CC
Subacute leukemia NOS
CC Excl: See code 203.0

√5ᵗʰ **208.8 Other leukemia of unspecified cell type** CC
CC Excl: See code 203.0

√5ᵗʰ **208.9 Unspecified leukemia** CC
Leukemia NOS
CC Excl: See code 203.0

BENIGN NEOPLASMS (210-229)

√4ᵗʰ **210 Benign neoplasm of lip, oral cavity, and pharynx**
EXCLUDES cyst (of):
jaw (526.0-526.2,526.89)
oral soft tissue (528.4)
radicular (522.8)

210.0 Lip
Frenulum labii
Lip (inner aspect) (mucosa) (vermilion border)
EXCLUDES labial commissure (210.4)
skin of lip (216.0)

210.1 Tongue
Lingual tonsil

N Newborn Age: 0 P Pediatric Age: 0-17 M Maternity Age: 12-55 A Adult Age: 15-124 CC CC Condition MC Major Complication CD Complex Dx HIV HIV Related Dx

42 — Volume 1 2007 ICD•9•CM

210.2   **Major salivary glands**

Gland: Gland:
   parotid   submandibular
   sublingual

EXCLUDES   *benign neoplasms of minor salivary*
        glands:
        NOS (210.4)
        buccal mucosa (210.4)
        lips (210.0)
        palate (hard) (soft) (210.4)
        tongue (210.1)
        tonsil, palatine (210.5)

210.3   **Floor of mouth**

210.4   **Other and unspecified parts of mouth**

Gingiva   Oral mucosa
Gum (upper) (lower)   Palate (hard) (soft)
Labial commissure   Uvula
Oral cavity NOS

EXCLUDES   *benign odontogenic neoplasms of bone*
        (213.0-213.1)
        developmental odontogenic cysts (526.0)
        mucosa of lips (210.0)
        nasopharyngeal [posterior] [superior]
          surface of soft palate (210.7)

210.5   **Tonsil**

Tonsil (faucial) (palatine)

EXCLUDES   *lingual tonsil (210.1)*
        pharyngeal tonsil (210.7)
        tonsillar:
        fossa (210.6)
        pillars (210.6)

210.6   **Other parts of oropharynx**

Branchial cleft or vestiges   Tonsillar:
Epiglottis, anterior aspect   fossa
Fauces NOS   pillars
Mesopharynx NOS   Vallecula

EXCLUDES   *epiglottis:*
        NOS (212.1)
        suprahyoid portion (212.1)

210.7   **Nasopharynx**

Adenoid tissue   Pharyngeal tonsil
Lymphadenoid tissue   Posterior nasal septum

210.8   **Hypopharynx**

Arytenoid fold   Postcricoidregion
Laryngopharynx   Pyriform fossa

210.9   **Pharynx, unspecified**

Throat NOS

√4ᵗʰ 211 Benign neoplasm of other parts of digestive system

EXCLUDES   ▶ *benign stromal tumors of digestive system*
        (215.5)◄

211.0   **Esophagus**

211.1   **Stomach**

Body ⎫
Cardia ⎬ of stomach
Fundus ⎭

Cardiac orifice
Pylorus

211.2   **Duodenum, jejunum, and ileum**

Small intestine NOS

EXCLUDES   *ampulla of Vater (211.5)*
        ileocecal valve (211.3)

211.3   **Colon**

Appendix   Ileocecal valve
Cecum   Large intestine NOS

EXCLUDES   *rectosigmoid junction (211.4)*

AHA: 3Q, '05, 17; 2Q, '05, 16; 4Q, '01, 56

DRG 188

211.4   **Rectum and anal canal**

Anal canal or sphincter   Rectosigmoid junction
Anus NOS

EXCLUDES   *anus:*
        margin (216.5)
        skin (216.5)
        perianal skin (216.5)

211.5   **Liver and biliary passages**

Ampulla of Vater   Gallbladder
Common bile duct   Hepatic duct
Cystic duct   Sphincter of Oddi

211.6   **Pancreas, except islets of Langerhans**

211.7   **Islets of Langerhans**

Islet cell tumor
Use additional code to identify any functional
   activity

211.8   **Retroperitoneum and peritoneum**

Mesentery   Omentum
Mesocolon   Retroperitoneal tissue

211.9   **Other and unspecified site**

Alimentary tract NOS
Digestive system NOS
Gastrointestinal tract NOS
Intestinal tract NOS
Intestine NOS
Spleen, not elsewhere classified

√4ᵗʰ 212 Benign neoplasm of respiratory and intrathoracic organs

212.0   **Nasal cavities, middle ear, and accessory sinuses**

Cartilage of nose   Sinus:
Eustachian tube   ethmoidal
Nares   frontal
Septum of nose   maxillary
                   sphenoidal

EXCLUDES   *auditory canal (external) (216.2)*
        bone of:
          ear (213.0)
          nose [turbinates] (213.0)
        cartilage of ear (215.0)
        ear (external) (skin) (216.2)
        nose NOS (229.8)
          skin (216.3)
        olfactory bulb (225.1)
        polyp of:
          accessory sinus (471.8)
          ear (385.30-385.35)
          nasal cavity (471.0)
        posterior margin of septum and
          choanae (210.7)

212.1   **Larynx**

Cartilage: Epiglottis (suprahyoid portion) NOS
   arytenoid   Glottis
   cricoid   Vocal cords (false) (true)
   cuneiform
   thyroid

EXCLUDES   *epiglottis, anterior aspect (210.6)*
        polyp of vocal cord or larynx (478.4)

212.2   **Trachea**

212.3   **Bronchus and lung**

Carina   Hilus of lung

212.4   **Pleura**

212.5   **Mediastinum**

212.6   **Thymus**

212.7   **Heart**

EXCLUDES   *great vessels (215.4)*

212.8   **Other specified sites**

212.9   **Site unspecified**

Respiratory organ NOS
Upper respiratory tract NOS

EXCLUDES   *intrathoracic NOS (229.8)*
        thoracic NOS (229.8)

√4ᵗʰ 213 Benign neoplasm of bone and articular cartilage

INCLUDES   cartilage (articular) (joint)
        periosteum

EXCLUDES   *cartilage of:*   *cartilage of:*
        ear (215.0)   *nose (212.0)*
        eyelid (215.0)   *exostosis NOS (726.91)*
        larynx (212.1)   *synovia (215.0-215.9)*

213.0   **Bones of skull and face**

EXCLUDES   *lower jaw bone (213.1)*

213.1   **Lower jaw bone**

√4ᵗʰ / √5ᵗʰ Additional Digit Required   Nonspecific PDx   Unacceptable PDx   Manifestation Code   **MCV** Major Cardiovascular Condition   ▶◀ Revised Text   ● New Code   ▲ Revised Code Title

Neoplasms

213.2–219.9

213.2 **Vertebral column, excluding sacrum and coccyx**
213.3 **Ribs, sternum, and clavicle**
213.4 **Scapula and long bones of upper limb**
213.5 **Short bones of upper limb**
213.6 **Pelvic bones, sacrum, and coccyx**
213.7 **Long bones of lower limb**
213.8 **Short bones of lower limb**
213.9 **Bone and articular cartilage, site unspecified**

√4ᵗʰ 214 **Lipoma**

INCLUDES
angiolipoma
fibrolipoma
hibernoma
lipoma (fetal) (infiltrating) (intramuscular)
myelolipoma
myxolipoma

DEF: Benign tumor frequently composed of mature fat cells; may occasionally be composed of fetal fat cells.

214.0 **Skin and subcutaneous tissue of face**
214.1 **Other skin and subcutaneous tissue**
214.2 **Intrathoracic organs**
214.3 **Intra-abdominal organs**
214.4 **Spermatic cord** ♂
214.8 **Other specified sites**
   AHA: 3Q, '94, 7
214.9 **Lipoma, unspecified site**

√4ᵗʰ 215 **Other benign neoplasm of connective and other soft tissue**

INCLUDES
blood vessel
bursa
fascia
ligament
muscle
peripheral, sympathetic, and parasympathetic
   nerves and ganglia
synovia
tendon (sheath)

EXCLUDES *cartilage:*
   articular (213.0-213.9)
   larynx (212.1)
   nose (212.0)
connective tissue of:
   breast (217)
   internal organ, except lipoma and
      hemangioma—code to benign neoplasm
      of the site
lipoma (214.0-214.9)

215.0 **Head, face, and neck**
215.2 **Upper limb, including shoulder**
215.3 **Lower limb, including hip**
215.4 **Thorax**
   EXCLUDES *heart (212.7)*
      mediastinum (212.5)
      thymus (212.6)
215.5 **Abdomen**
   Abdominal wall
   ►Benign stromal tumors of abdomen◄
   Hypochondrium
215.6 **Pelvis**
   Buttock   Inguinal region
   Groin   Perineum
   EXCLUDES *uterine:*
      leiomyoma (218.0-218.9)
      ligament, any (221.0)
215.7 **Trunk, unspecified**
   Back NOS   Flank NOS
215.8 **Other specified sites**
215.9 **Site unspecified**

√4ᵗʰ 216 **Benign neoplasm of skin**

INCLUDES
blue nevus   pigmented nevus
dermatofibroma   syringoadenoma
hydrocystoma   syringoma

EXCLUDES *skin of genital organs (221.0-222.9)*

AHA: 1Q, '00, 21

216.0 **Skin of lip**
   EXCLUDES *vermilion border of lip (210.0)*
216.1 **Eyelid, including canthus**
   EXCLUDES *cartilage of eyelid (215.0)*
216.2 **Ear and external auditory canal**
   Auricle (ear)   External meatus
   Auricular canal, external   Pinna
   EXCLUDES *cartilage of ear (215.0)*
216.3 **Skin of other and unspecified parts of face**
   Cheek, external   Nose, external
   Eyebrow   Temple
216.4 **Scalp and skin of neck**
   AHA: 3Q, '91, 12
216.5 **Skin of trunk, except scrotum**
   Axillary fold   Skin of:
   Perianal skin   buttock
   Skin of: chest wall
      abdominal wall   groin
      anus   perineum
      back   Umbilicus
      breast
   EXCLUDES *anal canal (211.4)*
      anus NOS (211.4)
      skin of scrotum (222.4)
216.6 **Skin of upper limb, including shoulder**
216.7 **Skin of lower limb, including hip**
216.8 **Other specified sites of skin**
216.9 **Skin, site unspecified**

217 **Benign neoplasm of breast**
   Breast (male) (female):   Breast (male) (female):
      connective tissue   soft parts
      glandular tissue
   EXCLUDES *adenofibrosis (610.2)*
      benign cyst of breast (610.0)
      fibrocystic disease (610.1)
      skin of breast (216.5)

AHA: 1Q, '00, 4

√4ᵗʰ 218 **Uterine leiomyoma**

INCLUDES
fibroid (bleeding) (uterine)
uterine:
   fibromyoma
   myoma

DEF: Benign tumor primarily derived from uterine smooth muscle tissue; may contain fibrous, fatty, or epithelial tissue; also called uterine fibroid or myoma.

218.0 **Submucous leiomyoma of uterus** ♀
218.1 **Intramural leiomyoma of uterus** ♀
   Interstitial leiomyoma of uterus
218.2 **Subserous leiomyoma of uterus** ♀
218.9 **Leiomyoma of uterus, unspecified** ♀
   AHA: 1Q, '03, 4

√4ᵗʰ 219 **Other benign neoplasm of uterus**
219.0 **Cervix uteri** ♀
219.1 **Corpus uteri** ♀
   Endometrium   Myometrium
   Fundus
219.8 **Other specified parts of uterus** ♀
219.9 **Uterus, part unspecified** ♀

Types of Uterine Fibroids

Types of Uterine Fibroids

N Newborn Age: 0   P Pediatric Age: 0-17   M Maternity Age: 12-55   A Adult Age: 15-124   CC CC Condition   MC Major Complication   CD Complex Dx   HIV HIV Related Dx

44 — Volume 1 • October 2006

2007 ICD•9•CM

220 Benign neoplasm of ovary ♀
Use additional code to identify any functional activity (256.0-256.1)

EXCLUDES   cyst:
     corpus albicans (620.2)
     corpus luteum (620.1)
     endometrial (617.1)
     follicular (atretic) (620.0)
     graafian follicle (620.0)
     ovarian NOS (620.2)
     retention (620.2)

√4th **221 Benign neoplasm of other female genital organs**
INCLUDES   adenomatous polyp
     benign teratoma

EXCLUDES   cyst:
     epoophoron (752.11)
     fimbrial (752.11)
     Gartner's duct (752.11)
     parovarian (752.11)

221.0 Fallopian tube and uterine ligaments ♀
     Oviduct
     Parametruim
     Uterine ligament (broad) (round) (uterosacral)
     Uterine tube

221.1 Vagina ♀

221.2 Vulva ♀
     Clitoris
     External female genitalia NOS
     Greater vestibular [Bartholin's] gland
     Labia (majora) (minora)
     Pudendum
     EXCLUDES   Bartholin's (duct) (gland) cyst (616.2)

221.8 Other specified sites of female genital organs ♀

221.9 Female genital organ, site unspecified ♀
     Female genitourinary tract NOS

√4th **222 Benign neoplasm of male genital organs**

222.0 Testis ♂
     Use additional code to identify any functional activity

222.1 Penis ♂
     Corpus cavernosum   Prepuce
     Glans penis

222.2 Prostate ♂
     EXCLUDES   adenomatous hyperplasia of prostate (600.20-600.21)
     prostatic:
       adenoma (600.20-600.21)
       enlargement (600.00-600.01)
       hypertrophy (600.00-600.01)

222.3 Epididymis ♂

222.4 Scrotum ♂
     Skin of scrotum

222.8 Other specified sites of male genital organs ♂
     Seminal vesicle
     Spermatic cord

222.9 Male genital organ, site unspecified ♂
     Male genitourinary tract NOS

Eyeball

Posterior segment
Vitreous
Optic nerve
Conjunctiva
Sclera
Lens
Cornea
Optic disc
Choroid
Sclera
Retina
Iris
Anterior chamber
Pars plana

√4th **223 Benign neoplasm of kidney and other urinary organs**

223.0 Kidney, except pelvis
     Kidney NOS
     EXCLUDES   renal:
       calyces (223.1)
       pelvis (223.1)

223.1 Renal pelvis

223.2 Ureter
     EXCLUDES   ureteric orifice of bladder (223.3)

223.3 Bladder

√5th **223.8 Other specified sites of urinary organs**

     223.81 Urethra
       EXCLUDES   urethral orifice of bladder (223.3)

     223.89 Other
       Paraurethral glands

223.9 Urinary organ, site unspecified
     Urinary system NOS

√4th **224 Benign neoplasm of eye**
     EXCLUDES   cartilage of eyelid (215.0)
       eyelid (skin) (216.1)
       optic nerve (225.1)
       orbital bone (213.0)

224.0 Eyeball, except conjunctiva, cornea, retina, and choroid
     Ciliary body   Sclera
     Iris   Uveal tract

224.1 Orbit
     EXCLUDES   bone of orbit (213.0)

224.2 Lacrimal gland

224.3 Conjunctiva

224.4 Cornea

224.5 Retina
     EXCLUDES   hemangioma of retina (228.03)

224.6 Choroid

224.7 Lacrimal duct
     Lacrimal sac   Nasolacrimal duct

224.8 Other specified parts of eye

224.9 Eye, part unspecified

√4th **225 Benign neoplasm of brain and other parts of nervous system**
     EXCLUDES   hemangioma (228.02)
       neurofibromatosis (237.7)
       peripheral, sympathetic, and parasympathetic nerves and ganglia (215.0-215.9)
       retrobulbar (224.1)

225.0 Brain

225.1 Cranial nerves
     Acoustic neuroma
     AHA: 4Q, '04, 113

225.2 Cerebral meninges
     Meninges NOS   Meningioma (cerebral)

225.3 Spinal cord
     Cauda equina

225.4 Spinal meninges
     Spinal meningioma

225.8 Other specified sites of nervous system

225.9 Nervous system, part unspecified
     Nervous system (central) NOS
     EXCLUDES   meninges NOS (225.2)

226 Benign neoplasm of thyroid glands
     Use additional code to identify any functional activity

√4th **227 Benign neoplasm of other endocrine glands and related structures**
     Use additional code to identify any functional activity
     EXCLUDES   ovary (220)   testis (222.0)
       pancreas (211.6)

227.0 Adrenal gland
     Suprarenal gland

227.1 Parathyroid gland

√4th √5th Additional Digit Required   Nonspecific PDx   Unacceptable PDx   Manifestation Code   **MCV** Major Cardiovascular Condition   ►◄ Revised Text   ● New Code   ▲ Revised Code Title

2007 ICD•9•CM   **Volume 1 — 45**

Neoplasms

227.3–232.9

227.3 Pituitary gland and craniopharyngeal duct (pouch)
Craniobuccal pouch   Rathke's pouch
Hypophysis   Sella turcica

227.4 Pineal gland
Pineal body

227.5 Carotid body

227.6 Aortic body and other paraganglia
Coccygeal body   Para-aortic body
Glomus jugulare
AHA: N-D, '84, 17

227.8 Other

227.9 Endocrine gland, site unspecified

√4ᵗʰ **228 Hemangioma and lymphangioma, any site**
INCLUDES angioma (benign) (cavernous) (congenital) NOS
cavernous nevus
glomus tumor
hemangioma (benign) (congenital)
EXCLUDES benign neoplasm of spleen, except hemangioma
and lymphangioma (211.9)
glomus jugulare (227.6)
nevus:
NOS (216.0-216.9)
blue or pigmented (216.0-216.9)
vascular (757.32)
AHA: 1Q, '00, 21

√5ᵗʰ **228.0 Hemangioma, any site**
AHA: J-F, '85, 19
DEF: A common benign tumor usually occurring in infancy;
composed of newly formed blood vessels due to malformation of
angioblastic tissue.

228.00 Of unspecified site
228.01 Of skin and subcutaneous tissue
228.02 Of intracranial structures
228.03 Of retina
228.04 Of intra-abdominal structures
Peritoneum   Retroperitoneal tissue
228.09 Of other sites
Systemic angiomatosis
AHA: 3Q, '91, 20

228.1 Lymphangioma, any site
Congenital lymphangioma   Lymphatic nevus

√4ᵗʰ **229 Benign neoplasm of other and unspecified sites**
229.0 Lymph nodes
EXCLUDES lymphangioma (228.1)
229.8 Other specified sites
Intrathoracic NOS   Thoracic NOS
229.9 Site unspecified

CARCINOMA IN SITU (230-234)
INCLUDES Bowen's disease
erythroplasia
Queyrat's erythroplasia
EXCLUDES leukoplakia—see Alphabetic Index
DEF: A neoplastic type; with tumor cells confined to epithelium of origin;
without further invasion.

√4ᵗʰ **230 Carcinoma in situ of digestive organs**
230.0 Lip, oral cavity, and pharynx
Gingiva   Oropharynx
Hypopharynx   Salivary gland or duct
Mouth [any part]   Tongue
Nasopharynx
EXCLUDES aryepiglottic fold or interarytenoid fold,
laryngeal aspect (231.0)
epiglottis:
NOS (231.0)
suprahyoid portion (231.0)
skin of lip (232.0)
230.1 Esophagus
230.2 Stomach
Body
Cardia } of stomach
Fundus
Cardiac orifice   Pylorus

230.3 Colon
Appendix   Ileocecal valve
Cecum   Large intestine NOS
EXCLUDES rectosigmoid junction (230.4)
230.4 Rectum
Rectosigmoid junction
230.5 Anal canal
Anal sphincter
230.6 Anus, unspecified
EXCLUDES anus:
margin (232.5)
skin (232.5)
perianal skin (232.5)
230.7 Other and unspecified parts of intestine
Duodenum   Jejunum
Ileum   Small intestine NOS
EXCLUDES ampulla of Vater (230.8)
230.8 Liver and biliary system
Ampulla of Vater   Gallbladder
Common bile duct   Hepatic duct
Cystic duct   Sphincter of Oddi
230.9 Other and unspecified digestive organs
Digestive organ NOS   Pancreas
Gastrointestinal tract NOS   Spleen

√4ᵗʰ **231 Carcinoma in situ of respiratory system**
231.0 Larynx
Cartilage: Epiglottis:
arytenoid   NOS
cricoid   posterior surface
cuneiform   suprahyoid portion
thyroid   Vocal cords (false) (true)
EXCLUDES aryepiglottic fold or interarytenoid fold:
NOS (230.0)
hypopharyngeal aspect (230.0)
marginal zone (230.0)
231.1 Trachea
231.2 Bronchus and lung
Carina
Hilus of lung
231.8 Other specified parts of respiratory system
Accessory sinuses   Nasal cavities
Middle ear   Pleura
EXCLUDES ear (external) (skin) (232.2)
nose NOS (234.8)
skin (232.3)
231.9 Respiratory system, part unspecified
Respiratory organ NOS

√4ᵗʰ **232 Carcinoma in situ of skin**
INCLUDES pigment cells
232.0 Skin of lip
EXCLUDES vermilion border of lip (230.0)
232.1 Eyelid, including canthus
232.2 Ear and external auditory canal
232.3 Skin of other and unspecified parts of face
232.4 Scalp and skin of neck
232.5 Skin of trunk, except scrotum
Anus, margin   Skin of:
Axillary fold   breast
Perianal skin   buttock
Skin of: chest wall
abdominal wall   groin
anus   perineum
back   Umbilicus
EXCLUDES anal canal (230.5)
anus NOS (230.6)
skin of genital organs (233.3, 233.5-233.6)
232.6 Skin of upper limb, including shoulder
232.7 Skin of lower limb, including hip
232.8 Other specified sites of skin
232.9 Skin, site unspecified

 Newborn Age: 0   Pediatric Age: 0-17   Maternity Age: 12-55   Adult Age: 15-124   CC Condition   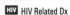 MC Major Complication   CD Complex Dx   HIV HIV Related Dx

46 — Volume 1   *2007 ICD•9•CM*

✓4ᵗʰ **233 Carcinoma in situ of breast and genitourinary system**

233.0 Breast
> EXCLUDES   *Paget's disease (174.0-174.9)*
> *skin of breast (232.5)*

233.1 Cervix uteri   ♀
▶Cervical intraepithelial glandular neoplasia◀
Cervical intraepithelial neoplasia III [CIN III]
Severe dysplasia of cervix
> EXCLUDES   *cervical intraepithelial neoplasia II*
> *[CIN II] (622.12)*
> *cytologic evidence of malignancy*
> *without histologic confirmation*
> ▶*(795.06)*◀
> *high grade squamous intraepithelial*
> *lesion (HGSIL) (795.04)*
> *moderate dysplasia of cervix (622.12)*

AHA: 3Q, '92, 7; 3Q, '92, 8; 1Q, '91, 11

233.2 Other and unspecified parts of uterus   ♀
233.3 Other and unspecified female genital organs   ♀
233.4 Prostate   ♂
233.5 Penis   ♂
233.6 Other and unspecified male genital organs   ♂
233.7 Bladder
233.9 Other and unspecified urinary organs

✓4ᵗʰ **234 Carcinoma in situ of other and unspecified sites**

234.0 Eye
> EXCLUDES   *cartilage of eyelid (234.8)*
> *eyelid (skin) (232.1)*
> *optic nerve (234.8)*
> *orbital bone (234.8)*

234.8 Other specified sites
Endocrine gland [any]

234.9 Site unspecified
Carcinoma in situ NOS

NEOPLASMS OF UNCERTAIN BEHAVIOR (235-238)

Note: Categories 235–238 classify by site certain
histomorphologically well-defined neoplasms, the
subsequent behavior of which cannot be predicted from
the present appearance.

✓4ᵗʰ **235 Neoplasm of uncertain behavior of digestive and respiratory systems**
> EXCLUDES ▶ *stromal tumors of uncertain behavior of*
> *digestive system (238.1)*◀

235.0 Major salivary glands
Gland: Gland:
parotid   submandibular
sublingual
> EXCLUDES   *minor salivary glands (235.1)*

235.1 Lip, oral cavity, and pharynx
Gingiva   Nasopharynx
Hypopharynx   Oropharynx
Minor salivary glands Tongue
Mouth
> EXCLUDES   *aryepiglottic fold or interarytenoid fold,*
> *laryngeal aspect (235.6)*
> *epiglottis:*
> *NOS (235.6)*
> *suprahyoid portion (235.6)*
> *skin of lip (238.2)*

235.2 Stomach, intestines, and rectum

235.3 Liver and biliary passages
Ampulla of Vater   Gallbladder
Bile ducts [any]   Liver

235.4 Retroperitoneum and peritoneum

235.5 Other and unspecified digestive organs
Anal: Esophagus
canal   Pancreas
sphincter   Spleen
Anus NOS
> EXCLUDES   *anus:*
> *margin (238.2)*
> *skin (238.2)*
> *perianal skin (238.2)*

235.6 Larynx
> EXCLUDES   *aryepiglottic fold or interarytenoid fold:*
> *NOS (235.1)*
> *hypopharyngeal aspect (235.1)*
> *marginal zone (235.1)*

235.7 Trachea, bronchus, and lung
235.8 Pleura, thymus, and mediastinum
235.9 Other and unspecified respiratory organs
Accessory sinuses   Nasal cavities
Middle ear   Respiratory organ NOS
> EXCLUDES   *ear (external) (skin) (238.2)*
> *nose (238.8)*
> *skin (238.2)*

✓4ᵗʰ **236 Neoplasm of uncertain behavior of genitourinary organs**

236.0 Uterus   ♀
236.1 Placenta   ♀
Chorioadenoma (destruens)
Invasive mole
Malignant hydatid(iform) mole

236.2 Ovary   ♀
Use additional code to identify any functional
activity

236.3 Other and unspecified female genital organs   ♀
236.4 Testis   ♂
Use additional code to identify any functional
activity

236.5 Prostate   ♂
236.6 Other and unspecified male genital organs   ♂
236.7 Bladder

✓5ᵗʰ **236.9 Other and unspecified urinary organs**
236.90 Urinary organ, unspecified
236.91 Kidney and ureter
236.99 Other

✓4ᵗʰ **237 Neoplasm of uncertain behavior of endocrine glands and nervous system**

237.0 Pituitary gland and craniopharyngeal duct
Use additional code to identify any functional
activity

237.1 Pineal gland
237.2 Adrenal gland
Suprarenal gland
Use additional code to identify any functional
activity

237.3 Paraganglia
Aortic body   Coccygeal body
Carotid body   Glomus jugulare

AHA: N-D, '84, 17

237.4 Other and unspecified endocrine glands
Parathyroid gland   Thyroid gland

237.5 Brain and spinal cord

237.6 Meninges
Meninges: Meninges:
NOS   spinal
cerebral

✓5ᵗʰ **237.7 Neurofibromatosis**
von Recklinghausen's disease
DEF: An inherited condition with developmental changes in the
nervous system, muscles, bones and skin; multiple soft tumors
(neurofibromas) distributed over the entire body.

237.70 Neurofibromatosis, unspecified
237.71 Neurofibromatosis, type 1 [von Recklinghausen's disease]
237.72 Neurofibromatosis, type 2 [acoustic neurofibromatosis]
DEF: Inherited condition with cutaneous lesions, benign
tumors of peripheral nerves and bilateral 8th nerve
masses.

237.9 Other and unspecified parts of nervous system
Cranial nerves
> EXCLUDES   *peripheral, sympathetic, and*
> *parasympathetic nerves and*
> *ganglia (238.1)*

✓4ᵗʰ Additional Digit Required   **Nonspecific PDx**   **Unacceptable PDx**   **Manifestation Code**   **MCV** Major Cardiovascular Condition   ▶◀ Revised Text   ● New Code   ▲ Revised Code Title

Neoplasms

238–239.9

√4ᵗʰ **238 Neoplasm of uncertain behavior of other and unspecified sites and tissues**

238.0 Bone and articular cartilage

EXCLUDES cartilage:
    ear (238.1)
    eyelid (238.1)
    larynx (235.6)
    nose (235.9)
    synovia (238.1)

AHA: 4Q, '04, 128

238.1 Connective and other soft tissue

Peripheral, sympathetic, and parasympathetic nerves and ganglia

▶Stromal tumors of digestive system◀

EXCLUDES cartilage (of):
    articular (238.0)
    larynx (235.6)
    nose (235.9)
    connective tissue of breast (238.3)

238.2 Skin

EXCLUDES anus NOS (235.5)
    skin of genital organs (236.3, 236.6)
    vermilion border of lip (235.1)

238.3 Breast

EXCLUDES skin of breast (238.2)

238.4 Polycythemia vera

DEF: Abnormal proliferation of all bone marrow elements, increased red cell mass and total blood volume; unknown etiology, frequently associated with splenomegaly, leukocytosis, and thrombocythemia.

238.5 Histiocytic and mast cells

Mast cell tumor NOS   Mastocytoma NOS

238.6 Plasma cells

Plasmacytoma NOS   Solitary myeloma

√5ᵗʰ **238.7 Other lymphatic and hematopoietic tissues**

EXCLUDES ▶ acute myelogenous leukemia (205.0)
    chronic myelomonocytic leukemia (205.1)◀
    myelofibrosis ▶(289.83)◀
    myelosclerosis NOS (289.89)
    myelosis:
      NOS (205.9)
      megakaryocytic (207.2)

AHA: 3Q, '01, 13; 1Q, '97, 5; 2Q, '89, 8

● **238.71 Essential thrombocythemia**

Essential hemorrhagic thrombocythemia
Essential thrombocytosis
Idiopathic (hemorrhagic) thrombocythemia
Primary thrombocytosis

● **238.72 Low grade myelodysplastic syndrome lesions**

Refractory anemia (RA)
Refractory anemia with ringed sideroblasts (RARS)
Refractory cytopenia with multilineage dysplasia (RCMD)
Refractory cytopenia with multilineage dysplasia and ringed sideroblasts (RCMD-RS)

DEF: Refractory anemia (RA): Form of bone marrow disorder (myelodysplastic syndrome) that interferes with red blood cell production in the bone marrow; malignancy unresponsive to hematinics; characteristic normal or hypercellular marrow with abnormal erythrocyte development and reticulocytopenia.

● **238.73 High grade myelodysplastic syndrome lesions**

Refractory anemia with excess blasts-1 (RAEB-1)
Refractory anemia with excess blasts-2 (RAEB-2)

● **238.74 Myelodysplastic syndrome with 5q deletion**

5q minus syndrome NOS

EXCLUDES constitutional 5q deletion (758.39)
    high grade myelodysplastic syndrome with 5q deletion (238.73)

● **238.75 Myelodysplastic syndrome, unspecified**

● **238.76 Myelofibrosis with myeloid metaplasia**

Agnogenic myeloid metaplasia
Idiopathic myelofibrosis (chronic)
Myelosclerosis with myeloid metaplasia
Primary myelofibrosis

EXCLUDES myelofibrosis NOS (289.83)
    myelophthisic anemia (284.2)
    myelophthisis (284.2)
    secondary myelofibrosis (289.83)

● **238.79 Other lymphatic and hematopoietic tissues**

Lymphoproliferative disease (chronic) NOS
Megakaryocytic myelosclerosis
Myeloproliferative disease (chronic) NOS
Panmyelosis (acute)

238.8 Other specified sites

Eye   Heart

EXCLUDES eyelid (skin) (238.2)
    cartilage (238.1)

238.9 Site unspecified

NEOPLASMS OF UNSPECIFIED NATURE (239)

√4ᵗʰ **239 Neoplasms of unspecified nature**

Note: Category 239 classifies by site neoplasms of unspecified morphology and behavior. The term "mass," unless otherwise stated, is not to be regarded as a neoplastic growth.

INCLUDES "growth" NOS   new growth NOS
    neoplasm NOS   tumor NOS

239.0 Digestive system

EXCLUDES anus:
    margin (239.2)
    skin (239.2)
    perianal skin (239.2)

239.1 Respiratory system

239.2 Bone, soft tissue, and skin

EXCLUDES anal canal (239.0)
    anus NOS (239.0)
    bone marrow (202.9)
    cartilage:
      larynx (239.1)
      nose (239.1)
    connective tissue of breast (239.3)
    skin of genital organs (239.5)
    vermilion border of lip (239.0)

239.3 Breast

EXCLUDES skin of breast (239.2)

239.4 Bladder

239.5 Other genitourinary organs

239.6 Brain

EXCLUDES cerebral meninges (239.7)
    cranial nerves (239.7)

239.7 Endocrine glands and other parts of nervous system

EXCLUDES peripheral, sympathetic, and parasympathetic nerves and ganglia (239.2)

239.8 Other specified sites

EXCLUDES eyelid (skin) (239.2)
    cartilage (239.2)
    great vessels (239.2)
    optic nerve (239.7)

239.9 Site unspecified

N Newborn Age: 0   P Pediatric Age: 0-17   M Maternity Age: 12-55   A Adult Age: 15-124   CC CC Condition   MC Major Complication   CD Complex Dx   HIV HIV Related Dx

48 — Volume 1 • October 2006   **2007 ICD•9•CM**

3. ENDOCRINE, NUTRITIONAL AND METABOLIC DISEASES, AND IMMUNITY DISORDERS (240-279)

> **EXCLUDES** *endocrine and metabolic disturbances specific to the fetus and newborn (775.0-775.9)*

Note: All neoplasms, whether functionally active or not, are classified in Chapter 2. Codes in Chapter 3 (i.e., 242.8, 246.0, 251-253, 255-259) may be used to identify such functional activity associated with any neoplasm, or by ectopic endocrine tissue.

DISORDERS OF THYROID GLAND (240-246)

✓4ᵗʰ 240 Simple and unspecified goiter
>DEF: An enlarged thyroid gland often caused by an inadequate dietary intake of iodine.

   240.0 Goiter, specified as simple
      Any condition classifiable to 240.9, specified as simple

   240.9 Goiter, unspecified
      Enlargement of thyroid
      Goiter or struma:
        NOS
        diffuse colloid
        endemic
      Goiter or struma:
        hyperplastic
        nontoxic (diffuse)
        parenchymatous
        sporadic
>   **EXCLUDES** *congenital (dyshormonogenic) goiter (246.1)*

✓4ᵗʰ 241 Nontoxic nodular goiter
>**EXCLUDES** *adenoma of thyroid (226)*
>*cystadenoma of thyroid (226)*

   241.0 Nontoxic uninodular goiter
      Thyroid nodule   Uninodular goiter (nontoxic)
>DEF: Enlarged thyroid, commonly due to decreased thyroid production, with single nodule; no clinical hypothyroidism.

   241.1 Nontoxic multinodular goiter
      Multinodular goiter (nontoxic)
>DEF: Enlarged thyroid, commonly due to decreased thyroid production with multiple nodules; no clinical hypothyroidism.

   241.9 Unspecified nontoxic nodular goiter
      Adenomatous goiter
      Nodular goiter (nontoxic) NOS
      Struma nodosa (simplex)

✓4ᵗʰ 242 Thyrotoxicosis with or without goiter
>**EXCLUDES** *neonatal thyrotoxicosis (775.3)*
>DEF: A condition caused by excess quantities of thyroid hormones being introduced into the tissues

The following fifth-digit subclassification is for use with category 242:
    0 without mention of thyrotoxic crisis or storm
    1 with mention of thyrotoxic crisis or storm

The Endocrine System

✓5ᵗʰ 242.0 Toxic diffuse goiter   `CC`
      Basedow's disease
      Exophthalmic or toxic goiter NOS
      Graves' disease
      Primary thyroid hyperplasia
    CC Excl: 017.50-017.56, 017.90-017.96, 240.0-246.9, 259.8-259.9

>DEF: Diffuse thyroid enlargement accompanied by hyperthyroidism, bulging eyes, and dermopathy.

✓5ᵗʰ 242.1 Toxic uninodular goiter   `CC`
      Thyroid nodule   } toxic or with
      Uninodular goiter }   hyperthyroidism

    CC Excl: See code 242.0

>DEF: Symptomatic hyperthyroidism with a single nodule on the enlarged thyroid gland. Abrupt onset of symptoms; including extreme nervousness, insomnia, weight loss, tremors, and psychosis or coma.

✓5ᵗʰ 242.2 Toxic multinodular goiter   `CC`
      Secondary thyroid hyperplasia
    CC Excl: See code 242.0

>DEF: Symptomatic hyperthyroidism with multiple nodules on the enlarged thyroid gland. Abrupt onset of symptoms; including extreme nervousness, insomnia, weight loss, tremors, and psychosis or coma

✓5ᵗʰ 242.3 Toxic nodular goiter, unspecified   `CC`
      Adenomatous goiter
      Nodular goiter   } toxic or with
      Struma nodosa }   hyperthyroidism

      Any condition classifiable to 241.9 specified as toxic or with hyperthyroidism
    CC Excl: See code 242.0

✓5ᵗʰ 242.4 Thyrotoxicosis from ectopic thyroid nodule   `CC`
    CC Excl: See code 242.0

✓5ᵗʰ 242.8 Thyrotoxicosis of other specified origin   `CC`
      Overproduction of thyroid-stimulating hormone [TSH]
      Thyrotoxicosis:
        factitia from ingestion of excessive thyroid material
      Use additional E code to identify cause, if drug-induced
    CC Excl: See code 242.0

✓5ᵗʰ 242.9 Thyrotoxicosis without mention of goiter or other cause   `CC`
      Hyperthyroidism NOS
      Thyrotoxicosis NOS
    CC Excl: See code 242.0

243 Congenital hypothyroidism
      Congenital thyroid insufficiency
      Cretinism (athyrotic) (endemic)
      Use additional code to identify associated mental retardation
>   **EXCLUDES** *congenital (dyshormonogenic) goiter (246.1)*
>DEF: Underproduction of thyroid hormone present from birth.

✓4ᵗʰ 244 Acquired hypothyroidism
>**INCLUDES** athyroidism (acquired)
>   hypothyroidism (acquired)
>   myxedema (adult) (juvenile)
>   thyroid (gland) insufficiency (acquired)

   244.0 Postsurgical hypothyroidism
>DEF: Underproduction of thyroid hormone due to surgical removal of all or part of the thyroid gland.

   244.1 Other postablative hypothyroidism
      Hypothyroidism following therapy, such as irradiation

`✓4ᵗʰ` `✓5ᵗʰ` **Additional Digit Required**   **Nonspecific PDx**   **Unacceptable PDx**   **Manifestation Code**   `MCV` Major Cardiovascular Condition   ►◄ Revised Text   ● New Code   ▲ Revised Code Title

2007 ICD•9•CM   **Volume 1 — 49**

244.2   Iodine hypothyroidism
Hypothyroidism resulting from administration or
     ingestion of iodide
Use additional E code to identify drug

244.3   Other iatrogenic hypothyroidism
Hypothyroidism resulting from:
     P-aminosalicylic acid [PAS]
     Phenylbutazone
     Resorcinol
Iatrogenic hypothyroidism NOS
Use additional E code to identify drug

244.8   Other specified acquired hypothyroidism
Secondary hypothyroidism NEC

AHA: J-A, '85, 9

244.9   Unspecified hypothyroidism
Hypothyroidism ⎫
Myxedema ⎭ primary or NOS

AHA: 3Q, '99, 19; 4Q, '96, 29

☑4ᵗʰ 245 Thyroiditis

245.0   Acute thyroiditis
Abscess of thyroid   Thyroiditis:
Thyroiditis: pyogenic
   nonsuppurative, acute   suppurative
Use additional code to identify organism
DEF: Inflamed thyroid caused by infection, with abscess and liquid
puris.

245.1   Subacute thyroiditis
Thyroiditis: Thyroiditis:
   de Quervain's   granulomatous
   giant cell   viral
DEF: Inflammation of the thyroid, characterized by fever and painful
enlargement of the thyroid gland, with granulomas in the gland.

245.2   Chronic lymphocytic thyroiditis
Hashimoto's disease
Struma lymphomatosa
Thyroiditis:
   autoimmune
   lymphocytic (chronic)
DEF: Autoimmune disease of thyroid; lymphocytes infiltrate the
gland and thyroid antibodies are produced; women more often
affected.

245.3   Chronic fibrous thyroiditis
Struma fibrosa   Thyroiditis:
Thyroiditis: ligneous
   invasive (fibrous)   Riedel's
DEF: Persistent fibrosing inflammation of thyroid with adhesions to
nearby structures; rare condition

245.4   Iatrogenic thyroiditis
Use additional code to identify cause
DEF: Thyroiditis resulting from treatment or intervention by
physician or in a patient intervention setting.

245.8   Other and unspecified chronic thyroiditis
Chronic thyroiditis:
   NOS
   nonspecific

245.9   Thyroiditis, unspecified
Thyroiditis NOS

☑4ᵗʰ 246 Other disorders of thyroid

246.0   Disorders of thyrocalcitonin secretion
Hypersecretion of calcitonin or thyrocalcitonin

246.1   Dyshormonogenic goiter
Congenital (dyshormonogenic) goiter
Goiter due to enzyme defect in synthesis of thyroid
     hormone
Goitrous cretinism (sporadic)

246.2   Cyst of thyroid
EXCLUDES   *cystadenoma of thyroid (226)*

246.3   Hemorrhage and infarction of thyroid

246.8   Other specified disorders of thyroid
Abnormality of thyroid-binding globulin
Atrophy of thyroid
Hyper-TBG-nemia
Hypo-TBG-nemia

246.9   Unspecified disorder of thyroid

DISEASES OF OTHER ENDOCRINE GLANDS (250-259)

☑4ᵗʰ 250 Diabetes mellitus
EXCLUDES   *gestational diabetes (648.8)*
hyperglycemia NOS (790.6)
neonatal diabetes mellitus (775.1)
nonclinical diabetes (790.29)

The following fifth-digit subclassification is for use with
category 250:
   **0   type II or unspecified type, not stated as
      uncontrolled**
     Fifth-digit 0 is for use for type II patients, even if the
       patient requires insulin
     Use additional code, if applicable, for associated long-
       term (current) insulin use V58.67
   1   type I [juvenile type], not stated as uncontrolled
   2   type II or unspecified type, uncontrolled
     Fifth-digit 2 is for use for type II patients, even if the
       patient requires insulin
     Use additional code, if applicable, for associated long-
       term (current) insulin use V58.67
   3   type I [juvenile type], uncontrolled

AHA: 4Q, '04, 56; 2Q, '04, 17; 2Q, '02, 13; 2Q,'01, 16; 2Q,'98, 15; 4Q, '97, 32;
2Q, '97, 14; 3Q, '96, 5; 4Q, '93, 19; 2Q, '92, 5; 3Q, '91, 3; 2Q, '90, 22;
N-D, '85, 11

DEF: Diabetes mellitus: Inability to metabolize carbohydrates, proteins, and
fats with insufficient secretion of insulin. Symptoms may be unremarkable,
with long-term complications, involving kidneys, nerves, blood vessels, and
eyes.

DEF: Uncontrolled diabetes: A nonspecific term indicating that the current
treatment regimen does not keep the blood sugar level of a patient within
acceptable levels.

⁸ **☑5ᵗʰ 250.0   Diabetes mellitus without mention**   `CC 1-3`
               of complication
Diabetes mellitus without mention of complication or
     manifestation classifiable to 250.1-250.9
Diabetes (mellitus) NOS
CC Excl: For code 250.01-250.03: 250.00-251.3, 259.8-259.9

AHA: ▶1Q, '06, 14;◀ 4Q, '97, 32; 3Q, '91, 3, 12; N-D, '85, 11;
For code 250.00: 1Q, '05, 15; 4Q, '04, 55; 4Q, '03, 105, 108; 2Q,
'03, 16; 1Q, '02, 7, 11; For code 250.01: 4Q, '04, 55; 4Q, '03, 110;
2Q, '03, 6; For code 250.02: 1Q, '03, 5

☑5ᵗʰ 250.1   Diabetes with ketoacidosis   `CC 1-3`
Diabetic:
   acidosis ⎫
   ketosis ⎭ without mention of coma

CC Excl: For code 250.11-250.13: 250.00-251.3, 259.8-259.9

AHA: 3Q, '91, 6; For code 250.11: 4Q, '03, 82

DEF: Diabetic hyperglycemic crisis causing ketone presence in
body fluids.

☑5ᵗʰ 250.2   Diabetes with hyperosmolarity   `CC 1-3`
Hyperosmolar (nonketotic) coma
CC Excl: For code 250.21-250.23: 250.00-251.3, 259.8-259.9

AHA: 4Q, '93, 19; 3Q, '91, 7

---

⁸   Questionable admission = 0

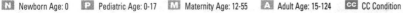

√5ᵗʰ **250.3 Diabetes with other coma** `CC 1-3`
Diabetic coma (with ketoacidosis)
Diabetic hypoglycemic coma
Insulin coma NOS
> **EXCLUDES** *diabetes with hyperosmolar coma (250.2)*

CC Excl: For code 250.31-250.33: See code 250.01

AHA: 3Q, '91, 7,12

DEF: Coma (not hyperosmolar) caused by hyperglycemia or hypoglycemia as complication of diabetes.

√5ᵗʰ **250.4 Diabetes with renal manifestations** `CC 1-3`
Use additional code to identify manifestation, as:
chronic kidney disease (585.1-585.9)
diabetic:
nephropathy NOS (583.81)
nephrosis (581.81)
intercapillary glomerulosclerosis (581.81)
Kimmelstiel-Wilson syndrome (581.81)

CC Excl: For code 250.41-250.43: See code 250.01

AHA: 3Q, '91, 8,12; S-O, '87, 9; S-O, '84, 3; **For code 250.40:** 1Q, '03, 20

DRG 331 For code 250.40

√5ᵗʰ **250.5 Diabetes with ophthalmic manifestations** `CC 1-3`
Use additional code to identify manifestation, as:
diabetic:
blindness (369.00-369.9)
cataract (366.41)
glaucoma (365.44)
macular edema (362.07)
retinal edema (362.07)
retinopathy (362.01-362.07)

CC Excl: For code 250.51-250.53: See code 250.01

AHA:►4Q, '05, 65;◄ 3Q, '91, 8; S-O, '85, 11 ;
For code 250.50: ►4Q, '05, 67◄

√5ᵗʰ **250.6 Diabetes with neurological manifestations** `CC 1-3`
Use additional code to identify manifestation, as:
diabetic:
amyotrophy (358.1)
gastroparalysis (536.3)
gastroparesis (536.3)
mononeuropathy (354.0-355.9)
neurogenic arthropathy (713.5)
peripheral autonomic neuropathy (337.1)
polyneuropathy (357.2)

CC Excl: For code 250.61-250.63: See code 250.01

AHA: 2Q, '93, 6; 2Q, '92, 15; 3Q, '91, 9; N-D, '84, 9; **For code 250.60:** 4Q, '03, 105; **For code 250.61:** 2Q, '04, 7

√5ᵗʰ **250.7 Diabetes with peripheral circulatory disorders** `CC 1-3`
Use additional code to identify manifestation, as:
diabetic:
gangrene (785.4)
peripheral angiopathy (443.81)

CC Excl: For code 250.71-250.73: See code 250.01

AHA: 1Q, '96, 10; 3Q, '94, 5; 2Q, '94, 17; 3Q, '91, 10, 12; 3Q, '90, 15; **For code 250.70:** 1Q, '04, 14

DRG 130 For code 250.70

DEF: Blood vessel damage or disease, usually in the feet, legs, or hands, as a complication of diabetes.

√5ᵗʰ **250.8 Diabetes with other specified manifestations** `CC 1-3`
Diabetic hypoglycemia
Hypoglycemic shock
Use additional code to identify manifestation, as:
any associated ulceration (707.10-707.9)
diabetic bone changes (731.8)
Use additional E code to identify cause, if drug-induced

CC Excl: For code 250.81-250.83: See code 250.01

AHA: 4Q, '00, 44; 4Q, '97, 43; 2Q, '97, 16; 4Q, '93, 20; 3Q, '91, 10; **For code 250.80:** 1Q, '04, 14

√5ᵗʰ **250.9 Diabetes with unspecified complication** `CC 1-3`
CC Excl: For code 250.91-250.93: See code 250.01

AHA: 2Q, '92, 15; 3Q, '91, 7, 12

√4ᵗʰ **251 Other disorders of pancreatic internal secretion**

251.0 Hypoglycemic coma `CC`
Iatrogenic hyperinsulinism
Non-diabetic insulin coma
Use additional E code to identify cause, if drug-induced
> **EXCLUDES** *hypoglycemic coma in diabetes mellitus (250.3)*

CC Excl: 250.00-251.3, 259.8-259.9

AHA: M-A, '85, 8

DEF: Coma induced by low blood sugar in non-diabetic patient.

251.1 Other specified hypoglycemia
Hyperinsulinism: Hyperplasia of pancreatic
NOS   islet beta cells NOS
ectopic
functional
> **EXCLUDES** *hypoglycemia:*
> *in diabetes mellitus (250.8)*
> *in infant of diabetic mother (775.0)*
> *hypoglycemic coma (251.0)*
> *neonatal hypoglycemia (775.6)*

Use additional E code to identify cause, if drug-induced

AHA: 1Q, '03, 10

DEF: Excessive production of insulin by the pancreas; associated with obesity and insulin-producing tumors.

251.2 Hypoglycemia, unspecified
Hypoglycemia: Hypoglycemia:
NOS   spontaneous
reactive
> **EXCLUDES** *hypoglycemia:*
> *with coma (251.0)*
> *in diabetes mellitus (250.8)*
> *leucine-induced (270.3)*

AHA: M-A, '85, 8

251.3 Postsurgical hypoinsulinemia `CC`
Hypoinsulinemia following complete or partial pancreatectomy
Postpancreatectomy hyperglycemia

CC Excl: See code 251.0

AHA: 3Q, '91, 6

251.4 Abnormality of secretion of glucagon
Hyperplasia of pancreatic islet alpha cells with glucagon excess

DEF: Production malfunction of a pancreatic hormone secreted by cells of the islets of Langerhans.

251.5 Abnormality of secretion of gastrin
Hyperplasia of pancreatic alpha cells with gastrin excess
Zollinger-Ellison syndrome

251.8 Other specified disorders of pancreatic internal secretion

AHA: 2Q, '98, 15; 3Q, '91, 6

251.9 Unspecified disorder of pancreatic internal secretion
Islet cell hyperplasia NOS

√4ᵗʰ / √5ᵗʰ Additional Digit Required Nonspecific PDx Unacceptable PDx Manifestation Code `MCV` Major Cardiovascular Condition ►◄ Revised Text ● New Code ▲ Revised Code Title

Dorsal View of Parathyroid Glands

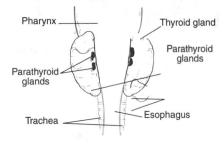

252 **Disorders of parathyroid gland** ✓4th

252.0 **Hyperparathyroidism** ✓5th

EXCLUDES   *ectopic hyperparathyroidism (259.3)*

DEF: Abnormally high secretion of parathyroid hormones causing bone deterioration, reduced renal function, kidney stones.

252.00 **Hyperparathyroidism, unspecified**

252.01 **Primary hyperparathyroidism**

Hyperplasia of parathyroid

DEF: Parathyroid dysfunction commonly caused by hyperplasia of two or more glands; characteristic hypercalcemia and increased parathyroid hormone levels.

252.02 **Secondary hyperparathyroidism, non-renal**

EXCLUDES   *secondary hyperparathyroidism (of renal origin) (588.81)*

AHA: 4Q, '04, 57-59

DEF: Underlying disease of nonrenal origin decreases blood levels of calcium causing the parathyroid to release increased levels of parathyroid hormone; parathyroid hormone levels return to normal once underlying condition is treated and blood calcium levels are normal.

252.08 **Other hyperparathyroidism**

Tertiary hyperparathyroidism

DEF: Tertiary hyperparathyroidism: chronic secondary hyperparathyroidism leads to adenomatous parathyroid causing irreversible abnormal production of parathyroid hormone (PTH); PTH remains high after the serum calcium levels are brought under control.

252.1 **Hypoparathyroidism**   CC

Parathyroiditis (autoimmune)

Tetany:

   parathyroid

   parathyroprival

EXCLUDES   *pseudohypoparathyroidism (275.4)*
pseudopseudohypoparathyroidism (275.4)
tetany NOS (781.7)
transitory neonatal hypoparathyroidism (775.4)

CC Excl: 252.00-252.9, 259.8-259.9

DEF: Abnormally low secretion of parathyroid hormones which causes decreased calcium and increased phosphorus in the blood. Resulting in muscle cramps, tetany, urinary frequency and cataracts.

252.8 **Other specified disorders of parathyroid gland**

Cyst
Hemorrhage } of parathyroid gland

252.9 **Unspecified disorder of parathyroid gland**

253 **Disorders of the pituitary gland and its hypothalamic control** ✓4th

INCLUDES   the listed conditions whether the disorder is in the pituitary or the hypothalamus

EXCLUDES   *Cushing's syndrome (255.0)*

253.0 **Acromegaly and gigantism**

Overproduction of growth hormone

DEF: Acromegaly: chronic, beginning in middle age; caused by hypersecretion of the pituitary growth hormone; produces enlarged parts of skeleton, especially the nose, ears, jaws, fingers and toes.

DEF: Gigantism: pituitary gigantism caused by excess growth of short flat bones; men may grow 78 to 80 inches tall.

253.1 **Other and unspecified anterior pituitary hyperfunction**

Forbes-Albright syndrome

EXCLUDES   *overproduction of:*
ACTH (255.3)
thyroid-stimulating hormone [TSH] (242.8)

AHA: J-A, '85, 9

DEF: Spontaneous galactorrhea-amenorrhea syndrome unrelated to pregnancy; usually related to presence of pituitary tumor.

253.2 **Panhypopituitarism**   CC

Cachexia, pituitary

Necrosis of pituitary (postpartum)

Pituitary insufficiency NOS

Sheehan's syndrome

Simmonds' disease

EXCLUDES   *iatrogenic hypopituitarism (253.7)*

CC Excl: 253.0-253.9, 259.8-259.9

DEF: Damage to or absence of pituitary gland leading to impaired sexual function, weight loss, fatigue, bradycardia, hypotension, pallor, depression, and impaired growth in children; called Simmonds' disease if cachexia is prominent.

253.3 **Pituitary dwarfism**

Isolated deficiency of (human) growth hormone [HGH]

Lorain-Levi dwarfism

DEF: Dwarfism with infantile physical characteristics due to abnormally low secretion of growth hormone and gonadotropin deficiency.

253.4 **Other anterior pituitary disorders**

Isolated or partial deficiency of an anterior pituitary hormone, other than growth hormone

Prolactin deficiency

AHA: J-A, '85, 9

253.5 **Diabetes insipidus**   CC

Vasopressin deficiency

EXCLUDES   *nephrogenic diabetes insipidus (588.1)*

CC Excl: 253.1-253.2, 253.4-253.9, 259.8-259.9

DEF: Metabolic disorder causing insufficient antidiuretic hormone release; symptoms include frequent urination, thirst, ravenous hunger, loss of weight, fatigue.

253.6 **Other disorders of neurohypophysis**

Syndrome of inappropriate secretion of antidiuretic hormone [ADH]

EXCLUDES   *ectopic antidiuretic hormone secretion (259.3)*

253.7 **Iatrogenic pituitary disorders**

Hypopituitarism: Hypopituitarism:
   hormone-induced   postablative
   hypophysectomy-induced   radiotherapy-induced

Use additional E code to identify cause

DEF: Pituitary dysfunction that results from drug therapy, radiation therapy, or surgery, causing mild to severe symptoms.

253.8 **Other disorders of the pituitary and other syndromes of diencephalohypophyseal origin**

Abscess of pituitary   Cyst of Rathke's pouch

Adiposogenital dystrophy   Fröhlich's syndrome

EXCLUDES   *craniopharyngioma (237.0)*

253.9 **Unspecified**

Dyspituitarism

N Newborn Age: 0   P Pediatric Age: 0-17   M Maternity Age: 12-55   A Adult Age: 15-124   CC CC Condition   MC Major Complication   CD Complex Dx   HIV HIV Related Dx

52 — Volume 1   2007 ICD•9•CM

✓4ᵗʰ **254 Diseases of thymus gland**

> **EXCLUDES**   aplasia or dysplasia with immunodeficiency (279.2)
> hypoplasia with immunodeficiency (279.2)
> myasthenia gravis (358.00-358.01)

254.0 Persistent hyperplasia of thymus
Hypertrophy of thymus
DEF: Continued abnormal growth of the twin lymphoid lobes that produce T lymphocytes.

254.1 Abscess of thymus   `CC`
CC Excl: 254.0–254.9, 259.5–259.9

254.8 Other specified diseases of thymus gland
Atrophy ⎫
Cyst   ⎬ of thymus

> **EXCLUDES**   thymoma (212.6)

254.9 Unspecified disease of thymus gland

✓4ᵗʰ **255 Disorders of adrenal glands**

> **INCLUDES**   the listed conditions whether the basic disorder is in the adrenals or is pituitary-induced

255.0 Cushing's syndrome   `CC`
Adrenal hyperplasia due to excess ACTH
Cushing's syndrome:
  NOS
  iatrogenic
  idiopathic
  pituitary-dependent
Ectopic ACTH syndrome
Iatrogenic syndrome of excess cortisol
Overproduction of cortisol
Use additional E code to identify cause, if drug-induced

> **EXCLUDES**   congenital adrenal hyperplasia (255.2)

CC Excl: 255.0-255.2, 259.8-259.9

DEF: Due to adrenal cortisol oversecretion or glucocorticoid medications; may cause fatty tissue of the face, neck and body; osteoporosis and curvature of spine, hypertension, diabetes mellitus, female genitourinary problems, male impotence, degeneration of muscle tissues, weakness.

✓5ᵗʰ **255.1 Hyperaldosteronism**
AHA: 4Q, '03, 48

DEF: Oversecretion of aldosterone causing fluid retention, hypertension.

▲   **255.10 Hyperaldosteronism, unspecified**
Aldosteronism NOS
▶Primary aldosteronism, unspecified◀

> **EXCLUDES**   Conn's syndrome (255.12)

255.11 Glucocorticoid-remediable aldosteronism
Familial aldosteronism type I

> **EXCLUDES**   Conn's syndrome (255.12)

DEF: A rare autosomal dominant familial form of primary aldosteronism in which the secretion of aldosterone is under the influence of adrenocortiotrophic hormone (ACTH) rather than the renin-angiotensin mechanism; characterized by moderate hypersecretion of aldosterone and suppressed plasma renin activity rapidly reversed by administration of glucocorticoids; symptoms include hypertension and mild hypokalemia.

255.12 Conn's syndrome
DEF: A type of primary aldosteronism caused by an adenoma of the glomerulosa cells in the adrenal cortex; presence of hypertension.

255.13 Bartter's syndrome
DEF: A cluster of symptoms caused by a defect in the ability of the kidney to reabsorb potassium; signs include alkalosis (hypokalemic alkalosis), increased aldosterone, increased plasma renin, and normal blood pressure; symptoms include muscle cramping, weakness, constipation, frequency of urination, and failure to grow; also known as urinary potassium wasting or juxtaglomerular cell hyperplasia.

255.14 Other secondary aldosteronism

255.2 Adrenogenital disorders
Achard-Thiers syndrome
Adrenogenital syndromes, virilizing or feminizing, whether acquired or associated with congenital adrenal hyperplasia consequent on inborn enzyme defects in hormone synthesis
Congenital adrenal hyperplasia
Female adrenal pseudohermaphroditism
Male:
  macrogenitosomia praecox
  sexual precocity with adrenal hyperplasia
Virilization (female) (suprarenal)

> **EXCLUDES**   adrenal hyperplasia due to excess ACTH (255.0)
> isosexual virilization (256.4)

255.3 Other corticoadrenal overactivity   `CC`
Acquired benign adrenal androgenic overactivity
Overproduction of ACTH
CC Excl: 017.60-017.66, 017.90-017.96, 255.3-255.9, 259.5-259.9

255.4 Corticoadrenal insufficiency   `CC`
Addisonian crisis   Adrenal:
Addison's disease NOS   crisis
Adrenal: hemorrhage
  atrophy (autoimmune)   infarction
  calcification   insufficiency NOS

> **EXCLUDES**   tuberculous Addison's disease (017.6)

CC Excl: See code 255.3

DEF: Underproduction of adrenal hormones causing low blood pressure.

255.5 Other adrenal hypofunction   `CC`
Adrenal medullary insufficiency

> **EXCLUDES**   Waterhouse-Friderichsen syndrome (meningococcal) (036.3)

CC Excl: See code 255.3

255.6 Medulloadrenal hyperfunction   `CC`
Catecholamine secretion by pheochromocytoma
CC Excl: See code 255.3

255.8 Other specified disorders of adrenal glands
Abnormality of cortisol-binding globulin

255.9 Unspecified disorder of adrenal glands

✓4ᵗʰ **256 Ovarian dysfunction**
AHA: 4Q, '00, 51

256.0 Hyperestrogenism   ♀
DEF: Excess secretion of estrogen by the ovaries; characterized by ovaries containing multiple follicular cysts filled with serous fluid.

256.1 Other ovarian hyperfunction   ♀
Hypersecretion of ovarian androgens
AHA: 3Q, '95, 15

256.2 Postablative ovarian failure   ♀
Ovarian failure: Ovarian failure:
  iatrogenic   postsurgical
  postirradiation
Use additional code for states associated with artificial menopause (627.4)

> **EXCLUDES**   acquired absence of ovary (V45.77)
> asymptomatic age-related (natural) postmenopausal status (V49.81)

AHA: 2Q, '02, 12

DEF: Failed ovarian function after medical or surgical intervention.

✓5ᵗʰ **256.3 Other ovarian failure**
Use additional code for states associated with natural menopause (627.2)

> **EXCLUDES**   asymptomatic age-related (natural) postmenopausal status (V49.81)

AHA: 4Q, '01, 41

256.31 Premature menopause   `A` ♀
DEF: Permanent cessation of ovarian function before the age of 40 occuring naturally of unknown cause.

✓4ᵗʰ ✓5ᵗʰ Additional Digit Required   Nonspecific PDx   Unacceptable PDx   Manifestation Code   `MCV` Major Cardiovascular Condition   ▶◀ Revised Text   ● New Code   ▲ Revised Code Title

2007 ICD•9•CM   October 2006 • Volume 1 — 53

256.39 Other ovarian failure ♀
    Delayed menarche
    Ovarian hypofunction
    Primary ovarian failure NOS

256.4 Polycystic ovaries ♀
    Isosexual virilization   Stein-Leventhal syndrome
    DEF: Multiple serous filled cysts of ovary; symptoms of infertility, hirsutism, oligomenorrhea or amenorrhea.

256.8 Other ovarian dysfunction ♀

256.9 Unspecified ovarian dysfunction ♀

✓4th **257 Testicular dysfunction**

257.0 Testicular hyperfunction ♂
    Hypersecretion of testicular hormones

257.1 Postablative testicular hypofunction ♂
    Testicular hypofunction: Testicular hypofunction:
      iatrogenic   postsurgical
      postirradiation

257.2 Other testicular hypofunction
    Defective biosynthesis of testicular androgen
    Eunuchoidism:
      NOS
      hypogonadotropic
    Failure:
      Leydig's cell, adult
      seminiferous tubule, adult
    Testicular hypogonadism
      EXCLUDES   azoospermia (606.0)

257.8 Other testicular dysfunction
    EXCLUDES   androgen insensitivity syndrome (259.5)

257.9 Unspecified testicular dysfunction ♂

✓4th **258 Polyglandular dysfunction and related disorders**

258.0 Polyglandular activity in multiple endocrine adenomatosis CC
    Wermer's syndrome
    CC Excl: 240.0-259.9

    DEF: Wermer's syndrome: A rare hereditary condition characterized by the presence of adenomas or hyperplasia in more than one endocrine gland causing premature aging.

258.1 Other combinations of endocrine dysfunction CC
    Lloyd's syndrome
    Schmidt's syndrome
    CC Excl: See code 258.0

258.8 Other specified polyglandular dysfunction CC
    CC Excl: See code 258.0

258.9 Polyglandular dysfunction, unspecified CC
    CC Excl: See code 258.0

✓4th **259 Other endocrine disorders**

259.0 Delay in sexual development and puberty, not elsewhere classified
    Delayed puberty

259.1 Precocious sexual development and puberty, not elsewhere classified P
    Sexual precocity: Sexual precocity:
      NOS   cryptogenic
      constitutional   idiopathic

259.2 Carcinoid syndrome CC
    Hormone secretion by carcinoid tumors
    CC Excl: 259.2-259.3, 259.5-259.9

    DEF: Presence of carcinoid tumors that spread to liver; characterized by cyanotic flushing of skin, diarrhea, bronchospasm, acquired tricuspid and pulmonary stenosis, sudden drops in blood pressure, edema, ascites.

259.3 Ectopic hormone secretion, not elsewhere classified
    Ectopic:
      antidiuretic hormone secretion [ADH]
      hyperparathyroidism
      EXCLUDES   ectopic ACTH syndrome (255.0)
    AHA: N-D, '85, 4

259.4 Dwarfism, not elsewhere classified
    Dwarfism:
      NOS
      constitutional
      EXCLUDES   dwarfism:
           achondroplastic (756.4)
           intrauterine (759.7)
           nutritional (263.2)
           pituitary (253.3)
           renal (588.0)
           progeria (259.8)

259.5 Androgen insensitivity syndrome
    Partial androgen insensitivity
    Reifenstein syndrome
    AHA: ▶4Q, '05, 53◄

    DEF: ▶X chromosome abnormality that prohibits the body from recognizing androgen; XY genotype with ambiguous genitalia; also called testicular feminization.◄

259.8 Other specified endocrine disorders
    Pineal gland dysfunction   Werner's syndrome
    Progeria

259.9 Unspecified endocrine disorder
    Disturbance: Infantilism NOS
      endocrine NOS
      hormone NOS

NUTRITIONAL DEFICIENCIES (260-269)
    EXCLUDES   deficiency anemias (280.0-281.9)

260 Kwashiorkor CC
    Nutritional edema with dyspigmentation of skin and hair
    CC Excl: 260-263.9

    DEF: Syndrome, particularly of children; excessive carbohydrate with inadequate protein intake, inhibited growth potential, anomalies in skin and hair pigmentation, edema and liver disease.

261 Nutritional marasmus CC
    Nutritional atrophy
    Severe calorie deficiency
    Severe malnutrition NOS
    CC Excl: See code 260

    DEF: Protein-calorie malabsorption or malnutrition of children; characterized by tissue wasting, dehydration, and subcutaneous fat depletion; may occur with infectious disease; also called infantile atrophy.

262 Other severe, protein-calorie malnutrition CC
    Nutritional edema without mention of dyspigmentation of skin and hair
    CC Excl: See code 260
    AHA: 4Q, '92, 24; J-A, '85, 12

✓4th **263 Other and unspecified protein-calorie malnutrition**
    AHA: 4Q, '92, 24

263.0 Malnutrition of moderate degree CC
    CC Excl: See code 260
    AHA: J-A, '85, 1
    DEF: Malnutrition characterized by biochemical changes in electrolytes, lipids, blood plasma.

263.1 Malnutrition of mild degree CC
    CC Excl: See code 260
    AHA: J-A, '85, 1

263.2 Arrested development following protein-calorie malnutrition CC
    Nutritional dwarfism
    Physical retardation due to malnutrition
    CC Excl: See code 260

263.8 Other protein-calorie malnutrition CC
    CC Excl: See code 260

N Newborn Age: 0   P Pediatric Age: 0-17   M Maternity Age: 12-55   A Adult Age: 15-124   CC CC Condition   MC Major Complication   CD Complex Dx   HIV HIV Related Dx

263.9 Unspecified protein-calorie malnutrition `CC`
Dystrophy due to malnutrition
Malnutrition (calorie) NOS
> **EXCLUDES** *nutritional deficiency NOS (269.9)*

CC Excl: See code 260

AHA: 4Q, '03, 109; N-D, '84, 19

✓4th 264 Vitamin A deficiency

264.0 With conjunctival xerosis
DEF: Vitamin A deficiency with conjunctival dryness.

264.1 With conjunctival xerosis and Bitot's spot
Bitot's spot in the young child
DEF: Vitamin A deficiency with conjunctival dryness, superficial spots of keratinized epithelium.

264.2 With corneal xerosis
DEF: Vitamin A deficiency with corneal dryness.

264.3 With corneal ulceration and xerosis
DEF: Vitamin A deficiency with corneal dryness, epithelial ulceration.

264.4 With keratomalacia
DEF: Vitamin A deficiency creating corneal dryness; progresses to corneal insensitivity, softness, necrosis; usually bilateral.

264.5 With night blindness
DEF: Vitamin A deficiency causing vision failure in dim light.

264.6 With xerophthalmic scars of cornea
DEF: Vitamin A deficiency with corneal scars from dryness.

264.7 Other ocular manifestations of vitamin A deficiency
Xerophthalmia due to vitamin A deficiency

264.8 Other manifestations of vitamin A deficiency
Follicular keratosis } due to vitamin A
Xeroderma } deficiency

264.9 Unspecified vitamin A deficiency
Hypovitaminosis A NOS

✓4th 265 Thiamine and niacin deficiency states

265.0 Beriberi
DEF: Inadequate vitamin B_1 (thiamine) intake, affects heart and peripheral nerves; individual may become edematous and develop cardiac disease due to the excess fluid; alcoholics and people with a diet of excessive polished rice prone to the disease.

265.1 Other and unspecified manifestations of thiamine deficiency
Other vitamin B_1 deficiency states

265.2 Pellagra

Deficiency:	Deficiency:
niacin (-tryptophan)	vitamin PP
nicotinamide	Pellagra (alcoholic)
nicotinic acid	

DEF: Niacin deficiency causing dermatitis, inflammation of mucous membranes, diarrhea, and psychic disturbances.

✓4th 266 Deficiency of B-complex components

266.0 Ariboflavinosis
Riboflavin [vitamin B_2] deficiency

AHA: S-O, '86, 10

DEF: Vitamin B_2 (riboflavin) deficiency marked by swollen lips and tongue fissures, corneal vascularization, scaling lesions, and anemia.

266.1 Vitamin B_6 deficiency

Deficiency:	Deficiency:
pyridoxal	pyridoxine
pyridoxamine	Vitamin B_6 deficiency syndrome

> **EXCLUDES** *vitamin B_6-responsive sideroblastic anemia (285.0)*

DEF: Vitamin B_6 deficiency causing skin, lip, and tongue disturbances, peripheral neuropathy; and convulsions in infants.

266.2 Other B-complex deficiencies

Deficiency:	Deficiency:
cyanocobalamin	vitamin B_{12}
folic acid	

> **EXCLUDES** *combined system disease with anemia (281.0-281.1)*
> *deficiency anemias (281.0-281.9)*
> *subacute degeneration of spinal cord with anemia (281.0-281.1)*

266.9 Unspecified vitamin B deficiency

267 Ascorbic acid deficiency
Deficiency of vitamin C
Scurvy
> **EXCLUDES** *scorbutic anemia (281.8)*

DEF: Vitamin C deficiency causing swollen gums, myalgia, weight loss, and weakness.

✓4th 268 Vitamin D deficiency
> **EXCLUDES** *vitamin D-resistant:*
> *osteomalacia (275.3)*
> *rickets (275.3)*

268.0 Rickets, active
> **EXCLUDES** *celiac rickets (579.0)*
> *renal rickets (588.0)*

DEF: Inadequate vitamin D intake, usually in pediatrics, that affects bones most involved with muscular action; may cause nodules on ends and sides of bones; delayed closure of fontanels in infants; symptoms may include muscle soreness, and profuse sweating.

268.1 Rickets, late effect
Any condition specified as due to rickets and stated to be a late effect or sequela of rickets
Use additional code to identify the nature of late effect
DEF: Distorted or demineralized bones as a result of vitamin D deficiency.

268.2 Osteomalacia, unspecified
DEF: Softening of bones due to decrease in calcium; marked by pain, tenderness, muscular weakness, anorexia, and weight loss.

268.9 Unspecified vitamin D deficiency
Avitaminosis D

✓4th 269 Other nutritional deficiencies

269.0 Deficiency of vitamin K `CC`
> **EXCLUDES** *deficiency of coagulation factor due to vitamin K deficiency (286.7)*
> *vitamin K deficiency of newborn (776.0)*

CC Excl: 269.0

269.1 Deficiency of other vitamins

Deficiency:	Deficiency:
vitamin E	vitamin P

269.2 Unspecified vitamin deficiency
Multiple vitamin deficiency NOS

269.3 Mineral deficiency, not elsewhere classified

Deficiency:	Deficiency:
calcium, dietary	iodine

> **EXCLUDES** *deficiency:*
> *calcium NOS (275.4)*
> *potassium (276.8)*
> *sodium (276.1)*

269.8 Other nutritional deficiency
> **EXCLUDES** *adult failure to thrive (783.7)*
> *failure to thrive in childhood (783.41)*
> *feeding problems (783.3)*
> *newborn (779.3)*

269.9 Unspecified nutritional deficiency

✓4th ✓5th Additional Digit Required   Nonspecific PDx   Unacceptable PDx   Manifestation Code   **MCV** Major Cardiovascular Condition   ▶◀ Revised Text   ● New Code   ▲ Revised Code Title

2007 ICD•9•CM   Volume 1 — 55

Endocrine, Nutritional and Metabolic, Immunity

270–272.0

OTHER METABOLIC AND IMMUNITY DISORDERS (270-279)

Use additional code to identify any associated mental retardation

✓4ᵗʰ 270 Disorders of amino-acid transport and metabolism

> **EXCLUDES**   *abnormal findings without manifest disease (790.0-796.9)*
> *disorders of purine and pyrimidine metabolism (277.1-277.2)*
> *gout (274.0-274.9)*

270.0 Disturbances of amino-acid transport

Cystinosis   Glycinuria (renal)
Cystinuria   Hartnup disease
Fanconi (-de Toni) (-Debré) syndrome

270.1 Phenylketonuria [PKU]

Hyperphenylalaninemia

DEF: Inherited metabolic condition causing excess phenylpyruvic and other acids in urine; results in mental retardation, neurological manifestations, including spasticity and tremors, light pigmentation, eczema, and mousy odor.

270.2 Other disturbances of aromatic amino-acid metabolism

Albinism   Hypertyrosinemia
Alkaptonuria   Indicanuria
Alkaptonuric ochronosis   Kynureninase defects
Disturbances of metabolism   Oasthouse urine disease
    of tyrosine and   Ochronosis
    tryptophan   Tyrosinosis
Homogentisic acid defects   Tyrosinuria
Hydroxykynureninuria   Waardenburg syndrome

> **EXCLUDES**   *vitamin B₆-deficiency syndrome (266.1)*

AHA: 3Q, '99, 20

270.3 Disturbances of branched-chain amino-acid metabolism

Disturbances of metabolism of leucine, isoleucine, and valine
Hypervalinemia
Intermittent branched-chain ketonuria
Leucine-induced hypoglycemia
Leucinosis
Maple syrup urine disease

AHA: 3Q, '00, 8

270.4 Disturbances of sulphur-bearing amino-acid metabolism

Cystathioninemia
Cystathioninuria
Disturbances of metabolism of methionine, homocystine, and cystathionine
Homocystinuria
Hypermethioninemia
Methioninemia

AHA: 1Q, '04, 6

270.5 Disturbances of histidine metabolism

Carnosinemia   Hyperhistidinemia
Histidinemia   Imidazole aminoaciduria

270.6 Disorders of urea cycle metabolism

Argininosuccinic aciduria
Citrullinemia
Disturbances of metabolism of ornithine, citrulline, argininosuccinic acid, arginine, and ammonia
Hyperammonemia
Hyperornithinemia

270.7 Other disturbances of straight-chain amino-acid metabolism

Glucoglycinuria
Glycinemia (with methyl-malonic acidemia)
Hyperglycinemia
Hyperlysinemia
Other disturbances of metabolism of glycine, threonine, serine, glutamine, and lysine
Pipecolic acidemia
Saccharopinuria

AHA: 3Q, '00, 8

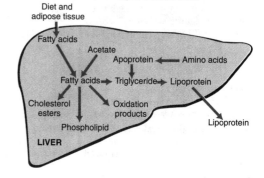

Lipid Metabolism

270.8 Other specified disorders of amino-acid metabolism

Alaninemia   Iminoacidopathy
Ethanolaminuria   Prolinemia
Glycoprolinuria   Prolinuria
Hydroxyprolinemia   Sarcosinemia
Hyperprolinemia

270.9 Unspecified disorder of amino-acid metabolism

✓4ᵗʰ 271 Disorders of carbohydrate transport and metabolism

> **EXCLUDES**   *abnormality of secretion of glucagon (251.4)*
> *diabetes mellitus (250.0-250.9)*
> *hypoglycemia NOS (251.2)*
> *mucopolysaccharidosis (277.5)*

271.0 Glycogenosis

Amylopectinosis
Glucose-6-phosphatase deficiency
Glycogen storage disease
McArdle's disease
Pompe's disease
von Gierke's disease

AHA: 1Q, '98, 5

271.1 Galactosemia

Galactose-1-phosphate uridyl transferase deficiency
Galactosuria

DEF: Any of three genetic disorders due to defective galactose metabolism; symptoms include failure to thrive in infancy, jaundice, liver and spleen damage, cataracts, and mental retardation.

271.2 Hereditary fructose intolerance

Essential benign fructosuria   Fructosemia

DEF: Chromosome recessive disorder of carbohydrate metabolism; in infants, occurs after dietary sugar introduced; characterized by enlarged spleen, yellowish cast to skin, and progressive inability to thrive.

271.3 Intestinal disaccharidase deficiencies and disaccharide malabsorption

Intolerance or malabsorption (congenital) (of):
    glucose-galactose
    lactose
    sucrose-isomaltose

271.4 Renal glycosuria

Renal diabetes

DEF: Persistent abnormal levels of glucose in urine, with normal blood glucose levels; caused by failure of the renal tubules to reabsorb glucose.

271.8 Other specified disorders of carbohydrate transport and metabolism

Essential benign pentosuria   Mannosidosis
Fucosidosis   Oxalosis
Glycolic aciduria   Xylosuria
Hyperoxaluria (primary)   Xylulosuria

271.9 Unspecified disorder of carbohydrate transport and metabolism

✓4ᵗʰ 272 Disorders of lipoid metabolism

> **EXCLUDES**   *localized cerebral lipidoses (330.1)*

272.0 Pure hypercholesterolemia

Familial hypercholesterolemia
Fredrickson Type IIa hyperlipoproteinemia
Hyperbetalipoproteinemia
Hyperlipidemia, Group A
Low-density-lipoid-type [LDL] hyperlipoproteinemia

AHA: ▶4Q, '05, 71◀

Ⓝ Newborn Age: 0   Ⓟ Pediatric Age: 0-17   Ⓜ Maternity Age: 12-55   Ⓐ Adult Age: 15-124   **CC** CC Condition   **MC** Major Complication   **CD** Complex Dx   **HIV** HIV Related Dx

56 — Volume 1 • February 2006   *2007 ICD•9•CM*

272.1 Pure hyperglyceridemia
Endogenous hyperglyceridemia
Fredrickson Type IV hyperlipoproteinemia
Hyperlipidemia, Group B
Hyperprebetalipoproteinemia
Hypertriglyceridemia, essential
Very-low-density-lipoid-type [VLDL]
hyperlipoproteinemia

272.2 Mixed hyperlipidemia
Broad- or floating-betalipoproteinemia
Fredrickson Type IIb or III hyperlipoproteinemia
Hypercholesterolemia with endogenous
hyperglyceridemia
Hyperbetalipoproteinemia with
prebetalipoproteinemia
Tubo-eruptive xanthoma
Xanthoma tuberosum
DEF: Elevated levels of lipoprotein, a complex of fats and proteins, in blood due to inherited metabolic disorder.

272.3 Hyperchylomicronemia
Bürger-Grütz syndrome
Fredrickson type I or V hyperlipoproteinemia
Hyperlipidemia, Group D
Mixed hyperglyceridemia

272.4 Other and unspecified hyperlipidemia
Alpha-lipoproteinemia
Combined hyperlipidemia
Hyperlipidemia NOS
Hyperlipoproteinemia NOS
AHA: 1Q, '05, 17

DEF: Hyperlipoproteinemia: elevated levels of transient chylomicrons in the blood which are a form of lipoproteins which transport dietary cholesterol and triglycerides from the small intestine to the blood.

272.5 Lipoprotein deficiencies
Abetalipoproteinemia
Bassen-Kornzweig syndrome
High-density lipoid deficiency
Hypoalphalipoproteinemia
Hypobetalipoproteinemia (familial)
DEF: Abnormally low levels of lipoprotein, a complex of fats and protein, in the blood.

272.6 Lipodystrophy
Barraquer-Simons disease
Progressive lipodystrophy
Use additional E code to identify cause, if iatrogenic
EXCLUDES intestinal lipodystrophy (040.2)
DEF: Disturbance of fat metabolism resulting in loss of fatty tissue in some areas of the body.

272.7 Lipidoses
Chemically-induced lipidosis
Disease:
Anderson's
Fabry's
Gaucher's
I cell [mucolipidosis I]
lipoid storage NOS
Niemann-Pick
pseudo-Hurler's or mucolipdosis III
triglyceride storage, Type I or II
Wolman's or triglyceride storage, Type III
Mucolipidosis II
Primary familial xanthomatosis
EXCLUDES cerebral lipidoses (330.1)
Tay-Sachs disease (330.1)
DEF: Lysosomal storage diseases marked by an abnormal amount of lipids in reticuloendothelial cells.

272.8 Other disorders of lipoid metabolism
Hoffa's disease or liposynovitis prepatellaris
Launois-Bensaude's lipomatosis
Lipoid dermatoarthritis

272.9 Unspecified disorder of lipoid metabolism

√4ᵗʰ **273 Disorders of plasma protein metabolism**
EXCLUDES agammaglobulinemia and
hypogammaglobulinemia (279.0-279.2)
coagulation defects (286.0-286.9)
hereditary hemolytic anemias (282.0-282.9)

273.0 Polyclonal hypergammaglobulinemia
Hypergammaglobulinemic purpura:
benign primary
Waldenström's
DEF: Elevated blood levels of gamma globulins, frequently found in patients with chronic infectious diseases.

273.1 Monoclonal paraproteinemia
Benign monoclonal hypergammaglobulinemia [BMH]
Monoclonal gammopathy:
NOS
associated with lymphoplasmacytic dyscrasias
benign
Paraproteinemia:
benign (familial)
secondary to malignant or inflammatory disease

273.2 Other paraproteinemias
Cryoglobulinemic: Mixed cryoglobulinemia
purpura
vasculitis

273.3 Macroglobulinemia   CC
Macroglobulinemia (idiopathic) (primary)
Waldenström's macroglobulinemia
CC Excl: 273.0-273.3, 273.8-273.9

DEF: Elevated blood levels of macroglobulins (plasma globulins of high weight); characterized by malignant neoplasms of bone marrow, spleen, liver, or lymph nodes; symptoms include weakness, fatigue, bleeding disorders, and vision problems.

273.4 Alpha-1-antitrypsin deficiency
AAT deficiency
DEF: Disorder of plasma protein metabolism that results in a deficiency of Alpha-1-antitrypsin, an acute-phase reactive protein, released into the blood in response to infection or injury to protect tissue against the harmful effect of enzymes.

273.8 Other disorders of plasma protein metabolism
Abnormality of transport protein
Bisalbuminemia
AHA: 2Q, '98, 11

273.9 Unspecified disorder of plasma protein metabolism

√4ᵗʰ **274 Gout**
EXCLUDES lead gout (984.0-984.9)
AHA: 2Q, '95, 4

DEF: Purine and pyrimidine metabolic disorders; manifested by hyperuricemia and recurrent acute inflammatory arthritis; monosodium urate or monohydrate crystals may be deposited in and around the joints, leading to joint destruction, and severe crippling.

274.0 Gouty arthropathy

√5ᵗʰ **274.1 Gouty nephropathy**
274.10 Gouty nephropathy, unspecified
AHA: N-D, '85, 15

274.11 Uric acid nephrolithiasis
DEF: Sodium urate stones in the kidney.

274.19 Other

√5ᵗʰ **274.8 Gout with other specified manifestations**
274.81 Gouty tophi of ear
DEF: Chalky sodium urate deposit in the ear due to gout; produces chronic inflammation of external ear.

274.82 Gouty tophi of other sites
Gouty tophi of heart

274.89 Other
Use additional code to identify
manifestations, as:
gouty:
iritis (364.11)
neuritis (357.4)

274.9 Gout, unspecified

√4ᵗʰ **275 Disorders of mineral metabolism**
EXCLUDES abnormal findings without manifest disease
(790.0-796.9)

√4ᵗʰ √5ᵗʰ Additional Digit Required   Nonspecific PDx   Unacceptable PDx   Manifestation Code   MCV Major Cardiovascular Condition   ▶◀ Revised Text   ● New Code   ▲ Revised Code Title

2007 ICD•9•CM   Volume 1 — 57

Endocrine, Nutritional and Metabolic, Immunity

275.0–276.9

275.0 Disorders of iron metabolism

Bronzed diabetes   Pigmentary cirrhosis (of liver)
Hemochromatosis

EXCLUDES   anemia:
      iron deficiency (280.0-280.9)
      sideroblastic (285.0)

AHA: 2Q, '97, 11

275.1 Disorders of copper metabolism

Hepatolenticular degeneration
Wilson's disease

275.2 Disorders of magnesium metabolism

Hypermagnesemia   Hypomagnesemia

275.3 Disorders of phosphorus metabolism

Familial hypophosphatemia   Vitamin D-resistant:
Hypophosphatasia   osteomalacia
                          rickets

✓5ᵗʰ 275.4 Disorders of calcium metabolism

EXCLUDES   parathyroid disorders (252.00-252.9)
      vitamin D deficiency (268.0-268.9)

AHA: 4Q, '97, 33

275.40 Unspecified disorder of calcium metabolism

275.41 Hypocalcemia

DEF: Abnormally decreased blood calcium level; symptoms include hyperactive deep tendon reflexes, muscle, abdominal cramps, and carpopedal spasm.

275.42 Hypercalcemia

AHA: 4Q, '03, 110

DEF: Abnormally increased blood calcium level; symptoms include muscle weakness, fatigue, nausea, depression, and constipation.

275.49 Other disorders of calcium metabolism

Nephrocalcinosis
Pseudohypoparathyroidism
Pseudopseudohypoparathyroidism

DEF: Nephrocalcinosis: calcium phosphate deposits in the tubules of the kidney with resultant renal insufficiency.

DEF: Pseudohypoparathyroidism: inherited disorder with signs and symptoms of hypoparathyroidism; caused by inadequate response to parathyroid hormone, not hormonal deficiency. Symptoms include muscle cramps, tetany, urinary frequency, blurred vision due to cataracts, and dry scaly skin.

DEF: Pseudopseudohypoparathyroidism: clinical manifestations of hypoparathyroidism without affecting blood calcium levels.

275.8 Other specified disorders of mineral metabolism

275.9 Unspecified disorder of mineral metabolism

✓4ᵗʰ 276 Disorders of fluid, electrolyte, and acid-base balance

EXCLUDES   diabetes insipidus (253.5)
      familial periodic paralysis (359.3)

276.0 Hyperosmolality and/or hypernatremia   CC

Sodium [Na] excess   Sodium [Na] overload

CC Excl: 276.0-276.9

276.1 Hyposmolality and/or hyponatremia   CC

Sodium [Na] deficiency

CC Excl: See code 276.0

DRG 296

276.2 Acidosis   CC

Acidosis: Acidosis:
   NOS   metabolic
   lactic   respiratory

EXCLUDES   diabetic acidosis (250.1)

CC Excl: See code 276.0

AHA: J-F, '87, 15

DEF: Disorder involves decrease of pH (hydrogen ion) concentration in blood and cellular tissues; caused by increase in acid and decrease in bicarbonate.

276.3 Alkalosis   CC

Alkalosis: Alkalosis:
   NOS   respiratory
   metabolic

CC Excl: See code 276.0

DEF: Accumulation of base (non-acid part of salt), or loss of acid without relative loss of base in body fluids; caused by increased arterial plasma bicarbonate concentration or loss of carbon dioxide due to hyperventilation.

276.4 Mixed acid-base balance disorder   CC

Hypercapnia with mixed acid-base disorder

CC Excl: See code 276.0

✓5ᵗʰ 276.5 Volume depletion

EXCLUDES   hypovolemic shock:
      postoperative (998.0)
      traumatic (958.4)

AHA: ▶4Q, '05, 54; 2Q, '05, 9;◀ ◀1Q, '03, 5, 22; 3Q, '02, 21; 4Q, '97, 30; 2Q, '88, 9

276.50 Volume depletion, unspecified   CC

CC Excl: See code 276.0

DEF: ▶Depletion of total body water (dehydration) and/or contraction of total intravascular plasma (hypovolemia).◀

276.51 Dehydration   CC

CC Excl: See code 276.0

DEF: ▶Depletion of total body water; blood volume may be normal while fluid is pulled from other tissues.◀

276.52 Hypovolemia   CC

Depletion of volume of plasma

CC Excl: See code 276.0

DRG 296

DEF: ▶Depletion of volume plasma; depletion of total blood volume.◀

276.6 Fluid overload   CC

Fluid retention

EXCLUDES   ascites (789.5)
      localized edema (782.3)

CC Excl: See code 276.0

276.7 Hyperpotassemia   CC

Hyperkalemia   Potassium [K]:
Potassium [K]:   intoxication
   excess   overload

CC Excl: See code 276.0

AHA: 1Q, '05, 9; 2Q,'01, 12

DRG 296

DEF: Elevated blood levels of potassium; symptoms include abnormal EKG readings, weakness; related to defective renal excretion.

276.8 Hypopotassemia

Hypokalemia   Potassium [K] deficiency

DEF: Decreased blood levels of potassium; symptoms include neuromuscular disorders.

276.9 Electrolyte and fluid disorders not elsewhere classified   CC

Electrolyte imbalance   Hypochloremia
Hyperchloremia

EXCLUDES   electrolyte imbalance:
      associated with hyperemesis
        gravidarum (643.1)
      complicating labor and delivery
        (669.0)
      following abortion and ectopic or
        molar pregnancy (634-638
        with .4, 639.4)

CC Excl: See code 276.0

AHA: J-F, '87, 15

N Newborn Age: 0   P Pediatric Age: 0-17   M Maternity Age: 12-55   A Adult Age: 15-124   CC CC Condition   MC Major Complication   CD Complex Dx   HIV HIV Related Dx

√4ᵗʰ 277 Other and unspecified disorders of metabolism

√5ᵗʰ 277.0 Cystic fibrosis
Fibrocystic disease of the pancreas
Mucoviscidosis

AHA: 4Q, '90, 16; 3Q, '90, 18

DEF: Generalized, genetic disorder of infants, children, and young adults marked by exocrine gland dysfunction; characterized by chronic pulmonary disease with excess mucus production, pancreatic deficiency, high levels of electrolytes in the sweat.

277.00 Without mention of meconium ileus `CC`
Cystic fibrosis NOS

CC Excl: 277.00-277.09

AHA: 2Q, '03, 12

277.01 With meconium ileus `CC` `N`
Meconium:
   ileus (of newborn)
   obstruction of intestine in mucoviscidosis

CC Excl: See code 277.00

277.02 With pulmonary manifestations `CC`
Cystic fibrosis with pulmonary exacerbation
Use additional code to identify any
   infectious organism present, such as:
     pseudomonas (041.7)

CC Excl: See code 277.00

277.03 With gastrointestinal manifestations `CC`
EXCLUDES *with meconium ileus (277.01)*

CC Excl: See code 277.00

AHA: 4Q, '02, 45

277.09 With other manifestations `CC`

CC Excl: See code 277.00

277.1 Disorders of porphyrin metabolism

Hematoporphyria	Porphyrinuria
Hematoporphyrinuria	Protocoproporphyria
Hereditary coproporphyria	Protoporphyria
Porphyria	Pyrroloporphyria

277.2 Other disorders of purine and pyrimidine metabolism
Hypoxanthine-guanine-phosphoribosyltransferase
   deficiency [HG-PRT deficiency]
Lesch-Nyhan syndrome
Xanthinuria
EXCLUDES *gout (274.0-274.9)*
orotic aciduric anemia (281.4)

√5ᵗʰ 277.3 Amyloidosis

AHA: 1Q, '96, 16

DEF: Conditions of diverse etiologies characterized by the accumulation of insoluble fibrillar proteins (amyloid) in various organs and tissues of the body, compromising vital functions.

277.30 Amyloidosis, unspecified
Amyloidosis NOS

277.31 Familial Mediterranean fever
Benign paroxysmal peritonitis
Hereditary amyloid nephropathy
Periodic familial polyserositis
Recurrent polyserositis

277.39 Other amyloidosis
Hereditary cardiac amyloidosis
Inherited systemic amyloidosis
Neuropathic (Portuguese) (Swiss)
   amyloidosis
Secondary amyloidosis

277.4 Disorders of bilirubin excretion

Hyperbilirubinemia:	Syndrome:
congenital	Dubin-Johnson
constitutional	Gilbert's
Syndrome:	Rotor's
Crigler-Najjar	

EXCLUDES *hyperbilirubinemias specific to the*
perinatal period (774.0-774.7)

277.5 Mucopolysaccharidosis

Gargoylism	Morquio-Brailsford disease
Hunter's syndrome	Osteochondrodystrophy
Hurler's syndrome	Sanfilippo's syndrome
Lipochondrodystrophy	Scheie's syndrome
Maroteaux-Lamy syndrome	

DEF: Metabolism disorders evidenced by excretion of various mucopolysaccharides in urine and infiltration of these substances into connective tissue, with resulting various defects of bone, cartilage and connective tissue.

277.6 Other deficiencies of circulating enzymes
Hereditary angioedema

277.7 Dysmetabolic syndrome X
Use additional code for associated manifestation,
   such as:
   cardiovascular disease (414.00-414.07)
   obesity (278.00-278.01)

AHA: 4Q, '01, 42

DEF: A specific group of metabolic disorders that are related to the state of insulin resistance (decreased cellular response to insulin) without elevated blood sugars; often related to elevated cholesterol and triglycerides, obesity, cardiovascular disease, and high blood pressure.

√5ᵗʰ 277.8 Other specified disorders of metabolism

AHA: 4Q, '03, 50; 2Q, '01, 18; S-O, '87, 9

277.81 Primary carnitine deficiency

277.82 Carnitine deficiency due to inborn errors of metabolism

277.83 Iatrogenic carnitine deficiency
Carnitine deficiency due to:
   hemodialysis
   valproic acid therapy

277.84 Other secondary carnitine deficiency

277.85 Disorders of fatty acid oxidation
Carnitine palmitoyltransferase deficiencies
   (CPT1, CPT2)
Glutaric aciduria type II (type IIA, IIB, IIC)
Long chain 3-hydroxyacyl CoA
   dehydrogenase deficiency (LCHAD)
Long chain/very long chain acyl CoA dehy-
   drogenase deficiency (LCAD, VLCAD)
Medium chain acyl CoA dehydrogenase
   deficiency (MCAD)
Short chain acyl CoA dehydrogenase
   deficiency (SCAD)
EXCLUDES *primary carnitine deficiency*
(277.81)

277.86 Peroxisomal disorders
Adrenomyeloneuropathy
Neonatal adrenoleukodystrophy
Rhizomelic chrondrodysplasia punctata
X-linked adrenoleukodystrophy
Zellweger syndrome
EXCLUDES *infantile Refsum disease*
(356.3)

277.87 Disorders of mitochondrial metabolism
Kearns-Sayre syndrome
Mitochondrial Encephalopathy, Lactic
   Acidosis and Stroke-like episodes
   (MELAS syndrome)
Mitochondrial Neurogastrointestinal
   Encephalopathy syndrome (MNGIE)
Myoclonus with Epilepsy and with Ragged
   Red Fibers (MERRF syndrome)
Neuropathy, Ataxia and Retinitis
   Pigmentosa (NARP syndrome)
Use additional code for associated conditions
EXCLUDES *disorders of pyruvate*
metabolism (271.8)
Leber's optic atrophy (377.16)
Leigh's subacute necrotizing
encephalopathy (330.8)
Reye's syndrome (331.81)

AHA: 4Q, '04, 62

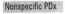

√4ᵗʰ / √5ᵗʰ Additional Digit Required   Nonspecific PDx   Unacceptable PDx   Manifestation Code   `MCV` Major Cardiovascular Condition   ◄► Revised Text   ● New Code   ▲ Revised Code Title

2007 ICD•9•CM   **October 2006 • Volume 1 — 59**

Endocrine, Nutritional and Metabolic, Immunity

277.89–279.9

277.89 Other specified disorders of metabolism
Hand-Schüller-Christian disease
Histiocytosis (acute) (chronic)
Histiocytosis X (chronic)
EXCLUDES   *histiocytosis:*
acute differentiated
progressive (202.5)
X, acute (progressive) (202.5)

277.9   Unspecified disorder of metabolism
Enzymopathy NOS

√4ᵗʰ 278 Overweight, obesity and other hyperalimentation
EXCLUDES   *hyperalimentation NOS (783.6)*
poisoning by vitamins NOS (963.5)
polyphagia (783.6)

√5ᵗʰ 278.0   Overweight and obesity
Use additional code to identify Body Mass Index (BMI),
if known ▶(V85.0-V85.54)◀
EXCLUDES   *adiposogenital dystrophy (253.8)*
obesity of endocrine origin NOS (259.9)
AHA: 4Q, '05, 97

     278.00 Obesity, unspecified
Obesity NOS
AHA: 4Q, '01, 42; 1Q, '99, 5, 6

     278.01 Morbid obesity
Severe obesity
AHA: 3Q, '03, 6-8
DEF: Increased weight beyond limits of skeletal and
physical requirements (125 percent or more over ideal
body weight), as a result of excess fat in subcutaneous
connective tissues.
DEF: BMI (body mass index) between 30.0 and 39.9.

     278.02 Overweight
AHA: 4Q, '05, 55
DEF: BMI (body mass index) between 25 and 29.9.

   278.1   Localized adiposity
Fat pad

   278.2   Hypervitaminosis A

   278.3   Hypercarotinemia
DEF: Elevated blood carotene level due to ingesting excess
carotenoids or the inability to convert carotenoids to vitamin A.

   278.4   Hypervitaminosis D
DEF: Weakness, fatigue, loss of weight, and other symptoms
resulting from ingesting excessive amounts of vitamin D.

   278.8   Other hyperalimentation

√4ᵗʰ 279 Disorders involving the immune mechanism

√5ᵗʰ 279.0   Deficiency of humoral immunity
DEF: Inadequate immune response to bacterial infections with
potential reinfection by viruses due to lack of circulating
immunoglobulins (acquired antibodies).

     279.00 Hypogammaglobulinemia, unspecified
Agammaglobulinemia NOS

     279.01 Selective IgA immunodeficiency

     279.02 Selective IgM immunodeficiency   [CC]
CC Excl: 279.02-279.9

     279.03 Other selective immunoglobulin   [CC]
deficiencies
Selective deficiency of IgG
CC Excl: See code 279.02

     279.04 Congenital hypogammaglobulinemia   [CC]
Agammaglobulinemia:
Bruton's type
X-linked
CC Excl: See code 279.02

     279.05 Immunodeficiency with increased IgM   [CC]
Immunodeficiency with hyper-IgM:
autosomal recessive
X-linked
CC Excl: See code 279.02

     279.06 Common variable immunodeficiency   [CC]
Dysgammaglobulinemia (acquired)
(congenital) (primary)
Hypogammaglobulinemia:
acquired primary
congenital non-sex-linked
sporadic
CC Excl: See code 279.02

     279.09 Other   [CC]
Transient hypogammaglobulinemia of infancy
CC Excl: See code 279.02

√5ᵗʰ 279.1   Deficiency of cell-mediated immunity

     279.10 Immunodeficiency with predominant   [CC]
T-cell defect, unspecified
CC Excl: See code 279.02
AHA: S-O, '87, 10

     279.11 DiGeorge's syndrome   [CC]
Pharyngeal pouch syndrome
Thymic hypoplasia
CC Excl: See code 279.02

DEF: Congenital disorder due to defective development of
the third and fourth pharyngeal pouches; results in
hypoplasia or aplasia of the thymus, parathyroid glands;
related to congenital heart defects, anomalies of the
great vessels, esophageal atresia, and abnormalities of
facial structures.

     279.12 Wiskott-Aldrich syndrome   [CC]
CC Excl: See code 279.02

DEF: A disease characterized by chronic conditions, such
as eczema, suppurative otitis media and anemia; it
results from an X-linked recessive gene and is classified
as an immune deficiency syndrome.

     279.13 Nezelof's syndrome   [CC]
Cellular immunodeficiency with abnormal
immunoglobulin deficiency
CC Excl: See code 279.02

DEF: Immune system disorder characterized by a pathological deficiency in cellular immunity and humoral antibodies resulting in inability to fight infectious diseases.

     279.19 Other   [CC]
EXCLUDES   *ataxia-telangiectasia (334.8)*
CC Excl: See code 279.02

   279.2   Combined immunity deficiency   [CC]
Agammaglobulinemia:
autosomal recessive
Swiss-type
x-linked recessive
Severe combined immunodeficiency [SCID]
Thymic:
alymophoplasia
aplasia or dysplasia with immunodeficiency
EXCLUDES   *thymic hypoplasia (279.11)*
CC Excl: See code 279.02

DEF: Agammaglobulinemia: No immunoglobulins in the blood.
DEF: Thymic alymphoplasia: Severe combined immunodeficiency;
result of failed lymphoid tissue development.

   279.3   Unspecified immunity deficiency   [CC]
CC Excl: See code 279.02

   279.4   Autoimmune disease, not elsewhere classified   [CC]
Autoimmune disease NOS
EXCLUDES   *transplant failure or rejection (996.80-*
996.89)
CC Excl: See code 279.02

   279.8   Other specified disorders involving the immune   [CC]
mechanism
Single complement [C_1-C_9] deficiency or dysfunction
CC Excl: See code 279.02

   279.9   Unspecified disorder of immune mechanism   [CC]
CC Excl: See code 279.02
AHA: 3Q, '92, 13

[N] Newborn Age: 0   [P] Pediatric Age: 0-17   [M] Maternity Age: 12-55   [A] Adult Age: 15-124   [CC] CC Condition   [MC] Major Complication   [CD] Complex Dx   [HIV] HIV Related Dx

4. DISEASES OF THE BLOOD AND BLOOD-FORMING ORGANS (280-289)

EXCLUDES *anemia complicating pregnancy or the puerperium (648.2)*

✓4th 280 Iron deficiency anemias

INCLUDES anemia:
asiderotic
hypochromic-microcytic
sideropenic

EXCLUDES *familial microcytic anemia (282.49)*

280.0 Secondary to blood loss (chronic) cc
Normocytic anemia due to blood loss
EXCLUDES *acute posthemorrhagic anemia (285.1)*
CC Excl: 280.0-285.9, 289.81-289.9, 517.3
AHA: 4Q, '93, 34

280.1 Secondary to inadequate dietary iron intake

280.8 Other specified iron deficiency anemias
Paterson-Kelly syndrome
Plummer-Vinson syndrome
Sideropenic dysphagia

280.9 Iron deficiency anemia, unspecified
Anemia:
achlorhydric
chlorotic
idiopathic hypochromic
iron [Fe] deficiency NOS

✓4th 281 Other deficiency anemias

281.0 Pernicious anemia
Anemia:
Addison's
Biermer's
congenital pernicious
Congenital intrinsic factor [Castle's] deficiency
EXCLUDES *combined system disease without mention of anemia (266.2)*
subacute degeneration of spinal cord without mention of anemia (266.2)
AHA: N-D, '84, 1; S-O, '84, 16
DEF: Chronic progressive anemia due to Vitamin B12 malabsorption; caused by lack of a secretion known as intrinsic factor, which is produced by the gastric mucosa of the stomach.

281.1 Other vitamin B_{12} deficiency anemia
Anemia:
vegan's
vitamin B_{12} deficiency (dietary)
due to selective vitamin B_{12} malabsorption with proteinuria
Syndrome:
Imerslund's
Imerslund-Gräsbeck
EXCLUDES *combined system disease without mention of anemia (266.2)*
subacute degeneration of spinal cord without mention of anemia (266.2)

281.2 Folate-deficiency anemia
Congenital folate malabsorption
Folate or folic acid deficiency anemia:
NOS
dietary
drug-induced
Goat's milk anemia
Nutritional megaloblastic anemia (of infancy)
Use additional E code to identify drug
DEF: Macrocytic anemia resembles pernicious anemia but without absence of hydrochloric acid secretions; responsive to folic acid therapy.

281.3 Other specified megaloblastic anemias not elsewhere classified
Combined B_{12} and folate-deficiency anemia
Refractory megaloblastic anemia
DEF: Megaloblasts predominant in bone marrow with few normoblasts; rare familial type associated with proteinuria and genitourinary tract anomalies.

281.4 Protein-deficiency anemia cc
Amino-acid-deficiency anemia
CC Excl: See code 280.0

281.8 Anemia associated with other specified nutritional deficiency cc
Scorbutic anemia
CC Excl: See code 280.0

281.9 Unspecified deficiency anemia
Anemia: Anemia:
dimorphic   nutritional NOS
macrocytic   simple chronic
megaloblastic NOS

✓4th 282 Hereditary hemolytic anemias
DEF: Escalated rate of erythrocyte destruction; similar to all anemias, occurs when imbalance exists between blood loss and blood production.

282.0 Hereditary spherocytosis
Acholuric (familial) jaundice
Congenital hemolytic anemia (spherocytic)
Congenital spherocytosis
Minkowski-Chauffard syndrome
Spherocytosis (familial)
EXCLUDES *hemolytic anemia of newborn (773.0-773.5)*
DEF: Hereditary, chronic illness marked by abnormal red blood cell membrane; symptoms include enlarged spleen, jaundice; and anemia in severe cases.

282.1 Hereditary elliptocytosis
Elliptocytosis (congenital)
Ovalocytosis (congenital) (hereditary)
DEF: Genetic hemolytic anemia characterized by malformed, elliptical erythrocytes; there is increased destruction of red cells with resulting anemia.

282.2 Anemias due to disorders of glutathione metabolism
Anemia:
6-phosphogluconic dehydrogenase deficiency
enzyme deficiency, drug-induced
erythrocytic glutathione deficiency
glucose-6-phosphate dehydrogenase [G-6-PD] deficiency
glutathione-reductase deficiency
hemolytic nonspherocytic (hereditary), type I
Disorder of pentose phosphate pathway
Favism

282.3 Other hemolytic anemias due to enzyme deficiency
Anemia:
hemolytic nonspherocytic (hereditary), type II
hexokinase deficiency
pyruvate kinase [PK] deficiency
triosephosphate isomerase deficiency

✓5th 282.4 Thalassemias
EXCLUDES *sickle-cell:*
disease (282.60-282.69)
trait (282.5)
AHA: 4Q, '03, 51
DEF: A group of inherited hemolytic disorders characterized by decreased production of at least one of the four polypeptide globin chains which results in defective hemoglobin synthesis; symptoms include severe anemia, expanded marrow spaces, transfusional and absorptive iron overload, impaired growth rate, thickened cranial bones, and pathologic fractures.

✓4th Additional Digit Required   Nonspecific PDx   Unacceptable PDx   Manifestation Code   MCV Major Cardiovascular Condition   ►◄ Revised Text   ● New Code   ▲ Revised Code Title

2007 ICD•9•CM   Volume 1 — 61

282.41　Sickle-cell thalassemia without crisis　`CC`
Sickle-cell thalassemia NOS
Thalassemia Hb-S disease without crisis
CC Excl: See code 280.0

282.42　Sickle-cell thalassemia with crisis　`CC`
Sickle-cell thalassemia with vaso-occlusive
pain
Thalassemia Hb-S disease with crisis
Use additional code for type of crisis, such as:
acute chest syndrome (517.3)
splenic sequestration (289.52)
CC Excl: See code 280.0

282.49　Other thalassemia　`CC`
Cooley's anemia
Hb-Bart's disease
Hereditary leptocytosis
Mediterranean anemia (with other
hemoglobinopathy)
Microdrepanocytosis
Thalassemia (alpha) (beta) (intermedia)
(major) (minima) (minor) (mixed) (trait)
(with other hemoglobinopathy)
Thalassemia NOS
CC Excl: See code 280.0

282.5　Sickle-cell trait
Hb-AS genotype　　　　Heterozygous:
Hemoglobin S [Hb-S] trait　　hemoglobin S
　　　　　　　　　　　　Hb-S
EXCLUDES　*that with other hemoglobinopathy
(282.60-282.69)*
that with thalassemia (282.49)
DEF: Heterozygous genetic makeup characterized by one gene for
normal hemoglobin and one for sickle-cell hemoglobin; clinical
disease rarely present.

√5ᵗʰ　282.6　Sickle-cell disease
Sickle-cell anemia
EXCLUDES　*sickle-cell thalassemia (282.41-282.42)*
sickle-cell trait (282.5)
DEF: Inherited blood disorder; sickle-shaped red blood cells are
hard and pointed, clogging blood flow; anemia characterized by,
periodic episodes of pain, acute abdominal discomfort, skin
ulcerations of the legs, increased infections; occurs primarily in
persons of African descent.

282.60　Sickle-cell disease, unspecified　`CC`
Sickle-cell anemia NOS
CC Excl: See code 280.0
AHA: 2Q, '97, 11

282.61　Hb-SS disease without crisis　`CC`
CC Excl: See code 280.0

282.62　Hb-SS disease with crisis　`CC`
Hb-SS disease with vaso-occlusive pain
Sickle-cell crisis NOS
Use additional code for type of crisis, such as:
acute chest syndrome (517.3)
splenic sequestration (289.52)
CC Excl: See code 280.0
AHA: 4Q, '03, 56; 2Q, '98, 8; 2Q, '91, 15

282.63　Sickle-cell/Hb-C disease without crisis　`CC`
Hb-S/Hb-C disease without crisis
CC Excl: See code 280.0

282.64　Sickle-cell/Hb-C disease with crisis　`CC`
Hb-S/Hb-C disease with crisis
Sickle-cell/Hb-C disease with vaso-occlusive
pain
Use additional code for type of crisis,
such as:
acute chest syndrome (517.3)
splenic sequestration (289.52)
CC Excl: See code 280.0
AHA: 4Q, '03, 51

282.68　Other sickle-cell disease without crisis　`CC`
Hb-S/Hb-D
Hb-S/Hb-E　　　　disease without
Sickle-cell/Hb-D　　　crisis
Sickle-cell/Hb-E
CC Excl: See code 280.0
AHA: 4Q, '03, 51

282.69　Other sickle-cell disease with crisis　`CC`
Hb-S/Hb-D
Hb-S/Hb-E　　　　disease with crisis
Sickle-cell/Hb-D
Sickle-cell/Hb-E
Other sickle-cell disease with vaso-occlusive
pain
Use additional code for type of crisis,
such as:
acute chest syndrome (517.3)
splenic sequestration (289.52)
CC Excl: See code 280.0

282.7　Other hemoglobinopathies
Abnormal hemoglobin NOS
Congenital Heinz-body anemia
Disease:
hemoglobin C [Hb-C]
hemoglobin D [Hb-D]
hemoglobin E [Hb-E]
hemoglobin Zurich [Hb-Zurich]
Hemoglobinopathy NOS
Hereditary persistence of fetal hemoglobin [HPFH]
Unstable hemoglobin hemolytic disease
EXCLUDES　*familial polycythemia (289.6)*
hemoglobin M [Hb-M] disease (289.7)
high-oxygen-affinity hemoglobin (289.0)
DEF: Any disorder of hemoglobin due to alteration of molecular
structure; may include overt anemia.

282.8　Other specified hereditary hemolytic anemias
Stomatocytosis

282.9　Hereditary hemolytic anemia, unspecified
Hereditary hemolytic anemia NOS

`N` Newborn Age: 0　`P` Pediatric Age: 0-17　`M` Maternity Age: 12-55　`A` Adult Age: 15-124　`CC` CC Condition　`MC` Major Complication　`CD` Complex Dx　`HIV` HIV Related Dx

62 — Volume 1　　　　　　　　　　　　　　　　　　　　　　　　　　　　　　　　　　*2007 ICD•9•CM*

Blood and Blood-Forming Organs

283–285.0

✓4ᵗʰ **283 Acquired hemolytic anemias**
DEF: Non-heriditary anemia characterized by premature destruction of red blood cells; caused by infectious organisms, poisons, and physical agents
AHA: N-D, '84, 1

283.0 Autoimmune hemolytic anemias CC
Autoimmune hemolytic disease (cold type) (warm type)
Chronic cold hemagglutinin disease
Cold agglutinin disease or hemoglobinuria
Hemolytic anemia:
cold type (secondary) (symptomatic)
drug-induced
warm type (secondary) (symptomatic)
Use additional E code to identify cause, if drug-induced
EXCLUDES Evans' syndrome (287.32)
hemolytic disease of newborn (773.0-773.5)
CC Excl: See code 280.0

✓5ᵗʰ **283.1 Non-autoimmune hemolytic anemias**
Use additional E code to identify cause
DEF: Hemolytic anemia and thrombocytopenia with acute renal failure; relatively rare condition; 50 percent of patients require renal dialysis.
AHA: 4Q, '93, 25

283.10 Non-autoimmune hemolytic anemia, unspecified CC
CC Excl: See code 280.0

283.11 Hemolytic-uremic syndrome CC
CC Excl: See code 280.0

283.19 Other non-autoimmune hemolytic anemias CC
Hemolytic anemia: Hemolytic anemia:
mechanical   toxic
microangiopathic
CC Excl: See code 280.0

283.2 Hemoglobinuria due to hemolysis from external causes CC
Acute intravascular hemolysis
Hemoglobinuria:
from exertion
march
paroxysmal (cold) (nocturnal)
due to other hemolysis
Marchiafava-Micheli syndrome
Use additional E code to identify cause
CC Excl: See code 280.0

283.9 Acquired hemolytic anemia, unspecified CC
Acquired hemolytic anemia NOS
Chronic idiopathic hemolytic anemia
CC Excl: See code 280.0

▲ ✓4ᵗʰ **284 Aplastic anemia and other bone marrow failure syndromes**
AHA: 1Q, '91, 14; N-D, '84, 1; S-O, '84, 16
DEF: Bone marrow failure to produce the normal amount of blood components; generally non-responsive to usual therapy.

✓5ᵗʰ **284.0 Constitutional aplastic anemia**
AHA: 1Q, '91, 14

284.01 Constitutional red blood cell aplasia
Aplasia, (pure) red cell:
congenital
of infants
primary
Blackfan-Diamond syndrome
Familial hypoplastic anemia

284.09 Other constitutional aplastic anemia
Fanconi's anemia
Pancytopenia with malformations

284.1 Pancytopenia
EXCLUDES pancytopenia (due to) (with):
aplastic anemia NOS (284.9)
bone marrow infiltration (284.2)
constitutional red blood cell aplasia (284.01)
drug induced (284.8)
hairy cell leukemia (202.4)
human immunodeficiency virus disease (042)
leukoerythroblastic anemia (284.2)
malformations (284.09)
myelodysplastic syndromes (238.72-238.75)
myeloproliferative disease (238.79)
other constitutional aplastic anemia (284.09)

284.2 Myelophthisis
Leukoerythroblastic anemia
Myelophthisic anemia
Code first the underlying disorder, such as:
malignant neoplasm of breast (174.0-174.9, 175.0-175.9)
tuberculosis (015.0-015.9)
EXCLUDES idiopathic myelofibrosis (238.76)
myelofibrosis NOS (289.83)
myelofibrosis with myeloid metaplasia (238.76)
primary myelofibrosis (238.76)
secondary myelofibrosis (289.83)

284.8 Other specified aplastic anemias CC
Aplastic anemia (due to):
chronic systemic disease
drugs
infection
radiation
toxic (paralytic)
Red cell aplasia (acquired) (adult) (pure) (with thymoma)
Use additional E code to identify cause
CC Excl: See code 280.0
AHA: 3Q, '05, 11; 1Q, '97, 5; 1Q, '92, 15; 1Q, '91, 14

284.9 Aplastic anemia, unspecified CC
Anemia:
aplastic (idiopathic) NOS
aregenerative
hypoplastic NOS
nonregenerative
Medullary hypoplasia
EXCLUDES refractory anemia ▶(238.72)◄
CC Excl: See code 280.0

✓4ᵗʰ **285 Other and unspecified anemias**
AHA: 1Q, '91, 14; N-D, '84, 1

285.0 Sideroblastic anemia CC
Anemia:
hypochromic with iron loading
sideroachrestic
sideroblastic: sideroblastic:
acquired   secondary (drug-induced)
congenital   (due to disease)
hereditary   sex-linked hypochromic
primary   vitamin B6-responsive
Pyridoxine-responsive (hypochromic) anemia
Use additional E code to identify cause, if drug induced
EXCLUDES refractory sideroblastic anemia ▶(238.72)◄
CC Excl: See code 280.0
DEF: Characterized by a disruption of final heme synthesis; results in iron overload of reticuloendothelial tissues.

Blood and Blood-Forming Organs

285.1–286.5

285.1 **Acute posthemorrhagic anemia** `cc`
   Anemia due to acute blood loss
   > **EXCLUDES** anemia due to chronic blood loss
   >   (280.0)
   >   blood loss anemia NOS (280.0)
   CC Excl: 280.0-285.9, 289.81-289.9, 958.2
   AHA: 2Q, '92, 15

▲ ✓5ᵗʰ **285.2** **Anemia of chronic disease**
   ▶Anemia in chronic illness◄
   AHA: 4Q, '00, 39

   285.21 Anemia in chronic kidney disease
        Anemia in end stage renal disease
        Erythropoietin-resistant anemia (EPO
             resistant anemia)
   285.22 Anemia in neoplastic disease
▲ **285.29 Anemia of other chronic disease**
        ▶Anemia in other chronic illness◄

285.8 **Other specified anemias**
   Anemia:
        dyserythropoietic (congenital)
        dyshematopoietic (congenital)
        von Jaksch's
   Infantile pseudoleukemia
   AHA: 1Q, '91, 16

285.9 **Anemia, unspecified**
   Anemia: Anemia:
        NOS   profound
        essential   progressive
        normocytic, not due secondary
             to blood loss Oligocythemia
   > **EXCLUDES** anemia (due to):
   >   blood loss:
   >   acute (285.1)
   >   chronic or unspecified (280.0)
   >   iron deficiency (280.0-280.9)
   AHA: 1Q, '02, 14; 2Q, '92, 16; M-A, '85, 13; N-D, '84, 1

✓4ᵗʰ **286 Coagulation defects**
   286.0 **Congenital factor VIII disorder** `cc`
        Antihemophilic globulin Hemophilia:
             [AHG] deficiency   A
        Factor VIII (functional)   classical
             deficiency   familial
        Hemophilia: hereditary
             NOS   Subhemophilia
        > **EXCLUDES** factor VIII deficiency with vascular
        >   defect (286.4)
        CC Excl: 286.0-287.9, 289.81-289.9
        DEF: Hereditary, sex-linked, results in missing antihemophilic
        globulin (AHG) (factor VIII); causes abnormal coagulation
        characterized by increased tendency to bleeding, large bruises of
        skin, soft tissue; may also be bleeding in mouth, nose,
        gastrointestinal tract; after childhood, hemorrhages in joints,
        resulting in swelling and impaired function.

   286.1 **Congenital factor IX disorder** `cc`
        Christmas disease
        Deficiency:
             factor IX (functional)
             plasma thromboplastin component [PTC]
        Hemophilia B
        CC Excl: See code 286.0
        DEF: Deficiency of plasma thromboplastin component (PTC) (factor
        IX) and plasma thromboplastin antecedent (PTA); PTC deficiency
        clinically indistinguishable from classical hemophilia; PTA
        deficiency found in both sexes.

286.2 **Congenital factor XI deficiency** `cc`
   Hemophilia C
   Plasma thromboplastin antecedent [PTA] deficiency
   Rosenthal's disease
   CC Excl: See code 286.0

286.3 **Congenital deficiency of other clotting factors** `cc`
   Congenital afibrinogenemia
   Deficiency:
        AC globulin factor:
             I [fibrinogen]
             II [prothrombin]
             V [labile]
             VII [stable]
             X [Stuart-Prower]
             XII [Hageman]
             XIII [fibrin stabilizing]
        Laki-Lorand factor
        proaccelerin
   Disease
        Owren's
        Stuart-Prower
   Dysfibrinogenemia (congenital)
   Dysprothrombinemia (constitutional)
   Hypoproconvertinemia
   Hypoprothrmbinemia (hereditary)
   Parahemophilia
   CC Excl: See code 286.0

286.4 **von Willebrand's disease** `cc`
   Angiohemophilia (A) (B)
   Constitutional thrombopathy
   Factor VIII deficiency with vascular defect
   Pseudohemophilia type B
   Vascular hemophilia
   von Willebrand's (-Jürgens') disease
   > **EXCLUDES** factor VIII deficiency:
   >   NOS (286.0)
   >   with functional defect (286.0)
   >   hereditary capillary fragility (287.8)
   CC Excl: See code 286.0
   DEF: Abnormal blood coagulation caused by deficient blood Factor
   VII; congenital; symptoms include excess or prolonged bleeding,
   such as hemorrhage during menstruation, following birthing, or
   after surgical procedure.

286.5 **Hemorrhagic disorder due to intrinsic
   circulating anticoagulants** `cc`
   Antithrombinemia
   Antithromboplastinemia
   Antithromboplastino-genemia
   Hyperheparinemia
   Increase in:
        anti-VIIIa
        anti-IXa
        anti-Xa
        anti-XIa
        antithrombin
   Secondary hemophilia
   Systemic lupus erythematosus [SLE] inhibitor
   CC Excl: See code 286.0
   AHA: 3Q, '92, 15; 3Q, '90, 14

`N` Newborn Age: 0   `P` Pediatric Age: 0-17   `M` Maternity Age: 12-55   `A` Adult Age: 15-124   `CC` CC Condition   `MC` Major Complication   `CD` Complex Dx   `HIV` HIV Related Dx

286.6 Defibrination syndrome `CC`
Afibrinogenemia, acquired
Consumption coagulopathy
Diffuse or disseminated intravascular coagulation [DIC syndrome]
Fibrinolytic hemorrhage, acquired
Hemorrhagic fibrinogenolysis
Pathologic fibrinolysis
Purpura:
    fibrinolytic
    fulminans
    EXCLUDES   *that complicating:*
            abortion (634-638 with .1, 639.1)
            pregnancy or the puerperium (641.3, 666.3)
            disseminated intravascular coagulation in newborn (776.2)

CC Excl: See code 286.0

AHA: 4Q, '93, 29

DEF: Characterized by destruction of circulating fibrinogen; often precipitated by other conditions, such as injury, causing release of thromboplastic particles in blood stream.

286.7 Acquired coagulation factor deficiency `CC`
Deficiency of coagulation factor due to:
    liver disease
    vitamin K deficiency
Hypoprothrombinemia, acquired
Use additional E code to identify cause, if drug induced
    EXCLUDES   *vitamin K deficiency of newborn (776.0)*

CC Excl: See code 286.0

AHA: 4Q, '93, 29

286.9 Other and unspecified coagulation defects `CC`
Defective coagulation NOS
Deficiency, coagulation factor NOS
Delay, coagulation
Disorder:
    coagulation
    hemostasis
    EXCLUDES   *abnormal coagulation profile (790.92)*
            hemorrhagic disease of newborn (776.0)
            that complicating:
               abortion (634-638 with .1, 639.1)
               pregnancy or the puerperium (641.3, 666.3)

CC Excl: See code 286.0

AHA: 4Q, '99, 22; 4Q, '93, 29

√4ᵗʰ **287 Purpura and other hemorrhagic conditions**
    EXCLUDES   *hemorrhagic thrombocythemia ▶(238.79)◀*
            purpura fulminans (286.6)

AHA: 1Q, '91, 14

287.0 Allergic purpura `CC`
Peliosis rheumatica   Purpura:
Purpura: rheumatica
    anaphylactoid   Schönlein-Henoch
    autoimmune   vascular
    Henoch's   Vasculitis, allergic
    nonthrombocytopenic:
        hemorrhagic
        idiopathic
    EXCLUDES   *hemorrhagic purpura (287.39)*
            purpura annularis telangiectodes (709.1)

CC Excl: See code 286.0

DEF: Any hemorrhagic condition, thrombocytic or nonthrombocytopenic in origin, caused by a presumed allergic reaction.

287.1 Qualitative platelet defects `CC`
Thrombasthenia (hemorrhagic) (hereditary)
Thrombocytasthenia
Thrombocytopathy (dystrophic)
Thrombopathy (Bernard-Soulier)
    EXCLUDES   *von Willebrand's disease (286.4)*

CC Excl: See code 286.0

287.2 Other nonthrombocytopenic purpuras `CC`
Purpura: Purpura:
    NOS   simplex
    senile

CC Excl: See code 286.0

√5ᵗʰ **287.3 Primary thrombocytopenia**
    EXCLUDES   *thrombotic thrombocytopenic purpura (446.6)*
            transient thrombocytopenia of newborn (776.1)

AHA: 4Q, '05, 56

DEF: Decrease in number of blood platelets in circulating blood and purpural skin hemorrhages.

287.30 Primary thrombocytopenia, unspecified `CC`
Megakaryocytic hypoplasia

CC Excl: 286.0-287.9, 289.81-289.9

287.31 Immune thrombocytopenic purpura `CC`
Idiopathic thrombocytopenic purpura
Tidal platelet dysgenesis

CC Excl: See code 287.30

AHA: 4Q, '05, 57

DEF: Tidal platelet dysgenesis: Platelet counts fluctuate from normal to very low within periods of 20 to 40 days and may involve autoimmune platelet destruction.

287.32 Evans' syndrome `CC`

CC Excl: See code 287.30

DEF: Combination of immunohemolytic anemia and autoimmune hemolytic anemia, sometimes with neutropenia.

287.33 Congenital and hereditary thrombocytopenic purpura `CC`
Congenital and hereditary thrombocytopenia
Thrombocytopenia with absent ●adii (TAR) syndrome
    EXCLUDES   *Wiskott-Aldrich syndrome (279.12)*

CC Excl: See code 287.30

DEF: Thrombocytopenia with absent radii (TAR) syndrome: autosomal recessive syndrome characterized by thrombocytopenia and bilateral radial aplasia; manifestations include skeletal, gastrointestinal, hematologic, and cardiac system abnormalities.

287.39 Other primary thrombocytopenia `CC`

CC Excl: See code 287.30

287.4 Secondary thrombocytopenia `CC`
Posttransfusion purpura
Thrombocytopenia (due to):
    dilutional
    drugs
    extracorporeal circulation of blood
    massive blood transfusion
    platelet alloimmunization
Use additional E code to identify cause
    EXCLUDES   *transient thrombocytopenia of newborn (776.1)*

CC Excl: See code 286.0

AHA: M-A, '85, 14

DEF: Reduced number of platelets in circulating blood as consequence of an underlying disease or condition.

√4ᵗʰ √5ᵗʰ Additional Digit Required   Nonspecific PDx   Unacceptable PDx   Manifestation Code   **MCV** Major Cardovascular Condition   ▶◀ Revised Text   ● New Code   ▲ Revised Code Title

Blood and Blood-Forming Organs

286.6-287.4

Blood and Blood Forming Organs

287.5–288.9

287.5 Thrombocytopenia, unspecified `CC`
CC Excl: See code 286.0

287.8 Other specified hemorrhagic conditions `CC`
Capillary fragility (hereditary)
Vascular pseudohemophilia
CC Excl: See code 286.0

287.9 Unspecified hemorrhagic conditions `CC`
Hemorrhagic diathesis (familial)
CC Excl: See code 286.0

✓4ᵗʰ **288 Diseases of white blood cells**
EXCLUDES   leukemia (204.0-208.9)
AHA: 1Q, '91, 14

▲ ✓5ᵗʰ **288.0 Neutropenia**
▶Decreased absolute neutrophil count (ANC)
Use additional code for any associated fever (780.6)◀
EXCLUDES ▶ neutropenic splenomegaly (289.53)◀
transitory neonatal neutropenia (776.7)
AHA: 3Q, '05, 11; 3Q, '99, 6; 2Q, '99, 9; 3Q, '96, 16; 2Q, '96, 6

DEF: Sudden, severe condition characterized by reduced number of white blood cells; results in sores in the throat, stomach or skin; symptoms include chills, fever; some drugs can bring on condition.

● **288.00 Neutropenia, unspecified**

● **288.01 Congenital neutropenia**
Congenital agranulocytosis
Infantile genetic agranulocytosis
Kostmann's syndrome

● **288.02 Cyclic neutropenia**
Cyclic hematopoiesis
Periodic neutropenia

● **288.03 Drug induced neutropenia**
Use additional E code to identify drug

● **288.04 Neutropenia due to infection**

● **288.09 Other neutropenia**
Agranulocytosis
Neutropenia:
immune
toxic

288.1 Functional disorders of polymorphonuclear `CC`
neutrophils
Chronic (childhood) granulomatous disease
Congenital dysphagocytosis
Job's syndrome
Lipochrome histiocytosis (familial)
Progressive septic granulomatosis
CC Excl: 288.00-288.9, 289.81-289.9

288.2 Genetic anomalies of leukocytes
Anomaly (granulation) (granulocyte) or syndrome:
Alder's (-Reilly)
Chédiak-Steinbrinck (-Higashi)
Jordan's
May-Hegglin
Pelger-Huet
Hereditary:
hypersegmentation
hyposegmentation
leukomelanopathy

288.3 Eosinophilia
Eosinophilia: Eosinophilia:
allergic   secondary
hereditary   Eosinophilic leukocytosis
idiopathic
EXCLUDES   Löffler's syndrome (518.3)
pulmonary eosinophilia (518.3)
AHA: 3Q, '00, 11

DEF: Elevated number of eosinophils in the blood; characteristic of allergic states and various parasitic infections.

● **288.4 Hemophagocytic syndromes**
Familial hemophagocytic lymphohistiocytosis
Familial hemophagocytic reticulosis
Hemophagocytic syndrome, infection-associated
Histiocytic syndromes
Macrophage activation syndrome

● ✓5ᵗʰ **288.5 Decreased white blood cell count**
EXCLUDES   neutropenia (288.01-288.09)

● **288.50 Leukocytopenia, unspecified**
Decreased leukocytes, unspecified
Decreased white blood cell count, unspecified
Leukopenia NOS

● **288.51 Lymphocytopenia**
Decreased lymphocytes

● **288.59 Other decreased white blood cell count**
Basophilic leukopenia
Eosinophilic leukopenia
Monocytopenia
Plasmacytopenia

● ✓5ᵗʰ **288.6 Elevated white blood cell count**
EXCLUDES   eosinophilia (288.3)

● **288.60 Leukocytosis, unspecified**
Elevated leukocytes, unspecified
Elevated white blood cell count, unspecified

● **288.61 Lymphocytosis (symptomatic)**
Elevated lymphocytes

● **288.62 Leukemoid reaction**
Basophilic leukemoid reaction
Lymphocytic leukemoid reaction
Monocytic leukemoid reaction
Myelocytic leukemoid reaction
Neutrophilic leukemoid reaction

● **288.63 Monocytosis (symptomatic)**
EXCLUDES   infectious mononucleosis (075)

● **288.64 Plasmacytosis**

● **288.65 Basophilia**

● **288.69 Other elevated white blood cell count**

288.8 Other specified disease of white blood cells
EXCLUDES ▶ decreased white blood cell counts
(288.50-288.59)
elevated white blood cell counts
(288.60-288.69)◀
immunity disorders (279.0-279.9)
AHA: M-A, '87, 12

288.9 Unspecified disease of white blood cells

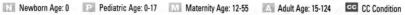 Ⓝ Newborn Age: 0   Ⓟ Pediatric Age: 0-17   Ⓜ Maternity Age: 12-55   Ⓐ Adult Age: 15-124   `CC` CC Condition   `MC` Major Complication   `CD` Complex Dx   `HIV` HIV Related Dx

66 — Volume 1 • October 2006 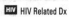   *2007 ICD•9•CM*

√4ᵗʰ **289 Other diseases of blood and blood-forming organs**

289.0　Polycythemia, secondary

High-oxygen-affinity hemoglobin

Polycythemia:
　acquired
　benign
　due to:
　　fall in plasma volume
　　high altitude

Polycythemia:
　emotional
　erythropoietin
　hypoxemic
　nephrogenous
　relative
　spurious
　stress

EXCLUDES　polycythemia:
　　　　　　neonatal (776.4)
　　　　　　primary (238.4)
　　　　　　vera (238.4)

DEF: Elevated number of red blood cells in circulating blood as result of reduced oxygen supply to the tissues.

289.1　Chronic lymphadenitis

Chronic:
　adenitis
　lymphadenitis 〕 any lymph node, except mesenteric

EXCLUDES　acute lymphadenitis (683)
　　　　　　mesenteric (289.2)
　　　　　　enlarged glands NOS (785.6)

DEF: Persistent inflammation of lymph node tissue; origin of infection is usually elsewhere.

289.2　Nonspecific mesenteric lymphadenitis

Mesenteric lymphadenitis (acute) (chronic)

DEF: Inflammation of the lymph nodes in peritoneal fold that encases abdominal organs; disease resembles acute appendicitis; unknown etiology.

289.3　Lymphadenitis, unspecified, except mesenteric

AHA: 2Q, '92, 8

289.4　Hypersplenism

"Big spleen" syndrome　　Hypersplenia
Dyssplenism

EXCLUDES　primary splenic neutropenia
　　　　　　▶(289.53)◀

DEF: An overactive spleen; it causes a deficiency of the peripheral blood components, an increase in bone marrow cells and sometimes a notable increase in the size of the spleen.

√5ᵗʰ **289.5　Other diseases of spleen**

289.50　Disease of spleen, unspecified

289.51　Chronic congestive splenomegaly

289.52　Splenic sequestration

Code first sickle-cell disease in crisis (282.42, 282.62, 282.64, 282.69)

AHA: 4Q, '03, 51

DEF: Blood is entrapped in the spleen due to vessel occlusion; most often associated with sickle-cell disease; spleen becomes enlarged and there is a sharp drop in hemoglobin.

289.53　Neutropenic splenomegaly

289.59　Other

Lien migrans
Perisplenitis
Splenic:
　abscess
　atrophy
　cyst

Splenic:
　fibrosis
　infarction
　rupture, nontraumatic
Splenitis
Wandering spleen

EXCLUDES　bilharzial splenic fibrosis
　　　　　　(120.0-120.9)
　　　　　　hepatolienal fibrosis (571.5)
　　　　　　splenomegaly NOS (789.2)

289.6　Familial polycythemia

Familial:
　benign polycythemia
　erythrocytosis

DEF: Elevated number of red blood cells.

289.7　Methemoglobinemia

Congenital NADH [DPNH]-methemoglobin-reductase deficiency
Hemoglobin M [Hb-M] disease
Methemoglobinemia:
　NOS
　acquired (with sulfhemoglobinemia)
　hereditary
　toxic
Stokvis' disease
Sulfhemoglobinemia
Use additional E code to identify cause

DEF: Presence in the blood of methemoglobin, a chemically altered form of hemoglobin; causes cyanosis, headache, dizziness, ataxia dyspnea, tachycardia, nausea, stupor, coma, and, rarely, death.

√5ᵗʰ **289.8　Other specified diseases of blood and blood-forming organs**

AHA: 4Q, '03, 56; 1Q, '02, 16; 2Q, '89, 8; M-A, '87, 12

DEF: Hypercoagulable states: a group of inherited or acquired abnormalities of specific proteins and anticoagulant factors; also called thromboembolic states or thrombotic disorders, these disorders result in the abnormal development of blood clots.

289.81　Primary hypercoagulable state　　CC

Activated protein C resistance
Antithrombin III deficiency
Factor V Leiden mutation
Lupus anticoagulant
Protein C deficiency
Protein S deficiency
Prothrombin gene mutation

CC Excl: 288.00-288.9, 289.81-289.9

DEF: Activated protein C resistance: decreased effectiveness of protein C to degrade factor V, necessary to inhibit clotting cascade; also called Factor V Leiden mutation.

DEF: Antithrombin III deficiency: deficiency in plasma antithrombin III one of six naturally occurring antithrombins that limit coagulation.

DEF: Factor V Leiden mutation: also called activated protein C resistance.

DEF: Lupus anticoagulant: deficiency in a circulating anticoagulant that inhibits the conversion of prothrombin into thrombin; autoimmune antibodies induce procoagulant surfaces in platelets; also called anti-phospholipid syndrome.

DEF: Protein C deficiency: deficiency of activated protein C which functions to bring the blood-clotting process into balance; same outcome as factor V Leiden mutation.

DEF: Protein S deficiency: similar to protein C deficiency; protein S is a vitamin K dependent cofactor in the activation of protein C.

DEF: Prothrombin gene mutation: increased levels of prothrombin, or factor II, a plasma protein that is converted to thrombin, which acts upon fibrinogen to form the fibrin.

√4ᵗʰ √5ᵗʰ Additional Digit Required　Nonspecific PDx　Unacceptable PDx　Manifestation Code　MCV Major Cardiovascular Condition　▶◀ Revised Text　● New Code　▲ Revised Code Title

289.82 Secondary hypercoagulable state `CC`
    CC Excl: See code 289.81

● — **289.83 Myelofibrosis**
    Myelofibrosis NOS
    Secondary myelofibrosis
    Code first the underlying disorder, such as:
      malignant neoplasm of breast (174.0-
        174.9, 175.0-175.9)

    EXCLUDES   *idiopathic myelofibrosis*
               (238.76)
           leukoerythroblastic anemia
               (284.2)
           myelofibrosis with myeloid
               metaplasia (238.76)
           myelophthisic anemia (284.2)
           myelophthisis (284.2)
           primary myelofibrosis (238.76)

289.89 Other specified diseases of blood and blood-forming organs
    Hypergammaglobulinemia
    Pseudocholinesterase deficiency

289.9 Unspecified diseases of blood and blood-forming organs
    Blood dyscrasia NOS
    Erythroid hyperplasia
    AHA: M-A, '85, 14

[N] Newborn Age: 0   [P] Pediatric Age: 0-17   [M] Maternity Age: 12-55   [A] Adult Age: 15-124   `CC` CC Condition   `MC` Major Complication   `CD` Complex Dx   `HIV` HIV Related Dx

68 — Volume 1 • October 2006   *2007 ICD•9•CM*

5. MENTAL DISORDERS (290-319)

PSYCHOSES (290-299)

EXCLUDES   *mental retardation (317-319)*

ORGANIC PSYCHOTIC CONDITIONS (290-294)

INCLUDES   psychotic organic brain syndrome

EXCLUDES   *nonpsychotic syndromes of organic etiology (310.0-310.9)*
psychoses classifiable to 295-298 and without impairment of orientation, comprehension, calculation, learning capacity, and judgment, but associated with physical disease, injury, or condition affecting the brain [eg., following childbirth] (295.0-298.8)

✓4ᵗʰ **290 Dementias**

Code first the associated neurological condition

EXCLUDES   *dementia due to alcohol (291.0-291.2)*
dementia due to drugs (292.82)
dementia not classified as senile, presenile, or arteriosclerotic (294.10-294.11)
psychoses classifiable to 295-298 occurring in the senium without dementia or delirium (295.0-298.8)
senility with mental changes of nonpsychotic severity (310.1)
transient organic psychotic conditions (293.0-293.9)

290.0 Senile dementia, uncomplicated   A

Senile dementia:
    NOS
    simple type

EXCLUDES   *mild memory disturbances, not amounting to dementia, associated with senile brain disease (310.1)*
senile dementia with:
    delirium or confusion (290.3)
    delusional [paranoid] features (290.20)
    depressive features (290.21)

AHA: 4Q, '99, 4

✓5ᵗʰ **290.1 Presenile dementia**

Brain syndrome with presenile brain disease

EXCLUDES   *arteriosclerotic dementia (290.40-290.43)*
dementia associated with other cerebral conditions (294.10-294.11)

AHA: N-D, '84, 20

290.10 Presenile dementia, uncomplicated   A HIV

Presenile dementia: Presenile dementia:
    NOS   simple type

290.11 Presenile dementia with delirium   A HIV

Presenile dementia with acute confusional state

AHA: 1Q, '88, 3

290.12 Presenile dementia with delusional   A HIV
    features

Presenile dementia, paranoid type

290.13 Presenile dementia with depressive   A HIV
    features

Presenile dementia, depressed type

✓5ᵗʰ **290.2 Senile dementia with delusional or depressive features**

EXCLUDES   *senile dementia:*
    NOS (290.0)
    with delirium and/or confusion (290.3)

290.20 Senile dementia with delusional   A
    features

Senile dementia, paranoid type
Senile psychosis NOS

290.21 Senile dementia with depressive   A
    features

290.3 Senile dementia with delirium   A

Senile dementia with acute confusional state

EXCLUDES   *senile:*
    dementia NOS (290.0)
    psychosis NOS (290.20)

✓5ᵗʰ **290.4 Vascular dementia**

Multi-infarct dementia or psychosis
Use additional code to identify cerebral atherosclerosis (437.0)

EXCLUDES   *suspected cases with no clear evidence of arteriosclerosis (290.9)*

AHA: 1Q, '88, 3

290.40 Vascular dementia, uncomplicated   A

Arteriosclerotic dementia:
    NOS
    simple type

290.41 Vascular dementia with delirium   A

Arteriosclerotic dementia with acute confusional state

290.42 Vascular dementia with delusions   A

Arteriosclerotic dementia, paranoid type

290.43 Vascular dementia with depressed   A
    mood

Arteriosclerotic dementia, depressed type

290.8 Other specified senile psychotic conditions

Presbyophrenic psychosis

290.9 Unspecified senile psychotic condition   A

✓4ᵗʰ **291 Alcohol induced mental disorders**

EXCLUDES   *alcoholism without psychosis (303.0-303.9)*

AHA: 1Q, '88, 3; S-O, '86, 3

291.0 Alcohol withdrawal delirium   CC

Alcoholic delirium   Delirium tremens

EXCLUDES   *alcohol withdrawal (291.81)*

CC Excl: 291.0-294.9, 303.00-305.03, 305.20-305.93, 790.3

AHA: 2Q, '91, 11

291.1 Alcohol induced persisting amnestic disorder   CC

Alcoholic polyneuritic psychosis
Korsakoff's psychosis, alcoholic
Wernicke-Korsakoff syndrome (alcoholic)

CC Excl: See code 291.0

AHA: 1Q, '88, 3

DEF: Prominent and lasting reduced memory span, disordered time appreciation and confabulation, occurring in alcoholics, as sequel to acute alcoholic psychosis.

291.2 Alcohol induced persisting dementia   CC

Alcoholic dementia NOS
Alcoholism associated with dementia NOS
Chronic alcoholic brain syndrome

CC Excl: See code 291.0

✓4ᵗʰ
✓5ᵗʰ Additional Digit Required   Nonspecific PDx   Unacceptable PDx   Manifestation Code   MCV Major Cardiovascular Condition   ►◄ Revised Text   ● New Code   ▲ Revised Code Title

2007 ICD•9•CM   Volume 1 — 69

Mental Disorders

291.3–292.9

291.3 Alcohol induced psychotic disorder with hallucinations `CC`

Alcoholic: Alcoholic:
hallucinosis (acute)   psychosis with hallucinosis

EXCLUDES   alcohol withdrawal with delirium
(291.0)
schizophrenia (295.0-295.9) and
paranoid states (297.0-297.9)
taking the form of chronic
hallucinosis with clear
consciousness in an alcoholic

CC Excl: See code 291.0

AHA: 2Q, '91, 11

DEF: Psychosis lasting less than six months with slight or no clouding of consciousness in which auditory hallucinations predominate.

291.4 Idiosyncratic alcohol intoxication `CC`

Pathologic: Pathologic:
alcohol intoxication   drunkenness

EXCLUDES   acute alcohol intoxication (305.0)
in alcoholism (303.0)
simple drunkenness (305.0)

CC Excl: See code 291.0

DEF: Unique behavioral patterns, like belligerence, after intake of relatively small amounts of alcohol; behavior not due to excess consumption.

291.5 Alcohol induced psychotic disorder with delusions

Alcoholic: Alcoholic:
paranoia   psychosis, paranoid type

EXCLUDES   nonalcoholic paranoid states (297.0-
297.9)
schizophrenia, paranoid type (295.3)

√5ᵗʰ **291.8 Other specified alcohol induced mental disorders**

AHA: 3Q, '94, 13; J-A, '85, 10

291.81 Alcohol withdrawal `CC`

Alcohol:
abstinence syndrome or symptoms
withdrawal syndrome or symptoms

EXCLUDES   alcohol withdrawal:
delirium (291.0)
hallucinosis (291.3)
delirium tremens (291.0)

CC Excl: 291.0-294.9, 303.00-305.03, 305.20-305.93, 790.3

AHA: 4Q, '96, 28; 2Q, '91, 11

291.82 Alcohol induced sleep disorders

Alcohol induced circadian rhythm sleep
disorders
Alcohol induced hypersomnia
Alcohol induced insomnia
Alcohol induced parasomnia

291.89 Other `CC`

Alcohol induced anxiety disorder
Alcohol induced mood disorder
Alcohol induced sexual dysfunction

CC Excl: See code 291.81

291.9 Unspecified alcohol induced mental disorders `CC`

Alcoholic:
mania NOS
psychosis NOS
Alcoholism (chronic) with psychosis
Alcohol related disorder NOS

CC Excl: See code 291.0

√4ᵗʰ **292 Drug induced mental disorders**

INCLUDES   organic brain syndrome associated with
consumption of drugs
Use additional code for any associated drug dependence
(304.0-304.9)
Use additional E code to identify drug

AHA: 3Q, '04, 8; 2Q, '91, 11; S-O, '86, 3

292.0 Drug withdrawal `CC`

Drug:
abstinence syndrome or symptoms
withdrawal syndrome or symptoms

CC Excl: See code 291.0

AHA: 1Q, '97, 12; 1Q, '88, 3

√5ᵗʰ **292.1 Drug induced psychotic disorders**

292.11 Drug induced psychotic disorder with delusions `CC`

Paranoid state induced by drugs

CC Excl: See code 291.0

292.12 Drug induced psychotic disorder with hallucinations `CC`

Hallucinatory state induced by drugs

EXCLUDES   states following LSD or other
hallucinogens, lasting
only a few days or less
["bad trips"] (305.3)

CC Excl: See code 291.0

292.2 Pathological drug intoxication `CC`

Drug reaction:
NOS   ⎫ resulting in brief
idiosyncratic   ⎬ psychotic states
pathologic   ⎭

EXCLUDES   expected brief psychotic reactions to
hallucinogens ["bad trips"] (305.3)
physiological side-effects of drugs (e.g.,
dystonias)

CC Excl: See code 291.0

√5ᵗʰ **292.8 Other specified drug induced mental disorders**

292.81 Drug induced delirium `CC`

CC Excl: See code 291.0

AHA: 1Q, '88, 3

292.82 Drug induced persisting dementia `CC`

CC Excl: See code 291.0

292.83 Drug induced persisting amnestic disorder `CC`

CC Excl: See code 291.0

292.84 Drug induced mood disorder `CC`

Depressive state induced by drugs

CC Excl: See code 291.0

292.85 Drug induced sleep disorders

Drug induced circadian rhythm sleep
disorder
Drug induced hypersomnia
Drug induced insomnia
Drug induced parasomnia

292.89 Other `CC`

Drug induced anxiety disorder
Drug induced organic personality syndrome
Drug induced sexual dysfunction
Drug intoxication

CC Excl: See code 291.0

292.9 Unspecified drug induced mental disorder `CC`

Drug related disorder NOS
Organic psychosis NOS due to or associated with
drugs

CC Excl: See code 291.0

`N` Newborn Age: 0   `P` Pediatric Age: 0-17   `M` Maternity Age: 12-55   `A` Adult Age: 15-124   `CC` CC Condition   `MC` Major Complication   `CD` Complex Dx   `HIV` HIV Related Dx

✓4ᵗʰ **293 Transient mental disorders due to conditions classified elsewhere**

> **INCLUDES**   transient organic mental disorders not associated with alcohol or drugs

Code first the associated physical or neurological condition

> **EXCLUDES**   *confusional state or delirium superimposed on senile dementia (290.3)*
> *dementia due to:*
>   *alcohol (291.0-291.9)*
>   *arteriosclerosis (290.40-290.43)*
>   *drugs (292.82)*
>   *senility (290.0)*

293.0 Delirium due to conditions classified elsewhere
> Acute:
>   confusional state
>   infective psychosis
>   organic reaction
>   posttraumatic organic psychosis
>   psycho-organic syndrome
> Acute psychosis associated with endocrine, metabolic, or cerebrovascular disorder
> Epileptic:
>   confusional state
>   twilight state

> **AHA:** 1Q, '88, 3
> **DRG** 425

293.1 Subacute delirium
> Subacute:
>   confusional state
>   infective psychosis
>   organic reaction
>   posttraumatic organic psychosis
>   psycho-organic syndrome
>   psychosis associated with endocrine or metabolic disorder

✓5ᵗʰ **293.8 Other specified transient mental disorders due to conditions classified elsewhere**

293.81 Psychotic disorder with delusions in **CC** **conditions classified elsewhere**
> Transient organic psychotic condition, paranoid type

> **CC Excl:** 291.0-294.9, 303.00-305.03, 305.20-305.93, 790.3

293.82 Psychotic disorder with hallucinations **CC** **in conditions classified elsewhere**
> Transient organic psychotic condition, hallucinatory type

> **CC Excl:** See code 293.81

293.83 Mood disorder in conditions classified **CC** **elsewhere**
> Transient organic psychotic condition, depressive type

> **CC Excl:** See code 293.81

293.84 Anxiety disorder in conditions **CC** **classified elsewhere**
> **CC Excl:** See code 293.81
> **AHA:** 4Q, '96, 29

293.89 Other
> Catatonic disorder in conditions classified elsewhere

293.9 Unspecified transient mental disorder in conditions classified elsewhere

Organic psychosis:	Organic psychosis:
infective NOS	transient NOS
posttraumatic NOS	Psycho-organic syndrome

✓4ᵗʰ **294 Persistent mental disorders due to conditions classified elsewhere**

> **INCLUDES**   organic psychotic brain syndromes (chronic), not elsewhere classified

> **AHA:** M-A, '85, 12

294.0 Amnestic disorder in conditions classified elsewhere
> Korsakoff's psychosis or syndrome (nonalcoholic)
> Code first underlying condition

> **EXCLUDES**   *alcoholic:*
>   *amnestic syndrome (291.1)*
>   *Korsakoff's psychosis (291.1)*

✓5ᵗʰ **294.1 Dementia in conditions classified elsewhere**
> Dementia of the Alzheimer's type
> *Code first any underlying physical condition, as:*
> dementia in:
>   Alzheimer's disease (331.0)
>   cerebral lipidoses (330.1)
>   dementia with Lewy bodies (331.82)
>   dementia with Parkinsonism (331.82)
>   epilepsy (345.0-345.9)
>   frontal dementia (331.19)
>   frontotemporal dementia (331.19)
>   general paresis [syphilis] (094.1)
>   hepatolenticular degeneration (275.1)
>   Huntington's chorea (333.4)
>   Jakob-Creutzfeldt disease (046.1)
>   multiple sclerosis (340)
>   Pick's disease of the brain (331.11)
>   polyarteritis nodosa (446.0)
>   syphilis (094.1)

> **EXCLUDES**   *dementia:*
>   *arteriosclerotic (290.40-290.43)*
>   *presenile (290.10-290.13)*
>   *senile (290.0)*
>   *epileptic psychosis NOS (294.8)*

> **AHA:** 4Q, '00, 40; 1Q, '99, 14; N-D, '85, 5

294.10 Dementia in conditions classified elsewhere without behavioral disturbance
> Dementia in conditions classified elsewhere NOS

294.11 Dementia in conditions classified elsewhere with behavioral disturbance
> Aggressive behavior
> Combative behavior
> Violent behavior
> Wandering off

> **AHA:** 4Q, '00, 41

294.8 Other persistent mental disorders due to conditions classified elsewhere
> Amnestic disorder NOS
> Dementia NOS
> Epileptic psychosis NOS
> Mixed paranoid and affective organic psychotic states
> Use additional code for associated epilepsy (345.0-345.9)

> **EXCLUDES**   *mild memory disturbances, not amounting to dementia (310.1)*

> **AHA:** 3Q, '03, 14; 1Q, '88, 5

294.9 Unspecified persistent mental disorders due **HIV** **to conditions classified elsewhere**
> Cognitive disorder NOS
> Organic psychosis (chronic)

OTHER PSYCHOSES (295-299)

Use additional code to identify any associated physical disease, injury, or condition affecting the brain with psychoses classifiable to 295-298

✓4ᵗʰ **295 Schizophrenic disorders**

> **INCLUDES**   schizophrenia of the types described in 295.0-295.9 occurring in children

> **EXCLUDES**   *childhood type schizophrenia (299.9)*
> *infantile autism (299.0)*

The following fifth-digit subclassification is for use with category 295:
> **0 unspecified**
> **1 subchronic**
> **2 chronic**
> **3 subchronic with acute exacerbation**
> **4 chronic with acute exacerbation**
> **5 in remission**

DEF: Group of disorders with disturbances in thought (delusions, hallucinations), mood (blunted, flattened, inappropriate affect), sense of self, relationship to world; also bizarre, purposeless behavior, repetitive activity, or inactivity.

✓4ᵗʰ Additional Digit Required   Nonspecific PDx   Unacceptable PDx   Manifestation Code   **MCV** Major Cardiovascular Condition   ►◄ Revised Text   ● New Code   ▲ Revised Code Title
✓5ᵗʰ

2007 ICD•9•CM   **February 2006 • Volume 1 — 71**

Mental Disorders

293–295

Mental Disorders

295.0–296.2

§ ✓5ᵗʰ **295.0**   **Simple type**   `CC 0-4`
Schizophrenia simplex
EXCLUDES   *latent schizophrenia (295.5)*
CC Excl: For codes 295.00-295.04; 295.00-301.9, 306.0-319

§ ✓5ᵗʰ **295.1**   **Disorganized type**   `CC 0-4`
Hebephrenia
Hebephrenic type schizophrenia
CC Excl: For codes 295.10-295.14: See code 295.0

DEF: Inappropriate behavior; results in extreme incoherence and disorganization of time, place and sense of social appropriateness; withdrawal from routine social interaction may occur.

§ ✓5ᵗʰ **295.2**   **Catatonic type**   `CC 1-4`
Catatonic (schizophrenia):   Schizophrenic:
   agitation   catalepsy
   excitation   catatonia
   excited type   flexibilitas cerea
   stupor
   withdrawn type
CC Excl: For codes 295.21-295.24: See code 295.0

DEF: Extreme changes in motor activity; one extreme is decreased response or reaction to the environment and the other is spontaneous activity.

§ ✓5ᵗʰ **295.3**   **Paranoid type**   `CC 0-4`
Paraphrenic schizophrenia
EXCLUDES   *involutional paranoid state (297.2)*
                paranoia (297.1)
                paraphrenia (297.2)
CC Excl: For codes 295.30–295.34: See code 295.0

▽ **DRG** 430 For code 295.34, 295.30

DEF: Preoccupied with delusional suspicions and auditory hallucinations related to single theme; usually hostile, grandiose, overly religious, occasionally hypochondriacal.

§ ✓5ᵗʰ **295.4**   **Schizophreniform disorder**   `CC 0-4`
Oneirophrenia   Schizophreniform:
Schizophreniform: psychosis, confusional type
   attack
EXCLUDES   *acute forms of schizophrenia of:*
                catatonic type (295.2)
                hebephrenic type (295.1)
                paranoid type (295.3)
                simple type (295.0)
                undifferentiated type (295.8)
CC Excl: For codes 295.40-295.44: See code 295.0

§ ✓5ᵗʰ **295.5**   **Latent schizophrenia**
Latent schizophrenic reaction
Schizophrenia:
   borderline
   incipient
   prepsychotic
   prodromal
   pseudoneurotic
   pseudopsychopathic
EXCLUDES   *schizoid personality (301.20-301.22)*
AHA: For code 295.50; ▶1Q, '06, 10◀

§ ✓5ᵗʰ **295.6**   **Residual type**   `CC 0-4`
Chronic undifferentiated schizophrenia
Restzustand (schizophrenic)
Schizophrenic residual state
CC Excl: For codes 295.60-295.64: See code 295.0

§ ✓5ᵗʰ **295.7**   **Schizoaffective disorder**   `CC 0-4`
Cyclic schizophrenia
Mixed schizophrenic and affective psychosis
Schizo-affective psychosis
Schizophreniform psychosis, affective type
CC Excl: For codes 295.70-295.74: See code 295.0

▽ **DRG** 430 For code 295.70

§ ✓5ᵗʰ **295.8**   **Other specified types of schizophrenia**   `CC 0-4`
Acute (undifferentiated) schizophrenia
Atypical schizophrenia
Cenesthopathic schizophrenia
EXCLUDES   *infantile autism (299.0)*
CC Excl: For codes 295.80-295.84: See code 295.0

§ ✓5ᵗʰ **295.9**   **Unspecified schizophrenia**   `CC 0-4`
Schizophrenia:
   NOS
   mixed NOS
   undifferentiated NOS
   undifferentiated type
Schizophrenic reaction NOS
Schizophreniform psychosis NOS
CC Excl: For codes 295.90-295.94: See code 295.0

AHA: 3Q, '95, 6

✓4ᵗʰ **296**   **Episodic mood disorders**
INCLUDES   episodic affective disorders
EXCLUDES   *neurotic depression (300.4)*
                reactive depressive psychosis (298.0)
                reactive excitation (298.1)

The following fifth-digit subclassification is for use with categories 296.0-296.6:
   0   **unspecified**
   1   **mild**
   2   **moderate**
   3   **severe, without mention of psychotic behavior**
   4   **severe, specified as with psychotic behavior**
   5   **in partial or unspecified remission**
   6   **in full remission**

AHA: M-A, '85, 14

✓5ᵗʰ **296.0**   **Bipolar I disorder, single manic episode**   `CC 4`
Hypomania (mild) NOS
Hypomanic psychosis
Mania (monopolar) NOS   ⎫
Manic-depressive psychosis   ⎬   single episode or
   or reaction: unspecified
   hypomanic
   manic   ⎭
EXCLUDES   *circular type, if there was a previous*
                attack of depression (296.4)
CC Excl: For code 296.04: See code 295.0

DEF: Mood disorder identified by hyperactivity; may show extreme agitation or exaggerated excitability; speech and thought processes may be accelerated.

✓5ᵗʰ **296.1**   **Manic disorder, recurrent episode**   `CC 4`
Any condition classifiable to 296.0, stated to be recurrent
EXCLUDES   *circular type, if there was a previous*
                attack of depression (296.4)
CC Excl: For code 296.14: See code 295.0

✓5ᵗʰ **296.2**   **Major depressive disorder, single episode**
Depressive psychosis   ⎫
Endogenous depression   ⎮
Involutional melancholia   ⎮
Manic-depressive psychosis or   ⎬   single episode or
   reaction, depressed type   ⎮   unspecified
Monopolar depression   ⎮
Psychotic depression   ⎭
EXCLUDES   *circular type, if previous attack was of*
                manic type (296.5)
                depression NOS (311)
                reactive depression (neurotic) (300.4)
                psychotic (298.0)
▽ **DRG** 430 For code 296.20

DEF: Mood disorder that produces depression; may exhibit as sadness, low self-esteem, or guilt feelings; other manifestations may be withdrawal from friends and family; interrupted sleep.

---

§   Requires fifth-digit. See category 295 for codes and definitions.

`N` Newborn Age: 0   `P` Pediatric Age: 0-17   `M` Maternity Age: 12-55   `A` Adult Age: 15-124   `CC` CC Condition   `MC` Major Complication   `CD` Complex Dx   `HIV` HIV Related Dx

Mental Disorders

√5ᵗʰ **296.3 Major depressive disorder, recurrent episode** CC 4
Any condition classifiable to 296.2, stated to be
recurrent
EXCLUDES circular type, if previous attack was of
manic type (296.5)
depression NOS (311)
reactive depression (neurotic) (300.4)
psychotic (298.0)
CC Excl: For code 296.34: See code 295.0
DRG 430 For code 296.30, 296.33 and 296.34

√5ᵗʰ **296.4 Bipolar I disorder, most recent episode (or current) manic** CC 4
Bipolar disorder, now manic
Manic-depressive psychosis, circular type but
currently manic
EXCLUDES brief compensatory or rebound mood
swings (296.99)
CC Excl: For code 296.44: See code 295.0

√5ᵗʰ **296.5 Bipolar I disorder, most recent episode (or current) depressed** CC 4
Bipolar disorder, now depressed
Manic-depressive psychosis, circular type but
currently depressed
EXCLUDES brief compensatory or rebound mood
swings (296.99)
CC Excl: For code 296.54: See code 295.0

√5ᵗʰ **296.6 Bipolar I disorder, most recent episode (or current) mixed** CC 4
Manic-depressive psychosis, circular type, mixed
CC Excl: For code 296.64: See code 295.0

296.7 Bipolar I disorder, most recent episode (or current) unspecified
Atypical bipolar affective disorder NOS
Manic-depressive psychosis, circular type, current
condition not specified as either manic or
depressive
DEF: Manic-depressive disorder referred to as bipolar because of
the mood range from manic to depressive.

√5ᵗʰ **296.8 Other and unspecified bipolar disorders**
296.80 Bipolar disorder, unspecified
Bipolar disorder NOS
Manic-depressive:
reaction NOS
syndrome NOS
296.81 Atypical manic disorder
296.82 Atypical depressive disorder
296.89 Other
Bipolar II disorder
Manic-depressive psychosis, mixed type

√5ᵗʰ **296.9 Other and unspecified episodic mood disorder**
EXCLUDES psychogenic affective psychoses
(298.0-298.8)
296.90 Unspecified episodic mood disorder
Affective psychosis NOS
Melancholia NOS
Mood disorder NOS
AHA: M-A, '85, 14
296.99 Other specified episodic mood disorder
Mood swings: Mood swings:
brief compensatory rebound

√4ᵗʰ **297 Delusional disorders**
INCLUDES paranoid disorders
EXCLUDES acute paranoid reaction (298.3)
alcoholic jealousy or paranoid state (291.5)
paranoid schizophrenia (295.3)
297.0 Paranoid state, simple
297.1 Delusional disorder
Chronic paranoid psychosis
Sander's disease
Systematized delusions
EXCLUDES paranoid personality disorder (301.0)

297.2 Paraphrenia
Involutional paranoid state
Late paraphrenia
Paraphrenia (involutional)
DEF: Paranoid schizophrenic disorder that persists over a
prolonged period but does not distort personality despite persistent
delusions.

297.3 Shared psychotic disorder
Folie à deux
Induced psychosis or paranoid disorder
DEF: Mental disorder two people share; first person with the
delusional disorder convinces second person because of a close
relationship and shared experiences to accept the delusions.

297.8 Other specified paranoid states
Paranoia querulans
Sensitiver Beziehungswahn
EXCLUDES acute paranoid reaction or state (298.3)
senile paranoid state (290.20)

297.9 Unspecified paranoid state
Paranoid: Paranoid:
disorder NOS reaction NOS
psychosis NOS state NOS
AHA: J-A, '85, 9

√4ᵗʰ **298 Other nonorganic psychoses**
INCLUDES psychotic conditions due to or provoked by:
emotional stress
environmental factors as major part of
etiology

298.0 Depressive type psychosis CC
Psychogenic depressive psychosis
Psychotic reactive depression
Reactive depressive psychosis
EXCLUDES manic-depressive psychosis, depressed
type (296.2-296.3)
neurotic depression (300.4)
reactive depression NOS (300.4)
CC Excl: See code 295.0

298.1 Excitative type psychosis
Acute hysterical psychosis Reactive excitation
Psychogenic excitation
EXCLUDES manic-depressive psychosis, manic
type (296.0-296.1)
DEF: Affective disorder similar to manic-depressive psychosis, in
the manic phase, seemingly brought on by stress.

298.2 Reactive confusion
Psychogenic confusion Psychogenic twilight state
EXCLUDES acute confusional state (293.0)
DEF: Confusion, disorientation, cloudiness in consciousness;
brought on by severe emotional upheaval.

298.3 Acute paranoid reaction CC
Acute psychogenic paranoid psychosis
Bouffée délirante
EXCLUDES paranoid states (297.0-297.9)
CC Excl: See code 295.0

298.4 Psychogenic paranoid psychosis CC
Protracted reactive paranoid psychosis
CC Excl: See code 295.0

298.8 Other and unspecified reactive psychosis
Brief psychotic disorder
Brief reactive psychosis NOS
Hysterical psychosis
Psychogenic psychosis NOS
Psychogenic stupor
EXCLUDES acute hysterical psychosis (298.1)

298.9 Unspecified psychosis HIV
Atypical psychosis
Psychosis NOS
Psychotic disorder NOS
DRG 430

√4th 299 Pervasive developmental disorders

> **EXCLUDES** *adult type psychoses occurring in childhood, as:*
> *affective disorders (296.0-296.9)*
> *manic-depressive disorders (296.0-296.9)*
> *schizophrenia (295.0-295.9)*

The following fifth-digit subclassification is for use with category 299:

0   **current or active state**
1   **residual state**

√5th 299.0 Autistic disorder   CC o

Childhood autism   Kanner's syndrome
Infantile psychosis

> **EXCLUDES** *disintegrative psychosis (299.1)*
> *Heller's syndrome (299.1)*
> *schizophrenic syndrome of childhood (299.9)*

CC Excl: For code 299.00: See code 295.0

DEF: Severe mental disorder of children, results in impaired social behavior; abnormal development of communicative skills, appears to be unaware of the need for emotional support and offers little emotional response to family members.

√5th 299.1 Childhood disintegrative disorder   CC o

Heller's syndrome
Use additional code to identify any associated neurological disorder

> **EXCLUDES** *infantile autism (299.0)*
> *schizophrenic syndrome of childhood (299.9)*

CC Excl: For code 299.10: See code 295.0

DEF: Mental disease of children identified by impaired development of reciprocal social skills, verbal and nonverbal communication skills, imaginative play.

√5th 299.8 Other specified pervasive developmental disorders   CC o

Asperger's disorder
Atypical childhood psychosis
Borderline psychosis of childhood

> **EXCLUDES** *simple stereotypes without psychotic disturbance (307.3)*

CC Excl: For code 299.80: See code 295.0

√5th 299.9 Unspecified pervasive developmental disorder   CC o

Child psychosis NOS
Pervasive developmental disorder NOS
Schizophrenia, childhood type NOS
Schizophrenic syndrome of childhood NOS

> **EXCLUDES** *schizophrenia of adult type occurring in childhood (295.0-295.9)*

CC Excl: For code 299.90: See code 295.0

NEUROTIC DISORDERS, PERSONALITY DISORDERS, AND OTHER NONPSYCHOTIC MENTAL DISORDERS (300-316)

√4th 300 Anxiety, dissociative and somatoform disorders

√5th 300.0 Anxiety states

> **EXCLUDES** *anxiety in:*
> *acute stress reaction (308.0)*
> *transient adjustment reaction (309.24)*
> *neurasthenia (300.5)*
> *psychophysiological disorders (306.0-306.9)*
> *separation anxiety (309.21)*

DEF: Mental disorder characterized by anxiety and avoidance behavior not particularly related to any specific situation or stimulus; symptoms include emotional instability, apprehension, fatigue.

300.00 Anxiety state, unspecified

Anxiety: Anxiety:
   neurosis   state (neurotic)
   reaction   Atypical anxiety disorder

AHA: 1Q, '02, 6

DRG 425

300.01 Panic disorder without agoraphobia

Panic: Panic:
   attack   state

> **EXCLUDES** *panic disorder with agoraphobia (300.21)*

DEF: Neurotic disorder characterized by recurrent panic or anxiety, apprehension, fear or terror; symptoms include shortness of breath, palpitations, dizziness, faintness or shakiness; fear of dying may persist or fear of other morbid consequences.

DRG 425

300.02 Generalized anxiety disorder

DRG 425

300.09 Other

√5th 300.1 Dissociative, conversion and factitious disorders

> **EXCLUDES** *adjustment reaction (309.0-309.9)*
> *anorexia nervosa (307.1)*
> *gross stress reaction (308.0-308.9)*
> *hysterical personality (301.50-301.59)*
> *psychophysiologic disorders (306.0-306.9)*

300.10 Hysteria, unspecified

300.11 Conversion disorder

Astasia-abasia,   Hysterical:
   hysterical   blindness
Conversion hysteria   deafness
   or reaction   paralysis

AHA: N-D, '85, 15

DRG 425

DEF: Mental disorder that impairs physical functions with no physiological basis; sensory motor symptoms include seizures, paralysis, temporary blindness; increase in stress or avoidance of unpleasant responsibilities may precipitate.

300.12 Dissociative amnesia

Hysterical amnesia

300.13 Dissociative fugue

Hysterical fugue

DEF: Dissociative hysteria; identified by loss of memory, flight from familiar surroundings; conscious activity is not associated with perception of surroundings, no later memory of episode.

300.14 Dissociative identity disorder

300.15 Dissociative disorder or reaction, unspecified

DEF: Hysterical neurotic episode; sudden but temporary changes in perceived identity, memory, consciousness, segregated memory patterns exist separate from dominant personality.

300.16 Factitious disorder with predominantly psychological signs and symptoms

Compensation neurosis
Ganser's syndrome, hysterical

DEF: A disorder characterized by the purposeful assumption of mental illness symptoms; the symptoms are not real, possibly representing what the patient imagines mental illness to be like, and are acted out more often when another person is present.

300.19 Other and unspecified factitious illness

Factitious disorder (with combined psychological and physical signs and symptoms) (with predominantly physical signs and symptoms) NOS

> **EXCLUDES** *multiple operations or hospital addiction syndrome (301.51)*

√5th 300.2 Phobic disorders

> **EXCLUDES** *anxiety state not associated with a specific situation or object (300.00-300.09)*
> *obsessional phobias (300.3)*

300.20 Phobia, unspecified

Anxiety-hysteria NOS
Phobia NOS

N Newborn Age: 0   P Pediatric Age: 0-17   M Maternity Age: 12-55   A Adult Age: 15-124   CC CC Condition   MC Major Complication   CD Complex Dx   HIV HIV Related Dx

300.21 Agoraphobia with panic disorder
Fear of:
open spaces
streets } with panic attacks
travel

Panic disorder with agoraphobia

EXCLUDES *agoraphobia without panic disorder (300.22)*
panic disorder without agoraphobia (300.01)

300.22 Agoraphobia without mention of panic attacks
Any condition classifiable to 300.21 without mention of panic attacks

300.23 Social phobia
Fear of: Fear of:
eating in public   washing in public
public speaking

300.29 Other isolated or specific phobias
Acrophobia   Claustrophobia
Animal phobias   Fear of crowds

300.3 Obsessive-compulsive disorders
Anancastic neurosis   Obsessional phobia [any]
Compulsive neurosis

EXCLUDES *obsessive-compulsive symptoms occurring in:*
endogenous depression (296.2-296.3)
organic states (eg., encephalitis)
schizophrenia (295.0-295.9)

300.4 Dysthymic disorder
Anxiety depression   Neurotic depressive state
Depression with anxiety Reactive depression
Depressive reaction

EXCLUDES *adjustment reaction with depressive symptoms (309.0-309.1)*
depression NOS (311)
manic-depressive psychosis, depressed type (296.2-296.3)
reactive depressive psychosis (298.0)

DEF: Depression without psychosis; less severe depression related to personal change or unexpected circumstances; also referred to as "reactional depression."

300.5 Neurasthenia
Fatigue neurosis   Psychogenic:
Nervous debility   general fatigue
Psychogenic:
asthenia
Use additional code to identify any associated physical disorder

EXCLUDES *anxiety state (300.00-300.09)*
neurotic depression (300.4)
psychophysiological disorders (306.0-306.9)
specific nonpsychotic mental disorders following organic brain damage (310.0-310.9)

DEF: Physical and mental symptoms caused primarily by what is known as mental exhaustion; symptoms include chronic weakness, fatigue.

300.6 Depersonalization disorder
Derealization (neurotic)
Neurotic state with depersonalization episode

EXCLUDES *depersonalization associated with:*
anxiety (300.00-300.09)
depression (300.4)
manic-depressive disorder or psychosis (296.0-296.9)
schizophrenia (295.0-295.9)

DEF: Dissociative disorder characterized by feelings of strangeness about self or body image; symptoms include dizziness, anxiety, fear of insanity, loss of reality of surroundings.

300.7 Hypochondriasis
Body dysmorphic disorder

EXCLUDES *hypochondriasis in:*
hysteria (300.10-300.19)
manic-depressive psychosis, depressed type (296.2-296.3)
neurasthenia (300.5)
obsessional disorder (300.3)
schizophrenia (295.0-295.9)

✓5ᵗʰ 300.8 Somatoform disorders

300.81 Somatization disorder
Briquet's disorder
Severe somatoform disorder

300.82 Undifferentiated somatoform disorder
Atypical somatoform disorder
Somatoform disorder NOS

AHA: 4Q, '96, 29

DEF: Disorders in which patients have symptoms that suggest an organic disease but no evidence of physical disorder after repeated testing.

300.89 Other somatoform disorders
Occupational neurosis, including writers' cramp
Psychasthenia
Psychasthenic neurosis

300.9 Unspecified nonpsychotic mental disorder
Psychoneurosis NOS

▽ **DRG** 425

✓4ᵗʰ 301 Personality disorders
INCLUDES character neurosis

Use additional code to identify any associated neurosis or psychosis, or physical condition

EXCLUDES *nonpsychotic personality disorder associated with organic brain syndromes (310.0-310.9)*

301.0 Paranoid personality disorder
Fanatic personality
Paranoid personality (disorder)
Paranoid traits

EXCLUDES *acute paranoid reaction (298.3)*
alcoholic paranoia (291.5)
paranoid schizophrenia (295.3)
paranoid states (297.0-297.9)

AHA: J-A, '85, 9

✓5ᵗʰ 301.1 Affective personality disorder

EXCLUDES *affective psychotic disorders (296.0-296.9)*
neurasthenia (300.5)
neurotic depression (300.4)

301.10 Affective personality disorder, unspecified
301.11 Chronic hypomanic personality disorder
Chronic hypomanic disorder
Hypomanic personality

301.12 Chronic depressive personality disorder
Chronic depressive disorder
Depressive character or personality

301.13 Cyclothymic disorder
Cycloid personality
Cyclothymia
Cyclothymic personality

✓5ᵗʰ 301.2 Schizoid personality disorder

EXCLUDES *schizophrenia (295.0-295.9)*

301.20 Schizoid personality disorder, unspecified
301.21 Introverted personality
301.22 Schizotypal personality disorder

301.3 Explosive personality disorder
Aggressive: Emotional instability
personality   (excessive)
reaction   Pathological emotionality
Aggressiveness   Quarrelsomeness

EXCLUDES *dyssocial personality (301.7)*
hysterical neurosis (300.10-300.19)

✓4ᵗʰ ✓5ᵗʰ Additional Digit Required   Nonspecific PDx   Unacceptable PDx   Manifestation Code   **MCV** Major Cardiovascular Condition   ▶◀ Revised Text   ● New Code   ▲ Revised Code Title

2007 ICD•9•CM   February 2006 • Volume 1 — 75

Mental Disorders

301.4–302.75

301.4 Obsessive-compulsive personality disorder
Anancastic personality
Obsessional personality
> **EXCLUDES**   obsessive-compulsive disorder (300.3)
>   phobic state (300.20-300.29)

√5ᵗʰ 301.5 Histrionic personality disorder
> **EXCLUDES**   hysterical neurosis (300.10-300.19)

DEF: Extreme emotional behavior, often theatrical; often concerned about own appeal; may demand attention, exhibit seductive behavior.

301.50 Histrionic personality disorder, unspecified
Hysterical personality NOS

301.51 Chronic factitious illness with physical symptoms
Hospital addiction syndrome
Multiple operations syndrome
Munchausen syndrome

301.59 Other histrionic personality disorder
Personality: Personality:
    emotionally unstable   psychoinfantile
    labile

301.6 Dependent personality disorder
Asthenic personality
Inadequate personality
Passive personality
> **EXCLUDES**   neurasthenia (300.5)
>   passive-aggressive personality (301.84)

DEF: Overwhelming feeling of helplessness; fears of abandonment may persist; difficulty in making personal decisions without confirmation by others; low self-esteem due to irrational sensitivity to criticism.

301.7 Antisocial personality disorder
Amoral personality
Asocial personality
Dyssocial personality
Personality disorder with predominantly sociopathic or asocial manifestation
> **EXCLUDES**   disturbance of conduct without
>   specifiable personality disorder
>   (312.0-312.9)
>   explosive personality (301.3)

AHA: S-O, '84, 16

DEF: Continuous antisocial behavior that violates rights of others; social traits include extreme aggression, total disregard for traditional social rules.

√5ᵗʰ 301.8 Other personality disorders
301.81 Narcissistic personality disorder
DEF: Grandiose fantasy or behavior, lack of social empathy, hypersensitive to the lack of others' judgment, exploits others; also sense of entitlement to have expectations met, need for continual admiration.

301.82 Avoidant personality disorder
DEF: Personality disorder marked by feelings of social inferiority; sensitivity to criticism, emotionally restrained due to fear of rejection.

301.83 Borderline personality disorder
DEF: Personality disorder characterized by unstable moods, self-image, and interpersonal relationships; uncontrolled anger, impulsive and self-destructive acts, fears of abandonment, feelings of emptiness and boredom, recurrent suicide threats or self-mutilation.

301.84 Passive-aggressive personality
DEF: Pattern of procrastination and refusal to meet standards; introduce own obstacles to success and exploit failure.

301.89 Other
Personality: Personality:
    eccentric   masochistic
    "haltlose" type   psychoneurotic
    immature
> **EXCLUDES**   psychoinfantile personality
>   (301.59)

301.9 Unspecified personality disorder
Pathological personality NOS
Personality disorder NOS
Psychopathic:
    constitutional state
    personality (disorder)

√4ᵗʰ 302 Sexual and gender identity disorders
> **EXCLUDES**   sexual disorder manifest in:
>   organic brain syndrome (290.0-294.9,
>   310.0-310.9)
>   psychosis (295.0-298.9)

302.0 Ego-dystonic sexual orientation
Ego-dystonic lesbianism
Sexual orientation conflict disorder
> **EXCLUDES**   homosexual pedophilia (302.2)

302.1 Zoophilia
Bestiality
DEF: A sociodeviant disorder marked by engaging in sexual intercourse with animals.

302.2 Pedophilia
DEF: A sociodeviant condition of adults characterized by sexual activity with children.

302.3 Transvestic fetishism
> **EXCLUDES**   trans-sexualism (302.5)

DEF: The desire to dress in clothing of opposite sex.

302.4 Exhibitionism
DEF: Sexual deviant behavior; exposure of genitals to strangers; behavior prompted by intense sexual urges and fantasies.

√5ᵗʰ 302.5 Trans-sexualism
> **EXCLUDES**   transvestism (302.3)

DEF: Gender identity disturbance; overwhelming desire to change anatomic sex, due to belief that individual is a member of the opposite sex.

302.50 With unspecified sexual history
302.51 With asexual history
302.52 With homosexual history
302.53 With heterosexual history

302.6 Gender identity disorder in children
Feminism in boys
Gender identity disorder NOS
> **EXCLUDES**   gender identity disorder in adult
>   (302.85)
>   trans-sexualism (302.50-302.53)
>   transvestism (302.3)

√5ᵗʰ 302.7 Psychosexual dysfunction
> **EXCLUDES**   impotence of organic origin (607.84)
>   normal transient symptoms from
>   ruptured hymen
>   transient or occasional failures of
>   erection due to fatigue, anxiety,
>   alcohol, or drugs

302.70 Psychosexual dysfunction, unspecified
Sexual dysfunction NOS

302.71 Hypoactive sexual desire disorder
> **EXCLUDES**   decreased sexual desire NOS
>   (799.81)

302.72 With inhibited sexual excitement
Female sexual arousal disorder
Frigidity
Impotence
Male erectile disorder

302.73 Female orgasmic disorder   ♀
302.74 Male orgasmic disorder   ♂
302.75 Premature ejaculation   ♂

N Newborn Age: 0   **P** Pediatric Age: 0-17   **M** Maternity Age: 12-55   **A** Adult Age: 15-124   **CC** CC Condition   **MC** Major Complication   **CD** Complex Dx   **HIV** HIV Related Dx

302.76 Dyspareunia, psychogenic ♀
DEF: Difficult or painful sex due to psychosomatic state.

302.79 With other specified psychosexual dysfunctions
Sexual aversion disorder

√5th **302.8 Other specified psychosexual disorders**

302.81 Fetishism
DEF: Psychosexual disorder noted for intense sexual urges and arousal precipitated by fantasies; use of inanimate objects, such as clothing, to stimulate sexual arousal, orgasm.

302.82 Voyeurism
DEF: Psychosexual disorder characterized by uncontrollable impulse to observe others, without their knowledge, who are nude or engaged in sexual activity.

302.83 Sexual masochism
DEF: Psychosexual disorder noted for need to achieve sexual gratification through humiliating or hurtful acts inflicted on self.

302.84 Sexual sadism
DEF: Psychosexual disorder noted for need to achieve sexual gratification through humiliating or hurtful acts inflicted on someone else.

302.85 Gender identity disorder in adolescents or adults
EXCLUDES gender identity disorder NOS (302.6)
gender identity disorder in children (302.6)

302.89 Other
Frotteurism
Nymphomania
Satyriasis

302.9 Unspecified psychosexual disorder
Paraphilia NOS
Pathologic sexuality NOS
Sexual deviation NOS
Sexual disorder NOS

√4th **303 Alcohol dependence syndrome**
Use additional code to identify any associated condition, as:
alcoholic psychoses (291.0-291.9)
drug dependence (304.0-304.9)
physical complications of alcohol, such as:
cerebral degeneration (331.7)
cirrhosis of liver (571.2)
epilepsy (345.0-345.9)
gastritis (535.3)
hepatitis (571.1)
liver damage NOS (571.3)
EXCLUDES drunkenness NOS (305.0)

The following fifth-digit subclassification is for use with category 303:
0 unspecified   2 episodic
1 continuous   3 in remission

AHA: 3Q, '95, 6; 2Q, '91, 9; 4Q, '88, 8; S-O, '86, 3

√5th **303.0 Acute alcoholic intoxication** CC 0-2
Acute drunkenness in alcoholism
CC Excl: For codes 303.00-303.02: 291.0-292.9, 303.00-305.03, 305.20-305.93, 790.3

√5th **303.9 Other and unspecified alcohol dependence** CC 0-2
Chronic alcoholism   Dipsomania
CC Excl: For codes 303.90-303.92: See code 303.0
AHA: 2Q, '02, 4; 2Q, '89, 9

√4th **304 Drug dependence**
EXCLUDES nondependent abuse of drugs (305.1-305.9)

The following fifth-digit subclassification is for use with category 304:
0 unspecified   2 episodic
1 continuous   3 in remission

AHA: 2Q, '91, 10; 4Q, '88, 8; S-O, '86, 3

√5th **304.0 Opioid type dependence** CC 0-2
Heroin   Opium alkaloids and their
Meperidine   derivatives
Methadone   Synthetics with morphine-like
Morphine   effects
Opium
CC Excl: For codes 304.00-304.02: See code 303.0

√5th **304.1 Sedative, hypnotic or anxiolytic dependence** CC 0-2
Barbiturates
Nonbarbiturate sedatives and tranquilizers with a similar effect:
chlordiazepoxide   meprobamate
diazepam   methaqualone
glutethimide
CC Excl: For codes 304.10-304.12: See code 303.0

√5th **304.2 Cocaine dependence** CC 0-2
Coca leaves and derivatives
CC Excl: For codes 304.20-304.22: See code 303.0

√5th **304.3 Cannabis dependence**
Hashish   Marihuana
Hemp

√5th **304.4 Amphetamine and other psychostimulant dependence** CC 0-2
Methylphenidate   Phenmetrazine
CC Excl: For codes 304.40-304.42: See code 303.0

√5th **304.5 Hallucinogen dependence** CC 0-2
Dimethyltryptamine [DMT]
Lysergic acid diethylamide [LSD] and derivatives
Mescaline
Psilocybin
CC Excl: For codes 304.50-304.52: See code 303.0

√5th **304.6 Other specified drug dependence** CC 0-2
Absinthe addiction
Glue sniffing
Inhalant dependence
Phencyclidine dependence
EXCLUDES tobacco dependence (305.1)
CC Excl: For codes 304.60-304.62: See code 303.0

√5th **304.7 Combinations of opioid type drug with any other** CC 0-2
CC Excl: For codes 304.70-304.72: See code 303.0
AHA: M-A, '86, 12

√5th **304.8 Combinations of drug dependence excluding opioid type drug** CC 0-2
CC Excl: For codes 304.80-304.82: See code 303.0
AHA: M-A, '86, 12

√5th **304.9 Unspecified drug dependence** CC 0-2
Drug addiction NOS   Drug dependence NOS
CC Excl: For codes 304.90-304.92: See code 303.0
AHA: For code 304.90: 4Q, '03, 103

√4th **305 Nondependent abuse of drugs**
Note: Includes cases where a person, for whom no other diagnosis is possible, has come under medical care because of the maladaptive effect of a drug on which he is not dependent and that he has taken on his own initiative to the detriment of his health or social functioning.
EXCLUDES alcohol dependence syndrome (303.0-303.9)
drug dependence (304.0-304.9)
drug withdrawal syndrome (292.0)
poisoning by drugs or medicinal substances (960.0-979.9)

The following fifth-digit subclassification is for use with codes 305.0, 305.2-305.9:
0 unspecified   2 episodic
1 continuous   3 in remission

AHA: 2Q, '91, 10; 4Q, '88, 8; S-O, '86, 3

Additional Digit Required Nonspecific PDx Unacceptable PDx Manifestation Code MCV Major Cardiovascular Condition ▶◀ Revised Text ● New Code ▲ Revised Code Title

Mental Disorders

305.0–306.9

§ ⍻5ᵗʰ **305.0** **Alcohol abuse**   `CC 0-2`
Drunkenness NOS
Excessive drinking of alcohol NOS
"Hangover" (alcohol)
Inebriety NOS
> **EXCLUDES** *acute alcohol intoxication in alcoholism (303.0)*
> *alcoholic psychoses (291.0-291.9)*

CC Excl: For codes 305.00-305.02: See code 303.0

AHA: 3Q, '96, 16

305.1 **Tobacco use disorder**
Tobacco dependence
> **EXCLUDES** *history of tobacco use (V15.82)*
> ▶*smoking complicating pregnancy (649.0)*
> *tobacco use disorder complicating pregnancy (649.0)*◀

AHA: 2Q, '96, 10; N-D, '84, 12

§ ⍻5ᵗʰ **305.2** **Cannabis abuse**

§ ⍻5ᵗʰ **305.3** **Hallucinogen abuse**   `CC 0-2`
Acute intoxication from hallucinogens ["bad trips"]
LSD reaction

CC Excl: For codes 305.30-305.32: See code 303.0

§ ⍻5ᵗʰ **305.4** **Sedative, hypnotic or anxiolytic abuse**   `CC 0-2`
CC Excl: For codes 305.40-305.42: See code 303.0

§ ⍻5ᵗʰ **305.5** **Opioid abuse**   `CC 0-2`
CC Excl: For codes 305.50-305.52: See code 303.0

§ ⍻5ᵗʰ **305.6** **Cocaine abuse**   `CC 0-2`
CC Excl: For codes 305.60-305.62: See code 303.0

AHA: For code 305.60: 1Q, '05, 6; 1Q, '93, 25

§ ⍻5ᵗʰ **305.7** **Amphetamine or related acting sympathomimetic abuse**   `CC 0-2`
CC Excl: For codes 305.70-305.72: See code 303.0

AHA: For code 305.70: 2Q, '03, 10–11

§ ⍻5ᵗʰ **305.8** **Antidepressant type abuse**

§ ⍻5ᵗʰ **305.9** **Other, mixed, or unspecified drug abuse**   `CC 0-2`
Caffeine intoxication
Inhalant abuse
"Laxative habit"
Misuse of drugs NOS
Nonprescribed use of drugs or patent medicinals
Phencyclidine abuse

CC Excl: For codes 305.90-305.92: See code 303.0

AHA: 3Q, '99, 20

⍻4ᵗʰ **306** **Physiological malfunction arising from mental factors**
> **INCLUDES** psychogenic:
> physical symptoms ⎫ not involving
> physiological ⎬ tissue
> manifestations ⎭ damage
> **EXCLUDES** *hysteria (300.11-300.19)*
> *physical symptoms secondary to a psychiatric disorder classified elsewhere*
> *psychic factors associated with physical conditions involving tissue damage classified elsewhere (316)*
> *specific nonpsychotic mental disorders following organic brain damage (310.0-310.9)*

DEF: Functional disturbances or interruptions due to mental or psychological causes; no tissue damage sustained in these conditions.

306.0 **Musculoskeletal**
Psychogenic paralysis
Psychogenic torticollis
> **EXCLUDES** *Gilles de la Tourette's syndrome (307.23)*
> *paralysis as hysterical or conversion reaction (300.11)*
> *tics (307.20-307.22)*

306.1 **Respiratory**
Psychogenic: Psychogenic:
   air hunger   hyperventilation
   cough   yawning
   hiccough
> **EXCLUDES** *psychogenic asthma (316 and 493.9)*

306.2 **Cardiovascular**
Cardiac neurosis
Cardiovascular neurosis
Neurocirculatory asthenia
Psychogenic cardiovascular disorder
> **EXCLUDES** *psychogenic paroxysmal tachycardia (316 and 427.2)*

AHA: J-A, '85, 14

DEF: Neurocirculatory asthenia: functional nervous and circulatory irregularities with palpitations, dyspnea, fatigue, rapid pulse, precordial pain, fear of effort, discomfort during exercise, anxiety; also called DaCosta's syndrome, Effort syndrome, Irritable or Soldier's Heart.

306.3 **Skin**
Psychogenic pruritus
> **EXCLUDES** *psychogenic:*
> *alopecia (316 and 704.00)*
> *dermatitis (316 and 692.9)*
> *eczema (316 and 691.8 or 692.9)*
> *urticaria (316 and 708.0-708.9)*

306.4 **Gastrointestinal**
Aerophagy
Cyclical vomiting, psychogenic
Diarrhea, psychogenic
Nervous gastritis
Psychogenic dyspepsia
> **EXCLUDES** *cyclical vomiting NOS (536.2)*
> *globus hystericus (300.11)*
> *mucous colitis (316 and 564.9)*
> *psychogenic:*
> *cardiospasm (316 and 530.0)*
> *duodenal ulcer (316 and 532.0-532.9)*
> *gastric ulcer (316 and 531.0-531.9)*
> *peptic ulcer NOS (316 and 533.0-533.9)*
> *vomiting NOS (307.54)*

AHA: 2Q, '89, 11

DEF: Aerophagy: excess swallowing of air, usually unconscious; related to anxiety; results in distended abdomen or belching, often interpreted by the patient as a physical disorder.

⍻5ᵗʰ **306.5** **Genitourinary**
> **EXCLUDES** *enuresis, psychogenic (307.6)*
> *frigidity (302.72)*
> *impotence (302.72)*
> *psychogenic dyspareunia (302.76)*

306.50 **Psychogenic genitourinary malfunction, unspecified**

306.51 **Psychogenic vaginismus**   ♀
Functional vaginismus

DEF: Psychogenic response resulting in painful contractions of vaginal canal muscles; can be severe enough to prevent sexual intercourse.

306.52 **Psychogenic dysmenorrhea**   ♀

306.53 **Psychogenic dysuria**

306.59 **Other**
AHA: M-A, '87, 11

306.6 **Endocrine**

306.7 **Organs of special sense**
> **EXCLUDES** *hysterical blindness or deafness (300.11)*
> *psychophysical visual disturbances (368.16)*

306.8 **Other specified psychophysiological malfunction**
Bruxism   Teeth grinding

306.9 **Unspecified psychophysiological malfunction**
Psychophysiologic disorder NOS
Psychosomatic disorder NOS

§ Requires fifth-digit. See category 305 for codes and definitions.

N Newborn Age: 0   P Pediatric Age: 0-17   M Maternity Age: 12-55   A Adult Age: 15-124   CC CC Condition   MC Major Complication   CD Complex Dx   HIV HIV Related Dx

☑4ᵗʰ 307 Special symptoms or syndromes, not elsewhere classified

Note: This category is intended for use if the psychopathology is manifested by a single specific symptom or group of symptoms which is not part of an organic illness or other mental disorder classifiable elsewhere.

> EXCLUDES those due to mental disorders classified elsewhere
> those of organic origin

307.0 Stuttering

> EXCLUDES dysphasia (784.5)
> lisping or lalling (307.9)
> retarded development of speech (315.31-315.39)

307.1 Anorexia nervosa `CC`

> EXCLUDES eating disturbance NOS (307.50)
> feeding problem (783.3)
> of nonorganic origin (307.59)
> loss of appetite (783.0)
> of nonorganic origin (307.59)

CC Excl: 306.4, 306.8-306.9, 307.1, 307.50-307.59, 309.22

AHA: 4Q, '89, 11

☑5ᵗʰ 307.2 Tics

> EXCLUDES nail-biting or thumb-sucking (307.9)
> stereotypes occurring in isolation (307.3)
> tics of organic origin (333.3)

DEF: Involuntary muscle response usually confined to the face, shoulders.

307.20 Tic disorder, unspecified
Tic disorder NOS

307.21 Transient tic disorder

307.22 Chronic motor or vocal tic disorder

307.23 Tourette's disorder
Motor-verbal tic disorder

DEF: Syndrome of facial and vocal tics in childhood; progresses to spontaneous or involuntary jerking, obscene utterances, other uncontrollable actions considered inappropriate.

307.3 Stereotypic movement disorder
Body-rocking   Spasmus nutans
Head banging   Stereotypes NOS

> EXCLUDES tics (307.20-307.23)
> of organic origin (333.3)

☑5ᵗʰ 307.4 Specific disorders of sleep of nonorganic origin

> EXCLUDES narcolepsy (347.00-347.11)
> organic hypersomnia (327.10-327.19)
> organic insomnia (327.00-327.09)
> those of unspecified cause (780.50-780.59)

307.40 Nonorganic sleep disorder, unspecified

307.41 Transient disorder of initiating or maintaining sleep
Hyposomnia ⎫ associated with inter-
Insomnia ⎬ mittent emotional
Sleeplessness ⎭ reactions or conflicts

307.42 Persistent disorder of initiating or maintaining sleep
Hyposomnia, insomnia, or sleeplessness associated with:
anxiety
conditioned arousal
depression (major) (minor)
psychosis
Idiopathic insomnia
Paradoxical insomnia
Primary insomnia
Psychophysiological insomnia

307.43 Transient disorder of initiating or maintaining wakefulness
Hypersomnia associated with acute or inter-mittent emotional reactions or conflicts

307.44 Persistent disorder of initiating or maintaining wakefulness
Hypersomnia associated with depression (major) (minor)
Insufficient sleep syndrome
Primary hypersomnia

> EXCLUDES sleep deprivation (V69.4)

307.45 Circadian rhythm sleep disorder of nonorganic origin

307.46 Sleep arousal disorder
Night terror disorder
Night terrors
Sleep terror disorder
Sleepwalking
Somnambulism

DEF: Sleepwalking marked by extreme terror, panic, screaming, confusion; no recall of event upon arousal; term may refer to simply the act of sleepwalking.

307.47 Other dysfunctions of sleep stages or arousal from sleep
Nightmare disorder
Nightmares:
NOS
REM-sleep type
Sleep drunkenness

307.48 Repetitive intrusions of sleep
Repetitive intrusion of sleep with:
atypical polysomnographic features
environmental disturbances
repeated REM-sleep interruptions

307.49 Other
"Short-sleeper"
Subjective insomnia complaint

☑5ᵗʰ 307.5 Other and unspecified disorders of eating

> EXCLUDES anorexia:
> nervosa (307-1)
> of unspecified cause (783.0)
> overeating, of unspecified cause (783.6)
> vomiting:
> NOS (787.0)
> cyclical (536.2)
> psychogenic (306.4)

307.50 Eating disorder, unspecified
Eating disorder NOS

307.51 Bulimia nervosa
Overeating of nonorganic origin

DEF: Mental disorder commonly characterized by binge eating followed by self-induced vomiting; perceptions of being fat; and fear the inability to stop eating voluntarily.

307.52 Pica
Perverted appetite of nonorganic origin

DEF: Compulsive eating disorder characterized by craving for substances, other than food; such as paint chips or dirt.

307.53 Rumination disorder
Regurgitation, of nonorganic origin, of food with reswallowing

> EXCLUDES obsessional rumination (300.3)

307.54 Psychogenic vomiting

307.59 Other
Feeding disorder of infancy or early childhood of nonorganic origin
Infantile feeding ⎫
     disturbances ⎬ of nonorganic
Loss of appetite ⎭ origin

307.6 Enuresis
Enuresis (primary) (secondary) of nonorganic origin

> EXCLUDES enuresis of unspecified cause (788.3)

DEF: Involuntary urination past age of normal control; also called bedwetting; no trace to biological problem; focus on psychological issues.

☑4ᵗʰ ☑5ᵗʰ Additional Digit Required   Nonspecific PDx   Unacceptable PDx   Manifestation Code   **MCV** Major Cardiovascular Condition   ▶◀ Revised Text   ● New Code   ▲ Revised Code Title

2007 ICD•9•CM   **Volume 1 — 79**

Mental Disorders

307.7–310.0

307.7 Encopresis

Encopresis (continuous) (discontinuous) of nonorganic origin

EXCLUDES encopresis of unspecified cause (787.6)

DEF: Inability to control bowel movements; cause traced to psychological, not biological, problems.

307.8 Pain disorders related to psychological factors

307.80 Psychogenic pain, site unspecified

307.81 Tension headache

EXCLUDES headache:
NOS (784.0)
migraine (346.0-346.9)

AHA: N-D, '85, 16

307.89 Other

Code first to ▶type or◀ site of pain

EXCLUDES pain disorder exclusively attributed to psychological factors (307.80)
psychogenic pain (307.80)

307.9 Other and unspecified special symptoms or syndromes, not elsewhere classified

Communication disorder NOS	Lisping
	Masturbation
Hair plucking	Nail-biting
Lalling	Thumb-sucking

308 Acute reaction to stress

INCLUDES catastrophic stress
combat fatigue
gross stress reaction (acute)
transient disorders in response to exceptional physical or mental stress which usually subside within hours or days

EXCLUDES adjustment reaction or disorder (309.0-309.9)
chronic stress reaction (309.1-309.9)

308.0 Predominant disturbance of emotions

Anxiety ⎫ as acute reaction to
Emotional crisis ⎬ exceptional
Panic state ⎭ [gross] stress

308.1 Predominant disturbance of consciousness

Fugues as acute reaction to exceptional [gross] stress

308.2 Predominant psychomotor disturbance

Agitation states ⎫ as acute reaction to exceptional
Stupor ⎭ [gross] stress

308.3 Other acute reactions to stress

Acute situational disturbance
Acute stress disorder

EXCLUDES prolonged posttraumatic emotional disturbance (309.81)

308.4 Mixed disorders as reaction to stress

308.9 Unspecified acute reaction to stress

309 Adjustment reaction

INCLUDES adjustment disorders
reaction (adjustment) to chronic stress

EXCLUDES acute reaction to major stress (308.0-308.9)
neurotic disorders (300.0-300.9)

309.0 Adjustment disorder with depressed mood

Grief reaction

EXCLUDES affective psychoses (296.0-296.9)
neurotic depression (300.4)
prolonged depressive reaction (309.1)
psychogenic depressive psychosis (298.0)

309.1 Prolonged depressive reaction

EXCLUDES affective psychoses (296.0-296.9)
brief depressive reaction (309.0)
neurotic depression (300.4)
psychogenic depressive psychosis (298.0)

309.2 With predominant disturbance of other emotions

309.21 Separation anxiety disorder

DEF: Abnormal apprehension by a child when physically separated from support environment; byproduct of abnormal symbiotic child-parent relationship.

309.22 Emancipation disorder of adolescence and early adult life

DEF: Adjustment reaction of late adolescence; conflict over independence from parental supervision; symptoms include difficulty in making decisions, increased reliance on parental advice, deliberate adoption of values in opposition of parents.

309.23 Specific academic or work inhibition

309.24 Adjustment disorder with anxiety

309.28 Adjustment disorder with mixed anxiety and depressed mood

Adjustment reaction with anxiety and depression

309.29 Other

Culture shock

309.3 Adjustment disorder with disturbance of conduct

Conduct disturbance ⎫ as adjustment reaction
Destructiveness ⎭

EXCLUDES destructiveness in child (312.9)
disturbance of conduct NOS (312.9)
dyssocial behavior without manifest psychiatric disorder (V71.01-V71.02)
personality disorder with predominantly sociopathic or asocial manifestations (301.7)

309.4 Adjustment disorder with mixed disturbance of emotions and conduct

309.8 Other specified adjustment reactions

309.81 Posttraumatic stress disorder

Chronic posttraumatic stress disorder
Concentration camp syndrome
Posttraumatic stress disorder NOS
▶Post-traumatic stress disorder (PTSD)◀

EXCLUDES acute stress disorder (308.3)
posttraumatic brain syndrome:
nonpsychotic (310.2)
psychotic (293.0-293.9)

DEF: Preoccupation with traumatic events beyond normal experience; events such as rape, personal assault, combat, natural disasters, accidents, torture precipitate disorder; also recurring flashbacks of trauma; symptoms include difficulty remembering, sleeping, or concentrating, and guilt feelings for surviving.

309.82 Adjustment reaction with physical symptoms

309.83 Adjustment reaction with withdrawal

Elective mutism as adjustment reaction
Hospitalism (in children) NOS

309.89 Other

309.9 Unspecified adjustment reaction

Adaptation reaction NOS
Adjustment reaction NOS

310 Specific nonpsychotic mental disorders due to brain damage

EXCLUDES neuroses, personality disorders, or other nonpsychotic conditions occurring in a form similar to that seen with functional disorders but in association with a physical condition (300.0-300.9, 301.0-301.9)

310.0 Frontal lobe syndrome

Lobotomy syndrome
Postleucotomy syndrome [state]

EXCLUDES postcontusion syndrome (310.2)

N Newborn Age: 0　　P Pediatric Age: 0-17　　M Maternity Age: 12-55　　A Adult Age: 15-124　　CC CC Condition　　MC Major Complication　　CD Complex Dx　　HIV HIV Related Dx

Mental Disorders

310.1 Personality change due to conditions classified elsewhere
Cognitive or personality change of other type, of nonpsychotic severity
Organic psychosyndrome of nonpsychotic severity
Presbyophrenia NOS
Senility with mental changes of nonpsychotic severity

> EXCLUDES *memory loss of unknown cause (780.93)*

AHA: ▶2Q, '05, 6◀

DEF: Personality disorder caused by organic factors, such as brain lesions, head trauma, or cerebrovascular accident (CVA).

310.2 Postconcussion syndrome
Postcontusion syndrome or encephalopathy
Posttraumatic brain syndrome, nonpsychotic
Status postcommotio cerebri

> EXCLUDES *frontal lobe syndrome (310.0)*
> *postencephalitic syndrome (310.8)*
> *any organic psychotic conditions following head injury (293.0-294.0)*

AHA: 4Q, '90, 24

DEF: Nonpsychotic disorder due to brain trauma, causes symptoms unrelated to any disease process; symptoms include amnesia, serial headaches, rapid heartbeat, fatigue, disrupted sleep patterns, inability to concentrate.

310.8 Other specified nonpsychotic mental disorders following organic brain damage
Mild memory disturbance
Postencephalitic syndrome
Other focal (partial) organic psychosyndromes

310.9 Unspecified nonpsychotic mental disorder following organic brain damage `HIV`
AHA: 4Q, '03, 103

311 Depressive disorder, not elsewhere classified
Depressive disorder NOS   Depression NOS
Depressive state NOS

> EXCLUDES *acute reaction to major stress with depressive symptoms (308.0)*
> *affective personality disorder (301.10-301.13)*
> *affective psychoses (296.0-296.9)*
> *brief depressive reaction (309.0)*
> *depressive states associated with stressful events (309.0-309.1)*
> *disturbance of emotions specific to childhood and adolescence, with misery and unhappiness (313.1)*
> *mixed adjustment reaction with depressive symptoms (309.4)*
> *neurotic depression (300.4)*
> *prolonged depressive adjustment reaction (309.1)*
> *psychogenic depressive psychosis (298.0)*

AHA: 4Q, '03, 75

✓4ᵗʰ 312 Disturbance of conduct, not elsewhere classified

> EXCLUDES *adjustment reaction with disturbance of conduct (309.3)*
> *drug dependence (304.0-304.9)*
> *dyssocial behavior without manifest psychiatric disorder (V71.01-V71.02)*
> *personality disorder with predominantly sociopathic or asocial manifestations (301.7)*
> *sexual deviations (302.0-302.9)*

The following fifth-digit subclassification is for use with categories 312.0-312.2:
 0 **unspecified**
 1 **mild**
 2 **moderate**
 3 **severe**

✓5ᵗʰ 312.0 Undersocialized conduct disorder, aggressive type
Aggressive outburst   Unsocialized aggressive
Anger reaction   disorder

DEF: Mental condition identified by behaviors disrespectful of others' rights and of age-appropriate social norms or rules; symptoms include bullying, vandalism, verbal and physical abusiveness, lying, stealing, defiance.

✓5ᵗʰ 312.1 Undersocialized conduct disorder, unaggressive type
Childhood truancy, unsocialized
Solitary stealing
Tantrums

✓5ᵗʰ 312.2 Socialized conduct disorder
Childhood truancy, socialized   Group delinquency

> EXCLUDES *gang activity without manifest psychiatric disorder (V71.01)*

✓5ᵗʰ 312.3 Disorders of impulse control, not elsewhere classified
312.30 Impulse control disorder, unspecified
312.31 Pathological gambling
312.32 Kleptomania
312.33 Pyromania
312.34 Intermittent explosive disorder
312.35 Isolated explosive disorder
312.39 Other
Trichotillomania

312.4 Mixed disturbance of conduct and emotions
Neurotic delinquency

> EXCLUDES *compulsive conduct disorder (312.3)*

✓5ᵗʰ 312.8 Other specified disturbances of conduct, not elsewhere classified
312.81 Conduct disorder, childhood onset type
312.82 Conduct disorder, adolescent onset type
312.89 Other conduct disorder
Conduct disorder of unspecified onset

312.9 Unspecified disturbance of conduct
Delinquency (juvenile)
Disruptive behavior disorder NOS

✓4ᵗʰ 313 Disturbance of emotions specific to childhood and adolescence

> EXCLUDES *adjustment reaction (309.0-309.9)*
> *emotional disorder of neurotic type (300.0-300.9)*
> *masturbation, nail-biting, thumbsucking, and other isolated symptoms (307.0-307.9)*

313.0 Overanxious disorder
Anxiety and fearfulness } of childhood and
Overanxious disorder   } adolescence

> EXCLUDES *abnormal separation anxiety (309.21)*
> *anxiety states (300.00-300.09)*
> *hospitalism in children (309.83)*
> *phobic state (300.20-300.29)*

313.1 Misery and unhappiness disorder

> EXCLUDES *depressive neurosis (300.4)*

✓5ᵗʰ 313.2 Sensitivity, shyness, and social withdrawal disorder

> EXCLUDES *infantile autism (299.0)*
> *schizoid personality (301.20-301.22)*
> *schizophrenia (295.0-295.9)*

313.21 Shyness disorder of childhood
Sensitivity reaction of childhood or adolescence

313.22 Introverted disorder of childhood
Social withdrawal }
Withdrawal   } of childhood or
reaction   } adolescence

313.23 Selective mutism

> EXCLUDES *elective mutism as adjustment reaction (309.83)*

310.1–313.23

✓4ᵗʰ Additional Digit Required   Nonspecific PDx   Unacceptable PDx   Manifestation Code   **MCV** Major Cardiovascular Condition   ▶◀ Revised Text   ● New Code   ▲ Revised Code Title

2007 ICD•9•CM   February 2006 • Volume 1 — 81

Mental Disorders

313.3–319

313.3 Relationship problems
Sibling jealousy
> EXCLUDES   *relationship problems associated with aggression, destruction, or other forms of conduct disturbance (312.0-312.9)*

✓5ᵗʰ **313.8 Other or mixed emotional disturbances of childhood or adolescence**

313.81 Oppositional defiant disorder
DEF: Mental disorder of children noted for pervasive opposition, defiance of authority.

313.82 Identity disorder
Identity problem
DEF: Distress of adolescents caused by inability to form acceptable self-identity; uncertainty about career choice, sexual orientation, moral values.

313.83 Academic underachievement disorder

313.89 Other   P
Reactive attachment disorder of infancy or early childhood

313.9 Unspecified emotional disturbance of childhood or adolescence   P
Mental disorder of infancy, childhood or adolescence NOS

✓4ᵗʰ **314 Hyperkinetic syndrome of childhood**
> EXCLUDES   *hyperkinesis as symptom of underlying disorder—code the underlying disorder*

✓5ᵗʰ **314.0 Attention deficit disorder**
Adult
Child
DEF: A behavioral disorder usually diagnosed at an early age; characterized by the inability to focus attention for a normal period of time.

314.00 Without mention of hyperactivity
Predominantly inattentive type
AHA: 1Q, '97, 8

314.01 With hyperactivity
Combined type
Overactivity NOS
Predominantly hyperactive/impulsive type
Simple disturbance of attention with overactivity
AHA: 1Q, '97, 8

314.1 Hyperkinesis with developmental delay
Developmental disorder of hyperkinesis
Use additional code to identify any associated neurological disorder

314.2 Hyperkinetic conduct disorder
Hyperkinetic conduct disorder without developmental delay
> EXCLUDES   *hyperkinesis with significant delays in specific skills (314.1)*

314.8 Other specified manifestations of hyperkinetic syndrome

314.9 Unspecified hyperkinetic syndrome
Hyperkinetic reaction of childhood or adolescence NOS
Hyperkinetic syndrome NOS

✓4ᵗʰ **315 Specific delays in development**
> EXCLUDES   *that due to a neurological disorder (320.0-389.9)*

✓5ᵗʰ **315.0 Specific reading disorder**

315.00 Reading disorder, unspecified

315.01 Alexia
DEF: Lack of ability to understand written language; manifestation of aphasia.

315.02 Developmental dyslexia
DEF: Serious impairment of reading skills unexplained in relation to general intelligence and teaching processes; it can be inherited or congenital.

315.09 Other
Specific spelling difficulty

315.1 Mathematics disorder
Dyscalculia

315.2 Other specific learning difficulties
Disorder of written expression
> EXCLUDES   *specific arithmetical disorder (315.1)*
> *specific reading disorder (315.00-315.09)*

✓5ᵗʰ **315.3 Developmental speech or language disorder**

315.31 Expressive language disorder
Developmental aphasia
Word deafness
> EXCLUDES   *acquired aphasia (784.3)*
> *elective mutism (309.83, 313.0, 313.23)*

315.32 Mixed receptive-expressive language disorder
AHA: ▶2Q, '05, 5;◀ 4Q, '96, 30

315.39 Other
Developmental articulation disorder
Dyslalia
Phonological disorder
> EXCLUDES   *lisping and lalling (307.9)*
> *stammering and stuttering (307.0)*

315.4 Developmental coordination disorder
Clumsiness syndrome   Specific motor development
Dyspraxia syndrome   disorder

315.5 Mixed development disorder
AHA: 2Q, '02, 11

315.8 Other specified delays in development

315.9 Unspecified delay in development
Developmental disorder NOS
Learning disorder NOS

316 Psychic factors associated with diseases classified elsewhere
Psychologic factors in physical conditions classified elsewhere
Use additional code to identify the associated physical condition, as:
psychogenic:
asthma (493.9)
dermatitis (692.9)
duodenal ulcer (532.0-532.9)
eczema (691.8, 692.9)
gastric ulcer (531.0-531.9)
mucous colitis (564.9)
paroxysmal tachycardia (427.2)
ulcerative colitis (556)
urticaria (708.0-708.9)
psychosocial dwarfism (259.4)
> EXCLUDES   *physical symptoms and physiological malfunctions, not involving tissue damage, of mental origin (306.0-306.9)*

MENTAL RETARDATION (317-319)
Use additional code(s) to identify any associated psychiatric or physical condition(s)

317 Mild mental retardation
High-grade defect
IQ 50-70
Mild mental subnormality

✓4ᵗʰ **318 Other specified mental retardation**

318.0 Moderate mental retardation
IQ 35-49
Moderate mental subnormality

318.1 Severe mental retardation
IQ 20-34   Severe mental subnormality

318.2 Profound mental retardation
IQ under 20   Profound mental subnormality

319 Unspecified mental retardation
Mental deficiency NOS   Mental subnormality NOS

N Newborn Age: 0   P Pediatric Age: 0-17   M Maternity Age: 12-55   A Adult Age: 15-124   CC CC Condition   MC Major Complication   CD Complex Dx   HIV HIV Related Dx

6. DISEASES OF THE NERVOUS SYSTEM AND SENSE ORGANS (320-389)

INFLAMMATORY DISEASES OF THE CENTRAL NERVOUS SYSTEM (320-326)

✓4ᵗʰ 320 Bacterial meningitis

INCLUDES
arachnoiditis ⎫
leptomeningitis ⎪
meningitis ⎪
meningoencephalitis ⎬ bacterial
meningomyelitis ⎪
pachymeningitis ⎭

AHA: J-F, '87, 6

DEF: Bacterial infection causing inflammation of the lining of the brain and/or spinal cord.

320.0 **Hemophilus meningitis**   CC
Meningitis due to Hemophilus influenzae [H. influenzae]
CC Excl: 003.21, 013.00-013.16, 036.0, 047.0-047.9, 049.0-049.1, 053.0, 054.72, 072.1, 090.42, 091.81, 094.2, 098.89, 100.81, 112.83, 114.2, 115.01, 115.11, 115.91, 130.0, 250.60-250.63, 250.80-250.93, 320.0-322.9, 349.89, 349.9, 357.0

320.1 **Pneumococcal meningitis**   CC
CC Excl: See code 320.0

320.2 **Streptococcal meningitis**   CC
CC Excl: See code 320.0

320.3 **Staphylococcal meningitis**   CC
CC Excl: See code 320.0

320.7 *Meningitis in other bacterial diseases classified elsewhere*   CC
Code first underlying disease, as:
actinomycosis (039.8)
listeriosis (027.0)
typhoid fever (002.0)
whooping cough (033.0-033.9)
EXCLUDES
meningitis (in):
epidemic (036.0)
gonococcal (098.82)
meningococcal (036.0)
salmonellosis (003.21)
syphilis:
NOS (094.2)
congenital (090.42)
meningovascular (094.2)
secondary (091.81)
tuberculous (013.0)
CC Excl: See code 320.0

✓5ᵗʰ 320.8 Meningitis due to other specified bacteria
320.81 **Anaerobic meningitis**   CC
Bacteroides (fragilis)
Gram-negative anaerobes
CC Excl: See code 320.0

320.82 **Meningitis due to gram-negative bacteria, not elsewhere classified**   CC
Aerobacter aerogenes pneumoniae
Escherichia coli [E. coli]
Friedländer bacillus
Klebsiella
Proteus morganii
Pseudomonas
EXCLUDES *gram-negative anaerobes (320.81)*
CC Excl: See code 320.0

320.89 **Meningitis due to other specified bacteria**   CC
Bacillus pyocyaneus
CC Excl: See code 320.0

320.9 **Meningitis due to unspecified bacterium**   CC
Meningitis: Meningitis:
bacterial NOS   pyogenic NOS
purulent NOS   suppurative NOS
CC Excl: See code 320.0

✓4ᵗʰ 321 Meningitis due to other organisms

AHA: J-F, '87, 6

DEF: Infection causing inflammation of the lining of the brain and/or spinal cord, due to organisms other than bacteria.

321.0 *Cryptococcal meningitis*   CC
Code first underlying disease (117.5)
CC Excl: See code 320.0

321.1 *Meningitis in other fungal diseases*   CC
Code first underlying disease (110.0-118)
EXCLUDES
meningitis in:
candidiasis (112.83)
coccidioidomycosis (114.2)
histoplasmosis (115.01, 115.11, 115.91)
CC Excl: See code 320.0

321.2 *Meningitis due to viruses not elsewhere classified*   CC
Code first underlying disease, as:
meningitis due to arbovirus (060.0-066.9)
EXCLUDES
meningitis (due to):
abacterial (047.0-047.9)
adenovirus (049.1)
aseptic NOS (047.9)
Coxsackie (virus)(047.0)
ECHO virus (047.1)
enterovirus (047.0-047.9)
herpes simplex virus (054.72)
herpes zoster virus (053.0)
lymphocytic choriomeningitis virus (049.0)
mumps (072.1)
viral NOS (047.9)
meningo-eruptive syndrome (047.1)
CC Excl: 003.21, 013.00-013.16, 036.0, 047.0-047.9, 049.0-049.1, 053.0, 054.72, 072.1, 090.42, 091.81, 094.2, 098.89, 100.81, 112.83, 114.2, 115.01, 115.11, 115.91, 130.0, 320.0-322.9, 349.89, 349.9, 357.0
AHA: 4Q, '04, 51

321.3 *Meningitis due to trypanosomiasis*   CC
Code first underlying disease (086.0-086.9)
CC Excl: 003.21, 013.00-013.16, 036.0, 047.0-047.9, 049.0-049.1, 053.0, 054.72, 072.1, 090.42, 091.81, 094.2, 098.89, 100.81, 112.83, 114.2, 115.01, 115.11, 115.91, 130.0, 250.60-250.63, 250.80-250.93, 320.0-320.9, 321.0-321.8, 322.0-322.9, 349.89, 349.9, 357.0

321.4 *Meningitis in sarcoidosis*   CC
Code first underlying disease (135)
CC Excl: See code 321.3

321.8 *Meningitis due to other nonbacterial organisms classified elsewhere*   CC
Code first underlying disease
EXCLUDES *leptospiral meningitis (100.81)*
CC Excl: See code 321.3

✓4ᵗʰ 322 Meningitis of unspecified cause

INCLUDES
arachnoiditis ⎫
leptomeningitis ⎬ with no organism
meningitis ⎪ specified as
pachymeningitis ⎭ cause

AHA: J-F, '87, 6

DEF: Infection causing inflammation of the lining of the brain and/or spinal cord, due to unspecified cause.

322.0 **Nonpyogenic meningitis**   CC
Meningitis with clear cerebrospinal fluid
CC Excl: See code 321.3

✓4ᵗʰ
✓5ᵗʰ   Additional Digit Required   Nonspecific PDx   Unacceptable PDx   Manifestation Code   MCV Major Cardiovascular Condition   ►◄ Revised Text   ● New Code   ▲ Revised Code Title

2007 ICD•9•CM   **Volume 1 — 83**

Nervous System and Sense Organs

322.1–323.9

322.1 Eosinophilic meningitis `CC`
CC Excl: See code 321.3

322.2 Chronic meningitis `CC`
CC Excl: See code 321.3

322.9 Meningitis, unspecified `CC`
CC Excl: See code 321.3

✓4ᵗʰ **323 Encephalitis, myelitis, and encephalomyelitis**
INCLUDES acute disseminated encephalomyelitis
meningoencephalitis, except bacterial
meningomyelitis, except bacterial
▶myelitis:◄
ascending
transverse
EXCLUDES ▶acute transverse myelitis NOS (341.20)
acute transverse myelitis in conditions classified
elsewhere (341.21)◄
bacterial:
meningoencephalitis (320.0-320.9)
meningomyelitis (320.0-320.9)
▶idiopathic transverse myelitis (341.22)◄
DEF: Encephalitis: inflammation of brain tissues.
DEF: Myelitis: inflammation of the spinal cord.
DEF: Encephalomyelitis: inflammation of brain and spinal cord.

▲ ✓5ᵗʰ **323.0 Encephalitis, myelitis, and encephalomyelitis
in viral diseases classified elsewhere**
Code first underlying disease, as:
cat-scratch disease (078.3)
infectious mononucleosis (075)
ornithosis (073.7)

● **323.01 *Encephalitis and encephalomyelitis in
viral diseases classified elsewhere***
EXCLUDES encephalitis (in):
arthropod-borne viral
(062.0-064)
herpes simplex (054.3)
mumps (072.2)
other viral diseases of
central nervous
system (049.8-049.9)
poliomyelitis (045.0-045.9)
rubella (056.01)
slow virus infections of
central nervous
system (046.0-046.9)
viral NOS (049.9)
West Nile (066.41)

● **323.02 *Myelitis in viral diseases classified
elsewhere***
EXCLUDES myelitis (in):
herpes simplex (054.74)
herpes zoster (053.14)
poliomyelitis (045.0-045.9)
rubella (056.01)
other viral diseases of
central nervous
system (049.8-049.9)

▲ **323.1 *Encephalitis, myelitis, and encephalomyelitis in
rickettsial diseases classified elsewhere***
Code first underlying disease (080-083.9)
DEF: Inflammation of the brain caused by rickettsial disease
carried by louse, tick, or mite.

▲ **323.2 *Encephalitis, myelitis, and encephalomyelitis in
protozoal diseases classified elsewhere***
Code first underlying disease, as:
malaria (084.0-084.9)
trypanosomiasis (086.0-086.9)
DEF: Inflammation of the brain caused by protozoal disease carried
by mosquitoes and flies.

▲ ✓5ᵗʰ **323.4 Other encephalitis, myelitis, and encephalomyelitis
due to infection classified elsewhere**
Code first underlying disease

● **323.41 *Other encephalitis and encephalomyelitis
due to infection classified elsewhere***
EXCLUDES encephalitis (in):
meningococcal (036.1)
syphilis:
NOS (094.81)
congenital (090.41)
toxoplasmosis (130.0)
tuberculosis (013.6)
meningoencephalitis due to
free-living ameba
[Naegleria] (136.2)

● **323.42 *Other myelitis due to infection classified
elsewhere***
EXCLUDES myelitis (in):
syphilis (094.89)
tuberculosis (013.6)

▲ ✓5ᵗʰ **323.5 Encephalitis, myelitis, and encephalomyelitis
following immunization procedures**
Use additional E code to identify vaccine

● **323.51 Encephalitis and encephalomyelitis
following immunization procedures**
Encephalitis postimmunization or
postvaccinal
Encephalomyelitis postimmunization or
postvaccinal

● **323.52 Myelitis following immunization procedures**
Myelitis postimmunization or postvaccinal

▲ ✓5ᵗʰ **323.6 Postinfectious encephalitis, myelitis, and
encephalomyelitis**
Code first underlying disease
DEF: Infection, inflammation of brain several weeks following the
outbreak of a systemic infection.

● **323.61 *Infectious acute disseminated
encephalomyelitis [ADEM]***
Acute necrotizing hemorrhagic
encephalopathy
EXCLUDES noninfectious acute
disseminated
encephalomyelitis
(ADEM) (323.81)

● **323.62 *Other postinfectious encephalitis and
encephalomyelitis***
EXCLUDES encephalitis:
postchickenpox (052.0)
postmeasles (055.0)

● **323.63 *Postinfectious myelitis***
EXCLUDES postchickenpox myelitis
(052.2)
herpes simplex myelitis
(054.74)
herpes zoster myelitis (053.14)

▲ ✓5ᵗʰ **323.7 Toxic encephalitis, myelitis, and encephalomyelitis**
Code first underlying cause, as:
carbon tetrachloride (982.1)
hydroxyquinoline derivatives (961.3)
lead (984.0-984.9)
mercury (985.0)
thallium (985.8)
AHA: 2Q, '97, 8

● **323.71 *Toxic encephalitis and encephalomyelitis***
● **323.72 *Toxic myelitis***

▲ ✓5ᵗʰ **323.8 Other causes of encephalitis, myelitis, and
encephalomyelitis**

● **323.81 Other causes of encephalitis and** `HIV`
encephalomyelitis
Noninfectious acute disseminated
encephalomyelitis (ADEM)

● **323.82 Other causes of myelitis** `HIV`
Transverse myelitis NOS

▲ **323.9 Unspecified cause of encephalitis, myelitis,** `HIV`
and encephalomyelitis
AHA: ▶1Q, '06, 8◄

N Newborn Age: 0   P Pediatric Age: 0-17   M Maternity Age: 12-55   A Adult Age: 15-124   CC CC Condition   MC Major Complication   CD Complex Dx   HIV HIV Related Dx

√4ᵗʰ **324 Intracranial and intraspinal abscess**

    324.0 Intracranial abscess   `CC`

        Abscess (embolic):   Abscess (embolic) of brain
          cerebellar   [any part]:
          cerebral   epidural
                              extradural
                              otogenic
                              subdural

           EXCLUDES   *tuberculous (013.3)*

        CC Excl: 006.5, 013.20-013.36, 250.60-250.63, 250.80-250.93, 324.0-325, 348.8-348.9

    324.1 Intraspinal abscess   `CC`

        Abscess (embolic) of spinal cord [any part]:
          epidural
          extradural
          subdural

           EXCLUDES   *tuberculous (013.5)*

        CC Excl: 006.5, 013.20-013.36, 250.60-250.63, 250.80-250.93, 324.1

    324.9 Of unspecified site   `CC`

        Extradural or subdural abscess NOS

        CC Excl: 006.5, 013.20-013.36, 250.60-250.63, 250.80-250.93, 324.0-325

325 Phlebitis and thrombophlebitis of intracranial venous sinuses   `CC`

    Embolism   of cavernous, lateral, or
    Endophlebitis   other intracranial
    Phlebitis, septic or suppurative   or unspecified
    Thrombophlebitis   intracranial
    Thrombosis   venous sinus

        EXCLUDES   *that specified as:*
                         complicating pregnancy, childbirth, or the
                              puerperium (671.5)
                        of nonpyogenic origin (437.6)

    CC Excl: See code 324.9

    DEF: Inflammation and formation of blood clot in a vein within the brain or its lining.

326 Late effects of intracranial abscess or pyogenic infection

    Note: This category is to be used to indicate conditions whose primary classification is to 320-325 [excluding 320.7, 321.0-321.8, ▶323.01-323.42,◀ 323.6-323.7] as the cause of late effects, themselves classifiable elsewhere. The "late effects" include conditions specified as such, or as sequelae, which may occur at any time after the resolution of the causal condition.
    Use additional code to identify condition, as:
        hydrocephalus (331.4)
        paralysis (342.0-342.9, 344.0-344.9)

▶ORGANIC SLEEP DISORDERS (327)◀

√4ᵗʰ **327 Organic sleep disorders**

    AHA: 4Q, '05, 59-64

√5ᵗʰ **327.0 Organic disorders of initiating and maintaining sleep [Organic insomnia]**

        EXCLUDES   *insomnia NOS (780.52)*
                     insomnia not due to a substance or
                        known physiological condition
                        (307.41-307.42)
                     insomnia with sleep apnea NOS
                        (780.51)

    327.00 Organic insomnia, unspecified

    327.01 Insomnia due to medical condition classified elsewhere
        Code first underlying condition
           EXCLUDES   *insomnia due to mental*
                        disorder (327.02)

    327.02 Insomnia due to mental disorder
        Code first mental disorder
           EXCLUDES   *alcohol induced insomnia*
                        (291.82)
                     drug induced insomnia
                        (292.85)

    327.09 Other organic insomnia

√5ᵗʰ **327.1 Organic disorder of excessive somnolence [Organic hypersomnia]**

        EXCLUDES   *hypersomnia NOS (780.54)*
                     hypersomnia not due to a substance or
                        known physiological condition
                        (307.43-307.44)
                     hypersomnia with sleep apnea NOS
                        (780.53)

    327.10 Organic hypersomnia, unspecified

    327.11 Idiopathic hypersomnia with long sleep time

    327.12 Idiopathic hypersomnia without long sleep time

    327.13 Recurrent hypersomnia
        Kleine-Levin syndrome
        Menstrual related hypersomnia

    327.14 Hypersomnia due to medical condition classified elsewhere
        Code first underlying condition
           EXCLUDES   *hypersomnia due to mental*
                        disorder (327.15)

    327.15 Hypersomnia due to mental disorder
        Code first mental disorder
           EXCLUDES   *alcohol induced hypersomnia*
                        (291.82)
                     drug induced hypersomnia
                        (292.85)

    327.19 Other organic hypersomnia

√5ᵗʰ **327.2 Organic sleep apnea**

        EXCLUDES   *Cheyne-Stokes breathing (786.04)*
                     hypersomnia with sleep apnea NOS
                        (780.53)
                     insomnia with sleep apnea NOS
                        (780.51)
                     sleep apnea in newborn (770.81-
                        770.82)
                     sleep apnea NOS (780.57)

    327.20 Organic sleep apnea, unspecified

    327.21 Primary central sleep apnea

    327.22 High altitude periodic breathing

    327.23 Obstructive sleep apnea (adult) (pediatric)

    327.24 Idiopathic sleep related nonobstructive alveolar hypoventilation
        Sleep related hypoxia

    327.25 Congenital central alveolar hypoventilation syndrome

    327.26 Sleep related hypoventilation/hypoxemia in conditions classifiable elsewhere
        Code first underlying condition

    327.27 Central sleep apnea in conditions classified elsewhere
        Code first underlying condition

    327.29 Other organic sleep apnea

√5ᵗʰ **327.3 Circadian rhythm sleep disorder**
        Organic disorder of sleep wake cycle
        Organic disorder of sleep wake schedule
        EXCLUDES   *alcohol induced circadian rhythm sleep*
                     disorder (291.82)
                     circadian rhythm sleep disorder of
                        nonorganic origin (307.45)
                     disruption of 24 hour sleep wake cycle
                        NOS (780.55)
                     drug induced circadian rhythm sleep
                        disorder (292.85)

    327.30 Circadian rhythm sleep disorder, unspecified

    327.31 Circadian rhythm sleep disorder, delayed sleep phase type

    327.32 Circadian rhythm sleep disorder, advanced sleep phase type

    327.33 Circadian rhythm sleep disorder, irregular sleep-wake type

√4ᵗʰ Additional Digit Required   Nonspecific PDx   Unacceptable PDx   Manifestation Code   **MCV** Major Cardiovascular Condition   ▶◀ Revised Text   ● New Code   ▲ Revised Code Title
√5ᵗʰ

Nervous System and Sense Organs

327.34–331.81

327.34 Circadian rhythm sleep disorder, free-running type

327.35 Circadian rhythm sleep disorder, jet lag type

327.36 Circadian rhythm sleep disorder, shift work type

327.37 *Circadian rhythm sleep disorder in conditions classified elsewhere*
Code first underlying condition

327.39 Other circadian rhythm sleep disorder

√5th **327.4** Organic parasomnia

EXCLUDES *alcohol induced parasomnia (291.82)*
drug induced parasomnia (292.85)
parasomnia not due to a known physiological condition (307.47)

327.40 Organic parasomnia, unspecified

327.41 Confusional arousals

327.42 REM sleep behavior disorder

327.43 Recurrent isolated sleep paralysis

327.44 *Parasomnia in conditions classified elsewhere*
Code first underlying condition

327.49 Other organic parasomnia

√5th **327.5** Organic sleep related movement disorders

EXCLUDES ▶ *restless legs syndrome (333.94)*◀
sleep related movement disorder NOS (780.58)

327.51 Periodic limb movement disorder
Periodic limb movement sleep disorder

327.52 Sleep related leg cramps

327.53 Sleep related bruxism

327.59 Other organic sleep related movement disorders

327.8 Other organic sleep disorders

HEREDITARY AND DEGENERATIVE DISEASES OF THE CENTRAL NERVOUS SYSTEM (330-337)

EXCLUDES *hepatolenticular degeneration (275.1)*
multiple sclerosis (340)
other demyelinating diseases of central nervous system (341.0-341.9)

√4th **330** Cerebral degenerations usually manifest in childhood
Use additional code to identify associated mental retardation

330.0 Leukodystrophy

Krabbe's disease
Leukodystrophy:
  NOS
  globoid cell
  metachromatic
  sudanophilic

Pelizaeus-Merzbacher disease
Sulfatide lipidosis

DEF: Hereditary disease of arylsulfatase or cerebroside sulfatase; characterized by a diffuse loss of myelin in CNS; infantile form causes blindness, motor disturbances, rigidity, mental deterioration and, occasionally, convulsions.

330.1 Cerebral lipidoses

Amaurotic (familial) idiocy
Disease:
  Batten
  Jansky-Bielschowsky
  Kufs'

Disease:
  Spielmeyer-Vogt
  Tay-Sachs
  Gangliosidosis

DEF: Genetic disorder causing abnormal lipid accumulation in the reticuloendothelial cells of the brain.

330.2 *Cerebral degeneration in generalized lipidoses*
Code first underlying disease, as:
Fabry's disease (272.7)
Gaucher's disease (272.7)
Niemann-Pick disease (272.7)
sphingolipidosis (272.7)

330.3 *Cerebral degeneration of childhood in other diseases classified elsewhere*
Code first underlying disease, as:
Hunter's disease (277.5)
mucopolysaccharidosis (277.5)

330.8 Other specified cerebral degenerations in childhood
Alpers' disease or gray-matter degeneration
Infantile necrotizing encephalomyelopathy
Leigh's disease
Subacute necrotizing encephalopathy or encephalomyelopathy
AHA: N-D, '85, 5

330.9 Unspecified cerebral degeneration in childhood

√4th **331** Other cerebral degenerations

331.0 Alzheimer's disease
AHA: 4Q, '00, 41; 4Q, '99, 7; N-D, '84, 20

DEF: Diffuse atrophy of cerebral cortex; causing a progressive decline in intellectual and physical functions, including memory loss, personality changes and profound dementia.

√5th **331.1** Frontotemporal dementia
Use additional code for associated behavioral disturbance (294.10-294.11)
AHA: 4Q, '03, 57

DEF: Rare, progressive degenerative brain disease, similar to Alzheimer's; cortical atrophy affects the frontal and temporal lobes.

331.11 Pick's disease
DEF: A less common form of progressive frontotemporal dementia with asymmetrical atrophy of the frontal and temporal regions of the cerebral cortex including abnormal rounded brain cells called Pick cells together with the presence of abnormal staining of protein (called tau) within the cells, called Pick bodies; symptoms include prominent apathy, deterioration of social skills, behavioral changes such as disinhibition and restlessness, echolalia, impairment of language, memory, and intellect, increased carelessness, poor personal hygiene, and decreased attention span.

331.19 Other frontotemporal dementia
Frontal dementia

331.2 Senile degeneration of brain
EXCLUDES *senility NOS (797)*

331.3 Communicating hydrocephalus
EXCLUDES *congenital hydrocephalus (741.0, 742.3)*
AHA: S-O, '85, 12

DEF: Subarachnoid hemorrhage and meningitis causing excess buildup of cerebrospinal fluid in cavities due to nonabsorption of fluid back through fluid pathways.

331.4 Obstructive hydrocephalus ⒸⒸ
Acquired hydrocephalus NOS
EXCLUDES *congenital hydrocephalus (741.0, 742.3)*
CC Excl: 250.60-250.63, 250.80-250.93, 331.3-331.7, 331.82-331.9, 348.8-348.9, 741.00-741.03, 742.3-742.4, 742.59-742.9
AHA: 4Q, '03, 106; 1Q, '99, 9

DEF: Obstruction of cerebrospinal fluid passage from brain into spinal canal.

331.7 *Cerebral degeneration in diseases classified elsewhere*
Code first underlying disease, as:
alcoholism (303.0-303.9)
beriberi (265.0)
cerebrovascular disease (430-438)
congenital hydrocephalus (741.0, 742.3)
myxedema (244.0-244.9)
neoplastic disease (140.0-239.9)
vitamin B_{12} deficiency (266.2)
EXCLUDES *cerebral degeneration in:*
Jakob-Creutzfeldt disease (046.1)
progressive multifocal leukoencephalopathy (046.3)
subacute spongiform encephalopathy (046.1)

√5th **331.8** Other cerebral degeneration
331.81 Reye's syndrome Ⓟ
DEF: Rare childhood illness, often developed after a bout of viral upper respiratory infection; characterized by vomiting, elevated serum transaminase, changes in liver and other viscera; symptoms may be followed by an encephalopathic phase with brain swelling, disturbances of consciousness and seizures; can be fatal.

Ⓝ Newborn Age: 0   Ⓟ Pediatric Age: 0-17   Ⓜ Maternity Age: 12-55   Ⓐ Adult Age: 15-124   ⒸⒸ CC Condition   ⓂⒸ Major Complication   ⒸⒹ Complex Dx   ⒽⒾⱽ HIV Related Dx

331.82 Dementia with Lewy bodies
Dementia with Parkinsonism
Lewy body dementia
Lewy body disease
Use additional code for associated behavioral disturbance (294.10-294.11)

AHA: 4Q, '03, 57

DEF: A cerebral dementia with neurophysiologic changes including increased hippocampal volume, hypoperfusion in the occipital lobes, and beta amyloid deposits with neurofibrillarity tangles, atrophy of cortex and brainstem, hallmark neuropsychologic characteristics are fluctuating cognition with pronounced variation in attention and alertness; recurrent hallucinations; and parkinsonism.

331.83 Mild cognitive impairment, so stated

EXCLUDES	altered mental status (780.97)
	cerebral degeneration (331.0-331.9)
	change in mental status (780.97)
	cognitive deficits following (late effects of) cerebral hemorrhage or infarction (438.0)
	cognitive impairment due to intracranial or head injury (850-854, 959.01)
	cognitive impairment due to late effect of intracranial injury (907.0)
	dementia (290.0-290.43, 294.8)
	mild memory disturbance (310.8)
	neurologic neglect syndrome (781.8)
	personality change, nonpsychotic (310.1)

331.89 Other
Cerebral ataxia

331.9 Cerebral degeneration, unspecified

√4ᵗʰ 332 Parkinson's disease

EXCLUDES	dementia with Parkinsonism (331.82)0

332.0 Paralysis agitans
Parkinsonism or Parkinson's disease:
NOS
idiopathic
primary

AHA: M-A, '87, 7

DEF: Form of parkinsonism; progressive, occurs in senior years; characterized by masklike facial expression; condition affects ability to stand erect, walk smoothly; weakened muscles, also tremble and involuntarily movement.

332.1 Secondary Parkinsonism
Neuroleptic-induced Parkinsonism
Parkinsonism due to drugs
Use additional E code to identify drug, if drug-induced

EXCLUDES	Parkinsonism (in):
	Huntington's disease (333.4)
	progressive supranuclear palsy (333.0)
	Shy-Drager syndrome (333.0)
	syphilitic (094.82)

√4ᵗʰ 333 Other extrapyramidal disease and abnormal movement disorders

INCLUDES	other forms of extrapyramidal, basal ganglia, or striatopallidal disease

EXCLUDES	abnormal movements of head NOS (781.0)
	sleep related movement disorders (327.51-327.59)

333.0 Other degenerative diseases of the basal ganglia
Atrophy or degeneration:
olivopontocerebellar [Déjérine-Thomas syndrome]
pigmentary pallidal [Hallervorden-Spatz disease]
striatonigral
Parkinsonian syndrome associated with:
idiopathic orthostatic hypotension
symptomatic orthostatic hypotension
Progressive supranuclear ophthalmoplegia
Shy-Drager syndrome

AHA: 3Q, '96, 8

333.1 Essential and other specified forms of tremor
Benign essential tremor
Familial tremor
Medication-induced postural tremor
Use additional E code to identify drug, if drug-induced

EXCLUDES	tremor NOS (781.0)

333.2 Myoclonus
Familial essential myoclonus
Progressive myoclonic epilepsy
Unverricht-Lundborg disease
Use additional E code to identify drug, if drug-induced

AHA: 3Q, '97, 4; M-A, '87, 12

DEF: Spontaneous movements or contractions of muscles.

333.3 Tics of organic origin
Use additional E code to identify drug, if drug-induced

EXCLUDES	Gilles de la Tourette's syndrome (307.23)
	habit spasm (307.22)
	tic NOS (307.20)

333.4 Huntington's chorea
DEF: Genetic disease characterized by chronic progressive mental deterioration; dementia and death within 15 years of onset.

333.5 Other choreas
Hemiballism(us)
Paroxysmal choreo-athetosis
Use additional E code to identify drug, if drug-induced

EXCLUDES	Sydenham's or rheumatic chorea (392.0-392.9)

▲ **333.6 Genetic torsion dystonia**
Dystonia:
deformans progressiva
musculorum deformans
(Schwalbe-) Ziehen-Oppenheim disease
DEF: Sustained muscular contractions, causing twisting and repetitive movements that result in abnormal postures of trunk and limbs; etiology unknown.

▲ **√5ᵗʰ 333.7 Acquired torsion dystonia**
● **333.71 Athetoid cerebral palsy**
Double athetosis (syndrome)
Vogt's disease

EXCLUDES	infantile cerebral palsy (343.0-343.9)

● **333.72 Acute dystonia due to drugs**
Acute dystonic reaction due to drugs
Neuroleptic induced acute dystonia
Use additional E code to identify drug

EXCLUDES	blepharospasm due to drugs (333.85)
	orofacial dyskinesia due to drugs (333.85)
	secondary Parkinsonism (332.1)
	subacute dyskinesia due to drugs (333.85)
	tardive dyskinesia (333.85)

● **333.79 Other acquired torsion dystonia**
√5ᵗʰ 333.8 Fragments of torsion dystonia
Use additional E code to identify drug, if drug-induced
333.81 Blepharospasm

EXCLUDES	▶ blepharospasm due to drugs (333.85)◀

DEF: Uncontrolled winking or blinking due to orbicularis oculi muscle spasm.

√4ᵗʰ / √5ᵗʰ Additional Digit Required   Nonspecific PDx   Unacceptable PDx   Manifestation Code   **MCV** Major Cardiovascular Condition   ▶◀ Revised Text   ● New Code   ▲ Revised Code Title

2007 ICD•9•CM   **October 2006 • Volume 1 — 87**

Nervous System and Sense Organs

331.82–333.81

Nervous System and Sense Organs

333.82–336.3

333.82 Orofacial dyskinesia
> EXCLUDES ▸ orofacial dyskinesia due to drugs (333.85)◂
> DEF: Uncontrolled movement of mouth or facial muscles.

333.83 Spasmodic torticollis
> EXCLUDES torticollis:
> NOS (723.5)
> hysterical (300.11)
> psychogenic (306.0)
> DEF: Uncontrolled movement of head due to spasms of neck muscle.

333.84 Organic writers' cramp
> EXCLUDES pychogenic (300.89)

333.85 Subacute dyskinesia due to drugs
> Blepharospasm due to drugs
> Orofacial dyskinesia due to drugs
> Tardive dyskinesia
> Use additional E code to identify drug
> EXCLUDES acute dystonia due to drugs (333.72)
> acute dystonic reaction due to drugs (333.72)
> secondary Parkinsonism (332.1)

333.89 Other

√5ᵗʰ 333.9 Other and unspecified extrapyramidal diseases and abnormal movement disorders

333.90 Unspecified extrapyramidal disease and abnormal movement disorder
> Medication-induced movement disorders NOS
> Use additional E code to identify drug, if drug-induced

333.91 Stiff-man syndrome

333.92 Neuroleptic malignant syndrome
> Use additional E code to identify drug
> EXCLUDES ▸ neuroleptic induced Parkinsonism (332.1)◂
> AHA: 4Q, '94, 37

333.93 Benign shuddering attacks
> AHA: 4Q, '94, 37

333.94 Restless legs syndrome [RLS]

333.99 Other
> Neuroleptic-induced acute akathisia
> Use additional E code to identify drug, if drug-induced
> AHA: 4Q, '04, 95; 2Q, '04, 12; 4Q, '94, 37

√4ᵗʰ 334 Spinocerebellar disease
> EXCLUDES olivopontocerebellar degeneration (333.0)
> peroneal muscular atrophy (356.1)

334.0 Friedreich's ataxia
> DEF: Genetic recessive disease of children; sclerosis of dorsal, lateral spinal cord columns; characterized by ataxia, speech impairment, swaying and irregular movements, with muscle paralysis, especially of lower limbs.

334.1 Hereditary spastic paraplegia

334.2 Primary cerebellar degeneration
> Cerebellar ataxia:
> Marie's
> Sanger-Brown
> Dyssynergia cerebellaris myoclonica
> Primary cerebellar degeneration:
> NOS
> hereditary
> sporadic
> AHA: M-A, '87, 9

334.3 Other cerebellar ataxia
> Cerebellar ataxia NOS
> Use additional E code to identify drug, if drug-induced

334.4 Cerebellar ataxia in diseases classified elsewhere
> Code first underlying disease, as:
> alcoholism (303.0-303.9)
> myxedema (244.0-244.9)
> neoplastic disease (140.0-239.9)

334.8 Other spinocerebellar diseases
> Ataxia-telangiectasia [Louis-Bar syndrome]
> Corticostriatal-spinal degeneration

334.9 Spinocerebellar disease, unspecified

√4ᵗʰ 335 Anterior horn cell disease

335.0 Werdnig-Hoffmann disease CC
> Infantile spinal muscular atrophy
> Progressive muscular atrophy of infancy
> CC Excl: 250.60-250.63, 250.80-250.93, 334.8-335.0, 335.10-337.9, 349.89-349.9
> DEF: Spinal muscle atrophy manifested in prenatal period or shortly after birth; symptoms include hypotonia, atrophy of skeletal muscle; death occurs in infancy.

√5ᵗʰ 335.1 Spinal muscular atrophy
335.10 Spinal muscular atrophy, unspecified CC
> CC Excl: See code 335.0

335.11 Kugelberg-Welander disease CC
> Spinal muscular atrophy:
> familial   juvenile
> CC Excl: See code 335.0
> DEF: Hereditary; juvenile muscle atrophy; appears during first two decades of life; due to lesions of anterior horns of spinal cord; includes wasting, diminution of lower body muscles and twitching.

335.19 Other CC
> Adult spinal muscular atrophy
> CC Excl: See code 335.0

√5ᵗʰ 335.2 Motor neuron disease
335.20 Amyotrophic lateral sclerosis CC A
> Motor neuron disease (bulbar) (mixed type)
> CC Excl: See code 335.0
> AHA: 4Q, '95, 81

335.21 Progressive muscular atrophy CC
> Duchenne-Aran muscular atrophy
> Progressive muscular atrophy (pure)
> CC Excl: See code 335.0

335.22 Progressive bulbar palsy CC
> CC Excl: See code 335.0

335.23 Pseudobulbar palsy CC
> CC Excl: See code 335.0

335.24 Primary lateral sclerosis CC
> CC Excl: See code 335.0

335.29 Other CC
> CC Excl: See code 335.0

335.8 Other anterior horn cell diseases CC
> CC Excl: See code 335.0

335.9 Anterior horn cell disease, unspecified CC
> CC Excl: See code 335.0

√4ᵗʰ 336 Other diseases of spinal cord

336.0 Syringomyelia and syringobulbia
> AHA: 1Q, '89, 10

336.1 Vascular myelopathies
> Acute infarction of spinal cord (embolic) (nonembolic)
> Arterial thrombosis of spinal cord
> Edema of spinal cord
> Hematomyelia
> Subacute necrotic myelopathy

336.2 Subacute combined degeneration of spinalcord in diseases classified elsewhere
> Code first underlying disease, as:
> pernicious anemia (281.0)
> other vitamin B_{12} deficiency anemia (281.1)
> vitamin B_{12} deficiency (266.2)

336.3 Myelopathy in other diseases classified elsewhere
> Code first underlying disease, as:
> myelopathy in neoplastic disease (140.0-239.9)
> EXCLUDES myelopathy in:
> intervertebral disc disorder (722.70-722.73)
> spondylosis (721.1, 721.41-721.42, 721.91)
> AHA: 3Q, '99, 5

N Newborn Age: 0   P Pediatric Age: 0-17   M Maternity Age: 12-55   A Adult Age: 15-124   CC CC Condition   MC Major Complication   CD Complex Dx   HIV HIV Related Dx

336.8 Other myelopathy
Myelopathy: Myelopathy:
   drug-induced   radiation-induced
Use additonal E code to identify cause

336.9 Unspecified disease of spinal cord `HIV`
Cord compression NOS   Myelopathy NOS
> EXCLUDES   *myelitis ▶(323.02, 323.1, 323.2,*
> *323.42, 323.52, 323.63, 323.72,*
> *323.82, 323.9)◀*
> *spinal (canal) stenosis (723.0, 724.00-*
> *724.09)*

✓4th **337 Disorders of the autonomic nervous system**
> INCLUDES   disorders of peripheral autonomic,
> sympathetic, parasympathetic, or
> vegetative system
> EXCLUDES   *familial dysautonomia [Riley-Day syndrome]*
> *(742.8)*

337.0 Idiopathic peripheral autonomic neuropathy
Carotid sinus syncope or syndrome
Cervical sympathetic dystrophy or paralysis

337.1 *Peripheral autonomic neuropathy in*
disorders classified elsewhere
Code first underlying disease, as:
   amyloidosis ▶(277.30-277.39)◀
   diabetes (250.6)
AHA: 2Q, '93, 6; 3Q, '91, 9; N-D, '84, 9

✓5th **337.2 Reflex sympathetic dystrophy**
AHA: 4Q, '93, 24

DEF: Disturbance of the sympathetic nervous system evidenced by sweating, pain, pallor and edema following injury to nerves or blood vessels.

337.20 Reflex sympathetic dystrophy, unspecified
337.21 Reflex sympathetic dystrophy of the upper limb
337.22 Reflex sympathetic dystrophy of the lower limb
337.29 Reflex sympathetic dystrophy of other specified site

337.3 Autonomic dysreflexia
Use additional code to identify the cause, such as:
   decubitus ulcer (707.00-707.09)
   fecal impaction (560.39)
   urinary tract infection (599.0)

AHA: 4Q, '98, 37

DEF: Noxious stimuli evokes paroxysmal hypertension, bradycardia, excess sweating, headache, pilomotor responses, facial flushing, and nasal congestion due to uncontrolled parasympathetic nerve response; usually occurs in patients with spinal cord injury above major sympathetic outflow tract (T₆).

337.9 Unspecified disorder of autonomic nervous system

▶PAIN (338)◀

● ✓4th **338 Pain, not elsewhere classified**
Use additional code to identify:
   pain associated with psychological factors (307.89)
> EXCLUDES   *generalized pain (780.96)*
> *localized pain, unspecified type—code to pain*
> *by site*
> *pain disorder exclusively attributed to*
> *psychological factors (307.80)*

● **338.0 Central pain syndrome**
Déjérine-Roussy syndrome
Myelopathic pain syndrome
Thalamic pain syndrome (hyperesthetic)

● ✓5th **338.1 Acute pain**
● **338.11 Acute pain due to trauma**
● **338.12 Acute post-thoracotomy pain**
Post-thoracotomy pain NOS
● **338.18 Other acute postoperative pain**
Postoperative pain NOS
● **338.19 Other acute pain**
> EXCLUDES   *neoplasm related acute pain*
> *(338.3)*

● ✓5th **338.2 Chronic pain**
> EXCLUDES   *causalgia (355.9)*
> *lower limb (355.71)*
> *upper limb (354.4)*
> *chronic pain syndrome (338.4)*
> *myofascial pain syndrome (729.1)*
> *neoplasm related chronic pain (338.3)*
> *reflex sympathetic dystrophy (337.20-*
> *337.29)*

● **338.21 Chronic pain due to trauma**
● **338.22 Chronic post-thoracotomy pain**
● **338.28 Other chronic postoperative pain**
● **338.29 Other chronic pain**

● **338.3 Neoplasm related pain (acute) (chronic)**
Cancer associated pain
Pain due to malignancy (primary) (secondary)
Tumor associated pain

● **338.4 Chronic pain syndrome**
Chronic pain associated with significant
psychosocial dysfunction

OTHER DISORDERS OF THE CENTRAL NERVOUS SYSTEM (340-349)

340 Multiple sclerosis `CC`
Disseminated or multiple sclerosis:
   NOS   cord
   brain stem   generalized
CC Excl: 250.60-250.63, 250.80-250.93, 340, 341.8-341.9

✓4th **341 Other demyelinating diseases of central nervous system**
341.0 Neuromyelitis optica
341.1 Schilder's disease
Baló's concentric sclerosis   Encephalitis periaxialis:
Encephalitis periaxialis: diffusa [Schilder's]
   concentrica [Baló's]

DEF: Chronic leukoencephalopathy of children and adolescents; symptoms include blindness, deafness, bilateral spasticity and progressive mental deterioration.

● ✓5th **341.2 Acute (transverse) myelitis**
> EXCLUDES   *acute (transverse) myelitis (in) (due to):*
> *following immunization procedures*
> *(323.52)*
> *infection classified elsewhere*
> *(323.42)*
> *postinfectious (323.63)*
> *protozoal diseases classified*
> *elsewhere (323.2)*
> *rickettsial diseases classified*
> *elsewhere (323.1)*
> *toxic (323.72)*
> *viral diseases classified elsewhere*
> *(323.02)*
> *transverse myelitis NOS (323.82)*

● **341.20 Acute (transverse) myelitis NOS**
● **341.21 *Acute (transverse) myelitis in conditions***
classified elsewhere
Code first underlying condition
● **341.22 Idiopathic transverse myelitis**

341.8 Other demyelinating diseases of central nervous system
Central demyelination of corpus callosum
Central pontine myelinosis
Marchiafava (-Bignami) disease

AHA: N-D, '87, 6

341.9 Demyelinating disease of central nervous `HIV`
system, unspecified

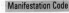

Nervous System and Sense Organs

342–345

√4th **342 Hemiplegia and hemiparesis**

Note: This category is to be used when hemiplegia (complete) (incomplete) is reported without further specification, or is stated to be old or long-standing but of unspecified cause. The category is also for use in multiple coding to identify these types of hemiplegia resulting from any cause.

EXCLUDES   congenital (343.1)
hemiplegia due to late effect of cerebrovascular accident (438.20-438.22)
infantile NOS (343.4)

The following fifth-digits are for use with codes 342.0-342.9:
0 **affecting unspecified side**
1 **affecting dominant side**
2 **affecting nondominant side**

AHA: 4Q, '94, 38

√5th **342.0 Flaccid hemiplegia**
√5th **342.1 Spastic hemiplegia**
√5th **342.8 Other specified hemiplegia**
√5th **342.9 Hemiplegia, unspecified**
AHA: 4Q, '98, 87

√4th **343 Infantile cerebral palsy**

INCLUDES   cerebral:
palsy NOS
spastic infantile paralysis
congenital spastic paralysis (cerebral)
Little's disease
paralysis (spastic) due to birth injury:
intracranial
spinal

EXCLUDES ▶ athetoid cerebral palsy (333.71)◄
hereditary cerebral paralysis, such as:
hereditary spastic paraplegia (334.1)
Vogt's disease ▶(333.71)◄
spastic paralysis specified as noncongenital or noninfantile (344.0-344.9)

343.0 Diplegic
Congenital diplegia
Congenital paraplegia
DEF: Paralysis affecting both sides of the body simultaneously.

343.1 Hemiplegic
Congenital hemiplegia
EXCLUDES   infantile hemiplegia NOS (343.4)

343.2 Quadriplegic   CC
Tetraplegic
CC Excl: 250.60-250.63, 250.80-250.93, 342.00-344.9, 348.8-348.9, 349.89-349.9, 742.59-742.9

343.3 Monoplegic

343.4 Infantile hemiplegia
Infantile hemiplegia (postnatal) NOS

343.8 Other specified infantile cerebral palsy

343.9 Infantile cerebral palsy, unspecified
Cerebral palsy NOS
AHA: 4Q, '05, 89

√4th **344 Other paralytic syndromes**

Note: This category is to be used when the listed conditions are reported without further specification or are stated to be old or long-standing but of unspecified cause. The category is also for use in multiple coding to identify these conditions resulting from any cause.

INCLUDES   paralysis (complete) (incomplete), except as classifiable to 342 and 343

EXCLUDES   congenital or infantile cerebral palsy (343.0-343.9)
hemiplegia (342.0-342.9)
congenital or infantile (343.1, 343.4)

√5th **344.0 Quadriplegia and quadriparesis**
344.00 Quadriplegia unspecified   CC
CC Excl: See code 343.2

AHA: 4Q, '03, 103; 4Q, '98, 38

344.01 C₁-C₄ complete   CC
CC Excl: See code 343.2

344.02 C₁-C₄ incomplete   CC
CC Excl: See code 343.2

344.03 C₅-C₇ complete   CC
CC Excl: See code 343.2

344.04 C₅-C₇ incomplete   CC
CC Excl: See code 343.2

344.09 Other   CC
CC Excl: See code 343.2

AHA: 1Q, '01, 12; 4Q, '98, 39

344.1 Paraplegia
Paralysis of both lower limbs   Paraplegia (lower)
AHA: 4Q, '03, 110;M-A, '87, 10

344.2 Diplegia of upper limbs
Diplegia (upper)   Paralysis of both upper limbs

√5th **344.3 Monoplegia of lower limb**
Paralysis of lower limb
EXCLUDES   monoplegia of lower limb due to late effect of cerebrovascular accident (438.40-438.42)

344.30 Affecting unspecified side
344.31 Affecting dominant side
344.32 Affecting nondominant side

√5th **344.4 Monoplegia of upper limb**
Paralysis of upper limb
EXCLUDES   monoplegia of upper limb due to late effect of cerebrovascular accident (438.30-438.32)

344.40 Affecting unspecified side
344.41 Affecting dominant side
344.42 Affecting nondominant side

344.5 Unspecified monoplegia

√5th **344.6 Cauda equina syndrome**
DEF: Dull pain and paresthesias in sacrum, perineum and bladder due to compression of spinal nerve roots; pain radiates down buttocks, back of thigh, calf of leg and into foot with prickling, burning sensations.
344.60 Without mention of neurogenic bladder
344.61 With neurogenic bladder
Acontractile bladder
Autonomic hyperreflexia of bladder
Cord bladder
Detrusor hyperreflexia
AHA: M-J, '87, 12; M-A, '87, 10

√5th **344.8 Other specified paralytic syndromes**
344.81 Locked-in state
AHA: 4Q, '93, 24

DEF: State of consciousness where patients are paralyzed and unable to respond to environmental stimuli; patients have eye movements, and stimuli can enter the brain but patients cannot respond to stimuli.

344.89 Other specified paralytic syndrome
AHA: 2Q, '99, 4

344.9 Paralysis, unspecified

▲ √4th **345 Epilepsy and recurrent seizures**

The following fifth-digit subclassification is for use with categories 345.0, .1, .4-.9:
0 **without mention of intractable epilepsy**
1 **with intractable epilepsy**

EXCLUDES   progressive myoclonic epilepsy (333.2)
AHA: 1Q, '93, 24; 2Q, '92, 8; 4Q, '92, 23

DEF: Brain disorder characterized by electrical-like disturbances; may include occasional impairment or loss of consciousness, abnormal motor phenomena and psychic or sensory disturbances.

N Newborn Age: 0   P Pediatric Age: 0-17   M Maternity Age: 12-55   A Adult Age: 15-124   CC CC Condition   MC Major Complication   CD Complex Dx   HIV HIV Related Dx

90 — Volume 1 • October 2006   2007 ICD•9•CM

√5ᵗʰ **345.0 Generalized nonconvulsive epilepsy** `CC 1`

Absences: Pykno-epilepsy
   atonic   Seizures:
   typical   akinetic
Minor epilepsy   atonic
Petit mal

CC Excl: For code 345.01: 250.60-250.63, 345.00-345.91, 348.8-348.9, 349.89, 349.9

AHA: For code 345.00: 1Q, '04, 18

√5ᵗʰ **345.1 Generalized convulsive epilepsy** `CC`

Epileptic seizures: Epileptic seizures:
   clonic   tonic-clonic
   myoclonic   Grand mal
   tonic   Major epilepsy

   EXCLUDES   *convulsions:*
            NOS ▶*(780.39)*◀
            infantile ▶*(780.39)*◀
            newborn (779.0)
            infantile spasms (345.6)

CC Excl: See code 345.01

AHA: 3Q, '97, 4

DEF: Convulsive seizures with tension of limbs (tonic) or rhythmic contractions (clonic).

345.2 Petit mal status `CC`

Epileptic absence status

CC Excl: 250.60-250.63, 250.80-250.93, 345.00-345.91, 348.8-348.9, 349.89, 349.9

DEF: Minor myoclonic spasms and sudden momentary loss of consciousness in epilepsy.

345.3 Grand mal status `CC`

Status epilepticus NOS

   EXCLUDES   *epilepsia partialis continua (345.7)*
            status:
              psychomotor (345.7)
              temporal lobe (345.7)

CC Excl: See code 345.2

AHA: ▶3Q, '05, 12◀

DEF: Sudden loss of consciousness followed by generalized convulsions in epilepsy.

▲ √5ᵗʰ **345.4 Localization-related (focal) (partial) epilepsy and epileptic syndromes with complex partial seizures** `CC 1`

Epilepsy:
   limbic system
   partial:
     secondarily generalized
     ▶with impairment of consciousness◀
     with memory and ideational disturbances
   psychomotor
   psychosensory
   temporal lobe
Epileptic automatism

CC Excl: For code 345.41: 250.60-250.63, 345.00-345.91, 348.8-348.9, 349.89, 349.9

▲ √5ᵗʰ **345.5 Localization-related (focal) (partial) epilepsy and epileptic syndromes with simple partial seizures** `CC 1`

Epilepsy:
   Bravais-Jacksonian NOS
   focal (motor) NOS
   Jacksonian NOS
   motor partial
   partial NOS:
     ▶without impairment of consciousness◀
   sensory-induced
   somatomotor
   somatosensory
   visceral
   visual

CC Excl: For code 345.51: See code 345.4

√5ᵗʰ **345.6 Infantile spasms** `CC 1`

Hypsarrhythmia   Salaam attacks
Lightning spasms

   EXCLUDES   *salaam tic (781.0)*

CC Excl: For code 345.61: See code 345.4

AHA: N-D, '84, 12

√5ᵗʰ **345.7 Epilepsia partialis continua** `CC 1`

Kojevnikov's epilepsy

CC Excl: For code 345.71: See code 345.4

DEF: Continuous muscle contractions and relaxation; result of abnormal neural discharge.

▲ √5ᵗʰ **345.8 Other forms of epilepsy and recurrent seizures** `CC 1`

Epilepsy: Epilepsy:
   cursive [running]   gelastic

CC Excl: For code 345.81: See code 345.4

√5ᵗʰ **345.9 Epilepsy, unspecified** `CC 1`

Epileptic convulsions, fits, or seizures NOS
▶Recurrent seizures NOS
Seizure disorder NOS◀

   EXCLUDES   ▶ *convulsion (convulsive) disorder (780.39)*◀
            convulsive seizure or fit NOS ▶*(780.39)*◀
            ▶*recurrent convulsions (780.39)*◀

CC Excl: For code 345.91: See code 345.4

AHA: N-D, '87, 12

√4ᵗʰ **346 Migraine**

DEF: Benign vascular headache of extreme pain; commonly associated with irritability, nausea, vomiting and often photophobia; premonitory visual hallucination of a crescent in the visual field (scotoma).

The following fifth-digit subclassification is for use with category 346:
   0 without mention of intractable migraine
   1 with intractable migraine, so stated

√5ᵗʰ **346.0 Classical migraine**

Migraine preceded or accompanied by transient focal neurological phenomena
Migraine with aura

√5ᵗʰ **346.1 Common migraine**

Atypical migraine   Sick headache

√5ᵗʰ **346.2 Variants of migraine**

Cluster headache   Migraine:
Histamine cephalgia   lower half
Horton's neuralgia   retinal
Migraine: Neuralgia:
   abdominal   ciliary
   basilar   migrainous

√5ᵗʰ **346.8 Other forms of migraine**

Migraine: Migraine:
   hemiplegic   ophthalmoplegic

√5ᵗʰ **346.9 Migraine, unspecified**

AHA: N-D, '85, 16

√4ᵗʰ **347 Cataplexy and narcolepsy**

DEF: Cataplexy: Sudden onset of muscle weakness with loss of tone and strength; caused by aggressive or spontaneous emotions.
DEF: Narcolepsy: Brief, recurrent, uncontrollable episodes of sound sleep.

√5ᵗʰ **347.0 Narcolepsy**

347.00 Without cataplexy
    Narcolepsy NOS

347.01 With cataplexy

√5ᵗʰ **347.1 Narcolepsy in conditions classified elsewhere**

   Code first underlying condition
347.10 Without cataplexy
347.11 With cataplexy

√4ᵗʰ **348 Other conditions of brain**

348.0 Cerebral cysts

Arachnoid cyst   Porencephaly, acquired
Porencephalic cyst   Pseudoporencephaly

   EXCLUDES   *porencephaly (congenital) (742.4)*

√4ᵗʰ ▲ Additional Digit Required   Nonspecific PDx   Unacceptable PDx   Manifestation Code   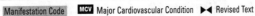 **MCV** Major Cardiovascular Condition   ▶◀ Revised Text   ● New Code   ▲ Revised Code Title

2007 ICD•9•CM   **October 2006 • Volume 1 — 91**

Nervous System and Sense Organs

348.1–349.9

348.1 Anoxic brain damage `CC`

> **EXCLUDES** *that occurring in:*
> *abortion (634-638 with .7, 639.8)*
> *ectopic or molar pregnancy (639.8)*
> *labor or delivery (668.2, 669.4)*
> *that of newborn (767.0, 768.0-768.9,*
> *772.1-772.2)*

Use additional E code to identify cause
CC Excl: 250.60-250.63, 250.80-250.93, 348.1-348.2, 349.89, 349.9

DEF: Brain injury due to lack of oxygen, other than birth trauma.

348.2 Benign intracranial hypertension
Pseudotumor cerebri

> **EXCLUDES** *hypertensive encephalopathy (437.2)*

DEF: Elevated pressure in brain due to fluid retention in brain cavities.

√5ᵗʰ **348.3 Encephalopathy, not elsewhere classified**
AHA: 4Q, '03, 58; 3Q, '97, 4

  348.30 Encephalopathy, unspecified `HIV`
  348.31 Metabolic encephalopathy `HIV`
    Septic encephalopathy

>   **EXCLUDES** ▶*toxic metabolic encepha-*
>   *lopathy (349.82)*◀

  348.39 Other encephalopathy `HIV`

>   **EXCLUDES** *encephalopathy:*
>   *alcoholic (291.2)*
>   *hepatic (572.2)*
>   *hypertensive (437.2)*
>   *toxic (349.82)*

348.4 Compression of brain
Compression
Herniation } brain (stem)
Posterior fossa compression syndrome
AHA: 4Q, '94, 37

DEF: Elevated pressure in brain due to blood clot, tumor, fracture, abscess, other condition.

348.5 Cerebral edema

DEF: Elevated pressure in the brain due to fluid retention in brain tissues.

348.8 Other conditions of brain
Cerebral: Cerebral:
  calcification   fungus
AHA: S-O, '87, 9

348.9 Unspecified condition of brain `HIV`

√4ᵗʰ **349 Other and unspecified disorders of the nervous system**

349.0 Reaction to spinal or lumbar puncture
Headache following lumbar puncture
AHA: 2Q, '99, 9; 3Q, '90, 18

349.1 Nervous system complications from `CC`
surgically implanted device

> **EXCLUDES** *immediate postoperative complications*
> *(997.00-997.09)*
> *mechanical complications of nervous*
> *system device (996.2)*

CC Excl: 250.60-250.63, 250.80-250.93, 349.1, 349.89, 349.9

Cranial Nerves

Olfactory bulb (I)
Optic nerve (II)
Oculomotor nerve (III)
Trochlear nerve (IV)
Trigeminal nerve (V)
Abducens nerve (VI)
Facial nerve (VII)
Pons
Vestibulocochlear nerve (VIII)
Glossopharyngeal nerve (IX)
Vagus nerve (X)
Accessory nerve (XI)
Hypoglossal nerve (XII)

349.2 Disorders of meninges, not elsewhere classified
Adhesions, meningeal (cerebral) (spinal)
Cyst, spinal meninges
Meningocele, acquired
Pseudomeningocele, acquired
AHA: ▶1Q, '06, 15;◀ 2Q, '98, 18; 3Q, '94, 4

√5ᵗʰ **349.8 Other specified disorders of nervous system**
  349.81 Cerebrospinal fluid rhinorrhea `CC`

>   **EXCLUDES** *cerebrospinal fluid otorrhea*
>   *(388.61)*

  CC Excl: 250.60-250.63, 250.80-250.93, 349.81, 349.89, 349.9

  DEF: Cerebrospinal fluid discharging from the nose; caused by fracture of frontal bone with tearing of dura mater and arachnoid.

  349.82 Toxic encephalopathy `CC`
  ▶Toxic metabolic encephalopathy◀
  Use additional E code to identify cause
  AHA: 4Q, '93, 29

  CC Excl: 013.60-013.66, 017.90-017.96, 036.1, 049.8-049.9, 052.0, 054.3, 062.0-062.9, 063.0-063.9, 072.2, 090.41, 094.81, 130.0, 250.60-250.63, 250.80-250.93, 323.01-323.9, 341.20-341.22, 348.30-348.39, 348.8-348.9, 349.82-349.89, 349.9

  DEF: Brain tissue degeneration due to toxic substance.

  349.89 Other

349.9 Unspecified disorders of nervous system `HIV`
Disorder of nervous system (central) NOS

Peripheral Nervous System

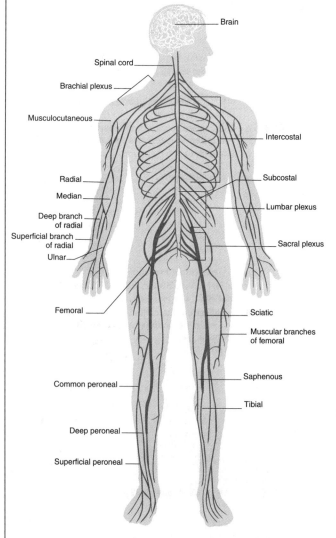

Brain
Spinal cord
Brachial plexus
Musculocutaneous
Intercostal
Radial
Subcostal
Median
Lumbar plexus
Deep branch of radial
Superficial branch of radial
Sacral plexus
Ulnar
Femoral
Sciatic
Muscular branches of femoral
Common peroneal
Saphenous
Tibial
Deep peroneal
Superficial peroneal

`N` Newborn Age: 0   `P` Pediatric Age: 0-17   `M` Maternity Age: 12-55   `A` Adult Age: 15-124   `CC` CC Condition   `MC` Major Complication   `CD` Complex Dx   `HIV` HIV Related Dx

DISORDERS OF THE PERIPHERAL NERVOUS SYSTEM (350-359)

EXCLUDES	diseases of:

diseases of:
 acoustic [8th] nerve (388.5)
 oculomotor [3rd, 4th, 6th] nerves (378.0-378.9)
 optic [2nd] nerve (377.0-377.9)
 peripheral autonomic nerves (337.0-337.9)

neuralgia
neuritis ⎬ NOS or "rheumatic" (729.2)
radiculitis

 peripheral neuritis in pregnancy (646.4)

✓4th 350 Trigeminal nerve disorders

> INCLUDES   disorders of 5th cranial nerve

350.1 Trigeminal neuralgia
 Tic douloureux   Trigeminal neuralgia NOS
 Trifacial neuralgia
> EXCLUDES   postherpetic (053.12)

350.2 Atypical face pain
350.8 Other specified trigeminal nerve disorders
350.9 Trigeminal nerve disorder, unspecified

✓4th 351 Facial nerve disorders
> INCLUDES   disorders of 7th cranial nerve
> EXCLUDES   that in newborn (767.5)

351.0 Bell's palsy
 Facial palsy
 DEF: Unilateral paralysis of face due to lesion on facial nerve; produces facial distortion.

351.1 Geniculate ganglionitis
 Geniculate ganglionitis NOS
> EXCLUDES   herpetic (053.11)
 DEF: Inflammation of tissue at bend in facial nerve.

351.8 Other facial nerve disorders
 Facial myokymia   Melkersson's syndrome
 AHA: 3Q, '02, 13

351.9 Facial nerve disorder, unspecified

✓4th 352 Disorders of other cranial nerves
352.0 Disorders of olfactory [1st] nerve
352.1 Glossopharyngeal neuralgia
 AHA: 2Q, '02, 8
 DEF: Pain between throat and ear along petrosal and jugular ganglia.

352.2 Other disorders of glossopharyngeal [9th] nerve
352.3 Disorders of pneumogastric [10th] nerve
 Disorders of vagal nerve
> EXCLUDES   paralysis of vocal cords or larynx (478.30-478.34)
 DEF: Nerve disorder affecting ear, tongue, pharynx, larynx, esophagus, viscera and thorax.

352.4 Disorders of accessory [11th] nerve
 DEF: Nerve disorder affecting palate, pharynx, larynx, thoracic viscera, sternocleidomastoid and trapezius muscles.

352.5 Disorders of hypoglossal [12th] nerve
 DEF: Nerve disorder affecting tongue muscles.

352.6 Multiple cranial nerve palsies
 Collet-Sicard syndrome   Polyneuritis cranialis

352.9 Unspecified disorder of cranial nerves

✓4th 353 Nerve root and plexus disorders
> EXCLUDES   conditions due to:
> intervertebral disc disorders (722.0-722.9)
> spondylosis (720.0-721.9)
> vertebrogenic disorders (723.0-724.9)

353.0 Brachial plexus lesions
 Cervical rib syndrome
 Costoclavicular syndrome
 Scalenus anticus syndrome
 Thoracic outlet syndrome
> EXCLUDES   brachial neuritis or radiculitis NOS (723.4)
> that in newborn (767.6)
 DEF: Acquired disorder in tissue along nerves in shoulder; causes corresponding motor and sensory dysfunction.

Trigeminal and Facial Nerve Branches

Temporal branches — Zygomatic branches — Buccal branches — Mandibular branch — Cervical branch — Branches of Facial Nerve (above) — Maxillary (V2) — Divisions of Trigeminal Nerve (below) — Ophthalmic (V1) — Trigeminal nerve (CN V) — Mandibulary (V3)

353.1 Lumbosacral plexus lesions
 DEF: Acquired disorder in tissue along nerves in lower back; causes corresponding motor and sensory dysfunction.

353.2 Cervical root lesions, not elsewhere classified
353.3 Thoracic root lesions, not elsewhere classified
353.4 Lumbosacral root lesions, not elsewhere classified
353.5 Neuralgic amyotrophy
 Parsonage-Aldren-Turner syndrome
353.6 Phantom limb (syndrome)
 DEF: Abnormal tingling or a burning sensation, transient aches, and intermittent or continuous pain perceived as originating in the absent limb.

353.8 Other nerve root and plexus disorders
353.9 Unspecified nerve root and plexus disorder

✓4th 354 Mononeuritis of upper limb and mononeuritis multiplex
 DEF: Inflammation of a single nerve; known as mononeuritis multiplex when several nerves in unrelated body areas are affected.

354.0 Carpal tunnel syndrome
 Median nerve entrapment
 Partial thenar atrophy
 DEF: Compression of median nerve by tendons; causes pain, tingling, numbness and burning sensation in hand.

354.1 Other lesion of median nerve
 Median nerve neuritis

354.2 Lesion of ulnar nerve
 Cubital tunnel syndrome
 Tardy ulnar nerve palsy

354.3 Lesion of radial nerve
 Acute radial nerve palsy
 AHA: N-D, '87, 6

354.4 Causalgia of upper limb
> EXCLUDES   causalgia:
> NOS (355.9)
> lower limb (355.71)
 DEF: Peripheral nerve damage, upper limb; usually due to injury; causes burning sensation and trophic skin changes.

354.5 Mononeuritis multiplex
 Combinations of single conditions classifiable to 354 or 355

354.8 Other mononeuritis of upper limb
354.9 Mononeuritis of upper limb, unspecified

✓4th 355 Mononeuritis of lower limb
355.0 Lesion of sciatic nerve
> EXCLUDES   sciatica NOS (724.3)
 AHA: 2Q, '89, 12
 DEF: Acquired disorder of sciatic nerve; causes motor and sensory dysfunction in back, buttock and leg.

355.1 Meralgia paresthetica
 Lateral cutaneous femoral nerve of thigh compression or syndrome
 DEF: Inguinal ligament entraps lateral femoral cutaneous nerve; causes tingling, pain and numbness along outer thigh.

355.2 Other lesion of femoral nerve

✓4th Additional Digit Required **✓5th** Nonspecific PDx Unacceptable PDx Manifestation Code **MCV** Major Cardiovascular Condition ▶◀ Revised Text ● New Code ▲ Revised Code Title

2007 ICD•9•CM   **Volume 1 — 93**

Nervous System and Sense Organs

355.3–358.9

355.3 Lesion of lateral popliteal nerve
Lesion of common peroneal nerve

355.4 Lesion of medial popliteal nerve

355.5 Tarsal tunnel syndrome
DEF: Compressed, entrapped posterior tibial nerve; causes tingling, pain and numbness in sole of foot.

355.6 Lesion of plantar nerve
Morton's metatarsalgia, neuralgia, or neuroma

✓5th **355.7 Other mononeuritis of lower limb**

    355.71 Causalgia of lower limb
      EXCLUDES   causalgia:
          NOS (355.9)
          upper limb (354.4)
      DEF: Dysfunction of lower limb peripheral nerve, usually due to injury; causes burning pain and trophic skin changes.

    355.79 Other mononeuritis of lower limb

355.8 Mononeuritis of lower limb, unspecified

355.9 Mononeuritis of unspecified site
Causalgia NOS
  EXCLUDES   causalgia:
    lower limb (355.71)
    upper limb (354.4)

✓4th **356 Hereditary and idiopathic peripheral neuropathy**

356.0 Hereditary peripheral neuropathy
Déjérine-Sottas disease

356.1 Peroneal muscular atrophy
Charcôt-Marie-Tooth disease
Neuropathic muscular atrophy
DEF: Genetic disorder, in muscles innervated by peroneal nerves; symptoms include muscle wasting in lower limbs and locomotor difficulties.

356.2 Hereditary sensory neuropathy
DEF: Inherited disorder in dorsal root ganglia, optic nerve, and cerebellum, causing sensory losses, shooting pains, and foot ulcers.

356.3 Refsum's disease
Heredopathia atactica polyneuritiformis
DEF: Genetic disorder of lipid metabolism; causes persistent, painful inflammation of nerves and retinitis pigmentosa.

356.4 Idiopathic progressive polyneuropathy

356.8 Other specified idiopathic peripheral neuropathy
Supranuclear paralysis

356.9 Unspecified

✓4th **357 Inflammatory and toxic neuropathy**

357.0 Acute infective polyneuritis   CC
Guillain-Barré syndrome   Postinfectious polyneuritis
CC Excl: 003.21, 013.00-013.16, 036.0, 036.89, 036.9, 041.81-041.89, 041.9, 047.0-047.9, 049.0-049.1, 053.0, 054.72, 072.1, 090.42, 091.81, 094.2, 098.89, 100.81, 112.83, 114.2, 115.01, 115.11, 115.91, 130.0, 139.8, 320.0-320.9, 321.0-321.8, 322.0-322.9, 349.89, 349.9, 357.0
AHA: 2Q, '98, 12
DEF: Guillain-Barré syndrome: acute demyelinaty polyneuropathy preceded by viral illness (i.e., herpes, cytomegalovirus [CMV], Epstein-Barr virus [EBV]) or a bacterial illness; areflexic motor paralysis with mild sensory disturbance and acellular rise in spinal fluid protein.

357.1 Polyneuropathy in collagen vasculardisease
Code first underlying disease, as:
  disseminated lupus erythematosus (710.0)
  polyarteritis nodosa (446.0)
  rheumatoid arthritis (714.0)

357.2 Polyneuropathy in diabetes
Code first underlying disease (250.6)
AHA: 4Q, '03, 105; 2Q, '92, 15; 3Q, '91, 9

357.3 Polyneuropathy in malignant disease
Code first underlying disease (140.0-208.9)

357.4 Polyneuropathy in other diseases classified elsewhere
Code first underlying disease, as:
  amyloidosis ▶(277.30-277.39)◄
  beriberi (265.0)
  ▶chronic uremia (585.9)◄
  deficiency of B vitamins (266.0-266.9)
  diphtheria (032.0-032.9)
  hypoglycemia (251.2)
  pellagra (265.2)
  porphyria (277.1)
  sarcoidosis (135)
  uremia ▶NOS (586)◄
  EXCLUDES   polyneuropathy in:
    herpes zoster (053.13)
    mumps (072.72)
AHA: 2Q, '98, 15

357.5 Alcoholic polyneuropathy

357.6 Polyneuropathy due to drugs
Use additional E code to identify drug

357.7 Polyneuropathy due to other toxic agents
Use additional E code to identify toxic agent

✓5th **357.8 Other**
AHA: 4Q, '02, 47; 2Q, '98, 12

  357.81 Chronic inflammatory demyelinating polyneuritis
    DEF: Inflammation of peripheral nerves resulting in destruction of myelin sheath; associated with diabetes mellitus, dys-proteinemias, renal failure and malnutrition; symptoms in-clude tingling, numbness, burning pain, diminished tendon reflexes, weakness, and atrophy in lower extremities.

  357.82 Critical illness polyneuropathy
    Acute motor neuropathy
    AHA: 4Q, '03, 111
    DEF: An acute axonal neuropathy, both sensory and motor, that is associated with Systemic Inflammatory Response Syndrome (SIRS).

  357.89 Other inflammatory and toxic neuropathy

357.9 Unspecified

✓4th **358 Myoneural disorders**

✓5th **358.0 Myasthenia gravis**
AHA: 4Q, '03, 59
DEF: Autoimmune disorder of acetylcholine at neuromuscular junction; causing fatigue of voluntary muscles.

  358.00 Myasthenia gravis without (acute) exacerbation   CC
    Myasthenia gravis NOS
    CC Excl: 250.60-250.63, 250.80-250.93, 349.89, 349.9, 358.00-358.1

  358.01 Myasthenia gravis with (acute) exacerbation   CC
    Myasthenia gravis in crisis
    CC Excl: See code 358.00
    AHA: 1Q, '05, 4; 4Q, '04, 139

358.1 Myasthenic syndromes in diseases classified elsewhere   CC

Amyotrophy   } from stated cause
Eaton-Lambert syndrome } classified elsewhere

Code first underlying disease, as:
  botulism (005.1)
  diabetes mellitus (250.6)
  hypothyroidism (244.0-244.9)
  malignant neoplasm (140.0-208.9)
  pernicious anemia (281.0)
  thyrotoxicosis (242.0-242.9)
CC Excl: See code 358.0

358.2 Toxic myoneural disorders
Use additional E code to identify toxic agent

358.8 Other specified myoneural disorders

358.9 Myoneural disorders, unspecified
AHA: 2Q, '02, 16

N Newborn Age: 0   P Pediatric Age: 0-17   M Maternity Age: 12-55   A Adult Age: 15-124   CC CC Condition   MC Major Complication   CD Complex Dx   HIV HIV Related Dx

94 — Volume 1 • October 2006   2007 ICD•9•CM

✓4th **359 Muscular dystrophies and other myopathies**
> EXCLUDES *idiopathic polymyositis (710.4)*

359.0 **Congenital hereditary muscular dystrophy** CC
> Benign congenital myopathy   Myotubular myopathy
> Central core disease   Nemaline body disease
> Centronuclear myopathy
> > EXCLUDES *arthrogryposis multiplex congenita (754.89)*

CC Excl: 250.60-250.63, 250.80-250.93, 349.89, 349.9, 359.0-359.1
DEF: Genetic disorder; causing progressive or nonprogressive muscle weakness.

359.1 **Hereditary progressive muscular dystrophy** CC
> Muscular dystrophy: Muscular dystrophy:
>   NOS   Gower's
>   distal   Landouzy-Déjérine
>   Duchenne   limb-girdle
>   Erb's   ocular
>   fascioscapulohumeral   oculopharyngeal

CC Excl: See code 359.0
DEF: Genetic degenerative, muscle disease; causes progressive weakness, wasting of muscle with no nerve involvement.

359.2 **Myotonic disorders**
> Dystrophia myotonica   Paramyotonia congenita
> Eulenburg's disease   Steinert's disease
> Myotonia congenita   Thomsen's disease

DEF: Impaired movement due to spasmatic, rigid muscles.

359.3 **Familial periodic paralysis**
> Hypokalemic familial periodic paralysis

DEF: Genetic disorder; characterized by rapidly progressive flaccid paralysis; attacks often occur after exercise or exposure to cold or dietary changes.

359.4 **Toxic myopathy**
> Use additional E code to identify toxic agent
AHA: 1Q, '88, 5
DEF: Muscle disorder caused by toxic agent.

359.5 *Myopathy in endocrine diseases classified elsewhere*
> Code first underlying disease, as:
>   Addison's disease (255.4)
>   Cushing's syndrome (255.0)
>   hypopituitarism (253.2)
>   myxedema (244.0-244.9)
>   thyrotoxicosis (242.0-242.9)
DEF: Muscle disorder secondary to dysfunction in hormone secretion.

359.6 *Symptomatic inflammatory myopathy in diseases classified elsewhere*
> Code first underlying disease, as:
>   amyloidosis ▶(277.30-277.39)◀
>   disseminated lupus erythematosus (710.0)
>   malignant neoplasm (140.0-208.9)
>   polyarteritis nodosa (446.0)
>   rheumatoid arthritis (714.0)
>   sarcoidosis (135)
>   scleroderma (710.1)
>   Sjögren's disease (710.2)

✓5th 359.8 **Other myopathies**
AHA: 4Q, '02, 47; 3Q, '90, 17

359.81 **Critical illness myopathy**
> Acute necrotizing myopathy
> Acute quadriplegic myopathy
> Intensive care (ICU) myopathy
> Myopathy of critical illness

359.89 **Other myopathies**

359.9 Myopathy, unspecified

DISORDERS OF THE EYE AND ADNEXA (360-379)

✓4th **360 Disorders of the globe**
> INCLUDES disorders affecting multiple structures of eye

✓5th 360.0 **Purulent endophthalmitis**
> EXCLUDES ▶ bleb associated endophthalmitis (379.63)◀

Eye

Sclera, Choroid (uvea), Cornea, Iris, Pupil, Anterior chamber, Posterior chamber, Ciliary body, Conjunctiva, Vitreous body, Lens, Hyaloid canal, Lamina cribosa, Optic nerve, Optic disk, Fovea, Retina — **Globe (Eyeball)**

Posterior Pole of Globe — Macula, Fovea, Optic disk — Ciliary body, Conjunctival veins, Canal of Schlemm, Trabecular mesh, Anterior chamber, Iris, Lens — **Flow of Aqueous Humor**

360.00 **Purulent endophthalmitis, unspecified**
360.01 **Acute endophthalmitis**
360.02 **Panophthalmitis**
360.03 **Chronic endophthalmitis**
360.04 **Vitreous abscess**

✓5th 360.1 **Other endophthalmitis**
> EXCLUDES ▶ bleb associated endophthalmitis (379.63)◀

360.11 **Sympathetic uveitis**
DEF: Inflammation of vascular layer of uninjured eye; follows injury to other eye.

360.12 **Panuveitis**
DEF: Inflammation of entire vascular layer of eye, including choroid, iris and ciliary body.

360.13 **Parasitic endophthalmitis NOS**
DEF: Parasitic infection causing inflammation of the entire eye.

360.14 **Ophthalmia nodosa**
DEF: Conjunctival inflammation caused by embedded hairs.

360.19 **Other**
> Phacoanaphylactic endophthalmitis

✓5th 360.2 **Degenerative disorders of globe**
AHA: 3Q, '91, 3

360.20 **Degenerative disorder of globe, unspecified**
360.21 **Progressive high (degenerative) myopia**
> Malignant myopia
DEF: Severe, progressive nearsightedness in adults, complicated by serious disease of the choroid; leads to retinal detachment and blindness.

360.23 **Siderosis**
DEF: Iron pigment deposits within tissue of eyeball; caused by high iron content of blood.

360.24 **Other metallosis**
> Chalcosis
DEF: Metal deposits, other than iron, within eyeball tissues.

✓4th ✓5th Additional Digit Required | Nonspecific PDx | Unacceptable PDx | Manifestation Code | MCV Major Cardiovascular Condition | ▶◀ Revised Text | ● New Code | ▲ Revised Code Title

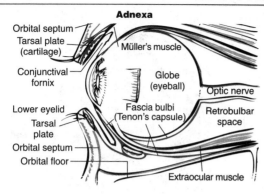

Adnexa

Orbital septum
Tarsal plate (cartilage)
Müller's muscle
Conjunctival fornix
Globe (eyeball)
Optic nerve
Lower eyelid
Fascia bulbi (Tenon's capsule)
Retrobulbar space
Tarsal plate
Orbital septum
Orbital floor
Extraocular muscle

360.29 Other
> EXCLUDES   xerophthalmia (264.7)

√5th **360.3 Hypotony of eye**
360.30 Hypotony, unspecified
> DEF: Low osmotic pressure causing lack of tone, tension and strength.

360.31 Primary hypotony
360.32 Ocular fistula causing hypotony
> DEF: Low intraocular pressure due to leak through abnormal passage.

360.33 Hypotony associated with other ocular disorders
360.34 Flat anterior chamber
> DEF: Low pressure behind cornea, causing compression.

√5th **360.4 Degenerated conditions of globe**
360.40 Degenerated globe or eye, unspecified
360.41 Blind hypotensive eye
> Atrophy of globe
> Phthisis bulbi
> DEF: Vision loss due to extremely low intraocular pressure.

360.42 Blind hypertensive eye
> Absolute glaucoma
> DEF: Vision loss due to painful, high intraocular pressure.

360.43 Hemophthalmos, except current injury
> EXCLUDES   traumatic (871.0-871.9, 921.0-921.9)
> DEF: Pool of blood within eyeball, not from current injury.

360.44 Leucocoria
> DEF: Whitish mass or reflex in the pupil behind lens; also called cat's eye reflex; often indicative of retinoblastoma.

√5th **360.5 Retained (old) intraocular foreign body, magnetic**
> EXCLUDES   current penetrating injury with magnetic foreign body (871.5)
> retained (old) foreign body of orbit (376.6)

360.50 Foreign body, magnetic, intraocular, unspecified
360.51 Foreign body, magnetic, in anterior chamber
360.52 Foreign body, magnetic, in iris or ciliary body
360.53 Foreign body, magnetic, in lens
360.54 Foreign body, magnetic, in vitreous
360.55 Foreign body, magnetic, in posterior wall
360.59 Foreign body, magnetic, in other or multiple sites

√5th **360.6 Retained (old) intraocular foreign body, nonmagnetic**
> Retained (old) foreign body:
> NOS
> nonmagnetic
> EXCLUDES   current penetrating injury with (nonmagnetic) foreign body (871.6)
> retained (old) foreign body in orbit (376.6)

360.60 Foreign body, intraocular, unspecified
360.61 Foreign body in anterior chamber
360.62 Foreign body in iris or ciliary body
360.63 Foreign body in lens
360.64 Foreign body in vitreous
360.65 Foreign body in posterior wall
360.69 Foreign body in other or multiple sites

√5th **360.8 Other disorders of globe**
360.81 Luxation of globe
> DEF: Displacement of eyeball.

360.89 Other

360.9 Unspecified disorder of globe

√4th **361 Retinal detachments and defects**
> DEF: Light-sensitive layer at back of eye, separates from blood supply; disrupting vision.

√5th **361.0 Retinal detachment with retinal defect**
> Rhegmatogenous retinal detachment
> EXCLUDES   detachment of retinal pigment epithelium (362.42-362.43)
> retinal detachment (serous) (without defect) (361.2)

361.00 Retinal detachment with retinal defect, unspecified
361.01 Recent detachment, partial, with single defect
361.02 Recent detachment, partial, with multiple defects
361.03 Recent detachment, partial, with giant tear
361.04 Recent detachment, partial, with retinal dialysis
> Dialysis (juvenile) of retina (with detachment)

361.05 Recent detachment, total or subtotal
361.06 Old detachment, partial
> Delimited old retinal detachment
361.07 Old detachment, total or subtotal

√5th **361.1 Retinoschisis and retinal cysts**
> EXCLUDES   juvenile retinoschisis (362.73)
> microcystoid degeneration of retina (362.62)
> parasitic cyst of retina (360.13)

361.10 Retinoschisis, unspecified
> DEF: Separation of retina due to degenerative process of aging; should not be confused with acute retinal detachment.

361.11 Flat retinoschisis
> DEF: Slow, progressive split of retinal sensory layers.

361.12 Bullous retinoschisis
> DEF: Fluid retention between split retinal sensory layers.

361.13 Primary retinal cysts
361.14 Secondary retinal cysts
361.19 Other
> Pseudocyst of retina

361.2 Serous retinal detachment
> Retinal detachment without retinal defect
> EXCLUDES   central serous retinopathy (362.41)
> retinal pigment epithelium detachment (362.42-362.43)

N Newborn Age: 0   P Pediatric Age: 0-17   M Maternity Age: 12-55   A Adult Age: 15-124   CC CC Condition   MC Major Complication   CD Complex Dx   HIV HIV Related Dx

96 — Volume 1 • October 2006   *2007 ICD•9•CM*

☑5ᵗʰ **361.3 Retinal defects without detachment**

> EXCLUDES *chorioretinal scars after surgery for detachment (363.30-363.35)*
> *peripheral retinal degeneration without defect (362.60-362.66)*

361.30 Retinal defect, unspecified
> Retinal break(s) NOS

361.31 Round hole of retina without detachment

361.32 Horseshoe tear of retina without detachment
> Operculum of retina without mention of detachment

361.33 Multiple defects of retina without detachment

☑5ᵗʰ **361.8 Other forms of retinal detachment**

361.81 Traction detachment of retina
> Traction detachment with vitreoretinal organization

361.89 Other
> AHA: 3Q, '99, 12

361.9 Unspecified retinal detachment
> AHA: N-D, '87, 10

☑4ᵗʰ **362 Other retinal disorders**

> EXCLUDES *chorioretinal scars (363.30-363.35)*
> *chorioretinitis (363.0-363.2)*

☑5ᵗʰ **362.0 Diabetic retinopathy**
> *Code first diabetes (250.5)*
> DEF: Retinal changes in diabetes of long duration; causes hemorrhages, microaneurysms, waxy deposits and proliferative noninflammatory degenerative disease of retina.
> AHA: 4Q, '05, 65; 3Q, '91, 8

362.01 Background diabetic retinopathy
> Diabetic retinal microaneurysms
> Diabetic retinopathy NOS

362.02 Proliferative diabetic retinopathy
> AHA: 3Q, '96, 5
>
> DEF: Occurrence of the ischemic effects of vessel blockages result in neovascularization; new blood vessels begin to form to compensate for restricted blood flow; multiple areas of the retina and inner vitreous may be affected.

362.03 Nonproliferative diabetic retinopathy NOS

362.04 Mild nonproliferative diabetic retinopathy
> DEF: Early stages of degenerative condition of the retina due to diabetes; microaneurysm formation; small balloon-like swelling of the retinal vessels.

362.05 Moderate nonproliferative diabetic retinopathy
> DEF: Stage of degenerative condition of the retina due to diabetes with pronounced microaneurysms; vessel blockages can occur.

362.06 Severe nonproliferative diabetic retinopathy
> AHA: 4Q, '05, 67
>
> DEF: Stage of degenerative condition of the retina due to diabetes in which vascular breakdown in the retina results in multiple vascular blockages, or "beadings," intraretinal hemorrhages can be numerous.

362.07 Diabetic macular edema
> Note: Code 362.07 must be used with a code for diabetic retinopathy (362.01-362.06)
> Diabetic retinal edema
> DEF: Leakage from retinal blood vessels causes swelling of the macula and impaired vision; exudates or plaques may develop in the posterior pole of the retina due to the breakdown of retinal vasculature.

☑5ᵗʰ **362.1 Other background retinopathy and retinal vascular changes**

362.10 Background retinopathy, unspecified
> AHA: ►1Q, '06, 12◄

362.11 Hypertensive retinopathy
> AHA: 3Q, '90, 3
> DEF: Retinal irregularities caused by systemic hypertension.

362.12 Exudative retinopathy
> Coats' syndrome
> AHA: 3Q, '99, 12

362.13 Changes in vascular appearance
> Vascular sheathing of retina
> Use additional code for any associated atherosclerosis (440.8)

362.14 Retinal microaneurysms NOS
> DEF: Microscopic dilation of retinal vessels in nondiabetic.

362.15 Retinal telangiectasia
> DEF: Dilation of blood vessels of the retina.

362.16 Retinal neovascularization NOS
> Neovascularization:
> choroidal
> subretinal
> DEF: New and abnormal vascular growth in the retina.

362.17 Other intraretinal microvascular abnormalities
> Retinal sclerosis   Retinal varices

362.18 Retinal vasculitis
> Eales' disease   Retinal:
> Retinal: perivasculitis
> arteritis   phlebitis
> endarteritis
> DEF: Inflammation of retinal blood vessels.

☑5ᵗʰ **362.2 Other proliferative retinopathy**

362.21 Retrolental fibroplasia
> DEF: Fibrous tissue in vitreous, from retina to lens, causing blindness; associated with premature infants requiring high amounts of oxygen.

362.29 Other nondiabetic proliferative retinopathy
> AHA: 3Q, '96, 5

☑5ᵗʰ **362.3 Retinal vascular occlusion**
> DEF: Obstructed blood flow to and from retina.

362.30 Retinal vascular occlusion, unspecified

362.31 Central retinal artery occlusion

362.32 Arterial branch occlusion

362.33 Partial arterial occlusion
> Hollenhorst plaque   Retinal microembolism

362.34 Transient arterial occlusion
> Amaurosis fugax
> AHA: 1Q, '00, 16

362.35 Central retinal vein occlusion
> AHA: 2Q, '93, 6

362.36 Venous tributary (branch) occlusion

362.37 Venous engorgement
> Occlusion:
> incipient ⎫ of retinal vein
> partial   ⎭

☑5ᵗʰ **362.4 Separation of retinal layers**
> EXCLUDES *retinal detachment (serous) (361.2)*
> *rhegmatogenous (361.00-361.07)*

362.40 Retinal layer separation, unspecified

362.41 Central serous retinopathy
> DEF: Serous-filled blister causing detachment of retina from pigment epithelium.

362.42 Serous detachment of retinal pigment epithelium
> Exudative detachment of retinal pigment epithelium
> DEF: Blister of fatty fluid causing detachment of retina from pigment epithelium.

362.43 Hemorrhagic detachment of retinal pigment epithelium
> DEF: Blood-filled blister causing detachment of retina from pigment epithelium.

Nervous System and Sense Organs

361.3–362.43

☑4ᵗʰ / ☑5ᵗʰ Additional Digit Required   Nonspecific PDx   Unacceptable PDx   Manifestation Code   **MCV** Major Cardiovascular Condition   ►◄ Revised Text   ● New Code   ▲ Revised Code Title

2007 ICD•9•CM   **October 2006 • Volume 1 — 97**

Nervous System and Sense Organs

362.5–363.11

√5th **362.5　Degeneration of macula and posterior pole**
　　　EXCLUDES　degeneration of optic disc (377.21-
　　　　　　　　377.24)
　　　　　　　hereditary retinal degeneration
　　　　　　　[dystrophy] (362.70-362.77)

362.50　**Macular degeneration (senile), unspecified**

362.51　**Nonexudative senile macular degeneration**
　　　　　Senile macular degeneration:
　　　　　　atrophic
　　　　　　dry

362.52　**Exudative senile macular degeneration**
　　　　　Kuhnt-Junius degeneration
　　　　　Senile macular degeneration:
　　　　　　disciform
　　　　　　wet
　　　　　DEF: Leakage in macular blood vessels with loss of
　　　　　visual acuity.

362.53　**Cystoid macular degeneration**
　　　　　Cystoid macular edema
　　　　　DEF: Retinal swelling and cyst formation in macula.

362.54　**Macular cyst, hole, or pseudohole**

362.55　**Toxic maculopathy**
　　　　　Use additional E code to identify drug, if
　　　　　drug induced

362.56　**Macular puckering**
　　　　　Preretinal fibrosis

362.57　**Drusen (degenerative)**
　　　　　DEF: White, hyaline deposits on Bruch's membrane
　　　　　(lamina basalis choroideae).

√5th **362.6　Peripheral retinal degenerations**
　　　EXCLUDES　hereditary retinal degeneration
　　　　　　　　[dystrophy] (362.70-362.77)
　　　　　　　retinal degeneration with retinal defect
　　　　　　　(361.00-361.07)

362.60　**Peripheral retinal degeneration, unspecified**

362.61　**Paving stone degeneration**
　　　　　DEF: Degeneration of peripheral retina; causes thinning
　　　　　through which choroid is visible.

362.62　**Microcystoid degeneration**
　　　　　Blessig's cysts　　Iwanoff's cysts

362.63　**Lattice degeneration**
　　　　　Palisade degeneration of retina
　　　　　DEF: Degeneration of retina; often bilateral, usually
　　　　　benign; characterized by lines intersecting at irregular
　　　　　intervals in peripheral retina; retinal thinning and retinal
　　　　　holes may occur.

362.64　**Senile reticular degeneration**
　　　　　DEF: Net-like appearance of retina; sign of degeneration.

362.65　**Secondary pigmentary degeneration**
　　　　　Pseudoretinitis pigmentosa

362.66　**Secondary vitreoretinal degenerations**

√5th **362.7　Hereditary retinal dystrophies**
　　　DEF: Genetically induced progressive changes in retina.

362.70　**Hereditary retinal dystrophy, unspecified**

362.71　*Retinal dystrophy in systemic or
　　　　cerebroretinal lipidoses*
　　　　　Code first underlying disease, as:
　　　　　　cerebroretinal lipidoses (330.1)
　　　　　　systemic lipidoses (272.7)

362.72　*Retinal dystrophy in other systemic
　　　　disorders and syndromes*
　　　　　Code first underlying disease, as:
　　　　　　Bassen-Kornzweig syndrome (272.5)
　　　　　　Refsum's disease (356.3)

362.73　**Vitreoretinal dystrophies**
　　　　　Juvenile retinoschisis

362.74　**Pigmentary retinal dystrophy**
　　　　　Retinal dystrophy, albipunctate
　　　　　Retinitis pigmentosa

362.75　**Other dystrophies primarily involving the
　　　　sensory retina**
　　　　　Progressive cone(-rod) dystrophy
　　　　　Stargardt's disease

362.76　**Dystrophies primarily involving the retinal
　　　　pigment epithelium**
　　　　　Fundus flavimaculatus
　　　　　Vitelliform dystrophy

362.77　**Dystrophies primarily involving Bruch's
　　　　membrane**
　　　　　Dystrophy:
　　　　　　hyaline
　　　　　　pseudoinflammatory foveal
　　　　　Hereditary drusen

√5th **362.8　Other retinal disorders**
　　　EXCLUDES　chorioretinal inflammations (363.0-
　　　　　　　　363.2)
　　　　　　　chorioretinal scars (363.30-363.35)

362.81　**Retinal hemorrhage**
　　　　　Hemorrhage:
　　　　　　preretinal
　　　　　　retinal (deep) (superficial)
　　　　　　subretinal
　　　　　AHA: 4Q, '96, 43

362.82　**Retinal exudates and deposits**

362.83　**Retinal edema**
　　　　　Retinal:
　　　　　　cotton wool spots
　　　　　　edema (localized) (macular) (peripheral)
　　　　　DEF: Retinal swelling due to fluid accumulation.

362.84　**Retinal ischemia**
　　　　　DEF: Reduced retinal blood supply.

362.85　**Retinal nerve fiber bundle defects**

362.89　**Other retinal disorders**

362.9　**Unspecified retinal disorder**

√4th **363　Chorioretinal inflammations, scars, and other disorders of
choroid**

√5th **363.0　Focal chorioretinitis and focal retinochoroiditis**
　　　EXCLUDES　focal chorioretinitis or retinochoroiditis in:
　　　　　　　　histoplasmosis (115.02, 115.12,
　　　　　　　　115.92)
　　　　　　　toxoplasmosis (130.2)
　　　　　　　congenital infection (771.2)

363.00　**Focal chorioretinitis, unspecified**
　　　　　Focal:
　　　　　　choroiditis or chorioretinitis NOS
　　　　　　retinitis or retinochoroiditis NOS

363.01　**Focal choroiditis and chorioretinitis,
　　　　juxtapapillary**

363.03　**Focal choroiditis and chorioretinitis of
　　　　other posterior pole**

363.04　**Focal choroiditis and chorioretinitis,
　　　　peripheral**

363.05　**Focal retinitis and retinochoroiditis,
　　　　juxtapapillary**
　　　　　Neuroretinitis

363.06　**Focal retinitis and retinochoroiditis,
　　　　macular or paramacular**

363.07　**Focal retinitis and retinochoroiditis of other
　　　　posterior pole**

363.08　**Focal retinitis and retinochoroiditis,
　　　　peripheral**

√5th **363.1　Disseminated chorioretinitis and disseminated
retinochoroiditis**
　　　EXCLUDES　disseminated choroiditis or
　　　　　　　　chorioretinitis in secondary
　　　　　　　　syphilis (091.51)
　　　　　　　neurosyphilitic disseminated retinitis or
　　　　　　　　retinochoroiditis (094.83)
　　　　　　　retinal (peri)vasculitis (362.18)

363.10　**Disseminated chorioretinitis, unspecified**
　　　　　Disseminated:
　　　　　　choroiditis or chorioretinitis NOS
　　　　　　retinitis or retinochoroiditis NOS

363.11　**Disseminated choroiditis and
　　　　chorioretinitis, posterior pole**

| N Newborn Age: 0 | P Pediatric Age: 0-17 | M Maternity Age: 12-55 | A Adult Age: 15-124 | CC CC Condition | MC Major Complication | CD Complex Dx | HIV HIV Related Dx |

98 — Volume 1　　　　　　　　　　　　　　　　　　　　　　　　　　　　　　　2007 ICD•9•CM

363.12 Disseminated choroiditis and chorioretinitis, peripheral

363.13 Disseminated choroiditis and chorioretinitis, generalized
> Code first any underlying disease, as:
> tuberculosis (017.3)

363.14 Disseminated retinitis and retinochoroiditis, metastatic

363.15 Disseminated retinitis and retinochoroiditis, pigment epitheliopathy
> Acute posterior multifocal placoid pigment epitheliopathy
> DEF: Widespread inflammation of retina and choroid; characterized by pigmented epithelium involvement.

✓5th **363.2 Other and unspecified forms of chorioretinitis and retinochoroiditis**
> EXCLUDES   panophthalmitis (360.02)
>   sympathetic uveitis (360.11)
>   uveitis NOS (364.3)

363.20 Chorioretinitis, unspecified
> Choroiditis NOS
> Retinitis NOS
> Uveitis, posterior NOS

363.21 Pars planitis
> Posterior cyclitis
> DEF: Inflammation of peripheral retina and ciliary body; characterized by bands of white cells.

363.22 Harada's disease
> DEF: Retinal detachment and bilateral widespread exudative choroiditis; symptoms include headache, vomiting, increased lymphocytes in cerebrospinal fluid; and temporary or permanent deafness may occur.

✓5th **363.3 Chorioretinal scars**
> Scar (postinflammatory) (postsurgical) (posttraumatic):
> choroid
> retina

363.30 Chorioretinal scar, unspecified

363.31 Solar retinopathy
> DEF: Retinal scarring caused by solar radiation.

363.32 Other macular scars

363.33 Other scars of posterior pole

363.34 Peripheral scars

363.35 Disseminated scars

✓5th **363.4 Choroidal degenerations**

363.40 Choroidal degeneration, unspecified
> Choroidal sclerosis NOS

363.41 Senile atrophy of choroid
> DEF: Wasting away of choroid; due to aging.

363.42 Diffuse secondary atrophy of choroid
> DEF: Wasting away of choroid in systemic disease.

363.43 Angioid streaks of choroid
> DEF: Degeneration of choroid; characterized by dark brown steaks radiating from optic disk; occurs with pseudoxanthoma, elasticum or Paget's disease.

✓5th **363.5 Hereditary choroidal dystrophies**
> Hereditary choroidal atrophy:
> partial [choriocapillaris]
> total [all vessels]

363.50 Hereditary choroidal dystrophy or atrophy, unspecified

363.51 Circumpapillary dystrophy of choroid, partial

363.52 Circumpapillary dystrophy of choroid, total
> Helicoid dystrophy of choroid

363.53 Central dystrophy of choroid, partial
> Dystrophy, choroidal:
> central areolar
> circinate

363.54 Central choroidal atrophy, total
> Dystrophy, choroidal:
> central gyrate
> serpiginous

363.55 Choroideremia
> DEF: Hereditary choroid degeneration, occurs in first decade; characterized by constricted visual field and ultimately blindness in males; less debilitating in females.

363.56 Other diffuse or generalized dystrophy, partial
> Diffuse choroidal sclerosis

363.57 Other diffuse or generalized dystrophy, total
> Generalized gyrate atrophy, choroid

✓5th **363.6 Choroidal hemorrhage and rupture**

363.61 Choroidal hemorrhage, unspecified

363.62 Expulsive choroidal hemorrhage

363.63 Choroidal rupture

✓5th **363.7 Choroidal detachment**

363.70 Choroidal detachment, unspecified

363.71 Serous choroidal detachment
> DEF: Detachment of choroid from sclera; due to blister of serous fluid.

363.72 Hemorrhagic choroidal detachment
> DEF: Detachment of choroid from sclera; due to blood-filled blister.

363.8 Other disorders of choroid
> AHA: ▶1Q, '06, 12◀

363.9 Unspecified disorder of choroid

✓4th **364 Disorders of iris and ciliary body**

✓5th **364.0 Acute and subacute iridocyclitis**
> Anterior uveitis
> Cyclitis   } acute,
> Iridocyclitis   subacute
> Iritis
>
> EXCLUDES   gonococcal (098.41)
>   herpes simplex (054.44)
>   herpes zoster (053.22)

364.00 Acute and subacute iridocyclitis, unspecified

364.01 Primary iridocyclitis

364.02 Recurrent iridocyclitis

364.03 Secondary iridocyclitis, infectious

364.04 Secondary iridocyclitis, noninfectious
> Aqueous: Aqueous:
> cells   flare
> fibrin

364.05 Hypopyon
> DEF: Accumulation of white blood cells between cornea and lens.

✓5th **364.1 Chronic iridocyclitis**
> EXCLUDES   posterior cyclitis (363.21)

364.10 Chronic iridocyclitis, unspecified

364.11 Chronic iridocyclitis in diseases classified elsewhere
> Code first underlying disease, as:
> sarcoidosis (135)
> tuberculosis (017.3)
> EXCLUDES   syphilitic iridocyclitis (091.52)
> DEF: Persistent inflammation of iris and ciliary body; due to underlying disease or condition.

✓5th **364.2 Certain types of iridocyclitis**
> EXCLUDES   posterior cyclitis (363.21)
>   sympathetic uveitis (360.11)

364.21 Fuchs' heterochromic cyclitis
> DEF: Chronic cyclitis characterized by differences in the color of the two irises; the lighter iris appears in the inflamed eye.

364.22 Glaucomatocyclitic crises
> DEF: One-sided form of secondary open angle glaucoma; recurrent, uncommon and of short duration; causes high intraocular pressure, rarely damage.

364.23 Lens-induced iridocyclitis
> DEF: Inflammation of iris; due to immune reaction to proteins in lens following trauma or other lens abnormality.

✓4th ✓5th Additional Digit Required   Nonspecific PDx   Unacceptable PDx   Manifestation Code   MCV Major Cardiovascular Condition   ▶◀ Revised Text   ● New Code   ▲ Revised Code Title

2007 ICD•9•CM   October 2006 • Volume 1 — 99

Nervous System and Sense Organs

364.24–365.41

364.24 Vogt-Koyanagi syndrome
DEF: Uveomeningitis with exudative iridocyclitis and choroiditis; causes depigmentation of hair and skin, detached retina; tinnitus and loss of hearing may occur.

364.3 Unspecified iridocyclitis
Uveitis NOS

√5ᵗʰ **364.4 Vascular disorders of iris and ciliary body**
364.41 Hyphema
Hemorrhage of iris or ciliary body
DEF: Hemorrhage in anterior chamber; also called hyphemia or "blood shot" eyes.

364.42 Rubeosis iridis
Neovascularization of iris or ciliary body
DEF: Blood vessel and connective tissue formation on surface of iris; symptomatic of diabetic retinopathy, central retinal vein occlusion and retinal detachment.

√5ᵗʰ **364.5 Degenerations of iris and ciliary body**
364.51 Essential or progressive iris atrophy
364.52 Iridoschisis
DEF: Splitting of the iris into two layers.

364.53 Pigmentary iris degeneration
Acquired heterochromia
Pigment dispersion syndrome } of iris
Translucency

364.54 Degeneration of pupillary margin
Atrophy of sphincter
Ectropion of pigment epithelium } of iris

364.55 Miotic cysts of pupillary margin
DEF: Serous-filled sacs in pupillary margin of iris.

364.56 Degenerative changes of chamber angle
364.57 Degenerative changes of ciliary body
364.59 Other iris atrophy
Iris atrophy (generalized) (sector shaped)

√5ᵗʰ **364.6 Cysts of iris, ciliary body, and anterior chamber**
EXCLUDES   miotic pupillary cyst (364.55)
parasitic cyst (360.13)
364.60 Idiopathic cysts
DEF: Fluid-filled sacs in iris or ciliary body; unknown etiology.

364.61 Implantation cysts
Epithelial down-growth, anterior chamber
Implantation cysts (surgical) (traumatic)
364.62 Exudative cysts of iris or anterior chamber
364.63 Primary cyst of pars plana
DEF: Fluid-filled sacs of outermost ciliary ring.

364.64 Exudative cyst of pars plana
DEF: Protein, fatty-filled sacs of outermost ciliary ring; due to fluid lead from blood vessels.

√5ᵗʰ **364.7 Adhesions and disruptions of iris and ciliary body**
EXCLUDES   flat anterior chamber (360.34)
364.70 Adhesions of iris, unspecified
Synechiae (iris) NOS
364.71 Posterior synechiae
DEF: Adhesion binding iris to lens.
364.72 Anterior synechiae
DEF: Adhesion binding the iris to cornea.
364.73 Goniosynechiae
Peripheral anterior synechiae
DEF: Adhesion binding the iris to cornea at the angle of the anterior chamber.
364.74 Pupillary membranes
Iris bombé   Pupillary:
Pupillary: seclusion
   occlusion
DEF: Membrane traversing the pupil and blocking vision.
364.75 Pupillary abnormalities
Deformed pupil   Rupture of sphincter, pupil
Ectopic pupil

364.76 Iridodialysis
DEF: Separation of the iris from the ciliary body base; due to trauma or surgical accident.
364.77 Recession of chamber angle
DEF: Receding of anterior chamber angle of the eye; restricts vision.

364.8 Other disorders of iris and ciliary body
Prolapse of iris NOS
EXCLUDES   prolapse of iris in recent wound (871.1)

364.9 Unspecified disorder of iris and ciliary body

√4ᵗʰ **365 Glaucoma**
EXCLUDES   blind hypertensive eye [absolute glaucoma] (360.42)
congenital glaucoma (743.20-743.22)
DEF: Rise in intraocular pressure which restricts blood flow; multiple causes.

√5ᵗʰ **365.0 Borderline glaucoma [glaucoma suspect]**
AHA: 1Q, '90, 8
365.00 Preglaucoma, unspecified
365.01 Open angle with borderline findings
Open angle with:
borderline intraocular pressure
cupping of optic discs
DEF: Minor block of aqueous outflow from eye.
365.02 Anatomical narrow angle
365.03 Steroid responders
365.04 Ocular hypertension
DEF: High fluid pressure within eye; no apparent cause.

√5ᵗʰ **365.1 Open-angle glaucoma**
365.10 Open-angle glaucoma, unspecified
Wide-angle glaucoma NOS
365.11 Primary open angle glaucoma
Chronic simple glaucoma
DEF: High intraocular pressure, despite free flow of aqueous.
365.12 Low tension glaucoma
365.13 Pigmentary glaucoma
DEF: High intraocular pressure; due to iris pigment granules blocking aqueous flow.
365.14 Glaucoma of childhood
Infantile or juvenile glaucoma
365.15 Residual stage of open angle glaucoma

√5ᵗʰ **365.2 Primary angle-closure glaucoma**
365.20 Primary angle-closure glaucoma, unspecified
365.21 Intermittent angle-closure glaucoma
Angle-closure glaucoma:
interval
subacute
DEF: Recurring attacks of high intraocular pressure; due to blocked aqueous flow.
365.22 Acute angle-closure glaucoma
DEF: Sudden, severe rise in intraocular pressure due to blockage in aqueous drainage.
365.23 Chronic angle-closure glaucoma
AHA: 2Q, '98, 16
365.24 Residual stage of angle-closure glaucoma

√5ᵗʰ **365.3 Corticosteroid-induced glaucoma**
DEF: Elevated intraocular pressure; due to long-term corticosteroid therapy.
365.31 Glaucomatous stage
365.32 Residual stage

√5ᵗʰ **365.4 Glaucoma associated with congenital anomalies, dystrophies, and systemic syndromes**
365.41 Glaucoma associated with chamber angle anomalies
Code first associated disorder, as:
Axenfeld's anomaly (743.44)
Rieger's anomaly or syndrome (743.44)

Ⓝ Newborn Age: 0   Ⓟ Pediatric Age: 0-17   Ⓜ Maternity Age: 12-55   Ⓐ Adult Age: 15-124   **CC** CC Condition   **MC** Major Complication   **CD** Complex Dx   **HIV** HIV Related Dx

100 — Volume 1   *2007 ICD•9•CM*

365.42 *Glaucoma associated with anomalies of iris*
　　　Code first associated disorder, as:
　　　　aniridia (743.45)
　　　　essential iris atrophy (364.51)

365.43 *Glaucoma associated with other anterior segment anomalies*
　　　Code first associated disorder, as:
　　　　microcornea (743.41)

365.44 *Glaucoma associated with systemic syndromes*
　　　Code first associated disease, as
　　　　neurofibromatosis (237.7)
　　　　Sturge-Weber (-Dimitri) syndrome (759.6)

✓5th 365.5 **Glaucoma associated with disorders of the lens**

365.51 **Phacolytic glaucoma**
　　　Use additional code for associated hypermature cataract (366.18)
　　　DEF: Elevated intraocular pressure; due to lens protein blocking aqueous flow.

365.52 **Pseudoexfoliation glaucoma**
　　　Use additional code for associated pseudoexfoliation of capsule (366.11)
　　　DEF: Glaucoma characterized by small grayish particles deposited on the lens.

365.59 **Glaucoma associated with other lens disorders**
　　　Use additional code for associated disorder, as:
　　　　dislocation of lens (379.33-379.34)
　　　　spherophakia (743.36)

✓5th 365.6 **Glaucoma associated with other ocular disorders**

365.60 **Glaucoma associated with unspecified ocular disorder**

365.61 **Glaucoma associated with pupillary block**
　　　Use additional code for associated disorder, as:
　　　　seclusion of pupil [iris bombé] (364.74)
　　　DEF: Acute, open-angle glaucoma caused by mature cataract; aqueous flow is blocked by lens material and macrophages.

365.62 **Glaucoma associated with ocular inflammations**
　　　Use additional code for associated disorder, as:
　　　　glaucomatocyclitic crises (364.22)
　　　　iridocyclitis (364.0-364.3)

365.63 **Glaucoma associated with vascular disorders**
　　　Use additional code for associated disorder, as:
　　　　central retinal vein occlusion (362.35)
　　　　hyphema (364.41)

Aqueous Misdirection Syndrome

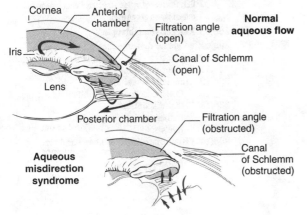

Cornea
Anterior chamber
Filtration angle (open)
Normal aqueous flow
Iris
Canal of Schlemm (open)
Lens
Posterior chamber
Filtration angle (obstructed)
Canal of Schlemm (obstructed)
Aqueous misdirection syndrome

365.64 **Glaucoma associated with tumors or cysts**
　　　Use additional code for associated disorder, as:
　　　　benign neoplasm (224.0-224.9)
　　　　epithelial down-growth (364.61)
　　　　malignant neoplasm (190.0-190.9)

365.65 **Glaucoma associated with ocular trauma**
　　　Use additional code for associated condition, as:
　　　　contusion of globe (921.3)
　　　　recession of chamber angle (364.77)

✓5th 365.8 **Other specified forms of glaucoma**

365.81 **Hypersecretion glaucoma**

365.82 **Glaucoma with increased episcleral venous pressure**

365.83 **Aqueous misdirection**
　　　Malignant glaucoma
　　　AHA: 4Q, '02, 48
　　　DEF: A form of glaucoma that occurs when aqueous humor flows into the posterior chamber of the eye (vitreous) rather than through the normal recycling channels into the anterior chamber.

365.89 **Other specified glaucoma**
　　　AHA: 2Q, '98, 16

365.9 **Unspecified glaucoma**
　　　AHA: 3Q, '03, 14; 2Q, '01, 16

✓4th 366 **Cataract**
　　DEF: A variety of conditions that create a cloudy, or calcified lens that obstructs vision.
　　EXCLUDES　congenital cataract (743.30-743.34)

✓5th 366.0 **Infantile, juvenile, and presenile cataract**

366.00 **Nonsenile cataract, unspecified**

366.01 **Anterior subcapsular polar cataract**
　　　DEF: Defect within the front, center lens surface.

366.02 **Posterior subcapsular polar cataract**
　　　DEF: Defect within the rear, center lens surface.

366.03 **Cortical, lamellar, or zonular cataract**
　　　DEF: Opacities radiating from center to edge of lens; appear as thin, concentric layers of lens.

366.04 **Nuclear cataract**

366.09 **Other and combined forms of nonsenile cataract**

✓5th 366.1 **Senile cataract**
　　AHA: 3Q, '91, 9; S-O, '85, 10

366.10 **Senile cataract, unspecified**
　　　AHA: 1Q, '03, 5

366.11 **Pseudoexfoliation of lens capsule**

366.12 **Incipient cataract**
　　　Cataract:　　　　　Cataract:
　　　　coronary　　　　　　punctate
　　　　immature NOS　　Water clefts
　　　DEF: Minor disorders of lens not affecting vision; due to aging.

366.13 **Anterior subcapsular polar senile cataract**

366.14 **Posterior subcapsular polar senile cataract**

366.15 **Cortical senile cataract**

366.16 **Nuclear sclerosis**
　　　Cataracta brunescens
　　　Nuclear cataract

366.17 **Total or mature cataract**

366.18 **Hypermature cataract**
　　　Morgagni cataract

366.19 **Other and combined forms of senile cataract**

Cataract

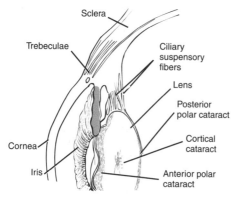

Sclera
Trebeculae
Ciliary suspensory fibers
Lens
Posterior polar cataract
Cortical cataract
Cornea
Iris
Anterior polar cataract

✓5ᵗʰ **366.2 Traumatic cataract**
366.20 Traumatic cataract, unspecified
366.21 Localized traumatic opacities
Vossius' ring
366.22 Total traumatic cataract
366.23 Partially resolved traumatic cataract

✓5ᵗʰ **366.3 Cataract secondary to ocular disorders**
366.30 Cataracta complicata, unspecified
366.31 Glaucomatous flecks (subcapsular)
Code first underlying glaucoma (365.0-365.9)
366.32 Cataract in inflammatory disorders
Code first underlying condition, as:
chronic choroiditis (363.0-363.2)
366.33 Cataract with neovascularization
Code first underlying condition, as:
chronic iridocyclitis (364.10)
366.34 Cataract in degenerative disorders
Sunflower cataract
Code first underlying condition, as:
chalcosis (360.24)
degenerative myopia (360.21)
pigmentary retinal dystrophy (362.74)

✓5ᵗʰ **366.4 Cataract associated with other disorders**
366.41 Diabetic cataract
Code first diabetes (250.5)
AHA: 3Q, '91, 9; S-O, '85, 11

366.42 Tetanic cataract
Code first underlying disease, as:
calcinosis (275.4)
hypoparathyroidism (252.1)
366.43 Myotonic cataract
Code first underlying disorder (359.2)
366.44 Cataract associated with other syndromes
Code first underlying condition, as:
craniofacial dysostosis (756.0)
galactosemia (271.1)
366.45 Toxic cataract
Drug-induced cataract
Use additional E code to identify drug or other toxic substance
366.46 Cataract associated with radiation and other physical influences
Use additional E code to identify cause

✓5ᵗʰ **366.5 After-cataract**
366.50 After-cataract, unspecified
Secondary cataract NOS
366.51 Soemmering's ring
DEF: A donut-shaped lens remnant and a capsule behind the pupil as a result of cataract surgery or trauma.
366.52 Other after-cataract, not obscuring vision
366.53 After-cataract, obscuring vision
366.8 Other cataract
Calcification of lens

366.9 Unspecified cataract

✓4ᵗʰ **367 Disorders of refraction and accommodation**
367.0 Hypermetropia
Far-sightedness   Hyperopia
DEF: Refraction error, called also hyperopia, focal point is posterior to retina; abnormally short anteroposterior diameter or subnormal refractive power; causes farsightedness.
367.1 Myopia
Near-sightedness
DEF: Refraction error, focal point is anterior to retina; causes near-sightedness.

✓5ᵗʰ **367.2 Astigmatism**
367.20 Astigmatism, unspecified
367.21 Regular astigmatism
367.22 Irregular astigmatism

✓5ᵗʰ **367.3 Anisometropia and aniseikonia**
367.31 Anisometropia
DEF: Eyes with refractive powers that differ by at least one diopter.
367.32 Aniseikonia
DEF: Eyes with unequal retinal imaging; usually due to refractive error.

367.4 Presbyopia
DEF: Loss of crystalline lens elasticity; causes errors of accommodation; due to aging.

✓5ᵗʰ **367.5 Disorders of accommodation**
367.51 Paresis of accommodation
Cycloplegia
DEF: Partial paralysis of ciliary muscle; causing focus problems.
367.52 Total or complete internal ophthalmoplegia
DEF: Total paralysis of ciliary muscle; large pupil incapable of focus.
367.53 Spasm of accommodation
DEF: Abnormal contraction of ciliary muscle; causes focus problems.

✓5ᵗʰ **367.8 Other disorders of refraction and accommodation**
367.81 Transient refractive change
367.89 Other
Drug-induced ⎤ disorders of refraction
Toxic   ⎦ and accommodation

367.9 Unspecified disorder of refraction and accommodation

✓4ᵗʰ **368 Visual disturbances**
EXCLUDES electrophysiological disturbances (794.11-794.14)

✓5ᵗʰ **368.0 Amblyopia ex anopsia**
DEF: Vision impaired due to disuse; esotropia often cause.
368.00 Amblyopia, unspecified
368.01 Strabismic amblyopia
Suppression amblyopia
368.02 Deprivation amblyopia
DEF: Decreased vision associated with suppressed retinal image of one eye.
368.03 Refractive amblyopia

✓5ᵗʰ **368.1 Subjective visual disturbances**
368.10 Subjective visual disturbance, unspecified
368.11 Sudden visual loss
368.12 Transient visual loss
Concentric fading   Scintillating scotoma
368.13 Visual discomfort
Asthenopia   Photophobia
Eye strain
368.14 Visual distortions of shape and size
Macropsia   Micropsia
Metamorphopsia

N Newborn Age: 0   P Pediatric Age: 0-17   M Maternity Age: 12-55   A Adult Age: 15-124   CC CC Condition   MC Major Complication   CD Complex Dx   HIV HIV Related Dx

102 — Volume 1

2007 ICD•9•CM

368.15 Other visual distortions and entoptic phenomena

Photopsia	Refractive:
Refractive:	polyopia
diplopia	Visual halos

368.16 Psychophysical visual disturbances

Visual:	Visual:
agnosia	hallucinations
disorientation	syndrome

368.2 Diplopia
Double vision

✓5th **368.3 Other disorders of binocular vision**
    368.30 Binocular vision disorder, unspecified
    368.31 Suppression of binocular vision
    368.32 Simultaneous visual perception without fusion
    368.33 Fusion with defective stereopsis
      DEF: Faulty depth perception though normal ability to focus.
    368.34 Abnormal retinal correspondence

✓5th **368.4 Visual field defects**
    368.40 Visual field defect, unspecified
    368.41 Scotoma involving central area

Scotoma:	Scotoma:
central	paracentral
centrocecal	

      DEF: Vision loss (blind spot) in central five degrees of visual field.
    368.42 Scotoma of blind spot area

Enlarged:	Paracecal scotoma
angioscotoma	
blind spot	

    368.43 Sector or arcuate defects

Scotoma:	Scotoma:
arcuate	Seidel
Bjerrum	

      DEF: Arc-shaped blind spot caused by retinal nerve damage.
    368.44 Other localized visual field defect

Scotoma:	Visual field defect:
NOS	nasal step
ring	peripheral

    368.45 Generalized contraction or constriction
    368.46 Homonymous bilateral field defects
      Hemianopsia (altitudinal) (homonymous)
      Quadrant anopia
      DEF: Disorders found in the corresponding vertical halves of the visual fields of both eyes.
    368.47 Heteronymous bilateral field defects

Hemianopsia:	Hemianopsia:
binasal	bitemporal

      DEF: Disorders in the opposite halves of the visual fields of both eyes.

✓5th **368.5 Color vision deficiencies**
Color blindness
    368.51 Protan defect
      Protanomaly   Protanopia
      DEF: Mild difficulty distinguishing green and red hues with shortened spectrum; sex-linked affecting one percent of males.
    368.52 Deutan defect
      Deuteranomaly   Deuteranopia
      DEF: Male-only disorder; difficulty in distinguishing green and red, no shortened spectrum.
    368.53 Tritan defect
      Tritanomaly   Tritanopia
      DEF: Difficulty in distinguishing blue and yellow; occurs often due to drugs, retinal detachment and central nervous system diseases.

    368.54 Achromatopsia
      Monochromatism (cone) (rod)
      DEF: Complete color blindness; caused by disease, injury to retina, optic nerve or pathway.
    368.55 Acquired color vision deficiencies
    368.59 Other color vision deficiencies

✓5th **368.6 Night blindness**
Nyctalopia
DEF: Nyctalopia: disorder of vision in dim light or night blindness.
    368.60 Night blindness, unspecified
    368.61 Congenital night blindness
      Hereditary night blindness
      Oguchi's disease
    368.62 Acquired night blindness
      EXCLUDES   *that due to vitamin A deficiency (264.5)*
    368.63 Abnormal dark adaptation curve

Abnormal threshold	} of cones or
Delayed adaptation	rods

    368.69 Other night blindness
    368.8 Other specified visual disturbances
      Blurred vision NOS
      AHA: 4Q, '02, 56

    368.9 Unspecified visual disturbance
      AHA: 1Q, '04, 15

✓4th **369 Blindness and low vision**
    Note: Visual impairment refers to a functional limitation of the eye (e.g., limited visual acuity or visual field). It should be distinguished from visual disability, indicating a limitation of the abilities of the individual (e.g., limited reading skills, vocational skills), and from visual handicap, indicating a limitation of personal and socioeconomic independence (e.g., limited mobility, limited employability).
    The levels of impairment defined in the table on the next page are based on the recommendations of the WHO Study Group on Prevention of Blindness (Geneva, November 6–10, 1972; WHO Technical Report Series 518), and of the International Council of Ophthalmology (1976).
    Note that definitions of blindness vary in different settings.
    For international reporting WHO defines blindness as profound impairment. This definition can be applied to blindness of one eye (369.1, 369.6) and to blindness of the individual (369.0).
    For determination of benefits in the U.S.A., the definition of legal blindness as severe impairment is often used. This definition applies to blindness of the individual only.
      EXCLUDES   *correctable impaired vision due to refractive errors (367.0-367.9)*

✓5th **369.0 Profound impairment, both eyes**
    369.00 Impairment level not further specified
      Blindness:
        NOS according to WHO definition
        both eyes
    369.01 Better eye: total impairment; lesser eye: total impairment
    369.02 Better eye: near-total impairment; lesser eye: not further specified
    369.03 Better eye: near-total impairment; lesser eye: total impairment
    369.04 Better eye: near-total impairment; lesser eye: near-total impairment
    369.05 Better eye: profound impairment; lesser eye: not further specified
    369.06 Better eye: profound impairment; lesser eye: total impairment
    369.07 Better eye: profound impairment; lesser eye: near-total impairment

✓4th ✓5th   Additional Digit Required   Nonspecific PDx   Unacceptable PDx   Manifestation Code   MCV Major Cardiovascular Condition   ▶◀ Revised Text   ● New Code   ▲ Revised Code Title

2007 ICD•9•CM   **Volume 1 — 103**

Nervous System and Sense Organs

369.08-370.04

369.08 Better eye: profound impairment; lesser eye: profound impairment

☑4ᵗʰ **369.1 Moderate or severe impairment, better eye, profound impairment lesser eye**

369.10 **Impairment level not further specified**
Blindness, one eye, low vision other eye

369.11 **Better eye: severe impairment; lesser eye: blind, not further specified**

369.12 **Better eye: severe impairment; lesser eye: total impairment**

369.13 **Better eye: severe impairment; lesser eye: near-total impairment**

369.14 **Better eye: severe impairment; lesser eye: profound impairment**

369.15 **Better eye: moderate impairment; lesser eye: blind, not further specified**

369.16 **Better eye: moderate impairment; lesser eye: total impairment**

369.17 **Better eye: moderate impairment; lesser eye: near-total impairment**

369.18 **Better eye: moderate impairment; lesser eye: profound impairment**

☑5ᵗʰ **369.2 Moderate or severe impairment, both eyes**

369.20 **Impairment level not further specified**
Low vision, both eyes NOS

369.21 **Better eye: severe impairment; lesser eye: not further specified**

369.22 **Better eye: severe impairment; lesser eye: severe impairment**

369.23 **Better eye: moderate impairment; lesser eye: not further specified**

369.24 **Better eye: moderate impairment; lesser eye: severe impairment**

369.25 **Better eye: moderate impairment; lesser eye: moderate impairment**

369.3 Unqualified visual loss, both eyes
EXCLUDES blindness NOS:
legal [U.S.A. definition] (369.4)
WHO definition (369.00)

369.4 Legal blindness, as defined in U.S.A.
Blindness NOS according to U.S.A. definition
EXCLUDES legal blindness with specification of impairment level (369.01-369.08, 369.11-369.14, 369.21-369.22)

☑5ᵗʰ **369.6 Profound impairment, one eye**

369.60 **Impairment level not further specified**
Blindness, one eye

369.61 **One eye: total impairment; other eye: not specified**

369.62 **One eye: total impairment; other eye: near-normal vision**

369.63 **One eye: total impairment; other eye: normal vision**

369.64 **One eye: near-total impairment; other eye: not specified**

369.65 **One eye: near-total impairment; other eye: near-normal vision**

369.66 **One eye: near-total impairment; other eye: normal vision**

369.67 **One eye: profound impairment; other eye: not specified**

369.68 **One eye: profound impairment; other eye: near-normal vision**

369.69 **One eye: profound impairment; other eye: normal vision**

☑5ᵗʰ **369.7 Moderate or severe impairment, one eye**

369.70 **Impairment level not further specified**
Low vision, one eye

369.71 **One eye: severe impairment; other eye: not specified**

Classification		LEVELS OF VISUAL IMPAIRMENT	Additional descriptors which may be encountered
"legal"	WHO	Visual acuity and/or visual field limitation (whichever is worse)	
	(NEAR-) NORMAL VISION	RANGE OF NORMAL VISION 20/10 20/13 20/16 20/20 20/25 2.0 1.6 1.25 1.0 0.8	
		NEAR-NORMAL VISION 20/30 20/40 20/50 20/60 0.7 0.6 0.5 0.4 0.3	
	LOW VISION	MODERATE VISUAL IMPAIRMENT 20/70 20/80 20/100 20/125 20/160 0.25 0.20 0.16 0.12	Moderate low vision
		SEVERE VISUAL IMPAIRMENT 20/200 20/250 20/320 20/400 0.10 0.08 0.06 0.05 Visual field: 20 degrees or less	Severe low vision, "Legal" blindness
LEGAL BLINDNESS (U.S.A.) both eyes	BLINDNESS (WHO) one or both eyes	PROFOUND VISUAL IMPAIRMENT 20/500 20/630 20/800 20/1000 0.04 0.03 0.025 0.02 Count fingers at: less than 3m (10 ft.) Visual field: 10 degrees or less	Profound low vision, Moderate blindness
		NEAR-TOTAL VISUAL IMPAIRMENT Visual acuity: less than 0.02 (20/1000) Count fingers at: 1m (3 ft.) or less Hand movements: 5m (15 ft.) or less Light projection, light perception Visual field: 5 degrees or less	Severe blindness, Near-total blindness
		TOTAL VISUAL IMPAIRMENT No light perception (NLP)	Total blindness

Visual acuity refers to best achievable acuity with correction.
Non-listed Snellen fractions may be classified by converting to the nearest decimal equivalent, e.g. 10/200 = 0.05, 6/30 = 0.20.
CF (count fingers) without designation of distance, may be classified to profound impairment.
HM (hand motion) without designation of distance, may be classified to near-total impairment.
Visual field measurements refer to the largest field diameter for a 1/100 white test object.

369.72 **One eye: severe impairment; other eye: near-normal vision**

369.73 **One eye: severe impairment; other eye: normal vision**

369.74 **One eye: moderate impairment; other eye: not specified**

369.75 **One eye: moderate impairment; other eye: near-normal vision**

369.76 **One eye: moderate impairment; other eye: normal vision**

369.8 Unqualified visual loss, one eye

369.9 Unspecified visual loss
AHA: 4Q, '02, 114; 3Q, '02, 20

☑4ᵗʰ **370 Keratitis**

☑5ᵗʰ **370.0 Corneal ulcer**
EXCLUDES that due to vitamin A deficiency (264.3)

370.00 **Corneal ulcer, unspecified**

370.01 **Marginal corneal ulcer**

370.02 **Ring corneal ulcer**

370.03 **Central corneal ulcer**

370.04 **Hypopyon ulcer**
Serpiginous ulcer
DEF: Corneal ulcer with an accumulation of pus in the eye's anterior chamber..

N Newborn Age: 0   P Pediatric Age: 0-17   M Maternity Age: 12-55   A Adult Age: 15-124   CC CC Condition   MC Major Complication   CD Complex Dx   HIV HIV Related Dx

370.05 Mycotic corneal ulcer
DEF: Fungal infection causing corneal tissue loss.

370.06 Perforated corneal ulcer
DEF: Tissue loss through all layers of cornea.

370.07 Mooren's ulcer
DEF: Tissue loss, with chronic inflammation, at junction of cornea and sclera; seen in elderly.

√5ᵗʰ **370.2 Superficial keratitis without conjunctivitis**
     EXCLUDES   dendritic [herpes simplex] keratitis (054.42)

370.20 Superficial keratitis, unspecified
370.21 Punctate keratitis
Thygeson's superficial punctate keratitis

DEF: Formation of cellular and fibrinous deposits (keratic precipitates) on posterior surface; deposits develop after injury or iridocyclitis.

370.22 Macular keratitis
Keratitis:	Keratitis:
areolar	stellate
nummular	striate

370.23 Filamentary keratitis
DEF: Keratitis characterized by twisted filaments of mucoid material on the cornea's surface.

370.24 Photokeratitis
Snow blindness
Welders' keratitis
AHA: 3Q, '96, 6

DEF: Painful, inflamed cornea; due to extended exposure to ultraviolet light.

√5ᵗʰ **370.3 Certain types of keratoconjunctivitis**
370.31 Phlyctenular keratoconjunctivitis
Phlyctenulosis
Use additional code for any associated tuberculosis (017.3)

DEF: Miniature blister on conjunctiva or cornea; associated with tuberculosis and malnutrition disorders.

370.32 Limbar and corneal involvement in vernal conjunctivitis
Use additional code for vernal conjunctivitis (372.13)

DEF: Corneal itching and inflammation in conjunctivitis; often limited to lining of eyelids.

370.33 Keratoconjunctivitis sicca, not specified as Sjögren's
     EXCLUDES   Sjögren's syndrome (710.2)

DEF: Inflammation of conjunctiva and cornea; characterized by "horny" looking tissue and excess blood in these areas; decreased flow of lacrimal (tear) is a contributing factor.

370.34 Exposure keratoconjunctivitis
AHA: 3Q, '96, 6

DEF: Incomplete closure of eyelid causing dry, inflamed eye.

370.35 Neurotrophic keratoconjunctivitis

√5ᵗʰ **370.4 Other and unspecified keratoconjunctivitis**
370.40 Keratoconjunctivitis, unspecified
Superficial keratitis with conjunctivitis NOS
370.44 Keratitis or keratoconjunctivitis in exanthema
Code first underlying condition (050.0-052.9)
     EXCLUDES   herpes simplex (054.43)
                 herpes zoster (053.21)
                  measles (055.71)

370.49 Other
     EXCLUDES   epidemic keratoconjunctivitis (077.1)

√5ᵗʰ **370.5 Interstitial and deep keratitis**
370.50 Interstitial keratitis, unspecified
370.52 Diffuse interstitial keratitis
Cogan's syndrome
DEF: Inflammation of cornea; with deposits in middle corneal layers; may obscure vision.

370.54 Sclerosing keratitis
DEF: Chronic corneal inflammation leading to opaque scarring.

370.55 Corneal abscess
DEF: Pocket of pus and inflammation on the cornea.

370.59 Other
     EXCLUDES   disciform herpes simplex keratitis (054.43)
                  syphilitic keratitis (090.3)

√5ᵗʰ **370.6 Corneal neovascularization**
370.60 Corneal neovascularization, unspecified
370.61 Localized vascularization of cornea
DEF: Limited infiltration of cornea by new blood vessels.

370.62 Pannus (corneal)
AHA: 3Q, '02, 20

DEF: Buildup of superficial vascularization and granulated tissue under epithelium of cornea.

370.63 Deep vascularization of cornea
DEF: Deep infiltration of cornea by new blood vessels.

370.64 Ghost vessels (corneal)

370.8 Other forms of keratitis
AHA: 3Q, '94, 5

370.9 Unspecified keratitis

√4ᵗʰ **371 Corneal opacity and other disorders of cornea**
√5ᵗʰ **371.0 Corneal scars and opacities**
     EXCLUDES   that due to vitamin A deficiency (264.6)
371.00 Corneal opacity, unspecified
Corneal scar NOS
371.01 Minor opacity of cornea
Corneal nebula
371.02 Peripheral opacity of cornea
Corneal macula not interfering with central vision
371.03 Central opacity of cornea
Corneal:
   leucoma } interfering with central
   macula } vision
371.04 Adherent leucoma
DEF: Dense, opaque corneal growth adhering to the iris; also spelled as leukoma.

371.05 Phthisical cornea
Code first underlying tuberculosis (017.3)

√5ᵗʰ **371.1 Corneal pigmentations and deposits**
371.10 Corneal deposit, unspecified
371.11 Anterior pigmentations
Stähli's lines
371.12 Stromal pigmentations
Hematocornea
371.13 Posterior pigmentations
Krukenberg spindle
371.14 Kayser-Fleischer ring
DEF: Copper deposits forming ring at outer edge of cornea; seen in Wilson's disease and other liver disorders.

371.15 Other deposits associated with metabolic disorders
371.16 Argentous deposits
DEF: Silver deposits in cornea.

√5ᵗʰ **371.2 Corneal edema**
371.20 Corneal edema, unspecified

√4ᵗʰ Additional Digit Required   Nonspecific PDx   Unacceptable PDx   Manifestation Code   **MCV** Major Cardiovascular Condition   ►◄ Revised Text   ● New Code   ▲ Revised Code Title

371.21 Idiopathic corneal edema
DEF: Corneal swelling and fluid retention of unknown cause.

371.22 Secondary corneal edema
DEF: Corneal swelling and fluid retention caused by an underlying disease, injury, or condition.

371.23 Bullous keratopathy
DEF: Corneal degeneration; characterized by recurring, rupturing epithelial "blisters;" ruptured blebs expose corneal nerves, cause great pain; occurs in glaucoma, iridocyclitis and Fuchs' epithelial dystrophy.

371.24 Corneal edema due to wearing of contact lenses

√5th **371.3 Changes of corneal membranes**
371.30 Corneal membrane change, unspecified
371.31 Folds and rupture of Bowman's membrane
371.32 Folds in Descemet's membrane
371.33 Rupture in Descemet's membrane

√5th **371.4 Corneal degenerations**
371.40 Corneal degeneration, unspecified
371.41 Senile corneal changes
    Arcus senilis   Hassall-Henle bodies
371.42 Recurrent erosion of cornea
    EXCLUDES   *Mooren's ulcer (370.07)*
371.43 Band-shaped keratopathy
DEF: Horizontal bands of superficial corneal calcium deposits.
371.44 Other calcerous degenerations of cornea
371.45 Keratomalacia NOS
    EXCLUDES   *that due to vitamin A deficiency (264.4)*
DEF: Destruction of the cornea by keratinization of the epithelium with ulceration and perforation of the cornea; seen in cases of vitamin A deficiency.
371.46 Nodular degeneration of cornea
    Salzmann's nodular dystrophy
371.48 Peripheral degenerations of cornea
    Marginal degeneration of cornea [Terrien's]
371.49 Other
    Discrete colliquative keratopathy

√5th **371.5 Hereditary corneal dystrophies**
DEF: Genetic disorder; leads to opacities, edema or lesions of cornea.
371.50 Corneal dystrophy, unspecified
371.51 Juvenile epithelial corneal dystrophy
371.52 Other anterior corneal dystrophies
    Corneal dystrophy: Corneal dystrophy:
      microscopic cystic   ring-like
371.53 Granular corneal dystrophy
371.54 Lattice corneal dystrophy
371.55 Macular corneal dystrophy
371.56 Other stromal corneal dystrophies
    Crystalline corneal dystrophy
371.57 Endothelial corneal dystrophy
    Combined corneal dystrophy
    Cornea guttata
    Fuchs' endothelial dystrophy
371.58 Other posterior corneal dystrophies
    Polymorphous corneal dystrophy

√5th **371.6 Keratoconus**
DEF: Bilateral bulging protrusion of anterior cornea; often due to noninflammatory thinning.
371.60 Keratoconus, unspecified
371.61 Keratoconus, stable condition
371.62 Keratoconus, acute hydrops

√5th **371.7 Other corneal deformities**
371.70 Corneal deformity, unspecified

371.71 Corneal ectasia
DEF: Bulging protrusion of thinned, scarred cornea.

371.72 Descemetocele
DEF: Protrusion of Descemet's membrane into cornea.

371.73 Corneal staphyloma
DEF: Protrusion of cornea into adjacent tissue.

√5th **371.8 Other corneal disorders**
371.81 Corneal anesthesia and hypoesthesia
DEF: Decreased or absent sensitivity of cornea.

371.82 Corneal disorder due to contact lens
    EXCLUDES   *corneal edema due to contact lens (371.24)*
DEF: Contact lens wear causing cornea disorder, excluding swelling.

371.89 Other
AHA: 3Q, '99, 12

371.9 Unspecified corneal disorder

√4th **372 Disorders of conjunctiva**
    EXCLUDES   *keratoconjunctivitis (370.3-370.4)*

√5th **372.0 Acute conjunctivitis**
372.00 Acute conjunctivitis, unspecified
372.01 Serous conjunctivitis, except viral
    EXCLUDES   *viral conjunctivitis NOS (077.9)*
372.02 Acute follicular conjunctivitis
    Conjunctival folliculosis NOS
    EXCLUDES   *conjunctivitis:*
        adenoviral (acute follicular) (077.3)
        epidemic hemorrhagic (077.4)
        inclusion (077.0)
        Newcastle (077.8)
        epidemic keratoconjunctivitis (077.1)
        pharyngoconjunctival fever (077.2)
DEF: Severe conjunctival inflammation with dense infiltrations of lymphoid tissues of inner eyelids; may be traced to a viral or chlamydial etiology.

372.03 Other mucopurulent conjunctivitis
    Catarrhal conjunctivitis
    EXCLUDES   *blennorrhea neonatorum (gonococcal) (098.40)*
        neonatal conjunctivitis(771.6)
        ophthalmia neonatorum NOS (771.6)
372.04 Pseudomembranous conjunctivitis
    Membranous conjunctivitis
    EXCLUDES   *diphtheritic conjunctivitis (032.81)*
DEF: Severe inflammation of conjunctiva; false membrane develops on inner surface of eyelid; membrane can be removed without harming epithelium, due to bacterial infections, toxic and allergic factors, and viral infections.

372.05 Acute atopic conjunctivitis
DEF: Sudden, severe conjunctivitis due to allergens.

√5th **372.1 Chronic conjunctivitis**
372.10 Chronic conjunctivitis, unspecified
372.11 Simple chronic conjunctivitis
372.12 Chronic follicular conjunctivitis
DEF: Persistent conjunctival inflammation with dense, localized infiltrations of lymphoid tissues of inner eyelids.

372.13 Vernal conjunctivitis
AHA: 3Q, '96, 8

372.14 Other chronic allergic conjunctivitis
AHA: 3Q, '96, 8

N Newborn Age: 0   P Pediatric Age: 0-17   M Maternity Age: 12-55   A Adult Age: 15-124   CC CC Condition   MC Major Complication   CD Complex Dx   HIV HIV Related Dx

372.15 *Parasitic conjunctivitis*
>> Code first underlying disease, as:
>> filariasis (125.0-125.9)
>> mucocutaneous leishmaniasis (085.5)

✓5ᵗʰ **372.2** **Blepharoconjunctivitis**
>> **372.20** **Blepharoconjunctivitis, unspecified**
>> **372.21** **Angular blepharoconjunctivitis**
>>> DEF: Inflammation at junction of upper and lower eyelids; may block lacrimal secretions.

>> **372.22** **Contact blepharoconjunctivitis**

✓5ᵗʰ **372.3** **Other and unspecified conjunctivitis**
>> **372.30** **Conjunctivitis, unspecified**
>> **372.31** *Rosacea conjunctivitis*
>>> Code first underlying rosacea dermatitis (695.3)

>> **372.33** *Conjunctivitis in mucocutaneous disease*
>>> Code first underlying disease, as:
>>> erythema multiforme (695.1)
>>> Reiter's disease (099.3)
>>> EXCLUDES ocular pemphigoid (694.61)

>> **372.39** **Other**

✓5ᵗʰ **372.4** **Pterygium**
>> EXCLUDES pseudopterygium (372.52)
>> DEF: Wedge-shaped, conjunctival thickening that advances from the inner corner of the eye toward the cornea.
>> **372.40** **Pterygium, unspecified**
>> **372.41** **Peripheral pterygium, stationary**
>> **372.42** **Peripheral pterygium, progressive**
>> **372.43** **Central pterygium**
>> **372.44** **Double pterygium**
>> **372.45** **Recurrent pterygium**

✓5ᵗʰ **372.5** **Conjunctival degenerations and deposits**
>> **372.50** **Conjunctival degeneration, unspecified**
>> **372.51** **Pinguecula**
>>> DEF: Proliferative spot on the bulbar conjunctiva located near the sclerocorneal junction, usually on the nasal side; it is seen in elderly people.

>> **372.52** **Pseudopterygium**
>>> DEF: Conjunctival scar joined to the cornea; it looks like a pterygium but is not attached to the tissue.

>> **372.53** **Conjunctival xerosis**
>>> EXCLUDES conjunctival xerosis due to vitamin A deficiency (264.0, 264.1, 264.7)
>>> DEF: Dry conjunctiva due to vitamin A deficiency; related to Bitot's spots; may develop into xerophthalmia and keratomalacia.

>> **372.54** **Conjunctival concretions**
>>> DEF: Calculus or deposit on conjunctiva.

>> **372.55** **Conjunctival pigmentations**
>>> Conjunctival argyrosis
>>> DEF: Color deposits in conjunctiva.

>> **372.56** **Conjunctival deposits**

✓5ᵗʰ **372.6** **Conjunctival scars**
>> **372.61** **Granuloma of conjunctiva**
>> **372.62** **Localized adhesions and strands of conjunctiva**
>>> DEF: Abnormal fibrous connections in conjunctiva.

>> **372.63** **Symblepharon**
>>> Extensive adhesions of conjunctiva
>>> DEF: Adhesion of the eyelids to the eyeball.

>> **372.64** **Scarring of conjunctiva**
>>> Contraction of eye socket (after enucleation)

✓5ᵗʰ **372.7** **Conjunctival vascular disorders and cysts**
>> **372.71** **Hyperemia of conjunctiva**
>>> DEF: Conjunctival blood vessel congestion causing eye redness.

>> **372.72** **Conjunctival hemorrhage**
>>> Hyposphagma
>>> Subconjunctival hemorrhage

>> **372.73** **Conjunctival edema**
>>> Chemosis of conjunctiva
>>> Subconjunctival edema
>>> DEF: Fluid retention and swelling in conjunctival tissue.

>> **372.74** **Vascular abnormalities of conjunctiva**
>>> Aneurysm(ata) of conjunctiva

>> **372.75** **Conjunctival cysts**
>>> DEF: Abnormal sacs of fluid in conjunctiva.

✓5ᵗʰ **372.8** **Other disorders of conjunctiva**
>> **372.81** **Conjunctivochalasis**
>>> AHA: 4Q, '00, 41
>>> DEF: Bilateral condition of redundant conjunctival tissue between globe and lower eyelid margin; may cover lower punctum, interferring with normal tearing.

>> **372.89** **Other disorders of conjunctiva**

372.9 *Unspecified disorder of conjunctiva*

✓4ᵗʰ **373** **Inflammation of eyelids**

✓5ᵗʰ **373.0** **Blepharitis**
>> EXCLUDES blepharoconjunctivitis (372.20-372.22)
>> **373.00** **Blepharitis, unspecified**
>> **373.01** **Ulcerative blepharitis**
>> **373.02** **Squamous blepharitis**

✓5ᵗʰ **373.1** **Hordeolum and other deep inflammation of eyelid**
>> DEF: Purulent, localized, staphylococcal infection in sebaceous glands of eyelids.
>> **373.11** **Hordeolum externum**
>>> Hordeolum NOS Stye
>>> DEF: Infection of the oil glands in the eyelash follicles.

>> **373.12** **Hordeolum internum**
>>> Infection of meibomian gland
>>> DEF: Infection of the oil gland of the eyelid margin.

>> **373.13** **Abscess of eyelid**
>>> Furuncle of eyelid
>>> DEF: Inflamed pocket of pus on the eyelid.

373.2 **Chalazion**
>> Meibomian (gland) cyst
>> EXCLUDES infected meibomian gland (373.12)
>> DEF: Chronic inflammation of the meibomian gland, causing an eyelid mass.

✓5ᵗʰ **373.3** **Noninfectious dermatoses of eyelid**
>> **373.31** **Eczematous dermatitis of eyelid**
>> **373.32** **Contact and allergic dermatitis of eyelid**
>> **373.33** **Xeroderma of eyelid**
>> **373.34** **Discoid lupus erythematosus of eyelid**

373.4 *Infective dermatitis of eyelid of types resulting in deformity*
>> Code first underlying disease, as:
>> leprosy (030.0-030.9)
>> lupus vulgaris (tuberculous) (017.0)
>> yaws (102.0-102.9)

373.5 *Other infective dermatitis of eyelid*
>> Code first underlying disease, as:
>> actinomycosis (039.3)
>> impetigo (684)
>> mycotic dermatitis (110.0-111.9)
>> vaccinia (051.0)
>> postvaccination (999.0)
>> EXCLUDES herpes:
>>> simplex (054.41)
>>> zoster (053.20)

✓4ᵗʰ / ✓5ᵗʰ Additional Digit Required   Nonspecific PDx   Unacceptable PDx   Manifestation Code   MCV Major Cardiovascular Condition   ►◄ Revised Text   ● New Code   ▲ Revised Code Title

2007 ICD•9•CM   Volume 1 — 107

Nervous System and Sense Organs

373.6–375.03

Entropion and Ectropion

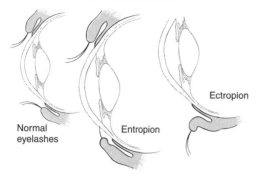

Ectropion

Normal eyelashes

Entropion

373.6 Parasitic infestation of eyelid
Code first underlying disease, as:
leishmaniasis (085.0-085.9)
loiasis (125.2)
onchocerciasis (125.3)
pediculosis (132.0)

373.8 Other inflammations of eyelids

373.9 Unspecified inflammation of eyelid

√4ᵗʰ **374 Other disorders of eyelids**

√5ᵗʰ **374.0 Entropion and trichiasis of eyelid**
DEF: Entropion: turning inward of eyelid edge toward eyeball.
DEF: Trichiasis: ingrowing eyelashes marked by irritation with possible distortion of sight.

374.00 Entropion, unspecified
374.01 Senile entropion A
374.02 Mechanical entropion
374.03 Spastic entropion
374.04 Cicatricial entropion
374.05 Trichiasis without entropion

√5ᵗʰ **374.1 Ectropion**
DEF: Turning outward (eversion) of eyelid edge; exposes palpebral conjunctiva; dryness irritation result.

374.10 Ectropion, unspecified
374.11 Senile ectropion A
374.12 Mechanical ectropion
374.13 Spastic ectropion
374.14 Cicatricial ectropion

√5ᵗʰ **374.2 Lagophthalmos**
DEF: Incomplete closure of eyes; causes dry eye and other complications.

374.20 Lagophthalmos, unspecified
374.21 Paralytic lagophthalmos
374.22 Mechanical lagophthalmos
374.23 Cicatricial lagophthalmos

√5ᵗʰ **374.3 Ptosis of eyelid**
374.30 Ptosis of eyelid, unspecified
AHA: 2Q, '96, 11

374.31 Paralytic ptosis
DEF: Drooping of upper eyelid due to nerve disorder.

374.32 Myogenic ptosis
DEF: Drooping of upper eyelid due to muscle disorder.

374.33 Mechanical ptosis
DEF: Outside force causes drooping of upper eyelid.

374.34 Blepharochalasis
Pseudoptosis
DEF: Loss of elasticity, thickened or indurated skin of eyelids associated with recurrent episodes of idiopathic edema causing intracellular tissue atrophy.

√5ᵗʰ **374.4 Other disorders affecting eyelid function**
EXCLUDES   blepharoclonus (333.81)
blepharospasm (333.81)
facial nerve palsy (351.0)
third nerve palsy or paralysis (378.51-378.52)
tic (psychogenic) (307.20-307.23)
organic (333.3)

374.41 Lid retraction or lag
374.43 Abnormal innervation syndrome
Jaw-blinking
Paradoxical facial movements

374.44 Sensory disorders
374.45 Other sensorimotor disorders
Deficient blink reflex

374.46 Blepharophimosis
Ankyloblepharon
DEF: Narrowing of palpebral fissure horizontally; caused by laterally displaced inner canthi; either acquired or congenital.

√5ᵗʰ **374.5 Degenerative disorders of eyelid and periocular area**
374.50 Degenerative disorder of eyelid, unspecified
374.51 Xanthelasma
Xanthoma (planum) (tuberosum) of eyelid
Code first underlying condition (272.0-272.9)
DEF: Fatty tumors of the eyelid linked to high fat content of blood.

374.52 Hyperpigmentation of eyelid
Chloasma   Dyspigmentation
DEF: Excess pigment of eyelid.

374.53 Hypopigmentation of eyelid
Vitiligo of eyelid
DEF: Lack of color pigment of the eyelid.

374.54 Hypertrichosis of eyelid
DEF: Excessive eyelash growth.

374.55 Hypotrichosis of eyelid
Madarosis of eyelid
DEF: Less than normal, or absent, eyelashes.

374.56 Other degenerative disorders of skin affecting eyelid

√5ᵗʰ **374.8 Other disorders of eyelid**
374.81 Hemorrhage of eyelid
EXCLUDES   black eye (921.0)

374.82 Edema of eyelid
Hyperemia of eyelid
DEF: Swelling and fluid retention in eyelid.

374.83 Elephantiasis of eyelid
DEF: Filarial disease causing dermatitis and enlargement of eyelid.

374.84 Cysts of eyelids
Sebaceous cyst of eyelid

374.85 Vascular anomalies of eyelid
374.86 Retained foreign body of eyelid
374.87 Dermatochalasis
DEF: Acquired form of connective tissue disorder associated with decreased elastic tissue and abnormal elastin formation resulting in loss of elasticity of the skin of the eyelid, generally associated with aging.

374.89 Other disorders of eyelid

374.9 Unspecified disorder of eyelid

√4ᵗʰ **375 Disorders of lacrimal system**

√5ᵗʰ **375.0 Dacryoadenitis**
375.00 Dacryoadenitis, unspecified
375.01 Acute dacryoadenitis
DEF: Severe, sudden inflammation of the lacrimal gland.

375.02 Chronic dacryoadenitis
DEF: Persistent inflammation of the lacrimal gland.

375.03 Chronic enlargement of lacrimal gland

N Newborn Age: 0   P Pediatric Age: 0-17   M Maternity Age: 12-55   A Adult Age: 15-124   CC CC Condition   MC Major Complication   CD Complex Dx   HIV HIV Related Dx

√5ᵗʰ **375.1 Other disorders of lacrimal gland**

    375.11 Dacryops

        DEF: Overproduction and constant flow of tears; may cause distended lacrimal duct.

    375.12 Other lacrimal cysts and cystic degeneration

    375.13 Primary lacrimal atrophy

    375.14 Secondary lacrimal atrophy

        DEF: Wasting away of the lacrimal gland due to another disease.

    375.15 Tear film insufficiency, unspecified

        Dry eye syndrome

        AHA: 3Q, '96, 6

        DEF: Eye dryness and irritation from insufficient tear production.

    375.16 Dislocation of lacrimal gland

√5ᵗʰ **375.2 Epiphora**

    DEF: Abnormal development of tears due to stricture of lacrimal passages.

    375.20 Epiphora, unspecified as to cause

    375.21 Epiphora due to excess lacrimation

        DEF: Tear overflow due to overproduction.

    375.22 Epiphora due to insufficient drainage

        DEF: Tear overflow due to blocked drainage.

√5ᵗʰ **375.3 Acute and unspecified inflammation of lacrimal passages**

        EXCLUDES   *neonatal dacryocystitis (771.6)*

    375.30 Dacryocystitis, unspecified

    375.31 Acute canaliculitis, lacrimal

    375.32 Acute dacryocystitis

        Acute peridacryocystitis

    375.33 Phlegmonous dacryocystitis

        DEF: Infection of the tear sac with pockets of pus.

√5ᵗʰ **375.4 Chronic inflammation of lacrimal passages**

    375.41 Chronic canaliculitis

    375.42 Chronic dacryocystitis

    375.43 Lacrimal mucocele

√5ᵗʰ **375.5 Stenosis and insufficiency of lacrimal passages**

    375.51 Eversion of lacrimal punctum

        DEF: Abnormal turning outward of the tear duct.

    375.52 Stenosis of lacrimal punctum

        DEF: Abnormal narrowing of the tear duct.

    375.53 Stenosis of lacrimal canaliculi

    375.54 Stenosis of lacrimal sac

        DEF: Abnormal narrowing of the tear sac.

    375.55 Obstruction of nasolacrimal duct, neonatal

        EXCLUDES   *congenital anomaly of nasolacrimal duct (743.65)*

        DEF: Acquired, abnormal obstruction of tear drainage system from the eye to the nose; in an infant.

    375.56 Stenosis of nasolacrimal duct, acquired

    375.57 Dacryolith

        DEF: Concretion or stone anywhere in lacrimal system.

√5ᵗʰ **375.6 Other changes of lacrimal passages**

    375.61 Lacrimal fistula

        DEF: Abnormal communication from the lacrimal system.

    375.69 Other

√5ᵗʰ **375.8 Other disorders of lacrimal system**

    375.81 Granuloma of lacrimal passages

        DEF: Abnormal nodules within lacrimal system.

    375.89 Other

    375.9 Unspecified disorder of lacrimal system

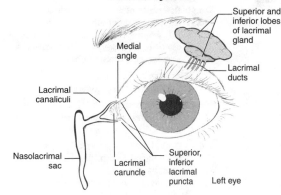

Lacrimal System

Superior and inferior lobes of lacrimal gland

Medial angle

Lacrimal ducts

Lacrimal canaliculi

Nasolacrimal sac

Lacrimal caruncle

Superior, inferior lacrimal puncta

Left eye

√4ᵗʰ **376 Disorders of the orbit**

√5ᵗʰ **376.0 Acute inflammation of orbit**

    376.00 Acute inflammation of orbit, unspecified

    376.01 Orbital cellulitis

        Abscess of orbit

        DEF: Infection of tissue between the orbital bone and eyeball.

    376.02 Orbital periostitis

        DEF: Inflammation of connective tissue covering the orbital bone.

    376.03 Orbital osteomyelitis

        DEF: Inflammation of the orbital bone.

    376.04 Tenonitis

√5ᵗʰ **376.1 Chronic inflammatory disorders of orbit**

    376.10 Chronic inflammation of orbit, unspecified

    376.11 Orbital granuloma

        Pseudotumor (inflammatory) of orbit

        DEF: Abnormal nodule between orbital bone and eyeball.

    376.12 Orbital myositis

        DEF: Painful inflammation of the muscles of the eye.

    376.13 *Parasitic infestation of orbit*

        Code first underlying disease, as:

        hydatid infestation of orbit (122.3, 122.6, 122.9)

        myiasis of orbit (134.0)

√5ᵗʰ **376.2 Endocrine exophthalmos**

    Code first underlying thyroid disorder (242.0-242.9)

    376.21 *Thyrotoxic exophthalmos*

        DEF: Painful inflammation of eye muscles.

    376.22 *Exophthalmic ophthalmoplegia*

        DEF: Inability to rotate eye as a result of bulging eyes.

√5ᵗʰ **376.3 Other exophthalmic conditions**

    376.30 Exophthalmos, unspecified

        DEF: Abnormal protrusion of eyeball.

    376.31 Constant exophthalmos

        DEF: Continuous, abnormal protrusion or bulging of eyeball.

    376.32 Orbital hemorrhage

        DEF: Bleeding behind the eyeball, causing it to bulge forward.

    376.33 Orbital edema or congestion

        DEF: Fluid retention behind eyeball, causing forward bulge.

    376.34 Intermittent exophthalmos

    376.35 Pulsating exophthalmos

        DEF: Bulge or protrusion; associated with a carotid-cavernous fistula.

    376.36 Lateral displacement of globe

        DEF: Abnormal displacement of the eyeball away from nose, toward temple.

√4ᵗʰ √5ᵗʰ Additional Digit Required   Nonspecific PDx   Unacceptable PDx   Manifestation Code   **MCV** Major Cardiovascular Condition   ▶◀ Revised Text   ● New Code   ▲ Revised Code Title

Nervous System and Sense Organs

376.4–377.73

√5th **376.4 Deformity of orbit**
376.40 Deformity of orbit, unspecified
376.41 Hypertelorism of orbit
DEF: Abnormal increase in interorbital distance; associated with congenital facial deformities; may be accompanied by mental deficiency.

376.42 Exostosis of orbit
DEF: Abnormal bony growth of orbit.

376.43 Local deformities due to bone disease
DEF: Acquired abnormalities of orbit; due to bone disease.

376.44 Orbital deformities associated with craniofacial deformities
376.45 Atrophy of orbit
DEF: Wasting away of bone tissue of orbit.

376.46 Enlargement of orbit
376.47 Deformity due to trauma or surgery
√5th **376.5 Enophthalmos**
DEF: Recession of eyeball deep into eye socket.

376.50 Enophthalmos, unspecified as to cause
376.51 Enophthalmos due to atrophy of orbital tissue
376.52 Enophthalmos due to trauma or surgery
376.6 Retained (old) foreign body following penetrating wound of orbit
Retrobulbar foreign body
√5th **376.8 Other orbital disorders**
376.81 Orbital cysts
Encephalocele of orbit
AHA: 3Q, '99, 13

376.82 Myopathy of extraocular muscles
DEF: Disease in the muscles that control eyeball movement.

376.89 Other
376.9 Unspecified disorder of orbit
√4th **377 Disorders of optic nerve and visual pathways**
√5th **377.0 Papilledema**
377.00 Papilledema, unspecified `CC`
CC Excl: 017.30-017.36, 017.90-017.96, 036.81, 250.50-250.53, 250.80-250.93, 377.00-377.03, 377.14, 377.24, 379.60-379.90, 379.99, 743.8-743.9

377.01 Papilledema associated with increased `CC` **intracranial pressure**
CC Excl: See code 377.00

377.02 Papilledema associated with decreased `CC` **ocular pressure**
CC Excl: See code 377.00

377.03 Papilledema associated with retinal disorder
377.04 Foster-Kennedy syndrome
DEF: Retrobulbar optic neuritis, central scotoma and optic atrophy; caused by tumors in frontal lobe of brain that press downward.

√5th **377.1 Optic atrophy**
377.10 Optic atrophy, unspecified
377.11 Primary optic atrophy
EXCLUDES   *neurosyphilitic optic atrophy (094.84)*

377.12 Postinflammatory optic atrophy
DEF: : Adverse effect of inflammation causing wasting away of eye.

377.13 Optic atrophy associated with retinal dystrophies
DEF: Progressive changes in retinal tissue due to metabolic disorder causing wasting away of eye.

377.14 Glaucomatous atrophy [cupping] of optic disc
377.15 Partial optic atrophy
Temporal pallor of optic disc
377.16 Hereditary optic atrophy
Optic atrophy: Optic atrophy:
dominant hereditary   Leber's
√5th **377.2 Other disorders of optic disc**
377.21 Drusen of optic disc
377.22 Crater-like holes of optic disc
377.23 Coloboma of optic disc
DEF: Ocular malformation caused by the failure of fetal fissure of optic stalk to close.

377.24 Pseudopapilledema
√5th **377.3 Optic neuritis**
EXCLUDES   *meningococcal optic neuritis (036.81)*
377.30 Optic neuritis, unspecified
377.31 Optic papillitis
DEF: Swelling and inflammation of the optic disc.

377.32 Retrobulbar neuritis (acute)
EXCLUDES   *syphilitic retrobulbar neuritis (094.85)*
DEF: Inflammation of optic nerve immediately behind the eyeball.

377.33 Nutritional optic neuropathy
DEF: Malnutrition causing optic nerve disorder.

377.34 Toxic optic neuropathy
Toxic amblyopia
DEF: Toxic substance causing optic nerve disorder.

377.39 Other
EXCLUDES   *ischemic optic neuropathy (377.41)*
√5th **377.4 Other disorders of optic nerve**
377.41 Ischemic optic neuropathy
DEF: Decreased blood flow affecting optic nerve.

377.42 Hemorrhage in optic nerve sheaths
DEF: Bleeding in meningeal lining of optic nerve.

377.43 Optic nerve hypoplasia
377.49 Other
Compression of optic nerve
√5th **377.5 Disorders of optic chiasm**
377.51 Associated with pituitary neoplasms and disorders
DEF: Abnormal pituitary growth causing disruption in nerve chain from retina to brain.

377.52 Associated with other neoplasms
DEF: Abnormal growth, other than pituitary, causing disruption in nerve chain from retina to brain.

377.53 Associated with vascular disorders
DEF: Vascular disorder causing disruption in nerve chain from retina to brain.

377.54 Associated with inflammatory disorders
DEF: Inflammatory disease causing disruption in nerve chain from retina to brain.

√5th **377.6 Disorders of other visual pathways**
377.61 Associated with neoplasms
377.62 Associated with vascular disorders
377.63 Associated with inflammatory disorders
√5th **377.7 Disorders of visual cortex**
EXCLUDES   *visual:*
agnosia (368.16)
hallucinations (368.16)
halos (368.15)
377.71 Associated with neoplasms
377.72 Associated with vascular disorders
377.73 Associated with inflammatory disorders

`N` Newborn Age: 0   `P` Pediatric Age: 0-17   `M` Maternity Age: 12-55   `A` Adult Age: 15-124   `CC` CC Condition   `MC` Major Complication   `CD` Complex Dx   `HIV` HIV Related Dx

110 — Volume 1 • October 2006   *2007 ICD•9•CM*

377.75 Cortical blindness
> DEF: Blindness due to brain disorder, rather than eye disorder.

377.9 Unspecified disorder of optic nerve and visual pathways

✓4ᵗʰ **378 Strabismus and other disorders of binocular eye movements**
> **EXCLUDES** *nystagmus and other irregular eye movements (379.50-379.59)*
>
> DEF: Misalignment of the eyes due to imbalance in extraocular muscles.

✓5ᵗʰ **378.0 Esotropia**
> Convergent concomitant strabismus
> **EXCLUDES** *intermittent esotropia (378.20-378.22)*
>
> DEF: Visual axis deviation created by one eye fixing upon an image and the other eye deviating inward.

378.00 Esotropia, unspecified
378.01 Monocular esotropia
378.02 Monocular esotropia with A pattern
378.03 Monocular esotropia with V pattern
378.04 Monocular esotropia with other noncomitancies
> Monocular esotropia with X or Y pattern

378.05 Alternating esotropia
378.06 Alternating esotropia with A pattern
378.07 Alternating esotropia with V pattern
378.08 Alternating esotropia with other noncomitancies
> Alternating esotropia with X or Y pattern

✓5ᵗʰ **378.1 Exotropia**
> Divergent concomitant strabismus
> **EXCLUDES** *intermittent exotropia (378.20, 378.23-378.24)*
>
> DEF: Visual axis deviation created by one eye fixing upon an image and the other eye deviating outward.

378.10 Exotropia, unspecified
378.11 Monocular exotropia
378.12 Monocular exotropia with A pattern
378.13 Monocular exotropia with V pattern
378.14 Monocular exotropia with other noncomitancies
> Monocular exotropia with X or Y pattern

378.15 Alternating exotropia
378.16 Alternating exotropia with A pattern
378.17 Alternating exotropia with V pattern
378.18 Alternating exotropia with other noncomitancies
> Alternating exotropia with X or Y pattern

✓5ᵗʰ **378.2 Intermittent heterotropia**
> **EXCLUDES** *vertical heterotropia (intermittent) (378.31)*
>
> DEF: Deviation of eyes seen only at intervals; it is also called strabismus.

Eye Musculature

Superior rectus
Superior oblique
Lateral rectus
Medial rectus
Inferior oblique
Inferior rectus

Muscles and actions (right eye)

R.   L.
Monocular (one eye only) esotropia (inward)

Monocular exotropia (outward)

Monocular hypertropia (upward)

378.20 Intermittent heterotropia, unspecified
> Intermittent: Intermittent:
> esotropia NOS   exotropia NOS

378.21 Intermittent esotropia, monocular
378.22 Intermittent esotropia, alternating
378.23 Intermittent exotropia, monocular
378.24 Intermittent exotropia, alternating

✓5ᵗʰ **378.3 Other and unspecified heterotropia**
378.30 Heterotropia, unspecified
378.31 Hypertropia
> Vertical heterotropia (constant) (intermittent)

378.32 Hypotropia
378.33 Cyclotropia
378.34 Monofixation syndrome
> Microtropia

378.35 Accommodative component in esotropia

✓5ᵗʰ **378.4 Heterophoria**
> DEF: Deviation occurring only when the other eye is covered.

378.40 Heterophoria, unspecified
378.41 Esophoria
378.42 Exophoria
378.43 Vertical heterophoria
378.44 Cyclophoria
378.45 Alternating hyperphoria

✓5ᵗʰ **378.5 Paralytic strabismus**
> DEF: Deviation of the eye due to nerve paralysis affecting muscle.

378.50 Paralytic strabismus, unspecified
378.51 Third or oculomotor nerve palsy, partial
> AHA: 3Q, '91, 9

378.52 Third or oculomotor nerve palsy, total
> AHA: 2Q, '89, 12

378.53 Fourth or trochlear nerve palsy
> AHA: 2Q, '01, 21

378.54 Sixth or abducens nerve palsy
> AHA: 2Q, '89, 12

378.55 External ophthalmoplegia
378.56 Total ophthalmoplegia

✓5ᵗʰ **378.6 Mechanical strabismus**
> DEF: Deviation of the eye due to an outside force upon the extraocular muscles.

378.60 Mechanical strabismus, unspecified
378.61 Brown's (tendon) sheath syndrome
> DEF: Congenital or acquired shortening of the anterior sheath of the superior oblique muscle; the eye is unable to move upward and inward; it is usually unilateral.

378.62 Mechanical strabismus from other musculofascial disorders
378.63 Limited duction associated with other conditions

✓5ᵗʰ **378.7 Other specified strabismus**
378.71 Duane's syndrome
> DEF: Congenital, affects one eye; due to abnormal fibrous bands attached to rectus muscle; inability to abduct affected eye with retraction of globe.

378.72 Progressive external ophthalmoplegia
> DEF: Paralysis progressing from one eye muscle to another.

378.73 Strabismus in other neuromuscular disorders

✓5ᵗʰ **378.8 Other disorders of binocular eye movements**
> **EXCLUDES** *nystagmus (379.50-379.56)*

378.81 Palsy of conjugate gaze
> DEF: Paralysis progressing from one eye muscle to another.

✓4ᵗʰ ✓5ᵗʰ Additional Digit Required   Nonspecific PDx   Unacceptable PDx   Manifestation Code   **MCV** Major Cardiovascular Condition   ▶◀ Revised Text   ● New Code   ▲ Revised Code Title

2007 ICD•9•CM   Volume 1 — 111

Nervous System and Sense Organs

378.82–379.55

378.82 Spasm of conjugate gaze
DEF: Muscle contractions impairing parallel movement of eye.

378.83 Convergence insufficiency or palsy
378.84 Convergence excess or spasm
378.85 Anomalies of divergence
378.86 Internuclear ophthalmoplegia
DEF: Eye movement anomaly due to brainstem lesion.

378.87 Other dissociated deviation of eye movements
Skew deviation

378.9 Unspecified disorder of eye movements
Ophthalmoplegia NOS   Strabismus NOS
AHA: 2Q, '01, 21

✓4th 379 Other disorders of eye

✓5th 379.0 Scleritis and episcleritis
EXCLUDES   syphilitic episcleritis (095.0)

379.00 Scleritis, unspecified
Episcleritis NOS

379.01 Episcleritis periodica fugax
DEF: Hyperemia (engorgement) of the sclera and overlying conjunctiva characterized by a sudden onset and short duration.

379.02 Nodular episcleritis
DEF: Inflammation of the outermost layer of the sclera, with formation of nodules.

379.03 Anterior scleritis
379.04 Scleromalacia perforans
DEF: Scleral thinning, softening and degeneration; seen with rheumatoid arthritis.

379.05 Scleritis with corneal involvement
Scleroperikeratitis

379.06 Brawny scleritis
DEF: Severe scleral inflammation with thickening corneal margins.

379.07 Posterior scleritis
Sclerotenonitis

379.09 Other
Scleral abscess

✓5th 379.1 Other disorders of sclera
EXCLUDES   blue sclera (743.47)

379.11 Scleral ectasia
Scleral staphyloma NOS
DEF: Protrusion of the contents of the eyeball where the sclera has thinned.

379.12 Staphyloma posticum
DEF: Ring-shaped protrusion or bulging of sclera and uveal tissue at posterior pole of eye.

379.13 Equatorial staphyloma
DEF: Ring-shaped protrusion or bulging of sclera and uveal tissue midway between front and back of eye.

379.14 Anterior staphyloma, localized
379.15 Ring staphyloma
379.16 Other degenerative disorders of sclera
379.19 Other

✓5th 379.2 Disorders of vitreous body
DEF: Disorder of clear gel that fills space between retina and lens.

379.21 Vitreous degeneration
Vitreous: Vitreous:
  cavitation   liquefaction
  detachment

379.22 Crystalline deposits in vitreous
Asteroid hyalitis   Synchysis scintillans

379.23 Vitreous hemorrhage
AHA: 3Q, '91, 15

379.24 Other vitreous opacities
Vitreous floaters

379.25 Vitreous membranes and strands
379.26 Vitreous prolapse
DEF: Slipping of vitreous from normal position.

379.29 Other disorders of vitreous
EXCLUDES   vitreous abscess (360.04)
AHA: 1Q, '99, 11

✓5th 379.3 Aphakia and other disorders of lens
EXCLUDES   after-cataract (366.50-366.53)

379.31 Aphakia
EXCLUDES   cataract extraction status (V45.61)
DEF: Absence of eye's crystalline lens.

379.32 Subluxation of lens
379.33 Anterior dislocation of lens
DEF: Lens displaced toward iris.

379.34 Posterior dislocation of lens
DEF: Lens displaced backward toward vitreous.

379.39 Other disorders of lens

✓5th 379.4 Anomalies of pupillary function
379.40 Abnormal pupillary function, unspecified
379.41 Anisocoria
DEF: Unequal pupil diameter.

379.42 Miosis (persistent), not due to miotics
DEF: Abnormal contraction of pupil less than 2 millimeters.

379.43 Mydriasis (persistent), not due to mydriatics
DEF: Morbid dilation of pupil.

379.45 Argyll Robertson pupil, atypical
Argyll Robertson phenomenon or pupil, nonsyphilitic
EXCLUDES   Argyll Robertson pupil (syphilitic) (094.89)
DEF: Failure of pupil to respond to light; affects both eyes; may be caused by diseases such as syphilis of the central nervous system or miosis.

379.46 Tonic pupillary reaction
Adie's pupil or syndrome

379.49 Other
Hippus   Pupillary paralysis

✓5th 379.5 Nystagmus and other irregular eye movements
379.50 Nystagmus, unspecified
AHA: 4Q, '02, 68; 2Q, '01, 21
DEF: Involuntary, rapid, rhythmic movement of eyeball; vertical, horizontal, rotatory or mixed; cause may be congenital, acquired, physiological, neurological, myopathic, or due to ocular diseases.

379.51 Congenital nystagmus
379.52 Latent nystagmus
379.53 Visual deprivation nystagmus
379.54 Nystagmus associated with disorders of the vestibular system
379.55 Dissociated nystagmus

Ear and Mastoid Process

Helix

Antihelix

Concha

External auditory meatus

Tragus

Mastoid process

Antitragus

N Newborn Age: 0   P Pediatric Age: 0-17   M Maternity Age: 12-55   A Adult Age: 15-124   CC CC Condition   MC Major Complication   CD Complex Dx   HIV HIV Related Dx

112 — Volume 1   *2007 ICD•9•CM*

379.56 **Other forms of nystagmus**
379.57 **Deficiencies of saccadic eye movements**
     Abnormal optokinetic response
     DEF: Saccadic eye movements; small, rapid, involuntary movements by both eyes simultaneously, due to changing point of fixation on visualized object.

379.58 **Deficiencies of smooth pursuit movements**
379.59 **Other irregularities of eye movements**
     Opsoclonus

● ✓5th 379.6 **Inflammation (infection) of postprocedural bleb**
     Postprocedural blebitis

●   379.60 **Inflammation (infection) of postprocedural bleb, unspecified**

●   379.61 **Inflammation (infection) of postprocedural bleb, stage 1**

●   379.62 **Inflammation (infection) of postprocedural bleb, stage 2**

●   379.63 **Inflammation (infection) of postprocedural bleb, stage 3**
     Bleb associated endophthalmitis

379.8 **Other specified disorders of eye and adnexa**
✓5th 379.9 **Unspecified disorder of eye and adnexa**
379.90 **Disorder of eye, unspecified**
379.91 **Pain in or around eye**
379.92 **Swelling or mass of eye**
379.93 **Redness or discharge of eye**
379.99 **Other ill-defined disorders of eye**
     EXCLUDES   *blurred vision NOS (368.8)*

DISEASES OF THE EAR AND MASTOID PROCESS (380-389)

✓4th 380 **Disorders of external ear**
✓5th 380.0 **Perichondritis and chondritis of pinna**
     Chondritis of auricle
     Perichondritis of auricle
380.00 **Perichondritis of pinna, unspecified**
380.01 **Acute perichondritis of pinna**
380.02 **Chronic perichondritis of pinna**
380.03 **Chondritis of pinna**
     AHA: 4Q, '04, 76
     DEF: Infection that has progressed into the cartilage; presents as indurated and edematous skin over the pinna; vascular compromise occurs with tissue necrosis and deformity.

✓5th 380.1 **Infective otitis externa**
380.10 **Infective otitis externa, unspecified**
     Otitis externa (acute):   Otitis externa (acute):
       NOS   hemorrhagica
       circumscribed   infective NOS
       diffuse
380.11 **Acute infection of pinna**
     EXCLUDES   *furuncular otitis externa (680.0)*
380.12 **Acute swimmers' ear**
     Beach ear   Tank ear
     DEF: Otitis externa due to swimming.
380.13 *Other acute infections of external ear*
     Code first underlying disease, as:
       erysipelas (035)
       impetigo (684)
       seborrheic dermatitis (690.10-690.18)
     EXCLUDES   *herpes simplex (054.73)*
                  herpes zoster (053.71)
380.14 **Malignant otitis externa**
     DEF: Severe necrotic otitis externa; due to bacteria.
380.15 *Chronic mycotic otitis externa*
     Code first underlying disease, as:
       aspergillosis (117.3)
       otomycosis NOS (111.9)
     EXCLUDES   *candidal otitis externa (112.82)*

380.16 **Other chronic infective otitis externa**
     Chronic infective otitis externa NOS
✓5th 380.2 **Other otitis externa**
380.21 **Cholesteatoma of external ear**
     Keratosis obturans of external ear (canal)
     EXCLUDES   *cholesteatoma NOS (385.30-385.35)*
                  postmastoidectomy (383.32)
     DEF: Cystlike mass filled with debris, including cholesterol; rare, congenital condition.
380.22 **Other acute otitis externa**
     Acute otitis externa: Acute otitis externa:
       actinic   eczematoid
       chemical   reactive
       contact
380.23 **Other chronic otitis externa**
     Chronic otitis externa NOS
✓5th 380.3 **Noninfectious disorders of pinna**
380.30 **Disorder of pinna, unspecified**
380.31 **Hematoma of auricle or pinna**
380.32 **Acquired deformities of auricle or pinna**
     EXCLUDES   *cauliflower ear (738.7)*
     AHA: 3Q, '03, 12
380.39 **Other**
     EXCLUDES   *gouty tophi of ear (274.81)*
380.4 **Impacted cerumen**
     Wax in ear
✓5th 380.5 **Acquired stenosis of external ear canal**
     Collapse of external ear canal
380.50 **Acquired stenosis of external ear canal, unspecified as to cause**
380.51 **Secondary to trauma**
     DEF: Narrowing of the external ear canal; due to trauma.
380.52 **Secondary to surgery**
     DEF: Postsurgical narrowing of the external ear canal.
380.53 **Secondary to inflammation**
     DEF: Narrowing of the external ear canal; due to chronic inflammation.
✓5th 380.8 **Other disorders of external ear**
380.81 **Exostosis of external ear canal**
380.89 **Other**
380.9 **Unspecified disorder of external ear**
✓4th 381 **Nonsuppurative otitis media and Eustachian tube disorders**
✓5th 381.0 **Acute nonsuppurative otitis media**
     Acute tubotympanic catarrh
     Otitis media, acute or subacute:
       catarrhal
       exudative
       transudative
       with effusion
     EXCLUDES   *otitic barotrauma (993.0)*
381.00 **Acute nonsuppurative otitis media, unspecified**
381.01 **Acute serous otitis media**
     Acute or subacute secretory otitis media
     DEF: Sudden, severe infection of the middle ear.
381.02 **Acute mucoid otitis media**
     Acute or subacute seromucinous otitis media
     Blue drum syndrome
     DEF: Sudden, severe infection of the middle ear, with mucous.
381.03 **Acute sanguinous otitis media**
     DEF: Sudden, severe infection of the middle ear, with blood.
381.04 **Acute allergic serous otitis media**
381.05 **Acute allergic mucoid otitis media**
381.06 **Acute allergic sanguinous otitis media**

✓4th ✓5th Additional Digit Required   Nonspecific PDx   Unacceptable PDx   Manifestation Code   **MCV** Major Cardiovascular Condition   ◄► Revised Text   ● New Code   ▲ Revised Code Title

2007 ICD•9•CM   October 2006 • Volume 1 — 113

Nervous System and Sense Organs

381.1–383.1

√5th **381.1 Chronic serous otitis media**
Chronic tubotympanic catarrh
381.10 Chronic serous otitis media, simple or unspecified
DEF: Persistent infection of the middle ear, without pus.

381.19 Other
Serosanguinous chronic otitis media

√5th **381.2 Chronic mucoid otitis media**
Glue ear
EXCLUDES   adhesive middle ear disease (385.10-385.19)
DEF: Chronic condition; characterized by viscous fluid in middle ear; due to obstructed Eustachian tube.
381.20 Chronic mucoid otitis media, simple or unspecified
381.29 Other
Mucosanguinous chronic otitis media

381.3 Other and unspecified chronic nonsuppurative otitis media
Otitis media, chronic: Otitis media, chronic:
allergic   seromucinous
exudative   transudative
secretory   with effusion

381.4 Nonsuppurative otitis media, not specified as acute or chronic
Otitis media: Otitis media:
allergic   seromucinous
catarrhal   serous
exudative   transudative
mucoid   with effusion
secretory

√5th **381.5 Eustachian salpingitis**
381.50 Eustachian salpingitis, unspecified
381.51 Acute Eustachian salpingitis
DEF: Sudden, severe inflammation of the Eustachian tube.

381.52 Chronic Eustachian salpingitis
DEF: Persistent inflammation of the Eustachian tube.

√5th **381.6 Obstruction of Eustachian tube**
Stenosis ⎫
Stricture ⎭ of Eustachian tube

381.60 Obstruction of Eustachian tube, unspecified
381.61 Osseous obstruction of Eustachian tube
Obstruction of Eustachian tube from cholesteatoma, polyp, or other osseous lesion
381.62 Intrinsic cartilagenous obstruction of Eustachian tube
DEF: Blockage of Eustachian tube; due to cartilage overgrowth.

381.63 Extrinsic cartilagenous obstruction of Eustachian tube
Compression of Eustachian tube

381.7 Patulous Eustachian tube
DEF: Distended, oversized Eustachian tube.

√5th **381.8 Other disorders of Eustachian tube**
381.81 Dysfunction of Eustachian tube
381.89 Other

381.9 Unspecified Eustachian tube disorder

√4th **382 Suppurative and unspecified otitis media**
√5th **382.0 Acute suppurative otitis media**
Otitis media, acute: Otitis media, acute:
necrotizing NOS   purulent
382.00 Acute suppurative otitis media without spontaneous rupture of ear drum
DEF: Sudden, severe inflammation of middle ear, with pus.

382.01 Acute suppurative otitis media with spontaneous rupture of ear drum
DEF: Sudden, severe inflammation of middle ear, with pressure tearing ear drum tissue.

382.02 Acute suppurative otitis media in diseases classified elsewhere
Code first underlying disease, as:
influenza (487.8)
scarlet fever (034.1)
EXCLUDES   postmeasles otitis (055.2)

382.1 Chronic tubotympanic suppurative otitis media
Benign chronic
suppurative otitis   ⎫ (with anterior
media   ⎬ perforation of
Chronic tubotympanic   ⎭ ear drum)
disease
DEF: Inflammation of tympanic cavity and auditory tube; with pus formation.

382.2 Chronic atticoantral suppurative otitis media
Chronic atticoantral   ⎫ (with posterior or superior
disease   ⎬ marginal perforation
Persistent mucosal   ⎭ of ear drum)
disease
DEF: Inflammation of upper tympanic membrane and mastoid antrum with pus formation.

382.3 Unspecified chronic suppurative otitis media
Chronic purulent otitis media
EXCLUDES   tuberculous otitis media (017.4)

382.4 Unspecified suppurative otitis media
Purulent otitis media NOS

382.9 Unspecified otitis media
Otitis media: Otitis media:
NOS   chronic NOS
acute NOS
AHA: N-D, '84, 16

√4th **383 Mastoiditis and related conditions**
√5th **383.0 Acute mastoiditis**
Abscess of mastoid   Empyema of mastoid
383.00 Acute mastoiditis without complications
DEF: Sudden, severe inflammation of mastoid air cells.

383.01 Subperiosteal abscess of mastoid   **CC**
CC Excl: 015.60-015.66, 017.40-017.46, 017.90-017.96, 383.00-388.9, 744.00, 744.02, 744.09, 744.29, 744.3
DEF: Pocket of pus within the mastoid bone.

383.02 Acute mastoiditis with other complications
Gradenigo's syndrome

383.1 Chronic mastoiditis
Caries of mastoid
Fistula of mastoid
EXCLUDES   tuberculous mastoiditis (015.6)
DEF: Persistent inflammation of the mastoid air cells.

Middle and Inner Ear

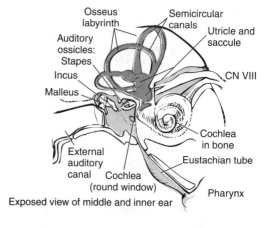

Exposed view of middle and inner ear

N Newborn Age: 0   P Pediatric Age: 0-17   M Maternity Age: 12-55   A Adult Age: 15-124   CC CC Condition   MC Major Complication   CD Complex Dx   HIV HIV Related Dx

114 — Volume 1   2007 ICD•9•CM

√5th **383.2 Petrositis**

Coalescing osteitis ⎫
Inflammation   ⎬ of petrous bone
Osteomyelitis   ⎭

383.20 Petrositis, unspecified
383.21 Acute petrositis
DEF: Sudden, severe inflammation of dense bone behind the ear.

383.22 Chronic petrositis
DEF: Persistent inflammation of dense bone behind the ear.

√5th **383.3 Complications following mastoidectomy**
383.30 Postmastoidectomy complication, unspecified **cc**
CC Excl: See code 383.01

383.31 Mucosal cyst of postmastoidectomy cavity
DEF: Mucous-lined cyst cavity following removal of mastoid bone.

383.32 Recurrent cholesteatoma of postmastoidectomy cavity
DEF: Cystlike mass of cell debris in cavity following removal of mastoid bone.

383.33 Granulations of postmastoidectomy cavity
Chronic inflammation of postmastoidectomy cavity
DEF: Granular tissue in cavity following removal of mastoid bone.

√5th **383.8 Other disorders of mastoid**
383.81 Postauricular fistula **cc**
CC Excl: See code 383.01
DEF: Abnormal passage behind mastoid cavity.

383.89 Other
383.9 Unspecified mastoiditis

√4th **384 Other disorders of tympanic membrane**
√5th **384.0 Acute myringitis without mention of otitis media**
384.00 Acute myringitis, unspecified
Acute tympanitis NOS
DEF: Sudden, severe inflammation of ear drum.

384.01 Bullous myringitis
Myringitis bullosa hemorrhagica
DEF: Type of viral otitis media characterized by the appearance of serous or hemorrhagic blebs on the tympanic membrane.

384.09 Other
384.1 Chronic myringitis without mention of otitis media
Chronic tympanitis
DEF: Persistent inflammation of ear drum; with no evidence of middle ear infection.

√5th **384.2 Perforation of tympanic membrane**
Perforation of ear drum: Perforation of ear drum:
NOS   postinflammatory
persistent posttraumatic
EXCLUDES otitis media with perforation of tympanic membrane (382.00-382.9)
traumatic perforation [current injury] (872.61)

384.20 Perforation of tympanic membrane, unspecified
384.21 Central perforation of tympanic membrane
384.22 Attic perforation of tympanic membrane
Pars flaccida

384.23 Other marginal perforation of tympanic membrane
384.24 Multiple perforations of tympanic membrane
384.25 Total perforation of tympanic membrane
√5th **384.8 Other specified disorders of tympanic membrane**
384.81 Atrophic flaccid tympanic membrane
Healed perforation of ear drum
384.82 Atrophic nonflaccid tympanic membrane
384.9 Unspecified disorder of tympanic membrane

√4th **385 Other disorders of middle ear and mastoid**
EXCLUDES mastoiditis (383.0-383.9)

√5th **385.0 Tympanosclerosis**
385.00 Tympanosclerosis, unspecified as to involvement
385.01 Tympanosclerosis involving tympanic membrane only
DEF: Tough, fibrous tissue impeding functions of ear drum.

385.02 Tympanosclerosis involving tympanic membrane and ear ossicles
DEF: Tough, fibrous tissue impeding functions of middle ear bones (stapes, malleus, incus).

385.03 Tympanosclerosis involving tympanic membrane, ear ossicles, and middle ear
DEF: Tough, fibrous tissue impeding functions of ear drum, middle ear bones and middle ear canal.

385.09 Tympanosclerosis involving other combination of structures
√5th **385.1 Adhesive middle ear disease**
Adhesive otitis   Otitis media:
Otitis media: fibrotic
chronic adhesive
EXCLUDES glue ear (381.20-381.29)
DEF: Adhesions of middle ear structures.

385.10 Adhesive middle ear disease, unspecified as to involvement
385.11 Adhesions of drum head to incus
385.12 Adhesions of drum head to stapes
385.13 Adhesions of drum head to promontorium
385.19 Other adhesions and combinations
√5th **385.2 Other acquired abnormality of ear ossicles**
385.21 Impaired mobility of malleus
Ankylosis of malleus
385.22 Impaired mobility of other ear ossicles
Ankylosis of ear ossicles, except malleus
385.23 Discontinuity or dislocation of ear ossicles
DEF: Disruption in auditory chain; created by malleus, incus and stapes.

385.24 Partial loss or necrosis of ear ossicles
DEF: Tissue loss in malleus, incus and stapes.

√4th
√5th Additional Digit Required   Nonspecific PDx   Unacceptable PDx   Manifestation Code   **MCV** Major Cardiovascular Condition   ◄► Revised Text   ● New Code   ▲ Revised Code Title

2007 ICD•9•CM   Volume 1 — 115

Nervous System and Sense Organs

385.3–387.0

Cholesteatoma

Middle ear chamber

Cholesteatoma sac   Ear drum

√5th **385.3 Cholesteatoma of middle ear and mastoid**

Cholesterosis
Epidermosis
Keratosis
Polyp
} of (middle) ear

EXCLUDES   cholesteatoma:
external ear canal (380.21)
recurrent of postmastoidectomy
cavity (383.32)

DEF: Cystlike mass of middle ear and mastoid antrum filled with debris, including cholesterol.

385.30 Cholesteatoma, unspecified
385.31 Cholesteatoma of attic
385.32 Cholesteatoma of middle ear
385.33 Cholesteatoma of middle ear and mastoid

AHA: 3Q, '00, 10

DEF: Cystlike mass of cell debris in middle ear and mastoid air cells behind ear.

385.35 Diffuse cholesteatosis

√5th **385.8 Other disorders of middle ear and mastoid**
385.82 Cholesterin granuloma

DEF: Granuloma formed of fibrotic tissue; contains cholesterol crystals surrounded by foreign-body cells; found in the middle ear and mastoid area.

385.83 Retained foreign body of middle ear

AHA: 3Q, '94, 7; N-D, '87, 9

385.89 Other

385.9 Unspecified disorder of middle ear and mastoid

√4th **386 Vertiginous syndromes and other disorders of vestibular system**

EXCLUDES   vertigo NOS (780.4)

AHA: M-A, '85, 12

√5th **386.0 Ménière's disease**

Endolymphatic hydrops
Lermoyez's syndrome
Ménière's syndrome or vertigo

DEF: Distended membranous labyrinth of middle ear from endolymphatic hydrops; causes ischemia, failure of nerve function; hearing and balance dysfunction; symptoms include fluctuating deafness, ringing in ears and dizziness.

386.00 Ménière's disease, unspecified
Ménière's disease (active)
386.01 Active Ménière's disease, cochleovestibular
386.02 Active Ménière's disease, cochlear
386.03 Active Ménière's disease, vestibular
386.04 Inactive Ménière's disease
Ménière's disease in remission

√5th **386.1 Other and unspecified peripheral vertigo**

EXCLUDES   epidemic vertigo (078.81)

386.10 Peripheral vertigo, unspecified

386.11 Benign paroxysmal positional vertigo
Benign paroxysmal positional nystagmus
386.12 Vestibular neuronitis
Acute (and recurrent) peripheral vestibulopathy

DEF: Transient benign vertigo, unknown cause; characterized by response to caloric stimulation on one side, nystagmus with rhythmic movement of eyes; normal auditory function present; occurs in young adults.

386.19 Other
Aural vertigo
Otogenic vertigo

386.2 Vertigo of central origin
Central positional nystagmus
Malignant positional vertigo

√5th **386.3 Labyrinthitis**
386.30 Labyrinthitis, unspecified
386.31 Serous labyrinthitis
Diffuse labyrinthitis

DEF: Inflammation of labyrinth; with fluid buildup.

386.32 Circumscribed labyrinthitis
Focal labyrinthitis
386.33 Suppurative labyrinthitis
Purulent labyrinthitis

DEF: Inflammation of labyrinth; with pus.

386.34 Toxic labyrinthitis

DEF: Inflammation of labyrinth; due to toxic reaction.

386.35 Viral labyrinthitis

√5th **386.4 Labyrinthine fistula**
386.40 Labyrinthine fistula, unspecified
386.41 Round window fistula
386.42 Oval window fistula
386.43 Semicircular canal fistula
386.48 Labyrinthine fistula of combined sites

√5th **386.5 Labyrinthine dysfunction**
386.50 Labyrinthine dysfunction, unspecified
386.51 Hyperactive labyrinth, unilateral

DEF: Abnormal increased sensitivity of labyrinth to stimuli such as sound, pressure or gravitational change, affecting one ear.

386.52 Hyperactive labyrinth, bilateral

DEF: Abnormal increased sensitivity of labyrinth to stimuli such as sound, pressure or gravitational change, affecting both ears.

386.53 Hypoactive labyrinth, unilateral

DEF: Abnormal decreased sensitivity of labyrinth to stimuli such as sound, pressure or gravitational change, affecting one ear.

386.54 Hypoactive labyrinth, bilateral

DEF: Abnormal decreased sensitivity of labyrinth to stimuli such as sound, pressure or gravitational change, affecting both ears.

386.55 Loss of labyrinthine reactivity, unilateral

DEF: Decreased function of the labyrinth sensors, affecting one ear

386.56 Loss of labyrinthine reactivity, bilateral

DEF: Decreased function of the labyrinth sensors, affecting both ears

386.58 Other forms and combinations

386.8 Other disorders of labyrinth

386.9 Unspecified vertiginous syndromes and labyrinthine disorders

√4th **387 Otosclerosis**

INCLUDES   otospongiosis

DEF: Synonym for otospongiosis, spongy bone formation in the labyrinth bones of the ear; it causes progressive hearing impairment.

387.0 Otosclerosis involving oval window, nonobliterative

DEF: Tough, fibrous tissue impeding functions of oval window.

N Newborn Age: 0   P Pediatric Age: 0-17   M Maternity Age: 12-55   A Adult Age: 15-124   CC CC Condition   MC Major Complication   CD Complex Dx   HIV HIV Related Dx

116 — Volume 1   *2007 ICD•9•CM*

387.1　**Otosclerosis involving oval window, obliterative**
　　　DEF: Tough, fibrous tissue blocking oval window.

387.2　**Cochlear otosclerosis**
　　　Otosclerosis involving:　Otosclerosis involving:
　　　　otic capsule　　　　round window
　　　DEF: Tough, fibrous tissue impeding functions of cochlea.

387.8　**Other otosclerosis**

387.9　**Otosclerosis, unspecified**

✓4th 388　**Other disorders of ear**

✓5th 388.0　**Degenerative and vascular disorders of ear**
　　388.00　**Degenerative and vascular disorders, unspecified**
　　388.01　**Presbyacusis**
　　　　DEF: Progressive, bilateral perceptive hearing loss caused by advancing age; it is also known as presbycusis.
　　388.02　**Transient ischemic deafness**
　　　　DEF: Restricted blood flow to auditory organs causing temporary hearing loss.

✓5th 388.1　**Noise effects on inner ear**
　　388.10　**Noise effects on inner ear, unspecified**
　　388.11　**Acoustic trauma (explosive) to ear**
　　　　Otitic blast injury
　　388.12　**Noise-induced hearing loss**

388.2　**Sudden hearing loss, unspecified**

✓5th 388.3　**Tinnitus**
　　　DEF: Abnormal noises in ear; may be heard by others beside the affected individual; noises include ringing, clicking, roaring and buzzing.
　　388.30　**Tinnitus, unspecified**
　　388.31　**Subjective tinnitus**
　　388.32　**Objective tinnitus**

✓5th 388.4　**Other abnormal auditory perception**
　　388.40　**Abnormal auditory perception, unspecified**
　　388.41　**Diplacusis**
　　　　DEF: Perception of a single auditory sound as two sounds at two different levels of intensity.
　　388.42　**Hyperacusis**
　　　　DEF: Exceptionally acute sense of hearing caused by such conditions as Bell's palsy; this term may also refer to painful sensitivity to sounds.
　　388.43　**Impairment of auditory discrimination**
　　　　DEF: Impaired ability to distinguish tone of sound.
　　388.44　**Recruitment**
　　　　DEF: Perception of abnormally increased loudness caused by a slight increase in sound intensity; it is a term used in audiology.

388.5　**Disorders of acoustic nerve**
　　Acoustic neuritis
　　Degeneration ⎫
　　Disorder 　 ⎬ of acoustic or eighth nerve
　　EXCLUDES　*acoustic neuroma (225.1)*
　　　　　　　syphilitic acoustic neuritis (094.86)

AHA: M-A, '87, 8

✓5th 388.6　**Otorrhea**
　　388.60　**Otorrhea, unspecified**
　　　　Discharging ear NOS
　　388.61　**Cerebrospinal fluid otorrhea**
　　　　EXCLUDES　*cerebrospinal fluid rhinorrhea (349.81)*
　　　　DEF: Spinal fluid leakage from ear.
　　388.69　**Other**
　　　　Otorrhagia

✓5th 388.7　**Otalgia**
　　388.70　**Otalgia, unspecified**
　　　　Earache NOS
　　388.71　**Otogenic pain**
　　388.72　**Referred pain**

388.8　**Other disorders of ear**

388.9　**Unspecified disorder of ear**

✓4th 389　**Hearing loss**

✓5th 389.0　**Conductive hearing loss**
　　　Conductive deafness
　　AHA: 4Q, '89, 5
　　DEF: Dysfunction in sound-conducting structures of external or middle ear causing hearing loss.
　　389.00　**Conductive hearing loss, unspecified**
　　389.01　**Conductive hearing loss, external ear**
　　389.02　**Conductive hearing loss, tympanic membrane**
　　389.03　**Conductive hearing loss, middle ear**
　　389.04　**Conductive hearing loss, inner ear**
　　389.08　**Conductive hearing loss of combined types**

✓5th 389.1　**Sensorineural hearing loss**
　　　Perceptive hearing loss or deafness
　　　EXCLUDES　*abnormal auditory perception (388.40-388.44)*
　　　　　　　psychogenic deafness (306.7)
　　AHA: 4Q, '89, 5
　　DEF: Nerve conduction causing hearing loss.
　　389.10　**Sensorineural hearing loss, unspecified**
　　　　AHA: 1Q, '93, 29
　　389.11　**Sensory hearing loss, bilateral** ▲
　　389.12　**Neural hearing loss, bilateral** ▲
　　389.14　**Central hearing loss, bilateral** ▲
　　389.15　**Sensorineural hearing loss, unilateral** ●
　　389.16　**Sensorineural hearing loss, asymmetrical** ●
　　389.18　**Sensorineural hearing loss of combined types, bilateral** ▲

389.2　**Mixed conductive and sensorineural hearing loss**
　　Deafness or hearing loss of type classifiable to 389.0 with type classifiable to 389.1

389.7　**Deaf mutism, not elsewhere classifiable**
　　Deaf, nonspeaking

389.8　**Other specified forms of hearing loss**

389.9　**Unspecified hearing loss**
　　Deafness NOS
　　AHA: 1Q, '04, 15

✓4th ✓5th Additional Digit Required　Nonspecific PDx　Unacceptable PDx　Manifestation Code　**MCV** Major Cardiovascular Condition　▶◀ Revised Text　● New Code　▲ Revised Code Title

7. DISEASES OF THE CIRCULATORY SYSTEM (390-459)

ACUTE RHEUMATIC FEVER (390-392)

DEF: Febrile disease occurs mainly in children or young adults following throat infection by group A *streptococci*; symptoms include fever, joint pain, lesions of heart, blood vessels and joint connective tissue, abdominal pain, skin changes, and chorea.

390 Rheumatic fever without mention of heart involvement
Arthritis, rheumatic, acute or subacute
Rheumatic fever (active) (acute)
Rheumatism, articular, acute or subacute
EXCLUDES *that with heart involvement (391.0-391.9)*

√4th **391 Rheumatic fever with heart involvement**
EXCLUDES *chronic heart diseases of rheumatic origin (398.0-398.9) unless rheumatic fever is also present or there is evidence of recrudescence or activity of the rheumatic process*

391.0 Acute rheumatic pericarditis
Rheumatic:
fever (active) (acute) with pericarditis
pericarditis (acute)
Any condition classifiable to 390 with pericarditis
EXCLUDES *that not specified as rheumatic (420.0-420.9)*
DEF: Sudden, severe inflammation of heart lining due to rheumatic fever.

391.1 Acute rheumatic endocarditis
Rheumatic:
endocarditis, acute
fever (active) (acute) with endocarditis or valvulitis
valvulitis acute
Any condition classifiable to 390 with endocarditis or valvulitis
DEF: Sudden, severe inflammation of heart cavities due to rheumatic fever.

391.2 Acute rheumatic myocarditis
Rheumatic fever (active) (acute) with myocarditis
Any condition classifiable to 390 with myocarditis
DEF: Sudden, severe inflammation of heart muscles due to rheumatic fever.

391.8 Other acute rheumatic heart disease
Rheumatic:
fever (active) (acute) with other or multiple types of heart involvement
pancarditis, acute
Any condition classifiable to 390 with other or multiple types of heart involvement

391.9 Acute rheumatic heart disease, unspecified
Rheumatic:
carditis, acute
fever (active) (acute) with unspecified type of heart involvement
heart disease, active or acute
Any condition classifiable to 390 with unspecified type of heart involvement

√4th **392 Rheumatic chorea**
INCLUDES Sydenham's chorea
EXCLUDES *chorea:*
NOS (333.5)
Huntington's (333.4)
DEF: Childhood disease linked with rheumatic fever and streptococcal infections; symptoms include spasmodic, involuntary movements of limbs or facial muscles, psychic symptoms, and irritability.

392.0 With heart involvement
Rheumatic chorea with heart involvement of any type classifiable to 391

392.9 Without mention of heart involvement

CHRONIC RHEUMATIC HEART DISEASE (393-398)

393 Chronic rheumatic pericarditis
Adherent pericardium, rheumatic
Chronic rheumatic:
mediastinopericarditis
myopericarditis
EXCLUDES *pericarditis NOS or not specified as rheumatic (423.0-423.9)*
DEF: Persistent inflammation of heart lining due to rheumatic heart disease.

√4th **394 Diseases of mitral valve**
EXCLUDES *that with aortic valve involvement (396.0-396.9)*

394.0 Mitral stenosis **CC**
Mitral (valve): Mitral (valve):
obstruction (rheumatic) stenosis NOS
CC Excl: 390, 391.8-391.9, 394.0-394.9, 396.0-396.9, 397.9, 398.90, 398.99, 424.0, 459.89, 459.9
DEF: Narrowing, of mitral valve between left atrium and left ventricle; due to rheumatic heart disease.

394.1 Rheumatic mitral insufficiency **CC**
Rheumatic mitral: Rheumatic mitral:
incompetence regurgitation
EXCLUDES *that not specified as rheumatic (424.0)*
CC Excl: See code 394.0
AHA: ▶2Q, '05, 14◀
DEF: Malfunction of mitral valve between left atrium and left ventricle; due to rheumatic heart disease.

394.2 Mitral stenosis with insufficiency **CC**
Mitral stenosis with incompetence or regurgitation
CC Excl: See code 394.0
DEF: A narrowing or stricture of the mitral valve situated between the left atrium and left ventricle. The stenosis interferes with blood flow from the atrium into the ventricle. If the valve does not completely close, it becomes insufficient (inadequate) and cannot prevent regurgitation (abnormal backward flow) into the atrium when the left ventricle contracts. This abnormal function is also called incompetence.

394.9 Other and unspecified mitral valve diseases **CC**
Mitral (valve): Mitral (valve):
disease (chronic) failure
CC Excl: See code 394.0

√4th **395 Diseases of aortic valve**
EXCLUDES *that not specified as rheumatic (424.1)*
that with mitral valve involvement (396.0-396.9)

395.0 Rheumatic aortic stenosis **CC**
Rheumatic aortic (valve) obstruction
CC Excl: 390, 391.8-391.9, 395.0-395.9, 396.0-396.9, 397.9, 398.90, 398.99, 424.1, 459.89, 459.9
AHA: 4Q, '88, 8
DEF: Narrowing of the aortic valve; results in backflow into ventricle; due to rheumatic heart disease.

395.1 Rheumatic aortic insufficiency **CC**
Rheumatic aortic: Rheumatic aortic:
incompetence regurgitation
CC Excl: See code 395.0
DEF: Malfunction of the aortic valve; results in backflow into left ventricle; due to rheumatic heart disease.

395.2 Rheumatic aortic stenosis with insufficiency **CC**
Rheumatic aortic stenosis with incompetence or regurgitation
CC Excl: See code 395.0
DEF: Malfunction and narrowing, of the aortic valve; results in backflow into left ventricle; due to rheumatic heart disease.

395.9 Other and unspecified rheumatic aortic diseases **CC**
Rheumatic aortic (valve) disease
CC Excl: See code 395.0

√4th √5th Additional Digit Required Nonspecific PDx Unacceptable PDx Manifestation Code **MCV** Major Cardiovascular Condition ▶◀ Revised Text ● New Code ▲ Revised Code Title

2007 ICD•9•CM February 2006 • Volume 1 — 119

Circulatory System

390–395.9

Circulatory System

396–402.91

✓4ᵗʰ **396 Diseases of mitral and aortic valves**

INCLUDES   involvement of both mitral and aortic valves, whether specified as rheumatic or not

AHA: N-D, '87, 8

396.0 Mitral valve stenosis and aortic valve stenosis CC
Atypical aortic (valve) stenosis
Mitral and aortic (valve) obstruction (rheumatic)
CC Excl: 390, 391.8-391.9, 394.0-394.9, 395.0-395.9, 396.0-396.9, 397.9, 398.90, 398.99, 424.0-424.1, 459.89, 459.9

396.1 Mitral valve stenosis and aortic valve insufficiency CC
CC Excl: See code 396.0

396.2 Mitral valve insufficiency and aortic valve stenosis CC
CC Excl: See code 396.0
AHA: 2Q, '00, 16

396.3 Mitral valve insufficiency and aortic valve insufficiency CC
Mitral and aortic (valve):   Mitral and aortic (valve):
   incompetence   regurgitation
CC Excl: See code 396.0

396.8 Multiple involvement of mitral and aortic valves CC
Stenosis and insufficiency of mitral or aortic valve with stenosis or insufficiency, or both, of the other valve
CC Excl: See code 396.0

396.9 Mitral and aortic valve diseases, unspecified CC
CC Excl: See code 396.0

✓4ᵗʰ **397 Diseases of other endocardial structures**

397.0 Diseases of tricuspid valve CC
Tricuspid (valve)   Tricuspid (valve)
  (rheumatic):   (rheumatic):
  disease   regurgitation
  insufficiency   stenosis
  obstruction
CC Excl: 397.0, 398.90, 398.99, 424.2, 459.89, 459.9
AHA: 2Q, '00, 16

DEF: Malfunction of the valve between right atrium and right ventricle; due to rheumatic heart disease.

397.1 Rheumatic diseases of pulmonary valve CC
EXCLUDES   that not specified as rheumatic (424.3)
CC Excl: 397.1, 398.90, 398.99, 424.3, 459.89, 459.9

397.9 Rheumatic diseases of endocardium, valve unspecified CC
Rheumatic:
  endocarditis (chronic)
  valvulitis (chronic)
EXCLUDES   that not specified as rheumatic (424.90-424.99)
CC Excl: 390, 391.1, 391.8-391.9, 394.0-394.9, 395.0-395.9, 397.1, 397.9, 398.90, 398.99, 421.0-421.9, 424.0-424.99, 459.89, 459.9

✓4ᵗʰ **398 Other rheumatic heart disease**

398.0 Rheumatic myocarditis CC
Rheumatic degeneration of myocardium
EXCLUDES   myocarditis not specified as rheumatic (429.0)
CC Excl: 390, 391.2-391.9, 398.0, 398.90, 398.99, 422.0, 422.90-422.99, 429.0, 429.71-429.79, 459.89, 459.9

DEF: Chronic inflammation of heart muscle; due to rheumatic heart disease.

✓5ᵗʰ **398.9 Other and unspecified rheumatic heart diseases**

398.90 Rheumatic heart disease, unspecified
Rheumatic:
  carditis
  heart disease NOS
EXCLUDES   carditis not specified as rheumatic (429.89)
heart disease NOS not specified as rheumatic (429.9)

398.91 Rheumatic heart failure (congestive) CC MC CD MCV
Rheumatic left ventricular failure
CC Excl: 398.90-398.99, 402.01, 402.11, 402.91, 428.0-428.9, 459.89, 459.9

AHA: 2Q, '05, 14; 1Q, '95, 6; 3Q, '88, 3

DEF: Decreased cardiac output, edema and hypertension; due to rheumatic heart disease.

398.99 Other

HYPERTENSIVE DISEASE (401-405)

EXCLUDES   that complicating pregnancy, childbirth, or the puerperium (642.0-642.9)
that involving coronary vessels (410.00-414.9)

AHA: 3Q, '90, 3; 2Q, '89, 12; S-O, '87, 9; J-A, '84, 11

✓4ᵗʰ **401 Essential hypertension**

INCLUDES   high blood pressure
hyperpiesia
hyperpiesis
hypertension (arterial) (essential) (primary) (systemic)
hypertensive vascular:
  degeneration
  disease

EXCLUDES   elevated blood pressure without diagnosis of hypertension (796.2)
pulmonary hypertension (416.0-416.9)
that involving vessels of:
  brain (430-438)
  eye (362.11)

AHA: 2Q, '92, 5

DEF: Hypertension that occurs without apparent organic cause; idiopathic.

401.0 Malignant CC
CC Excl: 401.0-405.99, 459.89, 459.9
AHA: M-J, '85, 19

DEF: Severe high arterial blood pressure; results in necrosis in kidney, retina, etc.; hemorrhages occur and death commonly due to uremia or rupture of cerebral vessel.

401.1 Benign
DEF: Mildly elevated arterial blood pressure.

401.9 Unspecified
AHA: 4Q, '05, 71; 3Q, '05, 8; 4Q, '04, 78; 4Q, '03, 105, 108, 111; 3Q, '03, 14; 2Q, '03, 16; 4Q, '97, 37

✓4ᵗʰ **402 Hypertensive heart disease**

INCLUDES   hypertensive:
  cardiomegaly
  cardiopathy
  cardiovascular disease
  heart (disease) (failure)
any condition classifiable to 429.0-429.3, 429.8, 429.9 due to hypertension
Use additional code to specify type of heart failure (428.0-428.43), if known

AHA: 4Q, '02, 49; 2Q, '93, 9; N-D, '84, 18

✓5ᵗʰ **402.0 Malignant**

402.00 Without heart failure CC
CC Excl: See code 401.0

402.01 With heart failure CC MC CD MCV
CC Excl: 398.91, 401.0-405.99, 428.0-428.9, 459.89, 459.9

✓5ᵗʰ **402.1 Benign**

402.10 Without heart failure

402.11 With heart failure CC MC CD MCV
CC Excl: See code 402.01

✓5ᵗʰ **402.9 Unspecified**

402.90 Without heart failure

402.91 With heart failure CC MC CD MCV
CC Excl: See code 402.01
AHA: 4Q, '02, 52; 1Q, '93, 19; 2Q, '89, 12
DRG 127

N Newborn Age: 0   P Pediatric Age: 0-17   M Maternity Age: 12-55   A Adult Age :15-124   CC CC Condition   MC Major Complication   CD Complex Dx   HIV HIV Related Dx

▲ ✓4ᵗʰ **403 Hypertensive chronic kidney disease**

INCLUDES   arteriolar nephritis
arteriosclerosis of:
  kidney
  renal arterioles
arteriosclerotic nephritis (chronic) (interstitial)
hypertensive:
  nephropathy
  renal failure
  uremia (chronic)
nephrosclerosis
renal sclerosis with hypertension
any condition classifiable to 585, 586, or 587
  with any condition classifiable to 401

EXCLUDES   *acute renal failure (584.5-584.9)*
renal disease stated as not due to hypertension
renovascular hypertension (405.0-405.9 with fifth-digit 1)

The following fifth-digit subclassification is for use with category 403:

▲ **0 with chronic kidney disease stage I through stage IV, or unspecified**
▶Use additional code to identify the stage of chronic kidney disease (585.1-585.4, 585.9) ◀

▲ **1 with chronic kidney disease stage V or end stage renal disease**
▶Use additional code to identify the stage of chronic kidney disease (585.5, 585.6) ◀

AHA: 4Q, '05, 68; 4Q, '92, 22; 2Q, '92, 5

✓5ᵗʰ **403.0 Malignant**   CC
CC Excl: 401.0-405.99, 459.89, 459.9

✓5ᵗʰ **403.1 Benign**   CC 1
CC Excl: For code 403.11: See code 403.0

✓5ᵗʰ **403.9 Unspecified**   CC 1
CC Excl: For code 403.91: See code 403.0

AHA: For code 403.91: 4Q, '05, 69; 1Q, '04, 14; 1Q, '03, 20; 2Q, '01, 11; 3Q, '91, 8

DRG 316 For code 403.91

▲ ✓4ᵗʰ **404 Hypertensive heart and chronic kidney disease**

INCLUDES   disease:
  cardiorenal
  cardiovascular renal
any condition classifiable to 402 with any condition classifiable to 403
Use additional code to specify type of heart failure (428.0-428.43), if known

The following fifth-digit subclassification is for use with category 404:

▲ **0 without heart failure and with chronic kidney disease stage I through stage IV, or unspecified**
▶Use additional code to identify the stage of chronic kidney disease (585.1-585.4, 585.9)◀

▲ **1 with heart failure and with chronic** MC CD MCV **kidney disease stage I through stage IV, or unspecified**
▶Use additional code to identify the stage of chronic kidney disease (585.1-585.4, 585.9)◀

▲ **2 without heart failure and with chronic kidney disease stage V or end stage renal disease**
▶Use additional code to identify the stage of chronic kidney disease (585.5, 585.6)◀

▲ **3 with heart failure and chronic kidney** MC CD MCV **disease stage V or end stage renal disease**
▶Use additional code to identify the stage of chronic kidney disease (585.5-585.6)◀

AHA: 4Q, '05, 68; 4Q, '02, 49; 3Q, '90, 3; J-A, '84, 14

✓5ᵗʰ **404.0 Malignant**   CC
CC Excl: See code 403.0

✓5ᵗʰ **404.1 Benign**   CC 1-3
CC Excl: For codes 404.11-404.13: See code 403.0

✓5ᵗʰ **404.9 Unspecified**   CC 1-3
CC Excl: For codes 404.91-404.93: See code 403.0

✓4ᵗʰ **405 Secondary hypertension**
AHA: 3Q, '90, 3; S-O, '87, 9, 11; J-A, '84, 14

DEF: High arterial blood pressure due to or with a variety of primary diseases, such as renal disorders, CNS disorders, endocrine, and vascular diseases.

✓5ᵗʰ **405.0 Malignant**
405.01 Renovascular   CC
CC Excl: 401.0-405.99, 459.89, 459.9

405.09 Other   CC
CC Excl: See code 405.01

✓5ᵗʰ **405.1 Benign**
405.11 Renovascular
405.19 Other

✓5ᵗʰ **405.9 Unspecified**
405.91 Renovascular
405.99 Other
AHA: 3Q, '00, 4

ISCHEMIC HEART DISEASE (410-414)

INCLUDES   that with mention of hypertension
Use additional code to identify presence of hypertension (401.0-405.9)

AHA: 3Q, '91, 10; J-A, '84, 5

✓4ᵗʰ **410 Acute myocardial infarction**

INCLUDES   cardiac infarction
coronary (artery):
  embolism
  occlusion
  rupture
  thrombosis
infarction of heart, myocardium, or ventricle
rupture of heart, myocardium, or ventricle
ST elevation (STEMI) and non-ST elevation (NSTEMI) myocardial infarction
any condition classifiable to 414.1-414.9 specified as acute or with a stated duration of 8 weeks or less

The following fifth-digit subclassification is for use with category 410:

0 episode of care unspecified
Use when the source document does not contain sufficient information for the assignment of fifth digit 1 or 2.

1 initial episode of care   MCV
Use fifth-digit 1 to designate the first episode of care (regardless of facility site) for a newly diagnosed myocardial infarction. The fifth-digit 1 is assigned regardless of the number of times a patient may be transferred during the initial episode of care.

2 subsequent episode of care
Use fifth-digit 2 to designate an episode of care following the initial episode when the patient is admitted for further observation, evaluation or treatment for a myocardial infarction that has received initial treatment, but is still less than 8 weeks old.

AHA: 4Q, '05, 69; 3Q, '01, 21; 3Q, '98, 15; 4Q, '97, 37; 3Q, '95, 9; 4Q, '92, 24; 1Q, '92,10; 3Q, '91, 18; 1Q, '91, 14; 3Q, '89, 3

DEF: A sudden insufficiency of blood supply to an area of the heart muscle; usually due to a coronary artery occlusion.

✓5ᵗʰ **410.0 Of anterolateral wall**   CC 1
ST elevation myocardial infarction (STEMI) of anterolateral wall
CC Excl: For code 410.01: 410.00-410.92, 459.89, 459.9

✓4ᵗʰ ✓5ᵗʰ Additional Digit Required   Nonspecific PDx   Unacceptable PDx   Manifestation Code   MCV Major Cardiovascular Condition   ▶◀ Revised Text   ● New Code   ▲ Revised Code Title

2007 ICD•9•CM   October 2006 • Volume 1 — 121

Circulatory System

410.1–411.89

Acute Myocardial Infarction

Anatomic Sites

- Anterolateral 410.0
- Other lateral 410.5
- Posterobasal 410.6
- Posterolateral 410.5
- Anteroseptal 410.1
- Inferoposterior 410.3
- Atrium only 410.8
- Septum only
- Apical 410.1
- Other and septum 410.4
- Papillary muscle

§ ☑5th **410.1** **Of other anterior wall** `CC 1`

Infarction:
- anterior (wall) NOS
- anteroapical
- anteroseptal

(with contiguous portion of intraventricular septum)

ST elevation myocardial infarction (STEMI) of other anterior wall

CC Excl: For code 410.11: See code 410.0

AHA: For code 410.11: 3Q, '03, 10

▽ **DRG** 121 and 122 For code 410.11

§ ☑5th **410.2** **Of inferolateral wall** `CC 1`

ST elevation myocardial infarction (STEMI) of inferolateral wall

CC Excl: For code 410.21: See code 410.0

§ ☑5th **410.3** **Of inferoposterior wall** `CC 1`

ST elevation myocardial infarction (STEMI) of inferoposterior wall

CC Excl: For code 410.31: See code 410.0

§ ☑5th **410.4** **Of other inferior wall** `CC 1`

Infarction:
- diaphragmatic wall
- NOS
- inferior (wall) NOS

(with contiguous portion of intraventricular septum)

ST elevation myocardial infarction (STEMI) of other inferior wall

CC Excl: For code 410.41: See code 410.0

AHA: 1Q, '00, 7, 26; 4Q, '99, 9; 3Q, '97, 10; **For code 410.41:** 2Q, '01, 8, 9

▽ **DRG** 122 For code 410.41

§ ☑5th **410.5** **Of other lateral wall** `CC 1`

Infarction:
- apical-lateral
- basal-lateral
- high lateral
- posterolateral

ST elevation myocardial infarction (STEMI) of other lateral wall

CC Excl: For code 410.51: See code 410.0

§ ☑5th **410.6** **True posterior wall infarction** `CC 1`

Infarction:
- posterobasal
- strictly posterior

ST elevation myocardial infarction (STEMI) of true posterior wall

CC Excl: For code 410.61: See code 410.0

§ ☑5th **410.7** **Subendocardial infarction** `CC 1`

Non-ST elevation myocardial infarction (NSTEMI)
Nontransmural infarction

CC Excl: For code 410.71: See code 410.0

AHA: 1Q, '00, 7; **For code 410.71:** 4Q, '05, 71; 2Q, '05, 19

▽ **DRG** 121 and 122 For code 410.71

§ ☑5th **410.8** **Of other specified sites** `CC 1`

Infarction of:
- atrium
- papillary muscle
- septum alone

ST elevation myocardial infarction (STEMI) of other specified sites

CC Excl: For code 410.81: See code 410.0

§ ☑5th **410.9** **Unspecified site** `CC 1`

Acute myocardial infarction NOS
Coronary occlusion NOS
Myocardial infarction NOS

CC Excl: For code 410.91: See code 410.0

AHA: 1Q, '96, 17; 1Q, '92, 9; **For code 410.91:** 2Q, '05, 18; 3Q, '02, 5

▽ **DRG** 121 and 122 For code 410.91

☑4th **411** **Other acute and subacute forms of ischemic heart disease**

AHA: 4Q, '94, 55; 3Q, '91, 24

411.0 **Postmyocardial infarction syndrome** `CC` `MC` `CD` `MCV`

Dressler's syndrome

CC Excl: 411.0, 411.81, 411.89, 459.89, 459.9

DEF: Complication developing several days/weeks after myocardial infarction; symptoms include fever, leukocytosis, chest pain, evidence of pericarditis, pleurisy, and pneumonitis; tendency to recur.

9 **411.1** **Intermediate coronary syndrome** `CC` `CD` `MCV`

Impending infarction   Preinfarction syndrome
Preinfarction angina   Unstable angina

EXCLUDES angina (pectoris) (413.9)
decubitus (413.0)

CC Excl: 410.00-410.92, 411.1-411.89, 413.0-413.9, 414.8-414.9, 459.89, 459.9

AHA: 4Q, '05, 105; 2Q, '04, 3; 1Q, '03, 12; 3Q, '01, 15; 2Q, '01, 7, 9; 4Q, '98, 86; 2Q, '96, 10; 3Q, '91, 24; 1Q, '91, 14; 3Q, '90, 6; 4Q, '89, 10

▽ **DRG** 140

DEF: A condition representing an intermediate stage between angina of effort and acute myocardial infarction. It is often documented by the physician as "unstable angina."

☑5th **411.8** **Other**

AHA: 3Q, '91, 18; 3Q, '89, 4

9 **411.81** **Acute coronary occlusion without myocardial infarction** `CC` `CD` `MCV`

Acute coronary (artery):
- embolism
- obstruction
- occlusion
- thrombosis

without or not resulting in myocardial infarction

EXCLUDES obstruction without infarction due to atherosclerosis (414.00-414.07)
occlusion without infarction due to atherosclerosis (414.00-414.07)

CC Excl: 410.00-410.92, 411.0-411.89, 413.0-413.9, 414.8-414.9, 459.89, 459.9

AHA: 3Q, '91, 24; 1Q, '91, 14

DEF: Interrupted blood flow to a portion of the heart; without tissue death.

411.89 **Other** `CC` `CD`

Coronary insufficiency (acute)
Subendocardial ischemia

CC Excl: See code 411.81

AHA: 3Q, '01, 14; 1Q, '92, 9

▽ **DRG** 140

---

9 MCV for DRGs 551 and 553 only.
§ Requires fifth-digit. See category 410 for codes and definitions.

`N` Newborn Age: 0   `P` Pediatric Age: 0-17   `M` Maternity Age: 12-55   `A` Adult Age :15-124   `CC` CC Condition   `MC` Major Complication   `CD` Complex Dx   `HIV` HIV Related Dx

412 Old myocardial infarction
　　Healed myocardial infarction
　　Past myocardial infarction diagnosed on ECG [EKG] or other special investigation, but currently presenting no symptoms
　　AHA: 2Q, '03, 10; 2Q, '01, 9; 3Q, '98, 15; 2Q, '91, 22; 3Q, '90, 7

✓4ᵗʰ 413 Angina pectoris
　　DEF: Severe constricting pain in the chest, often radiating from the precordium to the left shoulder and down the arm, due to ischemia of the heart muscle; usually caused by coronary disease; pain is often precipitated by effort or excitement.

　　413.0 Angina decubitus `CC`
　　　　Nocturnal angina
　　　　CC Excl: 410.00-410.92, 411.1-411.89, 413.0-413.9, 414.8-414.9, 459.89, 459.9

　　　　DEF: Angina occurring only in the recumbent position.

　　413.1 Prinzmetal angina `CC`
　　　　Variant angina pectoris
　　　　CC Excl: See code 413.0

　　　　DEF Angina occurring when patient is recumbent; associated with ST-segment elevations.

　　413.9 Other and unspecified angina pectoris `CC`
　　　　Angina:　　　　　　Anginal syndrome
　　　　　NOS　　　　　　Status anginosus
　　　　　cardiac　　　　　Stenocardia
　　　　　of effort　　　　Syncope anginosa
　　　　　　EXCLUDES　*preinfarction angina (411.1)*
　　　　CC Excl: See code 413.0
　　　　AHA: 3Q, '02, 4; 3Q, '91, 16; 3Q, '90, 6
　　　　▽ DRG 140

✓4ᵗʰ 414 Other forms of chronic ischemic heart disease
　　　　EXCLUDES　*arteriosclerotic cardiovascular disease [ASCVD] (429.2)*
　　　　　cardiovascular:
　　　　　　arteriosclerosis or sclerosis (429.2)
　　　　　　degeneration or disease (429.2)

　　✓5ᵗʰ 414.0 Coronary atherosclerosis
　　　　Arteriosclerotic heart disease [ASHD]
　　　　Atherosclerotic heart disease
　　　　Coronary (artery):
　　　　　arteriosclerosis
　　　　　arteritis or endarteritis
　　　　　atheroma
　　　　　sclerosis
　　　　　stricture
　　　　　　EXCLUDES　*embolism of graft (996.72)*
　　　　　　　occlusion NOS of graft (996.72)
　　　　　　　thrombus of graft (996.72)
　　　　AHA: 2Q, '97, 13; 2Q, '95, 17; 4Q, '94, 49; 2Q, '94, 13; 1Q, '94, 6; 3Q, '90, 7
　　　　DEF: A chronic condition marked by thickening and loss of elasticity of the coronary artery; caused by deposits of plaque containing cholesterol, lipoid material and lipophages.

　　　　414.00 Of unspecified type of vessel, native or graft `A`
　　　　　　AHA: 1Q, '04, 24; 2Q, '03, 16; 3Q, '01, 15; 4Q, '99, 4; 3Q, '97, 15; 4Q, '96, 31
　　　　　　▽ DRG 124, 125 and 132

　　　　414.01 Of native coronary artery `A`
　　　　　　AHA: 4Q, '05, 71; 2Q, '04, 3; 4Q, '03, 108; 3Q, '03, 9, 14; 3Q, '02, 4-9; 3Q, '01, 15; 2Q, '01, 8, 9; 3Q, '97, 15; 2Q, '96, 10; 4Q, '96, 31
　　　　　　▽ DRG 132, 124, and 125
　　　　　　DEF: Plaque deposits in natural heart vessels.

　　　　414.02 Of autologous vein bypass graft `A`
　　　　　　DEF: Plaque deposit in grafted vein originating within patient.

　　　　414.03 Of nonautologous biological bypass graft `A`
　　　　　　DEF: Plaque deposits in grafted vessel originating outside patient.

Arteries of the Heart

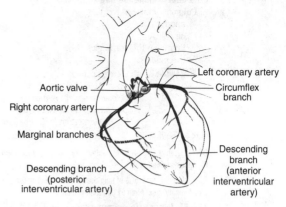

414.04 Of artery bypass graft `A`
　　Internal mammary artery
　　AHA: 4Q, '96, 31
　　DEF: Plaque deposits in grafted artery originating within patient.

414.05 Of unspecified type of bypass graft `A`
　　Bypass graft NOS
　　AHA: 3Q, '97, 15; 4Q, '96, 31

414.06 Of native coronary artery of transplanted heart
　　AHA: 4Q, '03, 60; 4Q, '02, 53

414.07 Of bypass graft (artery) (vein) of transplanted heart `A`

✓5ᵗʰ 414.1 Aneurysm and dissection of heart
　　AHA: 4Q, '02, 54

　　414.10 Aneurysm of heart (wall) `MC` `MCV`
　　　　Aneurysm (arteriovenous):
　　　　　mural
　　　　　ventricular

　　414.11 Aneurysm of coronary vessels `MC` `MCV`
　　　　Aneurysm (arteriovenous) of coronary vessels
　　　　AHA: 3Q, '03, 10; 1Q, '99, 17
　　　　DEF: Dilatation of all three-vessel wall layers forming a sac filled with blood.

　　414.12 Dissection of coronary artery `MC` `MCV`
　　　　DEF: A tear in the intimal arterial wall of a coronary artery resulting in the sudden intrusion of blood within the layers of the wall.

　　414.19 Other aneurysm of heart `MC` `MCV`
　　　　Arteriovenous fistula, acquired, of heart

414.8 Other specified forms of chronic ischemic heart disease
　　Chronic coronary insufficiency
　　Ischemia, myocardial (chronic)
　　Any condition classifiable to 410 specified as chronic, or presenting with symptoms after 8 weeks from date of infarction
　　　EXCLUDES　*coronary insufficiency (acute) (411.89)*
　　AHA: 3Q, '01, 15; 1Q, '92, 10; 3Q, '90, 7, 15; 2Q, '90, 19

414.9 Chronic ischemic heart disease, unspecified
　　Ischemic heart disease NOS

DISEASES OF PULMONARY CIRCULATION (415-417)

✓4ᵗʰ 415 Acute pulmonary heart disease
　　415.0 Acute cor pulmonale `CC` `CD` `MCV`
　　　　EXCLUDES　*cor pulmonale NOS (416.9)*
　　　　CC Excl: 415.0, 416.8-416.9, 459.89, 459.9
　　　　DEF: A heart-lung disease marked by dilation and failure of the right side of heart; due to pulmonary embolism; ventilatory function is impaired and pulmonary hypertension results within hours.

✓4ᵗʰ ✓5ᵗʰ Additional Digit Required　　`Nonspecific PDx`　Nonspecific PDx　`Unacceptable PDx`　Unacceptable PDx　`Manifestation Code`　Manifestation Code　　`MCV` Major Cardiovascular Condition　▶◀ Revised Text　● New Code　▲ Revised Code Title

2007 ICD•9•CM   **October 2006 • Volume 1 — 123**

✓5ᵗʰ 415.1 Pulmonary embolism and infarction
Pulmonary (artery) (vein):
  apoplexy
  embolism
  infarction (hemorrhagic)
  thrombosis

EXCLUDES   that complicating:
        abortion (634-638 with .6, 639.6)
        ectopic or molar pregnancy (639.6)
        pregnancy, childbirth, or the
          puerperium (673.0-673.8)

AHA: 4Q, '90, 25

DEF: Embolism: Closure of the pulmonary artery or branch; due to thrombosis (blood clot).

DEF: Infarction: Necrosis of lung tissue; due to obstructed arterial blood supply, most often by pulmonary embolism.

¹⁰ **415.11 Iatrogenic pulmonary**   CC MC CD MCV
        embolism and infarction
        CC Excl: 415.11, 415.19, 459.89, 459.9
        AHA: 4Q, '95, 58

¹⁰ **415.19 Other**   CC MC CD MCV
        CC Excl: 415.11, 415.19, 459.89, 459.9

✓4ᵗʰ 416 Chronic pulmonary heart disease
416.0 Primary pulmonary hypertension   CC MC
    Idiopathic pulmonary arteriosclerosis
    Pulmonary hypertension (essential) (idiopathic)
      (primary)
    CC Excl: 416.0, 416.8-416.9, 417.8-417.9, 459.89, 459.9

    DEF: A rare increase in pulmonary circulation, often resulting in right ventricular failure or fatal syncope.

416.1 Kyphoscoliotic heart disease
    DEF: High blood pressure within the lungs as a result of curvature of the spine.

416.8 Other chronic pulmonary heart diseases
    Pulmonary hypertension, secondary

416.9 Chronic pulmonary heart disease, unspecified
    Chronic cardiopulmonary disease
    Cor pulmonale (chronic) NOS

✓4ᵗʰ 417 Other diseases of pulmonary circulation
417.0 Arteriovenous fistula of pulmonary vessels
    EXCLUDES   congenital arteriovenous fistula (747.3)
    DEF: Abnormal communication between blood vessels within lung.

417.1 Aneurysm of pulmonary artery
    EXCLUDES   congenital aneurysm (747.3)

417.8 Other specified diseases of pulmonary circulation
    Pulmonary: Pulmonary:
      arteritis   endarteritis
    Rupture ⎫
    Stricture ⎬ of pulmonary vessel

417.9 Unspecified disease of pulmonary circulation

OTHER FORMS OF HEART DISEASE (420-429)

✓4ᵗʰ 420 Acute pericarditis
    INCLUDES   acute:
              mediastinopericarditis
              myopericarditis
              pericardial effusion
              pleuropericarditis
              pneumopericarditis
    EXCLUDES   acute rheumatic pericarditis (391.0)
              postmyocardial infarction syndrome [Dressler's]
                (411.0)

    DEF: Inflammation of the pericardium (heart sac); pericardial friction rub results from this inflammation and is heard as a scratchy or leathery sound.

Anatomy

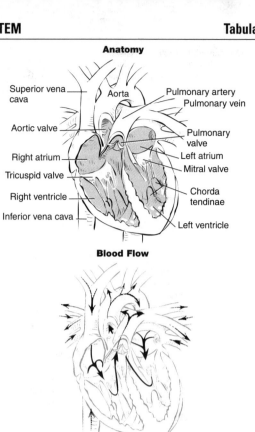

Blood Flow

420.0 Acute pericarditis in diseases   CC CD MCV
        classified elsewhere
    Code first underlying disease, as:
      actinomycosis (039.8)
      amebiasis (006.8)
      ▶chronic uremia (585.9)◀
      nocardiosis (039.8)
      tuberculosis (017.9)
      uremia ▶NOS (586)◀
    EXCLUDES   pericarditis (acute) (in):
              Coxsackie (virus) (074.21)
              gonococcal (098.83)
              histoplasmosis (115.0-115.9 with
                fifth-digit 3)
              meningococcal infection (036.41)
              syphilitic (093.81)
    CC Excl: 391.0, 393, 420.0-420.99, 423.8-423.9, 459.89, 459.9

✓5ᵗʰ 420.9 Other and unspecified acute pericarditis
    420.90 Acute pericarditis, unspecified   CC CD MCV
        Pericarditis (acute):   Pericarditis (acute):
          NOS   sicca
          infective NOS
        CC Excl: See code 420.0
        AHA: 2Q, '89, 12

    420.91 Acute idiopathic pericarditis   CC CD MCV
        Pericarditis, acute: Pericarditis, acute:
          benign   viral
          nonspecific
        CC Excl: See code 420.0

    420.99 Other   CC CD MCV
        Pericarditis (acute):   Pericarditis (acute):
          pneumococcal   suppurative
          purulent   Pneumopyopericardium
          staphylococcal   Pyopericardium
          streptococcal
        EXCLUDES   pericarditis in diseases
                  classified elsewhere
                  (420.0)
        CC Excl: See code 420.0

---

¹⁰ MCV as SDx only.

| N Newborn Age: 0 | P Pediatric Age: 0-17 | M Maternity Age: 12-55 | A Adult Age :15-124 | CC CC Condition | MC Major Complication | CD Complex Dx | HIV HIV Related Dx |

√4ᵗʰ **421 Acute and subacute endocarditis**

DEF: Bacterial inflammation of the endocardium (intracardiac area); major symptoms include fever, fatigue, heart murmurs, splenomegaly, embolic episodes and areas of infarction.

421.0 Acute and subacute bacterial endocarditis `CC` `CD` `HIV` `MCV`

Endocarditis (acute) (chronic) (subacute):
bacterial
infective NOS
lenta
malignant
purulent
septic

Endocarditis (acute) (chronic) (subacute):
ulcerative
vegetative
Infective aneurysm
Subacute bacterial endocarditis [SBE]

Use additional code to identify infectious organism [e.g., Streptococcus 041.0, Staphylococcus 041.1]

CC Excl: 391.1, 397.9, 421.0-421.9, 424.90-424.99, 459.89, 459.9

AHA: 1Q, '99, 12; 1Q, '91, 15

421.1 Acute and subacute infective endocarditis in diseases classified elsewhere `CC` `CD` `MCV`

Code first underlying disease, as:
blastomycosis (116.0)
Q fever (083.0)
typhoid (fever) (002.0)

EXCLUDES   endocarditis (in):
Coxsackie (virus) (074.22)
gonococcal (098.84)
histoplasmosis (115.0-115.9 with fifth-digit 4)
meningococcal infection (036.42)
monilial (112.81)

CC Excl: See code 421.0

421.9 Acute endocarditis, unspecified `CC` `CD` `HIV` `MCV`

Endocarditis
Myoendocarditis } acute or subacute
Periendocarditis

EXCLUDES   acute rheumatic endocarditis (391.1)

CC Excl: See code 421.0

√4ᵗʰ **422 Acute myocarditis**

EXCLUDES   acute rheumatic myocarditis (391.2)

DEF: Acute inflammation of the muscular walls of the heart (myocardium).

422.0 Acute myocarditis in diseases classified elsewhere `CC` `CD`

Code first underlying disease, as:
myocarditis (acute):
influenzal (487.8)
tuberculous (017.9)

EXCLUDES   myocarditis (acute) (due to):
aseptic, of newborn (074.23)
Coxsackie (virus) (074.23)
diphtheritic (032.82)
meningococcal infection (036.43)
syphilitic (093.82)
toxoplasmosis (130.3)

CC Excl: 391.2, 398.0, 422.0-422.99, 429.0, 429.71, 429.79, 459.89, 459.9

√5ᵗʰ **422.9 Other and unspecified acute myocarditis**

422.90 Acute myocarditis, unspecified `CC` `CD` `HIV`

Acute or subacute (interstitial) myocarditis

CC Excl: See code 422.0

422.91 Idiopathic myocarditis `CC` `CD` `HIV`

Myocarditis (acute or subacute):
Fiedler's
giant cell
isolated (diffuse) (granulomatous)
nonspecific granulomatous

CC Excl: See code 422.0

422.92 Septic myocarditis `CC` `CD` `HIV` `MCV`

Myocarditis, acute or subacute:
pneumococcal
staphylococcal

Use additional code to identify infectious organism [e.g., Staphylococcus 041.1]

EXCLUDES   myocarditis, acute or subacute:
in bacterial diseases classified elsewhere (422.0)
streptococcal (391.2)

CC Excl: See code 422.0

422.93 Toxic myocarditis `CC` `CD` `HIV`

CC Excl: See code 422.0

DEF: Inflammation of the heart muscle due to an adverse reaction to certain drugs or chemicals reaching the heart through the bloodstream.

422.99 Other `CC` `CD` `HIV`

CC Excl: See code 422.0

√4ᵗʰ **423 Other diseases of pericardium**

EXCLUDES   that specified as rheumatic (393)

423.0 Hemopericardium `CC` `CD` `MCV`

CC Excl: 423.0-423.9, 459.89, 459.9

DEF: Blood in the pericardial sac (pericardium).

423.1 Adhesive pericarditis `CC`

Adherent pericardium
Fibrosis of pericardium
Milk spots

Pericarditis:
adhesive
obliterative
Soldiers' patches

CC Excl: See code 423.0

DEF: Two layers of serous pericardium adhere to each other by fibrous adhesions.

423.2 Constrictive pericarditis `CC`

Concato's disease   Pick's disease of heart (and liver)

CC Excl: See code 423.0

DEF: Inflammation identified by a rigid, thickened and sometimes calcified pericardium; ventricles of the heart cannot be adequately filled and congestive heart failure may result.

423.8 Other specified diseases of pericardium

Calcification
Fistula } of pericardium

AHA: 2Q, '89, 12

423.9 Unspecified disease of pericardium

√4ᵗʰ **424 Other diseases of endocardium**

EXCLUDES   bacterial endocarditis (421.0-421.9)
rheumatic endocarditis (391.1, 394.0-397.9)
syphilitic endocarditis (093.20-093.24)

424.0 Mitral valve disorders `CC`

Mitral (valve):
incompetence
insufficiency } NOS of specified cause, except rheumatic
regurgitation

EXCLUDES   mitral (valve):
disease (394.9)
failure (394.9)
stenosis (394.0)
the listed conditions:
specified as rheumatic (394.1)
unspecified as to cause but with mention of:
diseases of aortic valve (396.0-396.9)
mitral stenosis or obstruction (394.2)

CC Excl: 394.0-394.9, 396.0-396.9, 424.0, 459.89, 459.9

AHA: 2Q, '00, 16; 3Q, '98, 11; N-D, '87, 8; N-D, '84, 8

√4ᵗʰ √5ᵗʰ   Additional Digit Required   Nonspecific PDx   Unacceptable PDx   Manifestation Code   `MCV` Major Cardiovascular Condition   ►◄ Revised Text   ● New Code   ▲ Revised Code Title

424.1   Aortic valve disorders `CC`

Aortic (valve):

incompetence
insufficiency   }   NOS of specified
regurgitation   cause, except
stenosis   rheumatic

> **EXCLUDES**   hypertrophic subaortic stenosis (425.1)
> that specified as rheumatic (395.0-395.9)
> that of unspecified cause but with
> mention of diseases of mitral
> valve (396.0-396.9)

CC Excl: 395.0-395.9, 396.0-396.9, 424.1, 459.89, 459.9

AHA: 4Q, '88, 8; N-D, '87, 8

424.2   Tricuspid valve disorders, specified as nonrheumatic `CC`

Tricuspid valve:

incompetence
insufficiency   }   of specified cause,
regurgitation   except
stenosis   rheumatic

> **EXCLUDES**   rheumatic or of unspecified cause (397.0)

CC Excl: 397.0, 424.2, 459.89, 459.9

424.3   Pulmonary valve disorders `CC`

Pulmonic: Pulmonic:
incompetence NOS   regurgitation NOS
insufficiency NOS   stenosis NOS

> **EXCLUDES**   that specified as rheumatic (397.1)

CC Excl: 397.1, 424.3, 459.89, 459.9

√5ᵗʰ 424.9   Endocarditis, valve unspecified

424.90   Endocarditis, valve unspecified, unspecified cause `CC` `CD` `MCV`

Endocarditis (chronic):
NOS
nonbacterial thrombotic

Valvular:

incompetence
insufficiency   }   of unspecified
regurgitation   valve,
stenosis   unspecified
                   cause

Valvulitis (chronic)

CC Excl: 424.90-424.99, 459.89, 459.9

424.91   *Endocarditis in diseases classified elsewhere* `CC` `CD`

Code first underlying disease as:
atypical verrucous endocarditis [Libman-
Sacks] (710.0)
disseminated lupus erythematosus (710.0)
tuberculosis (017.9)

> **EXCLUDES**   syphilitic (093.20-093.24)

CC Excl: See code 424.90

424.99   Other `CC`

Any condition classifiable to 424.90 with
specified cause, except rheumatic

> **EXCLUDES**   endocardial fibroelastosis
> (425.3)
> that specified as rheumatic
> (397.9)

CC Excl: See code 424.90

√4ᵗʰ 425   Cardiomyopathy

> **INCLUDES**   myocardiopathy

AHA: J-A, '85, 15

425.0   Endomyocardial fibrosis `CC`

CC Excl: 425.0-425.9, 459.89, 459.9

425.1   Hypertrophic obstructive cardiomyopathy `CC`

Hypertrophic subaortic stenosis (idiopathic)

CC Excl: See code 425.0

DEF: Cardiomyopathy marked by left ventricle hypertrophy, enlarged septum; results in obstructed blood flow.

Heart Valve Disorders

Valve stenosis (trouble opening)

Incompetent valve (trouble closing)

causes regurgitation (backflow of blood)

Insuficient valve (unable to close completely)

Shortened, fused chorda tendinae

Ventricular hypertrophy

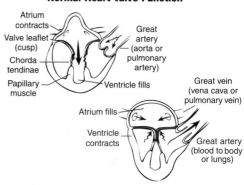

Normal Heart Valve Function

Atrium contracts

Valve leaflet (cusp)

Chorda tendinae

Papillary muscle

Great artery (aorta or pulmonary artery)

Ventricle fills

Atrium fills

Ventricle contracts

Great vein (vena cava or pulmonary vein)

Great artery (blood to body or lungs)

425.2   Obscure cardiomyopathy of Africa `CC` `CD`

Becker's disease
Idiopathic mural endomyocardial disease

CC Excl: See code 425.0

425.3   Endocardial fibroelastosis `CC` `CD`

Elastomyofibrosis

CC Excl: See code 425.0

DEF: A condition marked by left ventricle hypertrophy and
conversion of the endocardium into a thick fibroelastic coat;
capacity of the ventricle may be reduced, but is often increased.

425.4   Other primary cardiomyopathies `CC` `CD`

Cardiomyopathy: Cardiomyopathy:
NOS   idiopathic
congestive   nonobstructive
constrictive   obstructive
familial   restrictive
hypertrophic   Cardiovascular collagenosis

CC Excl: See code 425.0

AHA: 2Q, '05, 14; 1Q, '00, 22; 4Q, '97, 55; 2Q, '90, 19

425.5   Alcoholic cardiomyopathy `CC` `CD`

CC Excl: See code 425.0

AHA: S-O, '85, 15

DEF: Heart disease as result of excess alcohol consumption.

425.7   *Nutritional and metabolic cardiomyopathy* `CC` `CD`

Code first underlying disease, as:
amyloidosis ▶(277.30-277.39)◀
beriberi (265.0)
cardiac glycogenosis (271.0)
mucopolysaccharidosis (277.5)
thyrotoxicosis (242.0-242.9)

> **EXCLUDES**   gouty tophi of heart (274.82)

CC Excl: See code 425.0

`N` Newborn Age: 0   `P` Pediatric Age: 0-17   `M` Maternity Age: 12-55   `A` Adult Age :15-124   `CC` CC Condition   `MC` Major Complication   `CD` Complex Dx   `HIV` HIV Related Dx

Nerve Conduction of the Heart

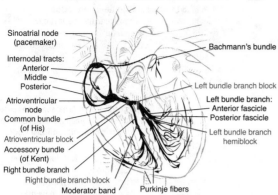

Normal and Long QT Electrocardiogram

425.8   Cardiomyopathy in other diseases classified CC CD
elsewhere
Code first underlying disease, as:
Friedreich's ataxia (334.0)
myotonia atrophica (359.2)
progressive muscular dystrophy (359.1)
sarcoidosis (135)
EXCLUDES   cardiomyopathy in Chagas' disease
(086.0)

CC Excl: See code 425.0

AHA: 2Q, '93, 9

425.9   Secondary cardiomyopathy, unspecified CC CD
CC Excl: See code 425.0

√4th **426 Conduction disorders**
DEF: Disruption or disturbance in the electrical impulses that regulate
heartbeats.

11 **426.0   Atrioventricular block, complete** CC MC MCV
Third degree atrioventricular block
CC Excl: 426.0-427.5, 427.89, 459.89, 459.9

√5th **426.1   Atrioventricular block, other and unspecified**
426.10   Atrioventricular block, unspecified MC
Atrioventricular [AV] block (incomplete)
(partial)
426.11   First degree atrioventricular block
Incomplete atrioventricular block, first degree
Prolonged P-R interval NOS
426.12   Mobitz (type) II atrioventricular CC MC
block
Incomplete atrioventricular block:
Mobitz (type) II
second degree, Mobitz (type) II
CC Excl: See code 426.0
DEF: Impaired conduction of excitatory impulse from
cardiac atrium to ventricle through AV node.
426.13   Other second degree atrioventricular CC MC
block
Incomplete atrioventricular block:
Mobitz (type) I [Wenckebach's]
second degree:
NOS
Mobitz (type) I
with 2:1 atrioventricular response [block]
Wenckebach's phenomenon
CC Excl: See code 426.0
DEF: Wenckebach's phenomenon: impulses generated at
constant rate to sinus node, P-R interval lengthens;
results in cycle of ventricular inadequacy and shortened
P-R interval; second-degree A-V block commonly called
"Mobitz type 1."

426.2   Left bundle branch hemiblock
Block:
left anterior fascicular
left posterior fascicular

426.3   Other left bundle branch block MC
Left bundle branch block:
NOS
anterior fascicular with posterior fascicular
complete
main stem

426.4   Right bundle branch block
AHA: 3Q, '00, 3

√5th **426.5   Bundle branch block, other and unspecified**
426.50   Bundle branch block, unspecified
426.51   Right bundle branch block and left MC
posterior fascicular block
426.52   Right bundle branch block and left MC
anterior fascicular block
11 **426.53   Other bilateral bundle branch** CC MC MCV
block
Bifascicular block NOS
Bilateral bundle branch block NOS
Right bundle branch with left bundle
branch block (incomplete) (main stem)
CC Excl: See code 426.0
11 **426.54   Trifascicular block** CC MC MCV
CC Excl: See code 426.0

426.6   Other heart block CC
Intraventricular block: Sinoatrial block
NOS   Sinoauricular block
diffuse
myofibrillar
CC Excl: See code 426.0

426.7   Anomalous atrioventricular excitation CC
Atrioventricular conduction:
accelerated
accessory
pre-excitation
Ventricular pre-excitation
Wolff-Parkinson-White syndrome
CC Excl: See code 426.0
DEF: Wolff-Parkinson-White: normal conduction pathway is
bypassed; results in short P-R interval on EKG; tendency to
supraventricular tachycardia.

√5th **426.8   Other specified conduction disorders**
426.81   Lown-Ganong-Levine syndrome CC
Syndrome of short P-R interval, normal QRS
complexes, and supraventricular
tachycardias
CC Excl: See code 426.0
426.82   Long QT syndrome
AHA: 4Q, '05, 72
DEF: Condition characterized by recurrent syncope,
malignant arrhythmias, and sudden death; characteristic
prolonged Q-T interval on electrocardiogram.
426.89   Other CC
Dissociation:
atrioventricular [AV]
interference
isorhythmic
Nonparoxysmal AV nodal tachycardia
CC Excl: See code 426.0

11 MCV for DRGs 547, 549, 553, 555, and 557 only.

√4th
√5th Additional Digit Required   Nonspecific PDx   Unacceptable PDx   Manifestation Code   MCV Major Cardiovascular Condition   ►◄ Revised Text   ● New Code   ▲ Revised Code Title

Circulatory System

426.9–428.1

426.9   Conduction disorder, unspecified `CC`
     Heart block NOS   Stokes-Adams syndrome
   CC Excl: See code 426.0

√4ᵗʰ 427 Cardiac dysrhythmias
   EXCLUDES   *that complicating:*
       abortion (634-638 with .7, 639.8)
       ectopic or molar pregnancy (639.8)
       labor or delivery (668.1, 669.4)

   AHA: J-A, '85, 15
   DEF: Disruption or disturbance in the rhythm of heartbeats.

427.0   Paroxysmal supraventricular tachycardia `CC` `MC`
     Paroxysmal tachycardia: Paroxysmal tachycardia:
       atrial [PAT]   junctional
       atrioventricular [AV]   nodal
   CC Excl: See code 426.0
   DEF: Rapid atrial rhythm.

427.1   Paroxysmal ventricular tachycardia `CC` `MC` `CD` `MCV`
     Ventricular tachycardia (paroxysmal)
   CC Excl: See code 426.0
   AHA: 3Q, '95, 9; M-A, '86, 11
   ▽ **DRG** 138
   DEF: Rapid ventricular rhythm.

427.2   Paroxysmal tachycardia, unspecified `CC` `MC`
     Bouveret-Hoffmann syndrome
     Paroxysmal tachycardia:
       essential
       NOS
   CC Excl: See code 426.0

√5ᵗʰ 427.3   Atrial fibrillation and flutter
   427.31 Atrial fibrillation `CC` `MC`
     CC Excl: See code 426.0
     AHA: 3Q, '05, 8; 4Q, '04, 78, 121; 3Q, '04, 7; 4Q, '03, 95, 105;
         1Q, '03, 8; 2Q, '99, 17; 3Q, '95, 8
     ▽ **DRG** 138
     DEF: Irregular, rapid atrial contractions.

   427.32 Atrial flutter `CC` `MC`
     CC Excl: See code 426.0
     AHA: 4Q, '03, 94
     ▽ **DRG** 138
     DEF: Regular, rapid atrial contractions.

√5ᵗʰ 427.4   Ventricular fibrillation and flutter
   427.41 Ventricular fibrillation `CC` `MC` `MCV`
     CC Excl: See code 426.0
     AHA: 3Q, '02, 5
     DEF: Irregular, rapid ventricular contractions.

   427.42 Ventricular flutter `CC` `MC`
     CC Excl: See code 426.0
     DEF: Regular, rapid, ventricular contractions.

427.5   Cardiac arrest `CC` `MC` `CD` `MCV`
     Cardiorespiratory arrest
   CC Excl: 427.0-427.5, 459.89, 459.9
   AHA: 3Q,'02, 5; 2Q, '00, 12; 3Q, '95, 8; 2Q, '88, 8

√5ᵗʰ 427.6   Premature beats
   427.60 Premature beats, unspecified
     Ectopic beats   Premature contractions
     Extrasystoles   or systoles NOS
     Extrasystolic arrhythmia
   427.61 Supraventricular premature beats
     Atrial premature beats, contractions, or
         systoles
   427.69 Other
     Ventricular premature beats, contractions,
         or systoles
     AHA: 4Q, '93, 42

√5ᵗʰ 427.8   Other specified cardiac dysrhythmias
   427.81 Sinoatrial node dysfunction
     Sinus bradycardia: Syndrome:
       persistent   sick sinus
       severe   tachycardia-
                 bradycardia
     EXCLUDES   *sinus bradycardia NOS*
                (427.89)
     AHA: 3Q, '00, 8
     DEF: Complex cardiac arrhythmia; appears as severe
     sinus bradycardia, sinus bradycardia with tachycardia,
     or sinus bradycardia with atrioventricular block.

   427.89 Other
     Rhythm disorder: Rhythm disorder:
       coronary sinus   nodal
       ectopic   Wandering (atrial)
                    pacemaker
     EXCLUDES   *carotid sinus syncope (337.0)*
                neonatal bradycardia (779.81)
                neonatal tachycardia (779.82)
                reflex bradycardia (337.0)
                tachycardia NOS (785.0)
     ▽ **DRG** 138

427.9   Cardiac dysrhythmia, unspecified
     Arrhythmia (cardiac) NOS
   AHA: 2Q, '89, 10

√4ᵗʰ 428 Heart failure
   Code, if applicable, heart failure due to hypertension first
   (402.0-402.9, with fifth-digit 1 or 404.0-404.9 with
   fifth-digit 1 or 3)
   EXCLUDES   *following cardiac surgery (429.4)*
          rheumatic (398.91)
          that complicating:
             abortion (634-638 with .7, 639.8)
             ectopic or molar pregnancy (639.8)
             labor or delivery (668.1, 669.4)
   AHA: 4Q, '02, 49; 3Q, '98, 5; 2Q, '90, 16; 2Q, '90, 19; 2Q, '89, 10; 3Q, '88, 3

428.0   Congestive heart failure, unspecified `CC` `MC` `CD` `MCV`
     Congestive heart disease
     Right heart failure (secondary to left heart failure)
     EXCLUDES   *fluid overload NOS (276.6)*
   CC Excl: 398.91, 402.01, 402.11, 402.91, 428.0-428.9, 459.89, 459.9, 518.4
   AHA: 4Q, '05, 120; 3Q, '05, 8; 1Q, '05, 5, 9; 1Q, '05, 5, 9; 4Q, '04, 140;
         3Q, '04, 7;4Q, '03, 109; 1Q, '03, 9; 4Q, '02, 52; 2Q, '01, 13; 4Q, '00,
         48; 2Q, '00, 16; 1Q, '00, 22; 4Q, '99, 4; 1Q, '99, 11; 4Q, '97, 55; 3Q,
         '97, 10; 3Q, '96, 9; 3Q, '91, 18; 3Q, '91, 19; 2Q, '89, 12
   ▽ **DRG** 121, 124 and 127
   DEF: Mechanical inadequacy; caused by inability of heart to pump
   and circulate blood; results in fluid collection in lungs,
   hypertension, congestion and edema of tissue.

428.1   Left heart failure `CC` `MC` `CD` `MCV`
     Acute edema of lung   }   with heart disease NOS
     Acute pulmonary edema   or heart failure
     Cardiac asthma   Left ventricular failure
   CC Excl: See code 428.0
   DEF: Mechanical inadequacy of left ventricle; causing fluid in lungs.

Echocardiography of Heart Failure

Four-chamber echocardiograms,
two-dimensional views.
LV: Left ventricle
RV: Right ventricle
RA: Right atrium
LA: Left atrium

Systolic dysfunction
with dilated LV

Diastolic dysfunction
with LV hypertrophy

`N` Newborn Age: 0   `P` Pediatric Age: 0-17   `M` Maternity Age: 12-55   `A` Adult Age :15-124   `CC` CC Condition   `MC` Major Complication   `CD` Complex Dx   `HIV` HIV Related Dx

✓5ᵗʰ 428.2 Systolic heart failure

> **EXCLUDES** *combined systolic and diastolic heart failure (428.40-428.43)*

DEF: Heart failure due to a defect in expulsion of blood caused by an abnormality in systolic function, or ventricular contractile dysfunction.

428.20 Unspecified `CC` `MC` `CD` `MCV`
CC Excl: See code 428.0

428.21 Acute `CC` `MC` `CD` `MCV`
CC Excl: See code 428.0

428.22 Chronic `CC` `MC` `CD` `MCV`
CC Excl: See code 428.0
AHA: 4Q, '05, 120

428.23 Acute on chronic `CC` `MC` `CD` `MCV`
CC Excl: See code 428.0
AHA: 1Q, '03, 9

✓5ᵗʰ 428.3 Diastolic heart failure

> **EXCLUDES** *combined systolic and diastolic heart failure (428.40-428.43)*

DEF: Heart failure due to resistance to ventricular filling caused by an abnormality in the diastolic function.

428.30 Unspecified `CC` `MC` `CD` `MCV`
CC Excl: See code 428.0
AHA: 4Q, '02, 52

428.31 Acute `CC` `MC` `CD` `MCV`
CC Excl: See code 428.0

428.32 Chronic `CC` `MC` `CD` `MCV`
CC Excl: See code 428.0

428.33 Acute on chronic `CC` `MC` `CD` `MCV`
CC Excl: See code 428.0

✓5ᵗʰ 428.4 Combined systolic and diastolic heart failure

428.40 Unspecified `CC` `MC` `CD` `MCV`
CC Excl: See code 428.0

428.41 Acute `CC` `MC` `CD` `MCV`
CC Excl: See code 428.0
AHA: 4Q, '04, 140

428.42 Chronic `CC` `MC` `CD` `MCV`
CC Excl: See code 428.0

428.43 Acute on chronic `CC` `MC` `CD` `MCV`
CC Excl: See code 428.0
AHA: 4Q, '02, 52

428.9 Heart failure, unspecified `CC` `MC` `CD` `MCV`
Cardiac failure NOS   Myocardial failure NOS
Heart failure NOS   Weak heart
CC Excl: See code 428.0
AHA: 2Q, '89, 10; N-D, '85, 14

✓4ᵗʰ 429 Ill-defined descriptions and complications of heart disease

429.0 Myocarditis, unspecified
Myocarditis:
  NOS
  chronic (interstitial)   } (with mention of
  fibroid   arteriosclerosis)
  senile
Use additional code to identify presence of arteriosclerosis

> **EXCLUDES** *acute or subacute (422.0-422.9)*
> *rheumatic (398.0)*
> *acute (391.2)*
> *that due to hypertension (402.0-402.9)*

429.1 Myocardial degeneration
Degeneration of heart or
  myocardium:
  fatty
  mural   } (with mention of
  muscular   arteriosclerosis)
Myocardial:
  degeneration
  disease
Use additional code to identify presence of arteriosclerosis

> **EXCLUDES** *that due to hypertension (402.0-402.9)*

429.2 Cardiovascular disease, unspecified
Arteriosclerotic cardiovascular disease [ASCVD]
Cardiovascular arteriosclerosis
Cardiovascular:
  degeneration
  disease   } (with mention of
  sclerosis   arteriosclerosis)
Use additional code to identify presence of arteriosclerosis

> **EXCLUDES** *that due to hypertension (402.0-402.9)*

429.3 Cardiomegaly
Cardiac: Ventricular dilatation
  dilatation
  hypertrophy

> **EXCLUDES** *that due to hypertension (402.0-402.9)*

429.4 Functional disturbances following cardiac surgery `CC` `CD`
Cardiac insufficiency } following cardiac surgery
Heart failure   or due to prosthesis
Postcardiotomy syndrome
Postvalvulotomy syndrome

> **EXCLUDES** *cardiac failure in the immediate postoperative period (997.1)*

CC Excl: 429.4, 429.71-429.79, 459.89, 459.9
AHA: 2Q, '02, 12; N-D, '85, 6

429.5 Rupture of chordae tendineae `CC` `MC` `CD` `MCV`
CC Excl: 429.5, 429.71, 429.79, 459.89, 459.9
DEF: Torn tissue, between heart valves and papillary muscles.

429.6 Rupture of papillary muscle `CC` `MC` `CD` `MCV`
CC Excl: 429.6-429.81, 459.89, 459.9
DEF: Torn muscle, between chordae tendineae and heart wall.

✓5ᵗʰ 429.7 Certain sequelae of myocardial infarction, not elsewhere classified
Use additional code to identify the associated myocardial infarction:
  with onset of 8 weeks or less (410.00-410.92)
  with onset of more than 8 weeks (414.8)

> **EXCLUDES** *congenital defects of heart (745, 746)*
> *coronary aneurysm (414.11)*
> *disorders of papillary muscle (429.6, 429.81)*
> *postmyocardial infarction syndrome (411.0)*
> *rupture of chordae tendineae (429.5)*

AHA: 3Q, '89, 5

429.71 Acquired cardiac septal defect `CC` `CD` `MCV` `A`

> **EXCLUDES** *acute septal infarction (410.00-410.92)*

CC Excl: 422.0-422.99, 429.0, 429.4-429.82, 459.89-459.9, 745.0-745.9, 746.89, 746.9, 747.83-747.9, 759.7-759.89
DEF: Abnormal communication, between opposite heart chambers; due to defect of septum; not present at birth.

429.79 Other `CC` `CD` `MCV` `A`
Mural thrombus (atrial) (ventricular), acquired, following myocardial infarction
CC Excl: See code 429.71
AHA: 1Q, '92, 10

✓5ᵗʰ 429.8 Other ill-defined heart diseases
429.81 Other disorders of papillary muscle `CC` `MC` `CD` `MCV`
Papillary muscle: Papillary muscle:
  atrophy   incompetence
  degeneration   incoordination
  dysfunction   scarring
CC Excl: 429.6, 429.71-429.79, 429.81, 459.89, 459.9

429.82 Hyperkinetic heart disease `CC` `CD`
CC Excl: 429.71-429.79, 429.82, 459.89, 459.9
DEF: Condition of unknown origin in young adults; marked by increased cardiac output at rest, increased rate of ventricular ejection; may lead to heart failure.

✓4ᵗʰ ✓5ᵗʰ Additional Digit Required   Nonspecific PDx   Unacceptable PDx   Manifestation Code   `MCV` Major Cardiovascular Condition ▶◀ Revised Text ● New Code ▲ Revised Code Title

2007 ICD•9•CM   October 2006 • Volume 1 — 129

Circulatory System

429.83–434.0

● **429.83 Takotsubo syndrome**
Broken heart syndrome
Reversible left ventricular dysfunction
following sudden emotional stress
Stress induced cardiomyopathy
Transient left ventricular apical ballooning
syndrome

429.89 Other
Carditis
EXCLUDES *that due to hypertension
(402.0-402.9)*
AHA: 3Q, '05, 14; 1Q, '92, 10

429.9 Heart disease, unspecified
Heart disease (organic) NOS   Morbus cordis NOS
EXCLUDES *that due to hypertension (402.0-402.9)*
AHA: 1Q, '93, 19

CEREBROVASCULAR DISEASE (430-438)

INCLUDES with mention of hypertension (conditions
classifiable to 401-405)
Use additional code to identify presence of hypertension
EXCLUDES *any condition classifiable to 430-434, 436, 437
occurring during pregnancy, childbirth, or
the puerperium, or specified as puerperal
(674.0)*

*iatrogenic cerebrovascular infarction or
hemorrhage (997.02)*
AHA: 1Q, '93, 27; 3Q, '91, 10; 3Q, '90, 3; 2Q, '89, 8; M-A, '85, 6

10 **430 Subarachnoid hemorrhage**   `CC` `MC` `MCV`
Meningeal hemorrhage   Ruptured:
Ruptured: (congenital) cerebral
berry aneurysm   aneurysm NOS
EXCLUDES *syphilitic ruptured cerebral aneurysm (094.87)*
CC Excl: 430, 432.9, 459.89, 459.9, 780.01-780.09, 800.00-801.99, 803.00-804.96,
850.0-852.19, 852.21-854.19
AHA: 4Q, '04, 77
DEF: Bleeding in space between brain and lining.

10 **431 Intracerebral hemorrhage**   `CC` `MC` `MCV`
Hemorrhage (of):   Hemorrhage (of):
basilar   internal capsule
bulbar   intrapontine
cerebellar   pontine
cerebral   subcortical
cerebromeningeal   ventricular
cortical   Rupture of blood vessel in brain
CC Excl: See code 430
AHA: 4Q, '04, 77
▼ **DRG** 014
DEF: Bleeding within the brain.

✓4ᵗʰ **432 Other and unspecified intracranial hemorrhage**
AHA: 4Q, '04, 7

10 **432.0 Nontraumatic extradural hemorrhage**   `CC` `MC` `MCV`
Nontraumatic epidural hemorrhage
CC Excl: See code 430
DEF: Bleeding, nontraumatic, between skull and brain lining.

Berry Aneurysms

Anterior communicating artery — 40 %
34%
Berry aneurysm
Internal carotid — 20 %
4%
Posterior cerebral arteries
Basilar artery
Vertebral arteries
Arrows depict blood flow

Cerebrovascular Arteries

Posterior parietal — Callosal-marginal
Parietal-occipital — Pericallosal
Calcarine — Anterior cerebral
Posterior cerebral — Anterior communicating
Anterior inferior cerebellar — Middle cerebral
— Ophthalmic
Posterior inferior cerebellar — Posterior communicating
Basilar — External carotid
Vertebral — Internal carotid
— Aorta

10 **432.1 Subdural hemorrhage**   `CC` `MC` `MCV`
Subdural hematoma, nontraumatic
CC Excl: See code 430
DEF: Bleeding, between outermost and other layers of brain lining.

10 **432.9 Unspecified intracranial hemorrhage**   `MC` `MCV`
Intracranial hemorrhage NOS

✓4ᵗʰ **433 Occlusion and stenosis of precerebral arteries**
INCLUDES embolism
narrowing   } of basilar, carotid, and
obstruction   vertebral arteries
thrombosis
EXCLUDES *insufficiency NOS of precerebral arteries
(435.0-435.9)*
The following fifth-digit subclassification is for use with
category 433:
0 without mention of cerebral infarction
1 with cerebral infarction   `MC` `MCV`
AHA: 2Q, '95, 14; 3Q, '90, 16
DEF: Blockage, stricture, arteries branching into brain.

10 ✓5ᵗʰ **433.0 Basilar artery**   `CC 1`
CC Excl: For code 433.01: 250.70-250.93, 433.00-433.91, 435.0,
459.89, 459.9

10 ✓5ᵗʰ **433.1 Carotid artery**   `CC 1`
CC Excl: For code 433.11: 250.70-250.93, 433.00-433.91, 459.89, 459.9
AHA: 1Q, '00, 16; For code 433.10: ▶1Q, '06, 17;◄1Q, '02, 7, 10
▼ **DRG** 015 For code 433.10

10 ✓5ᵗʰ **433.2 Vertebral artery**   `CC 1`
CC Excl: For code 433.21: 250.70-250.93, 433.00-433.91, 435.1, 459.89,
459.9

10 ✓5ᵗʰ **433.3 Multiple and bilateral**   `CC 1`
CC Excl: For code 443.30: ▶1Q, '06, 17;◄ For code 433.31: See code
433.11
AHA: 2Q, '02, 19
▼ **DRG** 015 For code 433.30

10 ✓5ᵗʰ **433.8 Other specified precerebral artery**   `CC 1`
CC Excl: For code 433.81: See code 433.01

1,10 ✓5ᵗʰ **433.9 Unspecified precerebral artery**
Precerebral artery NOS
CC Excl: For code 433.91: See code 433.01

✓4ᵗʰ **434 Occlusion of cerebral arteries**
The following fifth-digit subclassification is for use with
category 434:
0 without mention of cerebral infarction
1 with cerebral infarction
AHA: 2Q, '95, 14

10 ✓5ᵗʰ **434.0 Cerebral thrombosis**   `CC 1` `MC` `MCV`
Thrombosis of cerebral arteries
CC Excl: For code 434.01: 250.70-250.93, 434.00-434.91, 436, 459.89, 459.9
AHA: For code 434.01: 4Q, '04, 77

---

1 Nonspecific PDx=0
10 MCV as SDx only.

`N` Newborn Age: 0   `P` Pediatric Age: 0-17   `M` Maternity Age: 12-55   `A` Adult Age :15-124   `CC` CC Condition   `MC` Major Complication   `CD` Complex Dx   `HIV` HIV Related Dx

10 √5ᵗʰ **434.1 Cerebral embolism** `CC 1` `MC` `MCV`
CC Excl: For code 434.11: See code 434.01

AHA: For code 434.11: 4Q, '04, 77; 3Q, '97, 11

▽ **DRG** 014 For code 434.11

1,10 √5ᵗʰ **434.9 Cerebral artery occlusion, unspecified** `CC 1` `MC` `MCV`
CC Excl: For code 434.91: See code 434.01

AHA: For code 434.91: 4Q, '04, 77-78; 4Q, '98, 87

▽ **DRG** 014 For code 434.91

√4ᵗʰ **435 Transient cerebral ischemia**

INCLUDES   cerebrovascular insufficiency (acute) with transient focal neurological signs and symptoms
insufficiency of basilar, carotid, and vertebral
arteries
spasm of cerebral arteries

EXCLUDES   acute cerebrovascular insufficiency NOS (437.1)
that due to any condition classifiable to 433
(433.0-433.9)

435.0 Basilar artery syndrome
435.1 Vertebral artery syndrome
435.2 Subclavian steal syndrome
DEF: Cerebrovascular insufficiency, due to occluded subclavian
artery; symptoms include pain in mastoid and posterior head
regions, flaccid paralysis of arm and diminished or absent radial
pulse on affected side.

435.3 Vertebrobasilar artery syndrome
AHA: 4Q, '95, 60

DEF: Transient ischemic attack; due to brainstem dysfunction;
symptoms include confusion, vertigo, binocular blindness, diplopia,
unilateral or bilateral weakness and paresthesis of extremities.

435.8 Other specified transient cerebral ischemias
▽ **DRG** 524

435.9 Unspecified transient cerebral ischemia
Impending cerebrovascular accident
Intermittent cerebral ischemia
Transient ischemic attack [TIA]
AHA: N-D, '85, 12

▽ **DRG** 524

10 **436 Acute, but ill-defined, cerebrovascular disease** `CC` `MC` `MCV`

Apoplexy, apoplectic: Apoplexy, apoplectic:
NOS   seizure
attack   Cerebral seizure
cerebral

EXCLUDES   any condition classifiable to categories 430-435
cerebrovascular accident (434.91)
CVA (ischemic) (434.91)
embolic (434.11)
hemorrhagic (430, 431, 432.0-432.9)
thrombotic (434.01)
postoperative cerebrovascular accident (997.02)
stroke (ischemic) (434.91)
embolic (434.11)
hemorrhagic (430, 431, 432.0-432.9)
thrombotic (434.01)

CC Excl: 250.70-250.93, 430-432.9, 434.00-434.91, 436, 459.89-459.9, 780.01-780.09,
800.00-801.99, 803.00-804.96, 850.0-852.19, 852.21-854.19

AHA: 4Q, '04, 77; 4Q, '99, 3

▽ **DRG** 015

√4ᵗʰ **437 Other and ill-defined cerebrovascular disease**
437.0 Cerebral atherosclerosis `A`
Atheroma of cerebral arteries
Cerebral arteriosclerosis

437.1 Other generalized ischemic cerebrovascular disease
Acute cerebrovascular insufficiency NOS
Cerebral ischemia (chronic)

437.2 Hypertensive encephalopathy `CC`
CC Excl: 250.70-250.93, 437.2, 459.89, 459.9

AHA: J-A, '84, 14

DEF: Cerebral manifestations (such as visual disturbances and
headache) due to high blood pressure.

437.3 Cerebral aneurysm, nonruptured
Internal carotid artery, intracranial portion
Internal carotid artery NOS

EXCLUDES   congenital cerebral aneurysm,
nonruptured (747.81)
internal carotid artery, extracranial
portion (442.81)

437.4 Cerebral arteritis `CC`
CC Excl: 250.70-250.93, 437.4, 459.89, 459.9

AHA: 4Q, '99, 21

DEF: Inflammation of a cerebral artery or arteries.

437.5 Moyamoya disease `CC`
CC Excl: 250.70-250.93, 437.5, 459.89, 459.9

DEF: Cerebrovascular ischemia; vessels occlude and rupture
causing tiny hemorrhages at base of brain; predominantly affects
Japanese.

437.6 Nonpyogenic thrombosis of intracranial `CC`
venous sinus
EXCLUDES   pyogenic (325)
CC Excl: 250.70-250.93, 437.6, 459.89, 459.9

437.7 Transient global amnesia
AHA: 4Q, '92, 20

DEF: Episode of short-term memory loss, not often recurrent;
pathogenesis unknown; with no signs or symptoms of neurological
disorder.

437.8 Other
437.9 Unspecified
Cerebrovascular disease or lesion NOS

√4ᵗʰ **438 Late effects of cerebrovascular disease**
Note: This category is to be used to indicate conditions in
430-437 as the cause of late effects. The "late effects"
include conditions specified as such, as sequelae,
which may occur at any time after the onset of the
causal condition.
AHA: 4Q, '99, 4, 6, 7; 4Q, '98, 39, 88; 4Q, '97, 35, 37; 4Q, '92, 21;N-D, '86, 12;
M-A, '86, 7

438.0 Cognitive deficits
√5ᵗʰ **438.1 Speech and language deficits**
438.10 Speech and language deficit, unspecified
438.11 Aphasia
AHA: 4Q, '03, 105; 4Q, '97, 36

DEF: Impairment or absence of the ability to
communicate by speech, writing or signs or to
comprehend the spoken or written language due to
disease or injury to the brain. Total aphasia is the loss of
function of both sensory and motor areas of the brain.

438.12 Dysphasia
AHA: 4Q, '99, 3, 9

DEF: Impaired speech; marked by inability to sequence
language.

438.19 Other speech and language deficits
√5ᵗʰ **438.2 Hemiplegia/hemiparesis**
DEF: Paralysis of one side of the body.

438.20 Hemiplegia affecting unspecified side
AHA: 4Q, '03, 105; 4Q, '99, 3, 9

438.21 Hemiplegia affecting dominant side
438.22 Hemiplegia affecting nondominant side
AHA: 4Q, '03, 105; 1Q, '02, 16

√5ᵗʰ **438.3 Monoplegia of upper limb**
DEF: Paralysis of one limb or one muscle group.

438.30 Monoplegia of upper limb affecting
unspecified side
438.31 Monoplegia of upper limb affecting
dominant side

¹ Nonspecific PDx=0
¹⁰ MCV as SDx only.

√4ᵗʰ
√5ᵗʰ   Additional Digit Required   Nonspecific PDx   Unacceptable PDx   Manifestation Code   `MCV` Major Cardiovascular Condition ▶◀ Revised Text ● New Code ▲ Revised Code Title

2007 ICD•9•CM   October 2006 • Volume 1 — 131

Map of Major Arteries

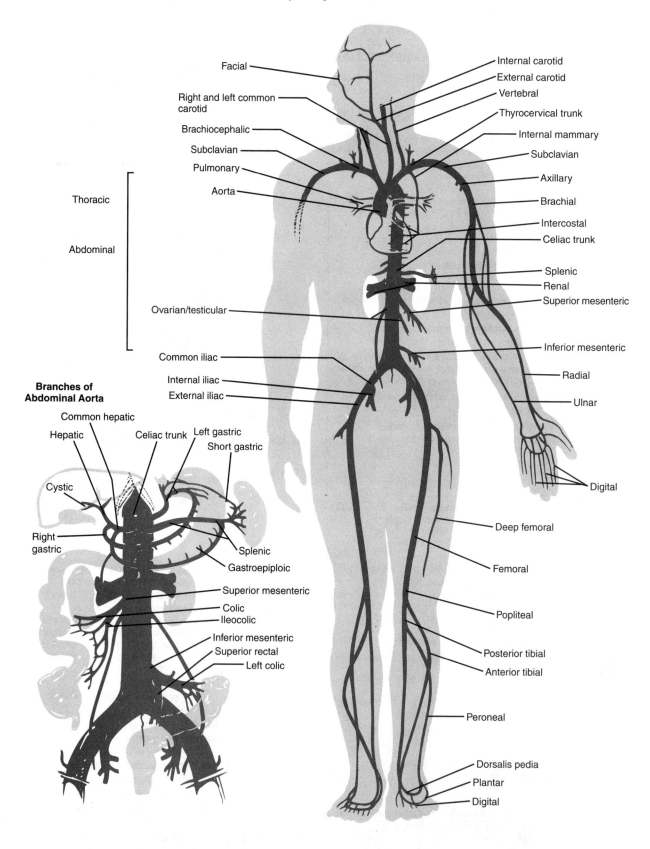

Facial

Right and left common carotid

Brachiocephalic

Subclavian

Pulmonary

Aorta

Thoracic

Abdominal

Ovarian/testicular

Common iliac

Internal iliac

External iliac

Internal carotid

External carotid

Vertebral

Thyrocervical trunk

Internal mammary

Subclavian

Axillary

Brachial

Intercostal

Celiac trunk

Splenic

Renal

Superior mesenteric

Inferior mesenteric

Radial

Ulnar

Digital

Deep femoral

Femoral

Popliteal

Posterior tibial

Anterior tibial

Peroneal

Dorsalis pedia

Plantar

Digital

Branches of Abdominal Aorta

Common hepatic

Hepatic

Celiac trunk

Left gastric

Short gastric

Cystic

Right gastric

Splenic

Gastroepiploic

Superior mesenteric

Colic

Ileocolic

Inferior mesenteric

Superior rectal

Left colic

| N | Newborn Age: 0 | P | Pediatric Age: 0-17 | M | Maternity Age: 12-55 | A | Adult Age :15-124 | CC | CC Condition | MC | Major Complication | CD | Complex Dx | HIV | HIV Related Dx |

132 — Volume 1

2007 ICD•9•CM

438.32 Monoplegia of upper limb affecting nondominant side

√5ᵗʰ **438.4 Monoplegia of lower limb**

438.40 Monoplegia of lower limb affecting unspecified side

438.41 Monoplegia of lower limb affecting dominant side

438.42 Monoplegia of lower limb affecting nondominant side

√5ᵗʰ **438.5 Other paralytic syndrome**

Use additional code to identify type of paralytic syndrome, such as:

locked-in state (344.81)

quadriplegia (344.00-344.09)

EXCLUDES *late effects of cerebrovascular accident with:*

hemiplegia/hemiparesis (438.20-438.22)

monoplegia of lower limb (438.40-438.42)

monoplegia of upper limb (438.30-438.32)

438.50 Other paralytic syndrome affecting unspecified side

438.51 Other paralytic syndrome affecting dominant side

438.52 Other paralytic syndrome affecting nondominant side

438.53 Other paralytic syndrome, bilateral

AHA: 4Q, '98, 39

438.6 Alterations of sensations

Use additional code to identify the altered sensation

438.7 Disturbances of vision

Use additional code to identify the visual disturbance

AHA: 4Q, '02, 56

√5ᵗʰ **438.8 Other late effects of cerebrovascular disease**

438.81 Apraxia

DEF: Inability to activate learned movements; no known sensory or motor impairment.

438.82 Dysphagia

DEF: Inability or difficulty in swallowing.

438.83 Facial weakness

Facial droop

438.84 Ataxia

AHA: 4Q, '02, 56

438.85 Vertigo

438.89 Other late effects of cerebrovascular disease

Use additional code to identify the late effect

AHA: 1Q, '05, 13; 4Q, '98, 39

438.9 Unspecified late effects of cerebrovascular disease

DISEASES OF ARTERIES, ARTERIOLES, AND CAPILLARIES (440-448)

√4ᵗʰ **440 Atherosclerosis**

INCLUDES arteriolosclerosis

arteriosclerosis (obliterans) (senile)

arteriosclerotic vascular disease

atheroma

degeneration:

arterial

arteriovascular

vascular

endarteritis deformans or obliterans

senile:

arteritis

endarteritis

EXCLUDES *atheroembolism (445.01-445.89)*

atherosclerosis of bypass graft of the extremities (440.30-440.32)

DEF: Stricture and reduced elasticity of an artery; due to plaque deposits.

440.0 Of aorta A

AHA: 2Q, '93, 7; 2Q, '93, 8; 4Q, '88, 8

440.1 Of renal artery A

EXCLUDES *atherosclerosis of renal arterioles (403.00-403.91)*

√5ᵗʰ **440.2 Of native arteries of the extremities**

EXCLUDES *atherosclerosis of bypass graft of the extremities (440.30-440.32)*

AHA: 4Q, '94, 49; 4Q, '93, 27; 4Q, '92, 25; 3Q, '90, 15; M-A, '87, 6

440.20 Atherosclerosis of the extremities, unspecified A

440.21 Atherosclerosis of the extremities with intermittent claudication A

DEF: Atherosclerosis; marked by pain, tension and weakness after walking; no symptoms while at rest.

440.22 Atherosclerosis of the extremities with rest pain A

INCLUDES any condition classifiable to 440.21

DEF: Atherosclerosis, marked by pain, tension and weakness while at rest.

440.23 Atherosclerosis of the extremities with ulceration A

INCLUDES any condition classifiable to 440.21 and 440.22

Use additional code for any associated ulceration (707.10-707.9)

AHA: 4Q, '00, 44

440.24 Atherosclerosis of the extremities with gangrene CC

INCLUDES any condition classifiable to 440.21, 440.22, and 440.23 with ischemic gangrene 785.4

▶Use additional code for any associated ulceration (707.10-707.9)◀

EXCLUDES *gas gangrene (040.0)*

CC Excl: 338.0-338.4, 440.24, 780.91-780.99, 785.4, 799.81-799.89

AHA: 4Q, '03, 109; 3Q, '03, 14; 4Q, '95, 54; 1Q, '95, 11

440.29 Other A

√5ᵗʰ **440.3 Of bypass graft of extremities**

EXCLUDES *atherosclerosis of native arteries of the extremities (440.21-440.24)*

embolism [occlusion NOS] [thrombus] of graft (996.74)

AHA: 4Q, '94, 49

440.30 Of unspecified graft A

440.31 Of autologous vein bypass graft A

440.32 Of nonautologous biological bypass graft A

440.8 Of other specified arteries A

EXCLUDES *basilar (433.0)*

carotid (433.1)

cerebral (437.0)

coronary (414.00-414.07)

mesenteric (557.1)

precerebral (433.0-433.9)

pulmonary (416.0)

vertebral (433.2)

440.9 Generalized and unspecified atherosclerosis A

Arteriosclerotic vascular disease NOS

EXCLUDES *arteriosclerotic cardiovascular disease [ASCVD] (429.2)*

√4ᵗʰ **441 Aortic aneurysm and dissection**

EXCLUDES *syphilitic aortic aneurysm (093.0)*

traumatic aortic aneurysm (901.0, 902.0)

√5ᵗʰ **441.0 Dissection of aorta**

AHA: 4Q, '89, 10

DEF: Dissection or splitting of wall of the aorta; due to blood entering through intimal tear or interstitial hemorrhage.

441.00 Unspecified site CC MC MCV

CC Excl: 250.70-250.93, 441.00-441.9, 459.89, 459.9

441.01 Thoracic CC MC MCV

CC Excl: See code 441.00

√4ᵗʰ √5ᵗʰ Additional Digit Required   Nonspecific PDx   Unacceptable PDx   Manifestation Code   MCV Major Cardiovascular Condition   ▶◀ Revised Text   ● New Code   ▲ Revised Code Title

2007 ICD•9•CM   October 2006 • Volume 1 — 133

Circulatory System

441.02–443.82

Thoracic and Abdominal Aortic Aneurysm

Thoracic aneurysm

Aorta

Abdominal aneurysm

441.02 Abdominal `CC` `MC` `MCV`
CC Excl: See code 441.00

441.03 Thoracoabdominal `CC` `MC` `MCV`
CC Excl: See code 441.00

441.1 Thoracic aneurysm, ruptured `CC` `MCV`
CC Excl: See code 441.00

441.2 Thoracic aneurysm without mention of rupture
AHA: 3Q, '92, 10

441.3 Abdominal aneurysm, ruptured `CC` `MCV`
CC Excl: See code 441.00

441.4 Abdominal aneurysm without mention of rupture
AHA: 4Q, '00, 64; 1Q, '99, 15, 16, 17; 3Q, '92, 10

441.5 Aortic aneurysm of unspecified site, ruptured `CC` `MCV`
    Rupture of aorta NOS
CC Excl: See code 441.00

441.6 Thoracoabdominal aneurysm, ruptured `CC` `MCV`
CC Excl: See code 441.00

441.7 Thoracoabdominal aneurysm, without mention of rupture

441.9 Aortic aneurysm of unspecified site without mention of rupture
Aneurysm
Dilatation } of aorta
Hyaline necrosis

✓4ᵗʰ 442 Other aneurysm
INCLUDES   aneurysm (ruptured) (cirsoid) (false) (varicose)
    aneurysmal varix
EXCLUDES   arteriovenous aneurysm or fistula:
    acquired (447.0)
    congenital (747.60-747.69)
    traumatic (900.0-904.9)

DEF: Dissection or splitting of arterial wall; due to blood entering through intimal tear or interstitial hemorrhage.

442.0 Of artery of upper extremity

442.1 Of renal artery

442.2 Of iliac artery
AHA: 1Q, '99, 16, 17

442.3 Of artery of lower extremity
Aneurysm:
    femoral } artery
    popliteal
AHA: 3Q, '02, 24-26; 1Q, '99, 16

✓5ᵗʰ 442.8 Of other specified artery
442.81 Artery of neck
Aneurysm of carotid artery (common) (external) (internal, extracranial portion)
EXCLUDES   internal carotid artery, intra-cranial portion (437.3)

442.82 Subclavian artery

442.83 Splenic artery

442.84 Other visceral artery
Aneurysm:
    celiac
    gastroduodenal
    gastroepiploic } artery
    hepatic
    pancreaticoduodenal
    superior mesenteric

442.89 Other
Aneurysm:
    mediastinal } artery
    spinal
EXCLUDES   cerebral (nonruptured) (437.3)
    congenital (747.81)
    ruptured (430)
    coronary (414.11)
    heart (414.10)
    pulmonary (417.1)

442.9 Of unspecified site

✓4ᵗʰ 443 Other peripheral vascular disease
443.0 Raynaud's syndrome
Raynaud's: Raynaud's:
  disease   phenomenon (secondary)
Use additional code to identify gangrene (785.4)
DEF: Constriction of the arteries, due to cold or stress; bilateral ischemic attacks of fingers, toes, nose or ears; symptoms include pallor, paresthesia and pain; more common in females.

443.1 Thromboangiitis obliterans [Buerger's disease]
Presenile gangrene
DEF: Inflammatory disease of extremity blood vessels, mainly the lower; occurs primarily in young men and leads to tissue ischemia and gangrene.

✓5ᵗʰ 443.2 Other arterial dissection
EXCLUDES   dissection of aorta (441.00-441.03)
    dissection of coronary arteries (414.12)
AHA: 4Q, '02, 54

443.21 Dissection of carotid artery

443.22 Dissection of iliac artery `MCV`

443.23 Dissection of renal artery

443.24 Dissection of vertebral artery

443.29 Dissection of other artery `MCV`

✓5ᵗʰ 443.8 Other specified peripheral vascular diseases
443.81 Peripheral angiopathy in diseases classified elsewhere
Code first underlying disease, as:
    diabetes mellitus (250.7)
AHA: 1Q, '04, 14; 3Q, '91, 10

443.82 Erythromelalgia
AHA: 4Q, '05, 73
DEF: Rare syndrome of paroxysmal vasodilation; maldistribution of blood flow causes redness, pain, increased skin temperature, and burning sensations in various parts of the body.

Arterial Diseases and Disorders

Lipids
Calcium deposits

Intimal proliferation

Atherosclerosis narrowing lumen

Thrombus (clot) forming in lumen

Organization of thrombus and recanalization

Embolus (from elsewhere) occluding lumen

Aneurysm bypasses lumen or...

...bulges from arterial wall

Arteriovenous fistula

`N` Newborn Age: 0   `P` Pediatric Age: 0-17   `M` Maternity Age: 12-55   `A` Adult Age :15-124   `CC` CC Condition   `MC` Major Complication   `CD` Complex Dx   `HIV` HIV Related Dx

443.89 Other

Acrocyanosis Erythrocyanosis

Acroparesthesia:
  simple [Schultze's type]
  vasomotor [Nothnagel's type]

EXCLUDES chilblains (991.5)
  frostbite (991.0-991.3)
  immersion foot (991.4)

443.9 Peripheral vascular disease, unspecified

Intermittent claudication NOS

Peripheral:
  angiopathy NOS
  vascular disease NOS

Spasm of artery

EXCLUDES atherosclerosis of the arteries of the
    extremities (440.20-440.22)
  spasm of cerebral artery (435.0-435.9)

AHA: 4Q, '92, 25; 3Q, '91, 10

DRG 130

√4ᵗʰ **444 Arterial embolism and thrombosis**

INCLUDES infarction:
    embolic
    thrombotic
  occlusion

EXCLUDES that complicating:
    abortion (634-638 with .6, 639.6)
    atheroembolism (445.01-445.89)
    ectopic or molar pregnancy (639.6)
    pregnancy, childbirth, or the pueperium
      (673.0-673.8)

AHA: 2Q, '92, 11; 4Q, '90, 27

444.0 Of abdominal aorta CC MCV

Aortic bifurcation syndrome Leriche's syndrome
Aortoiliac obstruction Saddle embolus

CC Excl: 250.70-250.93, 444.0, 444.89, 444.9, 459.89, 459.9

AHA: 2Q, '93, 7; 4Q, '90, 27

444.1 Of thoracic aorta CC MCV

Embolism or thrombosis of aorta (thoracic)

CC Excl: 250.70-250.93, 444.1, 444.89, 444.9, 459.89, 459.9

√5ᵗʰ **444.2 Of arteries of the extremities**

AHA: M-A, '87, 6

444.21 Upper extremity CC

CC Excl: 250.70-250.93, 444.21, 444.89, 444.9, 459.89, 459.9

444.22 Lower extremity CC

Arterial embolism or thrombosis:
  femoral
  peripheral NOS
  popliteal

EXCLUDES iliofemoral (444.81)

CC Excl: 250.70-250.93, 444.22, 444.89, 444.9, 459.89, 459.9

AHA: 3Q, '03, 10; 1Q, '03, 17; 3Q, '90, 16

√5ᵗʰ **444.8 Of other specified artery**

444.81 Iliac artery CC

CC Excl: 250.70-250.93, 444.81-444.9, 459.89, 459.9
AHA: 1Q, '03, 16

444.89 Other CC

EXCLUDES basilar (433.0)
  carotid (433.1)
  cerebral (434.0-434.9)
  coronary (410.00-410.92)
  mesenteric (557.0)
  ophthalmic (362.30-362.34)
  precerebral (433.0-433.9)
  pulmonary (415.19)
  renal (593.81)
  retinal (362.30-362.34)
  vertebral (433.2)

CC Excl: 250.70-250.93, 444.89, 444.9, 459.89, 459.9

444.9 Of unspecified artery CC

CC Excl: See code 444.89

√4ᵗʰ **445 Atheroembolism**

INCLUDES atherothrombotic microembolism
  cholesterol embolism

AHA: 4Q, '02, 57

√5ᵗʰ **445.0 Of extremities**

445.01 Upper extremity CC

CC Excl: 250.70-250.73, 250.80-250.83, 250.90-250.93, 444.89,
444.9, 445.01, 459.89, 459.9

445.02 Lower extremity CC

CC Excl: 250.70-250.73, 250.80-250.83, 250.90-250.93, 444.89,
444.9, 445.02, 459.89, 459.9

√5ᵗʰ **445.8 Of other sites**

10 **445.81 Kidney** CC MCV

▶Use additional code for any associated acute
renal failure or chronic kidney disease
(584, 585)◀

CC Excl: 250.70-250.73, 250.80-250.83, 250.90-250.93, 444.89,
444.9, 445.81, 459.89, 459.9

445.89 Other site CC

CC Excl: 250.70-250.73, 250.80-250.83, 250.90-250.93, 444.89,
444.9, 445.89, 459.9

√4ᵗʰ **446 Polyarteritis nodosa and allied conditions**

446.0 Polyarteritis nodosa CC

Disseminated necrotizing periarteritis
Necrotizing angiitis
Panarteritis (nodosa)
Periarteritis (nodosa)

CC Excl: 250.70-250.93, 446.0-446.7, 459.89, 459.9

DEF: Inflammation of small and mid-size arteries; symptoms related
to involved arteries in kidneys, muscles, gastrointestinal tract and
heart; results in tissue death.

**446.1 Acute febrile mucocutaneous lymph node syndrome
[MCLS]**

Kawasaki disease

DEF: Acute febrile disease of children; marked by erythema of
conjunctiva and mucous membranes of upper respiratory tract, skin
eruptions and edema.

√5ᵗʰ **446.2 Hypersensitivity angiitis**

EXCLUDES antiglomerular basement membrane
  disease without pulmonary
  hemorrhage (583.89)

446.20 Hypersensitivity angiitis, unspecified CC

CC Excl: See code 446.0

446.21 Goodpasture's syndrome CC

Antiglomerular basement membrane
  antibody-mediated nephritis with
  pulmonary hemorrhage
Use additional code to identify renal disease
  (583.81)

CC Excl: See code 446.0

DEF: Glomerulonephritis associated with hematuria,
progresses rapidly; results in death from renal failure.

446.29 Other specified hypersensitivity angiitis CC

CC Excl: See code 446.0

AHA: 1Q, '95, 3

446.3 Lethal midline granuloma CC

Malignant granuloma of face

CC Excl: See code 446.0

DEF: Granulomatous lesion; in nose or paranasal sinuses; often
fatal; occurs chiefly in males.

---

10 MCV as SDx only.

√4ᵗʰ √5ᵗʰ Additional Digit Required Nonspecific PDx Unacceptable PDx Manifestation Code MCV Major Cardiovascular Condition ▶◀ Revised Text ● New Code ▲ Revised Code Title

2007 ICD•9•CM **October 2006 • Volume 1 — 135**

Map of Major Veins

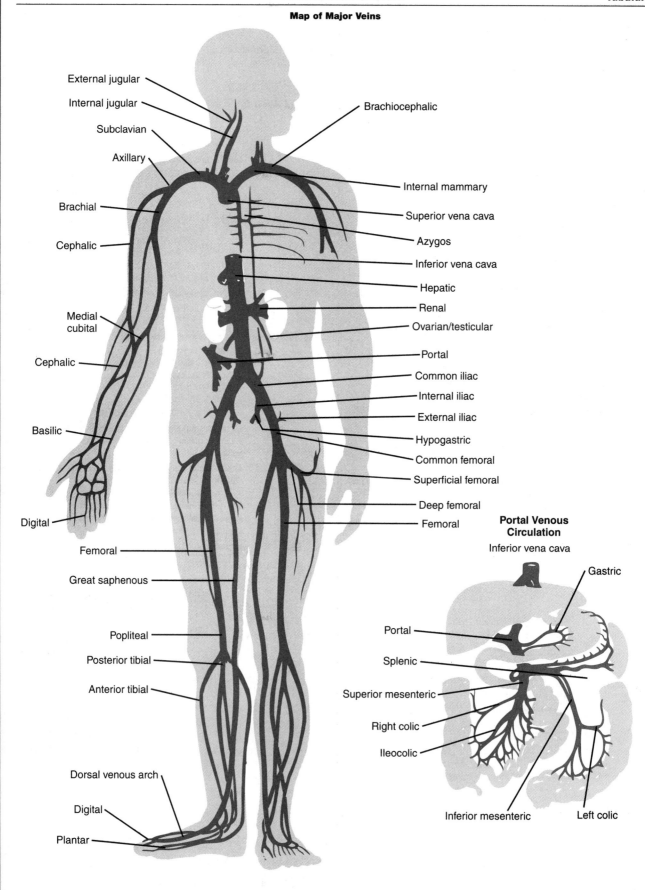

External jugular

Internal jugular

Subclavian

Axillary

Brachial

Cephalic

Medial cubital

Cephalic

Basilic

Digital

Femoral

Great saphenous

Popliteal

Posterior tibial

Anterior tibial

Dorsal venous arch

Digital

Plantar

Brachiocephalic

Internal mammary

Superior vena cava

Azygos

Inferior vena cava

Hepatic

Renal

Ovarian/testicular

Portal

Common iliac

Internal iliac

External iliac

Hypogastric

Common femoral

Superficial femoral

Deep femoral

Femoral

Portal Venous Circulation

Inferior vena cava

Gastric

Portal

Splenic

Superior mesenteric

Right colic

Ileocolic

Inferior mesenteric

Left colic

446.4 Wegener's granulomatosis   `cc`
Necrotizing respiratory granulomatosis
Wegener's syndrome
CC Excl: See code 446.0

AHA: 3Q, '00, 11

DEF: A disease occurring mainly in men; marked by necrotizing granulomas and ulceration of the upper respiratory tract; underlying condition is a vasculitis affecting small vessels and is possibly due to an immune disorder.

446.5 Giant cell arteritis   `cc`
Bagratuni's syndrome   Horton's disease
Cranial arteritis   Temporal arteritis
CC Excl: See code 446.0

DEF: Inflammation of arteries; due to giant cells affecting carotid artery branches, resulting in occlusion; symptoms include fever, headache and neurological problems; occurs in elderly.

446.6 Thrombotic microangiopathy   `cc`
Moschcowitz's syndrome
Thrombotic thrombocytopenic purpura
CC Excl: See code 446.0

DEF: Blockage of small blood vessels; due to hyaline deposits; symptoms include purpura, CNS disorders; results in protracted disease or rapid death.

446.7 Takayasu's disease   `cc`
Aortic arch arteritis
Pulseless disease
CC Excl: See code 446.0

DEF: Progressive obliterative arteritis of brachiocephalic trunk, left subclavian, and left common carotid arteries above aortic arch; results in ischemia in brain, heart and arm; pulses impalpable in head, neck and arms; more common in young adult females.

√4ᵗʰ 447 Other disorders of arteries and arterioles

447.0 Arteriovenous fistula, acquired
Arteriovenous aneurysm, acquired
> **EXCLUDES** cerebrovascular (437.3)
> coronary (414.19)
> pulmonary (417.0)
> surgically created arteriovenous shunt or fistula:
> complication (996.1, 996.61-996.62)
> status or presence (V45.1)
> traumatic (900.0-904.9)

DEF: Communication between an artery and vein caused by error in healing.

447.1 Stricture of artery
AHA: 2Q, '93, 8; M-A, '87, 6

447.2 Rupture of artery
Erosion
Fistula, except arteriovenous } of artery
Ulcer
> **EXCLUDES** traumatic rupture of artery (900.0-904.9)

447.3 Hyperplasia of renal artery
Fibromuscular hyperplasia of renal artery
DEF: Overgrowth of cells in muscular lining of renal artery.

447.4 Celiac artery compression syndrome
Celiac axis syndrome
Marable's syndrome

447.5 Necrosis of artery

447.6 Arteritis, unspecified
Aortitis NOS
Endarteritis NOS
> **EXCLUDES** arteritis, endarteritis:
> aortic arch (446.7)
> cerebral (437.4)
> coronary (414.00-414.07)
> deformans (440.0-440.9)
> obliterans (440.0-440.9)
> pulmonary (417.8)
> senile (440.0-440.9)
> polyarteritis NOS (446.0)
> syphilitic aortitis (093.1)

AHA: 1Q, '95, 3

447.8 Other specified disorders of arteries and arterioles
Fibromuscular hyperplasia of arteries, except renal

447.9 Unspecified disorders of arteries and arterioles

√4ᵗʰ 448 Disease of capillaries

448.0 Hereditary hemorrhagic telangiectasia
Rendu-Osler-Weber disease
DEF: Genetic disease with onset after puberty; results in multiple telangiectases, dilated venules on skin and mucous membranes; recurrent bleeding may occur.

448.1 Nevus, non-neoplastic
Nevus:
araneus
senile
spider
stellar
> **EXCLUDES** neoplastic (216.0-216.9)
> port wine (757.32)
> strawberry (757.32)

DEF: Enlarged or malformed blood vessels of skin; results in reddish swelling, skin patch, or birthmark.

448.9 Other and unspecified capillary diseases
Capillary:
hemorrhage
hyperpermeability
thrombosis
> **EXCLUDES** capillary fragility (hereditary) (287.8)

DISEASES OF VEINS AND LYMPHATICS, AND OTHER DISEASES OF CIRCULATORY SYSTEM (451-459)

√4ᵗʰ 451 Phlebitis and thrombophlebitis
> **INCLUDES** endophlebitis   periphlebitis
> inflammation, vein   suppurative phlebitis

Use additional E code to identify drug, if drug-induced
> **EXCLUDES** that complicating:
> abortion (634-638 with .7, 639.8)
> ectopic or molar pregnancy (639.8)
> pregnancy, childbirth, or the puerperium (671.0-671.9)
> that due to or following:
> implant or catheter device (996.61-996.62)
> infusion, perfusion, or transfusion (999.2)

AHA: 1Q, '92, 16

DEF: Inflammation of a vein (phlebitis) with formation of a thrombus (thrombophlebitis).

451.0 Of superficial vessels of lower extremities   `cc`
Saphenous vein (greater) (lesser)
CC Excl: 250.70-250.93, 451.0-451.9, 459.89, 459.9
AHA: 3Q, '91, 16

√5ᵗʰ 451.1 Of deep vessels of lower extremities
AHA: 3Q, '91, 16

451.11 Femoral vein (deep) (superficial)   `cc`
CC Excl: See code 451.0
▽ **DRG** 128

451.19 Other   `cc`
Femoropopliteal vein   Tibial vein
Popliteal vein
CC Excl: See code 451.0
▽ **DRG** 128

√4ᵗʰ / √5ᵗʰ **Additional Digit Required**   **Nonspecific PDx**   **Unacceptable PDx**   **Manifestation Code**   **MCV** Major Cardiovascular Condition   ►◄ Revised Text   ● New Code   ▲ Revised Code Title

Circulatory System

451.2–455.1

451.2   **Of lower extremities, unspecified** `CC`
CC Excl: See code 451.0
AHA: 4Q, '04, 80
DRG 128

✓5th **451.8**   **Of other sites**
> EXCLUDES   *intracranial venous sinus (325)*
>   *nonpyogenic (437.6)*
>   *portal (vein) (572.1)*

    451.81   **Iliac vein** `CC`
CC Excl: See code 451.0

    451.82   **Of superficial veins of upper extremities**
Antecubital vein   Cephalic vein
Basilic vein

    451.83   **Of deep veins of upper extremities**
Brachial vein   Ulnar vein
Radial vein

    451.84   **Of upper extremities, unspecified**
    451.89   **Other**
Axillary vein   Thrombophlebitis of
Jugular vein   breast (Mondor's
Subclavian vein   disease)

451.9   **Of unspecified site**

452   **Portal vein thrombosis** `CC`
Portal (vein) obstruction
> EXCLUDES   *hepatic vein thrombosis (453.0)*
>   *phlebitis of portal vein (572.1)*

CC Excl: 250.70-250.93, 452, 453.40-453.9, 459.89, 459.9
DEF: Formation of a blood clot in main vein of liver.

✓4th **453**   **Other venous embolism and thrombosis**
> EXCLUDES   *that complicating:*
>   *abortion (634-638 with .7, 639.8)*
>   *ectopic or molar pregnancy (639.8)*
>   *pregnancy, childbirth, or the puerperium*
>   *(671.0-671.9)*
>   *that with inflammation, phlebitis, and*
>   *thrombophlebitis (451.0-451.9)*

AHA: 1Q, '92, 16

    453.0   **Budd-Chiari syndrome** `CC`
Hepatic vein thrombosis
CC Excl: 250.70-250.93, 453.0, 453.40-453.9, 459.89, 459.9
DEF: Thrombosis or other obstruction of hepatic vein; symptoms include enlarged liver, extensive collateral vessels, intractable ascites and severe portal hypertension.

    453.1   **Thrombophlebitis migrans** `CC`
CC Excl: 250.70-250.93, 453.1, 453.40-453.9, 459.89, 459.9
DEF: Slow, advancing thrombophlebitis; appearing first in one vein then another.

    453.2   **Of vena cava** `CC` `MCV`
CC Excl: 250.70-250.93, 453.2, 453.40-453.9, 459.89, 459.9
DRG 128

    453.3   **Of renal vein** `CC`
CC Excl: 250.70-250.93, 453.3-453.9, 459.89, 459.9

✓5th   **453.4**   **Venous embolism and thrombosis of deep vessels of lower extremity**

       453.40   **Venous embolism and thrombosis of unspecified deep vessels of lower extremity** `CC`
Deep vein thrombosis NOS
DVT NOS
CC Excl: 250.70-250.93, 453.40-453.9, 453.40-453.9, 459.89-459.9

       453.41   **Venous embolism and thrombosis of deep vessels of proximal lower extremity** `CC`
Femoral   Thigh
Iliac   Upper leg NOS
Popliteal
CC Excl: See code 453.40
AHA: 4Q, '04, 79

       453.42   **Venous embolism and thrombosis of deep vessels of distal lower extremity** `CC`
Calf   Peroneal
Lower leg NOS   Tibial
CC Excl: See code 453.40

    453.8   **Of other specified veins** `CC`
> EXCLUDES   *cerebral (434.0-434.9)*
>   *coronary (410.00-410.92)*
>   *intracranial venous sinus (325)*
>   *nonpyogenic (437.6)*
>   *mesenteric (557.0)*
>   *portal (452)*
>   *precerebral (433.0-433.9)*
>   *pulmonary (415.19)*

CC Excl: 250.70-250.93, 453.8-453.9, 459.89, 459.9
AHA: 3Q, '91, 16; M-A, '87, 6
DRG 130

    453.9   **Of unspecified site** `CC`
Embolism of vein   Thrombosis (vein)
CC Excl: See code 453.8

✓4th **454**   **Varicose veins of lower extremities**
> EXCLUDES   *that complicating pregnancy, childbirth, or the*
>   *puerperium (671.0)*

AHA: 2Q, '91, 20
DEF: Dilated leg veins; due to incompetent vein valves that allow reversed blood flow and cause tissue erosion or weakness of wall; may be painful.

    454.0   **With ulcer** `A`
Varicose ulcer (lower extremity, any part)
Varicose veins with ulcer of lower extremity [any part] or of unspecified site
Any condition classifiable to 454.9 with ulcer or specified as ulcerated
AHA: 4Q, '99, 18

    454.1   **With inflammation** `A`
Stasis dermatitis
Varicose veins with inflammation of lower extremity [any part] or of unspecified site
Any condition classifiable to 454.9 with inflammation or specified as inflamed

    454.2   **With ulcer and inflammation** `A`
Varicose veins with ulcer and inflammation of lower extremity [any part] or of unspecified site
Any condition classifiable to 454.9 with ulcer and inflammation
DRG 188

    454.8   **With other complications**
Edema   Swelling
Pain
AHA: 4Q, '02, 58

    454.9   **Asymptomatic varicose veins** `A`
Phlebectasia   ⎫
Varicose veins   ⎬ of lower extremity [any part]
Varix   ⎭ or of unspecified site
Varicose veins NOS
AHA: 4Q, '02, 58

✓4th **455**   **Hemorrhoids**
> INCLUDES   hemorrhoids (anus) (rectum)
>   piles
>   varicose veins, anus or rectum
> EXCLUDES   *that complicating pregnancy, childbirth, or the*
>   *puerperium (671.8)*

DEF: Varicose condition of external hemorrhoidal veins causing painful swellings at the anus.

    455.0   **Internal hemorrhoids without mention of complication**
AHA: 3Q, '05, 17

    455.1   **Internal thrombosed hemorrhoids**

N Newborn Age: 0   P Pediatric Age: 0-17   M Maternity Age: 12-55   A Adult Age :15-124   `CC` CC Condition   `MC` Major Complication   `CD` Complex Dx   `HIV` HIV Related Dx

138 — Volume 1 • October 2006   **2007 ICD•9•CM**

455.2 Internal hemorrhoids with other complication

Internal hemorrhoids: Internal hemorrhoids:
bleeding   strangulated
prolapsed   ulcerated

AHA: ▶3Q, '05, 17;◀1Q, '03, 8

DRG 188

455.3 External hemorrhoids without mention of complication

AHA: ▶3Q, '05, 17◀

455.4 External thrombosed hemorrhoids

455.5 External hemorrhoids with other complication

External hemorrhoids: External hemorrhoids:
bleeding   strangulated
prolapsed   ulcerated

AHA:▶ 3Q, '05, 17;◀1Q, '03, 8

455.6 Unspecified hemorrhoids without mention of complication

Hemorrhoids NOS

455.7 Unspecified thrombosed hemorrhoids

Thrombosed hemorrhoids, unspecified whether internal or external

455.8 Unspecified hemorrhoids with other complication

Hemorrhoids, unspecified whether internal or external:
bleeding
prolapsed
strangulated
ulcerated

455.9 Residual hemorrhoidal skin tags

Skin tags, anus or rectum

√4ᵗʰ **456 Varicose veins of other sites**

456.0 Esophageal varices with bleeding   CC

CC Excl: 251.5, 456.0, 456.20, 459.89, 459.9, 530.20-530.21, 530.7, 530.82, 530.85, 531.00-534.91, 535.01, 535.11, 535.21, 535.31, 535.41, 535.51, 535.61, 537.83, 562.02-562.03, 562.12-562.13, 569.3, 569.85, 578.0-578.9

DEF: Distended, tortuous, veins of lower esophagus, usually due to portal hypertension.

456.1 Esophageal varices without mention of bleeding

√5ᵗʰ **456.2 Esophageal varices in diseases classified elsewhere**

Code first underlying cause, as:
cirrhosis of liver (571.0-571.9)
portal hypertension (572.3)

456.20 With bleeding   CC

CC Excl: 456.0, 456.20, 459.89, 459.9, 530.82

AHA: N-D, '85, 14

456.21 Without mention of bleeding

AHA: ▶3Q, '05, 15;◀2Q, '02, 4

456.3 Sublingual varices

DEF: Distended, tortuous veins beneath tongue.

456.4 Scrotal varices   ♂

Varicocele

456.5 Pelvic varices

Varices of broad ligament

456.6 Vulval varices   ♀

Varices of perineum

EXCLUDES   that complicating pregnancy, childbirth, or the puerperium (671.1)

456.8 Varices of other sites

Varicose veins of nasal septum (with ulcer)

EXCLUDES   placental varices (656.7)
retinal varices (362.17)
varicose ulcer of unspecified site (454.0)
varicose veins of unspecified site (454.9)

AHA: 2Q, '02, 4

√4ᵗʰ **457 Noninfectious disorders of lymphatic channels**

457.0 Postmastectomy lymphedema syndrome   A

Elephantiasis
Obliteration of lymphatic vessel } due to mastectomy

AHA: 2Q, '02, 12

DEF: Reduced lymphatic circulation following mastectomy; symptoms include swelling of the arm on the operative side.

457.1 Other lymphedema

Elephantiasis   Lymphedema:
(nonfilarial) NOS   praecox
Lymphangiectasis   secondary
Lymphedema: Obliteration, lymphatic vessel
acquired (chronic)

EXCLUDES   elephantiasis (nonfilarial):
congenital (757.0)
eyelid (374.83)
vulva (624.8)

AHA: 3Q, '04, 5

DEF: Fluid retention due to reduced lymphatic circulation; due to other than mastectomy.

457.2 Lymphangitis

Lymphangitis: Lymphangitis:
NOS   subacute
chronic

EXCLUDES   acute lymphangitis (682.0-682.9)

457.8 Other noninfectious disorders of lymphatic channels

Chylocele (nonfilarial)   Lymph node or vessel:
Chylous: fistula
ascites   infarction
cyst   rupture

EXCLUDES   chylocele:
filarial (125.0-125.9)
tunica vaginalis (nonfilarial) (608.84)

AHA: 1Q, '04, 5; 3Q, '03, 17

457.9 Unspecified noninfectious disorder of lymphatic channels

√4ᵗʰ **458 Hypotension**

INCLUDES   hypopiesis
EXCLUDES   cardiovascular collapse (785.50)
maternal hypotension syndrome (669.2)
shock (785.50-785.59)
Shy-Drager syndrome (333.0)

458.0 Orthostatic hypotension

Hypotension: Hypotension:
orthostatic (chronic)   postural

AHA: 3Q, '00, 8; 3Q, '91, 9

DEF: Low blood pressure; occurs when standing.

458.1 Chronic hypotension

Permanent idiopathic hypotension

DEF: Persistent low blood pressure.

√5ᵗʰ **458.2 Iatrogenic hypotension**

AHA: 4Q, '03, 60; 3Q, '02, 12; 4Q, '95, 57

DEF: Abnormally low blood pressure; due to medical treatment.

458.21 Hypotension of hemodialysis

Intra-dialytic hypotension

AHA: 4Q, '03, 61

458.29 Other iatrogenic hypotension

Postoperative hypotension

458.8 Other specified hypotension   MC

AHA: 4Q, '97, 37

458.9 Hypotension, unspecified   MC

Hypotension (arterial) NOS

√4ᵗʰ
√5ᵗʰ Additional Digit Required   Nonspecific PDx   Unacceptable PDx   Manifestation Code   MCV Major Cardiovascular Condition   ▶◀ Revised Text   ● New Code   ▲ Revised Code Title

2007 ICD•9•CM   February 2006 • Volume 1 — 139

Circulatory System

459–459.9

√4ᵗʰ **459 Other disorders of circulatory system**

    459.0 Hemorrhage, unspecified   CC

        Rupture of blood vessel NOS

        Spontaneous hemorrhage NEC

        EXCLUDES *hemorrhage:*

               gastrointestinal NOS (578.9)

               in newborn NOS (772.9)

               secondary or recurrent following

                    trauma (958.2)

               traumatic rupture of blood vessel

                    (900.0-904.9)

        CC Excl: 459.0, 459.89, 459.9

        AHA: 4Q, '90, 26

√5ᵗʰ **459.1 Postphlebitic syndrome**

        Chronic venous hypertension due to deep vein

           thrombosis

        EXCLUDES *chronic venous hypertension without*

               deep vein thrombosis (459.30-

               459.39)

        AHA: 4Q, '02, 58; 2Q, '91, 20

        DEF: Various conditions following deep vein thrombosis; including edema, pain, stasis dermatitis, cellulitis, varicose veins and ulceration of the lower leg.

        459.10 Postphlebitic syndrome without complications

           Asymptomatic postphlebitic syndrome

           Postphlebitic syndrome NOS

           459.11 Postphlebitic syndrome with ulcer

        459.12 Postphlebitic syndrome with inflammation

        459.13 Postphlebitic syndrome with ulcer and inflammation

        459.19 Postphlebitic syndrome with other complication

    459.2 Compression of vein

        Stricture of vein

        Vena cava syndrome (inferior) (superior)

√5ᵗʰ **459.3 Chronic venous hypertension (idiopathic)**

        Stasis edema

        EXCLUDES *chronic venous hypertension due to*

               deep vein thrombosis

               (459.10-459.9)

               varicose veins (454.0-454.9)

         AHA: 4Q, '02, 59

        459.30 Chronic venous hypertension without complications

           Asymptomatic chronic venous hypertension

           Chronic venous hypertension NOS

        459.31 Chronic venous hypertension with ulcer

           AHA: 4Q, '02, 43

        459.32 Chronic venous hypertension with inflammation

        459.33 Chronic venous hypertension with ulcer and inflammation

        459.39 Chronic venous hypertension with other complication

√5ᵗʰ **459.8 Other specified disorders of circulatory system**

        459.81 Venous (peripheral) insufficiency, unspecified

           Chronic venous insufficiency NOS

           Use additional code for any associated

               ulceration (707.10-707.9)

           AHA: 3Q, '04, 5; 2Q, '91, 20; M-A, '87, 6

           DEF: Insufficient drainage, venous blood, any part of body, results in edema or dermatosis.

           ▽ **DRG** 130

        459.89 Other

           Collateral circulation (venous), any site

           Phlebosclerosis

           Venofibrosis

    459.9 Unspecified circulatory system disorder

N Newborn Age: 0   P Pediatric Age: 0-17   M Maternity Age: 12-55   A Adult Age :15-124   CC CC Condition   MC Major Complication   CD Complex Dx   HIV HIV Related Dx

140 — Volume 1   *2007 ICD•9•CM*

8. DISEASES OF THE RESPIRATORY SYSTEM (460-519)

Use additional code to identify infectious organism

ACUTE RESPIRATORY INFECTIONS (460-466)

EXCLUDES *pneumonia and influenza (480.0-487.8)*

460 Acute nasopharyngitis [common cold]

Coryza (acute)
Nasal catarrh, acute
Nasopharyngitis:
  NOS
  acute

Nasopharyngitis:
  infective NOS
Rhinitis:
  acute
  infective

EXCLUDES *nasopharyngitis, chronic (472.2)*
pharyngitis:
  acute or unspecified (462)
  chronic (472.1)
rhinitis:
  allergic (477.0-477.9)
  chronic or unspecified (472.0)
sore throat:
  acute or unspecified (462)
  chronic (472.1)

AHA: 1Q, '88, 12

DEF: Acute inflammation of mucous membranes; extends from nares to pharynx.

✓4ᵗʰ 461 Acute sinusitis

INCLUDES
abscess
empyema
infection
inflammation
suppuration
} acute, of sinus
  (accessory)
  (nasal)

EXCLUDES *chronic or unspecified sinusitis (473.0-473.9)*

461.0 Maxillary
  Acute antritis

461.1 Frontal

461.2 Ethmoidal

461.3 Sphenoidal

461.8 Other acute sinusitis
  Acute pansinusitis

461.9 Acute sinusitis, unspecified
  Acute sinusitis NOS

462 Acute pharyngitis

Acute sore throat NOS
Pharyngitis (acute):
  NOS
  gangrenous
  infective
  phlegmonous
  pneumococcal

Pharyngitis (acute):
  staphylococcal
  suppurative
  ulcerative
Sore throat (viral) NOS
Viral pharyngitis

EXCLUDES *abscess:*
  peritonsillar [quinsy] (475)
  pharyngeal NOS (478.29)
  retropharyngeal (478.24)
chronic pharyngitis (472.1)
infectious mononucleosis (075)
that specified as (due to):
  Coxsackie (virus) (074.0)
  gonococcus (098.6)
  herpes simplex (054.79)
  influenza (487.1)
  septic (034.0)
  streptococcal (034.0)

AHA: 4Q, '99, 26; S-O, '85, 8

Respiratory System

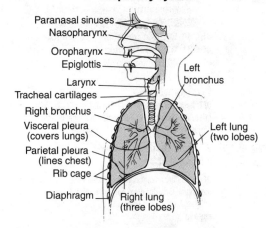

Paranasal sinuses
Nasopharynx
Oropharynx
Epiglottis
Larynx
Tracheal cartilages
Right bronchus
Visceral pleura (covers lungs)
Parietal pleura (lines chest)
Rib cage
Diaphragm
Left bronchus
Left lung (two lobes)
Right lung (three lobes)

463 Acute tonsillitis

Tonsillitis (acute):
  NOS
  follicular
  gangrenous
  infective
  pneumococcal

Tonsillitis (acute):
  septic
  staphylococcal
  suppurative
  ulcerative
  viral

EXCLUDES *chronic tonsillitis (474.0)*
hypertrophy of tonsils (474.1)
peritonsillar abscess [quinsy] (475)
sore throat:
  acute or NOS (462)
  septic (034.0)
streptococcal tonsillitis (034.0)

AHA: N-D, '84, 16

✓4ᵗʰ 464 Acute laryngitis and tracheitis

EXCLUDES *that associated with influenza (487.1)*
that due to Streptococcus (034.0)

✓5ᵗʰ 464.0 Acute laryngitis

Laryngitis (acute):
  NOS
  edematous
  Hemophilus influenzae [H. influenzae]
  pneumococcal
  septic
  suppurative
  ulcerative

EXCLUDES *chronic laryngitis (476.0-476.1)*
influenzal laryngitis (487.1)

464.00 Without mention of obstruction

464.01 With obstruction

✓5ᵗʰ 464.1 Acute tracheitis

Tracheitis (acute):
  NOS
  catarrhal

Tracheitis (acute):
  viral

EXCLUDES *chronic tracheitis (491.8)*

464.10 Without mention of obstruction

464.11 With obstruction   **CC**
CC Excl: 012.20-012.86, 017.90-017.96, 464.10-464.31, 519.8-519.9

✓5ᵗʰ 464.2 Acute laryngotracheitis

Laryngotracheitis (acute)
Tracheitis (acute) with laryngitis (acute)

EXCLUDES *chronic laryngotracheitis (476.1)*

464.20 Without mention of obstruction

464.21 With obstruction   **CC**
CC Excl: See code 464.11

✓4ᵗʰ Additional Digit Required   **Nonspecific PDx**   **Unacceptable PDx**   **Manifestation Code**   **MCV** Major Cardiovascular Condition   ▶◀ Revised Text   ● New Code   ▲ Revised Code Title

✓5th **464.3 Acute epiglottitis**
Viral epiglottitis
EXCLUDES *epiglottitis, chronic (476.1)*
464.30 Without mention of obstruction
464.31 With obstruction CC
CC Excl: See code 464.11

464.4 Croup
Croup syndrome
DEF: Acute laryngeal obstruction due to allergy, foreign body or infection; symptoms include barking cough, hoarseness and harsh, persistent high-pitched respiratory sound.

✓5th **464.5 Supraglottitis, unspecified**
AHA: 4Q, '01, 42

DEF: A rapidly advancing generalized upper respiratory infection of the lingual tonsillar area, epiglottic folds, false vocal cords, and the epiglottis; seen most commonly in children, but can affect people of any age.

464.50 Without mention of obstruction
AHA: 4Q, '01, 43

464.51 With obstruction

✓4th **465 Acute upper respiratory infections of multiple or unspecified sites**
EXCLUDES *upper respiratory infection due to:*
influenza (487.1)
Streptococcus (034.0)

465.0 Acute laryngopharyngitis
DEF: Acute infection of the vocal cords and pharynx.

465.8 Other multiple sites
Multiple URI

465.9 Unspecified site
Acute URI NOS
Upper respiratory infection (acute)

✓4th **466 Acute bronchitis and bronchiolitis**
INCLUDES that with:
bronchospasm
obstruction

466.0 Acute bronchitis
Bronchitis, acute   Bronchitis, acute
  or subacute: or subacute:
fibrinous   viral
membranous   with tracheitis
pneumococcal   Croupous bronchitis
purulent   Tracheobronchitis, acute
septic
EXCLUDES *acute bronchitis with chronic obstructive pulmonary disease (491.22)*

AHA: 4Q, '04, 137; 1Q, '04, 3; 4Q, '02, 46; 4Q, '96, 28; 4Q, '91, 24; 1Q, '88, 12

DRG 096

DEF: Acute inflammation of main branches of bronchial tree due to infectious or irritant agents; symptoms include cough with a varied production of sputum, fever, substernal soreness, and lung rales.

✓5th **466.1 Acute bronchiolitis**
Bronchiolitis (acute)   Capillary pneumonia
DEF: Acute inflammation of finer subdivisions of bronchial tree due to infectious or irritant agents; symptoms include cough with a varied production of sputum, fever, substernal soreness, and lung rales.

466.11 Acute bronchiolitis due to respiratory syncytial virus (RSV)
AHA: 1Q, '05, 10; 4Q, '96, 27

466.19 Acute bronchiolitis due to other infectious organisms
Use additional code to identify organism

OTHER DISEASES OF THE UPPER RESPIRATORY TRACT (470–478)

470 Deviated nasal septum
Deflected septum (nasal) (acquired)
EXCLUDES *congenital (754.0)*

✓4th **471 Nasal polyps**
EXCLUDES *adenomatous polyps (212.0)*

471.0 Polyp of nasal cavity
Polyp: Polyp:
choanal   nasopharyngeal

471.1 Polypoid sinus degeneration
Woakes' syndrome or ethmoiditis

471.8 Other polyp of sinus
Polyp of sinus:
accessory
ethmoidal
maxillary
sphenoidal

471.9 Unspecified nasal polyp
Nasal polyp NOS

✓4th **472 Chronic pharyngitis and nasopharyngitis**
472.0 Chronic rhinitis
Ozena   Rhinitis:
Rhinitis: hypertrophic
NOS   obstructive
atrophic   purulent
granulomatous   ulcerative
EXCLUDES *allergic rhinitis (477.0-477.9)*
DEF: Persistent inflammation of mucous membranes of nose.

472.1 Chronic pharyngitis
Chronic sore throat   Pharyngitis:
Pharyngitis: granular (chronic)
atrophic   hypertrophic

472.2 Chronic nasopharyngitis
EXCLUDES *acute or unspecified nasopharyngitis (460)*
DEF: Persistent inflammation of mucous membranes extending from nares to pharynx.

Upper Respiratory System

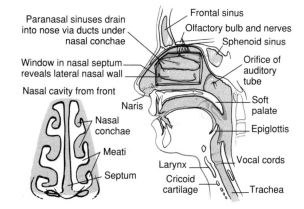

Paranasal sinuses drain into nose via ducts under nasal conchae
Frontal sinus
Olfactory bulb and nerves
Sphenoid sinus
Window in nasal septum reveals lateral nasal wall
Orifice of auditory tube
Nasal cavity from front
Naris
Soft palate
Nasal conchae
Epiglottis
Meati
Vocal cords
Larynx
Septum
Cricoid cartilage
Trachea

N Newborn Age: 0   P Pediatric Age: 0-17   M Maternity Age: 12-55   A Adult Age: 15-124   CC CC Condition   MC Major Complication   CD Complex Dx   HIV HIV Related Dx

142 — Volume 1 • February 2006

2007 ICD•9•CM

Respiratory System

473–478.30

Paranasal Sinuses

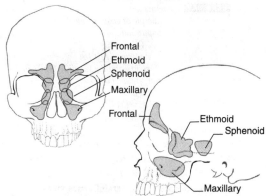

Frontal
Ethmoid
Sphenoid
Maxillary

Frontal
Ethmoid
Sphenoid
Maxillary

√4th 473 Chronic sinusitis

> **INCLUDES**   abscess
> empyema } (chronic) of sinus
> infection   (accessory) (nasal)
> suppuration

> **EXCLUDES**   *acute sinusitis (461.0-461.9)*

473.0 Maxillary
     Antritis (chronic)

473.1 Frontal

473.2 Ethmoidal
> **EXCLUDES**   *Woakes' ethmoiditis (471.1)*

473.3 Sphenoidal

473.8 Other chronic sinusitis
     Pansinusitis (chronic)

473.9 Unspecified sinusitis (chronic)
     Sinusitis (chronic) NOS

√4th 474 Chronic disease of tonsils and adenoids

√5th 474.0 Chronic tonsillitis and adenoiditis
> **EXCLUDES**   *acute or unspecified tonsillitis (463)*

AHA: 4Q, '97, 38

474.00 Chronic tonsillitis
474.01 Chronic adenoiditis
474.02 Chronic tonsillitis and adenoiditis

√5th 474.1 Hypertrophy of tonsils and adenoids
     Enlargement
     Hyperplasia } of tonsils or adenoids
     Hypertrophy

> **EXCLUDES**   *that with:*
> *adenoiditis (474.01)*
> *adenoiditis and tonsillitis (474.02)*
> *tonsillitis (474.00)*

474.10 Tonsils with adenoids
     AHA: 2Q, '05, 16

474.11 Tonsils alone
474.12 Adenoids alone

474.2 Adenoid vegetations
DEF: Fungus-like growth of lymph tissue between the nares and pharynx.

474.8 Other chronic disease of tonsils and adenoids
     Amygdalolith   Tonsillar tag
     Calculus, tonsil   Ulcer, tonsil
     Cicatrix of tonsil (and adenoid)

474.9 Unspecified chronic disease of tonsils and adenoids
     Disease (chronic) of tonsils (and adenoids)

475 Peritonsillar abscess   CC
     Abscess of tonsil   Quinsy
     Peritonsillar cellulitis

> **EXCLUDES**   *tonsillitis:*
> *acute or NOS (463)*
> *chronic (474.0)*

CC Excl: 475, 519.8-519.9

√4th 476 Chronic laryngitis and laryngotracheitis

476.0 Chronic laryngitis
     Laryngitis: Laryngitis:
        catarrhal   sicca
        hypertrophic

476.1 Chronic laryngotracheitis
     Laryngitis, chronic, with tracheitis (chronic)
     Tracheitis, chronic, with laryngitis
> **EXCLUDES**   *chronic tracheitis (491.8)*
> *laryngitis and tracheitis, acute or*
> *unspecified (464.00-464.51)*

√4th 477 Allergic rhinitis

> **INCLUDES**   allergic rhinitis (nonseasonal) (seasonal)
> hay fever
> spasmodic rhinorrhea

> **EXCLUDES**   *allergic rhinitis with asthma (bronchial) (493.0)*

DEF: True immunoglobulin E (IgE)-mediated allergic reaction of nasal mucosa; seasonal (typical hay fever) or perennial (year-round allergens: dust, food, dander).

477.0 Due to pollen
     Pollinosis

477.1 Due to food
     AHA: 4Q, '00, 42

477.2 Due to animal (cat) (dog) hair and dander
477.8 Due to other allergen
477.9 Cause unspecified
     AHA: 2Q, '97, 9

√4th 478 Other diseases of upper respiratory tract

478.0 Hypertrophy of nasal turbinates
DEF: Overgrowth, enlargement of shell-shaped bones, in nasal cavity.

√5th 478.1 Other diseases of nasal cavity and sinuses
> **EXCLUDES**   *varicose ulcer of nasal septum (456.8)*

●   **478.11 Nasal mucositis (ulcerative)**
     Use additional E code to identify adverse
     effects of therapy, such as:
     antineoplastic and immunosuppressive
     drugs (E930.7, E933.1)
     radiation therapy (E879.2)

●   **478.19 Other diseases of nasal cavity and sinuses**
     Abscess
     Necrosis } of nose (septum)
     Ulcer

     Cyst or mucocele of sinus (nasal)
     Rhinolith

√5th 478.2 Other diseases of pharynx, not elsewhere classified
478.20 Unspecified disease of pharynx
478.21 Cellulitis of pharynx or nasopharynx   CC
     CC Excl: 478.20-478.24, 519.8-519.9

478.22 Parapharyngeal abscess   CC
     CC Excl: See code 478.21

478.24 Retropharyngeal abscess   CC
     CC Excl: See code 478.21

     DEF: Purulent infection, behind pharynx and front of precerebral fascia.

478.25 Edema of pharynx or nasopharynx
478.26 Cyst of pharynx or nasopharynx
478.29 Other
     Abscess of pharynx or nasopharynx
> **EXCLUDES**   *ulcerative pharyngitis (462)*

√5th 478.3 Paralysis of vocal cords or larynx
DEF: Loss of motor ability of vocal cords or larynx; due to nerve or muscle damage.

478.30 Paralysis, unspecified   CC
     Laryngoplegia   Paralysis of glottis
     CC Excl: 478.30-478.34, 478.5, 478.70, 519.8-519.9

√4th Additional Digit Required   Nonspecific PDx   Unacceptable PDx   Manifestation Code   **MCV** Major Cardiovascular Condition   ►◄ Revised Text   ● New Code   ▲ Revised Code Title

Respiratory System

478.31–482.39

478.31 Unilateral, partial `CC`
CC Excl: See code 478.30

478.32 Unilateral, complete `CC`
CC Excl: See code 478.30

478.33 Bilateral, partial `CC`
CC Excl: See code 478.30

478.34 Bilateral, complete `CC`
CC Excl: See code 478.30

478.4 Polyp of vocal cord or larynx
> EXCLUDES   adenomatous polyps (212.1)

478.5 Other diseases of vocal cords

Abscess ⎫
Cellulitis ⎪
Granuloma ⎬ of vocal cords
Leukoplakia ⎭

Chorditis (fibrinous) (nodosa) (tuberosa)
Singers' nodes

478.6 Edema of larynx

Edema (of):   Edema (of):
   glottis   supraglottic
   subglottic

√5ᵗʰ 478.7 Other diseases of larynx, not elsewhere classified

478.70 Unspecified disease of larynx

478.71 Cellulitis and perichondritis of larynx
> DEF: Inflammation of deep soft tissues or lining of bone of the larynx.

478.74 Stenosis of larynx

478.75 Laryngeal spasm
Laryngismus (stridulus)
> DEF: Involuntary muscle contraction of the larynx.

478.79 Other

Abscess ⎫
Necrosis ⎪
Obstruction ⎬ of larynx
Pachyderma ⎪
Ulcer ⎭

> EXCLUDES   ulcerative laryngitis (464.00-464.01)

AHA: 3Q, '91, 20

478.8 Upper respiratory tract hypersensitivity reaction, site unspecified
> EXCLUDES   hypersensitivity reaction of lower respiratory tract, as:
>   extrinsic allergic alveolitis (495.0-495.9)
>   pneumoconiosis (500-505)

478.9 Other and unspecified diseases of upper respiratory tract

Abscess ⎫
Cicatrix ⎬ of trachea

Lungs

Right Lung (Three Lobes)   Trachea   **Left Lung (Two Lobes)**
Bronchopulmonary   S1   S3   Primary bronchus   Secondary bronchus
segments:
Upper lobe   S2   S1,2   S3   Upper lobe
              S5   S4, S5
Middle lobe   S4   S6
                        S7,8
Lower lobe   S8   Lower lobe
           S9   S7   S9
          S10   S10
Diaphragm

PNEUMONIA AND INFLUENZA (480-487)

> EXCLUDES   pneumonia:
>   allergic or eosinophilic (518.3)
>   aspiration:
>   NOS (507.0)
>   newborn (770.18)
>   solids and liquids (507.0-507.8)
>   congenital (770.0)
>   lipoid (507.1)
>   passive (514)
>   rheumatic (390)

√4ᵗʰ 480 Viral pneumonia

480.0 Pneumonia due to adenovirus

480.1 Pneumonia due to respiratory syncytial virus
AHA: 4Q, '96, 28; 1Q, '88, 12

480.2 Pneumonia due to parainfluenza virus

480.3 Pneumonia due to SARS-associated coronavirus `CC`
CC Excl: 011.00-012.16, 012.80-012.86, 017.90-017.96, 021.2, 031.0, 039.1, 115.05, 115.15, 115.95, 122.1, 130.4, 136.3, 480.0-487.1, 494.0-508.9, 517.1, 517.8, 518.89, 519.8-519.9, 748.61

AHA: 4Q, '03, 46-47

> DEF: A severe adult respiratory syndrome caused by the coronavirus, specified as inflammation of the lungs with consolidation.

480.8 Pneumonia due to other virus not elsewhere classified `HIV`
> EXCLUDES   congenital rubella pneumonitis (771.0)
>   influenza with pneumonia, any form (487.0)
>   pneumonia complicating viral diseases classified elsewhere (484.1-484.8)

480.9 Viral pneumonia, unspecified `HIV`
AHA: 3Q, '98, 5

481 Pneumococcal pneumonia [Streptococcus pneumoniae pneumonia] `CC` `MC` `HIV`
Lobar pneumonia, organism unspecified
CC Excl: 011.00-012.16, 012.80-012.86, 017.90-017.96, 021.2, 031.0, 039.1, 115.05, 115.15, 115.95, 122.1, 130.4, 136.3, 480.0-480.2, 480.8-487.1, 494.0-508.9, 517.1, 517.8, 518.89, 519.8-519.9, 748.61

AHA: 2Q, '98, 7; 4Q, '92, 19; 1Q, '92, 18; 1Q, '91, 13; 1Q, '88, 13; M-A, '85, 6

√4ᵗʰ 482 Other bacterial pneumonia
AHA: 4Q, '93, 39

482.0 Pneumonia due to Klebsiella pneumoniae `CC` `MC` `HIV`
CC Excl: See code 481

482.1 Pneumonia due to Pseudomonas `CC` `MC` `HIV`
CC Excl: See code 481
▽ DRG 079

482.2 Pneumonia due to Hemophilus influenzae [H. influenzae] `CC` `MC` `HIV`
CC Excl: See code 481

AHA: ▶2Q, '05, 19◄

√5ᵗʰ 482.3 Pneumonia due to Streptococcus
> EXCLUDES   Streptococcus pneumoniae (481)

AHA: 1Q, '88, 13

482.30 Streptococcus, unspecified `CC` `MC` `HIV`
CC Excl: See code 481

482.31 Group A `CC` `MC` `HIV`
CC Excl: See code 481

482.32 Group B `CC` `MC` `HIV`
CC Excl: See code 481

482.39 Other Streptococcus `CC` `MC` `HIV`
CC Excl: See code 481

 Newborn Age: 0   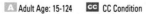 Pediatric Age: 0-17   Maternity Age: 12-55   Adult Age: 15-124   `CC` CC Condition   `MC` Major Complication   `CD` Complex Dx   `HIV` HIV Related Dx

144 — Volume 1 • February 2006   2007 ICD•9•CM

√5th **482.4 Pneumonia due to Staphylococcus**
AHA: 3Q, '91, 16

482.40 Pneumonia due to `CC` `MC` `HIV`
Staphylococcus, unspecified
CC Excl: See code 481

482.41 Pneumonia due to `CC` `MC` `HIV`
Staphylococcus aureus
CC Excl: See code 481

▽ DRG 079

482.49 Other Staphylococcus `CC` `MC` `HIV`
pneumonia
CC Excl: See code 481

√5th **482.8 Pneumonia due to other specified bacteria**
EXCLUDES *pneumonia, complicating infectious
disease classified elsewhere
(484.1-484.8)*

AHA: 3Q, '88, 11

482.81 Anaerobes `CC` `MC` `HIV`
Bacteroides (melaninogenicus)
Gram-negative anaerobes
CC Excl: See code 481

482.82 Escherichia coli [E. coli] `CC` `MC` `HIV`
CC Excl: See code 481

482.83 Other gram-negative bacteria `CC` `MC` `HIV`
Gram-negative pneumonia NOS
Proteus
Serratia marcescens
EXCLUDES *gram-negative anaerobes
(482.81)
Legionnaires' disease (482.84)*
CC Excl: See code 481

AHA: 2Q, '98, 5; 3Q, '94, 9

▽ DRG 079

482.84 Legionnaires' disease `CC` `HIV`
CC Excl: See code 481

AHA: 4Q, '97, 38

DEF: Severe and often fatal infection by Legionella
pneumophilia; symptoms include high fever,
gastrointestinal pain, headache, myalgia, dry cough, and
pneumonia; transmitted airborne via air conditioning
systems, humidifiers, water faucets, shower heads; not
person-to-person contact.

482.89 Other specified bacteria `CC` `MC` `HIV`
CC Excl: See code 481

AHA: 2Q, '97, 6

482.9 Bacterial pneumonia unspecified `CC` `MC` `HIV`
CC Excl: See code 481

AHA: 2Q, '98, 6; 2Q, '97, 6; 1Q, '94, 17

√4th **483 Pneumonia due to other specified organism**
AHA: N-D, '87, 5

483.0 Mycoplasma pneumoniae `CC` `MC`
Eaton's agent
Pleuropneumonia-like organism [PPLO]
CC Excl: See code 481

483.1 Chlamydia `CC` `MC`
CC Excl: See code 481

AHA: 4Q, '96, 31

483.8 Other specified organism `CC` `MC`
CC Excl: See code 481

√4th **484 Pneumonia in infectious diseases classified elsewhere**
EXCLUDES *influenza with pneumonia, any form (487.0)*

484.1 Pneumonia in cytomegalic inclusion disease `CC` `MC`
Code first underlying disease (078.5)
CC Excl: See code 481

484.3 Pneumonia in whooping cough `CC` `MC`
Code first underlying disease (033.0-033.9)
CC Excl: See code 481

484.5 Pneumonia in anthrax `CC` `MC`
Code first underlying disease (022.1)
CC Excl: See code 481

484.6 Pneumonia in aspergillosis `CC` `MC`
Code first underlying disease (117.3)
CC Excl: See code 481

AHA: 4Q, '97, 40

484.7 Pneumonia in other systemic mycoses `CC` `MC`
Code first underlying disease
EXCLUDES *pneumonia in:
candidiasis (112.4)
coccidioidomycosis (114.0)
histoplasmosis (115.0-115.9 with
fifth-digit 5)*
CC Excl: See code 481

484.8 Pneumonia in other infectious diseases `CC` `MC`
classified elsewhere
*Code first underlying disease, as:
Q fever (083.0)
typhoid fever (002.0)*
EXCLUDES *pneumonia in:
actinomycosis (039.1)
measles (055.1)
nocardiosis (039.1)
ornithosis (073.0)
Pneumocystis carinii (136.3)
salmonellosis (003.22)
toxoplasmosis (130.4)
tuberculosis (011.6)
tularemia (021.2)
varicella (052.1)*

CC Excl: See code 481

485 Bronchopneumonia, organism unspecified `CC` `MC`
Bronchopneumonia: Pneumonia:
hemorrhagic   lobular
terminal   segmental
Pleurobronchopneumonia
EXCLUDES *bronchiolitis (acute) (466.11-466.19)
chronic (491.8)
lipoid pneumonia (507.1)*
CC Excl: See code 481

√4th
√5th Additional Digit Required   Nonspecific PDx   Unacceptable PDx   Manifestation Code   `MCV` Major Cardiovascular Condition   ▶◀ Revised Text   ● New Code   ▲ Revised Code Title

2007 ICD•9•CM   Volume 1 — 145

Respiratory System

486–491.9

486 Pneumonia, organism unspecified   `CC` `MC` `HIV`

EXCLUDES   hypostatic or passive pneumonia (514)
influenza with pneumonia, any form (487.0)
inhalation or aspiration pneumonia due to
    foreign materials (507.0-507.8)
pneumonitis due to fumes and vapors (506.0)

CC Excl: See code 481

AHA: 4Q, '99, 6; 3Q, '99, 9; 3Q, '98, 7; 2Q, '98, 4, 5; 1Q, '98, 8; 3Q, '97, 9;
3Q, '94, 10; 3Q, '88, 11

▽ **DRG** 089 and 475

✓4ᵗʰ 487 Influenza

EXCLUDES   Hemophilus influenzae [H. influenzae]:
infection NOS (041.5)
laryngitis (464.00-464.01)
meningitis (320.0)

487.0 With pneumonia   `CC` `MC`

Influenza with pneumonia, any form
Influenzal:
    bronchopneumonia
    pneumonia
Use additional code to identify the type of
    pneumonia (480.0-480.9, 481, 482.0-482.9,
    483.0-483.8, 485)

CC Excl: See code 481

AHA: ▶1Q, '06, 18; 2Q, '05, 18◀

487.1 With other respiratory manifestations

Influenza NOS
Influenzal:
    laryngitis
    pharyngitis
    respiratory infection (upper) (acute)

AHA: ▶1Q, '06, 18;◀ 2Q, '05, 18; 4Q, '99, 26

487.8 With other manifestations

Encephalopathy due to influenza
Influenza with involvement of gastrointestinal tract
    EXCLUDES   "intestinal flu" [viral gastroenteritis]
        (008.8)

CHRONIC OBSTRUCTIVE PULMONARY DISEASE AND ALLIED CONDITIONS (490-496)

AHA: 3Q, '88, 5

490 Bronchitis, not specified as acute or chronic

Bronchitis NOS: Tracheobronchitis NOS
    catarrhal
    with tracheitis NOS
    EXCLUDES   bronchitis:
        allergic NOS (493.9)
        asthmatic NOS (493.9)
        due to fumes and vapors (506.0)

▽ **DRG** 096

✓4ᵗʰ 491 Chronic bronchitis

EXCLUDES   chronic obstructive asthma (493.2)

491.0 Simple chronic bronchitis

Catarrhal bronchitis, chronic
Smokers' cough

Bronchioli and Alveoli

To trachea
Pulmonary arteriole
Terminal bronchiolus
Elastic fibers
Capillary network over all alveioli
Alveoli
Alveolus

Interrelationship Between Chronic Airway Obstruction, Chronic Bronchitis, and Emphysema

Chronic Bronchitis 491
Chronic Airway Obstruction (COPD, NOS) 496
Emphysema 492

Shaded area:
Obstructive Chronic
Bronchitis (Chronic Bronchitis
with COPD) 491.20-491.21

491.1 Mucopurulent chronic bronchitis   `CC`

Bronchitis (chronic) (recurrent):
    fetid
    mucopurulent
    purulent

CC Excl: 491.1-491.9, 493.20-493.21

AHA: 3Q, '88, 12

DEF: Chronic bronchial infection characterized by both mucus and
pus secretions in the bronchial tree; recurs after asymptomatic
periods; signs are coughing, expectoration and secondary changes
in the lung.

✓5ᵗʰ 491.2 Obstructive chronic bronchitis

Bronchitis:
    emphysematous
    obstructive (chronic) (diffuse)
Bronchitis with:
    chronic airway obstruction
    emphysema
    EXCLUDES   asthmatic bronchitis (acute) NOS
        (493.9)
        chronic obstructive asthma (493.2)

AHA: 3Q, '97, 9; 4Q, '91, 25; 2Q, '91, 21

491.20 Without exacerbation   `CC`

Emphysema with chronic bronchitis

CC Excl: See code 491.1

AHA: 3Q, '97, 9

491.21 With (acute) exacerbation   `CC`

Acute exacerbation of chronic obstructive
    pulmonary disease [COPD]
Decompensated chronic obstructive
    pulmonary disease [COPD]
Decompensated chronic obstructive
    pulmonary disease [COPD] with
    exacerbation
    EXCLUDES   chronic obstructive asthma
        with acute exacerbation
        (493.22)

CC Excl: See code 491.1

AHA: 1Q, '04, 3; 3Q, '02, 18, 19; 4Q, '01, 43; 2Q, '96, 10

▽ **DRG** 088 and 475

491.22 With acute bronchitis   `CC`

CC Excl: See code 491.1

AHA: 4Q, '04, 82

▽ **DRG** 088

491.8 Other chronic bronchitis   `CC`

Chronic:
    tracheitis
    tracheobronchitis

CC Excl: See code 491.1

491.9 Unspecified chronic bronchitis   `CC`

CC Excl: See code 491.1

`N` Newborn Age: 0   `P` Pediatric Age: 0-17   `M` Maternity Age: 12-55   `A` Adult Age: 15-124   `CC` CC Condition   `MC` Major Complication   `CD` Complex Dx   `HIV` HIV Related Dx

✓4ᵗʰ **492 Emphysema**
AHA: 2Q, '91, 21

492.0 Emphysematous bleb
Giant bullous emphysema
Ruptured emphysematous bleb
Tension pneumatocele
Vanishing lung
AHA: 2Q, '93, 3

DEF: Formation of vesicle or bulla in emphysematous lung, more than one millimeter; contains serum or blood.

492.8 Other emphysema   `CC`
Emphysema (lung or   Emphysema (lung or
   pulmonary):   pulmonary):
   NOS   unilateral
   centriacinar   vesicular
   centrilobular   MacLeod's syndrome
   obstructive   Swyer-James syndrome
   panacinar   Unilateral hyperlucent lung
   panlobular

EXCLUDES   *emphysema:*
     with chronic bronchitis (491.20-
       491.22)
     compensatory (518.2)
     due to fumes and vapors (506.4)
     interstitial (518.1)
       newborn (770.2)
     mediastinal (518.1)
     surgical (subcutaneous) (998.81)
     traumatic (958.7)

CC Excl: 492.0, 492.8, 493.20-493.21

AHA: 1Q, '05, 4; 4Q, '93, 41; J-A, '84, 17

✓4ᵗʰ **493 Asthma**
EXCLUDES   *wheezing NOS (786.07)*

The following fifth-digit subclassification is for use with codes 493.0-493.2, 493.9:
   0 unspecified
   1 with status asthmaticus
   2 with (acute) exacerbation

AHA: 4Q, '04, 137; 4Q, '03, 62; 4Q, '01, 43; 4Q, '00, 42; 1Q, '91, 13; 3Q, '88, 9; J-A, '85, 8; N-D, '84, 17

DEF: Status asthmaticus: severe, intractable episode of asthma unresponsive to normal therapeutic measures.

✓5ᵗʰ **493.0 Extrinsic asthma**   `CC 1-2`
Asthma: Asthma:
   allergic with   hay
       stated cause   platinum
   atopic   Hay fever with asthma
   childhood

EXCLUDES   *asthma:*
     allergic NOS (493.9)
     detergent (507.8)
     miners' (500)
     wood (495.8)

CC Excl: For code 493.01 and 493.02: 493.00-493.92, 517.8, 518.89, 519.8-519.9

DEF: Transient stricture of airway diameters of bronchi; due to environmental factor; also called allergic (bronchial) asthma.

✓5ᵗʰ **493.1 Intrinsic asthma**   `CC 1-2`
Late-onset asthma
CC Excl: For code 493.11 and 493.12: See code 493.0

AHA: 3Q, '88, 9; M-A, '85, 7

DEF: Transient stricture, of airway diameters of bronchi; due to pathophysiological disturbances.

✓5ᵗʰ **493.2 Chronic obstructive asthma**   `CC`
Asthma with chronic obstructive pulmonary disease [COPD]
Chronic asthmatic bronchitis
EXCLUDES   *acute bronchitis (466.0)*
     chronic obstructive bronchitis (491.20-
       491.22)

CC Excl: For code 493.20 and 493.21: 491.1-493.92, 517.8, 518.89, 519.8-519.9; For code 493.22: 493.00-493.92, 517.8, 518.89, 519.8-519.9

AHA: 2Q, '91, 21; 2Q, '90, 20; For code 493.20: 4Q, '03, 108

DRG 088 For code 493.22

DEF: Persistent narrowing of airway diameters in the bronchial tree, restricting airflow and causing constant labored breathing.

✓5ᵗʰ **493.8 Other forms of asthma**
AHA: 4Q, '03, 62

493.81 Exercise induced bronchospasm
493.82 Cough variant asthma

✓5ᵗʰ **493.9 Asthma, unspecified**   `CC 1-2`
Asthma (bronchial) (allergic NOS)
Bronchitis:
   allergic
   asthmatic
CC Excl: For code 493.91 and 493.92: 493.00-493.92, 517.8, 518.89, 519.8-519.9

AHA: 4Q, '97, 40, For code 493.90: 4Q, '04, 137; 4Q, '03, 108; 4Q, '99, 25; 1Q, '97, 7; For code 493.91: 1Q, '05, 5; For code 493.92: 1Q, '03, 9

DRG 096 For code 493.90 and 493.92

✓4ᵗʰ **494 Bronchiectasis**
Bronchiectasis (fusiform) (postinfectious) (recurrent)
Bronchiolectasis
EXCLUDES   *congenital (748.61)*
     tuberculous bronchiectasis (current disease)
       (011.5)

AHA: 4Q, '00, 42

DEF: Dilation of bronchi; due to infection or chronic conditions; causes decreased lung capacity and recurrent infections of lungs.

494.0 Bronchiectasis without acute exacerbation
494.1 Bronchiectasis with acute exacerbation   `CC`
CC Excl: 017.90-017.96, 487.1, 494.1, 496, 506.1, 506.4, 506.9, 748.61

✓4ᵗʰ **495 Extrinsic allergic alveolitis**
INCLUDES   allergic alveolitis and pneumonitis due to inhaled organic dust particles of fungal, thermophilic actinomycete, or other origin

DEF: Pneumonitis due to particles inhaled into lung, often at workplace; symptoms include cough, chills, fever, increased heart and respiratory rates; develops within hours of exposure.

495.0 Farmers' lung   `CC`
CC Excl: 011.00-012.16, 012.80-012.86, 017.90-017.96, 021.2, 031.0, 039.1, 115.05, 115.15, 115.95, 122.1, 130.4, 136.3, 480.0-487.1, 494.0-508.9, 517.1, 517.8, 518.89, 519.8-519.9, 748.61

495.1 Bagassosis   `CC`
CC Excl: See code 495.0

495.2 Bird-fanciers' lung   `CC`
Budgerigar-fanciers' disease or lung
Pigeon-fanciers' disease or lung
CC Excl: See code 495.0

495.3 Suberosis   `CC`
Cork-handlers' disease or lung
CC Excl: See code 495.0

495.4 Malt workers' lung   `CC`
Alveolitis due to Aspergillus clavatus
CC Excl: See code 495.0

495.5 Mushroom workers' lung   `CC`
CC Excl: See code 495.0

495.6 Maple bark-strippers' lung   `CC`
Alveolitis due to Cryptostroma corticale
CC Excl: See code 495.0

✓4ᵗʰ ✓5ᵗʰ Additional Digit Required   Nonspecific PDx   Unacceptable PDx   Manifestation Code   `MCV` Major Cardiovascular Condition   ►◄ Revised Text   ● New Code   ▲ Revised Code Title

Respiratory System

495.7–508.8

495.7   "Ventilation" pneumonitis   `CC`

Allergic alveolitis due to fungal, thermophilic actinomycete, and other organisms growing in ventilation [air conditioning] systems

CC Excl: See code 495.0

495.8   Other specified allergic alveolitis and pneumonitis   `CC`

Cheese-washers' lung
Coffee workers' lung
Fish-meal workers' lung
Furriers' lung
Grain-handlers' disease or lung
Pituitary snuff-takers' disease
Sequoiosis or red-cedar asthma
Wood asthma

CC Excl: See code 495.0

495.9   Unspecified allergic alveolitis and pneumonitis   `CC`

Alveolitis, allergic (extrinsic)
Hypersensitivity pneumonitis

CC Excl: See code 495.0

496 Chronic airway obstruction, not elsewhere classified   `CC`

Note: This code is not to be used with any code from categories 491-493

Chronic:
   nonspecific lung disease
   obstructive lung disease
   obstructive pulmonary disease [COPD] NOS

EXCLUDES   chronic obstructive lung disease [COPD]
     specified (as) (with):
     allergic alveolitis (495.0-495.9)
     asthma (493.20-493.22)
     bronchiectasis (494.0-494.1)
     bronchitis (491.20-491.22)
       with emphysema (491.20-491.22)
       ▶decompensated (491.21)◀
     emphysema (492.0-492.8)

CC Excl: 017.90-017.96, 487.1, 494.0-494.1, 496, 506.1, 506.4, 506.9, 748.61

AHA: 4Q, '03, 109; 2Q, '00, 15; 2Q, '92, 16; 2Q, '91, 21; 3Q, '88, 56

PNEUMOCONIOSES AND OTHER LUNG DISEASES DUE TO EXTERNAL AGENTS (500-508)

DEF: Permanent deposits of particulate matter, within lungs; due to occupational or environmental exposure; results in chronic induration and fibrosis. (See specific listings in 500-508 code range)

500 Coal workers' pneumoconiosis   `A`

Anthracosilicosis   Coal workers' lung
Anthracosis   Miner's asthma
Black lung disease

501 Asbestosis   `A`

502 Pneumoconiosis due to other silica or silicates

Pneumoconiosis due to talc
Silicotic fibrosis (massive) of lung
Silicosis (simple) (complicated)

503 Pneumoconiosis due to other inorganic dust

Aluminosis (of lung)   Graphite fibrosis (of lung)
Baritosis   Siderosis
Bauxite fibrosis (of lung)   Stannosis
Berylliosis

504 Pneumonopathy due to inhalation of other dust

Byssinosis   Flax-dressers' disease
Cannabinosis

EXCLUDES   allergic alveolitis (495.0-495.9)
     asbestosis (501)
     bagassosis (495.1)
     farmers' lung (495.0)

505 Pneumoconiosis, unspecified

√4ᵗʰ **506 Respiratory conditions due to chemical fumes and vapors**

Use additional E code to identify cause

506.0   Bronchitis and pneumonitis due to fumes and vapors   `CC`

Chemical bronchitis (acute)

CC Excl: 011.00-011.96, 012.10-012.16, 012.80-012.86, 017.90-017.96, 021.2, 031.0, 039.1, 115.05, 115.15, 115.95, 122.1, 130.4, 136.3, 480.0-408.2, 480.8-487.1, 494.0-508.9, 517.1, 517.8, 518.89, 519.8-519.9, 748.61

506.1   Acute pulmonary edema due to fumes and vapors   `CC`

Chemical pulmonary edema (acute)

EXCLUDES   acute pulmonary edema NOS (518.4)
     chronic or unspecified pulmonary
       edema (514)

CC Excl: See code 506.0

AHA: 3Q, '88, 4

506.2   Upper respiratory inflammation due to fumes and vapors

AHA: 3Q, '05, 10

506.3   Other acute and subacute respiratory conditions due to fumes and vapors

506.4   Chronic respiratory conditions due to fumes and vapors

Emphysema (diffuse)
   (chronic)
Obliterative bronchiolitis   } due to inhalation of
   (chronic) (subacute)   chemical fumes
Pulmonary fibrosis   and vapors
   (chronic)

506.9   Unspecified respiratory conditions due to fumes and vapors

Silo-fillers' disease

√4ᵗʰ **507 Pneumonitis due to solids and liquids**

EXCLUDES   fetal aspiration pneumonitis (770.18)

AHA: 3Q, '91, 16

507.0   Due to inhalation of food or vomitus   `CC` `MC`

Aspiration pneumonia (due to):
   NOS
   food (regurgitated)
   gastric secretions
   milk
   saliva
   vomitus

CC Excl: See code 506.0

AHA: 1Q, '89, 10

DRG 079 and 475

507.1   Due to inhalation of oils and essences   `CC` `MC`

Lipoid pneumonia (exogenous)

EXCLUDES   endogenous lipoid pneumonia (516.8)

CC Excl: See code 506.0

507.8   Due to other solids and liquids   `CC` `MC`

Detergent asthma

CC Excl: See code 506.0

√4ᵗʰ **508 Respiratory conditions due to other and unspecified external agents**

Use additional E code to identify cause

508.0   Acute pulmonary manifestations due to radiation   `CC`

Radiation pneumonitis

CC Excl: See code 506.0

AHA: 2Q, '88, 4

508.1   Chronic and other pulmonary manifestations due to radiation   `CC`

Fibrosis of lung following radiation

CC Excl: See code 506.0

508.8   Respiratory conditions due to other specified external agents

---

`N` Newborn Age: 0   `P` Pediatric Age: 0-17   `M` Maternity Age: 12-55   `A` Adult Age: 15-124   `CC` CC Condition   `MC` Major Complication   `CD` Complex Dx   `HIV` HIV Related Dx

508.9   **Respiratory conditions due to unspecified external agent**

OTHER DISEASES OF RESPIRATORY SYSTEM (510-519)

√4th **510 Empyema**

Use additional code to identify infectious organism (041.0-041.9)

EXCLUDES   *abscess of lung (513.0)*

DEF: Purulent infection; within pleural space.

510.0   **With fistula**   `CC`

Fistula:
- bronchocutaneous
- bronchopleural
- hepatopleural
- mediastinal
- pleural
- thoracic

Any condition classifiable to 510.9 with fistula

CC Excl: 510.0-510.9, 517.8, 518.89, 519.8-519.9

DEF: Purulent infection of respiratory cavity; with communication from cavity to another structure.

510.9   **Without mention of fistula**   `CC`

Abscess: Pleurisy:
- pleura   septic
- thorax   seropurulent

Empyema (chest) (lung)   suppurative
   (pleura)   Pyopneumothorax

Fibrinopurulent pleurisy   Pyothorax

Pleurisy:
- purulent

CC Excl: See code 510.0

AHA: 3Q, '94, 6

√4th **511 Pleurisy**

EXCLUDES   *malignant pleural effusion (197.2)*
pleurisy with mention of tuberculosis,
current disease (012.0)

DEF: Inflammation of serous membrane of lungs and lining of thoracic cavity; causes exudation in cavity or membrane surface.

511.0   **Without mention of effusion or current tuberculosis**

Adhesion, lung or pleura   Pleurisy:
Calcification of pleura   NOS
Pleurisy (acute) (sterile):   pneumococcal
- diaphragmatic   staphylococcal
- fibrinous   streptococcal
- interlobar   Thickening of pleura

AHA: 3Q, '94, 5

511.1   **With effusion, with mention of a bacterial cause other than tuberculosis**   `CC`

Pleurisy with effusion (exudative) (serous):
- pneumococcal
- staphylococcal
- streptococcal
- other specified nontuberculous bacterial cause

CC Excl: 011.00-012.16, 012.80-012.86, 017.90-017.96, 511.0-511.9, 517.8, 518.89, 519.8-519.9

511.8   **Other specified forms of effusion, except tuberculous**   `CC`

Encysted pleurisy
Hemopneumothorax
Hemothorax
Hydropneumothorax
Hydrothorax

EXCLUDES   *traumatic (860.2-860.5, 862.29, 862.39)*

CC Excl: See code 511.1

AHA: 1Q, '97, 10

511.9   **Unspecified pleural effusion**   `CC`

Pleural effusion NOS
Pleurisy:
- exudative
- serofibrinous
- serous
- with effusion NOS

CC Excl: See code 511.1

AHA: 2Q, '03, 7; 3Q, '91, 19; 4Q, '89, 11

√4th **512 Pneumothorax**

DEF: Collapsed lung; due to gas or air in pleural space.

512.0   **Spontaneous tension pneumothorax**   `CC`

CC Excl: 512.0-512.1, 512.8, 517.8, 518.89, 519.8-519.9

AHA: 3Q, '94, 5

DEF: Leaking air from lung into lining causing collapse.

512.1   **Iatrogenic pneumothorax**   `CC`

Postoperative pneumothorax

CC Excl: See code 512.0

AHA: 4Q, '94, 40

DEF: Air trapped in the lining of the lung following surgery.

512.8   **Other spontaneous pneumothorax**   `CC`

Pneumothorax:
- NOS
- acute
- chronic

EXCLUDES   *pneumothorax:*
congenital (770.2)
traumatic (860.0-860.1, 860.4-
860.5)
tuberculous, current disease (011.7)

CC Excl: See code 512.0

AHA: 2Q, '93, 3

√4th **513 Abscess of lung and mediastinum**

513.0   **Abscess of lung**   `CC`

Abscess (multiple) of lung
Gangrenous or necrotic pneumonia
Pulmonary gangrene or necrosis

CC Excl: 006.4, 011.00-012.16, 012.80-012.86, 017.90-017.96, 513.0, 519.8-519.9

AHA: 2Q, '98, 7

513.1   **Abscess of mediastinum**   `CC`

CC Excl: 513.1, 519.8-519.9

514 Pulmonary congestion and hypostasis

Hypostatic: Pulmonary edema:
- bronchopneumonia   NOS
- pneumonia   chronic

Passive pneumonia
Pulmonary congestion
   (chronic) (passive)

EXCLUDES   *acute pulmonary edema:*
NOS (518.4)
with mention of heart disease or failure
(428.1)
▶*hypostatic pneumonia due to or specified as a*
specific type of pneumonia—code to the
type of pneumonia (480.0-480.9, 481,
482.0-482.49, 483.0-483.8, 485, 486,
487.0)◀

AHA: 2Q, '98, 6; 3Q, '88, 5

DEF: Excessive retention of interstitial fluid in the lungs and pulmonary vessels; due to poor circulation.

√4th √5th **Additional Digit Required**   **Nonspecific PDx**   **Unacceptable PDx**   **Manifestation Code**   `MCV` Major Cardiovascular Condition   ▶◀ Revised Text   ● New Code   ▲ Revised Code Title

2007 ICD•9•CM   **October 2006 • Volume 1 — 149**

Respiratory System

515 Postinflammatory pulmonary fibrosis `CC`
Cirrhosis of lung
Fibrosis of lung (atrophic)
(confluent) (massive)
(perialveolar) } chronic or unspecified
(peribronchial)
Induration of lung

CC Excl: 011.00-012.16, 012.80-012.86, 017.90-017.96, 494.0-508.9, 515-517, 517.2, 517.8, 518.89, 519.8-519.9, 748.61

DEF: Fibrosis and scarring of the lungs due to inflammatory reaction.

✓4ᵗʰ **516 Other alveolar and parietoalveolar pneumonopathy**

516.0 Pulmonary alveolar proteinosis `CC`
CC Excl: See code 515

DEF: Reduced ventilation; due to proteinaceous deposits on alveoli; symptoms include dyspnea, cough, chest pain, weakness, weight loss, and hemoptysis.

516.1 Idiopathic pulmonary hemosiderosis `CC`
Code first underlying disease (275.0)
Essential brown induration of lung
CC Excl: See code 515

DEF: Fibrosis of alveolar walls; marked by abnormal amounts hemosiderin in lungs; primarily affects children; symptoms include anemia, fluid in lungs, and blood in sputum; etiology unknown.

516.2 Pulmonary alveolar microlithiasis `CC`
CC Excl: See code 515

DEF: Small calculi in pulmonary alveoli resembling sand-like particles on x-ray.

516.3 Idiopathic fibrosing alveolitis `CC`
Alveolar capillary block
Diffuse (idiopathic) (interstitial) pulmonary fibrosis
Hamman-Rich syndrome
CC Excl: See code 515

516.8 Other specified alveolar and parietoalveolar pneumonopathies `CC`
Endogenous lipoid pneumonia
Interstitial pneumonia (desquamative) (lymphoid)
EXCLUDES *lipoid pneumonia, exogenous or unspecified (507.1)*
CC Excl: See code 515
AHA: 1Q, '92, 12

516.9 Unspecified alveolar and parietoalveolar pneumonopathy `CC`
CC Excl: See code 515

✓4ᵗʰ **517 Lung involvement in conditions classified elsewhere**
EXCLUDES *rheumatoid lung (714.81)*

517.1 Rheumatic pneumonia `CC`
Code first underlying disease (390)
CC Excl: 011.00-012.16, 012.80-012.86, 017.90-017.96, 480.0-480.2, 480.8-487.1, 494.0-508.9, 515-517.8, 518.89, 519.8-519.9, 748.61

517.2 Lung involvement in systemic sclerosis `CC`
Code first underlying disease (710.1)
CC Excl: 011.00-012.16, 012.80-012.86, 017.90-017.96, 494.0-508.9, 515-517, 517.2, 517.8, 518.89, 519.8-519.9, 748.61

517.3 Acute chest syndrome
Code first sickle-cell disease in crisis (282.42, 282.62, 282.64, 282.69)
AHA: 4Q, '03, 51, 56

517.8 Lung involvement in other diseases classified elsewhere `CC`
Code first underlying disease, as:
amyloidosis ▶(277.30-277.39)◀
polymyositis (710.4)
sarcoidosis (135)
Sjögren's disease (710.2)
systemic lupus erythematosus (710.0)
EXCLUDES *syphilis (095.1)*
CC Excl: See code 517.2
AHA: 2Q, '03, 7

✓4ᵗʰ **518 Other diseases of lung**

518.0 Pulmonary collapse `CC` `MC`
Atelectasis
Collapse of lung
Middle lobe syndrome
EXCLUDES *atelectasis:*
congenital (partial) (770.5)
primary (770.4)
tuberculous, current disease (011.8)
CC Excl: 518.0, 519.8-519.9
AHA: 4Q, '90, 25

518.1 Interstitial emphysema `CC`
Mediastinal emphysema
EXCLUDES *surgical (subcutaneous) emphysema (998.81)*
that in fetus or newborn (770.2)
traumatic emphysema (958.7)
CC Excl: 518.1, 519.8-519.9

DEF: Escaped air from the alveoli trapped in the interstices of the lung; trauma or cough may cause the disease.

518.2 Compensatory emphysema
DEF: Distention of all or part of the lung caused by disease processes or surgical intervention that decreased volume in another part of the lung; overcompensation reaction to the loss of capacity in another part of the lung.

518.3 Pulmonary eosinophilia
Eosinophilic asthma
Löffler's syndrome
Pneumonia:
allergic
eosinophilic
Tropical eosinophilia
DEF: Infiltration, into pulmonary parenchyma of eosinophilia; results in cough, fever, and dyspnea.

518.4 Acute edema of lung, unspecified `CC`
Acute pulmonary edema NOS
Pulmonary edema, postoperative
EXCLUDES *pulmonary edema:*
acute, with mention of heart disease or failure (428.1)
chronic or unspecified (514)
due to external agents (506.0-508.9)
CC Excl: 398.91, 428.0-428.9, 518.4, 519.8-519.9

DEF: Severe, sudden fluid retention within lung tissues.

`N` Newborn Age: 0   `P` Pediatric Age: 0-17   `M` Maternity Age: 12-55   `A` Adult Age: 15-124   `CC` CC Condition   `MC` Major Complication   `CD` Complex Dx   `HIV` HIV Related Dx

518.5 Pulmonary insufficiency following trauma and surgery `CC` `MC`

   Adult respiratory distress syndrome
   Pulmonary insufficiency following:
     shock
     surgery
     trauma
   Shock lung

   EXCLUDES   adult respiratory distress syndrome
                     associated with other conditions
                     (518.82)
                  pneumonia:
                     aspiration (507.0)
                     hypostatic (514)
                  respiratory failure in other conditions
                     (518.81, 518.83-518.84)

   CC Excl: 518.5, 519.8-519.9

   AHA: 4Q, '04, 139; 3Q, '88, 3; 3Q, '88, 7; S-O, '87, 1

518.6 Allergic bronchopulmonary aspergillosis `CC`
   CC Excl: 518.6, 519.8-519.9

   AHA: 4Q, '97, 39

   DEF: Noninvasive hypersensitive reaction; due to allergic reaction
   to *Aspergillus fumigatus* (mold).

● **518.7 Transfusion related acute lung injury [TRALI]** `CC`
   CC Excl: 518.7, 997.3, 997.91-997.99, 998.81, 998.83-998.9

✓5ᵗʰ **518.8 Other diseases of lung**

   518.81 Acute respiratory failure `CC` `MC`
      Respiratory failure NOS
      EXCLUDES   acute and chronic respiratory
                        failure (518.84)
                     acute respiratory distress
                        (518.82)
                     chronic respiratory failure
                        (518.83)
                     respiratory arrest (799.1)
                     respiratory failure, newborn
                        (770.84)

      CC Excl: 518.81-518.89, 519.8-519.9, 799.1

      AHA: 4Q, '05, 96; 2Q, '05, 19; 1Q, '05, 3-8; 1Q, '05, 3–8;
               4Q, '04, 139; 1Q, '03, 15; 4Q, '98, 41; 3Q, '91, 14;
               2Q, '91, 3; 4Q, '90, 25; 2Q, '90, 20; 3Q, '88, 7;
               3Q, '88, 10; S-O, '87, 1

      ▽ᴰᴿᴳ **DRG** 087 and 475

   518.82 Other pulmonary insufficiency, not `CC`
            elsewhere classified
      Acute respiratory distress
      Acute respiratory insufficiency
      Adult respiratory distress syndrome NEC
      EXCLUDES   adult respiratory distress
                        syndrome associated
                        with trauma and surgery
                        (518.5)
                     pulmonary insufficiency
                        following trauma and
                        surgery (518.5)
                     respiratory distress:
                        NOS (786.09)
                        newborn (770.89)
                        syndrome, newborn (769)
                        shock lung (518.5)

      CC Excl: See code 518.81

      AHA: 4Q, '03, 105; 2Q, '91, 21; 3Q, '88, 7

   518.83 Chronic respiratory failure `CC` `MC`
      CC Excl: See code 518.81

      AHA: 4Q, '05, 96; 4Q, '03, 103, 111

518.84 Acute and chronic respiratory `CC` `MC`
         failure
   Acute on chronic respiratory failure
   CC Excl: See code 518.81

   ▽ᴰᴿᴳ **DRG** 087 and 475

518.89 Other diseases of lung, not elsewhere
         classified
   Broncholithiasis   Lung disease NOS
   Calcification of lung   Pulmolithiasis
   AHA: 3Q, '90, 18; 4Q, '88, 6

   DEF: Broncholithiasis: calculi in lumen of transbronchial
   tree.

   DEF: Pulmolithiasis: calculi in lung.

✓4ᵗʰ **519 Other diseases of respiratory system**
   ✓5ᵗʰ **519.0 Tracheostomy complications**

      519.00 Tracheostomy complication, unspecified `CC`
         CC Excl: 519.00-519.19, 519.8-519.9

      519.01 Infection of tracheostomy `CC`
         Use additional code to identify type of
            infection, such as:
            abscess or cellulitis of neck (682.1)
            septicemia (038.0-038.9)
         Use additional code to identify organism
            (041.00-041.9)
         CC Excl: See code 519.00

         AHA: 4Q, '98, 41

      519.02 Mechanical complication of `CC`
               tracheostomy
         Tracheal stenosis due to tracheostomy
         CC Excl: See code 519.00

      519.09 Other tracheostomy complications `CC`
         Hemorrhage due to tracheostomy
         Tracheoesophageal fistula due to
            tracheostomy
         CC Excl: See code 519.00

   ✓5ᵗʰ **519.1 Other diseases of trachea and bronchus, not**
          elsewhere classified
      AHA: 3Q, '02, 18; 3Q, '88, 6

      ● **519.11 Acute bronchospasm**
         Bronchospasm NOS
         EXCLUDES   acute bronchitis with
                           bronchospasm (466.0)
                        asthma (493.00-493.92)
                        exercise induced
                           bronchospasm (493.81)

      ● **519.19 Other diseases of trachea and bronchus**
         Calcification ⎫
         Stenosis   ⎬ of bronchus or trachea
         Ulcer   ⎭

   519.2 Mediastinitis `CC`
      CC Excl: 519.2-519.3, 519.8-519.9

      DEF: Inflammation of tissue between organs behind sternum.

   519.3 Other diseases of mediastinum, not elsewhere
          classified
      Fibrosis   ⎫
      Hernia   ⎬ of mediastinum
      Retraction ⎭

   519.4 Disorders of diaphragm
      Diaphragmitis   Relaxation of diaphragm
      Paralysis of diaphragm
      EXCLUDES   congenital defect of diaphragm (756.6)
                     diaphragmatic hernia (551-553 with .3)
                     congenital (756.6)

   519.8 Other diseases of respiratory system, not elsewhere
          classified
      AHA: 4Q, '89, 12

   519.9 Unspecified disease of respiratory system
      Respiratory disease (chronic) NOS

✓4ᵗʰ✓5ᵗʰ Additional Digit Required   Nonspecific PDx   Unacceptable PDx   Manifestation Code   `MCV` Major Cardiovascular Condition   ▶◀ Revised Text   ● New Code   ▲ Revised Code Title

2007 ICD•9•CM   October 2006 • Volume 1 — 151

9. DISEASES OF THE DIGESTIVE SYSTEM (520-579)

DISEASES OF ORAL CAVITY, SALIVARY GLANDS, AND JAWS (520-529)

☑4ᵗʰ **520 Disorders of tooth development and eruption**

520.0 Anodontia
Absence of teeth (complete) (congenital) (partial)
Hypodontia
Oligodontia
EXCLUDES   *acquired absence of teeth (525.10-525.19)*

520.1 Supernumerary teeth
Distomolar
Fourth molar
Mesiodens
Paramolar
Supplemental teeth
EXCLUDES   *supernumerary roots (520.2)*

520.2 Abnormalities of size and form
Concrescence
Fusion   } of teeth
Gemination

Dens evaginatus   Microdontia
Dens in dente   Peg-shaped [conical] teeth
Dens invaginatus   Supernumerary roots
Enamel pearls   Taurodontism
Macrodontia   Tuberculum paramolare
EXCLUDES   *that due to congenital syphilis (090.5)*
tuberculum Carabelli, which is regarded as a normal variation

520.3 Mottled teeth
Mottling of enamel
Dental fluorosis   Nonfluoride enamel opacities

Digestive System

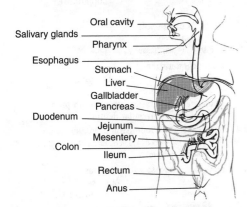

- Oral cavity
- Salivary glands
- Pharynx
- Esophagus
- Stomach
- Liver
- Gallbladder
- Pancreas
- Duodenum
- Jejunum
- Mesentery
- Colon
- Ileum
- Rectum
- Anus

The Oral Cavity

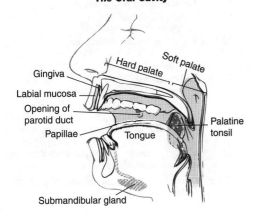

- Gingiva
- Labial mucosa
- Opening of parotid duct
- Papillae
- Hard palate
- Soft palate
- Tongue
- Palatine tonsil
- Submandibular gland

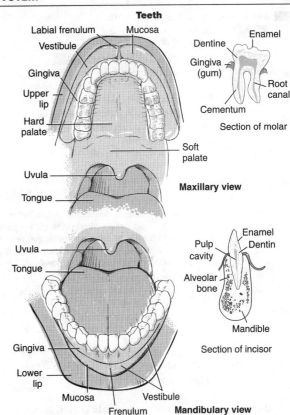

Teeth

- Labial frenulum
- Mucosa
- Vestibule
- Gingiva
- Upper lip
- Hard palate
- Soft palate
- Uvula
- Tongue
- Enamel
- Dentine
- Gingiva (gum)
- Root canal
- Cementum

Section of molar

Maxillary view

- Uvula
- Tongue
- Gingiva
- Lower lip
- Mucosa
- Vestibule
- Frenulum
- Enamel
- Dentin
- Pulp cavity
- Alveolar bone
- Mandible

Section of incisor

Mandibulary view

520.4 Disturbances of tooth formation
Aplasia and hypoplasia of cementum
Dilaceration of tooth
Enamel hypoplasia (neonatal) (postnatal) (prenatal)
Horner's teeth
Hypocalcification of teeth
Regional odontodysplasia
Turner's tooth
EXCLUDES   *Hutchinson's teeth and mulberry molars in congenital syphilis (090.5)*
mottled teeth (520.3)

520.5 Hereditary disturbances in tooth structure, not elsewhere classified
Amelogenesis
Dentinogenesis   } imperfecta
Odontogenesis

Dentinal dysplasia
Shell teeth

520.6 Disturbances in tooth eruption
Teeth: Tooth eruption:
  embedded   late
  impacted   obstructed
  natal   premature
  neonatal
  ▶prenatal◀
  primary [deciduous]:
    persistent
    shedding, premature
EXCLUDES   *exfoliation of teeth (attributable to disease of surrounding tissues) (525.0-525.19)*

AHA: ▶1Q, '06, 18;◀ 2Q, '05, 15

520.7 Teething syndrome

520.8 Other specified disorders of tooth development and eruption
Color changes during tooth formation
Pre-eruptive color changes
EXCLUDES   *posteruptive color changes (521.7)*

520.9 Unspecified disorder of tooth development and eruption

☑4ᵗʰ ☑5ᵗʰ   Additional Digit Required   **Nonspecific PDx**   **Unacceptable PDx**   **Manifestation Code**   **MCV** Major Cardiovascular Condition   ▶◀ Revised Text   ● New Code   ▲ Revised Code Title

Digestive System

521–522.9

√4ᵗʰ **521 Diseases of hard tissues of teeth**

√5ᵗʰ **521.0 Dental caries**
AHA: 4Q, '01, 44

521.00 Dental caries, unspecified

521.01 Dental caries limited to enamel
Initial caries   White spot lesion

521.02 Dental caries extending into dentine

521.03 Dental caries extending into pulp

521.04 Arrested dental caries

521.05 Odontoclasia
Infantile melanodontia
Melanodontoclasia

EXCLUDES *internal and external resorption of teeth (521.40-521.49)*

DEF: A pathological dental condition described as stained areas, loss of tooth substance, and hypoplasia linked to nutritional deficiencies during tooth development and to cariogenic oral conditions; synonyms are melanodontoclasia and infantile melanodontia.

521.06 Dental caries pit and fissure
►Primary dental caries, pit and fissure origin◄

521.07 Dental caries of smooth surface
►Primary dental caries, smooth surface origin◄

521.08 Dental caries of root surface
►Primary dental caries, root surface◄

521.09 Other dental caries
AHA: 3Q, '02, 14

√5ᵗʰ **521.1 Excessive attrition (approximal wear) (occlusal wear)**

521.10 Excessive attrition, unspecified

521.11 Excessive attrition, limited to enamel

521.12 Excessive attrition, extending into dentine

521.13 Excessive attrition, extending into pulp

521.14 Excessive attrition, localized

521.15 Excessive attrition, generalized

√5ᵗʰ **521.2 Abrasion**
Abrasion:
dentifrice
habitual
occupational } of teeth
ritual
traditional
Wedge defect NOS

521.20 Abrasion, unspecified

521.21 Abrasion, limited to enamel

521.22 Abrasion, extending into dentine

521.23 Abrasion, extending into pulp

521.24 Abrasion, localized

521.25 Abrasion, generalized

√5ᵗʰ **521.3 Erosion**
Erosion of teeth: Erosion of teeth:
NOS   idiopathic
due to: occupational
medicine
persistent vomiting

521.30 Erosion, unspecified

521.31 Erosion, limited to enamel

521.32 Erosion, extending into dentine

521.33 Erosion, extending into pulp

521.34 Erosion, localized

521.35 Erosion, generalized

√5ᵗʰ **521.4 Pathological resorption**
DEF: Loss of dentin and cementum due to disease process.

521.40 Pathological resorption, unspecified

521.41 Pathological resorption, internal

521.42 Pathological resorption, external

521.49 Other pathological resorption
Internal granuloma of pulp

521.5 Hypercementosis
Cementation hyperplasia
DEF: Excess deposits of cementum, on tooth root. Primary dental caries, root surface

521.6 Ankylosis of teeth
DEF: Adhesion of tooth to surrounding bone.

521.7 Intrinsic posteruptive color changes
Staining [discoloration] of teeth:
NOS
due to:
drugs
metals
pulpal bleeding
EXCLUDES *accretions [deposits] on teeth (523.6)*
extrinsic color changes (523.6)
pre-eruptive color changes (520.8)

√5ᵗʰ **521.8 Other specified diseases of hard tissues of teeth**

521.81 Cracked tooth
EXCLUDES *asymptomatic craze lines in enamel—omit code*
broken tooth due to trauma (873.63, 873.73)
fractured tooth due to trauma (873.63, 873.73)

521.89 Other specified diseases of hard tissues of teeth
Irradiated enamel
Sensitive dentin

521.9 Unspecified disease of hard tissues of teeth

√4ᵗʰ **522 Diseases of pulp and periapical tissues**

522.0 Pulpitis
Pulpal: Pulpitis:
abscess   chronic (hyperplastic)
polyp   (ulcerative)
Pulpitis: suppurative
acute

522.1 Necrosis of the pulp
Pulp gangrene
DEF: Death of pulp tissue.

522.2 Pulp degeneration
Denticles   Pulp stones
Pulp calcifications

522.3 Abnormal hard tissue formation in pulp
Secondary or irregular dentin

522.4 Acute apical periodontitis of pulpal origin
DEF: Severe inflammation of periodontal ligament due to pulpal inflammation or necrosis.

522.5 Periapical abscess without sinus
Abscess: Abscess:
dental   dentoalveolar
EXCLUDES *periapical abscess with sinus (522.7)*

522.6 Chronic apical periodontitis
Apical or periapical granuloma
Apical periodontitis NOS

522.7 Periapical abscess with sinus
Fistula: Fistula:
alveolar process   dental

522.8 Radicular cyst
Cyst: Cyst:
apical (periodontal)   radiculodental
periapical   residual radicular
EXCLUDES *lateral developmental or lateral periodontal cyst (526.0)*
DEF: Cyst in tissue around tooth apex due to chronic infection of granuloma around root.

522.9 Other and unspecified diseases of pulp and periapical tissues

N Newborn Age: 0   P Pediatric Age: 0-17   M Maternity Age: 12-55   A Adult Age: 15-124   CC CC Condition   MC Major Complication   CD Complex Dx   HIV HIV Related Dx

√4ᵗʰ **523 Gingival and periodontal diseases**

√5ᵗʰ **523.0 Acute gingivitis**

> EXCLUDES   *acute necrotizing ulcerative gingivitis (101)*
> *herpetic gingivostomatitis (054.2)*

●   **523.00 Acute gingivitis, plaque induced**
      Acute gingivitis NOS

●   **523.01 Acute gingivitis, non-plaque induced**

√5ᵗʰ **523.1 Chronic gingivitis**

    Gingivitis (chronic):   Gingivitis (chronic):
      desquamative   simple marginal
      hyperplastic   ulcerative

> EXCLUDES   *herpetic gingivostomatitis (054.2)*

●   **523.10 Chronic gingivitis, plaque induced**
      Chronic gingivitis NOS
      Gingivitis NOS

●   **523.11 Chronic gingivitis, non-plaque induced**

√5ᵗʰ **523.2 Gingival recession**

    Gingival recession (postinfective) (postoperative)

    523.20 Gingival recession, unspecified
    523.21 Gingival recession, minimal
    523.22 Gingival recession, moderate
    523.23 Gingival recession, severe
    523.24 Gingival recession, localized
    523.25 Gingival recession, generalized

▲ √5ᵗʰ **523.3 Aggressive and acute periodontitis**

    Acute:
      pericementitis
      pericoronitis

> EXCLUDES   *acute apical periodontitis (522.4)*
> *periapical abscess (522.5, 522.7)*

DEF: Severe inflammation, of tissues supporting teeth.

●   **523.30 Aggressive periodontitis, unspecified**
●   **523.31 Aggressive periodontitis, localized**
      Periodontal abscess
●   **523.32 Aggressive periodontitis, generalized**
●   **523.33 Acute periodontitis**

√5ᵗʰ **523.4 Chronic periodontitis**

    Chronic pericoronitis   Periodontitis:
    Pericementitis (chronic)   complex
                           simplex
                           NOS

> EXCLUDES   *chronic apical periodontitis (522.6)*

●   **523.40 Chronic periodontitis, unspecified**
●   **523.41 Chronic periodontitis, localized**
●   **523.42 Chronic periodontitis, generalized**

523.5 Periodontosis

523.6 Accretions on teeth

    Dental calculus: Deposits on teeth:
      subgingival   soft
      supragingival   tartar
    Deposits on teeth: tobacco
      betel   Extrinsic discoloration of teeth
      materia alba

> EXCLUDES   *intrinsic discoloration of teeth (521.7)*

DEF: Foreign material on tooth surface, usually plaque or calculus.

523.8 Other specified periodontal diseases

    Giant cell:
      epulis
      peripheral granuloma
    Gingival:
      cysts
      enlargement NOS
      fibromatosis
    Gingival polyp
    Periodontal lesions due to traumatic occlusion
    Peripheral giant cell granuloma

> EXCLUDES   *leukoplakia of gingiva (528.6)*

523.9 Unspecified gingival and periodontal disease
AHA: 3Q, '02, 14

√4ᵗʰ **524 Dentofacial anomalies, including malocclusion**

√5ᵗʰ **524.0 Major anomalies of jaw size**

> EXCLUDES   *hemifacial atrophy or hypertrophy (754.0)*
> *unilateral condylar hyperplasia or hypoplasia of mandible (526.89)*

    524.00 Unspecified anomaly
      DEF: Unspecified deformity of jaw size.

    524.01 Maxillary hyperplasia
      DEF: Overgrowth or over development of upper jaw bone.

    524.02 Mandibular hyperplasia
      DEF: Overgrowth or over development of lower jaw bone.

    524.03 Maxillary hypoplasia
      DEF: Incomplete or underdeveloped, upper jaw bone.

    524.04 Mandibular hypoplasia
      DEF: Incomplete or underdeveloped, lower jaw bone.

    524.05 Macrogenia
      DEF: Enlarged, jaw, especially chin; affects bone, soft tissue, or both.

    524.06 Microgenia
      DEF: Underdeveloped mandible, characterized by an extremely small chin.

    524.07 Excessive tuberosity of jaw
      ▶Entire maxillary tuberosity◀

    524.09 Other specified anomaly

√5ᵗʰ **524.1 Anomalies of relationship of jaw to cranial base**

    524.10 Unspecified anomaly
      Prognathism   Retrognathism
      DEF: Prognathism: protrusion of lower jaw.
      DEF: Retrognathism: jaw is located posteriorly to a normally positioned jaw; backward position of mandible.

    524.11 Maxillary asymmetry
      DEF: Absence of symmetry of maxilla.

    524.12 Other jaw asymmetry
    524.19 Other specified anomaly

√5ᵗʰ **524.2 Anomalies of dental arch relationship**

    ▶Anomaly of dental arch◀

> EXCLUDES   *hemifacial atrophy or hypertrophy (754.0)*
> *soft tissue impingement (524.81-524.82)*
> *unilateral condylar hyperplasia or hypoplasia of mandible (526.89)*

    524.20 Unspecified anomaly of dental arch relationship

▲   **524.21 Malocclusion, Angle's class I**
      Neutro-occlusion

▲   **524.22 Malocclusion, Angle's class II**
      Disto-occlusion Division I
      Disto-occlusion Division II

▲   **524.23 Malocclusion, Angle's class III**
      Mesio-occlusion

    524.24 Open anterior occlusal relationship
      ▶Anterior open bite◀

    524.25 Open posterior occlusal relationship
      ▶Posterior open bite◀

    524.26 Excessive horizontal overlap
      ▶Excessive horizontal overjet◀

    524.27 Reverse articulation
      Anterior articulation
      ▶Crossbite◀
      Posterior articulation

    524.28 Anomalies of interarch distance
      Excessive interarch distance
      Inadequate interarch distance

    524.29 Other anomalies of dental arch relationship
      ▶Other anomalies of dental arch◀

√4ᵗʰ Additional Digit Required   Nonspecific PDx   Unacceptable PDx   Manifestation Code   **MCV** Major Cardiovascular Condition   ▶◀ Revised Text   ● New Code   ▲ Revised Code Title

Angle's Classification of Malocclusion

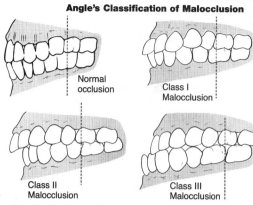

Normal occlusion

Class I Malocclusion

Class II Malocclusion

Class III Malocclusion

√5ᵗʰ **524.3 Anomalies of tooth position of fully erupted teeth**

EXCLUDES   *impacted or embedded teeth with abnormal position of such teeth or adjacent teeth (520.6)*

524.30 Unspecified anomaly of tooth position
Diastema of teeth NOS
Displacement of teeth NOS
Transposition of teeth NOS

524.31 Crowding of teeth

524.32 Excessive spacing of teeth

524.33 Horizontal displacement of teeth
►Tipped teeth◄
Tipping of teeth

524.34 Vertical displacement of teeth
►Extruded tooth◄
Infraeruption of teeth
►Intruded tooth◄
Supraeruption of teeth

524.35 Rotation of tooth/teeth

524.36 Insufficient interocclusal distance of teeth (ridge)
►Lack of adequate intermaxillary vertical dimension◄

524.37 Excessive interocclusal distance of teeth
►Excessive intermaxillary vertical dimension◄
Loss of occlusal vertical dimension

524.39 Other anomalies of tooth position

524.4 Malocclusion, unspecified
DEF: Malposition of top and bottom teeth; interferes with chewing.

√5ᵗʰ **524.5 Dentofacial functional abnormalities**

524.50 Dentofacial functional abnormality, unspecified

524.51 Abnormal jaw closure

524.52 Limited mandibular range of motion

524.53 Deviation in opening and closing of the mandible

524.54 Insufficient anterior guidance
►Insufficient anterior occlusal guidance◄

524.55 Centric occlusion maximum intercuspation discrepancy
►Centric occlusion of teeth discrepancy◄

524.56 Non-working side interference
►Balancing side interference◄

524.57 Lack of posterior occlusal support

524.59 Other dentofacial functional abnormalities
Abnormal swallowing   Sleep postures
Mouth breathing   Tongue, lip, or finger
                      habits

√5ᵗʰ **524.6 Temporomandibular joint disorders**

EXCLUDES   *current temporomandibular joint: dislocation (830.0-830.1) strain (848.1)*

524.60 Temporomandibular joint disorders, unspecified
Temporomandibular joint-pain-dysfunction syndrome [TMJ]

524.61 Adhesions and ankylosis (bony or fibrous)
DEF: Stiffening or union of temporomandibular joint due to bony or fibrous union across joint.

524.62 Arthralgia of temporomandibular joint
DEF: Pain in temporomandibular joint; not inflammatory in nature.

524.63 Articular disc disorder (reducing or non-reducing)

524.64 Temporomandibular joint sounds on opening and/or closing the jaw

524.69 Other specified temporomandibular joint disorders

√5ᵗʰ **524.7 Dental alveolar anomalies**

524.70 Unspecified alveolar anomaly

524.71 Alveolar maxillary hyperplasia
DEF: Excessive tissue formation in the dental alveoli of upper jaw.

524.72 Alveolar mandibular hyperplasia
DEF: Excessive tissue formation in the dental alveoli of lower jaw.

524.73 Alveolar maxillary hypoplasia
DEF: Incomplete or underdeveloped, alveolar tissue of upper jaw.

524.74 Alveolar mandibular hypoplasia
DEF: Incomplete or underdeveloped, alveolar tissue of lower jaw.

524.75 Vertical displacement of alveolus and teeth
Extrusion of alveolus and teeth

524.76 Occlusal plane deviation

524.79 Other specified alveolar anomaly

√5ᵗʰ **524.8 Other specified dentofacial anomalies**

524.81 Anterior soft tissue impingement

524.82 Posterior soft tissue impingement

524.89 Other specified dentofacial anomalies

524.9 Unspecified dentofacial anomalies

√4ᵗʰ **525 Other diseases and conditions of the teeth and supporting structures**

525.0 Exfoliation of teeth due to systemic causes
DEF: Deterioration of teeth and surrounding structures due to systemic disease.

√5ᵗʰ **525.1 Loss of teeth due to trauma, extraction, or periodontal disease**
Code first class of edentulism (525.40-525.44, 525.50-525.54)
AHA: 4Q, '05, 74; 4Q, '01, 44

525.10 Acquired absence of teeth, unspecified
Tooth extraction status, NOS

525.11 Loss of teeth due to trauma

525.12 Loss of teeth due to periodontal disease

525.13 Loss of teeth due to caries

525.19 Other loss of teeth

√5ᵗʰ **525.2 Atrophy of edentulous alveolar ridge**

525.20 Unspecified atrophy of edentulous alveolar ridge
Atrophy of the mandible NOS
Atrophy of the maxilla NOS

525.21 Minimal atrophy of the mandible

525.22 Moderate atrophy of the mandible

525.23 Severe atrophy of the mandible

525.24 Minimal atrophy of the maxilla

525.25 Moderate atrophy of the maxilla

525.26 Severe atrophy of the maxilla

525.3 Retained dental root

√5ᵗʰ **525.4 Complete edentulism**
Use additional code to identify cause of edentulism (525.10-525.19)
AHA: 4Q, '05, 74

525.40 Complete edentulism, unspecified
Edentulism NOS

525.41 Complete edentulism, class I

| N Newborn Age: 0 | P Pediatric Age: 0-17 | M Maternity Age: 12-55 | A Adult Age: 15-124 | CC CC Condition | MC Major Complication | CD Complex Dx | HIV HIV Related Dx |

525.42 **Complete edentulism, class II**

525.43 **Complete edentulism, class III**

525.44 **Complete edentulism, class IV**

√5ᵗʰ 525.5 **Partial edentulism**

> Use additional code to identify cause of edentulism (525.10-525.19)

> **AHA:** 4Q, '05, 74

525.50 **Partial edentulism, unspecified**

525.51 **Partial edentulism, class I**

525.52 **Partial edentulism, class II**

525.53 **Partial edentulism, class III**

525.54 **Partial edentulism, class IV**

● √5ᵗʰ 525.6 **Unsatisfactory restoration of tooth**

> Defective bridge, crown, fillings
> Defective dental restoration
> > **EXCLUDES**   *dental restoration status (V45.84)*
> > *unsatisfactory endodontic treatment (526.61-526.69)*

● 525.60 **Unspecified unsatisfactory restoration of tooth**

> Unspecified defective dental restoration

● 525.61 **Open restoration margins**

> Dental restoration failure of marginal integrity
> Open margin on tooth restoration

● 525.62 **Unrepairable overhanging of dental restorative materials**

> Overhanging of tooth restoration

● 525.63 **Fractured dental restorative material without loss of material**

> > **EXCLUDES**   *cracked tooth (521.81)*
> > *fractured tooth (873.63, 873.73)*

● 525.64 **Fractured dental restorative material with loss of material**

> > **EXCLUDES**   *cracked tooth (521.81)*
> > *fractured tooth (873.63, 873.73)*

● 525.65 **Contour of existing restoration of tooth biologically incompatible with oral health**

> Dental restoration failure of periodontal anatomical integrity
> Unacceptable contours of existing restoration
> Unacceptable morphology of existing restoration

● 525.66 **Allergy to existing dental restorative material**

> Use additional code to identify the specific type of allergy

● 525.67 **Poor aesthetics of existing restoration**

> Dental restoration aesthetically inadequate or displeasing

● 525.69 **Other unsatisfactory restoration of existing tooth**

525.8 **Other specified disorders of the teeth and supporting structures**

> Enlargement of alveolar ridge NOS
> Irregular alveolar process

525.9 **Unspecified disorder of the teeth and supporting structures**

√4ᵗʰ 526 **Diseases of the jaws**

526.0 **Developmental odontogenic cysts**

> Cyst: Cyst:
> dentigerous   lateral periodontal
> eruption   primordial
> follicular   Keratocyst
> lateral developmental
> > **EXCLUDES**   *radicular cyst (522.8)*

526.1 **Fissural cysts of jaw**

> Cyst: Cyst:
> globulomaxillary   median palatal
> incisor canal   nasopalatine
> median anterior maxillary   palatine of papilla
> > **EXCLUDES**   *cysts of oral soft tissues (528.4)*

526.2 **Other cysts of jaws**

> Cyst of jaw: Cyst of jaw:
> NOS   hemorrhagic
> aneurysmal   traumatic

526.3 **Central giant cell (reparative) granuloma**

> > **EXCLUDES**   *peripheral giant cell granuloma (523.8)*

526.4 **Inflammatory conditions**

> Abscess
> Osteitis
> Osteomyelitis (neonatal)   } of jaw (acute) (chronic) (suppurative)
> Periostitis
>
> Sequestrum of jaw bone
> > **EXCLUDES**   *alveolar osteitis (526.5)*

526.5 **Alveolitis of jaw**

> Alveolar osteitis   Dry socket
> **DEF:** Inflammation, of alveoli or tooth socket.

● √5ᵗʰ 526.6 **Periradicular pathology associated with previous endodontic treatment**

● 526.61 **Perforation of root canal space**

● 526.62 **Endodontic overfill**

● 526.63 **Endodontic underfill**

● 526.69 **Other periradicular pathology associated with previous endodontic treatment**

√5ᵗʰ 526.8 **Other specified diseases of the jaws**

526.81 **Exostosis of jaw**

> Torus mandibularis   Torus palatinus
> **DEF:** Spur or bony outgrowth on the jaw.

526.89 **Other**

> Cherubism
> Fibrous dysplasia
> Latent bone cyst   } of jaw(s)
> Osteoradionecrosis
>
> Unilateral condylar hyperplasia or hypoplasia of mandible

526.9 **Unspecified disease of the jaws**

√4ᵗʰ 527 **Diseases of the salivary glands**

527.0 **Atrophy**

> **DEF:** Wasting away, necrosis of salivary gland tissue.

527.1 **Hypertrophy**

> **DEF:** Overgrowth or overdeveloped salivary gland tissue.

527.2 **Sialoadenitis**

> Parotitis: Sialoangitis
> NOS   Sialodochitis
> allergic
> toxic
> > **EXCLUDES**   *epidemic or infectious parotitis (072.0-072.9)*
> > *uveoparotid fever (135)*
> **DEF:** Inflammation of salivary gland.

527.3 **Abscess**   **CC**

> **CC Excl:** 527.0-527.9, 537.89, 537.9

527.4 **Fistula**   **CC**

> > **EXCLUDES**   *congenital fistula of salivary gland (750.24)*
> **CC Excl:** See code 527.3

527.5 **Sialolithiasis**

> Calculus
> Stone } of salivary gland or duct
> Sialodocholithiasis

527.6 **Mucocele**

> Mucous:
> extravasation cyst of salivary gland
> retention cyst of salivary gland
> Ranula
> **DEF:** Dilated salivary gland cavity filled with mucous.

√4ᵗʰ
√5ᵗʰ Additional Digit Required   **Nonspecific PDx**   Unacceptable PDx   **Manifestation Code**   **MCV** Major Cardiovascular Condition   ▶◀ Revised Text   ● New Code   ▲ Revised Code Title

2007 ICD•9•CM   October 2006 • Volume 1 — 157

Digestive System

527.7–529.3

527.7 Disturbance of salivary secretion
Hyposecretion   Sialorrhea
Ptyalism   Xerostomia

527.8 Other specified diseases of the salivary glands
Benign lymphoepithelial lesion of salivary gland
Sialectasia
Sialosis
Stenosis ⎱ of salivary duct
Stricture ⎰

527.9 Unspecified disease of the salivary glands

✓4ᵗʰ **528 Diseases of the oral soft tissues, excluding lesions specific for gingiva and tongue**

▲ ✓5ᵗʰ **528.0 Stomatitis and mucositis (ulcerative)**

> **EXCLUDES** ▶ *cellulitis and abscess of mouth (528.3)*
> *diphtheritic stomatitis (032.0)*
> *epizootic stomatitis (078.4)*
> *gingivitis (523.0-523.1)*
> *oral thrush (112.0)*
> *Stevens-Johnson syndrome (695.1)*◀
> *stomatitis:*
>   *acute necrotizing ulcerative (101)*
>   *aphthous (528.2)*
>   *gangrenous (528.1)*
>   *herpetic (054.2)*
>   *Vincent's (101)*

AHA: 2Q, '99, 9

DEF: Stomatitis: Inflammation of oral mucosa; labial and buccal mucosa, tongue, palate, floor of the mouth, and gingivae.

● **528.00 Stomatitis and mucositis, unspecified**
Mucositis NOS
Ulcerative mucositis NOS
Ulcerative stomatitis NOS
Vesicular stomatitis NOS

● **528.01 Mucositis (ulcerative) due to antineoplastic therapy**
Use additional E code to identify adverse effects of therapy, such as:
antineoplastic and immunosuppressive drugs (E930.7, E933.1)
radiation therapy (E879.2)

● **528.02 Mucositis (ulcerative) due to other drugs**
Use additional E code to identify drug

● **528.09 Other stomatitis and mucositis (ulcerative)**

528.1 Cancrum oris
Gangrenous stomatitis   Noma
DEF: A severely gangrenous lesion of mouth due to fusospirochetal infection; destroys buccal, labial and facial tissues; can be fatal; found primarily in debilitated and malnourished children.

528.2 Oral aphthae
Aphthous stomatitis   Recurrent aphthous ulcer
Canker sore   Stomatitis herpetiformis
Periadenitis mucosa
  necrotica recurrens

> **EXCLUDES** *herpetic stomatitis (054.2)*

DEF: Small oval or round ulcers of the mouth marked by a grayish exudate and a red halo effect.

528.3 Cellulitis and abscess   CC
Cellulitis of mouth (floor)   Oral fistula
Ludwig's angina

> **EXCLUDES** *abscess of tongue (529.0)*
> *cellulitis or abscess of lip (528.5)*
> *fistula (of):*
>   *dental (522.7)*
>   *lip (528.5)*
>   *gingivitis ▶(523.00-523.11)◀*

CC Excl: 528.00-528.09, 528.3, 529.0, 529.2

528.4 Cysts
Dermoid cyst ⎤
Epidermoid cyst │
Epstein's pearl │ of mouth
Lymphoepithelial cyst ⎬
Nasoalveolar cyst │
Nasolabial cyst ⎦

> **EXCLUDES** *cyst:*   *cyst:*
> *gingiva (523.8)*   *tongue (529.8)*

528.5 Diseases of lips
Abscess ⎤
Cellulitis │ of lip(s)
Fistula ⎬
Hypertrophy ⎦

Cheilitis: Cheilodynia
  NOS   Cheilosis
  angular

> **EXCLUDES** *actinic cheilitis (692.79)*
> *congenital fistula of lip (750.25)*
> *leukoplakia of lips (528.6)*

AHA: S-O, '86, 10

528.6 Leukoplakia of oral mucosa, including tongue
Leukokeratosis of oral   Leukoplakia of:
  mucosa   gingiva
                                  lips
                                  tongue

> **EXCLUDES** *carcinoma in situ (230.0, 232.0)*
> *leukokeratosis nicotina palati (528.79)*

DEF: Thickened white patches of epithelium on mucous membranes of mouth.

✓5ᵗʰ **528.7 Other disturbances of oral epithelium, including tongue**

> **EXCLUDES** *carcinoma in situ (230.0, 232.0)*
> *leukokeratosis NOS (702)*

528.71 Minimal keratinized residual ridge mucosa
▶Minimal keratinization of alveolar ridge mucosa◀

528.72 Excessive keratinized residual ridge mucosa
▶Excessive keratinization of alveolar ridge mucosa◀

528.79 Other disturbances of oral epithelium, including tongue
Erythroplakia of mouth or tongue
Focal epithelial hyperplasia of mouth or tongue
Leukoedema of mouth or tongue
Leukokeratosis nicotina palate
▶Other oral epithelium disturbances◀

528.8 Oral submucosal fibrosis, including of tongue

528.9 Other and unspecified diseases of the oral soft tissues
Cheek and lip biting   Melanoplakia
Denture sore mouth   Papillary hyperplasia of palate
Denture stomatitis
Eosinophilic granuloma ⎤
Irritative hyperplasia │ of oral mucosa
Pyogenic granuloma ⎬
Ulcer (traumatic) ⎦

✓4ᵗʰ **529 Diseases and other conditions of the tongue**

529.0 Glossitis
Abscess ⎱ of tongue
Ulceration (traumatic) ⎰

> **EXCLUDES** *glossitis:*
> *benign migratory (529.1)*
> *Hunter's (529.4)*
> *median rhomboid (529.2)*
> *Moeller's (529.4)*

529.1 Geographic tongue
Benign migratory glossitis
Glossitis areata exfoliativa
DEF: Chronic glossitis; marked by filiform papillae atrophy and inflammation; no known etiology.

529.2 Median rhomboid glossitis
DEF: A noninflammatory, congenital disease characterized by rhomboid-like lesions at the middle third of the tongue's dorsal surface.

529.3 Hypertrophy of tongue papillae
Black hairy tongue   Hypertrophy of foliate papillae
Coated tongue   Lingua villosa nigra

| N Newborn Age: 0 | P Pediatric Age: 0-17 | M Maternity Age: 12-55 | A Adult Age: 15-124 | CC CC Condition | MC Major Complication | CD Complex Dx | HIV HIV Related Dx |

158 — Volume 1 • October 2006   **2007 ICD•9•CM**

529.4 Atrophy of tongue papillae
Bald tongue
Glazed tongue
Glossitis:
  Hunter's
Glossitis:
  Moeller's
Glossodynia exfoliativa
Smooth atrophic tongue

529.5 Plicated tongue
Fissured
Furrowed } tongue
Scrotal
EXCLUDES   *fissure of tongue, congenital (750.13)*
DEF: Cracks, fissures or furrows, on dorsal surface of tongue.

529.6 Glossodynia
Glossopyrosis   Painful tongue
EXCLUDES   *glossodynia exfoliativa (529.4)*

529.8 Other specified conditions of the tongue
Atrophy
Crenated
Enlargement } (of) tongue
Hypertrophy

Glossocele
Glossoptosis
EXCLUDES
erythroplasia of tongue (528.79)
leukoplakia of tongue (528.6)
macroglossia (congenital) (750.15)
microglossia (congenital) (750.16)
oral submucosal fibrosis (528.8)

529.9 Unspecified condition of the tongue

DISEASES OF ESOPHAGUS, STOMACH, AND DUODENUM
▶(530–538)◀

√4ᵗʰ 530 Diseases of esophagus
EXCLUDES   *esophageal varices (456.0-456.2)*

530.0 Achalasia and cardiospasm
Achalasia (of cardia)   Megaesophagus
Aperistalsis of esophagus
EXCLUDES   *congenital cardiospasm (750.7)*
DEF: Failure of smooth muscle fibers to relax, at gastrointestinal junctures; such as esophagogastric sphincter when swallowing.

√5ᵗʰ 530.1 Esophagitis
Abscess of esophagus
Esophagitis:
  NOS
  chemical
Esophagitis:
  peptic
  postoperative
  regurgitant
Use additional E code to identify cause, if induced by chemical
EXCLUDES   *tuberculous esophagitis (017.8)*
AHA: 4Q, '93, 27; 1Q, '92, 17; 3Q, '91, 20

530.10 Esophagitis, unspecified
AHA: 3Q, '05, 17

530.11 Reflux esophagitis
AHA: 4Q, '95, 82
DEF: Inflammation of lower esophagus; due to regurgitated gastric acid.

530.12 Acute esophagitis
AHA: 4Q, '01, 45
DEF: An acute inflammation of the mucous lining or submucosal coat of the esophagus.

530.19 Other esophagitis
AHA: 3Q, '01, 10

√5ᵗʰ 530.2 Ulcer of esophagus
Ulcer of esophagus:
  fungal
Ulcer of esophagus:
  peptic
Ulcer of esophagus due to ingestion of:
  aspirin   chemicals
  medicines
Use additional E code to identify cause, if induced by chemical or drug
AHA: 4Q, '03, 63

530.20 Ulcer of esophagus without bleeding
Ulcer of esophagus NOS

530.21 Ulcer of esophagus with bleeding `CC`
EXCLUDES   *bleeding esophageal varices (456.0, 456.20)*
CC Excl: 251.5, 456.0, 530.20-530.21, 530.7, 530.82, 530.85, 531.00-534.91, 535.01, 535.11, 535.21, 535.31, 535.41, 535.51, 535.61, 537.89-537.9, 562.02-562.03, 562.12-562.13, 569.3, 569.85, 578.0-578.9

530.3 Stricture and stenosis of esophagus
Compression of esophagus
Obstruction of esophagus
EXCLUDES   *congenital stricture of esophagus (750.3)*
AHA: 2Q, '01, 4; 2Q, '97, 3; 1Q, '88, 13

530.4 Perforation of esophagus `CC`
Rupture of esophagus
EXCLUDES   *traumatic perforation of esophagus (862.22, 862.32, 874.4-874.5)*
CC Excl: 530.4, 530.7-530.81, 530.83-530.9

530.5 Dyskinesia of esophagus
Corkscrew esophagus   Esophagospasm
Curling esophagus   Spasm of esophagus
EXCLUDES   *cardiospasm (530.0)*
AHA: 1Q, '88, 13; N-D, '84, 19
DEF: Difficulty performing voluntary esophageal movements.

530.6 Diverticulum of esophagus, acquired
Diverticulum, acquired:
  epiphrenic
  pharyngoesophageal
  pulsion
  subdiaphragmatic
Diverticulum, acquired:
  traction
  Zenker's
    (hypopharyngeal)
  Esophageal pouch, acquired
  Esophagocele, acquired
EXCLUDES   *congenital diverticulum of esophagus (750.4)*
AHA: J-F, '85, 3

530.7 Gastroesophageal laceration-hemorrhage syndrome `CC`
Mallory-Weiss syndrome
CC Excl: 251.5, 456.0, 530.20-530.21, 530.4, 530.7-530.85, 530.89-534.91, 535.01, 535.11, 535.21, 535.31, 535.41, 535.51, 535.61, 537.83, 562.02-562.03, 562.12-562.13, 569.3, 569.85, 578.0-578.9
DEF: Laceration of distal esophagus and proximal stomach due to vomiting, hiccups or other sustained activity.

√5ᵗʰ 530.8 Other specified disorders of esophagus
530.81 Esophageal reflux
Gastroesophageal reflux
EXCLUDES   *reflux esophagitis (530.11)*
AHA: 2Q, '01, 4; 1Q, '95, 7; 4Q, '92, 27
DEF: Regurgitation of the gastric contents into esophagus and possibly pharynx; where aspiration may occur between the vocal cords and down into the trachea.
DRG 182

530.82 Esophageal hemorrhage `CC`
EXCLUDES   *hemorrhage due to esophageal varices (456.0-456.2)*
CC Excl: 251.5, 456.0, 456.20, 459.89-459.9, 530.20-530.21, 530.7, 530.82, 530.85, 531.00-534.91, 535.01, 535.11, 535.21, 535.31, 535.41, 535.51, 535.61, 537.83, 562.02-562.03, 562.12-562.13, 569.3, 569.85, 578.0-578.9
AHA: 1Q, '05, 17

Esophagus

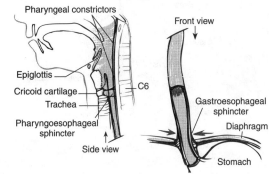

Pharyngeal constrictors
Front view
Epiglottis
Cricoid cartilage
C6
Trachea
Gastroesophageal sphincter
Pharyngoesophageal sphincter
Diaphragm
Side view
Stomach

√4ᵗʰ √5ᵗʰ Additional Digit Required   **Nonspecific PDx**   **Unacceptable PDx**   **Manifestation Code**   `MCV` Major Cardiovascular Condition   ▶◀ Revised Text   ● New Code   ▲ Revised Code Title

530.83 Esophageal leukoplakia

530.84 Tracheoesophageal fistula `CC`

> **EXCLUDES** *congenital tracheoesophageal fistula (750.3)*

CC Excl: 530.4, 530.7, 530.81, 530.83-530.9

530.85 Barrett's esophagus

AHA: 4Q, '03, 63

DEF: A metaplastic disorder in which specialized columnar epithelial cells replace the normal squamous epithelial cells; an acquired condition secondary to chronic gastroesophageal reflux damage to the mucosa; associated with increased risk of developing adenocarcinoma.

530.86 Infection of esophagostomy `CC`

> Use additional code to specify infection

CC Excl: 530.86-530.87, 536.40-536.49, 997.4, 997.91-997.99, 998.81, 998.83-998.9

530.87 Mechanical complication of esophagostomy `CC`

> Malfunction of esophagostomy

CC Excl: See code 530.8

530.89 Other

> **EXCLUDES** *Paterson-Kelly syndrome (280.8)*

530.9 Unspecified disorder of esophagus

√4ᵗʰ **531 Gastric ulcer**

> **INCLUDES** ulcer (peptic):
> prepyloric
> pylorus
> stomach

Use additional E code to identify drug, if drug-induced

> **EXCLUDES** *peptic ulcer NOS (533.0-533.9)*

The following fifth-digit subclassification is for use with category 531:

0 without mention of obstruction
1 with obstruction

AHA: 1Q, '91, 15; 4Q, '90, 27

DEF: Destruction of tissue in lumen of stomach due to action of gastric acid and pepsin on gastric mucosa decreasing resistance to ulcers.

√5ᵗʰ **531.0 Acute with hemorrhage** `CC`

CC Excl: 251.5, 456.0, 530.20-530.21, 530.7, 530.82, 530.85, 531.00-534.91, 535.01, 535.11, 535.21, 535.31, 535.41, 535.51, 535.61, 537.83, 537.89, 537.9, 562.02-562.03, 562.12-562.13, 569.3, 569.85, 578.0-578.9

AHA: N-D, '84, 15

√5ᵗʰ **531.1 Acute with perforation** `CC`

CC Excl: See code 531.0

√5ᵗʰ **531.2 Acute with hemorrhage and perforation** `CC`

CC Excl: See code 531.0

√5ᵗʰ **531.3 Acute without mention of hemorrhage or perforation** `CC 1`

CC Excl: For code 531.31: see code 531.0

√5ᵗʰ **531.4 Chronic or unspecified with hemorrhage** `CC`

CC Excl: See code 531.0

AHA: 4Q, '90, 22

▽ **DRG** 174 For code 531.40

√5ᵗʰ **531.5 Chronic or unspecified with perforation** `CC`

CC Excl: See code 531.0

Stomach

√5ᵗʰ **531.6 Chronic or unspecified with hemorrhage and perforation** `CC`

CC Excl: See code 531.0

√5ᵗʰ **531.7 Chronic without mention of hemorrhage or perforation** `CC 1`

CC Excl: For code 531.71: see code 531.0

√5ᵗʰ **531.9 Unspecified as acute or chronic, without mention of hemorrhage or perforation** `CC 1`

CC Excl: For code 531.91: see code 531.0

√4ᵗʰ **532 Duodenal ulcer**

> **INCLUDES** erosion (acute) of duodenum
> ulcer (peptic):
> duodenum
> postpyloric

Use additional E code to identify drug, if drug-induced

> **EXCLUDES** *peptic ulcer NOS (533.0-533.9)*

The following fifth-digit subclassification is for use with category 532:

0 without mention of obstruction
1 with obstruction

AHA: 4Q, '90, 27; 1Q, '91, 15

DEF: Ulcers in duodenum due to action of gastric acid and pepsin on mucosa decreasing resistance to ulcers.

√5ᵗʰ **532.0 Acute with hemorrhage** `CC`

CC Excl: 251.5, 456.0, 530.20-530.21, 530.7, 530.82, 530.85, 531.00-534.91, 535.01, 535.11, 535.21, 535.31, 535.41, 535.51, 535.61, 537.3, 537.83, 537.89, 537.9, 562.02-562.03, 562.12-562.13, 569.3, 569.85, 578.0-578.9

AHA: 4Q, '90, 22

√5ᵗʰ **532.1 Acute with perforation** `CC`

CC Excl: See code 532.0

√5ᵗʰ **532.2 Acute with hemorrhage and perforation** `CC`

CC Excl: See code 532.0

√5ᵗʰ **532.3 Acute without mention of hemorrhage or perforation** `CC 1`

CC Excl: For code 532.31: See code 532.0

√5ᵗʰ **532.4 Chronic or unspecified with hemorrhage** `CC`

CC Excl: See code 532.0

▽ **DRG** 174 For code 532.40

√5ᵗʰ **532.5 Chronic or unspecified with perforation** `CC`

CC Excl: See code 532.0

√5ᵗʰ **532.6 Chronic or unspecified with hemorrhage and perforation** `CC`

CC Excl: See code 532.0

√5ᵗʰ **532.7 Chronic without mention of hemorrhage or perforation** `CC 1`

CC Excl: For code 532.71: See code 532.0

√5ᵗʰ **532.9 Unspecified as acute or chronic, without mention of hemorrhage or perforation** `CC 1`

CC Excl: For code 532.91: See code 532.0

√4ᵗʰ **533 Peptic ulcer, site unspecified**

> **INCLUDES** gastroduodenal ulcer NOS   stress ulcer NOS
> peptic ulcer NOS

Use additional E code to identify drug, if drug-induced

> **EXCLUDES** *peptic ulcer:*
> *duodenal (532.0-532.9)*
> *gastric (531.0-531.9)*

The following fifth-digit subclassification is for use with category 533:

0 without mention of obstruction
1 with obstruction

AHA: 1Q, '91, 15; 4Q, '90, 27

DEF: Ulcer of mucous membrane of esophagus, stomach or duodenum due to gastric acid secretion.

√5ᵗʰ **533.0 Acute with hemorrhage** `CC`

CC Excl: See code 532.0

√5ᵗʰ **533.1 Acute with perforation** `CC`

CC Excl: See code 532.0

Ⓝ Newborn Age: 0   Ⓟ Pediatric Age: 0-17   Ⓜ Maternity Age: 12-55   Ⓐ Adult Age: 15-124   `CC` CC Condition   `MC` Major Complication   `CD` Complex Dx   `HIV` HIV Related Dx

160 — Volume 1 • February 2006   *2007 ICD•9•CM*

§ √5ᵗʰ **533.2 Acute with hemorrhage and perforation** `CC`
CC Excl: See code 532.0

§ √5ᵗʰ **533.3 Acute without mention of hemorrhage and perforation** `CC 1`
CC Excl: For code 533.31: See code 532.0

§ √5ᵗʰ **533.4 Chronic or unspecified with hemorrhage** `CC`
CC Excl: See code 532.0

§ √5ᵗʰ **533.5 Chronic or unspecified with perforation** `CC`
CC Excl: See code 532.0

§ √5ᵗʰ **533.6 Chronic or unspecified with hemorrhage and perforation** `CC`
CC Excl: See code 532.0

§ √5ᵗʰ **533.7 Chronic without mention of hemorrhage or perforation** `CC 1`
CC Excl: For code 533.71: See code 532.0
AHA: 2Q, '89, 16

§ √5ᵗʰ **533.9 Unspecified as acute or chronic, without mention of hemorrhage or perforation** `CC 1`
CC Excl: For code 533.91: See code 532.0

√4ᵗʰ **534 Gastrojejunal ulcer**

> INCLUDES   ulcer (peptic) or erosion: ulcer (peptic) or erosion:
>   anastomotic   jejunal
>   gastrocolic   marginal
>   gastrointestinal   stomal
>   gastrojejunal
>
> EXCLUDES   *primary ulcer of small intestine (569.82)*

The following fifth-digit subclassification is for use with category 534:
> **0 without mention of obstruction**
> **1 with obstruction**

AHA: 1Q, '91, 15; 4Q, '90, 27

√5ᵗʰ **534.0 Acute with hemorrhage** `CC`
CC Excl: 251.5, 456.0, 530.20-530.21, 530.7, 530.82, 530.85, 531.00-534.91, 535.01, 535.11, 535.21, 535.31, 535.41, 535.51, 535.61, 537.83, 537.89, 537.9, 562.02-562.03, 562.12-562.13, 569.3, 569.85, 578.0-578.9

√5ᵗʰ **534.1 Acute with perforation** `CC`
CC Excl: See code 534.0

√5ᵗʰ **534.2 Acute with hemorrhage and perforation** `CC`
CC Excl: See code 534.0

√5ᵗʰ **534.3 Acute without mention of hemorrhage or perforation** `CC 1`
CC Excl: For code 534.31: See code 534.0

√5ᵗʰ **534.4 Chronic or unspecified with hemorrhage** `CC`
CC Excl: See code 534.0

√5ᵗʰ **534.5 Chronic or unspecified with perforation** `CC`
CC Excl: See code 534.0

√5ᵗʰ **534.6 Chronic or unspecified with hemorrhage and perforation** `CC`
CC Excl: See code 534.0

√5ᵗʰ **534.7 Chronic without mention of hemorrhage or perforation** `CC 1`
CC Excl: For code 534.71: See code 534.0

√5ᵗʰ **534.9 Unspecified as acute or chronic, without mention of hemorrhage or perforation** `CC 1`
CC Excl: For code 534.91: See code 534.0

√4ᵗʰ **535 Gastritis and duodenitis**

The following fifth-digit subclassification is for use with category 535:
> **0 without mention of hemorrhage**
> **1 with hemorrhage**

AHA: 2Q, '92, 9; 4Q, '91, 25

√5ᵗʰ **535.0 Acute gastritis** `CC 1`
CC Excl: For code 535.01: 251.5, 456.0, 530.20-530.21, 530.7, 530.82, 530.85, 531.00-534.91, 535.01, 535.11, 535.21, 535.31, 535.41, 535.51, 535.61, 537.83, 562.02-562.03, 562.12-562.13, 569.3, 569.85, 578.0-578.9
AHA: 2Q, '92, 8; N-D, '86, 9

√5ᵗʰ **535.1 Atrophic gastritis** `CC 1`
> Gastritis: Gastritis:
>   atrophic-hyperplastic   chronic (atrophic)
CC Excl: For code 535.11: See code 535.01
AHA: 1Q, '94, 18
DEF: Inflammation of stomach, with mucous membrane atrophy and peptic gland destruction.

√5ᵗʰ **535.2 Gastric mucosal hypertrophy** `CC 1`
> Hypertrophic gastritis
CC Excl: For code 535.21: See code 535.01

√5ᵗʰ **535.3 Alcoholic gastritis** `CC 1`
CC Excl: For code 535.31: See code 535.01

√5ᵗʰ **535.4 Other specified gastritis** `CC 1`
> Gastritis: Gastritis:
>   allergic   superficial
>   bile induced   toxic
>   irritant
CC Excl: For code 535.41: See code 535.01
AHA: 4Q, '90, 27

√5ᵗʰ **535.5 Unspecified gastritis and gastroduodenitis** `CC 1`
CC Excl: For code 535.51: See code 535.01
AHA: For code 535.50: ▶3Q, '05, 17;◀ 4Q, '99, 25

√5ᵗʰ **535.6 Duodenitis** `CC 1`
CC Excl: For code 535.61: See code 535.01
AHA: For code 535.60: ▶3Q, '05, 17◀
DEF: Inflammation of intestine, between pylorus and jejunum.

√4ᵗʰ **536 Disorders of function of stomach**

> EXCLUDES   *functional disorders of stomach specified as psychogenic (306.4)*

536.0 Achlorhydria
DEF: Absence of gastric acid due to gastric mucosa atrophy; unresponsive to histamines; also known as gastric anacidity.

536.1 Acute dilatation of stomach `CC`
> Acute distention of stomach
CC Excl: 536.1

536.2 Persistent vomiting
> Habit vomiting   Uncontrollable vomiting
> Persistent vomiting [not of pregnancy]
> EXCLUDES   *excessive vomiting in pregnancy (643.0-643.9)*
>   *vomiting NOS (787.0)*

536.3 Gastroparesis
> Gastroparalysis
AHA: 2Q, '04, 7; 2Q, '01, 4; 4Q, '94, 42
DEF: Slight degree of paralysis within muscular coat of stomach.

√5ᵗʰ **536.4 Gastrostomy complications**
AHA: 4Q, '98, 42

> **536.40 Gastrostomy complication, unspecified** `CC`
> CC Excl: 530.86-530.87, 536.40-536.49, 997.4, 997.71, 997.91, 997.99, 998.81, 998.83-998.9

> **536.41 Infection of gastrostomy** `CC`
> Use additional code to specify type of infection, such as:
>   abscess or cellulitis of abdomen (682.2)
>   septicemia (038.0-038.9)
> Use additional code to identify organism (041.00-041.9)
> CC Excl: See code 536.40
> AHA: 4Q, '98, 42

> **536.42 Mechanical complication of gastrostomy** `CC`
> CC Excl: See code 536.40

> **536.49 Other gastrostomy complications** `CC`
> CC Excl: See code 536.40
> AHA: 4Q, '98, 42

---

§ Requires fifth digit. See category 533 for codes and definitions.

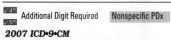

√4ᵗʰ Additional Digit Required   Nonspecific PDx   Unacceptable PDx   Manifestation Code   `MCV` Major Cardiovascular Condition   ▶◀ Revised Text   ● New Code   ▲ Revised Code Title

Digestive System

536.8–540.9

536.8 Dyspepsia and other specified disorders of function of stomach

Achylia gastrica
Hourglass contraction
  of stomach
Hyperacidity
Hyperchlorhydria
Hypochlorhydria
Indigestion
▶ Tachygastria ◀

> EXCLUDES   achlorhydria (536.0)
>   heartburn (787.1)

AHA: 2Q, '93, 6; 2Q, '89, 16; N-D, '84, 9

536.9 Unspecified functional disorder of stomach

Functional gastrointestinal:
  disorder
  disturbance
  irritation

√4ᵗʰ **537 Other disorders of stomach and duodenum**

537.0 Acquired hypertrophic pyloric stenosis   CC

Constriction
Obstruction } of pylorus, acquired or adult
Stricture

> EXCLUDES   congenital or infantile pyloric stenosis
>   (750.5)

CC Excl: 536.3, 536.8-536.9, 537.0, 537.3, 750.5, 750.8-750.9, 751.1, 751.5

AHA: 2Q, '01, 4; J-F, '85, 14

537.1 Gastric diverticulum

> EXCLUDES   congenital diverticulum of stomach
>   (750.7)

AHA: J-F, '85, 4

DEF: Herniated sac or pouch, within stomach or duodenum.

537.2 Chronic duodenal ileus

DEF: Persistent obstruction between pylorus and jejunum.

537.3 Other obstruction of duodenum   CC

Cicatrix
Stenosis } of duodenum
Stricture
Volvulus

> EXCLUDES   congenital obstruction of duodenum
>   (751.1)

CC Excl: 537.3, 750.8-750.9, 751.1, 751.5

537.4 Fistula of stomach or duodenum   CC

Gastrocolic fistula   Gastrojejunocolic fistula

CC Excl: 537.4, 750.8-750.9, 751.5

537.5 Gastroptosis

DEF: Downward displacement of stomach.

537.6 Hourglass stricture or stenosis of stomach

Cascade stomach

> EXCLUDES   congenital hourglass stomach (750.7)
>   hourglass contraction of stomach
>   (536.8)

√5ᵗʰ **537.8 Other specified disorders of stomach and duodenum**

AHA: 4Q, '91, 25

537.81 Pylorospasm

> EXCLUDES   congenital pylorospasm
>   (750.5)

DEF: Spasm of the pyloric sphincter.

Duodenum

537.82 Angiodysplasia of stomach and duodenum (without mention of hemorrhage)

AHA: 3Q, '96, 10; 4Q, '90, 4

537.83 Angiodysplasia of stomach and duodenum with hemorrhage   CC

CC Excl: 251.5, 456.0, 530.20-530.21, 530.7, 530.82, 530.85, 531.00-534.91, 535.01, 535.11, 535.21, 535.31, 535.41, 535.51, 535.61, 537.83, 562.02-562.03, 562.12-562.13, 569.3, 569.85, 578.0-578.9

DEF: Bleeding of stomach and duodenum due to vascular abnormalities.

537.84 Dieulafoy lesion (hemorrhagic) of stomach and duodenum   CC

CC Excl: 251.5, 456.0, 530.20-530.21, 530.7, 530.82, 530.85, 531.00-534.91, 535.01, 535.11, 535.21, 535.31, 535.41, 535.51, 535.61, 537.83-537.84, 562.02-562.03, 562.12-562.13, 569.3, 569.85, 578.0-578.9

AHA: 4Q, '02, 60

DEF: An abnormally large and convoluted submucosal artery protruding through a defect in the mucosa in the stomach or intestines that can erode the epithelium causing hemorrhaging; also called Dieulafoy's vascular malformation.

537.89 Other

Gastric or duodenal:
  prolapse
  rupture
Intestinal metaplasia of gastric mucosa
Passive congestion of stomach

> EXCLUDES   diverticula of duodenum
>   (562.00-562.01)
>   gastrointestinal hemorrhage
>   (578.0-578.9)

AHA: 3Q, '05, 15; N-D, '84, 7

537.9 Unspecified disorder of stomach and duodenum

● **538 Gastrointestinal mucositis (ulcerative)**

Use additional E code to identify adverse effects of therapy, such as:
antineoplastic and immunosuppressive drugs (E930.7, E933.1)
radiation therapy (E879.2)

> EXCLUDES   mucositis (ulcerative) of mouth and oral soft
>   tissue (528.00- 528.09)

APPENDICITIS (540-543)

√4ᵗʰ **540 Acute appendicitis**

AHA: N-D, '84, 19

DEF: Inflammation of vermiform appendix due to fecal obstruction, neoplasm or foreign body of appendiceal lumen; causes infection, edema and infarction of appendiceal wall; may result in mural necrosis, and perforation.

540.0 With generalized peritonitis   CC

Appendicitis (acute):
  fulminating
  gangrenous } with:
  obstructive   perforation
Cecitis (acute)   peritonitis (generalized)
                   rupture

Rupture of appendix

> EXCLUDES   acute appendicitis with peritoneal
>   abscess (540.1)

CC Excl: 537.89-543.9

540.1 With peritoneal abscess   CC

Abscess of appendix
With generalized peritonitis

CC Excl: See code 540.0

AHA: N-D, '84, 19

540.9 Without mention of peritonitis   CC

Acute:
  appendicitis:
    fulminating
    gangrenous } without mention of
    inflamed   perforation,
    obstructive   peritonitis, or rupture
    cecitis

CC Excl: See code 540.0

AHA: 1Q, '01, 15; 4Q, '97, 52

N Newborn Age: 0   P Pediatric Age: 0-17   M Maternity Age: 12-55   A Adult Age: 15-124   CC CC Condition   MC Major Complication   CD Complex Dx   HIV HIV Related Dx

Appendix

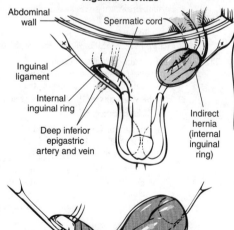

- Appendicular artery
- Mesoappendix
- Cecum
- Vermiform appendix

541 Appendicitis, unqualified
AHA: 2Q, '90, 26

542 Other appendicitis
Appendicitis: Appendicitis:
   chronic   relapsing
   recurrent   subacute

    EXCLUDES   *hyperplasia (lymphoid) of appendix (543.0)*
AHA: 1Q, '01, 15

√4ᵗʰ 543 Other diseases of appendix

543.0 Hyperplasia of appendix (lymphoid)
DEF: Proliferation of cells in appendix tissue.

543.9 Other and unspecified diseases of appendix
Appendicular or appendiceal:
   colic
   concretion
   fistula
   Diverticulum ⎫
   Fecalith   ⎬
   Intussusception ⎬ of appendix
   Mucocele   ⎬
   Stercolith   ⎭

HERNIA OF ABDOMINAL CAVITY (550-553)
   INCLUDES   hernia:
                 acquired
                 congenital, except diaphragmatic or hiatal

√4ᵗʰ 550 Inguinal hernia
   INCLUDES   bubonocele
                 inguinal hernia (direct) (double) (indirect)
                       (oblique) (sliding)
                 scrotal hernia

The following fifth-digit subclassification is for use with category 550:

   0 unilateral or unspecified (not specified as recurrent)
       Unilateral NOS
   1 unilateral or unspecified, recurrent
   2 bilateral (not specified as recurrent)
       Bilateral NOS
   3 bilateral, recurrent

AHA: N-D, '85, 12

DEF: Hernia protrusion of an abdominal organ or tissue through inguinal canal.
DEF: Indirect inguinal hernia: (external or oblique) leaves abdomen through deep inguinal ring, passes through inguinal canal lateral to the inferior epigastric artery.
DEF: Direct inguinal hernia: (internal) emerges between inferior epigastric artery and rectus muscle edge.

√5ᵗʰ 550.0 Inguinal hernia, with gangrene   CC
      Inguinal hernia with gangrene (and obstruction)
      CC Excl: 537.89-537.9, 550.00-550.93, 552.8-552.9, 553.8-553.9

√5ᵗʰ 550.1 Inguinal hernia, with obstruction, without mention of gangrene   CC
      Inguinal hernia with mention of incarceration, irreducibility, or strangulation
      CC Excl: See code 550.0

√5ᵗʰ 550.9 Inguinal hernia, without mention of obstruction or gangrene
      Inguinal hernia NOS
      AHA: For code 550.91: 3Q, '03, 10; 1Q, '03, 4

√4ᵗʰ 551 Other hernia of abdominal cavity, with gangrene
   INCLUDES   that with gangrene (and obstruction)

√5ᵗʰ 551.0 Femoral hernia with gangrene

551.00 Unilateral or unspecified (not specified as recurrent)   CC
      Femoral hernia NOS with gangrene
      CC Excl: 537.89-537.9, 551.00-551.03, 552.8-553.03, 553.8-553.9

551.01 Unilateral or unspecified, recurrent   CC
      CC Excl: See code 551.00

551.02 Bilateral (not specified as recurrent)   CC
      CC Excl: See code 551.00

551.03 Bilateral, recurrent   CC
      CC Excl: See code 551.00

551.1 Umbilical hernia with gangrene   CC
      Parumbilical hernia specified as gangrenous
      CC Excl: 537.89-537.9, 551.1-551.29, 552.1-552.29, 552.8-552.9, 553.1-553.29, 553.8-553.9

√5ᵗʰ 551.2 Ventral hernia with gangrene

551.20 Ventral, unspecified, with gangrene   CC
      CC Excl: See code 551.1

551.21 Incisional, with gangrene   CC
      Hernia:
        postoperative   ⎫ specified as
        recurrent, ventral ⎬ gangrenous
      CC Excl: See code 551.1

551.29 Other   CC
      Epigastric hernia specified as gangrenous
      CC Excl: See code 551.1

551.3 Diaphragmatic hernia with gangrene   CC
      Hernia:
        hiatal (esophageal) (sliding) ⎫
        paraesophageal   ⎬ specified as
        Thoracic stomach   ⎭ gangrenous

   EXCLUDES   *congenital diaphragmatic hernia (756.6)*
      CC Excl: 551.3, 552.3-552.9, 553.3, 553.8-553.9

Inguinal Hernias

- Abdominal wall
- Spermatic cord
- Inguinal ligament
- Internal inguinal ring
- Deep inferior epigastric artery and vein
- Indirect hernia (internal inguinal ring)
- Direct inguinal hernia (between deep inferior epigastric vessels and rectus fascia)
- Incarcerated hernia

√4ᵗʰ √5ᵗʰ Additional Digit Required   Nonspecific PDx   Unacceptable PDx   Manifestation Code   **MCV** Major Cardiovascular Condition   ◄► Revised Text   ● New Code   ▲ Revised Code Title

2007 ICD•9•CM   **Volume 1 — 163**

Femoral Hernia

Hernias of Abdominal Cavity

551.8 Hernia of other specified sites, with gangrene `CC`
Any condition classifiable to 553.8 if specified as gangrenous
CC Excl: 537.89, 537.9, 550.0-553.9

551.9 Hernia of unspecified site, with gangrene `CC`
Any condition classifiable to 553.9 if specified as gangrenous
CC Excl: See code 551.8

√4th **552 Other hernia of abdominal cavity, with obstruction, but without mention of gangrene**
    EXCLUDES   *that with mention of gangrene (551.0-551.9)*

√5th **552.0 Femoral hernia with obstruction**
Femoral hernia specified as incarcerated, irreducible, strangulated, or causing obstruction

552.00 Unilateral or unspecified (not specified as recurrent) `CC`
CC Excl: 537.89-537.9, 551.00-551.03, 552.00-552.03, 552.8-552.9, 553.00-553.03, 553.8-553.9

552.01 Unilateral or unspecified, recurrent `CC`
CC Excl: See code 552.00

552.02 Bilateral (not specified as recurrent) `CC`
CC Excl: See code 552.00

552.03 Bilateral, recurrent `CC`
CC Excl: See code 552.00

552.1 Umbilical hernia with obstruction `CC`
Parumbilical hernia specified as incarcerated, irreducible, strangulated, or causing obstruction
CC Excl: 551.1-551.29, 552.1-552.29, 552.8-552.9, 553.8-553.9

√5th **552.2 Ventral hernia with obstruction**
Ventral hernia specified as incarcerated, irreducible, strangulated, or causing obstruction

552.20 Ventral, unspecified, with obstruction `CC`
CC Excl: See code 552.1

552.21 Incisional, with obstruction `CC`
Hernia:
  postoperative ⎱ specified as incarcer-
  recurrent, ⎰ ated, irreducible,
  ventral   strangulated, or
                 causing
                 obstruction

CC Excl: See code 552.1
AHA: 3Q, '03, 11

552.29 Other `CC`
Epigastric hernia specified as incarcerated, irreducible, strangulated, or causing obstruction
CC Excl: See code 552.1

552.3 Diaphragmatic hernia with obstruction `CC`
Hernia:
  hiatal (esophageal) ⎱ specified as incarcerated,
    (sliding)   ⎰ irreducible,
  paraesophageal   ⎰ strangulated, or
  Thoracic stomach ⎰ causing obstruction
    EXCLUDES   *congenital diaphragmatic hernia (756.6)*
CC Excl: 551.3, 552.3-552.9, 553.3-553.9

552.8 Hernia of other specified sites, with obstruction `CC`
Any condition classifiable to 553.8 if specified as incarcerated, irreducible, strangulated, or causing obstruction
    EXCLUDES   *hernia due to adhesion with obstruction (560.81)*
CC Excl: 550.00-553.9
AHA: 1Q, '04, 10

552.9 Hernia of unspecified site, with obstruction `CC`
Any condition classifiable to 553.9 if specified as incarcerated, irreducible, strangulated, or causing obstruction
CC Excl: See code 552.8

√4th **553 Other hernia of abdominal cavity without mention of obstruction or gangrene**
    EXCLUDES   *the listed conditions with mention of:*
                   gangrene (and obstruction) (551.0-551.9)
                   obstruction (552.0-552.9)

√5th **553.0 Femoral hernia**

553.00 Unilateral or unspecified (not specified as recurrent)
Femoral hernia NOS

553.01 Unilateral or unspecified, recurrent

553.02 Bilateral (not specified as recurrent)

553.03 Bilateral, recurrent

553.1 Umbilical hernia
Parumbilical hernia

√5th **553.2 Ventral hernia**

553.20 Ventral, unspecified
AHA: 3Q, '03, 6

553.21 Incisional
Hernia: Hernia:
  postoperative   recurrent, ventral
AHA: 3Q, '03, 6

553.29 Other
Hernia: Hernia:
  epigastric   spigelian

553.3 Diaphragmatic hernia
Hernia:
  hiatal (esophageal) (sliding)
  paraesophageal
Thoracic stomach
    EXCLUDES   *congenital:*
                   diaphragmatic hernia (756.6)
                   hiatal hernia (750.6)
                   esophagocele (530.6)
AHA: 2Q, '01, 6; 1Q, '00, 6

`N` Newborn Age: 0   `P` Pediatric Age: 0-17   `M` Maternity Age: 12-55   `A` Adult Age: 15-124   `CC` CC Condition   `MC` Major Complication   `CD` Complex Dx   `HIV` HIV Related Dx

Digestive System

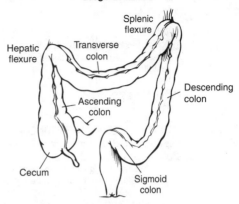

Diaphragmatic Hernias

Esophagus
Gastroesophageal junction (remains in place)
Stomach
Diaphragm
Gastroesophageal junction (slides up and down)
Paraesophageal Hiatal Hernia
Sliding Hiatal Hernia

Large Intestine

Splenic flexure
Hepatic flexure
Transverse colon
Descending colon
Ascending colon
Cecum
Sigmoid colon

553.8 Hernia of other specified sites

Hernia:
ischiatic
ischiorectal
lumbar
obturator

Hernia:
pudendal
retroperitoneal
sciatic
Other abdominal hernia of specified site

EXCLUDES *vaginal enterocele (618.6)*

553.9 Hernia of unspecified site

Enterocele
Epiplocele
Hernia:
NOS
interstitial

Hernia:
intestinal
intra-abdominal
Rupture (nontraumatic)
Sarcoepiplocele

NONINFECTIOUS ENTERITIS AND COLITIS (555-558)

✓4ᵗʰ 555 Regional enteritis

INCLUDES Crohn's disease
Granulomatous enteritis
EXCLUDES *ulcerative colitis (556)*
DEF: Inflammation of intestine; classified to site.

555.0 Small intestine

Ileitis:
regional
segmental
terminal

Regional enteritis or Crohn's disease of:
duodenum
ileum
jejunum

555.1 Large intestine

Colitis:
granulmatous
regional
transmural

Regional enteritis or Crohn's disease of:
colon
large bowel
rectum

AHA: 3Q, '99, 8

555.2 Small intestine with large intestine
Regional ileocolitis
AHA: 1Q, '03, 18

555.9 Unspecified site
Crohn's disease NOS   Regional enteritis NOS
AHA: ▶2Q, '05, 11;◀ 3Q, '99, 8; 4Q, '97, 42; 2Q, '97, 3

✓4ᵗʰ 556 Ulcerative colitis
AHA: 3Q, '99, 8
DEF: Chronic inflammation of mucosal lining of intestinal tract; may be single area or entire colon.

556.0 Ulcerative (chronic) enterocolitis
556.1 Ulcerative (chronic) ileocolitis
556.2 Ulcerative (chronic) proctitis
556.3 Ulcerative (chronic) proctosigmoiditis
556.4 Pseudopolyposis of colon
556.5 Left-sided ulcerative (chronic) colitis
556.6 Universal ulcerative (chronic) colitis
Pancolitis
556.8 Other ulcerative colitis
556.9 Ulcerative colitis, unspecified
Ulcerative enteritis NOS
AHA: 1Q, '03, 10

✓4ᵗʰ 557 Vascular insufficiency of intestine
EXCLUDES *necrotizing enterocolitis of the newborn (777.5)*
DEF: Inadequacy of intestinal vessels.

557.0 Acute vascular insufficiency of intestine `CC`
Acute:
hemorrhagic enterocolitis
ischemic colitis, enteritis, or enterocolitis
massive necrosis of intestine
Bowel infarction
Embolism of mesenteric artery
Fulminant enterocolitis
Hemorrhagic necrosis of intestine
Infarction of appendices epiploicae
Intestinal gangrene
Intestinal infarction (acute) (agnogenic) (hemorrhagic) (nonocclusive)
Mesenteric infarction (embolic) (thrombotic)
Necrosis of intestine
Terminal hemorrhagic enteropathy
Thrombosis of mesenteric artery
CC Excl: 557.0-557.1
DRG 188
AHA: 4Q, '01, 53

557.1 Chronic vascular insufficiency of intestine
Angina, abdominal
Chronic ischemic colitis, enteritis, or enterocolitis
Ischemic stricture of intestine
Mesenteric:
angina
artery syndrome (superior)
vascular insufficiency
AHA: 3Q, '96, 9; 4Q, '90, 4; N-D, '86, 11; N-D, '84, 7

557.9 Unspecified vascular insufficiency of intestine
Alimentary pain due to vascular insufficiency
Ischemic colitis, enteritis, or enterocolitis NOS
DRG 188

✓4ᵗʰ 558 Other and unspecified noninfectious gastroenteritis and colitis
EXCLUDES *infectious:*
colitis, enteritis, or gastroenteritis (009.0-009.1)
diarrhea (009.2-009.3)

558.1 Gastroenteritis and colitis due to radiation `CC`
Radiation enterocolitis
CC Excl: 558.1

558.2 Toxic gastroenteritis and colitis `CC`
Use additional E code to identify cause
CC Excl: 558.2

558.3 Allergic gastroenteritis and colitis
Use additional code to identify type of food allergy (V15.01-V15.05)
AHA: 1Q, '03, 12; 4Q, '00, 42
DEF: True immunoglobulin E (IgE)-mediated allergic reaction of the lining of the stomach, intestines, or colon to food proteins; causes nausea, vomiting, diarrhea, and abdominal cramping.

✓4ᵗʰ/✓5ᵗʰ Additional Digit Required   Nonspecific PDx   Unacceptable PDx   Manifestation Code   `MCV` Major Cardiovascular Condition   ◄► Revised Text   ● New Code   ▲ Revised Code Title

558.9 Other and unspecified noninfectious gastroenteritis and colitis

Colitis
Enteritis
Gastroenteritis } NOS, dietetic, or
Ileitis   noninfectious
Jejunitis
Sigmoiditis

AHA: 3Q, '99, 4, 6; N-D, '87, 7

▽ DRG 182

OTHER DISEASES OF INTESTINES AND PERITONEUM (560-569)

✓4ᵗʰ **560 Intestinal obstruction without mention of hernia**

EXCLUDES   duodenum (537.2-537.3)
inguinal hernia with obstruction (550.1)
intestinal obstruction complicating hernia
(552.0-552.9)
mesenteric:
    embolism (557.0)
    infarction (557.0)
    thrombosis (557.0)
neonatal intestinal obstruction (277.01, 777.1-
777.2, 777.4)

560.0 Intussusception   CC

Intussusception (colon) (intestine) (rectum)
Invagination of intestine or colon
EXCLUDES   intussusception of appendix (543.9)

CC Excl: 560.0-560.9, 569.89, 569.9

AHA: 4Q, '98, 82

DEF: Prolapse of a bowel section into adjacent section; occurs primarily in children; symptoms include paroxysmal pain, vomiting, presence of lower abdominal tumor and blood, and mucous passage from rectum.

560.1 Paralytic ileus   CC

Adynamic ileus
Ileus (of intestine) (of bowel) (of colon)
Paralysis of intestine or colon
EXCLUDES   gallstone ileus (560.31)

CC Excl: See code 560.0

AHA: J-F, '87, 13

DEF: Obstruction of ileus due to inhibited bowel motility.

▽ DRG 180

560.2 Volvulus   CC

Knotting
Strangulation } of intestine, bowel, or
Torsion   colon
Twist

CC Excl: See code 560.0

DEF: Entanglement of bowel; causes obstruction; may compromise bowel circulation.

✓5ᵗʰ **560.3 Impaction of intestine**

560.30 Impaction of intestine, unspecified   CC
Impaction of colon
CC Excl: See code 560.0

560.31 Gallstone ileus   CC
Obstruction of intestine by gallstone
CC Excl: See code 560.0

Volvulus and Diverticulitis

Knotted intestine (volvulus)

Diverticulum

560.39 Other   CC
Concretion of intestine
Enterolith
Fecal impaction
CC Excl: See code 560.0

AHA: 4Q, '98, 38

▽ DRG 180

✓5ᵗʰ **560.8 Other specified intestinal obstruction**

560.81 Intestinal or peritoneal adhesions   CC
with obstruction (postoperative)
(postinfection)
EXCLUDES   adhesions without obstruction
(568.0)

CC Excl: See code 560.0

AHA: 4Q, '95, 55; 3Q, '95, 6; N-D, '87, 9

DEF: Obstruction of peritoneum or intestine due to abnormal union of tissues.

▽ DRG 180

560.89 Other   CC
Acute pseudo-obstruction of intestine
Mural thickening causing obstruction
EXCLUDES   ischemic stricture of intestine
(557.1)

CC Excl: See code 560.0

AHA: 2Q, '97, 3; 1Q, '88, 6

▽ DRG 180

560.9 Unspecified intestinal obstruction   CC
Enterostenosis
Obstruction
Occlusion } of intestine or colon
Stenosis
Stricture

EXCLUDES   congenital stricture or stenosis of
intestine (751.1-751.2)

CC Excl: See code 560.0

▽ DRG 180

✓4ᵗʰ **562 Diverticula of intestine**
Use additional code to identify any associated:
peritonitis (567.0-567.9)
EXCLUDES   congenital diverticulum of colon (751.5)
diverticulum of appendix (543.9)
Meckel's diverticulum (751.0)

AHA: 4Q, '91, 25; J-F, '85, 1

✓5ᵗʰ **562.0 Small intestine**

562.00 Diverticulosis of small intestine (without
mention of hemorrhage)
Diverticulosis:
    duodenum
    ileum } without mention of
    jejunum   diverticulitis

DEF: Saclike herniations of mucous lining of small intestine.

562.01 Diverticulitis of small intestine (without
mention of hemorrhage)
Diverticulitis (with diverticulosis):
    duodenum
    ileum
    jejunum
    small intestine

DEF: Inflamed saclike herniations of mucous lining of small intestine.

562.02 Diverticulosis of small intestine with   CC
hemorrhage
CC Excl: 251.5, 456.0, 530.20-530.21, 530.7, 530.82, 530.85, 531.00-534.91, 535.01, 535.11, 535.21, 535.31, 535.41, 535.51, 535.61, 537.83, 562.02-562.03, 562.12-562.13, 569.3, 569.85, 578.0-578.9

562.03 Diverticulitis of small intestine with   CC
hemorrhage
CC Excl: See code 562.02

N Newborn Age: 0   P Pediatric Age: 0-17   M Maternity Age: 12-55   A Adult Age: 15-124   CC CC Condition   MC Major Complication   CD Complex Dx   HIV HIV Related Dx

166 — Volume 1 • February 2006   2007 ICD•9•CM

✓5th 562.1 Colon

562.10 **Diverticulosis of colon (without mention of hemorrhage)**

Diverticulosis:
NOS } without mention
intestine (large) } of
Diverticular disease } diverticulitis
(colon)

AHA: ▶3Q, '05, 17;◀ 3Q, '02, 15; 4Q, '90, 21; J-F, '85, 5

DEF: Saclike herniations of mucous lining of large intestine.

562.11 **Diverticulitis of colon (without mention of hemorrhage)**

Diverticulitis (with diverticulosis):
NOS
colon
intestine (large)

AHA: 1Q, '96, 14; J-F, '85, 5

DEF: Inflamed saclike herniations of mucosal lining of large intestine.

562.12 **Diverticulosis of colon with hemorrhage** CC

CC Excl: See code 562.02

DRG 174 and 182

562.13 **Diverticulitis of colon with hemorrhage** CC

CC Excl: See code 562.02

✓4th **564 Functional digestive disorders, not elsewhere classified**

EXCLUDES *functional disorders of stomach (536.0-536.9)*
those specified as psychogenic (306.4)

✓5th **564.0 Constipation**
AHA: 4Q, '01, 45

564.00 Constipation, unspecified

564.01 **Slow transit constipation**

DEF: Delay in the transit of fecal material through the colon secondary to smooth muscle dysfunction or decreased peristaltic contractions along the colon: also called colonic inertia or delayed transit.

564.02 **Outlet dysfunction constipation**

DEF: Failure to relax the paradoxical contractions of the striated pelvic floor muscles during the attempted defecation.

564.09 **Other constipation**

564.1 **Irritable bowel syndrome**

Irritable colon
Spastic colon

AHA: 1Q, '88, 6

DEF: Functional gastrointestinal disorder (FGID); symptoms following meals include diarrhea, constipation, abdominal pain; other symptoms include bloating, gas, distended abdomen, nausea, vomiting, appetite loss, emotional distress, and depression.

564.2 **Postgastric surgery syndromes**

Dumping syndrome Postgastrectomy syndrome
Jejunal syndrome Postvagotomy syndrome

EXCLUDES *malnutrition following gastrointestinal surgery (579.3)*
postgastrojejunostomy ulcer (534.0-534.9)

AHA: 1Q, '95, 11

564.3 **Vomiting following gastrointestinal surgery**

Vomiting (bilious) following gastrointestinal surgery

564.4 **Other postoperative functional disorders**

Diarrhea following gastrointestinal surgery

EXCLUDES *colostomy and enterostomy complications (569.60-569.69)*

564.5 **Functional diarrhea**

EXCLUDES *diarrhea:*
NOS (787.91)
psychogenic (306.4)

DEF: Diarrhea with no detectable organic cause.

564.6 **Anal spasm**

Proctalgia fugax

Anal Fistula and Abscess

564.7 **Megacolon, other than Hirschsprung's**

Dilatation of colon

EXCLUDES *megacolon:*
congenital [Hirschsprung's] (751.3)
toxic (556)

DEF: Enlarged colon; congenital or acquired; can occur acutely or become chronic.

✓5th 564.8 **Other specified functional disorders of intestine**

EXCLUDES *malabsorption (579.0-579.9)*

AHA: 1Q, '88, 6

564.81 **Neurogenic bowel**

AHA: 1Q, '01, 12; 4Q, '98, 45

DEF: Disorder of bowel due to spinal cord lesion above conus medullaris; symptoms include precipitous micturition, nocturia, catheter intolerance, headache, sweating, nasal obstruction and spastic contractions.

564.89 **Other functional disorders of intestine**

Atony of colon

564.9 Unspecified functional disorder of intestine

✓4th **565 Anal fissure and fistula**

565.0 **Anal fissure**

Tear of anus, nontraumatic

EXCLUDES *traumatic (863.89, 863.99)*

DEF: Ulceration of cleft at anal mucosa; causes pain, itching, bleeding, infection, and sphincter spasm; may occur with hemorrhoids.

565.1 **Anal fistula**

Fistula: Fistula:
anorectal rectum to skin
rectal

EXCLUDES *fistula of rectum to internal organs—*
see Alphabetic Index
ischiorectal fistula (566)
rectovaginal fistula (619.1)

DEF: Abnormal opening on cutaneous surface near anus; may lack connection with rectum.

566 Abscess of anal and rectal regions CC

Abscess: Cellulitis:
ischiorectal anal
perianal perirectal
perirectal rectal
Ischiorectal fistula

CC Excl: 566

✓4th
✓5th Additional Digit Required **Nonspecific PDx** **Unacceptable PDx** **Manifestation Code** **MCV** Major Cardiovascular Condition ▶◀ Revised Text ● New Code ▲ Revised Code Title

2007 ICD•9•CM **February 2006 • Volume 1 — 167**

Digestive System

567–569.0

Psoas Muscle Abscess

Psoas minor muscle
Psoas major muscle
Small intestine (ilium)
Peritoneal cavity
Small intestine (jejunum)
Abscess
Ascending colon
Ascending colon
Pelvic bone
Psoas major muscle
Psoas major muscle
Spinous process of L4
Erector spinae muscles

✓4ᵗʰ 567 Peritonitis and retroperitoneal infections

EXCLUDES   peritonitis:
    benign paroxysmal ▶(277.31)◀
    pelvic, female (614.5, 614.7)
    periodic familial ▶(277.31)◀
    puerperal (670)
    with or following:
      abortion (634-638 with .0, 639.0)
      appendicitis (540.0-540.1)
      ectopic or molar pregnancy (639.0)

DEF: Inflammation of the peritoneal cavity.

567.0 Peritonitis in infectious diseases classified elsewhere `CC`

    Code first underlying disease
    EXCLUDES   peritonitis:
      gonococcal (098.86)
      syphilitic (095.2)
      tuberculous (014.0)
CC Excl: 567.0-567.29, 567.38-567.9, 569.89, 569.9

567.1 Pneumococcal peritonitis `CC`
CC Excl: See code 567.0

✓5ᵗʰ 567.2 Other suppurative peritonitis
AHA: 4Q, '05, 74; 2Q, '01, 11, 12; 3Q, '99, 9; 2Q, '98, 19

    567.21 Peritonitis (acute) generalized `CC`
      Pelvic peritonitis, male
      CC Excl: See code 567.0

    567.22 Peritoneal abscess `CC`
      Abscess (of):   Abscess (of):
        abdominopelvic   retrocecal
        mesenteric   subdiaphragmatic
        omentum   subhepatic
        peritoneum   subphrenic
      CC Excl: See code 567.0

    567.23 Spontaneous bacterial peritonitis `CC`
      EXCLUDES ▶ bacterial peritonitis NOS (567.29)◀
      CC Excl: See code 567.0

    567.29 Other suppurative peritonitis `CC`
      Subphrenic peritonitis
      CC Excl: See code 567.0

✓5ᵗʰ 567.3 Retroperitoneal infections
AHA: 4Q, '05, 74

    567.31 Psoas muscle abscess `CC`
      CC Excl: 567.31, 728.0, 728.11-728.3, 728.81, 728.86

      DEF: Infection that extends into or around the psoas muscle that connects the lumbar vertebrae to the femur.

    567.38 Other retroperitoneal abscess `CC`
      AHA: 4Q, '05, 77
      CC Excl: See code 567.0

    567.39 Other retroperitoneal infections `CC`
      CC Excl: See code 567.0

✓5ᵗʰ 567.8 Other specified peritonitis
AHA: 4Q, '05, 74

567.81 Choleperitonitis `CC`
    Peritonitis due to bile
    CC Excl: See code 567.0

    DEF: Inflammation or infection due to presence of bile in the peritoneum resulting from rupture of the bile passages or gallbladder.

567.82 Sclerosing mesenteritis `CC`
    Fat necrosis of peritoneum
    (Idiopathic) sclerosing mesenteric fibrosis
    Mesenteric lipodystrophy
    Mesenteric panniculitis
    Retractile mesenteritis
    CC Excl: See code 567.0

    AHA: 4Q, '05, 77

    DEF: Inflammatory processes involving the mesenteric fat; progresses to fibrosis and necrosis of tissue.

567.89 Other specified peritonitis `CC`
    Chronic proliferative peritonitis
    Mesenteric saponification
    Peritonitis due to urine
    CC Excl: See code 567.0

567.9 Unspecified peritonitis `CC`
    Peritonitis NOS
    Peritonitis of unspecified cause
    CC Excl: See code 567.0
    AHA: 1Q, '04, 10

✓4ᵗʰ 568 Other disorders of peritoneum

568.0 Peritoneal adhesions (postoperative) (postinfection)
    Adhesions (of):   Adhesions (of):
      abdominal (wall)   mesenteric
      diaphragm   omentum
      intestine   stomach
      male pelvis   Adhesive bands
    EXCLUDES   adhesions:
      pelvic, female (614.6)
      with obstruction:
        duodenum (537.3)
        intestine (560.81)
    AHA: 3Q, '03, 7, 11; 4Q, '95, 55; 3Q, '95, 7; S-O, '85, 11
    DEF: Abnormal union of tissues in peritoneum.

✓5ᵗʰ 568.8 Other specified disorders of peritoneum

    568.81 Hemoperitoneum (nontraumatic) `CC`
      CC Excl: 568.81

    568.82 Peritoneal effusion (chronic)
      EXCLUDES   ascites NOS (789.5)
      DEF: Persistent leakage of fluid within peritoneal cavity.

    568.89 Other
      Peritoneal: Peritoneal:
        cyst   granuloma

568.9 Unspecified disorder of peritoneum

✓4ᵗʰ 569 Other disorders of intestine

569.0 Anal and rectal polyp
    Anal and rectal polyp NOS
    EXCLUDES   adenomatous anal and rectal polyp (211.4)

Rectum and Anus

Rectum
Sigmoid colon
Rectosigmoid junction
Inferior rectal valve
Levator ani muscle
Internal rectal venous plexus
Anal columns
External sphincter:
  deep
  subcutaneous
Internal sphincter
Pectinate line

| N Newborn Age: 0 | P Pediatric Age: 0-17 | M Maternity Age: 12-55 | A Adult Age: 15-124 | CC CC Condition | MC Major Complication | CD Complex Dx | HIV HIV Related Dx |

168 — Volume 1 • October 2006   2007 ICD•9•CM

569.1 Rectal prolapse

Procidentia:
   anus (sphincter)
   rectum (sphincter)
Proctoptosis

Prolapse:
   anal canal
   rectal mucosa

   EXCLUDES *prolapsed hemorrhoids (455.2, 455.5)*

569.2 Stenosis of rectum and anus

Stricture of anus (sphincter)

569.3 Hemorrhage of rectum and anus `cc`

   EXCLUDES *gastrointestinal bleeding NOS (578.9)*
                  melena (578.1)

CC Excl: 251.5, 456.0, 530.20-530.21, 530.7, 530.82, 530.85, 531.00-534.91, 535.01, 535.11, 535.21, 535.31, 535.41, 535.51, 535.61, 537.83, 562.02-562.03, 562.12-562.13, 569.3, 569.85, 578.0-578.9

AHA: ▶3Q, '05, 17◀

✓5ᵗʰ 569.4 Other specified disorders of rectum and anus

569.41 Ulcer of anus and rectum

Solitary ulcer ⎫ of anus (sphincter) or
Stercoral ulcer ⎬ rectum (sphincter)

569.42 Anal or rectal pain

AHA: 1Q, '03, 8; 1Q, '96, 13

569.49 Other

Granuloma ⎫ of rectum (sphincter)
Rupture ⎬

Hypertrophy of anal papillae
Proctitis NOS

   EXCLUDES *fistula of rectum to:*
                internal organs—see
                Alphabetic Index
                skin (565.1)
                hemorrhoids (455.0-455.9)
                incontinence of sphincter ani
                  (787.6)

569.5 Abscess of intestine `cc`

   EXCLUDES *appendiceal abscess (540.1)*

CC Excl: 569.5

✓5ᵗʰ 569.6 Colostomy and enterostomy complications

AHA: 4Q, '95, 58

DEF: Complication in a surgically created opening, from intestine to surface skin.

569.60 Colostomy and enterostomy complication, unspecified `cc`

CC Excl: 569.60-569.69

569.61 Infection of colostomy or enterostomy `cc`

Use additional code to identify organism
   (041.00-041.9)
Use additional code to specify type of
   infection, such as:
      abscess or cellulitis of abdomen (682.2)
      septicemia (038.0-038.9)

CC Excl: see code 569.60

569.62 Mechanical complication of colostomy and enterostomy `cc`

Malfunction of colostomy and
   enterostomy

CC Excl: 530.86-530.87, 536.40-536.49, 569.60-569.69, 997.4, 997.71, 997.91-997.99, 998.81, 998.83-998.9

AHA: ▶2Q, '05, 11◀; 1Q, '03, 10; 4Q, '98, 44

569.69 Other complication `cc`

Fistula   Prolapse
Hernia

CC Excl: see code 569.60

AHA: 3Q, '98, 16

✓5ᵗʰ 569.8 Other specified disorders of intestine

AHA: 4Q, '91, 25

569.81 Fistula of intestine, excluding rectum and anus

Fistula:
   abdominal wall
   enterocolic

Fistula:
   enteroenteric
   ileorectal

   EXCLUDES *fistula of intestine to internal*
                organs—see Alphabetic
                Index
                persistent postoperative fistula
                (998.6)

AHA: 3Q, '99, 8

569.82 Ulceration of intestine

Primary ulcer of intestine
Ulceration of colon

   EXCLUDES *that with perforation (569.83)*

569.83 Perforation of intestine `cc`

CC Excl: 569.83

569.84 Angiodysplasia of intestine (without mention of hemorrhage)

AHA: 3Q, '96, 10; 4Q, '90, 4; 4Q, '90, 21

DEF: Small vascular abnormalities of the intestinal tract without bleeding problems.

569.85 Angiodysplasia of intestine with hemorrhage `cc`

CC Excl: 251.5, 456.0, 530.20-530.21, 530.7, 530.82, 530.85, 531.00-534.91, 535.01, 535.11, 535.21, 535.31, 535.41, 535.51, 535.61, 537.83, 562.02-562.03, 562.12-562.13, 569.3, 569.85, 578.0-578.9

AHA: 3Q, '96, 9

DEF: Small vascular abnormalities of the intestinal tract with bleeding problems.

569.86 Dieulafoy lesion (hemorrhagic) of intestine `cc`

CC Excl: See 569.85

AHA: 4Q, '02, 60-61

569.89 Other

Enteroptosis
Granuloma ⎫ of intestine
Prolapse ⎬

Pericolitis
Perisigmoiditis
Visceroptosis

   EXCLUDES *gangrene of intestine,*
                mesentery, or omentum
                (557.0)
                hemorrhage of intestine NOS
                (578.9)
                obstruction of intestine (560.0-
                560.9)

AHA: 3Q, '96, 9

569.9 Unspecified disorder of intestine

OTHER DISEASES OF DIGESTIVE SYSTEM (570-579)

570 Acute and subacute necrosis of liver `cc`

Acute hepatic failure
Acute or subacute hepatitis, not specified as infective
Necrosis of liver (acute) (diffuse) (massive) (subacute)
Parenchymatous degeneration of liver
Yellow atrophy (liver) (acute) (subacute)

   EXCLUDES *icterus gravis of newborn (773.0-773.2)*
                serum hepatitis (070.2-070.3)
                that with:
                  abortion (634-638 with .7, 639.8)
                  ectopic or molar pregnancy (639.8)
                  pregnancy, childbirth, or the puerperium
                    (646.7)
                viral hepatitis (070.0-070.9)

CC Excl: 570, 573.4-573.9

AHA: ▶2Q, '05, 9;◀ 1Q, '00, 22

✓4ᵗʰ ✓5ᵗʰ Additional Digit Required   **Nonspecific PDx**   **Unacceptable PDx**   **Manifestation Code**   **MCV** Major Cardiovascular Condition   ▶◀ Revised Text   ● New Code   ▲ Revised Code Title

2007 ICD•9•CM

February 2006 • Volume 1 — 169

569.1–570

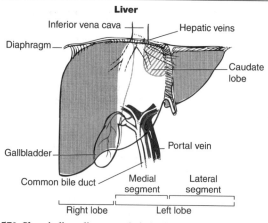

Liver

Inferior vena cava
Hepatic veins
Diaphragm
Caudate lobe
Gallbladder
Portal vein
Common bile duct
Medial segment
Lateral segment
Right lobe
Left lobe

✓4ᵗʰ **571 Chronic liver disease and cirrhosis**

571.0 Alcoholic fatty liver   A

571.1 Acute alcoholic hepatitis   A
Acute alcoholic liver disease
AHA: 2Q, '02, 4

571.2 Alcoholic cirrhosis of liver   CC A
Florid cirrhosis
Laennec's cirrhosis (alcoholic)
CC Excl: 571.2, 573.8-573.9
AHA: 2Q, '02, 4; 1Q, '02, 3; N-D, '85, 14
DEF: Fibrosis and dysfunction, of liver; due to alcoholic liver disease.

571.3 Alcoholic liver damage, unspecified   A

✓5ᵗʰ **571.4 Chronic hepatitis**
EXCLUDES   *viral hepatitis (acute) (chronic) (070.0-070.9)*

571.40 Chronic hepatitis, unspecified

571.41 Chronic persistent hepatitis

571.49 Other   CC
Chronic hepatitis:
  active
  aggressive
Recurrent hepatitis
CC Excl: 571.49-571.9, 573.8-573.9
AHA: 3Q, '99, 19; N-D, '85, 14

571.5 Cirrhosis of liver without mention of alcohol   CC
Cirrhosis of liver:
  NOS
  cryptogenic
  macronodular
  micronodular
  posthepatitic

Cirrhosis of liver:
  postnecrotic
  Healed yellow atrophy
    (liver)
  Portal cirrhosis
CC Excl: See code 571.49
DEF: Fibrosis and dysfunction of liver; not alcohol related.

571.6 Biliary cirrhosis   CC
Chronic nonsuppurative destructive cholangitis
Cirrhosis:
  cholangitic
  cholestatic
CC Excl: See code 571.49

571.8 Other chronic nonalcoholic liver disease
Chronic yellow atrophy (liver)
Fatty liver, without mention of alcohol
AHA: 2Q, '96, 12

571.9 Unspecified chronic liver disease without mention of alcohol

✓4ᵗʰ **572 Liver abscess and sequelae of chronic liver disease**

572.0 Abscess of liver   CC
EXCLUDES   *amebic liver abscess (006.3)*
CC Excl: 006.3, 572.0-572.1, 573.8-573.9

572.1 Portal pyemia   CC
Phlebitis of portal vein   Pylephlebitis
Portal thrombophlebitis   Pylethrombophlebitis
CC Excl: See code 572.0
DEF: Inflammation of portal vein or branches; may be due to intestinal disease; symptoms include fever, chills, jaundice, sweating, and abscess in various body parts.

572.2 Hepatic coma   CC
Hepatic encephalopathy
Hepatocerebral intoxication
Portal-systemic encephalopathy
CC Excl: 572.2, 573.8-573.9
AHA: 2Q, '05, 9; 1Q, '02, 3; 3Q, '95, 14

572.3 Portal hypertension
AHA: 3Q, '05, 15
DEF: Abnormally high blood pressure in the portal vein.

572.4 Hepatorenal syndrome   CC
EXCLUDES   *that following delivery (674.8)*
CC Excl: 572.4, 573.8-573.9
AHA: 3Q, '93, 15
DEF: Hepatic and renal failure characterized by cirrhosis with ascites or obstructive jaundice, oliguria, and low sodium concentration.

572.8 Other sequelae of chronic liver disease

✓4ᵗʰ **573 Other disorders of liver**
EXCLUDES   *amyloid or lardaceous degeneration of liver*
    ▶*(277.39)*◄
congenital cystic disease of liver (751.62)
glycogen infiltration of liver (271.0)
hepatomegaly NOS (789.1)
portal vein obstruction (452)

573.0 Chronic passive congestion of liver
DEF: Blood accumulation in liver tissue.

573.1 Hepatitis in viral diseases classified elsewhere   CC
Code first underlying disease as:
  Coxsackie virus disease (074.8)
  cytomegalic inclusion virus disease (078.5)
  infectious mononucleosis (075)
EXCLUDES   *hepatitis (in):*
    mumps (072.71)
    viral (070.0-070.9)
    yellow fever (060.0-060.9)
CC Excl: 573.1-573.3, 573.8-573.9

573.2 Hepatitis in other infectious diseases classified elsewhere   CC
Code first underlying disease, as:
  malaria (084.9)
EXCLUDES   *hepatitis in:*
    late syphilis (095.3)
    secondary syphilis (091.62)
    toxoplasmosis (130.5)
CC Excl: See code 573.1

573.3 Hepatitis, unspecified   CC
Toxic (noninfectious) hepatitis
Use additional E code to identify cause
CC Excl: See code 573.1
AHA: 3Q, '98, 3, 4; 4Q, '90, 26

573.4 Hepatic infarction   CC
CC Excl: 570, 573.4-573.9

573.8 Other specified disorders of liver
Hepatoptosis

573.9 Unspecified disorder of liver

N Newborn Age: 0   P Pediatric Age: 0-17   M Maternity Age: 12-55   A Adult Age: 15-124   CC CC Condition   MC Major Complication   CD Complex Dx   HIV HIV Related Dx

Digestive System

574–575.12

Gallbladder and Bile Ducts

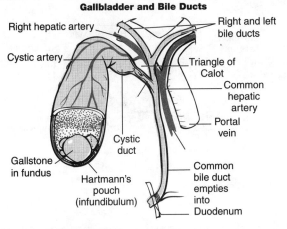

- Right hepatic artery
- Cystic artery
- Gallstone in fundus
- Cystic duct
- Hartmann's pouch (infundibulum)
- Right and left bile ducts
- Triangle of Calot
- Common hepatic artery
- Portal vein
- Common bile duct empties into Duodenum

✓4ᵗʰ **574 Cholelithiasis**

The following fifth-digit subclassification is for use with category 574:

    0 **without mention of obstruction**
    1 **with obstruction**

✓5ᵗʰ **574.0 Calculus of gallbladder with acute cholecystitis** `CC`

    Biliary calculus
    Calculus of cystic duct } with acute cholecystitis
    Cholelithiasis

    Any condition classifiable to 574.2 with acute cholecystitis

    CC Excl: For code 574.00: 574.00-574.21, 574.40, 574.60-574.61, 574.80-574.81, 575.0, 575.10-575.12, 575.9, 576.8-576.9;
    CC Excl: For code 574.01: 574.00-574.21, 574.60-574.61, 574.80-574.81, 575.0, 575.10-575.12, 575.9, 576.8-576.9

    AHA: 4Q, '96, 32

✓5ᵗʰ **574.1 Calculus of gallbladder with other cholecystitis** `CC`

    Biliary calculus
    Calculus of cystic duct } with cholecystitis
    Cholelithiasis

    Cholecystitis with cholelithiasis NOS
    Any condition classifiable to 574.2 with cholecystitis (chronic)

    CC Excl: See code 574.01

    AHA: 3Q, '99, 9; 4Q, '96, 32, 69; 2Q, '96, 13; **For code 574.10:** 1Q, '03, 5

✓5ᵗʰ **574.2 Calculus of gallbladder without mention of cholecystitis** `CC 1`

    Biliary: Cholelithiasis NOS
      calculus NOS   Colic (recurrent) of
      colic NOS   gallbladder
    Calculus of cystic duct   Gallstone (impacted)

    CC Excl: For code 574.21: See code 574.01

    AHA: For code 574.20: 1Q, '88, 14

✓5ᵗʰ **574.3 Calculus of bile duct with acute cholecystitis** `CC`

    Calculus of bile
      duct [any] } with acute
    Choledocholithiasis   cholecystitis

    Any condition classifiable to 574.5 with acute cholecystitis

    CC Excl: 574.30-575.12, 576.8-576.9

✓5ᵗʰ **574.4 Calculus of bile duct with other cholecystitis** `CC`

    Calculus of bile duct
      [any] } with cholecystitis
    Choledocholithiasis   (chronic)

    Any condition classifiable to 574.5 with cholecystitis (chronic)

    CC Excl: See code 574.3

✓5ᵗʰ **574.5 Calculus of bile duct without mention of cholecystitis** `CC`

    Calculus of: Choledocholithiasis
      bile duct [any]   Hepatic:
      common duct   colic (recurrent)
      hepatic duct   lithiasis

    CC Excl: See code 574.3

    AHA: 3Q, '94, 11

✓5ᵗʰ **574.6 Calculus of gallbladder and bile duct with acute cholecystitis** `CC`

    Any condition classifiable to 574.0 and 574.3

    CC Excl: 574.60-574.61, 575.0-575.12, 575.9, 576.8-576.9

    AHA: 4Q, '96, 32

✓5ᵗʰ **574.7 Calculus of gallbladder and bile duct with other cholecystitis** `CC`

    Any condition classifiable to 574.1 and 574.4

    CC Excl: 574.30-575.12, 576.8-576.9

    AHA: 4Q, '96, 32

✓5ᵗʰ **574.8 Calculus of gallbladder and bile duct with acute and chronic cholecystitis** `CC`

    Any condition classifiable to 574.6 and 574.7

    CC Excl: 574.80-574.81, 575.0-575.12, 575.9, 576.8-576.9

    AHA: 4Q, '96, 32

✓5ᵗʰ **574.9 Calculus of gallbladder and bile duct without cholecystitis** `CC`

    Any condition classifiable to 574.2 and 574.5

    CC Excl: See code 574.7

    AHA: 4Q, '96, 32

✓4ᵗʰ **575 Other disorders of gallbladder**

    575.0 Acute cholecystitis `CC`

      Abscess of gallbladder
      Angiocholecystitis
      Cholecystitis:
        emphysematous (acute) } without mention
        gangrenous   of calculus
        suppurative
      Empyema of gallbladder
      Gangrene of gallbladder

      EXCLUDES *that with:*
        acute and chronic cholecystitis (575.12)
        choledocholithiasis (574.3)
        choledocholithiasis and cholelithiasis (574.6)
        cholelithiasis (574.0)

    CC Excl: 574.60-574.61, 574.80-574.81, 575.0-575.12, 575.9, 576.8-576.9

    AHA: 3Q, '91, 17

✓5ᵗʰ **575.1 Other cholecystitis**

      Cholecystitis:
        NOS   } without mention
        chronic   of calculus

      EXCLUDES *that with:*
        choledocholithiasis (574.4)
        choledocholithiasis and cholelithiasis (574.8)
        cholelithiasis (574.1)

    AHA: 4Q, '96, 32

    575.10 Cholecystitis, unspecified
      Cholecystitis NOS

    575.11 Chronic cholecystitis

    575.12 Acute and chronic cholecystitis `CC`

      CC Excl: 575.0, 575.10-575.12, 575.9, 576.8-576.9

      AHA: 4Q, '97, 52; 4Q, '96, 32

✓4ᵗʰ / ✓5ᵗʰ **Additional Digit Required**   **Nonspecific PDx**   **Unacceptable PDx**   **Manifestation Code**   **MCV** Major Cardiovascular Condition   ►◄ Revised Text   ● New Code   ▲ Revised Code Title

575.2　Obstruction of gallbladder　`CC`

Occlusion
Stenosis　} of cystic duct or gallbladder without
Stricture　　mention of calculus

EXCLUDES　*that with calculus (574.0-574.2 with fifth-digit 1)*

CC Excl: 575.2-575.9, 576.8-576.9

575.3　Hydrops of gallbladder　`CC`

Mucocele of gallbladder

CC Excl: See code 575.2

AHA: 2Q, '89, 13

DEF: Serous fluid accumulation in bladder.

575.4　Perforation of gallbladder　`CC`

Rupture of cystic duct or gallbladder

CC Excl: See code 575.2

575.5　Fistula of gallbladder　`CC`

Fistula:　　　　　　Fistula:
　cholecystoduodenal　cholecystoenteric

CC Excl: See code 575.2

575.6　Cholesterolosis of gallbladder

Strawberry gallbladder

AHA: 4Q, '90, 17

DEF: Cholesterol deposits in gallbladder tissue.

575.8　Other specified disorders of gallbladder

Adhesions
Atrophy
Cyst　　　　　　(of) cystic duct or
Hypertrophy　　　　gallbladder
Nonfunctioning
Ulcer

Biliary dyskinesia

EXCLUDES　*Hartmann's pouch of intestine (V44.3)*
nonvisualization of gallbladder (793.3)

AHA: 4Q, '90, 26; 2Q, '89, 13

575.9　Unspecified disorder of gallbladder

✓4ᵗʰ **576　Other disorders of biliary tract**

EXCLUDES　*that involving the:*
cystic duct (575.0-575.9)
gallbladder (575.0-575.9)

576.0　Postcholecystectomy syndrome

AHA: 1Q, '88, 10

DEF: Jaundice or abdominal pain following cholecystectomy.

576.1　Cholangitis　`CC`

Cholangitis:　　　　Cholangitis:
　NOS　　　　　　　recurrent
　acute　　　　　　sclerosing
　ascending　　　　secondary
　chronic　　　　　stenosing
　primary　　　　　suppurative

CC Excl: 576.1, 576.8-576.9

AHA: 2Q, '99, 13

576.2　Obstruction of bile duct

Occlusion　} of bile duct, except cystic
Stenosis　　duct, without mention
Stricture　　of calculus

EXCLUDES　*congenital (751.61)*
that with calculus (574.3-574.5 with fifth-digit 1)

AHA: 3Q, '03, 17-18; 1Q, '01, 8; 2Q, '99, 13

576.3　Perforation of bile duct　`CC`

Rupture of bile duct, except cystic duct

CC Excl: 576.3-576.4, 576.8-576.9

576.4　Fistula of bile duct　`CC`

Choledochoduodenal fistula

CC Excl: See code 576.3

576.5　Spasm of sphincter of Oddi

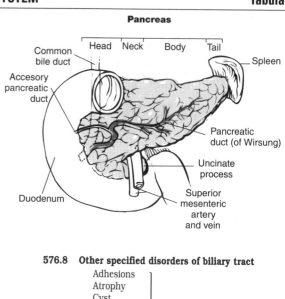

Pancreas

576.8　Other specified disorders of biliary tract

Adhesions
Atrophy
Cyst　　　　} of bile duct [any]
Hypertrophy
Stasis
Ulcer

EXCLUDES　*congenital choledochal cyst (751.69)*

AHA: 3Q, '03, 17; 2Q, '99, 14

576.9　Unspecified disorder of biliary tract

✓4ᵗʰ **577　Diseases of pancreas**

577.0　Acute pancreatitis　`CC`

Abscess of pancreas　Pancreatitis:
Necrosis of pancreas:　　acute (recurrent)
　acute　　　　　　　apoplectic
　infective　　　　　hemorrhagic
Pancreatitis:　　　　　subacute
　NOS　　　　　　　suppurative

EXCLUDES　*mumps pancreatitis (072.3)*

CC Excl: 577.0-577.1, 577.8-577.9

AHA: 3Q, '99, 9; 2Q, '98, 19; 2Q, '96, 13; 2Q, '89, 9

577.1　Chronic pancreatitis

Chronic pancreatitis:　Pancreatitis:
　NOS　　　　　　　painless
　infectious　　　　　recurrent
　interstitial　　　　relapsing

AHA: 1Q, '01, 8; 2Q, '96, 13; 3Q, '94, 11

577.2　Cyst and pseudocyst of pancreas　`CC`

CC Excl: 577.2, 577.8-577.9

577.8　Other specified diseases of pancreas

Atrophy
Calculus　　} of pancreas
Cirrhosis
Fibrosis

Pancreatic:
　infantilism
　necrosis:
　　NOS
　　aseptic
　　fat
Pancreatolithiasis

EXCLUDES　*fibrocystic disease of pancreas (277.00-277.09)*
islet cell tumor of pancreas (211.7)
pancreatic steatorrhea (579.4)

AHA: 1Q, '01, 8

577.9　Unspecified disease of pancreas

`N` Newborn Age: 0　`P` Pediatric Age: 0-17　`M` Maternity Age: 12-55　`A` Adult Age: 15-124　`CC` CC Condition　`MC` Major Complication　`CD` Complex Dx　`HIV` HIV Related Dx

Digestive System

✓4ᵗʰ 578 Gastrointestinal hemorrhage

> **EXCLUDES** *that with mention of:*
> *angiodysplasia of stomach and duodenum (537.83)*
> *angiodysplasia of intestine (569.85)*
> *diverticulitis, intestine:*
> *large (562.13)*
> *small (562.03)*
> *diverticulosis, intestine:*
> *large (562.12)*
> *small (562.02)*
> *gastritis and duodenitis (535.0-535.6)*
> *ulcer:*
> *duodenal, gastric, gastrojejuunal or peptic (531.00-534.91)*

AHA: 2Q, '92, 9; 4Q, '90, 20

578.0 Hematemesis   `CC`
Vomiting of blood
CC Excl: 251.5, 456.0, 530.20-530.21, 530.7, 530.82, 530.85, 531.00-534.91, 535.01, 535.11, 535.21, 535.31, 535.41, 535.51, 535.61, 537.83, 562.02-562.03, 562.12-562.13, 569.3, 569.85, 578.0-578.9

AHA: 2Q, '02, 4

578.1 Blood in stool   `CC`
Melena
> **EXCLUDES** *melena of the newborn (772.4, 777.3)*
> *occult blood (792.1)*

CC Excl: See code 578.0

AHA: 2Q, '92, 8

▽ **DRG 174**

578.9 Hemorrhage of gastrointestinal tract, unspecified   `CC`
Gastric hemorrhage
Intestinal hemorrhage
CC Excl: See code 578.0

AHA: ▶3Q, '05, 17;◀ N-D, '86, 9

▽ **DRG 174**

✓4ᵗʰ 579 Intestinal malabsorption

579.0 Celiac disease

Celiac:	Gee (-Herter) disease
crisis	Gluten enteropathy
infantilism	Idiopathic steatorrhea
rickets	Nontropical sprue

DEF: Malabsorption syndrome due to gluten consumption; symptoms include fetid, bulky, frothy, oily stools; distended abdomen, gas, weight loss, asthenia, electrolyte depletion and vitamin B, D and K deficiency.

579.1 Tropical sprue
Sprue: Tropical steatorrhea
NOS
tropical
DEF: Diarrhea, occurs in tropics; may be due to enteric infection and malnutrition.

579.2 Blind loop syndrome
Postoperative blind loop syndrome
DEF: Obstruction or impaired passage in small intestine due to alterations, from strictures or surgery; causes stasis, abnormal bacterial flora, diarrhea, weight loss, multiple vitamin deficiency, and megaloblastic anemia.

579.3 Other and unspecified postsurgical nonabsorption   `CC`
Hypoglycemia ⎫ following gastrointestinal
Malnutrition ⎭ surgery

CC Excl: 579.3-579.9

AHA: 4Q, '03, 104

579.4 Pancreatic steatorrhea
DEF: Excess fat in feces due to absence of pancreatic juice in intestine.

579.8 Other specified intestinal malabsorption
Enteropathy: Steatorrhea (chronic)
exudative
protein-losing

AHA: 1Q, '88, 6

579.9 Unspecified intestinal malabsorption
Malabsorption syndrome NOS

AHA: 4Q, '04, 59

578–579.9

✓4ᵗʰ Additional Digit Required   Nonspecific PDx   Unacceptable PDx   Manifestation Code   `MCV` Major Cardiovascular Condition   ▶◀ Revised Text   ● New Code   ▲ Revised Code Title
✓5ᵗʰ

2007 ICD•9•CM   **February 2006 • Volume 1 — 173**

10. DISEASES OF THE GENITOURINARY SYSTEM (580-629)

Kidney

Nephron

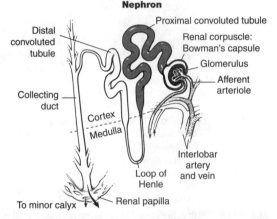

NEPHRITIS, NEPHROTIC SYNDROME, AND NEPHROSIS (580-589)

> **EXCLUDES** ▶ hypertensive chronic kidney disease (403.00-403.91, 404.00-404.93)◀

√4ᵗʰ **580 Acute glomerulonephritis**

INCLUDES acute nephritis

DEF: Acute, severe inflammation in tuft of capillaries that filter the kidneys.

580.0 With lesion of proliferative glomerulonephritis `CC`
Acute (diffuse) proliferative glomerulonephritis
Acute poststreptococcal glomerulonephritis

CC Excl: 016.00-016.06, 016.30-016.36, 016.90-016.96, 017.90-
017.96, 098.10, 098.19, 098.30-098.31, 098.89, 112.2, 131.00,
131.8-131.9, 250.40-250.43, 250.80-250.93, 274.10, 274.19,
580.0-591, 593.0-593.2, 593.89, 593.9, 599.7-599.9

580.4 With lesion of rapidly progressive glomerulonephritis `CC`
Acute nephritis with lesion of necrotizing
glomerulitis

CC Excl: See code 580.0

DEF: Acute glomerulonephritis; progresses to ESRD with diffuse
epithelial proliferation.

√5ᵗʰ **580.8 With other specified pathological lesion in kidney**

580.81 Acute glomerulonephritis in diseases
classified elsewhere `CC`
Code first underlying disease, as:
infectious hepatitis (070.0-070.9)
mumps (072.79)
subacute bacterial endocarditis (421.0)
typhoid fever (002.0)
CC Excl: See code 580.0

580.89 Other `CC`
Glomerulonephritis, acute, with lesion of:
exudative nephritis
interstitial (diffuse) (focal) nephritis
CC Excl: 016.00-016.06, 016.30-016.36, 016.90-016.96,
017.90-017.96, 098.10, 098.19, 098.30-098.31, 098.89,
112.2, 131.00, 131.8-131.9, 274.10, 274.19, 580.0-591,
593.0-593.2, 593.89, 593.9, 599.7-599.9

580.9 Acute glomerulonephritis with unspecified `CC`
pathological lesion in kidney
Glomerulonephritis:
NOS
hemorrhagic }
Nephritis } specified as acute
Nephropathy

CC Excl: 016.00-016.06, 016.30-016.36, 016.90-016.96, 017.90-
017.96, 098.10, 098.19, 098.30-098.31, 098.89, 112.2, 131.00,
131.8-131.9, 250.40-250.43, 250.80-250.93, 274.10, 274.19, 580.0-591,
593.0-593.2, 593.89, 593.9, 599.7-599.9

√4ᵗʰ **581 Nephrotic syndrome**

DEF: Disease process marked by symptoms such as; extensive edema, notable
proteinuria, hypoalbuminemia, and susceptibility to intercurrent infections.

581.0 With lesion of proliferative glomerulonephritis `CC`
CC Excl: See code 580.9

581.1 With lesion of membranous glomerulonephritis `CC`
Epimembranous nephritis
Idiopathic membranous glomerular disease
Nephrotic syndrome with lesion of:
focal glomerulosclerosis
sclerosing membranous glomerulonephritis
segmental hyalinosis
CC Excl: See code 580.9

581.2 With lesion of membranoproliferative `CC`
glomerulonephritis
Nephrotic syndrome with lesion (of):
endothelial
hypocomplementemic
persistent
lobular } glomerulonephritis
mesangiocapillary
mixed membranous and
proliferative

CC Excl: See code 580.9

DEF: Glomerulonephritis combined with clinical features of
nephrotic syndrome; characterized by uneven thickening of
glomerular capillary walls and mesangial cell increase; slowly
progresses to ESRD.

581.3 With lesion of minimal change `CC`
glomerulonephritis
Foot process disease
Lipoid nephrosis
Minimal change:
glomerular disease
glomerulitis
nephrotic syndrome
CC Excl: See code 580.9

√4ᵗʰ **581.8 With other specified pathological lesion in kidney**

581.81 Nephrotic syndrome in diseases
classified elsewhere `CC`
Code first underlying disease, as:
amyloidosis ▶(277.30-277.39)◀
diabetes mellitus (250.4)
malaria (084.9)
polyarteritis (446.0)
systemic lupus erythematosus (710.0)
EXCLUDES nephrosis in epidemic
hemorrhagic fever
(078.6)

CC Excl: See code 580.9

AHA: 3Q, '91, 8,12; S-O, '85, 3

581.89 Other `CC`
Glomerulonephritis with edema and lesion
of:
exudative nephritis
interstitial (diffuse) (focal) nephritis
CC Excl: See code 580.9

√4ᵗʰ / √5ᵗʰ Additional Digit Required   Nonspecific PDx   Unacceptable PDx   Manifestation Code   `MCV` Major Cardiovascular Condition   ▶◀ Revised Text   ● New Code   ▲ Revised Code Title

Genitourinary System

581.9–583.9

581.9   Nephrotic syndrome with unspecified pathological lesion in kidney   `CC`
Glomerulonephritis with edema NOS
Nephritis:
     nephrotic NOS
     with edema NOS
Nephrosis NOS
Renal disease with edema NOS
CC Excl: See code 580.9

✓4ᵗʰ **582   Chronic glomerulonephritis**
      `INCLUDES`   chronic nephritis
DEF: Slow progressive type of nephritis characterized by inflammation of the capillary loops in the glomeruli of the kidney, which leads to renal failure.

582.0   With lesion of proliferative glomerulonephritis
Chronic (diffuse) proliferative glomerulonephritis

582.1   With lesion of membranous glomerulonephritis
Chronic glomerulonephritis:
     membranous
     sclerosing
Focal glomerulosclerosis
Segmental hyalinosis
AHA: S-O, '84, 16

582.2   With lesion of membranoproliferative glomerulonephritis
Chronic glomerulonephritis:
     endothelial
     hypocomplementemic persistent
     lobular
     membranoproliferative
     mesangiocapillary
     mixed membranous and proliferative
DEF: Chronic glomerulonephritis with mesangial cell proliferation.

582.4   With lesion of rapidly progressive glomerulonephritis
Chronic nephritis with lesion of necrotizing glomerulitis
DEF: Chronic glomerulonephritisrapidly progresses to ESRD; marked by diffuse epithelial proliferation.

✓5ᵗʰ **582.8   With other specified pathological lesion in kidney**
    582.81   Chronic glomerulonephritis in diseases classified elsewhere
       Code first underlying disease, as:
         amyloidosis ▶(277.30-277.39)◀
         systemic lupus erythematosus (710.0)
    582.89   Other
       Chronic glomerulonephritis with lesion of:
         exudative nephritis
         interstitial (diffuse) (focal) nephritis

582.9   Chronic glomerulonephritis with unspecified pathological lesion in kidney
Glomerulonephritis: ⎫
     NOS   ⎪
     hemorrhagic   ⎬ specified as chronic
Nephritis   ⎪
Nephropathy   ⎭
AHA: 2Q, '01, 12

✓4ᵗʰ **583   Nephritis and nephropathy, not specified as acute or chronic**
      `INCLUDES`   "renal disease" so stated, not specified as acute or chronic but with stated pathology or cause

583.0   With lesion of proliferative glomerulonephritis
Proliferative: Proliferative:
   glomerulonephritis   nephritis NOS
   (diffuse) NOS   nephropathy NOS

583.1   With lesion of membranous glomerulonephritis
Membranous:
     glomerulonephritis NOS
     nephritis NOS
Membranous nephropathy NOS
DEF: Kidney inflammation or dysfunction with deposits on glomerular capillary basement membranes.

583.2   With lesion of membranoproliferative glomerulonephritis
Membranoproliferative:
     glomerulonephritis NOS
     nephritis NOS
     nephropathy NOS
Nephritis NOS, with lesion of:
     hypocomplementemic   ⎫
       persistent   ⎪
     lobular   ⎬ glomerulonephritis
     mesangiocapillary   ⎪
     mixed membranous   ⎪
       and proliferative   ⎭
DEF: Kidney inflammation or dysfunction with mesangial cell proliferation.

583.4   With lesion of rapidly progressive glomerulonephritis   `CC`
Necrotizing or rapidly progressive:
     glomerulitis NOS
     glomerulonephritis NOS
     nephritis NOS
     nephropathy NOS
Nephritis, unspecified, with lesion of necrotizing glomerulitis
CC Excl: See code 580.9
DEF: Kidney inflammation or dysfunction; rapidly progresses to ESRD marked by diffuse epithelial proliferation.

583.6   With lesion of renal cortical necrosis
Nephritis NOS   ⎫ with (renal) cortical
Nephropathy NOS   ⎭   necrosis
Renal cortical necrosis NOS

583.7   With lesion of renal medullary necrosis
Nephritis NOS   ⎫ with (renal) medullary
Nephropathy NOS   ⎭   [papillary] necrosis

✓5ᵗʰ **583.8   With other specified pathological lesion in kidney**
    583.81   Nephritis and nephropathy, not specified as acute or chronic, in diseases classified elsewhere
       Code first underlying disease, as:
         amyloidosis ▶(277.30-277.39)◀
         diabetes mellitus (250.4)
         gonococcal infection (098.19)
         Goodpasture's syndrome (446.21)
         systemic lupus erythematosus (710.0)
         tuberculosis (016.0)
       `EXCLUDES`   gouty nephropathy (274.10)
                 syphilitic nephritis (095.4)
      AHA: 2Q, '03, 7; 3Q, '91, 8; S-O, '85, 3

    583.89   Other
       Glomerulitis   ⎫ with lesion of:
       Glomerulonephritis   ⎪   exudative
       Nephritis   ⎬   nephritis
       Nephropathy   ⎪   interstitial
       Renal disease   ⎭   nephritis

583.9   With unspecified pathological lesion in kidney
Glomerulitis   ⎫
Glomerulonephritis   ⎬ NOS
Nephritis   ⎪
Nephropathy   ⎭
      `EXCLUDES`   *nephropathy complicating pregnancy, labor, or the puerperium (642.0-642.9, 646.2)*
                renal disease NOS with no stated cause (593.9)

`N` Newborn Age: 0   `P` Pediatric Age: 0-17   `M` Maternity Age: 12-55   `A` Adult Age: 15-124   `CC` CC Condition   `MC` Major Complication   `CD` Complex Dx   `HIV` HIV Related Dx

√4ᵗʰ **584 Acute renal failure**

> EXCLUDES   *following labor and delivery (669.3)*
> *posttraumatic (958.5)*
> *that complicating:*
>   *abortion (634-638 with .3, 639.3)*
>   *ectopic or molar pregnancy (639.3)*

AHA: 1Q, '93, 18; 2Q, '92, 5; 4Q, '92, 22

DEF: State resulting from increasing urea and related substances from the blood (azotemia), often with urine output of less than 500 ml per day.

584.5 With lesion of tubular necrosis CC MC
> Lower nephron nephrosis
> Renal failure with (acute) tubular necrosis
> Tubular necrosis:
>   NOS
>   acute

CC Excl: 250.40-250.43, 250.80-250.93, 274.10, 274.19, 580.0-591, 593.0-593.2, 593.89, 593.9, 599.7-599.9, 753.0-753.3, 753.9

DEF: Acute decline in kidney efficiency with destruction of tubules.

584.6 With lesion of renal cortical necrosis CC MC
CC Excl: See code 584.5

DEF: Acute decline in kidney efficiency with destruction of renal tissues that filter blood.

584.7 With lesion of renal medullary [papillary] necrosis CC MC
> Necrotizing renal papillitis

CC Excl: See code 584.5

DEF: Acute decline in kidney efficiency with destruction of renal tissues that collect urine.

584.8 With other specified pathological lesion in kidney CC MC
CC Excl: 250.40-250.43, 250.80-250.93, 274.10, 274.19, 580.0-591, 593.0-593.2, 593.89, 593.9, 599.7-599.9

AHA: N-D, '85, 1

584.9 Acute renal failure, unspecified CC MC
CC Excl: 250.40-250.43, 250.80-250.93, 274.10, 274.19, 580.0-591, 593.0-593.2, 593.89-593.9, 599.7-599.9, 753.0-753.3, 753.9

AHA: 2Q, '05, 18; 2Q, '03, 7; 1Q, '03, 22; 3Q, '02, 21, 28; 2Q, '01, 14; 1Q, '00, 22; 3Q, '96, 9; 4Q, '88, 1

▽ **DRG** 316

√4ᵗʰ **585 Chronic kidney disease [CKD]**
> Chronic uremia
> ▶Code first hypertensive chronic kidney disease, if applicable, (403.00-403.91, 404.00-404.94)◀
> Use additional code to identify kidney transplant status, if applicable (V42.0)
> Use additional code to identify manifestation as:
>   uremic:
>   neuropathy (357.4)
>   pericarditis (420.0)

AHA: 4Q, '05, 68, 77; 1Q, '04, 5; 4Q, '03, 61, 111; 2Q, '03, 7; 2Q, '01, 12, 13; 1Q, '01, 3; 4Q, '98, 55; 3Q, '98, 6, 7; 2Q, '98, 20; 3Q, '96, 9; 1Q, '93, 18; 3Q, '91, 8; 4Q, '89, 1; N-D, '85, 15; S-O, '84, 3

585.1 Chronic kidney disease, Stage I CC
CC Excl: 250.40-250.43, 250.80-250.83, 250.90-250.93, 274.10, 274.19, 580.0-591, 593.0-593.2, 593.89-593.9, 599.7-599.9, 753.0-753.3, 753.9

DEF: Some kidney damage; normal or slightly increased GFR (> 90).

585.2 Chronic kidney disease, Stage II (mild) CC
CC Excl: See code 585.1

DEF: Kidney damage with mild decrease in GFR (60–89).

585.3 Chronic kidney disease, Stage III (moderate) CC
CC Excl: See code 585.1

AHA: 4Q, '05, 69

DEF: Kidney damage with moderate decrease in GFR (30–59).

585.4 Chronic kidney disease, Stage IV (severe) CC
CC Excl: See code 585.1

DEF: Kidney damage with severe decrease in GFR (15–29).

585.5 Chronic kidney disease, Stage V CC
> EXCLUDES ▶ *chronic kidney disease, stage V requiring chronic dialysis (585.6)*◀

CC Excl: See code 585.1

DEF: Kidney failure with GFR value of less than 15.

585.6 End stage renal disease CC
> ▶Chronic kidney disease requiring chronic dialysis◀

CC Excl: See code 585.1

AHA: 4Q, '05, 79

DEF: Federal government indicator of a stage V CKD patient undergoing treatment by dialysis or transplantation.

585.9 Chronic kidney disease, unspecified CC
> Chronic renal disease
> Chronic renal failure NOS
> Chronic renal insufficiency

CC Excl: See code 585.1

AHA: 4Q, '05, 79

586 Renal failure, unspecified
> Uremia NOS

> EXCLUDES   *following labor and delivery (669.3)*
> *posttraumatic renal failure (958.5)*
> *that complicating:*
>   *abortion (634-638 with .3, 639.3)*
>   *ectopic or molar pregnancy (639.3)*
> *uremia:*
>   *extrarenal (788.9)*
>   *prerenal (788.9)*
>   *with any condition classifiable to 401 (403.0-403.9 with fifth-digit 1)*

AHA: 3Q, '98, 6; 1Q, '93, 18; 1Q, '88, 3

DEF: Renal failure: kidney functions cease; malfunction may be due to inability to excrete metabolized substances or retain level of electrolytes.

DEF: Uremia: excess urea, creatinine and other nitrogenous products of protein and amino acid metabolism in blood due to reduced excretory function in bilateral kidney disease; also called azotemia.

587 Renal sclerosis, unspecified
> Atrophy of kidney   Renal:
> Contracted kidney   cirrhosis
>   fibrosis

> EXCLUDES   *nephrosclerosis (arteriolar) (arteriosclerotic) (403.00-403.91)*
>   *with hypertension (403.00-403.91)*

√4ᵗʰ **588 Disorders resulting from impaired renal function**

588.0 Renal osteodystrophy
> Azotemic osteodystrophy
> Phosphate-losing tubular disorders
> Renal:
>   dwarfism   infantilism
>   rickets

DEF: Bone disorder that results in various bone diseases such as osteomalacia, osteoporosis or osteosclerosis; caused by impaired renal function, an abnormal level of phosphorus in the blood and impaired stimulation of the parathyroid.

588.1 Nephrogenic diabetes insipidus
> EXCLUDES   *diabetes insipidus NOS (253.5)*

DEF: Type of diabetes due to renal tubules inability to reabsorb water; not responsive to vasopressin; may develop into chronic renal insufficiency.

√5ᵗʰ **588.8 Other specified disorders resulting from impaired renal function**
> EXCLUDES   *secondary hypertension (405.0-405.9)*

588.81 Secondary hyperparathyroidism (of renal origin)
> Secondary hyperparathyroidism NOS

AHA: 4Q, '04, 58-59

DEF: Parathyroid dysfunction caused by chronic renal failure; phosphate clearance is impaired, phosphate is released from bone, vitamin D is not produced, intestinal calcium absorption is low, and blood levels of calcium are lowered causing excessive production of parathyroid hormone.

√4ᵗʰ √5ᵗʰ Additional Digit Required   Nonspecific PDx   Unacceptable PDx   Manifestation Code   **MCV** Major Cardiovascular Condition   ▶◀ Revised Text   ● New Code   ▲ Revised Code Title

Genitourinary System

588.89–593.4

588.89 Other specified disorders resulting from impaired renal function
Hypokalemic nephropathy

588.9 Unspecified disorder resulting from impaired renal function

✓4th **589 Small kidney of unknown cause**

589.0 Unilateral small kidney

589.1 Bilateral small kidneys

589.9 Small kidney, unspecified

OTHER DISEASES OF URINARY SYSTEM (590-599)

✓4th **590 Infections of kidney**
Use additional code to identify organism, such as Escherichia coli [E. coli] (041.4)

✓5th **590.0 Chronic pyelonephritis**
Chronic pyelitis
Chronic pyonephrosis
Code if applicable, any casual condition first

590.00 Without lesion of renal medullary necrosis

590.01 With lesion of renal medullary necrosis

✓5th **590.1 Acute pyelonephritis**
Acute pyelitis   Acute pyonephrosis

590.10 Without lesion of renal medullary necrosis CC
CC Excl: 016.00-016.06, 016.30-016.36, 016.90-016.96, 017.90-017.96, 098.10, 098.19, 098.30-098.31, 098.89, 112.2, 131.00, 131.8-131.9, 250.40-250.43, 250.80-250.93, 274.10, 274.19, 580.0-591, 593.0-593.2, 593.89, 593.9, 599.0, 599.7-599.9

🔻 DRG 320

590.11 With lesion of renal medullary necrosis CC
CC Excl: See code 590.10

590.2 Renal and perinephric abscess CC
Abscess: Abscess:
  kidney   perirenal
  nephritic   Carbuncle of kidney
CC Excl: See code 590.10

590.3 Pyeloureteritis cystica CC
Infection of renal pelvis and ureter
Ureteritis cystica
CC Excl: 016.00-016.06, 016.30-016.36, 016.90-016.96, 017.90-017.96, 098.10, 098.19, 098.30-098.31, 098.89, 112.2, 131.00, 131.8-131.9, 274.10, 274.19, 580.0-591, 593.0-593.2, 593.89, 593.9, 599.0, 599.7-599.9

DEF: Inflammation and formation of submucosal cysts in the kidney, pelvis, and ureter.

✓5th **590.8 Other pyelonephritis or pyonephrosis, not specified as acute or chronic**

590.80 Pyelonephritis, unspecified CC
Pyelitis NOS
Pyelonephritis NOS
CC Excl: See code 590.3

AHA: 1Q, '98, 10; 4Q, '97, 40

🔻 DRG 320

590.81 Pyelitis or pyelonephritis in diseases classified elsewhere CC
Code first underlying disease, as:
tuberculosis (016.0)
CC Excl: See code 590.3

590.9 Infection of kidney, unspecified CC
EXCLUDES   urinary tract infection NOS (599.0)
CC Excl: See code 590.3

Genitourinary System

Genitourinary System
Inferior vena cava — Aorta — Left kidney — Right kidney — Ureter — Anterior division of internal iliac artery — Ovarian or testicular artery and vein — Superior and Inferior vesicular arteries — Urinary bladder — Ureteral orifice — Urogenital diaphragm — Urethra

591 Hydronephrosis CC
Hydrocalycosis   Hydroureteronephrosis
Hydronephrosis
EXCLUDES   congenital hydronephrosis (753.29)
hydroureter (593.5)

CC Excl: See code 590.3

AHA: 2Q, '98, 9

DEF: Distention of kidney and pelvis, with urine build-up due to ureteral obstruction; pyonephrosis may result.

✓4th **592 Calculus of kidney and ureter**
EXCLUDES   nephrocalcinosis (275.4)

592.0 Calculus of kidney
Nephrolithiasis NOS   Staghorn calculus
Renal calculus or stone   Stone in kidney
EXCLUDES   uric acid nephrolithiasis (274.11)

AHA: 1Q, '00, 4

592.1 Calculus of ureter CC
Ureteric stone
Ureterolithiasis
CC Excl: 592.0-592.9, 593.3-593.5, 593.89-594.9, 599.60-599.9

AHA: 2Q, '98, 9; 1Q, '98, 10; 1Q, '91, 11

592.9 Urinary calculus, unspecified
AHA: 1Q, '98, 10; 4Q, '97, 40

✓4th **593 Other disorders of kidney and ureter**

593.0 Nephroptosis
Floating kidney   Mobile kidney

593.1 Hypertrophy of kidney

593.2 Cyst of kidney, acquired
Cyst (multiple) (solitary) of kidney, not congenital
Peripelvic (lymphatic) cyst
EXCLUDES   calyceal or pyelogenic cyst of kidney (591)
congenital cyst of kidney (753.1)
polycystic (disease of) kidney (753.1)

AHA: 4Q, '90, 3

DEF: Abnormal, fluid-filled sac in the kidney, not present at birth.

593.3 Stricture or kinking of ureter
Angulation
Constriction } of ureter (post-operative)

Stricture of pelviureteric junction
AHA: 2Q, '98, 9

DEF: Stricture or knot in tube connecting kidney to bladder.

593.4 Other ureteric obstruction
Idiopathic retroperitoneal fibrosis
Occlusion NOS of ureter
EXCLUDES   that due to calculus (592.1)

AHA: 2Q, '97, 4

N Newborn Age: 0   P Pediatric Age: 0-17   M Maternity Age: 12-55   A Adult Age: 15-124   CC CC Condition   MC Major Complication   CD Complex Dx   HIV HIV Related Dx

593.5 Hydroureter `CC`

> EXCLUDES   congenital hydroureter (753.22)
> hydroureteronephrosis (591)

CC Excl: 593.3-593.5, 593.89, 593.9, 595.0-595.9, 596.8-596.9, 599.0, 599.60-599.9, 753.4-753.5, 753.9

593.6 Postural proteinuria

> Benign postural proteinuria
> Orthostatic proteinuria
> EXCLUDES   proteinuria NOS (791.0)

DEF: Excessive amounts of serum protein in the urine caused by the body position, e.g., orthostatic and lordotic.

√5ᵗʰ **593.7 Vesicoureteral reflux**

AHA: 4Q, '94, 42

DEF: Backflow of urine, from bladder into ureter due to obstructed bladder neck.

593.70 Unspecified or without reflux nephropathy
593.71 With reflux nephropathy, unilateral
593.72 With reflux nephropathy, bilateral
593.73 With reflux nephropathy NOS

√5ᵗʰ **593.8 Other specified disorders of kidney and ureter**

593.81 Vascular disorders of kidney

> Renal (artery):   Renal (artery):
> embolism   thrombosis
> hemorrhage   Renal infarction

593.82 Ureteral fistula

> Intestinoureteral fistula
> EXCLUDES   fistula between ureter and
> female genital tract
> (619.0)

DEF: Abnormal communication, between tube connecting kidney to bladder and another structure.

593.89 Other

> Adhesions, kidney   Polyp of ureter
> or ureter   Pyelectasia
> Periureteritis   Ureterocele
> EXCLUDES   tuberculosis of ureter (016.2)
> ureteritis cystica (590.3)

593.9 Unspecified disorder of kidney and ureter

> Acute renal disease
> Acute renal insufficiency
> Renal disease NOS
> Salt-losing nephritis or syndrome
> EXCLUDES   chronic renal insufficiency (585.9)
> cystic kidney disease (753.1)
> nephropathy, so stated (583.0-583.9)
> renal disease:
> arising in pregnancy or the
> puerperium (642.1-642.2,
> 642.4-642.7, 646.2)
> not specified as acute or chronic, but
> with stated pathology or cause
> (583.0-583.9)

AHA: ▶4Q, '05, 79;◀ 1Q, '93, 17

▽ **DRG 331**

√4ᵗʰ **594 Calculus of lower urinary tract**

594.0 Calculus in diverticulum of bladder

DEF: Stone or mineral deposit in abnormal sac on the bladder wall.

594.1 Other calculus in bladder

> Urinary bladder stone
> EXCLUDES   staghorn calculus (592.0)

DEF: Stone or mineral deposit in bladder.

594.2 Calculus in urethra

DEF: Stone or mineral deposit in tube that empties urine from bladder.

594.8 Other lower urinary tract calculus

AHA: J-F, '85, 16

594.9 Calculus of lower urinary tract, unspecified

> EXCLUDES   calculus of urinary tract NOS (592.9)

√4ᵗʰ **595 Cystitis**

> EXCLUDES   prostatocystitis (601.3)
> Use additional code to identify organism, such as Escherichia coli [E. coli] (041.4)

595.0 Acute cystitis `CC`

> EXCLUDES   trigonitis (595.3)

CC Excl: 016.10-016.16, 016.30-016.36, 016.90-016.96, 017.90-017.96, 098.0, 098.11, 098.2, 098.39, 098.89, 112.2, 131.00, 131.8-131.9, 593.3-593.5, 593.89, 593.9, 595.0-595.9, 596.8-596.9, 599.0, 599.60-599.9

AHA: 2Q, '99, 15

DEF: Acute inflammation of bladder.

595.1 Chronic interstitial cystitis `CC`

> Hunner's ulcer   Submucous cystitis
> Panmural fibrosis of bladder

CC Excl: See code 595.0

DEF: Inflamed lesion affecting bladder wall; symptoms include urinary frequency, pain on bladder filling, nocturia, and distended bladder.

595.2 Other chronic cystitis `CC`

> Chronic cystitis NOS   Subacute cystitis
> EXCLUDES   trigonitis (595.3)

CC Excl: See code 595.0

DEF: Persistent inflammation of bladder.

595.3 Trigonitis

> Follicular cystitis   Urethrotrigonitis
> Trigonitis (acute) (chronic)

DEF: Inflammation of the triangular area of the bladder called the trigonum vesicae.

595.4 Cystitis in diseases classified elsewhere `CC`

> Code first underlying disease, as:
> actinomycosis (039.8)
> amebiasis (006.8)
> bilharziasis (120.0-120.9)
> Echinococcus infestation (122.3, 122.6)
> EXCLUDES   cystitis:
> diphtheritic (032.84)
> gonococcal (098.11, 098.31)
> monilial (112.2)
> trichomonal (131.09)
> tuberculous (016.1)

CC Excl: See code 595.0

√5ᵗʰ **595.8 Other specified types of cystitis**

595.81 Cystitis cystica `CC`

CC Excl: See code 595.0

DEF: Inflammation of the bladder characterized by formation of multiple cysts.

595.82 Irradiation cystitis `CC`

> Use additional E code to identify cause

CC Excl: See code 595.0

DEF: Inflammation of the bladder due to effects of radiation.

595.89 Other `CC`

> Abscess of bladder   Cystitis:
> Cystitis: emphysematous
> bullous   glandularis

CC Excl: See code 595.0

595.9 Cystitis, unspecified `CC`

CC Excl: See code 595.0

√4ᵗʰ √5ᵗʰ Additional Digit Required   Nonspecific PDx   Unacceptable PDx   Manifestation Code   `MCV` Major Cardiovascular Condition   ▶◀ Revised Text   ● New Code   ▲ Revised Code Title

Genitourinary System

596–597.0

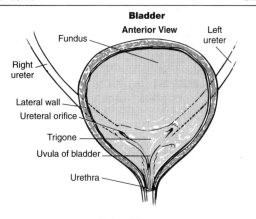

Bladder
Anterior View

- Fundus
- Right ureter
- Left ureter
- Lateral wall
- Ureteral orifice
- Trigone
- Uvula of bladder
- Urethra

Lateral View

- Urachus
- Left ureter
- Peritoneum
- Pubic bone
- Urogenital diaphragm

✓4ᵗʰ **596 Other disorders of bladder**

Use additional code to identify urinary incontinence (625.6, 788.30-788.39)

AHA: M-A, '87, 10

596.0 Bladder neck obstruction `CC`

Contracture (acquired)
Obstruction (acquired) } of bladder neck or vesicourethral orifice
Stenosis (acquired)

EXCLUDES congenital (753.6)

CC Excl: 185, 188.0-188.9, 189.3-189.9, 596.0, 596.4, 596.51-596.59, 596.8-596.9, 600.00-600.9, 601.0-602.9

AHA: 3Q, '02, 28; 2Q, '01, 14; N-D, '86, 10

DEF: Bladder outlet and vesicourethral obstruction; occurs more often in males as a consequence of benign prostatic hypertrophy or prostatic cancer; may also occur in either sex due to strictures, following radiation, cystoscopy, catheterization, injury, infection, blood clots, bladder cancer, impaction or disease compressing bladder neck.

596.1 Intestinovesical fistula `CC`

Fistula: Fistula:
enterovesical   vesicoenteric
vesicocolic   vesicorectal

CC Excl: 098.0, 098.2, 098.39, 098.89, 596.1-596.2, 596.8-596.9, 599.7-599.9, 788.1

DEF: Abnormal communication, between intestine and bladder.

596.2 Vesical fistula, not elsewhere classified `CC`

Fistula: Fistula:
bladder NOS   vesicocutaneous
urethrovesical   vesicoperineal

EXCLUDES fistula between bladder and female genital tract (619.0)

CC Excl: See code 596.1

DEF: Abnormal communication between bladder and another structure.

596.3 Diverticulum of bladder

Diverticulitis
Diverticulum (acquired) (false) } of bladder

EXCLUDES that with calculus in diverticulum of bladder (594.0)

DEF: Abnormal pouch in bladder wall.

596.4 Atony of bladder `CC`

High compliance bladder
Hypotonicity
Inertia } of bladder

EXCLUDES neurogenic bladder (596.54)

CC Excl: 596.4, 596.51-596.59, 596.8-596.9, 599.7-599.9, 788.1

DEF: Distended, bladder with loss of expulsive force; linked to CNS disease.

✓5ᵗʰ **596.5 Other functional disorders of bladder**

EXCLUDES cauda equina syndrome with neurogenic bladder (344.61)

596.51 Hypertonicity of bladder

Hyperactivity
Overactive bladder

DEF: Abnormal tension of muscular wall of bladder; may appear after surgery of voluntary nerve.

596.52 Low bladder compliance

DEF: Low bladder capacity; causes increased pressure and frequent urination.

596.53 Paralysis of bladder

DEF: Impaired bladder motor function due to nerve or muscle damage.

596.54 Neurogenic bladder NOS

AHA: 1Q, '01, 12

DEF: Unspecified dysfunctional bladder due to lesion of central, peripheral nervous system; may result in incontinence, residual urine retention, urinary infection, stones and renal failure.

596.55 Detrusor sphincter dyssynergia

DEF: Instability of the urinary bladder sphincter muscle associated with urinary incontinence..

596.59 Other functional disorder of bladder

Detrusor instability

DEF: Detrusor instability: instability of bladder; marked by uninhibited contractions often leading to incontinence.

596.6 Rupture of bladder, nontraumatic `CC`

CC Excl: 596.6-596.9, 599.7-599.9, 788.1

596.7 Hemorrhage into bladder wall `CC`

Hyperemia of bladder

EXCLUDES acute hemorrhagic cystitis (595.0)

CC Excl: See code 596.6

596.8 Other specified disorders of bladder

Bladder: Bladder:
calcified   hemorrhage
contracted   hypertrophy

EXCLUDES cystocele, female (618.01-618.02, 618.09, 618.2-618.4)
hernia or prolapse of bladder, female (618.01-618.02, 618.09, 618.2-618.4)

AHA: J-F, '85, 8

596.9 Unspecified disorder of bladder

AHA: J-F, '85, 8

✓4ᵗʰ **597 Urethritis, not sexually transmitted, and urethral syndrome**

EXCLUDES nonspecific urethritis, so stated (099.4)

597.0 Urethral abscess `CC`

Abscess: Abscess of:
periurethral   Cowper's gland
urethral (gland)   Littré's gland
Abscess of: Periurethral cellulitis
bulbourethral gland

EXCLUDES urethral caruncle (599.3)

CC Excl: 098.0, 098.2, 098.39, 098.89, 099.40-099.49, 112.2, 131.00, 131.02, 131.8-131.9, 597.0-598.01, 598.8-599.0, 599.60-599.9, 607.1-607.83, 607.85-607.9, 608.4-608.81, 608.85, 608.87-608.89, 752.61-752.69, 752.81-752.9, 753.6-753.9, 788.1

DEF: Pocket of pus in tube that empties urine from the bladder.

Ⓝ Newborn Age: 0   Ⓟ Pediatric Age: 0-17   Ⓜ Maternity Age: 12-55   Ⓐ Adult Age: 15-124   `CC` CC Condition   `MC` Major Complication   `CD` Complex Dx   `HIV` HIV Related Dx

180 — Volume 1   *2007 ICD•9•CM*

√5ᵗʰ **597.8 Other urethritis**

    597.80 Urethritis, unspecified

    597.81 Urethral syndrome NOS

    597.89 Other

        Adenitis, Skene's glands

        Cowperitis

        Meatitis, urethral

        Ulcer, urethra (meatus)

        Verumontanitis

        EXCLUDES *trichomonal (131.02)*

√4ᵗʰ **598 Urethral stricture**

Use additional code to identify urinary incontinence (625.6, 788.30-788.39)

    INCLUDES pinhole meatus

        stricture of urinary meatus

    EXCLUDES *congenital stricture of urethra and urinary meatus (753.6)*

DEF: Narrowing of tube that empties urine from bladder.

√5ᵗʰ **598.0 Urethral stricture due to infection**

    598.00 Due to unspecified infection

    598.01 Due to infective diseases classified elsewhere

        Code first underlying disease, as:

          gonococcal infection (098.2)

          schistosomiasis (120.0-120.9)

          syphilis (095.8)

    598.1 Traumatic urethral stricture   CC

    Stricture of urethra: Stricture of urethra:

    late effect of injury   postobstetric

    EXCLUDES *postoperative following surgery on genitourinary tract (598.2)*

CC Excl: 098.0, 098.2, 098.39, 098.89, 131.02, 598.1-598.9, 599.60-599.9, 752.61-752.65, 752.69, 753.6-753.9, 788.1

    598.2 Postoperative urethral stricture   CC

    Postcatheterization stricture of urethra

CC Excl: See code 598.1

AHA: 3Q, '97, 6

    598.8 Other specified causes of urethral stricture

AHA: N-D, '84, 9

    598.9 Urethral stricture, unspecified

√4ᵗʰ **599 Other disorders of urethra and urinary tract**

    599.0 Urinary tract infection, site not specified   CC

    EXCLUDES *candidiasis of urinary tract (112.2)*

        urinary tract infection of newborn (771.82)

Use additional code to identify organism, such as Escherichia coli [E. coli] (041.4)

CC Excl: 098.2, 098.39, 098.89, 099.40-099.49, 112.2, 131.00, 131.8-131.9, 590.10-590.9, 591, 593.89, 593.9, 595.0-595.9, 599.0, 599.6-599.9, 788.1, 996.64

AHA: 3Q, '05, 12; 2Q, '04, 13; 4Q, '03, 79; 4Q, '99, 6; 2Q, '99, 15;1Q, '98, 5; 2Q, '96, 7; 4Q, '96, 33; 2Q, '95, 7; 1Q, '92, 13

▽ DRG 320

    599.1 Urethral fistula

    Fistula:

        urethroperineal

        urethrorectal

    Urinary fistula NOS

    EXCLUDES *fistula:*

        urethroscrotal (608.89)

        urethrovaginal (619.0)

        urethrovesicovaginal (619.0)

AHA: 3Q, '97, 6

    599.2 Urethral diverticulum

DEF: Abnormal pouch in urethral wall.

    599.3 Urethral caruncle

    Polyp of urethra

    599.4 Urethral false passage   CC

CC Excl: 597.0-598.9, 599.1-599.9, 607.1-607.83, 607.85-607.9, 608.4-608.81, 608.85, 608.87-608.89, 752.61-752.69, 752.81-752.9, 753.9, 788.1

DEF: Abnormal opening in urethra due to surgery; trauma or disease.

    599.5 Prolapsed urethral mucosa

    Prolapse of urethra

    Urethrocele

    EXCLUDES *urethrocele, female (618.03, 618.09, 618.2-618.4)*

√5ᵗʰ **599.6 Urinary obstruction**

Use additional code to identify urinary incontinence (625.6, 788.30-788.39)

    EXCLUDES *obstructive nephropathy NOS (593.89)*

AHA: 4Q, '05, 80

    599.60 Urinary obstruction, unspecified   CC

        Obstructive uropathy NOS

        Urinary (tract) obstruction NOS

CC Excl: 185, 188.0-188.9, 189.2-189.9, 274.11, 344.61, 592.1-592.9, 593.3-593.5, 593.89-596.0, 596.51-596.59, 596.8-602.9, 753.0-753.9, 788.1

    599.69 Urinary obstruction, not elsewhere classified   CC

        ▶Code, if applicable, any causal condition first, such as:

        hyperplasia of prostate (600.0-600.9 with fifth-digit 1)◀

    CC Excl: See code 599.60

    599.7 Hematuria   CC

    Hematuria (benign) (essential)

    EXCLUDES *hemoglobinuria (791.2)*

CC Excl: 592.0-592.9, 593.89, 593.9, 594.0-594.9, 596.6-596.7, 599.7-599.9

AHA: 1Q, '00, 5; 3Q, '95, 8

DEF: Blood in urine.

√5ᵗʰ **599.8 Other specified disorders of urethra and urinary tract**

Use additional code to identify urinary incontinence (625.6, 788.30-788.39), if present

    EXCLUDES *symptoms and other conditions classifiable to 788.0-788.2, 788.4-788.9, 791.0-791.9*

    599.81 Urethral hypermobility

DEF: Hyperactive urethra.

    599.82 Intrinsic (urethral) spincter deficiency [ISD]

AHA: 2Q, '96, 15

DEF: Malfunctioning urethral sphincter.

    599.83 Urethral instability

DEF: Inconsistent functioning of urethra.

    599.84 Other specified disorders of urethra

        Rupture of urethra (nontraumatic)

        Urethral:

          cyst

          granuloma

DEF: Rupture of urethra due to herniation or breaking down of tissue; not due to trauma.

DEF: Urethral cyst: abnormal sac in urethra; usually fluid filled.

DEF: Granuloma: inflammatory cells forming small nodules in urethra.

    599.89 Other specified disorders of urinary tract

    599.9 Unspecified disorder of urethra and urinary tract

√4ᵗʰ Additional Digit Required   Nonspecific PDx   Unacceptable PDx   Manifestation Code   MCV Major Cardiovascular Condition   ▶◀ Revised Text   ● New Code   ▲ Revised Code Title
√5ᵗʰ

2007 ICD•9•CM   October 2006 • Volume 1 — 181

Genitourinary System

600–601.3

DISEASES OF MALE GENITAL ORGANS (600-608)

✓4ᵗʰ **600 Hyperplasia of prostate**

　　INCLUDES ▶enlarged prostate◀

AHA: 3Q, '05, 20; 4Q, '00, 43; 3Q, '94, 12; 3Q, '92, 7; N-D, '86, 10

DEF: Fibrostromal proliferation in periurethral glands, causes blood in urine; etiology unknown.

✓5ᵗʰ **600.0　Hypertrophy (benign) of prostate**
　　　　Benign prostatic hypertrophy
　　　　Enlargement of prostate
　　　　Smooth enlarged prostate
　　　　Soft enlarged prostate

AHA: 3Q, '05, 20; 4Q, '03, 63; 1Q, '03, 6; 3Q, '02, 28; 2Q, '01, 14

▲　**600.00　Hypertrophy (benign) of prostate** 　A ♂
　　　　　without urinary obstruction and other
　　　　　lower urinary tract symptoms [LUTS]
　　　　　Hypertrophy (benign) of prostate NOS

▲　**600.01　Hypertrophy (benign) of prostate** 　A ♂
　　　　　with urinary obstruction and other
　　　　　urinary tract symptoms [LUTS]
　　　　　Hypertrophy (benign) of prostate with
　　　　　　urinary retention
　　　　　▶Use additional code to identify symptoms:
　　　　　　incomplete bladder emptying (788.21)
　　　　　　nocturia (788.43)
　　　　　　straining on urination (788.65)
　　　　　　urinary frequency (788.41)
　　　　　　urinary hesitancy (788.64)
　　　　　　urinary incontinence (788.30-788.39)
　　　　　　urinary obstruction (599.69)
　　　　　　urinary retention (788.20)
　　　　　　urinary urgency (788.63)
　　　　　　weak urinary stream (788.62)◀

　　　　AHA: 4Q, '03, 64

✓5ᵗʰ **600.1　Nodular prostate**
　　　　Hard, firm prostate
　　　　Multinodular prostate
　　　　　EXCLUDES　malignant neoplasm of prostate (185)

AHA: 4Q, '03, 63

DEF: Hard, firm nodule in prostate.

600.10　Nodular prostate without urinary 　A ♂
　　　　　obstruction
　　　　　Nodular prostate NOS

600.11　Nodular prostate with urinary 　A ♂
　　　　　obstruction
　　　　　Nodular prostate with urinary retention

✓5ᵗʰ **600.2　Benign localized hyperplasia of prostate**
　　　　Adenofibromatous hypertrophy of prostate
　　　　Adenoma of prostate
　　　　Fibroadenoma of prostate
　　　　Fibroma of prostate
　　　　Myoma of prostate
　　　　Polyp of prostate
　　　　　EXCLUDES　benign neoplasms of prostate (222.2)
　　　　　　　　　　hypertrophy of prostate (600.00-
　　　　　　　　　　　600.01)
　　　　　　　　　　malignant neoplasm of prostate (185)

AHA: 4Q, '03, 63

DEF: Benign localized hyperplasia is a clearly defined epithelial tumor. Other terms used for this condition are adenofibromatous hypertrophy of prostate, adenoma of prostate, fibroadenoma of prostate, fibroma of prostate, myoma of prostate, and polyp of prostate.

▲　**600.20　Benign localized hyperplasia of** 　A ♂
　　　　　prostate without urinary obstruction
　　　　　and other lower urinary tract symptoms
　　　　　[LUTS]
　　　　　Benign localized hyperplasia of prostate
　　　　　　NOS

Male Pelvic Organs

▲　**600.21　Benign localized hyperplasia of** 　A ♂
　　　　　prostate with urinary obstruction and
　　　　　other lower urinary tract symptoms [LUTS]
　　　　　Benign localized hyperplasia of prostate
　　　　　　with urinary retention
　　　　　▶Use additional code to identify symptoms:
　　　　　　incomplete bladder emptying (788.21)
　　　　　　nocturia (788.43)
　　　　　　straining on urination (788.65)
　　　　　　urinary frequency (788.41)
　　　　　　urinary hesitancy (788.64)
　　　　　　urinary incontinence (788.30-788.39)
　　　　　　urinary obstruction (599.69)
　　　　　　urinary retention (788.20)
　　　　　　urinary urgency (788.63)
　　　　　　weak urinary stream (788.62)◀

600.3　Cyst of prostate 　A ♂

DEF: Sacs of fluid, which differentiate this from either nodular or adenomatous tumors.

✓5ᵗʰ **600.9　Hyperplasia of prostate, unspecified**
　　　　Median bar
　　　　Prostatic obstruction NOS

AHA: 4Q, '03, 63

▲　**600.90　Hyperplasia of prostate, unspecified,** 　A ♂
　　　　　without urinary obstruction and other
　　　　　lower urinary tract symptoms [LUTS]
　　　　　Hyperplasia of prostate NOS

▲　**600.91　Hyperplasia of prostate, unspecified,** 　A ♂
　　　　　with urinary obstruction and other
　　　　　lower urinary tract symptoms [LUTS]
　　　　　Hyperplasia of prostate, unspecified, with
　　　　　　urinary retention
　　　　　▶Use additional code to identify symptoms:
　　　　　　incomplete bladder emptying (788.21)
　　　　　　nocturia (788.43)
　　　　　　straining on urination (788.65)
　　　　　　urinary frequency (788.41)
　　　　　　urinary hesitancy (788.64)
　　　　　　urinary incontinence (788.30-788.39)
　　　　　　urinary obstruction (599.69)
　　　　　　urinary retention (788.20)
　　　　　　urinary urgency (788.63)
　　　　　　weak urinary stream (788.62)◀

✓4ᵗʰ **601 Inflammatory diseases of prostate**
　　　　Use additional code to identify organism, such as
　　　　　Staphylococcus (041.1), or Streptococcus (041.0)

601.0　Acute prostatitis 　CC A ♂
　　　　CC Excl: 098.12, 098.32, 098.89, 112.2, 131.00, 131.03, 131.8-131.9,
　　　　600.00-602.9

601.1　Chronic prostatitis 　A ♂

601.2　Abscess of prostate 　CC A ♂
　　　　CC Excl: See code 601.0

601.3　Prostatocystitis 　CC A ♂
　　　　CC Excl: See code 601.0

N Newborn Age: 0　　P Pediatric Age: 0-17　　M Maternity Age: 12-55　　A Adult Age: 15-124　　CC CC Condition　　MC Major Complication　　CD Complex Dx　　HIV HIV Related Dx

601.4 *Prostatitis in diseases classified elsewhere* A ♂

Code first underlying disease, as:
actinomycosis (039.8)
blastomycosis (116.0)
syphilis (095.8)
tuberculosis (016.5)

EXCLUDES   prostatitis:
gonococcal (098.12, 098.32)
monilial (112.2)
trichomonal (131.03)

601.8 **Other specified inflammatory diseases of prostate** A ♂

Prostatitis: Prostatitis:
cavitary   granulomatous
diverticular

601.9 Prostatitis, unspecified A ♂

Prostatitis NOS

✓4ᵗʰ **602 Other disorders of prostate**

602.0 **Calculus of prostate** A ♂

Prostatic stone
DEF: Stone or mineral deposit in prostate.

602.1 **Congestion or hemorrhage of prostate** CC A ♂

CC Excl: See code 601.0
DEF: Bleeding or fluid collection in prostate.

602.2 **Atrophy of prostate** A ♂

602.3 **Dysplasia of prostate** ♂

Prostatic intraepithelial neoplasia I (PIN I)
Prostatic intraepithelial neoplasia II (PIN II)

EXCLUDES   prostatic intraepithelial neoplasia III
(PIN III) (233.4)

AHA: 4Q, '01, 46

DEF: Abnormality of shape and size of the intraepithelial tissues of the prostate; pre-malignant condition characterized by stalks and absence of a basilar cell layer; synonyms are intraductal dysplasia, large acinar atypical hyperplasia, atypical primary hyperplasia, hyperplasia with malignant changes, marked atypia, or duct-acinar dysplasia.

602.8 **Other specified disorders of prostate** A ♂

Fistula
Infarction } of prostate
Stricture

Periprostatic adhesions

602.9 Unspecified disorder of prostate A ♂

✓4ᵗʰ **603 Hydrocele**

INCLUDES   hydrocele of spermatic cord, testis, or tunica vaginalis

EXCLUDES   congenital (778.6)

DEF: Circumscribed collection of fluid in tunica vaginalis, spermatic cord or testis.

603.0 **Encysted hydrocele**

603.1 **Infected hydrocele** CC

Use additional code to identify organism
CC Excl: 112.2, 131.00, 131.8-131.9, 603.0-603.9

603.8 **Other specified types of hydrocele**

603.9 **Hydrocele, unspecified**

✓4ᵗʰ **604 Orchitis and epididymitis**

Use additional code to identify organism, such as Escherichia coli [E. coli] (041.4), Staphylococcus (041.1), or Streptococcus (041.0)

604.0 **Orchitis, epididymitis, and epididymo-orchitis, with abscess** CC ♂

Abscess of epididymis or testis
CC Excl: 072.0, 098.13-098.14, 098.33-098.34, 098.89, 112.2, 131.00, 131.8-131.9, 604.0-604.99

Common Inguinal Canal Anomalies

✓5ᵗʰ **604.9** **Other orchitis, epididymitis, and epididymo-orchitis, without mention of abscess**

604.90 **Orchitis and epididymitis, unspecified** ♂

604.91 *Orchitis and epididymitis in diseases classified elsewhere* ♂

Code first underlying disease, as:
diphtheria (032.89)
filariasis (125.0-125.9)
syphilis (095.8)

EXCLUDES   orchitis:
gonococcal (098.13, 098.33)
mumps (072.0)
tuberculous (016.5)
tuberculous epididymitis (016.4)

604.99 **Other** ♂

605 Redundant prepuce and phimosis ♂

Adherent prepuce   Phimosis (congenital)
Paraphimosis   Tight foreskin

DEF: Constriction of preputial orifice causing inability of the prepuce to be drawn back over the glans; it may be congenital or caused by infection.

✓4ᵗʰ **606 Infertility, male**

AHA: 2Q, '96, 9

606.0 **Azoospermia** A ♂

Absolute infertility   Infertility due to:
Infertility due to: spermatogenic arrest
germinal (cell) aplasia   (complete)

DEF: Absence of spermatozoa in the semen or inability to produce spermatozoa.

606.1 **Oligospermia** A ♂

Infertility due to:
germinal cell desquamation
hypospermatogenesis
incomplete spermatogenic arrest

DEF: Insufficient number of sperm in semen.

606.8 **Infertility due to extratesticular causes** A ♂

Infertility due to: Infertility due to:
drug therapy   radiation
infection   systemic disease
obstruction of efferent
ducts

606.9 **Male infertility, unspecified** A ♂

✓4ᵗʰ **607 Disorders of penis**

EXCLUDES   phimosis (605)

607.0 **Leukoplakia of penis** ♂

Kraurosis of penis

EXCLUDES   carcinoma in situ of penis (233.5)
erythroplasia of Queyrat (233.5)

DEF: White, thickened patches on glans penis.

607.1 **Balanoposthitis** ♂

Balanitis
Use additional code to identify organism
DEF: Inflammation of glans penis and prepuce.

✓4ᵗʰ / ✓5ᵗʰ Additional Digit Required   Nonspecific PDx   Unacceptable PDx   Manifestation Code   MCV Major Cardiovascular Condition   ◄ Revised Text   ● New Code   ▲ Revised Code Title

2007 ICD•9•CM   **Volume 1 — 183**

Genitourinary System

607.2–608.9

607.2 Other inflammatory disorders of penis ♂

Abscess
Boil
Carbuncle
Cellulitis } of corpus cavernosum or penis

Cavernitis (penis)
Use additional code to identify organism

EXCLUDES   *herpetic infection (054.13)*

607.3 Priapism ♂

Painful erection
DEF: Prolonged penile erection without sexual stimulation.

√5ᵗʰ **607.8 Other specified disorders of penis**

607.81 Balanitis xerotica obliterans ♂

Induratio penis plastica
DEF: Inflammation of the glans penis, caused by stricture of the opening of the prepuce.

607.82 Vascular disorders of penis ♂

Embolism
Hematoma
  (nontraumatic)
Hemorrhage
Thrombosis } of corpus cavernosum or penis

607.83 Edema of penis ♂

DEF: Fluid retention within penile tissues.

607.84 Impotence of organic origin A ♂

EXCLUDES   *nonorganic (302.72)*
AHA: 3Q, '91, 11

DEF: Physiological cause interfering with erection.

607.85 Peyronie's disease ♂

AHA: 4Q, '03, 64
DEF: A severe curvature of the erect penis due to fibrosis of the cavernous sheaths.

607.89 Other ♂

Atrophy
Fibrosis
Hypertrophy
Ulcer (chronic) } of corpus cavernosum or penis

607.9 Unspecified disorder of penis ♂

√4ᵗʰ **608 Other disorders of male genital organs**

608.0 Seminal vesiculitis ♂

Abscess
Cellulitis } of seminal vesicle

Vesiculitis (seminal)
Use additional code to identify organism

EXCLUDES   *gonococcal infection (098.14, 098.34)*

DEF: Inflammation of seminal vesicle.

608.1 Spermatocele ♂

DEF: Cystic enlargement of the epididymis or the testis; the cysts contain spermatozoa.

√5ᵗʰ **608.2 Torsion of testis**

DEF: Twisted or rotated testis; may compromise blood flow.

• **608.20 Torsion of testis, unspecified** ♂
• **608.21 Extravaginal torsion of spermatic cord** ♂
• **608.22 Intravaginal torsion of spermatic cord** ♂
• **608.23 Torsion of appendix testis** ♂
• **608.24 Torsion of appendix epididymis** ♂

Torsion of Testes

Spermatic cord

Torsion of testis

Testes after correction showing bilateral fixation

608.3 Atrophy of testis ♂

608.4 Other inflammatory disorders of male genital organs ♂

Abscess
Boil
Carbuncle
Cellulitis } of scrotum, spermatic cord, testis [except abscess], tunica vaginalis, or vas deferens

Vasitis
Use additional code to identify organism

EXCLUDES   *abscess of testis (604.0)*

√5ᵗʰ **608.8 Other specified disorders of male genital organs**

608.81 Disorders of male genital organs in diseases classified elsewhere ♂

Code first underlying disease, as:
filariasis (125.0-125.9)
tuberculosis (016.5)

608.82 Hematospermia ♂

AHA: 4Q, '01, 46
DEF: Presence of blood in the ejaculate; relatively common, affecting men of any age after puberty; cause is often difficult to determine since the semen originates in several organs, often the result of a viral or bacterial infection and inflammation.

608.83 Vascular disorders ♂

Hematoma
  (non-
  traumatic)
Hemorrhage
Thrombosis } of seminal vesicle, spermatic cord, testis, scrotum, tunica vaginalis, or vas deferens

Hematocele NOS, male
AHA: 4Q, '03, 110

608.84 Chylocele of tunica vaginalis ♂

DEF: Chylous effusion into tunica vaginalis; due to infusion of lymphatic fluids.

608.85 Stricture ♂

Stricture of:
  spermatic cord
  tunica vaginalis
Stricture of:
  vas deferens

608.86 Edema ♂

608.87 Retrograde ejaculation ♂

AHA: 4Q, '01, 46
DEF: Condition where the semen travels to the bladder rather than out through the urethra due to damaged nerves causing the bladder neck to remain open during ejaculation.

608.89 Other ♂

Atrophy
Fibrosis
Hypertrophy
Ulcer } of seminal vesicle, spermatic cord, testis, scrotum, tunica vaginalis, or vas deferens

EXCLUDES   *atrophy of testis (608.3)*

608.9 Unspecified disorder of male genital organs ♂

N Newborn Age: 0   P Pediatric Age: 0-17   M Maternity Age: 12-55   A Adult Age: 15-124   CC CC Condition   MC Major Complication   CD Complex Dx   HIV HIV Related Dx

184 — Volume 1 • October 2006   *2007 ICD•9•CM*

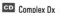

DISORDERS OF BREAST (610-611)

☑4ᵗʰ 610 Benign mammary dysplasias

610.0 Solitary cyst of breast
Cyst (solitary) of breast

610.1 Diffuse cystic mastopathy   [A]
Chronic cystic mastitis   Fibrocystic disease of
Cystic breast   breast

DEF: Extensive formation of nodular cysts in breast tissue; symptoms include tenderness, change in size and hyperplasia of ductal epithelium.

610.2 Fibroadenosis of breast
Fibroadenosis of breast: Fibroadenosis of breast:
NOS   diffuse
chronic   periodic
cystic   segmental

DEF: Non-neoplastic nodular condition of breast.

610.3 Fibrosclerosis of breast
DEF: Fibrous tissue in breast.

610.4 Mammary duct ectasia
Comedomastitis   Mastitis:
Duct ectasia   periductal
                    plasma cell

DEF: Atrophy of duct epithelium; causes distended collecting ducts of mammary gland; drying up of breast secretion, intraductal inflammation and periductal and interstitial chronic inflammatory reaction.

610.8 Other specified benign mammary dysplasias
Mazoplasia   Sebaceous cyst of breast

610.9 Benign mammary dysplasia, unspecified

☑4ᵗʰ 611 Other disorders of breast
EXCLUDES   that associated with lactation or the puerperium (675.0-676.9)

611.0 Inflammatory disease of breast
Abscess (acute) (chronic)   Mastitis (acute) (subacute)
 (nonpuerperal) of: (nonpuerperal):
   areola   NOS
   breast   infective
   Mammillary fistula   retromammary
                     submammary

EXCLUDES   carbuncle of breast (680.2)
                chronic cystic mastitis (610.1)
                neonatal infective mastitis (771.5)
                thrombophlebitis of breast [Mondor's disease] (451.89)

611.1 Hypertrophy of breast
Gynecomastia   Hypertrophy of breast:
Hypertrophy of breast: massive pubertal
NOS

611.2 Fissure of nipple

611.3 Fat necrosis of breast
Fat necrosis (segmental) of breast

DEF: Splitting of neutral fats in adipose tissue cells as a result of trauma; a firm circumscribed mass is then formed in the breast.

611.4 Atrophy of breast

611.5 Galactocele

611.6 Galactorrhea not associated with childbirth

☑5ᵗʰ 611.7 Signs and symptoms in breast

611.71 Mastodynia
Pain in breast

611.72 Lump or mass in breast   [CC]
CC Excl: 610.0-610.9, 611.0-611.9
AHA: 2Q, '03, 4-5

611.79 Other
Induration of breast   Nipple discharge
Inversion of nipple   Retraction of nipple

611.8 Other specified disorders of breast
Hematoma (nontraumatic) ⎫
Infarction   ⎬ of breast
                      ⎭
Occlusion of breast duct
Subinvolution of breast (postlactational) (postpartum)

611.9 Unspecified breast disorder

INFLAMMATORY DISEASE OF FEMALE PELVIC ORGANS (614-616)

Use additional code to identify organism, such as Staphylococcus (041.1), or Streptococcus (041.0)

EXCLUDES   that associated with pregnancy, abortion, childbirth, or the puerperium (630-676.9)

☑4ᵗʰ 614 Inflammatory disease of ovary, fallopian tube, pelvic cellular tissue, and peritoneum

EXCLUDES   endometritis (615.0-615.9)
          major infection following delivery (670)
          that complicating:
            abortion (634-638 with .0, 639.0)
            ectopic or molar pregnancy (639.0)
            pregnancy or labor (646.6)

614.0 Acute salpingitis and oophoritis   [CC] ♀
Any condition classifiable to 614.2, specified as acute or subacute

CC Excl: 016.60-016.96, 017.90-017.96, 098.15-098.17, 098.35-098.37, 098.89, 112.2, 131.00, 131.8-131.9, 614.0-615.9, 616.8-616.9, 625.8-625.9, 629.20-629.9, 752.81-752.9

DEF: Acute inflammation, of ovary and fallopian tube.

614.1 Chronic salpingitis and oophoritis   ♀
Hydrosalpinx   Salpingitis:
Salpingitis: isthmica nodosa
follicularis
Any condition classifiable to 614.2, specified as chronic

DEF: Persistent inflammation of ovary and fallopian tube.

614.2 Salpingitis and oophoritis not specified as acute, subacute, or chronic   ♀
Abscess (of):   Pyosalpinx
   fallopian tube   Perisalpingitis
   ovary   Salpingitis
   tubo-ovarian   Salpingo-oophoritis
Oophoritis   Tubo-ovarian inflammatory
Perioophoritis   disease

EXCLUDES   gonococcal infection (chronic) (098.37)
                acute (098.17)
                tuberculous (016.6)

AHA: 2Q, '91, 5

614.3 Acute parametritis and pelvic cellulitis   [CC] ♀
Acute inflammatory pelvic disease
Any condition classifiable to 614.4, specified as acute

CC Excl: See code 614.0

DEF: Parametritis: inflammation of the parametrium; pelvic cellulitis is a synonym for parametritis.

614.4 Chronic or unspecified parametritis and pelvic cellulitis   ♀
Abscess (of):
   broad ligament   ⎫
   parametrium   ⎬ chronic or NOS
   pelvis, female |
   pouch of Douglas ⎭

Chronic inflammatory pelvic disease
Pelvic cellulitis, female

EXCLUDES   tuberculous (016.7)

614.5 Acute or unspecified pelvic peritonitis, female [CC] ♀
CC Excl: See code 614.0

AHA: ▶4Q, '05, 74◀

☑4ᵗʰ/☑5ᵗʰ Additional Digit Required   Nonspecific PDx   Unacceptable PDx   Manifestation Code   [MCV] Major Cardiovascular Condition   ▶◀ Revised Text   ● New Code   ▲ Revised Code Title

Genitourinary System

610–614.5

Genitourinary System

614.6–616.9

Female Genitourinary System

614.6 Pelvic peritoneal adhesions, female (postoperative) (postinfection) ♀

Adhesions: Adhesions:
  peritubal   tubo-ovarian

Use additional code to identify any associated infertility (628.2)

AHA: 3Q, '03, 6; 1Q, '03, 4; 3Q, '95, 7; 3Q, '94, 12

DEF: Fibrous scarring abnormally joining structures within abdomen.

614.7 Other chronic pelvic peritonitis, female ♀
EXCLUDES tuberculous(016.7)

614.8 Other specified inflammatory disease of female pelvic organs and tissues ♀

614.9 Unspecified inflammatory disease of female pelvic organs and tissues ♀
Pelvic infection or inflammation, female NOS
Pelvic inflammatory disease [PID]

✓4th 615 Inflammatory diseases of uterus, except cervix
EXCLUDES following delivery (670)
hyperplastic endometritis (621.30-621.33)
that complicating:
  abortion (634-638 with .0, 639.0)
  ectopic or molar pregnancy (639.0)
  pregnancy or labor (646.6)

615.0 Acute   CC ♀
Any condition classifiable to 615.9, specified as acute or subacute

CC Excl: 016.60-016.96, 017.90-017.96, 098.15-098.17, 098.35-098.37, 098.89, 112.2, 131.00, 131.8-131.9, 614.0-616.0, 616.8-616.9, 621.8-621.9, 625.8-625.9, 629.20-629.9, 752.81-752.9

615.1 Chronic ♀
Any condition classifiable to 615.9, specified as chronic

615.9 Unspecified inflammatory disease of uterus ♀
Endometritis   Myometritis
Endomyometritis   Perimetritis
Intrauterine infection   Pyometra
Metritis   Uterine abscess

✓4th 616 Inflammatory disease of cervix, vagina, and vulva
EXCLUDES that complicating:
  abortion (634-638 with .0, 639.0)
  ectopic or molar pregnancy (639.0)
  pregnancy, childbirth, or the puerperium (646.6)

616.0 Cervicitis and endocervicitis ♀
Cervicitis   } with or without mention of
Endocervicitis }   erosion or ectropion
Nabothian (gland) cyst or follicle
EXCLUDES erosion or ectropion without mention of cervicitis (622.0)

✓5th 616.1 Vaginitis and vulvovaginitis
DEF: Inflammation or infection of vagina or external female genitalia.

616.10 Vaginitis and vulvovaginitis, unspecified ♀
Vaginitis:
  NOS
  postirradiation
Vulvitis NOS
Vulvovaginitis NOS
Use additional code to identify organism, such as Escherichia coli [E. coli] (041.4), Staphylococcus (041.1), or Streptococcus (041.0)
EXCLUDES noninfective leukorrhea (623.5)
postmenopausal or senile vaginitis (627.3)

616.11 Vaginitis and vulvovaginitis in diseases classified elsewhere ♀
Code first underlying disease, as:
  pinworm vaginitis (127.4)
EXCLUDES herpetic vulvovaginitis (054.11)
monilial vulvovaginitis (112.1)
trichomonal vaginitis or vulvovaginitis (131.01)

616.2 Cyst of Bartholin's gland ♀
Bartholin's duct cyst
DEF: Fluid-filled sac within gland of vaginal orifice.

616.3 Abscess of Bartholin's gland   CC ♀
Vulvovaginal gland abscess
CC Excl: 016.70-016.96, 017.90-017.96, 112.1-112.2, 131.00-131.01, 131.8-131.9, 616.10-616.9, 624.3-624.9, 625.8-625.9, 629.20-629.9, 752.81-752.9

616.4 Other abscess of vulva   CC ♀
Abscess   }
Carbuncle } of vulva
Furuncle   }
CC Excl: See code 616.3

✓5th 616.5 Ulceration of vulva
616.50 Ulceration of vulva, unspecified ♀
Ulcer NOS of vulva

616.51 Ulceration of vulva in diseases classified elsewhere ♀
Code first underlying disease, as:
  Behçet's syndrome (136.1)
  tuberculosis (016.7)
EXCLUDES vulvar ulcer (in):
  gonococcal (098.0)
  herpes simplex (054.12)
  syphilitic (091.0)

✓5th 616.8 Other specified inflammatory diseases of cervix, vagina, and vulva
EXCLUDES noninflammatory disorders of:
  cervix (622.0-622.9)
  vagina (623.0-623.9)
  vulva (624.0-624.9)

● 616.81 Mucositis (ulcerative) of cervix, vagina, and vulva ♀
Use additional E code to identify adverse effects of therapy, such as:
  antineoplastic and immunosuppressive drugs (E930.7, E933.1)
  radiation therapy (E879.2)

● 616.89 Other inflammatory disease of cervix, vagina and vulva ♀
Caruncle, vagina or labium
Ulcer, vagina

616.9 Unspecified inflammatory disease of cervix, vagina, and vulva ♀

N Newborn Age: 0   P Pediatric Age: 0-17   M Maternity Age: 12-55   A Adult Age: 15-124   CC CC Condition   MC Major Complication   CD Complex Dx   HIV HIV Related Dx

186 — Volume 1 • October 2006   2007 ICD•9•CM

OTHER DISORDERS OF FEMALE GENITAL TRACT (617-629)

√4ᵗʰ **617 Endometriosis**

617.0 Endometriosis of uterus　♀
　　Adenomyosis　　　　Endometriosis:
　　Endometriosis:　　　　internal
　　　cervix　　　　　　　myometrium
　　EXCLUDES *stromal endometriosis (236.0)*
　　AHA: 3Q, '92, 7
　　DEF: Aberrant uterine mucosal tissue; creating products of menses and inflamed uterine tissues.

617.1 Endometriosis of ovary　♀
　　Chocolate cyst of ovary
　　Endometrial cystoma of ovary
　　DEF: Aberrant uterine tissue; creating products of menses and inflamed ovarian tissues.

617.2 Endometriosis of fallopian tube　♀
　　DEF: Aberrant uterine tissue; creating products of menses and inflamed tissues of fallopian tubes.

617.3 Endometriosis of pelvic peritoneum　♀
　　Endometriosis:　　　　Endometriosis:
　　　broad ligament　　　　parametrium
　　　cul-de-sac (Douglas')　round ligament
　　DEF: Aberrant uterine tissue; creating products of menses and inflamed peritoneum tissues.

617.4 Endometriosis of rectovaginal septum and vagina ♀
　　DEF: Aberrant uterine tissue; creating products of menses and inflamed tissues in and behind vagina.

617.5 Endometriosis of intestine　♀
　　Endometriosis:　　　　Endometriosis:
　　　appendix　　　　　　rectum
　　　colon
　　DEF: Aberrant uterine tissue; creating products of menses and inflamed intestinal tissues.

617.6 Endometriosis in scar of skin　♀
617.8 Endometriosis of other specified sites　♀
　　Endometriosis:　　　　Endometriosis:
　　　bladder　　　　　　umbilicus
　　　lung　　　　　　　vulva

617.9 Endometriosis, site unspecified　♀

√4ᵗʰ **618 Genital prolapse**
　Use additional code to identify urinary incontinence (625.6, 788.31, 788.33-788.39)
　　EXCLUDES *that complicating pregnancy, labor, or delivery (654.4)*

√5ᵗʰ **618.0 Prolapse of vaginal walls without mention of uterine prolapse**
　　EXCLUDES *that with uterine prolapse (618.2-618.4)*
　　　　　　　enterocele (618.6)
　　　　　　　vaginal vault prolapse following hysterectomy (618.5)

　　618.00 Unspecified prolapse of vaginal walls　♀
　　　　Vaginal prolapse NOS
　　618.01 Cystocele, midline　♀
　　　　Cystocele NOS
　　　　DEF: Defect in the pubocervical fascia, the supportive layer of the bladder, causing bladder drop and herniated into the vagina along the midline.

Common Sites of Endometriosis

Common sites of endometriosis, in descending order of frequency:
(1) ovary
(2) cul de sac
(3) utersacral ligaments
(4) broad ligaments
(5) fallopian tube
(6) uterovesical fold
(7) round ligament
(8) vermiform appedix
(9) vagina
(10) rectovaginal septum

Vaginal Midline Cystocele

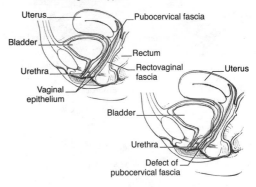

618.02 Cystocele, lateral　♀
　　Paravaginal
　　DEF: Loss of support of the lateral attachment of the vagina at the arcus tendinous results in bladder drop; bladder herniates into the vagina laterally; also called paravaginal defect.

618.03 Urethrocele　♀
618.04 Rectocele　♀
　　Proctocele
618.05 Perineocele　♀
618.09 Other prolapse of vaginal walls without mention of uterine prolapse　♀
　　Cystourethrocele

618.1 Uterine prolapse without mention of vaginal wall prolapse　♀
　　Descensus uteri　　　Uterine prolapse:
　　Uterine prolapse:　　　first degree
　　　NOS　　　　　　　second degree
　　　complete　　　　　third degree
　　EXCLUDES *that with mention of cystocele, urethrocele, or rectocele (618.2-618.4)*

618.2 Uterovaginal prolapse, incomplete　♀
　　DEF: Downward displacement of uterus downward into vagina.

618.3 Uterovaginal prolapse, complete　♀
　　DEF: Downward displacement of uterus exposed within external genitalia.

618.4 Uterovaginal prolapse, unspecified　♀
618.5 Prolapse of vaginal vault after hysterectomy　♀
618.6 Vaginal enterocele, congenital or acquired　♀
　　Pelvic enterocele, congenital or acquired
　　DEF: Vaginal vault hernia formed by the loop of the small intestine protruding into the rectal vaginal pouch; can also accompany uterine prolapse or follow hysterectomy.

618.7 Old laceration of muscles of pelvic floor　♀

Vaginal Lateral Cystocele

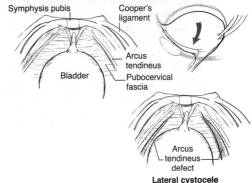

Lateral cystocele

Additional Digit Required　**Nonspecific PDx**　**Unacceptable PDx**　**Manifestation Code**　**MCV** Major Cardiovascular Condition　▶◀ Revised Text　● New Code　▲ Revised Code Title

2007 ICD•9•CM　　　　　　　　　　　　　　　　　　　　　　　　**Volume 1 — 187**

Genitourinary System

618.8–621.2

Types of Vaginal Hernias

Urethrocele

Uterus
Bladder
Rectum
Urethra
Urethrocele
Vaginal canal

Cystocele

Uterus
Bladder
Rectum
Urethra
Cystocele
Vaginal canal

Rectocele

Uterus
Bladder
Rectum
Urethra
Rectocele
Vaginal canal

Enterocele

Uterus
Bladder
Rectum
Urethra
Terminal ileum
Vaginal canal

Uterus and Ovaries

Fundus of uterus
Uterine (fallopian tube)
Ligament of ovary
Ovary
Uterosacral ligament
Cervix
Vagina
Mesosalpinx
Mesovarium
Suspensory ligaments
Body
Fimbria
Ovary
Broad ligament

✓5ᵗʰ 618.8 Other specified genital prolapse

618.81 Incompetence or weakening of pubocervical tissue ♀

618.82 Incompetence or weakening of rectovaginal tissue ♀

618.83 Pelvic muscle wasting ♀
Disuse atrophy of pelvic muscles and anal sphincter

618.84 Cervical stump prolapse ♀

618.89 Other specified genital prolapse ♀

618.9 Unspecified genital prolapse ♀

✓4ᵗʰ 619 Fistula involving female genital tract
EXCLUDES vesicorectal and intestinovesical fistula (596.1)

619.0 Urinary-genital tract fistula, female ♀
Fistula:
cervicovesical
ureterovaginal
urethrovaginal
urethrovesicovaginal

Fistula:
uteroureteric
uterovesical
vesicocervicovaginal
vesicovaginal

619.1 Digestive-genital tract fistula, female ♀
Fistula:
intestinouterine
intestinovaginal
rectovaginal

Fistula:
rectovulval
sigmoidovaginal
uterorectal

619.2 Genital tract-skin fistula, female ♀
Fistula:
uterus to abdominal wall

Fistula:
vaginoperineal

619.8 Other specified fistulas involving female genital tract ♀
Fistula:
cervix
cul-de-sac (Douglas')

Fistula:
uterus
vagina

619.9 Unspecified fistula involving female genital tract ♀

✓4ᵗʰ 620 Noninflammatory disorders of ovary, fallopian tube, and broad ligament
EXCLUDES hydrosalpinx (614.1)

620.0 Follicular cyst of ovary ♀
Cyst of graafian follicle
DEF: Fluid-filled, encapsulated cyst due to occluded follicle duct that secretes hormones into ovaries.

620.1 Corpus luteum cyst or hematoma ♀
Corpus luteum hemorrhage or rupture
Lutein cyst
DEF: Fluid-filled cyst due to serous developing from corpus luteum or clotted blood.

620.2 Other and unspecified ovarian cyst ♀
Cyst:
NOS
corpus albicans
retention NOS } of ovary
serous
theca-lutein
Simple cystoma of ovary
EXCLUDES cystadenoma (benign) (serous) (220)
developmental cysts (752.0)
neoplastic cysts (220)
polycystic ovaries (256.4)
Stein-Leventhal syndrome (256.4)

620.3 Acquired atrophy of ovary and fallopian tube ♀
Senile involution of ovary

620.4 Prolapse or hernia of ovary and fallopian tube ♀
Displacement of ovary and fallopian tube
Salpingocele

620.5 Torsion of ovary, ovarian pedicle, or fallopian tube ♀
Torsion:
accessory tube

Torsion:
hydatid of Morgagni

620.6 Broad ligament laceration syndrome ♀
Masters-Allen syndrome

620.7 Hematoma of broad ligament CC ♀
Hematocele, broad ligament
CC Excl: 620.6-620.9, 625.8-625.9, 629.20-629.9, 752.81-752.9
DEF: Blood within peritoneal fold that supports uterus.

620.8 Other noninflammatory disorders of ovary, fallopian tube, and broad ligament ♀
Cyst
Polyp } of broad ligament or fallopian tube

Infarction
Rupture } of ovary or fallopian tube

Hematosalpinx
EXCLUDES hematosalpinx in ectopic pregnancy (639.2)
peritubal adhesions (614.6)
torsion of ovary, ovarian pedicle, or fallopian tube (620.5)

620.9 Unspecified noninflammatory disorder of ovary, fallopian tube, and broad ligament ♀

✓4ᵗʰ 621 Disorders of uterus, not elsewhere classified

621.0 Polyp of corpus uteri ♀
Polyp:
endometrium

Polyp:
uterus NOS
EXCLUDES cervical polyp NOS (622.7)

621.1 Chronic subinvolution of uterus ♀
EXCLUDES puerperal (674.8)
AHA: 1Q, '91, 11
DEF: Abnormal size of uterus after delivery; the uterus does not return to its normal size after the birth of a child.

621.2 Hypertrophy of uterus ♀
Bulky or enlarged uterus
EXCLUDES puerperal (674.8)

N Newborn Age: 0   P Pediatric Age: 0-17   M Maternity Age: 12-55   A Adult Age: 15-124   CC CC Condition   MC Major Complication   CD Complex Dx   HIV HIV Related Dx

✓5ᵗʰ **621.3 Endometrial hyperplasia**
Hyperplasia (adenomatous) (cystic) (glandular) of endometrium
DEF: Abnormal cystic overgrowth of endometrial tissue.

621.30 Endometrial hyperplasia, unspecified ♀
Endometrial hyperplasia NOS

621.31 Simple endometrial hyperplasia without atypia ♀

621.32 Complex endometrial hyperplasia without atypia ♀

621.33 Endometrial hyperplasia with atypia ♀

621.4 Hematometra ♀
Hemometra
EXCLUDES   that in congenital anomaly (752.2-752.3)

DEF: Accumulated blood in uterus.

621.5 Intrauterine synechiae ♀
Adhesions of uterus   Band(s) of uterus

621.6 Malposition of uterus ♀
Anteversion
Retroflexion } of uterus
Retroversion
EXCLUDES   malposition complicating pregnancy, labor, or delivery (654.3-654.4)

621.7 Chronic inversion of uterus ♀
EXCLUDES   current obstetrical trauma (665.2)
prolapse of uterus (618.1-618.4)

621.8 Other specified disorders of uterus, not elsewhere classified ♀
Atrophy, acquired
Cyst
Fibrosis NOS } of uterus
Old laceration (postpartum)
Ulcer
EXCLUDES   bilharzial fibrosis (120.0-120.9)
endometriosis (617.0)
fistulas (619.0-619.8)
inflammatory diseases (615.0-615.9)

621.9 Unspecified disorder of uterus ♀

✓4ᵗʰ **622 Noninflammatory disorders of cervix**
EXCLUDES   abnormality of cervix complicating pregnancy, labor, or delivery (654.5-654.6)
fistula (619.0-619.8)

622.0 Erosion and ectropion of cervix ♀
Eversion } of cervix
Ulcer
EXCLUDES   that in chronic cervicitis (616.0)

DEF: Ulceration or turning outward of uterine cervix.

✓5ᵗʰ **622.1 Dysplasia of cervix (uteri)**
EXCLUDES   abnormal results from cervical cytologic examination without histologic confirmation (795.00-795.09)
carcinoma in situ of cervix (233.1)
cervical intraepithelial neoplasia III [CIN III] (233.1)

AHA: 1Q, '91, 11
DEF: Abnormal cell structures in portal between uterus and vagina.

622.10 Dysplasia of cervix, unspecified ♀
Anaplasia of cervix   Cervical dysplasia
Cervical atypism   NOS

622.11 Mild dysplasia of cervix ♀
Cervical intraepithelial neoplasia I [CIN I]

622.12 Moderate dysplasia of cervix ♀
Cervical intraepithelial neoplasia II [CIN II]
EXCLUDES   carcinoma in situ of cervix (233.1)
cervical intraepithelial neo-plasia III [CIN III] (233.1)
severe dysplasia (233.1)

622.2 Leukoplakia of cervix (uteri) ♀
EXCLUDES   carcinoma in situ of cervix (233.1)

DEF: Thickened, white patches on portal between uterus and vagina.

622.3 Old laceration of cervix ♀
Adhesions
Band(s) } of cervix
Cicatrix (postpartum)
EXCLUDES   current obstetrical trauma (665.3)

DEF: Scarring or other evidence of old wound on cervix.

622.4 Stricture and stenosis of cervix ♀
Atresia (acquired)
Contracture } of cervix
Occlusion
Pinpoint os uteri
EXCLUDES   congenital (752.49)
that complicating labor (654.6)

622.5 Incompetence of cervix ♀
EXCLUDES   complicating pregnancy (654.5)
that affecting fetus or newborn (761.0)

DEF: Inadequate functioning of cervix; marked by abnormal widening during pregnancy; causing miscarriage.

622.6 Hypertrophic elongation of cervix ♀
DEF: Overgrowth of cervix tissues extending down into vagina.

622.7 Mucous polyp of cervix ♀
Polyp NOS of cervix
EXCLUDES   adenomatous polyp of cervix (219.0)

622.8 Other specified noninflammatory disorders of cervix ♀
Atrophy (senile)
Cyst
Fibrosis } of cervix
Hemorrhage
EXCLUDES   endometriosis (617.0)
fistula (619.0-619.8)
inflammatory diseases (616.0)

622.9 Unspecified noninflammatory disorder of cervix ♀

✓4ᵗʰ **623 Noninflammatory disorders of vagina**
EXCLUDES   abnormality of vagina complicating pregnancy, labor, or delivery (654.7)
congenital absence of vagina (752.49)
congenital diaphragm or bands (752.49)
fistulas involving vagina (619.0-619.8)

623.0 Dysplasia of vagina ♀
EXCLUDES   carcinoma in situ of vagina (233.3)

623.1 Leukoplakia of vagina ♀
DEF: Thickened white patches on vaginal canal.

623.2 Stricture or atresia of vagina ♀
Adhesions (postoperative) (postradiation) of vagina
Occlusion of vagina
Stenosis, vagina
Use additional E code to identify any external cause
EXCLUDES   congenital atresia or stricture (752.49)

623.3 Tight hymenal ring ♀
Rigid hymen
Tight hymenal ring } acquired or congenital
Tight introitus
EXCLUDES   imperforate hymen (752.42)

623.4 Old vaginal laceration ♀
EXCLUDES   old laceration involving muscles of pelvic floor (618.7)

DEF: Scarring or other evidence of old wound on vagina.

623.5 Leukorrhea, not specified as infective ♀
Leukorrhea NOS of vagina
Vaginal discharge NOS
EXCLUDES   trichomonal (131.00)

DEF: Viscid whitish discharge, from vagina.

✓4ᵗʰ
✓5ᵗʰ
Additional Digit Required   Nonspecific PDx   Unacceptable PDx   Manifestation Code   MCV Major Cardiovascular Condition   ▶◀ Revised Text   ● New Code   ▲ Revised Code Title

2007 ICD•9•CM   Volume 1 — 189

Genitourinary System

621.3–623.5

Genitourinary System

623.6–627.2

623.6 **Vaginal hematoma** ♀
> **EXCLUDES** *current obstetrical trauma (665.7)*

623.7 **Polyp of vagina** ♀

623.8 **Other specified noninflammatory disorders of vagina** ♀
> Cyst
> Hemorrhage } of vagina

623.9 **Unspecified noninflammatory disorder of vagina** ♀

√4ᵗʰ **624 Noninflammatory disorders of vulva and perineum**
> **EXCLUDES** *abnormality of vulva and perineum complicating pregnancy, labor, or delivery (654.8)*
> *condyloma acuminatum (078.1)*
> *fistulas involving:*
> *perineum — see Alphabetic Index*
> *vulva (619.0-619.8)*
> *vulval varices (456.6)*
> *vulvar involvement in skin conditions (690-709.9)*

624.0 **Dystrophy of vulva** ♀
> Kraurosis
> Leukoplakia } of vulva
> **EXCLUDES** *carcinoma in situ of vulva (233.3)*

624.1 **Atrophy of vulva** ♀

624.2 **Hypertrophy of clitoris** ♀
> **EXCLUDES** *that in endocrine disorders (255.2, 256.1)*

624.3 **Hypertrophy of labia** ♀
> Hypertrophy of vulva NOS
> DEF: Overgrowth of fleshy folds on either side of vagina.

624.4 **Old laceration or scarring of vulva** ♀
> DEF: Scarring or other evidence of old wound on external female genitalia.

624.5 **Hematoma of vulva** ♀
> **EXCLUDES** *that complicating delivery (664.5)*
> DEF: Blood in tissue of external genitalia.

624.6 **Polyp of labia and vulva** ♀

624.8 **Other specified noninflammatory disorders of vulva and perineum** ♀
> Cyst
> Edema } of vulva
> Stricture
> AHA: 1Q, '03, 13; 1Q, '95, 8

624.9 **Unspecified noninflammatory disorder of vulva and perineum** ♀

√4ᵗʰ **625 Pain and other symptoms associated with female genital organs**

625.0 **Dyspareunia** ♀
> **EXCLUDES** *psychogenic dyspareunia (302.76)*
> DEF: Difficult or painful sexual intercourse.

625.1 **Vaginismus** ♀
> Colpospasm   Vulvismus
> **EXCLUDES** *psychogenic vaginismus (306.51)*
> DEF: Vaginal spasms; due to involuntary contraction of musculature; prevents intercourse.

625.2 **Mittelschmerz** ♀
> Intermenstrual pain   Ovulation pain
> DEF: Pain occurring between menstrual periods.

625.3 **Dysmenorrhea** ♀
> Painful menstruation
> **EXCLUDES** *psychogenic dysmenorrhea (306.52)*
> AHA: 2Q, '94, 12

625.4 **Premenstrual tension syndromes** ♀
> Menstrual: Premenstrual dysphoric disorder
>   migraine   Premenstrual syndrome
>   molimen   Premenstrual tension NOS
> AHA: 4Q, '03, 116

625.5 **Pelvic congestion syndrome** ♀
> Congestion-fibrosis syndrome   Taylor's syndrome
> DEF: Excessive accumulation of blood in vessels of pelvis; may occur after orgasm; causes abnormal menstruation, lower back pain and vaginal discharge.

625.6 **Stress incontinence, female** ♀
> **EXCLUDES** *mixed incontinence (788.33)*
> *stress incontinence, male (788.32)*
> DEF: Involuntary leakage of urine due to insufficient sphincter control; occurs upon sneezing, laughing, coughing, sudden movement or lifting.

625.8 **Other specified symptoms associated with female genital organs** ♀
> AHA: N-D, '85, 16

625.9 **Unspecified symptom associated with female genital organs** ♀

√4ᵗʰ **626 Disorders of menstruation and other abnormal bleeding from female genital tract**
> **EXCLUDES** *menopausal and premenopausal bleeding (627.0)*
> *pain and other symptoms associated with menstrual cycle (625.2-625.4)*
> *postmenopausal bleeding (627.1)*

626.0 **Absence of menstruation** ♀
> Amenorrhea (primary) (secondary)

626.1 **Scanty or infrequent menstruation** ♀
> Hypomenorrhea   Oligomenorrhea

626.2 **Excessive or frequent menstruation** ♀
> Heavy periods   Menorrhagia
> Menometrorrhagia   Plymenorrhea
> **EXCLUDES** *premenopausal(627.0)*
> *that in puberty (626.3)*

626.3 **Puberty bleeding** ♀
> Excessive bleeding associated with onset of menstrual periods
> Pubertal menorrhagia

626.4 **Irregular menstrual cycle** ♀
> Irregular: Irregular:
>   bleeding NOS   periods
>   menstruation

626.5 **Ovulation bleeding** ♀
> Regular intermenstrual bleeding

626.6 **Metrorrhagia** ♀
> Bleeding unrelated to menstrual cycle
> Irregular intermenstrual bleeding

626.7 **Postcoital bleeding** ♀
> DEF: Bleeding from vagina after sexual intercourse.

626.8 **Other** ♀
> Dysfunctional or functional uterine hemorrhage NOS
> Menstruation:
>   retained
>   suppression of

626.9 **Unspecified** ♀

√4ᵗʰ **627 Menopausal and postmenopausal disorders**
> **EXCLUDES** *asymptomatic age-related (natural) postmenopausal status (V49.81)*

627.0 **Premenopausal menorrhagia** ♀
> Excessive bleeding associated with onset of menopause
> Menorrhagia:
>   climacteric
>   menopausal
>   preclimacteric

627.1 **Postmenopausal bleeding** ♀

627.2 **Symptomatic menopausal or female climacteric states** ♀
> Symptoms, such as flushing, sleeplessness, headache, lack of concentration, associated with the menopause

---

N Newborn Age: 0   P Pediatric Age: 0-17   M Maternity Age: 12-55   A Adult Age: 15-124   CC CC Condition   MC Major Complication   CD Complex Dx   HIV HIV Related Dx

627.3 Postmenopausal atrophic vaginitis ♀
Senile (atrophic) vaginitis

627.4 Symptomatic states associated with artificial menopause ♀
Postartificial menopause syndromes
Any condition classifiable to 627.1, 627.2, or 627.3 which follows induced menopause
DEF: Conditions arising after hysterectomy.

627.8 Other specified menopausal and postmenopausal disorders ♀
EXCLUDES premature menopause NOS (256.31)

627.9 Unspecified menopausal and postmenopausal disorder ♀

✓4ᵗʰ **628 Infertility, female**
INCLUDES primary and secondary sterility
AHA: 2Q, '96, 9; 1Q, '95, 7

DEF: Infertility: inability to conceive for at least one year with regular intercourse.

DEF: Primary infertility: occurring in patients who have never conceived.

DEF: Secondary infertility: occurring in patients who have previously conceived.

628.0 Associated with anovulation ♀
Anovulatory cycle
Use additional code for any associated Stein-Leventhal syndrome (256.4)

628.1 Of pituitary-hypothalamic origin ♀
Code first underlying cause, as:
adiposogenital dystrophy (253.8)
anterior pituitary disorder (253.0-253.4)

628.2 Of tubal origin ♀
Infertility associated with congenital anomaly of tube
Tubal:
block
occlusion
stenosis
Use additional code for any associated peritubal adhesions (614.6)

628.3 Of uterine origin ♀
Infertility associated with congenital anomaly of uterus
Nonimplantation
Use additional code for any associated tuberculous endometritis (016.7)

628.4 Of cervical or vaginal origin ♀
Infertility associated with:
anomaly of cervical mucus
congenital structural anomaly
dysmucorrhea

628.8 Of other specified origin ♀
628.9 Of unspecified origin ♀

✓4ᵗʰ **629 Other disorders of female genital organs**
629.0 Hematocele, female, not elsewhere classified ♀
EXCLUDES hematocele or hematoma:
broad ligament (620.7)
fallopian tube (620.8)
that associated with ectopic pregnancy (633.00-633.91)
uterus (621.4)
vagina (623.6)
vulva (624.5)

629.1 Hydrocele, canal of Nuck ♀
Cyst of canal of Nuck (acquired)
EXCLUDES congenital (752.41)

✓5ᵗʰ **629.2 Female genital mutilation status** ♀
Female circumcision status
▶Female genital cutting◀
AHA: 4Q, '04, 88

629.20 Female genital mutilation status, unspecified ♀
▶Female genital cutting status, unspecified◀
Female genital mutilation status NOS

629.21 Female genital mutilation Type I status ♀
Clitorectomy status
▶Female genital cutting Type I status◀
DEF: Female genital mutilation involving clitorectomy, with part or all of the clitoris removed.

629.22 Female genital mutilation Type II status ♀
Clitorectomy with excision of labia minora status
▶Female genital cutting Type II status◀
AHA: 4Q, '04, 90
DEF: Female genital mutilation involving clitoris and the labia minora amputation.

629.23 Female genital mutilation Type III status ♀
▶Female genital cutting Type III status◀
Infibulation status
AHA: 4Q, '04, 90
DEF: Female genital mutilation involving removal, most or all of the labia minora excised, labia majora incised which is then made into a hood of skin over the urethral and vaginal opening.

● **629.29 Other female genital mutilation status** ♀
Female genital cutting Type IV status
Female genital mutilation Type IV status
Other female genital cutting status

✓5ᵗʰ **629.8 Other specified disorders of female genital organs**
● **629.81 Habitual aborter without current pregnancy** ♀
EXCLUDES habitual aborter with current pregnancy (646.3)

● **629.89 Other specified disorders of female genital organs** ♀

629.9 Unspecified disorder of female genital organs ♀

11. COMPLICATIONS OF PREGNANCY, CHILDBIRTH, AND THE PUERPERIUM (630-677)

ECTOPIC AND MOLAR PREGNANCY (630-633)
Use additional code from category 639 to identify any complications

630 Hydatidiform mole Ⓜ♀
Trophoblastic disease NOS   Vesicularmole
> **EXCLUDES** *chorioadenoma (destruens) (236.1)*
> *chorionepithelioma (181)*
> *malignant hydatidiform mole (236.1)*

DEF: Abnormal product of pregnancy; marked by mass of cysts resembling bunch of grapes due to chorionic villi proliferation, and dissolution; must be surgically removed.

631 Other abnormal product of conception Ⓜ♀
Blighted ovum   Mole:
Mole: fleshy
  NOS   stone
  carneous

632 Missed abortion Ⓜ♀
Early fetal death before completion of 22 weeks' gestation with retention of dead fetus
Retained products of conception, not following spontaneous or induced abortion or delivery
> **EXCLUDES** *failed induced abortion (638.0-638.9)*
> *fetal death (intrauterine) (late) (656.4)*
> *missed delivery (656.4)*
> *that with abnormal product of conception (630, 631)*

AHA: 1Q, '01, 5

√4ᵗʰ 633 Ectopic pregnancy
> **INCLUDES** ruptured ectopic pregnancy

AHA: 4Q, '02, 61

DEF: Fertilized egg develops outside uterus.

√5ᵗʰ 633.0 Abdominal pregnancy
Intraperitoneal pregnancy

633.00 Abdominal pregnancy without intrauterine pregnancy Ⓜ♀

633.01 Abdominal pregnancy with intrauterine pregnancy Ⓜ♀

√5ᵗʰ 633.1 Tubal pregnancy
Fallopian pregnancy
Rupture of (fallopian) tube due to pregnancy
Tubal abortion

AHA: 2Q, '90, 27

633.10 Tubal pregnancy without intrauterine pregnancy Ⓜ♀

633.11 Tubal pregnancy with intrauterine pregnancy Ⓜ♀

√5ᵗʰ 633.2 Ovarian pregnancy

633.20 Ovarian pregnancy without intrauterine pregnancy ♀

633.21 Ovarian pregnancy with intrauterine pregnancy Ⓜ♀

√5ᵗʰ 633.8 Other ectopic pregnancy
Pregnancy: Pregnancy:
  cervical   intraligamentous
  combined   mesometric
  cornual   mural

633.80 Other ectopic pregnancy without intrauterine pregnancy Ⓜ♀

633.81 Other ectopic pregnancy with intrauterine pregnancy Ⓜ♀

√5ᵗʰ 633.9 Unspecified ectopic pregnancy

633.90 Unspecified ectopic pregnancy without intrauterine pregnancy Ⓜ♀

633.91 Unspecified ectopic pregnancy with intrauterine pregnancy Ⓜ♀

Ectopic Pregnancy Sites

Tubal
Ovarian
Mesometric
Abdominal
Cervical

OTHER PREGNANCY WITH ABORTIVE OUTCOME (634-639)

The following fourth-digit subdivisions are for use with categories 634-638:

.0 Complicated by genital tract and pelvic infection
Endometritis
Salpingo-oophoritis
Sepsis NOS
Septicemia NOS
Any condition classifiable to 639.0, with condition classifiable to 634-638
> **EXCLUDES** *urinary tract infection (634-638 with .7)*

.1 Complicated by delayed or excessive hemorrhage
Afibrinogenemia
Defibrination syndrome
Intravascular hemolysis
Any condition classifiable to 639.1, with condition classifiable to 634-638

.2 Complicated by damage to pelvic organs and tissues
Laceration, perforation, or tear of:
  bladder
  uterus
Any condition classifiable to 639.2, with condition classifiable to 634-638

.3 Complicated by renal failure
Oliguria
Uremia
Any condition classifiable to 639.3, with condition classifiable to 634-638

.4 Complicated by metabolic disorder
Electrolyte imbalance with conditions classifiable to 634-638

.5 Complicated by shock
Circulatory collapse
Shock (postoperative) (septic)
Any condition classifiable to 639.5, with condition classifiable to 634-638

.6 Complicated by embolism
Embolism:
  NOS
  amniotic fluid
  pulmonary
Any condition classifiable to 639.6, with condition classifiable to 634-638

.7 With other specified complications
Cardiac arrest or failure
Urinary tract infection
Any condition classifiable to 639.8, with condition classifiable to 634-638

.8 With unspecified complication

.9 Without mention of complication

▣ Additional Digit Required   **Nonspecific PDx**   **Unacceptable PDx**   **Manifestation Code**   **MCV** Major Cardiovascular Condition   ▶◀ Revised Text   ● New Code   ▲ Revised Code Title

2007 ICD•9•CM   **Volume 1 — 193**

§ ✓4ᵗʰ **634 Spontaneous abortion**

Requires fifth-digit to identify stage:
  0 unspecified
  1 incomplete
  2 complete

INCLUDES miscarriage
      spontaneous abortion

AHA: 2Q, '91, 16

DEF: Spontaneous premature expulsion of the products of conception from the uterus.

✓5ᵗʰ **634.0 Complicated by genital tract and pelvic infection** cc M ♀
  CC Excl: 634.00-638.9, 640.00-641.23, 646.80-646.93, 648.90-650, 669.40-669.44, 669.80-669.94

✓5ᵗʰ **634.1 Complicated by delayed or excessive hemorrhage** cc M ♀
  CC Excl: See code 634.0
  AHA: For Code 634.11: 1Q, '03, 6

✓5ᵗʰ **634.2 Complicated by damage to pelvic organs or tissues** cc M ♀
  CC Excl: See code 634.0

✓5ᵗʰ **634.3 Complicated by renal failure** cc M ♀
  CC Excl: See code 634.0

✓5ᵗʰ **634.4 Complicated by metabolic disorder** cc M ♀
  CC Excl: See code 634.0

✓5ᵗʰ **634.5 Complicated by shock** cc M ♀
  CC Excl: See code 634.0

✓5ᵗʰ **634.6 Complicated by embolism** cc M ♀
  CC Excl: See code 634.0

✓5ᵗʰ **634.7 With other specified complications** cc M ♀
  CC Excl: See code 634.0

✓5ᵗʰ **634.8 With unspecified complication** cc M ♀
  CC Excl: See code 634.0

✓5ᵗʰ **634.9 Without mention of complication** cc M ♀
  CC Excl: See code 634.0

§ ✓4ᵗʰ **635 Legally induced abortion**

Requires fifth-digit to identify stage:
  0 unspecified
  1 incomplete
  2 complete

INCLUDES abortion or termination of pregnancy:
      elective
      legal
      therapeutic

EXCLUDES *menstrual extraction or regulation (V25.3)*

AHA: 2Q, '94, 14

DEF: Intentional expulsion of products of conception from uterus performed by medical professionals inside boundaries of law.

✓5ᵗʰ **635.0 Complicated by genital tract and pelvic infection** M ♀

✓5ᵗʰ **635.1 Complicated by delayed or excessive hemorrhage** M ♀

✓5ᵗʰ **635.2 Complicated by damage to pelvic organs or tissues** M ♀

✓5ᵗʰ **635.3 Complicated by renal failure** M ♀

✓5ᵗʰ **635.4 Complicated by metabolic disorder** M ♀

✓5ᵗʰ **635.5 Complicated by shock** M ♀

✓5ᵗʰ **635.6 Complicated by embolism** M ♀

✓5ᵗʰ **635.7 With other specified complications** M ♀

✓5ᵗʰ **635.8 With unspecified complication** M ♀

✓5ᵗʰ **635.9 Without mention of complication** M ♀
  AHA: For code 635.92; 2Q, '94, 14

§ ✓4ᵗʰ **636 Illegally induced abortion**

Requires fifth-digit to identify stage:
  0 unspecified
  1 incomplete
  2 complete

INCLUDES abortion:
      criminal
      illegal
      self-induced

DEF: Intentional expulsion of products of conception from uterus; outside boundaries of law.

✓5ᵗʰ **636.0 Complicated by genital tract and pelvic infection** M ♀

✓5ᵗʰ **636.1 Complicated by delayed or excessive hemorrhage** M ♀

✓5ᵗʰ **636.2 Complicated by damage to pelvic organs or tissues** M ♀

✓5ᵗʰ **636.3 Complicated by renal failure** M ♀

✓5ᵗʰ **636.4 Complicated by metabolic disorder** M ♀

✓5ᵗʰ **636.5 Complicated by shock** M ♀

✓5ᵗʰ **636.6 Complicated by embolism** M ♀

✓5ᵗʰ **636.7 With other specified complications** M ♀

✓5ᵗʰ **636.8 With unspecified complication** M ♀

✓5ᵗʰ **636.9 Without mention of complication** M ♀

§ ✓4ᵗʰ **637 Unspecified abortion**

Requires fifth-digit to identify stage:
  0 unspecified
  1 incomplete
  2 complete

INCLUDES abortion NOS
      retained products of conception following
        abortion, not classifiable elsewhere

✓5ᵗʰ **637.0 Complicated by genital tract and pelvic infection** M ♀

✓5ᵗʰ **637.1 Complicated by delayed or excessive hemorrhage** M ♀

✓5ᵗʰ **637.2 Complicated by damage to pelvic organs or tissues** M ♀

✓5ᵗʰ **637.3 Complicated by renal failure** M ♀

✓5ᵗʰ **637.4 Complicated by metabolic disorder** M ♀

✓5ᵗʰ **637.5 Complicated by shock** M ♀

✓5ᵗʰ **637.6 Complicated by embolism** M ♀

✓5ᵗʰ **637.7 With other specified complications** M ♀

✓5ᵗʰ **637.8 With unspecified complication** M ♀

✓5ᵗʰ **637.9 Without mention of complication** M ♀

§ ✓4ᵗʰ **638 Failed attempted abortion**

INCLUDES failure of attempted induction of (legal) abortion

EXCLUDES *incomplete abortion (634.0-637.9)*

DEF: Continued pregnancy despite an attempted legal abortion.

638.0 Complicated by genital tract and pelvic infection M ♀

638.1 Complicated by delayed or excessive hemorrhage M ♀

638.2 Complicated by damage to pelvic organs or tissues M ♀

638.3 Complicated by renal failure M ♀

638.4 Complicated by metabolic disorder M ♀

638.5 Complicated by shock M ♀

638.6 Complicated by embolism M ♀

638.7 With other specified complications M ♀

638.8 With unspecified complication M ♀

638.9 Without mention of complication M ♀

§ See beginning of section 634-639 for fourth-digit definitions.

N Newborn Age: 0   P Pediatric Age: 0-17   M Maternity Age: 12-55   A Adult Age: 15-124   cc CC Condition   MC Major Complication   CD Complex Dx   HIV HIV Related Dx

✓4ᵗʰ **639 Complications following abortion and ectopic and molar pregnancies**

Note: This category is provided for use when it is required to classify separately the complications classifiable to the fourth-digit level in categories 634-638; for example:

a) when the complication itself was responsible for an episode of medical care, the abortion, ectopic or molar pregnancy itself having been dealt with at a previous episode

b) when these conditions are immediate complications of ectopic or molar pregnancies classifiable to 630-633 where they cannot be identified at fourth-digit level.

639.0   Genital tract and pelvic infection   cc M ♀

Endometritis
Parametritis
Pelvic peritonitis
Salpingitis   } following conditions classifiable to 630-638
Salpingo-oophoritis
Sepsis NOS
Septicemia NOS

> **EXCLUDES**   *urinary tract infection (639.8)*

CC Excl: 639.0, 639.2-641.23, 646.80-646.93, 648.90-650, 669.40-669.44, 669.80-669.94

639.1   Delayed or excessive hemorrhage   cc M ♀

Afibrinogenemia
Defibrination syndrome   } following conditions classifiable to 630-638
Intravascular hemolysis

CC Excl: 639.1-639.9, 640.00-640.93, 641.00-641.23, 646.80-646.93, 648.90-648.94, 650, 669.40-669.44, 669.80-669.94

639.2   Damage to pelvic organs and tissues   cc M ♀

Laceration, perforation, or tear of:
  bladder
  bowel
  broad ligament   } following conditions classifiable to 630-638
  cervix
  periurethral tissue
  uterus
  vagina

CC Excl: 639.2-639.9, 640.00-640.93, 641.00-641.23, 646.80-646.93, 648.90-648.94, 650, 669.40-669.44, 669.80-669.94

639.3   Renal failure   cc M ♀

Oliguria
Renal:
  failure (acute)   } following conditions classifiable to 630-638
  shutdown
  tubular necrosis
Uremia

CC Excl: See code 639.2

639.4   Metabolic disorders   cc M ♀

Electrolyte imbalance following conditions classifiable to 630-638

CC Excl: See code 639.2

639.5   Shock   cc M ♀

Circulatory collapse
Shock (postoperative)   } following conditions classifiable to 630-638
  (septic)

CC Excl: See code 639.2

639.6   Embolism   cc M ♀

Embolism:
  NOS
  air
  amniotic fluid
  blood-clot
  fat   } following conditions classifiable to 630-638
  pulmonary
  pyemic
  septic
  soap

CC Excl: See code 639.2

639.8   Other specified complications following abortionor ectopic and molar pregnancy   cc M ♀

Acute yellow atrophy or necrosis of liver
Cardiac arrest or failure   } following conditions classifiable to 630-638
Cerebral anoxia
Urinary tract infection

CC Excl: See code 639.2

639.9   Unspecified complication following abortion orectopic and molar pregnancy   cc M ♀

Complication(s) not further specified following conditions classifiable to 630-638

CC Excl: See code 639.2

COMPLICATIONS MAINLY RELATED TO PREGNANCY ▶(640-649)◀

> **INCLUDES**   the listed conditions even if they arose or were present during labor, delivery, or the puerperium

AHA: 2Q, '90, 11

The following fifth-digit subclassification is for use with categories ▶640-649◀ to denote the current episode of care. Valid fifth-digits are in [brackets] under each code.

0   unspecified as to episode of care or not applicable

1   delivered, with or without mention of antepartum condition
  Antepartum condition with delivery
  Delivery NOS (with mention of antepartum complication during current episode of care)
  Intrapartum obstetric condition (with mention of antepartum complication during current episode of care)
  Pregnancy, delivered (with mention of antepartum complication during current episode of care)

2   delivered, with mention of postpartum complication
  Delivery with mention of puerperal complication during current episode of care

3   antepartum condition or complication
  Antepartum obstetric condition, not delivered during the current episode of care

4   postpartum condition or complication
  Postpartum or puerperal obstetric condition or complication following delivery that occurred:
    during previous episode of care
    outside hospital, with subsequent admission for observation or care

✓4ᵗʰ **640 Hemorrhage in early pregnancy**

> **INCLUDES**   hemorrhage before completion of 22 weeks' gestation

✓5ᵗʰ **640.0   Threatened abortion**   cc M ♀
[0,1,3]   **CC Excl:** 640.00-640.93, 641.00-641.13, 646.80-646.93, 648.90-648.94, 650, 669.40-669.44, 669.80-669.94

DEF: Bloody discharge during pregnancy; cervix may be dilated and pregnancy is threatened, but the pregnancy is not terminated.

✓5ᵗʰ **640.8   Other specified hemorrhage in early**   cc M ♀
[0,1,3]   **pregnancy**
  CC Excl: See code 640.0

✓4ᵗʰ Additional Digit Required   Nonspecific PDx   Unacceptable PDx   Manifestation Code   **MCV** Major Cardiovascular Condition   ▶◀ Revised Text   ● New Code   ▲ Revised Code Title

2007 ICD•9•CM   **October 2006 • Volume 1 — 195**

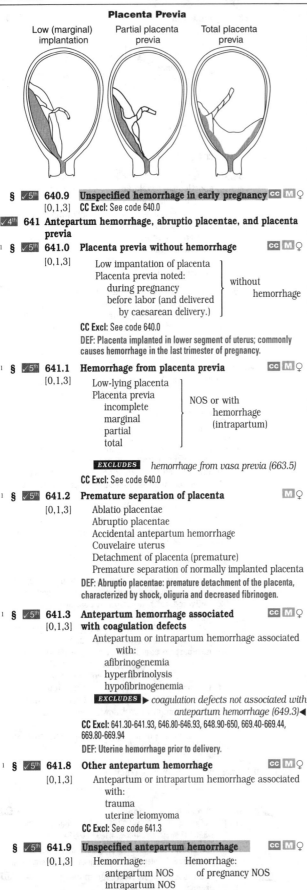

Placenta Previa

Low (marginal) implantation   Partial placenta previa   Total placenta previa

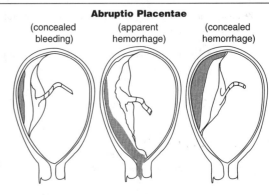

Abruptio Placentae

(concealed bleeding)   (apparent hemorrhage)   (concealed hemorrhage)

§ ✓5ᵗʰ **640.9 Unspecified hemorrhage in early pregnancy** CC M ♀
[0,1,3]   CC Excl: See code 640.0

✓4ᵗʰ **641 Antepartum hemorrhage, abruptio placentae, and placenta previa**

¹ § ✓5ᵗʰ **641.0 Placenta previa without hemorrhage** CC M ♀
[0,1,3]

Low impantation of placenta
Placenta previa noted:
   during pregnancy
   before labor (and delivered
      by caesarean delivery.)   } without hemorrhage

CC Excl: See code 640.0

DEF: Placenta implanted in lower segment of uterus; commonly causes hemorrhage in the last trimester of pregnancy.

¹ § ✓5ᵗʰ **641.1 Hemorrhage from placenta previa** CC M ♀
[0,1,3]

Low-lying placenta
Placenta previa
  incomplete
  marginal   } NOS or with hemorrhage (intrapartum)
  partial
  total

EXCLUDES   *hemorrhage from vasa previa (663.5)*

CC Excl: See code 640.0

¹ § ✓5ᵗʰ **641.2 Premature separation of placenta** M ♀
[0,1,3]

Ablatio placentae
Abruptio placentae
Accidental antepartum hemorrhage
Couvelaire uterus
Detachment of placenta (premature)
Premature separation of normally implanted placenta

DEF: Abruptio placentae: premature detachment of the placenta, characterized by shock, oliguria and decreased fibrinogen.

¹ § ✓5ᵗʰ **641.3 Antepartum hemorrhage associated** CC M ♀
[0,1,3] **with coagulation defects**

Antepartum or intrapartum hemorrhage associated
  with:
    afibrinogenemia
    hyperfibrinolysis
    hypofibrinogenemia

EXCLUDES ▶ *coagulation defects not associated with antepartum hemorrhage (649.3)*◀

CC Excl: 641.30-641.93, 646.80-646.93, 648.90-650, 669.40-669.44, 669.80-669.94

DEF: Uterine hemorrhage prior to delivery.

¹ § ✓5ᵗʰ **641.8 Other antepartum hemorrhage** CC M ♀
[0,1,3]

Antepartum or intrapartum hemorrhage associated
  with:
    trauma
    uterine leiomyoma

CC Excl: See code 641.3

§ ✓5ᵗʰ **641.9 Unspecified antepartum hemorrhage** CC M ♀
[0,1,3]

Hemorrhage: Hemorrhage:
  antepartum NOS   of pregnancy NOS
  intrapartum NOS

CC Excl: See code 641.3

✓4ᵗʰ **642 Hypertension complicating pregnancy, childbirth, and the puerperium**

¹ § ✓5ᵗʰ **642.0 Benign essential hypertension complicating** M ♀
[0-4] **pregnancy, childbirth, and the puerperium**

Hypertension: specified as complicating,
  benign essential   or as a reason for
  chronic NOS   obstetric care during
  essential   pregnancy, childbirth,
  pre-existing NOS   or the puerperium

¹ § ✓5ᵗʰ **642.1 Hypertension secondary to renal disease,** M ♀
[0-4] **complicating pregnancy, childbirth, and the puerperium**

Hypertension secondary to renal disease, specified
  as complicating, or as a reason for obstetric
  care during pregnancy, childbirth, or the
  puerperium

¹ § ✓5ᵗʰ **642.2 Other pre-existing hypertension complicating** M ♀
[0-4] **pregnancy, childbirth, and the puerperium**

Hypertensive: specified as
  ▶chronic kidney◀   complicating, or
    disease   as a reason for
  heart and ▶chronic   obstetric care
    kidney◀ disease   during pregnancy,
  heart disease   childbirth, or the
  Malignant hypertension   puerperium

¹ § ✓5ᵗʰ **642.3 Transient hypertension of pregnancy** M ♀
[0-4]

Gestational hypertension
Transient hypertension, so described, in pregnancy,
  childbirth, or the puerperium

AHA: 3Q, '90, 4

¹ § ✓5ᵗʰ **642.4 Mild or unspecified pre-eclampsia** CC M ♀
[0-4]

Hypertension in pregnancy, childbirth, or the
  puerperium, not specified as pre-existing, with
  either albuminuria or edema, or both; mild or
  unspecified
Pre-eclampsia: Toxemia (pre-eclamptic):
  NOS   NOS
  mild   mild

EXCLUDES   *albuminuria in pregnancy, without mention of hypertension (646.2)*
edema in pregnancy, without mention of hypertension (646.1)

CC Excl: 642.00-642.94, 646.10-646.14, 646.80-646.93, 648.90-650, 669.40-669.44, 669.80-669.94

¹ § ✓5ᵗʰ **642.5 Severe pre-eclampsia** CC M ♀
[0-4]

Hypertension in pregnancy, childbirth, or the
  puerperium, not specified as pre-existing, with
  either albuminuria or edema, or both; specified
  as severe
Pre-eclampsia, severe
Toxemia (pre-eclamptic), severe

CC Excl: See code 642.4

AHA: N-D, '85, 3

¹ Nonspecific PDx=0
§ Requires fifth-digit. Valid digits are in [brackets] under each code. See beginning of section 640-649 for codes and definitions.

N Newborn Age: 0   P Pediatric Age: 0-17   M Maternity Age: 12-55   A Adult Age: 15-124   CC CC Condition   MC Major Complication   CD Complex Dx   HIV HIV Related Dx

¹ § ✓5ᵗʰ **642.6** **Eclampsia**   CC M ♀
[0-4]   Toxemia:
       eclamptic
       with convulsions
    CC Excl: See code 642.4

¹ § ✓5ᵗʰ **642.7** **Pre-eclampsia or eclampsia superimposed** CC M ♀
[0-4] **on pre-existing hypertension**
       Conditions classifiable to 642.4-642.6, with
         conditions classifiable to 642.0-642.2
    CC Excl: See code 642.4

¹ § ✓5ᵗʰ **642.9** **Unspecified hypertension complicating** M ♀
[0-4]   **pregnancy, childbirth, or the puerperium**
       Hypertension NOS, without mention of albuminuria
         or edema, complicating pregnancy, childbirth,
         or the puerperium

✓4ᵗʰ **643 Excessive vomiting in pregnancy**

    INCLUDES hyperemesis
           vomiting: } arising during
            persistent   } pregnancy
            vicious   }
          hyperemesis gravidarum

¹ § ✓5ᵗʰ **643.0** **Mild hyperemesis gravidarum** M ♀
[0,1,3]   Hyperemesis gravidarum, mild or unspecified,
         starting before the end of the 22nd week of
         gestation
    DEF: Detrimental vomiting and nausea.

¹ § ✓5ᵗʰ **643.1** **Hyperemesis gravidarum with metabolic** M ♀
[0,1,3] **disturbance**
       Hyperemesis gravidarum, starting before the end of
         the 22nd week of gestation, with metabolic
         disturbance, such as:
         carbohydrate depletion
         dehydration
         electrolyte imbalance

¹ § ✓5ᵗʰ **643.2** **Late vomiting of pregnancy** M ♀
[0,1,3]   Excessive vomiting starting after 22 completed
         weeks of gestation

¹ § ✓5ᵗʰ **643.8** **Other vomiting complicating pregnancy** M ♀
[0,1,3]   Vomiting due to organic disease or other cause,
         specified as complicating pregnancy, or as a
         reason for obstetric care during pregnancy
       Use additional code to specify cause

¹ § ✓5ᵗʰ **643.9** **Unspecified vomiting of pregnancy** M ♀
[0,1,3]   Vomiting as a reason for care during pregnancy,
         length of gestation unspecified

✓4ᵗʰ **644 Early or threatened labor**

¹ § ✓5ᵗʰ **644.0** **Threatened premature labor** CC M ♀
[0,3]   Premature labor after 22 weeks, but before 37
         completed weeks of gestation without delivery
       EXCLUDES that occurring before 22 completed
                 weeks of gestation (640.0)
    CC Excl: 644.00-644.21, 646.80-646.93, 648.90-650, 669.40-669.44,
    669.80-669.94

¹ § ✓5ᵗʰ **644.1** **Other threatened labor** CC M ♀
[0,3]   False labor:
       NOS
       after 37 completed weeks of   } without
         gestation   } delivery
       Threatened labor NOS   }
    CC Excl: See code 644.0

¹ § ✓5ᵗʰ **644.2** **Early onset of delivery** M ♀
[0,1]   Onset (spontaneous) of   }
       delivery   } before 37 completed
       Premature labor with   } weeks of gestation
       onset of delivery   }
    AHA: 2Q, '91, 16

✓4ᵗʰ **645 Late pregnancy**
    AHA: 4Q, '00, 43; 4Q, '91, 26

§ ✓5ᵗʰ **645.1** **Post term pregnancy** M ♀
[0,1,3]   Pregnancy over 40 completed weeks to 42
         completed weeks gestation

§ ✓5ᵗʰ **645.2** **Prolonged pregnancy** M ♀
[0,1,3]   Pregnancy which has advanced beyond 42
         completed weeks gestation

✓4ᵗʰ **646 Other complications of pregnancy, not elsewhere classified**
    Use additional code(s) to further specify complication
    AHA: 4Q, '95, 59

¹ § ✓5ᵗʰ **646.0** **Papyraceous fetus** M ♀
[0,1,3]
    DEF: Fetus that dies in the second trimester of pregnancy and is
    retained in the uterus, with subsequent atrophy and mummification;
    commonly occurs in twin pregnancy, nonviable fetus becomes
    compressed by growth of living twin and exhibits parchment-like
    skin.

¹ § ✓5ᵗʰ **646.1** **Edema or excessive weight gain in pregnancy,** M ♀
[0-4] **without mention of hypertension**
       Gestational edema
       Maternal obesity syndrome
       EXCLUDES that with mention of hypertension
                 (642.0-642.9)

¹ § ✓5ᵗʰ **646.2** **Unspecified renal disease in pregnancy,** M ♀
[0-4] **without mention of hypertension**
       Albuminuria   } in pregnancy or the
       Nephropathy NOS   } puerperium
       Renal disease NOS   } without mention of
       Uremia   } hypertension

       Gestational proteinuria
       EXCLUDES that with mention of hypertension
                 (642.0-642.9)

¹ § ✓5ᵗʰ **646.3** **Habitual aborter** M ♀
[0,1,3]   EXCLUDES with current abortion (634.0-634.9)
                 without current pregnancy (629.9)
    DEF: Three or more consecutive spontaneous abortions.

¹ § ✓5ᵗʰ **646.4** **Peripheral neuritis in pregnancy** M ♀
[0-4]

¹ § ✓5ᵗʰ **646.5** **Asymptomatic bacteriuria in pregnancy** M ♀
[0-4]

¹ § ✓5ᵗʰ **646.6** **Infections of genitourinary tract in** CC M ♀
[0-4] **pregnancy**
       Conditions classifiable to 590, 595, 597, 599.0, 616
         complicating pregnancy, childbirth, or the
         puerperium
       Conditions classifiable to 614.0-614.5, 614.7-614.9,
         615 complicating pregnancy or labor
       EXCLUDES major puerperal infection (670)
    CC Excl: 646.60-646.64, 646.80-646.93, 648.90-648.94,
    650, 669.40-669.44, 669.80-669.94
    AHA: For code 646.63: 4Q, '04, 90

¹ § ✓5ᵗʰ **646.7** **Liver disorders in pregnancy** CC M ♀
[0,1,3]   Acute yellow atrophy of   }
         liver (obstetric) (true)   } of pregnancy
       Icterus gravis   }
       Necrosis of liver   }

       EXCLUDES hepatorenal syndrome following
                 delivery (674.8)
                 viral hepatitis (647.6)
    CC Excl: 646.70-646.93, 648.90-650, 669.40-669.44, 669.80-669.94

¹ § ✓5ᵗʰ **646.8** **Other specified complications of pregnancy** M ♀
[0-4]   Fatigue during pregnancy
       Herpes gestationis
       Insufficient weight gain of pregnancy
    AHA: 3Q, '98, 16; J-F, '85, 15

¹ § ✓5ᵗʰ **646.9** **Unspecified complication of pregnancy** M ♀
[0,1,3]

---

¹ Nonspecific PDx=0
§ Requires fifth-digit. Valid digits are in [brackets] under each code. See beginning of section 640-649 for codes and definitions.

 Additional Digit Required   Nonspecific PDx   Unacceptable PDx   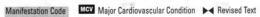 Manifestation Code   **MCV** Major Cardiovascular Condition   ►◄ Revised Text   ● New Code   ▲ Revised Code Title

Complications of Pregnancy, Childbirth & Puerperium (side margin)

647–649.6 (side margin)

✓4ᵗʰ **647 Infectious and parasitic conditions in the mother classifiable elsewhere, but complicating pregnancy, childbirth, or the puerperium**

> INCLUDES   the listed conditions when complicating the pregnant state, aggravated by the pregnancy, or when a main reason for obstetric care

> EXCLUDES   *those conditions in the mother known or suspected to have affected the fetus (655.0-655.9)*

Use additional code(s) to further specify complication

¹ § ✓5ᵗʰ **647.0 Syphilis**   M ♀
[0-4]   Conditions classifiable to 090-097

¹ § ✓5ᵗʰ **647.1 Gonorrhea**   M ♀
[0-4]   Conditions classifiable to 098

¹ § ✓5ᵗʰ **647.2 Other venereal diseases**   M ♀
[0-4]   Conditions classifiable to 099

¹ § ✓5ᵗʰ **647.3 Tuberculosis**   CC M ♀
[0-4]   Conditions classifiable to 010-018

> CC Excl: 646.80-646.93, 647.30-647.34, 648.90-650, 669.40-669.44, 669.80-669.94

¹ § ✓5ᵗʰ **647.4 Malaria**   CC M ♀
[0-4]   Conditions classifiable to 084

> CC Excl: 646.80-646.93, 647.30-647.34, 648.90-650, 669.40-669.44, 669.80-669.94

¹ § ✓5ᵗʰ **647.5 Rubella**   M ♀
[0-4]   Conditions classifiable to 056

¹ § ✓5ᵗʰ **647.6 Other viral diseases**   M ♀
[0-4]   Conditions classifiable to 042 and 050-079, except 056

> AHA: J-F, '85, 15

¹ § ✓5ᵗʰ **647.8 Other specified infectious and parasitic**   M ♀
[0-4]   **diseases**

§ ✓5ᵗʰ **647.9 Unspecified infection or infestation**   M ♀
[0-4]

✓4ᵗʰ **648 Other current conditions in the mother classifiable elsewhere, but complicating pregnancy, childbirth, or the puerperium**

> INCLUDES   the listed conditions when complicating the pregnant state, aggravated by the pregnancy, or when a main reason for obstetric care

> EXCLUDES   *those conditions in the mother known or suspected to have affected the fetus (655.0-665.9)*

Use additional code(s) to identify the condition

¹ § ✓5ᵗʰ **648.0 Diabetes mellitus**   CC M ♀
[0-4]   Conditions classifiable to 250

> EXCLUDES   *gestational diabetes (648.8)*

> CC Excl: 646.80-646.93, 648.00-648.04, 648.90-650, 669.40-669.44, 669.80-669.94

> AHA: 3Q, '91, 5, 11

¹ § ✓5ᵗʰ **648.1 Thyroid dysfunction**   M ♀
[0-4]   Conditions classifiable to 240-246

¹ § ✓5ᵗʰ **648.2 Anemia**   CC M ♀
[0-4]   Conditions classifiable to 280-285

> CC Excl: 646.80-646.93, 648.20-648.24, 648.90-650, 669.40-669.44, 669.80-669.94

> AHA: For Code 648.22: 1Q, '02, 14

¹ § ✓5ᵗʰ **648.3 Drug dependence**   CC M ♀
[0-4]   Conditions classifiable to 304

> CC Excl: 646.80-646.93, 648.30-648.34, 648.90-650, 669.40-669.44, 669.80-669.94

> AHA: 2Q, '98, 13; 4Q, '88, 8

¹ § ✓5ᵗʰ **648.4 Mental disorders**   M ♀
[0-4]   Conditions classifiable to 290-303, ▶305.0, 305.2-305.9, 306-316, 317-319◀

> AHA: 2Q, '98, 13; 4Q, '95, 63

¹ § ✓5ᵗʰ **648.5 Congenital cardiovascular disorders**   CC M ♀
[0-4]   Conditions classifiable to 745-747

> CC Excl: 646.80-646.93, 648.50-648.64, 648.90-648.94, 650, 669.40-669.44, 669.80-669.94

¹ § ✓5ᵗʰ **648.6 Other cardiovascular diseases**   CC M ♀
[0-4]   Conditions classifiable to 390-398, 410-429

> EXCLUDES   *cerebrovascular disorders in the puerperium (674.0) peripartum cardiomyopathy (674.5) venous complications (671.0-671.9)*

> CC Excl: See code 648.5

> AHA: 3Q, '98, 11

¹ § ✓5ᵗʰ **648.7 Bone and joint disorders of back, pelvis, and**   M ♀
[0-4]   **lower limbs**
     Conditions classifiable to 720-724, and those classifiable to 711-719 or 725-738, specified as affecting the lower limbs

¹ § ✓5ᵗʰ **648.8 Abnormal glucose tolerance**   M ♀
[0-4]   Conditions classifiable to 790.21-790.29
     Gestational diabetes
     Use additional code, if applicable, for associated long-term (current) insulin use (V58.67)

> AHA: 3Q, '91, 5; For code 648.83: 4Q, '04, 56

> DEF: Glucose intolerance arising in pregnancy, resolving at end of pregnancy.

¹ § ✓5ᵗʰ **648.9 Other current conditions classifiable**   M ♀
     elsewhere
[0-4]   Conditions classifiable to 440-459
     Nutritional deficiencies [conditions classifiable to 260-269]

> AHA: 4Q, '04, 88; N-D, '87, 10; For code 648.91: 1Q, '02, 14; For code 648.93: 4Q, '04, 90

● ✓4ᵗʰ **649 Other conditions or status of the mother complicating pregnancy, childbirth, or the puerperium**

● § ✓5ᵗʰ **649.0 Tobacco use disorder complicating pregnancy,** M ♀
[0-4]   **childbirth, or the puerperium**
     Smoking complicating pregnancy, childbirth, or the puerperium

● § ✓5ᵗʰ **649.1 Obesity complicating pregnancy, childbirth,** M ♀
[0-4]   **or the puerperium**
     Use additional code to identify the obesity (278.00, 278.01)

● § ✓5ᵗʰ **649.2 Bariatric surgery status complicating** M ♀
[0-4]   **pregnancy, childbirth, or the puerperium**
     Gastric banding status complicating pregnancy, childbirth, or the puerperium
     Gastric bypass status for obesity complicating pregnancy, childbirth, or the puerperium
     Obesity surgery status complicating pregnancy, childbirth, or the puerperium

● § ✓5ᵗʰ **649.3 Coagulation defects complicating pregnancy,** M ♀
[0-4]   **childbirth, or the puerperium**
     Conditions classifiable to 286
     Use additional code to identify the specific coagulation defect (286.0-286.9)

> EXCLUDES   *coagulation defects causing antepartum hemorrhage (641.3) postpartum coagulation defects (666.3)*

● § ✓5ᵗʰ **649.4 Epilepsy complicating pregnancy,** M ♀
[0-4]   **childbirth, or the puerperium**
     Conditions classifiable to 345
     Use additional code to identify the specific type of epilepsy (345.00-345.91)

> EXCLUDES   *eclampsia (642.6)*

● § ✓5ᵗʰ **649.5 Spotting complicating pregnancy** M ♀
[0,1,3]   EXCLUDES   *antepartum hemorrhage (641.0-641.9) hemorrhage in early pregnancy (640.0-640.9)*

● § ✓5ᵗʰ **649.6 Uterine size date discrepancy** M ♀
[0-4]

---

¹   Nonspecific PDx=0

§   Requires fifth-digit. Valid digits are in [brackets] under each code. See beginning of section 640-649 for codes and definitions.

N Newborn Age: 0   P Pediatric Age: 0-17   M Maternity Age: 12-55   A Adult Age: 15-124   CC CC Condition   MC Major Complication   CD Complex Dx   HIV HIV Related Dx

NORMAL DELIVERY, AND OTHER INDICATIONS FOR CARE IN PREGNANCY, LABOR, AND DELIVERY (650-659)

The following fifth-digit subclassification is for use with categories 651-659 to denote the current episode of care. Valid fifth-digits are in [brackets] under each code.

0 unspecified as to episode of care or not applicable
1 delivered, with or without mention of antepartum condition
2 delivered, with mention of postpartum complication
3 antepartum condition or complication
4 postpartum condition or complication

650 Normal delivery M♀

Delivery requiring minimal or no assistance, with or without episiotomy, without fetal manipulation [e.g., rotation version] or instrumentation [forceps] of spontaneous, cephalic, vaginal, full-term, single, live-born infant. This code is for use as a single diagnosis code and is not to be used with any other code in the range 630-676.

> **EXCLUDES** breech delivery (assisted) (spontaneous) NOS (652.2)
> delivery by vacuum extractor, forceps, cesarean section, or breech extraction, without specified complication (669.5-669.7)

Use additional code to indicate outcome of delivery (V27.0)

AHA: 2Q, '02, 10; 3Q, '01, 12; 3Q, '00, 5; 4Q, '95, 28, 59

✓4th 651 Multiple gestation

¹ § ✓5th **651.0 Twin pregnancy** M♀
[0,1,3]

¹ § ✓5th **651.1 Triplet pregnancy** M♀
[0,1,3]

¹ § ✓5th **651.2 Quadruplet pregnancy** M♀
[0,1,3]

¹ § ✓5th **651.3 Twin pregnancy with fetal loss and retention** M♀
[0,1,3] **of one fetus**

¹ § ✓5th **651.4 Triplet pregnancy with fetal loss and** M♀
[0,1,3] **retention of one or more fetus(es)**

¹ § ✓5th **651.5 Quadruplet pregnancy with fetal loss and** M♀
[0,1,3] **retention of one or more fetus(es)**

¹ § ✓5th **651.6 Other multiple pregnancy with fetal loss and** M♀
[0,1,3] **retention of one or more fetus(es)**

§ ✓5th **651.7 Multiple gestation following (elective) fetal** M♀
[0,1,3] **reduction**

Fetal reduction of multiple fetuses reduced to single fetus

AHA: For code 651.71: ▶4Q, '05, 81◀

¹ § ✓5th **651.8 Other specified multiple gestation** M♀
[0,1,3]

§ ✓5th **651.9 Unspecified multiple gestation** M♀
[0,1,3]

✓4th 652 Malposition and malpresentation of fetus

Code first any associated obstructed labor (660.0)

¹ § ✓5th **652.0 Unstable lie** M♀
[0,1,3] **DEF:** Changing fetal position.

Malposition and Malpresentation

Breech

Shoulder (arm prolapse)

Mother's pelvis

Face (mentum)

Compound (extremity together with head)

Oblique

Cephalopelvic Disproportion

Pubic symphysis

Cephalopelvic disproportion due to: Contraction of pelvic inlet, or large fetus, or hydrocephalus

Ischial tuberosity

Contraction of pelvic outlet (from below)

Pubic symphysis

Pelvic inlet from above

¹ § ✓5th **652.1 Breech or other malpresentation successfully** M♀
[0,1,3] **converted to cephalic presentation**
Cephalic version NOS

¹ § ✓5th **652.2 Breech presentation without mention of** M♀
[0,1,3] **version**
Breech delivery (assisted) (spontaneous) NOS
Buttocks presentation
Complete breech
Frank breech
> **EXCLUDES** footling presentation (652.8)
> incomplete breech (652.8)

DEF: Fetal presentation of buttocks or feet at birth canal.

¹ § ✓5th **652.3 Transverse or oblique presentation** M♀
[0,1,3] Oblique lie   Transverse lie
> **EXCLUDES** transverse arrest of fetal head (660.3)

¹ § ✓5th **652.4 Face or brow presentation** M♀
[0,1,3] Mentum presentation

¹ § ✓5th **652.5 High head at term** M♀
[0,1,3] Failure of head to enter pelvic brim

¹ § ✓5th **652.6 Multiple gestation with malpresentation of** M♀
[0,1,3] **one fetus or more**

¹ § ✓5th **652.7 Prolapsed arm** M♀
[0,1,3]

¹ § ✓5th **652.8 Other specified malposition or** M♀
[0,1,3] **malpresentation**
Compound presentation

§ ✓5th **652.9 Unspecified malposition or malpresentation** M♀
[0,1,3]

✓4th 653 Disproportion

Code first any associated obstructed labor (660.1)

¹ § ✓5th **653.0 Major abnormality of bony pelvis, not further** M♀
[0,1,3] **specified**
Pelvic deformity NOS

¹ § ✓5th **653.1 Generally contracted pelvis** M♀
[0,1,3] Contracted pelvis NOS

¹ § ✓5th **653.2 Inlet contraction of pelvis** M♀
[0,1,3] Inlet contraction (pelvis)

¹ § ✓5th **653.3 Outlet contraction of pelvis** M♀
[0,1,3] Outlet contraction (pelvis)

¹ § ✓5th **653.4 Fetopelvic disproportion** M♀
[0,1,3] Cephalopelvic disproportion NOS
Disproportion of mixed maternal and fetal origin, with normally formed fetus

¹ § ✓5th **653.5 Unusually large fetus causing disproportion** M♀
[0,1,3] Disproportion of fetal origin with normally formed fetus
Fetal disproportion NOS
> **EXCLUDES** that when the reason for medical care was concern for the fetus (656.6)

¹ § ✓5th **653.6 Hydrocephalic fetus causing disproportion** M♀
[0,1,3] > **EXCLUDES** that when the reason for medical care was concern for the fetus (655.0)

¹ § ✓5th **653.7 Other fetal abnormality causing disproportion** M♀
[0,1,3] Conjoined twins   Fetal:
Fetal: myelomeningocele
ascites   sacral teratoma
hydrops   tumor

---

¹ Nonspecific PDx=0
§ Requires fifth-digit. Valid digits are in [brackets] under each code. See beginning of section 640-649 for codes and definitions.

✓4th ✓5th Additional Digit Required **Nonspecific PDx** **Unacceptable PDx** **Manifestation Code** **MCV** Major Cardiovascular Condition ▶◀ Revised Text ● New Code ▲ Revised Code Title

2007 ICD•9•CM   February 2006 • Volume 1 — 199

Complications of Pregnancy, Childbirth & Puerperium

653.8–656.9

[1] § √5th **653.8 Disproportion of other origin** Ⓜ ♀
[0,1,3]
     EXCLUDES   shoulder (girdle) dystocia (660.4)

§ √5th **653.9 Unspecified disproportion** Ⓜ ♀
[0,1,3]

√4th **654 Abnormality of organs and soft tissues of pelvis**
    INCLUDES   the listed conditions during pregnancy,
                      childbirth, or the puerperium
    Code first any associated obstructed labor (660.2)

[1] § √5th **654.0 Congenital abnormalities of uterus** Ⓜ ♀
[0-4]
    Double uterus   Uterus bicornis

[1] § √5th **654.1 Tumors of body of uterus** Ⓜ ♀
[0-4]
    Uterine fibroids

[1] § √5th **654.2 Previous cesarean delivery** Ⓜ ♀
[0,1,3]
    Uterine scar from previous cesarean delivery
    AHA: 1Q, '92, 8

[1] § √5th **654.3 Retroverted and incarcerated gravid uterus** Ⓜ ♀
[0-4]

    DEF: Retroverted: tilted back uterus; no change in angle of
    longitudinal axis.

    DEF: Incarcerated: immobile, fixed uterus.

[1] § √5th **654.4 Other abnormalities in shape or position of** Ⓜ ♀
[0-4]   **gravid uterus and of neighboring structures**
    Cystocele   Prolapse of gravid uterus
    Pelvic floor repair   Rectocele
    Pendulous abdomen   Rigid pelvic floor

[1] § √5th **654.5 Cervical incompetence** Ⓜ ♀
[0-4]
    Presence of Shirodkar suture with or without
            mention of cervical incompetence

    DEF: Abnormal cervix; tendency to dilate in second trimester;
    causes premature fetal expulsion.

    DEF: Shirodkar suture: purse-string suture used to artificially close
    incompetent cervix.

[1] § √5th **654.6 Other congenital or acquired abnormality of** Ⓜ ♀
[0-4]   **cervix**
    Cicatricial cervix   Rigid cervix (uteri)
    Polyp of cervix   Stenosis or stricture of
    Previous surgery to cervix   cervix
                            Tumor of cervix

[1] § √5th **654.7 Congenital or acquired abnormality of vagina** Ⓜ ♀
[0-4]
    Previous surgery to vagina   Stricture of vagina
    Septate vagina   Tumor of vagina
    Stenosis of vagina (acquired) (congenital)

[1] § √5th **654.8 Congenital or acquired abnormality of vulva** Ⓜ ♀
[0-4]
    Fibrosis of perineum   Rigid perineum
    Persistent hymen   Tumor of vulva
    Previous surgery to
           perineum or vulva
      EXCLUDES   varicose veins of vulva (671.1)
    AHA: 1Q, '03, 14

§ √5th **654.9 Other and unspecified** Ⓜ ♀
[0-4]
    Uterine scar NEC

√4th **655 Known or suspected fetal abnormality affecting**
    management of mother
    INCLUDES   the listed conditions in the fetus as a reason
                    for observation or obstetrical care of the
                    mother, or for termination of pregnancy
    AHA: 3Q, '90, 4

[1] § √5th **655.0 Central nervous system malformation in fetus** Ⓜ ♀
[0,1,3]
    Fetal or suspected fetal:
       anencephaly
       hydrocephalus
       spina bifida (with myelomeningocele)

[1] § √5th **655.1 Chromosomal abnormality in fetus** Ⓜ ♀
[0,1,3]

[1] § √5th **655.2 Hereditary disease in family possibly** Ⓜ ♀
[0,1,3]   **affecting fetus**

[1] § √5th **655.3 Suspected damage to fetus from viral** Ⓜ ♀
[0,1,3]   **disease in the mother**
    Suspected damage to fetus from maternal rubella

[1] § √5th **655.4 Suspected damage to fetus from other** Ⓜ ♀
[0,1,3]   **disease in the mother**
    Suspected damage to fetus from maternal:
       alcohol addiction
       listeriosis
       toxoplasmosis

[1] § √5th **655.5 Suspected damage to fetus from drugs** Ⓜ ♀
[0,1,3]

[1] § √5th **655.6 Suspected damage to fetus from radiation** Ⓜ ♀
[0,1,3]

[1] § √5th **655.7 Decreased fetal movements** Ⓜ ♀
[0,1,3]   AHA: 4Q, '97, 41

[1] § √5th **655.8 Other known or suspected fetal abnormality,** Ⓜ ♀
[0,1,3]   **not elsewhere classified**
    Suspected damage to fetus from:
       environmental toxins
       intrauterine contraceptive device

§ √5th **655.9 Unspecified** Ⓜ ♀
[0,1,3]

√4th **656 Other fetal and placental problems affecting management of**
    mother

[1] § √5th **656.0 Fetal-maternal hemorrhage** Ⓜ ♀
[0,1,3]
    Leakage (microscopic) of fetal blood into maternal
       circulation

[1] § √5th **656.1 Rhesus isoimmunization** Ⓜ ♀
[0,1,3]
    Anti-D [Rh] antibodies
    Rh incompatibility

    DEF: Antibodies developing against Rh factor; mother with Rh
    negative develops antibodies against Rh positive fetus.

[1] § √5th **656.2 Isoimmunization from other and unspecified** Ⓜ ♀
[0,1,3]   **blood-group incompatibility**
    ABO isoimmunization.

[1] § √5th **656.3 Fetal distress** Ⓜ ♀
[0,1,3]
    Fetal metabolic acidemia
      EXCLUDES   abnormal fetal acid-base balance
                    (656.8)
                  abnormality in fetal heart rate or
                    rhythm (659.7)
                  fetal bradycardia (659.7)
                  fetal tachycardia (659.7)
                  meconium in liquor (656.8)
    AHA: N-D, '86, 4

    DEF: Life-threatening disorder; fetal anoxia, hemolytic disease and
    other miscellaneous diseases cause fetal distress.

[1] § √5th **656.4 Intrauterine death** Ⓜ ♀
[0,1,3]
    Fetal death:
       NOS
       after completion of 22 weeks' gestation
       late
    Missed delivery
      EXCLUDES   missed abortion (632)

[1] § √5th **656.5 Poor fetal growth** Ⓜ ♀
[0,1,3]
    "Light-for-dates"
    "Placental insufficiency"
    "Small-for-dates"

[1] § √5th **656.6 Excessive fetal growth** Ⓜ ♀
[0,1,3]
    "Large-for-dates"

[1] § √5th **656.7 Other placental conditions** Ⓜ ♀
[0,1,3]
    Abnormal placenta
    Placental infarct
      EXCLUDES   placental polyp (674.4)
                  placentitis (658.4)

[1] § √5th **656.8 Other specified fetal and placental problems** Ⓜ ♀
[0,1,3]
    Abnormal acid-base balance
    Intrauterine acidosis
    Lithopedian
    Meconium in liquor

    DEF: Lithopedion: Calcified fetus; not expelled by mother.

[1] § √5th **656.9 Unspecified fetal and placental problem** Ⓜ ♀
[0,1,3]

---

[1]   Nonspecific PDx=0
§   Requires fifth-digit. Valid digits are in [brackets] under each code. See beginning of section 640-649 for codes and definitions.

Ⓝ Newborn Age: 0   Ⓟ Pediatric Age: 0-17   Ⓜ Maternity Age: 12-55   Ⓐ Adult Age: 15-124   CC CC Condition   MC Major Complication   CD Complex Dx   HIV HIV Related Dx

¹ ☑4ᵗʰ **657 Polyhydramnios**   M ♀
     [0,1,3]
     § ☑5ᵗʰ Use 0 as fourth-digit for this category
       Hydramnios
       AHA: 4Q, '91, 26
       DEF: Excess amniotic fluid.

☑4ᵗʰ **658 Other problems associated with amniotic cavity and membranes**
       EXCLUDES   *amniotic fluid embolism (673.1)*

¹ § ☑5ᵗʰ **658.0 Oligohydramnios**   M ♀
     [0,1,3]
       Oligohydramnios without mention of rupture of membranes
       DEF: Deficient amount of amniotic fluid.

¹ § ☑5ᵗʰ **658.1 Premature rupture of membranes**   M ♀
     [0,1,3]
       Rupture of amniotic sac less than 24 hours prior to the onset of labor
       AHA: For code 658.13: 1Q, '01, 5; 4Q, '98, 77

¹ § ☑5ᵗʰ **658.2 Delayed delivery after spontaneous or unspecified rupture of membranes**   M ♀
     [0,1,3]
       Prolonged rupture of membranes NOS
       Rupture of amniotic sac 24 hours or more prior to the onset of labor

¹ § ☑5ᵗʰ **658.3 Delayed delivery after artificial rupture of membranes**   M ♀
     [0,1,3]

¹ § ☑5ᵗʰ **658.4 Infection of amniotic cavity**   M ♀
     [0,1,3]
       Amnionitis   Membranitis
       Chorioamnionitis   Placentitis

¹ § ☑5ᵗʰ **658.8 Other**   M ♀
     [0,1,3]
       Amnion nodosum   Amniotic cyst

§ ☑5ᵗʰ **658.9 Unspecified**   M ♀
     [0,1,3]

☑4ᵗʰ **659 Other indications for care or intervention related to labor and delivery, not elsewhere classified**

¹ § ☑5ᵗʰ **659.0 Failed mechanical induction**   M ♀
     [0,1,3]
       Failure of induction of labor by surgical or other instrumental methods

¹ § ☑5ᵗʰ **659.1 Failed medical or unspecified induction**   M ♀
     [0,1,3]
       Failed induction NOS
       Failure of induction of labor by medical methods, such as oxytocic drugs

¹ § ☑5ᵗʰ **659.2 Maternal pyrexia during labor, unspecified**   M ♀
     [0,1,3]   DEF: Fever during labor.

¹ § ☑5ᵗʰ **659.3 Generalized infection during labor**   CC M ♀
     [0,1,3]
       Septicemia during labor
       CC Excl: 646.80-646.93, 648.90-650, 659.30-659.33, 669.40-669.44, 669.80-669.94

¹ § ☑5ᵗʰ **659.4 Grand multiparity**   M ♀
     [0,1,3]
       EXCLUDES   *supervision only, in pregnancy (V23.3)*
          without current pregnancy (V61.5)
       DEF: Having borne six or more children previously.

¹ § ☑5ᵗʰ **659.5 Elderly primigravida**   M ♀
     [0,1,3]
       First pregnancy in a woman who will be 35 years of age or older at expected date of delivery
       EXCLUDES   *supervision only, in pregnancy (V23.81)*
       AHA: 3Q, '01, 12

¹ § ☑5ᵗʰ **659.6 Elderly multigravida**   M ♀
     [0,1,3]
       Second or more pregnancy in a woman who will be 35 years of age or older at expected date of delivery
       EXCLUDES   *elderly primigravida 659.5*
          supervision only, in pregnancy (V23.82)
       AHA: 3Q, '01, 12

¹ § ☑5ᵗʰ **659.7 Abnormality in fetal heart rate or rhythm**   M ♀
     [0,1,3]
       Depressed fetal heart tones
       Fetal:
          bradycardia
          tachycardia
       Fetal heart rate decelerations
       Non-reassuring fetal heart rate or rhythm
       AHA: 4Q, '98, 48

¹ § ☑5ᵗʰ **659.8 Other specified indications for care or intervention related to labor and delivery**   M ♀
     [0,1,3]
       Pregnancy in a female less than 16 years old at expected date of delivery
       Very young maternal age
       AHA: 3Q, '01, 12

§ ☑5ᵗʰ **659.9 Unspecified indication for care or intervention related to labor and delivery**   M ♀
     [0,1,3]

COMPLICATIONS OCCURRING MAINLY IN THE COURSE OF LABOR AND DELIVERY (660-669)

The following fifth-digit subclassification is for use with categories 660-669 to denote the current episode of care. Valid fifth-digits are in [brackets] under each code.

     0   unspecified as to episode of care or not applicable
     1   delivered, with or without mention of antepartum condition
     2   delivered, with mention of postpartum complication
     3   antepartum condition or complication
     4   postpartum condition or complication

☑4ᵗʰ **660 Obstructed labor**
     AHA: 3Q, '95, 10

¹ § ☑5ᵗʰ **660.0 Obstruction caused by malposition of fetus at onset of labor**   M ♀
     [0,1,3]
       Any condition classifiable to 652, causing obstruction during labor
       Use additional code from 652.0-652.9 to identify condition

¹ § ☑5ᵗʰ **660.1 Obstruction by bony pelvis**   M ♀
     [0,1,3]
       Any condition classifiable to 653, causing obstruction during labor
       Use additional code from 653.0-653.9 to identify condition

¹ § ☑5ᵗʰ **660.2 Obstruction by abnormal pelvic soft tissues**   M ♀
     [0,1,3]
       Prolapse of anterior lip of cervix
       Any condition classifiable to 654, causing obstruction during labor
       Use additional code from 654.0-654.9 to identify condition

¹ § ☑5ᵗʰ **660.3 Deep transverse arrest and persistent occipitoposterior position**   M ♀
     [0,1,3]

¹ § ☑5ᵗʰ **660.4 Shoulder (girdle) dystocia**   M ♀
     [0,1,3]
       Impacted shoulders
       DEF: Obstructed labor due to impacted fetal shoulders.

¹ § ☑5ᵗʰ **660.5 Locked twins**   M ♀
     [0,1,3]

¹ § ☑5ᵗʰ **660.6 Failed trial of labor, unspecified**   M ♀
     [0,1,3]
       Failed trial of labor, without mention of condition or suspected condition

¹ § ☑5ᵗʰ **660.7 Failed forceps or vacuum extractor, unspecified**   M ♀
     [0,1,3]
       Application of ventouse or forceps, without mention of condition

¹ § ☑5ᵗʰ **660.8 Other causes of obstructed labor**   M ♀
     [0,1,3]
       Use additional code to identify condition
       AHA: 4Q, '04, 88

¹ § ☑5ᵗʰ **660.9 Unspecified obstructed labor**   M ♀
     [0,1,3]
       Dystocia: Dystocia:
          NOS   maternal NOS
          fetal NOS

---

¹   Nonspecific PDx=0
§   Requires fifth-digit. Valid digits are in [brackets] under each code. See beginning of section 640-649 for codes and definitions.

 Additional Digit Required   Nonspecific PDx   Unacceptable PDx   Manifestation Code   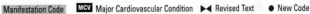 **MCV** Major Cardiovascular Condition   ▶◀ Revised Text   ● New Code   ▲ Revised Code Title

Complications of Pregnancy, Childbirth & Puerperium

661–665.2

√4ᵗʰ **661 Abnormality of forces of labor**

¹ § √5ᵗʰ **661.0 Primary uterine inertia** Ⓜ♀
[0,1,3]
Failure of cervical dilation
Hypotonic uterine dysfunction, primary
Prolonged latent phase of labor
DEF: Lack of efficient contractions during labor causing prolonged labor.

¹ § √5ᵗʰ **661.1 Secondary uterine inertia** Ⓜ♀
[0,1,3]
Arrested active phase of labor
Hypotonic uterine dysfunction, secondary

¹ § √5ᵗʰ **661.2 Other and unspecified uterine inertia** Ⓜ♀
[0,1,3]
Desultory labor
Irregular labor
Poor contractions
Slow slope active phase of labor

¹ § √5ᵗʰ **661.3 Precipitate labor** Ⓜ♀
[0,1,3] **DEF:** Rapid labor and delivery.

¹ § √5ᵗʰ **661.4 Hypertonic, incoordinate, or prolonged** Ⓜ♀
[0,1,3] **uterine contractions**
Cervical spasm
Contraction ring (dystocia)
Dyscoordinate labor
Hourglass contraction of uterus
Hypertonic uterine dysfunction
Incoordinate uterine action
Retraction ring (Bandl's) (pathological)
Tetanic contractions
Uterine dystocia NOS
Uterine spasm

§ √5ᵗʰ **661.9 Unspecified abnormality of labor** Ⓜ♀
[0,1,3]

√4ᵗʰ **662 Long labor**

¹ § √5ᵗʰ **662.0 Prolonged first stage** Ⓜ♀
[0,1,3]

¹ § √5ᵗʰ **662.1 Prolonged labor, unspecified** Ⓜ♀
[0,1,3]

¹ § √5ᵗʰ **662.2 Prolonged second stage** Ⓜ♀
[0,1,3]

¹ § √5ᵗʰ **662.3 Delayed delivery of second twin, triplet, etc.** Ⓜ♀
[0,1,3]

√4ᵗʰ **663 Umbilical cord complications**

¹ § √5ᵗʰ **663.0 Prolapse of cord** Ⓜ♀
[0,1,3]
Presentation of cord
DEF: Abnormal presentation of fetus; marked by protruding umbilical cord during labor; can cause fetal death.

¹ § √5ᵗʰ **663.1 Cord around neck, with compression** Ⓜ♀
[0,1,3]
Cord tightly around neck

¹ § √5ᵗʰ **663.2 Other and unspecified cord entanglement,** Ⓜ♀
[0,1,3] **with compression**
Entanglement of cords of twins in mono-amniotic sac
Knot in cord (with compression)

¹ § √5ᵗʰ **663.3 Other and unspecified cord entanglement,** Ⓜ♀
[0,1,3] **without mention of compression**
AHA: For code 663.31: 2Q, '03, 9

¹ § √5ᵗʰ **663.4 Short cord** Ⓜ♀
[0,1,3]

¹ § √5ᵗʰ **663.5 Vasa previa** Ⓜ♀
[0,1,3]
DEF: Abnormal presentation of fetus marked by blood vessels of umbilical cord in front of fetal head.

¹ § √5ᵗʰ **663.6 Vascular lesions of cord** Ⓜ♀
[0,1,3]
Bruising of cord
Hematoma of cord
Thrombosis of vessels of cord

¹ § √5ᵗʰ **663.8 Other umbilical cord complications** Ⓜ♀
[0,1,3]
Velamentous insertion of umbilical cord

§ √5ᵗʰ **663.9 Unspecified umbilical cord complication** Ⓜ♀
[0,1,3]

Perineal Lacerations

First degree
Second degree
Anus
Third degree
Fourth degree

√4ᵗʰ **664 Trauma to perineum and vulva during delivery**
[INCLUDES] damage from instruments
that from extension of episiotomy
AHA: 1Q, '92, 11; N-D, '84, 10

¹ § √5ᵗʰ **664.0 First-degree perineal laceration** Ⓜ♀
[0,1,4]
Perineal laceration, rupture, or tear involving:
fourchette
hymen
labia
skin
vagina
vulva

¹ § √5ᵗʰ **664.1 Second-degree perineal laceration** Ⓜ♀
[0,1,4]
Perineal laceration, rupture, or tear (following episiotomy) involving:
pelvic floor
perineal muscles
vaginal muscles
[EXCLUDES] that involving anal sphincter (664.2)

¹ § √5ᵗʰ **664.2 Third-degree perineal laceration** Ⓜ♀
[0,1,4]
Perineal laceration, rupture, or tear (following episiotomy) involving:
anal sphincter
rectovaginal septum
sphincter NOS
[EXCLUDES] that with anal or rectal mucosal laceration (664.3)

¹ § √5ᵗʰ **664.3 Fourth-degree perineal laceration** Ⓜ♀
[0,1,4]
Perineal laceration, rupture, or tear as classifiable to 664.2 and involving also:
anal mucosa
rectal mucosa

§ √5ᵗʰ **664.4 Unspecified perineal laceration** Ⓜ♀
[0,1,4]
Central laceration
AHA: 1Q, '92, 8

¹ § √5ᵗʰ **664.5 Vulval and perineal hematoma** Ⓜ♀
[0,1,4] **AHA:** N-D, '84, 10

¹ § √5ᵗʰ **664.8 Other specified trauma to perineum and vulva** Ⓜ♀
[0,1,4]

§ √5ᵗʰ **664.9 Unspecified trauma to perineum and vulva** Ⓜ♀
[0,1,4]

√4ᵗʰ **665 Other obstetrical trauma**
[INCLUDES] damage from instruments

¹ § √5ᵗʰ **665.0 Rupture of uterus before onset of labor** cc Ⓜ♀
[0,1,3]
CC Excl: 646.80-646.93, 648.90-650, 655.70-655.73, 665.00-665.11, 665.50-665.54, 665.80-665.94, 669.40-669.44, 669.80-669.94

¹ § √5ᵗʰ **665.1 Rupture of uterus during labor** cc Ⓜ♀
[0,1]
Rupture of uterus NOS
CC Excl: See code 665.0

¹ § √5ᵗʰ **665.2 Inversion of uterus** Ⓜ♀
[0,2,4]

---

¹ Nonspecific PDx=0
§ Requires fifth-digit. Valid digits are in [brackets] under each code. See beginning of section 640-649 for codes and definitions.

Ⓝ Newborn Age: 0   Ⓟ Pediatric Age: 0-17   Ⓜ Maternity Age: 12-55   Ⓐ Adult Age: 15-124   cc CC Condition   MC Major Complication   CD Complex Dx   HIV HIV Related Dx

[1] § √5th **665.3 Laceration of cervix**   M ♀
[0,1,4]

[1] § √5th **665.4 High vaginal laceration**   M ♀
[0,1,4]   Laceration of vaginal wall or sulcus without mention of perineal laceration

[1] § √5th **665.5 Other injury to pelvic organs**   M ♀
[0,1,4]
   Injury to: Injury to:
     bladder   urethra
   AHA: M-A, '87, 10

[1] § √5th **665.6 Damage to pelvic joints and ligaments**   M ♀
[0,1,4]   Avulsion of inner symphyseal cartilage
   Damage to coccyx
   Separation of symphysis (pubis)
   AHA: N-D, '84, 12

[1] § √5th **665.7 Pelvic hematoma**   M ♀
[0,1,2,4]   Hematoma of vagina

[1] § √5th **665.8 Other specified obstetrical trauma**   M ♀
[0-4]

§ √5th **665.9 Unspecified obstetrical trauma**   M ♀
[0-4]

√4th **666 Postpartum hemorrhage**
   AHA: 1Q, '88, 14

[1] § √5th **666.0 Third-stage hemorrhage**   M ♀
[0,2,4]   Hemorrhage associated with retained, trapped, or adherent placenta
   Retained placenta NOS

[1] § √5th **666.1 Other immediate postpartum hemorrhage**   M ♀
[0,2,4]   Atony of uterus ▶with hemorrhage◀
   Hemorrhage within the first 24 hours following delivery of placenta
   Postpartum hemorrhage (atonic) NOS
    EXCLUDES ▶ *atony of uterus without hemorrhage (669.8)*◀

[1] § √5th **666.2 Delayed and secondary postpartum**   M ♀
[0,2,4] **hemorrhage**
   Hemorrhage:
     after the first 24 hours following delivery
     associated with retained portions of placenta or membranes
   Postpartum hemorrhage specified as delayed or secondary
   Retained products of conception NOS, following delivery

[1] § √5th **666.3 Postpartum coagulation defects**   CC 2,4 M ♀
[0,2,4]
   Postpartum: Postpartum:
     afibrinogenemia   fibrinolysis
   CC Excl: For codes 666.32-666.34: 646.80-646.93, 648.90-650, 666.00-666.34, 669.40-669.44, 669.80-669.94

√4th **667 Retained placenta or membranes, without hemorrhage**
   AHA: 1Q, '88, 14
   DEF: Postpartum condition resulting from failure to expel placental membrane tissues due to failed contractions of uterine wall.

[1] § √5th **667.0 Retained placenta without hemorrhage**   M ♀
[0,2,4]
   Placenta accreta
   Retained placenta: without
     NOS   hemorrhage
     total

[1] § √5th **667.1 Retained portions of placenta or membranes,**   M ♀
[0,2,4] **without hemorrhage**
   Retained products of conception following delivery, without hemorrhage

√4th **668 Complications of the administration of anesthetic or other sedation in labor and delivery**
   INCLUDES complications arising from the administration of a general or local anesthetic, analgesic, or other sedation in labor and delivery
   EXCLUDES *reaction to spinal or lumbar puncture (349.0)*
     spinal headache (349.0)
   Use additional code(s) to further specify complication

[1] § √5th **668.0 Pulmonary complications**   CC M ♀
[0-4]
   Inhalation [aspiration] of stomach contents or secretions ⎫
   Mendelson's syndrome   ⎬ following anesthesia or other sedation in labor or delivery
   Pressure collapse of lung   ⎭
   CC Excl: 646.80-646.93, 648.90-650, 668.00-668.04, 669.40-669.44, 669.80-669.94

[1] § √5th **668.1 Cardiac complications**   CC M ♀
[0-4]   Cardiac arrest or failure following anesthesia or other sedation in labor and delivery
   CC Excl: 646.80-646.93, 648.90-650, 668.10-668.14, 669.40-669.44, 669.80-669.94

[1] § √5th **668.2 Central nervous system complications**   CC M ♀
[0-4]   Cerebral anoxia following anesthesia or other sedation in labor and delivery
   CC Excl: 646.80-646.93, 648.90-650, 668.20-668.24, 669.40-669.44, 669.80-669.94

[1] § √5th **668.8 Other complications of anesthesia or**   CC M ♀
[0-4] **other sedation in labor and delivery**
   CC Excl: 646.80-646.93, 648.90-650, 668.80-94, 668,669.40-669.44, 669.80-669.94
   AHA: 2Q, '99, 9

§ √5th **668.9 Unspecified complication of anesthesia**   CC M ♀
[0-4] **and other sedation**
   CC Excl: See code 668.8

√4th **669 Other complications of labor and delivery, not elsewhere classified**

[1] § √5th **669.0 Maternal distress**   M ♀
[0-4]   Metabolic disturbance in labor and delivery

[1] § √5th **669.1 Shock during or following labor and**   CC M ♀
[0-4] **delivery**
   Obstetric shock
   CC Excl: 646.80-646.93, 648.90-650, 669.10-669.14, 669.40-669.44, 669.80-669.94

[1] § √5th **669.2 Maternal hypotension syndrome**   M ♀
[0-4]
   DEF: Low arterial blood pressure, in mother, during labor and delivery.

[1] § √5th **669.3 Acute renal failure following labor and**   CC M ♀
[0,2,4] **delivery**
   CC Excl: 646.80-646.93, 648.90-650, 669.30-669.44, 669.80-669.94

[1] § √5th **669.4 Other complications of obstetrical surgery**   M ♀
[0-4] **and procedures**
   Cardiac: ⎫
     arrest   ⎬ following cesarean or other obstetrical surgery or procedure, including delivery NOS
     failure   ⎪
   Cerebral anoxia ⎭
   EXCLUDES *complications of obstetrical surgical wounds (674.1-674.3)*

[1] § √5th **669.5 Forceps or vacuum extractor delivery**   M ♀
[0,1] **without mention of indication**
   Delivery by ventouse, without mention of indication

[1] § √5th **669.6 Breech extraction, without mention of**   M ♀
[0,1] **indication**
   EXCLUDES *breech delivery NOS (652.2)*

[1] § √5th **669.7 Cesarean delivery, without mention of**   M ♀
[0,1] **indication**
   AHA: For code 669.71: 1Q, '01, 11

[1] § √5th **669.8 Other complications of labor and delivery**   M ♀
[0-4]

§ √5th **669.9 Unspecified complication of labor and delivery**   M ♀
[0-4]

---

[1] Nonspecific PDx=0
§ Requires fifth-digit. Valid digits are in [brackets] under each code. See beginning of section 640-649 for codes and definitions.

√4th Additional Digit Required   Nonspecific PDx   Unacceptable PDx   Manifestation Code   **MCV** Major Cardiovascular Condition   ▶◀ Revised Text   ● New Code   ▲ Revised Code Title

Complications of Pregnancy, Childbirth & Puerperium

670–674.2

COMPLICATIONS OF THE PUERPERIUM (670–677)

Note: Categories 671 and 673-676 include the listed conditions even if they occur during pregnancy or childbirth.

The following fifth-digit subclassification is for use with categories 670-676 to denote the current episode of care. Valid fifth-digits are in [brackets] under each code.

    0   unspecified as to episode of care or not applicable
    1   delivered, with or without mention of antepartum condition
    2   delivered, with mention of postpartum complication
    3   antepartum condition or complication
    4   postpartum condition or complication

¹ √4ᵗʰ **670 Major puerperal infection**   CC M♀
    [0,2,4]
     § √5ᵗʰ Use 0 as fourth-digit for this category

      Puerperal: Puerperal:
       endometritis   peritonitis
       fever (septic)   pyemia
       pelvic: salpingitis
         cellulitis   septicemia
         sepsis

     EXCLUDES   infection following abortion (639.0)
                 minor genital tract infection following delivery (646.6)
                 puerperal pyrexia NOS (672)
                 puerperal fever NOS (672)
                 puerperal pyrexia of unknown origin (672)
                 urinary tract infection following delivery (646.6)

    CC Excl: 646.80-646.93, 648.90-650, 669.40-669.44, 669.80-669.94, 670.00-670.04

    AHA: 4Q, '91, 26; 2Q, '91, 7

    DEF: Infection and inflammation, following childbirth.

√4ᵗʰ **671 Venous complications in pregnancy and the puerperium**

¹ § √5ᵗʰ **671.0 Varicose veins of legs**   M♀
    [0-4]   Varicose veins NOS
         DEF: Distended, tortuous veins on legs associated with pregnancy.

¹ § √5ᵗʰ **671.1 Varicose veins of vulva and perineum**   M♀
    [0-4]
         DEF: Distended, tortuous veins on external female genitalia associated with pregnancy.

¹ § √5ᵗʰ **671.2 Superficial thrombophlebitis**   CC M♀
    [0-4]   Thrombophlebitis (superficial)
         CC Excl: 646.80-646.93, 648.90-650, 669.40-669.44, 669.80-669.94, 671.20-671.94

¹ § √5ᵗʰ **671.3 Deep phlebothrombosis, antepartum**   CC M♀
    [0,1,3]   Deep-vein thrombosis, antepartum
         CC Excl: See code 671.2

¹ § √5ᵗʰ **671.4 Deep phlebothrombosis, postpartum**   CC M♀
    [0,2,4]   Deep-vein thrombosis, postpartum
           Pelvic thrombophlebitis, postpartum
           Phlegmasia alba dolens (puerperal)
         CC Excl: See code 671.2

¹ § √5ᵗʰ **671.5 Other phlebitis and thrombosis**   M♀
    [0-4]   Cerebral venous thrombosis
           Thrombosis of intracranial venous sinus

¹ § √5ᵗʰ **671.8 Other venous complications**   M♀
    [0-4]   Hemorrhoids

§ √5ᵗʰ **671.9 Unspecified venous complication**   M♀
    [0-4]   Phlebitis NOS
           Thrombosis NOS

¹ √4ᵗʰ **672 Pyrexia of unknown origin during the puerperium**   M♀
    [0,2,4]
     § √5ᵗʰ Use 0 as fourth-digit for this category

      Postpartum fever NOS
      Puerperal fever NOS
      Puerperal pyrexia NOS

    AHA: 4Q, '91, 26

    DEF: Fever of unknown origin experienced by the mother after childbirth.

√4ᵗʰ **673 Obstetrical pulmonary embolism**
    INCLUDES   pulmonary emboli in pregnancy, childbirth, or the puerperium, or specified as puerperal
    EXCLUDES   embolism following abortion (639.6)

¹ § √5ᵗʰ **673.0 Obstetrical air embolism**   CC M♀
    [0-4]
         CC Excl: 646.80-646.93, 648.90-648.94, 650, 669.40-669.44, 669.80-669.94, 673.00-673.84

         DEF: Sudden blocking of pulmonary artery with air or nitrogen bubbles during puerperium.

¹ § √5ᵗʰ **673.1 Amniotic fluid embolism**   CC M♀
    [0-4]
         CC Excl: See code 673.0

         DEF: Sudden onset of pulmonary artery blockage from amniotic fluid entering the mother's circulation near the end of pregnancy due to strong uterine contractions.

¹ § √5ᵗʰ **673.2 Obstetrical blood-clot embolism**   CC M♀
    [0-4]   Puerperal pulmonary embolism NOS
         CC Excl: See code 673.0

    AHA: For code 673.24: 1Q, '05, 6

         DEF: Blood clot blocking artery in the lung; associated with pregnancy.

¹ § √5ᵗʰ **673.3 Obstetrical pyemic and septic embolism**   CC M♀
    [0-4]
         CC Excl: See code 673.0

¹ § √5ᵗʰ **673.8 Other pulmonary embolism**   CC M♀
    [0-4]   Fat embolism
         CC Excl: See code 673.0

√4ᵗʰ **674 Other and unspecified complications of the puerperium, not elsewhere classified**

¹ § √5ᵗʰ **674.0 Cerebrovascular disorders in the puerperium**   CC M♀
    [0-4]   Any condition classifiable to 430-434, 436-437 occurring during pregnancy, childbirth, or the puerperium, or specified as puerperal
       EXCLUDES   intracranial venous sinus thrombosis (671.5)
         CC Excl: 646.80-646.93, 648.90-650, 669.40-669.44, 669.80-669.94, 674.00-674.04, 674.50-674.54

¹ § √5ᵗʰ **674.1 Disruption of cesarean wound**   CC 0,2 M♀
    [0,2,4]   Dehiscence or disruption of uterine wound
       EXCLUDES   uterine rupture before onset of labor (665.0)
                  uterine rupture during labor (665.1)
         CC Excl: For Codes 674.10 and 674.12: 646.80-646.93, 648.90-650, 669.40-669.44, 669.80-669.94, 674.10, 674.34

¹ § √5ᵗʰ **674.2 Disruption of perineal wound**   CC M♀
    [0,2,4]   Breakdown of perineum
           Disruption of wound of:
             episiotomy
             perineal laceration
           Secondary perineal tear
         CC Excl: 646.80-646.93, 648.90-650, 669.40-669.44, 669.80-669.94, 674.10, 674.34

    AHA: For code 674.24: 1Q, '97, 9

¹ Nonspecific PDx=0
§ Requires fifth-digit. Valid digits are in [brackets] under each code. See beginning of section 640-649 for codes and definitions.

N Newborn Age: 0   P Pediatric Age: 0-17   M Maternity Age: 12-55   A Adult Age: 15-124   CC CC Condition   MC Major Complication   CD Complex Dx   HIV HIV Related Dx

204 — Volume 1   2007 ICD•9•CM

¹ § √5ᵗʰ **674.3 Other complications of obstetrical surgical**   M ♀
[0,2,4] **wounds**

Hematoma
Hemorrhage   } of cesarean section or perineal
Infection   wound

EXCLUDES   damage from instruments in delivery (664.0-665.9)

AHA: 2Q, '91, 7

¹ § √5ᵗʰ **674.4 Placental polyp**   M ♀
[0,2,4]

¹ § √5ᵗʰ **674.5 Peripartum cardiomyopathy**   CC M ♀
[0-4]   Postpartum cardiomyopathy

CC Excl: 646.80-646.93, 648.90-650, 669.40-669.44, 669.80-669.94, 674.00-674.04, 674.50-674.54

AHA: 4Q, '03, 65

DEF: Any structural or functional abnormality of the ventricular myocardium, non-inflammatory disease of obscure or unknown etiology with onset during the postpartum period.

¹ § √5ᵗʰ **674.8 Other**   M ♀
[0,2,4]   Hepatorenal syndrome, following delivery
Postpartum:
     subinvolution of uterus
     uterine hypertrophy

AHA: 3Q, '98, 16

§ √5ᵗʰ **674.9 Unspecified**   M ♀
[0,2,4]   Sudden death of unknown cause during the puerperium

√4ᵗʰ **675 Infections of the breast and nipple associated with childbirth**
INCLUDES   the listed conditions during pregnancy, childbirth, or the puerperium

¹ § √5ᵗʰ **675.0 Infections of nipple**   M ♀
[0-4]   Abscess of nipple

¹ § √5ᵗʰ **675.1 Abscess of breast**   CC 0-2 M ♀
[0-4]   Abscess:
     mammary
     subareolar
     submammary
     purulent
     retromammary
     submammary

CC Excl: For codes 675.10-675.12: 646.80-646.93, 648.90-650, 669.40-669.44, 669.80-669.94, 675.00-675.94

¹ § √5ᵗʰ **675.2 Nonpurulent mastitis**   M ♀
[0-4]   Lymphangitis of breast
Mastitis:
     NOS
     interstitial
     parenchymatous

¹ § √5ᵗʰ **675.8 Other specified infections of the breast and**   M ♀
[0-4] **nipple**

¹ § √5ᵗʰ **675.9 Unspecified infection of the breast and nipple**   M ♀
[0-4]

√4ᵗʰ **676 Other disorders of the breast associated with childbirth and disorders of lactation**
INCLUDES   the listed conditions during pregnancy, the puerperium, or lactation

¹ § √5ᵗʰ **676.0 Retracted nipple**   M ♀
[0-4]

Lactation Process: Ejection Reflex Arc

¹ § √5ᵗʰ **676.1 Cracked nipple**   M ♀
[0-4]   Fissure of nipple

¹ § √5ᵗʰ **676.2 Engorgement of breasts**   M ♀
[0-4]

DEF: Abnormal accumulation of milk in ducts of breast.

¹ § √5ᵗʰ **676.3 Other and unspecified disorder of breast**   M ♀
[0-4]

¹ § √5ᵗʰ **676.4 Failure of lactation**   M ♀
[0-4]   Agalactia
DEF: Abrupt ceasing of milk secretion by breast.

¹ § √5ᵗʰ **676.5 Suppressed lactation**   M ♀
[0-4]

¹ § √5ᵗʰ **676.6 Galactorrhea**   M ♀
[0-4]   **EXCLUDES**   galactorrhea not associated with childbirth (611.6)
DEF: Excessive or persistent milk secretion by breast; may be in absence of nursing.

¹ § √5ᵗʰ **676.8 Other disorders of lactation**   M ♀
[0-4]   Galactocele
DEF: Galactocele: Obstructed mammary gland, creating retention cyst, results in milk-filled cysts enlarging mammary gland.

§ √5ᵗʰ **676.9 Unspecified disorder of lactation**   M ♀
[0-4]

677 Late effect of complication of pregnancy, childbirth, and the puerperium   ♀

Note: This category is to be used to indicate conditions in 632-648.9 and 651-676.9 as the cause of the late effect, themselves classifiable elsewhere. The "late effects" include conditions specified as such, or as sequelae, which may occur at any time after puerperium.
Code first any sequelae

AHA: 1Q, '97, 9; 4Q, '94, 42

---

¹   Nonspecific   PDx=0
§   Requires fifth-digit. Valid digits are in [brackets] under each code. See beginning of section 640-649 for codes and definitions.

√4ᵗʰ √5ᵗʰ Additional Digit Required   Nonspecific PDx   Unacceptable PDx   Manifestation Code   **MCV** Major Cardiovascular Condition   ►◄ Revised Text   ● New Code   ▲ Revised Code Title

2007 ICD•9•CM   **Volume 1 — 205**

Skin and Subcutaneous Tissue

680–681.11

12. DISEASES OF THE SKIN AND SUBCUTANEOUS TISSUE
(680-709)

Skin and Subcutaneous Layer

INFECTIONS OF SKIN AND SUBCUTANEOUS TISSUE (680-686)

> **EXCLUDES**   *certain infections of skin classified under "Infectious and Parasitic Diseases," such as:*
> *erysipelas (035)*
> *erysipeloid of Rosenbach (027.1)*
> *herpes:*
>   *simplex (054.0-054.9)*
>   *zoster (053.0-053.9)*
> *molluscum contagiosum (078.0)*
> *viral warts (078.1)*

✓4ᵗʰ 680 Carbuncle and furuncle

> **INCLUDES**   boil
>   furunculosis

DEF: Carbuncle: necrotic boils in skin and subcutaneous tissue of neck or back mainly due to staphylococcal infection.

DEF: Furuncle: circumscribed inflammation of corium and subcutaneous tissue due to staphylococcal infection.

680.0 Face   `CC`
     Ear [any part]
     Face [any part, except eye]
     Nose (septum)
     Temple (region)

> **EXCLUDES**   *eyelid (373.13)*
> *lacrimal apparatus (375.31)*
> *orbit (376.01)*

CC Excl: 017.00-017.06, 017.90-017.96, 040.82-041.9, 680.0, 680.8-680.9, 686.00-686.9, 705.83, 709.8, V09.0-V09.91

680.1 Neck   `CC`
CC Excl: 017.00-017.06, 017.90-017.96, 040.82-041.9, 680.1, 680.8-680.9, 686.00-686.9, 705.83, 709.8, V09.0-V09.91

680.2 Trunk   `CC`
     Abdominal wall
     Back [any part, except buttocks]
     Breast
     Chest wall
     Flank
     Groin
     Pectoral region
     Perineum
     Umbilicus

> **EXCLUDES**   *buttocks (680.5)*
> *external genital organs:*
>   *female (616.4)*
>   *male (607.2, 608.4)*

CC Excl: 017.00-017.06, 017.90-017.96, 040.82-041.9, 680.2, 680.8-680.9, 686.00-686.9, 705.83, 709.8, V09.0-V09.91

680.3 Upper arm and forearm   `CC`
     Arm [any part, except hand]
     Axilla
     Shoulder

CC Excl: 017.00-017.06, 017.90-017.96, 040.82-041.9, 680.3, 680.8-680.9, 686.00-686.9, 705.83, 709.8, V09.0-V09.91

680.4 Hand   `CC`
     Finger [any]
     Thumb
     Wrist

CC Excl: 017.00-017.06, 017.90-017.96, 040.82-041.9, 680.4, 680.8-680.9, 686.00-686.9, 705.83, 709.8, V09.0-V09.91

680.5 Buttock   `CC`
     Anus
     Gluteal region

CC Excl: 017.00-017.06, 017.90-017.96, 040.82-041.9, 680.5, 680.8-680.9, 686.00-686.9, 705.83, 709.8, V09.0-V09.91

680.6 Leg, except foot   `CC`
     Ankle   Knee
     Hip   Thigh

CC Excl: 017.00-017.06, 017.90-017.96, 040.82-041.9, 680.6, 680.8-680.9, 686.00-686.9, 705.83, 709.8, V09.0-V09.91

680.7 Foot   `CC`
     Heel
     Toe

CC Excl: 017.00-017.06, 017.90-017.96, 040.82-041.9, 680.7-680.9, 686.00-686.9, 705.83, 709.8, V09.0-V09.91

680.8 Other specified sites   `CC`
     Head [any part, except face]
     Scalp

> **EXCLUDES**   *external genital organs:*
>   *female (616.4)*
>   *male (607.2, 608.4)*

CC Excl: 017.00-017.06, 017.90-017.96, 040.82-041.9, 680.8-680.9, 686.00-686.9, 705.83, 709.8, V09.0-V09.91

680.9 Unspecified site   `CC`
     Boil NOS   Furuncle NOS
     Carbuncle NOS

CC Excl: See code 680.8

✓4ᵗʰ 681 Cellulitis and abscess of finger and toe

> **INCLUDES**   that with lymphangitis

Use additional code to identify organism, such as Staphylococcus (041.1)

AHA: 2Q, '91, 5; J-F, '87, 12

DEF: Acute suppurative inflammation and edema in subcutaneous tissue or muscle of finger or toe.

✓5ᵗʰ 681.0 Finger

     681.00 Cellulitis and abscess, unspecified

     681.01 Felon
         Pulp abscess   Whitlow

> **EXCLUDES**   *herpetic whitlow (054.6)*

         DEF: Painful abscess of fingertips caused by infection in the closed space of terminal phalanx.

     681.02 Onychia and paronychia of finger
         Panaritium } of finger
         Perionychia

         DEF: Onychia: inflammation of nail matrix; causes nail loss.

         DEF: Paronychia: inflammation of tissue folds around nail.

✓5ᵗʰ 681.1 Toe

     681.10 Cellulitis and abscess, unspecified
         AHA: 1Q, '05, 14

     681.11 Onychia and paronychia of toe
         Panaritium } of toe
         Perionychia

✓4ᵗʰ ✓5ᵗʰ Additional Digit Required   Nonspecific PDx   Unacceptable PDx   Manifestation Code   `MCV` Major Cardiovascular Condition   ▶◀ Revised Text   ● New Code   ▲ Revised Code Title

Skin and Subcutaneous Tissue

681.9–684

681.9   **Cellulitis and abscess of unspecified digit**
       Infection of nail NOS

✓4ᵗʰ **682 Other cellulitis and abscess**

> INCLUDES   abscess (acute)   } (with lymphangitis)
>   cellulitis (diffuse)   } except of
>   lymphangitis, acute } finger or toe

Use additional code to identify organism, such as
Staphylococcus (041.1)

> EXCLUDES   *lymphangitis (chronic) (subacute) (457.2)*

AHA: 2Q, '91, 5; J-F, '87, 12; S-O, '85, 10

DEF: Cellulitis: Acute suppurative inflammation of deep subcutaneous tissue and sometimes muscle due to infection of wound, burn or other lesion.

682.0   **Face**   CC
      Cheek, external   Nose, external
      Chin   Submandibular
      Forehead   Temple (region)

> EXCLUDES   *ear [any part] (380.10-380.16)*
>   *eyelid (373.13)*
>   *lacrimal apparatus (375.31)*
>   *lip (528.5)*
>   *mouth (528.3)*
>   *nose (internal) (478.1)*
>   *orbit (376.01)*

CC Excl: 017.00-017.06, 017.90-017.96, 040.82-041.9, 682.0, 682.8-682.9, 686.00-686.9, 705.83, 709.8, V09.0-V09.91

682.1   **Neck**   CC
CC Excl: 017.00-017.06, 017.90-017.96, 040.89, 041.00-041.89, 041.9, 682.1, 682.8-682.9, 686.00-686.01, 686.09, 686.1-686.9, 705.83, 709.8, V09.0-V09.91

682.2   **Trunk**   CC
      Abdominal wall   Groin
      Back [any part, except   Pectoral region
          buttock]   Perineum
      Chest wall   Umbilicus, except newborn
      Flank

> EXCLUDES   *anal and rectal regions (566)*
>   *breast:*
>   *NOS (611.0)*
>   *puerperal (675.1)*
>   *external genital organs:*
>   *female (616.3-616.4)*
>   *male (604.0, 607.2, 608.4)*
>   *umbilicus, newborn (771.4)*

CC Excl: 017.00-017.06, 017.90-017.96, 040.82-041.9, 682.2, 682.8-682.9, 686.00-686.9, 705.83, 709.8, V09.0-V09.91

AHA: 4Q, '98, 42

682.3   **Upper arm and forearm**   CC
      Arm [any part, except hand]
      Axilla
      Shoulder

> EXCLUDES   *hand (682.4)*

CC Excl: 017.00-017.06, 017.90-017.96, 040.82-041.9, 682.3, 682.8-682.9, 686.00-686.9, 705.83, 709.8, V09.0-V09.91

AHA: 2Q, '03, 7

682.4   **Hand, except fingers and thumb**   CC
      Wrist

> EXCLUDES   *finger and thumb (681.00-681.02)*

682.5   **Buttock**   CC
      Gluteal region

> EXCLUDES   *anal and rectal regions (566)*

CC Excl: 017.00-017.06, 017.90-017.96, 040.82-041.9, 682.5, 682.8-682.9, 686.00-686.9, 705.83, 709.8, V09.0-V09.91

682.6   **Leg, except foot**   CC
      Ankle   Knee
      Hip   Thigh

CC Excl: 017.00-017.06, 017.90-017.96, 040.82-041.9, 682.6, 682.8-682.9, 686.00-686.9, 705.83, 709.8, V09.0-V09.91

AHA: 3Q, '04, 5; 4Q, '03, 108

682.7   **Foot, except toes**   CC
      Heel

> EXCLUDES   *toe (681.10-681.11)*

CC Excl: 017.00-017.06, 017.90-017.96, 040.82-041.9, 682.7-682.9, 686.00-686.9, 705.83, 709.8, V09.0-V09.91

682.8   **Other specified sites**   CC
      Head [except face]
      Scalp

> EXCLUDES   *face (682.0)*

CC Excl: 017.00-017.06, 017.90-017.96, 040.82-041.9, 682.8-682.9, 686.00-686.9, 705.83, 709.8, V09.0-V09.91

682.9   **Unspecified site**   CC
      Abscess NOS   Lymphangitis, acute NOS
      Cellulitis NOS

> EXCLUDES   *lymphangitis NOS (457.2)*

CC Excl: See code 682.8

683 Acute lymphadenitis
      Abscess (acute)   }
      Adenitis, acute   } lymph gland or node,
      Lymphadenitis, acute } except mesenteric

Use additional code to identify organism, such as
Staphylococcus (041.1)

> EXCLUDES   *enlarged glands NOS (785.6)*
>   *lymphadenitis:*
>   *chronic or subacute, except mesenteric (289.1)*
>   *mesenteric (acute) (chronic) (subacute) (289.2)*
>   *unspecified (289.3)*

DEF: Acute inflammation of lymph nodes due to primary infection located elsewhere in the body.

684 Impetigo   CC
      Impetiginization of other dermatoses
      Impetigo (contagiosa) [any site] [any organism]:
          bullous
          circinate
          neonatorum
          simplex
      Pemphigus neonatorum

> EXCLUDES   *impetigo herpetiformis (694.3)*

CC Excl: 684, 686.00-686.9, 709.8

DEF: Infectious skin disease commonly occurring in children; caused by group A streptococci or *Staphylococcus aureus*; skin lesions usually appear on the face and consist of subcorneal vesicles and bullae that burst and form yellow crusts.

Lymphatic System of Head and Neck

Schematic of lymph node

Afferent vessels (in)
Blood vessels
Hilum
Efferent vessel (out)

Jugulodigastric
Submental
Submandibular
Jugulomyohyoid
Anterior cervical
Superficial parotid
Occipital

Lymphatic drainage of the head, neck, and face

N Newborn Age: 0   P Pediatric Age: 0-17   M Maternity Age: 12-55   A Adult Age: 15-124   CC CC Condition   MC Major Complication   CD Complex Dx   HIV HIV Related Dx

208 — Volume 1   *2007 ICD•9•CM*

Stages of Pilonidal Disease

- Normal follicle
- Stretched follicle
- Infected follicle
- Acute abscess
- Chronic abscess
- Epithelial tube

√4ᵗʰ 685 Pilonidal cyst

INCLUDES   fistula } coccygeal or pilonidal
      sinus

DEF: Hair-containing cyst or sinus in the tissues of the sacrococcygeal area; often drains through opening at the postanal dimple.

685.0 With abscess   CC
     CC Excl: 685.0-685.1, 709.8

685.1 Without mention of abscess

√4ᵗʰ 686 Other local infections of skin and subcutaneous tissue
Use additional code to identify any infectious organism (041.0-041.8)

√5ᵗʰ 686.0 Pyoderma
Dermatitis: Dermatitis:
   purulent   suppurative
   septic

DEF: Nonspecific purulent skin disease related most to furuncles, pustules, or possibly carbuncles.

686.00 Pyoderma, unspecified

686.01 Pyoderma gangrenosum
     AHA: 4Q, '97, 42

DEF: Persistent debilitating skin disease, characterized by irregular, boggy, blue-red ulcerations, with central healing and undermined edges.

686.09 Other pyoderma

686.1 Pyogenic granuloma
Granuloma:
   septic
   suppurative
   telangiectaticum
     EXCLUDES   pyogenic granuloma of oral mucosa (528.9)

DEF: Solitary polypoid capillary hemangioma often asociated with local irritation, trauma, and superimposed inflammation; located on the skin and gingival or oral mucosa.

686.8 Other specified local infections of skin and subcutaneous tissue
Bacterid (pustular)   Ecthyma
Dermatitis vegetans   Perlèche
     EXCLUDES   dermatitis infectiosa eczematoides (690.8)
            panniculitis (729.30-729.39)

686.9 Unspecified local infection of skin and subcutaneous tissue
Fistula of skin NOS
Skin infection NOS
     EXCLUDES   fistula to skin from internal organs — see Alphabetic Index

OTHER INFLAMMATORY CONDITIONS OF SKIN AND SUBCUTANEOUS TISSUE (690-698)
EXCLUDES   panniculitis (729.30-729.39)

√4ᵗʰ 690 Erythematosquamous dermatosis
EXCLUDES   eczematous dermatitis of eyelid (373.31)
            parakeratosis variegata (696.2)
            psoriasis (696.0-696.1)
            seborrheic keratosis (702.11-702.19)

√5ᵗʰ 690.1 Seborrheic dermatitis
AHA: 4Q, '95, 58

690.10 Seborrheic dermatitis, unspecified
Seborrheic dermatitis NOS

690.11 Seborrhea capitis   P
Cradle cap

690.12 Seborrheic infantile dermatitis   P

690.18 Other seborrheic dermatitis

690.8 Other erythematosquamous dermatosis

√4ᵗʰ 691 Atopic dermatitis and related conditions
DEF: Atopic dermatitis: chronic, pruritic, inflammatory skin disorder found on the face and antecubital and popliteal fossae; noted in persons with a hereditary predisposition to pruritus, and often accompanied by allergic rhinitis, hay fever, asthma, and extreme itching; also called allergic dermatitis, allergic or atopic eczema, or disseminated neurodermatitis.

691.0 Diaper or napkin rash
Ammonia dermatitis   Diaper or napkin:
Diaper or napkin: rash
   dermatitis   Psoriasiform napkin eruption
   erythema

691.8 Other atopic dermatitis and related conditions
Atopic dermatitis   Eczema:
Besnier's prurigo   intrinsic (allergic)
Eczema: Neurodermatitis:
   atopic   atopic
   flexural   diffuse (of Brocq)

√4ᵗʰ 692 Contact dermatitis and other eczema
INCLUDES   dermatitis: eczema (acute) (chronic):
         NOS   NOS
         contact   allergic
         occupational   erythematous
         venenata   occupational
EXCLUDES   allergy NOS (995.3)
            contact dermatitis of eyelids (373.32)
            dermatitis due to substances taken internally (693.0-693.9)
            eczema of external ear (380.22)
            perioral dermatitis (695.3)
            urticarial reactions (708.0-708.9, 995.1)

DEF: Contact dermatitis: acute or chronic dermatitis caused by initial irritant effect of a substance, or by prior sensitization to a substance coming once again in contact with skin.

692.0 Due to detergents

692.1 Due to oils and greases

692.2 Due to solvents
Dermatitis due to solvents of:
   chlorocompound
   cyclohexane
   ester } group
   glycol
   hydrocarbon
   ketone

√4ᵗʰ √5ᵗʰ Additional Digit Required   Nonspecific PDx   Unacceptable PDx   Manifestation Code   MCV Major Cardiovascular Condition   ▶◀ Revised Text   ● New Code   ▲ Revised Code Title

2007 ICD•9•CM   **Volume 1 — 209**

692.3   Due to drugs and medicines in contact with skin

Dermatitis (allergic)   Dermatitis (allergic)
   (contact) due to: (contact) due to:
    arnica   neomycin
    fungicides   pediculocides
    iodine   phenols
    keratolytics   scabicides
    mercurials   any drug applied to skin
Dermatitis medicamentosa due to drug applied to
   skin
Use additional E code to identify drug

   EXCLUDES   *allergy NOS due to drugs ▶(995.27)◀*
               dermatitis due to ingested drugs
                  (693.0)
               dermatitis medicamentosa NOS (693.0)

692.4   Due to other chemical products

Dermatitis due to:
   acids
   adhesive plaster
   alkalis
   caustics
   dichromate
   insecticide
   nylon
   plastic
   rubber
AHA: 2Q, '89, 16

692.5   Due to food in contact with skin

Dermatitis, contact,   Dermatitis, contact,
   due to: due to:
   cereals   fruit
   fish   meat
   flour   milk

   EXCLUDES   *dermatitis due to:*
               dyes (692.89)
               ingested foods (693.1)
               preservatives (692.89)

692.6   Due to plants [except food]

Dermatitis due to:
   lacquer tree [Rhus verniciflua]
   poison:
      ivy [Rhus toxicodendron]
      oak [Rhus diversiloba]
      sumac [Rhus venenata]
      vine [Rhus radicans]
   primrose [Primula]
   ragweed [Senecio jacobae]
   other plants in contact with the skin

   EXCLUDES   *allergy NOS due to pollen (477.0)*
               nettle rash (708.8)

√5ᵗʰ **692.7   Due to solar radiation**

   EXCLUDES   *sunburn due to other ultraviolet*
               radiation exposure (692.82)

692.70   Unspecified dermatitis due to sun

692.71   Sunburn

First degree sunburn
Sunburn NOS
AHA: 4Q, '01, 47

692.72   Acute dermatitis due to solar radiation

Berlogue dermatitis
Photoallergic response
Phototoxic response
Polymorphus light eruption
Acute solar skin damage NOS

   EXCLUDES   *sunburn (692.71, 692.76-*
               692.77)
Use additional E code to identify drug, if
   drug induced

DEF: Berloque dermatitis: Phytophotodermatitis due to
sun exposure after use of a product containing bergamot
oil; causes red patches, which may turn brown.

DEF: Photoallergic response: Dermatitis due to
hypersensitivity to the sun; causes papulovesicular,
eczematous or exudative eruptions.

DEF: Phototoxic response: Chemically induced sensitivity
to sun causes burn-like reaction, occasionally
vesiculation and subsequent hyperpigmentation.

DEF: Polymorphous light eruption: Inflammatory skin
eruptions due to sunlight exposure; eruptions differ in
size and shape.

DEF: Acute solar skin damage (NOS): Rapid, unspecified
injury to skin from sun.

692.73   Actinic reticuloid and actinic granuloma

DEF: Actinic reticuloid: Dermatosis aggravated by light,
causes chronic eczema-like eruption on exposed skin
which extends to other unexposed surfaces; occurs in
the eldery.

DEF: Actinic granuloma: Inflammatory response of skin to
sun causing small nodule of microphages.

**692.74   Other chronic dermatitis due to solar
            radiation**

Chronic solar skin damage NOS
Solar elastosis

   EXCLUDES   *actinic [solar] keratosis (702.0)*

DEF: Solar elastosis: Premature aging of skin of light-
skinned people; causes inelasticity, thinning or
thickening, wrinkling, dryness, scaling and
hyperpigmentation.

DEF: Chronic solar skin damage (NOS): Chronic skin
impairment due to exposure to the sun, not otherwise
specified.

**692.75   Disseminated superficial actinic
            porokeratosis [DSAP]**

DEF: Autosomal dominant skin condition occurring in
skin that has been overexposed to the sun. Primarily
affects women over the age of 16; characterized by
numerous superficial annular, keratotic, brownish-red
spots or thickenings with depressed centers and sharp,
ridged borders. High risk that condition will evolve into
squamous cell carcinoma.

AHA: 4Q, '00, 43

692.76   Sunburn of second degree

AHA: 4Q, '01, 47

692.77   Sunburn of third degree

AHA: 4Q, '01, 47

692.79   Other dermatitis due to solar radiation

Hydroa aestivale
Photodermatitis   }
Photosensitiveness   } (due to sun)

Solar skin damage NOS

√5ᵗʰ **692.8   Due to other specified agents**

692.81   Dermatitis due to cosmetics

692.82   Dermatitis due to other radiation

Infrared rays   Tanning bed
Light, except   Ultraviolet rays, except
   from sun   from sun
Radiation NOS   X-rays

   EXCLUDES   *solar radiation (692.70-692.79)*
AHA: 4Q, '01, 47; 3Q, '00, 5

692.83   Dermatitis due to metals

Jewelry

Ⓝ Newborn Age: 0   Ⓟ Pediatric Age: 0-17   Ⓜ Maternity Age: 12-55   Ⓐ Adult Age: 15-124   CC CC Condition   MC Major Complication   CD Complex Dx   HIV HIV Related Dx

210 — Volume 1 • October 2006   *2007 ICD•9•CM*

692.84 Due to animal (cat) (dog) dander
> Due to animal (cat) (dog) hair

692.89 Other
> Dermatitis due to: Dermatitis due to:
> cold weather   hot weather
> dyes   preservatives
>> **EXCLUDES** *allergy (NOS) (rhinitis) due to animal hair or dander (477.2)*
>> *allergy to dust (477.8)*
>> *sunburn (692.71, 692.76-692.77)*

692.9 Unspecified cause
> Dermatitis:
> NOS
> contact NOS
> venenata NOS
> Eczema NOS

√4ᵗʰ **693 Dermatitis due to substances taken internally**
> **EXCLUDES** *adverse effect NOS of drugs and medicines ▶(995.20)◄*
> *allergy NOS (995.3)*
> *contact dermatitis (692.0-692.9)*
> *urticarial reactions (708.0-708.9, 995.1)*

DEF: Inflammation of skin due to ingested substance.

693.0 Due to drugs and medicines
> Dermatitis medicamentosa NOS
> Use additional E code to identify drug
>> **EXCLUDES** *that due to drugs in contact with skin (692.3)*

693.1 Due to food

693.8 Due to other specified substances taken internally

693.9 Due to unspecified substance taken internally
>> **EXCLUDES** *dermatitis NOS (692.9)*

√4ᵗʰ **694 Bullous dermatoses**

694.0 Dermatitis herpetiformis
> Dermatosis herpetiformis
> Duhring's disease
> Hydroa herpetiformis
>> **EXCLUDES** *herpes gestationis (646.8)*
>> *dermatitis herpetiformis:*
>> *juvenile (694.2)*
>> *senile (694.5)*

DEF: Chronic, relapsing multisystem disease manifested most in the cutaneous system; seen as an extremely pruritic eruption of various combinations of lesions that frequently heal leaving hyperpigmentation or hypopigmentation and occasionally scarring; usually associated with an asymptomatic gluten-sensitive enteropathy, and immunogenic factors are believed to play a role in its origin.

694.1 Subcorneal pustular dermatosis
> Sneddon-Wilkinson disease or syndrome

DEF: Chronic relapses of sterile pustular blebs beneath the horny skin layer of the trunk and skin folds; resembles dermatitis herpetiformis.

694.2 Juvenile dermatitis herpetiformis
> Juvenile pemphigoid

694.3 Impetigo herpetiformis

DEF: Rare dermatosis associated with pregnancy; marked by itching pustules in third trimester, hypocalcemia, tetany, fever and lethargy; may result in maternal or fetal death.

694.4 Pemphigus   `CC`
> Pemphigus: Pemphigus:
> NOS   malignant
> erythematosus   vegetans
> foliaceus   vulgaris
>> **EXCLUDES** *pemphigus neonatorum (684)*

CC Excl: 694.4-694.9, 709.8

DEF: Chronic, relapsing, sometimes fatal skin diseases; causes vesicles, bullae; autoantibodies against intracellular connections cause acantholysis.

694.5 Pemphigoid   `CC`
> Benign pemphigus NOS
> Bullous pemphigoid
> Herpes circinatus bullosus
> Senile dermatitis herpetiformis

CC Excl: See code 694.4

√5ᵗʰ **694.6 Benign mucous membrane pemphigoid**
> Cicatricial pemphigoid
> Mucosynechial atrophic bullous dermatitis

694.60 Without mention of ocular involvement

694.61 With ocular involvement
> Ocular pemphigus

DEF: Mild self-limiting, subepidermal blistering of mucosa including the conjunctiva, seen predominantly in the elderly. It produces adhesions and scarring.

694.8 Other specified bullous dermatoses
>> **EXCLUDES** *herpes gestationis (646.8)*

694.9 Unspecified bullous dermatoses

√4ᵗʰ **695 Erythematous conditions**

695.0 Toxic erythema   `CC`
> Erythema venenatum

CC Excl: 695.0-695.4, 709.8

695.1 Erythema multiforme
> Erythema iris
> Herpes iris
> Lyell's syndrome
> Scalded skin syndrome
> Stevens-Johnson syndrome
> Toxic epidermal necrolysis

DEF: Symptom complex with a varied skin eruption pattern of macular, bullous, papular, nodose, or vesicular lesions on the neck, face, and legs; gastritis and rheumatic pains are also noticeable, first-seen symptoms; complex is secondary to a number of factors, including infections, ingestants, physical agents, malignancy and pregnancy.

695.2 Erythema nodosum
>> **EXCLUDES** *tuberculous erythema nodosum (017.1)*

DEF: Panniculitis (an inflammatory reaction of the subcutaneous fat) of women, usually seen as a hypersensitivity reaction to various infections, drugs, sarcoidosis, and specific enteropathies; the acute stage is often associated with other symptoms, including fever, malaise, and arthralgia; the lesions are pink to blue in color, appear in crops as tender nodules and are found on the front of the legs below the knees.

695.3 Rosacea
> Acne:
> erythematosa
> rosacea
> Perioral dermatitis
> Rhinophyma

DEF: Chronic skin disease, usually of the face, characterized by persistent erythema and sometimes by telangiectasis with acute episodes of edema, engorgement papules, and pustules.

695.4 Lupus erythematosus
> Lupus:
> erythematodes (discoid)
> erythematosus (discoid), not disseminated
>> **EXCLUDES** *lupus (vulgaris) NOS (017.0)*
>> *systemic [disseminated] lupus erythematosus (710.0)*

DEF: Group of connective tissue disorders occurring as various cutaneous diseases of unknown origin; it primarily affects women between the ages of 20 and 40.

√5ᵗʰ **695.8 Other specified erythematous conditions**

695.81 Ritter's disease
> Dermatitis exfoliativa neonatorum

DEF: Infectious skin disease of infants and young children marked by eruptions ranging from a localized bullous type to widespread development of easily ruptured fine vesicles and bullae; results in exfoliation of large planes of skin and leaves raw areas; also called staphylococcal scalded skin syndrome.

√4ᵗʰ √5ᵗʰ Additional Digit Required   Nonspecific PDx   Unacceptable PDx   Manifestation Code   `MCV` Major Cardiovascular Condition   ▶◀ Revised Text   ● New Code   ▲ Revised Code Title

Skin and Subcutaneous Tissue

695.89–701.0

695.89 Other
Erythema intertrigo
Intertrigo
Pityriasis rubra (Hebra)
EXCLUDES   *mycotic intertrigo (111.0-111.9)*

AHA:: S-O, '86, 10

695.9 Unspecified erythematous condition
Erythema NOS   Erythroderma (secondary)

✓4ᵗʰ **696 Psoriasis and similar disorders**

696.0 Psoriatic arthropathy   CC
CC Excl: 015.80-015.96, 017.90-017.96, 036.82, 056.71, 098.50-098.51, 098.59, 098.89, 696.0, 711.00-714.0, 715.00, 715.09-715.10, 715.18-716.99, 718.00-718.08, 719.00-719.09, 719.10, 719.18-719.99
DEF: Psoriasis associated with inflammatory arthritis; often involves interphalangeal joints.

696.1 Other psoriasis
Acrodermatitis continua   Psoriasis:
Dermatitis repens   NOS
                           any type, except
                           arthropathic
EXCLUDES   *psoriatic arthropathy (696.0)*

696.2 Parapsoriasis
Parakeratosis variegata
Parapsoriasis lichenoides chronica
Pityriasis lichenoides et varioliformis
DEF: Erythrodermas similar to lichen, planus and psoriasis; symptoms include redness and itching; resistant to treatment.

696.3 Pityriasis rosea
Pityriasis circinata (et maculata)
DEF: Common, self-limited rash of unknown etiology marked by a solitary erythematous, salmon or fawn-colored herald plaque on the trunk, arms or thighs; followed by development of papular or macular lesions that tend to peel and form a scaly collarette.

696.4 Pityriasis rubra pilaris
Devergie's disease   Lichen ruber acuminatus
EXCLUDES   *pityriasis rubra (Hebra) (695.89)*
DEF: Inflammatory disease of hair follicles; marked by firm, red lesions topped by horny plugs; may form patches; occurs on fingers elbows, knees.

696.5 Other and unspecified pityriasis
Pityriasis: Pityriasis:
   NOS   streptogenes
   alba
EXCLUDES   *pityriasis:*
         simplex (690.18)
         versicolor (111.0)

696.8 Other

✓4ᵗʰ **697 Lichen**
EXCLUDES   *lichen:*
         obtusus corneus (698.3)
         pilaris (congenital) (757.39)
         ruber acuminatus (696.4)
         sclerosus et atrophicus (701.0)
         scrofulosus (017.0)
         simplex chronicus (698.3)
         spinulosus (congenital) (757.39)
         urticatus (698.2)

697.0 Lichen planus
Lichen: Lichen:
   planopilaris   ruber planus
DEF: Inflammatory, pruritic skin disease; marked by angular, flat-top, violet-colored papules; may be acute and widespread or chronic and localized.

697.1 Lichen nitidus
Pinkus' disease
DEF: Chronic, inflammatory, usually asymptomatic skin disorder, characterized by numerous glistening, flat-topped, discrete, smooth, skin-colored micropapules most often on penis, lower abdomen, inner thighs, wrists, forearms, breasts and buttocks.

697.8 Other lichen, not elsewhere classified
Lichen: Lichen:
   ruber moniliforme   striata

697.9 Lichen, unspecified

✓4ᵗʰ **698 Pruritus and related conditions**
EXCLUDES   *pruritus specified as psychogenic (306.3)*
DEF: Pruritus: Intense, persistent itching due to irritation of sensory nerve endings from organic or psychogenic causes.

698.0 Pruritus ani
Perianal itch

698.1 Pruritus of genital organs

698.2 Prurigo
Lichen urticatus   Prurigo:
Prurigo: mitis
   NOS   simplex
   Hebra's   Urticaria papulosa (Hebra)
EXCLUDES   *prurigo nodularis (698.3)*

698.3 Lichenification and lichen simplex chronicus
Hyde's disease
Neurodermatitis (circumscripta) (local)
Prurigo nodularis
EXCLUDES   *neurodermatitis, diffuse (of Brocq)*
                (691.8)
DEF: Lichenification: thickening of skin due to prolonged rubbing or scratching.

DEF: Lichen simplex chronicus: eczematous dermatitis, of face, neck, extremities, scrotum, vulva, and perianal region due to repeated itching, rubbing and scratching; spontaneous or evolves with other dermatoses.

698.4 Dermatitis factitia [artefacta]
Dermatitis ficta
Neurotic excoriation
Use additional code to identify any associated mental disorder
DEF: Various types of self-inflicted skin lesions characterized in appearance as an erythema to a gangrene.

698.8 Other specified pruritic conditions
Pruritus: Winter itch
   hiemalis
   senilis

698.9 Unspecified pruritic disorder
Itch NOS   Pruritus NOS

OTHER DISEASES OF SKIN AND SUBCUTANEOUS TISSUE (700-709)

EXCLUDES   *conditions confined to eyelids (373.0-374.9)*
             congenital conditions of skin, hair, and nails
                (757.0-757.9)

700 Corns and callosities
Callus   Clavus
DEF: Corns: Conical or horny thickening of skin on toes, due to friction, pressure from shoes and hosiery; pain and inflammation may develop.

DEF: Callosities: Localized overgrowth (hyperplasia) of the horny epidermal layer due to pressure or friction.

✓4ᵗʰ **701 Other hypertrophic and atrophic conditions of skin**
EXCLUDES   *dermatomyositis (710.3)*
             hereditary edema of legs (757.0)
             scleroderma (generalized) (710.1)

701.0 Circumscribed scleroderma
Addison's keloid   Morphea
Dermatosclerosis, localized   Scleroderma, circum-
Lichen sclerosus   scribed or localized
   et atrophicus
DEF: Thickened, hardened, skin and subcutaneous tissue; may involve musculoskeletal system.

N Newborn Age: 0   P Pediatric Age: 0-17   M Maternity Age: 12-55   A Adult Age: 15-124   CC CC Condition   MC Major Complication   CD Complex Dx   HIV HIV Related Dx

212 — Volume 1   *2007 ICD•9•CM*

701.1 Keratoderma, acquired
  Acquired:
    ichthyosis
    keratoderma palmaris et plantaris
  Elastosis perforans serpiginosa
  Hyperkeratosis:
    NOS
    follicularis in cutem penetrans
    palmoplantaris climacterica
  Keratoderma:
    climactericum
    tylodes, progressive
  Keratosis (blennorrhagica)

  | EXCLUDES | Darier's disease [keratosis follicularis] (congenital) (757.39)
  | | keratosis:
  | | arsenical (692.4)
  | | gonococcal (098.81)

  AHA: 4Q, '94, 48

701.2 Acquired acanthosis nigricans
  Keratosis nigricans

  DEF: Diffuse velvety hyperplasia of the spinous skin layer of the axilla and other body folds marked by gray, brown, or black pigmentation; in adult form it is often associated with an internal carcinoma (malignant acanthosis nigricans) in a benign, nevoid form it is relatively generalized; benign juvenile form with obesity is sometimes caused by an endocrine disturbance.

701.3 Striae atrophicae
  Atrophic spots of skin
  Atrophoderma maculatum
  Atrophy blanche (of Milian)
  Degenerative colloid atrophy
  Senile degenerative atrophy
  Striae distensae

  DEF: Bands of atrophic, depressed, wrinkled skin associated with stretching of skin from pregnancy, obesity, or rapid growth during puberty.

701.4 Keloid scar
  Cheloid
  Hypertrophic scar
  Keloid

  DEF: Overgrowth of scar tissue due to excess amounts of collagen during connective tissue repair; occurs mainly on upper trunk, face.

701.5 Other abnormal granulation tissue
  Excessive granulation

701.8 Other specified hypertrophic and atrophic conditions of skin
  Acrodermatitis atrophicans chronica
  Atrophia cutis senilis
  Atrophoderma neuriticum
  Confluent and reticulate papillomatosis
  Cutis laxa senilis
  Elastosis senilis
  Folliculitis ulerythematosa reticulata
  Gougerot-Carteaud syndrome or disease

701.9 Unspecified hypertrophic and atrophic conditions of skin
  Skin tag   Atrophoderma

✓4ᵗʰ 702 Other dermatoses
  | EXCLUDES | carcinoma in situ (232.0-232.9)

  702.0 Actinic keratosis
    AHA: 1Q, '92, 18

    DEF: Wart-like growth, red or skin-colored; may form a cutaneous horn.

✓5ᵗʰ 702.1 Seborrheic keratosis
    DEF: Common, benign, lightly pigmented, warty growth composed of basaloid cells.

    702.11 Inflamed seborrheic keratosis
      AHA: 4Q, '94, 48

    702.19 Other seborrheic keratosis
      Seborrheic keratosis NOS

702.8 Other specified dermatoses

✓4ᵗʰ 703 Diseases of nail
  | EXCLUDES | congenital anomalies (757.5)
  | | onychia and paronychia (681.02, 681.11)

  703.0 Ingrowing nail
    Ingrowing nail with infection   Unguis incarnatus
    | EXCLUDES | infection, nail NOS (681.9)

  703.8 Other specified diseases of nail
    Dystrophia unguium   Onychauxis
    Hypertrophy of nail   Onychogryposis
    Koilonychia   Onycholysis
    Leukonychia (punctata) (striata)

  703.9 Unspecified disease of nail

✓4ᵗʰ 704 Diseases of hair and hair follicles
  | EXCLUDES | congenital anomalies (757.4)

✓5ᵗʰ 704.0 Alopecia
  | EXCLUDES | madarosis (374.55)
  | | syphilitic alopecia (091.82)

  DEF: Lack of hair, especially on scalp; often called baldness; may be partial or total; occurs at any age.

  704.00 Alopecia, unspecified
    Baldness
    Loss of hair

  704.01 Alopecia areata
    Ophiasis

    DEF: Alopecia areata: usually reversible, inflammatory, patchy hair loss found in beard or scalp.

    DEF: Ophiasis: alopecia areata of children; marked by band around temporal and occipital scalp margins.

  704.02 Telogen effluvium
    DEF: Shedding of hair from premature telogen development in follicles due to stress, including shock, childbirth, surgery, drugs or weight loss.

  704.09 Other
    Folliculitis decalvans
    Hypotrichosis:
      NOS
      postinfectional NOS
    Pseudopelade

704.1 Hirsutism
  Hypertrichosis: Polytrichia
    NOS
  lanuginosa, acquired
  | EXCLUDES | hypertrichosis of eyelid (374.54)

  DEF: Excess hair growth; often in unexpected places and amounts.

704.2 Abnormalities of the hair
  Atrophic hair   Trichiasis:
  Clastothrix   NOS
  Fragilitas crinium   cicatrical
                            Trichorrhexis (nodosa)
  | EXCLUDES | trichiasis of eyelid (374.05)

704.3 Variations in hair color
  Canities (premature)   Poliosis:
  Grayness, hair (premature)   NOS
  Heterochromia of hair   circumscripta, acquired

704.8 Other specified diseases of hair and hair follicles
  Folliculitis: Sycosis:
    NOS   NOS
    abscedens et suffodiens   barbae [not parasitic]
    pustular   lupoid
  Perifolliculitis: vulgaris
    NOS
    capitis abscedens et suffodiens
    scalp

704.9 Unspecified disease of hair and hair follicles

✓4ᵗʰ 705 Disorders of sweat glands
  705.0 Anhidrosis
    Hypohidrosis   Oligohidrosis
    DEF: Lack or deficiency of ability to sweat.

✓4ᵗʰ ✓5ᵗʰ Additional Digit Required   Nonspecific PDx   Unacceptable PDx   Manifestation Code   **MCV** Major Cardiovascular Condition   ►◄ Revised Text   ● New Code   ▲ Revised Code Title

2007 ICD•9•CM   Volume 1 — 213

Skin and Subcutaneous Tissue

705.1–707.09

705.1 Prickly heat

Heat rash   Sudamina
Miliaria rubra (tropicalis)

✓5ᵗʰ 705.2 Focal hyperhidrosis

> **EXCLUDES** *generalized (secondary) hyperhidrosis (780.8)*

705.21 Primary focal hyperhidrosis

Focal hyperhidrosis   Hyperhidrosis of:
  NOS   axilla
Hyperhidrosis NOS   face
                         palms
                         soles

AHA: 4Q, '04, 91

DEF: A rare condition that is a disorder of the sweat glands resulting in excessive production of sweat; occurs in the absence of any underlying or causative condition and is almost always focal, confined to one or more specific areas of the body.

705.22 Secondary focal hyperhidrosis

Frey's syndrome

AHA: 4Q, '04, 91

DEF: Secondary focal hyperhidrosis: a symptom of an underlying disease process resulting in excessive sweating beyond what the body requires to maintain thermal control, confined to one or more specific areas of the body.
DEF: Frey's syndrome: an auriculotemporal syndrome due to lesion on the parotid gland; characteristic redness and excessive sweating on the cheek in connection with eating.

✓5ᵗʰ 705.8 Other specified disorders of sweat glands

705.81 Dyshidrosis

Cheiropompholyx   Pompholyx
DEF: Vesicular eruption, on hands, feet causing itching and burning.

705.82 Fox-Fordyce disease

DEF: Chronic, usually pruritic disease chiefly of women evidenced by small follicular papular eruptions, especially in the axillary and pubic areas; develops from the closure and rupture of the affected apocrine glands' intraepidermal portion of the ducts.

705.83 Hidradenitis

Hidradenitis suppurativa
DEF: Inflamed sweat glands.

705.89 Other

Bromhidrosis   Granulosis rubra nasi
Chromhidrosis   Urhidrosis

> **EXCLUDES** *generalized hyperhidrosis (780.8)*
> *hidrocystoma (216.0-216.9)*

DEF: Bromhidrosis: foul-smelling axillary sweat due to decomposed bacteria.
DEF: Chromhidrosis: secretion of colored sweat.
DEF: Granulosis rubra nasi: ideopathic condition of children; causes redness, sweating around nose, face and chin; tends to end by puberty.
DEF: Urhidrosis: urinous substance, such as uric acid, in sweat; occurs in uremia.

705.9 Unspecified disorder of sweat glands

Disorder of sweat glands NOS

✓4ᵗʰ 706 Diseases of sebaceous glands

706.0 Acne varioliformis

Acne: Acne:
  frontalis   necrotica
DEF: Rare form of acne characterized by persistent brown papulo-pustules usually on the brow and temporoparietal part of the scalp.

706.1 Other acne

Acne: Acne:
  NOS   vulgaris
  conglobata   Blackhead
  cystic   Comedo
  pustular

> **EXCLUDES** *acne rosacea (695.3)*

Four Stages of Decubitus Ulcers

First Stage
Nonblanchable erythema

Second Stage
Partial thickness skin loss involving epidermis, dermis, or both

Third Stage
Full thickness skin loss extending through subcutaneous tissue

Fourth Stage
Full thickness skin loss extending to muscle and bone

706.2 Sebaceous cyst

Atheroma, skin   Wen
Keratin cyst
DEF: Benign epidermal cyst, contains sebum and keratin; presents as firm, circumscribed nodule.

706.3 Seborrhea

> **EXCLUDES** *seborrhea:*
> *capitis (690.11)*
> *sicca (690.18)*
> *seborrheic*
> *dermatitis (690.10)*
> *keratosis (702.11-702.19)*

DEF: Seborrheic dermatitis marked by excessive secretion of sebum; the sebum forms an oily coating, crusts, or scales on the skin; it is also called hypersteatosis.

706.8 Other specified diseases of sebaceous glands

Asteatosis (cutis)
Xerosis cutis

706.9 Unspecified disease of sebaceous glands

✓4ᵗʰ 707 Chronic ulcer of skin

> **INCLUDES** non-infected sinus of skin
> non-healing ulcer
> **EXCLUDES** *specific infections classified under "Infectious and Parasitic Diseases" (001.0-136.9)*
> *varicose ulcer (454.0, 454.2)*

AHA: 4Q, '04, 92

✓5ᵗʰ 707.0 Decubitus ulcer

Bed sore   Plaster ulcer
Decubitus ulcer [any site] Pressure ulcer

AHA: 1Q, '04, 14; 4Q, '03, 110; 4Q, '99, 20; 1Q, '96, 15; 3Q, '90, 15; N-D, '87, 9

707.00 Unspecified site `CC` `MC`
CC Excl: 707.0, 707.8-707.9, 709.8

707.01 Elbow `CC` `MC`
CC Excl: See code 707.00

707.02 Upper back `CC` `MC`
Shoulder blades
CC Excl: See code 707.00

707.03 Lower back `CC` `MC`
Sacrum
CC Excl: See code 707.00
AHA: 1Q, '05, 16

707.04 Hip `CC` `MC`
CC Excl: See code 707.00

707.05 Buttock `CC` `MC`
CC Excl: See code 707.00

707.06 Ankle `CC` `MC`
CC Excl: See code 707.00

707.07 Heel `CC` `MC`
CC Excl: See code 707.00
AHA: 1Q, '05, 16

707.09 Other site `CC` `MC`
Head
CC Excl: See code 707.00

| N | Newborn Age: 0 | P | Pediatric Age: 0-17 | M | Maternity Age: 12-55 | A | Adult Age: 15-124 | CC | CC Condition | MC | Major Complication | CD | Complex Dx | HIV | HIV Related Dx |

√5ᵗʰ **707.1 Ulcer of lower limbs, except decubitus**

Ulcer, chronic:
neurogenic ⎤
trophic   ⎦ of lower limb

Code, if applicable, any causal condition first:
atherosclerosis of the extremities with ulceration (440.23)
chronic venous hypertension with ulcer (459.31)
chronic venous hypertension with ulcer and inflammation (459.33)
diabetes mellitus (250.80-250.83)
postphlebitic syndrome with ulcer (459.11)
postphlebitic syndrome with ulcer and inflammation (459.13)

AHA: 4Q, '00, 44; 4Q, '99, 15

707.10 Ulcer of lower limb, unspecified ᶜᶜ
CC Excl: 440.23, 707.10-707.9, 709.8
AHA: 3Q, '04, 5; 4Q, '02, 43

707.11 Ulcer of thigh ᶜᶜ
CC Excl: See code 707.10

707.12 Ulcer of calf ᶜᶜ
CC Excl: See code 707.10

707.13 Ulcer of ankle ᶜᶜ
CC Excl: See code 707.10

707.14 Ulcer of heel and midfoot ᶜᶜ
Plantar surface of midfoot
CC Excl: See code 707.10

707.15 Ulcer of other part of foot ᶜᶜ
Toes
CC Excl: See code 707.10

707.19 Ulcer of other part of lower limb ᶜᶜ
CC Excl: See code 707.10

707.8 Chronic ulcer of other specified sites
Ulcer, chronic:
neurogenic ⎤
trophic   ⎦ of other specified sites

707.9 Chronic ulcer of unspecified site
Chronic ulcer NOS
Trophic ulcer NOS
Tropical ulcer NOS
Ulcer of skin NOS

√4ᵗʰ **708 Urticaria**
EXCLUDES edema:
angioneurotic (995.1)
Quincke's (995.1)
hereditary angioedema (277.6)
urticaria:
giant (995.1)
papulosa (Hebra) (698.2)
pigmentosa (juvenile) (congenital) (757.33)

DEF: Skin disorder marked by raised edematous patches of skin or mucous membrane with intense itching; also called hives.

708.0 Allergic urticaria

708.1 Idiopathic urticaria

708.2 Urticaria due to cold and heat
Thermal urticaria

708.3 Dermatographic urticaria
Dermatographia   Factitial urticaria

708.4 Vibratory urticaria

708.5 Cholinergic urticaria

708.8 Other specified urticaria
Nettle rash   Urticaria:
Urticaria: recurrent periodic
chronic

708.9 Urticaria, unspecified
Hives NOS

Cutaneous Lesions

Surface Lesions
Fissure   Polyp growth   Ulcer

Solid Lesions
Flat macule   Slightly elevated wheal   Solid papule

Sac Lesions
Cyst   Clear fluid vesicle   Pustule

√4ᵗʰ **709 Other disorders of skin and subcutaneous tissue**

√5ᵗʰ **709.0 Dyschromia**
EXCLUDES albinism (270.2)
pigmented nevus (216.0-216.9)
that of eyelid (374.52-374.53)

DEF: Pigment disorder of skin or hair.

709.00 Dyschromia, unspecified

709.01 Vitiligo
DEF: Persistent, progressive development of nonpigmented white patches on otherwise normal skin.

709.09 Other

709.1 Vascular disorders of skin
Angioma serpiginosum
Purpura (primary)annularis telangiectodes

709.2 Scar conditions and fibrosis of skin
Adherent scar (skin)   Fibrosis, skin NOS
Cicatrix   Scar NOS
Disfigurement (due to scar)
EXCLUDES keloid scar (701.4)

AHA: N-D, '84, 19

709.3 Degenerative skin disorders
Calcinosis: Degeneration, skin
circumscripta   Deposits, skin
cutis   Senile dermatosis NOS
Colloid milium   Subcutaneous calcification

709.4 Foreign body granuloma of skin and subcutaneous tissue
EXCLUDES residual foreign body without granuloma of skin and subcutaneous tissue (729.6)
that of muscle (728.82)

709.8 Other specified disorders of skin
Epithelial hyperplasia
Menstrual dermatosis
Vesicular eruption

AHA: N-D, '87, 6

DEF: Epithelial hyperplasia: increased number of epitheleal cells.

DEF: Vesicular eruption: liquid-filled structures appearing through skin.

709.9 Unspecified disorder of skin and subcutaneous tissue
Dermatosis NOS

√4ᵗʰ
√5ᵗʰ Additional Digit Required   Nonspecific PDx   Unacceptable PDx   Manifestation Code   **MCV** Major Cardiovascular Condition   ◄► Revised Text   ● New Code   ▲ Revised Code Title

2007 ICD•9•CM   Volume 1 — 215

13. DISEASES OF THE MUSCULOSKELETAL SYSTEM AND CONNECTIVE TISSUE (710-739)

Joint Structures

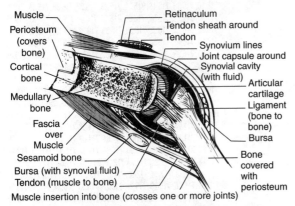

Muscle
Periosteum (covers bone)
Cortical bone
Medullary bone
Fascia over Muscle
Sesamoid bone
Bursa (with synovial fluid)
Tendon (muscle to bone)
Muscle insertion into bone (crosses one or more joints)

Retinaculum
Tendon sheath around
Tendon
Synovium lines
Joint capsule around
Synovial cavity (with fluid)
Articular cartilage
Ligament (bone to bone)
Bursa
Bone covered with periosteum

The following fifth-digit subclassification is for use with categories 711-712, 715-716, 718-719, and 730:

0 site unspecified

1 shoulder region
   Acromioclavicular joint(s)
   Clavicle
   Glenohumeral joint(s)
   Scapula
   Sternoclavicular joint(s)

2 upper arm
   Elbow joint
   Humerus

3 forearm
   Radius
   Ulna
   Wrist joint

4 hand
   Carpus
   Metacarpus
   Phalanges [fingers]

5 pelvic region and thigh
   Buttock
   Femur
   Hip (joint)

6 lower leg
   Fibula   Patella
   Knee joint   Tibia

7 ankle and foot
   Ankle joint   Phalanges, foot
   Digits [toes]   Tarsus
   Metatarsus   Other joints in foot

8 other specified sites
   Head   Skull
   Neck   Trunk
   Ribs   Vertebral column

9 multiple sites

ARTHROPATHIES AND RELATED DISORDERS (710-719)

> **EXCLUDES**   *disorders of spine (720.0-724.9)*

√4ᵗʰ **710 Diffuse diseases of connective tissue**
> **INCLUDES**   all collagen diseases whose effects are not mainly confined to a single system
> **EXCLUDES**   *those affecting mainly the cardiovascular system, i.e., polyarteritis nodosa and allied conditions (446.0-446.7)*

710.0 Systemic lupus erythematosus   `CC`
   Disseminated lupus erythematosus
   Libman-Sacks disease
   Use additional code to identify manifestation, as:
     endocarditis (424.91)
     nephritis (583.81)
       chronic (582.81)
     nephrotic syndrome (581.81)
> **EXCLUDES**   *lupus erythematosus (discoid) NOS (695.4)*

CC Excl: 710.0

AHA: 2Q, '03, 7-8; 2Q, '97, 8

DEF: A chronic multisystemic inflammatory disease affecting connective tissue; marked by anemia, leukopenia, muscle and joint pains, fever, rash of a butterfly pattern around cheeks and forehead area; of unknown etiology.

710.1 Systemic sclerosis   `CC`
   Acrosclerosis   Progressive systemic sclerosis
   CRST syndrome   Scleroderma
> **EXCLUDES**   *circumscribed scleroderma (701.0)*
   Use additional code to identify manifestation, as:
     lung involvement (517.2)
     myopathy (359.6)

CC Excl: 710.1

AHA: 1Q, '88, 6

DEF: Systemic disease, involving excess fibrotic collagen build-up; symptoms include thickened skin; fibrotic degenerative changes in various organs; and vascular abnomalities; condition occurs more often in females.

710.2 Sicca syndrome
   Keratoconjunctivitis sicca   Sjögren's disease
DEF: Autoimmune disease; associated with keratoconjunctivitis, laryngopharyngitis, rhinitis, dry mouth, enlarged parotid gland, and chronic polyarthritis.

710.3 Dermatomyositis   `CC`
   Poikilodermatomyositis
   Polymyositis with skin involvement
CC Excl: 710.3

DEF: Polymyositis associated with flat-top purple papules on knuckles; marked by upper eyelid rash, edema of eyelids and orbit area, red rash on forehead, neck, shoulders, trunk and arms; symptoms include fever, weight loss aching muscles; visceral cancer (in individuals older than 40).

710.4 Polymyositis   `CC`
CC Excl: 710.4

DEF: Chronic, progressive, inflammatory skeletal muscle disease; causes weakness of limb girdles, neck, pharynx; may precede or follow scleroderma, Sjogren's disease, systemic lupus erythematosus, arthritis, or malignancy.

710.5 Eosinophilia myalgia syndrome   `CC`
   Toxic oil syndrome
     Use additional E code to identify drug, if drug induced
CC Excl: 292.0-293.9, 710.5

AHA: 4Q, '92, 21

DEF: Eosinophilia myalgia syndrome (EMS): inflammatory, multisystem fibrosis; associated with ingesting elementary L-tryptophan; symptoms include myalgia, weak limbs and bulbar muscles, distal sensory loss, areflexia, arthralgia, cough, fever, fatigue, skin rashes, myopathy, and eosinophil counts greater than 1000/microliter.

DEF: Toxic oil syndrome: syndrome similar to EMS due to ingesting contaminated cooking oil.

√4ᵗʰ / √5ᵗʰ Additional Digit Required   Nonspecific PDx   Unacceptable PDx   Manifestation Code   `MCV` Major Cardiovascular Condition   ►◄ Revised Text   ● New Code   ▲ Revised Code Title

2007 ICD•9•CM   **Volume 1 — 217**

710.8 Other specified diffuse diseases of connective tissue `CC`
Multifocal fibrosclerosis (idiopathic) NEC
Systemic fibrosclerosing syndrome
CC Excl: 710.8
AHA: M-A, '87, 12

710.9 Unspecified diffuse connective tissue disease
Collagen disease NOS

`✓4ᵗʰ` **711 Arthropathy associated with infections**

> `INCLUDES` arthritis
> arthropathy } associated with
> polyarthritis } conditions
> polyarthropathy } classifiable below

> `EXCLUDES` *rheumatic fever (390)*

The following fifth-digit subclassification is for use with category 711; valid digits are in [brackets] under each code. See list at beginning of chapter for definitions.
    0 site unspecified
    1 shoulder region
    2 upper arm
    3 forearm
    4 hand
    5 pelvic region and thigh
    6 lower leg
    7 ankle and foot
    8 other specified sites
    9 multiple sites

AHA: 1Q, '92, 17

§ `✓5ᵗʰ` **711.0 Pyogenic arthritis** `CC`
[0-9]   Arthritis or polyarthritis (due to):
    coliform [Escherichia coli]
    Hemophilus influenzae [H. influenzae]
    pneumococcal
    Pseudomonas
    staphylococcal
    streptococcal
    Pyarthrosis
    Use additional code to identify infectious organism
    (041.0-041.8)
CC Excl: For code 711.00: 015.80-015.96, 017.90-017.96, 036.82, 056.71, 098.50-098.51, 098.59, 098.89, 711.00-714.0, 715.00, 715.09-715.10, 715.18-716.99, 718.00-718.08, 719.00-719.10, 719.18-719.99 **For code 711.01:** 015.80-015.96, 017.90-017.96, 036.82, 056.71, 098.50-098.51, 098.59, 098.89, 711.00-711.01, 711.08-711.11, 711.18-711.21, 711.28-711.31, 711.38-711.41, 711.48-711.51, 711.58-711.61, 711.68-711.71, 711.78-711.81, 711.88-711.91, 711.98-711.99, 712.10-712.11, 712.18-712.21, 712.28-712.31, 712.38-712.81, 712.88-712.91, 712.98-712.99, 713.0-713.8, 714.0, 715.00, 715.09-715.11, 715.18-715.21, 715.28-715.31, 715.38-715.91, 715.98, 716.00-716.01, 716.08-716.11, 716.18-716.21, 716.28-716.31, 716.38-716.41, 716.48-716.51, 716.58-716.61, 716.68-716.81, 716.88-716.91, 716.98-716.91, 718.00-718.01, 718.08, 719.00-719.01, 719.08-719.11, 719.18-719.21, 719.28-719.31, 719.38-719.41, 719.48-719.51, 719.58-719.61, 719.68-719.7, 719.80-719.81, 719.88-719.91, 719.98-719.99

For code 711.02: 015.80-015.96, 017.90-017.96, 036.82, 056.71, 098.50-098.51, 098.59, 098.89, 711.00, 711.02, 711.08-711.10, 711.12, 711.18-711.20, 711.22, 711.28-711.30, 711.32, 711.38-711.40, 711.42, 711.48-711.50, 711.52, 711.58-711.60, 711.62, 711.68-711.70, 711.72, 711.78-711.80, 711.82, 711.88-711.90, 711.92, 711.98-711.99, 712.10, 712.12, 712.18-712.20, 712.22, 712.28-712.30, 712.32, 712.38-712.80, 712.82, 712.88-712.90, 712.92, 712.98-712.99, 713.0-713.8, 714.0, 715.00, 715.09-715.10, 715.12, 715.18, 715.20, 715.22, 715.28, 715.30, 715.32, 715.38-715.90, 715.92, 715.98, 716.00, 716.02, 716.08-716.10, 716.12, 716.18-716.20, 716.22, 716.28-716.30, 716.32, 716.38-716.40, 716.42, 716.48-716.50, 716.52, 716.58-716.60, 716.62, 716.68, 716.80, 716.82, 716.88-716.90, 716.92, 716.98-716.99, 718.00, 718.02, 718.08, 719.00, 719.02, 719.08-719.10, 719.12, 719.18-719.20, 719.22, 719.28-719.30, 719.32, 719.38-719.40, 719.42, 719.48-719.50, 719.52, 719.58-719.60, 719.62, 719.68-719.7, 719.80, 719.82, 719.88-719.90, 719.92, 719.98-719.99 **For code 711.03:** 015.80-015.96, 017.90-017.96, 036.82, 056.71, 098.50-098.51, 098.59, 098.89, 711.00, 711.03, 711.08-711.10, 711.13, 711.18-711.20, 711.23, 711.28-711.30, 711.33, 711.38-711.40, 711.43, 711.48-

711.50, 711.53, 711.58-711.60, 711.63, 711.68-711.70, 711.73, 711.78-711.80, 711.83, 711.88-711.90, 711.93, 711.98-711.99, 712.10, 712.13, 712.18-712.20, 712.23, 712.28-712.30, 712.33, 712.38-712.80, 712.83, 712.88-712.90, 712.93, 712.98-712.99, 713.0-713.8, 714.0, 715.00, 715.09-715.10, 715.13, 715.18, 715.20, 715.23, 715.28, 715.30, 715.33, 715.38-715.90, 715.93, 715.98, 716.00, 716.03, 716.08-716.10, 716.13, 716.18-716.20, 716.23, 716.28-716.30, 716.33, 716.38-716.40, 716.43, 716.48-716.50, 716.53, 716.58-716.60, 716.63, 716.68, 716.80, 716.83, 716.88-716.90, 716.93, 716.98-716.99, 718.00, 718.03, 718.08, 719.00, 719.03, 719.08-719.10, 719.13, 719.18-719.20, 719.23, 719.28-719.30, 719.33, 719.38-719.40, 719.43, 719.48-719.50, 719.53, 719.58-719.60, 719.63, 719.68-719.7, 719.80, 719.83, 719.88-719.90, 719.93, 719.98-719.99 **For code 711.04:** 015.80-015.96, 017.90-017.96, 036.82, 056.71, 098.50-098.51, 098.59, 098.89, 711.00, 711.04, 711.08-711.10, 711.14, 711.18-711.20, 711.24, 711.28-711.30, 711.34, 711.38-711.40, 711.44, 711.48-711.50, 711.54, 711.58-711.60, 711.64, 711.68-711.70, 711.74, 711.78-711.80, 711.84, 711.88-711.90, 711.94, 711.98-711.99, 712.10, 712.14, 712.18-712.20, 712.24, 712.28-712.30, 712.34, 712.38-712.80, 712.84, 712.88-712.90, 712.94, 712.98-712.99, 713.0-713.8, 714.0, 715.00-715.10, 715.14, 715.18, 715.20, 715.24, 715.28, 715.30, 715.34, 715.38-715.90, 715.94, 715.98, 716.00, 716.04, 716.08-716.10, 716.14, 716.18-716.20, 716.24, 716.28-716.30, 716.34, 716.38-716.40, 716.44, 716.48-716.50, 716.54, 716.58-716.60, 716.64, 716.68, 716.80, 716.84, 716.88-716.90, 716.94, 716.98-716.99, 718.00, 718.04, 718.08, 719.00, 719.04, 719.08-719.10, 719.14, 719.18-719.20, 719.24, 719.28-719.30, 719.34, 719.38-719.40, 719.44, 719.48-719.50, 719.54, 719.58-719.60, 719.64, 719.68-719.7, 719.80, 719.84, 719.88-719.90, 719.94, 719.98-719.99: **For code 711.05:** 015.80-015.96, 017.90-017.96, 036.82, 056.71, 098.50-098.51, 098.59, 098.89, 711.00, 711.05, 711.08-711.10, 711.15, 711.18-711.20, 711.25, 711.28-711.30, 711.35, 711.38-711.40, 711.45, 711.48-711.50, 711.55, 711.58-711.60, 711.65, 711.68-711.70, 711.75, 711.78-711.80, 711.85, 711.88-711.90, 711.95, 711.98-711.99, 712.10, 712.15, 712.18-712.20, 712.25, 712.28-712.30, 712.35, 712.38-712.80, 712.85, 712.88-712.90, 712.95, 712.98-712.99, 713.0-713.8, 714.0, 715.00, 715.09-715.10, 715.15, 715.18, 715.20, 715.25, 715.28, 715.30, 715.35, 715.38-715.90, 715.95, 715.98, 716.00, 716.05, 716.08-716.10, 716.15, 716.18-716.20, 716.25, 716.28-716.30, 716.35, 716.38-716.40, 716.45, 716.48-716.50, 716.55, 716.58-716.60, 716.65, 716.68, 716.80, 716.85, 716.88-716.90, 716.95, 716.98-716.99, 718.00, 718.05, 718.08, 719.00, 719.05, 719.08-719.10, 719.15, 719.18-719.20, 719.25, 719.28-719.30, 719.35, 719.38-719.40, 719.45, 719.48-719.50, 719.55, 719.58-719.60, 719.65, 719.68-719.7, 719.80, 719.85, 719.88-719.90, 719.95, 719.98-719.99 **For code 711.06:** 015.80-015.96, 017.90-017.96, 036.82, 056.71, 098.50-098.51, 098.59, 098.89, 711.00, 711.06, 711.08-711.10, 711.16, 711.18-711.20, 711.26, 711.28-711.30, 711.36, 711.38-711.40, 711.46, 711.48-711.50, 711.56, 711.58-711.60, 711.66, 711.68-711.70, 711.76, 711.78-711.80, 711.86, 711.88-711.90, 711.96, 711.98-711.99, 712.10, 712.16, 712.18-712.20, 712.26, 712.28-712.30, 712.36, 712.38-712.80, 712.86, 712.88-712.90, 712.96, 712.98-712.99, 713.0-713.8, 714.0, 715.00, 715.09-715.10, 715.16, 715.18, 715.20, 715.26, 715.28, 715.30, 715.36, 715.38-715.90, 715.96, 715.98, 716.00, 716.06, 716.08-716.10, 716.16, 716.18-716.20, 716.26, 716.28-716.30, 716.36, 716.38-716.40, 716.46, 716.48-716.50, 716.56, 716.58-716.60, 716.66, 716.68, 716.80, 716.86, 716.88-716.90, 716.96, 716.98-716.99, 718.00, 718.08, 719.00, 719.06, 719.08-719.10, 719.16, 719.18-719.20, 719.26, 719.28-719.30, 719.36, 719.38-719.40, 719.46, 719.48-719.50, 719.56, 719.58-719.60, 719.66, 719.68-719.7, 719.80, 719.86, 719.88-719.90, 719.96, 719.98-719.99 **For code 711.07:** 015.80-015.96, 017.90-017.96, 036.82, 056.71, 098.50-098.51, 098.59, 098.89, 711.00, 711.07-711.10, 711.17-711.20, 711.27-711.30, 711.37-711.40, 711.47-711.50, 711.57-711.60, 711.67-711.70, 711.77-711.80, 711.87-711.90, 711.97-711.99, 712.10, 712.17-712.20, 712.27-712.30, 712.37-712.80, 712.87-712.90, 712.97-712.99, 713.0-713.8, 714.0, 715.00, 715.09-715.10, 715.17-715.18, 715.20, 715.27-715.28, 715.30, 715.37-715.90, 715.97-715.98, 716.00, 716.07-716.10, 716.17-716.20, 716.27-716.30, 716.37-716.40, 716.47-716.50, 716.57-716.60, 716.67-716.68, 716.80, 716.87-716.90, 716.97-716.99, 718.00, 718.07-718.08, 719.00, 719.07-719.10, 719.17-719.20, 719.27-719.30, 719.37-719.40, 719.47-719.50, 719.57-719.60, 719.67-719.7, 719.80, 719.87-719.90, 719.97-719.99 **For code 711.08:** 015.80-015.96, 017.90-017.96, 036.82, 056.71, 098.50-098.51, 098.59, 098.89, 711.00-714.0, 715.00, 715.09-715.10, 715.18-716.99, 718.00-718.08, 719.00-719.10, 719.18-719.99 **For code 711.09:** See code 711.08

AHA: 1Q, '92, 16; 1Q, '91, 15

DEF: Infectious arthritis caused by various bacteria; marked by inflamed synovial membranes, and purulent effusion in joints.

§ Requires fifth-digit. Valid digits are in [brackets] under each code. See beginning of section 710-739 for codes and definitions.

`N` Newborn Age: 0   `P` Pediatric Age: 0-17   `M` Maternity Age: 12-55   `A` Adult Age: 15-124   `CC` CC Condition   `MC` Major Complication   `CD` Complex Dx   `HIV` HIV Related Dx

§ ✓5ᵗʰ **711.1** *Arthropathy associated with Reiter's disease and*
[0-9]   *nonspecific urethritis*

     Code first underlying disease as:
       nonspecific urethritis (099.4)
       Reiter's disease (099.3)

     DEF: Reiter's disease: joint disease marked by diarrhea, urethritis,
conjunctivitis, keratosis and arthritis; of unknown etiology; affects
young males.

     DEF: Urethritis: inflamed urethra.

§ ✓5ᵗʰ **711.2** *Arthropathy in Behçet's syndrome*
[0-9]   *Code first underlying disease (136.1)*

     DEF: Behçet's syndrome: Chronic inflammatory disorder, of
unknown etiology; affects small blood vessels; causes ulcers of
oral and pharyngeal mucous membranes and genitalia, skin
lesions, retinal vasculitis, optic atrophy and severe uveitis.

§ ✓5ᵗʰ **711.3** *Postdysenteric arthropathy*
[0-9]   *Code first underlying disease as:*
       dysentery (009.0)
       enteritis, infectious (008.0-009.3)
       paratyphoid fever (002.1-002.9)
       typhoid fever (002.0)
       EXCLUDES   *salmonella arthritis (003.23)*

§ ✓5ᵗʰ **711.4** *Arthropathy associated with other bacterial*
[0-9]   *diseases*

     Code first underlying disease as:
       diseases classifiable to 010-040, 090-099, except
         as in 711.1, 711.3, and 713.5
       leprosy (030.0-030.9)
       tuberculosis (015.0-015.9)
       EXCLUDES   *gonococcal arthritis (098.50)*
                   meningococcal arthritis (036.82)

§ ✓5ᵗʰ **711.5** *Arthropathy associated with other viral diseases*
[0-9]   *Code first underlying disease as:*
       diseases classifiable to 045-049, 050-079, 480,
         487
       O'nyong nyong (066.3)
       EXCLUDES   *that due to rubella (056.71)*

§ ✓5ᵗʰ **711.6** *Arthropathy associated with mycoses*   **CC**
[0-9]   *Code first underlying disease (110.0-118)*

     CC Excl: **For code 711.60:** See code 711.08: **For code 711.61:** 015.80-
015.96, 017.90-017.96, 036.82, 056.71, 098.50-098.51, 098.59, 098.89,
711.00-711.01, 711.08-711.11, 711.18-711.21, 711.28-711.31, 711.38-
711.41, 711.48-711.51, 711.58-711.61, 711.68-711.71, 711.78-711.81,
711.88-711.91, 711.98-711.99, 712.10-712.11, 712.18-712.21, 712.28-
712.31, 712.38-712.81, 712.88-712.91, 712.98-712.99, 713.0-713.8, 714.0,
715.00, 715.09-715.11, 715.18-715.21, 715.28, 715.30-715.31, 715.38-
715.91, 715.98, 716.00-716.01, 716.08-716.11, 716.18-716.21, 716.28-
716.31, 716.38-716.41, 716.48-716.51, 716.58-716.61, 716.68, 716.80-
716.81, 716.88-716.91, 716.98-716.99, 718.00-718.01, 718.08, 719.00-
719.01, 719.08-719.11, 719.18-719.21, 719.28-719.31, 719.38-719.41,
719.48-719.51, 719.58-719.61, 719.68-719.7, 719.80-719.81, 719.88-
719.91, 719.98-719.99; **For code 711.62:** 015.80-015.96, 017.90-017.96,
036.82, 056.71, 098.50-098.51, 098.59, 098.89, 711.00, 711.02, 711.08-
711.10, 711.12, 711.18-711.20, 711.22, 711.28-711.30, 711.32, 711.38-
711.40, 711.42, 711.48-711.50, 711.52, 711.58-711.60, 711.62, 711.68-
711.70, 711.72, 711.78-711.80, 711.82, 711.88-711.90, 711.92,
711.98-711.99, 712.10, 712.12, 712.18-712.20, 712.22, 712.28-712.30,
712.32, 712.38-712.80, 712.82, 712.88-712.90, 712.92, 712.98-712.99,
713.0-713.8, 714.0, 715.00, 715.09-715.10, 715.12, 715.18, 715.20, 715.22,
715.28, 715.30, 715.32, 715.38-715.90, 715.92, 715.98, 716.00, 716.02,
716.08-716.10, 716.12, 716.18-716.20, 716.22, 716.28-716.30, 716.32,
716.38-716.40, 716.42, 716.48-716.50, 716.52, 716.58-716.60, 716.62,
716.68, 716.80, 716.82, 716.88-716.90, 716.92, 716.98-716.99, 718.00,
718.02, 718.08, 719.00, 719.02, 719.08-719.10, 719.12, 719.18-719.20,
719.22, 719.28-719.30, 719.32, 719.38-719.40, 719.42, 719.48-719.50,
719.52, 719.58-719.60, 719.62, 719.68-719.7, 719.80, 719.82, 719.88-
719.90, 719.92, 719.98-719.99; **For code 711.63:** 015.80-015.96, 017.90-
017.96, 036.82, 056.71, 098.50-098.51, 098.59, 098.89, 711.00, 711.03,
711.08-711.10, 711.13, 711.18-711.20, 711.23, 711.28-711.30, 711.33,

711.38-711.40, 711.43, 711.48-711.50, 711.53, 711.58-711.60, 711.63,
711.68-711.70, 711.73, 711.78-711.80, 711.83, 711.88-711.90, 711.93,
711.98-711.99, 712.10, 712.13, 712.18-712.20, 712.23, 712.28-712.30,
712.33, 712.38-712.80, 712.83, 712.88-712.90, 712.93, 712.98-712.99,
713.0-713.8, 714.0, 715.00, 715.09-715.10, 715.13, 715.18, 715.20, 715.23,
715.28, 715.30, 715.33, 715.38-715.90, 715.93, 715.98, 716.00, 716.03,
716.08-716.10, 716.13, 716.18-716.20, 716.23, 716.28-716.30, 716.33,
716.38-716.40, 716.43, 716.48-716.50, 716.53, 716.58-716.60, 716.63,
716.68, 716.80, 716.83, 716.88-716.90, 716.93, 716.98-716.99, 718.00,
718.03, 718.08, 719.00, 719.03, 719.08-719.10, 719.13, 719.18-719.20,
719.23, 719.28-719.30, 719.33, 719.38-719.40, 719.43, 719.48-719.50,
719.53, 719.58-719.60, 719.63, 719.68-719.7, 719.80, 719.83, 719.88-
719.90, 719.93, 719.98-719.99 **For code 711.64:** 015.80-015.96, 017.90-
017.96, 036.82, 056.71, 098.50-098.51, 098.59, 098.89, 711.00, 711.04,
711.08-711.10, 711.14, 711.18-711.20, 711.24, 711.28-711.30, 711.34,
711.38-711.40, 711.44, 711.48-711.50, 711.58-711.60, 711.64, 711.68-
711.70, 711.74, 711.78-711.80, 711.84, 711.88-711.90, 711.94, 711.98-
711.99, 712.10, 712.14, 712.18-712.20, 712.24, 712.28-712.30, 712.34,
712.38-712.80, 712.84, 712.88-712.90, 712.94, 712.98-712.99, 713.0-713.8,
714.0, 715.00-715.10, 715.14, 715.18, 715.20, 715.24, 715.28, 715.30,
715.34, 715.38-715.90, 715.94, 715.98, 716.00, 716.04, 716.08-716.10,
716.14, 716.18-716.20, 716.24, 716.28-716.30, 716.34, 716.38-716.40,
716.44, 716.48-716.50, 716.54, 716.58-716.60, 716.64, 716.68, 716.80,
716.84, 716.88-716.90, 716.94, 716.98-716.99, 718.00, 718.04, 718.08,
719.00, 719.04, 719.08-719.10, 719.14, 719.18-719.20, 719.24, 719.28-
719.30, 719.34, 719.38-719.40, 719.44, 719.48-719.50, 719.54, 719.58-
719.60, 719.64, 719.68-719.7, 719.80, 719.84, 719.88-719.90, 719.94,
719.98-719.99 **For code 711.65:** 015.80-015.96, 017.90-017.96, 036.82,
056.71, 098.50-098.51, 098.59, 098.89, 711.00, 711.05, 711.08-711.10,
711.15, 711.18-711.20, 711.25, 711.28-711.30, 711.35, 711.38-711.40,
711.45, 711.48-711.50, 711.55, 711.58-711.60, 711.65, 711.68-711.70,
711.75, 711.78-711.80, 711.85, 711.88-711.90, 711.95, 711.98-711.99,
712.10, 712.15, 712.18-712.20, 712.25, 712.28-712.30, 712.35, 712.38-
712.80, 712.85, 712.88-712.90, 712.95, 712.98-712.99, 713.0-713.8, 714.0,
715.00, 715.09-715.10, 715.15, 715.18, 715.20, 715.25, 715.28, 715.30,
715.35, 715.38-715.90, 715.95, 715.98, 716.00, 716.05, 716.08-716.10,
716.15, 716.18-716.20, 716.25, 716.28-716.30, 716.35, 716.38-716.40,
716.45, 716.48-716.50, 716.55, 716.58-716.60, 716.65, 716.68, 716.80,
716.85, 716.88-716.90, 716.95, 716.98-716.99, 718.00, 718.05, 718.08,
719.00, 719.05, 719.08-719.10, 719.15, 719.18-719.20, 719.25, 719.28-
719.30, 719.35, 719.38-719.40, 719.45, 719.48-719.50, 719.55, 719.58-
719.60, 719.65, 719.68-719.7, 719.80, 719.85, 719.88-719.90, 719.95,
719.98-719.99
For code 711.66: 015.80-015.96, 017.90-017.96, 036.82, 056.71, 098.50-
098.51, 098.59, 098.89, 711.00, 711.06, 711.08-711.10, 711.16, 711.18-
711.20, 711.26, 711.28-711.30, 711.36, 711.38-711.40, 711.46, 711.48-
711.50, 711.56, 711.58-711.60, 711.66, 711.68-711.70, 711.76, 711.78-
711.80, 711.86, 711.88-711.90, 711.96, 711.98-711.99, 712.10, 712.16,
712.18-712.20, 712.26, 712.28-712.30, 712.36, 712.38-712.80, 712.86,
712.88-712.90, 712.96, 712.98-712.99, 713.0-713.8, 714.0, 715.00, 715.09-
715.10, 715.16, 715.18, 715.20, 715.26, 715.28, 715.30, 715.36, 715.38-
715.90, 715.96, 715.98, 716.00, 716.06, 716.08-716.10, 716.16, 716.18-
716.20, 716.26, 716.28-716.30, 716.36, 716.38-716.40, 716.46, 716.48-
716.50, 716.56, 716.58-716.60, 716.66, 716.68, 716.80, 716.86, 716.88-
716.90, 716.96, 716.98-716.99, 718.00, 718.08, 719.00, 719.06, 719.08-
719.10, 719.16, 719.18-719.20, 719.26, 719.28-719.30, 719.36, 719.38-
719.40, 719.46, 719.48-719.50, 719.56, 719.58-719.60, 719.66, 719.68-
719.7, 719.80, 719.86, 719.88-719.90, 719.96, 719.98-719.99 **For code
711.67:** 015.80-015.96, 017.90-017.96, 036.82, 056.71, 098.50-098.51,
098.59, 098.89, 711.00, 711.07-711.10, 711.17-711.20, 711.27-711.30,
711.37-711.40, 711.47-711.50, 711.57-711.60, 711.67-711.70, 711.77-
711.80, 711.87-711.90, 711.97-711.99, 712.10, 712.17-712.20, 712.27-
712.30, 712.37-712.80, 712.87-712.90, 712.97-712.99, 713.0-713.8, 714.0,
715.00, 715.09-715.10, 715.17-715.18, 715.20, 715.27-715.28, 715.30,
715.37-715.90, 715.97-715.98, 716.00, 716.07-716.10, 716.17-716.20,
716.27-716.30, 716.37-716.40, 716.47-716.50, 716.57-716.60, 716.67-
716.80, 716.87-716.90, 716.97-716.99, 718.00, 718.07-718.08, 719.00,
719.07-719.10, 719.17-719.20, 719.27-719.30, 719.37-719.40, 719.47-
719.50, 719.57-719.60, 719.67-719.7, 719.80, 719.87-719.90, 719.97-
719.99 **For code 711.68:** 015.80-015.96, 017.90-017.96, 036.82, 056.71,
098.50-098.51, 098.59, 098.89, 711.00-711.99, 712.10-712.99, 713.0-713.8,
714.0, 715.00, 715.09-715.10, 715.18-715.98, 716.00-716.99, 718.00-
718.08, 719.00-719.10, 719.18-719.99 **For code 711.69:** See code 711.68

---

§   Requires fifth-digit. Valid digits are in [brackets] under each code. See beginning of section 710-739 for codes and definitions.

✓4ᵗʰ / ✓5ᵗʰ   Additional Digit Required   Nonspecific PDx   Unacceptable PDx   Manifestation Code   **MCV** Major Cardiovascular Condition   ▶◀ Revised Text   ● New Code   ▲ Revised Code Title

Musculoskeletal and Connective Tissue

711.7–714.0

§ ✓5ᵗʰ **711.7** *Arthropathy associated with helminthiasis*
[0-9]   *Code first underlying disease as:*
         filariasis (125.0-125.9)

§ ✓5ᵗʰ **711.8** *Arthropathy associated with other infectious and parasitic diseases*
[0-9]   *Code first underlying disease as:*
         diseases classifiable to 080-088, 100-104, 130-136
     EXCLUDES   arthropathy associated with sarcoidosis (713.7)

     AHA: 4Q, '91, 15; 3Q, '90, 14

§ ✓5ᵗʰ **711.9** **Unspecified infective arthritis**
[0-9]   Infective arthritis or polyarthritis (acute) (chronic) (subacute) NOS

✓4ᵗʰ **712 Crystal arthropathies**
     INCLUDES   crystal-induced arthritis and synovitis
     EXCLUDES   gouty arthropathy (274.0)
     DEF: Joint disease due to urate crystal deposit in joints or synovial membranes.

The following fifth-digit subclassification is for use with category 712; valid digits are in [brackets] under each code. See list at beginning of chapter for definitions.
     0 site unspecified
     1 shoulder region
     2 upper arm
     3 forearm
     4 hand
     5 pelvic region and thigh
     6 lower leg
     7 ankle and foot
     8 other specified sites
     9 multiple sites

§ ✓5ᵗʰ **712.1** *Chondrocalcinosis due to dicalcium phosphate crystals*
[0-9]   Chondrocalcinosis due to dicalcium phosphate crystals (with other crystals)
     Code first underlying disease (275.4)

§ ✓5ᵗʰ **712.2** *Chondrocalcinosis due to pyrophosphate crystals*
[0-9]   *Code first underlying disease (275.4)*

§ ✓5ᵗʰ **712.3** *Chondrocalcinosis, unspecified*
[0-9]   *Code first underlying disease (275.4)*

§ ✓5ᵗʰ **712.8** **Other specified crystal arthropathies**
[0-9]

§ ✓5ᵗʰ **712.9** **Unspecified crystal arthropathy**
[0-9]

✓4ᵗʰ **713 Arthropathy associated with other disorders classified elsewhere**
     INCLUDES
         arthritis
         arthropathy   associated with
         polyarthritis   conditions
         polyarthropathy   classifiable below

713.0 *Arthropathy associated with other endocrine and metabolic disorders*
     Code first underlying disease as:
         acromegaly (253.0)
         hemochromatosis (275.0)
         hyperparathyroidism (252.00-252.08)
         hypogammaglobulinemia (279.00-279.09)
         hypothyroidism (243-244.9)
         lipoid metabolism disorder (272.0-272.9)
         ochronosis (270.2)
     EXCLUDES   arthropathy associated with:
         amyloidosis (713.7)
         crystal deposition disorders, except gout (712.1-712.9)
         diabetic neuropathy (713.5)
         gouty arthropathy (274.0)

713.1 *Arthropathy associated with gastrointestinal conditions other than infections*
     Code first underlying disease as:
         regional enteritis (555.0-555.9)
         ulcerative colitis (556)

713.2 *Arthropathy associated with hematological disorders*
     Code first underlying disease as:
         hemoglobinopathy (282.4-282.7)
         hemophilia (286.0-286.2)
         leukemia (204.0-208.9)
         malignant reticulosis (202.3)
         multiple myelomatosis (203.0)
     EXCLUDES   arthropathy associated with Henoch-Schönlein purpura (713.6)

713.3 *Arthropathy associated with dermatological disorders*
     Code first underlying disease as:
         erythema multiforme (695.1)
         erythema nodosum (695.2)
     EXCLUDES   psoriatic arthropathy (696.0)

713.4 *Arthropathy associated with respiratory disorders*
     Code first underlying disease as:
         diseases classifiable to 490-519
     EXCLUDES   arthropathy associated with respiratory infections (711.0, 711.4-711.8)

713.5 *Arthropathy associated with neurological disorders*
     Charcôt's arthropathy ⎱ associated with diseases
     Neuropathic arthritis ⎰ classifiable elsewhere
     Code first underlying disease as:
         neuropathic joint disease [Charcôt's joints]:
         NOS (094.0)
         diabetic (250.6)
         syringomyelic (336.0)
         tabetic [syphilitic] (094.0)

713.6 *Arthropathy associated with hypersensitivity reaction*
     Code first underlying disease as:
         Henoch (-Schönlein) purpura (287.0)
         serum sickness (999.5)
     EXCLUDES   allergic arthritis NOS (716.2)

713.7 *Other general diseases with articular involvement*
     Code first underlying disease as:
         amyloidosis ▶(277.30-277.39)◀
         familial Mediterranean fever ▶(277.31)◀
         sarcoidosis (135)

     AHA: 2Q, '97, 12

713.8 *Arthropathy associated with other condition classifiable elsewhere*
     Code first underlying disease as:
         conditions classifiable elsewhere except as in 711.1-711.8, 712, and 713.0-713.7

✓4ᵗʰ **714 Rheumatoid arthritis and other inflammatory polyarthropathies**
     EXCLUDES   rheumatic fever (390)
         rheumatoid arthritis of spine NOS (720.0)

     AHA: 2Q, '95, 3

714.0 **Rheumatoid arthritis**
     Arthritis or polyarthritis:
         atrophic
         rheumatic (chronic)
     Use additional code to identify manifestation, as:
         myopathy (359.6)
         polyneuropathy (357.1)
     EXCLUDES   juvenile rheumatoid arthritis NOS (714.30)

     AHA: 1Q, '90, 5

     DEF: Chronic systemic disease principally of joints, manifested by inflammatory changes in articular structures and synovial membranes, atrophy, and loss in bone density.

---

§   Requires fifth-digit. Valid digits are in [brackets] under each code. See beginning of section 710-739 for codes and definitions.

| **N** Newborn Age: 0 | **P** Pediatric Age: 0-17 | **M** Maternity Age: 12-55 | **A** Adult Age: 15-124 | **CC** CC Condition | **MC** Major Complication | **CD** Complex Dx | **HIV** HIV Related Dx |

714.1 Felty's syndrome `cc`
Rheumatoid arthritis with splenoadenomegaly and leukopenia
CC Excl: 036.82, 056.71, 711.00-714.4, 715.00, 715.09-715.10, 715.18-716.99, 718.00-718.08, 719.00-719.10, 719.18-719.99

DEF: Syndrome marked by rheumatoid arthritis, splenomegaly, leukopenia, pigmented spots on lower extremity skin, anemia, and thrombocytopenia.

714.2 Other rheumatoid arthritis with visceral or systemic involvement `cc`
Rheumatoid carditis
CC Excl: See code 714.1

✓5ᵗʰ **714.3 Juvenile chronic polyarthritis**
DEF: Rheumatoid arthritis of more than one joint; lasts longer than six weeks in age 17 or younger; symptoms include fever, erythematous rash, weight loss, lymphadenopathy, hepatosplenomegaly and pericarditis.

     714.30 Polyarticular juvenile rheumatoid arthritis, chronic or unspecified `cc`
         Juvenile rheumatoid arthritis NOS
         Still's disease
         CC Excl: See code 714.1

     714.31 Polyarticular juvenile rheumatoid arthritis, acute `cc`
         CC Excl: See code 714.1

     714.32 Pauciarticular juvenile rheumatoid arthritis `cc`
         CC Excl: See code 714.1

     714.33 Monoarticular juvenile rheumatoid arthritis `cc`
         CC Excl: See code 714.1

714.4 Chronic postrheumatic arthropathy
Chronic rheumatoid nodular fibrositis
Jaccoud's syndrome
DEF: Persistent joint disorder; follows previous rheumatic infection.

✓5ᵗʰ **714.8 Other specified inflammatory polyarthropathies**
     714.81 Rheumatoid lung
         Caplan's syndrome
         Diffuse interstitial rheumatoid disease of lung
         Fibrosing alveolitis, rheumatoid
         DEF: Lung disorders associated with rheumatoid arthritis.

     714.89 Other

714.9 Unspecified inflammatory polyarthropathy
Inflammatory polyarthropathy or polyarthritis NOS
EXCLUDES polyarthropathy NOS (716.5)

✓4ᵗʰ **715 Osteoarthrosis and allied disorders**
Note: Localized, in the subcategories below, includes bilateral involvement of the same site.
INCLUDES arthritis or polyarthritis:
     degenerative
     hypertrophic
     degenerative joint disease
     osteoarthritis
EXCLUDES Marie-Strümpell spondylitis (720.0)
     osteoarthrosis [osteoarthritis] of spine (721.0-721.9)

The following fifth-digit subclassification is for use with category 715; valid digits are in [brackets] under each code. See list at beginning of chapter for definitions.
   0 site unspecified
   1 shoulder region
   2 upper arm
   3 forearm
   4 hand
   5 pelvic region and thigh
   6 lower leg
   7 ankle and foot
   8 other specified sites
   9 multiple sites

§ ✓5ᵗʰ **715.0 Osteoarthrosis, generalized**
[0,4,9]   Degenerative joint disease, involving multiple joints
     Primary generalized hypertrophic osteoarthrosis
DEF: Chronic noninflammatory arthritis; marked by degenerated articular cartilage and enlarged bone; symptoms include pain and stiffness with activity; occurs among elderly.

§ ✓5ᵗʰ **715.1 Osteoarthrosis, localized, primary**
[0-8]   Localized osteoarthropathy, idiopathic

§ ✓5ᵗʰ **715.2 Osteoarthrosis, localized, secondary**
[0-8]   Coxae malum senilis

§ ✓5ᵗʰ **715.3 Osteoarthrosis, localized, not specified whether primary or secondary**
[0-8]
     Otto's pelvis
AHA: For code 715.35: 3Q, '04, 12; 2Q, '04, 15; For code 715.36: 4Q, '03, 118; 2Q, '95, 5

§ ✓5ᵗʰ **715.8 Osteoarthrosis involving, or with mention of more than one site, but not specified as generalized**
[0,9]

¹ § ✓5ᵗʰ **715.9 Osteoarthrosis, unspecified whether generalized or localized**
[0-8]
AHA: For code 715.90: 2Q, '97, 12

✓4ᵗʰ **716 Other and unspecified arthropathies**
EXCLUDES cricoarytenoid arthropathy (478.79)
The following fifth-digit subclassification is for use with category 716; valid digits are in [brackets] under each code. See list at beginning of chapter for definitions.
   0 site unspecified
   1 shoulder region
   2 upper arm
   3 forearm
   4 hand
   5 pelvic region and thigh
   6 lower leg
   7 ankle and foot
   8 other specified sites
   9 multiple sites

AHA: 2Q, '95, 3

§ ✓5ᵗʰ **716.0 Kaschin-Beck disease**
[0-9]   Endemic polyarthritis
DEF: Chronic degenerative disease of spine and peripheral joints; occurs in eastern Siberian, northern Chinese, and Korean youth; may be a mycotoxicosis caused by eating cereals infected with fungus.

§ ✓5ᵗʰ **716.1 Traumatic arthropathy**
[0-9]   **AHA:** For Code 716.11: 1Q, '02, 9

---

¹ Nonspecific PDx=0
§ Requires fifth-digit. Valid digits are in [brackets] under each code. See beginning of section 710-739 for codes and definitions.

✓4ᵗʰ Additional Digit Required   Nonspecific PDx   Unacceptable PDx   Manifestation Code   **MCV** Major Cardiovascular Condition   ◄ Revised Text   ● New Code   ▲ Revised Code Title

2007 ICD•9•CM   **Volume 1 — 221**

§ ✓5ᵗʰ **716.2** **Allergic arthritis**
[0-9]   **EXCLUDES**   *arthritis associated with Henoch-Schönlein purpura or serum sickness (713.6)*

§ ✓5ᵗʰ **716.3** **Climacteric arthritis**   ♀
[0-9]   Menopausal arthritis
DEF: Ovarian hormone deficiency; causes pain in small joints, shoulders, elbows or knees; affects females at menopause; also called arthropathia ovaripriva.

§ ✓5ᵗʰ **716.4** **Transient arthropathy**
[0-9]   **EXCLUDES**   *palindromic rheumatism (719.3)*

§ ✓5ᵗʰ **716.5** **Unspecified polyarthropathy or polyarthritis**
[0-9]

§ ✓5ᵗʰ **716.6** **Unspecified monoarthritis**
[0-8]   Coxitis

§ ✓5ᵗʰ **716.8** **Other specified arthropathy**
[0-9]

§ ✓5ᵗʰ **716.9** **Arthropathy, unspecified**
[0-9]   Arthritis ⎫
         Arthropathy ⎬ (acute) (chronic) (subacute)

         Articular rheumatism (chronic)
         Inflammation of joint NOS

✓4ᵗʰ **717 Internal derangement of knee**

    INCLUDES   degeneration ⎫
         rupture, old ⎬ of articular cartilage or
         tear, old ⎭ meniscus of knee

    EXCLUDES   *acute derangement of knee (836.0-836.6)*
         ankylosis (718.5)
         contracture (718.4)
         current injury (836.0-836.6)
         deformity (736.4-736.6)
         recurrent dislocation (718.3)

    717.0 **Old bucket handle tear of medial meniscus**
         Old bucket handle tear of unspecified cartilage

    717.1 **Derangement of anterior horn of medial meniscus**

    717.2 **Derangement of posterior horn of medial meniscus**

    717.3 **Other and unspecified derangement of medial meniscus**
         Degeneration of internal semilunar cartilage

✓5ᵗʰ **717.4** **Derangement of lateral meniscus**
         717.40 **Derangement of lateral meniscus, unspecified**
         717.41 **Bucket handle tear of lateral meniscus**
         717.42 **Derangement of anterior horn of lateral meniscus**
         717.43 **Derangement of posterior horn of lateral meniscus**
         717.49 **Other**

    717.5 **Derangement of meniscus, not elsewhere classified**
         Congenital discoid meniscus
         Cyst of semilunar cartilage
         Derangement of semilunar cartilage NOS

Disruption and Tears of Meniscus

Bucket-handle   Flap-type   Peripheral   Radial

Horizontal cleavage   Vertical   Congenital discoid meniscus

Internal Derangements of Knee

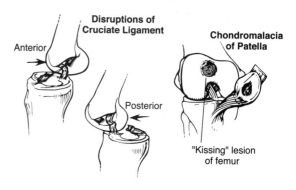

Disruptions of Cruciate Ligament
Anterior
Posterior

Chondromalacia of Patella

"Kissing" lesion of femur

    717.6 **Loose body in knee**
         Joint mice, knee
         Rice bodies, knee (joint)
         DEF: The presence in the joint synovial area of a small, frequently calcified, loose body created from synovial membrane, organized fibrin fragments of articular cartilage or arthritis osteophytes.

    717.7 **Chondromalacia of patella**
         Chondromalacia patellae
         Degeneration [softening] of articular cartilage of patella
         AHA: M-A, '85, 14; N-D, '84, 9

         DEF: Softened patella cartilage.

✓5ᵗʰ **717.8** **Other internal derangement of knee**
         717.81 **Old disruption of lateral collateral ligament**
         717.82 **Old disruption of medial collateral ligament**
         717.83 **Old disruption of anterior cruciate ligament**
         717.84 **Old disruption of posterior cruciate ligament**
         717.85 **Old disruption of other ligaments of knee**
              Capsular ligament of knee
         717.89 **Other**
              Old disruption of ligaments NOS

    717.9 **Unspecified internal derangement of knee**
         Derangement NOS of knee

✓4ᵗʰ **718 Other derangement of joint**
    EXCLUDES   *current injury (830.0-848.9)*
         jaw (524.60-524.69)

The following fifth-digit subclassification is for use with category 718; valid digits are in [brackets] under each code. See list at beginning of chapter for definitions.
    0   site unspecified
    1   shoulder region
    2   upper arm
    3   forearm
    4   hand
    5   pelvic region and thigh
    6   lower leg
    7   ankle and foot
    8   other specified sites
    9   multiple sites

§ ✓5ᵗʰ **718.0** **Articular cartilage disorder**
[0-5,7-9]   Meniscus: Meniscus:
         disorder   tear, old
         rupture, old   Old rupture of ligament(s) of joint NOS
    EXCLUDES   *articular cartilage disorder:*
         in ochronosis (270.2)
         knee (717.0-717.9)
         chondrocalcinosis (275.4)
         metastatic calcification (275.4)

§ Requires fifth-digit. Valid digits are in [brackets] under each code. See beginning of section 710-739 for codes and definitions.

N Newborn Age: 0   **P** Pediatric Age: 0-17   **M** Maternity Age: 12-55   **A** Adult Age: 15-124   **CC** CC Condition   **MC** Major Complication   **CD** Complex Dx   **HIV** HIV Related Dx

§ ✓5th **718.1 Loose body in joint**
[0-5,7-9]   Joint mice
> EXCLUDES   *knee (717.6)*

AHA: For code 718.17: 2Q, '01, 15

DEF: Calcified loose bodies in synovial fluid; due to arthritic osteophytes.

§ ✓5th **718.2 Pathological dislocation**
[0-9]   Dislocation or displacement of joint, not recurrent and not current injury
Spontaneous dislocation (joint)

§ ✓5th **718.3 Recurrent dislocation of joint**
[0-9]   **AHA:** N-D, '87, 7

2 § ✓5th **718.4 Contracture of joint**
[0-9]   **AHA:** 4Q, '98, 40

1 § ✓5th **718.5 Ankylosis of joint**
[0-9]   Ankylosis of joint (fibrous) (osseous)
> EXCLUDES   *spine (724.9)*
> *stiffness of joint without mention of ankylosis (719.5)*

DEF: Immobility and solidification, of joint; due to disease, injury or surgical procedure.

§ ✓5th **718.6 Unspecified intrapelvic protrusion of acetabulum**
[0,5]   Protrusio acetabuli, unspecified

DEF: Sinking of the floor of acetabulum; causing femoral head to protrude, limits hip movement; of unknown etiology.

1 § ✓5th **718.7 Developmental dislocation of joint**
[0-9]
> EXCLUDES   *congenital dislocation of joint (754.0-755.8)*
> *traumatic dislocation of joint (830-839)*

AHA: 4Q, '01, 48

§ ✓5th **718.8 Other joint derangement, not elsewhere classified**
[0-9]   Flail joint (paralytic)   Instability of joint
> EXCLUDES   *deformities classifiable to 736 (736.0-736.9)*

AHA: For code 718.81: 2Q, '00, 14

§ ✓5th **718.9 Unspecified derangement of joint**
[0-5,7-9] > EXCLUDES   *knee (717.9)*

✓4th **719 Other and unspecified disorders of joint**
> EXCLUDES   *jaw (524.60-524.69)*

The following fifth-digit subclassification is for use with codes 719.0-719.6, 719.8-719.9; valid digits are in [brackets] under each code. See list at beginning of chapter for definitions.

   0 site unspecified
   1 shoulder region
   2 upper arm
   3 forearm
   4 hand
   5 pelvic region and thigh
   6 lower leg
   7 ankle and foot
   8 other specified sites
   9 multiple sites

§ ✓5th **719.0 Effusion of joint**
[0-9]   Hydrarthrosis
Swelling of joint, with or without pain
> EXCLUDES   *intermittent hydrarthrosis (719.3)*

§ ✓5th **719.1 Hemarthrosis**
[0-9]   > EXCLUDES   *current injury (840.0-848.9)*

§ ✓5th **719.2 Villonodular synovitis**
[0-9]
DEF: Overgrowth of synovial tissue, especially at knee joint; due to macrophage infiltration of giant cells in synovial villi and fibrous nodules.

Joint Derangements and Disorders

| Joint contracture | Ankylosis of joint | Synovial effusion (fluid) | Hemarthrosis (blood) |

§ ✓5th **719.3 Palindromic rheumatism**
[0-9]   Hench-Rosenberg syndrome
Intermittent hydrarthrosis

DEF: Recurrent episodes of afebrile arthritis and periarthritis marked by their complete disappearance after a few days or hours; causes swelling, redness, and disability usually affecting only one joint; no known cause; affects adults of either sex.

§ ✓5th **719.4 Pain in joint**
[0-9]   Arthralgia

AHA: For code 719.46: 1Q, '01, 3

§ ✓5th **719.5 Stiffness of joint, not elsewhere classified**
[0-9]

§ ✓5th **719.6 Other symptoms referable to joint**
[0-9]   Joint crepitus   Snapping hip

AHA: 1Q, '94, 15

719.7 Difficulty in walking
> EXCLUDES   *abnormality of gait (781.2)*

AHA: 2Q, '04, 15; 4Q, '03, 66

§ ✓5th **719.8 Other specified disorders of joint**
[0-9]   Calcification of joint   Fistula of joint
> EXCLUDES   *temporomandibular joint-pain-dysfunction syndrome [Costen's syndrome] (524.60)*

§ ✓5th **719.9 Unspecified disorder of joint**
[0-9]

DORSOPATHIES (720-724)
> EXCLUDES   *curvature of spine (737.0-737.9)*
> *osteochondrosis of spine (juvenile) (732.0)*
> *adult (732.8)*

✓4th **720 Ankylosing spondylitis and other inflammatory spondylopathies**

720.0 Ankylosing spondylitis
Rheumatoid arthritis of spine NOS
Spondylitis:
   Marie-Strümpell
   rheumatoid

DEF: Rheumatoid arthritis of spine and sacroiliac joints; fusion and deformity in spine follows; affects mainly males; cause unknown.

720.1 Spinal enthesopathy
Disorder of peripheral ligamentous or muscular attachments of spine
Romanus lesion

DEF: Tendinous or muscular vertebral bone attachment abnormality.

720.2 Sacroiliitis, not elsewhere classified
Inflammation of sacroiliac joint NOS

DEF: Pain due to inflammation in joint, at juncture of sacrum and hip.

---

1 Nonspecific PDx=0
2 Nonspecific PDx=9
§ Requires fifth-digit. Valid digits are in [brackets] under each code. See beginning of section 710-739 for codes and definitions.

 Additional Digit Required   Nonspecific PDx   Unacceptable PDx   Manifestation Code   **MCV** Major Cardiovascular Condition   ▶◀ Revised Text   ● New Code   ▲ Revised Code Title

✓5th **720.8 Other inflammatory spondylopathies**

720.81 Inflammatory spondylopathies in diseases classified elsewhere
Code first underlying disease as:
tuberculosis (015.0)

720.89 Other

720.9 Unspecified inflammatory spondylopathy
Spondylitis NOS

✓4th **721 Spondylosis and allied disorders**
AHA: 2Q, '89, 14

DEF: Degenerative changes in spinal joint.

721.0 Cervical spondylosis without myelopathy
Cervical or cervicodorsal: Cervical or cervicodorsal:
arthritis   spondylarthritis
osteoarthritis

721.1 Cervical spondylosis with myelopathy
Anterior spinal artery compression syndrome
Spondylogenic compression of cervical spinal cord
Vertebral artery compression syndrome

721.2 Thoracic spondylosis without myelopathy
Thoracic: Thoracic:
arthritis   spondylarthritis
osteoarthritis

721.3 Lumbosacral spondylosis without myelopathy
Lumbar or lumbosacral: Lumbar or lumbosacral:
arthritis   spondylarthritis
osteoarthritis

AHA: 4Q, '02, 107

▽ **DRG** 243

✓5th **721.4 Thoracic or lumbar spondylosis with myelopathy**

721.41 Thoracic region
Spondylogenic compression of thoracic
spinal cord

721.42 Lumbar region
Spondylogenic compression of lumbar
spinal cord

721.5 Kissing spine
Baastrup's syndrome

DEF: Compression of spinous processes of adjacent vertebrae; due to mutual contact.

721.6 Ankylosing vertebral hyperostosis

721.7 Traumatic spondylopathy
Kümmell's disease or spondylitis

721.8 Other allied disorders of spine

✓5th **721.9 Spondylosis of unspecified site**

721.90 Without mention of myelopathy
Spinal:
arthritis (deformans) (degenerative)
(hypertrophic)
osteoarthritis NOS
Spondylarthrosis NOS

721.91 With myelopathy
Spondylogenic compression of spinal cord
NOS

Normal Anatomy of Vertebral Disc

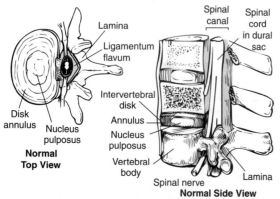

Lamina
Ligamentum flavum
Spinal canal
Spinal cord in dural sac
Intervertebral disk
Annulus
Nucleus pulposus
Disk annulus
Nucleus pulposus
Vertebral body
Spinal nerve
Lamina
Normal Top View
Normal Side View

Derangement of Vertebral Disc

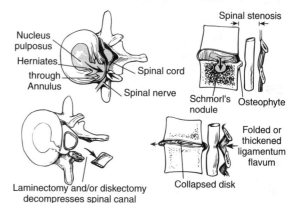

Nucleus pulposus
Herniates through Annulus
Spinal cord
Spinal nerve
Spinal stenosis
Schmorl's nodule
Osteophyte
Folded or thickened ligamentum flavum
Collapsed disk
Laminectomy and/or diskectomy decompresses spinal canal

✓4th **722 Intervertebral disc disorders**
AHA: 1Q, '88, 10

722.0 Displacement of cervical intervertebral disc without myelopathy
Neuritis (brachial) or radiculitis due to displacement
or rupture of cervical intervertebral disc
Any condition classifiable to 722.2 of the cervical or
cervicothoracic intervertebral disc

✓5th **722.1 Displacement of thoracic or lumbar intervertebral disc without myelopathy**

722.10 Lumbar intervertebral disc without myelopathy
Lumbago or sciatica due to displacement of
intervertebral disc
Neuritis or radiculitis due to displacement
or rupture of lumbar intervertebral
disc
Any condition classifiable to 722.2 of the
lumbar or lumbosacral intervertebral
disc

AHA: 3Q, '03, 12; 1Q, '03, 7; 4Q, '02, 107

▽ **DRG** 243

722.11 Thoracic intervertebral disc without myelopathy
Any condition classifiable to 722.2 of
thoracic intervertebral disc

722.2 Displacement of intervertebral disc, site unspecified, without myelopathy
Discogenic syndrome NOS
Herniation of nucleus pulposus NOS
Intervertebral disc NOS:
extrusion
prolapse
protrusion
rupture
Neuritis or radiculitis due to displacement or
rupture of intervertebral disc

✓5th **722.3 Schmorl's nodes**

DEF: Irregular bone defect in the margin of the vertebral body;
causes herniation into end plate of vertebral body.

722.30 Unspecified region
722.31 Thoracic region
722.32 Lumbar region
722.39 Other

722.4 Degeneration of cervical intervertebral disc
Degeneration of cervicothoracic intervertebral disc

✓5th **722.5 Degeneration of thoracic or lumbar intervertebral disc**

722.51 Thoracic or thoracolumbar intervertebral disc

722.52 Lumbar or lumbosacral intervertebral disc

AHA: 4Q, '04, 133

▽ **DRG** 243

N Newborn Age: 0   P Pediatric Age: 0-17   M Maternity Age: 12-55   A Adult Age: 15-124   CC CC Condition   MC Major Complication   CD Complex Dx   HIV HIV Related Dx

722.6   **Degeneration of intervertebral disc, site unspecified**
     Degenerative disc disease NOS
     Narrowing of intervertebral disc or space NOS

✓5ᵗʰ **722.7**   **Intervertebral disc disorder with myelopathy**
     722.70 Unspecified region
     722.71 Cervical region
     722.72 Thoracic region
     722.73 Lumbar region

✓5ᵗʰ **722.8**   **Postlaminectomy syndrome**
     AHA: J-F, '87, 7

     DEF: Spinal disorder due to spinal laminectomy surgery.

     722.80 Unspecified region   `CC`
         CC Excl: 722.51-722.93

     722.81 Cervical region   `CC`
         CC Excl: See code 722.80

     722.82 Thoracic region   `CC`
         CC Excl: See code 722.80

     722.83 Lumbar region   `CC`
         CC Excl: See code 722.80

         AHA: 2Q, '97, 15

✓5ᵗʰ **722.9**   **Other and unspecified disc disorder**
     Calcification of intervertebral cartilage or disc
     Discitis
     722.90 Unspecified region
         AHA: N-D, '84, 19

     722.91 Cervical region
     722.92 Thoracic region
     722.93 Lumbar region

✓4ᵗʰ **723 Other disorders of cervical region**
     EXCLUDES   conditions due to:
         intervertebral disc disorders (722.0-722.9)
         spondylosis (721.0-721.9)

AHA: 3Q, '94, 14; 2Q, '89, 14

  723.0   **Spinal stenosis in cervical region**
     AHA: 4Q, '03, 101

  723.1   **Cervicalgia**
     Pain in neck
     DEF: Pain in cervical spine or neck region.

  723.2   **Cervicocranial syndrome**
     Barré-Liéou syndrome
     Posterior cervical sympathetic syndrome
     DEF: Neurologic disorder of upper cervical spine and nerve roots.

Spinal Stenosis in Cervical Region

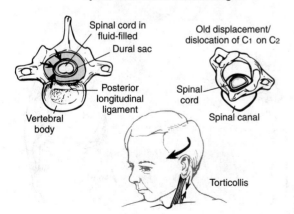

Spinal cord in fluid-filled Dural sac
Old displacement/ dislocation of C₁ on C₂
Posterior longitudinal ligament
Spinal cord
Vertebral body
Spinal canal
Torticollis

723.3   **Cervicobrachial syndrome (diffuse)**
     AHA: N-D, '85, 12

     DEF: Complex of symptoms due to scalenus anterior muscle compressing the brachial plexus; pain radiates from shoulder to arm or back of neck.

723.4   **Brachial neuritis or radiculitis NOS**   `CC`
     Cervical radiculitis
     Radicular syndrome of upper limbs
     CC Excl: 722.6-722.71, 722.80-722.81, 722.90-722.91, 723.0-723.9

723.5   **Torticollis, unspecified**   `CC`
     Contracture of neck
     EXCLUDES   congenital (754.1)
         due to birth injury (767.8)
         hysterical (300.11)
         ocular torticollis (781.93)
         psychogenic (306.0)
         spasmodic (333.83)
         traumatic, current (847.0)
     CC Excl: 053.71, 722.6-722.71, 722.80-722.81, 722.90-722.91, 723.0-723.9
     AHA: 2Q, '01, 21; 1Q, '95, 7

     DEF: Abnormally positioned neck relative to head; due to cervical muscle or fascia contractions; also called wryneck.

723.6   **Panniculitis specified as affecting neck**
     DEF: Inflammation of the panniculus adiposus (subcutaneous fat) in the neck.

723.7   **Ossification of posterior longitudinal ligament in cervical region**

723.8   **Other syndromes affecting cervical region**
     Cervical syndrome NEC
     Klippel's disease
     Occipital neuralgia
     AHA: 1Q, '00, 7

723.9   **Unspecified musculoskeletal disorders and symptoms referable to neck**
     Cervical (region) disorder NOS

✓4ᵗʰ **724 Other and unspecified disorders of back**
     EXCLUDES   collapsed vertebra (code to cause, e.g., osteoporosis, 733.00-733.09)
         conditions due to:
         intervertebral disc disorders (722.0-722.9)
         spondylosis (721.0-721.9)

AHA: 2Q, '89, 14

✓5ᵗʰ **724.0**   **Spinal stenosis, other than cervical**
     724.00 Spinal stenosis, unspecified region
     724.01 Thoracic region
     724.02 Lumbar region
         AHA: 4Q, '99, 13

         ▽ **DRG** 243

     724.09 Other

724.1   **Pain in thoracic spine**

724.2   **Lumbago**
     Low back pain   Lumbalgia
     Low back syndrome
     AHA: N-D, '85, 12

     ▽ **DRG** 243

724.3   **Sciatica**
     Neuralgia or neuritis of sciatic nerve
     EXCLUDES   specified lesion of sciatic nerve (355.0)
     AHA: 2Q, '89, 12

724.4   **Thoracic or lumbosacral neuritis or radiculitis, unspecified**
     Radicular syndrome of lower limbs
     AHA: 2Q, '99, 3

724.5   **Backache, unspecified**
     Vertebrogenic (pain) syndrome NOS
     ▽ **DRG** 243

724.6   **Disorders of sacrum**
     Ankylosis ⎫
     Instability ⎬ lumbosacral or sacroiliac (joint)

√5ᵗʰ **724.7 Disorders of coccyx**
   724.70 Unspecified disorder of coccyx
   724.71 Hypermobility of coccyx
   724.79 Other
      Coccygodynia

  724.8 Other symptoms referable to back
     Ossification of posterior longitudinal ligament NOS
     Panniculitis specified as sacral or affecting back

  724.9 Other unspecified back disorders
     Ankylosis of spine NOS
     Compression of spinal nerve root NEC
     Spinal disorder NOS
     EXCLUDES   *sacroiliitis (720.2)*

RHEUMATISM, EXCLUDING THE BACK (725-729)
    INCLUDES   disorders of muscles and tendons and their
               attachments, and of other soft tissues

725 Polymyalgia rheumatica
  DEF: Joint and muscle pain, pelvis, and shoulder girdle stiffness, high
  sedimentation rate and temporal arteritis; occurs in elderly.

√4ᵗʰ **726 Peripheral enthesopathies and allied syndromes**
    Note: Enthesopathies are disorders of peripheral ligamentous
    or muscular attachments.
    EXCLUDES   *spinal enthesopathy (720.1)*
  726.0 Adhesive capsulitis of shoulder
√5ᵗʰ **726.1 Rotator cuff syndrome of shoulder and allied
    disorders**
   **726.10 Disorders of bursae and tendons in shoulder
      region, unspecified**
      Rotator cuff syndrome NOS
      Supraspinatus syndrome NOS
     AHA: 2Q, '01, 11

   726.11 Calcifying tendinitis of shoulder
   726.12 Bicipital tenosynovitis
   726.19 Other specified disorders
      EXCLUDES   *complete rupture of rotator
              cuff, nontraumatic
              (727.61)*
  **726.2 Other affections of shoulder region, not elsewhere
    classified**
     Periarthritis of shoulder
     Scapulohumeral fibrositis
√5ᵗʰ **726.3 Enthesopathy of elbow region**
   726.30 Enthesopathy of elbow, unspecified
   726.31 Medial epicondylitis
   726.32 Lateral epicondylitis
      Epicondylitis NOS   Tennis elbow
      Golfers' elbow
   726.33 Olecranon bursitis
      Bursitis of elbow
   726.39 Other
  726.4 Enthesopathy of wrist and carpus
     Bursitis of hand or wrist
     Periarthritis of wrist
  726.5 Enthesopathy of hip region
     Bursitis of hip   Psoas tendinitis
     Gluteal tendinitis   Trochanteric tendinitis
     Iliac crest spur
√5ᵗʰ **726.6 Enthesopathy of knee**
   726.60 Enthesopathy of knee, unspecified
      Bursitis of knee NOS
   726.61 Pes anserinus tendinitis or bursitis
      DEF: Inflamed tendons of sartorius, gracilis and
      semitendinosus muscles of medial aspect of knee.
   726.62 Tibial collateral ligament bursitis
      Pellegrini-Stieda syndrome
   726.63 Fibular collateral ligament bursitis
   726.64 Patellar tendinitis
   726.65 Prepatellar bursitis

   726.69 Other
      Bursitis:
       infrapatellar
       subpatellar
√5ᵗʰ **726.7 Enthesopathy of ankle and tarsus**
   **726.70 Enthesopathy of ankle and tarsus,
      unspecified**
      Metatarsalgia NOS
     EXCLUDES   *Morton's metatarsalgia (355.6)*
   726.71 Achilles bursitis or tendinitis
   726.72 Tibialis tendinitis
      Tibialis (anterior) (posterior) tendinitis
   726.73 Calcaneal spur
      DEF: Overgrowth of calcaneous bone; causes pain on
      walking; due to chronic avulsion injury of plantar fascia
      from calcaneus.
   726.79 Other
      Peroneal tendinitis
  726.8 Other peripheral enthesopathies
√5ᵗʰ **726.9 Unspecified enthesopathy**
   726.90 Enthesopathy of unspecified site
      Capsulitis NOS
      Periarthritis NOS
      Tendinitis NOS
   726.91 Exostosis of unspecified site
      Bone spur NOS
     AHA: 2Q, '01, 15

√4ᵗʰ **727 Other disorders of synovium, tendon, and bursa**
√5ᵗʰ **727.0 Synovitis and tenosynovitis**
   727.00 Synovitis and tenosynovitis, unspecified
      Synovitis NOS
      Tenosynovitis NOS

Bunion

Normal metatarsophalangeal joint

Exostosis

Ganglia

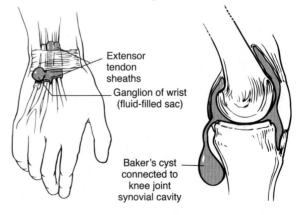

Extensor tendon sheaths

Ganglion of wrist (fluid-filled sac)

Baker's cyst connected to knee joint synovial cavity

N Newborn Age: 0 P Pediatric Age: 0-17 M Maternity Age: 12-55 A Adult Age: 15-124 CC CC Condition MC Major Complication CD Complex Dx HIV HIV Related Dx

226 — Volume 1   *2007 ICD•9•CM*

727.01 Synovitis and tenosynovitis in diseases classified elsewhere
Code first underlying disease as:
tuberculosis (015.0-015.9)
EXCLUDES crystal-induced (275.4)
gonococcal (098.51)
gouty (274.0)
syphilitic (095.7)

727.02 Giant cell tumor of tendon sheath

727.03 Trigger finger (acquired)
DEF: Stenosing tenosynovitis or nodule in flexor tendon; cessation of flexion or extension movement in finger, followed by snapping into place.

727.04 Radial styloid tenosynovitis
de Quervain's disease

727.05 Other tenosynovitis of hand and wrist

727.06 Tenosynovitis of foot and ankle

727.09 Other

727.1 Bunion
DEF: Enlarged first metatarsal head due to inflamed bursa; results in laterally displaced great toe.

727.2 Specific bursitides often of occupational origin
Beat: Miners':
elbow   elbow
hand   knee
knee
Chronic crepitant synovitis of wrist

727.3 Other bursitis
Bursitis NOS
EXCLUDES bursitis:
gonococcal (098.52)
subacromial (726.19)
subcoracoid (726.19)
subdeltoid (726.19)
syphilitic (095.7)
"frozen shoulder" (726.0)

727.4 Ganglion and cyst of synovium, tendon, and bursa
727.40 Synovial cyst, unspecified
EXCLUDES that of popliteal space (727.51)
AHA: 2Q, '97, 6
727.41 Ganglion of joint
727.42 Ganglion of tendon sheath
727.43 Ganglion, unspecified
727.49 Other
Cyst of bursa

727.5 Rupture of synovium
727.50 Rupture of synovium, unspecified
727.51 Synovial cyst of popliteal space
Baker's cyst (knee)
727.59 Other

727.6 Rupture of tendon, nontraumatic
727.60 Nontraumatic rupture of unspecified tendon
727.61 Complete rupture of rotator cuff
727.62 Tendons of biceps (long head)
727.63 Extensor tendons of hand and wrist
727.64 Flexor tendons of hand and wrist
727.65 Quadriceps tendon
727.66 Patellar tendon
727.67 Achilles tendon
727.68 Other tendons of foot and ankle
727.69 Other

727.8 Other disorders of synovium, tendon, and bursa
727.81 Contracture of tendon (sheath)
Short Achilles tendon (acquired)
727.82 Calcium deposits in tendon and bursa
Calcification of tendon NOS
Calcific tendinitis NOS
EXCLUDES peripheral ligamentous or muscular attachments (726.0-726.9)

727.83 Plica syndrome
Plica knee
AHA: 4Q, '00, 44
DEF: A fold in the synovial tissue that begins to form before birth, creating a septum between two pockets of synovial tissue; two most common plicae are the medial patellar plica and the suprapatellar plica. Plica syndrome, or plica knee, refers to symptomatic plica. Experienced by females more commonly than males.

727.89 Other
Abscess of bursa or tendon
EXCLUDES xanthomatosis localized to tendons (272.7)
AHA: 2Q, '89, 15

727.9 Unspecified disorder of synovium, tendon, and bursa

728 Disorders of muscle, ligament, and fascia
EXCLUDES enthesopathies (726.0-726.9)
muscular dystrophies (359.0-359.1)
myoneural disorders (358.00-358.9)
myopathies (359.2-359.9)
old disruption of ligaments of knee (717.81-717.89)

728.0 Infective myositis CC
Myositis:
purulent
suppurative
EXCLUDES myositis:
epidemic (074.1)
interstitial (728.81)
syphilitic (095.6)
tropical (040.81)
CC Excl: 567.31, 728.0, 728.11-728.3, 728.81, 728.86
DEF: Inflamed connective septal tissue of muscle.

728.1 Muscular calcification and ossification
728.10 Calcification and ossification, unspecified
Massive calcification (paraplegic)
728.11 Progressive myositis ossificans
DEF: Progressive myositic disease; marked by bony tissue formed by voluntary muscle; occurs among very young.
728.12 Traumatic myositis ossificans
Myositis ossificans (circumscripta)
728.13 Postoperative heterotopic calcification
DEF: Abnormal formation of calcium deposits in muscular tissue after surgery, marked by a corresponding loss of muscle tone and tension.
728.19 Other
Polymyositis ossificans

728.2 Muscular wasting and disuse atrophy, not elsewhere classified
Amyotrophia NOS
Myofibrosis
EXCLUDES neuralgic amyotrophy (353.5)
pelvic muscle wasting and disuse atrophy (618.83)
progressive muscular atrophy (335.0-335.9)

728.3 Other specific muscle disorders
Arthrogryposis
Immobility syndrome (paraplegic)
EXCLUDES arthrogryposis multiplex congenita (754.89)
stiff-man syndrome (333.91)

728.4 Laxity of ligament
728.5 Hypermobility syndrome

Musculoskeletal and Connective Tissue

728.6–729.79

728.6   Contracture of palmar fascia   A
    Dupuytren's contracture

DEF: Dupuytren's contracture: flexion deformity of finger, due to shortened, thickened fibrosing of palmar fascia; cause unknown; associated with long-standing epilepsy; occurs more often in males.

✓5ᵗʰ 728.7   Other fibromatoses

728.71   Plantar fascial fibromatosis
    Contracture of plantar fascia
    Plantar fasciitis (traumatic)

DEF: Plantar fascia fibromatosis; causes nodular swelling and pain; not associated with contractures.

728.79   Other
    Garrod's or knuckle pads
    Nodular fasciitis
    Pseudosarcomatous fibromatosis
       (proliferative) (subcutaneous)

DEF: Knuckle pads: Pea-size nodules on dorsal surface of interphalangeal joints; new growth of fibrous tissue with thickened dermis and epidermis.

✓5ᵗʰ 728.8   Other disorders of muscle, ligament, and fascia

728.81   Interstitial myositis

DEF: Inflammation of septal connective parts of muscle tissue.

728.82   Foreign body granuloma of muscle
    Talc granuloma of muscle

728.83   Rupture of muscle, nontraumatic

728.84   Diastasis of muscle
    Diastasis recti (abdomen)

     EXCLUDES   diastasis recti complicating pregnancy, labor, and delivery (665.8)

DEF: Muscle separation, such as recti abdominis after repeated pregnancies.

728.85   Spasm of muscle

728.86   Necrotizing fasciitis   CC
    Use additional code to identify:
       infectious organism (041.00-041.89)
       gangrene (785.4), if applicable

CC Excl: 567.31, 728.0, 728.11-728.3, 728.81, 728.86, 728.88

AHA: 4Q, '95, 54

DEF: Fulminating infection begins with extensive cellulitis, spreads to superficial and deep fascia; causes thrombosis of subcutaneous vessels, and gangrene of underlying tissue.

728.87   Muscle weakness (generalized)

     EXCLUDES   generalized weakness (780.79)

AHA: 1Q, '05, 13; 4Q, '03, 66

728.88   Rhabdomyolysis   CC

CC Excl: 567.31, 728.0, 728.11-728.3, 728.81, 728.86, 728.88

AHA: 4Q, '03, 66

DEF: A disintegration or destruction of muscle; an acute disease characterized by the excretion of myoglobin into the urine.

728.89   Other
    Eosinophilic fasciitis
    Use additional E code to identify drug, if
       drug induced

AHA: 3Q, '02, 28; 2Q, '01, 14, 15

DEF: Eosinophilic fasciitis: inflammation of fascia of extremities associated with eosinophilia, edema, and swelling; occurs alone or as part of myalgia syndrome.

728.9   Unspecified disorder of muscle, ligament, and fascia
AHA: 4Q, '88, 11

✓4ᵗʰ 729   Other disorders of soft tissues

     EXCLUDES   acroparesthesia (443.89)
         carpal tunnel syndrome (354.0)
         disorders of the back (720.0-724.9)
         entrapment syndromes (354.0-355.9)
         palindromic rheumatism (719.3)
         periarthritis (726.0-726.9)
         psychogenic rheumatism (306.0)

729.0   Rheumatism, unspecified and fibrositis

DEF: General term describes diseases of muscle, tendon, nerve, joint, or bone; symptoms include pain and stiffness.

729.1   Myalgia and myositis, unspecified
    Fibromyositis NOS

DEF: Myalgia: muscle pain.

DEF: Myositis: inflamed voluntary muscle.

DEF: Fibromyositis: inflamed fibromuscular tissue.

729.2   Neuralgia, neuritis, and radiculitis, unspecified

     EXCLUDES   brachial radiculitis (723.4)
         cervical radiculitis (723.4)
         lumbosacral radiculitis (724.4)
         mononeuritis (354.0-355.9)
         radiculitis due to intervertebral disc
           involvement (722.0-722.2, 722.7)
         sciatica (724.3)

DEF: Neuralgia: paroxysmal pain along nerve; symptoms include brief pain and tenderness at point nerve exits.

DEF: Neuritis: inflamed nerve, symptoms include paresthesia, paralysis and loss of reflexes at nerve site.

DEF: Radiculitis: inflamed nerve root.

✓5ᵗʰ 729.3   Panniculitis, unspecified

DEF: Inflammatory reaction of subcutaneous fat; causes nodules; often develops in abdominal region.

729.30   Panniculitis, unspecified site
    Weber-Christian disease

DEF: Febrile, nodular, nonsuppurative, relapsing inflammation of subcutaneous fat.

729.31   Hypertrophy of fat pad, knee
    Hypertrophy of infrapatellar fat pad

729.39   Other site

     EXCLUDES   panniculitis specified as
         (affecting):
         back (724.8)
         neck (723.6)
         sacral (724.8)

729.4   Fasciitis, unspecified

     EXCLUDES   necrotizing fasciitis (728.86)
         nodular fasciitis (728.79)

AHA: 2Q, '94, 13

729.5   Pain in limb

729.6   Residual foreign body in soft tissue

     EXCLUDES   foreign body granuloma:
         muscle (728.82)
         skin and subcutaneous tissue (709.4)

● ✓5ᵗʰ 729.7   Nontraumatic compartment syndrome

     EXCLUDES   compartment syndrome NOS (958.90)
         traumatic compartment syndrome
           (958.90-958.99)

● 729.71   Nontraumatic compartment syndrome of upper extremity
    Nontraumatic compartment syndrome of shoulder, arm, forearm, wrist, hand, and fingers

● 729.72   Nontraumatic compartment syndrome of lower extremity
    Nontraumatic compartment syndrome of hip, buttock, thigh, leg, foot, and toes

● 729.73   Nontraumatic compartment syndrome of abdomen

● 729.79   Nontraumatic compartment syndrome of other sites

| N Newborn Age: 0   P Pediatric Age: 0-17   M Maternity Age: 12-55   A Adult Age: 15-124   CC CC Condition   MC Major Complication   CD Complex Dx   HIV HIV Related Dx

228 — Volume 1 • October 2006   **2007 ICD•9•CM**

√5ᵗʰ **729.8　Other musculoskeletal symptoms referable to limbs**

729.81　Swelling of limb
　　AHA: 4Q, '88, 6

729.82　Cramp

729.89　Other

　　　EXCLUDES　　*abnormality of gait (781.2)*
　　　　　　　　　　　tetany (781.7)
　　　　　　　　　　　transient paralysis of limb
　　　　　　　　　　　　(781.4)

　　AHA: 4Q, '88, 12

729.9　Other and unspecified disorders of soft tissue
　　Polyalgia

OSTEOPATHIES, CHONDROPATHIES, AND ACQUIRED MUSCULOSKELETAL DEFORMITIES (730-739)

√4ᵗʰ **730　Osteomyelitis, periostitis, and other infections involving bone**

　　　EXCLUDES　　*jaw (526.4-526.5)*
　　　　　　　　　　　petrous bone (383.2)

　　Use additional code to identify organism, such as
　　　Staphylococcus (041.1)

The following fifth-digit subclassification is for use with category 730; valid digits are in [brackets] under each code. See list at beginning of chapter for definitions.

　　0　site unspecified
　　1　shoulder region
　　2　upper arm
　　3　forearm
　　4　hand
　　5　pelvic region and thigh
　　6　lower leg
　　7　ankle and foot
　　8　other specified sites
　　9　multiple sites

AHA: 4Q, '97, 43

DEF: Osteomyelitis: bacterial inflammation of bone tissue and marrow.

DEF: Periostitis: inflammation of specialized connective tissue; causes swelling of bone and aching pain.

¹　√5ᵗʰ **730.0　Acute osteomyelitis**　　`cc`
　　[0-9]　　Abscess of any bone except accessory sinus, jaw, or
　　　　　　　mastoid
　　　　　Acute or subacute osteomyelitis, with or without
　　　　　　mention of periostitis
　　　　▶Use additional code to identify major osseous defect,
　　　　　if applicable (731.3)◀

　CC Excl: For code **730.00**: 015.50-015.56, 015.70-015.76, 015.90-015.96, 017.90-017.96, 730.00-730.99, 730.80-730.99 **For code 730.01**: 015.50-015.56, 015.70-015.76, 015.90-015.96, 017.90-017.96, 730.00, 730.08-730.11, 730.18-730.21, 730.28-730.31, 730.38-730.39, 730.80-730.81, 730.88-730.91, 730.98-730.99 **For code 730.02**: 015.50-015.56, 015.70-015.76, 015.90-015.96, 017.90-017.96, 730.00, 730.08-730.10, 730.12, 730.18-730.20, 730.22, 730.28-730.30, 730.32, 730.38-730.39, 730.80, 730.82, 730.88-730.90, 730.92, 730.98-730.99 **For code 730.03**: 015.50-015.56, 015.70-015.76, 015.90-015.96, 017.90-017.96, 730.00, 730.08-730.10, 730.13, 730.18-730.20, 730.23, 730.28-730.30, 730.33, 730.38-730.39, 730.80, 730.83, 730.88-730.90, 730.93, 730.98-730.99: **For code 730.04**: 015.50-015.56, 015.70-015.76, 015.90-015.96, 017.90-017.96, 730.00, 730.08-730.10, 730.14, 730.18-730.20, 730.24, 730.28-730.30, 730.34, 730.38-730.39, 730.80, 730.84, 730.88-730.90, 730.94, 730.98-730.99 **For code 730.05**: 015.10-015.16, 015.50-015.56, 015.70-015.76, 015.90-015.96, 017.90-017.96, 730.00, 730.08-730.10, 730.15, 730.18-730.20, 730.25, 730.28-730.30, 730.35, 730.38-730.39, 730.80, 730.85, 730.88-730.90, 730.95, 730.98-730.99 **For code 730.06**: 015.20-015.56, 015.70-015.76, 015.90-015.96, 017.90-017.96, 730.00, 730.08-730.10, 730.16, 730.18-730.20, 730.26, 730.28-730.30, 730.36, 730.38-730.39, 730.80, 730.86, 730.88-730.90, 730.96, 730.98-730.99 **For code 730.07**: 015.50-015.56, 015.70-015.76, 015.90-015.96, 017.90-017.96, 730.00, 730.08-730.10, 730.17-730.20, 730.27-730.30, 730.37-730.39, 730.80, 730.87-730.90, 730.97-730.99 **For code 730.08**: 015.00-015.06, 015.50-015.56, 015.70-015.76, 015.90-015.96, 017.90-017.96, 730.00-730.39, 730.80-730.99 **For code 730.09**: 015.50-015.56, 015.70-015.76, 015.90-015.96, 017.90-017.96, 730.00-730.39, 730.80-730.99

　　AHA: For code **730.06**: 1Q, '02, 4; For code **730.07**: 1Q, '04, 14

---

¹　√5ᵗʰ **730.1　Chronic osteomyelitis**
　　[0-9]　　Brodie's abscess
　　　　　　Chronic or old osteomyelitis, with or without
　　　　　　　mention of periostitis
　　　　　　Sequestrum of bone
　　　　　　Sclerosing osteomyelitis of Garré
　　　　▶Use additional code to identify major osseous defect,
　　　　　if applicable (731.3)◀

　　　　　EXCLUDES　　*aseptic necrosis of bone (733.40-*
　　　　　　　　　　　　733.49)

　AHA: For code **730.17**: 3Q, '00, 4

¹　√5ᵗʰ **730.2　Unspecified osteomyelitis**
　　[0-9]　　Osteitis or osteomyelitis NOS, with or without
　　　　　　　mention of periostitis
　　　　▶Use additional code to identify major osseous defect,
　　　　　if applicable (731.3)◀

¹　√5ᵗʰ **730.3　Periostitis without mention of osteomyelitis**
　　[0-9]　　Abscess of periosteum ⎫ without mention of
　　　　　　Periostosis　　　　　 ⎬　 osteomyelitis

　　　　　EXCLUDES　　*that in secondary syphilis (091.61)*

√5ᵗʰ **730.7　*Osteopathy resulting from poliomyelitis***
　　[0-9]　　*Code first underlying disease (045.0-045.9)*

√5ᵗʰ **730.8　*Other infections involving bone in diseases***　`cc`
　　[0-9]　　***classified elsewhere***
　　　　　　Code first underlying disease as:
　　　　　　　tuberculosis (015.0-015.9)
　　　　　　　typhoid fever (002.0)

　　　　　EXCLUDES　　*syphilis of bone NOS (095.5)*

　CC Excl: For code **730.80**: See code 730.09 CC Excl: For code **730.81**: 015.50-015.56, 015.70-015.76, 015.90-015.96, 017.90-017.96, 730.00-730.01, 730.08-730.11, 730.18-730.21, 730.28-730.31, 730.38-730.39, 730.80, 730.88-730.91, 730.98-730.99 **For code 730.82**: 015.50-015.56, 015.70-015.76, 015.90-015.96, 017.90-017.96, 730.00, 730.02, 730.08-730.10, 730.12, 730.18-730.20, 730.22, 730.28-730.30, 730.32, 730.38-730.39, 730.80, 730.88-730.90, 730.92, 730.98-730.99: **For code 730.83**: 015.50-015.56, 015.70-015.76, 015.90-015.96, 017.90-017.96, 730.00, 730.03, 730.08-730.10, 730.13, 730.18-730.20, 730.23, 730.28-730.30, 730.33, 730.38-730.39, 730.80, 730.88-730.90, 730.93, 730.98-730.99: **For code 730.84**: 015.50-015.56, 015.70-015.76, 015.90-015.96, 017.90-017.96, 730.00, 730.04, 730.08-730.10, 730.14, 730.18-730.20, 730.24, 730.28-730.30, 730.34, 730.38-730.39, 730.80, 730.88-730.90, 730.94, 730.98-730.99 **For code 730.85**: 015.10-015.16, 015.50-015.56, 015.70-015.76, 015.90-015.96, 017.90-017.96, 730.00, 730.05, 730.08-730.10, 730.15, 730.18-730.20, 730.25, 730.28-730.30, 730.35, 730.38-730.39, 730.80, 730.88-730.90, 730.95, 730.98-730.99 **For code 730.86**: 015.20-015.26, 015.50-015.56, 015.70-015.76, 015.90-015.96, 017.90-017.96, 730.00, 730.06, 730.08-730.10, 730.16, 730.18-730.20, 730.26, 730.28-730.30, 730.36, 730.38-730.39, 730.80, 730.88-730.90, 730.96, 730.98-730.99 **For code 730.87**: 015.50-015.56, 015.70-015.76, 015.90-015.96, 017.90-017.96, 730.00, 730.07-730.10, 730.17-730.20, 730.27-730.30, 730.37-730.39, 730.80, 730.88-730.90, 730.97-730.99 **For code 730.88**: 015.00-015.06, 015.50-015.56, 015.70-015.76, 015.90-015.96, 017.90-017.96, 730.00-730.39, 730.80-730.99: **For code 730.89**: 015.50-015.56, 015.70-015.76, 015.90-015.96, 017.90-017.96, 730.00-730.39, 730.80-730.99

　　AHA: 2Q, '97, 16; 3Q, '91, 10

√5ᵗʰ **730.9　Unspecified infection of bone**　`cc`
　　[0-9]　　CC Excl: For code **730.90**: See code 730.89 **For code 730.91**: 015.50-015.56, 015.70-015.76, 015.90-015.96, 017.90-017.96, 730.00-730.01, 730.08-730.11, 730.18-730.21, 730.28-730.31, 730.38-730.39, 730.80-730.81, 730.88-730.90, 730.98-730.99 **For code 730.92**: 015.50-015.56, 015.70-015.76, 015.90-015.96, 017.90-017.96, 730.00, 730.02, 730.08-730.10, 730.12, 730.18-730.20, 730.22, 730.28-730.30, 730.32, 730.38-730.39, 730.80, 730.82, 730.88-730.90, 730.98-730.99 **For code 730.93**: 015.50-015.56, 015.70-015.76, 015.90-015.96, 017.90-017.96, 730.00, 730.03, 730.08-730.10, 730.13, 730.18-730.20, 730.23, 730.28-730.30, 730.33, 730.38-730.39, 730.80, 730.83, 730.88-730.90, 730.98-730.99 **For code 730.94**: 015.50-015.56, 015.70-015.76, 015.90-015.96, 017.90-017.96, 730.00, 730.04, 730.08-730.10, 730.14, 730.18-730.20, 730.24, 730.28-730.30, 730.34, 730.38-730.39, 730.80, 730.84, 730.88-730.90, 730.98-730.99: **For code 730.95**: 015.10-015.16, 015.50-015.56, 015.70-015.76, 015.90-015.96, 017.90-017.96, 730.00, 730.05, 730.08-730.10, 730.15, 730.18-730.20, 730.25, 730.28-730.30, 730.35, 730.38-730.39, 730.80, 730.85, 730.88-730.90, 730.98-730.99 **For code 730.96**: 015.20-015.26, 015.50-015.56, 015.70-015.76, 015.90-015.96, 017.90-017.96, 730.00, 730.06, 730.08-730.10, 730.16, 730.18-730.20, 730.26, 730.28-730.30, 730.36, 730.38-730.39, 730.80, 730.86, 730.88-730.90, 730.98-730.99: **For code 730.97**: 015.50-015.56, 015.70-015.76, 015.90-015.96, 017.90-017.96, 730.00, 730.07-730.10, 730.17-730.20, 730.27-730.30, 730.37-730.39, 730.80, 730.87-730.90, 730.99: **For code 730.98**: 015.00-015.06, 015.50-015.56, 015.70-015.76, 015.90-015.96, 017.90-017.96, 730.00-730.39, 730.80-730.99 **For code 730.99**: 015.50-015.56, 015.70-015.76, 015.90-015.96, 017.90-017.96, 730.00-730.39, 730.80-730.99

---

¹ Nonspecific PDx=0

√4ᵗʰ / √5ᵗʰ　Additional Digit Required　　`Nonspecific PDx`　　`Unacceptable PDx`　　`Manifestation Code`　　`MCV` Major Cardiovascular Condition　▶◀ Revised Text　● New Code　▲ Revised Code Title

2007 ICD•9•CM　　　　　　　　　　　　　　　　　　　　　　　October 2006 • Volume 1 — 229

Slipped Femoral Epiphysis

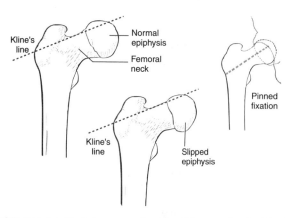

✓4ᵗʰ 731 Osteitis deformans and osteopathies associated with other disorders classified elsewhere

DEF: Osteitis deformans: Bone disease marked by episodes of increased bone loss, excessive repair attempts follow; causes weakened, deformed bones with increased mass, bowed long bones, deformed flat bones, pain and pathological fractures; may be fatal if associated with congestive heart failure, giant cell tumors or bone sarcoma; also called Paget's disease.

731.0 Osteitis deformans without mention of bone tumor
Paget's disease of bone

731.1 *Osteitis deformans in diseases classified elsewhere*
Code first underlying disease as:
malignant neoplasm of bone (170.0-170.9)

731.2 Hypertrophic pulmonary osteoarthropathy
Bamberger-Marie disease

DEF: Clubbing, of fingers and toes; related to enlarged ends of long bones; due to chronic lung and heart disease.

731.3 Major osseous defects
Code first underlying disease, if known, such as:
aseptic necrosis (733.40-733.49)
malignant neoplasm of bone (170.0-170.9)
osteomyelitis (730.00-730.29)
osteoporosis (733.00-733.09)
peri-prosthetic osteolysis (996.45)

731.8 *Other bone involvement in diseases classified elsewhere*
Code first underlying disease as:
diabetes mellitus (250.8)
Use additional code to specify bone condition, such as:
acute osteomyelitis (730.00-730.09)
AHA: 1Q, '04, 14; 4Q, '97, 43; 2Q, '97, 16

✓4ᵗʰ 732 Osteochondropathies

DEF: Conditions related to both bone and cartilage, or conditions in which cartilage is converted to bone (enchondral ossification).

732.0 Juvenile osteochondrosis of spine
Juvenile osteochondrosis (of):
marginal or vertebral epiphysis (of Scheuermann)
spine NOS
Vertebral epiphysitis
EXCLUDES adolescent postural kyphosis (737.0)

732.1 Juvenile osteochondrosis of hip and pelvis
Coxa plana
Ischiopubic synchondrosis (of van Neck)
Osteochondrosis (juvenile) of:
acetabulum
head of femur (of Legg-Calvé-Perthes)
iliac crest (of Buchanan)
symphysis pubis (of Pierson)
Pseudocoxalgia

732.2 Nontraumatic slipped upper femoral epiphysis
Slipped upper femoral epiphysis NOS

732.3 Juvenile osteochondrosis of upper extremity
Osteochondrosis (juvenile) of:
capitulum of humerus (of Panner)
carpal lunate (of Kienbock)
hand NOS
head of humerus (of Haas)
heads of metacarpals (of Mauclaire)
lower ulna (of Burns)
radial head (of Brailsford)
upper extremity NOS

732.4 Juvenile osteochondrosis of lower extremity, excluding foot
Osteochondrosis (juvenile) of:
lower extremity NOS
primary patellar center (of Köhler)
proximal tibia (of Blount)
secondary patellar center (of Sinding-Larsen)
tibial tubercle (of Osgood-Schlatter)
Tibia vara

732.5 Juvenile osteochondrosis of foot
Calcaneal apophysitis
Epiphysitis, os calcis
Osteochondrosis (juvenile) of:
astragalus (of Diaz)
calcaneum (of Sever)
foot NOS
metatarsal
second (of Freiberg)
fifth (of Iselin)
os tibiale externum (of Haglund)
tarsal navicular (of Köhler)

732.6 Other juvenile osteochondrosis
Apophysitis ⎫
Epiphysitis ⎬ specified as juvenile,
Osteochondritis ⎪ of other site,
Osteochondrosis ⎭ or site NOS

732.7 Osteochondritis dissecans

732.8 Other specified forms of osteochondropathy
Adult osteochondrosis of spine

732.9 Unspecified osteochondropathy
Apophysitis ⎫ NOS
Epiphysitis ⎬ not specified as adult
Osteochondritis ⎪ or juvenile, of
Osteochondrosis ⎭ unspecified site

✓4ᵗʰ 733 Other disorders of bone and cartilage
EXCLUDES bone spur (726.91)
cartilage of, or loose body in, joint (717.0-717.9, 718.0-718.9)
giant cell granuloma of jaw (526.3)
osteitis fibrosa cystica generalisata (252.01)
osteomalacia (268.2)
polyostotic fibrous dysplasia of bone (756.54)
prognathism, retrognathism (524.1)
xanthomatosis localized to bone (272.7)

✓5ᵗʰ 733.0 Osteoporosis
►Use additional code to identify major osseous defect, if applicable (731.3)◄

DEF: Bone mass reduction that ultimately results in fractures after minimal trauma; dorsal kyphosis or loss of height often occur.

733.00 Osteoporosis, unspecified
Wedging of vertebra NOS
AHA: 3Q, '01, 19; 2Q, '98, 12

733.01 Senile osteoporosis
Postmenopausal osteoporosis

733.02 Idiopathic osteoporosis

733.03 Disuse osteoporosis

733.09 Other
Drug-induced osteoporosis
Use additional E code to identify drug
AHA: 4Q, '03, 108

N Newborn Age: 0   P Pediatric Age: 0-17   M Maternity Age: 12-55   A Adult Age: 15-124   CC CC Condition   MC Major Complication   CD Complex Dx   HIV HIV Related Dx

√5ᵗʰ **733.1 Pathologic fracture**
Spontaneous fracture
EXCLUDES *stress fracture (733.93-733.95)*
traumatic fracture (800-829)
AHA: 4Q, '93, 25; N-D, '86, 10; N-D, '85, 16

DEF: Fracture due to bone structure weakening by pathological processes (e.g., osteoporosis, neoplasms and osteomalacia).

733.10 Pathologic fracture, unspecified site `CC`
CC Excl: 733.10-733.19, 733.93-733.95

733.11 Pathologic fracture of humerus `CC`
CC Excl: See code 733.10

733.12 Pathologic fracture of distal radius and ulna `CC`
Wrist NOS
CC Excl: See code 733.10

733.13 Pathologic fracture of vertebrae `CC`
Collapse of vertebra NOS
CC Excl: See code 733.10
AHA: 3Q, '99, 5
▽ **DRG** 239

733.14 Pathologic fracture of neck of femur `CC`
Femur NOS   Hip NOS
CC Excl: See code 733.10
AHA: 1Q, '01, 1; 1Q, '96, 16

733.15 Pathologic fracture of other specified part of femur `CC`
CC Excl: See code 733.10
AHA: 2Q, '98, 12

733.16 Pathologic fracture of tibia or fibula `CC`
Ankle NOS
CC Excl: See code 733.10

733.19 Pathologic fracture of other specified site `CC`
CC Excl: See code 733.10

√4ᵗʰ **733.2 Cyst of bone**
733.20 Cyst of bone (localized), unspecified
733.21 Solitary bone cyst
Unicameral bone cyst
733.22 Aneurysmal bone cyst
DEF: Solitary bone lesion, bulges into periosteum; marked by calcified rim.

733.29 Other
Fibrous dysplasia (monostotic)
EXCLUDES *cyst of jaw (526.0-526.2, 526.89)*
osteitis fibrosa cystica (252.01)
polyostotic fibrousdyplasia of bone (756.54)

733.3 Hyperostosis of skull
Hyperostosis interna frontalis
Leontiasis ossium
DEF: Abnormal bone growth on inner aspect of cranial bones.

√5ᵗʰ **733.4 Aseptic necrosis of bone**
EXCLUDES *osteochondropathies (732.0-732.9)*
▶Use additional code to identify major osseous defect, if applicable (731.3)◀
DEF: Infarction of bone tissue due to a nonfectious etiology, such as a fracture, ischemic disorder or administration of immunosuppressive drugs; leads to degenerative joint disease or nonunion of fractures.

733.40 Aseptic necrosis of bone, site unspecified
733.41 Head of humerus
733.42 Head and neck of femur
Femur NOS
EXCLUDES *Legg-Calvé-Perthes disease (732.1)*

733.43 Medial femoral condyle
733.44 Talus
733.49 Other
733.5 Osteitis condensans
Piriform sclerosis of ilium
DEF: Idiopathic condition marked by low back pain; associated with oval or triangular sclerotic, opaque bone next to sacroiliac joints in the ileum.

733.6 Tietze's disease
Costochondral junction syndrome
Costochondritis
DEF: Painful, idiopathic, nonsuppurative, swollen costal cartilage sometimes confused with cardiac symptoms because the anterior chest pain resembles that of coronary artery disease.

733.7 Algoneurodystrophy
Disuse atrophy of bone   Sudeck's atrophy
DEF: Painful, idiopathic.

√5ᵗʰ **733.8 Malunion and nonunion of fracture**
AHA: 2Q, '94, 5

733.81 Malunion of fracture `CC`
CC Excl: 733.81-733.82

733.82 Nonunion of fracture `CC`
Pseudoarthrosis (bone)
CC Excl: See code 733.81

√5ᵗʰ **733.9 Other and unspecified disorders of bone and cartilage**
733.90 Disorder of bone and cartilage, unspecified
733.91 Arrest of bone development or growth
Epiphyseal arrest
733.92 Chondromalacia
Chondromalacia:
NOS
localized, except patella
systemic
tibial plateau
EXCLUDES *chondromalacia of patella (717.7)*
DEF: Articular cartilage softening.

733.93 Stress fracture of tibia or fibula `CC`
Stress reaction of tibia or fibula
CC Excl: 733.10-733.19, 733.93-733.95
AHA: 4Q, '01, 48

733.94 Stress fracture of the metatarsals `CC`
Stress reaction of metatarsals
CC Excl: See code 733.93
AHA: 4Q, '01, 48

733.95 Stress fracture of other bone `CC`
Stress reaction of other bone
CC Excl: See code 733.93
AHA: 4Q, '01, 48

733.99 Other
Diaphysitis
Hypertrophy of bone
Relapsing polychondritis
AHA: J-F, '87, 14

734 Flat foot
Pes planus (acquired)
Talipes planus (acquired)
EXCLUDES *congenital (754.61)*
rigid flat foot (754.61)
spastic (everted) flat foot (754.61)

√4ᵗʰ **735 Acquired deformities of toe**
EXCLUDES *congenital (754.60-754.69, 755.65-755.66)*

735.0 Hallux valgus (acquired)
DEF: Angled displacement of the great toe, causing it to ride over or under other toes.

√4ᵗʰ / √5ᵗʰ Additional Digit Required   Nonspecific PDx   Unacceptable PDx   Manifestation Code   `MCV` Major Cardiovascular Condition   ▶◀ Revised Text   ● New Code   ▲ Revised Code Title

Musculoskeletal and Connective Tissue

735.1–736.6

Acquired Deformities of Toe

Hallux valgus

Hallux varus

Hallux malleus (hammer of big toe)

Hammertoe

735.1   Hallux varus (acquired)
DEF: Angled displacement of the great toe toward the body midline, away from the other toes.

735.2   Hallux rigidus
DEF: Limited flexion movement at metatarsophalangeal joint of great toe; due to degenerative joint disease.

735.3   Hallux malleus
DEF: Extended proximal phalanx, flexed distal phalanges, of great toe; foot resembles claw or hammer.

735.4   Other hammer toe (acquired)

735.5   Claw toe (acquired)
DEF: Hyperextended proximal phalanges, flexed middle and distal phalanges.

735.8   Other acquired deformities of toe

735.9   Unspecified acquired deformity of toe

✓4ᵗʰ 736   Other acquired deformities of limbs
EXCLUDES   congenital (754.3-755.9)

✓5ᵗʰ 736.0   Acquired deformities of forearm, excluding fingers

736.00   Unspecified deformity
Deformity of elbow, forearm, hand, or wrist (acquired) NOS

736.01   Cubitus valgus (acquired)
DEF: Deviation of the elbow away from the body midline upon extension; it occurs when the palm is turning outward.

736.02   Cubitus varus (acquired)
DEF: Elbow joint displacement angled laterally; when the forearm is extended, it is deviated toward the midline of the body; also called "gun stock" deformity.

736.03   Valgus deformity of wrist (acquired)
DEF: Abnormal angulation away from the body midline.

736.04   Varus deformity of wrist (acquired)
DEF: Abnormal angulation toward the body midline.

736.05   Wrist drop (acquired)
DEF: Inability to extend the hand at the wrist due to extensor muscle paralysis

736.06   Claw hand (acquired)
DEF: Flexion and atrophy of the hand and fingers; found in ulnar nerve lesions, syringomyelia, and leprosy.

736.07   Club hand, acquired
DEF: Twisting of the hand out of shape or position; caused by the congenital absence of the ulna or radius.

736.09   Other

736.1   Mallet finger
DEF: Permanently flexed distal phalanx.

✓5ᵗʰ 736.2   Other acquired deformities of finger
736.20   Unspecified deformity
Deformity of finger (acquired) NOS

736.21   Boutonniere deformity
DEF: A deformity of the finger caused by flexion of the proximal interphalangeal joint and hyperextension of the distal joint; also called buttonhole deformity.

736.22   Swan-neck deformity
DEF: Flexed distal and hyperextended proximal interphalangeal joint.

736.29   Other
EXCLUDES   trigger finger (727.03)
AHA: ▶2Q, '05, 7;◀ 2Q, '89, 13

✓5ᵗʰ 736.3   Acquired deformities of hip
736.30   Unspecified deformity
Deformity of hip (acquired) NOS

736.31   Coxa valga (acquired)
DEF: Increase of at least 140 degrees in the angle formed by the axis of the head and the neck of the femur, and the axis of its shaft.

736.32   Coxa vara (acquired)
DEF: The bending downward of the neck of the femur; causing difficulty in movement; a right angle or less may be formed by the axis of the head and neck of the femur, and the axis of its shaft.

736.39   Other
AHA: 2Q, '91, 18

✓5ᵗʰ 736.4   Genu valgum or varum (acquired)
736.41   Genu valgum (acquired)
DEF: Abnormally close together and an abnormally large space between the ankles; also called "knock-knees."

736.42   Genu varum (acquired)
DEF: Abnormally separated knees and the inward bowing of the legs; it is also called "bowlegs."

736.5   Genu recurvatum (acquired)
DEF: Hyperextended knees; also called "backknee."

736.6   Other acquired deformities of knee
Deformity of knee (acquired) NOS

Acquired Deformities of Forearm

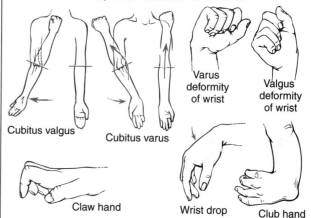

Cubitus valgus

Cubitus varus

Varus deformity of wrist

Valgus deformity of wrist

Claw hand

Wrist drop

Club hand

N Newborn Age: 0   **P** Pediatric Age: 0-17   **M** Maternity Age: 12-55   **A** Adult Age: 15-124   **CC** CC Condition   **MC** Major Complication   **CD** Complex Dx   **HIV** HIV Related Dx

232 — Volume 1 • February 2006   *2007 ICD•9•CM*

Acquired Deformities of Hip

Genu valga (knock-knee)

Normal angle   Coxa valga   Coxa vara

Genu vara (bowleg)

Acquired Deformities of Lower Limb

Equinovarus

Cavus deformity

Cavovarus

Genu recurvatum

Axis of Deformity (may be multiple)

Dorsal

Valgus   Varus

Plantar

Equinus Calcaneus

√5ʰ 736.7 Other acquired deformities of ankle and foot

> *EXCLUDES*   deformities of toe (acquired) (735.0-735.9)
> pes planus (acquired) (734)

736.70 Unspecified deformity of ankle and foot, acquired

736.71 Acquired equinovarus deformity
Clubfoot, acquired
> *EXCLUDES*   clubfoot not specified as acquired (754.5-754.7)

736.72 Equinus deformity of foot, acquired
DEF: A plantar flexion deformity that forces people to walk on their toes.

736.73 Cavus deformity of foot
> *EXCLUDES*   that with claw foot (736.74)

DEF: Abnormally high longitudinal arch of the foot.

736.74 Claw foot, acquired
DEF: High foot arch with hyperextended toes at metatarsophalangeal joint and flexed toes at distal joints; also called "main en griffe."

736.75 Cavovarus deformity of foot, acquired
DEF: Inward turning of the heel from the midline of the leg and an abnormally high longitudinal arch.

736.76 Other calcaneus deformity
736.79 Other
Acquired:
   pes
   talipes   } not elsewhere classified

√5ʰ 736.8 Acquired deformities of other parts of limbs
736.81 Unequal leg length (acquired)
736.89 Other
Deformity (acquired):
   arm or leg, not elsewhere classified
   shoulder

736.9 Acquired deformity of limb, site unspecified

√4ʰ 737 Curvature of spine
> *EXCLUDES*   congenital (754.2)

737.0 Adolescent postural kyphosis
> *EXCLUDES*   osteochondrosis of spine (juvenile) (732.0)
> adult (732.8)

√5ʰ 737.1 Kyphosis (acquired)
737.10 Kyphosis (acquired) (postural)
737.11 Kyphosis due to radiation
737.12 Kyphosis, postlaminectomy
AHA: J-F, '87, 7

737.19 Other
> *EXCLUDES*   that associated with conditions classifiable elsewhere (737.41)

√5ʰ 737.2 Lordosis (acquired)
DEF: Swayback appearance created by an abnormally increased spinal curvature; it is also referred to as "hollow back" or "saddle back."

737.20 Lordosis (acquired) (postural)
737.21 Lordosis, postlaminectomy
737.22 Other postsurgical lordosis
737.29 Other
> *EXCLUDES*   that associated with conditions classifiable elsewhere (737.42)

√5ʰ 737.3 Kyphoscoliosis and scoliosis
DEF: Kyphoscoliosis: backward and lateral curvature of the spinal column; it is found in vertebral osteochondrosis.

DEF: Scoliosis: an abnormal deviation of the spine to the left or right of the midline

737.30 Scoliosis [and kyphoscoliosis], idiopathic
AHA: 3Q, '03, 19

737.31 Resolving infantile idiopathic scoliosis
737.32 Progressive infantile idiopathic scoliosis
AHA: 3Q, '02, 12

737.33 Scoliosis due to radiation
737.34 Thoracogenic scoliosis
737.39 Other
> *EXCLUDES*   that associated with conditions classifiable elsewhere (737.43)
> that in kyphoscoliotic heart disease (416.1)

AHA: 2Q, '02, 16

Kyphosis and Lordosis

Kyphosis (hump)

Lordosis (concave)

√4ʰ / √5ʰ Additional Digit Required   Nonspecific PDx   Unacceptable PDx   Manifestation Code   MCV Major Cardiovascular Condition   ►◄ Revised Text   ● New Code   ▲ Revised Code Title

2007 ICD•9•CM   Volume 1 — 233

Musculoskeletal and Connective Tissue

737.4–739.9

Scoliosis and Kyphoscoliosis

Scoliosis

Kyphoscoliosis

√5ᵗʰ 737.4   Curvature of spine associated with other conditions
  Code first associated condition as:
   Charcôt-Marie-Tooth disease (356.1)
   mucopolysaccharidosis (277.5)
   neurofibromatosis (237.7)
   osteitis deformans (731.0)
   osteitis fibrosa cystica (252.01)
   osteoporosis (733.00-733.09)
   poliomyelitis (138)
   tuberculosis [Pott's curvature] (015.0)

  737.40   Curvature of spine, unspecified
  737.41   Kyphosis
  737.42   Lordosis
  737.43   Scoliosis

737.8   Other curvatures of spine

737.9   Unspecified curvature of spine
  Curvature of spine (acquired) (idiopathic) NOS
  Hunchback, acquired
   EXCLUDES *deformity of spine NOS (738.5)*

√4ᵗʰ 738   Other acquired deformity
  EXCLUDES *congenital (754.0-756.9, 758.0-759.9)*
       dentofacial anomalies (524.0-524.9)

738.0   Acquired deformity of nose
  Deformity of nose (acquired)
  Overdevelopment of nasal bones
   EXCLUDES *deflected or deviated nasal septum*
        (470)

√5ᵗʰ 738.1   Other acquired deformity of head
  738.10   Unspecified deformity
  738.11   Zygomatic hyperplasia
   DEF: Abnormal enlargement of the zygoma (processus
   zygomaticus temporalis).

  738.12   Zygomatic hypoplasia
   DEF: Underdevelopment of the zygoma (processus
   zygomaticus temporalis).

  738.19   Other specified deformity
   AHA: ▶1Q, '06, 6;◀ 2Q, '03, 13

738.2   Acquired deformity of neck

738.3   Acquired deformity of chest and rib
  Deformity: Pectus:
   chest (acquired) carinatum, acquired
   rib (acquired)   excavatum, acquired

738.4   Acquired spondylolisthesis
  Degenerative spondylolisthesis
  Spondylolysis, acquired
   EXCLUDES *congenital (756.12)*

  DEF: Vertebra displaced forward over another; due to bilateral
  defect in vertebral arch, eroded articular surface of posterior facts
  and elongated pedicle between fifth lumbar vertebra and sacrum.

738.5   Other acquired deformity of back or spine
  Deformity of spine NOS
   EXCLUDES *curvature of spine (737.0-737.9)*

738.6   Acquired deformity of pelvis
  Pelvic obliquity
   EXCLUDES *intrapelvic protrusion of acetabulum*
        (718.6)
       that in relation to labor and delivery
        (653.0-653.4, 653.8-653.9)

  DEF: Pelvic obliquity: slanting or inclination of the pelvis at an
  angle between 55 and 60 degrees between the plane of the pelvis
  and the horizontal plane.

738.7   Cauliflower ear
  DEF: Abnormal external ear; due to injury, subsequent
  perichondritis.

738.8   Acquired deformity of other specified site
  Deformity of clavicle
  AHA: 2Q, '01, 15

738.9   Acquired deformity of unspecified site

√4ᵗʰ 739   Nonallopathic lesions, not elsewhere classified
   INCLUDES segmental dysfunction
       somatic dysfunction

  DEF: Disability, loss of function or abnormality of a body part that is neither
  classifiable to a particular system nor brought about therapeutically to
  counteract another disease.

739.0   Head region
  Occipitocervical region

739.1   Cervical region
  Cervicothoracic region

739.2   Thoracic region
  Thoracolumbar region

739.3   Lumbar region
  Lumbosacral region

739.4   Sacral region
  Sacrococcygeal region Sacroiliac region

739.5   Pelvic region
  Hip region   Pubic region

739.6   Lower extremities

739.7   Upper extremities
  Acromioclavicular region
  Sternoclavicular region

739.8   Rib cage
  Costochondral region Sternochondral region
  Costovertebral region

739.9   Abdomen and other
  AHA: 2Q, '89, 14

N Newborn Age: 0 **P** Pediatric Age: 0-17 **M** Maternity Age: 12-55 **A** Adult Age: 15-124 **CC** CC Condition **MC** Major Complication **CD** Complex Dx **HIV** HIV Related Dx

14. CONGENITAL ANOMALIES (740-759)

✓4th **740 Anencephalus and similar anomalies**

740.0 Anencephalus
Acrania   Hemicephaly
Amyelencephalus   Hemianencephaly
DEF: Fetus without cerebrum, cerebellum and flat bones of skull.

740.1 Craniorachischisis
DEF: Congenital slit in cranium and vertebral column

740.2 Iniencephaly
DEF: Spinal cord passes through enlarged occipital bone (foramen magnum); absent vertebral bone layer and spinal processes; resulting in both reduction in number and proper fusion of the vertebrae.

✓4th **741 Spina bifida**
    EXCLUDES *spina bifida occulta (756.17)*

The following fifth-digit subclassification is for use with category 741:

0 unspecified region
1 cervical region
2 dorsal [thoracic] region
3 lumbar region

AHA: 3Q, '94, 7

DEF: Lack of closure of spinal cord's bony encasement; marked by cord protrusion into lumbosacral area; evident by elevated alpha-fetoprotein of amniotic fluid

✓5th **741.0 With hydrocephalus**   `CC`
Arnold-Chiari syndrome, type II
Any condition classifiable to 741.9 with any
    condition classifiable to 742.3
Chiari malformation, type II
CC Excl: 741.00-741.93, 742.59-742.9, 759.7-759.89

AHA: 4Q, '97, 51; 4Q, '94, 37; S-O, '87, 10

✓5th **741.9 Without mention of hydrocephalus**   `CC`
Hydromeningocele (spinal)   Myelocystocele
Hydromyelocele   Rachischisis
Meningocele (spinal)   Spina bifida (aperta)
Meningomyelocele   Syringomyelocele
Myelocele
CC Excl: See code 741.0

✓4th **742 Other congenital anomalies of nervous system**
    EXCLUDES *congenital central alveolar hypoventilation
                 syndrome (327.25)*

742.0 Encephalocele
Encephalocystocele
Encephalomyelocele
Hydroencephalocele
Hydromeningocele, cranial
Meningocele, cerebral
Meningoencephalocele
AHA: 4Q, '94, 37
DEF: Brain tissue protrudes through skull defect.

Spina Bifida

Normal Ventricles and Hydrocephalus

742.1 Microcephalus
Hydromicrocephaly
Micrencephaly
DEF: Extremely small head or brain.

742.2 Reduction deformities of brain
Absence
Agenesis
Aplasia   } of part of brain
Hypoplasia

Agyria   Holoprosencephaly
Arhinencephaly   Microgyria
AHA: 3Q, '03, 15; 4Q, '94, 37

742.3 Congenital hydrocephalus
Aqueduct of Sylvius:
    anomaly
    obstruction, congenital
    stenosis
Atresia of foramina of Magendie and Luschka
Hydrocephalus in newborn
    EXCLUDES *hydrocephalus:
                 acquired (331.3-331.4)
                 due to congenital toxoplasmosis
                    (771.2)
                 with any condition classifiable to
                    741.9 (741.0)*

AHA: ▶4Q, '05, 83◀

DEF: Fluid accumulation within the skull; involves subarachnoid (external) or ventricular (internal) brain spaces.

742.4 Other specified anomalies of brain
Congenital cerebral cyst   Multiple anomalies of brain
Macroencephaly   NOS
Macrogyria   Porencephaly
Megalencephaly   Ulegyria
AHA: 1Q, '99, 9; 3Q, '92, 12

✓5th **742.5 Other specified anomalies of spinal cord**

742.51 Diastematomyelia
DEF: Congenital anomaly often associated with spina bifida; the spinal cord is separated into halves by a bony tissue resembling a "spike" (a spicule), each half surrounded by a dural sac.

✓4th ✓5th Additional Digit Required   Nonspecific PDx   Unacceptable PDx   Manifestation Code   MCV Major Cardiovascular Condition   ▶◀ Revised Text   ● New Code   ▲ Revised Code Title

2007 ICD•9•CM   February 2006 • Volume 1 — 235

742.53 Hydromyelia

Hydrorhachis

DEF: Dilated central spinal cord canal; characterized by increased fluid accumulation.

742.59 Other

Amyelia
Atelomyelia
Congenital anomaly of spinal meninges
Defective development of cauda equina
Hypoplasia of spinal cord
Myelatelia
Myelodysplasia

AHA: 2Q, '91, 14; 1Q, '89, 10

742.8 Other specified anomalies of nervous system

Agenesis of nerve
Displacement of brachial plexus
Familial dysautonomia
Jaw-winking syndrome
Marcus-Gunn syndrome
Riley-Day syndrome

EXCLUDES   neurofibromatosis (237.7)

742.9 Unspecified anomaly of brain, spinal cord, and nervous system

Anomaly
Congenital:
  disease   of: brain
  lesion   nervous system
Deformity   spinal cord

√4th **743 Congenital anomalies of eye**

√5th **743.0 Anophthalmos**

DEF: Complete absence of the eyes or the presence of vestigial eyes.

743.00 Clinical anophthalmos, unspecified

Agenesis   } of eye
Congenital absence

Anophthalmos NOS

743.03 Cystic eyeball, congenital

743.06 Cryptophthalmos

DEF: Eyelids continue over eyeball, results in apparent absence of eyelids.

√5th **743.1 Microphthalmos**

Dysplasia   } of eye
Hypoplasia

Rudimentary eye

DEF: Abnormally small eyeballs, may be opacities of cornea and lens, scarring of choroid and retina.

743.10 Microphthalmos, unspecified

743.11 Simple microphthalmos

743.12 Microphthalmos associated with other anomalies of eye and adnexa

√5th **743.2 Buphthalmos**

Glaucoma: Hydrophthalmos
  congenital
  newborn

EXCLUDES   glaucoma of childhood (365.14)
            traumatic glaucoma due to birth injury (767.8)

DEF: Distended, enlarged fibrous coats of eye; due to intraocular pressure of congenital glaucoma.

743.20 Buphthalmos, unspecified

743.21 Simple buphthalmos

743.22 Buphthalmos associated with other ocular anomalies

Keratoglobus, congenital   } associated with
Megalocornea   buphthalmos

√5th **743.3 Congenital cataract and lens anomalies**

EXCLUDES   infantile cataract (366.00-366.09)

DEF: Opaque eye lens.

743.30 Congenital cataract, unspecified

743.31 Capsular and subcapsular cataract

743.32 Cortical and zonular cataract

743.33 Nuclear cataract

743.34 Total and subtotal cataract, congenital

743.35 Congenital aphakia

Congenital absence of lens

743.36 Anomalies of lens shape

Microphakia   Spherophakia

743.37 Congenital ectopic lens

743.39 Other

√5th **743.4 Coloboma and other anomalies of anterior segment**

DEF: Coloboma: ocular tissue defect associated with defect of ocular fetal intraocular fissure; may cause small pit on optic disk, major defects of iris, ciliary body, choroid, and retina.

743.41 Anomalies of corneal size and shape

Microcornea

EXCLUDES   that associated with buphthalmos (743.22)

743.42 Corneal opacities, interfering with vision, congenital

743.43 Other corneal opacities, congenital

743.44 Specified anomalies of anterior chamber, chamber angle, and related structures

Anomaly: Anomaly:
  Axenfeld's   Rieger's
  Peters'

743.45 Aniridia

AHA: 3Q, '02, 20

DEF: Incompletely formed or absent iris; affects both eyes; dominant trait; also called congenital hyperplasia of iris.

743.46 Other specified anomalies of iris and ciliary body

Anisocoria, congenital   Coloboma of iris
Atresia of pupil   Corectopia

743.47 Specified anomalies of sclera

743.48 Multiple and combined anomalies of anterior segment

743.49 Other

√5th **743.5 Congenital anomalies of posterior segment**

743.51 Vitreous anomalies

Congenital vitreous opacity

743.52 Fundus coloboma

DEF: Absent retinal and choroidal tissue; occurs in lower fundus; a bright white ectatic zone of exposed sclera extends into and changes the optic disk.

743.53 Chorioretinal degeneration, congenital

743.54 Congenital folds and cysts of posterior segment

743.55 Congenital macular changes

743.56 Other retinal changes, congenital

AHA: 3Q, '99, 12

743.57 Specified anomalies of optic disc

Coloboma of optic disc (congenital)

743.58 Vascular anomalies

Congenital retinal aneurysm

743.59 Other

N Newborn Age: 0   P Pediatric Age: 0-17   M Maternity Age: 12-55   A Adult Age: 15-124   CC CC Condition   MC Major Complication   CD Complex Dx   HIV HIV Related Dx

√5ᵗʰ **743.6 Congenital anomalies of eyelids, lacrimal system, and orbit**

743.61 Congenital ptosis
DEF: Drooping of eyelid.

743.62 Congenital deformities of eyelids
Ablepharon
Absence of eyelid
Accessory eyelid
Congenital:
   ectropion
   entropion
AHA: 1Q, '00, 22

743.63 Other specified congenital anomalies of eyelid
Absence, agenesis, of cilia

743.64 Specified congenital anomalies of lacrimal gland

743.65 Specified congenital anomalies of lacrimal passages
Absence, agenesis of:
   lacrimal apparatus
   punctum lacrimale
Accessory lacrimal canal

743.66 Specified congenital anomalies of orbit

743.69 Other
Accessory eye muscles

743.8 Other specified anomalies of eye
EXCLUDES   congenital nystagmus (379.51)
            ocular albinism (270.2)
           ▶optic nerve hypoplasia (377.43)◀
           retinitis pigmentosa (362.74)

743.9 Unspecified anomaly of eye
Congenital:
   anomaly NOS   } of eye [any part]
   deformity NOS

√4ᵗʰ **744 Congenital anomalies of ear, face, and neck**
EXCLUDES   anomaly of:
        cervical spine (754.2, 756.10-756.19)
        larynx (748.2-748.3)
        nose (748.0-748.1)
        parathyroid gland (759.2)
        thyroid gland (759.2)
        cleft lip (749.10-749.25)

√5ᵗʰ **744.0 Anomalies of ear causing impairment of hearing**
EXCLUDES   congenital deafness without mention of
           cause (389.0-389.9)

744.00 Unspecified anomaly of ear with impairment of hearing

744.01 Absence of external ear
Absence of:
   auditory canal (external)
   auricle (ear) (with stenosis or atresia of
     auditory canal)

744.02 Other anomalies of external ear with impairment of hearing
Atresia or stricture of auditory canal
   (external)

744.03 Anomaly of middle ear, except ossicles
Atresia or stricture of osseous meatus (ear)

744.04 Anomalies of ear ossicles
Fusion of ear ossicles

744.05 Anomalies of inner ear
Congenital anomaly of:
   membranous labyrinth
   organ of Corti

744.09 Other
Absence of ear, congenital

744.1 Accessory auricle
Accessory tragus   Supernumerary:
Polyotia   ear
Preauricular appendage   lobule
DEF: Redundant tissue or structures of ear.

√5ᵗʰ **744.2 Other specified anomalies of ear**
EXCLUDES   that with impairment of hearing
           (744.00-744.09)

744.21 Absence of ear lobe, congenital

744.22 Macrotia
DEF: Abnormally large pinna of ear.

744.23 Microtia
DEF: Hypoplasia of pinna; associated with absent or
closed auditory canal.

744.24 Specified anomalies of Eustachian tube
Absence of Eustachian tube

744.29 Other
Bat ear   Prominence of auricle
Darwin's tubercle Ridge ear
Pointed ear
EXCLUDES   preauricular sinus (744.46)

744.3 Unspecified anomaly of ear
Congenital:
   anomaly NOS   } of ear, not elsewhere
   deformity NOS   classified

√5ᵗʰ **744.4 Branchial cleft cyst or fistula; preauricular sinus**

744.41 Branchial cleft sinus or fistula
Branchial:
   sinus (external) (internal)
   vestige
DEF: Cyst due to failed closure of embryonic branchial
cleft.

744.42 Branchial cleft cyst

744.43 Cervical auricle

744.46 Preauricular sinus or fistula

744.47 Preauricular cyst

744.49 Other
Fistula (of):   Fistula (of):
   auricle, congenital   cervicoaural

744.5 Webbing of neck
Pterygium colli
DEF: Thick, triangular skinfold, stretches from lateral side of neck
across shoulder; associated with Turner's and Noonan's syndromes.

√5ᵗʰ **744.8 Other specified anomalies of face and neck**

744.81 Macrocheilia
Hypertrophy of lip, congenital
DEF: Abnormally large lips.

744.82 Microcheilia
DEF: Abnormally small lips.

744.83 Macrostomia
DEF: Bilateral or unilateral anomaly, of mouth due to
malformed maxillary and mandibular processes; results
in mouth extending toward ear.

744.84 Microstomia
DEF: Abnormally small mouth.

744.89 Other
EXCLUDES   congenital fistula of lip
           (750.25)
           musculoskeletal anomalies
           (754.0-754.1, 756.0)

744.9 Unspecified anomalies of face and neck
Congenital:
   anomaly NOS   } of face [any part] or
   deformity NOS   neck [any part]

Congenital Anomalies

743.6–744.9

√4ᵗʰ Additional Digit Required   Nonspecific PDx   Unacceptable PDx   Manifestation Code   MSP Medicare Secondary Payer   ▶◀ Revised Text   ● New Code   ▲ Revised Code Title

2007 ICD•9•CM   October 2006 • Volume 1 — 237

Congenital Anomalies

745–746.1

Heart Defects

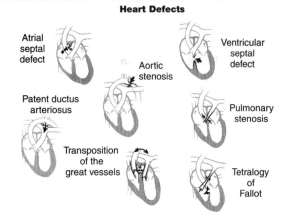

Atrial septal defect

Ventricular septal defect

Aortic stenosis

Patent ductus arteriosus

Pulmonary stenosis

Transposition of the great vessels

Tetralogy of Fallot

√4th **745 Bulbus cordis anomalies and anomalies of cardiac septal closure**

745.0 Common truncus [CC]

Absent septum ⎤ between aorta and
Communication (abnormal) ⎦ pulmonary artery

Aortic septal defect
Common aortopulmonary trunk
Persistent truncus arteriosus
CC Excl: 429.71, 429.79, 745.0-745.9, 746.89, 746.9, 747.83-747.9, 759.7-759.89

√5th **745.1 Transposition of great vessels**

745.10 Complete transposition of great vessels [CC]
Transposition of great vessels:
NOS
classical
CC Excl: See code 745.0

745.11 Double outlet right ventricle [CC]
Dextratransposition of aorta
Incomplete transposition of great vessels
Origin of both great vessels from right ventricle
Taussig-Bing syndrome or defect
CC Excl: See code 745.0

745.12 Corrected transposition of great vessels [CC]
CC Excl: See code 745.0

745.19 Other [CC]
CC Excl: See code 745.0

745.2 Tetralogy of Fallot [CC]
Fallot's pentalogy
Ventricular septal defect with pulmonary stenosis or atresia, dextraposition of aorta, and hypertrophy of right ventricle
EXCLUDES *Fallot's triad (746.09)*
CC Excl: See code 745.0

DEF: Obstructed cardiac outflow causes pulmonary stenosis, interventricular septal defect and right ventricular hypertrophy.

745.3 Common ventricle [CC]
Cor triloculare biatriatum
Single ventricle
CC Excl: See code 745.0

745.4 Ventricular septal defect [CC]
Eisenmenger's defect or complex
Gerbo dedefect
Interventricular septal defect
Left ventricular-right atrial communication
Roger's disease
EXCLUDES *common atrioventricular canal type (745.69)*
single ventricle (745.3)
CC Excl: See code 745.0

745.5 Ostium secundum type atrial septal defect
Defect: Patent or persistent:
atrium secundum   foramen ovale
fossa ovalis   ostium secundum
Lutembacher's syndrome
DEF: Opening in atrial septum due to failure of the septum secundum and the endocardial cushions to fuse; there is a rim of septum surrounding the defect.

√5th **745.6 Endocardial cushion defects**
DEF: Atrial and/or ventricular septal defects causing abnormal fusion of cushions in atrioventricular canal.

745.60 Endocardial cushion defect, unspecified type [CC]
CC Excl: See code 745.0

DEF: Septal defect due to imperfect fusion of endocardial cushions.

745.61 Ostium primum defect
Persistent ostium primum
DEF: Opening in low, posterior septum primum; causes cleft in basal portion of atrial septum; associated with cleft mitral valve.

745.69 Other [CC]
Absence of atrial septum
Atrioventricular canal type ventricular septal defect
Common atrioventricular canal
Common atrium
CC Excl: See code 745.0

745.7 Cor biloculare [CC]
Absence of atrial and ventricular septa
CC Excl: See code 745.0

DEF: Atrial and ventricular septal defect; marked by heart with two cardiac chambers (one atrium, one ventricle), and one atrioventricular valve.

745.8 Other

745.9 Unspecified defect of septal closure
Septal defect NOS

√4th **746 Other congenital anomalies of heart**
EXCLUDES *endocardial fibroelastosis (425.3)*

√5th **746.0 Anomalies of pulmonary valve**
EXCLUDES *infundibular or subvalvular pulmonic stenosis (746.83)*
tetralogy of Fallot (745.2)

746.00 Pulmonary valve anomaly, unspecified

746.01 Atresia, congenital [CC]
Congenital absence of pulmonary valve
CC Excl: 746.00-746.09, 746.89, 746.9, 747.83-747.9, 759.7-759.89

746.02 Stenosis, congenital [CC]
CC Excl: See code 746.01
AHA: 1Q, '04, 16
DEF: Stenosis of opening between pulmonary artery and right ventricle; causes obstructed blood outflow from right ventricle.

746.09 Other
Congenital insufficiency of pulmonary valve
Fallot's triad or trilogy

746.1 Tricuspid atresia and stenosis, congenital [CC]
Absence of tricuspid valve
CC Excl: 746.1-746.7, 746.89, 746.9, 747.83-747.9, 759.7-759.89

[N] Newborn Age: 0   [P] Pediatric Age: 0-17   [M] Maternity Age: 12-55   [A] Adult Age: 15-124   [CC] CC Condition   [MC] Major Complication   [CD] Complex Dx   [HIV] HIV Related Dx

746.2 Ebstein's anomaly `CC`

CC Excl: See code 746.1

DEF: Malformation of the tricuspid valve characterized by septal and posterior leaflets attaching to the wall of the right ventricle; causing the right ventricle to fuse with the atrium producing a large right atrium and a small ventricle; causes a malfunction of the right ventricle with accompanying complications such as heart failure and abnormal cardiac rhythm.

746.3 Congenital stenosis of aortic valve `CC`

Congenital aortic stenosis

> EXCLUDES   congenital:
> subaortic stenosis (746.81)
> supravalvular aortic stenosis
> (747.22)

CC Excl: See code 746.1

AHA: 4Q, '88, 8

DEF: Stenosis of orifice of aortic valve; obstructs blood outflow from left ventricle.

746.4 Congenital insufficiency of aortic valve `CC`

Bicuspid aortic valve
Congenital aortic insufficiency

CC Excl: See code 746.1

DEF: Impaired functioning of aortic valve due to incomplete closure; causes backflow (regurgitation) of blood from aorta to left ventricle.

746.5 Congenital mitral stenosis `CC`

Fused commissure
Parachute deformity   } of mitral valve
Supernumerary cusps

CC Excl: See code 746.1

DEF: Stenosis of left atrioventricular orifice.

746.6 Congenital mitral insufficiency `CC`

CC Excl: See code 746.1

DEF: Impaired functioning of mitral valve due to incomplete closure; causes backflow of blood from left ventricle to left atrium.

746.7 Hypoplastic left heart syndrome `CC`

Atresia, or marked hypoplasia, of aortic orifice or valve, with hypoplasia of ascending aorta and defective development of left ventricle (with mitral valve atresia)

CC Excl: See code 746.1

√5ᵗʰ **746.8 Other specified anomalies of heart**

746.81 Subaortic stenosis `CC`

CC Excl: 746.81-746.84, 746.89, 746.9, 747.83-747.9, 759.7-759.89

DEF: Stenosis, of left ventricular outflow tract due to fibrous tissue ring or septal hypertrophy below aortic valve.

746.82 Cor triatriatum `CC`

CC Excl: See code 746.81

DEF: Transverse septum divides left atrium due to failed resorption of embryonic common pulmonary vein; results in three atrial chambers.

746.83 Infundibular pulmonic stenosis `CC`

Subvalvular pulmonic stenosis

CC Excl: See code 746.81

DEF: Stenosis of right ventricle outflow tract within infundibulum due to fibrous diaphragm below valve or long, narrow fibromuscular channel.

746.84 Obstructive anomalies of heart, not elsewhere classified `CC`

Uhl's disease

CC Excl: See code 746.81

746.85 Coronary artery anomaly

Anomalous origin or communication of coronary artery
Arteriovenous malformation of coronary artery
Coronary artery:
   absence
   arising from aorta or pulmonary trunk
   single

AHA: N-D, '85, 3

746.86 Congenital heart block `CC`

Complete or incomplete atrioventricular [AV] block

CC Excl: 746.86, 746.89, 746.9, 747.83, 747.89, 747.9, 759.7-759.89

DEF: Impaired conduction of electrical impulses; due to maldeveloped junctional tissue.

746.87 Malposition of heart and cardiac apex

Abdominal heart   Levocardia (isolated)
Dextrocardia   Mesocardia
Ectopia cordis

> EXCLUDES   dextrocardia with complete
> transposition of viscera
> (759.3)

746.89 Other

Atresia   } of cardiac vein
Hypoplasia

Congenital: Congenital:
  cardiomegaly   pericardial defect
  diverticulum, left ventricle

AHA: 3Q, '00, 3; 1Q, '99, 11; J-F, '85, 3

746.9 Unspecified anomaly of heart

Congenital:
  anomaly of heart NOS
  heart disease NOS

√4ᵗʰ **747 Other congenital anomalies of circulatory system**

747.0 Patent ductus arteriosus

Patent ductus Botalli
Persistent ductus arteriosus

DEF: Open lumen in ductus arteriosus causes arterial blood recirculation in lungs; inhibits blood supply to aorta; symptoms such as shortness of breath more noticeable upon activity.

√5ᵗʰ **747.1 Coarctation of aorta**

DEF: Localized deformity of aortic media seen as a severe constriction of the vessel lumen; major symptom is high blood pressure in the arms and low pressure in the legs; a CVA, rupture of the aorta, bacterial endocarditis or congestive heart failure can follow if left untreated.

747.10 Coarctation of aorta (preductal) (postductal) `CC`

Hypoplasia of aortic arch

CC Excl: No Exclusions

AHA: 1Q, '99, 11; 4Q, '88, 8

747.11 Interruption of aortic arch `CC`

CC Excl: 747.10-747.22, 747.83-747.9, 759.7-759.89

√4ᵗʰ ⁄ √5ᵗʰ Additional Digit Required   Nonspecific PDx   Unacceptable PDx   Manifestation Code   `MCV` Major Cardiovascular Condition   ▶◀ Revised Text   ● New Code   ▲ Revised Code Title

Congenital Anomalies

747.2–747.83

✓5ᵗʰ **747.2 Other anomalies of aorta**

747.20 Anomaly of aorta, unspecified

747.21 Anomalies of aortic arch
Anomalous origin, right subclavian artery
Dextraposition of aorta
Double aortic arch
Kommerell's diverticulum
Overriding aorta
Persistent:
    convolutions, aortic arch
    right aortic arch
Vascular ring
> **EXCLUDES** *hypoplasia of aortic arch (747.10)*

AHA: 1Q, '03, 15

747.22 Atresia and stenosis of aorta   **CC**
Absence ⎫
Aplasia ⎬ of aorta
Hypoplasia ⎪
Stricture ⎭

Supra (valvular)-aortic stenosis
> **EXCLUDES** *congenital aortic (valvular) stenosis or stricture, so stated (746.3)*
> *hypoplasia of aorta in hypoplastic left heart syndrome (746.7)*

CC Excl: See code 747.11

747.29 Other
Aneurysm of sinus of Valsalva
Congenital:
    aneurysm ⎫
    dilation ⎬ of aorta

747.3 Anomalies of pulmonary artery
Agenesis ⎫
Anomaly ⎪
Atresia ⎪
Coarctation ⎬ of pulmonary artery
Hypoplasia ⎪
Stenosis ⎭
Pulmonary arteriovenous aneurysm
AHA: 1Q, '04, 16; 1Q, '94, 15; 4Q, '88, 8

✓5ᵗʰ **747.4 Anomalies of great veins**

747.40 Anomaly of great veins, unspecified
Anomaly NOS of: Anomaly NOS of:
  pulmonary veins   vena cava

747.41 Total anomalous pulmonary venous connection
Total anomalous pulmonary venous return [TAPVR]:
    subdiaphragmatic
    supradiaphragmatic

747.42 Partial anomalous pulmonary venous connection
Partial anomalous pulmonary venous return

747.49 Other anomalies of great veins
Absence ⎫ of vena cava
Congenital stenosis ⎬ (inferior)
           (superior)
Persistent:
    left posterior cardinal vein
    left superior vena cava
Scimitar syndrome
Transposition of pulmonary veins NOS

747.5 Absence or hypoplasia of umbilical artery
Single umbilical artery

✓5ᵗʰ **747.6 Other anomalies of peripheral vascular system**
Absence ⎫
Anomaly ⎬ of artery or vein, NEC
Atresia ⎭

Arteriovenous aneurysm (peripheral)
Arteriovenous malformation of the peripheral
    vascular system
Congenital:
    aneurysm (peripheral)   stricture, artery
    phlebectasia   varix
Multiple renal arteries
> **EXCLUDES** *anomalies of:*
> *cerebral vessels (747.81)*
> *pulmonary artery (747.3)*
> *congenital retinal aneurysm (743.58)*
> *hemangioma (228.00-228.09)*
> *lymphangioma (228.1)*

747.60 Anomaly of the peripheral vascular system, unspecified site

747.61 Gastrointestinal vessel anomaly
AHA: 3Q, '96, 10

747.62 Renal vessel anomaly

747.63 Upper limb vessel anomaly

747.64 Lower limb vessel anomaly

747.69 Anomalies of other specified sites of peripheral vascular system

✓5ᵗʰ **747.8 Other specified anomalies of circulatory system**

747.81 Anomalies of cerebrovascular system
Arteriovenous malformation of brain
Cerebral arteriovenous aneurysm, congenital
Congenital anomalies of cerebral vessels
> **EXCLUDES** *ruptured cerebral (arteriovenous) aneurysm (430)*

747.82 Spinal vessel anomaly
Arteriovenous malformation of spinal vessel
AHA: 3Q, '95, 5

747.83 Persistent fetal circulation   **N**
Persistent pulmonary hypertension
Primary pulmonary hypertension of newborn
AHA: 4Q, '02, 62

DEF: A return to fetal-type circulation due to constriction of pulmonary arterioles and opening of the ductus arteriosus and foramen ovale, right-to-left shunting occurs, oxygenation of the blood does not occur, and the lungs remain constricted after birth; PFC is seen in term or post-term infants causes include asphyxiation, meconium aspiration syndrome, acidosis, sepsis, and developmental immaturity.

Persistent Fetal Circulation

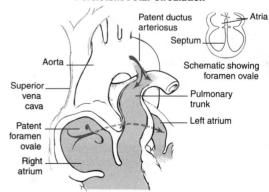

N Newborn Age: 0   **P** Pediatric Age: 0-17   **M** Maternity Age: 12-55   **A** Adult Age: 15-124   **CC** CC Condition   **MC** Major Complication   **CD** Complex Dx   **HIV** HIV Related Dx

240 — Volume 1   *2007 ICD•9•CM*

747.89 Other

Aneurysm, congenital, specified site not elsewhere classified

> **EXCLUDES**   *congenital aneurysm:*
> *coronary (746.85)*
> *peripheral (747.6)*
> *pulmonary (747.3)*
> *retinal (743.58)*

AHA: 4Q, '02, 63

747.9 Unspecified anomaly of circulatory system

√4th **748 Congenital anomalies of respiratory system**

> **EXCLUDES**   *congenital central alveolar hypoventilation syndrome (327.25)*
> *congenital defect of diaphragm (756.6)*

748.0 Choanal atresia

Atresia   } of nares (anterior)
Congenital stenosis }   (posterior)

DEF: Occluded posterior nares (choana), bony or membranous due to failure of embryonic bucconasal membrane to rupture.

748.1 Other anomalies of nose

Absent nose	Congenital:
Accessory nose	notching of tip of nose
Cleft nose	perforation of wall of
Congenital:	nasal sinus
deformity of nose	Deformity of wall of nasal
	sinus

> **EXCLUDES**   *congenital deviation of nasal septum (754.0)*

748.2 Web of larynx

Web of larynx: Web of larynx:
  NOS   subglottic
  glottic

DEF: Malformed larynx; marked by thin, translucent, or thick, fibrotic spread between vocal folds; affects speech.

748.3 Other anomalies of larynx, trachea, and bronchus

Absence or agenesis of:	Congenital:
bronchus	dilation, trachea
larynx	stenosis:
trachea	larynx
Anomaly(of):	trachea
cricoid cartilage	tracheocele
epiglottis	Diverticulum:
thyroid cartilage	bronchus
tracheal cartilage	trachea
Atresia (of):	Fissure of epiglottis
epiglottis	Laryngocele
glottis	Posterior cleft of cricoid
larynx	cartilage (congenital)
trachea	Rudimentary tracheal
Cleft thyroid, cartilage,	bronchus
congenital	Stridor, laryngeal, congenital

AHA: 1Q, '99, 14

748.4 Congenital cystic lung   `CC`

Disease, lung:	Honeycomb lung, congenital
cystic, congenital	
polycystic, congenital	

> **EXCLUDES**   *acquired or unspecified cystic lung (518.89)*

CC Excl: 748.4-748.9
DEF: Enlarged air spaces of lung parenchyma.

748.5 Agenesis, hypoplasia, and dysplasia of lung   `CC`

Absence of lung (fissures) (lobe)	
(lobe)	Hypoplasia of lung
Aplasia of lung	Sequestration of lung

CC Excl: See code 748.4

√5th **748.6 Other anomalies of lung**

748.60 Anomaly of lung, unspecified

748.61 Congenital bronchiectasis   `CC`

CC Excl: 494.0-494.1, 496, 506.1, 506.4, 506.9, 748.61

748.69 Other

Accessory lung (lobe)
Azygos lobe (fissure), lung

748.8 Other specified anomalies of respiratory system

Abnormal communication between pericardial and pleural sacs
Anomaly, pleural folds
Atresia of nasopharynx
Congenital cyst of mediastinum

748.9 Unspecified anomaly of respiratory system

Anomaly of respiratory system NOS

√4th **749 Cleft palate and cleft lip**

√5th **749.0 Cleft palate**

749.00 Cleft palate, unspecified

749.01 Unilateral, complete

749.02 Unilateral, incomplete

Cleft uvula

749.03 Bilateral, complete

749.04 Bilateral, incomplete

√5th **749.1 Cleft lip**

Cheiloschisis   Harelip
Congenital fissure of lip   Labium leporinum

749.10 Cleft lip, unspecified

749.11 Unilateral, complete

749.12 Unilateral, incomplete

749.13 Bilateral, complete

749.14 Bilateral, incomplete

√5th **749.2 Cleft palate with cleft lip**

Cheilopalatoschisis

749.20 Cleft palate with cleft lip, unspecified

749.21 Unilateral, complete

749.22 Unilateral, incomplete

749.23 Bilateral, complete

AHA: 1Q, '96, 14

749.24 Bilateral, incomplete

749.25 Other combinations

√4th **750 Other congenital anomalies of upper alimentary tract**

> **EXCLUDES**   *dentofacial anomalies (524.0-524.9)*

750.0 Tongue tie

Ankyloglossia

DEF: Restricted tongue movement due to lingual frenum extending toward tip of tongue. Tongue may be fused to mouth floor affecting speech.

Cleft Lip and Palate

Unilateral cleft lip

No cleft palate

Cleft lip with cleft alveolar ridge

No cleft palate

Unilateral cleft lip and cleft palate
Alveolar ridge
Cleft palate

Prolabium

Bilateral cleft lip and cleft palate

Isolated cleft palate

√4th √5th Additional Digit Required   Nonspecific PDx   Unacceptable PDx   Manifestation Code   **MCV** Major Cardiovascular Condition   ►◄ Revised Text   ● New Code   ▲ Revised Code Title

2007 ICD•9•CM   **Volume 1 — 241**

Congenital Anomalies   **747.89–750.0**

Congenital Anomalies

750.1–751.61

✓5th **750.1   Other anomalies of tongue**

750.10 Anomaly of tongue, unspecified

750.11 Aglossia
 DEF: Absence of tongue.

750.12 Congenital adhesions of tongue

750.13 Fissure of tongue
 Bifid tongue   Double tongue

750.15 Macroglossia
 Congenital hypertrophy of tongue

750.16 Microglossia
 Hypoplasia of tongue

750.19 Other

✓5th **750.2   Other specified anomalies of mouth and pharynx**

750.21 Absence of salivary gland

750.22 Accessory salivary gland

750.23 Atresia, salivary duct
 Imperforate salivary duct

750.24 Congenital fistula of salivary gland

750.25 Congenital fistula of lip
 Congenital (mucus) lip pits

750.26 Other specified anomalies of mouth
 Absence of uvula

750.27 Diverticulum of pharynx
 Pharyngeal pouch

750.29 Other specified anomalies of pharynx
 Imperforate pharynx

750.3   Tracheoesophageal fistula, esophageal atresia and stenosis
 Absent esophagus   Congenital fistula:
 Atresia of esophagus   esophagobronchial
 Congenital: esophagotracheal
  esophageal ring   Imperforate esophagus
  stenosis of esophagus   Webbed esophagus
  stricture of esophagus

750.4   Other specified anomalies of esophagus
 Dilatation, congenital
 Displacement, congenital
 Diverticulum   } (of) esophagus
 Duplication
 Giant

 Esophageal pouch
 EXCLUDES congenital hiatus hernia (750.6)
 AHA: J-F, '85, 3

750.5   Congenital hypertrophic pyloric stenosis
 Congenital or infantile:
  constriction ⎤
  hypertrophy   ⎥
  spasm   ⎬ of pylorus
  stenosis   ⎥
  stricture   ⎦

 DEF: Obstructed pylorus due to overgrowth of pyloric muscle.

750.6   Congenital hiatus hernia
 Displacement of cardia through esophageal hiatus
 EXCLUDES congenital diaphragmatic hernia (756.6)

750.7   Other specified anomalies of stomach
 Congenital:
  cardiospasm
  hourglass stomach
 Displacement of stomach
 Diverticulum of stomach, congenital
 Duplication of stomach
 Megalogastria
 Microgastria
 Transposition of stomach

750.8   Other specified anomalies of upper alimentary tract

750.9   Unspecified anomaly of upper alimentary tract
 Congenital:
  anomaly NOS ⎤ of upper alimentary tract [any
  deformity NOS⎦   part, except tongue]

✓4th **751 Other congenital anomalies of digestive system**

751.0   Meckel's diverticulum
 Meckel's diverticulum (displaced) (hypertrophic)
 Persistent:
  omphalomesenteric duct
  vitelline duct

 AHA: 1Q, '04, 10

 DEF: Malformed sacs or appendages of ileum of small intestine;
 can cause strangulation, volvulus and intussusception.

751.1   Atresia and stenosis of small intestine P
 Atresia of: Atresia of:
  duodenum   intestine NOS
  ileum
 Congenital:
  absence   ⎤
  obstruction ⎥ of small intestine or
  stenosis   ⎬ intestine NOS
  stricture   ⎦

 Imperforate jejunum

**751.2   Atresia and stenosis of large intestine, rectum, P
 and anal canal**
 Absence: Congenital or infantile:
  anus (congenital)   obstruction of large
  appendix, congenital   intestine
  large intestine, congenital occlusion of anus
  rectum   stricture of anus
 Atresia of: Imperforate:
  anus   anus
  colon   rectum
  rectum   Stricture of rectum,
                          congenital

 AHA: 2Q, '98, 16

751.3   Hirschsprung's disease and other congenital functional disorders of colon
 Aganglionosis   Congenital megacolon
 Congenital dilation of colon Macrocolon

 DEF: Hirschsprung's disease: enlarged or dilated colon
 (megacolon), with absence of ganglion cells in the narrowed wall
 distally; causes inability to defecate.

751.4   Anomalies of intestinal fixation
 Congenital adhesions: Rotation of cecum or colon:
  omental, anomalous   failure of
  peritoneal   incomplete
 Jackson's membrane   insufficient
 Malrotation of colon   Universal mesentery

751.5   Other anomalies of intestine
 Congenital diverticulum, colon Megaloappendix
 Dolichocolon   Megaloduodenum
 Duplication of: Microcolon
  anus   Persistent cloaca
  appendix   Transposition of:
  cecum   appendix
  intestine   colon
 Ectopic anus   intestine

 AHA: 3Q, '02, 11; 3Q, '01, 8

✓5th **751.6   Anomalies of gallbladder, bile ducts, and liver**

751.60 Unspecified anomaly of gallbladder, bile ducts, and liver

751.61 Biliary atresia P
 Congenital:
  absence   ⎤
  hypoplasia   ⎥ of bile duct (common)
  obstruction ⎬ or passage
  stricture   ⎦

 AHA: S-O, '87, 8

N Newborn Age: 0   **P** Pediatric Age: 0-17   **M** Maternity Age: 12-55   **A** Adult Age: 15-124   **CC** CC Condition   **MC** Major Complication   **CD** Complex Dx   **HIV** HIV Related Dx

242 — Volume 1   *2007 ICD•9•CM*

751.62 Congenital cystic disease of liver
Congenital polycystic disease of liver
Fibrocystic disease of liver

751.69 Other anomalies of gallbladder, bile ducts, and liver

Absence of:	Duplication of:
gallbladder, congenital	biliary duct
liver (lobe)	cystic duct
Accessory:	gallbladder
hepatic ducts	liver
liver	Floating:
Congenital:	gallbladder
choledochal cyst	liver
hepatomegaly	Intrahepatic
	gallbladder

AHA: S-O, '87, 8

751.7 Anomalies of pancreas
Absence
Accessory
Agenesis   } (of) pancreas
Annular
Hypoplasia

Ectopic pancreatic tissue   Pancreatic heterotopia
  EXCLUDES   *diabetes mellitus:*
    congenital (250.0-250.9)
    neonatal (775.1)
    fibrocystic disease of pancreas
    (277.00-277.09)

751.8 Other specified anomalies of digestive system
Absence (complete) (partial) of alimentary tract NOS
Duplication   } of digestive organs NOS
Malposition, congenital
  EXCLUDES   *congenital diaphragmatic hernia*
    (756.6)
    congenital hiatus hernia (750.6)

751.9 Unspecified anomaly of digestive system
Congenital:
anomaly NOS   } of digestive system NOS
deformity NOS

√4th **752 Congenital anomalies of genital organs**
  EXCLUDES   *syndromes associated with anomalies in the*
    number and form of chromosomes (758.0-
    758.9)
    testicular feminization syndrome (259.5)

752.0 Anomalies of ovaries   ♀
Absence, congenital
Accessory
Ectopic   } (of) ovary
Streak

√5th **752.1 Anomalies of fallopian tubes and broad ligaments**

752.10 Unspecified anomaly of fallopian tubes and broad ligaments   ♀

752.11 Embryonic cyst of fallopian tubes and broad ligaments   ♀
Cyst:
epoophoron
fimbrial
parovarian
AHA: S-O, '85, 13

752.19 Other   ♀
Absence
Accessory   } (of) fallopian tube or
Atresia   broad ligament

752.2 Doubling of uterus   ♀
Didelphic uterus
Doubling of uterus [any degree] (associated with doubling of cervix and vagina)

752.3 Other anomalies of uterus   ♀
Absence, congenital
Agenesis
Aplasia   } (of) uterus
Bicornuate

Uterus unicornis
Uterus with only one functioning horn

√5th **752.4 Anomalies of cervix, vagina, and external female genitalia**

752.40 Unspecified anomaly of cervix, vagina, and external female genitalia   ♀

752.41 Embryonic cyst of cervix, vagina, and external female genitalia   ♀
Cyst of:
canal of Nuck, congenital
Gartner's duct
vagina, embryonal
vulva, congenital
DEF: Embryonic fluid-filled cysts, of cervix, vagina or external female genitalia.

752.42 Imperforate hymen   ♀
DEF: Complete closure of membranous fold around external opening of vagina.

752.49 Other anomalies of cervix, vagina, and external female genitalia   ♀
Absence   } of cervix, clitoris, vagina,
Agenesis   or vulva
Congenital stenosis or stricture of:
cervical canal
vagina
  EXCLUDES   *double vagina associated with*
    total duplication (752.2)

√5th **752.5 Undescended and retractile testicle**
AHA: 4Q, '96, 33

752.51 Undescended testis   ♂
Cryptorchism
Ectopic testis

752.52 Retractile testis   ♂

√5th **752.6 Hypospadias and epispadias and other penile anomalies**
AHA: 4Q, '96, 34, 35

752.61 Hypospadias   ♂
AHA: 4Q, '03, 67-68; 3Q, '97, 6
DEF: Abnormal opening of urethra on the ventral surface of the penis or perineum; also a rare defect of vagina.

752.62 Epispadias   ♂
Anaspadias
DEF: Urethra opening on dorsal surface of penis; in females appears as a slit in the upper wall of urethra.

752.63 Congenital chordee   ♂
DEF: Ventral bowing of penis due to fibrous band along corpus spongiosum; occurs with hypospadias.

Hypospadias and Epispadias

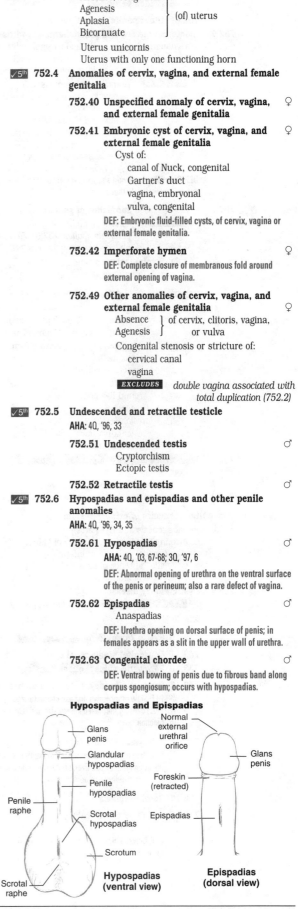

Hypospadias (ventral view)   Epispadias (dorsal view)

√4th Additional Digit Required   Nonspecific PDx   Unacceptable PDx   Manifestation Code   **MCV** Major Cardiovascular Condition   ▶◀ Revised Text   ● New Code   ▲ Revised Code Title

2007 ICD•9•CM   **Volume 1 — 243**

Congenital Anomalies

752.64–753.9

752.64 Micropenis ♂

752.65 Hidden penis ♂

752.69 Other penile anomalies ♂

752.7 Indeterminate sex and pseudohermaphroditism

Gynandrism   Pseudohermaphroditism
Hermaphroditism   (male) (female)
Ovotestis   Pure gonadal dysgenesis

EXCLUDES   *pseudohermaphroditism:*
female, with adrenocortical disorder
(255.2)
male, with gonadal disorder (257.8)
with specified chromosomal
anomaly (758.0-758.9)
testicular feminization syndrome
(259.5)

DEF: Pseudohermaphroditism: presence of gonads of one sex and external genitalia of other sex.

√5ᵗʰ 752.8 Other specified anomalies of genital organs

EXCLUDES   *congenital hydrocele (778.6)*
penile anomalies (752.61-752.69)
phimosis or paraphimosis (605)

752.81 Scrotal transposition ♂
AHA: 4Q, '03, 67-68

752.89 Other specified anomalies of genital organs

Absence of: Fusion of testes
   prostate   Hypoplasia of testis
   spermatic cord   Monorchism
   vas deferens   Polyorchism
Anorchism
Aplasia (congenital) of:
   prostate
   round ligament
   testicle
Atresia of:
   ejaculatory duct
   vas deferens

752.9 Unspecified anomaly of genital organs

Congenital:
   anomaly NOS } of genital organ,
   deformity NOS   not elsewhere classified

√4ᵗʰ 753 Congenital anomalies of urinary system

753.0 Renal agenesis and dysgenesis

Atrophy of kidney: Atrophy of kidney:
   congenital   infantile
Congenital absence of kidney(s)
Hypoplasia of kidney(s)

√5ᵗʰ 753.1 Cystic kidney disease

EXCLUDES   *acquired cyst of kidney (593.2)*
AHA: 4Q, '90, 3

753.10 Cystic kidney disease, unspecified

753.11 Congenital single renal cyst

753.12 Polycystic kidney, unspecified type

753.13 Polycystic kidney, autosomal dominant
DEF: Slow progressive disease characterized by bilateral cysts causing increased kidney size and impaired function.

753.14 Polycystic kidney, autosomal recessive
DEF: Rare disease characterized by multiple cysts involving kidneys and liver, producing renal and hepatic failure in childhood or adolescence.

753.15 Renal dysplasia

753.16 Medullary cystic kidney
Nephronopthisis
DEF: Diffuse kidney disease results in uremia onset prior to age 20.

753.17 Medullary sponge kidney
DEF: Dilated collecting tubules; usually asymptomatic but calcinosis in tubules may cause renal insufficiency.

753.19 Other specified cystic kidney disease
Multicystic kidney

√5ᵗʰ 753.2 Obstructive defects of renal pelvis and ureter
AHA: 4Q, '96, 35

753.20 Unspecified obstructive defect of renal pelvis and ureter

753.21 Congenital obstruction of ureteropelvic junction
DEF: Stricture at junction of ureter and renal pelvis.

753.22 Congenital obstruction of ureterovesical junction
Adynamic ureter   Congenital hydroureter
DEF: Stricture at junction of ureter and bladder.

753.23 Congenital ureterocele

753.29 Other

753.3 Other specified anomalies of kidney

Accessory kidney   Fusion of kidneys
Congenital: Giant kidney
   calculus of kidney   Horseshoe kidney
   displaced kidney   Hyperplasia of kidney
Discoid kidney   Lobulation of kidney
Double kidney with   Malrotation of kidney
   double pelvis   Trifid kidney (pelvis)
Ectopic kidney

753.4 Other specified anomalies of ureter

Absent ureter   Double ureter
Accessory ureter   Ectopic ureter
Deviation of ureter   Implantation, anomalous
Displaced ureteric   of ureter
   orifice

753.5 Exstrophy of urinary bladder

Ectopia vesicae
Extroversion of bladder
DEF: Absence of lower abdominal and anterior bladder walls with posterior bladder wall protrusion.

753.6 Atresia and stenosis of urethra and bladder neck

Congenital obstruction: Imperforate urinary
   bladder neck   meatus
   urethra   Impervious urethra
Congenital stricture of: Urethral valve formation
   urethra (valvular)
   urinary meatus
   vesicourethral orifice

753.7 Anomalies of urachus

Cyst
Fistula   } (of) urachussinus
Patent

Persistent umbilical sinus

753.8 Other specified anomalies of bladder and urethra

Absence, congenital of: Congenital urethrorectal
   bladder   fistula
   urethra   Congenital prolapse of:
Accessory: bladder (mucosa)
   bladder   urethra
   urethra   Double:
Congenital: urethra
   diverticulum of bladder   urinary meatus
   hernia of bladder

753.9 Unspecified anomaly of urinary system

Congenital:
   anomaly NOS } of urinary system [any part,
   deformity NOS   except urachus]

 Newborn Age: 0   Pediatric Age: 0-17   Maternity Age: 12-55   Adult Age: 15-124   CC Condition   Major Complication   Complex Dx   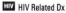 HIV Related Dx

244 — Volume 1   2007 ICD•9•CM

✓4ᵗʰ **754 Certain congenital musculoskeletal deformities**
> **INCLUDES** nonteratogenic deformities which are considered to be due to intrauterine malposition and pressure

754.0 Of skull, face, and jaw
> Asymmetry of face   Dolichocephaly
> Compression facies   Plagiocephaly
> Depressions in skull   Potter's facies
> Deviation of nasal   Squashed or bent nose,
>   septum, congenital   congenital
> **EXCLUDES** dentofacial anomalies (524.0-524.9)
>   syphilitic saddle nose (090.5)

754.1 Of sternocleidomastoid muscle
> Congenital sternomastoid torticollis
> Congenital wryneck
> Contracture of sternocleidomastoid (muscle)
> Sternomastoid tumor

754.2 Of spine
> Congenital postural:
>   lordosis   scoliosis

✓5ᵗʰ **754.3 Congenital dislocation of hip**

> **754.30 Congenital dislocation of hip, unilateral**
>> Congenital dislocation of hip NOS

> **754.31 Congenital dislocation of hip, bilateral**

> **754.32 Congenital subluxation of hip, unilateral**
>> Congenital flexion deformity, hip or thigh
>> Predislocation status of hip at birth
>> Preluxation of hip, congenital

> **754.33 Congenital subluxation of hip, bilateral**

> **754.35 Congenital dislocation of one hip with subluxation of other hip**

✓5ᵗʰ **754.4 Congenital genu recurvatum and bowing of long bones of leg**

> **754.40 Genu recurvatum**
>> DEF: Backward curving of knee joint.

> **754.41 Congenital dislocation of knee (with genu recurvatum)**

> **754.42 Congenital bowing of femur**

> **754.43 Congenital bowing of tibia and fibula**

> **754.44 Congenital bowing of unspecified long bones of leg**

✓5ᵗʰ **754.5 Varus deformities of feet**
> **EXCLUDES** acquired (736.71, 736.75, 736.79)

> **754.50 Talipes varus**
>> Congenital varus deformity of foot, unspecified
>> Pes varus
>> DEF: Inverted foot marked by outer sole resting on ground.

> **754.51 Talipes equinovarus**
>> Equinovarus (congenital)
>> DEF: Elevated, outward rotation of heel; also called clubfoot.

> **754.52 Metatarsus primus varus**
>> DEF: Malformed first metatarsal bone, with bone angled toward body.

> **754.53 Metatarsus varus**

> **754.59 Other**
>> Talipes calcaneovarus

✓5ᵗʰ **754.6 Valgus deformities of feet**
> **EXCLUDES** valgus deformity of foot (acquired) (736.79)

> **754.60 Talipes valgus**
>> Congenital valgus deformity of foot, unspecified

> **754.61 Congenital pes planus**
>> Congenital rocker bottom flat foot
>> Flat foot, congenital
>> **EXCLUDES** pes planus (acquired) (734)

> **754.62 Talipes calcaneovalgus**

> **754.69 Other**
>> Talipes: Talipes:
>>   equinovalgus   planovalgus

✓5ᵗʰ **754.7 Other deformities of feet**
> **EXCLUDES** acquired (736.70-736.79)

> **754.70 Talipes, unspecified**
>> Congenital deformity of foot NOS

> **754.71 Talipes cavus**
>> Cavus foot (congenital)

> **754.79 Other**
>> Asymmetric talipes
>> Talipes:
>>   calcaneus
>>   equinus

✓5ᵗʰ **754.8 Other specified nonteratogenic anomalies**

> **754.81 Pectus excavatum**
>> Congenital funnel chest

> **754.82 Pectus carinatum**
>> Congenital pigeon chest [breast]

> **754.89 Other**
>> Club hand (congenital)
>> Congenital:
>>   deformity of chest wall
>>   dislocation of elbow
>> Generalized flexion contractures of lower limb joints, congenital
>> Spade-like hand (congenital)

✓4ᵗʰ **755 Other congenital anomalies of limbs**
> **EXCLUDES** those deformities classifiable to 754.0-754.8

✓5ᵗʰ **755.0 Polydactyly**

> **755.00 Polydactyly, unspecified digits**
>> Supernumerary digits

> **755.01 Of fingers**
>> Accessory fingers

> **755.02 Of toes**
>> Accessory toes

✓5ᵗʰ **755.1 Syndactyly**
> Symphalangy   Webbing of digits

> **755.10 Of multiple and unspecified sites**

> **755.11 Of fingers without fusion of bone**

> **755.12 Of fingers with fusion of bone**

> **755.13 Of toes without fusion of bone**

> **755.14 Of toes with fusion of bone**

✓5ᵗʰ **755.2 Reduction deformities of upper limb**

> **755.20 Unspecified reduction deformity of upper limb**
>> Ectromelia NOS } of upper limb
>> Hemimelia NOS }
>>
>> Shortening of arm, congenital

> **755.21 Transverse deficiency of upper limb**
>> Amelia of upper limb
>> Congenital absence of:
>>   fingers, all (complete or partial)
>>   forearm, including hand and fingers
>>   upper limb, complete
>> Congenital amputation of upper limb
>> Transverse hemimelia of upper limb

> **755.22 Longitudinal deficiency of upper limb, not elsewhere classified**
>> Phocomelia NOS of upper limb
>> Rudimentary arm

Additional Digit Required   Nonspecific PDx   Unacceptable PDx   Manifestation Code   **MCV** Major Cardiovascular Condition   ▶◀ Revised Text   ● New Code   ▲ Revised Code Title

2007 ICD•9•CM   **Volume 1 — 245**

755.23 Longitudinal deficiency, combined, involving humerus, radius, and ulna (complete or incomplete)
Congenital absence of arm and forearm (complete or incomplete) with or without metacarpal deficiency and/or phalangeal deficiency, incomplete
Phocomelia, complete, of upper limb

755.24 Longitudinal deficiency, humeral, complete or partial (with or without distal deficiencies, incomplete)
Congenital absence of humerus (with or without absence of some [but not all] distal elements)
Proximal phocomelia of upper limb

755.25 Longitudinal deficiency, radioulnar, complete or partial (with or without distal deficiencies, incomplete)
Congenital absence of radius and ulna (with or without absence of some [but not all] distal elements)
Distal phocomelia of upper limb

755.26 Longitudinal deficiency, radial, complete or partial (with or without distal deficiencies, incomplete)
Agenesis of radius
Congenital absence of radius (with or without absence of some [but not all] distal elements)

755.27 Longitudinal deficiency, ulnar, complete or partial (with or without distal deficiencies, incomplete)
Agenesis of ulna
Congenital absence of ulna (with or without absence of some [but not all] distal elements)

755.28 Longitudinal deficiency, carpals or metacarpals, complete or partial (with or without incomplete phalangeal deficiency)

755.29 Longitudinal deficiency, phalanges, complete or partial
Absence of finger, congenital
Aphalangia of upper limb, terminal, complete or partial
> **EXCLUDES** *terminal deficiency of all five digits (755.21)*
> *transverse deficiency of phalanges (755.21)*

✓5ᵗʰ **755.3 Reduction deformities of lower limb**

755.30 Unspecified reduction deformity of lower limb
Ectromelia NOS ⎱ of lower limb
Hemimelia NOS ⎰
Shortening of leg, congenital

755.31 Transverse deficiency of lower limb
Amelia of lower limb
Congenital absence of:
foot
leg, including foot and toes
lower limb, complete
toes, all, complete
Transverse hemimelia of lower limb

755.32 Longitudinal deficiency of lower limb, not elsewhere classified
Phocomelia NOS of lower limb

755.33 Longitudinal deficiency, combined, involving femur, tibia, and fibula (complete or incomplete)
Congenital absence of thigh and (lower) leg (complete or incomplete) with or without metacarpal deficiency and/or phalangeal deficiency, incomplete
Phocomelia, complete, of lower limb

755.34 Longitudinal deficiency, femoral, complete or partial (with or without distal deficiencies, incomplete)
Congenital absence of femur (with or without absence of some [but not all] distal elements)
Proximal phocomelia of lower limb

755.35 Longitudinal deficiency, tibiofibular, complete or partial (with or without distal deficiencies, incomplete)
Congenital absence of tibia and fibula (with or without absence of some [but not all] distal elements)
Distal phocomelia of lower limb

755.36 Longitudinal deficiency, tibia, complete or partial (with or without distal deficiencies, incomplete)
Agenesis of tibia
Congenital absence of tibia (with or without absence of some [but not all] distal elements)

755.37 Longitudinal deficiency, fibular, complete or partial (with or without distal deficiencies, incomplete)
Agenesis of fibula
Congenital absence of fibula (with or without absence of some [but not all] distal elements)

755.38 Longitudinal deficiency, tarsals or metatarsals, complete or partial (with or without incomplete phalangeal deficiency)

755.39 Longitudinal deficiency, phalanges, complete or partial
Absence of toe, congenital
Aphalangia of lower limb, terminal, complete or partial
> **EXCLUDES** *terminal deficiency of all five digits (755.31)*
> *transverse deficiency of phalanges (755.31)*

755.4 Reduction deformities, unspecified limb
Absence, congenital (complete or partial) of limb NOS
Amelia ⎫
Ectromelia ⎬ of unspecified limb
Hemimelia ⎪
Phocomelia ⎭

✓5ᵗʰ **755.5 Other anomalies of upper limb, including shoulder girdle**

755.50 Unspecified anomaly of upper limb

755.51 Congenital deformity of clavicle

755.52 Congenital elevation of scapula
Sprengel's deformity

755.53 Radioulnar synostosis
DEF: Osseous adhesion of radius and ulna.

755.54 Madelung's deformity
DEF: Distal ulnar overgrowth or radial shortening; also called carpus curvus.

755.55 Acrocephalosyndactyly
Apert's syndrome
DEF: Premature cranial suture fusion (craniostenosis); marked by cone-shaped or pointed (acrocephaly) head and webbing of the fingers (syndactyly); it is very similar to craniofacial dysostosis.

N Newborn Age: 0   **P** Pediatric Age: 0-17   **M** Maternity Age: 12-55   **A** Adult Age: 15-124   **CC** CC Condition   **MC** Major Complication   **CD** Complex Dx   **HIV** HIV Related Dx

246 — Volume 1   2007 ICD•9•CM

755.56 Accessory carpal bones

755.57 Macrodactylia (fingers)
DEF: Abnormally large fingers, toes.

755.58 Cleft hand, congenital
Lobster-claw hand
DEF: Extended separation between fingers into metacarpus; also may refer to large fingers and absent middle fingers of hand.

755.59 Other
Cleidocranial dysostosis
Cubitus:
valgus, congenital
varus, congenital
> EXCLUDES   club hand (congenital) (754.89)
>   congenital dislocation of elbow
>   (754.89)

√5th 755.6 Other anomalies of lower limb, including pelvic girdle

755.60 Unspecified anomaly of lower limb

755.61 Coxa valga, congenital
DEF: Abnormally wide angle between the neck and shaft of the femur.

755.62 Coxa vara, congenital
DEF: Diminished angle between neck and shaft of femur.

755.63 Other congenital deformity of hip (joint)
Congenital anteversion of femur (neck)
> EXCLUDES   congenital dislocation of hip
>   (754.30-754.35)

AHA: 1Q, '94, 15; S-O, '84, 15

755.64 Congenital deformity of knee (joint)
Congenital:
absence of patella
genu valgum [knock-knee]
genu varum [bowleg]
Rudimentary patella

755.65 Macrodactylia of toes
DEF: Abnormally large toes.

755.66 Other anomalies of toes
Congenital: Congenital:
hallux valgus   hammer toe
hallux varus

755.67 Anomalies of foot, not elsewhere classified
Astragaloscaphoid synostosis
Calcaneonavicular bar
Coalition of calcaneus
Talonavicular synostosis
Tarsal coalitions

755.69 Other
Congenital:
angulation of tibia
deformity (of):
ankle (joint)
sacroiliac (joint)
fusion of sacroiliac joint

755.8 Other specified anomalies of unspecified limb

755.9 Unspecified anomaly of unspecified limb
Congenital:
anomaly NOS ⎫
deformity NOS ⎭ of unspecified limb
> EXCLUDES   reduction deformity of unspecified
>   limb (755.4)

√4th 756 Other congenital musculoskeletal anomalies
> EXCLUDES   those deformities classifiable to 754.0-754.8

756.0 Anomalies of skull and face bones
Absence of skull bones	Imperfect fusion of skull
Acrocephaly	Oxycephaly
Congenital deformity	Platybasia
of forehead	Premature closure of
Craniosynostosis	cranial sutures
Crouzon's disease	Tower skull
Hypertelorism	Trigonocephaly

> EXCLUDES   acrocephalosyndactyly [Apert's
>   syndrome] (755.55)
>   dentofacial anomalies (524.0-524.9)
>   skull defects associated with brain
>   anomalies, such as:
>   anencephalus (740.0)
>   encephalocele (742.0)
>   hydrocephalus (742.3)
>   microcephalus (742.1)

AHA: 3Q, '98, 9; 3Q, '96, 15

√5th 756.1 Anomalies of spine

756.10 Anomaly of spine, unspecified

756.11 Spondylolysis, lumbosacral region
Prespondylolisthesis (lumbosacral)
DEF: Bilateral or unilateral defect through the pars interarticularis of a vertebra causes spondylolisthesis.

756.12 Spondylolisthesis
DEF: Downward slipping of lumbar vertebra over next vertebra; usually related to pelvic deformity.

756.13 Absence of vertebra, congenital

756.14 Hemivertebra
DEF: Incomplete development of one side of a vertebra.

756.15 Fusion of spine [vertebra], congenital

756.16 Klippel-Feil syndrome
DEF: Short, wide neck; limits range of motion due to abnormal number of cervical vertebra or fused hemivertebrae.

756.17 Spina bifida occulta
> EXCLUDES   spina bifida (aperta) (741.0-
>   741.9)

DEF: Spina bifida marked by a bony spinal canal defect without a protrusion of the cord or meninges; it is diagnosed by radiography and has no symptoms.

756.19 Other
Platyspondylia   Supernumerary vertebra

756.2 Cervical rib
Supernumerary rib in the cervical region
DEF: Costa cervicalis: extra rib attached to cervical vertebra.

756.3 Other anomalies of ribs and sternum
Congenital absence of:	Congenital:
rib	fissure of sternum
sternum	fusion of ribs
	Sternum bifidum

> EXCLUDES   nonteratogenic deformity of chest wall
>   (754.81-754.89)

756.4 Chondrodystrophy
Achondroplasia	Enchondromatosis
Chondrodystrophia (fetalis)	Ollier's disease
Dyschondroplasia	

> EXCLUDES   lipochondrodystrophy [Hurler's
>   syndrome] (277.5)
>   Morquio's disease (277.5)

AHA: 2Q, '02, 16; S-O, '87, 10

DEF: Abnormal development of cartilage.

√4th √5th Additional Digit Required   Nonspecific PDx   Unacceptable PDx   Manifestation Code   **MCV** Major Cardiovascular Condition   ▶◀ Revised Text   ● New Code   ▲ Revised Code Title

2007 ICD•9•CM   **Volume 1 — 247**

Congenital Anomalies

755.56—756.4

Congenital Anomalies

756.5–757.6

✓5ᵗʰ **756.5 Osteodystrophies**

756.50 Osteodystrophy, unspecified

756.51 Osteogenesis imperfecta
Fragilitas ossium   Osteopsathyrosis

DEF: A collagen disorder commonly characterized by brittle, osteoporotic, easily fractured bones, hypermobility of joints, blue sclerae, and a tendency to hemorrhage.

756.52 Osteopetrosis

DEF: Abnormally dense bone, optic atrophy, hepatosplenomegaly, deafness; sclerosing depletes bone marrow and nerve foramina of skull; often fatal.

756.53 Osteopoikilosis

DEF: Multiple sclerotic foci on ends of long bones, stippling in round, flat bones; identified by x-ray.

756.54 Polyostotic fibrous dysplasia of bone

DEF: Fibrous tissue displaces bone results in segmented ragged-edge café-au-lait spots; occurs in girls of early puberty.

756.55 Chondroectodermal dysplasia
Ellis-van Creveld syndrome

DEF: Inadequate enchondral bone formation; impaired development of hair and teeth, polydactyly, and cardiac septum defects.

756.56 Multiple epiphyseal dysplasia

756.59 Other
Albright (-McCune)-Sternberg syndrome

756.6 Anomalies of diaphragm
Absence of diaphragm   Eventration of diaphragm
Congenital hernia:
diaphragmatic
foramen of Morgagni
EXCLUDES   congenital hiatus hernia (750.6)

✓5ᵗʰ **756.7 Anomalies of abdominal wall**

756.70 Anomaly of abdominal wall, unspecified

756.71 Prune belly syndrome
Eagle-Barrett syndrome
Prolapse of bladder mucosa
AHA: 4Q, '97, 44

DEF: Prune belly syndrome: absence of lower rectus abdominis muscle and lower and medial oblique muscles; results in dilated bladder and ureters, dysplastic kidneys and hydronephrosis; more common in male infants with undescended testicles.

756.79 Other congenital anomalies of abdominal wall
Exomphalos   Omphalocele
Gastroschisis
EXCLUDES   umbilical hernia (551-553 with .1)

DEF: Exomphalos: umbilical hernia prominent navel.

DEF: Gastroschisis: fissure of abdominal wall, results in protruding small or large intestine.

DEF: Omphalocele: hernia of umbilicus due to impaired abdominal wall; results in membrane-covered intestine protruding through peritoneum and amnion.

✓5ᵗʰ **756.8 Other specified anomalies of muscle, tendon, fascia, and connective tissue**

756.81 Absence of muscle and tendon
Absence of muscle (pectoral)

756.82 Accessory muscle

756.83 Ehlers-Danlos syndrome

DEF: Danlos syndrome: connective tissue disorder causes hyperextended skin and joints; results in fragile blood vessels with bleeding, poor wound healing and subcutaneous pseudotumors.

756.89 Other
Amyotrophia congenita
Congenital shortening of tendon
AHA: 3Q, '99, 16

756.9 Other and unspecified anomalies of musculoskeletal system
Congenital:
anomaly NOS } of musculoskeletal system,
deformity NOS }   not elsewhere classified

✓4ᵗʰ **757 Congenital anomalies of the integument**
INCLUDES   anomalies of skin, subcutaneous tissue, hair, nails, and breast
EXCLUDES   hemangioma (228.00-228.09)
pigmented nevus (216.0-216.9)

757.0 Hereditary edema of legs
Congenital lymphedema
Hereditary trophedema
Milroy's disease

757.1 Ichthyosis congenita
Congenital ichthyosis
Harlequin fetus
Ichthyosiform erythroderma

DEF: Overproduction of skin cells causes scaling of skin; may result in stillborn fetus or death soon after birth.

757.2 Dermatoglyphic anomalies
Abnormal palmar creases

DEF: Abnormal skin-line patterns of fingers, palms, toes and soles; initial finding of possible chromosomal abnormalities.

✓5ᵗʰ **757.3 Other specified anomalies of skin**

757.31 Congenital ectodermal dysplasia

DEF: Tissues and structures originate in embryonic ectoderm; includes anhidrotic and hidrotic ectodermal dysplasia and EEC syndrome.

757.32 Vascular hamartomas
Birthmarks   Strawberry nevus
Port-wine stain

DEF: Benign tumor of blood vessels; due to malformed angioblastic tissues.

757.33 Congenital pigmentary anomalies of skin
Congenital poikiloderma
Urticaria pigmentosa
Xeroderma pigmentosum
EXCLUDES   albinism (270.2)

757.39 Other
Accessory skin tags, congenital
Congenital scar
Epidermolysis bullosa
Keratoderma (congenital)
EXCLUDES   pilonidal cyst (685.0-685.1)

757.4 Specified anomalies of hair
Congenital: Congenital:
alopecia   hypertrichosis
atrichosis   monilethrix
beaded hair   Persistent lanugo

757.5 Specified anomalies of nails
Anonychia   Congenital:
Congenital: leukonychia
clubnail   onychauxis
koilonychia   pachyonychia

757.6 Specified anomalies of breast
Absent
Accessory   } breast or nipple
Supernumerary
Hypoplasia of breast
EXCLUDES   absence of pectoral muscle (756.81)

N Newborn Age: 0   P Pediatric Age: 0-17   M Maternity Age: 12-55   A Adult Age: 15-124   CC CC Condition   MC Major Complication   CD Complex Dx   HIV HIV Related Dx

248 — Volume 1   2007 ICD•9•CM

757.8 **Other specified anomalies of the integument**

757.9 **Unspecified anomaly of the integument**

Congenital:

anomaly NOS }

deformity NOS } of integument

√4ᵗʰ **758 Chromosomal anomalies**

> **INCLUDES** syndromes associated with anomalies in the number and form of chromosomes

Use additional codes for conditions associated with the chromosomal anomalies

758.0 **Down's syndrome**

Mongolism	Trisomy:
Translocation Down's	21 or 22
syndrome	G

758.1 **Patau's syndrome**

Trisomy:	Trisomy:
13	D₁

DEF: Trisomy of 13th chromosome; characteristic failure to thrive, severe mental impairment, seizures, abnormal eyes, low-set ears and sloped forehead.

758.2 **Edwards' syndrome**

Trisomy:	Trisomy:
18	E₃

DEF: Trisomy of 18th chromosome; characteristic mental and physical impairments; mainly affects females.

√5ᵗʰ 758.3 **Autosomal deletion syndromes**

758.31 **Cri-du-chat syndrome**

Deletion 5p

DEF: Hereditary congenital syndrome caused by a microdeletion of short arm of chromosome 5; characterized by catlike cry in newborn, microencephaly, severe mental deficiency, and hypertelorism.

758.32 **Velo-cardio-facial syndrome**

Deletion 22q11.2

DEF: Microdeletion syndrome affecting multiple organs; characteristic cleft palate, heart defects, elongated face with almond-shaped eyes, wide nose, small ears, weak immune systems, weak musculature, hypothyroidism, short stature, and scoliosis; deletion at q11.2 on the long arm of the chromosome 22.

758.33 **Other microdeletions**

Miller-Dieker syndrome

Smith-Magenis syndrome

DEF: Miller-Dieker syndrome: deletion from the short arm of chromosome 17; characteristic mental retardation, speech and motor development delays, neurological complications, and multiple abnormalities affecting the kidneys, heart, gastrointestinal tract, and other organ; death in infancy or early childhood.

DEF: Smith-Magenis syndrome: deletion in a certain area of chromosome 17 that results in craniofacial changes, speech delay, hoarse voice, hearing loss in many, and behavioral problems, such as self-destructive head banging, wrist biting, and tearing at nails.

758.39 **Other autosomal deletions**

758.4 **Balanced autosomal translocation in normal individual**

758.5 **Other conditions due to autosomal anomalies**

Accessory autosomes NEC

758.6 **Gonadal dysgenesis**

Ovarian dysgenesis	XO syndrome
Turner's syndrome	

> **EXCLUDES** pure gonadal dysgenesis (752.7)

758.7 **Klinefelter's syndrome**   ♂

XXY syndrome

DEF: Impaired embryonic development of seminiferous tubes; results in small testes, azoospermia, infertility and enlarged mammary glands.

√5ᵗʰ 758.8 **Other conditions due to chromosome anomalies**

758.81 **Other conditions due to sex chromosome anomalies**

758.89 **Other**

758.9 **Conditions due to anomaly of unspecified chromosome**

√4ᵗʰ **759 Other and unspecified congenital anomalies**

759.0 **Anomalies of spleen**

Aberrant }

Absent } spleen

Accessory }

Congenital splenomegaly

Ectopic spleen

Lobulation of spleen

759.1 **Anomalies of adrenal gland**

Aberrant }

Absent } adrenal gland

Accessory }

> **EXCLUDES** adrenogenital disorders (255.2)
> congenital disorders of steroid metabolism (255.2)

759.2 **Anomalies of other endocrine glands**

Absent parathyroid gland	Persistent thyroglossal
Accessory thyroid gland	or thyrolingual duct
	Thyroglossal (duct) cyst

> **EXCLUDES** congenital:
> goiter (246.1)
> hypothyroidism (243)

759.3 **Situs inversus**

Situs inversus or transversus:	Transposition of
abdominalis	viscera:
thoracis	abdominal
	thoracic

> **EXCLUDES** dextrocardia without mention of complete transposition (746.87)

DEF: Laterally transposed thoracic and abdominal viscera.

759.4 **Conjoined twins**

Craniopagus	Thoracopagus
Dicephalus	Xiphopagus
Pygopagus	

759.5 **Tuberous sclerosis**

Bourneville's disease   Epiloia

DEF: Hamartomas of brain, retina and viscera, impaired mental ability, seizures and adenoma sebaceum.

759.6 **Other hamartoses, not elsewhere classified**

Syndrome:	Syndrome:
Peutz-Jeghers	von Hippel-Lindau
Sturge-Weber (-Dimitri)	

> **EXCLUDES** neurofibromatosis (237.7)

AHA: 3Q, '92, 12

DEF: Peutz-Jeghers: hereditary syndrome characterized by hamartomas of small intestine.

DEF: Sturge-Weber: congenital syndrome characterized by unilateral port-wine stain over trigeminal nerve, underlying meninges and cerebral cortex.

DEF: von Hipple-Lindau: hereditary syndrome of congenital angiomatosis of the retina and cerebellum.

√4ᵗʰ
√5ᵗʰ Additional Digit Required   Nonspecific PDx   Unacceptable PDx   Manifestation Code   **MCV** Major Cardiovascular Condition   ▶◀ Revised Text   ● New Code   ▲ Revised Code Title

2007 ICD•9•CM   **Volume 1 — 249**

Congenital Anomalies

759.7–759.9

759.7 Multiple congenital anomalies, so described

Congenital:
     anomaly, multiple NOS
     NOS

Congenital:
     deformity, multiple

√5th **759.8 Other specified anomalies**

AHA: S-O, '87, 9; S-O, '85, 11

759.81 Prader-Willi syndrome

759.82 Marfan syndrome

AHA: 3Q, '93, 11

759.83 Fragile X syndrome

AHA: 4Q, '94, 41

759.89 Other

Congenital malformation syndromes affecting multiple systems, not elsewhere classified
Laurence-Moon-Biedl syndrome

AHA: ▶2Q, '05, 17;◀ 2Q, '04, 12; 1Q, '01, 3; 3Q, '99, 17, 18; 3Q, '98, 8

759.9 Congenital anomaly, unspecified

 Newborn Age: 0   Pediatric Age: 0-17   Maternity Age: 12-55   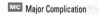 Adult Age: 15-124   **CC** CC Condition   **MC** Major Complication   **CD** Complex Dx   **HIV** HIV Related Dx

250 — Volume 1 • February 2006   *2007 ICD•9•CM*

15. CERTAIN CONDITIONS ORIGINATING IN THE PERINATAL PERIOD (760-779)

INCLUDES   conditions which have their origin in the perinatal period, before birth through the first 28 days after birth, even though death or morbidity occurs later

Use additional code(s) to further specify condition

MATERNAL CAUSES OF PERINATAL MORBIDITY AND MORTALITY (760-763)

AHA: 2Q, '89, 14; 3Q, '90, 5

✓4th **760 Fetus or newborn affected by maternal conditions which may be unrelated to present pregnancy**

INCLUDES   the listed maternal conditions only when specified as a cause of mortality or morbidity of the fetus or newborn

EXCLUDES   *maternal endocrine and metabolic disorders affecting fetus or newborn (775.0-775.9)*

AHA: 1Q, '94, 8; 2Q, '92, 12; N-D, '84, 11

760.0 Maternal hypertensive disorders
Fetus or newborn affected by maternal conditions classifiable to 642

760.1 Maternal renal and urinary tract diseases
Fetus or newborn affected by maternal conditions classifiable to 580-599

760.2 Maternal infections
Fetus or newborn affected by maternal infectious disease classifiable to 001-136 and 487, but fetus or newborn not manifesting that disease
EXCLUDES   *congenital infectious diseases (771.0-771.8)*
maternal genital tract and other localized infections (760.8)

760.3 Other chronic maternal circulatory and respiratory diseases
Fetus or newborn affected by chronic maternal conditions classifiable to 390-459, 490-519, 745-748

760.4 Maternal nutritional disorders
Fetus or newborn affected by:
maternal disorders classifiable to 260-269
maternal malnutrition NOS
EXCLUDES   *fetal malnutrition (764.10-764.29)*

760.5 Maternal injury
Fetus or newborn affected by maternal conditions classifiable to 800-995

760.6 Surgical operation on mother
EXCLUDES   *cesarean section for present delivery (763.4)*
damage to placenta from amniocentesis, cesarean section, or surgical induction (762.1)
previous surgery to uterus or pelvic organs (763.89)

✓5th **760.7 Noxious influences affecting fetus or newborn via placenta or breast milk**
Fetus or newborn affected by noxious substance transmitted via placenta or breast milk
EXCLUDES   *anesthetic and analgesic drugs administered during labor and delivery (763.5)*
drug withdrawal syndrome in newborn (779.5)

AHA: 3Q, '91, 21

760.70 Unspecified noxious substance
Fetus or newborn affected by:
Drug NEC

760.71 Alcohol
Fetal alcohol syndrome

760.72 Narcotics

760.73 Hallucinogenic agents

760.74 Anti-infectives
Antibiotics
Antifungals

760.75 Cocaine
AHA: 3Q, '94, 6; 2Q, '92, 12; 4Q, '91, 26

760.76 Diethylstilbestrol [DES]
AHA: 4Q, '94, 45

760.77 Anticonvulsants   N
Carbamazepine   Phenytoin
Phenobarbital   Valproic acid
AHA: ▶4Q, '05, 82◀

760.78 Antimetabolic agents   N
Methotrexate   Statins
Retinoic acid
AHA: ▶4Q, '05, 82-83◀

760.79 Other
Fetus or newborn affected by:
immune sera ⎫
medicinal agents ⎪ transmitted via
NEC ⎬ placenta
toxic substance NEC ⎭ or breast

760.8 Other specified maternal conditions affecting fetus or newborn
Maternal genital tract and other localized infection affecting fetus or newborn, but fetus or newborn not manifesting that disease
EXCLUDES   *maternal urinary tract infection affecting fetus or newborn (760.1)*

760.9 Unspecified maternal condition affecting fetus or newborn

✓4th **761 Fetus or newborn affected by maternal complications of pregnancy**
INCLUDES   the listed maternal conditions only when specified as a cause of mortality or morbidity of the fetus or newborn

761.0 Incompetent cervix
DEF: Inadequate functioning of uterine cervix.

761.1 Premature rupture of membranes

761.2 Oligohydramnios
EXCLUDES   *that due to premature rupture of membranes (761.1)*
DEF: Deficient amniotic fluid.

761.3 Polyhydramnios
Hydramnios (acute) (chronic)
DEF: Excess amniotic fluid.

761.4 Ectopic pregnancy
Pregnancy: Pregnancy:
abdominal   tubal
intraperitoneal

761.5 Multiple pregnancy
Triplet (pregnancy)   Twin (pregnancy)

761.6 Maternal death

761.7 Malpresentation before labor
Breech presentation ⎫
External version ⎪
Oblique lie ⎬ before labor
Transverse lie ⎪
Unstable lie ⎭

761.8 Other specified maternal complications of pregnancy affecting fetus or newborn
Spontaneous abortion, fetus

761.9 Unspecified maternal complication of pregnancy affecting fetus or newborn

✓4th ✓5th Additional Digit Required   Nonspecific PDx   Unacceptable PDx   Manifestation Code   MCV Major Cardiovascular Condition   ▶◀ Revised Text   ● New Code   ▲ Revised Code Title

2007 ICD•9•CM   February 2006 • Volume 1 — 251

Conditions in the Perinatal Period

762–763.9

☑4ᵗʰ **762 Fetus or newborn affected by complications of placenta, cord, and membranes**

> INCLUDES the listed maternal conditions only when specified as a cause of mortality or morbidity in the fetus or newborn

AHA: 1Q, '94, 8

762.0 Placenta previa   N

> DEF: Placenta developed in lower segment of uterus; causes hemorrhaging in last trimester.

762.1 Other forms of placental separation and hemorrhage   N

> Abruptio placentae
> Antepartum hemorrhage
> Damage to placenta from amniocentesis, cesarean section, or surgical induction
> Maternal blood loss
> Premature separation of placenta
> Rupture of marginal sinus

762.2 Other and unspecified morphological and functional abnormalities of placenta   N

> Placental:
>   dysfunction
>   infarction
>   insufficiency

762.3 Placental transfusion syndromes   N

> Placental and cord abnormality resulting in twin-to-twin or other transplacental transfusion
> Use additional code to indicate resultant condition in fetus or newborn:
>   fetal blood loss (772.0)
>   polycythemia neonatorum (776.4)

762.4 Prolapsed cord   N

> Cord presentation

762.5 Other compression of umbilical cord   N

> Cord around neck
> Entanglement of cord
> Knot in cord
> Torsion of cord

AHA: 2Q, '03, 9

762.6 Other and unspecified conditions of umbilical cord   N

> Short cord
> Thrombosis
> Varices   ⎱
> Velamentous insertion   ⎰ of umbilical cord
> Vasa previa

> EXCLUDES infection of umbilical cord (771.4)
>   single umbilical artery (747.5)

762.7 Chorioamnionitis   N

> Amnionitis
> Membranitis
> Placentitis

> DEF: Inflamed fetal membrane.

762.8 Other specified abnormalities of chorion and amnion   N

762.9 Unspecified abnormality of chorion and amnion   N

☑4ᵗʰ **763 Fetus or newborn affected by other complications of labor and delivery**

> INCLUDES the listed conditions only when specified as a cause of mortality or morbidity in the fetus or newborn

AHA: 1Q, '94, 8

763.0 Breech delivery and extraction   N

763.1 Other malpresentation, malposition, and disproportion during labor and delivery   N

> Fetus or newborn affected by:
>   abnormality of bony pelvis
>   contracted pelvis
>   persistent occipitoposterior position
>   shoulder presentation
>   transverse lie
>   conditions classifiable to 652, 653, and 660

763.2 Forceps delivery   N

> Fetus or newborn affected by forceps extraction

763.3 Delivery by vacuum extractor   N

763.4 Cesarean delivery   N

> EXCLUDES placental separation or hemorrhage from cesarean section (762.1)

763.5 Maternal anesthesia and analgesia   N

> Reactions and intoxications from maternal opiates and tranquilizers during labor and delivery

> EXCLUDES drug withdrawal syndrome in newborn (779.5)

763.6 Precipitate delivery   N

> Rapid second stage

763.7 Abnormal uterine contractions   N

> Fetus or newborn affected by:
>   contraction ring
>   hypertonic labor
>   hypotonic uterine dysfunction
>   uterine inertia or dysfunction
>   conditions classifiable to 661, except 661.3

☑5ᵗʰ **763.8 Other specified complications of labor and delivery affecting fetus or newborn**

AHA: 4Q, '98, 46

763.81 Abnormality in fetal heart rate or rhythm before the onset of labor   N

763.82 Abnormality in fetal heart rate or rhythm during labor   N

> AHA: 4Q, '98, 46

763.83 Abnormality in fetal heart rate or rhythm, unspecified as to time of onset   N

763.84 Meconium passage during delivery

> EXCLUDES meconium aspiration (770.11, 770.12)
>   meconium staining (779.84)

> AHA: ▶4Q, '05, 83◀

> DEF: ▶Fetal intestinal activity that increases in response to a distressed state during delivery; anal sphincter relaxes, and meconium is passed into the amniotic fluid.◀

763.89 Other specified complications of labor and delivery affecting fetus or newborn   N

> Fetus or newborn affected by:
>   abnormality of maternal soft tissues
>   destructive operation on live fetus to facilitate delivery
>   induction of labor (medical)
>   previous surgery to uterus or pelvic organs
>   other conditions classifiable to 650-669
>   other procedures used in labor and delivery

763.9 Unspecified complication of labor and delivery affecting fetus or newborn   N

N Newborn Age: 0   P Pediatric Age: 0-17   M Maternity Age: 12-55   A Adult Age: 15-124   CC CC Condition   MC Major Complication   CD Complex Dx   HIV HIV Related Dx

OTHER CONDITIONS ORIGINATING IN THE PERINATAL PERIOD (764-779)

The following fifth-digit subclassification is for use with category 764 and codes 765.0-765.1 to denote birthweight:

0 unspecified [weight]
1 less than 500 grams
2 500-749 grams
3 750-999 grams
4 1,000-1,249 grams
5 1,250-1,499 grams
6 1,500-1,749 grams
7 1,750-1,999 grams
8 2,000-2,499 grams
9 2,500 grams and over

✓4th **764 Slow fetal growth and fetal malnutrition**
AHA: 3Q, '04, 4; 4Q, '02, 63; 1Q, '94, 8; 2Q, '91, 19; 2Q, '89, 15

✓5th **764.0 "Light-for-dates" without mention of fetal malnutrition**
Infants underweight for gestational age
"Small-for-dates"

✓5th **764.1 "Light-for-dates" with signs of fetal malnutrition**
Infants "light-for-dates" classifiable to 764.0, who in addition show signs of fetal malnutrition, such as dry peeling skin and loss of subcutaneous tissue

✓5th **764.2 Fetal malnutrition without mention of "light-for-dates"**
Infants, not underweight for gestational age, showing signs of fetal malnutrition, such as dry peeling skin and loss of subcutaneous tissue
Intrauterine malnutrition

✓5th **764.9 Fetal growth retardation, unspecified**
Intrauterine growth retardation
AHA: For code 764.97: 1Q, '97, 6

✓4th **765 Disorders relating to short gestation and low birthweight**
INCLUDES the listed conditions, without further specification, as causes of mortality, morbidity, or additional care, in fetus or newborn
AHA: 1Q, '97, 6; 1Q, '94, 8; 2Q, '91, 19; 2Q, '89, 15

✓5th **765.0 Extreme immaturity** CC 1-8
Note: Usually implies a birthweight of less than 1000 grams.
Use additional code for weeks of gestation (765.20-765.29)
CC Excl: For codes 765.01-765.08: 764.00-765.29, 767.8-767.9, 779.8, 779.81-779.89
AHA: 3Q, '04, 4; 4Q, '02, 63; For code 765.03: 4Q, '01, 51

✓5th **765.1 Other preterm infants**
Note: Usually implies a birthweight of 1000-2499 grams.
Prematurity NOS
Prematurity or small size, not classifiable to 765.0 or as "light-for-dates" in 764
Use additional code for weeks of gestation (765.20-765.29)
AHA: 3Q, '04, 4; 4Q, '02, 63; For code 765.10: 1Q, '94, 14; For code 765.17: 1Q, '97, 6; For code 765.18: 4Q, '02, 64

✓5th **765.2 Weeks of gestation**
AHA: 3Q, '04, 4; 4Q, '02, 63

765.20 Unspecified weeks of gestation
765.21 Less than 24 completed weeks of gestation
765.22 24 completed weeks of gestation
765.23 25-26 completed weeks of gestation
765.24 27-28 completed weeks of gestation
765.25 29-30 completed weeks of gestation
765.26 31-32 completed weeks of gestation
765.27 33-34 completed weeks of gestation

765.28 35-36 completed weeks of gestation
AHA: 4Q, '02, 64

765.29 37 or more completed weeks of gestation

✓4th **766 Disorders relating to long gestation and high birthweight**
INCLUDES the listed conditions, without further specification, as causes of mortality, morbidity, or additional care, in fetus or newborn

766.0 Exceptionally large baby
Note: Usually implies a birthweight of 4500 grams or more.

766.1 Other "heavy-for-dates" infants
Other fetus or infant "heavy-" or "large-for-dates" regardless of period of gestation

✓5th **766.2 Late infant, not "heavy-for-dates"**

766.21 Post-term infant
Infant with gestation period over 40 completed weeks to 42 completed weeks
AHA: 4Q, '03, 69

766.22 Prolonged gestation of infant
Infant with gestation period over 42 completed weeks
Postmaturity NOS

✓4th **767 Birth trauma**

767.0 Subdural and cerebral hemorrhage CC
Subdural and cerebral hemorrhage, whether described as due to birth trauma or to intrapartum anoxia or hypoxia
Subdural hematoma (localized)
Tentorial tear
Use additional code to identify cause
EXCLUDES *intraventricular hemorrhage (772.10-772.14)*
subarachnoid hemorrhage (772.2)
CC Excl: 767.0, 767.8-767.9, 779.81-779.89

✓5th **767.1 Injuries to scalp**
AHA: 4Q, '03, 69

767.11 Epicranial subaponeurotic hemorrhage (massive) CC
Subgaleal hemorrhage
CC Excl: 767.0-767.11, 767.8-767.9, 779.81-779.89
DEF: A hemorrhage that occurs within the space between the galea aponeurotica, or epicranial aponeurosis, a thin tendinous structure that is attached to the skull laterally and provides an insertion site for the occipitalis posteriorly and the frontalis muscle anteriorly, and the periosteum of the skull.

767.19 Other injuries to scalp
Caput succedaneum
Cephalhematoma
Chignon (from vacuum extraction)

767.2 Fracture of clavicle

Epicranial Subaponeurosis

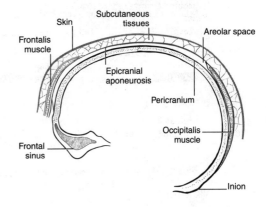

✓4th ✓5th Additional Digit Required   Nonspecific PDx   Unacceptable PDx   Manifestation Code   MCV Major Cardiovascular Condition   ►◄ Revised Text   ● New Code   ▲ Revised Code Title

2007 ICD•9•CM   Volume 1 — 253

Conditions in the Perinatal Period

767.3–770.15

767.3 Other injuries to skeleton   N
Fracture of:
   long bones
   skull
   EXCLUDES   *congenital dislocation of hip*
        (754.30-754.35)
        fracture of spine, congenital (767.4)

767.4 Injury to spine and spinal cord   N
   Dislocation
   Fracture   } of spine or spinal cord
   Laceration   due to birth trauma
   Rupture

767.5 Facial nerve injury   N
   Facial palsy

767.6 Injury to brachial plexus   N
   Palsy or paralysis:
      brachial
      Erb (-Duchenne)
      Klumpke (-Déjérine)

767.7 Other cranial and peripheral nerve injuries   N
   Phrenic nerve paralysis

767.8 Other specified birth trauma   N
   Eye damage   Rupture of:
   Hematoma of: liver
      liver (subcapsular)   spleen
      testes   Scalpel wound
      vulva   Traumatic glaucoma
   EXCLUDES   *hemorrhage classifiable to 772.0-772.9*

767.9 Birth trauma, unspecified   N
   Birth injury NOS

✓4ᵗʰ **768 Intrauterine hypoxia and birth asphyxia**
   Use only when associated with newborn morbidity
   classifiable elsewhere
   EXCLUDES ▶ *acidemia NOS of newborn (775.81)*
        acidosis NOS of newborn (775.81)
        cerebral ischemia NOS (779.2)
        hypoxia NOS of newborn (770.88)
        mixed metabolic and respiratory acidosis of
          newborn (775.81)
        respiratory arrest of newborn (770.87)◀

AHA: 4Q, '92, 20

DEF: Oxygen intake insufficiency due to interrupted placental circulation or premature separation of placenta.

768.0 Fetal death from asphyxia or anoxia before onset of labor or at unspecified time   N

768.1 Fetal death from asphyxia or anoxia during labor   N

768.2 Fetal distress before onset of labor, in liveborn infant   N
   Fetal metabolic acidemia before onset of labor, in
      liveborn infant

▲ **768.3 Fetal distress first noted during labor and delivery, in liveborn infant**   N
   Fetal metabolic acidemia first noted during labor
      ▶and delivery,◀ in liveborn infant

768.4 Fetal distress, unspecified as to time of onset, in liveborn infant   N
   Fetal metabolic acidemia unspecified as to time of
      onset, in liveborn infant
   AHA: N-D, '86, 10

768.5 Severe birth asphyxia   CC N
   Birth asphyxia with neurologic involvement
   EXCLUDES ▶ *hypoxic-ischemic encephalopathy [HIE]*
        (768.7)◀
   CC Excl: 768.5-770.9, 779.81-779.89
   AHA: N-D, '86, 3

768.6 Mild or moderate birth asphyxia   N
   Birth asphyxia (without mention of neurologic
      involvement)
   EXCLUDES ▶ *hypoxic-ischemic encephalopathy [HIE]*
        (768.7)◀
   AHA: N-D, '86, 3

● **768.7 Hypoxic-ischemic encephalopathy [HIE]**   N

768.9 Unspecified birth asphyxia in liveborn infant   N
   Anoxia
   Asphyxia   } NOS, in liveborn infant

769 Respiratory distress syndrome   CC N
   Cardiorespiratory distress syndrome of newborn
   Hyaline membrane disease (pulmonary)
   Idiopathic respiratory distress syndrome [IRDS or RDS] of
      newborn
   Pulmonary hypoperfusion syndrome
   EXCLUDES   *transient tachypnea of newborn (770.6)*

CC Excl: See code 768.5

AHA: 1Q, '89, 10; N-D, '86, 6

DEF: Severe chest contractions upon air intake and expiratory grunting; infant appears blue due to oxygen deficiency and has rapid respiratory rate; formerly called hyaline membrane disease.

✓4ᵗʰ **770 Other respiratory conditions of fetus and newborn**

770.0 Congenital pneumonia   CC N
   Infective pneumonia acquired prenatally
   EXCLUDES   *pneumonia from infection acquired*
        after birth (480.0-486)

CC Excl: See code 768.5

AHA: 1Q, '05, 10

✓5ᵗʰ **770.1 Fetal and newborn aspiration**
   EXCLUDES   *aspiration of postnatal stomach*
        contents (770.85, 770.86)
        meconium passage during delivery
          (763.84)
        meconium staining (779.84)

AHA: 4Q, '05, 83

770.10 Fetal and newborn aspiration, unspecified   N

770.11 Meconium aspiration without respiratory symptoms   N
   Meconium aspiration NOS

770.12 Meconium aspiration with respiratory symptoms   CC N
   Meconium aspiration pneumonia
   Meconium aspiration pneumonitis
   Meconium aspiration syndrome NOS
   Use additional code to identify any
      secondary pulmonary hypertension
      (416.8), if applicable

CC Excl: See code 768.5

DEF: Meconium aspiration syndrome: aspiration of fetal intestinal material during or prior to delivery, usually a complication of placental insufficiency, causing pneumonitis and bronchial obstruction (inflammatory reaction of lungs).

770.13 Aspiration of clear amniotic fluid without respiratory symptoms   N
   Aspiration of clear amniotic fluid NOS

770.14 Aspiration of clear amniotic fluid with respiratory symptoms   CC N
   Aspiration of clear amniotic fluid with
      pneumonia
   Aspiration of clear amniotic fluid with
      pneumonitis
   Use additional code to identify any
      secondary pulmonary hypertension
      (416.8), if applicable

CC Excl: See code 768.5

770.15 Aspiration of blood without respiratory symptoms   N
   Aspiration of blood NOS

| N Newborn Age: 0 | P Pediatric Age: 0-17 | M Maternity Age: 12-55 | A Adult Age: 15-124 | CC CC Condition | MC Major Complication | CD Complex Dx | HIV HIV Related Dx |

770.16 Aspiration of blood with respiratory symptoms `CC` `N`
Aspiration of blood with pneumonia
Aspiration of blood with pneumonitis
Use additional code to identify any
secondary pulmonary hypertension
(416.8), if applicable
CC Excl: See code 768.5

770.17 Other fetal and newborn aspiration without respiratory symptoms `N`

770.18 Other fetal and newborn aspiration with respiratory symptoms `CC` `N`
Other aspiration pneumonia
Other aspiration pneumonitis
Use additional code to identify any
secondary pulmonary hypertension
(416.8), if applicable
CC Excl: See code 768.5

770.2 Interstitial emphysema and related conditions `CC` `N`
Pneumomediastinum ⎫
Pneumopericardium ⎬ originating in the
Pneumothorax ⎭ perinatal period
CC Excl: See code 768.5

770.3 Pulmonary hemorrhage `CC` `N`
Hemorrhage:
alveolar (lung) ⎫
intra-alveolar (lung) ⎬ originating in the
massive pulmonary ⎭ perinatal period
CC Excl: See code 768.5

770.4 Primary atelectasis `CC` `N`
Pulmonary immaturity NOS
CC Excl: See code 768.5

DEF: Alveoli fail to expand causing insufficient air intake by newborn.

770.5 Other and unspecified atelectasis `CC` `N`
Atelectasis:
NOS ⎫
partial ⎬ originating in the
secondary ⎥ perinatal period
Pulmonary collapse ⎭
CC Excl: See code 768.5

770.6 Transitory tachypnea of newborn `N`
Idiopathic tachypnea of newborn
Wet lung syndrome
EXCLUDES respiratory distress syndrome (769)
AHA: 4Q, '95, 4; 1Q, '94, 12; 3Q, '93, 7; 1Q, '89, 10; N-D, '86, 6
DEF: Quick, shallow breathing of newborn; short-term problem.

770.7 Chronic respiratory disease arising in the perinatal period `CC`
Bronchopulmonary dysplasia
Interstitial pulmonary fibrosis of prematurity
Wilson-Mikity syndrome
CC Excl: See code 768.5
AHA: 2Q, '91, 19; N-D, '86, 11

`√5th` **770.8 Other respiratory problems after birth**
EXCLUDES ▶ mixed metabolic and respiratory acidosis of newborn (775.81)◀
AHA: 4Q, '02, 65; 2Q, '98, 10; 2Q, '96, 10

770.81 Primary apnea of newborn `N`
Apneic spells of newborn NOS
Essential apnea of newborn
Sleep apnea of newborn
DEF: Cessation of breathing when a neonate makes no respiratory effort for 15 seconds, resulting in cyanosis and bradycardia.

770.82 Other apnea of newborn `N`
Obstructive apnea of newborn

770.83 Cyanotic attacks of newborn `N`

770.84 Respiratory failure of newborn `CC` `N`
EXCLUDES respiratory distress syndrome (769)
CC Excl: See code 768.5

770.85 Aspiration of postnatal stomach contents without respiratory symptoms `N`
Aspiration of postnatal stomach contents NOS
AHA: 4Q, '05, 83

770.86 Aspiration of postnatal stomach contents with respiratory symptoms `CC` `N`
Aspiration of postnatal stomach contents with pneumonia
Aspiration of postnatal stomach contents with pneumonitis
Use additional code to identify any
secondary pulmonary hypertension
(416.8), if applicable
CC Excl: See code 768.5
AHA: 4Q, '05, 83

● **770.87 Respiratory arrest of newborn** `N`
● **770.88 Hypoxemia of newborn** `N`
Hypoxia NOS of newborn

770.89 Other respiratory problems after birth `N`

770.9 Unspecified respiratory condition of fetus and newborn `N`

`√4th` **771 Infections specific to the perinatal period**
INCLUDES infections acquired before or during birth or via the umbilicus or during the first 28 days after birth
EXCLUDES congenital pneumonia (770.0)
congenital syphilis (090.0-090.9)
maternal infectious disease as a cause of mortality or morbidity in fetus or newborn, but fetus or newborn not manifesting the disease (760.2)
ophthalmia neonatorum due to gonococcus (098.40)
other infections not specifically classified to this category
AHA: N-D, '85, 4

771.0 Congenital rubella `CC` `N`
Congenital rubella pneumonitis
CC Excl: 771.0-771.2, 779.81-779.89

771.1 Congenital cytomegalovirus infection `CC` `N`
Congenital cytomegalic inclusion disease
CC Excl: See code 771.0

771.2 Other congenital infections `N`
Congenital: Congenital:
herpes simplex   toxoplasmosis
listeriosis   tuberculosis
malaria

771.3 Tetanus neonatorum `CC` `N`
Tetanus omphalitis
EXCLUDES hypocalcemic tetany (775.4)
CC Excl: 771.3, 779.81-779.89

DEF: Severe infection of central nervous system; due to exotoxin of tetanus bacillus from navel infection prompted by nonsterile technique during umbilical ligation.

771.4 Omphalitis of the newborn `N`
Infection:
navel cord
umbilical stump
EXCLUDES tetanus omphalitis (771.3)
DEF: Inflamed umbilicus.

771.5 Neonatal infective mastitis `N`
EXCLUDES noninfective neonatal mastitis (778.7)

`√4th` `√5th` Additional Digit Required   Nonspecific PDx   Unacceptable PDx   Manifestation Code   `MCV` Major Cardiovascular Condition   ▶◀ Revised Text   ● New Code   ▲ Revised Code Title

Conditions in the Perinatal Period

771.6–774.0

771.6 Neonatal conjunctivitis and dacryocystitis [N]
Ophthalmia neonatorum NOS
> EXCLUDES   ophthalmia neonatorum due to gonococcus (098.40)

771.7 Neonatal Candida infection [N]
Neonatal moniliasis
Thrush in newborn

√5ᵗʰ 771.8 Other infection specific to the perinatal period
Use additional code to identify organism (041.00-041.9)
AHA: 4Q, '02, 66

771.81 Septicemia [sepsis] of newborn [CC] [N]
CC Excl: 771.4-771.89, 776.0-776.9, 779.81-779.89

771.82 Urinary tract infection of newborn [N]

771.83 Bacteremia of newborn [CC] [N]
CC Excl: See code 771.81

771.89 Other infections specific to the perinatal period [N]
Intra-amniotic infection of fetus NOS
Infection of newborn NOS

√4ᵗʰ 772 Fetal and neonatal hemorrhage
> EXCLUDES   hematological disorders of fetus and newborn (776.0-776.9)

772.0 Fetal blood loss [N]
Fetal blood loss from:
  cut end of co-twin's cord
  placenta
  ruptured cord
  vasa previa
Fetal exsanguination
Fetal hemorrhage into:
  co-twin
  mother's circulation

√5ᵗʰ 772.1 Intraventricular hemorrhage
Intraventricular hemorrhage from any perinatal cause
AHA: 4Q, '01, 49; 3Q, '92, 8; 4Q, '88, 8

772.10 Unspecified grade [CC] [N]
CC Excl: 772.0-772.2, 772.8-772.9, 776.0-776.9, 779.81-779.89

772.11 Grade I [CC] [N]
Bleeding into germinal matrix
CC Excl: See code 772.10

772.12 Grade II [CC] [N]
Bleeding into ventricle
CC Excl: See code 772.10

772.13 Grade III [CC] [N]
Bleeding with enlargement of ventricle
CC Excl: See code 772.10
AHA: 4Q, '01, 51

772.14 Grade IV [CC] [N]
Bleeding into cerebral cortex
CC Excl: See code 772.10

772.2 Subarachnoid hemorrhage [CC] [N]
Subarachnoid hemorrhage from any perinatal cause
> EXCLUDES   subdural and cerebral hemorrhage (767.0)
CC Excl: 772.0-772.2, 772.8-772.9, 776.0-776.9, 779.7-779.89

772.3 Umbilical hemorrhage after birth [N]
Slipped umbilical ligature

772.4 Gastrointestinal hemorrhage [CC] [N]
> EXCLUDES   swallowed maternal blood (777.3)
CC Excl: 772.0, 772.4-772.5, 772.8-772.9, 776.0-776.9, 779.81-779.89

772.5 Adrenal hemorrhage [CC] [N]
CC Excl: See code 772.4

772.6 Cutaneous hemorrhage [N]
Bruising
Ecchymoses
Petechiae } in fetus or newborn
Superficial hematoma

772.8 Other specified hemorrhage of fetus or newborn [N]
> EXCLUDES   hemorrhagic disease of newborn (776.0)
> pulmonary hemorrhage (770.3)

772.9 Unspecified hemorrhage of newborn [N]

√4ᵗʰ 773 Hemolytic disease of fetus or newborn, due to isoimmunization
DEF: Hemolytic anemia of fetus or newborn due to maternal antibody formation against fetal erythrocytes; infant blood contains nonmaternal antigen.

773.0 Hemolytic disease due to Rh isoimmunization [CC] [N]
Anemia
Erythroblastosis (fetalis)
Hemolytic disease (fetus)
  (newborn)
} due to RH:
  antibodies
  isoimmunization
  maternal/fetal
    incompatibility

Rh hemolytic disease
Rh isoimmunization
CC Excl: 773.0-773.5, 779.81-779.89

773.1 Hemolytic disease due to ABO isoimmunization [CC] [N]
ABO hemolytic disease   ABO isoimmunization
Anemia
Erythroblastosis (fetalis)
Hemolytic disease (fetus)
  (newborn)
Jaundice
} due to ABO:
  antibodies
  isoimmunization
  maternal/fetal
    incompatibility
CC Excl: See code 773.0
AHA: 3Q, '92, 8
DEF: Incompatible Rh fetal-maternal blood grouping; prematurely destroys red blood cells; detected by Coombs test.

773.2 Hemolytic disease due to other and unspecified isoimmunization [CC] [N]
Eythroblastosis (fetalis) (neonatorum) NOS
Hemolytic disease (fetus) (newborn) NOS
Jaundice or anemia due to other and unspecified blood-group incompatibility
CC Excl: See code 773.0
AHA: 1Q, '94, 13

773.3 Hydrops fetalis due to isoimmunization [CC] [N]
Use additional code to identify type of isoimmunization (773.0-773.2)
CC Excl: See code 773.0
DEF: Massive edema of entire body and severe anemia; may result in fetal death or stillbirth.

773.4 Kernicterus due to isoimmunization [CC] [N]
Use additional code to identify type of isoimmunization (773.0-773.2)
CC Excl: See code 773.0
DEF: Complication of erythroblastosis fetalis associated with severe neural symptoms, high blood bilirubin levels and nerve cell destruction; results in bilirubin-pigmented gray matter of central nervous system.

773.5 Late anemia due to isoimmunization [N]

√4ᵗʰ 774 Other perinatal jaundice

774.0 *Perinatal jaundice from hereditary hemolyticanemias* [CC] [N]
Code first underlying disease (282.0-282.9)
CC Excl: 774.0-774.7, 779.81-779.89

[N] Newborn Age: 0   [P] Pediatric Age: 0-17   [M] Maternity Age: 12-55   [A] Adult Age: 15-124   [CC] CC Condition   [MC] Major Complication   [CD] Complex Dx   [HIV] HIV Related Dx

774.1 Perinatal jaundice from other excessive hemolysis CC N

Fetal or neonatal jaundice from:
   bruising
   drugs or toxins transmitted from mother
   infection
   polycythemia
   swallowed maternal blood
Use additional code to identify cause
   EXCLUDES   *jaundice due to isoimmunization (773.0-773.2)*

CC Excl: See code 774.0

774.2 Neonatal jaundice associated with preterm delivery CC N

Hyperbilirubinemia of prematurity
Jaundice due to delayed conjugation associated with preterm delivery

CC Excl: See code 774.0

AHA: 3Q, '91, 21

✓5th **774.3 Neonatal jaundice due to delayed conjugation from other causes**

   774.30 Neonatal jaundice due to delayed conjugation, cause unspecified CC N

   CC Excl: See code 774.0

   DEF: Jaundice of newborn with abnormal bilirubin metabolism; causes excess accumulated unconjugated bilirubin in blood.

   774.31 Neonatal jaundice due to delayed conjugation in diseases classified elsewhere CC N

      Code first underlying diseases as:
         congenital hypothyroidism (243)
         Crigler-Najjar syndrome (277.4)
         Gilbert's syndrome (277.4)

   CC Excl: See code 774.0

   774.39 Other CC N

      Jaundice due to delayed conjugation from causes, such as:
         breast milk inhibitors
         delayed development of conjugating system

   CC Excl: See code 774.0

774.4 Perinatal jaundice due to hepatocellular damage CC N

Fetal or neonatal hepatitis
Giant cell hepatitis
Inspissated bile syndrome

CC Excl: See code 774.0

774.5 Perinatal jaundice from other causes CC N

Code first underlying cause as:
   congenital obstruction of bile duct (751.61)
   galactosemia (271.1)
   mucoviscidosis (277.00-277.09)

CC Excl: See code 774.0

774.6 Unspecified fetal and neonatal jaundice N

Icterus neonatorum
Neonatal hyperbilirubinemia (transient)
Physiologic jaundice NOS in newborn
   EXCLUDES   *that in preterm infants (774.2)*

AHA: 1Q, '94, 13; 2Q, '89, 15

774.7 Kernicterus not due to isoimmunization CC N

Bilirubin encephalopathy
Kernicterus of newborn NOS
   EXCLUDES   *kernicterus due to isoimmunization (773.4)*

CC Excl: See code 774.0

✓4th **775 Endocrine and metabolic disturbances specific to the fetus and newborn**

   INCLUDES   transitory endocrine and metabolic disturbances caused by the infant's response to maternal endocrine and metabolic factors, its removal from them, or its adjustment to extrauterine existence

775.0 Syndrome of "infant of a diabetic mother" N

Maternal diabetes mellitus affecting fetus or newborn (with hypoglycemia)

AHA: 1Q, '04, 7-8; 3Q, '91, 5

775.1 Neonatal diabetes mellitus CC N

Diabetes mellitus syndrome in newborn infant

CC Excl: 775.0-775.9, 779.81-779.89

AHA: 3Q, '91, 6

775.2 Neonatal myasthenia gravis CC N

CC Excl: See code 775.1

775.3 Neonatal thyrotoxicosis CC N

Neonatal hyperthyroidism (transient)

CC Excl: See code 775.1

775.4 Hypocalcemia and hypomagnesemia of newborn CC N

Cow's milk hypocalcemia
Hypocalcemic tetany, neonatal
Neonatal hypoparathyroidism
Phosphate-loading hypocalcemia

CC Excl: See code 775.1

775.5 Other transitory neonatal electrolyte disturbances CC N

Dehydration, neonatal

CC Excl: See code 775.1

AHA: 1Q, '05, 9

775.6 Neonatal hypoglycemia CC N

   EXCLUDES   *infant of mother with diabetes mellitus (775.0)*

CC Excl: See code 775.1

AHA: 1Q, '94, 8

775.7 Late metabolic acidosis of newborn CC N

CC Excl: See code 775.1

▲ **775.8 Other neonatal endocrine and metabolic disturbances**

●   **775.81 Other acidosis of newborn** N

      Acidemia NOS of newborn
      Acidosis of newborn NOS
      Mixed metabolic and respiratory acidosis of newborn

●   **775.89 Other neonatal endocrine and metabolic disturbances** N

      Amino-acid metabolic disorders described as transitory

775.9 Unspecified endocrine and metabolic disturbances specific to the fetus and newborn N

✓4th **776 Hematological disorders of fetus and newborn**

   INCLUDES   disorders specific to the fetus or newborn

776.0 Hemorrhagic disease of newborn CC N

Hemorrhagic diathesis of newborn
Vitamin K deficiency of newborn
   EXCLUDES   *fetal or neonatal hemorrhage (772.0-772.9)*

CC Excl: 776.0-776.9, 779.81-779.89

776.1 Transient neonatal thrombocytopenia CC N

Neonatal thrombocytopenia due to:
   exchange transfusion
   idiopathic maternal thrombocytopenia
   isoimmunization

CC Excl: See code 776.0

DEF: Temporary decrease in blood platelets of newborn.

✓4th ✓5th Additional Digit Required   Nonspecific PDx   Unacceptable PDx   Manifestation Code   MCV Major Cardiovascular Condition   ▶◀ Revised Text   ● New Code   ▲ Revised Code Title

Conditions in the Perinatal Period

776.2–779.3

776.2   **Disseminated intravascular coagulation in newborn**   `CC` `N`

CC Excl: See code 776.0

DEF: Disseminated intravascular coagulation of newborn: clotting disorder due to excess thromboplastic agents in blood as a result of disease or trauma; causes blood clotting within vessels and reduces available elements necessary for blood coagulation.

776.3   **Other transient neonatal disorders of coagulation**   `CC` `N`

Transient coagulation defect, newborn

CC Excl: See code 776.0

776.4   **Polycythemia neonatorum**   `N`

Plethora of newborn   Polycythemia due to:
Polycythemia due to: maternal-fetal transfusion
   donor twin transfusion

DEF: Abnormal increase of total red blood cells of newborn.

776.5   **Congenital anemia**   `N`

Anemia following fetal blood loss

EXCLUDES   anemia due to isoimmunization (773.0-773.2, 773.5)
      hereditary hemolytic anemias (282.0-282.9)

776.6   **Anemia of prematurity**   `N`

776.7   **Transient neonatal neutropenia**   `N`

Isoimmune neutropenia
Maternal transfer neutropenia

EXCLUDES   congenital neutropenia (nontransient) ▶(288.01)◀

DEF: Decreased neutrophilic leukocytes in blood of newborn.

776.8   **Other specified transient hematological disorders**   `N`

776.9   **Unspecified hematological disorder specific to fetus or newborn**   `N`

✓4ᵗʰ **777 Perinatal disorders of digestive system**

INCLUDES   disorders specific to the fetus and newborn
EXCLUDES   intestinal obstruction classifiable to 560.0-560.9

777.1   **Meconium obstruction**   `CC` `N`

Congenital fecaliths   Meconium ileus NOS
Delayed passage of meconium   Meconium plug syndrome

EXCLUDES   meconium ileus in cystic fibrosis (277.01)

CC Excl: 777.1-777.9, 779.81-779.89

DEF: Meconium blocked digestive tract of newborn.

777.2   **Intestinal obstruction due to inspissated milk**   `CC` `N`

CC Excl: See code 777.1

777.3   **Hematemesis and melena due to swallowed maternal blood**   `N`

Swallowed blood syndrome in newborn

EXCLUDES   that not due to swallowed maternal blood (772.4)

777.4   **Transitory ileus of newborn**   `N`

EXCLUDES   Hirschsprung's disease (751.3)

777.5   **Necrotizing enterocolitis in fetus or newborn**   `CC` `N`

Pseudomembranous enterocolitis in newborn

CC Excl: See code 777.1

DEF: Acute inflammation of small intestine due to pseudomembranous plaque over ulceration; may be due to aggressive antibiotic therapy.

777.6   **Perinatal intestinal perforation**   `CC` `N`

Meconium peritonitis

CC Excl: See code 777.1

777.8   **Other specified perinatal disorders of digestive system**   `N`

777.9   **Unspecified perinatal disorder of digestive system**   `N`

✓4ᵗʰ **778 Conditions involving the integument and temperature regulation of fetus and newborn**

778.0   **Hydrops fetalis not due to isoimmunization**   `CC` `N`

Idiopathic hydrops

EXCLUDES   hydrops fetalis due to isoimmunization (773.3)

CC Excl: 778.0, 779.81-779.89

DEF: Edema of entire body, unrelated to immune response.

778.1   **Sclerema neonatorum**   `N`

Subcutaneous fat necrosis

DEF: Diffuse, rapidly progressing white, waxy, nonpitting hardening of tissue, usually of legs and feet, life-threatening; found in preterm or debilitated infants; unknown etiology.

778.2   **Cold injury syndrome of newborn**   `N`

778.3   **Other hypothermia of newborn**   `N`

778.4   **Other disturbances of temperature regulation of newborn**   `N`

Dehydration fever in newborn
Environmentally-induced pyrexia
Hyperthermia in newborn
Transitory fever of newborn

778.5   **Other and unspecified edema of newborn**   `N`

Edema neonatorum

778.6   **Congenital hydrocele**   `N`

Congenital hydrocele of tunica vaginalis

778.7   **Breast engorgement in newborn**   `N`

Noninfective mastitis of newborn

EXCLUDES   infective mastitis of newborn (771.5)

778.8   **Other specified conditions involving the integument of fetus and newborn**   `N`

Urticaria neonatorum

EXCLUDES   impetigo neonatorum (684)
     pemphigus neonatorum (684)

778.9   **Unspecified condition involving the integument and temperature regulation of fetus and newborn**   `N`

✓4ᵗʰ **779 Other and ill-defined conditions originating in the perinatal period**

779.0   **Convulsions in newborn**   `CC` `N`

Fits
Seizures   } in newborn

CC Excl: 779.0-779.1, 779.81-779.89

AHA: N-D, '94, 11

779.1   **Other and unspecified cerebral irritability in newborn**   `CC` `N`

CC Excl: See code 779.0

779.2   **Cerebral depression, coma, and other abnormal cerebral signs**   `N`

▶Cerebral ischemia NOS of newborn◀
CNS dysfunction in newborn NOS

EXCLUDES ▶ cerebral ischemia due to birth trauma (767.0)
     intrauterine cerebral ischemia (768.2-768.9)
     intraventricular hemorrhage (772.10-772.14)◀

779.3   **Feeding problems in newborn**   `CC` `N`

Regurgitation of food
Slow feeding   } in newborn
Vomiting

CC Excl: 779.3

AHA: 2Q, '89, 15

`N` Newborn Age: 0   `P` Pediatric Age: 0-17   `M` Maternity Age: 12-55   `A` Adult Age: 15-124   `CC` CC Condition   `MC` Major Complication   `CD` Complex Dx   `HIV` HIV Related Dx

779.4   **Drug reactions and intoxications specific**   `CC` `N`
to newborn
     Gray syndrome from chloramphenicol
         administration in newborn
     EXCLUDES   *fetal alcohol syndrome (760.71)*
                 reactions and intoxications from
                   maternal opiates and
                   tranquilizers (763.5)

     CC Excl: 779.4-779.5

779.5   **Drug withdrawal syndrome in newborn**   `N`
     Drug withdrawal syndrome in infant of dependent
         mother
     EXCLUDES   *fetal alcohol syndrome (760.71)*

     AHA: 3Q, '94, 6

779.6   **Termination of pregnancy (fetus)**   `N`
     Fetal death due to:
         induced abortion
         termination of pregnancy
     EXCLUDES   *spontaneous abortion (fetus) (761.8)*

779.7   **Periventricular leukomalacia**   `CC`
     CC Excl: 772.0-772.2, 772.8, 772.9, 776.0-776.9, 779.7-779.89

     AHA: 4Q, '01, 50, 51

     DEF: Necrosis of white matter adjacent to lateral ventricles with
     the formation of cysts; cause of PVL has not been firmly
     established, but thought to be related to inadequate blood flow in
     certain areas of the brain.

`√5ᵗʰ` **779.8**   **Other specified conditions originating in the**
perinatal period
     AHA: 4Q, '02, 67; 1Q, '94, 15

     779.81 Neonatal bradycardia   `N`
         EXCLUDES   *abnormality in fetal heart rate*
                   or rhythm complicating
                   labor and delivery
                   (763.81-763.83)
                   bradycardia due to birth
                   asphyxia (768.5-768.9)

779.82 Neonatal tachycardia   `N`
     EXCLUDES   *abnormality in fetal heart rate*
               or rhythm complicating
                labor and delivery
                (763.81-763.83)

779.83 Delayed separation of umbilical cord   `N`
     AHA: 4Q, '03, 71

779.84 Meconium staining   `N`
     EXCLUDES   *meconium aspiration (770.11,*
               770.12)
               meconium passage during
               delivery (763.84)

     AHA: 4Q, '05, 83, 88

779.85 Cardiac arrest of newborn   `N`
779.89 Other specified conditions originating   `N`
in the perinatal period
     Use additional code to specify condition
     AHA: ▶1Q, '06, 18; 2Q, '05, 15;◀ 1Q, '05, 9

779.9   **Unspecified condition originating in the**   `N`
perinatal period
     Congenital debility NOS
     Stillbirth NEC

`√4ᵗʰ`
`√5ᵗʰ` Additional Digit Required   Nonspecific PDx   Unacceptable PDx   Manifestation Code   `MCV` Major Cardiovascular Condition   ►◄ Revised Text   ● New Code   ▲ Revised Code Title

2007 ICD•9•CM   **October 2006 • Volume 1 — 259**

16. SYMPTOMS, SIGNS, AND ILL-DEFINED CONDITIONS (780-799)

This section includes symptoms, signs, abnormal results of laboratory or other investigative procedures, and ill-defined conditions regarding which no diagnosis classifiable elsewhere is recorded.

Signs and symptoms that point rather definitely to a given diagnosis are assigned to some category in the preceding part of the classification. In general, categories 780-796 include the more ill-defined conditions and symptoms that point with perhaps equal suspicion to two or more diseases or to two or more systems of the body, and without the necessary study of the case to make a final diagnosis. Practically all categories in this group could be designated as "not otherwise specified," or as "unknown etiology," or as "transient." The Alphabetic Index should be consulted to determine which symptoms and signs are to be allocated here and which to more specific sections of the classification; the residual subcategories numbered .9 are provided for other relevant symptoms which cannot be allocated elsewhere in the classification.

The conditions and signs or symptoms included in categories 780-796 consist of: (a) cases for which no more specific diagnosis can be made even after all facts bearing on the case have been investigated; (b) signs or symptoms existing at the time of initial encounter that proved to be transient and whose causes could not be determined; (c) provisional diagnoses in a patient who failed to return for further investigation or care; (d) cases referred elsewhere for investigation or treatment before the diagnosis was made; (e) cases in which a more precise diagnosis was not available for any other reason; (f) certain symptoms which represent important problems in medical care and which it might be desired to classify in addition to a known cause.

SYMPTOMS (780-789)

AHA: 1Q, '91, 12; 2Q, '90, 3; 2Q, '90, 5; 2Q, '90, 15; M-A, '85, 3

✓4ᵗʰ 780 General symptoms

✓5ᵗʰ 780.0 Alteration of consciousness

EXCLUDES   coma:
        diabetic (250.2-250.3)
        hepatic (572.2)
        originating in the perinatal period
            (779.2)

AHA: 4Q, '92, 20

780.01 Coma   cc

CC Excl: 070.0-070.9, 250.00-251.3, 338.0-338.4, 348.8-348.9, 349.89, 349.9, 430-432.9, 572.2, 780.01-780.09, 780.2, 780.4, 780.91-780.99, 799.81-799.89, 800.00-801.99, 803.00-804.96, 850.0-852.19, 852.21-854.19

AHA: 3Q, '96, 16

DEF: State of unconsciousness from which the patient cannot be awakened.

780.02 Transient alteration of awareness

DEF: Temporary, recurring spells of reduced consciousness.

780.03 Persistent vegetative state   cc

CC Excl: See code 780.01

DEF: Persistent wakefulness without consciousness due to nonfunctioning cerebral cortex.

780.09 Other

Drowsiness	Stupor
Semicoma	Unconsciousness
Somnolence	

780.1 Hallucinations   cc

Hallucinations:	Hallucinations:
NOS	olfactory
auditory	tactile
gustatory	

EXCLUDES   those associated with mental
            disorders, as functional
            psychoses (295.0-298.9)
        organic brain syndromes (290.0-294.9,
            310.0-310.9)
        visual hallucinations (368.16)

CC Excl: 338.0-338.4, 780.1, 780.4, 780.91-780.99, 799.81-799.89

DEF: Perception of external stimulus in absence of stimulus; inability to distinguish between real and imagined.

780.2 Syncope and collapse

Blackout	(Near) (Pre) syncope
Fainting	Vasovagal attack

EXCLUDES   carotid sinus syncope (337.0)
        heat syncope (992.1)
        neurocirculatory asthenia (306.2)
        orthostatic hypotension (458.0)
        shock NOS (785.50)

AHA: 1Q, '02, 6; 3Q, '00, 12; 3Q, '95, 14; N-D, '85, 12

DEF: Sudden unconsciousness due to reduced blood flow to brain.

✓5ᵗʰ 780.3 Convulsions

EXCLUDES   convulsions:
            epileptic (345.10-345.91)
            in newborn (779.0)

AHA: 2Q, '97, 8; 1Q, '97, 12; 3Q, '94, 9; 1Q, '93, 24; 4Q, '92, 23; N-D, '87, 12

DEF: Sudden, involuntary contractions of the muscles.

780.31 Febrile convulsions (simple), unspecified   cc
        Febrile seizure ▶NOS◀

CC Excl: 338.0-338.4, 345.00-345.91, 348.81-348.9, 349.89, 349.9, 779.0-779.1, 780.31, 780.39, 780.91-780.99, 799.81-799.89

AHA: 4Q, '97, 45

780.32 Complex febrile convulsions   cc
        Febrile seizure:
            atypical
            complex
            complicated

EXCLUDES   status epilepticus (345.3)

CC Excl: See code 780.31

780.39 Other convulsions   cc
        Convulsive disorder NOS
        Fit NOS
        ▶Recurrent convulsions NOS◀
        Seizure NOS

CC Excl: See code 780.31

AHA: 4Q, '04, 51; 1Q, '03, 7; 2Q, '99, 17; 4Q, '98, 39

780.4 Dizziness and giddiness

Light-headedness	Vertigo NOS

EXCLUDES   Ménière's disease and other specified
            vertiginous syndromes (386.0-
            386.9)

AHA: 2Q, '03, 11; 3Q, '00, 12; 2Q, '97, 9; 2Q, '91, 17

DEF: Whirling sensations in head with feeling of falling.

✓5ᵗʰ 780.5 Sleep disturbances

EXCLUDES   circadian rhythm sleep disorders
            (327.30-327.39)
        organic hypersomnia (327.10-327.19)
        organic insomnia (327.00-327.09)
        organic sleep apnea (327.20-327.29)
        organic sleep related movement
            disorders (327.51-327.59)
        parasomnias (327.40-327.49)
        that of nonorganic origin (307.40-
            307.49)

AHA: 4Q, '05, 59

780.50 Sleep disturbance, unspecified

780.51 Insomnia with sleep apnea, unspecified

DEF: Transient cessation of breathing disturbing sleep.

780.52 Insomnia, unspecified

DEF: Inability to maintain adequate sleep cycle.

780.53 Hypersomnia with sleep apnea, unspecified

AHA: 1Q, '93, 28; N-D, '85, 4

DEF: Autonomic response inhibited during sleep; causes insufficient oxygen intake, acidosis and pulmonary hypertension.

780.54 Hypersomnia, unspecified

DEF: Prolonged sleep cycle.

780.55 Disruptions of 24 hour sleep wake cycle, unspecified

✓4ᵗʰ ✓5ᵗʰ Additional Digit Required   Nonspecific PDx   Unacceptable PDx   Manifestation Code   MCV Major Cardiovascular Condition   ▶◀ Revised Text   ● New Code   ▲ Revised Code Title

2007 ICD•9•CM   October 2006 • Volume 1 — 261

Symptoms, Signs, and Ill-Defined Conditions

780.56–781.0

780.56 Dysfunctions associated with sleep stages or arousal from sleep

780.57 Unspecified sleep apnea
AHA: 1Q, '01, 6 ; 1Q, '97, 5; 1Q, '93, 28

780.58 Sleep related movement disorder, unspecified
> EXCLUDES ▶ restless legs syndrome (333.94)◀
AHA: 4Q, '04, 95

780.59 Other

780.6 Fever

Chills with fever	Hyperpyrexia NOS
Fever NOS	Pyrexia
Fever of unknown origin (FUO)	Pyrexia of unknown origin

▶Code first underlying condition when associated fever is present, such as with:
leukemia (codes from categories 204-208)
neutropenia (288.00-288.09)
sickle-cell disease (282.60-282.69)◀
EXCLUDES pyrexia of unknown origin (during):
in newborn (778.4)
labor (659.2)
the puerperium (672)
AHA: 3Q, '05, 16; 3Q, '00,13; 4Q, '99, 26; 2Q, '91, 8
DEF: Elevated body temperature; no known cause.

✓5ᵗʰ **780.7 Malaise and fatigue**
EXCLUDES debility, unspecified (799.3)
fatigue (during):
combat (308.0-308.9)
heat (992.6)
pregnancy (646.8)
neurasthenia (300.5)
senile asthenia (797)
AHA: 4Q, '88, 12; M-A, '87, 8

780.71 Chronic fatigue syndrome
AHA: 4Q, '98, 48
DEF: Persistent fatigue, symptoms include weak muscles, sore throat, lymphadenitis, headache, depression and mild fever; no known cause; also called chronic mononucleosis, benign myalgic encephalomyelitis, Iceland disease and neurosthenia.

780.79 Other malaise and fatigue

Asthenia NOS	Postviral (asthenic) syndrome
Lethargy	Tiredness

AHA: 4Q, '04, 78; 1Q, '00, 6; 4Q, '99, 26
DEF: Asthenia: Any weakness, lack of strength or loss of energy, especially neuromuscular.
DEF: Lethargy: Listlessness, drowsiness, stupor and apathy.
DEF: Malaise: Vague feeling of debility or lack of good health.
DEF: Postviral (asthenic) syndrome: Listlessness, drowsiness, stupor and apathy; follows acute viral infection.
DEF: Tiredness: General exhaustion or fatigue.

780.8 Generalized hyperhidrosis
Diaphoresis
Excessive sweating
Secondary hyperhidrosis
EXCLUDES focal (localized) (primary) (secondary) hyperhidrosis (705.21-705.22)
Frey's syndrome (705.22)
DEF: Excessive sweating, appears as droplets on skin; general or localized.

✓5ᵗʰ **780.9 Other general symptoms**
EXCLUDES hypothermia:
NOS (accidental) (991.6)
due to anesthesia (995.89)
of newborn (778.2-778.3)
memory disturbance as part of a pattern of mental disorder
AHA: 4Q, '02, 67; 4Q, '99, 10; 3Q, '93, 11; N-D, '85, 12

780.91 Fussy infant (baby) [P]

780.92 Excessive crying of infant (baby) [N]
EXCLUDES excessive crying of child, adolescent or adult (780.95)

780.93 Memory loss
Amnesia (retrograde)
Memory loss NOS
EXCLUDES mild memory disturbance due to organic brain damage (310.1)
transient global amnesia (437.7)
AHA: 4Q, '03, 71

780.94 Early satiety
AHA: 4Q, '03, 72
DEF: The premature feeling of being full; mechanism of satiety is mutlifactorial.

▲ **780.95 Excessive crying of child, adolescent, or adult**
EXCLUDES excessive crying of infant (baby) (780.92)
AHA: 4Q, '05, 89

● **780.96 Generalized pain**
Pain NOS

● **780.97 Altered mental status**
Change in mental status
EXCLUDES altered level of consciousness (780.01-780.09)
altered mental status due to known condition—code to condition
delirium NOS (780.09)

780.99 Other general symptoms
Chill(s) NOS
Hypothermia, not associated with low environmental temperature
AHA: 4Q, '03, 103

✓4ᵗʰ **781 Symptoms involving nervous and musculoskeletal systems**
EXCLUDES depression NOS (311)
disorders specifically relating to:
back (724.0-724.9)
hearing (388.0-389.9)
joint (718.0-719.9)
limb (729.0-729.9)
neck (723.0-723.9)
vision (368.0-369.9)
pain in limb (729.5)

781.0 Abnormal involuntary movements

Abnormal head movements	Spasms NOS
Fasciculation	Tremor NOS

EXCLUDES abnormal reflex (796.1)
chorea NOS (333.5)
infantile spasms (345.60-345.61)
spastic paralysis (342.1, 343.0-344.9)
specified movement disorders classifiable to 333 (333.0-333.9)
that of nonorganic origin (307.2-307.3)

[N] Newborn Age: 0   [P] Pediatric Age: 0-17   [M] Maternity Age: 12-55   [A] Adult Age: 15-124   [CC] CC Condition   [MC] Major Complication   [CD] Complex Dx   [HIV] HIV Related Dx

262 — Volume 1 • October 2006   2007 ICD•9•CM

781.1 Disturbances of sensation of smell and taste

Anosmia   Parosmia
Parageusia

DEF: Anosmia: loss of sense of smell due to organic factors, including loss of olfactory nerve conductivity, cerebral disease, nasal fossae formation and peripheral olfactory nerve diseases; can also be psychological disorder.

DEF: Parageusia: distorted sense of taste, or bad taste in mouth.

DEF: Parosmia: distorted sense of smell.

781.2 Abnormality of gait

Gait: Gait:
  ataxic   spastic
  paralytic   staggering

EXCLUDES   *ataxia:*
    NOS (781.3)
    locomotor (progressive) (094.0)
    difficulty in walking (719.7)

AHA: 2Q, '05, 6; 2Q, '04, 15

DEF: Abnormal, asymmetric gait.

781.3 Lack of coordination

Ataxia NOS   Muscular incoordination

EXCLUDES   *ataxic gait (781.2)*
    cerebellar ataxia (334.0-334.9)
    difficulty in walking (719.7)
    vertigo NOS (780.4)

AHA: 4Q, '04, 51; 3Q, '97, 12

781.4 Transient paralysis of limb

Monoplegia, transient NOS

EXCLUDES   *paralysis (342.0-344.9)*

781.5 Clubbing of fingers

DEF: Enlarged soft tissue of distal fingers.

781.6 Meningismus

Dupré's syndrome   Meningism

AHA: 3Q, '00,13; J-F, '87, 7

DEF: Condition with signs and symptoms that resemble meningeal irritation; it is associated with febrile illness and dehydration with no evidence of infection.

781.7 Tetany   CC

Carpopedal spasm

EXCLUDES   *tetanus neonatorum (771.3)*
    tetany:
      hysterical (300.11)
      newborn (hypocalcemic) (775.4)
      parathyroid (252.1)
      psychogenic (306.0)

CC Excl: 037, 332.0-334.4, 338.0-338.4, 342.10-342.12, 771.3, 780.91-780.99, 781.7, 799.81-799.89

DEF: Nerve and muscle hyperexcitability; symptoms include muscle spasms, twitching, cramps, laryngospasm with inspiratory stridor, hyperreflexia and choreiform movements.

781.8 Neurologic neglect syndrome

Asomatognosia   Left-sided neglect
Hemi-akinesia   Sensory extinction
Hemi-inattention   Sensory neglect
Hemispatial neglect   Visuospatial neglect

AHA: 4Q, '94, 37

√5ᵗʰ 781.9 Other symptoms involving nervous and musculoskeletal systems

AHA: 4Q, '00, 45

781.91 Loss of height

EXCLUDES   *osteoporosis (733.00-733.09)*

781.92 Abnormal posture

781.93 Ocular torticollis

AHA: 4Q, '02, 68

DEF: Abnormal head posture as a result of a contracted state of cervical muscles to correct a visual disturbance; either double vision or a visual field defect.

781.94 Facial weakness

Facial droop

EXCLUDES   *facial weakness due to late effect of cerebrovascular accident (438.83)*

AHA: 4Q, '03, 72

781.99 Other symptoms involving nervous and musculoskeletal systems

√4ᵗʰ 782 Symptoms involving skin and other integumentary tissue

EXCLUDES   *symptoms relating to breast (611.71-611.79)*

782.0 Disturbance of skin sensation

Anesthesia of skin   Numbness
Burning or prickling sensation   Paresthesia
Hyperesthesia   Tingling
Hypoesthesia

782.1 Rash and other nonspecific skin eruption

Exanthem

EXCLUDES   *vesicular eruption (709.8)*

782.2 Localized superficial swelling, mass, or lump

Subcutaneous nodules

EXCLUDES   *localized adiposity (278.1)*

782.3 Edema

Anasarca
Dropsy
Localized edema NOS

EXCLUDES   *ascites (789.5)*
    edema of:
      newborn NOS (778.5)
      pregnancy (642.0-642.9, 646.1)
    fluid retention (276.6)
    hydrops fetalis (773.3, 778.0)
    hydrothorax (511.8)
    nutritional edema (260, 262)

AHA: 2Q, '00, 18

DEF: Edema: excess fluid in intercellular body tissue.

DEF: Anasarca: massive edema in all body tissues.

DEF: Dropsy: serous fluid accumulated in body cavity or cellular tissue.

DEF: Localized edema: edema in specific body areas.

782.4 Jaundice, unspecified, not of newborn

Cholemia NOS
Icterus NOS

EXCLUDES   *jaundice in newborn (774.0-774.7)*
    due to isoimmunization (773.0-773.2, 773.4)

DEF: Bilirubin deposits of skin, causing yellow cast.

782.5 Cyanosis

EXCLUDES   *newborn (770.83)*

DEF: Deficient oxygen of blood; causes blue cast to skin.

√5ᵗʰ 782.6 Pallor and flushing

782.61 Pallor

782.62 Flushing

Excessive blushing

782.7 Spontaneous ecchymoses

Petechiae

EXCLUDES   *ecchymosis in fetus or newborn (772.6)*
    purpura (287.0-287.9)

DEF: Hemorrhagic spots of skin; resemble freckles.

782.8 Changes in skin texture

Induration } of skin
Thickening

782.9 Other symptoms involving skin and integumentary tissues

√4ᵗʰ 783 Symptoms concerning nutrition, metabolism, and development

783.0 Anorexia

Loss of appetite

EXCLUDES   *anorexia nervosa (307.1)*
    loss of appetite of nonorganic origin (307.59)

√4ᵗʰ √5ᵗʰ Additional Digit Required   Nonspecific PDx   Unacceptable PDx   Manifestation Code   **MCV** Major Cardiovascular Condition   ►◄ Revised Text   ● New Code   ▲ Revised Code Title

2007 ICD•9•CM   **Volume 1 — 263**

Symptoms, Signs, and Ill-Defined Conditions

783.1–785.3

783.1 Abnormal weight gain

> EXCLUDES   excessive weight gain in pregnancy
> (646.1)
> obesity (278.00)
> morbid (278.01)

√5ᵗʰ 783.2 Abnormal loss of weight and underweight
Use additional code to identify Body Mass Index
(BMI), if known ▶(V85.0-V85.54)◀
AHA: 4Q, '00, 45

783.21 Loss of weight
AHA: 4Q, '05, 96

783.22 Underweight
AHA: 4Q, '05, 96

783.3 Feeding difficulties and mismanagement
Feeding problem (elderly) (infant)

> EXCLUDES   feeding disturbance or problems:
> in newborn (779.3)
> of nonorganic origin (307.50-307.59

AHA: 3Q, '97, 12

**√5ᵗʰ 783.4 Lack of expected normal physiological development
in childhood**

> EXCLUDES   delay in sexual development and
> puberty (259.0)
> gonadal dysgenesis (758.6)
> pituitary dwarfism (253.3)
> slow fetal growth and fetal malnutrition
> (764.00-764.99)
> specific delays in mental development
> (315.0-315.9)

AHA: 4Q, '00, 45; 3Q, '97, 4

**783.40 Lack of normal physiological development,
unspecified**
Inadequate development
Lack of development

783.41 Failure to thrive   **P**
Failure to gain weight
AHA: 1Q, '03, 12

DEF: Organic failure to thrive: acute or chronic illness
that interferes with nutritional intake, absorption,
metabolism excretion and energy requirements.
Nonorganic FTT is symptom of neglect or abuse.

783.42 Delayed milestones   **P**
Late talker   Late walker

783.43 Short stature
Growth failure   Lack of growth
Growth retardation   Physical retardation

DEF: Constitutional short stature: stature inconsistent
with chronological age. Genetic short stature is when
skeletal maturation matches chronological age.

783.5 Polydipsia
Excessive thirst

783.6 Polyphagia
Excessive eating   Hyperalimentation NOS

> EXCLUDES   disorders of eating of nonorganic origin
> (307.50-307.59)

783.7 Adult failure to thrive   **A**

**783.9 Other symptoms concerning nutrition, metabolism,
and development**
Hypometabolism

> EXCLUDES   abnormal basal metabolic rate (794.7)
> dehydration (276.51)
> other disorders of fluid, electrolyte, and
> acid-base balance (276.0-276.9)

AHA: 2Q, '04, 3

√4ᵗʰ 784 Symptoms involving head and neck

> EXCLUDES   encephalopathy NOS (348.30)
> specific symptoms involving neck classifiable to
> 723 (723.0-723.9)

784.0 Headache
Facial pain   Pain in head NOS

> EXCLUDES   atypical face pain (350.2)
> migraine (346.0-346.9)
> tension headache (307.81)

AHA: 3Q, '00, 13; 1Q, '90, 4; 3Q, '92, 14

784.1 Throat pain

> EXCLUDES   dysphagia (787.2)
> neck pain (723.1)
> sore throat (462)
> chronic (472.1)

784.2 Swelling, mass, or lump in head and neck
Space-occupying lesion, intracranial NOS
AHA: 1Q, '03, 8

784.3 Aphasia

> EXCLUDES ▶ aphasia due to late effects of
> cerebrovascular disease
> (438.11)◀
> developmental aphasia (315.31)

AHA: 4Q, '04, 78; 4Q, '98, 87; 3Q, '97, 12

DEF: Inability to communicate through speech, written word, or
sign language.

√5ᵗʰ 784.4 Voice disturbance

784.40 Voice disturbance, unspecified

784.41 Aphonia
Loss of voice

784.49 Other
Change in voice   Hypernasality
Dysphonia   Hyponasality
Hoarseness

784.5 Other speech disturbance
Dysarthria   Slurred speech
Dysphasia

> EXCLUDES   stammering and stuttering (307.0)
> that of nonorganic origin (307.0, 307.9)

√5ᵗʰ 784.6 Other symbolic dysfunction

> EXCLUDES   developmental learning delays (315.0-
> 315.9)

784.60 Symbolic dysfunction, unspecified

784.61 Alexia and dyslexia
Alexia (with agraphia)

DEF: Alexia: Inability to understand written word due to
central brain lesion.

DEF: Dyslexia: Ability to recognize letters but inability to
read, spell, and write words; genetic.

784.69 Other
Acalculia   Agraphia NOS
Agnosia   Apraxia

784.7 Epistaxis
Hemorrhage from nose   Nosebleed
AHA: 3Q, '04, 7

784.8 Hemorrhage from throat

> EXCLUDES   hemoptysis (786.3)

√5ᵗʰ 784.9 Other symptoms involving head and neck

784.91 Postnasal drip

784.99 Other symptoms involving head and neck
Choking sensation   Mouth breathing
Halitosis   Sneezing

√4ᵗʰ 785 Symptoms involving cardiovascular system

> EXCLUDES   heart failure NOS (428.9)

785.0 Tachycardia, unspecified
Rapid heart beat

> EXCLUDES   neonatal tachycardia (779.82)
> paroxysmal tachycardia (427.0-427.2)

AHA: 2Q, '03, 11

DEF: Excessively rapid heart rate.

785.1 Palpitations
Awareness of heart beat

> EXCLUDES   specified dysrhythmias (427.0-427.9)

785.2 Undiagnosed cardiac murmurs
Heart murmurs NOS
AHA: 4Q, '92, 16

785.3 Other abnormal heart sounds
Cardiac dullness, increased or decreased
Friction fremitus, cardiac
Precordial friction

N Newborn Age: 0   **P** Pediatric Age: 0-17   **M** Maternity Age: 12-55   **A** Adult Age: 15-124   **CC** CC Condition   **MC** Major Complication   **CD** Complex Dx   **HIV** HIV Related Dx

785.4 Gangrene `CC`
Gangrene:
  NOS
  spreading cutaneous
Gangrenous cellulitis
Phagedena
Code first any associated underlying condition

> `EXCLUDES` gangrene of certain sites — see
>   Alphabetic Index
>   gangrene with atherosclerosis of the
>   extremities (440.24)
>   gas gangrene (040.0

CC Excl: 338.0-338.4, 440.24, 780.91-780.99, 785.4, 799.81-799.89
AHA: 1Q, '04, 14; 3Q, '91, 12; 3Q, '90, 15; M-A, '86, 12
DEF: Gangrene: necrosis of skin tissue due to bacterial infection, diabetes, embolus and vascular supply loss.
DEF: Gangrenous cellulitis: group A streptococcal infection; begins with severe cellulitis, spreads to superficial and deep fascia; produces gangrene of underlying tissues.

√5th **785.5 Shock without mention of trauma**
785.50 Shock, unspecified `CC` `MC` `CD` `MCV`
Failure of peripheral circulation
CC Excl: 338.0-338.4, 780.91-780.99, 785.50-785.59, 785.9, 799.81-799.89
AHA: 2Q, '96, 10
DEF: Peripheral circulatory failure due to heart insufficiencies.

785.51 Cardiogenic shock `CC` `MC` `CD` `MCV`
CC Excl: See code 785.50
AHA: 3Q, '05, 14
DEF: Shock syndrome: associated with myocardial infarction, cardiac tamponade and massive pulmonary embolism; symptoms include mental confusion, reduced blood pressure, tachycardia, pallor and cold, clammy skin.

785.52 Septic shock `CC`
Shock:
  endotoxic
  gram-negative
Code first:
  systemic inflammatory response
    syndrome due to infectious process
    with organ dysfunction (995.92)
CC Excl: See code 785.50
AHA: 2Q, '05, 18-19; 4Q, '03, 73, 79

785.59 Other `CC`
Shock:
  hypovolemic

> `EXCLUDES` shock (due to):
>   anesthetic (995.4)
>   anaphylactic (995.0)
>   due to serum (999.4)
>   electric (994.8)
>   following abortion (639.5)
>   lightning (994.0)
>   obstetrical (669.1)
>   postoperative (998.0)
>   traumatic (958.4)

CC Excl: see code 785.50
AHA: 2Q, '00, 3

785.6 Enlargement of lymph nodes
Lymphadenopathy   "Swollen glands"

> `EXCLUDES` lymphadenitis (chronic) (289.1-289.3)
>   acute (683)

785.9 Other symptoms involving cardiovascular system
Bruit (arterial)   Weak pulse

√4th **786 Symptoms involving respiratory system and other chest symptoms**
√5th **786.0 Dyspnea and respiratory abnormalities**
786.00 Respiratory abnormality, unspecified
786.01 Hyperventilation

> `EXCLUDES` hyperventilation, psychogenic
>   (306.1)

DEF: Rapid breathing causes carbon dioxide loss from blood.

786.02 Orthopnea
DEF: Difficulty breathing except in upright position.

786.03 Apnea `CC`

> `EXCLUDES` apnea of newborn (770.81, 770.82)
>   sleep apnea (780.51, 780.53, 780.57)

CC Excl: 518.81-518.84, 519.8, 519.9, 786.03, 786.04, 799.1
AHA: 4Q, '98, 50
DEF: Cessation of breathing.

786.04 Cheyne-Stokes respiration `CC`
CC Excl: 518.81-518.84, 519.8, 519.9, 786.03, 786.04, 799.1
AHA: 4Q, '98, 50
DEF: Rhythmic increase of depth and frequency of breathing with apnea; occurs in frontal lobe and diencephalic dysfunction.

786.05 Shortness of breath
AHA: 4Q, '99, 25; 1Q, '99, 6; 4Q, '98, 50
DEF: Inability to take in sufficient oxygen.

786.06 Tachypnea

> `EXCLUDES` transitory tachypnea of
>   newborn (770.6)

AHA: 4Q, '98, 50
DEF: Abnormal rapid respiratory rate; called hyperventilation.

786.07 Wheezing

> `EXCLUDES` asthma (493.00-493.92)

AHA: 4Q, '98, 50
DEF: Stenosis of respiratory passageway; causes whistling sound; due to asthma, coryza, croup, emphysema, hay fever, edema, and pleural effusion.

786.09 Other
Respiratory: Respiratory:
  distress   insufficiency

> `EXCLUDES` respiratory distress:
>   following trauma and
>   surgery (518.5)
>   newborn (770.89)
>   syndrome (newborn) (769)
>   adult (518.5)
>   respiratory failure (518.81,
>   518.83-518.84)
>   newborn (770.84)

AHA: 4Q, '05, 90; 2Q, '98, 10; 1Q, '97, 7; 1Q, '90, 9

786.1 Stridor

> `EXCLUDES` congenital laryngeal stridor (748.3)

DEF: Obstructed airway causes harsh sound.

786.2 Cough

> `EXCLUDES` cough:
>   psychogenic (306.1)
>   smokers' (491.0)
>   with hemorrhage (786.3)

AHA: 4Q, '99, 26

786.3 Hemoptysis `CC`
Cough with hemorrhage
Pulmonary hemorrhage NOS

> `EXCLUDES` pulmonary hemorrhage of newborn
>   (770.3)

CC Excl: 338.0-338.4, 780.91-780.99, 786.3-786.4, 786.9, 799.81-799.89
AHA: 4Q, '90, 26
DEF: Coughing up blood or blood-stained sputum.

786.4 Abnormal sputum
Abnormal:
  amount
  color   (of) sputum
  odor
  Excessive

√5th **786.5 Chest pain**
786.50 Chest pain, unspecified
AHA: 1Q, '03, 6; 1Q, '02, 4; 4Q, '99, 25

▽ `DRG` 125

786.51 Precordial pain
DEF: Chest pain over heart and lower thorax.

Symptoms, Signs, and Ill-Defined Conditions

785.4–786.51

√4th Additional Digit Required   `Nonspecific PDx`   `Unacceptable PDx`   `Manifestation Code`   `MCV` Major Cardiovascular Condition   ▶◀ Revised Text   ● New Code   ▲ Revised Code Title
√5th

786.52 Painful respiration
Pain:
    anterior chest wall
    pleuritic
    Pleurodynia
    EXCLUDES   *epidemic pleurodynia (074.1)*
    AHA: N-D, '84, 17

786.59 Other
Discomfort
Pressure   } in chest
Tightness
    EXCLUDES   *pain in breast (611.71)*
    AHA: 1Q, '02, 6
    DRG 125

786.6 Swelling, mass, or lump in chest
    EXCLUDES   *lump in breast (611.72)*

786.7 Abnormal chest sounds
Abnormal percussion, chest   Rales
Friction sounds, chest   Tympany, chest
    EXCLUDES   *wheezing (786.07)*

786.8 Hiccough
    EXCLUDES   *psychogenic hiccough (306.1)*

786.9 Other symptoms involving respiratory system and chest
Breath-holding spell

✓4ᵗʰ **787 Symptoms involving digestive system**
    EXCLUDES   *constipation (564.00-564.09)*
       pylorospasm (537.81)
       congenital (750.5)

✓5ᵗʰ **787.0 Nausea and vomiting**
Emesis
    EXCLUDES   *hematemesis NOS (578.0)*
       vomiting:
         bilious, following gastrointestinal
           surgery (564.3)
         cyclical (536.2)
           psychogenic (306.4)
         excessive, in pregnancy (643.0-
           643.9)
         habit (536.2)
         of newborn (779.3)
         psychogenic NOS (307.54)
    AHA: M-A, '85, 11

787.01 Nausea with vomiting
    AHA: 1Q, '03, 5
    DRG 182

787.02 Nausea alone
    AHA: 3Q, '00, 12; 2Q, '97, 9

787.03 Vomiting alone

787.1 Heartburn
Pyrosis   Waterbrash
    EXCLUDES   *dyspepsia or indigestion (536.8)*
    AHA: 2Q, '01, 6

787.2 Dysphagia
Difficulty in swallowing
    AHA: 4Q, '03, 103, 109; 2Q, '01, 4

787.3 Flatulence, eructation, and gas pain
Abdominal distention (gaseous)
Bloating
Tympanites (abdominal) (intestinal)
    EXCLUDES   *aerophagy (306.4)*
    DEF: Flatulence: excess air or gas in intestine or stomach.
    DEF: Eructation: belching, expelling gas through mouth.
    DEF: Gas pain: gaseous pressure affecting gastrointestinal system.

787.4 Visible peristalsis
Hyperperistalsis
    DEF: Increase in involuntary movements of intestines.

787.5 Abnormal bowel sounds
Absent bowel sounds   Hyperactive bowel sounds

787.6 Incontinence of feces
Encopresis NOS
Incontinence of sphincter ani
    EXCLUDES   *that of nonorganic origin (307.7)*
    AHA: 1Q, '97, 9

787.7 Abnormal feces
Bulky stools
    EXCLUDES   *abnormal stool content (792.1)*
       melena:
         NOS (578.1)
         newborn (772.4, 777.3)

✓5ᵗʰ **787.9 Other symptoms involving digestive system**
    EXCLUDES   *gastrointestinal hemorrhage (578.0-*
          578.9)
       intestinal obstruction (560.0-560.9)
       specific functional digestive disorders:
         esophagus (530.0-530.9)
         stomach and duodenum (536.0-
           536.9)
       those not elsewhere classified
         (564.00-564.9)

787.91 Diarrhea
Diarrhea NOS
    AHA: 4Q, '95, 54

787.99 Other
Change in bowel habits
Tenesmus (rectal)
    DEF: Tenesmus: Painful, ineffective straining at the rectum with limited passage of fecal matter.

✓4ᵗʰ **788 Symptoms involving urinary system**
    EXCLUDES   *hematuria (599.7)*
       nonspecific findings on examination of the urine
         (791.0-791.9)
       small kidney of unknown cause (589.0-589.9)
       uremia NOS (586)
       ▶*urinary obstruction (599.60, 599.69)*◀

788.0 Renal colic
Colic (recurrent) of: Colic (recurrent) of:
    kidney   ureter
    AHA: 3Q, '04, 8
    DEF: Kidney pain.

788.1 Dysuria
Painful urination   Strangury

✓5ᵗʰ **788.2 Retention of urine**
▶Code, if applicable, any causal condition first,
    such as:
      hyperplasia of prostate (600.0-600.9 with fifth-
        digit 1)◀
    DEF: Accumulation of urine in the bladder due to inability to void

788.20 Retention of urine, unspecified   **CC**
    CC Excl: 274.11, 338.0-338.4, 344.61, 593.3-593.5, 596.0,
    596.4- 596.59, 596.8-596.9, 599.60-599.69, 600.00-602.9,
    753.0-753.9,-780.91-780.99, 788.20-788.29, 788.61-788.69,
    788.9, 799.81-799.89
    AHA: 2Q, '04, 18; 3Q, '03, 12-13; 1Q, '03, 6; 3Q, '96, 10

788.21 Incomplete bladder emptying

788.29 Other specified retention of urine   **CC**
    CC Excl: See code 788.20

✓5ᵗʰ **788.3 Urinary incontinence**
Code, if applicable, any causal condition first,
    such as:
      congenital ureterocele (753.23)
      genital prolapse (618.00-618.9)
    ▶hyperplasia of prostate (600.0-600.9 with fifth-
       digit 1)◀
    EXCLUDES   *that of nonorganic origin (307.6)*
    AHA: 4Q, '92, 22

788.30 Urinary incontinence, unspecified
Enuresis NOS

788.31 Urge incontinence
    AHA: 1Q, '00, 19
    DEF: Inability to control urination, upon urge to urinate.

 Newborn Age: 0   Pediatric Age: 0-17   Maternity Age: 12-55   Adult Age: 15-124   **CC** CC Condition   **MC** Major Complication   **CD** Complex Dx   **HIV** HIV Related Dx

788.32 Stress incontinence, male ♂
> EXCLUDES   *stress incontinence, female (625.6)*

DEF: Inability to control urination associated with weak sphincter in males.

788.33 Mixed incontinence, (male) (female)
Urge and stress
DEF: Urge, stress incontinence: involuntary discharge of urine due to anatomic displacement.

788.34 Incontinence without sensory awareness
DEF: Involuntary discharge of urine without sensory warning.

788.35 Post-void dribbling
DEF: Involuntary discharge of residual urine after voiding.

788.36 Nocturnal enuresis
DEF: Involuntary discharge of urine during the night.

788.37 Continuous leakage
DEF: Continuous, involuntary urine seepage.

788.38 Overflow incontinence
DEF: Leakage caused by pressure of retained urine in the bladder after the bladder has fully contracted due to weakened bladder muscles or an obstruction of the urethra.

788.39 Other urinary incontinence

✓5ᵗʰ **788.4 Frequency of urination and polyuria**
▶Code, if applicable, any causal condition first, such as:
hyperplasia of prostate (600.0-600.9 with fifth-digit 1)◄

788.41 Urinary frequency
Frequency of micturition

788.42 Polyuria
DEF: Excessive urination.

788.43 Nocturia
DEF: Urination affecting sleep patterns.

788.5 Oliguria and anuria
Deficient secretion of urine
Suppression of urinary secretion
> EXCLUDES   *that complicating:*
> *abortion (634-638 with .3, 639.3)*
> *ectopic or molar pregnancy (639.3)*
> *pregnancy, childbirth, or the puerperium (642.0-642.9, 646.2)*

DEF: Oliguria: diminished urinary secretion related to fluid intake.
DEF: Anuria: lack of urinary secretion due to renal failure or obstructed urinary tract.

✓5ᵗʰ **788.6 Other abnormality of urination**
▶Code, if applicable, any causal condition first, such as:
hyperplasia of prostate (600.0-600.9 with fifth-digit 1)◄

788.61 Splitting of urinary stream
Intermittent urinary stream

788.62 Slowing of urinary stream
Weak stream

788.63 Urgency of urination
> EXCLUDES   *urge incontinence (788.31, 788.33)*

AHA: 4Q, '03, 74

DEF: Feeling of intense need to urinate; abrupt sensation of imminent urination.

● **788.64 Urinary hesitancy**
● **788.65 Straining on urination**
788.69 Other

788.7 Urethral discharge
Penile discharge   Urethrorrhea

788.8 Extravasation of urine
DEF: Leaking or infiltration of urine into tissues.

788.9 Other symptoms involving urinary system
Extrarenal uremia   Vesical:
Vesical: tenesmus
pain
AHA: 1Q, '05, 12; 4Q, '88, 1

✓4ᵗʰ **789 Other symptoms involving abdomen and pelvis**
> EXCLUDES   *symptoms referable to genital organs:*
> *female (625.0-625.9)*
> *male (607.0-608.9)*
> *psychogenic (302.70-302.79)*

The following fifth-digit subclassification is to be used for codes 789.0, 789.3, 789.4, 789.6:
  0 **unspecified site**
  1 **right upper quadrant**
  2 **left upper quadrant**
  3 **right lower quadrant**
  4 **left lower quadrant**
  5 **periumbilic**
  6 **epigastric**
  7 **generalized**
  9 **other specified site**
    Multiple sites

✓5ᵗʰ **789.0 Abdominal pain**
Colic: Colic:
NOS   infantile
Cramps, abdominal
> EXCLUDES   *renal colic (788.0)*

AHA: 1Q, '95, 3; For code 789.06: 1Q, '02, 5

789.1 Hepatomegaly
Enlargement of liver

789.2 Splenomegaly
Enlargement of spleen

✓5ᵗʰ **789.3 Abdominal or pelvic swelling, mass, or lump**
Diffuse or generalized swelling or mass:
abdominal NOS
umbilical
> EXCLUDES   *abdominal distention (gaseous) (787.3)*
> *ascites (789.5)*

✓5ᵗʰ **789.4 Abdominal rigidity**

789.5 Ascites   CC
Fluid in peritoneal cavity
CC Excl: 338.0-338.4, 780.91-780.99, 789.30-789.5, 789.9, 799.81-799.89
AHA: 2Q, '05, 8; 4Q, '89, 11
DEF: Serous fluid effusion and accumulation in abdominal cavity.

✓5ᵗʰ **789.6 Abdominal tenderness**
Rebound tenderness

789.9 Other symptoms involving abdomen and pelvis
Umbilical: Umbilical:
bleeding   discharge

NONSPECIFIC ABNORMAL FINDINGS (790-796)
AHA: 2Q, '90, 16

✓4ᵗʰ **790 Nonspecific findings on examination of blood**
> EXCLUDES   *abnormality of:*
> *platelets (287.0-287.9)*
> *thrombocytes (287.0-287.9)*
> *white blood cells ▶(288.00-288.9)◄*

✓5ᵗʰ **790.0 Abnormality of red blood cells**
> EXCLUDES   *anemia:*
> *congenital (776.5)*
> *newborn, due to isoimmunization (773.0-773.2, 773.5)*
> *of premature infant (776.6)*
> *other specified types (280.0-285.9)*
> *hemoglobin disorders (282.5-282.7)*
> *polycythemia:*
> *familial (289.6)*
> *neonatorum (776.4)*
> *secondary (289.0)*
> *vera (238.4)*

AHA: 4Q, '00, 46

790.01 Precipitous drop in hematocrit
Drop in hematocrit

✓4ᵗʰ ✓5ᵗʰ Additional Digit Required | Nonspecific PDx | Unacceptable PDx | Manifestation Code | MCV Major Cardiovascular Condition | ▶◄ Revised Text | ● New Code | ▲ Revised Code Title

Symptoms, Signs, and Ill-Defined Conditions

790.09–791.9

790.09 Other abnormality of red blood cells
Abnormal red cell morphology NOS
Abnormal red cell volume NOS
Anisocytosis
Poikilocytosis

790.1 Elevated sedimentation rate

✓5th **790.2 Abnormal glucose**
EXCLUDES   *diabetes mellitus (250.00-250.93)*
dysmetabolic syndrome X (277.7)
gestational diabetes (648.8)
glycosuria (791.5)
hypoglycemia (251.2)
that complicating pregnancy, childbirth, or puerperium (648.8)
AHA: 4Q, '03, 74; 3Q, '91, 5

790.21 Impaired fasting glucose
Elevated fasting glucose

790.22 Impaired glucose tolerance test (oral)
Elevated glucose tolerance test

790.29 Other abnormal glucose
Abnormal glucose NOS
Abnormal non-fasting glucose
▶Hyperglycemia NOS◄
Pre-diabetes NOS
AHA: 2Q, '05, 21

790.3 Excessive blood level of alcohol
Elevated blood-alcohol
AHA: S-O, '86, 3

790.4 Nonspecific elevation of levels of transaminase or lactic acid dehydrogenase [LDH]

790.5 Other nonspecific abnormal serum enzyme levels
Abnormal serum level of:
acid phosphatase
alkaline phosphatase
amylase
lipase
EXCLUDES   *deficiency of circulating enzymes (277.6)*

790.6 Other abnormal blood chemistry
Abnormal blood level of: Abnormal blood level of:
cobalt   lithium
copper   magnesium
iron   mineral
▶lead◄   zinc
EXCLUDES   *abnormality of electrolyte or acid-base balance (276.0-276.9)*
hypoglycemia NOS (251.2)
▶*lead poisoning (984.0-984.9)*◄
specific finding indicating abnormality of:
amino-acid transport and metabolism (270.0-270.9)
carbohydrate transport and metabolism (271.0-271.9)
lipid metabolism (272.0-272.9)
uremia NOS (586)
AHA: 4Q, '88, 1

790.7 Bacteremia   CC
EXCLUDES   *bacteremia of newborn (771.83)*
septicemia (038)
Use additional code to identify organism (041)
CC Excl: 338.0-338.4, 780.91-780.99, 790.7-790.99, 799.81-799.89
AHA: 2Q, '03, 7; 4Q, '93, 29; 3Q, '88, 12
DEF: Laboratory finding of bacteria in the blood in the absence of two or more signs of sepsis; transient in nature, progresses to septicemia with severe infectious process.
DRG 416

790.8 Viremia, unspecified
AHA: 4Q, '88, 10
DEF: Presence of a virus in the blood stream.

✓5th **790.9 Other nonspecific findings on examination of blood**
AHA: 4Q, '93, 29

790.91 Abnormal arterial blood gases

790.92 Abnormal coagulation profile
Abnormal or prolonged:
bleeding time
coagulation time
partial thromboplastin time [PTT]
prothrombintime [PT]
EXCLUDES   *coagulation (hemorrhagic) disorders (286.0-286.9)*

790.93 Elevated prostate specific antigen, [PSA]   A ♂

790.94 Euthyroid sick syndrome
AHA: 4Q, '97, 45
DEF: Transient alteration of thyroid hormone metabolism due to nonthyroid illness or stress.

790.95 Elevated C-reactive protein [CRP]
DEF: Inflammation in an arterial wall results in elevated C-reactive protein (CRP) in the blood; CRP is a recognized risk factor in cardiovascular disease.

790.99 Other
AHA: 2Q, '03, 14

✓4th **791 Nonspecific findings on examination of urine**
EXCLUDES   *hematuria NOS (599.7)*
specific findings indicating abnormality of:
amino-acid transport and metabolism (270.0-270.9)
carbohydrate transport and metabolism (271.0-271.9)

791.0 Proteinuria
Albuminuria
Bence-Jones proteinuria
EXCLUDES   *postural proteinuria (593.6)*
that arising during pregnancy or the puerperium (642.0-642.9, 646.2)
AHA: 3Q, '91, 8
DEF: Excess protein in urine.

791.1 Chyluria   CC
EXCLUDES   *filarial (125.0-125.9)*
CC Excl: 338.0-338.4, 780.91-780.99, 791.1, 791.9, 799.81-799.89
DEF: Excess chyle in urine.

791.2 Hemoglobinuria
DEF: Free hemoglobin in blood due to rapid hemolysis of red blood cells.

791.3 Myoglobinuria   CC
CC Excl: 338.0-338.4, 780.91-780.99, 791.2-791.3, 791.9, 799.81-799.89
DEF: Myoglobin (oxygen-transporting pigment) in urine.

791.4 Biliuria
DEF: Bile pigments in urine.

791.5 Glycosuria
EXCLUDES   *renal glycosuria (271.4)*
DEF: Sugar in urine.

791.6 Acetonuria
Ketonuria
DEF: Excess acetone in urine.

791.7 Other cells and casts in urine

791.9 Other nonspecific findings on examination of urine
Crystalluria   Elevated urine levels of:
Elevated urine levels of: indolacetic acid
17-ketosteroids   vanillylmandelic acid [VMA]
catecholamines   Melanuria
AHA: 1Q, '05, 12

N Newborn Age: 0   P Pediatric Age: 0-17   M Maternity Age: 12-55   A Adult Age: 15-124   CC CC Condition   MC Major Complication   CD Complex Dx   HIV HIV Related Dx

268 — Volume 1 • October 2006   2007 ICD•9•CM

√4ᵗʰ **792 Nonspecific abnormal findings in other body substances**

> EXCLUDES *that in chromosomal analysis (795.2)*

792.0 Cerebrospinal fluid

792.1 Stool contents
Abnormal stool color   Occult stool
Fat in stool   Pus in stool
Mucus in stool

> EXCLUDES *blood in stool [melena] (578.1)*
> *newborn (772.4, 777.3)*

AHA: 2Q, '92, 9

792.2 Semen   ♂
Abnormal spermatozoa

> EXCLUDES *azoospermia (606.0)*
> *oligospermia (606.1)*

792.3 Amniotic fluid   M ♀
AHA: N-D, '86, 4
DEF: Nonspecific abnormal findings in amniotic fluid.

792.4 Saliva

> EXCLUDES *that in chromosomal analysis (795.2)*

792.5 Cloudy (hemodialysis) (peritoneal) dialysis effluent
AHA: 4Q, '00, 46

792.9 Other nonspecific abnormal findings in body substances
Peritoneal fluid   Synovial fluid
Pleural fluid   Vaginal fluids

√4ᵗʰ **793 Nonspecific abnormal findings on radiological and other examination of body structure**

> INCLUDES nonspecific abnormal findings of:
> thermography
> ultrasound examination [echogram]
> x-ray examination

> EXCLUDES *abnormal results of function studies and radioisotope scans (794.0-794.9)*

793.0 Skull and head

> EXCLUDES *nonspecific abnormal echoencephalogram (794.01)*

793.1 Lung field
Coin lesion ⎫
Shadow   ⎬ (of) lung

DEF: Coin lesion of lung: coin-shaped, solitary pulmonary nodule.

793.2 Other intrathoracic organ
Abnormal: Abnormal:
echocardiogram   ultrasound cardiogram
heart shadow   Mediastinal shift

793.3 Biliary tract
Nonvisualization of gallbladder

793.4 Gastrointestinal tract

793.5 Genitourinary organs
Filling defect: Filling defect:
bladder   ureter
kidney

793.6 Abdominal area, including retroperitoneum

793.7 Musculoskeletal system

√5ᵗʰ **793.8 Breast**
AHA: 4Q, '01, 51

793.80 Abnormal mammogram, unspecified

793.81 Mammographic microcalcification

> EXCLUDES ▶ *mammographic calcification (793.89)*
> *mammographic calculus (793.89)*◀

DEF: Calcium and cellular debris deposits in the breast that cannot be felt but can be detected on a mammogram; can be a sign of cancer, benign conditions, or changes in the breast tissue as a result of inflammation, injury, or obstructed duct.

793.89 Other abnormal findings on radiological examination of breast
▶Mammographic calcification
Mammographic calculus◀

√5ᵗʰ **793.9 Other**

> EXCLUDES *abnormal finding by radioisotope localization of placenta (794.9)*

● **793.91 Image test inconclusive due to excess body fat**
Use additional code to identify Body Mass Index (BMI), if known (V85.0-V85.54)

● **793.99 Other nonspecific abnormal findings on radiological and other examinations of body structure**
Abnormal:
placental finding by x-ray or ultrasound method
radiological findings in skin and subcutaneous tissue

√4ᵗʰ **794 Nonspecific abnormal results of function studies**

> INCLUDES radioisotope:
> scans
> uptake studies
> scintiphotography

√5ᵗʰ **794.0 Brain and central nervous system**
794.00 Abnormal function study, unspecified
794.01 Abnormal echoencephalogram
794.02 Abnormal electroencephalogram [EEG]
794.09 Other
Abnormal brain scan

√5ᵗʰ **794.1 Peripheral nervous system and special senses**
794.10 Abnormal response to nerve stimulation, unspecified
794.11 Abnormal retinal function studies
Abnormal electroretinogram [ERG]
794.12 Abnormal electro-oculogram [EOG]
794.13 Abnormal visually evoked potential
794.14 Abnormal oculomotor studies
794.15 Abnormal auditory function studies
AHA: 1Q, '04, 15-16
794.16 Abnormal vestibular function studies
794.17 Abnormal electromyogram [EMG]

> EXCLUDES *that of eye (794.14)*

794.19 Other

794.2 Pulmonary
Abnormal lung scan   Reduced:
Reduced: vital capacity
ventilatory capacity

√5ᵗʰ **794.3 Cardiovascular**
794.30 Abnormal function study, unspecified
794.31 Abnormal electrocardiogram [ECG] [EKG]

> EXCLUDES *long QT syndrome (426.82)*

794.39 Other
Abnormal: Abnormal:
ballistocardiogram   vectorcardiogram
phonocardiogram

794.4 Kidney
Abnormal renal function test

794.5 Thyroid
Abnormal thyroid: Abnormal thyroid:
scan   uptake

794.6 Other endocrine function study

794.7 Basal metabolism
Abnormal basal metabolic rate [BMR]

794.8 Liver
Abnormal liver scan

794.9 Other
Bladder   Placenta
Pancreas   Spleen

√4ᵗʰ Additional Digit Required Nonspecific PDx Unacceptable PDx Manifestation Code MCV Major Cardiovascular Condition ▶◀ Revised Text ● New Code ▲ Revised Code Title
√5ᵗʰ

Symptoms, Signs, and Ill-Defined Conditions

795–795.89

✓4th **795 Other and nonspecific abnormal cytological, histological, immunological and DNA test findings**

> EXCLUDES   *nonspecific abnormalities of red blood cells (790.01-790.09)*

✓5th **795.0 Abnormal Papanicolaou smear of cervix and cervical HPV**

Abnormal thin preparation smear of cervix
Abnormal cervical cytology

> EXCLUDES   *carcinoma in-situ of cervix (233.1)*
> *cervical intraepithelial neoplasia I (CIN I) (622.11)*
> *cervical intraepithelial neoplasia II (CIN II) (622.12)*
> *cervical intraepithelial neoplasia III (CIN III) (233.1)*
> *dysplasia (histologically confirmed) of cervix (uteri) NOS (622.10)*
> *mild dysplasia (histologically confirmed) (622.11)*
> *moderate dysplasia (histologically confirmed) (622.12)*
> *severe dysplasia (histologically confirmed) (233.1)*

AHA: 4Q, '02, 69

795.00 Abnormal glandular Papanicolaou smear of cervix ♀
Atypical endocervical cells NOS
Atypical endometrial cells NOS
Atypical glandular cells NOS

795.01 Papanicolaou smear of cervix with atypical squamous cells of undetermined significance [ASC-US] ♀

795.02 Papanicolaou smear of cervix with atypical squamous cells cannot exclude high grade squamous intraepithelial lesion [ASC-H] ♀

795.03 Papanicolaou smear of cervix with low grade squamous intraepithelial lesion [LGSIL] ♀

795.04 Papanicolaou smear of cervix with high grade squamous intraepithelial lesion [HGSIL] ♀

795.05 Cervical high risk human papillomavirus [HPV] DNA test positive ♀

795.06 Papanicolaou smear of cervix with cytologic evidence of malignancy ♀

795.08 Unsatisfactory smear ♀
Inadequate sample

795.09 Other abnormal Papanicolaou smear of cervix and cervical HPV ♀
Cervical low risk human papillomavirus (HPV) DNA test positive
Use additional code for associated human papillomavirus (079.4)

> EXCLUDES   *encounter for Papanicolaou cervical smear to confirm findings of recent normal smear following initial abnormal smear (V72.32)*

795.1 Nonspecific abnormal Papanicolaou smear of other site

795.2 Nonspecific abnormal findings on chromosomal analysis
Abnormal karyotype

✓5th **795.3 Nonspecific positive culture findings**
Positive culture findings in:
nose   throat
sputum   wound

> EXCLUDES   *that of:*
> *blood (790.7-790.8)*
> *urine (791.9)*

795.31 Nonspecific positive findings for anthrax
Positive findings by nasal swab
AHA: 4Q, '02, 70

795.39 Other nonspecific positive culture findings

795.4 Other nonspecific abnormal histological findings

795.5 Nonspecific reaction to tuberculin skin test without active tuberculosis
Abnormal result of   Tuberculin (skin test):
   Mantoux test   positive
PPD positive   reactor

795.6 False positive serological test for syphilis
False positive Wassermann reaction

✓5th **795.7 Other nonspecific immunological findings**

> EXCLUDES   ▶ *abnormal tumor markers (795.81-795.89)*
> *elevated prostate specific antigen [PSA] (790.93)*
> *elevated tumor associated antigens (795.81-795.89)*◀
> *isoimmunization, in pregnancy (656.1-656.2)*
> *affecting fetus or newborn (773.0-773.2)*

AHA: 2Q, '93, 6

795.71 Nonspecific serologic evidence of human immunodeficiency virus [HIV]
Inclusive human immunodeficiency [HIV] test (adult) (infant)
Note: This code is **only** to be used when a test finding is reported as nonspecific. Asymptomatic positive findings are coded to V08. If any HIV infection symptom or condition is present, see code 042. Negative findings are not coded.

> EXCLUDES   *acquired immunodeficiency syndrome [AIDS] (042)*
> *asymptomatic human immuno-deficiency virus, [HIV] infection status (V08)*
> *HIV infection, symptomatic (042)*
> *human immunodeficiency virus [HIV] disease (042)*
> *positive (status) NOS (V08)*

AHA: 2Q, '04, 11; 1Q, '93, 21; 1Q, '93, 22; 2Q, '92, 11; J-A, '87, 24

795.79 Other and unspecified nonspecific immunological findings
Raised antibody titer
Raised level of immunoglobulins

✓5th **795.8 Abnormal tumor markers**
Elevated tumor associated antigens [TAA]
Elevated tumor specific antigens [TSA]

> EXCLUDES   *elevated prostate specific antigen [PSA] (790.93)*

795.81 Elevated carcinoembryonic antigen [CEA]

795.82 Elevated cancer antigen 125 [CA 125]

795.89 Other abnormal tumor markers

N Newborn Age: 0   P Pediatric Age: 0-17   M Maternity Age: 12-55   A Adult Age: 15-124   CC CC Condition   MC Major Complication   CD Complex Dx   HIV HIV Related Dx

√4th **796 Other nonspecific abnormal findings**

796.0 Nonspecific abnormal toxicological findings
Abnormal levels of heavy metals or drugs in blood, urine, or other tissue
> EXCLUDES   *excessive blood level of alcohol (790.3)*

AHA: 1Q, '97, 16

796.1 Abnormal reflex

796.2 Elevated blood pressure reading without diagnosis of hypertension
Note: This category is to be used to record an episode of elevated blood pressure in a patient in whom no formal diagnosis of hypertension has been made, or as an incidental finding.

AHA: 2Q, '03, 11; 3Q, '90, 4; J-A, '84, 12

796.3 Nonspecific low blood pressure reading

796.4 Other abnormal clinical findings
AHA: 1Q, '97, 16

796.5 Abnormal finding on antenatal screening ♀ M
AHA: 4Q, '97, 46

796.6 Abnormal findings on neonatal screening N
> EXCLUDES   *nonspecific serologic evidence of human immunodeficiency virus [HIV] (795.71)*

AHA: 4Q, '04, 99

796.9 Other

ILL-DEFINED AND UNKNOWN CAUSES OF MORBIDITY AND MORTALITY (797-799)

797 Senility without mention of psychosis

Old age	Senile:
Senescence	debility
Senile asthenia	exhaustion

> EXCLUDES   *senile psychoses (290.0-290.9)*

√4th **798 Sudden death, cause unknown**

798.0 Sudden infant death syndrome P

Cot death	Sudden death of nonspecific
Crib death	cause in infancy

DEF: Death of infant under age one due to nonspecific cause.

798.1 Instantaneous death

798.2 Death occurring in less than 24 hours from onset of symptoms, not otherwise explained
Death known not to be violent or instantaneous, for which no cause could be discovered
Died without sign of disease

798.9 Unattended death
Death in circumstances where the body of the deceased was found and no cause could be discovered
Found dead

√4th **799 Other ill-defined and unknown causes of morbidity and mortality**

√5th **799.0 Asphyxia and hypoxemia**
> EXCLUDES   *asphyxia and hypoxemia (due to):*
> *carbon monoxide (986)*
> *hypercapnia (786.09)*
> *inhalation of food or foreign body (932-934.9)*
> *newborn (768.0-768.9)*
> *traumatic (994.7)*

799.01 Asphyxia CC
CC Excl: 338.0-338.4, 518.81-518.84, 780.91-780.99, 798.0, 799.01-799.1, 799.81-799.89

AHA: 4Q, '05, 90

DEF: Lack of oxygen in inspired air, causing a deficiency of oxygen in tissues (hypoxia) and elevated levels of arterial carbon dioxide (hypercapnia).

799.02 Hypoxemia CC
CC Excl: See code 799.01

AHA: 4Q, '05, 90

DEF: Deficient oxygenation of the blood.

799.1 Respiratory arrest CC
Cardiorespiratory failure
> EXCLUDES   *cardiac arrest (427.5)*
> *failure of peripheral circulation (785.50)*
> *respiratory distress:*
> *NOS (786.09)*
> *acute (518.82)*
> *following trauma and surgery (518.5)*
> *newborn (770.89)*
> *syndrome (newborn) (769)*
> *adult (following trauma and surgery) (518.5)*
> *other (518.82)*
> *respiratory failure (518.81, 518.83-518.84)*
> *newborn (770.84)*
> *respiratory insufficiency (786.09)*
> *acute (518.82)*

CC Excl: 338.0-338.4, 518.81-518.84, 780.91-780.99, 798.0, 799.01-799.1, 799.81-799.89

799.2 Nervousness
"Nerves"

799.3 Debility, unspecified
> EXCLUDES   *asthenia (780.79)*
> *nervous debility (300.5)*
> *neurasthenia (300.5)*
> *senile asthenia (797)*

799.4 Cachexia CC
Wasting disease
►Code first underlying condition, if known◄
CC Excl: 780.91-780.99, 799.3-799.4, 799.81-799.89
AHA: 3Q, '90, 17
DEF: General ill health and poor nutrition.

√5th **799.8 Other ill-defined conditions**

799.81 Decreased libido A
Decreased sexual desire
> EXCLUDES   *psychosexual dysfunction with inhibited sexual desire (302.71)*

AHA: 4Q, '03, 75

799.89 Other ill-defined conditions

799.9 Other unknown and unspecified cause
Undiagnosed disease, not specified as to site or system involved
Unknown cause of morbidity or mortality
AHA: 1Q, '98,.4; 1Q, '90, 20

√4th √5th Additional Digit Required   Nonspecific PDx   Unacceptable PDx   Manifestation Code   MCV Major Cardiovascular Condition ►◄ Revised Text ● New Code ▲ Revised Code Title

2007 ICD•9•CM   **October 2006 • Volume 1 — 271**

17. INJURY AND POISONING (800-999)

Use E code(s) to identify the cause and intent of the injury or poisoning (E800-E999)

Note:

1. The principle of multiple coding of injuries should be followed wherever possible. Combination categories for multiple injuries are provided for use when there is insufficient detail as to the nature of the individual conditions, or for primary tabulation purposes when it is more convenient to record a single code; otherwise, the component injuries should be coded separately.

   Where multiple sites of injury are specified in the titles, the word "with" indicates involvement of both sites, and the word "and" indicates involvement of either or both sites. The word "finger" includes thumb.

2. Categories for "late effect" of injuries are to be found at 905-909.

FRACTURES (800-829)

EXCLUDES   *malunion (733.81)*
nonunion (733.82)
pathological or spontaneous fracture (733.10-733.19)
stress fractures (733.93-733.95)

The terms "condyle," "coronoid process," "ramus," and "symphysis" indicate the portion of the bone fractured, not the name of the bone involved.

The descriptions "closed" and "open" used in the fourth-digit subdivisions include the following terms:

closed (with or without delayed healing):

comminuted	impacted
depressed	linear
elevated	simple
fissured	slipped epiphysis
fracture NOS	spiral
greenstick	

open (with or without delayed healing):

compound	puncture
infected	with foreign body
missile	

A fracture not indicated as closed or open should be classified as closed.

AHA: 4Q, '90, 26; 3Q, '90, 5; 3Q, '90, 13; 2Q, '90, 7; 2Q, '89, 15, S-O, '85, 3

FRACTURE OF SKULL (800-804)

The following fifth-digit subclassification is for use with the appropriate codes in categories 800, 801, 803, and 804:

  0 **unspecified state of consciousness**
  1 **with no loss of consciousness**
  2 **with brief [less than one hour] loss of consciousness**
  3 **with moderate [1-24 hours] loss of consciousness**
  4 **with prolonged [more than 24 hours] loss of consciousness and return to pre-existing conscious level**
  5 **with prolonged [more than 24 hours] loss of consciousness, without return to pre-existing conscious level**
    Use fifth-digit 5 to designate when a patient is unconscious and dies before regaining consciousness, regardless of the duration of the loss of consciousness
  6 **with loss of consciousness of unspecified duration**
  9 **with concussion, unspecified**

√4ᵗʰ **800 Fracture of vault of skull**
     INCLUDES   frontal bone
                     parietal bone

AHA: 4Q,'96, 36

DEF: Fracture of bone that forms skull dome and protects brain.

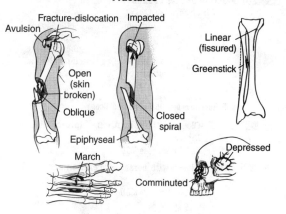

Fractures

√5ᵗʰ **800.0 Closed without mention of intracranial injury**   CC
CC Excl: 800.00-801.99, 803.00-804.99, 829.0-829.1, 850.0-852.19, 852.21-854.19, 873.8-873.9, 879.8-879.9, 905.0, 925.1-925.2, 929.0-929.9, 958.8, 959.01, 959.09, 959.8-959.9

√5ᵗʰ **800.1 Closed with cerebral laceration and contusion**   CC
CC Excl: See code 800.0

√5ᵗʰ **800.2 Closed with subarachnoid, subdural, and extradural hemorrhage**   CC
CC Excl: See code 800.0

√5ᵗʰ **800.3 Closed with other and unspecified intracranial hemorrhage**   CC
CC Excl: See code 800.0

√5ᵗʰ **800.4 Closed with intracranial injury of other and unspecified nature**   CC
CC Excl: See code 800.0

√5ᵗʰ **800.5 Open without mention of intracranial injury**   CC
CC Excl: See code 800.0

√5ᵗʰ **800.6 Open with cerebral laceration and contusion**   CC
CC Excl: See code 800.0

√5ᵗʰ **800.7 Open with subarachnoid, subdural, and extradural hemorrhage**   CC
CC Excl: See code 800.0

√5ᵗʰ **800.8 Open with other and unspecified intracranial hemorrhage**   CC
CC Excl: See code 800.0

√5ᵗʰ **800.9 Open with intracranial injury of other and unspecified nature**   CC
CC Excl: See code 800.0

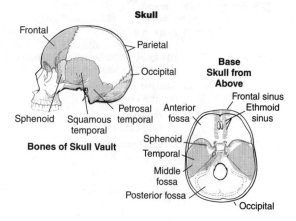

Skull

√4ᵗʰ √5ᵗʰ Additional Digit Required   Nonspecific PDx   Unacceptable PDx   Manifestation Code   **MCV** Major Cardiovascular Condition   ▶◀ Revised Text   ● New Code   ▲ Revised Code Title

2007 ICD•9•CM   **Volume 1 — 273**

Injury and Poisoning

801–802.6

✓4th **801 Fracture of base of skull**

INCLUDES   fossa: sinus:
                 anterior   ethmoid
                 middle   frontal
                 posterior   sphenoid bone
                 occiput bone   temporal bone
                 orbital roof

AHA: 4Q, '96, 36

DEF: Fracture of bone that forms skull floor.

§ ✓5th **801.0**   **Closed without mention of intracranial**   CC
                 injury
                 CC Excl: See code 800.0

§ ✓5th **801.1**   **Closed with cerebral laceration and**   CC
                 contusion
                 CC Excl: See code 800.0

                 AHA: 4Q, '96, 36

§ ✓5th **801.2**   **Closed with subarachnoid, subdural, and**   CC
                 extradural hemorrhage
                 CC Excl: See code 800.0

§ ✓5th **801.3**   **Closed with other and unspecified**   CC
                 intracranial hemorrhage
                 CC Excl: See code 800.0

§ ✓5th **801.4**   **Closed with intracranial injury of other**   CC
                 and unspecified nature
                 CC Excl: See code 800.0

§ ✓5th **801.5**   **Open without mention of intracranial injury**   CC
                 CC Excl: See code 800.0

§ ✓5th **801.6**   **Open with cerebral laceration and**   CC
                 contusion
                 CC Excl: See code 800.0

§ ✓5th **801.7**   **Open with subarachnoid, subdural, and**   CC
                 extradural hemorrhage
                 CC Excl: See code 800.0

§ ✓5th **801.8**   **Open with other and unspecified**   CC
                 intracranial hemorrhage
                 CC Excl: See code 800.0

§ ✓5th **801.9**   **Open with intracranial injury of other and**   CC
                 unspecified nature
                 CC Excl: See code 800.0

✓4th **802 Fracture of face bones**

       AHA: 4Q, '96, 36

       802.0   **Nasal bones, closed**

       802.1   **Nasal bones, open**   CC
                 CC Excl: 800.00-802.1, 803.00-804.99, 829.0-829.1, 850.0-852.19, 852.21-854.19, 873.8-873.9, 879.8-879.9, 905.0, 925.1-925.2, 929.0-929.9, 958.8-959.09, 959.8-959.9

   ✓5th **802.2**   **Mandible, closed**
                 Inferior maxilla   Lower jaw (bone)

           802.20   **Unspecified site**   CC
                   CC Excl: 800.00-801.99, 802.20-802.5, 803.00-804.99, 829.0-830.1, 850.0-852.19, 852.21-854.19, 873.8-873.9, 879.8-879.9, 905.0, 925.1-925.2, 929.0-929.9, 958.8-959.09, 959.8-959.9

           802.21   **Condylar process**   CC
                   CC Excl: See code 802.20

           802.22   **Subcondylar**   CC
                   CC Excl: See code 802.20

           802.23   **Coronoid process**   CC
                   CC Excl: See code 802.20

Facial Fractures

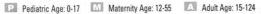

LeFort Fracture Types

Frontal bone, Nasal bone, Orbital floor, Zygomatic bone (malar) and arch, Subcondylar, Body, Angle, Maxilla, Symphysis, Parasymphysis

Type III, Type II, Type I

Common Fracture Sites of Mandible

          802.24   **Ramus, unspecified**   CC
                   CC Excl: See code 802.20

           802.25   **Angle of jaw**   CC
                   CC Excl: See code 802.20

           802.26   **Symphysis of body**   CC
                   CC Excl: See code 802.20

           802.27   **Alveolar border of body**   CC
                   CC Excl: See code 802.20

           802.28   **Body, other and unspecified**   CC
                   CC Excl: See code 802.20

           802.29   **Multiple sites**   CC
                   CC Excl: See code 802.20

   ✓5th **802.3**   **Mandible, open**

           802.30   **Unspecified site**   CC
                   CC Excl: See code 802.20

           802.31   **Condylar process**   CC
                   CC Excl: See code 802.20

           802.32   **Subcondylar**   CC
                   CC Excl: See code 802.20

           802.33   **Coronoid process**   CC
                   CC Excl: See code 802.20

           802.34   **Ramus, unspecified**   CC
                   CC Excl: See code 802.20

           802.35   **Angle of jaw**   CC
                   CC Excl: See code 802.20

           802.36   **Symphysis of body**   CC
                   CC Excl: See code 802.20

           802.37   **Alveolar border of body**   CC
                   CC Excl: See code 802.20

           802.38   **Body, other and unspecified**   CC
                   CC Excl: See code 802.20

           802.39   **Multiple sites**   CC
                   CC Excl: See code 802.20

       802.4   **Malar and maxillary bones, closed**   CC
                 Superior maxilla   Zygoma
                 Upper jaw (bone)   Zygomatic arch
                 CC Excl: See code 802.20

       802.5   **Malar and maxillary bones, open**   CC
                 CC Excl: See code 802.20

       802.6   **Orbital floor (blow-out), closed**   CC
                 CC Excl: 800.00-801.99, 802.6-804.99, 829.0-829.1, 850.0-852.19, 852.21-854.19, 873.8-873.9, 879.8-879.9, 905.0, 925.1-925.2, 929.0-929.9, 958.8-959.09, 959.8-959.9

---

§   Requires fifth-digit. See beginning of section 800-804 for codes and definitions.

N Newborn Age: 0   P Pediatric Age: 0-17   M Maternity Age: 12-55   A Adult Age: 15-124   CC CC Condition   MC Major Complication   CD Complex Dx   HIV HIV Related Dx

Injury and Poisoning

802.7   **Orbital floor (blow-out), open**   `CC`
CC Excl: See code 802.6

802.8   **Other facial bones, closed**   `CC`
Alveolus   Palate
Orbit:
   NOS
   part other than roof or floor
   EXCLUDES   orbital:
          floor (802.6)
          roof (801.0-801.9)
CC Excl: See code 802.6

802.9   **Other facial bones, open**   `CC`
CC Excl: See code 802.6

√4th **803**   **Other and unqualified skull fractures**
   INCLUDES   skull NOS   skull multiple NOS
AHA: 4Q, '96, 36

§ √5th **803.0**   **Closed without mention of intracranial injury**   `CC`
CC Excl: 800.00-801.99, 803.00-804.99, 829.0-829.1, 850.0-852.19, 852.21-854.19, 873.8-873.9, 879.8-879.9, 905.0, 925.1-925.2, 929.0-929.9, 958.8-959.09, 959.8-959.9

§ √5th **803.1**   **Closed with cerebral laceration and contusion**   `CC`
CC Excl: See code 803.0

§ √5th **803.2**   **Closed with subarachnoid, subdural, and extradural hemorrhage**   `CC`
CC Excl: See code 803.0

§ √5th **803.3**   **Closed with other and unspecified intracranial hemorrhage**   `CC`
CC Excl: See code 803.0

§ √5th **803.4**   **Closed with intracranial injury of other and unspecified nature**   `CC`
CC Excl: See code 803.0

§ √5th **803.5**   **Open without mention of intracranial injury**   `CC`
CC Excl: See code 803.0

§ √5th **803.6**   **Open with cerebral laceration and contusion**   `CC`
CC Excl: See code 803.0

§ √5th **803.7**   **Open with subarachnoid, subdural, and extradural hemorrhage**   `CC`
CC Excl: See code 803.0

§ √5th **803.8**   **Open with other and unspecified intracranial hemorrhage**   `CC`
CC Excl: See code 803.0

§ √5th **803.9**   **Open with intracranial injury of other and unspecified nature**   `CC`
CC Excl: See code 803.0

√4th **804**   **Multiple fractures involving skull or face with other bones**
AHA: 4Q, '96, 36

§ √5th **804.0**   **Closed without mention of intracranial injury**   `CC`
CC Excl: See code 803.0

§ √5th **804.1**   **Closed with cerebral laceration and contusion**   `CC`
CC Excl: See code 803.0
AHA: For code 804.10: ►1Q, '06, 6◄

§ √5th **804.2**   **Closed with subarachnoid, subdural, and extradural hemorrhage**   `CC`
CC Excl: See code 803.0

§ √5th **804.3**   **Closed with other and unspecified intracranial hemorrhage**   `CC`
CC Excl: See code 803.0

§ √5th **804.4**   **Closed with intracranial injury of other and unspecified nature**   `CC`
CC Excl: See code 803.0

§ √5th **804.5**   **Open without mention of intracranial injury**   `CC`
CC Excl: See code 803.0

§ √5th **804.6**   **Open with cerebral laceration and contusion**   `CC`
CC Excl: See code 803.0

§ √5th **804.7**   **Open with subarachnoid, subdural, and extradural hemorrage**   `CC`
CC Excl: See code 803.0

§ √5th **804.8**   **Open with other and unspecified intracranial hemorrhage**   `CC`
CC Excl: See code 803.0

§ √5th **804.9**   **Open with intracranial injury of other and unspecified nature**   `CC`
CC Excl: See code 803.0

FRACTURE OF NECK AND TRUNK (805-809)

√4th **805**   **Fracture of vertebral column without mention of spinal cord injury**
   INCLUDES   neural arch   transverse process
               spine   vertebra
               spinous process

The following fifth-digit subclassification is for use with codes 805.0-805.1:
   0   cervical vertebra, unspecified level
   1   first cervical vertebra
   2   second cervical vertebra
   3   third cervical vertebra
   4   fourth cervical vertebra
   5   fifth cervical vertebra
   6   sixth cervical vertebra
   7   seventh cervical vertebra
   8   multiple cervical vertebrae

√5th **805.0**   **Cervical, closed**   `CC`
Atlas   Axis
CC Excl: 805.00-805.18, 805.8-806.19, 806.8-806.9, 829.0-829.1, 839.00-839.18, 839.40, 839.49-839.50, 839.59, 839.69, 839.79-839.9, 847.0, 847.9, 848.8-848.9, 879.8-879.9, 905.1, 926.11, 929.0-929.9, 952.00-952.09, 952.8-952.9, 958.8-958.99, 959.11-959.19, 959.8-959.9
▽ DRG 243

√5th **805.1**   **Cervical, open**   `CC`
CC Excl: See code 805.0

805.2   **Dorsal [thoracic], closed**   `CC`
CC Excl: 805.2-805.3, 805.8-805.9, 806.20-806.39, 806.8-806.9, 829.0-829.1, 839.21, 839.31, 839.40, 839.49-839.50, 839.59, 839.69, 839.79-839.9, 847.1, 847.9, 848.8-848.9, 879.8-879.9, 905.1, 926.11, 929.0-929.9, 952.10-952.19, 952.8-952.9, 958.8-958.99, 959.11-959.19, 959.8-959.9

805.3   **Dorsal [thoracic], open**   `CC`
CC Excl: See code 805.2

805.4   **Lumbar, closed**   `CC`
CC Excl: 805.4-805.5, 805.8-805.9, 806.4-806.5, 806.8-806.9, 829.0-829.1, 839.20, 839.30, 839.40, 839.49-839.50, 839.59, 839.69, 839.79-839.9, 847.2, 847.9, 848.8-848.9, 879.8-879.9, 905.1, 926.11, 929.0-929.9, 952.2, 952.8-952.9, 958.8-958.99, 959.11-959.19, 959.8-959.9
AHA: 4Q, '99, 12
▽ DRG 243

805.5   **Lumbar, open**   `CC`
CC Excl: See code 805.4

805.6   **Sacrum and coccyx, closed**   `CC`
CC Excl: 805.6-805.9, 806.60-806.9, 829.0-829.1, 839.40-839.59, 839.69, 839.79-839.9, 846.0-846.9, 847.3-847.9, 848.5-848.9, 879.8-879.9, 905.1, 926.11, 929.0-929.9, 952.3-952.9, 958.8-958.99, 959.11-959.19, 959.8-959.9

---

§ Requires fifth-digit. See beginning of section 800-804 for codes and definitions.

√4th Additional Digit Required   Nonspecific PDx   Unacceptable PDx   Manifestation Code   **MCV** Major Cardiovascular Condition   ►◄ Revised Text   ● New Code   ▲ Revised Code Title

Vertebral Column

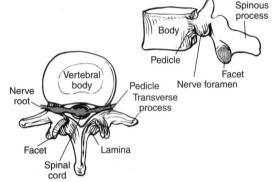

805.7 **Sacrum and coccyx, open** `CC`
CC Excl: See code 805.6

805.8 **Unspecified, closed** `CC`
CC Excl: 733.10-733.19, 733.93-733.95, 805.00-805.9, 806.00-806.9, 829.0-829.1, 839.00-839.59, 839.69, 839.79, 839.8-839.9, 846.0-846.9, 847.0-847.9, 848.5-848.9, 879.8-879.9, 905.1, 926.11, 929.0, 929.9, 952.00-952.9, 958.8-958.99, 959.11-959.19, 959.8-959.9

805.9 **Unspecified, open** `CC`
CC Excl: See code 805.8

√4ᵗʰ **806 Fracture of vertebral column with spinal cord injury**

INCLUDES   any condition classifiable to 805 with:
   complete or incomplete transverse lesion (of cord)
   hematomyelia
   injury to:
      cauda equina
      nerve
   paralysis
   paraplegia
   quadriplegia
   spinal concussion

√5ᵗʰ **806.0** **Cervical, closed**

806.00 C_1-C_4 level with unspecified spinal cord injury `CC`
   Cervical region NOS with spinal cord injury NOS
   CC Excl: 733.10-733.19, 733.93-733.95, 805.00-805.18, 805.8-806.19, 806.8-806.9, 829.0-829.1, 839.00-839.18, 839.40, 839.49-839.50, 839.59, 839.69, 839.79-839.9, 847.9, 848.8-848.9, 879.8-879.9, 905.1, 926.11, 929.0-929.9, 952.00-952.09, 952.8-952.9, 958.8-958.99, 959.11-959.19, 959.8-959.9

806.01 C_1-C_4 level with complete lesion of cord `CC`
CC Excl: See code 806.00

806.02 C_1-C_4 level with anterior cord syndrome `CC`
CC Excl: See code 806.00

806.03 C_1-C_4 level with central cord Syndrome `CC`
CC Excl: See code 806.00

806.04 C_1-C_4 level with other specified spinal cord injury `CC`
   C_1-C_4 level with:
      incomplete spinal cord lesion NOS
      posterior cord syndrome
   CC Excl: See code 806.00

806.05 C_5-C_7 level with unspecified spinal cord injury `CC`
CC Excl: See code 806.00

806.06 C_5-C_7 level with complete lesion of cord `CC`
CC Excl: See code 806.00

806.07 C_5-C_7 level with anterior cord syndrome `CC`
CC Excl: See code 806.00

806.08 C_5-C_7 level with central cord syndrome `CC`
CC Excl: See code 806.00

806.09 C_5-C_7 level with other specified spinal cord injury `CC`
   C_5-C_7 level with:
      incomplete spinal cord lesion NOS
      posterior cord syndrome
   CC Excl: See code 806.00

√5ᵗʰ **806.1** **Cervical, open**

806.10 C_1-C_4 level with unspecified spinal cord injury `CC`
CC Excl: See code 806.00

806.11 C_1-C_4 level with complete lesion of cord `CC`
CC Excl: See code 806.00

806.12 C_1-C_4 level with anterior cord syndrome `CC`
CC Excl: See code 806.00

806.13 C_1-C_4 level with central cord syndrome `CC`
CC Excl: See code 806.00

806.14 C_1-C_4 level with other specified spinal cord injury `CC`
   C_1-C_4 level with:
      incomplete spinal cord lesion NOS
      posterior cord syndrome
   CC Excl: See code 806.00

806.15 C_5-C_7 level with unspecified spinal cord injury `CC`
CC Excl: See code 806.00

806.16 C_5-C_7 level with complete lesion of cord `CC`
CC Excl: See code 806.00

806.17 C_5-C_7 level with anterior cord syndrome `CC`
CC Excl: See code 806.00

806.18 C_5-C_7 level with central cord syndrome `CC`
CC Excl: See code 806.00

806.19 C_5-C_7 level with other specified spinal cord injury `CC`
   C_5-C_7 level with:
      incomplete spinal cord lesion NOS
      posterior cord syndrome
   CC Excl: See code 806.00

N Newborn Age: 0   **P** Pediatric Age: 0-17   **M** Maternity Age: 12-55   **A** Adult Age: 15-124   `CC` CC Condition   `MC` Major Complication   `CD` Complex Dx   `HIV` HIV Related Dx

√5th **806.2** **Dorsal [thoracic], closed**

806.20 **T₁-T₆ level with unspecified spinal cord injury** `CC`

> Thoracic region NOS with spinal cord injury NOS

CC Excl: 733.10-733.19, 733.93-733.95, 805.2-805.3, 805.8-805.9, 806.20-806.39, 806.8-806.9, 829.0-829.1, 839.21, 839.31-839.40, 839.49-839.50, 839.59, 839.69, 839.79, 839.8-839.9, 847.1, 847.9, 848.8-848.9, 879.8-879.9, 905.1, 926.11, 929.0, 929.9, 952.10-952.19, 952.8-952.9, 958.8-958.99, 959.11-959.19, 959.8-959.9

806.21 **T₁-T₆ level with complete lesion of cord** `CC`

CC Excl: See code 806.20

806.22 **T₁-T₆ level with anterior cord syndrome** `CC`

CC Excl: See code 806.20

806.23 **T₁-T₆ level with central cord syndrome** `CC`

CC Excl: See code 806.20

806.24 **T₁-T₆ level with other specified spinal cord injury** `CC`

> T₁-T₆ level with:
> incomplete spinal cord lesion NOS
> posterior cord syndrome

CC Excl: See code 806.20

806.25 **T₇-T₁₂ level with unspecified spinal cord injury** `CC`

CC Excl: See code 806.20

806.26 **T₇-T₁₂ level with complete lesion of cord** `CC`

CC Excl: See code 806.20

806.27 **T₇-T₁₂ level with anterior cord syndrome** `CC`

CC Excl: See code 806.20

806.28 **T₇-T₁₂ level with central cord syndrome** `CC`

CC Excl: See code 806.20

806.29 **T₇-T₁₂ level with other specified spinal cord injury** `CC`

> T₇-T₁₂ level with:
> incomplete spinal cord lesion NOS
> posterior cord syndrome

CC Excl: See code 806.20

√5th **806.3** **Dorsal [thoracic], open**

806.30 **T₁-T₆ level with unspecified spinal cord injury** `CC`

CC Excl: See code 806.20

806.31 **T₁-T₆ level with complete lesion of cord** `CC`

CC Excl: See code 806.20

806.32 **T₁-T₆ level with anteriorr cord syndrome** `CC`

CC Excl: See code 806.20

806.33 **T₁-T₆ level with centralr cord syndrome** `CC`

CC Excl: See code 806.20

806.34 **T₁-T₆ level with other specified spinal cord injury** `CC`

> T₁-T₆ level with:
> incomplete spinal cord lesion NOS
> posterior cord syndrome

CC Excl: See code 806.20

806.35 **T₇-T₁₂ level with unspecified spinal cord injury** `CC`

CC Excl: See code 806.20

806.36 **T₇-T₁₂ level with complete lesion of cord** `CC`

CC Excl: See code 806.20

806.37 **T₇-T₁₂ level with anterior cord syndrome** `CC`

CC Excl: See code 806.20

806.38 **T₇-T₁₂ level with central cord syndrome** `CC`

CC Excl: See code 806.20

806.39 **T₇-T₁₂ level with other specified spinal cord injury** `CC`

> T₇-T₁₂ level with:
> incomplete spinal cord lesion NOS
> posterior cord syndrome

CC Excl: See code 806.20

806.4 **Lumbar, closed** `CC`

CC Excl: 733.10-733.19, 733.93-733.95, 805.4-805.5, 805.8-805.9, 806.4-806.5, 806.8-806.9, 829.0-829.1, 839.20, 839.30, 839.40, 839.49-839.50, 839.59, 839.69, 839.79, 839.8-839.9, 847.2, 847.9, 848.8-848.9, 879.8-879.9, 905.1, 926.11, 929.0, 929.9, 952.2, 952.8-952.9, 958.8-958.99, 959.11-959.19, 959.8-959.9

AHA: 4Q, '99, 11, 13

806.5 **Lumbar, open** `CC`

CC Excl: See code 806.4

√5th **806.6** **Sacrum and coccyx, closed**

806.60 **With unspecified spinal cord injury** `CC`

CC Excl: 733.10-733.19, 733.93-733.95, 805.6-805.9, 806.60-806.9, 829.0-829.1, 839.40-839.59, 839.69, 839.79, 839.8-839.9, 846.0-846.9, 847.0, 847.3-847.9, 848.5-848.9, 879.8-879.9, 905.1, 926.11, 929.0, 929.9, 952.3-952.9, 958.8-958.99, 959.11-959.19, 959.8-959.9

806.61 **With complete cauda equina lesion** `CC`

CC Excl: See code 806.60

806.62 **With other cauda equina injury** `CC`

CC Excl: See code 806.60

806.69 **With other spinal cord injury** `CC`

CC Excl: See code 806.60

√5th **806.7** **Sacrum and coccyx, open**

806.70 **With unspecified spinal cord injury** `CC`

CC Excl: See code 806.60

806.71 **With complete cauda equina lesion** `CC`

CC Excl: See code 806.60

806.72 **With other cauda equina injury** `CC`

CC Excl: See code 806.60

806.79 **With other spinal cord injury** `CC`

CC Excl: See code 806.60

806.8 **Unspecified, closed** `CC`

CC Excl: 733.10-733.19, 733.93-733.95, 805.00-805.09, 806.00-806.9, 829.0-829.1, 839.00-839.59, 839.69, 839.79, 839.8-839.9, 846.0-846.9, 847.0-847.9, 848.5-848.9, 879.8-879.9, 905.1, 926.11, 929.0, 929.9, 952.00-952.9, 958.8-958.99, 959.11-959.19, 959.8-959.9

806.9 **Unspecified, open** `CC`

CC Excl: See code 806.8

√4th 807 Fracture of rib(s), sternum, larynx, and trachea

The following fifth-digit subclassification is for use with codes 807.0-807.1:

0	rib(s), unspecified	5	five ribs
1	one rib	6	six ribs
2	two ribs	7	seven ribs
3	three ribs	8	eight or more ribs
4	four ribs	9	multiple ribs, unspecified

√5th 807.0 Rib(s), closed   `CC 4-9`
CC Excl: For codes 807.04-807.09: 807.00-807.19, 807.4, 819.0-819.1, 828.0-829.1, 848.8-848.9, 879.8-879.9, 929.0-929.9, 958.8-958.99, 959.8-959.9

√5th 807.1 Rib(s), open   `CC`
CC Excl: 807.00-807.19, 807.4, 819.0-819.1, 828.0-829.1, 848.8-848.9, 879.8-879.9, 929.0-929.9, 958.8-958.99, 959.8-959.9

807.2 Sternum, closed   `CC`
CC Excl: 807.2-807.4, 829.0-829.1, 848.8-848.9, 879.8-879.9, 929.0, 929.9, 958.8-958.99, 959.8-959.9
DEF: Break in flat bone (breast bone) in anterior thorax.

807.3 Sternum, open   `CC`
CC Excl: See code 807.2
DEF: Break, with open wound, in flat bone in mid anterior thorax.

807.4 Flail chest   `CC`
CC Excl: 807.00-807.4, 829.0-829.1, 848.8-848.9, 879.8-879.9, 929.0, 929.9, 958.8-958.99, 959.8-959.9

807.5 Larynx and trachea, closed   `CC`
  Hyoid bone   Trachea
  Thyroid cartilage
CC Excl: 807.5-807.6, 829.0-829.1, 848.8-848.9, 879.8-879.9, 929.0, 929.9, 958.8-958.99, 959.8-959.9

807.6 Larynx and trachea, open   `CC`
CC Excl: See code 807.5

√4th 808 Fracture of pelvis

808.0 Acetabulum, closed   `CC`
CC Excl: 733.10-733.19, 733.93-733.95, 808.0-808.1, 808.43-808.49, 808.53-809.1, 829.0-829.1, 835.00-835.13, 843.0-843.9, 846.0-846.9, 879.8-879.9, 929.0-929.9, 958.8-958.99, 959.6, 959.8-959.9

808.1 Acetabulum, open   `CC`
CC Excl: 808.0-808.1, 808.43-808.49, 808.53-809.1, 829.0-829.1, 835.00-835.13, 843.0-843.9, 846.0-846.9, 848.5-848.9, 879.8-879.9, 929.0-929.9, 958.8-958.99, 959.6, 959.8-959.9

808.2 Pubis, closed   `CC`
CC Excl: 733.10-733.19, 733.93-733.95, 808.2-808.3, 808.43-808.49, 808.53-809.1, 829.0-829.1, 835.00-835.13, 843.0-843.9, 846.0-846.9, 848.5-848.9, 879.8-879.9, 929.0-929.9, 958.8-958.99, 959.6, 959.8-959.9

808.3 Pubis, open   `CC`
CC Excl: See code 808.2

Ribs, Sternum, Larynx, and Trachea

Hyoid bone — Mandible
Laryngeal cartilage
Clavicle — Cricoid cartilage
— Trachea
— Manubrium of sternum
— Sternum
Rib cage — Xiphoid process
— Costal cartilages

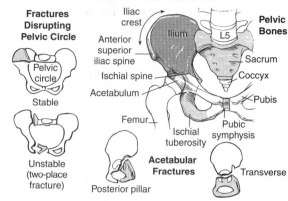

Pelvis and Pelvic Fractures

Fractures Disrupting Pelvic Circle
Pelvic circle
Stable
Unstable (two-place fracture)

Iliac crest
Ilium
L5
Anterior superior iliac spine
Ischial spine
Acetabulum
Femur
Ischial tuberosity
Acetabular Fractures
Posterior pillar
Sacrum
Coccyx
Pubis
Pubic symphysis
Transverse
Pelvic Bones

√5th 808.4 Other specified part, closed
  808.41 Ilium
  808.42 Ischium
  808.43 Multiple pelvic fractures with   `CC`
    disruption of pelvic circle
    CC Excl: 733.10-733.19, 733.93-733.95, 808.0-809.1, 829.0-829.1, 835.00-835.13, 843.0-843.9, 846.0-846.9, 848.5-848.9, 879.8-879.9, 929.0-929.9, 958.8-958.99, 959.6, 959.8-959.9

  808.49 Other   `CC`
    Innominate bone
    Pelvic rim
    CC Excl: See code 808.43

√5th 808.5 Other specified part, open
  808.51 Ilium   `CC`
    CC Excl: 733.10-733.19, 733.93-733.95, 808.41, 808.43-808.49, 808.51, 808.53-809.1, 829.0-829.1, 835.00-835.13, 843.0-843.9, 846.0-846.9, 848.5-848.9, 879.8-879.9, 929.0-929.9, 958.8-958.99, 959.6, 959.8-959.9

  808.52 Ischium   `CC`
    CC Excl: 733.10-733.19, 733.93-733.95, 808.42-808.49, 808.52-809.1, 829.0-829.1, 835.00-835.13, 843.0-843.9, 846.0-846.9, 848.5-848.9, 879.8-879.9, 929.0-929.9, 958.8-958.99, 959.6, 959.8-959.9

  808.53 Multiple pelvic fractures with   `CC`
    disruption of pelvic circle
    CC Excl: 733.10-733.19, 733.93-733.95, 808.0-809.1, 829.0-829.1, 835.00-835.13, 843.0-843.9, 846.0-846.9, 848.5-848.9, 879.8-879.9, 929.0-929.9, 958.8-958.99, 959.6, 959.8-959.9

  808.59 Other   `CC`
    CC Excl: See code 808.53

  808.8 Unspecified, closed   `CC`
    CC Excl: See code 808.53

  808.9 Unspecified, open   `CC`
    CC Excl: See code 808.53

√4th 809 Ill-defined fractures of bones of trunk
  `INCLUDES` bones of trunk with other bones except those of skull and face
    multiple bones of trunk
  `EXCLUDES` *multiple fractures of:*
    pelvic bones alone (808.0-808.9)
    ribs alone (807.0-807.1, 807.4)
    ribs or sternum with limb bones (819.0-819.1, 828.0-828.1)
    skull or face with other bones (804.0-804.9)

  809.0 Fracture of bones of trunk, closed
  809.1 Fracture of bones of trunk, open

`N` Newborn Age: 0   `P` Pediatric Age: 0-17   `M` Maternity Age: 12-55   `A` Adult Age: 15-124   `CC` CC Condition   `MC` Major Complication   `CD` Complex Dx   `HIV` HIV Related Dx

FRACTURE OF UPPER LIMB (810-819)

✓4ᵗʰ **810 Fracture of clavicle**

> INCLUDES   collar bone
> interligamentous part of clavicle

The following fifth-digit subclassification is for use with category 810:

> **0 unspecified part**
> Clavicle NOS
> **1 sternal end of clavicle**
> **2 shaft of clavicle**
> **3 acromial end of clavicle**

✓5ᵗʰ **810.0 Closed**

✓5ᵗʰ **810.1 Open**

✓4ᵗʰ **811 Fracture of scapula**

> INCLUDES   shoulder blade

The following fifth-digit subclassification is for use with category 811:

> **0 unspecified part**
> **1 acromial process**
> Acromion (process)
> **2 coracoid process**
> **3 glenoid cavity and neck of scapula**
> **9 other**

✓5ᵗʰ **811.0 Closed**

✓5ᵗʰ **811.1 Open**

✓4ᵗʰ **812 Fracture of humerus**

✓5ᵗʰ **812.0 Upper end, closed**

> **812.00 Upper end, unspecified part**
> Proximal end   Shoulder
> **812.01 Surgical neck**
> Neck of humerus NOS
> **812.02 Anatomical neck**
> **812.03 Greater tuberosity**
> **812.09 Other**
> Head   Upper epiphysis
> Lesser tuberosity

✓5ᵗʰ **812.1 Upper end, open**

> **812.10 Upper end, unspecified part**
> **812.11 Surgical neck**
> **812.12 Anatomical neck**
> **812.13 Greater tuberosity**
> **812.19 Other**

✓5ᵗʰ **812.2 Shaft or unspecified part, closed**

> **812.20 Unspecified part of humerus**
> Humerus NOS   Upper arm NOS
> Lesser tuberosity
> **812.21 Shaft of humerus**
> AHA: ►4Q, '05, 129;◄ 3Q, '99, 14

✓5ᵗʰ **812.3 Shaft or unspecified part, open**

> **812.30 Unspecified part of humerus**
> **812.31 Shaft of humerus**

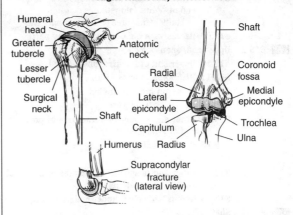

Right Humerus, Anterior View

✓5ᵗʰ **812.4 Lower end, closed**

> Distal end of humerus   Elbow
> **812.40 Lower end, unspecified part**
> **812.41 Supracondylar fracture of humerus**
> **812.42 Lateral condyle**
> External condyle
> **812.43 Medial condyle**
> Internal epicondyle
> **812.44 Condyle(s), unspecified**
> Articular process NOS
> Lower epiphysis NOS
> **812.49 Other**
> Multiple fractures of lower end
> Trochlea

✓5ᵗʰ **812.5 Lower end, open**

> **812.50 Lower end, unspecified part**
> **812.51 Supracondylar fracture of humerus**
> **812.52 Lateral condyle**
> **812.53 Medial condyle**
> **812.54 Condyle(s), unspecified**
> **812.59 Other**

✓4ᵗʰ **813 Fracture of radius and ulna**

✓5ᵗʰ **813.0 Upper end, closed**

> Proximal end
> **813.00 Upper end of forearm, unspecified**
> **813.01 Olecranon process of ulna**
> **813.02 Coronoid process of ulna**
> **813.03 Monteggia's fracture**
> DEF: Fracture near the head of the ulnar shaft, causing dislocation of the radial head.
> **813.04 Other and unspecified fractures of proximal end of ulna (alone)**
> Multiple fractures of ulna, upper end
> **813.05 Head of radius**
> **813.06 Neck of radius**

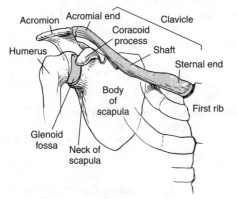

Right Clavicle and Scapula, Anterior View

Right Radius and Ulna, Anterior View

✓4ᵗʰ ✓5ᵗʰ Additional Digit Required   Nonspecific PDx   Unacceptable PDx   Manifestation Code   **MCV** Major Cardiovascular Condition   ►◄ Revised Text   ● New Code   ▲ Revised Code Title

2007 ICD•9•CM   **February 2006 • Volume 1 — 279**

813.07 Other and unspecified fractures of proximal end of radius (alone)

Multiple fractures of radius, upper end

813.08 Radius with ulna, upper end [any part]

✓5th **813.1 Upper end, open**

813.10 Upper end of forearm, unspecified

813.11 Olecranon process of ulna

813.12 Coronoid process of ulna

813.13 Monteggia's fracture

813.14 Other and unspecified fractures of proximal end of ulna (alone)

813.15 Head of radius

813.16 Neck of radius

813.17 Other and unspecified fractures of proximal end of radius (alone)

813.18 Radius with ulna, upper end [any part]

✓5th **813.2 Shaft, closed**

813.20 Shaft, unspecified

813.21 Radius (alone)

813.22 Ulna (alone)

813.23 Radius with ulna

✓5th **813.3 Shaft, open**

813.30 Shaft, unspecified

813.31 Radius (alone)

813.32 Ulna (alone)

813.33 Radius with ulna

✓5th **813.4 Lower end, closed**

Distal end

813.40 Lower end of forearm, unspecified

813.41 Colles' fracture

Smith's fracture

DEF: Break of lower end of radius; associated with backward movement of the radius lower section.

813.42 Other fractures of distal end of radius (alone)

Dupuytren's fracture, radius
Radius, lower end

DEF: Dupuytren's fracture: fracture and dislocation of the forearm; the fracture is of the radius above the wrist, and the dislocation is of the ulna at the lower end.

813.43 Distal end of ulna (alone)

Ulna:
head   lower epiphysis
lower end   styloid process

813.44 Radius with ulna, lower end

813.45 Torus fracture of radius

AHA: 4Q, '02, 70

✓5th **813.5 Lower end, open**

813.50 Lower end of forearm, unspecified

813.51 Colles' fracture

813.52 Other fractures of distal end of radius (alone)

813.53 Distal end of ulna (alone)

813.54 Radius with ulna, lower end

✓5th **813.8 Unspecified part, closed**

813.80 Forearm, unspecified

813.81 Radius (alone)

AHA: 2Q, '98, 19

813.82 Ulna (alone)

813.83 Radius with ulna

✓5th **813.9 Unspecified part, open**

813.90 Forearm, unspecified

813.91 Radius (alone)

813.92 Ulna (alone)

813.93 Radius with ulna

Hand Fractures

✓4th **814 Fracture of carpal bone(s)**

The following fifth-digit subclassification is for use with category 814:

0 carpal bone, unspecified
Wrist NOS

1 navicular [scaphoid] of wrist

2 lunate [semilunar] bone of wrist

3 triquetral [cuneiform] bone of wrist

4 pisiform

5 trapezium bone [larger multangular]

6 trapezoid bone [smaller multangular]

7 capitate bone [os magnum]

8 hamate [unciform] bone

9 other

✓5th **814.0 Closed**

✓5th **814.1 Open**

✓4th **815 Fracture of metacarpal bone(s)**

INCLUDES   hand [except finger]
metacarpus

The following fifth-digit subclassification is for use with category 815:

0 metacarpal bone(s), site unspecified

1 base of thumb [first] metacarpal
Bennett's fracture

2 base of other metacarpal bone(s)

3 shaft of metacarpal bone(s)

4 neck of metacarpal bone(s)

9 multiple sites of metacarpus

✓5th **815.0 Closed**

✓5th **815.1 Open**

✓4th **816 Fracture of one or more phalanges of hand**

INCLUDES   finger(s) thumb

The following fifth-digit subclassification is for use with category 816:

0 phalanx or phalanges, unspecified

1 middle or proximal phalanx or phalanges

2 distal phalanx or phalanges

3 multiple sites

✓5th **816.0 Closed**

✓5th **816.1 Open**

AHA: For code 816.12: 4Q, '03, 77

✓4th **817 Multiple fractures of hand bones**

INCLUDES   metacarpal bone(s) with phalanx or phalanges
of same hand

817.0 Closed

817.1 Open

✓4th **818 Ill-defined fractures of upper limb**

INCLUDES   arm NOS
multiple bones of same upper limb

EXCLUDES   *multiple fractures of:*
metacarpal bone(s) with phalanx or phalanges (817.0-817.1)
phalanges of hand alone (816.0-816.1)
radius with ulna (813.0-813.9)

N Newborn Age: 0   P Pediatric Age: 0-17   M Maternity Age: 12-55   A Adult Age: 15-124   CC CC Condition   MC Major Complication   CD Complex Dx   HIV HIV Related Dx

818.0   **Closed**

818.1   **Open**

√4ᵗʰ   **819   Multiple fractures involving both upper limbs, and upper limb with rib(s) and sternum**

     INCLUDES   arm(s) with rib(s) or sternum
                     both arms [any bones]

819.0   **Closed**

819.1   **Open**

FRACTURE OF LOWER LIMB (820-829)

√4ᵗʰ   **820   Fracture of neck of femur**

√5ᵗʰ   **820.0   Transcervical fracture, closed**

     820.00   Intracapsular section, unspecified   `cc`

         CC Excl: 733.10-733.19, 733.93-733.95, 820.00-821.39,
         827.0-829.1, 843.0-843.9, 848.8-848.9, 879.8-879.9, 929.0-
         929.9, 958.8, 959.6, 959.8-959.9

     820.01   Epiphysis (separation) (upper)   `cc`

         Transepiphyseal

         CC Excl: See code 820.00

     820.02   Midcervical section   `cc`

         Transcervical NOS

         CC Excl: See code 820.00

         AHA: 3Q, '03, 12

     820.03   Base of neck   `cc`

         Cervicotrochanteric section

         CC Excl: See code 820.00

     820.09   Other   `cc`

         Head of femur
         Subcapital

         CC Excl: See code 820.00

√5ᵗʰ   **820.1   Transcervical fracture, open**

     820.10   Intracapsular section, unspecified   `cc`

         CC Excl: See code 820.00

     820.11   Epiphysis (separation) (upper)   `cc`

         CC Excl: See code 820.00

     820.12   Midcervical section   `cc`

         CC Excl: See code 820.00

     820.13   Base of neck   `cc`

         CC Excl: See code 820.00

     820.19   Other   `cc`

         CC Excl: See code 820.00

√5ᵗʰ   **820.2   Pertrochanteric fracture, closed**

     820.20   Trochanteric section, unspecified   `cc`

         Trochanter: Trochanter:
           NOS   lesser
           greater

         CC Excl: See code 820.00

     820.21   Intertrochanteric section   `cc`

         CC Excl: See code 820.00

     820.22   Subtrochanteric section   `cc`

         CC Excl: See code 820.00

√5ᵗʰ   **820.3   Pertrochanteric fracture, open**

     820.30   Trochanteric section, unspecified   `cc`

         CC Excl: See code 820.00

     820.31   Intertrochanteric section   `cc`

         CC Excl: See code 820.00

     820.32   Subtrochanteric section   `cc`

         CC Excl: See code 820.00

     820.8   Unspecified part of neck of femur, closed   `cc`

         Hip NOS   Neck of femur NOS

         CC Excl: See code 820.00

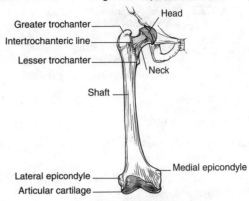

Right Femur, Anterior View

Greater trochanter — Head
Intertrochanteric line
Lesser trochanter — Neck
Shaft
Lateral epicondyle — Medial epicondyle
Articular cartilage

     820.9   Unspecified part of neck of femur, open   `cc`

         CC Excl: See code 820.00

√4ᵗʰ   **821   Fracture of other and unspecified parts of femur**

√5ᵗʰ   **821.0   Shaft or unspecified part, closed**

     821.00   Unspecified part of femur   `cc`

         Thigh   Upper leg

         EXCLUDES   hip NOS (820.8)

         CC Excl: See code 820.00

     821.01   Shaft   `cc`

         CC Excl: See code 820.00

         AHA: 1Q, '99, 5

√5ᵗʰ   **821.1   Shaft or unspecified part, open**

     821.10   Unspecified part of femur   `cc`

         CC Excl: See code 820.00

     821.11   Shaft   `cc`

         CC Excl: See code 820.00

√5ᵗʰ   **821.2   Lower end, closed**

         Distal end

     821.20   Lower end, unspecified part

     821.21   Condyle, femoral

     821.22   Epiphysis, lower (separation)

     821.23   Supracondylar fracture of femur

     821.29   Other

         Multiple fractures of lower end

√5ᵗʰ   **821.3   Lower end, open**

     821.30   Lower end, unspecified part

     821.31   Condyle, femoral

     821.32   Epiphysis, lower (separation)

     821.33   Supracondylar fracture of femur

     821.39   Other

√4ᵗʰ   **822   Fracture of patella**

     822.0   Closed

     822.1   Open

Right Tibia and Fibula, Anterior View

Patella
Tibial plateau
Tibial tubercle
Shaft of fibula
Tibia
Lateral (fibular) malleolus — Medial (tibial) malleolus
Pott's fracture

√4ᵗʰ √5ᵗʰ Additional Digit Required   Nonspecific PDx   Unacceptable PDx   Manifestation Code   MCV Major Cardiovascular Condition   ►◄ Revised Text   ● New Code   ▲ Revised Code Title

2007 ICD•9•CM   Volume 1 — 281

✓4ᵗʰ **823 Fracture of tibia and fibula**

    EXCLUDES *Dupuytren's fracture (824.4-824.5)*
                   ankle (824.4-824.5)
                   radius (813.42, 813.52)
                   Pott's fracture (824.4-824.5)
                   that involving ankle (824.0-824.9)

The following fifth-digit subclassification is for use with category 823:

    0 tibia alone
    1 fibula alone
    2 fibula with tibia

✓5ᵗʰ **823.0 Upper end, closed**
        Head   Tibia:
        Proximal end   condyles
                        tuberosity

✓5ᵗʰ **823.1 Upper end, open**

✓5ᵗʰ **823.2 Shaft, closed**

✓5ᵗʰ **823.3 Shaft, open**

✓5ᵗʰ **823.4 Torus fracture**
        AHA: 4Q, '02, 70

        DEF: A bone deformity in children, occurring commonly in the tibia and fibula, in which the bone bends and buckles but does not fracture.

✓5ᵗʰ **823.8 Unspecified part, closed**
        Lower leg NOS
        AHA: For code 823.82: 1Q, '97, 8

✓5ᵗʰ **823.9 Unspecified part, open**

✓4ᵗʰ **824 Fracture of ankle**

    824.0 Medial malleolus, closed
        Tibia involving: Tibia involving:
           ankle   malleolus
        AHA: 1Q, '04, 9

    824.1 Medial malleolus, open

    824.2 Lateral malleolus, closed
        Fibula involving:
           ankle
           malleolus
        AHA: 2Q, '02, 3

    824.3 Lateral malleolus, open

    824.4 Bimalleolar, closed
        Dupuytren's fracture, fibula   Pott's fracture

        DEF: Bimalleolar, closed: Breaking of both nodules (malleoli) on either side of ankle joint, without an open wound.

        DEF: Dupuytren's fracture (Pott's fracture): The breaking of the farthest end of the lower leg bone (fibula), with injury to the farthest end joint of the other lower leg bone (tibia).

    824.5 Bimalleolar, open

    824.6 Trimalleolar, closed
        Lateral and medial malleolus with anterior or posterior lip of tibia

    824.7 Trimalleolar, open

Torus Fracture

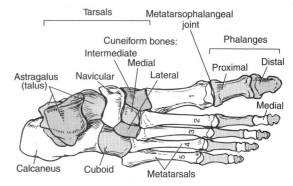

Fibula — Tibia — Diaphysis

Torus, bulging, fracture

Direction of force

Anterior views of torus compression fracture

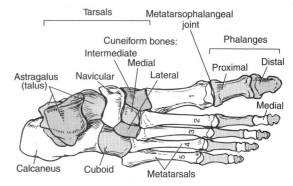

Right Foot, Dorsal

Tarsals — Metatarsophalangeal joint

Cuneiform bones: — Phalanges
  Intermediate — Medial — Proximal — Distal
Astragalus (talus) — Navicular — Lateral — Medial
Calcaneus — Cuboid — Metatarsals

    824.8 Unspecified, closed
        Ankle NOS
        AHA: 3Q, '00, 12

    824.9 Unspecified, open

✓4ᵗʰ **825 Fracture of one or more tarsal and metatarsal bones**

    825.0 Fracture of calcaneus, closed
        Heel bone   Os calcis

    825.1 Fracture of calcaneus, open

✓5ᵗʰ **825.2 Fracture of other tarsal and metatarsal bones, closed**

        825.20 Unspecified bone(s) of foot [except toes]
                Instep

        825.21 Astragalus
                Talus

        825.22 Navicular [scaphoid], foot

        825.23 Cuboid

        825.24 Cuneiform, foot

        825.25 Metatarsal bone(s)

        825.29 Other
                Tarsal with metatarsal bone(s) only
                EXCLUDES *calcaneus (825.0)*

✓5ᵗʰ **825.3 Fracture of other tarsal and metatarsal bones, open**

        825.30 Unspecified bone(s) of foot [except toes]

        825.31 Astragalus

        825.32 Navicular [scaphoid], foot

        825.33 Cuboid

        825.34 Cuneiform, foot

        825.35 Metatarsal bone(s)

        825.39 Other

✓4ᵗʰ **826 Fracture of one or more phalanges of foot**
        INCLUDES toe(s)

    826.0 Closed

    826.1 Open

✓4ᵗʰ **827 Other, multiple, and ill-defined fractures of lower limb**
        INCLUDES leg NOS
                     multiple bones of same lower limb
        EXCLUDES *multiple fractures of:*
                 ankle bones alone (824.4-824.9)
                 phalanges of foot alone (826.0-826.1)
                 tarsal with metatarsal bones (825.29, 825.39)
                 tibia with fibula (823.0-823.9 with fifth-digit 2)

    827.0 Closed

    827.1 Open

✓4ᵗʰ **828 Multiple fractures involving both lower limbs, lower with upper limb, and lower limb(s) with rib(s) and sternum**
        INCLUDES arm(s) with leg(s) [any bones]
                     both legs [any bones]
                     leg(s) with rib(s) or sternum

    828.0 Closed

    828.1 Open

N Newborn Age: 0   **P** Pediatric Age: 0-17   **M** Maternity Age: 12-55   **A** Adult Age: 15-124   **CC** CC Condition   **MC** Major Complication   **CD** Complex Dx   **HIV** HIV Related Dx

Injury and Poisoning

✓4th **829 Fracture of unspecified bones**

    829.0   Unspecified bone, closed

    829.1   Unspecified bone, open

DISLOCATION (830-839)

INCLUDES   displacement
             subluxation

EXCLUDES   *congenital dislocation (754.0-755.8)*
             pathological dislocation (718.2)
             recurrent dislocation (718.3)

The descriptions "closed" and "open," used in the fourth-digit subdivisions, include the following terms:

closed:	open:
complete	compound
dislocation NOS	infected
partial	with foreign body
simple	
uncomplicated	

A dislocation not indicated as closed or open should be classified as closed.

AHA: 3Q, '90, 12

✓4th **830 Dislocation of jaw**

     INCLUDES   jaw (cartilage) (meniscus)
                mandible
                maxilla (inferior)
                temporomandibular (joint)

    830.0   **Closed dislocation**

    830.1   **Open dislocation**

✓4th **831 Dislocation of shoulder**

     EXCLUDES   *sternoclavicular joint (839.61, 839.71)*
               sternum (839.61, 839.71)

The following fifth-digit subclassification is for use with category 831:

    0 shoulder, unspecified
         Humerus NOS
    1 anterior dislocation of humerus
    2 posterior dislocation of humerus
    3 inferior dislocation of humerus
    4 acromioclavicular (joint)
         Clavicle
    9 other
         Scapula

✓5th   831.0   **Closed dislocation**

✓5th   831.1   **Open dislocation**

✓4th **832 Dislocation of elbow**

The following fifth-digit subclassification is for use with category 832:

    0 elbow unspecified
    1 anterior dislocation of elbow
    2 posterior dislocation of elbow
    3 medial dislocation of elbow
    4 lateral dislocation of elbow
    9 other

✓5th   832.0   **Closed dislocation**

✓5th   832.1   **Open dislocation**

✓4th **833 Dislocation of wrist**

The following fifth-digit subclassification is for use with category 833:

    0 wrist, unspecified part
         Carpal (bone)
         Radius, distal end
    1 radioulnar (joint), distal
    2 radiocarpal (joint)
    3 midcarpal (joint)
    4 carpometacarpal (joint)
    5 metacarpal (bone), proximal end
    9 other
         Ulna, distal end

✓5th   833.0   **Closed dislocation**

✓5th   833.1   **Open dislocation**

✓4th **834 Dislocation of finger**

     INCLUDES   finger(s)   thumb
                phalanx of hand

The following fifth-digit subclassification is for use with category 834:

    0 finger, unspecified part
    1 metacarpophalangeal (joint)
         Metacarpal (bone), distal end
    2 interphalangeal (joint), hand

✓5th   834.0   **Closed dislocation**

✓5th   834.1   **Open dislocation**

✓4th **835 Dislocation of hip**

The following fifth-digit subclassification is for use with category 835:

    0 dislocation of hip, unspecified
    1 posterior dislocation
    2 obturator dislocation
    3 other anterior dislocation

✓5th   835.0   **Closed dislocation**

✓5th   835.1   **Open dislocation**

✓4th **836 Dislocation of knee**

     EXCLUDES   *dislocation of knee:*
                old or pathological (718.2)
                recurrent (718.3)
             internal derangement of knee joint (717.0-717.5,
                717.8-717.9)
             old tear of cartilage or meniscus of knee (717.0-
                717.5, 717.8-717.9)

    836.0   **Tear of medial cartilage or meniscus of knee, current**

         Bucket handle tear:
           NOS   } current injury
           medial meniscus

    836.1   **Tear of lateral cartilage or meniscus of knee, current**

    836.2   **Other tear of cartilage or meniscus of knee, current**

         Tear of:
           cartilage
           (semilunar) } current injury, not specified
           meniscus   as medial or lateral

    836.3   **Dislocation of patella, closed**

    836.4   **Dislocation of patella, open**

✓5th   836.5   **Other dislocation of knee, closed**

         836.50 **Dislocation of knee, unspecified**
         836.51 **Anterior dislocation of tibia, proximal end**
                Posterior dislocation of femur, distal end
         836.52 **Posterior dislocation of tibia, proximal end**
                Anterior dislocation of femur, distal end
         836.53 **Medial dislocation of tibia, proximal end**
         836.54 **Lateral dislocation of tibia, proximal end**
         836.59 **Other**

✓5th   836.6   **Other dislocation of knee, open**

         836.60 **Dislocation of knee, unspecified**
         836.61 **Anterior dislocation of tibia, proximal end**
         836.62 **Posterior dislocation of tibia, proximal end**
         836.63 **Medial dislocation of tibia, proximal end**
         836.64 **Lateral dislocation of tibia, proximal end**
         836.69 **Other**

✓4th **837 Dislocation of ankle**

     INCLUDES   astragalus
                fibula, distal end
                navicular, foot
                scaphoid, foot
                tibia, distal end

    837.0   **Closed dislocation**

    837.1   **Open dislocation**

829–837.1

✓4th ✓5th Additional Digit Required   Nonspecific PDx   Unacceptable PDx   Manifestation Code   MCV Major Cardiovascular Condition   ►◄ Revised Text   ● New Code   ▲ Revised Code Title

2007 ICD•9•CM   Volume 1 — 283

Injury and Poisoning

838–841.9

√4ᵗʰ **838 Dislocation of foot**

> The following fifth-digit subclassification is for use with category 838:
>
> 0   foot, unspecified
> 1   tarsal (bone), joint unspecified
> 2   midtarsal (joint)
> 3   tarsometatarsal (joint)
> 4   metatarsal (bone), joint unspecified
> 5   metatarsophalangeal (joint)
> 6   interphalangeal (joint), foot
> 9   other
> > Phalanx of foot
> > Toe(s)

√5ᵗʰ **838.0   Closed dislocation**

√5ᵗʰ **838.1   Open dislocation**   `CC 9`
     CC Excl: No Exclusions

√4ᵗʰ **839 Other, multiple, and ill-defined dislocations**

√5ᵗʰ **839.0   Cervical vertebra, closed**
     Cervical spine   Neck

    839.00   Cervical vertebra, unspecified   `CC`
       CC Excl: 805.00-805.18, 806.00-806.19, 806.8-806.9, 839.00-839.18, 847.0, 848.8-848.9, 879.8-879.9, 929.0, 929.9, 952.00-952.09, 958.8-958.99, 959.8-959.9

    839.01   First cervical vertebra   `CC`
       CC Excl: See code 839.00

    839.02   Second cervical vertebra   `CC`
       CC Excl: See code 839.00

    839.03   Third cervical vertebra   `CC`
       CC Excl: See code 839.00

    839.04   Fourth cervical vertebra   `CC`
       CC Excl: See code 839.00

    839.05   Fifth cervical vertebra   `CC`
       CC Excl: See code 839.00

    839.06   Sixth cervical vertebra   `CC`
       CC Excl: See code 839.00

    839.07   Seventh cervical vertebra   `CC`
       CC Excl: See code 839.00

    839.08   Multiple cervical vertebrae   `CC`
       CC Excl: See code 839.00

√5ᵗʰ **839.1   Cervical vertebra, open**

    839.10   Cervical vertebra, unspecified   `CC`
       CC Excl: See code 839.00

    839.11   First cervical vertebra   `CC`
       CC Excl: See code 839.00

    839.12   Second cervical vertebra   `CC`
       CC Excl: See code 839.00

    839.13   Third cervical vertebra   `CC`
       CC Excl: See code 839.00

    839.14   Fourth cervical vertebra   `CC`
       CC Excl: See code 839.00

    839.15   Fifth cervical vertebra   `CC`
       CC Excl: See code 839.00

    839.16   Sixth cervical vertebra   `CC`
       CC Excl: See code 839.00

    839.17   Seventh cervical vertebra   `CC`
       CC Excl: See code 839.00

    839.18   Multiple cervical vertebrae   `CC`
       CC Excl: See code 839.00

√5ᵗʰ **839.2   Thoracic and lumbar vertebra, closed**
    839.20   Lumbar vertebra
    839.21   Thoracic vertebra
       Dorsal [thoracic] vertebra

√5ᵗʰ **839.3   Thoracic and lumbar vertebra, open**
    839.30   Lumbar vertebra
    839.31   Thoracic vertebra

√5ᵗʰ **839.4   Other vertebra, closed**
    839.40   Vertebra, unspecified site
       Spine NOS
    839.41   Coccyx
    839.42   Sacrum
       Sacroiliac (joint)
    839.49   Other

√5ᵗʰ **839.5   Other vertebra, open**
    839.50   Vertebra, unspecified site
    839.51   Coccyx
    839.52   Sacrum
    839.59   Other

√5ᵗʰ **839.6   Other location, closed**
    839.61   Sternum
       Sternoclavicular joint
    839.69   Other
       Pelvis

√5ᵗʰ **839.7   Other location, open**
    839.71   Sternum
    839.79   Other

    839.8   Multiple and ill-defined, closed
       Arm
       Back
       Hand
       Multiple locations, except fingers or toes alone
       Other ill-defined locations
       Unspecified location

    839.9   Multiple and ill-defined, open

SPRAINS AND STRAINS OF JOINTS AND ADJACENT MUSCLES (840-848)

`INCLUDES`	avulsion	
	hemarthrosis	of:
	laceration	joint capsule
	rupture	ligament
	sprain	muscle
	strain	tendon
	tear	

`EXCLUDES`   *laceration of tendon in open wounds (880-884 and 890-894 with .2)*

√4ᵗʰ **840 Sprains and strains of shoulder and upper arm**
    840.0   Acromioclavicular (joint) (ligament)
    840.1   Coracoclavicular (ligament)
    840.2   Coracohumeral (ligament)
    840.3   Infraspinatus (muscle) (tendon)
    840.4   Rotator cuff (capsule)
       `EXCLUDES`   *complete rupture of rotator cuff, nontraumatic (727.61)*
    840.5   Subscapularis (muscle)
    840.6   Supraspinatus (muscle) (tendon)
    840.7   Superior glenoid labrum lesion
       SLAP lesion
       AHA: 4Q,'01, 52

       DEF: Detachment injury of the superior aspect of the glenoid labrum which is the ring of fibrocartilage attached to the rim of the glenoid cavity of the scapula.

    840.8   Other specified sites of shoulder and upper arm
    840.9   Unspecified site of shoulder and upper arm
       Arm NOS   Shoulder NOS

√4ᵗʰ **841 Sprains and strains of elbow and forearm**
    841.0   Radial collateral ligament
    841.1   Ulnar collateral ligament
    841.2   Radiohumeral (joint)
    841.3   Ulnohumeral (joint)
    841.8   Other specified sites of elbow and forearm
    841.9   Unspecified site of elbow and forearm
       Elbow NOS

`N` Newborn Age: 0   `P` Pediatric Age: 0-17   `M` Maternity Age: 12-55   `A` Adult Age: 15-124   `CC` CC Condition   `MC` Major Complication   `CD` Complex Dx   `HIV` HIV Related Dx

✓4ᵗʰ 842 Sprains and strains of wrist and hand
　　✓5ᵗʰ 842.0　Wrist
　　　　842.00　Unspecified site
　　　　842.01　Carpal (joint)
　　　　842.02　Radiocarpal (joint) (ligament)
　　　　842.09　Other
　　　　　　Radioulnar joint, distal
　　✓5ᵗʰ 842.1　Hand
　　　　842.10　Unspecified site
　　　　842.11　Carpometacarpal (joint)
　　　　842.12　Metacarpophalangeal (joint)
　　　　842.13　Interphalangeal (joint)
　　　　842.19　Other
　　　　　　Midcarpal (joint)

✓4ᵗʰ 843 Sprains and strains of hip and thigh
　　843.0　Iliofemoral (ligament)
　　843.1　Ischiocapsular (ligament)
　　843.8　Other specified sites of hip and thigh
　　843.9　Unspecified site of hip and thigh
　　　　Hip NOS　　　　Thigh NOS

✓4ᵗʰ 844 Sprains and strains of knee and leg
　　844.0　Lateral collateral ligament of knee
　　844.1　Medial collateral ligament of knee
　　844.2　Cruciate ligament of knee
　　844.3　Tibiofibular (joint) (ligament), superior
　　844.8　Other specified sites of knee and leg
　　844.9　Unspecified site of knee and leg
　　　　Knee NOS　　　　Leg NOS

✓4ᵗʰ 845 Sprains and strains of ankle and foot
　　✓5ᵗʰ 845.0　Ankle
　　　　845.00　Unspecified site
　　　　　　AHA: 2Q, '02, 3
　　　　845.01　Deltoid (ligament), ankle
　　　　　　Internal collateral (ligament), ankle
　　　　845.02　Calcaneofibular (ligament)
　　　　845.03　Tibiofibular (ligament), distal
　　　　　　AHA: 1Q, '04, 9
　　　　845.09　Other
　　　　　　Achilles tendon
　　✓5ᵗʰ 845.1　Foot
　　　　845.10　Unspecified site
　　　　845.11　Tarsometatarsal (joint) (ligament)
　　　　845.12　Metatarsophalangeal (joint)
　　　　845.13　Interphalangeal (joint), toe
　　　　845.19　Other

✓4ᵗʰ 846 Sprains and strains of sacroiliac region
　　846.0　Lumbosacral (joint) (ligament)
　　846.1　Sacroiliac ligament
　　846.2　Sacrospinatus (ligament)
　　846.3　Sacrotuberous (ligament)
　　846.8　Other specified sites of sacroiliac region
　　846.9　Unspecified site of sacroiliac region

✓4ᵗʰ 847 Sprains and strains of other and unspecified parts of back
　　EXCLUDES　lumbosacral (846.0)
　　847.0　Neck
　　　　Anterior longitudinal (ligament), cervical
　　　　Atlanto-axial (joints)
　　　　Atlanto-occipital (joints)
　　　　Whiplash injury
　　　　EXCLUDES　neck injury NOS (959.0)
　　　　　　　　　　thyroid region (848.2)
　　847.1　Thoracic
　　847.2　Lumbar
　　847.3　Sacrum
　　　　Sacrococcygeal (ligament)
　　847.4　Coccyx
　　847.9　Unspecified site of back
　　　　Back NOS

✓4ᵗʰ 848 Other and ill-defined sprains and strains
　　848.0　Septal cartilage of nose
　　848.1　Jaw
　　　　Temporomandibular (joint) (ligament)
　　848.2　Thyroid region
　　　　Cricoarytenoid (joint) (ligament)
　　　　Cricothyroid (joint) (ligament)
　　　　Thyroid cartilage
　　848.3　Ribs
　　　　Chondrocostal } without mention of
　　　　　(joint)　　　　injury to
　　　　Costal cartilage } sternum
　　✓5ᵗʰ 848.4　Sternum
　　　　848.40　Unspecified site
　　　　848.41　Sternoclavicular (joint) (ligament)
　　　　848.42　Chondrosternal (joint)
　　　　848.49　Other
　　　　　　Xiphoid cartilage
　　848.5　Pelvis
　　　　Symphysis pubis
　　　　EXCLUDES　that in childbirth (665.6)
　　848.8　Other specified sites of sprains and strains
　　848.9　Unspecified site of sprain and strain

INTRACRANIAL INJURY, EXCLUDING THOSE WITH SKULL FRACTURE (850-854)

　　EXCLUDES　intracranial injury with skull fracture (800-801
　　　　　　　　　and 803-804, except .0 and .5)
　　　　　　　　open wound of head without intracranial injury
　　　　　　　　　(870.0-873.9)
　　　　　　　　skull fracture alone (800-801 and 803-804 with
　　　　　　　　　.0, .5)

The description "with open intracranial wound," used in the fourth-digit subdivisions, includes those specified as open or with mention of infection or foreign body.

The following fifth-digit subclassification is for use with categories 851-854:
　0　unspecified state of consciousness
　1　with no loss of consciousness
　2　with brief [less than one hour] loss of consciousness
　3　with moderate [1-24 hours] loss of consciousness
　4　with prolonged [more than 24 hours] loss of consciousness and return to pre-existing conscious level
　5　with prolonged [more than 24 hours] loss of consciousness, without return to pre-existing conscious level
　　　Use fifth-digit 5 to designate when a patient is unconscious and dies before regaining consciousness, regardless of the duration of the loss of consciousness
　6　with loss of consciousness of unspecified duration
　9　with concussion, unspecified

AHA: 1Q, '93, 22

✓4ᵗʰ 850 Concussion
　　INCLUDES　commotio cerebri
　　EXCLUDES　concussion with:
　　　　　　　　cerebral laceration or contusion (851.0-851.9)
　　　　　　　　cerebral hemorrhage (852-853)
　　　　　　　　head injury NOS (959.01)

AHA: 2Q, '96, 6; 4Q, '90, 24

✓4ᵗʰ Additional Digit Required　Nonspecific PDx　Unacceptable PDx　Manifestation Code　**MCV** Major Cardiovascular Condition　▶◀ Revised Text　● New Code　▲ Revised Code Title

2007 ICD•9•CM　　　　　　　　　　　　　　　　　　　　　　　**Volume 1 — 285**

Injury and Poisoning

850.0–852.3

850.0 With no loss of consciousness `cc`
Concussion with mental confusion or disorientation, without loss of consciousness
CC Excl: 800.00-800.99, 801.00-801.99, 803.00-803.99, 804.00-804.99, 850.0-850.9, 851.00-851.99, 852.00-852.19, 852.21-852.59, 853.00-853.19, 854.00-854.19, 873.8-873.9, 879.8-879.9, 905.0, 925.1-925.2, 929.0, 929.9, 958.8, 959.01, 959.09, 959.8-959.9

✓5th **850.1 With brief loss of consciousness**
Loss of consciousness for less than one hour
AHA: 4Q, '03, 76; 1Q, '99, 10; 2Q, '92, 5

850.11 With loss of consciousness of 30 minutes or less `cc`
CC Excl: See code 850.0

850.12 With loss of consciousness from 31 to 59 minutes `cc`
CC Excl: See code 850.0

850.2 With moderate loss of consciousness `cc`
Loss of consciousness for 1-24 hours
CC Excl: See code 850.0

850.3 With prolonged loss of consciousness and return to pre-existing conscious level `cc`
Loss of consciousness for more than 24 hours with complete recovery
CC Excl: See code 850.0

850.4 With prolonged loss of consciousness, without return to pre-existing conscious level `cc`
CC Excl: See code 850.0

850.5 With loss of consciousness of unspecified duration `cc`
CC Excl: See code 850.0

850.9 Concussion, unspecified `cc`
CC Excl: See code 850.0

Brain

Corpus callosum
Cerebrum
Hypothalamus
Interventricular foramen
Fornix
Third ventricle
Pineal body
Optic chiasm
Corpora quadrigemina
Cerebral aqueduct
Hypophysis
Pons
Vermis
Mamillary body
Fourth ventricle
Peduncle
Median aperture
Medulla oblangata
Spinal cord

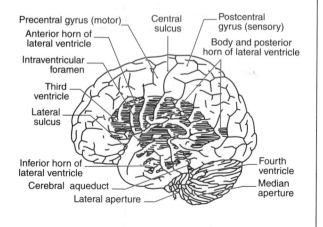

Precentral gyrus (motor)
Central sulcus
Postcentral gyrus (sensory)
Anterior horn of lateral ventricle
Body and posterior horn of lateral ventricle
Intraventricular foramen
Third ventricle
Lateral sulcus
Inferior horn of lateral ventricle
Fourth ventricle
Median aperture
Cerebral aqueduct
Lateral aperture

✓4th **851 Cerebral laceration and contusion**
AHA: 4Q, '96, 36; 1Q, '93, 22; 4Q, '90, 24

§ ✓5th **851.0 Cortex (cerebral) contusion without mention of open intracranial wound** `cc`
CC Excl: See code 850.0

§ ✓5th **851.1 Cortex (cerebral) contusion with open intracranial wound** `cc`
CC Excl: See code 850.0
AHA: 1Q, '92, 9

§ ✓5th **851.2 Cortex (cerebral) laceration without mention of open intracranial wound** `cc`
CC Excl: See code 850.0

§ ✓5th **851.3 Cortex (cerebral) laceration with open intracranial wound** `cc`
CC Excl: See code 850.0

§ ✓5th **851.4 Cerebellar or brain stem contusion without mention of open intracranial wound** `cc`
CC Excl: See code 850.0

§ ✓5th **851.5 Cerebellar or brain stem contusion with open intracranial wound** `cc`
CC Excl: See code 850.0

§ ✓5th **851.6 Cerebellar or brain stem laceration without mention of open intracranial wound** `cc`
CC Excl: See code 850.0

§ ✓5th **851.7 Cerebellar or brain stem laceration with open intracranial wound** `cc`
CC Excl: See code 850.0

§ ✓5th **851.8 Other and unspecified cerebral laceration and contusion, without mention of open intracranial wound** `cc`
Brain (membrane) NOS
CC Excl: See code 850.0
AHA: 4Q, '96, 37

§ ✓5th **851.9 Other and unspecified cerebral laceration and contusion, with open intracranial wound** `cc`
CC Excl: See code 850.0

✓4th **852 Subarachnoid, subdural, and extradural hemorrhage, following injury**
EXCLUDES *Cerebral contusion or laceration (with hemorrhage) (851.0-851.9)*
DEF: Bleeding from lining of brain; due to injury.

§ ✓5th **852.0 Subarachnoid hemorrhage following injury without mention of open intracranial wound** `cc`
Middle meningeal hemorrhage following injury
CC Excl: See code 850.0

§ ✓5th **852.1 Subarachnoid hemorrhage following injury with open intracranial wound** `cc`
CC Excl: See code 850.0

§ ✓5th **852.2 Subdural hemorrhage following injury without mention of open intracranial wound** `cc`
CC Excl: For code 852.20: 800.00-801.99, 803.00-804.99, 850.0-854.19, 873.8-873.9, 879.8-879.9, 905.0, 925.1-925.2, 929.0-929.9, 958.8-959.09, 959.8-959.9 For code 852.21-852.29: 800.00-801.99, 803.00-804.99, 850.0-852.19, 852.21-854.19, 873.8-873.9, 879.8-879.9, 905.0, 925.1-925.2, 929.0-929.9, 958.8-959.09, 959.8-959.9
AHA: 4Q, '96, 43

§ ✓5th **852.3 Subdural hemorrhage following injury with open intracranial wound** `cc`
CC Excl: See code 852.21

---

§ Requires fifth-digit. See beginning of section 850-854 for codes and definitions.

`N` Newborn Age: 0   `P` Pediatric Age: 0-17   `M` Maternity Age: 12-55   `A` Adult Age: 15-124   `CC` CC Condition   `MC` Major Complication   `CD` Complex Dx   `HIV` HIV Related Dx

§ ✓5ᵗʰ **852.4** **Extradural hemorrhage following injury without mention of open intracranial wound** `CC`
     Epidural hematoma following injury
     CC Excl: See code 852.21

§ ✓5ᵗʰ **852.5** **Extradural hemorrhage following injury with open intracranial wound** `CC`
     CC Excl: See code 852.21

✓4ᵗʰ **853 Other and unspecified intracranial hemorrhage following injury**

§ ✓5ᵗʰ **853.0** **Without mention of open intracranial wound** `CC`
     Cerebral compression due to injury
     Intracranial hematoma following injury
     Traumatic cerebral hemorrhage
     CC Excl: See code 852.21
     AHA: 3Q, '90, 14

§ ✓5ᵗʰ **853.1** **With open intracranial wound** `CC`
     CC Excl: See code 852.21

✓4ᵗʰ **854 Intracranial injury of other and unspecified nature**
     `INCLUDES` brain injury NOS
               cavernous sinus
               intracranial injury
     `EXCLUDES` *any condition classifiable to 850-853*
               head injury NOS (959.01)
     AHA: 1Q, '99, 10; 2Q, '92, 6

§ ✓5ᵗʰ **854.0** **Without mention of open intracranial wound** `CC`
     CC Excl: See code 852.21
     AHA: For code 854.00: 2Q, '05, 6

§ ✓5ᵗʰ **854.1** **With open intracranial wound** `CC`
     CC Excl: See code 852.21

INTERNAL INJURY OF THORAX, ABDOMEN, AND PELVIS (860-869)

     `INCLUDES` blast injuries
               blunt trauma
               bruise
               concussion injuries
                  (except cerebral)
               crushing   } of internal organs
               hematoma
               laceration
               puncture
               tear
               traumatic rupture
     `EXCLUDES` *concussion NOS (850.0-850.9)*
               flail chest (807.4)
               foreign body entering through orifice (930.0-939.9)
               injury to blood vessels (901.0-902.9)
     The description "with open wound," used in the fourth-digit subdivisions, includes those with mention of infection or foreign body.

✓4ᵗʰ **860 Traumatic pneumothorax and hemothorax**
     AHA: 2Q, '93, 4
     DEF: Traumatic pneumothorax: air or gas leaking into pleural space of lung due to trauma.
     DEF: Traumatic hemothorax: blood buildup in pleural space of lung due to trauma.

     860.0 **Pneumothorax without mention of open wound into thorax** `CC`
         CC Excl: 860.0-860.5, 861.20-861.32, 862.29, 862.39, 862.8-862.9, 875.0-875.1, 879.8-879.9, 929.0, 929.9, 958.7-958.99, 959.8-959.9

     860.1 **Pneumothorax with open wound into thorax** `CC`
         CC Excl: See code 860.0

     860.2 **Hemothorax without mention of open wound into thorax** `CC`
         CC Excl: See code 860.0

     860.3 **Hemothorax with open wound into thorax** `CC`
         CC Excl: See code 860.0

     860.4 **Pneumohemothorax without mention of open wound into thorax** `CC`
         CC Excl: See code 860.0

     860.5 **Pneumohemothorax with open wound into thorax** `CC`
         CC Excl: See code 860.0

✓4ᵗʰ **861 Injury to heart and lung**
     `EXCLUDES` *injury to blood vessels of thorax (901.0-901.9)*

✓5ᵗʰ **861.0** **Heart, without mention of open wound into thorax**
     AHA: 1Q, '92, 9

     861.00 **Unspecified injury**
     861.01 **Contusion** `CC`
         Cardiac contusion   Myocardial contusion
         CC Excl: 861.00-861.13, 862.29, 862.39, 862.8-862.9, 875.0-875.1, 879.8-879.9, 929.0, 929.9, 958.7-958.99, 959.8-959.9
         DEF: Bruising within the pericardium with no mention of open wound.

     861.02 **Laceration without penetration of heart chambers** `CC` `MCV`
         CC Excl: See code 861.01
         DEF: Tearing injury of heart tissue, without penetration of chambers; no open wound.

     861.03 **Laceration with penetration of heart chambers** `CC` `MCV`
         CC Excl: See code 861.01

✓5ᵗʰ **861.1** **Heart, with open wound into thorax**
     861.10 **Unspecified injury** `CC` `MCV`
         CC Excl: See code 861.01

     861.11 **Contusion** `CC` `MCV`
         CC Excl: See code 861.01

     861.12 **Laceration without penetration of heart chambers** `CC` `MCV`
         CC Excl: See code 861.01

     861.13 **Laceration with penetration of heart chambers** `CC` `MCV`
         CC Excl: See code 861.01

✓5ᵗʰ **861.2** **Lung, without mention of open wound into thorax**
     861.20 **Unspecified injury**
     861.21 **Contusion**
         DEF: Bruising of lung without mention of open wound.

     861.22 **Laceration** `CC`
         CC Excl: 861.20-861.32, 862.29, 862.39, 862.8-862.9, 875.0-875.1, 879.8-879.9, 929.0, 929.9, 958.7-958.99, 959.8-959.9

✓5ᵗʰ **861.3** **Lung, with open wound into thorax**
     861.30 **Unspecified injury** `CC`
         CC Excl: See code 861.22

     861.31 **Contusion** `CC`
         CC Excl: See code 861.22

     861.32 **Laceration** `CC`
         CC Excl: See code 861.22

✓4ᵗʰ **862 Injury to other and unspecified intrathoracic organs**
     `EXCLUDES` *injury to blood vessels of thorax (901.0-901.9)*

     862.0 **Diaphragm, without mention of open wound into cavity**
     862.1 **Diaphragm, with open wound into cavity** `CC`
         CC Excl: 862.0-862.1, 862.29, 862.39-862.9, 875.0-875.1, 879.8-879.9, 929.0-929.9, 958.7-958.99, 959.8-959.9

---

§ Requires fifth-digit. See beginning of section 850-854 for codes and definitions.

✓4ᵗʰ ✓5ᵗʰ Additional Digit Required   `Nonspecific PDx`   `Unacceptable PDx`   `Manifestation Code`   `MCV` Major Cardiovascular Condition   ▶◀ Revised Text   ● New Code   ▲ Revised Code Title

2007 ICD•9•CM   October 2006 • Volume 1 — 287

✓5ᵗʰ **862.2** **Other specified intrathoracic organs, without mention of open wound into cavity**
    862.21 Bronchus `CC`
      CC Excl: 862.21, 862.29, 862.31, 862.39-862.9, 875.0-875.1, 879.8-879.9, 929.0-929.9, 958.7-958.99, 959.9-959.9
    862.22 Esophagus `CC`
      CC Excl: 862.22-862.29, 862.32-862.9, 875.0-875.1, 879.8-879.9, 929.0-929.9, 958.7-958.99, 959.9-959.9
    862.29 Other `CC`
      Pleura
      Thymus gland
      CC Excl: 862.29, 862.39-862.9, 875.0-875.1, 879.8-879.9, 929.0-929.9, 958.7-958.99, 959.9-959.9

✓5ᵗʰ **862.3** **Other specified intrathoracic organs, with open wound into cavity**
    862.31 Bronchus `CC`
      CC Excl: 862.21, 862.29, 862.31, 862.39-862.9, 875.0-875.1, 879.8-879.9, 929.0-929.9, 958.7-958.99, 959.9-959.9
    862.32 Esophagus `CC`
      CC Excl: 862.22-862.29, 862.32-862.9, 875.0-875.1, 879.8-879.9, 929.0-929.9, 958.7-958.99, 959.9-959.9
    862.39 Other `CC`
      CC Excl: 862.29, 862.39-862.9, 875.0-875.1, 879.8-879.9, 929.0-929.9, 958.7-958.99, 959.9-959.9

862.8 **Multiple and unspecified intrathoracic organs, without mention of open wound into cavity**
    Crushed chest
    Multiple intrathoracic organs

10 **862.9** **Multiple and unspecified intrathoracic organs, with open wound into cavity** `CC` `MCV`
    CC Excl: See code 862.39

✓4ᵗʰ **863 Injury to gastrointestinal tract**
    EXCLUDES *anal sphincter laceration during delivery (664.2)*
      bile duct (868.0-868.1 with fifth-digit 2)
      gallbladder (868.0-868.1 with fifth-digit 2)

863.0 **Stomach, without mention of open wound into cavity**

863.1 **Stomach, with open wound into cavity** `CC`
    CC Excl: 863.0-863.1, 863.80, 863.89-863.90, 863.99, 868.00, 868.03-868.10, 868.13-868.19, 869.0-869.1, 879.2-879.9, 929.0, 929.9, 958.8-958.99, 959.8-959.9

✓5ᵗʰ **863.2** **Small intestine, without mention of open wound into cavity**
    863.20 Small intestine, unspecified site
    863.21 Duodenum
    863.29 Other

✓5ᵗʰ **863.3** **Small intestine, with open wound into cavity**
    863.30 Small intestine, unspecified site `CC`
      CC Excl: 863.20-863.39, 863.80, 863.89-863.90, 863.99, 868.00, 868.03-868.10, 868.13-868.19, 869.0-869.1, 879.2-879.9, 929.0, 929.9, 958.8-958.99, 959.8-959.9
    863.31 Duodenum `CC`
      CC Excl: 863.21, 863.31, 863.39, 863.80, 863.89-863.90, 863.99, 868.00, 868.03-868.10, 868.13-868.19, 869.0-869.1, 879.2-879.9, 929.0, 929.9, 958.8-958.99, 959.8-959.9
    863.39 Other `CC`
      CC Excl: See Code 863.30

✓5ᵗʰ **863.4** **Colon or rectum, without mention of open wound into cavity**
    863.40 Colon, unspecified site
    863.41 Ascending [right] colon
    863.42 Transverse colon
    863.43 Descending [left] colon
    863.44 Sigmoid colon
    863.45 Rectum
    863.46 Multiple sites in colon and rectum
    863.49 Other

✓5ᵗʰ **863.5** **Colon or rectum, with open wound into cavity**
    863.50 Colon, unspecified site `CC`
      CC Excl: 863.40-863.80, 863.89-863.90, 863.99, 868.00, 868.03-868.10, 868.13-869.1, 879.2-879.9, 929.0-929.9, 958.8-958.99, 959.8-959.9
    863.51 Ascending [right] colon `CC`
      CC Excl: See code 863.50
    863.52 Transverse colon `CC`
      CC Excl: See code 863.50
    863.53 Descending [left] colon `CC`
      CC Excl: See code 863.50
    863.54 Sigmoid colon `CC`
      CC Excl: See code 863.50
    863.55 Rectum `CC`
      CC Excl: See code 863.50
    863.56 Multiple sites in colon and rectum `CC`
      CC Excl: See code 863.50
    863.59 Other `CC`
      CC Excl: See code 863.50

✓5ᵗʰ **863.8** **Other and unspecified gastrointestinal sites, without mention of open wound into cavity**
    863.80 Gastrointestinal tract, unspecified site
    863.81 Pancreas, head
    863.82 Pancreas, body
    863.83 Pancreas, tail
    863.84 Pancreas, multiple and unspecified sites
    863.85 Appendix
    863.89 Other
      Intestine NOS

✓5ᵗʰ **863.9** **Other and unspecified gastrointestinal sites, with open wound into cavity**
    863.90 Gastrointestinal tract, unspecified site `CC`
      CC Excl: 863.80-863.84, 863.89-863.94, 863.99, 868.00, 868.03-868.10, 868.13-868.19, 869.0-869.1, 879.2-879.9, 929.0, 929.9, 958.8-958.99, 959.8-959.9
    863.91 Pancreas, head `CC`
      CC Excl: 863.80-863.84, 863.91-863.94, 863.99, 868.00, 868.03-868.10, 868.13-868.19, 869.0-869.1, 879.2-879.9, 929.0, 929.9, 958.8-958.99, 959.8-959.9
    863.92 Pancreas, body `CC`
      CC Excl: See code 863.91
    863.93 Pancreas, tail `CC`
      CC Excl: See code 863.91
    863.94 Pancreas, multiple and unspecified sites `CC`
      CC Excl: See code 863.91
    863.95 Appendix `CC`
      CC Excl: 863.80, 863.85, 863.95, 863.99, 868.00, 868.03-868.10, 868.13-868.19, 869.0-869.1, 879.2-879.9, 929.0, 929.9, 958.99, 959.8-959.9
    863.99 Other `CC`
      CC Excl: 863.80, 863.99, 868.00, 868.03-868.10, 868.13-868.19, 869.0-869.1, 879.2-879.9, 929.0, 929.9, 958.8-958.99, 959.8-959.9

10 MCV as SDx only

N Newborn Age: 0   P Pediatric Age: 0-17   M Maternity Age: 12-55   A Adult Age: 15-124   CC CC Condition   MC Major Complication   CD Complex Dx   HIV HIV Related Dx

288 — Volume 1 • October 2006   2007 ICD•9•CM

√4ᵗʰ **864 Injury to liver**

The following fifth-digit subclassification is for use with category 864:

0 unspecified injury
1 hematoma and contusion
2 laceration, minor
    Laceration involving capsule only, or without significant involvement of hepatic parenchyma [i.e., less than 1 cm deep]
3 laceration, moderate
    Laceration involving parenchyma but without major disruption of parenchyma [i.e., less than 10 cm long and less than 3 cm deep]
4 laceration, major
    Laceration with significant disruption of hepatic parenchyma [i.e., 10 cm long and 3 cm deep]
    Multiple moderate lacerations, with or without hematoma
    Stellate lacerations of liver
5 laceration, unspecified
9 other

√5ᵗʰ **864.0 Without mention of open wound into cavity** `cc`
    CC Excl: 863.80, 863.99-864.19, 868.00, 868.03-868.10, 868.13-869.1, 879.2-879.9, 929.0-929.9, 958.8-958.99, 959.8-959.9

√5ᵗʰ **864.1 With open wound into cavity** `cc`
    CC Excl: See code 864.0

√4ᵗʰ **865 Injury to spleen**

The following fifth-digit subclassification is for use with category 865:

0 unspecified injury
1 hematoma without rupture of capsule
2 capsular tears, without major disruption of parenchyma
3 laceration extending into parenchyma
4 massive parenchymal disruption
9 other

√5ᵗʰ **865.0 Without mention of open wound into cavity** `cc`
    CC Excl: 865.00-865.19, 868.00, 868.03-868.10, 868.13-869.1, 879.2-879.9, 929.0-929.9, 958.8-958.99, 959.8-959.9

√5ᵗʰ **865.1 With open wound into cavity** `cc`
    CC Excl: See code 865.0

√4ᵗʰ **866 Injury to kidney**

The following fifth-digit subclassification is for use with category 866:

0 unspecified injury
1 hematoma without rupture of capsule
2 laceration
3 complete disruption of kidney parenchyma

√5ᵗʰ **866.0 Without mention of open wound into cavity** `cc`
    CC Excl: 866.00-866.13, 868.00, 868.03-868.10, 868.13-868.19, 869.0-869.1, 879.2-879.9, 929.0, 929.9, 958.8-958.99, 959.8-959.9

√5ᵗʰ **866.1 With open wound into cavity** `cc`
    CC Excl: See code 866.0

√4ᵗʰ **867 Injury to pelvic organs**
    EXCLUDES *injury during delivery (664.0-665.9)*

867.0 Bladder and urethra, without mention of open wound into cavity `cc`
    CC Excl: 867.0-867.1, 867.6-868.00, 868.03-868.10, 868.13-869.1, 879.2-879.9, 929.0-929.9, 958.8-958.99, 959.8-959.9
    AHA: N-D, '85, 15

867.1 Bladder and urethra, with open wound into cavity `cc`
    CC Excl: See code 867.0

867.2 Ureter, without mention of open wound into cavity `cc`
    CC Excl: 867.2-867.3, 867.6-868.00, 868.03-868.10, 868.13-869.1, 879.2-879.9, 929.0-929.9, 958.8-958.99, 959.8-959.9

867.3 Ureter, with open wound into cavity `cc`
    CC Excl: See code 867.2

867.4 Uterus, without mention of open wound into cavity `cc`♀
    CC Excl: 867.4-868.00, 868.03-868.10, 868.13-869.1, 879.2-879.9, 929.0-929.9, 958.8-958.99, 959.8-959.9

867.5 Uterus, with open wound into cavity `cc`♀
    CC Excl: See code 867.4

867.6 Other specified pelvic organs, without mention of open wound into cavity `cc`
    Fallopian tube   Seminal vesicle
    Ovary   Vas deferens
    Prostate
    CC Excl: 867.6-868.00, 868.03-868.10, 868.13-869.1, 879.2-879.9, 929.0-929.9, 958.8-958.99, 959.8-959.9

867.7 Other specified pelvic organs, with open wound into cavity `cc`
    CC Excl: See code 867.6

867.8 Unspecified pelvic organ, without mention of open wound into cavity `cc`
    CC Excl: See code 867.6

867.9 Unspecified pelvic organ, with open wound into cavity `cc`
    CC Excl: See code 867.6

√4ᵗʰ **868 Injury to other intra-abdominal organs**

The following fifth-digit subclassification is for use with category 868:

0 unspecified intra-abdominal organ
1 adrenal gland
2 bile duct and gallbladder
3 peritoneum
4 retroperitoneum
9 other and multiple intra-abdominal organs

√5ᵗʰ **868.0 Without mention of open wound into cavity** `cc`
    CC Excl: For code **868.00**: 868.00, 868.03-868.10, 868.13-869.1, 879.2-879.9, 929.0-929.9, 958.8-958.99, 959.8-959.9 For code **868.01**: 868.00-868.01, 868.03-868.11, 868.13-869.1, 879.2-879.9, 929.0-929.9, 958.8-958.99, 959.8-959.9 For code **868.02**: 868.00, 868.02-868.10, 868.13-869.1, 879.2-879.9, 929.0-929.9, 958.8-958.99, 959.8-959.9 For codes **868.03-868.09**: See Code 868.00

√5ᵗʰ **868.1 With open wound into cavity** `cc`
    CC Excl: For code **868.10**: See code 868.03 For code **868.11**: 868.00, 868.01, 868.03-868.11, 868.13-868.19, 869.0-869.1, 879.2-879.9, 929.0, 929.9, 958.8-958.99, 959.8-959.9 For code **868.12**: 868.00, 868.03-868.10, 868.12-868.19, 869.0-869.1, 879.2-879.9, 929.0, 929.9, 958.8-958.99, 959.8-959.9 For codes **868.13-868.19**: See Code 868.10

√4ᵗʰ **869 Internal injury to unspecified or ill-defined organs**
    INCLUDES internal injury NOS
        multiple internal injury NOS

869.0 Without mention of open wound into cavity `cc`
    CC Excl: See code 868.10

869.1 With open wound into cavity `cc`
    CC Excl: See code 868.10
    AHA: 2Q, '89, 15

√4ᵗʰ Additional Digit Required   Nonspecific PDx   Unacceptable PDx   Manifestation Code   `MCV` Major Cardiovascular Condition ▶◀ Revised Text ● New Code ▲ Revised Code Title

OPEN WOUND (870-897)

INCLUDES	animal bite
	avulsion
	cut
	laceration
	puncture wound
	traumatic amputation

EXCLUDES	*burn (940.0-949.5)*
	crushing (925-929.9)
	puncture of internal organs (860.0-869.1)
	superficial injury (910.0-919.9)
	that incidental to:
	dislocation (830.0-839.9)
	fracture (800.0-829.1)
	internal injury (860.0-869.1)
	intracranial injury (851.0-854.1)

Note: The description "complicated" used in the fourth-digit subdivisions includes those with mention of delayed healing, delayed treatment, foreign body, or infection. Use additional code to identify infection

AHA: 4Q, '01, 52

OPEN WOUND OF HEAD, NECK, AND TRUNK (870-879)

√4th **870 Open wound of ocular adnexa**

870.0 Laceration of skin of eyelid and periocular area

870.1 Laceration of eyelid, full-thickness, not involving lacrimal passages

870.2 Laceration of eyelid involving lacrimal passages

870.3 Penetrating wound of orbit, without mention of foreign body `CC`
CC Excl: 870.0-871.9, 879.8-879.9, 929.0-929.9, 958.8-958.99, 959.8-959.9

870.4 Penetrating wound of orbit with foreign body `CC`
EXCLUDES	*retained (old) foreign body in orbit (376.6)*
CC Excl: See code 870.3

870.8 Other specified open wounds of ocular adnexa `CC`
CC Excl: See code 870.3

870.9 Unspecified open wound of ocular adnexa `CC`
CC Excl: See code 870.3

√4th **871 Open wound of eyeball**
EXCLUDES	*2nd cranial nerve [optic] injury (950.0-950.9)*
	3rd cranial nerve [oculomotor] injury (951.0)

871.0 Ocular laceration without prolapse of intraocular tissue `CC`
CC Excl: See code 870.3
AHA: 3Q, '96, 7
DEF: Tear in ocular tissue without displacing structures.

871.1 Ocular laceration with prolapse or exposure of intraocular tissue `CC`
CC Excl: See code 870.3

871.2 Rupture of eye with partial loss of intraocular tissue `CC`
CC Excl: See code 870.3
DEF: Forcible tearing of eyeball, with tissue loss.

871.3 Avulsion of eye `CC`
Traumatic enucleation
CC Excl: See code 870.3
DEF: Traumatic extraction of eyeball from socket.

871.4 Unspecified laceration of eye `CC`
CC Excl: See code 870.3

871.5 Penetration of eyeball with magnetic foreign body
EXCLUDES	*retained (old) magnetic foreign body in globe (360.50-360.59)*

871.6 Penetration of eyeball with (nonmagnetic) foreign body
EXCLUDES	*retained (old) (nonmagnetic) foreign body in globe (360.60-360.69)*

871.7 Unspecified ocular penetration

871.9 Unspecified open wound of eyeball `CC`
CC Excl: See code 870.3

√4th **872 Open wound of ear**

√5th **872.0 External ear, without mention of complication**
872.00 External ear, unspecified site
872.01 Auricle, ear
Pinna
DEF: Open wound of fleshy, outer ear.

872.02 Auditory canal
DEF: Open wound of passage from external ear to eardrum.

√5th **872.1 External ear, complicated**
872.10 External ear, unspecified site
872.11 Auricle, ear
872.12 Auditory canal

√5th **872.6 Other specified parts of ear, without mention of complication**
872.61 Ear drum
Drumhead   Tympanic membrane
872.62 Ossicles
872.63 Eustachian tube
DEF: Open wound of channel between nasopharynx and tympanic cavity.

872.64 Cochlea
DEF: Open wound of snail shell shaped tube of inner ear.

872.69 Other and multiple sites

√5th **872.7 Other specified parts of ear, complicated**
872.71 Ear drum
872.72 Ossicles `CC`
CC Excl: 872.00-872.9, 879.8-879.9, 929.0, 929.9, 958.8-958.99, 959.8-959.9

872.73 Eustachian tube `CC`
CC Excl: See code 872.72

872.74 Cochlea `CC`
CC Excl: See code 872.72

872.79 Other and multiple sites

872.8 Ear, part unspecified, without mention of complication
Ear NOS

872.9 Ear, part unspecified, complicated

√4th **873 Other open wound of head**
873.0 Scalp, without mention of complication
873.1 Scalp, complicated

√5th **873.2 Nose, without mention of complication**
873.20 Nose, unspecified site
873.21 Nasal septum
DEF: Open wound between nasal passages.

873.22 Nasal cavity
DEF: Open wound of nostrils.

873.23 Nasal sinus
DEF: Open wound of mucous-lined respiratory cavities.

873.29 Multiple sites

√5th **873.3 Nose, complicated**
873.30 Nose, unspecified site
873.31 Nasal septum
873.32 Nasal cavity
873.33 Nasal sinus `CC`
CC Excl: 873.20-873.39, 879.8-879.9, 929.0, 929.9, 958.8-958.99, 959.8-959.9

873.39 Multiple sites

N Newborn Age: 0	P Pediatric Age: 0-17	M Maternity Age: 12-55	A Adult Age: 15-124	CC CC Condition	MC Major Complication	CD Complex Dx	HIV HIV Related Dx

290 — Volume 1

2007 ICD•9•CM

√5ᵗʰ **873.4 Face, without mention of complication**
  873.40 Face, unspecified site
  873.41 Cheek
  873.42 Forehead
      Eyebrow
      AHA: 4Q, '96, 43
  873.43 Lip
  873.44 Jaw
  873.49 Other and multiple sites

√5ᵗʰ **873.5 Face, complicated**
  873.50 Face, unspecified site
  873.51 Cheek
  873.52 Forehead
  873.53 Lip
  873.54 Jaw
  873.59 Other and multiple sites

√5ᵗʰ **873.6 Internal structures of mouth, without mention of complication**
  873.60 Mouth, unspecified site
  873.61 Buccal mucosa
      DEF: Open wound of inside of cheek.
  873.62 Gum (alveolar process)
▲ 873.63 Tooth (broken) (fractured) (due to trauma)
      EXCLUDES ▶ cracked tooth (521.81)◀
      AHA: 1Q, '04, 17
  873.64 Tongue and floor of mouth
  873.65 Palate
      DEF: Open wound of roof of mouth.
  873.69 Other and multiple sites

√5ᵗʰ **873.7 Internal structures of mouth, complicated**
  873.70 Mouth, unspecified site
  873.71 Buccal mucosa
  873.72 Gum (alveolar process)
▲ 873.73 Tooth (broken) (fractured) (due to trauma)
      EXCLUDES ▶ cracked tooth (521.81)◀
      AHA: 1Q, '04, 17
  873.74 Tongue and floor of mouth
  873.75 Palate
  873.79 Other and multiple sites

  873.8 Other and unspecified open wound of head without mention of complication
      Head NOS
  873.9 Other and unspecified open wound of head, complicated CC
      CC Excl: 847.0, 873.40-873.79, 873.9, 874.8-874.9, 879.8-879.9, 929.0, 929.9, 958.8-958.99, 959.8-959.9

√4ᵗʰ **874 Open wound of neck**
√5ᵗʰ **874.0 Larynx and trachea, without mention of complication**
  874.00 Larynx with trachea CC
      CC Excl: 847.0, 874.00-874.12, 874.8-874.9, 879.8-879.9, 929.0, 929.9, 958.8-958.99, 959.8-959.9
  874.01 Larynx CC
      CC Excl: See code 874.00
  874.02 Trachea CC
      CC Excl: See code 874.00

√5ᵗʰ **874.1 Larynx and trachea, complicated**
  874.10 Larynx with trachea CC
      CC Excl: See code 874.00
  874.11 Larynx CC
      CC Excl: See code 874.00
  874.12 Trachea CC
      CC Excl: See code 874.00

  874.2 Thyroid gland, without mention of complication

  874.3 Thyroid gland, complicated CC
      CC Excl: 847.0, 874.2-874.3, 874.8-874.9, 879.8-879.9, 929.0, 929.9, 958.8-958.99, 959.8-959.9
  874.4 Pharynx, without mention of complication
      Cervical esophagus
  874.5 Pharynx, complicated CC
      CC Excl: 847.0, 874.4-874.9, 879.8-879.9, 929.0, 929.9, 958.8-958.99, 959.8-959.9
  874.8 Other and unspecified parts, without mention of complication
      Nape of neck   Throat NOS
      Supraclavicular region
  874.9 Other and unspecified parts, complicated

√4ᵗʰ **875 Open wound of chest (wall)**
      EXCLUDES   open wound into thoracic cavity (860.0-862.9)
                 traumatic pneumothorax and hemothorax
                 (860.1, 860.3, 860.5)
      AHA: 3Q, '93, 17
  875.0 Without mention of complication CC
      CC Excl: 847.1, 862.29, 862.39, 862.8-862.9, 875.0-875.1, 879.8-879.9, 929.0, 929.9, 958.7-958.99, 959.8-959.9
  875.1 Complicated CC
      CC Excl: See code 875.0

√4ᵗʰ **876 Open wound of back**
      INCLUDES   loin
                 lumbar region
      EXCLUDES   open wound into thoracic cavity (860.0-862.9)
                 traumatic pneumothorax and hemothorax
                 (860.1, 860.3, 860.5)
  876.0 Without mention of complication
  876.1 Complicated

√4ᵗʰ **877 Open wound of buttock**
      INCLUDES   sacroiliac region
  877.0 Without mention of complication
  877.1 Complicated

√4ᵗʰ **878 Open wound of genital organs (external), including traumatic amputation**
      EXCLUDES   injury during delivery (664.0-665.9)
                 internal genital organs (867.0-867.9)
  878.0 Penis, without mention of complication ♂
  878.1 Penis, complicated ♂
  878.2 Scrotum and testes, without mention of complication ♂
  878.3 Scrotum and testes, complicated ♂
  878.4 Vulva, without mention of complication ♀
      Labium (majus) (minus)
  878.5 Vulva, complicated ♀
  878.6 Vagina, without mention of complication ♀
  878.7 Vagina, complicated ♀
  878.8 Other and unspecified parts, without mention of complication
  878.9 Other and unspecified parts, complicated

√4ᵗʰ **879 Open wound of other and unspecified sites, except limbs**
  879.0 Breast, without mention of complication
  879.1 Breast, complicated
  879.2 Abdominal wall, anterior, without mention of complication
      Abdominal wall NOS   Pubic region
      Epigastric region   Umbilical region
      Hypogastric region
      AHA: 2Q, '91, 22
  879.3 Abdominal wall, anterior, complicated
  879.4 Abdominal wall, lateral, without mention of complication
      Flank   Iliac (region)
      Groin   Inguinal region
      Hypochondrium
  879.5 Abdominal wall, lateral, complicated

√4ᵗʰ / √5ᵗʰ Additional Digit Required   Nonspecific PDx   Unacceptable PDx   Manifestation Code   MCV Major Cardiovascular Condition   ▶◀ Revised Text   ● New Code   ▲ Revised Code Title

Injury and Poisoning

879.6–897.0

879.6   **Other and unspecified parts of trunk, without mention of complication**
  Pelvic region   Trunk NOS
  Perineum

879.7   **Other and unspecified parts of trunk, complicated**

879.8   **Open wound(s) (multiple) of unspecified site(s) without mention of complication**
  Multiple open wounds NOS   Open wound NOS

879.9   **Open wound(s) (multiple) of unspecified site(s), complicated**

OPEN WOUND OF UPPER LIMB (880-887)
AHA: N-D, '85, 5

✓4th **880 Open wound of shoulder and upper arm**

The following fifth-digit subclassification is for use with category 880:
  0   shoulder region
  1   scapular region
  2   axillary region
  3   upper arm
  9   multiple sites

✓5th   **880.0**   **Without mention of complication**
✓5th   **880.1**   **Complicated**
✓5th   **880.2**   **With tendon involvement**

✓4th **881 Open wound of elbow, forearm, and wrist**

The following fifth-digit subclassification is for use with category 881:
  0   forearm
  1   elbow
  2   wrist

✓5th   **881.0**   **Without mention of complication**
✓5th   **881.1**   **Complicated**
✓5th   **881.2**   **With tendon involvement**

✓4th **882 Open wound of hand except finger(s) alone**
  882.0   **Without mention of complication**
  882.1   **Complicated**
  882.2   **With tendon involvement**

✓4th **883 Open wound of finger(s)**
  INCLUDES   fingernail
               thumb (nail)
  883.0   **Without mention of complication**
  883.1   **Complicated**
  883.2   **With tendon involvement**

✓4th **884 Multiple and unspecified open wound of upper limb**
  INCLUDES   arm NOS
               multiple sites of one upper limb
               upper limb NOS
  884.0   **Without mention of complication**
  884.1   **Complicated**
  884.2   **With tendon involvement**

✓4th **885 Traumatic amputation of thumb (complete) (partial)**
  INCLUDES   thumb(s) (with finger(s) of either hand)
  885.0   **Without mention of complication**
          AHA: 1Q, '03, 7
  885.1   **Complicated**

✓4th **886 Traumatic amputation of other finger(s) (complete) (partial)**
  INCLUDES   finger(s) of one or both hands, without mention of thumb(s)
  886.0   **Without mention of complication**
  886.1   **Complicated**

✓4th **887 Traumatic amputation of arm and hand (complete) (partial)**
  887.0   **Unilateral, below elbow, without mention of complication**   CC
          CC Excl: 880.00-887.7, 929.0-929.9, 958.8-958.99, 959.8-959.9
  887.1   **Unilateral, below elbow, complicated**   CC
          CC Excl: See code 887.0

887.2   **Unilateral, at or above elbow, without mention of complication**   CC
        CC Excl: See code 887.0

887.3   **Unilateral, at or above elbow, complicated**   CC
        CC Excl: See code 887.0

887.4   **Unilateral, level not specified, without mention of complication**   CC
        CC Excl: See code 887.0

887.5   **Unilateral, level not specified, complicated**   CC
        CC Excl: See code 887.0

887.6   **Bilateral [any level], without mention of complication**   CC
        One hand and other arm
        CC Excl: See code 887.0

887.7   **Bilateral [any level], complicated**   CC
        CC Excl: See code 887.0

OPEN WOUND OF LOWER LIMB (890-897)
AHA: N-D, '85, 5

✓4th **890 Open wound of hip and thigh**
  890.0   **Without mention of complication**
  890.1   **Complicated**
  890.2   **With tendon involvement**

✓4th **891 Open wound of knee, leg [except thigh], and ankle**
  INCLUDES   leg NOS
               multiple sites of leg, except thigh
  EXCLUDES   *that of thigh (890.0-890.2)*
               with multiple sites of lower limb (894.0-894.2)
  891.0   **Without mention of complication**
  891.1   **Complicated**
  891.2   **With tendon involvement**

✓4th **892 Open wound of foot except toe(s) alone**
  INCLUDES   heel
  892.0   **Without mention of complication**
  892.1   **Complicated**
  892.2   **With tendon involvement**

✓4th **893 Open wound of toe(s)**
  INCLUDES   toenail
  893.0   **Without mention of complication**
  893.1   **Complicated**
  893.2   **With tendon involvement**

✓4th **894 Multiple and unspecified open wound of lower limb**
  INCLUDES   lower limb NOS
               multiple sites of one lower limb, with thigh
  894.0   **Without mention of complication**
  894.1   **Complicated**
  894.2   **With tendon involvement**

✓4th **895 Traumatic amputation of toe(s) (complete) (partial)**
  INCLUDES   toe(s) of one or both feet
  895.0   **Without mention of complication**
  895.1   **Complicated**

✓4th **896 Traumatic amputation of foot (complete) (partial)**
  896.0   **Unilateral, without mention of complication**   CC
          CC Excl: 890.0-897.7, 929.0-929.9, 958.8-958.99, 959.8-959.9
  896.1   **Unilateral, complicated**   CC
          CC Excl: See code 896.0
  896.2   **Bilateral, without mention of complication**   CC
          EXCLUDES   *one foot and other leg (897.6-897.7)*
          CC Excl: See code 896.0
  896.3   **Bilateral, complicated**   CC
          CC Excl: See code 896.0

✓4th **897 Traumatic amputation of leg(s) (complete) (partial)**
  897.0   **Unilateral, below knee, without mention of complication**   CC
          CC Excl: See code 896.0

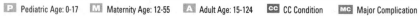
N Newborn Age: 0   P Pediatric Age: 0-17   M Maternity Age: 12-55   A Adult Age: 15-124   CC CC Condition   MC Major Complication   CD Complex Dx   HIV HIV Related Dx

292 — Volume 1   *2007 ICD•9•CM*

897.1   Unilateral, below knee, complicated   `CC`
CC Excl: See code 896.0

897.2   Unilateral, at or above knee, without mention of complication   `CC`
CC Excl: See code 896.0

897.3   Unilateral, at or above knee, complicated   `CC`
CC Excl: See code 896.0

897.4   Unilateral, level not specified, without mention of complication   `CC`
CC Excl: See code 896.0

897.5   Unilateral, level not specified, complicated   `CC`
CC Excl: See code 896.0

897.6   Bilateral [any level], without mention of complication   `CC`
> One foot and other leg

CC Excl: See code 896.0

897.7   Bilateral [any level], complicated   `CC`
CC Excl: See code 896.0
AHA: 3Q, '90, 5

INJURY TO BLOOD VESSELS (900-904)

INCLUDES   arterial hematoma
avulsion
cut   of blood vessel,
laceration   secondary to
rupture   other injuries
traumatic aneurysm   e.g., fracture
or fistula (arteri-   or open
ovenous)   wound

EXCLUDES   accidental puncture or laceration during medical procedure (998.2)
intracranial hemorrhage following injury (851.0-854.1)

AHA: 3Q, '90, 5

√4ᵗʰ **900 Injury to blood vessels of head and neck**

√5ᵗʰ **900.0**   Carotid artery

900.00 Carotid artery, unspecified   `CC`
CC Excl: 900.00, 900.82-900.9, 904.9, 929.0-929.9, 958.8-958.99, 959.8-959.9

900.01 Common carotid artery   `CC`
CC Excl: See code 900.00

900.02 External carotid artery   `CC`
CC Excl: See code 900.00

900.03 Internal carotid artery   `CC`
CC Excl: See code 900.00

900.1   Internal jugular vein   `CC`
CC Excl: 900.82-900.9, 904.9, 929.0-929.9, 958.8-958.99, 959.8-959.9

√5ᵗʰ **900.8**   Other specified blood vessels of head and neck

900.81 External jugular vein
> Jugular vein NOS

CC Excl: See code 900.1

900.82 Multiple blood vessels of head and neck   `CC`
CC Excl: See code 900.1

900.89 Other   `CC`
CC Excl: See code 900.1

900.9   Unspecified blood vessel of head and neck   `CC`
CC Excl: See code 900.1

√4ᵗʰ **901 Injury to blood vessels of thorax**
EXCLUDES   traumatic hemothorax (860.2-860.5)

901.0   Thoracic aorta   `CC`
CC Excl: 901.0, 904.9, 929.0, 929.9, 958.8-958.99, 959.8-959.9

901.1   Innominate and subclavian arteries   `CC`
CC Excl: 901.1, 904.9, 929.0, 929.9, 958.8-958.99, 959.8-959.9

901.2   Superior vena cava   `CC`
CC Excl: 901.2, 904.9, 929.0, 929.9, 958.8-958.99, 959.8-959.9

901.3   Innominate and subclavian veins   `CC`
CC Excl: 901.3, 904.9, 929.0, 929.9, 958.8-958.99, 959.8-959.9

√5ᵗʰ **901.4**   Pulmonary blood vessels

901.40 Pulmonary vessel(s), unspecified

901.41 Pulmonary artery   `CC`
CC Excl: 901.40, 901.41, 904.9, 929.0, 929.9, 958.8-958.99, 959.8-959.9

901.42 Pulmonary vein   `CC`
CC Excl: 901.40, 901.42, 904.9, 929.0, 929.9, 958.8-958.99, 959.8-959.9

√5ᵗʰ **901.8**   Other specified blood vessels of thorax

901.81 Intercostal artery or vein

901.82 Internal mammary artery or vein

901.83 Multiple blood vessels of thorax   `CC`
CC Excl: 904.9, 929.0, 929.9, 958.8-958.99, 959.8-959.9

901.89 Other
> Azygos vein
> Hemiazygos vein

901.9   Unspecified blood vessel of thorax

√4ᵗʰ **902 Injury to blood vessels of abdomen and pelvis**

902.0   Abdominal aorta   `CC`
CC Excl: 902.0, 902.87, 902.89, 902.9, 904.9, 929.0, 929.9, 958.8-958.99, 959.8-959.9

√5ᵗʰ **902.1**   Inferior vena cava

902.10 Inferior vena cava, unspecified   `CC`
CC Excl: 902.10, 902.87-902.9, 904.9, 929.0, 929.9, 958.8-958.99, 959.8-959.9

902.11 Hepatic veins   `CC`
CC Excl: 902.11, 902.87-902.9, 904.9, 929.0, 929.9, 958.8-958.99, 959.8-959.9

902.19 Other   `CC`
CC Excl: 902.19, 902.87-902.9, 904.9, 929.0, 929.9, 958.8-958.99, 959.8-959.9

√5ᵗʰ **902.2**   Celiac and mesenteric arteries

902.20 Celiac and mesenteric arteries, unspecified   `CC`
CC Excl: 902.20, 902.87-902.9, 904.9, 929.0, 929.9, 958.8-958.99, 959.8-959.9

902.21 Gastric artery

902.22 Hepatic artery   `CC`
CC Excl: 902.22, 902.87, 902.89, 902.9, 904.9, 929.0, 929.9, 958.8-958.99, 959.8-959.9

902.23 Splenic artery   `CC`
CC Excl: 902.23, 902.87-902.9, 904.9, 929.0, 929.9, 958.8-958.99, 959.8-959.9

902.24 Other specified branches of celiac axis   `CC`
CC Excl: 902.24, 902.87-902.9, 904.9, 929.0, 929.9, 958.8-958.99, 959.8-959.9

902.25 Superior mesenteric artery (trunk)   `CC`
CC Excl: 902.25, 902.87-902.9, 904.9, 929.0, 929.9, 958.8-958.99, 959.8-959.9

902.26 Primary branches of superior mesenteric artery   `CC`
> Ileocolic artery

CC Excl: 902.26, 902.87-902.9, 904.9, 929.0, 929.9, 958.8-958.99, 959.8-959.9

902.27 Inferior mesenteric artery   `CC`
CC Excl: 902.27, 902.87-902.9, 904.9, 929.0, 929.9, 958.8-958.99, 959.8-959.9

√4ᵗʰ / √5ᵗʰ Additional Digit Required   Nonspecific PDx   Unacceptable PDx   Manifestation Code   `MCV` Major Cardiovascular Condition   ▶◀ Revised Text   ● New Code   ▲ Revised Code Title

2007 ICD•9•CM   **Volume 1 — 293**

Injury and Poisoning

902.29–905.6

902.29 Other `CC`
> CC Excl: 902.29, 902.87-902.9, 904.9, 929.0, 929.9, 958.8-958.99, 959.8-959.9

✓5th **902.3 Portal and splenic veins**

902.31 Superior mesenteric vein and primary subdivisions `CC`
> Ileocolic vein
> CC Excl: 902.31, 902.87-902.9, 904.9, 929.0, 929.9, 958.8-958.99, 959.8-959.9

902.32 Inferior mesenteric vein `CC`
> CC Excl: 902.32, 902.87-902.9, 904.9, 929.0, 929.9, 958.8-958.99, 959.8-959.9

902.33 Portal vein `CC`
> CC Excl: 902.33, 902.87-902.9, 904.9, 929.0, 929.9, 958.8-958.99, 959.8-959.9

902.34 Splenic vein `CC`
> CC Excl: 902.34, 902.87-902.9, 904.9, 929.0, 929.9, 958.8-958.99, 959.8-959.9

902.39 Other `CC`
> Cystic vein   Gastric vein
> CC Excl: 902.39, 902.87, 902.9, 904.9, 929.0, 929.9, 958.8-958.99, 959.8-959.9

✓5th **902.4 Renal blood vessels**

902.40 Renal vessel(s), unspecified `CC`
> CC Excl: 902.40, 902.87-902.9, 904.9, 929.0, 929.9, 958.8-958.99, 959.8-959.9

902.41 Renal artery `CC`
> CC Excl: 902.41, 902.87-902.9, 904.9, 929.0, 929.9, 958.8-958.99, 959.8-959.9

902.42 Renal vein `CC`
> CC Excl: 902.42, 902.87-902.9, 904.9, 929.0, 929.9, 958.8-958.99, 959.8-959.9

902.49 Other `CC`
> Suprarenal arteries
> CC Excl: 902.49, 902.87-902.9, 904.9, 929.0, 929.9, 958.8-958.99, 959.8-959.9

✓5th **902.5 Iliac blood vessels**

902.50 Iliac vessel(s), unspecified `CC`
> CC Excl: 902.50, 902.53-902.54, 902.59, 902.87-902.9, 904.9, 929.0, 929.9, 958.8-958.99, 959.8-959.9

902.51 Hypogastric artery `CC`
> CC Excl: 902.51, 902.87-902.9, 904.9, 929.0, 929.9, 958.8-958.99, 959.8-959.9

902.52 Hypogastric vein `CC`
> CC Excl: 902.52, 902.87, 902.9, 904.9, 929.0, 929.9, 958.8-958.99, 959.8-959.9

902.53 Iliac artery `CC`
> CC Excl: 902.50, 902.53, 902.59, 902.87-902.9, 904.9, 929.0, 929.9, 958.8-958.99, 959.8-959.9

902.54 Iliac vein `CC`
> CC Excl: 902.50, 902.54, 902.59, 902.87-902.9, 904.9, 929.0, 929.9, 958.8-958.99, 959.8-959.9

902.55 Uterine artery ♀
902.56 Uterine vein ♀
902.59 Other `CC`
> CC Excl: 902.50, 902.53-902.54, 902.59, 902.87-902.9, 904.9, 929.0, 929.9, 958.8-958.99, 959.8-959.9

✓5th **902.8 Other specified blood vessels of abdomen and pelvis**

902.81 Ovarian artery ♀
902.82 Ovarian vein ♀
902.87 Multiple blood vessels of abdomen and pelvis `CC`
> CC Excl: 902.87-902.9, 904.9, 929.0, 929.9, 958.8-958.99, 959.8-959.9

902.89 Other

902.9 Unspecified blood vessel of abdomen and pelvis

✓4th **903 Injury to blood vessels of upper extremity**

✓5th **903.0 Axillary blood vessels**

903.00 Axillary vessel(s), unspecified
903.01 Axillary artery
903.02 Axillary vein

903.1 Brachial blood vessels
903.2 Radial blood vessels
903.3 Ulnar blood vessels
903.4 Palmar artery
903.5 Digital blood vessels
903.8 Other specified blood vessels of upper extremity
> Multiple blood vessels of upper extremity

903.9 Unspecified blood vessel of upper extremity

✓4th **904 Injury to blood vessels of lower extremity and unspecified sites**

904.0 Common femoral artery `CC`
> Femoral artery above profunda origin
> CC Excl: No exclusions

904.1 Superficial femoral artery
904.2 Femoral veins
904.3 Saphenous veins
> Saphenous vein (greater) (lesser)

✓5th **904.4 Popliteal blood vessels**

904.40 Popliteal vessel(s), unspecified
904.41 Popliteal artery
904.42 Popliteal vein

✓5th **904.5 Tibial blood vessels**

904.50 Tibial vessel(s), unspecified
904.51 Anterior tibial artery
904.52 Anterior tibial vein
904.53 Posterior tibial artery
904.54 Posterior tibial vein

904.6 Deep plantar blood vessels
904.7 Other specified blood vessels of lower extremity
> Multiple blood vessels of lower extremity

904.8 Unspecified blood vessel of lower extremity
904.9 Unspecified site
> Injury to blood vessel NOS

LATE EFFECTS OF INJURIES, POISONINGS, TOXIC EFFECTS, AND OTHER EXTERNAL CAUSES (905-909)

> Note: These categories are to be used to indicate conditions classifiable to 800-999 as the cause of late effects, which are themselves classified elsewhere. The "late effects" include those specified as such, or as sequelae, which may occur at any time after the acute injury.

✓4th **905 Late effects of musculoskeletal and connective tissue injuries**
> AHA: 1Q, '95, 10; 2Q, '94, 3

905.0 Late effect of fracture of skull and face bones
> Late effect of injury classifiable to 800-804
> AHA: 3Q, '97, 12

905.1 Late effect of fracture of spine and trunk without mention of spinal cord lesion
> Late effect of injury classifiable to 805, 807-809

905.2 Late effect of fracture of upper extremities
> Late effect of injury classifiable to 810-819

905.3 Late effect of fracture of neck of femur
> Late effect of injury classifiable to 820

905.4 Late effect of fracture of lower extremities
> Late effect of injury classifiable to 821-827

905.5 Late effect of fracture of multiple and unspecified bones
> Late effect of injury classifiable to 828-829

905.6 Late effect of dislocation
> Late effect of injury classifiable to 830-839

`N` Newborn Age: 0   `P` Pediatric Age: 0-17   `M` Maternity Age: 12-55   `A` Adult Age: 15-124   `CC` CC Condition   `MC` Major Complication   `CD` Complex Dx   `HIV` HIV Related Dx

905.7   **Late effect of sprain and strain without mention of tendon injury**
Late effect of injury classifiable to 840-848, except tendon injury

905.8   **Late effect of tendon injury**
Late effect of tendon injury due to:
open wound [injury classifiable to 880-884 with .2, 890-894 with .2]
sprain and strain [injury classifiable to 840-848]
AHA: 2Q, '89, 13; 2Q, '89, 15

905.9   **Late effect of traumatic amputation**
Late effect of injury classifiable to 885-887, 895-897
   EXCLUDES   *late amputation stump complication (997.60-997.69)*

✓4ᵗʰ **906 Late effects of injuries to skin and subcutaneous tissues**

906.0   **Late effect of open wound of head, neck, and trunk**
Late effect of injury classifiable to 870-879

906.1   **Late effect of open wound of extremities without mention of tendon injury**
Late effect of injury classifiable to 880-884, 890-894 except .2

906.2   **Late effect of superficial injury**
Late effect of injury classifiable to 910-919

906.3   **Late effect of contusion**
Late effect of injury classifiable to 920-924

906.4   **Late effect of crushing**
Late effect of injury classifiable to 925-929

906.5   **Late effect of burn of eye, face, head, and neck**
Late effect of injury classifiable to 940-941
AHA: 4Q, '04, 76

906.6   **Late effect of burn of wrist and hand**
Late effect of injury classifiable to 944
AHA: 4Q, '94, 22

906.7   **Late effect of burn of other extremities**
Late effect of injury classifiable to 943 or 945
AHA: 4Q, '94, 22

906.8   **Late effect of burns of other specified sites**
Late effect of injury classifiable to 942, 946-947
AHA: 4Q, '94, 22

906.9   **Late effect of burn of unspecified site**
Late effect of injury classifiable to 948-949
AHA: 4Q, '94, 22

✓4ᵗʰ **907 Late effects of injuries to the nervous system**

907.0   **Late effect of intracranial injury without mention of skull fracture**
Late effect of injury classifiable to 850-854
AHA: 4Q, '03, 103; 3Q, '90, 14

907.1   **Late effect of injury to cranial nerve**
Late effect of injury classifiable to 950-951

907.2   **Late effect of spinal cord injury**
Late effect of injury classifiable to 806, 952
AHA: 4Q, '03, 103; 4Q, '98, 38

907.3   **Late effect of injury to nerve root(s), spinal plexus(es), and other nerves of trunk**
Late effect of injury classifiable to 953-954

907.4   **Late effect of injury to peripheral nerve of shoulder girdle and upper limb**
Late effect of injury classifiable to 955

907.5   **Late effect of injury to peripheral nerve of pelvic girdle and lower limb**
Late effect of injury classifiable to 956

907.9   **Late effect of injury to other and unspecified nerve**
Late effect of injury classifiable to 957

✓4ᵗʰ **908 Late effects of other and unspecified injuries**

908.0   **Late effect of internal injury to chest**
Late effect of injury classifiable to 860-862

908.1   **Late effect of internal injury to intra-abdominal organs**
Late effect of injury classifiable to 863-866, 868

908.2   **Late effect of internal injury to other internal organs**
Late effect of injury classifiable to 867 or 869

908.3   **Late effect of injury to blood vessel of head, neck, and extremities**
Late effect of injury classifiable to 900, 903-904

908.4   **Late effect of injury to blood vessel of thorax, abdomen, and pelvis**
Late effect of injury classifiable to 901-902

908.5   **Late effect of foreign body in orifice**
Late effect of injury classifiable to 930-939

908.6   **Late effect of certain complications of trauma**
Late effect of complications classifiable to 958

908.9   **Late effect of unspecified injury**
Late effect of injury classifiable to 959
AHA: 3Q, '00, 4

✓4ᵗʰ **909 Late effects of other and unspecified external causes**

909.0   **Late effect of poisoning due to drug, medicinal or biological substance**
Late effect of conditions classifiable to 960-979
   EXCLUDES   *late effect of adverse effect of drug, medicinal or biological substance (909.5)*
AHA: 4Q, '03, 103

909.1   **Late effect of toxic effects of nonmedical substances**
Late effect of conditions classifiable to 980-989

909.2   **Late effect of radiation**
Late effect of conditions classifiable to 990

909.3   **Late effect of complications of surgical and medical care**
Late effect of conditions classifiable to 996-999
AHA: 1Q, '93, 29

909.4   **Late effect of certain other external causes**
Late effect of conditions classifiable to 991-994

909.5   **Late effect of adverse effect of drug, medical or biological substance**
   EXCLUDES   *late effect of poisoning due to drug, medicinal or biological substance (909.0)*
AHA: 4Q, '94, 48

909.9   **Late effect of other and unspecified external causes**

SUPERFICIAL INJURY (910-919)

   EXCLUDES   *burn (blisters) (940.0-949.5)*
contusion (920-924.9)
foreign body:
granuloma (728.82)
inadvertently left in operative wound (998.4)
residual in soft tissue (729.6)
insect bite, venomous (989.5)
open wound with incidental foreign body (870.0-897.7)

AHA: 2Q, '89, 15

✓4ᵗʰ **910 Superficial injury of face, neck, and scalp except eye**
   INCLUDES   cheek   lip
              ear   nose
              gum   throat
   EXCLUDES   *eye and adnexa (918.0-918.9)*

910.0   **Abrasion or friction burn without mention of infection**

910.1   **Abrasion or friction burn, infected**

910.2   **Blister without mention of infection**

910.3   **Blister, infected**

910.4   **Insect bite, nonvenomous, without mention of infection**

910.5   **Insect bite, nonvenomous, infected**

910.6   **Superficial foreign body (splinter) without major open wound and without mention of infection**

910.7   **Superficial foreign body (splinter) without major open wound, infected**

✓4ᵗʰ ✓5ᵗʰ Additional Digit Required   Nonspecific PDx   Unacceptable PDx   Manifestation Code   **MCV** Major Cardiovascular Condition   ►◄ Revised Text   ● New Code   ▲ Revised Code Title

2007 ICD•9•CM   **Volume 1 — 295**

Injury and Poisoning

910.8–917.9

910.8 Other and unspecified superficial injury of face, neck, and scalp without mention of infection

910.9 Other and unspecified superficial injury of face, neck, and scalp, infected

√4ᵗʰ **911 Superficial injury of trunk**

INCLUDES	abdominal wall	interscapular region
	anus	labium (majus) (minus)
	back	penis
	breast	perineum
	buttock	scrotum
	chest wall	testis
	flank	vagina
	groin	vulva

EXCLUDES   hip (916.0-916.9)
            scapular region (912.0-912.9)

911.0 Abrasion or friction burn without mention of infection

AHA: 3Q, '01, 10

911.1 Abrasion or friction burn, infected

911.2 Blister without mention of infection

911.3 Blister, infected

911.4 Insect bite, nonvenomous, without mention of infection

911.5 Insect bite, nonvenomous, infected

911.6 Superficial foreign body (splinter) without major open wound and without mention of infection

911.7 Superficial foreign body (splinter) without major open wound, infected

911.8 Other and unspecified superficial injury of trunk without mention of infection

911.9 Other and unspecified superficial injury of trunk, infected

√4ᵗʰ **912 Superficial injury of shoulder and upper arm**

INCLUDES	axilla	scapular region

912.0 Abrasion or friction burn without mention of infection

912.1 Abrasion or friction burn, infected

912.2 Blister without mention of infection

912.3 Blister, infected

912.4 Insect bite, nonvenomous, without mention of infection

912.5 Insect bite, nonvenomous, infected

912.6 Superficial foreign body (splinter) without major open wound and without mention of infection

912.7 Superficial foreign body (splinter) without major open wound, infected

912.8 Other and unspecified superficial injury of shoulder and upper arm without mention of infection

912.9 Other and unspecified superficial injury of shoulder and upper arm, infected

√4ᵗʰ **913 Superficial injury of elbow, forearm, and wrist**

913.0 Abrasion or friction burn without mention of infection

913.1 Abrasion or friction burn, infected

913.2 Blister without mention of infection

913.3 Blister, infected

913.4 Insect bite, nonvenomous, without mention of infection

913.5 Insect bite, nonvenomous, infected

913.6 Superficial foreign body (splinter) without major open wound and without mention of infection

913.7 Superficial foreign body (splinter) without major open wound, infected

913.8 Other and unspecified superficial injury of elbow, forearm, and wrist without mention of infection

913.9 Other and unspecified superficial injury of elbow, forearm, and wrist, infected

√4ᵗʰ **914 Superficial injury of hand(s) except finger(s) alone**

914.0 Abrasion or friction burn without mention of infection

914.1 Abrasion or friction burn, infected

914.2 Blister without mention of infection

914.3 Blister, infected

914.4 Insect bite, nonvenomous, without mention of infection

914.5 Insect bite, nonvenomous, infected

914.6 Superficial foreign body (splinter) without major open wound and without mention of infection

914.7 Superficial foreign body (splinter) without major open wound, infected

914.8 Other and unspecified superficial injury of hand without mention of infection

914.9 Other and unspecified superficial injury of hand, infected

√4ᵗʰ **915 Superficial injury of finger(s)**

INCLUDES	fingernail	thumb (nail)

915.0 Abrasion or friction burn without mention of infection

915.1 Abrasion or friction burn, infected

915.2 Blister without mention of infection

915.3 Blister, infected

915.4 Insect bite, nonvenomous, without mention of infection

915.5 Insect bite, nonvenomous, infected

915.6 Superficial foreign body (splinter) without major open wound and without mention of infection

915.7 Superficial foreign body (splinter) without major open wound, infected

915.8 Other and unspecified superficial injury of fingers without mention of infection

AHA: 3Q, '01, 10

915.9 Other and unspecified superficial injury of fingers, infected

√4ᵗʰ **916 Superficial injury of hip, thigh, leg, and ankle**

916.0 Abrasion or friction burn without mention of infection

916.1 Abrasion or friction burn, infected

916.2 Blister without mention of infection

916.3 Blister, infected

916.4 Insect bite, nonvenomous, without mention of infection

916.5 Insect bite, nonvenomous, infected

916.6 Superficial foreign body (splinter) without major open wound and without mention of infection

916.7 Superficial foreign body (splinter) without major open wound, infected

916.8 Other and unspecified superficial injury of hip, thigh, leg, and ankle without mention of infection

916.9 Other and unspecified superficial injury of hip, thigh, leg, and ankle, infected

√4ᵗʰ **917 Superficial injury of foot and toe(s)**

INCLUDES	heel	toenail

917.0 Abrasion or friction burn without mention of infection

917.1 Abrasion or friction burn, infected

917.2 Blister without mention of infection

917.3 Blister, infected

917.4 Insect bite, nonvenomous, without mention of infection

917.5 Insect bite, nonvenomous, infected

917.6 Superficial foreign body (splinter) without major open wound and without mention of infection

917.7 Superficial foreign body (splinter) without major open wound, infected

917.8 Other and unspecified superficial injury of foot and toes without mention of infection

AHA: 1Q, '03, 13

917.9 Other and unspecified superficial injury of foot and toes, infected

AHA: 1Q, '03, 13

N Newborn Age: 0   **P** Pediatric Age: 0-17   **M** Maternity Age: 12-55   **A** Adult Age: 15-124   **CC** CC Condition   **MC** Major Complication   **CD** Complex Dx   **HIV** HIV Related Dx

☑4th **918 Superficial injury of eye and adnexa**
  EXCLUDES *burn (940.0-940.9)*
       foreign body on external eye (930.0-930.9)

918.0 **Eyelids and periocular area**
  Abrasion   Superficial foreign body
  Insect bite   (splinter)

918.1 **Cornea**
  Corneal abrasion   Superficial laceration
  EXCLUDES *corneal injury due to contact lens*
       (371.82)

918.2 **Conjunctiva**

918.9 **Other and unspecified superficial injuries of eye**
  Eye (ball) NOS

☑4th **919 Superficial injury of other, multiple, and unspecified sites**
  EXCLUDES *multiple sites classifiable to the same three-digit*
       category (910.0-918.9)

919.0 **Abrasion or friction burn without mention of infection**

919.1 **Abrasion or friction burn, infected**

919.2 **Blister without mention of infection**

919.3 **Blister, infected**

919.4 **Insect bite, nonvenomous, without mention of infection**

919.5 **Insect bite, nonvenomous, infected**

919.6 **Superficial foreign body (splinter) without major open wound and without mention of infection**

919.7 **Superficial foreign body (splinter) without major open wound, infected**

919.8 **Other and unspecified superficial injury without mention of infection**

919.9 **Other and unspecified superficial injury, infected**

CONTUSION WITH INTACT SKIN SURFACE (920-924)

  INCLUDES bruise   } without fracture or open
       hematoma }   wound

  EXCLUDES *concussion (850.0-850.9)*
       hemarthrosis (840.0-848.9)
       internal organs (860.0-869.1)
       that incidental to:
         crushing injury (925-929.9)
         dislocation (830.0-839.9)
         fracture (800.0-829.1)
         internal injury (860.0-869.1)
         intracranial injury (850.0-854.1)
         nerve injury (950.0-957.9)
         open wound (870.0-897.7)

920 Contusion of face, scalp, and neck except eye(s)
  Cheek   Mandibular joint area
  Ear (auricle)   Nose
  Gum   Throat
  Lip

☑4th **921 Contusion of eye and adnexa**
  921.0 **Black eye, not otherwise specified**
  921.1 **Contusion of eyelids and periocular area**
  921.2 **Contusion of orbital tissues**
  921.3 **Contusion of eyeball**
    AHA: J-A, '85, 16
  921.9 **Unspecified contusion of eye**
    Injury of eye NOS

☑4th **922 Contusion of trunk**
  922.0 **Breast**
  922.1 **Chest wall**
  922.2 **Abdominal wall**
    Flank   Groin
  ☑5th 922.3 **Back**
    AHA: 4Q, '96, 39
    922.31 **Back**
      EXCLUDES *interscapular region (922.33)*
      AHA: 3Q, '99, 14
    922.32 **Buttock**
    922.33 **Interscapular region**

922.4 **Genital organs**
  Labium (majus) (minus) Vulva
  Penis   Vagina
  Perineum   Testis
  Scrotum

922.8 **Multiple sites of trunk**
922.9 **Unspecified part**
  Trunk NOS

☑4th **923 Contusion of upper limb**
  ☑5th 923.0 **Shoulder and upper arm**
    923.00 **Shoulder region**
    923.01 **Scapular region**
    923.02 **Axillary region**
    923.03 **Upper arm**
    923.09 **Multiple sites**
  ☑5th 923.1 **Elbow and forearm**
    923.10 **Forearm**
    923.11 **Elbow**
  ☑5th 923.2 **Wrist and hand(s), except finger(s) alone**
    923.20 **Hand(s)**
    923.21 **Wrist**
  923.3 **Finger**
    Fingernail   Thumb (nail)
  923.8 **Multiple sites of upper limb**
  923.9 **Unspecified part of upper limb**
    Arm NOS

☑4th **924 Contusion of lower limb and of other and unspecified sites**
  ☑5th 924.0 **Hip and thigh**
    924.00 **Thigh**
    924.01 **Hip**
  ☑5th 924.1 **Knee and lower leg**
    924.10 **Lower leg**
    924.11 **Knee**
  ☑5th 924.2 **Ankle and foot, excluding toe(s)**
    924.20 **Foot**
      Heel
    924.21 **Ankle**
  924.3 **Toe**
    Toenail
  924.4 **Multiple sites of lower limb**
  924.5 **Unspecified part of lower limb**
    Leg NOS
  924.8 **Multiple sites, not elsewhere classified**
    AHA: 1Q, '03, 7
  924.9 **Unspecified site**

CRUSHING INJURY (925-929)

Use additional code to identify any associated injuries, such as:
  fractures (800-829)
  internal injuries (860.0-869.1)
  intracranial injuries (850.0-854.1)
AHA: 4Q, '03, 77; 2Q, '93, 7

☑4th **925 Crushing injury of face, scalp, and neck**
  Cheek   Pharynx
  Ear   Throat
  Larynx
  925.1 **Crushing injury of face and scalp** CC
    Cheek   Ear
    CC Excl: 873.8-873.9, 905.0, 925.1-925.2, 929.0, 929.9, 958.8-959.09, 959.8-959.9
  925.2 **Crushing injury of neck** CC
    Larynx   Throat
    Pharynx
    CC Excl: 873.8-873.9, 905.0, 925.1-925.2, 929.0, 929.9, 958.8-959.09, 959.8-959.9

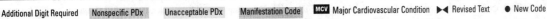
☑4th ☑5th Additional Digit Required Nonspecific PDx Unacceptable PDx Manifestation Code MCV Major Cardiovascular Condition ▶◀ Revised Text ● New Code ▲ Revised Code Title

2007 ICD•9•CM Volume 1 — 297

Injury and Poisoning

926–940.9

✓4ᵗʰ **926 Crushing injury of trunk**

    926.0   **External genitalia**

        Labium (majus) (minus)   Testis

        Penis   Vulva

        Scrotum

    ✓5ᵗʰ **926.1**   **Other specified sites**

        926.11   **Back**

        926.12   **Buttock**

        926.19   **Other**

              Breast

    926.8   **Multiple sites of trunk**

    926.9   **Unspecified site**

        Trunk NOS

✓4ᵗʰ **927 Crushing injury of upper limb**

    ✓5ᵗʰ **927.0**   **Shoulder and upper arm**

        927.00   **Shoulder region**

        927.01   **Scapular region**

        927.02   **Axillary region**

        927.03   **Upper arm**

        927.09   **Multiple sites**

    ✓5ᵗʰ **927.1**   **Elbow and forearm**

        927.10   **Forearm**

        927.11   **Elbow**

    ✓5ᵗʰ **927.2**   **Wrist and hand(s), except finger(s) alone**

        927.20   **Hand(s)**

        927.21   **Wrist**

    927.3   **Finger(s)**

        AHA: 4Q, '03, 77

    927.8   **Multiple sites of upper limb**

    927.9   **Unspecified site**

        Arm NOS

✓4ᵗʰ **928 Crushing injury of lower limb**

    ✓5ᵗʰ **928.0**   **Hip and thigh**

        928.00   **Thigh**

        928.01   **Hip**

    ✓5ᵗʰ **928.1**   **Knee and lower leg**

        928.10   **Lower leg**

        928.11   **Knee**

    ✓5ᵗʰ **928.2**   **Ankle and foot, excluding toe(s) alone**

        928.20   **Foot**

              Heel

        928.21   **Ankle**

    928.3   **Toe(s)**

    928.8   **Multiple sites of lower limb**

    928.9   **Unspecified site**

        Leg NOS

✓4ᵗʰ **929 Crushing injury of multiple and unspecified sites**

    929.0   **Multiple sites, not elsewhere classified**   **CC**

        CC Excl: 929.0, 929.9, 958.8-958.99, 959.8-959.9

    929.9   **Unspecified site**

EFFECTS OF FOREIGN BODY ENTERING THROUGH ORIFICE (930–939)

    EXCLUDES   *foreign body:*

        granuloma (728.82)

        inadvertently left in operative wound (998.4,
            998.7)

        in open wound (800-839, 851-897)

        residual in soft tissues (729.6)

        superficial without major open wound (910-
            919 with .6 or .7)

✓4ᵗʰ **930 Foreign body on external eye**

    EXCLUDES   *foreign body in penetrating wound of:*

        eyeball (871.5-871.6)

            retained (old) (360.5-360.6)

        ocular adnexa (870.4)

            retained (old) (376.6)

    930.0   **Corneal foreign body**

    930.1   **Foreign body in conjunctival sac**

    930.2   **Foreign body in lacrimal punctum**

    930.8   **Other and combined sites**

    930.9   **Unspecified site**

        External eye NOS

931 Foreign body in ear

    Auditory canal   Auricle

932 Foreign body in nose

    Nasal sinus   Nostril

✓4ᵗʰ **933 Foreign body in pharynx and larynx**

    933.0   **Pharynx**

        Nasopharynx   Throat NOS

    933.1   **Larynx**

        Asphyxia due to foreign body

        Choking due to:

           food (regurgitated)

           phlegm

✓4ᵗʰ **934 Foreign body in trachea, bronchus, and lung**

    934.0   **Trachea**

    934.1   **Main bronchus**

        AHA: 3Q, '02, 18

    934.8   **Other specified parts**

        Bronchioles   Lung

    934.9   **Respiratory tree, unspecified**

        Inhalation of liquid or vomitus, lower respiratory
           tract NOS

✓4ᵗʰ **935 Foreign body in mouth, esophagus, and stomach**

    935.0   **Mouth**

    935.1   **Esophagus**

        AHA: 1Q, '88, 13

    935.2   **Stomach**

936 Foreign body in intestine and colon

937 Foreign body in anus and rectum

    Rectosigmoid (junction)

938 Foreign body in digestive system, unspecified

    Alimentary tract NOS

    Swallowed foreign body

✓4ᵗʰ **939 Foreign body in genitourinary tract**

    939.0   **Bladder and urethra**

    939.1   **Uterus, any part**   ♀

        EXCLUDES   *intrauterine contraceptive device:*

           complications from (996.32, 996.65)

           presence of (V45.51)

    939.2   **Vulva and vagina**   ♀

    939.3   **Penis**   ♂

    939.9   **Unspecified site**

BURNS (940–949)

    INCLUDES   burns from:

        electrical heating appliance

        electricity

        flame

        hot object

        lightning

        radiation

        chemical burns (external) (internal)

        scalds

    EXCLUDES   *friction burns (910-919 with .0, .1)*

        sunburn (692.71, 692.76-692.77)

    AHA: 4Q, 94, 22; 2Q, '90, 7; 4Q, '88, 3; M-A, '86, 9

✓4ᵗʰ **940 Burn confined to eye and adnexa**

    940.0   **Chemical burn of eyelids and periocular area**

    940.1   **Other burns of eyelids and periocular area**

    940.2   **Alkaline chemical burn of cornea and conjunctival sac**

    940.3   **Acid chemical burn of cornea and conjunctival sac**

    940.4   **Other burn of cornea and conjunctival sac**

    940.5   **Burn with resulting rupture and destruction of eyeball**

    940.9   **Unspecified burn of eye and adnexa**

N Newborn Age: 0   **P** Pediatric Age: 0-17   **M** Maternity Age: 12-55   **A** Adult Age: 15-124   **CC** CC Condition   **MC** Major Complication   **CD** Complex Dx   **HIV** HIV Related Dx

298 — Volume 1   *2007 ICD•9•CM*

√4th **941 Burn of face, head, and neck**

EXCLUDES mouth (947.0)

The following fifth-digit subclassification is for use with category 941:

0 face and head, unspecified site
1 ear [any part]
2 eye (with other parts of face, head, and neck)
3 lip(s)
4 chin
5 nose (septum)
6 scalp [any part]
  Temple (region)
7 forehead and cheek
8 neck
9 multiple sites [except with eye] of face, head, and neck

AHA: 4Q, '94, 22; M-A, '86, 9

√5th **941.0 Unspecified degree**
√5th **941.1 Erythema [first degree]**
AHA: For code 941.19: ▶3Q, '05, 10◀

√5th **941.2 Blisters, epidermal loss [second degree]**
√5th **941.3 Full-thickness skin loss [third degree NOS]**
√5th **941.4 Deep necrosis of underlying tissues [deep third degree] without mention of loss of a body part**
√5th **941.5 Deep necrosis of underlying tissues [deep third degree] with loss of a body part**

√4th **942 Burn of trunk**

EXCLUDES scapular region (943.0-943.5 with fifth-digit 6)

The following fifth-digit subclassification is for use with category 942:

0 trunk, unspecified site
1 breast
2 chest wall, excluding breast and nipple
3 abdominal wall
  Flank   Groin
4 back [any part]
  Buttock
  Interscapular region
5 genitalia
  Labium (majus) (minus)   Scrotum
  Penis   Testis
  Perineum   Vulva
9 other and multiple sites of trunk

AHA: 4Q, '94, 22; M-A, '86, 9

√5th **942.0 Unspecified degree**
√5th **942.1 Erythema [first degree]**
√5th **942.2 Blisters, epidermal loss [second degree]**
√5th **942.3 Full-thickness skin loss [third degree NOS]**
√5th **942.4 Deep necrosis of underlying tissues [deep third degree] without mention of loss of a body part**
√5th **942.5 Deep necrosis of underlying tissues [deep third degree] with loss of a body part**

√4th **943 Burn of upper limb, except wrist and hand**

The following fifth-digit subclassification is for use with category 943:

0 upper limb, unspecified site
1 forearm
2 elbow
3 upper arm
4 axilla
5 shoulder
6 scapular region
9 multiple sites of upper limb, except wrist and hand

AHA: 4Q, '94, 22; M-A, '86, 9

√5th **943.0 Unspecified degree**
√5th **943.1 Erythema [first degree]**
√5th **943.2 Blisters, epidermal loss [second degree]**
√5th **943.3 Full-thickness skin loss [third degree NOS]**

√5th **943.4 Deep necrosis of underlying tissues [deep third degree] without mention of loss of a body part**
√5th **943.5 Deep necrosis of underlying tissues [deep third degree] with loss of a body part**

√4th **944 Burn of wrist(s) and hand(s)**

The following fifth-digit subclassification is for use with category 944:

0 hand, unspecified site
1 single digit [finger (nail)] other than thumb
2 thumb (nail)
3 two or more digits, not including thumb
4 two or more digits including thumb
5 palm
6 back of hand
7 wrist
8 multiple sites of wrist(s) and hand(s)

√5th **944.0 Unspecified degree**
√5th **944.1 Erythema [first degree]**
√5th **944.2 Blisters, epidermal loss [second degree]**
√5th **944.3 Full-thickness skin loss [third degree NOS]**
√5th **944.4 Deep necrosis of underlying tissues [deep third degree] without mention of loss of a body part**
√5th **944.5 Deep necrosis of underlying tissues [deep third degree] with loss of a body part**

√4th **945 Burn of lower limb(s)**

The following fifth-digit subclassification is for use with category 945:

0 lower limb [leg], unspecified site
1 toe(s) (nail)
2 foot
3 ankle
4 lower leg
5 knee
6 thigh [any part]
9 multiple sites of lower limb(s)

AHA: 4Q, '94, 22; M-A, '86, 9

√5th **945.0 Unspecified degree**
√5th **945.1 Erythema [first degree]**
√5th **945.2 Blisters, epidermal loss [second degree]**
√5th **945.3 Full-thickness skin loss [third degree NOS]**
√5th **945.4 Deep necrosis of underlying tissues [deep third degree] without mention of loss of a body part**
√5th **945.5 Deep necrosis of underlying tissues [deep third degree] with loss of a body part**

√4th **946 Burns of multiple specified sites**

INCLUDES burns of sites classifiable to more than one three-digit category in 940-945

EXCLUDES multiple burns NOS (949.0-949.5)

AHA: 4Q, '94, 22; M-A, '86, 9

946.0 Unspecified degree
946.1 Erythema [first degree]
946.2 Blisters, epidermal loss [second degree]
946.3 Full-thickness skin loss [third degree NOS]
946.4 Deep necrosis of underlying tissues [deep third degree] without mention of loss of a body part
946.5 Deep necrosis of underlying tissues [deep third degree] with loss of a body part

√4th **947 Burn of internal organs**

INCLUDES burns from chemical agents (ingested)

AHA: 4Q, '94, 22; M-A, '86, 9

947.0 Mouth and pharynx
  Gum   Tongue
947.1 Larynx, trachea, and lung
947.2 Esophagus
947.3 Gastrointestinal tract
  Colon   Small intestine
  Rectum   Stomach
947.4 Vagina and uterus   ♀

√4th Additional Digit Required   Nonspecific PDx   Unacceptable PDx   Manifestation Code   MCV Major Cardiovascular Condition   ▶◀ Revised Text   ● New Code   ▲ Revised Code Title

947.8   **Other specified sites**

947.9   Unspecified site

√4ᵗʰ **948 Burns classified according to extent of body surface involved**

> Note: This category is to be used when the site of the burn is unspecified, or with categories 940-947 when the site is specified.

> **EXCLUDES**   sunburn (692.71, 692.76-692.77)

The following fifth-digit subclassification is for use with category 948 to indicate the percent of body surface with third degree burn; valid digits are in [brackets] under each code:

> 0   less than 10 percent or unspecified
> 1   10-19%
> 2   20-29%
> 3   30-39%
> 4   40-49%
> 5   50-59%
> 6   60-69%
> 7   70-79%
> 8   80-89%
> 9   90% or more of body surface

AHA: 4Q, '94, 22; 4Q, '88, 3; M-A, '86, 9; N-D, '84, 13

√5ᵗʰ **948.0**   **Burn [any degree] involving less than 10 percent of**
[0]   **body surface**

√5ᵗʰ **948.1**   **10-19 percent of body surface**
[0-1]

√5ᵗʰ **948.2**   **20-29 percent of body surface**
[0-2]

√5ᵗʰ **948.3**   **30-39 percent of body surface**
[0-3]

√5ᵗʰ **948.4**   **40-49 percent of body surface**
[0-4]

√5ᵗʰ **948.5**   **50-59 percent of body surface**
[0-5]

√5ᵗʰ **948.6**   **60-69 percent of body surface**
[0-6]

√5ᵗʰ **948.7**   **70-79 percent of body surface**
[0-7]

√5ᵗʰ **948.8**   **80-89 percent of body surface**
[0-8]

√5ᵗʰ **948.9**   **90 percent or more of body surface**
[0-9]

Burns

Degrees of Burns

First (redness)   Second (blistering)   Third (fill thickness)   Deep Third (deep necrosis)   Eschar

Rule of Nines Estimation of Total Body Surface Burned

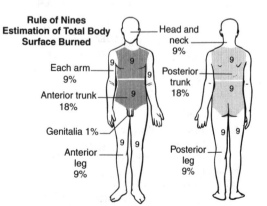

Head and neck 9%
Each arm 9%
Anterior trunk 18%
Genitalia 1%
Anterior leg 9%
Posterior trunk 18%
Posterior leg 9%

√4ᵗʰ **949 Burn, unspecified**

> **INCLUDES**   burn NOS multiple burns NOS
> **EXCLUDES**   burn of unspecified site but with statement of the extent of body surface involved (948.0-948.9)

AHA: 4Q, '94, 22; M-A, '86, 9

949.0   **Unspecified degree**

949.1   **Erythema [first degree]**

949.2   **Blisters, epidermal loss [second degree]**

949.3   **Full-thickness skin loss [third degree NOS]**

949.4   **Deep necrosis of underlying tissues [deep third degree] without mention of loss of a body part**

949.5   **Deep necrosis of underlying tissues [deep third degree] with loss of a body part**

INJURY TO NERVES AND SPINAL CORD (950-957)

> **INCLUDES**   division of nerve
> lesion in continuity
> traumatic neuroma   } (with open wound)
> traumatic transient paralysis

> **EXCLUDES**   accidental puncture or laceration during medical procedure (998.2)

√4ᵗʰ **950 Injury to optic nerve and pathways**

950.0   **Optic nerve injury**
Second cranial nerve

950.1   **Injury to optic chiasm**

950.2   **Injury to optic pathways**

950.3   **Injury to visual cortex**

950.9   **Unspecified**
Traumatic blindness NOS

√4ᵗʰ **951 Injury to other cranial nerve(s)**

951.0   **Injury to oculomotor nerve**
Third cranial nerve

951.1   **Injury to trochlear nerve**
Fourth cranial nerve

951.2   **Injury to trigeminal nerve**
Fifth cranial nerve

951.3   **Injury to abducens nerve**
Sixth cranial nerve

951.4   **Injury to facial nerve**
Seventh cranial nerve

951.5   **Injury to acoustic nerve**
Auditory nerve
Eighth cranial nerve
Traumatic deafness NOS

951.6   **Injury to accessory nerve**
Eleventh cranial nerve

951.7   **Injury to hypoglossal nerve**
Twelfth cranial nerve

951.8   **Injury to other specified cranial nerves**
Glossopharyngeal [9th cranial] nerve
Olfactory [1st cranial] nerve
Pneumogastric [10th cranial] nerve
Traumatic anosmia NOS
Vagus [10th cranial] nerve

951.9   Injury to unspecified cranial nerve

√4ᵗʰ **952 Spinal cord injury without evidence of spinal bone injury**

√5ᵗʰ **952.0**   **Cervical**

952.00   **C_1-C_4 level with unspecified spinal cord** CC **injury**
Spinal cord injury, cervical region NOS
CC Excl: 805.00-805.18, 805.8-806.19, 806.8-806.9, 839.00-839.18, 839.40, 839.49-839.50, 839.59, 839.69, 839.79-839.9, 847.9, 905.1, 926.11, 952.00-952.09, 952.8-952.9, 958.8-958.99, 959.11-959.19, 959.8-959.9

N Newborn Age: 0   P Pediatric Age: 0-17   M Maternity Age: 12-55   A Adult Age: 15-124   CC CC Condition   MC Major Complication   CD Complex Dx   HIV HIV Related Dx

300 — Volume 1   *2007 ICD•9•CM*

Spinal Nerve Roots

952.01 C₁-C₄ level with complete lesion of spinal cord `CC`
CC Excl: See code 952.00

952.02 C₁-C₄ level with anterior cord syndrome `CC`
CC Excl: See code 952.00

952.03 C₁-C₄ level with central cord syndrome `CC`
CC Excl: See code 952.00

952.04 C₁-C₄ level with other specified spinal cord injury `CC`
Incomplete spinal cord lesion at C₁-C₄ level:
NOS
with posterior cord syndrome
CC Excl: See code 952.00

952.05 C₅-C₇ level with unspecified spinal cord injury `CC`
CC Excl: See code 952.00

952.06 C₅-C₇ level with complete lesion of spinal cord `CC`
CC Excl: See code 952.00

952.07 C₅-C₇ level with anterior cord syndrome `CC`
CC Excl: See code 952.00

952.08 C₅-C₇ level with central cord syndrome `CC`
CC Excl: See code 952.00

952.09 C₅-C₇ level with other specified spinal cord injury `CC`
Incomplete spinal cord lesion at C₅-C₇ level:
NOS
with posterior cord syndrome
CC Excl: See code 952.00

√5ᵗʰ **952.1** Dorsal [thoracic]

952.10 T₁-T₆ level with unspecified spinal cord injury `CC`
Spinal cord injury, thoracic region NOS
CC Excl: 805.8-805.9, 806.20-806.39, 839.40, 839.49-839.50, 839.59, 839.69, 839.79, 839.8-839.9, 847.9, 905.1, 926.11, 952.10-952.19, 952.8-952.9, 958.8-958.99, 959.11-959.19, 959.8-959.9

952.11 T₁-T₆ level with complete lesion of spinal cord `CC`
CC Excl: See code 952.10

952.12 T₁-T₆ level with anterior cord syndrome `CC`
CC Excl: See code 952.10

952.13 T₁-T₆ level with central cord syndrome `CC`
CC Excl: See code 952.10

952.14 T₁-T₆ level with other specified spinal cord injury `CC`
Incomplete spinal cord lesion at T₁-T₆ level:
NOS
with posterior cord syndrome
CC Excl: See code 952.10

952.15 T₇-T₁₂ level with unspecified spinal cord injury `CC`
CC Excl: See code 952.10

952.16 T₇-T₁₂ level with complete lesion of spinal cord `CC`
CC Excl: See code 952.10

952.17 T₇-T₁₂ level with anterior cord syndrome `CC`
CC Excl: See code 952.10

952.18 T₇-T₁₂ level with central cord syndrome `CC`
CC Excl: See code 952.10

952.19 T₇-T₁₂ level with other specified spinal cord injury `CC`
Incomplete spinal cord lesion at T₇-T₁₂ level:
NOS
with posterior cord syndrome
CC Excl: See code 952.10

952.2 Lumbar `CC`
CC Excl: 805.8-805.9, 806.4-806.5, 839.40, 839.49-839.50, 839.59, 839.69, 839.79-839.9, 847.9, 905.1, 926.11, 952.2, 952.8-952.9, 958.8-958.99, 959.11-959.19, 959.8-959.9

952.3 Sacral `CC`
CC Excl: 805.8-805.9, 806.60-806.79, 839.40, 839.49-839.50, 839.59, 839.69, 839.79-839.9, 847.9, 905.1, 926.11, 952.3-952.4, 952.8-952.9, 958.8-958.99, 959.11-959.19, 959.8-959.9

952.4 Cauda equina `CC`
CC Excl: See code 952.3

952.8 Multiple sites of spinal cord `CC`
CC Excl: 805.8-805.9, 839.40, 839.49-839.50, 839.59, 839.69, 839.79-839.9, 847.9, 905.1, 926.11, 952.8-952.9, 958.8-958.99, 959.11-959.19, 959.8-959.9

952.9 Unspecified site of spinal cord `CC`
CC Excl: See Code 952.8

√4ᵗʰ **953 Injury to nerve roots and spinal plexus**

953.0 Cervical root `CC`
CC Excl: 953.8-953.9, 958.8, 959.8-959.9

953.1 Dorsal root `CC`
CC Excl: See code 953.0

953.2 Lumbar root `CC`
CC Excl: See code 953.0

953.3 Sacral root `CC`
CC Excl: See code 953.0

953.4 Brachial plexus `CC`
CC Excl: See code 953.0

953.5 Lumbosacral plexus `CC`
CC Excl: See code 953.0

953.8 Multiple sites `CC`
CC Excl: See code 953.0

953.9 Unspecified site `CC`
CC Excl: See code 953.0

√4ᵗʰ **954 Injury to other nerve(s) of trunk, excluding shoulder and pelvic girdles**

954.0 Cervical sympathetic

954.1 Other sympathetic
Celiac ganglion or plexus   Splanchnic nerve(s)
Inferior mesenteric plexus   Stellate ganglion

954.8 Other specified nerve(s) of trunk

954.9 Unspecified nerve of trunk

√4ᵗʰ **955 Injury to peripheral nerve(s) of shoulder girdle and upper limb**

955.0 Axillary nerve

955.1 Median nerve

955.2 Ulnar nerve

955.3 Radial nerve

955.4 Musculocutaneous nerve

955.5 Cutaneous sensory nerve, upper limb

955.6 Digital nerve

955.7 Other specified nerve(s) of shoulder girdle and upper limb

955.8 Multiple nerves of shoulder girdle and upper limb

955.9 Unspecified nerve of shoulder girdle and upper limb

√4ᵗʰ √5ᵗʰ Additional Digit Required   Nonspecific PDx   Unacceptable PDx   Manifestation Code   `MCV` Major Cardiovascular Condition   ◄► Revised Text   ● New Code   ▲ Revised Code Title

2007 ICD•9•CM   Volume 1 — 301

Injury and Poisoning

956–959.12

✓4th **956 Injury to peripheral nerve(s) of pelvic girdle and lower limb**
    956.0 **Sciatic nerve**
    956.1 **Femoral nerve**
    956.2 **Posterior tibial nerve**
    956.3 **Peroneal nerve**
    956.4 **Cutaneous sensory nerve, lower limb**
    956.5 **Other specified nerve(s) of pelvic girdle and lower limb**
    956.8 **Multiple nerves of pelvic girdle and lower limb**
    956.9 **Unspecified nerve of pelvic girdle and lower limb**

✓4th **957 Injury to other and unspecified nerves**
    957.0 **Superficial nerves of head and neck**
    957.1 **Other specified nerve(s)**
    957.8 **Multiple nerves in several parts**
        Multiple nerve injury NOS
    957.9 **Unspecified site**
        Nerve injury NOS

CERTAIN TRAUMATIC COMPLICATIONS AND UNSPECIFIED INJURIES (958-959)

✓4th **958 Certain early complications of trauma**
    EXCLUDES *adult respiratory distress syndrome (518.5)*
        flail chest (807.4)
        shock lung (518.5)
        that occurring during or following medical procedures (996.0-999.9)

    958.0 **Air embolism** CC
        Pneumathemia
        EXCLUDES *that complicating:*
            abortion (634-638 with .6, 639.6)
            ectopic or molar pregnancy (639.6)
            pregnancy, childbirth, or the puerperium (673.0)
        CC Excl: 958.0, 958.8-958.99, 959.8-959.9, 997.91, 997.99, 998.81, 998.83-999.1
        DEF: Arterial obstruction due to introduction of air bubbles into the veins following surgery or trauma.

    958.1 **Fat embolism** CC
        EXCLUDES *that complicating:*
            abortion (634-638 with .6, 639.6)
            pregnancy, childbirth, or the puerperium (673.8)
        CC Excl: 958.1, 958.8-958.99, 959.8-959.9, 997.91, 997.99, 998.81, 998.83-998.9
        DEF: Arterial blockage due to the entrance of fat in circulatory system, after fracture of large bones or administration of corticosteroids.

    958.2 **Secondary and recurrent hemorrhage** CC
        CC Excl: 958.2, 958.8-958.99, 959.8-959.9, 997.91, 997.99, 998.81, 998.83-998.9

    958.3 **Posttraumatic wound infection, not elsewhere classified** CC
        EXCLUDES *infected open wounds–code to complicated open wound of site*
        CC Excl: 958.3, 958.8-958.99, 959.8-959.9, 997.91, 997.99, 998.81, 998.83-998.9
        AHA: 4Q, '01, 53; S-O, '85, 10

    958.4 **Traumatic shock** CC
        Shock (immediate) (delayed) following injury
        EXCLUDES *shock:*
            anaphylactic (995.0)
              due to serum (999.4)
            anesthetic (995.4)
            electric (994.8)
            following abortion (639.5)
            lightning (994.0)
            nontraumatic NOS (785.50)
            obstetric (669.1)
            postoperative (998.0)
        CC Excl: 958.4, 958.8-958.99, 959.8-959.9, 997.91, 997.99, 998.81, 998.83-998.9
        DEF: Shock, immediate or delayed following injury.

    958.5 **Traumatic anuria** CC
        Crush syndrome
        Renal failure following crushing
        EXCLUDES *that due to a medical procedure (997.5)*
        CC Excl: 958.5, 958.8-958.99, 959.8-959.9, 995.4, 997.91, 997.99, 998.0, 998.11-998.13, 998.81, 998.83-998.9
        DEF: Complete suppression of urinary secretion by kidneys due to trauma.

    958.6 **Volkmann's ischemic contracture**
        Posttraumatic muscle contracture
        DEF: Muscle deterioration due to loss of blood supply from injury or tourniquet; causes muscle contraction and results in inability to extend the muscles fully.

    958.7 **Traumatic subcutaneous emphysema** CC
        EXCLUDES *subcutaneous emphysema resulting from a procedure (998.81)*
        CC Excl: 860.0-860.5, 861.20-861.32, 862.0-862.1, 862.29, 862.31-862.9, 875.0-875.1, 958.7-958.99, 959.8-959.9, 997.91, 997.99, 998.81, 998.83-998.9

    958.8 **Other early complications of trauma**
        AHA: 2Q, '92, 13
        DEF: Compartmental syndrome is abnormal pressure in confined anatomical space, as in swollen muscle restricted by fascia.

• ✓5th   **958.9** **Traumatic compartment syndrome**
        EXCLUDES *nontraumatic compartment syndrome (729.71-729.79)*

•   958.90 **Compartment syndrome, unspecified**
•   958.91 **Traumatic compartment syndrome of upper extremity**
        Traumatic compartment syndrome of shoulder, arm, forearm, wrist, hand, and fingers
    958.92 **Traumatic compartment syndrome of lower extremity**
        Traumatic compartment syndrome of hip, buttock, thigh, leg, foot, and toes
•   958.93 **Traumatic compartment syndrome of abdomen**
•   958.99 **Traumatic compartment syndrome of other sites**

✓4th **959 Injury, other and unspecified**
    INCLUDES injury NOS
    EXCLUDES *injury NOS of:*
        blood vessels (900.0-904.9)
        eye (921.0-921.9)
        internal organs (860.0-869.1)
        intracranial sites (854.0-854.1)
        nerves (950.0-951.9, 953.0-957.9)
        spinal cord (952.0-952.9)

✓5th   **959.0** **Head, face and neck**
    959.01 **Head injury, unspecified**
        EXCLUDES *concussion (850.1-850.9)*
            with head injury NOS (850.1-850.9)
            head injury NOS with loss of consciousness (850.1-850.5)
            specified intracranial injuries (850.0-854.1)
        AHA: 4Q, '97, 46

    959.09 **Injury of face and neck**
        Cheek   Mouth
        Ear   Nose
        Eyebrow   Throat
        Lip
        AHA: 4Q, '97, 46

✓5th   **959.1** **Trunk**
        EXCLUDES *scapular region (959.2)*
        AHA: 4Q, '03, 78; 1Q, '99, 10
    959.11 **Other injury of chest wall**
    959.12 **Other injury of abdomen**

N Newborn Age: 0   P Pediatric Age: 0-17   M Maternity Age: 12-55   A Adult Age: 15-124   CC CC Condition   MC Major Complication   CD Complex Dx   HIV HIV Related Dx

959.13 **Fracture of corpus cavernosum penis**　♂

959.14 **Other injury of external genitals**

959.19 **Other injury of other sites of trunk**
　　　Injury of trunk NOS

959.2 **Shoulder and upper arm**
　　Axilla　　　　　　　　Scapular region

959.3 **Elbow, forearm, and wrist**
　　AHA: 1Q, '97, 8

959.4 **Hand, except finger**

959.5 **Finger**
　　Fingernail　　　　　　Thumb (nail)

959.6 **Hip and thigh**
　　Upper leg

959.7 **Knee, leg, ankle, and foot**

959.8 **Other specified sites, including multiple**
　　　EXCLUDES　　*multiple sites classifiable to the same*
　　　　　　　　　　　four-digit category (959.0-959.7)

959.9 **Unspecified site**

POISONING BY DRUGS, MEDICINAL AND BIOLOGICAL SUBSTANCES (960-979)

INCLUDES　　overdose of these substances
　　　　　　wrong substance given or taken in error

EXCLUDES　　*adverse effects ["hypersensitivity," "reaction,"*
　　　　　　etc.] of correct substance properly
　　　　　　administered. Such cases are to be
　　　　　　classified according to the nature of the
　　　　　　adverse effect, such as:
　　　　　　adverse effect NOS ▶(995.20)◀
　　　　　　allergic lymphadenitis (289.3)
　　　　　　aspirin gastritis (535.4)
　　　　　　blood disorders (280.0-289.9)
　　　　　　dermatitis:
　　　　　　　contact (692.0-692.9)
　　　　　　　due to ingestion (693.0-693.9)
　　　　　　nephropathy (583.9)
　　　　　　[The drug giving rise to the adverse effect may
　　　　　　　be identified by use of categories E930-
　　　　　　　E949.]
　　　　　　drug dependence (304.0-304.9)
　　　　　　drug reaction and poisoning affecting the
　　　　　　　newborn (760.0-779.9)
　　　　　　nondependent abuse of drugs (305.0-305.9)
　　　　　　pathological drug intoxication (292.2)
　　　Use additional code to specify the effects of the poisoning
　　AHA: 2Q, '90, 11

✓4th **960 Poisoning by antibiotics**
　　EXCLUDES　　*antibiotics:*
　　　　　　ear, nose, and throat (976.6)
　　　　　　eye (976.5)
　　　　　　local (976.0)

960.0 **Penicillins**
　　Ampicillin　　　　　　Cloxacillin
　　Carbenicillin　　　　　Penicillin G

960.1 **Antifungal antibiotics**
　　Amphotericin B　　　　Nystatin
　　Griseofulvin　　　　　Trichomycin
　　　EXCLUDES　　*preparations intended for topical use*
　　　　　　(976.0-976.9)

960.2 **Chloramphenicol group**
　　Chloramphenicol　　　Thiamphenicol

960.3 **Erythromycin and other macrolides**
　　Oleandomycin　　　　　Spiramycin

960.4 **Tetracycline group**
　　Doxycycline　　　　　Oxytetracycline
　　Minocycline

960.5 **Cephalosporin group**
　　Cephalexin　　　　　　Cephaloridine
　　Cephaloglycin　　　　　Cephalothin

960.6 **Antimycobacterial antibiotics**
　　Cycloserine　　　　　Rifampin
　　Kanamycin　　　　　　Streptomycin

960.7 **Antineoplastic antibiotics**
　　Actinomycin such as:
　　Bleomycin　　　　　　Daunorubicin
　　Cactinomycin　　　　　Mitomycin
　　Dactinomycin

960.8 **Other specified antibiotics**

960.9 **Unspecified antibiotic**

✓4th **961 Poisoning by other anti-infectives**
　　EXCLUDES　　*anti-infectives:*
　　　　　　ear, nose, and throat (976.6)
　　　　　　eye (976.5)
　　　　　　local (976.0)

961.0 **Sulfonamides**
　　Sulfadiazine　　　　　Sulfamethoxazole
　　Sulfafurazole

961.1 **Arsenical anti-infectives**

961.2 **Heavy metal anti-infectives**
　　Compounds of:　　　Compounds of:
　　　antimony　　　　　　lead
　　　bismuth　　　　　　mercury
　　　EXCLUDES　　*mercurial diuretics (974.0)*

961.3 **Quinoline and hydroxyquinoline derivatives**
　　Chiniofon　　　　　　Diiodohydroxyquin
　　　EXCLUDES　　*antimalarial drugs (961.4)*

961.4 **Antimalarials and drugs acting on other blood protozoa**
　　Chloroquine　　　　　Proguanil [chloroguanide]
　　Cycloguanil　　　　　Pyrimethamine
　　Primaquine　　　　　Quinine

961.5 **Other antiprotozoal drugs**
　　Emetine

961.6 **Anthelmintics**
　　Hexylresorcinol　　　Thiabendazole
　　Piperazine

961.7 **Antiviral drugs**
　　Methisazone
　　　EXCLUDES　　*amantadine (966.4)*
　　　　　　cytarabine (963.1)
　　　　　　idoxuridine (976.5)

961.8 **Other antimycobacterial drugs**
　　Ethambutol　　　　　Para-aminosalicylic acid
　　Ethionamide　　　　　derivatives
　　Isoniazid　　　　　　Sulfones

961.9 **Other and unspecified anti-infectives**
　　Flucytosine
　　Nitrofuran derivatives

✓4th **962 Poisoning by hormones and synthetic substitutes**
　　EXCLUDES　　*oxytocic hormones (975.0)*

962.0 **Adrenal cortical steroids**
　　Cortisone derivatives　Fluorinated corticosteroids
　　Desoxycorticosterone derivatives

962.1 **Androgens and anabolic congeners**
　　Methandriol　　　　　Oxymetholone
　　Nandrolone　　　　　Testosterone

962.2 **Ovarian hormones and synthetic substitutes**
　　Contraceptives, oral
　　Estrogens
　　Estrogens and progestogens, combined
　　Progestogens

962.3 **Insulins and antidiabetic agents**
　　Acetohexamide　　　　Insulin
　　Biguanide derivatives,　Phenformin
　　　oral　　　　　　　Sulfonylurea derivatives,
　　Chlorpropamide　　　　oral
　　Glucagon　　　　　　Tolbutamide
　　AHA: M-A, '85, 8

962.4 **Anterior pituitary hormones**
　　Corticotropin
　　Gonadotropin
　　Somatotropin [growth hormone]

962.5 **Posterior pituitary hormones**
　　Vasopressin
　　　EXCLUDES　　*oxytocic hormones (975.0)*

962.6 **Parathyroid and parathyroid derivatives**

✓4th ✓5th **Additional Digit Required**　　**Nonspecific PDx**　　**Unacceptable PDx**　　**Manifestation Code**　　**MCV** Major Cardiovascular Condition　▶◀ Revised Text　● New Code　▲ Revised Code Title

2007 ICD•9•CM　　　　　　　　　　　　　　　　　　　　　October 2006 • Volume 1 — **303**

Injury and Poisoning

962.7–967.9

962.7 Thyroid and thyroid derivatives
Dextrothyroxin   Liothyronine
Levothyroxine sodium   Thyroglobulin

962.8 Antithyroid agents
Iodides   Thiourea
Thiouracil

962.9 Other and unspecified hormones and synthetic substitutes

✓4th **963 Poisoning by primarily systemic agents**

963.0 Antiallergic and antiemetic drugs
Antihistamines   Diphenylpyraline
Chlorpheniramine   Thonzylamine
Diphenhydramine   Tripelennamine
   EXCLUDES   *phenothiazine-based tranquilizers (969.1)*

963.1 Antineoplastic and immunosuppressive drugs
Azathioprine   Cytarabine
Busulfan   Fluorouracil
Chlorambucil   Mercaptopurine
Cyclophosphamide   thio-TEPA
   EXCLUDES   *antineoplastic antibiotics (960.7)*

963.2 Acidifying agents

963.3 Alkalizing agents

963.4 Enzymes, not elsewhere classified
Penicillinase

963.5 Vitamins, not elsewhere classified
Vitamin A   Vitamin D
   EXCLUDES   *nicotinic acid (972.2)*
               vitamin K (964.3)

963.8 Other specified systemic agents
Heavy metal antagonists

963.9 Unspecified systemic agent

✓4th **964 Poisoning by agents primarily affecting blood constituents**

964.0 Iron and its compounds
Ferric salts
Ferrous sulfate and other ferrous salts

964.1 Liver preparations and other antianemic agents
Folic acid

964.2 Anticoagulants
Coumarin   Phenindione
Heparin   Warfarin sodium
AHA: 1Q, '94, 22

964.3 Vitamin K [phytonadione]

964.4 Fibrinolysis-affecting drugs
Aminocaproic acid   Streptokinase
Streptodornase   Urokinase

964.5 Anticoagulant antagonists and other coagulants
Hexadimethrine   Protamine sulfate

964.6 Gamma globulin

964.7 Natural blood and blood products
Blood plasma   Packed red cells
Human fibrinogen   Whole blood
   EXCLUDES   *transfusion reactions (999.4-999.8)*

964.8 Other specified agents affecting blood constituents
Macromolecular blood substitutes
Plasma expanders

964.9 Unspecified agent affecting blood constituents

✓4th **965 Poisoning by analgesics, antipyretics, and antirheumatics**
   EXCLUDES   *drug dependence (304.0-304.9)*
               nondependent abuse (305.0-305.9)

✓5th **965.0 Opiates and related narcotics**

965.00 Opium (alkaloids), unspecified

965.01 Heroin
Diacetylmorphine

965.02 Methadone

965.09 Other
Codeine [methylmorphine]
Meperidine [pethidine]
Morphine

965.1 Salicylates
Acetylsalicylic acid [aspirin]
Salicylic acid salts
AHA: N-D, '94, 15

965.4 Aromatic analgesics, not elsewhere classified
Acetanilid   Phenacetin [acetophenetidin]
Paracetamol [acetaminophen]

965.5 Pyrazole derivatives
Aminophenazone [aminopyrine]
Phenylbutazone

✓5th **965.6 Antirheumatics [antiphlogistics]**
   EXCLUDES   *salicylates (965.1)*
              steroids (962.0-962.9)
AHA: 4Q, '98, 50

965.61 Propionic acid derivatives
Fenoprofen
Flurbiprofen
Ibuprofen
Ketoprofen
Naproxen
Oxaprozin
AHA: 4Q, '98, 50

965.69 Other antirheumatics
Gold salts
Indomethacin

965.7 Other non-narcotic analgesics
Pyrabital

965.8 Other specified analgesics and antipyretics
Pentazocine

965.9 Unspecified analgesic and antipyretic

✓4th **966 Poisoning by anticonvulsants and anti-Parkinsonism drugs**

966.0 Oxazolidine derivatives
Paramethadione
Trimethadione

966.1 Hydantoin derivatives
Phenytoin

966.2 Succinimides
Ethosuximide
Phensuximide

966.3 Other and unspecified anticonvulsants
Primidone
   EXCLUDES   *barbiturates (967.0)*
              sulfonamides (961.0)

966.4 Anti-Parkinsonism drugs
Amantadine
Ethopropazine [profenamine]
Levodopa [L-dopa]

✓4th **967 Poisoning by sedatives and hypnotics**
   EXCLUDES   *drug dependence (304.0-304.9)*
              nondependent abuse (305.0-305.9)

967.0 Barbiturates
Amobarbital [amylobarbitone]
Barbital [barbitone]
Butabarbital [butabarbitone]
Pentobarbital [pentobarbitone]
Phenobarbital [phenobarbitone]
Secobarbital [quinalbarbitone]
   EXCLUDES   *thiobarbiturate anesthetics (968.3)*

967.1 Chloral hydrate group

967.2 Paraldehyde

967.3 Bromine compounds
Bromide
Carbromal (derivatives)

967.4 Methaqualone compounds

967.5 Glutethimide group

967.6 Mixed sedatives, not elsewhere classified

967.8 Other sedatives and hypnotics

967.9 Unspecified sedative or hypnotic
Sleeping:
    drug
    pill   } NOS
    tablet

N Newborn Age: 0   P Pediatric Age: 0-17   M Maternity Age: 12-55   A Adult Age: 15-124   CC CC Condition   MC Major Complication   CD Complex Dx   HIV HIV Related Dx

304 — Volume 1   *2007 ICD•9•CM*

☑4ᵗʰ 968 Poisoning by other central nervous system depressants and anesthetics

> EXCLUDES drug dependence (304.0-304.9)
> nondependent abuse (305.0-305.9)

968.0 Central nervous system muscle-tone depressants
Chlorphenesin (carbamate)　Methocarbamol
Mephenesin

968.1 Halothane

968.2 Other gaseous anesthetics
Ether
Halogenated hydrocarbon derivatives, except halothane
Nitrous oxide

968.3 Intravenous anesthetics
Ketamine
Methohexital [methohexitone]
Thiobarbiturates, such as thiopental sodium

968.4 Other and unspecified general anesthetics

968.5 Surface [topical] and infiltration anesthetics
Cocaine　Procaine
Lidocaine [lignocaine]　Tetracaine
AHA: 1Q, '93, 25

968.6 Peripheral nerve- and plexus-blocking anesthetics

968.7 Spinal anesthetics

968.9 Other and unspecified local anesthetics

☑4ᵗʰ 969 Poisoning by psychotropic agents

> EXCLUDES drug dependence (304.0-304.9)
> nondependent abuse (305.0-305.9)

969.0 Antidepressants
Amitriptyline
Imipramine
Monoamine oxidase [MAO] inhibitors

969.1 Phenothiazine-based tranquilizers
Chlorpromazine　Prochlorperazine
Fluphenazine　Promazine

969.2 Butyrophenone-based tranquilizers
Haloperidol　Trifluperidol
Spiperone

969.3 Other antipsychotics, neuroleptics, and major tranquilizers

969.4 Benzodiazepine-based tranquilizers
Chlordiazepoxide　Lorazepam
Diazepam　Medazepam
Flurazepam　Nitrazepam

969.5 Other tranquilizers
Hydroxyzine　Meprobamate

969.6 Psychodysleptics [hallucinogens]
Cannabis (derivatives)　Mescaline
Lysergide [LSD]　Psilocin
Marihuana (derivatives)　Psilocybin

969.7 Psychostimulants
Amphetamine
Caffeine
> EXCLUDES central appetite depressants (977.0)
AHA: 2Q, '03, 11

969.8 Other specified psychotropic agents

969.9 Unspecified psychotropic agent

☑4ᵗʰ 970 Poisoning by central nervous system stimulants

970.0 Analeptics
Lobeline　Nikethamide

970.1 Opiate antagonists
Levallorphan　Naloxone
Nalorphine

970.8 Other specified central nervous system stimulants
AHA: 1Q, '05, 6

970.9 Unspecified central nervous system stimulant

☑4ᵗʰ 971 Poisoning by drugs primarily affecting the autonomic nervous system

971.0 Parasympathomimetics [cholinergics]
Acetylcholine　Pilocarpine
Anticholinesterase:
organophosphorus
reversible

971.1 Parasympatholytics [anticholinergics and antimuscarinics] and spasmolytics
Atropine　Quaternary ammonium
Homatropine　derivatives
Hyoscine [scopolamine]
> EXCLUDES papaverine (972.5)

971.2 Sympathomimetics [adrenergics]
Epinephrine [adrenalin]　Levarterenol [noradrenalin]

971.3 Sympatholytics [antiadrenergics]
Phenoxybenzamine　Tolazolinehydrochloride

971.9 Unspecified drug primarily affecting autonomic nervous system

☑4ᵗʰ 972 Poisoning by agents primarily affecting the cardiovascular system

972.0 Cardiac rhythm regulators
Practolol　Propranolol
Procainamide　Quinidine
> EXCLUDES lidocaine (968.5)

972.1 Cardiotonic glycosides and drugs of similar action
Digitalis glycosides　Strophanthins
Digoxin

972.2 Antilipemic and antiarteriosclerotic drugs
Clofibrate　Nicotinic acid derivatives

972.3 Ganglion-blocking agents
Pentamethonium bromide

972.4 Coronary vasodilators
Dipyridamole　Nitrites
Nitrates [nitroglycerin]

972.5 Other vasodilators
Cyclandelate　Papaverine
Diazoxide
> EXCLUDES nicotinic acid (972.2)

972.6 Other antihypertensive agents
Clonidine　Rauwolfia alkaloids
Guanethidine　Reserpine

972.7 Antivaricose drugs, including sclerosing agents
Sodium morrhuate　Zinc salts

972.8 Capillary-active drugs
Adrenochrome derivatives　Metaraminol

972.9 Other and unspecified agents primarily affecting the cardiovascular system

☑4ᵗʰ 973 Poisoning by agents primarily affecting the gastrointestinal system

973.0 Antacids and antigastric secretion drugs
Aluminum hydroxide　Magnesium trisilicate
AHA: 1Q, '03, 19

973.1 Irritant cathartics
Bisacodyl　Phenolphthalein
Castor oil

973.2 Emollient cathartics
Dioctyl sulfosuccinates

973.3 Other cathartics, including intestinal atonia drugs
Magnesium sulfate

973.4 Digestants
Pancreatin　Pepsin
Papain

973.5 Antidiarrheal drugs
Kaolin　Pectin
> EXCLUDES anti-infectives (960.0-961.9)

973.6 Emetics

973.8 Other specified agents primarily affecting the gastrointestinal system

973.9 Unspecified agent primarily affecting the gastrointestinal system

☑4ᵗʰ 974 Poisoning by water, mineral, and uric acid metabolism drugs

974.0 Mercurial diuretics
Chlormerodrin　Mersalyl
Mercaptomerin

974.1 Purine derivative diuretics
Theobromine　Theophylline
> EXCLUDES aminophylline [theophylline ethylenediamine] (975.7)
> caffeine (969.7)

☑4ᵗʰ ☑5ᵗʰ Additional Digit Required　Nonspecific PDx　Unacceptable PDx　Manifestation Code　MCV Major Cardiovascular Condition　▶◀ Revised Text　● New Code　▲ Revised Code Title

2007 ICD•9•CM　　Volume 1 — 305

974.2 Carbonic acid anhydrase inhibitors
Acetazolamide

974.3 Saluretics
Benzothiadiazides   Chlorothiazide group

974.4 Other diuretics
Ethacrynic acid   Furosemide

974.5 Electrolytic, caloric, and water-balance agents

974.6 Other mineral salts, not elsewhere classified

974.7 Uric acid metabolism drugs
Allopurinol   Probenecid
Colchicine

✓4th **975 Poisoning by agents primarily acting on the smooth and skeletal muscles and respiratory system**

975.0 Oxytocic agents
Ergot alkaloids   Prostaglandins
Oxytocin

975.1 Smooth muscle relaxants
Adiphenine   Metaproterenol [orciprenaline]
EXCLUDES *papaverine (972.5)*

975.2 Skeletal muscle relaxants

975.3 Other and unspecified drugs acting on muscles

975.4 Antitussives
Dextromethorphan   Pipazethate

975.5 Expectorants
Acetylcysteine   Terpin hydrate
Guaifenesin

975.6 Anti-common cold drugs

975.7 Antiasthmatics
Aminophylline [theophylline ethylenediamine]

975.8 Other and unspecified respiratory drugs

✓4th **976 Poisoning by agents primarily affecting skin and mucous membrane, ophthalmological, otorhinolaryngological, and dental drugs**

976.0 Local anti-infectives and anti-inflammatory drugs

976.1 Antipruritics

976.2 Local astringents and local detergents

976.3 Emollients, demulcents, and protectants

976.4 Keratolytics, keratoplastics, other hair treatment drugs and preparations

976.5 Eye anti-infectives and other eye drugs
Idoxuridine

976.6 Anti-infectives and other drugs and preparations for ear, nose, and throat

976.7 Dental drugs topically applied
EXCLUDES *anti-infectives (976.0)*
local anesthetics (968.5)

976.8 Other agents primarily affecting skin and mucous membrane
Spermicides [vaginal contraceptives]

976.9 Unspecified agent primarily affecting skin and mucous membrane

✓4th **977 Poisoning by other and unspecified drugs and medicinal substances**

977.0 Dietetics
Central appetite depressants

977.1 Lipotropic drugs

977.2 Antidotes and chelating agents, not elsewhere classified

977.3 Alcohol deterrents

977.4 Pharmaceutical excipients
Pharmaceutical adjuncts

977.8 Other specified drugs and medicinal substances
Contrast media used for diagnostic x-ray procedures
Diagnostic agents and kits

977.9 Unspecified drug or medicinal substance

✓4th **978 Poisoning by bacterial vaccines**

978.0 BCG

978.1 Typhoid and paratyphoid

978.2 Cholera

978.3 Plague

978.4 Tetanus

978.5 Diphtheria

978.6 Pertussis vaccine, including combinations with a pertussis component

978.8 Other and unspecified bacterial vaccines

978.9 Mixed bacterial vaccines, except combinations with a pertussis component

✓4th **979 Poisoning by other vaccines and biological substances**
EXCLUDES *gamma globulin (964.6)*

979.0 Smallpox vaccine

979.1 Rabies vaccine

979.2 Typhus vaccine

979.3 Yellow fever vaccine

979.4 Measles vaccine

979.5 Poliomyelitis vaccine

979.6 Other and unspecified viral and rickettsial vaccines
Mumps vaccine

979.7 Mixed viral-rickettsial and bacterial vaccines, except combinations with a pertussis component
EXCLUDES *combinations with a pertussis component (978.6)*

979.9 Other and unspecified vaccines and biological substances

TOXIC EFFECTS OF SUBSTANCES CHIEFLY NONMEDICINAL AS TO SOURCE (980-989)

EXCLUDES *burns from chemical agents (ingested) (947.0-947.9)*
localized toxic effects indexed elsewhere (001.0-799.9)
respiratory conditions due to external agents (506.0-508.9)

Use additional code to specify the nature of the toxic effect

✓4th **980 Toxic effect of alcohol**

980.0 Ethyl alcohol
Denatured alcohol   Grain alcohol
Ethanol
Use additional code to identify any associated:
acute alcohol intoxication (305.0)
in alcoholism (303.0)
drunkenness (simple) (305.0)
pathological (291.4)

AHA: 3Q, '96, 16

980.1 Methyl alcohol
Methanol   Wood alcohol

980.2 Isopropyl alcohol
Dimethyl carbinol   Rubbing alcohol
Isopropanol

980.3 Fusel oil
Alcohol: Alcohol:
amyl   propyl
butyl

980.8 Other specified alcohols

980.9 Unspecified alcohol

981 Toxic effect of petroleum products
Benzine   Petroleum:
Gasoline   ether
Kerosene   naphtha
Paraffin wax   spirit

✓4th **982 Toxic effect of solvents other than petroleum-based**

982.0 Benzene and homologues

982.1 Carbon tetrachloride

982.2 Carbon disulfide
Carbon bisulfide

982.3 Other chlorinated hydrocarbon solvents
Tetrachloroethylene   Trichloroethylene
EXCLUDES *chlorinated hydrocarbon preparations other than solvents (989.2)*

982.4 Nitroglycol

982.8 Other nonpetroleum-based solvents
Acetone

N Newborn Age: 0 P Pediatric Age: 0-17 M Maternity Age: 12-55 A Adult Age: 15-124 CC CC Condition MC Major Complication CD Complex Dx HIV HIV Related Dx

306 — Volume 1

2007 ICD•9•CM

✓4th **983 Toxic effect of corrosive aromatics, acids, and caustic alkalis**

983.0 Corrosive aromatics
Carbolic acid or phenol
Cresol

983.1 Acids
Acid: Acid:
  hydrochloric   sulfuric
  nitric

983.2 Caustic alkalis
Lye   Sodium hydroxide
Potassium hydroxide

983.9 Caustic, unspecified

✓4th **984 Toxic effect of lead and its compounds (including fumes)**
INCLUDES   that from all sources except medicinal
            substances

984.0 Inorganic lead compounds
Lead dioxide   Lead salts

984.1 Organic lead compounds
Lead acetate
Tetraethyl lead

984.8 Other lead compounds

984.9 Unspecified lead compound

✓4th **985 Toxic effect of other metals**
INCLUDES   that from all sources except medicinal
            substances

985.0 Mercury and its compounds
Minamata disease

985.1 Arsenic and its compounds

985.2 Manganese and its compounds

985.3 Beryllium and its compounds

985.4 Antimony and its compounds

985.5 Cadmium and its compounds

985.6 Chromium

985.8 Other specified metals
Brass fumes   Iron compounds
Copper salts   Nickel compounds
AHA: 1Q, '88, 5

985.9 Unspecified metal

986 Toxic effect of carbon monoxide
Carbon monoxide from any source

✓4th **987 Toxic effect of other gases, fumes, or vapors**

987.0 Liquefied petroleum gases
Butane   Propane

987.1 Other hydrocarbon gas

987.2 Nitrogen oxides
Nitrogen dioxide   Nitrous fumes

987.3 Sulfur dioxide

987.4 Freon
Dichloromonofluoromethane

987.5 Lacrimogenic gas
Bromobenzyl cyanide   Ethyliodoacetate
Chloroacetophenone

987.6 Chlorine gas

987.7 Hydrocyanic acid gas

987.8 Other specified gases, fumes, or vapors
Phosgene   Polyester fumes

987.9 Unspecified gas, fume, or vapor
AHA: ▶3Q, '05, 10◀

✓4th **988 Toxic effect of noxious substances eaten as food**
EXCLUDES   allergic reaction to food, such as:
        gastroenteritis (558.3)
        rash (692.5, 693.1)
      food poisoning (bacterial) (005.0-005.9)
      toxic effects of food contaminants, such as:
        aflatoxin and other mycotoxin (989.7)
        mercury (985.0)

988.0 Fish and shellfish

988.1 Mushrooms

988.2 Berries and other plants

988.8 Other specified noxious substances eaten as food

988.9 Unspecified noxious substance eaten as food

✓4th **989 Toxic effect of other substances, chiefly nonmedicinal as to source**

989.0 Hydrocyanic acid and cyanides
Potassium cyanide   Sodium cyanide
EXCLUDES   gas and fumes (987.7)

989.1 Strychnine and salts

989.2 Chlorinated hydrocarbons
Aldrin   DDT
Chlordane   Dieldrin
EXCLUDES   chlorinated hydrocarbon solvents
          (982.0-982.3)

989.3 Organophosphate and carbamate
Carbaryl   Parathion
Dichlorvos   Phorate
Malathion   Phosdrin

989.4 Other pesticides, not elsewhere classified
Mixtures of insecticides

989.5 Venom
Bites of venomous snakes, lizards, and spiders
Tick paralysis

989.6 Soaps and detergents

989.7 Aflatoxin and other mycotoxin [food contaminants]

✓5th **989.8 Other substances, chiefly nonmedicinal as to source**
AHA: 4Q, '95, 60

  989.81 Asbestos
    EXCLUDES   asbestosis (501)
           exposure to asbestos (V15.84)

  989.82 Latex

  989.83 Silicone
    EXCLUDES   silicone used in medical
           devices, implants and
           grafts (996.00-996.79)

  989.84 Tobacco

  989.89 Other

989.9 Unspecified substance, chiefly nonmedicinal as to source

OTHER AND UNSPECIFIED EFFECTS OF EXTERNAL CAUSES (990-995)

990 Effects of radiation, unspecified
Complication of: Radiation sickness
phototherapy
radiation therapy
EXCLUDES   specified adverse effects of radiation. Such
         conditions are to be classified according to
         the nature of the adverse effect, as:
         burns (940.0-949.5)
         dermatitis (692.7-692.8)
         leukemia (204.0-208.9)
         pneumonia (508.0)
         sunburn (692.71, 692.76-692.77)
         [The type of radiation giving rise to the adverse
         effect may be identified by use of the E
         codes.]

✓4th **991 Effects of reduced temperature**

991.0 Frostbite of face

991.1 Frostbite of hand

991.2 Frostbite of foot

991.3 Frostbite of other and unspecified sites

991.4 Immersion foot
Trench foot
DEF: Paresthesia, edema, blotchy cyanosis of foot, the skin is soft (macerated), pale and wrinkled, and the sole is swollen with surface ridging and following sustained immersion in water.

991.5 Chilblains
Erythema pernio   Perniosis
DEF: Red, swollen, itchy skin; follows damp cold exposure; also associated with pruritus and a burning feeling, in hands, feet, ears, and face in children, legs and toes in women, and hands and fingers in men.

✓4th ✓5th **Additional Digit Required**   **Nonspecific PDx**   **Unacceptable PDx**   **Manifestation Code**   MCV Major Cardiovascular Condition   ▶◀ Revised Text   ● New Code   ▲ Revised Code Title

2007 ICD•9•CM   **February 2006 • Volume 1 — 307**

Injury and Poisoning

991.6–995.1

991.6　Hypothermia
Hypothermia (accidental)

> EXCLUDES　hypothermia following anesthesia
> (995.89)
> hypothermia not associated with low
> environmental temperature
> (780.99)

DEF: Reduced body temperature due to low environmental temperatures.

991.8　Other specified effects of reduced temperature

991.9　Unspecified effect of reduced temperature
Effects of freezing or excessive cold NOS

√4ᵗʰ **992　Effects of heat and light**

> EXCLUDES　burns (940.0-949.5)
> diseases of sweat glands due to heat (705.0-705.9)
> malignant hyperpyrexia following anesthesia (995.86)
> sunburn (692.71, 692.76-692.77)

992.0　Heat stroke and sunstroke
Heat apoplexy　　　　Siriasis
Heat pyrexia　　　　Thermoplegia
Ictus solaris

DEF: Headache, vertigo, cramps and elevated body temperature due to high environmental temperatures.

992.1　Heat syncope
Heat collapse

992.2　Heat cramps

992.3　Heat exhaustion, anhydrotic
Heat prostration due to water depletion

> EXCLUDES　that associated with salt depletion (992.4)

992.4　Heat exhaustion due to salt depletion
Heat prostration due to salt (and water) depletion

992.5　Heat exhaustion, unspecified
Heat prostration NOS

992.6　Heat fatigue, transient

992.7　Heat edema

DEF: Fluid retention due to high environmental temperatures.

992.8　Other specified heat effects

992.9　Unspecified

√4ᵗʰ **993　Effects of air pressure**

993.0　Barotrauma, otitic
Aero-otitis media
Effects of high altitude on ears

DEF: Ringing ears, deafness, pain and vertigo due to air pressure changes.

993.1　Barotrauma, sinus
Aerosinusitis
Effects of high altitude on sinuses

993.2　Other and unspecified effects of high altitude
Alpine sickness　　　Hypobaropathy
Andes disease　　　　Mountain sickness
Anoxia due to high altitude

AHA: 3Q, '88, 4

993.3　Caisson disease
Bends　　　　　　　　Decompression sickness
Compressed-air disease　Divers' palsy or paralysis

DEF: Rapid reduction in air pressure while breathing compressed air; symptoms include skin lesions, joint pains, respiratory and neurological problems.

993.4　Effects of air pressure caused by explosion

993.8　Other specified effects of air pressure

993.9　Unspecified effect of air pressure

√4ᵗʰ **994　Effects of other external causes**

> EXCLUDES　certain adverse effects not elsewhere classified (995.0-995.8)

994.0　Effects of lightning
Shock from lightning　Struck by lightning NOS

> EXCLUDES　burns (940.0-949.5)

994.1　Drowning and nonfatal submersion
Bathing cramp
Immersion

AHA: 3Q, '88, 4

994.2　Effects of hunger
Deprivation of food
Starvation

994.3　Effects of thirst
Deprivation of water

994.4　Exhaustion due to exposure

994.5　Exhaustion due to excessive exertion
Overexertion

994.6　Motion sickness
Air sickness
Seasickness
Travel sickness

994.7　Asphyxiation and strangulation
Suffocation (by):
bedclothes
cave-in
constriction
mechanical
plastic bag
pressure
strangulation

> EXCLUDES　asphyxia from:
> carbon monoxide (986)
> inhalation of food or foreign body (932-934.9)
> other gases, fumes, and vapors (987.0-987.9)

994.8　Electrocution and nonfatal effects of electric current
Shock from electric current

> EXCLUDES　electric burns (940.0-949.5)

994.9　Other effects of external causes
Effects of:
abnormal gravitational [G] forces or states
weightlessness

√4ᵗʰ **995　Certain adverse effects not elsewhere classified**

> EXCLUDES　complications of surgical and medical care (996.0-999.9)

995.0　Other anaphylactic shock
Allergic shock　⎫
Anaphylactic　　⎬　NOS or due to adverse effect of
　reaction　　　⎪　　correct medicinal substance
Anaphylaxis　　⎭　　properly administered

Use additional E code to identify external cause, such as:
adverse effects of correct medicinal substance properly administered [E930-E949]

> EXCLUDES　anaphylactic reaction to serum (999.4)
> anaphylactic shock due to adverse food reaction (995.60-995.69)

AHA: 4Q, '93, 30

DEF: Immediate sensitivity response after exposure to specific antigen; results in life-threatening respiratory distress; usually followed by vascular collapse, shock, urticaria, angioedema and pruritus.

995.1　Angioneurotic edema
Giant urticaria

> EXCLUDES　urticaria:
> due to serum (999.5)
> other specified (698.2, 708.0-708.9, 757.33)

DEF: Circulatory response of deep dermis, subcutaneous or submucosal tissues; causes localized edema and wheals.

Ⓝ Newborn Age: 0　　Ⓟ Pediatric Age: 0-17　　Ⓜ Maternity Age: 12-55　　Ⓐ Adult Age: 15-124　　CC CC Condition　　MC Major Complication　　CD Complex Dx　　HIV HIV Related Dx

Injury and Poisoning

▲ ✓5th **995.2 Other and unspecified adverse effect of drug, medicinal and biological substance**

Adverse effect
Allergic reaction
Hypersensitivity
Idiosyncrasy
} (due) to correct medicinal substance properly administered

Drug:
  hypersensitivity NOS

Drug:
  reaction NOS

> **EXCLUDES** pathological drug intoxication (292.2)

AHA: 2Q, '97, 12; 3Q, '95, 13; 3Q, '92, 16

- **995.20 Unspecified adverse effect of unspecified drug, medicinal and biological substance**

- **995.21 Arthus phenomenon**
  Arthus reaction

- **995.22 Unspecified adverse effect of anesthesia**

- **995.23 Unspecified adverse effect of insulin**

- **995.27 Other drug allergy**
  Drug allergy NOS
  Drug hypersensitivity NOS

- **995.29 Unspecified adverse effect of other drug, medicinal and biological substance**

995.3 Allergy, unspecified

Allergic reaction NOS   Idiosyncrasy NOS
Hypersensitivity NOS

> **EXCLUDES** allergic reaction NOS to correct medicinal substance properly administered ▶(995.27)◀
> ▶allergy to existing dental restorative materials (525.66)◀
> specific types of allergic reaction, such as:
> allergic diarrhea (558.3)
> dermatitis (691.0-693.9)
> hayfever (477.0-477.9)

995.4 Shock due to anesthesia   **CC**

Shock due to anesthesia in which the correct substance was properly administered

> **EXCLUDES** complications of anesthesia in labor or delivery (668.0-668.9)
> overdose or wrong substance given (968.0-969.9)
> postoperative shock NOS (998.0)
> specified adverse effects of anesthesia classified elsewhere, such as:
> anoxic brain damage (348.1)
> hepatitis (070.0-070.9), etc.
> unspecified adverse effect of anesthesia ▶(995.22)◀

CC Excl: 958.4, 995.4, 997.91-998.13, 998.81, 998.83-998.9

✓5th **995.5 Child maltreatment syndrome**

Use additional code(s), if applicable, to identify any associated injuries
Use additional E code to identify:
nature of abuse (E960-E968)
perpetrator (E967.0-E967.9)

AHA: 1Q, '98, 11

995.50 Child abuse, unspecified   **P**

995.51 Child emotional/psychological abuse   **P**
AHA: 4Q, '96, 38, 40

995.52 Child neglect (nutritional)   **P**
AHA: 4Q, '96, 38, 40

995.53 Child sexual abuse   **P**
AHA: 4Q, '96, 39, 40

995.54 Child physical abuse   **P**
Battered baby or child syndrome
> **EXCLUDES** shaken infant syndrome (995.55)
AHA: 3Q, '99, 14; 4Q, '96, 39, 40

995.55 Shaken infant syndrome   **P**
Use additional code(s) to identify any associated injuries
AHA: 4Q, '96, 40, 43

995.59 Other child abuse and neglect   **P**
Multiple forms of abuse

✓5th **995.6 Anaphylactic shock due to adverse food reaction**
Anaphylactic shock due to nonpoisonous foods
AHA: 4Q, '93, 30

995.60 Due to unspecified food
995.61 Due to peanuts
995.62 Due to crustaceans
995.63 Due to fruits and vegetables
995.64 Due to tree nuts and seeds
995.65 Due to fish
995.66 Due to food additives
995.67 Due to milk products
995.68 Due to eggs
995.69 Due to other specified food

995.7 Other adverse food reactions, not elsewhere classified
Use additional code to identify the type of reaction, such as:
hives (708.0)   wheezing (786.07)
> **EXCLUDES** anaphylactic shock due to adverse food reaction (995.60-995.69)
> asthma (493.0, 493.9)
> dermatitis due to food (693.1)
> in contact with skin (692.5)
> gastroenteritis and colitis due to food (558.3)
> rhinitis due to food (477.1)

✓5th **995.8 Other specified adverse effects, not elsewhere classified**

995.80 Adult maltreatment, unspecified   **A**
Abused person NOS
Use additional code to identify:
any associated injury
perpetrator (E967.0-E967.9)
AHA: 4Q, '96, 41, 43

995.81 Adult physical abuse   **A**
Battered: Battered:
person syndrome NEC   spouse
man   woman
Use additional code to identify:
any association injury
nature of abuse (E960-E968)
perpetrator (E967.0-E967.9)
AHA: 4Q, '96, 42, 43

995.82 Adult emotional/psychological abuse   **A**
Use additional E code to identify perpetrator (E967.0-E967.9)

995.83 Adult sexual abuse   **A**
Use additional code(s) to identify:
any associated injury
perpetrator (E967.0-E967.9)

995.84 Adult neglect (nutritional)   **A**
Use addition code(s) to identify:
intent of neglect (E904.0, E968.4)
perpetrator (E967.0-E967.9)

995.85 Other adult abuse and neglect   **A**
Multiple forms of abuse and neglect
Use additional code(s) to identify
any associated injury
intent of neglect (E904.0, E968.4)
nature of abuse (E960-E968)
perpetrator (E967.0-E967.9)

995.86 Malignant hyperthermia   **CC**
Malignant hyperpyrexia due to anesthesia
CC Excl: 958.4, 995.4, 995.86, 997.91-998.13, 998.81, 998.83-998.9
AHA: 4Q, '98, 51

995.89 Other
Hypothermia due to anesthesia
AHA: 2Q, '04, 18; 3Q, '03, 12

995.2–995.89

✓4th ✓5th Additional Digit Required   Nonspecific PDx   Unacceptable PDx   Manifestation Code   **MCV** Major Cardiovascular Condition   ▶◀ Revised Text   ● New Code   ▲ Revised Code Title

Injury and Poisoning

995.9–996.0

Continuum of Illness Due to Infection

Bacteremia → Septicemia → Sepsis

Severe Sepsis with Septic Shock ← Severe Sepsis

↓

MODS (Multiple Organ Dysfunction Syndrome) → Death

✓5ᵗʰ 995.9 Systemic inflammatory response syndrome (SIRS)
AHA: 2Q, '04, 16; 4Q, '02, 71

DEF: Clinical response to infection or trauma that can trigger an acute inflammatory reaction and progresses to coagulation, impaired fibrinolysis, and organ failure; manifested by two or more of the following symptoms: fever, tachycardia, tachypnea, leukocytosis or leukopenia.

995.90 Systemic inflammatory response syndrome, unspecified `CC`
SIRS NOS
CC Excl: 003.1, 020.2, 036.2, 038.0-038.9, 040.82-041.9, 054.5, 139.8, 995.90-995.94, V09.0-V09.91

▲ **995.91 Sepsis** `CC`
▶Systemic inflammatory response syndrome due to infectious process without acute organ dysfunction◀
▶Code first underlying infection◀
EXCLUDES ▶ *sepsis with acute organ dysfunction (995.92)*
sepsis with multiple organ dysfunction (995.92)
severe sepsis (995.92)◀
CC Excl: See code 995.90
AHA: 2Q, '04, 16; 4Q, '03, 79

▲ **995.92 Severe sepsis** `CC`
▶Sepsis with acute organ dysfunction
Sepsis with multiple organ dysfunction (MOD)
Systemic inflammatory response syndrome due to infectious process with acute organ dysfunction
Code first underlying infection◀
Use additional code to specify ▶acute◀ organ dysfunction, such as:
acute renal failure (584.5-584.9)
acute respiratory failure (518.81)
critical illness myopathy (359.81)
critical illness polyneuropathy (357.82)
▶disseminated intravascular coagulopathy [DIC] (286.6)◀
encephalopathy (348.31)
hepatic failure (570)
septic shock (785.52)
CC Excl: See code 995.90
AHA: 2Q, '05, 18-19; 1Q, '05, 7; 1Q, '05, 7; 2Q, '04, 16; 4Q, '03, 73, 79

▲ **995.93 Systemic inflammatory response syndrome due to noninfectious process without acute organ dysfunction** `CC`
▶Code first underlying conditions, such as:
acute pancreatitis (577.0)
trauma◀
EXCLUDES ▶ *systemic inflammatory response syndrome due to noninfectious process with acute organ dysfunction (995.94)◀*
CC Excl: See code 995.90

▲ **995.94 Systemic inflammatory response syndrome due to noninfectious process with acute organ dysfunction** `CC`
▶Code first underlying conditions, such as:
acute pancreatitis (577.0)
trauma◀
Use additional code to specify ▶acute◀ organ dysfunction, such as:
acute renal failure (584.5-584.9)
acute respiratory failure (518.81)
critical illness myopathy (359.81)
critical illness polyneuropathy (357.82)
▶disseminated intravascular coagulopathy [DIC] syndrome (286.6)◀
encephalopathy (348.31)
hepatic failure (570)
EXCLUDES ▶ *severe sepsis (995.92)◀*
CC Excl: See code 995.90
AHA: 4Q, '03, 79

COMPLICATIONS OF SURGICAL AND MEDICAL CARE, NOT ELSEWHERE CLASSIFIED (996-999)

EXCLUDES *adverse effects of medicinal agents (001.0-799.9, 995.0-995.8)*
burns from local applications and irradiation (940.0-949.5)
complications of:
conditions for which the procedure was performed
surgical procedures during abortion, labor, and delivery (630-676.9)
poisoning and toxic effects of drugs and chemicals (960.0-989.9)
postoperative conditions in which no complications are present, such as:
artificial opening status (V44.0-V44.9)
closure of external stoma (V55.0-V55.9)
fitting of prosthetic device (V52.0-V52.9)
specified complications classified elsewhere
anesthetic shock (995.4)
electrolyte imbalance (276.0-276.9)
postlaminectomy syndrome (722.80-722.83)
postmastectomy lymphedema syndrome (457.0)
postoperative psychosis (293.0-293.9)
any other condition classified elsewhere in the Alphabetic Index when described as due to a procedure

✓4ᵗʰ 996 Complications peculiar to certain specified procedures
INCLUDES complications, not elsewhere classified, in the use of artificial substitutes [e.g., Dacron, metal, Silastic, Teflon] or natural sources [e.g., bone] involving:
anastomosis (internal)
graft (bypass) (patch)
implant
internal device:
catheter   fixation
electronic   prosthetic
reimplant
transplant
EXCLUDES *accidental puncture or laceration during procedure (998.2)*
complications of internal anastomosis of:
gastrointestinal tract (997.4)
urinary tract (997.5)
mechanical complication of respirator (V46.14)
other specified complications classified elsewhere, such as:
hemolytic anemia (283.1)
functional cardiac disturbances (429.4)
serum hepatitis (070.2-070.3)
AHA: 1Q, '94, 3

✓5ᵗʰ 996.0 Mechanical complication of cardiac device, implant, and graft
Breakdown (mechanical)   Obstruction, mechanical
Displacement   Perforation
Leakage   Protrusion
AHA: 2Q, '93, 9

`N` Newborn Age: 0   `P` Pediatric Age: 0-17   `M` Maternity Age: 12-55   `A` Adult Age: 15-124   `CC` CC Condition   `MC` Major Complication   `CD` Complex Dx   `HIV` HIV Related Dx

996.00 Unspecified device, implant, and graft `CC`
CC Excl: 996.00, 996.04, 996.61-996.62, 996.70-996.74, 997.91, 997.99, 998.81, 998.83-998.9

996.01 Due to cardiac pacemaker (electrode) `CC`
CC Excl: 996.01, 997.91, 997.99, 998.81, 998.83-998.9
AHA: 2Q, '99, 11

996.02 Due to heart valve prosthesis `CC`
CC Excl: 996.02, 997.91, 997.99, 998.81, 998.83-998.9

996.03 Due to coronary bypass graft `CC`
> EXCLUDES atherosclerosis of graft (414.02, 414.03)
> embolism [occlusion NOS] [thrombus] of graft (996.72)

CC Excl: 996.03, 997.91, 997.99, 998.81, 998.83-998.9
AHA: 2Q, '95, 17; N-D, '86, 5

996.04 Due to automatic implantable cardiac defibrillator `CC`
CC Excl: 996.04, 997.91, 997.99, 998.81, 998.83-998.9
AHA: 2Q, '05, 3

996.09 Other `CC`
CC Excl: 996.09, 997.91, 997.99, 998.81, 998.83-998.9
AHA: 2Q, '93, 9

996.1 Mechanical complication of other vascular device, implant, and graft `CC`
Mechanical complications involving:
aortic (bifurcation) graft (replacement)
arteriovenous:
dialysis catheter
fistula } surgically created
shunt
balloon (counterpulsation) device, intra-aortic
carotid artery bypass graft
femoral-popliteal bypass graft
umbrella device, vena cava
> EXCLUDES atherosclerosis of biological graft (440.30-440.32)
> embolism [occlusion NOS] [thrombus] of (biological) (synthetic) graft (996.74)
> peritoneal dialysis catheter (996.56)

CC Excl: 996.1, 997.91, 997.99, 998.81, 998.83-998.9
AHA: ▶1Q, '06, 10;◀ 2Q, '05, 8; 1Q, '02, 13; 1Q, '95, 3

996.2 Mechanical complication of nervous system device, implant, and graft `CC`
Mechanical complications involving:
dorsal column stimulator
electrodes implanted in brain [brain "pacemaker"]
peripheral nerve graft
ventricular (communicating) shunt
CC Excl: 996.2, 996.63, 996.75, 997.91, 997.99, 998.81, 998.83-998.9
AHA: 2Q, '99, 4; S-O, '87, 10

✓5ᵗʰ **996.3 Mechanical complication of genitourinary device, implant, and graft**
AHA: 3Q, '01, 13; S-O, '85, 3

996.30 Unspecified device, implant, and graft `CC`
CC Excl: 996.30, 996.64-996.65, 996.76, 997.91, 997.99, 998.81, 998.83-998.9

996.31 Due to urethral [indwelling] catheter

996.32 Due to intrauterine contraceptive device ♀

996.39 Other `CC`
Cystostomy catheter
Prosthetic reconstruction of vas deferens
Repair (graft) of ureter without mention of resection
> EXCLUDES complications due to:
> external stoma of urinary tract (997.5)
> internal anastomosis of urinary tract (997.5)

CC Excl: 996.39, 996.64-996.65, 996.76, 997.91, 997.99, 998.81, 998.83-998.9

✓5ᵗʰ **996.4 Mechanical complication of internal orthopedic device, implant, and graft**
Mechanical complications involving:
external (fixation) device utilizing internal screw(s), pin(s) or other methods of fixation
grafts of bone, cartilage, muscle, or tendon
internal (fixation) device such as nail, plate, rod, etc.
Use additional code to identify prosthetic joint with mechanical complication (V43.60-V43.69)
> EXCLUDES complications of external orthopedic device, such as:
> pressure ulcer due to cast (707.00-707.09)

AHA: 4Q, '05, 91; 2Q, '99, 10; 2Q, '98, 19; 2Q, '96, 11; 3Q, '95, 16; N-D, '85, 11

996.40 Unspecified mechanical complication of internal orthopedic device, implant, and graft `CC`
CC Excl: 996.40-996.49, 996.66-996.67, 996.77-996.78, 997.91-997.99, 998.81, 991.83-998.9

996.41 Mechanical loosening of prosthetic joint `CC`
Aseptic loosening
CC Excl: See code 996.40
AHA: 4Q, '05, 112

996.42 Dislocation of prosthetic joint `CC`
Instability of prosthetic joint
Subluxation of prosthetic joint
CC Excl: See code 996.40

996.43 Prosthetic joint implant failure `CC`
Breakage (fracture) of prosthetic joint
CC Excl: See code 996.40

996.44 Peri-prosthetic fracture around prosthetic joint `CC`
CC Excl: See code 996.40
AHA: 4Q, '05, 93

996.45 Peri-prosthetic osteolysis `CC`
▶Use additional code to identify major osseous defect, if applicable (731.3)◀
CC Excl: See code 996.40

996.46 Articular bearing surface wear of prosthetic joint `CC`
CC Excl: See code 996.40

996.47 Other mechanical complication of prosthetic joint implant `CC`
Mechanical complication of prosthetic joint NOS
CC Excl: See code 996.40

996.49 Other mechanical complication of other internal orthopedic device, implant, and graft `CC`
> EXCLUDES mechanical complication of prosthetic joint implant (996.41-996.47)

CC Excl: See code 996.40

✓5ᵗʰ **996.5 Mechanical complication of other specified prosthetic device, implant, and graft**
Mechanical complications involving:
prosthetic implant in:
bile duct   chin
breast   orbit of eye
nonabsorbable surgical material NOS
other graft, implant, and internal device, not elsewhere classified
AHA: 1Q, '98, 11

996.51 Due to corneal graft `CC`
CC Excl: 996.51, 997.91, 997.99

✓4ᵗʰ ✓5ᵗʰ Additional Digit Required | Nonspecific PDx | Unacceptable PDx | Manifestation Code | `MCV` Major Cardiovascular Condition | ▶◀ Revised Text | ● New Code | ▲ Revised Code Title

2007 ICD·9·CM | October 2006 • Volume 1 — 311

Injury and Poisoning

996.52–996.7

996.52 Due to graft of other tissue, not elsewhere classified `CC`

Skin graft failure or rejection

> **EXCLUDES** failure of artificial skin graft (996.55)
>
> failure of decellularized allodermis (996.55)
>
> sloughing of temporary skin allografts or xenografts (pigskin)—omit code

CC Excl: 996.52, 996.55, 997.91, 997.99

AHA: 1Q, '96, 10

996.53 Due to ocular lens prosthesis `CC`

> **EXCLUDES** contact lenses—code to condition

CC Excl: 996.53, 997.91, 997.99

AHA: 1Q, '00, 9

996.54 Due to breast prosthesis `CC`

Breast capsule (prosthesis)

Mammary implant

CC Excl: 996.54, 997.91, 997.99

AHA: 2Q, '98, 14; 3Q, '92, 4

996.55 Due to artificial skin graft and decellularized allodermis `CC`

Dislodgement	Non-adherence
Displacement	Poor incorporation
Failure	Shearing

CC Excl: 996.52, 996.55-996.60, 996.68-996.69, 996.70, 996.79, 997.91, 997.99

AHA: 4Q, '98, 52

996.56 Due to peritoneal dialysis catheter `CC`

> **EXCLUDES** mechanical complication of arteriovenous dialysis catheter (996.1)

CC Excl: 996.56-996.60, 996.68-996.70, 996.79, 997.91, 997.99

AHA: 4Q, '98, 54

996.57 Due to insulin pump `CC`

CC Excl: 996.00-996.30, 996.39-996.79, 997.91-997.99, 998.81, 998.83-998.9

AHA: 4Q, '03, 81-82

996.59 Due to other implant and internal device, not elsewhere classified `CC`

Nonabsorbable surgical material NOS

Prosthetic implant in:
  bile duct
  chin
  orbit of eye

CC Excl: 996.59-996.60, 996.68-996.70, 996.79, 997.91-997.99

AHA: 2Q, '99, 13; 3Q, '94, 7

√5ᵗʰ **996.6 Infection and inflammatory reaction due to internal prosthetic device, implant, and graft**

Infection (causing obstruction)	due to (presence of) any device, implant, and graft classi-
Inflammation	fiable to 996.0-996.5

Use additional code to identify specified infections

AHA: 2Q, '89, 16; J-F, '87, 14

996.60 Due to unspecified device, implant, and graft `CC`

CC Excl: 996.00-996.30, 996.39, 996.4-996.79, 997.91-997.99, 998.81, 998.83-998.9

996.61 Due to cardiac device, implant, and graft `CC` `MCV`

Cardiac pacemaker or defibrillator:
  electrode(s), lead(s)
  pulse generator
  subcutaneous pocket
Coronary artery bypass graft
Heart valve prosthesis

CC Excl: 996.00-996.1, 996.52, 996.55-996.62, 996.68-996.74, 996.79, 997.91, 997.99, 998.81, 998.83-998.9

996.62 Due to other vascular device, implant, and graft `CC` `MC` `MCV`

Arterial graft
Arteriovenous fistula or shunt
Infusion pump
Vascular catheter (arterial) (dialysis) (venous)

CC Excl: See code 996.61

AHA: 2Q, '04, 16; 1Q, '04, 5; 4Q, '03, 107, 111; 2Q, '03, 7; 2Q, '94, 13

996.63 Due to nervous system device, implant, and graft `CC`

Electrodes implanted in brain
Peripheral nerve graft
Spinal canal catheter
Ventricular (communicating) shunt (catheter)

CC Excl: 996.2, 996.52, 996.55-996.60, 996.63, 996.68-996.70, 996.75, 996.79, 997.91, 997.99, 998.81, 998.83-998.9

996.64 Due to indwelling urinary catheter `CC`

Use additional code to identify specified infections, such as:
  Cystitis (595.0-595.9)
  Sepsis (038.0-038.9)

CC Excl: 599.0, 996.30, 996.39, 996.56-996.60, 996.64-996.65, 996.68-996.70, 996.76, 996.79, 997.91, 997.99, 998.81, 998.83-998.9

AHA: 3Q, '93, 6

▽ DRG 331

996.65 Due to other genitourinary device, implant, and graft `CC`

Intrauterine contraceptive device

CC Excl: 996.30, 996.39, 996.52, 996.55-996.60, 996.64-996.65, 996.68-996.70, 996.76, 996.79, 997.91, 997.99, 998.81, 998.83-998.9

AHA: 1Q, '00, 15

996.66 Due to internal joint prosthesis `CC`

Use additional code to identify infected prosthetic joint (V43.60-V43.69)

CC Excl: 996.40-996.49, 996.52, 996.55-996.60, 996.66-996.70, 996.77-996.79, 997.91-997.99, 998.81, 998.83-998.9

AHA: 4Q, '05, 91, 113; 2Q, '91, 18

996.67 Due to other internal orthopedic device, implant, and graft `CC`

Bone growth stimulator (electrode)
Internal fixation device (pin) (rod) (screw)

CC Excl: See code 996.66

996.68 Due to peritoneal dialysis catheter `CC`

Exit-site infection or inflammation

CC Excl: 996.56-996.60, 996.68-996.70, 996.79, 997.91, 997.99

AHA: 4Q, '98, 54

996.69 Due to other internal prosthetic device, implant, and graft `CC`

Breast prosthesis	Prosthetic orbital
Ocular lens prosthesis	implant

CC Excl: 996.00-996.30, 996.39-996.79, 997.91-997.99, 998.81, 998.83-998.9

AHA: 4Q, '03, 108; 4Q, '98, 52

√5ᵗʰ **996.7 Other complications of internal (biological) (synthetic) prosthetic device, implant, and graft**

Complication NOS	
occlusion NOS	
Embolism	due to (presence of) any
Fibrosis	device, implant, and
Hemorrhage	graft classifiable to
Pain	996.0-996.5
Stenosis	
Thrombus	

▶Use additional code to identify complication, such as:
  pain due to presence of device, implant or graft (338.18-338.19, 338.28-338.29)◀

> **EXCLUDES** transplant rejection (996.8)

AHA: 4Q, '05, 94; 1Q, '89, 9; N-D, '86, 5

`N` Newborn Age: 0	`P` Pediatric Age: 0-17	`M` Maternity Age: 12-55	`A` Adult Age: 15-124	`CC` CC Condition	`MC` Major Complication	`CD` Complex Dx	`HIV` HIV Related Dx

996.70 Due to unspecified device, implant, and `CC`
graft
  CC Excl: See code 996.69

996.71 Due to heart valve prosthesis `CC`
  CC Excl: 996.00, 996.02, 996.09, 996.1, 996.52, 996.55-996.62,
  996.68-996.74, 996.79, 997.91-997.99, 998.81, 998.83-998.9

996.72 Due to other cardiac device, `CC` `MC` `MCV`
implant, and graft
  Cardiac pacemaker or defibrillator:
    electrode(s), lead(s)
    subcutaneous pocket
  Coronary artery bypass (graft)
    EXCLUDES occlusion due to athero-
            sclerosis (414.02-414.06)
  CC Excl: 996.00-996.02, 996.04, 996.09, 996.1, 996.52,
  996.55-996.62, 996.68-996.74, 996.79, 997.91-997.99,
  998.81, 998.83-998.9
  AHA: 3Q, '01, 20

996.73 Due to renal dialysis device, implant, `CC`
and graft
  CC Excl: 996.1, 996.52, 996.55-996.60, 996.68-996.70,
  996.73, 996.79, 997.91, 997.99, 998.81, 998.83-998.9
  AHA: 2Q, '91, 18

996.74 Due to other vascular device, implant, `CC`
and graft
    EXCLUDES occlusion of biological graft
            due to atherosclerosis
            (440.30-440.32)
  CC Excl: See code 996.71
  AHA: 1Q, '03, 16, 17

996.75 Due to nervous system device, implant, `CC`
and graft
  CC Excl: 996.2, 996.52, 996.55-996.60, 996.63, 996.68-
  996.70, 996.75, 996.79, 997.91, 997.99, 998.81, 998.83-998.9

996.76 Due to genitourinary device, implant, `CC`
and graft
  CC Excl: 996.30, 996.39, 996.52, 996.55-996.60, 996.64-
  996.65, 996.68-996.70, 996.76, 996.79, 997.91, 997.99,
  998.81, 998.83-998.9
  AHA: 1Q, '00, 15

996.77 Due to internal joint prosthesis `CC`
  CC Excl: 996.40-996.49, 996.52, 996.55-996.60, 996.66-
  996.67, 996.69-996.70, 996.77-996.79, 997.91-997.99, 998.81,
  998.83-998.9
  AHA: 4Q, '05, 91

996.78 Due to other internal orthopedic `CC`
device, implant, and graft
  CC Excl: See code 996.77
  AHA: 2Q, '03, 14

996.79 Due to other internal prosthetic `CC`
device, implant, and graft
  CC Excl: 996.00-996.30, 996.39, 996.4-996.79, 997.91,
  997.99, 998.81, 998.83-998.9
  AHA: 2Q, '04, 7; 1Q, '01, 8; 3Q, '95, 14; 3Q, '92, 4

√5th **996.8 Complications of transplanted organ**
  Transplant failure or rejection
  Use additional code to identify nature of
  complication, such as:
  Cytomegalovirus (CMV) infection (078.5)
  AHA: 3Q, '01, 12; 3Q, '93, 3, 4; 2Q, '93, 11; 1Q, '93, 24

996.80 Transplanted organ, unspecified `CC`
  CC Excl: 996.80, 996.87, 997.91, 997.99

996.81 Kidney `CC`
  CC Excl: 996.81, 997.91, 997.99
  AHA: 3Q, '03, 16; 3Q, '98, 6, 7; 3Q, '94, 8; 2Q, '94, 9;
    1Q, '93, 24
  DRG 331

996.82 Liver `CC`
  CC Excl: 996.82, 997.91, 997.99
  AHA: 3Q, '03, 17; 3Q, '98, 3, 4

996.83 Heart `CC` `MCV`
  CC Excl: 996.83, 997.91, 997.99
  AHA: 3Q, '03, 16; 4Q, '02, 53; 3Q, '98, 5

996.84 Lung `CC`
  CC Excl: 996.84, 997.91, 997.99
  AHA: 2Q, '03, 12; 3Q, '98, 5

996.85 Bone marrow `CC`
  Graft-versus-host disease (acute) (chronic)
  CC Excl: 996.85, 997.91, 997.99
  AHA: 4Q, '90, 4

996.86 Pancreas `CC`
  CC Excl: 996.86, 997.91, 997.99

996.87 Intestine `CC`
  CC Excl: 996.80, 996.87, 997.91, 997.99

996.89 Other specified transplanted organ `CC`
  CC Excl: 996.89, 997.91, 997.99
  AHA: 3Q, '94, 5

√5th **996.9 Complications of reattached extremity or body part**

996.90 Unspecified extremity `CC`
  CC Excl: 996.90, 997.91, 997.99, 998.81, 998.83-998.9

996.91 Forearm `CC`
  CC Excl: 996.91, 997.91, 997.99, 998.81, 998.83-998.9

996.92 Hand `CC`
  CC Excl: 996.92, 997.91, 997.99, 998.81, 998.83-998.9

996.93 Finger(s) `CC`
  CC Excl: 996.93, 997.91, 997.99, 998.81, 998.83-998.9

996.94 Upper extremity, other and unspecified `CC`
  CC Excl: 996.94, 997.91, 997.99, 998.81, 998.83-998.9

996.95 Foot and toe(s) `CC`
  CC Excl: 996.95, 997.91, 997.99, 998.81, 998.83-998.9

996.96 Lower extremity, other and unspecified `CC`
  CC Excl: 996.96, 997.91, 997.99, 998.81, 998.83-998.9

996.99 Other specified body part `CC`
  CC Excl: 996.99, 997.91, 997.99, 998.81, 998.83-998.9

√4th **997 Complications affecting specified body systems, not elsewhere classified**
  Use additional code to identify complications
    EXCLUDES the listed conditions when specified as:
            causing shock (998.0)
            complications of:
              anesthesia:
                adverse effect (001.0-799.9, 995.0-
                  995.8)
                in labor or delivery (668.0-668.9)
                poisoning (968.0-969.9)
              implanted device or graft (996.0-996.9)
              obstetrical procedures (669.0-669.4)
              reattached extremity (996.90-996.96)
              transplanted organ (996.80-996.89)
  AHA: 1Q, '94, 4; 1Q, '93, 26

√5th **997.0 Nervous system complications**
  CC Excl: For codes 997.00-997.09: 997.00-997.09, 997.91, 997.99,
  998.81, 998.83, 998.89, 998.9

997.00 Nervous system complication, `CC`
unspecified

997.01 Central nervous system complication `CC`
  Anoxic brain damage
  Cerebral hypoxia
    EXCLUDES cerebrovascular hemorrhage or
            infarction (997.02)
  AHA: ▶1Q, '06, 15◀

997.02 Iatrogenic cerebrovascular infarction or `CC`
hemorrhage
  Postoperative stroke
  AHA: 2Q, '04, 8; 4Q, '95, 57

997.09 Other nervous system complications `CC`

√4th √5th Additional Digit Required | Nonspecific PDx | Unacceptable PDx | Manifestation Code | `MCV` Major Cardiovascular Condition | ▶◀ Revised Text | ● New Code | ▲ Revised Code Title

Injury and Poisoning

997.1–997.69

997.1 Cardiac complications `cc`

Cardiac:
    arrest
    insufficiency } during or resulting
Cardiorespiratory failure   from a procedure
Heart failure

EXCLUDES *the listed conditions as long-term effects of cardiac surgery or due to the presence of cardiac prosthetic device (429.4)*

CC Excl: 997.1, 997.91, 997.99, 998.81, 998.83-998.9

AHA: 2Q, '02, 12

997.2 Peripheral vascular complications `cc`

Phlebitis or thrombophlebitis during or resulting from a procedure

EXCLUDES *the listed conditions due to:*
implant or catheter device (996.62)
infusion, perfusion, or transfusion (999.2)
complications affecting blood vessels (997.71-997.79)

CC Excl: 997.2, 997.79, 997.91, 997.99, 998.81, 998.83-998.9

AHA: 1Q, '03, 6; 3Q, '02, 24-26

997.3 Respiratory complications `cc`

Mendelson's syndrome } resulting from a
Pneumonia (aspiration)   procedure

EXCLUDES *iatrogenic [postoperative] pneumothorax (512.1)*
iatrogenic pulmonary embolism (415.11)
Mendelson's syndrome in labor and delivery (668.0)
specified complications classified elsewhere, such as:
adult respiratory distress syndrome (518.5)
pulmonary edema, postoperative (518.4)
respiratory insufficiency, acute, postoperative (518.5)
shock lung (518.5)
tracheostomy complications (519.00-519.09)
▶*transfusion related acute lung injury [TRALI] (518.7)*◀

CC Excl: 518.7, 997.3, 997.91, 997.99, 998.81, 998.83, 998.83-998.9
AHA: 1Q, '97, 10; 2Q, '93, 3; 2Q, '93, 9; 4Q, '90, 25
DEF: Mendelson's syndrome: acid pneumonitis due to aspiration of gastric acids, may occur after anesthesia or sedation.

997.4 Digestive system complications `cc`

Complications of:
    intestinal (internal) anastomosis and bypass, not elsewhere classified, except that involving urinary tract
Hepatic failure
Hepatorenal syndrome } specified as due to
Intestinal obstruction NOS   a procedure

EXCLUDES *gastrostomy complications (536.40-536.49)*
specified gastrointestinal complications classified elsewhere, such as:
blind loop syndrome (579.2)
colostomy and enterostomy complications (569.60-569.69)
gastrojejunal ulcer (534.0-534.9)
infection of esophagostomy (530.86)
infection of external stoma (569.61)
mechanical complication of esophagostomy (530.87)
pelvic peritoneal adhesions, female (614.6)
peritoneal adhesions (568.0)
peritoneal adhesions with obstruction (560.81)
postcholecystectomy syndrome (576.0)
postgastric surgery syndromes (564.2)
vomiting following gastrointestinal surgery (564.3)

CC Excl: 530.86-530.87, 536.40-536.49, 997.4, 997.71, 997.91-997.99, 998.81, 998.83-998.9
AHA: 2Q, '01, 4-6; 3Q, '99, 4; 2Q, '99, 14; 3Q, '97, 7; 1Q, '97, 11; 2Q, '95, 7; 1Q, '93, 26; 3Q, '92, 15; 2Q, '89, 15; 1Q, '88, 14
▽ **DRG** 188

997.5 Urinary complications `cc`

Complications of:
    external stoma of urinary tract
    internal anastomosis and bypass of urinary tract, including that involving intestinal tract
Oliguria or anuria
Renal:
    failure (acute) } specified as due to
    insufficiency (acute)   procedure
Tubular necrosis (acute)

EXCLUDES *specified complications classified elsewhere, such as:*
postoperative stricture of:
ureter (593.3)
urethra (598.2)

CC Excl: 997.5, 997.72, 997.91, 997.99, 998.81, 998.83-998.9
AHA: 3Q, '03, 13; 3Q, '96, 10, 15; 4Q, '95, 73; 1Q, '92, 13; 2Q, '89, 16; M-A, '87, 10; S-O, '85, 3
▽ **DRG** 331

✓5ᵗʰ **997.6 Amputation stump complication**

EXCLUDES *admission for treatment for a current traumatic amputation — code to complicated traumatic amputation*
phantom limb (syndrome) (353.6)

AHA: 4Q, '95, 82

997.60 Unspecified complication

997.61 Neuroma of amputation stump

DEF: Hyperplasia generated nerve cell mass following amputation.

997.62 Infection (chronic) `cc`

Use additional code to identify the organism
CC Excl: 997.60, 997.62, 997.69, 997.91, 997.99, 998.81, 998.83-998.9
AHA: 1Q, '05, 15 4Q, '96, 46

997.69 Other

AHA: 1Q, '05, 15

| N Newborn Age: 0 | P Pediatric Age: 0-17 | M Maternity Age: 12-55 | A Adult Age: 15-124 | CC CC Condition | MC Major Complication | CD Complex Dx | HIV HIV Related Dx |

314 — Volume 1 • October 2006   **2007 ICD•9•CM**

☑5ᵗʰ **997.7 Vascular complications of other vessels**

>EXCLUDES peripheral vascular complications (997.2)

997.71 Vascular complications of mesenteric artery `cc`
CC Excl: 997.2, 997.71-997.79, 997.91, 997.99, 998.81 998.83-998.9
AHA: 4Q, '01, 53

997.72 Vascular complications of renal artery `cc`
CC Excl: See code 997.71

997.79 Vascular complications of other vessels `cc`
CC Excl: See code 997.71

☑5ᵗʰ **997.9 Complications affecting other specified body systems, not elsewhere classified** `cc`

>EXCLUDES specified complications classified elsewhere, such as:
broad ligament laceration syndrome (620.6)
postartificial menopause syndrome (627.4)
postoperative stricture of vagina (623.2)

997.91 Hypertension
>EXCLUDES essential hypertension (401.0-401.9)

AHA: 4Q, '95, 57

997.99 Other `cc`
Vitreous touch syndrome
CC Excl: 997.91, 997.99, 998.81, 998.83-998.9
AHA: 2Q, '94, 12; 1Q, '94, 17

DEF: Vitreous touch syndrome: vitreous protruding through pupil and attaches to corneal epithelium; causes aqueous fluid in vitreous body; marked by corneal edema, loss of lucidity; complication of cataract surgery.

☑4ᵗʰ **998 Other complications of procedures, not elsewhere classified**
AHA: 1Q, '94, 4

998.0 Postoperative shock `cc`
Collapse NOS
Shock (endotoxic) (hypo-volemic) (septic) } during or resulting from a surgical procedure

>EXCLUDES shock:
anaphylactic due to serum (999.4)
anesthetic (995.4)
electric (994.8)
following abortion (639.5)
obstetric (669.1)
traumatic (958.4)

CC Excl: 958.4, 995.4, 997.91-998.13, 998.81, 998.83-998.9

☑5ᵗʰ **998.1 Hemorrhage or hematoma or seroma complicating a procedure**
>EXCLUDES hemorrhage, hematoma, or seroma:
complicating cesarean section or puerperal perineal wound (674.3)

998.11 Hemorrhage complicating a procedure `cc`
CC Excl: 456.0, 456.20, 530.81-530.83, 530.89, 531.00-531.01, 531.20-531.21, 531.40-531.41, 531.60-531.61, 532.00-532.01, 532.20-532.21, 532.40-532.41, 532.60-532.61, 533.00-533.01, 533.20-533.21, 533.40-533.41, 533.60-533.61, 534.00-534.01, 534.20-534.21, 534.40-534.41, 534.60-534.61, 535.01, 535.11, 535.21, 535.31, 535.41, 535.51, 535.61, 537.83, 562.02-562.03, 562.12-562.13, 569.3, 569.85, 578.0-578.1, 578.9, 772.4, 997.91-998.13, 998.81, 998.89, 998.9
AHA: 3Q, '03, 13; 1Q, '03, 4; 4Q, '97, 52; 1Q, '97, 10

998.12 Hematoma complicating a procedure `cc`
CC Excl: see code 998.11
AHA: 1Q, '03, 6; 3Q, '02, 24, 26

998.13 Seroma complicating a procedure `cc`
CC Excl: See code 998.11
AHA: 4Q, '96, 46; 1Q, '93, 26; 2Q, '92, 15; S-O, '87, 8

998.2 Accidental puncture or laceration during a procedure `cc`
Accidental perforation by catheter or other instrument during a procedure on:
blood vessel
nerve
organ
>EXCLUDES iatrogenic [postoperative] pneumothorax (512.1)
puncture or laceration caused by implanted device intentionally left in operation wound (996.0-996.5)
specified complications classified elsewhere, such as:
broad ligament laceration syndrome (620.6)
trauma from instruments during delivery (664.0-665.9)

CC Excl: 997.91, 997.99, 998.2, 998.81, 998.83-998.9
AHA: ▶1Q, '06, 15;◀ 3Q, '02, 24, 26; 3Q, '94, 6; 3Q, '90, 17; 3Q, '90, 18

☑5ᵗʰ **998.3 Disruption of operation wound**
Dehiscence
Rupture } of operation wound
>EXCLUDES disruption of:
cesarean wound (674.1)
perineal wound, puerperal (674.2)
AHA: 4Q, '02, 73; 1Q, '93, 19

998.31 Disruption of internal operation wound `cc`
CC Excl: 997.91-997.99, 998.31, 998.32, 998.81-998.89, 998.9

998.32 Disruption of external operation wound `cc`
Disruption of operation wound NOS
CC Excl: See code 998.31
AHA: ▶1Q, '06, 8;◀ 1Q, '05, 11; 4Q, '03, 104, 106

998.4 Foreign body accidentally left during a procedure `cc`
Adhesions
Obstruction
Perforation } due to foreign body accidentally left in operative wound or body cavity during a procedure
>EXCLUDES obstruction or perforation caused by implanted device intentionally left in body (996.0-996.5)
CC Excl: 997.91, 997.99, 998.4, 998.81, 998.83-998.9
AHA: 1Q, '89, 9

☑5ᵗʰ **998.5 Postoperative infection**
>EXCLUDES ▶ bleb associated endophthalmitis (379.63)◀
infection due to:
implanted device (996.60-996.69)
infusion, perfusion, or transfusion (999.3)
postoperative obstetrical wound infection (674.3)

998.51 Infected postoperative seroma `cc`
Use additional code to identify organism
CC Excl: 997.91, 997.99, 998.51-998.59, 998.81, 998.83-998.9
AHA: 4Q, '96, 46

998.59 Other postoperative infection `cc`
Abscess:
intra-abdominal
stitch
subphrenic
wound
Septicemia } postoperative
Use additional code to identify infection
CC Excl: See code 998.51
AHA: 4Q, '04, 76; 4Q, '03, 104, 106-107; 3Q, '98, 3; 3Q, '95, 5; 2Q, '95, 7; 3Q, '94, 6; 1Q, '93, 19; J-F, '87, 14

998.6 Persistent postoperative fistula `cc`
CC Excl: 997.91, 997.99, 998.6, 998.81, 998.83-998.9
AHA: J-F, '87, 14

☑4ᵗʰ/☑5ᵗʰ Additional Digit Required   Nonspecific PDx   Unacceptable PDx   Manifestation Code   `MCV` Major Cardiovascular Condition   ▶◀ Revised Text   ● New Code   ▲ Revised Code Title

Injury and Poisoning

998.7–999.9

998.7 Acute reaction to foreign substance accidentally left during a procedure `CC`

Peritonitis: Peritonitis:
  aseptic   chemical

CC Excl: 997.91, 997.99, 998.7, 998.81, 998.83-998.9

✓5th 998.8 Other specified complications of procedures, not elsewhere classified

AHA: 4Q, '94, 46; 1Q, '89, 9

998.81 Emphysema (subcutaneous) (surgical) resulting from a procedure

998.82 Cataract fragments in eye following cataract surgery

998.83 Non-healing surgical wound `CC`

CC Excl: 997.91, 997.99, 998.81, 998.83, 998.89, 998.9

AHA 4Q, '96, 47

998.89 Other specified complications `CC`

CC Excl: See code 998.83

AHA: 3Q, '05, 16; 3Q, '99, 13; 2Q, '98, 16

998.9 Unspecified complication of procedure, not elsewhere classified `CC`

Postoperative complication NOS

> EXCLUDES   *complication NOS of obstetrical, surgery or procedure (669.4)*

CC Excl: See code 998.83

AHA: 4Q, '93, 37

✓4th 999 Complications of medical care, not elsewhere classified

> INCLUDES   complications, not elsewhere classified, of:
>   dialysis (hemodialysis) (peritoneal) (renal)
>   extracorporeal circulation
>   hyperalimentation therapy
>   immunization
>   infusion
>   inhalation therapy
>   injection
>   inoculation
>   perfusion
>   transfusion
>   vaccination
>   ventilation therapy

> EXCLUDES   *specified complications classified elsewhere such as:*
>   *complications of implanted device (996.0-996.9)*
>   *contact dermatitis due to drugs (692.3)*
>   *dementia dialysis (294.8)*
>   *transient (293.9)*
>   *dialysis disequilibrium syndrome (276.0-276.9)*
>   *poisoning and toxic effects of drugs and chemicals (960.0-989.9)*
>   *postvaccinal encephalitis ▶(323.51)◀*
>   *water and electrolyte imbalance (276.0-276.9)*

999.0 Generalized vaccinia

DEF: Skin eruption, self-limiting; follows vaccination; due to transient viremia with virus localized in skin.

999.1 Air embolism `CC`

Air embolism to any site following infusion, perfusion, or transfusion

> EXCLUDES   *embolism specified as:*
>   *complicating:*
>   *abortion (634-638 with .6, 639.6)*
>   *ectopic or molar pregnancy (639.6)*
>   *pregnancy, childbirth, or the puerperium (673.0)*
>   *due to implanted device (996.7)*
>   *traumatic (958.0)*

CC Excl: 958.0, 999.1

999.2 Other vascular complications `CC`

Phlebitis
Thromboembolism } following infusion, perfusion, or transfusion
Thrombophlebitis

> EXCLUDES   *the listed conditions when specified as:*
>   *due to implanted device (996.61-996.62. 996.72-996.74)*
>   *postoperative NOS (997.2, 997.71-997.79)*

CC Excl: 999.2

AHA: 2Q, '97, 5

999.3 Other infection `CC`

Infection
Sepsis } following infusion, injection, transfusion, or vaccination
Septicemia

> EXCLUDES   *the listed conditions when specified as:*
>   *due to implanted device (996.60-996.69)*
>   *postoperative NOS (998.51-998.59)*

CC Excl: 999.3

AHA: 2Q, '01, 11, 12; 2Q, '97, 5; J-F, '87, 14

999.4 Anaphylactic shock due to serum `CC`

> EXCLUDES   *shock:*
>   *allergic NOS (995.0)*
>   *anaphylactic:*
>   *NOS (995.0)*
>   *due to drugs and chemicals (995.0)*

CC Excl: 999.4

DEF: Life-threatening hypersensitivity to foreign serum; causes respiratory distress, vascular collapse, and shock.

999.5 Other serum reaction `CC`

Intoxication by serum   Serum sickness
Protein sickness   Urticaria due to serum
Serum rash

> EXCLUDES   *serum hepatitis (070.2-070.3)*

CC Excl: 999.5

DEF: Serum sickness: Hypersensitivity to foreign serum; causes fever, hives, swelling, and lymphadenopathy.

999.6 ABO incompatibility reaction `CC`

Incompatible blood transfusion
Reaction to blood group incompatibility in infusion or transfusion

CC Excl: 999.6

999.7 Rh incompatibility reaction `CC`

Elevation of Rh titer
Reactions due to Rh factor in infusion or transfusion

CC Excl: 999.7

999.8 Other transfusion reaction `CC`

Septic shock due to transfusion
Transfusion reaction NOS

> EXCLUDES   *postoperative shock (998.0)*
>   ▶*transfusion related acute lung injury [TRALI] (518.7)*◀

CC Excl: 999.8

AHA: 3Q, '00, 9

999.9 Other and unspecified complications of medical care, not elsewhere classified

Complications, not elsewhere classified, of:
electroshock
inhalation   } therapy
ultrasound
ventilation

Unspecified misadventure of medical care

> EXCLUDES   *unspecified complication of:*
>   *phototherapy (990)*
>   *radiation therapy (999)*

AHA: 1Q, '03, 19; 2Q, '97, 5

N Newborn Age: 0   P Pediatric Age: 0-17   M Maternity Age: 12-55   A Adult Age: 15-124   CC CC Condition   MC Major Complication   CD Complex Dx   HIV HIV Related Dx

SUPPLEMENTARY CLASSIFICATION OF FACTORS INFLUENCING HEALTH STATUS AND CONTACT WITH HEALTH SERVICES ▶(V01-V86)◀

This classification is provided to deal with occasions when circumstances other than a disease or injury classifiable to categories 001-999 (the main part of ICD) are recorded as "diagnoses" or "problems." This can arise mainly in three ways:

a) When a person who is not currently sick encounters the health services for some specific purpose, such as to act as a donor of an organ or tissue, to receive prophylactic vaccination, or to discuss a problem which is in itself not a disease or injury. This will be a fairly rare occurrence among hospital inpatients, but will be relatively more common among hospital outpatients and patients of family practitioners, health clinics, etc.

b) When a person with a known disease or injury, whether it is current or resolving, encounters the health care system for a specific treatment of that disease or injury (e.g., dialysis for renal disease; chemotherapy for malignancy; cast change).

c) When some circumstance or problem is present which influences the person's health status but is not in itself a current illness or injury. Such factors may be elicited during population surveys, when the person may or may not be currently sick, or be recorded as an additional factor to be borne in mind when the person is receiving care for some current illness or injury classifiable to categories 001-999.

In the latter circumstances the V code should be used only as a supplementary code and should not be the one selected for use in primary, single cause tabulations. Examples of these circumstances are a personal history of certain diseases, or a person with an artificial heart valve in situ.

     AHA: J-F, '87, 8

PERSONS WITH POTENTIAL HEALTH HAZARDS RELATED TO COMMUNICABLE DISEASES (V01-V06)

> **EXCLUDES**   *family history of infectious and parasitic diseases (V18.8)*
> *personal history of infectious and parasitic diseases (V12.0)*

✓4th **V01 Contact with or exposure to communicable diseases**

     V01.0 Cholera
         Conditions classifiable to 001

     V01.1 Tuberculosis
         Conditions classifiable to 010-018

     V01.2 Poliomyelitis
         Conditions classifiable to 045

     V01.3 Smallpox
         Conditions classifiable to 050

     V01.4 Rubella
         Conditions classifiable to 056

     V01.5 Rabies
         Conditions classifiable to 071

     V01.6 Venereal diseases
         Conditions classifiable to 090-099

✓5th **V01.7 Other viral diseases**
         Conditions classifiable to 042-078 and V08, except as above

         AHA: 2Q, '92, 11

       [3] **V01.71 Varicella**

       [3] **V01.79 Other viral diseases**

✓5th **V01.8 Other communicable diseases**
         Conditions classifiable to 001-136, except as above

         AHA: J-A, '87, 24

         V01.81 Anthrax
            AHA: 4Q, '02, 70, 78

       [3] **V01.82 Exposure to SARS-associated coronavirus**
            AHA: 4Q, '03, 46-47

       [3] **V01.83 Escherichia coli (E. coli)**

       [3] **V01.84 Meningococcus**

         V01.89 Other communicable diseases

     V01.9 Unspecified communicable disease

✓4th **V02 Carrier or suspected carrier of infectious diseases**
     AHA: 3Q, '95, 18; 3Q, '94, 4

     V02.0 Cholera
     V02.1 Typhoid
     V02.2 Amebiasis
     V02.3 Other gastrointestinal pathogens
     V02.4 Diphtheria

✓5th **V02.5 Other specified bacterial diseases**

         V02.51 Group B streptococcus
            AHA: 1Q, '02, 14; 4Q, '98, 56

         V02.52 Other streptococcus

         V02.59 Other specified bacterial diseases
            Meningococcal   Staphylococcal

✓5th **V02.6 Viral hepatitis**
         Hepatitis Australian-antigen [HAA] [SH] carrier
         Serum hepatitis carrier

         V02.60 Viral hepatitis carrier, unspecified
            AHA: 4Q, '97, 47

         V02.61 Hepatitis B carrier
            AHA: 4Q, '97, 47

         V02.62 Hepatitis C carrier
            AHA: 4Q, '97, 47

         V02.69 Other viral hepatitis carrier
            AHA: 4Q, '97, 47

     V02.7 Gonorrhea
     V02.8 Other venereal diseases
     V02.9 Other specified infectious organism
         AHA: 3Q, '95, 18; 1Q, '93, 22; J-A, '87, 24

✓4th **V03 Need for prophylactic vaccination and inoculation against bacterial diseases**

> **EXCLUDES**   *vaccination not carried out (V64.00-V64.09)*
> *vaccines against combinations of diseases (V06.0-V06.9)*

     V03.0 Cholera alone
     V03.1 Typhoid-paratyphoid alone [TAB]
     V03.2 Tuberculosis [BCG]
     V03.3 Plague
     V03.4 Tularemia
     V03.5 Diphtheria alone
     V03.6 Pertussis alone
     V03.7 Tetanus toxoid alone

✓5th **V03.8 Other specified vaccinations against single bacterial diseases**

         V03.81 Hemophilus influenza, type B [Hib]
         V03.82 Streptococcus pneumoniae [pneumococcus]
         V03.89 Other specified vaccination
            AHA: 2Q, '00, 9

     V03.9 Unspecified single bacterial disease

✓4th **V04 Need for prophylactic vaccination and inoculation against certain viral diseases**

> **EXCLUDES**   *vaccines against combinations of diseases (V06.0-V06.9)*

     V04.0 Poliomyelitis
     V04.1 Smallpox
     V04.2 Measles alone
     V04.3 Rubella alone
     V04.4 Yellow fever
     V04.5 Rabies
     V04.6 Mumps alone
     V04.7 Common cold

✓5th **V04.8 Other viral diseases**
     AHA: 4Q, '03, 83

         V04.81 Influenza
         V04.82 Respiratory syncytial virus (RSV)
         V04.89 Other viral diseases

---

[3] These V codes may be used as principal diagnosis on Medicare patients.

✓4th   ✓5th   Additional Digit Required   Nonspecific PDx   Unacceptable PDx   Manifestation Code   **MCV** Major Cardiovascular Condition   ▶◀ Revised Text   ● New Code   ▲ Revised Code Title

2007 ICD•9•CM   October 2006 • Volume 1 — 317

V Codes

V05–V09.91

☑4th **V05 Need for other prophylactic vaccination and inoculation against single diseases**

> EXCLUDES   *vaccines against combinations of diseases (V06.0-V06.9)*

V05.0 Athropod-borne viral encephalitis

V05.1 Other arthropod-borne viral diseases

V05.2 Leishmaniasis

V05.3 Viral hepatitis

V05.4 Varicella
> Chickenpox

V05.8 Other specified disease
> AHA: 1Q, '01, 4; 3Q, '91, 20

V05.9 Unspecified single disease

☑4th **V06 Need for prophylactic vaccination and inoculation against combinations of diseases**

> Note: Use additional single vaccination codes from categories V03-V05 to identify any vaccinations not included in a combination code.

V06.0 Cholera with typhoid-paratyphoid [cholera+TAB]

V06.1 Diphtheria-tetanus-pertussis, combined [DTP] [DTaP]
> AHA: 4Q, '03, 83; 3Q, '98, 13

V06.2 Diphtheria-tetanus-pertussis with typhoid-paratyphoid [DTP+TAB]

V06.3 Diphtheria-tetanus-pertussis with poliomyelitis [DTP+polio]

V06.4 Measles-mumps-rubella [MMR]

V06.5 Tetanus-diphtheria [Td] [DT]
> AHA: 4Q, '03, 83

V06.6 Streptococcus pneumoniae [pneumococcus] and influenza

V06.8 Other combinations
> EXCLUDES   *multiple single vaccination codes (V03.0-V05.9)*
> AHA: 1Q, '94, 19

V06.9 Unspecified combined vaccine

PERSONS WITH NEED FOR ISOLATION, OTHER POTENTIAL HEALTH HAZARDS AND PROPHYLACTIC MEASURES (V07-V09)

☑4th **V07 Need for isolation and other prophylactic measures**

> EXCLUDES   *prophylactic organ removal (V50.41-V50.49)*

3 **V07.0 Isolation**
> Admission to protect the individual from his surroundings or for isolation of individual after contact with infectious diseases

V07.1 Desensitization to allergens

V07.2 Prophylactic immunotherapy
> Administration of:
> antivenin
> immune sera [gamma globulin]
> RhoGAM
> tetanus antitoxin

☑5th **V07.3 Other prophylactic chemotherapy**

V07.31 Prophylactic fluoride administration

3 **V07.39 Other prophylactic chemotherapy**
> EXCLUDES   *maintenance chemotherapy following disease ▶(V58.11)◀*

V07.4 Hormone replacement therapy (postmenopausal) ♀

3 **V07.8 Other specified prophylactic measure**
> AHA: 1Q, '92, 11

V07.9 Unspecified prophylactic measure

V08 Asymptomatic human immunodeficiency virus [HIV] infection status

> HIV positive NOS

> Note: This code is *only* to be used when no HIV infection symptoms or conditions are present. If any HIV infection symptoms or conditions are present, see code 042.

> EXCLUDES   *AIDS (042)*
> *human immunodeficiency virus [HIV] disease (042)*
> *exposure to HIV (V01.79)*
> *nonspecific serologic evidence of HIV (795.71)*
> *symptomatic human immunodeficiency virus [HIV] infection (042)*

> AHA: 2Q, '04, 11; 2Q, '99, 8; 3Q, '95, 18

☑4th **V09 Infection with drug-resistant microorganisms**

> Note: This category is intended for use as an additional code for infectious conditions classified elsewhere to indicate the presence of drug-resistance of the infectious organism.

> AHA: 3Q, '94, 4; 4Q, '93, 22

V09.0 Infection with microorganisms resistant to penicillins
> Methicillin-resistant staphylococcus aureus (MRSA)
> AHA: 4Q, '03, 104, 106

V09.1 Infection with microorganisms resistant to cephalosporins and other B-lactam antibiotics

V09.2 Infection with microorganisms resistant to macrolides

V09.3 Infection with microorganisms resistant to tetracyclines

V09.4 Infection with microorganisms resistant to aminoglycosides

☑5th **V09.5 Infection with microorganisms resistant to quinolones and fluoroquinolones**

V09.50 Without mention of resistance to multiple quinolones and fluoroquinoles

V09.51 With resistance to multiple quinolones and fluoroquinoles

V09.6 Infection with microorganisms resistant to sulfonamides

☑5th **V09.7 Infection with microorganisms resistant to other specified antimycobacterial agents**
> EXCLUDES   *Amikacin (V09.4)*
> *Kanamycin (V09.4)*
> *Streptomycin [SM] (V09.4)*

V09.70 Without mention of resistance to multiple antimycobacterial agents

V09.71 With resistance to multiple antimycobacterial agents

☑5th **V09.8 Infection with microorganisms resistant to other specified drugs**
> Vancomycin (glycopeptide) intermediate staphylococcus aureus (VISA/GISA)
> Vancomycin (glycopeptide) resistant enterococcus (VRE)
> Vancomycin (glycopeptide) resistant staphylococcus aureus (VRSA/GRSA)

V09.80 Without mention of resistance to multiple drugs

V09.81 With resistance to multiple drugs

☑5th **V09.9 Infection with drug-resistant microorganisms, unspecified**
> Drug resistance, NOS

V09.90 Without mention of multiple drug resistance

V09.91 With multiple drug resistance
> Multiple drug resistance NOS

---

3 These V codes may be used as principal diagnosis on Medicare patients.

N Newborn Age: 0   P Pediatric Age: 0-17   M Maternity Age: 12-55   A Adult Age: 15-124   CC CC Condition   MC Major Complication   CD Complex Dx   HIV HIV Related Dx

PERSONS WITH POTENTIAL HEALTH HAZARDS RELATED TO PERSONAL AND FAMILY HISTORY (V10-V19)

> **EXCLUDES**   *obstetric patients where the possibility that the fetus might be affected is the reason for observation or management during pregnancy (655.0-655.9)*

AHA: J-F, '87, 1

✓4th V10 Personal history of malignant neoplasm
AHA: 4Q, '02, 80; 4Q, '98, 69; 1Q, '95, 4; 3Q, '92, 5; M-J, '85, 10; 2Q, '90, 9

  ✓5th V10.0 Gastrointestinal tract
History of conditions classifiable to 140-159

- **V10.00 Gastrointestinal tract, unspecified**
- **V10.01 Tongue**
- **V10.02 Other and unspecified oral cavity and pharynx**
- **V10.03 Esophagus**
- **V10.04 Stomach**
- **V10.05 Large intestine**
  AHA: 3Q, '99, 7; 1Q, '95, 4
- **V10.06 Rectum, rectosigmoid junction, and anus**
- **V10.07 Liver**
- **V10.09 Other**
  AHA: 4Q, '03, 111

  ✓5th V10.1 Trachea, bronchus, and lung
History of conditions classifiable to 162

- **V10.11 Bronchus and lung**
- **V10.12 Trachea**

  ✓5th V10.2 Other respiratory and intrathoracic organs
History of conditions classifiable to 160, 161, 163-165

- **V10.20 Respiratory organ, unspecified**
- **V10.21 Larynx**
  AHA: 4Q, '03, 108, 110
- **V10.22 Nasal cavities, middle ear, and accessory sinuses**
- **V10.29 Other**

  V10.3 Breast
History of conditions classifiable to 174 and 175
AHA: 2Q, '03, 5; 4Q, '01, 66; 4Q, '98, 65; 4Q, '97, 50; 1Q, '91, 16; 1Q, '90, 21

  ✓5th V10.4 Genital organs
History of conditions classifiable to 179-187

- **V10.40 Female genital organ, unspecified** ♀
- **V10.41 Cervix uteri** ♀
- **V10.42 Other parts of uterus** ♀
- **V10.43 Ovary** ♀
- **V10.44 Other female genital organs** ♀
- **V10.45 Male genital organ, unspecified** ♂
- **V10.46 Prostate** ♂
- **V10.47 Testis** ♂
- **V10.48 Epididymis** ♂
- **V10.49 Other male genital organs** ♂

  ✓5th V10.5 Urinary organs
History of conditions classifiable to 188 and 189

- **V10.50 Urinary organ, unspecified**
- **V10.51 Bladder**
- **V10.52 Kidney**
  AHA: 2Q, '04, 4
  > **EXCLUDES**   *renal pelvis (V10.53)*
- **V10.53 Renal pelvis**
  AHA: 4Q, '01, 55
- **V10.59 Other**

  ✓5th V10.6 Leukemia
Conditions classifiable to 204-208
> **EXCLUDES**   *leukemia in remission (204-208)*
AHA: 2Q, '92, 13; 4Q, '91, 26; 4Q, '90, 3

- **V10.60 Leukemia, unspecified**
- **V10.61 Lymphoid leukemia**
- **V10.62 Myeloid leukemia**
- **V10.63 Monocytic leukemia**
- **V10.69 Other**

  ✓5th V10.7 Other lymphatic and hematopoietic neoplasms
Conditions classifiable to 200-203
> **EXCLUDES**   *listed conditions in 200-203 in remission*
AHA: M-J, '85, 18

- **V10.71 Lymphosarcoma and reticulosarcoma**
- **V10.72 Hodgkin's disease**
- **V10.79 Other**

  ✓5th V10.8 Personal history of malignant neoplasm of other sites
History of conditions classifiable to 170-173, 190-195

- **V10.81 Bone**
  AHA: 2Q, '03, 13
- **V10.82 Malignant melanoma of skin**
- **V10.83 Other malignant neoplasm of skin**
- **V10.84 Eye**
- **V10.85 Brain**
  AHA: 1Q, '01, 6
- **V10.86 Other parts of nervous system**
  > **EXCLUDES**   *peripheral sympathetic, and parasympathetic nerves (V10.89)*
- **V10.87 Thyroid**
- **V10.88 Other endocrine glands and related structures**
- **V10.89 Other**

  V10.9 Unspecified personal history of malignant neoplasm

✓4th V11 Personal history of mental disorder

  V11.0 Schizophrenia
> **EXCLUDES**   *that in remission (295.0-295.9 with fifth-digit 5)*

  V11.1 Affective disorders
Personal history of manic-depressive psychosis
> **EXCLUDES**   *that in remission (296.0-296.6 with fifth-digit 5, 6)*

  V11.2 Neurosis

  V11.3 Alcoholism

  V11.8 Other mental disorders

  V11.9 Unspecified mental disorder

✓4th V12 Personal history of certain other diseases
AHA: 3Q, '92, 11

  ✓5th V12.0 Infectious and parasitic diseases
> **EXCLUDES**   *personal history of infectious diseases specific to a body system*

- **V12.00 Unspecified infectious and parasitic disease**
- **V12.01 Tuberculosis**
- **V12.02 Poliomyelitis**
- **V12.03 Malaria**
- **V12.09 Other**

  V12.1 Nutritional deficiency

  V12.2 Endocrine, metabolic, and immunity disorders
> **EXCLUDES**   *history of allergy (V14.0-V14.9, V15.01-V15.09)*

  V12.3 Diseases of blood and blood-forming organs

  ✓5th V12.4 Disorders of nervous system and sense organs

- **V12.40 Unspecified disorder of nervous system and sense organs**
- **V12.41 Benign neoplasm of the brain**
  AHA: 4Q, '97, 48
- **V12.42 Infections of the central nervous system**
  Encephalitis   Meningitis
  AHA: ►4Q, '05, 95◄
- **V12.49 Other disorders of nervous system and sense organs**
  AHA: 4Q, '98, 59

  ✓5th V12.5 Diseases of circulatory system
AHA: 4Q, '95, 61
> **EXCLUDES**   *old myocardial infarction (412) postmyocardial infarction syndrome (411.0)*

- **V12.50 Unspecified circulatory disease**

✓4th ✓5th Additional Digit Required   Nonspecific PDx   Unacceptable PDx   Manifestation Code   **MCV** Major Cardiovascular Condition   ►◄ Revised Text   ● New Code   ▲ Revised Code Title

2007 ICD•9•CM   **February 2006 • Volume 1 — 319**

V Codes

V12.51–V15.9

V12.51 Venous thrombosis and embolism
Pulmonary embolism
AHA: 4Q, '03, 108; 1Q, '02, 15

V12.52 Thrombophlebitis

V12.59 Other
AHA: 4Q, '99, 4; 4Q, '98, 88; 4Q, '97, 37

✓5th **V12.6 Diseases of respiratory system**
EXCLUDES   tuberculosis (V12.01)

V12.60 Unspecified disease of respiratory system

V12.61 Pneumonia (recurrent)
AHA: ▶4Q, '05, 95◄

V12.69 Other diseases of respiratory system

✓5th **V12.7 Diseases of digestive system**
AHA: 1Q, '95, 3; 2Q, '89, 16

V12.70 Unspecified digestive disease

V12.71 Peptic ulcer disease

V12.72 Colonic polyps
AHA: 3Q, '02, 15

V12.79 Other

✓4th **V13 Personal history of other diseases**

✓5th **V13.0 Disorders of urinary system**

V13.00 Unspecified urinary disorder

V13.01 Urinary calculi

V13.02 Urinary (tract) infection
AHA: ▶4Q, '05, 95◄

V13.03 Nephrotic syndrome
AHA: ▶4Q, '05, 95◄

V13.09 Other

V13.1 Trophoblastic disease   ♀
EXCLUDES   supervision during a current pregnancy (V23.1)

✓5th **V13.2 Other genital system and obstetric disorders**
EXCLUDES   supervision during a current pregnancy of a woman with poor obstetric history (V23.0-V23.9)
habitual aborter (646.3)
without current pregnancy (629.9)

V13.21 Personal history of pre-term labor   ♀
EXCLUDES   current pregnancy with history of pre-term labor (V23.41)
AHA: 4Q, '02, 78

V13.29 Other genital system and obstetric disorders   ♀

V13.3 Diseases of skin and subcutaneous tissue

V13.4 Arthritis

V13.5 Other musculoskeletal disorders

✓5th **V13.6 Congenital malformations**
AHA: 4Q, '98, 63

V13.61 Hypospadias   ♂

V13.69 Other congenital malformations
AHA: 1Q, '04, 16

V13.7 Perinatal problems
EXCLUDES   low birth weight status (V21.30-V21.35)

V13.8 Other specified diseases

V13.9 Unspecified disease

✓4th **V14 Personal history of allergy to medicinal agents**

V14.0 Penicillin

V14.1 Other antibiotic agent

V14.2 Sulfonamides

V14.3 Other anti-infective agent

V14.4 Anesthetic agent

V14.5 Narcotic agent

V14.6 Analgesic agent

V14.7 Serum or vaccine

V14.8 Other specified medicinal agents

V14.9 Unspecified medicinal agent

✓4th **V15 Other personal history presenting hazards to health**

✓5th **V15.0 Allergy, other than to medicinal agents**
EXCLUDES   allergy to food substance used as base for medicinal agent (V14.0-V14.9)
AHA: 4Q, '00, 42, 49

V15.01 Allergy to peanuts

V15.02 Allergy to milk products
EXCLUDES   lactose intolerance (271.3)
AHA: 1Q, '03, 12

V15.03 Allergy to eggs

V15.04 Allergy to seafood
Seafood (octopus) (squid) ink
Shellfish

V15.05 Allergy to other foods
Food additives   Nuts other than peanuts

V15.06 Allergy to insects
Bugs
Insect bites and stings
Spiders

V15.07 Allergy to latex
Latex sensitivity

V15.08 Allergy to radiographic dye
Contrast media used for diagnostic x-ray procedures

V15.09 Other allergy, other than to medicinal agents

V15.1 Surgery to heart and great vessels
EXCLUDES   replacement by transplant or other means (V42.1-V42.2, V43.2-V43.4)
AHA: 1Q, '04, 16

V15.2 Surgery to other major organs
EXCLUDES   replacement by transplant or other means (V42.0-V43.8)

V15.3 Irradiation
Previous exposure to therapeutic or other ionizing radiation

✓5th **V15.4 Psychological trauma**
EXCLUDES   history of condition classifiable to 290-316 (V11.0-V11.9)

V15.41 History of physical abuse
Rape
AHA: 3Q, '99, 15

V15.42 History of emotional abuse
Neglect
AHA: 3Q, '99, 15

V15.49 Other
AHA: 3Q, '99, 15

V15.5 Injury

V15.6 Poisoning

V15.7 Contraception
EXCLUDES   current contraceptive management (V25.0-V25.4)
presence of intrauterine contraceptive device as incidental finding (V45.5)

✓5th **V15.8 Other specified personal history presenting hazards to health**
AHA: 4Q, '95, 62

V15.81 Noncompliance with medical treatment
AHA: 2Q, '03, 7; 2Q, '01, 11, 12, 13; 2Q, '99, 17; 2Q, '97, 11; 1Q, '97, 12; 3Q, '96, 9

V15.82 History of tobacco use
EXCLUDES   tobacco dependence (305.1)

V15.84 Exposure to asbestos

V15.85 Exposure to potentially hazardous body fluids

V15.86 Exposure to lead

V15.87 History of extracorporeal membrane oxygenation [ECMO]
AHA: 4Q, '03, 84

V15.88 History of fall
At risk for falling
AHA: ▶4Q, '05, 95◄

V15.89 Other
AHA: 1Q, '90, 21; N-D, '84, 12

V15.9 Unspecified personal history presenting hazards to health

---

N Newborn Age: 0   P Pediatric Age: 0-17   M Maternity Age: 12-55   A Adult Age: 15-124   CC CC Condition   MC Major Complication   CD Complex Dx   HIV HIV Related Dx

✓4th **V16 Family history of malignant neoplasm**
　　V16.0　**Gastrointestinal tract**
　　　　　Family history of condition classifiable to 140-159
　　　　　AHA: 1Q, '99, 4

　　V16.1　**Trachea, bronchus, and lung**
　　　　　Family history of condition classifiable to 162

　　V16.2　**Other respiratory and intrathoracic organs**
　　　　　Family history of condition classifiable to 160-161,
　　　　　　　163-165

　　V16.3　**Breast**
　　　　　Family history of condition classifiable to 174
　　　　　AHA: 4Q, '04, 107; 2Q, '03, 4; 2Q, '00, 8; 1Q, '92, 11

✓5th **V16.4**　**Genital organs**
　　　　　Family history of condition classifiable to 179-187
　　　　　AHA: 4Q, '97, 48

　　　　　V16.40 Genital organ, unspecified
　　　　　V16.41 Ovary
　　　　　V16.42 Prostate
　　　　　V16.43 Testis
　　　　　V16.49 Other

✓5th **V16.5**　**Urinary organs**
　　　　　Family history of condition classifiable to 189
　　　　　V16.51 Kidney
　　　　　V16.59 Other

　　V16.6　**Leukemia**
　　　　　Family history of condition classifiable to 204-208

　　V16.7　**Other lymphatic and hematopoietic neoplasms**
　　　　　Family history of condition classifiable to 200-203

　　V16.8　**Other specified malignant neoplasm**
　　　　　Family history of other condition classifiable to 140-
　　　　　　199

　　V16.9　**Unspecified malignant neoplasm**

✓4th **V17 Family history of certain chronic disabling diseases**
　　V17.0　**Psychiatric condition**
　　　　　EXCLUDES　family history of mental retardation
　　　　　　　　　　　(V18.4)

　　V17.1　**Stroke (cerebrovascular)**
　　V17.2　**Other neurological diseases**
　　　　　Epilepsy　　　　　　Huntington's chorea
　　V17.3　**Ischemic heart disease**
　　V17.4　**Other cardiovascular diseases**
　　　　　AHA: 1Q, '04, 6
　　V17.5　**Asthma**
　　V17.6　**Other chronic respiratory conditions**
　　V17.7　**Arthritis**
✓5th **V17.8**　**Other musculoskeletal diseases**
　　　　　V17.81 Osteoporosis
　　　　　　AHA: 4Q, '05, 95

　　　　　V17.89 Other musculoskeletal diseases
✓4th **V18 Family history of certain other specific conditions**
　　V18.0　**Diabetes mellitus**
　　　　　AHA: 1Q, '04, 8
　　V18.1　**Other endocrine and metabolic diseases**
　　V18.2　**Anemia**
　　V18.3　**Other blood disorders**
　　V18.4　**Mental retardation**
✓5th **V18.5**　**Digestive disorders**
　　　　　V18.51 Colonic polyps
　　　　　　EXCLUDES　family history of malignant
　　　　　　　　　　　neoplasm of
　　　　　　　　　　　gastrointestinal tract
　　　　　　　　　　　(V16.0)

●　　　　　**V18.59 Other digestive disorders**
✓5th **V18.6**　**Kidney diseases**
　　　　　V18.61 Polycystic kidney
　　　　　V18.69 Other kidney diseases
　　V18.7　**Other genitourinary diseases**
　　V18.8　**Infectious and parasitic diseases**
　　V18.9　**Genetic disease carrier**
　　　　　AHA: 4Q, '05, 95

[3] These V codes may be used as principal diagnosis on Medicare patients.

✓4th **V19 Family history of other conditions**
　　V19.0　**Blindness or visual loss**
　　V19.1　**Other eye disorders**
　　V19.2　**Deafness or hearing loss**
　　V19.3　**Other ear disorders**
　　V19.4　**Skin conditions**
　　V19.5　**Congenital anomalies**
　　V19.6　**Allergic disorders**
　　V19.7　**Consanguinity**
　　V19.8　**Other condition**

PERSONS ENCOUNTERING HEALTH SERVICES IN CIRCUMSTANCES RELATED TO REPRODUCTION AND DEVELOPMENT (V20-V29)

✓4th **V20 Health supervision of infant or child**
　[3]　**V20.0**　**Foundling**　　　　　　　　　P
　　V20.1　**Other healthy infant or child receiving care**　P
　　　　　Medical or nursing care supervision of healthy infant
　　　　　　in cases of:
　　　　　　maternal illness, physical or psychiatric
　　　　　　socioeconomic adverse condition at home
　　　　　　too many children at home preventing or
　　　　　　　interfering with normal care
　　　　　AHA: 1Q, '00, 25; 3Q, '89, 14

　　V20.2　**Routine infant or child health check**　　P
　　　　　Developmental testing of infant or child
　　　　　Immunizations appropriate for age
　　　　　▶Initial and subsequent routine newborn check◀
　　　　　Routine vision and hearing testing
　　　　　Use additional code(s) to identify:
　　　　　　special screening examination(s) performed
　　　　　　　(V73.0-V82.9)
　　　　　　EXCLUDES　special screening for developmental
　　　　　　　　　　　handicaps (V79.3)
　　　　　AHA: 1Q, '04, 15

✓4th **V21 Constitutional states in development**
　　V21.0　**Period of rapid growth in childhood**
　　V21.1　**Puberty**
　　V21.2　**Other adolescence**
✓5th **V21.3**　**Low birth weight status**
　　　　　EXCLUDES　history of perinatal problems
　　　　　AHA: 4Q, '00, 51

　　　　　V21.30 Low birth weight status, unspecified
　　　　　**V21.31 Low birth weight status, less than 500
　　　　　　grams**
　　　　　V21.32 Low birth weight status, 500-999 grams
　　　　　V21.33 Low birth weight status, 1000-1499 grams
　　　　　V21.34 Low birth weight status, 1500-1999 grams
　　　　　V21.35 Low birth weight status, 2000-2500 grams
　　V21.8　**Other specified constitutional states in
　　　　　development**
　　V21.9　**Unspecified constitutional state in development**
✓4th **V22 Normal pregnancy**
　　　　　EXCLUDES　pregnancy examination or test, pregnancy
　　　　　　　　　　　unconfirmed (V72.40)

　　V22.0　**Supervision of normal first pregnancy**　　♀
　　　　　AHA: 3Q, '99, 16

　　V22.1　**Supervision of other normal pregnancy**　　♀
　　　　　AHA: 3Q, '99, 16

　　V22.2　**Pregnant state, incidental**　　　　　♀
　　　　　Pregnant state NOS
✓4th **V23 Supervision of high-risk pregnancy**
　　　　　AHA: 1Q, '90, 10
　　V23.0　**Pregnancy with history of infertility**　　M♀
　　V23.1　**Pregnancy with history of trophoblastic
　　　　　disease**　　　　　　　　　　　　M♀
　　　　　Pregnancy with history of:
　　　　　　hydatidiform mole　　　　vesicular mole
　　　　　　EXCLUDES　that without current pregnancy (V13.1)

✓4th
✓5th　Additional Digit Required　　Nonspecific PDx　　Unacceptable PDx　　Manifestation Code　　MCV Major Cardiovascular Condition　▶◀ Revised Text　● New Code　▲ Revised Code Title

2007 ICD•9•CM　　　　　　　　　　　　　　　　　　　　　**October 2006 • Volume 1 — 321**

V23.2 Pregnancy with history of abortion M ♀
Pregnancy with history of conditions classifiable to 634-638
EXCLUDES habitual aborter:
care during pregnancy (646.3)
that without current pregnancy (629.9)

V23.3 Grand multiparity M ♀
EXCLUDES care in relation to labor and delivery (659.4)
that without current pregnancy (V61.5)

√5ᵗʰ **V23.4 Pregnancy with other poor obstetric history**
Pregnancy with history of other conditions classifiable to 630-676

V23.41 Pregnancy with history of pre-term labor M ♀
AHA: 4Q, '02, 79

V23.49 Pregnancy with other poor obstetric history M ♀

V23.5 Pregnancy with other poor reproductive history M ♀
Pregnancy with history of stillbirth or neonatal death

V23.7 Insufficient prenatal care CC M ♀
History of little or no prenatal care
CC Excl: V22.0-V23.9

√5ᵗʰ **V23.8 Other high-risk pregnancy**
AHA: 4Q, '98, 56, 63

V23.81 Elderly primigravida CC M ♀
First pregnancy in a woman who will be 35 years of age or older at expected date of delivery
EXCLUDES elderly primigravida complicating pregnancy (659.5)
CC Excl: See code V23.7

V23.82 Elderly multigravida CC M ♀
Second or more pregnancy in a woman who will be 35 years of age or older at expected date of delivery
EXCLUDES elderly multigravida complicating pregnancy (659.6)
CC Excl: See code V23.7

V23.83 Young primigravida CC M ♀
First pregnancy in a female less than 16 years old at expected date of delivery
EXCLUDES young primigravida complicating pregnancy (659.8)
CC Excl: See code V23.7

V23.84 Young multigravida CC M ♀
Second or more pregnancy in a female less than 16 years old at expected date of delivery
EXCLUDES young multigravida complicating pregnancy (659.8)

V23.89 Other high-risk pregnancy CC M ♀
CC Excl: See code V23.7

V23.9 Unspecified high-risk pregnancy CC M ♀
CC Excl: See code V23.7

√4ᵗʰ **V24 Postpartum care and examination**

³ **V24.0 Immediately after delivery** M ♀
Care and observation in uncomplicated cases

V24.1 Lactating mother ♀
Supervision of lactation

V24.2 Routine postpartum follow-up ♀

√4ᵗʰ **V25 Encounter for contraceptive management**
AHA: 4Q, '92, 24

√5ᵗʰ **V25.0 General counseling and advice**

V25.01 Prescription of oral contraceptives ♀

V25.02 Initiation of other contraceptive measures
Fitting of diaphragm
Prescription of foams, creams, or other agents
AHA: 3Q, '97, 7

V25.03 Encounter for emergency contraceptive counseling and prescription
Encounter for postcoital contraceptive counseling and prescription
AHA: 4Q, '03, 84

V25.09 Other
Family planning advice

V25.1 Insertion of intrauterine contraceptive device ♀

³ **V25.2 Sterilization**
Admission for interruption of fallopian tubes or vas deferens

³ **V25.3 Menstrual extraction** ♀
Menstrual regulation

√5ᵗʰ **V25.4 Surveillance of previously prescribed contraceptive methods**
Checking, reinsertion, or removal of contraceptive device
Repeat prescription for contraceptive method
Routine examination in connection with contraceptive maintenance
EXCLUDES presence of intrauterine contraceptive device as incidental finding (V45.5)

V25.40 Contraceptive surveillance, unspecified

V25.41 Contraceptive pill ♀

V25.42 Intrauterine contraceptive device ♀
Checking, reinsertion, or removal of intrauterine device

V25.43 Implantable subdermal contraceptive ♀

V25.49 Other contraceptive method
AHA: 3Q, '97, 7

V25.5 Insertion of implantable subdermal contraceptive ♀
AHA: 3Q, '92, 9

V25.8 Other specified contraceptive management
Postvasectomy sperm count
EXCLUDES sperm count following sterilization reversal (V26.22)
sperm count for fertility testing (V26.21)
AHA: 3Q, '96, 9

V25.9 Unspecified contraceptive management

√4ᵗʰ **V26 Procreative management**

³ **V26.0 Tuboplasty or vasoplasty after previous sterilization**
AHA: 2Q, '95, 10

V26.1 Artificial insemination ♀

√5ᵗʰ **V26.2 Investigation and testing**
EXCLUDES postvasectomy sperm count (V25.8)
AHA: 4Q, '00, 56

V26.21 Fertility testing
Fallopian insufflation
Sperm count for fertility testing
EXCLUDES genetic counseling and testing ▶(V26.31-V26.39)◀

V26.22 Aftercare following sterilization reversal
Fallopian insufflation following sterilization reversal
Sperm count following sterilization reversal

V26.29 Other investigation and testing
AHA: 2Q, '96, 9; N-D, '85, 15

√5ᵗʰ **V26.3 Genetic counseling and testing**
EXCLUDES fertility testing (V26.21)
▶nonprocreative genetic screening (V82.71, V82.79)◀
AHA: 4Q, '05, 96

---

³ These V codes may be used as principal diagnosis on Medicare patients.

N Newborn Age: 0   P Pediatric Age: 0-17   M Maternity Age: 12-55   A Adult Age: 15-124   CC CC Condition   MC Major Complication   CD Complex Dx   HIV HIV Related Dx

▲   **V26.31 Testing of female for genetic disease carrier status** ♀

▲   **V26.32 Other genetic testing of female** ♀
> ▶Use additional code to identify habitual aborter (629.81, 646.3)◀

V26.33 Genetic counseling

●   **V26.34 Testing of male for genetic disease carrier status** ♂

●   **V26.35 Encounter for testing of male partner of habitual aborter** ♂

●   **V26.39 Other genetic testing of male** ♂

V26.4 General counseling and advice

✓5ᵗʰ **V26.5 Sterilization status**

V26.51 Tubal ligation status ♀
> **EXCLUDES**   *infertility not due to previous tubal ligation (628.0-628.9)*

V26.52 Vasectomy status ♂

V26.8 Other specified procreative management

V26.9 Unspecified procreative management

✓4ᵗʰ **V27 Outcome of delivery**
> Note: This category is intended for the coding of the outcome of delivery on the mother's record.

AHA: 2Q, '91, 16

V27.0 Single liveborn M♀
> **AHA:** 4Q, '05, 81; 2Q, '03, 9; 2Q, '02, 10; 1Q, '01, 10; 3Q, '00, 5; 4Q, '98, 77; 4Q, '95, 59; 1Q, '92, 9

V27.1 Single stillborn M♀

V27.2 Twins, both liveborn M♀

V27.3 Twins, one liveborn and one stillborn M♀

V27.4 Twins, both stillborn M♀

V27.5 Other multiple birth, all liveborn M♀

V27.6 Other multiple birth, some liveborn M♀

V27.7 Other multiple birth, all stillborn M♀

V27.9 Unspecified outcome of delivery M♀

> Single birth
> Multiple birth } outcome to infant unspecified

▲ ✓4ᵗʰ **V28 Encounter for antenatal screening of mother**
> **EXCLUDES**   *abnormal findings on screening — code to findings*
> *routine prenatal care (V22.0-V23.9)*

AHA: 1Q, '04, 11

V28.0 Screening for chromosomal anomalies by amniocentesis M♀

V28.1 Screening for raised alpha-fetoprotein levels in amniotic fluid M♀

V28.2 Other screening based on amniocentesis M♀

V28.3 Screening for malformation using ultrasonics ♀

V28.4 Screening for fetal growth retardation using ultrasonics ♀

V28.5 Screening for isoimmunization ♀

V28.6 Screening for Streptococcus B M♀
> **AHA:** 4Q, '97, 46

V28.8 Other specified antenatal screening ♀
> **AHA:** 3Q, '99, 16

V28.9 Unspecified antenatal screening ♀

✓4ᵗʰ **V29 Observation and evaluation of newborns and infants for suspected condition not found**
> Note: This category is to be used for newborns, within the neonatal period, (the first 28 days of life) who are suspected of having an abnormal condition resulting from exposure from the mother or the birth process, but without signs or symptoms, and, which after examination and observation, is found not to exist.

AHA: 1Q, '00, 25; 4Q, '94, 47; 1Q, '94, 9; 4Q, '92, 21

³ **V29.0 Observation for suspected infectious condition** N
> **AHA:** 1Q, '01, 10

³ **V29.1 Observation for suspected neurological condition** N

³ **V29.2 Observation for suspected respiratory condition** N

V29.3 Observation for suspected genetic or metabolic condition N
> **AHA:** 2Q, '05, 21; 4Q, '98, 59, 68

³ **V29.8 Observation for other specified suspected condition** N
> **AHA:** 2Q, '03, 15

V29.9 Observation for unspecified suspected condition N
> **AHA:** 1Q, '02, 6

LIVEBORN INFANTS ACCORDING TO TYPE OF BIRTH (V30-V39)

> Note: These categories are intended for the coding of liveborn infants who are consuming health care [e.g., crib or bassinet occupancy].

The following fourth-digit subdivisions are for use with categories V30-V39:
> ✓5ᵗʰ **0 Born in hospital** N
> **1 Born before admission to hospital** N
> **2 Born outside hospital and not hospitalized**

The following two fifth-digits are for use with the fourth-digit .0, Born in hospital:
> **0 delivered without mention of cesarean delivery**
> **1 delivered by cesarean delivery**

AHA: 1Q, '01, 10

4 ✓4ᵗʰ **V30 Single liveborn**
> **AHA:** 2Q, '03, 9; 4Q, '98, 46, 59; 1Q, '94, 9; For code **V30.00**: 1Q, '04, 8, 16; 4Q, '03, 68; For code **V30.01**: 4Q, '05, 88

4 ✓4ᵗʰ **V31 Twin, mate liveborn**
> **AHA:** 3Q, '92, 10

4 ✓4ᵗʰ **V32 Twin, mate stillborn**

4 ✓4ᵗʰ **V33 Twin, unspecified**

4 ✓4ᵗʰ **V34 Other multiple, mates all liveborn**

4 ✓4ᵗʰ **V35 Other multiple, mates all stillborn**

4 ✓4ᵗʰ **V36 Other multiple, mates live and stillborn**

4 ✓4ᵗʰ **V37 Other multiple, unspecified**

5 ✓4ᵗʰ **V39 Unspecified**

PERSONS WITH A CONDITION INFLUENCING THEIR HEALTH STATUS (V40-V49)

> Note: These categories are intended for use when these conditions are recorded as "diagnoses" or "problems."

✓4ᵗʰ **V40 Mental and behavioral problems**

V40.0 Problems with learning

V40.1 Problems with communication [including speech]

V40.2 Other mental problems

V40.3 Other behavioral problems

V40.9 Unspecified mental or behavioral problem

✓4ᵗʰ **V41 Problems with special senses and other special functions**

V41.0 Problems with sight

V41.1 Other eye problems

V41.2 Problems with hearing

V41.3 Other ear problems

V41.4 Problems with voice production

V41.5 Problems with smell and taste

V41.6 Problems with swallowing and mastication

V41.7 Problems with sexual function
> **EXCLUDES**   *marital problems (V61.10)*
> *psychosexual disorders (302.0-302.9)*

---

³ These V codes may be used as principal diagnosis on Medicare patients.
⁴ These codes with the fourth digit of 0 or 1, may be used as a principal diagnosis for Medicare patients.
⁵ These V codes are acceptable as principal diagnosis with the fourth digit of 0.

✓4ᵗʰ
✓5ᵗʰ
Additional Digit Required   Nonspecific PDx   Unacceptable PDx   Manifestation Code   **MCV** Major Cardiovascular Condition   ▶◀ Revised Text   ● New Code   ▲ Revised Code Title

2007 ICD•9•CM   **October 2006 • Volume 1 — 323**

V26.31–V41.7

V41.8 Other problems with special functions

V41.9 Unspecified problem with special functions

√4th **V42 Organ or tissue replaced by transplant**

> INCLUDES   homologous or heterologous (animal) (human) transplant organ status

AHA: 3Q, '98, 3, 4

V42.0 Kidney   `CC`
CC Excl: 996.80-996.81, 996.87, V42.0, V42.89-V42.9
AHA: 1Q, '03, 10; 3Q, '01, 12

V42.1 Heart   `CC`
CC Excl: 996.80, 996.83, 996.87, V42.1, V42.89-V42.9
AHA: 3Q, '03, 16; 3Q, '01, 13

V42.2 Heart valve   `CC`
CC Excl: 996.71, V42.2, V42.89-V42.9

V42.3 Skin

V42.4 Bone

V42.5 Cornea

V42.6 Lung   `CC`
CC Excl: 996.80, 996.84, 996.87, V42.6, V42.89-V42.9

V42.7 Liver   `CC`
CC Excl: 996.80, 996.82, 996.87, 996.87, V42.7, V42.89-V42.9

√5th **V42.8 Other specified organ or tissue**
AHA: 4Q, '98, 64; 4Q, '97, 49

   V42.81 Bone marrow   `CC`
CC Excl: 996.80, 996.85, 996.87, V42.9

   V42.82 Peripheral stem cells   `CC`
CC Excl: 996.80, 996.87, V42.9

   V42.83 Pancreas   `CC`
CC Excl: 996.80, 996.86-996.87, V42.83, V42.9
AHA: 1Q, '03, 10; 2Q, '01, 16

   V42.84 Intestines   `CC`
CC Excl: 996.80, 996.89, V42.84-V42.9
AHA: 4Q, '00, 48, 50

   V42.89 Other   `CC`
CC Excl: 996.80, 996.87-996.89, V42.89-V42.9

V42.9 Unspecified organ or tissue

√4th **V43 Organ or tissue replaced by other means**

> INCLUDES   organ or tissue assisted by other means
> replacement of organ by:
>   artificial device
>   mechanical device
>   prosthesis

> EXCLUDES   cardiac pacemaker in situ (V45.01)
>   fitting and adjustment of prosthetic device
>   (V52.0-V52.9)
>   renal dialysis status (V45.1)

V43.0 Eye globe

V43.1 Lens
     Pseudophakos
AHA: 4Q, '98, 65

√5th **V43.2 Heart**
AHA: 4Q, '03, 85

   V43.21 Heart assist device   `CC`
CC Excl: 996.80, 996.83, 996.87, V42.1, V43.21-V43.22

   V43.22 Fully implantable artificial heart   `CC`
CC Excl: See code V43.21

V43.3 Heart valve
AHA: 3Q, '02, 13, 14

V43.4 Blood vessel

V43.5 Bladder

√5th **V43.6 Joint**
AHA: 4Q, '05, 91

   V43.60 Unspecified joint
   V43.61 Shoulder
   V43.62 Elbow
   V43.63 Wrist

   V43.64 Hip
AHA: 4Q, '05, 93, 112; 2Q, '04, 15

   V43.65 Knee

   V43.66 Ankle

   V43.69 Other

V43.7 Limb

√5th **V43.8 Other organ or tissue**

   V43.81 Larynx
AHA: 4Q, '95, 55

   V43.82 Breast
AHA: 4Q, '95, 55

   V43.83 Artificial skin

   V43.89 Other

√4th **V44 Artificial opening status**

> EXCLUDES   artificial openings requiring attention or
>   management (V55.0-V55.9)

V44.0 Tracheostomy
AHA: 4Q, '03, 103, 107, 111; 1Q, '01, 6

V44.1 Gastrostomy
AHA: 4Q, '03, 103, 107-108, 110; 1Q, '01, 12; 3Q, '97, 12; 1Q, '93, 26

V44.2 Ileostomy

V44.3 Colostomy
AHA: 4Q, '03, 110

V44.4 Other artificial opening of gastrointestinal tract

√5th **V44.5 Cystostomy**

   V44.50 Cystostomy, unspecified
   V44.51 Cutaneous-vesicostomy
   V44.52 Appendico-vesicostomy
   V44.59 Other cystostomy

V44.6 Other artificial opening of urinary tract
     Nephrostomy   Urethrostomy
     Ureterostomy

V44.7 Artificial vagina

V44.8 Other artificial opening status

V44.9 Unspecified artificial opening status

√4th **V45 Other postprocedural states**

> EXCLUDES   aftercare management (V51-V58.9)
>   malfunction or other complication — code to
>   condition

AHA: 4Q, '03, 85

√5th **V45.0 Cardiac device in situ**

> EXCLUDES   artificial heart (V43.22)
>   heart assist device (V43.21)

   V45.00 Unspecified cardiac device
   V45.01 Cardiac pacemaker
   V45.02 Automatic implantable cardiac defibrillator
   V45.09 Other specified cardiac device
       Carotid sinus pacemaker in situ

V45.1 Renal dialysis status   `CC`
     Hemodialysis status
     Patient requiring intermittent renal dialysis
     Peritoneal dialysis status
     Presence of arterial-venous shunt (for dialysis)

> EXCLUDES   admission for dialysis treatment or
>   session (V56.0)

CC Excl: 996.73, V45.1
AHA: 4Q, '05, 96; 2Q, '03, 7; 2Q, '01, 12, 13

V45.2 Presence of cerebrospinal fluid drainage device
     Cerebral ventricle (communicating) shunt, valve, or
     device in situ

> EXCLUDES   malfunction (996.2)

AHA: 4Q, '03, 106

V45.3 Intestinal bypass or anastomosis status

> EXCLUDES ▶ bariatric surgery status (V45.86)
>   gastric bypass status (V45.86)
>   obesity surgery status (V45.86)◄

V45.4 Arthrodesis status
AHA: N-D, '84, 18

`N` Newborn Age: 0   `P` Pediatric Age: 0-17   `M` Maternity Age: 12-55   `A` Adult Age: 15-124   `CC` CC Condition   `MC` Major Complication   `CD` Complex Dx   `HIV` HIV Related Dx

✓5th **V45.5　Presence of contraceptive device**

> EXCLUDES　*checking, reinsertion, or removal of device (V25.42)*
> *complication from device (996.32)*
> *insertion of device (V25.1)*

V45.51　Intrauterine contraceptive device　　♀

V45.52　Subdermal contraceptive implant

V45.59　Other

✓5th **V45.6　States following surgery of eye and adnexa**

> Cataract extraction
> Filtering bleb   } state following eye surgery
> Surgical eyelid adhesion

> EXCLUDES　*aphakia (379.31)*
> *artificial eye globe (V43.0)*

AHA: 4Q, '98, 65; 4Q, '97, 49

V45.61　Cataract extraction status

> Use additional code for associated artificial lens status (V43.1)

V45.69　Other states following surgery of eye and adnexa

AHA: 2Q, '01, 16; 1Q, '98, 10; 4Q, '97, 19

✓5th **V45.7　Acquired absence of organ**

AHA: 4Q, '98, 65; 4Q, '97, 50

3 **V45.71　Acquired absence of breast**

AHA: 4Q, '01, 66; 4Q, '97, 50

V45.72　Acquired absence of intestine (large) (small)

V45.73　Acquired absence of kidney

V45.74　Other parts of urinary tract

> Bladder
> AHA: 4Q, '00, 51

V45.75　Stomach

AHA: 4Q, '00, 51

V45.76　Lung

AHA: 4Q, '00, 51

V45.77　Genital organs

> EXCLUDES　*female genital mutilation status ▶(629.20-629.29)◀*
> AHA: 1Q, '03, 13, 14; 4Q, '00, 51

V45.78　Eye

AHA: 4Q, '00, 51

V45.79　Other acquired absence of organ

AHA: 4Q, '00, 51

✓5th **V45.8　Other postprocedural status**

V45.81　Aortocoronary bypass status

AHA: 4Q, '03, 105; 3Q, '01, 15; 3Q, '97, 16

V45.82　Percutaneous transluminal coronary angioplasty status

V45.83　Breast implant removal status

AHA: 4Q, '95, 55

V45.84　Dental restoration status

> Dental crowns status
> Dental fillings status
> AHA: 4Q, '01, 54

V45.85　Insulin pump status

V45.86　Bariatric surgery status

> Gastric banding status
> Gastric bypass status for obesity
> Obesity surgery status
> EXCLUDES　*bariatric surgery status complicating pregnancy, childbirth or the puerperium (649.2)*
> *intestinal bypass or anastomosis status (V45.3)*

V45.89　Other

> Presence of neuropacemaker or other electronic device
> EXCLUDES　*artificial heart valve in situ (V43.3)*
> *vascular prosthesis in situ (V43.4)*

AHA: 1Q, '95, 11

✓4th **V46　Other dependence on machines**

V46.0　Aspirator

✓5th **V46.1　Respirator [Ventilator]**

> Iron lung
> AHA: 4Q, '05, 96; 4Q, '03, 103; 1Q, '01, 12; J-F, '87, 7 3

3 **V46.11　Dependence on respirator, status**　　CC

> CC Excl: V46.0-V46.9
> AHA: 4Q, '04, 100

3 **V46.12　Encounter for respirator dependence during power failure**　　CC

> CC Excl: See code V46.11
> AHA: 4Q, '04, 100

3 **V46.13　Encounter for weaning from respirator [ventilator]**　　CC

> CC Excl: See code V46.11

3 **V46.14　Mechanical complication of respirator [ventilator]**　　CC

> Mechanical failure of respirator [ventilator]
> CC Excl: See code V46.11

V46.2　Supplemental oxygen

> Long-term oxygen therapy
> AHA: 4Q, '03, 108; 4Q, '02, 79

V46.8　Other enabling machines

> Hyperbaric chamber
> Possum [Patient-Operated-Selector-Mechanism]
> EXCLUDES　*cardiac pacemaker (V45.0)*
> *kidney dialysis machine (V45.1)*

V46.9　Unspecified machine dependence

✓4th **V47　Other problems with internal organs**

V47.0　Deficiencies of internal organs

V47.1　Mechanical and motor problems with internal organs

V47.2　Other cardiorespiratory problems

> Cardiovascular exercise intolerance with pain (with):
> at rest
> less than ordinary activity
> ordinary activity

V47.3　Other digestive problems

V47.4　Other urinary problems

V47.5　Other genital problems

V47.9　Unspecified

✓4th **V48　Problems with head, neck, and trunk**

V48.0　Deficiencies of head

> EXCLUDES　*deficiencies of ears, eyelids, and nose (V48.8)*

V48.1　Deficiencies of neck and trunk

V48.2　Mechanical and motor problems with head

V48.3　Mechanical and motor problems with neck and trunk

V48.4　Sensory problem with head

V48.5　Sensory problem with neck and trunk

V48.6　Disfigurements of head

V48.7　Disfigurements of neck and trunk

V48.8　Other problems with head, neck, and trunk

V48.9　Unspecified problem with head, neck, or trunk

✓4th **V49　Other conditions influencing health status**

V49.0　Deficiencies of limbs

V49.1　Mechanical problems with limbs

V49.2　Motor problems with limbs

V49.3　Sensory problems with limbs

V49.4　Disfigurements of limbs

V49.5　Other problems of limbs

---

3 These V codes may be used as principal diagnosis on Medicare patients.

✓4th
✓5th　Additional Digit Required　　Nonspecific PDx　　Unacceptable PDx　　Manifestation Code　　MCV Major Cardiovascular Condition　　▶◀ Revised Text　　● New Code　　▲ Revised Code Title

V Codes

V49.6–V53.4

✓5ᵗʰ **V49.6 Upper limb amputation status**
AHA: 4Q, '05, 94; 4Q, '98, 42; 4Q, '94, 39

V49.60 Unspecified level
V49.61 Thumb
V49.62 Other finger(s)
AHA: ▶2Q, '05, 7◀

V49.63 Hand
V49.64 Wrist
Disarticulation of wrist
V49.65 Below elbow
V49.66 Above elbow
Disarticulation of elbow
V49.67 Shoulder
Disarticulation of shoulder

✓5ᵗʰ **V49.7 Lower limb amputation status**
AHA: ▶4Q, '05, 94; ◀ 4Q, '98, 42; 4Q, '94, 39

V49.70 Unspecified level
V49.71 Great toe
V49.72 Other toe(s)
V49.73 Foot
V49.74 Ankle
Disarticulation of ankle
V49.75 Below knee
V49.76 Above knee
Disarticulation of knee
AHA: ▶2Q, '05, 14◀

V49.77 Hip
Disarticulation of hip

✓5ᵗʰ **V49.8 Other specified conditions influencing health status**
AHA: 4Q, '00, 51

V49.81 Asymptomatic postmenopausal status (age-related) (natural) A ♀
EXCLUDES menopausal and premenopausal disorder (627.0-627.9)
postsurgical menopause (256.2)
premature menopause (256.31)
symptomatic menopause (627.0-627.9)
AHA: 4Q, '02, 79; 4Q, '00, 54

V49.82 Dental sealant status
AHA: 4Q, '01, 54

V49.83 Awaiting organ transplant status CC
CC Excl: V49.83

V49.84 Bed confinement status
AHA: ▶ 4Q, '05, 96◀

V49.89 Other specified conditions influencing health status
AHA: ▶ 4Q, '05, 94◀

V49.9 Unspecified

PERSONS ENCOUNTERING HEALTH SERVICES FOR SPECIFIC PROCEDURES AND AFTERCARE (V50-V59)

Note: Categories V51-V58 are intended for use to indicate a reason for care in patients who may have already been treated for some disease or injury not now present, or who are receiving care to consolidate the treatment, to deal with residual states, or to prevent recurrence.
EXCLUDES follow-up examination for medical surveillance following treatment (V67.0-V67.9)

✓4ᵗʰ **V50 Elective surgery for purposes other than remedying health states**
³ **V50.0 Hair transplant**
³ **V50.1 Other plastic surgery for unacceptable cosmetic appearance**
Breast augmentation or reduction
Face-lift
EXCLUDES plastic surgery following healed injury or operation (V51)

³ **V50.2 Routine or ritual circumcision** ♂
Circumcision in the absence of significant medical indication
V50.3 Ear piercing
✓5ᵗʰ **V50.4 Prophylactic organ removal**
EXCLUDES organ donations (V59.0-V59.9)
therapeutic organ removal — code to condition
AHA: 4Q, '94, 44
³ **V50.41 Breast**
AHA: 4Q, '04, 107
³ **V50.42 Ovary** ♀
³ **V50.49 Other**
V50.8 Other
V50.9 Unspecified

³ **V51 Aftercare involving the use of plastic surgery**
Plastic surgery following healed injury or operation
EXCLUDES cosmetic plastic surgery (V50.1)
plastic surgery as treatment for current injury — code to condition
repair of scarred tissue — code to scar

✓4ᵗʰ **V52 Fitting and adjustment of prosthetic device and implant**
INCLUDES removal of device
EXCLUDES malfunction or complication of prosthetic device (996.0-996.7)
status only, without need for care (V43.0-V43.8)
AHA: ▶4Q, '05, 94; ◀ 4Q, '95, 55 ; 1Q, '90, 7
³ **V52.0 Artificial arm (complete) (partial)**
³ **V52.1 Artificial leg (complete) (partial)**
³ **V52.2 Artificial eye**
³ **V52.3 Dental prosthetic device**
³ **V52.4 Breast prosthesis and implant** ♀
EXCLUDES admission for implant insertion (V50.1)
AHA: 4Q, '95, 80, 81
³ **V52.8 Other specified prosthetic device**
AHA: 2Q, '02, 12, 16
V52.9 Unspecified prosthetic device

✓4ᵗʰ **V53 Fitting and adjustment of other device**
INCLUDES removal of device
replacement of device
EXCLUDES status only, without need for care (V45.0-V45.8)
✓5ᵗʰ **V53.0 Devices related to nervous system and special senses**
AHA: 4Q, '98, 66; 4Q, '97, 51
³ **V53.01 Fitting and adjustment of cerebral ventricular (communicating) shunt**
AHA: 4Q, '97, 51
³ **V53.02 Neuropacemaker (brain) (peripheral nerve) (spinal cord)**
³ **V53.09 Fitting and adjustment of other devices related to nervous system and special senses**
Auditory substitution device
Visual substitution device
AHA: 2Q, '99, 4
V53.1 Spectacles and contact lenses
V53.2 Hearing aid
✓5ᵗʰ **V53.3 Cardiac device**
Reprogramming
AHA: 3Q, '92, 3; 1Q, '90, 7; M-J, '87, 8 ; N-D, '84, 18
V53.31 Cardiac pacemaker
EXCLUDES mechanical complication of cardiac pacemaker (996.01)
AHA: 1Q, '02, 3
V53.32 Automatic implantable cardiac defibrillator
AHA: ▶3Q, '05, 8◀
V53.39 Other cardiac device
V53.4 Orthodontic devices

³ These V codes may be used as principal diagnosis on Medicare patients.

N Newborn Age: 0   P Pediatric Age: 0-17   M Maternity Age: 12-55   A Adult Age: 15-124   CC CC Condition   MC Major Complication   CD Complex Dx   HIV HIV Related Dx

V53.5 Other intestinal appliance

> EXCLUDES   *colostomy (V55.3)*
> *ileostomy (V55.2)*
> *other artificial opening of digestive tract (V55.4)*

V53.6 Urinary devices

Urinary catheter

> EXCLUDES   *cystostomy (V55.5)*
> *nephrostomy (V55.6)*
> *ureterostomy (V55.6)*
> *urethrostomy (V55.6)*

V53.7 Orthopedic devices

Orthopedic:	Orthopedic:
brace	corset
cast	shoes

> EXCLUDES   *other orthopedic aftercare (V54)*

V53.8 Wheelchair

√5ᵗʰ **V53.9 Other and unspecified device**

AHA: 2Q, '03, 6

V53.90 Unspecified device

V53.91 Fitting and adjustment of insulin pump

Insulin pump titration

V53.99 Other device

√4ᵗʰ **V54 Other orthopedic aftercare**

> EXCLUDES   *fitting and adjustment of orthopedic devices (V53.7)*
> *malfunction of internal orthopedic device (996.40-996.49)*
> *other complication of nonmechanical nature (996.60-996.79)*

AHA: 3Q, '95, 3

√5ᵗʰ **V54.0 Aftercare involving internal fixation device**

> EXCLUDES   *malfunction of internal orthopedic device (996.40-996.49)*
> *other complication of nonmechanical nature (996.60-996.79)*
> *removal of external fixation device (V54.89)*

AHA: 4Q, '03, 87

[3] **V54.01 Encounter for removal of internal fixation device**

[3] **V54.02 Encounter for lengthening/adjustment of growth rod**

[3] **V54.09 Other aftercare involving internal fixation device**

√5ᵗʰ **V54.1 Aftercare for healing traumatic fracture**

> EXCLUDES   ▶*aftercare for amputation stump (V54.89)*◀

AHA: 4Q, '02, 80

[3] **V54.10 Aftercare for healing traumatic fracture of arm, unspecified**

[3] **V54.11 Aftercare for healing traumatic fracture of upper arm**

[3] **V54.12 Aftercare for healing traumatic fracture of lower arm**

[3] **V54.13 Aftercare for healing traumatic fracture of hip**

AHA: 4Q, '03, 103, 105; 2Q, '03, 16

[3] **V54.14 Aftercare for healing traumatic fracture of leg, unspecified**

[3] **V54.15 Aftercare for healing traumatic fracture of upper leg**

> EXCLUDES   *aftercare for healing traumatic fracture of hip (V54.13)*

[3] **V54.16 Aftercare for healing traumatic fracture of lower leg**

[3] **V54.17 Aftercare for healing traumatic fracture of vertebrae**

[3] **V54.19 Aftercare for healing traumatic fracture of other bone**

AHA: 1Q, '05, 13; 4Q, '02, 80

√5ᵗʰ **V54.2 Aftercare for healing pathologic fracture**

AHA: 4Q, '02, 80

[3] **V54.20 Aftercare for healing pathologic fracture of arm, unspecified**

[3] **V54.21 Aftercare for healing pathologic fracture of upper arm**

[3] **V54.22 Aftercare for healing pathologic fracture of lower arm**

[3] **V54.23 Aftercare for healing pathologic fracture of hip**

[3] **V54.24 Aftercare for healing pathologic fracture of leg, unspecified**

[3] **V54.25 Aftercare for healing pathologic fracture of upper leg**

> EXCLUDES   *aftercare for healing pathologic fracture of hip (V54.23)*

[3] **V54.26 Aftercare for healing pathologic fracture of lower leg**

[3] **V54.27 Aftercare for healing pathologic fracture of vertebrae**

AHA: 4Q, '03, 108

[3] **V54.29 Aftercare for healing pathologic fracture of other bone**

AHA: 4Q, '02, 80

√5ᵗʰ **V54.8 Other orthopedic aftercare**

AHA: 3Q, '01, 19; 4Q, '99, 5

[3] **V54.81 Aftercare following joint replacement**

Use additional code to identify joint replacement site (V43.60-V43.69)

AHA: 2Q, '04, 15; 4Q, '02, 80

[3] **V54.89 Other orthopedic aftercare**

Aftercare for healing fracture NOS

V54.9 Unspecified orthopedic aftercare

√4ᵗʰ **V55 Attention to artificial openings**

> INCLUDES   adjustment or repositioning of catheter
> closure
> passage of sounds or bougies
> reforming
> removal or replacement of catheter
> toilet or cleansing

> EXCLUDES   *complications of external stoma (519.00-519.09, 569.60-569.69, 997.4, 997.5)*
> *status only, without need for care (V44.0-V44.9)*

[3] **V55.0 Tracheostomy**

[3] **V55.1 Gastrostomy**

AHA: 4Q, '99, 9; 3Q, '97, 7, 8; 1Q, '96, 14; 3Q, '95, 13

[3] **V55.2 Ileostomy**

[3] **V55.3 Colostomy**

AHA: 2Q, '05, 4; 3Q, '97, 9

[3] **V55.4 Other artificial opening of digestive tract**

AHA: 2Q, '05, 14; 1Q, '03, 10

[3] **V55.5 Cystostomy**

[3] **V55.6 Other artificial opening of urinary tract**

Nephrostomy	Urethrostomy
Ureterostomy	

[3] **V55.7 Artificial vagina**

[3] **V55.8 Other specified artificial opening**

V55.9 Unspecified artificial opening

√4ᵗʰ **V56 Encounter for dialysis and dialysis catheter care**

Use additional code to identify the associated condition

> EXCLUDES   *dialysis preparation — code to condition*

AHA: 4Q, '98, 66; 1Q, '93, 29

[3] **V56.0 Extracorporeal dialysis**

Dialysis (renal) NOS

> EXCLUDES   *dialysis status (V45.1)*

AHA: 4Q, '05, 79; 1Q, '04, 23; 4Q, '00, 40; 3Q, '98, 6; 2Q, '98, 20

---

[3]   These V codes may be used as principal diagnosis on Medicare patients.

√4ᵗʰ
√5ᵗʰ Additional Digit Required   Nonspecific PDx   Unacceptable PDx   Manifestation Code   **MCV** Major Cardiovascular Condition   ▶◀ Revised Text   ● New Code   ▲ Revised Code Title

2007 ICD•9•CM   October 2006 • Volume 1 — 327

⁶ **V56.1 Fitting and adjustment of extracorporeal dialysis catheter**
Removal or replacement of catheter
Toilet or cleansing
Use additional code for any concurrent extracorporeal dialysis (V56.0)
AHA: 2Q, '98, 20

V56.2 Fitting and adjustment of peritoneal dialysis catheter
Use additional code for any concurrent peritoneal dialysis (V56.8)
AHA: 4Q, '98, 55

√5ᵗʰ **V56.3 Encounter for adequacy testing for dialysis**
AHA: 4Q, '00, 55

     V56.31 Encounter for adequacy testing for hemodialysis

     V56.32 Encounter for adequacy testing for peritoneal dialysis
Peritoneal equilibration test

³ **V56.8 Other dialysis**
Peritoneal dialysis
AHA: 4Q, '98, 55

√4ᵗʰ **V57 Care involving use of rehabilitation procedures**
Use additional code to identify underlying condition
AHA: 1Q, '02, 19; 3Q, '97, 12; 1Q, '90, 6; S-O, '86, 3

V57.0 Breathing exercises

⁶ **V57.1 Other physical therapy**
Therapeutic and remedial exercises, except breathing
AHA: 2Q, '04, 15; 4Q, '02, 56; 4Q, '99, 5

√5ᵗʰ **V57.2 Occupational therapy and vocational rehabilitation**

     ⁶ **V57.21 Encounter for occupational therapy**
AHA: 4Q, '99, 7

     ⁶ **V57.22 Encounter for vocational therapy**

⁶ **V57.3 Speech therapy**
AHA: 4Q, '97, 36

V57.4 Orthoptic training

√5ᵗʰ **V57.8 Other specified rehabilitation procedure**

     V57.81 Orthotic training
Gait training in the use of artificial limbs

     ⁶ **V57.89 Other**
Multiple training or therapy
AHA: 4Q, '03, 105-106, 108; 2Q, '03, 16; 1Q, '02, 16; 3Q, '01, 21; 3Q, '97, 11, 12; S-O, '86, 4

⁶ **V57.9 Unspecified rehabilitation procedure**

√4ᵗʰ **V58 Encounter for other and unspecified procedures and aftercare**
EXCLUDES   convalescence and palliative care (V66)

³ **V58.0 Radiotherapy**
Encounter or admission for radiotherapy
EXCLUDES   encounter for radioactive implant — code to condition
radioactive iodine therapy — code to condition
AHA: 3Q, '92, 5; 2Q, '90, 7; J-F, '87, 13

√5ᵗʰ **V58.1 Encounter for antineoplastic chemotherapy and immunotherapy**
Encounter or admission for chemotherapy
EXCLUDES   chemotherapy and immunotherapy for nonneoplastic conditions — code to condition
prophylactic chemotherapy against disease which has never been present (V03.0-V07.9)
AHA: 1Q, '04, 13; 2Q, '03, 16; 3Q, '93, 4; 2Q, '92, 6; 2Q, '91, 17; 2Q, '90, 7; S-O, '84, 5

³ **V58.11 Encounter for antineoplastic chemotherapy**
AHA: 4Q, '05, 98

³ **V58.12 Encounter for antineoplastic immunotherapy**
AHA: 4Q, '05, 98

V58.2 Blood transfusion, without reported diagnosis

▲ √5ᵗʰ **V58.3 Attention to dressings and sutures**
►Change or removal of wound packing◄
EXCLUDES   ►attention to drains (V58.49)
planned postoperative wound closure (V58.41)◄
AHA: 2Q, '05, 14

● **V58.30 Encounter for change or removal of nonsurgical wound dressing**
Encounter for change or removal of wound dressing NOS

● **V58.31 Encounter for change or removal of surgical wound dressing**

● **V58.32 Encounter for removal of sutures**
Encounter for removal of staples

√5ᵗʰ **V58.4 Other aftercare following surgery**
Note: Codes from this subcategory should be used in conjunction with other aftercare codes to fully identify the reason for the aftercare encounter
EXCLUDES   aftercare following sterilization reversal surgery (V26.22)
attention to artificial openings (V55.0-V55.9)
orthopedic aftercare (V54.0-V54.9)
AHA: 4Q, '99, 9; N-D, '87, 9

⁷ **V58.41 Encounter for planned postoperative wound closure**
EXCLUDES   disruption of operative wound (998.3)
►encounter for dressings and suture aftercare (V58.30-V58.32)◄
AHA: 4Q, '99, 15

⁷ **V58.42 Aftercare following surgery for neoplasm**
Conditions classifiable to 140-239
AHA: 4Q, '02, 80

⁷ **V58.43 Aftercare following surgery for injury and trauma**
Conditions classifiable to 800-999
EXCLUDES   aftercare for healing traumatic fracture (V54.10-V54.19)
AHA: 4Q, '02, 80

⁷ **V58.44 Aftercare following organ transplant**
Use additional code to identify the organ transplanted (V42.0-V42.9)
AHA: 4Q, '04, 101

⁷ **V58.49 Other specified aftercare following surgery**
►Change or removal of drains◄
AHA: 1Q, '96, 8, 9

⁷ **V58.5 Orthodontics**
EXCLUDES   fitting and adjustment of orthodontic device (V53.4)

√5ᵗʰ **V58.6 Long-term (current) drug use**
EXCLUDES   drug abuse (305.00-305.93)
drug dependence (304.00-304.93)
hormone replacement therapy (postmenopausal) (V07.4)
AHA: 4Q, '03, 85; 4Q, '02, 84; 3Q, '02, 15; 4Q, '95, 61

⁷ **V58.61 Long-term (current) use of anticoagulants**
EXCLUDES   long-term (current) use of aspirin (V58.66)
AHA   3Q, '04, 7; 4Q, '03, 108; 3Q, '02, 13-16; 1Q, '02, 15, 16

V58.62 Long-term (current) use of antibiotics
AHA: 4Q, '98, 59

V58.63 Long-term (current) use of antiplatelets/antithrombotics
EXCLUDES   long-term (current) use of aspirin (V58.66)

---

³ These V codes may be used as principal diagnosis on Medicare patients.
⁶ Rehabilitation codes acceptable as a principal diagnosis when accompanied by a secondary diagnosis reflecting the condition treated.
⁷ These V codes are acceptable as principal diagnosis and group to DRGs 465-466.

🄽 Newborn Age: 0   🄿 Pediatric Age: 0-17   🄼 Maternity Age: 12-55   🄰 Adult Age: 15-124   CC CC Condition   MC Major Complication   CD Complex Dx   HIV HIV Related Dx

V58.64 **Long-term (current) use of non-steroidal anti-inflammatories (NSAID)**
EXCLUDES   *long-term (current) use of aspirin (V58.66)*

V58.65 **Long-term (current) use of steroids**

V58.66 **Long-term (current) use of aspirin**
AHA: 4Q, '04, 102

V58.67 **Long-term (current) use of insulin**
AHA: 4Q, '04, 55-56, 103

7 V58.69 **Long-term (current) use of other medications**
High-risk medications
AHA: 2Q, '04, 10; 1Q, '04, 13; 1Q, '03, 11; 2Q, '00, 8; 3Q, '99, 13; 2Q, '99, 17; 1Q, '97, 12; 2Q, '96, 7

✓5th V58.7 **Aftercare following surgery to specified body systems, not elsewhere classified**
Note: Codes from this subcategory should be used in conjunction with other aftercare codes to fully identify the reason for the aftercare encounter
EXCLUDES   *aftercare following organ transplant (V58.44)*
aftercare following surgery for neoplasm (V58.42)
AHA: 4Q, '03, 104; 4Q, '02, 80

7 V58.71 **Aftercare following surgery of the sense organs, NEC**
Conditions classifiable to 360-379, 380-389

7 V58.72 **Aftercare following surgery of the nervous system, NEC**
Conditions classifiable to 320-359
EXCLUDES   *aftercare following surgery of the sense organs, NEC (V58.71)*

7 V58.73 **Aftercare following surgery of the circulatory system, NEC**
Conditions classifiable to 390-459
AHA: 4Q, '03, 105

7 V58.74 **Aftercare following surgery of the respiratory system, NEC**
Conditions classifiable to 460-519

7 V58.75 **Aftercare following surgery of the teeth, oral cavity and digestive system, NEC**
Conditions classifiable to 520-579
AHA: ▶2Q, '05, 14◄

7 V58.76 **Aftercare following surgery of the genitourinary system, NEC**
Conditions classifiable to 580-629
EXCLUDES   *aftercare following sterilization reversal (V26.22)*
AHA: 1Q, '05, 11-12

7 V58.77 **Aftercare following surgery of the skin and subcutaneous tissue, NEC**
Conditions classifiable to 680-709

7 V58.78 **Aftercare following surgery of the musculoskeletal system, NEC**
Conditions classifiable to 710-739

✓5th V58.8 **Other specified procedures and aftercare**
AHA: 4Q, '94, 45; 2Q, '94, 8

7 V58.81 **Fitting and adjustment of vascular catheter**
Removal or replacement of catheter
Toilet or cleansing
EXCLUDES   *complication of renal dialysis (996.73)*
complication of vascular catheter (996.74)
dialysis preparation — code to condition
encounter for dialysis (V56.0-V56.8)
fitting and adjustment of dialysis catheter (V56.1)

7 V58.82 **Fitting and adjustment of nonvascular catheter, NEC**
Removal or replacement of catheter
Toilet or cleansing
EXCLUDES   *fitting and adjustment of peritoneal dialysis catheter (V56.2)*
fitting and adjustment of urinary catheter (V53.6)

7 V58.83 **Encounter for therapeutic drug monitoring**
Use additional code for any associated long-term (current) drug use (V58.61-V58.69)
EXCLUDES   *blood-drug testing for medicolegal reasons (V70.4)*
AHA: 2Q, '04, 10; 1Q, '04, 13; 4Q, '03, 85; 4Q, '02, 84; 3Q, '02, 13-16
DEF: Drug monitoring: Measurement of the level of a specific drug in the body or measurement of a specific function to assess effectiveness of a drug.

V58.89 **Other specified aftercare**
AHA: 4Q, '98, 59

7 V58.9 **Unspecified aftercare**

✓4th V59 **Donors**
EXCLUDES   *examination of potential donor (V70.8)*
self-donation of organ or tissue — code to condition
AHA: 4Q, '95, 62; 1Q, '90, 10; N-D, '84, 8

✓5th V59.0 **Blood**
V59.01 **Whole blood**
V59.02 **Stem cells**
V59.09 **Other**

3 V59.1 **Skin**
3 V59.2 **Bone**
3 V59.3 **Bone marrow**
3 V59.4 **Kidney**
3 V59.5 **Cornea**
3 V59.6 **Liver**

✓5th V59.7 **Egg (oocyte) (ovum)**
AHA: ▶4Q, '05, 99◄

V59.70 **Egg (oocyte) (ovum) donor, unspecified**   ♀
V59.71 **Egg (oocyte) (ovum) donor, under age 35, anonymous recipient**   ♀
Egg donor, under age 35 NOS
V59.72 **Egg (oocyte) (ovum) donor, under age 35, designated recipient**   ♀
V59.73 **Egg (oocyte) (ovum) donor, age 35 and over, anonymous recipient**   ♀
Egg donor, age 35 and over NOS
V59.74 **Egg (oocyte) (ovum) donor, age 35 and over, designated recipient**   ♀

3 V59.8 **Other specified organ or tissue**
AHA: 3Q, '02, 20

3 V59.9 **Unspecified organ or tissue**

PERSONS ENCOUNTERING HEALTH SERVICES IN OTHER CIRCUMSTANCES (V60-V69)

✓4th V60 **Housing, household, and economic circumstances**

V60.0 **Lack of housing**
Hobos	Transients
Social migrants	Vagabonds
Tramps	

V60.1 **Inadequate housing**
Lack of heating	Technical defects in home preventing adequate care
Restriction of space	

V60.2 **Inadequate material resources**
Economic problem	Poverty NOS

V60.3 **Person living alone**

---

3 These V codes may be used as principal diagnosis on Medicare patients.
7 These V codes are acceptable as principal diagnosis and group to DRGs 465-466.

✓4th
✓5th Additional Digit Required   Nonspecific PDx   Unacceptable PDx   Manifestation Code   MCV Major Cardiovascular Condition   ▶◄ Revised Text   ● New Code   ▲ Revised Code Title

V Codes

V60.4–V63.9

V60.4   No other household member able to render care
Person requiring care (has) (is):
family member too handicapped, ill, or otherwise
unsuited to render care
partner temporarily away from home
temporarily away from usual place of abode
EXCLUDES   *holiday relief care (V60.5)*

V60.5   Holiday relief care
Provision of health care facilities to a person
normally cared for at home, to enable relatives
to take a vacation

V60.6   Person living in residential institution
Boarding school resident

V60.8   Other specified housing or economic circumstances

V60.9   Unspecified housing or economic circumstance

√4ᵗʰ **V61   Other family circumstances**
INCLUDES   when these circumstances or fear of them,
affecting the person directly involved or
others, are mentioned as the reason,
justified or not, for seeking or receiving
medical advice or care

AHA: 1Q, '90, 9

V61.0   Family disruption
Divorce   Estrangement

√5ᵗʰ **V61.1   Counseling for marital and partner problems**
EXCLUDES   *problems related to:*
psychosexual disorders (302.0-302.9)
sexual function (V41.7)

V61.10   Counseling for marital and partner problems, unspecified
Marital conflict
Marital relationship problem
Partner conflict
Partner relationship problem

V61.11   Counseling for victim of spousal and partner abuse
EXCLUDES   *encounter for treatment of current injuries due to abuse (995.80-995.85)*

V61.12   Counseling for perpetrator of spousal and partner abuse

√5ᵗʰ **V61.2   Parent-child problems**
V61.20   Counseling for parent-child problem, unspecified
Concern about behavior of child
Parent-child conflict
Parent-child relationship problem

³ **V61.21   Counseling for victim of child abuse**
Child battering   Child neglect
EXCLUDES   *current injuries due to abuse (995.50-995.59)*

V61.22   Counseling for perpetrator of parental child abuse
EXCLUDES   *counseling for non-parental abuser (V62.83)*

V61.29   Other
Problem concerning adopted or foster child
AHA: 3Q, '99, 16

V61.3   Problems with aged parents or in-laws

√5ᵗʰ **V61.4   Health problems within family**
V61.41   Alcoholism in family
V61.49   Other
Care of   } sick or handicapped person
Presence of   }   in family or household

V61.5   Multiparity
V61.6   Illegitimacy or illegitimate pregnancy   M ♀
V61.7   Other unwanted pregnancy   M ♀
V61.8   Other specified family circumstances
Problems with family members NEC
Sibling relationship problem

V61.9   Unspecified family circumstance

√4ᵗʰ **V62   Other psychosocial circumstances**
INCLUDES   those circumstances or fear of them, affecting
the person directly involved or others,
mentioned as the reason, justified or not,
for seeking or receiving medical advice or
care
EXCLUDES   *previous psychological trauma (V15.41-V15.49)*

V62.0   Unemployment
EXCLUDES   *circumstances when main problem is economic inadequacy or poverty (V60.2)*

V62.1   Adverse effects of work environment

V62.2   Other occupational circumstances or maladjustment
Career choice problem
Dissatisfaction with employment
Occupational problem

V62.3   Educational circumstances
Academic problem
Dissatisfaction with school environment
Educational handicap

V62.4   Social maladjustment
Acculturation problem   Social:
Cultural deprivation   isolation
Political, religious, or   persecution
sex discrimination

V62.5   Legal circumstances
Imprisonment   Litigation
Legal investigation   Prosecution

V62.6   Refusal of treatment for reasons of religion or conscience

√5ᵗʰ **V62.8   Other psychological or physical stress, not elsewhere classified**
V62.81   Interpersonal problems, not elsewhere classified
Relational problem NOS

V62.82   Bereavement, uncomplicated
EXCLUDES   *bereavement as adjustment reaction (309.0)*

V62.83   Counseling for perpetrator of physical/sexual abuse
EXCLUDES   *counseling for perpetrator of parental child abuse (V61.22)*
counseling for perpetrator of spousal and partner abuse (V61.12)

V62.84   Suicidal ideation
EXCLUDES   *suicidal tendencies (300.9)*
AHA: ▶4Q, '05, 96◀
DEF:▶ Thoughts of committing suicide; no actual attempt of suicide has been made.◀

V62.89   Other
Borderline intellectual functioning
Life circumstance problems
Phase of life problems
Religious or spiritual problem

V62.9   Unspecified psychosocial circumstance

√5ᵗʰ **V63   Unavailability of other medical facilities for care**
AHA: 1Q, '91, 21

V63.0   Residence remote from hospital or other health care facility

V63.1   Medical services in home not available
EXCLUDES   *no other household member able to render care (V60.4)*
AHA: 4Q, '01, 67; 1Q, '01, 12

V63.2   Person awaiting admission to adequate facility elsewhere

V63.8   Other specified reasons for unavailability of medical facilities
Person on waiting list undergoing social agency investigation

V63.9   Unspecified reason for unavailability of medical facilities

---

³ These V codes may be used as principal diagnosis on Medicare patients.

N Newborn Age: 0   P Pediatric Age: 0-17   M Maternity Age: 12-55   A Adult Age: 15-124   CC CC Condition   MC Major Complication   CD Complex Dx   HIV HIV Related Dx

√4ᵗʰ **V64 Persons encountering health services for specific procedures, not carried out**

√5ᵗʰ **V64.0 Vaccination not carried out**
AHA: 4Q, '05, 99

    V64.00 Vaccination not carried out, unspecified reason

    V64.01 Vaccination not carried out because of acute illness

    V64.02 Vaccination not carried out because of chronic illness or condition

    V64.03 Vaccination not carried out because of immune compromised state

    V64.04 Vaccination not carried out because of allergy to vaccine or component

    V64.05 Vaccination not carried out because of caregiver refusal

    V64.06 Vaccination not carried out because of patient refusal

    V64.07 Vaccination not carried out for religious reasons

    V64.08 Vaccination not carried out because patient had disease being vaccinated against

    V64.09 Vaccination not carried out for other reason

V64.1 Surgical or other procedure not carried out because of contraindication

V64.2 Surgical or other procedure not carried out because of patient's decision
AHA: 2Q, '01, 8

V64.3 Procedure not carried out for other reasons

√5ᵗʰ **V64.4 Closed surgical procedure converted to open procedure**
AHA: 4Q, '03, 87; 4Q, '98, 68; 4Q, '97, 52

    V64.41 Laparoscopic surgical procedure converted to open procedure

    V64.42 Thoracoscopic surgical procedure converted to open procedure

    V64.43 Arthroscopic surgical procedure converted to open procedure

√4ᵗʰ **V65 Other persons seeking consultation**

³ **V65.0 Healthy person accompanying sick person**
Boarder

√5ᵗʰ **V65.1 Person consulting on behalf of another person**
Advice or treatment for nottending third party
EXCLUDES *concern (normal) about sick person in family (V61.41-V61.49)*
AHA: 4Q, '03, 84

    V65.11 Pediatric pre-birth visit for expectant M ♀ **mother**

    V65.19 Other person consulting on behalf of another person

³ **V65.2 Person feigning illness**
Malingerer   Peregrinating patient
AHA: 3Q, '99, 20

V65.3 Dietary surveillance and counseling
Dietary surveillance and counseling (in):
  NOS   gastritis
  colitis   hypercholesterolemia
  diabetes mellitus hypoglycemia
  food allergies or obesity
    intolerance
▶Use additional code to identify Body Mass Index (BMI), if known (V85.0-V85.54)◀
AHA: 4Q, '05, 96

√5ᵗʰ **V65.4 Other counseling, not elsewhere classified**
Health: Health:
  advice   instruction
  education
EXCLUDES *counseling (for):*
    contraception (V25.40-V25.49)
    genetic ▶(V26.31-V26.39)◀
    on behalf of third party (V65.11-V65.19)
    procreative management (V26.4)

    V65.40 Counseling NOS

    V65.41 Exercise counseling

    V65.42 Counseling on substance use and abuse

    V65.43 Counseling on injury prevention

    V65.44 Human immunodeficiency virus [HIV] counseling

    V65.45 Counseling on other sexually transmitted diseases

    V65.46 Encounter for insulin pump training

    V65.49 Other specified counseling
AHA: 2Q, '00, 8

V65.5 Person with feared complaint in whom no diagnosis was made
Feared condition not demonstrated
Problem was normal state
"Worried well"

V65.8 Other reasons for seeking consultation
EXCLUDES *specified symptoms*
AHA: 3Q, '92, 4

V65.9 Unspecified reason for consultation

√4ᵗʰ **V66 Convalescence and palliative care**

³ **V66.0 Following surgery**

³ **V66.1 Following radiotherapy**

³ **V66.2 Following chemotherapy**

³ **V66.3 Following psychotherapy and other treatment for mental disorder**

³ **V66.4 Following treatment of fracture**

V66.5 Following other treatment

³ **V66.6 Following combined treatment**

V66.7 Encounter for palliative care
End of life care   Terminal care
Hospice care
Code first underlying disease
AHA: 2Q, '05, 9; 4Q, '03, 107; 1Q, '98, 11; 4Q, '96, 47, 48

V66.9 Unspecified convalescence
AHA: 4Q, '99, 8

√4ᵗʰ **V67 Follow-up examination**
INCLUDES surveillance only following completed treatment
EXCLUDES *surveillance of contraception (V25.40-V25.49)*
AHA: 2Q, '03, 5

√5ᵗʰ **V67.0 Following surgery**
AHA: 4Q, '00, 56; 4Q, '98, 69; 4Q, '97, 50; 2Q, '95, 8; 1Q, '95, 4; 3Q, '92, 11

    ⁷ **V67.00 Following surgery, unspecified**

    ⁷ **V67.01 Follow-up vaginal pap smear** ♀
Vaginal pap-smear, status-post
    hysterectomy for malignant condition
Use additional code to identify:
  acquired absence of uterus (V45.77)
  personal history of malignant neoplasm (V10.40-V10.44)
EXCLUDES *vaginal pap smear status-post hysterectomy for non-malignant condition (V76.47)*

    ⁷ **V67.09 Following other surgery**
EXCLUDES *sperm count following sterilization reversal (V26.22)*
    sperm count for fertility testing (V26.21)
AHA: 3Q, '03, 16; 3Q, '02, 15

³ **V67.1 Following radiotherapy**

³ **V67.2 Following chemotherapy**
Cancer chemotherapy follow-up

³ **V67.3 Following psychotherapy and other treatment for mental disorder**

---

³ These V codes may be used as principal diagnosis on Medicare patients.
⁷ These V codes are acceptable as principal diagnosis and group to DRGs 465-466.

√4ᵗʰ
√5ᵗʰ Additional Digit Required   Nonspecific PDx   Unacceptable PDx   Manifestation Code   MCV Major Cardiovascular Condition ▶◀ Revised Text ● New Code ▲ Revised Code Title

2007 ICD•9•CM   October 2006 • Volume 1 — 331

[7] **V67.4 Following treatment of healed fracture**
> EXCLUDES   *current (healing) fracture aftercare (V54.0-V54.9)*

AHA: 1Q, '90, 7

✓5th **V67.5 Following other treatment**
    [3] **V67.51 Following completed treatment with high-risk medications, not elsewhere classified**
> EXCLUDES   *long-term (current) drug use (V58.61-V58.69)*

AHA: 1Q, '99, 5, 6;4Q, '95, 61 ; 1Q, '90, 18

    [3] **V67.59 Other**
[3] **V67.6 Following combined treatment**
V67.9 Unspecified follow-up examination

✓4th **V68 Encounters for administrative purposes**

V68.0 Issue of medical certificates
Issue of medical certificate of:
   cause of death
   fitness
   incapacity
> EXCLUDES   *encounter for general medical examination (V70.0-V70.9)*

V68.1 Issue of repeat prescriptions
Issue of repeat prescription for:
   appliance   medications
   glasses
> EXCLUDES   *repeat prescription for contraceptives (V25.41-V25.49)*

V68.2 Request for expert evidence
✓5th **V68.8 Other specified administrative purpose**
    V68.81 Referral of patient without examination or treatment
    V68.89 Other
V68.9 Unspecified administrative purpose

✓4th **V69 Problems related to lifestyle**
AHA: 4Q, '94, 48

V69.0 Lack of physical exercise
V69.1 Inappropriate diet and eating habits
> EXCLUDES   *anorexia nervosa (307.1)*
> *bulimia (783.6)*
> *malnutrition and other nutritional deficiencies (260-269.9)*
> *other and unspecified eating disorders (307.50-307.59)*

V69.2 High-risk sexual behavior
V69.3 Gambling and betting
> EXCLUDES   *pathological gambling (312.31)*

V69.4 Lack of adequate sleep
Sleep deprivation
> EXCLUDES   *insomnia (780.52)*

V69.5 Behavioral insomnia of childhood   P
AHA: ▶4Q, '05, 99◄

DEF: ▶Behaviors on the part of the child or caregivers that cause negative compliance with a child's sleep schedule; results in lack of adequate sleep.◄

V69.8 Other problems related to lifestyle
Self-damaging behavior
V69.9 Problem related to lifestyle, unspecified

PERSONS WITHOUT REPORTED DIAGNOSIS ENCOUNTERED DURING EXAMINATION AND INVESTIGATION OF INDIVIDUALS AND POPULATIONS ▶(V70-V82)◄

Note: Nonspecific abnormal findings disclosed at the time of these examinations are classifiable to categories 790-796.

✓4th **V70 General medical examination**
Use additional code(s) to identify any special screening examination(s) performed (V73.0-V82.9)

V70.0 Routine general medical examination at a health care facility
Health checkup
> EXCLUDES   *health checkup of infant or child (V20.2)*
> *pre-procedural general physical examination (V72.83)*

[3] **V70.1 General psychiatric examination, requested by the authority**
V70.2 General psychiatric examination, other and unspecified
V70.3 Other medical examination for administrative purposes
General medical examination for:
   admission to old age home
   adoption
   camp
   driving license
   immigration and naturalization
   insurance certification
   marriage
   prison
   school admission
   sports competition
> EXCLUDES   *attendance for issue of medical certificates (V68.0)*
> *pre-employment screening (V70.5)*

AHA: 1Q, '90, 6

[3] **V70.4 Examination for medicolegal reasons**
Blood-alcohol tests   Paternity testing
Blood-drug tests
> EXCLUDES   *examination and observation following:*
> *accidents (V71.3, V71.4)*
> *assault (V71.6)*
> *rape (V71.5)*

[3] **V70.5 Health examination of defined subpopulations**
Armed forces personnel   Prisoners
Inhabitants of institutions   Prostitutes
Occupational health   Refugees
   examinations   School children
Pre-employment screening   Students
Preschool children

V70.6 Health examination in population surveys
> EXCLUDES   *special screening (V73.0-V82.9)*

[3] **V70.7 Examination of participant in clinical trial**
Examination of participant or control in clinical research
AHA: 4Q, '01, 55

V70.8 Other specified general medical examinations
Examination of potential donor of organ or tissue
V70.9 Unspecified general medical examination

✓4th **V71 Observation and evaluation for suspected conditions not found**
> INCLUDES   This category is to be used when persons without a diagnosis are suspected of having an abnormal condition, without signs or symptoms, which requires study, but after examination and observation, is found not to exist. This category is also for use for administrative and legal observation status.

AHA: 4Q, '94, 47; 2Q, '90, 5; M-A, '87, 1

✓5th **V71.0 Observation for suspected mental condition**
    [3] **V71.01 Adult antisocial behavior**   A
       Dyssocial behavior or gang activity in adult without manifest psychiatric disorder
    [3] **V71.02 Childhood or adolescent antisocial behavior**
       Dyssocial behavior or gang activity in child or adolescent without manifest psychiatric disorder
    [3] **V71.09 Other suspected mental condition**
[3] **V71.1 Observation for suspected malignant neoplasm**
[3] **V71.2 Observation for suspected tuberculosis**
[3] **V71.3 Observation following accident at work**
[3] **V71.4 Observation following other accident**
Examination of individual involved in motor vehicle traffic accident
AHA: ▶1Q, '06, 9◄

---

[3] These V codes may be used as principal diagnosis on Medicare patients.
[7] These V codes are acceptable as principal diagnosis and group to DRGs 465-466.

N Newborn Age: 0   P Pediatric Age: 0-17   M Maternity Age: 12-55   A Adult Age: 15-124   CC CC Condition   MC Major Complication   CD Complex Dx   HIV HIV Related Dx

3 **V71.5 Observation following alleged rape or seduction**
Examination of victim or culprit

3 **V71.6 Observation following other inflicted injury**
Examination of victim or culprit

3 **V71.7 Observation for suspected cardiovascular disease**
AHA: 1Q, '04, 6; 3Q, '90, 10; S-O, '87, 10

✓5th **V71.8 Observation and evaluation for other specified suspected conditions**
AHA: 4Q, '00, 54 ; 1Q, '90, 19

  3 **V71.81 Abuse and neglect**
EXCLUDES adult abuse and neglect (995.80-995.85)
child abuse and neglect (995.50-995.59)
AHA: 4Q, '00, 55

  3 **V71.82 Observation and evaluation for suspected exposure to anthrax**
AHA: 4Q, '02, 70, 85

  3 **V71.83 Observation and evaluation for suspected exposure to other biological agent**
AHA: 4Q, '03, 47

  3 **V71.89 Other specified suspected conditions**
AHA: 2Q, '03, 15

V71.9 Observation for unspecified suspected condition
AHA: 1Q, '02, 6

✓4th **V72 Special investigations and examinations**
INCLUDES routine examination of specific system
EXCLUDES general medical examination (V70.0-V70.4)
general screening examination of defined population groups (V70.5, V70.6, V70.7)
routine examination of infant or child (V20.2)
Use additional code(s) to identify any special screening examination(s) performed (V73.0-V82.9)

3 **V72.0 Examination of eyes and vision**
AHA: 1Q, '04, 15

✓5th **V72.1 Examination of ears and hearing**
AHA: 1Q, '04, 15

  • **V72.11 Encounter for hearing examination following failed hearing screening**

  • **V72.19 Other examination of ears and hearing**

V72.2 Dental examination

✓5th **V72.3 Gynecological examination**
EXCLUDES cervical Papanicolaou smear without general gynecological examination (V76.2)
routine examination in contraceptive management (V25.40-V25.49)

  3 **V72.31 Routine gynecological examination** ♀
General gynecological examination with or without Papanicolaou cervical smear
Pelvic examination (annual) (periodic)
Use additional code to identify routine vaginal Papanicolaou smear (V76.47)
AHA: 4Q, '05, 9

  3 **V72.32 Encounter for Papanicolaou cervical smear to confirm findings of recent normal smear following initial abnormal smear** ♀

✓5th **V72.4 Pregnancy examination or test**
AHA: 4Q, '05, 98

  3 **V72.40 Pregnancy examination or test, pregnancy unconfirmed** ♀
Possible pregnancy, not (yet) confirmed

  3 **V72.41 Pregnancy examination or test, negative result** ♀

  3 **V72.42 Pregnancy examination or test, positive result** ♀ M

V72.5 Radiological examination, not elsewhere classified
Routine chest x-ray
EXCLUDES examination for suspected tuberculosis (V71.2)
AHA: 1Q, '90, 19

V72.6 Laboratory examination
EXCLUDES that for suspected disorder (V71,0-V71.9)
AHA: 1Q, '90, 22

V72.7 Diagnostic skin and sensitization tests
Allergy tests   Skin tests for hypersensitivity
EXCLUDES diagnostic skin tests for bacterial diseases (V74.0-V74.9)

✓5th **V72.8 Other specified examinations**

  3 **V72.81 Pre-operative cardiovascular examination**
Pre-procedural cardiovascular examination

  3 **V72.82 Pre-operative respiratory examination**
Pre-procedural respiratory examination
AHA: 3Q, '96, 14

  3 **V72.83 Other specified pre-operative examination**
Other pre-procedural examination
Pre-procedural general physical examination
EXCLUDES routine general medical examination (V70.0)
AHA: 3Q, '96, 14

  V72.84 Pre-operative examination, unspecified
Pre-procedural examination, unspecified

  V72.85 Other specified examination
AHA: 4Q, '05, 96; 1Q, '04, 12

  V72.86 Encounter for blood typing

V72.9 Unspecified examination

✓4th **V73 Special screening examination for viral and chlamydial diseases**
AHA: 1Q, '04, 11

V73.0 Poliomyelitis
V73.1 Smallpox
V73.2 Measles
V73.3 Rubella
V73.4 Yellow fever
V73.5 Other arthropod-borne viral diseases
Dengue fever   Viral encephalitis:
Hemorrhagic fever   mosquito-borne
     tick-borne
V73.6 Trachoma
✓5th **V73.8 Other specified viral and chlamydial diseases**
V73.88 Other specified chlamydial diseases
V73.89 Other specified viral diseases
✓5th **V73.9 Unspecified viral and chlamydial disease**
V73.98 Unspecified chlamydial disease
V73.99 Unspecified viral disease

✓4th **V74 Special screening examination for bacterial and spirochetal diseases**
INCLUDES diagnostic skin tests for these diseases
AHA: 1Q, '04, 11

V74.0 Cholera
V74.1 Pulmonary tuberculosis
V74.2 Leprosy [Hansen's disease]
V74.3 Diphtheria
V74.4 Bacterial conjunctivitis
V74.5 Venereal disease
V74.6 Yaws
V74.8 Other specified bacterial and spirochetal diseases
Brucellosis   Tetanus
Leptospirosis   Whooping cough
Plague
V74.9 Unspecified bacterial and spirochetal disease

3 These V codes may be used as principal diagnosis on Medicare patients.

V Codes

V75–V82.0

✓4th **V75 Special screening examination for other infectious diseases**
AHA: 1Q, '04, 11

    V75.0 Rickettsial diseases
    V75.1 Malaria
    V75.2 Leishmaniasis
    V75.3 Trypanosomiasis
        Chagas' disease   Sleeping sickness
    V75.4 Mycotic infections
    V75.5 Schistosomiasis
    V75.6 Filariasis
    V75.7 Intestinal helminthiasis
    V75.8 Other specified parasitic infections
    V75.9 Unspecified infectious disease

✓4th **V76 Special screening for malignant neoplasms**
AHA: 1Q, '04, 11

    V76.0 Respiratory organs
   ✓5th **V76.1 Breast**
      AHA: 4Q, '98, 67

      V76.10 Breast screening, unspecified
      V76.11 Screening mammogram for high-risk patient ♀
        AHA: 2Q, '03, 4

      V76.12 Other screening mammogram
        AHA: 2Q, '03, 3-4

      V76.19 Other screening breast examination
    V76.2 Cervix ♀
      Routine cervical Papanicolaou smear
      EXCLUDES *that as part of a general gynecological examination (V72.31)*

    V76.3 Bladder
   ✓5th **V76.4 Other sites**
      V76.41 Rectum
      V76.42 Oral cavity
      V76.43 Skin
      V76.44 Prostate ♂
      V76.45 Testis ♂
      V76.46 Ovary ♀
        AHA: 4Q, '00, 52

      V76.47 Vagina ♀
        Vaginal pap smear status-post hysterectomy for non-malignant condition
        Use additional code to identify acquired absence of uterus (V45.77)
        EXCLUDES *vaginal pap smear status-post hysterectomy for malignant condition (V67.01)*
        AHA: 4Q, '00, 52

      V76.49 Other sites
        AHA: 1Q, '99, 4

   ✓5th **V76.5 Intestine**
      AHA: 4Q, '00, 52

      V76.50 Intestine, unspecified
      V76.51 Colon
        EXCLUDES *rectum (V76.41)*
        AHA: 4Q, '01, 56

      V76.52 Small intestine
   ✓5th **V76.8 Other neoplasm**
      AHA: 4Q, '00, 52

      V76.81 Nervous system
      V76.89 Other neoplasm
    V76.9 Unspecified

✓4th **V77 Special screening for endocrine, nutritional, metabolic, and immunity disorders**
AHA: 1Q, '04, 11

    V77.0 Thyroid disorders
    V77.1 Diabetes mellitus

    V77.2 Malnutrition
    V77.3 Phenylketonuria [PKU]
    V77.4 Galactosemia
    V77.5 Gout
    V77.6 Cystic fibrosis
        Screening for mucoviscidosis
    V77.7 Other inborn errors of metabolism
    V77.8 Obesity
   ✓5th **V77.9 Other and unspecified endocrine, nutritional, metabolic, and immunity disorders**
      AHA: 4Q, '00, 53

      V77.91 Screening for lipoid disorders
        Screening for cholesterol level
        Screening for hypercholesterolemia
        Screening for hyperlipidemia

      V77.99 Other and unspecified endocrine, nutritional, metabolic, and immunity disorders

✓4th **V78 Special screening for disorders of blood and blood-forming organs**
AHA: 1Q, '04, 11

    V78.0 Iron deficiency anemia
    V78.1 Other and unspecified deficiency anemia
    V78.2 Sickle cell disease or trait
    V78.3 Other hemoglobinopathies
    V78.8 Other disorders of blood and blood-forming organs
    V78.9 Unspecified disorder of blood and blood-forming organs

✓4th **V79 Special screening for mental disorders and developmental handicaps**
AHA: 1Q, '04, 11

    V79.0 Depression
    V79.1 Alcoholism
    V79.2 Mental retardation
    V79.3 Developmental handicaps in early childhood
    V79.8 Other specified mental disorders and developmental handicaps
    V79.9 Unspecified mental disorder and developmental handicap

✓4th **V80 Special screening for neurological, eye, and ear diseases**
AHA: 1Q, '04, 11

    V80.0 Neurological conditions
    V80.1 Glaucoma
    V80.2 Other eye conditions
        Screening for: Screening for:
          cataract   senile macular lesions
          congenital anomaly of eye
        EXCLUDES *general vision examination (V72.0)*

    V80.3 Ear diseases
        EXCLUDES *general hearing examination (V72.1)*

✓4th **V81 Special screening for cardiovascular, respiratory, and genitourinary diseases**
AHA: 1Q, '04, 11

    V81.0 Ischemic heart disease
    V81.1 Hypertension
    V81.2 Other and unspecified cardiovascular conditions
    V81.3 Chronic bronchitis and emphysema
    V81.4 Other and unspecified respiratory conditions
        EXCLUDES *screening for:*
          lung neoplasm (V76.0)
          pulmonary tuberculosis (V74.1)

    V81.5 Nephropathy
        Screening for asymptomatic bacteriuria
    V81.6 Other and unspecified genitourinary conditions

✓4th **V82 Special screening for other conditions**
AHA: 1Q, '04, 11

    V82.0 Skin conditions

N Newborn Age: 0   **P** Pediatric Age: 0-17   **M** Maternity Age: 12-55   **A** Adult Age: 15-124   **CC** CC Condition   **MC** Major Complication   **CD** Complex Dx   **HIV** HIV Related Dx

V82.1   **Rheumatoid arthritis**

V82.2   **Other rheumatic disorders**

V82.3   **Congenital dislocation of hip**

V82.4   **Maternal postnatal screening for chromosomal anomalies** ♀

> EXCLUDES   *antenatal screening by amniocentesis (V28.0)*

V82.5   **Chemical poisoning and other contamination**
Screening for:
heavy metal poisoning
ingestion of radioactive substance
poisoning from contaminated water supply
radiation exposure

V82.6   **Multiphasic screening**

● √5ᵗʰ **V82.7**   **Genetic screening**

> EXCLUDES   *genetic testing for procreative management (V26.31-V26.32)*

●   **V82.71 Screening for genetic disease carrier status**

●   **V82.79 Other genetic screening**

√5ᵗʰ **V82.8**   **Other specified conditions**
AHA: 4Q, '00, 53

V82.81 Osteoporosis
Use additional code to identify:
hormone replacement therapy
(postmenopausal) status (V07.4)
postmenopausal (age-related) (natural)
status (V49.81)
AHA: 4Q, '00, 54

V82.89 Other specified conditions

V82.9   **Unspecified condition**

▶GENETICS (V83-V84)◀

√4ᵗʰ **V83 Genetic carrier status**
AHA: 4Q, '02, 79; 4Q, '01, 54

√5ᵗʰ **V83.0**   **Hemophilia A carrier**
V83.01 Asymptomatic hemophilia A carrier
V83.02 Symptomatic hemophilia A carrier

√5ᵗʰ **V83.8**   **Other genetic carrier status**
V83.81 Cystic fibrosis gene carrier
V83.89 Other genetic carrier status

√4ᵗʰ **V84 Genetic susceptibility to disease**

> INCLUDES   confirmed abnormal gene

Use additional code, if applicable, for any associated family history of the disease (V16-V19)
AHA: 4Q, '04, 106

√5ᵗʰ **V84.0**   **Genetic susceptibility to malignant neoplasm**
Code first, if applicable, any current malignant neoplasms (140.0-195.8, 200.0-208.9, 230.0-234.9)
Use additional code, if applicable, for any personal history of malignant neoplasm (V10.0-V10.9)

V84.01 Genetic susceptibility to malignant neoplasm of breast
AHA: 4Q, '04, 107

V84.02 Genetic susceptibility to malignant neoplasm of ovary ♀

V84.03 Genetic susceptibility to malignant neoplasm of prostate ♂

V84.04 Genetic susceptibility to malignant neoplasm of endometrium ♀

V84.09 Genetic susceptibility to other malignant neoplasm

V84.8   **Genetic susceptibility to other disease**

▶BODY MASS INDEX (V85)◀

▲ √4ᵗʰ **V85 Body Mass Index [BMI]**
Kilograms per meters squared
Note: BMI adult codes are for use for persons over 20 years old
AHA: 4Q, '05, 97

V85.0   **Body Mass Index less than 19, adult** `A`

V85.1   **Body Mass Index between 19-24, adult** `A`

√5ᵗʰ **V85.2**   **Body Mass Index between 25-29, adult**
V85.21 Body Mass Index 25.0-25.9, adult `A`
V85.22 Body Mass Index 26.0-26.9, adult `A`
V85.23 Body Mass Index 27.0-27.9, adult `A`
V85.24 Body Mass Index 28.0-28.9, adult `A`
V85.25 Body Mass Index 29.0-29.9, adult `A`

√5ᵗʰ **V85.3**   **Body Mass Index between 30-39, adult**
V85.30 Body Mass Index 30.0-30.9, adult `A`
V85.31 Body Mass Index 31.0-31.9, adult `A`
V85.32 Body Mass Index 32.0-32.9, adult `A`
V85.33 Body Mass Index 33.0-33.9, adult `A`
V85.34 Body Mass Index 34.0-34.9, adult `A`
V85.35 Body Mass Index 35.0-35.9, adult `A`
V85.36 Body Mass Index 36.0-36.9, adult `A`
V85.37 Body Mass Index 37.0-37.9, adult `A`
V85.38 Body Mass Index 38.0-38.9, adult `A`
V85.39 Body Mass Index 39.0-39.9, adult `A`

V85.4   **Body Mass Index 40 and over, adult** `A`

● √5ᵗʰ **V85.5**   **Body Mass Index, pediatric**
Note: BMI pediatric codes are for use for persons age 2-20 years old. These percentiles are based on the growth charts published by the Centers for Disease Control and Prevention (CDC)

●   **V85.51 Body Mass Index, pediatric, less than 5th percentile for age** `P`

●   **V85.52 Body Mass Index, pediatric, 5th percentile to less than 85th percentile for age** `P`

●   **V85.53 Body Mass Index, pediatric, 85th percentile to less than 95th percentile for age** `P`

●   **V85.54 Body Mass Index, pediatric, greater than or equal to 95th percentile for age** `P`

▶ESTROGEN RECEPTOR STATUS (V86)◀

● √4ᵗʰ **V86 Estrogen receptor status**
Code first malignant neoplasm of breast (174.0-174.9, 175.0-175.9)

●   **V86.0**   **Estrogen receptor positive status [ER+]**

●   **V86.1**   **Estrogen receptor negative status [ER-]**

√4ᵗʰ √5ᵗʰ Additional Digit Required   Nonspecific PDx   Unacceptable PDx   Manifestation Code   `MCV` Major Cardiovascular Condition   ▶◀ Revised Text   ● New Code   ▲ Revised Code Title

2007 ICD•9•CM   **October 2006 • Volume 1 — 335**

SUPPLEMENTARY CLASSIFICATION OF EXTERNAL CAUSES OF INJURY AND POISONING (E800-E999)

This section is provided to permit the classification of environmental events, circumstances, and conditions as the cause of injury, poisoning, and other adverse effects. Where a code from this section is applicable, it is intended that it shall be used in addition to a code from one of the main chapters of ICD-9-CM, indicating the nature of the condition. Certain other conditions which may be stated to be due to external causes are classified in Chapters 1 to 16 of ICD-9-CM. For these, the "E" code classification should be used as an additional code for more detailed analysis.

Machinery accidents [other than those connected with transport] are classifiable to category E919, in which the fourth-digit allows a broad classification of the type of machinery involved. If a more detailed classification of type of machinery is required, it is suggested that the "Classification of Industrial Accidents according to Agency," prepared by the International Labor Office, be used in addition. This is reproduced in Appendix D for optional use.

Categories for "late effects" of accidents and other external causes are to be found at E929, E959, E969, E977, E989, and E999.

DEFINITIONS AND EXAMPLES RELATED TO TRANSPORT ACCIDENTS

(a) A **transport accident** (E800-E848) is any accident involving a device designed primarily for, or being used at the time primarily for, conveying persons or goods from one place to another.

> INCLUDES   accidents involving:
> aircraft and spacecraft (E840-E845)
> watercraft (E830-E838)
> motor vehicle (E810-E825)
> railway (E800-E807)
> other road vehicles (E826-E829)

In classifying accidents which involve more than one kind of transport, the above order of precedence of transport accidents should be used.

Accidents involving agricultural and construction machines, such as tractors, cranes, and bulldozers, are regarded as transport accidents only when these vehicles are under their own power on a highway [otherwise the vehicles are regarded as machinery]. Vehicles which can travel on land or water, such as hovercraft and other amphibious vehicles, are regarded as watercraft when on the water, as motor vehicles when on the highway, and as off-road motor vehicles when on land, but off the highway.

> EXCLUDES   *accidents:*
> *in sports which involve the use of transport but where the transport vehicle itself was not involved in the accident*
> *involving vehicles which are part of industrial equipment used entirely on industrial premises*
> *occurring during transportation but unrelated to the hazards associated with the means of transportation [e.g., injuries received in a fight on board ship; transport vehicle involved in a cataclysm such as an earthquake]*
> *to persons engaged in the maintenance or repair of transport equipment or vehicle not in motion, unlesss injured by another vehicle in motion*

(b) A **railway accident** is a transport accident involving a railway train or other railway vehicle operated on rails, whether in motion or not.

> EXCLUDES   *accidents:*
> *in repair shops*
> *in roundhouse or on turntable*
> *on railway premises but not involving a train or other railway vehicle*

(c) A **railway train** or **railway vehicle** is any device with or without cars coupled to it, desiged for traffic on a railway.

> INCLUDES   interurban:
> electric car ⎤ (operated chiefly on its
> streetcar   ⎟ own right-of-way,
>   ⎟ not open to other
>   ⎦ traffic)
>
> railway train, any power [diesel] [electric] [steam]
> funicular
> monorail or two-rail
> subterranean or elevated
> other vehicle designed to run on a railway track

> EXCLUDES   *interurban electric cars [streetcars] specified to be operating on a right-of-way that forms part of the public street or highway [definition (n)]*

(d) A **railway** or **railroad** is a right-of-way designed for traffic on rails, which is used by carriages or wagons transporting passengers or freight, and by other rolling stock, and which is not open to other public vehicular traffic.

(e) A **motor vehicle accident** is a transport accident involving a motor vehicle. It is defined as a motor vehicle traffic accident or as a motor vehicle nontraffic accident according to whether the accident occurs on a public highway or elsewhere.

> EXCLUDES   *injury or damage due to cataclysm*
> *injury or damage while a motor vehicle, not under its own power, is being loaded on, or unloaded from, another conveyance*

(f) A **motor vehicle traffic accident** is any motor vehicle accident occurring on a public highway [i.e., originating, terminating, or involving a vehicle partially on the highway]. A motor vehicle accident is assumed to have occurred on the highway unless another place is specified, except in the case of accidents involving only off-road motor vehicles which are classified as nontraffic accidents unless the contrary is stated.

(g) A **motor vehicle nontraffic accident** is any motor vehicle accident which occurs entirely in any place other than a public highway.

(h) A **public highway [trafficway]** or **street** is the entire width between property lines [or other boundary lines] of every way or place, of which any part is open to the use of the public for purposes of vehicular traffic as a matter of right or custom. A **roadway** is that part of the public highway designed, improved, and ordinarily used, for vehicular travel.

> INCLUDES   approaches (public) to:
> docks
> public building
> station

> EXCLUDES   *driveway (private)*
> *parking lot*
> *ramp*
> *roads in:*
> *airfield*
> *farm*
> *industrial premises*
> *mine*
> *private grounds*
> *quarry*

E Codes

(i) A **motor vehicle** is any mechanically or electrically powered device, not operated on rails, upon which any person or property may be transported or drawn upon a highway. Any object such as a trailer, coaster, sled, or wagon being towed by a motor vehicle is considerd a part of the motor vehicle.

INCLUDES   automobile [any type]
           bus
           construction machinery, farm and industrial machinery, steam roller, tractor, army tank, highway grader, or similar vehicle on wheels or treads, while in transport under own power
           fire engine (motorized)
           motorcycle
           motorized bicycle [moped] or scooter
           trolley bus not operating on rails
           truck
           van

EXCLUDES   *devices used solely to move persons or materials within the confines of a building and its premises, such as:*
           building elevator
           coal car in mine
           electric baggage or mail truck used solely within a railroad station
           electric truck used solely within an industrial plant
           moving overhead crane

(j) A **motorcycle** is a two-wheeled motor vehicle having one or two riding saddles and sometimes having a third wheel for the support of a sidecar. The sidecar is considered part of the motorcycle.

INCLUDES   motorized:
           bicycle [moped]
           scooter
           tricycle

(k) An **off-road motor vehicle** is a motor vehicle of special design, to enable it to negotiate rough or soft terrain or snow. Examples of special design are high construction, special wheels and tires, driven by treads, or support on a cushion of air.

INCLUDES   all terrain vehicle [ATV]
           army tank
           hovercraft, on land or swamp
           snowmobile

(l) A **driver** of a motor vehicle is the occupant of the motor vehicle operating it or intending to operate it. A **motorcyclist** is the driver of a motorcycle. Other authorized occupants of a motor vehicle are **passengers**.

(m) An **other road vehicle** is any device, except a motor vehicle, in, on, or by which any person or property may be transported on a highway.

INCLUDES   animal carrying a person or goods
           animal-drawn vehicles
           animal harnessed to conveyance
           bicycle [pedal cycle]
           streetcar
           tricycle (pedal)

EXCLUDES   *pedestrian conveyance [definition (q)]*

(n) A **streetcar** is a device designed and used primarily for transporting persons within a municipality, running on rails, usually subject to normal traffic control signals, and operated principally on a right-of-way that forms part of the traffic way. A trailer being towed by a streetcar is considered a part of the streetcar.

INCLUDES   interurban or intraurban electric or streetcar, when specified to be operating on a street or public highway
           tram (car)
           trolley (car)

(o) A **pedal cycle** is any road transport vehicle operated solely by pedals.

INCLUDES   bicycle
           pedal cycle
           tricycle

EXCLUDES   *motorized bicycle [definition (i)]*

(p) A **pedal cyclist** is any person riding on a pedal cycle or in a sidecar attached to such a vehicle.

(q) A **pedestrian conveyance** is any human powered device by which a pedestrian may move other than by walking or by which a walking person may move another pedestrian.

INCLUDES   baby carriage
           coaster wagon
           ice skates
           perambulator
           pushcart
           pushchair
           roller skates
           scooter
           skateboard
           skis
           sled
           wheelchair

(r) A **pedestrian** is any person involved in an accident who was not at the time of the accident riding in or on a motor vehicle, railroad train, streetcar, animal-drawn or other vehicle, or on a bicycle or animal.

INCLUDES   person:
           changing tire of vehicle
           in or operating a pedestrian conveyance
           making adjustment to motor of vehicle
           on foot

(s) A **watercraft** is any device for transporting passengers or goods on the water.

(t) A **small boat** is any watercraft propelled by paddle, oars, or small motor, with a passenger capacity of less than ten.

INCLUDES   boat NOS
           canoe
           coble
           dinghy
           punt
           raft
           rowboat
           rowing shell
           scull
           skiff
           small motorboat

EXCLUDES   *barge*
           lifeboat (used after abandoning ship)
           raft (anchored) being used as a diving platform
           yacht

(u) An **aircraft** is any device for transporting passengers or goods in the air.

INCLUDES   airplane [any type]
           balloon
           bomber
           dirigible
           glider (hang)
           military aircraft
           parachute

(v) A **commercial transport aircraft** is any device for collective passenger or freight transportation by air, whether run on commercial lines for profit or by government authorities, with the exception of military craft.

    Fourth-digit Required   ▶◀ Revised Text   ● New Code   ▲ Revised Code Title

RAILWAY ACCIDENTS (E800-E807)

Note: For definitions of railway accident and related terms see definitions (a) to (d).

> EXCLUDES   accidents involving railway train and:
>   aircraft (E840.0-E845.9)
>   motor vehicle (E810.0-E825.9)
>   watercraft (E830.0-E838.9)

The following fourth-digit subdivisions are for use with categories E800-E807 to identify the injured person:

.0 Railway employee
> Any person who by virtue of his employment in connection with a railway, whether by the railway company or not, is at increased risk of involvement in a railway accident, such as:
>   catering staff of train
>   driver
>   guard
>   porter
>   postal staff on train
>   railway fireman
>   shunter
>   sleeping car attendant

.1 Passenger on railway
> Any authorized person traveling on a train, except a railway employee.
>
> > EXCLUDES   intending passenger waiting at station (.8)
> >
> > unauthorized rider on railway vehicle (.8)

.2 Pedestrian
> See definition (r)

.3 Pedal cyclist
> See definition (p)

.8 Other specified person
> Intending passenger or bystander waiting at station
> Unauthorized rider on railway vehicle

.9 Unspecified person

✓4ᵗʰ E800 Railway accident involving collision with rolling stock

> INCLUDES   collision between railway trains or railway vehicles, any kind
> collision NOS on railway
> derailment with antecedent collision with rolling stock or NOS

✓4ᵗʰ E801 Railway accident involving collision with other object

> INCLUDES   collision of railway train with:
>   buffers
>   fallen tree on railway
>   gates
>   platform
>   rock on railway
>   streetcar
>   other nonmotor vehicle
>   other object
>
> > EXCLUDES   collision with:
> >   aircraft (E840.0-E842.9)
> >   motor vehicle (E810.0-E810.9, E820.0-E822.9)

✓4ᵗʰ E802 Railway accident involving derailment without antecedent collision

✓4ᵗʰ E803 Railway accident involving explosion, fire, or burning

> > EXCLUDES   explosion or fire, with antecedent derailment (E802.0-E802.9)
> > explosion or fire, with mention of antecedent collision (E800.0-E801.9)

✓4ᵗʰ E804 Fall in, on, or from railway train

> INCLUDES   fall while alighting from or boarding railway train
>
> > EXCLUDES   fall related to collision, derailment, or explosion of railway train (E800.0-E803.9)

✓4ᵗʰ E805 Hit by rolling stock

> INCLUDES   crushed
> injured
> killed   } by railway train or part
> knocked down
> run over
>
> > EXCLUDES   pedestrian hit by object set in motion by railway train (E806.0-E806.9)

✓4ᵗʰ E806 Other specified railway accident

> INCLUDES   hit by object falling in railway train
> injured by door or window on railway train
> nonmotor road vehicle or pedestrian hit by object set in motion by railway train
> railway train hit by falling:
>   earth NOS
>   rock
>   tree
>   other object
>
> > EXCLUDES   railway accident due to cataclysm (E908-E909)

✓4ᵗʰ E807 Railway accident of unspecified nature

> INCLUDES   found dead } on railway right-of-way
> injured   NOS
>
> railway accident NOS

MOTOR VEHICLE TRAFFIC ACCIDENTS (E810-E819)

Note: For definitions of motor vehicle traffic accident, and related terms, see definitions (e) to (k).

> EXCLUDES   accidents involving motor vehicle and aircraft (E840.0-E845.9)

The following fourth-digit subdivisions are for use with categories E810-E819 to identify the injured person:

.0 Driver of motor vehicle other than motorcycle
> See definition (1)

.1 Passenger in motor vehicle other than motorcycle
> See definition (1)

.2 Motorcyclist
> See definition (1)

.3 Passenger on motorcycle
> See definition (1)

.4 Occupant of streetcar

.5 Rider of animal; occupant of animal-drawn vehicle

.6 Pedal cyclist
> See definition (p)

.7 Pedestrian
> See definition (r)

.8 Other specified person
> Occupant of vehicle other than above
> Person in railway train involved in accident
> Unauthorized rider of motor vehicle

.9 Unspecified person

✓4ᵗʰ E810 Motor vehicle traffic accident involving collision with train

> > EXCLUDES   motor vehicle collision with object set in motion by railway train (E815.0-E815.9)
> > railway train hit by object set in motion by motor vehicle (E818.0-E818.9)

✓4ᵗʰ E811 Motor vehicle traffic accident involving re-entrant collision with another motor vehicle

> INCLUDES   collision between motor vehicle which accidentally leaves the roadway then re-enters the same roadway, or the opposite roadway on a divided highway, and another motor vehicle
>
> > EXCLUDES   collision on the same roadway when none of the motor vehicles involved have left and re-entered the highway (E812.0-E812.9)

✓4ᵗʰ Fourth-digit Required   ►◄ Revised Text   ● New Code   ▲ Revised Code Title

E Codes

E812–E819

§ ☑4ᵗʰ **E812 Other motor vehicle traffic accident involving collision with motor vehicle**

INCLUDES   collision with another motor vehicle parked, stopped, stalled, disabled, or abandoned on the highway
motor vehicle collision NOS

EXCLUDES   *collision with object set in motion by another motor vehicle (E815.0-E815.9)*
re-entrant collision with another motor vehicle (E811.0-E811.9)

§ ☑4ᵗʰ **E813 Motor vehicle traffic accident involving collision with other vehicle**

INCLUDES   collision between motor vehicle, any kind, and:
other road (nonmotor transport) vehicle, such as:
    animal carrying a person
    animal-drawn vehicle
    pedal cycle
    streetcar

EXCLUDES   *collision with:*
    object set in motion by nonmotor road vehicle (E815.0-E815.9)
    pedestrian (E814.0-E814.9)
nonmotor road vehicle hit by object set in motion by motor vehicle (E818.0-E818.9)

§ ☑4ᵗʰ **E814 Motor vehicle traffic accident involving collision with pedestrian**

INCLUDES   collision between motor vehicle, any kind, and pedestrian
pedestrian dragged, hit, or run over by motor vehicle, any kind

EXCLUDES   *pedestrian hit by object set in motion by motor vehicle (E818.0-E818.9)*

§ ☑4ᵗʰ **E815 Other motor vehicle traffic accident involving collision on the highway**

INCLUDES   collision (due to loss of control) (on highway) between motor vehicle, any kind, and:
    abutment (bridge) (overpass)
    animal (herded) (unattended)
    fallen stone, traffic sign, tree, utility pole
    guard rail or boundary fence
    interhighway divider
    landslide (not moving)
    object set in motion by railway train or road vehicle (motor) (nonmotor)
    object thrown in front of motor vehicle
    other object, fixed, movable, or moving
    safety island
    temporary traffic sign or marker
    wall of cut made for road

EXCLUDES   *collision with:*
    any object off the highway (resulting from loss of control) (E816.0-E816.9)
    any object which normally would have been off the highway and is not stated to have been on it (E816.0-E816.9)
    motor vehicle parked, stopped, stalled, disabled, or abandoned on highway (E812.0-E812.9)
    moving landslide (E909)
motor vehicle hit by object:
    set in motion by railway train or road vehicle (motor) (nonmotor) (E818.0-E818.9)
    thrown into or on vehicle (E818.0-E818.9)

§ ☑4ᵗʰ **E816 Motor vehicle traffic accident due to loss of control, without collision on the highway**

INCLUDES   motor vehicle:
    failing to make curve   and:
    going out of control   coliding with
    (due to):   object off
        blowout   the high-
        burst tire   way
        driver falling   overturning
          asleep   stopping
        driver inattention   abruptly
        excessive speed   off the
        failure of mech-   highway
          anical part

EXCLUDES   *collision on highway following loss of control (E810.0-E815.9)*
loss of control of motor vehicle following collision on the highway (E810.0-E815.9)

§ ☑4ᵗʰ **E817 Noncollision motor vehicle traffic accident while boarding or alighting**

INCLUDES   fall down stairs of motor bus
fall from car in street
injured by moving part of the vehicle   while boarding or alighting
trapped by door of motor bus

§ ☑4ᵗʰ **E818 Other noncollision motor vehicle traffic accident**

INCLUDES   accidental poisoning from exhaust gas generated by
breakage of any part of
explosion of any part of
fall, jump, or being accidentally pushed from
fire starting in   motor vehicle
hit by object thrown into or on   while in motion
injured by being thrown against some part of, or object in
injury from moving part of
object falling in or on
object thrown on

collision of railway train or road vehicle except motor vehicle, with object set in motion by motor vehicle
motor vehicle hit by object set in motion by railway train or road vehicle (motor) (nonmotor)
pedestrian, railway train, or road vehicle (motor) (nonmotor) hit by object set in motion by motor vehicle

EXCLUDES   *collision between motor vehicle and:*
    object set in motion by railway train or road vehicle (motor) (nonmotor) (E815.0-E815.9)
    object thrown towards the motor vehicle (E815.0-E815.9)
person overcome by carbon monoxide generated by stationary motor vehicle off the roadway with motor running (E868.2)

§ ☑4ᵗʰ **E819 Motor vehicle traffic accident of unspecified nature**

INCLUDES   motor vehicle traffic accident NOS
traffic accident NOS

---

§   Requires fourth-digit. See beginning of section E810-E819 for codes and definitions.

☑4ᵗʰ Fourth-digit Required   ►◄ Revised Text   ● New Code   ▲ Revised Code Title

MOTOR VEHICLE NONTRAFFIC ACCIDENTS (E820-E825)

Note: For definitions of motor vehicle nontraffic accident and related terms see definition (a) to (k).

`INCLUDES` accidents involving motor vehicles being used in recreational or sporting activities off the highway

collision and noncollision motor vehicle accidents occurring entirely off the highway

`EXCLUDES` *accidents involving motor vehicle and:*
aircraft (E840.0-E845.9)
watercraft (E830.0-E838.9)
accidents, not on the public highway, involving agricultural and construction machinery but not involving another motor vehicle (E919.0, E919.2, E919.7)

The following fourth-digit subdivisions are for use with categories E820-E825 to identify the injured person:

.0 Driver of motor vehicle other than motorcycle
See definition (l)

.1 Passenger in motor vehicle other than motorcycle
See definition (l)

.2 Motorcyclist
See definition (l)

.3 Passenger on motorcycle
See definition (l)

.4 Occupant of streetcar

.5 Rider of animal; occupant of animal-drawn vehicle

.6 Pedal cyclist
See definition (p)

.7 Pedestrian
See definition (r)

.8 Other specified person
Occupant of vehicle other than above
Person on railway train involved in accident
Unauthorized rider of motor vehicle

.9 Unspecified person

`√4ᵗʰ` **E820 Nontraffic accident involving motor-driven snow vehicle**

`INCLUDES` breakage of part of ⎫
fall from ⎪ motor-driven
hit by ⎬ snow
overturning of ⎪ vehicle (not
run over or dragged by ⎭ on public
highway)

collision of motor-driven snow vehicle with:
animal (being ridden) (-drawn vehicle)
another off-road motor vehicle
other motor vehicle, not on public highway
railway train
other object, fixed or movable
injury caused by rough landing of motor-driven snow vehicle (after leaving ground on rough terrain)

`EXCLUDES` *accident on the public highway involving motor driven snow vehicle (E810.0-E819.9)*

`√4ᵗʰ` **E821 Nontraffic accident involving other off-road motor vehicle**

`INCLUDES` breakage of part of ⎫
fall from ⎪ off-road motor
hit by ⎬ vehicle,
overturning of ⎪ except snow
run over or dragged by ⎪ vehicle (not
thrown against some ⎪ on public
part of or object in ⎭ highway)

collision with:
animal (being ridden) (-drawn vehicle)
another off-road motor vehicle, except snow vehicle
other motor vehicle, not on public highway
other object, fixed or movable

`EXCLUDES` *accident on public highway involving off-road motor vehicle (E810.0-E819.9)*
collision between motor driven snow vehicle and other off-road motor vehicle (E820.0-E820.9)
hovercraft accident on water (E830.0-E838.9)

`√4ᵗʰ` **E822 Other motor vehicle nontraffic accident involving collision with moving object**

`INCLUDES` collision, not on public highway, between motor vehicle, except off-road motor vehicle and:
animal
nonmotor vehicle
other motor vehicle, except off-road motor vehicle
pedestrian
railway train
other moving object

`EXCLUDES` *collision with:*
motor-driven snow vehicle (E820.0-E820.9)
other off-road motor vehicle (E821.0-E821.9)

`√4ᵗʰ` **E823 Other motor vehicle nontraffic accident involving collision with stationary object**

`INCLUDES` collision, not on public highway, between motor vehicle, except off-road motor vehicle, and any object, fixed or movable, but not in motion

`√4ᵗʰ` **E824 Other motor vehicle nontraffic accident while boarding and alighting**

`INCLUDES` fall ⎫ while boarding or
injury from moving ⎪ alighting from
part of motor ⎬ motor vehicle,
vehicle ⎪ except off-road
trapped by door of ⎪ motor vehicle, not
motor vehicle ⎭ on public highway

§ ☑4ᵗʰ **E825 Other motor vehicle nontraffic accident of other and unspecified nature**

INCLUDES

accidental poisoning from carbon monoxide generated by	
breakage of any part of	
explosion of any part of	
fall, jump, or being accidentally pushed from	motor vehicle while in motion, not on public highway
fire starting in	
hit by object thrown into, towards, or on	
injured by being thrown against some part of, or object in	
injury from moving part of	
object falling in or on	

motor vehicle nontraffic accident NOS

EXCLUDES　*fall from or in stationary motor vehicle (E884.9, E885.9)*
overcome by carbon monoxide or exhaust gas generated by stationary motor vehicle off the roadway with motor running (E868.2)
struck by falling object from or in stationary motor vehicle (E916)

OTHER ROAD VEHICLE ACCIDENTS (E826-E829)

Note: Other road vehicle accidents are transport accidents involving road vehicles other than motor vehicles. For definitions of other road vehicle and related terms see definitions (m) to (o).

INCLUDES　accidents involving other road vehicles being used in recreational or sporting activities

EXCLUDES　*collision of other road vehicle [any] with:*
aircraft (E840.0-E845.9)
motor vehicle (E813.0-E813.9, E820.0-E822.9)
railway train (E801.0-E801.9)

The following fourth-digit subdivisions are for use with categories E826-E829 to identify the injured person.

　.0 **Pedestrian**
　　　See definition (r)
　.1 **Pedal cyclist**
　　　See definition (p)
　.2 **Rider of animal**
　.3 **Occupant of animal-drawn vehicle**
　.4 **Occupant of streetcar**
　.8 **Other specified person**
　.9 **Unspecified person**

☑4ᵗʰ **E826 Pedal cycle accident**

[0-9]　INCLUDES

breakage of any part of pedal cycle
collision between pedal cycle and:
　animal (being ridden) (herded) (unattended)
　another pedal cycle
　any pedestrian
　nonmotor road vehicle
　other object, fixed, movable, or moving, not set in motion by motor vehicle, railway train, or aircraft
entanglement in wheel of pedal cycle
fall from pedal cycle
hit by object falling or thrown on the pedal cycle
pedal cycle accident NOS
pedal cycle overturned

☑4ᵗʰ **E827 Animal-drawn vehicle accident**

[0,2-4,8,9]　INCLUDES

breakage of any part of vehicle
collision between animal-drawn vehicle and:
　animal (being ridden) (herded) (unattended)
　nonmotor road vehicle, except pedal cycle
　pedestrian, pedestrian conveyance, or pedestrian vehicle
　other object, fixed, movable, or moving, not set in motion by motor vehicle, railway train, or aircraft

fall from	
knocked down by	
overturning of	animal-drawn vehicle
run over by	
thrown from	

EXCLUDES　*collision of animal-drawn vehicle with pedal cycle (E826.0-E826.9)*

☑4ᵗʰ **E828 Accident involving animal being ridden**

[0,2,4,8,9]　INCLUDES

collision between animal being ridden and:
　another animal
　nonmotor road vehicle, except pedal cycle, and animal-drawn vehicle
　pedestrian, pedestrian conveyance, or pedestrian vehicle
　other object, fixed, movable, or moving, not set in motion by motor vehicle, railway train, or aircraft

fall from	
knocked down by	animal being ridden
thrown from	
trampled by	

ridden animal stumbled and fell

EXCLUDES　*collision of animal being ridden with:*
animal-drawn vehicle (E827.0-E827.9)
pedal cycle (E826.0-E826.9)

☑4ᵗʰ **E829 Other road vehicle accidents**

[0,4,8,9]　INCLUDES

accident while boarding or alighting from	
blow from object in	streetcar
breakage of any part of	nonmotor road vehicle not classifiable to E826-E828
caught in door of-	
derailment of	
fall in, on, or from	
fire in	

collision between streetcar or nonmotor road vehicle, except as in E826-E828, and:
　animal (not being ridden)
　another nonmotor road vehicle not classifiable to E826-E828
　pedestrian
　other object, fixed, movable, or moving, not set in motion by motor vehicle, railway train, or aircraft
nonmotor road vehicle accident NOS
streetcar accident NOS

EXCLUDES　*collision with:*
animal being ridden (E828.0-E828.9)
animal-drawn vehicle (E827.0-E827.9)
pedal cycle (E826.0-E826.9)

§　Requires fourth-digit. Valid digits are in [brackets] under each code. See beginning of section E820-E825 for codes and definitions.

☑4ᵗʰ Fourth-digit Required　►◄ Revised Text　● New Code　▲ Revised Code Title

6 — E Codes　　　　　　　　　　　　　　　　　　　　　　　　　　　　　*2007 ICD•9•CM*

WATER TRANSPORT ACCIDENTS (E830-E838)

Note: For definitions of water transport accident and related terms see definitions (a), (s), and (t).

INCLUDES   watercraft accidents in the course of recreational activities

EXCLUDES   *accidents involving both aircraft, including objects set in motion by aircraft, and watercraft (E840.0-E845.9)*

The following fourth-digit subdivisions are for use with categories E830-E838 to identify the injured person:

.0 Occupant of small boat, unpowered

.1 Occupant of small boat, powered
See definition (t)
> **EXCLUDES** *water skier (.4)*

.2 Occupant of other watercraft — crew
Persons:
> engaged in operation of watercraft
> providing passenger services [cabin attendants, ship's physician, catering personnel]
> working on ship during voyage in other capacity [musician in band, operators of shops and beauty parlors]

.3 Occupant of other watercraft — other than crew
> Passenger
> Occupant of lifeboat, other than crew, after abandoning ship

.4 Water skier

.5 Swimmer

.6 Dockers, stevedores
> Longshoreman employed on the dock in loading and unloading ships

.8 Other specified person
> Immigration and custom officials on board ship
> Person:
>> accompanying passenger or member of crew visiting boat
> Pilot (guiding ship into port)

.9 Unspecified person

✓4ᵗʰ E830 Accident to watercraft causing submersion

INCLUDES   submersion and drowning due to:
> boat overturning
> boat submerging
> falling or jumping from burning ship
> falling or jumping from crushed watercraft
> ship sinking
> other accident to watercraft

✓4ᵗʰ E831 Accident to watercraft causing other injury

INCLUDES   any injury, except submersion and drowning, as a result of an accident to watercraft
> burned while ship on fire
> crushed between ships in collision
> crushed by lifeboat after abandoning ship
> fall due to collision or other accident to watercraft
> hit by falling object due to accident to watercraft
> injured in watercraft accident involving collision
> struck by boat or part thereof after fall or jump from damaged boat

EXCLUDES   *burns from localized fire or explosion on board ship (E837.0-E837.9)*

✓4ᵗʰ E832 Other accidental submersion or drowning in water transport accident

INCLUDES   submersion or drowning as a result of an accident other than accident to the watercraft, such as:
> fall:
>> from gangplank
>> from ship
>> overboard
> thrown overboard by motion of ship
> washed overboard

EXCLUDES   *submersion or drowning of swimmer or diver who voluntarily jumps from boat not involved in an accident (E910.0-E910.9)*

✓4ᵗʰ E833 Fall on stairs or ladders in water transport

EXCLUDES   *fall due to accident to watercraft (E831.0-E831.9)*

✓4ᵗʰ E834 Other fall from one level to another in water transport

EXCLUDES   *fall due to accident to watercraft (E831.0-E831.9)*

✓4ᵗʰ E835 Other and unspecified fall in water transport

EXCLUDES   *fall due to accident to watercraft (E831.0-E831.9)*

✓4ᵗʰ E836 Machinery accident in water transport

INCLUDES   injuries in water transport caused by:
> deck
> engine room
> galley } machinery
> laundry
> loading

✓4ᵗʰ E837 Explosion, fire, or burning in watercraft

INCLUDES   explosion of boiler on steamship
> localized fire on ship

EXCLUDES   *burning ship (due to collision or explosion) resulting in:*
> *submersion or drowning (E830.0-E830.9)*
> *other injury (E831.0-E831.9)*

✓4ᵗʰ E838 Other and unspecified water transport accident

INCLUDES   accidental poisoning by gases or fumes on ship
> atomic power plant malfunction in watercraft
> crushed between ship and stationary object [wharf]
> crushed between ships without accident to watercraft
> crushed by falling object on ship or while loading or unloading
> hit by boat while water skiing
> struck by boat or part thereof (after fall from boat)
> watercraft accident NOS

AIR AND SPACE TRANSPORT ACCIDENTS (E840-E845)

Note: For definition of aircraft and related terms see definitions (u) and (v).

The following fourth-digit subdivisions are for use with categories E840-E845 to identify the injured person. Valid fourth digits are in [brackets] under codes E842-E845.

.0 Occupant of spacecraft

.1 Occupant of military aircraft, any

Crew in military aircraft [air force] [army] [national guard] [navy]

Passenger (civilian) (military) in military aircraft [air force] [army] [national guard] [navy]

Troops in military aircraft [air force] [army] [national guard] [navy]

> **EXCLUDES** *occupants of aircraft operated under jurisdiction of police departments (.5)*
> *parachutist (.7)*

.2 Crew of commercial aircraft (powered) in surface to surface transport

.3 Other occupant of commercial aircraft (powered) in surface to surface transport

Flight personnel:
not part of crew
on familiarization flight
Passenger on aircraft (powered) NOS

.4 Occupant of commercial aircraft (powered) in surface to air transport

Occupant [crew] [passenger] of aircraft (powered) engaged in activities, such as:

aerial spraying (crops) (fire retardants)
air drops of emergency supplies
air drops of parachutists, except from military craft
crop dusting
lowering of construction material [bridge or telephone pole]
sky writing

.5 Occupant of other powered aircraft

Occupant [crew][passenger] of aircraft [powered] engaged in activities, such as:

aerobatic flying
aircraft racing
rescue operation
storm surveillance
traffic surveillance
Occupant of private plane NOS

.6 Occupant of unpowered aircraft, except parachutist

Occupant of aircraft classifiable to E842

.7 Parachutist (military) (other)

Person making voluntary descent

> **EXCLUDES** *person making descent after accident to aircraft (.1-.6)*

.8 Ground crew, airline employee

Persons employed at airfields (civil) (military) or launching pads, not occupants of aircraft

.9 Other person

✓4th E840 Accident to powered aircraft at takeoff or landing

> **INCLUDES**
> collision of aircraft with any object, fixed, movable, or moving
> crash
> explosion on aircraft
> fire on aircraft
> forced landing
> } while taking off or landing

✓4th E841 Accident to powered aircraft, other and unspecified

> **INCLUDES**
> aircraft accident NOS
> aircraft crash or wreck NOS
> any accident to powered aircraft while in transit or when not specified whether in transit, taking off, or landing
> collision of aircraft with another aircraft, bird, or any object, while in transit
> explosion on aircraft while in transit
> fire on aircraft while in transit

✓4th E842 Accident to unpowered aircraft

[6-9]

> **INCLUDES**
> any accident, except collision with powered aircraft, to:
> balloon
> glider
> hang glider
> kite carrying a person
> hit by object falling from unpowered aircraft

✓4th E843 Fall in, on, or from aircraft

[0-9]

> **INCLUDES**
> accident in boarding or alighting from aircraft, any kind
> fall in, on, or from aircraft [any kind], while in transit, taking off, or landing, except when as a result of an accident to aircraft

✓4th E844 Other specified air transport accidents

[0-9]

> **INCLUDES**
> hit by:
> aircraft
> object falling from aircraft
> injury by or from:
> machinery on aircraft
> rotating propeller
> voluntary parachute descent
> poisoning by carbon monoxide from aircraft while in transit
> } without accident to aircraft
> sucked into jet
> any accident involving other transport vehicle (motor) (nonmotor) due to being hit by object set in motion by aircraft (powered)

> **EXCLUDES** *air sickness (E903)*
> *effects of:*
> *high altitude (E902.0-E902.1)*
> *pressure change (E902.0-E902.1)*
> *injury in parachute descent due to accident to aircraft (E840.0-E842-9)*

✓4th E845 Accident involving spacecraft

[0,8,9]

> **INCLUDES** launching pad accident
> **EXCLUDES** *effects of weightlessness in spacecraft (E928.0)*

VEHICLE ACCIDENTS NOT ELSEWHERE CLASSIFIABLE (E846-E848)

E846 Accidents involving powered vehicles used solely within the buildings and premises of industrial or commercial establishment

Accident to, on, or involving:
- battery powered airport passenger vehicle
- battery powered trucks (baggage) (mail)
- coal car in mine
- logging car
- self propelled truck, industrial
- station baggage truck (powered)
- tram, truck, or tub (powered) in mine or quarry

Collision with:
- pedestrian
- other vehicle or object within premises

Explosion of ⎫
Fall from   ⎬ powered vehicle, industrial
Overturning of   ⎬   or commercial
Struck by   ⎭

EXCLUDES   accidental poisoning by exhaust gas from vehicle not elsewhere classifiable (E868.2)
injury by crane, lift (fork), or elevator (E919.2)

E847 Accidents involving cable cars not running on rails

Accident to, on, or involving:
- cable car, not on rails
- ski chair-lift
- ski-lift with gondola
- téléférique

Breakage of cable

Caught or dragged by ⎫
Fall or jump from   ⎬ cable car, not on rails
Object thrown from or in ⎭

E848 Accidents involving other vehicles, not elsewhere classifiable

Accident to, on, or involving:
- ice yacht
- land yacht
- nonmotor, nonroad vehicle NOS

✓4ᵗʰ E849 Place of occurrence

The following category is for use to denote the place where the injury or poisoning occurred.

E849.0 Home

Apartment	Private:
Boarding house	garage
Farm house	garden
Home premises	home
House (residential)	walk
Noninstitutional	Swimming pool in private
place of residence	house or garden
Private:	Yard of home
driveway	

EXCLUDES   home under construction but not yet occupied (E849.3)
institutional place of residence (E849.7)

E849.1 Farm

Farm:
- buildings
- land under cultivation

EXCLUDES   farm house and home premises of farm (E849.0)

E849.2 Mine and quarry

Gravel pit	Tunnel under
Sand pit	construction

E849.3 Industrial place and premises

Building under	Industrial yard
construction	Loading platform (factory)
Dockyard	(store)
Dry dock	Plant, industrial
Factory	Railway yard
building	Shop (place of work)
premises	Warehouse
Garage (place of work)	Workhouse

E849.4 Place for recreation and sport

Amusement park	Public park
Baseball field	Racecourse
Basketball court	Resort NOS
Beach resort	Riding school
Cricket ground	Rifle range
Fives court	Seashore resort
Football field	Skating rink
Golf course	Sports palace
Gymnasium	Stadium
Hockey field	Swimming pool, public
Holiday camp	Tennis court
Ice palace	Vacation resort
Lake resort	
Mountain resort	
Playground, including school playground	

EXCLUDES   that in private house or garden (E849.0)

E849.5 Street and highway

E849.6 Public building

Building (including adjacent grounds) used by the general public or by a particular group of the public, such as:

airport	music hall
bank	nightclub
café	office
casino	office building
church	opera house
cinema	post office
clubhouse	public hall
courthouse	radio broadcasting station
dance hall	restaurant
garage building (for	school (state) (public)
car storage)	(private)
hotel	shop, commercial
market (grocery or	station (bus) (railway)
other	store
commodity)	theater
movie house	

EXCLUDES   home garage (E849.0)
industrial building or workplace (E849.3)

E849.7 Residential institution

Children's home	Old people's home
Dormitory	Orphanage
Hospital	Prison
Jail	Reform school

E849.8 Other specified places

Beach NOS	Pond or pool (natural)
Canal	Prairie
Caravan site NOS	Public place NOS
Derelict house	Railway line
Desert	Reservoir
Dock	River
Forest	Sea
Harbor	Seashore NOS
Hill	Stream
Lake NOS	Swamp
Mountain	Trailer court
Parking lot	Woods
Parking place	

E849.9 Unspecified place

✓4ᵗʰ Fourth-digit Required   ▶◀ Revised Text   ● New Code   ▲ Revised Code Title

ACCIDENTAL POISONING BY DRUGS, MEDICINAL SUBSTANCES, AND BIOLOGICALS (E850-E858)

INCLUDES   accidental overdose of drug, wrong drug given or taken in error, and drug taken inadvertently

accidents in the use of drugs and biologicals in medical and surgical procedures

EXCLUDES   *administration with suicidal or homicidal intent or intent to harm, or in circumstances classifiable to E980-E989 (E950.0-E950.5, E962.0, E980.0-E980.5)*

correct drug properly administered in therapeutic or prophylactic dosage, as the cause of adverse effect (E930.0-E949.9)

See Alphabetic Index for more complete list of specific drugs to be classified under the fourth-digit subdivisions. The American Hospital Formulary numbers can be used to classify new drugs listed by the American Hospital Formulary Service (AHFS). See Appendix C.

✓4ᵗʰ E850 Accidental poisoning by analgesics, antipyretics, and antirheumatics

    E850.0 Heroin
        Diacetylmorphine

    E850.1 Methadone

    E850.2 Other opiates and related narcotics
        Codeine [methylmorphine]   Morphine
        Meperidine [pethidine]   Opium (alkaloids)

    E850.3 Salicylates
        Acetylsalicylic acid [aspirin]
        Amino derivatives of salicylic acid
        Salicylic acid salts

    E850.4 Aromatic analgesics, not elsewhere classified
        Acetanilid
        Paracetamol [acetaminophen]
        Phenacetin [acetophenetidin]

    E850.5 Pyrazole derivatives
        Aminophenazone [amidopyrine]
        Phenylbutazone

    E850.6 Antirheumatics [antiphlogistics]
        Gold salts   Indomethacin
        EXCLUDES   *salicylates (E850.3)*
                  steroids (E858.0)

    E850.7 Other non-narcotic analgesics
        Pyrabital

    E850.8 Other specified analgesics and antipyretics
        Pentazocine

    E850.9 Unspecified analgesic or antipyretic

E851 Accidental poisoning by barbiturates
    Amobarbital [amylobarbitone]   Pentobarbital [pentobarbitone]
    Barbital [barbitone]   Phenobarbital [phenobarbitone]
    Butabarbital [butabarbitone]   Secobarbital [quinalbarbitone]
    EXCLUDES   *thiobarbiturates (E855.1)*

✓4ᵗʰ E852 Accidental poisoning by other sedatives and hypnotics

    E852.0 Chloral hydrate group

    E852.1 Paraldehyde

    E852.2 Bromine compounds
        Bromides   Carbromal (derivatives)

    E852.3 Methaqualone compounds

    E852.4 Glutethimide group

    E852.5 Mixed sedatives, not elsewhere classified

    E852.8 Other specified sedatives and hypnotics

    E852.9 Unspecified sedative or hypnotic
        Sleeping:
          drug
          pill   } NOS
          tablet

✓4ᵗʰ E853 Accidental poisoning by tranquilizers

    E853.0 Phenothiazine-based tranquilizers
        Chlorpromazine   Prochlorperazine
        Fluphenazine   Promazine

    E853.1 Butyrophenone-based tranquilizers
        Haloperidol   Trifluperidol
        Spiperone

    E853.2 Benzodiazepine-based tranquilizers
        Chlordiazepoxide   Lorazepam
        Diazepam   Medazepam
        Flurazepam   Nitrazepam

    E853.8 Other specified tranquilizers
        Hydroxyzine   Meprobamate

    E853.9 Unspecified tranquilizer

✓4ᵗʰ E854 Accidental poisoning by other psychotropic agents

    E854.0 Antidepressants
        Amitriptyline
        Imipramine
        Monoamine oxidase [MAO] inhibitors

    E854.1 Psychodysleptics [hallucinogens]
        Cannabis derivatives   Mescaline
        Lysergide [LSD]   Psilocin
        Marihuana (derivatives)   Psilocybin

    E854.2 Psychostimulants
        Amphetamine   Caffeine
        EXCLUDES   *central appetite depressants (E858.8)*

    E854.3 Central nervous system stimulants
        Analeptics   Opiate antagonists

    E854.8 Other psychotropic agents

✓4ᵗʰ E855 Accidental poisoning by other drugs acting on central and autonomic nervous system

    E855.0 Anticonvulsant and anti-Parkinsonism drugs
        Amantadine
        Hydantoin derivatives
        Levodopa [L-dopa]
        Oxazolidine derivatives [paramethadione] [trimethadione]
        Succinimides

    E855.1 Other central nervous system depressants
        Ether
        Gaseous anesthetics
        Halogenated hydrocarbon derivatives
        Intravenous anesthetics
        Thiobarbiturates, such as thiopental sodium

    E855.2 Local anesthetics
        Cocaine   Procaine
        Lidocaine [lignocaine]   Tetracaine

    E855.3 Parasympathomimetics [cholinergics]
        Acetylcholine   Pilocarpine
        Anticholinesterase:
          organophosphorus
          reversible

    E855.4 Parasympatholytics [anticholinergics and antimuscarinics] and spasmolytics
        Atropine
        Homatropine
        Hyoscine [scopolamine]
        Quaternary ammonium derivatives

    E855.5 Sympathomimetics [adrenergics]
        Epinephrine [adrenalin]
        Levarterenol [noradrenalin]

    E855.6 Sympatholytics [antiadrenergics]
        Phenoxybenzamine
        Tolazoline hydrochloride

    E855.8 Other specified drugs acting on central and autonomic nervous systems

    E855.9 Unspecified drug acting on central and autonomic nervous systems

E856 Accidental poisoning by antibiotics

E857 Accidental poisoning by other anti-infectives

✓4ᵗʰ E858 Accidental poisoning by other drugs

    E858.0 Hormones and synthetic substitutes

    E858.1 Primarily systemic agents

    E858.2 Agents primarily affecting blood constituents

    E858.3 Agents primarily affecting cardiovascular system

    E858.4 Agents primarily affecting gastrointestinal system

---

✓4ᵗʰ Fourth-digit Required   ▶◀ Revised Text   ● New Code   ▲ Revised Code Title

E858.5   Water, mineral, and uric acid metabolism drugs

E858.6   Agents primarily acting on the smooth and skeletal muscles and respiratory system

E858.7   Agents primarily affecting skin and mucous membrane, ophthalmological, otorhinolaryngological, and dental drugs

E858.8   Other specified drugs
     Central appetite depressants

E858.9   Unspecified drug

ACCIDENTAL POISONING BY OTHER SOLID AND LIQUID SUBSTANCES, GASES, AND VAPORS (E860-E869)

Note: Categories in this section are intended primarily to indicate the external cause of poisoning states classifiable to 980-989. They may also be used to indicate external causes of localized effects classifiable to 001-799.

√4ᵗʰ **E860 Accidental poisoning by alcohol, not elsewhere classified**

E860.0   Alcoholic beverages
     Alcohol in preparations intended for consumption

E860.1   Other and unspecified ethyl alcohol and its products
     Denatured alcohol   Grain alcohol NOS
     Ethanol NOS   Methylated spirit

E860.2   Methyl alcohol
     Methanol   Wood alcohol

E860.3   Isopropyl alcohol
     Dimethyl carbinol   Rubbing alcohol subsitute
     Isopropanol   Secondary propyl alcohol

E860.4   Fusel oil
     Alcohol: Alcohol:
       amyl   propyl
       butyl

E860.8   Other specified alcohols

E860.9   Unspecified alcohol

√4ᵗʰ **E861 Accidental poisoning by cleansing and polishing agents, disinfectants, paints, and varnishes**

E861.0   Synthetic detergents and shampoos

E861.1   Soap products

E861.2   Polishes

E861.3   Other cleansing and polishing agents
     Scouring powders

E861.4   Disinfectants
     Household and other disinfectants not ordinarily used on the person
     EXCLUDES   *carbolic acid or phenol (E864.0)*

E861.5   Lead paints

E861.6   Other paints and varnishes
     Lacquers   Paints, other than lead
     Oil colors   White washes

E861.9   Unspecified

√4ᵗʰ **E862 Accidental poisoning by petroleum products, other solvents and their vapors, not elsewhere classified**

E862.0   Petroleum solvents
     Petroleum: Petroleum:
       ether   naphtha
       benzine

E862.1   Petroleum fuels and cleaners
     Antiknock additives to petroleum fuels
     Gas oils
     Gasoline or petrol
     Kerosene
     EXCLUDES   *kerosene insecticides (E863.4)*

E862.2   Lubricating oils

E862.3   Petroleum solids
     Paraffin wax

E862.4   Other specified solvents
     Benzene

E862.9   Unspecified solvent

√4ᵗʰ **E863 Accidental poisoning by agricultural and horticultural chemical and pharmaceutical preparations other than plant foods and fertilizers**
     EXCLUDES   *plant foods and fertilizers (E866.5)*

E863.0   Insecticides of organochlorine compounds
     Benzene hexachloride   Dieldrin
     Chlordane   Endrine
     DDT   Toxaphene

E863.1   Insecticides of organophosphorus compounds
     Demeton   Parathion
     Diazinon   Phenylsulphthion
     Dichlorvos   Phorate
     Malathion   Phosdrin
     Methyl parathion

E863.2   Carbamates
     Aldicarb   Propoxur
     Carbaryl

E863.3   Mixtures of insecticides

E863.4   Other and unspecified insecticides
     Kerosene insecticides

E863.5   Herbicides
     2, 4-Dichlorophenoxyacetic acid [2, 4-D]
     2, 4, 5-Trichlorophenoxyacetic acid [2, 4, 5-T]
     Chlorates
     Diquat
     Mixtures of plant foods and fertilizers with herbicides
     Paraquat

E863.6   Fungicides
     Organic mercurials (used in seed dressing)
     Pentachlorophenols

E863.7   Rodenticides
     Fluoroacetates   Warfarin
     Squill and derivatives   Zinc phosphide
     Thallium

E863.8   Fumigants
     Cyanides   Phosphine
     Methyl bromide

E863.9   Other and unspecified

√4ᵗʰ **E864 Accidental poisoning by corrosives and caustics, not elsewhere classified**
     EXCLUDES   *those as components of disinfectants (E861.4)*

E864.0   Corrosive aromatics
     Carbolic acid or phenol

E864.1   Acids
     Acid: Acid:
       hydrochloric   sulfuric
       nitric

E864.2   Caustic alkalis
     Lye

E864.3   Other specified corrosives and caustics

E864.4   Unspecified corrosives and caustics

√4ᵗʰ **E865 Accidental poisoning from poisonous foodstuffs and poisonous plants**
     INCLUDES   any meat, fish, or shellfish
           plants, berries, and fungi eaten as, or in mistake for, food, or by a child
     EXCLUDES   *anaphylactic shock due to adverse food reaction (995.60-995.69)*
           food poisoning (bacterial) (005.0-005.9)
           poisoning and toxic reactions to venomous plants (E905.6-E905.7)

E865.0   Meat

E865.1   Shellfish

E865.2   Other fish

E865.3   Berries and seeds

E865.4   Other specified plants

E865.5   Mushrooms and other fungi

E865.8   Other specified foods

E865.9   Unspecified foodstuff or poisonous plant

✓4ᵗʰ **E866 Accidental poisoning by other and unspecified solid and liquid substances**

> EXCLUDES   *these substances as a component of:*
> *medicines (E850.0-E858.9)*
> *paints (E861.5-E861.6)*
> *pesticides (E863.0-E863.9)*
> *petroleum fuels (E862.1)*

E866.0 **Lead and its compounds and fumes**

E866.1 **Mercury and its compounds and fumes**

E866.2 **Antimony and its compounds and fumes**

E866.3 **Arsenic and its compounds and fumes**

E866.4 **Other metals and their compounds and fumes**

> Beryllium (compounds)   Iron (compounds)
> Brass fumes   Manganese (compounds)
> Cadmium (compounds)   Nickel (compounds)
> Copper salts   Thallium (compounds)

E866.5 **Plant foods and fertilizers**

> EXCLUDES   *mixtures with herbicides (E863.5)*

E866.6 **Glues and adhesives**

E866.7 **Cosmetics**

E866.8 **Other specified solid or liquid substances**

E866.9 **Unspecified solid or liquid substance**

E867 Accidental poisoning by gas distributed by pipeline

> Carbon monoxide from incomplete combustion of piped gas
> Coal gas NOS
> Liquefied petroleum gas distributed through pipes (pure or mixed with air)
> Piped gas (natural) (manufactured)

✓4ᵗʰ **E868 Accidental poisoning by other utility gas and other carbon monoxide**

E868.0 **Liquefied petroleum gas distributed in mobile containers**

> Butane
> Liquefied hydrocarbon gas NOS } or carbon monoxide from incomplete combustion of these gases
> Propane

E868.1 **Other and unspecified utility gas**

> Acetylene
> Gas NOS used for lighting, heating, or cooking } or carbon monoxide from incomplete combustion of these gases
> Water gas

E868.2 **Motor vehicle exhaust gas**

> Exhaust gas from:
> farm tractor, not in transit
> gas engine
> motor pump
> motor vehicle, not in transit
> any type of combustion engine not in watercraft

> EXCLUDES   *poisoning by carbon monoxide from:*
> *aircraft while in transit (E844.0-E844.9)*
> *motor vehicle while in transit (E818.0-E818.9)*
> *watercraft whether or not in transit (E838.0-E838.9)*

E868.3 **Carbon monoxide from incomplete combustion of other domestic fuels**

> Carbon monoxide from incomplete combustion of:
> coal
> coke } in domestic stove or fireplace
> kerosene
> wood

> EXCLUDES   *carbon monoxide from smoke and fumes due to conflagration (E890.0-E893.9)*

E868.8 **Carbon monoxide from other sources**

> Carbon monoxide from:
> blast furnace gas
> incomplete combustion of fuels in industrial use
> kiln vapor

E868.9 **Unspecified carbon monoxide**

✓4ᵗʰ **E869 Accidental poisoning by other gases and vapors**

> EXCLUDES   *effects of gases used as anesthetics (E855.1, E938.2)*
> *fumes from heavy metals (E866.0-E866.4)*
> *smoke and fumes due to conflagration or explosion (E890.0-E899)*

E869.0 **Nitrogen oxides**

E869.1 **Sulfur dioxide**

E869.2 **Freon**

E869.3 **Lacrimogenic gas [tear gas]**

> Bromobenzyl cyanide   Ethyliodoacetate
> Chloroacetophenone

E869.4 **Second-hand tobacco smoke**

E869.8 **Other specified gases and vapors**

> Chlorine   Hydrocyanic acid gas

E869.9 **Unspecified gases and vapors**

MISADVENTURES TO PATIENTS DURING SURGICAL AND MEDICAL CARE (E870-E876)

> EXCLUDES   *accidental overdose of drug and wrong drug given in error (E850.0-E858.9)*
> *surgical and medical procedures as the cause of abnormal reaction by the patient, without mention of misadventure at the time of procedure (E878.0-E879.9)*

✓4ᵗʰ **E870 Accidental cut, puncture, perforation, or hemorrhage during medical care**

E870.0 **Surgical operation**

E870.1 **Infusion or transfusion**

E870.2 **Kidney dialysis or other perfusion**

E870.3 **Injection or vaccination**

E870.4 **Endoscopic examination**

E870.5 **Aspiration of fluid or tissue, puncture, and catheterization**

> Abdominal paracentesis   Lumbar puncture
> Aspirating needle biopsy   Thoracentesis
> Blood sampling

> EXCLUDES   *heart catheterization (E870.6)*

E870.6 **Heart catheterization**

E870.7 **Administration of enema**

E870.8 **Other specified medical care**

E870.9 **Unspecified medical care**

✓4ᵗʰ **E871 Foreign object left in body during procedure**

E871.0 **Surgical operation**

E871.1 **Infusion or transfusion**

E871.2 **Kidney dialysis or other perfusion**

E871.3 **Injection or vaccination**

E871.4 **Endoscopic examination**

E871.5 **Aspiration of fluid or tissue, puncture, and catheterization**

> Abdominal paracentesis   Lumbar puncture
> Aspiration needle biopsy   Thoracentesis
> Blood sampling

> EXCLUDES   *heart catheterization (E871.6)*

E871.6 **Heart catheterization**

E871.7 **Removal of catheter or packing**

E871.8 **Other specified procedures**

E871.9 **Unspecified procedure**

✓4ᵗʰ **E872 Failure of sterile precautions during procedure**

E872.0 **Surgical operation**

E872.1 **Infusion or transfusion**

E872.2 **Kidney dialysis and other perfusion**

E872.3 **Injection or vaccination**

E872.4 **Endoscopic examination**

E872.5 **Aspiration of fluid or tissue, puncture, and catheterization**

> Abdominal paracentesis   Lumbar puncture
> Aspiration needle biopsy   Thoracentesis
> Blood sampling

> EXCLUDES   *heart catheterization (E872.6)*

E872.6 Heart catheterization

E872.8 Other specified procedures

E872.9 Unspecified procedure

✓4ᵗʰ **E873 Failure in dosage**

> EXCLUDES *accidental overdose of drug, medicinal or biological substance (E850.0-E858.9)*

E873.0 Excessive amount of blood or other fluid during transfusion or infusion

E873.1 Incorrect dilution of fluid during infusion

E873.2 Overdose of radiation in therapy

E873.3 Inadvertent exposure of patient to radiation during medical care

E873.4 Failure in dosage in electroshock or insulin-shock therapy

E873.5 Inappropriate [too hot or too cold] temperature in local application and packing

E873.6 Nonadministration of necessary drug or medicinal substance

E873.8 Other specified failure in dosage

E873.9 Unspecified failure in dosage

✓4ᵗʰ **E874 Mechanical failure of instrument or apparatus during procedure**

E874.0 Surgical operation

E874.1 Infusion and transfusion
    Air in system

E874.2 Kidney dialysis and other perfusion

E874.3 Endoscopic examination

E874.4 Aspiration of fluid or tissue, puncture, and catheterization
    Abdominal paracentesis   Lumbar puncture
    Aspiration needle biopsy   Thoracentesis
    Blood sampling

> EXCLUDES *heart catheterization (E874.5)*

E874.5 Heart catheterization

E874.8 Other specified procedures

E874.9 Unspecified procedure

✓4ᵗʰ **E875 Contaminated or infected blood, other fluid, drug, or biological substance**

> INCLUDES presence of:
>   bacterial pyrogens
>   endotoxin-producing bacteria
>   serum hepatitis-producing agent

E875.0 Contaminated substance transfused or infused

E875.1 Contaminated substance injected or used for vaccination

E875.2 Contaminated drug or biological substance administered by other means

E875.8 Other

E875.9 Unspecified

✓4ᵗʰ **E876 Other and unspecified misadventures during medical care**

E876.0 Mismatched blood in transfusion

E876.1 Wrong fluid in infusion

E876.2 Failure in suture and ligature during surgical operation

E876.3 Endotracheal tube wrongly placed during anesthetic procedure

E876.4 Failure to introduce or to remove other tube or instrument

> EXCLUDES *foreign object left in body during procedure (E871.0-E871.9)*

E876.5 Performance of inappropriate operation

E876.8 Other specified misadventures during medical care
    Performance of inappropriate treatment NEC

E876.9 Unspecified misadventure during medical care

SURGICAL AND MEDICAL PROCEDURES AS THE CAUSE OF ABNORMAL REACTION OF PATIENT OR LATER COMPLICATION, WITHOUT MENTION OF MISADVENTURE AT THE TIME OF PROCEDURE (E878-E879)

> INCLUDES procedures as the cause of abnormal reaction, such as:
>   displacement or malfunction of prosthetic device
>   hepatorenal failure, postoperative
>   malfunction of external stoma
>   postoperative intestinal obstruction
>   rejection of transplanted organ

> EXCLUDES *anesthetic management properly carried out as the cause of adverse effect (E937.0-E938.9)*
> *infusion and transfusion, without mention of misadventure in the technique of procedure (E930.0-E949.9)*

✓4ᵗʰ **E878 Surgical operation and other surgical procedures as the cause of abnormal reaction of patient, or of later complication, without mention of misadventure at the time of operation**

E878.0 Surgical operation with transplant of whole organ
Transplantation of:	Transplantation of:
heart	liver
kidney	

E878.1 Surgical operation with implant of artificial internal device
| Cardiac pacemaker | Heart valve prosthesis |
| Electrodes implanted in brain | Internal orthopedic device |

E878.2 Surgical operation with anastomosis, bypass, or graft, with natural or artificial tissues used as implant
Anastomosis:	Graft of blood vessel,
arteriovenous	tendon, or skin
gastrojejunal	

> EXCLUDES *external stoma (E878.3)*

E878.3 Surgical operation with formation of external stoma
Colostomy	Gastrostomy
Cystostomy	Ureterostomy
Duodenostomy	

E878.4 Other restorative surgery

E878.5 Amputation of limb(s)

E878.6 Removal of other organ (partial) (total)

E878.8 Other specified surgical operations and procedures

E878.9 Unspecified surgical operations and procedures

✓4ᵗʰ **E879 Other procedures, without mention of misadventure at the time of procedure, as the cause of abnormal reaction of patient, or of later complication**

E879.0 Cardiac catheterization

E879.1 Kidney dialysis

E879.2 Radiological procedure and radiotherapy

> EXCLUDES *radio-opaque dyes for diagnostic x-ray procedures (E947.8)*

E879.3 Shock therapy
    Electroshock therapy
    Insulin-shock therapy

E879.4 Aspiration of fluid
    Lumbar puncture
    Thoracentesis

E879.5 Insertion of gastric or duodenal sound

E879.6 Urinary catheterization

E879.7 Blood sampling

E879.8 Other specified procedures
    Blood transfusion

E879.9 Unspecified procedure

✓4ᵗʰ Fourth-digit Required   ▶◀ Revised Text   ● New Code   ▲ Revised Code Title

ACCIDENTAL FALLS (E880-E888)

> EXCLUDES   *falls (in or from):*
> *burning building (E890.8, E891.8)*
> *into fire (E890.0-E899)*
> *into water (with submersion or drowning) (E910.0-E910.9)*
> *machinery (in operation) (E919.0-E919.9)*
> *on edged, pointed, or sharp object (E920.0-E920.9)*
> *transport vehicle (E800.0-E845.9)*
> *vehicle not elsewhere classifiable (E846-E848)*

✓4ᵗʰ **E880 Fall on or from stairs or steps**

    E880.0 Escalator

    E880.1 Fall on or from sidewalk curb
> EXCLUDES   *fall from moving sidewalk (E885.9)*

    E880.9 Other stairs or steps

✓4ᵗʰ **E881 Fall on or from ladders or scaffolding**

    E881.0 Fall from ladder

    E881.1 Fall from scaffolding

E882 Fall from or out of building or other structure

Fall from:	Fall from:
balcony	turret
bridge	viaduct
building	wall
flagpole	window
tower	Fall through roof

> EXCLUDES   *collapse of a building or structure (E916)*
> *fall or jump from burning building (E890.8, E891.8)*

✓4ᵗʰ **E883 Fall into hole or other opening in surface**

> INCLUDES

fall into:	fall into:
cavity	shaft
dock	swimming pool
hole	tank
pit	well
quarry	

> EXCLUDES   *fall into water NOS (E910.9)*
> *that resulting in drowning or submersion without mention of injury (E910.0-E910.9)*

    E883.0 Accident from diving or jumping into water [swimming pool]
Strike or hit:
against bottom when jumping or diving into water
wall or board of swimming pool
water surface
> EXCLUDES   *diving with insufficient air supply (E913.2)*
> *effects of air pressure from diving (E902.2)*

    E883.1 Accidental fall into well

    E883.2 Accidental fall into storm drain or manhole

    E883.9 Fall into other hole or other opening in surface

✓4ᵗʰ **E884 Other fall from one level to another**

    E884.0 Fall from playground equipment
> EXCLUDES   *recreational machinery (E919.8)*

    E884.1 Fall from cliff

    E884.2 Fall from chair

    E884.3 Fall from wheelchair

    E884.4 Fall from bed

    E884.5 Fall from other furniture

    E884.6 Fall from commode
Toilet

    E884.9 Other fall from one level to another

Fall from:	Fall from:
embankment	stationary vehicle
haystack	tree

✓4ᵗʰ **E885 Fall on same level from slipping, tripping, or stumbling**

    E885.0 Fall from (nonmotorized) scooter

    E885.1 Fall from roller skates
In-line skates

    E885.2 Fall from skateboard

    E885.3 Fall from skis

    E885.4 Fall from snowboard

    E885.9 Fall from other slipping, tripping, or stumbling
Fall on moving sidewalk

✓4ᵗʰ **E886 Fall on same level from collision, pushing, or shoving, by or with other person**
> EXCLUDES   *crushed or pushed by a crowd or human stampede (E917.1, E917.6)*

    E886.0 In sports
Tackles in sports
> EXCLUDES   *kicked, stepped on, struck by object, in sports (E917.0, E917.5)*

    E886.9 Other and unspecified
Fall from collision of pedestrian (conveyance) with another pedestrian (conveyance)

E887 Fracture, cause unspecified

✓4ᵗʰ **E888 Other and unspecified fall**
Accidental fall NOS   Fall on same level NOS

    E888.0 Fall resulting in striking against sharp object
Use additional external cause code to identify object (E920)

    E888.1 Fall resulting in striking against other object

    E888.8 Other fall

    E888.9 Unspecified fall
Fall NOS

ACCIDENTS CAUSED BY FIRE AND FLAMES (E890-E899)

> INCLUDES   asphyxia or poisoning due to conflagration or ignition
> burning by fire
> secondary fires resulting from explosion

> EXCLUDES   *arson (E968.0)*
> *fire in or on:*
> *machinery (in operation) (E919.0-E919.9)*
> *transport vehicle other than stationary vehicle (E800.0-E845.9)*
> *vehicle not elsewhere classifiable (E846-E848)*

✓4ᵗʰ **E890 Conflagration in private dwelling**

> INCLUDES

conflagration in:	conflagration in:
apartment	lodging house
boarding house	mobile home
camping place	private garage
caravan	rooming house
farmhouse	tenement
house	

conflagration originating from sources classifiable to E893-E898 in the above buildings

    E890.0 Explosion caused by conflagration

    E890.1 Fumes from combustion of polyvinylchloride [PVC] and similar material in conflagration

    E890.2 Other smoke and fumes from conflagration
Carbon monoxide ⎫
Fumes NOS   ⎬ from conflagration in private building
Smoke NOS   ⎭

    E890.3 Burning caused by conflagration

    E890.8 Other accident resulting from conflagration
Collapse of   ⎫
Fall from   ⎬ burning private building
Hit by object falling from ⎪
Jump from   ⎭

    E890.9 Unspecified accident resulting from conflagration in private dwelling

E Codes

✓4ᵗʰ E891 Conflagration in other and unspecified building or structure

Conflagration in:	Conflagration in:
barn	farm outbuildings
church	hospital
convalescent and other	hotel
residential home	school
dormitory of educational	store
institution	theater
factory	

Conflagration originating from sources classifiable to E893-E898, in the above buildings

E891.0 Explosion caused by conflagration

E891.1 Fumes from combustion of polyvinylchloride [PVC] and similar material in conflagration

E891.2 Other smoke and fumes from conflagration

Carbon monoxide ⎫ from conflagration in
Fumes NOS ⎬ building or
Smoke NOS ⎭ structure

E891.3 Burning caused by conflagration

E891.8 Other accident resulting from conflagration

Collapse of ⎫
Fall from ⎬ burning building or
Hit by object falling from ⎪ structure
Jump from ⎭

E891.9 Unspecified accident resulting from conflagration of other and unspecified building or structure

E892 Conflagration not in building or structure

Fire (uncontrolled) (in) (of):	Fire (uncontrolled) (in) (of):
forest	prairie
grass	transport vehicle [any],
hay	except while in
lumber	transit
mine	tunnel

✓4ᵗʰ E893 Accident caused by ignition of clothing

> EXCLUDES   ignition of clothing:
> *from highly inflammable material (E894)*
> *with conflagration (E890.0-E892)*

E893.0 From controlled fire in private dwelling

Ignition of clothing from:
normal fire (charcoal) (coal) ⎫ in private
(electric) (gas) (wood) in: ⎬ dwelling
brazier ⎪ (as listed
fireplace ⎪ in E890)
furnace ⎪
stove ⎭

E893.1 From controlled fire in other building or structure

Ignition of clothing from:
normal fire (charcoal) ⎫
(coal) (electric) ⎬ in other building or
(gas) (wood) in: ⎪ structure (as
brazier ⎪ listed in E81)
fireplace ⎪
furnace ⎪
stove ⎭

E893.2 From controlled fire not in building or structure

Ignition of clothing from:
bonfire (controlled)
brazier fire (controlled), not in building or structure
trash fire (controlled)

> EXCLUDES   *conflagration not in building (E892)*
> *trash fire out of control (E892)*

E893.8 From other specified sources

Ignition of clothing from:	Ignition of clothing from:
blowlamp	cigarette
blowtorch	lighter
burning bedspread	matches
candle	pipe
cigar	welding torch

E893.9 Unspecified source

Ignition of clothing (from controlled fire NOS) (in building NOS) NOS

E894 Ignition of highly inflammable material

Ignition of:
benzine ⎫
gasoline ⎪
fat ⎬ (with ignition of clothing)
kerosene ⎪
paraffin ⎪
petrol ⎭

> EXCLUDES   *ignition of highly inflammable material with:*
> *conflagration (E890.0-E892)*
> *explosion (E923.0-E923.9)*

E895 Accident caused by controlled fire in private dwelling

Burning by (flame of) normal fire
(charcoal) (coal) (electric) ⎫
(gas) (wood) in: ⎬ in private dwelling (as
brazier ⎪ listed in E890)
fireplace ⎪
furnace ⎪
stove ⎭

> EXCLUDES   *burning by hot objects not producing fire or*
> *flames (E924.0-E924.9)*
> *ignition of clothing from these sources (E893.0)*
> *poisoning by carbon monoxide from incomplete*
> *combustion of fuel (E867-E868.9)*
> *that with conflagration (E890.0-E890.9)*

E896 Accident caused by controlled fire in other and unspecified building or structure

Burning by (flame of) normal fire (charcoal) (coal) (electric)
(gas) (wood) in: ⎫
brazier ⎪ in other building or structure (as
fireplace ⎬ listed in E891)
furnace ⎪
stove ⎭

> EXCLUDES   *burning by hot objects not producing fire or*
> *flames (E924.0-E924.9)*
> *ignition of clothing from these sources (E893.1)*
> *poisoning by carbon monoxide from incomplete*
> *combustion of fuel (E867-E868.9)*
> *that with conflagration (E891.0-E891.9)*

E897 Accident caused by controlled fire not in building or structure

Burns from flame of: ⎫
bonfire ⎪
brazier fire, not in building or structure ⎬ controlled
trash fire ⎭

> EXCLUDES   *ignition of clothing from these sources (E893.2)*
> *trash fire out of control (E892)*
> *that with conflagration (E892)*

✓4ᵗʰ E898 Accident caused by other specified fire and flames

> EXCLUDES   *conflagration (E890.0-E892)*
> *that with ignition of:*
> *clothing (E893.0-E893.9)*
> *highly inflammable material (E894)*

E898.0 Burning bedclothes

Bed set on fire NOS

E898.1 Other

Burning by:	Burning by:
blowlamp	lamp
blowtorch	lighter
candle	matches
cigar	pipe
cigarette	welding torch
fire in room NOS	

E899 Accident caused by unspecified fire

Burning NOS

ACCIDENTS DUE TO NATURAL AND ENVIRONMENTAL FACTORS (E900-E909)

✓4ᵗʰ E900 Excessive heat

E900.0 Due to weather conditions

Excessive heat as the external cause of:
ictus solaris   sunstroke
siriasis

E900.1 Of man-made origin

Heat (in):	Heat (in):
boiler room	generated in transport
drying room	vehicle
factory	kitchen
furnace room	

E900.9 Of unspecified origin

✓4ᵗʰ **E901 Excessive cold**

E901.0 Due to weather conditions

Excessive cold as the cause of:
chilblains NOS
immersion foot

E901.1 Of man-made origin

Contact with or inhalation of:
dry ice
liquid air
liquid hydrogen
liquid nitrogen
Prolonged exposure in:
deep freeze unit
refrigerator

E901.8 Other specified origin

E901.9 Of unspecified origin

✓4ᵗʰ **E902 High and low air pressure and changes in air pressure**

E902.0 Residence or prolonged visit at high altitude

Residence or prolonged visit at high altitude as the
cause of:
Acosta syndrome
Alpine sickness
altitude sickness
Andes disease
anoxia, hypoxia
barotitis, barodontalgia, barosinusitis, otitic
barotrauma
hypobarism, hypobaropathy
mountain sickness
range disease

E902.1 In aircraft

Sudden change in air pressure in aircraft during
ascent or descent as the cause of:
aeroneurosis
aviators' disease

E902.2 Due to diving

High air pressure from		as the cause of:
rapid descent in water		caisson disease
Reduction in atmospheric		divers' disease
pressure while		divers' palsy or
surfacing from deep		paralysis
water diving		

E902.8 Due to other specified causes

Reduction in atmospheric pressure whilesurfacing
from underground

E902.9 Unspecified cause

E903 Travel and motion

✓4ᵗʰ **E904 Hunger, thirst, exposure, and neglect**

EXCLUDES any condition resulting from homicidal intent
(E968.0-E968.9)
hunger, thirst, and exposure resulting from
accidents connected with transport
(E800.0-E848)

E904.0 Abandonment or neglect of infants and helpless persons

Exposure to weather	} resulting from
conditions	abandonment
Hunger or thirst	or neglect

Desertion of newborn
Inattention at or after birth
Lack of care (helpless person) (infant)

EXCLUDES criminal [purposeful] neglect (E968.4)

E904.1 Lack of food

Lack of food as the cause of:
inanition
insufficient nourishment
starvation

EXCLUDES hunger resulting from abandonment or
neglect (E904.0)

E904.2 Lack of water

Lack of water as the cause of:
dehydration   inanition

EXCLUDES dehydration due to acute fluid loss
(276.51)

E904.3 Exposure (to weather conditions), not elsewhere classifiable

| Exposure NOS | Struck by hailstones |
| Humidity | |

EXCLUDES struck by lightning (E907)

E904.9 Privation, unqualified

Destitution

✓4ᵗʰ **E905 Venomous animals and plants as the cause of poisoning and toxic reactions**

INCLUDES chemical released by animal
insects
release of venom through fangs, hairs, spines,
tentacles, and other venom apparatus

EXCLUDES eating of poisonous animals or plants (E865.0-E865.9)

E905.0 Venomous snakes and lizards

Cobra	Mamba
Copperhead snake	Rattlesnake
Coral snake	Sea snake
Fer de lance	Snake (venomous)
Gila monster	Viper
Krait	Water moccasin

EXCLUDES bites of snakes and lizards known to
be nonvenomous (E906.2)

E905.1 Venomous spiders

| Black widow spider | Tarantula (venomous) |
| Brown spider | |

E905.2 Scorpion

E905.3 Hornets, wasps, and bees

Yellow jacket

E905.4 Centipede and venomous millipede (tropical)

E905.5 Other venomous arthropods

| Sting of: | Sting of: |
| ant | caterpillar |

E905.6 Venomous marine animals and plants

Puncture by sea	Sting of:
urchin spine	sea anemone
Sting of:	sea cucumber
coral	other marine animal
jelly fish	or plant
nematocysts	

EXCLUDES bites and other injuries caused by
nonvenomous marine animal
(E906.2-E906.8)
bite of sea snake (venomous) (E905.0)

E905.7 Poisoning and toxic reactions caused by other plants

Injection of poisons or toxins into or through skin by
plant thorns, spines, or other mechanisms

EXCLUDES puncture wound NOS by plant thorns
or spines (E920.8)

E905.8 Other specified

E905.9 Unspecified

| Sting NOS | Venomous bite NOS |

✓4ᵗʰ **E906 Other injury caused by animals**

EXCLUDES poisoning and toxic reactions caused by
venomous animals and insects (E905.0-
E905.9)
road vehicle accident involving animals (E827.0-
E828.9)
tripping or falling over an animal (E885.9)

✓4ᵗʰ Fourth-digit Required   ►◄ Revised Text   ● New Code   ▲ Revised Code Title

E906.0 Dog bite

E906.1 Rat bite

E906.2 Bite of nonvenomous snakes and lizards

E906.3 Bite of other animal except arthropod

Cats	Rodents, except rats
Moray eel	Shark

E906.4 Bite of nonvenomous arthropod

    Insect bite NOS

E906.5 Bite by unspecified animal

    Animal bite NOS

E906.8 Other specified injury caused by animal

    Butted by animal

    Fallen on by horse or other animal, not being ridden

    Gored by animal

    Implantation of quills of porcupine

    Pecked by bird

    Run over by animal, not being ridden

    Stepped on by animal, not being ridden

        EXCLUDES *injury by animal being ridden (E828.0-E828.9)*

E906.9 Unspecified injury caused by animal

E907 Lightning

    EXCLUDES *injury from:*
        fall of tree or other object caused by lightning (E916)
        fire caused by lightning (E890.0-E892)

✓4ᵗʰ E908 Cataclysmic storms, and floods resulting from storms

    EXCLUDES *collapse of dam or man-made structure causing flood (E909.3)*

E908.0 Hurricane

    Storm surge

    "Tidal wave" caused by storm action

    Typhoon

E908.1 Tornado

    Cyclone

    Twisters

E908.2 Floods

    Torrential rainfall

    Flash flood

        EXCLUDES *collapse of dam or man-made structure causing flood (E909.3)*

E908.3 Blizzard (snow) (ice)

E908.4 Dust storm

E908.8 Other cataclysmic storms

    Cloudburst

E908.9 Unspecified cataclysmic storms, and floods resulting from storms

    Storm NOS

✓4ᵗʰ E909 Cataclysmic earth surface movements and eruptions

E909.0 Earthquakes

E909.1 Volcanic eruptions

    Burns from lava

    Ash inhalation

E909.2 Avalanche, landslide, or mudslide

E909.3 Collapse of dam or man-made structure

E909.4 Tidalwave caused by earthquake

    Tidalwave NOS

    Tsunami

        EXCLUDES *tidalwave caused by tropical storm (E908.0)*

E909.8 Other cataclysmic earth surface movements and eruptions

E909.9 Unspecified cataclysmic earth surface movements and eruptions

ACCIDENTS CAUSED BY SUBMERSION, SUFFOCATION, AND FOREIGN BODIES (E910-E915)

✓4ᵗʰ E910 Accidental drowning and submersion

    INCLUDES immersion
            swimmers' cramp

    EXCLUDES *diving accident (NOS) (resulting in injury except drowning) (E883.0)*
        diving with insufficient air supply (E913.2)
        drowning and submersion due to:
            cataclysm (E908-E909)
            machinery accident (E919.0-E919.9)
            transport accident (E800.0-E845.9)
        effect of high and low air pressure (E902.2)
        injury from striking against objects while in running water (E917.2)

E910.0 While water-skiing

    Fall from water skis with submersion or drowning

        EXCLUDES *accident to water-skier involving a watercraft and resulting in submersion or other injury (E830.4, E831.4)*

E910.1 While engaged in other sport or recreational activity with diving equipment

Scuba diving NOS	Underwater spear
Skin diving NOS	fishing NOS

E910.2 While engaged in other sport or recreational activity without diving equipment

    Fishing or hunting, except from boat or with diving equipment

    Ice skating

    Playing in water

    Surfboarding

    Swimming NOS

    Voluntarily jumping from boat, not involved in accident, for swim NOS

    Wading in water

        EXCLUDES *jumping into water to rescue another person (E910.3)*

E910.3 While swimming or diving for purposes other than recreation or sport

    Marine salvage

    Pearl diving

    Placement of fishing nets   (with diving

    Rescue (attempt) of   equipment)

        another person

    Underwater construction

        or repairs

E910.4 In bathtub

E910.8 Other accidental drowning or submersion

Drowning in:	Drowning in:
quenching tank	swimming pool

E910.9 Unspecified accidental drowning or submersion

    Accidental fall into water NOS

    Drowning NOS

E911 Inhalation and ingestion of food causing obstruction of respiratory tract or suffocation

    Aspiration and inhalation of food [any] (into respiratory tract) NOS

    Asphyxia by
    Choked on   } food [including bone, seed in
    Suffocation by   food, regurgitated food]

    Compression of trachea
    Interruption of respiration   } by food lodged in
    Obstruction of respiration   esophagus

    Obstruction of pharynx by food (bolus)

        EXCLUDES *injury, except asphyxia and obstruction of respiratory passage, caused by food (E915)*
        obstruction of esophagus by food without mention of asphyxia or obstruction of respiratory passage (E915)

E912 Inhalation and ingestion of other object causing obstruction of respiratory tract or suffocation

Aspiration and inhalation of foreign body except food (into respiratory tract) NOS

Foreign object [bean] [marble] in nose

Obstruction of pharynx by foreign body

Compression

Interruption of respiration } by foreign body in

Obstruction of respiration } esophagus

> **EXCLUDES** *injury, except asphyxia and obstruction of respiratory passage, caused by foreign body (E915)*
> *obstruction of esophagus by foreign body without mention of asphyxia or obstruction in respiratory passage (E915)*

✓4ᵗʰ E913 Accidental mechanical suffocation

> **EXCLUDES** *mechanical suffocation from or by:*
> *accidental inhalation or ingestion of:*
> *food (E911)*
> *foreign object (E912)*
> *cataclysm (E908-E909)*
> *explosion (E921.0-E921.9, E923.0-E923.9)*
> *machinery accident (E919.0-E919.9)*

E913.0 In bed or cradle

> **EXCLUDES** *suffocation by plastic bag (E913.1)*

E913.1 By plastic bag

E913.2 Due to lack of air (in closed place)

Accidentally closed up in refrigerator or other airtight enclosed space

Diving with insufficient air supply

> **EXCLUDES** *suffocation by plastic bag (E913.1)*

E913.3 By falling earth or other substance

Cave-in NOS

> **EXCLUDES** *cave-in caused by cataclysmic earth surface movements and eruptions (E909)*
> *struck by cave-in without asphyxiation or suffocation (E916)*

E913.8 Other specified means

Accidental hanging, except in bed or cradle

E913.9 Unspecified means

Asphyxia, mechanical NOS   Suffocation NOS

Strangulation NOS

E914 Foreign body accidentally entering eye and adnexa

> **EXCLUDES** *corrosive liquid (E924.1)*

E915 Foreign body accidentally entering other orifice

> **EXCLUDES** *aspiration and inhalation of foreign body, any, (into respiratory tract) NOS (E911-E912)*

OTHER ACCIDENTS (E916-E928)

E916 Struck accidentally by falling object

Collapse of building, except on fire

Falling:

rock

snowslide NOS

stone

tree

Object falling from:

machine, not in operation

stationary vehicle

Code first:

collapse of building on fire (E890.0-E891.9)

falling object in:

cataclysm (E908-E909)

machinery accidents (E919.0-E919.9)

transport accidents (E800.0-E845.9)

vehicle accidents not elsewhere classifiable (E846-E848)

object set in motion by:

explosion (E921.0-E921.9, E923.0-E923.9)

firearm (E922.0-E922.9)

projected object (E917.0-E917.9)

✓4ᵗʰ E917 Striking against or struck accidentally by objects or persons

> **INCLUDES** bumping into or against
> colliding with
> kicking against } object (moving) (projected) (stationary)
> stepping on
> struck by } pedestrian conveyance person

> **EXCLUDES** *fall from:*
> *collision with another person, except when caused by a crowd (E886.0-E886.9)*
> *stumbling over object (E885.9)*
> *fall resulting in striking against object (E888.0, E888.1)*
> *injury caused by:*
> *assault (E960.0-E960.1, E967.0-E967.9)*
> *cutting or piercing instrument (E920.0-E920.9)*
> *explosion (E921.0-E921.9, E923.0-E923.9)*
> *firearm (E922.0-E922.9)*
> *machinery (E919.0-E919.9)*
> *transport vehicle (E800.0-E845.9)*
> *vehicle not elsewhere classifiable (E846-E848)*

E917.0 In sports without subsequent fall

Kicked or stepped on during game (football) (rugby)

Struck by hit or thrown ball

Struck by hockey stick or puck

E917.1 Caused by a crowd, by collective fear or panic without subsequent fall

Crushed

Pushed } by crowd or human stampede

Stepped on

E917.2 In running water without subsequent fall

> **EXCLUDES** *drowning or submersion (E910.0-E910.9)*
> *that in sports (E917.0, E917.5)*

E917.3 Furniture without subsequent fall

> **EXCLUDES** *fall from furniture (E884.2, E884.4-E884.5)*

E917.4 Other stationary object without subsequent fall

Bath tub

Fence

Lamp-post

E917.5 Object in sports with subsequent fall

Knocked down while boxing

E917.6 Caused by a crowd, by collective fear or panic with subsequent fall

E917.7 Furniture with subsequent fall

> **EXCLUDES** *fall from furniture (E884.2, E884.4-E884.5)*

E917.8 Other stationary object with subsequent fall

Bath tub

Fence

Lamp-post

E917.9 Other striking against with or without subsequent fall

E918 Caught accidentally in or between objects

Caught, crushed, jammed, or pinched in or between moving or stationary objects, such as:

escalator

folding object

hand tools, appliances, or implements

sliding door and door frame

under packing crate

washing machine wringer

> **EXCLUDES** *injury caused by:*
> *cutting or piercing instrument (E920.0-E920.9)*
> *machinery (E919.0-E919.9)*
> *transport vehicle (E800.0-E845.9)*
> *vehicle not elsewhere classifiable (E846-E848)*
> *struck accidentally by:*
> *falling object (E916)*
> *object (moving) (projected) (E917.0-E917.9)*

✓4ᵗʰ Fourth-digit Required   ►◄ Revised Text   ● New Code   ▲ Revised Code Title

☑4ᵗʰ **E919 Accidents caused by machinery**

INCLUDES

burned by
caught in (moving parts of)
collapse of
crushed by
cut or pierced by
drowning or submersion
    caused by
explosion of, on, in
fall from or into moving
    part of   } machinery
fire starting in or on   (accident)
mechanical suffocation
    caused by
object falling from, on, in
    motion by
overturning of
pinned under
run over by
struck by
thrown from

caught between machinery and other object
machinery accident NOS

EXCLUDES

accidents involving machinery, not in operation
    (E884.9, E916-E918)
injury caused by:
    electric current in connection with machinery
        (E925.0-E925.9)
    escalator (E880.0, E918)
    explosion of pressure vessel in connection
        with machinery (E921.0-E921.9)
    moving sidewalk (E885.9)
    powered hand tools, appliances, and
        implements (E916-E918, E920.0-
        E921.9, E923.0-E926.9)
    transport vehicle accidents involving
        machinery (E800.0-E848)
    poisoning by carbon monoxide generated by
        machine (E868.8)

E919.0 Agricultural machines

Animal-powered   Farm tractor
    agricultural machine   Harvester
Combine   Hay mower or rake
Derrick, hay   Reaper
Farm machinery NOS   Thresher

EXCLUDES   that in transport under own power on
    the highway (E810.0-E819.9)
that being towed by another vehicle on
    the highway (E810.0-E819.9,
    E827.0-E827.9, E829.0-E829.9)
that involved in accident classifiable to
    E820-E829 (E820.0-E829.9)

E919.1 Mining and earth-drilling machinery

Bore or drill (land) (seabed)   Shaft lift
Shaft hoist   Under-cutter

EXCLUDES   coal car, tram, truck, and tub in mine
    (E846)

E919.2 Lifting machines and appliances

Chain hoist
Crane
Derrick   } except in
Elevator (building) (grain)   agricultural
Forklift truck   or mining
Lift   operations
Pulley block
Winch

EXCLUDES   that being towed by another vehicle on
    the highway (E810.0-E819.9,
    E827.0-E827.9, E829.0-829.9)
that in transport under own power on
    the highway (E810.0-E819.9)
that involved in accident classifiable to
    E820-E829 (E820.0-E829.9)

E919.3 Metalworking machines

Abrasive wheel   Metal:
Forging machine   drilling machine
Lathe   milling machine
Mechanical shears   power press
        rolling-mill
        sawing machine

E919.4 Woodworking and forming machines

Band saw   Overhead plane
Bench saw   Powered saw
Circular saw   Radial saw
Molding machine   Sander

EXCLUDES   hand saw (E920.1)

E919.5 Prime movers, except electrical motors

Gas turbine
Internal combustion engine
Steam engine
Water driven turbine

EXCLUDES   that being towed by other vehicle on
    the highway (E810.0-E819.9,
    E827.0-E827.9, E829.0-E829.9)
that in transport under own power on
    the highway (E810.0-E819.9)

E919.6 Transmission machinery

Transmission: Transmission:
    belt   pinion
    cable   pulley
    chain   shaft
    gear

E919.7 Earth moving, scraping, and other excavating machines

Bulldozer   Steam shovel
Road scraper

EXCLUDES   that being towed by other vehicle on
    the highway (E810.0-E819.9,
    E827.0-E827.9, E829.0-E829.9)
that in transport under own power on
    the highway (E810.0-E819.9)

E919.8 Other specified machinery

Machines for manufacture of:
    clothing
    foodstuffs and beverages
    paper
Printing machine
Recreational machinery
Spinning, weaving, and textile machines

E919.9 Unspecified machinery

☑4ᵗʰ **E920 Accidents caused by cutting and piercing instruments or objects**

INCLUDES   object:
                              edged
accidental injury (by) }   pointed
                              sharp

E920.0 Powered lawn mower

E920.1 Other powered hand tools

Any powered hand tool [compressed air] [electric]
    [explosive cartridge] [hydraulic power], such as:
    drill
    hand saw
    hedge clipper
    rivet gun
    snow blower
    staple gun

EXCLUDES   band saw (E919.4)
    bench saw (E919.4)

E920.2 Powered household appliances and implements

Blender   Electric:
Electric: fan
    beater or mixer   knife
    can opener   sewing machine
        Garbage disposal appliance

E920.3 Knives, swords, and daggers

E920.4 Other hand tools and implements

Axe	Paper cutter
Can opener NOS	Pitchfork
Chisel	Rake
Fork	Scissors
Hand saw	Screwdriver
Hoe	Sewing machine, not powered
Ice pick	Shovel
Needle (sewing)	

E920.5 Hypodermic needle

    Contaminated needle
    Needle stick

E920.8 Other specified cutting and piercing instruments or objects

Arrow	Nail
Broken glass	Plant thorn
Dart	Splinter
Edge of stiff paper	Tin can lid
Lathe turnings	

> **EXCLUDES**   *animal spines or quills (E906.8)*
> *flying glass due to explosion (E921.0-E923.9)*

E920.9 Unspecified cutting and piercing instrument or object

✓4th **E921 Accident caused by explosion of pressure vessel**

> **INCLUDES**   accidental explosion of pressure vessels, whether or not part of machinery

> **EXCLUDES**   *explosion of pressure vessel on transport vehicle (E800.0-E845.9)*

E921.0 Boilers

E921.1 Gas cylinders

    Air tank
    Pressure gas tank

E921.8 Other specified pressure vessels

Aerosol can	Pressure cooker
Automobile tire	

E921.9 Unspecified pressure vessel

✓4th **E922 Accident caused by firearm, and air gun missile**

E922.0 Handgun

Pistol	Revolver

> **EXCLUDES**   *Verey pistol (E922.8)*

E922.1 Shotgun (automatic)

E922.2 Hunting rifle

E922.3 Military firearms

Army rifle	Machine gun

E922.4 Air gun

    BB gun
    Pellet gun

E922.5 Paintball gun

E922.8 Other specified firearm missile

    Verey pistol [flare]

E922.9 Unspecified firearm missile

    Gunshot wound NOS
    Shot NOS

✓4th **E923 Accident caused by explosive material**

> **INCLUDES**   flash burns and other injuries resulting from explosion of explosive material
> ignition of highly explosive material with explosion

> **EXCLUDES**   *explosion:*
> *in or on machinery (E919.0-E919.9)*
> *on any transport vehicle, except stationary motor vehicle (E800.0-E848)*
> *with conflagration (E890.0, E891.0,E892)*
> *secondary fires resulting from explosion (E890.0-E899)*

E923.0 Fireworks

E923.1 Blasting materials

    Blasting cap
    Detonator
    Dynamite
    Explosive [any] used in blasting operations

E923.2 Explosive gases

Acetylene	Fire damp
Butane	Gasoline fumes
Coal gas	Methane
Explosion in mine NOS	Propane

E923.8 Other explosive materials

Bomb	Torpedo
Explosive missile	Explosion in munitions:
Grenade	dump
Mine	factory
Shell	

E923.9 Unspecified explosive material

    Explosion NOS

✓4th **E924 Accident caused by hot substance or object, caustic or corrosive material, and steam**

> **EXCLUDES**   *burning NOS (E899)*
> *chemical burn resulting from swallowing a corrosive substance (E860.0-E864.4)*
> *fire caused by these substances and objects (E890.0-E894)*
> *radiation burns (E926.0-E926.9)*
> *therapeutic misadventures (E870.0-E876.9)*

E924.0 Hot liquids and vapors, including steam

    Burning or scalding by:
      boiling water
      hot or boiling liquids not primarily caustic or corrosive
      liquid metal
      steam
      other hot vapor

> **EXCLUDES**   *hot (boiling) tap water (E924.2)*

E924.1 Caustic and corrosive substances

Burning by:	Burning by:
acid [any kind]	corrosive substance
ammonia	lye
caustic oven cleaner	vitriol
or other substance	

E924.2 Hot (boiling) tap water

E924.8 Other

    Burning by:
      heat from electric heating appliance
      hot object NOS
      light bulb
      steam pipe

E924.9 Unspecified

✓4th **E925 Accident caused by electric current**

> **INCLUDES**   electric current from exposed wire, faulty appliance, high voltage cable, live rail, or open electric socket as the cause of:
>   burn
>   cardiac fibrillation
>   convulsion
>   electric shock
>   electrocution
>   puncture wound
>   respiratory paralysis

> **EXCLUDES**   *burn by heat from electrical appliance (E924.8)*
> *lightning (E907)*

E925.0 Domestic wiring and appliances

E925.1 Electric power generating plants, distribution stations, transmission lines

    Broken power line

E925.2 Industrial wiring, appliances, and electrical machinery

Conductors	Electrical equipment and
Control apparatus	machinery
	Transformers

E925.8 Other electric current

    Wiring and appliances in or on:
      farm [not farmhouse]
      outdoors
      public building
      residential institutions
      schools

✓4th Fourth-digit Required   ▶◀ Revised Text   ● New Code   ▲ Revised Code Title

E925.9 Unspecified electric current
Burns or other injury from electric current NOS
Electric shock NOS
Electrocution NOS

☑️4ᵗʰ E926 Exposure to radiation

> EXCLUDES *abnormal reaction to or complication of treatment without mention of misadventure (E879.2)*
> *atomic power plant malfunction in water transport (E838.0-E838.9)*
> *misadventure to patient in surgical and medical procedures (E873.2-E873.3)*
> *use of radiation in war operations (E996-E997.9)*

E926.0 Radiofrequency radiation

Overexposure to:	from:
microwave radiation	high-powered radio and television transmitters
radar radiation	industrial
radiofrequency	radiofrequency
radiofrequency radiation [any]	induction heaters radar installations

E926.1 Infrared heaters and lamps
Exposure to infrared radiation from heaters and lamps as the cause of:
blistering
burning
charring
inflammatory change

> EXCLUDES *physical contact with heater or lamp (E924.8)*

E926.2 Visible and ultraviolet light sources

Arc lamps	Oxygas welding torch
Black light sources	Sun rays
Electrical welding arc	Tanning bed

> EXCLUDES *excessive heat from these sources (E900.1-E900.9)*

E926.3 X-rays and other electromagnetic ionizing radiation

Gamma rays	X-rays (hard) (soft)

E926.4 Lasers

E926.5 Radioactive isotopes

Radiobiologicals	Radiopharmaceuticals

E926.8 Other specified radiation
Artificially accelerated beams of ionized particles generated by:
betatrons
synchrotrons

E926.9 Unspecified radiation
Radiation NOS

E927 Overexertion and strenuous movements

Excessive physical exercise	Strenuous movements in:
Overexertion (from):	recreational activities
lifting	other activities
pulling	
pushing	

☑️4ᵗʰ E928 Other and unspecified environmental and accidental causes

E928.0 Prolonged stay in weightless environment
Weightlessness in spacecraft (simulator)

E928.1 Exposure to noise

Noise (pollution)	Supersonic waves
Sound waves	

E928.2 Vibration

E928.3 Human bite

E928.4 External constriction caused by hair

E928.5 External constriction caused by other object

E928.8 Other

E928.9 Unspecified accident

Accident NOS	
Blow NOS	stated as accidentally
Casualty (not due to war)	inflicted
Decapitation	

Knocked down	
Killed	stated as accidentally
Injury [any part of body, or unspecified]	inflicted, but not otherwise specified
Mangled	
Wound	

> EXCLUDES *fracture, cause unspecified (E887)*
> *injuries undetermined whether accidentally or purposely inflicted (E980.0-E989)*

LATE EFFECTS OF ACCIDENTAL INJURY (E929)

Note: This category is to be used to indicate accidental injury as the cause of death or disability from late effects, which are themselves classifiable elsewhere. The "late effects" include conditions reported as such, or as sequelae which may occur at any time after the attempted suicide or self-inflicted injury.

☑️4ᵗʰ E929 Late effects of accidental injury

> EXCLUDES *late effects of:*
> *surgical and medical procedures (E870.0-E879.9)*
> *therapeutic use of drugs and medicines (E930.0-E949.9)*

E929.0 Late effects of motor vehicle accident
Late effects of accidents classifiable to E810-E825

E929.1 Late effects of other transport accident
Late effects of accidents classifiable to E800-E807, E826-E838, E840-E848

E929.2 Late effects of accidental poisoning
Late effects of accidents classifiable to E850-E858, E860-E869

E929.3 Late effects of accidental fall
Late effects of accidents classifiable to E880-E888

E929.4 Late effects of accident caused by fire
Late effects of accidents classifiable to E890-E899

E929.5 Late effects of accident due to natural and environmental factors
Late effects of accidents classifiable to E900-E909

E929.8 Late effects of other accidents
Late effects of accidents classifiable to E910-E928.8

E929.9 Late effects of unspecified accident
Late effects of accidents classifiable to E928.9

DRUGS, MEDICINAL AND BIOLOGICAL SUBSTANCES CAUSING ADVERSE EFFECTS IN THERAPEUTIC USE (E930-E949)

> INCLUDES correct drug properly administered in therapeutic or prophylactic dosage, as the cause of any adverse effect including allergic or hypersensitivity reactions

> EXCLUDES *accidental overdose of drug and wrong drug given or taken in error (E850.0-E858.9)*
> *accidents in the technique of administration of drug or biological substance, such as accidental puncture during injection, or contamination of drug (E870.0-E876.9)*
> *administration with suicidal or homicidal intent or intent to harm, or in circumstances classifiable to E980-E989 (E950.0-E950.5, E962.0, E980.0-E980.5)*

See Alphabetic Index for more complete list of specific drugs to be classified under the fourth-digit subdivisions. The American Hospital Formulary numbers can be used to classify new drugs listed by the American Hospital Formulary Service (AHFS). See Appendix C.

☑️4ᵗʰ E930 Antibiotics

> EXCLUDES *that used as eye, ear, nose, and throat [ENT], and local anti-infectives (E946.0-E946.9)*

☑️4ᵗʰ Fourth-digit Required   ▶◀ Revised Text   ● New Code   ▲ Revised Code Title

E Codes

E930.0–E934.4

E930.0 Penicillins
Natural
Synthetic
Semisynthetic, such as:
  ampicillin
Semisynthetic, such as:
  cloxacillin
  nafcillin
  oxacillin

E930.1 Antifungal antibiotics
Amphotericin B
Griseofulvin
Hachimycin [trichomycin]
Nystatin

E930.2 Chloramphenicol group
Chloramphenicol
Thiamphenicol

E930.3 Erythromycin and other macrolides
Oleandomycin
Spiramycin

E930.4 Tetracycline group
Doxycycline
Minocycline
Oxytetracycline

E930.5 Cephalosporin group
Cephalexin
Cephaloglycin
Cephaloridine
Cephalothin

E930.6 Antimycobacterial antibiotics
Cycloserine
Kanamycin
Rifampin
Streptomycin

E930.7 Antineoplastic antibiotics
Actinomycins, such as:
  Bleomycin
  Cactinomycin
  Dactinomycin
Actinomycins, such as:
  Daunorubicin
  Mitomycin
EXCLUDES *other antineoplastic drugs (E933.1)*

E930.8 Other specified antibiotics

E930.9 Unspecified antibiotic

√4ᵗʰ **E931 Other anti-infectives**
EXCLUDES *ENT, and local anti-infectives (E946.0-E946.9)*

E931.0 Sulfonamides
Sulfadiazine
Sulfafurazole
Sulfamethoxazole

E931.1 Arsenical anti-infectives

E931.2 Heavy metal anti-infectives
Compounds of:
  antimony
  bismuth
Compounds of:
  lead
  mercury
EXCLUDES *mercurial diuretics (E944.0)*

E931.3 Quinoline and hydroxyquinoline derivatives
Chiniofon
Diiodohydroxyquin
EXCLUDES *antimalarial drugs (E931.4)*

E931.4 Antimalarials and drugs acting on other blood protozoa
Chloroquine phosphate
Cycloguanil
Primaquine
Proguanil [chloroguanide]
Pyrimethamine
Quinine (sulphate)

E931.5 Other antiprotozoal drugs
Emetine

E931.6 Anthelmintics
Hexylresorcinol
Male fern oleoresin
Piperazine
Thiabendazole

E931.7 Antiviral drugs
Methisazone
EXCLUDES *amantadine (E936.4)*
cytarabine (E933.1)
idoxuridine (E946.5)

E931.8 Other antimycobacterial drugs
Ethambutol
Ethionamide
Isoniazid
Para-aminosalicylic
  acid derivatives
Sulfones

E931.9 Other and unspecified anti-infectives
Flucytosine
Nitrofuranderivatives

√4ᵗʰ **E932 Hormones and synthetic substitutes**

E932.0 Adrenal cortical steroids
Cortisone derivatives
Desoxycorticosterone derivatives
Fluorinated corticosteroid

E932.1 Androgens and anabolic congeners
Nandrolone phenpropionate
Oxymetholone
Testosterone and preparations

E932.2 Ovarian hormones and synthetic substitutes
Contraceptives, oral
Estrogens
Estrogens and progestogens combined
Progestogens

E932.3 Insulins and antidiabetic agents
Acetohexamide
Biguanide derivatives, oral
Chlorpropamide
Glucagon
Insulin
Phenformin
Sulfonylurea
  derivatives,
  oral
Tolbutamide
EXCLUDES *adverse effect of insulin administered for shock therapy (E879.3)*

E932.4 Anterior pituitary hormones
Corticotropin
Gonadotropin
Somatotropin [growth hormone]

E932.5 Posterior pituitary hormones
Vasopressin
EXCLUDES *oxytocic agents (E945.0)*

E932.6 Parathyroid and parathyroid derivatives

E932.7 Thyroid and thyroid derivatives
Dextrothyroxine
Levothyroxine sodium
Liothyronine
Thyroglobulin

E932.8 Antithyroid agents
Iodides
Thiouracil
Thiourea

E932.9 Other and unspecified hormones and synthetic substitutes

√4ᵗʰ **E933 Primarily systemic agents**

E933.0 Antiallergic and antiemetic drugs
Antihistamines
Chlorpheniramine
Diphenhydramine
Diphenylpyraline
Thonzylamine
Tripelennamine
EXCLUDES *phenothiazine-based tranquilizers (E939.1)*

E933.1 Antineoplastic and immunosuppressive drugs
Azathioprine
Busulfan
Chlorambucil
Cyclophosphamide
Cytarabine
Fluorouracil
Mechlorethamine hydrochloride
Mercaptopurine
Triethylenethiophosphoramide [thio-TEPA]
EXCLUDES *antineoplastic antibiotics (E930.7)*

E933.2 Acidifying agents

E933.3 Alkalizing agents

E933.4 Enzymes, not elsewhere classified
Penicillinase

E933.5 Vitamins, not elsewhere classified
Vitamin A
Vitamin D
EXCLUDES *nicotinic acid (E942.2)*
vitamin K (E934.3)

E933.8 Other systemic agents, not elsewhere classified
Heavy metal antagonists

E933.9 Unspecified systemic agent

√4ᵗʰ **E934 Agents primarily affecting blood constituents**

E934.0 Iron and its compounds
Ferric salts
Ferrous sulphate and other ferrous salts

E934.1 Liver preparations and other antianemic agents
Folic acid

E934.2 Anticoagulants
Coumarin
Heparin
Phenindione
Prothrombin synthesis
  inhibitor
Warfarin sodium

E934.3 Vitamin K [phytonadione]

E934.4 Fibrinolysis-affecting drugs
Aminocaproic acid
Streptodornase
Streptokinase
Urokinase

√4ᵗʰ Fourth-digit Required   ▶◀ Revised Text   ● New Code   ▲ Revised Code Title

E Codes

E934.5–E941.0

E934.5 Anticoagulant antagonists and other coagulants
Hexadimethrine bromide
Protamine sulfate

E934.6 Gamma globulin

E934.7 Natural blood and blood products
Blood plasma   Packed red cells
Human fibrinogen   Whole blood

E934.8 Other agents affecting blood constituents
Macromolecular blood substitutes

E934.9 Unspecified agent affecting blood constituents

✓4ᵗʰ **E935 Analgesics, antipyretics, and antirheumatics**

E935.0 Heroin
Diacetylmorphine

E935.1 Methadone

E935.2 Other opiates and related narcotics
Codeine [methylmorphine]   Morphine
Meperidine [pethidine]   Opium (alkaloids)

E935.3 Salicylates
Acetylsalicylic acid [aspirin]
Amino derivatives of salicylic acid
Salicylic acid salts

E935.4 Aromatic analgesics, not elsewhere classified
Acetanilid
Paracetamol [acetaminophen]
Phenacetin [acetophenetidin]

E935.5 Pyrazole derivatives
Aminophenazone [aminopyrine]
Phenylbutazone

E935.6 Antirheumatics [antiphlogistics]
Gold salts   Indomethacin
    EXCLUDES salicylates (E935.3)
                  steroids (E932.0)

E935.7 Other non-narcotic analgesics
Pyrabital

E935.8 Other specified analgesics and antipyretics
Pentazocine

E935.9 Unspecified analgesic and antipyretic

✓4ᵗʰ **E936 Anticonvulsants and anti-Parkinsonism drugs**

E936.0 Oxazolidine derivatives
Paramethadione
Trimethadione

E936.1 Hydantoin derivatives
Phenytoin

E936.2 Succinimides
Ethosuximide
Phensuximide

E936.3 Other and unspecified anticonvulsants
Beclamide
Primidone

E936.4 Anti-Parkinsonism drugs
Amantadine
Ethopropazine [profenamine]
Levodopa [L-dopa]

✓4ᵗʰ **E937 Sedatives and hypnotics**

E937.0 Barbiturates
Amobarbital [amylobarbitone]
Barbital [barbitone]
Butabarbital [butabarbitone]
Pentobarbital [pentobarbitone]
Phenobarbital [phenobarbitone]
Secobarbital [quinalbarbitone]
    EXCLUDES thiobarbiturates (E938.3)

E937.1 Chloral hydrate group

E937.2 Paraldehyde

E937.3 Bromine compounds
Bromide
Carbromal (derivatives)

E937.4 Methaqualone compounds

E937.5 Glutethimide group

E937.6 Mixed sedatives, not elsewhere classified

E937.8 Other sedatives and hypnotics

E937.9 Unspecified
Sleeping:
drug ⎫
pill ⎬ NOS
tablet ⎭

✓4ᵗʰ **E938 Other central nervous system depressants and anesthetics**

E938.0 Central nervous system muscle-tone depressants
Chlorphenesin (carbamate)
Mephenesin
Methocarbamol

E938.1 Halothane

E938.2 Other gaseous anesthetics
Ether
Halogenated hydrocarbon derivatives, except
    halothane
Nitrous oxide

E938.3 Intravenous anesthetics
Ketamine
Methohexital [methohexitone]
Thiobarbiturates, such as thiopental sodium

E938.4 Other and unspecified general anesthetics

E938.5 Surface and infiltration anesthetics
Cocaine   Procaine
Lidocaine [lignocaine] Tetracaine

E938.6 Peripheral nerve- and plexus-blocking anesthetics

E938.7 Spinal anesthetics

E938.9 Other and unspecified local anesthetics

✓4ᵗʰ **E939 Psychotropic agents**

E939.0 Antidepressants
Amitriptyline
Imipramine
Monoamine oxidase [MAO] inhibitors

E939.1 Phenothiazine-based tranquilizers
Chlorpromazine   Prochlorperazine
Fluphenazine   Promazine
Phenothiazine

E939.2 Butyrophenone-based tranquilizers
Haloperidol   Trifluperidol
Spiperone

E939.3 Other antipsychotics, neuroleptics, and major tranquilizers

E939.4 Benzodiazepine-based tranquilizers
Chlordiazepoxide   Lorazepam
Diazepam   Medazepam
Flurazepam   Nitrazepam

E939.5 Other tranquilizers
Hydroxyzine   Meprobamate

E939.6 Psychodysleptics [hallucinogens]
Cannabis (derivatives)   Mescaline
Lysergide [LSD]   Psilocin
Marihuana (derivatives) Psilocybin

E939.7 Psychostimulants
Amphetamine   Caffeine
    EXCLUDES central appetite depressants (E947.0)

E939.8 Other psychotropic agents

E939.9 Unspecified psychotropic agent

✓4ᵗʰ **E940 Central nervous system stimulants**

E940.0 Analeptics
Lobeline   Nikethamide

E940.1 Opiate antagonists
Levallorphan   Naloxone
Nalorphine

E940.8 Other specified central nervous system stimulants

E940.9 Unspecified central nervous system stimulant

✓4ᵗʰ **E941 Drugs primarily affecting the autonomic nervous system**

E941.0 Parasympathomimetics [cholinergics]
Acetylcholine
Anticholinesterase:
    organophosphorus
    reversible
Pilocarpine

▨4ᵗʰ Fourth-digit Required   ▶◀ Revised Text   ● New Code   ▲ Revised Code Title

E941.1 Parasympatholytics [anticholinergics and antimuscarinics] and spasmolytics
Atropine Hyoscine [scopalamine]
Homatropine Quaternary ammonium derivatives
EXCLUDES papaverine (E942.5)

E941.2 Sympathomimetics [adrenergics]
Epinephrine [adrenalin] Levarterenol [noradrenalin]

E941.3 Sympatholytics [antiadrenergics]
Phenoxybenzamine
Tolazolinehydrochloride

E941.9 Unspecified drug primarily affecting the autonomic nervous system

✓4th **E942 Agents primarily affecting the cardiovascular system**

E942.0 Cardiac rhythm regulators
Practolol Propranolol
Procainamide Quinidine

E942.1 Cardiotonic glycosides and drugs of similar action
Digitalis glycosides Strophanthins
Digoxin

E942.2 Antilipemic and antiarteriosclerotic drugs
Cholestyramine Nicotinic acid derivatives
Clofibrate Sitosterols
EXCLUDES dextrothyroxine (E932.7)

E942.3 Ganglion-blocking agents
Pentamethonium bromide

E942.4 Coronary vasodilators
Dipyridamole Nitrites
Nitrates [nitroglycerin] Prenylamine

E942.5 Other vasodilators
Cyclandelate Hydralazine
Diazoxide Papaverine

E942.6 Other antihypertensive agents
Clonidine Rauwolfia alkaloids
Guanethidine Reserpine

E942.7 Antivaricose drugs, including sclerosing agents
Monoethanolamine Zinc salts

E942.8 Capillary-active drugs
Adrenochrome derivatives
Bioflavonoids
Metaraminol

E942.9 Other and unspecified agents primarily affecting the cardiovascular system

✓4th **E943 Agents primarily affecting gastrointestinal system**

E943.0 Antacids and antigastric secretion drugs
Aluminum hydroxide
Magnesium trisilicate

E943.1 Irritant cathartics
Bisacodyl Phenolphthalein
Castor oil

E943.2 Emollient cathartics
Sodium dioctyl sulfosuccinate

E943.3 Other cathartics, including intestinal atonia drugs
Magnesium sulfate

E943.4 Digestants
Pancreatin Pepsin
Papain

E943.5 Antidiarrheal drugs
Bismuth subcarbonate Pectin or Kaolin
EXCLUDES anti-infectives (E930.0-E931.9)

E943.6 Emetics

E943.8 Other specified agents primarily affecting the gastrointestinal system

E943.9 Unspecified agent primarily affecting the gastrointestinal system

✓4th **E944 Water, mineral, and uric acid metabolism drugs**

E944.0 Mercurial diuretics
Chlormerodrin Mercurophylline
Mercaptomerin Mersalyl

E944.1 Purine derivative diuretics
Theobromine Theophylline
EXCLUDES aminophylline [theophylline ethylenediamine] (E945.7)

E944.2 Carbonic acid anhydrase inhibitors
Acetazolamide

E944.3 Saluretics
Benzothiadiazides Chlorothiazide group

E944.4 Other diuretics
Ethacrynic acid Furosemide

E944.5 Electrolytic, caloric, and water-balance agents

E944.6 Other mineral salts, not elsewhere classified

E944.7 Uric acid metabolism drugs
Cinchophen and congeners Phenoquin
Colchicine Probenecid

✓4th **E945 Agents primarily acting on the smooth and skeletal muscles and respiratory system**

E945.0 Oxytocic agents
Ergot alkaloids
Prostaglandins

E945.1 Smooth muscle relaxants
Adiphenine
Metaproterenol [orciprenaline]
EXCLUDES papaverine (E942.5)

E945.2 Skeletal muscle relaxants
Alcuronium chloride
Suxamethonium chloride

E945.3 Other and unspecified drugs acting on muscles

E945.4 Antitussives
Dextromethorphan Pipazethate hydrochloride

E945.5 Expectorants
Acetylcysteine Ipecacuanha
Cocillana Terpin hydrate
Guaifenesin [glyceryl guaiacolate]

E945.6 Anti-common cold drugs

E945.7 Antiasthmatics
Aminophylline [theophylline ethylenediamine]

E945.8 Other and unspecified respiratory drugs

✓4th **E946 Agents primarily affecting skin and mucous membrane, ophthalmological, otorhinolaryngological, and dental drugs**

E946.0 Local anti-infectives and anti-inflammatory drugs

E946.1 Antipruritics

E946.2 Local astringents and local detergents

E946.3 Emollients, demulcents, and protectants

E946.4 Keratolytics, kerstoplastics, other hair treatment drugs and preparations

E946.5 Eye anti-infectives and other eye drugs
Idoxuridine

E946.6 Anti-infectives and other drugs and preparations for ear, nose, and throat

E946.7 Dental drugs topically applied

E946.8 Other agents primarily affecting skin and mucous membrane
Spermicides

E946.9 Unspecified agent primarily affecting skin and mucous membrane

✓4th **E947 Other and unspecified drugs and medicinal substances**

E947.0 Dietetics

E947.1 Lipotropic drugs

E947.2 Antidotes and chelating agents, not elsewhere classified

E947.3 Alcohol deterrents

E947.4 Pharmaceutical excipients

E947.8 Other drugs and medicinal substances
Contrast media used for diagnostic x-ray procedures
Diagnostic agents and kits

E947.9 Unspecified drug or medicinal substance

✓4th **E948 Bacterial vaccines**

E948.0 BCG vaccine

✓4th Fourth-digit Required ►◄ Revised Text ● New Code ▲ Revised Code Title

E948.1 Typhoid and paratyphoid

E948.2 Cholera

E948.3 Plague

E948.4 Tetanus

E948.5 Diphtheria

E948.6 Pertussis vaccine, including combinations with a pertussis component

E948.8 Other and unspecified bacterial vaccines

E948.9 Mixed bacterial vaccines, except combinations with a pertussis component

✓4ᵗʰ E949 Other vaccines and biological substances

> EXCLUDES   gamma globulin (E934.6)

E949.0 Smallpox vaccine

E949.1 Rabies vaccine

E949.2 Typhus vaccine

E949.3 Yellow fever vaccine

E949.4 Measles vaccine

E949.5 Poliomyelitis vaccine

E949.6 Other and unspecified viral and rickettsial vaccines
Mumps vaccine

E949.7 Mixed viral-rickettsial and bacterial vaccines, except combinations with a pertussis component

> EXCLUDES   combinations with a pertussis component (E948.6)

E949.9 Other and unspecified vaccines and biological substances

SUICIDE AND SELF-INFLICTED INJURY (E950-E959)

> INCLUDES   injuries in suicide and attempted suicide
> self-inflicted injuries specified as intentional

✓4ᵗʰ E950 Suicide and self-inflicted poisoning by solid or liquid substances

E950.0 Analgesics, antipyretics, and antirheumatics

E950.1 Barbiturates

E950.2 Other sedatives and hypnotics

E950.3 Tranquilizers and other psychotropic agents

E950.4 Other specified drugs and medicinal substances

E950.5 Unspecified drug or medicinal substance

E950.6 Agricultural and horticultural chemical and pharmaceutical preparations other than plant foods and fertilizers

E950.7 Corrosive and caustic substances
Suicide and self-inflicted poisoning by substances classifiable to E864

E950.8 Arsenic and its compounds

E950.9 Other and unspecified solid and liquid substances

✓4ᵗʰ E951 Suicide and self-inflicted poisoning by gases in domestic use

E951.0 Gas distributed by pipeline

E951.1 Liquefied petroleum gas distributed in mobile containers

E951.8 Other utility gas

✓4ᵗʰ E952 Suicide and self-inflicted poisoning by other gases and vapors

E952.0 Motor vehicle exhaust gas

E952.1 Other carbon monoxide

E952.8 Other specified gases and vapors

E952.9 Unspecified gases and vapors

✓4ᵗʰ E953 Suicide and self-inflicted injury by hanging, strangulation, and suffocation

E953.0 Hanging

E953.1 Suffocation by plastic bag

E953.8 Other specified means

E953.9 Unspecified means

E954 Suicide and self-inflicted injury by submersion [drowning]

✓4ᵗʰ E955 Suicide and self-inflicted injury by firearms, air guns and explosives

E955.0 Handgun

E955.1 Shotgun

E955.2 Hunting rifle

E955.3 Military firearms

E955.4 Other and unspecified firearm
Gunshot NOS   Shot NOS

E955.5 Explosives

E955.6 Air gun
BB gun   Pellet gun

E955.7 Paintball gun

E955.9 Unspecified

E956 Suicide and self-inflicted injury by cutting and piercing instrument

✓4ᵗʰ E957 Suicide and self-inflicted injuries by jumping from high place

E957.0 Residential premises

E957.1 Other man-made structures

E957.2 Natural sites

E957.9 Unspecified

✓4ᵗʰ E958 Suicide and self-inflicted injury by other and unspecified means

E958.0 Jumping or lying before moving object

E958.1 Burns, fire

E958.2 Scald

E958.3 Extremes of cold

E958.4 Electrocution

E958.5 Crashing of motor vehicle

E958.6 Crashing of aircraft

E958.7 Caustic substances, except poisoning

> EXCLUDES   poisoning by caustic substance (E950.7)

E958.8 Other specified means

E958.9 Unspecified means

E959 Late effects of self-inflicted injury

> Note: This category is to be used to indicate circumstances classifiable to E950-E958 as the cause of death or disability from late effects, which are themselves classifiable elsewhere. The "late effects" include conditions reported as such, or as sequelae which may occur at any time after the attempted suicide or self-inflicted injury.

HOMICIDE AND INJURY PURPOSELY INFLICTED BY OTHER PERSONS (E960-E969)

> INCLUDES   injuries inflicted by another person with intent
> to injure or kill, by any means

> EXCLUDES   injuries due to:
> legal intervention (E970-E978)
> operations of war (E990-E999)
> terrorism (E979)

✓4ᵗʰ E960 Fight, brawl, rape

E960.0 Unarmed fight or brawl
Beatings NOS
Brawl or fight with hands, fists, feet
Injured or killed in fight NOS

> EXCLUDES   homicidal:
> injury by weapons (E965.0-E966, E969)
> strangulation (E963)
> submersion (E964)

E960.1 Rape

E961 Assault by corrosive or caustic substance, except poisoning
Injury or death purposely caused by corrosive or caustic substance, such as:
acid [any]
corrosive substance
vitriol

> EXCLUDES   burns from hot liquid (E968.3)
> chemical burns from swallowing a corrosive substance (E962.0-E962.9)

✓4ᵗʰ Fourth-digit Required   ▶◀ Revised Text   ● New Code   ▲ Revised Code Title

E Codes

E962–E978

✓4ᵗʰ **E962 Assault by poisoning**

    E962.0 Drugs and medicinal substances

        Homicidal poisoning by any drug or medicinal substance

    E962.1 Other solid and liquid substances

    E962.2 Other gases and vapors

    E962.9 Unspecified poisoning

E963 Assault by hanging and strangulation

    Homicidal (attempt):   Homicidal (attempt):
      garrotting or ligature   strangulation
      hanging   suffocation

E964 Assault by submersion [drowning]

✓4ᵗʰ **E965 Assault by firearms and explosives**

    E965.0 Handgun

        Pistol   Revolver

    E965.1 Shotgun

    E965.2 Hunting rifle

    E965.3 Military firearms

    E965.4 Other and unspecified firearm

    E965.5 Antipersonnel bomb

    E965.6 Gasoline bomb

    E965.7 Letter bomb

    E965.8 Other specified explosive

        Bomb NOS (placed in):   Dynamite
          car
          house

    E965.9 Unspecified explosive

E966 Assault by cutting and piercing instrument

    Assassination (attempt), homicide (attempt) by any instrument classifiable under E920

    Homicidal:
      cut
      puncture } any part of body
      stab
    Stabbed

✓4ᵗʰ **E967 Perpetrator of child and adult abuse**

    Note: Selection of the correct perpetrator code is based on the relationship between the perpetrator and the victim

    E967.0 By father, stepfather, or boyfriend

        Male partner of child's parent or guardian

    E967.1 By other specified person

    E967.2 By mother, stepmother, or girlfriend

        Female partner of child's parent or guardian

    E967.3 By spouse or partner

        Abuse of spouse or partner by ex-spouse or ex-partner

    E967.4 By child

    E967.5 By sibling

    E967.6 By grandparent

    E967.7 By other relative

    E967.8 By non-related caregiver

    E967.9 By unspecified person

✓4ᵗʰ **E968 Assault by other and unspecified means**

    E968.0 Fire

        Arson
        Homicidal burns NOS

        EXCLUDES   burns from hot liquid (E968.3)

    E968.1 Pushing from a high place

    E968.2 Striking by blunt or thrown object

    E968.3 Hot liquid

        Homicidal burns by scalding

    E968.4 Criminal neglect

        Abandonment of child, infant, or other helpless person with intent to injure or kill

    E968.5 Transport vehicle

        Being struck by other vehicle or run down with intent to injure
        Pushed in front of, thrown from, or dragged by moving vehicle with intent to injure

    E968.6 Air gun

        BB gun
        Pellet gun

    E968.7 Human bite

    E968.8 Other specified means

    E968.9 Unspecified means

        Assassination (attempt) NOS
        Homicidal (attempt):
          injury NOS
          wound NOS
        Manslaughter (nonaccidental)
        Murder (attempt) NOS
        Violence, non-accidental

E969 Late effects of injury purposely inflicted by other person

    Note: This category is to be used to indicate circumstances classifiable to E960-E968 as the cause of death or disability from late effects, which are themselves classifiable elsewhere. The "late effects" include conditions reported as such, or as sequelae which may occur at any time after injury purposely inflicted by another person.

LEGAL INTERVENTION (E970-E978)

    INCLUDES   injuries inflicted by the police or other law-enforcing agents, including military on duty, in the course of arresting or attempting to arrest lawbreakers, suppressing disturbances, maintaining order, and other legal action
        legal execution

    EXCLUDES   *injuries caused by civil insurrections (E990.0-E999)*

E970 Injury due to legal intervention by firearms

    Gunshot wound   Injury by:
    Injury by: rifle pellet or
      machine gun   rubber bullet
      revolver   shot NOS

E971 Injury due to legal intervention by explosives

    Injury by: Injury by:
      dynamite   grenade
      explosive shell   mortar bomb

E972 Injury due to legal intervention by gas

    Asphyxiation by gas   Poisoning by gas
    Injury by tear gas

E973 Injury due to legal intervention by blunt object

    Hit, struck by: Hit, struck by:
      baton (nightstick)   stave
      blunt object

E974 Injury due to legal intervention by cutting and piercing instrument

    Cut   Injured by bayonet
    Incised wound   Stab wound

E975 Injury due to legal intervention by other specified means

    Blow   Manhandling

E976 Injury due to legal intervention by unspecified means

E977 Late effects of injuries due to legal intervention

    Note: This category is to be used to indicate circumstances classifiable to E970-E976 as the cause of death or disability from late effects, which are themselves classifiable elsewhere. The "late effects" include conditions reported as such, or as sequelae, which may occur at any time after the injury due to legal intervention.

E978 Legal execution

    All executions performed at the behest of the judiciary or ruling authority [whether permanent or temporary] as:
    asphyxiation by gas
    beheading, decapitation (by guillotine)
    capital punishment
    electrocution
    hanging
    poisoning
    shooting
    other specified means

✓4ᵗʰ Fourth-digit Required   ►◄ Revised Text   ● New Code   ▲ Revised Code Title

TERRORISM (E979)

√4ᵗʰ **E979 Terrorism**

Injuries resulting from the unlawful use of force or violence against persons or property to intimidate or coerce a Government, the civilian population, or any segment thereof, in furtherance of political or social objective

E979.0 Terrorism involving explosion of marine weapons

Depth-charge
Marine mine
Mine NOS, at sea or in harbour
Sea-based artillery shell
Torpedo
Underwater blast

E979.1 Terrorism involving destruction of aircraft

Aircraft used as a weapon
Aircraft:
  burned
  exploded
  shot down
Crushed by falling aircraft

E979.2 Terrorism involving other explosions and fragments

Antipersonnel bomb (fragments)
Blast NOS
Explosion (of):
  artillery shell
  breech-block
  cannon block
  mortar bomb
  munitions being used in terrorism
  NOS
Fragments from:
  artillery shell
  bomb
  grenade
  guided missile
  land-mine
  rocket
  shell
  shrapnel
Mine NOS

E979.3 Terrorism involving fires, conflagration and hot substances

Burning building or structure:
  collapse of
  fall from
  hit by falling object in
  jump from
Conflagration NOS
Fire (causing):
  Asphyxia
  Burns
  NOS
  Other injury
Melting of fittings and furniture in burning
Petrol bomb
Smouldering building or structure

E979.4 Terrorism involving firearms

Bullet:
  carbine
  machine gun
  pistol
  rifle
  rubber (rifle)
Pellets (shotgun)

E979.5 Terrorism involving nuclear weapons

Blast effects
Exposure to ionizing radiation from nuclear weapon
Fireball effects
Heat from nuclear weapon
Other direct and secondary effects of nuclear weapons

E979.6 Terrorism involving biological weapons

Anthrax
Cholera
Smallpox

E979.7 Terrorism involving chemical weapons

Gases, fumes, chemicals
Hydrogen cyanide
Phosgene
Sarin

E979.8 Terrorism involving other means

Drowning and submersion
Lasers
Piercing or stabbing instruments
Terrorism NOS

E979.9 Terrorism, secondary effects

Note: This code is for use to identify conditions occurring subsequent to a terrorist attack not those that are due to the initial terrorist act

EXCLUDES *late effect of terrorist attack (E999.1)*

INJURY UNDETERMINED WHETHER ACCIDENTALLY OR PURPOSELY INFLICTED (E980-E989)

Note: Categories E980-E989 are for use when it is unspecified or it cannot be determined whether the injuries are accidental (unintentional), suicide (attempted), or assault.

√4ᵗʰ **E980 Poisoning by solid or liquid substances, undetermined whether accidentally or purposely inflicted**

E980.0 Analgesics, antipyretics, and antirheumatics

E980.1 Barbiturates

E980.2 Other sedatives and hypnotics

E980.3 Tranquilizers and other psychotropic agents

E980.4 Other specified drugs and medicinal substances

E980.5 Unspecified drug or medicinal substance

E980.6 Corrosive and caustic substances

Poisoning, undetermined whether accidental or purposeful, by substances classifiable to E864

E980.7 Agricultural and horticultural chemical and pharmaceutical preparations other than plant foods and fertilizers

E980.8 Arsenic and its compounds

E980.9 Other and unspecified solid and liquid substances

√4ᵗʰ **E981 Poisoning by gases in domestic use, undetermined whether accidentally or purposely inflicted**

E981.0 Gas distributed by pipeline

E981.1 Liquefied petroleum gas distributed in mobile containers

E981.8 Other utility gas

√4ᵗʰ **E982 Poisoning by other gases, undetermined whether accidentally or purposely inflicted**

E982.0 Motor vehicle exhaust gas

E982.1 Other carbon monoxide

E982.8 Other specified gases and vapors

E982.9 Unspecified gases and vapors

√4ᵗʰ **E983 Hanging, strangulation, or suffocation, undetermined whether accidentally or purposely inflicted**

E983.0 Hanging

E983.1 Suffocation by plastic bag

E983.8 Other specified means

E983.9 Unspecified means

E984 Submersion [drowning], undetermined whether accidentally or purposely inflicted

√4ᵗʰ **E985 Injury by firearms, air guns and explosives, undetermined whether accidentally or purposely inflicted**

E985.0 Handgun

E985.1 Shotgun

E985.2 Hunting rifle

E985.3 Military firearms

E985.4 Other and unspecified firearm

E985.5 Explosives

E985.6 Air gun

  BB gun   Pellet gun

E985.7 Paintball gun

√4ᵗʰ Fourth-digit Required   ▶◀ Revised Text   ● New Code   ▲ Revised Code Title

E986 Injury by cutting and piercing instruments, undetermined whether accidentally or purposely inflicted

✓4ᵗʰ E987 Falling from high place, undetermined whether accidentally or purposely inflicted

E987.0 **Residential premises**

E987.1 **Other man-made structures**

E987.2 **Natural sites**

E987.9 **Unspecified site**

✓4ᵗʰ E988 Injury by other and unspecified means, undetermined whether accidentally or purposely inflicted

E988.0 **Jumping or lying before moving object**

E988.1 **Burns, fire**

E988.2 **Scald**

E988.3 **Extremes of cold**

E988.4 **Electrocution**

E988.5 **Crashing of motor vehicle**

E988.6 **Crashing of aircraft**

E988.7 **Caustic substances, except poisoning**

E988.8 **Other specified means**

E988.9 **Unspecified means**

E989 Late effects of injury, undetermined whether accidentally or purposely inflicted

> Note: This category is to be used to indicate circumstances classifiable to E980-E988 as the cause of death or disability from late effects, which are themselves classifiable elsewhere. The "late effects" include conditions reported as such, or as sequelae, which may occur at any time after injury, undetermined whether accidentally or purposely inflicted.

INJURY RESULTING FROM OPERATIONS OF WAR (E990-E999)

INCLUDES	injuries to military personnel and civilians caused by war and civil insurrections and occurring during the time of war and insurrection
EXCLUDES	*accidents during training of military personnel manufacture of war material and transport, unless attributable to enemy action*

✓4ᵗʰ E990 Injury due to war operations by fires and conflagrations

INCLUDES	asphyxia, burns, or other injury originating from fire caused by a fire-producing device or indirectly by any conventional weapon

E990.0 **From gasoline bomb**

E990.9 **From other and unspecified source**

✓4ᵗʰ E991 Injury due to war operations by bullets and fragments

E991.0 **Rubber bullets (rifle)**

E991.1 **Pellets (rifle)**

E991.2 **Other bullets**

> Bullet [any, except rubber bullets and pellets]
>> carbine
>> machine gun
>> pistol
>> rifle
>> shotgun

E991.3 **Antipersonnel bomb (fragments)**

E991.9 **Other and unspecified fragments**

Fragments from:	Fragments from:
artillery shell	land mine
bombs, except	rockets
anti-personnel	shell
grenade	Shrapnel
guided missile	

E992 Injury due to war operations by explosion of marine weapons

Depth charge	Sea-based artillery shell
Marine mines	Torpedo
Mine NOS, at sea or in harbor	Underwater blast

E993 Injury due to war operations by other explosion

Accidental explosion of munitions being used in war	Explosion of: artillery shell breech block
Accidental explosion of own weapons	cannon block mortar bomb
Air blast NOS	Injury by weapon burst
Blast NOS	
Explosion NOS	

E994 Injury due to war operations by destruction of aircraft

Airplane:	Airplane:
burned	shot down
exploded	Crushed by falling airplane

E995 Injury due to war operations by other and unspecified forms of conventional warfare

Battle wounds
Bayonet injury
Drowned in war operations

E996 Injury due to war operations by nuclear weapons

Blast effects
Exposure to ionizing radiation from nuclear weapons
Fireball effects
Heat
Other direct and secondary effects of nuclear weapons

✓4ᵗʰ E997 Injury due to war operations by other forms of unconventional warfare

E997.0 **Lasers**

E997.1 **Biological warfare**

E997.2 **Gases, fumes, and chemicals**

E997.8 **Other specified forms of unconventional warfare**

E997.9 **Unspecified form of unconventional warfare**

E998 Injury due to war operations but occurring after cessation of hostilities

> Injuries due to operations of war but occurring after cessation of hostilities by any means classifiable under E990-E997
>
> Injuries by explosion of bombs or mines placed in the course of operations of war, if the explosion occurred after cessation of hostilities

✓4ᵗʰ E999 Late effect of injury due to war operations and terrorism

> Note: This category is to be used to indicate circumstances classifiable to E979, E990-E998 as the cause of death or disability from late effects, which are themselves classifiable elsewhere. The "late effects" include conditions reported as such, or as sequelae, which may occur at any time after the injury, resulting from operations of war or terrorism

E999.0 **Late effect of injury due to war operations**

E999.1 **Late effect of injury due to terrorism**

■4ᵗʰ Fourth-digit Required   ▶◀ Revised Text   ● New Code   ▲ Revised Code Title

Official ICD-9-CM Government Appendixes

MORPHOLOGY OF NEOPLASMS

The World Health Organization has published an adaptation of the International Classification of Diseases for oncology (ICD-O). It contains a coded nomenclature for the morphology of neoplasms, which is reproduced here for those who wish to use it in conjunction with Chapter 2 of the International Classification of Diseases, 9th Revision, Clinical Modification.

The morphology code numbers consist of five digits; the first four identify the histological type of the neoplasm and the fifth indicates its behavior. The one-digit behavior code is as follows:

/0 Benign

/1 Uncertain whether benign or malignant
    Borderline malignancy

/2 Carcinoma in situ
    Intraepithelial
    Noninfiltrating
    Noninvasive

/3 Malignant, primary site

/6 Malignant, metastatic site
    Secondary site

/9 Malignant, uncertain whether primary or metastatic site

In the nomenclature below, the morphology code numbers include the behavior code appropriate to the histological type of neoplasm, but this behavior code should be changed if other reported information makes this necessary. For example, "chordoma (M9370/3) is assumed to be malignant; the term "benign chordoma" should be coded M9370/0. Similarly, "superficial spreading adenocarcinoma (M8143/3)" described as "noninvasive" should be coded M8143/2 and "melanoma (M8720/3)" described as "secondary" should be coded M8720/6.

The following table shows the correspondence between the morphology code and the different sections of Chapter 2:

Morphology Code Histology/Behavior		ICD-9-CM Chapter 2	
Any	0	210-229	Benign neoplasms
M8000-M8004	1	239	Neoplasms of unspecified nature
M8010+	1	235-238	Neoplasms of uncertain behavior
Any	2	230-234	Carcinoma in situ
Any	3	140-195 200-208	Malignant neoplasms, stated or presumed to be primary
Any	6	196-198	Malignant neoplasms, stated or presumed to be secondary

The ICD-O behavior digit /9 is inapplicable in an ICD context, since all malignant neoplasms are presumed to be primary (/3) or secondary (/6) according to other information on the medical record.

Only the first-listed term of the full ICD-O morphology nomenclature appears against each code number in the list below. The ICD-9-CM Alphabetical Index (Volume 2), however, includes all the ICD-O synonyms as well as a number of other morphological names still likely to be encountered on medical records but omitted from ICD-O as outdated or otherwise undesirable.

A coding difficulty sometimes arises where a morphological diagnosis contains two qualifying adjectives that have different code numbers. An example is "transitional cell epidermoid carcinoma." "Transitional cell carcinoma NOS" is M8120/3 and "epidermoid carcinoma NOS" is M8070/3. In such circumstances, the higher number (M8120/3 in this example) should be used, as it is usually more specific.

CODED NOMENCLATURE FOR MORPHOLOGY OF NEOPLASMS

M800	**Neoplasms NOS**
M8000/0	Neoplasm, benign
M8000/1	Neoplasm, uncertain whether benign or malignant
M8000/3	Neoplasm, malignant
M8000/6	Neoplasm, metastatic
M8000/9	Neoplasm, malignant, uncertain whether primary or metastatic
M8001/0	Tumor cells, benign
M8001/1	Tumor cells, uncertain whether benign or malignant
M8001/3	Tumor cells, malignant
M8002/3	Malignant tumor, small cell type
M8003/3	Malignant tumor, giant cell type
M8004/3	Malignant tumor, fusiform cell type
M801-M804	**Epithelial neoplasms NOS**
M8010/0	Epithelial tumor, benign
M8010/2	Carcinoma in situ NOS
M8010/3	Carcinoma NOS
M8010/6	Carcinoma, metastatic NOS
M8010/9	Carcinomatosis
M8011/0	Epithelioma, benign
M8011/3	Epithelioma, malignant
M8012/3	Large cell carcinoma NOS
M8020/3	Carcinoma, undifferentiated type NOS
M8021/3	Carcinoma, anaplastic type NOS
M8022/3	Pleomorphic carcinoma
M8030/3	Giant cell and spindle cell carcinoma
M8031/3	Giant cell carcinoma
M8032/3	Spindle cell carcinoma
M8033/3	Pseudosarcomatous carcinoma
M8034/3	Polygonal cell carcinoma
M8035/3	Spheroidal cell carcinoma
M8040/1	Tumorlet
M8041/3	Small cell carcinoma NOS
M8042/3	Oat cell carcinoma
M8043/3	Small cell carcinoma, fusiform cell type
M805-M808	**Papillary and squamous cell neoplasms**
M8050/0	Papilloma NOS (except Papilloma of urinary bladder M8120/1)
M8050/2	Papillary carcinoma in situ
M8050/3	Papillary carcinoma NOS
M8051/0	Verrucous papilloma
M8051/3	Verrucous carcinoma NOS
M8052/0	Squamous cell papilloma
M8052/3	Papillary squamous cell carcinoma
M8053/0	Inverted papilloma
M8060/0	Papillomatosis NOS

M8070/2	Squamous cell carcinoma in situ NOS
M8070/3	Squamous cell carcinoma NOS
M8070/6	Squamous cell carcinoma, metastatic NOS
M8071/3	Squamous cell carcinoma, keratinizing type NOS
M8072/3	Squamous cell carcinoma, large cell, nonkeratinizing type
M8073/3	Squamous cell carcinoma, small cell, nonkeratinizing type
M8074/3	Squamous cell carcinoma, spindle cell type
M8075/3	Adenoid squamous cell carcinoma
M8076/2	Squamous cell carcinoma in situ with questionable stromal invasion
M8076/3	Squamous cell carcinoma, microinvasive
M8080/2	Queyrat's erythroplasia
M8081/2	Bowen's disease
M8082/3	Lymphoepithelial carcinoma
M809-M811	**Basal cell neoplasms**
M8090/1	Basal cell tumor
M8090/3	Basal cell carcinoma NOS
M8091/3	Multicentric basal cell carcinoma
M8092/3	Basal cell carcinoma, morphea type
M8093/3	Basal cell carcinoma, fibroepithelial type
M8094/3	Basosquamous carcinoma
M8095/3	Metatypical carcinoma
M8096/0	Intraepidermal epithelioma of Jadassohn
M8100/0	Trichoepithelioma
M8101/0	Trichofolliculoma
M8102/0	Tricholemmoma
M8110/0	Pilomatrixoma
M812-M813	**Transitional cell papillomas and carcinomas**
M8120/0	Transitional cell papilloma NOS
M8120/1	Urothelial papilloma
M8120/2	Transitional cell carcinoma in situ
M8120/3	Transitional cell carcinoma NOS
M8121/0	Schneiderian papilloma
M8121/1	Transitional cell papilloma, inverted type
M8121/3	Schneiderian carcinoma
M8122/3	Transitional cell carcinoma, spindle cell type
M8123/3	Basaloid carcinoma
M8124/3	Cloacogenic carcinoma
M8130/3	Papillary transitional cell carcinoma
M814-M838	**Adenomas and adenocarcinomas**
M8140/0	Adenoma NOS
M8140/1	Bronchial adenoma NOS
M8140/2	Adenocarcinoma in situ
M8140/3	Adenocarcinoma NOS
M8140/6	Adenocarcinoma, metastatic NOS
M8141/3	Scirrhous adenocarcinoma
M8142/3	Linitis plastica
M8143/3	Superficial spreading adenocarcinoma
M8144/3	Adenocarcinoma, intestinal type
M8145/3	Carcinoma, diffuse type
M8146/0	Monomorphic adenoma
M8147/0	Basal cell adenoma
M8150/0	Islet cell adenoma
M8150/3	Islet cell carcinoma
M8151/0	Insulinoma NOS
M8151/3	Insulinoma, malignant
M8152/0	Glucagonoma NOS
M8152/3	Glucagonoma, malignant
M8153/1	Gastrinoma NOS

Appendix A: Morphology of Neoplasms

M8153/3	Gastrinoma, malignant
M8154/3	Mixed islet cell and exocrine adenocarcinoma
M8160/0	Bile duct adenoma
M8160/3	Cholangiocarcinoma
M8161/0	Bile duct cystadenoma
M8161/3	Bile duct cystadenocarcinoma
M8170/0	Liver cell adenoma
M8170/3	Hepatocellular carcinoma NOS
M8180/0	Hepatocholangioma, benign
M8180/3	Combined hepatocellular carcinoma and cholangiocarcinoma
M8190/0	Trabecular adenoma
M8190/3	Trabecular adenocarcinoma
M8191/0	Embryonal adenoma
M8200/0	Eccrine dermal cylindroma
M8200/3	Adenoid cystic carcinoma
M8201/3	Cribriform carcinoma
M8210/0	Adenomatous polyp NOS
M8210/3	Adenocarcinoma in adenomatous polyp
M8211/0	Tubular adenoma NOS
M8211/3	Tubular adenocarcinoma
M8220/0	Adenomatous polyposis coli
M8220/3	Adenocarcinoma in adenomatous polyposis coli
M8221/0	Multiple adenomatous polyps
M8230/3	Solid carcinoma NOS
M8231/3	Carcinoma simplex
M8240/1	Carcinoid tumor NOS
M8240/3	Carcinoid tumor, malignant
M8241/1	Carcinoid tumor, argentaffin NOS
M8241/3	Carcinoid tumor, argentaffin, malignant
M8242/1	Carcinoid tumor, nonargentaffin NOS
M8242/3	Carcinoid tumor, nonargentaffin, malignant
M8243/3	Mucocarcinoid tumor, malignant
M8244/3	Composite carcinoid
M8250/1	Pulmonary adenomatosis
M8250/3	Bronchiolo-alveolar adenocarcinoma
M8251/0	Alveolar adenoma
M8251/3	Alveolar adenocarcinoma
M8260/0	Papillary adenoma NOS
M8260/3	Papillary adenocarcinoma NOS
M8261/1	Villous adenoma NOS
M8261/3	Adenocarcinoma in villous adenoma
M8262/3	Villous adenocarcinoma
M8263/0	Tubulovillous adenoma
M8270/0	Chromophobe adenoma
M8270/3	Chromophobe carcinoma
M8280/0	Acidophil adenoma
M8280/3	Acidophil carcinoma
M8281/0	Mixed acidophil-basophil adenoma
M8281/3	Mixed acidophil-basophil carcinoma
M8290/0	Oxyphilic adenoma
M8290/3	Oxyphilic adenocarcinoma
M8300/0	Basophil adenoma
M8300/3	Basophil carcinoma
M8310/0	Clear cell adenoma
M8310/3	Clear cell adenocarcinoma NOS
M8311/1	Hypernephroid tumor
M8312/3	Renal cell carcinoma
M8313/0	Clear cell adenofibroma
M8320/3	Granular cell carcinoma
M8321/0	Chief cell adenoma
M8322/0	Water-clear cell adenoma
M8322/3	Water-clear cell adenocarcinoma
M8323/0	Mixed cell adenoma
M8323/3	Mixed cell adenocarcinoma
M8324/0	Lipoadenoma
M8330/0	Follicular adenoma
M8330/3	Follicular adenocarcinoma NOS
M8331/3	Follicular adenocarcinoma, well differentiated type

M8332/3	Follicular adenocarcinoma, trabecular type
M8333/0	Microfollicular adenoma
M8334/0	Macrofollicular adenoma
M8340/3	Papillary and follicular adenocarcinoma
M8350/3	Nonencapsulated sclerosing carcinoma
M8360/1	Multiple endocrine adenomas
M8361/1	Juxtaglomerular tumor
M8370/0	Adrenal cortical adenoma NOS
M8370/3	Adrenal cortical carcinoma
M8371/0	Adrenal cortical adenoma, compact cell type
M8372/0	Adrenal cortical adenoma, heavily pigmented variant
M8373/0	Adrenal cortical adenoma, clear cell type
M8374/0	Adrenal cortical adenoma, glomerulosa cell type
M8375/0	Adrenal cortical adenoma, mixed cell type
M8380/0	Endometrioid adenoma NOS
M8380/1	Endometrioid adenoma, borderline malignancy
M8380/3	Endometrioid carcinoma
M8381/0	Endometrioid adenofibroma NOS
M8381/1	Endometrioid adenofibroma, borderline malignancy
M8381/3	Endometrioid adenofibroma, malignant

M839-M842 Adnexal and skin appendage neoplasms

M8390/0	Skin appendage adenoma
M8390/3	Skin appendage carcinoma
M8400/0	Sweat gland adenoma
M8400/1	Sweat gland tumor NOS
M8400/3	Sweat gland adenocarcinoma
M8401/0	Apocrine adenoma
M8401/3	Apocrine adenocarcinoma
M8402/0	Eccrine acrospiroma
M8403/0	Eccrine spiradenoma
M8404/0	Hidrocystoma
M8405/0	Papillary hydradenoma
M8406/0	Papillary syringadenoma
M8407/0	Syringoma NOS
M8410/0	Sebaceous adenoma
M8410/3	Sebaceous adenocarcinoma
M8420/0	Ceruminous adenoma
M8420/3	Ceruminous adenocarcinoma

M843 Mucoepidermoid neoplasms

M8430/1	Mucoepidermoid tumor
M8430/3	Mucoepidermoid carcinoma

M844-M849 Cystic, mucinous, and serous neoplasms

M8440/0	Cystadenoma NOS
M8440/3	Cystadenocarcinoma NOS
M8441/0	Serous cystadenoma NOS
M8441/1	Serous cystadenoma, borderline malignancy
M8441/3	Serous cystadenocarcinoma NOS
M8450/0	Papillary cystadenoma NOS
M8450/1	Papillary cystadenoma, borderline malignancy
M8450/3	Papillary cystadenocarcinoma NOS
M8460/0	Papillary serous cystadenoma NOS
M8460/1	Papillary serous cystadenoma, borderline malignancy
M8460/3	Papillary serous cystadenocarcinoma
M8461/0	Serous surface papilloma NOS
M8461/1	Serous surface papilloma, borderline malignancy
M8461/3	Serous surface papillary carcinoma
M8470/0	Mucinous cystadenoma NOS
M8470/1	Mucinous cystadenoma, borderline malignancy

M8470/3	Mucinous cystadenocarcinoma NOS
M8471/0	Papillary mucinous cystadenoma NOS
M8471/1	Papillary mucinous cystadenoma, borderline malignancy
M8471/3	Papillary mucinous cystadenocarcinoma
M8480/0	Mucinous adenoma
M8480/3	Mucinous adenocarcinoma
M8480/6	Pseudomyxoma peritonei
M8481/3	Mucin-producing adenocarcinoma
M8490/3	Signet ring cell carcinoma
M8490/6	Metastatic signet ring cell carcinoma

M850-M854 Ductal, lobular, and medullary neoplasms

M8500/2	Intraductal carcinoma, noninfiltrating NOS
M8500/3	Infiltrating duct carcinoma
M8501/2	Comedocarcinoma, noninfiltrating
M8501/3	Comedocarcinoma NOS
M8502/3	Juvenile carcinoma of the breast
M8503/0	Intraductal papilloma
M8503/2	Noninfiltrating intraductal papillary adenocarcinoma
M8504/0	Intracystic papillary adenoma
M8504/2	Noninfiltrating intracystic carcinoma
M8505/0	Intraductal papillomatosis NOS
M8506/0	Subareolar duct papillomatosis
M8510/3	Medullary carcinoma NOS
M8511/3	Medullary carcinoma with amyloid stroma
M8512/3	Medullary carcinoma with lymphoid stroma
M8520/2	Lobular carcinoma in situ
M8520/3	Lobular carcinoma NOS
M8521/3	Infiltrating ductular carcinoma
M8530/3	Inflammatory carcinoma
M8540/3	Paget's disease, mammary
M8541/3	Paget's disease and infiltrating duct carcinoma of breast
M8542/3	Paget's disease, extramammary (except Paget's disease of bone)

M855 Acinar cell neoplasms

M8550/0	Acinar cell adenoma
M8550/1	Acinar cell tumor
M8550/3	Acinar cell carcinoma

M856-M858 Complex epithelial neoplasms

M8560/3	Adenosquamous carcinoma
M8561/0	Adenolymphoma
M8570/3	Adenocarcinoma with squamous metaplasia
M8571/3	Adenocarcinoma with cartilaginous and osseous metaplasia
M8572/3	Adenocarcinoma with spindle cell metaplasia
M8573/3	Adenocarcinoma with apocrine metaplasia
M8580/0	Thymoma, benign
M8580/3	Thymoma, malignant

M859-M867 Specialized gonadal neoplasms

M8590/1	Sex cord-stromal tumor
M8600/0	Thecoma NOS
M8600/3	Theca cell carcinoma
M8610/0	Luteoma NOS
M8620/1	Granulosa cell tumor NOS
M8620/3	Granulosa cell tumor, malignant
M8621/1	Granulosa cell-theca cell tumor
M8630/0	Androblastoma, benign
M8630/1	Androblastoma NOS
M8630/3	Androblastoma, malignant
M8631/0	Sertoli-Leydig cell tumor
M8632/1	Gynandroblastoma
M8640/0	Tubular androblastoma NOS
M8640/3	Sertoli cell carcinoma
M8641/0	Tubular androblastoma with lipid storage

M8650/0	Leydig cell tumor, benign	M8813/0	Fascial fibroma	M8990/1	Mesenchymoma NOS
M8650/1	Leydig cell tumor NOS	M8813/3	Fascial fibrosarcoma	M8990/3	Mesenchymoma, malignant
M8650/3	Leydig cell tumor, malignant	M8814/3	Infantile fibrosarcoma	M8991/3	Embryonal sarcoma
M8660/0	Hilar cell tumor	M8820/0	Elastofibroma	**M900-M903**	**Fibroepithelial neoplasms**
M8670/0	Lipid cell tumor of ovary	M8821/1	Aggressive fibromatosis	M9000/0	Brenner tumor NOS
M8671/0	Adrenal rest tumor	M8822/1	Abdominal fibromatosis	M9000/1	Brenner tumor, borderline
M868-M871	**Paragangliomas and glomus**	M8823/1	Desmoplastic fibroma		malignancy
	tumors	M8830/0	Fibrous histiocytoma NOS	M9000/3	Brenner tumor, malignant
M8680/1	Paraganglioma NOS	M8830/1	Atypical fibrous histiocytoma	M9010/0	Fibroadenoma NOS
M8680/3	Paraganglioma, malignant	M8830/3	Fibrous histiocytoma, malignant	M9011/0	Intracanalicular fibroadenoma NOS
M8681/1	Sympathetic paraganglioma	M8831/0	Fibroxanthoma NOS	M9012/0	Pericanalicular fibroadenoma
M8682/1	Parasympathetic paraganglioma	M8831/1	Atypical fibroxanthoma	M9013/0	Adenofibroma NOS
M8690/1	Glomus jugulare tumor	M8831/3	Fibroxanthoma, malignant	M9014/0	Serous adenofibroma
M8691/1	Aortic body tumor	M8832/0	Dermatofibroma NOS	M9015/0	Mucinous adenofibroma
M8692/1	Carotid body tumor	M8832/1	Dermatofibroma protuberans	M9020/0	Cellular intracanalicular
M8693/1	Extra-adrenal paraganglioma NOS	M8832/3	Dermatofibrosarcoma NOS		fibroadenoma
M8693/3	Extra-adrenal paraganglioma,	**M884**	**Myxomatous neoplasms**	M9020/1	Cystosarcoma phyllodes NOS
	malignant	M8840/0	Myxoma NOS	M9020/3	Cystosarcoma phyllodes, malignant
M8700/0	Pheochromocytoma NOS	M8840/3	Myxosarcoma	M9030/0	Juvenile fibroadenoma
M8700/3	Pheochromocytoma, malignant	**M885-M888**	**Lipomatous neoplasms**	**M904**	**Synovial neoplasms**
M8710/3	Glomangiosarcoma	M8850/0	Lipoma NOS	M9040/0	Synovioma, benign
M8711/0	Glomus tumor	M8850/3	Liposarcoma NOS	M9040/3	Synovial sarcoma NOS
M8712/0	Glomangioma	M8851/0	Fibrolipoma	M9041/3	Synovial sarcoma, spindle cell type
M872-M879	**Nevi and melanomas**	M8851/3	Liposarcoma, well differentiated	M9042/3	Synovial sarcoma, epithelioid cell
M8720/0	Pigmented nevus NOS		type		type
M8720/3	Malignant melanoma NOS	M8852/0	Fibromyxolipoma	M9043/3	Synovial sarcoma, biphasic type
M8721/3	Nodular melanoma	M8852/3	Myxoid liposarcoma	M9044/3	Clear cell sarcoma of tendons and
M8722/0	Balloon cell nevus	M8853/3	Round cell liposarcoma		aponeuroses
M8722/3	Balloon cell melanoma	M8854/3	Pleomorphic liposarcoma	**M905**	**Mesothelial neoplasms**
M8723/0	Halo nevus	M8855/3	Mixed type liposarcoma	M9050/0	Mesothelioma, benign
M8724/0	Fibrous papule of the nose	M8856/3	Intramuscular lipoma	M9050/3	Mesothelioma, malignant
M8725/0	Neuronevus	M8857/0	Spindle cell lipoma	M9051/0	Fibrous mesothelioma, benign
M8726/0	Magnocellular nevus	M8860/0	Angiomyolipoma	M9051/3	Fibrous mesothelioma, malignant
M8730/0	Nonpigmented nevus	M8860/3	Angiomyoliposarcoma	M9052/0	Epithelioid mesothelioma, benign
M8730/3	Amelanotic melanoma	M8861/0	Angiolipoma NOS	M9052/3	Epithelioid mesothelioma,
M8740/0	Junctional nevus	M8861/1	Angiolipoma, infiltrating		malignant
M8740/3	Malignant melanoma in junctional	M8870/0	Myelolipoma	M9053/0	Mesothelioma, biphasic type,
	nevus	M8880/0	Hibernoma		benign
M8741/2	Precancerous melanosis NOS	M8881/0	Lipoblastomatosis	M9053/3	Mesothelioma, biphasic type,
M8741/3	Malignant melanoma in	**M889-M892**	**Myomatous neoplasms**		malignant
	precancerous melanosis	M8890/0	Leiomyoma NOS	M9054/0	Adenomatoid tumor NOS
M8742/2	Hutchinson's melanotic freckle	M8890/1	Intravascular leiomyomatosis	**M906-M909**	**Germ cell neoplasms**
M8742/3	Malignant melanoma in	M8890/3	Leiomyosarcoma NOS	M9060/3	Dysgerminoma
	Hutchinson's melanotic freckle	M8891/1	Epithelioid leiomyoma	M9061/3	Seminoma NOS
M8743/3	Superficial spreading melanoma	M8891/3	Epithelioid leiomyosarcoma	M9062/3	Seminoma, anaplastic type
M8750/0	Intradermal nevus	M8892/1	Cellular leiomyoma	M9063/3	Spermatocytic seminoma
M8760/0	Compound nevus	M8893/0	Bizarre leiomyoma	M9064/3	Germinoma
M8761/1	Giant pigmented nevus	M8894/0	Angiomyoma	M9070/3	Embryonal carcinoma NOS
M8761/3	Malignant melanoma in giant	M8894/3	Angiomyosarcoma	M9071/3	Endodermal sinus tumor
	pigmented nevus	M8895/0	Myoma	M9072/3	Polyembryoma
M8770/0	Epithelioid and spindle cell nevus	M8895/3	Myosarcoma	M9073/1	Gonadoblastoma
M8771/3	Epithelioid cell melanoma	M8900/0	Rhabdomyoma NOS	M9080/0	Teratoma, benign
M8772/3	Spindle cell melanoma NOS	M8900/3	Rhabdomyosarcoma NOS	M9080/1	Teratoma NOS
M8773/3	Spindle cell melanoma, type A	M8901/3	Pleomorphic rhabdomyosarcoma	M9080/3	Teratoma, malignant NOS
M8774/3	Spindle cell melanoma, type B	M8902/3	Mixed type rhabdomyosarcoma	M9081/3	Teratocarcinoma
M8775/3	Mixed epithelioid and spindle cell	M8903/0	Fetal rhabdomyoma	M9082/3	Malignant teratoma,
	melanoma	M8904/0	Adult rhabdomyoma		undifferentiated type
M8780/0	Blue nevus NOS	M8910/3	Embryonal rhabdomyosarcoma	M9083/3	Malignant teratoma, intermediate
M8780/3	Blue nevus, malignant	M8920/3	Alveolar rhabdomyosarcoma		type
M8790/0	Cellular blue nevus	**M893-M899**	**Complex mixed and stromal**	M9084/0	Dermoid cyst
M880	**Soft tissue tumors and**		**neoplasms**	M9084/3	Dermoid cyst with malignant
	sarcomas NOS	M8930/3	Endometrial stromal sarcoma		transformation
M8800/0	Soft tissue tumor, benign	M8931/1	Endolymphatic stromal myosis	M9090/0	Struma ovarii NOS
M8800/3	Sarcoma NOS	M8932/0	Adenomyoma	M9090/3	Struma ovarii, malignant
M8800/9	Sarcomatosis NOS	M8940/0	Pleomorphic adenoma	M9091/1	Strumal carcinoid
M8801/3	Spindle cell sarcoma	M8940/3	Mixed tumor, malignant NOS	**M910**	**Trophoblastic neoplasms**
M8802/3	Giant cell sarcoma (except of bone	M8950/3	Mullerian mixed tumor	M9100/0	Hydatidiform mole NOS
	M9250/3)	M8951/3	Mesodermal mixed tumor	M9100/1	Invasive hydatidiform mole
M8803/3	Small cell sarcoma	M8960/1	Mesoblastic nephroma	M9100/3	Choriocarcinoma
M8804/3	Epithelioid cell sarcoma	M8960/3	Nephroblastoma NOS	M9101/3	Choriocarcinoma combined with
M881-M883	**Fibromatous neoplasms**	M8961/3	Epithelial nephroblastoma		teratoma
M8810/0	Fibroma NOS	M8962/3	Mesenchymal nephroblastoma	M9102/3	Malignant teratoma, trophoblastic
M8810/3	Fibrosarcoma NOS	M8970/3	Hepatoblastoma	**M911**	**Mesonephromas**
M8811/0	Fibromyxoma	M8980/3	Carcinosarcoma NOS	M9110/0	Mesonephroma, benign
M8811/3	Fibromyxosarcoma	M8981/3	Carcinosarcoma, embryonal type	M9110/1	Mesonephric tumor
M8812/0	Periosteal fibroma	M8982/3	Myoepithelioma	M9110/3	Mesonephroma, malignant
M8812/3	Periosteal fibrosarcoma	M8990/0	Mesenchymoma, benign	M9111/1	Endosalpingioma

Appendix A: Morphology of Neoplasms

M912-M916 Blood vessel tumors
M9120/0 Hemangioma NOS
M9120/3 Hemangiosarcoma
M9121/0 Cavernous hemangioma
M9122/0 Venous hemangioma
M9123/0 Racemose hemangioma
M9124/3 Kupffer cell sarcoma
M9130/0 Hemangioendothelioma, benign
M9130/1 Hemangioendothelioma NOS
M9130/3 Hemangioendothelioma, malignant
M9131/0 Capillary hemangioma
M9132/0 Intramuscular hemangioma
M9140/3 Kaposi's sarcoma
M9141/0 Angiokeratoma
M9142/0 Verrucous keratotic hemangioma
M9150/0 Hemangiopericytoma, benign
M9150/1 Hemangiopericytoma NOS
M9150/3 Hemangiopericytoma, malignant
M9160/0 Angiofibroma NOS
M9161/1 Hemangioblastoma

M917 Lymphatic vessel tumors
M9170/0 Lymphangioma NOS
M9170/3 Lymphangiosarcoma
M9171/0 Capillary lymphangioma
M9172/0 Cavernous lymphangioma
M9173/0 Cystic lymphangioma
M9174/0 Lymphangiomyoma
M9174/1 Lymphangiomyomatosis
M9175/0 Hemolymphangioma

M918-M920 Osteomas and osteosarcomas
M9180/0 Osteoma NOS
M9180/3 Osteosarcoma NOS
M9181/3 Chondroblastic osteosarcoma
M9182/3 Fibroblastic osteosarcoma
M9183/3 Telangiectatic osteosarcoma
M9184/3 Osteosarcoma in Paget's disease of bone
M9190/3 Juxtacortical osteosarcoma
M9191/0 Osteoid osteoma NOS
M9200/0 Osteoblastoma

M921-M924 Chondromatous neoplasms
M9210/0 Osteochondroma
M9210/1 Osteochondromatosis NOS
M9220/0 Chondroma NOS
M9220/1 Chondromatosis NOS
M9220/3 Chondrosarcoma NOS
M9221/0 Juxtacortical chondroma
M9221/3 Juxtacortical chondrosarcoma
M9230/0 Chondroblastoma NOS
M9230/3 Chondroblastoma, malignant
M9240/3 Mesenchymal chondrosarcoma
M9241/0 Chondromyxoid fibroma

M925 Giant cell tumors
M9250/1 Giant cell tumor of bone NOS
M9250/3 Giant cell tumor of bone, malignant
M9251/1 Giant cell tumor of soft parts NOS
M9251/3 Malignant giant cell tumor of soft parts

M926 Miscellaneous bone tumors
M9260/3 Ewing's sarcoma
M9261/3 Adamantinoma of long bones
M9262/0 Ossifying fibroma

M927-M934 Odontogenic tumors
M9270/0 Odontogenic tumor, benign
M9270/1 Odontogenic tumor NOS
M9270/3 Odontogenic tumor, malignant
M9271/0 Dentinoma
M9272/0 Cementoma NOS
M9273/0 Cementoblastoma, benign
M9274/0 Cementifying fibroma
M9275/0 Gigantiform cementoma
M9280/0 Odontoma NOS
M9281/0 Compound odontoma
M9282/0 Complex odontoma
M9290/0 Ameloblastic fibro-odontoma
M9290/3 Ameloblastic odontosarcoma
M9300/0 Adenomatoid odontogenic tumor

M9301/0 Calcifying odontogenic cyst
M9310/0 Ameloblastoma NOS
M9310/3 Ameloblastoma, malignant
M9311/0 Odontoameloblastoma
M9312/0 Squamous odontogenic tumor
M9320/0 Odontogenic myxoma
M9321/0 Odontogenic fibroma NOS
M9330/0 Ameloblastic fibroma
M9330/3 Ameloblastic fibrosarcoma
M9340/0 Calcifying epithelial odontogenic tumor

M935-M937 Miscellaneous tumors
M9350/1 Craniopharyngioma
M9360/1 Pinealoma
M9361/1 Pineocytoma
M9362/3 Pineoblastoma
M9363/0 Melanotic neuroectodermal tumor
M9370/3 Chordoma

M938-M948 Gliomas
M9380/3 Glioma, malignant
M9381/3 Gliomatosis cerebri
M9382/3 Mixed glioma
M9383/1 Subependymal glioma
M9384/1 Subependymal giant cell astrocytoma
M9390/0 Choroid plexus papilloma NOS
M9390/3 Choroid plexus papilloma, malignant
M9391/3 Ependymoma NOS
M9392/3 Ependymoma, anaplastic type
M9393/1 Papillary ependymoma
M9394/1 Myxopapillary ependymoma
M9400/3 Astrocytoma NOS
M9401/3 Astrocytoma, anaplastic type
M9410/3 Protoplasmic astrocytoma
M9411/3 Gemistocytic astrocytoma
M9420/3 Fibrillary astrocytoma
M9421/3 Pilocytic astrocytoma
M9422/3 Spongioblastoma NOS
M9423/3 Spongioblastoma polare
M9430/3 Astroblastoma
M9440/3 Glioblastoma NOS
M9441/3 Giant cell glioblastoma
M9442/3 Glioblastoma with sarcomatous component
M9443/3 Primitive polar spongioblastoma
M9450/3 Oligodendroglioma NOS
M9451/3 Oligodendroglioma, anaplastic type
M9460/3 Oligodendroblastoma
M9470/3 Medulloblastoma NOS
M9471/3 Desmoplastic medulloblastoma
M9472/3 Medullomyoblastoma
M9480/3 Cerebellar sarcoma NOS
M9481/3 Monstrocellular sarcoma

M949-M952 Neuroepitheliomatous neoplasms
M9490/0 Ganglioneuroma
M9490/3 Ganglioneuroblastoma
M9491/0 Ganglioneuromatosis
M9500/3 Neuroblastoma NOS
M9501/3 Medulloepithelioma NOS
M9502/3 Teratoid medulloepithelioma
M9503/3 Neuroepithelioma NOS
M9504/3 Spongioneuroblastoma
M9505/1 Ganglioglioma
M9506/0 Neurocytoma
M9507/0 Pacinian tumor
M9510/3 Retinoblastoma NOS
M9511/3 Retinoblastoma, differentiated type
M9512/3 Retinoblastoma, undifferentiated type
M9520/3 Olfactory neurogenic tumor
M9521/3 Esthesioneurocytoma
M9522/3 Esthesioneuroblastoma
M9523/3 Esthesioneuroepithelioma

M953 Meningiomas
M9530/0 Meningioma NOS
M9530/1 Meningiomatosis NOS

M9530/3 Meningioma, malignant
M9531/0 Meningotheliomatous meningioma
M9532/0 Fibrous meningioma
M9533/0 Psammomatous meningioma
M9534/0 Angiomatous meningioma
M9535/0 Hemangioblastic meningioma
M9536/0 Hemangiopericytic meningioma
M9537/0 Transitional meningioma
M9538/1 Papillary meningioma
M9539/3 Meningeal sarcomatosis

M954-M957 Nerve sheath tumor
M9540/0 Neurofibroma NOS
M9540/1 Neurofibromatosis NOS
M9540/3 Neurofibrosarcoma
M9541/0 Melanotic neurofibroma
M9550/0 Plexiform neurofibroma
M9560/0 Neurilemmoma NOS
M9560/1 Neurinomatosis
M9560/3 Neurilemmoma, malignant
M9570/0 Neuroma NOS

M958 Granular cell tumors and alveolar soft part sarcoma
M9580/0 Granular cell tumor NOS
M9580/3 Granular cell tumor, malignant
M9581/3 Alveolar soft part sarcoma

M959-M963 Lymphomas, NOS or diffuse
M9590/0 Lymphomatous tumor, benign
M9590/3 Malignant lymphoma NOS
M9591/3 Malignant lymphoma, non Hodgkin's type
M9600/3 Malignant lymphoma, undifferentiated cell type NOS
M9601/3 Malignant lymphoma, stem cell type
M9602/3 Malignant lymphoma, convoluted cell type NOS
M9610/3 Lymphosarcoma NOS
M9611/3 Malignant lymphoma, lymphoplasmacytoid type
M9612/3 Malignant lymphoma, immunoblastic type
M9613/3 Malignant lymphoma, mixed lymphocytic-histiocytic NOS
M9614/3 Malignant lymphoma, centroblastic-centrocytic, diffuse
M9615/3 Malignant lymphoma, follicular center cell NOS
M9620/3 Malignant lymphoma, lymphocytic, well differentiated NOS
M9621/3 Malignant lymphoma, lymphocytic, intermediate differentiation NOS
M9622/3 Malignant lymphoma, centrocytic
M9623/3 Malignant lymphoma, follicular center cell, cleaved NOS
M9630/3 Malignant lymphoma, lymphocytic, poorly differentiated NOS
M9631/3 Prolymphocytic lymphosarcoma
M9632/3 Malignant lymphoma, centroblastic type NOS
M9633/3 Malignant lymphoma, follicular center cell, noncleaved NOS

M964 Reticulosarcomas
M9640/3 Reticulosarcoma NOS
M9641/3 Reticulosarcoma, pleomorphic cell type
M9642/3 Reticulosarcoma, nodular

M965-M966 Hodgkin's disease
M9650/3 Hodgkin's disease NOS
M9651/3 Hodgkin's disease, lymphocytic predominance
M9652/3 Hodgkin's disease, mixed cellularity
M9653/3 Hodgkin's disease, lymphocytic depletion NOS
M9654/3 Hodgkin's disease, lymphocytic depletion, diffuse fibrosis
M9655/3 Hodgkin's disease, lymphocytic depletion, reticular type

M9656/3	*Hodgkin's disease, nodular sclerosis NOS*
M9657/3	*Hodgkin's disease, nodular sclerosis, cellular phase*
M9660/3	*Hodgkin's paragranuloma*
M9661/3	*Hodgkin's granuloma*
M9662/3	*Hodgkin's sarcoma*
M969	**Lymphomas, nodular or follicular**
M9690/3	*Malignant lymphoma, nodular NOS*
M9691/3	*Malignant lymphoma, mixed lymphocytic-histiocytic, nodular*
M9692/3	*Malignant lymphoma, centroblastic-centrocytic, follicular*
M9693/3	*Malignant lymphoma, lymphocytic, well differentiated, nodular*
M9694/3	*Malignant lymphoma, lymphocytic, intermediate differentiation, nodular*
M9695/3	*Malignant lymphoma, follicular center cell, cleaved, follicular*
M9696/3	*Malignant lymphoma, lymphocytic, poorly differentiated, nodular*
M9697/3	*Malignant lymphoma, centroblastic type, follicular*
M9698/3	*Malignant lymphoma, follicular center cell, noncleaved, follicular*
M970	**Mycosis fungoides**
M9700/3	*Mycosis fungoides*
M9701/3	*Sezary's disease*
M971-M972	**Miscellaneous reticuloendothelial neoplasms**
M9710/3	*Microglioma*
M9720/3	*Malignant histiocytosis*
M9721/3	*Histiocytic medullary reticulosis*
M9722/3	*Letterer-Siwe's disease*

M973	**Plasma cell tumors**
M9730/3	*Plasma cell myeloma*
M9731/0	*Plasma cell tumor, benign*
M9731/1	*Plasmacytoma NOS*
M9731/3	*Plasma cell tumor, malignant*
M974	**Mast cell tumors**
M9740/1	*Mastocytoma NOS*
M9740/3	*Mast cell sarcoma*
M9741/3	*Malignant mastocytosis*
M975	**Burkitt's tumor**
M9750/3	*Burkitt's tumor*
M980-M994	**Leukemias**
M980	**Leukemias NOS**
M9800/3	*Leukemia NOS*
M9801/3	*Acute leukemia NOS*
M9802/3	*Subacute leukemia NOS*
M9803/3	*Chronic leukemia NOS*
M9804/3	*Aleukemic leukemia NOS*
M981	**Compound leukemias**
M9810/3	*Compound leukemia*
M982	**Lymphoid leukemias**
M9820/3	*Lymphoid leukemia NOS*
M9821/3	*Acute lymphoid leukemia*
M9822/3	*Subacute lymphoid leukemia*
M9823/3	*Chronic lymphoid leukemia*
M9824/3	*Aleukemic lymphoid leukemia*
M9825/3	*Prolymphocytic leukemia*
M983	**Plasma cell leukemias**
M9830/3	*Plasma cell leukemia*
M984	**Erythroleukemias**
M9840/3	*Erythroleukemia*
M9841/3	*Acute erythremia*
M9842/3	*Chronic erythremia*
M985	**Lymphosarcoma cell leukemias**
M9850/3	*Lymphosarcoma cell leukemia*

M986	**Myeloid leukemias**
M9860/3	*Myeloid leukemia NOS*
M9861/3	*Acute myeloid leukemia*
M9862/3	*Subacute myeloid leukemia*
M9863/3	*Chronic myeloid leukemia*
M9864/3	*Aleukemic myeloid leukemia*
M9865/3	*Neutrophilic leukemia*
M9866/3	*Acute promyelocytic leukemia*
M987	**Basophilic leukemias**
M9870/3	*Basophilic leukemia*
M988	**Eosinophilic leukemias**
M9880/3	*Eosinophilic leukemia*
M989	**Monocytic leukemias**
M9890/3	*Monocytic leukemia NOS*
M9891/3	*Acute monocytic leukemia*
M9892/3	*Subacute monocytic leukemia*
M9893/3	*Chronic monocytic leukemia*
M9894/3	*Aleukemic monocytic leukemia*
M990-M994	**Miscellaneous leukemias**
M9900/3	*Mast cell leukemia*
M9910/3	*Megakaryocytic leukemia*
M9920/3	*Megakaryocytic myelosis*
M9930/3	*Myeloid sarcoma*
M9940/3	*Hairy cell leukemia*
M995-M997	**Miscellaneous myeloproliferative and lymphoproliferative disorders**
M9950/1	*Polycythemia vera*
M9951/1	*Acute panmyelosis*
M9960/1	*Chronic myeloproliferative disease*
M9961/1	*Myelosclerosis with myeloid metaplasia*
M9962/1	*Idiopathic thrombocythemia*
M9970/1	*Chronic lymphoproliferative disease*

Appendix B
was officially deleted
October 1, 2004

CLASSIFICATION OF DRUGS BY AMERICAN HOSPITAL FORMULARY SERVICE LIST NUMBER AND THEIR ICD-9-CM EQUIVALENTS

The coding of adverse effects of drugs is keyed to the continually revised Hospital Formulary of the American Hospital Formulary Service (AHFS) published under the direction of the American Society of Hospital Pharmacists.

The following section gives the ICD-9-CM diagnosis code for each AHFS list.

AHFS* List		ICD-9-CM Diagnosis Code
4:00	ANTIHISTAMINE DRUGS	963.0
8:00	ANTI-INFECTIVE AGENTS	
8:04	Amebacides	961.5
	hydroxyquinoline derivatives	961.3
	arsenical anti-infectives	961.1
8:08	Anthelmintics	961.6
	quinoline derivatives	961.3
8:12.04	Antifungal Antibiotics	960.1
	nonantibiotics	961.9
8:12.06	Cephalosporins	960.5
8:12.08	Chloramphenicol	960.2
8:12.12	The Erythromycins	960.3
8:12.16	The Penicillins	960.0
8:12.20	The Streptomycins	960.6
8:12.24	The Tetracyclines	960.4
8:12.28	Other Antibiotics	960.8
	antimycobacterial antibiotics	960.6
	macrolides	960.3
8:16	Antituberculars	961.8
	antibiotics	960.6
8:18	Antivirals	961.7
8:20	Plasmodicides (antimalarials)	961.4
8:24	Sulfonamides	961.0
8:26	The Sulfones	961.8
8:28	Treponemicides	961.2
8:32	Trichomonacides	961.5
	hydroxyquinoline derivatives	961.3
	nitrofuran derivatives	961.9
8:36	Urinary Germicides	961.9
	quinoline derivatives	961.3
8:40	Other Anti-Infectives	961.9
10:00	ANTINEOPLASTIC AGENTS	963.1
	antibiotics	960.7
	progestogens	962.2
12:00	AUTONOMIC DRUGS	
12:04	Parasympathomimetic (Cholinergic) Agents	971.0
12:08	Parasympatholytic (Cholinergic Blocking) Agents	971.1
12:12	Sympathomimetic (Adrenergic) Agents	971.2
12:16	Sympatholytic (Adrenergic Blocking) Agents	971.3
12:20	Skeletal Muscle Relaxants	975.2
	central nervous system muscle-tone depressants	968.0
16:00	BLOOD DERIVATIVES	964.7
20:00	BLOOD FORMATION AND COAGULATION	
20:04	Antianemia Drugs	964.1
20:04.04	Iron Preparations	964.0
20:04.08	Liver and Stomach Preparations	964.1
20:12.04	Anticoagulants	964.2
20:12.08	Antiheparin Agents	964.5
20:12.12	Coagulants	964.5
20:12.16	Hemostatics	964.5
	capillary-active drugs	972.8
	fibrinolysis-affecting agents	964.4
	natural products	964.7
24:00	CARDIOVASCULAR DRUGS	
24:04	Cardiac Drugs	972.9
	cardiotonic agents	972.1
	rhythm regulators	972.0
24:06	Antilipemic Agents	972.2
	thyroid derivatives	962.7
24:08	Hypotensive Agents	972.6
	adrenergic blocking agents	971.3
	ganglion-blocking agents	972.3
	vasodilators	972.5
24:12	Vasodilating Agents	972.5
	coronary	972.4
	nicotinic acid derivatives	972.2

AHFS* List		ICD-9-CM Diagnosis Code
24:16	Sclerosing Agents	972.7
28:00	CENTRAL NERVOUS SYSTEM DRUGS	
28:04	General Anesthetics	968.4
	gaseous anesthetics	968.2
	halothane	968.1
	intravenous anesthetics	968.3
28:08	Analgesics and Antipyretics	965.9
	antirheumatics	965.61-965.69
	aromatic analgesics	965.4
	non-narcotics NEC	965.7
	opium alkaloids	965.00
	heroin	965.01
	methadone	965.02
	specified type NEC	965.09
	pyrazole derivatives	965.5
	salicylates	965.1
	specified type NEC	965.8
28:10	Narcotic Antagonists	970.1
28:12	Anticonvulsants	966.3
	barbiturates	967.0
	benzodiazepine-based tranquilizers	969.4
	bromides	967.3
	hydantoin derivatives	966.1
	oxazolidine derivative	966.0
	succinimides	966.2
28:16.04	Antidepressants	969.0
28:16.08	Tranquilizers	969.5
	benzodiazepine-based	969.4
	butyrophenone-based	969.2
	major NEC	969.3
	phenothiazine-based	969.1
28:16.12	Other Psychotherapeutic Agents	969.8
28:20	Respiratory and Cerebral Stimulants	970.9
	analeptics	970.0
	anorexigenic agents	977.0
	psychostimulants	969.7
	specified type NEC	970.8
28:24	Sedatives and Hypnotics	967.9
	barbiturates	967.0
	benzodiazepine-based tranquilizers	969.4
	chloral hydrate group	967.1
	glutethamide group	967.5
	intravenous anesthetics	968.3
	methaqualone	967.4
	paraldehyde	967.2
	phenothiazine-based tranquilizers	969.1
	specified type NEC	967.8
	thiobarbiturates	968.3
	tranquilizer NEC	969.5
36:00	DIAGNOSTIC AGENTS	977.8
40:00	ELECTROLYTE, CALORIC, AND WATER BALANCE AGENTS NEC	974.5
40:04	Acidifying Agents	963.2
40:08	Alkalinizing Agents	963.3
40:10	Ammonia Detoxicants	974.5
40:12	Replacement Solutions NEC	974.5
	plasma volume expanders	964.8
40:16	Sodium-Removing Resins	974.5
40:18	Potassium-Removing Resins	974.5
40:20	Caloric Agents	974.5
40:24	Salt and Sugar Substitutes	974.5
40:28	Diuretics NEC	974.4
	carbonic acid anhydrase inhibitors	974.2
	mercurials	974.0
	purine derivatives	974.1
	saluretics	974.3
40:36	Irrigating Solutions	974.5
40:40	Uricosuric Agents	974.7
44:00	ENZYMES NEC	963.4
	fibrinolysis-affecting agents	964.4
	gastric agents	973.4

Appendix C: Classification of Drugs by AHFS List

AHFS* List	ICD-9-CM Diagnosis Code
48:00 EXPECTORANTS AND COUGH PREPARATIONS	
antihistamine agents	963.0
antitussives	975.4
codeine derivatives	965.09
expectorants	975.5
narcotic agents NEC	965.09
52:00 EYE, EAR, NOSE, AND THROAT PREPARATIONS	
52:04 Anti-Infectives	
ENT	976.6
ophthalmic	976.5
52:04.04 Antibiotics	
ENT	976.6
ophthalmic	976.5
52:04.06 Antivirals	
ENT	976.6
ophthalmic	976.5
52:04.08 Sulfonamides	
ENT	976.6
ophthalmic	976.5
52:04.12 Miscellaneous Anti-Infectives	
ENT	976.6
ophthalmic	976.5
52:08 Anti-Inflammatory Agents	
ENT	976.6
ophthalmic	976.5
52:10 Carbonic Anhydrase Inhibitors	974.2
52:12 Contact Lens Solutions	976.5
52:16 Local Anesthetics	968.5
52:20 Miotics	971.0
52:24 Mydriatics	
adrenergics	971.2
anticholinergics	971.1
antimuscarinics	971.1
parasympatholytics	971.1
spasmolytics	971.1
sympathomimetics	971.2
52:28 Mouth Washes and Gargles	976.6
52:32 Vasoconstrictors	971.2
52:36 Unclassified Agents	
ENT	976.6
ophthalmic	976.5
56:00 GASTROINTESTINAL DRUGS	
56:04 Antacids and Absorbents	973.0
56:08 Anti-Diarrhea Agents	973.5
56:10 Antiflatulents	973.8
56:12 Cathartics NEC	973.3
emollients	973.2
irritants	973.1
56:16 Digestants	973.4
56:20 Emetics and Antiemetics	
antiemetics	963.0
emetics	973.6
56:24 Lipotropic Agents	977.1
60:00 GOLD COMPOUNDS	965.69
64:00 HEAVY METAL ANTAGONISTS	963.8
68:00 HORMONES AND SYNTHETIC SUBSTITUTES	
68:04 Adrenals	962.0
68:08 Androgens	962.1
68:12 Contraceptives	962.2
68:16 Estrogens	962.2
68:18 Gonadotropins	962.4
68:20 Insulins and Antidiabetic Agents	962.3
68:20.08 Insulins	962.3
68:24 Parathyroid	962.6
68:28 Pituitary	
anterior	962.4
posterior	962.5
68:32 Progestogens	962.2
68:34 Other Corpus Luteum Hormones	962.2
68:36 Thyroid and Antithyroid	
antithyroid	962.8
thyroid	962.7

AHFS* List	ICD-9-CM Diagnosis Code
72:00 LOCAL ANESTHETICS NEC	968.9
topical (surface) agents	968.5
infiltrating agents (intradermal) (subcutaneous) (submucosal)	968.5
nerve blocking agents (peripheral) (plexus) (regional)	968.6
spinal	968.7
76:00 OXYTOCICS	975.0
78:00 RADIOACTIVE AGENTS	990
80:00 SERUMS, TOXOIDS, AND VACCINES	
80:04 Serums	979.9
immune globulin (gamma) (human)	964.6
80:08 Toxoids NEC	978.8
diphtheria	978.5
and tetanus	978.9
with pertussis component	978.6
tetanus	978.4
and diphtheria	978.9
with pertussis component	978.6
80:12 Vaccines NEC	979.9
bacterial NEC	978.8
with	
other bacterial component	978.9
pertussis component	978.6
viral and rickettsial component	979.7
rickettsial NEC	979.6
with	
bacterial component	979.7
pertussis component	978.6
viral component	979.7
viral NEC	979.6
with	
bacterial component	979.7
pertussis component	978.6
rickettsial component	979.7
84:00 SKIN AND MUCOUS MEMBRANE PREPARATIONS	
84:04 Anti-Infectives	976.0
84:04.04 Antibiotics	976.0
84:04.08 Fungicides	976.0
84:04.12 Scabicides and Pediculicides	976.0
84:04.16 Miscellaneous Local Anti-Infectives	976.0
84:06 Anti-Inflammatory Agents	976.0
84:08 Antipruritics and Local Anesthetics	
antipruritics	976.1
local anesthetics	968.5
84:12 Astringents	976.2
84:16 Cell Stimulants and Proliferants	976.8
84:20 Detergents	976.2
84:24 Emollients, Demulcents, and Protectants	976.3
84:28 Keratolytic Agents	976.4
84:32 Keratoplastic Agents	976.4
84:36 Miscellaneous Agents	976.8
86:00 SPASMOLYTIC AGENTS	975.1
antiasthmatics	975.7
papaverine	972.5
theophyllin	974.1
88:00 VITAMINS	
88:04 Vitamin A	963.5
88:08 Vitamin B Complex	963.5
hematopoietic vitamin	964.1
nicotinic acid derivatives	972.2
88:12 Vitamin C	963.5
88:16 Vitamin D	963.5
88:20 Vitamin E	963.5
88:24 Vitamin K Activity	964.3
88:28 Multivitamin Preparations	963.5
92:00 UNCLASSIFIED THERAPEUTIC AGENTS	977.8

* American Hospital Formulary Service

CLASSIFICATION OF INDUSTRIAL ACCIDENTS ACCORDING TO AGENCY
Annex B to the Resolution concerning Statistics of Employment Injuries adopted by the Tenth International Conference of Labor Statisticians on 12 October 1962

1 MACHINES

11 Prime-Movers, except Electrical Motors
111 *Steam engines*
112 *Internal combustion engines*
119 *Others*
12 Transmission Machinery
121 *Transmission shafts*
122 *Transmission belts, cables, pulleys, pinions, chains, gears*
129 *Others*
13 Metalworking Machines
131 *Power presses*
132 *Lathes*
133 *Milling machines*
134 *Abrasive wheels*
135 *Mechanical shears*
136 *Forging machines*
137 *Rolling-mills*
139 *Others*
14 Wood and Assimilated Machines
141 *Circular saws*
142 *Other saws*
143 *Molding machines*
144 *Overhand planes*
149 *Others*
15 Agricultural Machines
151 *Reapers (including combine reapers)*
152 *Threshers*
159 *Others*
16 Mining Machinery
161 *Under-cutters*
169 *Others*
19 Other Machines Not Elsewhere Classified
191 *Earth-moving machines, excavating and scraping machines, except means of transport*
192 *Spinning, weaving and other textile machines*
193 *Machines for the manufacture of foodstuffs and beverages*
194 *Machines for the manufacture of paper*
195 *Printing machines*
199 *Others*

2 MEANS OF TRANSPORT AND LIFTING EQUIPMENT

21 Lifting Machines and Appliances
211 *Cranes*
212 *Lifts and elevators*
213 *Winches*
214 *Pulley blocks*
219 *Others*
22 Means of Rail Transport
221 *Inter-urban railways*
222 *Rail transport in mines, tunnels, quarries, industrial establishments, docks, etc.*
229 *Others*
23 Other Wheeled Means of Transport, Excluding Rail Transport
231 *Tractors*
232 *Lorries*
233 *Trucks*
234 *Motor vehicles, not elsewhere classified*
235 *Animal-drawn vehicles*
236 *Hand-drawn vehicles*
239 *Others*
24 Means of Air Transport
25 Means of Water Transport
251 *Motorized means of water transport*
252 *Non-motorized means of water transport*
26 Other Means of Transport
261 *Cable-cars*
262 *Mechanical conveyors, except cable-cars*
269 *Others*

3 OTHER EQUIPMENT

31 Pressure Vessels
311 *Boilers*
312 *Pressurized containers*
313 *Pressurized piping and accessories*
314 *Gas cylinders*
315 *Caissons, diving equipment*
319 *Others*
32 Furnaces, Ovens, Kilns
321 *Blast furnaces*
322 *Refining furnaces*
323 *Other furnaces*
324 *Kilns*
325 *Ovens*
33 Refrigerating Plants
34 Electrical Installations, Including Electric Motors, but Excluding Electric Hand Tools
341 *Rotating machines*
342 *Conductors*
343 *Transformers*
344 *Control apparatus*
349 *Others*
35 Electric Hand Tools
36 Tools, Implements, and Appliances, Except Electric Hand Tools
361 *Power-driven hand tools, except electric hand tools*
362 *Hand tools, not power-driven*
369 *Others*
37 Ladders, Mobile Ramps
38 Scaffolding
39 Other Equipment, Not Elsewhere Classified

4 MATERIALS, SUBSTANCES AND RADIATIONS

41 Explosives
42 Dusts, Gases, Liquids and Chemicals, Excluding Explosives
421 *Dusts*
422 *Gases, vapors, fumes*
423 *Liquids, not elsewhere classified*
424 *Chemicals, not elsewhere classified*
43 Flying Fragments
44 Radiations
441 *Ionizing radiations*
449 *Others*
49 Other Materials and Substances Not Elsewhere Classified

5 WORKING ENVIRONMENT

51 Outdoor
511 *Weather*
512 *Traffic and working surfaces*
513 *Water*
519 *Others*
52 Indoor
521 *Floors*
522 *Confined quarters*
523 *Stairs*
524 *Other traffic and working surfaces*
525 *Floor openings and wall openings*
526 *Environmental factors (lighting, ventilation, temperature, noise, etc.)*
529 *Others*
53 Underground
531 *Roofs and faces of mine roads and tunnels, etc.*
532 *Floors of mine roads and tunnels, etc.*
533 *Working-faces of mines, tunnels, etc.*
534 *Mine shafts*
535 *Fire*
536 *Water*
539 *Others*

6 OTHER AGENCIES, NOT ELSEWHERE CLASSIFIED

61 Animals
611 *Live animals*
612 *Animal products*
69 Other Agencies, Not Elsewhere Classified

7 AGENCIES NOT CLASSIFIED FOR LACK OF SUFFICIENT DATA

LIST OF THREE-DIGIT CATEGORIES

1. INFECTIOUS AND PARASITIC DISEASES

Intestinal infectious diseases (001-009)
001 Cholera
002 Typhoid and paratyphoid fevers
003 Other salmonella infections
004 Shigellosis
005 Other food poisoning (bacterial)
006 Amebiasis
007 Other protozoal intestinal diseases
008 Intestinal infections due to other organisms
009 Ill-defined intestinal infections

Tuberculosis (010-018)
010 Primary tuberculous infection
011 Pulmonary tuberculosis
012 Other respiratory tuberculosis
013 Tuberculosis of meninges and central nervous system
014 Tuberculosis of intestines, peritoneum, and mesenteric glands
015 Tuberculosis of bones and joints
016 Tuberculosis of genitourinary system
017 Tuberculosis of other organs
018 Miliary tuberculosis

Zoonotic bacterial diseases (020-027)
020 Plague
021 Tularemia
022 Anthrax
023 Brucellosis
024 Glanders
025 Melioidosis
026 Rat-bite fever
027 Other zoonotic bacterial diseases

Other bacterial diseases (030-042)
030 Leprosy
031 Diseases due to other mycobacteria
032 Diphtheria
033 Whooping cough
034 Streptococcal sore throat and scarlatina
035 Erysipelas
036 Meningococcal infection
037 Tetanus
038 Septicemia
039 Actinomycotic infections
040 Other bacterial diseases
041 Bacterial infection in conditions classified elsewhere and of unspecified site

Human immunodeficiency virus (042)
042 Human immunodeficiency virus [HIV] disease

Poliomyelitis and other non-arthropod-borne viral diseases of central nervous system (045-049)
045 Acute poliomyelitis
046 Slow virus infection of central nervous system
047 Meningitis due to enterovirus
048 Other enterovirus diseases of central nervous system
049 Other non-arthropod-borne viral diseases of central nervous system

Viral diseases accompanied by exanthem (050-057)
050 Smallpox
051 Cowpox and paravaccinia
052 Chickenpox
053 Herpes zoster
054 Herpes simplex
055 Measles
056 Rubella
057 Other viral exanthemata

Arthropod-borne viral diseases (060-066)
060 Yellow fever
061 Dengue
062 Mosquito-borne viral encephalitis
063 Tick-borne viral encephalitis
064 Viral encephalitis transmitted by other and unspecified arthropods
065 Arthropod-borne hemorrhagic fever
066 Other arthropod-borne viral diseases

Other diseases due to viruses and Chlamydiae (070-079)
070 Viral hepatitis
071 Rabies
072 Mumps
073 Ornithosis
074 Specific diseases due to Coxsackievirus
075 Infectious mononucleosis
076 Trachoma
077 Other diseases of conjunctiva due to viruses and Chlamydiae
078 Other diseases due to viruses and Chlamydiae
079 Viral infection in conditions classified elsewhere and of unspecified site

Rickettsioses and other arthropod-borne diseases (080-088)
080 Louse-borne [epidemic] typhus
081 Other typhus
082 Tick-borne rickettsioses
083 Other rickettsioses
084 Malaria
085 Leishmaniasis
086 Trypanosomiasis
087 Relapsing fever
088 Other arthropod-borne diseases

Syphilis and other venereal diseases (090-099)
090 Congenital syphilis
091 Early syphilis, symptomatic
092 Early syphilis, latent
093 Cardiovascular syphilis
094 Neurosyphilis
095 Other forms of late syphilis, with symptoms
096 Late syphilis, latent
097 Other and unspecified syphilis
098 Gonococcal infections
099 Other venereal diseases

Other spirochetal diseases (100-104)
100 Leptospirosis
101 Vincent's angina
102 Yaws
103 Pinta
104 Other spirochetal infection

Mycoses (110-118)
110 Dermatophytosis
111 Dermatomycosis, other and unspecified
112 Candidiasis
114 Coccidioidomycosis
115 Histoplasmosis
116 Blastomycotic infection
117 Other mycoses
118 Opportunistic mycoses

Helminthiases (120-129)
120 Schistosomiasis [bilharziasis]
121 Other trematode infections
122 Echinococcosis
123 Other cestode infection
124 Trichinosis
125 Filarial infection and dracontiasis
126 Ancylostomiasis and necatoriasis
127 Other intestinal helminthiases
128 Other and unspecified helminthiases
129 Intestinal parasitism, unspecified

Other infectious and parasitic diseases (130-136)
130 Toxoplasmosis
131 Trichomoniasis
132 Pediculosis and phthirus infestation
133 Acariasis
134 Other infestation
135 Sarcoidosis
136 Other and unspecified infectious and parasitic diseases

Late effects of infectious and parasitic diseases (137-139)
137 Late effects of tuberculosis
138 Late effects of acute poliomyelitis
139 Late effects of other infectious and parasitic diseases

2. NEOPLASMS

Malignant neoplasm of lip, oral cavity, and pharynx (140-149)
140 Malignant neoplasm of lip
141 Malignant neoplasm of tongue
142 Malignant neoplasm of major salivary glands
143 Malignant neoplasm of gum
144 Malignant neoplasm of floor of mouth
145 Malignant neoplasm of other and unspecified parts of mouth
146 Malignant neoplasm of oropharynx
147 Malignant neoplasm of nasopharynx
148 Malignant neoplasm of hypopharynx
149 Malignant neoplasm of other and ill-defined sites within the lip, oral cavity, and pharynx

Malignant neoplasm of digestive organs and peritoneum (150-159)
150 Malignant neoplasm of esophagus
151 Malignant neoplasm of stomach
152 Malignant neoplasm of small intestine, including duodenum
153 Malignant neoplasm of colon
154 Malignant neoplasm of rectum, rectosigmoid junction, and anus
155 Malignant neoplasm of liver and intrahepatic bile ducts
156 Malignant neoplasm of gallbladder and extrahepatic bile ducts
157 Malignant neoplasm of pancreas
158 Malignant neoplasm of retroperitoneum and peritoneum
159 Malignant neoplasm of other and ill-defined sites within the digestive organs and peritoneum

Malignant neoplasm of respiratory and intrathoracic organs (160-165)
160 Malignant neoplasm of nasal cavities, middle ear, and accessory sinuses
161 Malignant neoplasm of larynx
162 Malignant neoplasm of trachea, bronchus, and lung
163 Malignant neoplasm of pleura
164 Malignant neoplasm of thymus, heart, and mediastinum
165 Malignant neoplasm of other and ill-defined sites within the respiratory system and intrathoracic organs

Malignant neoplasm of bone, connective tissue, skin, and breast (170-176)
170 Malignant neoplasm of bone and articular cartilage
171 Malignant neoplasm of connective and other soft tissue
172 Malignant melanoma of skin
173 Other malignant neoplasm of skin
174 Malignant neoplasm of female breast
175 Malignant neoplasm of male breast
176 Kaposi's sarcoma

Malignant neoplasm of genitourinary organs (179-189)
179 Malignant neoplasm of uterus, part unspecified
180 Malignant neoplasm of cervix uteri
181 Malignant neoplasm of placenta
182 Malignant neoplasm of body of uterus
183 Malignant neoplasm of ovary and other uterine adnexa
184 Malignant neoplasm of other and unspecified female genital organs
185 Malignant neoplasm of prostate

Appendix E: List of Three-Digit Categories

186 Malignant neoplasm of testis
187 Malignant neoplasm of penis and other male genital organs
188 Malignant neoplasm of bladder
189 Malignant neoplasm of kidney and other unspecified urinary organs

Malignant neoplasm of other and unspecified sites (190-199)
190 Malignant neoplasm of eye
191 Malignant neoplasm of brain
192 Malignant neoplasm of other and unspecified parts of nervous system
193 Malignant neoplasm of thyroid gland
194 Malignant neoplasm of other endocrine glands and related structures
195 Malignant neoplasm of other and ill-defined sites
196 Secondary and unspecified malignant neoplasm of lymph nodes
197 Secondary malignant neoplasm of respiratory and digestive systems
198 Secondary malignant neoplasm of other specified sites
199 Malignant neoplasm without specification of site

Malignant neoplasm of lymphatic and hematopoietic tissue (200-208)
200 Lymphosarcoma and reticulosarcoma
201 Hodgkin's disease
202 Other malignant neoplasm of lymphoid and histiocytic tissue
203 Multiple myeloma and immunoproliferative neoplasms
204 Lymphoid leukemia
205 Myeloid leukemia
206 Monocytic leukemia
207 Other specified leukemia
208 Leukemia of unspecified cell type

Benign neoplasms (210-229)
210 Benign neoplasm of lip, oral cavity, and pharynx
211 Benign neoplasm of other parts of digestive system
212 Benign neoplasm of respiratory and intrathoracic organs
213 Benign neoplasm of bone and articular cartilage
214 Lipoma
215 Other benign neoplasm of connective and other soft tissue
216 Benign neoplasm of skin
217 Benign neoplasm of breast
218 Uterine leiomyoma
219 Other benign neoplasm of uterus
220 Benign neoplasm of ovary
221 Benign neoplasm of other female genital organs
222 Benign neoplasm of male genital organs
223 Benign neoplasm of kidney and other urinary organs
224 Benign neoplasm of eye
225 Benign neoplasm of brain and other parts of nervous system
226 Benign neoplasm of thyroid gland
227 Benign neoplasm of other endocrine glands and related structures
228 Hemangioma and lymphangioma, any site
229 Benign neoplasm of other and unspecified sites

Carcinoma in situ (230-234)
230 Carcinoma in situ of digestive organs
231 Carcinoma in situ of respiratory system
232 Carcinoma in situ of skin
233 Carcinoma in situ of breast and genitourinary system
234 Carcinoma in situ of other and unspecified sites

Neoplasms of uncertain behavior (235-238)
235 Neoplasm of uncertain behavior of digestive and respiratory systems

236 Neoplasm of uncertain behavior of genitourinary organs
237 Neoplasm of uncertain behavior of endocrine glands and nervous system
238 Neoplasm of uncertain behavior of other and unspecified sites and tissues

Neoplasms of unspecified nature (239)
239 Neoplasm of unspecified nature

3. ENDOCRINE, NUTRITIONAL AND METABOLIC DISEASES, AND IMMUNITY DISORDERS

Disorders of thyroid gland (240-246)
240 Simple and unspecified goiter
241 Nontoxic nodular goiter
242 Thyrotoxicosis with or without goiter
243 Congenital hypothyroidism
244 Acquired hypothyroidism
245 Thyroiditis
246 Other disorders of thyroid

Diseases of other endocrine glands (250-259)
250 Diabetes mellitus
251 Other disorders of pancreatic internal secretion
252 Disorders of parathyroid gland
253 Disorders of the pituitary gland and its hypothalamic control
254 Diseases of thymus gland
255 Disorders of adrenal glands
256 Ovarian dysfunction
257 Testicular dysfunction
258 Polyglandular dysfunction and related disorders
259 Other endocrine disorders

Nutritional deficiencies (260-269)
260 Kwashiorkor
261 Nutritional marasmus
262 Other severe protein-calorie malnutrition
263 Other and unspecified protein-calorie malnutrition
264 Vitamin A deficiency
265 Thiamine and niacin deficiency states
266 Deficiency of B-complex components
267 Ascorbic acid deficiency
268 Vitamin D deficiency
269 Other nutritional deficiencies

Other metabolic disorders and immunity disorders (270-279)
270 Disorders of amino-acid transport and metabolism
271 Disorders of carbohydrate transport and metabolism
272 Disorders of lipid metabolism
273 Disorders of plasma protein metabolism
274 Gout
275 Disorders of mineral metabolism
276 Disorders of fluid, electrolyte, and acid-base balance
277 Other and unspecified disorders of metabolism
278 Overweight, obesity and other hyperalimentation
279 Disorders involving the immune mechanism

4. DISEASES OF BLOOD AND BLOOD-FORMING ORGANS (280-289)
280 Iron deficiency anemias
281 Other deficiency anemias
282 Hereditary hemolytic anemias
283 Acquired hemolytic anemias
284 Aplastic anemia
285 Other and unspecified anemias
286 Coagulation defects
287 Purpura and other hemorrhagic conditions
288 Diseases of white blood cells
289 Other diseases of blood and blood-forming organs

5. MENTAL DISORDERS

Organic psychotic conditions (290-294)
290 Senile and presenile organic psychotic conditions
291 Alcoholic psychoses
292 Drug psychoses
293 Transient organic psychotic conditions
294 Other organic psychotic conditions (chronic)

Other psychoses (295-299)
295 Schizophrenic psychoses
296 Affective psychoses
297 Paranoid states
298 Other nonorganic psychoses
299 Psychoses with origin specific to childhood

Neurotic disorders, personality disorders, and other nonpsychotic mental disorders (300-316)
300 Neurotic disorders
301 Personality disorders
302 Sexual deviations and disorders
303 Alcohol dependence syndrome
304 Drug dependence
305 Nondependent abuse of drugs
306 Physiological malfunction arising from mental factors
307 Special symptoms or syndromes, not elsewhere classified
308 Acute reaction to stress
309 Adjustment reaction
310 Specific nonpsychotic mental disorders following organic brain damage
311 Depressive disorder, not elsewhere classified
312 Disturbance of conduct, not elsewhere classified
313 Disturbance of emotions specific to childhood and adolescence
314 Hyperkinetic syndrome of childhood
315 Specific delays in development
316 Psychic factors associated with diseases classified elsewhere

Mental retardation (317-319)
317 Mild mental retardation
318 Other specified mental retardation
319 Unspecified mental retardation

6. DISEASES OF THE NERVOUS SYSTEM AND SENSE ORGANS

Inflammatory diseases of the central nervous system (320-326)
320 Bacterial meningitis
321 Meningitis due to other organisms
322 Meningitis of unspecified cause
323 Encephalitis, myelitis, and encephalomyelitis
324 Intracranial and intraspinal abscess
325 Phlebitis and thrombophlebitis of intracranial venous sinuses
326 Late effects of intracranial abscess or pyogenic infection

Organic Sleep Disorders (327)
327 Organic sleep disorders

Hereditary and degenerative diseases of the central nervous system (330-337)
330 Cerebral degenerations usually manifest in childhood
331 Other cerebral degenerations
332 Parkinson's disease
333 Other extrapyramidal diseases and abnormal movement disorders
334 Spinocerebellar disease
335 Anterior horn cell disease
336 Other diseases of spinal cord
337 Disorders of the autonomic nervous system

Pain (338)
338 Pain, not elsewhere classified

Other disorders of the central nervous system (340-349)
340 Multiple sclerosis
341 Other demyelinating diseases of central nervous system
342 Hemiplegia and hemiparesis
343 Infantile cerebral palsy
344 Other paralytic syndromes
345 Epilepsy and recurrent seizures
346 Migraine
347 Cataplexy and narcolepsy
348 Other conditions of brain
349 Other and unspecified disorders of the nervous system

Disorders of the peripheral nervous system (350-359)
350 Trigeminal nerve disorders
351 Facial nerve disorders
352 Disorders of other cranial nerves
353 Nerve root and plexus disorders
354 Mononeuritis of upper limb and mononeuritis multiplex
355 Mononeuritis of lower limb
356 Hereditary and idiopathic peripheral neuropathy
357 Inflammatory and toxic neuropathy
358 Myoneural disorders
359 Muscular dystrophies and other myopathies

Disorders of the eye and adnexa (360-379)
360 Disorders of the globe
361 Retinal detachments and defects
362 Other retinal disorders
363 Chorioretinal inflammations and scars and other disorders of choroid
364 Disorders of iris and ciliary body
365 Glaucoma
366 Cataract
367 Disorders of refraction and accommodation
368 Visual disturbances
369 Blindness and low vision
370 Keratitis
371 Corneal opacity and other disorders of cornea
372 Disorders of conjunctiva
373 Inflammation of eyelids
374 Other disorders of eyelids
375 Disorders of lacrimal system
376 Disorders of the orbit
377 Disorders of optic nerve and visual pathways
378 Strabismus and other disorders of binocular eye movements
379 Other disorders of eye

Diseases of the ear and mastoid process (380-389)
380 Disorders of external ear
381 Nonsuppurative otitis media and Eustachian tube disorders
382 Suppurative and unspecified otitis media
383 Mastoiditis and related conditions
384 Other disorders of tympanic membrane
385 Other disorders of middle ear and mastoid
386 Vertiginous syndromes and other disorders of vestibular system
387 Otosclerosis
388 Other disorders of ear
389 Hearing loss

7. DISEASES OF THE CIRCULATORY SYSTEM

Acute rheumatic fever (390-392)
390 Rheumatic fever without mention of heart involvement
391 Rheumatic fever with heart involvement
392 Rheumatic chorea

Chronic rheumatic heart disease (393-398)
393 Chronic rheumatic pericarditis
394 Diseases of mitral valve
395 Diseases of aortic valve
396 Diseases of mitral and aortic valves
397 Diseases of other endocardial structures
398 Other rheumatic heart disease

Hypertensive disease (401-405)
401 Essential hypertension
402 Hypertensive heart disease
403 Hypertensive kidney disease
404 Hypertensive heart and kidney disease
405 Secondary hypertension

Ischemic heart disease (410-414)
410 Acute myocardial infarction
411 Other acute and subacute form of ischemic heart disease
412 Old myocardial infarction
413 Angina pectoris
414 Other forms of chronic ischemic heart disease

Diseases of pulmonary circulation (415-417)
415 Acute pulmonary heart disease
416 Chronic pulmonary heart disease
417 Other diseases of pulmonary circulation

Other forms of heart disease (420-429)
420 Acute pericarditis
421 Acute and subacute endocarditis
422 Acute myocarditis
423 Other diseases of pericardium
424 Other diseases of endocardium
425 Cardiomyopathy
426 Conduction disorders
427 Cardiac dysrhythmias
428 Heart failure
429 Ill-defined descriptions and complications of heart disease

Cerebrovascular disease (430-438)
430 Subarachnoid hemorrhage
431 Intracerebral hemorrhage
432 Other and unspecified intracranial hemorrhage
433 Occlusion and stenosis of precerebral arteries
434 Occlusion of cerebral arteries
435 Transient cerebral ischemia
436 Acute but ill-defined cerebrovascular disease
437 Other and ill-defined cerebrovascular disease
438 Late effects of cerebrovascular disease

Diseases of arteries, arterioles, and capillaries (440-448)
440 Atherosclerosis
441 Aortic aneurysm and dissection
442 Other aneurysm
443 Other peripheral vascular disease
444 Arterial embolism and thrombosis
445 Atheroembolism
446 Polyarteritis nodosa and allied conditions
447 Other disorders of arteries and arterioles
448 Diseases of capillaries

Diseases of veins and lymphatics, and other diseases of circulatory system (451-459)
451 Phlebitis and thrombophlebitis
452 Portal vein thrombosis
453 Other venous embolism and thrombosis
454 Varicose veins of lower extremities
455 Hemorrhoids
456 Varicose veins of other sites
457 Noninfective disorders of lymphatic channels
458 Hypotension
459 Other disorders of circulatory system

8. DISEASES OF THE RESPIRATORY SYSTEM

Acute respiratory infections (460-466)
460 Acute nasopharyngitis [common cold]
461 Acute sinusitis
462 Acute pharyngitis
463 Acute tonsillitis
464 Acute laryngitis and tracheitis
465 Acute upper respiratory infections of multiple or unspecified sites
466 Acute bronchitis and bronchiolitis

Other diseases of upper respiratory tract (470-478)
470 Deviated nasal septum
471 Nasal polyps
472 Chronic pharyngitis and nasopharyngitis
473 Chronic sinusitis
474 Chronic disease of tonsils and adenoids
475 Peritonsillar abscess
476 Chronic laryngitis and laryngotracheitis
477 Allergic rhinitis
478 Other diseases of upper respiratory tract

Pneumonia and influenza (480-487)
480 Viral pneumonia
481 Pneumococcal pneumonia [Streptococcus pneumoniae pneumonia]
482 Other bacterial pneumonia
483 Pneumonia due to other specified organism
484 Pneumonia in infectious diseases classified elsewhere
485 Bronchopneumonia, organism unspecified
486 Pneumonia, organism unspecified
487 Influenza

Chronic obstructive pulmonary disease and allied conditions (490-496)
490 Bronchitis, not specified as acute or chronic
491 Chronic bronchitis
492 Emphysema
493 Asthma
494 Bronchiectasis
495 Extrinsic allergic alveolitis
496 Chronic airways obstruction, not elsewhere classified

Pneumoconioses and other lung diseases due to external agents (500-508)
500 Coal workers' pneumoconiosis
501 Asbestosis
502 Pneumoconiosis due to other silica or silicates
503 Pneumoconiosis due to other inorganic dust
504 Pneumopathy due to inhalation of other dust
505 Pneumoconiosis, unspecified
506 Respiratory conditions due to chemical fumes and vapors
507 Pneumonitis due to solids and liquids
508 Respiratory conditions due to other and unspecified external agents

Other diseases of respiratory system (510-519)
510 Empyema
511 Pleurisy
512 Pneumothorax
513 Abscess of lung and mediastinum
514 Pulmonary congestion and hypostasis
515 Postinflammatory pulmonary fibrosis
516 Other alveolar and parietoalveolar pneumopathy
517 Lung involvement in conditions classified elsewhere
518 Other diseases of lung
519 Other diseases of respiratory system

9. DISEASES OF THE DIGESTIVE SYSTEM

Diseases of oral cavity, salivary glands, and jaws (520-529)
520 Disorders of tooth development and eruption
521 Diseases of hard tissues of teeth
522 Diseases of pulp and periapical tissues
523 Gingival and periodontal diseases
524 Dentofacial anomalies, including malocclusion
525 Other diseases and conditions of the teeth and supporting structures
526 Diseases of the jaws
527 Diseases of the salivary glands

Appendix E: List of Three-Digit Categories

528 Diseases of the oral soft tissues, excluding lesions specific for gingiva and tongue
529 Diseases and other conditions of the tongue

Diseases of esophagus, stomach, and duodenum (530-538)
530 Diseases of esophagus
531 Gastric ulcer
532 Duodenal ulcer
533 Peptic ulcer, site unspecified
534 Gastrojejunal ulcer
535 Gastritis and duodenitis
536 Disorders of function of stomach
537 Other disorders of stomach and duodenum
538 Gastrointestinal mucositis (ulcerative)

Appendicitis (540-543)
540 Acute appendicitis
541 Appendicitis, unqualified
542 Other appendicitis
543 Other diseases of appendix

Hernia of abdominal cavity (550-553)
550 Inguinal hernia
551 Other hernia of abdominal cavity, with gangrene
552 Other hernia of abdominal cavity, with obstruction, but without mention of gangrene
553 Other hernia of abdominal cavity without mention of obstruction or gangrene

Noninfective enteritis and colitis (555-558)
555 Regional enteritis
556 Ulcerative colitis
557 Vascular insufficiency of intestine
558 Other noninfective gastroenteritis and colitis

Other diseases of intestines and peritoneum (560-569)
560 Intestinal obstruction without mention of hernia
562 Diverticula of intestine
564 Functional digestive disorders, not elsewhere classified
565 Anal fissure and fistula
566 Abscess of anal and rectal regions
567 Peritonitis and retroperitoneal infections
568 Other disorders of peritoneum
569 Other disorders of intestine

Other diseases of digestive system (570-579)
570 Acute and subacute necrosis of liver
571 Chronic liver disease and cirrhosis
572 Liver abscess and sequelae of chronic liver disease
573 Other disorders of liver
574 Cholelithiasis
575 Other disorders of gallbladder
576 Other disorders of biliary tract
577 Diseases of pancreas
578 Gastrointestinal hemorrhage
579 Intestinal malabsorption

10. DISEASES OF THE GENITOURINARY SYSTEM

Nephritis, nephrotic syndrome, and nephrosis (580-589)
580 Acute glomerulonephritis
581 Nephrotic syndrome
582 Chronic glomerulonephritis
583 Nephritis and nephropathy, not specified as acute or chronic
584 Acute renal failure
585 Chronic kidney disease (CKD)
586 Renal failure, unspecified
587 Renal sclerosis, unspecified
588 Disorders resulting from impaired renal function
589 Small kidney of unknown cause

Other diseases of urinary system (590-599)
590 Infections of kidney
591 Hydronephrosis
592 Calculus of kidney and ureter
593 Other disorders of kidney and ureter

594 Calculus of lower urinary tract
595 Cystitis
596 Other disorders of bladder
597 Urethritis, not sexually transmitted, and urethral syndrome
598 Urethral stricture
599 Other disorders of urethra and urinary tract

Diseases of male genital organs (600-608)
600 Hyperplasia of prostate
601 Inflammatory diseases of prostate
602 Other disorders of prostate
603 Hydrocele
604 Orchitis and epididymitis
605 Redundant prepuce and phimosis
606 Infertility, male
607 Disorders of penis
608 Other disorders of male genital organs

Disorders of breast (610-611)
610 Benign mammary dysplasias
611 Other disorders of breast

Inflammatory disease of female pelvic organs (614-616)
614 Inflammatory disease of ovary, fallopian tube, pelvic cellular tissue, and peritoneum
615 Inflammatory diseases of uterus, except cervix
616 Inflammatory disease of cervix, vagina, and vulva

Other disorders of female genital tract (617-629)
617 Endometriosis
618 Genital prolapse
619 Fistula involving female genital tract
620 Noninflammatory disorders of ovary, fallopian tube, and broad ligament
621 Disorders of uterus, not elsewhere classified
622 Noninflammatory disorders of cervix
623 Noninflammatory disorders of vagina
624 Noninflammatory disorders of vulva and perineum
625 Pain and other symptoms associated with female genital organs
626 Disorders of menstruation and other abnormal bleeding from female genital tract
627 Menopausal and postmenopausal disorders
628 Infertility, female
629 Other disorders of female genital organs

11. COMPLICATIONS OF PREGNANCY, CHILDBIRTH AND THE PUERPERIUM

Ectopic and molar pregnancy and other pregnancy with abortive outcome (630-639)
630 Hydatidiform mole
631 Other abnormal product of conception
632 Missed abortion
633 Ectopic pregnancy
634 Spontaneous abortion
635 Legally induced abortion
636 Illegally induced abortion
637 Unspecified abortion
638 Failed attempted abortion
639 Complications following abortion and ectopic and molar pregnancies

Complications mainly related to pregnancy (640-649)
640 Hemorrhage in early pregnancy
641 Antepartum hemorrhage, abruptio placentae, and placenta previa
642 Hypertension complicating pregnancy, childbirth, and the puerperium
643 Excessive vomiting in pregnancy
644 Early or threatened labor
645 Prolonged pregnancy
646 Other complications of pregnancy, not elsewhere classified
647 Infective and parasitic conditions in the mother classifiable elsewhere but complicating pregnancy, childbirth, and the puerperium

648 Other current conditions in the mother classifiable elsewhere but complicating pregnancy, childbirth, and the puerperium
649 Other conditions or status of the mother complicating pregnancy, childbirth, or puerperium

Normal delivery, and other indications for care in pregnancy, labor, and delivery (650-659)
650 Normal delivery
651 Multiple gestation
652 Malposition and malpresentation of fetus
653 Disproportion
654 Abnormality of organs and soft tissues of pelvis
655 Known or suspected fetal abnormality affecting management of mother
656 Other fetal and placental problems affecting management of mother
657 Polyhydramnios
658 Other problems associated with amniotic cavity and membranes
659 Other indications for care or intervention related to labor and delivery and not elsewhere classified

Complications occurring mainly in the course of labor and delivery (660-669)
660 Obstructed labor
661 Abnormality of forces of labor
662 Long labor
663 Umbilical cord complications
664 Trauma to perineum and vulva during delivery
665 Other obstetrical trauma
666 Postpartum hemorrhage
667 Retained placenta or membranes, without hemorrhage
668 Complications of the administration of anesthetic or other sedation in labor and delivery
669 Other complications of labor and delivery, not elsewhere classified

Complications of the puerperium (670-677)
670 Major puerperal infection
671 Venous complications in pregnancy and the puerperium
672 Pyrexia of unknown origin during the puerperium
673 Obstetrical pulmonary embolism
674 Other and unspecified complications of the puerperium, not elsewhere classified
675 Infections of the breast and nipple associated with childbirth
676 Other disorders of the breast associated with childbirth, and disorders of lactation
677 Late effect of complication of pregnancy, childbirth, and the puerperium

12. DISEASES OF THE SKIN AND SUBCUTANEOUS TISSUE

Infections of skin and subcutaneous tissue (680-686)
680 Carbuncle and furuncle
681 Cellulitis and abscess of finger and toe
682 Other cellulitis and abscess
683 Acute lymphadenitis
684 Impetigo
685 Pilonidal cyst
686 Other local infections of skin and subcutaneous tissue

Other inflammatory conditions of skin and subcutaneous tissue (690-698)
690 Erythematosquamous dermatosis
691 Atopic dermatitis and related conditions
692 Contact dermatitis and other eczema
693 Dermatitis due to substances taken internally
694 Bullous dermatoses
695 Erythematous conditions
696 Psoriasis and similar disorders

697 Lichen
698 Pruritus and related conditions

Other diseases of skin and subcutaneous tissue (700-709)
700 Corns and callosities
701 Other hypertrophic and atrophic conditions of skin
702 Other dermatoses
703 Diseases of nail
704 Diseases of hair and hair follicles
705 Disorders of sweat glands
706 Diseases of sebaceous glands
707 Chronic ulcer of skin
708 Urticaria
709 Other disorders of skin and subcutaneous tissue

13. DISEASES OF THE MUSCULOSKELETAL SYSTEM AND CONNECTIVE TISSUE

Arthropathies and related disorders (710-719)
710 Diffuse diseases of connective tissue
711 Arthropathy associated with infections
712 Crystal arthropathies
713 Arthropathy associated with other disorders classified elsewhere
714 Rheumatoid arthritis and other inflammatory polyarthropathies
715 Osteoarthrosis and allied disorders
716 Other and unspecified arthropathies
717 Internal derangement of knee
718 Other derangement of joint
719 Other and unspecified disorder of joint

Dorsopathies (720-724)
720 Ankylosing spondylitis and other inflammatory spondylopathies
721 Spondylosis and allied disorders
722 Intervertebral disc disorders
723 Other disorders of cervical region
724 Other and unspecified disorders of back

Rheumatism, excluding the back (725-729)
725 Polymyalgia rheumatica
726 Peripheral enthesopathies and allied syndromes
727 Other disorders of synovium, tendon, and bursa
728 Disorders of muscle, ligament, and fascia
729 Other disorders of soft tissues

Osteopathies, chondropathies, and acquired musculoskeletal deformities (730-739)
730 Osteomyelitis, periostitis, and other infections involving bone
731 Osteitis deformans and osteopathies associated with other disorders classified elsewhere
732 Osteochondropathies
733 Other disorders of bone and cartilage
734 Flat foot
735 Acquired deformities of toe
736 Other acquired deformities of limbs
737 Curvature of spine
738 Other acquired deformity
739 Nonallopathic lesions, not elsewhere classified

14. CONGENITAL ANOMALIES
740 Anencephalus and similar anomalies
741 Spina bifida
742 Other congenital anomalies of nervous system
743 Congenital anomalies of eye
744 Congenital anomalies of ear, face, and neck
745 Bulbus cordis anomalies and anomalies of cardiac septal closure
746 Other congenital anomalies of heart
747 Other congenital anomalies of circulatory system
748 Congenital anomalies of respiratory system
749 Cleft palate and cleft lip
750 Other congenital anomalies of upper alimentary tract

751 Other congenital anomalies of digestive system
752 Congenital anomalies of genital organs
753 Congenital anomalies of urinary system
754 Certain congenital musculoskeletal deformities
755 Other congenital anomalies of limbs
756 Other congenital musculoskeletal anomalies
757 Congenital anomalies of the integument
758 Chromosomal anomalies
759 Other and unspecified congenital anomalies

15. CERTAIN CONDITIONS ORIGINATING IN THE PERINATAL PERIOD

Maternal causes of perinatal morbidity and mortality (760-763)
760 Fetus or newborn affected by maternal conditions which may be unrelated to present pregnancy
761 Fetus or newborn affected by maternal complications of pregnancy
762 Fetus or newborn affected by complications of placenta, cord, and membranes
763 Fetus or newborn affected by other complications of labor and delivery

Other conditions originating in the perinatal period (764-779)
764 Slow fetal growth and fetal malnutrition
765 Disorders relating to short gestation and unspecified low birthweight
766 Disorders relating to long gestation and high birthweight
767 Birth trauma
768 Intrauterine hypoxia and birth asphyxia
769 Respiratory distress syndrome
770 Other respiratory conditions of fetus and newborn
771 Infections specific to the perinatal period
772 Fetal and neonatal hemorrhage
773 Hemolytic disease of fetus or newborn, due to isoimmunization
774 Other perinatal jaundice
775 Endocrine and metabolic disturbances specific to the fetus and newborn
776 Hematological disorders of fetus and newborn
777 Perinatal disorders of digestive system
778 Conditions involving the integument and temperature regulation of fetus and newborn
779 Other and ill-defined conditions originating in the perinatal period

16. SYMPTOMS, SIGNS, AND ILL-DEFINED CONDITIONS

Symptoms (780-789)
780 General symptoms
781 Symptoms involving nervous and musculoskeletal systems
782 Symptoms involving skin and other integumentary tissue
783 Symptoms concerning nutrition, metabolism, and development
784 Symptoms involving head and neck
785 Symptoms involving cardiovascular system
786 Symptoms involving respiratory system and other chest symptoms
787 Symptoms involving digestive system
788 Symptoms involving urinary system
789 Other symptoms involving abdomen and pelvis

Nonspecific abnormal findings (790-796)
790 Nonspecific findings on examination of blood
791 Nonspecific findings on examination of urine
792 Nonspecific abnormal findings in other body substances

793 Nonspecific abnormal findings on radiological and other examination of body structure
794 Nonspecific abnormal results of function studies
795 Nonspecific abnormal histological and immunological findings
796 Other nonspecific abnormal findings

Ill-defined and unknown causes of morbidity and mortality (797-799)
797 Senility without mention of psychosis
798 Sudden death, cause unknown
799 Other ill-defined and unknown causes of morbidity and mortality

17. INJURY AND POISONING

Fracture of skull (800-804)
800 Fracture of vault of skull
801 Fracture of base of skull
802 Fracture of face bones
803 Other and unqualified skull fractures
804 Multiple fractures involving skull or face with other bones

Fracture of spine and trunk (805-809)
805 Fracture of vertebral column without mention of spinal cord lesion
806 Fracture of vertebral column with spinal cord lesion
807 Fracture of rib(s), sternum, larynx, and trachea
808 Fracture of pelvis
809 Ill-defined fractures of bones of trunk

Fracture of upper limb (810-819)
810 Fracture of clavicle
811 Fracture of scapula
812 Fracture of humerus
813 Fracture of radius and ulna
814 Fracture of carpal bone(s)
815 Fracture of metacarpal bone(s)
816 Fracture of one or more phalanges of hand
817 Multiple fractures of hand bones
818 Ill-defined fractures of upper limb
819 Multiple fractures involving both upper limbs, and upper limb with rib(s) and sternum

Fracture of lower limb (820-829)
820 Fracture of neck of femur
821 Fracture of other and unspecified parts of femur
822 Fracture of patella
823 Fracture of tibia and fibula
824 Fracture of ankle
825 Fracture of one or more tarsal and metatarsal bones
826 Fracture of one or more phalanges of foot
827 Other, multiple, and ill-defined fractures of lower limb
828 Multiple fractures involving both lower limbs, lower with upper limb, and lower limb(s) with rib(s) and sternum
829 Fracture of unspecified bones

Dislocation (830-839)
830 Dislocation of jaw
831 Dislocation of shoulder
832 Dislocation of elbow
833 Dislocation of wrist
834 Dislocation of finger
835 Dislocation of hip
836 Dislocation of knee
837 Dislocation of ankle
838 Dislocation of foot
839 Other, multiple, and ill-defined dislocations

Sprains and strains of joints and adjacent muscles (840-848)
840 Sprains and strains of shoulder and upper arm
841 Sprains and strains of elbow and forearm
842 Sprains and strains of wrist and hand
843 Sprains and strains of hip and thigh

844 Sprains and strains of knee and leg
845 Sprains and strains of ankle and foot
846 Sprains and strains of sacroiliac region
847 Sprains and strains of other and unspecified parts of back
848 Other and ill-defined sprains and strains

Intracranial injury, excluding those with skull fracture (850-854)
850 Concussion
851 Cerebral laceration and contusion
852 Subarachnoid, subdural, and extradural hemorrhage, following injury
853 Other and unspecified intracranial hemorrhage following injury
854 Intracranial injury of other and unspecified nature

Internal injury of chest, abdomen, and pelvis (860-869)
860 Traumatic pneumothorax and hemothorax
861 Injury to heart and lung
862 Injury to other and unspecified intrathoracic organs
863 Injury to gastrointestinal tract
864 Injury to liver
865 Injury to spleen
866 Injury to kidney
867 Injury to pelvic organs
868 Injury to other intra-abdominal organs
869 Internal injury to unspecified or ill-defined organs

Open wound of head, neck, and trunk (870-879)
870 Open wound of ocular adnexa
871 Open wound of eyeball
872 Open wound of ear
873 Other open wound of head
874 Open wound of neck
875 Open wound of chest (wall)
876 Open wound of back
877 Open wound of buttock
878 Open wound of genital organs (external), including traumatic amputation
879 Open wound of other and unspecified sites, except limbs

Open wound of upper limb (880-887)
880 Open wound of shoulder and upper arm
881 Open wound of elbow, forearm, and wrist
882 Open wound of hand except finger(s) alone
883 Open wound of finger(s)
884 Multiple and unspecified open wound of upper limb
885 Traumatic amputation of thumb (complete) (partial)
886 Traumatic amputation of other finger(s) (complete) (partial)
887 Traumatic amputation of arm and hand (complete) (partial)

Open wound of lower limb (890-897)
890 Open wound of hip and thigh
891 Open wound of knee, leg [except thigh], and ankle
892 Open wound of foot except toe(s) alone
893 Open wound of toe(s)
894 Multiple and unspecified open wound of lower limb
895 Traumatic amputation of toe(s) (complete) (partial)
896 Traumatic amputation of foot (complete) (partial)
897 Traumatic amputation of leg(s) (complete) (partial)

Injury to blood vessels (900-904)
900 Injury to blood vessels of head and neck
901 Injury to blood vessels of thorax
902 Injury to blood vessels of abdomen and pelvis
903 Injury to blood vessels of upper extremity
904 Injury to blood vessels of lower extremity and unspecified sites

Late effects of injuries, poisonings, toxic effects, and other external causes (905-909)
905 Late effects of musculoskeletal and connective tissue injuries
906 Late effects of injuries to skin and subcutaneous tissues
907 Late effects of injuries to the nervous system
908 Late effects of other and unspecified injuries
909 Late effects of other and unspecified external causes

Superficial injury (910-919)
910 Superficial injury of face, neck, and scalp except eye
911 Superficial injury of trunk
912 Superficial injury of shoulder and upper arm
913 Superficial injury of elbow, forearm, and wrist
914 Superficial injury of hand(s) except finger(s) alone
915 Superficial injury of finger(s)
916 Superficial injury of hip, thigh, leg, and ankle
917 Superficial injury of foot and toe(s)
918 Superficial injury of eye and adnexa
919 Superficial injury of other, multiple, and unspecified sites

Contusion with intact skin surface (920-924)
920 Contusion of face, scalp, and neck except eye(s)
921 Contusion of eye and adnexa
922 Contusion of trunk
923 Contusion of upper limb
924 Contusion of lower limb and of other and unspecified sites

Crushing injury (925-929)
925 Crushing injury of face, scalp, and neck
926 Crushing injury of trunk
927 Crushing injury of upper limb
928 Crushing injury of lower limb
929 Crushing injury of multiple and unspecified sites

Effects of foreign body entering through orifice (930-939)
930 Foreign body on external eye
931 Foreign body in ear
932 Foreign body in nose
933 Foreign body in pharynx and larynx
934 Foreign body in trachea, bronchus, and lung
935 Foreign body in mouth, esophagus, and stomach
936 Foreign body in intestine and colon
937 Foreign body in anus and rectum
938 Foreign body in digestive system, unspecified
939 Foreign body in genitourinary tract

Burns (940-949)
940 Burn confined to eye and adnexa
941 Burn of face, head, and neck
942 Burn of trunk
943 Burn of upper limb, except wrist and hand
944 Burn of wrist(s) and hand(s)
945 Burn of lower limb(s)
946 Burns of multiple specified sites
947 Burn of internal organs
948 Burns classified according to extent of body surface involved
949 Burn, unspecified

Injury to nerves and spinal cord (950-957)
950 Injury to optic nerve and pathways
951 Injury to other cranial nerve(s)
952 Spinal cord injury without evidence of spinal bone injury
953 Injury to nerve roots and spinal plexus
954 Injury to other nerve(s) of trunk excluding shoulder and pelvic girdles
955 Injury to peripheral nerve(s) of shoulder girdle and upper limb

956 Injury to peripheral nerve(s) of pelvic girdle and lower limb
957 Injury to other and unspecified nerves

Certain traumatic complications and unspecified injuries (958-959)
958 Certain early complications of trauma
959 Injury, other and unspecified

Poisoning by drugs, medicinals and biological substances (960-979)
960 Poisoning by antibiotics
961 Poisoning by other anti-infectives
962 Poisoning by hormones and synthetic substitutes
963 Poisoning by primarily systemic agents
964 Poisoning by agents primarily affecting blood constituents
965 Poisoning by analgesics, antipyretics, and antirheumatics
966 Poisoning by anticonvulsants and anti-Parkinsonism drugs
967 Poisoning by sedatives and hypnotics
968 Poisoning by other central nervous system depressants and anesthetics
969 Poisoning by psychotropic agents
970 Poisoning by central nervous system stimulants
971 Poisoning by drugs primarily affecting the autonomic nervous system
972 Poisoning by agents primarily affecting the cardiovascular system
973 Poisoning by agents primarily affecting the gastrointestinal system
974 Poisoning by water, mineral, and uric acid metabolism drugs
975 Poisoning by agents primarily acting on the smooth and skeletal muscles and respiratory system
976 Poisoning by agents primarily affecting skin and mucous membrane, ophthalmological, otorhinolaryngological, and dental drugs
977 Poisoning by other and unspecified drugs and medicinals
978 Poisoning by bacterial vaccines
979 Poisoning by other vaccines and biological substances

Toxic effects of substances chiefly nonmedicinal as to source (980-989)
980 Toxic effect of alcohol
981 Toxic effect of petroleum products
982 Toxic effect of solvents other than petroleum-based
983 Toxic effect of corrosive aromatics, acids, and caustic alkalis
984 Toxic effect of lead and its compounds (including fumes)
985 Toxic effect of other metals
986 Toxic effect of carbon monoxide
987 Toxic effect of other gases, fumes, or vapors
988 Toxic effect of noxious substances eaten as food
989 Toxic effect of other substances, chiefly nonmedicinal as to source

Other and unspecified effects of external causes (990-995)
990 Effects of radiation, unspecified
991 Effects of reduced temperature
992 Effects of heat and light
993 Effects of air pressure
994 Effects of other external causes
995 Certain adverse effects, not elsewhere classified

Complications of surgical and medical care, not elsewhere classified (996-999)
996 Complications peculiar to certain specified procedures
997 Complications affecting specified body systems, not elsewhere classified
998 Other complications of procedures, not elsewhere classified

999 Complications of medical care, not elsewhere classified

SUPPLEMENTARY CLASSIFICATION OF FACTORS INFLUENCING HEALTH STATUS AND CONTACT WITH HEALTH SERVICES

Persons with potential health hazards related to communicable diseases (V01-V09)

V01 Contact with or exposure to communicable diseases
V02 Carrier or suspected carrier of infectious diseases
V03 Need for prophylactic vaccination and inoculation against bacterial diseases
V04 Need for prophylactic vaccination and inoculation against certain viral diseases
V05 Need for other prophylactic vaccination and inoculation against single diseases
V06 Need for prophylactic vaccination and inoculation against combinations of diseases
V07 Need for isolation and other prophylactic measures
V08 Asymptomatic human immunodeficiency virus [HIV] infection status
V09 Infection with drug-resistant microorganisms

Persons with potential health hazards related to personal and family history (V10-V19)

V10 Personal history of malignant neoplasm
V11 Personal history of mental disorder
V12 Personal history of certain other diseases
V13 Personal history of other diseases
V14 Personal history of allergy to medicinal agents
V15 Other personal history presenting hazards to health
V16 Family history of malignant neoplasm
V17 Family history of certain chronic disabling diseases
V18 Family history of certain other specific conditions
V19 Family history of other conditions

Persons encountering health services in circumstances related to reproduction and development (V20-V29)

V20 Health supervision of infant or child
V21 Constitutional states in development
V22 Normal pregnancy
V23 Supervision of high-risk pregnancy
V24 Postpartum care and examination
V25 Encounter for contraceptive management
V26 Procreative management
V27 Outcome of delivery
V28 Antenatal screening
V29 Observation and evaluation of newborns and infants for suspected condition not found

Liveborn infants according to type of birth (V30-V39)

V30 Single liveborn
V31 Twin, mate liveborn
V32 Twin, mate stillborn
V33 Twin, unspecified
V34 Other multiple, mates all liveborn
V35 Other multiple, mates all stillborn
V36 Other multiple, mates live- and stillborn
V37 Other multiple, unspecified
V39 Unspecified

Persons with a condition influencing their health status (V40-V49)

V40 Mental and behavioral problems
V41 Problems with special senses and other special functions
V42 Organ or tissue replaced by transplant
V43 Organ or tissue replaced by other means
V44 Artificial opening status
V45 Other postprocedural states
V46 Other dependence on machines
V47 Other problems with internal organs
V48 Problems with head, neck, and trunk
V49 Problems with limbs and other problems

Persons encountering health services for specific procedures and aftercare (V50-V59)

V50 Elective surgery for purposes other than remedying health states
V51 Aftercare involving the use of plastic surgery
V52 Fitting and adjustment of prosthetic device
V53 Fitting and adjustment of other device
V54 Other orthopedic aftercare
V55 Attention to artificial openings
V56 Encounter for dialysis and dialysis catheter care
V57 Care involving use of rehabilitation procedures
V58 Encounter for other and unspecified procedures and aftercare
V59 Donors

Persons encountering health services in other circumstances (V60-V69)

V60 Housing, household, and economic circumstances
V61 Other family circumstances
V62 Other psychosocial circumstances
V63 Unavailability of other medical facilities for care
V64 Persons encountering health services for specific procedures, not carried out
V65 Other persons seeking consultation
V66 Convalescence and palliative care
V67 Follow-up examination
V68 Encounters for administrative purposes
V69 Problems related to lifestyle

Persons without reported diagnosis encountered during examination and investigation of individuals and populations (V70-V82)

V70 General medical examination
V71 Observation and evaluation for suspected conditions not found
V72 Special investigations and examinations
V73 Special screening examination for viral and chlamydial diseases
V74 Special screening examination for bacterial and spirochetal diseases
V75 Special screening examination for other infectious diseases
V76 Special screening for malignant neoplasms
V77 Special screening for endocrine, nutritional, metabolic, and immunity disorders
V78 Special screening for disorders of blood and blood-forming organs
V79 Special screening for mental disorders and developmental handicaps
V80 Special screening for neurological, eye, and ear diseases
V81 Special screening for cardiovascular, respiratory, and genitourinary diseases
V82 Special screening for other conditions

Genetics (V83-V84)

V83 Genetic carrier status
V84 Genetic susceptibility to disease

Body mass index (V85)

V85 Body Mass Index

Estrogen receptor status (V86)

V86 Estrogen receptor status

SUPPLEMENTARY CLASSIFICATION OF EXTERNAL CAUSES OF INJURY AND POISONING

Railway accidents (E800-E807)

E800 Railway accident involving collision with rolling stock
E801 Railway accident involving collision with other object
E802 Railway accident involving derailment without antecedent collision
E803 Railway accident involving explosion, fire, or burning
E804 Fall in, on, or from railway train
E805 Hit by rolling stock
E806 Other specified railway accident
E807 Railway accident of unspecified nature

Motor vehicle traffic accidents (E810-E819)

E810 Motor vehicle traffic accident involving collision with train
E811 Motor vehicle traffic accident involving re-entrant collision with another motor vehicle
E812 Other motor vehicle traffic accident involving collision with another motor vehicle
E813 Motor vehicle traffic accident involving collision with other vehicle
E814 Motor vehicle traffic accident involving collision with pedestrian
E815 Other motor vehicle traffic accident involving collision on the highway
E816 Motor vehicle traffic accident due to loss of control, without collision on the highway
E817 Noncollision motor vehicle traffic accident while boarding or alighting
E818 Other noncollision motor vehicle traffic accident
E819 Motor vehicle traffic accident of unspecified nature

Motor vehicle nontraffic accidents (E820-E825)

E820 Nontraffic accident involving motor-driven snow vehicle
E821 Nontraffic accident involving other off-road motor vehicle
E822 Other motor vehicle nontraffic accident involving collision with moving object
E823 Other motor vehicle nontraffic accident involving collision with stationary object
E824 Other motor vehicle nontraffic accident while boarding and alighting
E825 Other motor vehicle nontraffic accident of other and unspecified nature

Other road vehicle accidents (E826-E829)

E826 Pedal cycle accident
E827 Animal-drawn vehicle accident
E828 Accident involving animal being ridden
E829 Other road vehicle accidents

Water transport accidents (E830-E838)

E830 Accident to watercraft causing submersion
E831 Accident to watercraft causing other injury
E832 Other accidental submersion or drowning in water transport accident
E833 Fall on stairs or ladders in water transport
E834 Other fall from one level to another in water transport
E835 Other and unspecified fall in water transport
E836 Machinery accident in water transport
E837 Explosion, fire, or burning in watercraft
E838 Other and unspecified water transport accident

Air and space transport accidents (E840-E845)

E840 Accident to powered aircraft at takeoff or landing
E841 Accident to powered aircraft, other and unspecified
E842 Accident to unpowered aircraft
E843 Fall in, on, or from aircraft
E844 Other specified air transport accidents
E845 Accident involving spacecraft

Vehicle accidents, not elsewhere classifiable (E846-E849)

E846 Accidents involving powered vehicles used solely within the buildings and premises of an industrial or commercial establishment
E847 Accidents involving cable cars not running on rails
E848 Accidents involving other vehicles, not elsewhere classifiable
E849 Place of occurrence

Accidental poisoning by drugs, medicinal substances, and biologicals (E850-E858)

E850 Accidental poisoning by analgesics, antipyretics, and antirheumatics
E851 Accidental poisoning by barbiturates
E852 Accidental poisoning by other sedatives and hypnotics
E853 Accidental poisoning by tranquilizers
E854 Accidental poisoning by other psychotropic agents
E855 Accidental poisoning by other drugs acting on central and autonomic nervous systems
E856 Accidental poisoning by antibiotics
E857 Accidental poisoning by anti-infectives
E858 Accidental poisoning by other drugs

Accidental poisoning by other solid and liquid substances, gases, and vapors (E860-E869)

E860 Accidental poisoning by alcohol, not elsewhere classified
E861 Accidental poisoning by cleansing and polishing agents, disinfectants, paints, and varnishes
E862 Accidental poisoning by petroleum products, other solvents and their vapors, not elsewhere classified
E863 Accidental poisoning by agricultural and horticultural chemical and pharmaceutical preparations other than plant foods and fertilizers
E864 Accidental poisoning by corrosives and caustics, not elsewhere classified
E865 Accidental poisoning from poisonous foodstuffs and poisonous plants
E866 Accidental poisoning by other and unspecified solid and liquid substances
E867 Accidental poisoning by gas distributed by pipeline
E868 Accidental poisoning by other utility gas and other carbon monoxide
E869 Accidental poisoning by other gases and vapors

Misadventures to patients during surgical and medical care (E870-E876)

E870 Accidental cut, puncture, perforation, or hemorrhage during medical care
E871 Foreign object left in body during procedure
E872 Failure of sterile precautions during procedure
E873 Failure in dosage
E874 Mechanical failure of instrument or apparatus during procedure
E875 Contaminated or infected blood, other fluid, drug, or biological substance
E876 Other and unspecified misadventures during medical care

Surgical and medical procedures as the cause of abnormal reaction of patient or later complication, without mention of misadventure at the time of procedure (E878-E879)

E878 Surgical operation and other surgical procedures as the cause of abnormal reaction of patient, or of later complication, without mention of misadventure at the time of operation
E879 Other procedures, without mention of misadventure at the time of procedure, as the cause of abnormal reaction of patient, or of later complication

Accidental falls (E880-E888)

E880 Fall on or from stairs or steps
E881 Fall on or from ladders or scaffolding
E882 Fall from or out of building or other structure
E883 Fall into hole or other opening in surface
E884 Other fall from one level to another
E885 Fall on same level from slipping, tripping, or stumbling
E886 Fall on same level from collision, pushing or shoving, by or with other person
E887 Fracture, cause unspecified
E888 Other and unspecified fall

Accidents caused by fire and flames (E890-E899)

E890 Conflagration in private dwelling
E891 Conflagration in other and unspecified building or structure
E892 Conflagration not in building or structure
E893 Accident caused by ignition of clothing
E894 Ignition of highly inflammable material
E895 Accident caused by controlled fire in private dwelling
E896 Accident caused by controlled fire in other and unspecified building or structure
E897 Accident caused by controlled fire not in building or structure
E898 Accident caused by other specified fire and flames
E899 Accident caused by unspecified fire

Accidents due to natural and environmental factors (E900-E909)

E900 Excessive heat
E901 Excessive cold
E902 High and low air pressure and changes in air pressure
E903 Travel and motion
E904 Hunger, thirst, exposure, and neglect
E905 Venomous animals and plants as the cause of poisoning and toxic reactions
E906 Other injury caused by animals
E907 Lightning
E908 Cataclysmic storms, and floods resulting from storms
E909 Cataclysmic earth surface movements and eruptions

Accidents caused by submersion, suffocation, and foreign bodies (E910-E915)

E910 Accidental drowning and submersion
E911 Inhalation and ingestion of food causing obstruction of respiratory tract or suffocation
E912 Inhalation and ingestion of other object causing obstruction of respiratory tract or suffocation
E913 Accidental mechanical suffocation
E914 Foreign body accidentally entering eye and adnexa
E915 Foreign body accidentally entering other orifice

Other accidents (E916-E928)

E916 Struck accidentally by falling object
E917 Striking against or struck accidentally by objects or persons
E918 Caught accidentally in or between objects
E919 Accidents caused by machinery
E920 Accidents caused by cutting and piercing instruments or objects
E921 Accident caused by explosion of pressure vessel
E922 Accident caused by firearm missile
E923 Accident caused by explosive material
E924 Accident caused by hot substance or object, caustic or corrosive material, and steam
E925 Accident caused by electric current
E926 Exposure to radiation
E927 Overexertion and strenuous movements
E928 Other and unspecified environmental and accidental causes

Late effects of accidental injury (E929)

E929   Late effects of accidental injury

Drugs, medicinal and biological substances causing adverse effects in therapeutic use (E930-E949)

E930 Antibiotics
E931 Other anti-infectives
E932 Hormones and synthetic substitutes
E933 Primarily systemic agents
E934 Agents primarily affecting blood constituents
E935 Analgesics, antipyretics, and antirheumatics
E936 Anticonvulsants and anti-Parkinsonism drugs
E937 Sedatives and hypnotics
E938 Other central nervous system depressants and anesthetics
E939 Psychotropic agents
E940 Central nervous system stimulants
E941 Drugs primarily affecting the autonomic nervous system
E942 Agents primarily affecting the cardiovascular system
E943 Agents primarily affecting gastrointestinal system
E944 Water, mineral, and uric acid metabolism drugs
E945 Agents primarily acting on the smooth and skeletal muscles and respiratory system
E946 Agents primarily affecting skin and mucous membrane, ophthalmological, otorhinolaryngological, and dental drugs
E947 Other and unspecified drugs and medicinal substances
E948 Bacterial vaccines
E949 Other vaccines and biological substances

Suicide and self-inflicted injury (E950-E959)

E950 Suicide and self-inflicted poisoning by solid or liquid substances
E951 Suicide and self-inflicted poisoning by gases in domestic use
E952 Suicide and self-inflicted poisoning by other gases and vapors
E953 Suicide and self-inflicted injury by hanging, strangulation, and suffocation
E954 Suicide and self-inflicted injury by submersion [drowning]
E955 Suicide and self-inflicted injury by firearms and explosives
E956 Suicide and self-inflicted injury by cutting and piercing instruments
E957 Suicide and self-inflicted injuries by jumping from high place
E958 Suicide and self-inflicted injury by other and unspecified means
E959 Late effects of self-inflicted injury

Homicide and injury purposely inflicted by other persons (E960-E969)

E960 Fight, brawl, and rape
E961 Assault by corrosive or caustic substance, except poisoning
E962 Assault by poisoning
E963 Assault by hanging and strangulation
E964 Assault by submersion [drowning]
E965 Assault by firearms and explosives
E966 Assault by cutting and piercing instrument
E967 Child and adult battering and other maltreatment
E968 Assault by other and unspecified means
E969 Late effects of injury purposely inflicted by other person

Legal intervention (E970-E978)

E970 Injury due to legal intervention by firearms
E971 Injury due to legal intervention by explosives
E972 Injury due to legal intervention by gas
E973 Injury due to legal intervention by blunt object
E974 Injury due to legal intervention by cutting and piercing instruments
E975 Injury due to legal intervention by other specified means
E976 Injury due to legal intervention by unspecified means
E977 Late effects of injuries due to legal intervention
E978 Legal execution

Appendix E: List of Three-Digit Categories

Terrorism (E979)
E979 Terrorism

Injury undetermined whether accidentally or purposely inflicted (E980-E989)
E980 Poisoning by solid or liquid substances, undetermined whether accidentally or purposely inflicted
E981 Poisoning by gases in domestic use, undetermined whether accidentally or purposely inflicted
E982 Poisoning by other gases, undetermined whether accidentally or purposely inflicted
E983 Hanging, strangulation, or suffocation, undetermined whether accidentally or purposely inflicted
E984 Submersion [drowning], undetermined whether accidentally or purposely inflicted

E985 Injury by firearms and explosives, undetermined whether accidentally or purposely inflicted
E986 Injury by cutting and piercing instruments, undetermined whether accidentally or purposely inflicted
E987 Falling from high place, undetermined whether accidentally or purposely inflicted
E988 Injury by other and unspecified means, undetermined whether accidentally or purposely inflicted
E989 Late effects of injury, undetermined whether accidentally or purposely inflicted

Injury resulting from operations of war (E990-E999)
E990 Injury due to war operations by fires and conflagrations

E991 Injury due to war operations by bullets and fragments
E992 Injury due to war operations by explosion of marine weapons
E993 Injury due to war operations by other explosion
E994 Injury due to war operations by destruction of aircraft
E995 Injury due to war operations by other and unspecified forms of conventional warfare
E996 Injury due to war operations by nuclear weapons
E997 Injury due to war operations by other forms of unconventional warfare
E998 Injury due to war operations but occurring after cessation of hostilities
E999 Late effects of injury due to war operations

A

Abbe operation
construction of vagina 70.61
intestinal anastomosis — *see* Anastomosis, intestine
Abciximab, infusion 99.20
Abdominocentesis 54.91
Abdominohysterectomy 68.49 ▲
laparoscopic 68.41 ●
Abdominoplasty 86.83
Abdominoscopy 54.21
Abdominouterotomy 68.0
obstetrical 74.99
Abduction, arytenoid 31.69
Ablation
biliary tract (lesion) by ERCP 51.64
endometrial (hysteroscopic) 68.23
inner ear (cryosurgery) (ultrasound) 20.79
by injection 20.72
lesion
esophagus 42.39
endoscopic 42.33
heart
by peripherally inserted catheter 37.34
endovascular approach 37.34
maze procedure (Cox-maze)
endovascular approach 37.34
open (trans-thoracic) approach 37.33
trans-thoracic approach 37.33
intestine
large 45.49
endoscopic 45.43
large intestine 45.49
endoscopic 45.43
liver 50.26 ●
laparoscopic 50.25 ●
open 50.23 ●
percutaneous 50.24 ●
lung 32.26 ●
open 32.23 ●
percutaneous 32.24 ●
thoracoscopic 32.25 ●
renal 55.35 ●
laparoscopic 55.34 ●
open 55.32 ●
percutaneous 55.33 ●
pituitary 07.69
by
Cobalt 60 92.32
implantation (strontium-yttrium) (Y) NEC 07.68
transfrontal approach 07.64
transphenoidal approach 07.65
proton beam (Bragg peak) 92.33
prostate
by
cryoablation 60.62
laser, transurethral 60.21
radical cryosurgical ablation (RCSA) 60.62
radiofrequency thermotherapy 60.97
transurethral needle ablation (TUNA) 60.97
tissue
heart — *see* Ablation, lesion, heart ●
liver — *see* Ablation, lesion, liver ●
lung — *see* Ablation, lesion, lung ●
renal — *see* Ablation, lesion, renal ●
Abortion, therapeutic 69.51
by
aspiration curettage 69.51
dilation and curettage 69.01
hysterectomy — *see* Hysterectomy
hysterotomy 74.91
insertion
laminaria 69.93
prostaglandin suppository 96.49

Abortion, therapeutic — *continued*
by — *continued*
intra-amniotic injection (saline) 75.0
Abrasion
corneal epithelium 11.41
for smear or culture 11.21
epicardial surface 36.39
pleural 34.6
skin 86.25
Abscission, cornea 11.49
Absorptiometry
photon (dual) (single) 88.98
Aburel operation (intra-amniotic injection for abortion) 75.0
Accouchement forcé 73.99
Acetabulectomy 77.85
Acetabuloplasty NEC 81.40
with prosthetic implant 81.52
Achillorrhaphy 83.64
delayed 83.62
Achillotenotomy 83.11
plastic 83.85
Achillotomy 83.11
plastic 83.85
Acid peel, skin 86.24
Acromionectomy 77.81
Acromioplasty 81.83
for recurrent dislocation of shoulder 81.82
partial replacement 81.81
total replacement 81.80
Actinotherapy 99.82
Activities of daily living (ADL)
therapy 93.83
training for the blind 93.78
Acupuncture 99.92
for anesthesia 99.91
with smouldering moxa 93.35
Adams operation
advancement of round ligament 69.22
crushing of nasal septum 21.88
excision of palmar fascia 82.35
Adenectomy — *see also* Excision, by site
prostate NEC 60.69
retropubic 60.4
Adenoidectomy (without tonsillectomy) 28.6
with tonsillectomy 28.3
Adhesiolysis — *see also* Lysis, adhesions
for collapse of lung 33.39
middle ear 20.23
Adipectomy 86.83
Adjustment
cardiac pacemaker program (reprogramming) — *omit code*
cochlear prosthetic device (external components) 95.49
dental 99.97
gastric restrictive device (laparoscopic) 44.98
occlusal 24.8
spectacles 95.31
Administration (of) — *see also* Injection
Activase® 99.10 ●
adhesion barrier substance 99.77
Alteplase (tPA, generic) 99.10 ●
Anistreplase (tPA, generic) 99.10 ●
antitoxins NEC 99.58
botulism 99.57
diphtheria 99.58
gas gangrene 99.58
scarlet fever 99.58
tetanus 99.56
Bender Visual-Motor Gestalt test 94.02
Benton Visual Retention test 94.02
DrotAA 00.11 ●
Eminase® 99.10 ●
inhaled nitric oxide 00.12
intelligence test or scale (Stanford-Binet) (Wechsler) (adult) (children) 94.01
Minnesota Multiphasic Personality Inventory (MMPI) 94.02

Administration — *see also* Injection — *continued*
MMPI (Minnesota Multiphasic Personality Inventory) 94.02
neuroprotective agent 99.75
psychologic test 94.02
Retavase® 99.10 ●
Reteplase (tPA, generic) 99.10 ●
Stanford-Binet test 94.01
Streptase® 99.10 ●
Streptokinase (tPA, generic) 99.10 ●
Tenecteplase (tPA, generic) 99.10 ●
TNKase™ 99.10 ●
toxoid
diphtheria 99.36
with tetanus and pertussis, combined (DTP) 99.39
tetanus 99.38
with diphtheria and pertussis, combined (DTP) 99.39
vaccine (*see also* Vaccination)
BCG 99.33
measles-mumps-rubella (MMR) 99.48
poliomyelitis 99.41
TAB 99.32
Wechsler
Intelligence Scale (adult) (children) 94.01
Memory Scale 94.02
Xigris® 00.11 ●
Adrenalectomy (unilateral) 07.22
with partial removal of remaining gland 07.29
bilateral 07.3
partial 07.29
subtotal 07.29
complete 07.3
partial NEC 07.29
remaining gland 07.3
subtotal NEC 07.29
total 07.3
Adrenalorrhaphy 07.44
Adrenalotomy (with drainage) 07.41
Advancement
extraocular muscle 15.12
multiple (with resection or recession) 15.3
eyelid muscle 08.59
eye muscle 15.12
multiple (with resection or recession) 15.3
graft — *see* Graft
leaflet (heart) 35.10
pedicle (flap) 86.72
profundus tendon (Wagner) 82.51
round ligament 69.22
tendon 83.71
hand 82.51
profundus (Wagner) 82.51
Wagner (profundus tendon) 82.51
Albee operation
bone peg, femoral neck 78.05
graft for slipping patella 78.06
sliding inlay graft, tibia 78.07
Albert operation (arthrodesis of knee) 81.22
Aldridge (-Studdiford) operation (urethral sling) 59.5
Alexander-Adams operation (shortening of round ligaments) 69.22
Alexander operation
prostatectomy
perineal 60.62
suprapubic 60.3
shortening of round ligaments 69.22
Alimentation, parenteral 99.29
Allograft — *see* Graft
Almoor operation (extrapetrosal drainage) 20.22
Altemeier operation (perineal rectal pull-through) 48.49
Alveolectomy (interradicular) (intraseptal) (radical) (simple) (with graft) (with implant) 24.5
Alveoloplasty (with graft or implant) 24.5

Alveolotomy (apical) 24.0
Ambulatory cardiac monitoring (ACM) 89.50
Ammon operation (dacryocystotomy) 09.53
Amniocentesis (transuterine) (diagnostic) 75.1
with intra-amniotic injection of saline 75.0
Amniography 87.81
Amnioinfusion 75.37
Amnioscopy, internal 75.31
Amniotomy 73.09
to induce labor 73.01
Amputation (cineplastic) (closed flap) (guillotine) (kineplastic) (open) 84.91
abdominopelvic 84.19
above-elbow 84.07
above-knee (AK) 84.17
ankle (disarticulation) 84.13
through malleoli of tibia and fibula 84.14
arm NEC 84.00
through
carpals 84.03
elbow (disarticulation) 84.06
forearm 84.05
humerus 84.07
shoulder (disarticulation) 84.08
wrist (disarticulation) 84.04
upper 84.07
Batch-Spittler-McFaddin (knee disarticulation) 84.16
below-knee (BK) NEC 84.15
conversion into above-knee amputation 84.17
Boyd (hip disarticulation) 84.18
Burgess operation (amputation of ankle) 84.14
Callander's (knee disarticulation) 84.16
carpals 84.03
cervix 67.4
Chopart's (midtarsal) 84.12
clitoris 71.4
Dieffenbach (hip disarticulation) 84.18
Dupuytren's (shoulder disarticulation) 84.08
ear, external 18.39
elbow (disarticulation) 84.06
finger, except thumb 84.01
thumb 84.02
foot (middle) 84.12
forearm 84.05
forefoot 84.12
forequarter 84.09
Gordon-Taylor (hindquarter) 84.19
Gritti-Stokes (knee disarticulation) 84.16
Guyon (ankle) 84.13
hallux 84.11
hand 84.03
Hey's (foot) 84.12
hindquarter 84.19
hip (disarticulation) 84.18
humerus 84.07
interscapulothoracic 84.09
interthoracoscapular 84.09
King-Steelquist (hindquarter) 84.19
Kirk (thigh) 84.17
knee (disarticulation) 84.16
Kutler (revision of current traumatic amputation of finger) 84.01
Larry (shoulder disarticulation) 84.08
leg NEC 84.10
above knee (AK) 84.17
below knee (BK) 84.15
through
ankle (disarticulation) 84.13
femur (AK) 84.17
foot 84.12
hip (disarticulation) 84.18
tibia and fibula (BK) 84.15
Lisfranc
foot 84.12

☑ Additional Digit Required — Refer to the Tabular List for Digit Selection
▽ Subterms under main terms may continue to next column or page

2007 ICD-9-CM   ▶◀ Revised Text   ● New Line   ▲ Revised Code   October 2006 · Volume 3 — 1

Abbe operation — Amputation

Amputation — *continued*
  Lisfranc — *continued*
    shoulder (disarticulation) 84.08
  Littlewood (forequarter) 84.09
  lower limb NEC (*see also* Amputation, leg) 84.10
  Mazet (knee disarticulation) 84.16
  metacarpal 84.03
  metatarsal 84.11
    head (bunionectomy) 77.59
  metatarsophalangeal (joint) 84.11
  midtarsal 84.12
  nose 21.4
  penis (circle) (complete) (flap) (partial) (radical) 64.3
  Pirogoff's (ankle amputation through malleoli of tibia and fibula) 84.14
  ray
    finger 84.01
    foot 84.11
    toe (metatarsal head) 84.11
  root (tooth) (apex) 23.73
    with root canal therapy 23.72
  shoulder (disarticulation) 84.08
  Sorondo-Ferré (hindquarter) 84.19
  S.P. Rogers (knee disarticulation) 84.16
  supracondyler, above-knee 84.17
  supramalleolar, foot 84.14
  Syme's (ankle amputation through malleoli of tibia and fibula) 84.14
  thigh 84.17
  thumb 84.02
  toe (through metatarsophalangeal joint) 84.11
  transcarpal 84.03
  transmetatarsal 84.12
  upper limb NEC (*see also* Amputation, arm) 84.00
  wrist (disarticulation) 84.04
Amygdalohippocampotomy 01.39
Amygdalotomy 01.39
Analysis
  cardiac rhythm device (CRT-D) (CRT-P) (AICD) (pacemaker) — *see* Interrogation
  character 94.03
  gastric 89.39
  psychologic 94.31
  transactional
    group 94.44
    individual 94.39
Anastomosis
  abdominal artery to coronary artery 36.17
  accessory-facial nerve 04.72
  accessory-hypoglossal nerve 04.73
  anus (with formation of endorectal ileal pouch) 45.95
  aorta (descending)-pulmonary (artery) 39.0
  aorta-renal artery 39.24
  aorta-subclavian artery 39.22
  aortoceliac 39.26
  aorto(ilio)femoral 39.25
  aortomesenteric 39.26
  appendix 47.99
  arteriovenous NEC 39.29
    for renal dialysis 39.27
  artery (suture of distal to proximal end) 39.31
    with
      bypass graft 39.29
        extracranial-intracranial [EC-IC] 39.28
      excision or resection of vessel — *see* Arteriectomy, with anastomosis, by site
    revision 39.49
  bile ducts 51.39
  bladder NEC 57.88
    with
      isolated segment of intestine 57.87 [45.50]

Anastomosis — *continued*
  bladder — *continued*
    with — *continued*
      isolated segment of intestine — *continued*
        colon (sigmoid) 57.87 [45.52]
        ileum 57.87 [45.51]
        open loop of ileum 57.87 [45.51]
      to intestine 57.88
        ileum 57.87 [45.51]
  bowel (*see also* Anastomosis, intestine) 45.90
  bronchotracheal 33.48
  bronchus 33.48
  carotid-subclavian artery 39.22
  caval-mesenteric vein 39.1
  caval-pulmonary artery 39.21
  cervicoesophageal 42.59
  colohypopharyngeal (intrathoracic) 42.55
    antesternal or antethoracic 42.65
  common bile duct 51.39
  common pulmonary trunk and left atrium (posterior wall) 35.82
  cystic bile duct 51.39
  cystocolic 57.88
  epididymis to vas deferens 63.83
  esophagocolic (intrathoracic) NEC 42.56
    with interposition 42.55
    antesternal or antethoracic NEC 42.66
      with interposition 42.65
  esophagocologastric (intrathoracic) 42.55
    antesternal or antethoracic 42.65
  esophagoduodenal (intrathoracic) NEC 42.54
    with interposition 42.53
  esophagoenteric (intrathoracic) NEC (*see also* Anastomosis, esophagus, to intestinal segment) 42.54
    antesternal or antethoracic NEC (*see also* Anastomosis, esophagus, antesternal, to intestinal segment) 42.64
  esophagoesophageal (intrathoracic) 42.51
    antesternal or antethoracic 42.61
  esophagogastric (intrathoracic) 42.52
    antesternal or antethoracic 42.62
  esophagus (intrapleural) (intrathoracic) (retrosternal) NEC 42.59
    with
      gastrectomy (partial) 43.5
        complete or total 43.99
      interposition (of) NEC 42.58
        colon 42.55
        jejunum 42.53
        small bowel 42.53
    antesternal or antethoracic NEC 42.69
      with
        interposition (of) NEC 42.68
          colon 42.65
          jejunal loop 42.63
          small bowel 42.63
          rubber tube 42.68
      to intestinal segment NEC 42.64
        with interposition 42.68
          colon NEC 42.66
            with interposition 42.65
          small bowel NEC 42.64
            with interposition 42.63
      to intestinal segment (intrathoracic) NEC 42.54
        with interposition 42.58
          antesternal or antethoracic NEC 42.64
            with interposition 42.68
          colon (intrathoracic) NEC 42.56
            with interposition 42.55
            antesternal or antethoracic 42.66
              with interposition 42.65

Anastomosis — *continued*
  esophagus — *continued*
    to intestinal segment — *continued*
      small bowel NEC 42.54
        with interposition 42.53
        antesternal or antethoracic 42.64
          with interposition 42.63
  facial-accessory nerve 04.72
  facial-hypoglossal nerve 04.71
  fallopian tube 66.73
    by reanastomosis 66.79
  gallbladder 51.35
    to
      hepatic ducts 51.31
      intestine 51.32
      pancreas 51.33
      stomach 51.34
  gastroepiploic artery to coronary artery 36.17
  hepatic duct 51.39
  hypoglossal-accessory nerve 04.73
  hypoglossal-facial nerve 04.71
  ileal loop to bladder 57.87 [45.51]
  ileoanal 45.95
  ileorectal 45.93
  inferior vena cava and portal vein 39.1
  internal mammary artery (to)
    coronary artery (single vessel) 36.15
      double vessel 36.16
    myocardium 36.2
  intestine 45.90
    large-to-anus 45.95
    large-to-large 45.94
    large-to-rectum 45.94
    large-to-small 45.93
    small-to-anus 45.95
    small-to-large 45.93
    small-to-rectal stump 45.92
    small-to-small 45.91
  intrahepatic 51.79
  intrathoracic vessel NEC 39.23
  kidney (pelvis) 55.86
  lacrimal sac to conjunctiva 09.82
  left-to-right (systemic-pulmonary artery) 39.0
  lymphatic (channel) (peripheral) 40.9
  mesenteric-caval 39.1
  mesocaval 39.1
  nasolacrimal 09.81
  nerve (cranial) (peripheral) NEC 04.74
    accessory-facial 04.72
    accessory-hypoglossal 04.73
    hypoglossal-facial 04.71
  pancreas (duct) (to) 52.96
    bile duct 51.39
    gall bladder 51.33
    intestine 52.96
    jejunum 52.96
    stomach 52.96
  pleurothecal (with valve) 03.79
  portacaval 39.1
  portal vein to inferior vena cava 39.1
  pulmonary-aortic (Pott's) 39.0
  pulmonary artery and superior vena cava 39.21
  pulmonary-innominate artery (Blalock) 39.0
  pulmonary-subclavian artery (Blalock-Taussig) 39.0
  pulmonary vein and azygos vein 39.23
  pyeloileocutaneous 56.51
  pyelourecterovesical 55.86
  radial artery 36.19
  rectum, rectal NEC 48.74
    stump to small intestine 45.92
  renal (pelvis) 55.86
    vein and splenic vein 39.1
  renoportal 39.1
  salpingothecal (with valve) 03.79
  splenic to renal veins 39.1
  splenorenal (venous) 39.1
    arterial 39.26

Anastomosis — *continued*
  subarachnoid-peritoneal (with valve) 03.71
  subarachnoid-ureteral (with valve) 03.72
  subclavian-aortic 39.22
  superior vena cava to pulmonary artery 39.21
  systemic-pulmonary artery 39.0
  thoracic artery (to)
    coronary artery (single) 36.15
      double 36.16
    myocardium 36.2
  ureter (to) NEC 56.79
    bladder 56.74
    colon 56.71
    ileal pouch (bladder) 56.51
    ileum 56.71
    intestine 56.71
    skin 56.61
  ureterocalyceal 55.86
  ureterocolic 56.71
  ureterovesical 56.74
  urethra (end-to-end) 58.44
  vas deferens 63.82
  veins (suture of proximal to distal end) (with bypass graft) 39.29
    with excision or resection of vessel — *see* Phlebectomy, with anastomosis, by site
    mesenteric to vena cava 39.1
    portal to inferior vena cava 39.1
    revision 39.49
    splenic and renal 39.1
  ventricle, ventricular (intracerebral) (with valve) (*see also* Shunt, ventricular) 02.2
  ventriculoatrial (with valve) 02.32
  ventriculocaval (with valve) 02.32
  ventriculomastoid (with valve) 02.31
  ventriculopleural (with valve) 02.33
  vesicle — *see* Anastomosis, bladder
Anderson operation (tibial lengthening) 78.37
Anel operation (dilation of lacrimal duct) 09.42
Anesthesia
  acupuncture for 99.91
  cryoanalgesia, nerve (cranial) (peripheral) 04.2
  spinal — *omit code*
Aneurysmectomy 38.60
  with
    anastomosis 38.30
      abdominal
        artery 38.36
        vein 38.37
      aorta (arch) (ascending) (descending) 38.34
      head and neck NEC 38.32
      intracranial NEC 38.31
      lower limb
        artery 38.38
        vein 38.39
      thoracic NEC 38.35
      upper limb (artery) (vein) 38.33
    graft replacement (interposition) 38.40
      abdominal
        aorta 38.44
        artery 38.46
        vein 38.47
      aorta (arch) (ascending) (descending thoracic)
        abdominal 38.44
        thoracic 38.45
        thoracoabdominal 38.45 [38.44]
      head and neck NEC 38.42
      intracranial NEC 38.41
      lower limb
        artery 38.48
        vein 38.49
      thoracic NEC 38.45
      upper limb (artery) (vein) 38.43

Aneurysmectomy — *continued*
abdominal
artery 38.66
vein 38.67
aorta (arch) (ascending) (descending) 38.64
atrial, auricular 37.32
head and neck NEC 38.62
heart 37.32
intracranial NEC 38.61
lower limb
artery 38.68
vein 38.69
sinus of Valsalva 35.39
thoracic NEC 38.65
upper limb (artery) (vein) 38.63
ventricle (myocardium) 37.32
Aneurysmoplasty — *see* Aneurysmorrhaphy
Aneurysmorrhaphy NEC 39.52
by or with
anastomosis — *see* Aneurysmectomy, with anastomosis, by site
clipping 39.51
coagulation 39.52
electrocoagulation 39.52
endovascular graft
abdominal aorta 39.71
lower extremity artery(s) 39.79
thoracic aorta 39.73
upper extremity artery(s) 39.79
excision or resection (*see also* Aneurysmectomy, by site)
with
anastomosis — *see* Aneurysmectomy, with anastomosis, by site
graft replacement — *see* Aneurysmectomy, with graft replacement, by site
filipuncture 39.52
graft replacement — *see* Aneurysmectomy, with graft replacement, by site
methyl methacrylate 39.52
suture 39.52
wiring 39.52
wrapping 39.52
Matas' 39.52
Aneurysmotomy — *see* Aneurysmectomy
Angiectomy
with
anastomosis 38.30
abdominal
artery 38.36
vein 38.37
aorta (arch) (ascending) (descending) 38.34
head and neck NEC 38.32
intracranial NEC 38.31
lower limb
artery 38.38
vein 38.39
thoracic vessel NEC 38.35
upper limb (artery) (vein) 38.33
graft replacement (interposition) 38.40
abdominal
aorta 38.44
artery 38.46
vein 38.47
aorta (arch) (ascending) (descending thoracic)
abdominal 38.44
thoracic 38.45
thoracoabdominal 38.45 [38.44]
head and neck NEC 38.42
intracranial NEC 38.41
lower limb
artery 38.48
vein 38.49
thoracic vessel NEC 38.45

Angiectomy — *continued*
with — *continued*
graft replacement — *continued*
upper limb (artery) (vein) 38.43
Angiocardiography (selective) 88.50
carbon dioxide (negative contrast) 88.58
combined right and left heart 88.54
left heart (aortic valve) (atrium) (ventricle) (ventricular outflow tract) 88.53
combined with right heart 88.54
right heart (atrium) (pulmonary valve) (ventricle) (ventricular outflow tract) 88.52
combined with left heart 88.54
vena cava (inferior) (superior) 88.51
Angiography (arterial) — *see also* Arteriography 88.40
by radioisotope — *see* Scan, radioisotope, by site
by ultrasound — *see* Ultrasonography, by site
basilar 88.41
brachial 88.49
carotid (internal) 88.41
celiac 88.47
cerebral (posterior circulation) 88.41
coronary NEC 88.57
eye (fluorescein) 95.12
femoral 88.48
heart 88.50
intra-abdominal NEC 88.47
intracranial 88.41
intrathoracic vessels NEC 88.44
lower extremity NEC 88.48
neck 88.41
placenta 88.46
pulmonary 88.43
renal 88.45
specified artery NEC 88.49
transfemoral 88.48
upper extremity NEC 88.49
veins — *see* Phlebography
vertebral 88.41
Angioplasty (laser) — *see also* Repair, blood vessel

Note — Also use 00.40, 00.41, 00.42, or 00.43 to show the total number of vessels treated. ▶Use code 00.44 once to show procedure on a bifurcated vessel.◀ In addition, use 00.45, 00.46, 00.47, or 00.48 to show the number of vascular stents inserted.

balloon (percutaneous transluminal) NEC 39.50
coronary artery 00.66
multiple vessels
coronary 36.09
open chest approach 36.03
percutaneous transluminal (balloon) 00.66
percutaneous transluminal (balloon)
basilar 00.61
carotid 00.61
cerebral (intracranial) 00.62
cerebrovascular
cerebral (intracranial) 00.62
precerebral (extracranial) 00.61
carotid 00.61
coronary (balloon) 00.66
femoropopliteal 39.50
iliac 39.50
lower extremity NOS 39.50
mesenteric 39.50
peripheral NEC 39.50
precerebral (extracranial) 00.61
carotid 00.61
renal 39.50
subclavian 39.50
upper extremity NOS 39.50
vertebral 00.61
specified site 39.50
cerebrovascular
cerebral (intracranial) 00.62
precerebral (extracranial) 00.61

Angioplasty — *see also* Repair, blood vessel — *continued*
specified site — *continued*
peripheral 39.50
Angiorrhaphy 39.30
artery 39.31
vein 39.32
Angioscopy, percutaneous 38.22
eye (fluorescein) 95.12
Angiotomy 38.00
abdominal
artery 38.06
vein 38.07
aorta (arch) (ascending) (descending) 38.04
head and neck NEC 38.02
intracranial NEC 38.01
lower limb
artery 38.08
vein 38.09
thoracic NEC 38.05
upper limb (artery) (vein) 38.03
Angiotripsy 39.98
Ankylosis, production of — *see* Arthrodesis
Annuloplasty (heart) (posteromedial) 35.33
Anoplasty 49.79
with hemorrhoidectomy 49.46
Anoscopy 49.21
Antibiogram — *see* Examination, microscopic
Antiembolic filter, vena cava 38.7
Antiphobic treatment 94.39
Antrectomy
mastoid 20.49
maxillary 22.39
radical 22.31
pyloric 43.6
Antrostomy — *see* Antrotomy
Antrotomy (exploratory) (nasal sinus) 22.2
Caldwell-Luc (maxillary sinus) 22.39
with removal of membrane lining 22.31
intranasal 22.2
with external approach (Caldwell-Luc) 22.39
radical 22.31
maxillary (simple) 22.2
with Caldwell-Luc approach 22.39
with removal of membrane lining 22.31
external (Caldwell-Luc approach) 22.39
with removal of membrane lining 22.31
radical (with removal of membrane lining) 22.31
Antrum window operation — *see* Antrotomy, maxillary
Aorticopulmonary window operation 39.59
Aortogram, aortography (abdominal) (retrograde) (selective) (translumbar) 88.42
Aortoplasty (aortic valve) (gusset type) 35.11
Aortotomy 38.04
Apexcardiogram (with ECG lead) 89.57
Apheresis, therapeutic — *see* category 99.7 ☑
Apicectomy
lung 32.3
petrous pyramid 20.59
tooth (root) 23.73
with root canal therapy 23.72
Apicoectomy 23.73
with root canal therapy 23.72
Apicolysis (lung) 33.39
Apicostomy, alveolar 24.0
Aponeurectomy 83.42
hand 82.33
Aponeurorrhaphy — *see also* Suture, tendon 83.64

Aponeurorrhaphy — *see also* Suture, tendon — *continued*
hand (*see also* Suture, tendon, hand) 82.45
Aponeurotomy 83.13
hand 82.11
Appendectomy (with drainage) 47.09
incidental 47.19
laparoscopic 47.11
laparoscopic 47.01
Appendicectomy (with drainage) 47.09
incidental 47.19
laparoscopic 47.11
laparoscopic 47.01
Appendicocecostomy 47.91
Appendicoenterostomy 47.91
Appendicolysis 54.59
with appendectomy 47.09
laparoscopic 47.01
other 47.09
laparoscopic 54.51
Appendicostomy 47.91
closure 47.92
Appendicotomy 47.2
Application
adhesion barrier substance 99.77
anti-shock trousers 93.58
arch bars (orthodontic) 24.7
for immobilization (fracture) 93.55
barrier substance, adhesion 99.77
Barton's tongs (skull) (with synchronous skeletal traction) 02.94
bone growth stimulator (surface) (transcutaneous) 99.86
bone morphogenetic protein (Infuse™) (OP-1™) (recombinant) (rhBMP) 84.52
Bryant's traction 93.44
with reduction of fracture or dislocation — *see* Reduction, fracture *and* Reduction, dislocation
Buck's traction 93.46
caliper tongs (skull) (with synchronous skeletal traction) 02.94
cast (fiberglass) (plaster) (plastic) NEC 93.53
with reduction of fracture or dislocation — *see* Reduction, fracture *and* Reduction, dislocation
spica 93.51
cervical collar 93.52
with reduction of fracture or dislocation — *see* Reduction, fracture *and* Reduction, dislocation
clamp, cerebral aneurysm (Crutchfield) (Silverstone) 39.51
croupette, croup tent 93.94
crown (artificial) 23.41
Crutchfield tongs (skull) (with synchronous skeletal traction) 02.94
Dunlop's traction 93.44
with reduction of fracture or dislocation — *see* Reduction, fracture *and* Reduction, dislocation
elastic stockings 93.59
electronic gaiter 93.59
external fixator device (bone) 78.10
carpal, metacarpal 78.14
clavicle 78.11
computer assisted (dependent) 84.73 ●
femur 78.15
fibula 78.17
humerus 78.12
hybrid device or system 84.73
Ilizarov type 84.72
monoplanar system or device 84.71
patella 78.16
pelvic 78.19
phalanges (foot) (hand) 78.19

☑ Additional Digit Required — Refer to the Tabular List for Digit Selection

▼ Subterms under main terms may continue to next column or page

2007 ICD-9-CM

▶◀ Revised Text

● New Line

▲ Revised Code

October 2006 · Volume 3 — 3

Application — *continued*
external fixator device — *continued*
radius 78.13
ring device or system 84.72
scapula 78.11
Sheffield type 84.72
specified site NEC 78.19
tarsal, metatarsal 78.18
thorax (ribs) (sternum) 78.11
tibia 78.17
ulna 78.13
vertebrae 78.19
forceps, with delivery — *see* Delivery, forceps
graft — *see* Graft
gravity (G-) suit 93.59
intermittent pressure device 93.59
Jewett extension brace 93.59
Jobst pumping unit (reduction of edema) 93.59
Lyman Smith traction 93.44
with reduction of fracture or dislocation — *see* Reduction, fracture *and* Reduction, dislocation
MAST (military anti-shock trousers) 93.58
Minerva jacket 93.52
minifixator device (bone) — *see* category 78.1 ☑
neck support (molded) 93.52
obturator (orthodontic) 24.7
orthodontic appliance (obturator) (wiring) 24.7
pelvic sling 93.44
with reduction of fracture or dislocation — *see* Reduction, fracture *and* Reduction, dislocation
peridontal splint (orthodontic) 24.7
plaster jacket 93.51
Minerva 93.52
pressure
dressing (bandage) (Gibney) (Robert Jones') (Shanz) 93.56
trousers (anti-shock) (MAST) 93.58
prosthesis for missing ear 18.71
Russell's traction 93.44
with reduction of fracture or dislocation — *see* Reduction, fracture *and* Reduction, dislocation
splint, for immobilization (plaster) (pneumatic) (tray) 93.54
with fracture reduction — *see* Reduction, fracture
stereotactic head frame 93.59
strapping (non-traction) 93.59   ●
substance, adhesion barrier 99.77
Thomas collar 93.52
with reduction of fracture or dislocation — *see* Reduction, fracture *and* Reduction, dislocation
traction
with reduction of fracture or dislocation — *see* Reduction, fracture *and* Reduction, dislocation
adhesive tape (skin) 93.46
boot 93.46
Bryant's 93.44
Buck's 93.46
Cotrel's 93.42
Dunlop's 93.44
gallows 93.46
Lyman Smith 93.44
Russell's 93.44
skeletal NEC 93.44
intermittent 93.43
skin, limbs NEC 93.46
spinal NEC 93.42
with skull device (halo) (caliper) (Crutchfield) (Gardner-Wells) (Vinke) (tongs) 93.41

Application — *continued*
traction — *continued*
spinal — *continued*
with skull device — *continued*
with synchronous insertion 02.94
Thomas' splint 93.45
Unna's paste boot 93.53
vasopneumatic device 93.58
Velpeau dressing 93.59
Vinke tongs (skull) (with synchronous skeletal traction) 02.94
wound dressing NEC 93.57
Aquapheresis 99.78
Arc lamp — *see* Photocoagulation
Arrest
bone growth (epiphyseal) 78.20
by stapling — *see* Stapling, epiphyseal plate
femur 78.25
fibula 78.27
humerus 78.22
radius 78.23
tibia 78.27
ulna 78.23
cardiac, induced (anoxic) (circulatory) 39.63
circulatory, induced (anoxic) 39.63
hemorrhage — *see* Control, hemorrhage
Arslan operation (fenestration of inner ear) 20.61
Arteriectomy 38.60
with
anastomosis 38.30
abdominal 38.36
aorta (arch) (ascending) (descending thoracic) 38.34
head and neck NEC 38.32
intracranial NEC 38.31
lower limb 38.38
thoracic NEC 38.35
upper limb 38.33
graft replacement (interposition) 38.40
abdominal
aorta 38.44
aorta (arch) (ascending) (descending thoracic)
abdominal 38.44
thoracic 38.45
thoracoabdominal 38.45 [38.44]
head and neck NEC 38.42
intracranial NEC 38.41
lower limb 38.48
thoracic NEC 38.45
upper limb 38.43
abdominal 38.66
aorta (arch) (ascending) (descending) 38.64
head and neck NEC 38.62
intracranial NEC 38.61
lower limb 38.68
thoracic NEC 38.65
upper limb 38.63
Arteriography (contrast) (fluoroscopic) (retrograde) 88.40
by
radioisotope — *see* Scan, radioisotope
ultrasound (Doppler) — *see* Ultrasonography, by site
aorta (arch) (ascending) (descending) 88.42
basilar 88.41
brachial 88.49
carotid (internal) 88.41
cerebral (posterior circulation) 88.41
coronary (direct) (selective) NEC 88.57
double catheter technique (Judkins) (Ricketts and Abrams) 88.56
single catheter technique (Sones) 88.55

Arteriography — *continued*
Doppler (ultrasonic) — *see* Ultrasonography, by site
femoral 88.48
head and neck 88.41
intra-abdominal NEC 88.47
intrathoracic NEC 88.44
lower extremity 88.48
placenta 88.46
pulmonary 88.43
radioisotope — *see* Scan, radioisotope
renal 88.45
specified site NEC 88.49
superior mesenteric artery 88.47
transfemoral 88.48
ultrasound — *see* Ultrasonography, by site
upper extremity 88.49
Arterioplasty — *see* Repair, artery
Arteriorrhaphy 39.31
Arteriotomy 38.00
abdominal 38.06
aorta (arch) (ascending) (descending) 38.04
head and neck NEC 38.02
intracranial NEC 38.01
lower limb 38.08
thoracic NEC 38.05
upper limb 38.03
Arteriovenostomy 39.29
for renal dialysis 39.27
Arthrectomy 80.90
ankle 80.97
elbow 80.92
foot and toe 80.98
hand and finger 80.94
hip 80.95
intervertebral disc — *see* category 80.5 ☑
knee 80.96
semilunar cartilage 80.6
shoulder 80.91
specified site NEC 80.99
spine NEC 80.99
wrist 80.93
Arthrocentesis 81.91
for arthrography — *see* Arthrogram
Arthrodesis (compression) (extra-articular) (intra-articular) (with bone graft) (with fixation device) 81.20
ankle 81.11
carporadial 81.25
cricoarytenoid 31.69
elbow 81.24
finger 81.28
foot NEC 81.17
hip 81.21
interphalangeal
finger 81.28
toe NEC 77.58
claw toe repair 77.57
hammer toe repair 77.56
ischiofemoral 81.21
knee 81.22
lumbosacral, lumbar NEC 81.08
ALIF (anterior lumbar interbody fusion) 81.06
anterior (interbody), anterolateral technique 81.06
lateral transverse process technique 81.07
PLIF (posterior lumbar interbody fusion) 81.08
posterior (interbody), posterolateral technique 81.08
TLIF (transforaminal lumbar interbody fusion) 81.08
McKeever (metatarsophalangeal) 81.16
metacarpocarpal 81.26
metacarpophalangeal 81.27
metatarsophalangeal 81.16
midtarsal 81.14
plantar 81.11
sacroiliac 81.08
shoulder 81.23
specified joint NEC 81.29

Arthrodesis — *continued*
spinal (*see also* Fusion, spinal) 81.00
subtalar 81.13
tarsometatarsal 81.15
tibiotalar 81.11
toe NEC 77.58
claw toe repair 77.57
hammer toe repair 77.56
triple 81.12
wrist 81.26
Arthroendoscopy — *see* Arthroscopy
Arthroereisis, subtalar joint 81.18
Arthrogram, arthrography 88.32
temporomandibular 87.13
Arthrolysis 93.26
Arthroplasty (with fixation device) (with traction) 81.96
ankle 81.49
carpals 81.75
with prosthetic implant 81.74
carpocarpal, carpometacarpal 81.75
with prosthetic implant 81.74
Carroll and Taber (proximal interphalangeal joint) 81.72
cup (partial hip) 81.52
Curtis (interphalangeal joint) 81.72
elbow 81.85
with prosthetic replacement (total) 81.84
femoral head NEC 81.40
with prosthetic implant 81.52
finger(s) 81.72
with prosthetic implant 81.71
foot (metatarsal) with joint replacement 81.57
Fowler (metacarpophalangeal joint) 81.72
hand (metacarpophalangeal) (interphalangeal) 81.72
with prosthetic implant 81.71
hip (with bone graft) 81.40
cup (partial hip) 81.52
femoral head NEC 81.40
with prosthetic implant 81.52
with total replacement 81.51
partial replacement 81.52
total replacement 81.51
interphalangeal joint 81.72
with prosthetic implant 81.71
Kessler (carpometacarpal joint) 81.74
knee (*see also* Repair, knee) 81.47
prosthetic replacement (bicompartmental) (hemijoint) (partial) (total) (tricompartmental) (unicompartmental) 81.54
revision 81.55
metacarpophalangeal joint 81.72
with prosthetic implant 81.71
shoulder 81.83
for recurrent dislocation 81.82
prosthetic replacement (partial) 81.81
total 81.80
temporomandibular 76.5
toe NEC 77.58
for hallux valgus repair 77.59
with prosthetic replacement 81.57
wrist 81.75
with prosthetic implant 81.74
total replacement 81.73
Arthroscopy 80.20
ankle 80.27
elbow 80.22
finger 80.24
foot 80.28
hand 80.24
hip 80.25
knee 80.26
shoulder 80.21
specified site NEC 80.29
toe 80.28
wrist 80.23
Arthrotomy — *see also* Arthrotomy 80.10
Arthrotomy 80.10

☑ Additional Digit Required — Refer to the Tabular List for Digit Selection   ▽ Subterms under main terms may continue to next column or page

4 — Volume 3 • October 2006   ▶◀ Revised Text   ● New Line   ▲ Revised Code   *2007 ICD-9-CM*

Arthrotomy — *continued*
as operative approach — *omit code*
with
arthrography — *see* Arthrogram
arthroscopy — *see* Arthroscopy
injection of drug 81.92
removal of prosthesis (*see also* Removal, prosthesis, joint
structures) 80.00
ankle 80.17
elbow 80.12
foot and toe 80.18
hand and finger 80.14
hip 80.15
knee 80.16
shoulder 80.11
specified site NEC 80.19
spine 80.19
wrist 80.13
Artificial
insemination 69.92
kidney 39.95
rupture of membranes 73.09
Arytenoidectomy 30.29
Arytenoidopexy 31.69
Asai operation (larynx) 31.75
Aspiration
abscess — *see* Aspiration, by site
anterior chamber, eye (therapeutic)
12.91
diagnostic 12.21
aqueous (eye) (humor) (therapeutic)
12.91
diagnostic 12.21
ascites 54.91
Bartholin's gland (cyst) (percutaneous)
71.21
biopsy — *see* Biopsy, by site
bladder (catheter) 57.0
percutaneous (needle) 57.11
bone marrow (for biopsy) 41.31
from donor for transplant 41.91
stem cell 99.79
branchial cleft cyst 29.0
breast 85.91
bronchus 96.05
with lavage 96.56
bursa (percutaneous) 83.94
hand 82.92
calculus, bladder 57.0
cataract 13.3
with
phacoemulsification 13.41
phacofragmentation 13.43
posterior route 13.42
chest 34.91
cisternal 01.01
cranial (puncture) 01.09
craniobuccal pouch 07.72
craniopharyngioma 07.72
cul-de-sac (abscess) 70.0
curettage, uterus 69.59
after abortion or delivery 69.52
diagnostic 69.59
to terminate pregnancy 69.51
cyst — *see* Aspiration, by site
diverticulum, pharynx 29.0
endotracheal 96.04
with lavage 96.56
extradural 01.09
eye (anterior chamber) (therapeutic)
12.91
diagnostic 12.21
fallopian tube 66.91
fascia 83.95
hand 82.93
gallbladder (percutaneous) 51.01
hematoma (*see also* Aspiration, by
site)
obstetrical 75.92
incisional 75.91
hydrocele, tunica vaginalis 61.91
hygroma — *see* Aspiration, by site
hyphema 12.91
hypophysis 07.72

Aspiration — *continued*
intracranial space (epidural) (extradural) (subarachnoid) (subdural)
(ventricular) 01.09
through previously implanted
catheter or reservoir (Ommaya) (Rickham) 01.02
joint 81.91
for arthrography — *see* Arthrogram
kidney (cyst) (pelvis) (percutaneous)
(therapeutic) 55.92
diagnostic 55.23
liver (percutaneous) 50.91
lung (percutaneous) (puncture) (needle) (trocar) 33.93
middle ear 20.09
with intubation 20.01
muscle 83.95
hand 82.93
nail 86.01
nasal sinus 22.00
by puncture 22.01
through natural ostium 22.02
nasotracheal 96.04
with lavage 96.56
orbit, diagnostic 16.22
ovary 65.91
percutaneous — *see* Aspiration, by
site
pericardium (wound) 37.0
pituitary gland 07.72
pleural cavity 34.91
prostate (percutaneous) 60.91
Rathke's pouch 07.72
seminal vesicles 60.71
seroma — *see* Aspiration, by site
skin 86.01
soft tissue NEC 83.95
hand 82.93
spermatocele 63.91
spinal (puncture) 03.31
spleen (cyst) 41.1
stem cell 99.79
subarachnoid space (cerebral) 01.09
subcutaneous tissue 86.01
subdural space (cerebral) 01.09
tendon 83.95
hand 82.93
testis 62.91
thymus 07.92
thyroid (field) (gland) 06.01
postoperative 06.02
trachea 96.04
with lavage 96.56
percutaneous 31.99
tunica vaginalis (hydrocele) (percutaneous) 61.91
vitreous (and replacement) 14.72
diagnostic 14.11
Assessment
fitness to testify 94.11
mental status 94.11
nutritional status 89.39
personality 94.03
temperament 94.02
vocational 93.85
Assistance
cardiac (*see also* Resuscitation, cardiac)
extracorporeal circulation 39.61
endotracheal respiratory — *see* category 96.7 ☑
hepatic, extracorporeal 50.92
respiratory (endotracheal) (mechanical) — *see* Ventilation, mechanical
Astragalectomy 77.98
Asymmetrogammagram — *see* Scan,
radioisotope
Atherectomy
cerebrovascular — *see* Angioplasty
coronary — *see* Angioplasty
peripheral 39.50
Atriocommissuropexy (mitral valve)
35.12
Atrioplasty NEC 37.99

Atrioplasty — *continued*
combined with repair of valvular and
ventricular septal defects — *see*
Repair, endocardial cushion defect
septum (heart) NEC 35.71
Atrioseptopexy — *see also* Repair, atrial
septal defect 35.71
Atrioseptoplasty — *see also* Repair,
atrial septal defect 35.71
Atrioseptostomy (balloon) 35.41
Atriotomy 37.11
Atrioventriculostomy (cerebral-heart)
02.32
Attachment
eye muscle
orbicularis oculi to eyebrow 08.36
rectus to frontalis 15.9
pedicle (flap) graft 86.74
hand 86.73
lip 27.57
mouth 27.57
pharyngeal flap (for cleft palate repair)
27.62
secondary or subsequent 27.63
retina — *see* Reattachment, retina
Atticoantrostomy (ear) 20.49
Atticoantrotomy (ear) 20.49
Atticotomy (ear) 20.23
Audiometry (Békésy 5-tone) (impedance)
(stapedial reflex response) (subjective) 95.41
Augmentation
bladder 57.87
breast — *see* Mammoplasty, augmentation
buttock ("fanny-lift") 86.89
chin 76.68
genioplasty 76.68
mammoplasty — *see* Mammoplasty,
augmentation
outflow tract (pulmonary valve) (gusset
type) 35.26
in total repair of tetralogy of Fallot
35.81
vocal cord(s) 31.0
Auriculectomy 18.39
Autograft — *see* Graft
Autologous — *see* Blood, transfusion
Autopsy 89.8
Autotransfusion (whole blood) — *see*
Blood, transfusion
Autotransplant, autotransplantation
— *see also* Reimplantation
adrenal tissue (heterotopic) (orthotopic) 07.45
kidney 55.61
lung — *see* Transplant, transplantation, lung 33.5 ☑
ovary 65.72
laparoscopic 65.75
pancreatic tissue 52.81
parathyroid tissue (heterotopic) (orthotopic) 06.95
thyroid tissue (heterotopic) (orthotopic) 06.94
tooth 23.5
Avulsion, nerve (cranial) (peripheral)
NEC 04.07
acoustic 04.01
phrenic 33.31
sympathetic 05.29
Azygography 88.63

B

Bacterial smear — *see* Examination,
microscopic
Baffes operation (interatrial transposition of venous return) 35.91
Baffle, atrial or interatrial 35.91
Balanoplasty 64.49
Baldy-Webster operation (uterine suspension) 69.22
Ballistocardiography 89.59

Balloon
angioplasty — *see* Angioplasty, balloon
pump, intra-aortic 37.61
systostomy (atrial) 35.41
Ball operation
herniorrhaphy — *see* Repair, hernia,
inguinal
undercutting 49.02
Bandage 93.57
elastic 93.56
Banding
gastric 44.68
vertical 44.68
pulmonary artery 38.85
Bankhart operation (capsular repair into
glenoid, for shoulder dislocation)
81.82
Bardenheuer operation (ligation of innominate artery) 38.85
Barium swallow 87.61
Barkan operation (goniotomy) 12.52
with goniopuncture 12.53
Barr operation (transfer of tibialis posterior tendon) 83.75
Barsky operation (closure of cleft hand)
82.82
Basal metabolic rate 89.39
Basiotripsy 73.8
Bassett operation (vulvectomy with inguinal lymph node dissection)
71.5 *[40.3]*
Bassini operation — *see* Repair, hernia,
inguinal
Batch-Spittler-McFaddin operation
(knee disarticulation) 84.16
Batista operation (partial ventriculectomy) (ventricular reduction) (ventricular remodeling) 37.35
Bearing surface, hip replacement
ceramic-on-ceramic 00.76
ceramic-on-polyethylene 00.77   ●
metal-on-metal 00.75
metal on polyethylene 00.74
Beck-Jianu operation (permanent gastrostomy) 43.19
Beck operation
aorta-coronary sinus shunt 36.39
epicardial poudrage 36.39
Behavior modification 94.33
Bell-Beuttner operation (subtotal abdominal hysterectomy) 68.39
laparoscopic 68.31
Belsey operation (esophagogastric
sphincter) 44.65
Benenenti operation (rotation of bulbous urethra) 58.49
Berke operation (levator resection of
eyelid) 08.33
Bicuspidization of heart valve 35.10
aortic 35.11
mitral 35.12
Bicycle dynamometer 93.01
Biesenberger operation (size reduction
of breast, bilateral) 85.32
unilateral 85.31
Bifurcation, bone — *see also* Osteotomy
77.30
Bigelow operation (litholapaxy) 57.0
Bililite therapy (ultraviolet) 99.82
Billroth I operation (partial gastrectomy
with gastroduodenostomy) 43.6
Billroth II operation (partial gastrectomy
with gastrojejunostomy) 43.7
Binnie operation (hepatopexy) 50.69
Biofeedback, psychotherapy 94.39
Biopsy
abdominal wall 54.22
adenoid 28.11
adrenal gland NEC 07.11
closed 07.11
open 07.12
percutaneous (aspiration) (needle)
07.11
alveolus 24.12
anus 49.23

☑ Additional Digit Required — Refer to the Tabular List for Digit Selection   ▽ Subterms under main terms may continue to next column or page

6 — Volume 3   ▶◀ Revised Text   ● New Line   ▲ Revised Code   *2007 ICD-9-CM*

Bisection — *see also* Excision — *continued*
  stapes foot plate 19.19
    with incus replacement 19.11
Blalock-Hanlon operation (creation of atrial septal defect) 35.42
Blalock operation (systemic-pulmonary anastomosis) 39.0
Blalock-Taussig operation (subclavian-pulmonary anastomosis) 39.0
Blascovic operation (resection and advancement of levator palpebrae superioris) 08.33
Blepharectomy 08.20
Blepharoplasty — *see also* Reconstruction, eyelid 08.70
  extensive 08.44
Blepharorrhaphy 08.52
  division or severing 08.02
Blepharotomy 08.09
Blind rehabilitation therapy NEC 93.78
Block
  caudal — *see* Injection, spinal
  celiac ganglion or plexus 05.31
  dissection
    breast
      bilateral 85.46
      unilateral 85.45
    bronchus 32.6
    larynx 30.3
    lymph nodes 40.50
    neck 40.40
    vulva 71.5
  epidural, spinal — *see* Injection, spinal
  gasserian ganglion 04.81
  intercostal nerves 04.81
  intrathecal — *see* Injection, spinal
  nerve (cranial) (peripheral) NEC 04.81
  paravertebral stellate ganglion 05.31
  peripheral nerve 04.81
  spinal nerve root (intrathecal) — *see* Injection, spinal
  stellate (ganglion) 05.31
  subarachnoid, spinal — *see* Injection, spinal
  sympathetic nerve 05.31
  trigeminal nerve 04.81
Blood
  flow study, Doppler-type (ultrasound) — *see* Ultrasonography
  patch, spine (epidural) 03.95
  transfusion
    antihemophilic factor 99.06
    autologous
      collected prior to surgery 99.02
      intraoperative 99.00
      perioperative 99.00
      postoperative 99.00
      previously collected 99.02
      salvage 99.00
    blood expander 99.08
    blood surrogate 99.09
    coagulation factors 99.06
    exchange 99.01
    granulocytes 99.09
    hemodilution 99.03
    other substance 99.09
    packed cells 99.04
    plasma 99.07
    platelets 99.05
    serum, other 99.07
    thrombocytes 99.05
Blount operation
  femoral shortening (with blade plate) 78.25
  by epiphyseal stapling 78.25
Boari operation (bladder flap) 56.74
Bobb operation (cholelithotomy) 51.04
Bone
  age studies 88.33
  mineral density study 88.98
Bonney operation (abdominal hysterectomy) 68.49 ▲
  laparoscopic 68.41 ●
Borthen operation (iridotasis) 12.63

Bost operation
  plantar dissection 80.48
  radiocarpal fusion 81.26
Bosworth operation
  arthroplasty for acromioclavicular separation 81.83
  fusion of posterior lumbar and lumbosacral spine 81.08
  for pseudarthrosis 81.38
  resection of radial head ligaments (for tennis elbow) 80.92
  shelf procedure, hip 81.40
Bottle repair of hydrocele, tunica-vaginalis 61.2
Boyd operation (hip disarticulation) 84.18
Brachytherapy
  intravascular 92.27
Brauer operation (cardiolysis) 37.10
Breech extraction — *see* Extraction, breech
Bricker operation (ileoureterostomy) 56.51
Brisement (forcé) 93.26
Bristow operation (repair of shoulder dislocation) 81.82
Brockman operation (soft tissue release for clubfoot) 83.84
Brock operation (pulmonary valvotomy) 35.03
Bronchogram, bronchography 87.32
  endotracheal 87.31
  transcricoid 87.32
Bronchoplasty 33.48
Bronchorrhaphy 33.41
Bronchoscopy NEC 33.23
  with biopsy 33.24
    lung 33.27
      brush 33.24
  fiberoptic 33.22
    with biopsy 33.24
      lung 33.27
        brush 33.24
  through tracheostomy 33.21
    with biopsy 33.24
      lung 33.27
        brush 33.24
Bronchospirometry 89.38
Bronchostomy 33.0
  closure 33.42
Bronchotomy 33.0
Browne (-Denis) operation (hypospadias repair) 58.45
Brunschwig operation (temporary gastrostomy) 43.19
Buckling, scleral 14.49
  with
    air tamponade 14.49
    implant (silicone) (vitreous) 14.41
    resection of sclera 14.49
    vitrectomy 14.49
    vitreous implant (silicone) 14.41
Bunionectomy (radical) 77.59
  with
    arthrodesis 77.52
    osteotomy of first metatarsal 77.51
    resection of joint with prosthetic implant 77.59
    soft tissue correction NEC 77.53
Bunnell operation (tendon transfer) 82.56
Burch procedure (retropubic urethral suspension for urinary stress incontinence) 59.5
Burgess operation (amputation of ankle) 84.14
Burn dressing 93.57
Burr holes 01.24
Bursectomy 83.5
  hand 82.31
Bursocentesis 83.94
  hand 82.92
Bursotomy 83.03
  hand 82.03
Burying of fimbriae in uterine wall 66.97 ●

Bypass
  abdominal-coronary artery 36.17
  aortocoronary (catheter stent) (with prosthesis) (with saphenous vein graft) (with vein graft) 36.10
    one coronary vessel 36.11
    two coronary vessels 36.12
    three coronary vessels 36.13
    four coronary vessels 36.14
  arterial (graft) (mandril grown graft) (vein graft) NEC 39.29
    carotid-cerebral 39.28
    carotid-vertebral 39.28
    extracranial-intracranial [EC-IC] 39.28
    intra-abdominal NEC 39.26
    intrathoracic NEC 39.23
    peripheral NEC 39.29
  cardiopulmonary 39.61
    open 39.61
    percutaneous (closed) 39.66
  carotid-cerebral 39.28
  carotid-vertebral 39.28
  coronary (*see also* Bypass, aortocoronary) 36.10
  extracranial-intracranial [EC-IC] 39.28
  gastric 44.39
    high 44.31
    laparoscopic 44.38
    Printen and Mason 44.31
  gastroduodenostomy (Jaboulay's) 44.39
    laparoscopic 44.38
  gastroenterostomy 44.39
    laparoscopic 44.38
  gastroepiploic-coronary artery 36.17
  gastrogastrostomy 44.39
  gastrojejunostomy 44.39
    laparoscopic 44.38
  graft, pressurized treatment 00.16
  heart-lung (complete) (partial) 39.61
    open 39.61
    percutaneous (closed) 39.66
  high gastric 44.31
  ileo-jejunal 45.91
  internal mammary-coronary artery (single) 36.15
    double vessel 36.16
  jejunal-ileum 45.91
  pulmonary 39.61
    open 39.61
    percutaneous (closed) 39.66
  shunt
    intestine
      large-to-large 45.94
      small-to-large 45.93
      small-to-small 45.91
    stomach 44.39
      high gastric 44.31
      laparoscopic 44.38
  terminal ileum 45.93
  vascular (arterial) (graft) (mandril grown graft) (vein graft) NEC 39.29
    aorta-carotid-brachial 39.22
    aorta-iliac-femoral 39.25
    aorta-renal 39.24
    aorta-subclavian-carotid 39.22
    aortic-superior mesenteric 39.26
    aortocarotid 39.22
    aortoceliac 39.26
    aortocoronary (*see also* Bypass, aortocoronary) 36.10
    aortofemoral 39.25
    aortofemoral-popliteal 39.25
    aortoiliac 39.25
      to popliteal 39.25
    aortoiliofemoral 39.25
    aortomesenteric 39.26
    aortopopliteal 39.25
    aortorenal 39.24
    aortosubclavian 39.22
    axillary-brachial 39.29
    axillary-femoral (superficial) 39.29
    axillofemoral (superficial) 39.29
    carotid-cerebral 39.28
    carotid to subclavian artery 39.22

Bypass — *continued*
  vascular — *continued*
    carotid-vertebral 39.28
    common hepatic-common iliac-renal 39.26
    coronary (*see also* Bypass, aorto-coronary) 36.10
    extracranial-intracranial [EC-IC] 39.28
    femoral-femoral 39.29
    femoroperoneal 39.29
    femoropopliteal (reversed saphenous vein) (saphenous) 39.29
    femorotibial (anterior) (posterior) 39.29
    iliofemoral 39.25
    ilioiliac 39.26
    internal mammary-coronary artery (single) 36.15
      double vessel 36.16
    intra-abdominal (arterial) NEC 39.26
      venous NEC 39.1
    intrathoracic NEC 39.23
    peripheral artery NEC 39.29
    popliteal-tibial 39.29
    renal artery 39.24
    splenorenal (venous) 39.1
      arterial 39.26
    subclavian-axillary 39.29
    subclavian-carotid 39.22
    subclavian-subclavian 39.22
    Y graft to renal arteries 39.24

C

Caldwell-Luc operation (maxillary sinusotomy) 22.39
  with removal of membrane lining 22.31
Caldwell operation (sulcus extension) 24.91
Calibration, urethra 89.29
Calicectomy (renal) 55.4
Callander operation (knee disarticulation) 84.16
Caloric test, vestibular function 95.44
Calycectomy (renal) 55.4
Calyco-ileoneocystostomy 55.86
Calycotomy (renal) 55.11
Campbell operation
  bone block, ankle 81.11
  fasciotomy (iliac crest) 83.14
  reconstruction of anterior cruciate ligament 81.45
Campimetry 95.05
Canaliculodacryocystorhinostomy 09.81
Canaliculoplasty 09.73
Canaliculorhinostomy 09.81
Canaloplasty, external auditory meatus 18.6
Cannulation — *see also* Insertion, catheter
  ampulla of Vater 51.99
  antrum 22.01
  arteriovenous 39.93
  artery 38.91
  caval-mesenteric vein 39.1
  cisterna chyli 40.61
  Eustachian tube 20.8
  lacrimal apparatus 09.42
  lymphatic duct, left (thoracic) 40.61
  nasal sinus (by puncture) 22.01
    through natural ostium 22.02
  pancreatic duct 52.92
    by retrograde endoscopy (ERP) 52.93
  renoportal 39.1
  sinus (nasal) (by puncture) 22.01
    through natural ostium 22.02
  splenorenal (venous) 39.1
    arterial 39.26
  thoracic duct (cervical approach) (thoracic approach) 40.61
Cannulization — *see* Cannulation
Canthocystostomy 09.82

☑ Additional Digit Required — Refer to the Tabular List for Digit Selection   ▽ Subterms under main terms may continue to next column or page

2007 ICD-9-CM   ▶◀ Revised Text   ● New Line   ▲ Revised Code   October 2006 • Volume 3 — 7

Bisection — Canthocystostomy

Canthoplasty 08.59
Canthorrhaphy 08.52
  division or severing 08.02
Canthotomy 08.51
Capsulectomy
  joint (see also Arthrectomy) 80.90
  kidney 55.91
  lens 13.65
    with extraction of lens 13.51
  ovary 65.29
    laparoscopic 65.25
Capsulo-iridectomy 13.65
Capsuloplasty — see Arthroplasty
Capsulorrhaphy 81.96
  with arthroplasty — see Arthroplasty
  ankle 81.94
  foot 81.94
  lower extremity NEC 81.95
  upper extremity 81.93
Capsulotomy
  joint (see also Division, joint capsule) 80.40
    for claw toe repair 77.57
  lens 13.64
    with
      discission of lens 13.2
      removal of foreign body 13.02
        by magnet extraction 13.01
Cardiac
  mapping 37.27
  massage (external) (closed chest) 99.63
    open chest 37.91
  retraining 93.36
Cardiac support device (CSD) 37.41
Cardiectomy (stomach) 43.5
Cardiocentesis 37.0
Cardiography — see also Angiocardiography 88.50
Cardiolysis 37.10
Cardiomyopexy 36.39
Cardiomyotomy 42.7
Cardio-omentopexy 36.39
Cardiopericardiopexy 36.39
Cardioplasty (stomach and esophagus) 44.65
  stomach alone 44.66
    laparoscopic 44.67
Cardioplegia 39.63
Cardiopneumopexy 36.39
Cardiorrhaphy 37.49
Cardioschisis 37.12
Cardiosplenopexy 36.39
Cardiotomy (exploratory) 37.11
Cardiovalvulotomy — see Valvulotomy, heart
Cardioversion (external) 99.62
  atrial 99.61
Carotid pulse tracing with ECG lead 89.56
Carpectomy (partial) 77.84
  total 77.94
Carroll and Taber arthroplasty (proximal interphalangeal joint) 81.72
Casting (for immobilization) NEC 93.53
  with fracture-reduction — see Reduction, fracture
Castration
  female (oophorectomy, bilateral) 65.51
    laparoscopic 65.53
  male 62.41
C.A.T. (computerized axial tomography) — see also Scan, C.A.T. 88.38
Catheterization — see also Insertion, catheter
  arteriovenous 39.93
  artery 38.91
  bladder, indwelling 57.94
    percutaneous (cystostomy) 57.17
    suprapubic NEC 57.18
  bronchus 96.05
    with lavage 96.56
  cardiac (right) 37.21
    combined left and right 37.23
    left 37.22
      combined with right heart 37.23

Catheterization — see also Insertion, catheter — continued
  cardiac — continued
    right 37.21
      combined with left heart 37.23
  central venous NEC 38.93
    peripherally inserted central catheter (PICC) 38.93
  chest 34.04
    revision (with lysis of adhesions) 34.04
  Eustachian tube 20.8
  heart (right) 37.21
    combined left and right 37.23
    left 37.22
      combined with right heart 37.23
    right 37.21
      combined with left heart 37.23
  hepatic vein 38.93
  inferior vena cava 38.93
  intercostal space (with water seal), for drainage 34.04
    revision (with lysis of adhesions) 34.04
  lacrimonasal duct 09.44
  laryngeal 96.05
  nasolacrimal duct 09.44
  pancreatic cyst 52.01
  renal vein 38.93
  Swan-Ganz (pulmonary) 89.64
  transtracheal for oxygenation 31.99
  umbilical vein 38.92
  ureter (to kidney) 59.8
    for retrograde pyelogram 87.74
  urethra, indwelling 57.94
  vein NEC 38.93
    for renal dialysis 38.95
Cattell operation (herniorrhaphy) 53.51
Cauterization — see also Destruction, lesion, by site
  anus NEC 49.39
    endoscopic 49.31
  Bartholin's gland 71.24
  broad ligament 69.19
  bronchus 32.09
    endoscopic 32.01
  canaliculi 09.73
  cervix 67.32
  chalazion 08.25
  choroid plexus 02.14
  conjunctiva 10.33
    lesion 10.32
  cornea (fistula) (ulcer) 11.42
  ear, external 18.29
  endometrial implant — see Excision, lesion, by site
  entropion 08.41
  esophagus 42.39
    endoscopic 42.33
  eyelid 08.25
    for entropion or ectropion 08.41
  fallopian tube 66.61
    by endoscopy (hysteroscopy) (laparoscopy) 66.29
  hemorrhoids 49.43
  iris 12.41
  lacrimal
    gland 09.21
    punctum 09.72
      for eversion 09.71
    sac 09.6
  larynx 30.09
  liver 50.29
  lung 32.29
    endoscopic 32.28
  meibomian gland 08.25
  nose, for epistaxis (with packing) 21.03
  ovary 65.29
    laparoscopic 65.25
  palate (bony) 27.31
  pannus (superficial) 11.42
  pharynx 29.39
  punctum, lacrimal 09.72
    for eversion 09.71
  rectum 48.32

Cauterization — see also Destruction, lesion, by site — continued
  rectum — continued
    radical 48.31
  round ligament 69.19
  sclera 12.84
    with iridectomy 12.62
  skin 86.3
  subcutaneous tissue 86.3
  tonsillar fossa 28.7
  urethra 58.39
    endoscopic 58.31
  uterosacral ligament 69.19
  uterotubal ostia 66.61
  uterus 68.29
  vagina 70.33
  vocal cords 30.09
  vulva 71.3
Cavernoscopy 34.21
Cavernostomy 33.1
Cavernotomy, kidney 55.39
Cavography (inferior vena cava) 88.51
Cecectomy (with resection of terminal ileum) 45.72
Cecocoloplicopexy 46.63
Cecocolostomy 45.94
Cecofixation 46.64
Ceco-ileostomy 45.93
Cecopexy 46.64
Cecoplication 46.62
Cecorrhaphy 46.75
Cecosigmoidostomy 45.94
Cecostomy (tube) — see also Colostomy 46.10
Cecotomy 45.03
Celiocentesis 54.91
Celioscopy 54.21
Celiotomy, exploratory 54.11
Cell block and Papanicolaou smear — see Examination, microscopic
Cephalogram 87.17
  dental 87.12
  orthodontic 87.12
Cephalometry, cephalometrics 87.17
  echo 88.78
  orthodontic 87.12
  ultrasound (sonar) 88.78
  x-ray 87.81
Cephalotomy, fetus 73.8
Cerclage
  anus 49.72
  cervix 67.59
    transabdominal 67.51
    transvaginal 67.59
  isthmus uteri (cervix) 67.59
  retinal reattachment (see also Buckling, scleral) 14.49
  sclera (see also Buckling, scleral) 14.49
Cervicectomy (with synchronous colporrhaphy) 67.4
Cervicoplasty 67.69
Cesarean section 74.99
  classical 74.0
  corporeal 74.0
  extraperitoneal 74.2
  fundal 74.0
  laparotrachelotomy 74.1
  Latzko 74.2
  low cervical 74.1
  lower uterine segment 74.1
  peritoneal exclusion 74.4
  specified type NEC 74.4
  supravesical 74.2
  transperitoneal 74.4
    classical 74.0
    low cervical 74.1
  upper uterine segment 74.0
  vaginal 74.4
  Waters 74.2
Chandler operation (hip fusion) 81.21
Change — see also Replacement
  cast NEC 97.13
    lower limb 97.12

Change — see also Replacement — continued
  cast — continued
    upper limb 97.11
  cystostomy catheter or tube 59.94
  gastrostomy tube 97.02
  length
    bone — see either category 78.2 ☑ Shortening, bone or category 78.3 ☑ Lengthening, bone
    muscle 83.85
      hand 82.55
    tendon 83.85
      hand 82.55
  nephrostomy catheter or tube 55.93
  pyelostomy catheter or tube 55.94
  tracheostomy tube 97.23
  ureterostomy catheter or tube 59.93
  urethral catheter, indwelling 57.95
Character analysis, psychologic 94.03
Charles operation (correction of lymphedema) 40.9
Charnley operation (compression arthrodesis)
  ankle 81.11
  hip 81.21
  knee 81.22
Cheatle-Henry operation — see Repair, hernia, femoral
Check
  automatic implantable cardioverter/defibrillatory (AICD) (interrogation only) 89.49
  CRT-D (cardiac resynchronization defibrillator) (interrogation only) 89.49
  CRT-P (cardiac resynchronization pacemaker) (interrogation only) 89.45
  pacemaker, artificial (cardiac) (function) (interrogation only) (rate) 89.45
    amperage threshold 89.48
    artifact wave form 89.46
    electrode impedance 89.47
    voltage threshold 89.48
  vision NEC 95.09
Cheiloplasty 27.59
Cheilorrhaphy 27.51
Cheilostomatoplasty 27.59
Cheilotomy 27.0
Chemical peel, skin 86.24
Chemocauterization — see also Destruction, lesion, by site
  corneal epithelium 11.41
  palate 27.31
Chemodectomy 39.8
Chemoembolization 99.25
Chemolysis
  nerve (peripheral) 04.2
  spinal canal structure 03.8
Chemoneurolysis 04.2
Chemonucleolysis (nucleus pulposus) 80.52
Chemopallidectomy 01.42
Chemopeel (skin) 86.24
Chemosurgery
  esophagus 42.39
    endoscopic 42.33
  Mohs' 86.24
  skin (superficial) 86.24
  stomach 43.49
    endoscopic 43.41
Chemothalamectomy 01.41
Chemotherapy — see also Immunotherapy
  for cancer NEC 99.25
    brain wafer implantation 00.10
    implantation of chemotherapeutic agent 00.10
    interstitial implantation 00.10
    intracavitary implantation 00.10
    wafer chemotherapy 00.10
  Antabuse 94.25
  lithium 94.22
  methadone 94.25

Chemotherapy — *see also*
  Immunotherapy — *continued*
  palate (bony) 27.31
Chevalier-Jackson operation (partial
  laryngectomy) 30.29
Child operation (radical subtotal pancreatectomy) 52.53
Cholangiocholangiostomy 51.39
Cholangiocholecystocholedochectomy
  51.22
Cholangio-enterostomy 51.39
Cholangiogastrostomy 51.39
Cholangiogram 87.54
  endoscopic retrograde (ERC) 51.11
  intraoperative 87.53
  intravenous 87.52
  percutaneous hepatic 87.51
  transhepatic 87.53
Cholangiography — *see also* Cholan-
  giogram 87.54
Cholangiojejunostomy (intrahepatic)
  51.39
**Cholangiopancreatography, endoscopic
  retrograde** (ERCP) 51.10
Cholangiostomy 51.59
Cholangiotomy 51.59
Cholecystectomy
  partial 51.21
    laparoscopic 51.24
  total 51.22
    laparoscopic 51.23
Cholecystenterorrhaphy 51.91
Cholecystocecostomy 51.32
Cholecystocholangiogram 87.59
Cholecystocolostomy 51.32
Cholecystoduodenostomy 51.32
Cholecystoenterostomy (Winiwater)
  51.32
Cholecystogastrostomy 51.34
Cholecystogram 87.59
Cholecystoileostomy 51.32
Cholecystojejunostomy (Roux-en-Y)
  (with jejunojejunostomy) 51.32
Cholecystopancreatostomy 51.33
Cholecystopexy 51.99
Cholecystorrhaphy 51.91
Cholecystostomy NEC 51.03
  by trocar 51.02
Cholecystotomy 51.04
  percutaneous 51.01
Choledochectomy 51.63
Choledochoduodenostomy 51.36
Choledochoenterostomy 51.36
Choledochojejunostomy 51.36
Choledocholithotomy 51.41
  endoscopic 51.88
Choledocholithotripsy 51.41
  endoscopic 51.88
Choledochopancreatostomy 51.39
Choledochoplasty 51.72
Choledochorrhaphy 51.71
Choledochoscopy 51.11
Choledochostomy 51.51
Choledochotomy 51.51
Cholelithotomy 51.04
Chondrectomy 80.90
  ankle 80.97
  elbow 80.92
  foot and toe 80.98
  hand and finger 80.94
  hip 80.95
  intervertebral cartilage — *see* category
    80.5 ☑
  knee (semilunar cartilage) 80.6
  nasal (submucous) 21.5
  semilunar cartilage (knee) 80.6
  shoulder 80.91
  specified site NEC 80.99
  spine — *see* category 80.5 ☑
  wrist 80.93
Chondroplasty — *see* Arthroplasty
Chondrosternoplasty (for pectus excavatum repair) 34.74
Chondrotomy — *see also* Division, cartilage 80.40
  nasal 21.1

Chopart operation (midtarsal amputation) 84.12
Chordectomy, vocal 30.22
Chordotomy (spinothalmic) (anterior)
  (posterior) NEC 03.29
  percutaneous 03.21
  stereotactic 03.21
Ciliarotomy 12.55
Ciliectomy (ciliary body) 12.44
  eyelid margin 08.20
Cinch, cinching
  for scleral buckling (*see also* Buckling,
    scleral) 14.49
  ocular muscle (oblique) (rectus) 15.22
    multiple (two or more muscles)
      15.4
Cineangiocardiography — *see also* Angiocardiography 88.50
Cineplasty, cineplastic prosthesis
  amputation — *see* Amputation
  arm 84.44
  biceps 84.44
  extremity 84.40
    lower 84.48
    upper 84.44
  leg 84.48
Cineradiograph — *see* Radiography
Cingulumotomy (brain) (percutaneous
  radiofrequency) 01.32
Circumcision (male) 64.0
  female 71.4
CISH (classic infrafascial SEMM hysterectomy) 68.31
Clagett operation (closure of chest wall
  following open flap drainage) 34.72
Clamp and cautery, hemorrhoids 49.43
Clamping
  aneurysm (cerebral) 39.51
  blood vessel — *see* Ligation, blood
    vessel
  ventricular shunt 02.43
Clavicotomy 77.31
  fetal 73.8
Claviculectomy (partial) 77.81
  total 77.91
Clayton operation (resection of
  metatarsal heads and bases of
  phalanges) 77.88
Cleaning, wound 96.59
Clearance
  bladder (transurethral) 57.0
  pelvic
    female 68.8
    male 57.71
  prescalene fat pad 40.21
  renal pelvis (transurethral) 56.0
  ureter (transurethral) 56.0
Cleidotomy 77.31
  fetal 73.8
Clipping
  aneurysm (basilar) (carotid) (cerebel-
    lar) (cerebellopontine) (commu-
    nicating artery) (vertebral) 39.51
  arteriovenous fistula 39.53
  frenulum, frenum
    labia (lips) 27.91
    lingual (tongue) 25.91
  tip of uvula 27.72
Clitoridectomy 71.4
Clitoridotomy 71.4
Clivogram 87.02
Closure — *see also* Repair
  abdominal wall 54.63
    delayed (granulating wound) 54.62
    secondary 54.61
    tertiary 54.62
  amputation stump, secondary 84.3
  aorticopulmonary fenestration (fistula)
    39.59
  appendicostomy 47.92
  artificial opening
    bile duct 51.79
    bladder 57.82
    bronchus 33.42
    common duct 51.72
    esophagus 42.83

Closure — *see also* Repair —
  continued
  artificial opening — *continued*
    gallbladder 51.92
    hepatic duct 51.79
    intestine 46.50
      large 46.52
      small 46.51
    kidney 55.82
    larynx 31.62
    rectum 48.72
    stomach 44.62
    thorax 34.72
    trachea 31.72
    ureter 56.83
    urethra 58.42
  atrial septal defect (*see also* Repair,
    atrial septal defect) 35.71
    with umbrella device (King-Mills
      type) 35.52
    combined with repair of valvular
      and ventricular septal defects
      — *see* Repair, endocardial
      cushion defect
  bronchostomy 33.42
  cecostomy 46.52
  cholecystostomy 51.92
  cleft hand 82.82
  colostomy 46.52
  cystostomy 57.82
  diastema (alveolar) (dental) 24.8
  disrupted abdominal wall (postopera-
    tive) 54.61
  duodenostomy 46.51
  encephalocele 02.12
  endocardial cushion defect (*see also*
    Repair, endocardial cushion de-
    fect) 35.73
  enterostomy 46.50
  esophagostomy 42.83
  fenestration
    aorticopulmonary 39.59
    septal, heart (*see also* Repair,
      heart, septum) 35.70
  filtering bleb, corneoscleral (postglau-
    coma) 12.66
  fistula
    abdominothoracic 34.83
    anorectal 48.73
    anovaginal 70.73
    antrobuccal 22.71
    anus 49.73
    aorticopulmonary (fenestration)
      39.59
    aortoduodenal 39.59
    appendix 47.92
    biliary tract 51.79
    bladder NEC 57.84
    branchial cleft 29.52
    bronchocutaneous 33.42
    bronchoesophageal 33.42
    bronchomediastinal 34.73
    bronchopleural 34.73
    bronchopleurocutaneous 34.73
    bronchopleuromediastinal 34.73
    bronchovisceral 33.42
    bronchus 33.42
    cecosigmoidal 46.76
    cerebrospinal fluid 02.12
    cervicoaural 18.79
    cervicosigmoidal 67.62
    cervicovesical 57.84
    cervix 67.62
    cholecystocolic 51.93
    cholecystoduodenal 51.93
    cholecystoenteric 51.93
    cholecystogastric 51.93
    cholecystojejunal 51.93
    cisterna chyli 40.63
    colon 46.76
    colovaginal 70.72
    common duct 51.72
    cornea 11.49
      with lamellar graft (homograft)
        11.62
      autograft 11.61

Closure — *see also* Repair —
  continued
  fistula — *continued*
    diaphragm 34.83
    duodenum 46.72
    ear drum 19.4
    ear, middle 19.9
    enterocolic 46.74
    enterocutaneous 46.74
    enterouterine 69.42
    enterovaginal 70.74
    enterovesical 57.83
    esophagobronchial 33.42
    esophagocutaneous 42.84
    esophagopleurocutaneous 34.73
    esophagotracheal 31.73
    esophagus NEC 42.84
    fecal 46.79
    gallbladder 51.93
    gastric NEC 44.63
    gastrocolic 44.63
    gastroenterocolic 44.63
    gastroesophageal 42.84
    gastrojejunal 44.63
    gastrojejunocolic 44.63
    heart valve — *see* Repair, heart,
      valve
    hepatic duct 51.79
    hepatopleural 34.73
    hepatopulmonary 34.73
    ileorectal 46.74
    ileosigmoidal 46.74
    ileovesical 57.83
    ileum 46.74
    in ano 49.73
    intestine 46.79
      large 46.76
      small NEC 46.74
    intestinocolonic 46.74
    intestinoureteral 56.84
    intestinouterine 69.42
    intestinovaginal 70.74
    intestinovesical 57.83
    jejunum 46.74
    kidney 55.83
    lacrimal 09.99
    laryngotracheal 31.62
    larynx 31.62
    lymphatic duct, left (thoracic)
      40.63
    mastoid (antrum) 19.9
    mediastinobronchial 34.73
    mediastinocutaneous 34.73
    mouth (external) 27.53
    nasal 21.82
      sinus 22.71
    nasolabial 21.82
    nasopharyngeal 21.82
    oroantral 22.71
    oronasal 21.82
    oval window (ear) 20.93
    pancreaticoduodenal 52.95
    perilymph 20.93
    perineorectal 48.73
    perineosigmoidal 46.76
    perineourethroscrotal 58.43
    perineum 71.72
    perirectal 48.93
    pharyngoesophageal 29.53
    pharynx NEC 29.53
    pleura, pleural NEC 34.93
    pleurocutaneous 34.73
    pleuropericardial 37.49
    pleuroperitoneal 34.83
    pulmonoperitoneal 34.83
    rectolabial 48.73
    rectoureteral 56.84
    rectourethral 58.43
    rectovaginal 70.73
    rectovesical 57.83
    rectovesicovaginal 57.83
    rectovulvar 48.73
    rectum NEC 48.73
    renal 55.83
    reno-intestinal 55.83
    round window 20.93

Closure — see also Repair — continued

fistula — continued
salivary (gland) (duct) 26.42
scrotum 61.42
sigmoidovaginal 70.74
sigmoidovesical 57.83
splenocolic 41.95
stomach NEC 44.63
thoracic duct 40.63
thoracoabdominal 34.83
thoracogastric 34.83
thoracointestinal 34.83
thorax NEC 34.73
trachea NEC 31.73
tracheoesophageal 31.73
tympanic membrane (see also Tympanoplasty) 19.4
umbilicourinary 57.51
ureter 56.84
ureterocervical 56.84
ureterorectal 56.84
ureterosigmoidal 56.84
ureterovaginal 56.84
ureterovesical 56.84
urethra 58.43
urethroperineal 58.43
urethroperineovesical 57.84
urethrorectal 58.43
urethroscrotal 58.43
urethrovaginal 58.43
uteroenteric 69.42
uterointestinal 69.42
uterorectal 69.42
uteroureteric 56.84
uterovaginal 69.42
uterovesical 57.84
vagina 70.75
vaginocutaneous 70.75
vaginoenteric 70.74
vaginoperineal 70.75
vaginovesical 57.84
vesicocervicovaginal 57.84
vesicocolic 57.83
vesicocutaneous 57.84
vesicoenteric 57.83
vesicometrorectal 57.83
vesicoperineal 57.84
vesicorectal 57.83
vesicosigmoidal 57.83
vesicosigmoidovaginal 57.83
vesicoureteral 56.84
vesicouretero vaginal 56.84
vesicourethral 57.84
vesicourethrorectal 57.83
vesicouterine 57.84
vesicovaginal 57.84
vulva 71.72
vulvorectal 48.73
foramen ovale (patent) 35.71
with
prosthesis (open heart technique) 35.51
closed heart technique 35.52
tissue graft 35.61
gastroduodenostomy 44.5
gastrojejunostomy 44.5
gastrostomy 44.62
ileostomy 46.51
jejunostomy 46.51
laceration (see also Suture, by site)
liver 50.61
laparotomy, delayed 54.62
meningocele (spinal) 03.51
cerebral 02.12
myelomeningocele 03.52
nephrostomy 55.82
palmar cleft 82.82
patent ductus arteriosus 38.85
pelviostomy 55.82
peptic ulcer (bleeding) (perforated) 44.40
perforation
ear drum (see also Tympanoplasty) 19.4
esophagus 42.82

Closure — see also Repair — continued

perforation — continued
nasal septum 21.88
tympanic membrane (see also Tympanoplasty) 19.4
proctostomy 48.72
punctum, lacrimal (papilla) 09.91
pyelostomy 55.82
rectostomy 48.72
septum defect (heart) (see also Repair, heart, septum) 35.70
sigmoidostomy 46.52
skin (V-Y type) 86.59
stoma
bile duct 51.79
bladder 57.82
bronchus 33.42
common duct 51.72
esophagus 42.83
gallbladder 51.92
hepatic duct 51.79
intestine 46.50
large 46.52
small 46.51
kidney 55.82
larynx 31.62
rectum 48.72
stomach 44.62
thorax 34.72
trachea 31.72
ureter 56.83
urethra 58.42
thoracostomy 34.72
tracheostomy 31.72
ulcer (bleeding) (peptic) (perforated) 44.40
duodenum 44.42
gastric 44.41
intestine (perforated) 46.79
skin 86.59
stomach 44.41
ureterostomy 56.83
urethrostomy 58.42
vagina 70.8
vascular
percutaneous puncture — omit code
vesicostomy 57.22
wound (see also Suture, by site)
with graft — see Graft
with tissue adhesive 86.59

Coagulation, electrocoagulation — see also Destruction, lesion, by site
aneurysm (cerebral) (peripheral vessel) 39.52
arteriovenous fistula 39.53
brain tissue (incremental) (radio-frequency) 01.59
broad ligament 69.19
cervix 67.32
ear
external 18.29
inner 20.79
middle 20.51
fallopian tube 66.61
gasserian ganglion 04.05
nose for epistaxis (with packing) 21.03
ovary 65.29
laparoscopic 65.25
pharynx (by diathermy) 29.39
prostatic bed 60.94
rectum (polyp) 48.32
radical 48.31
retina (for)
destruction of lesion 14.21
reattachment 14.51
repair of tear 14.31
round ligament 69.19
semicircular canals 20.79
spinal cord (lesion) 03.4
urethrovesical junction, transurethral 57.49
uterosacral ligament 69.19
uterus 68.29
vagina 70.33

Coagulation, electrocoagulation — see also Destruction, lesion, by site — continued
vulva 71.3
Coating, aneurysm of brain 39.52
Cobalt-60 therapy (treatment) 92.23
Coccygectomy (partial) 77.89
total 77.99
Coccygotomy 77.39
"Cocked hat" procedure (metacarpal lengthening and transfer of local flap) 82.69
Cockett operation (varicose vein)
lower limb 38.59
upper limb 38.53
Cody tack (perforation of footplate) 19.0
Coffey operation (uterine suspension) (Meig's modification) 69.22
Colectomy (partial) (segmental) (subtotal) 45.79
cecum (with terminal ileum) 45.72
left (Hartmann) (lower) (radical) 45.75
multiple segmental 45.71
right (radical) 45.73
sigmoid 45.76
terminal ileum with cecum 45.72
total 45.8
transverse 45.74
Cole operation (anterior tarsal wedge osteotomy) 77.28
Collapse, lung, surgical 33.39
by
destruction of phrenic nerve 33.31
pneumoperitoneum 33.33
pneumothorax, artificially-induced 33.32
thoracoplasty 33.34
Collection, sperm for artificial insemination 99.96
Collis-Nissen operation (hiatal hernia repair with esophagogastroplasty) 53.80
Colocentesis 45.03
Colocolostomy 45.94
proximal to distal segment 45.79
Colocystoplasty 57.87 [45.52]
Colofixation 46.64
Coloileotomy 45.00
Colonna operation
adductor tenotomy (first stage) 83.12
hip arthroplasty (second stage) 81.40
reconstruction of hip (second stage) 81.40
Colonoscopy 45.23
with biopsy 45.25
rectum 48.24
fiberoptic (flexible) 45.23
intraoperative 45.21
through stoma (artificial) 45.22
transabdominal 45.21
Colopexy 46.63
Coloplication 46.64
Coloproctostomy 45.94
Colorectosigmoidostomy 45.94
Colorectostomy 45.94
Colorrhaphy 46.75
Coloscopy — see Colonoscopy
Colosigmoidostomy 45.94
Colostomy (ileo-ascending) (ileo-transverse) (perineal) (transverse) 46.10
with anterior rectal resection 48.62
delayed opening 46.14
loop 46.03
permanent (magnetic) 46.13
temporary 46.11
Colotomy 45.03
Colpectomy 70.4
Colpoceliocentesis 70.0
Colpocentesis 70.0
Colpocleisis (complete) (partial) 70.8
Colpohysterectomy 68.59
laparoscopically assisted (LAVH) 68.51
Colpoperineoplasty 70.79
with repair of urethrocele 70.50
Colpoperineorrhaphy 70.71
following delivery 75.69

Colpopexy 70.77
Colpoplasty 70.79
Colpopoiesis 70.61
Colporrhaphy 70.71
for repair of
cystocele 70.51
with rectocele 70.50
enterocele 70.92
rectocele 70.52
with cystocele 70.50
urethrocele 70.51
anterior (cystocele repair) 70.51
posterior (rectocele repair) 70.52
Colposcopy 70.21
Colpotomy 70.14
for pelvic peritoneal drainage 70.12
Commando operation (radical glossectomy) 25.4
Commissurotomy
closed heart technique — see Valvulotomy, heart
open heart technique — see Valvuloplasty, heart
Compression, trigeminal nerve 04.02
Conchectomy 21.69
Conchotomy 21.1
Conduction study, nerve 89.15
Conduitogram, ileum 87.78
Condylectomy — see category 77.8 ☑
mandible 76.5
Condylotomy NEC — see also Division, joint capsule 80.40
mandible (open) 76.62
closed 76.61
Conization
cervix (knife) (sharp) (biopsy) 67.2
by
cryosurgery 67.33
electroconization 67.32
Conjunctivocystorhinostomy 09.82
with insertion of tube or stent 09.83
Conjunctivodacryocystorhinostomy (CDCR) 09.82
with insertion of tube or stent 09.83
Conjunctivodacryocystostomy 09.82
with insertion of tube or stent 09.83
Conjunctivoplasty 10.49
Conjunctivorhinostomy 09.82
with insertion of tube or stent 09.83
Constriction of globe, for scleral buckling — see also Buckling, scleral 14.49
Construction
auricle, ear (with graft) (with implant) 18.71
ear
auricle (with graft) (with implant) 18.71
meatus (osseous) (skin-lined) 18.6
endorectal ileal pouch (J-pouch) (H-pouch) (S-pouch) (with anastomosis to anus) 45.95
esophagus, artificial — see Anastomosis, esophagus
ileal bladder (open) 56.51
closed 57.87 [45.51]
ileal conduit 56.51
larynx, artificial 31.75
patent meatus (ear) 18.6
penis (rib graft) (skin graft) (myocutaneous flap) 64.43
pharyngeal valve, artificial 31.75
urethra 58.46
vagina, artificial 70.61
venous valves (peripheral) 39.59
Consultation 89.09
comprehensive 89.07
limited (single organ system) 89.06
specified type NEC 89.08
Continuous positive airway pressure (CPAP) 93.90
Control
atmospheric pressure and composition NEC 93.98
antigen-free air conditioning 93.98
decompression chamber 93.97

☑ Additional Digit Required — Refer to the Tabular List for Digit Selection   ﹀ Subterms under main terms may continue to next column or page

10 — Volume 3   ▶◀ Revised Text   ● New Line   ▲ Revised Code   *2007 ICD-9-CM*

Control — *continued*
  atmospheric pressure and composition
      — *continued*
    mountain sanatorium 93.98
  epistaxis 21.00
    by
      cauterization (and packing)
          21.03
      coagulation (with packing) 21.03
      electrocoagulation (with packing) 21.03
      excision of nasal mucosa with
          grafting 21.07
      ligation of artery 21.09
        ethmoidal 21.04
        external carotid 21.06
        maxillary (transantral) 21.05
      packing (nasal) (anterior) 21.01
        posterior (and anterior) 21.02
      specified means NEC 21.09
  hemorrhage 39.98
    abdominal cavity 54.19
    adenoids (postoperative) 28.7
    anus (postoperative) 49.95
    bladder (postoperative) 57.93
    chest 34.09
    colon 45.49
      endoscopic 45.43
    duodenum (ulcer) 44.49
      by
        embolization (transcatheter)
            44.44
        suture (ligation) 44.42
      endoscopic 44.43
    esophagus 42.39
      endoscopic 42.33
    gastric (ulcer) 44.49
      by
        embolization (transcatheter)
            44.44
        suture (ligation) 44.41
      endoscopic 44.43
    intrapleural 34.09
      postoperative (recurrent) 34.03
    laparotomy site 54.12
    nose (*see also* Control, epistaxis)
        21.00
    peptic (ulcer) 44.49
      by
        embolization (transcatheter)
            44.44
        suture (ligation) 44.40
      endoscopic 44.43
    pleura, pleural cavity 34.09
      postoperative (recurrent) 34.03
    postoperative NEC 39.98
    postvascular surgery 39.41
    prostate 60.94
    specified site NEC 39.98
    stomach — *see* Control, hemorrhage, gastric
    thorax NEC 34.09
      postoperative (recurrent) 34.03
    thyroid (postoperative) 06.02
    tonsils (postoperative) 28.7
Conversion
  anastomosis — *see* Revision, anastomosis
  cardiac rhythm NEC 99.69
    to sinus rhythm 99.62
  gastrostomy to jejunostomy (endoscopic) 44.32
  obstetrical position — *see* Version
Cooling, gastric 96.31
CorCap™ 37.41
Cordectomy, vocal 30.22
Cordopexy, vocal 31.69
Cordotomy
  spinal (bilateral) NEC 03.29
    percutaneous 03.21
  vocal 31.3
Corectomy 12.12
Corelysis 12.35
Coreoplasty 12.35
Corneoconjunctivoplasty 11.53
Corpectomy, (vertebral) 80.99   ●

Corpectomy, — *continued*
  with diskectomy 80.99   ●
Correction — *see also* Repair
  atresia
    esophageal 42.85
      by magnetic forces 42.99
    external meatus (ear) 18.6
    nasopharynx, nasopharyngeal 29.4
    rectum 48.0
    tricuspid 35.94
  atrial septal defect (*see also* Repair,
      atrial septal defect) 35.71
    combined with repair of valvular
        and ventricular septal defects
        — *see* Repair, endocardial
        cushion defect
  blepharoptosis (*see also* Repair, blepharoptosis) 08.36
  bunionette (with osteotomy) 77.54
  chordee 64.42
  claw toe 77.57
  cleft
    lip 27.54
    palate 27.62
  clubfoot NEC 83.84
  coarctation of aorta
    with
      anastomosis 38.34
      graft replacement 38.44
  cornea NEC 11.59
    refractive NEC 11.79
      epikeratophakia 11.76
      keratomileusis 11.71
      keratophakia 11.72
      radial keratotomy 11.75
  esophageal atresia 42.85
    by magnetic forces 42.99
  everted lacrimal punctum 09.71
  eyelid
    ptosis (*see also* Repair, blepharoptosis) 08.36
    retraction 08.38
  fetal defect 75.36
  forcible, of musculoskeletal deformity
      NEC 93.29
  hammer toe 77.56
  hydraulic pressure, open surgery for
      penile inflatable prosthesis
      64.99
    urinary artificial sphincter 58.99
  intestinal malrotation 46.80
    large 46.82
    small 46.81
  inverted uterus — *see* Repair, inverted
      uterus
  lymphedema (of limb) 40.9
    excision with graft 40.9
    obliteration of lymphatics 40.9
    transplantation of autogenous
        lymphatics 40.9
  nasopharyngeal atresia 29.4
  overlapping toes 77.58
  palate (cleft) 27.62
  prognathism NEC 76.64
  prominent ear 18.5
  punctum (everted) 09.71
  spinal pseudarthrosis — *see* Refusion,
      spinal
  syndactyly 86.85
  tetralogy of Fallot
    one-stage 35.81
    partial — *see* specific procedure
    total 35.81
  total anomalous pulmonary venous
      connection
    one-stage 35.82
    partial — *see* specific procedure
    total 35.82
  transposition, great arteries, total
      35.84
  tricuspid atresia 35.94
  truncus arteriosus
    one-stage 35.83
    partial — *see* specific procedure
    total 35.83
  ureteropelvic junction 55.87

Correction — *see also* Repair —
    continued
  ventricular septal defect (*see also* Repair, ventricular septal defect)
      35.72
    combined with repair of valvular
        and atrial septal defects —
        see Repair, endocardial
        cushion defect
Costectomy 77.91
  with lung excision — *see* Excision,
      lung
  associated with thoracic operation —
      omit code
Costochondrectomy 77.91
  associated with thoracic operation —
      omit code
Costosternoplasty (pectus excavatum
      repair) 34.74
Costotomy 77.31
Costotransversectomy 77.91
  associated with thoracic operation —
      omit code
Counseling (for) NEC 94.49
  alcoholism 94.46
  drug addiction 94.45
  employers 94.49
  family (medical) (social) 94.49
  marriage 94.49
  ophthalmologic (with instruction)
      95.36
  pastoral 94.49
Countershock, cardiac NEC 99.62
Coventry operation (tibial wedge osteotomy) 77.27
CPAP (continuous positive airway pressure) 93.90
Craniectomy 01.25
  linear (opening of cranial suture)
      02.01
  reopening of site 01.23
  strip (opening of cranial suture) 02.01
Cranioclasis, fetal 73.8
Cranioplasty 02.06
  with synchronous repair of encephalocele 02.12
Craniotomy 01.24
  as operative approach — *omit code*
  for decompression of fracture 02.02
  fetal 73.8
  reopening of site 01.23
Craterization, bone — *see* Excision,
    lesion, bone 77.60
Crawford operation (tarso-frontalis sling
    of eyelid) 08.32
Creation — *see also* Formation
  cardiac device (defibrillator) (pacemaker) pocket
    with initial insertion of cardiac device — *omit code*
    new site (skin) (subcutaneous)
        37.79
  conduit
    ileal (urinary) 56.51
    left ventricle and aorta 35.93
    right atrium and pulmonary artery
        35.94
    right ventricle and pulmonary (distal) artery 35.92
      in repair of
        pulmonary artery atresia
            35.92
        transposition of great vessels
            35.92
        truncus arteriosus 35.83
  endorectal ileal pouch (J-pouch) (H-pouch) (S-pouch) (with anastomosis to anus) 45.95
  esophagogastric sphincteric competence NEC 44.66
    laparoscopic 44.67
  Hartmann pouch — *see* Colectomy,
      by site
  interatrial fistula 35.42
  pericardial window 37.12
  pleural window, for drainage 34.09

Creation — *see also* Formation —
    continued
  pocket
    cardiac device (defibrillator) (pacemaker)
      with initial insertion of cardiac
          device — *omit code*
      new site (skin) (subcutaneous)
          37.79
    loop recorder 37.79
    thalamic stimulator pulse generator
      with initial insertion of battery
          package — *omit code*
      new site (skin) (subcutaneous)
          86.09
  shunt (*see also* Shunt)
    arteriovenous fistula, for dialysis
        39.93
    left-to-right (systemic to pulmonary
        circulation) 39.0
  subcutaneous tunnel for esophageal
      anastomosis 42.86
    with anastomosis — *see* Anastomosis, esophagus, antesternal
  syndactyly (finger) (toe) 86.89
  thalamic stimulator pulse generator
      pocket
    with initial insrtion of battery
        package — *omit code*
    new site (skin) (subcutaneous)
        86.09
  tracheoesophageal fistula 31.95
  window
    pericardial 37.12
    pleura, for drainage 34.09
Credé maneuver 73.59
Cricoidectomy 30.29
Cricothyreotomy (for assistance in
    breathing) 31.1
Cricothyroidectomy 30.29
Cricothyrostomy 31.1
Cricothyrotomy (for assistance in
    breathing) 31.1
Cricotomy (for assistance in breathing)
    31.1
Cricotracheotomy (for assistance in
    breathing) 31.1
Crisis intervention 94.35
Croupette, croup tent 93.94
Crown, dental (ceramic) (gold) 23.41
Crushing
  bone — *see* category 78.4 ☑
  calculus
    bile (hepatic) passage 51.49
      endoscopic 51.88
    bladder (urinary) 57.0
    pancreatic duct 52.09
      endoscopic 52.94
    fallopian tube (*see also* Ligation, fallopian tube) 66.39
  ganglion — *see* Crushing, nerve
  hemorrhoids 49.45
  nasal septum 21.88
  nerve (cranial) (peripheral) NEC 04.03
    acoustic 04.01
    auditory 04.01
    phrenic 04.03
      for collapse of lung 33.31
    sympathetic 05.0
    trigeminal 04.02
    vestibular 04.01
  vas deferens 63.71
Cryoablation — *see* Ablation
Cryoanalgesia
  nerve (cranial) (peripheral) 04.2
Cryoconization, cervix 67.33
Cryodestruction — *see* Destruction, lesion, by site
Cryoextraction, lens — *see also* Extraction, cataract, intracapsular 13.19
Cryohypophysectomy (complete) (total)
    — *see also* Hypophysectomy 07.69
Cryoleucotomy 01.32
Cryopexy, retinal — *see* Cryotherapy,
    retina

☑ Additional Digit Required — Refer to the Tabular List for Digit Selection   ⓦ Subterms under main terms may continue to next column or page

2007 ICD-9-CM   ▶◀ Revised Text   ● New Line   ▲ Revised Code   **October 2006 · Volume 3 — 11**

Cryoprostatectomy 60.62
Cryoretinopexy (for)
  reattachment 14.52
  repair of tear or defect 14.32
Cryosurgery — see Cryotherapy
Cryothalamectomy 01.41
Cryotherapy — see also Destruction, lesion, by site
  bladder 57.59
  brain 01.59
  cataract 13.19
  cervix 67.33
  choroid — see Cryotherapy, retina
  ciliary body 12.72
  corneal lesion (ulcer) 11.43
    to reshape cornea 11.79
  ear
    external 18.29
    inner 20.79
  esophagus 42.39
    endoscopic 42.33
  eyelid 08.25
  hemorrhoids 49.44
  iris 12.41
  nasal turbinates 21.61
  palate (bony) 27.31
  prostate 60.62
  retina (for)
    destruction of lesion 14.22
    reattachment 14.52
    repair of tear 14.32
  skin 86.3
  stomach 43.49
    endoscopic 43.41
  subcutaneous tissue 86.3
  turbinates (nasal) 21.61
  warts 86.3
    genital 71.3
Cryptectomy (anus) 49.39
  endoscopic 49.31
Cryptorchidectomy (unilateral) 62.3
  bilateral 62.41
Cryptotomy (anus) 49.39
  endoscopic 49.31
Cuirass 93.99
Culdocentesis 70.0
Culdoplasty 70.92
Culdoscopy (exploration) (removal of foreign body or lesion) 70.22
Culdotomy 70.12
Culp-Deweerd operation (spiral flap pyeloplasty) 55.87
Culp-Scardino operation (ureteral flap pyeloplasty) 55.87
Culture (and sensitivity) — see Examination, microscopic
Curettage (with packing) (with secondary closure) — see also Dilation and curettage
  adenoids 28.6
  anus 49.39
    endoscopic 49.31
  bladder 57.59
    transurethral 57.49
  bone (see also Excision, lesion, bone) 77.60
  brain 01.59
  bursa 83.39
    hand 82.29
  cartilage (see also Excision, lesion, joint) 80.80
  cerebral meninges 01.51
  chalazion 08.25
  conjunctiva (trachoma follicles) 10.33
  corneal epithelium 11.41
    for smear or culture 11.21
  ear, external 18.29
  eyelid 08.25
  joint (see also Excision, lesion, joint) 80.80
  meninges (cerebral) 01.51
    spinal 03.4
  muscle 83.32
    hand 82.22
  nerve (peripheral) 04.07
    sympathetic 05.29

Curettage — see also Dilation and curettage — continued
  sclera 12.84
  skin 86.3
  spinal cord (meninges) 03.4
  subgingival 24.31
  tendon 83.39
    sheath 83.31
      hand 82.21
  uterus (with dilation) 69.09
    aspiration (diagnostic) NEC 69.59
      after abortion or delivery 69.52
      to terminate pregnancy 69.51
    following delivery or abortion 69.02
Curette evacuation, lens 13.2
Curtis operation (interphalangeal joint arthroplasty) 81.72
Cutaneolipectomy 86.83
Cutdown, venous 38.94
Cutting
  nerve (cranial) (peripheral) NEC 04.03
    acoustic 04.01
    auditory 04.01
    root, spinal 03.1
    sympathetic 05.0
    trigeminal 04.02
    vestibular 04.01
  pedicle (flap) graft 86.71
  pylorus (with wedge resection) 43.3
  spinal nerve root 03.1
  ureterovesical orifice 56.1
  urethral sphincter 58.5
CVP (central venous pressure monitoring) 89.62
Cyclectomy (ciliary body) 12.44
  eyelid margin 08.20
Cyclicotomy 12.55
Cycloanemization 12.74
Cyclocryotherapy 12.72
Cyclodialysis (initial) (subsequent) 12.55
Cyclodiathermy (penetrating) (surface) 12.71
Cycloelectrolysis 12.71
Cyclophotocoagulation 12.73
Cyclotomy 12.55
Cystectomy — see also Excision, lesion, by site
  gallbladder — see Cholecystectomy
  urinary (partial) (subtotal) 57.6
    complete (with urethrectomy) 57.79
    radical 57.71
      with pelvic exenteration (female) 68.8
    total (with urethrectomy) 57.79
Cystocolostomy 57.88
Cystogram, cystography NEC 87.77
Cystolitholapaxy 57.0
Cystolithotomy 57.19
Cystometrogram 89.22
Cystopexy NEC 57.89
Cystoplasty NEC 57.89
Cystoproctostomy 57.88
Cystoprostatectomy, radical 57.71
Cystopyelography 87.74
Cystorrhaphy 57.81
Cystoscopy (transurethral) 57.32
  for
    control of hemorrhage
      bladder 57.93
      prostate 60.94
    retrograde pyelography 87.74
  with biopsy 57.33
  ileal conduit 56.35
  through stoma (artificial) 57.31
Cystostomy
  closed (suprapubic) (percutaneous) 57.17
  open (suprapubic) 57.18
  percutaneous (closed) (suprapubic) 57.17
  suprapubic
    closed 57.17
    open 57.18
Cystotomy (open) (for removal of calculi) 57.19

Cystourethrogram (retrograde) (voiding) 87.76
Cystourethropexy (by) 59.79
  levator muscle sling 59.71
  retropubic suspension 59.5
  suprapubic suspension 59.4
Cystourethroplasty 57.85
Cystourethroscopy 57.32
  with biopsy
    bladder 57.33
    ureter 56.33
Cytology — see Examination, microscopic

D

Dacryoadenectomy 09.20
  partial 09.22
  total 09.23
Dacryoadenotomy 09.0
Dacryocystectomy (complete) (partial) 09.6
Dacryocystogram 87.05
Dacryocystorhinostomy (DCR) (by intubation) (external) (intranasal) 09.81
Dacryocystostomy 09.53
Dacryocystosyringotomy 09.53
Dacryocystotomy 09.53
Dahlman operation (excision of esophageal diverticulum) 42.31
Dana operation (posterior rhizotomy) 03.1
Danforth operation (fetal) 73.8
Darrach operation (ulnar resection) 77.83
Davis operation (intubated ureterotomy) 56.2
Deaf training 95.49
Debridement
  abdominal wall 54.3
  bone (see also Excision, lesion, bone) 77.60
    fracture — see Debridement, open fracture
  brain 01.59
  burn (skin) 86.28
    excisional 86.22
    nonexcisional 86.28
  bursa 83.5
  cerebral meninges 01.51
  dental 96.54
  fascia 83.39
  flap graft 86.75
  graft (flap) (pedicle) 86.75
  heart valve (calcified) — see Valvuloplasty, heart
  infection (skin) 86.28
    excisional 86.22
    nail (bed) (fold) 86.27
    nonexcisional 86.28
  joint — see Excision, lesion, joint
  meninges (cerebral) 01.51
    spinal 03.4
  muscle 83.45
    hand 82.36
  nail (bed) (fold) 86.27
  nerve (peripheral) 04.07
  open fracture (compound) 79.60
    arm NEC 79.62
    carpal, metacarpal 79.63
    facial bone 76.2
    femur 79.65
    fibula 79.66
    foot NEC 79.67
    hand NEC 79.63
    humerus 79.61
    leg NEC 79.66
    phalanges
      foot 79.68
      hand 79.64
    radius 79.62
    specified site NEC 79.69
    tarsal, metatarsal 79.67
    tibia 79.66
    ulna 79.62
  patella 77.66
  pedicle graft 86.75

Debridement — continued
  skin or subcutaneous tissue (burn) (infection) (wound) 86.28
    cardioverter/defibrillator (automatic) pocket 37.79 ▲
    excisional 86.22
    graft 86.75
    nail, nail bed, or nail fold 86.27
    nonexcisional 86.28
    pacemaker pocket 37.79
    pocket
      cardiac device NEC 37.79 ●
      cardiac pacemaker 37.79
      cardioverter/defibrillator (automatic) 37.79 ▲
  skull 01.25
    compound fracture 02.02
  spinal cord (meninges) 03.4
  VersaJet™ 86.28 ●
  wound (skin) 86.28
    excisional 86.22
    nonexcisional 86.28
Decapitation, fetal 73.8
Decapsulation, kidney 55.91
Declotting — see also Removal, thrombus
  arteriovenous cannula or shunt 39.49
Decompression
  anus (imperforate) 48.0
  biliary tract 51.49
    by intubation 51.43
      endoscopic 51.87
      percutaneous 51.98
  brain 01.24
  carpal tunnel 04.43
  cauda equina 03.09
  chamber 93.97
  colon 96.08
    by incision 45.03
    endoscopic (balloon) 46.85
  common bile duct 51.42
    by intubation 51.43
      endoscopic 51.87
      percutaneous 51.98
  cranial 01.24
    for skull fracture 02.02
  endolymphatic sac 20.79
  ganglion (peripheral) NEC 04.49
    cranial NEC 04.42
  gastric 96.07
  heart 37.0
  intestine 96.08
    by incision 45.00
    endoscopic (balloon) 46.85
  intracranial 01.24
  labyrinth 20.79
  laminectomy 03.09
  laminotomy 03.09
  median nerve 04.43
  muscle 83.02
    hand 82.02
  nerve (peripheral) NEC 04.49
    auditory 04.42
    cranial NEC 04.42
    median 04.43
    trigeminal (root) 04.41
  orbit (see also Orbitotomy) 16.09
  pancreatic duct 52.92
    endoscopic 52.93
  pericardium 37.0
  rectum 48.0
  skull fracture 02.02
  spinal cord (canal) 03.09
  tarsal tunnel 04.44
  tendon (sheath) 83.01
    hand 82.01
  thoracic outlet
    by
      myotomy (division of scalenus anticus muscle) 83.19
      tenotomy 83.13
  trigeminal (nerve root) 04.41
Decortication
  arterial 05.25
  brain 01.51
  cerebral meninges 01.51

Decortication — *continued*
  heart 37.31
  kidney 55.91
  lung (partial) (total) 34.51
  nasal turbinates — *see* Turbinectomy
  nose 21.89
  ovary 65.29
    laparoscopic 65.25
  periarterial 05.25
  pericardium 37.31
  ventricle, heart (complete) 37.31
Decoy, E2F 00.16
Deepening
  alveolar ridge 24.5
  buccolabial sulcus 24.91
  lingual sulcus 24.91
Defatting, flap or pedicle graft 86.75
Defibrillation, electric (external) (internal) 99.62
  automatic cardioverter / defibrillator
    — *see* category 37.9 ☑
de Grandmont operation (tarsectomy)
    08.35
Delaying of pedicle graft 86.71
Delivery (with)
  assisted spontaneous 73.59
  breech extraction (assisted) 72.52
    partial 72.52
      with forceps to aftercoming head
        72.51
    total 72.54
      with forceps to aftercoming head
        72.53
    unassisted (spontaneous delivery)
      — *omit code*
  cesarean section — *see* Cesarean
    section
  Credé maneuver 73.59
  De Lee maneuver 72.4
  forceps 72.9
    application to aftercoming head
      (Piper) 72.6
    with breech extraction
      partial 72.51
      total 72.53
    Barton's 72.4
    failed 73.3
    high 72.39
      with episiotomy 72.31
    low (outlet) 72.0
      with episiotomy 72.1
    mid 72.29
      with episiotomy 72.21
    outlet (low) 72.0
      with episiotomy 72.1
    rotation of fetal head 72.4
    trial 73.3
  instrumental NEC 72.9
    specified NEC 72.8
  key-in-lock rotation 72.4
  Kielland rotation 72.4
  Malström's extraction 72.79
    with episiotomy 72.71
  manually assisted (spontaneous)
    73.59
  spontaneous (unassisted) 73.59
    assisted 73.59
  vacuum extraction 72.79
    with episiotomy 72.71
Delorme operation
  pericardiectomy 37.31
  proctopexy 48.76
  repair of prolapsed rectum 48.76
  thoracoplasty 33.34
Denervation
  aortic body 39.8
  carotid body 39.8
  facet, percutaneous (radiofrequency)
    03.96
  ovarian 65.94
  paracervical uterine 69.3
  uterosacral 69.3
Denker operation (radical maxillary
    antrotomy) 22.31
Dennis-Barco operation — *see* Repair,
    hernia, femoral

Denonvillier operation (limited rhino-
    plasty) 21.86
Densitometry, bone (serial) (radiograph-
    ic) 88.98
Depilation, skin 86.92
Derlacki operation (tympanoplasty) 19.4
Dermabond 86.59
Dermabrasion (laser) 86.25
  for wound debridement 86.28
Derotation — *see* Reduction, torsion
Desensitization
  allergy 99.12
  psychologic 94.33
Desmotomy — *see also* Division, liga-
    ment 80.40
Destruction
  breast 85.20
  chorioretinopathy (*see also* Destruc-
    tion, lesion, choroid) 14.29
  ciliary body 12.74
  epithelial downgrowth, anterior
    chamber 12.93
  fallopian tube 66.39
    with
      crushing (and ligation) 66.31
        by endoscopy (laparoscopy)
          66.21
      division (and ligation) 66.32
        by endoscopy (culdoscopy)
          (hysteroscopy) (la-
          paroscopy) (perito-
          neoscopy) 66.22
      ligation 66.39
        with
          crushing 66.31
            by endoscopy (la-
              paroscopy) 66.21
          division 66.32
            by endoscopy (cul-
              doscopy) (hys-
              teroscopy) (la-
              paroscopy) (peri-
              toneoscopy)
              66.22
  fetus 73.8
  hemorrhoids 49.49
    by
      cryotherapy 49.44
      sclerotherapy 49.42
  inner ear NEC 20.79
    by injection 20.72
  intervertebral disc (NOS) 80.50
    by injection 80.52
    by other specified method 80.59
    herniated (nucleus pulposus) 80.51
  lacrimal sac 09.6
  lesion (local)
    anus 49.39
      endoscopic 49.31
    Bartholin's gland 71.24
      by
        aspiration 71.21
        excision 71.24
        incision 71.22
        marsupialization 71.23
    biliary ducts 51.69
      endoscopic 51.64
    bladder 57.59
      transurethral 57.49
    bone — *see* Excision, lesion, bone
    bowel — *see* Destruction, lesion,
      intestine
    brain (transtemporal approach)
      NEC 01.59
      by stereotactic radiosurgery
        92.30
        cobalt 60 92.32
        linear accelerator (LINAC)
          92.31
        multi-source 92.32
        particle beam 92.33
        particulate 92.33
        radiosurgery NEC 92.39
        single source photon 92.31
    breast NEC 85.20
    bronchus NEC 32.09

Destruction — *continued*
  lesion — *continued*
    bronchus — *continued*
      endoscopic 32.01
    cerebral NEC 01.59
      meninges 01.51
    cervix 67.39
      by
        cauterization 67.32
        cryosurgery, cryoconization
          67.33
        electroconization 67.32
    choroid 14.29
      by
        cryotherapy 14.22
        diathermy 14.21
        implantation of radiation
          source 14.27
        photocoagulation 14.25
          laser 14.24
          xenon arc 14.23
        radiation therapy 14.26
    ciliary body (nonexcisional) 12.43
      by excision 12.44
    conjunctiva 10.32
      by excision 10.31
    cornea NEC 11.49
      by
        cryotherapy 11.43
        electrocauterization 11.42
        thermocauterization 11.42
    cul-de-sac 70.32
    duodenum NEC 45.32
      by excision 45.31
      endoscopic 45.30
      endoscopic 45.30
    esophagus (chemosurgery)
      (cryosurgery) (electroresec-
      tion) (fulguration) NEC 42.39
      by excision 42.32
      endoscopic 42.33
      endoscopic 42.33
    eye NEC 16.93
    eyebrow 08.25
    eyelid 08.25
      excisional — *see* Excision, le-
        sion, eyelid
    heart 37.33
      by catheter ablation 37.34
    intestine (large) 45.49
      by excision 45.41
        endoscopic 45.43
          polypectomy 45.42
      endoscopic 45.43
        polypectomy 45.42
      small 45.34
        by excision 45.33
    intranasal 21.31
    iris (nonexcisional) NEC 12.41
      by excision 12.42
    kidney 55.39
      by marsupialization 55.31
    lacrimal sac 09.6
    larynx 30.09
    liver 50.29
    lung 32.29
      endoscopic 32.28
    meninges (cerebral) 01.51
      spinal 03.4
    nerve (peripheral) 04.07
      sympathetic 05.29
    nose 21.30
      intranasal 21.31
      specified NEC 21.32
    ovary
      by
        aspiration 65.91
        excision 65.29
          laparoscopic 65.25
      cyst by rupture (manual) 65.93
    palate (bony) (local) 27.31
      wide 27.32
    pancreas 52.22
      by marsupialization 52.3
      endoscopic 52.21
    pancreatic duct 52.22

Destruction — *continued*
  lesion — *continued*
    pancreatic duct — *continued*
      endoscopic 52.21
    penis 64.2
    pharynx (excisional) NEC 29.39
    pituitary gland
      by stereotactic radiosurgery
        92.30
        cobalt 60 92.32
        linear accelerator (LINAC)
          92.31
        multi-source 92.32
        particle beam 92.33
        particulate 92.33
        radiosurgery NEC 92.39
        single source photon 92.31
    rectum (local) 48.32
      by
        cryosurgery 48.34
        electrocoagulation 48.32
        excision 48.35
        fulguration 48.32
        laser (Argon) 48.33
      polyp 48.36
      radical 48.31
    retina 14.29
      by
        cryotherapy 14.22
        diathermy 14.21
        implantation of radiation
          source 14.27
        photocoagulation 14.25
          laser 14.24
          xenon arc 14.23
        radiation therapy 14.26
    salivary gland NEC 26.29
      by marsupialization 26.21
    sclera 12.84
    scrotum 61.3
    skin NEC 86.3
    sphincter of Oddi 51.69
      endoscopic 51.64
    spinal cord (meninges) 03.4
    spleen 41.42
      by marsupialization 41.41
    stomach NEC 43.49
      by excision 43.42
      endoscopic 43.41
      endoscopic 43.41
    subcutaneous tissue NEC 86.3
    testis 62.2
    tongue 25.1
    urethra (excisional) 58.39
      endoscopic 58.31
    uterus 68.29
  nerve (cranial) (peripheral) (by
    cryoanalgesia) by radiofrequen-
    cy) 04.2
    sympathetic, by injection of neu-
      rolytic agent 05.32
  neuroma
    acoustic 04.01
      by craniotomy 04.01
      by stereotactic radiosurgery
        92.30
        cobalt 60 92.32
        linear accelerator (LINAC)
          92.31
        multi-source 92.32
        particle beam 92.33
        particulate 92.33
        radiosurgery NEC 92.39
        single source photon 92.31
    cranial 04.07
    Morton's 04.07
    peripheral
      Morton's 04.07
  prostate (prostatic tissue)
    by
      cryotherapy 60.62
      microwave 60.96
      radiofrequency 60.97
      transurethral microwave ther-
        motherapy (TUMT) 60.96

Decortication — Destruction

☑ Additional Digit Required — Refer to the Tabular List for Digit Selection   � Subterms under main terms may continue to next column or page

2007 ICD-9-CM   ▶◀ Revised Text   ● New Line   ▲ Revised Code   **Volume 3 — 13**

Destruction — *continued*
  prostate — *continued*
    transurethral needle ablation (TU-NA) 60.97
    TULIP (transurethral (ultrasound) guided laser induced prostatectomy) 60.21
    TUMT (transurethral microwave thermotherapy) 60.96
    TUNA (transurethral needle ablation) 60.97
  semicircular canals, by injection 20.72
  vestibule, by injection 20.72
Detachment, uterosacral ligaments 69.3
Determination
  mental status (clinical) (medicolegal) (psychiatric) NEC 94.11
    psychologic NEC 94.09
  vital capacity (pulmonary) 89.37
Detorsion
  intestine (twisted) (volvulus) 46.80
    large 46.82
      endoscopic (balloon) 46.85
    small 46.81
  kidney 55.84
  ovary 65.95
  spermatic cord 63.52
    with orchiopexy 62.5
  testis 63.52
    with orchiopexy 62.5
  volvulus 46.80
    endoscopic (balloon) 46.85
Detoxification therapy 94.25
  alcohol 94.62
    with rehabilitation 94.63
    combined alcohol and drug 94.68
      with rehabilitation 94.69
  drug 94.65
    with rehabilitation 94.66
    combined alcohol and drug 94.68
      with rehabilitation 94.69
Devascularization, stomach 44.99
Device
  CorCap™ 37.41
  external fixator — *see* Fixator, external
Dewebbing
  esophagus 42.01
  syndactyly (fingers) (toes) 86.85
Dextrorotation — *see* Reduction, torsion
Dialysis
  hemodiafiltration, hemofiltration (extracorporeal) 39.95
  kidney (extracorporeal) 39.95
  liver 50.92
  peritoneal 54.98
  renal (extracorporeal) 39.95
Diaphanoscopy
  nasal sinuses 89.35
  skull (newborn) 89.16
Diaphysectomy — *see* category 77.8 ☑
Diathermy 93.34
  choroid — *see* Diathermy, retina
  nasal turbinates 21.61
  retina
    for
      destruction of lesion 14.21
      reattachment 14.51
      repair of tear 14.31
    surgical — *see* Destruction, lesion, by site
  turbinates (nasal) 21.61
Dickson-Diveley operation (tendon transfer and arthrodesis to correct claw toe) 77.57
Dickson operation (fascial transplant) 83.82
Dieffenbach operation (hip disarticulation) 84.18
Dilation
  achalasia 42.92
  ampulla of Vater 51.81
    endoscopic 51.84
  anus, anal (sphincter) 96.23

Dilation — *continued*
  biliary duct
    endoscopic 51.84
    pancreatic duct 52.99
      endoscopic 52.98
    percutaneous (endoscopy) 51.98
  sphincter
    of Oddi 51.81
      endoscopic 51.84
    pancreatic 51.82
      endoscopic 51.85
  bladder 96.25
    neck 57.92
  bronchus 33.91
  cervix (canal) 67.0
    obstetrical 73.1
    to assist delivery 73.1
  choanae (nasopharynx) 29.91
  colon (endoscopic) (balloon) 46.85
  colostomy stoma 96.24
  duodenum (endoscopic) (balloon) 46.85
  endoscopic — *see* Dilation, by site
  enterostomy stoma 96.24
  esophagus (by bougie) (by sound) 42.92
  fallopian tube 66.96
  foreskin (newborn) 99.95
  frontonasal duct 96.21
  gastrojejunostomy site, endoscopic 44.22
  heart valve — *see* Valvulotomy, heart
  ileostomy stoma 96.24
  ileum (endoscopic) (balloon) 46.85
  intestinal stoma (artificial) 96.24
  intestine (endoscopic) (balloon) 46.85
  jejunum (endoscopic) (balloon) 46.85
  lacrimal
    duct 09.42
    punctum 09.41
  larynx 31.98
  lymphatic structure(s) (peripheral) 40.9
  nares 21.99
  nasolacrimal duct (retrograde) 09.43
    with insertion of tube or stent 09.44
  nasopharynx 29.91
  pancreatic duct 52.99
    endoscopic 52.98
  pharynx 29.91
  prostatic urethra (transurethral) (balloon) 60.95
  punctum, lacrimal papilla 09.41
  pylorus
    by incision 44.21
    endoscopic 44.22
  rectum 96.22
  salivary duct 26.91
  sphenoid ostia 22.52
  sphincter
    anal 96.23
    cardiac 42.92
    of Oddi 51.81
      endoscopic 51.84
    pancreatic 51.82
      endoscopic 51.85
  pylorus, endoscopic 44.22
    by incision 44.21
  Stenson's duct 26.91
  trachea 31.99
  ureter 59.8
    meatus 56.91
  ureterovesical orifice 59.8
  urethra 58.6
    prostatic (transurethral) (balloon) 60.95
  urethrovesical junction 58.6
  vagina (instrumental) (manual) NEC 96.16
  vesical neck 57.92
  Wharton's duct 26.91
  Wirsung's duct 52.99
    endoscopic 52.98
Dilation and curettage, uterus (diagnostic) 69.09

Dilation and curettage, uterus — *continued*
  after
    abortion 69.02
    delivery 69.02
  to terminate pregnancy 69.01
Diminution, ciliary body 12.74
Disarticulation 84.91
  ankle 84.13
  elbow 84.06
  finger, except thumb 84.01
    thumb 84.02
  hip 84.18
  knee 84.16
  shoulder 84.08
  thumb 84.02
  toe 84.11
  wrist 84.04
Discectomy — *see* Diskectomy
Discission
  capsular membrane 13.64
  cataract (Wheeler knife) (Ziegler knife) 13.2
    congenital 13.69
    secondary membrane 13.64
  iris 12.12
  lens (capsule) (Wheeler knife) (Ziegler knife) (with capsulotomy) 13.2
  orbitomaxillary, radical 16.51
  pupillary 13.2
  secondary membrane (after cataract) 13.64
  vitreous strands (posterior approach) 14.74
    anterior approach 14.73
Discogram, diskogram 87.21
Discolysis (by injection) 80.52
Diskectomy (discectomy), intervertebral 80.51
  with corpectomy 80.99 ●
  herniated (nucleus pulposus) 80.51
  percutaneous 80.59
Dispensing (with fitting)
  contact lens 95.32
  low vision aids NEC 95.33
  spectacles 95.31
Dissection — *see also* Excision
  aneurysm 38.60
  artery-vein-nerve bundle 39.91
  branchial cleft fistula or sinus 29.52
  bronchus 32.1
  femoral hernia 53.29
  groin, radical 40.54
  larynx block (en bloc) 30.3
  mediastinum with pneumonectomy 32.5
  neck, radical 40.40
    with laryngectomy 30.4
    bilateral 40.42
    unilateral 40.41
  orbital fibrous bands 16.92
  pterygium (with reposition) 11.31
  radical neck — *see* Dissection, neck, radical
  retroperitoneal NEC 59.00
  thoracic structures (block) (en bloc) (radical) (brachial plexus, bronchus, lobe of lung, ribs, and sympathetic nerves) 32.6
  vascular bundle 39.91
Distention, bladder (therapeutic) (intermittent) 96.25
Diversion
  biliopancreatic (BPD) 43.7 *[45.51] [45.91]*
    with duodenal switch 43.89 *[45.51] [45.91]*
  urinary
    cutaneous 56.61
    ileal conduit 56.51
    internal NEC 56.71
    uretero-ileostomy 56.51
  ureter to
    intestine 56.71
    skin 56.61
Diversional therapy 93.81

Diverticulectomy
  bladder (suprapubic) 57.59
    transurethral approach 57.49
  duodenum 45.31
    endoscopic 45.30
  esophagomyotomy 42.7
  esophagus 42.31
    endoscopic 42.33
  hypopharyngeal (by cricopharyngeal myotomy) 29.32
  intestine
    large 45.41
      endoscopic 45.43
    small 45.33
  kidney 55.39
  Meckel's 45.33
  pharyngeal (by cricopharyngeal myotomy) 29.32
  pharyngoesophageal (by cricopharyngeal myotomy) 29.32
  stomach 43.42
    endoscopic 43.41
  urethra 58.39
    endoscopic 58.31
Division
  Achilles tendon 83.11
  adductor tendon (hip) 83.12
  adhesions — *see* Lysis, adhesions
  angle of mandible (open) 76.62
    closed 76.61
  anterior synechiae 12.32
  aponeurosis 83.13
  arcuate ligament (spine) — *omit code*
  arteriovenous fistula (with ligation) 39.53
  artery (with ligation) 38.80
    abdominal 38.86
    aorta (arch) (ascending) (descending) 38.84
    head and neck NEC 38.82
    intracranial NEC 38.81
    lower limb 38.88
    thoracic NEC 38.85
    upper limb 38.83
  bladder neck 57.91
  blepharorrhaphy 08.02
  blood vessels, cornea 10.1
  bone (*see also* Osteotomy) 77.30
  brain tissue 01.32
    cortical adhesions 02.91
  canaliculus 09.52
  canthorrhaphy 08.02
  cartilage 80.40
    ankle 80.47
    elbow 80.42
    foot and toe 80.48
    hand and finger 80.44
    hip 80.45
    knee 80.46
    shoulder 80.41
    specified site NEC 80.49
    spine 80.49
    wrist 80.43
  cerebral tracts 01.32
  chordae tendineae 35.32
  common wall between posterior left atrium and coronary sinus (with roofing of resultant defect with patch graft) 35.82
  congenital web
    larynx 31.98
    pharynx 29.54
  endometrial synechiae 68.21
  fallopian tube — *see* Ligation, fallopian tube
  fascia 83.14
    hand 82.12
  frenulum, frenum
    labial 27.91
    lingual 25.91
    tongue 25.91
  ganglion, sympathetic 05.0
  glossopharyngeal nerve 29.92
  goniosynechiae 12.31
  hypophyseal stalk (*see also* Hypophysectomy, partial) 07.63

☑ Additional Digit Required — Refer to the Tabular List for Digit Selection
▽ Subterms under main terms may continue to next column or page
14 — Volume 3 · October 2006
▶◀ Revised Text ● New Line ▲ Revised Code
2007 ICD-9-CM

Division — *continued*
iliotibial band 83.14
isthmus
  horseshoe kidney 55.85
  thyroid 06.91
joint capsule 80.40
  ankle 80.47
  elbow 80.42
  foot and toe 80.48
  hand and finger 80.44
  hip 80.45
  knee 80.46
  shoulder 80.41
  specified site NEC 80.49
  wrist 80.43
labial frenum 27.91
lacrimal ductules 09.0
laryngeal nerve (external) (recurrent) (superior) 31.91
ligament 80.40
  ankle 80.47
  arcuate (spine) — *omit code*
  canthal 08.36
  elbow 80.42
  foot and toe 80.48
  hand and finger 80.44
  hip 80.45
  knee 80.46
  palpebrae 08.36
  shoulder 80.41
  specified site NEC 80.49
  spine 80.49
    arcuate — *omit code*
    flavum — *omit code*
  uterosacral 69.3
  wrist 80.43
ligamentum flavum (spine) — *omit code*
meninges (cerebral) 01.31
muscle 83.19
  hand 82.19
nasolacrimal duct stricture (with drainage) 09.59
nerve (cranial) (peripheral) NEC 04.03
  acoustic 04.01
  adrenal gland 07.42
  auditory 04.01
  glossopharyngeal 29.92
  lacrimal branch 05.0
  laryngeal (external) (recurrent) (superior) 31.91
  phrenic 04.03
    for collapse of lung 33.31
  root, spinal or intraspinal 03.1
  sympathetic 05.0
  tracts
    cerebral 01.32
    spinal cord 03.29
      percutaneous 03.21
  trigeminal 04.02
  vagus (*see also* Vagotomy) 44.00
  vestibular 04.01
otosclerotic process or material, middle ear 19.0
papillary muscle (heart) 35.31
patent ductus arteriosus 38.85
penile adhesions 64.93
posterior synechiae 12.33
pylorus (with wedge resection) 43.3
rectum (stricture) 48.91
scalenus anticus muscle 83.19
Skene's gland 71.3
soft tissue NEC 83.19
  hand 82.19
sphincter
  anal (external) (internal) 49.59
    left lateral 49.51
    posterior 49.52
  cardiac 42.7
  of Oddi 51.82
    endoscopic 51.85
  pancreatic 51.82
    endoscopic 51.85
spinal
  cord tracts 03.29
    percutaneous 03.21

Division — *continued*
spinal — *continued*
  nerve root 03.1
symblepharon (with insertion of conformer) 10.5
synechiae
  endometrial 68.21
  iris (posterior) 12.33
    anterior 12.32
tarsorrhaphy 08.02
tendon 83.13
  Achilles 83.11
  adductor (hip) 83.12
  hand 82.11
trabeculae carneae cordis (heart) 35.35
tympanum 20.23
uterosacral ligaments 69.3
vaginal septum 70.14
vas deferens 63.71
vein (with ligation) 38.80
  abdominal 38.87
  head and neck NEC 38.82
  intracranial NEC 38.81
  lower limb 38.89
    varicose 38.59
  thoracic NEC 38.85
  upper limb 38.83
  varicose 38.50
    abdominal 38.57
    head and neck NEC 38.52
    intracranial NEC 38.51
    lower limb 38.59
    thoracic NEC 38.55
    upper limb 38.53
vitreous, cicatricial bands (posterior approach) 14.74
  anterior approach 14.73
Doleris operation (shortening of round ligaments) 69.22
D'Ombrain operation (excision of pterygium with corneal graft) 11.32
Domestic tasks therapy 93.83
Dopplergram, Doppler flow mapping — *see also* Ultrasonography
  aortic arch 88.73
  head and neck 88.71
  heart 88.72
  thorax NEC 88.73
Dorrance operation (push-back operation for cleft palate) 27.62
Dotter operation (transluminal angioplasty) 39.59
Douche, vaginal 96.44
Douglas' operation (suture of tongue to lip for micrognathia) 25.59
Doyle operation (paracervical uterine denervation) 69.3
Drainage
  by
    anastomosis — *see* Anastomosis
    aspiration — *see* Aspiration
    incision — *see* Incision
  abdomen 54.19
    percutaneous 54.91
  abscess (*see also* Drainage, by site *and* Incision, by site)
    appendix 47.2
      with appendectomy 47.09
        laparoscopic 47.01
    parapharyngeal (oral) (transcervical) 28.0
    peritonsillar (oral) (transcervical) 28.0
    retropharyngeal (oral) (transcervical) 28.0
    thyroid (field) (gland) 06.09
      percutaneous (needle) 06.01
      postoperative 06.02
    tonsil, tonsillar (oral) (transcervical) 28.0
  antecubital fossa 86.04
  appendix 47.91
    with appendectomy 47.09
      laparoscopic 47.01
    abscess 47.2

Drainage — *continued*
appendix — *continued*
  abscess — *continued*
    with appendectomy 47.09
      laparoscopic 47.01
axilla 86.04
bladder (without incision) 57.0
  by indwelling catheter 57.94
  percutaneous suprapubic (closed) 57.17
  suprapubic NEC 57.18
buccal space 27.0
bursa 83.03
  by aspiration 83.94
  hand 82.92
  hand 82.03
    by aspiration 82.92
  radial 82.03
  ulnar 82.03
cerebrum, cerebral (meninges) (ventricle) (incision) (trephination) 01.39
  by
    anastomosis — *see* Shunt, ventricular
    aspiration 01.09
      through previously implanted catheter 01.02
chest (closed) 34.04
  open (by incision) 34.09
cranial sinus (incision) (trephination) 01.21
  by aspiration 01.09
cul-de-sac 70.12
  by aspiration 70.0
cyst (*see also* Drainage, by site *and* Incision, by site)
  pancreas (by catheter) 52.01
    by marsupialization 52.3
    internal (anastomosis) 52.4
  pilonidal 86.03
  spleen, splenic (by marsupialization) 41.41
duodenum (tube) 46.39
  by incision 45.01
ear
  external 18.09
  inner 20.79
  middle (by myringotomy) 20.09
    with intubation 20.01
epidural space, cerebral (incision) (trephination) 01.24
  by aspiration 01.09
extradural space, cerebral (incision) (trephination) 01.24
  by aspiration 01.09
extraperitoneal 54.0
facial region 27.0
fascial compartments, head and neck 27.0
fetal hydrocephalic head (needling) (trocar) 73.8
gallbladder 51.04
  by
    anastomosis 51.35
    aspiration 51.01
    incision 51.04
groin region (abdominal wall) (inguinal) 54.0
  skin 86.04
  subcutaneous tissue 86.04
hematoma — *see* Drainage, by site *and* Incision, by site
hydrocephalic head (needling) (trocar) 73.8
hypochondrium 54.0
  intra-abdominal 54.19
iliac fossa 54.0
infratemporal fossa 27.0
intracranial space (epidural) (extradural) (incision) (trephination) 01.24
  by aspiration 01.09
  subarachnoid or subdural (incision) (trephination) 01.31
    by aspiration 01.09

Drainage — *continued*
intraperitoneal 54.19
  percutaneous 54.91
kidney (by incision) 55.01
  by
    anastomosis 55.86
    catheter 59.8
  pelvis (by incision) 55.11
liver 50.0
  by aspiration 50.91
Ludwig's angina 27.0
lung (by incision) 33.1
  by punch (needle) (trocar) 33.93
midpalmar space 82.04
mouth floor 27.0
mucocele, nasal sinus 22.00
  by puncture 22.01
  through natural ostium 22.02
omentum 54.19
  percutaneous 54.91
ovary (aspiration) 65.91
  by incision 65.09
  laparoscopic 65.01
palmar space (middle) 82.04
pancreas (by catheter) 52.01
  by anastomosis 52.96
parapharyngeal 28.0
paronychia 86.04
parotid space 27.0
pelvic peritoneum (female) 70.12
  male 54.19
pericardium 37.0
perigastric 54.19
  percutaneous 54.91
perineum
  female 71.09
  male 86.04
perisplenic tissue 54.19
  percutaneous 54.91
peritoneum 54.19
  pelvic (female) 70.12
  percutaneous 54.91
peritonsillar 28.0
pharyngeal space, lateral 27.0
pilonidal cyst or sinus 86.03
pleura (closed) 34.04
  open (by incision) 34.09
popliteal space 86.04
postural 93.99
postzygomatic space 27.0
pseudocyst, pancreas 52.3
  by anastomosis 52.4
pterygopalatine fossa 27.0
retropharyngeal 28.0
scrotum 61.0
skin 86.04
spinal (canal) (cord) 03.09
  by anastomosis — *see* Shunt, spinal
  diagnostic 03.31
spleen 41.2
  cyst (by marsupialization) 41.41
subarachnoid space, cerebral (incision) (trephination) 01.31
  by aspiration 01.09
subcutaneous tissue 86.04
subdiaphragmatic 54.19
  percutaneous 54.91
subdural space, cerebral (incision) (trephination) 01.31
  by aspiration 01.09
subhepatic space 54.19
  percutaneous 54.91
sublingual space 27.0
submental space 27.0
subphrenic space 54.19
  percutaneous 54.91
supraclavicular fossa 86.04
temporal pouches 27.0
tendon (sheath) 83.01
  hand 82.01
thenar space 82.04
thorax (closed) 34.04
  open (by incision) 34.09
thyroglossal tract (by incision) 06.09
  by aspiration 06.01

Note — Also use 00.40, 00.41, 00.42,
or 00.43 to show the total number of
vessels treated. ▶Use code 00.44 once
to show procedure on a bifurcated vessel.◀ In addition, use 00.45, 00.46,
00.47, or 00.48 to show the number of
vascular stents inserted.

Note — Also use 00.40, 00.41, 00.42,
or 00.43 to show the total number of
vessels treated. ▶Use code 00.44 once
to show prcoedure on a bifurcated vessel.◀ In addition, use 00.45, 00.46,
00.47, or 00.48 to show the number of
vascular stents inserted.

☑ Additional Digit Required — Refer to the Tabular List for Digit Selection   ▽ Subterms under main terms may continue to next column or page

16 — Volume 3 • October 2006   ▶◀ Revised Text   ● New Line   ▲ Revised Code   **2007 ICD-9-CM**

Endoprosthesis
  bile duct 51.87
  femoral head (bipolar) 81.52
Endoscopy
  with biopsy — see Biopsy, by site,
    closed
  anus 49.21
  biliary tract (operative) 51.11
    by retrograde cholangiography
      (ERC) 51.11
    by retrograde cholangiopancreatog-
      raphy (ERCP) 51.10
    intraoperative 51.11
    percutaneous (via T-tube or other
      tract) 51.98
      with removal of common duct
        stones 51.96
  bladder 57.32
    through stoma (artificial) 57.31
  bronchus NEC 33.23
    with biopsy 33.24
    fiberoptic 33.22
    through stoma (artificial) 33.21
  colon 45.23
    through stoma (artificial) 45.22
    transabdominal (operative) 45.21
  cul-de-sac 70.22
  ear 18.11
  esophagus NEC 42.23
    through stoma (artificial) 42.22
    transabdominal (operative) 42.21
  ileum 45.13
    through stoma (artificial) 45.12
    transabdominal (operative) 45.11
  intestine NEC 45.24
    large 45.24
      fiberoptic (flexible) 45.23
      through stoma (artificial) 45.22
      transabdominal (intraoperative)
        45.21
    small 45.13
      esophagogastroduodenoscopy
        (EGD) 45.13
        with closed biopsy 45.16
      through stoma (artificial) 45.12
      transabdominal (operative)
        45.11
  jejunum 45.13
    through stoma (artificial) 45.12
    transabdominal (operative) 45.11
  kidney 55.21
  larynx 31.42
    through stoma (artificial) 31.41
  lung — see Bronchoscopy
  mediastinum (transpleural) 34.22
  nasal sinus 22.19
  nose 21.21
  pancreatic duct 52.13
  pelvis 55.22
  peritoneum 54.21
  pharynx 29.11
  rectum 48.23
    through stoma (artificial) 48.22
    transabdominal (operative) 48.21
  sinus, nasal 22.19
  stomach NEC 44.13
    through stoma (artificial) 44.12
    transabdominal (operative) 44.11
  thorax (transpleural) 34.21
  trachea NEC 31.42
    through stoma (artificial) 31.41
  transpleural
    mediastinum 34.22
    thorax 34.21
  ureter 56.31
  urethra 58.22
  uterus 68.12
  vagina 70.21
Enema (transanal) NEC 96.39
  for removal of impacted feces 96.38
ENG (electronystagmogram) 95.24
Enlargement
  aortic lumen, thoracic 38.14
  atrial septal defect (pre-existing) 35.41

Enlargement — continued
  atrial septal defect — continued
    in repair of total anomalous pul-
      monary venous connection
      35.82
  eye socket 16.64
  foramen ovale (pre-existing) 35.41
    in repair of total anomalous pul-
      monary venous connection
      35.82
  intestinal stoma 46.40
    large intestine 46.43
    small intestine 46.41
  introitus 96.16
  orbit (eye) 16.64
  palpebral fissure 08.51
  punctum 09.41
  sinus tract (skin) 86.89
Enterectomy NEC 45.63
Enteroanastomosis
  large-to-large intestine 45.94
  small-to-large intestine 45.93
  small-to-small intestine 45.91
Enterocelectomy 53.9
  female 70.92
  vaginal 70.92
Enterocentesis 45.00
  duodenum 45.01
  large intestine 45.03
  small intestine NEC 45.02
Enterocholecystostomy 51.32
Enteroclysis (small bowel) 96.43
Enterocolectomy NEC 45.79
Enterocolostomy 45.93
Enteroentectropy 46.99
Enteroenterostomy 45.90
  small-to-large intestine 45.93
  small-to-small intestine 45.91
Enterogastrostomy 44.39
  laparoscopic 44.38
Enterolithotomy 45.00
Enterolysis 54.59
  laparoscopic 54.51
Enteropancreatostomy 52.96
Enterorrhaphy 46.79
  large intestine 46.75
  small intestine 46.73
Enterostomy NEC 46.39
  cecum (see also Colostomy) 46.10
  colon (transverse) (see also Colostomy)
    46.10
    loop 46.03
  delayed opening 46.31
  duodenum 46.39
    loop 46.01
  feeding NEC 46.39
    percutaneous (endoscopic) 46.32
    ileum (Brooke) (Dragstedt) 46.20
      loop 46.01
  jejunum (feeding) 46.39
    loop 46.01
    percutaneous (endoscopic) 46.32
  sigmoid colon (see also Colostomy)
    46.10
    loop 46.03
  transverse colon (see also Colostomy)
    46.10
    loop 46.03
Enterotomy 45.00
  large intestine 45.03
  small intestine 45.02
Enucleation — see also Excision, lesion,
    by site
  cyst
    broad ligament 69.19
    dental 24.4
    liver 50.29
    ovarian 65.29
      laparoscopic 65.25
    parotid gland 26.29
    salivary gland 26.29
    skin 86.3
    subcutaneous tissue 86.3
  eyeball 16.49
    with implant (into Tenon's capsule)
      16.42

Enucleation — see also Excision, lesion,
    by site — continued
  eyeball — continued
    with implant — continued
      with attachment of muscles
        16.41
EOG (electro-oculogram) 95.22
Epicardiectomy 36.39
Epididymectomy 63.4
  with orchidectomy (unilateral) 62.3
    bilateral 62.41
Epididymogram 87.93
Epididymoplasty 63.59
Epididymorrhaphy 63.81
Epididymotomy 63.92
Epididymovasostomy 63.83
Epiglottidectomy 30.21
Epikeratophakia 11.76
Epilation
  eyebrow (forceps) 08.93
    cryosurgical 08.92
    electrosurgical 08.91
  eyelid (forceps) NEC 08.93
    cryosurgical 08.92
    electrosurgical 08.91
  skin 86.92
Epiphysiodesis — see also Arrest, bone
  growth — see category 78.2 ☑
Epiphysiolysis — see also Arrest, bone
  growth — see category 78.2 ☑
Epiploectomy 54.4
Epiplopexy 54.74
Epiplorrhaphy 54.74
Episioperineoplasty 71.79
Episioperineorrhaphy 71.71
  obstetrical 75.69
Episioplasty 71.79
Episioproctotomy 73.6
Episiorrhaphy 71.71
  for obstetrical laceration 75.69
  following routine episiotomy — see
    Episiotomy
Episiotomy (with subsequent episiorrha-
    phy) 73.6
  high forceps 72.31
  low forceps 72.1
  mid forceps 72.21
  nonobstetrical 71.09
  outlet forceps 72.1
EPS (electrophysiologic stimulation)
  as part of intraoperative testing — ●
    omit code ●
  catheter based invasive electrophys-●
    iologic testing 37.26
  device interrogation only without ●
    arrhythmia induction (bedside●
    check) 89.45-89.49
  noninvasive programmed electrical ●
    stimulation (NIPS) 37.20 ●
Eptifibatide, infusion 99.20
Equalization, leg
  lengthening — see category 78.3 ☑
  shortening — see category 78.2 ☑
Equilibration (occlusal) 24.8
Equiloudness balance 95.43
ERC (endoscopic retrograde cholangiog-
    raphy) 51.11
ERCP (endoscopic retrograde cholan-
    giopancreatography) 51.10
  cannulation of pancreatic duct 52.93
ERG (electroretinogram) 95.21
ERP (endoscopic retrograde pancreatog-
    raphy) 52.13
Eruption, tooth, surgical 24.6
Erythrocytapheresis, therapeutic 99.73
Escharectomy 86.22
Escharotomy 86.09
Esophageal voice training (post-laryn-
    gectomy) 93.73
Esophagectomy 42.40
  abdominothoracocervical (combined)
    (synchronous) 42.42
  partial or subtotal 42.41
  total 42.42
Esophagocologastrostomy (intratho-
    racic) 42.55

Esophagocologastrostomy —
    continued
  antesternal or antethoracic 42.65
Esophagocolostomy (intrathoracic) NEC
    42.56
  with interposition of colon 42.55
  antesternal or antethoracic NEC 42.66
    with interposition of colon 42.65
Esophagoduodenostomy (intrathoracic)
    NEC 42.54
  with
    complete gastrectomy 43.99
    interposition of small bowel 42.53
Esophagoenterostomy (intrathoracic)
    NEC — see also Anastomosis,
    esophagus, to intestinal segment
    42.54
  antesternal or antethoracic (see also
    Anastomosis, esophagus, an-
    testernal, to intestinal segment)
    42.64
Esophagoesophagostomy (intrathoracic)
    42.51
  antesternal or antethoracic 42.61
Esophagogastrectomy 43.99
Esophagogastroduodenoscopy (EGD)
    45.13
  with closed biopsy 45.16
  through stoma (artificial) 45.12
  transabdominal (operative) 45.11
Esophagogastromyotomy 42.7
Esophagogastropexy 44.65
Esophagogastroplasty 44.65
Esophagogastroscopy NEC 44.13
  through stoma (artificial) 44.12
  transabdominal (operative) 44.11
Esophagogastrostomy (intrathoracic)
    42.52
  with partial gastrectomy 43.5
  antesternal or antethoracic 42.62
Esophagoileostomy (intrathoracic) NEC
    42.54
  with interposition of small bowel
    42.53
  antesternal or antethoracic NEC 42.64
    with interposition of small bowel
      42.63
Esophagojejunostomy (intrathoracic)
    NEC 42.54
  with
    complete gastrectomy 43.99
    interposition of small bowel 42.53
  antesternal or antethoracic NEC 42.64
    with interposition of small bowel
      42.63
Esophagomyotomy 42.7
Esophagoplasty NEC 42.89
Esophagorrhaphy 42.82
Esophagoscopy NEC 42.23
  by incision (operative) 42.21
  with closed biopsy 42.24
  through stoma (artificial) 42.22
  transabdominal (operative) 42.21
Esophagostomy 42.10
  cervical 42.11
  thoracic 42.19
Esophagotomy NEC 42.09
Estes operation (ovary) 65.72
  laparoscopic 65.75
Estlander operation (thoracoplasty)
    33.34
ESWL (extracorporeal shockwave
    lithotripsy) NEC 98.59
  bile duct 98.52
  bladder 98.51
  gallbladder 98.52
  kidney 98.51
  Kock pouch (urinary diversion) 98.51
  renal pelvis 98.51
  specified site NEC 98.59
  ureter 98.51
Ethmoidectomy 22.63
Ethmoidotomy 22.51
Evacuation
  abscess — see Drainage, by site

☑ Additional Digit Required — Refer to the Tabular List for Digit Selection ▽ Subterms under main terms may continue to next column or page

2007 ICD-9-CM ►◄ Revised Text ● New Line ▲ Revised Code October 2006 · Volume 3 — 17

Evacuation — *continued*
  anterior chamber (eye) (aqueous) (hyphema) 12.91
  cyst (*see also* Excision, lesion, by site)
    breast 85.91
    kidney 55.01
    liver 50.29
  hematoma (*see also* Incision, hematoma)
    obstetrical 75.92
      incisional 75.91
  hemorrhoids (thrombosed) 49.47
  pelvic blood clot (by incision) 54.19
    by
        culdocentesis 70.0
        culdoscopy 70.22
  retained placenta
    with curettage 69.02
    manual 75.4
  streptothrix from lacrimal duct 09.42
Evaluation (of)
  audiological 95.43
  cardiac rhythm device (CRT-D) (CRT-P) (AICD) (pacemaker) — *see* Interrogation
  criminal responsibility, psychiatric 94.11
  functional (physical therapy) 93.01
  hearing NEC 95.49
  orthotic (for brace fitting) 93.02
  prosthetic (for artificial limb fitting) 93.03
  psychiatric NEC 94.19
    commitment 94.13
  psychologic NEC 94.08
  testimentary capacity, psychiatric 94.11
Evans operation (release of clubfoot) 83.84
Evisceration
  eyeball 16.39
    with implant (into scleral shell) 16.31
  ocular contents 16.39
    with implant (into scleral shell) 16.31
  orbit (*see also* Exenteration, orbit) 16.59
  pelvic (anterior) (posterior) (partial) (total) (female) 68.8
    male 57.71
Evulsion
  nail (bed) (fold) 86.23
  skin 86.3
  subcutaneous tissue 86.3
Examination (for)
  breast
    manual 89.36
    radiographic NEC 87.37
    thermographic 88.85
    ultrasonic 88.73
  cervical rib (by x-ray) 87.43
  colostomy stoma (digital) 89.33
  dental (oral mucosa) (peridontal) 89.31
    radiographic NEC 87.12
  enterostomy stoma (digital) 89.33
  eye 95.09
    color vision 95.06
    comprehensive 95.02
    dark adaptation 95.07
    limited (with prescription of spectacles) 95.01
    under anesthesia 95.04
  fetus, intrauterine 75.35
  general physical 89.7
  glaucoma 95.03
  gynecological 89.26
  hearing 95.47

Examination — *continued*
  microscopic (specimen) (of) 91.9 ☑

> *Note* — *Use the following fourth-digit subclassification with categories 90–91 to identify type of examination:*
> 1   *bacterial smear*
> 2   *culture*
> 3   *culture and sensitivity*
> 4   *parasitology*
> 5   *toxicology*
> 6   *cell block and Papanicolaou smear*
> 9   *other microsopic examination*

    adenoid 90.3 ☑
    adrenal gland 90.1 ☑
    amnion 91.4 ☑
    anus 90.9 ☑
    appendix 90.9 ☑
    bile ducts 91.0 ☑
    bladder 91.3 ☑
    blood 90.5 ☑
    bone 91.5 ☑
      marrow 90.6 ☑
    brain 90.0 ☑
    breast 91.6 ☑
    bronchus 90.4 ☑
    bursa 91.5 ☑
    cartilage 91.5 ☑
    cervix 91.4 ☑
    chest wall 90.4 ☑
    chorion 91.4 ☑
    colon 90.9 ☑
    cul-de-sac 91.1 ☑
    dental 90.8 ☑
    diaphragm 90.4 ☑
    duodenum 90.8 ☑
    ear 90.3 ☑
    endocrine gland NEC 90.1 ☑
    esophagus 90.8 ☑
    eye 90.2 ☑
    fallopian tube 91.4 ☑
    fascia 91.5 ☑
    female genital tract 91.4 ☑
    fetus 91.4 ☑
    gallbladder 91.0 ☑
    hair 91.6 ☑
    ileum 90.9 ☑
    jejunum 90.9 ☑
    joint fluid 91.5 ☑
    kidney 91.2 ☑
    large intestine 90.9 ☑
    larynx 90.3 ☑
    ligament 91.5 ☑
    liver 91.0 ☑
    lung 90.4 ☑
    lymph (node) 90.7 ☑
    meninges 90.0 ☑
    mesentery 91.1 ☑
    mouth 90.8 ☑
    muscle 91.5 ☑
    musculoskeletal system 91.5 ☑
    nails 91.6 ☑
    nerve 90.0 ☑
    nervous system 90.0 ☑
    nose 90.3 ☑
    omentum 91.1 ☑
    operative wound 91.7 ☑
    ovary 91.4 ☑
    pancreas 91.0 ☑
    parathyroid gland 90.1 ☑
    penis 91.3 ☑
    perirenal tissue 91.2 ☑
    peritoneum (fluid) 91.1 ☑
    periureteral tissue 91.2 ☑
    perivesical (tissue) 91.3 ☑
    pharynx 90.3 ☑
    pineal gland 90.1 ☑
    pituitary gland 90.1 ☑
    placenta 91.4 ☑
    pleura (fluid) 90.4 ☑

Examination — *continued*
  microscopic — *continued*
    prostate 91.3 ☑
    rectum 90.9 ☑
    retroperitoneum 91.1 ☑
    semen 91.3 ☑
    seminal vesicle 91.3 ☑
    sigmoid 90.9 ☑
    skin 91.6 ☑
    small intestine 90.9 ☑
    specified site NEC 91.8 ☑
    spinal fluid 90.0 ☑
    spleen 90.6 ☑
    sputum 90.4 ☑
    stomach 90.8 ☑
    stool 90.9 ☑
    synovial membrane 91.5 ☑
    tendon 91.5 ☑
    thorax NEC 90.4 ☑
    throat 90.3 ☑
    thymus 90.1 ☑
    thyroid gland 90.1 ☑
    tonsil 90.3 ☑
    trachea 90.4 ☑
    ureter 91.2 ☑
    urethra 91.3 ☑
    urine 91.3 ☑
    uterus 91.4 ☑
    vagina 91.4 ☑
    vas deferens 91.3 ☑
    vomitus 90.8 ☑
    vulva 91.4 ☑
  neurologic 89.13
  neuro-ophthalmology 95.03
  ophthalmoscopic 16.21
  panorex, mandible 87.12
  pelvic (manual) 89.26
    instrumental (by pelvimeter) 88.25
    pelvimetric 88.25
  physical, general 89.7
  postmortem 89.8
  rectum (digital) 89.34
    endoscopic 48.23
      through stoma (artificial) 48.22
      transabdominal 48.21
  retinal disease 95.03
  specified type (manual) NEC 89.39
  thyroid field, postoperative 06.02
  uterus (digital) 68.11
    endoscopic 68.12
  vagina 89.26
    endoscopic 70.21
  visual field 95.05
Exchange transfusion 99.01
  intrauterine 75.2
Excision
  aberrant tissue — *see* Excision, lesion, by site of tissue origin
  abscess — *see* Excision, lesion, by site
  accessory tissue (*see also* Excision, lesion, by site of tissue origin)
    lung 32.29
      endoscopic 32.28
    spleen 41.93
  adenoids (tag) 28.6
    with tonsillectomy 28.3
  adenoma — *see* Excision, lesion, by site
  adrenal gland (*see also* Adrenalectomy) 07.22
  ampulla of Vater (with reimplantation of common duct) 51.62
  anal papilla 49.39
    endoscopic 49.31
  aneurysm (arteriovenous) (*see also* Aneurysmectomy) 38.60
    coronary artery 36.91
    heart 37.32
    myocardium 37.32
    sinus of Valsalva 35.39
    ventricle (heart) 37.32
  anus (complete) (partial) 49.6
  aortic subvalvular ring 35.35
  apocrine gland 86.3
  aponeurosis 83.42

Excision — *continued*
  aponeurosis — *continued*
    hand 82.33
  appendiceal stump 47.09
    laparoscopic 47.01
  appendices epiploicae 54.4
  appendix (*see also* Appendectomy) 47.01, 47.09
    epididymis 63.3
    testis 62.2
  arcuate ligament (spine) — omit code
  arteriovenous fistula (*see also* Aneurysmectomy) 38.60
  artery (*see also* Arteriectomy) 38.60
  Baker's cyst, knee 83.39
  Bartholin's gland 71.24
  basal ganglion 01.59
  bile duct 51.69
    endoscopic 51.64
  bladder (*see also* Cystectomy)
  bleb (emphysematous), lung 32.29
    endoscopic 32.28
  blood vessel (*see also* Angiectomy) 38.60
  bone (ends) (partial), except facial — *see* category 77.8 ☑
    for graft (autograft) (homograft) — *see* category 77.7 ☑
    facial NEC 76.39
      total 76.45
        with reconstruction 76.44
    fragments (chips) (*see also* Incision, bone) 77.10
    joint (*see also* Arthrotomy) 80.10
    necrotic (*see also* Sequestrectomy, bone) 77.00
    heterotopic, from
      muscle 83.32
        hand 82.22
      skin 86.3
      tendon 83.31
        hand 82.21
    mandible 76.31
      with arthrodesis — *see* Arthrodesis
      total 76.42
        with reconstruction 76.41
    spur — *see* Excision, lesion, bone
    total, except facial — *see* category 77.9 ☑
      facial NEC 76.45
        with reconstruction 76.44
      mandible 76.42
        with reconstruction 76.41
  brain 01.59
    hemisphere 01.52
    lobe 01.53
  branchial cleft cyst or vestige 29.2
  breast (*see also* Mastectomy) 85.41
    aberrant tissue 85.24
    accessory 85.24
    ectopic 85.24
    nipple 85.25
      accessory 85.24
    segmental 85.23
    supernumerary 85.24
    wedge 85.21
  broad ligament 69.19
  bronchogenic cyst 32.09
    endoscopic 32.01
  bronchus (wide sleeve) NEC 32.1
  buccal mucosa 27.49
  bulbourethral gland 58.92
  bulbous tuberosities (mandible) (maxilla) (fibrous) (osseous) 24.31
  bunion (*see also* Bunionectomy) 77.59
  bunionette (with osteotomy) 77.54
  bursa 83.5
    hand 82.31
  canal of Nuck 69.19
  cardioma 37.33
  carotid body (lesion) (partial) (total) 39.8

☑ Additional Digit Required — Refer to the Tabular List for Digit Selection   ▼ Subterms under main terms may continue to next column or page

18 — Volume 3   ►◄ Revised Text   ● New Line   ▲ Revised Code   **2007 ICD-9-CM**

☑ Additional Digit Required — Refer to the Tabular List for Digit Selection   ▽ Subterms under main terms may continue to next column or page

2007 ICD-9-CM   ▶◀ Revised Text   ● New Line   ▲ Revised Code   **Volume 3 — 19**

Excision — continued
  lesion — continued
    bone — continued
      patella 77.66
      pelvic 77.69
      phalanges (foot) (hand) 77.69
      radius 77.63
      scapula 77.61
      skull 01.6
      specified site NEC 77.69
      tarsal, metatarsal 77.68
      thorax (ribs) (sternum) 77.61
      tibia 77.67
      ulna 77.63
      vertebrae 77.69
    brain (transtemporal approach) NEC 01.59
      by stereotactic radiosurgery 92.30
        cobalt 60 92.32
        linear accelerator (LINAC) 92.31
        multi-source 92.32
        particle beam 92.33
        particulate 92.33
        radiosurgery NEC 92.39
        single source photon 92.31
    breast (segmental) (wedge) 85.21
    broad ligament 69.19
    bronchus NEC 32.09
      endoscopic 32.01
    cerebral (cortex) NEC 01.59
      meninges 01.51
    cervix (myoma) 67.39
    chest wall 34.4
    choroid plexus 02.14
    ciliary body 12.44
    colon 45.41
      endoscopic NEC 45.43
        polypectomy 45.42
    conjunctiva 10.31
    cornea 11.49
    cranium 01.6
    cul-de-sac (Douglas') 70.32
    dental (jaw) 24.4
    diaphragm 34.81
    duodenum (local) 45.31
      endoscopic 45.30
    ear, external 18.29
      radical 18.31
    endometrium 68.29
    epicardium 37.31
    epididymis 63.3
    epiglottis 30.09
    esophagus NEC 42.32
      endoscopic 42.33
    eyebrow (skin) 08.20
    eye, eyeball 16.93
      anterior segment NEC 12.40
    eyelid 08.20
      by
        halving procedure 08.24
        wedge resection 08.24
      major
        full-thickness 08.24
        partial-thickness 08.23
      minor 08.22
    fallopian tube 66.61
    fascia 83.39
      hand 82.29
    groin region (abdominal wall) (inguinal) 54.3
      skin 86.3
      subcutaneous tissue 86.3
    gum 24.31
    heart 37.33
    hepatic duct 51.69
    inguinal canal 54.3
    intestine
      large 45.41
        endoscopic NEC 45.43
          polypectomy 45.42
      small NEC 45.33
    intracranial NEC 01.59
    intranasal 21.31
    intraspinal 03.4

Excision — continued
  lesion — continued
    iris 12.42
    jaw 76.2
      dental 24.4
    joint 80.80
      ankle 80.87
      elbow 80.82
      foot and toe 80.88
      hand and finger 80.84
      hip 80.85
      knee 80.86
      shoulder 80.81
      specified site NEC 80.89
      spine 80.89
      wrist 80.83
    kidney 55.39
      with partial nephrectomy 55.4
    labia 71.3
    lacrimal
      gland (frontal approach) 09.21
      passage 09.6
      sac 09.6
    larynx 30.09
    ligament (joint) (see also Excision, lesion, joint) 80.80
      broad 69.19
      round 69.19
      uterosacral 69.19
    lip 27.43
      by wide excision 27.42
    liver 50.29
    lung NEC 32.29
      by lung volume reduction surgery 32.22
      by wide excision 32.3
      endoscopic 32.28
    lymph structure(s) (channel) (vessel) NEC 40.29
      node — see Excision, lymph, node
    mammary duct 85.21
    mastoid (bone) 20.49
    mediastinum 34.3
    meninges (cerebral) 01.51
      spinal 03.4
    mesentery 54.4
    middle ear 20.51
    mouth NEC 27.49
    muscle 83.32
      hand 82.22
      ocular 15.13
    myocardium 37.33
    nail 86.23
    nasal sinus 22.60
      antrum 22.62
        with Caldwell-Luc approach 22.61
        specified approach NEC 22.62
      ethmoid 22.63
      frontal 22.42
      maxillary 22.62
        with Caldwell-Luc approach 22.61
        specified approach NEC 22.62
      sphenoid 22.64
    nasopharynx 29.3 ☑
    nerve (cranial) (peripheral) 04.07
      sympathetic 05.29
    nonodontogenic 24.31
    nose 21.30
      intranasal 21.31
      polyp 21.31
      skin 21.32
      specified site NEC 21.32
    odontogenic 24.4
    omentum 54.4
    orbit 16.92
    ovary 65.29
      by wedge resection 65.22
        laparoscopic 65.24
      that by laparoscope 65.25
    palate (bony) 27.31
      by wide excision 27.32

Excision — continued
  lesion — continued
    palate — continued
      soft 27.49
    pancreas (local) 52.22
      endoscopic 52.21
    parathyroid 06.89
    parotid gland or duct NEC 26.29
    pelvic wall 54.3
    pelvirectal tissue 48.82
    penis 64.2
    pericardium 37.31
    perineum (female) 71.3
      male 86.3
    periprostatic tissue 60.82
    perirectal tissue 48.82
    perirenal tissue 59.91
    peritoneum 54.4
    perivesical tissue 59.91
    pharynx 29.39
      diverticulum 29.32
    pineal gland 07.53
    pinna 18.29
      radical 18.31
    pituitary (gland) (see also Hypophysectomy, partial) 07.63
      by stereotactic radiosurgery 92.30
        cobalt 60 92.32
        linear accelerator (LINAC) 92.31
        multi-source 92.32
        particle beam 92.33
        particulate 92.33
        radiosurgery NEC 92.39
        single source photon 92.31
    pleura 34.59
    pouch of Douglas 70.32
    preauricular (ear) 18.21
    presacral 54.4
    prostate (transurethral) 60.61
    pulmonary (fibrosis) 32.29
      endoscopic 32.28
    rectovaginal septum 48.82
    rectum 48.35
      polyp (endoscopic) 48.36
    retroperitoneum 54.4
    salivary gland or duct NEC 26.29
      en bloc 26.32
    sclera 12.84
    scrotum 61.3
    sinus (nasal) — see Excision, lesion, nasal sinus
    Skene's gland 71.3
    skin 86.3
      breast 85.21
      nose 21.32
      radical (wide) (involving underlying or adjacent structure) (with flap closure) 86.4
      scrotum 61.3
    skull 01.6
    soft tissue NEC 83.39
      hand 82.29
    spermatic cord 63.3
    sphincter of Oddi 51.62
      endoscopic 51.64
    spinal cord (meninges) 03.4
    spleen (cyst) 41.42
    stomach NEC 43.42
      endoscopic 43.41
        polyp 43.41
      polyp (endoscopic) 43.41
    subcutaneous tissue 86.3
      breast 85.21
    subgingival 24.31
    sweat gland 86.3
    tendon 83.39
      hand 82.29
      ocular 15.13
      sheath 83.31
        hand 82.21
    testis 62.2
    thorax 34.4
    thymus 07.81
    thyroid 06.31

Excision — continued
  lesion — continued
    thyroid — continued
      substernal or transsternal route 06.51
    tongue 25.1
    tonsil 28.92
    trachea 31.5
    tunica vaginalis 61.92
    ureter 56.41
    urethra 58.39
      endoscopic 58.31
    uterine ligament 69.19
    uterosacral ligament 69.19
    uterus 68.29
    vagina 70.33
    vein 38.60
      abdominal 38.67
      head and neck NEC 38.62
      intracranial NEC 38.61
      lower limb 38.69
      thoracic NEC 38.65
      upper limb 38.63
    ventricle (heart) 37.33
    vocal cords 30.09
    vulva 71.3
  ligament (see also Arthrectomy) 80.90
    broad 69.19
    round 69.19
    uterine 69.19
    uterosacral 69.19
  ligamentum flavum (spine) — omit code
  lingual tonsil 28.5
  lip 27.43
  liver (partial) 50.22
  loose body
    bone — see Sequestrectomy, bone
    joint 80.10
  lung (complete) (with mediastinal dissection) 32.5
    accessory or ectopic tissue 32.29
      endoscopic 32.28
    segmental 32.3
    specified type NEC 32.29
      endoscopic 32.28
    volume reduction surgery 32.22
      biologic lung volume reduction ● (BLVR) — see category ● 33.7 ☑ ●
    wedge 32.29
  lymphangioma (simple) (see also Excision, lymph, lymphatic node) 40.29
  lymph, lymphatic
    drainage area 40.29
      radical — see Excision, lymph, node, radical
      regional (with lymph node, skin, subcutaneous tissue, and fat) 40.3
    node (simple) NEC 40.29
      with
        lymphatic drainage area (including skin, subcutaneous tissue, and fat) 40.3
        mastectomy — see Mastectomy, radical
        muscle and deep fascia — see Excision, lymph, node, radical
      axillary 40.23
        radical 40.51
        regional (extended) 40.3
      cervical (deep) (with excision of scalene fat pad) 40.21
        with laryngectomy 30.4
        radical (including muscle and deep fascia) 40.40
          bilateral 40.42
          unilateral 40.41
        regional (extended) 40.3
        superficial 40.29
      groin 40.24
        radical 40.54

☑ Additional Digit Required — Refer to the Tabular List for Digit Selection
▽ Subterms under main terms may continue to next column or page
2007 ICD-9-CM
▶◀ Revised Text ● New Line ▲ Revised Code
Volume 3 — 21

Exercise — *continued*
  musculoskeletal
    active NEC 93.12
    passive NEC 93.17
  neurologic 89.13
  passive musculoskeletal NEC 93.17
  resistive 93.13
Exfoliation, skin, by chemical 86.24
Exostectomy — *see also* Excision, lesion, bone 77.60
  first metatarsal (hallux valgus repair) — *see* Bunionectomy
  hallux valgus repair (with wedge osteotomy) — *see* Bunionectomy
Expiratory flow rate 89.38
Explant, explantation — *see* Removal
Exploration — *see also* Incision
  abdomen 54.11
  abdominal wall 54.0
  adrenal (gland) 07.41
    field 07.00
      bilateral 07.02
      unilateral 07.01
  artery 38.00
    abdominal 38.06
    aorta (arch) (ascending) (descending) 38.04
    head and neck NEC 38.02
    intracranial NEC 38.01
    lower limb 38.08
    thoracic NEC 38.05
    upper limb 38.03
  auditory canal, external 18.02
  axilla 86.09
  bile duct(s) 51.59
    for relief of obstruction 51.49
      endoscopic 51.84
    common duct 51.51
      for
        relief of obstruction 51.42
          endoscopic 51.84
          removal of calculus 51.41
            endoscopic 51.88
      endoscopic 51.11
      laparoscopic 51.11
  bladder (by incision) 57.19
    endoscopic 57.32
      through stoma (artificial) 57.31
  bone (*see also* Incision, bone) 77.10
  brain (tissue) 01.39
  breast 85.0
  bronchus 33.0
    endoscopic — *see* Bronchoscopy
  bursa 83.03
    hand 82.03
  carotid body 39.8
  carpal tunnel 04.43
  choroid 14.9
  ciliary body 12.44
  colon 45.03
  common bile duct 51.51
    for
      relief of obstruction 51.42
        endoscopic 51.84
      removal of calculus 51.41
        endoscopic 51.88
    endoscopic 51.11
  coronary artery 36.99
  cranium 01.24
  cul-de-sac 70.12
    endoscopic 70.22
  disc space 03.09
  duodenum 45.01
  endoscopic — *see* Endoscopy, by site
  epididymis 63.92
  esophagus (by incision) NEC 42.09
    endoscopic — *see* Esophagoscopy
  ethmoid sinus 22.51
  eyelid 08.09
  fallopian tube 66.01
  fascia 83.09
    hand 82.09
  flank 54.0
  fossa (superficial) NEC 86.09
    pituitary 07.71
  frontal sinus 22.41

Exploration — *see also* Incision — *continued*
  frontonasal duct 96.21
  gallbladder 51.04
  groin (region) (abdominal wall) (inguinal) 54.0
    skin and subcutaneous tissue 86.09
  heart 37.11
  hepatic duct 51.59
  hypophysis 07.72
  ileum 45.02
  inguinal canal (groin) 54.0
  intestine (by incision) NEC 45.00
    large 45.03
    small 45.02
  intrathoracic 34.02
  jejunum 45.02
  joint structures (*see also* Arthrotomy) 80.10
  kidney 55.01
    pelvis 55.11
  labia 71.09
  lacrimal
    gland 09.0
    sac 09.53
  laparotomy site 54.12
  larynx (by incision) 31.3
    endoscopic 31.42
  liver 50.0
  lung (by incision) 33.1
  lymphatic structure(s) (channel) (node) (vessel) 40.0
  mastoid 20.21
  maxillary antrum or sinus (Caldwell-Luc approach) 22.39
  mediastinum 34.1
    endoscopic 34.22
  middle ear (transtympanic) 20.23
  muscle 83.02
    hand 82.02
  neck (*see also* Exploration, thyroid) 06.09
  nerve (cranial) (peripheral) NEC 04.04
    auditory 04.01
    root (spinal) 03.09
  nose 21.1
  orbit (*see also* Orbitotomy) 16.09
  pancreas 52.09
    endoscopic 52.13
  pancreatic duct 52.09
    endoscopic 52.13
  pelvis (by laparotomy) 54.11
    by colpotomy 70.12
  penis 64.92
  perinephric area 59.09
  perineum (female) 71.09
    male 86.09
  peripheral vessels
    lower limb
      artery 38.08
      vein 38.09
    upper limb (artery) (vein) 38.03
  periprostatic tissue 60.81
  perirenal tissue 59.09
  perivesical tissue 59.19
  petrous pyramid air cells 20.22
  pilonidal sinus 86.03
  pineal (gland) 07.52
    field 07.51
  pituitary (gland) 07.72
    fossa 07.71
  pleura 34.09
  popliteal space 86.09
  prostate 60.0
  rectum (*see also* Proctoscopy) 48.23
    by incision 48.0
  retroperitoneum 54.0
  retropubic 59.19
  salivary gland 26.0
  sclera (by incision) 12.89
  scrotum 61.0
  shunt
    ventriculoperitoneal at
      peritoneal site 54.95
      ventricular site 02.41

Exploration — *see also* Incision — *continued*
  sinus
    ethmoid 22.51
    frontal 22.41
    maxillary (Caldwell-Luc approach) 22.39
    sphenoid 22.52
    tract, skin and subcutaneous tissue 86.09
  skin 86.09
  soft tissue NEC 83.09
    hand 82.09
  spermatic cord 63.93
  sphenoidal sinus 22.52
  spinal (canal) (nerve root) 03.09
  spleen 41.2
  stomach (by incision) 43.0
    endoscopic — *see* Gastroscopy
  subcutaneous tissue 86.09
  subdiaphragmatic space 54.11
  superficial fossa 86.09
  tarsal tunnel 04.44
  tendon (sheath) 83.01
    hand 82.01
  testes 62.0
  thymus (gland) 07.92
    field 07.91
  thyroid (field) (gland) (by incision) 06.09
    postoperative 06.02
  trachea (by incision) 31.3
    endoscopic — *see* Tracheoscopy
  tunica vaginalis 61.0
  tympanum 20.09
    transtympanic route 20.23
  ureter (by incision) 56.2
    endoscopic 56.31
  urethra (by incision) 58.0
    endoscopic 58.22
  uterus (corpus) 68.0
    cervix 69.95
    digital 68.11
    postpartal, manual 75.7
  vagina (by incision) 70.14
    endoscopic 70.21
  vas deferens 63.6
  vein 38.00
    abdominal 38.07
    head and neck NEC 38.02
    intracranial NEC 38.01
    lower limb 38.09
    thoracic NEC 38.05
    upper limb 38.03
  vulva (by incision) 71.09
Exposure — *see also* Incision, by site
  tooth (for orthodontic treatment) 24.6
Expression, trachoma follicles 10.33
Exsanguination transfusion 99.01
Extension
  buccolabial sulcus 24.91
  limb, forced 93.25
  lingual sulcus 24.91
  mandibular ridge 76.43
Exteriorization
  esophageal pouch 42.12
  intestine 46.03
    large 46.03
    small 46.01
  maxillary sinus 22.9
  pilonidal cyst or sinus (open excision) (with partial closure) 86.21
Extirpation — *see also* Excision, by site
  aneurysm — *see* Aneurysmectomy
  arteriovenous fistula — *see* Aneurysmectomy
  lacrimal sac 09.6
  larynx 30.3
    with radical neck dissection (with synchronous thyroidectomy) (with synchronous tracheostomy) 30.4
  nerve, tooth (*see also* Therapy, root canal) 23.70
  varicose vein (peripheral) (lower limb) 38.59

Extirpation — *see also* Excision, by site — *continued*
  varicose vein — *continued*
    upper limb 38.53
Extracorporeal
  circulation (regional), except hepatic 39.61
    hepatic 50.92
    percutaneous 39.66
  hemodialysis 39.95
  membrane oxygenation (ECMO) 39.65
  photopheresis, therapeutic 99.88
  shockwave lithotripsy (ESWL) NEC 98.59
    bile duct 98.52
    bladder 98.51
    gallbladder 98.52
    kidney 98.51
    renal pelvis 98.51
    specified site NEC 98.59
    ureter 98.51
Extracranial-intracranial bypass [EC-IC] 39.28
Extraction
  breech (partial) 72.52
    with forceps to aftercoming head 72.51
    total 72.54
      with forceps to aftercoming head 72.53
  cataract 13.19
    after cataract (by)
      capsulectomy 13.65
      capsulotomy 13.64
      discission 13.64
      excision 13.65
      iridocapsulectomy 13.65
      mechanical fragmentation 13.66
      needling 13.64
      phacofragmentation (mechanical) 13.66
    aspiration (simple) (with irrigation) 13.3
    cryoextraction (intracapsular approach) 13.19
      temporal inferior route (in presence of fistulization bleb) 13.11
    curette evacuation (extracapsular approach) 13.2
    emulsification (and aspiration) 13.41
    erysiphake (intracapsular approach) 13.19
      temporal inferior route (in presence of fistulization bleb) 13.11
    extracapsular approach (with iridectomy) NEC 13.59
      by temporal inferior route (in presence of fistulization bleb) 13.51
      aspiration (simple) (with irrigation) 13.3
      curette evacuation 13.2
      emulsification (and aspiration) 13.41
      linear extraction 13.2
      mechanical fragmentation with aspiration by
        posterior route 13.42
        specified route NEC 13.43
      phacoemulsification (ultrasonic) (with aspiration) 13.41
      phacofragmentation (mechanical)
        with aspiration by
          posterior route 13.42
          specified route NEC 13.43
        ultrasonic (with aspiration) 13.41
      rotoextraction (mechanical) with aspiration by
        posterior route 13.42
        specified route NEC 13.43

☑ Additional Digit Required — Refer to the Tabular List for Digit Selection   ▽ Subterms under main terms may continue to next column or page

22 — Volume 3   ►◄ Revised Text   ● New Line   ▲ Revised Code   *2007 ICD-9-CM*

Extraction — *continued*
  cataract — *continued*
    intracapsular (combined) (simple)
      (with iridectomy) (with suc-
      tion) (with zonulolysis) 13.19
      by temporal inferior route (in
        presence of fistulization
        bleb) 13.11
    linear extraction (extracapsular
      approach) 13.2
    phacoemulsification (and aspira-
      tion) 13.41
    phacofragmentation (mechanical)
      with aspiration by
        posterior route 13.42
        specified route NEC 13.43
      ultrasonic 13.41
    rotoextraction (mechanical)
      with aspiration by
        posterior route 13.42
        specified route NEC 13.43
    secondary membranous (after
      cataract) (by)
      capsulectomy 13.65
      capsulotomy 13.64
      discission 13.64
      excision 13.65
      iridocapsulectomy 13.65
      mechanical fragmentation 13.66
      needling 13.64
      phacofragmentation (mechani-
        cal) 13.66
  common duct stones (percutaneous)
    (through sinus tract) (with bas-
    ket) 51.96
  foreign body — *see* Removal, foreign
    body
  kidney stone(s), percutaneous 55.03
    with fragmentation procedure
      55.04
  lens (eye) (*see also* Extraction,
    cataract) 13.19
  Malström's 72.79
    with episiotomy 72.71
  menstrual, menses 69.6
  milk from lactating breast (manual)
    (pump) 99.98
  tooth (by forceps) (multiple) (single)
    NEC 23.09
    with mucoperiosteal flap elevation
      23.19
    deciduous 23.01
    surgical NEC (*see also* Removal,
      tooth, surgical) 23.19
  vacuum, fetus 72.79
    with episiotomy 72.71
  vitreous (*see also* Removal, vitreous)
    14.72

F

Face lift 86.82
Facetectomy 77.89
Facilitation, intraocular circulation
  NEC 12.59
Failed (trial) forceps 73.3
Family
  counselling (medical) (social) 94.49
  therapy 94.42
Farabeuf operation (ischiopubiotomy)
  77.39
Fasanella-Servatt operation (blepharop-
  tosis repair) 08.35
Fasciaplasty — *see* Fascioplasty
Fascia sling operation — *see* Operation,
  sling
Fasciectomy 83.44
  for graft 83.43
    hand 82.34
  hand 82.35
    for graft 82.34
  palmar (release of Dupuytren's con-
    tracture) 82.35
Fasciodesis 83.89
  hand 82.89
Fascioplasty — *see also* Repair, fascia
  83.89

Fascioplasty — *see also* Repair, fascia
  — *continued*
  hand (*see also* Repair, fascia, hand)
    82.89
Fasciorrhaphy — *see* Suture, fascia
Fasciotomy 83.14
  Dupuytren's 82.12
    with excision 82.35
  Dwyer 83.14
  hand 82.12
  Ober-Yount 83.14
  orbital (*see also* Orbitotomy) 16.09
  palmar (release of Dupuytren's con-
    tracture) 82.12
    with excision 82.35
Fenestration
  aneurysm (dissecting), thoracic aorta
    39.54
  aortic aneurysm 39.54
  cardiac valve 35.10
  chest wall 34.01
  ear
    inner (with graft) 20.61
      revision 20.62
    tympanic 19.55
  labyrinth (with graft) 20.61
  Lempert's (endaural) 19.9
  operation (aorta) 39.54
  oval window, ear canal 19.55
  palate 27.1
  pericardium 37.12
  semicircular canals (with graft) 20.61
  stapes foot plate (with vein graft)
    19.19
    with incus replacement 19.11
  tympanic membrane 19.55
  vestibule (with graft) 20.61
Ferguson operation (hernia repair) 53.00
Fetography 87.81
Fetoscopy 75.31
Fiberoscopy — *see* Endoscopy, by site
Fibroidectomy, uterine 68.29
Fick operation (perforation of foot plate)
  19.0
Filipuncture (aneurysm) (cerebral) 39.52
Filleting
  hammer toe 77.56
  pancreas 52.3
Filling, tooth (amalgam) (plastic) (silicate) 23.2
  root canal (*see also* therapy, root
    canal) 23.70
Fimbriectomy — *see also* Salpingectomy, partial 66.69
  Uchida (with tubal ligation) 66.32
Finney operation (pyloroplasty) 44.29
Fissurectomy, anal 49.39
  endoscopic 49.31
  skin (subcutaneous tissue) 49.04
Fistulectomy — *see also* Closure, fistula,
  by site
  abdominothoracic 34.83
  abdominouterine 69.42
  anus 49.12
  appendix 47.92
  bile duct 51.79
  biliary tract NEC 51.79
  bladder (transurethral approach)
    57.84
  bone (*see also* Excision, lesion, bone)
    77.60
  branchial cleft 29.52
  bronchocutaneous 33.42
  bronchoesophageal 33.42
  bronchomediastinal 34.73
  bronchopleural 34.73
  bronchopleurocutaneous 34.73
  bronchopleuromediastinal 34.73
  bronchovisceral 33.42
  cervicosigmoidal 67.62
  cholecystogastroenteric 51.93
  cornea 11.49
  diaphragm 34.83
  enterouterine 69.42
  esophagopleurocutaneous 34.73
  esophagus NEC 42.84

Fistulectomy — *see also* Closure, fistula,
  by site — *continued*
  fallopian tube 66.73
  gallbladder 51.93
  gastric NEC 44.63
  hepatic duct 51.79
  hepatopleural 34.73
  hepatopulmonary 34.73
  intestine
    large 46.76
    small 46.74
  intestinouterine 69.42
  joint (*see also* Excision, lesion, joint)
    80.80
  lacrimal
    gland 09.21
    sac 09.6
  laryngotracheal 31.62
  larynx 31.62
  mediastinocutaneous 34.73
  mouth NEC 27.53
  nasal 21.82
    sinus 22.71
  nasolabial 21.82
  nasopharyngeal 21.82
  oroantral 22.71
  oronasal 21.82
  pancreas 52.95
  perineorectal 71.72
  perineosigmoidal 71.72
  perirectal, not opening into rectum
    48.93
  pharyngoesophageal 29.53
  pharynx NEC 29.53
  pleura 34.73
  rectolabial 71.72
  rectourethral 58.43
  rectouterine 69.42
  rectovaginal 70.73
  rectovesical 57.83
  rectovulvar 71.72
  rectum 48.73
  salivary (duct) (gland) 26.42
  scrotum 61.42
  skin 86.3
  stomach NEC 44.63
  subcutaneous tissue 86.3
  thoracoabdominal 34.83
  thoracogastric 34.83
  thoracointestinal 34.83
  thorax NEC 34.73
  trachea NEC 31.73
  tracheoesophageal 31.73
  ureter 56.84
  urethra 58.43
  uteroenteric 69.42
  uterointestinal 69.42
  uterorectal 69.42
  uterovaginal 69.42
  vagina 70.75
  vesicosigmoidovaginal 57.83
  vocal cords 31.62
  vulvorectal 71.72
Fistulization
  appendix 47.91
  arteriovenous 39.27
  cisterna chyli 40.62
  endolymphatic sac (for decompression)
    20.79
  esophagus, external 42.10
    cervical 42.11
    specified technique NEC 42.19
  interatrial 35.41
  labyrinth (for decompression) 20.79
  lacrimal sac into nasal cavity 09.81
  larynx 31.29
  lymphatic duct, left (thoracic) 40.62
  orbit 16.09
  peritoneal 54.93
  salivary gland 26.49
  sclera 12.69
    by trephination 12.61
    with iridectomy 12.65
  sinus, nasal NEC 22.9
  subarachnoid space 02.2
  thoracic duct 40.62

Fistulization — *continued*
  trachea 31.29
  tracheoesophageal 31.95
  urethrovaginal 58.0
  ventricle, cerebral (*see also* Shunt,
    ventricular) 02.2
Fistulogram
  abdominal wall 88.03
  chest wall 87.38
  retroperitoneum 88.14
  specified site NEC 88.49   ●
Fistulotomy, anal 49.11
Fitting
  arch bars (orthodontic) 24.7
    for immobilization (fracture) 93.55
  artificial limb 84.40
  contact lens 95.32
  denture (total) 99.97
    bridge (fixed) 23.42
      removable 23.43
    partial (fixed) 23.42
      removable 23.43
  hearing aid 95.48
  obturator (orthodontic) 24.7
  ocular prosthetics 95.34
  orthodontic
    appliance 24.7
    obturator 24.7
    wiring 24.7
  orthotic device 93.23
  periodontal splint (orthodontic) 24.7
  prosthesis, prosthetic device
    above knee 84.45
    arm 84.43
      lower (and hand) 84.42
      upper (and shoulder) 84.41
    below knee 84.46
    hand (and lower arm) 84.42
    leg 84.47
      above knee 84.45
      below knee 84.46
    limb NEC 84.40
    ocular 95.34
    penis (external) 64.94
    shoulder (and upper arm) 84.41
  spectacles 95.31
Five-in-one repair, knee 81.42
Fixation
  bone
    external, without reduction 93.59
      with fracture reduction — *see*
        Reduction, fracture
      cast immobilization NEC 93.53
      external fixator — *see* Fixator,
        external
      splint 93.54
      traction (skeletal) NEC 93.44
        intermittent 93.43
    internal (without fracture reduc-
      tion) 78.50
      with fracture reduction — *see*
        Reduction, fracture
      carpal, metacarpal 78.54
      clavicle 78.51
      femur 78.55
      fibula 78.57
      humerus 78.52
      patella 78.56
      pelvic 78.59
      phalanges (foot) (hand) 78.59
      radius 78.53
      scapula 78.51
      specified site NEC 78.59
      tarsal, metatarsal 78.58
      thorax (ribs) (sternum) 78.51
      tibia 78.57
      ulna 78.53
      vertebrae 78.59
  breast (pendulous) 85.6
  cardinal ligaments 69.22
  cervical collar 93.52
  duodenum 46.62
    to abdominal wall 46.61
  external (without manipulation for re-
    duction) 93.59

☑ Additional Digit Required — Refer to the Tabular List for Digit Selection   ▽ Subterms under main terms may continue to next column or page

2007 ICD-9-CM   ►◄ Revised Text   ● New Line   ▲ Revised Code   **October 2006 · Volume 3 — 23**

☑ Additional Digit Required — Refer to the Tabular List for Digit Selection　　　　　　　　　　　　　　∇ Subterms under main terms may continue to next column or page

24 — Volume 3 · October 2006　　　　▶◀ Revised Text　　　● New Line　　　▲ Revised Code　　　**2007 ICD-9-CM**

Fusion — Graft, grafting

☑ Additional Digit Required — Refer to the Tabular List for Digit Selection   ▽ Subterms under main terms may continue to next column or page

2007 ICD-9-CM   ▶◀ Revised Text   ● New Line   ▲ Revised Code   **Volume 3 — 25**

☑ Additional Digit Required — Refer to the Tabular List for Digit Selection   ▽ Subterms under main terms may continue to next column or page

26 — Volume 3   ▶◀ Revised Text   ● New Line   ▲ Revised Code   *2007 ICD-9-CM*

Index

High forceps delivery — Implant, implantation

High forceps delivery 72.39
  with episiotomy 72.31
Hill-Allison operation (hiatal hernia repair, transpleural approach) 53.80
Hinging, mitral valve 35.12
His bundle recording 37.29
Hitchcock operation (anchoring tendon of biceps) 83.88
Hofmeister operation (gastrectomy) 43.7
Hoke operation
  midtarsal fusion 81.14
  triple arthrodesis 81.12
Holth operation
  iridencleisis 12.63
  sclerectomy 12.65
Homan operation (correction of lymphedema) 40.9
Homograft — see Graft
Homotransplant, homotransplantation — see Transplant
Hosiery, elastic 93.59
Hutch operation (ureteroneocystostomy) 56.74
Hybinette-Eden operation (glenoid bone block) 78.01
Hydrocelectomy
  canal of Nuck (female) 69.19
    male 63.1
  round ligament 69.19
  spermatic cord 63.1
  tunica vaginalis 61.2
Hydrotherapy 93.33
  assisted exercise in pool 93.31
  whirlpool 93.32
Hymenectomy 70.31
Hymenoplasty 70.76
Hymenorrhaphy 70.76
Hymenotomy 70.11
Hyperalimentation (parenteral) 99.15
Hyperbaric oxygenation 93.95
  wound 93.59
Hyperextension, joint 93.25
Hyperthermia NEC 93.35
  for cancer treatment (interstitial) (local) (radiofrequency) (regional) (ultrasound) (whole-body) 99.85
Hypnodrama, psychiatric 94.32
Hypnosis (psychotherapeutic) 94.32
  for anesthesia — omit code
Hypnotherapy 94.32
Hypophysectomy (complete) (total) 07.69
  partial or subtotal 07.63
    transfrontal approach 07.61
    transsphenoidal approach 07.62
  specified approach NEC 07.68
  transfrontal approach (complete) (total) 07.64
    partial 07.61
  transsphenoidal approach (complete) (total) 07.65
    partial 07.62
Hypothermia (central) (local) 99.81
  gastric (cooling) 96.31
    freezing 96.32
  systemic (in open heart surgery) 39.62
Hypotympanotomy 20.23
Hysterectomy 68.9
  abdominal 68.49 ▲
    laparoscopic (total) [TLH] 68.41 ●
    partial or subtotal (supracervical) (supravaginal) 68.39
    radical (modified) (Wertheim's) 68.69 ▲
      laparoscopic (total) [TLRH] 68.61 ●
    supracervical 68.39 ●
      classic infrafascial SEMM hysterectomy (CISH) 68.31
      laparoscopically assisted (LASH) 68.31
  vaginal (complete) (partial) (subtotal) (total) 68.59
    laparoscopically assisted (LAVH) 68.51
    radical (Schauta) 68.79 ▲
      laparoscopic [LRVH] 68.71 ●

Hysterocolpectomy (radical) (vaginal) 68.79 ▲
  abdominal 68.69 ▲
    laparoscopic 68.61 ●
  laparoscopic 68.71 ●
Hysterogram NEC 87.85
  percutaneous 87.84
Hysterolysis 54.59
  laparoscopic 54.51
Hysteromyomectomy 68.29
Hysteropexy 69.22
Hysteroplasty 69.49
Hysterorrhaphy 69.41
Hysterosalpingography gas (contrast) 87.82
  opaque dye (contrast) 87.83
Hysterosalpingostomy 66.74
Hysteroscopy 68.12
  with
    ablation
      endometrial 68.23
    biopsy 68.16
Hysterotomy (with removal of foreign body) (with removal of hydatidiform mole) 68.0
  for intrauterine transfusion 75.2
  obstetrical 74.99
    for termination of pregnancy 74.91
Hysterotrachelectomy 67.4
Hysterotracheloplasty 69.49
Hysterotrachelorrhaphy 69.41
Hysterotrachelotomy 69.95

I

ICCE (intracapsular cataract extraction) 13.19
Ileal
  bladder
    closed 57.87 [45.51]
    open (ileoureterostomy) 56.51
  conduit (ileoureterostomy) 56.51
Ileocecostomy 45.93
Ileocolectomy 45.73
Ileocolostomy 45.93
Ileocolotomy 45.00
Ileocystoplasty (isolated segment anastomosis) (open loop) 57.87 [45.51]
Ileoduodenotomy 45.01
Ileoectomy (partial) 45.62
  with cecectomy 45.72
Ileoentectropy 46.99
Ileoesophagostomy 42.54
Ileoileostomy 45.91
  proximal to distal segment 45.62
Ileoloopogram 87.78
Ileopancreatostomy 52.96
Ileopexy 46.61
Ileoproctostomy 45.93
Ileorectostomy 45.93
Ileorrhaphy 46.73
Ileoscopy 45.13
  through stoma (artificial) 45.12
  transabdominal (operative) 45.11
Ileosigmoidostomy 45.93
Ileostomy 46.20
  continent (permanent) 46.22
    for urinary diversion 56.51
  delayed opening 46.24
  Hendon (temporary) 46.21
  loop 46.01
  Paul (temporary) 46.21
  permanent 46.23
    continent 46.22
  repair 46.41
  revision 46.41
  tangential (temporary) 46.21
  temporary 46.21
  transplantation to new site 46.23
  tube (temporary) 46.21
  ureteral
    external 56.51
    internal 56.71
Ileotomy 45.02
Ileotransversostomy 45.93
Ileoureterostomy (Bricker's) (ileal bladder) 56.51

Imaging (diagnostic)
  diagnostic, not elsewhere classified 88.90
  endovascular ultrasound — see Imaging, intravascular ultrasound
  intraoperative
    iMRI — see Imaging, magnetic resonance
    intravascular — see Imaging, intravascular ultrasound
  intravascular ultrasound (IVUS) 00.29
    aorta 00.22
    aortic arch 00.22
    carotid vessel 00.21
    cerebral vessel, extracranial 00.21
    coronary vessel 00.24
    intrathoracic vessel 00.22
    other specified vessel 00.28
    peripheral vessel 00.23
    renal vessel 00.25
    vena cava (inferior) (superior) 00.22
  magnetic resonance (nuclear) (proton) NEC 88.97
    abdomen 88.97
    bladder (urinary) 88.95
    bone marrow blood supply 88.94
    brain (brain stem) 88.91
      intraoperative (iMRI) 88.96
      real-time 88.96
    chest (hilar) (mediastinal) 88.92
    computer assisted surgery (CAS) with MR/MRA 00.32
    extremity (upper) (lower) 88.94
    eye orbit 88.97
    face 88.97
    head NEC 88.97
    musculoskeletal 88.94
    myocardium 88.92
    neck 88.97
    orbit of eye 88.97
    prostate 88.95
    specified site NEC 88.97
    spinal canal (cord) (spine) 88.93
Immobilization (by)
  with fracture-reduction — see Reduction, fracture
  bandage 93.59
  bone 93.53
  cast NEC 93.53
    with reduction of fracture or dislocation — see Reduction, fracture, and Reduction, dislocation
  device NEC 93.59
  pressure dressing 93.56
  splint (plaster) (tray) 93.54
    with reduction of fracture or dislocation — see Reduction, fracture, and Reduction, dislocation
  stereotactic head frame 93.59
  strapping (non-traction) 93.59 ●
Immunization — see also Vaccination
  allergy 99.12
  autoimmune disease 99.13
  BCG 99.33
  brucellosis 99.55
  cholera 99.31
  diphtheria 99.36
  DPT 99.39
  epidemic parotitis 99.46
  German measles 99.47
  Hemophilus influenzae 99.52
  influenza 99.52
  measles 99.45
  meningococcus 99.55
  mumps 99.46
  pertussis 99.37
  plague 99.34
  poliomyelitis 99.41
  rabies 99.44
  rubella 99.47
  salmonella 99.55
  smallpox 99.42
  staphylococcus 99.55

Immunization — see also Vaccination — continued
  TAB 99.32
  tetanus 99.38
  triple vaccine 99.48
  tuberculosis 99.33
  tularemia 99.35
  typhoid-paratyphoid 99.32
  typhus 99.55
  viral NEC 99.55
  whooping cough 99.37
  yellow fever 99.43
Immunoadsorption
  extracorporeal (ECI) 99.76
Immunotherapy, antineoplastic 99.28
  C-Parvum 99.28
  Interferon 99.28
  interleukin-2 (low-dose) 99.28
    high-dose 00.15
  Levamisole 99.28
  Proleukin (low-dose) 99.28
    high-dose 00.15
  Thymosin 99.28
Implant, implantation
  abdominal artery to coronary artery 36.17
  artery
    aortic branches to heart muscle 36.2
    mammary to ventricular wall (Vineberg) 36.2
  baffle, atrial or interatrial 35.91
  biliary fistulous tract into stomach or intestine 51.39
  bipolar endoprosthesis (femoral head) 81.52
  bladder sphincter, artificial (inflatable) 58.93
  blood vessels to myocardium 36.2
  bone growth stimulator (invasive) (percutaneous) (semi-invasive) — see category 78.9 ☑
  bone morphogenetic protein (Infuse™) (OP-1™) (recombinant) (rhBMP) 84.52
  bone void filler 84.55
    that with kyphoplasty 81.66
    that with vertebroplasty 81.65
  breast (for augmentation) (bilateral) 85.54
    unilateral 85.53
  cardiac resynchronization device
    defibrillator ▶(biventricular) (BiV ICD) (BiV pacemaker with defibrillator) (BiV pacing with defibrillator)◀ (CRT-D) (device and one or more leads) (total system) 00.51
      left ventricular coronary venous lead only 00.52
      pulse generator only 00.54
    pacemaker ▶(BiV) (biventricular)◀ (CRT-P) (device and one or more leads) (total system) 00.50
      left ventricular coronary venous lead only 00.52
      pulse generator only 00.53
  cardiac support device (CSD) 37.41
  cardiomyostimulation system 37.67
  cardioverter/defibrillator (automatic) 37.94
    leads only (patch electrodes) (sensing) (pacing) 37.95
    pulse generator only 37.96
    total system 37.94
  chest wall (mesh) (silastic) 34.79
  chin (polyethylene) (silastic) 76.68
  cochlear (electrode) 20.96
    prosthetic device (electrode and receiver) 20.96
      channel (single) 20.97
        multiple 20.98
      electrode only 20.99
      internal coil only 20.99
  CorCap™ 37.41

☑ Additional Digit Required — Refer to the Tabular List for Digit Selection   ▽ Subterms under main terms may continue to next column or page

2007 ICD-9-CM   ▶◀ Revised Text   ● New Line   ▲ Revised Code   October 2006 • Volume 3 — 27

Implant, implantation — *continued*
cornea 11.73
CRT-D ▶(biventricular defibrillator)
(BiV ICD) (BiV pacemaker with
defibrillator) (BiV pacing with
defibrillator)◀ (cardiac resynchronization defibrillator) (device and one or more leads)
00.51
left ventricular coronary venous
lead only 00.52
pulse generator only 00.54
CRT-P ▶(biventricular pacemaker)
(BiV pacemaker)◀ (cardiac
resynchronization pacemaker)
(device and one or more leads)
00.50
left ventricular coronary venous
lead only 00.52
pulse generator only 00.53
custodis eye 14.41
dental (endosseous) (prosthetic) 23.6
device
adjustable gastric band and port
44.95
bronchial device NOS 33.79 ●
bronchial substance NOS 33.79 ●
bronchial valve 33.71 ●
cardiac support device (CSD) 37.41
CorCap™ 37.41
epicardial support device 37.41
Lap-Band™ 44.95
left atrial appendage 37.90
left atrial filter 37.90
left atrial occluder 37.90
prosthetic cardiac support device
37.41
subcutaneous for intracardiac ●
hemodynamic monitoring ●
00.57 ●
vascular access 86.07
ventricular support device 37.41
diaphragmatic pacemaker 34.85
Dynesys® 84.59 ●
electrode(s)
brain 02.93
depth 02.93
foramen ovale 02.93
sphenoidal 02.96
cardiac (initial) (transvenous) 37.70
atrium (initial) 37.73
replacement 37.76
atrium and ventricle (initial)
37.72
replacement 37.76
epicardium (sternotomy or thoracotomy approach) 37.74
left ventricular coronary venous
system 00.52
temporary transvenous pacemaker system 37.78
during and immediately following cardiac surgery
39.64
ventricle (initial) 37.71
replacement 37.76
depth 02.93
foramen ovale 02.96
gastric 04.92 ●
heart (*see also* Implant, elec-
trode(s), cardiac) 37.70
intracranial 02.93
osteogenic (invasive) for bone
growth stimulation — *see*
category 78.9 ☑
peripheral nerve 04.92
sacral nerve 04.92
sphenoidal 02.96
spine 03.93
electroencephalographic receiver
brain 02.93
intracranial 02.93
electronic stimulator
anus (subcutaneous) 49.92
bladder 57.96

Implant, implantation — *continued*
electronic stimulator — *continued*
bone growth (invasive) (percutaneous) (semi-invasive)
78.9 ☑
brain — *see* Implant, neurostimulator, brain
carotid sinus 39.8
cochlear 20.96
channel (single) 20.97
multiple 20.98
gastric 04.92 ●
intracranial — *see* Implant, neurostimulator, intracranial
peripheral nerve — *see* Implant,
neurostimulator, peripheral
nerve
phrenic nerve 34.85
skeletal muscle 83.92
spine — *see* Implant, neurostimulator, spine
ureter 56.92
electrostimulator — *see* Implant,
electronic stimulator, by site
endoprosthesis
bile duct 51.87
femoral head (bipolar) 81.52
pancreatic duct 52.93
endosseous (dental) 23.6
epidural pegs 02.93
epikeratoprosthesis 11.73
estradiol (pellet) 99.23
eye (Iowa type) 16.61
integrated 16.41
facial bone, synthetic (alloplastic)
76.92
fallopian tube (Mulligan hood) (silastic
tube) (stent) 66.93
into uterus 66.74
gastroepiploic artery to coronary
artery 36.17
half-heart 37.62
hearing device, electromagnetic 20.95
heart
artificial 37.52
total replacement system 37.52
assist system NEC 37.62
external 37.65
extrinsic 37.68
implantable 37.66
non-implantable 37.62
percutaneous external 37.68
pVAD 37.68
auxiliary ventricle 37.62
cardiac support device (CSD) 37.41
circulatory assist system — *see*
Implant, heart, assist system
CorCap™ 37.41
epicardial support device 37.41
pacemaker (*see also* Implant,
pacemaker, cardiac) 37.80
prosthetic cardiac support device
37.41
total replacement system 37.52
valve(s)
prosthesis or synthetic device
(partial) (synthetic) (total)
35.20
aortic 35.22
mitral 35.24
pulmonary 35.26
tricuspid 35.28
tissue graft 35.20
aortic 35.21
mitral 35.23
pulmonary 35.25
tricuspid 35.27
ventricular support device 37.41
inert material
breast (for augmentation) (bilateral)
85.54
unilateral 85.53
larynx 31.0
nose 21.85
orbit (eye socket) 16.69
reinsertion 16.62

Implant, implantation — *continued*
inert material — *continued*
scleral shell (cup) (with evisceration
of eyeball) 16.31
reinsertion 16.62
Tenon's capsule (with enucleation
of eyeball) 16.42
with attachment of muscles
16.41
reinsertion 16.62
urethra 59.79
vocal cord(s) 31.0
infusion pump 86.06
interbody spinal fusion device 84.51
intracardiac hemodynamic monitor, ●
subcutaneous 00.57 ●
joint (prosthesis) (silastic) (Swanson
type) NEC 81.96
ankle (total) 81.56
revision 81.59
carpocarpal, carpometacarpal
81.74
elbow (total) 81.84
revision 81.97
extremity (bioelectric) (cineplastic)
(kineplastic) 84.40
lower 84.48
revision 81.59
upper 84.44
revision 81.97
femoral (bipolar endoprosthesis)
81.52
revision NOS 81.53
acetabular and femoral components (total) 00.70
acetabular component only
00.71
acetabular liner and/or
femoral head only
00.73
femoral component only
00.72
femoral head only and/or
acetabular liner 00.73
total (acetabular and femoral
components) 00.70
finger 81.71
hand (metacarpophalangeal) (interphalangeal) 81.71
revision 81.97
hip (partial) 81.52
revision NOS 81.53
acetabular and femoral components (total) 00.70
acetabular component only
00.71
acetabular liner and/or
femoral head only
00.73
femoral component only
00.72
femoral head only and/or
acetabular liner 00.73
partial
acetabular component
only 00.71
acetabular liner and/or
femoral head only
00.73
femoral component only
00.72
femoral head only and/or
acetabular liner
00.73
total (acetabular and femoral
components) 00.70
total 81.51
revision (acetabular and
femoral components)
00.70
interphalangeal 81.71
revision 81.97
knee (partial) (total) 81.54
revision NOS 81.55
femoral component 00.82

Implant, implantation — *continued*
joint — *continued*
knee — *continued*
revision — *continued*
partial
femoral component 00.82
patellar component 00.83
tibial component 00.81
tibial insert 00.84
patellar component 00.83
tibial component 00.81
tibial insert 00.84
total (all components) 00.80
metacarpophalangeal 81.71
revision 81.97
shoulder (partial) 81.81
revision 81.97
total replacement 81.80
toe 81.57
for hallux valgus repair 77.59
revision 81.59
wrist (partial) 81.74
revision 81.97
total replacement 81.73
kidney, mechanical 55.97
Lap-Band™ 44.95
larynx 31.0
leads (cardiac) — *see* Implant, elec-
trode(s), cardiac
limb lengthening device, internal
(NOS) 84.54
with kinetic distraction 84.53
mammary artery
in ventricle (Vineberg) 36.2
to coronary artery (single vessel)
36.15
double vessel 36.16
M-Brace™ 84.59 ●
Mulligan hood, fallopian tube 66.93
nerve (peripheral) 04.79
neuropacemaker — *see* Implant, neurostimulator, by site
neurostimulator
brain 02.93
electrodes
brain 02.93
gastric 04.92 ●
intracranial 02.93
peripheral nerve 04.92
sacral nerve 04.92
spine 03.93
intracranial 02.93
peripheral nerve 04.92
pulse generator 86.96
dual array 86.95
rechargeable 86.98
single array 86.94
rechargeable 86.97
spine 03.93
nose 21.85
Ommaya reservoir 02.2
orbit 16.69
reinsertion 16.62
outflow tract prosthesis (heart) (gusset
type)
in
pulmonary valvuloplasty 35.26
total repair of tetralogy of Fallot
35.81
ovary into uterine cavity 65.72
laparoscopic 65.75
pacemaker
brain — *see* Implant, neurostimulator, brain
cardiac (device) (initial) (permanent)
(replacement) 37.80
dual-chamber device (initial)
37.83
replacement 37.87
resynchronization device
▶(biventricular pacemak-
er) (BiV pacemaker)◀
(CRT-P)
device only (initial) (replacement) 00.53

☑ Additional Digit Required — Refer to the Tabular List for Digit Selection   ▽ Subterms under main terms may continue to next column or page

28 — Volume 3 • October 2006   ▶◀ Revised Text   ● New Line   ▲ Revised Code   *2007 ICD-9-CM*

Implant, implantation — *continued*
pacemaker — *continued*
  cardiac — *continued*
    resynchronization device —
      continued
      total system (device and one
        or more leads) 00.50
      transvenous lead into left
        ventricular coronary
        venous system 00.52
    single-chamber device (initial)
      37.81
      rate responsive 37.82
      replacement 37.85
        rate responsive 37.86
    temporary transvenous pace-
      maker system 37.78
      during and immediately fol-
        lowing cardiac surgery
        39.64
carotid sinus 39.8
diaphragm 34.85
gastric 04.92 ●
intracranial — *see* Implant, neurostimulator, intracranial
neural — *see* Implant, neurostimulator, by site
peripheral nerve — *see* Implant,
  neurostimulator, peripheral
  nerve
spine — *see* Implant, neurostimulator, spine
pancreas (duct) 52.96
penis, prosthesis (internal)
  inflatable 64.97
  non-inflatable 64.95
port, vascular access device 86.07
premaxilla 76.68
progesterone (subdermal) 99.23
prosthesis, prosthetic device
  acetabulum (Aufranc-Turner) 81.52
  ankle (total) 81.56
  arm (bioelectric) (cineplastic)
    (kineplastic) 84.44
  breast (Cronin) (Dow-Corning)
    (Perras-Pappillon) (bilateral)
    85.54
    unilateral 85.53
  cardiac support device (CSD) (Cor-
    Cap™) 37.41
  cochlear 20.96
    channel (single) 20.97
    multiple 20.98
  extremity (bioelectric) (cineplastic)
    (kineplastic) 84.40
    lower 84.48
    upper 84.44
  fallopian tube (Mulligan hood)
    (stent) 66.93
  femoral head (Austin-Moore) (bipo-
    lar) (Eicher) (Thompson)
    81.52
    revision NOS 81.53
      acetabular and femoral com-
        ponents (total) 00.70
      acetabular component only
        00.71
      acetabular liner and/or
        femoral head only
        00.73
      femoral component only
        00.72
      femoral head only and/or
        acetabular liner
        00.73
      partial
        acetabular component
          only 00.71
        acetabular liner and/or
          femoral head only
          00.73
        femoral component only
          00.72
        femoral head only and/or
          acetabular liner
          00.73

Implant, implantation — *continued*
prosthesis, prosthetic device — *continued*
  femoral head — *continued*
    revision — *continued*
      total (acetabular and femoral
        components) 00.70
  joint (Swanson type) NEC 81.96
    ankle (total) 81.56
    carpocarpal, carpometacarpal
      81.74
    elbow (total) 81.84
    finger 81.71
    hand (metacarpophalangeal)
      (interphalangeal) 81.71
    hip (partial) 81.52
      revision NOS 81.53
        acetabular and femoral
          components (total)
          00.70
        acetabular component
          only 00.71
        acetabular liner and/or
          femoral head only
          00.73
        femoral component only
          00.72
        femoral head only and/or
          acetabular liner
          00.73
        partial
          acetabular component
            only 00.71
          acetabular liner
            and/or femoral
            head only 00.73
          femoral component on-
            ly 00.72
          femoral head only
            and/or acetabu-
            lar liner 00.73
        total (acetabular and
          femoral compo-
          nents) 00.70
      total 81.51
      revision (acetabular and
        femoral compo-
        nents) 00.70
    interphalangeal 81.71
    knee (partial) (total) 81.54
      revision NOS 81.55
        femoral component 00.82
        partial
          femoral component
            00.82
          patellar component
            00.83
          tibial component 00.81
          tibial insert 00.84
        patellar component 00.83
        tibial component 00.81
        tibial insert 00.84
        total (all components)
          00.80
    metacarpophalangeal 81.71
    shoulder (partial) 81.81
      total 81.80
    spine NEC 84.59
      interspinous process decom-
        pression device 84.58
    toe 81.57
      for hallux valgus repair
        77.59
    wrist (partial) 81.74
      total 81.73
  leg (bioelectric) (cineplastic) (kine-
    plastic) 84.48
  lens 13.91 ●
  outflow tract (heart) (gusset type)
    in
      pulmonary valvuloplasty
        35.26
      total repair of tetralogy of
        Fallot 35.81
  penis (internal) (non-inflatable)
    64.95

Implant, implantation — *continued*
prosthesis, prosthetic device — *continued*
  penis — *continued*
    inflatable (internal) 64.97
    skin (dermal regenerative) (matrix)
      86.67
    testicular (bilateral) (unilateral)
      62.7
  pulsation balloon (phase-shift) 37.61
  pump, infusion 86.06
  radial artery 36.19
  radioactive isotope 92.27
  radium (radon) 92.27
  retinal attachment 14.41
    with buckling 14.41
  Rickham reservoir 02.2
  silicone
    breast (bilateral) 85.54
      unilateral 85.53
    skin (for filling of defect) 86.02
      for augmentation NEC 86.89
  stimoceiver — *see* Implant, neurostim-
    ulator, by site
  subdural
    grids 02.93
    strips 02.93
  Swanson prosthesis (joint) (silastic)
    NEC 81.96
    carpocarpal, carpometacarpal
      81.74
    finger 81.71
    hand (metacarpophalangeal) (inter-
      phalangeal) 81.71
    interphalangeal 81.71
    knee (partial) (total) 81.54
      revision 81.55
    metacarpophalangeal 81.71
    toe 81.57
      for hallux valgus repair 77.59
    wrist (partial) 81.74
      total 81.73
  systemic arteries into myocardium
    (Vineberg type operation) 36.2
  Tandem™ heart 37.68
  telescope (IMT) (miniature) 13.91 ●
  testicular prosthesis (bilateral) (unilat-
    eral) 62.7
  tissue expander (skin) NEC 86.93
    breast 85.95
  tissue mandril (for vascular graft)
    39.99
    with
      blood vessel repair 39.56
      vascular bypass or shunt — *see*
        Bypass, vascular
  tooth (bud) (germ) 23.5
    prosthetic 23.6
  umbrella, vena cava 38.7
  ureters into
    bladder 56.74
    intestine 56.71
      external diversion 56.51
    skin 56.61
  urethra
    for repair of urinary stress inconti-
      nence
      collagen 59.72
      fat 59.72
      polytef 59.72
  urethral sphincter, artificial (inflat-
    able) 58.93
  urinary sphincter, artificial (inflatable)
    58.93
  vascular access device 86.07
  vitreous (silicone) 14.75
    for retinal reattachment 14.41
      with buckling 14.41
  vocal cord(s) (paraglottic) 31.98
  X Stop™ 84.58 ●
Implosion (psychologic desensitization)
  94.33
Incision (and drainage)
  with
    exploration — *see* Exploration

Incision — *continued*
  with — *continued*
    removal of foreign body — *see* Re-
      moval, foreign body
  abdominal wall 54.0
    as operative approach — *omit code*
  abscess (*see also* Incision, by site)
    appendix 47.2
      with appendectomy 47.09
        laparoscopic 47.01
    extraperitoneal 54.0
    ischiorectal 49.01
    lip 27.0
    omental 54.19
    perianal 49.01
    perigastric 54.19
    perisplenic 54.19
    peritoneal NEC 54.19
      pelvic (female) 70.12
    retroperitoneal 54.0
    sclera 12.89
    skin 86.04
    subcutaneous tissue 86.04
    subdiaphragmatic 54.19
    subhepatic 54.19
    subphrenic 54.19
    vas deferens 63.6
  adrenal gland 07.41
  alveolus, alveolar bone 24.0
  antecubital fossa 86.09
  anus NEC 49.93
    fistula 49.11
    septum 49.91
  appendix 47.2
  artery 38.00
    abdominal 38.06
    aorta (arch) (ascending) (de-
      scending) 38.04
    head and neck NEC 38.02
    intracranial NEC 38.01
    lower limb 38.08
    thoracic NEC 38.05
    upper limb 38.03
  atrium (heart) 37.11
  auditory canal or meatus, external
    18.02
  auricle 18.09
  axilla 86.09
  Bartholin's gland or cyst 71.22
  bile duct (with T or Y tube insertion)
    NEC 51.59
    for
      exploration 51.59
      relief of obstruction 51.49
    common (exploratory) 51.51
      for
        relief of obstruction NEC
          51.42
        removal of calculus 51.41
  bladder 57.19
    neck (transurethral) 57.91
    percutaneous suprapubic (closed)
      57.17
    suprapubic NEC 57.18
  blood vessel (*see also* Angiotomy)
    38.00
  bone 77.10
    alveolus, alveolar 24.0
    carpals, metacarpals 77.14
    clavicle 77.11
    facial 76.09
    femur 77.15
    fibula 77.17
    humerus 77.12
    patella 77.16
    pelvic 77.19
    phalanges (foot) (hand) 77.19
    radius 77.13
    scapula 77.11
    skull 01.24
    specified site NEC 77.19
    tarsals, metatarsals 77.18
    thorax (ribs) (sternum) 77.11
    tibia 77.17
    ulna 77.13
    vertebrae 77.19

☑ Additional Digit Required — Refer to the Tabular List for Digit Selection   ▽ Subterms under main terms may continue to next column or page

2007 ICD-9-CM   ▶◀ Revised Text   ● New Line   ▲ Revised Code   October 2006 · Volume 3 — 29

Incision — *continued*
brain 01.39
  cortical adhesions 02.91
breast (skin) 85.0
  with removal of tissue expander 85.96
bronchus 33.0
buccal space 27.0
bulbourethral gland 58.91
bursa 83.03
  hand 82.03
  pharynx 29.0
carotid body 39.8
cerebral (meninges) 01.39
  epidural or extradural space 01.24
  subarachnoid or subdural space 01.31
cerebrum 01.39
cervix 69.95
  to
    assist delivery 73.93
    replace inverted uterus 75.93
chalazion 08.09
  with removal of capsule 08.21
cheek 86.09
chest wall (for extrapleural drainage) (for removal of foreign body) 34.01
  as operative approach — *omit code*
common bile duct (for exploration) 51.51
  for
    relief of obstruction 51.42
    removal of calculus 51.41
common wall between posterior left atrium and coronary sinus (with roofing of resultant defect with patch graft) 35.82
conjunctiva 10.1
cornea 11.1
  radial (refractive) 11.75
cranial sinus 01.21
craniobuccal pouch 07.72
cul-de-sac 70.12
cyst
  dentigerous 24.0
  radicular (apical) (periapical) 24.0
Dührssen's (cervix, to assist delivery) 73.93
duodenum 45.01
ear
  external 18.09
  inner 20.79
  middle 20.23
endocardium 37.11
endolymphatic sac 20.79
epididymis 63.92
epidural space, cerebral 01.24
epigastric region 54.0
  intra-abdominal 54.19
esophagus, esophageal NEC 42.09
  web 42.01
exploratory — *see* Exploration
extradural space (cerebral) 01.24
extrapleural 34.01
eyebrow 08.09
eyelid 08.09
  margin (trichiasis) 08.01
face 86.09
fallopian tube 66.01
fascia 83.09
  with division 83.14
    hand 82.12
  hand 82.09
    with division 82.12
fascial compartments, head and neck 27.0
fistula, anal 49.11
flank 54.0
furuncle — *see* Incision, by site
gallbladder 51.04
gingiva 24.0
gluteal 86.09
groin region (abdominal wall) (inguinal) 54.0
  skin 86.09

Incision — *continued*
groin region — *continued*
  subcutaneous tissue 86.09
gum 24.0
hair follicles 86.09
heart 37.10
  valve — *see* Valvulotomy
hematoma (*see also* Incision, by site)
  axilla 86.04
  broad ligament 69.98
  ear 18.09
  episiotomy site 75.91
  fossa (superficial) NEC 86.04
  groin region (abdominal wall) (inguinal) 54.0
    skin 86.04
    subcutaneous tissue 86.04
  laparotomy site 54.12
  mediastinum 34.1
  perineum (female) 71.09
    male 86.04
  popliteal space 86.04
  scrotum 61.0
  skin 86.04
  space of Retzius 59.19
  subcutaneous tissue 86.04
  vagina (cuff) 70.14
    episiotomy site 75.91
    obstetrical NEC 75.92
hepatic ducts 51.59
hordeolum 08.09
hygroma (*see also* Incision, by site)
  cystic 40.0
hymen 70.11
hypochondrium 54.0
  intra-abdominal 54.19
hypophysis 07.72
iliac fossa 54.0
infratemporal fossa 27.0
ingrown nail 86.09
intestine 45.00
  large 45.03
  small 45.02
intracerebral 01.39
intracranial (epidural space) (extradural space) 01.24
  subarachnoid or subdural space 01.31
intraperitoneal 54.19
ischiorectal tissue 49.02
  abscess 49.01
joint structures (*see also* Arthrotomy) 80.10
kidney 55.01
  pelvis 55.11
labia 71.09
lacrimal
  canaliculus 09.52
  gland 09.0
  passage NEC 09.59
  punctum 09.51
  sac 09.53
larynx NEC 31.3
ligamentum flavum (spine) — *omit code*
liver 50.0
lung 33.1
lymphangioma 40.0
lymphatic structure (channel) (node) (vessel) 40.0
mastoid 20.21
mediastinum 34.1
meibomian gland 08.09
meninges (cerebral) 01.31
  spinal 03.09
midpalmar space 82.04
mouth NEC 27.92
  floor 27.0
muscle 83.02
  with division 83.19
    hand 82.19
  hand 82.02
    with division 82.19
myocardium 37.11
nailbed or nailfold 86.09
nasolacrimal duct (stricture) 09.59

Incision — *continued*
neck 86.09
nerve (cranial) (peripheral) NEC 04.04
  root (spinal) 03.1
nose 21.1
omentum 54.19
orbit (*see also* Orbitotomy) 16.09
ovary 65.09
  laparoscopic 65.01
palate 27.1
palmar space (middle) 82.04
pancreas 52.09
pancreatic sphincter 51.82
  endoscopic 51.85
parapharyngeal (oral) (transcervical) 28.0
paronychia 86.09
parotid
  gland or duct 26.0
  space 27.0
pelvirectal tissue 48.81
penis 64.92
perianal (skin) (tissue) 49.02
  abscess 49.01
perigastric 54.19
perineum (female) 71.09
  male 86.09
peripheral vessels
  lower limb
    artery 38.08
    vein 38.09
  upper limb (artery) (vein) 38.03
periprostatic tissue 60.81
perirectal tissue 48.81
perirenal tissue 59.09
perisplenic 54.19
peritoneum 54.95
  by laparotomy 54.19
  pelvic (female) 70.12
    male 54.19
periureteral tissue 59.09
periurethral tissue 58.91
perivesical tissue 59.19
petrous pyramid (air cells) (apex) (mastoid) 20.22
pharynx, pharyngeal (bursa) 29.0
  space, lateral 27.0
pilonidal sinus (cyst) 86.03
pineal gland 07.52
pituitary (gland) 07.72
pleura NEC 34.09
popliteal space 86.09
postzygomatic space 27.0
pouch of Douglas 70.12
prostate (perineal approach) (transurethral approach) 60.0
pterygopalatine fossa 27.0
pulp canal (tooth) 24.0
Rathke's pouch 07.72
rectovaginal septum 48.81
rectum 48.0
  stricture 48.91
renal pelvis 55.11
retroperitoneum 54.0
retropharyngeal (oral) (transcervical) 28.0
salivary gland or duct 26.0
sclera 12.89
scrotum 61.0
sebaceous cyst 86.04
seminal vesicle 60.72
sinus — *see* Sinusotomy
Skene's duct or gland 71.09
skin 86.09
  with drainage 86.04
  breast 85.0
  cardiac pacemaker pocket, new site 37.79
  ear 18.09
  nose 21.1
  subcutaneous tunnel for pulse generator lead wire 86.99
    with initial procedure — *omit code*
  thalamic stimulator pulse generator pocket, new site 86.09

Incision — *continued*
skin — *continued*
  thalamic stimulator pulse generator pocket, new site — *continued*
    with initial insertion of battery package — *omit code*
  tunnel, subcutaneous for pulse generator lead wire 86.99
    with initial procedure — *omit code*
skull (bone) 01.24
soft tissue NEC 83.09
  with division 83.19
    hand 82.19
  hand 82.09
    with division 82.19
space of Retzius 59.19
spermatic cord 63.93
sphincter of Oddi 51.82
  endoscopic 51.85
spinal
  cord 03.09
  nerve root 03.1
spleen 41.2
stomach 43.0
stye 08.09
subarachnoid space, cerebral 01.31
subcutaneous tissue 86.09
  with drainage 86.04
  tunnel
    esophageal 42.86
      with anastomosis — *see* Anastomosis, esophagus, antesternal
    pulse generator lead wire 86.99
      with initial procedure — *omit code*
subdiaphragmatic space 54.19
subdural space, cerebral 01.31
sublingual space 27.0
submandibular space 27.0
submaxillary 86.09
  with drainage 86.04
submental space 27.0
subphrenic space 54.19
supraclavicular fossa 86.09
  with drainage 86.04
sweat glands, skin 86.04
temporal pouches 27.0
tendon (sheath) 83.01
  with division 83.13
    hand 82.11
  hand 82.01
    with division 82.11
testis 62.0
thenar space 82.04
thymus 07.92
thyroid (field) (gland) NEC 06.09
  postoperative 06.02
tongue NEC 25.94
  for tongue tie 25.91
tonsil 28.0
trachea NEC 31.3
tunica vaginalis 61.0
umbilicus 54.0
urachal cyst 54.0
ureter 56.2
urethra 58.0
uterus (corpus) 68.0
  for termination of pregnancy 74.91
  cervix 69.95
  septum (congenital) 68.22
uvula 27.71
vagina (cuff) (septum) (stenosis) 70.14
  for
    incisional hematoma (episiotomy) 75.91
    obstetrical hematoma NEC 75.92
  pelvic abscess 70.12
vas deferens 63.6
vein 38.00
  abdominal 38.07
  head and neck NEC 38.02
  intracranial NEC 38.01

Incision — *continued*
vein — *continued*
lower limb 38.09
thoracic NEC 38.05
upper limb 38.03
vertebral column 03.09
vulva 71.09
obstetrical 75.92
web, esophageal 42.01
Incudectomy NEC 19.3
with
stapedectomy (*see also* Stapedectomy) 19.19
tympanoplasty — *see* Tympanoplasty
Incudopexy 19.19
Incudostapediopexy 19.19
with incus replacement 19.11
Indentation, sclera, for buckling — *see also* Buckling, scleral 14.49
Indicator dilution flow measurement 89.68
Induction
abortion
by
D and C 69.01
insertion of prostaglandin suppository 96.49
intra-amniotic injection (prostaglandin) (saline) 75.0
labor
medical 73.4
surgical 73.01
intra- and extra-amniotic injection 73.1
stripping of membranes 73.1
Inflation
belt wrap 93.99
Eustachian tube 20.8
fallopian tube 66.8
with injection of therapeutic agent 66.95
Infolding, sclera, for buckling — *see also* Buckling, scleral 14.49
Infraction, turbinates (nasal) 21.62
Infundibulectomy
hypophyseal (*see also* Hypophysectomy, partial) 07.63
ventricle (heart) (right) 35.34
in total repair of tetralogy of Fallot 35.81
Infusion (intra-arterial) (intravenous)
Abciximab 99.20
antibiotic
oxazolidinone class 00.14
antineoplastic agent (chemotherapeutic) 99.25
biological response modifier [BRM] 99.28
cintredekin besudotox 99.28 ●
high-dose interleukin-2 00.15
low-dose interleukin-2 99.28
biological response modifier [BRM], antineoplastic agent 99.28
cintredekin besudotox 99.28 ●
high-dose interleukin-2 00.15
low-dose interleukin-2 99.28
cancer chemotherapy agent NEC 99.25
cintredekin besudotox 99.28 ●
drotrecogin alfa (activated) 00.11
electrolytes 99.18
enzymes, thrombolytic (streptokinase) (tissue plasminogen activator) (TPA) (urokinase)
direct coronary artery 36.04
intravenous 99.10
Eptifibatide 99.20
GP IIb/IIIa inhibitor 99.20
hormone substance NEC 99.24
human B-type natriuretic peptide (hBNP) 00.13
immunosuppressive antibody therapy 00.18
nesiritide 00.13

Infusion — *continued*
neuroprotective agent 99.75
nimodipine 99.75
nutritional substance — *see* Nutrition
platelet inhibitor
direct coronary artery 36.04
intravenous 99.20
Proleukin (low-dose) 99.28
high-dose 00.15
prophylactic substance NEC 99.29
radioimmunoconjugate 92.28
radioimmunotherapy 92.28
radioisotope (liquid brachytherapy) (liquid I-125) 92.20
recombinant protein 00.11
reteplase 99.10
therapeutic substance NEC 99.29
thrombolytic agent (enzyme) (streptokinase) 99.10
with percutaneous transluminal angioplasty

Note: Also use 00.40, 00.41, 00.42, or 00.43 to show the total number of vessels treated.

coronary 00.66
non-coronary vessel(s) 39.50
specified site NEC 39.50
direct intracoronary artery 36.04
tirofiban (HCl) 99.20
vaccine
tumor 99.28
vasopressor 00.17
Injection (into) (hypodermically) (intramuscularly) (intravenously) (acting locally or systemically)
Actinomycin D, for cancer chemotherapy 99.25
adhesion barrier substance 99.77
alcohol
nerve — *see* Injection, nerve
spinal 03.8
anterior chamber, eye (air) (liquid) (medication) 12.92
antibiotic 99.21
oxazolidinone class 00.14
anticoagulant 99.19
anti-D (Rhesus) globulin 99.11
antidote NEC 99.16
anti-infective NEC 99.22
antineoplastic agent (chemotherapeutic) NEC 99.25
biological response modifier [BRM] 99.28
cintredekin besudotox 99.28 ●
high-dose interleukin-2 00.15
low-dose interleukin-2 99.28
antivenin 99.16
barrier substance, adhesion 99.77
BCG
for chemotherapy 99.25
vaccine 99.33
biological response modifier [BRM], antineoplastic agent 99.28
cintredekin besudotox 99.28 ●
high-dose interleukin-2 00.15
low-dose interleukin-2 99.28
bone marrow 41.92
transplant — *see* Transplant, bone, marrow
breast (therapeutic agent) 85.92
inert material (silicone) (bilateral) 85.52
unilateral 85.51
bursa (therapeutic agent) 83.96
hand 82.94
cancer chemotherapeutic agent 99.25
caudal — *see* Injection, spinal
cintredekin besudotox 99.28 ●
cortisone 99.23
costochondral junction 81.92
dinoprost-tromethine, intraamniotic 75.0
ear, with alcohol 20.72
electrolytes 99.18

Injection — *continued*
enzymes, thrombolytic (streptokinase) (tissue plasminogen activator) (TPA) (urokinase)
direct coronary artery 36.04
intravenous 99.10
epidural, spinal — *see* Injection, spinal
esophageal varices or blood vessel (endoscopic) (sclerosing agent) 42.33
Eustachian tube (inert material) 20.8
eye (orbit) (retrobulbar) 16.91
anterior chamber 12.92
subconjunctival 10.91
fascia 83.98
hand 82.96
gamma globulin 99.14
ganglion, sympathetic 05.39
ciliary 12.79
paravertebral stellate 05.39
gel, adhesion barrier — *see* Injection, adhesion barrier substance
globulin
anti-D (Rhesus) 99.11
gamma 99.14
Rh immune 99.11
heart 37.92
heavy metal antagonist 99.16
hemorrhoids (sclerosing agent) 49.42
hormone NEC 99.24
human B-type natriuretic peptide (hBNP) 00.13
immune sera 99.14
inert material — *see* Implant, inert material
inner ear, for destruction 20.72
insulin 99.17
intervertebral space for herniated disc 80.52
intra-amniotic
for induction of
abortion 75.0
labor 73.1
intrathecal — *see* Injection, spinal
joint (therapeutic agent) 81.92
temporomandibular 76.96
kidney (cyst) (therapeutic substance) NEC 55.96
larynx 31.0
ligament (joint) (therapeutic substance) 81.92
liver 50.94
lung, for surgical collapse 33.32
Methotrexate, for cancer chemotherapy 99.25
nerve (cranial) (peripheral) 04.80
agent NEC 04.89
alcohol 04.2
anesthetic for analgesia 04.81
for operative anesthesia — *omit code*
neurolytic 04.2
phenol 04.2
laryngeal (external) (recurrent) (superior) 31.91
optic 16.91
sympathetic 05.39
alcohol 05.32
anesthetic for analgesia 05.31
neurolytic agent 05.32
phenol 05.32
nesiritide 00.13
neuroprotective agent 99.75
nimodipine 99.75
orbit 16.91
pericardium 37.93
peritoneal cavity
air 54.96
locally-acting therapeutic substance 54.97
platelet inhibitor
direct coronary artery 36.04
intravenous 99.20
prophylactic substance NEC 99.29
prostate 60.92

Injection — *continued*
radioimmunoconjugate 92.28
radioimmunotherapy 92.28
radioisotopes (intracavitary) (intravenous) 92.28
renal pelvis (cyst) 55.96
retrobulbar (therapeutic substance) 16.91
for anesthesia — *omit code*
Rh immune globulin 99.11
RhoGAM 99.11
sclerosing agent NEC 99.29
esophageal varices (endoscopic) 42.33
hemorrhoids 49.42
pleura 34.92
treatment of malignancy (cytotoxic agent) 34.92 [99.25]
with tetracycline 34.92 [99.21]
varicose vein 39.92
vein NEC 39.92
semicircular canals, for destruction 20.72
silicone — *see* Implant, inert material
skin (sclerosing agent) (filling material) 86.02
soft tissue 83.98
hand 82.96
spinal (canal) NEC 03.92
alcohol 03.8
anesthetic agent for analgesia 03.91
for operative anesthesia — *omit code*
contrast material (for myelogram) 87.21
destructive agent NEC 03.8
neurolytic agent NEC 03.8
phenol 03.8
proteolytic enzyme (chymopapain) (chymodiactin) 80.52
saline (hypothermic) 03.92
steroid 03.92
spinal nerve root (intrathecal) — *see* Injection, spinal
steroid NEC 99.23
subarachnoid, spinal — *see* Injection, spinal
subconjunctival 10.91
tendon 83.97
hand 82.95
testis 62.92
therapeutic agent NEC 99.29
thoracic cavity 34.92
thrombolytic agent (enzyme) (streptokinase) 99.10
with percutaneous transluminal angioplasty

Note: Also use 00.40, 00.41, 00.42, or 00.43 to show the total number of vessels treated.

coronary 00.66
non-coronary vessel(s) 39.50
specified site NEC 39.50
direct intracoronary artery 36.04
trachea 31.94
tranquilizer 99.26
tunica vaginalis (with aspiration) 61.91
tympanum 20.94
urethra (inert material)
for repair of urinary stress incontinence
collagen implant 59.72
endoscopic injection of implant 59.72
fat implant 59.72
polytef implant 59.72
vaccine
tumor 99.28
varices, esophagus (endoscopic) (sclerosing agent) 42.33
varicose vein (sclerosing agent) 39.92
esophagus (endoscopic) 42.33
vestibule, for destruction 20.72

Incision — Injection

☑ Additional Digit Required — Refer to the Tabular List for Digit Selection   ▽ Subterms under main terms may continue to next column or page

2007 ICD-9-CM   ▶◀ Revised Text   ● New Line   ▲ Revised Code   **October 2006 · Volume 3 — 31**

☑ Additional Digit Required — Refer to the Tabular List for Digit Selection   ▽ Subterms under main terms may continue to next column or page

32 — Volume 3 • October 2006   ▶◀ Revised Text   ● New Line   ▲ Revised Code   *2007 ICD-9-CM*

☑ Additional Digit Required — Refer to the Tabular List for Digit Selection   ▽ Subterms under main terms may continue to next column or page

2007 ICD-9-CM   ▶◀ Revised Text   ● New Line   ▲ Revised Code   October 2006 · Volume 3 — 33

Insertion — *continued*
  prosthesis, prosthetic device — *continued*
    spine — *continued*
      artificial disc, — *continued*
        lumbar, lumbosacral — *continued*
          total 84.65
          thoracic (partial) (total) 84.63
        other device 84.59
    testicular (bilateral) (unilateral) 62.7
    toe 81.57
      hallux valgus repair 77.59
  pseudophakos (*see also* Insertion, lens) 13.70
  pump, infusion 86.06
  radioactive isotope 92.27
  radium 92.27
  radon seeds 92.27
  Reuter bobbin (with intubation) 20.01
  Rickham reservoir 02.2
  Rosen prosthesis (for urinary incontinence) 59.79
  Scribner shunt 39.93
  Sengstaken-Blakemore tube 96.06
  sensor ▶(lead)◀
    intra-arterial, for continuous blood gas monitoring 89.60
    intracardiac hemodynamic monitoring 00.56 ●
  sieve, vena cava 38.7
  skeletal muscle stimulator 83.92
  skull
    plate 02.05
    stereotactic frame 93.59
    tongs (Barton) (caliper) (Garder Wells) (Vinke) (with synchronous skeletal traction) 02.94
  spacer (cement) (joint) 84.56
    spine 84.51
  sphenoidal electrodes 02.96
  spine
    bone void filler
      that with kyphoplasty 81.66
      that with vertebroplasty 81.65
    cage (BAK) 84.51
    interbody spinal fusion device 84.51
    interspinous process decompression device 84.58
    non-fusion stabilization device ● 84.59 ●
    spacer 84.51
  Spitz-Holter valve 02.2
  Steinmann pin 93.44
    with reduction of fracture or dislocation — *see* Reduction, fracture *and* Reduction, dislocation
  stent(s) (stent graft)
    artery (bare) (bonded) (drug-coated) (non-drug-eluting)

Note — Also use 00.40, 00.41, 00.42, or 00.43 to show the total number of vessels treated. ▶Use code 00.44 once to show procedure on a bifurcated vessel.◀ In addition, use 00.45, 00.46, 00.47, or 00.48 to show the number of vascular stents inserted.

      basilar 00.64
      carotid 00.63
      cerebrovascular
        cerebral (intracranial) 00.65
        precerebral (extracranial) 00.64
          carotid 00.63
      coronary (bare) (bonded) (drug-coated) (non-drug-eluting) 36.06
        drug-eluting 36.07
      extracranial 00.64
        carotid 00.63
        intracranial 00.65

Insertion — *continued*
  stent(s) — *continued*
    artery — *continued*
      non-coronary vessel
        basilar 00.64
        carotid 00.63
        extracranial 00.64
        intracranial 00.65
        peripheral 39.90
          bare, drug-coated 39.90
          drug-eluting 00.55
        vertebral 00.64
    bile duct 51.43
      endoscopic 51.87
      percutaneous transhepatic 51.98
    coronary (artery) (bare) (bonded) (drug-coated) (non-drug-eluting) 36.06

Note — Also use 00.40, 00.41, 00.42, or 00.43 to show the total number of vessels treated. ▶Use code 00.44 once to show procedure on a bifurcated vessel.◀ In addition, use 00.45, 00.46, 00.47, or 00.48 to show the number of vascular stents inserted.

      drug-eluting 36.07
    esophagus (endoscopic) (fluoroscopic) 42.81
    mesenteric 39.90 ●
      bare, drug-coated 39.90 ●
      drug-eluting 00.55 ●
    non-coronary vessel

Note — Also use 00.40, 00.41, 00.42, or 00.43 to show the total number of vessels treated. ▶Use code 00.44 once to show procedure on a bifurcated vessel.◀ In addition, use 00.45, 00.46, 00.47, or 00.48 to show the number of vascular stents inserted.

      with angioplasty or atherectomy 39.50
      with bypass — *omit code*
      basilar 00.64
      carotid 00.63
      extracranial 00.64
      intracranial 00.65
      mesenteric 39.90 ●
        bare, drug-coated 39.90 ●
        drug-eluting 00.55 ●
      peripheral 39.90
        bare, drug-coated 39.90
        drug-eluting 00.55
      renal 39.90 ●
        bare, drug-coated 39.90 ●
        drug-eluting 00.55 ●
      vertebral 00.64
    pancreatic duct 52.92
      endoscopic 52.93
    peripheral vessel 39.90

Note — Also use 00.40, 00.41, 00.42, or 00.43 to show the total number of vessels treated. ▶Use code 00.44 once to show procedure on a bifurcated vessel.◀ In addition, use 00.45, 00.46, 00.47, or 00.48 to show the number of vascular stents inserted.

      bare, drug-coated 39.90
      drug-eluting 00.55
    precerebral 00.64

Note — Also use 00.40, 00.41, 00.42, or 00.43 to show the total number of vessels treated. ▶Use code 00.44 once to show procedure on a bifurcated vessel.◀ In addition, use 00.45, 00.46, 00.47, or 00.48 to show the number of vascular stents inserted.

      renal 39.90 ●
        bare, drug-coated 39.90 ●
        drug-eluting 00.55 ●

Insertion — *continued*
  stent(s) — *continued*
    subclavian 39.90

Note — Also use 00.40, 00.41, 00.42, or 00.43 to show the total number of vessels treated. ▶Use code 00.44 once to show procedure on a bifurcated vessel.◀ In addition, use 00.45, 00.46, 00.47, or 00.48 to show the number of vascular stents inserted.

      bare, drug-coated 39.90
      drug-eluting 00.55
    tracheobronchial 96.05
    vertebral 00.64

Note — Also use 00.40, 00.41, 00.42, or 00.43 to show the total number of vessels treated. ▶Use code 00.44 once to show procedure on a bifurcated vessel.◀ In addition, use 00.45, 00.46, 00.47, or 00.48 to show the number of vascular stents inserted.

    stimoceiver — *see* Implant, neurostimulator, by site
    stimulator for bone growth — *see* category 78.9 ☑
    subdural
      grids 02.93
      strips 02.93
    suppository
      prostaglandin (for abortion) 96.49
      vagina 96.49
    Swan-Ganz catheter (pulmonary) 89.64
    tampon
      esophagus 96.06
      uterus 69.91
      vagina 96.14
        after delivery or abortion 75.8
    Tandem™ heart 37.68
    telescope (IMT) (miniature) 13.91 ●
    testicular prosthesis (bilateral) (unilateral) 62.7
    tissue expander (skin) NEC 86.93
      breast 85.95
    tissue mandril (peripheral vessel) (Dacron) (Spark's type) 39.99
      with
        blood vessel repair 39.56
        vascular bypass or shunt — *see* Bypass, vascular
    tongs, skull (with synchronous skeletal traction) 02.94
    totally implanted device for bone growth (invasive) — *see* category 78.9 ☑
    tube (*see also* Catheterization and Intubation)
      bile duct 51.43
        endoscopic 51.87
      chest 34.04
        revision (with lysis of adhesions) 34.04
      endotracheal 96.04
      esophagus (nonoperative) (Sengstaken) 96.06
        permanent (silicone) (Souttar) 42.81
      feeding
        esophageal 42.81
        gastric 96.6
        nasogastric 96.6
      gastric
        by gastrostomy — *see* category 43.1 ☑
        for
          decompression, intestinal 96.07
          feeding 96.6
      intercostal (with water seal), for drainage 34.04
        revision (with lysis of adhesions) 34.04
      Miller-Abbott (for intestinal decompression) 96.08
      nasobiliary (drainage) 51.86

Insertion — *continued*
  tube (*see also* Catheterization and Intubation) — *continued*
    nasogastric (for intestinal decompression) NEC 96.07
    naso-intestinal 96.08
    nasopancreatic drainage (endoscopic) 52.97
    pancreatic duct 52.92
      endoscopic 52.93
    rectum 96.09
    stomach (nasogastric) (for intestinal decompression) NEC 96.07
      for feeding 96.6
    tracheobronchial 96.05
  umbrella device
    atrial septum (King-Mills) 35.52
    vena cava (Mobitz-Uddin) 38.7
  ureteral stent (transurethral) 59.8
    with ureterotomy 59.8 *[56.2]*
  urinary sphincter, artificial (AUS) (inflatable) 58.93
  vaginal mold 96.15
  valve
    bronchus 33.71 ●
    Holter 02.2
    Hufnagel — *see* Replacement, heart valve
    pharyngeal (artificial) 31.75
    Spitz-Holter 02.2
    vas deferens 63.95
  vascular access device, totally implantable 86.07
  vena cava sieve or umbrella 38.7
  Vinke tongs (skull) (with synchronous skeletal traction) 02.94
  X Stop™ 84.58 ●
Instillation
  bladder 96.49
  digestive tract, except gastric gavage 96.43
  genitourinary NEC 96.49
  radioisotope (intracavitary) (intravenous) 92.28
  thoracic cavity 34.92 ●
Insufflation
  Eustachian tube 20.8
  fallopian tube (air) (dye) (gas) (saline) 66.8
    for radiography — *see* Hysterosalpingography
    therapeutic substance 66.95
  lumbar retroperitoneal, bilateral 88.15
Intercricothyroidotomy (for assistance in breathing) 31.1
Intermittent positive pressure breathing (IPPB) 93.91
Interposition operation
  antesternal or antethoracic NEC (*see also* Anastomosis, esophagus, antesternal, with, interposition) 42.68
  esophageal reconstruction (intrathoracic) (retrosternal) NEC (*see also* Anastomosis, esophagus, with, interposition) 42.58
  uterine suspension 69.21
Interrogation
  cardioverter-defibrillator, automatic (AICD)
    with catheter based invasive ● electrophysiologic testing ● 37.26 ●
    with NIPS (arrhythmia induction) 37.20 ▲
    interrogation only (bedside device check) 89.49
  CRT-D (cardiac resynchronization defibrillator)
    with catheter based invasive ● electrophysiologic testing ● 37.26 ●
    with NIPS (arrhythmia induction) 37.20 ▲

Interrogation — *continued*
  CRT-D — *continued*
    interrogation only (bedside device check) 89.49
  CRT-P (cardiac resynchronization pacemaker)
    with catheter based invasive electrophysiologic testing ● 37.26
    with NIPS (arrhythmia induction) ▲ 37.20
    interrogation only (bedside device check) 89.45
  pacemaker
    with catheter based invasive electrophysiologic testing ● 37.26
    with NIPS (arrhythmia induction) ▲ 37.20
    interrogation only (bedside device check) 89.45
Interruption
  vena cava (inferior) (superior) 38.7
Interview (evaluation) (diagnostic)
  medical, except psychiatric 89.05
    brief (abbreviated history) 89.01
    comprehensive (history and evaluation of new problem) 89.03
    limited (interval history) 89.02
    specified type NEC 89.04
  psychiatric NEC 94.19
    follow-up 94.19
    initial 94.19
    pre-commitment 94.13
Intimectomy 38.10
  abdominal 38.16
  aorta (arch) (ascending) (descending) 38.14
  head and neck NEC 38.12
  intracranial NEC 38.11
  lower limb 38.18
  thoracic NEC 38.15
  upper limb 38.13
Introduction
  orthodontic appliance 24.7
  therapeutic substance (acting locally or systemically) NEC 99.29
    bursa 83.96
      hand 82.94
    fascia 83.98
      hand 82.96
    heart 37.92
    joint 81.92
      temporomandibular 76.96
    ligament (joint) 81.92
    pericardium 37.93
    soft tissue NEC 83.98
      hand 82.96
    tendon 83.97
      hand 82.95
    vein 39.92
Intubation — *see also* Catheterization and Insertion
  bile duct(s) 51.59
    common 51.51
      endoscopic 51.87
    endoscopic 51.87
  esophagus (nonoperative) (Sengstaken) 96.06
    permanent tube (silicone) (Souttar) 42.81
  Eustachian tube 20.8
  intestine (for decompression) 96.08
  lacrimal for
    dilation 09.42
    tear drainage, intranasal 09.81
  larynx 96.05
  nasobiliary (drainage) 51.86
  nasogastric
    for
      decompression, intestinal 96.07
      feeding 96.6
    naso-intestinal 96.08
  nasolacrimal (duct) (with irrigation) 09.44

Intubation — *see also* Catheterization and Insertion — *continued*
  nasopancreatic drainage (endoscopic) 52.97
  respiratory tract NEC 96.05
  small intestine (Miller-Abbott) 96.08
  stomach (nasogastric) (for intestinal decompression) NEC 96.07
    for feeding 96.6
  trachea 96.04
  ventriculocisternal 02.2
Invagination, diverticulum
  gastric 44.69
    laparoscopic 44.68
  pharynx 29.59
  stomach 44.69
    laparoscopic 44.68
Inversion
  appendix 47.99
  diverticulum
    gastric 44.69
      laparoscopic 44.68
    intestine
      large 45.49
        endoscopic 45.43
      small 45.34
    stomach 44.69
      laparoscopic 44.68
  tunica vaginalis 61.49
Ionization, medical 99.27
Iontherapy 99.27
Iontophoresis 99.27
Iridectomy (basal) (buttonhole) (optical) (peripheral) (total) 12.14
  with
    capsulectomy 13.65
    cataract extraction — *see* Extraction, cataract
    filtering operation (for glaucoma) NEC 12.65
    scleral
      fistulization 12.65
      thermocauterization 12.62
      trephination 12.61
Iridencleisis 12.63
Iridesis 12.63
Irido-capsulectomy 13.65
Iridocyclectomy 12.44
Iridocystectomy 12.42
Iridodesis 12.63
Iridoplasty NEC 12.39
Iridosclerectomy 12.65
Iridosclerotomy 12.69
Iridotasis 12.63
Iridotomy 12.12
  by photocoagulation 12.12
  for iris bombé 12.11
  with transfixion 12.11
  specified type NEC 12.12
Iron lung 93.99
Irradiation
  gamma, stereotactic 92.32
Irrigation
  anterior chamber (eye) 12.91
  bronchus NEC 96.56
  canaliculus 09.42
  catheter
    ureter 96.46
    urinary, indwelling NEC 96.48
    vascular 96.57
    ventricular 02.41
    wound 96.58
  cholecystostomy 96.41
  cornea 96.51
    with removal of foreign body 98.21
  corpus cavernosum 64.98
  cystostomy 96.47
  ear (removal of cerumen) 96.52
  enterostomy 96.36
  eye 96.51
    with removal of foreign body 98.21
  gastrostomy 96.36
  lacrimal
    canaliculi 09.42
    punctum 09.41
  muscle 83.02

Irrigation — *continued*
  muscle — *continued*
    hand 82.02
  nasal
    passages 96.53
    sinus 22.00
  nasolacrimal duct 09.43
    with insertion of tube or stent 09.44
  nephrostomy 96.45
  peritoneal 54.25
  pyelostomy 96.45
  rectal 96.39
  stomach 96.33
  tendon (sheath) 83.01
    hand 82.01
  trachea NEC 96.56
  traumatic cataract 13.3
  tube
    biliary NEC 96.41
    nasogastric NEC 96.34
    pancreatic 96.42
  ureterostomy 96.46
  ventricular shunt 02.41
  wound (cleaning) NEC 96.59
Irving operation (tubal ligation) 66.32
Irwin operation — *see also* Osteotomy 77.30
Ischiectomy (partial) 77.89
  total 77.99
Ischiopubiotomy 77.39
Isolation
  after contact with infectious disease 99.84
  ileal loop 45.51
  intestinal segment or pedicle flap
    large 45.52
    small 45.51
Isthmectomy, thyroid — *see also* Thyroidectomy, partial 06.39

J

Jaboulay operation (gastroduodenostomy) 44.39
  laparoscopic 44.38
Janeway operation (permanent gastrostomy) 43.19
Jatene operation (arterial switch) 35.84
Jejunectomy 45.62
Jejunocecostomy 45.93
Jejunocholecystostomy 51.32
Jejunocolostomy 45.93
Jejunoileostomy 45.91
Jejunojejunostomy 45.91
Jejunopexy 46.61
Jejunorrhaphy 46.73
Jejunostomy (feeding) 46.39
  delayed opening 46.31
  loop 46.01
  percutaneous (endoscopic) (PEJ) 46.32
  revision 46.41
Jejunotomy 45.02
Johanson operation (urethral reconstruction) 58.46
Jones operation
  claw toe (transfer of extensor hallucis longus tendon) 77.57
    modified (with arthrodesis) 77.57
  dacryocystorhinostomy 09.81
  hammer toe (interphalangeal fusion) 77.56
  modified (tendon transfer with arthrodesis) 77.57
  repair of peroneal tendon 83.88
Joplin operation (exostectomy with tendon transfer) 77.53

K

Kader operation (temporary gastrostomy) 43.19
Kasai portoenterostomy 51.37
Kaufman operation (for urinary stress incontinence) 59.79
Kazanjiian operation (buccal vestibular sulcus extension) 24.91

Kehr operation (hepatopexy) 50.69
Keller operation (bunionectomy) 77.59
Kelly (-Kennedy) operation (urethrovesical plication) 59.3
Kelly-Stoeckel operation (urethrovesical plication) 59.3
Kelotomy 53.9
Keratectomy (complete) (partial) (superficial) 11.49
  for pterygium 11.39
  with corneal graft 11.32
Keratocentesis (for hyphema) 12.91
Keratomileusis 11.71
Keratophakia 11.72
Keratoplasty (tectonic) (with autograft) (with homograft) 11.60
  lamellar (nonpenetrating) (with homograft) 11.62
    with autograft 11.61
  penetrating (full-thickness) (with homograft) 11.64
    with autograft 11.63
  perforating — *see* Keratoplasty, penetrating
  refractive 11.71
  specified type NEC 11.69
Keratoprosthesis 11.73
Keratotomy (delimiting) (posterior) 11.1
  radial (refractive) 11.75
Kerr operation (low cervical cesarean section) 74.1
Kessler operation (arthroplasty, carpometacarpal joint) 81.74
Kidner operation (excision of accessory navicular bone) (with tendon transfer) 77.98
Killian operation (frontal sinusotomy) 22.41
Kineplasty — *see* Cineplasty
King-Steelquist operation (hind-quarter amputation) 84.19
Kirk operation (amputation through thigh) 84.17
Kockogram (ileal conduitogram) 87.78
Kockoscopy 45.12
Kock pouch
  bowel anastomosis — *omit code*
  continent ileostomy 46.22
  cutaneous uretero-ileostomy 56.51
  ESWL (extracorporeal shockwave lithotripsy) 98.51
  removal, calculus 57.19
  revision, cutaneous uretero-ileostomy 56.52
  urinary diversion procedure 56.51
Kondoleon operation (correction of lymphedema) 40.9
Krause operation (sympathetic denervation) 05.29
Kroener operation (partial salpingectomy) 66.69
Kroenlein operation (lateral orbitotomy) 16.01
Krönig operation (low cervical cesarean section) 74.1
Krukenberg operation (reconstruction of below-elbow amputation) 82.89
Kuhnt-Szymanowski operation (ectropion repair with lid reconstruction) 08.44
Kyphoplasty 81.66

L

Labbe operation (gastrotomy) 43.0
Labiectomy (bilateral) 71.62
  unilateral 71.61
Labyrinthectomy (transtympanic) 20.79
Labyrinthotomy (transtympanic) 20.79
Ladd operation (mobilization of intestine) 54.95
Lagrange operation (iridosclerectomy) 12.65
Lambrinudi operation (triple arthrodesis) 81.12
Laminectomy (decompression) (for exploration) 03.09

Laminectomy — *continued*
  as operative approach — *omit code*
  with
    excision of herniated intervertebral
      disc (nucleus pulposus)
      80.51
    excision of other intraspinal lesion
      (tumor) 03.4
    reopening of site 03.02
Laminography — *see* Radiography
Laminoplasty, expansile 03.09
Laminotomy (decompression) (for exploration) 03.09
  as operative approach — *omit code*
  reopening of site 03.02
Langenbeck operation (cleft palate repair) 27.62
Laparoamnioscopy 75.31
Laparorrhaphy 54.63
Laparoscopy 54.21
  with
    biopsy (intra-abdominal) 54.24
      uterine ligaments 68.15
      uterus 68.16
    destruction of fallopian tubes —
      see Destruction, fallopian
      tube
Laparotomy NEC 54.19
  as operative approach — *omit code*
  exploratory (pelvic) 54.11
  reopening of recent operative site (for
    control of hemorrhage) (for exploration) (for incision of
    hematoma) 54.12
Laparotrachelotomy 74.1
Lapidus operation (bunionectomy with
  metatarsal osteotomy) 77.51
Larry operation (shoulder disarticulation) 84.08
Laryngectomy
  with radical neck dissection (with
    synchronous thyroidectomy)
    (with synchronous tracheostomy) 30.4
  complete (with partial laryngectomy)
    (with synchronous tracheostomy) 30.3
    with radical neck dissection (with
      synchronous thyroidectomy)
      (with synchronous tracheostomy) 30.4
  frontolateral partial (extended) 30.29
  glottosupraglottic partial 30.29
  lateral partial 30.29
  partial (frontolateral) (glottosupraglottic) (lateral) (submucous)
    (supraglottic) (vertical) 30.29
  radical (with synchronous thyroidectomy) (with synchronous tracheostomy) 30.4
  submucous (partial) 30.29
  supraglottic partial 30.29
  total (with partial pharyngectomy)
    (with synchronous tracheostomy) 30.3
    with radical neck dissection (with
      synchronous thyroidectomy)
      (with synchronous tracheostomy) 30.4
  vertical partial 30.29
  wide field 30.3
Laryngocentesis 31.3
Laryngoesophagectomy 30.4
Laryngofissure 30.29
Laryngogram 87.09
  contrast 87.07
Laryngopharyngectomy (with synchronous tracheostomy) 30.3
  radical (with synchronous thyroidectomy) 30.4
Laryngopharyngoesophagectomy (with
  synchronous tracheostomy) 30.3
  with radical neck dissection (with
    synchronous thyroidectomy)
    30.4
Laryngoplasty 31.69

Laryngorrhaphy 31.61
Laryngoscopy (suspension) (through artificial stoma) 31.42
Laryngostomy (permanent) 31.29
  revision 31.63
  temporary (emergency) 31.1
Laryngotomy 31.3
Laryngotracheobronchoscopy 33.23
  with biopsy 33.24
Laryngotracheoscopy 31.42
Laryngotracheostomy (permanent)
  31.29
  temporary (emergency) 31.1
Laryngotracheotomy (temporary) 31.1
  permanent 31.29
Laser — *see also* Coagulation, Destruction, and Photocoagulation by site
  angioplasty, percutaneous transluminal 39.59
    coronary — *see* Angioplasty, coronary
Lash operation
  internal cervical os repair 67.59
  laparoscopic supracervical hysterectomy 68.31
LASIK (laser-assisted in situ keratomileusis) 11.71
Latzko operation
  cesarean section 74.2
  colpocleisis 70.8
Lavage
  antral 22.00
  bronchus NEC 96.56
    diagnostic (endoscopic) bronchoalveolar lavage (BAL)
      33.24
  endotracheal 96.56
  gastric 96.33
  lung (total) (whole) 33.99
    diagnostic (endoscopic) bronchoalveolar lavage (BAL)
      33.24
  nasal sinus(es) 22.00
    by puncture 22.01
    through natural ostium 22.02
  peritoneal (diagnostic) 54.25
  trachea NEC 96.56
Leadbetter operation (urethral reconstruction) 58.46
Leadbetter-Politano operation
  (ureteroneocystostomy) 56.74
LEEP (loop electrosurgical excision procedure) of cervix 67.32
Le Fort operation (colpocleisis) 70.8
LeMesurier operation (cleft lip repair)
  27.54
Lengthening
  bone (with bone graft) 78.30
    for reconstruction of thumb 82.69
    femur 78.35
    specified site NEC (*see also* category 78.3 ☑)
    tibia 78.37
    ulna 78.33
  extraocular muscle NEC 15.21
    multiple (two or more muscles)
      15.4
  fascia 83.89
    hand 82.89
  hamstring NEC 83.85
  heel cord 83.85
  leg
    femur 78.35
    tibia 78.37
  levator palpebrae muscle 08.38
  muscle 83.85
    extraocular 15.21
      multiple (two or more muscles)
        15.4
    hand 82.55
  palate 27.62
    secondary or subsequent 27.63
  tendon 83.85
    for claw toe repair 77.57
    hand 82.55

Leriche operation (periarterial sympathectomy) 05.25
Leucotomy, leukotomy 01.32
Leukopheresis, therapeutic 99.72
Lid suture operation (blepharoptosis)
  08.31
Ligation
  adrenal vessel (artery) (vein) 07.43
  aneurysm 39.52
  appendages, dermal 86.26
  arteriovenous fistula 39.53
    coronary artery 36.99
  artery 38.80
    for control of epistaxis — *see* Control, epistaxis
    abdominal 38.86
    adrenal 07.43
    aorta (arch) (ascending) (descending) 38.84
    coronary (anomalous) 36.99
    ethmoidal 21.04
    external carotid 21.06
    head and neck NEC 38.82
    intracranial NEC 38.81
    lower limb 38.88
    maxillary (transantral) 21.05
    middle meningeal 02.13
    thoracic NEC 38.85
    thyroid 06.92
    upper limb 38.83
  atrium, heart 37.99
  auricle, heart 37.99
  bleeding vessel — *see* Control, hemorrhage
  blood vessel 38.80
    abdominal
      artery 38.86
      vein 38.87
    adrenal 07.43
    aorta (arch) (ascending) (descending) 38.84
    esophagus 42.91
      endoscopic 42.33
    head and neck NEC 38.82
    intracranial NEC 38.81
    lower limb
      artery 38.88
      vein 38.89
    meningeal (artery) (longitudinal sinus) 02.13
    thoracic NEC 38.85
    thyroid 06.92
    upper limb (artery) (vein) 38.83
  bronchus 33.92
  cisterna chyli 40.64
  coronary
    artery (anomalous) 36.99
    sinus 36.39
  dermal appendage 86.26
  ductus arteriosus, patent 38.85
  esophageal vessel 42.91
    endoscopic 42.33
  ethmoidal artery 21.04
  external carotid artery 21.06
  fallopian tube (bilateral) (remaining)
    (solitary) 66.39
    by endoscopy (culdoscopy) (hysteroscopy) (laparoscopy)
      (peritoneoscopy) 66.29
    with
      crushing 66.31
        by endoscopy (laparoscopy)
          66.21
      division 66.32
        by endoscopy (culdoscopy)
          (laparoscopy) (peritoneoscopy) 66.22
    Falope ring 66.39
      by endoscopy (laparoscopy)
        66.29
    unilateral 66.92
  fistula, arteriovenous 39.53
    coronary artery 36.99
  gastric
    artery 38.86
    varices 44.91

Ligation — *continued*
  gastric — *continued*
    varices — *continued*
      endoscopic 43.41
  hemorrhoids 49.45
  longitudinal sinus (superior) 02.13
  lymphatic (channel) (peripheral) 40.9
    thoracic duct 40.64
  maxillary artery 21.05
  meningeal vessel 02.13
  spermatic
    cord 63.72
      varicocele 63.1
    vein (high) 63.1
  splenic vessels 38.86
  subclavian artery 38.85
  superior longitudinal sinus 02.13
  supernumerary digit 86.26
  thoracic duct 40.64
  thyroid vessel (artery) (vein) 06.92
  toes (supernumerary) 86.26
  tooth 93.55
    impacted 24.6
  ulcer (peptic) (base) (bed) (bleeding
    vessel) 44.40
    duodenal 44.42
    gastric 44.41
  ureter 56.95
  varices
    esophageal 42.91
      endoscopic 42.33
    gastric 44.91
      endoscopic 43.41
    peripheral vein (lower limb) 38.59
      upper limb 38.53
  varicocele 63.1
  vas deferens 63.71
  vein 38.80
    abdominal 38.87
    adrenal 07.43
    head and neck NEC 38.82
    intracranial NEC 38.81
    lower limb 38.89
    spermatic, high 63.1
    thoracic NEC 38.85
    thyroid 06.92
    upper limb 38.83
    varicose 38.50
      abdominal 38.57
      esophagus 42.91
        endoscopic 42.33
      gastric 44.91
        endoscopic 43.41
      head and neck NEC 38.52
      intracranial NEC 38.51
      lower limb 38.59
      stomach 44.91
      thoracic NEC 38.55
      upper limb 38.53
  vena cava, inferior 38.7
  venous connection between anomalous vein 35.82
    left innominate vein 35.82
    superior vena cava 35.82
  wart 86.26
Light coagulation — *see* Photocoagulation
Lindholm operation (repair of ruptured
  tendon) 83.88
Lingulectomy, lung 32.3
Linton operation (varicose vein) 38.59
Lipectomy (subcutaneous tissue) (abdominal) (submental) 86.83
Liposuction 86.83
Lip reading training 95.49
Lip shave 27.43
Lisfranc operation
  foot amputation 84.12
  shoulder disarticulation 84.08
Litholapaxy, bladder 57.0
  by incision 57.19
Lithotomy
  bile passage 51.49
  bladder (urinary) 57.19
  common duct 51.41
    percutaneous 51.96

☑ Additional Digit Required — Refer to the Tabular List for Digit Selection   ⏳ Subterms under main terms may continue to next column or page

36 — Volume 3   ▶◀ Revised Text   ● New Line   ▲ Revised Code   *2007 ICD-9-CM*

Lithotomy — *continued*
  gallbladder 51.04
  hepatic duct 51.49
  kidney 55.01
    percutaneous 55.03
  ureter 56.2
Lithotripsy
  bile duct NEC 51.49
    extracorporeal shockwave (ESWL)
      98.52
  bladder 57.0
    with ultrasonic fragmentation
      57.0 [59.95]
    extracorporeal shockwave (ESWL)
      98.51
  extracorporeal shockwave (ESWL) NEC
    98.59
    bile duct 98.52
    bladder (urinary) 98.51
    gallbladder 98.52
    kidney 98.51
    Kock pouch 98.51
    renal pelvis 98.51
    specified site NEC 98.59
    ureter 98.51
  gallbladder NEC 51.04
    endoscopic 51.88
    extracorporeal shockwave (ESWL)
      98.52
  kidney 56.0
    extracorporeal shockwave (ESWL)
      98.51
    percutaneous nephrostomy with
      fragmentation (laser) (ultra-
      sound) 55.04
  renal pelvis 56.0
    extracorporeal shockwave (ESWL)
      98.51
    percutaneous nephrostomy with
      fragmentation (laser) (ultra-
      sound) 55.04
  ureter 56.0
    extracorporeal shockwave
      (ESWL) 98.51
Littlewood operation (forequarter ampu-
    tation) 84.09
LLETZ (large loop excision of the trans-
    formation zone) of cervix 67.32
Lloyd-Davies operation (abdominoper-
    ineal resection) 48.5
Lobectomy
  brain 01.53
    partial 01.59
  liver (with partial excision of adjacent
    lobes) 50.3
  lung (complete) 32.4
    partial 32.3
    segmental (with resection of adja-
      cent lobes) 32.4
  thyroid (total) (unilateral) (with re-
    moval of isthmus) (with removal
    of portion of remaining lobe)
    06.2
    partial (*see also* Thyroidectomy,
      partial) 06.39
    substernal 06.51
    subtotal (*see also* Thyroidectomy,
      partial) 06.39
Lobotomy, brain 01.32
Localization, placenta 88.78
  by RISA injection 92.17
Longmire operation (bile duct anastomo-
    sis) 51.39
Loop ileal stoma — *see also* Ileostomy
    46.01
Loopogram 87.78
Looposcopy (ileal conduit) 56.35
Lord operation
  dilation of anal canal for hemorrhoids
    49.49
  hemorrhoidectomy 49.49
  orchidopexy 62.5
Lower GI series (x-ray) 87.64
Lucas and Murray operation (knee
  arthrodesis with plate) 81.22

Lumpectomy
  breast 85.21
  specified site — *see* Excision, lesion,
    by site
Lymphadenectomy (simple) — *see also*
    Excision, lymph, node 40.29
Lymphadenotomy 40.0
Lymphangiectomy (radical) — *see also*
    Excision, lymph, node, by site,
    radical 40.50
Lymphangiogram
  abdominal 88.04
  cervical 87.08
  intrathoracic 87.34
  lower limb 88.36
  pelvic 88.04
  upper limb 88.34
Lymphangioplasty 40.9
Lymphangiorrhaphy 40.9
Lymphangiotomy 40.0
Lymphaticostomy 40.9
  thoracic duct 40.62
Lysis
  adhesions

  Note:
  blunt — *omit code*
  digital — *omit code*
  manual — *omit code*
  mechanical — *omit code*
  without instrumentation — *omit code*
  ---

    abdominal 54.59
      laparoscopic 54.51
    appendiceal 54.59
      laparoscopic 54.51
    artery-vein-nerve bundle 39.91
    biliary tract 54.59
      laparoscopic 54.51
    bladder (neck) (intraluminal) 57.12
      external 59.11
        laparoscopic 59.12
      transurethral 57.41
    blood vessels 39.91
    bone — *see* category 78.4 ☑
    bursa 83.91
      by stretching or manipulation
        93.28
      hand 82.91
    cartilage of joint 93.26
    chest wall 33.99
    choanae (nasopharynx) 29.54
    conjunctiva 10.5
    corneovitreal 12.34
    cortical (brain) 02.91
    ear, middle 20.23
    Eustachean tube 20.8
    extraocular muscle 15.7
    extrauterine 54.59
      laparoscopic 54.51
    eyelid 08.09
      and conjunctiva 10.5
    eye muscle 15.7
    fallopian tube 65.89
      laparoscopic 65.81
    fascia 83.91
      hand 82.91
        by stretching or manipula-
          tion 93.26
    gallbladder 54.59
      laparoscopic 54.51
    ganglion (peripheral) NEC 04.49
      cranial NEC 04.42
    hand 82.91
      by stretching or manipulation
        93.26
    heart 37.10
    intestines 54.59
      laparoscopic 54.51
    iris (posterior) 12.33
      anterior 12.32
    joint (capsule) (structure) (*see also*
      Division, joint capsule) 80.40
    kidney 59.02
      laparoscopic 59.03
    labia (vulva) 71.01
    larynx 31.92
    liver 54.59

Lysis — *continued*
  adhesions — *continued*
    liver — *continued*
      laparoscopic 54.51
    lung (for collapse of lung) 33.39
    mediastinum 34.99
    meninges (spinal) 03.6
      cortical 02.91
    middle ear 20.23
    muscle 83.91
      by stretching or manipulation
        93.91
      extraocular 15.7
      hand 82.91
        by stretching or manipula-
          tion 93.26
    nasopharynx 29.54
    nerve (peripheral) NEC 04.49
      cranial NEC 04.42
      roots, spinal 03.6
      trigeminal 04.41
    nose, nasal 21.91
    ocular muscle 15.7
    ovary 65.89
      laparoscopic 65.81
    pelvic 54.59
      laparoscopic 54.51
    penile 64.93
    pericardium 37.12
    perineal (female) 71.01
    peripheral vessels 39.91
    perirectal 48.81
    perirenal 59.02
      laparoscopic 59.03
    peritoneum (pelvic) 54.59
      laparoscopic 54.51
    periureteral 59.02
      laparoscopic 59.03
    perivesical 59.11
      laparoscopic 59.12
    pharynx 29.54
    pleura (for collapse of lung) 33.39
    spermatic cord 63.94
    spinal (cord) (meninges) (nerve
      roots) 03.6
    spleen 54.59
      laparoscopic 54.51
    tendon 83.91
      by stretching or manipulation
        93.27
      hand 82.91
        by stretching or manipula-
          tion 93.26
    thorax 34.99
    tongue 25.93
    trachea 31.92
    tubo-ovarian 65.89
      laparoscopic 65.81
    ureter 59.02
      with freeing or repositioning of
        ureter 59.02
      intraluminal 56.81
      laparoscopic 59.03
    urethra (intraluminal) 58.5
    uterus 54.59
      intraluminal 68.21
      laparoscopic 54.51
      peritoneal 54.59
        laparoscopic 54.51
    vagina (intraluminal) 70.13
    vitreous (posterior approach) 14.74
      anterior approach 14.73
    vulva 71.01
  goniosynechiae (with injection of air
    or liquid) 12.31
  synechiae (posterior) 12.33
    anterior (with injection of air or
      liquid) 12.32

M

Madlener operation (tubal ligation)
    66.31
Magnet extraction
  foreign body
    anterior chamber, eye 12.01
    choroid 14.01

Magnet extraction — *continued*
  foreign body — *continued*
    ciliary body 12.01
    conjunctiva 98.22
    cornea 11.0
    eye, eyeball NEC 98.21
      anterior segment 12.01
      posterior segment 14.01
      intraocular (anterior segment)
        12.01
    iris 12.01
    lens 13.01
    orbit 98.21
    retina 14.01
    sclera 12.01
    vitreous 14.01
Magnetic resonance imaging (nuclear)
    — *see* Imaging, magnetic resonance
Magnuson (-Stack) operation (arthro-
    plasty for recurrent shoulder dislo-
    cation) 81.82
Malleostapediopexy 19.19
  with incus replacement 19.11
Malström's vacuum extraction 72.79
  with episiotomy 72.71
Mammaplasty — *see* Mammoplasty
Mammectomy — *see also* Mastectomy
  subcutaneous (unilateral) 85.34
    with synchronous implant 85.35
    bilateral 85.36
Mammilliplasty 85.87
Mammography NEC 87.37
Mammoplasty 85.89
  with
    full-thickness graft 85.83
    muscle flap 85.85
    pedicle graft 85.84
    split-thickness graft 85.82
  amputative (reduction) (bilateral)
    85.32
    unilateral 85.31
  augmentation 85.50
    with
      breast implant (bilateral) 85.54
        unilateral 85.53
      injection into breast (bilateral)
        85.52
        unilateral 85.51
  reduction (bilateral) 85.32
    unilateral 85.31
  revision 85.89
  size reduction (gynecomastia) (bilater-
    al) 85.32
    unilateral 85.31
Mammotomy 85.0
**Manchester (-Donald) (-Fothergill) op-
    eration** (uterine suspension) 69.22
Mandibulectomy (partial) 76.31
  total 76.42
    with reconstruction 76.41
Maneuver (method)
  Bracht 72.52
  Credé 73.59
  De Lee (key-in-lock) 72.4
  Kristeller 72.54
  Loveset's (extraction of arms in breech
    birth) 72.52
  Mauriceau (-Smellie-Veit) 72.52
  Pinard (total breech extraction) 72.54
  Prague 72.52
  Ritgen 73.59
  Scanzoni (rotation) 72.4
  Van Hoorn 72.52
  Wigand-Martin 72.52
Manipulation
  with reduction of fracture or disloca-
    tion — *see* Reduction, fracture
    and Reduction, dislocation
  enterostomy stoma (with dilation)
    96.24
  intestine (intra-abdominal) 46.80
    large 46.82
    small 46.81
  joint
    adhesions 93.26
      temporomandibular 76.95

Lithotomy — Manipulation

☑ Additional Digit Required — Refer to the Tabular List for Digit Selection   ▼ Subterms under main terms may continue to next column or page

2007 ICD-9-CM   ▶◀ Revised Text   ● New Line   ▲ Revised Code   **Volume 3 — 37**

☑ Additional Digit Required — Refer to the Tabular List for Digit Selection   ⦚ Subterms under main terms may continue to next column or page

38 — Volume 3 · October 2006   ▶◀ Revised Text   ● New Line   ▲ Revised Code   *2007 ICD-9-CM*

☑ Additional Digit Required — Refer to the Tabular List for Digit Selection   ▽ Subterms under main terms may continue to next column or page

40 — Volume 3 · October 2006   ▶◀ Revised Text   ● New Line   ▲ Revised Code   **2007 ICD-9-CM**

Operation — *continued*
Fontan (creation of conduit between right atrium and pulmonary artery) 35.94
Fothergill (-Donald) (uterine suspension) 69.22
Fowler
   arthroplasty of metacarpophalangeal joint 81.72
   release (mallet finger repair) 82.84
   tenodesis (hand) 82.85
   thoracoplasty 33.34
Fox (entropion repair with wedge resection) 08.43
Franco (suprapubic cystotomy) 57.19
Frank (permanent gastrostomy) 43.19
Frazier (-Spiller) (subtemporal trigeminal rhizotomy) 04.02
Fredet-Ramstedt (pyloromyotomy) (with wedge resection) 43.3
Frenckner (intrapetrosal drainage) 20.22
Frickman (abdominal proctopexy) 48.75
Frommel (shortening of uterosacral ligaments) 69.22
Gabriel (abdominoperineal resection of rectum) 48.5
gallbladder NEC 51.99
ganglia NEC 04.99
   sympathetic 05.89
Gant (wedge osteotomy of trochanter) 77.25
Garceau (tibial tendon transfer) 83.75
Gardner (spinal meningocele repair) 03.51
gastric NEC 44.99
Gelman (release of clubfoot) 83.84
genital organ NEC
   female 71.9
   male 64.99
Ghormley (hip fusion) 81.21
Gifford
   destruction of lacrimal sac 09.6
   keratotomy (delimiting) 11.1
Gill
   arthrodesis of shoulder 81.23
   laminectomy 03.09
Gilliam (uterine suspension) 69.22
Gill-Stein (carporadial arthrodesis) 81.25
Girdlestone
   laminectomy with spinal fusion 81.00
   muscle transfer for claw toe 77.57
   resection of femoral head and neck (without insertion of joint prosthesis) 77.85
     with replacement prosthesis — *see* Implant, joint, hip
   resection of hip prosthesis 80.05
     with replacement prosthesis — *see* Implant, joint, hip
Girdlestone-Taylor (muscle transfer for claw toe repair) 77.57
glaucoma NEC 12.79
Glenn (anastomosis of superior vena cava to right pulmonary artery) 39.21
globus pallidus NEC 01.42
Goebel-Frangenheim-Stoeckel (urethrovesical suspension) 59.4
Goldner (clubfoot release) 80.48
Goldthwait
   ankle stabilization 81.11
   patella stabilization 81.44
   tendon transfer for patella dislocation 81.44
Goodall-Power (vagina) 70.4
Gordon-Taylor (hindquarter amputation) 84.19
Graber-Duvernay (drilling femoral head) 77.15
Green (scapulopexy) 78.41
Grice (subtalar arthrodesis) 81.13

Operation — *continued*
Gritti-Stokes (knee disarticulation) 84.16
Gross (herniorrhaphy) 53.49
gum NEC 24.39
Guyon (amputation of ankle) 84.13
Hagner (epididymotomy) 63.92
Halsted — *see* Repair, hernia, inguinal
Hampton (anastomosis small intestine to rectal stump) 45.92
hanging hip (muscle release) 83.19
harelip 27.54
Harrison-Richardson (vaginal suspension) 70.77
Hartmann — *see* Colectomy, by site
Hauser
   achillotenotomy 83.11
   bunionectomy with adductor tendon transfer 77.53
   stabilization of patella 81.44
Heaney (vaginal hysterectomy) 68.59
   laparoscopically assisted (LAVH) 68.51
heart NEC 37.99
   valve NEC 35.99
     adjacent structure NEC 35.39
Hegar (perineorrhaphy) 71.79
Heine (cyclodialysis) 12.55
Heineke-Mikulicz (pyloroplasty) — *see* category 44.2 ☑
Heller (esophagomyotomy) 42.7
Hellström (transplantation of aberrant renal vessel) 39.55
hemorrhoids NEC 49.49
Henley (jejunal transposition) 43.81
hepatic NEC 50.99
hernia — *see* Repair, hernia
Hey (amputation of foot) 84.12
Hey-Groves (reconstruction of anterior cruciate ligament) 81.45
Heyman (soft tissue release for clubfoot) 83.84
Heyman-Herndon (-Strong) (correction of metatarsus varus) 80.48
Hibbs (lumbar spinal fusion) — *see* Fusion, lumbar
Higgins — *see* Repair, hernia, femoral
Hill-Allison (hiatal hernia repair, transpleural approach) 53.80
Hitchcock (anchoring tendon of biceps) 83.88
Hofmeister (gastrectomy) 43.7
Hoke
   midtarsal fusion 81.14
   triple arthrodesis 81.12
Holth
   iridencleisis 12.63
   sclerectomy 12.65
Homan (correction of lymphedema) 40.9
Hutch (ureteroneocystostomy) 56.74
Hybinette-eden (glenoid bone block) 78.01
hymen NEC 70.91
hypopharynx NEC 29.99
hypophysis NEC 07.79
ileal loop 56.51
ileum NEC 46.99
intestine NEC 46.99
iris NEC 12.97
   inclusion 12.63
Irving (tubal ligation) 66.32
Irwin (*see also* Osteotomy) 77.30
Jaboulay (gastroduodenostomy) 44.39
   laparoscopic 44.38
Janeway (permanent gastrostomy) 43.19
Jatene (arterial switch) 35.84
jejunum NEC 46.99
Johanson (urethral reconstruction) 58.46
joint (capsule) (ligament) (structure) NEC 81.99
   facial NEC 76.99

Operation — *continued*
Jones
   claw toe (transfer of extensor hallucis longus tendon) 77.57
     modified (with arthrodesis) 77.57
   dacryocystorhinostomy 09.81
   hammer toe (interphalangeal fusion) 77.56
     modified (tendon transfer with arthrodesis) 77.57
   repair of peroneal tendon 83.88
Joplin (exostectomy with tendon transfer) 77.53
Kader (temporary gastrostomy) 43.19
Kaufman (for urinary stress incontinence) 59.79
Kazanjiian (buccal vestibular sulcus extension) 24.91
Kehr (hepatopexy) 50.69
Keller (bunionectomy) 77.59
Kelly (-Kennedy) (urethrovesical plication) 59.3
Kelly-Stoeckel (urethrovesical plication) 59.3
Kerr (cesarean section) 74.1
Kessler (arthroplasty, carpometacarpal joint) 81.74
Kidner (excision of accessory navicular bone) (with tendon transfer) 77.98
kidney NEC 55.99
Killian (frontal sinusotomy) 22.41
King-Steelquist (hindquarter amputation) 84.19
Kirk (amputation through thigh) 84.17
Kock pouch
   bowel anastomosis — *omit code*
   continent ileostomy 46.22
   cutaneous uretero-ileostomy 56.51
   ESWL (electrocorporeal shockwave lithotripsy) 98.51
   removal, calculus 57.19
   revision, cutaneous uretero-ileostomy 56.52
   urinary diversion procedure 56.51
Kondoleon (correction of lymphedema) 40.9
Krause (sympathetic denervation) 05.29
Kroener (partial salpingectomy) 66.69
Kroenlein (lateral orbitotomy) 16.01
Krönig (low cervical cesarean section) 74.1
Krukenberg (reconstruction of below-elbow amputation) 82.89
Kuhnt-Szymanowski (ectropion repair with lid reconstruction) 08.44
Labbe (gastrotomy) 43.0
labia NEC 71.8
lacrimal
   gland 09.3
   system NEC 09.99
Ladd (mobilization of intestine) 54.95
Lagrange (iridosclerectomy) 12.65
Lambrinudi (triple arthrodesis) 81.12
Langenbeck (cleft palate repair) 27.62
Lapidus (bunionectomy with metatarsal osteotomy) 77.51
Larry (shoulder disarticulation) 84.08
Lash
   internal cervical os repair 67.59
   laparoscopic supracervical hysterectomy 68.31
Latzko
   cesarean section, extraperitoneal 74.2
   colpocleisis 70.8
Leadbetter (urethral reconstruction) 58.46
Leadbetter-Politano (ureteroneocystostomy) 56.74
Le Fort (colpocleisis) 70.8
LeMesurier (cleft lip repair) 27.54
lens NEC 13.90 ▲

Operation — *continued*
Leriche (periarterial sympathectomy) 05.25
levator muscle sling
   eyelid ptosis repair 08.33
   urethrovesical suspension 59.71
   urinary stress incontinence 59.71
lid suture (blepharoptosis) 08.31
ligament NEC 81.99
   broad NEC 69.98
   round NEC 69.98
   uterine NEC 69.98
Lindholm (repair of ruptured tendon) 83.88
Linton (varicose vein) 38.59
lip NEC 27.99
Lisfranc
   foot amputation 84.12
   shoulder disarticulation 84.08
Littlewood (forequarter amputation) 84.09
   liver NEC 50.99
Lloyd-Davies (abdominoperineal resection) 48.5
Longmire (bile duct anastomosis) 51.39
Lord
   dilation of anal canal for hemorrhoids 49.49
   hemorrhoidectomy 49.49
   orchidopexy 62.5
Lucas and Murray (knee arthrodesis with plate) 81.22
lung NEC 33.99
lung volume reduction 32.22
   biologic lung volume reduction (BLVR) — *see* category 33.7 ☑ ●
lymphatic structure(s) NEC 40.9
   duct, left (thoracic) NEC 40.69
Madlener (tubal ligation) 66.31
Magnuson (-Stack) (arthroplasty for recurrent shoulder dislocation) 81.82
male genital organs NEC 64.99
Manchester (-Donald) (-Fothergill) (uterine suspension) 69.22
mandible NEC 76.99
   orthognathic 76.64
Marckwald operation (cervical os repair) 67.59
Marshall-Marchetti (-Krantz) (retropubic urethral suspension) 59.5
Matas (aneurysmorrhaphy) 39.52
Mayo
   bunionectomy 77.59
   herniorrhaphy 53.49
   vaginal hysterectomy 68.59
     laparoscopically assisted (LAVH) 68.51
maze procedure (ablation or destruction of heart tissue)
   by incision (open) 37.33
   by peripherally inserted catheter 37.34
   endovascular approach 37.34
   trans-thoracic approach 37.33
Mazet (knee disarticulation) 84.16
McBride (bunionectomy with soft tissue correction) 77.53
McBurney — *see* Repair, hernia, inguinal
McCall (enterocele repair) 70.92
McCauley (release of clubfoot) 83.84
McDonald (encirclement suture, cervix) 67.59
McIndoe (vaginal construction) 70.61
McKeever (fusion of first metatarsophalangeal joint for hallux valgus repair) 77.52
McKissock (breast reduction) 85.33
McReynolds (transposition of pterygium) 11.31
McVay
   femoral hernia — *see* Repair, hernia, femoral

☑ Additional Digit Required — Refer to the Tabular List for Digit Selection   ▽ Subterms under main terms may continue to next column or page

2007 ICD-9-CM   ▶◀ Revised Text   ● New Line   ▲ Revised Code   **October 2006 • Volume 3 — 41**

Operation — *continued*

McVay — *continued*
  inguinal hernia — *see* Repair, hernia, inguinal
  meninges (spinal) NEC 03.99
    cerebral NEC 02.99
  mesentery NEC 54.99
Mikulicz (exteriorization of intestine) (first stage) 46.03
  second stage 46.04
Miles (complete proctectomy) 48.5
Millard (cheiloplasty) 27.54
Miller
  midtarsal arthrodesis 81.14
  urethrovesical suspension 59.4
Millin-Read (urethrovesical suspension) 59.4
Mitchell (hallux valgus repair) 77.51
Mohs (chemosurgical excision of skin) 86.24
Moore (arthroplasty) 81.52
Moschowitz
  enterocele repair 70.92
  herniorrhaphy — *see* Repair, hernia, femoral
  sigmoidopexy 46.63
mouth NEC 27.99
Muller (banding of pulmonary artery) 38.85
Mumford (partial claviculectomy) 77.81
muscle NEC 83.99
  extraocular — *see* Operation, extraocular
  hand NEC 82.99
  papillary heart NEC 35.31
musculoskeletal system NEC 84.99
Mustard (interatrial transposition of venous return) 35.91
nail (finger) (toe) NEC 86.99
nasal sinus NEC 22.9
nasopharynx NEC 29.99
nerve (cranial) (peripheral) NEC 04.99
  adrenal NEC 07.49
  sympathetic NEC 05.89
nervous system NEC 05.9
Nicola (tenodesis for recurrent dislocation of shoulder) 81.82
nipple NEC 85.99
Nissen (fundoplication of stomach) 44.66
  laparoscopic 44.67
Noble (plication of small intestine) 46.62
node (lymph) NEC 40.9
Norman Miller (vaginopexy) 70.77
Norton (extraperitoneal cesarean operation) 74.2
nose, nasal NEC 21.99
  sinus NEC 22.9
Ober (-Yount) (gluteal-iliotibial fasciotomy) 83.14
obstetric NEC 75.99
ocular NEC 16.99
  muscle — *see* Operation, extraocular muscle
O'Donoghue (triad knee repair) 81.43
Olshausen (uterine suspension) 69.22
omentum NEC 54.99
ophthalmologic NEC 16.99
oral cavity NEC 27.99
orbicularis muscle sling 08.36
orbit NEC 16.98
oropharynx NEC 29.99
orthodontic NEC 24.8
orthognathic NEC 76.69
Oscar Miller (midtarsal arthrodesis) 81.14
Osmond-Clark (soft tissue release with peroneus brevis tendon transfer) 83.75
ovary NEC 65.99
Oxford (for urinary incontinence) 59.4
palate NEC 27.99
palpebral ligament sling 08.36
Panas (linear proctotomy) 48.0

Operation — *continued*

Pancoast (division of trigeminal nerve at foramen ovale) 04.02
pancreas NEC 52.99
pantaloon (revision of gastric anastomosis) 44.5
papillary muscle (heart) NEC 35.31
Paquin (ureteroneocystostomy) 56.74
parathyroid gland(s) NEC 06.99
parotid gland or duct NEC 26.99
Partsch (marsupialization of dental cyst) 24.4
Pattee (auditory canal) 18.6
Peet (splanchnic resection) 05.29
Pemberton
  osteotomy of ilium 77.39
  rectum (mobilization and fixation for prolapse repair) 48.76
penis NEC 64.98
Pereyra (paraurethral suspension) 59.6
pericardium NEC 37.99
perineum (female) NEC 71.8
  male NEC 86.99
perirectal tissue NEC 48.99
perirenal tissue NEC 59.92
peritoneum NEC 54.99
periurethral tissue NEC 58.99
perivesical tissue NEC 59.92
pharyngeal flap (cleft palate repair) 27.62
  secondary or subsequent 27.63
pharynx, pharyngeal (pouch) NEC 29.99
pineal gland NEC 07.59
Pinsker (obliteration of nasoseptal telangiectasia) 21.07
Piper (forceps) 72.6
Pirogoff (ankle amputation through malleoli of tibia and fibula) 84.14
pituitary gland NEC 07.79
plastic — *see* Repair, by site
pleural cavity NEC 34.99
Politano-Leadbetter (ureteroneocystostomy) 56.74
pollicization (with nerves and blood supply) 82.61
Polya (gastrectomy) 43.7
Pomeroy (ligation and division of fallopian tubes) 66.32
Poncet
  lengthening of Achilles tendon 83.85
  urethrostomy, perineal 58.0
Porro (cesarean section) 74.99
posterior chamber (eye) NEC 14.9
Potts-Smith (descending aorta-left pulmonary artery anastomosis) 39.0
Printen and Mason (high gastric bypass) 44.31
prostate NEC (*see also* Prostatectomy) 60.69
  specified type 60.99
pterygium 11.39
  with corneal graft 11.32
Puestow (pancreaticojejunostomy) 52.96
pull-through NEC 48.49
pulmonary NEC 33.99
push-back (cleft palate repair) 27.62
Putti-Platt (capsulorrhaphy of shoulder for recurrent dislocation) 81.82
pyloric exclusion 44.39
  laparoscopic 44.38
pyriform sinus NEC 29.99
"rabbit ear" (anterior urethropexy) (Tudor) 59.79
Ramadier (intrapetrosal drainage) 20.22
Ramstedt (pyloromyotomy) (with wedge resection) 43.3
Rankin
  exteriorization of intestine 46.03

Operation — *continued*

Rankin — *continued*
  proctectomy (complete) 48.5
Rashkind (balloon septostomy) 35.41
Rastelli (creation of conduit between right ventricle and pulmonary artery) 35.92
  in repair of
    pulmonary artery atresia 35.92
    transposition of great vessels 35.92
    truncus arteriosus 35.83
Raz-Pereyra procedure (bladder neck suspension) 59.79
rectal NEC 48.99
rectocele NEC 70.52
re-entry (aorta) 39.54
renal NEC 55.99
respiratory (tract) NEC 33.99
retina NEC 14.9
Ripstein (repair of rectal prolapse) 48.75
Rodney Smith (radical subtotal pancreatectomy) 52.53
Roux-en-Y
  bile duct 51.36
  cholecystojejunostomy 51.32
  esophagus (intrathoracic) 42.54
  gastroenterostomy 44.39
    laparoscopic 44.38
  gastrojejunostomy 44.39
    laparoscopic 44.38
  pancreaticojejunostomy 52.96
Roux-Goldthwait (repair of patellar dislocation) 81.44
Roux-Herzen-Judine (jejunal loop interposition) 42.63
Ruiz-Mora (proximal phalangectomy for hammer toe) 77.99
Russe (bone graft of scaphoid) 78.04
Saemisch (corneal section) 11.1
salivary gland or duct NEC 26.99
Salter (innominate osteotomy) 77.39
Sauer-Bacon (abdominoperineal resection) 48.5
Schanz (femoral osteotomy) 77.35
Schauta (-Amreich) (radical vaginal hysterectomy) 68.79   ▲
  laparoscopic 68.71   ●
Schede (thoracoplasty) 33.34
Scheie
  cautery of sclera 12.62
  sclerostomy 12.62
Schlatter (total gastrectomy) 43.99
Schroeder (endocervical excision) 67.39
Schuchardt (nonobstetrical episiotomy) 71.09
Schwartze (simple mastoidectomy) 20.41
sclera NEC 12.89
Scott
  intestinal bypass for obesity 45.93
  jejunocolostomy (bypass) 45.93
scrotum NEC 61.99
Seddon-Brooks (transfer of pectoralis major tendon) 83.75
Semb (apicolysis of lung) 33.39
seminal vesicle NEC 60.79
Senning (correction of transposition of great vessels) 35.91
Sever (division of soft tissue of arm) 83.19
Sewell (heart) 36.2
sex transformation NEC 64.5
Sharrard (iliopsoas muscle transfer) 83.77
shelf (hip arthroplasty) 81.40
Shirodkar (encirclement suture, cervix) 67.59
sigmoid NEC 46.99
Silver (bunionectomy) 77.59
Sistrunk (excision of thyroglossal cyst) 06.7
Skene's gland NEC 71.8
skin NEC 86.99

Operation — *continued*

skull NEC 02.99
sling
  eyelid
    fascia lata, palpebral 08.36
    frontalis fascial 08.32
    levator muscle 08.33
    orbicularis muscle 08.36
    palpebral ligament, fascia lata 08.36
    tarsus muscle 08.35
  fascial (fascia lata)
    for facial weakness (trigeminal nerve paralysis) 86.81
    eye 08.32
    palpebral ligament 08.36
    tongue 25.59
  tongue (fascial) 25.59
  urethra (suprapubic) 59.4
    retropubic 59.5
  urethrovesical 59.5
Slocum (pes anserinus transfer) 81.47
Sluder (tonsillectomy) 28.2
Smith (open osteotomy of mandible) 76.62
Smith-Peterson (radiocarpal arthrodesis) 81.25
Smithwick (sympathectomy) 05.29
Soave (endorectal pull-through) 48.41
soft tissue NEC 83.99
  hand 82.99
Sonneberg (inferior maxillary neurectomy) 04.07
Sorondo-Ferré (hindquarter amputation) 84.19
Soutter (iliac crest fasciotomy) 83.14
Spalding-Richardson (uterine suspension) 69.22
spermatic cord NEC 63.99
sphincter of Oddi NEC 51.89
spinal (canal) (cord) (structures) NEC 03.99
Spinelli (correction of inverted uterus) 75.93
Spivack (permanent gastrostomy) 43.19
spleen NEC 41.99
S.P. Rogers (knee disarticulation) 84.16
Ssabanejew-Frank (permanent gastrostomy) 43.19
Stacke (simple mastoidectomy) 20.41
Stallard (conjunctivocystorhinostomy) 09.82
  with insertion of tube or stent 09.83
Stamm (-Kader) (temporary gastrostomy) 43.19
Steinberg 44.5
Steindler
  fascia stripping (for cavus deformity) 83.14
  flexorplasty (elbow) 83.77
  muscle transfer 83.77
sterilization NEC
  female (*see also* specific operation) 66.39
  male (*see also* Ligation, vas deferens) 63.70
Stewart (renal plication with pyeloplasty) 55.87
stomach NEC 44.99
Stone (anoplasty) 49.79
Strassman (metroplasty) 69.49
  metroplasty (Jones modification) 69.49
  uterus 68.22
Strayer (gastrocnemius recession) 83.72
stress incontinence — *see* Repair, stress incontinence
Stromeyer-Little (hepatotomy) 50.0
Strong (unbridling of celiac artery axis) 39.91
Sturmdorf (conization of cervix) 67.2
subcutaneous tissue NEC 86.99

☑ Additional Digit Required — Refer to the Tabular List for Digit Selection   ▽ Subterms under main terms may continue to next column or page

42 — Volume 3 · October 2006   ▶◀ Revised Text   ● New Line   ▲ Revised Code   **2007 ICD-9-CM**

Osteotomy — continued
  carpals, metacarpals — continued
    wedge 77.24
  clavicle 77.31
    wedge 77.21
  facial bone NEC 76.69
  femur 77.35
    wedge 77.25
  fibula 77.37
    wedge 77.27
  humerus 77.32
    wedge 77.22
  mandible (segmental) (subapical)
    76.64
    angle (open) 76.62
      closed 76.61
    body 76.63
    Gigli saw 76.61
    ramus (open) 76.62
      closed 76.61
  maxilla (segmental) 76.65
    total 76.66
  metatarsal 77.38
    wedge 77.28
      for hallux valgus repair 77.51
  patella 77.36
    wedge 77.26
  pelvic 77.39
    wedge 77.29
  phalanges (foot) (hand) 77.39
    for repair of
      bunion — see Bunionectomy
      bunionette 77.54
      hallux valgus — see Bunionecto-
        my
    wedge 77.29
      for repair of
        bunion — see Bunionectomy
        bunionette 77.54
        hallux valgus — see
          Bunionectomy
  radius 77.33
    wedge 77.23
  scapula 77.31
    wedge 77.21
  specified site NEC 77.39
    wedge 77.29
  tarsal 77.38
    wedge 77.28
  thorax (ribs) (sternum) 77.31
    wedge 77.21
  tibia 77.37
    wedge 77.27
  toe 77.39
    for repair of
      bunion — see Bunionectomy
      bunionette 77.54
      hallux valgus — see Bunionecto-
        my
    wedge 77.29
      for repair of
        bunion — see Bunionectomy
        bunionette 77.54
        hallux valgus — see
          Bunionectomy
  ulna 77.33
    wedge 77.23
  vertebrae 77.39
    wedge 77.29
Otonecrectomy (inner ear) 20.79
Otoplasty (external) 18.79
  auditory canal or meatus 18.6
  auricle 18.79
  cartilage 18.79
    reconstruction 18.71
  prominent or protruding 18.5
Otoscopy 18.11
Outfolding, sclera, for buckling — see
  also Buckling, scleral 14.49
Outfracture, turbinates (nasal) 21.62
Output and clearance, circulatory
  92.05
Overdistension, bladder (therapeutic)
  96.25
Overlapping, sclera, for buckling — see
  also Buckling, scleral 14.49

Oversewing
  pleural bleb 32.21
  ulcer crater (peptic) 44.40
    duodenum 44.42
    stomach 44.41
Oxford operation (for urinary incontinence) 59.4
Oximetry
  fetal pulse 75.38
Oxygenation 93.96
  extracorporeal membrane (ECMO)
    39.65
  hyperbaric 93.95
    wound 93.59
Oxygen therapy (catalytic) (pump) 93.96
  hyperbaric 93.95

P

Pacemaker
  cardiac (see also Insertion, pacemak-
    er, cardiac)
    intraoperative (temporary) 39.64
    temporary (during and immediately
      following cardiac surgery)
      39.64
Packing — see also Insertion, pack
  auditory canal 96.11
  nose, for epistaxis (anterior) 21.01
    posterior (and anterior) 21.02
  rectal 96.19
  sella turcica 07.79
  vaginal 96.14
Palatoplasty 27.69
  for cleft palate 27.62
    secondary or subsequent 27.63
Palatorrhaphy 27.61
  for cleft palate 27.62
Pallidectomy 01.42
Pallidoansotomy 01.42
Pallidotomy 01.42
  by stereotactic radiosurgery 92.32
    cobalt 60 92.32
    linear accelerator (LINAC) 92.31
    multi-source 92.32
    particle beam 92.33
    particulate 92.33
    radiosurgery NEC 92.39
    single source photon 92.31
Panas operation (linear proctotomy) 48.0
Pancoast operation (division of trigemi-
  nal nerve at foramen ovale) 04.02
Pancreatectomy (total) (with syn-
  chronous duodenectomy) 52.6
  partial NEC 52.59
    distal (tail) (with part of body)
      52.52
    proximal (head) (with part of body)
      (with synchronous duodenec-
      tomy) 52.51
    radical 52.53
      subtotal 52.53
  radical 52.7
    subtotal 52.53
Pancreaticocystoduodenostomy 52.4
Pancreaticocystoenterostomy 52.4
Pancreaticocystogastrostomy 52.4
Pancreaticocystojejunostomy 52.4
Pancreaticoduodenectomy (total) 52.6
  partial NEC 52.59
    proximal 52.51
    radical subtotal 52.53
  radical (one-stage) (two-stage) 52.7
    subtotal 52.53
Pancreaticoduodenostomy 52.96
Pancreaticoenterostomy 52.96
Pancreaticogastrostomy 52.96
Pancreaticoileostomy 52.96
Pancreaticojejunostomy 52.96
Pancreatoduodenectomy (total) 52.6
  partial NEC 52.59
  radical (one-stage) (two-stage) 52.7
    subtotal 52.53
Pancreatogram 87.66
  endoscopic retrograde (ERP) 52.13
Pancreatolithotomy 52.09
  endoscopic 52.94

Pancreatotomy 52.09
Pancreolithotomy 52.09
  endoscopic 52.94
Panendoscopy 57.32
  specified site, other than bladder —
    see Endoscopy, by site
  through artificial stoma 57.31
Panhysterectomy (abdominal)
  68.49   ▲
  laparoscopic 68.41   ●
  vaginal 68.59
    laparoscopically assisted (LAVH)
      68.51
Panniculectomy 86.83
Panniculotomy 86.83
Pantaloon operation (revision of gastric
  anastomosis) 44.5
Papillectomy, anal 49.39
  endoscopic 49.31
Papillotomy (pancreas) 51.82
  endoscopic 51.85
Paquin operation (ureteroneocystostomy) 56.74
Paracentesis
  abdominal (percutaneous) 54.91
  anterior chamber, eye 12.91
  bladder 57.11
  cornea 12.91
  eye (anterior chamber) 12.91
  thoracic, thoracis 34.91
  tympanum 20.09
    with intubation 20.01
Parasitology — see Examination, microscopic
Parathyroidectomy (partial) (subtotal)
  NEC 06.89
  complete 06.81
  ectopic 06.89
  global removal 06.81
  mediastinal 06.89
  total 06.81
Parenteral nutrition, total 99.15
  peripheral 99.15
Parotidectomy 26.30
  complete 26.32
  partial 26.31
  radical 26.32
Partsch operation (marsupialization of
  dental cyst) 24.4
Passage — see Insertion and Intubation
Passage of sounds, urethra 58.6
Patch
  blood, spinal (epidural) 03.95
  graft — see Graft
  spinal, blood (epidural) 03.95
  subdural, brain 02.12
Patellapexy 78.46
Patellaplasty NEC 78.46
Patellectomy 77.96
  partial 77.86
Pattee operation (auditory canal) 18.6
Pectenotomy — see also Sphincteroto-
  my, anal 49.59
Pedicle flap — see Graft, skin, pedicle
Peet operation (splanchnic resection)
  05.29
PEG (percutaneous endoscopic gastrosto-
  my) 43.11
PEJ (percutaneous endoscopic jejunosto-
  my) 46.32
Pelvectomy, kidney (partial) 55.4
Pelvimetry 88.25
  gynecological 89.26
Pelviolithotomy 55.11
Pelvioplasty, kidney 55.87
Pelviostomy 55.12
  closure 55.82
Pelviotomy 77.39
  to assist delivery 73.94
Pelvi-ureteroplasty 55.87
Pemberton operation
  osteotomy of ilium 77.39
  rectum (mobilization and fixation for
    prolapse repair) 48.76
Penectomy 64.3

Pereyra operation (paraurethral suspension) 59.6
Perforation
  stapes footplate 19.0
Perfusion NEC 39.97
  for
    chemotherapy NEC 99.25
    hormone therapy NEC 99.24
  carotid artery 39.97
  coronary artery 39.97
  head 39.97
  hyperthermic (lymphatic), localized
    region or site 93.35
  intestine (large) (local) 46.96
    small 46.95
  kidney, local 55.95
  limb (lower) (upper) 39.97
  liver, localized 50.93
  neck 39.97
  subarachnoid (spinal cord) (refrigerat-
    ed saline) 03.92
  total body 39.96
Pericardiectomy 37.31
Pericardiocentesis 37.0
Pericardiolysis 37.12
Pericardioplasty 37.49
Pericardiorrhaphy 37.49
Pericardiostomy (tube) 37.12
Pericardiotomy 37.12
Peridectomy 10.31
Perilimbal suction 89.11
Perimetry 95.05
Perineoplasty 71.79
Perineorrhaphy 71.71
  obstetrical laceration (current) 75.69
Perineotomy (nonobstetrical) 71.09
  to assist delivery — see Episiotomy
Periosteotomy — see also Incision, bone
  77.10
  facial bone 76.09
Perirectofistulectomy 48.93
Peritectomy 10.31
Peritomy 10.1
Peritoneocentesis 54.91
Peritoneoscopy 54.21
Peritoneotomy 54.19
Peritoneumectomy 54.4
Phacoemulsification (ultrasonic) (with
  aspiration) 13.41
Phacofragmentation (mechanical) (with
  aspiration) 13.43
  posterior route 13.42
  ultrasonic 13.41
Phalangectomy (partial) 77.89
  claw toe 77.57
  cockup toe 77.58
  hammer toe 77.56
  overlapping toe 77.58
  total 77.99
Phalangization (fifth metacarpal) 82.81
Pharyngeal flap operation (cleft palate
  repair) 27.62
  secondary or subsequent 27.63
Pharyngectomy (partial) 29.33
  with laryngectomy 30.3
Pharyngogram 87.09
  contrast 87.06
Pharyngolaryngectomy 30.3
Pharyngoplasty (with silastic implant)
  29.4
  for cleft palate 27.62
    secondary or subsequent 27.63
Pharyngorrhaphy 29.51
  for cleft palate 27.62
Pharyngoscopy 29.11
Pharyngotomy 29.0
Phenopeel (skin) 86.24
Phlebectomy 38.60
  with
    anastomosis 38.30
      abdominal 38.37
      head and neck NEC 38.32
      intracranial NEC 38.31
      lower limb 38.39
      thoracic NEC 38.35
      upper limb 38.33

☑ Additional Digit Required — Refer to the Tabular List for Digit Selection
  ▽ Subterms under main terms may continue to next column or page
44 — Volume 3 · October 2006
▶◀ Revised Text   ● New Line   ▲ Revised Code
2007 ICD-9-CM

Phlebectomy — continued
with — continued
- graft replacement 38.4 ☑
  - abdominal 38.47
  - head and neck NEC 38.42
  - intracranial NEC 38.41
  - lower limb 38.49
  - thoracic NEC 38.45
  - upper limb 38.43
- abdominal 38.67
- head and neck NEC 38.62
- intracranial NEC 38.61
- lower limb 38.69
- thoracic NEC 38.65
- upper limb 38.63
- varicose 38.50
  - abdominal 38.57
  - head and neck NEC 38.52
  - intracranial NEC 38.51
  - lower limb 38.59
  - thoracic NEC 38.55
  - upper limb 38.53

Phlebogoniostomy 12.52
Phlebography (contrast) (retrograde) 88.60
- by radioisotope — see Scan, radioisotope, by site
- adrenal 88.65
- femoral 88.66
- head 88.61
- hepatic 88.64
- impedance 88.68
- intra-abdominal NEC 88.65
- intrathoracic NEC 88.63
- lower extremity NEC 88.66
- neck 88.61
- portal system 88.64
- pulmonary 88.62
- specified site NEC 88.67
- vena cava (inferior) (superior) 88.51

Phleborrhaphy 39.32
Phlebotomy 38.99
Phonocardiogram, with ECG lead 89.55
Photochemotherapy NEC 99.83
- extracorporeal 99.88

Photocoagulation
- ciliary body 12.73
- eye, eyeball 16.99
- iris 12.41
- macular hole — see Photocoagulation, retina
- orbital lesion 16.92
- retina
  - for
    - destruction of lesion 14.25
    - reattachment 14.55
    - repair of tear or defect 14.35
  - laser (beam)
    - for
      - destruction of lesion 14.24
      - reattachment 14.54
      - repair of tear or defect 14.34
  - xenon arc
    - for
      - destruction of lesion 14.23
      - reattachment 14.53
      - repair of tear or defect 14.33

Photography 89.39
- fundus 95.11
Photopheresis, therapeutic 99.88
Phototherapy NEC 99.83
- newborn 99.83
- ultraviolet 99.82
Phrenemphraxis 04.03
- for collapse of lung 33.31
Phrenicectomy 04.03
- for collapse of lung 33.31
Phrenicoexeresis 04.03
- for collapse of lung 33.31
Phrenicotomy 04.03
- for collapse of lung 33.31
Phrenicotripsy 04.03
- for collapse of lung 33.31
Phrenoplasty 34.84
Physical medicine — see Therapy, physical

Physical therapy — see Therapy, physical
Physiotherapy, chest 93.99
PICC (peripherally inserted central catheter) 38.93
Piercing ear, external (pinna) 18.01
Pigmenting, skin 86.02
Pilojection (aneurysm) (Gallagher) 39.52
Pinealectomy (complete) (total) 07.54
- partial 07.53
Pinealotomy (with drainage) 07.52
Pinning
- bone — see Fixation, bone, internal
- ear 18.5
Pinsker operation (obliteration of nasoseptal telangiectasia) 21.07
Piper operation (forceps) 72.6
Pirogoff operation (ankle amputation through malleoli of tibia and fibula) 84.14
Pituitectomy (complete) (total) — see also Hypophysectomy 07.69
Placentogram, placentography 88.46
- with radioisotope (RISA) 92.17
Planing, skin 86.25
Plantation, tooth (bud) (germ) 23.5
- prosthetic 23.6
Plasma exchange 99.07
Plasmapheresis, therapeutic 99.71
Plastic repair — see Repair, by site
Plasty — see also Repair, by site
- bladder neck (V-Y) 57.85
- skin (without graft) 86.89
- subcutaneous tissue 86.89
Platelet inhibitor (GP IIb/IIIa inhibitor only), infusion 99.20
Plateletpheresis, therapeutic 99.74
Play
- psychotherapy 94.36
- therapy 93.81
Pleating
- eye muscle 15.22
  - multiple (two or more muscles) 15.4
- sclera, for buckling (see also Buckling, scleral) 14.49
Plethysmogram (carotid) 89.58
- air-filled (pneumatic) 89.58
- capacitance 89.58
- cerebral 89.58
- differential 89.58
- oculoplethysmogram 89.58
- penile 89.58
- photoelectric 89.58
- regional 89.58
- respiratory function measurement (body) 89.38
- segmental 89.58
- strain-gauge 89.58
- thoracic impedance 89.38
- venous occlusion 89.58
- water-filled 89.58
Plethysmography
- CaverMap™ 89.58   ●
- penile 89.58
Pleurectomy NEC 34.59
Pleurocentesis 34.91
Pleurodesis 34.6
- chemical 34.92
  - with cancer chemotherapy substance 34.92 [99.25]
  - tetracycline 34.92 [99.21]
Pleurolysis (for collapse of lung) 33.39
Pleuropexy 34.99
Pleurosclerosis 34.6
- chemical 34.92
  - with cancer chemotherapy substance 34.92 [99.25]
  - tetracycline 34.92 [99.21]
Pleurotomy 34.09
Plexectomy
- choroid 02.14
- hypogastric 05.24
Plication
- aneurysm
  - heart 37.32

Plication — continued
- annulus, heart valve 35.33
- bleb (emphysematous), lung 32.21
- broad ligament 69.22
- diaphragm (for hernia repair) (thoracic approach) (thoracoabdominal approach) 53.81
- eye muscle (oblique) (rectus) 15.22
  - multiple (two or more muscles) 15.4
- fascia 83.89
  - hand 82.89
- inferior vena cava 38.7
- intestine (jejunum) (Noble) 46.62
- Kelly (-Stoeckel) (urethrovesical junction) 59.3
- levator, for blepharoptosis 08.34
- ligament (see also Arthroplasty) 81.96
  - broad 69.22
  - round 69.22
  - uterosacral 69.22
- mesentery 54.75
- round ligament 69.22
- sphincter, urinary bladder 57.85
- stomach 44.69
  - laparoscopic 44.68
- superior vena cava 38.7
- tendon 83.85
  - hand 82.55
- tricuspid valve (with repositioning) 35.14
- ureter 56.89
- urethra 58.49
- urethrovesical junction 59.3
- vein (peripheral) 39.59
- vena cava (inferior) (superior) 38.7
- ventricle (heart)
  - aneurysm 37.32
Plicotomy, tympanum 20.23
Plombage, lung 33.39
Pneumocentesis 33.93
Pneumocisternogram 87.02
Pneumoencephalogram 87.01
Pneumogram, pneumography
- extraperitoneal 88.15
- mediastinal 87.33
- orbit 87.14
- pelvic 88.13
- peritoneum NEC 88.13
- presacral 88.15
- retroperitoneum 88.15
Pneumogynecography 87.82
Pneumomediastinography 87.33
Pneumonectomy (complete) (extended) (radical) (standard) (total) (with mediastinal dissection) 32.5
- partial
  - complete excision, one lobe 32.4
  - resection (wedge), one lobe 32.3
Pneumonolysis (for collapse of lung) 33.39
Pneumonotomy (with exploration) 33.1
Pneumoperitoneum (surgically-induced) 54.96
- for collapse of lung 33.33
- pelvic 88.12
Pneumothorax (artificial) (surgical) 33.32
- intrapleural 33.32
Pneumoventriculogram 87.02
Politano-Leadbetter operation (ureteroneocystostomy) 56.74
Politerization, Eustachian tube 20.8
Pollicization (with carry over of nerves and blood supply) 82.61
Polya operation (gastrectomy) 43.7
Polypectomy — see also Excision, lesion, by site
- esophageal 42.32
  - endoscopic 42.33
- gastric (endoscopic) 43.41
- large intestine (colon) 45.42
- nasal 21.31
- rectum (endoscopic) 48.36
Polysomnogram 89.17
Pomeroy operation (ligation and division of fallopian tubes) 66.32

Poncet operation
- lengthening of Achilles tendon 83.85
- urethrostomy, perineal 58.0
Porro operation (cesarean section) 74.99
Portoenterostomy (Kasai) 51.37
Positrocephalogram 92.11
Positron emission tomography (PET) — see Scan, radioisotope
Postmortem examination 89.8
Potts-Smith operation (descending aorta-left pulmonary artery anastomosis) 39.0
Poudrage
- intrapericardial 36.39
- pleural 34.6
PPN (peripheral parenteral nutrition) 99.15
Preparation (cutting), pedicle (flap) graft 86.71
Preputiotomy 64.91
Prescription for glasses 95.31
Pressure support
- ventilation [PSV] — see category 96.7 ☑
Pressurized
- graft treatment 00.16
Printen and Mason operation (high gastric bypass) 44.31
Probing
- canaliculus, lacrimal (with irrigation) 09.42
- lacrimal
  - canaliculi 09.42
  - punctum (with irrigation) 09.41
  - nasolacrimal duct (with irrigation) 09.43
    - with insertion of tube or stent 09.44
- salivary duct (for dilation of duct) (for removal of calculus) 26.91
  - with incision 26.0
Procedure — see also specific procedure
- diagnostic NEC
  - abdomen (region) 54.29
  - adenoid 28.19
  - adrenal gland 07.19
  - alveolus 24.19
  - amnion 75.35
  - anterior chamber, eye 12.29
  - anus 49.29
  - appendix 45.28
  - biliary tract 51.19
  - bladder 57.39
  - blood vessel (any site) 38.29
  - bone 78.80
    - carpal, metacarpal 78.84
    - clavicle 78.81
    - facial 76.19
    - femur 78.85
    - fibula 78.87
    - humerus 78.82
    - marrow 41.38
    - patella 78.86
    - pelvic 78.89
    - phalanges (foot) (hand) 78.89
    - radius 78.83
    - scapula 78.81
    - specified site NEC 78.89
    - tarsal, metatarsal 78.88
    - thorax (ribs) (sternum) 78.81
    - tibia 78.87
    - ulna 78.83
    - vertebrae 78.89
  - brain 01.18
  - breast 85.19
  - bronchus 33.29
  - buccal 27.24
  - bursa 83.29
  - canthus 08.19
  - cecum 45.28
  - cerebral meninges 01.18
  - cervix 67.19
  - chest wall 34.28
  - choroid 14.19
  - ciliary body 12.29
  - clitoris 71.19

☑ Additional Digit Required — Refer to the Tabular List for Digit Selection   ▽ Subterms under main terms may continue to next column or page

2007 ICD-9-CM   ▶◀ Revised Text   ● New Line   ▲ Revised Code   **October 2006 · Volume 3 — 45**

Procedure — *see also* specific procedure
— *continued*
diagnostic — *continued*
colon 45.28
conjunctiva 10.29
cornea 11.29
cul-de-sac 70.29
dental 24.19
diaphragm 34.28
duodenum 45.19
ear
external 18.19
inner and middle 20.39
epididymis 63.09
esophagus 42.29
Eustachian tube 20.39
extraocular muscle or tendon
15.09
eye 16.29
anterior chamber 12.29
posterior chamber 14.19
eyeball 16.29
eyelid 08.19
fallopian tube 66.19
fascia (any site) 83.29
fetus 75.35
gallbladder 51.19
ganglion (cranial) (peripheral) 04.19
sympathetic 05.19
gastric 44.19
globus pallidus 01.18
gum 24.19
heart 37.29
hepatic 50.19
hypophysis 07.19
ileum 45.19
intestine 45.29
large 45.28
small 45.19
iris 12.29
jejunum 45.19
joint (capsule) (ligament) (structure)
NEC 81.98
facial 76.19
kidney 55.29
labia 71.19
lacrimal (system) 09.19
large intestine 45.28
larynx 31.48
ligament 81.98
uterine 68.19
liver 50.19
lung 33.29
lymphatic structure (channel)
(gland) (node) (vessel) 40.19
mediastinum 34.29
meninges (cerebral) 01.18
spinal 03.39
mouth 27.29
muscle 83.29
extraocular (oblique) (rectus)
15.09
papillary (heart) 37.29
nail 86.19
nasopharynx 29.19
nerve (cranial) (peripheral) NEC
04.19
sympathetic 05.19
nipple 85.19
nose, nasal 21.29
sinus 22.19
ocular 16.29
muscle 15.09
omentum 54.29
ophthalmologic 16.29
oral (cavity) 27.29
orbit 16.29
orthodontic 24.19
ovary 65.19
laparoscopic 65.14
palate 27.29
pancreas 52.19
papillary muscle (heart) 37.29
parathyroid gland 06.19
penis 64.19
perianal tissue 49.29

Procedure — *see also* specific procedure
— *continued*
diagnostic — *continued*
pericardium 37.29
periprostatic tissue 60.18
perirectal tissue 48.29
perirenal tissue 59.29
peritoneum 54.29
periurethral tissue 58.29
perivesical tissue 59.29
pharynx 29.19
pineal gland 07.19
pituitary gland 07.19
pleura 34.28
posterior chamber, eye 14.19
prostate 60.18
pulmonary 33.29
rectosigmoid 48.29
rectum 48.29
renal 55.29
respiratory 33.29
retina 14.19
retroperitoneum 59.29
salivary gland or duct 26.19
sclera 12.29
scrotum 61.19
seminal vesicle 60.19
sigmoid 45.28
sinus, nasal 22.19
skin 86.19
skull 01.19
soft tissue 83.29
spermatic cord 63.09
sphincter of Oddi 51.19
spine, spinal (canal) (cord)
(meninges) (structure) 03.39
spleen 41.39
stomach 44.19
subcutaneous tissue 86.19
sympathetic nerve 05.19
tarsus 09.19
tendon NEC 83.29
extraocular 15.09
testicle 62.19
thalamus 01.18
thoracic duct 40.19
thorax 34.28
thymus 07.19
thyroid gland 06.19
tongue 25.09
tonsils 28.19
tooth 24.19
trachea 31.49
tunica vaginalis 61.19
ureter 56.39
urethra 58.29
uterus and supporting structures
68.19
uvula 27.29
vagina 70.29
vas deferens 63.09
vesical 57.39
vessel (blood) (any site) 38.29
vitreous 14.19
vulva 71.19
fistulizing, sclera NEC 12.69
miscellaneous (nonoperative) NEC
99.99
respiratory (nonoperative) NEC 93.99
surgical — *see* Operation
Proctectasis 96.22
Proctectomy (partial) — *see also* Resection, rectum 48.69
abdominoperineal 48.5
complete (Miles) (Rankin) 48.5
pull-through 48.49
Proctoclysis 96.37
Proctolysis 48.99
Proctopexy (Delorme) 48.76
abdominal (Ripstein) 48.75
Proctoplasty 48.79
Proctorrhaphy 48.71
Proctoscopy 48.23
with biopsy 48.24
through stoma (artificial) 48.22
transabdominal approach 48.21

Proctosigmoidectomy — *see also* Resection, rectum 48.69
Proctosigmoidopexy 48.76
Proctosigmoidoscopy (rigid) 48.23
with biopsy 48.24
flexible 45.24
through stoma (artificial) 48.22
transabdominal approach 48.21
Proctostomy 48.1
Proctotomy (decompression) (linear) 48.0
Production — *see also* Formation and Creation
atrial septal defect 35.42
subcutaneous tunnel for esophageal anastomosis 42.86
with anastomosis — *see* Anastomosis, esophagus, antesternal
Prognathic recession 76.64
Prophylaxis, dental (scaling) (polishing) 96.54
Prostatectomy (complete) (partial) NEC 60.69
loop 60.29
perineal 60.62
radical (any approach) 60.5
retropubic (punch) (transcapsular) 60.4
suprapubic (punch) (transvesical) 60.3
transcapsular NEC 60.69
retropubic 60.4
transperineal 60.62
transurethral 60.29
ablation (contact) (noncontact) by laser 60.21
electrovaporization 60.29
enucleative 60.29
resection of prostate (TURP) 60.29
ultrasound guided laser induced (TULIP) 60.21
transvesical punch (suprapubic) 60.3
Prostatocystotomy 60.0
Prostatolithotomy 60.0
Prostatotomy (perineal) 60.0
Prostatovesiculectomy 60.5
Protection (of)
individual from his surroundings 99.84
surroundings from individual 99.84
Psychoanalysis 94.31
Psychodrama 94.43
Psychotherapy NEC 94.39
biofeedback 94.39
exploratory verbal 94.37
group 94.44
for psychosexual dysfunctions 94.41
play 94.36
psychosexual dysfunctions 94.34
supportive verbal 94.38
PTCA (percutaneous transluminal coronary angioplasty) — *see* Angioplasty, balloon, coronary
Ptyalectasis 26.91
Ptyalithotomy 26.0
Ptyalolithotomy 26.0
Pubiotomy 77.39
assisting delivery 73.94
Pubococcygeoplasty 59.71
Puestow operation (pancreaticojejunostomy) 52.96
Pull-through
abdomino-anal 48.49
abdominoperineal 48.49
Duhamel type 48.65
endorectal 48.41
Pulmowrap 93.99
Pulpectomy — *see also* Therapy, root canal 23.70
Pulpotomy — *see also* Therapy, root canal 23.70
Pump-oxygenator, for extracorporeal circulation 39.61
percutaneous 39.66
Punch
operation
bladder neck, transurethral 57.49

Punch — *continued*
operation — *continued*
prostate — *see* Prostatectomy
resection, vocal cords 30.22
Puncture
antrum (nasal) (bilateral) (unilateral) 22.01
artery NEC 38.98
for
arteriography (*see also* Arteriography) 88.40
coronary arteriography (*see also* Arteriography, coronary) 88.57
percutaneous vascular closure — *omit code*
bladder, suprapubic (for drainage) NEC 57.18
needle 57.11
percutaneous (suprapubic) 57.17
bursa 83.94
hand 82.92
cisternal 01.01
with contrast media 87.02
cranial 01.09
with contrast media 87.02
craniobuccal pouch 07.72
craniopharyngioma 07.72
fallopian tube 66.91
fontanel, anterior 01.09
heart 37.0
for intracardiac injection 37.92
hypophysis 07.72
iris 12.12
joint 81.91
kidney (percutaneous) 55.92
larynx 31.98
lumbar (diagnostic) (removal of dye) 03.31
lung (for aspiration) 33.93
nasal sinus 22.01
pericardium 37.0
pituitary gland 07.72
pleural cavity 34.91
Rathke's pouch 07.72
spinal 03.31
spleen 41.1
for biopsy 41.32
sternal (for bone marrow biopsy) 41.31
donor for bone marrow transplant 41.91
vein NEC 38.99
for
phlebography (*see also* Phlebography) 88.60
transfusion — *see* Transfusion
ventricular shunt tubing 01.02
Pupillotomy 12.35
Push-back operation (cleft palate repair) 27.62
Putti-Platt operation (capsulorrhaphy of shoulder for recurrent dislocation) 81.82
pVAD (percutaneous ventricular assist device) 37.68
Pyelogram (intravenous) 87.73
infusion (continuous) (diuretic) 87.73
percutaneous 87.75
retrograde 87.74
Pyeloileostomy 56.71
Pyelolithotomy 55.11
Pyeloplasty 55.87
Pyelorrhaphy 55.81
Pyeloscopy 55.22
Pyelostolithotomy, percutaneous 55.03
Pyelostomy 55.12
closure 55.82
Pyelotomy 55.11
Pyeloureteroplasty 55.87
Pylorectomy 43.6
Pyloroduodenotomy — *see* category 44.2 ☑
Pyloromyotomy (Ramstedt) (with wedge resection) 43.3
Pyloroplasty (Finney) (Heineke-Mikulicz) 44.29

☑ Additional Digit Required — Refer to the Tabular List for Digit Selection   ▽ Subterms under main terms may continue to next column or page

46 — Volume 3   ▶◀ Revised Text   ● New Line   ▲ Revised Code   *2007 ICD-9-CM*

Pyloroplasty — continued
 dilation, endoscopic 44.22
  by incision 44.21
 not elsewhere classified 44.29
 revision 44.29
Pylorostomy — see Gastrostomy

Q

Quadrant resection of breast 85.22
Quadricepsplasty (Thompson) 83.86
Quarantine 99.84
Quenuthoracoplasty 77.31
Quotient, respiratory 89.38

R

Rabbit ear (Tudor) **operation** 59.79
Rachicentesis 03.31
Rachitomy 03.09
Radiation therapy — see also Therapy, radiation
 teleradiotherapy — see Teleradiotherapy
Radical neck dissection — see Dissection, neck
Radicotomy 03.1
Radiculectomy 03.1
Radiculotomy 03.1
Radiography (diagnostic) NEC 88.39
 abdomen, abdominal (flat plate) NEC 88.19
  wall (soft tissue) NEC 88.09
 adenoid 87.09
 ankle (skeletal) 88.28
  soft tissue 88.37
 bone survey 88.31
 bronchus 87.49
 chest (routine) 87.44
  wall NEC 87.39
 clavicle 87.43
 computer assisted surgery (CAS) with fluoroscopy 00.33
 contrast (air) (gas) (radio-opaque substance) NEC
  abdominal wall 88.03
  arteries (by fluoroscopy) — see Arteriography
  bile ducts NEC 87.54
  bladder NEC 87.77
  brain 87.02
  breast 87.35
  bronchus NEC (transcricoid) 87.32
   endotracheal 87.31
  epididymis 87.93
  esophagus 87.61
  fallopian tubes
   gas 87.82
   opaque dye 87.83
  fistula (sinus tract) (see also Radiography, contrast, by site)
   abdominal wall 88.03
   chest wall 87.38
  gallbladder NEC 87.59
  intervertebral disc(s) 87.21
  joints 88.32
  larynx 87.07
  lymph — see Lymphangiogram
  mammary ducts 87.35
  mediastinum 87.33
  nasal sinuses 87.15
  nasolacrimal ducts 87.05
  nasopharynx 87.06
  orbit 87.14
  pancreas 87.66
  pelvis
   gas 88.12
   opaque dye 88.11
  peritoneum NEC 88.13
  retroperitoneum NEC 88.15
  seminal vesicles 87.91
  sinus tract (see also Radiography, contrast, by site)
   abdominal wall 88.03
   chest wall 87.38
   nose 87.15
  skull 87.02

Radiography — continued
 contrast — continued
  spinal disc(s) 87.21
  trachea 87.32
  uterus
   gas 87.82
   opaque dye 87.83
  vas deferens 87.94
  veins (by fluoroscopy) — see Phlebography
  vena cava (inferior) (superior) 88.51
 dental NEC 87.12
 diaphragm 87.49
 digestive tract NEC 87.69
  barium swallow 87.61
  lower GI series 87.64
  small bowel series 87.63
  upper GI series 87.62
 elbow (skeletal) 88.22
  soft tissue 88.35
 epididymis NEC 87.95
 esophagus 87.69
  barium-swallow 87.61
 eye 95.14
 face, head, and neck 87.09
 facial bones 87.16
 fallopian tubes 87.85
 foot 88.28
 forearm (skeletal) 88.22
  soft tissue 88.35
 frontal area, facial 87.16
 genital organs
  female NEC 87.89
  male NEC 87.99
 hand (skeletal) 88.23
  soft tissue 88.35
 head NEC 87.09
 heart 87.49
 hip (skeletal) 88.26
  soft tissue 88.37
 intestine NEC 87.65
 kidney-ureter-bladder (KUB) 87.79
 knee (skeletal) 88.27
  soft tissue 88.37
 KUB (kidney-ureter-bladder) 87.79
 larynx 87.09
 lower leg (skeletal) 88.27
  soft tissue 88.37
 lower limb (skeletal) NEC 88.29
  soft tissue NEC 88.37
 lung 87.49
 mandible 87.16
 maxilla 87.16
 mediastinum 87.49
 nasal sinuses 87.16
 nasolacrimal duct 87.09
 nasopharynx 87.09
 neck NEC 87.09
 nose 87.16
 orbit 87.16
 pelvis (skeletal) 88.26
  pelvimetry 88.25
  soft tissue 88.19
 prostate NEC 87.92
 retroperitoneum NEC 88.16
 ribs 87.43
 root canal 87.12
 salivary gland 87.09
 seminal vesicles NEC 87.92
 shoulder (skeletal) 88.21
  soft tissue 88.35
 skeletal NEC 88.33
  series (whole or complete) 88.31
 skull (lateral, sagittal or tangential projection) NEC 87.17
 spine NEC 87.29
  cervical 87.22
  lumbosacral 87.24
  sacrococcygeal 87.24
  thoracic 87.23
 sternum 87.43
 supraorbital area 87.16
 symphysis menti 87.16
 teeth NEC 87.12
  full-mouth 87.11
 thigh (skeletal) 88.27

Radiography — continued
 thigh — continued
  soft tissue 88.37
 thyroid region 87.09
 tonsils and adenoids 87.09
 trachea 87.49
 ultrasonic — see Ultrasonography
 upper arm (skeletal) 88.21
  soft tissue 88.35
 upper limb (skeletal) NEC 88.24
  soft tissue NEC 88.35
 urinary system NEC 87.79
 uterus NEC 87.85
  gravid 87.81
 uvula 87.09
 vas deferens NEC 87.95
 wrist 88.23
 zygomaticomaxillary complex 87.16
Radioimmunotherapy 92.28
Radioisotope
 scanning — see Scan, radioisotope
 therapy — see Therapy, radioisotope
Radiology
 diagnostic — see Radiography
 therapeutic — see Therapy, radiation
Radiosurgery, stereotactic 92.30
 cobalt 60 92.32
 linear accelerator (LINAC) 92.31
 multi-source 92.32
 particle beam 92.33
 particulate 92.33
 radiosurgery NEC 92.39
 single source photon 92.31
Raising, pedicle graft 86.71
Ramadier operation (intrapetrosal drainage) 20.22
Ramisection (sympathetic) 05.0
Ramstedt operation (pyeloromyotomy) (with wedge resection) 43.3
Range of motion testing 93.05
Rankin operation
 exteriorization of intestine 46.03
 proctectomy (complete) 48.5
Rashkind operation (balloon septostomy) 35.41
Rastelli operation (creation of conduit between right ventricle and pulmonary artery) 35.92
 in repair of
  pulmonary artery atresia 35.92
  transposition of great vessels 35.92
  truncus arteriosus 35.83
Raz-Pereyra procedure (bladder neck suspension) 59.79
RCSA (radical cryosurgical ablation) of prostate 60.62
Readjustment — see Adjustment
Reamputation, stump 84.3
Reanastomosis — see Anastomosis
Reattachment
 amputated ear 18.72
 ankle 84.27
 arm (upper) NEC 84.24
 choroid and retina NEC 14.59
  by
   cryotherapy 14.52
   diathermy 14.51
   electrocoagulation 14.51
   photocoagulation 14.55
    laser 14.54
    xenon arc 14.53
 ear (amputated) 18.72
 extremity 84.29
  ankle 84.27
  arm (upper) NEC 84.24
  fingers, except thumb 84.22
   thumb 84.21
  foot 84.26
  forearm 84.23
  hand 84.23
  leg (lower) NEC 84.27
  thigh 84.28
  thumb 84.21
  toe 84.25
  wrist 84.23
 finger 84.22

Reattachment — continued
 finger — continued
  thumb 84.21
 foot 84.26
 forearm 84.23
 hand 84.23
 joint capsule (see also Arthroplasty) 81.96
 leg (lower) NEC 84.27
 ligament (see also Arthroplasty)
  uterosacral 69.22
 muscle 83.74
  hand 82.54
  papillary (heart) 35.31
 nerve (peripheral) 04.79
 nose (amputated) 21.89
 papillary muscle (heart) 35.31
 penis (amputated) 64.45
 retina (and choroid) NEC 14.59
  by
   cryotherapy 14.52
   diathermy 14.51
   electrocoagulation 14.51
   photocoagulation 14.55
    laser 14.54
    xenon arc 14.53
 tendon (to tendon) 83.73
  hand 82.53
  to skeletal attachment 83.88
   hand 82.85
 thigh 84.28
 thumb 84.21
 toe 84.25
 tooth 23.5
 uterosacral ligament(s) 69.22
 vessels (peripheral) 39.59
  renal, aberrant 39.55
 wrist 84.23
Recession
 extraocular muscle 15.11
  multiple (two or more muscles) (with advancement or resection) 15.3
 gastrocnemius tendon (Strayer operation) 83.72
 levator palpebrae (superioris) muscle 08.38
 prognathic jaw 76.64
 tendon 83.72
  hand 82.52
Reclosure — see also Closure
 disrupted abdominal wall (postoperative) 54.61
Reconstruction (plastic) — see also Construction and Repair, by site
 alveolus, alveolar (process) (ridge) (with graft or implant) 24.5
 artery (graft) — see Graft, artery
 artificial stoma, intestine 46.40
 auditory canal (external) 18.6
 auricle (ear) 18.71
 bladder 57.87
  with
   ileum 57.87 [45.51]
   sigmoid 57.87 [45.52]
 bone, except facial (see also Osteoplasty) 78.40
  facial NEC 76.46
   with total ostectomy 76.44
  mandible 76.43
   with total mandibulectomy 76.41
 breast, total 85.7
 bronchus 33.48
 canthus (lateral) 08.59
 cardiac annulus 35.33
 chest wall (mesh) (silastic) 34.79
 cleft lip 27.54
 conjunctival cul-de-sac 10.43
  with graft (buccal mucous membrane) (free) 10.42
 cornea NEC 11.79
 diaphragm 34.84
 ear (external) (auricle) 18.71
  external auditory canal 18.6

Reconstruction — *see also* Construction and Repair, by site — *continued*
 ear — *continued*
  meatus (new) (osseous skin-lined) 18.6
  ossicles 19.3
  prominent or protruding 18.5
 eyebrow 08.70
 eyelid 08.70
  with graft or flap 08.69
   hair follicle 08.63
   mucous membrane 08.62
   skin 08.61
   tarsoconjunctival (one-stage) (two-stage) 08.64
  full-thickness 08.74
   involving lid margin 08.73
  partial-thickness 08.72
   involving lid margin 08.71
 eye socket 16.64
  with graft 16.63
 fallopian tube 66.79
 foot and toes (with fixation device) 81.57
  with prosthetic implant 81.57
 frontonasal duct 22.79
 hip (total) (with prosthesis) 81.51
 intraoral 27.59
 joint — *see* Arthroplasty
 lymphatic (by transplantation) 40.9
 mandible 76.43
  with total mandibulectomy 76.41
 mastoid cavity 19.9
 mouth 27.59
 nipple NEC 85.87
 nose (total) (with arm flap) (with forehead flap) 21.83
 ossicles (graft) (prosthesis) NEC 19.3
  with
   stapedectomy 19.19
   tympanoplasty 19.53
 pelvic floor 71.79
 penis (rib graft) (skin graft) (myocutaneous flap) 64.44
 pharynx 29.4
 scrotum (with pedicle flap) (with rotational flap) 61.49
 skin (plastic) (without graft) NEC 86.89
  with graft — *see* Graft, skin
 subcutaneous tissue (plastic) (without skin graft) NEC 86.89
  with graft — *see* Graft, skin
 tendon pulley — (with graft) (with local tissue) 83.83
  for opponensplasty 82.71
  hand 82.71
 thumb (osteoplastic) (with bone graft) (with skin graft) 82.69
 trachea (with graft) 31.75
 umbilicus 53.49
 ureteropelvic junction 55.87
 urethra 58.46
 vagina 70.62
 vas deferens, surgically divided 63.82
Recontour, gingiva 24.2
Recreational therapy 93.81
Rectectomy — *see also* Resection, rectum 48.69
Rectopexy (Delorme) 48.76
 abdominal (Ripstein) 48.75
Rectoplasty 48.79
Rectorectostomy 48.74
Rectorrhaphy 48.71
Rectosigmoidectomy — *see also* Resection, rectum 48.69
 transsacral 48.61
Rectosigmoidostomy 45.94
Rectostomy 48.1
 closure 48.72
Red cell survival studies 92.05
Reduction
 adipose tissue 86.83
 batwing arms 86.83
 breast (bilateral) 85.32
  unilateral 85.31

Reduction — *continued*
 bulbous tuberosities (mandible) (maxilla) (fibrous) (osseous) 24.31
 buttocks 86.83
 diastasis, ankle mortise (closed) 79.77
  open 79.87
 dislocation (of joint) (manipulation) (with cast) (with splint) (with traction device) (closed) 79.70
  with fracture — *see* Reduction, fracture, by site
  ankle (closed) 79.77
   open 79.87
  elbow (closed) 79.72
   open 79.82
  finger (closed) 79.74
   open 79.84
  foot (closed) 79.78
   open 79.88
  hand (closed) 79.74
   open 79.84
  hip (closed) 79.75
   open 79.85
  knee (closed) 79.76
   open 79.86
  open (with external fixation) (with internal fixation) 79.80
   specified site NEC 79.89
  shoulder (closed) 79.71
   open 79.81
  specified site (closed) NEC 79.79
   open 79.89
  temporomandibular (closed) 76.93
   open 76.94
  toe (closed) 79.78
   open 79.88
  wrist (closed) 79.73
   open 79.83
 elephantiasis, scrotum 61.3
 epistaxis (*see also* Control, epistaxis) 21.00
 fracture (bone) (with cast) (with splint) (with traction device) (closed) 79.00
  with internal fixation 79.10
  alveolar process (with stabilization of teeth)
   mandible (closed) 76.75
    open 76.77
   maxilla (closed) 76.73
    open 76.77
  ankle — *see* Reduction, fracture, leg
  arm (closed) NEC 79.02
   with internal fixation 79.12
   open 79.22
    with internal fixation 79.32
  blow-out — *see* Reduction, fracture, orbit
  carpal, metacarpal (closed) 79.03
   with internal fixation 79.13
   open 79.23
    with internal fixation 79.33
  epiphysis — *see* Reduction, separation
  facial (bone) NEC 76.70
   closed 76.78
   open 76.79
  femur (closed) 79.05
   with internal fixation 79.15
   open 79.25
    with internal fixation 79.35
  fibula (closed) 79.06
   with internal fixation 79.16
   open 79.26
    with internal fixation 79.36
  foot (closed) NEC 79.07
   with internal fixation 79.17
   open 79.27
    with internal fixation 79.37
  hand (closed) NEC 79.03
   with internal fixation 79.13
   open 79.23
    with internal fixation 79.33

Reduction — *continued*
 fracture — *continued*
  humerus (closed) 79.01
   with internal fixation 79.11
   open 79.21
    with internal fixation 79.31
  jaw (lower) (*see also* Reduction, fracture, mandible)
   upper — *see* Reduction, fracture, maxilla
  larynx 31.64
  leg (closed) NEC 79.06
   with internal fixation 79.16
   open 79.26
    with internal fixation 79.36
  malar 76.71
   open 76.72
  mandible (with dental wiring) (closed) 76.75
   open 76.76
  maxilla (with dental wiring) (closed) 76.73
   open 76.74
  nasal (closed) 21.71
   open 21.72
  open 79.20
   with internal fixation 79.30
   specified site NEC 79.29
    with internal fixation 79.39
  orbit (rim) (wall) (closed) 76.78
   open 76.79
  patella (open) (with internal fixation) 79.36
  phalanges
   foot (closed) 79.08
    with internal fixation 79.18
    open 79.28
     with internal fixation 79.38
   hand (closed) 79.04
    with internal fixation 79.14
    open 79.24
     with internal fixation 79.34
  radius (closed) 79.02
   with internal fixation 79.12
   open 79.22
    with internal fixation 79.32
  skull 02.02
  specified site (closed) NEC 79.09
   with internal fixation 79.19
   open 79.29
    with internal fixation 79.39
  spine 03.53
  tarsal, metatarsal (closed) 79.07
   with internal fixation 79.17
   open 79.27
    with internal fixation 79.37
  tibia (closed) 79.06
   with internal fixation 79.16
   open 79.26
    with internal fixation 79.36
  ulna (closed) 79.02
   with internal fixation 79.12
   open 79.22
    with internal fixation 79.32
  vertebra 03.53
  zygoma, zygomatic arch (closed) 76.71
   open 76.72
  fracture-dislocation — *see* Reduction, fracture
 heart volume 37.35
 hemorrhoids (manual) 49.41
 hernia (*see also* Repair, hernia)
  manual 96.27
 intussusception (open) 46.80
  with
   fluoroscopy 96.29
   ionizing radiation enema 96.29
   ultrasonography guidance 96.29
  hydrostatic 96.29
  large intestine 46.82
   endoscopic (balloon) 46.85
  pneumatic 96.29
  small intestine 46.81

Reduction — *continued*
 lung volume 32.22
  biologic lung volume reduction (BLVR) — *see* category 33.7 ☑ ●
 malrotation, intestine (manual) (surgical) 46.80
  large 46.82
   endoscopic (balloon) 46.85
  small 46.81
 mammoplasty (bilateral) 85.32
  unilateral 85.31
 prolapse
  anus (operative) 49.94
  colostomy (manual) 96.28
  enterostomy (manual) 96.28
  ileostomy (manual) 96.28
  rectum (manual) 96.26
  uterus
   by pessary 96.18
   surgical 69.22
 ptosis overcorrection 08.37
 retroversion, uterus by pessary 96.18
 separation, epiphysis (with internal fixation) (closed) 79.40
  femur (closed) 79.45
   open 79.55
  fibula (closed) 79.46
   open 79.56
  humerus (closed) 79.41
   open 79.51
  open 79.50
  specified site (closed) NEC (*see also* category) 79.4 ☑
   open — *see* category 79.5 ☑
  tibia (closed) 79.46
   open 79.56
 size
  abdominal wall (adipose) (pendulous) 86.83
  arms (adipose) (batwing) 86.83
  breast (bilateral) 85.32
   unilateral 85.31
  buttocks (adipose) 86.83
  finger (macrodactyly repair) 82.83
  skin 86.83
  subcutaneous tissue 86.83
  thighs (adipose) 86.83
 torsion
  intestine (manual) (surgical) 46.80
   large 46.82
    endoscopic (balloon) 46.85
   small 46.81
  kidney pedicle 55.84
  omentum 54.74
  spermatic cord 63.52
   with orchiopexy 62.5
  testis 63.52
   with orchiopexy 62.5
  uterus NEC 69.98
   gravid 75.99
 ventricular 37.35
 volvulus
  intestine 46.80
   large 46.82
    endoscopic (balloon) 46.85
   small 46.81
  stomach 44.92
Reefing, joint capsule — *see also* Arthroplasty 81.96
Re-entry operation (aorta) 39.54
Re-establishment, continuity — *see also* Anastomosis
 bowel 46.50
 fallopian tube 66.79
 vas deferens 63.82
Referral (for)
 psychiatric aftercare (halfway house) (outpatient clinic) 94.52
 psychotherapy 94.51
 rehabilitation
  alcoholism 94.53
  drug addiction 94.54
  psychologic NEC 94.59
  vocational 94.55

☑ Additional Digit Required — Refer to the Tabular List for Digit Selection   ▽ Subterms under main terms may continue to next column or page

48 — Volume 3 · October 2006   ▶◀ Revised Text   ● New Line   ▲ Revised Code   *2007 ICD-9-CM*

Reformation
cardiac pacemaker pocket, new site (skin) (subcutaneous) 37.79
cardioverter/defibrillator (automatic) pocket, new site (skin) (subcutaneous) 37.99
chamber of eye 12.99

Refracture
bone (for faulty union) (see also Osteoclasis) 78.70
nasal bones 21.88

Refusion
spinal, NOS 81.30

Note: Also use either 81.62, 81.63, or 81.64 as an additional code to show the total number of vertebrae fused

atlas-axis (anterior) (transoral) (posterior) 81.31
cervical (C$_2$ level or below) NEC 81.32
  anterior (interbody), anterolateral technique 81.32
  C$_1$-C$_2$ level (anterior) (posterior) 81.31
  posterior (interbody), posterolateral technique 81.33
craniocervical (anterior) (transoral) (posterior) 81.31
dorsal, dorsolumbar NEC 81.35
  anterior (interbody) anterolateral technique 81.34
  posterior (interbody), posterolateral technique 81.35
lumbar, lumbosacral NEC 81.38
  anterior (interbody), anterolateral technique 81.36
  anterior lumbar interbody fusion (ALIF) 81.36
  lateral transverse process technique 81.37
  posterior lumbar interbody fusion (PLIF) 81.38
  posterior (interbody), posterolateral technique 81.38
  transforaminal lumbar interbody fusion (TLIF) 81.38
number of vertebrae — see codes 81.62-81.64
occiput — C$_2$ (anterior) (transoral) (posterior) 81.31
refusion NEC 81.39

Regional blood flow study 92.05
Regulation, menstrual 69.6
Rehabilitation programs NEC 93.89
alcohol 94.61
  with detoxification 94.63
  combined alcohol and drug 94.67
    with detoxification 94.69
drug 94.64
  with detoxification 94.66
  combined drug and alcohol 94.67
    with detoxification 94.69
sheltered employment 93.85
vocational 93.85

Reimplantation
adrenal tissue (heterotopic) (orthotopic) 07.45
artery 39.59
  renal, aberrant 39.55
bile ducts following excision of ampulla of Vater 51.62
extremity — see Reattachment, extremity
fallopian tube into uterus 66.74
kidney 55.61
lung 33.5 ☑
ovary 65.72
  laparoscopic 65.75
pancreatic tissue 52.81
parathyroid tissue (heterotopic) (orthotopic) 06.95
pulmonary artery for hemitruncus repair 35.83
renal vessel, aberrant 39.55
testis in scrotum 62.5

Reimplantation — continued
thyroid tissue (heterotopic) (orthotopic) 06.94
tooth 23.5
ureter into bladder 56.74

Reinforcement — see also Repair, by site
sclera NEC 12.88
  with graft 12.87

Reinsertion — see also Insertion or Revision
cystostomy tube 59.94
fixation device (internal) (see also Fixation, bone, internal) 78.50
heart valve (prosthetic) 35.95
Holter (-Spitz) valve 02.42
implant (expelled) (extruded)
  eyeball (with conjunctival graft) 16.62
  orbital 16.62
nephrostomy tube 55.93
pyelostomy tube 55.94
ureteral stent (transurethral) 59.8
  with ureterotomy 59.8 *[56.2]*
ureterostomy tube 59.93
valve
  heart (prosthetic) 35.95
  ventricular (cerebral) 02.42

Relaxation — see also Release training 94.33

Release
carpal tunnel (for nerve decompression) 04.43
celiac artery axis 39.91
central slip, extensor tendon hand (mallet finger repair) 82.84
chordee 64.42
clubfoot NEC 83.84
de Quervain's tenosynovitis 82.01
Dupuytren's contracture (by palmar fasciectomy) 82.35
  by fasciotomy (subcutaneous) 82.12
    with excision 82.35
Fowler (mallet finger repair) 82.84
joint (capsule) (adherent) (constrictive) (see also Division, joint capsule) 80.40
laryngeal 31.92
ligament (see also Division, ligament) 80.40
  median arcuate 39.91
median arcuate ligament 39.91
muscle (division) 83.19
  hand 82.19
nerve (peripheral) NEC 04.49
  cranial NEC 04.42
  trigeminal 04.41
pressure, intraocular 12.79
scar tissue
  skin 86.84
  stoma — see Revision, stoma
tarsal tunnel 04.44
tendon 83.13
  hand 82.11
    extensor, central slip (repair mallet finger) 82.84
  sheath 83.01
    hand 82.01
tenosynovitis 83.01
  abductor pollicis longus 82.01
  de Quervain's 82.01
  external pollicis brevis 82.01
  hand 82.01
torsion
  intestine 46.80
    large 46.82
      endoscopic (balloon) 46.85
    small 46.81
  kidney pedicle 55.84
  ovary 65.95
  testes 63.52
transverse carpal ligament (for nerve decompression) 04.43
trigger finger or thumb 82.01
urethral stricture 58.5

Release — continued
Volkmann's contracture
  excision of scar, muscle 83.32
  fasciotomy 83.14
  muscle transplantation 83.77
web contracture (skin) 86.84

Relief — see Release

Relocation — see also Revision
cardiac device (CRT-D) (CRT-P) (defibrillator) (pacemaker) pocket, new site (skin) (subcutaneous) 37.79
CRT-D pocket 37.79
CRT-P pocket 37.79
subcutaneous device pocket NEC 86.09

Remobilization
joint 93.16
stapes 19.0

Remodel
ventricle 37.35

Removal — see also Excision
Abrams bar (chest wall) 34.01
abscess — see Incision, by site
adenoid tag(s) 28.6
anal sphincter
  with revision 49.75
  without revision 49.76
arch bars (orthodontic) 24.8
  immobilization device 97.33
arterial graft or prosthesis 39.49
arteriovenous shunt (device) 39.43
  with creation of new shunt 39.42
Barton's tongs (skull) 02.95
  with synchronous replacement 02.94
bladder sphincter, artificial 58.99
  with replacement 58.93
blood clot (see also Incision, by site)
  bladder (by incision) 57.19
    without incision 57.0
  kidney (without incision) 56.0
    by incision 55.01
  ureter
    by incision 56.2
bone fragment (chip) (see also Incision, bone) 77.10
  joint (see also Arthrotomy) 80.10
  necrotic (see also Sequestrectomy, bone) 77.00
    joint (see also Arthrotomy) 80.10
  skull 01.25
    with debridement compound fracture 02.02
bone growth stimulator — see category 78.6 ☑
bony spicules, spinal canal 03.53
brace 97.88
breast implant 85.94
  tissue expander 85.96
bronchial device or substance   ●
  endoscopic 33.78   ●
calcareous deposit
  bursa 83.03
    hand 82.03
  tendon, intratendinous 83.39
    hand 82.29
calcification, heart valve leaflets — see Valvuloplasty, heart
calculus
  bile duct (by incision) 51.49
    endoscopic 51.88
    laparoscopic 51.88
    percutaneous 51.98
  bladder (by incision) 57.19
    without incision 57.0
  common duct (by incision) 51.41
    endoscopic 51.88
    laparoscopic 51.88
    percutaneous 51.96
  gallbladder 51.04
    endoscopic 51.88
    laparoscopic 51.88
  kidney (by incision) 55.01
    without incision (transurethral) 56.0

Removal — see also Excision — continued
calculus — continued
  kidney — continued
    percutaneous 55.03
      with fragmentation (ultrasound) 55.04
    renal pelvis (by incision) 55.11
      percutaneous nephrostomy 55.03
        with fragmentation 55.04
    transurethral 56.0
  lacrimal
    canaliculi 09.42
      by incision 09.52
    gland 09.3
      by incision 09.0
    passage(s) 09.49
      by incision 09.59
    punctum 09.41
      by incision 09.51
    sac 09.49
      by incision 09.53
  pancreatic duct (by incision) 52.09
    endoscopic 52.94
  perirenal tissue 59.09
  pharynx 29.39
  prostate 60.0
  salivary gland (by incision) 26.0
    by probe 26.91
  ureter (by incision) 56.2
    without incision 56.0
  urethra (by incision) 58.0
    without incision 58.6
caliper tongs (skull) 02.95
cannula
  for extracorporeal membrane oxygenation (ECMO) — omit code
cardiac pacemaker (device) (initial) (permanent) (cardiac resynchronization device, CRT-P) 37.89
  with replacement
    cardiac resynchronization pacemaker (CRT-P)
      device only 00.53
      total system 00.50
    dual-chamber 37.87
    single-chamber device 37.85
      rate responsive 37.86
cardioverter/defibrillator pulse generator without replacement (cardiac resynchronization defibrillator device (CRT-D) 37.79 ▲
cast 97.88
  with reapplication 97.13
  lower limb 97.12
  upper limb 97.11
catheter (indwelling) (see also Removal, tube)
  bladder 97.64
  cranial cavity 01.27
  middle ear (tympanum) 20.1
  ureter 97.62
  urinary 97.64
  ventricular (cerebral) 02.43
    with synchronous replacement 02.42
cerclage material, cervix 69.96
cerumen, ear 96.52
corneal epithelium 11.41
  for smear or culture 11.21
coronary artery obstruction (thrombus) 36.09
  direct intracoronary artery infusion 36.04
  open chest approach 36.03

☑ Additional Digit Required — Refer to the Tabular List for Digit Selection   ▽ Subterms under main terms may continue to next column or page

2007 ICD-9-CM   ▶◀ Revised Text   ● New Line   ▲ Revised Code   October 2006 · Volume 3 — 49

Removal — *see also* Excision — *continued*
coronary artery obstruction — *continued*
percutaneous transluminal (balloon) 00.66

Note — Also use 00.40, 00.41, 00.42, or 00.43 to show the total number of vessels treated. ▶Use code 00.44 once to show procedure on a bifurcated vessel.◀ In addition, use 00.45, 00.46, 00.47, or 00.48 to show the number of vascular stents inserted.

Crutchfield tongs (skull) 02.95
with synchronous replacement 02.94
cyst (*see also* Excision, lesion, by site)
dental 24.4
lung 32.29
endoscopic 32.28
cystic duct remnant 51.61
decidua (by)
aspiration curettage 69.52
curettage (D and C) 69.02
manual 75.4
dental wiring (immobilization device) 97.33
orthodontic 24.8
device (therapeutic) NEC 97.89
for musculoskeletal immobilization NEC 97.88
abdomen NEC 97.86
bronchus 33.78 ●
valve 33.78 ●
digestive system NEC 97.59
drainage — *see* Removal, tube
external fixation device 97.88
mandibular NEC 97.36
minifixator (bone) — *see* category 78.6 ☑
genital tract NEC 97.79
head and neck NEC 97.39
intrauterine contraceptive 97.71
spine 80.09
thorax NEC 97.49
trunk NEC 97.87
urinary system NEC 97.69
diaphragm, vagina 97.73
drainage device — *see* Removal, tube
dye, spinal canal 03.31
ectopic fetus (from) 66.02
abdominal cavity 74.3
extraperitoneal (intraligamentous) 74.3
fallopian tube (by salpingostomy) 66.02
by salpingotomy 66.01
with salpingectomy 66.62
intraligamentous 74.3
ovarian 74.3
peritoneal (following uterine or tubal rupture) 74.3
site NEC 74.3
tubal (by salpingostomy) 66.02
by salpingotomy 66.01
with salpingectomy 66.62
electrodes
bone growth stimulator — *see* category 78.6 ☑
brain 01.22
depth 01.22
with synchronous replacement 02.93
foramen ovale 01.22
with synchronous replacement 02.93
sphenoidal — *omit code*
with synchronous replacement 02.96
cardiac pacemaker (atrial) (transvenous) (ventricular) 37.77
with replacement 37.76
depth 01.22
with synchronous replacement 02.93

Removal — *see also* Excision — *continued*
electrodes — *continued*
epicardial (myocardial) 37.77
with replacement (by)
atrial and/or ventricular lead(s) (electrode) 37.76
epicardial lead 37.74
epidural pegs 01.22
with synchronous replacement 02.93
foramen ovale 01.22
with synchronous replacement 02.93
gastric 04.93 ●
with synchronous replacement ●
04.92 ●
intracranial 01.22
with synchronous replacement 02.93
peripheral nerve 04.93
with synchronous replacement 04.92
sacral nerve 04.93
sphenoidal — *omit code*
with synchronous replacement 02.96
spinal 03.94
with synchronous replacement 03.93
temporary transvenous pacemaker system — *omit code*
electroencephalographic receiver (brain) (intracranial) 01.22
with synchronous replacement 02.93
electronic
stimulator — *see* Removal, neurostimulator, by site
bladder 57.98
bone 78.6 ☑
skeletal muscle 83.93
with synchronous replacement 83.92
ureter 56.94
electrostimulator — *see* Removal, electronic, stimulator, by site
embolus 38.00
with endarterectomy — *see* Endarterectomy
abdominal
artery 38.06
vein 38.07
aorta (arch) (ascending) (descending) 38.04
arteriovenous shunt or cannula 39.49
bovine graft 39.49
head and neck vessel
endovascular approach 39.74 ●
open approach, intracranial ●
vessels 38.01 ●
open approach, other vessels ●
of head and neck 38.02 ●
intracranial vessel
endovascular approach 39.74 ●
open approach, intracranial ●
vessels 38.01 ●
open approach, other vessels ●
of head and neck 38.02 ●
lower limb
artery 38.08
vein 38.09
pulmonary (artery) (vein) 38.05
thoracic vessel NEC 38.05
upper limb (artery) (vein) 38.03
embryo — *see* Removal, ectopic fetus
encircling tube, eye (episcleral) 14.6
epithelial downgrowth, anterior chamber 12.93
external fixation device 97.88
mandibular NEC 97.36
minifixator (bone) — *see* category 78.6 ☑

Removal — *see also* Excision — *continued*
extrauterine embryo — *see* Removal, ectopic fetus
eyeball 16.49
with implant 16.42
with attachment of muscles 16.41
fallopian tube — *see* Salpingectomy
feces (impacted) (by flushing) (manual) 96.38
fetus, ectopic — *see* Removal, ectopic fetus
fingers, supernumerary 86.26
fixation device
external 97.88
mandibular NEC 97.36
minifixator (bone) — *see* category 78.6 ☑
internal 78.60
carpal, metacarpal 78.64
clavicle 78.61
facial (bone) 76.97
femur 78.65
fibula 78.67
humerus 78.62
patella 78.66
pelvic 78.69
phalanges (foot) (hand) 78.69
radius 78.63
scapula 78.61
specified site NEC 78.69
tarsal, metatarsal 78.68
thorax (ribs) (sternum) 78.61
tibia 78.67
ulna 78.63
vertebrae 78.69
foreign body NEC (*see also* Incision, by site) 98.20
abdominal (cavity) 54.92
wall 54.0
adenoid 98.13
by incision 28.91
alveolus, alveolar bone 98.22
by incision 24.0
antecubital fossa 98.27
by incision 86.05
anterior chamber 12.00
by incision 12.02
with use of magnet 12.01
anus (intraluminal) 98.05
by incision 49.93
artifical stoma (intraluminal) 98.18
auditory canal, external 18.02
axilla 98.27
by incision 86.05
bladder (without incision) 57.0
by incision 57.19
bone, except fixation device (*see also* Incision, bone) 77.10
alveolus, alveolar 98.22
by incision 24.0
brain 01.39
without incision into brain 01.24
breast 85.0
bronchus (intraluminal) 98.15
by incision 33.0
bursa 83.03
hand 82.03
canthus 98.22
by incision 08.51
cerebral meninges 01.31
cervix (intraluminal) NEC 98.16
penetrating 69.97
choroid (by incision) 14.00
with use of magnet 14.01
without use of magnet 14.02
ciliary body (by incision) 12.00
with use of magnet 12.01
without use of magnet 12.02
conjunctiva (by magnet) 98.22
by incision 10.0
cornea 98.21
by
incision 11.1

Removal — *see also* Excision — *continued*
foreign body (*see also* Incision, by site) — *continued*
cornea — *continued*
by — *continued*
magnet 11.0
duodenum 98.03
by incision 45.01
ear (intraluminal) 98.11
with incision 18.09
epididymis 63.92
esophagus (intraluminal) 98.02
by incision 42.09
extrapleural (by incision) 34.01
eye, eyeball (by magnet) 98.21
anterior segment (by incision) 12.00
with use of magnet 12.01
without use of magnet 12.02
posterior segment (by incision) 14.00
with use of magnet 14.01
without use of magnet 14.02
superficial 98.21
eyelid 98.22
by incision 08.09
fallopian tube
by salpingostomy 66.02
by salpingotomy 66.01
fascia 83.09
hand 82.09
foot 98.28
gall bladder 51.04
groin region (abdominal wall) (inguinal) 54.0
gum 98.22
by incision 24.0
hand 98.26
head and neck NEC 98.22
heart 37.11
internal fixation device — *see* Removal, fixation device, internal
intestine
by incision 45.00
large (intraluminal) 98.04
by incision 45.03
small (intraluminal) 98.03
by incision 45.02
intraocular (by incision) 12.00
with use of magnet 12.01
without use of magnet 12.02
iris (by incision) 12.00
with use of magnet 12.01
without use of magnet 12.02
joint structures (*see also* Arthrotomy) 80.10
kidney (transurethral) (by endoscopy) 56.0
by incision 55.01
pelvis (transurethral) 56.0
by incision 55.11
labia 98.23
by incision 71.09
lacrimal
canaliculi 09.42
by incision 09.52
gland 09.3
by incision 09.0
passage(s) 09.49
by incision 09.59
punctum 09.41
by incision 09.51
sac 09.49
by incision 09.53
large intestine (intraluminal) 98.04
by incision 45.03
larynx (intraluminal) 98.14
by incision 31.3
lens 13.00
by incision 13.02
with use of magnet 13.01
liver 50.0
lower limb, except foot 98.29
foot 98.28

☑ Additional Digit Required — Refer to the Tabular List for Digit Selection
Subterms under main terms may continue to next column or page
50 — Volume 3 • October 2006
▶◀ Revised Text
● New Line
▲ Revised Code
2007 ICD-9-CM

☑ Additional Digit Required — Refer to the Tabular List for Digit Selection   ꟻ Subterms under main terms may continue to next column or page

2007 ICD-9-CM   ▶◀ Revised Text   ● New Line   ▲ Revised Code   **October 2006 · Volume 3 — 51**

Removal — *see also* Excision — *continued*

patella — *continued*
  partial 77.86
pectus deformity implant device 34.01
pelvic viscera, en masse (female) 68.8
  male 57.71
pessary, vagina NEC 97.74
pharynx (partial) 29.33
phlebolith — *see* Removal, embolus
placenta (by)
  aspiration curettage 69.52
  D and C 69.02
  manual 75.4
plaque, dental 96.54
plate, skull 02.07
  with synchronous replacement 02.05
polyp (*see also* Excision, lesion, by site)
  esophageal 42.32
    endoscopic 42.33
  gastric (endoscopic) 43.41
  intestine 45.41
    endoscopic 45.42
  nasal 21.31
prosthesis
  bile duct 51.95
    nonoperative 97.55
  cochlear prosthetic device 20.99
  dental 97.35
  eye 97.31
  facial bone 76.99
  fallopian tube 66.94
    with synchronous replacement 66.93
  joint structures 80.00
    ankle 80.07
    elbow 80.02
    foot and toe 80.08
    hand and finger 80.04
    hip 80.05
    knee 80.06
    shoulder 80.01
    specified site NEC 80.09
    spine 80.09
    wrist 80.03
  lens 13.8
  penis (internal) without replacement 64.96
  Rosen (urethra) 59.99
  testicular, by incision 62.0
  urinary sphincter, artificial 58.99
    with replacement 58.93
pseudophakos 13.8
pterygium 11.39
  with corneal graft 11.32
pulse generator
  cardiac pacemaker 37.86
  cardioverter/defibrillator 37.79 ▲
  neurostimulator — *see* Removal, neurostimulator, pulse generator
pump assist device, heart 37.64
  with replacement 37.63
  nonoperative 97.44
radioactive material — *see* Removal, foreign body, by site
redundant skin, eyelid 08.86
rejected organ
  kidney 55.53
  testis 62.42
reservoir, ventricular (Ommaya) (Rickham) 02.43
  with synchronous replacement 02.42
retained placenta (by)
  aspiration curettage 69.52
  D and C 69.02
  manual 75.4
retinal implant 14.6
rhinolith 21.31
rice bodies, tendon sheaths 83.01
  hand 82.01

Removal — *see also* Excision — *continued*

Roger-Anderson minifixator device (bone) — *see* category 78.6 ☑
root, residual (tooth) (buried) (retained) 23.11
Rosen prosthesis (urethra) 59.99
scleral buckle or implant 14.6
Scribner shunt 39.43
secondary membranous cataract (with iridectomy) 13.65
secundines (by)
  aspiration curettage 69.52
  D and C 69.02
  manual 75.4
sequestrum — *see* Sequestrectomy
seton, anus 49.93
Shepard's tube (ear) 20.1
Shirodkar suture, cervix 69.96
shunt
  arteriovenous 39.43
    with creation of new shunt 39.42
  lumbar-subarachnoid NEC 03.98
  pleurothecal 03.98
  salpingothecal 03.98
  spinal (thecal) NEC 03.98
  subarachnoid-peritoneal 03.98
  subarachnoid-ureteral 03.98
silastic tubes
  ear 20.1
  fallopian tubes 66.94
    with synchronous replacement 66.93
skin
  necrosis or slough 86.28
    excisional 86.22
    superficial layer (by dermabrasion) 86.25
skull tongs 02.95
  with synchronous replacement 02.94
spacer (cement) (joint) 84.57
splint 97.88
stent
  bile duct 97.55
  larynx 31.98
  ureteral 97.62
  urethral 97.65
stimoceiver — *see* Removal, neurostimulator
subdural
  grids 01.22
  strips 01.22
supernumerary digit(s) 86.26
suture(s) NEC 97.89
  by incision — *see* Incision, by site
  abdominal wall 97.83
  genital tract 97.79
  head and neck 97.38
  thorax 97.43
  trunk NEC 97.84
symblepharon — *see* Repair, symblepharon
temporary transvenous pacemaker system — omit code
testis (unilateral) 62.3
  bilateral 62.41
  remaining or solitary 62.42
thrombus 38.00
  with endarterectomy — *see* Endarterectomy
  abdominal
    artery 38.06
    vein 38.07
  aorta (arch) (ascending) (descending) 38.04
  arteriovenous shunt or cannula 39.49
  bovine graft 39.49
  coronary artery 36.09
  head and neck vessel NEC 38.02
  intracranial vessel NEC 38.01
  lower limb
    artery 38.08
    vein 38.09

Removal — *see also* Excision — *continued*

thrombus — *continued*
  pulmonary (artery) (vein) 38.05
  thoracic vessel NEC 38.05
  upper limb (artery) (vein) 38.03
tissue expander (skin) NEC 86.05
  breast 85.96
toes, supernumerary 86.26
tongs, skull 02.95
  with synchronous replacement 02.94
tonsil tag 28.4
tooth (by forceps) (multiple) (single) NEC 23.09
  deciduous 23.01
  surgical NEC 23.19
    impacted 23.19
    residual root 23.11
    root apex 23.73
      with root canal therapy 23.72
trachoma follicles 10.33
T-tube (bile duct) 97.55
tube
  appendix 97.53
  bile duct (T-tube) NEC 97.55
  cholecystostomy 97.54
  cranial cavity 01.27
  cystostomy 97.63
  ear (button) 20.1
  gastrostomy 97.51
  large intestine 97.53
  liver 97.55
  mediastinum 97.42
  nephrostomy 97.61
  pancreas 97.56
  peritoneum 97.82
  pleural cavity 97.41
  pyelostomy 97.61
  retroperitoneum 97.81
  small intestine 97.52
  thoracotomy 97.41
  tracheostomy 97.37
  tympanostomy 20.1
  tympanum 20.1
  ureterostomy 97.62
ureteral splint (stent) 97.62
urethral sphincter, artificial 58.99
  with replacement 58.93
urinary sphincter, artificial 58.99
  with replacement 58.93
utricle 20.79
valve
  vas deferens 63.85
  ventricular (cerebral) 02.43
vascular graft or prosthesis 39.49
ventricular shunt or reservoir 02.43
  with synchronous replacement 02.42
Vinke tongs (skull) 02.95
  with synchronous replacement 02.94
vitreous (with replacement) 14.72
  anterior approach (partial) 14.71
  open sky technique 14.71
Wagner-Brooker minifixator device (bone) — *see* category 78.6 ☑
wiring, dental (immobilization device) 97.33
  orthodontic 24.8

Renipuncture (percutaneous) 55.92

Renogram 92.03

Renotransplantation NEC 55.69

> *Note* — To report donor source:
> cadaver 00.93
> *live non-related donor 00.92*
> *live related donor 00.91*
> *live unrelated donor 00.92*

Reopening — *see also* Incision, by site
blepharorrhaphy 08.02
canthorrhaphy 08.02
cilia base 08.71
craniotomy or craniectomy site 01.23
fallopian tube (divided) 66.79
iris in anterior chambers 12.97

Reopening — *see also* Incision, by site — *continued*

laminectomy or laminotomy site 03.02
laparotomy site 54.12
osteotomy site (*see also* Incision, bone) 77.10
  facial bone 76.09
tarsorrhaphy 08.02
thoracotomy site (for control of hemorrhage) (for examination) (for exploration) 34.03
thyroid field wound (for control of hemorrhage) (for examination) (for exploration) (for removal of hematoma) 06.02

Repacking — *see* Replacement, pack, by site

Repair

abdominal wall 54.72
adrenal gland 07.44
alveolus, alveolar (process) (ridge) (with graft) (with implant) 24.5
anal sphincter 49.79
  artificial sphincter
    implantation 49.75
    revision 49.75
  laceration (by suture) 49.71
    obstetric (current) 75.62
    old 49.79
aneurysm (false) (true) 39.52
  by or with
    clipping 39.51
    coagulation 39.52
    coil (endovascular approach) 39.79
      head and neck 39.72
    electrocoagulation 39.52
    with
      anastomosis — *see* Aneurysmectomy, with anastomosis, by site
      graft replacement — *see* Aneurysmectomy, with graft replacement, by site
      excision or resection of vessel (*see also* Aneurysmectomy, by site)
  endovascular graft 39.79
    abdominal aorta 39.71
    head and neck 39.72
    lower extremity artery(s) 39.79
    thoracic aorta 39.73
    upper extremity artery(s) 39.79
  filipuncture 39.52
  graft replacement — *see* Aneurysmectomy, with graft replacement, by site
  ligation 39.52
  liquid tissue adhesive (glue) 39.79
    endovascular approach 39.79
      head and neck 39.72
  methyl methacrylate 39.52
    endovascular approach 39.79
      head and neck 39.72
  occlusion 39.52
    endovascular approach 39.79
      head and neck 39.72
  suture 39.52
  trapping 39.52
  wiring 39.52
  wrapping (gauze) (methyl methacrylate) (plastic) 39.52
  coronary artery 36.91
  heart 37.32
  sinus of Valsalva 35.39
  thoracic aorta (dissecting), by fenestration 39.54

Repair — *continued*
anomalous pulmonary venous connection (total)
  one-stage 35.82
  partial — *see* specific procedure
  total 35.82
anus 49.79
  laceration (by suture) 49.71
    obstetric (current) 75.62
    old 49.79
aorta 39.31
aorticopulmonary window 39.59
arteriovenous fistula 39.53
  by or with
    clipping 39.53
    coagulation 39.53
    coil (endovascular approach) 39.79
      head and neck vessels 39.72
    division 39.53
    excision or resection (*see also* Aneurysmectomy, by site)
      with
        anastomosis — *see* Aneurysmectomy, with anastomosis, by site
        graft replacement — *see* Aneurysmectomy, with graft replacement, by site
    ligation 39.53
      coronary artery 36.99
    occlusion 39.53
      endovascular approach 39.79
        head and neck 39.72
    suture 39.53
artery NEC 39.59
  by
    endovascular approach
      abdominal aorta 39.71
      head and neck (embolization or occlusion) 39.72
      other repair (of aneurysm) 39.79
      percutaneous repair of intracranial vessel(s) (for stent insertion) 00.62

Note — Also use 00.40, 00.41, 00.42, or 00.43 to show the total number of vessels treated. ▶Use code 00.44 once to show procedure on a bifurcated vessel.◀ In addition, use 00.45, 00.46, 00.47, or 00.48 to show the number of vascular stents inserted.

      percutaneous repair of precerebral (extracranial) vessel(s) (for stent insertion) 00.61

Note — Also use 00.40, 00.41, 00.42, or 00.43 to show the total number of vessels treated. ▶Use code 00.44 once to show procedure on a bifurcated vessel.◀ In addition, use 00.45, 00.46, 00.47, or 00.48 to show the number of vascular stents inserted.

      thoracic aorta 39.73
      non-coronary percutaneous transluminal angioplasty or atherectomy

Note — Also use 00.40, 00.41, 00.42, or 00.43 to show the total number of vessels treated. ▶Use code 00.44 once to show procedure on a bifurcated vessel.◀ In addition, use 00.45, 00.46, 00.47, or 00.48 to show the number of vascular stents inserted.

      basilar 00.61
      carotid 00.61
      femoropopliteal 39.50
      iliac 39.50
      lower extremity NOS 39.50
      mesenteric 39.50

Repair — *continued*
artery — *continued*
  by — *continued*
    non-coronary percutaneous transluminal angioplasty or atherectomy — *continued*
      renal 39.50
      upper extremity NOS 39.50
      vertebral 00.61
  with
    patch graft 39.58
      with excision or resection of vessel — *see* Arteriectomy, with graft replacement, by site
      synthetic (Dacron) (Teflon) 39.57
      tissue (vein) (autogenous) (homograft) 39.56
    suture 39.31
  coronary NEC 36.99
    by angioplasty — *see* Angioplasty, coronary
    by atherectomy — *see* Angioplasty, coronary
artificial opening — *see* Repair, stoma
atrial septal defect 35.71
  with
    prosthesis (open heart technique) 35.51
      closed heart technique 35.52
    tissue graft 35.61
  combined with repair of valvular and ventricular septal defects — *see* Repair, endocardial cushion defect
  in total repair of total anomalous pulmonary venous connection 35.82
atrioventricular canal defect (any type) 35.73
  with
    prosthesis 35.54
    tissue graft 35.63
bifid digit (finger) 82.89
bile duct NEC 51.79
  laceration (by suture) NEC 51.79
    common bile duct 51.71
bladder NEC 57.89
  for stress incontinence — *see* Repair, stress incontinence
  exstrophy 57.86
  laceration (by suture) 57.81
    obstetric (current) 75.61
    old 57.89
  neck 57.85
blepharophimosis 08.59
blepharoptosis 08.36
  by
    frontalis muscle technique (with)
      fascial sling 08.32
      suture 08.31
    levator muscle technique 08.34
      with resection or advancement 08.33
    orbicularis oculi muscle sling 08.36
    tarsal technique 08.35
blood vessel NEC 39.59
  with
    patch graft 39.58
      with excision or resection — *see* Angiectomy, with graft replacement
      synthetic (Dacron) (Teflon) 39.57
      tissue (vein) (autogenous) (homograft) 39.56
    resection — *see* Angiectomy
    suture 39.30
  coronary artery NEC 36.99
    by angioplasty — *see* Angioplasty, coronary
    by atherectomy — *see* Angioplasty, coronary

Repair — *continued*
blood vessel — *continued*
  peripheral vessel NEC 39.59
    by angioplasty 39.50

Note — Also use 00.40, 00.41, 00.42, or 00.43 to show the total number of vessels treated. ▶Use code 00.44 once to show procedure on a bifurcated vessel.◀ In addition, use 00.45, 00.46, 00.47, or 00.48 to show the number of vascular stents inserted.

    by atherectomy 39.50

Note — Also use 00.40, 00.41, 00.42, or 00.43 to show the total number of vessels treated. ▶Use code 00.44 once to show procedure on a bifurcated vessel.◀ In addition, use 00.45, 00.46, 00.47, or 00.48 to show the number of vascular stents inserted.

    by endovascular approach 39.79
  bone NEC (*see also* Osteoplasty) — *see* category 78.4 ☑
    by synostosis technique — *see* Arthrodesis
    for malunion, nonunion, or delayed union of fracture — *see* Repair, fracture, malunion or nonunion
  accessory sinus 22.79
  cranium NEC 02.06
    with
      flap (bone) 02.03
      graft (bone) 02.04
  nasal 21.89
  skull NEC 02.06
    with
      flap (bone) 02.03
      graft (bone) 02.04
bottle, hydrocele of tunica vaginalis 61.2
brain (trauma) NEC 02.92
breast (plastic) (*see also* Mammoplasty) 85.89
broad ligament 69.29
bronchus NEC 33.48
  laceration (by suture) 33.41
bunionette (with osteotomy) 77.54
canaliculus, lacrimal 09.73
canthus (lateral) 08.59
cardiac pacemaker NEC 37.89
  electrode(s) (lead) NEC 37.75
cardioverter/defibrillator (automatic) pocket (skin) (subcutaneous) 37.99
cerebral meninges 02.12
cervix 67.69
  internal os 67.59
    transabdominal 67.51
    transvaginal 67.59
  laceration (by suture) 67.61
    obstetric (current) 75.51
    old 67.69
chest wall (mesh) (silastic) NEC 34.79
chordae tendineae 35.32
choroid NEC 14.9
  with retinal repair — *see* Repair, retina
cisterna chyli 40.69
claw toe 77.57
cleft
  hand 82.82
  laryngotracheal 31.69
  lip 27.54
  palate 27.62
    secondary or subsequent 27.63
coarctation of aorta — *see* Excision, coarctation of aorta
cochlear prosthetic device 20.99
  external components only 95.49
cockup toe 77.58
colostomy 46.43
conjunctiva NEC 10.49
  with scleral repair 12.81
  laceration 10.6
    with repair of sclera 12.81

Repair — *continued*
conjunctiva — *continued*
  late effect of trachoma 10.49
cornea NEC 11.59
  with
    conjunctival flap 11.53
    transplant — *see* Keratoplasty
  postoperative dehiscence 11.52
coronary artery NEC 36.99
  by angioplasty — *see* Angioplasty, coronary
  by atherectomy — *see* Angioplasty, coronary
cranium NEC 02.06
  with
    flap (bone) 02.03
    graft (bone) 02.04
cusp, valve — *see* Repair, heart, valve
cystocele 70.51
  and rectocele 70.50
dental arch 24.8
diaphragm NEC 34.84
diastasis recti 83.65
diastematomyelia 03.59
ear (external) 18.79
  auditory canal or meatus 18.6
  auricle NEC 18.79
  cartilage NEC 18.79
  laceration (by suture) 18.4
  lop ear 18.79
  middle NEC 19.9
  prominent or protruding 18.5
ectropion 08.49
  by or with
    lid reconstruction 08.44
    suture (technique) 08.42
    thermocauterization 08.41
    wedge resection 08.43
encephalocele (cerebral) 02.12
endocardial cushion defect 35.73
  with
    prosthesis (grafted to septa) 35.54
    tissue graft 35.63
enterocele (female) 70.92
  male 53.9
enterostomy 46.40
entropion 08.49
  by or with
    lid reconstruction 08.44
    suture (technique) 08.42
    thermocauterization 08.41
    wedge resection 08.43
epicanthus (fold) 08.59
epididymis (and spermatic cord) NEC 63.59
  with vas deferens 63.89
epiglottis 31.69
episiotomy
  routine following delivery — *see* Episiotomy
  secondary 75.69
epispadias 58.45
esophagus, esophageal NEC 42.89
  fistula NEC 42.84
  stricture 42.85
exstrophy of bladder 57.86
eyebrow 08.89
  linear 08.81
eye, eyeball 16.89
  multiple structures 16.82
  rupture 16.82
  socket 16.64
    with graft 16.63
eyelid 08.89
  full-thickness 08.85
    involving lid margin 08.84
  laceration 08.81
    full-thickness 08.85
      involving lid margin 08.84
    partial-thickness 08.83
      involving lid margin 08.82
  linear 08.81
  partial-thickness 08.83
    involving lid margin 08.82
  retraction 08.38

☑ Additional Digit Required — Refer to the Tabular List for Digit Selection   ▽ Subterms under main terms may continue to next column or page

2007 ICD-9-CM   ▶◀ Revised Text   ● New Line   ▲ Revised Code   **October 2006 · Volume 3 — 53**

Repair — *continued*
fallopian tube (with prosthesis) 66.79
  by
    anastomosis 66.73
    reanastomosis 66.79
    reimplantation into
      ovary 66.72
      uterus 66.74
    suture 66.71
false aneurysm — *see* Repair,
  aneurysm
fascia 83.89
  by or with
    arthroplasty — *see* Arthroplasty
    graft (fascial) (muscle) 83.82
      hand 82.72
      tendon 83.81
        hand 82.79
    suture (direct) 83.65
      hand 82.46
  hand 82.89
    by
      graft NEC 82.79
        fascial 82.72
        muscle 82.72
      suture (direct) 82.46
  joint — *see* Arthroplasty
filtering bleb (corneal) (scleral) (by excision) 12.82
  by
    corneal graft (*see also* Kerato-
      plasty) 11.60
    scleroplasty 12.82
    suture 11.51
      with conjunctival flap 11.53
fistula (*see also* Closure, fistula)
  anovaginal 70.73
  arteriovenous 39.53
    clipping 39.53
    coagulation 39.53
      endovascular approach
        39.79
        head and neck 39.72
    division 39.53
    excision or resection (*see also*
      Aneurysmectomy, by site)
      with
        anastomosis — *see*
          Aneurysmectomy,
          with anasto-mosis,
          by site
        graft replacement — *see*
          Aneurysmectomy,
          with graft replace-
          ment, by site
    ligation 39.53
    coronary artery 36.99
    occlusion 39.53
      endovascular approach
        39.79
        head and neck 39.72
    suture 39.53
  cervicovesical 57.84
  cervix 67.62
  choledochoduodenal 51.72
  colovaginal 70.72
  enterovaginal 70.74
  enterovesical 57.83
  esophagocutaneous 42.84
  ileovesical 57.83
  intestinovaginal 70.74
  intestinovesical 57.83
  oroantral 22.71
  perirectal 48.93
  pleuropericardial 37.49
  rectovaginal 70.73
  rectovesical 57.83
  rectovesicovaginal 57.83
  scrotum 61.42
  sigmoidovaginal 70.74
  sinus
    nasal 22.71
    of Valsalva 35.39
  splenocolic 41.95
  urethroperineovesical 57.84
  urethrovesical 57.84

Repair — *continued*
fistula (*see also* Closure, fistula) —
  continued
  urethrovesicovaginal 57.84
  uterovesical 57.84
  vagina NEC 70.75
  vaginocutaneous 70.75
  vaginoenteric NEC 70.74
  vaginoileal 70.74
  vaginoperineal 70.75
  vaginovesical 57.84
  vesicocervicovaginal 57.84
  vesicocolic 57.83
  vesicocutaneous 57.84
  vesicoenteric 57.83
  vesicointestinal 57.83
  vesicometrorectal 57.83
  vesicoperineal 57.84
  vesicorectal 57.83
  vesicosigmoidal 57.83
  vesicosigmoidovaginal 57.83
  vesicourethral 57.84
  vesicourethrorectal 57.83
  vesicouterine 57.84
  vesicovaginal 57.84
  vulva 71.72
  vulvorectal 48.73
foramen ovale (patent) 35.71
  with
    prosthesis (open heart tech-
      nique) 35.51
    closed heart technique 35.52
    tissue graft 35.61
fracture (*see also* Reduction, fracture)
  larynx 31.64
  malunion or nonunion (delayed)
    NEC — *see* category 78.4 ☑
    with
      graft — *see* Graft, bone
      insertion (of)
        bone growth stimulator
          (invasive) — *see*
          category 78.9 ☑
        internal fixation device
          78.5 ☑
      manipulation for realignment
        — *see* Reduction, frac-
        ture, by site, closed
    osteotomy
      with
        correction of alignment
          — *see* category
          77.3 ☑
        with internal fixa-
          tion device —
          see categories
          77.3 ☑ *[78.5]* ☑
        with intramed-
          ullary rod —
          see categories
          77.3 ☑ *[78.5]* ☑
    replacement arthroplasty —
      see Arthroplasty
    sequestrectomy — *see* catego-
      ry 77.0 ☑
    Sofield type procedure —
      see categories
      77.3 ☑ *[78.5]* ☑
    synostosis technique — *see*
      Arthrodesis
  vertebra 03.53
funnel chest (with implant) 34.74
gallbladder 51.91
gastroschisis 54.71
great vessels NEC 39.59
  laceration (by suture) 39.30
    artery 39.31
    vein 39.32
hallux valgus NEC 77.59
  resection of joint with prosthetic
    implant 77.59
hammer toe 77.56
hand 82.89
  with graft or implant 82.79
    fascia 82.72
    muscle 82.72

Repair — *continued*
hand — *continued*
  with graft or implant — *contin-*
    ued
    tendon 82.79
heart 37.49
  assist system 37.63
  septum 35.70
    with
      prosthesis 35.50
      tissue graft 35.60
    atrial 35.71
      with
        prosthesis (open heart
          technique) 35.51
        closed heart technique
          35.52
        tissue graft 35.61
      combined with repair of
        valvular and ventricu-
        lar septal defects —
        see Repair, endocardial
        cushion defect
      in total repair of
        tetralogy of Fallot 35.81
        total anomalous pul-
          monary venous
          connection 35.82
        truncus arteriosus 35.83
    combined with repair of valvular
      defect — *see* Repair, endo-
      cardial cushion defect
    ventricular 35.72
      with
        prosthesis ▶(open heart
          technique)◀ 35.53
        closed heart tech-   ●
          nique 35.55   ●
        tissue graft 35.62
      combined with repair of
        valvular and atrial
        septal defects — *see*
        Repair, endocardial
        cushion defect
      in total repair of
        tetralogy of Fallot 35.81
        total anomalous pul-
          monary venous
          connection 35.82
        truncus arteriosus 35.83
  total replacement system 37.52
    implantable battery 37.54
    implantable controller 37.54
    thoracic unit 37.53
    transcutaneous energy transfer
      (TET) device 37.54
  valve (cusps) (open heart tech-
    nique) 35.10
    with prosthesis or tissue graft
      35.20
    aortic (without replacement)
      35.11
      with
        prosthesis 35.22
        tissue graft 35.21
      combined with repair of atrial
        and ventricular septal de-
        fects — *see* Repair, endo-
        cardial cushion defect
    mitral (without replacement)
      35.12
      with
        prosthesis 35.24
        tissue graft 35.23
    pulmonary (without replace-
      ment) 35.13
      with
        prosthesis 35.26
        in total repair of tetral-
          ogy of Fallot
          35.81
        tissue graft 35.25
    tricuspid (without replacement)
      35.14
      with
        prosthesis 35.28

Repair — *continued*
heart — *continued*
  valve — *continued*
    tricuspid — *continued*
      with — *continued*
        tissue graft 35.27
hepatic duct 51.79
hernia NEC 53.9
  anterior abdominal wall NEC 53.59
    with prosthesis or graft 53.69
  colostomy 46.42
  crural 53.29
  cul-de-sac (Douglas') 70.92
  diaphragmatic
    abdominal approach 53.7
    thoracic, thoracoabdominal ap-
      proach 53.80
  epigastric 53.59
    with prosthesis or graft 53.69
  esophageal hiatus
    abdominal approach 53.7
    thoracic, thoracoabdominal ap-
      proach 53.80
  fascia 83.89
    hand 82.89
  femoral (unilateral) 53.29
    with prosthesis or graft 53.21
    bilateral 53.39
      with prosthesis or graft 53.31
  Ferguson 53.00
  Halsted 53.00
  Hill-Allison (hiatal hernia repair,
    transpleural approach) 53.80
  hypogastric 53.59
    with prosthesis or graft 53.69
  incisional 53.51
    with prosthesis or graft 53.61
  inguinal (unilateral) 53.00
    with prosthesis or graft 53.05
    bilateral 53.10
      with prosthesis or graft 53.17
      direct 53.11
        with prosthesis or graft
          53.14
      direct and indirect 53.13
        with prosthesis or graft
          53.16
      indirect 53.12
        with prosthesis or graft
          53.15
    direct (unilateral) 53.01
      with prosthesis or graft 53.03
      and indirect (unilateral)
        53.01
        with prosthesis or graft
          53.03
      bilateral 53.13
        with prosthesis or graft
          53.16
      bilateral 53.11
        with prosthesis or graft
          53.14
    indirect (unilateral) 53.02
      with prosthesis or graft 53.04
      and direct (unilateral) 53.01
        with prosthesis or graft
          53.03
      bilateral 53.13
        with prosthesis or graft
          53.16
      bilateral 53.12
        with prosthesis or graft
          53.15
  internal 53.9
  ischiatic 53.9
  ischiorectal 53.9
  lumbar 53.9
  manual 96.27
  obturator 53.9
  omental 53.9
  paraesophageal 53.7
  parahiatal 53.7
  paraileostomy 46.41
  parasternal 53.82
  paraumbilical 53.49
    with prosthesis 53.41

☑ Additional Digit Required — Refer to the Tabular List for Digit Selection   ⚐ Subterms under main terms may continue to next column or page

Repair — *continued*
hernia — *continued*
   pericolostomy 46.42
   perineal (enterocele) 53.9
   preperitoneal 53.29
   pudendal 53.9
   retroperitoneal 53.9
   sciatic 53.9
   scrotal — *see* Repair, hernia, inguinal
   spigelian 53.59
      with prosthesis or graft 53.69
   umbilical 53.49
      with prosthesis 53.41
   uveal 12.39
   ventral 53.59
      incisional 53.51
         with prosthesis or graft 53.61
hydrocele
   round ligament 69.19
   spermatic cord 63.1
   tunica vaginalis 61.2
hymen 70.76
hypospadias 58.45
ileostomy 46.41
ingrown toenail 86.23
intestine, intestinal NEC 46.79
   fistula — *see* Closure, fistula, intestine
   laceration
      large intestine 46.75
      small intestine NEC 46.73
   stoma — *see* Repair, stoma
inverted uterus NEC 69.29
   manual
      nonobstetric 69.94
      obstetric 75.94
   obstetrical
      manual 75.94
      surgical 75.93
   vaginal approach 69.23
iris (rupture) NEC 12.39
jejunostomy 46.41
joint (capsule) (cartilage) NEC (*see also* Arthroplasty) 81.96
kidney NEC 55.89
knee (joint) NEC 81.47
   collateral ligaments 81.46
   cruciate ligaments 81.45
   five-in-one 81.42
   triad 81.43
labia — *see* Repair, vulva
laceration — *see* Suture, by site
lacrimal system NEC 09.99
   canaliculus 09.73
   punctum 09.72
      for eversion 09.71
laryngostomy 31.62
laryngotracheal cleft 31.69
larynx 31.69
   fracture 31.64
   laceration 31.61
leads (cardiac) NEC 37.75
ligament (*see also* Arthroplasty) 81.96
   broad 69.29
   collateral, knee NEC 81.46
   cruciate, knee NEC 81.45
   round 69.29
   uterine 69.29
lip NEC 27.59
   cleft 27.54
   laceration (by suture) 27.51
liver NEC 50.69
   laceration 50.61
lop ear 18.79
lung NEC 33.49
lymphatic (channel) (peripheral) NEC 40.9
   duct, left (thoracic) NEC 40.69
macrodactyly 82.83
mallet finger 82.84
mandibular ridge 76.64
mastoid (antrum) (cavity) 19.9
meninges (cerebral) NEC 02.12
   spinal NEC 03.59
      meningocele 03.51

Repair — *continued*
meninges — *continued*
   spinal — *continued*
      myelomeningocele 03.52
meningocele (spinal) 03.51
   cranial 02.12
mesentery 54.75
mouth NEC 27.59
   laceration NEC 27.52
muscle NEC 83.87
   by
      graft or implant (fascia) (muscle) 83.82
      hand 82.72
      tendon 83.81
         hand 82.79
      suture (direct) 83.65
         hand 82.46
      transfer or transplantation (muscle) 83.77
         hand 82.58
   hand 82.89
      by
         graft or implant NEC 82.79
            fascia 82.72
         suture (direct) 82.46
         transfer or transplantation (muscle) 82.58
musculotendinous cuff, shoulder 83.63
myelomeningocele 03.52
nasal
   septum (perforation) NEC 21.88
   sinus NEC 22.79
      fistula 22.71
nasolabial flaps (plastic) 21.86
nasopharyngeal atresia 29.4
nerve (cranial) (peripheral) NEC 04.79
   old injury 04.76
   revision 04.75
   sympathetic 05.81
nipple NEC 85.87
nose (external) (internal) (plastic) NEC (*see also* Rhinoplasty) 21.89
   laceration (by suture) 21.81
notched lip 27.59
omentum 54.74
omphalocele 53.49
   with prosthesis 53.41
orbit 16.89
   wound 16.81
ostium
   primum defect 35.73
      with
         prosthesis 35.54
         tissue graft 35.63
   secundum defect 35.71
      with
         prosthesis (open heart technique) 35.51
            closed heart technique 35.52
         tissue graft 35.61
ovary 65.79
   with tube 65.73
      laparoscopic 65.76
overlapping toe 77.58
pacemaker
   cardiac
      device (permanent) 37.89
      electrode(s) (leads) NEC 37.75
      pocket (skin) (subcutaneous) 37.79
palate NEC 27.69
   cleft 27.62
      secondary or subsequent 27.63
   laceration (by suture) 27.61
pancreas NEC 52.95
   Wirsung's duct 52.99
papillary muscle (heart) 35.31
patent ductus arteriosus 38.85
pectus deformity (chest) (carinatum) (excavatum) 34.74
pelvic floor NEC 70.79
   obstetric laceration (current) 75.69
      old 70.79

Repair — *continued*
penis NEC 64.49
   for epispadias or hypospadias 58.45
   inflatable prosthesis 64.99
   laceration 64.41
pericardium 37.49
perineum (female) 71.79
   laceration (by suture) 71.71
      obstetric (current) 75.69
         old 71.79
   male NEC 86.89
      laceration (by suture) 86.59
peritoneum NEC 54.73
   by suture 54.64
pharynx NEC 29.59
   laceration (by suture) 29.51
   plastic 29.4
pleura NEC 34.93
postcataract wound dehiscence 11.52
   with conjunctival flap 11.53
pouch of Douglas 70.52
primum ostium defect 35.73
   with
      prosthesis 35.54
      tissue graft 35.63
prostate 60.93
ptosis, eyelid — *see* Repair, blepharoptosis
punctum, lacrimal NEC 09.72
   for correction of eversion 09.71
quadriceps (mechanism) 83.86
rectocele (posterior colporrhaphy) 70.52
   and cystocele 70.50
rectum NEC 48.79
   laceration (by suture) 48.71
   prolapse NEC 48.76
      abdominal, approach 48.75
retina, retinal
   detachment 14.59
      by
         cryotherapy 14.52
         diathermy 14.51
         photocoagulation 14.55
            laser 14.54
            xenon arc 14.53
         scleral buckling (*see also* Buckling, scleral) 14.49
   tear or defect 14.39
      by
         cryotherapy 14.32
         diathermy 14.31
         photocoagulation 14.35
            laser 14.34
            xenon arc 14.33
retroperitoneal tissue 54.73
rotator cuff ▶(graft)◀ (suture) 83.63
round ligament 69.29
ruptured tendon NEC 83.88
   hand 82.86
salivary gland or duct NEC 26.49
sclera, scleral 12.89
   fistula 12.82
   staphyloma NEC 12.86
      with graft 12.85
scrotum 61.49
sinus
   nasal NEC 22.79
   of Valsalva (aneurysm) 35.39
skin (plastic) (without graft) 86.89
   laceration (by suture) 86.59
skull NEC 02.06
   with
      flap (bone) 02.03
      graft (bone) 02.04
spermatic cord NEC 63.59
   laceration (by suture) 63.51
sphincter ani 49.79
   laceration (by suture) 49.71
      obstetric (current) 75.62
         old 49.79
spina bifida NEC 03.59
   meningocele 03.51
   myelomeningocele 03.52

Repair — *continued*
spinal (cord) (meninges) (structures) NEC 03.59
   meningocele 03.51
   myelomeningocele 03.52
spleen 41.95
sternal defect 78.41
stoma
   bile duct 51.79
   bladder 57.22
   bronchus 33.42
   common duct 51.72
   esophagus 42.89
   gallbladder 51.99
   hepatic duct 51.79
   intestine 46.40
      large 46.43
      small 46.41
   kidney 55.89
   larynx 31.63
   rectum 48.79
   stomach 44.69
      laparoscopic 44.68
   thorax 34.79
   trachea 31.74
   ureter 56.62
   urethra 58.49
stomach NEC 44.69
   laceration (by suture) 44.61
   laparoscopic 44.68
stress incontinence (urinary) NEC 59.79
   by
      anterior urethropexy 59.79
      Burch 59.5
      cystourethropexy (with levator muscle sling) 59.71
      injection of implant (collagen) (fat) (polytef) 59.72
      paraurethral suspension (Pereyra) 59.6
      periurethral suspension 59.6
      plication of urethrovesical junction 59.3
      pubococcygeal sling 59.71
      retropubic urethral suspension 59.5
      suprapubic sling 59.4
      tension free vaginal tape 59.79
      urethrovesical suspension 59.4
         gracilis muscle transplant 59.71
      levator muscle sling 59.71
subcutaneous tissue (plastic) (without skin graft) 86.89
   laceration (by suture) 86.59
supracristal defect (heart) 35.72
   with
      prosthesis ▶(open heart technique)◀ 35.53
         closed heart technique 35.55 ●
      tissue graft 35.62 ●
symblepharon NEC 10.49
   by division (with insertion of conformer) 10.5
   with free graft 10.41
syndactyly 86.85
synovial membrane, joint — *see* Arthroplasty
telecanthus 08.59
tendon 83.88
   by or with
      arthroplasty — *see* Arthroplasty
      graft or implant (tendon) 83.81
         fascia 83.82
            hand 82.72
         hand 82.79
         muscle 83.82
            hand 82.72
      suture (direct) (immediate) (primary) (*see also* Suture, tendon) 83.64
         hand 82.45
      transfer or transplantation (tendon) 83.75

☑ Additional Digit Required — Refer to the Tabular List for Digit Selection   ▽ Subterms under main terms may continue to next column or page

2007 ICD-9-CM   ▶◀ Revised Text   ● New Line   ▲ Revised Code   October 2006 · Volume 3 — 55

Repair — *continued*
  tendon — *continued*
    by or with — *continued*
      transfer or transplantation — *continued*
        hand 82.56
      hand 82.86
        by
          graft or implant (tendon) 82.79
          suture (direct) (immediate) (primary) (*see also* Suture, tendon, hand) 82.45
          transfer or transplantation (tendon) 82.56
  rotator cuff (direct suture) 83.63
  ruptured NEC 83.88
    hand 82.86
  sheath (direct suture) 83.61
    hand 82.41
  testis NEC 62.69
  tetralogy of Fallot
    partial — *see* specific procedure
    total (one-stage) 35.81
  thoracic duct NEC 40.69
  thoracostomy 34.72
  thymus (gland) 07.93
  tongue NEC 25.59
  tooth NEC 23.2
    by
      crown (artificial) 23.41
      filling (amalgam) (plastic) (silicate) 23.2
      inlay 23.3
  total anomalous pulmonary venous connection
    partial — *see* specific procedure
    total (one-stage) 35.82
  trachea NEC 31.79
    laceration (by suture) 31.71
  tricuspid atresia 35.94
  truncus arteriosus
    partial — *see* specific procedure
    total (one-stage) 35.83
  tunica vaginalis 61.49
    laceration (by suture) 61.41
  tympanum — *see* Tympanoplasty
  ureter NEC 56.89
    laceration (by suture) 56.82
  ureterocele 56.89
  urethra NEC 58.49
    laceration (by suture) 58.41
      obstetric (current) 75.61
      old 58.49
    meatus 58.47
  urethrocele (anterior colporrhaphy) (female) 70.51
    and rectocele 70.50
  urinary sphincter, artificial (component) 58.99
  urinary stress incontinence — *see* Repair, stress incontinence
  uterus, uterine 69.49
    inversion — *see* Repair, inverted uterus
    laceration (by suture) 69.41
      obstetric (current) 75.50
      old 69.49
    ligaments 69.29
      by
        interposition 69.21
        plication 69.22
  uvula 27.73
    with synchronous cleft palate repair 27.62
  vagina, vaginal (cuff) (wall) NEC 70.79
    anterior 70.51
      with posterior repair 70.50
    cystocele 70.51
      and rectocele 70.50
    enterocele 70.92
    laceration (by suture) 70.71
      obstetric (current) 75.69
      old 70.79
    posterior 70.52

Repair — *continued*
  vagina, vaginal — *continued*
    posterior — *continued*
      with anterior repair 70.50
      rectocele 70.52
        and cystocele 70.50
      urethrocele 70.51
        and rectocele 70.50
  varicocele 63.1
  vas deferens 63.89
    by
      anastomosis 63.82
        to epididymis 63.83
      reconstruction 63.82
    laceration (by suture) 63.81
  vein NEC 39.59
    by
      endovascular approach
        head and neck (embolization or occlusion) 39.72
    with
      patch graft 39.58
        with excision or resection of vessel — *see* Phlebectomy, with graft replacement, by site
        synthetic (Dacron) (Teflon) 39.57
        tissue (vein) (autogenous) (homograft) 39.56
      suture 39.32
  ventricular septal defect 35.72
    with
      prosthesis ▶(open heart technique)◀ 35.53
      closed heart technique ● 35.55 ●
      in total repair of tetralogy of Fallot 35.81
      tissue graft 35.62
    combined with repair of valvular and atrial septal defects — *see* Repair, endocardial cushion defect
    in total repair of
      tetralogy of Fallot 35.81
      truncus arteriosus 35.83
  vertebral arch defect (spina bifida) 03.59
  vulva NEC 71.79
    laceration (by suture) 71.71
      obstetric (current) 75.69
      old 71.79
  Wirsung's duct 52.99
  wound (skin) (without graft) 86.59
    abdominal wall 54.63
      dehiscence 54.61
    postcataract dehiscence (corneal) 11.52

Replacement
  acetabulum (with prosthesis) 81.52
  ankle, total 81.56
    revision 81.59
  aortic valve (with prosthesis) 35.22
    with tissue graft 35.21
  artery — *see* Graft, artery
  bag — *see* Replacement, pack or bag
  Barton's tongs (skull) 02.94
  bladder
    with
      ileal loop 57.87 [45.51]
      sigmoid 57.87 [45.52]
    sphincter, artificial 58.93
  bronchial device NOS 33.79 ●
  bronchial substance NOS 33.79 ●
  bronchial valve 33.71 ●
  caliper tongs (skull) 02.94
  cannula
    arteriovenous shunt 39.94
    pancreatic duct 97.05
    vessel-to-vessel (arteriovenous) 39.94

Replacement — *continued*
  cardiac resynchronization device
    defibrillator ▶(biventricular defibrillator) (BiV ICD) (BiV pacemaker with defibrillator) (BiV pacing with defibrillator)◀ (CRT-D) (device and one or more leads) (total system) 00.51
      left ventricular coronary venous lead only 00.52
      pulse generator only 00.54
    pacemaker ▶(biventricular pacemaker) (BiV pacemaker)◀ (CRT-P) (device and one or more leads) (total system) 00.50
      left ventricular coronary venous lead only 00.52
      pulse generator only 00.53
  cardioverter/defibrillator (total system) 37.94
    leads only (electrodes) (sensing) (pacing) 37.97
    pulse generator only 37.98
  cast NEC 97.13
    lower limb 97.12
    upper limb 97.11
  catheter
    bladder (indwelling) 57.95
    cystostomy 59.94
    ventricular shunt (cerebral) 02.42
    wound 97.15
  CRT-D ▶(biventricular defibrillator) (BiV ICD) (BiV pacemaker with defibrillator) (BiV pacing with defibrillator)◀ (cardiac resynchronization defibrillator) (device and one or more leads) 00.51
    left ventricular coronary venous lead only 00.52
    pulse generator only 00.54
  CRT-P ▶(biventricular pacemaker) (BiV pacemaker)◀ (cardiac resynchronization pacemaker) (device and one or more leads) 00.50
    left ventricular coronary venous lead only 00.52
    pulse generator only 00.53
  Crutchfield tongs (skull) 02.94
  cystostomy tube (catheter) 59.94
  device ●
    subcutaneous for intracardiac ● hemodynamic monitoring ● 00.57 ●
  diaphragm, vagina 97.24
  disc — *see* Replacement, intervertebral disc
  drain (*see also* Replacement, tube)
    vagina 97.26
    vulva 97.26
    wound, musculoskeletal or skin 97.16
  ear (prosthetic) 18.71
  elbow (joint), total 81.84
  electrode(s) — *see* Implant, electrode or lead by site or name of device
  brain
    depth 02.93
    foramen ovale 02.93
    sphenoidal 02.96
  depth 02.93
  foramen ovale 02.93
  gastric 04.92 ●
  intracranial 02.93
  pacemaker — *see* Replacement, pacemaker, electrode(s)
  peripheral nerve 04.92
  sacral nerve 04.92
  sphenoidal 02.96
  spine 03.93
  electroencephalographic receiver (brain) (intracranial) 02.93

Replacement — *continued*
  electronic
    cardioverter/defibrillator — *see* Replacement, cardioverter/defibrillator
    leads (electrode) (s) — *see* Replacement, electrode(s)
    stimulator (*see also* Implant, electronic stimulator, by site)
      bladder 57.97
      muscle (skeletal) 83.92
      ureter 56.93
  electrostimulator — *see* Implant, electronic stimulator by site
  enterostomy device (tube)
    large intestine 97.04
    small intestine 97.03
  epidural pegs 02.93
  femoral head, by prosthesis 81.52
    revision 81.53
  Gardner Wells tongs (skull) 02.94
  gastric band, laparoscopic 44.96
  gastric port device (subcutaneous) 44.96
  graft — *see* Graft
  halo traction device (skull) 02.94
  Harrington rod (with refusion of spine) — *see* Refusion, spinal
  heart
    artificial
      total replacement system 37.52
        implantable battery 37.54
        implantable controller 37.54
        thoracic unit 37.53
        transcutaneous energy transfer (TET) device 37.54
    total replacement system 37.52
      implantable battery 37.54
      implantable controller 37.54
      thoracic unit 37.53
      transcutaneous energy transfer (TET) device 37.54
    valve (with prosthesis) (with tissue graft) 35.20
      aortic (with prosthesis) 35.22
        with tissue graft 35.21
      mitral (with prosthesis) 35.24
        with tissue graft 35.23
      poppet (prosthetic) 35.95
      pulmonary (with prosthesis) 35.26
        with tissue graft 35.25
        in total repair of tetralogy of Fallot 35.81
      tricuspid (with prosthesis) 35.28
        with tissue graft 35.27
  hip (partial) (with fixation device) (with prosthesis) (with traction) 81.52
    acetabulum 81.52
      revision 81.53
    femoral head 81.52
      revision 81.53
    total 81.51
      revision 81.53
  intervertebral disc
    artificial, NOS 84.60
      cervical 84.62
        nucleus 84.61
        partial 84.61
        total 84.62
      lumbar, lumbosacral 84.65
        nucleus 84.64
        partial 84.64
        total 84.65
      thoracic (partial) (total) 84.63
  inverted uterus — *see* Repair, inverted uterus
  iris NEC 12.39
  kidney, mechanical 55.97
  knee (bicompartmental) (hemijoint) (partial) (total) (tricompartmental) (unicompartmental) 81.54
    revision 81.55
  laryngeal stent 31.93

☑ Additional Digit Required — Refer to the Tabular List for Digit Selection   ▽ Subterms under main terms may continue to next column or page

2007 ICD-9-CM   ▶◀ Revised Text   ● New Line   ▲ Revised Code   October 2006 • Volume 3 — 57

Replacement — Resection

Resection — see also Excision, by site — continued
  joint structure NEC (see also Arthrectomy) 80.90
  kidney (segmental) (wedge) 55.4
  larynx (see also Laryngectomy)
    submucous 30.29
  lesion — see Excision, lesion, by site
  levator palpebrae muscle 08.33
  ligament (see also Arthrectomy) 80.90
    broad 69.19
    round 69.19
    uterine 69.19
  lip (wedge) 27.43
  liver (partial) (wedge) 50.22
    lobe (total) 50.3
    total 50.4
  lung (wedge) NEC 32.29
    endoscopic 32.28
    segmental (any part) 32.3
    volume reduction 32.22
      biologic lung volume reduction ●
        (BLVR) — see category ●
        33.7 ☑ ●
  meninges (cerebral) 01.51
    spinal 03.4
  mesentery 54.4
  muscle 83.45
    for graft 83.43
      hand 82.34
    extraocular 15.13
      with
        advancement or recession of other eye muscle 15.3
        suture of original insertion 15.13
    levator palpebrae 08.33
    Müller's, for blepharoptosis 08.35
    orbicularis oculi 08.20
    tarsal, for blepharoptosis 08.35
    hand 82.36
      for graft 82.34
    ocular — see Resection, muscle, extraocular
  myocardium 37.33
  nasal septum (submucous) 21.5
  nerve (cranial) (peripheral) NEC 04.07
    phrenic 04.03
      for collapse of lung 33.31
    sympathetic 05.29
    vagus — see Vagotomy
  nose (complete) (extended) (partial) (radical) 21.4
  omentum 54.4
  orbitomaxillary, radical 16.51
  ovary (see also Oophorectomy, wedge) 65.22
    laparoscopic 65.24
  palate (bony) (local) 27.31
    by wide excision 27.32
    soft 27.49
  pancreas (total) (with synchronous duodenectomy) 52.6
    partial NEC 52.59
      distal (tail) (with part of body) 52.52
      proximal (head) (with part of body) (with synchronous duodenectomy) 52.51
      radical subtotal 52.53
    radical (one-stage) (two-stage) 52.7
    subtotal 52.53
  pancreaticoduodenal (see also Pancreatectomy) 52.6
  pelvic viscera (en masse) (female) 68.8
    male 57.71
  penis 64.3
  pericardium (partial) (for)
    chronic constrictive pericarditis 37.31
    drainage 37.12
    removal of adhesions 37.31
  peritoneum 54.4
  pharynx (partial) 29.33
  phrenic nerve 04.03

Resection — see also Excision, by site — continued
  phrenic nerve — continued
    for collapse of lung 33.31
  prostate (see also Prostatectomy)
    transurethral (punch) 60.29
  pterygium 11.39
  radial head 77.83
  rectosigmoid (see also Resection, rectum) 48.69
  rectum (partial) NEC 48.69
    with
      pelvic exenteration 68.8
      transsacral sigmoidectomy 48.61
    abdominoendorectal (combined) 48.5
    abdominoperineal 48.5
      pull-through NEC 48.49
        Duhamel type 48.65
    anterior 48.63
      with colostomy (synchronous) 48.62
    Duhamel 48.65
    endorectal 48.41
      combined abdominal 48.5
    posterior 48.64
    pull-through NEC 48.49
      endorectal 48.41
    submucosal (Soave) 48.41
      combined abdominal 48.5
  rib (transaxillary) 77.91
    as operative approach — omit code
    incidental to thoracic operation — omit code
  right ventricle (heart), for infundibular stenosis 35.34
  root (tooth) (apex) 23.73
    with root canal therapy 23.72
    residual or retained 23.11
  round ligament 69.19
  sclera 12.65
    with scleral buckling (see also Buckling, scleral) 14.49
    lamellar (for retinal reattachment) 14.49
    with implant 14.41
  scrotum 61.3
  soft tissue NEC 83.49
    hand 82.39
  sphincter of Oddi 51.89
  spinal cord (meninges) 03.4
  splanchnic 05.29
  splenic flexure (colon) 45.75
  sternum 77.81
  stomach (partial) (sleeve) (subtotal) NEC (see also Gastrectomy) 43.89
    with anastomosis NEC 43.89
      esophagogastric 43.5
      gastroduodenal 43.6
      gastrogastric 43.89
      gastrojejunal 43.7
    complete or total NEC 43.99
      with intestinal interposition 43.91
    fundus 43.89
    radical NEC 43.99
      with intestinal interposition 43.91
    wedge 43.42
      endoscopic 43.41
  submucous
    larynx 30.29
    nasal septum 21.5
    vocal cords 30.22
  synovial membrane (complete) (partial) (see also Synovectomy) 80.70
  tarsolevator 08.33
  tendon 83.42
    hand 82.33
  thoracic structures (block) (en bloc) (radical) (brachial plexus, bronchus, lobes of lung, ribs, and sympathetic nerves) 32.6
  thorax 34.4

Resection — see also Excision, by site — continued
  tongue 25.2
    wedge 25.1
  tooth root 23.73
    with root canal therapy 23.72
    apex (abscess) 23.73
      with root canal therapy 23.72
    residual or retained 23.11
  trachea 31.5
  transurethral
    bladder NEC 57.49
    prostate 60.29
  transverse colon 45.74
  turbinates — see Turbinectomy
  ureter (partial) 56.41
    total 56.42
  uterus — see Hysterectomy
  vein — see Phlebectomy
  ventricle (heart) 37.35
    infundibula 35.34
  vesical neck 57.59
    transurethral 57.49
  vocal cords (punch) 30.22
Respirator, volume-controlled (Bennett) (Byrd) — see Ventilation
Restoration
  cardioesophageal angle 44.66
    laparoscopic 44.67
  dental NEC 23.49
    by
      application of crown (artificial) 23.41
      insertion of bridge (fixed) 23.42
      removable 23.43
  extremity — see Reattachment, extremity
  eyebrow 08.70
    with graft 08.63
  eye socket 16.64
    with graft 16.63
  tooth NEC 23.2
    by
      crown (artificial) 23.41
      filling (amalgam) (plastic) (silicate) 23.2
      inlay 23.3
Restrictive
  gastric band, laparoscopic 44.95
Resurfacing, hip 00.86 ●
  acetabulum 00.87 ●
    with femoral head 00.85 ●
  femoral head 00.86 ●
    with acetabulum 00.85 ●
  partial NOS 00.85 ●
    acetabulum 00.87 ●
    femoral head 00.86 ●
  total (acetabulum and femoral head) ●
    00.85 ●
Resuscitation
  artificial respiration 93.93
  cardiac 99.60
    cardioversion 99.62
      atrial 99.61
    defibrillation 99.62
    external massage 99.63
      open chest 37.91
    intracardiac injection 37.92
  cardiopulmonary 99.60
  endotracheal intubation 96.04
  manual 93.93
  mouth-to-mouth 93.93
  pulmonary 93.93
Resuture
  abdominal wall 54.61
  cardiac septum prosthesis 35.95
  chest wall 34.71
  heart valve prosthesis (poppet) 35.95
  wound (skin and subcutaneous tissue) (without graft) NEC 86.59
Retavase, infusion 99.10
Reteplase, infusion 99.10
Retinaculotomy NEC — see also Division, ligament 80.40
  carpal tunnel (flexor) 04.43

Retraining
  cardiac 93.36
  vocational 93.85
Retrogasserian neurotomy 04.02
Revascularization
  cardiac (heart muscle) (myocardium) (direct) 36.10
    with
      bypass anastomosis
        abdominal artery to coronary artery 36.17
        aortocoronary (catheter stent) (homograft) (prosthesis) (saphenous vein graft) 36.10
        one coronary vessel 36.11
        two coronary vessels 36.12
        three coronary vessels 36.13
        four coronary vessels 36.14
        gastroepiploic artery to coronary artery 36.17
        internal mammary-coronary artery (single vessel) 36.15
        double vessel 36.16
        specified type NEC 36.19
        thoracic artery-coronary artery (single vessel) 36.15
        double vessel 36.16
      implantation of artery into heart (muscle) (myocardium) (ventricle) 36.2
    indirect 36.2
    specified type NEC 36.39
    transmyocardial
      endoscopic 36.33 ●
      endovascular 36.34 ●
      open chest 36.31
      percutaneous 36.34 ▲
      specified type NEC 36.32 ▲
      thoracoscopic 36.33 ▲
Reversal, intestinal segment 45.50
  large 45.52
  small 45.51
Revision
  amputation stump 84.3
    current traumatic — see Amputation
  anastomosis
    biliary tract 51.94
    blood vessel 39.49
    gastric, gastrointestinal (with jejunal interposition) 44.5
    intestine (large) 46.94
      small 46.93
    pleurothecal 03.97
    pyelointestinal 56.72
    salpingothecal 03.97
    subarachnoid-peritoneal 03.97
    subarachnoid-ureteral 03.97
    ureterointestinal 56.72
  ankle replacement (prosthesis) 81.59
  anterior segment (eye) wound (operative) NEC 12.83
  arteriovenous shunt (cannula) (for dialysis) 39.42
  arthroplasty — see Arthroplasty
  bone flap, skull 02.06
  breast implant 85.93
  bronchostomy 33.42
  bypass graft (vascular) 39.49
    abdominal-coronary artery 36.17
    aortocoronary (catheter stent) (with prosthesis) (with saphenous vein graft) (with vein graft) 36.10
      one coronary vessel 36.11
      three coronary vessels 36.13
      four coronary vessels 36.14
      two coronary vessels 36.12
    CABG — see Revision, aortocoronary bypass graft

☑ Additional Digit Required — Refer to the Tabular List for Digit Selection   ᵀᴮⁿ Subterms under main terms may continue to next column or page

58 — Volume 3 · October 2006   ▶◀ Revised Text   ● New Line   ▲ Revised Code   *2007 ICD-9-CM*

Revision — Rhytidectomy

☑ Additional Digit Required — Refer to the Tabular List for Digit Selection
▽ Subterms under main terms may continue to next column or page
60 — Volume 3 · October 2006
▶◀ Revised Text
● New Line
▲ Revised Code
2007 ICD-9-CM

Shock therapy — *continued*
subconvulsive 94.26
Shortening
bone (fusion) 78.20
femur 78.25
specified site NEC — *see category*
78.2 ☑
tibia 78.27
ulna 78.23
endopelvic fascia 69.22
extraocular muscle NEC 15.22
multiple (two or more muscles) 15.4
eyelid margin 08.71
eye muscle NEC 15.22
multiple (two or more muscles)
(with lengthening) 15.4
finger (macrodactyly repair) 82.83
heel cord 83.85
levator palpebrae muscle 08.33
ligament (*see also* Arthroplasty)
round 69.22
uterosacral 69.22
muscle 83.85
extraocular 15.22
multiple (two or more muscles)
15.4
hand 82.55
sclera (for repair of retinal detachment) 14.59
by scleral buckling (*see also* Buckling, scleral) 14.49
tendon 83.85
hand 82.55
ureter (with reimplantation) 56.41
Shunt — *see also* Anastomosis and Bypass, vascular
abdominovenous 54.94
aorta-coronary sinus 36.39
aorta (descending)-pulmonary (artery)
39.0
aortocarotid 39.22
aortoceliac 39.26
aortofemoral 39.25
aortoiliac 39.25
aortoiliofemoral 39.25
aortomesenteric 39.26
aorto-myocardial (graft) 36.2
aortorenal 39.24
aortosubclavian 39.22
apicoaortic 35.93
arteriovenous NEC 39.29
for renal dialysis (by)
anastomosis 39.27
external cannula 39.93
ascending aorta to pulmonary artery
(Waterston) 39.0
axillary-femoral 39.29
carotid-carotid 39.22
carotid-subclavian 39.22
caval-mesenteric 39.1
corpora cavernosa-corpus spongiosum
64.98
corpora-saphenous 64.98
descending aorta to pulmonary artery
(Potts-Smith) 39.0
endolymphatic (-subarachnoid) 20.71
endolymph-perilymph 20.71
extracranial-intracranial (EC-IC) 39.28
femoroperoneal 39.29
femoropopliteal 39.29
iliofemoral 39.25
ilioiliac 39.25
intestinal
large-to-large 45.94
small-to-large 45.93
small-to-small 45.91
left subclavian to descending aorta
(Blalock-Park) 39.0
left-to-right (systemic-pulmonary
artery) 39.0
left ventricle (heart) (apex) and aorta
35.93
lienorenal 39.1
lumbar-subarachnoid (with valve)
NEC 03.79
mesocaval 39.1

Shunt — *see also* Anastomosis and
Bypass, vascular — *continued*
peritoneal-jugular 54.94
peritoneo-vascular 54.94
peritoneovenous 54.94
pleuroperitoneal 34.05
pleurothecal (with valve) 03.79
portacaval (double) 39.1
portal-systemic 39.1
portal vein to vena cava 39.1
pulmonary-innominate 39.0
pulmonary vein to atrium 35.82
renoportal 39.1
right atrium and pulmonary artery
35.94
right ventricle and pulmonary artery
(distal) 35.92
in repair of
pulmonary artery atresia 35.92
transposition of great vessels
35.92
truncus arteriosus 35.83
salpingothecal (with valve) 03.79
semicircular-subarachnoid 20.71
spinal (thecal) (with valve) NEC 03.79
subarachnoid-peritoneal 03.71
subarachnoid-ureteral 03.72
splenorenal (venous) 39.1
arterial 39.26
subarachnoid-peritoneal (with valve)
03.71
subarachnoid-ureteral (with valve)
03.72
subclavian-pulmonary 39.0
subdural-peritoneal (with valve) 02.34
superior mesenteric-caval 39.1
systemic-pulmonary 39.0
transjugular intrahepatic portosystemic [TIPS] 39.1
vena cava to pulmonary artery (Green)
39.21
ventricular (cerebral) (with valve) 02.2
to
abdominal cavity or organ 02.34
bone marrow 02.39
cervical subarachnoid space
02.2
circulatory system 02.32
cisterna magna 02.2
extracranial site NEC 02.39
gallbladder 02.34
head or neck structure 02.31
intracerebral site NEC 02.2
lumbar site 02.39
mastoid 02.31
nasopharynx 02.31
thoracic cavity 02.33
ureter 02.35
urinary system 02.35
venous system 02.32
ventriculoatrial (with valve) 02.32
ventriculocaval (with valve) 02.32
ventriculocisternal (with valve) 02.2
ventriculolumbar (with valve) 02.39
ventriculomastoid (with valve) 02.31
ventriculonasopharyngeal 02.31
ventriculopleural (with valve) 02.33
Sialoadenectomy (parotid) (sublingual)
(submaxillary) 26.30
complete 26.32
partial 26.31
radical 26.32
Sialoadenolithotomy 26.0
Sialoadenotomy 26.0
Sialodochoplasty NEC 26.49
Sialogram 87.09
Sialolithotomy 26.0
Sieve, vena cava 38.7
Sigmoid bladder 57.87 *[45.52]*
Sigmoidectomy 45.76
Sigmoidomyotomy 46.91
Sigmoidopexy (Moschowitz) 46.63
Sigmoidoproctectomy — *see also* Resec-
tion, rectum 48.69
Sigmoidoproctostomy 45.94
Sigmoidorectostomy 45.94

Sigmoidorrhaphy 46.75
Sigmoidoscopy (rigid) 48.23
with biopsy 45.25
flexible 45.24
through stoma (artificial) 45.22
transabdominal 45.21
Sigmoidosigmoidostomy 45.94
proximal to distal segment 45.76
Sigmoidostomy — *see also* Colostomy
46.10
Sigmoidotomy 45.03
Sign language 93.75
Silver operation (bunionectomy) 77.59
Sinogram
abdominal wall 88.03
chest wall 87.38
retroperitoneum 88.14
Sinusectomy (nasal) (complete) (partial)
(with turbinectomy) 22.60
antrum 22.62
with Caldwell-Luc approach 22.61
ethmoid 22.63
frontal 22.42
maxillary 22.62
with Caldwell-Luc approach 22.61
sphenoid 22.64
Sinusotomy (nasal) 22.50
antrum (intranasal) 22.2
with external approach (Caldwell-
Luc) 22.39
radical (with removal of membrane lining) 22.31
ethmoid 22.51
frontal 22.41
maxillary (intranasal) 22.2
external approach (Caldwell-Luc)
22.39
radical (with removal of membrane lining) 22.31
multiple 22.53
perinasal 22.50
sphenoid 22.52
Sistrunk operation (excision of thyroglossal cyst) 06.7
Size reduction
abdominal wall (adipose) (pendulous)
86.83
arms (adipose) (batwing) 86.83
breast (bilateral) 85.32
unilateral 85.31
buttocks (adipose) 86.83
skin 86.83
subcutaneous tissue 86.83
thighs (adipose) 86.83
Skeletal series (x-ray) 88.31
Sling — *see also* Operation, sling
fascial (fascia lata)
for facial weakness (trigeminal
nerve paralysis) 86.81
mouth 86.81
orbicularis (mouth) 86.81
tongue 25.59
levator muscle (urethrocystopexy)
59.71
pubococcygeal 59.71
rectum (puborectalis) 48.76
tongue (fascial) 25.59
Slitting
canaliculus for
passage of tube 09.42
removal of streptothrix 09.42
lens 13.2
prepuce (dorsal) (lateral) 64.91
Slocum operation (pes anserinus
transfer) 81.47
Sluder operation (tonsillectomy) 28.2
Small bowel series (x-ray) 87.63
Smith operation (open osteotomy of
mandible) 76.62
Smith-Peterson operation (radiocarpal
arthrodesis) 81.25
Smithwick operation (sympathectomy)
05.29
Snaring, polyp, colon (endoscopic) 45.42
Snip, punctum (with dilation) 09.51

Soave operation (endorectal pull-
through) 48.41
Somatotherapy, psychiatric NEC 94.29
Sonneberg operation (inferior maxillary
neurectomy) 04.07
Sorondo-Ferré operation (hindquarter
amputation) 84.19
Soutter operation (iliac crest fasciotomy)
83.14
Spaulding-Richardson operation (uterine suspension) 69.22
Spectrophotometry NEC 89.39
blood 89.39
placenta 89.29
urine 89.29
Speech therapy NEC 93.75
Spermatocelectomy 63.2
Spermatocystectomy 60.73
Spermatocystotomy 60.72
Sphenoidectomy 22.64
Sphenoidotomy 22.52
Sphincterectomy, anal 49.6
Sphincteroplasty
anal 49.79
obstetrical laceration (current)
75.62
old 49.79
bladder neck 57.85
pancreas 51.83
sphincter of Oddi 51.83
Sphincterorrhaphy, anal 49.71
obstetrical laceration (current) 75.62
old 49.79
Sphincterotomy
anal (external) (internal) 49.59
left lateral 49.51
posterior 49.52
bladder (neck) (transurethral) 57.91
choledochal 51.82
endoscopic 51.85
iris 12.12
pancreatic 51.82
endoscopic 51.85
sphincter of Oddi 51.82
endoscopic 51.85
transduodenal ampullary 51.82
endoscopic 51.85
Spinal anesthesia — *omit code*
Spinelli operation (correction of inverted
uterus) 75.93
Spirometry (incentive) (respiratory) 89.37
Spivack operation (permanent gastrostomy) 43.19
Splanchnicectomy 05.29
Splanchnicotomy 05.0
Splenectomy (complete) (total) 41.5
partial 41.43
Splenogram 88.64
radioisotope 92.05
Splenolysis 54.59
laparoscopic 54.51
Splenopexy 41.95
Splenoplasty 41.95
Splenoportogram (by splenic arteriography) 88.64
Splenorrhaphy 41.95
Splenotomy 41.2
Splinting
dental (for immobilization) 93.55
orthodontic 24.7
musculoskeletal 93.54
ureteral 56.2
Splitting — *see also* Division
canaliculus 09.52
lacrimal papilla 09.51
spinal cord tracts 03.29
percutaneous 03.21
tendon sheath 83.01
hand 82.01
Spondylosyndesis — *see also* Fusion,
spinal 81.00
S.P. Rogers operation (knee disartitula-
tion) 84.16
Ssabanejew-Frank operation (permanent gastrostomy) 43.19

☑ Additional Digit Required — Refer to the Tabular List for Digit Selection   ▽ Subterms under main terms may continue to next column or page

2007 ICD-9-CM   ▶◀ Revised Text   ● New Line   ▲ Revised Code   **Volume 3 — 61**

Stabilization, joint — see also
  Arthrodesis patella (for recurrent dislocation) 81.44
Stab, intercostal 34.09
Stacke operation (simple mastoidectomy) 20.41
Stallard operation (conjunctivocystorhinostomy) 09.82
  with insertion of tube or stent 09.83
Stamm (-Kader) operation (temporary gastrostomy) 43.19
Stapedectomy 19.19
  with incus replacement (homograft) (prosthesis) 19.11
  revision 19.29
    with incus replacement 19.21
Stapediolysis 19.0
Stapling
  artery 39.31
  blebs, lung (emphysematous) 32.21
  diaphysis (see also Stapling, epiphyseal plate) 78.20
  epiphyseal plate 78.20
    femur 78.25
    fibula 78.27
    humerus 78.22
    radius 78.23
    specified site NEC 78.29
    tibia 78.27
    ulna 78.23
  gastric varices 44.91
  graft — see Graft
  vein 39.32
STARR (stapled transanal rectal resection) 70.52
Steinberg operation 44.5
Steindler operation
  fascia stripping (for cavus deformity) 83.14
  flexorplasty (elbow) 83.77
  muscle transfer 83.77
Stereotactic head frame application 93.59
Stereotactic radiosurgery 92.30
  cobalt 60 92.32
  linear accelerator (LINAC) 92.31
  multi-source 92.32
  particle beam 92.33
  particulate 92.33
  radiosurgery NEC 92.39
  single source photon 92.31
Sterilization
  female (see also specific operation) 66.39
  male NEC (see also Ligation, vas deferens) 63.70
Sternotomy 77.31
  as operative approach — omit code
  for bone marrow biopsy 41.31
Stewart operation (renal plication with pyeloplasty) 55.87
Stimulation (electronic) — see also Implant, electronic stimulator
  bone growth (percutaneous) — see category 78.9 ☑
    transcutaneous (surface) 99.86
  cardiac (external) 99.62
    internal 37.91
  carotid sinus 99.64
  CaverMap™ 89.58 ●
  defibrillator
    as part of intraoperative testing ●
      — omit code ●
    catheter based invasive electro- ●
      physiologic testing 37.26 ●
    device interrogation only without ●
      arrhythmia induction (bed- ●
      side check) 89.45-89.49 ●
    non-invasive programmed electrical stimulation (NIPS) 37.20 ▲
  electrophysiologic, cardiac
    as part of intraoperative testing ●
      — omit code ●
    catheter based invasive electro- ●
      physiologic testing 37.26 ●

Stimulation — see also Implant, electronic stimulator — continued
  electrophysiologic, cardiac — continued
    device interrogation only without ●
      arrhythmia induction (bed- ●
      side check) 89.45-89.49 ●
    noninvasive programmed electri- ●
      cal stimulation (NIPS) ●
      37.20 ●
  nerve
    CaverMap™ 89.58 ●
    penile 89.58 ●
    peripheral or spinal cord, transcutaneous 93.39 ●
Stitch, Kelly-Stoeckel (urethra) 59.3
Stomatoplasty 27.59
Stomatorrhaphy 27.52
Stone operation (anoplasty) 49.79
Strapping (non-traction) 93.59 ●
Strassman operation (metroplasty) 69.49
Strayer operation (gastrocnemius recession) 83.72
Stretching
  eyelid (with elongation) 08.71
  fascia 93.28
  foreskin 99.95
  iris 12.63
  muscle 93.27
  nerve (cranial) (peripheral) 04.91
  tendon 93.27
Stripping
  bone (see also Incision, bone) 77.10
  carotid sinus 39.8
  cranial suture 02.01
  fascia 83.14
    hand 82.12
  membranes for surgical induction of labor 73.1
  meninges (cerebral) 01.51
    spinal 03.4
  saphenous vein, varicose 38.59
  subdural membrane (cerebral) 01.51
    spinal 03.4
  varicose veins (lower limb) 38.59
    upper limb 38.53
  vocal cords 30.09
Stromeyer-Little operation (hepatotomy) 50.0
Strong operation (unbridling of celiac artery axis) 39.91
Stryker frame 93.59
Study
  bone mineral density 88.98
  bundle of His 37.29
  color vision 95.06
  conduction, nerve (median) 89.15
  dark adaptation, eye 95.07
  electrophysiologic stimulation and recording, cardiac
    as part of intraoperative testing ●
      — omit code ●
    catheter based invasive electro- ●
      physiologic testing 37.26 ●
    device interrogation only without ●
      arrhythmia induction (bed- ●
      side check) 89.45-89.49 ●
    noninvasive programmed electri- ●
      cal stimulation (NIPS) ●
      37.20 ●
  function (see also Function, study)
    radioisotope — see Scan, radioisotope
  lacrimal flow (radiographic) 87.05
  ocular motility 95.15
  pulmonary function — see categories 89.37-89.38
  radiographic — see Radiography
  radio-iodinated triolein 92.04
  renal clearance 92.03
  spirometer 89.37
  tracer (see also Scan, radioisotope eye (P^{32})) 95.16
  ultrasonic — see Ultrasonography

Study — continued
  visual field 95.05
  xenon flow NEC 92.19
    cardiovascular 92.05
    pulmonary 92.15
Sturmdorf operation (conization of cervix) 67.2
Submucous resection
  larynx 30.29
  nasal septum 21.5
Summerskill operation (dacryocystorhinostomy by intubation) 09.81
Surgery
  computer assisted (CAS) 00.39
    CAS with CT/CTA 00.31
    CAS with fluoroscopy 00.33
    CAS with MR/MRA 00.32
    CAS with multiple datasets 00.35
      imageless 00.34
    other CAS 00.39
  IGS — see Surgery, computer assisted
  image guided — see Surgery, computer assisted
  navigation (CT-free, IGN image guided, imageless) — see Surgery, computer assisted
Surmay operation (jejunostomy) 46.39
Suspension
  balanced, for traction 93.45
  bladder NEC 57.89
  diverticulum, pharynx 29.59
  kidney 55.7
  Olshausen (uterus) 69.22
  ovary 65.79
  paraurethral (Pereyra) 59.6
  periurethral 59.6
  urethra (retropubic) (sling) 59.5
  urethrovesical
    Goebel-Frangenheim-Stoeckel 59.4
    gracilis muscle transplant 59.71
    levator muscle sling 59.71
    Marshall-Marchetti (-Krantz) 59.5
    Millin-Read 59.4
    suprapubic 59.4
  uterus (abdominal or vaginal approach) 69.22
  vagina 70.77
Suture (laceration)
  abdominal wall 54.63
    secondary 54.61
  adenoid fossa 28.7
  adrenal (gland) 07.44
  aneurysm (cerebral) (peripheral) 39.52
  anus 49.71
    obstetric laceration (current) 75.62
      old 49.79
  aorta 39.31
  aponeurosis (see also Suture, tendon) 83.64
  arteriovenous fistula 39.53
  artery 39.31
    percutaneous puncture closure — omit code
  bile duct 51.79
  bladder 57.81
    obstetric laceration (current) 75.61
  blood vessel NEC 39.30
    artery 39.31
      percutaneous puncture closure — omit code
    vein 39.32
  breast (skin) 85.81
  bronchus 33.41
  bursa 83.99
    hand 82.99
  canaliculus 09.73
  cecum 46.75
  cerebral meninges 02.11
  cervix (traumatic laceration) 67.61
    internal os, encirclement 67.59
    obstetric laceration (current) 75.51
      old 67.69
  chest wall 34.71
  cleft palate 27.62
  clitoris 71.4
  colon 46.75

Suture — continued
  common duct 51.71
  conjunctiva 10.6
  cornea 11.51
    with conjunctival flap 11.53
  corneoscleral 11.51
    with conjunctival flap 11.53
  diaphragm 34.82
  duodenum 46.71
    ulcer (bleeding) (perforated) 44.42
      endoscopic 44.43
  dura mater (cerebral) 02.11
    spinal 03.59
  ear, external 18.4
  enterocele 70.92
  entropion 08.42
  epididymis (and)
    spermatic cord 63.51
    vas deferens 63.81
  episiotomy — see Episiotomy
  esophagus 42.82
  eyeball 16.89
  eyebrow 08.81
  eyelid 08.81
    with entropion or ectropion repair 08.42
  fallopian tube 66.71
  fascia 83.65
    hand 82.46
    to skeletal attachment 83.89
      hand 82.89
  gallbladder 51.91
  ganglion, sympathetic 05.81
  gingiva 24.32
  great vessel 39.30
    artery 39.31
    vein 39.32
  gum 24.32
  heart 37.49
  hepatic duct 51.79
  hymen 70.76
  ileum 46.73
  intestine 46.79
    large 46.75
    small 46.73
  jejunum 46.73
  joint capsule 81.96
    with arthroplasty — see Arthroplasty
    ankle 81.94
    foot 81.94
    lower extremity NEC 81.95
    upper extremity 81.93
  kidney 55.81
  labia 71.71
  laceration — see Suture, by site
  larynx 31.61
  ligament 81.96
    with arthroplasty — see Arthroplasty
    ankle 81.94
    broad 69.29
    Cooper's 54.64
    foot and toes 81.94
    gastrocolic 54.73
    knee 81.95
    lower extremity NEC 81.95
    sacrouterine 69.29
    upper extremity 81.93
    uterine 69.29
  ligation — see Ligation
  lip 27.51
  liver 50.61
  lung 33.43
  meninges (cerebral) 02.11
    spinal 03.59
  mesentery 54.75
  mouth 27.52
  muscle 83.65
    hand 82.46
    ocular (oblique) (rectus) 15.7
  nerve (cranial) (peripheral) 04.3
    sympathetic 05.81
  nose (external) (internal) 21.81
    for epistaxis 21.09
  obstetric laceration NEC 75.69

☑ Additional Digit Required — Refer to the Tabular List for Digit Selection   ⩔ Subterms under main terms may continue to next column or page

62 — Volume 3 · October 2006   ▶◀ Revised Text   ● New Line   ▲ Revised Code   2007 ICD-9-CM

Suture — Tenomyoplasty

☑ Additional Digit Required — Refer to the Tabular List for Digit Selection   ▽ Subterms under main terms may continue to next column or page

2007 ICD-9-CM   ▶◀ Revised Text   ● New Line   ▲ Revised Code   October 2006 • Volume 3 — 65

Transfusion — *continued*
exchange — *continued*
in utero (with hysterotomy) 75.2
exsanguination 99.01
gamma globulin 99.14
granulocytes 99.09
hemodilution 99.03
intrauterine 75.2
packed cells 99.04
plasma 99.07
platelets 99.05
replacement, total 99.01
serum NEC 99.07
substitution 99.01
thrombocytes 99.05
Transillumination
nasal sinuses 89.35
skull (newborn) 89.16
Translumbar aortogram 88.42
Transplant, transplantation

> *Note* — To report donor source:
> *cadaver 00.93*
> *live non-related donor 00.92*
> *live related donor 00.91*
> *live unrelated donor 00.92*

artery 39.59
renal, aberrant 39.55
autotransplant — *see* Reimplantation
blood vessel 39.59
renal, aberrant 39.55
bone (*see also* Graft, bone) 78.00
marrow 41.00
allogeneic 41.03
with purging 41.02
allograft 41.03
with purging 41.02
autograft 41.01
with purging 41.09
autologous 41.01
with purging 41.09
stem cell
allogeneic (hematopoietic) 41.05
with purging 41.08
autologous (hematopoietic) 41.04
with purging 41.07
cord blood 41.06
stem cell
allogeneic (hematopoietic) 41.05
with purging 41.08
autologous (hematopoietic) 41.04
with purging 41.07
cord blood 41.06
combined heart-lung 33.6
conjunctiva, for pterygium 11.39
corneal (*see also* Keratoplasty) 11.60
dura 02.12
fascia 83.82
hand 82.72
finger (replacing absent thumb) (same hand) 82.61
to
finger, except thumb 82.81
opposite hand (with amputation) 82.69 [84.01]
gracilis muscle (for) 83.77
anal incontinence 49.74
urethrovesical suspension 59.71
hair follicles
eyebrow 08.63
eyelid 08.63
scalp 86.64
heart (orthotopic) 37.51
combined with lung 33.6
ileal stoma to new site 46.23
intestine 46.97
islets of Langerhans (cells) 52.86
allotransplantation of cells 52.85
autotransplantation of cells 52.84
heterotransplantation of cells 52.85
homotransplantation of cells 52.84
kidney NEC 55.69
liver 50.59

Transplant, transplantation — *continued*
liver — *continued*
auxiliary (permanent) (temporary) (recipient's liver in situ) 50.51
cells into spleen via percutaneous catheterization 38.91
lung 33.50
bilateral 33.52
combined with heart 33.6
double 33.52
single 33.51
unilateral 33.51
lymphatic structure(s) (peripheral) 40.9
mammary artery to myocardium or ventricular wall 36.2
muscle 83.77
gracilis (for) 83.77
anal incontinence 49.74
urethrovesical suspension 59.71
hand 82.58
temporalis 83.77
with orbital exenteration 16.59
nerve (cranial) (peripheral) 04.6
ovary 65.92
pancreas 52.80
heterotransplant 52.83
homotransplant 52.82
islets of Langerhans (cells) 52.86
allotransplantation of cells 52.85
autotransplanation of cells 52.84
islets of Langerhans
heterotransplantation of cells 52.85
homotransplantation of cells 52.84
reimplantation 52.81
pes anserinus (tendon) (repair of knee) 81.47
renal NEC 55.69
vessel, aberrant 39.55
salivary duct opening 26.49
skin — *see* Graft, skin
spermatic cord 63.53
spleen 41.94
stem cell
allogeneic (hematopoietic) 41.05
with purging 41.08
autologous (hematopoietic) 41.04
with purging 41.07
cord blood 41.06
tendon 83.75
hand 82.56
pes anserinus (repair of knee) 81.47
superior rectus (blepharoptosis) 08.36
testis to scrotum 62.5
thymus 07.94
thyroid tissue 06.94
toe (replacing absent thumb) (with amputation) 82.69 [84.11]
to finger, except thumb 82.81 [84.11]
tooth 23.5
ureter to
bladder 56.74
ileum (external diversion) 56.51
internal diversion only 56.71
intestine 56.71
skin 56.61
vein (peripheral) 39.59
renal, aberrant 39.55
vitreous 14.72
anterior approach 14.71
Transposition
extraocular muscles 15.5
eyelash flaps 08.63
eye muscle (oblique) (rectus) 15.5
finger (replacing absent thumb) (same hand) 82.61

Transposition — *continued*
finger — *continued*
to
finger, except thumb 82.81
opposite hand (with amputation) 82.69 [84.01]
interatrial venous return 35.91
jejunal (Henley) 43.81
joint capsule (*see also* Arthroplasty) 81.96
muscle NEC 83.79
extraocular 15.5
hand 82.59
nerve (cranial) (peripheral) (radial anterior) (ulnar) 04.6
nipple 85.86
pterygium 11.31
tendon NEC 83.76
hand 82.57
vocal cords 31.69
Transureteroureterostomy 56.75
Transversostomy — *see also* Colostomy 46.10
Trapping, aneurysm (cerebral) 39.52
Trauner operation (lingual sulcus extension) 24.91
Trephination, trephining
accessory sinus — *see* Sinusotomy
corneoscleral 12.89
cranium 01.24
nasal sinus — *see* Sinusotomy
sclera (with iridectomy) 12.61
Trial (failed) forceps 73.3
Trigonectomy 57.6
Trimming, amputation stump 84.3
Triple arthrodesis 81.12
Trochanterplasty 81.40
Tsuge operation (macrodactyly repair) 82.83
Tuck, tucking — *see also* Plication
eye muscle 15.22
multiple (two or more muscles) 15.4
levator palpebrae, for blepharoptosis 08.34
Tudor "rabbit ear" operation (anterior urethropexy) 59.79
Tuffier operation
apicolysis of lung 33.39
vaginal hysterectomy 68.59
laparoscopically assisted (LAVH) 68.51
TULIP (transurethral ultrasound guided laser induced prostatectomy) 60.21
TUMT (transurethral microwave thermotherapy) of prostate 60.96
TUNA (transurethral needle ablation) of prostate 60.97
Tunnel, subcutaneous (antethoracic) 42.86
with esophageal anastomosis 42.68
esophageal 42.86
with anastomosis — *see* Anastomosis, esophagus, antesternal
pulse generator lead wire 86.99
with initial procedure — *omit code*
Turbinectomy (complete) (partial) NEC 21.69
by
cryosurgery 21.61
diathermy 21.61
with sinusectomy — *see* Sinusectomy
Turco operation (release of joint capsules in clubfoot) 80.48
TURP (transurethral resection of prostate) 60.29
Tylectomy (breast) (partial) 85.21
Tympanectomy 20.59
with tympanoplasty — *see* Tympanoplasty
Tympanogram 95.41
Tympanomastoidectomy 20.42
Tympanoplasty (type I) (with graft) 19.4
with
air pocket over round window 19.54

Tympanoplasty — *continued*
with — *continued*
fenestra in semicircular canal 19.55
graft against
incus or malleus 19.52
mobile and intact stapes 19.53
incudostapediopexy 19.52
epitympanic, type I 19.4
revision 19.6
type
II (graft against incus or malleus) 19.52
III (graft against mobile and intact stapes) 19.53
IV (air pocket over round window) 19.54
V (fenestra in semicircular canal) 19.55
Tympanosympathectomy 20.91
Tympanotomy 20.09
with intubation 20.01

U

Uchida operation (tubal ligation with or without fimbriectomy) 66.32
UFR (uroflowmetry) 89.24
Ultrafiltration 99.78
hemodiafiltration 39.95
hemodialysis (kidney) 39.95
removal, plasma water 99.78
therapeutic plasmapheresis 99.71
Ultrasonography
abdomen 88.76
aortic arch 88.73
biliary tract 88.74
breast 88.73
deep vein thrombosis 88.77
digestive system 88.74
eye 95.13
head and neck 88.71
heart 88.72
intestine 88.74
intravascular — *see* Ultrasound, intravascular (IVUS)
lung 88.73
midline shift, brain 88.71
multiple sites 88.79
peripheral vascular system 88.77
retroperitoneum 88.76
therapeutic — *see* Ultrasound
thorax NEC 88.73
total body 88.79
urinary system 88.75
uterus 88.79
gravid 88.78
Ultrasound
diagnostic — *see* Ultrasonography
fragmentation (of)
cataract (with aspiration) 13.41
urinary calculus, stones (Kock pouch) 59.95
heart (intravascular) 88.72
intracardiac (heart chambers) (ICE) 37.28
intravascular (coronary vessels) (IVUS) 00.24
non-invasive 88.72
inner ear 20.79
intravascular (IVUS) 00.29
aorta 00.22
aortic arch 00.22
cerebral vessel, extracranial 00.21
coronary vessel 00.24
intrathoracic vessel 00.22
other specified vessel 00.28
peripheral vessel 00.23
renal vessel 00.25
vena cava (inferior) (superior) 00.22
therapeutic
head 00.01
heart 00.02
neck 00.01
other therapeutic ultrasound 00.09
peripheral vascular vessels 00.03
vessels of head and neck 00.01

☑ Additional Digit Required — Refer to the Tabular List for Digit Selection ▽ Subterms under main terms may continue to next column or page

☑ Additional Digit Required — Refer to the Tabular List for Digit Selection   ▽ Subterms under main terms may continue to next column or page

2007 ICD-9-CM   ▶◀ Revised Text   ● New Line   ▲ Revised Code   **Volume 3 — 67**

Vitrectomy (mechanical) (posterior approach) 14.74
  with scleral buckling 14.49
    anterior approach 14.73
Vocational
  assessment 93.85
  retraining 93.85
  schooling 93.82
Voice training (postlaryngectomy) 93.73
von Kraske operation (proctectomy) 48.64
Voss operation (hanging hip operation) 83.19
Vulpius (-Compere) operation (lengthening of gastrocnemius muscle) 83.85
Vulvectomy (bilateral) (simple) 71.62
  partial (unilateral) 71.61
  radical (complete) 71.5
  unilateral 71.61
V-Y operation (repair)
  bladder 57.89
    neck 57.85
  ectropion 08.44
  lip 27.59
  skin (without graft) 86.89
  subcutaneous tissue (without skin graft) 86.89
  tongue 25.59

W

Wada test (hemispheric function) 89.10
Wardill operation 27.62
Ward-Mayo operation (vaginal hysterectomy) 68.59
  laparoscopically assisted (LAVH) 68.51
Washing — *see* Lavage and Irrigation
Waterston operation (aorta-right pulmonary artery anastomosis) 39.0

Watkins (-Wertheim) operation (uterus interposition) 69.21
Watson-Jones operation
  hip arthrodesis 81.21
  reconstruction of lateral ligaments, ankle 81.49
  shoulder arthrodesis (extra-articular) 81.23
  tenoplasty 83.88
Webbing (syndactylization) 86.89
Weir operation
  appendicostomy 47.91
  correction of nostrils 21.86
Wertheim operation (radical hysterectomy) 68.69 ▲
  laparoscopic 68.61 ●
West operation (dacryocystorhinostomy) 09.81
Wheeler operation
  entropion repair 08.44
  halving procedure (eyelid) 08.24
Whipple operation (radical pancreaticoduodenectomy) 52.7
  Child modification (radical subtotal pancreatectomy) 52.53
  Rodney Smith modification (radical subtotal pancreatectomy) 52.53
Whitehead operation
  glossectomy, radical 25.4
  hemorrhoidectomy 49.46
White operation (lengthening of tendo calcaneus by incomplete tenotomy) 83.11
Whitman operation
  foot stabilization (talectomy) 77.98
  hip reconstruction 81.40
  repair of serratus anterior muscle 83.87

Whitman operation — *continued*
  talectomy 77.98
  trochanter wedge osteotomy 77.25
Wier operation (entropion repair) 08.44
Williams-Richardson operation (vaginal construction) 70.61
Wilms operation (thoracoplasty) 33.34
Wilson operation (angulation osteotomy for hallux valgus) 77.51
Window operation
  antrum (nasal sinus) — *see* Antrotomy, maxillary
  aorticopulmonary 39.59
  bone cortex (*see also* Incision, bone) 77.10
    facial 76.09
  nasoantral — *see* Antrotomy, maxillary
  pericardium 37.12
  pleura 34.09
Winiwarter operation (cholecystoenterostomy) 51.32
Wiring
  aneurysm 39.52
  dental (for immobilization) 93.55
    with fracture-reduction — *see* Reduction, fracture
  orthodontic 24.7
Wirsungojejunostomy 52.96
Witzel operation (temporary gastrostomy) 43.19
Woodward operation (release of high riding scapula) 81.83
Wrapping, aneurysm (gauze) (methyl methacrylate) (plastic) 39.52

X

Xenograft 86.65

Xerography, breast 87.36
Xeromammography 87.36
Xiphoidectomy 77.81
X-ray
  chest (routine) 87.44
    wall NEC 87.39
  contrast — *see* Radiography, contrast
  diagnostic — *see* Radiography
  injection of radio-opaque substance — *see* Radiography, contrast
  skeletal series, whole or complete 88.31
  therapeutic — *see* Therapy, radiation

Y

Young operation
  epispadias repair 58.45
  tendon transfer (anterior tibialis) (repair of flat foot) 83.75
Yount operation (division of iliotibial band) 83.14

Z

Zancolli operation
  capsuloplasty 81.72
  tendon transfer (biceps) 82.56
Ziegler operation (iridectomy) 12.14
Zonulolysis (with lens extraction) — *see also* Extraction, cataract, intracapsular 13.19
Z-plasty
  epicanthus 08.59
  eyelid (*see also* Reconstruction, eyelid) 08.70
  hypopharynx 29.4
  skin (scar) (web contracture) 86.84
    with excision of lesion 86.3

☑ Additional Digit Required — Refer to the Tabular List for Digit Selection   ▽ Subterms under main terms may continue to next column or page

68 — Volume 3 · October 2006   ▶◀ Revised Text   ● New Line   ▲ Revised Code   *2007 ICD-9-CM*

00. PROCEDURES AND INTERVENTIONS, NOT ELSEWHERE CLASSIFIED (00)

√3rd **00**   **Procedures and interventions, not elsewhere classified**

√4th **00.0**   **Therapeutic ultrasound**

> EXCLUDES   diagnostic ultrasound (non-invasive)
> (88.71-88.79)
> intracardiac echocardiography [ICE]
> (heart chamber(s)) (37.28)
> intravascular imaging (adjunctive)
> (00.21-00.29)

AHA: 4Q, '02, 90

DEF: Interventional treatment modality using lower frequency and higher intensity levels of ultrasound energy than used in diagnostic ultrasound modality for the purpose of limiting intimal hyperpalsia, or restenosis, associated with atherosclerotic vascular disease.

00.01   **Therapeutic ultrasound of vessels of head and neck**
Anti-restenotic ultrasound
Intravascular non-ablative ultrasound

> EXCLUDES   diagnostic ultrasound of:
> eye (95.13)
> head and neck (88.71)
> that of inner ear (20.79)
> ultrasonic:
> angioplasty of non-coronary
> vessel (39.50)
> embolectomy (38.01, 38.02)
> endarterectomy (38.11,
> 38.12)
> thrombectomy (38.01, 38.02)

00.02   **Therapeutic ultrasound of heart**
Anti-restenotic ultrasound
Intravascular non-ablative ultrasound

> EXCLUDES   diagnostic ultrasound of heart
> (88.72)
> ultrasonic ablation of heart
> lesion (37.34)
> ultrasonic angioplasty of
> coronary vessels
> (00.66, 36.09)

00.03   **Therapeutic ultrasound of peripheral vascular vessels**
Anti-restenotic ultrasound
Intravascular non-ablative ultrasound

> EXCLUDES   diagnostic ultrasound of
> peripheral vascular
> system (88.77)
> ultrasonic angioplasty of:
> non-coronary vessel (39.50)

00.09   **Other therapeutic ultrasound**

> EXCLUDES   ultrasonic:
> fragmentation of urinary
> stones (59.95)
> percutaneous nephrostomy
> with fragmentation
> (55.04)
> physical therapy (93.35)
> transurethral guided laser
> induced prostatec-
> tomy (TULIP) (60.21)

√4th **00.1**   **Pharmaceuticals**

00.10   **Implantation of chemotherapeutic agent**
Brain wafer chemotherapy
Interstitial/intracavitary

> EXCLUDES   injection or infusion of cancer
> chemotherapeutic
> substance (99.25)

AHA: 4Q, '02, 93

DEF: Brain wafer chemotherapy: Placement of wafers containing antineoplastic agent against the wall of the resection cavity subsequent to the surgeon completing a tumor excision to deliver chemotherapy directly to the tumor site; used to treat glioblastoma multiforme (GBM).

00.11   **Infusion of drotrecogin alfa (activated)**
Infusion of recombinant protein
AHA: 4Q, '02, 93

00.12   **Administration of inhaled nitric oxide**
Nitric oxide therapy
AHA: 4Q, '02, 94

00.13   **Injection or infusion of nesiritide**
Human B-type natriuretic peptide (hBNP)
AHA: 4Q, '02, 94

00.14   **Injection or infusion of oxazolidinone class of antibiotics**
Linezolid injection
AHA: 4Q, '02, 95

00.15   **High-dose infusion interleukin-2 [IL-2]**
Infusion (IV bolus, CIV) interleukin
Injection of aldesleukin

> EXCLUDES   low-dose infusion interleukin-2
> (99.28)

AHA: 4Q, '03, 92

DEF: A high-dose anti-neoplastic therapy using a biological response modifier (BRM); the body naturally produces substances called interleukins, which are multi-function cytokines in the generation of an immune response.

00.16   **Pressurized treatment of venous bypass graft [conduit] with pharmaceutical substance**
Ex-vivo treatment of vessel
Hyperbaric pressurized graft [conduit]

DEF: Ex-vivo process of delivering small nucleic acid molecules that block protein transcription factors essential for the expression of genes controlling cell proliferation into graft tissue under nondistending pressure; reduces intimal hyperplasia and vein graft failure.

00.17   **Infusion of vasopressor agent**

00.18   **Infusion of immunosuppressive antibody therapy during induction phase of solid organ transplantation**
Monoclonal antibody therapy
Polyclonal antibody therapy
AHA: ▶4Q, '05, 101◀

√4th **00.2**   **Intravascular imaging of blood vessels**
Note: Real-time imaging of lumen of blood vessel(s) using sound waves
Endovascular ultrasonography
Intravascular [ultrasound] imaging of blood vessels
Intravascular ultrasound (IVUS)
Code also any synchronous diagnostic or therapeutic procedures

> EXCLUDES   adjunct vascular system procedures,
> number of vessels treated (00.40-
> 00.43)
> diagnostic procedures on blood vessels
> (38.21-38.29)
> diagnostic ultrasound of peripheral
> vascular system (88.77)
> magnetic resonance imaging (MRI)
> (88.91-88.97)
> therapeutic ultrasound (00.01-00.09)

00.21   **Intravascular imaging of extracranial cerebral vessels**
Common carotid vessels and branches
Intravascular ultrasound (IVUS), extracranial cerebral vessels

> EXCLUDES   diagnostic ultrasound
> (non-invasive) of head
> and neck (88.71)

00.22   **Intravascular imaging of intrathoracic vessels**
Aorta and aortic arch
Intravascular ultrasound (IVUS), intrathoracic vessels
Vena cava (superior) (inferior)

> EXCLUDES   diagnostic ultrasound
> (non-invasive) of other
> sites of thorax (88.73)

Procedures and Interventions, NEC

00.23–00.50

00.23   Intravascular imaging of peripheral vessels
Imaging of:
     vessels of arm(s)
     vessels of leg(s)
Intravascular ultrasound (IVUS), peripheral vessels
> **EXCLUDES**   diagnostic ultrasound (non-invasive) of peripheral vascular system (88.77)

00.24   Intravascular imaging of coronary vessels
Intravascular ultrasound (IVUS), coronary vessels
> **EXCLUDES**   diagnostic ultrasound (non-invasive) of heart (88.72)
> intracardiac echocardiography [ICE] (ultrasound of heart chamber(s)) (37.28)

00.25   Intravascular imaging of renal vessels
Intravascular ultrasound (IVUS), renal vessels
Renal artery
> **EXCLUDES**   diagnostic ultrasound (non-invasive) of urinary system (88.75)

00.28   Intravascular imaging, other specified vessel(s)

00.29   Intravascular imagining unspecified vessel(s)

✓4ᵗʰ **00.3   Computer assisted surgery [CAS]**
CT-free navigation
Image guided navigation (IGN)
Image guided surgery (IGS)
Imageless navigation
Code also diagnostic or therapeutic procedure
> **EXCLUDES**   stereotactic frame application only (93.59)

00.31   Computer assisted surgery with CT/CTA
AHA: 4Q, '04, 113

00.32   Computer assisted surgery with MR/MRA
AHA: 4Q, '04, 113

00.33   Computer assisted surgery with fluoroscopy

00.34   Imageless computer assisted surgery

00.35   Computer assisted surgery with multiple datasets

00.39   Other computer assisted surgery
Computer assisted surgery NOS

✓4ᵗʰ **00.4   Adjunct vascular system procedures**
Note: These codes can apply to both coronary and peripheral vessels. These codes are to be used in conjunction with other therapeutic procedure codes to provide additional information on the number of vessels upon which a procedure was performed and/or the number of stents inserted. As appropriate, code both the number of vessels operated on (00.40-00.43), and the number of stents inserted (00.45-00.48).
Code also any:
     angioplasty or atherectomy (00.61-00.62, 00.66, 39.50)
     endarterectomy (38.10-38.18)
     insertion of vascular stent(s) (00.55, 00.63-00.65, 36.06-36.07, 39.90)
     other removal of coronary artery obstruction (36.09)
AHA: 4Q, '05, 101

00.40   Procedure on single vessel
Number of vessels, unspecified
> **EXCLUDES**   (aorto)coronary bypass (36.10-36.19)
> intravascular imaging of blood vessels (00.21-00.29)
AHA: 4Q, '05, 71, 106

00.41   Procedure on two vessels
> **EXCLUDES**   (aorto)coronary bypass (36.10-36.19)
> intravascular imaging of blood vessels (00.21-00.29)
AHA: 4Q, '05, 105

00.42   Procedure on three vessels
> **EXCLUDES**   (aorto)coronary bypass (36.10-36.19)
> intravascular imaging of blood vessels (00.21-00.29)

00.43   Procedure on four or more vessels
> **EXCLUDES**   (aorto)coronary bypass (36.10-36.19)
> intravascular imaging of blood vessels (00.21-00.29)

● **00.44   Procedure on vessel bifurcation**
Note: This code is to be used to identify the presence of a vessel bifurcation; it does not describe a specific bifurcation stent. Use this code only once per operative episode, irrespective of the number of bifurcations in vessels.

00.45   Insertion of one vascular stent
Number of stents, unspecified
AHA: 4Q, '05, 71

00.46   Insertion of two vascular stents
AHA: 4Q, '05, 105-106

00.47   Insertion of three vascular stents

00.48   Insertion of four or more vascular stents

✓4ᵗʰ **00.5   Other cardiovascular procedures**
AHA: 4Q, '02, 95

00.50   Implantation of cardiac resynchronization pacemaker without mention of defibrillation, total system [CRT-P]
▶Note: Device testing during procedure—omit code◀
▶Biventricular pacemaker◀
Biventricular pacing without internal cardiac defibrillator
▶BiV pacemaker◀
Implantation of cardiac resynchronization (biventricular) pulse generator pacing device, formation of pocket, transvenous leads including placement of lead into left ventricular coronary venous system, and intraoperative procedures for evaluation of lead signals
That with CRT-P generator and one or more leads
> **EXCLUDES**   implantation of cardiac resynchronization defibrillator, total system [CRT-D] (00.51)
> insertion or replacement of any type pacemaker device (37.80-37.87)
> replacement of cardiac resynchronization: defibrillator, pulse generator only [CRT-D] (00.54)
> pacemaker, pulse generator only [CRT-P] (00.53)
AHA: 3Q, '05, 3-9; 4Q, '02, 100

DEF: Cardiac resynchronization pacemaker: CRT-P, or biventricular pacing, adds a third lead to traditional pacemaker designs that connects to the left ventricle. The device provides electrical stimulation to the right atrium, right ventricle, and left ventricle, and coordinates ventricular contractions to improve cardiac output.

BI Bilateral Procedure   **NC** Non-covered Procedure   **LC** Limited Coverage Procedure   ▶◀ Revised Text   ● New Code   ▲ Revised Code Title

00.51 **Implantation of cardiac resynchronization defibrillator, total system [CRT-D]**
▶Note: Device testing during procedure—*omit code*◀
▶BiV defibrillator
Biventricular defibrillator◀
Biventricular pacing with internal cardiac defibrillator
▶BiV ICD
BiV pacemaker with defibrillator
BiV pacing with defibrillator◀
Implantation of cardiac resynchronization (biventricular) pulse generator with defibrillator [AICD], formation of pocket, transvenous leads, including placement of lead into left ventricular coronary venous system, intraoperative procedures for evaluation of lead signals, and obtaining defibrillator threshold measurements
That with CRT-D generator and one or more leads

EXCLUDES *implantation of cardiac resynchronization pacemaker, total system [CRT-P] (00.50)*
implantation or replacement of automatic cardioverter/ defibrillator, total system [AICD] (37.94)
replacement of cardiac resynchronization defibrillator, pulse generator only [CRT-D] (00.54)

AHA: 3Q, '05, 3-9; 4Q, '02, 99, 100

00.52 **Implantation or replacement of transvenous lead [electrode] into left ventricular coronary venous system**
EXCLUDES *implantation of cardiac resynchronization: defibrillator, total system [CRT-D] (00.51) pacemaker, total system [CRT-P] (00.50) initial insertion of transvenous lead [electrode] (37.70-37.72) replacement of transvenous atrial and/or ventricular lead(s) [electrodes] (37.76)*

00.53 **Implantation or replacement of cardiac resynchronization pacemaker, pulse generator only [CRT-P]**
▶Note: Device testing during procedure—*omit code*◀
Implantation of CRT-P device with removal of any existing CRT-P or other pacemaker device
EXCLUDES *implantation of cardiac resynchronization pacemaker, total system [CRT-P] (00.50) implantation or replacement of cardiac resynchronization defibrillator, pulse generator only [CRT-D] (00.54) insertion or replacement of any type pacemaker device (37.80-37.87)*

AHA: 3Q, '05, 3-9

00.54 **Implantation or replacement of cardiac resynchronization defibrillator, pulse generator device only [CRT-D]**
▶Note: Device testing during procedure—*omit code*◀
Implantation of CRT-D device with removal of any existing CRT-D, CRT-P, pacemaker, or defibrillator device
EXCLUDES *implantation of automatic cardioverter/defibrillator pulse generator only (37.96) implantation of cardiac resynchronization defibrillator, total system [CRT-D] (00.51) implantation or replacement of cardiac resynchron- ization pacemaker, pulse generator only [CRT-P] (00.53)*

AHA: 3Q, '05, 3-9; 4Q, '02, 100

00.55 **Insertion of drug-eluting peripheral vessel stent(s)**
Endograft(s)
Endovascular graft(s)
Stent graft(s)
Code also any:
angioplasty or atherectomy of other non-coronary vessel(s) (39.50)
number of vascular stents inserted (00.45-00.48)
number of vessels treated (00.40-00.43)
▶procedure on vessel bifurcation (00.44)◀
EXCLUDES *drug-coated peripheral stents, e.g., heparin coated (39.90) insertion of cerebrovascular stent(s) (00.63-00.65) insertion of drug-eluting coronary artery stent (36.07) insertion of non-drug-eluting stent(s): coronary artery (36.06) peripheral vessel (39.90) that for aneurysm repair (39.71-39.79)*

AHA: 4Q, '02, 101

00.56 **Insertion or replacement of implantable pressure sensor (lead) for intracardiac hemodynamic monitoring**
Code also any associated implantation or replacement of monitor (00.57)
EXCLUDES *circulatory monitoring (blood gas, arterial or venous pressure, cardiac output and coronary blood flow) (89.60-89.69)*

00.57 **Implantation or replacement of subcutaneous device for intracardiac hemodynamic monitoring**
Implantation of monitoring device with formation of subcutaneous pocket and connection to intracardiac pressure sensor (lead)
Code also any associated insertion or replacement of implanted pressure sensor (lead) (00.56)

Procedures and Interventions, NEC

00.6–00.66

√4ᵗʰ **00.6**   **Procedures on blood vessels**

00.61   **Percutaneous angioplasty or atherectomy of precerebral (extracranial) vessel(s)**

Basilar
Carotid
Vertebral
Code also any:
     injection or infusion of thrombolytic agent (99.10)
     number of vascular stents inserted (00.45-00.48)
     number of vessels treated (00.40-00.43)
     percutaneous insertion of carotid artery stent(s) (00.63)
     percutaneous insertion of other precerebral artery stent(s) (00.64)
     ▶procedure on vessel bifurcation (00.44)◀

EXCLUDES   *angioplasty or atherectomy of other non-coronary vessel(s) (39.50)*
     removal of cerebrovascular obstruction of vessel(s) by open approach (38.01-38.02, 38.11-38.12, 38.31-38.32, 38.41-38.42)

00.62   **Percutaneous angioplasty or atherectomy intracranial vessel(s)**   NC

Code also any:
     injection or infusion of thrombolytic agent (99.10)
     number of vascular stents inserted (00.45-00.48)
     number of vessels treated (00.40-00.43)
     percutaneous insertion of intracranial stent(s) (00.65)
     ▶procedure on vessel bifurcation (00.44)◀

EXCLUDES   *angioplasty or atherectomy of other non-coronary vessel(s) (39.50)*
     removal of cerebrovascular obstruction of vessel(s) by open approach (38.01-38.02, 38.11-38.12, 38.31-38.32, 38.41-38.42)

00.63   **Percutaneous insertion of carotid artery stent(s)**

Includes the use of any embolic protection device, distal protection device, filter device, or stent delivery system
Non-drug-eluting stent
Code also any:
     number of vascular stents inserted (00.45-00.48)
     number of vessels treated (00.40-00.43)
     percutaneous angioplasty or atherectomy of precerebral vessel(s) (00.61)
     ▶procedure on vessel bifurcation (00.44)◀

EXCLUDES   *angioplasty or atherectomy of other non-coronary vessel(s) (39.50)*
     insertion of drug-eluting peripheral vessel stent(s) (00.55)

00.64   **Percutaneous insertion of other precerebral (extracranial) artery stent(s)**

Includes the use of any embolic protection device, distal protection device, filter device, or stent delivery system
Basilar stent
Vertebral stent
Code also any:
     number of vascular stents inserted (00.45-00.48)
     number of vessels treated (00.40-00.43)
     percutaneous angioplasty or atherectomy of precerebral vessel(s) (00.61)
     ▶procedure on vessel bifurcation (00.44)◀

EXCLUDES   *angioplasty or atherectomy of other non-coronary vessel(s) (39.50)*
     insertion of drug-eluting peripheral vessel stent(s) (00.55)

00.65   **Percutaneous insertion of intracranial vascular stent(s)**

Includes the use of any embolic protection device, distal protection device, filter device, or stent delivery system
Code also any:
     number of vascular stents inserted (00.45-00.48)
     number of vessels treated (00.40-00.43)
     percutaneous angioplasty or atherectomy of intracranial vessel(s) (00.62)
     ▶procedure on vessel bifurcation (00.44)◀

EXCLUDES   *angioplasty or atherectomy of other non-coronary vessel(s) (39.50)*
     insertion of drug-eluting peripheral vessel stent(s) (00.55)

00.66   **Percutaneous transluminal coronary angioplasty [PTCA] or coronary atherectomy**

Balloon angioplasty of coronary artery
Coronary atherectomy
Percutaneous coronary angioplasty NOS
PTCA NOS
Code also any:
     injection or infusion of thrombolytic agent (99.10)
     insertion of coronary artery stent(s) (36.06-36.07)
     intracoronary artery thrombolytic infusion (36.04)
     number of vascular stents inserted (00.45-00.48)
     number of vessels treated (00.40-00.43)
     ▶procedure on vessel bifurcation (00.44)◀

AHA: 4Q, '05, 71, 101; **The following references pertain to deleted PTCA codes (36.01, 36.02, 36.05):** 1Q, '04, 10; 3Q, '03, 9; 4Q, '02, 114; 3Q, '02, 19; 1Q, '01, 9; 2Q, '01, 24; 1Q, '00, 11; 1Q, '99, 17; 4Q, '98, 74, 85; 1Q, '97, 3; 1Q, '94, 3; 3Q, '91, 24

DEF: Balloon angioplasty: Insertion of catheter with inflation of balloon to flatten plaque and widen vessels.

PTCA (Balloon Angioplasty)

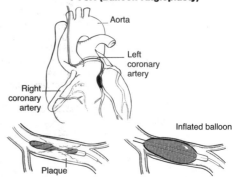

BI Bilateral Procedure   NC Non-covered Procedure   LC Limited Coverage Procedure   ▶◀ Revised Text   ● New Code   ▲ Revised Code Title

72 — Volume 3 • October 2006   *2007 ICD•9•CM*

√4ᵗʰ **00.7   Other hip procedures**
AHA: 4Q, '05, 106

00.70   Revision of hip replacement, both `BI`
acetabular and femoral components
     Total hip revision
     Code also any:
       removal of (cement) (joint) spacer (84.57)
       type of bearing surface, if known
         ▶(00.74-00.77)◀

       `EXCLUDES`   *revision of hip replacement,*
                acetabular component
                only (00.71)
              revision of hip replacement,
                femoral component only
                (00.72)
              revision of hip replacement,
                not otherwise specified
                (81.53)
              revision with replacement of
                acetabular liner and/or
                femoral head only
                (00.73)

     AHA: 4Q, '05, 113

00.71   Revision of hip replacement, `BI`
acetabular component
     Partial, acetabular component only
     That with:
       exchange of acetabular cup and liner
       exchange of femoral head
     Code also any type of bearing surface, if
       known ▶(00.74-00.77)◀

       `EXCLUDES`   *revision of hip replacement,*
                both acetabular and
                femoral components
                (00.70)
              revision of hip replacement,
                femoral component
                (00.72)
              revision of hip replacement,
                not otherwise specified
                (81.53)
              revision with replacement of
                acetabular liner and/or
                femoral head only
                (00.73)

     AHA: 4Q, '05, 112

00.72   Revision of hip replacement, femoral `BI`
component
     Partial, femoral component only
     That with:
       exchange of acetabular liner
       exchange of femoral stem and head
     Code also any type of bearing surface, if
       known ▶(00.74-00.77)◀

       `EXCLUDES`   *revision of hip replacement,*
                acetabular component
                (00.71)
              revision of hip replacement,
                both acetabular and
                femoral components
                (00.70)
              revision of hip replacement,
                not otherwise specified
                (81.53)
              revision with replacement of
                acetabular liner and/or
                femoral head only
                (00.73)

00.73   Revision of hip replacement, acetabular `BI`
liner and/or femoral head only
     Code also any type of bearing surface, if
       known ▶(00.74-00.77)◀

00.74   Hip replacement bearing surface, metal
on polyethylene

00.75   Hip replacement bearing surface,
metal-on-metal

00.76   Hip replacement bearing surface,
ceramic-on-ceramic
     AHA: 4Q, '05, 112

● **00.77   Hip replacement bearing surface,**
ceramic-on-polyethylene

▲ √4ᵗʰ **00.8   Other knee and hip procedures**
     Note: Report up to two components using 00.81-
     00.83 to describe revision of knee
     replacements. If all three components are
     revised, report 00.80.
     AHA: 4Q, '05, 113

00.80   Revision of knee replacement, total `BI`
(all components)
     Replacement of femoral, tibial, and patellar
       components (all components)
     Code also any removal of (cement) (joint)
       spacer (84.57)

       `EXCLUDES`   *revision of only one or two*
                components (tibial,
                femoral or patellar
                component) (00.81-
                00.84)

00.81   Revision of knee replacement, tibial `BI`
component
     Replacement of tibial baseplate and tibial
       insert (liner)

       `EXCLUDES`   *revision of knee replacement,*
                total (all components)
                (00.80)

     AHA: 4Q, '05, 117

00.82   Revision of knee replacement, femoral `BI`
component
     That with replacement of tibial insert (liner)

       `EXCLUDES`   *revision of knee replacement,*
                total (all components)
                (00.80)

     AHA: 4Q, '05, 117

00.83   Revision of knee replacement, `BI`
patellar component

       `EXCLUDES`   *revision of knee replacement,*
                total (all components)
                (00.80)

00.84   Revision of total knee replacement, `BI`
tibial insert (liner)
     Replacement of tibial insert (liner)

       `EXCLUDES`   *that with replacement of tibial*
                component (tibial
                baseplate and liner)
                (00.81)

● **00.85   Resurfacing hip, total, acetabulum** `BI`
and femoral head
     Hip resurfacing arthroplasty, total

● **00.86   Resurfacing hip, partial, femoral head** `BI`
     Hip resurfacing arthroplasty, NOS
     Hip resurfacing arthroplasty, partial,
       femoral head

       `EXCLUDES`   *that with resurfacing of*
                acetabulum (00.85)

● **00.87   Resurfacing hip, partial, acetabulum** `BI`
     Hip resurfacing arthroplasty, partial,
       acetabulum

       `EXCLUDES`   *that with resurfacing of*
                femoral head (00.85)

√4ᵗʰ **00.9   Other procedures and interventions**

00.91   Transplant from live related donor
     Code also organ transplant procedure

00.92   Transplant from live non-related donor
     Code also organ transplant procedure
     AHA: 4Q, '04, 117

00.93   Transplant from cadaver
     Code also organ transplant procedure

√3ʳᵈ
√4ᵗʰ Additional Digit Required   Nonspecific OR Procedure   Valid OR Procedure   Non-OR Procedure   Adjunct Code

Operations on the Nervous System

01–01.39

1. OPERATIONS ON THE NERVOUS SYSTEM (01-05)

✓3rd **01**   **Incision and excision of skull, brain, and cerebral meninges**

  ✓4th **01.0**   **Cranial puncture**

    01.01   **Cisternal puncture**

         Cisternal aspiration

         Cisternal tap

         EXCLUDES   *pneumocisternogram (87.02)*

         DEF: Needle insertion through subarachnoid space to withdraw cerebrospinal fluid.

    01.02   **Ventriculopuncture through previously implanted catheter**

         Puncture of ventricular shunt tubing

         DEF: Piercing of artificial, fluid-diverting tubing in the brain for withdrawal of cerebrospinal fluid.

    01.09   **Other cranial puncture**

         Aspiration of:

           subarachnoid space

           subdural space

         Cranial aspiration NOS

         Puncture of anterior fontanel

         Subdural tap (through fontanel)

  ✓4th **01.1**   **Diagnostic procedures on skull, brain, and cerebral meninges**

    01.11   **Closed [percutaneous] [needle] biopsy of cerebral meninges**

         Burr hole approach

         DEF: Needle excision of tissue sample through skin into cerebral membranes; no other procedure performed.

    01.12   **Open biopsy of cerebral meninges**

         DEF: Open surgical excision of tissue sample from cerebral membrane.

    01.13   **Closed [percutaneous] [needle] biopsy of brain**

         Burr hole approach

         Stereotactic method

         AHA: M-A, '87, 9

         DEF: Removal by needle of brain tissue sample through skin.

    01.14   **Open biopsy of brain**

         DEF: Open surgical excision of brain tissue sample.

    01.15   **Biopsy of skull**

    01.18   **Other diagnostic procedures on brain and cerebral meninges** ●

         EXCLUDES   *cerebral:*

           arteriography (88.41)

           thermography (88.81)

         contrast radiogram of brain (87.01-87.02)

         echoencephalogram (88.71)

         electroencephalogram (89.14)

         microscopic examination of specimen from nervous system and of spinal fluid (90.01-90.09)

         neurologic examination (89.13)

         phlebography of head and neck (88.61)

         pneumoencephalogram (87.01)

         radioisotope scan:

           cerebral (92.11)

           head NEC (92.12)

         tomography of head:

           C.A.T. scan (87.03)

           other (87.04)

         AHA: 3Q, '98, 12

    01.19   **Other diagnostic procedures on skull**

         EXCLUDES   *transillumination of skull (89.16)*

           x-ray of skull (87.17)

  ✓4th **01.2**   **Craniotomy and craniectomy**

         EXCLUDES   *decompression of skull fracture (02.02)*

           exploration of orbit (16.01-16.09)

           that as operative approach — omit code

         AHA: 1Q, '91, 1

         DEF: Craniotomy: Incision into skull.

         DEF: Craniectomy: Excision of part of skull.

    01.21   **Incision and drainage of cranial sinus**

         DEF: Incision for drainage, including drainage of air cavities in skull bones.

    01.22   **Removal of intracranial neurostimulator lead(s)**

         Code also any removal of neurostimulator pulse generator (86.05)

         EXCLUDES   *removal with synchronous replacement (02.93)*

    01.23   **Reopening of craniotomy site**

         DEF: Reopening of skull incision.

    01.24   **Other craniotomy**

         Cranial: Craniotomy with

           decompression   removal of:

           exploration   epidural abscess

           trephination   extradural hematoma

         Craniotomy NOS   foreign body of skull

         EXCLUDES   *removal of foreign body with incision into brain (01.39)*

         AHA: 2Q, '91, 14

    01.25   **Other craniectomy**

         Debridement of skull NOS

         Sequestrectomy of skull

         EXCLUDES   *debridement of compound fracture of skull (02.02)*

           strip craniectomy (02.01)

         AHA: ▶1Q, '06, 6◀

    01.26   **Insertion of catheter(s) into cranial cavity or tissue** ▲

         Code also any concomitant procedure (e.g. resection (01.59))

         EXCLUDES   ▶ *placement of intracerebral catheter(s) via burr hole(s) (01.28)*◀

         AHA: 4Q, '05, 117-118

    01.27   **Removal of catheter(s) from cranial cavity or tissue** ▲

         AHA: 4Q, '05, 117-118

    01.28   **Placement of intracerebral catheter(s) via burr hole(s)**

         Convection enhanced delivery

         Stereotactic placement of intracerebral catheter(s)

         Code also infusion of medication

         EXCLUDES   *insertion of catheter(s) into cranial cavity or tissue(s) (01.26)*

  ✓4th **01.3**   **Incision of brain and cerebral meninges**

    01.31   **Incision of cerebral meninges**

         Drainage of:

           intracranial hygroma

           subarachnoid abscess (cerebral)

           subdural empyema

    01.32   **Lobotomy and tractotomy**

         Division of: Percutaneous

           brain tissue   (radiofrequency)

           cerebral tracts   cingulotomy

         DEF: Lobotomy: Incision of nerve fibers of brain lobe, usually frontal.

         DEF: Tractotomy: Severing of a nerve fiber group to relieve pain.

    01.39   **Other incision of brain**

         Amygdalohippocampotomy

         Drainage of intracerebral hematoma

         Incision of brain NOS

         EXCLUDES   *division of cortical adhesions (02.91)*

BI Bilateral Procedure   **NC** Non-covered Procedure   **LC** Limited Coverage Procedure   ▶◀ Revised Text   ● New Code   ▲ Revised Code Title

74 — Volume 3 • October 2006   **2007 ICD•9•CM**

Operations on the Nervous System

01.4–02.41

✓4th **01.4   Operations on thalamus and globus pallidus**

    01.41   Operations on thalamus

        Chemothalamectomy   Thalamotomy

        EXCLUDES   *that by stereotactic radiosurgery (92.30-92.39)*

    01.42   Operations on globus pallidus

        Pallidoansectomy   Pallidotomy

        EXCLUDES   *that by stereotactic radiosurgery (92.30-92.39)*

✓4th **01.5   Other excision or destruction of brain and meninges**

    AHA: 4Q, '93, 33

    01.51   Excision of lesion or tissue of cerebral meninges

        Decortication

        Resection   of (cerebral)

        Stripping of subdural   meninges

        membrane

        EXCLUDES   *biopsy of cerebral meninges (01.11-01.12)*

    01.52   Hemispherectomy

        DEF: Removal of one half of the brain. Most often performed for malignant brain tumors or intractable epilepsy.

    01.53   Lobectomy of brain

        DEF: Excision of a brain lobe.

    01.59   Other excision or destruction of lesion or tissue of brain

        Curettage of brain

        Debridement of brain

        Marsupialization of brain cyst

        Transtemporal (mastoid) excision of brain tumor

        EXCLUDES   *biopsy of brain (01.13-01.14)*

                 that by stereotactic radiosurgery (92.30-92.39)

        AHA: 4Q, '05, 118; 3Q, '99, 7; 1Q, '99, 9; 3Q, '98, 12; 1Q, '98, 6

  01.6   Excision of lesion of skull

    Removal of granulation tissue of cranium

    EXCLUDES   *biopsy of skull (01.15)*

              sequestrectomy (01.25)

✓3rd **02   Other operations on skull, brain, and cerebral meninges**

✓4th **02.0   Cranioplasty**

    EXCLUDES   *that with synchronous repair of encephalocele (02.12)*

    02.01   Opening of cranial suture

        Linear craniectomy

        Strip craniectomy

        DEF: Opening of the lines of junction between the bones of the skull for removal of strips of skull bone.

    02.02   Elevation of skull fracture fragments

        Debridement of compound fracture of skull

        Decompression of skull fracture

        Reduction of skull fracture

        Code also any synchronous debridement of brain (01.59)

        EXCLUDES   *debridement of skull NOS (01.25)*

                 removal of granulation tissue of cranium (01.6)

    02.03   Formation of cranial bone flap

        Repair of skull with flap

    02.04   Bone graft to skull

        Pericranial graft (autogenous) (heterogenous)

    02.05   Insertion of skull plate

        Replacement of skull plate

    02.06   Other cranial osteoplasty

        Repair of skull NOS

        Revision of bone flap of skull

        AHA: ▶1Q, '06, 6◀ 1Q, '05, 11; 3Q, '98, 9

        DEF: Plastic surgery repair of skull bones.

    02.07   Removal of skull plate

        EXCLUDES   *removal with synchronous replacement (02.05)*

✓4th **02.1   Repair of cerebral meninges**

    EXCLUDES   *marsupialization of cerebral lesion (01.59)*

    02.11   Simple suture of dura mater of brain

    02.12   Other repair of cerebral meninges

        Closure of fistula of cerebrospinal fluid

        Dural graft

        Repair of encephalocele including synchronous cranioplasty

        Repair of meninges NOS

        Subdural patch

    02.13   Ligation of meningeal vessel

        Ligation of:

          longitudinal sinus

          middle meningeal artery

    02.14   Choroid plexectomy

        Cauterization of choroid plexus

        DEF: Excision or destruction of the ependymal cells that form the membrane lining in the third, fourth, and lateral ventricles of the brain and secrete cerebrospinal fluid.

  02.2   Ventriculostomy

    Anastomosis of ventricle to:

      cervical subarachnoid space

      cisterna magna

    Insertion of Holter valve

    Ventriculocisternal intubation

    DEF: Surgical creation of an opening of ventricle; often performed to drain cerebrospinal fluid in treating hydrocephalus.

✓4th **02.3   Extracranial ventricular shunt**

    INCLUDES   that with insertion of valve

    DEF: Placement of shunt or creation of artificial passage leading from skull cavities to site outside skull to relieve excess cerebrospinal fluid created in the chorioid plexuses of the third and fourth ventricles of the brain.

    02.31   Ventricular shunt to structure in head and neck

        Ventricle to nasopharynx shunt

        Ventriculomastoid anastomosis

    02.32   Ventricular shunt to circulatory system

        Ventriculoatrial anastomosis

        Ventriculocaval shunt

    02.33   Ventricular shunt to thoracic cavity

        Ventriculopleural anastomosis

    02.34   Ventricular shunt to abdominal cavity and organs

        Ventriculocholecystostomy

        Ventriculoperitoneostomy

    02.35   Ventricular shunt to urinary system

        Ventricle to ureter shunt

    02.39   Other operations to establish drainage of ventricle

        Ventricle to bone marrow shunt

        Ventricular shunt to extracranial site NEC

✓4th **02.4   Revision, removal, and irrigation of ventricular shunt**

    EXCLUDES   *revision of distal catheter of ventricular shunt (54.95)*

    02.41   Irrigation and exploration of ventricular shunt

        Exploration of ventriculoperitoneal shunt at ventricular site

        Re-programming of ventriculoperitoneal shunt

Operations on the Nervous System

02.42–03.32

02.42   **Replacement of ventricular shunt**
Reinsertion of Holter valve
Replacement of ventricular catheter
Revision of ventriculoperitoneal shunt at
ventricular site

AHA: N-D, '86, 8

02.43   **Removal of ventricular shunt**

AHA: N-D, '86, 8

√4ᵗʰ **02.9**   **Other operations on skull, brain, and cerebral meninges**

EXCLUDES   *operations on:*
pineal gland (07.17, 07.51-07.59)
*pituitary gland [hypophysis] (07.13-
07.15, 07.61-07.79)*

02.91   **Lysis of cortical adhesions**

DEF: Breaking up of fibrous structures in brain outer layer.

02.92   **Repair of brain**

02.93   **Implantation or replacement of intracranial neurostimulator lead(s)**
Implantation, insertion, placement, or
replacement of intracranial:
brain pacemaker [neuropacemaker]
depth electrodes
epidural pegs
electroencephalographic receiver
foramen ovale electrodes
intracranial electrostimulator
subdural grids
subdural strips
Code also any insertion of neurostimulator
pulse generator ▶(86.94-86.98)◀

AHA: 4Q, '97, 57; 4Q, '92, 28

02.94   **Insertion or replacement of skull tongs or halo traction device**

AHA: 3Q, '01, 8; 3Q, '96, 14

DEF: Halo traction device: Metal or plastic band
encircles the head or neck secured to the skull with four
pins and attached to a metal chest plate by rods;
provides support and stability for the head and neck.

DEF: Skull tongs: Device inserted into each side of the
skull used to apply parallel traction to the long axis of
the cervical spine.

02.95   **Removal of skull tongs or halo traction device**

02.96   **Insertion of sphenoidal electrodes**

AHA: 4Q, '92, 28

02.99   **Other**

EXCLUDES   *chemical shock therapy (94.24)*
electroshock therapy:
subconvulsive (94.26)
other (94.27)

Laminotomy with Decompression

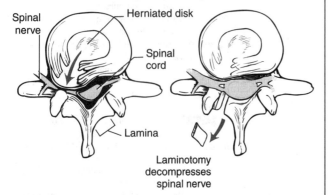

√3ʳᵈ **03**   **Operations on spinal cord and spinal canal structures**
Code also any application or administration of an adhesion
barrier substance (99.77)

√4ᵗʰ **03.0**   **Exploration and decompression of spinal canal structures**

03.01   **Removal of foreign body from spinal canal**

03.02   **Reopening of laminectomy site**

03.09   **Other exploration and decompression of spinal canal**
Decompression:
laminectomy   laminotomy
Expansile laminoplasty
Exploration of spinal nerve root
Foraminotomy

EXCLUDES   *drainage of spinal fluid by*
anastomosis (03.71-03.79)
laminectomy with excision of
intervertebral disc (80.51)
spinal tap (03.31)
that as operative approach —
omit code

AHA: 3Q, '04, 6; 4Q, '02, 109; 2Q, '02, 15; 4Q, '99, 14; 2Q, '97,
6; 2Q, '95, 9; 2Q, '95, 10; 2Q, '90, 22; S-Q, '86, 12

DEF: Decompression of spinal canal: Excision of bone
pieces, hematoma or other lesion to relieve spinal cord
pressure.

DEF: Expansile laminoplasty: Lamina is incised at the
level of the pedicle to relieve pressure; no tissue is
excised.

DEF: Foraminotomy: Removal of root opening between
vertebrae to relieve nerve root pressure.

03.1   **Division of intraspinal nerve root**
Rhizotomy

DEF: Rhizotomy: Surgical severing of spinal nerve roots within
spinal canal for pain relief.

√4ᵗʰ **03.2**   **Chordotomy**

DEF: Chordotomy: Surgical cutting of lateral spinothalamic tract of
spinal cord to relieve pain.

03.21   **Percutaneous chordotomy**
Stereotactic chordotomy

DEF: Percutaneous chordotomy: Insertion of hollow needle through
skin to interrupt spinal nerve root.

DEF: Stereotactic chordotomy: Use of three-dimensional imaging to
locate spinal nerve root for surgical interruption.

03.29   **Other chordotomy**
Chordotomy NOS
Tractotomy (one-stage) (two-stage) of spinal
cord
Transection of spinal cord tracts

DEF: Tractotomy (one stage) (two stages) of the spinal cord:
Surgical incision or severing of a nerve tract of spinal cord.

DEF: Transection of spinal cord tracts: Use of transverse incision to
divide spinal nerve root.

√4ᵗʰ **03.3**   **Diagnostic procedures on spinal cord and spinal canal structures**

03.31   **Spinal tap**
Lumbar puncture for removal of dye

EXCLUDES   *lumbar puncture for injection*
of dye [myelogram]
(87.21)

AHA: 2Q, '90, 22

DEF: Puncture into lumbar subarachnoid space to tap
cerebrospinal fluid.

03.32   **Biopsy of spinal cord or spinal meninges**

BI Bilateral Procedure   **NC** Non-covered Procedure   **LC** Limited Coverage Procedure   ▶◀ Revised Text   ● New Code   ▲ Revised Code Title

76 — Volume 3 • October 2006   *2007 ICD•9•CM*

03.39　Other diagnostic procedures on spinal cord and spinal canal structures

> EXCLUDES　*microscopic examination of specimen from nervous system or of spinal fluid (90.01-90.09)*
> *x-ray of spine (87.21-87.29)*

03.4　Excision or destruction of lesion of spinal cord or spinal meninges

Curettage
Debridement
Marsupialization of cyst
Resection
} of spinal cord or spinal meninges

> EXCLUDES　*biopsy of spinal cord or meninges (03.32)*

AHA: 3Q, '95, 5

√4ᵗʰ　03.5　Plastic operations on spinal cord structures

03.51　Repair of spinal meningocele

Repair of meningocele NOS

DEF: Restoration of hernial protrusion of spinal meninges through defect in vertebral column.

03.52　Repair of spinal myelomeningocele

DEF: Restoration of hernial protrusion of spinal cord and meninges through defect in vertebral column.

03.53　Repair of vertebral fracture

Elevation of spinal bone fragments
Reduction of fracture of vertebrae
Removal of bony spicules from spinal canal

> EXCLUDES　*kyphoplasty (81.66)*
> *vertebroplasty (81.65)*

AHA: 4Q, '04, 126; 2Q, '02, 14; 4Q, '99, 11, 12, 13; 3Q, '96, 14

03.59　Other repair and plastic operations on spinal cord structures

Repair of:
diastematomyelia
spina bifida NOS
spinal cord NOS
spinal meninges NOS
vertebral arch defect

03.6　Lysis of adhesions of spinal cord and nerve roots

AHA: 2Q, '98, 18

√4ᵗʰ　03.7　Shunt of spinal theca

> INCLUDES　that with valve

DEF: Surgical passage created from spinal cord dura mater to another channel.

03.71　Spinal subarachnoid-peritoneal shunt

03.72　Spinal subarachnoid-ureteral shunt

03.79　Other shunt of spinal theca

Lumbar-subarachnoid shunt NOS
Pleurothecal anastomosis
Salpingothecal anastomosis

AHA: 1Q, '97, 7

03.8　Injection of destructive agent into spinal canal

√4ᵗʰ　03.9　Other operations on spinal cord and spinal canal structures

03.90　Insertion of catheter into spinal canal for infusion of therapeutic or palliative substances

Insertion of catheter into epidural, subarachnoid, or subdural space of spine with intermittent or continuous infusion of drug (with creation of any reservoir)
Code also any implantation of infusion pump (86.06)

03.91　Injection of anesthetic into spinal canal for analgesia

> EXCLUDES　*that for operative anesthesia — omit code*

AHA: 3Q, '00, 15; 1Q, '99, 8; 2Q, '98, 18

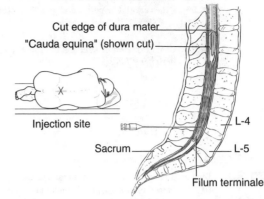

Lumbar Spinal Puncture

Cut edge of dura mater
"Cauda equina" (shown cut)
Injection site
Sacrum
L-4
L-5
Filum terminale

03.92　Injection of other agent into spinal canal

Intrathecal injection of steroid
Subarachnoid perfusion of refrigerated saline

> EXCLUDES　*injection of:*
> *contrast material for myelogram (87.21)*
> *destructive agent into spinal canal (03.8)*

AHA: 2Q, '03, 6; 3Q, '00, 15; 2Q, '98, 18

03.93　Implantation or replacement of spinal neurostimulator lead(s)

Code also any insertion of neurostimulator pulse generator ▶(86.94-86.98)◀

AHA: 1Q, '00, 19

03.94　Removal of spinal neurostimulator lead(s)

Code also any removal of neurostimulator pulse generator (86.05)

03.95　Spinal blood patch

DEF: Injection of blood into epidural space to patch hole in outer spinal membrane when blood clots.

03.96　Percutaneous denervation of facet

03.97　Revision of spinal thecal shunt

AHA: 2Q, '99, 4

03.98　Removal of spinal thecal shunt

03.99　Other

√3ʳᵈ　04　Operations on cranial and peripheral nerves

√4ᵗʰ　04.0　Incision, division, and excision of cranial and peripheral nerves

> EXCLUDES　*opticociliary neurectomy (12.79)*
> *sympathetic ganglionectomy (05.21-05.29)*

04.01　Excision of acoustic neuroma

That by craniotomy

> EXCLUDES　*that by stereotactic radiosurgery (92.3)*

AHA: 2Q, '98, 20; 2Q, '95, 8; 4Q, '92, 26

04.02　Division of trigeminal nerve

Retrogasserian neurotomy

DEF: Transection of sensory root fibers of trigeminal nerve for relief of trigeminal neuralgia.

04.03　Division or crushing of other cranial and peripheral nerves

> EXCLUDES　*that of:*
> *glossopharyngeal nerve (29.92)*
> *laryngeal nerve (31.91)*
> *nerves to adrenal glands (07.42)*
> *phrenic nerve for collapse of lung (33.31)*
> *vagus nerve (44.00-44.03)*

AHA: 2Q, '98, 20

04.04　Other incision of cranial and peripheral nerves

√3ʳᵈ
√4ᵗʰ Additional Digit Required　　Nonspecific OR Procedure　　Valid OR Procedure　　Non-OR Procedure　　Adjunct Code

Operations on the Nervous System

04.05–05.22

04.05 Gasserian ganglionectomy

04.06 Other cranial or peripheral ganglionectomy

> EXCLUDES   sympathetic ganglionectomy (05.21-05.29)

04.07 Other excision or avulsion of cranial and peripheral nerves

Curettage
Debridement } of peripheral nerve
Resection

Excision of peripheral neuroma [Morton's]

> EXCLUDES   biopsy of cranial or peripheral nerve (04.11-04.12)

AHA: 2Q, '95, 8; 4Q, '92, 26

✓4th **04.1 Diagnostic procedures on peripheral nervous system**

04.11 Closed [percutaneous] [needle] biopsy of cranial or peripheral nerve or ganglion

04.12 Open biopsy of cranial or peripheral nerve or ganglion

04.19 Other diagnostic procedures on cranial and peripheral nerves and ganglia

> EXCLUDES   microscopic examination of specimen from nervous system (90.01-90.09)
> neurologic examination (89.13)

04.2 Destruction of cranial and peripheral nerves

Destruction of cranial or peripheral nerves by:
  cryoanalgesia
  injection of neurolytic agent
  radiofrequency
Radiofrequency ablation

AHA: 3Q, '02, 10, 11; 4Q, '95, 74

DEF: Radiofrequency ablation: High frequency radio waves are applied to injure the nerve resulting in interruption of the pain signal.

04.3 Suture of cranial and peripheral nerves

✓4th **04.4 Lysis of adhesions and decompression of cranial and peripheral nerves**

04.41 Decompression of trigeminal nerve root

04.42 Other cranial nerve decompression

AHA: 3Q, '02, 13

04.43 Release of carpal tunnel

04.44 Release of tarsal tunnel

04.49 Other peripheral nerve or ganglion decompression or lysis of adhesions

Peripheral nerve neurolysis NOS

04.5 Cranial or peripheral nerve graft

Release of Carpal Tunnel

Median nerve

(Deep) transverse carpal ligament being cut

04.6 Transposition of cranial and peripheral nerves

Nerve transplantation

DEF: Relocation of cranial or peripheral nerves without detaching or severing them.

✓4th **04.7 Other cranial or peripheral neuroplasty**

04.71 Hypoglossal-facial anastomosis

DEF: Surgical connection of hypoglossal nerve to facial nerve.

04.72 Accessory-facial anastomosis

DEF: Surgical connection of accessory nerve to facial nerve.

04.73 Accessory-hypoglossal anastomosis

DEF: Surgical connection of accessory nerve to hypoglossal nerve.

04.74 Other anastomosis of cranial or peripheral nerve

04.75 Revision of previous repair of cranial and peripheral nerves

04.76 Repair of old traumatic injury of cranial and peripheral nerves

04.79 Other neuroplasty

AHA: ▶1Q, '06, 11◀

✓4th **04.8 Injection into peripheral nerve**

> EXCLUDES   destruction of nerve (by injection of neurolytic agent) (04.2)

04.80 Peripheral nerve injection, not otherwise specified

04.81 Injection of anesthetic into peripheral nerve for analgesia

> EXCLUDES   that for operative anesthesia — omit code

AHA: 1Q, '00, 7

04.89 Injection of other agent, except neurolytic

> EXCLUDES   injection of neurolytic agent (04.2)

✓4th **04.9 Other operations on cranial and peripheral nerves**

04.91 Neurectasis

DEF: Surgical stretching of peripheral or cranial nerve.

04.92 Implantation or replacement of peripheral neurostimulator lead(s)

Code also any insertion of neurostimulator pulse generator ▶(86.94-86.98)◀

AHA: 2Q, '04, 7; 3Q, '01, 16; 2Q, '00, 22; 3Q, '96, 12

DEF: Placement of or removal and replacement of neurostimulator lead(s) during the same episode.

04.93 Removal of peripheral neurostimulator lead(s)

Code also any removal of neurostimulator pulse generator (86.05)

AHA: 3Q, '01, 16

04.99 Other

✓3rd **05 Operations on sympathetic nerves or ganglia**

> EXCLUDES   paracervical uterine denervation (69.3)

05.0 Division of sympathetic nerve or ganglion

> EXCLUDES   that of nerves to adrenal glands (07.42)

✓4th **05.1 Diagnostic procedures on sympathetic nerves or ganglia**

05.11 Biopsy of sympathetic nerve or ganglion

05.19 Other diagnostic procedures on sympathetic nerves or ganglia

✓4th **05.2 Sympathectomy**

DEF: Sympathectomy: Division of nerve pathway at a specific site of a sympathetic nerve.

05.21 Sphenopalatine ganglionectomy

05.22 Cervical sympathectomy

BI Bilateral Procedure   NC Non-covered Procedure   LC Limited Coverage Procedure   ▶◀ Revised Text   ● New Code   ▲ Revised Code Title

05.23   **Lumbar sympathectomy**
DEF: Excision, resection of lumbar chain nerve group to relieve causalgia, Raynaud's disease, or lower extremity thromboangiitis.

05.24   **Presacral sympathectomy**
DEF: Excision or resection of hypogastric nerve network.

05.25   **Periarterial sympathectomy**
DEF: Removal of arterial sheath containing sympathetic nerve fibers.

05.29   **Other sympathectomy and ganglionectomy**
Excision or avulsion of sympathetic nerve NOS
Sympathetic ganglionectomy NOS
> EXCLUDES   biopsy of sympathetic nerve or ganglion (05.11)
> opticociliary neurectomy (12.79)
> periarterial sympathectomy (05.25)
> tympanosympathectomy (20.91)

✓4th **05.3**   **Injection into sympathetic nerve or ganglion**
> EXCLUDES   injection of ciliary sympathetic ganglion (12.79)

05.31   **Injection of anesthetic into sympathetic nerve for analgesia**

05.32   **Injection of neurolytic agent into sympathetic nerve**

05.39   **Other injection into sympathetic nerve or ganglion**

✓4th **05.8**   **Other operations on sympathetic nerves or ganglia**

05.81   **Repair of sympathetic nerve or ganglion**

05.89   **Other**

05.9   **Other operations on nervous system**

Operations on the Endocrine System

06–06.99

2. OPERATIONS ON THE ENDOCRINE SYSTEM (06-07)

√3rd **06**   **Operations on thyroid and parathyroid glands**

     INCLUDES   incidental resection of hyoid bone

√4th **06.0**   **Incision of thyroid field**

     EXCLUDES   *division of isthmus (06.91)*

    06.01   **Aspiration of thyroid field**

       Percutaneous or needle drainage of thyroid field

        EXCLUDES   *aspiration biopsy of thyroid (06.11)*

                 drainage by incision (06.09)

                 postoperative aspiration of field (06.02)

    06.02   **Reopening of wound of thyroid field**

       Reopening of wound of thyroid field for:

        control of (postoperative) hemorrhage

        examination

        exploration

        removal of hematoma

    06.09   **Other incision of thyroid field**

       Drainage of hematoma

       Drainage of thyroglossal tract

       Exploration: } by incision

        neck

        thyroid (field)

       Removal of foreign body

       Thyroidotomy NOS

        EXCLUDES   *postoperative exploration (06.02)*

                 removal of hematoma by aspiration (06.01)

√4th **06.1**   **Diagnostic procedures on thyroid and parathyroid glands**

    06.11   **Closed [percutaneous] [needle] biopsy of thyroid gland**

       Aspiration biopsy of thyroid

       DEF: Insertion of needle-type device for removal of thyroid tissue sample.

    06.12   **Open biopsy of thyroid gland**

    06.13   **Biopsy of parathyroid gland**

    06.19   **Other diagnostic procedures on thyroid and parathyroid glands**

        EXCLUDES   *radioisotope scan of:*

                 parathyroid (92.13)

                 thyroid (92.01)

                 soft tissue x-ray of thyroid field (87.09)

Thyroidectomy

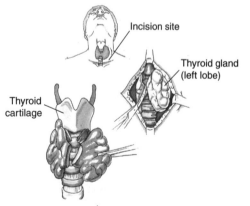

Incision site

Thyroid gland (left lobe)

Thyroid cartilage

06.2   **Unilateral thyroid lobectomy**

       Complete removal of one lobe of thyroid (with removal of isthmus or portion of other lobe)

       Hemithyroidectomy

        EXCLUDES   *partial substernal thyroidectomy (06.51)*

       DEF: Excision of thyroid lobe.

√4th **06.3**   **Other partial thyroidectomy**

    06.31   **Excision of lesion of thyroid**

        EXCLUDES   *biopsy of thyroid (06.11-06.12)*

       DEF: Removal of growth on thyroid.

    06.39   **Other**

       Isthmectomy   Partial thyroidectomy NOS

        EXCLUDES   *partial substernal thyroidectomy (06.51)*

06.4   **Complete thyroidectomy**

        EXCLUDES   *complete substernal thyroidectomy (06.52)*

                 that with laryngectomy (30.3-30.4)

√4th **06.5**   **Substernal thyroidectomy**

       DEF: Removal of thyroid tissue below breastbone.

    06.50   **Substernal thyroidectomy, not otherwise specified**

    06.51   **Partial substernal thyroidectomy**

    06.52   **Complete substernal thyroidectomy**

06.6   **Excision of lingual thyroid**

       Excision of thyroid by:

        submental route

        transoral route

       DEF: Excision of thyroid tissue at base of tongue.

06.7   **Excision of thyroglossal duct or tract**

√4th **06.8**   **Parathyroidectomy**

       DEF: Removal of parathyroid glands.

    06.81   **Complete parathyroidectomy**

    06.89   **Other parathyroidectomy**

       Parathyroidectomy NOS

       Partial parathyroidectomy

        EXCLUDES   *biopsy of parathyroid (06.13)*

√4th **06.9**   **Other operations on thyroid (region) and parathyroid**

    06.91   **Division of thyroid isthmus**

       Transection of thyroid isthmus

       DEF: Cutting or division of tissue at narrowest point of thyroid.

    06.92   **Ligation of thyroid vessels**

    06.93   **Suture of thyroid gland**

    06.94   **Thyroid tissue reimplantation**

       Autotransplantation of thyroid tissue

       DEF: Placement of thyroid tissue graft into functional site.

       DEF: Autotransplantation of thyroid tissue: Tissue graft from patient thyroid tissue to another site on thyroid.

    06.95   **Parathyroid tissue reimplantation**

       Autotransplantation of parathyroid tissue

       DEF: Placement of parathyroid tissue graft into functional site.

       DEF: Autotransplantation of parathyroid tissue: Use of patient parathyroid tissue for graft.

    06.98   **Other operations on thyroid glands**

    06.99   **Other operations on parathyroid glands**

BI Bilateral Procedure   NC Non-covered Procedure   LC Limited Coverage Procedure   ▶◀ Revised Text   ● New Code   ▲ Revised Code Title

Operations on the Endocrine System　　**07–07.68**

✓3rd **07** **Operations on other endocrine glands**

INCLUDES　operations on:
　　　　　adrenal glands　　pituitary gland
　　　　　pineal gland　　　thymus

EXCLUDES　operations on:
　　　　　aortic and carotid bodies (39.8)
　　　　　ovaries (65.0-65.99)
　　　　　pancreas (52.01-52.99)
　　　　　testes (62.0-62.99)

✓4th **07.0** **Exploration of adrenal field**

EXCLUDES　incision of adrenal (gland) (07.41)

　　07.00 **Exploration of adrenal field, not otherwise specified**

　　07.01 **Unilateral exploration of adrenal field**

　　　　DEF: Investigation of one adrenal gland for diagnostic reasons.

　　07.02 **Bilateral exploration of adrenal field**

　　　　DEF: Investigation of both adrenal glands for diagnostic reasons.

✓4th **07.1** **Diagnostic procedures on adrenal glands, pituitary gland, pineal gland, and thymus**

　　07.11 **Closed [percutaneous] [needle] biopsy of adrenal gland**

　　07.12 **Open biopsy of adrenal gland**

　　07.13 **Biopsy of pituitary gland, transfrontal approach**

　　　　DEF: Excision of pituitary gland tissue for exam through frontal bone.

　　07.14 **Biopsy of pituitary gland, transsphenoidal approach**

　　　　DEF: Excision of pituitary gland tissue for exam through sphenoid bone.

　　07.15 **Biopsy of pituitary gland, unspecified approach**

　　07.16 **Biopsy of thymus**

　　07.17 **Biopsy of pineal gland**

　　07.19 **Other diagnostic procedures on adrenal glands, pituitary gland, pineal gland, and thymus**

　　　　EXCLUDES　microscopic examination of specimen from endocrine gland (90.11-90.19)
　　　　　　　　　radioisotope scan of pituitary gland (92.11)

✓4th **07.2** **Partial adrenalectomy**

　　07.21 **Excision of lesion of adrenal gland**

　　　　EXCLUDES　biopsy of adrenal gland (07.11-07.12)

　　07.22 **Unilateral adrenalectomy**
　　　　Adrenalectomy NOS

　　　　EXCLUDES　excision of remaining adrenal gland (07.3)

　　　　DEF: Excision of one adrenal gland.

　　07.29 **Other partial adrenalectomy**
　　　　Partial adrenalectomy NOS

　　　　AHA: ▶2Q, '05, 4◀

　　07.3 **Bilateral adrenalectomy**
　　　　Excision of remaining adrenal gland

　　　　EXCLUDES　bilateral partial adrenalectomy (07.29)

✓4th **07.4** **Other operations on adrenal glands, nerves, and vessels**

　　07.41 **Incision of adrenal gland**
　　　　Adrenalotomy (with drainage)

　　07.42 **Division of nerves to adrenal glands**

　　07.43 **Ligation of adrenal vessels**

　　07.44 **Repair of adrenal gland**

　　07.45 **Reimplantation of adrenal tissue**
　　　　Autotransplantation of adrenal tissue

　　　　DEF: Autotransplantation of adrenal tissue: Use of tissue graft from the patient's own body.

　　07.49 **Other**

✓4th **07.5** **Operations on pineal gland**

　　07.51 **Exploration of pineal field**

　　　　EXCLUDES　that with incision of pineal gland (07.52)

　　07.52 **Incision of pineal gland**

　　07.53 **Partial excision of pineal gland**

　　　　EXCLUDES　biopsy of pineal gland (07.17)

　　07.54 **Total excision of pineal gland**
　　　　Pinealectomy (complete) (total)

　　07.59 **Other operations on pineal gland**

✓4th **07.6** **Hypophysectomy**

　　DEF: Excision, destruction of pituitary gland.

　　07.61 **Partial excision of pituitary gland, transfrontal approach**

　　　　Cryohypophysectomy, partial ⎫
　　　　Division of hypophyseal stalk ⎪
　　　　Excision of lesion of pituitary [hypophysis] ⎬ transfrontal approach
　　　　Hypophysectomy, subtotal ⎪
　　　　Infundibulectomy, hypophyseal ⎭

　　　　EXCLUDES　biopsy of pituitary gland, transfrontal approach (07.13)

　　　　DEF: Removal of pituitary gland, partial, through frontal bone.

　　07.62 **Partial excision of pituitary gland, transsphenoidal approach**

　　　　EXCLUDES　biopsy of pituitary gland, transsphenoidal approach (07.14)

　　　　DEF: Removal of pituitary gland, partial, through sphenoid bone.

　　07.63 **Partial excision of pituitary gland, unspecified approach**

　　　　EXCLUDES　biopsy of pituitary gland NOS (07.15)

　　07.64 **Total excision of pituitary gland, transfrontal approach**

　　　　Ablation of pituitary by implantation (strontiumyttrium) ⎫
　　　　　　　　　　　　　　　　　⎬ transfrontal approach
　　　　Cryohypophysectomy, complete ⎭

　　　　DEF: Removal of pituitary gland, total, through frontal bone.

　　07.65 **Total excision of pituitary gland, transsphenoidal approach**

　　　　DEF: Removal of pituitary gland, total, through sphenoid bone.

　　07.68 **Total excision of pituitary gland, other specified approach**

　　　　DEF: Destroy or remove pituitary gland by a specified approach, other than those listed.

Operations on the Endocrine System

07.69–07.99

07.69 **Total excision of pituitary gland, unspecified approach**
Hypophysectomy NOS
Pituitectomy NOS

√4ᵗʰ 07.7 **Other operations on hypophysis**

07.71 **Exploration of pituitary fossa**
EXCLUDES   exploration with incision of pituitary gland (07.72)
DEF: Exploration of region of pituitary gland.

07.72 **Incision of pituitary gland**
Aspiration of: Aspiration of:
craniobuccal pouch   pituitary gland
craniopharyngioma   Rathke's pouch
hypophysis

07.79 **Other**
Insertion of pack into sella turcica

√4ᵗʰ 07.8 **Thymectomy**

07.80 **Thymectomy, not otherwise specified**

07.81 **Partial excision of thymus**
EXCLUDES   biopsy of thymus (07.16)

07.82 **Total excision of thymus**

√4ᵗʰ 07.9 **Other operations on thymus**

07.91 **Exploration of thymus field**
EXCLUDES   exploration with incision of thymus (07.92)

07.92 **Incision of thymus**

07.93 **Repair of thymus**

07.94 **Transplantation of thymus**
DEF: Placement of thymus tissue grafts into functional area of gland.

07.99 **Other**
Thymopexy

BI Bilateral Procedure   NC Non-covered Procedure   LC Limited Coverage Procedure   ►◄ Revised Text   ● New Code   ▲ Revised Code Title

Operations on the Eye

08–08.72

3. OPERATIONS ON THE EYE (08-16)

✓3rd **08 Operations on eyelids**
> INCLUDES operations on the eyebrow

✓4th **08.0 Incision of eyelid**

08.01 Incision of lid margin
> DEF: Cutting into eyelid edge.

08.02 Severing of blepharorrhaphy
> DEF: Freeing of eyelids previously sutured shut.

08.09 Other incision of eyelid

✓4th **08.1 Diagnostic procedures on eyelid**

08.11 Biopsy of eyelid

08.19 Other diagnostic procedures on eyelid

✓4th **08.2 Excision or destruction of lesion or tissue of eyelid**
> Code also any synchronous reconstruction (08.61-08.74)
> EXCLUDES biopsy of eyelid (08.11)

08.20 Removal of lesion of eyelid, not otherwise specified
> Removal of meibomian gland NOS

08.21 Excision of chalazion

08.22 Excision of other minor lesion of eyelid
> Excision of: Excision of:
>   verruca   wart

08.23 Excision of major lesion of eyelid, partial-thickness
> Excision involving one-fourth or more of lid margin, partial-thickness
> DEF: Excision of lesion not in all eyelid layers.

08.24 Excision of major lesion of eyelid, full-thickness
> Excision involving one-fourth or more of lid margin, full-thickness
> Wedge resection of eyelid
> DEF: Excision of growth in all eyelid layers, full thickness.

08.25 Destruction of lesion of eyelid

✓4th **08.3 Repair of blepharoptosis and lid retraction**

08.31 Repair of blepharoptosis by frontalis muscle technique with suture
> DEF: Correction of drooping upper eyelid with suture of frontalis muscle.

08.32 Repair of blepharoptosis by frontalis muscle technique with fascial sling
> DEF: Correction of drooping upper eyelid with fascial tissue sling of frontalis muscle.

08.33 Repair of blepharoptosis by resection or advancement of levator muscle or aponeurosis
> DEF: Correction of drooping upper eyelid with levator muscle, extended, cut, or by expanded tendon.

08.34 Repair of blepharoptosis by other levator muscle techniques

08.35 Repair of blepharoptosis by tarsal technique
> DEF: Correction of drooping upper eyelid with tarsal muscle.

08.36 Repair of blepharoptosis by other techniques
> Correction of eyelid ptosis NOS
> Orbicularis oculi muscle sling for correction of blepharoptosis

08.37 Reduction of overcorrection of ptosis
> DEF: Correction, release of previous plastic repair of drooping eyelid.

08.38 Correction of lid retraction
> DEF: Fixing of withdrawn eyelid into normal position.

✓4th **08.4 Repair of entropion or ectropion**

08.41 Repair of entropion or ectropion by thermocauterization
> DEF: Restoration of eyelid margin to normal position with heat cautery.

08.42 Repair of entropion or ectropion by suture technique
> DEF: Restoration of eyelid margin to normal position by suture.

08.43 Repair of entropion or ectropion with wedge resection
> DEF: Restoration of eyelid margin to normal position by removing tissue.

08.44 Repair of entropion or ectropion with lid reconstruction
> DEF: Reconstruction of eyelid margin.

08.49 Other repair of entropion or ectropion

✓4th **08.5 Other adjustment of lid position**

08.51 Canthotomy
> DEF: Incision into outer canthus of eye.

08.52 Blepharorrhaphy
> Canthorrhaphy   Tarsorrhaphy
> DEF: Suture together of eyelids, partial or repair; done to shorten palpebral fissure or protect cornea.

08.59 Other
> Canthoplasty NOS
> Repair of epicanthal fold

✓4th **08.6 Reconstruction of eyelid with flaps or grafts**
> EXCLUDES that associated with repair of entropion and ectropion (08.44)

08.61 Reconstruction of eyelid with skin flap or graft
> DEF: Rebuild of eyelid by graft or flap method.

08.62 Reconstruction of eyelid with mucous membrane flap or graft
> DEF: Rebuild of eyelid with mucous membrane by graft or flap method.

08.63 Reconstruction of eyelid with hair follicle graft
> DEF: Rebuild of eyelid with hair follicle graft.

08.64 Reconstruction of eyelid with tarsoconjunctival flap
> Transfer of tarsoconjunctival flap from opposing lid
> DEF: Recreation of eyelid with tarsoconjunctival tissue.

08.69 Other reconstruction of eyelid with flaps or grafts

✓4th **08.7 Other reconstruction of eyelid**
> EXCLUDES that associated with repair of entropion and ectropion (08.44)

08.70 Reconstruction of eyelid, not otherwise specified
> AHA: 2Q, '96, 11

08.71 Reconstruction of eyelid involving lid margin, partial-thickness
> DEF: Repair of eyelid margin not using all lid layers.

08.72 Other reconstruction of eyelid, partial-thickness
> DEF: Reshape of eyelid not using all lid layers.

Operations on the Eye

08.73–10.1

08.73   **Reconstruction of eyelid involving lid margin, full-thickness**

DEF: Repair of eyelid and margin using all tissue layers.

08.74   **Other reconstruction of eyelid, full-thickness**

DEF: Other repair of eyelid using all tissue layers.

√4th **08.8**   **Other repair of eyelid**

08.81   **Linear repair of laceration of eyelid or eyebrow**

08.82   **Repair of laceration involving lid margin, partial-thickness**

DEF: Repair of laceration not involving all layers of eyelid margin.

08.83   **Other repair of laceration of eyelid, partial thickness**

DEF: Repair of eyelid tear not involving all eyelid layers.

08.84   **Repair of laceration involving lid margin, full-thickness**

DEF: Repair of eyelid margin tear involving all margin layers.

08.85   **Other repair of laceration of eyelid, full-thickness**

DEF: Repair of eyelid tear involving all layers.

08.86   **Lower eyelid rhytidectomy**

DEF: Removal of wrinkles from lower eyelid.

08.87   **Upper eyelid rhytidectomy**

AHA: 2Q, '96, 11

DEF: Removal of wrinkles from upper eyelid.

08.89   **Other eyelid repair**

AHA: 1Q, '00, 22

√4th **08.9**   **Other operations on eyelids**

08.91   **Electrosurgical epilation of eyelid**

DEF: Electrical removal of eyelid hair roots.

08.92   **Cryosurgical epilation of eyelid**

DEF: Removal of eyelid hair roots by freezing.

08.93   **Other epilation of eyelid**

08.99   **Other**

√3rd **09**   **Operations on lacrimal system**

√4th **09.0**   **Incision of lacrimal gland**

Incision of lacrimal cyst (with drainage)

√4th **09.1**   **Diagnostic procedures on lacrimal system**

09.11   **Biopsy of lacrimal gland**

09.12   **Biopsy of lacrimal sac**

09.19   **Other diagnostic procedures on lacrimal system**

EXCLUDES   contrast dacryocystogram (87.05)

soft tissue x-ray of nasolacrimal duct (87.09)

√4th **09.2**   **Excision of lesion or tissue of lacrimal gland**

09.20   **Excision of lacrimal gland, not otherwise specified**

09.21   **Excision of lesion of lacrimal gland**

EXCLUDES   biopsy of lacrimal gland (09.11)

09.22   **Other partial dacryoadenectomy**

EXCLUDES   biopsy of lacrimal gland (09.11)

DEF: Excision, partial, of tear gland.

09.23   **Total dacryoadenectomy**

DEF: Excision, total, of tear gland.

09.3   **Other operations on lacrimal gland**

√4th **09.4**   **Manipulation of lacrimal passage**

INCLUDES   removal of calculus

that with dilation

EXCLUDES   contrast dacryocystogram (87.05)

09.41   **Probing of lacrimal punctum**

DEF: Exploration of tear duct entrance with flexible rod.

09.42   **Probing of lacrimal canaliculi**

DEF: Exploration of tear duct with flexible rod.

09.43   **Probing of nasolacrimal duct**

EXCLUDES   that with insertion of tube or stent (09.44)

DEF: Exploration of passage between tear sac and nose with flexible rod.

09.44   **Intubation of nasolacrimal duct**

Insertion of stent into nasolacrimal duct

AHA: 2Q, '94, 11

09.49   **Other manipulation of lacrimal passage**

√4th **09.5**   **Incision of lacrimal sac and passages**

09.51   **Incision of lacrimal punctum**

09.52   **Incision of lacrimal canaliculi**

09.53   **Incision of lacrimal sac**

DEF: Cutting into lacrimal pouch of tear gland.

09.59   **Other incision of lacrimal passages**

Incision (and drainage) of nasolacrimal duct NOS

09.6   **Excision of lacrimal sac and passage**

EXCLUDES   biopsy of lacrimal sac (09.12)

DEF: Removal of pouch and passage of tear gland.

09.7   **Repair of canaliculus and punctum**

EXCLUDES   repair of eyelid (08.81-08.89)

09.71   **Correction of everted punctum**

DEF: Repair of an outwardly turned tear duct entrance.

09.72   **Other repair of punctum**

09.73   **Repair of canaliculus**

√4th **09.8**   **Fistulization of lacrimal tract to nasal cavity**

09.81   **Dacryocystorhinostomy [DCR]**

DEF: Creation of entrance between tear gland and nasal passage for tear flow.

09.82   **Conjunctivocystorhinostomy**

Conjunctivodacryocystorhinostomy [CDCR]

EXCLUDES   that with insertion of tube or stent (09.83)

DEF: Creation of tear drainage path from lacrimal sac to nasal cavity through conjunctiva.

09.83   **Conjunctivorhinostomy with insertion of tube or stent**

DEF: Creation of passage between eye sac membrane and nasal cavity with tube or stent.

√4th **09.9**   **Other operations on lacrimal system**

09.91   **Obliteration of lacrimal punctum**

DEF: Destruction, total of tear gland opening in eyelid.

09.99   **Other**

AHA: 2Q, '94, 11

√3rd **10**   **Operations on conjunctiva**

10.0   **Removal of embedded foreign body from conjunctiva by incision**

EXCLUDES   removal of:

embedded foreign body without incision (98.22)

superficial foreign body (98.21)

10.1   **Other incision of conjunctiva**

BI Bilateral Procedure   NC Non-covered Procedure   LC Limited Coverage Procedure   ▶◀ Revised Text   ● New Code   ▲ Revised Code Title

10.2 Diagnostic procedures on conjunctiva
    10.21 Biopsy of conjunctiva
    10.29 Other diagnostic procedures on conjunctiva

10.3 Excision or destruction of lesion or tissue of conjunctiva
    10.31 Excision of lesion or tissue of conjunctiva
       Excision of ring of conjunctiva around cornea
       EXCLUDES *biopsy of conjunctiva (10.21)*
       AHA: 4Q, '00, 41; 3Q, '96, 7

       DEF: Removal of growth or tissue from eye membrane.

    10.32 Destruction of lesion of conjunctiva
       EXCLUDES *excision of lesion (10.31)*
              thermocauterization for entropion (08.41)

       DEF: Destruction of eye membrane growth; not done by excision.

    10.33 Other destructive procedures on conjunctiva
       Removal of trachoma follicles

10.4 Conjunctivoplasty
    DEF: Correction of conjunctiva by plastic surgery.

    10.41 Repair of symblepharon with free graft
       AHA: 3Q, '96, 7

    10.42 Reconstruction of conjunctival cul-de-sac with free graft
       EXCLUDES *revision of enucleation socket with graft (16.63)*

       DEF: Rebuilding of eye membrane fold with graft of unattached tissue.

    10.43 Other reconstruction of conjunctival cul-de-sac
       EXCLUDES *revision of enucleation socket (16.64)*

    10.44 Other free graft to conjunctiva
    10.49 Other conjunctivoplasty
       EXCLUDES *repair of cornea with conjunctival flap (11.53)*

10.5 Lysis of adhesions of conjunctiva and eyelid
    Division of symblepharon (with insertion of conformer)

10.6 Repair of laceration of conjunctiva
    EXCLUDES *that with repair of sclera (12.81)*

10.9 Other operations on conjunctiva
    10.91 Subconjunctival injection
       AHA: 3Q, '96, 7

    10.99 Other

11 Operations on cornea
    11.0 Magnetic removal of embedded foreign body from cornea
       EXCLUDES *that with incision (11.1)*

    11.1 Incision of cornea
       Incision of cornea for removal of foreign body

    11.2 Diagnostic procedures on cornea
       11.21 Scraping of cornea for smear or culture
       11.22 Biopsy of cornea
       11.29 Other diagnostic procedures on cornea

    11.3 Excision of pterygium
       11.31 Transposition of pterygium
          DEF: Cutting into membranous structure extending from eye membrane to cornea and suturing it in a downward position.

11.32 Excision of pterygium with corneal graft
    DEF: Surgical removal and repair of membranous structure extending from eye membrane to cornea using corneal tissue transplant.

11.39 Other excision of pterygium

11.4 Excision or destruction of tissue or other lesion of cornea
    11.41 Mechanical removal of corneal epithelium
       That by chemocauterization
       EXCLUDES *that for smear or culture (11.21)*
       AHA: 3Q, '02, 20

       DEF: Removal of outer layer of cornea by mechanical means.

    11.42 Thermocauterization of corneal lesion
       DEF: Destruction of corneal lesion by electrical cautery.

    11.43 Cryotherapy of corneal lesion
       DEF: Destruction of corneal lesion with cold therapy.

    11.49 Other removal or destruction of corneal lesion
       Excision of cornea NOS
       EXCLUDES *biopsy of cornea (11.22)*

11.5 Repair of cornea
    11.51 Suture of corneal laceration
       AHA: 3Q, '96, 7

    11.52 Repair of postoperative wound dehiscence of cornea
       DEF: Repair of ruptured postoperative corneal wound.

    11.53 Repair of corneal laceration or wound with conjunctival flap
       DEF: Correction corneal wound or tear with conjunctival tissue.

    11.59 Other repair of cornea

11.6 Corneal transplant
    EXCLUDES *excision of pterygium with corneal graft (11.32)*

    11.60 Corneal transplant, not otherwise specified
       Note: To report donor sources — see codes 00.91-00.93
       Keratoplasty NOS

    11.61 Lamellar keratoplasty with autograft
       DEF: Restoration of sight using patient's own corneal tissue, partial thickness.

    11.62 Other lamellar keratoplasty
       AHA: S-O, '85, 6

       DEF: Restoration of sight using donor corneal tissue, partial thickness.

    11.63 Penetrating keratoplasty with autograft
       Perforating keratoplasty with autograft

    11.64 Other penetrating keratoplasty
       Perforating keratoplasty (with homograft)

    11.69 Other corneal transplant

11.7 Other reconstructive and refractive surgery on cornea
    11.71 Keratomileusis   NC
       DEF: Restoration of corneal shape by removing portion of cornea, freezing, reshaping curve and reattaching it.

    11.72 Keratophakia   NC
       DEF: Correction of eye lens loss by dissecting the central zone of the cornea and replacing it with a thickened graft of the cornea.

    11.73 Keratoprosthesis
       DEF: Placement of corneal artificial implant.

    11.74 Thermokeratoplasty
       DEF: Reshaping and reforming cornea by heat application.

√3ʳᵈ ‖ √4ᵗʰ Additional Digit Required   Nonspecific OR Procedure   Valid OR Procedure   Non-OR Procedure   Adjunct Code

11.75   **Radial keratotomy**   NC
DEF: Incisions around cornea radius to correct nearsightedness.

11.76   **Epikeratophakia**   NC
DEF: Repair lens loss by cornea graft sutured to central corneal zone.

11.79   **Other**

√4th **11.9**   **Other operations on cornea**
11.91   **Tattooing of cornea**
11.92   **Removal of artificial implant from cornea**
11.99   **Other**
AHA: 3Q, '02, 20

√3rd **12**   **Operations on iris, ciliary body, sclera, and anterior chamber**
EXCLUDES   operations on cornea (11.0-11.99)

√4th **12.0**   **Removal of intraocular foreign body from anterior segment of eye**
12.00   **Removal of intraocular foreign body from anterior segment of eye, not otherwise specified**
12.01   **Removal of intraocular foreign body from anterior segment of eye with use of magnet**
12.02   **Removal of intraocular foreign body from anterior segment of eye without use of magnet**

√4th **12.1**   **Iridotomy and simple iridectomy**
EXCLUDES   iridectomy associated with:
cataract extraction (13.11-13.69)
removal of lesion (12.41-12.42)
scleral fistulization (12.61-12.69)
12.11   **Iridotomy with transfixion**
12.12   **Other iridotomy**
Corectomy
Discission of iris
Iridotomy NOS
DEF: Corectomy: Incision into iris (also called iridectomy).
12.13   **Excision of prolapsed iris**
DEF: Removal of downwardly placed portion of iris.
12.14   **Other iridectomy**
Iridectomy (basal) (peripheral) (total)
DEF: Removal, partial or total of iris.

√4th **12.2**   **Diagnostic procedures on iris, ciliary body, sclera, and anterior chamber**
12.21   **Diagnostic aspiration of anterior chamber of eye**
DEF: Suction withdrawal of fluid from anterior eye chamber for diagnostic reasons.
12.22   **Biopsy of iris**
12.29   **Other diagnostic procedures on iris, ciliary body, sclera, and anterior chamber**

√4th **12.3**   **Iridoplasty and coreoplasty**
DEF: Correction or abnormal iris or pupil by plastic surgery.
12.31   **Lysis of goniosynechiae**
Lysis of goniosynechiae by injection of air or liquid
DEF: Freeing of fibrous structures between cornea and iris by injecting air or liquid.
12.32   **Lysis of other anterior synechiae**
Lysis of anterior synechiae:
NOS
by injection of air or liquid
12.33   **Lysis of posterior synechiae**
Lysis of iris adhesions NOS
12.34   **Lysis of corneovitreal adhesions**
DEF: Release of adhesions of cornea and vitreous body.

12.35   **Coreoplasty**
Needling of pupillary membrane
DEF: Correction of an iris defect.

12.39   **Other iridoplasty**

√4th **12.4**   **Excision or destruction of lesion of iris and ciliary body**
12.40   **Removal of lesion of anterior segment of eye, not otherwise specified**
12.41   **Destruction of lesion of iris, nonexcisional**
Destruction of lesion of iris by:
cauterization
cryotherapy
photocoagulation
12.42   **Excision of lesion of iris**
EXCLUDES   biopsy of iris (12.22)
12.43   **Destruction of lesion of ciliary body, nonexcisional**
12.44   **Excision of lesion of ciliary body**

√4th **12.5**   **Facilitation of intraocular circulation**
12.51   **Goniopuncture without goniotomy**
DEF: Stab incision into anterior chamber of eye to relieve optic pressure.
12.52   **Goniotomy without goniopuncture**
DEF: Incision into Schlemm's canal to drain aqueous and relieve pressure.
12.53   **Goniotomy with goniopuncture**
12.54   **Trabeculotomy ab externo**
DEF: Incision into supporting connective tissue strands of eye capsule, via exterior approach.
12.55   **Cyclodialysis**
DEF: Creation of passage between anterior chamber and suprachoroidal space.
12.59   **Other facilitation of intraocular circulation**

√4th **12.6**   **Scleral fistulization**
EXCLUDES   exploratory sclerotomy (12.89)
12.61   **Trephination of sclera with iridectomy**
DEF: Cut around sclerocornea to remove part of the iris.
12.62   **Thermocauterization of sclera with iridectomy**
DEF: Destruction of outer eyeball layer with partial excision of iris using heat.
12.63   **Iridencleisis and iridotasis**
DEF: Creation of permanent drain in iris by transposing or stretching iris tissue.
12.64   **Trabeculectomy ab externo**
DEF: Excision of supporting connective tissue strands of eye capsule, via exterior approach.

Trabeculectomy Ab Externo

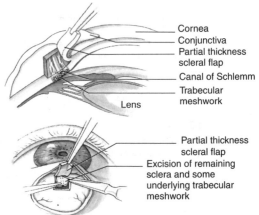

Cornea
Conjunctiva
Partial thickness scleral flap
Canal of Schlemm
Trabecular meshwork
Lens
Partial thickness scleral flap
Excision of remaining sclera and some underlying trabecular meshwork

 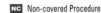

12.65　Other scleral fistulization with iridectomy
Holth's sclerectomy
DEF: Creation of outer eyeball layer passage with partial excision of iris.

12.66　Postoperative revision of scleral fistulization procedure
Revision of filtering bleb
EXCLUDES repair of fistula (12.82)
AHA: 2Q, '01, 16

12.69　Other fistulizing procedure

√4ᵗʰ 12.7　Other procedures for relief of elevated intraocular pressure

12.71　Cyclodiathermy
DEF: Destruction of ciliary body tissue with heat.

12.72　Cyclocryotherapy
DEF: Destruction of ciliary body tissue by freezing.

12.73　Cyclophotocoagulation
DEF: Destruction of ciliary body tissue by high energy light source.

12.74　Diminution of ciliary body, not otherwise specified

12.79　Other glaucoma procedures
AHA: 2Q, '98, 16

√4ᵗʰ 12.8　Operations on sclera
EXCLUDES those associated with:
retinal reattachment (14.41-14.59)
scleral fistulization (12.61-12.69)

12.81　Suture of laceration of sclera
Suture of sclera with synchronous repair of conjunctiva

12.82　Repair of scleral fistula
EXCLUDES postoperative revision of scleral fistulization procedure (12.66)

12.83　Revision of operative wound of anterior segment, not elsewhere classified
EXCLUDES postoperative revision of scleral fistulization procedure (12.66)

12.84　Excision or destruction of lesion of sclera

12.85　Repair of scleral staphyloma with graft
DEF: Repair of protruding outer eyeball layer with a graft.

12.86　Other repair of scleral staphyloma

12.87　Scleral reinforcement with graft
DEF: Restoration of outer eyeball shape with tissue graft.

12.88　Other scleral reinforcement

12.89　Other operations on sclera
Exploratory sclerotomy

√4ᵗʰ 12.9　Other operations on iris, ciliary body, and anterior chamber

12.91　Therapeutic evacuation of anterior chamber
Paracentesis of anterior chamber
EXCLUDES diagnostic aspiration (12.21)

12.92　Injection into anterior chamber
Injection of:
air ⎫
liquid ⎬ into anterior chamber
medication ⎭
AHA: J-A, '84, 1

12.93　Removal or destruction of epithelial downgrowth from anterior chamber
EXCLUDES that with iridectomy (12.41-12.42)
DEF: Excision or destruction of epithelial overgrowth in anterior eye chamber.

12.97　Other operations on iris
12.98　Other operations on ciliary body
12.99　Other operations on anterior chamber

√3ʳᵈ 13　Operations on lens

√4ᵗʰ 13.0　Removal of foreign body from lens
EXCLUDES removal of pseudophakos (13.8)

13.00　Removal of foreign body from lens, not otherwise specified

13.01　Removal of foreign body from lens with use of magnet

13.02　Removal of foreign body from lens without use of magnet

√4ᵗʰ 13.1　Intracapsular extraction of lens
Code also any synchronous insertion of pseudophakos (13.71)
AHA: S-O, '85, 6

13.11　Intracapsular extraction of lens by temporal inferior route
DEF: Extraction of lens and capsule via anterior approach through outer side of eyeball.

13.19　Other intracapsular extraction of lens
Cataract extraction NOS
Cryoextraction of lens
Erysiphake extraction of cataract
Extraction of lens NOS

13.2　Extracapsular extraction of lens by linear extraction technique
AHA: S-O, '85, 6
DEF: Excision of lens without the posterior capsule at junction between the cornea and outer eyeball layer by means of a linear incision.

13.3　Extracapsular extraction of lens by simple aspiration (and irrigation) technique
Irrigation of traumatic cataract
AHA: S-O, '85, 6
DEF: Removal of lens without the posterior capsule by suctioning and flushing out the area.

√4ᵗʰ 13.4　Extracapsular extraction of lens by fragmentation and aspiration technique
AHA: S-O, '85, 6
DEF: Removal of lens after division into smaller pieces with posterior capsule left intact.

13.41　Phacoemulsification and aspiration of cataract
AHA: 3Q, '96, 4; 1Q, '94, 16

13.42　Mechanical phacofragmentation and aspiration of cataract by posterior route
Code also any synchronous vitrectomy (14.74)

Extraction of Lens
(with insertion of intraocular lens prosthesis)

Iris

Lens cataract removed

Iris

Lens

Intraocular lens insertion

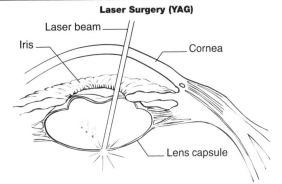

Laser Surgery (YAG)

Laser beam

Iris

Cornea

Lens capsule

13.43   **Mechanical phacofragmentation and other aspiration of cataract**

✓4th **13.5**   **Other extracapsular extraction of lens**
Code also any synchronous insertion of pseudophakos (13.71)
AHA: S-O, '85, 6

13.51   **Extracapsular extraction of lens by temporal inferior route**
DEF: Removal of lens through outer eyeball with posterior capsule left intact.

13.59   **Other extracapsular extraction of lens**

✓4th **13.6**   **Other cataract extraction**
Code also any synchronous insertion of pseudophakos (13.71)
AHA: S-O, '85, 6

13.64   **Discission of secondary membrane [after cataract]**
DEF: Breaking up of fibrotic lens capsule developed after previous lens extraction.

13.65   **Excision of secondary membrane [after cataract]**
Capsulectomy
DEF: Capsulectomy: Excision of lens capsule membrane after previous lens extraction.

13.66   **Mechanical fragmentation of secondary membrane [after cataract]**
DEF: Breaking up and removal of fibrotic lens capsule developed after previous lens extraction.

13.69   **Other cataract extraction**

✓4th **13.7**   **Insertion of prosthetic lens [pseudophakos]**
EXCLUDES ▶ implantation of intraocular telescope prosthesis (13.91) ◀
AHA: J-A, '84, 1
DEF: Insertion of ocular implant, following lens extraction.

13.70   **Insertion of pseudophakos, not otherwise specified**

13.71   **Insertion of intraocular lens prosthesis at time of cataract extraction, one-stage**
Code also synchronous extraction of cataract (13.11-13.69)
AHA: 3Q, '96, 4

13.72   **Secondary insertion of intraocular lens prosthesis**

13.8   **Removal of implanted lens**
Removal of pseudophakos

✓4th **13.9**   **Other operations on lens**
AHA: 1Q, '00, 9

●   **13.90**   **Operation on lens, not elsewhere classified**

●   **13.91**   **Implantation of intraocular telescope prosthesis**
Implantable miniature telescope
INCLUDES removal of lens, any method
EXCLUDES secondary insertion of ocular implant (16.61)

✓3rd **14**   **Operations on retina, choroid, vitreous, and posterior chamber**

✓4th **14.0**   **Removal of foreign body from posterior segment of eye**
EXCLUDES removal of surgically implanted material (14.6)

14.00   **Removal of foreign body from posterior segment of eye, not otherwise specified**

14.01   **Removal of foreign body from posterior segment of eye with use of magnet**

14.02   **Removal of foreign body from posterior segment of eye without use of magnet**

✓4th **14.1**   **Diagnostic procedures on retina, choroid, vitreous, and posterior chamber**

14.11   **Diagnostic aspiration of vitreous**

14.19   **Other diagnostic procedures on retina, choroid, vitreous, and posterior chamber**

✓4th **14.2**   **Destruction of lesion of retina and choroid**
INCLUDES destruction of chorioretinopathy or isolated chorioretinal lesion
EXCLUDES that for repair of retina (14.31-14.59)
DEF: Destruction of damaged retina and choroid tissue.

14.21   **Destruction of chorioretinal lesion by diathermy**

14.22   **Destruction of chorioretinal lesion by cryotherapy**

14.23   **Destruction of chorioretinal lesion by xenon arc photocoagulation**

14.24   **Destruction of chorioretinal lesion by laser photocoagulation**

14.25   **Destruction of chorioretinal lesion by photocoagulation of unspecified type**

14.26   **Destruction of chorioretinal lesion by radiation therapy**

14.27   **Destruction of chorioretinal lesion by implantation of radiation source**

14.29   **Other destruction of chorioretinal lesion**
Destruction of lesion of retina and choroid NOS

✓4th **14.3**   **Repair of retinal tear**
INCLUDES repair of retinal defect
EXCLUDES repair of retinal detachment (14.41-14.59)

14.31   **Repair of retinal tear by diathermy**

14.32   **Repair of retinal tear by cryotherapy**

14.33   **Repair of retinal tear by xenon arc photocoagulation**

14.34   **Repair of retinal tear by laser photocoagulation**
AHA: 1Q, '94, 17

14.35   **Repair of retinal tear by photocoagulation of unspecified type**

14.39   **Other repair of retinal tear**

✓4th **14.4**   **Repair of retinal detachment with scleral buckling and implant**
DEF: Placement of material around eye to indent sclera and close a hole or tear or to reduce vitreous traction.

14.41   **Scleral buckling with implant**
AHA: 3Q, '96, 6

14.49   **Other scleral buckling**
Scleral buckling with:
air tamponade
resection of sclera
vitrectomy
AHA: 1Q, '94, 16

BI Bilateral Procedure   **NC** Non-covered Procedure   **LC** Limited Coverage Procedure   ▶◀ Revised Text   ● New Code   ▲ Revised Code Title

✓4th **14.5** **Other repair of retinal detachment**
     INCLUDES   that with drainage

     14.51 **Repair of retinal detachment with diathermy**

     14.52 **Repair of retinal detachment with cryotherapy**

     14.53 **Repair of retinal detachment with xenon arc photocoagulation**

     14.54 **Repair of retinal detachment with laser photocoagulation**
        AHA: N-D, '87, 10

     14.55 **Repair of retinal detachment with photocoagulation of unspecified type**

     14.59 **Other**

   14.6 **Removal of surgically implanted material from posterior segment of eye**

✓4th **14.7** **Operations on vitreous**

     14.71 **Removal of vitreous, anterior approach**
        Open sky technique
        Removal of vitreous, anterior approach (with replacement)

        DEF: Removal of all or part of the eyeball fluid via the anterior segment of the eyeball.

     14.72 **Other removal of vitreous**
        Aspiration of vitreous by posterior sclerotomy

     14.73 **Mechanical vitrectomy by anterior approach**
        AHA: 3Q, '96, 4, 5

        DEF: Removal of abnormal tissue in eyeball fluid to control fibrotic overgrowth in severe intraocular injury.

     14.74 **Other mechanical vitrectomy**
        ▶Posterior approach◀
        AHA: 3Q, '96, 4, 5

     14.75 **Injection of vitreous substitute**
        EXCLUDES   that associated with removal (14.71-14.72)
        AHA: 1Q, '98, 6; 3Q, '96, 4, 5; 1Q, '94, 17

     14.79 **Other operations on vitreous**
        AHA: 3Q, '99, 12; 1Q, '99, 11; 1Q, '98, 6

   14.9 **Other operations on retina, choroid, and posterior chamber**
        AHA: 3Q, '96, 5

✓3rd **15** **Operations on extraocular muscles**

✓4th **15.0** **Diagnostic procedures on extraocular muscles or tendons**

     15.01 **Biopsy of extraocular muscle or tendon**

     15.09 **Other diagnostic procedures on extraocular muscles and tendons**

✓4th **15.1** **Operations on one extraocular muscle involving temporary detachment from globe**

     15.11 **Recession of one extraocular muscle**
        AHA: 3Q, '96, 3

        DEF: Detachment of exterior eye muscle with posterior reattachment to correct strabismus.

     15.12 **Advancement of one extraocular muscle**
        DEF: Detachment of exterior eye muscle with forward reattachment to correct strabismus.

     15.13 **Resection of one extraocular muscle**

     15.19 **Other operations on one extraocular muscle involving temporary detachment from globe**
        EXCLUDES   transposition of muscle (15.5)

✓4th **15.2** **Other operations on one extraocular muscle**

     15.21 **Lengthening procedure on one extraocular muscle**
        DEF: Extension of exterior eye muscle length.

Lengthening Procedure on One Extraocular Muscle

Shortening Procedure on One Extraocular Muscle

     15.22 **Shortening procedure on one extraocular muscle**
        DEF: Shortening of exterior eye muscle.

     15.29 **Other**

   15.3 **Operations on two or more extraocular muscles involving temporary detachment from globe, one or both eyes**
        AHA: 3Q, '96, 3

   15.4 **Other operations on two or more extraocular muscles, one or both eyes**

   15.5 **Transposition of extraocular muscles**
        EXCLUDES   that for correction of ptosis (08.31-08.36)
        DEF: Relocation of exterior eye muscle to a more functional site.

   15.6 **Revision of extraocular muscle surgery**
        DEF: Repair of previous exterior eye muscle surgery.

   15.7 **Repair of injury of extraocular muscle**
        Freeing of entrapped extraocular muscle
        Lysis of adhesions of extraocular muscle
        Repair of laceration of extraocular muscle, tendon, or Tenon's capsule

   15.9 **Other operations on extraocular muscles and tendons**

✓3rd **16** **Operations on orbit and eyeball**
     EXCLUDES   reduction of fracture of orbit (76.78-76.79)

✓4th **16.0** **Orbitotomy**

     16.01 **Orbitotomy with bone flap**
        Orbitotomy with lateral approach
        DEF: Incision into orbital bone with insertion of small bone piece.

     16.02 **Orbitotomy with insertion of orbital implant**
        EXCLUDES   that with bone flap (16.01)

     16.09 **Other orbitotomy**

Operations on the Eye

16.1–16.99

16.1 Removal of penetrating foreign body from eye, not otherwise specified

> EXCLUDES removal of nonpenetrating foreign body (98.21)

DEF: Removal of foreign body from an unspecified site in eye.

✓4ᵗʰ 16.2 Diagnostic procedures on orbit and eyeball

16.21 Ophthalmoscopy

16.22 Diagnostic aspiration of orbit

16.23 Biopsy of eyeball and orbit

16.29 Other diagnostic procedures on orbit and eyeball

> EXCLUDES examination of form and structure of eye (95.11-95.16)
> general and subjective eye examination (95.01-95.09)
> microscopic examination of specimen from eye (90.21-90.29)
> objective functional tests of eye (95.21-95.26)
> ocular thermography (88.82)
> tonometry (89.11)
> x-ray of orbit (87.14, 87.16)

✓4ᵗʰ 16.3 Evisceration of eyeball

DEF: Removal of eyeball, leaving sclera and occasionally cornea.

16.31 Removal of ocular contents with synchronous implant into scleral shell

DEF: Removal of eyeball leaving outer eyeball layer with ocular implant into shell.

16.39 Other evisceration of eyeball

✓4ᵗʰ 16.4 Enucleation of eyeball

DEF: Removal of entire eyeball after severing eye muscles and optic nerves.

16.41 Enucleation of eyeball with synchronous implant into Tenon's capsule with attachment of muscles

Integrated implant of eyeball

DEF: Removal of eyeball with insertion of ocular implant and muscle attachment.

16.42 Enucleation of eyeball with other synchronous implant

16.49 Other enucleation of eyeball

Removal of eyeball NOS

✓4ᵗʰ 16.5 Exenteration of orbital contents

16.51 Exenteration of orbit with removal of adjacent structures

Radical orbitomaxillectomy

DEF: Removal of contents of bony cavity of eye as well as related tissues and structures.

DEF: Radical orbitomaxillectomy: Removal of contents of bony cavity of eye, related tissues and structures, and a portion of maxillary bone.

16.52 Exenteration of orbit with therapeutic removal of orbital bone

16.59 Other exenteration of orbit

Evisceration of orbit NOS
Exenteration of orbit with temporalis muscle transplant

✓4ᵗʰ 16.6 Secondary procedures after removal of eyeball

> EXCLUDES that with synchronous:
> enucleation of eyeball (16.41-16.42)
> evisceration of eyeball (16.31)

16.61 Secondary insertion of ocular implant

DEF: Insertion of ocular implant after previous eye removal.

16.62 Revision and reinsertion of ocular implant

DEF: Reimplant or correction of ocular implant.

16.63 Revision of enucleation socket with graft

DEF: Implant of tissue to correct socket after eye removal.

16.64 Other revision of enucleation socket

16.65 Secondary graft to exenteration cavity

DEF: Implant of tissue in place of eye after removal.

16.66 Other revision of exenteration cavity

16.69 Other secondary procedures after removal of eyeball

✓4ᵗʰ 16.7 Removal of ocular or orbital implant

16.71 Removal of ocular implant

16.72 Removal of orbital implant

✓4ᵗʰ 16.8 Repair of injury of eyeball and orbit

16.81 Repair of wound of orbit

> EXCLUDES reduction of orbital fracture (76.78-76.79)
> repair of extraocular muscles (15.7)

16.82 Repair of rupture of eyeball

Repair of multiple structures of eye

> EXCLUDES repair of laceration of:
> cornea (11.51-11.59)
> sclera (12.81)

16.89 Other repair of injury of eyeball or orbit

✓4ᵗʰ 16.9 Other operations on orbit and eyeball

> EXCLUDES irrigation of eye (96.51)
> prescription and fitting of low vision aids (95.31-95.33)
> removal of:
> eye prosthesis NEC (97.31)
> nonpenetrating foreign body from eye without incision (98.21)

16.91 Retrobulbar injection of therapeutic agent

> EXCLUDES injection of radiographic contrast material (87.14)
> opticociliary injection (12.79)

16.92 Excision of lesion of orbit

> EXCLUDES biopsy of orbit (16.23)

16.93 Excision of lesion of eye, unspecified structure

> EXCLUDES biopsy of eye NOS (16.23)

16.98 Other operations on orbit

16.99 Other operations on eyeball

BI Bilateral Procedure   NC Non-covered Procedure   LC Limited Coverage Procedure   ▶◀ Revised Text   ● New Code   ▲ Revised Code Title

4. OPERATIONS ON THE EAR (18-20)

✓3rd 18 Operations on external ear

INCLUDES   operations on:
> external auditory canal
> skin and cartilage of:
>> auricle
>> meatus

✓4th 18.0 Incision of external ear

EXCLUDES   removal of intraluminal foreign body (98.11)

18.01 Piercing of ear lobe
> Piercing of pinna

18.02 Incision of external auditory canal

18.09 Other incision of external ear

✓4th 18.1 Diagnostic procedures on external ear

18.11 Otoscopy

DEF: Exam of the ear with instrument designed for visualization.

18.12 Biopsy of external ear

18.19 Other diagnostic procedures on external ear

EXCLUDES   microscopic examination of specimen from ear (90.31-90.39)

✓4th 18.2 Excision or destruction of lesion of external ear

18.21 Excision of preauricular sinus
> Radical excision of preauricular sinus or cyst

EXCLUDES   excision of preauricular remnant [appendage] (18.29)

DEF: Excision of preauricular sinus or cyst with adjacent tissues.

18.29 Excision or destruction of other lesion of external ear
> Cauterization
> Coagulation
> Cryosurgery   } of external ear
> Curettage
> Electrocoagulation
> Enucleation

> Excision of:
>> exostosis of external auditory canal
>> preauricular remnant [appendage]
> Partial excision of ear

EXCLUDES   biopsy of external ear (18.12)
> radical excision of lesion (18.31)
> removal of cerumen (96.52)

✓4th 18.3 Other excision of external ear

EXCLUDES   biopsy of external ear (18.12)

18.31 Radical excision of lesion of external ear

EXCLUDES   radical excision of preauricular sinus (18.21)

DEF: Removal of damaged, diseased ear and adjacent tissue.

18.39 Other
> Amputation of external ear

EXCLUDES   excision of lesion (18.21-18.29, 18.31)

18.4 Suture of laceration of external ear

18.5 Surgical correction of prominent ear
> Ear:
>> pinning
>> setback

DEF: Reformation of protruding outer ear.

18.6 Reconstruction of external auditory canal
> Canaloplasty of external auditory meatus
> Construction [reconstruction] of external meatus of ear:
>> osseous portion
>> skin-lined portion (with skin graft)

DEF: Repair of outer ear canal.

✓4th 18.7 Other plastic repair of external ear

18.71 Construction of auricle of ear
> Prosthetic appliance for absent ear
> Reconstruction:
>> auricle
>> ear

DEF: Reformation or repair of external ear flap.

18.72 Reattachment of amputated ear

18.79 Other plastic repair of external ear
> Otoplasty NOS   Repair of lop ear
> Postauricular skin graft

AHA: 3Q, '03, 12

DEF: Postauricular skin graft: Graft repair behind ear.

DEF: Repair of lop ear: Reconstruction of ear that is at right angle to head.

18.9 Other operations on external ear

EXCLUDES   irrigation of ear (96.52)
> packing of external auditory canal (96.11)
> removal of:
>> cerumen (96.52)
>> foreign body (without incision) (98.11)

✓3rd 19 Reconstructive operations on middle ear

19.0 Stapes mobilization
> Division, otosclerotic:
>> material
>> process
> Remobilization of stapes
> Stapediolysis
> Transcrural stapes mobilization

EXCLUDES   that with synchronous stapedectomy (19.11-19.19)

DEF: Repair of innermost bone of middle ear to enable movement and response to sound.

✓4th 19.1 Stapedectomy

EXCLUDES   revision of previous stapedectomy (19.21-19.29)
> stapes mobilization only (19.0)

DEF: Removal of innermost bone of middle ear.

19.11 Stapedectomy with incus replacement
> Stapedectomy with incus:
>> homograft
>> prosthesis

DEF: Removal of innermost bone of middle ear with autograft or prosthesis replacement.

19.19 Other stapedectomy

Stapedectomy with Incus Replacement

Area excised   Tissue seal on oval window

Operations on the Ear

19.2–20.72

✓4th **19.2 Revision of stapedectomy**

    19.21 Revision of stapedectomy with incus replacement

    19.29 Other revision of stapedectomy

19.3 Other operations on ossicular chain
    Incudectomy NOS
    Ossiculectomy NOS
    Reconstruction of ossicles, second stage

DEF: Incudectomy: Excision of middle bone of middle ear, not otherwise specified.

DEF: Ossiculectomy: Excision of middle ear bones, not otherwise specified.

DEF: Reconstruction of ossicles, second stage: Repair of middle ear bones following previous surgery.

19.4 Myringoplasty
    Epitympanic, type I   Myringoplasty by:
    Myringoplasty by: graft
       cauterization   Tympanoplasty (type I)

DEF: Epitympanic, type I: Repair over or upon eardrum.

DEF: Myringoplasty by cauterization: Plastic repair of tympanic membrane of eardrum by heat.

DEF: Graft: Plastic repair using implanted tissue.

DEF: Tympanoplasty (type I): Reconstruction of eardrum to restore hearing.

✓4th **19.5 Other tympanoplasty**

    19.52 Type II tympanoplasty
        Closure of perforation with graft against incus or malleus

    19.53 Type III tympanoplasty
        Graft placed in contact with mobile and intact stapes
        AHA: M-A, '85, 15

    19.54 Type IV tympanoplasty
        Mobile footplate left exposed with air pocket between round window and graft

    19.55 Type V tympanoplasty
        Fenestra in horizontal semicircular canal covered by graft

19.6 Revision of tympanoplasty

DEF: Repair or correction of previous plastic surgery on eardrum.

19.9 Other repair of middle ear
    Closure of mastoid fistula
    Mastoid myoplasty
    Obliteration of tympanomastoid cavity

DEF: Closure of mastoid fistula: Closing of abnormal channel in mastoid.

DEF: Mastoid myoplasty: Restoration or repair of mastoid muscle.

DEF: Obliteration of tympanomastoid cavity: Removal, total, of functional elements of middle ear.

✓3rd **20 Other operations on middle and inner ear**

✓4th **20.0 Myringotomy**

DEF: Myringotomy: Puncture of tympanic membrane or eardrum, also called tympanocentesis

    20.01 Myringotomy with insertion of tube
        Myringostomy

    20.09 Other myringotomy
        Aspiration of middle ear NOS

20.1 Removal of tympanostomy tube

✓4th **20.2 Incision of mastoid and middle ear**

    20.21 Incision of mastoid

    20.22 Incision of petrous pyramid air cells

    20.23 Incision of middle ear
        Atticotomy
        Division of tympanum
        Lysis of adhesions of middle ear

        EXCLUDES   *division of otosclerotic process (19.0)*
                stapediolysis (19.0)
                that with stapedectomy (19.11-19.19)

✓4th **20.3 Diagnostic procedures on middle and inner ear**

    20.31 Electrocochleography

    DEF: Measure of electric potential of eighth cranial nerve by electrode applied sound.

    20.32 Biopsy of middle and inner ear

    20.39 Other diagnostic procedures on middle and inner ear
        EXCLUDES   *auditory and vestibular function tests (89.13, 95.41-95.49)*
                microscopic examination of specimen from ear (90.31-90.39)

✓4th **20.4 Mastoidectomy**
    Code also any:
        skin graft (18.79)
        tympanoplasty (19.4-19.55)
    EXCLUDES   *that with implantation of cochlear prosthetic device (20.96-20.98)*

DEF: Mastoidectomy: Excision of bony protrusion behind ear.

    20.41 Simple mastoidectomy

    20.42 Radical mastoidectomy

    20.49 Other mastoidectomy
        Atticoantrostomy
        Mastoidectomy:
            NOS
            modified radical

    DEF: Atticoantrotomy: Opening of cavity of mastoid bone and middle ear.

✓4th **20.5 Other excision of middle ear**
    EXCLUDES   *that with synchronous mastoidectomy (20.41-20.49)*

    20.51 Excision of lesion of middle ear
        EXCLUDES   *biopsy of middle ear (20.32)*

    20.59 Other
        Apicectomy of petrous pyramid
        Tympanectomy

✓4th **20.6 Fenestration of inner ear**

    20.61 Fenestration of inner ear (initial)
        Fenestration of:
          labyrinth   with graft (skin)
          semicircular canals   (vein)
          vestibule

        EXCLUDES   *that with tympanoplasty, type V (19.55)*

    DEF: Creation of inner ear opening.

    20.62 Revision of fenestration of inner ear

✓4th **20.7 Incision, excision, and destruction of inner ear**

    20.71 Endolymphatic shunt

    DEF: Insertion of tube to drain fluid in inner ear cavities.

    20.72 Injection into inner ear
        Destruction by injection (alcohol):
          inner ear
          semicircular canals
          vestibule

BI Bilateral Procedure   **NC** Non-covered Procedure   **LC** Limited Coverage Procedure   ▶◀ Revised Text   ● New Code   ▲ Revised Code Title

20.79 Other incision, excision, and destruction of inner ear

Decompression of labyrinth
Drainage of inner ear
Fistulization:
    endolymphatic sac
    labyrinth
Incision of endolymphatic sac
Labyrinthectomy (transtympanic)
Opening of bony labyrinth
Perilymphatic tap

> **EXCLUDES** *biopsy of inner ear (20.32)*

DEF: Decompression of labyrinth: Controlled relief of pressure in cavities of inner ear.

DEF: Drainage of inner ear: Removal of fluid from inner ear.

DEF: Fistulization of endolymphatic sac: Creation of passage to fluid sac in inner ear cavities.

DEF: Fistulization of labyrinth: Creation of passage to inner ear cavities.

DEF: Incision of endolymphatic sac: Cutting into fluid sac in inner ear cavities.

DEF: Labyrinthectomy (transtympanic): Excision of cavities across eardrum.

DEF: Opening of bony labyrinth: Cutting into inner ear bony cavities.

DEF: Perilymphatic tap: Puncture or incision into fluid sac of inner ear cavities.

20.8 Operations on Eustachian tube

Catheterization
Inflation
Injection (Teflon paste)
Insufflation (boric acid-
    salicylic acid)
Intubation
Politzerization
    } of Eustachian tube

DEF: Catheterization: Passing catheter into passage between pharynx and middle ear.

DEF: Inflation: Blowing air, gas or liquid into passage between pharynx and middle ear to inflate.

DEF: Injection (Teflon paste): Forcing fluid (Teflon paste) into passage between pharynx and middle ear.

DEF: Insufflation (boric acid-salicylic acid): Blowing gas or liquid into passage between pharynx and middle ear.

DEF: Intubation: Placing tube into passage between pharynx and middle ear.

DEF: Politzerization: Inflating passage between pharynx and middle ear with Politzer bag.

✓4th 20.9 Other operations on inner and middle ear

20.91 Tympanosympathectomy

DEF: Excision or chemical suppression of impulses of middle ear nerves.

20.92 Revision of mastoidectomy

AHA: 2Q, '98, 20

DEF: Correction of previous removal of mastoid cells from temporal or mastoid bone.

20.93 Repair of oval and round windows

Closure of fistula: Closure of fistula:
    oval window   round window
    perilymph

DEF: Restoration of middle ear openings.

20.94 Injection of tympanum

20.95 Implantation of electromagnetic hearing device

Bone conduction hearing device

> **EXCLUDES** *cochlear prosthetic device (20.96-20.98)*

AHA: 4Q, '89, 5

20.96 Implantation or replacement of cochlear prosthetic device, not otherwise specified

Implantation of receiver (within skull) and insertion of electrode(s) in the cochlea

> **INCLUDES** mastoidectomy
> **EXCLUDES** *electromagnetic hearing device (20.95)*

AHA: 4Q, '89, 5

20.97 Implantation or replacement of cochlear prosthetic device, single channel

Implantation of receiver (within skull) and insertion of electrode in the cochlea

> **INCLUDES** mastoidectomy
> **EXCLUDES** *electromagnetic hearing device (20.95)*

AHA: 4Q, '89, 5

20.98 Implantation or replacement of cochlear prosthetic device, multiple channel

Implantation of receiver (within skull) and insertion of electrodes in the cochlea

> **INCLUDES** mastoidectomy
> **EXCLUDES** *electromagnetic hearing device (20.95)*

AHA: 4Q, '89, 5

20.99 Other operations on middle and inner ear

Repair or removal of cochlear prosthetic device (receiver) (electrode)

> **EXCLUDES** *adjustment (external components) of cochlear prosthetic device (95.49)*
> *fitting of hearing aid (95.48)*

AHA: 4Q, '89, 7

Operations on the Nose, Mouth, and Pharynx

21–21.87

5. OPERATIONS ON THE NOSE, MOUTH, AND PHARYNX (21-29)

√3rd **21** Operations on nose
　　INCLUDES operations on:
　　　　bone }
　　　　skin } of nose

AHA: 1Q, '94, 5

√4th **21.0** Control of epistaxis
　　21.00 Control of epistaxis, not otherwise specified
　　21.01 Control of epistaxis by anterior nasal packing
　　21.02 Control of epistaxis by posterior (and anterior) packing
　　21.03 Control of epistaxis by cauterization (and packing)
　　21.04 Control of epistaxis by ligation of ethmoidal arteries
　　21.05 Control of epistaxis by (transantral) ligation of the maxillary artery
　　21.06 Control of epistaxis by ligation of the external carotid artery
　　21.07 Control of epistaxis by excision of nasal mucosa and skin grafting of septum and lateral nasal wall
　　21.09 Control of epistaxis by other means

21.1 Incision of nose
　　Chondrotomy　　Nasal septotomy
　　Incision of skin of nose
　　DEF: Chondrotomy: Incision or division of nasal cartilage.
　　DEF: Nasal septotomy: Incision into bone dividing nose into two chambers.

√4th **21.2** Diagnostic procedures on nose
　　21.21 Rhinoscopy
　　　　DEF: Visualization of nasal passage with nasal speculum.
　　21.22 Biopsy of nose
　　21.29 Other diagnostic procedures on nose
　　　　EXCLUDES microscopic examination of specimen from nose (90.31-90.39)
　　　　　　nasal:
　　　　　　　function study (89.12)
　　　　　　　x-ray (87.16)
　　　　　　　rhinomanometry (89.12)

√4th **21.3** Local excision or destruction of lesion of nose
　　　　EXCLUDES biopsy of nose (21.22)
　　　　　　nasal fistulectomy (21.82)
　　21.30 Excision or destruction of lesion of nose, not otherwise specified
　　21.31 Local excision or destruction of intranasal lesion
　　　　Nasal polypectomy
　　21.32 Local excision or destruction of other lesion of nose
　　　　AHA: 2Q, '89, 16

21.4 Resection of nose
　　Amputation of nose

21.5 Submucous resection of nasal septum
　　DEF: Resection, partial, of nasal septum with mucosa reimplanted after excision.

√4th **21.6** Turbinectomy
　　DEF: Removal, partial, or total of turbinate bones; inferior turbinate is most often excised.
　　21.61 Turbinectomy by diathermy or cryosurgery
　　　　DEF: Destruction of turbinate bone by heat or freezing.

Excision of Turbinate

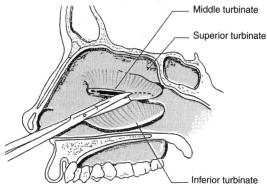

　　21.62 Fracture of the turbinates
　　　　DEF: Surgical breaking of turbinate bones.
　　21.69 Other turbinectomy
　　　　EXCLUDES turbinectomy associated with sinusectomy (22.31-22.39, 22.42, 22.60-22.64)

√4th **21.7** Reduction of nasal fracture
　　21.71 Closed reduction of nasal fracture
　　21.72 Open reduction of nasal fracture

√4th **21.8** Repair and plastic operations on the nose
　　21.81 Suture of laceration of nose
　　21.82 Closure of nasal fistula
　　　　Nasolabial
　　　　Nasopharyngeal } fistulectomy
　　　　Oronasal
　　　　DEF: Sealing off crack or hole between nose and lip, nose and pharynx, or nose and mouth.
　　21.83 Total nasal reconstruction
　　　　Reconstruction of nose with:
　　　　　arm flap
　　　　　forehead flap
　　　　DEF: Reformation, plastic, of nasal structure with tissue flap from arm or forehead.
　　21.84 Revision rhinoplasty
　　　　Rhinoseptoplasty
　　　　Twisted nose rhinoplasty
　　　　DEF: Rhinoseptoplasty: Repair of nose and the bone dividing the nose into two chambers.
　　　　DEF: Twisted nose rhinoplasty: Repair of nose alignment following reconstructive surgery.
　　21.85 Augmentation rhinoplasty
　　　　Augmentation rhinoplasty with:
　　　　　graft
　　　　　synthetic implant
　　　　DEF: Implant of tissue or synthetic graft to enlarge nose.
　　21.86 Limited rhinoplasty
　　　　Plastic repair of nasolabial flaps
　　　　Tip rhinoplasty
　　　　DEF: Plastic repair of nasolabial flaps: Reconstruction of nasal area above lips.
　　　　DEF: Tip rhinoplasty: Reconstruction or restoration of nasal tip.
　　21.87 Other rhinoplasty
　　　　Rhinoplasty NOS

21.88   Other septoplasty
Crushing of nasal septum
Repair of septal perforation
> EXCLUDES   septoplasty associated with
> submucous resection of
> septum (21.5)

DEF: Crushing of nasal septum: Division and
reconstruction of defects in bone dividing nasal
chambers.

DEF: Repair of septal perforation: Repair of hole in bone
dividing nasal chambers with adjacent tissue.

21.89   Other repair and plastic operations on nose
Reattachment of amputated nose

√4ᵗʰ **21.9   Other operations on nose**

21.91   Lysis of adhesions of nose
Posterior nasal scrub

DEF: Posterior nasal scrub: Clearing out of abnormal
adhesions in posterior nasal area.

21.99   Other
> EXCLUDES   dilation of frontonasal duct
> (96.21)
> irrigation of nasal passages
> (96.53)
> removal of:
> intraluminal foreign body
> without incision
> (98.12)
> nasal packing (97.32)
> replacement of nasal packing
> (97.21)

√3ʳᵈ **22   Operations on nasal sinuses**

√4ᵗʰ **22.0   Aspiration and lavage of nasal sinus**

**22.00   Aspiration and lavage of nasal sinus, not
otherwise specified**

**22.01   Puncture of nasal sinus for aspiration or
lavage**

**22.02   Aspiration or lavage of nasal sinus through
natural ostium**

DEF: Withdrawal of fluid and washing of nasal cavity
through natural opening.

√4ᵗʰ **22.1   Diagnostic procedures on nasal sinus**

**22.11   Closed [endoscopic] [needle] biopsy of nasal
sinus**

22.12   Open biopsy of nasal sinus

**22.19   Other diagnostic procedures on nasal
sinuses**
Endoscopy without biopsy
> EXCLUDES   transillumination of sinus
> (89.35)
> x-ray of sinus (87.15-87.16)

22.2   Intranasal antrotomy
> EXCLUDES   antrotomy with external approach
> (22.31-22.39)

DEF: Incision of intranasal sinus.

√4ᵗʰ **22.3   External maxillary antrotomy**

22.31   Radical maxillary antrotomy
Removal of lining membrane of maxillary
sinus using Caldwell-Luc approach

DEF: Caldwell-Luc approach: Removal of membrane
lining the maxillary cavity through incision above canine
teeth.

22.39   Other external maxillary antrotomy
Exploration of maxillary antrum with
Caldwell-Luc approach

√4ᵗʰ **22.4   Frontal sinusotomy and sinusectomy**

22.41   Frontal sinusotomy

22.42   Frontal sinusectomy
Excision of lesion of frontal sinus
Obliteration of frontal sinus (with fat)
> EXCLUDES   biopsy of nasal sinus (22.11-
> 22.12)

√4ᵗʰ **22.5   Other nasal sinusotomy**

22.50   Sinusotomy, not otherwise specified

22.51   Ethmoidotomy

22.52   Sphenoidotomy

22.53   Incision of multiple nasal sinuses

√4ᵗʰ **22.6   Other nasal sinusectomy**
> INCLUDES   that with incidental turbinectomy
> EXCLUDES   biopsy of nasal sinus (22.11-22.12)

22.60   Sinusectomy, not otherwise specified

**22.61   Excision of lesion of maxillary sinus with
Caldwell-Luc approach**

**22.62   Excision of lesion of maxillary sinus with
other approach**

22.63   Ethmoidectomy

DEF: Removal of ethmoid cells and bone, partial or total
includes excising mucosal lining, partial or total.

22.64   Sphenoidectomy

DEF: Removal of wedge shaped sphenoid bone at base of
brain.

√4ᵗʰ **22.7   Repair of nasal sinus**

22.71   Closure of nasal sinus fistula
Repair of oro-antral fistula

22.79   Other repair of nasal sinus
Reconstruction of frontonasal duct
Repair of bone of accessory sinus

22.9   Other operations on nasal sinuses
Exteriorization of maxillary sinus
Fistulization of sinus
> EXCLUDES   dilation of frontonasal duct (96.21)

DEF: Exteriorization of maxillary sinus: Creation of external
maxillary cavity opening.

DEF: Fistulization of sinus: Creation of fistula canal in nasal cavity.

√3ʳᵈ **23   Removal and restoration of teeth**

√4ᵗʰ **23.0   Forceps extraction of tooth**

23.01   Extraction of deciduous tooth

23.09   Extraction of other tooth
Extraction of tooth NOS

√4ᵗʰ **23.1   Surgical removal of tooth**

23.11   Removal of residual root

23.19   Other surgical extraction of tooth
Odontectomy NOS
Removal of impacted tooth
Tooth extraction with elevation of
mucoperiosteal flap

23.2   Restoration of tooth by filling

23.3   Restoration of tooth by inlay

DEF: Restoration of tooth by cementing in a molded filling.

√4ᵗʰ **23.4   Other dental restoration**

23.41   Application of crown

23.42   Insertion of fixed bridge

23.43   Insertion of removable bridge

23.49   Other

23.5   Implantation of tooth

DEF: Insertion of a sound tooth to replace extracted tooth.

23.6   Prosthetic dental implant
Endosseous dental implant

DEF: Implant of artificial denture within bone covering tooth socket.

√4ᵗʰ **23.7   Apicoectomy and root canal therapy**

23.70   Root canal, not otherwise specified

23.71   Root canal therapy with irrigation

√3ʳᵈ / √4ᵗʰ Additional Digit Required   Nonspecific OR Procedure   Valid OR Procedure   Non-OR Procedure   Adjunct Code

Operations on the Nose, Mouth, and Pharynx

23.72–26.0

23.72   **Root canal therapy with apicoectomy**

DEF: Removal of tooth root to treat damaged root canal tissue.

23.73   **Apicoectomy**

√3ʳᵈ **24**   **Other operations on teeth, gums, and alveoli**

24.0   **Incision of gum or alveolar bone**

Apical alveolotomy

√4ᵗʰ **24.1**   **Diagnostic procedures on teeth, gums, and alveoli**

24.11   **Biopsy of gum**

24.12   **Biopsy of alveolus**

24.19   **Other diagnostic procedures on teeth, gums, and alveoli**

> EXCLUDES   *dental:*
> *examination (89.31)*
> *x-ray:*
> *full-mouth (87.11)*
> *other (87.12)*
> *microscopic examination of dental specimen (90.81-90.89)*

24.2   **Gingivoplasty**

Gingivoplasty with bone or soft tissue graft

DEF: Repair of gum tissue.

√4ᵗʰ **24.3**   **Other operations on gum**

24.31   **Excision of lesion or tissue of gum**

> EXCLUDES   *biopsy of gum (24.11)*
> *excision of odontogenic lesion (24.4)*

24.32   **Suture of laceration of gum**

24.39   **Other**

24.4   **Excision of dental lesion of jaw**

Excision of odontogenic lesion

24.5   **Alveoloplasty**

Alveolectomy (interradicular) (intraseptal) (radical) (simple) (with graft or implant)

> EXCLUDES   *biopsy of alveolus (24.12)*
> *en bloc resection of alveolar process and palate (27.32)*

DEF: Repair or correction of bony tooth socket.

24.6   **Exposure of tooth**

24.7   **Application of orthodontic appliance**

Application, insertion, or fitting of:
arch bars	orthodontic wiring
orthodontic obturator	periodontal splint

> EXCLUDES   *nonorthodontic dental wiring (93.55)*

24.8   **Other orthodontic operation**

Closure of diastema (alveolar) (dental)	Removal of arch bars Repair of dental arch
Occlusal adjustment	

> EXCLUDES   *removal of nonorthodontic wiring (97.33)*

√4ᵗʰ **24.9**   **Other dental operations**

24.91   **Extension or deepening of buccolabial or lingual sulcus**

24.99   **Other**

> EXCLUDES   *dental:*
> *debridement (96.54)*
> *examination (89.31)*
> *prophylaxis (96.54)*
> *scaling and polishing (96.54)*
> *wiring (93.55)*
> *fitting of dental appliance [denture] (99.97)*
> *microscopic examination of dental specimen (90.81-90.89)*
> *removal of dental:*
> *packing (97.34)*
> *prosthesis (97.35)*
> *wiring (97.33)*
> *replacement of dental packing (97.22)*

√3ʳᵈ **25**   **Operations on tongue**

√4ᵗʰ **25.0**   **Diagnostic procedures on tongue**

25.01   **Closed [needle] biopsy of tongue**

25.02   **Open biopsy of tongue**

Wedge biopsy

25.09   **Other diagnostic procedures on tongue**

25.1   **Excision or destruction of lesion or tissue of tongue**

> EXCLUDES   *biopsy of tongue (25.01-25.02)*
> *frenumectomy:*
> *labial (27.41)*
> *lingual (25.92)*

AHA: 2Q, '02, 5

25.2   **Partial glossectomy**

25.3   **Complete glossectomy**

Glossectomy NOS

Code also any neck dissection (40.40-40.42)

25.4   **Radical glossectomy**

Code also any:
neck dissection (40.40-40.42)
tracheostomy (31.1-31.29)

√4ᵗʰ **25.5**   **Repair of tongue and glossoplasty**

25.51   **Suture of laceration of tongue**

25.59   **Other repair and plastic operations on tongue**

Fascial sling of tongue
Fusion of tongue (to lip)
Graft of mucosa or skin to tongue

> EXCLUDES   *lysis of adhesions of tongue (25.93)*

AHA: 1Q, '97, 5

√4ᵗʰ **25.9**   **Other operations on tongue**

25.91   **Lingual frenotomy**

> EXCLUDES   *labial frenotomy (27.91)*

DEF: Extension of groove between cheek and lips or cheek and tongue.

25.92   **Lingual frenectomy**

> EXCLUDES   *labial frenectomy (27.41)*

DEF: Frenectomy: Removal of vertical membrane attaching tongue to floor of mouth.

25.93   **Lysis of adhesions of tongue**

25.94   **Other glossotomy**

25.99   **Other**

√3ʳᵈ **26**   **Operations on salivary glands and ducts**

> INCLUDES   operations on:
> lesser salivary
> parotid
> sublingual
> submaxillary   } gland and duct

Code also any neck dissection (40.40-40.42)

26.0   **Incision of salivary gland or duct**

BI Bilateral Procedure   **NC** Non-covered Procedure   **LC** Limited Coverage Procedure   ▶◀ Revised Text   ● New Code   ▲ Revised Code Title

96 — Volume 3   *2007 ICD•9•CM*

✓4th **26.1** **Diagnostic procedures on salivary glands and ducts**
    26.11 **Closed [needle] biopsy of salivary gland or duct**
    26.12 **Open biopsy of salivary gland or duct**
    26.19 **Other diagnostic procedures on salivary glands and ducts**
      EXCLUDES   *x-ray of salivary gland (87.09)*

✓4th **26.2** **Excision of lesion of salivary gland**
    26.21 **Marsupialization of salivary gland cyst**
      DEF: Creation of pouch of salivary gland cyst to drain and promote healing.
    26.29 **Other excision of salivary gland lesion**
      EXCLUDES   *biopsy of salivary gland (26.11-26.12)*
           salivary fistulectomy (26.42)

✓4th **26.3** **Sialoadenectomy**
    DEF: Removal of salivary gland.
    26.30 **Sialoadenectomy, not otherwise specified**
    26.31 **Partial sialoadenectomy**
    26.32 **Complete sialoadenectomy**
      En bloc excision of salivary gland lesion
      Radical sialoadenectomy

✓4th **26.4** **Repair of salivary gland or duct**
    26.41 **Suture of laceration of salivary gland**
    26.42 **Closure of salivary fistula**
      DEF: Closing of abnormal opening in salivary gland.
    26.49 **Other repair and plastic operations on salivary gland or duct**
      Fistulization of salivary gland
      Plastic repair of salivary gland or duct NOS
      Transplantation of salivary duct opening

✓4th **26.9** **Other operations on salivary gland or duct**
    26.91 **Probing of salivary duct**
    26.99 **Other**

✓3rd **27** **Other operations on mouth and face**
    INCLUDES   operations on:
      lips
      palate
      soft tissue of face and mouth, except tongue and gingiva
    EXCLUDES   operations on:
      gingiva (24.0-24.99)
      tongue (25.01-25.99)

    27.0 **Drainage of face and floor of mouth**
      Drainage of: Drainage of:
      facial region (abscess)   Ludwig's angina
      fascial compartment of face
      EXCLUDES   *drainage of thyroglossal tract (06.09)*

    27.1 **Incision of palate**

✓4th **27.2** **Diagnostic procedures on oral cavity**
    27.21 **Biopsy of bony palate**
    27.22 **Biopsy of uvula and soft palate**
    27.23 **Biopsy of lip**
    27.24 **Biopsy of mouth, unspecified structure**
    27.29 **Other diagnostic procedures on oral cavity**
      EXCLUDES   *soft tissue x-ray (87.09)*

✓4th **27.3** **Excision of lesion or tissue of bony palate**
    27.31 **Local excision or destruction of lesion or tissue of bony palate**
      Local excision or destruction of palate by:
      cautery   cryotherapy
      chemotherapy
      EXCLUDES   *biopsy of bony palate (27.21)*
    27.32 **Wide excision or destruction of lesion or tissue of bony palate**
      En bloc resection of alveolar process and palate

✓4th **27.4** **Excision of other parts of mouth**
    27.41 **Labial frenectomy**
      EXCLUDES   *division of labial frenum (27.91)*
      DEF: Removal of mucous membrane fold of lip.
    27.42 **Wide excision of lesion of lip**
    27.43 **Other excision of lesion or tissue of lip**
    27.49 **Other excision of mouth**
      EXCLUDES   *biopsy of mouth NOS (27.24)*
           excision of lesion of:
           palate (27.31-27.32)
           tongue (25.1)
           uvula (27.72)
           fistulectomy of mouth (27.53)
           frenectomy of:
           lip (27.41)
           tongue (25.92)
      AHA: ▶2Q, '05, 8◀

✓4th **27.5** **Plastic repair of mouth**
      EXCLUDES   *palatoplasty (27.61-27.69)*
    27.51 **Suture of laceration of lip**
    27.52 **Suture of laceration of other part of mouth**
    27.53 **Closure of fistula of mouth**
      EXCLUDES   *fistulectomy:*
           nasolabial (21.82)
           oro-antral (22.71)
           oronasal (21.82)
    27.54 **Repair of cleft lip**
    27.55 **Full-thickness skin graft to lip and mouth**
    27.56 **Other skin graft to lip and mouth**
    27.57 **Attachment of pedicle or flap graft to lip and mouth**
      AHA: 1Q, '96, 14
      DEF: Repair of lip or mouth with tissue pedicle or flap still connected to original vascular base.
    27.59 **Other plastic repair of mouth**

✓4th **27.6** **Palatoplasty**
    27.61 **Suture of laceration of palate**
    27.62 **Correction of cleft palate**
      Correction of cleft palate by push-back operation
      EXCLUDES   *revision of cleft palate repair (27.63)*
    27.63 **Revision of cleft palate repair**
      Secondary:
      attachment of pharyngeal flap
      lengthening of palate
      AHA: 1Q, '96, 14
    27.64 **Insertion of palatal implant**
      DEF: Nonabsorbable polyester implants into the soft palate at the back of the roof of the mouth; one implant placed at the soft palate midline and two are positioned on either side; to support and stiffen the palate reducing vibration (snoring).
    27.69 **Other plastic repair of palate**
      Code also any insertion of palatal implant (27.64)
      EXCLUDES   *fistulectomy of mouth (27.53)*
      AHA: 3Q, '99, 22; 1Q, '97, 14; 3Q, '92, 18

✓4th **27.7** **Operations on uvula**
    27.71 **Incision of uvula**
    27.72 **Excision of uvula**
      EXCLUDES   *biopsy of uvula (27.22)*
    27.73 **Repair of uvula**
      EXCLUDES   *that with synchronous cleft palate repair (27.62)*
           uranostaphylorrhaphy (27.62)

Operations on the Nose, Mouth, and Pharynx

26.1–27.73

✓3rd ✓4th Additional Digit Required   Nonspecific OR Procedure   Valid OR Procedure   Non-OR Procedure   Adjunct Code

Operations on the Nose, Mouth, and Pharynx

27.79–29.99

27.79   **Other operations on uvula**
AHA: 3Q, '92, 18

✓4ᵗʰ 27.9   **Other operations on mouth and face**

27.91   **Labial frenotomy**
Division of labial frenum
EXCLUDES   *lingual frenotomy (25.91)*
DEF: Division of labial frenum: Cutting and separating mucous membrane fold of lip.

27.92   **Incision of mouth, unspecified structure**
EXCLUDES   *incision of:*
gum (24.0)
palate (27.1)
salivary gland or duct (26.0)
tongue (25.94)
uvula (27.71)

27.99   **Other operations on oral cavity**
Graft of buccal sulcus
EXCLUDES   *removal of:*
intraluminal foreign body (98.01)
penetrating foreign body from mouth without incision (98.22)
DEF: Graft of buccal sulcus: Implant of tissue into groove of interior cheek lining.

✓3ʳᵈ 28   **Operations on tonsils and adenoids**

28.0   **Incision and drainage of tonsil and peritonsillar structures**
Drainage (oral) (transcervical) of:
parapharyngeal
peritonsillar   } abscess
retropharyngeal
tonsillar

✓4ᵗʰ 28.1   **Diagnostic procedures on tonsils and adenoids**

28.11   **Biopsy of tonsils and adenoids**

28.19   **Other diagnostic procedures on tonsils and adenoids**
EXCLUDES   *soft tissue x-ray (87.09)*

28.2   **Tonsillectomy without adenoidectomy**
AHA: 1Q, '97, 5; 2Q, '90, 23

28.3   **Tonsillectomy with adenoidectomy**
AHA: ▶2Q, '05, 16◀

28.4   **Excision of tonsil tag**

28.5   **Excision of lingual tonsil**

28.6   **Adenoidectomy without tonsillectomy**
Excision of adenoid tag

28.7   **Control of hemorrhage after tonsillectomy and adenoidectomy**
AHA: ▶2Q, '05, 16◀

✓4ᵗʰ 28.9   **Other operations on tonsils and adenoids**

28.91   **Removal of foreign body from tonsil and adenoid by incision**
EXCLUDES   *that without incision (98.13)*

28.92   **Excision of lesion of tonsil and adenoid**
EXCLUDES   *biopsy of tonsil and adenoid (28.11)*

28.99   **Other**

✓3ʳᵈ 29   **Operations on pharynx**
INCLUDES   operations on: operations on:
hypopharynx   pharyngeal pouch
nasopharynx   pyriform sinus
oropharynx

29.0   **Pharyngotomy**
Drainage of pharyngeal bursa
EXCLUDES   *incision and drainage of retropharyngeal abscess (28.0)*
removal of foreign body (without incision) (98.13)

✓4ᵗʰ 29.1   **Diagnostic procedures on pharynx**

29.11   **Pharyngoscopy**

29.12   **Pharyngeal biopsy**
Biopsy of supraglottic mass

29.19   **Other diagnostic procedures on pharynx**
EXCLUDES   *x-ray of nasopharynx:*
contrast (87.06)
other (87.09)

29.2   **Excision of branchial cleft cyst or vestige**
EXCLUDES   *branchial cleft fistulectomy (29.52)*

✓4ᵗʰ 29.3   **Excision or destruction of lesion or tissue of pharynx**
AHA: 2Q, '89, 18

29.31   **Cricopharyngeal myotomy**
EXCLUDES   *that with pharyngeal diverticulectomy (29.32)*
DEF: Removal of outward pouching of throat.

29.32   **Pharyngeal diverticulectomy**

29.33   **Pharyngectomy (partial)**
EXCLUDES   *laryngopharyngectomy (30.3)*

29.39   **Other excision or destruction of lesion or tissue of pharynx**

29.4   **Plastic operation on pharynx**
Correction of nasopharyngeal atresia
EXCLUDES   *pharyngoplasty associated with cleft palate repair (27.62-27.63)*
AHA: 3Q, '99, 22; 1Q, '97, 5; 3Q, '92, 18
DEF: Correction of nasopharyngeal atresia: Construction of normal opening for throat stricture behind nose.

✓4ᵗʰ 29.5   **Other repair of pharynx**

29.51   **Suture of laceration of pharynx**

29.52   **Closure of branchial cleft fistula**
DEF: Sealing off an abnormal opening of the branchial fissure in throat.

29.53   **Closure of other fistula of pharynx**
Pharyngoesophageal fistulectomy

29.54   **Lysis of pharyngeal adhesions**

29.59   **Other**
AHA: 2Q, '89, 18

✓4ᵗʰ 29.9   **Other operations on pharynx**

29.91   **Dilation of pharynx**
Dilation of nasopharynx

29.92   **Division of glossopharyngeal nerve**

29.99   **Other**
EXCLUDES   *insertion of radium into pharynx and nasopharynx (92.27)*
removal of intraluminal foreign body (98.13)

BI Bilateral Procedure   NC Non-covered Procedure   LC Limited Coverage Procedure   ▶◀ Revised Text   ● New Code   ▲ Revised Code Title

6. OPERATIONS ON THE RESPIRATORY SYSTEM (30-34)

√3rd **30**   **Excision of larynx**

√4th **30.0**   **Excision or destruction of lesion or tissue of larynx**

30.01   **Marsupialization of laryngeal cyst**

DEF: Incision of cyst of larynx with the edges sutured open to create pouch.

30.09   **Other excision or destruction of lesion or tissue of larynx**

Stripping of vocal cords

> **EXCLUDES**   *biopsy of larynx (31.43)*
> *laryngeal fistulectomy (31.62)*
> *laryngotracheal fistulectomy (31.62)*

30.1   **Hemilaryngectomy**

DEF: Excision of one side (half) of larynx.

√4th **30.2**   **Other partial laryngectomy**

30.21   **Epiglottidectomy**

30.22   **Vocal cordectomy**

Excision of vocal cords

30.29   **Other partial laryngectomy**

Excision of laryngeal cartilage

30.3   **Complete laryngectomy**

Block dissection of larynx (with thyroidectomy) (with synchronous tracheostomy)

Laryngopharyngectomy

> **EXCLUDES**   *that with radical neck dissection (30.4)*

30.4   **Radical laryngectomy**

Complete [total] laryngectomy with radical neck dissection (with thyroidectomy) (with synchronous tracheostomy)

√3rd **31**   **Other operations on larynx and trachea**

31.0   **Injection of larynx**

Injection of inert material into larynx or vocal cords

31.1   **Temporary tracheostomy**

Tracheotomy for assistance in breathing

AHA: 1Q, '97, 6

√4th **31.2**   **Permanent tracheostomy**

31.21   **Mediastinal tracheostomy**

DEF: Placement of artificial breathing tube in windpipe through mediastinum, for long-term use.

31.29   **Other permanent tracheostomy**

> **EXCLUDES**   *that with laryngectomy (30.3-30.4)*

AHA: ▶2Q, '05, 8;◀ 2Q, '02, 6

31.3   **Other incision of larynx or trachea**

> **EXCLUDES**   *that for assistance in breathing (31.1-31.29)*

√4th **31.4**   **Diagnostic procedures on larynx and trachea**

31.41   **Tracheoscopy through artificial stoma**

> **EXCLUDES**   *that with biopsy (31.43-31.44)*

DEF: Exam by scope of trachea through an artificial opening.

Temporary Tracheostomy

Closed Endoscopic Biopsy of Larynx

Laryngoscope

Trachea

Palate

Growth on vocal cord

31.42   **Laryngoscopy and other tracheoscopy**

> **EXCLUDES**   *that with biopsy (31.43-31.44)*

31.43   **Closed [endoscopic] biopsy of larynx**

31.44   **Closed [endoscopic] biopsy of trachea**

31.45   **Open biopsy of larynx or trachea**

31.48   **Other diagnostic procedures on larynx**

> **EXCLUDES**   *contrast laryngogram (87.07)*
> *microscopic examination of specimen from larynx (90.31-90.39)*
> *soft tissue x-ray of larynx NEC (87.09)*

31.49   **Other diagnostic procedures on trachea**

> **EXCLUDES**   *microscopic examination of specimen from trachea (90.41-90.49)*
> *x-ray of trachea (87.49)*

31.5   **Local excision or destruction of lesion or tissue of trachea**

> **EXCLUDES**   *biopsy of trachea (31.44-31.45)*
> *laryngotracheal fistulectomy (31.62)*
> *tracheoesophageal fistulectomy (31.73)*

√4th **31.6**   **Repair of larynx**

31.61   **Suture of laceration of larynx**

31.62   **Closure of fistula of larynx**

Laryngotracheal fistulectomy

Take-down of laryngostomy

DEF: Laryngotracheal fistulectomy: Excision and closing of passage between voice box and trachea.

DEF: Take-down of laryngostomy: Removal of laryngostomy tube and restoration of voice box.

31.63   **Revision of laryngostomy**

31.64   **Repair of laryngeal fracture**

DEF: Alignment and positioning of harder structures of larynx such as hyoid bone; following fracture.

31.69   **Other repair of larynx**

Arytenoidopexy

Cordopexy

Graft of larynx

Transposition of vocal cords

> **EXCLUDES**   *construction of artificial larynx (31.75)*

DEF: Arytenoidopexy: Fixation of pitcher-shaped cartilage in voice box.

DEF: Graft of larynx: Implant of graft tissue into voice box.

DEF: Transposition of the vocal cords: Placement of vocal cords into more functional positions.

√4th **31.7**   **Repair and plastic operations on trachea**

31.71   **Suture of laceration of trachea**

√3rd √4th Additional Digit Required   Nonspecific OR Procedure   Valid OR Procedure   Non-OR Procedure   Adjunct Code

Operations on the Respiratory System

31.72   Closure of external fistula of trachea
Closure of tracheotomy

31.73   Closure of other fistula of trachea
Tracheoesophageal fistulectomy
EXCLUDES   *laryngotracheal fistulectomy (31.62)*

DEF: Tracheoesophageal fistulectomy: Excision and closure of abnormal opening between windpipe and esophagus.

31.74   Revision of tracheostomy

31.75   Reconstruction of trachea and construction of artificial larynx
Tracheoplasty with artificial larynx

31.79   Other repair and plastic operations on trachea

✓4ᵗʰ **31.9   Other operations on larynx and trachea**

31.91   Division of laryngeal nerve

31.92   Lysis of adhesions of trachea or larynx

31.93   Replacement of laryngeal or tracheal stent

DEF: Removal and substitution of tubed molding into larynx or trachea.

31.94   Injection of locally-acting therapeutic substance into trachea

31.95   Tracheoesophageal fistulization

DEF: Creation of passage between trachea and esophagus.

31.98   Other operations on larynx

Dilation
Division of congenital web ⎫ of larynx
Removal of keel or stent ⎭

EXCLUDES   *removal of intraluminal foreign body from larynx without incision (98.14)*

DEF: Dilation: Increasing larynx size by stretching.

DEF: Division of congenital web: Cutting and separating congenital membranes around larynx.

DEF: Removal of keel or stent: Removal of prosthetic device from larynx.

31.99   Other operations on trachea
EXCLUDES   *removal of:*
intraluminal foreign body from trachea without incision (98.15)
tracheostomy tube (97.37)
replacement of tracheostomy tube (97.23)
tracheostomy toilette (96.55)

AHA: 1Q, '97, 14

✓3ʳᵈ **32   Excision of lung and bronchus**
INCLUDES   rib resection
sternotomy
sternum-splitting ⎫ as operative
incision ⎬ approach
thoracotomy ⎭

Code also any synchronous bronchoplasty (33.48)

DEF: Rib resection: Cutting of ribs to access operative field.

DEF: Sternotomy: Cut through breastbone as an operative approach.

DEF: Sternum-splitting incision: Breaking through breastbone to access operative field.

✓4ᵗʰ **32.0   Local excision or destruction of lesion or tissue of bronchus**
EXCLUDES   *biopsy of bronchus (33.24-33.25)*
bronchial fistulectomy (33.42)

AHA: 4Q, '88, 11

Lung Volume Reduction

32.01   Endoscopic excision or destruction of lesion or tissue of bronchus

32.09   Other local excision or destruction of lesion or tissue of bronchus
EXCLUDES   *that by endoscopic approach (32.01)*

32.1   Other excision of bronchus
Resection (wide sleeve) of bronchus
EXCLUDES   *radical dissection [excision] of bronchus (32.6)*

DEF: Resection (wide sleeve) of bronchus: Excision and partial, lengthwise removal of a lung branch.

✓4ᵗʰ **32.2   Local excision or destruction of lesion or tissue of lung**

32.21   Plication of emphysematous bleb
DEF: Stitching of a swollen vesicle into folds or tuck.

32.22   Lung volume reduction surgery   LC
AHA: 1Q, '97, 6; 3Q, '96, 20; 4Q, '95, 64

DEF: Excision of portion of lung(s) to reduce respiratory effort in moderate to severe emphysema.

●   **32.23   Open ablation of lung lesion or tissue**
●   **32.24   Percutaneous ablation of lung lesion or tissue**
●   **32.25   Thoracoscopic ablation of lung lesion or tissue**
●   **32.26   Other and unspecified ablation of lung lesion or tissue**

32.28   Endoscopic excision or destruction of lesion or tissue of lung
EXCLUDES ▶ *ablation of lung lesion or tissue:*
open (32.23)
other (32.26)
percutaneous (32.24)
thoracoscopic (32.25)◀
biopsy of lung (33.26-33.27)

32.29   Other local excision or destruction of lesion or tissue of lung
Resection of lung: Resection of lung:
NOS   wedge
EXCLUDES ▶ *ablation of lung lesion or tissue:*
open (32.23)
other (32.26)
percutaneous (32.24)
thoracoscopic (32.25)◀
biopsy of lung (33.26-33.27)
that by endoscopic approach (32.28)
wide excision of lesion of lung (32.3)

AHA: 3Q, '99, 3

32.3   Segmental resection of lung
Partial lobectomy

BI Bilateral Procedure   NC Non-covered Procedure   LC Limited Coverage Procedure   ▶◀ Revised Text   ● New Code   ▲ Revised Code Title

100 — Volume 3 • October 2006   ***2007 ICD•9•CM***

32.4   Lobectomy of lung
> Lobectomy with segmental resection of adjacent lobes of lung
> > EXCLUDES   *that with radical dissection [excision] of thoracic structures (32.6)*

32.5   Complete pneumonectomy
> Excision of lung NOS
> Pneumonectomy (with mediastinal dissection)
> AHA: 1Q, '99, 6

32.6   Radical dissection of thoracic structures
> Block [en bloc] dissection of bronchus, lobe of lung, brachial plexus, intercostal structure, ribs (transverse process), and sympathetic nerves

32.9   Other excision of lung
> > EXCLUDES   *biopsy of lung and bronchus (33.24-33.27)*
> > *pulmonary decortication (34.51)*

√3rd 33   Other operations on lung and bronchus
> INCLUDES
> rib resection
> sternotomy   } as operative
> sternum-splitting incision   approach
> thoracotomy

33.0   Incision of bronchus

33.1   Incision of lung
> > EXCLUDES   *puncture of lung (33.93)*

√4th 33.2   Diagnostic procedures on lung and bronchus

33.21   Bronchoscopy through artificial stoma
> > EXCLUDES   *that with biopsy (33.24, 33.27)*
> DEF: Visual exam of lung and its branches via tube through artificial opening.

33.22   Fiber-optic bronchoscopy
> > EXCLUDES   *that with biopsy (33.24, 33.27)*
> AHA: 1Q, '04, 4
> DEF: Exam of lung and bronchus via flexible optical instrument for visualization.

33.23   Other bronchoscopy
> > EXCLUDES   *that for:*
> > *aspiration (96.05)*
> > *biopsy (33.24, 33.27)*
> AHA: 3Q, '02, 18; 1Q, '99, 6

33.24   Closed [endoscopic] biopsy of bronchus
> Bronchoscopy (fiberoptic) (rigid) with:
> brush biopsy of "lung"
> brushing or washing for specimen collection
> excision (bite) biopsy
> Diagnostic bronchoalveolar lavage (BAL)
> > EXCLUDES   *closed biopsy of lung, other than brush biopsy of "lung" (33.26, 33.27)*
> > *whole lung lavage (33.99)*
> AHA: 3Q, '04, 9; 3Q, '02, 16; 4Q, '92, 27; 3Q, '91, 15
> DEF: Bronchoalveolar lavage (BAL): Saline is introduced into the subsegment of a lobe and retrieved using gentle suction; also called 'liquid biopsy'.
> DEF: Brush biopsy: Obtaining cell or tissue samples via bristled instrument without incision.

Bronchoscopy with Bite Biopsy

33.25   Open biopsy of bronchus
> > EXCLUDES   *open biopsy of lung (33.28)*

33.26   Closed [percutaneous] [needle] biopsy of lung
> > EXCLUDES   *endoscopic biopsy of lung (33.27)*
> AHA: 3Q, '92, 12

33.27   Closed endoscopic biopsy of lung
> Fiber-optic (flexible) bronchoscopy with fluoroscopic guidance with biopsy
> Transbronchial lung biopsy
> > EXCLUDES   *brush biopsy of "lung" (33.24)*
> > *percutaneous biopsy of lung (33.26)*
> AHA: 3Q, '04, 9; 3Q, '02, 16; 4Q, '92, 27; 3Q, '91, 15; S-O, '86, 11

33.28   Open biopsy of lung
> AHA: 3Q, '99, 3; 3Q, '92, 12

33.29   Other diagnostic procedures on lung and bronchus
> > EXCLUDES   *contrast bronchogram:*
> > *endotracheal (87.31)*
> > *other (87.32)*
> > *lung scan (92.15)*
> > *magnetic resonance imaging (88.92)*
> > *microscopic examination of specimen from bronchus or lung (90.41-90.49)*
> > *routine chest x-ray (87.44)*
> > *ultrasonography of lung (88.73)*
> > *vital capacity determination (89.37)*
> > *x-ray of bronchus or lung NOS (87.49)*

√4th 33.3   Surgical collapse of lung

33.31   Destruction of phrenic nerve for collapse of lung
> DEF: Therapeutic deadening or destruction of diaphragmatic nerve to collapse the lung.

33.32   Artificial pneumothorax for collapse of lung
> Thoracotomy for collapse of lung
> DEF: Forcing air or gas into diaphragmatic space to achieve therapeutic collapse of lung.
> DEF: Thoracotomy for collapse of lung: Incision into chest for therapeutic collapse of lung.

33.33   Pneumoperitoneum for collapse of lung
> DEF: Forcing air or gas into abdominal serous membrane to achieve therapeutic collapse of lung.

33.34   Thoracoplasty
> DEF: Removal of ribs for therapeutic collapse of lungs.

33.39   Other surgical collapse of lung
> Collapse of lung NOS

√4th 33.4   Repair and plastic operation on lung and bronchus

33.41   Suture of laceration of bronchus

33.42   Closure of bronchial fistula
> Closure of bronchostomy
> Fistulectomy:
> bronchocutaneous
> bronchoesophageal
> bronchovisceral
> > EXCLUDES   *closure of fistula:*
> > *bronchomediastinal (34.73)*
> > *bronchopleural (34.73)*
> > *bronchopleuromediastinal (34.73)*
> DEF: Closure of bronchostomy: Removal of bronchostomy tube and repair of surgical wound.
> DEF: Fistulectomy: Closure of abnormal passage.
> Bronchocutaneous: Between skin and lung branch.
> Bronchoesophagus: Between esophagus and lung branch.
> Bronchovisceral: Between an internal organ and lung branch.

Operations on the Respiratory System

33.43–34.27

33.43   **Closure of laceration of lung**

33.48   **Other repair and plastic operations on bronchus**

33.49   **Other repair and plastic operations on lung**
> *EXCLUDES*   closure of pleural fistula (34.73)

√4ᵗʰ **33.5**   **Lung transplant**
> Note: To report donor source — *see* codes 00.91-00.93
>
> Code also cardiopulmonary bypass [extracorporeal circulation] [heart-lung machine] [39.61]
>
> *EXCLUDES*   combined heart-lung transplantation (33.6)

AHA: 4Q, '95, 75

33.50   **Lung transplantation, not otherwise specified**   `LC`

33.51   **Unilateral lung transplantation**   `LC`

33.52   **Bilateral lung transplantation**   `LC`
> Double-lung transplantation
> En bloc transplantation
> DEF: Sequential excision and implant of both lungs.

33.6   **Combined heart-lung transplantation**   `LC`
> Note: To report donor source — *see* codes 00.91-00.93
>
> Code also cardiopulmonary bypass [extracorporeal circulation] [heart-lung machine] (39.61)

● √4ᵗʰ **33.7**   **Endoscopic insertion, replacement, and removal of therapeutic device or substances in bronchus or lung**
> Biologic lung volume reduction (BLVR)
> *EXCLUDES*   insertion of tracheobronchial stent (96.05)

● **33.71**   **Endoscopic insertion or replacement of bronchial valve(s)**
> Endobronchial airflow redirection valve
> Intrabronchial airflow redirection valve

● **33.78**   **Endoscopic removal of bronchial device(s) or substances**

● **33.79**   **Endoscopic insertion of other bronchial device or substances**
> Biologic lung volume reduction NOS (BLVR)

√4ᵗʰ **33.9**   **Other operations on lung and bronchus**

33.91   **Bronchial dilation**
> AHA: 1Q, '97, 14

33.92   **Ligation of bronchus**
> DEF: Tying off of a lung branch.

33.93   **Puncture of lung**
> *EXCLUDES*   needle biopsy (33.26)
> DEF: Piercing of lung with surgical instrument.

33.98   **Other operations on bronchus**
> *EXCLUDES*   bronchial lavage (96.56)
> removal of intraluminal foreign body from bronchus without incision (98.15)

33.99   **Other operations on lung**
> Whole lung lavage
> *EXCLUDES*   other continuous mechanical ventilation (96.70-96.72)
> respiratory therapy (93.90-93.99)

AHA: 3Q, '02, 17

√3ʳᵈ **34**   **Operations on chest wall, pleura, mediastinum, and diaphragm**
> *EXCLUDES*   operations on breast (85.0-85.99)

√4ᵗʰ **34.0**   **Incision of chest wall and pleura**
> *EXCLUDES*   that as operative approach — omit code

34.01   **Incision of chest wall**
> Extrapleural drainage
> *EXCLUDES*   incision of pleura (34.09)

AHA: 3Q, '00, 12; 1Q, '92, 13

DEF: Extrapleural drainage: Incision to drain fluid from external pleura.

34.02   **Exploratory thoracotomy**

34.03   **Reopening of recent thoracotomy site**

34.04   **Insertion of intercostal catheter for drainage**
> Chest tube
> Closed chest drainage
> Revision of intercostal catheter (chest tube) (with lysis of adhesions)

AHA: 2Q, '03, 7; 1Q, '99, 10; 2Q, '99, 12; 1Q, '95, 5; 1Q, '92, 12

DEF: Insertion of catheter between ribs for drainage.

34.05   **Creation of pleuroperitoneal shunt**
> AHA: 4Q, '94, 50

34.09   **Other incision of pleura**
> Creation of pleural window for drainage
> Intercostal stab
> Open chest drainage
> *EXCLUDES*   thoracoscopy (34.21)
> thoracotomy for collapse of lung (33.32)

AHA: 3Q, '02, 22; 1Q, '94, 7; 4Q, '94, 50

DEF: Creation of pleural window: Creation of circumscribed drainage hole in serous membrane of chest.

DEF: Intercostal stab: Creation of penetrating stab wound between ribs.

DEF: Open chest drainage: Insertion of tube through ribs and serous membrane of chest for drainage.

34.1   **Incision of mediastinum**
> *EXCLUDES*   mediastinoscopy (34.22)
> mediastinotomy associated with pneumonectomy (32.5)

√4ᵗʰ **34.2**   **Diagnostic procedures on chest wall, pleura, mediastinum, and diaphragm**

34.21   **Transpleural thoracoscopy**
> AHA: 3Q, '02, 27

DEF: Exam of chest through serous membrane using scope.

34.22   **Mediastinoscopy**
> Code also any lymph node biopsy (40.11)
> DEF: Exam of lung cavity and heart using scope.

34.23   **Biopsy of chest wall**

34.24   **Pleural biopsy**
> AHA: 3Q, '02, 22, 27; 1Q, '92, 14

34.25   **Closed [percutaneous] [needle] biopsy of mediastinum**

34.26   **Open biopsy of mediastinum**

34.27   **Biopsy of diaphragm**

`BI` Bilateral Procedure   `NC` Non-covered Procedure   `LC` Limited Coverage Procedure   ▶◀ Revised Text   ● New Code   ▲ Revised Code Title

102 — Volume 3 • October 2006   *2007 ICD•9•CM*

34.28 Other diagnostic procedures on chest wall, pleura, and diaphragm

> EXCLUDES   angiocardiography (88.50-88.58)
> aortography (88.42)
> arteriography of:
>> intrathoracic vessels NEC (88.44)
>> pulmonary arteries (88.43)
>
> microscopic examination of specimen from chest wall, pleura, and diaphragm (90.41-90.49)
> phlebography of:
>> intrathoracic vessels NEC (88.63)
>> pulmonary veins (88.62)
>
> radiological examinations of thorax:
>> C.A.T. scan (87.41)
>> diaphragmatic x-ray (87.49)
>> intrathoracic lymphangiogram (87.34)
>> routine chest x-ray (87.44)
>> sinogram of chest wall (87.38)
>> soft tissue x-ray of chest wall NEC (87.39)
>> tomogram of thorax NEC (87.42)
>> ultrasonography of thorax (88.73)

34.29 Other diagnostic procedures on mediastinum

> EXCLUDES   mediastinal:
>> pneumogram (87.33)
>> x-ray NEC (87.49)

34.3 Excision or destruction of lesion or tissue of mediastinum

> EXCLUDES   biopsy of mediastinum (34.25-34.26)
> mediastinal fistulectomy (34.73)

34.4 Excision or destruction of lesion of chest wall

Excision of lesion of chest wall NOS (with excision of ribs)

> EXCLUDES   biopsy of chest wall (34.23)
> costectomy not incidental to thoracic procedure (77.91)
> excision of lesion of:
>> breast (85.20-85.25)
>> cartilage (80.89)
>> skin (86.2-86.3)
>
> fistulectomy (34.73)

√4ᵗʰ 34.5 Pleurectomy

34.51 Decortication of lung

DEF: Removal of thickened serous membrane for lung expansion.

34.59 Other excision of pleura

Excision of pleural lesion

> EXCLUDES   biopsy of pleura (34.24)
> pleural fistulectomy (34.73)

34.6 Scarification of pleura

Pleurosclerosis

> EXCLUDES   injection of sclerosing agent (34.92)

AHA: 1Q, '92, 12

DEF: Destruction of fluid-secreting serous membrane cells of chest.

√4ᵗʰ 34.7 Repair of chest wall

34.71 Suture of laceration of chest wall

> EXCLUDES   suture of skin and subcutaneous tissue alone (86.59)

34.72 Closure of thoracostomy

34.73 Closure of other fistula of thorax

Closure of:
> bronchopleural
> bronchopleurocutaneous } fistula
> bronchopleuromediastinal

34.74 Repair of pectus deformity

Repair of:
> pectus carinatum
> pectus excavatum } (with implant)

AHA: 2Q, '04, 6

DEF: Pectus carinatum repair: Restoration of prominent chest bone defect with implant.

DEF: Pectus excavatum: Restoration of depressed chest bone defect with implant.

34.79 Other repair of chest wall

Repair of chest wall NOS

AHA: 2Q, '04, 6; J-F, '87, 13

√4ᵗʰ 34.8 Operations on diaphragm

34.81 Excision of lesion or tissue of diaphragm

> EXCLUDES   biopsy of diaphragm (34.27)

34.82 Suture of laceration of diaphragm

34.83 Closure of fistula of diaphragm

> Thoracicoabdominal
> Thoracicogastric } fistulectomy
> Thoracicointestinal

DEF: Fistulectomy: Closure of abnormal passage.

34.84 Other repair of diaphragm

> EXCLUDES   repair of diaphragmatic hernia (53.7-53.82)

34.85 Implantation of diaphragmatic pacemaker

34.89 Other operations on diaphragm

√4ᵗʰ 34.9 Other operations on thorax

34.91 Thoracentesis

AHA: S-O, '85, 6

DEF: Puncture of pleural cavity for fluid aspiration, also called pleurocentesis.

34.92 Injection into thoracic cavity

Chemical pleurodesis
Injection of cytotoxic agent or tetracycline
►Instillation into thoracic cavity◄
Requires additional code for any cancer chemotherapeutic substance (99.25)

> EXCLUDES   that for collapse of lung (33.32)

AHA: 1Q, '92, 12; 2Q, '89, 17

DEF: Chemical pleurodesis: Tetracycline hydrochloride injections to create adhesions between parietal and visceral pleura for treatment of pleural effusion.

34.93 Repair of pleura

34.99 Other

> EXCLUDES   removal of:
>> mediastinal drain (97.42)
>> sutures (97.43)
>> thoracotomy tube (97.41)

AHA: 1Q, '00, 17; 1Q, '88, 9

DEF: Pleural tent: Extrapleural mobilization of parietal pleura that allows draping of membrane over visceral pleura to eliminate intrapleural dead space and seal visceral pleura.

Operations on the Respiratory System

34.28–34.99

√3ʳᵈ √4ᵗʰ Additional Digit Required   Nonspecific OR Procedure   Valid OR Procedure   Non-OR Procedure   Adjunct Code

Operations on the Cardiovascular System

35–35.42

7. OPERATIONS ON THE CARDIOVASCULAR SYSTEM (35-39)

✓3ʳᵈ **35 Operations on valves and septa of heart**

INCLUDES   sternotomy (median) (transverse) thoracotomy } as operative approach

Code also cardiopulmonary bypass [extracorporeal circulation] [heart-lung machine] (39.61)

✓4ᵗʰ **35.0 Closed heart valvotomy**

EXCLUDES   percutaneous (balloon) valvuloplasty (35.96)

DEF: Incision into valve to restore function.

35.00 Closed heart valvotomy, unspecified valve
35.01 Closed heart valvotomy, aortic valve
35.02 Closed heart valvotomy, mitral valve
35.03 Closed heart valvotomy, pulmonary valve
35.04 Closed heart valvotomy, tricuspid valve

✓4ᵗʰ **35.1 Open heart valvuloplasty without replacement**

INCLUDES   open heart valvotomy

Code also cardiopulmonary bypass, if performed [extracorporeal circulation] [heart-lung machine] (39.61)

EXCLUDES   that associated with repair of: endocardial cushion defect (35.54,35.63,35.73) percutaneous (balloon) valvuloplasty (35.96) valvular defect associated with atrial and ventricular septal defects (35.54, 35.63, 35.73)

DEF: Incision into heart for plastic repair of valve without replacing valve.

35.10 Open heart valvuloplasty without replacement, unspecified valve
35.11 Open heart valvuloplasty of aortic valve without replacement
35.12 Open heart valvuloplasty of mitral valve without replacement

AHA: 1Q, '97, 13

35.13 Open heart valvuloplasty of pulmonary valve without replacement
35.14 Open heart valvuloplasty of tricuspid valve without replacement

✓4ᵗʰ **35.2 Replacement of heart valve**

INCLUDES   excision of heart valve with replacement

Code also cardiopulmonary bypass [extracorporeal circulation] [heart-lung machine] (39.61)

EXCLUDES   that associated with repair of: endocardial cushion defect (35.54,35.63, 35.73) valvular defect associated with atrial and ventricular septal defects (35.54, 35.63, 35.73)

DEF: Removal and replacement of valve with tissue from patient, animal, other human, or prosthetic (synthetic) valve.

35.20 Replacement of unspecified heart valve
Repair of unspecified heart valve with tissue graft or prosthetic implant

35.21 Replacement of aortic valve with tissue graft
Repair of aortic valve with tissue graft (autograft) (heterograft) (homograft)

AHA: 2Q, '97, 8

35.22 Other replacement of aortic valve
Repair of aortic valve with replacement:
NOS
prosthetic (partial) (synthetic) (total)

AHA: 1Q, '96, 11

35.23 Replacement of mitral valve with tissue graft
Repair of mitral valve with tissue graft (autograft) (heterograft) (homograft)

35.24 Other replacement of mitral valve
Repair of mitral valve with replacement:
NOS
prosthetic (partial) (synthetic) (total)

AHA: 4Q, '97, 55

35.25 Replacement of pulmonary valve with tissue graft
Repair of pulmonary valve with tissue graft (autograft) (heterograft) (homograft)

AHA: 1Q, '04, 16; 2Q, '97, 8

35.26 Other replacement of pulmonary valve
Repair of pulmonary valve with replacement:
NOS
prosthetic (partial) (synthetic) (total)

35.27 Replacement of tricuspid valve with tissue graft
Repair of tricuspid valve with tissue graft (autograft) (heterograft) (homograft)

35.28 Other replacement of tricuspid valve
Repair of tricuspid valve with replacement:
NOS
prosthetic (partial) (synthetic) (total)

✓4ᵗʰ **35.3 Operations on structures adjacent to heart valves**

Code also cardiopulmonary bypass [extracorporeal circulation] [heart-lung machine] (39.61)

35.31 Operations on papillary muscle
Division
Reattachment } of papillary muscle
Repair

35.32 Operations on chordae tendineae
Division } chordae tendineae
Repair

35.33 Annuloplasty
Plication of annulus

AHA: 1Q, '97, 13; 1Q, '88, 10

DEF: Plication of annulus: Tuck stitched in valvular ring for tightening.

35.34 Infundibulectomy
Right ventricular infundibulectomy

DEF: Infundibulectomy: Excision of funnel-shaped heart passage.

DEF: Right ventricular infundibulectomy: Excision of funnel-shaped passage in right upper heart chamber.

35.35 Operations on trabeculae carneae cordis
Division } of trabeculae carneae
Excision } cordis

Excision of aortic subvalvular ring

35.39 Operations on other structures adjacent to valves of heart
Repair of sinus of Valsalva (aneurysm)

✓4ᵗʰ **35.4 Production of septal defect in heart**

35.41 Enlargement of existing atrial septal defect
Rashkind procedure
Septostomy (atrial) (balloon)

DEF: Enlargement of partition wall defect in lower heart chamber to improve function.

DEF: Rashkind procedure: Enlargement of partition wall defect between the two lower heart chambers by balloon catheter.

35.42 Creation of septal defect in heart
Blalock-Hanlon operation

DEF: Blalock-Hanlon operation: Removal of partition wall defect in lower heart chamber.

BI Bilateral Procedure   NC Non-covered Procedure   LC Limited Coverage Procedure   ▶◀ Revised Text   ● New Code   ▲ Revised Code Title

✓4ᵗʰ **35.5 Repair of atrial and ventricular septa with prosthesis**

> INCLUDES   repair of septa with synthetic implant or patch

Code also cardiopulmonary bypass [extracorporeal circulation] [heart-lung machine] (39.61)

35.50 Repair of unspecified septal defect of heart with prosthesis

> EXCLUDES   *that associated with repair of:*
> *endocardial cushion defect (35.54)*
> *septal defect associated with valvular defect (35.54)*

35.51 Repair of atrial septal defect with prosthesis, open technique

Atrioseptoplasty
Correction of atrial septal defect
Repair:
  foramen ovale (patent)
  ostium secundum defect
} with prosthesis

> EXCLUDES   *that associated with repair of:*
> *atrial septal defect associated with valvular and ventricular septal defects (35.54)*
> *endocardial cushion defect (35.54)*

DEF: Repair of opening or weakening in septum separating the atria; prosthesis implanted through heart incision.

35.52 Repair of atrial septal defect with prosthesis, closed technique

Insertion of atrial septal umbrella [King-Mills]
AHA: 2Q, '05, 17; 3Q, '98, 11

DEF: Correction of partition wall defect in lower heart chamber with artificial material; without incision into heart.

DEF: Insertion of atrial septal umbrella (King-Mills): Correction of partition wall defect in lower heart chamber with atrial septal umbrella.

▲ **35.53 Repair of ventricular septal defect with prosthesis, open technique**

Correction of ventricular septal defect
Repair of supracristal defect
} with prosthesis

> EXCLUDES   *that associated with repair of:*
> *endocardial cushion defect (35.54)*
> *ventricular defect associated with valvular and atrial septal defects (35.54)*

35.54 Repair of endocardial cushion defect with prosthesis

Repair:
  atrioventricular canal
  ostium primum defect
  valvular defect associated with atrial and ventricular
} with prosthesis (grafted to septa)

> EXCLUDES   *repair of isolated:*
> *atrial septal defect (35.51-35.52)*
> *valvular defect (35.20, 35.22, 35.24, 35.26, 35.28)*
> *ventricular septal defect (35.53)*

● **35.55 Repair of ventricular septal defect with prosthesis, closed technique**

✓4ᵗʰ **35.6 Repair of atrial and ventricular septa with tissue graft**

Code also cardiopulmonary bypass [extracorporeal circulation] [heart-lung machine] (39.61)

35.60 Repair of unspecified septal defect of heart with tissue graft

> EXCLUDES   *that associated with repair of:*
> *endocardial cushion defect (35.63)*
> *septal defect associated with valvular defect (35.63)*

35.61 Repair of atrial septal defect with tissue graft

Atrioseptoplasty
Correction of atrial septal defect
Repair:
  foramen ovale (patent)
  ostium secundum defect
} with tissue graft

> EXCLUDES   *that associated with repair of:*
> *atrial septal defect associated with valvular and ventricular septal defects (35.63)*
> *endocardial cushion defect (35.63)*

35.62 Repair of ventricular septal defect with tissue graft

Correction of ventricular septal defect
Repair of supracristal defect
} with tissue graft

> EXCLUDES   *that associated with repair of:*
> *endocardial cushion defect (35.63)*
> *ventricular defect associated with valvular and atrial septal defects (35.63)*

35.63 Repair of endocardial cushion defect with tissue graft

Repair of:
  atrioventricular canal
  ostium primum defect
  valvular defect associated with atrial and ventricular septal defects
} with tissue graft

> EXCLUDES   *repair of isolated:*
> *atrial septal defect (35.61)*
> *valvular defect (35.20-35.21, 35.23, 35.25, 35.27)*
> *ventricular septal defect (35.62)*

✓4ᵗʰ **35.7 Other and unspecified repair of atrial and ventricular septa**

Code also cardiopulmonary bypass [extracorporeal circulation] [heart-lung machine] (39.61)

35.70 Other and unspecified repair of unspecified septal defect of heart

Repair of septal defect NOS

> EXCLUDES   *that associated with repair of:*
> *endocardial cushion defect (35.73)*
> *septal defect associated with valvular defect (35.73)*

Operations on the Cardiovascular System

35.5–35.70

Operations on the Cardiovascular System

35.71–35.95

35.71 Other and unspecified repair of atrial septal defect

Repair NOS:
atrial septum
foramen ovale (patent)
ostium secundum defect

> EXCLUDES that associated with repair of:
> atrial septal defect assoc-
> iated with valvular
> and ventricular septal
> defects (35.73)
> endocardial cushion defect
> (35.73)

35.72 Other and unspecified repair of ventricular septal defect

Repair NOS:
supracristal defect
ventricular septum

> EXCLUDES that associated with repair of:
> endocardial cushion defect
> (35.73)
> ventricular septal defect
> associated with valvular
> and atrial septal defects
> (35.73)

35.73 Other and unspecified repair of endocardial cushion defect

Repair NOS:
atrioventricular canal
ostium primum defect
valvular defect associated with atrial and
ventricular septal defects

> EXCLUDES repair of isolated:
> atrial septal defect (35.71)
> valvular defect (35.20,
> 35.22, 35.24, 35.26,
> 35.28)
> ventricular septal defect
> (35.72)

✓4ᵗʰ **35.8 Total repair of certain congenital cardiac anomalies**

Note: For partial repair of defect [e.g. repair of atrial septal defect in tetralogy of Fallot] — code to specific procedure

35.81 Total repair of tetralogy of Fallot

One-stage total correction of tetralogy of
Fallot with or without:
commissurotomy of pulmonary valve
infundibulectomy
outflow tract prosthesis
patch graft of outflow tract
prosthetic tube for pulmonary artery
repair of ventricular septal defect (with
prosthesis)
take-down of previous systemic-
pulmonary artery anastomosis

35.82 Total repair of total anomalous pulmonary venous connection

One-stage total correction of total
anomalous pulmonary venous
connection with or without:
anastomosis between (horizontal)
common pulmonary trunk and
posterior wall of left atrium (side-
to-side)
enlargement of foramen ovale
incision [excision] of common wall
between posterior left atrium and
coronary sinus and roofing of
resultant defect with patch graft
(synthetic)
ligation of venous connection (descending
anomalous vein) (to left innominate
vein) (to superior vena cava)
repair of atrial septal defect (with
prosthesis)

35.83 Total repair of truncus arteriosus

One-stage total correction of truncus
arteriosus with or without:
construction (with aortic homograft) (with
prosthesis) of a pulmonary artery
placed from right ventricle to
arteries supplying the lung
ligation of connections between aorta and
pulmonary artery
repair of ventricular septal defect (with
prosthesis)

35.84 Total correction of transposition of great vessels, not elsewhere classified

Arterial switch operation [Jatene]
Total correction of transposition of great
arteries at the arterial level by
switching the great arteries, including
the left or both coronary arteries,
implanted in the wall of the
pulmonary artery

> EXCLUDES baffle operation [Mustard]
> [Senning] (35.91)
> creation of shunt between
> right ventricle and
> pulmonary artery
> [Rastelli] (35.92)

✓4ᵗʰ **35.9 Other operations on valves and septa of heart**

Code also cardiopulmonary bypass, if performed
[extracorporeal circulation] [heart-lung
machine] (39.61)

35.91 Interatrial transposition of venous return

Baffle: Baffle:
atrial   interatrial
Mustard's operation
Resection of atrial septum and insertion of
patch to direct systemic venous return
to tricuspid valve and pulmonary
venous return to mitral valve

DEF: Atrial baffle: Correction of venous flow of abnormal
or deviated lower heart chamber.
DEF: Interatrial baffle: Correction of venous flow
between abnormal lower heart chambers.
DEF: Mustard's operation: Creates intra-atrial baffle
using pericardial tissue to correct transposition of the
great vessels.

35.92 Creation of conduit between right ventricle and pulmonary artery

Creation of shunt between right ventricle
and (distal) pulmonary artery

> EXCLUDES that associated with total
> repair of truncus
> arteriosus (35.83)

35.93 Creation of conduit between left ventricle and aorta

Creation of apicoaortic shunt
Shunt between apex of left ventricle and aorta

35.94 Creation of conduit between atrium and pulmonary artery

Fontan procedure

35.95 Revision of corrective procedure on heart

Replacement of prosthetic heart valve poppet
Resuture of prosthesis of:
septum   valve

> EXCLUDES complete revision — code to
> specific procedure
> replacement of prosthesis or
> graft of:
> septum (35.50-35.63)
> valve (35.20-35.28)

DEF: Replacement of prosthetic heart valve poppet:
Removal and replacement of valve-supporting prosthesis.
DEF: Resuture of prosthesis of septum: Restitching of
prosthesis in partition wall.
DEF: Resuture of prosthesis of valve: Restitching of
prosthetic valve.

BI Bilateral Procedure   NC Non-covered Procedure   LC Limited Coverage Procedure   ▶◀ Revised Text   ● New Code   ▲ Revised Code Title

35.96 Percutaneous valvuloplasty

Percutaneous balloon valvuloplasty

AHA: 3Q, '04, 10; M-J, '86, 6; N-D, '85, 10

DEF: Repair of valve with catheter.

DEF: Percutaneous balloon valvuloplasty: Repair of valve with inflatable catheter.

35.98 Other operations on septa of heart

35.99 Other operations on valves of heart

✓3rd **36 Operations on vessels of heart**

INCLUDES sternotomy (median)
(transverse)
thoracotomy } as operative approach

Code also any:

injection or infusion of platelet inhibitor (99.20)

injection or infusion of thrombolytic agent (99.10)

Code also cardiopulmonary bypass, if performed [extracorporeal circulation] [heart-lung machine] (39.61)

✓4th **36.0 Removal of coronary artery obstruction and insertion of stent(s)**

AHA: 4Q, '95, 66; 2Q, '94, 13; 1Q, '94, 3; 2Q, '90, 23; N-D, '86, 8

36.03 Open chest coronary artery angioplasty

Coronary (artery):
endarterectomy (with patch graft)
thromboendarterectomy (with patch graft)

Open surgery for direct relief of coronary artery obstruction

Code also any:

insertion of drug-eluting coronary stent(s) (36.07)

insertion of non-drug-eluting coronary stent(s) (36.06)

number of vascular stents inserted (00.45-00.48)

number of vessels treated (00.40-00.43)

▶procedure on vessel bifurcation (00.44)◀

EXCLUDES that with coronary artery bypass graft (36.10-36.19)

AHA: 2Q, '01, 24; 3Q, '93, 7

DEF: Endarterectomy (with patch graft): Excision of thickened material within coronary artery; repair with patch graft.

DEF: Thromboendarterectomy (with patch graft): Excision of blood clot and thickened material within coronary artery; repair with patch graft.

DEF: Open surgery for direct relief of coronary artery obstruction: Removal of coronary artery obstruction through opening in chest.

36.04 Intracoronary artery thrombolytic infusion

That by direct coronary artery injection, infusion, or catheterization

enzyme infusion

platelet inhibitor

EXCLUDES infusion of platelet inhibitor (99.20)

infusion of thrombolytic agent (99.10)

that associated with any procedure in 36.03

AHA: 4Q, '05, 102; 4Q, '02, 114; 3Q, '02, 20; 2Q, '01, 24; 4Q, '98, 85; 1Q, '97, 3; 4Q, '95, 67

DEF: Infusion of clot breaking solution into intracoronary artery.

Coronary Bypass

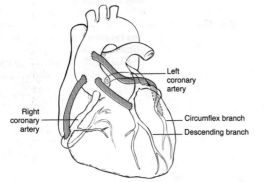

Left coronary artery

Right coronary artery

Circumflex branch

Descending branch

Transmyocardial Revascularization

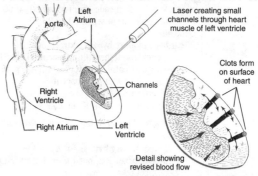

Aorta

Left Atrium

Laser creating small channels through heart muscle of left ventricle

Right Ventricle

Channels

Clots form on surface of heart

Right Atrium

Left Ventricle

Detail showing revised blood flow

36.06 Insertion of non-drug-eluting coronary artery stent(s)

Bare stent(s) Endovascular graft(s)

Bonded stent(s) Stent graft(s)

Drug-coated stent(s), e.g., heparin coated

Endograft(s)

Code also any:

number of vascular stents inserted (00.45-00.48)

number of vessels treated (00.40-00.43)

open chest coronary artery angioplasty (36.03)

percutaneous transluminal coronary angioplasty [PTCA] or coronary atherectomy (00.66)

▶procedure on vessel bifurcation (00.44)◀

EXCLUDES insertion of drug-eluting coronary artery stent(s) (36.07)

AHA: 4Q, '05, 71; 2Q, '04, 3; 4Q, '02, 101; 1Q,'01, 9; 2Q, '01, 24; 1Q, '00, 11; 1Q, '99, 17

DEF: Percutaneous implant via catheter of metal stent, to enlarge, maintain lumen size of coronary artery.

36.07 Insertion of drug-eluting coronary artery stent(s)

Endograft(s) Stent graft(s)

Endovascular graft(s)

Code also any:

number of vascular stents inserted (00.45-00.48)

number of vessels treated (00.40-00.43)

open chest coronary artery angioplasty (36.03)

percutaneous transluminal coronary angioplasty [PTCA] or coronary atherectomy (00.66)

▶procedure on vessel bifurcation (00.44)◀

EXCLUDES drug-coated stents, e.g., heparin coated (36.06)

insertion of non-drug-eluting coronary artery stent(s) (36.06)

AHA: 4Q, '05, 105-106; 4Q, '02, 101

DEF: Drug-eluting stent technology developed to prevent the accumulation of scar tissue that can narrow reopened coronary arteries. A special polymer is used to coat the drug onto the stent, which slowly releases into the coronary artery wall tissue.

36.09 Other removal of coronary artery obstruction

Coronary angioplasty NOS

Code also any:

number of vascular stents inserted (00.45-00.48)

number of vessels treated (00.40-00.43)

▶procedure on vessel bifurcation (00.44)◀

EXCLUDES that by open angioplasty (36.03)

that by percutaneous transluminal coronary angioplasty [PTCA] or coronary atherectomy (00.66)

Operations on the Cardiovascular System

36.1–37.20

✓4th **36.1** **Bypass anastomosis for heart revascularization**
Note: Do not assign codes from series 00.40-00.43 with codes from series 36.10-36.19
Code also:
cardiopulmonary bypass [extracorporeal circulation] [heart-lung machine] (39.61)
pressurized treatment of venous bypass graft [conduit] with pharmaceutical substance, if performed (00.16)

AHA: 2Q, '96, 7; 3Q, '95, 7; 3Q, '93, 8; 1Q, '91, 7; 2Q, '90, 24; 4Q, '89, 3

DEF: Insertion of tube to bypass blocked coronary artery, correct coronary blood flow.

36.10 **Aortocoronary bypass for heart revascularization, not otherwise specified**
Direct revascularization:
cardiac
coronary   } with catheter stent, prosthesis, or vein graft
heart muscle
myocardial

Heart revascularization NOS
AHA: 2Q, '96, 7

36.11 **(Aorto)coronary bypass of one coronary artery**
AHA: 3Q, '02, 4, 9; 4Q, '89, 3

36.12 **(Aorto)coronary bypass of two coronary arteries**
AHA: 3Q, '02, 8; 4Q, '99, 15; 2Q, '96, 7; 3Q, '97, 14; 4Q, '89, 3

36.13 **(Aorto)coronary bypass of three coronary arteries**
AHA: 3Q, '02, 6, 7, 9; 2Q, '96, 7; 4Q, '89, 3

36.14 **(Aorto)coronary bypass of four or more coronary arteries**
AHA: 3Q, '02, 5; 2Q, '96, 7; 4Q, '89, 3

36.15 **Single internal mammary-coronary artery bypass**
Anastomosis (single):
mammary artery to coronary artery
thoracic artery to coronary artery
AHA: 3Q, '02, 4-9; 4Q, '99, 15; 3Q, '97, 14; 2Q, '96, 7

36.16 **Double internal mammary-coronary artery bypass**
Anastomosis, double:
mammary artery to coronary artery
thoracic artery to coronary artery
AHA: 3Q, '02, 6, 8, 9; 2Q, '96, 7

36.17 **Abdominal-coronary artery bypass**
Anastomosis:
gastroepiploic artery to coronary artery
AHA: 3Q, '97, 14; 4Q, '96, 64

36.19 **Other bypass anastomosis for heart revascularization**
AHA: 2Q, '96, 7

36.2 **Heart revascularization by arterial implant**
Implantation of:
aortic branches [ascending aortic branches] into heart muscle
blood vessels into myocardium
internal mammary artery [internal thoracic artery] into:
heart muscle
myocardium
ventricle
ventricular wall
Indirect heart revascularization NOS

✓4th **36.3** **Other heart revascularization**

36.31 **Open chest transmyocardial revascularization**
DEF: Transmyocardial revascularization (TMR): Laser creation of channels through myocardium allows oxygenated blood flow from sinusoids to myocardial tissue.

36.32 **Other transmyocardial revascularization**
AHA: 4Q, '98, 74

● **36.33** **Endoscopic transmyocardial revascularization**
Robot-assisted transmyocardial revascularization
Thoracoscopic transmyocardial revascularization

● **36.34** **Percutaneous transmyocardial revascularization**
Endovascular transmyocardial revascularization

36.39 **Other heart revascularization**
Abrasion of epicardium
Cardio-omentopexy
Intrapericardial poudrage
Myocardial graft: Myocardial graft:
mediastinal fat   pectoral muscles
omentum
DEF: Cardio-omentopexy: Suture of omentum segment to heart after drawing segment through incision in diaphragm to improve blood supply.
DEF: Intrapericardial poudrage: Application of powder to heart lining to promote fusion.

✓4th **36.9** **Other operations on vessels of heart**
Code also cardiopulmonary bypass [extracorporeal circulation] [heart-lung machine] (39.61)

36.91 **Repair of aneurysm of coronary vessel**

36.99 **Other operations on vessels of heart**
Exploration
Incision   } of coronary artery
Ligation

Repair of arteriovenous fistula
AHA: 3Q, '03, 18; 1Q, '94, 3

✓3rd **37** **Other operations on heart and pericardium**
Code also any injection or infusion of platelet inhibitor (99.20)

37.0 **Pericardiocentesis**
DEF: Puncture of the heart lining to withdraw fluid.

✓4th **37.1** **Cardiotomy and pericardiotomy**
Code also cardiopulmonary bypass [extracorporeal circulation] [heart-lung machine] (39.61)

37.10 **Incision of heart, not otherwise specified**
Cardiolysis NOS

37.11 **Cardiotomy**
Incision of: Incision of:
atrium   myocardium
endocardium   ventricle

37.12 **Pericardiotomy**
Pericardial window   Pericardiolysis
operation   Pericardiotomy
DEF: Pericardial window operation: Incision into heart lining for drainage.
DEF: Pericardiolysis: Destruction of heart tissue lining.

✓4th **37.2** **Diagnostic procedures on heart and pericardium**

● **37.20** **Non-invasive programmed electrical stimulation [NIPS]**
EXCLUDES   *catheter based invasive electrophysiologic testing (37.26)*
device interrogation only without arrhythmia induction (bedside check) (89.45-89.49)
that as part of intraoperative testing—omit code

BI Bilateral Procedure   NC Non-covered Procedure   LC Limited Coverage Procedure   ►◄ Revised Text   ● New Code   ▲ Revised Code Title

Intracardiac Echocardiography

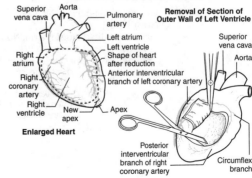

Superior vena cava
Aorta
Inferior vena cava
Right atrium
Left atrium
Left ventricle
Right ventricle
Inferior vena cava
Femoral vein access
Miniaturized ultrasound transducer

37.21 Right heart cardiac catheterization
Cardiac catheterization NOS

EXCLUDES   *that with catheterization of left heart (37.23)*

AHA: 3Q, '04, 10; 3Q, '03, 9; 2Q, '90, 23; M-J, '87, 11

37.22 Left heart cardiac catheterization

EXCLUDES   *that with catheterization of right heart (37.23)*

AHA: 4Q, '05, 71; 3Q, '05, 14; 3Q, '04, 10; 2Q, '04, 3; 1Q, '00, 21; 2Q, '90, 23; 4Q, '88, 4; M-J, '87, 11

37.23 Combined right and left heart cardiac catheterization

AHA: 2Q, '05, 17; 3Q, '04, 10; 2Q, '01, 8; 1Q, '00, 20; 3Q, '98, 11; 2Q, '90, 23; M-J, '87, 11

37.24 Biopsy of pericardium
37.25 Biopsy of heart

AHA: 3Q, '03, 16; 3Q, '94, 8

37.26 Catheter based invasive electrophysiologic testing
Electrophysiologic studies [EPS]
Code also any concomitant procedure

EXCLUDES   *device interrogation only without arrhythmia induction (bedside check) (89.45-89.49)*
His bundle recording (37.29)
▶*non-invasive programmed electrical stimulation (NIPS) (37.20)*
that as part of intraoperative testing—omit code◀

AHA: 3Q, '03, 23; 2Q, '03, 19; 1Q, '02, 8, 9; 1Q, '99, 3; 2Q, '97, 10; 3Q, '90, 11

DEF: Diagnostic mapping and measurement of intracardiac electrical activity; requires inserting three to six catheters into heart blood vessels and positioning catheters under fluoroscopic guidance to determine site of the tachycardia or abnormal impulse pathway; may also be used to terminate arrhythmias.

37.27 Cardiac mapping
Code also any concomitant procedure

EXCLUDES   *electrocardiogram (89.52)*
His bundle recording (37.29)

37.28 Intracardiac echocardiography
Echocardiography of heart chambers
ICE
Code also any synchronous Doppler flow mapping (88.72)

EXCLUDES   *intravascular imaging of coronary vessels (intravascular ultrasound) (IVUS) (00.24)*

AHA: 4Q, '01, 62

DEF: Creation of a two-dimensional graphic of heart using endoscopic echocardiographic equipment.

37.29 Other diagnostic procedures on heart and pericardium

EXCLUDES   *angiocardiography (88.50-88.58)*
cardiac function tests (89.41-89.69)
cardiovascular radioisotopic scan and function study (92.05)
coronary arteriography (88.55-88.57)
diagnostic pericardiocentesis (37.0)
diagnostic ultrasound of heart (88.72)
x-ray of heart (87.49)

AHA: S-O, '87, 3

✓4th 37.3 Pericardiectomy and excision of lesion of heart
Code also cardiopulmonary bypass [extracorporeal circulation] [heart-lung machine] (39.61)

37.31 Pericardiectomy
Excision of:
adhesions of pericardium
constricting scar of:
epicardium
pericardium

DEF: Excision of a portion of heart lining.

37.32 Excision of aneurysm of heart
Repair of aneurysm of heart

37.33 Excision or destruction of other lesion or tissue of heart, open approach
Ablation of heart tissue (cryoablation) (electrocurrent) (laser) (microwave) (radiofrequency) (resection), open chest approach
Cox-maze procedure
Maze procedure
Modified maze procedure, trans-thoracic approach

EXCLUDES   *ablation, excision or destruction of lesion or tissue of heart, endovascular approach (37.34)*

AHA: 4Q, '03, 93-94; 2Q, '94, 12

37.34 Excision or destruction of other lesion or tissue of heart, other approach
Ablation of heart tissue (cryoablation) (electrocurrent) (laser) (microwave) (radiofrequency) (resection), via peripherally inserted catheter
Modified maze procedure, endovascular approach

AHA: 4Q, '03, 93-95; 1Q, '00, 20

DEF: Destruction of heart tissue or lesion by freezing, electric current or resection.

37.35 Partial ventriculectomy   NC
Ventricular reduction surgery
Ventricular remodeling
Code also any synchronous:
mitral valve repair (35.02, 35.12)
mitral valve replacement (35.23-35.24)

AHA: 4Q, '97, 54, 55

DEF: Removal of elliptical slice of ventricle between anterior and posterior papillary muscle; also called Batiste operation.

Ventricular Reduction Surgery

Superior vena cava
Aorta
Pulmonary artery
Left atrium
Left ventricle
Shape of heart after reduction
Anterior interventricular branch of left coronary artery
Right atrium
Right coronary artery
Right ventricle
New apex
Apex
Enlarged Heart

Removal of Section of Outer Wall of Left Ventricle
Superior vena cava
Aorta
Posterior interventricular branch of right coronary artery
Circumflex branch

Operations on the Cardiovascular System

37.4–37.67

√4ᵗʰ **37.4 Repair of heart and pericardium**
AHA: 2Q, '90, 24

37.41 Implantation of prosthetic cardiac support device around the heart
Cardiac support device (CSD)
Epicardial support device
Fabric (textile) (mesh) device
Ventricular support device on surface of heart
Code also any:
cardiopulmonary bypass [extracorporeal circulation] [heart-lung machine] if performed (39.61)
mitral valve repair (35.02, 35.12)
mitral valve replacement (35.23-35.24)
transesophageal echocardiography (88.72)
EXCLUDES circulatory assist systems (37.61-37.68)

AHA: 4Q, '05, 119-120

DEF: Cardiac support device: any device implanted around the ventricles of the heart for cardiac support

DEF: Fabric (textile) (mesh) device: textile mesh net sutured around the heart for support.

37.49 Other repair of heart and pericardium

√4ᵗʰ **37.5 Heart replacement procedures**
AHA: 4Q, '03, 96

37.51 Heart transplantation LC
EXCLUDES combined heart-lung transplantation (33.6)

AHA: 2Q, '05, 14

37.52 Implantation of total replacement heart system NC
Artificial heart
Implantation of fully implantable total replacement heart system, including ventriculectomy
EXCLUDES implantation of heart assist system [VAD] (37.62, 37.65, 37.66)

37.53 Replacement or repair of thoracic unit of total replacement heart system NC
EXCLUDES replacement and repair of heart assist system [VAD] (37.63)

37.54 Replacement or repair of other implantable component of total replacement heart system NC
Implantable battery
Implantable controller
Transcutaneous energy transfer [TET] device
EXCLUDES replacement and repair of heart assist system [VAD] (37.63)
replacement or repair of thoracic unit of total replacement heart system (37.53)

√4ᵗʰ **37.6 Implantation of heart and circulatory assist system**
EXCLUDES implantation of prosthetic cardiac support system (37.41)

AHA: 4Q, '95, 68
DEF: Implant of device for assisting heart in circulating blood.

37.61 Implant of pulsation balloon
AHA: 3Q, '05, 14

37.62 Insertion of non-implantable heart assist system
Insertion of heart assist system, NOS
Insertion of heart pump
EXCLUDES implantation of total replacement heart system (37.52)
insertion of percutaneous external heart assist device (37.68)

AHA: 4Q, '03, 116; 2Q, '90, 25

37.63 Repair of heart assist system
Replacement of parts of an existing ventricular assist device (VAD)
EXCLUDES replacement or repair of other implantable component of total replacement heart system [artificial heart] (37.54)
replacement or repair of thoracic unit of total replacement heart system [artificial heart] (37.53)

37.64 Removal of heart assist system
EXCLUDES explantation [removal] of percutaneous external heart assist device (97.44)
that with replacement of implant (37.63)
nonoperative removal of heart assist system (97.44)

37.65 Implant of external heart assist system
Note: Device (outside the body but connected to heart) with external circulation and pump
INCLUDES open chest (sternotomy) procedure for cannulae attachments
EXCLUDES implantation of total replacement heart system (37.52)
implant of pulsation balloon (37.61)
insertion of percutaneous external heart assist device (37.68)

DEF: Insertion of short-term circulatory support device with pump outside body.

37.66 Insertion of implantable heart assist system LC
Note: Device directly connected to the heart and implanted in the upper left quadrant of peritoneal cavity.
► This device can be used for either destination therapy (DT) or bridge-to-transplant (BTT).◄
Axial flow heart assist system
Diagonal pump heart assist system
Left ventricular assist device (LVAD)
Pulsatile heart assist system
Right ventricular assist device (RVAD)
Rotary pump heart assist system
Transportable, implantable heart assist system
Ventricular assist device (VAD) not otherwise specified
EXCLUDES implantation of total replacement heart system [artificial heart] (37.52)
implant of pulsation balloon (37.61)
insertion of percutaneous external heart assist device (37.68)

AHA: 4Q, '03, 116; 1Q, '98, 8
DEF: Insertion of long-term circulatory support device with pump in body.

37.67 Implantation of cardiomyostimulation system
Note: Two-step open procedure consisting of tranfer of one end of the latissimus dorsi muscle; wrapping it around the heart; rib resection; implantation of epicardial cardiac pacing leads into the right ventricle; tunneling and pocket creation for the cardiomyostimulator.
AHA: 4Q, '98, 75; 1Q, '98, 8

BI Bilateral Procedure   NC Non-covered Procedure   LC Limited Coverage Procedure   ►◄ Revised Text   ● New Code   ▲ Revised Code Title

37.68 **Insertion of percutaneous external heart assist device**
> Circulatory assist device
> Extrinsic heart assist device
> pVAD
> Percutaneous heart assist device
> > INCLUDES   percutaneous [femoral] insertion of cannulae attachments

▲   ✓4th **37.7** **Insertion, revision, replacement, and removal of leads; insertion of temporary pacemaker system; or revision of cardiac device pocket**
> Code also any insertion and replacement of pacemaker device (37.80-37.87)
> > EXCLUDES   *implantation or replacement of transvenous lead [electrode] into left ventricular cardiac venous system (00.52)*

AHA: 1Q, '94, 16; 3Q, '92, 3; M-J, '87, 1

12 **37.70** **Initial insertion of lead [electrode], not otherwise specified**
> > EXCLUDES   *insertion of temporary transvenous pacemaker system (37.78)*
> > *replacement of atrial and/or ventricular lead(s) (37.76)*

12 **37.71** **Initial insertion of transvenous lead [electrode] into ventricle**
> > EXCLUDES   *insertion of temporary transvenous pacemaker system (37.78)*
> > *replacement of atrial and/or ventricular lead(s) (37.76)*

13 **37.72** **Initial insertion of transvenous leads [electrodes] into atrium and ventricle**
> > EXCLUDES   *insertion of temporary transvenous pacemaker system (37.78)*
> > *replacement of atrial and/or ventricular lead(s) (37.76)*

AHA: 2Q, '97, 4

12 **37.73** **Initial insertion of transvenous lead [electrode] into atrium**
> > EXCLUDES   *insertion of temporary transvenous pacemaker system (37.78)*
> > *replacement of atrial and/or ventricular lead(s) (37.76)*

15 **37.74** **Insertion or replacement of epicardial lead [electrode] into epicardium**
> Insertion or replacement of epicardial lead by:
> > sternotomy   thoracotomy
> > EXCLUDES   *replacement of atrial and/or ventricular lead(s) (37.76)*

AHA: 3Q, '05, 3-9

37.75 **Revision of lead [electrode]**
> Repair of electrode [removal with re-insertion]
> Repositioning of ▶lead(s) (AICD) (cardiac device) (CRT-D) (CRT-P) (defibrillator) (pacemaker) (pacing) (sensing) [electrode]◀
> Revision of lead NOS
> > EXCLUDES   *repositioning of temporary transvenous pacemaker system — omit code*

AHA: 3Q, '05, 8; 2Q, '99, 11

14 **37.76** **Replacement of transvenous atrial and/or ventricular lead(s) [electrode]**
> Removal or abandonment of existing transvenous or epicardial lead(s) with transvenous lead(s) replacement
> > EXCLUDES   *replacement of epicardial lead [electrode] (37.74)*

AHA: 3Q, '05, 3-92

37.77 **Removal of lead(s) [electrode] without replacement**
> Removal:
> > epicardial lead (transthoracic approach)
> > transvenous lead(s)
> > EXCLUDES   *removal of temporary transvenous pacemaker system — omit code that with replacement of: atrial and/or ventricular lead(s) [electrode] (37.76) epicardial lead [electrode] (37.74)*

37.78 **Insertion of temporary transvenous pacemaker system**
> > EXCLUDES   *intraoperative cardiac pacemaker (39.64)*

AHA: 3Q, '05, 7; 3Q, '93, 12; 1Q, '89, 2

37.79 **Revision or relocation of cardiac device pocket**
> Debridement and reforming pocket (skin and subcutaneous tissue)
> ▶Insertion of loop recorder◀
> Relocation of pocket [creation of new pocket] pacemaker or CRT-P
> ▶Removal of cardiac device/pulse generator without replacement
> Removal of the implantable hemodynamic pressure sensor [lead] and monitor device
> Removal without replacement of cardiac resynchronization defibrillator device
> Repositioning of implantable hemodynamic pressure sensor [lead] and monitor device
> Repositioning of pulse generator
> Revision of cardioverter/defibrillator (automatic) pocket
> Revision of pocket for intracardiac hemodynamic monitoring
> Revision or relocation of CRT-D pocket◀
> Revision or relocation of pacemaker, defibrillator, or other implanted cardiac device pocket
> > EXCLUDES   ▶ *removal of loop recorder (86.05)◀*

AHA: 3Q, '05, 3-9

✓4th **37.8** **Insertion, replacement, removal, and revision of pacemaker device**
> ▶Note: Device testing during procedure—*omit code*◀
> Code also any lead insertion, lead replacement, lead removal and/or lead revision (37.70-37.77)
> > EXCLUDES   *implantation of cardiac resynchronization pacemaker, total system [CRT-P] (00.50) implantation or replacement of cardiac resynchronization pacemaker pulse generator only [CRT-P] (00.53)*

AHA: M-J, '87, 1

37.80 **Insertion of permanent pacemaker, initial or replacement, type of device not specified**

16 **37.81** **Initial insertion of single-chamber device, not specified as rate responsive**
> > EXCLUDES   *replacement of existing pacemaker device (37.85-37.87)*

16 **37.82** **Initial insertion of single-chamber device, rate responsive**
> Rate responsive to physiologic stimuli other than atrial rate
> > EXCLUDES   *replacement of existing pacemaker device (37.85-37.87)*

---

12 Valid OR procedure code if accompanied by one of the following codes: 37.80, 37.81, 37.82, 37.85, 37.86, 37.87
13 Valid OR procedure code if accompanied by one of the following codes: 37.80, 37.83
14 Valid OR procedure code if accompanied by one of the following codes: 37.80, 37.85, 37.86, 37.87
15 Valid OR procedure code if accompanied by one of the following codes: 37.80, 37.81, 37.82, 37.83, 37.85, 37.86, 37.87
16 Valid OR procedure code if accompanied by one of the following codes: 37.72, 37.76

✓3rd
✓4th Additional Digit Required   Nonspecific OR Procedure   Valid OR Procedure   Non-OR Procedure   Adjunct Code

Operations on the Cardiovascular System

37.83–37.98

Insertion of Pacemaker

Automatic Implantable Cardioverter/Defibrillator

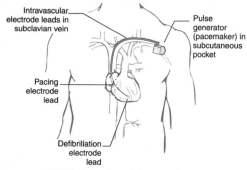

[17] **37.83 Initial insertion of dual-chamber device**
Atrial ventricular sequential device
EXCLUDES *replacement of existing pacemaker device (37.85-37.87)*

AHA: 2Q, '97, 4

37.85 Replacement of any type pacemaker device with single-chamber device, not specified as rate responsive

37.86 Replacement of any type pacemaker device with single-chamber device, rate responsive
Rate responsive to physiologic stimuli other than atrial rate

37.87 Replacement of any type pacemaker device with dual-chamber device
Atrial ventricular sequential device

37.89 Revision or removal of pacemaker device
Removal without replacement of cardiac re-synchronization pacemaker device [CRT-P]
Repair of pacemaker device
EXCLUDES *removal of temporary transvenous pacemaker system — omit code*
replacement of existing pacemaker device (37.85-37.87)
replacement of existing pacemaker device with CRT-P pacemaker device (00.53)

AHA: N-D, '86, 1

[✓4th] **37.9 Other operations on heart and pericardium**
AHA: 3Q, '90, 11

37.90 Insertion of left atrial appendage device
Left atrial filter   Transseptal catheter
Left atrial occluder   technique
AHA: 4Q, '04, 121

DEF: Implantation of a filtering device within the left atrial appendage (LAA) to block emboli from exiting the LAA causing stroke or systemic thromboembolism.

37.91 Open chest cardiac massage
EXCLUDES *closed chest cardiac massage (99.63)*

AHA: 4Q, '88, 12

DEF: Massage of heart through opening in chest wall to reinstate or maintain circulation.

Left Atrial Appendage Device Insertion

37.92 Injection of therapeutic substance into heart

37.93 Injection of therapeutic substance into pericardium

37.94 Implantation or replacement of automatic cardioverter/defibrillator, total system [AICD]
▶Note: Device testing during procedure— *omit code*◀
Implantation of defibrillator with leads (epicardial patches), formation of pocket (abdominal fascia) (subcutaneous), any transvenous leads, intra-operative procedures for evaluation of lead signals, and obtaining defibrillator threshold measurements
Techniques:
lateral thoracotomy
medial sternotomy
subxiphoid procedure
Code also extracorporeal circulation, if performed (39.61)
Code also any concomitant procedure [e.g., coronary bypass] (36.01-36.19)
EXCLUDES *implantation of cardiac resynchronization defibrillator, total system [CRT-D] (00.51)*

AHA: 2Q, '03, 19; 3Q, '01, 5-7; 3Q, '99, 12; 1Q, '99, 3; 3Q, '90, 11; S-O, '87, 5

DEF: Direct insertion, of defibrillator/cardioverter system to deliver shock and restore heart rhythm.

37.95 Implantation of automatic cardioverter/defibrillator lead(s) only
AHA: 3Q, '90, 11

37.96 Implantation of automatic cardioverter/ defibrillator pulse generator only
▶Note: Device testing during procedure— *omit code*◀
EXCLUDES *implantation or replacement of cardiac resynchronization defibrillator, pulse generator device only [CRT-D] (00.54)*

AHA: 3Q, '90, 11

37.97 Replacement of automatic cardioverter/defibrillator lead(s) only
EXCLUDES ▶ *replacement of epicardial lead [electrode] into epicardium (37.74)*
replacement of transvenous lead [electrode] into left ventricular coronary venous system (00.52)◀

AHA: 3Q, '05, 3-9; 3Q, '90, 11

37.98 Replacement of automatic cardioverter defibrillator pulse generator only
▶Note: Device testing during procedure— *omit code*◀
EXCLUDES *replacement of cardiac resynchronization defibrillator, pulse generator device only [CRT-D] (00.54)*

AHA: 1Q, '99, 3; 3Q, '90, 11

[17] Valid OR procedure code if accompanied by one of the following codes: 37.70, 37.71, 37.73, 37.76

BI Bilateral Procedure   NC Non-covered Procedure   LC Limited Coverage Procedure   ▶◀ Revised Text   ● New Code   ▲ Revised Code Title

37.99   Other

> EXCLUDES   cardiac retraining (93.36)
> conversion of cardiac rhythm
> (99.60-99.69)
> implantation of prosthetic
> cardiac support device
> (37.41)
> insertion of left atrial appen-
> dage device (37.90)
> maze procedure (Cox-maze),
> open (37.33)
> maze procedure, endovascular
> approach (37.34)
> ►repositioning of pulse
> generator (37.79)
> revision of lead(s) (37.75)
> revision or relocation of
> pacemaker, defibrillator
> or other implanted
> cardiac device pocket
> (37.79)◄

AHA: 3Q, '05, 5; 2Q, '05, 14; 1Q, '97, 12; 1Q, '94, 19;
3Q, '90, 11; 1Q, '89, 11

√3ʳᵈ   38   Incision, excision, and occlusion of vessels

Code also any application or administration of an adhesion
barrier substance (99.77)
Code also cardiopulmonary bypass [extracorporeal
circulation] [heart-lung machine] (39.61)

> EXCLUDES   that of coronary vessels ►(00.66, 36.03, 36.04,
> 36.09, 36.10-36.99)◄

The following fourth-digit subclassification is for use with
appropriate categories in section 38.0, 38.1, 38.3, 38.5, 38.6,
and 38.8 according to site. Valid fourth-digits are in [brackets]
under each code.

0   unspecified
1   intracranial vessels
   Cerebral (anterior) (middle)
   Circle of Willis
   Posterior communicating artery
2   other vessels of head and neck
   Carotid artery (common) (external) (internal)
   Jugular vein (external) (internal)
3   upper limb vessels
   Axillary   Radial
   Brachial   Ulnar
4   aorta
5   other thoracic vessels
   Innominate   Subclavian
   Pulmonary (artery) (vein) Vena cava, superior
6   abdominal arteries
   Celiac   Mesenteric
   Gastric   Renal
   Hepatic   Splenic
   Iliac   Umbilical
> EXCLUDES   abdominal aorta (4)
7   abdominal veins
   Iliac   Splenic
   Portal   Vena cava (inferior)
   Renal
8   lower limb arteries
   Femoral (common) Popliteal
   (superficial)   Tibial
9   lower limb veins
   Femoral   Saphenous
   Popliteal   Tibial

Endarterectomy of Aortic Bifurcation

Aorta (shown sectioned)
Plaque
Femoral artery
Plaque removed

18 § √4ᵗʰ   38.0   Incision of vessel
[0-9]
   Embolectomy   Thrombectomy
> EXCLUDES   ►endovascular removal of obstruction
> from head and neck vessel(s)
> (39.74)◄
> puncture or catheterization of any:
> artery (38.91, 38.98)
> vein (38.92-38.95, 38.99)

AHA: 2Q, '98, 23; For code 38.08 and 38.09: 1Q, '03, 17

18 § √4ᵗʰ   38.1   Endarterectomy
[0-6,8]
   Endarterectomy with:
      embolectomy
      patch graft
      temporary bypass during procedure
      thrombectomy
   Code also any:
      number of vascular stents inserted (00.45-00.48)
      number of vessels treated (00.40-00.43)
      ►procedure on vessel bifurcation (00.44)◄

AHA: 1Q, '00, 16; 2Q, '99, 5; 2Q, '95, 16; For code 38.12: 1Q, '02, 10

DEF: Excision of tunica intima of artery to relieve arterial walls
thickened by plaque or chronic inflammation.

√4ᵗʰ   38.2   Diagnostic procedures on blood vessels
> EXCLUDES   adjunct vascular system procedures
> (00.40-00.43)

38.21   Biopsy of blood vessel
38.22   Percutaneous angioscopy
> EXCLUDES   angioscopy of eye (95.12)

DEF: Exam, with fiberoptic catheter inserted through peripheral artery to visualize inner lining of blood vessels.

**38.29   Other diagnostic procedures on blood
vessels**
> EXCLUDES   blood vessel thermography
> (88.86)
> circulatory monitoring (89.61-
> 89.69)
> contrast:
> angiocardiography (88.50-
> 88.58)
> arteriography (88.40-88.49)
> phlebography (88.60-88.67)
> impedance phlebography
> (88.68)
> peripheral vascular
> ultrasonography (88.77)
> plethysmogram (89.58)

AHA: 3Q, '00, 16; 1Q, '99, 7

18 § √4ᵗʰ   38.3   Resection of vessel with anastomosis
[0-9]
   Angiectomy
   Excision of:
      aneurysm (arteriovenous) } with anastomosis
      blood vessel (lesion)

DEF: Reconstruction and reconnection of vessel after partial
excision.

---

§ Requires fourth-digit. Valid digits are in [brackets] under each code. See category 38 for definitions.
18 Nonspecific OR procedure = 0

√3ʳᵈ
√4ᵗʰ   Additional Digit Required | Nonspecific OR Procedure | | Valid OR Procedure | | Non-OR Procedure | | Adjunct Code |

Operations on the Cardiovascular System

38.4–38.98

[18] §§ ✓4th **38.4**   **Resection of vessel with replacement**
[0-9]

    Angiectomy
    Excision of:
      aneurysm (arteriovenous) or   } with replacement
      blood vessel (lesion)

    ▶Partial resection with replacement◀
    EXCLUDES   *endovascular repair of aneurysm (39.71-39.79)*

Requires the use of one of the following fourth-digit
subclassifications to identify site:

0   unspecified site

1   intracranial vessels
    Cerebral (anterior) (middle)
    Circle of Willis
    Posterior communicating artery

2   other vessels of head and neck
    Carotid artery (common) (external) (internal)
    Jugular vein (external) (internal)

3   upper limb vessels
    Axillary   Radial
    Brachial   Ulnar

4   aorta, abdominal
    Code also any thoracic vessel involvement
      (thoracoabdominal procedure) (38.45)

5   thoracic vessel
    Aorta (thoracic)
    Innominate   Subclavian
    Pulmonary (artery) (vein)   Vena cava, superior
    Code also any abdominal aorta involvement
      (thoracoabdominal procedure) (38.44)

6   abdominal arteries
    Celiac   Mesenteric
    Gastric   Renal
    Hepatic   Splenic
    Iliac   Umbilical
    EXCLUDES   *abdominal aorta (4)*

7   abdominal veins
    Iliac   Splenic
    Portal   Vena cava (inferior)
    Renal

8   lower limb arteries
    Femoral (common) (superficial)
    Tibial

9   lower limb veins
    Femoral   Saphenous
    Popliteal   Tibial

AHA: 2Q, '99, 5, 6

DEF: Excision of aneurysm (arteriovenous): Excision and
replacement of segment of stretched or bulging blood vessel.
DEF: Excision of blood vessel (lesion): Excision and replacement of
segment of vessel containing lesion.

[18] § ✓4th **38.5**   **Ligation and stripping of varicose veins**
[0-3,5,7,9]   **EXCLUDES**   *ligation of varices:*
            esophageal (42.91)
            gastric (44.91)

AHA: For code 38.59: 2Q, '97, 7

DEF: Ligation of varicose veins: Typing off vein with thread or wire
to eliminate blood flow; stripping involves excising length of vein.

[18] § ✓4th **38.6**   **Other excision of vessels**
[0-9]

    Excision of blood vessel (lesion) NOS
    EXCLUDES   *excision of vessel for aortocoronary*
              bypass (36.10-36.14)
            excision with:
              anastomosis (38.30-38.39)
              graft replacement (38.40-38.49)
              implant (38.40-38.49)

AHA: 3Q, '90, 17

38.7   **Interruption of the vena cava**
    Insertion of implant or sieve in vena cava
    Ligation of vena cava (inferior) (superior)
    Plication of vena cava
    AHA: 2Q, '94, 9; S-O, '85, 5

DEF: Interruption of the blood flow through the venous heart vessels
to prevent clots from reaching the chambers of the heart by means
of implanting a sieve or implant, separating off a portion or by
narrowing the venous blood vessels.

Methods of Vessel Anastomoses

End-to-end   Side-to-side

Oblique cut   Fish mouth

Funnelization   End-to-side

[18] § ✓4th **38.8**   **Other surgical occlusion of vessels**
[0-9]

    Clamping
    Division
    Ligation   } of blood vessel
    Occlusion

    EXCLUDES   *adrenal vessels (07.43)*
            esophageal varices (42.91)
            gastric or duodenal vessel for ulcer
              (44.40-44.49)
            gastric varices (44.91)
            meningeal vessel (02.13)
            percutaneous transcatheter infusion
              embolization (99.29)
            spermatic vein for varicocele (63.1)
            surgical occlusion of vena cava (38.7)
            that for chemoembolization (99.25)
            that for control of (postoperative)
              hemorrhage:
              anus (49.95)
              bladder (57.93)
              following vascular procedure (39.41)
              nose (21.00-21.09)
              prostate (60.94)
              tonsil (28.7)
              thyroid vessel (06.92)

    AHA: 2Q, '90, 23; M-A, '87, 9; **For code 38.85:** 1Q, '03, 15;
         For code 38.86: 1Q, '05, 14; N-D, '87, 4

✓4th **38.9**   **Puncture of vessel**
    EXCLUDES   *that for circulatory monitoring*
              (89.60-89.69)

38.91   **Arterial catheterization**
    AHA: 1Q, '05, 14; 1Q, '97, 3; 1Q, '95, 3; 2Q, '91, 15; 2Q, '90, 23

38.92   **Umbilical vein catheterization**

38.93   **Venous catheterization, not elsewhere**
    classified
    EXCLUDES   *that for cardiac catheterization*
              (37.21-37.23)
              that for renal dialysis (38.95)

    AHA: 3Q, '00, 9; 2Q, '98, 24; 1Q, '96, 3; 2Q, '96, 15; 3Q, '91,
         13; 4Q, '90, 14; 2Q, '90, 24; 3Q, '88, 13

38.94   **Venous cutdown**
    DEF: Incision of vein to place needle or catheter.

38.95   **Venous catheterization for renal dialysis**
    EXCLUDES   *insertion of totally implantable*
              vascular access device
              [VAD] (86.07)

    AHA: 3Q, '98, 13; 2Q, '94, 11

38.98   **Other puncture of artery**
    EXCLUDES   *that for:*
              arteriography (88.40-88.49)
              coronary arteriography
               (88.55-88.57)

---

§   Requires fourth-digit. Valid digits are in [brackets] under each code. See category 38 for definitions.
§§ Requires fourth-digit. Valid digits are in [brackets] under each code. See subcategory 38.4 for definitions.
[18] Nonspecific OR procedure = 0

BI Bilateral Procedure   **NC** Non-covered Procedure   **LC** Limited Coverage Procedure   ▶◀ Revised Text   ● New Code   ▲ Revised Code Title

Typical Venous Cutdown

Vein mobilized, opened by oblique cut, catheter inserted

Distal vein tied

Saphenous vein (typical site) accessed by transverse incision

38.99   Other puncture of vein

Phlebotomy

> **EXCLUDES**   *that for:*
> *angiography (88.60-88.68)*
> *extracorporeal circulation (39.61, 50.92):*
> *injection or infusion of:*
> *sclerosing solution (39.92)*
> *therapeutic or prophylactic substance (99.11-99.29)*
> *perfusion (39.96, 39.97)*
> *phlebography (88.60-88.68)*
> *transfusion (99.01-99.09)*

AHA: 4Q, '94, 50; 1Q, '88, 11

√3rd 39   Other operations on vessels

> **EXCLUDES**   *those on coronary vessels (36.0-36.99)*

39.0   Systemic to pulmonary artery shunt

Descending aorta-pulmonary artery }
Left to right   } anastomosis
Subclavian-pulmonary   } (graft)

Code also cardiopulmonary bypass [extracorporeal circulation] [heart-lung machine] (39.61)

DEF: Descending aorta-pulmonary artery anastomosis (graft): Connection of descending main heart artery to pulmonary artery.

DEF: Left to right anastomosis (graft): Connection of systemic arterial blood vessel to venous pulmonary system.

DEF: Subclavian-pulmonary anastomosis (graft): Connection of subclavian artery to pulmonary artery

39.1   Intra-abdominal venous shunt

Anastomosis:
mesocaval
portacaval
portal vein to inferior vena cava
splenic and renal veins
transjugular intrahepatic portosystemic shunt [TIPS]

> **EXCLUDES**   *peritoneovenous shunt (54.94)*

AHA: 2Q, '02, 4; 4Q, '94, 50; 4Q, '93, 31; 2Q, '93, 8

DEF: Connection of two venous blood vessels within abdominal cavity.

√4th 39.2   Other shunt or vascular bypass

Code also pressurized treatment of venous bypass graft [conduit] with pharmaceutical substance, if performed (00.16)

DEF: Creation of supplemental blood flow to area with inadequate blood supply due to disease or injury of vessels.

39.21   Caval-pulmonary artery anastomosis

Code also cardiopulmonary bypass (39.61)

39.22   Aorta-subclavian-carotid bypass

Bypass (arterial):
aorta to carotid and brachial
aorta to subclavian and carotid
carotid to subclavian

39.23   Other intrathoracic vascular shunt or bypass

Intrathoracic (arterial) bypass graft NOS

> **EXCLUDES**   *coronary artery bypass (36.10-36.19)*

39.24   Aorta-renal bypass

39.25   Aorta-iliac-femoral bypass

Bypass: Bypass:
aortofemoral   aortopopliteal
aortoiliac   iliofemoral [iliac-femoral]
aortoiliac to popliteal

AHA: 1Q, '03, 16; 4Q, '90, 27; 1Q, '88, 10

39.26   Other intra-abdominal vascular shunt or bypass

Bypass:
aortoceliac
aortic-superior mesenteric
common hepatic-common iliac-renal
Intra-abdominal arterial bypass graft NOS

> **EXCLUDES**   *peritoneovenous shunt (54.94)*

39.27   Arteriovenostomy for renal dialysis

Anastomosis for renal dialysis
Formation of (peripheral) arteriovenous fistula for renal [kidney] dialysis
Code also any renal dialysis (39.95)

AHA: ▶1Q, '06, 10◀

39.28   Extracranial-intracranial (EC-IC) vascular bypass   **NC**

AHA: 2Q, '92, 7; 4Q, '91, 22

39.29   Other (peripheral) vascular shunt or bypass

Bypass (graft):
axillary-brachial
axillary-femoral [axillofemora] (superficial)
brachial
femoral-femoral
femoroperoneal
femoropopliteal (arteries)
femorotibial (anterior) (posterior)
popliteal
vascular NOS

> **EXCLUDES**   *peritoneovenous shunt (54.94)*

AHA: 1Q, '03, 17; 2Q, '02, 8; 1Q, '02, 13; S-O, '85, 13

√4th 39.3   Suture of vessel

Repair of laceration of blood vessel

> **EXCLUDES**   *any other vascular puncture closure device — omit code*
> *suture of aneurysm (39.52)*
> *that for control of hemorrhage (postoperative):*
> *anus (49.95)*
> *bladder (57.93)*
> *following vascular procedure (39.41)*
> *nose (21.00-21.09)*
> *prostate (60.94)*
> *tonsil (28.7)*

39.30   Suture of unspecified blood vessel

39.31   Suture of artery

39.32   Suture of vein

√4th 39.4   Revision of vascular procedure

39.41   Control of hemorrhage following vascular surgery

> **EXCLUDES**   *that for control of hemorrhage (postoperative):*
> *anus (49.95)*
> *bladder (57.93)*
> *nose (21.00-21.09)*
> *prostate (60.94)*
> *tonsil (28.7)*

39.42   Revision of arteriovenous shunt for renal dialysis

Conversion of renal dialysis:
end-to-end anastomosis to end-to-side
end-to-side anastomosis to end-to-end
vessel-to-vessel cannula to arteriovenous shunt
Removal of old arteriovenous shunt and creation of new shunt

> **EXCLUDES**   *replacement of vessel-to-vessel cannula (39.94)*

AHA: 2Q, '94, 15; 4Q, '93, 33

39.43   Removal of arteriovenous shunt for renal dialysis

> **EXCLUDES**   *that with replacement [revision] of shunt (39.42)*

√3rd
√4th Additional Digit Required   Nonspecific OR Procedure   Valid OR Procedure   Non-OR Procedure   Adjunct Code

Operations on the Cardiovascular System

39.49–39.62

39.49   **Other revision of vascular procedure**
Declotting (graft)
Revision of:
   anastomosis of blood vessel
   vascular procedure (previous)
AHA: 2Q, '98, 17; 1Q, '97, 3; 2Q, '94, 15
DEF: Declotting (graft): Removal of clot from graft.

✓4ᵗʰ **39.5**   **Other repair of vessels**

39.50   **Angioplasty or atherectomy of other non-coronary vessel(s)**
Percutaneous transluminal angioplasty (PTA) of non-coronary vessels:
   lower extremity vessels
   mesenteric artery
   renal artery
   upper extremity vessels
Code also any:
   injection or infusion of thrombolytic agent (99.10)
   insertion of non-coronary stent(s) or stent grafts(s) (39.90)
   number of vascular stents inserted (00.45-00.48)
   number of vessels treated (00.40-00.43)
   ▶procedure on vessel bifurcation (00.44)◀
   EXCLUDES   *percutaneous angioplasty or atherectomy of precerebral or cerebral vessel(s) (00.61-00.62)*
AHA: 3Q, '03, 10; 1Q, '02, 13; 2Q, '01, 23; 2Q, '00, 10; 1Q, '00, 12; 2Q, '98, 17; 1Q, '97, 3; 4Q, '96, 63; 4Q, '95, 66

39.51   **Clipping of aneurysm**
   EXCLUDES   *clipping of arteriovenous fistula (39.53)*

39.52   **Other repair of aneurysm**
Repair of aneurysm by:
   coagulation   wiring
   electrocoagulation   wrapping
   filipuncture
   methyl methacrylate
   suture
   EXCLUDES   *endovascular repair of aneurysm (39.71-39.79)*
     re-entry operation (aorta) (39.54)
     that with:
       graft replacement (38.40-38.49)
       resection (38.30-38.49, 38.60-38.69)
AHA: 3Q, '02, 25, 26; 1Q, '99, 15, 16, 17; 1Q, '88, 10
DEF: Application of device in abnormally stretched blood vessel to prevent movement of material collected in vessel.
DEF: Repair of aneurysm by: Coagulation: Clotting or solidifying. Electrocoagulation: Electrically produced clotting. Filipuncture: Insertion of wire or thread. Methyl methacrylate: Injection or insertion of plastic material. Suture: Stitching. Wiring: Insertion of wire. Wrapping: Compression.

39.53   **Repair of arteriovenous fistula**
Embolization of carotid cavernous fistula
Repair of arteriovenous fistula by:
   clipping
   coagulation
   ligation and division
   EXCLUDES   *repair of:*
     arteriovenous shunt for renal dialysis (39.42)
     head and neck vessels, endovascular approach (39.72)
     that with:
       graft replacement (38.40-38.49)
       resection (38.30-38.49, 38.60-38.69)
AHA: 1Q, '00, 8
DEF: Correction of arteriovenous fistula by application of clamps, causing coagulation or by tying off and dividing the connection.

39.54   **Re-entry operation (aorta)**
Fenestration of dissecting aneurysm of thoracic aorta
Code also cardiopulmonary bypass [extracorporeal circulation] [heart-lung machine] (39.61)
DEF: Re-entry operation: Creation of passage between stretched wall of the vessel and major arterial channel to heart.
DEF: Fenestration of dissecting aneurysm of thoracic aorta: Creation of passage between stretched arterial heart vessel and functional part of vessel.

39.55   **Reimplantation of aberrant renal vessel**
DEF: Reimplant of renal vessel into normal position.

39.56   **Repair of blood vessel with tissue patch graft**
   EXCLUDES   *that with resection (38.40-38.49)*
AHA: 1Q, '04, 16

39.57   **Repair of blood vessel with synthetic patch graft**
   EXCLUDES   *that with resection (38.40-38.49)*

39.58   **Repair of blood vessel with unspecified type of patch graft**
   EXCLUDES   *that with resection (38.40-38.49)*

39.59   **Other repair of vessel**
Aorticopulmonary window operation
Arterioplasty NOS
Construction of venous valves (peripheral)
Plication of vein (peripheral)
Reimplantation of artery
Code also cardiopulmonary bypass [extracorporeal circulation] [heart-lung machine] (39.61)
   EXCLUDES   *interruption of the vena cava (38.7)*
     reimplantation of renal artery (39.55)
     that with:
       graft (39.56-39.58)
       resection (38.30-38.49, 38.60-38.69)
AHA: 4Q, '93, 31; 2Q, '89, 17; N-D, '86, 8; S-O, '85, 5; M-A, '85, 15
DEF: Aorticopulmonary window operation: Repair of abnormal opening between major heart arterial vessel above valves and pulmonary artery.
DEF: Construction of venous valves (peripheral): Reconstruction of valves within peripheral veins.
DEF: Plication of vein (peripheral): Shortening of peripheral vein.
DEF: Reimplantation of artery: Reinsertion of artery into its normal position.

✓4ᵗʰ **39.6**   **Extracorporeal circulation and procedures auxiliary to heart surgery**
AHA: 1Q, '95, 5

39.61   **Extracorporeal circulation auxiliary to open heart surgery**
Artificial heart and lung
Cardiopulmonary bypass
Pump oxygenator
   EXCLUDES   *extracorporeal hepatic assistance (50.92)*
     extracorporeal membrane oxygenation [ECMO] (39.65)
     hemodialysis (39.95)
     percutaneous cardiopulmonary bypass (39.66)
AHA: 1Q, '04, 16; 3Q, '02, 5; 4Q, '97, 55; 3Q, '97, 14; 2Q, '97, 8; 2Q, '90, 24

39.62   **Hypothermia (systemic) incidental to open heart surgery**

BI Bilateral Procedure   **NC** Non-covered Procedure   **LC** Limited Coverage Procedure   ▶◀ Revised Text   ● New Code   ▲ Revised Code Title

39.63   Cardioplegia

Arrest: Arrest:
  anoxic   circulatory

DEF: Purposely inducing electromechanical cardiac arrest.

39.64   Intraoperative cardiac pacemaker

Temporary pacemaker used during and immediately following cardiac surgery

AHA: 1Q, '89, 2; M-J, '87, 3

39.65   Extracorporeal membrane oxygenation [ECMO]

EXCLUDES   extracorporeal circulation auxiliary to open heart surgery (39.61)
percutaneous cardiopulmonary bypass (39.66)

AHA: 2Q, '90, 23; 2Q, '89, 17; 4Q, '88, 5

DEF: Creation of closed-chest, heart-lung bypass or Bard cardiopulmonary assist system with tube insertion.

39.66   Percutaneous cardiopulmonary bypass

Closed chest

EXCLUDES   extracorporeal circulation auxiliary to open heart surgery (39.61)
extracorporeal hepatic assistance (50.92)
extracorporeal membrane oxygenation [ECMO] (39.65)
hemodialysis (39.95)

AHA: 3Q, '96, 11

DEF: Use of mechanical pump system to oxygenate and pump blood throughout the body via catheter in the femoral artery and vein.

✓4ᵗʰ **39.7   Endovascular repair of vessel**

Endoluminal repair

EXCLUDES   angioplasty or atherectomy of other non-coronary vessel(s) (39.50)
insertion of non-drug-eluting peripheral vessel stent(s) (39.90)
other repair of aneurysm (39.52)
percutaneous insertion of carotid artery stent(s) (00.63)
percutaneous insertion of intracranial stent(s) (00.65)
percutaneous insertion of other precerebral artery stent(s) (00.64)
resection of abdominal aorta with replacement (38.44)
resection of lower limb arteries with replacement (38.48)
resection of thoracic aorta with replacement (38.45)
resection of upper limb vessels with replacement (38.43)

39.71   Endovascular implantation of graft in abdominal aorta

Endovascular repair of abdominal aortic aneurysm with graft
Stent graft(s)

AHA: 1Q, '02, 13; 4Q, '00, 63, 64

DEF: Replacement of a section of abdominal aorta with mesh graft; via catheters inserted through femoral arteries.

Endovascular Repair of Abdominal Aortic Aneurysm

39.72   Endovascular repair or occlusion of head and neck vessels

Coil embolization or occlusion
Endograft(s)
Endovascular graft(s)
Liquid tissue adhesive (glue) embolization or occlusion
Other implant or substance for repair, embolization or occlusion
That for repair of aneurysm, arteriovenous malformation [AVM] or fistula

EXCLUDES ▶ mechanical thrombectomy of pre-cerebral and cerebral vessels (39.74)◀

AHA: 4Q, '02, 103

DEF: Coil embolization or occlusion: Utilizing x-ray guidance a neuro-microcatheter is guided from entry in the femoral artery in the groin to the site of the aneurysm of the head and neck vessels for delivery of micro-coils that stop blood flow to the arteriovenous malfomation (AVM).

39.73   Endovascular implantation of graft in thoracic aorta

Endograft(s)
Endovascular graft(s)
Endovascular repair of defect of thoracic aorta with graft(s) or device(s)
Stent graft(s) or device(s)
That for repair of aneurysm, dissection, or injury

EXCLUDES   fenestration of dissecting aneurysm of thoracic aorta (39.54)

AHA: 4Q, '05, 120

DEF: Intravascular transcatheter deployment of an expanding stent-graft for repair of thoracic aortic aneurysm, performed without opening the chest.

39.74   Endovascular removal of obstruction from head and neck vessel(s)

Endovascular embolectomy
Endovascular thrombectomy of pre-cerebral and cerebral vessels
Mechanical embolectomy or thrombectomy
Code also:
any injection or infusion of thrombolytic agent (99.10)
number of vessels treated (00.40-00.43)
procedure on vessel bifurcation (00.44)

EXCLUDES   endarterectomy of intracranial vessels and other vessels of head and neck (38.11-38.12)
occlusive endovascular repair of head or neck vessels (39.72)
open embolectomy or thrombectomy (38.01-38.02)

External Arteriovenous Shunt

Cephalic vein

Radial artery

39.79   **Other endovascular repair (of aneurysm) of other vessels**

Coil embolization or occlusion
Endograft(s)
Endovascular graft(s)
Liquid tissue adhesive (glue) embolization or occlusion
Other implant or substance for repair, embolization or occlusion

> EXCLUDES   *endovascular implantation of graft in thoracic aorta (39.73)*
> *endovascular repair or occlusion of head and neck vessels (39.72)*
> *insertion of drug-eluting peripheral vessel stent(s) (00.55)*
> *insertion of non-drug-eluting peripheral vessel stent(s) (for other than aneurysm repair) (39.90)*
> *non-endovascular repair of arteriovenous fistula (39.53)*
> *other surgical occlusion of vessels–see category 38.8*
> *percutaneous transcatheter infusion (99.29)*
> *transcatheter embolization for gastric or duodenal bleeding (44.44)*

AHA: 4Q, '02, 103; 3Q, '01, 17,18; 4Q, '00, 64

39.8   **Operations on carotid body and other vascular bodies**

Chemodectomy   Glomectomy, carotid
Denervation of: Implantation into carotid body:
   aortic body   electronic stimulator
   carotid body   pacemaker

> EXCLUDES   *excision of glomus jugulare (20.51)*

DEF: Chemodectomy: Removal of a chemoreceptor vascular body.
DEF: Denervation of aortic body: Destruction of nerves attending the major heart blood vessels.
DEF: Destruction of carotid body: Destruction of nerves of carotid artery.
DEF: Glomectomy, carotid: Removal of the carotid artery framework.

√4ᵗʰ   **39.9**   **Other operations on vessels**

39.90   **Insertion of non-drug-eluting peripheral vessel stent(s)**

Bare stent(s)
Bonded stent(s)
Drug-coated stent(s), i.e., heparin coated
Endograft(s)
Endovascular graft(s)
Endovascular recanalization techniques
Stent graft(s)
Code also any:
   non-coronary angioplasty or atherectomy (39.50)
   number of vascular stents inserted (00.45-00.48)
   number of vessels treated (00.40-00.43)
   ▶procedure on vessel bifurcation (00.44)◀

> EXCLUDES   *insertion of drug-eluting, peripheral vessel stent(s) (00.55)*
> *percutaneous insertion of carotid artery stent(s) (00.63)*
> *percutaneous insertion of intracranial stent(s) (00.65)*
> *percutaneous insertion of other precerebral artery stent(s) (00.64)*
> *that for aneurysm repair (39.71-39.79)*

AHA: 4Q, '02, 101; 1Q, '00, 12; 4Q, '96, 63

39.91   **Freeing of vessel**

Dissection and freeing of adherent tissue:
   artery-vein-nerve bundle
   vascular bundle

AHA: 3Q, '02, 12

39.92   **Injection of sclerosing agent into vein**

> EXCLUDES   *injection:*
> *esophageal varices (42.33)*
> *hemorrhoids (49.42)*

AHA: 2Q, '92, 17

39.93   **Insertion of vessel-to-vessel cannula**

Formation of:
   arteriovenous: } by external
     fistula
     shunt   cannula
Code also any renal dialysis (39.95)

AHA: 3Q, '88, 13; S-O, '85, 5 & 12

39.94   **Replacement of vessel-to-vessel cannula**

Revision of vessel-to-vessel cannula

39.95   **Hemodialysis**

Artificial kidney   Hemodiafiltration
Hemofiltration   Renal dialysis

> EXCLUDES   *peritoneal dialysis (54.98)*

AHA: 1Q, '04, 22; 4Q, '03, 111; 2Q, '01, 2-14; 4Q, '00, 40; 2Q, '98, 20; S-O, '86, 11

DEF: Filtration process to treat acute and chronic renal failure by eliminating toxic end products of nitrogen metabolism from blood.

39.96   **Total body perfusion**

Code also substance perfused (99.21-99.29)

39.97   **Other perfusion**

Perfusion NOS   Perfusion, local
Perfusion, local   [regional] of:
   [regional] of: lower limb
   carotid artery   neck
   coronary artery   upper limb
   head
Code also substance perfused (99.21-99.29)

> EXCLUDES   *perfusion of:*
> *kidney (55.95)*
> *large intestine (46.96)*
> *liver (50.93)*
> *small intestine (46.95)*

AHA: 3Q, '96, 11

39.98   **Control of hemorrhage, not otherwise specified**

Angiotripsy
Control of postoperative hemorrhage NOS
Venotripsy

> EXCLUDES   *control of hemorrhage (postoperative):*
> *anus (49.95)*
> *bladder (57.93)*
> *following vascular procedure (39.41)*
> *nose (21.00-21.09)*
> *prostate (60.94)*
> *tonsil (28.7)*
> *that by:*
> *ligation (38.80-38.89)*
> *suture (39.30-39.32)*

DEF: Angiotripsy: Clamping of tissue to stop arterial blood flow.

DEF: Venotripsy: Clamping of tissue to stop venous blood flow.

39.99   **Other operations on vessels**

> EXCLUDES   *injection or infusion of therapeutic or prophylactic substance (99.11-99.29)*
> *transfusion of blood and blood components (99.01-99.09)*

AHA: 1Q, '89, 11

B1 Bilateral Procedure   NC Non-covered Procedure   LC Limited Coverage Procedure   ▶◀ Revised Text   ● New Code   ▲ Revised Code Title

8. OPERATIONS ON THE HEMIC AND LYMPHATIC SYSTEMS (40-41)

√3rd **40 Operations on lymphatic system**

40.0 Incision of lymphatic structures

√4th **40.1 Diagnostic procedures on lymphatic structures**

40.11 Biopsy of lymphatic structure

40.19 Other diagnostic procedures on lymphatic structures

> EXCLUDES *lymphangiogram:*
> *abdominal (88.04)*
> *cervical (87.08)*
> *intrathoracic (87.34)*
> *lower limb (88.36)*
> *upper limb (88.34)*
> *microscopic examination of*
> *specimen (90.71-90.79)*
> *radioisotope scan (92.16)*
> *thermography (88.89)*

√4th **40.2 Simple excision of lymphatic structure**

> EXCLUDES *biopsy of lymphatic structure (40.11)*

DEF: Removal of lymphatic structure only.

40.21 Excision of deep cervical lymph node

AHA: 4Q, '99, 16

40.22 Excision of internal mammary lymph node

40.23 Excision of axillary lymph node

AHA: 2Q, '02, 7

40.24 Excision of inguinal lymph node

40.29 Simple excision of other lymphatic structure

> Excision of:
> cystic hygroma
> lymphangioma
> Simple lymphadenectomy

AHA: 1Q, '99, 6

DEF: Lymphangioma: Removal of benign congenital lymphatic malformation.

DEF: Simple lymphadenectomy: Removal of lymph node.

40.3 Regional lymph node excision

> Extended regional lymph node excision
> Regional lymph node excision with excision of lymphatic drainage area including skin, subcutaneous tissue, and fat

AHA: 2Q, '92, 7

DEF: Extended regional lymph node excision: Removal of lymph node group, including area around nodes.

√4th **40.4 Radical excision of cervical lymph nodes**

> Resection of cervical lymph nodes down to muscle and deep fascia
> EXCLUDES *that associated with radical laryngectomy (30.4)*

40.40 Radical neck dissection, not otherwise specified

40.41 Radical neck dissection, unilateral

AHA: ▶2Q, '05, 8;◀ 2Q, '99, 6

DEF: Dissection, total, of cervical lymph nodes on one side of neck.

40.42 Radical neck dissection, bilateral

DEF: Dissection, total, of cervical lymph nodes on both sides of neck.

√4th **40.5 Radical excision of other lymph nodes**

> EXCLUDES *that associated with radical mastectomy (85.45-85.48)*

40.50 Radical excision of lymph nodes, not otherwise specified

> Radical (lymph) node dissection NOS

40.51 Radical excision of axillary lymph nodes

40.52 Radical excision of periaortic lymph nodes

40.53 Radical excision of iliac lymph nodes

40.54 Radical groin dissection

40.59 Radical excision of other lymph nodes

> EXCLUDES *radical neck dissection (40.40-40.42)*

√4th **40.6 Operations on thoracic duct**

40.61 Cannulation of thoracic duct

DEF: Placement of cannula in main lymphatic duct of chest.

40.62 Fistulization of thoracic duct

DEF: Creation of passage in main lymphatic duct of chest.

40.63 Closure of fistula of thoracic duct

DEF: Closure of fistula in main lymphatic duct of chest.

40.64 Ligation of thoracic duct

DEF: Tying off main lymphatic duct of chest.

40.69 Other operations on thoracic duct

40.9 Other operations on lymphatic structures

> Anastomosis
> Dilation
> Ligation
> Obliteration   of peripheral
> Reconstruction   lymphatics
> Repair
> Transplantation

> Correction of lymphedema of limb, NOS
> EXCLUDES *reduction of elephantiasis of scrotum (61.3)*

√3rd **41 Operations on bone marrow and spleen**

√4th **41.0 Bone marrow or hematopoietic stem cell transplant**

> Note: To report donor source — see codes 00.91-00.93
> EXCLUDES *aspiration of bone marrow from donor (41.91)*

AHA: 4Q, '00, 64; 1Q, '91, 3; 4Q, '91, 26

41.00 Bone marrow transplant, not otherwise specified

[19] **41.01 Autologous bone marrow transplant without purging** NC

> EXCLUDES *that with purging (41.09)*

DEF: Transplant of patient's own bone marrow.

[20] **41.02 Allogeneic bone marrow transplant with purging** NC

> Allograft of bone marrow with in vitro removal (purging) of T-cells

DEF: Transplant of bone marrow from donor to patient after donor marrow purged of undesirable cells.

[20] **41.03 Allogeneic bone marrow transplant without purging** NC

> Allograft of bone marrow NOS

[19] **41.04 Autologous hematopoietic stem cell transplant without purging** NC

> EXCLUDES *that with purging (41.07)*

AHA: 4Q, '94, 52

[20] **41.05 Allogeneic hematopoietic stem cell transplant without purging** NC

> EXCLUDES *that with purging (41.08)*

AHA: 4Q, '97, 55

---

[19] Non-covered procedure only when the following diagnoses are present as either principal or secondary diagnosis: 204.00, 205.00, 205.10, 205.11, 206.00, 207.00, 208.00

[20] Non-covered procedure only when the following diagnoses are present as either principal or secondary diagnosis: 203.00, 203.01

√3rd
√4th Additional Digit Required   Nonspecific OR Procedure   Valid OR Procedure   Non-OR Procedure   Adjunct Code

Operations on the Hemic and Lymphatic Systems

40–41.05

Partial Splenectomy

Total Splenectomy

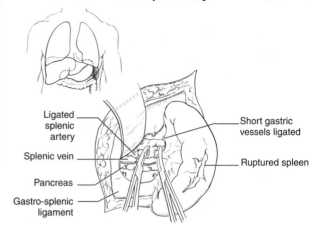

41.06   Cord blood stem cell transplant
AHA: 4Q, '97, 56

[19] **41.07   Autologous hematopoietic stem cell transplant with purging**   NC
Cell depletion

[20] **41.08   Allogeneic hematopoietic stem cell transplant with purging**   NC
Cell depletion

[19] **41.09   Autologous bone marrow transplant with purging**   NC
With extracorporeal purging of malignant cells from marrow
Cell depletion

41.1   Puncture of spleen
EXCLUDES   aspiration biopsy of spleen (41.32)

41.2   Splenotomy

✓4th **41.3   Diagnostic procedures on bone marrow and spleen**

41.31   Biopsy of bone marrow

41.32   Closed [aspiration] [percutaneous] biopsy of spleen
Needle biopsy of spleen

41.33   Open biopsy of spleen

41.38   Other diagnostic procedures on bone marrow
EXCLUDES   microscopic examination of specimen from bone marrow (90.61-90.69)
radioisotope scan (92.05)

41.39   Other diagnostic procedures on spleen
EXCLUDES   microscopic examination of specimen from spleen (90.61-90.69)
radioisotope scan (92.05)

✓4th **41.4   Excision or destruction of lesion or tissue of spleen**
Code also any application or administration of an adhesion barrier substance (99.77)
EXCLUDES   excision of accessory spleen (41.93)

41.41   Marsupialization of splenic cyst
DEF: Incision of cyst of spleen with edges sutured open to create pouch.

41.42   Excision of lesion or tissue of spleen
EXCLUDES   biopsy of spleen (41.32-41.33)

41.43   Partial splenectomy
DEF: Removal of spleen, partial.

41.5   Total splenectomy
Splenectomy NOS
Code also any application or administration of an adhesion barrier substance (99.77)

✓4th **41.9   Other operations on spleen and bone marrow**
Code also any application or administration of an adhesion barrier substance (99.77)

41.91   Aspiration of bone marrow from donor for transplant
EXCLUDES   biopsy of bone marrow (41.31)
AHA: 1Q, '91, 3

41.92   Injection into bone marrow
EXCLUDES   bone marrow transplant (41.00-41.03)
AHA: 3Q, '96, 17

41.93   Excision of accessory spleen

41.94   Transplantation of spleen

41.95   Repair and plastic operations on spleen

41.98   Other operations on bone marrow

41.99   Other operations on spleen

---

[19] Non-covered procedure only when the following diagnoses are present as either principal or secondary diagnosis: 204.00, 205.00, 205.10, 205.11, 206.00, 207.00, 208.00
[20] Non-covered procedure only when the following diagnoses are present as either principal or secondary diagnosis: 203.00, 203.01

B1 Bilateral Procedure   NC Non-covered Procedure   LC Limited Coverage Procedure   ▶◀ Revised Text   ● New Code   ▲ Revised Code Title

120 — Volume 3   2007 ICD•9•CM

9. OPERATIONS ON THE DIGESTIVE SYSTEM (42-54)

√3rd **42 Operations on esophagus**

√4th **42.0 Esophagotomy**

42.01 Incision of esophageal web

DEF: Cutting into congenital esophageal membrane.

42.09 Other incision of esophagus

Esophagotomy NOS

EXCLUDES   esophagomyotomy (42.7)
esophagostomy (42.10-42.19)

√4th **42.1 Esophagostomy**

42.10 Esophagostomy, not otherwise specified

42.11 Cervical esophagostomy

DEF: Creation of opening into upper region of esophagus.

42.12 Exteriorization of esophageal pouch

DEF: Transfer of section of esophageal pouch to exterior of the body.

42.19 Other external fistulization of esophagus

Thoracic esophagostomy
Code also any resection (42.40-42.42)

√4th **42.2 Diagnostic procedures on esophagus**

42.21 Operative esophagoscopy by incision

DEF: Esophageal examination with an endoscope through incision.

42.22 Esophagoscopy through artificial stoma

EXCLUDES   that with biopsy (42.24)

42.23 Other esophagoscopy

EXCLUDES   that with biopsy (42.24)

AHA: 1Q, '00, 20; 3Q, '98, 11

42.24 Closed [endoscopic] biopsy of esophagus

Brushing or washing for specimen collection
Esophagoscopy with biopsy
Suction biopsy of the esophagus

EXCLUDES   esophagogastroduodenoscopy [EGD] with closed biopsy (45.16)

DEF: Scope passed through mouth and throat to obtain biopsy specimen, usually by brushing and swabbing.

42.25 Open biopsy of esophagus

42.29 Other diagnostic procedures on esophagus

EXCLUDES   barium swallow (87.61)
esophageal manometry (89.32)
microscopic examination of specimen from esophagus (90.81-90.89)

AHA: 3Q, '96, 12

√4th **42.3 Local excision or destruction of lesion or tissue of esophagus**

42.31 Local excision of esophageal diverticulum

42.32 Local excision of other lesion or tissue of esophagus

EXCLUDES   biopsy of esophagus (42.24-42.25)
esophageal fistulectomy (42.84)

42.33 Endoscopic excision or destruction of lesion or tissue of esophagus

Ablation of esophageal neoplasm
Control of esophageal bleeding
Esophageal polypectomy   } by endoscopic approach
Esophageal varices
Injection of esophageal varices

EXCLUDES   biopsy of esophagus (42.24-42.25)
fistulectomy (42.84)
open ligation of esophageal varices (42.91)

42.39 Other destruction of lesion or tissue of esophagus

EXCLUDES   that by endoscopic approach (42.33)

√4th **42.4 Excision of esophagus**

EXCLUDES   esophagogastrectomy NOS (43.99)

42.40 Esophagectomy, not otherwise specified

42.41 Partial esophagectomy

Code also any synchronous:
anastomosis other than end-to-end (42.51-42.69)
esophagostomy (42.10-42.19)
gastrostomy (43.11-43.19)

DEF: Surgical removal of any part of esophagus.

42.42 Total esophagectomy

Code also any synchronous:
gastrostomy (43.11-43.19)
interposition or anastomosis other than end-to-end (42.51-42.69)

EXCLUDES   esophagogastrectomy (43.99)

AHA: 4Q, '88, 11

DEF: Surgical removal of entire esophagus.

√4th **42.5 Intrathoracic anastomosis of esophagus**

Code also any synchronous:
esophagectomy (42.40-42.42)
gastrostomy (43.1)

DEF: Connection of esophagus to conduit within chest.

42.51 Intrathoracic esophagoesophagostomy

DEF: Connection of both ends of esophagus within chest cavity.

42.52 Intrathoracic esophagogastrostomy

DEF: Connection of esophagus to stomach within chest; follows esophagogastrectomy.

42.53 Intrathoracic esophageal anastomosis with interposition of small bowel

42.54 Other intrathoracic esophagoenterostomy

Anastomosis of esophagus to intestinal segment NOS

42.55 Intrathoracic esophageal anastomosis with interposition of colon

42.56 Other intrathoracic esophagocolostomy

Esophagocolostomy NOS

42.58 Intrathoracic esophageal anastomosis with other interposition

Construction of artificial esophagus
Retrosternal formation of reversed gastric tube

DEF: Construction of artificial esophagus: Creation of artificial esophagus.

DEF: Retrosternal anastomosis of reversed gastric tube: Formation of gastric tube behind breastbone.

Operations on the Digestive System

42.59–43.5

42.59   **Other intrathoracic anastomosis of esophagus**

AHA: 4Q, '88, 11

√4ᵗʰ **42.6**   **Antesternal anastomosis of esophagus**

Code also any synchronous:
esophagectomy (42.40-42.42)
gastrostomy (43.1)

42.61   **Antesternal esophagoesophagostomy**

42.62   **Antesternal esophagogastrostomy**

42.63   **Antesternal esophageal anastomosis with interposition of small bowel**

42.64   **Other antesternal esophagoenterostomy**

Antethoracic:
esophagoenterostomy
esophagoileostomy
esophagojejunostomy

42.65   **Antesternal esophageal anastomosis with interposition of colon**

DEF: Connection of esophagus with colon segment.

42.66   **Other antesternal esophagocolostomy**

Antethoracic esophagocolostomy

42.68   **Other antesternal esophageal anastomosis with interposition**

42.69   **Other antesternal anastomosis of esophagus**

42.7   **Esophagomyotomy**

DEF: Division of esophageal muscle, usually distal.

√4ᵗʰ **42.8**   **Other repair of esophagus**

42.81   **Insertion of permanent tube into esophagus**

AHA: 1Q, '97, 15

42.82   **Suture of laceration of esophagus**

42.83   **Closure of esophagostomy**

42.84   **Repair of esophageal fistula, not elsewhere classified**

EXCLUDES   repair of fistula:
bronchoesophageal (33.42)
esophagopleurocutaneous (34.73)
pharyngoesophageal (29.53)
tracheoesophageal (31.73)

42.85   **Repair of esophageal stricture**

42.86   **Production of subcutaneous tunnel without esophageal anastomosis**

DEF: Surgical formation of esophageal passage, without cutting, and reconnection.

42.87   **Other graft of esophagus**

EXCLUDES   antesternal esophageal
anastomosis with
interposition of:
colon (42.65)
small bowel (42.63)
antesternal esophageal
anastomosis with other
interposition (42.68)
intrathoracic esophageal
anastomosis with
interposition of:
colon (42.55)
small bowel (42.53)
intrathoracic esophageal
anastomosis with other
interposition (42.58)

42.89   **Other repair of esophagus**

√4ᵗʰ **42.9**   **Other operations on esophagus**

42.91   **Ligation of esophageal varices**

EXCLUDES   that by endoscopic approach (42.33)

DEF: Destruction of dilated veins by suture strangulation.

42.92   **Dilation of esophagus**

Dilation of cardiac sphincter

EXCLUDES   intubation of esophagus (96.03, 96.06-96.08)

DEF: Passing of balloon or hydrostatic dilators through esophagus to enlarge esophagus and relieve obstruction.

42.99   **Other**

EXCLUDES   insertion of Sengstaken tube (96.06)
intubation of esophagus (96.03, 96.06-96.08)
removal of intraluminal foreign
body from esophagus
without incision (98.02)
tamponade of esophagus (96.06)

√3ʳᵈ **43**   **Incision and excision of stomach**

Code also any application or administration of an adhesion barrier substance (99.77)

43.0   **Gastrotomy**

EXCLUDES   gastrostomy (43.11-43.19)
that for control of hemorrhage (44.49)

AHA: 3Q, '89, 14

√4ᵗʰ **43.1**   **Gastrostomy**

AHA: S-O, '85, 5

43.11   **Percutaneous [endoscopic] gastrostomy [PEG]**

Percutaneous transabdominal gastrostomy

DEF: Endoscopic positioning of tube through abdominal wall into stomach.

43.19   **Other gastrostomy**

EXCLUDES   percutaneous [endoscopic]
gastrostomy [PEG]
(43.11)

AHA: 1Q, '92, 14; 3Q, '89, 14

43.3   **Pyloromyotomy**

DEF: Cutting into longitudinal and circular muscular membrane between stomach and small intestine.

√4ᵗʰ **43.4**   **Local excision or destruction of lesion or tissue of stomach**

43.41   **Endoscopic excision or destruction of lesion or tissue of stomach**

Gastric polypectomy by endoscopic approach
Gastric varices by endoscopic approach

EXCLUDES   biopsy of stomach (44.14-44.15)
control of hemorrhage (44.43)
open ligation of gastric varices (44.91)

AHA: 3Q, '96, 10

43.42   **Local excision of other lesion or tissue of stomach**

EXCLUDES   biopsy of stomach (44.14-44.15)
gastric fistulectomy (44.62-44.63)
partial gastrectomy (43.5-43.89)

43.49   **Other destruction of lesion or tissue of stomach**

EXCLUDES   that by endoscopic approach (43.41)

AHA: N-D, '87, 5; S-O, '85, 6

43.5   **Partial gastrectomy with anastomosis to esophagus**

Proximal gastrectomy

BI Bilateral Procedure   NC Non-covered Procedure   LC Limited Coverage Procedure   ▶◀ Revised Text   ● New Code   ▲ Revised Code Title

Biliopancreatic Diversion Without Duodenal Switch

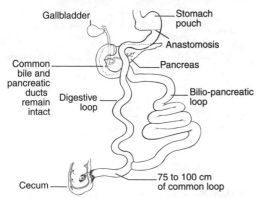

Partial Gastrectomy with Anastomosis to Duodenum

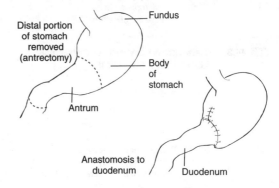

43.6   **Partial gastrectomy with anastomosis to duodenum**
Billroth I operation   Gastropylorectomy
Distal gastrectomy

43.7   **Partial gastrectomy with anastomosis to jejunum**
Billroth II operation
AHA: 3Q, '03, 7

✓4th **43.8**   **Other partial gastrectomy**
    43.81   **Partial gastrectomy with jejunal transposition**
       Henley jejunal transposition operation
       Code also any synchronous intestinal resection (45.51)
    43.89   **Other**
       Partial gastrectomy with bypass gastrogastrostomy
       Sleeve resection of stomach
AHA: 3Q, '03, 6-8

✓4th **43.9**   **Total gastrectomy**
    43.91   **Total gastrectomy with intestinal interposition**
    43.99   **Other total gastrectomy**
       Complete gastroduodenectomy
       Esophagoduodenostomy with complete gastrectomy
       Esophagogastrectomy NOS
       Esophagojejunostomy with complete gastrectomy
       Radical gastrectomy

✓3rd **44**   **Other operations on stomach**
Code also any application or administration of an adhesion barrier substance (99.77)

✓4th **44.0**   **Vagotomy**
    44.00   **Vagotomy, not otherwise specified**
       Division of vagus nerve NOS
       DEF: Cutting of vagus nerve to reduce acid production.
    44.01   **Truncal vagotomy**
       DEF: Surgical removal of vagus nerve segment near stomach branches.

44.02   **Highly selective vagotomy**
Parietal cell vagotomy
Selective proximal vagotomy
DEF: Cutting select gastric branches of vagus nerve to reduce acid production and preserve other nerve functions.

44.03   **Other selective vagotomy**

✓4th **44.1**   **Diagnostic procedures on stomach**
    44.11   **Transabdominal gastroscopy**
       Intraoperative gastroscopy
       EXCLUDES   *that with biopsy (44.14)*
    44.12   **Gastroscopy through artificial stoma**
       EXCLUDES   *that with biopsy (44.14)*
    44.13   **Other gastroscopy**
       EXCLUDES   *that with biopsy (44.14)*
       AHA: 1Q, '88, 15; N-D, '87, 5
    44.14   **Closed [endoscopic] biopsy of stomach**
       Brushing or washing for specimen collection
       EXCLUDES   *esophagogastroduodenoscopy [EGD] with closed biopsy (45.16)*
       AHA: 1Q, '88, 15; N-D, '87, 5
    44.15   **Open biopsy of stomach**
    44.19   **Other diagnostic procedures on stomach**
       EXCLUDES   *gastric lavage (96.33)*
               microscopic examination of specimen from stomach (90.81-90.89)
               upper GI series (87.62)

✓4th **44.2**   **Pyloroplasty**
    44.21   **Dilation of pylorus by incision**
       DEF: Cutting and suturing pylorus to relieve obstruction.
    44.22   **Endoscopic dilation of pylorus**
       Dilation with balloon endoscope
       Endoscopic dilation of gastrojejunostomy site
       AHA: 2Q, '01, 17

Biliopancreatic Diversion with Duodenal Switch

Types of Vagotomy Procedures

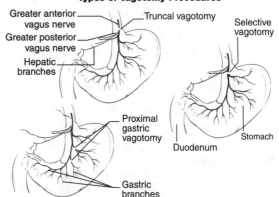

✓3rd ✓4th Additional Digit Required   Nonspecific OR Procedure   Valid OR Procedure   Non-OR Procedure   Adjunct Code

Operations on the Digestive System

44.29–44.69

44.29   Other pyloroplasty
Pyloroplasty NOS
Revision of pylorus
AHA: 3Q, '99, 3

✓4ᵗʰ **44.3   Gastroenterostomy without gastrectomy**
44.31   High gastric bypass
Printen and Mason gastric bypass
AHA: M-J, '85, 17

DEF: Connection of middle part of small intestine to upper stomach to divert food passage from upper intestine.

44.32   Percutaneous [endoscopic] gastrojejunostomy
Endoscopic conversion of gastrostomy to jejunostomy
DEF: Percutaneous placement of a thin feeding tube through a gastrostomy tube and then pulling the tube into the proximal end of the jejunum.

44.38   Laparoscopic gastroenterostomy
Bypass:
gastroduodenostomy
gastroenterostomy
gastrogastrostomy
Laparoscopic gastrojejunostomy without gastrectomy NEC
EXCLUDES   gastroenterostomy, open approach (44.39)

44.39   Other gastroenterostomy
Bypass:
gastroduodenostomy
gastroenterostomy
gastrogastrostomy
Gastrojejunostomy without gastrectomy NOS
AHA: 3Q, '03, 6; 1Q, '01, 16, 17

✓4ᵗʰ **44.4   Control of hemorrhage and suture of ulcer of stomach or duodenum**
44.40   Suture of peptic ulcer, not otherwise specified
44.41   Suture of gastric ulcer site
EXCLUDES   ligation of gastric varices (44.91)
44.42   Suture of duodenal ulcer site
AHA: J-F, '87, 11
44.43   Endoscopic control of gastric or duodenal bleeding
AHA: 2Q, '04, 12; 2Q, '92, 17; N-D, '87, 4
44.44   Transcatheter embolization for gastric or duodenal bleeding
EXCLUDES   surgical occlusion of abdominal vessels (38.86-38.87)
AHA: 1Q, '88, 15; N-D, '87, 4

DEF: Therapeutic blocking of stomach or upper small intestine blood vessel to stop hemorrhaging; accomplished by introducing various substances using a catheter.

44.49   Other control of hemorrhage of stomach or duodenum
That with gastrotomy

44.5   Revision of gastric anastomosis
Closure of:
gastric anastomosis
gastroduodenostomy
gastrojejunostomy
Pantaloon operation

✓4ᵗʰ **44.6   Other repair of stomach**
44.61   Suture of laceration of stomach
EXCLUDES   that of ulcer site (44.41)
44.62   Closure of gastrostomy

Roux-en-Y Operation (Gastrojejunostomy without gastrectomy)

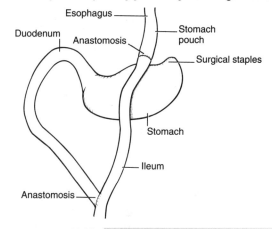

44.63   Closure of other gastric fistula
Closure of:
gastrocolic fistula
gastrojejunocolic fistula
44.64   Gastropexy
AHA: M-J, '85, 17

DEF: Suturing of stomach into position.

44.65   Esophagogastroplasty
Belsey operation
Esophagus and stomach cardioplasty
AHA: M-J, '85, 17

44.66   Other procedures for creation of esophagogastric sphincteric competence
Fundoplication
Gastric cardioplasty
Nissen's fundoplication
Restoration of cardio-esophageal angle
EXCLUDES   that by laparoscopy (44.67)
AHA: 2Q, '03, 12; 2Q, '01, 3, 5, 6; 3Q, '98, 10; M-J, '85, 17

44.67   Laparoscopic procedures for creation of esophagogastric sphincteric competence
Fundoplication
Gastric cardioplasty
Nissen's fundoplication
Restoration of cardio-esophageal angle

44.68   Laparoscopic gastroplasty
Banding
Silastic vertical banding
Vertical banded gastroplasty (VBG)
Code also any synchronous laparoscopic gastroenterostomy (44.38)
EXCLUDES   insertion, laparoscopic adjustable gastric band (restrictive procedure) (44.95)
other repair of stomach, open approach (44.61-44.65, 44.69)

44.69   Other
Inversion of gastric diverticulum
Repair of stomach NOS
AHA: 3Q, '03, 8; 2Q, '01, 3; 3Q, '99, 3; M-J, '85, 17; N-D, '84, 13

DEF: Inversion of gastric diverticulum: Turning stomach inward to repair outpouch of wall.

B1 Bilateral Procedure   **NC** Non-covered Procedure   **LC** Limited Coverage Procedure   ▶◀ Revised Text   ● New Code   ▲ Revised Code Title

124 — Volume 3   *2007 ICD•9•CM*

√4th **44.9** **Other operations on stomach**

44.91 **Ligation of gastric varices**

EXCLUDES *that by endoscopic approach (43.41)*

DEF: Destruction of dilated veins by suture or strangulation.

44.92 **Intraoperative manipulation of stomach**

Reduction of gastric volvulus

44.93 **Insertion of gastric bubble (balloon)** NC

44.94 **Removal of gastric bubble (balloon)**

44.95 **Laparoscopic gastric restrictive procedure**

Adjustable gastric band and port insertion

EXCLUDES *laparoscopic gastroplasty (44.68)*

other repair of stomach (44.69)

44.96 **Laparoscopic revision of gastric restrictive procedure**

Revision or replacement of:
adjustable gastric band
subcutaneous gastric port device

44.97 **Laparoscopic removal of gastric restrictive device(s)**

Removal of either or both:
adjustable gastric band
subcutaneous port device

EXCLUDES *nonoperative removal of gastric restrictive device(s) (97.86)*

open removal of gastric restrictive device(s) (44.99)

44.98 **(Laparoscopic) adjustment of size of adjustable gastric restrictive device**

Infusion of saline for device tightening
Withdrawal of saline for device loosening
Code also any:
abdominal ultrasound (88.76)
abdominal wall fluoroscopy (88.09)
barium swallow (87.61)

44.99 **Other**

EXCLUDES *change of gastrostomy tube (97.02)*

dilation of cardiac sphincter (42.92)

gastric:
cooling (96.31)
freezing (96.32)
gavage (96.35)
hypothermia (96.31)
lavage (96.33)

insertion of nasogastric tube (96.07)

irrigation of gastrostomy (96.36)

irrigation of nasogastric tube (96.34)

removal of:
gastrostomy tube (97.51)
intraluminal foreign body from stomach without incision (98.03)

replacement of:
gastrostomy tube (97.02)
(naso-)gastric tube (97.01)

AHA: 3Q, '04, 5

√3rd **45** **Incision, excision, and anastomosis of intestine**

Code also any application or administration of an adhesion barrier substance (99.77)

√4th **45.0** **Enterotomy**

EXCLUDES *duodenocholedochotomy (51.41-51.42, 51.51)*

that for destruction of lesion (45.30-45.34)

that of exteriorized intestine (46.14, 46.24, 46.31)

45.00 **Incision of intestine not otherwise specified**

45.01 **Incision of duodenum**

45.02 **Other incision of small intestine**

45.03 **Incision of large intestine**

EXCLUDES *proctotomy (48.0)*

√4th **45.1** **Diagnostic procedures on small intestine**

Code also any laparotomy (54.11-54.19)

45.11 **Transabdominal endoscopy of small intestine**

Intraoperative endoscopy of small intestine

EXCLUDES *that with biopsy (45.14)*

DEF: Endoscopic exam of small intestine through abdominal wall.

DEF: Intraoperative endoscope of small intestine: Endoscopic exam of small intestine during surgery.

45.12 **Endoscopy of small intestine through artificial stoma**

EXCLUDES *that with biopsy (45.14)*

AHA: M-J, '85, 17

45.13 **Other endoscopy of small intestine**

Esophagogastroduodenoscopy [EGD]

EXCLUDES *that with biopsy (45.14, 45.16)*

AHA: 3Q, '04, 5; N-D, '87, 5

45.14 **Closed [endoscopic] biopsy of small intestine**

Brushing or washing for specimen collection

EXCLUDES *esophagogastroduodenoscopy [EGD] with closed biopsy (45.16)*

45.15 **Open biopsy of small intestine**

AHA: ▶2Q, '05, 12◀

45.16 **Esophagogastroduodenoscopy [EGD] with closed biopsy**

Biopsy of one or more sites involving esophagus, stomach, and/or duodenum

AHA: ▶3Q, '05, 17;◀ 2Q, '01, 9

45.19 **Other diagnostic procedures on small intestine**

EXCLUDES *microscopic examination of specimen from small intestine (90.91-90.99)*

radioisotope scan (92.04)

ultrasonography (88.74)

x-ray (87.61-87.69)

√4th **45.2** **Diagnostic procedures on large intestine**

Code also any laparotomy (54.11-54.19)

45.21 **Transabdominal endoscopy of large intestine**

Intraoperative endoscopy of large intestine

EXCLUDES *that with biopsy (45.25)*

DEF: Endoscopic exam of large intestine through abdominal wall.

DEF: Intraoperative endoscopy of large intestine: Endoscopic exam of large intestine during surgery.

Esophagogastroduodenoscopy

Esophagus

Duodenum

Stomach

√3rd √4th Additional Digit Required   Nonspecific OR Procedure   Valid OR Procedure   Non-OR Procedure   Adjunct Code

45.22 Endoscopy of large intestine through artificial stoma

> EXCLUDES   *that with biopsy (45.25)*

DEF: Endoscopic exam of large intestine lining from rectum to cecum via colostomy stoma.

45.23 Colonoscopy

Flexible fiberoptic colonoscopy

> EXCLUDES   *endoscopy of large intestine through artificial stoma (45.22)*
> *flexible sigmoidoscopy (45.24)*
> *rigid proctosigmoidoscopy (48.23)*
> *transabdominal endoscopy of large intestine (45.21)*

AHA: ▶3Q, '05, 17;◀ S-O, '85, 5

DEF: Endoscopic exam of descending colon, splenic flexure, transverse colon, hepatic flexure and cecum.

45.24 Flexible sigmoidoscopy

Endoscopy of descending colon

> EXCLUDES   *rigid proctosigmoidoscopy (48.23)*

DEF: Endoscopic exam of anus, rectum and sigmoid colon.

45.25 Closed [endoscopic] biopsy of large intestine

Biopsy, closed, of unspecified intestinal site
Brushing or washing for specimen collection
Colonoscopy with biopsy

> EXCLUDES   *proctosigmoidoscopy with biopsy (48.24)*

AHA: 1Q, '03, 10

45.26 Open biopsy of large intestine
45.27 Intestinal biopsy, site unspecified
45.28 Other diagnostic procedures on large intestine
45.29 Other diagnostic procedures on intestine, site unspecified

> EXCLUDES   *microscopic examination of specimen (90.91-90.99)*
> *scan and radioisotope function study (92.04)*
> *ultrasonography (88.74)*
> *x-ray (87.61-87.69)*

✓4ᵗʰ **45.3 Local excision or destruction of lesion or tissue of small intestine**

45.30 Endoscopic excision or destruction of lesion of duodenum

> EXCLUDES   *biopsy of duodenum (45.14-45.15)*
> *control of hemorrhage (44.43)*
> *fistulectomy (46.72)*

45.31 Other local excision of lesion of duodenum

> EXCLUDES   *biopsy of duodenum (45.14-45.15)*
> *fistulectomy (46.72)*
> *multiple segmental resection (45.61)*
> *that by endoscopic approach (45.30)*

45.32 Other destruction of lesion of duodenum

> EXCLUDES   *that by endoscopic approach (45.30)*

AHA: N-D, '87, 5; S-O, '85, 6

45.33 Local excision of lesion or tissue of small intestine, except duodenum

Excision of redundant mucosa of ileostomy

> EXCLUDES   *biopsy of small intestine (45.14-45.15)*
> *fistulectomy (46.74)*
> *multiple segmental resection (45.61)*

45.34 Other destruction of lesion of small intestine, except duodenum

✓4ᵗʰ **45.4 Local excision or destruction of lesion or tissue of large intestine**

AHA: N-D, '87, 11

45.41 Excision of lesion or tissue of large intestine

Excision of redundant mucosa of colostomy

> EXCLUDES   *biopsy of large intestine (45.25-45.27)*
> *endoscopic polypectomy of large intestine (45.42)*
> *fistulectomy (46.76)*
> *multiple segmental resection (45.71)*
> *that by endoscopic approach (45.42-45.43)*

45.42 Endoscopic polypectomy of large intestine

> EXCLUDES   *that by open approach (45.41)*

AHA: ▶2Q, '05, 16;◀ 2Q, '90, 25

DEF: Endoscopic removal of polyp from large intestine.

45.43 Endoscopic destruction of other lesion or tissue of large intestine

Endoscopic ablation of tumor of large intestine
Endoscopic control of colonic bleeding

> EXCLUDES   *endoscopic polypectomy of large intestine (45.42)*

AHA: 4Q, '02, 61

45.49 Other destruction of lesion of large intestine

> EXCLUDES   *that by endoscopic approach (45.43)*

✓4ᵗʰ **45.5 Isolation of intestinal segment**

Code also any synchronous:
anastomosis other than end-to-end (45.90-45.94)
enterostomy (46.10-46.39)

45.50 Isolation of intestinal segment, not otherwise specified

Isolation of intestinal pedicle flap
Reversal of intestinal segment

DEF: Isolation of small intestinal pedicle flap: Separation of intestinal pedicle flap.

DEF: Reversal of intestinal segment: Separation of intestinal segment.

45.51 Isolation of segment of small intestine

Isolation of ileal loop
Resection of small intestine for interposition

AHA: ▶2Q, '05, 12;◀ 3Q, '03, 6-8; 2Q, '03, 11; 3Q, '00, 7

45.52 Isolation of segment of large intestine

Resection of colon for interposition

Colectomy

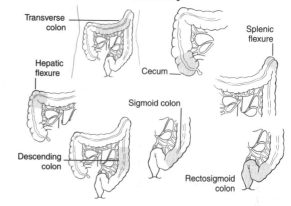

Transverse colon
Hepatic flexure
Descending colon
Splenic flexure
Cecum
Sigmoid colon
Rectosigmoid colon

| BI Bilateral Procedure | NC Non-covered Procedure | LC Limited Coverage Procedure | ▶◀ Revised Text | ● New Code | ▲ Revised Code Title |

✓4ᵗʰ 45.6 Other excision of small intestine
Code also any synchronous:
  anastomosis other than end-to-end (45.90-45.93,
    45.95)
  colostomy (46.10-46.13)
  enterostomy (46.10-46.39)
> **EXCLUDES**   cecectomy (45.72)
>   enterocolectomy (45.79)
>   gastroduodenectomy (43.6-43.99)
>   ileocolectomy (45.73)
>   pancreatoduodenectomy (52.51-52.7)

45.61 Multiple segmental resection of small intestine
Segmental resection for multiple traumatic
  lesions of small intestine

45.62 Other partial resection of small intestine
Duodenectomy   Jejunectomy
Ileectomy
> **EXCLUDES**   duodenectomy with
>   synchronous
>   pancreatectomy (52.51-
>   52.7)
>   resection of cecum and
>   terminal ileum (45.72)

AHA: 1Q, '04, 10; 1Q, '03, 18

45.63 Total removal of small intestine

✓4ᵗʰ 45.7 Partial excision of large intestine
Code also any synchronous:
  anastomosis other than end-to-end (45.92-45.94)
  enterostomy (46.10-46.39)

AHA: 4Q, '92, 27

45.71 Multiple segmental resection of large intestine
Segmental resection for multiple traumatic
  lesions of large intestine

45.72 Cecectomy
Resection of cecum and terminal ileum

45.73 Right hemicolectomy
Ileocolectomy
Right radical colectomy

AHA: 3Q, '99, 10

45.74 Resection of transverse colon

45.75 Left hemicolectomy
> **EXCLUDES**   proctosigmoidectomy (48.41-
>   48.69)
>   second stage Mikulicz
>   operation (46.04)

DEF: Excision of left descending large intestine.

45.76 Sigmoidectomy

AHA: 1Q, '96, 9; 3Q, '89, 15

45.79 Other partial excision of large intestine
Enterocolectomy NEC

AHA: 1Q, '03, 18; 3Q, '97, 9; 2Q, '91, 16

45.8 Total intra-abdominal colectomy
Excision of cecum, colon, and sigmoid
> **EXCLUDES**   coloproctectomy (48.41-48.69)

Intestinal Anastomosis

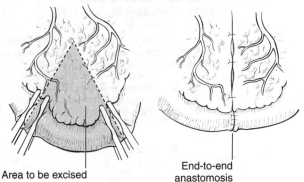

Area to be excised   End-to-end
anastomosis

✓4ᵗʰ 45.9 Intestinal anastomosis
Code also any synchronous resection (45.31-45.8,
  48.41-48.69)
> **EXCLUDES**   end-to-end anastomosis — omit code

45.90 Intestinal anastomosis, not otherwise specified

45.91 Small-to-small intestinal anastomosis
AHA: 3Q, '03, 6-8; M-J, '85, 17

45.92 Anastomosis of small intestine to rectal stump
Hampton procedure

45.93 Other small-to-large intestinal anastomosis
AHA: 1Q, '03, 18; N-D, '86, 11

45.94 Large-to-large intestinal anastomosis
> **EXCLUDES**   rectorectostomy (48.74)

AHA: 3Q, '89, 15

45.95 Anastomosis to anus
Formation of endorectal ileal pouch (J-
  pouch) (H-pouch) (S-pouch) with
  anastomosis of small intestine to anus

AHA: ▶2Q, '05, 13◀

✓3ʳᵈ 46 Other operations on intestine
Code also any application or administration of an adhesion
  barrier substance (99.77)

✓4ᵗʰ 46.0 Exteriorization of intestine
> **INCLUDES**   loop enterostomy
>   multiple stage resection of intestine

DEF: Bringing intestinal segment to body surface.

46.01 Exteriorization of small intestine
Loop ileostomy

46.02 Resection of exteriorized segment of small intestine

46.03 Exteriorization of large intestine
Exteriorization of intestine NOS
First stage Mikulicz exteriorization of
  intestine
Loop colostomy

46.04 Resection of exteriorized segment of large intestine
Resection of exteriorized segment of
  intestine NOS
Second stage Mikulicz operation

✓4ᵗʰ 46.1 Colostomy
Code also any synchronous resection (45.49, 45.71-
  45.79, 45.8)
> **EXCLUDES**   loop colostomy (46.03)
>   that with abdominoperineal resection of
>   rectum (48.5)
>   that with synchronous anterior rectal
>   resection (48.62)

DEF: Creation of opening from large intestine through abdominal
wall to body surface.

46.10 Colostomy, not otherwise specified
46.11 Temporary colostomy
46.13 Permanent colostomy
46.14 Delayed opening of colostomy

✓4ᵗʰ 46.2 Ileostomy
Code also any synchronous resection (45.34, 45.61-
  45.63)
> **EXCLUDES**   loop ileostomy (46.01)

DEF: Creation of artificial anus by bringing ileum through
abdominal wall to body surface.

46.20 Ileostomy, not otherwise specified
46.21 Temporary ileostomy
46.22 Continent ileostomy
AHA: M-J, '85, 17

DEF: Creation of opening from third part of small intestine
through abdominal wall, with pouch outside abdomen.

46.23 Other permanent ileostomy
46.24 Delayed opening of ileostomy

✓4ᵗʰ **46.3**   **Other enterostomy**
     Code also any synchronous resection (45.61-45.8)

   46.31   **Delayed opening of other enterostomy**

   46.32   **Percutaneous (endoscopic) jejunostomy [PEJ]**

      DEF: Endoscopic placement of tube in midsection of small intestine through abdominal wall.

   46.39   **Other**
      Duodenostomy   Feeding enterostomy
      AHA: 3Q, '89, 15

✓4ᵗʰ **46.4**   **Revision of intestinal stoma**
     DEF: Revision of opening surgically created from intestine through abdominal wall, to skin surface.

   46.40   **Revision of intestinal stoma, not otherwise specified**
      Plastic enlargement of intestinal stoma
      Reconstruction of stoma of intestine
      Release of scar tissue of intestinal stoma
      EXCLUDES   *excision of redundant mucosa (45.41)*

   46.41   **Revision of stoma of small intestine**
      EXCLUDES   *excision of redundant mucosa (45.33)*

      AHA: ▶2Q, '05, 11◀

   46.42   **Repair of pericolostomy hernia**

   46.43   **Other revision of stoma of large intestine**
      EXCLUDES   *excision of redundant mucosa (45.41)*

      AHA: 2Q, '02, 9

✓4ᵗʰ **46.5**   **Closure of intestinal stoma**
     Code also any synchronous resection (45.34, 45.49, 45.61-45.8)

   46.50   **Closure of intestinal stoma, not otherwise specified**

   46.51   **Closure of stoma of small intestine**

   46.52   **Closure of stoma of large intestine**
      Closure or take-down of cecostomy
      Closure or take-down of colostomy
      Closure or take-down of sigmoidostomy
      AHA: ▶2Q, '05, 4;◀ 3Q, '97, 9; 2Q, '91, 16; N-D, '87, 8

✓4ᵗʰ **46.6**   **Fixation of intestine**

   46.60   **Fixation of intestine not otherwise specified**
      Fixation of intestine to abdominal wall

   46.61   **Fixation of small intestine to abdominal wall**
      Ileopexy

   46.62   **Other fixation of small intestine**
      Noble plication of small intestine
      Plication of jejunum

      DEF: Noble plication of small intestine: Fixing small intestine into place with tuck in small intestine.
      DEF: Plication of jejunum: Fixing small intestine into place with tuck in midsection.

   46.63   **Fixation of large intestine to abdominal wall**
      Cecocoloplicopexy
      Sigmoidopexy   (Moschowitz)

   46.64   **Other fixation of large intestine**
      Cecofixation   Colofixation

✓4ᵗʰ **46.7**   **Other repair of intestine**
      EXCLUDES   *closure of:*
          ulcer of duodenum (44.42)
          vesicoenteric fistula (57.83)

   46.71   **Suture of laceration of duodenum**

   46.72   **Closure of fistula of duodenum**

   46.73   **Suture of laceration of small intestine, except duodenum**

   46.74   **Closure of fistula of small intestine, except duodenum**
      EXCLUDES   *closure of:*
          artificial stoma (46.51)
          vaginal fistula (70.74)
          repair of gastrojejunocolic fistula (44.63)

   46.75   **Suture of laceration of large intestine**

   46.76   **Closure of fistula of large intestine**
      EXCLUDES   *closure of:*
          gastrocolic fistula (44.63)
          rectal fistula (48.73)
          sigmoidovesical fistula (57.83)
          stoma (46.52)
          vaginal fistula (70.72-70.73)
          vesicocolic fistula (57.83)
          vesicosigmoidovaginal fistula (57.83)

      AHA: 3Q, '99, 8

   46.79   **Other repair of intestine**
      Duodenoplasty
      AHA: 3Q, '02, 11

✓4ᵗʰ **46.8**   **Dilation and manipulation of intestine**
     AHA: 1Q, '03, 14

   46.80   **Intra-abdominal manipulation of intestine, not otherwise specified**
      Correction of intestinal malrotation
      Reduction of:
          intestinal torsion
          intestinal volvulus
          intussusception
      EXCLUDES   *reduction of intussusception with:*
          fluoroscopy (96.29)
          ionizing radiation enema (96.29)
          ultrasonography guidance (96.29)

      AHA: 4Q, '98, 82

      DEF: Correction of intestinal malrotation: Repair of abnormal rotation.
      DEF: Reduction of:
         Intestinal torsion: Repair of twisted segment.
         Intestinal volvulus: Repair of a knotted segment.
         Intussusception: Repair of prolapsed segment.

   46.81   **Intra-abdominal manipulation of small intestine**

   46.82   **Intra-abdominal manipulation of large intestine**

   46.85   **Dilation of intestine**
      Dilation (balloon) of duodenum
      Dilation (balloon) of jejunum
      Endoscopic dilation (balloon) of large intestine
      That through rectum or colostomy
      AHA: 3Q, '89, 15

✓4ᵗʰ **46.9**   **Other operations on intestines**

   46.91   **Myotomy of sigmoid colon**

   46.92   **Myotomy of other parts of colon**

   46.93   **Revision of anastomosis of small intestine**

   46.94   **Revision of anastomosis of large intestine**

   46.95   **Local perfusion of small intestine**
      Code also substance perfused (99.21-99.29)

   46.96   **Local perfusion of large intestine**
      Code also substance perfused (99.21-99.29)

   46.97   **Transplant of intestine**   **LC**
      Note: To report donor source — see codes 00.91-00.93
      AHA: 4Q, '00, 66

BI Bilateral Procedure   **NC** Non-covered Procedure   **LC** Limited Coverage Procedure   ▶◀ Revised Text   ● New Code   ▲ Revised Code Title

46.99   Other
Ileoentectropy
> **EXCLUDES**   *diagnostic procedures on*
> *intestine (45.11-45.29)*
> *dilation of enterostomy stoma*
> *(96.24)*
> *intestinal intubation (96.08)*
> *removal of:*
> *intraluminal foreign body*
> *from large intestine*
> *without incision*
> *(98.04)*
> *intraluminal foreign body*
> *from small intestine*
> *without incision*
> *(98.03)*
> *tube from large intestine*
> *(97.53)*
> *tube from small intestine*
> *(97.52)*
> *replacement of:*
> *large intestine tube or*
> *enterostomy device*
> *(97.04)*
> *small intestine tube or*
> *enterostomy device*
> *(97.03)*

AHA: 3Q, '99, 11; 1Q, '89, 11

✓3rd **47   Operations on appendix**
> **INCLUDES**   appendiceal stump
Code also any application or administration of an adhesion
barrier substance (99.77)

✓4th **47.0   Appendectomy**
> **EXCLUDES**   *incidental appendectomy, so described*
> *(47.11, 47.19)*

AHA: 4Q, '96, 64; 3Q, '92, 12

47.01   Laparoscopic appendectomy
AHA: 1Q, '01, 15; 4Q, '96, 64

47.09   Other appendectomy
AHA: 4Q, '97, 52

✓4th **47.1   Incidental appendectomy**
DEF: Removal of appendix during abdominal surgery as
prophylactic measure, without significant appendiceal pathology.

47.11   Laparoscopic incidental appendectomy
47.19   Other incidental appendectomy
AHA: 4Q, '96, 65

47.2   Drainage of appendiceal abscess
> **EXCLUDES**   *that with appendectomy (47.0)*

✓4th **47.9   Other operations on appendix**
47.91   Appendicostomy
47.92   Closure of appendiceal fistula
47.99   Other
Anastomosis of appendix
> **EXCLUDES**   *diagnostic procedures on*
> *appendix (45.21-45.29)*

AHA: 3Q, '01, 16

✓3rd **48   Operations on rectum, rectosigmoid, and perirectal tissue**
Code also any application or administration of an adhesion
barrier substance (99.77)

48.0   Proctotomy
Decompression of imperforate anus
Panas' operation [linear proctotomy]
> **EXCLUDES**   *incision of perirectal tissue (48.81)*

AHA: 3Q, '99, 8

DEF: Incision into rectal portion of large intestine.

DEF: Decompression of imperforate anus: opening a closed anus by
means of an incision.

DEF: Panas' operation (linear proctotomy): Linear incision into
rectal portion of large intestine

48.1   Proctostomy

✓4th **48.2   Diagnostic procedures on rectum, rectosigmoid, and
perirectal tissue**
48.21   Transabdominal proctosigmoidoscopy
Intraoperative proctosigmoidoscopy
> **EXCLUDES**   *that with biopsy (48.24)*

**48.22   Proctosigmoidoscopy through artificial
stoma**
> **EXCLUDES**   *that with biopsy (48.24)*

48.23   Rigid proctosigmoidoscopy
> **EXCLUDES**   *flexible sigmoidoscopy (45.24)*

AHA: 1Q, '01, 8

DEF: Endoscopic exam of anus, rectum and lower
sigmoid colon.

48.24   Closed [endoscopic] biopsy of rectum
Brushing or washing for specimen collection
Proctosigmoidoscopy with biopsy
AHA: 1Q, '03, 14

48.25   Open biopsy of rectum
48.26   Biopsy of perirectal tissue
**48.29   Other diagnostic procedures on rectum,
rectosigmoid, and perirectal tissue**
> **EXCLUDES**   *digital examination of rectum*
> *(89.34)*
> *lower GI series (87.64)*
> *microscopic examination of*
> *specimen from rectum*
> *(90.91-90.99)*

✓4th **48.3   Local excision or destruction of lesion or tissue of
rectum**
**48.31   Radical electrocoagulation of rectal lesion
or tissue**
DEF: Destruction of lesion or tissue of large intestine,
rectal part.

**48.32   Other electrocoagulation of rectal lesion or
tissue**
AHA: 2Q, '98, 18

**48.33   Destruction of rectal lesion or tissue by
laser**
**48.34   Destruction of rectal lesion or tissue by
cryosurgery**
48.35   Local excision of rectal lesion or tissue
> **EXCLUDES**   *biopsy of rectum (48.24-48.25)*
> *[endoscopic] polypectomy of*
> *rectum (48.36)*
> *excision of perirectal tissue*
> *(48.82)*
> *hemorrhoidectomy (49.46)*
> *rectal fistulectomy (48.73)*

48.36   [Endoscopic] polypectomy of rectum
AHA: 4Q, '95, 65

✓4th **48.4   Pull-through resection of rectum**
Code also any synchronous anastomosis other than
end-to-end (45.90, 45.92-45.95)
48.41   Soave submucosal resection of rectum
Endorectal pull-through operation
DEF: Soave submucosal resection: Resection of
submucosal rectal part of large intestine by pull-through
technique.

DEF: Endorectal pull-through operation: Resection of
interior large intestine by pull-through technique.

48.49   Other pull-through resection of rectum
Abdominoperineal pull-through
Altemeier operation
Swenson proctectomy
> **EXCLUDES**   *Duhamel abdominoperineal*
> *pull-through (48.65)*

AHA: 3Q, '01, 8; 2Q, '99, 13

DEF: Abdominoperineal pull-through: Resection of large
intestine, latter part, by pull-through of abdomen,
scrotum or vulva and anus.

DEF: Swenson proctectomy: Excision of large intestine,
rectal by pull-through and preserving muscles that close
the anus.

✓3rd
✓4th Additional Digit Required   Nonspecific OR Procedure   Valid OR Procedure   Non-OR Procedure   Adjunct Code

Operations on the Digestive System

48.5–49.23

48.5 Abdominoperineal resection of rectum
INCLUDES with synchronous colostomy
Combined abdominoendorectal resection
Complete proctectomy
Code also any synchronous anastomosis other than
end-to-end (45.90, 45.92-45.95)
> EXCLUDES *Duhamel abdominoperineal pull-*
> *through (48.65)*
> *that as part of pelvic exenteration*
> *(68.8)*

AHA: 2Q, '97, 5

DEF: Rectal excision through cavities formed by abdomen, anus,
vulva or scrotum.

✓4ᵗʰ 48.6 Other resection of rectum
Code also any synchronous anastomosis other than
end-to-end (45.90, 45.92-45.95)

48.61 Transsacral rectosigmoidectomy
DEF: Excision through sacral bone area of sigmoid and
last parts of large intestine.

**48.62 Anterior resection of rectum with
synchronous colostomy**
DEF: Resection of front terminal end of large intestine
and creation of colostomy.

48.63 Other anterior resection of rectum
> EXCLUDES *that with synchronous*
> *colostomy (48.62)*

AHA: 1Q, '96, 9

48.64 Posterior resection of rectum
48.65 Duhamel resection of rectum
Duhamel abdominoperineal pull-through
48.69 Other
Partial proctectomy
Rectal resection NOS

AHA: ▶2Q, '05, 13;◀ J-F, '87, 11; N-D, '86, 11

✓4ᵗʰ 48.7 Repair of rectum
> EXCLUDES *repair of:*
> *current obstetric laceration (75.62)*
> *vaginal rectocele (70.50, 70.52)*

48.71 Suture of laceration of rectum
48.72 Closure of proctostomy
48.73 Closure of other rectal fistula
> EXCLUDES *fistulectomy:*
> *perirectal (48.93)*
> *rectourethral (58.43)*
> *rectovaginal (70.73)*
> *rectovesical (57.83)*
> *rectovesicovaginal (57.83)*

48.74 Rectorectostomy
Rectal anastomosis NOS
DEF: Connection of two cut portions of large intestine,
rectal end.

48.75 Abdominal proctopexy
Frickman procedure
Ripstein repair of rectal prolapse
DEF: Fixation of rectum to adjacent abdominal structures.

48.76 Other proctopexy
Delorme repair of prolapsed rectum
Proctosigmoidopexy
Puborectalis sling operation
> EXCLUDES *manual reduction of rectal*
> *prolapse (96.26)*

DEF: Delorme repair of prolapsed rectum: Fixation of
collapsed large intestine, rectal part.

DEF: Proctosigmoidopexy: Suturing of twisted large
intestine, rectal part.

DEF: Puborectalis sling operation: Fixation of large
intestine, rectal part by forming puborectalis muscle into
sling.

48.79 Other repair of rectum
Repair of old obstetric laceration of rectum
> EXCLUDES *anastomosis to:*
> *large intestine (45.94)*
> *small intestine (45.92-*
> *45.93)*
> *repair of:*
> *current obstetrical*
> *laceration (75.62)*
> *vaginal rectocele (70.50,*
> *70.52)*

✓4ᵗʰ 48.8 Incision or excision of perirectal tissue or lesion
INCLUDES pelvirectal tissue
rectovaginal septum
48.81 Incision of perirectal tissue
Incision of rectovaginal septum
48.82 Excision of perirectal tissue
> EXCLUDES *perirectal biopsy (48.26)*
> *perirectofistulectomy (48.93)*
> *rectal fistulectomy (48.73)*

✓4ᵗʰ 48.9 Other operations on rectum and perirectal tissue
48.91 Incision of rectal stricture
48.92 Anorectal myectomy
DEF: Excision of anorectal muscle.
48.93 Repair of perirectal fistula
> EXCLUDES *that opening into rectum*
> *(48.73)*

DEF: Closure of abdominal passage in tissue around
large intestine, rectal part.

48.99 Other
> EXCLUDES *digital examination of rectum*
> *(89.34)*
> *dilation of rectum (96.22)*
> *insertion of rectal tube (96.09)*
> *irrigation of rectum (96.38-*
> *96.39)*
> *manual reduction of rectal*
> *prolapse (96.26)*
> *proctoclysis (96.37)*
> *rectal massage (99.93)*
> *rectal packing (96.19)*
> *removal of:*
> *impacted feces (96.38)*
> *intraluminal foreign body*
> *from rectum without*
> *incision (98.05)*
> *rectal packing (97.59)*
> *transanal enema (96.39)*

✓3ʳᵈ 49 Operations on anus
Code also any application or administration of an adhesion
barrier substance (99.77)

✓4ᵗʰ 49.0 Incision or excision of perianal tissue
49.01 Incision of perianal abscess
AHA: ▶2Q, '05, 10◀

49.02 Other incision of perianal tissue
Undercutting of perianal tissue
> EXCLUDES *anal fistulotomy (49.11)*

49.03 Excision of perianal skin tags
49.04 Other excision of perianal tissue
> EXCLUDES *anal fistulectomy (49.12)*
> *biopsy of perianal tissue*
> *(49.22)*

AHA: 1Q, '01, 8

✓4ᵗʰ 49.1 Incision or excision of anal fistula
> EXCLUDES *closure of anal fistula (49.73)*

49.11 Anal fistulotomy
49.12 Anal fistulectomy

✓4ᵗʰ 49.2 Diagnostic procedures on anus and perianal tissue
49.21 Anoscopy
49.22 Biopsy of perianal tissue
49.23 Biopsy of anus

BI Bilateral Procedure   NC Non-covered Procedure   LC Limited Coverage Procedure   ▶◀ Revised Text   ● New Code   ▲ Revised Code Title

49.29   **Other diagnostic procedures on anus and perianal tissue**
> EXCLUDES   *microscopic examination of specimen from anus (90.91-90.99)*

√4ᵗʰ 49.3   **Local excision or destruction of other lesion or tissue of anus**
> Anal cryptotomy
> Cauterization of lesion of anus
> EXCLUDES   *biopsy of anus (49.23)*
>   *control of (postoperative) hemorrhage of anus (49.95)*
>   *hemorrhoidectomy (49.46)*

49.31   **Endoscopic excision or destruction of lesion or tissue of anus**

49.39   **Other local excision or destruction of lesion or tissue of anus**
> EXCLUDES   *that by endoscopic approach (49.31)*
> AHA: 1Q, '01, 8

√4ᵗʰ 49.4   **Procedures on hemorrhoids**

49.41   **Reduction of hemorrhoids**
> DEF: Manual manipulation to reduce hemorrhoids.

49.42   **Injection of hemorrhoids**

49.43   **Cauterization of hemorrhoids**
> Clamp and cautery of hemorrhoids

49.44   **Destruction of hemorrhoids by cryotherapy**

49.45   **Ligation of hemorrhoids**

49.46   **Excision of hemorrhoids**
> Hemorrhoidectomy NOS

49.47   **Evacuation of thrombosed hemorrhoids**
> DEF: Removal of clotted material from hemorrhoid.

49.49   **Other procedures on hemorrhoids**
> Lord procedure

√4ᵗʰ 49.5   **Division of anal sphincter**

49.51   **Left lateral anal sphincterotomy**

49.52   **Posterior anal sphincterotomy**

49.59   **Other anal sphincterotomy**
> Division of sphincter NOS

49.6   **Excision of anus**

√4ᵗʰ 49.7   **Repair of anus**
> EXCLUDES   *repair of current obstetric laceration (75.62)*

49.71   **Suture of laceration of anus**

49.72   **Anal cerclage**
> DEF: Encircling anus with ring or sutures.

49.73   **Closure of anal fistula**
> EXCLUDES   *excision of anal fistula (49.12)*

49.74   **Gracilis muscle transplant for anal incontinence**
> DEF: Moving pubic attachment of gracilis muscle to restore anal control.

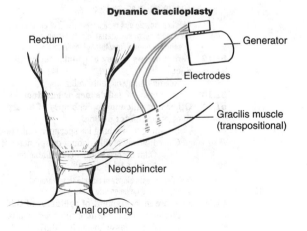

Dynamic Graciloplasty

49.75   **Implantation or revision of artificial anal sphincter**
> Removal with subsequent replacement
> Replacement during same or subsequent operative episode
> AHA: 4Q, '02, 105

49.76   **Removal of artificial anal sphincter**
> Explantation or removal without replacement
> EXCLUDES   *revision with implantation during same operative episode (49.75)*
> AHA: 4Q, '02, 105

49.79   **Other repair of anal sphincter**
> Repair of old obstetric laceration of anus
> EXCLUDES   *anoplasty with synchronous hemorrhoidectomy (49.46)*
>   *repair of current obstetric laceration (75.62)*
> AHA: 2Q, '98, 16; 1Q, '97, 9

√4ᵗʰ 49.9   **Other operations on anus**
> EXCLUDES   *dilation of anus (sphincter) (96.23)*

49.91   **Incision of anal septum**

49.92   **Insertion of subcutaneous electrical anal stimulator**

49.93   **Other incision of anus**
> Removal of:
>   foreign body from anus with incision
>   seton from anus
> EXCLUDES   *anal fistulotomy (49.11)*
>   *removal of intraluminal foreign body without incision (98.05)*

49.94   **Reduction of anal prolapse**
> EXCLUDES   *manual reduction of rectal prolapse (96.26)*
> DEF: Manipulation of displaced anal tissue to normal position.

49.95   **Control of (postoperative) hemorrhage of anus**

49.99   **Other**

√3ʳᵈ 50   **Operations on liver**
> Code also any application or administration of an adhesion barrier substance (99.77)

50.0   **Hepatotomy**
> Incision of abscess of liver
> Removal of gallstones from liver
> Stromeyer-Little operation

√4ᵗʰ 50.1   **Diagnostic procedures on liver**

50.11   **Closed (percutaneous) (needle) biopsy of liver**
> Diagnostic aspiration of liver
> AHA: ▶3Q, '05, 24◀ 4Q, '88, 12

50.12   **Open biopsy of liver**
> Wedge biopsy
> AHA: ▶3Q, '05, 24; 2Q, '05, 13◀

Closed Liver Biopsy

Inserted along midaxillary line
8
9
10
11
(12 behind)

Operations on the Digestive System

50.19–51.15

Liver Biopsy (Open, Wedge)

Right lobe — Left lobe

Liver — Caudate lobe — Gallbladder

Typical wedge biopsy sites

50.19   **Other diagnostic procedures on liver**
Laparoscopic liver biopsy
EXCLUDES   *liver scan and radioisotope function study (92.02)*
microscopic examination of specimen from liver (91.01-91.09)

√4th **50.2**   **Local excision or destruction of liver tissue or lesion**

50.21   **Marsupialization of lesion of liver**
DEF: Exteriorizing lesion by incision and suturing cut edges to skin to create opening.

50.22   **Partial hepatectomy**
Wedge resection of liver
EXCLUDES   *biopsy of liver (50.11-50.12)*
hepatic lobectomy (50.3)

● **50.23**   **Open ablation of liver lesion or tissue**
● **50.24**   **Percutaneous ablation of liver lesion or tissue**
● **50.25**   **Laparoscopic ablation of liver lesion or tissue**
● **50.26**   **Other and unspecified ablation of liver lesion or tissue**

50.29   **Other destruction of lesion of liver**
Cauterization ⎫
Enucleation ⎬ of hepatic lesion
Evacuation ⎭
EXCLUDES ▶ *ablation of liver lesion or tissue:*
laparoscopic (50.25)
open (50.23)
other (50.26)
percutaneous (50.24)◀
percutaneous aspiration of lesion (50.91)
AHA: 2Q, '03, 9

50.3   **Lobectomy of liver**
Total hepatic lobectomy with partial excision of other lobe

50.4   **Total hepatectomy**

√4th **50.5**   **Liver transplant**
Note: To report donor source — see codes 00.91-00.93
50.51   **Auxiliary liver transplant**   NC
Auxiliary hepatic transplantation leaving patient's own liver in situ
50.59   **Other transplant of liver**   LC

√4th **50.6**   **Repair of liver**
50.61   **Closure of laceration of liver**
50.69   **Other repair of liver**
Hepatopexy

√4th **50.9**   **Other operations on liver**
EXCLUDES   *lysis of adhesions (54.5)*
50.91   **Percutaneous aspiration of liver**
EXCLUDES   *percutaneous biopsy (50.11)*
DEF: Incision into liver through body wall to withdraw fluid.

50.92   **Extracorporeal hepatic assistance**
Liver dialysis
AHA: 2Q, '01, 21
DEF: Devices used outside body to assist liver function.

50.93   **Localized perfusion of liver**
50.94   **Other injection of therapeutic substance into liver**
50.99   **Other**

√3rd **51**   **Operations on gallbladder and biliary tract**
INCLUDES   operations on:
    ampulla of Vater
    common bile duct
    cystic duct
    hepatic duct
    intrahepatic bile duct
    sphincter of Oddi
Code also any application or administration of an adhesion barrier substance (99.77)

√4th **51.0**   **Cholecystotomy and cholecystostomy**
51.01   **Percutaneous aspiration of gallbladder**
Percutaneous cholecystotomy for drainage
That by: needle or catheter
EXCLUDES   *needle biopsy (51.12)*

51.02   **Trocar cholecystostomy**
AHA: 3Q, '89, 18
DEF: Creating opening in gallbladder with catheter.

51.03   **Other cholecystostomy**
51.04   **Other cholecystotomy**
Cholelithotomy NOS

√4th **51.1**   **Diagnostic procedures on biliary tract**
EXCLUDES   *that for endoscopic procedures classifiable to 51.64, 51.84-51.88, 52.14, 52.21, 52.93 -52.94, 52.97-52.98*
AHA: 2Q, '97, 7

51.10   **Endoscopic retrograde cholangiopancreatography [ERCP]**
EXCLUDES   *endoscopic retrograde: cholangiography [ERC] (51.11)*
pancreatography [ERP] (52.13)
AHA: 4Q, '03, 118; 3Q, '03, 17; 1Q, '01, 8; 2Q, '99, 13
DEF: Endoscopic and radioscopic exam of pancreatic and common bile ducts with contrast material injected in opposite direction of normal flow through catheter.

51.11   **Endoscopic retrograde cholangiography [ERC]**
Laparoscopic exploration of common bile duct
EXCLUDES   *endoscopic retrograde: cholangiopancreatography [ERCP] (51.10)*
pancreatography [ERP] (52.13)
AHA: 1Q, '96, 12; 3Q, '89, 18; 4Q, '88, 7
DEF: Endoscopic and radioscopic exam of common bile ducts with contrast material injected in opposite direction of normal flow through catheter.

51.12   **Percutaneous biopsy of gallbladder or bile ducts**
Needle biopsy of gallbladder

51.13   **Open biopsy of gallbladder or bile ducts**
51.14   **Other closed [endoscopic] biopsy of biliary duct or sphincter of Oddi**
Brushing or washing for specimen collection
Closed biopsy of biliary duct or sphincter of Oddi by procedures classifiable to 51.10-51.11, 52.13
DEF: Endoscopic biopsy of muscle tissue around pancreatic and common bile ducts.

51.15   **Pressure measurement of sphincter of Oddi**
Pressure measurement of sphincter by procedures classifiable to 51.10-51.11, 52.13
DEF: Pressure measurement tests of muscle tissue surrounding pancreatic and common bile ducts.

BI Bilateral Procedure   NC Non-covered Procedure   LC Limited Coverage Procedure   ▶◀ Revised Text   ● New Code   ▲ Revised Code Title

Laparoscopic Cholecystectomy by Laser

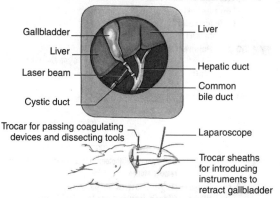

Gallbladder
Liver
Laser beam
Cystic duct
Liver
Hepatic duct
Common bile duct
Trocar for passing coagulating devices and dissecting tools
Laparoscope
Trocar sheaths for introducing instruments to retract gallbladder

51.19 Other diagnostic procedures on biliary tract

> *EXCLUDES*   biliary tract x-ray (87.51-87.59)
> microscopic examination of specimen from biliary tract (91.01-91.09)

√4ᵗʰ 51.2 Cholecystectomy

AHA: 1Q, '93, 17; 4Q, '91, 26; 3Q, '89, 18

51.21 Other partial cholecystectomy

Revision of prior cholecystectomy

> *EXCLUDES*   that by laparoscope (51.24)

AHA: 4Q, '96, 69

51.22 Cholecystectomy

> *EXCLUDES*   laparoscopic cholecystectomy (51.23)

AHA: 4Q, '97, 52; 2Q, '91, 16

51.23 Laparoscopic cholecystectomy

That by laser

AHA: 3Q, '98, 10; 4Q, '97, 52; 1Q, '96, 12; 2Q, '95, 11; 4Q, '91, 26

DEF: Endoscopic removal of gallbladder.

51.24 Laparoscopic partial cholecystectomy

AHA: 4Q, '96, 69

√4ᵗʰ 51.3 Anastomosis of gallbladder or bile duct

> *EXCLUDES*   resection with end-to-end anastomosis (51.61-51.69)

51.31 Anastomosis of gallbladder to hepatic ducts
51.32 Anastomosis of gallbladder to intestine
51.33 Anastomosis of gallbladder to pancreas
51.34 Anastomosis of gallbladder to stomach
51.35 Other gallbladder anastomosis

Gallbladder anastomosis NOS

51.36 Choledochoenterostomy

DEF: Connection of common bile duct to intestine.

51.37 Anastomosis of hepatic duct to gastrointestinal tract

Kasai portoenterostomy

AHA: 2Q, '02, 12

DEF: Kaisi portoenterostomy: A duct to drain bile from the liver is formed by anastomosing the porta hepatis to a loop of bowel.

51.39 Other bile duct anastomosis

Anastomosis of bile duct NOS
Anastomosis of unspecified bile duct to:
    intestine   pancreas
    liver   stomach

√4ᵗʰ 51.4 Incision of bile duct for relief of obstruction

51.41 Common duct exploration for removal of calculus

> *EXCLUDES*   percutaneous extraction (51.96)

AHA: 1Q, '96, 12; 3Q, '89, 18; 4Q, '88, 7

51.42 Common duct exploration for relief of other obstruction

AHA: 3Q, '89, 18

51.43 Insertion of choledochohepatic tube for decompression

Hepatocholedochostomy

AHA: 3Q, '89, 18; 4Q, '88, 7

51.49 Incision of other bile ducts for relief of obstruction

AHA: 3Q, '89, 18

√4ᵗʰ 51.5 Other incision of bile duct

> *EXCLUDES*   that for relief of obstruction (51.41-51.49)

51.51 Exploration of common duct

Incision of common bile duct

AHA: 2Q, '97, 16; 1Q, '96, 12

51.59 Incision of other bile duct

AHA: 2Q, '97, 16; 3Q, '89, 18

√4ᵗʰ 51.6 Local excision or destruction of lesion or tissue of biliary ducts and sphincter of Oddi

Code also anastomosis other than end-to-end (51.31, 51.36-51.39)

> *EXCLUDES*   biopsy of bile duct (51.12-51.13)

51.61 Excision of cystic duct remnant

AHA: 3Q, '89, 18

51.62 Excision of ampulla of Vater (with reimplantation of common duct)
51.63 Other excision of common duct

Choledochectomy

> *EXCLUDES*   fistulectomy (51.72)

51.64 Endoscopic excision or destruction of lesion of biliary ducts or sphincter of Oddi

Excision or destruction of lesion of biliary duct by procedures classifiable to 51.10-51.11, 52.13

51.69 Excision of other bile duct

Excision of lesion of bile duct NOS

> *EXCLUDES*   fistulectomy (51.79)

√4ᵗʰ 51.7 Repair of bile ducts

51.71 Simple suture of common bile duct
51.72 Choledochoplasty

Repair of fistula of common bile duct

51.79 Repair of other bile ducts

Closure of artificial opening of bile duct NOS
Suture of bile duct NOS

> *EXCLUDES*   operative removal of prosthetic device (51.95)

√4ᵗʰ 51.8 Other operations on biliary ducts and sphincter of Oddi

51.81 Dilation of sphincter of Oddi

Dilation of ampulla of Vater

> *EXCLUDES*   that by endoscopic approach (51.84)

DEF: Dilation of muscle around common bile and pancreatic ducts; to mitigate constriction obstructing bile flow.

51.82 Pancreatic sphincterotomy

Incision of pancreatic sphincter
Transduodenal ampullary sphincterotomy

> *EXCLUDES*   that by endoscopic approach (51.85)

DEF: Pancreatic sphincterotomy: Division of muscle around common bile and pancreatic ducts.

DEF: Transduodenal ampullary sphincterotomy: Incision into muscle around common bile and pancreatic ducts; closing approach through first section of small intestine.

51.83 Pancreatic sphincteroplasty
51.84 Endoscopic dilation of ampulla and biliary duct

Dilation of ampulla and biliary duct by procedures classifiable to 51.10-51.11, 52.13

51.85 Endoscopic sphincterotomy and papillotomy

Sphincterotomy and papillotomy by procedures classifiable to 51.10-51.11, 52.13

AHA: 4Q, '03, 118; 3Q, '03, 17; 2Q, '97, 7

DEF: Incision of muscle around common bile and pancreatic ducts and closing the duodenal papilla.

√3ʳᵈ
√4ᵗʰ **Additional Digit Required**   Nonspecific OR Procedure   Valid OR Procedure   Non-OR Procedure   Adjunct Code

Operations on the Digestive System

51.86–52.4

51.86 Endoscopic insertion of nasobiliary drainage tube
Insertion of nasobiliary tube by procedures classifiable to 51.10-51.11, 52.13

51.87 Endoscopic insertion of stent (tube) into bile duct
Endoprosthesis of bile duct
Insertion of stent into bile duct by procedures classifiable to 51.10-51.11, 52.13
> EXCLUDES   nasobiliary drainage tube (51.86)
> replacement of stent (tube) (97.05)

AHA: 3Q, '03, 17

51.88 Endoscopic removal of stone(s) from biliary tract
Laparoscopic removal of stone(s) from biliary tract
Removal of biliary tract stone(s) by procedures classifiable to 51.10-51.11, 52.13
> EXCLUDES   percutaneous extraction of common duct stones (51.96)

AHA: 2Q, '00, 11; 2Q, '97, 7

51.89 Other operations on sphincter of Oddi

√4ᵗʰ **51.9 Other operations on biliary tract**

51.91 Repair of laceration of gallbladder
51.92 Closure of cholecystostomy
51.93 Closure of other biliary fistula
Cholecystogastroenteric fistulectomy

51.94 Revision of anastomosis of biliary tract
51.95 Removal of prosthetic device from bile duct
> EXCLUDES   nonoperative removal (97.55)

51.96 Percutaneous extraction of common duct stones

AHA: 4Q, '88, 7

51.98 Other percutaneous procedures on biliary tract
Percutaneous biliary endoscopy via existing T-tube or other tract for:
dilation of biliary duct stricture
removal of stone(s) except common duct stone
exploration (postoperative)
Percutaneous transhepatic biliary drainage
> EXCLUDES   percutaneous aspiration of gallbladder (51.01)
> percutaneous biopsy and/or collection of specimen by brushing or washing (51.12)
> percutaneous removal of common duct stone(s) (51.96)

AHA: 1Q, '97, 14; 3Q, '89, 18; N-D, '87, 1

51.99 Other
Insertion or replacement of biliary tract prosthesis
> EXCLUDES   biopsy of gallbladder (51.12-51.13)
> irrigation of cholecystostomy and other biliary tube (96.41)
> lysis of peritoneal adhesions (54.5)
> nonoperative removal of:
> cholecystostomy tube (97.54)
> tube from biliary tract or liver (97.55)

√3ʳᵈ **52 Operations on pancreas**
> INCLUDES   operations on pancreatic duct
Code also any application or administration of an adhesion barrier substance (99.77)

√4ᵗʰ **52.0 Pancreatotomy**
52.01 Drainage of pancreatic cyst by catheter
52.09 Other pancreatotomy
Pancreatolithotomy
> EXCLUDES   drainage by anastomosis (52.4, 52.96)
> incision of pancreatic sphincter (51.82)
> marsupialization of cyst (52.3)

DEF: Pancreatolithotomy: Incision into pancreas to remove stones.

√4ᵗʰ **52.1 Diagnostic procedures on pancreas**
52.11 Closed [aspiration] [needle] [percutaneous] biopsy of pancreas
52.12 Open biopsy of pancreas
52.13 Endoscopic retrograde pancreatography [ERP]
> EXCLUDES   endoscopic retrograde:
> cholangiography [ERC] (51.11)
> cholangiopancreatography [ERCP] (51.10)
> that for procedures classifiable to 51.14-51.15, 51.64, 51.84-51.88, 52.14, 52.21, 52.92-52.94, 52.97-52.98

52.14 Closed [endoscopic] biopsy of pancreatic duct
Closed biopsy of pancreatic duct by procedures classifiable to 51.10-51.11, 52.13

52.19 Other diagnostic procedures on pancreas
> EXCLUDES   contrast pancreatogram (87.66)
> endoscopic retrograde pancreatography [ERP] (52.13)
> microscopic examination of specimen from pancreas (91.01-91.09)

√4ᵗʰ **52.2 Local excision or destruction of pancreas and pancreatic duct**
> EXCLUDES   biopsy of pancreas (52.11-52.12, 52.14)
> pancreatic fistulectomy (52.95)

52.21 Endoscopic excision or destruction of lesion or tissue of pancreatic duct
Excision or destruction of lesion or tissue of pancreatic duct by procedures classifiable to 51.10-51.11, 52.13

52.22 Other excision or destruction of lesion or tissue of pancreas or pancreatic duct

52.3 Marsupialization of pancreatic cyst
> EXCLUDES   drainage of cyst by catheter (52.01)

DEF: Incision into pancreas and suturing edges to form pocket; promotes drainage and healing.

52.4 Internal drainage of pancreatic cyst
Pancreaticocystoduodenostomy
Pancreaticocystogastrostomy
Pancreaticocystojejunostomy

DEF: Withdrawing fluid from pancreatic cyst by draining it through a created passage to another organ.

DEF: Pancreaticocystoduodenostomy: Creation of passage from pancreatic cyst to first portion of small intestine.

DEF: Pancreaticocystogastrostomy: Creation of passage from pancreatic cyst to stomach.

DEF: Pancreaticocystojejunostomy: Creation of passage from pancreatic cyst to midsection of small intestine.

BI Bilateral Procedure   NC Non-covered Procedure   LC Limited Coverage Procedure   ►◄ Revised Text   ● New Code   ▲ Revised Code Title

134 — Volume 3   *2007 ICD•9•CM*

√4th **52.5 Partial pancreatectomy**
>   EXCLUDES   *pancreatic fistulectomy (52.95)*

52.51 Proximal pancreatectomy
> Excision of head of pancreas (with part of body)
> Proximal pancreatectomy with synchronous duodenectomy

52.52 Distal pancreatectomy
> Excision of tail of pancreas (with part of body)

52.53 Radical subtotal pancreatectomy

52.59 Other partial pancreatectomy

52.6 Total pancreatectomy
> Pancreatectomy with synchronous duodenectomy

AHA: 4Q, '96, 71

52.7 Radical pancreaticoduodenectomy
> One-stage pancreaticoduodenal resection with choledochojejunal anastomosis, pancreaticojejunal anastomosis, and gastrojejunostomy
> Two-stage pancreaticoduodenal resection (first stage) (second stage)
> Radical resection of the pancreas
> Whipple procedure
>   EXCLUDES   *radical subtotal pancreatectomy (52.53)*

AHA: 1Q, '01, 13

DEF: Whipple procedure: pancreaticoduodenectomy involving the removal of the head of the pancreas and part of the small intestines; pancreaticojejunostomy, choledochojejunal anastomosis, and gastrojejunostomy included in the procedure.

√4th **52.8 Transplant of pancreas**
> Note: To report donor source—*see* codes 00.91-00.93

21 **52.80 Pancreatic transplant, not otherwise specified** NC

52.81 Reimplantation of pancreatic tissue

21 **52.82 Homotransplant of pancreas** NC

52.83 Heterotransplant of pancreas NC

52.84 Autotransplantation of cells of islets of Langerhans
> Homotransplantation of islet cells of pancreas

AHA: 4Q, '96, 70, 71

DEF: Transplantation of Islet cells from pancreas to another location of same patient.

52.85 Allotransplantation of cells of islets of Langerhans
> Heterotransplantation of islet cells of pancreas

AHA: 4Q, '96, 70, 71

DEF: Transplantation of Islet cells from one individual to another.

52.86 Transplantation of cells of islets of Langerhans, not otherwise specified

AHA: 4Q, '96, 70

√4th **52.9 Other operations on pancreas**

DEF: Placement of tube into pancreatic duct, without an endoscope.

52.92 Cannulation of pancreatic duct
>   EXCLUDES   *that by endoscopic approach (52.93)*

52.93 Endoscopic insertion of stent (tube) into pancreatic duct
> Insertion of cannula or stent into pancreatic duct by procedures classifiable to 51.10-51.11, 52.13
>   EXCLUDES   *endoscopic insertion of nasopancreatic drainage tube (52.97)*
>   *replacement of stent (tube) (97.05)*

AHA: 2Q, '97, 7

52.94 Endoscopic removal of stone(s) from pancreatic duct
> Removal of stone(s) from pancreatic duct by procedures classifiable to 51.10-51.11, 52.13

52.95 Other repair of pancreas
> Fistulectomy } of pancreas
> Simple suture

52.96 Anastomosis of pancreas
> Anastomosis of pancreas (duct) to:
> intestine   stomach
> jejunum
>   EXCLUDES   *anastomosis to:*
>   *bile duct (51.39)*
>   *gallbladder (51.33)*

52.97 Endoscopic insertion of nasopancreatic drainage tube
> Insertion of nasopancreatic drainage tube by procedures classifiable to 51.10-51.11, 52.13
>   EXCLUDES   *drainage of pancreatic cyst by catheter (52.01)*
>   *replacement of stent (tube) (97.05)*

52.98 Endoscopic dilation of pancreatic duct
> Dilation of Wirsung's duct by procedures classifiable to 51.10-51.11, 52.13

52.99 Other
> Dilation of pancreatic [Wirsung's] duct } by open
> Repair of pancreatic [Wirsung's] duct } approach
>   EXCLUDES   *irrigation of pancreatic tube (96.42)*
>   *removal of pancreatic tube (97.56)*

√3rd **53 Repair of hernia**
>   INCLUDES   herniaplasty   herniotomy
>   herniorrhaphy
> Code also any application or administration of an adhesion barrier substance (99.77)
>   EXCLUDES   *manual reduction of hernia (96.27)*

AHA: 3Q, '94, 8

DEF: Repair of hernia: Restoration of abnormally protruding organ or tissue.
DEF: Herniorrhaphy: Repair of hernia.
DEF: Herniotomy: Division of constricted, strangulated, irreducible hernia.

√4th **53.0 Unilateral repair of inguinal hernia**

53.00 Unilateral repair of inguinal hernia, not otherwise specified
> Inguinal herniorrhaphy NOS

AHA: 3Q, '03, 10

53.01 Repair of direct inguinal hernia

AHA: 4Q, '96, 66

Indirect Repair of Hernia

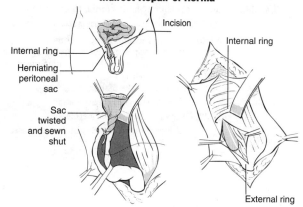

Incision
Internal ring
Internal ring
Herniating peritoneal sac
Sac twisted and sewn shut
External ring

---

21 Noncovered procedure unless a diagnosis code is present from 250.00-250.93.

Operations on the Digestive System

53.02–54.19

53.02   **Repair of indirect inguinal hernia**

53.03   **Repair of direct inguinal hernia with graft or prosthesis**

53.04   **Repair of indirect inguinal hernia with graft or prosthesis**

53.05   **Repair of inguinal hernia with graft or prosthesis, not otherwise specified**

✓4th **53.1**   **Bilateral repair of inguinal hernia**

53.10   **Bilateral repair of inguinal hernia, not otherwise specified**

53.11   **Bilateral repair of direct inguinal hernia**

53.12   **Bilateral repair of indirect inguinal hernia**

53.13   **Bilateral repair of inguinal hernia, one direct and one indirect**

53.14   **Bilateral repair of direct inguinal hernia with graft or prosthesis**

53.15   **Bilateral repair of indirect inguinal hernia with graft or prosthesis**

53.16   **Bilateral repair of inguinal hernia, one direct and one indirect, with graft or prosthesis**

53.17   **Bilateral inguinal hernia repair with graft or prosthesis, not otherwise specified**

✓4th **53.2**   **Unilateral repair of femoral hernia**

53.21   **Unilateral repair of femoral hernia with graft or prosthesis**

53.29   **Other unilateral femoral herniorrhaphy**

✓4th **53.3**   **Bilateral repair of femoral hernia**

53.31   **Bilateral repair of femoral hernia with graft or prosthesis**

53.39   **Other bilateral femoral herniorrhaphy**

✓4th **53.4**   **Repair of umbilical hernia**

> EXCLUDES   *repair of gastroschisis (54.71)*

53.41   **Repair of umbilical hernia with prosthesis**

53.49   **Other umbilical herniorrhaphy**

✓4th **53.5**   **Repair of other hernia of anterior abdominal wall (without graft or prosthesis)**

53.51   **Incisional hernia repair**

> AHA: 3Q, '03, 6

53.59   **Repair of other hernia of anterior abdominal wall**

> Repair of hernia: Repair of hernia:
>   epigastric   spigelian
>   hypogastric   ventral

> AHA: 3Q, '03, 6; 3Q, '96, 15

✓4th **53.6**   **Repair of other hernia of anterior abdominal wall with graft or prosthesis**

53.61   **Incisional hernia repair with prosthesis**

> AHA: 3Q, '03, 11

53.69   **Repair of other hernia of anterior abdominal wall with prosthesis**

53.7   **Repair of diaphragmatic hernia, abdominal approach**

✓4th **53.8**   **Repair of diaphragmatic hernia, thoracic approach**

> DEF: Repair of diaphragmatic hernia though abdomen and thorax.

53.80   **Repair of diaphragmatic hernia with thoracic approach, not otherwise specified**

> Thoracoabdominal repair of diaphragmatic hernia

53.81   **Plication of the diaphragm**

> DEF: Tuck repair of diaphragmatic hernia.

53.82   **Repair of parasternal hernia**

> DEF: Repair of hernia protruding into breastbone area.

53.9   **Other hernia repair**

> Repair of hernia: Repair of hernia:
>   ischiatic   omental
>   ischiorectal   retroperitoneal
>   lumbar   sciatic
>   obturator

> EXCLUDES   *relief of strangulated hernia with exteriorization of intestine (46.01, 46.03)*
> *repair of pericolostomy hernia (46.42)*
> *repair of vaginal enterocele (70.92)*

✓3rd **54**   **Other operations on abdominal region**

> INCLUDES   operations on: operations on:
>   epigastric region   male pelvic cavity
>   flank   mesentery
>   groin region   omentum
>   hypochondrium   peritoneum
>   inguinal region   retroperitoneal
>   loin region   tissue space

> Code also any application or administration of an adhesion barrier substance (99.77)

> EXCLUDES   *female pelvic cavity (69.01-70.92)*
> *hernia repair (53.00-53.9)*
> *obliteration of cul-de-sac (70.92)*
> *retroperitoneal tissue dissection (59.00-59.09)*
> *skin and subcutaneous tissue of abdominal wall (86.01-86.99)*

54.0   **Incision of abdominal wall**

> Drainage of:
>   abdominal wall
>   extraperitoneal abscess
>   retroperitoneal abscess

> EXCLUDES   *incision of peritoneum (54.95)*
> *laparotomy (54.11-54.19)*

> AHA: ▶4Q, '05, 77;◀ 1Q, '97, 11; N-D, '87, 12

✓4th **54.1**   **Laparotomy**

> AHA: 1Q, '92, 13

> DEF: Incision into abdomen.

54.11   **Exploratory laparotomy**

> EXCLUDES   *exploration incidental to intra-abdominal surgery — omit code*

> AHA: 3Q, '89, 14; 4Q, '88, 12

> DEF: Exam of peritoneal cavity through incision into abdomen.

54.12   **Reopening of recent laparotomy site**

> Reopening of recent laparotomy site for:
>   control of hemorrhage
>   exploration
>   incision of hematoma

54.19   **Other laparotomy**

> Drainage of intraperitoneal abscess or hematoma

> EXCLUDES   *culdocentesis (70.0)*
> *drainage of appendiceal abscess (47.2)*
> *exploration incidental to intra-abdominal surgery — omit code*
> *Ladd operation (54.95)*
> *percutaneous drainage of abdomen (54.91)*
> *removal of foreign body (54.92)*

> AHA: 3Q, '03, 17

BI Bilateral Procedure   **NC** Non-covered Procedure   **LC** Limited Coverage Procedure   ▶◀ Revised Text   ● New Code   ▲ Revised Code Title

136 — Volume 3 • February 2006   *2007 ICD•9•CM*

✓4ᵗʰ **54.2**　**Diagnostic procedures of abdominal region**

54.21　**Laparoscopy**

Peritoneoscopy

EXCLUDES　　laparoscopic cholecystectomy (51.23)

that incidental to destruction of fallopian tubes (66.21-66.29)

DEF: Endoscopic exam of peritoneal cavity through abdominal incision.

54.22　**Biopsy of abdominal wall or umbilicus**

54.23　**Biopsy of peritoneum**

Biopsy of:

mesentery

omentum

peritoneal implant

EXCLUDES　　closed biopsy of:

omentum (54.24)

peritoneum (54.24)

54.24　**Closed [percutaneous] [needle] biopsy of intra-abdominal mass**

Closed biopsy of:

omentum

peritoneal implant

peritoneum

EXCLUDES　　that of:

fallopian tube (66.11)

ovary (65.11)

uterine ligaments (68.15)

uterus (68.16)

AHA: 4Q, '97, 57

54.25　**Peritoneal lavage**

Diagnostic peritoneal lavage

EXCLUDES　　peritoneal dialysis (54.98)

AHA: 2Q, '98, 19; 4Q, '93, 28

DEF: Irrigation of peritoneal cavity with siphoning of liquid contents for analysis.

54.29　**Other diagnostic procedures on abdominal region**

EXCLUDES　　abdominal lymphangiogram (88.04)

abdominal x-ray NEC (88.19)

angiocardiography of venae cavae (88.51)

C.A.T. scan of abdomen (88.01)

contrast x-ray of abdominal cavity (88.11-88.15)

intra-abdominal arteriography NEC (88.47)

microscopic examination of peritoneal and retroperitoneal specimen (91.11-91.19)

phlebography of:

intra-abdominal vessels NEC (88.65)

portal venous system (88.64)

sinogram of abdominal wall (88.03)

soft tissue x-ray of abdominal wall NEC (88.09)

tomography of abdomen NEC (88.02)

ultrasonography of abdomen and retroperitoneum (88.76)

54.3　**Excision or destruction of lesion or tissue of abdominal wall or umbilicus**

Debridement of abdominal wall

Omphalectomy

EXCLUDES　　biopsy of abdominal wall or umbilicus (54.22)

size reduction operation (86.83)

that of skin of abdominal wall (86.22, 86.26, 86.3)

AHA: 1Q, '89, 11

54.4　**Excision or destruction of peritoneal tissue**

Excision of:

appendices epiploicae

falciform ligament

gastrocolic ligament

lesion of:

mesentery

omentum

peritoneum

presacral lesion NOS

retroperitoneal lesion NOS

EXCLUDES　　biopsy of peritoneum (54.23)

endometrectomy of cul-de-sac (70.32)

✓4ᵗʰ **54.5**　**Lysis of peritoneal adhesions**

Freeing of adhesions of:

biliary tract

intestines

liver

pelvic peritoneum

peritoneum

spleen

uterus

EXCLUDES　　lysis of adhesions of:

bladder (59.11)

fallopian tube and ovary (65.81, 65.89)

kidney (59.02)

ureter (59.02-59.03)

AHA: 3Q, '94, 8; 4Q, '90, 18

54.51　**Laparoscopic lysis of peritoneal adhesions**

AHA: 3Q, '03, 6-7; 4Q, '96, 65

54.59　**Other lysis of peritoneal adhesions**

AHA: 3Q, '03, 11; 1Q, '03, 14; 4Q, '96, 66

✓4ᵗʰ **54.6**　**Suture of abdominal wall and peritoneum**

54.61　**Reclosure of postoperative disruption of abdominal wall**

54.62　**Delayed closure of granulating abdominal wound**

Tertiary subcutaneous wound closure

DEF: Closure of outer layers of abdominal wound; follows procedure to close initial layers of wound.

54.63　**Other suture of abdominal wall**

Suture of laceration of abdominal wall

EXCLUDES　　closure of operative wound — omit code

54.64　**Suture of peritoneum**

Secondary suture of peritoneum

EXCLUDES　　closure of operative wound — omit code

✓4ᵗʰ **54.7**　**Other repair of abdominal wall and peritoneum**

54.71　**Repair of gastroschisis**

AHA: 2Q, '02, 9

DEF: Repair of congenital fistula of abdominal wall.

54.72　**Other repair of abdominal wall**

54.73　**Other repair of peritoneum**

Suture of gastrocolic ligament

Operations on the Digestive System

54.74   **Other repair of omentum**
Epiplorrhaphy
Graft of omentum
Omentopexy
Reduction of torsion of omentum
> EXCLUDES   cardio-omentopexy (36.39)

AHA: J-F, '87, 11

DEF: Epiplorrhaphy: Suture of abdominal serous membrane.

DEF: Graft of omentum: Implantation of tissue into abdominal serous membrane.

DEF: Omentopexy: Anchoring of abdominal serous membrane.

DEF: Reduction of torsion of omentum: Reduction of twisted abdominal serous membrane.

54.75   **Other repair of mesentery**
Mesenteric plication
Mesenteropexy

DEF: Creation of folds in mesentery for shortening.

DEF: Mesenteriopexy: Fixation of torn, incised mesentery.

√4ᵗʰ **54.9**   **Other operations of abdominal region**
> EXCLUDES   removal of ectopic pregnancy (74.3)

54.91   **Percutaneous abdominal drainage**
Paracentesis
> EXCLUDES   creation of cutaneoperitoneal fistula (54.93)

AHA: 3Q, '99, 9; 2Q, '99, 14; 3Q, '98, 12; 1Q, '92, 14; 2Q, '90, 25

DEF: Puncture for removal of fluid.

54.92   **Removal of foreign body from peritoneal cavity**

AHA: 1Q, '89, 11

54.93   **Creation of cutaneoperitoneal fistula**

AHA: 2Q, '95, 10; N-D, '84, 6

DEF: Creation of opening between skin and peritoneal cavity.

54.94   **Creation of peritoneovascular shunt**
Peritoneovenous shunt

AHA: 1Q, '94, 7; 1Q, '88, 9; S-O, '85, 6

DEF: Peritoneal vascular shunt: Construction of shunt to connect peritoneal cavity with vascular system.

DEF: Peritoneovenous shunt: Construction of shunt to connect peritoneal cavity with vein.

54.95   **Incision of peritoneum**
Exploration of ventriculoperitoneal shunt at peritoneal site
Ladd operation
Revision of distal catheter of ventricular shunt
Revision of ventriculoperitoneal shunt at peritoneal site
> EXCLUDES   that incidental to laparotomy (54.11-54.19)

AHA: 4Q, '95, 65

DEF: Ladd operation: Peritoneal attachment of incompletely rotated cecum, obstructing duodenum.

54.96   **Injection of air into peritoneal cavity**
Pneumoperitoneum
> EXCLUDES   that for:
> collapse of lung (33.33)
> radiography (88.12-88.13, 88.15)

54.97   **Injection of locally-acting therapeutic substance into peritoneal cavity**
> EXCLUDES   peritoneal dialysis (54.98)

54.98   **Peritoneal dialysis**
> EXCLUDES   peritoneal lavage (diagnostic) (54.25)

AHA: 4Q, '93, 28; N-D, '84, 6

DEF: Separation of blood elements by diffusion through membrane.

54.99   **Other**
> EXCLUDES   removal of:
> abdominal wall sutures (97.83)
> peritoneal drainage device (97.82)
> retroperitoneal drainage device (97.81)

AHA: 1Q, '99, 4

BI Bilateral Procedure   NC Non-covered Procedure   LC Limited Coverage Procedure   ▶◀ Revised Text   ● New Code   ▲ Revised Code Title

Operations on the Urinary System

55–55.4

10. OPERATIONS ON THE URINARY SYSTEM (55-59)

✓3rd 55   Operations on kidney

INCLUDES   operations on renal pelvis
Code also any application or administration of an adhesion barrier substance (99.77)
EXCLUDES   perirenal tissue (59.00-59.09, 59.21-59.29, 59.91-59.92)

✓4th 55.0   Nephrotomy and nephrostomy
EXCLUDES   drainage by:
     anastomosis (55.86)
     aspiration (55.92)

55.01   Nephrotomy
Evacuation of renal cyst
Exploration of kidney
Nephrolithotomy
DEF: Nephrotomy: Incision into kidney.
DEF: Evacuation of renal cyst: Draining contents of cyst.
DEF: Exploration of kidney: Exploration through incision.
DEF: Nephrolithotomy: Removal of kidney stone through incision.

55.02   Nephrostomy
AHA: 2Q, '97, 4

55.03   Percutaneous nephrostomy without fragmentation
Nephrostolithotomy, percutaneous (nephroscopic)
Percutaneous removal of kidney stone(s) by:
     forceps extraction (nephroscopic)
     basket extraction
Pyelostolithotomy, percutaneous (nephroscopic)
With placement of catheter down ureter
EXCLUDES   percutaneous removal by fragmentation (55.04)
     repeat nephroscopic removal during current episode (55.92)

AHA: 2Q, '96, 5

DEF: Insertion of tube through abdominal wall without breaking up stones.

DEF: Nephrostolithotomy: Insertion of tube through the abdominal wall to remove stones.

DEF: Basket extraction: Removal, percutaneous of stone with grasping forceps.

DEF: Pyelostolithotomy: Removal, percutaneous of stones from funnel-shaped portion of kidney.

55.04   Percutaneous nephrostomy with fragmentation
Percutaneous nephrostomy with disruption of kidney stone by ultrasonic energy and extraction (suction) through endoscope
With placement of catheter down ureter
With fluoroscopic guidance
EXCLUDES   repeat fragmentation during current episode (59.95)

AHA: 1Q, '89, 1; S-O, '86, 11

DEF: Insertion of tube through abdominal wall into kidney to break up stones.

✓4th 55.1   Pyelotomy and pyelostomy
EXCLUDES   drainage by anastomosis (55.86)
     percutaneous pyelostolithotomy (55.03)
     removal of calculus without incision (56.0)

55.11   Pyelotomy
Exploration of renal pelvis
Pyelolithotomy

55.12   Pyelostomy
Insertion of drainage tube into renal pelvis

✓4th 55.2   Diagnostic procedures on kidney

55.21   Nephroscopy
DEF: Endoscopic exam of renal pelvis; retrograde through ureter, percutaneous or open exposure.

55.22   Pyeloscopy
DEF: Fluoroscopic exam of kidney pelvis, calyces and ureters; follows IV or retrograde injection of contrast.

55.23   Closed [percutaneous] [needle] biopsy of kidney
Endoscopic biopsy via existing nephrostomy, nephrotomy, pyelostomy, or pyelotomy

55.24   Open biopsy of kidney
55.29   Other diagnostic procedures on kidney
EXCLUDES   microscopic examination of specimen from kidney (91.21-91.29)
     pyelogram:
         intravenous (87.73)
         percutaneous (87.75)
         retrograde (87.74)
     radioisotope scan (92.03)
     renal arteriography (88.45)
     tomography:
         C.A.T scan (87.71)
         other (87.72)

✓4th 55.3   Local excision or destruction of lesion or tissue of kidney

55.31   Marsupialization of kidney lesion
DEF: Exteriorization of lesion by incising anterior wall and suturing cut edges to create open pouch.

55.32   Open ablation of renal lesion or tissue
55.33   Percutaneous ablation of renal lesion or tissue
55.34   Laparoscopic ablation of renal lesion or tissue
55.35   Other and unspecified ablation of renal lesion or tissue
55.39   Other local destruction or excision of renal lesion or tissue
Obliteration of calyceal diverticulum
EXCLUDES   ▶ ablation of renal lesion or tissue:
     laparoscopic (55.34)
     open (55.32)
     other (55.35)
     percutaneous (55.33)◄
     biopsy of kidney (55.23-55.24)
     partial nephrectomy (55.4)
     percutaneous aspiration of kidney (55.92)
     wedge resection of kidney (55.4)

55.4   Partial nephrectomy
Calycectomy
Wedge resection of kidney
Code also any synchronous resection of ureter (56.40-56.42)
DEF: Surgical removal of a part of the kidney.

DEF: Calycectomy: Removal of indentations in kidney.

✓4th **55.5 Complete nephrectomy**
Code also any synchronous excision of:
adrenal gland (07.21-07.3)
bladder segment (57.6)
lymph nodes (40.3, 40.52-40.59)

55.51 Nephroureterectomy
Nephroureterectomy with bladder cuff
Total nephrectomy (unilateral)
EXCLUDES *removal of transplanted kidney (55.53)*

AHA: ▶2Q, '05, 4◀

DEF: Complete removal of the kidney and all or portion of the ureter.

DEF: Nephroureterectomy with bladder cuff: Removal of kidney, ureter, and portion of bladder attached to ureter.

DEF: Total nephrectomy (unilateral): Complete excision of one kidney.

55.52 Nephrectomy of remaining kidney
Removal of solitary kidney
EXCLUDES *removal of transplanted kidney (55.53)*

55.53 Removal of transplanted or rejected kidney

55.54 Bilateral nephrectomy
EXCLUDES *complete nephrectomy NOS (55.51)*

DEF: Removal of both kidneys same operative session.

✓4th **55.6 Transplant of kidney**
Note: To report donor source — see codes 00.91-00.93

55.61 Renal autotransplantation

55.69 Other kidney transplantation
AHA: ▶4Q, '04, 117;◀ 4Q, '96, 71

55.7 Nephropexy
Fixation or suspension of movable [floating] kidney

✓4th **55.8 Other repair of kidney**

55.81 Suture of laceration of kidney

55.82 Closure of nephrostomy and pyelostomy

DEF: Removal of tube from kidney and closure of site of tube insertion.

55.83 Closure of other fistula of kidney

55.84 Reduction of torsion of renal pedicle

DEF: Restoration of twisted renal pedicle into normal position.

55.85 Symphysiotomy for horseshoe kidney

DEF: Division of congenitally malformed kidney into two parts.

55.86 Anastomosis of kidney
Nephropyeloureterostomy
Pyeloureterovesical anastomosis
Ureterocalyceal anastomosis
EXCLUDES *nephrocystanastomosis NOS (56.73)*

DEF: Nephropyeloureterostomy: Creation of passage between kidney and ureter.

DEF: Pyeloureterovesical anastomosis: Creation of passage between kidney and bladder.

DEF: Ureterocalyceal anastomosis: Creation of passage between ureter and kidney indentations.

55.87 Correction of ureteropelvic junction

55.89 Other

✓4th **55.9 Other operations on kidney**
EXCLUDES *lysis of perirenal adhesions (59.02)*

55.91 Decapsulation of kidney
Capsulectomy ⎱
Decortication ⎰ of kidney

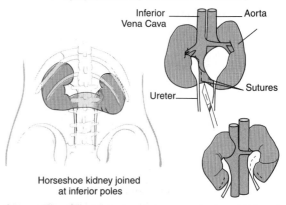
Symphysiostomy for Horseshoe Kidney

Inferior Vena Cava — Aorta
Ureter — Sutures

Horseshoe kidney joined at inferior poles

55.92 Percutaneous aspiration of kidney (pelvis)
Aspiration of renal cyst   Renipuncture
EXCLUDES *percutaneous biopsy of kidney (55.23)*

AHA: N-D, '84, 20

DEF: Insertion of needle into kidney to withdraw fluid.

55.93 Replacement of nephrostomy tube

55.94 Replacement of pyelostomy tube

55.95 Local perfusion of kidney

DEF: Fluid passage through kidney.

55.96 Other injection of therapeutic substance into kidney
Injection into renal cyst

55.97 Implantation or replacement of mechanical kidney

55.98 Removal of mechanical kidney

55.99 Other
EXCLUDES *removal of pyelostomy or nephrostomy tube (97.61)*

✓3rd **56 Operations on ureter**
Code also any application or administration of an adhesion barrier substance (99.77)

56.0 Transurethral removal of obstruction from ureter and renal pelvis
Removal of:
blood clot ⎫
calculus   ⎬ from ureter or renal pelvis
foreign body ⎭ without incision
EXCLUDES *manipulation without removal of obstruction (59.8)*
that by incision (55.11,56.2)
transurethral insertion of ureteral stent for passage of calculus (59.8)

AHA: 1Q, '89, 1; S-O, '86, 12

DEF: Removal of obstruction by tube inserted through urethra to ureter.

56.1 Ureteral meatotomy

DEF: Incision into ureteral meatus to enlarge passage.

56.2 Ureterotomy
Incision of ureter for: Incision of ureter for:
drainage   removal of calculus
exploration
EXCLUDES *cutting of ureterovesical orifice (56.1)*
removal of calculus without incision (56.0)
transurethral insertion of ureteral stent for passage of calculus (59.8)
urinary diversion (56.51-56.79)

AHA: S-O, '86, 10

BI Bilateral Procedure   **NC** Non-covered Procedure   **LC** Limited Coverage Procedure   ▶◀ Revised Text   ● New Code   ▲ Revised Code Title

140 — Volume 3 • February 2006   *2007 ICD•9•CM*

√4ᵗʰ **56.3** **Diagnostic procedures on ureter**

56.31 **Ureteroscopy**

56.32 **Closed percutaneous biopsy of ureter**
> EXCLUDES   *endoscopic biopsy of ureter (56.33)*

56.33 **Closed endoscopic biopsy of ureter**
Cystourethroscopy with ureteral biopsy
Transurethral biopsy of ureter
Ureteral endoscopy with biopsy through ureterotomy
Ureteroscopy with biopsy
> EXCLUDES   *percutaneous biopsy of ureter (56.32)*

56.34 **Open biopsy of ureter**

56.35 **Endoscopy (cystoscopy) (looposcopy) of ileal conduit**
DEF: Endoscopic exam of created opening between ureters and one end of small intestine; other end used to form artificial opening.

56.39 **Other diagnostic procedures on ureter**
> EXCLUDES   *microscopic examination of specimen from ureter (91.21-91.29)*

√4ᵗʰ **56.4** **Ureterectomy**
Code also anastomosis other than end-to-end (56.51-56.79)
> EXCLUDES   *fistulectomy (56.84)*
> *nephroureterectomy (55.51-55.54)*

56.40 **Ureterectomy, not otherwise specified**

56.41 **Partial ureterotomy**
Excision of lesion of ureter
Shortening of ureter with reimplantation
> EXCLUDES   *biopsy of ureter (56.32-56.34)*

56.42 **Total ureterectomy**

√4ᵗʰ **56.5** **Cutaneous uretero-ileostomy**

56.51 **Formation of cutaneous uretero-ileostomy**
Construction of ileal conduit
External ureteral ileostomy
Formation of open ileal bladder
Ileal loop operation
Ileoureterostomy (Bricker's) (ileal bladder)
Transplantation of ureter into ileum with external diversion
> EXCLUDES   *closed ileal bladder (57.87)*
> *replacement of ureteral defect by ileal segment (56.89)*

DEF: Creation of urinary passage by connecting the terminal end of small intestine to ureter then connected to opening through abdominal wall.

DEF: Construction of ileal conduit: Formation of conduit from terminal end of small intestine.

56.52 **Revision of cutaneous uretero-ileostomy**
AHA: 3Q, '96, 15; 4Q, '88, 7

√4ᵗʰ **56.6** **Other external urinary diversion**

56.61 **Formation of other cutaneous ureterostomy**
Anastomosis of ureter to skin
Ureterostomy NOS

56.62 **Revision of other cutaneous ureterostomy**
Revision of ureterostomy stoma
> EXCLUDES   *nonoperative removal of ureterostomy tube (97.62)*

√4ᵗʰ **56.7** **Other anastomosis or bypass of ureter**
> EXCLUDES   *ureteropyelostomy (55.86)*

56.71 **Urinary diversion to intestine**
Anastomosis of ureter to intestine
Internal urinary diversion NOS
Code also any synchronous colostomy (46.10-46.13)
> EXCLUDES   *external ureteral ileostomy (56.51)*

56.72 **Revision of ureterointestinal anastomosis**
> EXCLUDES   *revision of external ureteral ileostomy (56.52)*

56.73 **Nephrocystanastomosis, not otherwise specified**
DEF: Connection of kidney to bladder.

56.74 **Ureteroneocystostomy**
Replacement of ureter with bladder flap
Ureterovesical anastomosis
DEF: Transfer of ureter to another site in bladder.
DEF: Ureterovesical anastomosis: Implantation of ureter into bladder.

56.75 **Transureteroureterostomy**
> EXCLUDES   *ureteroureterostomy associated with partial resection (56.41)*

DEF: Separating one ureter and joining the ends to the opposite ureter.

56.79 **Other**

√4ᵗʰ **56.8** **Repair of ureter**

56.81 **Lysis of intraluminal adhesions of ureter**
> EXCLUDES   *lysis of periureteral adhesions (59.01-59.02)*
> *ureterolysis (59.02-59.03)*

DEF: Destruction of adhesions within urethral cavity.

56.82 **Suture of laceration of ureter**

56.83 **Closure of ureterostomy**

56.84 **Closure of other fistula of ureter**

56.85 **Ureteropexy**

56.86 **Removal of ligature from ureter**

56.89 **Other repair of ureter**
Graft of ureter
Replacement of ureter with ileal segment implanted into bladder
Ureteroplication
DEF: Graft of ureter: Tissue from another site for graft replacement or repair of ureter.
DEF: Replacement of ureter with ileal segment implanted into bladder and ureter replacement with terminal end of small intestine.
DEF: Ureteroplication: Creation of tucks in ureter.

√4ᵗʰ **56.9** **Other operations on ureter**

56.91 **Dilation of ureteral meatus**

56.92 **Implantation of electronic ureteral stimulator**

56.93 **Replacement of electronic ureteral stimulator**

56.94 **Removal of electronic ureteral stimulator**
> EXCLUDES   *that with synchronous replacement (56.93)*

56.95 **Ligation of ureter**

56.99 **Other**
> EXCLUDES   *removal of ureterostomy tube and ureteral catheter (97.62)*
> *ureteral catheterization (59.8)*

√3ʳᵈ **57** **Operations on urinary bladder**
Code also any application or administration of an adhesion barrier substance (99.77)
> EXCLUDES   *perivesical tissue (59.11-59.29, 59.91-59.92)*
> *ureterovesical orifice (56.0-56.99)*

57.0 **Transurethral clearance of bladder**
Drainage of bladder without incision
Removal of:
  blood clot
  calculus   } from bladder without incision
  foreign body
> EXCLUDES   *that by incision (57.19)*

AHA: S-O, '86, 11

DEF: Insertion of device through urethra to cleanse bladder.

Operations on the Urinary System

56.3–57.0

Operations on the Urinary System

57.1–57.6

✓4ᵗʰ 57.1   **Cystotomy and cystostomy**

> **EXCLUDES**   *cystotomy and cystostomy as operative approach — omit code*

DEF: Cystotomy: Incision of bladder.

DEF: Cystostomy: Creation of opening into bladder.

57.11   **Percutaneous aspiration of bladder**

57.12   **Lysis of intraluminal adhesions with incision into bladder**

> **EXCLUDES**   *transurethral lysis of intraluminal adhesions (57.41)*

DEF: Incision into bladder to destroy lesions.

57.17   **Percutaneous cystostomy**

Closed cystostomy
Percutaneous suprapubic cystostomy

> **EXCLUDES**   *removal of cystostomy tube (97.63)*
> *replacement of cystostomy tube (59.94)*

DEF: Incision through body wall into bladder to insert tube.

DEF: Percutaneous (closed) suprapubic cystostomy: Incision above pubic arch, through body wall, into the bladder to insert tube.

57.18   **Other suprapubic cystostomy**

> **EXCLUDES**   *percutaneous cystostomy (57.17)*
> *removal of cystostomy tube (97.63)*
> *replacement of cystostomy tube (59.94)*

57.19   **Other cystotomy**

Cystolithotomy

> **EXCLUDES**   *percutaneous cystostomy (57.17)*
> *suprapubic cystostomy (57.18)*

AHA: 4Q, '95, 73; S-O, '86, 11

✓4ᵗʰ 57.2   **Vesicostomy**

> **EXCLUDES**   *percutaneous cystostomy (57.17)*
> *suprapubic cystostomy (57.18)*

57.21   **Vesicostomy**

Creation of permanent opening from bladder to skin using a bladder flap

DEF: Creation of permanent opening from the bladder to the skin.

57.22   **Revision or closure of vesicostomy**

> **EXCLUDES**   *closure of cystostomy (57.82)*

✓4ᵗʰ 57.3   **Diagnostic procedures on bladder**

57.31   **Cystoscopy through artificial stoma**

57.32   **Other cystoscopy**

Transurethral cystoscopy

> **EXCLUDES**   *cystourethroscopy with ureteral biopsy (56.33)*
> *retrograde pyelogram (87.74)*
> *that for control of hemorrhage (postoperative):*
> *bladder (57.93)*
> *prostate (60.94)*

AHA: 1Q, '01, 14

57.33   **Closed [transurethral] biopsy of bladder**

57.34   **Open biopsy of bladder**

AHA: ▶2Q, '05, 12◀

Transurethral Cystourethroscopy

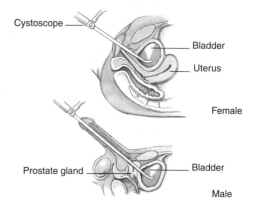

Cystoscope — Bladder — Uterus
Female
Prostate gland — Bladder
Male

57.39   **Other diagnostic procedures on bladder**

> **EXCLUDES**   *cystogram NEC (87.77)*
> *microscopic examination of specimen from bladder (91.31-91.39)*
> *retrograde cystourethrogram (87.76)*
> *therapeutic distention of bladder (96.25)*

✓4ᵗʰ 57.4   **Transurethral excision or destruction of bladder tissue**

DEF: Destruction of bladder tissue with instrument inserted into urethra.

57.41   **Transurethral lysis of intraluminal adhesions**

57.49   **Other transurethral excision or destruction of lesion or tissue of bladder**

Endoscopic resection of bladder lesion

> **EXCLUDES**   *transurethral biopsy of bladder (57.33)*
> *transurethral fistulectomy (57.83-57.84)*

✓4ᵗʰ 57.5   **Other excision or destruction of bladder tissue**

> **EXCLUDES**   *that with transurethral approach (57.41-57.49)*

57.51   **Excision of urachus**

Excision of urachal sinus of bladder

> **EXCLUDES**   *excision of urachal cyst of abdominal wall (54.3)*

57.59   **Open excision or destruction of other lesion or tissue of bladder**

Endometrectomy of bladder
Suprapubic excision of bladder lesion

> **EXCLUDES**   *biopsy of bladder (57.33-57.34)*
> *fistulectomy of bladder (57.83-57.84)*

DEF: Endometrectomy of bladder: Removal of inner lining.

DEF: Suprapubic excision of bladder lesion: Removal of lesion by excision above suprapubic bone arch.

57.6   **Partial cystectomy**

Excision of bladder dome
Trigonectomy
Wedge resection of bladder

BI Bilateral Procedure   **NC** Non-covered Procedure   **LC** Limited Coverage Procedure   ▶◀ Revised Text   ● New Code   ▲ Revised Code Title

142 — Volume 3 • February 2006   **2007 ICD•9•CM**

√4ᵗʰ **57.7** **Total cystectomy**

INCLUDES total cystectomy with urethrectomy

57.71 **Radical cystectomy**
Pelvic exenteration in male
Removal of bladder, prostate, seminal
vesicles and fat
Removal of bladder, urethra, and fat in a
female
Code also any:
lymph node dissection (40.3, 40.5)
urinary diversion (56.51-56.79)

EXCLUDES *that as part of pelvic*
exenteration in female
(68.8)

DEF: Radical cystectomy: Removal of bladder and
surrounding tissue.

DEF: Pelvic exenteration in male: Excision of bladder,
prostate, seminal vessels and fat.

57.79 **Other total cystectomy**

√4ᵗʰ **57.8** **Other repair of urinary bladder**

EXCLUDES *repair of:*
current obstetric laceration (75.61)
cystocele (70.50-70.51)
that for stress incontinence (59.3-59.79)

57.81 **Suture of laceration of bladder**

57.82 **Closure of cystostomy**

57.83 **Repair of fistula involving bladder and
intestine**

Rectovesicovaginal ⎫
Vesicosigmoidovaginal ⎭ fistulectomy

57.84 **Repair of other fistula of bladder**

Cervicovesical ⎫
Urethroperineovesical ⎪
Uterovesical ⎬ fistulectomy
Vaginovesical ⎭

EXCLUDES *vesicoureterovaginal*
fistulectomy (56.84)

57.85 **Cystourethroplasty and plastic repair of
bladder neck**

Plication of sphincter of urinary bladder
V-Y plasty of bladder neck

DEF: Cystourethroplasty: Reconstruction of narrowed
portion of bladder.

DEF: Plication of sphincter or urinary bladder: Creation of
tuck in bladder sphincter.

DEF: V-Y plasty of bladder neck: Surgical reconstruction
of the narrowed portion of bladder by V-Y technique.

57.86 **Repair of bladder exstrophy**

DEF: Surgical correction of a congenital bladder wall
defect.

57.87 **Reconstruction of urinary bladder**

Anastomosis of bladder with isolated
segment of ileum
Augmentation of bladder
Replacement of bladder with ileum or
sigmoid [closed ileal bladder]
Code also resection of intestine (45.50-
45.52)

AHA: ▶2Q, '05, 12;◀ 2Q, '03, 11; 3Q, '00, 7

DEF: Anastomosis of bladder with isolated segment of
ileum: Creation of connection between bladder and
separated terminal end of small intestine.

57.88 **Other anastomosis of bladder**

Anastomosis of bladder to intestine NOS
Cystocolic anastomosis

EXCLUDES *formation of closed ileal*
bladder (57.87)

57.89 **Other repair of bladder**

Bladder suspension, not elsewhere classified
Cystopexy NOS
Repair of old obstetric laceration of bladder

EXCLUDES *repair of current obstetric*
laceration (75.61)

√4ᵗʰ **57.9** **Other operations on bladder**

57.91 **Sphincterotomy of bladder**
Division of bladder neck
AHA: 2Q, '90, 26

57.92 **Dilation of bladder neck**

57.93 **Control of (postoperative) hemorrhage of
bladder**

57.94 **Insertion of indwelling urinary catheter**

57.95 **Replacement of indwelling urinary catheter**

57.96 **Implantation of electronic bladder
stimulator** NC

57.97 **Replacement of electronic bladder
stimulator** NC

57.98 **Removal of electronic bladder stimulator**

EXCLUDES *that with synchronous*
replacement (57.97)

57.99 **Other**

EXCLUDES *irrigation of:*
cystostomy (96.47)
other indwelling urinary
catheter (96.48)
lysis of external adhesions
(59.11)
removal of:
cystostomy tube (97.63)
other urinary drainage
device (97.64)
therapeutic distention of
bladder (96.25)

√3ʳᵈ **58** **Operations on urethra**

INCLUDES operations on:
bulbourethral gland [Cowper's gland]
periurethral tissue
Code also any application or administration of an adhesion
barrier substance (99.77)

58.0 **Urethrotomy**

Excision of urethral septum
Formation of urethrovaginal fistula
Perineal urethrostomy
Removal of calculus from urethra by incision

EXCLUDES *drainage of bulbourethral gland or*
periurethral tissue (58.91)
internal urethral meatotomy (58.5)
removal of urethral calculus without
incision (58.6)

58.1 **Urethral meatotomy**

EXCLUDES *internal urethral meatotomy (58.5)*

DEF: Incision of urethra to enlarge passage.

√4ᵗʰ **58.2** **Diagnostic procedures on urethra**

58.21 **Perineal urethroscopy**

58.22 **Other urethroscopy**

58.23 **Biopsy of urethra**

58.24 **Biopsy of periurethral tissue**
DEF: Removal for biopsy of tissue around urethra.

58.29 **Other diagnostic procedures on urethra and
periurethral tissue**

EXCLUDES *microscopic examination of*
specimen from urethra
(91.31-91.39)
retrograde cystourethrogram
(87.76)
urethral pressure profile
(89.25)
urethral sphincter
electromyogram (89.23)

√3ʳᵈ √4ᵗʰ Additional Digit Required   Nonspecific OR Procedure   Valid OR Procedure   Non-OR Procedure   Adjunct Code

Operations on the Urinary System

57.7–58.29

Operations on the Urinary System

58.3–59.3

✓4ᵗʰ **58.3**   **Excision or destruction of lesion or tissue of urethra**

> **EXCLUDES**   *biopsy of urethra (58.23)*
> *excision of bulbourethral gland (58.92)*
> *fistulectomy (58.43)*
> *urethrectomy as part of:*
>   *complete cystectomy (57.79)*
>   *pelvic evisceration (68.8)*
>   *radical cystectomy (57.71)*

   58.31   **Endoscopic excision or destruction of lesion or tissue of urethra**

       Fulguration of urethral lesion

   58.39   **Other local excision or destruction of lesion or tissue of urethra**

       Excision of:
         congenital valve
         lesion   } of urethra
         stricture

       Urethrectomy
> **EXCLUDES**   *that by endoscopic appoach (58.31)*

✓4ᵗʰ **58.4**   **Repair of urethra**

> **EXCLUDES**   *repair of current obstetric laceration (75.61)*

   58.41   **Suture of laceration of urethra**

   58.42   **Closure of urethrostomy**

   58.43   **Closure of other fistula of urethra**
> **EXCLUDES**   *repair of urethroperineovesical fistula (57.84)*

   58.44   **Reanastomosis of urethra**

       Anastomosis of urethra

       DEF: Repair of severed urethra.

   58.45   **Repair of hypospadias or epispadias**

       AHA: 3Q, '97, 6; 4Q, '96, 35

       DEF: Repair of abnormal urethral opening.

   58.46   **Other reconstruction of urethra**

       Urethral construction

   58.47   **Urethral meatoplasty**

       DEF: Reconstruction of urethral opening.

   58.49   **Other repair of urethra**

       Benenenti rotation of bulbous urethra
       Repair of old obstetric laceration of urethra
       Urethral plication
> **EXCLUDES**   *repair of:*
>   *current obstetric laceration (75.61)*
>   *urethrocele (70.50-70.51)*

   58.5   **Release of urethral stricture**

       Cutting of urethral sphincter
       Internal urethral meatotomy
       Urethrolysis

       AHA: 1Q, '97, 13

   58.6   **Dilation of urethra**

       Dilation of urethrovesical junction
       Passage of sounds through urethra
       Removal of calculus from urethra without incision
> **EXCLUDES**   *urethral calibration (89.29)*

       AHA: 1Q, '01, 14; 1Q, '97, 13

✓4ᵗʰ **58.9**   **Other operations on urethra and periurethral tissue**

   58.91   **Incision of periurethral tissue**

       Drainage of bulbourethral gland

       DEF: Incision of tissue around urethra.

   58.92   **Excision of periurethral tissue**
> **EXCLUDES**   *biopsy of periurethral tissue (58.24)*
> *lysis of periurethral adhesions (59.11-59.12)*

   58.93   **Implantation of artificial urinary sphincter [AUS]**

       Placement of inflatable:
         urethral sphincter
         bladder sphincter
       Removal with replacement of sphincter device [AUS]
       With pump and/or reservoir

   58.99   **Other**

       Repair of inflatable sphincter pump and/or reservoir
       Surgical correction of hydraulic pressure of inflatable sphincter device
       Removal of inflatable urinary sphincter without replacement
> **EXCLUDES**   *removal of:*
>   *intraluminal foreign body from urethra without incision (98.19)*
>   *urethral stent (97.65)*

✓3ʳᵈ **59**   **Other operations on urinary tract**

       Code also any application or administration of an adhesion barrier substance (99.77)

✓4ᵗʰ **59.0**   **Dissection of retroperitoneal tissue**

   59.00   **Retroperitoneal dissection, not otherwise specified**

   59.02   **Other lysis of perirenal or periureteral adhesions**
> **EXCLUDES**   *that by laparoscope (59.03)*

   59.03   **Laparoscopic lysis of perirenal or periureteral adhesions**

   59.09   **Other incision of perirenal or periureteral tissue**

       Exploration of perinephric area
       Incision of perirenal abscess

       DEF: Exploration of the perinephric area: Exam of tissue around the kidney by incision.

       DEF: Incision of perirenal abscess: Incising abscess in tissue around kidney.

✓4ᵗʰ **59.1**   **Incision of perivesical tissue**

       DEF: Incising tissue around bladder.

   59.11   **Other lysis of perivesical adhesions**

   59.12   **Laparoscopic lysis of perivesical adhesions**

   59.19   **Other incision of perivesical tissue**

       Exploration of perivesical tissue
       Incision of hematoma of space of Retzius
       Retropubic exploration

✓4ᵗʰ **59.2**   **Diagnostic procedures on perirenal and perivesical tissue**

   59.21   **Biopsy of perirenal or perivesical tissue**

   59.29   **Other diagnostic procedures on perirenal tissue, perivesical tissue, and retroperitoneum**
> **EXCLUDES**   *microscopic examination of specimen from:*
>   *perirenal tissue (91.21-91.29)*
>   *perivesical tissue (91.31-91.39)*
>   *retroperitoneum NEC (91.11-91.19)*
>   *retroperitoneal x-ray (88.14-88.16)*

   59.3   **Plication of urethrovesical junction**

       Kelly-Kennedy operation on urethra
       Kelly-Stoeckel urethral plication

       DEF: Suturing a tuck in tissues around urethra at junction with bladder; changes angle of junction and provides support.

BI Bilateral Procedure   **NC** Non-covered Procedure   **LC** Limited Coverage Procedure   ▶◀ Revised Text   ● New Code   ▲ Revised Code Title

144 — Volume 3   *2007 ICD•9•CM*

59.4   Suprapubic sling operation
>   Goebel-Frangenheim-Stoeckel urethrovesical
>   suspension
>   Millin-Read urethrovesical suspension
>   Oxford operation for urinary incontinence
>   Urethrocystopexy by suprapubic suspension

DEF: Suspension of urethra from suprapubic periosteum to restore support to bladder and urethra.

59.5   Retropubic urethral suspension
>   Burch procedure
>   Marshall-Marchetti-Krantz operation
>   Suture of periurethral tissue to symphysis pubis
>   Urethral suspension NOS

AHA: 1Q, '97, 11

DEF: Suspension of urethra from pubic bone with suture placed from symphysis pubis to paraurethral tissues; elevates urethrovesical angle, restores urinary continence.

59.6   Paraurethral suspension
>   Pereyra paraurethral suspension
>   Periurethral suspension

DEF: Suspension of bladder neck from fibrous membranes of anterior abdominal wall; upward traction applied; changes angle of urethra, improves urinary control.

√4ᵗʰ 59.7   Other repair of urinary stress incontinence

59.71   Levator muscle operation for urethrovesical suspension
>   Cystourethropexy with levator muscle sling
>   Gracilis muscle transplant for
>   urethrovesical suspension
>   Pubococcygeal sling

59.72   Injection of implant into urethra and/or bladder neck
>   Collagen implant
>   Endoscopic injection of implant
>   Fat implant
>   Polytef implant

AHA: 4Q, '95, 72, 73

DEF: Injection of collagen into submucosal tissues to increase tissue bulk and improve urinary control.

59.79   Other
>   Anterior urethropexy
>   Repair of stress incontinence NOS
>   Tudor "rabbit ear" urethropexy

AHA: 2Q, '01, 20; 1Q, '00, 14, 15, 19

DEF: Pubovaginal sling for treatment of stress incontinence: A strip of fascia is harvested and the vaginal epithelium is mobilized and then sutured to the midline at the urethral level to the rectus muscle to create a sling supporting the bladder.

DEF: Vaginal wall sling with bone anchors for treatment of stress incontinence: A sling for the bladder is formed by a suture attachment of vaginal wall to the abdominal wall. In addition, a suture is run from the vagina to a bone anchor placed in the pubic bone.

DEF: Transvaginal endoscopic bladder neck suspension for treatment of stress incontinence: Endoscopic surgical suturing of the vaginal epithelium and the pubocervical fascia at the bladder neck level on both sides of the urethra. Two supporting sutures are run from the vagina to an anchor placed in the pubic bone on each side.

59.8   Ureteral catheterization
>   Drainage of kidney by catheter
>   Insertion of ureteral stent
>   Ureterovesical orifice dilation
>   Code also any ureterotomy (56.2)

EXCLUDES   that for:
>   transurethral removal of calculus or
>   clot from ureter and renal
>   pelvis (56.0)
>   retrograde pyelogram (87.74)

AHA: ▶2Q, '05, 12;◀ 2Q, '03, 11; 3Q, '00, 7; 1Q, '89, 1; S-O, '86, 10

√4ᵗʰ 59.9   Other operations on urinary system
EXCLUDES   nonoperative removal of therapeutic
>   device (97.61-97.69)

59.91   Excision of perirenal or perivesical tissue
EXCLUDES   biopsy of perirenal or
>   perivesical tissue (59.21)

59.92   Other operations on perirenal or perivesical tissue

59.93   Replacement of ureterostomy tube
>   Change of ureterostomy tube
>   Reinsertion of ureterostomy tube
EXCLUDES   nonoperative removal of
>   ureterostomy tube
>   (97.62)

59.94   Replacement of cystostomy tube
EXCLUDES   nonoperative removal of
>   cystostomy tube (97.63)

59.95   Ultrasonic fragmentation of urinary stones
>   Shattered urinary stones
EXCLUDES   percutaneous nephrostomy
>   with fragmentation
>   (55.04)
>   shockwave disintegration
>   (98.51)

AHA: 1Q, '89, 1; S-O, '86, 11

59.99   Other
EXCLUDES   instillation of medication into
>   urinary tract (96.49)
>   irrigation of urinary tract
>   (96.45-96.48)

Operations on the Male Genital Organs

60–60.79

11. OPERATIONS ON THE MALE GENITAL ORGANS (60-64)

√3ʳᵈ **60 Operations on prostate and seminal vesicles**

Code also any application or administration of an adhesion barrier substance (99.77)

INCLUDES operations on periprostatic tissue
EXCLUDES *that associated with radical cystectomy (57.71)*

60.0 Incision of prostate ♂

Drainage of prostatic abscess
Prostatolithotomy
EXCLUDES *drainage of periprostatic tissue only (60.81)*

√4ᵗʰ **60.1 Diagnostic procedures on prostate and seminal vesicles**

60.11 Closed [percutaneous] [needle] biopsy of prostate ♂

Approach:
  transrectal   Punch biopsy
  transurethral

DEF: Excision of prostate tissue by closed technique for biopsy.

60.12 Open biopsy of prostate ♂
60.13 Closed [percutaneous] biopsy of seminal vesicles ♂

Needle biopsy of seminal vesicles

60.14 Open biopsy of seminal vesicles ♂
60.15 Biopsy of periprostatic tissue ♂
60.18 Other diagnostic procedures on prostate and periprostatic tissue ♂

EXCLUDES *microscopic examination of specimen from prostate (91.31-91.39)*
x-ray of prostate (87.92)

60.19 Other diagnostic procedures on seminal vesicles ♂

EXCLUDES *microscopic examination of specimen from seminal vesicles (91.31-91.39)*
x-ray:
contrast seminal vesiculogram (87.91)
other (87.92)

√4ᵗʰ **60.2 Transurethral prostatectomy**

EXCLUDES *local excision of lesion of prostate (60.61)*

AHA: 2Q, '94, 9; 3Q, '92, 13

60.21 Transurethral (ultrasound) guided laser induced prostatectomy (TULIP) ♂

Ablation (contact) (noncontact) by laser
AHA: 4Q, '95, 7

60.29 Other transurethral prostatectomy ♂

Excision of median bar by transurethral approach
Transurethral electrovaporization of prostate (TEVAP)
Transurethral enucleative procedure
Transurethral prostatectomy NOS
Transurethral resection of prostate (TURP)

DEF: Excision of median bar by transurethral approach: Removal of fibrous structure of prostate.

DEF: Transurethral enucleative procedure: Transurethral prostatectomy.

AHA: 3Q, '97, 3

Transurethral Prostatectomy

Resectoscope

Adenomatous prostate

60.3 Suprapubic prostatectomy ♂

Transvesical prostatectomy
EXCLUDES *local excision of lesion of prostate (60.61)*
radical prostatectomy (60.5)

DEF: Resection of prostate through incision in abdomen above pubic arch.

60.4 Retropubic prostatectomy ♂

EXCLUDES *local excision of lesion of prostate (60.61)*
radical prostatectomy (60.5)

DEF: Removal of the prostate using an abdominal approach with direct cutting into prostatic capsule.

60.5 Radical prostatectomy ♂

Prostatovesiculectomy
Radical prostatectomy by any approach
EXCLUDES *cystoprostatectomy (57.71)*

AHA: 3Q, '93, 12

DEF: Removal of prostate, epididymis and vas ampullae.
DEF: Prostatovesiculectomy: Removal of prostate and epididymis.

√4ᵗʰ **60.6 Other prostatectomy**

60.61 Local excision of lesion of prostate ♂

Excision of prostatic lesion by any approach
EXCLUDES *biopsy of prostate (60.11-60.12)*

60.62 Perineal prostatectomy ♂

Cryoablation of prostate
Cryoprostatectomy
Cryosurgery of prostate
Radical cryosurcial ablation of prostate (RCSA)
EXCLUDES *local excision of lesion of prostate (60.61)*

AHA: 4Q, '95, 71

DEF: Excision of prostate tissue through incision between scrotum and anus.

60.69 Other ♂

√4ᵗʰ **60.7 Operations on seminal vesicles**

60.71 Percutaneous aspiration of seminal vesicle ♂

EXCLUDES *needle biopsy of seminal vesicle (60.13)*

60.72 Incision of seminal vesicle ♂
60.73 Excision of seminal vesicle ♂

Excision of Müllerian duct cyst
Spermatocystectomy
EXCLUDES *biopsy of seminal vesicle (60.13-60.14)*
prostatovesiculectomy (60.5)

60.79 Other operations on seminal vesicles ♂

BI Bilateral Procedure   NC Non-covered Procedure   LC Limited Coverage Procedure   ▶◀ Revised Text   ● New Code   ▲ Revised Code Title

√4th **60.8**   **Incision or excision of periprostatic tissue**

    60.81   **Incision of periprostatic tissue**   ♂

      Drainage of periprostatic abscess

    60.82   **Excision of periprostatic tissue**   ♂

      Excision of lesion of periprostatic tissue

      EXCLUDES   *biopsy of periprostatic tissue (60.15)*

√4th **60.9**   **Other operations on prostate**

    60.91   **Percutaneous aspiration of prostate**   ♂

      EXCLUDES   *needle biopsy of prostate (60.11)*

    60.92   **Injection into prostate**   ♂

    60.93   **Repair of prostate**   ♂

    60.94   **Control of (postoperative) hemorrhage of prostate**   ♂

      Coagulation of prostatic bed

      Cystoscopy for control of prostatic hemorrhage

    60.95   **Transurethral balloon dilation of the prostatic urethra**   ♂

      AHA: 4Q, '91, 23

      DEF: Insertion and inflation of balloon to stretch prostate passage.

    60.96   **Transurethral destruction of prostate tissue by microwave thermotherapy**   ♂

      Transurethral microwave thermotherapy (TUMT) of prostate

      EXCLUDES   *Prostatectomy:*
        other (60.61-60.69)
        radical (60.5)
        retropubic (60.4)
        suprapubic (60.3)
        transurethral (60.21-60.29)

      AHA: 4Q, '00, 67

    60.97   **Other transurethral destruction of prostate tissue by other thermotherapy**   ♂

      Radiofrequency thermotherapy

      Transurethral needle ablation (TUNA) of prostate

      EXCLUDES   *Prostatectomy:*
        other (60.61-60.69)
        radical (60.5)
        retropubic (60.4)
        suprapubic (60.3)
        transurethral (60.21-60.29)

      AHA: 4Q, '00, 67

    60.99   **Other**   ♂

      EXCLUDES   *prostatic massage (99.94)*

      AHA: 3Q, '90, 12

√3rd **61**   **Operations on scrotum and tunica vaginalis**

    61.0   **Incision and drainage of scrotum and tunica vaginalis**   ♂

      EXCLUDES   *percutaneous aspiration of hydrocele (61.91)*

√4th **61.1**   **Diagnostic procedures on scrotum and tunica vaginalis**

    61.11   **Biopsy of scrotum or tunica vaginalis**   ♂

    61.19   **Other diagnostic procedures on scrotum and tunica vaginalis**   ♂

    61.2   **Excision of hydrocele (of tunica vaginalis)**   ♂

      Bottle repair of hydrocele of tunica vaginalis

      EXCLUDES   *percutaneous aspiration of hydrocele (61.91)*

      DEF: Removal of fluid collected in serous membrane of testes.

Hydrocelectomy

Scrotal skin incised · Sac opened · Fluid-filled sac mobilized · Excess tissue trimmed · Testis · Remaining sacular tissue folded back and sewn to itself to preclude recurrence ("bottle" procedure)

    61.3   **Excision or destruction of lesion or tissue of scrotum**   ♂

      Fulguration of lesion ⎫
      Reduction of elephantiasis ⎬ of scrotum
      Partial scrotectomy ⎭

      EXCLUDES   *biopsy of scrotum (61.11)*
        scrotal fistulectomy (61.42)

√4th **61.4**   **Repair of scrotum and tunica vaginalis**

    61.41   **Suture of laceration of scrotum and tunica vaginalis**   ♂

    61.42   **Repair of scrotal fistula**   ♂

    61.49   **Other repair of scrotum and tunica vaginalis**   ♂

      Reconstruction with rotational or pedicle flaps

√4th **61.9**   **Other operations on scrotum and tunica vaginalis**

    61.91   **Percutaneous aspiration of tunica vaginalis**   ♂

      Aspiration of hydrocele of tunica vaginalis

    61.92   **Excision of lesion of tunica vaginalis other than hydrocele**   ♂

      Excision of hematocele of tunica vaginalis

      DEF: Removal of blood collected in tunica vaginalis.

    61.99   **Other**   ♂

      EXCLUDES   *removal of foreign body from scrotum without incision (98.24)*

√3rd **62**   **Operations on testes**

    62.0   **Incision of testis**   ♂

√4th **62.1**   **Diagnostic procedures on testes**

    62.11   **Closed [percutaneous] [needle] biopsy of testis**   ♂

    62.12   **Open biopsy of testis**   ♂

    62.19   **Other diagnostic procedures on testes**   ♂

    62.2   **Excision or destruction of testicular lesion**   ♂

      Excision of appendix testis

      Excision of cyst of Morgagni in the male

      Excision of hydatid of Morgagni in the male

      EXCLUDES   *biopsy of testis (62.11-62.12)*

    62.3   **Unilateral orchiectomy**   ♂

      Orchidectomy (with epididymectomy) NOS

√4th **62.4**   **Bilateral orchiectomy**

      Male castration

      Radical bilateral orchiectomy (with epididymectomy)

      Code also any synchronous lymph node dissection (40.3, 40.5)

      DEF: Removal of both testes.

      DEF: Radical bilateral orchiectomy (with epididymectomy): Excision of both testes and structures that store sperm.

    62.41   **Removal of both testes at same operative episode**   ♂

      Bilateral orchidectomy NOS

    62.42   **Removal of remaining testis**   ♂

      Removal of solitary testis

62.5   **Orchiopexy** ♂

Mobilization and replacement of testis in scrotum
Orchiopexy with detorsion of testis
Torek (-Bevan) operation (orchidopexy) (first stage)
(second stage)
Transplantation to and fixation of testis in scrotum

DEF: Fixation of testis in scrotum.

DEF: Orchiopexy with detorsion of testis: Fixation and placement of testis in scrotum after correcting angle.

DEF: Torek operation (first stage) (second stage): Transfer of congenitally undescended testis from inguinal canal to scrotum.

DEF: Transplantation to and fixation of testis in scrotum: Transfer of displaced testis to scrotum.

✓4th **62.6**   **Repair of testes**

EXCLUDES   *reduction of torsion (63.52)*

62.61   **Suture of laceration of testis** ♂

62.69   **Other repair of testis** ♂
Testicular graft

62.7   **Insertion of testicular prosthesis** ♂

✓4th **62.9**   **Other operations on testes**

62.91   **Aspiration of testis** ♂
EXCLUDES   *percutaneous biopsy of testis (62.11)*

62.92   **Injection of therapeutic substance into testis** ♂

62.99   **Other** ♂

✓3rd **63**   **Operations on spermatic cord, epididymis, and vas deferens**

✓4th **63.0**   **Diagnostic procedures on spermatic cord, epididymis, and vas deferens**

63.01   **Biopsy of spermatic cord, epididymis, or vas deferens** ♂

63.09   **Other diagnostic procedures on spermatic cord, epididymis, and vas deferens** ♂
EXCLUDES   *contrast epididymogram (87.93)*
contrast vasogram (87.94)
other x-ray of epididymis and vas deferens (87.95)

63.1   **Excision of varicocele and hydrocele of spermatic cord** ♂
High ligation of spermatic vein
Hydrocelectomy of canal of Nuck

DEF: Removal of a swollen vein and collected fluid from spermatic cord.

DEF: High ligation of spermatic vein: Tying off of spermatic vein.

DEF: Hydrocelectomy of canal of Nuck: Removal of fluid collected from serous membrane of inguinal canal.

Varicocelectomy

Ligated veins
Pampiniform plexus
Ligated veins
Vas deferens
Artery

63.2   **Excision of cyst of epididymis** ♂
Spermatocelectomy

63.3   **Excision of other lesion or tissue of spermatic cord and epididymis** ♂
Excision of appendix epididymis
EXCLUDES   *biopsy of spermatic cord or epididymis (63.01)*

63.4   **Epididymectomy** ♂
EXCLUDES   *that synchronous with orchiectomy (62.3-62.42)*

✓4th **63.5**   **Repair of spermatic cord and epididymis**

63.51   **Suture of laceration of spermatic cord and epididymis** ♂

63.52   **Reduction of torsion of testis or spermatic cord** ♂
EXCLUDES   *that associated with orchiopexy (62.5)*

DEF: Correction of twisted testicle or spermatic cord.

63.53   **Transplantation of spermatic cord** ♂

63.59   **Other repair of spermatic cord and epididymis** ♂

63.6   **Vasotomy** ♂
Vasostomy

DEF: Vasotomy: Incision of ducts carrying sperm from testicles.

DEF: Vasostomy: Creation of an opening into duct.

✓4th **63.7**   **Vasectomy and ligation of vas deferens**

63.70   **Male sterilization procedure, not otherwise specified** NC ♂

63.71   **Ligation of vas deferens** NC ♂
Crushing of vas deferens
Division of vas deferens

63.72   **Ligation of spermatic cord** NC ♂

63.73   **Vasectomy** NC ♂
AHA: 2Q, '98, 13

✓4th **63.8**   **Repair of vas deferens and epididymis**

63.81   **Suture of laceration of vas deferens and epididymis** ♂

63.82   **Reconstruction of surgically divided vas deferens** ♂

63.83   **Epididymovasostomy** ♂
DEF: Creation of new connection between vas deferens and epididymis.

63.84   **Removal of ligature from vas deferens** ♂

63.85   **Removal of valve from vas deferens** ♂

63.89   **Other repair of vas deferens and epididymis** ♂

✓4th **63.9**   **Other operations on spermatic cord, epididymis, and vas deferens**

63.91   **Aspiration of spermatocele** ♂
DEF: Puncture of cystic distention of epididymis.

63.92   **Epididymotomy** ♂
DEF: Incision of epididymis.

63.93   **Incision of spermatic cord** ♂
DEF: Incision into sperm storage structure.

63.94   **Lysis of adhesions of spermatic cord** ♂

63.95   **Insertion of valve in vas deferens** ♂

63.99   **Other** ♂

✓3rd **64**   **Operations on penis**
INCLUDES   operations on:
corpora cavernosa
glans penis
prepuce

64.0   **Circumcision** ♂
DEF: Removal of penis foreskin.

B1 Bilateral Procedure   NC Non-covered Procedure   LC Limited Coverage Procedure   ►◄ Revised Text   ● New Code   ▲ Revised Code Title

✓4th **64.1 Diagnostic procedures on the penis**
  64.11 Biopsy of penis   ♂
  64.19 Other diagnostic procedures on penis   ♂
64.2 Local excision or destruction of lesion of penis   ♂
  EXCLUDES *biopsy of penis (64.11)*
64.3 Amputation of penis   ♂
✓4th **64.4 Repair and plastic operation on penis**
  64.41 Suture of laceration of penis   ♂
  64.42 Release of chordee   ♂
    AHA: 4Q, '96, 34

    DEF: Correction of downward displacement of penis.

  64.43 Construction of penis   ♂
  64.44 Reconstruction of penis   ♂
  64.45 Replantation of penis   ♂
    Reattachment of amputated penis
  64.49 Other repair of penis   ♂
    EXCLUDES *repair of epispadias and*
                  hypospadias (58.45)
64.5 Operations for sex transformation, not   NC ♂
elsewhere classified
✓4th **64.9 Other operations on male genital organs**
  64.91 Dorsal or lateral slit of prepuce   ♂
  64.92 Incision of penis   ♂
  64.93 Division of penile adhesions   ♂
  64.94 Fitting of external prosthesis of penis   ♂
    Penile prosthesis NOS
  64.95 Insertion or replacement of non-inflatable ♂
  penile prosthesis
    Insertion of semi-rigid rod prosthesis into
      shaft of penis
    EXCLUDES *external penile prosthesis*
                  (64.94)
                  inflatable penile prosthesis
                  (64.97)
                  plastic repair, penis (64.43-
                  64.49)
                  that associated with:
                  construction (64.43)
                  reconstruction (64.44)

64.96 Removal of internal prosthesis of penis   ♂
    Removal without replacement of non-
      inflatable or inflatable penile
      prosthesis
64.97 Insertion or replacement of inflatable   ♂
penile prosthesis
    Insertion of cylinders into shaft of penis and
      placement of pump and reservoir
    EXCLUDES *external penile prosthesis*
                  (64.94)
                  non-inflatable penile
                  prosthesis (64.95)
                  plastic repair, penis (64.43-
                  64.49)
64.98 Other operations on penis   ♂
    Corpora cavernosa-corpus spongiosum
      shunt
    Corpora-saphenous shunt
    Irrigation of corpus cavernosum
    EXCLUDES *removal of foreign body:*
                  intraluminal (98.19)
                  without incision (98.24)
                  stretching of foreskin (99.95)

  AHA: 3Q, '92, 9

  DEF: Corpora cavernosa-corpus spongiosum shunt:
  Insertion of shunt between erectile tissues of penis.

  DEF: Corpora-saphenous shunt: Insertion of shunt
  between erectile tissue and vein of penis.

  DEF: Irrigation of corpus cavernosum: Washing of
  erectile tissue forming dorsum and side of penis.

64.99 Other   ♂
    EXCLUDES *collection of sperm for artificial*
                  insemination (99.96)

| ✓3rd / ✓4th Additional Digit Required | Nonspecific OR Procedure | Valid OR Procedure | Non-OR Procedure | Adjunct Code |

2007 ICD•9•CM   **Volume 3 — 149**

Operations on the Male Genital Organs

64.1–64.99

Operations on the Female Genital Organs

65–65.99

12. OPERATIONS ON THE FEMALE GENITAL ORGANS (65-71)

√3rd **65   Operations on ovary**

Code also any application or administration of an adhesion barrier substance (99.77)

√4th **65.0   Oophorotomy**

Salpingo-oophorotomy

DEF: Incision into ovary.

DEF: Salpingo-oophorotomy: Incision into ovary and the fallopian tube.

65.01   Laparoscopic oophorotomy   ♀

65.09   Other oophorotomy   ♀

√4th **65.1   Diagnostic procedures on ovaries**

65.11   Aspiration biopsy of ovary   ♀

65.12   Other biopsy of ovary   ♀

65.13   Laparoscopic biopsy of ovary   ♀

AHA: 4Q, '96, 67

65.14   Other laparoscopic diagnostic procedures on   ovaries   ♀

65.19   Other diagnostic procedures on ovaries   ♀

EXCLUDES   microscopic examination of specimen from ovary (91.41-91.49)

√4th **65.2   Local excision or destruction of ovarian lesion or tissue**

65.21   Marsupialization of ovarian cyst   ♀

EXCLUDES   that by laparoscope (65.23)

DEF: Exteriorized cyst to outside by incising anterior wall and suturing cut edges to create open pouch.

65.22   Wedge resection of ovary   ♀

EXCLUDES   that by laparoscope (65.24)

65.23   Laparoscopic marsupialization of ovarian cyst   ♀

65.24   Laparoscopic wedge resection of ovary   ♀

65.25   Other laparoscopic local excision or destruction of ovary   ♀

65.29   Other local excision or destruction of ovary   ♀

Bisection   ⎫
Cauterization   ⎬ of ovary
Partial excision   ⎭

EXCLUDES   biopsy of ovary (65.11-65.13)
that by laparoscope (65.25)

√4th **65.3   Unilateral oophorectomy**

65.31   Laparoscopic unilateral oophorectomy   ♀

65.39   Other unilateral oophorectomy   ♀

EXCLUDES   that by laparoscope (65.31)

AHA: 4Q, '96, 66

√4th **65.4   Unilateral salpingo-oophorectomy**

65.41   Laparoscopic unilateral salpingo-oophorectomy   ♀

AHA: 4Q, '96, 67

65.49   Other unilateral salpingo-oophorectomy   ♀

Oophorectomy

√4th **65.5   Bilateral oophorectomy**

65.51   Other removal of both ovaries at same operative episode   ♀

Female castration

EXCLUDES   that by laparoscope (65.53)

65.52   Other removal of remaining ovary   ♀

Removal of solitary ovary

EXCLUDES   that by laparoscope (65.54)

65.53   Laparoscopic removal of both ovaries at same operative eisode   ♀

65.54   Laparoscopic removal of remaining ovary   ♀

√4th **65.6   Bilateral salpingo-oophorectomy**

65.61   Other removal of both ovaries and tubes at same operative episode   ♀

EXCLUDES   that by laparoscope (65.53)

AHA: 4Q, '96, 65

65.62   Other removal of remaining ovary and tube   ♀

Removal of solitary ovary and tube

EXCLUDES   that by laparoscope (65.54)

65.63   Laparoscopic removal of both ovaries and tubes at the same operative episode   ♀

AHA: 4Q, '96, 68

65.64   Laparoscopic removal of remaining ovary and tube   ♀

√4th **65.7   Repair of ovary**

EXCLUDES   salpingo-oophorostomy (66.72)

65.71   Other simple suture of ovary   ♀

EXCLUDES   that by laparoscope (65.74)

65.72   Other reimplantation of ovary   ♀

EXCLUDES   that by laparoscope (65.75)

DEF: Grafting and repositioning of ovary at same site.

65.73   Other salpingo-oophoroplasty   ♀

EXCLUDES   that by laparoscope (65.76)

65.74   Laparoscopic simple suture of ovary   ♀

65.75   Laparoscopic reimplantation of ovary   ♀

65.76   Laparoscopic salpingo-oophoroplasty   ♀

65.79   Other repair of ovary   ♀

Oophoropexy

√4th **65.8   Lysis of adhesions of ovary and fallopian tube**

65.81   Laparoscopic lysis of adhesions of ovary and fallopian tube   ♀

AHA: 4Q, '96, 67

65.89   Other lysis of adhesions of ovary and fallopian tube   ♀

EXCLUDES   that by laparoscope (65.81)

√4th **65.9   Other operations on ovary**

65.91   Aspiration of ovary   ♀

EXCLUDES   aspiration biopsy of ovary (65.11)

65.92   Transplantation of ovary   ♀

EXCLUDES   reimplantation of ovary (65.72, 65.75)

65.93   Manual rupture of ovarian cyst   ♀

DEF: Breaking up an ovarian cyst using manual technique or blunt instruments.

65.94   Ovarian denervation   ♀

DEF: Destruction of nerve tracts to ovary.

65.95   Release of torsion of ovary   ♀

65.99   Other   ♀

Ovarian drilling

AHA: N-D, '86, 9

BI Bilateral Procedure   NC Non-covered Procedure   LC Limited Coverage Procedure   ►◄ Revised Text   ● New Code   ▲ Revised Code Title

Endoscopic Ligation of Fallopian Tubes

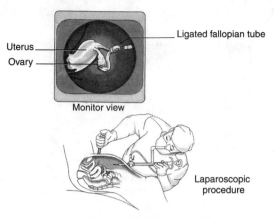

Ligated fallopian tube

Uterus

Ovary

Monitor view

Laparoscopic procedure

√3rd **66**   **Operations on fallopian tubes**
Code also any application or administration of an adhesion barrier substance (99.77)

√4th **66.0**   **Salpingotomy and salpingostomy**
    66.01   **Salpingotomy**   ♀
    66.02   **Salpingostomy**   ♀

√4th **66.1**   **Diagnostic procedures on fallopian tubes**
    66.11   **Biopsy of fallopian tube**   ♀
    66.19   **Other diagnostic procedures on fallopian tubes**   ♀
       EXCLUDES   *microscopic examination of specimen from fallopian tubes (91.41-91.49)*
              radiography of fallopian tubes (87.82-87.83, 87.85)
              Rubin's test (66.8)

√4th **66.2**   **Bilateral endoscopic destruction or occlusion of fallopian tubes**
      INCLUDES   bilateral endoscopic destruction or occlusion of fallopian tubes by:
          culdoscopy   laparoscopy
          endoscopy   peritoneoscopy
          hysteroscopy
         endoscopic destruction of solitary fallopian tube

DEF: Endoscopic blockage or destruction of both fallopian tubes.

DEF: Bilateral endoscopic destruction or occlusion of fallopian tubes by:

   Culdoscopy: Endoscopic insertion through posterior structure of vagina.

   Hysteroscopy: Endoscopic insertion through uterus.

   Laparoscopy: Endoscopic insertion through abdomen.

   Peritoneoscopy: Endoscopic insertion through abdominal serous membrane cavity.

   Endoscopic destruction of solitary fallopian tube: Endoscopic destruction of one fallopian tube.

    66.21   **Bilateral endoscopic ligation and crushing of fallopian tubes**   NC ♀
    66.22   **Bilateral endoscopic ligation and division of fallopian tubes**   NC ♀
    66.29   **Other bilateral endoscopic destruction or occlusion of fallopian tubes**   NC ♀

√4th **66.3**   **Other bilateral destruction or occlusion of fallopian tubes**
      INCLUDES   destruction of solitary fallopian tube
      EXCLUDES   *endoscopic destruction or occlusion of fallopian tubes (66.21-66.29)*
    66.31   **Other bilateral ligation and crushing of fallopian tubes**   NC ♀
    66.32   **Other bilateral ligation and division of fallopian tubes**   NC ♀
       Pomeroy operation
    66.39   **Other bilateral destruction or occlusion of fallopian tubes**   NC ♀
       Female sterilization operation NOS

   66.4   **Total unilateral salpingectomy**   ♀

√4th **66.5**   **Total bilateral salpingectomy**
      EXCLUDES   *bilateral partial salpingectomy for sterilization (66.39)*
              that with oophorectomy (65.61-65.64)
    66.51   **Removal of both fallopian tubes at same operative episode**   ♀
    66.52   **Removal of remaining fallopian tube**   ♀
       Removal of solitary fallopian tube

√4th **66.6**   **Other salpingectomy**
      INCLUDES   salpingectomy by:
          cauterization
          coagulation
          electrocoagulation
          excision
      EXCLUDES   *fistulectomy (66.73)*
    66.61   **Excision or destruction of lesion of fallopian tube**   ♀
       EXCLUDES   *biopsy of fallopian tube (66.11)*
    66.62   **Salpingectomy with removal of tubal pregnancy**   ♀
       Code also any synchronous oophorectomy (65.31, 65.39)
       AHA: 3Q, '95, 15; S-O, '85, 14
    66.63   **Bilateral partial salpingectomy, not otherwise specified**   ♀
    66.69   **Other partial salpingectomy**   ♀

√4th **66.7**   **Repair of fallopian tube**
    66.71   **Simple suture of fallopian tube**   ♀
    66.72   **Salpingo-oophorostomy**   ♀
    66.73   **Salpingo-salpingostomy**   ♀
    66.74   **Salpingo-uterostomy**   ♀
    66.79   **Other repair of fallopian tube**   ♀
       Graft of fallopian tube
       Reopening of divided fallopian tube
       Salpingoplasty
       AHA: 2Q, '95, 10

       DEF: Graft of fallopian: Repair of fallopian tube with implanted graft.

       DEF: Reopening of divided fallopian tube: Reconnection of severed fallopian tube to restore patency.

       DEF: Salpingoplasty: Plastic reconstruction of fallopian tube defect.

   66.8   **Insufflation of fallopian tube**   ♀
       Insufflation of fallopian tube with:
          air
          dye
          gas
          saline
       Rubin's test
      EXCLUDES   *insufflation of therapeutic agent (66.95)*
             that for hysterosalpingography (87.82-87.83)

       DEF: Forceful blowing of gas or liquid into fallopian tubes.

       DEF: Rubin's test: Introduction of carbon dioxide gas into fallopian tubes.

√3rd √4th Additional Digit Required   Nonspecific OR Procedure   Valid OR Procedure   Non-OR Procedure   Adjunct Code

Operations on the Female Genital Organs   66.9–68.0

√4th **66.9**   **Other operations on fallopian tubes**

66.91   **Aspiration of fallopian tube** ♀

66.92   **Unilateral destruction or occlusion of fallopian tube** ♀

EXCLUDES   *that of solitary tube (66.21-66.39)*

66.93   **Implantation or replacement of prosthesis of fallopian tube** ♀

66.94   **Removal of prosthesis of fallopian tube** ♀

66.95   **Insufflation of therapeutic agent into fallopian tubes** ♀

66.96   **Dilation of fallopian tube** ♀

66.97   **Burying of fimbriae in uterine wall** ♀

DEF: Implantation of fallopian tube, fringed edges into uterine wall.

66.99   **Other** ♀

EXCLUDES   *lysis of adhesions of ovary and tube (65.81, 65.89)*

AHA: 2Q, '94, 11

√3rd **67**   **Operations on cervix**

Code also any application or administration of an adhesion barrier substance (99.77)

67.0   **Dilation of cervical canal** ♀

EXCLUDES   *dilation and curettage (69.01-69.09)*
that for induction of labor (73.1)

√4th **67.1**   **Diagnostic procedures on cervix**

67.11   **Endocervical biopsy** ♀

EXCLUDES   *conization of cervix (67.2)*

67.12   **Other cervical biopsy** ♀

Punch biopsy of cervix NOS

EXCLUDES   *conization of cervix (67.2)*

67.19   **Other diagnostic procedures on cervix** ♀

EXCLUDES   *microscopic examination of specimen from cervix (91.41-91.49)*

67.2   **Conization of cervix** ♀

EXCLUDES   *that by:*
cryosurgery (67.33)
electrosurgery (67.32)

DEF: Removal of cone-shaped section from distal cervix; cervical function preserved.

√4th **67.3**   **Other excision or destruction of lesion or tissue of cervix**

67.31   **Marsupialization of cervical cyst** ♀

DEF: Incision and then suturing open of a cyst in the neck of the uterus.

67.32   **Destruction of lesion of cervix by cauterization** ♀

Electroconization of cervix
LEEP (loop electrosurgical excision procedure)
LLETZ (large loop excision of the transformation zone)

AHA: 1Q, '98, 3

DEF: Destruction of lesion of uterine neck by applying intense heat.

DEF: Electroconization of cervix: Electrocautery excision of multilayer cone-shaped section from uterine neck.

67.33   **Destruction of lesion of cervix by cryosurgery** ♀

Cryoconization of cervix

DEF: Destruction of lesion of uterine neck by freezing.

DEF: Cryoconization of cervix: Excision by freezing of multilayer cone-shaped section of abnormal tissue in uterine neck.

67.39   **Other excision or destruction of lesion or tissue of cervix** ♀

EXCLUDES   *biopsy of cervix (67.11-67.12)*
cervical fistulectomy (67.62)
conization of cervix (67.2)

Cerclage of Cervix

Suture material is inserted around cervix and tightened

Uterus

Cervix and cervical canal

Cervix and cervical canal

67.4   **Amputation of cervix** ♀

Cervicectomy with synchronous colporrhaphy

DEF: Excision of lower uterine neck.

DEF: Cervicectomy with synchronous colporrhaphy: Excision of lower uterine neck with suture of vaginal stump.

√4th **67.5**   **Repair of internal cervical os**

AHA: 4Q, '01, 63; 3Q, '00, 11

DEF: Repair of cervical opening defect.

67.51   **Transabdominal cerclage of cervix** ♀

67.59   **Other repair of internal cervical os** ♀

Cerclage of isthmus uteri
McDonald operation
Shirodkar operation
Transvaginal cerclage

EXCLUDES   *laparoscopically assisted supracervical hysterectomy [LASH] (68.31)*
transabdominal cerclage of cervix (67.51)

DEF: Cerclage of isthmus uteri: Placement of encircling suture between neck and body of uterus.

DEF: Shirodkar operation: Placement of purse-string suture in internal cervical opening.

√4th **67.6**   **Other repair of cervix**

EXCLUDES   *repair of current obstetric laceration (75.51)*

67.61   **Suture of laceration of cervix** ♀

67.62   **Repair of fistula of cervix** ♀

Cervicosigmoidal fistulectomy

EXCLUDES   *fistulectomy:*
cervicovesical (57.84)
ureterocervical (56.84)
vesicocervicovaginal (57.84)

DEF: Closure of fistula in lower uterus.

DEF: Cervicosigmoidal fistulectomy: Excision of abnormal passage between uterine neck and torsion of large intestine.

67.69   **Other repair of cervix** ♀

Repair of old obstetric laceration of cervix

√3rd **68**   **Other incision and excision of uterus**

Code also any application or administration of an adhesion barrier substance (99.77)

68.0   **Hysterotomy** ♀

Hysterotomy with removal of hydatidiform mole

EXCLUDES   *hysterotomy for termination of pregnancy (74.91)*

DEF: Incision into the uterus.

BI Bilateral Procedure   NC Non-covered Procedure   LC Limited Coverage Procedure   ◄ Revised Text   ● New Code   ▲ Revised Code Title

✓4ᵗʰ 68.1   **Diagnostic procedures on uterus and supporting structures**

     68.11   **Digital examination of uterus**   ♀
         EXCLUDES   *pelvic examination, so described (89.26)*
         postpartal manual exploration of uterine cavity (75.7)

     68.12   **Hysteroscopy**   ♀
         EXCLUDES   *that with biopsy (68.16)*

     68.13   **Open biopsy of uterus**   ♀
         EXCLUDES   *closed biopsy of uterus (68.16)*

     68.14   **Open biopsy of uterine ligaments**   ♀
         EXCLUDES   *closed biopsy of uterine ligaments (68.15)*

     68.15   **Closed biopsy of uterine ligaments**   ♀
         Endoscopic (laparoscopy) biopsy of uterine adnexa, except ovary and fallopian tube

     68.16   **Closed biopsy of uterus**   ♀
         Endoscopic (laparoscopy) (hysteroscopy) biopsy of uterus
         EXCLUDES   *open biopsy of uterus (68.13)*

     68.19   **Other diagnostic procedures on uterus and supporting structures**   ♀
         EXCLUDES   *diagnostic:*
         aspiration curettage (69.59)
         dilation and curettage (69.09)
         microscopic examination of specimen from uterus (91.41-91.49)
         pelvic examination (89.26)
         radioisotope scan of:
         placenta (92.17)
         uterus (92.19)
         ultrasonography of uterus (88.78-88.79)
         x-ray of uterus (87.81-87.89)

✓4ᵗʰ 68.2   **Excision or destruction of lesion or tissue of uterus**

     68.21   **Division of endometrial synechiae**   ♀
         Lysis of intraluminal uterine adhesions
         DEF: Separation of uterine adhesions.
         DEF: Lysis of intraluminal uterine adhesion: Surgical destruction of adhesive, fibrous structures inside uterine cavity.

     68.22   **Incision or excision of congenital septum of uterus**   ♀

     68.23   **Endometrial ablation**   ♀
         Dilation and curettage
         Hysteroscopic endometrial ablation
         AHA: 4Q, '96, 68
         DEF: Removal or destruction of uterine lining; usually by electrocautery or loop electrosurgical excision procedure (LEEP).

     68.29   **Other excision or destruction of lesion of uterus**   ♀
         Uterine myomectomy
         EXCLUDES   *biopsy of uterus (68.13)*
         uterine fistulectomy (69.42)
         AHA: 1Q, '96, 14

Vaginal Hysterectomy

Total hysterectomy (uterus only removed)

Total hysterectomy with bilateral salpingectomy (uterus and tubes removed)

Total hysterectomy with bilateral salpingo-oophorectomy (uterus, tubes, and ovaries removed)

✓4ᵗʰ 68.3   **Subtotal abdominal hysterectomy**

     68.31   **Laparoscopic supracervical hysterectomy [LSH]**   ♀
         Classic infrafascial SEMM hysterectomy [CISH]
         Laparoscopically assisted supracervical hysterectomy [LASH]
         AHA: 4Q, '03, 98-99
         DEF: A hysterectomy that spares the cervix and maintains the integrity of the pelvic floor; SEMM version of the supracervical hysterectomy, also called the classic infrafascial SEMM hysterectomy [CISH], the cardinal ligaments, or lateral cervical ligaments that merge with the pelvic diaphragm remain intact.

     68.39   **Other and unspecified subtotal abdominal hysterectomy**   ♀
         Supracervical hysterectomy
         EXCLUDES   *classic infrafascial SEMM hysterectomy [CISH] (68.31)*
         laparoscopic supracervical hysterectomy [LSH] (68.31)
         AHA: 4Q, '03, 98

✓4ᵗʰ 68.4   **Total abdominal hysterectomy**
     Code also any synchronous removal of tubes and ovaries ►(65.31-65.64)◄
         EXCLUDES   ► *laparoscopic total abdominal hysterectomy (68.41)*
         radical abdominal hysterectomy, any approach (68.61-68.69)◄
     AHA: 4Q, '96, 65
     DEF: Complete excision of uterus and uterine neck through abdominal approach.

     68.41   **Laparoscopic total abdominal hysterectomy**   ♀
         Total laparoscopic hysterectomy [TLH]

     68.49   **Other and unspecified total abdominal hysterectomy**   ♀
         Hysterectomy:
         extended

✓4ᵗʰ 68.5   **Vaginal hysterectomy**
     Code also any synchronous:
     removal of tubes and ovaries (65.31-65.64)
     repair of cystocele or rectocele (70.50-70.52)
     repair of pelvic floor (70.79)
     DEF: Complete excision of the uterus by a vaginal approach.

     68.51   **Laparoscopically assisted vaginal hysterectomy (LAVH)**   ♀
         AHA: 4Q, '96, 68

     68.59   **Other and unspecified vaginal hysterectomy**   ♀
         EXCLUDES   *laparoscopically assisted vaginal hysterectomy (68.51)*
         radical vaginal hysterectomy (68.71-68.79)

✓4ᵗʰ 68.6   **Radical abdominal hysterectomy**
     Code also any synchronous:
     lymph gland dissection (40.3, 40.5)
     removal of tubes and ovaries ►(65.31-65.64)◄
         EXCLUDES   *pelvic evisceration (68.8)*
     DEF: Excision of uterus, loose connective tissue and smooth muscle around uterus and vagina via abdominal approach.

     68.61   **Laparoscopic radical abdominal hysterectomy**   ♀
         Laparoscopic modified radical hysterectomy
         Total laparoscopic radical hysterectomy [TLRH]

     68.69   **Other and unspecified radical abdominal hysterectomy**   ♀
         Modified radical hysterectomy
         Wertheim's operation
         EXCLUDES   *laparoscopic total abdominal hysterectomy (68.41)*
         laparoscopic radical abdominal hysterectomy (68.61)

Operations on the Female Genital Organs

68.7–69.96

✓4th **68.7 Radical vaginal hysterectomy**
Code also any synchronous:
lymph gland dissection (40.3, 40.5)
removal of tubes and ovaries ▶(65.31-65.64)◀
> EXCLUDES ▶ *abdominal hysterectomy, any approach (68.31-68.39, 68.41-68.49, 68.61-68.69, 68.9)◀*

DEF: Excision of uterus, loose connective tissue and smooth muscle around uterus and vagina via vaginal approach.

● **68.71 Laparoscopic radical vaginal hysterectomy [LRVH]** ♀

● **68.79 Other and unspecified radical vaginal hysterectomy** ♀
Hysterocolpectomy
Schauta operation

68.8 Pelvic evisceration ♀
Removal of ovaries, tubes, uterus, vagina, bladder, and urethra (with removal of sigmoid colon and rectum)
Code also any synchronous:
colostomy (46.10-46.13)
lymph gland dissection (40.3, 40.5)
urinary diversion (56.51-56.79)

68.9 Other and unspecified hysterectomy ♀
Hysterectomy NOS
> EXCLUDES *abdominal hysterectomy, any approach ▶(68.31-68.39, 68.41-68.49, 68.61-68.69)◀*
> *vaginal hysterectomy, any approach ▶(68.51-68.59, 68.71-68.79)◀*

✓3rd **69 Other operations on uterus and supporting structures**
Code also any application or administration of an adhesion barrier substance (99.77)

✓4th **69.0 Dilation and curettage of uterus**
> EXCLUDES *aspiration curettage of uterus (69.51-69.59)*

DEF: Stretching of uterine neck to scrape tissue from walls.

69.01 Dilation and curettage for termination of pregnancy ♀
AHA: 1Q, '98, 4

69.02 Dilation and curettage following delivery or abortion ♀
AHA: 3Q, '93, 6

69.09 Other dilation and curettage ♀
Diagnostic D and C
AHA: 1Q, '98, 4

✓4th **69.1 Excision or destruction of lesion or tissue of uterus and supporting structures**

69.19 Other excision or destruction of uterus and supporting structures ♀
> EXCLUDES *biopsy of uterine ligament (68.14)*

Dilation and Curettage

Cervix (being dilated)
Fallopian tube
Ovary
Curetting endometrium
Cervix
Vagina

✓4th **69.2 Repair of uterine supporting structures**

69.21 Interposition operation ♀
Watkins procedure
DEF: Repositioning or realignment of bladder and uterus.

69.22 Other uterine suspension ♀
Hysteropexy
Manchester operation
Plication of uterine ligament
DEF: Hysteropexy: Fixation or anchoring of uterus.

DEF: Manchester operation: Fixation or anchoring of uterus with supportive banding tissue of uterine neck and vagina.

DEF: Plication of uterine ligament: Creation of tucks in suppurative uterine banding tissue.

69.23 Vaginal repair of chronic inversion of uterus ♀
DEF: Repositioning of inverted uterus via vaginal approach.

69.29 Other repair of uterus and supporting structures ♀

69.3 Paracervical uterine denervation ♀

✓4th **69.4 Uterine repair**
> EXCLUDES *repair of current obstetric laceration (75.50-75.52)*

69.41 Suture of laceration of uterus ♀

69.42 Closure of fistula of uterus ♀
> EXCLUDES *uterovesical fistulectomy (57.84)*

69.49 Other repair of uterus ♀
Repair of old obstetric laceration of uterus

✓4th **69.5 Aspiration curettage of uterus**
> EXCLUDES *menstrual extraction (69.6)*

69.51 Aspiration curettage of uterus for termination of pregnancy ♀
Therapeutic abortion NOS

69.52 Aspiration curettage following delivery or abortion ♀

69.59 Other aspiration curettage of uterus ♀
AHA: 1Q, '98, 7

69.6 Menstrual extraction or regulation ♀
DEF: Induction of menstruation by low pressure suction.

69.7 Insertion of intrauterine contraceptive device ♀

✓4th **69.9 Other operations on uterus, cervix, and supporting structures** ♀
> EXCLUDES *obstetric dilation or incision of cervix (73.1, 73.93)*

69.91 Insertion of therapeutic device into uterus ♀
> EXCLUDES *insertion of:*
> *intrauterine contraceptive device (69.7)*
> *laminaria (69.93)*
> *obstetric insertion of bag, bougie, or pack (73.1)*

69.92 Artificial insemination ♀

69.93 Insertion of laminaria ♀
DEF: Placement of laminaria, a sea kelp, in cervical os to induce labor; applied for six to 12 hours.

69.94 Manual replacement of inverted uterus ♀
> EXCLUDES *that in immediate postpartal period (75.94)*

69.95 Incision of cervix ♀
> EXCLUDES *that to assist delivery (73.93)*

69.96 Removal of cerclage material from cervix
DEF: Removal of ring inserted to restore uterine neck competency.

BI Bilateral Procedure   NC Non-covered Procedure   LC Limited Coverage Procedure   ▶◀ Revised Text   ● New Code   ▲ Revised Code Title

154 — Volume 3 • October 2006

2007 ICD•9•CM

69.97   **Removal of other penetrating foreign body from cervix** ♀
> EXCLUDES   *removal of intraluminal foreign body from cervix (98.16)*

69.98   **Other operations on supporting structures of uterus** ♀
> EXCLUDES   *biopsy of uterine ligament (68.14)*

69.99   **Other operations on cervix and uterus** ♀
> EXCLUDES   *removal of:*
> *foreign body (98.16)*
> *intrauterine contraceptive device (97.71)*
> *obstetric bag, bougie, or pack (97.72)*
> *packing (97.72)*

√3rd **70**   **Operations on vagina and cul-de-sac**
> Code also any application or administration of an adhesion barrier substance (99.77)

70.0   **Culdocentesis** ♀
AHA: 2Q, '90, 26

DEF: Insertion of needle into upper vaginal vault encircling cervix to withdraw fluid.

√4th **70.1**   **Incision of vagina and cul-de-sac**
    70.11   **Hymenotomy** ♀
    70.12   **Culdotomy** ♀
       DEF: Incision into pocket between terminal end of large intestine and posterior uterus.

    70.13   **Lysis of intraluminal adhesions of vagina** ♀

    70.14   **Other vaginotomy** ♀
       Division of vaginal septum
       Drainage of hematoma of vaginal cuff
       DEF: Division of vaginal septum: Incision into partition of vaginal walls.

       DEF: Drainage of hematoma of vaginal cuff: Incision into vaginal tissue to drain collected blood.

√4th **70.2**   **Diagnostic procedures on vagina and cul-de-sac**
    70.21   **Vaginoscopy** ♀
    70.22   **Culdoscopy** ♀
       DEF: Endoscopic exam of pelvic viscera through incision in posterior vaginal wall.

    70.23   **Biopsy of cul-de-sac** ♀
    70.24   **Vaginal biopsy** ♀
    70.29   **Other diagnostic procedures on vagina and cul-de-sac** ♀

√4th **70.3**   **Local excision or destruction of vagina and cul-de-sac**
    70.31   **Hymenectomy** ♀
    70.32   **Excision or destruction of lesion of cul-de-sac** ♀
       Endometrectomy of cul-de-sac
> EXCLUDES   *biopsy of cul-de-sac (70.23)*

    70.33   **Excision or destruction of lesion of vagina** ♀
> EXCLUDES   *biopsy of vagina (70.24)*
> *vaginal fistulectomy (70.72-70.75)*

70.4   **Obliteration and total excision of vagina** ♀
    Vaginectomy
> EXCLUDES   *obliteration of vaginal vault (70.8)*

DEF: Vaginectomy: Removal of vagina.

√4th **70.5**   **Repair of cystocele and rectocele**
    70.50   **Repair of cystocele and rectocele** ♀
       DEF: Repair of anterior and posterior vaginal wall bulges.

    70.51   **Repair of cystocele** ♀
       Anterior colporrhaphy (with urethrocele repair)
       AHA: N-D, '84, 20

    70.52   **Repair of rectocele** ♀
       Posterior colporrhaphy
       AHA: ▶1Q, '06, 12◀

√4th **70.6**   **Vaginal construction and reconstruction**
    70.61   **Vaginal construction** ♀
    70.62   **Vaginal reconstruction** ♀
       AHA: N-D, '84, 20

√4th **70.7**   **Other repair of vagina**
> EXCLUDES   *lysis of intraluminal adhesions (70.13)*
> *repair of current obstetric laceration (75.69)*
> *that associated with cervical amputation (67.4)*

    70.71   **Suture of laceration of vagina** ♀
       AHA: N-D, '84, 20

    70.72   **Repair of colovaginal fistula** ♀
       DEF: Correction of abnormal opening between midsection of large intestine and vagina.

    70.73   **Repair of rectovaginal fistula** ♀
       DEF: Correction of abnormal opening between last section of large intestine and vagina.

    70.74   **Repair of other vaginoenteric fistula** ♀
       DEF: Correction of abnormal opening between vagina and intestine; other than mid or last sections.

    70.75   **Repair of other fistula of vagina** ♀
> EXCLUDES   *repair of fistula:*
> *rectovesicovaginal (57.83)*
> *ureterovaginal (56.84)*
> *urethrovaginal (58.43)*
> *uterovaginal (69.42)*
> *vesicocervicovaginal (57.84)*
> *vesicosigmoidovaginal (57.83)*
> *vesicoureterovaginal (56.84)*
> *vesicovaginal (57.84)*

    70.76   **Hymenorrhaphy** ♀
       DEF: Closure of vagina with suture of hymenal ring or hymenal remnant flaps.

    70.77   **Vaginal suspension and fixation** ♀
       DEF: Repair of vaginal protrusion, sinking or laxity by suturing vagina into position.

    70.79   **Other repair of vagina** ♀
       Colpoperineoplasty
       Repair of old obstetric laceration of vagina

70.8   **Obliteration of vaginal vault** ♀
    LeFort operation
    DEF: LeFort operation: Uniting or sewing together vaginal walls.

√4th **70.9**   **Other operations on vagina and cul-de-sac**
    70.91   **Other operations on vagina** ♀
> EXCLUDES   *insertion of:*
> *diaphragm (96.17)*
> *mold (96.15)*
> *pack (96.14)*
> *pessary (96.18)*
> *suppository (96.49)*
> *removal of:*
> *diaphragm (97.73)*
> *foreign body (98.17)*
> *pack (97.75)*
> *pessary (97.74)*
> *replacement of:*
> *diaphragm (97.24)*
> *pack (97.26)*
> *pessary (97.25)*
> *vaginal dilation (96.16)*
> *vaginal douche (96.44)*

    70.92   **Other operations on cul-de-sac** ♀
       Obliteration of cul-de-sac
       Repair of vaginal enterocele
       AHA: 4Q, '94, 54

       DEF: Repair of vaginal enterocele: Elimination of herniated cavity within pouch between last part of large intestine and posterior uterus.

√3rd Additional Digit Required   Nonspecific OR Procedure   Valid OR Procedure   Non-OR Procedure   Adjunct Code

Operations on the Female Genital Organs

71–71.9

✓3ʳᵈ **71 Operations on vulva and perineum**
Code also any application or administration of an adhesion barrier substance (99.77)

✓4ᵗʰ **71.0 Incision of vulva and perineum**

    71.01 Lysis of vulvar adhesions ♀

    71.09 Other incision of vulva and perineum ♀
Enlargement of introitus NOS

        EXCLUDES *removal of foreign body without incision (98.23)*

✓4ᵗʰ **71.1 Diagnostic procedures on vulva**

    71.11 Biopsy of vulva ♀

    71.19 Other diagnostic procedures on vulva ♀

✓4ᵗʰ **71.2 Operations on Bartholin's gland**

    71.21 Percutaneous aspiration of Bartholin's gland (cyst) ♀

    71.22 Incision of Bartholin's gland (cyst) ♀

    71.23 Marsupialization of Bartholin's gland (cyst) ♀
DEF: Incision and suturing opening of a cyst in Bartholin's gland.

    71.24 Excision or other destruction of Bartholin's gland (cyst) ♀

    71.29 Other operations on Bartholin's gland ♀

  71.3 Other local excision or destruction of vulva and perineum ♀
Division of Skene's gland

      EXCLUDES *biopsy of vulva (71.11)*
vulvar fistulectomy (71.72)

  71.4 Operations on clitoris ♀
Amputation of clitoris
Clitoridotomy
Female circumcision

DEF: Amputation of clitoris: Removal of clitoris.

DEF: Clitoridotomy: Incision into clitoris.

DEF: Female circumcision: Incision of skin fold over clitoris.

  71.5 Radical vulvectomy ♀
Code also any synchronous lymph gland dissection (40.3, 40.5)

DEF: Removal of over 80 percent of deep tissue from vulva, including tissue of abdomen, groin, labia minora, labia majora, clitoris, mons veneris, and terminal portions of urethra, vagina and other vulvar organs.

✓4ᵗʰ **71.6 Other vulvectomy**

    71.61 Unilateral vulvectomy ♀

    71.62 Bilateral vulvectomy ♀
Vulvectomy NOS

Marsupialization

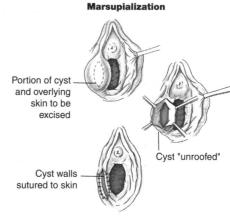

Portion of cyst and overlying skin to be excised

Cyst "unroofed"

Cyst walls sutured to skin

✓4ᵗʰ **71.7 Repair of vulva and perineum**

      EXCLUDES *repair of current obstetric laceration (75.69)*

    71.71 Suture of laceration of vulva or perineum ♀

    71.72 Repair of fistula of vulva or perineum ♀

        EXCLUDES *repair of fistula:*
urethroperineal (58.43)
urethroperineovesical (57.84)
vaginoperineal (70.75)

    71.79 Other repair of vulva and perineum ♀
Repair of old obstetric laceration of vulva or perineum

      AHA: 1Q, '97, 9

  71.8 Other operations on vulva ♀

      EXCLUDES *removal of:*
foreign body without incision (98.23)
packing (97.75)
replacement of packing (97.26)

  71.9 Other operations on female genital organs ♀
AHA: 4Q, '04, 90; 1Q, '03, 13

BI Bilateral Procedure   NC Non-covered Procedure   LC Limited Coverage Procedure   ▶◀ Revised Text   ● New Code   ▲ Revised Code Title

156 — Volume 3   *2007 ICD•9•CM*

13. OBSTETRICAL PROCEDURES (72-75)

√3rd **72　Forceps, vacuum, and breech delivery**

72.0　Low forceps operation　　♀
　　　Outlet forceps operation

72.1　Low forceps operation with episiotomy　　♀
　　　Outlet forceps operation with episiotomy

√4th **72.2　Mid forceps operation**

　　72.21　Mid forceps operation with episiotomy　♀

　　72.29　Other mid forceps operation　♀

√4th **72.3　High forceps operation**

　　72.31　High forceps operation with episiotomy　♀

　　72.39　Other high forceps operation　♀

72.4　Forceps rotation of fetal head　　♀
　　　DeLee maneuver
　　　Key-in-lock rotation
　　　Kielland rotation
　　　Scanzoni's maneuver
　　　Code also any associated forceps extraction (72.0-72.39)

√4th **72.5　Breech extraction**

　　72.51　Partial breech extraction with forceps to aftercoming head　♀

　　72.52　Other partial breech extraction　♀

　　72.53　Total breech extraction with forceps to aftercoming head　♀

　　72.54　Other total breech extraction　♀

72.6　Forceps application to aftercoming head　　♀
　　　Piper forceps operation
　　　EXCLUDES　*partial breech extraction with forceps to aftercoming head (72.51)*
　　　　　total breech extraction with forceps to aftercoming head (72.53)

√4th **72.7　Vacuum extraction**
　　　INCLUDES　Malström's extraction

　　72.71　Vacuum extraction with episiotomy　♀

　　72.79　Other vacuum extraction　♀

72.8　Other specified instrumental delivery　　♀

72.9　Unspecified instrumental delivery　　♀

√3rd **73　Other procedures inducing or assisting delivery**

√4th **73.0　Artificial rupture of membranes**

　　73.01　Induction of labor by artificial rupture of membranes　♀
　　　　　Surgical induction NOS
　　　　　EXCLUDES　*artificial rupture of membranes after onset of labor (73.09)*

　　　　　AHA: 3Q, '00, 5

　　73.09　Other artificial rupture of membranes　♀
　　　　　Artificial rupture of membranes at time of delivery

Breech Extraction

Breech
presentation

Delivery
of legs

Baby rotated
for delivery
of arms

Umbilicus

73.1　Other surgical induction of labor　　♀
　　　Induction by cervical dilation
　　　EXCLUDES　*injection for abortion (75.0)*
　　　　　insertion of suppository for abortion (96.49)

√4th **73.2　Internal and combined version and extraction**

　　73.21　Internal and combined version without extraction　♀
　　　　　Version NOS

　　73.22　Internal and combined version with extraction　♀

73.3　Failed forceps　　♀
　　　Application of forceps without delivery
　　　Trial forceps

73.4　Medical induction of labor　　♀
　　　EXCLUDES　*medication to augment active labor — omit code*

√4th **73.5　Manually assisted delivery**　　♀

　　73.51　Manual rotation of fetal head　♀

　　73.59　Other manually assisted delivery　♀
　　　　　Assisted spontaneous delivery
　　　　　Credé maneuver
　　　　　AHA: 4Q, '98, 76

73.6　Episiotomy　　♀
　　　Episioproctotomy
　　　Episiotomy with subsequent episiorrhaphy
　　　EXCLUDES　*that with:*
　　　　　high forceps (72.31)
　　　　　low forceps (72.1)
　　　　　mid forceps (72.21)
　　　　　outlet forceps (72.1)
　　　　　vacuum extraction (72.71)

　　　AHA: 1Q, '92, 10

73.8　Operations on fetus to facilitate delivery　　♀
　　　Clavicotomy on fetus
　　　Destruction of fetus
　　　Needling of hydrocephalic head

√4th **73.9　Other operations assisting delivery**

　　73.91　External version　♀

　　73.92　Replacement of prolapsed umbilical cord　♀

　　73.93　Incision of cervix to assist delivery　♀
　　　　　Dührssen's incisions

　　73.94　Pubiotomy to assist delivery　♀
　　　　　Obstetrical symphysiotomy

　　73.99　Other　♀
　　　　　EXCLUDES　*dilation of cervix, obstetrical, to induce labor (73.1)*
　　　　　　insertion of bag or bougie to induce labor (73.1)
　　　　　　removal of cerclage material (69.96)

√3rd **74　Cesarean section and removal of fetus**
　　　Code also any synchronous:
　　　　hysterectomy (68.3-68.4, 68.6, 68.8)
　　　　myomectomy (68.29)
　　　　sterilization (66.31-66.39, 66.63)

74.0　Classical cesarean section　　♀
　　　Transperitoneal classical cesarean section

74.1　Low cervical cesarean section　　♀
　　　Lower uterine segment cesarean section
　　　AHA: 1Q, '01, 11

74.2　Extraperitoneal cesarean section　　♀
　　　Supravesical cesarean section

74.3 **Removal of extratubal ectopic pregnancy** ♀
Removal of:
    ectopic abdominal pregnancy
    fetus from peritoneal or extraperitoneal cavity
        following uterine or tubal rupture
    EXCLUDES *that by salpingostomy (66.02)*
        that by salpingotomy (66.01)
        that with synchronous salpingectomy
        (66.62)

AHA: 4Q, '92, 25; 2Q, '90, 25; 2Q, '90, 27; 1Q, '89, 11

74.4 **Cesarean section of other specified type** ♀
Peritoneal exclusion cesareansection
Transperitoneal cesarean section NOS
Vaginal cesarean section

✓4th **74.9** **Cesarean section of unspecified type**
    74.91 **Hysterotomy to terminate pregnancy** ♀
        Therapeutic abortion by hysterotomy
    74.99 **Other cesarean section of unspecified** ♀
        type
        Cesarean section NOS
        Obstetrical abdominouterotomy
        Obstetrical hysterotomy

✓3rd **75** **Other obstetric operations**
  75.0 **Intra-amniotic injection for abortion** ♀
    Injection of:
      prostaglandin } for induction of
      saline   abortion
    Termination of pregnancy by intrauterine injection
    EXCLUDES *insertion of prostaglandin suppository*
        for abortion (96.49)

  75.1 **Diagnostic amniocentesis** ♀
  75.2 **Intrauterine transfusion** ♀
    Exchange transfusion in utero
    Insertion of catheter into abdomen of fetus for
        transfusion
    Code also any hysterotomy approach (68.0)

✓4th **75.3** **Other intrauterine operations on fetus and amnion**
    Code also any hysterotomy approach (68.0)
    75.31 **Amnioscopy** ♀
        Fetoscopy
        Laparoamnioscopy
    75.32 **Fetal EKG (scalp)** ♀
    75.33 **Fetal blood sampling and biopsy** ♀
    75.34 **Other fetal monitoring** ♀
        Antepartum fetal nonstress test
        Fetal monitoring, not otherwise specified
        EXCLUDES *fetal pulse oximetry (75.38)*

Amniocentesis

Aspiration of amniotic fluid

75.35 **Other diagnostic procedures on fetus** ♀
    and amnion
    Intrauterine pressure determination
    EXCLUDES *amniocentesis (75.1)*
        diagnostic procedures on
        gravid uterus and
        placenta (87.81, 88.46,
        88.78, 92.17)

75.36 **Correction of fetal defect** ♀
75.37 **Amnioinfusion**
    Code also injection of antibiotic (99.21)
AHA: 4Q, '98, 76

75.38 **Fetal pulse oximetry**
    Transcervical fetal oxygen saturation
        monitoring
    Transcervical fetal SpO_2 monitoring
DEF: Single-use sensor inserted through the birth canal
and positioned to rest against the fetal cheek, forehead,
or temple; infrared beam of light aimed at the fetal skin
is reflected back through the sensor for analysis.

AHA: 4Q, '01, 64

75.4 **Manual removal of retained placenta** ♀
    EXCLUDES *aspiration curettage (69.52)*
        dilation and curettage (69.02)

✓4th **75.5** **Repair of current obstetric laceration of uterus**
    75.50 **Repair of current obstetric laceration of** ♀
        uterus, not otherwise specified
    75.51 **Repair of current obstetric laceration** ♀
        of cervix
    75.52 **Repair of current obstetric laceration** ♀
        of corpus uteri

✓4th **75.6** **Repair of other current obstetric laceration**
AHA: 1Q, '92, 11

    75.61 **Repair of current obstetric laceration** ♀
        of bladder and urethra
    75.62 **Repair of current obstetric laceration of** ♀
        rectum and sphincter ani
    75.69 **Repair of other current obstetric** ♀
        laceration
        Episioperineorrhaphy
        Repair of:
          pelvic floor
          perineum
          vagina
          vulva
        Secondary repair of episiotomy
        EXCLUDES *repair of routine episiotomy*
        (73.6)

75.7 **Manual exploration of uterine cavity,** ♀
  postpartum
75.8 **Obstetric tamponade of uterus or vagina** ♀
    EXCLUDES *antepartum tamponade (73.1)*

✓4th **75.9** **Other obstetric operations**
    75.91 **Evacuation of obstetrical incisional** ♀
        hematoma of perineum
        Evacuation of hematoma of:
          episiotomy
          perineorrhaphy
    75.92 **Evacuation of other hematoma of** ♀
        vulva or vagina
    75.93 **Surgical correction of inverted uterus** ♀
        Spintelli operation
        EXCLUDES *vaginal repair of chronic*
        inversion of uterus
        (69.23)
    75.94 **Manual replacement of inverted uterus** ♀
    75.99 **Other** ♀

BI Bilateral Procedure   NC Non-covered Procedure   LC Limited Coverage Procedure   ▶◀ Revised Text   ● New Code   ▲ Revised Code Title

14. OPERATIONS ON THE MUSCULOSKELETAL SYSTEM
(76-84)

√3rd 76   **Operations on facial bones and joints**

> **EXCLUDES**   accessory sinuses (22.00-22.9)
> nasal bones (21.00-21.99)
> skull (01.01-02.99)

√4th 76.0   **Incision of facial bone without division**

76.01   **Sequestrectomy of facial bone**
Removal of necrotic bone chip from facial bone

76.09   **Other incision of facial bone**
Reopening of osteotomy site of facial bone

> **EXCLUDES**   osteotomy associated with orthognathic surgery (76.61-76.69)
> removal of internal fixation device (76.97)

√4th 76.1   **Diagnostic procedures on facial bones and joints**

76.11   **Biopsy of facial bone**

76.19   **Other diagnostic procedures on facial bones and joints**

> **EXCLUDES**   contrast arthrogram of temporomandibular joint (87.13)
> other x-ray (87.11-87.12, 87.14-87.16)

AHA: N-D, '87, 12

76.2   **Local excision or destruction of lesion of facial bone**

> **EXCLUDES**   biopsy of facial bone (76.11)
> excision of odontogenic lesion (24.4)

√4th 76.3   **Partial ostectomy of facial bone**

76.31   **Partial mandibulectomy**
Hemimandibulectomy

> **EXCLUDES**   that associated with temporomandibular arthroplasty (76.5)

AHA: ▶2Q, '05, 8◀

DEF: Excision, partial of lower jawbone.

DEF: Hemimandibulectomy: Excision of one-half of lower jawbone.

76.39   **Partial ostectomy of other facial bone**
Hemimaxillectomy (with bonegraft or prosthesis)

AHA: J-F, '87, 14

DEF: Excision, partial of facial bone; other than lower jawbone.

DEF: Hemimaxillectomy (with bone graft or prosthesis): Excision of one side of upper jawbone and restoration with bone graft or prosthesis.

√4th 76.4   **Excision and reconstruction of facial bones**

76.41   **Total mandibulectomy with synchronous reconstruction**

76.42   **Other total mandibulectomy**

76.43   **Other reconstruction of mandible**

> **EXCLUDES**   genioplasty (76.67-76.68)
> that with synchronous total mandibulectomy (76.41)

AHA: 2Q, '03, 13

76.44   **Total ostectomy of other facial bone with synchronous reconstruction**

AHA: 3Q, '93, 6

DEF: Excision, facial bone, total with reconstruction during same operative session.

76.45   **Other total ostectomy of other facial bone**

76.46   **Other reconstruction of other facial bone**

> **EXCLUDES**   that with synchronous total ostectomy (76.44)

76.5   **Temporomandibular arthroplasty**

AHA: 4Q, '99, 20

√4th 76.6   **Other facial bone repair and orthognathic surgery**
Code also any synchronous:
bone graft (76.91)
synthetic implant (76.92)

> **EXCLUDES**   reconstruction of facial bones (76.41-76.46)

76.61   **Closed osteoplasty [osteotomy] of mandibular ramus**
Gigli saw osteotomy

DEF: Reshaping and restoration of lower jawbone projection; closed surgical field.

DEF: Gigli saw osteotomy: Plastic repair using a flexible wire with saw teeth.

76.62   **Open osteoplasty [osteotomy] of mandibular ramus**

76.63   **Osteoplasty [osteotomy] of body of mandible**

76.64   **Other orthognathic surgery on mandible**
Mandibular osteoplasty NOS
Segmental or subapical osteotomy

AHA: 2Q, '04, 9, 10

76.65   **Segmental osteoplasty [osteotomy] of maxilla**
Maxillary osteoplasty NOS

76.66   **Total osteoplasty [osteotomy] of maxilla**

76.67   **Reduction genioplasty**
Reduction mentoplasty

DEF: Reduction of protruding chin or lower jawbone.

76.68   **Augmentation genioplasty**
Mentoplasty:
NOS
with graft or implant

DEF: Extension of the lower jawbone to a functional position by means of plastic surgery.

76.69   **Other facial bone repair**
Osteoplasty of facial bone NOS

√4th 76.7   **Reduction of facial fracture**

> **INCLUDES**   internal fixation

Code also any synchronous:
bone graft (76.91)
synthetic implant (76.92)

> **EXCLUDES**   that of nasal bones (21.71-21.72)

76.70   **Reduction of facial fracture, not otherwise specified**

76.71   **Closed reduction of malar and zygomatic fracture**

76.72   **Open reduction of malar and zygomatic fracture**

76.73   **Closed reduction of maxillary fracture**

76.74   **Open reduction of maxillary fracture**

76.75   **Closed reduction of mandibular fracture**

76.76   **Open reduction of mandibular fracture**

76.77   **Open reduction of alveolar fracture**
Reduction of alveolar fracture with stabilization of teeth

76.78   **Other closed reduction of facial fracture**
Closed reduction of orbital fracture

> **EXCLUDES**   nasal bone (21.71)

76.79   **Other open reduction of facial fracture**
Open reduction of orbit rim or wall

> **EXCLUDES**   nasal bone (21.72)

√4th 76.9   **Other operations on facial bones and joints**

76.91   **Bone graft to facial bone**

Autogenous
Bone bank   } graft to facial bone
Heterogenous

76.92   **Insertion of synthetic implant in facial bone**
Alloplastic implant to facial bone

Operations on the Musculoskeletal System

76.93–77.7

76.93   **Closed reduction of temporomandibular dislocation**

76.94   **Open reduction of temporomandibular dislocation**

76.95   **Other manipulation of temporomandibular joint**

76.96   **Injection of therapeutic substance into temporomandibular joint**

76.97   **Removal of internal fixation device from facial bone**

> EXCLUDES   *removal of:*
> *dental wiring (97.33)*
> *external mandibular*
> *fixation device NEC*
> *(97.36)*

76.99   **Other**

√3rd **77**   **Incision, excision, and division of other bones**

> EXCLUDES   *laminectomy for decompression (03.09)*
> *operations on:*
> *accessory sinuses (22.00-22.9)*
> *ear ossicles (19.0-19.55)*
> *facial bones (76.01-76.99)*
> *joint structures (80.00-81.99)*
> *mastoid (19.9-20.99)*
> *nasal bones (21.00-21.99)*
> *skull (01.01-02.99)*

The following fourth-digit subclassification is for use with appropriate categories in section 77 to identify the site. Valid fourth-digit categories are in [brackets] under each code.

  0   **unspecified site**
  1   **scapula, clavicle, and thorax [ribs and sternum]**
  2   **humerus**
  3   **radius and ulna**
  4   **carpals and metacarpals**
  5   **femur**
  6   **patella**
  7   **tibia and fibula**
  8   **tarsals and metatarsals**
  9   **other**
       Pelvic bones
       Phalanges (of foot) (of hand)
       Vertebrae

18 § √4th **77.0**   **Sequestrectomy**
    [0-9]   DEF: Excision and removal of dead bone.

§ √4th **77.1**   **Other incision of bone without division**
    [0-9]   Reopening of osteotomy site
> EXCLUDES   *aspiration of bone marrow, (41.31, 41.91)*
> *removal of internal fixation device (78.60-78.69)*

     AHA: For code 77.17: 1Q, '02, 3

     DEF: Incision into bone without division of site.

18 § √4th **77.2**   **Wedge osteotomy**
    [0-9]   EXCLUDES   *that for hallux valgus (77.51)*

     DEF: Removal of wedge-shaped piece of bone.

§ √4th **77.3**   **Other division of bone**
    [0-9]   Osteoarthrotomy
> EXCLUDES   *clavicotomy of fetus (73.8)*
> *laminotomy or incision of vertebra (03.01-03.09)*
> *pubiotomy to assist delivery (73.94)*
> *sternotomy incidental to thoracic operation — omit code*

§ √4th **77.4**   **Biopsy of bone**
    [0-9]   AHA: 2Q, '98, 12

√4th **77.5**   **Excision and repair of bunion and other toe deformities**

Repair of Hammer Toe

77.51   **Bunionectomy with soft tissue correction and osteotomy of the first metatarsal**
     DEF: Incision and removal of big toe bony prominence and reconstruction with soft tissue.

77.52   **Bunionectomy with soft tissue correction and arthrodesis**
     DEF: Removal of big toe bony prominence and reconstruction with soft tissue and joint fixation.

77.53   **Other bunionectomy with soft tissue correction**

77.54   **Excision or correction of bunionette**
     That with osteotomy
     DEF: Resection of fifth metatarsal head via exposure of joint; includes imbrication of capsule.

77.56   **Repair of hammer toe**
     Fusion
     Phalangectomy (partial)   } of hammer
     Filleting   toe
     DEF: Repair of clawlike toe defect by joint fusion, or partial removal of toe via traction technique.

77.57   **Repair of claw toe**
     Fusion
     Phalangectomy (partial)   }
     Capsulotomy   of claw toe
     Tendon lengthening
     DEF: Repair of clawlike toe defect by joint fusion, partial removal of toe, joint capsule incision or lengthening of fibrous muscle attachment.

77.58   **Other excision, fusion, and repair of toes**
     Cockup toe repair
     Overlapping toe repair
     That with use of prosthetic materials

77.59   **Other bunionectomy**
     Resection of hallux valgus joint with insertion of prosthesis
     DEF: Resection of hallux valgus joint with insertion of prosthesis: Cutting away part of big toe with prosthesis insertion to correct bony prominence.

18 § √4th **77.6**   **Local excision of lesion or tissue of bone**
    [0-9]   EXCLUDES   *biopsy of bone (77.40-77.49)*
> *debridement of compound fracture (79.60-79.69)*

     AHA: For code 77.61: 3Q, '01, 9; **For code 77.65:** 4Q, '04, 128; S-O, '85, 4; **For code 77.67:** 1Q, '02, 3; 1Q, '99, 8; **For code 77.69:** 2Q, '00, 18

18 § √4th **77.7**   **Excision of bone for graft**
    [0-9]   **AHA:** 4Q, '99, 11, 13; **For code 77.71:** 3Q, '03, 19; **For code 77.79:** 2Q, '03, 13; 4Q, '02, 107, 109-110; 2Q, '02, 16; 2Q, '00 12, 13; 4Q, '99, 11, 13

---

§   Requires fourth-digit. Valid digits are in [brackets] under each code. See category 77 for definitions.
18   Nonspecific OR procedure=0

BI Bilateral Procedure   NC Non-covered Procedure   LC Limited Coverage Procedure   ►◄ Revised Text   ● New Code   ▲ Revised Code Title

18 § ✓4th **77.8** **Other partial ostectomy**
[0-9]   Condylectomy
> EXCLUDES   amputation (84.00-84.19, 84.91)
> arthrectomy (80.90-80.99)
> excision of bone ends associated with:
> arthrodesis (81.00-81.29)
> arthroplasty (81.51-81.59, 81.71-
> 81.81, 81.84)
> excision of cartilage (80.5-80.6, 80.80-
> 80.99)
> excision of head of femur with syn-
> chronous replacement (00.70-
> 00.73, 81.51-81.53)
> hemilaminectomy (03.01-03.09)
> laminectomy (03.01-03.09)
> ostectomy for hallux valgus (77.51-
> 77.59)
> partial amputation:
> finger (84.01)
> thumb (84.02)
> toe (84.11)
> resection of ribs incidental to thoracic
> operation — omit code
> that incidental to other operation —
> omit code

AHA: For code 77.89: 2Q, '02, 8

18 § ✓4th **77.9** **Total ostectomy**
[0-9]   EXCLUDES   amputation of limb (84.00-84.19, 84.91)
> that incidental to other operation —
> omit code

✓3rd **78** **Other operations on bones, except facial bones**
> EXCLUDES   operations on:
> accessory sinuses (22.00-22.9)
> facial bones (76.01-76.99)
> joint structures (80.00-81.99)
> nasal bones (21.00-21.99)
> skull (01.01-02.99)

The following fourth-digit subclassification is for use with categories in
section 78 to identify the site. Valid fourth-digit categories are in
[brackets] under each code.

0   **unspecified site**
1   **scapula, clavicle, and thorax [ribs and sternum]**
2   **humerus**
3   **radius and ulna**
4   **carpals and metacarpals**
5   **femur**
6   **patella**
7   **tibia and fibula**
8   **tarsals and metatarsals**
9   **other**
 Pelvic bones   Vertebrae
 Phalanges (of foot) (of hand)

18 ✓4th **78.0** **Bone graft**
[0-9]   Bone:
bank graft
graft (autogenous) (heterogenous)
That with debridement of bone graft site (removal of
sclerosed, fibrous, or necrotic bone or tissue)
Transplantation of bone
Code also any excision of bone for graft (77.70-
77.79)
> EXCLUDES   that for bone lengthening (78.30-78.39)

AHA: 2Q, '02, 11; 2Q, '98, 12; 3Q, '94, 10; 1Q, '91, 3

18 ✓4th **78.1** **Application of external fixator device**
[0-9]   Fixator with insertion of pins/wires/screws into
bone
Code also any type of fixator device, if known
(84.71-84.73)
> EXCLUDES   other immobilization, pressure, and
> attention to wound (93.51-93.59)

AHA: 2Q, '94, 4; For code 78.12: ▶4Q, '05, 129◀

18 ✓4th **78.2** **Limb shortening procedures**
[0,2-5,7-9] Epiphyseal stapling
Open epiphysiodesis
Percutaneous epiphysiodesis
Resection/osteotomy

18 ✓4th **78.3** **Limb lengthening procedures**
[0,2-5,7-9] Bone graft with or without internal fixation devices
or osteotomy
Distraction technique with or without
corticotomy/osteotomy
Code also any application of an external fixation
device (78.10-78.19)

18 ✓4th **78.4** **Other repair or plastic operations on bone**
[0-9]   Other operation on bone NEC
Repair of malunion or nonunion fracture NEC
> EXCLUDES   application of external fixation device
> (78.10-78.19)
> limb lengthening procedures (78.30-
> 78.39)
> limb shortening procedures (78.20-78.29)
> osteotomy (77.3)
> reconstruction of thumb (82.61-82.69)
> repair of pectus deformity (34.74)
> repair with bone graft (78.00-78.09)

AHA: 3Q, '91, 20; 4Q, '88, 11; **For code 78.41:** 2Q, '02, 16;
For code 78.47: 3Q, '91, 20; **For code 78.49:** 3Q, '04, 9;
2Q, '03, 22; 3Q, '02, 12; 2Q, '02, 14, 15; 4Q, '99, 22; 1Q, '97, 5

18 ✓4th **78.5** **Internal fixation of bone without fracture**
[0-9]   **reduction**
Internal fixation of bone (prophylactic)
Reinsertion of internal fixation device
Revision of displaced or broken fixation device
> EXCLUDES   arthroplasty and arthrodesis
> (81.00-81.85)
> bone graft (78.00-78.09)
> limb shortening procedures (78.20-
> 78.29)
> that for fracture reduction (79.10-79.19,
> 79.30-79.59)

AHA: 2Q, '99, 11; 2Q, '94, 4; **For Code 78.59:** 3Q, '04, 6; 2Q, '03, 15;
4Q, '99, 13

✓4th **78.6** **Removal of implanted devices from bone**
[0-9]   External fixator device (invasive)
Internal fixation device
Removal of bone growth stimulator (invasive)
Removal of internal limb lengthening device
> EXCLUDES   removal of cast, splint, and traction
> device (Kirschner wire)
> (Steinmann pin) (97.88)
> removal of skull tongs or halo traction
> device (02.95)

AHA: 1Q, '00, 15; **For Code 78.67** 2Q, '03, 14;
For Code 78.69: 4Q, '02, 110; 2Q, '00, 18

18 ✓4th **78.7** **Osteoclasis**
[0-9]   DEF: Surgical breaking or rebreaking of bone.

18 ✓4th **78.8** **Diagnostic procedures on bone, not elsewhere**
[0-9]   **classified**
> EXCLUDES   biopsy of bone (77.40-77.49)
> magnetic resonance imaging (88.94)
> microscopic examination of specimen
> from bone (91.51-91.59)
> radioisotope scan (92.14)
> skeletal x-ray (87.21-87.29, 87.43,
> 88.21-88.33)
> thermography (88.83)

18 ✓4th **78.9** **Insertion of bone growth stimulator**
[0-9]   Insertion of:
bone stimulator (electrical) to aid bone healing
osteogenic electrodes for bone growth stimulation
totally implanted device (invasive)
> EXCLUDES   non-invasive (transcutaneous) (surface)
> stimulator (99.86)

§ Requires fourth-digit. Valid digits are in [brackets] under each code. See category 77 for definitions.
18 Nonspecific OR procedure=0

✓3rd
✓4th   Additional Digit Required Nonspecific OR Procedure Valid OR Procedure Non-OR Procedure Adjunct Code

√3rd **79   Reduction of fracture and dislocation**

INCLUDES   application of cast or splint
reduction with insertion of traction device
(Kirschner wire) (Steinmann pin)

Code also any:
application of external fixator device (78.10-78.19)
type of fixator device, if known (84.71-84.73)

EXCLUDES   *external fixation alone for immobilization of*
fracture (93.51-93.56, 93.59)
internal fixation without reduction of fracture
(78.50-78.59)
operations on:
facial bones(76.70-76.79)
nasal bones (21.71-21.72)
orbit (76.78-76.79)
skull (02.02)
vertebrae (03.53)
removal of cast or splint (97.88)
replacement of cast or splint (97.11-97.14)
traction alone for reduction of fracture (93.41-
93.46)

The following fourth-digit subclassification is for use with appropriate
categories in section 79 to identify the site. Valid fourth-digit
categories are in [brackets] under each code.

    0   **unspecified site**
    1   **humerus**
    2   **radius and ulna**
        Arm NOS
    3   **carpals and metacarpals**
        Hand NOS
    4   **phalanges of hand**
    5   **femur**
    6   **tibia and fibula**
        Leg NOS
    7   **tarsals and metatarsals**
        Foot NOS
    8   **phalanges of foot**
    9   **other specified bone**

√4th **79.0   Closed reduction of fracture without internal**
[0-9]   **fixation**

EXCLUDES   *that for separation of epiphysis*
(79.40-79.49)

AHA: 2Q, '94, 3; 3Q, '89, 17; 4Q, '88, 11;
For code 79.01: ►4Q, '05, 129;◄ **For code 79.05:** 3Q, '89, 16

DEF: Manipulative realignment of fracture; without incision or
internal fixation.

18   √4th **79.1   Closed reduction of fracture with internal**
[0-9]   **fixation**

EXCLUDES   *that for separation of epiphysis*
(79.40-79.49)

AHA: 2Q, '94, 4; 4Q, '93, 35; 1Q, '93, 27

DEF: Manipulative realignment of fracture; with internal fixation but
without incision.

18   √4th **79.2   Open reduction of fracture without internal**
[0-9]   **fixation**

EXCLUDES   *that for separation of epiphysis*
(79.50-79.59)

AHA: 2Q, '94, 3

18   √4th **79.3   Open reduction of fracture with internal**
[0-9]   **fixation**

EXCLUDES   *that for separation of epiphysis*
(79.50-79.59)

AHA: 2Q, '98, 12; 3Q, '94, 10; 2Q, '94, 3; 4Q, '93, 35

DEF: Realignment of fracture with incision and internal fixation.

18   √4th **79.4   Closed reduction of separated epiphysis**
[0-2,5,6,9] Reduction with or without internal fixation

DEF: Manipulative reduction of expanded joint end of long bone to
normal position without incision.

18   √4th **79.5   Open reduction of separated epiphysis**
[0-2,5,6,9] Reduction with or without internal fixation

DEF: Reduction of expanded joint end of long bone with incision.

18   Nonspecific OR procedure=0

---

18   √4th **79.6   Debridement of open fracture site**
[0-9]   Debridement of compound fracture

AHA: 3Q, '95, 12; 3Q, '89, 16
DEF: Removal of damaged tissue at fracture site.

√4th **79.7   Closed reduction of dislocation**

INCLUDES   closed reduction (with external
traction device)

EXCLUDES   *closed reduction of dislocation of*
temporomandibular joint (76.93)

DEF: Manipulative reduction of displaced joint without incision;
with or without external traction.

79.70   Closed reduction of dislocation of
unspecified site
79.71   Closed reduction of dislocation of shoulder
79.72   Closed reduction of dislocation of elbow
79.73   Closed reduction of dislocation of wrist
79.74   Closed reduction of dislocation of hand and
finger
79.75   Closed reduction of dislocation of hip
79.76   Closed reduction of dislocation of knee

AHA: N-D, '86, 7

79.77   Closed reduction of dislocation of ankle
79.78   Closed reduction of dislocation of foot and toe
79.79   Closed reduction of dislocation of other
specified sites

18   √4th **79.8   Open reduction of dislocation**

INCLUDES   open reduction (with internal and
external fixation devices)

EXCLUDES   *open reduction of dislocation of*
temporomandibular joint (76.94)

DEF: Reduction of displaced joint via incision; with or without
internal and external fixation.

79.80   Open reduction of dislocation of
unspecified site
79.81   Open reduction of dislocation of shoulder
79.82   Open reduction of dislocation of elbow
79.83   Open reduction of dislocation of wrist
79.84   Open reduction of dislocation of hand and
finger
79.85   Open reduction of dislocation of hip
79.86   Open reduction of dislocation of knee
79.87   Open reduction of dislocation of ankle
79.88   Open reduction of dislocation of foot and toe
79.89   Open reduction of dislocation of other
specified sites

18   √4th **79.9   Unspecified operation on bone injury**
[0-9]

√3rd **80   Incision and excision of joint structures**

INCLUDES   operations on:
capsule of joint
cartilage
condyle
ligament
meniscus
synovial membrane

EXCLUDES   *cartilage of:*
ear (18.01-18.9)
nose (21.00-21.99)
temporomandibular joint (76.01-76.99)

The following fourth-digit subclassification is for use with appropriate
categories in section 80 to identify the site:

    0   **unspecified site**
    1   **shoulder**
    2   **elbow**
    3   **wrist**
    4   **hand and finger**
    5   **hip**
    6   **knee**
    7   **ankle**
    8   **foot and toe**
    9   **other specified sites**
        Spine

BI Bilateral Procedure   NC Non-covered Procedure   LC Limited Coverage Procedure   ►◄ Revised Text   ● New Code   ▲ Revised Code Title

¹⁸ § ✓4ᵗʰ **80.0   Arthrotomy for removal of prosthesis**

Code also any:
insertion of (cement) (joint) spacer (84.56)
removal of (cement) (joint) spacer (84.57)

AHA: For code 80.06: 2Q, '97, 10

DEF: Incision into joint to remove prosthesis.

¹⁸ § ✓4ᵗʰ **80.1   Other arthrotomy**

Arthrostomy

EXCLUDES   *that for:*
arthrography (88.32)
arthroscopy (80.20-80.29)
injection of drug (81.92)
operative approach — omit code

DEF: Incision into joint; other than to remove prosthesis.
DEF: Arthrostomy: Creation of opening into joint.

¹⁸ § ✓4ᵗʰ **80.2   Arthroscopy**

AHA: 3Q, '93, 5

§ ✓4ᵗʰ **80.3   Biopsy of joint structure**

Aspiration biopsy

AHA: For code 80.39: 3Q, '05, 13-14

¹⁸ § ✓4ᵗʰ **80.4   Division of joint capsule, ligament, or cartilage**

Goldner clubfoot release
Heyman-Herndon(-Strong) correction of metatarsus varus
Release of:
adherent or constrictive joint capsule
joint
ligament

EXCLUDES   *symphysiotomy to assist delivery (73.94)*
that for:
carpal tunnel syndrome (04.43)
tarsal tunnel syndrome (04.44)

AHA: For code 80.49: 2Q, '02, 16

DEF: Incision and separation of joint tissues, including capsule, fibrous bone attachment or cartilage.

✓4ᵗʰ **80.5   Excision or destruction of intervertebral disc**

80.50   Excision or destruction of intervertebral disc, unspecified

Unspecified as to excision or destruction

80.51   Excision of intervertebral disc

Code also any concurrent spinal fusion (81.00-81.08)
Diskectomy
Level:
cervical
thoracic
lumbar (lumbosacral)
Removal of herniated nucleus pulposus
That by laminotomy or hemilaminectomy
That with decompression of spinal nerve root at same level
Requires additional code for any concomitant decompression of spinal nerve root at different level from excision site

EXCLUDES   *intervertebral chemonucleolysis (80.52)*
laminectomy for exploration of intraspinal canal (03.09)
laminotomy for decompression of spinal nerve root only (03.09)
that for insertion of (non-fusion) spinal disc replacement device (84.60-84.69)
▶*that with corpectomy, (vertebral) (80.99)*◀

AHA:▶ 1Q, '06, 12;◀ 4Q, '04, 133; 3Q, '03, 12; 1Q, '96, 7; 2Q, '95, 9; 2Q, '90, 27; S-O, '86, 12

DEF: Diskectomy: Removal of intervertebral disc.
DEF: Removal of a herniated nucleus pulposus: Removal of displaced intervertebral disc, central part.

80.52   Intervertebral chemonucleolysis

With aspiration of disc fragments
With diskography
Injection of proteolytic enzyme into intervertebral space (chymopapain)

EXCLUDES   *injection of anesthestic substance (03.91)*
injection of other substances (03.92)

DEF: Destruction of intervertebral disc via injection of enzyme.

80.59   Other destruction of intervertebral disc

Destruction NEC
That by laser

AHA: 3Q, '02, 10

80.6   Excision of semilunar cartilage of knee

Excision of meniscus of knee

AHA: 2Q, '03, 18; 3Q, '00, 4; 2Q, '96, 3; 1Q, '93, 23

¹⁸ § ✓4ᵗʰ **80.7   Synovectomy**

Complete or partial resection of synovial membrane

EXCLUDES   *excision of Baker's cyst (83.39)*

DEF: Excision of inner membrane of joint capsule.

¹⁸ § ✓4ᵗʰ **80.8   Other local excision or destruction of lesion of joint**

¹⁸ § ✓4ᵗʰ **80.9   Other excision of joint**

EXCLUDES   *cheilectomy of joint (77.80-77.89)*
excision of bone ends (77.80-77.89)

✓3ʳᵈ **81   Repair and plastic operations on joint structures**

✓4ᵗʰ **81.0   Spinal fusion**

INCLUDES   arthrodesis of spine with:
bone graft
internal fixation

Code also any:
insertion of interbody spinal fusion device (84.51)
insertion of recombinant bone morphogenetic protein (84.52)
Code also the total number of vertebrae fused (81.62-81.64)

EXCLUDES   *corrections of pseudarthrosis of spine (81.30-81.39)*
refusion of spine (81.30-81.39)

AHA: 4Q, '03, 99

DEF: Spinal fusion: Immobilization of spinal column.

DEF: Anterior interbody fusion: Arthrodesis by excising disc and cartilage end plates with bone graft insertion between two vertebrae.

DEF: Lateral fusion: Arthrodesis by decorticating and bone grafting lateral surface of zygapophysial joint, pars interarticularis and transverse process.

DEF: Posterior fusion: Arthrodesis by decorticating and bone grafting of neural arches between right and left zygapophysial joints.

DEF: Posterolateral fusion: Arthrodesis by decorticating and bone grafting zygapophysial joint, pars interarticularis and transverse processes

81.00   Spinal fusion, not otherwise specified

81.01   Atlas-axis spinal fusion

Craniocervical fusion ⎫ by anterior trans-
C1-C2 fusion   ⎬ oral or poster-
Occiput C2 fusion   ⎭ ior technique

81.02   Other cervical fusion, anterior technique

Arthrodesis of C2 level or below:
anterior (interbody) technique
anterolateral technique

AHA: 4Q, '03, 101; 1Q, '01, 6; 1Q, '96, 7

81.03   Other cervical fusion, posterior technique

Arthrodesis of C2 level or below:
posterior (interbody) technique
posterolateral technique

---

§ Requires fourth-digit. Valid digits are in [brackets] under each code. See category 80 for definitions.
¹⁸ Nonspecific OR procedure=0

| ✓3ʳᵈ ✓4ᵗʰ Additional Digit Required | Nonspecific OR Procedure | Valid OR Procedure | Non-OR Procedure | Adjunct Code |

Operations on the Musculoskeletal System

81.04–81.35

Types of Grafts for Anterior Arthrodesis

Subtalar Joint Arthroereisis

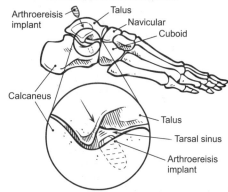

81.04   Dorsal and dorsolumbar fusion, anterior technique

   Arthrodesis of thoracic or thoracolumbar region:
   anterior (interbody) technique
   anterolateral technique

   AHA: 3Q, '03, 19

81.05   Dorsal and dorsolumbar fusion, posterior technique

   Arthrodesis of thoracic or thoracolumbar region:
   posterior (interbody) technique
   posterolateral technique

   AHA: 2Q, '02, 16; 4Q, '99, 11

81.06   Lumbar and lumbosacral fusion, anterior technique

   Anterior lumbar interbody fusion (ALIF)
   Arthrodesis of lumbar or lumbosacral region:
   anterior (interbody) technique
   anterolateral technique

   AHA: 4Q, '05, 122; 4Q, '02, 107; 4Q, '99, 11

81.07   Lumbar and lumbosacral fusion, lateral transverse process technique

   AHA: 4Q, '02, 108

81.08   Lumbar and lumbosacral fusion, posterior technique

   Arthrodesis of lumbar or lumbosacral region:
   posterior (interbody) technique
   posterolateral technique
   Posterior lumbar interbody fusion (PLIF)
   Transforaminal lumbar interbody fusion (TLIF)

   AHA: ▶1Q, '06, 12, 13;◀ 4Q, '05, 122-123; 4Q, '02, 107, 109; 2Q, '00, 12, 13; 4Q, '99, 13; 2Q, '95, 9

✓4th **81.1   Arthrodesis and arthroereisis of foot and ankle**

   INCLUDES   arthrodesis of foot and ankle with:
   bone graft
   external fixation device

   DEF: Fixation of foot or ankle joints.

   81.11   Ankle fusion
      Tibiotalar fusion

   81.12   Triple arthrodesis
      Talus to calcaneus and calcaneus to cuboid and navicular

   81.13   Subtalar fusion
      EXCLUDES   arthroereisis (81.18)

   81.14   Midtarsal fusion

   81.15   Tarsometatarsal fusion

   81.16   Metatarsophalangeal fusion

   81.17   Other fusion of foot

   81.18   Subtalar joint arthroereisis

      AHA: 4Q, '05, 124

   DEF: Insertion of an endoprostheses to limit excessive valgus motion of the subtalar joint; nonfusion procedure to prevent pronation.

✓4th **81.2   Arthrodesis of other joint**

   INCLUDES   arthrodesis with:
   bone graft
   external fixation device
   excision of bone ends and compression

   81.20   Arthrodesis of unspecified joint
   81.21   Arthrodesis of hip
   81.22   Arthrodesis of knee
   81.23   Arthrodesis of shoulder
   81.24   Arthrodesis of elbow
   81.25   Carporadial fusion
   81.26   Metacarpocarpal fusion
   81.27   Metacarpophalangeal fusion
   81.28   Interphalangeal fusion
   81.29   Arthrodesis of other specified joints

✓4th **81.3   Refusion of spine**

   INCLUDES   arthrodesis of spine with:
   bone graft
   internal fixation
   correction of pseudarthrosis of spine
   Code also any:
   insertion of interbody spinal fusion device (84.51)
   insertion of recombinant bone morphogenetic protein (84.52)
   Code also the total number of vertebrae fused (81.62-81.64)

   AHA: 4Q, '03, 99; 4Q, '01, 64

   81.30   Refusion of spine, not otherwise specified

   81.31   Refusion of atlas-axis spine

      Craniocervical fusion
      C1-C2 fusion   } by anterior transoral or posterior technique
      Occiput C2 fusion

   81.32   Refusion of other cervical spine, anterior technique
      Arthrodesis of C2 level or below:
      anterior (interbody) technique
      anterolateral technique

   81.33   Refusion of other cervical spine, posterior technique
      Arthrodesis of C2 level or below:
      posterior (interbody) technique
      posterolateral technique

   81.34   Refusion of dorsal and dorsolumbar spine, anterior technique
      Arthrodesis of thoracic or thoracolumbar region:
      anterior (interbody) technique
      anterolateral technique

   81.35   Refusion of dorsal and dorsolumbar spine, posterior technique
      Arthrodesis of thoracic or thoracolumbar region:
      posterior (interbody) technique
      posterolateral technique

BI Bilateral Procedure   NC Non-covered Procedure   LC Limited Coverage Procedure   ▶◀ Revised Text   ● New Code   ▲ Revised Code Title

Partial Hip Replacement

Acetabulum remains intact

Prosthesis

Total Hip Replacement

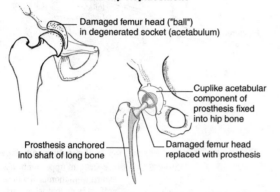

Damaged femur head ("ball") in degenerated socket (acetabulum)

Cuplike acetabular component of prosthesis fixed into hip bone

Prosthesis anchored into shaft of long bone

Damaged femur head replaced with prosthesis

81.36 Refusion of lumbar and lumbosacral spine, anterior technique
Anterior lumbar interbody fusion (ALIF)
Arthrodesis of lumbar or lumbosacral region:
anterior (interbody) technique
anterolateral technique
AHA: 4Q, '05, 122-123

81.37 Refusion of lumbar and lumbosacral spine, lateral transverse process technique

81.38 Refusion of lumbar and lumbosacral spine, posterior technique
Arthrodesis of lumbar or lumbosacral region:
posterior (interbody) technique
posterolateral technique
Posterior lumbar interbody fusion (PLIF)
Transforaminal lumbar interbody fusion (TLIF)
AHA: 4Q, '05, 122-123; 4Q, '02, 110

81.39 Refusion of spine, not elsewhere classified

√4th **81.4 Other repair of joint of lower extremity**
INCLUDES   arthroplasty of lower extremity with:
external traction or fixation
graft of bone (chips) or cartilage
internal fixation device
AHA: S-O, '85, 4

81.40 Repair of hip, not elsewhere classified
81.42 Five-in-one repair of knee
Medial meniscectomy, medial collateral ligament repair, vastus medialis advancement, semitendinosus advancement, and pes anserinus transfer

81.43 Triad knee repair
Medial meniscectomy with repair of the anterior cruciate ligament and the medial collateral ligament
O'Donoghue procedure

81.44 Patellar stabilization
Roux-Goldthwait operation for recurrent dislocation of patella
DEF: Roux-Goldthwait operation: Stabilization of patella via lateral ligament transposed at insertion beneath undisturbed medial insertion; excision of capsule ellipse and medial patella retinaculum; capsule reefed for lateral patella hold.

81.45 Other repair of the cruciate ligaments
AHA: M-A, '87, 12

81.46 Other repair of the collateral ligaments
81.47 Other repair of knee
AHA: 2Q, '03, 18; 1Q, '00, 12, 13; 1Q, '96, 3; 3Q, '93, 5

81.49 Other repair of ankle
AHA: 2Q, '01, 15; 3Q, '00, 4

√4th **81.5 Joint replacement of lower extremity**
INCLUDES   arthroplasty of lower extremity with:
external traction or fixation
graft of bone (chips) or cartilage
internal fixation device or prosthesis
removal of cement spacer
AHA: S-O, '85, 4

81.51 Total hip replacement   BI
Replacement of both femoral head and acetabulum by prosthesis
Total reconstruction of hip
Code also any type of bearing surface, if known ▶(00.74-00.77)◀
AHA: 4Q, '04, 113; 2Q, '91, 18
DEF: Repair of both surfaces of hip joint with prosthesis.

81.52 Partial hip replacement   BI
Bipolar endoprosthesis
Code also any type of bearing surface, if known ▶(00.74-00.77)◀
AHA: 2Q, '91, 18
DEF: Repair of single surface of hip joint with prosthesis.

81.53 Revision of hip replacement, not otherwise specified   BI
Revision of hip replacement, not specified as to component(s) replaced, (acetabular, femoral or both)
Code also any:
removal of (cement) (joint) spacer (84.57)
type of bearing surface, if known
▶(00.74-00.77)◀
EXCLUDES   revision of hip replacement, components specified (00.70-00.73)
AHA: 4Q, '05, 125; 3Q, '97, 12

81.54 Total knee replacement   BI
Bicompartmental
Tricompartmental
Unicompartmental (hemijoint)
DEF: Repair of a knee joint with prosthetic implant in one, two, or three compartments.

Total Knee Replacement

Condyle component

Femur

Prosthesis

Patella

Tibia

Plateau component

81.55 Revision of knee replacement, not otherwise specified `B1`

Code also any removal of (cement) (joint) spacer (84.57)

EXCLUDES arthrodesis of knee (81.22)
revision of knee replacement,
components specified
(00.80-00.84)

AHA: 4Q, '05, 113; 2Q, '97, 10

81.56 Total ankle replacement `B1`

81.57 Replacement of joint of foot and toe

81.59 Revision of joint replacement of lower extremity, not elsewhere classified

✓4th **81.6 Other procedures on spine**

Note: Number of vertebrae
The vertebral spine consists of 25 vertebrae in the following order and number:
Cervical: C1 (atlas), C2 (axis), C3, C4, C5, C6, C7
Thoracic or Dorsal: T1, T2, T3, T4, T5, T6, T7, T8, T9, T10, T11, T12
Lumbar and Sacral: L1, L2, L3, L4, L5, S1
Coders should report only one code from the series 81.62-81.64 to show the total number of vertebrae fused on the patient.
Code also the level and approach of the fusion or refusion (81.00-81.08, 81.30-81.39)

AHA: 4Q, '03, 99
DEF: A combined posterior and anterior fusion performed by a surgeon through one incision: lateral transverse, posterior, or anterior.

81.62 Fusion or refusion of 2-3 vertebrae
AHA: ▶1Q, '06, 12, 13;◀ 4Q, '05, 123; 4Q, '03, 99

81.63 Fusion or refusion of 4-8 vertebrae
AHA: 4Q, '03, 99-101

81.64 Fusion or refusion of 9 or more vertebrae
AHA: 4Q, '03, 99

81.65 Vertebroplasty

Injection of bone void filler (cement) (poly-methylmethacrylate) (PMMA) into the diseased or fractured vertebral body

EXCLUDES kyphoplasty (81.66)

81.66 Kyphoplasty

Insertion of inflatable balloon, bone tamp, or other device to create a cavity for partial restoration of height of diseased or fractured vertebral body prior to injection of bone void filler (cement) (polymethylmethacrylate) (PMMA)

EXCLUDES vertebroplasty (81.65)

AHA: 4Q, '04, 126

✓4th **81.7 Arthroplasty and repair of hand, fingers, and wrist**

INCLUDES arthroplasty of hand and finger with:
external traction or fixation
graft of bone (chips) or cartilage
internal fixation device or prosthesis

EXCLUDES operations on muscle, tendon, and fascia of hand (82.01-82.99)

DEF: Plastic surgery of hand, fingers and wrist joints.

81.71 Arthroplasty of metacarpophalangeal and interphalangeal joint with implant

81.72 Arthroplasty of metacarpophalangeal and interphalangeal joint without implant
AHA: 1Q, '93, 28

81.73 Total wrist replacement

81.74 Arthroplasty of carpocarpal or carpometacarpal joint with implant

81.75 Arthroplasty of carpocarpal or carpometacarpal joint without implant
AHA: 3Q, '93, 8

81.79 Other repair of hand, fingers, and wrist

Vertebroplasty

Lamina

Body

Spinous process

Lateral view of fractured body of thoracic vertebra

Injection of bone cement into fracture site

Kyphoplasty

Vertebral body

Inflatable balloon catheter

Inflated balloon

Fractured vertebra

Disc

The cavity is filled with bone cement

✓4th **81.8 Arthroplasty and repair of shoulder and elbow**

INCLUDES arthroplasty of upper limb NEC with:
external traction or fixation
graft of bone (chips) or cartilage
internal fixation device or prosthesis

81.80 Total shoulder replacement

81.81 Partial shoulder replacement

81.82 Repair of recurrent dislocation of shoulder
AHA: 3Q, '95, 15

81.83 Other repair of shoulder
Revision of arthroplasty of shoulder
AHA: 1Q, '02, 9; 4Q, '01, 51; 2Q, '00, 14; 3Q, '93, 5

81.84 Total elbow replacement

81.85 Other repair of elbow

✓4th **81.9 Other operations on joint structures**

81.91 Arthrocentesis
Joint aspiration

EXCLUDES that for:
arthrography (88.32)
biopsy of joint structure (80.30-80.39)
injection of drug (81.92)

DEF: Insertion of needle to withdraw fluid from joint.

81.92 Injection of therapeutic substance into joint or ligament
AHA: 2Q, '00, 14; 3Q, '89, 16

Arthrocentesis

Needle access into fluid filled knee joint

Femur

Patella (kneecap)

Fluid-filled joint capsule

Tibia

`B1` Bilateral Procedure   `NC` Non-covered Procedure   `LC` Limited Coverage Procedure   ▶◀ Revised Text   ● New Code   ▲ Revised Code Title

166 — Volume 3 • October 2006   *2007 ICD•9•CM*

81.93   Suture of capsule or ligament of upper extremity

> EXCLUDES   that associated with arthroplasty (81.71-81.75, 81.80-81.81, 81.84)

81.94   Suture of capsule or ligament of ankle and foot

> EXCLUDES   that associated with arthroplasty (81.56-81.59)

81.95   Suture of capsule or ligament of other lower extremity

> EXCLUDES   that associated with arthroplasty (81.51-81.55, 81.59)

81.96   Other repair of joint

81.97   Revision of joint replacement of upper extremity

    Partial   Total

    Removal of cement spacer

AHA: 1Q, '04, 12

81.98   Other diagnostic procedures on joint structures

> EXCLUDES   arthroscopy (80.20-80.29)
> biopsy of joint structure (80.30-80.39)
> microscopic examination of specimen from joint (91.51-91.59)
> thermography (88.83)
> x-ray (87.21-87.29, 88.21-88.33)

81.99   Other

AHA: ▶4Q, '05, 124◀

√3rd **82   Operations on muscle, tendon, and fascia of hand**

> INCLUDES   operations on:
> aponeurosis
> synovial membrane (tendon sheath)
> tendon sheath

√4th **82.0   Incision of muscle, tendon, fascia, and bursa of hand**

82.01   Exploration of tendon sheath of hand

    Incision of   } tendon sheath
    Removal of rice bodies in   of hand

> EXCLUDES   division of tendon (82.11)

DEF: Incision into and exploring the hand's muscle and its accompanying supportive, connective tissue, bands, and sacs.

82.02   Myotomy of hand

> EXCLUDES   myotomy for division (82.19)

DEF: Incision into hand muscle.

82.03   Bursotomy of hand

82.04   Incision and drainage of palmar or thenar space

82.09   Other incision of soft tissue of hand

> EXCLUDES   incision of skin and subcutaneous tissue alone (86.01-86.09)

AHA: N-D, '87, 10

√4th **82.1   Division of muscle, tendon, and fascia of hand**

82.11   Tenotomy of hand

    Division of tendon of hand

82.12   Fasciotomy of hand

    Division of fascia of hand

82.19   Other division of soft tissue of hand

    Division of muscle of hand

√4th **82.2   Excision of lesion of muscle, tendon, and fascia of hand**

82.21   Excision or lesion of tendon sheath of hand

    Ganglionectomy of tendon sheath (wrist)

82.22   Excision of lesion of muscle of hand

82.29   Excision of other lesion of soft tissue of hand

> EXCLUDES   excision of lesion of skin and subcutaneous tissue (86.21-86.3)

√4th **82.3   Other excision of soft tissue of hand**

    Code also any skin graft (86.61-86.62, 86.73)

> EXCLUDES   excision of skin and subcutaneous tissue (86.21-86.3)

82.31   Bursectomy of hand

82.32   Excision of tendon of hand for graft

DEF: Resection and excision of fibrous tissue connecting bone to hand muscle for grafting.

82.33   Other tenonectomy of hand

    Tenosynovectomy of hand

> EXCLUDES   excision of lesion of:
> tendon (82.29)
> sheath (82.21)

DEF: Removal of fibrous bands connecting muscle to bone of hand.

DEF: Tenosynovectomy of hand: Excision of fibrous band connecting muscle and bone of hand and removal of coverings.

82.34   Excision of muscle or fascia of hand for graft

82.35   Other fasciectomy of hand

    Release of Dupuytren's contracture

> EXCLUDES   excision of lesion of fascia (82.29)

DEF: Excision of fibrous connective tissue; other than for grafting or removing lesion.

DEF: Release of Dupuytren's contracture: Excision of fibrous connective tissue to correct flexion of fingers.

82.36   Other myectomy of hand

> EXCLUDES   excision of lesion of muscle (82.22)

82.39   Other excision of soft tissue of hand

> EXCLUDES   excision of skin (86.21-86.3)
> excision of soft tissue lesion (82.29)

√4th **82.4   Suture of muscle, tendon, and fascia of hand**

82.41   Suture of tendon sheath of hand

82.42   Delayed suture of flexor tendon of hand

DEF: Suture of fibrous band between flexor muscle and bone; following initial repair.

82.43   Delayed suture of other tendon of hand

82.44   Other suture of flexor tendon of hand

> EXCLUDES   delayed suture of flexor tendon of hand (82.42)

82.45   Other suture of other tendon of hand

> EXCLUDES   delayed suture of other tendon of hand (82.43)

82.46   Suture of muscle or fascia of hand

√4th **82.5   Transplantation of muscle and tendon of hand**

AHA: 1Q, '93, 28

82.51   Advancement of tendon of hand

DEF: Detachment of fibrous connective muscle band and bone with reattachment at advanced point of hand.

82.52   Recession of tendon of hand

DEF: Detachment of fibrous band of muscle and bone with reattachment at drawn-back point of hand.

82.53   Reattachment of tendon of hand

82.54   Reattachment of muscle of hand

82.55   Other change in hand muscle or tendon length

82.56   Other hand tendon transfer or transplantation

> EXCLUDES   pollicization of thumb (82.61)
> transfer of finger, except thumb (82.81)

AHA: 2Q, '99, 10; 4Q, '98, 40

√3rd √4th Additional Digit Required   Nonspecific OR Procedure   Valid OR Procedure   Non-OR Procedure   Adjunct Code

82.57 Other hand tendon transposition
AHA: 1Q, '93, 28; 3Q, '93, 8

82.58 Other hand muscle transfer or transplantation

82.59 Other hand muscle transposition

✓4th **82.6 Reconstruction of thumb**
INCLUDES digital transfer to act as thumb
Code also any amputation for digital transfer (84.01, 84.11)

82.61 Pollicization operation carrying over nerves and blood supply
DEF: Creation or reconstruction of a thumb with another digit, commonly the index finger.

82.69 Other reconstruction of thumb
"Cocked-hat" procedure [skin flap and bone]
Grafts:
bone
skin (pedicle) } to thumb

✓4th **82.7 Plastic operation on hand with graft or implant**
82.71 Tendon pulley reconstruction
Reconstruction for opponensplasty
DEF: Reconstruction of fibrous band between muscle and bone of hand.

82.72 Plastic operation on hand with graft of muscle or fascia

82.79 Plastic operation on hand with other graft or implant
Tendon graft to hand
AHA: J-F, '87, 6

✓4th **82.8 Other plastic operations on hand**
82.81 Transfer of finger, except thumb
EXCLUDES pollicization of thumb (82.61)
AHA: ▶2Q, '05, 7◀

82.82 Repair of cleft hand
DEF: Correction of fissure defect of hand.

82.83 Repair of macrodactyly
DEF: Reduction in size of abnormally large fingers.

82.84 Repair of mallet finger
DEF: Repair of flexed little finger.

82.85 Other tenodesis of hand
Tendon fixation of hand NOS
DEF: Fixation of fibrous connective band between muscle and bone of hand.

82.86 Other tenoplasty of hand
Myotenoplasty of hand
DEF: Myotenoplasty of hand: Plastic repair of muscle and fibrous band connecting muscle to bone.

82.89 Other plastic operations on hand
Plication of fascia
Repair of fascial hernia
EXCLUDES that with graft or implant (82.71-82.79)

✓4th **82.9 Other operations on muscle, tendon, and fascia of hand**
EXCLUDES diagnostic procedures on soft tissue of hand (83.21-83.29)

82.91 Lysis of adhesions of hand
Freeing of adhesions of fascia, muscle, and tendon of hand
EXCLUDES decompression of carpal tunnel (04.43)
that by stretching or manipulation only (93.26)

82.92 Aspiration of bursa of hand
82.93 Aspiration of other soft tissue of hand
EXCLUDES skin and subcutaneous tissue (86.01)

82.94 Injection of therapeutic substance into bursa of hand

82.95 Injection of therapeutic substance into tendon of hand

82.96 Other injection of locally-acting therapeutic substance into soft tissue of hand
EXCLUDES subcutaneous or intramuscular injection (99.11-99.29)

82.99 Other operations on muscle, tendon, and fascia of hand

✓3rd **83 Operations on muscle, tendon, fascia, and bursa, except hand**
INCLUDES operations on:
aponeurosis
synovial membrane of bursa and tendon sheaths
tendon sheaths
EXCLUDES diaphragm (34.81-34.89)
hand (82.01-82.99)
muscles of eye (15.01-15.9)

✓4th **83.0 Incision of muscle, tendon, fascia, and bursa**
83.01 Exploration of tendon sheath
Incision of tendon sheath
Removal of rice bodies from tendon sheath
DEF: Incision of external covering of fibrous cord for exam.
DEF: Removal of rice bodies from tendon sheath: Incision and removal of small bodies resembling grains of rice.

83.02 Myotomy
EXCLUDES cricopharyngeal myotomy (29.31)
AHA: 2Q, '89, 18

83.03 Bursotomy
Removal of calcareous deposit of bursa
EXCLUDES aspiration of bursa (percutaneous) (83.94)

83.09 Other incision of soft tissue
Incision of fascia
EXCLUDES incision of skin and subcutaneous tissue alone (86.01-86.09)

✓4th **83.1 Division of muscle, tendon, and fascia**
83.11 Achillotenotomy
83.12 Adductor tenotomy of hip
DEF: Incision into fibrous attachment between adductor muscle and hip bone.

83.13 Other tenotomy
Aponeurotomy   Tendon transection
Division of tendon Tenotomy for thoracic
Tendon release   outlet decompression
DEF: Aponeurotomy: Incision and separation of fibrous cords attaching a muscle to bone to aid movement.
DEF: Division of tendon: Separation of fibrous band connecting muscle to bone.
DEF: Tendon release: Surgical detachment of fibrous band from muscle and/or bone.
DEF: Tendon transection: Incision across width of fibrous bands between muscle and bone.
DEF: Tenotomy for thoracic outlet decompression: Incision of fibrous muscle with separation from bone to relieve compressed thoracic outlet.

83.14 Fasciotomy
Division of fascia
Division of iliotibial band
Fascia stripping
Release of Volkmann's contracture by fasciotomy
AHA: 3Q, '98, 8
DEF: Division of fascia: Incision to separate fibrous connective tissue.
DEF: Division of iliotibial band: Incision to separate fibrous band connecting tibial bone to muscle in flank.
DEF: Fascia stripping: Incision and lengthwise separation of fibrous connective tissue.
DEF: Release of Volkmann's contracture by fasciotomy: Divisional incision of connective tissue to correct defect in flexion of finger(s).

BI Bilateral Procedure   NC Non-covered Procedure   LC Limited Coverage Procedure   ▶◀ Revised Text   ● New Code   ▲ Revised Code Title

168 — Volume 3 • February 2006   2007 ICD•9•CM

83.19 **Other division of soft tissue**
Division of muscle
Muscle release
Myotomy for thoracic outlet decompression
Myotomy with division
Scalenotomy
Transection of muscle

✓4th **83.2** **Diagnostic procedures on muscle, tendon, fascia, and bursa, including that of hand**

83.21 **Biopsy of soft tissue**
EXCLUDES *biopsy of chest wall (34.23)*
biopsy of skin and subcutaneous tissue (86.11)

83.29 **Other diagnostic procedures on muscle, tendon, fascia, and bursa, including that of hand**
EXCLUDES *microscopic examination of specimen (91.51-91.-59)*
soft tissue x-ray (87.09, 87.38-87.39, 88.09, 88.35, 88.37)
thermography of muscle (88.84)

✓4th **83.3** **Excision of lesion of muscle, tendon, fascia, and bursa**
EXCLUDES *biopsy of soft tissue (83.21)*

83.31 **Excision of lesion of tendon sheath**
Excision of ganglion of tendon sheath, except of hand

83.32 **Excision of lesion of muscle**
Excision of:
heterotopic bone
muscle scar for release of Volkmann's contracture
myositis ossificans
DEF: Heterotopic bone: Bone lesion in muscle.
DEF: Muscle scar for release of Volkmann's contracture: Scarred muscle tissue interfering with finger flexion.
DEF: Myositis ossificans: Bony deposits in muscle.

83.39 **Excision of lesion of other soft tissue**
Excision of Baker's cyst
EXCLUDES *bursectomy (83.5)*
excision of lesion of skin and subcutaneous tissue (86.3)
synovectomy (80.70-80.79)
AHA: 2Q, '05, 3; 2Q, '97, 6

✓4th **83.4** **Other excision of muscle, tendon, and fascia**
83.41 **Excision of tendon for graft**
83.42 **Other tenonectomy**
Excision of: Tenosynovectomy
aponeurosis
tendon sheath
83.43 **Excision of muscle or fascia for graft**
83.44 **Other fasciectomy**
DEF: Excision of fascia; other than for graft.
83.45 **Other myectomy**
Debridement of muscle NOS
Scalenectomy
AHA: 1Q, '99, 8
DEF: Scalenectomy: Removal of thoracic scaleni muscle tissue.
83.49 **Other excision of soft tissue**

83.5 **Bursectomy**
AHA: 2Q, '99, 11

✓4th **83.6** **Suture of muscle, tendon, and fascia**
83.61 **Suture of tendon sheath**
83.62 **Delayed suture of tendon**
83.63 **Rotator cuff repair**
AHA: ▶1Q, '06, 6;◀ 2Q, '93, 8
DEF: Repair of musculomembranous structure around shoulder joint capsule.

83.64 **Other suture of tendon**
Achillorrhaphy   Aponeurorrhaphy
EXCLUDES *delayed suture of tendon (83.62)*
DEF: Achillorrhaphy: Suture of fibrous band connecting Achilles tendon to heel bone.
DEF: Aponeurorrhaphy: Suture of fibrous cords connecting muscle to bone.

83.65 **Other suture of muscle or fascia**
Repair of diastasis recti

✓4th **83.7** **Reconstruction of muscle and tendon**
EXCLUDES *reconstruction of muscle and tendon associated with arthroplasty*

83.71 **Advancement of tendon**
DEF: Detaching fibrous cord between muscle and bone with reattachment at advanced point.

83.72 **Recession of tendon**
DEF: Detaching fibrous cord between muscle and bone with reattachment at drawn-back point.

83.73 **Reattachment of tendon**
83.74 **Reattachment of muscle**
83.75 **Tendon transfer or transplantation**
83.76 **Other tendon transposition**
83.77 **Muscle transfer or transplantation**
Release of Volkmann's contracture by muscle transplantation
83.79 **Other muscle transposition**

✓4th **83.8** **Other plastic operations on muscle, tendon, and fascia**
EXCLUDES *plastic operations on muscle, tendon, and fascia associated with arthroplasty*

83.81 **Tendon graft**
83.82 **Graft of muscle or fascia**
AHA: 3Q, '01, 9

83.83 **Tendon pulley reconstruction**
DEF: Reconstruction of fibrous cord between muscle and bone; at any site other than hand.

83.84 **Release of clubfoot, not elsewhere classified**
Evans operation on clubfoot

83.85 **Other change in muscle or tendon length**
Hamstring lengthening
Heel cord shortening
Plastic achillotenotomy
Tendon plication
DEF: Plastic achillotenotomy: Increase in heel cord length.
DEF: Tendon plication: Surgical tuck of tendon.

83.86 **Quadricepsplasty**
DEF: Correction of quadriceps femoris muscle.

83.87 **Other plastic operations on muscle**
Musculoplasty   Myoplasty
AHA: 1Q, '97, 9

83.88 **Other plastic operations on tendon**
Myotenoplasty   Tenodesis
Tendon fixation   Tenoplasty

83.89 **Other plastic operations on fascia**
Fascia lengthening
Fascioplasty
Plication of fascia

✓4th **83.9** **Other operations on muscle, tendon, fascia, and bursa**
EXCLUDES *nonoperative:*
manipulation (93.25-93.29)
stretching (93.27-93.29)

83.91 **Lysis of adhesions of muscle, tendon, fascia, and bursa**
EXCLUDES *that for tarsal tunnel syndrome (04.44)*
DEF: Separation of created fibrous structures from muscle, connective tissues, bands and sacs.

Operations on the Musculoskeletal System

83.19–83.91

Operations on the Musculoskeletal System

83.92–84.17

83.92 **Insertion or replacement of skeletal muscle stimulator**

Implantation, insertion, placement, or replacement of skeletal muscle:
electrodes
stimulator

AHA: 2Q, '99, 10

83.93 **Removal of skeletal muscle stimulator**

83.94 **Aspiration of bursa**

83.95 **Aspiration of other soft tissue**

> EXCLUDES   *that of skin and subcutaneous tissue (86.01)*

83.96 **Injection of therapeutic substance into bursa**

83.97 **Injection of therapeutic substance into tendon**

83.98 **Injection of locally-acting therapeutic substance into other soft tissue**

> EXCLUDES   *subcutaneous or intramuscular injection (99.11-99.29)*

83.99 **Other operations on muscle, tendon, fascia, and bursa**

Suture of bursa

√3ʳᵈ **84** **Other procedures on musculoskeletal system**

√4ᵗʰ **84.0** **Amputation of upper limb**

> EXCLUDES   *revision of amputation stump (84.3)*

84.00 **Upper limb amputation, not otherwise specified**

Closed flap amputation
Kineplastic amputation
Open or guillotine amputation
Revision of current traumatic amputation
} of upper limb NOS

DEF: Closed flap amputation: Sewing a created skin flap over stump end of upper limb.

DEF: Kineplastic amputation: Amputation and preparation of stump of upper limb to permit movement.

DEF: Open or guillotine amputation: Straight incision across upper limb; used when primary closure is contraindicated.

DEF: Revision of current traumatic amputation: Reconstruction of traumatic amputation of upper limb to enable closure.

84.01 **Amputation and disarticulation of finger**

> EXCLUDES   *ligation of supernumerary finger (86.26)*

84.02 **Amputation and disarticulation of thumb**

84.03 **Amputation through hand**

Amputation through carpals

84.04 **Disarticulation of wrist**

84.05 **Amputation through forearm**

Forearm amputation

84.06 **Disarticulation of elbow**

DEF: Amputation of forearm through elbow joint.

84.07 **Amputation through humerus**

Upper arm amputation

84.08 **Disarticulation of shoulder**

DEF: Amputation of arm through shoulder joint.

84.09 **Interthoracoscapular amputation**

Forequarter amputation

DEF: Removal of upper arm, shoulder bone and collarbone.

√4ᵗʰ **84.1** **Amputation of lower limb**

> EXCLUDES   *revision of amputation stump (84.3)*

84.10 **Lower limb amputation, not otherwise specified**

Closed flap amputation
Kineplastic amputation
Open or guillotine amputation
Revision of current traumatic amputation
} of lower limb NOS

DEF: Closed flap amputation: Sewing a created skin flap over stump of lower limb.

DEF: Kineplastic amputation: Amputation and preparation of stump of lower limb to permit movement.

DEF: Open or guillotine amputation: Straight incision across lower limb; used when primary closure is contraindicated.

DEF: Revision of current traumatic amputation: Reconstruction of traumatic amputation of lower limb to enable closure.

84.11 **Amputation of toe**

Amputation through metatarsophalangeal joint
Disarticulation of toe
Metatarsal head amputation
Ray amputation of foot (disarticulation of the metatarsal head of the toe extending across the forefoot, just proximal to the metatarsophalangeal crease)

> EXCLUDES   *ligation of supernumerary toe (86.26)*

AHA: ▶2Q, '05, 7;◀ 4Q, '99, 19

84.12 **Amputation through foot**

Amputation of forefoot
Amputation through middle of foot
Chopart's amputation
Midtarsal amputation
Transmetatarsal amputation (amputation of the forefoot, including the toes)

> EXCLUDES   *Ray amputation of foot (84.11)*

AHA: 4Q, '99, 19

DEF: Amputation of forefoot: Removal of foot in front of joint between toes and body of foot.

DEF: Chopart's amputation: Removal of foot with retention of heel, ankle and other associated ankle bones.

DEF: Midtarsal amputation: Amputation of foot through tarsals.

DEF: Transmetatarsal amputation: Amputation of foot through metatarsals.

84.13 **Disarticulation of ankle**

DEF: Removal of foot through ankle bone.

84.14 **Amputation of ankle through malleoli of tibia and fibula**

84.15 **Other amputation below knee**

Amputation of leg through tibia and fibula NOS

84.16 **Disarticulation of knee**

Batch, Spitler, and McFaddin amputation
Mazet amputation
S.P. Roger's amputation

DEF: Removal of lower leg through knee joint.

84.17 **Amputation above knee**

Amputation of leg through femur
Amputation of thigh
Conversion of below-knee amputation into above-knee amputation
Supracondylar above-knee amputation

AHA: 1Q, '05, 16; 1Q, '05, 16; 3Q, '03, 14

BI Bilateral Procedure	**NC** Non-covered Procedure	**LC** Limited Coverage Procedure	▶◀ Revised Text ● New Code ▲ Revised Code Title

84.18 Disarticulation of hip

DEF: Removal of leg through hip joint.

84.19 Abdominopelvic amputation

Hemipelvectomy

Hindquarter amputation

DEF: Removal of leg and portion of pelvic bone.

DEF: Hemipelvectomy: Removal of leg and lateral pelvis.

√4th **84.2 Reattachment of extremity**

AHA: 1Q, '95, 8

84.21 Thumb reattachment

84.22 Finger reattachment

84.23 Forearm, wrist, or hand reattachment

84.24 Upper arm reattachment

Reattachment of arm NOS

84.25 Toe reattachment

84.26 Foot reattachment

84.27 Lower leg or ankle reattachment

Reattachment of leg NOS

84.28 Thigh reattachment

84.29 Other reattachment

84.3 Revision of amputation stump

Reamputation

Secondary closure } of stump

Trimming

EXCLUDES   revision of current traumatic amputation [revision by further amputation of current injury] (84.00-84.19, 84.91)

AHA: 4Q, '99, 15; 2Q, '98, 15; 4Q, '88, 12

√4th **84.4 Implantation or fitting of prosthetic limb device**

84.40 Implantation or fitting of prosthetic limb device, not otherwise specified

84.41 Fitting of prosthesis of upper arm and shoulder

84.42 Fitting of prosthesis of lower arm and hand

84.43 Fitting of prosthesis of arm, not otherwise specified

84.44 Implantation of prosthetic device of arm

84.45 Fitting of prosthesis above knee

84.46 Fitting of prosthesis below knee

84.47 Fitting of prosthesis of leg, not otherwise specified

84.48 Implantation of prosthetic device of leg

√4th **84.5 Implantation of other musculoskeletal devices and substances**

EXCLUDES   insertion of (non-fusion) spinal disc replacement device (84.60-84.69)

84.51 Insertion of interbody spinal fusion device

Insertion of:

cages (carbn, ceramic, metal, plastic or titanium)

interbody fusion cage

synthetic cages or spacers

threaded bone dowels

Code also refusion of spine (81.30-81.39)

Code also spinal fusion (81.00-81.08)

AHA: 4Q, '05, 123; 1Q, '04, 21; 4Q, '02, 108-110

84.52 Insertion of recombinant bone morphogenetic protein

rhBMP

That via collagen sponge, coral, ceramic and other carriers

Code also primary procedure performed:

fracture repair (79.00-79.99)

spinal fusion (81.00-81.08)

spinal refusion (81.30-81.39)

AHA: 4Q, '02, 110

DEF: Surgical implantation of bone morphogenetic proteins (BMP) and recombinant BMP (rhBMP) to induce new bone growth formation; clinical applications include delayed unions and nonunions, fractures, and spinal fusions.

Spinal Fusion with Metal Cage

Metal cages support spine until fusion occurs

Lateral view

Anterior view

Spinal fusion with metal cages

Detail

84.53 Implantation of internal limb lengthening device with kinetic distraction

Code also limb lengthening procedure (78.30-78.39)

84.54 Implantation of other internal limb lengthening device

Implantation of internal limb lengthening device, not otherwise specified (NOS)

Code also limb lengthening procedure (78.30-78.39)

84.55 Insertion of bone void filler

Insertion of:

acrylic cement (PMMA)

bone void cement

calcium based bone void filler

polymethylmethacrylate (PMMA)

EXCLUDES   that with kyphoplasty (81.66) that with vertebroplasty (81.65)

AHA: 4Q, '04, 128

84.56 Insertion of (cement) spacer

Insertion of joint spacer

AHA: 4Q, '05, 124

DEF: Implantation of an interspinous process decompressive (IPD) device between the spinous processes to limit extension; nonfusion, posterior approach procedure.

84.57 Removal of (cement) spacer

Removal of joint spacer

AHA: 4Q, '05, 113, 124-125

84.58 Implantation of interspinous process decompression device

EXCLUDES   fusion of spine (81.00-81.08, 81.30-81.39)

AHA: 4Q, '05, 126

84.59 Insertion of other spinal devices

▶Insertion of non-fusion spinal stabilization device◀

√4th **84.6 Replacement of spinal disc**

INCLUDES   non-fusion arthroplasty of the spine with insertion of artificial disc prosthesis

84.60 Insertion of spinal disc prosthesis, not otherwise specified

Replacement of spinal disc, NOS

INCLUDES   diskectomy (discectomy)

84.61 Insertion of partial spinal disc prosthesis, cervical

Nuclear replacement device, cervical

Partial artificial disc prosthesis (flexible), cervical

Replacement of nuclear disc (nucleus pulposus), cervical

INCLUDES   diskectomy (discectomy)

√3rd √4th Additional Digit Required   Nonspecific OR Procedure   Valid OR Procedure   Non-OR Procedure   Adjunct Code

Operations on the Musculoskeletal System

84.62–84.99

84.62 Insertion of total spinal disc prosthesis, cervical
Replacement of cervical spinal disc, NOS
Replacement of total spinal disc, cervical
Total artificial disc prosthesis (flexible), cervical
INCLUDES diskectomy (discectomy)

84.63 Insertion of spinal disc prosthesis, thoracic
Artificial disc prosthesis (flexible), thoracic
Replacement of thoracic spinal disc, partial or total
INCLUDES diskectomy (discectomy)

84.64 Insertion of partial spinal disc prosthesis, lumbosacral
Nuclear replacement device, lumbar
Partial artificial disc prosthesis (flexible), lumbar
Replacement of nuclear disc (nucleus pulposus), lumbar
INCLUDES diskectomy (discectomy)

84.65 Insertion of total spinal disc prosthesis, lumbosacral
Replacement of lumbar spinal disc, NOS
Replacement of total spinal disc, lumbar
Total artificial disc prosthesis (flexible), lumbar
INCLUDES diskectomy (discectomy)
AHA: 4Q, '04, 133

84.66 Revision or replacement of artificial spinal disc prosthesis, cervical
Removal of (partial) (total) spinal disc prosthesis with synchronous insertion of new (partial) (total) spinal disc prosthesis, cervical
Repair of previously inserted spinal disc prosthesis, cervical

84.67 Revision or replacement of artificial spinal disc prosthesis, thoracic
Removal of (partial) (total) spinal disc prosthesis with synchronous insertion of new (partial) (total) spinal disc prosthesis, thoracic
Repair of previously inserted spinal disc prosthesis, thoracic

84.68 Revision or replacement of artificial spinal disc prosthesis, lumbosacral
Removal of (partial) (total) spinal disc prosthesis with synchronous insertion of new (partial) (total) spinal disc prosthesis, lumbosacral
Repair of previously inserted spinal disc prosthesis, lumbosacral

84.69 Revision or replacement of artificial spinal disc prosthesis, not otherwise specified
Removal of (partial) (total) spinal disc prosthesis with synchronous insertion of new (partial) (total) spinal disc prosthesis
Repair of previously inserted spinal disc prosthesis

√4ᵗʰ **84.7 Adjunct codes for external fixator devices**
Code also any primary procedure performed:
application of external fixator device (78.10, 78.12-78.13, 78.15, 78.17-78.19)
reduction of fracture and dislocation (79.00-79.89)
AHA: 4Q, '05, 127-129

84.71 Application of external fixator device, monoplanar system
EXCLUDES other hybrid device or system (84.73)
ring device or system (84.72)
AHA: 4Q, '05, 129

DEF: Instrumentation that provides percutaneous neutralization, compression, and /or distraction of bone in a single plane by applying force within that plane.

84.72 Application of external fixator device, ring system
Ilizarov type
Sheffield type
EXCLUDES monoplanar device or system (84.71)
other hybrid device or system (84.73)

DEF: Instrumentation that provides percutaneous neutralization, compression, and/or distraction of bone through 360 degrees of force application.

84.73 Application of hybrid external fixator device
►Computer (assisted) (dependent) external fixator device◄
Hybrid system using both ring and monoplanar devices
EXCLUDES monoplanar device or system, when used alone (84.71)
ring device or system, when used alone (84.72)

DEF: Instrumentation that provides percutaneous neutralization, compression, and /or distraction of bone by applying multiple external forces using monoplanar and ring device combinations.

√4ᵗʰ **84.9 Other operations on musculoskeletal system**
EXCLUDES nonoperative manipulation (93.25-93.29)

84.91 Amputation, not otherwise specified
84.92 Separation of equal conjoined twins
84.93 Separation of unequal conjoined twins
Separation of conjoined twins NOS
84.99 Other

External Fixator Devices

Monoplanar   Ring system

Hybrid

BI Bilateral Procedure   **NC** Non-covered Procedure   **LC** Limited Coverage Procedure   ►◄ Revised Text   ● New Code   ▲ Revised Code Title

172 — Volume 3 • October 2006   2007 *ICD•9•CM*

15. OPERATIONS ON THE INTEGUMENTARY SYSTEM (85-86)

√3rd **85 Operations on the breast**

INCLUDES operations on the skin and subcutaneous tissue of:

breast ⎫ female or
previous mastectomy site ⎬ male

revision of previous mastectomy site

85.0 Mastotomy

Incision of breast (skin)
Mammotomy

EXCLUDES aspiration of breast (85.91)
removal of implant (85.94)

AHA: 1Q, '04, 3; 2Q, '90, 27

√4th **85.1 Diagnostic procedures on breast**

85.11 Closed [percutaneous] [needle] biopsy of breast

AHA: 2Q, '00, 10; 3Q, '89, 17

DEF: Mammatome biopsy: Excision of breast tissue using a needle inserted through a small incision; followed by a full cut circle of tissue surrounding the core biopsy to obtain; multiple contiguous directional sampling for definitive diagnosis and staging of cancer.

85.12 Open biopsy of breast

AHA: 3Q, '89, 17; M-A, '86, 11

DEF: Excision of breast tissue for examination.

85.19 Other diagnostic procedures on breast

EXCLUDES mammary ductogram (87.35)
mammography NEC (87.37)
manual examination (89.36)
microscopic examination of
specimen (91.61-91.69)
thermography (88.85)
ultrasonography (88.73)
xerography (87.36)

√4th **85.2 Excision or destruction of breast tissue**

EXCLUDES mastectomy (85.41-85.48)
reduction mammoplasty (85.31-85.32)

85.20 Excision or destruction of breast tissue, not otherwise specified

85.21 Local excision of lesion of breast

Lumpectomy
Removal of area of fibrosis from breast

EXCLUDES biopsy of breast (85.11-85.12)

AHA: 2Q, '90, 27; 3Q, '89, 17; M-A, '86, 11

85.22 Resection of quadrant of breast

85.23 Subtotal mastectomy

EXCLUDES quadrant resection (85.22)

AHA: 2Q, '92, 7

DEF: Excision of a large portion of breast tissue.

85.24 Excision of ectopic breast tissue

Excision of accessory nipple

DEF: Excision of breast tissue outside normal breast region.

85.25 Excision of nipple

EXCLUDES excision of accessory nipple
(85.24)

√4th **85.3 Reduction mammoplasty and subcutaneous mammectomy**

AHA: 4Q, '95, 79, 80

85.31 Unilateral reduction mammoplasty

Unilateral:
amputative mammoplasty
size reduction mammoplasty

85.32 Bilateral reduction mammoplasty

Amputative mammoplasty
Biesenberger operation
Reduction mammoplasty (for gynecomastia)

85.33 Unilateral subcutaneous mammectomy with synchronous implant

EXCLUDES that without synchronous
implant (85.34)

DEF: Removal of mammary tissue, leaving skin and nipple intact with implant of prosthesis.

85.34 Other unilateral subcutaneous mammectomy

Removal of breast tissue with preservation of skin and nipple
Subcutaneous mammectomy NOS

DEF: Excision of mammary tissue, leaving skin and nipple intact.

85.35 Bilateral subcutaneous mammectomy with synchronous implant

EXCLUDES that without synchronous
implant (85.36)

DEF: Excision of mammary tissue, both breasts, leaving skin and nipples intact; with prosthesis.

85.36 Other bilateral subcutaneous mammectomy

√4th **85.4 Mastectomy**

85.41 Unilateral simple mastectomy

Mastectomy: Mastectomy:
NOS complete

DEF: Removal of one breast.

85.42 Bilateral simple mastectomy

Bilateral complete mastectomy

DEF: Removal of both breasts.

85.43 Unilateral extended simple mastectomy

Extended simple mastectomy NOS
Modified radical mastectomy
Simple mastectomy with excision of regional lymph nodes

AHA: 2Q, '92, 7; 3Q, '91, 24; 2Q, '91, 21

DEF: Removal of one breast and lymph nodes under arm.

85.44 Bilateral extended simple mastectomy

AHA: 2Q, '92, 7; 3Q, '91, 24; 2Q, '91, 21

85.45 Unilateral radical mastectomy

Excision of breast, pectoral muscles, and regional lymph nodes [axillary, clavicular, supraclavicular]
Radical mastectomy NOS

AHA: 2Q, '91, 21

DEF: Removal of one breast and regional lymph nodes, pectoral muscle and adjacent tissue.

Mastectomy

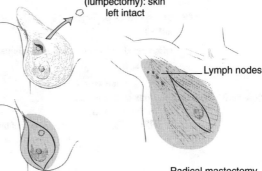

Partial mastectomy (lumpectomy): skin left intact

Lymph nodes

Simple mastectomy

Radical mastectomy

√3rd
√4th Additional Digit Required · Nonspecific OR Procedure · Valid OR Procedure · Non-OR Procedure · Adjunct Code

Operations on the Integumentary System

85.46–86.05

85.46 Bilateral radical mastectomy
AHA: 2Q, '91, 21

85.47 Unilateral extended radical mastectomy
Excision of breast, muscles, and lymph
nodes [axillary, clavicular,
supraclavicular, internal mammary,
and mediastinal]
Extended radical mastectomy NOS

DEF: Removal of one breast, regional and middle chest
lymph nodes, chest muscle and adjacent tissue.

85.48 Bilateral extended radical mastectomy
DEF: Removal of both breasts, regional and middle chest
lymph nodes, chest muscle and adjacent tissue.

√4th **85.5 Augmentation mammoplasty**
EXCLUDES   *that associated with subcutaneous
mammectomy (85.33, 85.35)*
AHA: 3Q, '97, 12; 4Q, '95, 76, 80

DEF: Plastic surgery to increase breast size.

**85.50 Augmentation mammoplasty, not otherwise
specified**

**85.51 Unilateral injection into breast for
augmentation**

**85.52 Bilateral injection into breast for
augmentation**
Injection into breast for augmentation NOS

85.53 Unilateral breast implant
AHA: 2Q, '00 18; 2Q, '98, 14

85.54 Bilateral breast implant
Breast implant NOS

85.6 Mastopexy
DEF: Anchoring of pendulous breast.

85.7 Total reconstruction of breast
AHA: 4Q, '95, 77; 1Q, '93, 27

√4th **85.8 Other repair and plastic operations on breast**
EXCLUDES   *that for:*
augmentation (85.50-85.54)
reconstruction (85.7)
reduction (85.31-85.32)
AHA: 4Q, '95, 77

85.81 Suture of laceration of breast
85.82 Split-thickness graft to breast
85.83 Full-thickness graft to breast
AHA: 4Q, '95, 77

85.84 Pedicle graft to breast
AHA: 4Q, '95, 77

DEF: Implantation of transferred muscle tissue still
connected to vascular source.

85.85 Muscle flap graft to breast
AHA: 4Q, '95, 77

DEF: Relocation of nipple.

85.86 Transposition of nipple
AHA: 4Q, '95, 78

85.87 Other repair or reconstruction of nipple
AHA: 4Q, '95, 78

85.89 Other mammoplasty
√4th **85.9 Other operations on the breast**
85.91 Aspiration of breast
EXCLUDES   *percutaneous biopsy of breast
(85.11)*

85.92 Injection of therapeutic agent into breast
EXCLUDES   *that for augmentation of
breast (85.51-85.52)*

85.93 Revision of implant of breast
AHA: 2Q, '98, 14; 4Q, '95, 76

85.94 Removal of implant of breast
AHA: 2Q, '98, 14; 3Q, '92, 4

85.95 Insertion of breast tissue expander
Insertion (soft tissue) of tissue expander
(one or more) under muscle or
platysma to develop skin flaps for
donor use

85.96 Removal of breast tissue expander(s)
AHA: 2Q, '00, 18; 4Q, '95, 77

85.99 Other
√3rd **86 Operations on skin and subcutaneous tissue**
INCLUDES   operations on: operations on:
hair follicles   subcutaneous fat pads
male perineum   sudoriferous glands
nails   superficial fossae
sebaceous glands

EXCLUDES   *those on skin of:*
anus (49.01-49.99)
breast (mastectomy site) (85.0-85.99)
ear (18.01-18.9)
eyebrow (08.01-08.99)
eyelid (08.01-08.99)
female perineum (71.01-71.9)
lips (27.0-27.99)
nose (21.00-21.99)
penis (64.0-64.99)
scrotum (61.0-61.99)
vulva (71.01-71.9)

√4th **86.0 Incision of skin and subcutaneous tissue**
86.01 Aspiration of skin and subcutaneous tissue
Aspiration of:
abscess } of nail, skin, or
hematoma } subcutaneous
seroma } tissue
AHA: 3Q, '89, 16

**86.02 Injection or tattooing of skin lesion or
defect**
Insertion } of filling material
Injection }
Pigmenting of skin

DEF: Pigmenting of skin: Adding color to skin.

86.03 Incision of pilonidal sinus or cyst
EXCLUDES   *marsupialization (86.21)*

**86.04 Other incision with drainage of skin and
subcutaneous tissue**
EXCLUDES   *drainage of:*
*fascial compartments of
face and mouth (27.0)*
*palmar or thenar space
(82.04)*
*pilonidal sinus or cyst
(86.03)*
AHA: 4Q, '04, 76

**86.05 Incision with removal of foreign body or
device from skin and subcutaneous tissue**
Removal of loop recorder
Removal of neurostimulator pulse generator
(single array, dual array)
Removal of tissue expander(s) from skin or
soft tissue other than breast tissue
EXCLUDES   *removal of foreign body
without incision (98.20-
98.29)*
AHA: 2Q, '96, 15; N-D, '87, 10; N-D, '86, 9

BI Bilateral Procedure   NC Non-covered Procedure   LC Limited Coverage Procedure   ►◄ Revised Text   ● New Code   ▲ Revised Code Title

86.06   **Insertion of totally implantable infusion pump**

Code also any associated catheterization

> EXCLUDES   *insertion of totally implantable vascular access device (86.07)*

AHA: 2Q, '99, 4; 4Q, '90, 14

86.07   **Insertion of totally implantable vascular access device [VAD]**

Totally implanted port

> EXCLUDES   *insertion of totally implantable infusion pump (86.06)*

AHA: 1Q, '01, 13; 1Q, '96, 3; 2Q, '94, 11; 3Q, '91, 13; 4Q, '90, 15

DEF: Placement of vascular access infusion catheter system under skin to allow for frequent manual infusions into blood vessel.

86.09   **Other incision of skin and subcutaneous tissue**

Creation of thalamic stimulator pulse generator pocket, new site

Escharotomy

Exploration:
  sinus tract, skin
  superficial fossa

Relocation of subcutaneous device pocket NEC

Reopening subcutaneous pocket for device revision without replacement

Undercutting of hair follicle

> EXCLUDES   *that of:*
> *cardiac pacemaker pocket, new site (37.79)*
> *creation of loop recorder pocket, new site and insertion/relocation of device (37.79)*
> *creation of pocket for implantable, patient-activated cardiac event recorder and insertion/relocation of device (37.79)*
> *fascial compartments of face and mouth (27.0)*
> *removal of catheter from cranial cavity (01.27)*

AHA: 1Q, '05, 17; 2Q, '04, 7, 8; 4Q, '00, 68; 4Q, '99, 21; 4Q, '97, 57; 3Q, '89, 17; N-D, '86, 1; N-D, '84, 6

√4ᵗʰ **86.1**   **Diagnostic procedures on skin and subcutaneous tissue**

86.11   **Biopsy of skin and subcutaneous tissue**

86.19   **Other diagnostic procedures on skin and subcutaneous tissue**

> EXCLUDES   *microscopic examination of specimen from skin and subcutaneous tissue (91.61-91.79)*

√4ᵗʰ **86.2**   **Excision or destruction of lesion or tissue of skin and subcutaneous tissue**

86.21   **Excision of pilonidal cyst or sinus**

Marsupialization of cyst

> EXCLUDES   *incision of pilonidal cyst or sinus (86.03)*

DEF: Marsupialization of cyst: Incision of cyst and suturing edges to skin to open site.

86.22   **Excisional debridement of wound, infection, or burn**

Removal by excision of:
  devitalized tissue
  necrosis
  slough

> EXCLUDES   *debridement of:*
> *abdominal wall (wound) (54.3)*
> *bone (77.60-77.69)*
> *muscle (83.45)*
> *of hand (82.36)*
> *nail (bed) (fold) (86.27)*
> *nonexcisional debridement of wound, infection, or burn (86.28)*
> *open fracture site (79.60-79.69)*
> *pedicle or flap graft (86.75)*

AHA: 1Q, '05, 14; 4Q, '04, 138; 3Q, '02, 23; 2Q, '00, 9; 1Q, '99, 8; 2Q, '92, 17; 3Q, '91, 18; 3Q, '89, 16; 4Q, '88, 5; N-D, '86, 1

86.23   **Removal of nail, nailbed, or nail fold**

86.24   **Chemosurgery of skin**

Chemical peel of skin

DEF: Chemicals applied to destroy skin tissue.

DEF: Chemical peel of skin: Chemicals used to peel skin layers.

86.25   **Dermabrasion**

That with laser

> EXCLUDES   *dermabrasion of wound to remove embedded debris (86.28)*

DEF: Removal of wrinkled or scarred skin; with fine sandpaper, wire, brushes or laser.

86.26   **Ligation of dermal appendage**

> EXCLUDES   *excision of preauricular appendage (18.29)*

DEF: Tying off extra skin.

86.27   **Debridement of nail, nail bed, or nail fold**

Removal of:
  necrosis
  slough

> EXCLUDES   *removal of nail, nail bed, or nail fold (86.23)*

86.28   **Nonexcisional debridement of wound, infection, or burn**

Debridement NOS

Maggot therapy

Removal of devitalized tissue, necrosis, and slough by such methods as:
  brushing
  irrigation (under pressure)
  scrubbing
  washing
▶Water scalpel (jet)◀

AHA: 1Q, '05, 14; 2Q, '04, 5, 6; 4Q, '03, 110; 2Q, '03, 15; 3Q, '02, 23; 2Q, '01, 18; 3Q, '91, 18; 4Q, '88, 5

DEF: Removal of damaged skin; by methods other than excision.

86.3   **Other local excision or destruction of lesion or tissue of skin and subcutaneous tissue**

Destruction of skin by:	Destruction of skin by:
cauterization	fulguration
cryosurgery	laser beam

That with Z-plasty

> EXCLUDES   *adipectomy (86.83)*
> *biopsy of skin (86.11)*
> *wide or radical excision of skin (86.4)*
> *Z-plasty without excision (86.84)*

AHA: 1Q, '96, 15; 2Q, '90, 27; 1Q, '89, 12; 3Q, '89, 18; 4Q, '88, 7

Operations on the Integumentary System

86.4–86.82

86.4   **Radical excision of skin lesion**

Wide excision of skin lesion involving underlying or adjacent structure

Code also any lymph node dissection (40.3-40.5)

✓4ᵗʰ 86.5   **Suture or other closure of skin and subcutaneous tissue**

86.51   **Replantation of scalp**

86.59   **Closure of skin and subcutaneous tissue of other sites**

Adhesives (surgical) (tissue)

Staples

Sutures

> EXCLUDES   *application of adhesive strips (butterfly) — omit code*

AHA: 4Q, '99, 23

✓4ᵗʰ 86.6   **Free skin graft**

> INCLUDES   excision of skin for autogenous graft
>
> EXCLUDES   *construction or reconstruction of:*
> *penis (64.43-64.44)*
> *trachea (31.75)*
> *vagina (70.61-70.62)*

DEF: Transplantation of skin to another site.

86.60   **Free skin graft, not otherwise specified**

86.61   **Full-thickness skin graft to hand**

> EXCLUDES   *heterograft (86.65)*
> *homograft (86.66)*

86.62   **Other skin graft to hand**

> EXCLUDES   *heterograft (86.65)*
> *homograft (86.66)*

86.63   **Full-thickness skin graft to other sites**

> EXCLUDES   *heterograft (86.65)*
> *homograft (86.66)*

86.64   **Hair transplant**

> EXCLUDES   *hair follicle transplant to eyebrow or eyelash (08.63)*

86.65   **Heterograft to skin**

Pigskin graft   Porcine graft

> EXCLUDES   *application of dressing only (93.57)*

AHA: 3Q,'02, 23

DEF: Implantation of nonhuman tissue.

86.66   **Homograft to skin**

Graft to skin of:

amnionic membrane ⎫
skin   ⎬ from donor

DEF: Implantation of tissue from human donor.

86.67   **Dermal regenerative graft**

Artificial skin, NOS

Creation of "neodermis"

Decellularized allodermis

Integumentary matrix implants

Prosthetic implant of dermal layer of skin

Regenerate dermal layer of skin

> EXCLUDES   *heterograft to skin (86.65)*
> *homograft to skin (86.66)*

AHA: 4Q, '98, 76, 79

DEF: Replacement of dermis and epidermal layer of skin by cultured or regenerated autologous tissue; used to treat full-thickness or deep partial-thickness burns; also called cultured epidermal autograft (CEA).

86.69   **Other skin graft to other sites**

> EXCLUDES   *heterograft (86.65)*
> *homograft (86.66)*

AHA: 4Q, '99, 15

✓4ᵗʰ 86.7   **Pedicle grafts or flaps**

> EXCLUDES   *construction or reconstruction of:*
> *penis (64.43-64.44)*
> *trachea (31.75)*
> *vagina (70.61-70.62)*

DEF: Full thickness skin and subcutaneous tissue partially attached to the body by a narrow strip of tissue so that it retains its blood supply. The unattached portion is sutured to the defect.

86.70   **Pedicle or flap graft, not otherwise specified**

86.71   **Cutting and preparation of pedicle grafts or flaps**

Elevation of pedicle from its bed

Flap design and raising

Partial cutting of pedicle or tube

Pedicle delay

> EXCLUDES   *pollicization or digital transfer (82.61,82.81)*
> *revision of pedicle (86.75)*

AHA: 4Q, '01, 66

DEF: Elevation of pedicle from its bed: Separation of tissue implanted from its bed.

DEF: Flap design and raising: Planing and elevation of tissue to be implanted.

DEF: Pedicle delay: Elevation and preparation of tissue still attached to vascular bed; delayed implant.

86.72   **Advancement of pedicle graft**

AHA: 3Q, '99, 9, 10

86.73   **Attachment of pedicle or flap graft to hand**

> EXCLUDES   *pollicization or digital transfer (82.61, 82.81)*

86.74   **Attachment of pedicle or flap graft to other sites**

Attachment by:	Attachment by:
advanced flap	rotating flap
double pedicled flap	sliding flap
pedicle graft	tube graft

AHA: 3Q, '99, 9; 1Q, '96, 15

DEF: Attachment by:

Advanced flap: Sliding tissue implant into new position.

Double pedicle flap: Implant connected to two vascular beds.

Pedicle graft: Implant connected to vascular bed.

Rotating flap: Implant rotated along curved incision.

Sliding flap: Sliding implant to site.

Tube graft: Double tissue implant to form tube with base connected to original site.

86.75   **Revision of pedicle or flap graft**

Debridement ⎫ of pedicle or flap
Defatting   ⎬ graft

DEF: Connection of implant still attached to its vascular tissue.

✓4ᵗʰ 86.8   **Other repair and reconstruction of skin and subcutaneous tissue**

DEF: Revision and tightening of excess, wrinkled facial skin.

86.81   **Repair for facial weakness**

86.82   **Facial rhytidectomy**

Face lift

> EXCLUDES   *rhytidectomy of eyelid (08.86-08.87)*

BI   Bilateral Procedure   NC   Non-covered Procedure   LC   Limited Coverage Procedure   ▶◀ Revised Text   ● New Code   ▲ Revised Code Title

176 — Volume 3   *2007 ICD•9•CM*

86.83 Size reduction plastic operation
Liposuction
Reduction of adipose tissue of:
abdominal wall (pendulous)
arms (batwing)
buttock
thighs (trochanteric lipomatosis)
> **EXCLUDES** breast (85.31-85.32)

DEF: Excision and plastic repair of excess skin and underlying tissue.

86.84 Relaxation of scar or web contracture of skin
Z-plasty of skin
> **EXCLUDES** Z-plasty with excision of lesion (86.3)

86.85 Correction of syndactyly

DEF: Plastic repair of webbed fingers or toes.

86.86 Onychoplasty

DEF: Plastic repair of nail or nail bed.

86.89 Other repair and reconstruction of skin and subcutaneous tissue
> **EXCLUDES** mentoplasty (76.67-76.68)

AHA: 4Q, '02, 107; 1Q, '00, 26; 2Q, '98, 20; 2Q, '93, 11; 2Q, '92, 17

√4ᵗʰ **86.9 Other operations on skin and subcutaneous tissue**

86.91 Excision of skin for graft
Excision of skin with closure of donor site
> **EXCLUDES** that with graft at same operative episode (86.60-86.69)

86.92 Electrolysis and other epilation of skin
> **EXCLUDES** epilation of eyelid (08.91-08.93)

86.93 Insertion of tissue expander
Insertion (subcutaneous) (soft tissue) of expander (one or more) in scalp (subgaleal space), face, neck, trunk except breast, and upper and lower extremities for development of skin flaps for donor use
> **EXCLUDES** flap graft preparation (86.71)
> tissue expander, breast (85.95)

86.94 Insertion or replacement of single array neurostimulator pulse generator, not specified as rechargeable
Pulse generator (single array, single channel) for intracranial, spinal, and peripheral neurostimulator
Code also any associated lead implantation (02.93, 03.93, 04.92)
> **EXCLUDES** insertion or replacement of single array rechargeable neurostimulator pulse generator (86.97)

AHA: 4Q, '04, 135

86.95 Insertion or replacement of dual array neurostimulator pulse generator, not specified as rechargeable
Pulse generator (dual array, dual channel) for intracranial, spinal, and peripheral neurostimulator
Code also any associated lead implantation (02.93, 03.93, 04.92)
> **EXCLUDES** insertion or replacement of dual array rechargeable neurostimulator pulse generator (86.98)

86.96 Insertion or replacement of other neurostimulator pulse generator
Code also any associated lead implantation (02.93, 03.93, 04.92)
> **EXCLUDES** insertion of dual array neurostimulator pulse generator (86.95, 86.98)
> insertion of single array neurostimulator pulse generator (86.94, 86.97)

86.97 Insertion or replacement of single array rechargeable neurostimulator pulse generator
Rechargeable pulse generator (single array, single channel) for intracranial, spinal, and peripheral neurostimulator
Code also any associated lead implantation (02.93, 03.93, 04.92)

AHA: ▶4Q, '05, 130◀

86.98 Insertion or replacement of dual array rechargeable neurostimulator pulse generator
Rechargeable pulse generator (dual array, dual channel) for intracranial, spinal, and peripheral neurostimulator
Code also any associated lead implantation (02.93, 03.93, 04.92)

AHA: ▶4Q, '05, 130◀

86.99 Other
> **EXCLUDES** removal of sutures from:
> abdomen (97.83)
> head and neck (97.38)
> thorax (97.43)
> trunk NEC (97.84)
> wound catheter:
> irrigation (96.58)
> replacement (97.15)

AHA: 4Q, '97, 57; N-D, '86, 1

Diagnostic and Therapeutic Procedures

87–87.49

16. MISCELLANEOUS DIAGNOSTIC AND THERAPEUTIC PROCEDURES (87-99)

√3ʳᵈ **87 Diagnostic radiology**

√4ᵗʰ **87.0 Soft tissue x-ray of face, head, and neck**

> **EXCLUDES** *angiography (88.40-88.68)*

87.01 Pneumoencephalogram
DEF: Radiographic exam of cerebral ventricles and subarachnoid spaces; with injection of air or gas for contrast.

87.02 Other contrast radiogram of brain and skull
Pneumocisternogram
Pneumoventriculogram
Posterior fossa myelogram
DEF: Pneumocisternogram: radiographic exam of subarachnoid spaces after injection of gas or contrast.

DEF: Pneumoventriculography: radiographic exam of cerebral ventricles after injection of gas or contrast.

DEF: Posterior fossa myelogram: radiographic exam of posterior channel of spinal cord after injection of gas or contrast.

87.03 Computerized axial tomography of head
C.A.T. scan of head
AHA: ▶3Q, '05, 12;◀ 3Q, '99, 7

87.04 Other tomography of head

87.05 Contrast dacryocystogram
DEF: Radiographic exam of tear sac after injection of contrast.

87.06 Contrast radiogram of nasopharynx

87.07 Contrast laryngogram

87.08 Cervical lymphangiogram
DEF: Radiographic exam of lymph vessels of neck; with or without contrast.

87.09 Other soft tissue x-ray of face, head, and neck

Noncontrast x-ray of:	Noncontrast x-ray of:
adenoid	salivary gland
larynx	thyroid region
nasolacrimal duct	uvula
nasopharynx	

> **EXCLUDES** *x-ray study of eye (95.14)*

√4ᵗʰ **87.1 Other x-ray of face, head, and neck**

> **EXCLUDES** *angiography (88.40-88.68)*

87.11 Full-mouth x-ray of teeth

87.12 Other dental x-ray
Orthodontic cephalogram or cephalometrics
Panorex examination of mandible
Root canal x-ray

87.13 Temporomandibular contrast arthrogram

87.14 Contrast radiogram of orbit

87.15 Contrast radiogram of sinus

87.16 Other x-ray of facial bones

X-ray of:	X-ray of:
frontal area	orbit
mandible	supraorbital area
maxilla	symphysis menti
nasal sinuses	zygomaticomaxillary
nose	complex

87.17 Other x-ray of skull
Lateral projection ⎫
Sagittal projection ⎬ of skull
Tangential projection ⎭

DEF: Lateral projection: Side to side view of head.

DEF: Sagittal projection: View of body in plane running midline from front to back.

DEF: Tangential projection: Views from adjacent skull surfaces.

√4ᵗʰ **87.2 X-ray of spine**

87.21 Contrast myelogram
DEF: Radiographic exam of space between middle and outer spinal cord coverings after injection of contrast.

87.22 Other x-ray of cervical spine

87.23 Other x-ray of thoracic spine

87.24 Other x-ray of lumbosacral spine
Sacrococcygeal x-ray

87.29 Other x-ray of spine
Spinal x-ray NOS

√4ᵗʰ **87.3 Soft tissue x-ray of thorax**

> **EXCLUDES** *angiocardiography (88.50-88.58)*
> *angiography (88.40-88.68)*

87.31 Endotracheal bronchogram
DEF: Radiographic exam of lung, main branch, with contrast introduced through windpipe.

87.32 Other contrast bronchogram
Transcricoid bronchogram
DEF: Transcricoid bronchogram: Radiographic exam of lung, main branch, with contrast introduced through cartilage of neck.

87.33 Mediastinal pneumogram
DEF: Radiographic exam of cavity containing heart, esophagus and adjacent structures.

87.34 Intrathoracic lymphangiogram
DEF: Radiographic exam of lymphatic vessels within chest; with or without contrast.

87.35 Contrast radiogram of mammary ducts
DEF: Radiographic exam of mammary ducts; with contrast.

87.36 Xerography of breast
DEF: Radiographic exam of breast via selenium-coated plates.

87.37 Other mammography
AHA: 3Q, '89, 17; 2Q, '90, 28; N-D, '87, 1

87.38 Sinogram of chest wall
Fistulogram of chest wall
DEF: Fistulogram of chest wall: Radiographic exam of abnormal opening in chest.

87.39 Other soft tissue x-ray of chest wall

√4ᵗʰ **87.4 Other x-ray of thorax**

> **EXCLUDES** *angiocardiography (88.50-88.58)*
> *angiography (88.40-88.68)*

87.41 Computerized axial tomography of thorax
C.A.T. scan ⎫
Crystal linea scan of x-ray beam ⎪
Electronic subtraction ⎬ of thorax
Photoelectric response ⎪
Tomography with use of computer, x-rays, and camera ⎭

87.42 Other tomography of thorax
Cardiac tomogram
DEF: Radiographic exam of chest plane.

87.43 X-ray of ribs, sternum, and clavicle
Examination for:
cervical rib
fracture

87.44 Routine chest x-ray, so described
X-ray of chest NOS

87.49 Other chest x-ray

X-ray of:	X-ray of:
bronchus NOS	lung NOS
diaphragm NOS	mediastinum NOS
heart NOS	trachea NOS

BI Bilateral Procedure   **NC** Non-covered Procedure   **LC** Limited Coverage Procedure   ▶◀ Revised Text   ● New Code   ▲ Revised Code Title

178 — Volume 3 • February 2006   *2007 ICD•9•CM*

✓4th **87.5 Biliary tract x-ray**

87.51 Percutaneous hepatic cholangiogram
AHA: 2Q, '90, 28; N-D, '87, 1

DEF: Radiographic exam of bile tract of gallbladder; with needle injection of contrast into bile duct of liver.

87.52 Intravenous cholangiogram
DEF: Radiographic exam of bile ducts; with intravenous contrast injection.

87.53 Intraoperative cholangiogram
AHA: 1Q, '96, 12; 2Q, '90, 28; 3Q, '89, 18; 4Q, '88, 7

DEF: Radiographic exam of bile ducts; with contrast; following gallbladder removal.

87.54 Other cholangiogram

87.59 Other biliary tract x-ray
Cholecystogram

✓4th **87.6 Other x-ray of digestive system**

87.61 Barium swallow
87.62 Upper GI series
87.63 Small bowel series
87.64 Lower GI series
87.65 Other x-ray of intestine
87.66 Contrast pancreatogram
87.69 Other digestive tract x-ray

✓4th **87.7 X-ray of urinary system**
EXCLUDES angiography of renal vessels (88.45, 88.65)

87.71 Computerized axial tomography of kidney
C.A.T. scan of kidney

87.72 Other nephrotomogram
DEF: Radiographic exam of kidney plane.

87.73 Intravenous pyelogram
Diuretic infusion pyelogram
DEF: Radiographic exam of lower kidney, with intravenous contrast injection.

DEF: Diuretic infusion pyelogram: Radiographic exam of lower kidney with diuretic contrast.

87.74 Retrograde pyelogram
87.75 Percutaneous pyelogram
87.76 Retrograde cystourethrogram
DEF: Radiographic exam of bladder and urethra with contrast injected through catheter into bladder.

87.77 Other cystogram
87.78 Ileal conduitogram
AHA: M-J, '87, 11

DEF: Radiographic exam of passage created between ureter and artificial opening into abdomen.

87.79 Other x-ray of the urinary system
KUB x-ray

Ureteropyelography

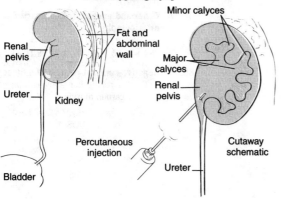

Minor calyces
Fat and abdominal wall
Renal pelvis
Major calyces
Ureter
Kidney
Renal pelvis
Percutaneous injection
Cutaway schematic
Ureter
Bladder

✓4th **87.8 X-ray of female genital organs**

87.81 X-ray of gravid uterus   ♀
Intrauterine cephalometry by x-ray

87.82 Gas contrast hysterosalpingogram   ♀
DEF: Radiographic exam of uterus and fallopian tubes; with gas contrast.

87.83 Opaque dye contrast hysterosal-pingogram   ♀

87.84 Percutaneous hysterogram   ♀
DEF: Radiographic exam of uterus with contrast injected through body wall.

87.85 Other x-ray of fallopian tubes and uterus   ♀
87.89 Other x-ray of female genital organs   ♀

✓4th **87.9 X-ray of male genital organs**

87.91 Contrast seminal vesiculogram   ♂
87.92 Other x-ray of prostate and seminal vesicles   ♂
87.93 Contrast epididymogram   ♂
87.94 Contrast vasogram   ♂
87.95 Other x-ray of epididymis and vas deferens   ♂
87.99 Other x-ray of male genital organs   ♂

✓3rd **88 Other diagnostic radiology and related techniques**

✓4th **88.0 Soft tissue x-ray of abdomen**
EXCLUDES angiography (88.40-88.68)

88.01 Computerized axial tomography of abdomen
C.A.T. scan of abdomen
EXCLUDES C.A.T. scan of kidney (87.71)
AHA: 2Q, '98, 13

88.02 Other abdomen tomography
EXCLUDES nephrotomogram (87.72)

88.03 Sinogram of abdominal wall
Fistulogram of abdominal wall
DEF: Radiographic exam of abnormal abdominal passage.

88.04 Abdominal lymphangiogram
DEF: Radiographic exam of abdominal lymphatic vessels; with contrast.

88.09 Other soft tissue x-ray of abdominal wall

✓4th **88.1 Other x-ray of abdomen**
88.11 Pelvic opaque dye contrast radiography
88.12 Pelvic gas contrast radiography
Pelvic pneumoperitoneum
88.13 Other peritoneal pneumogram
88.14 Retroperitoneal fistulogram
88.15 Retroperitoneal pneumogram
88.16 Other retroperitoneal x-ray
88.19 Other x-ray of abdomen
Flat plate of abdomen
AHA: 3Q, '99, 9

✓4th **88.2 Skeletal x-ray of extremities and pelvis**
EXCLUDES contrast radiogram of joint (88.32)

88.21 Skeletal x-ray of shoulder and upper arm
88.22 Skeletal x-ray of elbow and forearm
88.23 Skeletal x-ray of wrist and hand
88.24 Skeletal x-ray of upper limb, not otherwise specified
88.25 Pelvimetry
DEF: Imaging of pelvic bones to measure pelvic capacity.

88.26 Other skeletal x-ray of pelvis and hip
88.27 Skeletal x-ray of thigh, knee, and lower leg
88.28 Skeletal x-ray of ankle and foot
88.29 Skeletal x-ray of lower limb, not otherwise specified

✓3rd✓4th Additional Digit Required   Nonspecific OR Procedure   Valid OR Procedure   Non-OR Procedure   Adjunct Code

Diagnostic and Therapeutic Procedures

87.5–88.29

Diagnostic and Therapeutic Procedures

88.3–88.58

√4ᵗʰ **88.3** **Other x-ray**

88.31 **Skeletal series**
X-ray of whole skeleton

88.32 **Contrast arthrogram**
EXCLUDES *that of temporomandibular joint (87.13)*

88.33 **Other skeletal x-ray**
EXCLUDES *skeletal x-ray of:*
extremities and pelvis (88.21-88.29)
face, head, and neck (87.11-87.17)
spine (87.21-87.29)
thorax (87.43)

88.34 **Lymphangiogram of upper limb**

88.35 **Other soft tissue x-ray of upper limb**

88.36 **Lymphangiogram of lower limb**

88.37 **Other soft tissue x-ray of lower limb**
EXCLUDES *femoral angiography (88.48, 88.66)*

88.38 **Other computerized axial tomography**
C.A.T. scan NOS
EXCLUDES *C.A.T. scan of:*
abdomen (88.01)
head (87.03)
kidney (87.71)
thorax (87.41)
AHA: ▶3Q, '05, 13-14◀

88.39 **X-ray, other and unspecified**

√4ᵗʰ **88.4** **Arteriography using contrast material**
Note: The fourth-digit subclassification identifies the site to be viewed, not the site of injection.
INCLUDES angiography of arteries
arterial puncture for injection of contrast material
radiography of arteries (by fluoroscopy)
retrograde arteriography
EXCLUDES *arteriography using:*
radioisotopes or radionuclides (92.01-92.19)
ultrasound (88.71-88.79)
fluorescein angiography of eye (95.12)
AHA: N-D, '85, 14

DEF: Electromagnetic wave photography of arteries; with contrast.

88.40 **Arteriography using contrast material, unspecified site**

88.41 **Arteriography of cerebral arteries**
Angiography of:
basilar artery
carotid (internal)
posterior cerebral circulation
vertebral artery
AHA: 1Q, '00, 16; 1Q, '99, 7; 1Q, '97, 3

88.42 **Aortography**
Arteriography of aorta and aortic arch
AHA: 1Q, '99, 17

88.43 **Arteriography of pulmonary arteries**

88.44 **Arteriography of other intrathoracic vessels**
EXCLUDES *angiocardiography (88.50-88.58)*
arteriography of coronary arteries (88.55-88.57)

88.45 **Arteriography of renal arteries**

88.46 **Arteriography of placenta** ♀
Placentogram using contrast material

88.47 **Arteriography of other intra-abdominal arteries**
AHA: 1Q, '00, 18; N-D, '87, 4

88.48 **Arteriography of femoral and other lower extremity arteries**
AHA: 3Q, '03, 10; 1Q, '03, 17; 2Q, '96, 6; 2Q, '89, 17

88.49 **Arteriography of other specified sites**

√4ᵗʰ **88.5** **Angiocardiography using contrast material**
INCLUDES arterial puncture and insertion of arterial catheter for injection of contrast material
cineangiocardiography
selective angiocardiography
Code also synchronous cardiac catheterization (37.21-37.23)
EXCLUDES *angiography of pulmonary vessels (88.43, 88.62)*
AHA: 3Q, '92, 10; M-J, '87, 11

DEF: Electromagnetic wave photography of heart and great vessels; with contrast.

88.50 **Angiocardiography, not otherwise specified**

88.51 **Angiocardiography of venae cavae**
Inferior vena cavography
Phlebography of vena cava (inferior) (superior)

88.52 **Angiocardiography of right heart structures**
Angiocardiography of:
pulmonary valve
right atrium
right ventricle (outflow tract)
EXCLUDES *that combined with left heart angiocardiography (88.54)*

88.53 **Angiocardiography of left heart structures**
Angiocardiography of:
aortic valve
left atrium
left ventricle (outflow tract)
EXCLUDES *that combined with right heart angiocardiography (88.54)*
AHA: ▶4Q, '05, 71; 3Q, '05, 14;◀ 1Q, '00, 20; 4Q, '88, 4

88.54 **Combined right and left heart angiocardiography**

88.55 **Coronary arteriography using a single catheter**
Coronary arteriography by Sones technique
Direct selective coronary arteriography using a single catheter
AHA: 3Q, '02, 20

88.56 **Coronary arteriography using two catheters**
Coronary arteriography by:
Judkins technique
Ricketts and Abrams technique
Direct selective coronary arteriography using two catheters
AHA: 1Q, '00, 20; 4Q, '88, 4

88.57 **Other and unspecified coronary arteriography**
Coronary arteriography NOS
AHA: ▶4Q, '05, 71; 3Q, '05, 14; 2Q, '05, 17;◀ 1Q, '00, 21

88.58 **Negative-contrast cardiac roentgenography**
Cardiac roentgenography with injection of carbon dioxide

BI Bilateral Procedure **NC** Non-covered Procedure **LC** Limited Coverage Procedure ▶◀ Revised Text ● New Code ▲ Revised Code Title

180 — Volume 3 • February 2006

2007 ICD•9•CM

√4ᵗʰ **88.6**   **Phlebography**

Note: The fourth-digit subclassification (88.60-88.67) identifies the site to be viewed, not the site of injection.

INCLUDES   angiography of veins
radiography of veins (by fluoroscopy)
retrograde phlebography
venipuncture for injection of contrast material
venography using contrast material

EXCLUDES   *angiography using:*
radioisotopes or radionuclides (92.01-92.19)
ultrasound (88.71-88.79)
fluorescein angiography of eye (95.12)

DEF: Electromagnetic wave photography of veins; with contrast.

88.60   **Phlebography using contrast material, unspecified site**

88.61   **Phlebography of veins of head and neck using contrast material**

88.62   **Phlebography of pulmonary veins using contrast material**

88.63   **Phlebography of other intrathoracic veins using contrast material**

88.64   **Phlebography of the portal venous system using contrast material**
Splenoportogram (by splenic arteriography)

88.65   **Phlebography of other intra-abdominal veins using contrast material**

88.66   **Phlebography of femoral and other lower extremity veins using contrast material**

88.67   **Phlebography of other specified sites using contrast material**

88.68   **Impedance phlebography**

√4ᵗʰ **88.7**   **Diagnostic ultrasound**

INCLUDES   echography
non-invasive ultrasound
ultrasonic angiography
ultrasonography

EXCLUDES   *intravascular imaging (adjunctive) (IVUS) (00.21-00.29)*
therapeutic ultrasound (00.01-00.09)

DEF: Graphic recording of anatomical structures via high frequency, sound-wave imaging and computer graphics.

88.71   **Diagnostic ultrasound of head and neck**
Determination of midline shift of brain
Echoencephalography

EXCLUDES   *eye (95.13)*

AHA: 1Q, '02, 10; 1Q, '92, 11

88.72   **Diagnostic ultrasound of heart**
Echocardiography
Transesophageal echocardiography

EXCLUDES   *echocardiography of heart chambers (37.28)*
intracardiac echocardiography (ICE) (37.28)
intravascular (IVUS) imaging of coronary vessels (00.24)

AHA: ▶3Q, '05, 14; 2Q, '05, 17;◀ 4Q, '04, 121; 1Q, '04, 16; 1Q, '00, 20, 21; 1Q, '99, 6; 3Q, '98, 11

88.73   **Diagnostic ultrasound of other sites of thorax**
Aortic arch ⎫
Breast   ⎬ ultrasonography
Lung   ⎭

88.74   **Diagnostic ultrasound of digestive system**

88.75   **Diagnostic ultrasound of urinary system**

88.76   **Diagnostic ultrasound of abdomen and retroperitoneum**

AHA: 2Q, '99, 14

88.77   **Diagnostic ultrasound of peripheral vascular system**
Deep vein thrombosis ultrasonic scanning

EXCLUDES   *adjunct vascular system procedures (00.40-00.43)*

AHA: 4Q, '99, 17; 1Q, '99, 12; 1Q, '92, 11

88.78   **Diagnostic ultrasound of gravid uterus** ♀
Intrauterine cephalometry:
echo
ultrasonic
Placental localization by ultrasound

88.79   **Other diagnostic ultrasound**
Ultrasonography of:
multiple sites
nongravid uterus
total body

√4ᵗʰ **88.8**   **Thermography**

DEF: Infrared photography to determine various body temperatures.

88.81   **Cerebral thermography**

88.82   **Ocular thermography**

88.83   **Bone thermography**
Osteoarticular thermography

88.84   **Muscle thermography**

88.85   **Breast thermography**

88.86   **Blood vessel thermography**
Deep vein thermography

88.89   **Thermographay of other sites**
Lymph gland thermography
Thermography NOS

√4ᵗʰ **88.9**   **Other diagnostic imaging**

88.90   **Diagnostic imaging, not elsewhere classified**

88.91   **Magnetic resonance imaging of brain and brain stem**

EXCLUDES   *intraoperative magnetic resonance imaging (88.96)*
real-time magnetic resonance imaging (88.96)

88.92   **Magnetic resonance imaging of chest and myocardium**
For evaluation of hilar and mediastinal lymphadenopathy

88.93   **Magnetic resonance imaging of spinal canal**
Spinal cord levels:
cervical
thoracic
lumbar (lumbosacral)
Spinal cord
Spine

88.94   **Magnetic resonance imaging of musculoskeletal**
Bone marrow blood supply
Extremities (upper) (lower)

88.95   **Magnetic resonance imaging of pelvis, prostate, and bladder**

88.96   **Other intraoperative magnetic resonance imaging**
iMRI
Real-time magnetic resonance imaging

AHA: 4Q, '02, 111

88.97   **Magnetic resonance imaging of other and unspecified sites**
Abdomen   Face
Eye orbit   Neck

Diagnostic and Therapeutic Procedures

88.98–89.37

88.98   Bone mineral density studies
Dual photon absorptiometry
Quantitative computed tomography (CT) studies
Radiographic densitometry
Single photon absorptiometry
DEF: Dual photon absorptiometry: Measurement of bone mineral density by comparing dissipation of emission from two separate photoelectric energy peaks.

DEF: Quantitative computed tomography (CT) studies: Computer assisted analysis of x-ray absorption through bone to determine density.

DEF: Radiographic densiometry: Measurement of bone mineral density by degree of bone radiopacity.

DEF: Single photon absorptiometry: Measurement of bone mineral density by degree of dissipation of emission from one photoelectric energy peaks emitted by gadolinium 153.

√3ʳᵈ **89   Interview, evaluation, consultation, and examination**

√4ᵗʰ **89.0   Diagnostic interview, consultation, and evaluation**
EXCLUDES   *psychiatric diagnostic interview (94.11-94.19)*

89.01   Interview and evaluation, described as brief
Abbreviated history and evaluation

89.02   Interview and evaluation, described as limited
Interval history and evaluation

89.03   Interview and evaluation, described as comprehensive
History and evaluation of new problem

89.04   Other interview and evaluation

89.05   Diagnostic interview and evaluation, not otherwise specified

89.06   Consultation, described as limited
Consultation on a single organ system

89.07   Consultation, described as comprehensive

89.08   Other consultation

89.09   Consulation, not otherwise specified

√4ᵗʰ **89.1   Anatomic and physiologic measurements and manual examinations — nervous system and sense organs**
EXCLUDES   *ear examination (95.41-95.49)*
eye examination (95.01-95.26)
the listed procedures when done as part of a general physical examination (89.7)

89.10   Intracarotid amobarbital test
Wada test
DEF: Amobarbital injections into internal carotid artery to induce hemiparalysis to determine the hemisphere that controls speech and language.

89.11   Tonometry
DEF: Pressure measurements inside eye.

89.12   Nasal function study
Rhinomanometry
DEF: Rhinomanometry: Measure of degree of nasal cavity obstruction.

89.13   Neurologic examination

89.14   Electroencephalogram
EXCLUDES   *that with polysomnogram (89.17)*

AHA: ▶3Q, '05, 12◀

DEF: Recording of electrical currents in brain via electrodes to detect epilepsy, lesions and other encephalopathies.

89.15   Other nonoperative neurologic function tests
AHA: 3Q, '95, 5; 2Q, '91, 14; J-F, '87, 16; N-D, '84, 6

89.16   Transillumination of newborn skull
DEF: Light passed through newborn skull for diagnostic purposes.

89.17   Polysomnogram
Sleep recording
DEF: Graphic studies of sleep patterns.

89.18   Other sleep disorder function tests
Multiple sleep latency test [MSLT]

89.19   Video and radio-telemetered electroencephalographic monitoring
Radiographic ⎫
Video   ⎬ EEG Monitoring
             ⎭

AHA: 1Q, '92, 17; 2Q, '90, 27

√4ᵗʰ **89.2   Anatomic and physiologic measurements and manual examinations — genitourinary system**
EXCLUDES   *the listed procedures when done as part of a general physical examination (89.7)*

AHA: 1Q, '90, 27

89.21   Urinary manometry
Manometry through:
indwelling ureteral catheter
nephrostomy
pyelostomy
ureterostomy
DEF: Measurement of urinary pressure.

DEF: Manometry through:

Indwelling urinary catheter: Semipermanent urinary catheter.
Nephrostomy: Opening into pelvis of kidney.
Pyelostomy: Opening in lower kidney.
Ureterostomy: Opening into ureter.

89.22   Cystometrogram
DEF: Pressure recordings at various stages of bladder filling.

89.23   Urethral sphincter electromyogram

89.24   Uroflowmetry [UFR]
DEF: Continuous recording of urine flow.

89.25   Urethral pressure profile [UPP]

89.26   Gynecological examination   ♀
Pelvic examination

89.29   Other nonoperative genitourinary system measurements
Bioassay of urine   Urine chemistry
Renal clearance
AHA: N-D, '84, 6

√4ᵗʰ **89.3   Other anatomic and physiologic measurements and manual examinations**
EXCLUDES   *the listed procedures when done as part of a general physical examination (89.7)*

89.31   Dental examination
Oral mucosal survey
Periodontal survey

89.32   Esophageal manometry
AHA: 3Q, '96, 13

DEF: Measurement of esophageal fluid and gas pressures.

89.33   Digital examination of enterostomy stoma
Digital examination of colostomy stoma

89.34   Digital examination of rectum

89.35   Transillumination of nasal sinuses

89.36   Manual examination of breast

89.37   Vital capacity determination
DEF: Measurement of expelled gas volume after full inhalation.

BI Bilateral Procedure   **NC** Non-covered Procedure   **LC** Limited Coverage Procedure   ▶◀ Revised Text   ● New Code   ▲ Revised Code Title

182 — Volume 3 • February 2006   *2007 ICD•9•CM*

89.38 **Other nonoperative respiratory measurements**

Plethysmography for measurement of respiratory function

Thoracic impedance plethysmography

AHA: S-O, '87, 6

DEF: Plethysmography for measurement of respiratory function: Registering changes in respiratory function as noted in blood circulation.

89.39 **Other nonoperative measurements and examinations**

[14] C-Urea breath test

Basal metabolic rate [BMR]

Gastric:

analysis

function NEC

EXCLUDES   body measurement (93.07)
cardiac tests (89.41-89.69)
fundus photography (95.11)
limb length measurement (93.06)

AHA: 2Q, '01, 9; 3Q, '00, 9; 3Q, '96, 12; 1Q, '94, 18; N-D, '84, 6

✓4ᵗʰ **89.4** **Cardiac stress tests, pacemaker and defibrillator checks**

89.41 **Cardiovascular stress test using treadmill**

AHA: 1Q, '88, 11

89.42 **Masters' two-step stress test**

AHA: 1Q, '88, 11

89.43 **Cardiovascular stress test using bicycle ergometer**

AHA: 1Q, '88, 11

DEF: Electrocardiogram during exercise on bicycle with device capable of measuring muscular, metabolic and respiratory effects of exercise.

89.44 **Other cardiovascular stress test**

Thallium stress test with or without transesophageal pacing

89.45 **Artificial pacemaker rate check**

Artificial pacemaker function check NOS

Bedside device check of pacemaker or cardiac resynchronization pacemaker [CRT-P]

Interrogation only without arrhythmia induction

EXCLUDES ▶ catheter based invasive electrophysiologic testing (37.26)◀
non-invasive programmed electrical stimulation [NIPS] (arrhythmia induction) ▶(37.20)◀

AHA: 1Q, '02, 3

89.46 **Artificial pacemaker artifact wave form check**

89.47 **Artificial pacemaker electrode impedance check**

89.48 **Artificial pacemaker voltage or amperage threshold check**

89.49 **Automatic implantable cardioverter/ defibrillator (AICD) check**

Bedside check of an AICD or cardiac resyn- chronization defibrillator [CRT-D]

Checking pacing thresholds of device

Interrogation only without arrhythmia induction

EXCLUDES ▶ catheter based invasive electrophysiologic testing (37.26)◀
non-invasive programmed electrical stimulation [NIPS] (arrhythmia induction) ▶(37.20)◀

AHA: 4Q, '04, 136

✓4ᵗʰ **89.5** **Other nonoperative cardiac and vascular diagnostic procedures**

EXCLUDES   fetal EKG (75.32)

89.50 **Ambulatory cardiac monitoring**

Analog devices [Holter-type]

AHA: 4Q, '99, 21; 4Q, '91, 23

89.51 **Rhythm electrocardiogram**

Rhythm EKG (with one to three leads)

89.52 **Electrocardiogram**

ECG NOS   EKG (with 12 or more leads)

AHA: 1Q, '88, 11; S-O, '87, 6

89.53 **Vectorcardiogram (with ECG)**

89.54 **Electrographic monitoring**

Telemetry

EXCLUDES   ambulatory cardiac monitoring (89.50)
electrographic monitoring during surgery — omit code

AHA: 4Q, '91, 23; 1Q, '88, 11

DEF: Evaluation of heart electrical activity by continuous screen monitoring.

DEF: Telemetry: Evaluation of heart electrical activity; with radio signals at distance from patient.

89.55 **Phonocardiogram with ECG lead**

89.56 **Carotid pulse tracing with ECG lead**

EXCLUDES   oculoplethysmography (89.58)

89.57 **Apexcardiogram (with ECG lead)**

AHA: J-F, '87, 16

89.58 **Plethysmogram**

Penile plethysmography with nerve stimulation

EXCLUDES   plethysmography (for):
measurement of respiratory function (89.38)
thoracic impedance (89.38)

AHA: S-O, '87, 7

DEF: Determination and recording of blood pressure variations present or passing through an organ.

89.59 **Other nonoperative cardiac and vascular measurements**

AHA: 3Q, '05, 21; 3Q, '03, 23; 2Q, '92, 12

✓4ᵗʰ **89.6** **Circulatory monitoring**

EXCLUDES   electrocardiographic monitoring during surgery — omit code
▶ implantation or replacement of subcutaneous device for intracardiac hemodynamic monitoring (00.57)
insertion or replacement of implantable pressure sensor (lead) for intracardiac hemodynamic monitoring (00.56)◀

AHA: M-J, '87, 11

89.60 **Continuous intra-arterial blood gas monitoring**

Insertion of blood gas monitoring system and continuous monitoring of blood gases through an intra-arterial sensor

AHA: 4Q, '02, 111

89.61 **Systemic arterial pressure monitoring**

89.62 **Central venous pressure monitoring**

89.63 **Pulmonary artery pressure monitoring**

EXCLUDES   pulmonary artery wedge monitoring (89.64)

89.64 **Pulmonary artery wedge monitoring**

Pulmonary capillary wedge [PCW] monitoring

Swan-Ganz catheterization

DEF: Monitoring pulmonary artery pressure via catheter inserted through right lower and upper heart chambers into pulmonary artery and advancing the balloon-tip to wedge it in the distal pulmonary artery branch.

Diagnostic and Therapeutic Procedures

89.38–89.64

Diagnostic and Therapeutic Procedures

89.65–92.09

Central Venous Pressure Monitoring

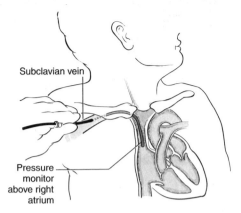

Subclavian vein

Pressure monitor above right atrium

89.65 **Measurement of systemic arterial blood gases**
> **EXCLUDES**   *continuous intra-arterial blood gas monitoring (89.60)*

89.66 **Measurement of mixed venous blood gases**

89.67 **Monitoring of cardiac output by oxygen consumption technique**
> Fick method
> DEF: Fick method: Indirect measure of cardiac output through blood volume flow over pulmonary capillaries; determines oxygen absorption by measurement of arterial oxygen content versus venous oxygen content.

89.68 **Monitoring of cardiac output by other technique**
> Cardiac output monitor by thermodilution indicator
> DEF: Cardiac output monitor by thermodilution indicator: Injection of ice cold dextrose solution into right lower heart chamber; temperature sensitive catheter monitors disappearance from beat to beat to measure expelled blood volume.

89.69 **Monitoring of coronary blood flow**
> Coronary blood flow monitoring by coincidence counting technique

89.7 **General physical examination**

89.8 **Autopsy**

√3rd **90** **Microscopic examination - I**

The following fourth-digit subclassification is for use with categories in section 90 to identify type of examination:
1 bacterial smear
2 culture
3 culture and sensitivity
4 parasitology
5 toxicology
6 cell block and Papanicolaou smear
9 other microscopic examination

√4th **90.0** **Microscopic examination of specimen from nervous system and of spinal fluid**

√4th **90.1** **Microscopic examination of specimen from endocrine gland, not elsewhere classified**

√4th **90.2** **Microscopic examination of specimen from eye**

√4th **90.3** **Microscopic examination of specimen from ear, nose, throat, and larynx**

√4th **90.4** **Microscopic examination of specimen from trachea, bronchus, pleura, lung, and other thoracic specimen, and of sputum**

√4th **90.5** **Microscopic examination of blood**

√4th **90.6** **Microscopic examination of specimen from spleen and of bone marrow**

√4th **90.7** **Microscopic examination of specimen from lymph node and of lymph**

√4th **90.8** **Microscopic examination of specimen from upper gastrointestinal tract and of vomitus**

√4th **90.9** **Microscopic examination of specimen from lower gastrointestinal tract and of stool**

√3rd **91** **Microscopic examination - II**

The following fourth-digit subclassification is for use with categories in section 91 to identify type of examination:
1 bacterial smear
2 culture
3 culture and sensitivity
4 parasitology
5 toxicology
6 cell block and Papanicolaou smear
9 other microscopic examination

√4th **91.0** **Microscopic examination of specimen from liver, biliary tract, and pancreas**

√4th **91.1** **Microscopic examination of peritoneal and retroperitoneal specimen**

√4th **91.2** **Microscopic examination of specimen from kidney, ureter, perirenal and periureteral tissue**

√4th **91.3** **Microscopic examination of specimen from bladder, urethra, prostate, seminal vesicle, perivesical tissue, and of urine and semen**

√4th **91.4** **Microscopic examination of specimen from female genital tract**   ♀
> Amnionic sac   Fetus

√4th **91.5** **Microscopic examination of specimen from musculoskeletal system and of joint fluid**
> Microscopic examination of:
> bone   ligament
> bursa   muscle
> cartilage   synovial membrane
> fascia   tendon

√4th **91.6** **Microscopic examination of specimen from skin and other integument**
> Microscopic examination of:
> hair
> nails
> skin
> **EXCLUDES**   *mucous membrane — code to organ site that of operative wound (91.71-91.79)*

√4th **91.7** **Microscopic examination of specimen from operative wound**

√4th **91.8** **Microscopic examination of specimen from other site**

√4th **91.9** **Microscopic examination of specimen from unspecified site**

√3rd **92** **Nuclear medicine**

√4th **92.0** **Radioisotope scan and function study**

92.01 **Thyroid scan and radioisotope function studies**
> Iodine-131 uptake   Radio-iodine uptake
> Protein-bound iodine

92.02 **Liver scan and radioisotope function study**

92.03 **Renal scan and radioisotope function study**
> Renal clearance study

92.04 **Gastrointestinal scan and radioisotope function study**
> Radio-cobalt B$_{12}$ Schilling test
> Radio-iodinated triolein study

92.05 **Cardiovascular and hematopoietic scan and radioisotope function study**
> Bone marrow
> Cardiac output
> Circulation time   } scan or function study
> Radionuclide cardiac ventriculogram
> Spleen
>
> AHA: 2Q, '92, 7; 1Q, '88, 11

92.09 **Other radioisotope function studies**

BI Bilateral Procedure   NC Non-covered Procedure   LC Limited Coverage Procedure   ►◄ Revised Text   ● New Code   ▲ Revised Code Title

✓4ᵗʰ **92.1** **Other radioisotope scan**

92.11 **Cerebral scan**
Pituitary

92.12 **Scan of other sites of head**
EXCLUDES   *eye (95.16)*

92.13 **Parathyroid scan**

92.14 **Bone scan**

92.15 **Pulmonary scan**

92.16 **Scan of lymphatic system**

92.17 **Placental scan**   ♀

92.18 **Total body scan**

92.19 **Scan of other sites**

✓4ᵗʰ **92.2** **Therapeutic radiology and nuclear medicine**
EXCLUDES   *that for:*
ablation of pituitary gland (07.64-07.69)
destruction of chorioretinal lesion (14.26-14.27)

AHA: 3Q, '92, 5

DEF: Radiation and nuclear isotope treatment of diseased tissue.

92.20 **Infusion of liquid brachytherapy radioisotope**
I-125 radioisotope
Intracavitary brachytherapy
INCLUDES   removal of radioisotope

AHA: ▶4Q, '05, 117-118◄

92.21 **Superficial radiation**
Contact radiation [up to 150 KVP]

92.22 **Orthovoltage radiation**
Deep radiation [200-300 KVP]

92.23 **Radioisotopic teleradiotherapy**
Teleradiotherapy using:
cobalt-60
iodine-125
radioactive cesium

92.24 **Teleradiotherapy using photons**
Megavoltage NOS   Use of:
Supervoltage NOS   Betatron
linear accelerator

92.25 **Teleradiotherapy using electrons**
Beta particles

92.26 **Teleradiotherapy of other particulate radiation**
Neutrons   Protons NOS

92.27 **Implantation or insertion of radioactive elements**
Intravascular brachytherapy
Code also incision of site
EXCLUDES   *infusion of liquid brachytherapy radioisotope (92.20)*

AHA: 1Q, '04, 3-4; 1Q, '00, 11, 12; 3Q, '94, 11; 1Q, '88, 4

92.28 **Injection or instillation of radioisotopes**
Injection or infusion of radioimmunoconjugate
Intracavitary injection or instillation
Intravenous injection or instillation
Iodine-131 [I-131] tositumomab
Radioimmunotherapy
Ytrium-90 [Y-90] ibritumomab tiuxetan
EXCLUDES   *infusion of liquid brachytherapy radioisotope (92.20)*

92.29 **Other radiotherapeutic procedure**

✓4ᵗʰ **92.3** **Stereotactic radiosurgery**
Code also stereotactic head frame application (93.59)
EXCLUDES   *stereotactic biopsy*

AHA: 4Q, '98, 79; 4Q, '95, 70

DEF: Ablation of deep intracranial lesions; single procedure; placement of head frame for 3-D analysis of lesion, followed by radiation treatment from helmet attached to frame.

92.30 **Stereotactic radiosurgery, not otherwise specified**

92.31 **Single source photon radiosurgery**
High energy x-rays
Linear accelerator (LINAC)

92.32 **Multi-source photon radiosurgery**
Cobalt 60 radiation
Gamma irradiation

AHA: 4Q, '04, 113

92.33 **Particulate radiosurgery**
Particle beam radiation (cyclotron)
Proton accelerator

92.39 **Stereotactic radiosurgery, not elsewhere classified**

✓3ʳᵈ **93** **Physical therapy, respiratory therapy, rehabilitation, and related procedures**

✓4ᵗʰ **93.0** **Diagnostic physical therapy**
AHA: N-D, '86, 7

93.01 **Functional evaluation**

93.02 **Orthotic evaluation**

93.03 **Prosthetic evaluation**

93.04 **Manual testing of muscle function**
AHA: J-F, '87, 16

93.05 **Range of motion testing**
AHA: J-F, '87, 16

93.06 **Measurement of limb length**

93.07 **Body measurement**
Girth measurement
Measurement of skull circumference

93.08 **Electromyography**
EXCLUDES   *eye EMG (95.25)*
that with polysomnogram (89.17)
urethral sphincter EMG (89.23)

AHA: J-F, '87, 16

DEF: Graphic recording of electrical activity of muscle.

93.09 **Other diagnostic physical therapy procedure**

✓4ᵗʰ **93.1** **Physical therapy exercises**
AHA: J-F, '87, 16; N-D, '86, 7

93.11 **Assisting exercise**
EXCLUDES   *assisted exercise in pool (93.31)*

93.12 **Other active musculoskeletal exercise**

93.13 **Resistive exercise**

93.14 **Training in joint movements**

93.15 **Mobilization of spine**

93.16 **Mobilization of other joints**
EXCLUDES   *manipulation of temporomandibular joint (76.95)*

93.17 **Other passive musculoskeletal exercise**

93.18 **Breathing exercise**

93.19 **Exercise, not elsewhere classified**

✓4ᵗʰ **93.2** **Other physical therapy musculoskeletal manipulation**
AHA: N-D, '86, 7

93.21 **Manual and mechanical traction**
EXCLUDES   *skeletal traction (93.43-93.44)*
skin traction (93.45-93.46)
spinal traction (93.41-93.42)

93.22 **Ambulation and gait training**

93.23 **Fitting of orthotic device**

93.24 **Training in use of prosthetic or orthotic device**
Training in crutch walking

93.25 **Forced extension of limb**

93.26 **Manual rupture of joint adhesions**
DEF: Therapeutic application of force to rupture adhesions restricting movement.

✓3ʳᵈ
✓4ᵗʰ Additional Digit Required   Nonspecific OR Procedure   Valid OR Procedure   Non-OR Procedure   Adjunct Code

Diagnostic and Therapeutic Procedures

93.27–93.81

93.27   **Stretching of muscle or tendon**

93.28   **Stretching of fascia**

93.29   **Other forcible correction of deformity**
     AHA: N-D, '85, 11

✓4ᵗʰ **93.3**   **Other physical therapy therapeutic procedures**

93.31   **Assisted exercise in pool**

93.32   **Whirlpool treatment**

93.33   **Other hydrotherapy**

93.34   **Diathermy**

93.35   **Other heat therapy**
     Acupuncture with smouldering moxa
     Hot packs
     Hyperthermia NEC
     Infrared irradiation
     Moxibustion
     Paraffin bath
     EXCLUDES   *hyperthermia for treatment of*
         cancer (99.85)
     DEF: Moxibustion: Igniting moxa, a Chinese plant, for
     counterirritation of skin.
     DEF: Paraffin bath: Hot wax treatment.

93.36   **Cardiac retraining**
     DEF: Cardiac rehabilitation regimen following
     myocardial infarction or coronary bypass graft
     procedure.

93.37   **Prenatal training**
     Training for natural childbirth

93.38   **Combined physical therapy without
     mention of the components**

93.39   **Other physical therapy**
     AHA: 2Q, '05, 6; 4Q, '03, 105 -106, 108-110; 3Q, '97, 12;
     3Q, '91, 15

✓4ᵗʰ **93.4**   **Skeletal traction and other traction**

93.41   **Spinal traction using skull device**
     Traction using: Traction using:
       caliper tongs   halo device
       Crutchfield tongs   Vinke tongs
     EXCLUDES   *insertion of tongs or halo*
         traction device (02.94)
     AHA: 3Q, '01, 8; 3Q, '96, 14; 2Q, '94, 3
     DEF: Applying device to head to exert pulling force on
     spine.

93.42   **Other spinal traction**
     Cotrel's traction
     EXCLUDES   *cervical collar (93.52)*
     DEF: Pulling force exerted on spine without skull device.

93.43   **Intermittent skeletal traction**

93.44   **Other skeletal traction**
     Bryant's
     Dunlop's
     Lyman Smith } traction
     Russell's

93.45   **Thomas' splint traction**
     DEF: Thomas splint: Placement of ring around thigh,
     attached to rods running length of leg for therapeutic
     purposes.

93.46   **Other skin traction of limbs**
     Adhesive tape traction   Buck's traction
     Boot traction   Gallows traction

✓4ᵗʰ **93.5**   **Other immobilization, pressure, and attention to
     wound**
     EXCLUDES   *external fixator device (84.71-84.73)*
         wound cleansing (96.58-96.59)

93.51   **Application of plaster jacket**
     EXCLUDES   *Minerva jacket (93.52)*

93.52   **Application of neck support**
     Application of:
       cervical collar
       Minerva jacket
       molded neck support

93.53   **Application of other cast**

93.54   **Application of splint**
     Plaster splint   Tray splint
     EXCLUDES   *periodontal splint (24.7)*

93.55   **Dental wiring**
     EXCLUDES   *that for orthodontia (24.7)*

93.56   **Application of pressure dressing**
     Application of:
       Gibney bandage
       Robert Jones' bandage
       Shanz dressing

93.57   **Application of other wound dressing**
     Porcine wound dressing
     AHA: 3Q, '02, 23

93.58   **Application of pressure trousers**
     Application of:
       anti-shock trousers
       MAST trousers
       vasopneumatic device
     AHA: 3Q, '96, 13

93.59   **Other immobilization, pressure, and
     attention to wound**
     Elastic stockings
     Electronic gaiter
     Intermittent pressure device
     Oxygenation of wound (hyperbaric)
     Stereotactic head frame application
     ▶Strapping (non-traction)◀
     Velpeau dressing
     AHA: 3Q, '99, 7; 1Q, '99, 12, 13; 1Q, '91, 11; 1Q, '89, 12

✓4ᵗʰ **93.6**   **Osteopathic manipulative treatment**

93.61   **Osteopathic manipulative treatment for
     general mobilization**
     General articulatory treatment

93.62   **Osteopathic manipulative treatment using
     high-velocity, low-amplitude forces**
     Thrusting forces

93.63   **Osteopathic manipulative treatment using
     low-velocity, high-amplitude forces**
     Springing forces

93.64   **Osteopathic manipulative treatment using
     isotonic, isometric forces**

93.65   **Osteopathic manipulative treatment using
     indirect forces**

93.66   **Osteopathic manipulative treatment to
     move tissue fluids**
     Lymphatic pump

93.67   **Other specified osteopathic manipulative
     treatment**

✓4ᵗʰ **93.7**   **Speech and reading rehabilitation and rehabilitation
     of the blind**

93.71   **Dyslexia training**

93.72   **Dysphasia training**
     DEF: Speech training to coordinate and arrange words in
     proper sequence.

93.73   **Esophageal speech training**
     DEF: Speech training after voice box removal; sound is
     produced by vibration of air column in esophagus against
     the cricopharangeal sphincter.

93.74   **Speech defect training**

93.75   **Other speech training and therapy**
     AHA: 4Q, '03, 105, 109; 4Q, '97, 36; 3Q, '97, 12

93.76   **Training in use of lead dog for the blind**

93.77   **Training in braille or Moon**

93.78   **Other rehabilitation for the blind**

✓4ᵗʰ **93.8**   **Other rehabilitation therapy**

93.81   **Recreational therapy**
     Diversional therapy   Play therapy
     EXCLUDES   *play psychotherapy (94.36)*

BI Bilateral Procedure   NC Non-covered Procedure   LC Limited Coverage Procedure   ▶◀ Revised Text   ● New Code   ▲ Revised Code Title

93.82 Educational therapy
Education of bed-bound children
Special schooling for the handicapped

93.83 Occupational therapy
Daily living activities therapy
EXCLUDES   *training in activities of daily living for the blind (93.78)*
AHA: ▶2Q, '05, 6;◀ 4Q, '03, 105-106, 108, 110; 3Q, '97, 12

93.84 Music therapy

93.85 Vocational rehabilitation
Sheltered employment
Vocational:
   assessment
   retraining
   training

93.89 Rehabilitation, not elsewhere classified
AHA: ▶2Q, '05, 6◀

✓4th **93.9 Respiratory therapy**
EXCLUDES   *insertion of airway (96.01-96.05)*
other continuous mechanical ventilation (96.70-96.72)

93.90 Continuous positive airway pressure [CPAP]
Bi-level airway pressure
Non-invasive positive pressure (NIPPV)
AHA: 3Q, '04, 3; 1Q, '02, 12, 13; 3Q, '98, 14; 4Q, '91, 21

DEF: Noninvasive ventilation support system that augments the ability to breathe spontaneously without the insertion of an endotracheal tube or tracheostomy.

93.91 Intermittent positive pressure breathing [IPPB]
AHA: 4Q, '91, 21

93.93 Nonmechanical methods of resuscitation
Artificial respiration
Manual resuscitation
Mouth-to-mouth resuscitition
AHA: 2Q, '03, 17

93.94 Respiratory medication administered by nebulizer
Mist therapy

93.95 Hyperbaric oxygenation
EXCLUDES   *oxygenation of wound (93.59)*

93.96 Other oxygen enrichment
Catalytic oxygen therapy
Cytoreductive effect
Oxygenators
Oxygen therapy
EXCLUDES   *oxygenation of wound (93.59)*

93.97 Decompression chamber

93.98 Other control of atmospheric pressure and composition
Antigen-free air conditioning
Helium therapy
EXCLUDES   *inhaled nitric oxide therapy (INO) (00.12)*
AHA: 1Q, '02, 14

93.99 Other respiratory procedures
Continuous negative pressure ventilation [CNP]
Postural drainage
AHA: 4Q, '03, 108; 3Q, '99, 11; 4Q, '91, 22

✓3rd **94 Procedures related to the psyche**
✓4th **94.0 Psychologic evaluation and testing**
94.01 Administration of intelligence test
Administration of:
   Stanford-Binet
   Wechsler Adult Intelligence Scale
   Wechsler Intelligence Scale for Children

94.02 Administration of psychologic test
Administration of:
   Bender Visual-Motor Gestalt Test
   Benton Visual Retention Test
   Minnesota Multiphasic Personality Inventory
   Wechsler Memory Scale

94.03 Character analysis

94.08 Other psychologic evaluation and testing

94.09 Psychologic mental status determination, not otherwise specified

✓4th **94.1 Psychiatric interviews, consultations, and evaluations**
94.11 Psychiatric mental status determination
Clinical psychiatric mental status determination
Evaluation for criminal responsibility
Evaluation for testimentary capacity
Medicolegal mental status determination
Mental status determination NOS

94.12 Routine psychiatric visit, not otherwise specified

94.13 Psychiatric commitment evaluation
Pre-commitment interview

94.19 Other psychiatric interview and evaluation
Follow-up psychiatric interview NOS

✓4th **94.2 Psychiatric somatotherapy**
DEF: Biological treatment of mental disorders.

94.21 Narcoanalysis
Narcosynthesis

94.22 Lithium therapy

94.23 Neuroleptic therapy

94.24 Chemical shock therapy

94.25 Other psychiatric drug therapy
AHA: S-O, '86, 4

94.26 Subconvulsive electroshock therapy

94.27 Other electroshock therapy
Electroconvulsive therapy (ECT)
EST

94.29 Other psychiatric somatotherapy

✓4th **94.3 Individual psychotherapy**
94.31 Psychoanalysis

94.32 Hypnotherapy
Hypnodrome
Hypnosis

94.33 Behavior therapy
Aversion therapy
Behavior modification
Desensitization therapy
Extinction therapy
Relaxation training
Token economy

94.34 Individual therapy for psychosexual dysfunction
EXCLUDES   *that performed in group setting (94.41)*

94.35 Crisis intervention

94.36 Play psychotherapy

94.37 Exploratory verbal psychotherapy

94.38 Supportive verbal psychotherapy

94.39 Other individual psychotherapy
Biofeedback

✓4th **94.4 Other psychotherapy and counselling**
94.41 Group therapy for psychosexual dysfunction
94.42 Family therapy
94.43 Psychodrama
94.44 Other group therapy
94.45 Drug addiction counselling
94.46 Alcoholism counselling
94.49 Other counselling

Diagnostic and Therapeutic Procedures   93.82–94.49

✓4th **94.5** Referral for psychologic rehabilitation

94.51 Referral for psychotherapy

94.52 Referral for psychiatric aftercare
That in:
halfway house
outpatient (clinic) facility

94.53 Referral for alcoholism rehabilitation

94.54 Referral for drug addiction rehabilitation

94.55 Referral for vocational rehabilitation

94.59 Referral for other psychologic rehabilitation

✓4th **94.6** Alcohol and drug rehabilitation and detoxification
AHA: 2Q, '91, 12

94.61 Alcohol rehabilitation
DEF: Program designed to restore social and physical functioning, free of the dependence of alcohol.

94.62 Alcohol detoxification
DEF: Treatment of physical symptoms during withdrawal from alcohol dependence.

94.63 Alcohol rehabilitation and detoxification

94.64 Drug rehabilitation
DEF: Program designed to restore social and physical functioning, free of the dependence of drugs.

94.65 Drug detoxification
DEF: Treatment of physical symptoms during withdrawal from drug dependence.

94.66 Drug rehabilitation and detoxification

94.67 Combined alcohol and drug rehabilitation

94.68 Combined alcohol and drug detoxification

94.69 Combined alcohol and drug rehabilitation and detoxification

✓3rd **95** Ophthalmologic and otologic diagnosis and treatment

✓4th **95.0** General and subjective eye examination

95.01 Limited eye examination
Eye examination with prescription of spectacles

95.02 Comprehensive eye examination
Eye examination covering all aspects of the visual system

95.03 Extended ophthalmologic work-up
Examination (for):
glaucoma
neuro-ophthalmology
retinal disease

95.04 Eye examination under anesthesia
Code also type of examination

95.05 Visual field study

95.06 Color vision study

95.07 Dark adaptation study
DEF: Exam of eye's adaption to dark.

95.09 Eye examination, not otherwise specified
Vision check NOS

✓4th **95.1** Examinations of form and structure of eye

95.11 Fundus photography

95.12 Fluorescein angiography or angioscopy of eye

95.13 Ultrasound study of eye

95.14 X-ray study of eye

95.15 Ocular motility study

95.16 P_{32} and other tracer studies of eye

✓4th **95.2** Objective functional tests of eye
EXCLUDES that with polysomnogram (89.17)

95.21 Electroretinogram [ERG]

95.22 Electro-oculogram [EOG]

95.23 Visual evoked potential [VEP]
DEF: Measuring and recording evoked visual responses of body and senses.

95.24 Electronystagmogram [ENG]
DEF: Monitoring of brain waves to record induced and spontaneous eye movements.

95.25 Electromyogram of eye [EMG]

95.26 Tonography, provocative tests, and other glaucoma testing

✓4th **95.3** Special vision services

95.31 Fitting and dispensing of spectacles

95.32 Prescription, fitting, and dispensing of contact lens

95.33 Dispensing of other low vision aids

95.34 Ocular prosthetics

95.35 Orthoptic training

95.36 Ophthalmologic counselling and instruction
Counselling in:
adaptation to visual loss
use of low vision aids

✓4th **95.4** Nonoperative procedures related to hearing

95.41 Audiometry
Békésy 5-tone audiometry
Impedance audiometry
Stapedial reflex response
Subjective audiometry
Tympanogram

95.42 Clinical test of hearing
Tuning fork test
Whispered speech test

95.43 Audiological evaluation
Audiological evaluation by:
Bárány noise machine
blindfold test
delayed feedback
masking
Weber lateralization

95.44 Clinical vestibular function tests
Thermal test of vestibular function

95.45 Rotation tests
Bárány chair
DEF: Irrigation of ear canal with warm or cold water to evaluate vestibular function.

95.46 Other auditory and vestibular function tests

95.47 Hearing examination, not otherwise specified

95.48 Fitting of hearing aid
EXCLUDES implantation of electromagnetic hearing device (20.95)
AHA: 4Q, '89, 5

95.49 Other nonoperative procedures related to hearing
Adjustment (external components) of cochlear prosthetic device

✓3rd **96** Nonoperative intubation and irrigation

✓4th **96.0** Nonoperative intubation of gastrointestinal and respiratory tracts

96.01 Insertion of nasopharyngeal airway

96.02 Insertion of oropharyngeal airway

96.03 Insertion of esophageal obturator airway

BI Bilateral Procedure **NC** Non-covered Procedure **LC** Limited Coverage Procedure ▶◀ Revised Text ● New Code ▲ Revised Code Title

Endotracheal Intubation

- Laryngoscope
- Larynx
- Trachea
- Balloon inflated above carina

96.04 Insertion of endotracheal tube
AHA: 4Q, '05, 88; 3Q, '05, 10; 2Q, '05, 19

96.05 Other intubation of respiratory tract
> EXCLUDES ▶ *endoscopic insertion or replacement of bronchial device or substance (33.71, 33.79)◀*
AHA: 1Q, '97, 14

96.06 Insertion of Sengstaken tube
Esophageal tamponade
DEF: Insertion of Sengstaken tube: Nonsurgical emergency measure to stop esophageal bleeding using compression exerted by inflated balloons; additional tube ports to aspirate blood and clots.

96.07 Insertion of other (naso-) gastric tube
Intubation for decompression
EXCLUDES *that for enteral infusion of nutritional substance (96.6)*

96.08 Insertion of (naso-) intestinal tube
Miller-Abbott tube (for decompression)

96.09 Insertion of rectal tube
Replacement of rectal tube

√4th **96.1 Other nonoperative insertion**
EXCLUDES *nasolacrimal intubation (09.44)*
96.11 Packing of external auditory canal
96.14 Vaginal packing ♀
96.15 Insertion of vaginal mold ♀
96.16 Other vaginal dilation ♀
96.17 Insertion of vaginal diaphragm ♀
96.18 Insertion of other vaginal pessary ♀
96.19 Rectal packing

√4th **96.2 Nonoperative dilation and manipulation**
96.21 Dilation of frontonasal duct
96.22 Dilation of rectum
96.23 Dilation of anal sphincter
96.24 Dilation and manipulation of enterostomy stoma
96.25 Therapeutic distention of bladder
Intermittent distention of bladder
96.26 Manual reduction of rectal prolapse
96.27 Manual reduction of hernia
96.28 Manual reduction of enterostomy prolapse
AHA: N-D, '87, 11
96.29 Reduction of intussusception of alimentary tract
With:
  fluoroscopy
  ionizing radiation enema
  ultrasonography guidance
Hydrostatic reduction
Pneumatic reduction
EXCLUDES *intra-abdominal manipulation of intestine, not other-wise specified (46.80)*
AHA: 4Q, '98, 82

√4th **96.3 Nonoperative alimentary tract irrigation, cleaning, and local instillation**
96.31 Gastric cooling
Gastric hypothermia
DEF: Reduction of internal stomach temperature.

96.32 Gastric freezing
96.33 Gastric lavage
96.34 Other irrigation of (naso-)gastric tube
96.35 Gastric gavage
DEF: Food forced into stomach.

96.36 Irrigation of gastrostomy or enterostomy
96.37 Proctoclysis
DEF: Slow introduction of large amounts of fluids into lower large intestine.7

96.38 Removal of impacted feces
Removal of impaction:
  by flushing manually
96.39 Other transanal enema
Rectal irrigation
EXCLUDES *reduction of intussusception of alimentary tract by ionizing radiation enema (96.29)*

√4th **96.4 Nonoperative irrigation, cleaning, and local instillation of other digestive and genitourinary organs**
96.41 Irrigation of cholecystostomy and other biliary tube
96.42 Irrigation of pancreatic tube
96.43 Digestive tract instillation, except gastric gavage
96.44 Vaginal douche ♀
96.45 Irrigation of nephrostomy and pyelostomy
96.46 Irrigation of ureterostomy and ureteral catheter
96.47 Irrigation of cystostomy
96.48 Irrigation of other indwelling urinary catheter
96.49 Other genitourinary instillation
Insertion of prostaglandin suppository
AHA: 1Q, '01, 5

√4th **96.5 Other nonoperative irrigation and cleaning**
96.51 Irrigation of eye
Irrigation of cornea
EXCLUDES *irrigation with removal of foreign body (98.21)*
96.52 Irrigation of ear
Irrigation with removal of cerumen
96.53 Irrigation of nasal passages
96.54 Dental scaling, polishing, and debridement
Dental prophylaxis   Plaque removal
96.55 Tracheostomy toilette
96.56 Other lavage of bronchus and trachea
EXCLUDES *diagnostic bronchoalveolar lavage (BAL) (33.24) whole lung lavage (33.99)*
AHA: 3Q, '02, 18
96.57 Irrigation of vascular catheter
AHA: 3Q, '93, 5
96.58 Irrigation of wound catheter
96.59 Other irrigation of wound
Wound cleaning NOS
EXCLUDES *debridement (86.22, 86.27-86.28)*
AHA: S-O, '85, 7

96.6 Enteral infusion of concentrated-nutritional substances

✓4th **96.7**   **Other continuous mechanical ventilation**

INCLUDES   Endotracheal respiratory assistance
Intermittent mandatory ventilation [IMV]
Positive end expiratory pressure [PEEP]
Pressure support ventilation [PSV]
That by tracheostomy
Weaning of an intubated (endotracheal tube) patient

EXCLUDES   *bi-level airway pressure (93.90)*
continuous negative pressure ventilation [CNP] (iron lung) (cuirass) (93.99)
continuous positive airway pressure [CPAP] (93.90)
intermittent positive pressure breathing [IPPB] (93.91)
non-invasive positive pressure (NIPPV) (93.90)
that by face mask (93.90-93.99)
that by nasal cannula (93.90-93.99)
that by nasal catheter (93.90-93.99)

Code also any associated:
endotracheal tube insertion (96.04)
tracheostomy (31.1-31.29)

Note: **Endotracheal intubation**

To calculate the number of hours (duration) of continuous mechanical ventilation during a hospitalization, begin the count from the start of the (endotracheal) intubation. The duration ends with (endotracheal) extubation.

If a patient is intubated prior to admission, begin counting the duration from the time of the admission. If a patient is transferred (discharged) while intubated, the duration would end at the time of transfer (discharge).

For patients who begin on (endotracheal) intubation and subsequently have a tracheostomy performed for mechanical ventilation, the duration begins with the (endotracheal) intubation and ends when the mechanical ventilation is turned off (after the weaning period).

Tracheostomy

To calculate the number of hours of continuous mechanical ventilation during a hospitalization, begin counting the duration when mechanical ventilation is started. The duration ends when the mechanical ventilator is turned off (after the weaning period).

If a patient has received a tracheostomy prior to admission and is on mechanical ventilation at the time of admission, begin counting the duration from the time of admission. If a patient is transferred (discharged) while still on mechanical ventilation via tracheostomy, the duration would end at the time of the transfer (discharge).

AHA: 3Q, '04, 3; 2Q, '92, 13; 4Q, '91, 16; 4Q, '91, 18; 4Q, '91, 21

96.70   **Continuous mechanical ventilation of unspecified duration**
Mechanical ventilation NOS

96.71   **Continuous mechanical ventilation for less than 96 consecutive hours**
AHA: ▶3Q, '05, 10;◀ 3Q, '04, 11; 2Q, '02, 19; 1Q, '02, 12; 1Q, '01, 6

96.72   **Continuous mechanical ventilation for 96 consecutive hours or more**
AHA: ▶2Q, '05, 19;◀ 1Q, '04, 23

✓3rd **97**   **Replacement and removal of therapeutic appliances**

✓4th **97.0**   **Nonoperative replacement of gastrointestinal appliance**

97.01   **Replacement of (naso-)gastric or esophagostomy tube**

97.02   **Replacement of gastrostomy tube**
AHA: 1Q, '97, 11

97.03   **Replacement of tube or enterostomy device of small intestine**
AHA: 1Q, '03, 10

97.04   **Replacement of tube or enterostomy device of large intestine**

97.05   **Replacement of stent (tube) in biliary or pancreatic duct**
AHA: 2Q, '99, 13

✓4th **97.1**   **Nonoperative replacement of musculoskeletal and integumentary system appliance**

97.11   **Replacement of cast on upper limb**

97.12   **Replacement of cast on lower limb**

97.13   **Replacement of other cast**

97.14   **Replacement of other device for musculoskeletal immobilization**

97.15   **Replacement of wound catheter**

97.16   **Replacement of wound packing or drain**
EXCLUDES   *repacking of:*
dental wound (97.22)
vulvar wound (97.26)

✓4th **97.2**   **Other nonoperative replacement**

97.21   **Replacement of nasal packing**

97.22   **Replacement of dental packing**

97.23   **Replacement of tracheostomy tube**
AHA: N-D, '87, 11

97.24   **Replacement and refitting of vagina diaphragm** ♀

97.25   **Replacement of other vaginal pessary** ♀

97.26   **Replacement of vaginal or vulvar packing or drain** ♀

97.29   **Other nonoperative replacements**
AHA: 3Q, '99, 9; 3Q, '98, 12

✓4th **97.3**   **Nonoperative removal of therapeutic device from head and neck**

97.31   **Removal of eye prosthesis**
EXCLUDES   *removal of ocular implant (16.71)*
removal of orbital implant (16.72)

97.32   **Removal of nasal packing**

97.33   **Removal of dental wiring**

97.34   **Removal of dental packing**

97.35   **Removal of dental prosthesis**

97.36   **Removal of other external mandibular fixation device**

97.37   **Removal of tracheostomy tube**

97.38   **Removal of sutures from head and neck**

97.39   **Removal of other therapeutic device from head and neck**
EXCLUDES   *removal of skull tongs (02.94)*

✓4th **97.4**   **Nonoperative removal of therapeutic device from thorax**

97.41   **Removal of thoracotomy tube or pleural cavity drain**
AHA: 1Q, '99, 10

97.42   **Removal of mediastinal drain**

Intraaortic Balloon Pump

Transverse aorta
Descending aorta
Aorta
Balloon pump in inflated phase
Thoracic aorta
Diaphragm
Femoral artery access
Abdominal aorta

BI Bilateral Procedure   NC Non-covered Procedure   LC Limited Coverage Procedure   ▶◀ Revised Text   ● New Code   ▲ Revised Code Title

190 — Volume 3 • February 2006   *2007 ICD•9•CM*

97.43 Removal of sutures from thorax

97.44 Nonoperative removal of heart assist system
Explantation [removal] of circulatory assist device
Explantation [removal] of percutaneous external heart assist device
Removal of extrinsic heart assist device
Removal of pVAD
Removal of percutaneous heart assist device

AHA: 4Q, '01, 65

DEF: Non-invasive removal of ventricular assist systems, or intraaortic balloon pump, which is a balloon catheter placed into the descending thoracic aorta and timed to inflate and deflate with the patient's own heart rhythm to aid in blood circulation.

97.49 Removal of other device from thorax

AHA: N-D, '86, 9

✓4th **97.5** Nonoperative removal of therapeutic device from digestive system

97.51 Removal of gastrostomy tube

97.52 Removal of tube from small intestine

97.53 Removal of tube from large intestine or appendix

97.54 Removal of cholecystostomy tube

97.55 Removal of T-tube, other bile duct tube, or liver tube
Removal of bile duct stent

AHA: 1Q, '01, 8

97.56 Removal of pancreatic tube or drain

97.59 Removal of other device from digestive system
Removal of rectal packing

✓4th **97.6** Nonoperative removal of therapeutic device from urinary system

97.61 Removal of pyelostomy and nephrostomy tube

DEF: Nonsurgical removal of tubes from lower part of kidney.

97.62 Removal of ureterostomy tube and ureteral catheter

97.63 Removal of cystostomy tube

97.64 Removal of other urinary drainage device
Removal of indwelling urinary catheter

97.65 Removal of urethral stent

97.69 Removal of other device from urinary system

✓4th **97.7** Nonoperative removal of therapeutic device from genital system

97.71 Removal of intrauterine contraceptive device ♀

97.72 Removal of intrauterine pack ♀

97.73 Removal of vaginal diaphragm ♀

97.74 Removal of other vaginal pessary ♀

97.75 Removal of vaginal or vulvar packing ♀

97.79 Removal of other device from genital tract
Removal of sutures

✓4th **97.8** Other nonoperative removal of therapeutic device

97.81 Removal of retroperitoneal drainage device

97.82 Removal of peritoneal drainage device

AHA: 2Q, '90, 28; S-O, '86, 12

97.83 Removal of abdominal wall sutures

97.84 Removal of sutures from trunk, not elsewhere classified

97.85 Removal of packing from trunk, not elsewhere classified

97.86 Removal of other device from abdomen

97.87 Removal of other device from trunk

97.88 Removal of external immobilization device
Removal of: Removal of:
brace   splint
cast

97.89 Removal of other therapeutic device

✓3rd **98** Nonoperative removal of foreign body or calculus

✓4th **98.0** Removal of intraluminal foreign body from digestive system without incision
EXCLUDES   *removal of therapeutic device (97.51-97.59)*

DEF: Retrieval of foreign body from digestive system lining without incision.

98.01 Removal of intraluminal foreign body from mouth without incision

98.02 Removal of intraluminal foreign body from esophagus without incision

98.03 Removal of intraluminal foreign body from stomach and small intestine without incision

98.04 Removal of intraluminal foreign body from large intestine without incision

98.05 Removal of intraluminal foreign body from rectum and anus without incision

✓4th **98.1** Removal of intraluminal foreign body from other sites without incision
EXCLUDES   *removal of therapeutic device (97.31-97.49, 97.61-97.89)*

98.11 Removal of intraluminal foreign body from ear without incision

98.12 Removal of intraluminal foreign body from nose without incision

98.13 Removal of intraluminal foreign body from pharynx without incision

98.14 Removal of intraluminal foreign body from larynx without incision

98.15 Removal of intraluminal foreign body from trachea and bronchus without incision

98.16 Removal of intraluminal foreign body from uterus without incision ♀
EXCLUDES   *removal of intrauterine contraceptive device (97.71)*

98.17 Removal of intraluminal foreign body from vagina without incision ♀

98.18 Removal of intraluminal foreign body from artificial stoma without incision

98.19 Removal of intraluminal foreign body from urethra without incision

✓4th **98.2** Removal of other foreign body without incision
EXCLUDES   *removal of intraluminal foreign body (98.01-98.19)*

98.20 Removal of foreign body, not otherwise specified

98.21 Removal of superficial foreign body from eye without incision

98.22 Removal of other foreign body without incision from head and neck
Removal of embedded foreign body from eyelid or conjunctiva without incision

98.23 Removal of foreign body from vulva without incision ♀

98.24 Removal of foreign body from scrotum or penis without incision ♂

Diagnostic and Therapeutic Procedures

98.25–99.19

Extracorporeal Shock Wave Lithotripsy

Radiographic monitors

Shock wave exit area

Water cushion

Shock wave entry area

Lithotripsy unit

Kidney

98.25 **Removal of other foreign body without incision from trunk except scrotum, penis, or vulva**

98.26 **Removal of foreign body from hand without incision**
AHA: N-D, '87, 10

98.27 **Removal of foreign body without incision from upper limb, except hand**

98.28 **Removal of foreign body from foot without incision**

98.29 **Removal of foreign body without incision from lower limb, except foot**

√4ᵗʰ **98.5** **Extracorporeal shockwave lithotripsy [ESWL]**
Lithotriptor tank procedure
Disintegration of stones by extracorporeal induced shockwaves
That with insertion of stent

DEF: Breaking of stones with high voltage condenser device synchronized with patient R waves.

98.51 **Extracorporeal shockwave lithotripsy [ESWL] of the kidney, ureter and/or bladder**
AHA: 4Q, '95, 73; 1Q, '89, 2

98.52 **Extracorporeal shockwave lithotripsy [ESWL] of the gallbladder and/or bile duct** NC

98.59 **Extracorporeal shockwave lithotripsy of other sites** NC

√3ʳᵈ **99** **Other nonoperative procedures**

√4ᵗʰ **99.0** **Transfusion of blood and blood components**
Use additional code for that done via catheter or cutdown (38.92-38.94)

99.00 **Perioperative autologous transfusion of whole blood or blood components**
Intraoperative blood collection
Postoperative blood collection
Salvage
AHA: 4Q, '95, 69

DEF: Salvaging patient blood with reinfusion during perioperative period.

99.01 **Exchange transfusion**
Transfusion: exsanguination
Transfusion: replacement
AHA: 2Q, '89, 15

DEF: Repetitive withdrawal of blood, replaced by donor blood.

99.02 **Transfusion of previously collected autologous blood**
Blood component
AHA: 4Q, '95, 69; 1Q, '90, 10; J-A, '85, 16

DEF: Transfusion with patient's own previously withdrawn and stored blood.

99.03 **Other transfusion of whole blood**
Transfusion: blood NOS hemodilution
Transfusion: NOS

99.04 **Transfusion of packed cells**

99.05 **Transfusion of platelets**
Transfusion of thrombocytes

99.06 **Transfusion of coagulation factors**
Transfusion of antihemophilic factor

99.07 **Transfusion of other serum**
Transfusion of plasma
EXCLUDES injection [transfusion] of:
antivenin (99.16)
gamma globulin (99.14)

99.08 **Transfusion of blood expander**
Transfusion of Dextran

99.09 **Transfusion of other substance**
Transfusion of:
blood surrogate
granulocytes
EXCLUDES transplantation [transfusion] of bone marrow (41.0)

√4ᵗʰ **99.1** **Injection or infusion of therapeutic or prophylactic substance**
INCLUDES injection or infusion given:
hypodermically
intramuscularly
intravenously } acting locally or systemically

99.10 **Injection or infusion of thrombolytic agent**
►Alteplase
Anistreplase
Reteplase◄
Streptokinase
►Tenecteplase◄
Tissue plasminogen activator (TPA)
Urokinase
EXCLUDES aspirin — omit code
GP IIb/IIIa platelet inhibitors (99.20)
heparin (99.19)
warfarin — omit code
AHA: 4Q, '05, 101-103; 2Q, '01, 7-9, 23; 4Q, '98, 83

99.11 **Injection of Rh immune globulin**
Injection of:
Anti-D (Rhesus) globulin
RhoGAM

99.12 **Immunization for allergy**
Desensitization

99.13 **Immunization for autoimmune disease**

99.14 **Injection of gamma globulin**
Injection of immune sera

99.15 **Parenteral infusion of concentrated nutritional substances**
Hyperalimentation
Total parenteral nutrition [TPN]
Peripheral parenteral nutrition [PPN]
AHA: 4Q, '03, 104

DEF: Administration of greater than necessary amount of nutrients via other than the alimentary canal (e.g., infusion).

99.16 **Injection of antidote**
Injection of: antivenin
Injection of: heavy metal antagonist

99.17 **Injection of insulin**

99.18 **Injection or infusion of electrolytes**

99.19 **Injection of anticoagulant**
EXCLUDES infusion of drotrecogin alfa (activated) (00.11)

BI Bilateral Procedure   NC Non-covered Procedure   LC Limited Coverage Procedure   ►◄ Revised Text   ● New Code   ▲ Revised Code Title

192 — Volume 3 • October 2006   2007 ICD•9•CM

✓4ᵗʰ **99.2**   **Injection or infusion of other therapeutic or prophylactic substance**

> **INCLUDES**   injection or infusion given:
>
> hypodermically
> intramuscularly }   acting locally or
> intravenously   systemically

Use additional code for:

injection (into):   injection (into):
   breast (85.92)   kidney (55.96)
   bursa (82.94, 83.96)   liver (50.94)
   intraperitoneal   orbit (16.91)
     (cavity) (54.97)   other sites — see
   intrathecal (03.92)   Alphabetic Index
   joint (76.96, 81.92)
perfusion: perfusion:
   NOS (39.97)   liver (50.93)
   intestine (46.95, 46.96)   total body (39.96)
   kidney (55.95)

99.20   **Injection or infusion of platelet inhibitor**
Glycoprotein IIb/IIIa inhibitor
GP IIb-IIIa inhibitor
GP IIb/IIIa inhibitor

> **EXCLUDES**   infusion of heparin (99.19)
> injection or infusion of thrombolytic agent (99.10)

AHA: 2Q, '04, 3; 4Q, '02, 114; 4Q, '98, 85

99.21   **Injection of antibiotic**

> **EXCLUDES**   injection or infusion of oxazolidinone class of antibiotics (00.14)

AHA: 4Q, '98, 76; 2Q, '90, 24; M-A, '87, 9

99.22   **Injection of other anti-infective**

> **EXCLUDES**   injection or infusion of oxazolidinone class of antibiotics (00.14)

99.23   **Injection of steroid**
Injection of cortisone
Subdermal implantation of progesterone
AHA: 3Q, '00, 15; 1Q, '99, 8; 3Q, '96, 7; 3Q, '92, 9; S-O, '85, 7

99.24   **Injection of other hormone**
AHA: ▶1Q, '06, 9◀

99.25   **Injection or infusion of cancer chemotherapeutic substance**
Chemoembolization
Injection or infusion of antineoplastic agent

> **EXCLUDES**   immunotherapy, antineoplastic (00.15, 99.28)
> implantation of chemotherapeutic agent (00.10)
> injection of radioisotope (92.28)
> injection or infusion of biological response modifier [BRM] as an antineoplastic agent (99.28)

AHA: 2Q, '03, 6, 16; 4Q, '02, 93; 1Q, '99, 4; 1Q, '98, 6; 3Q, '96, 11; 4Q, '95, 67; 2Q, '92, 7; 1Q, '92, 12; 1Q, '88, 8; N-D, '86, 11

99.26   **Injection of tranquilizer**

99.27   **Iontophoresis**
DEF: Iontophoresis: Introduction of soluble salts into tissues via electric current.

99.28   **Injection or infusion of biological response modifier [BRM] as an antineoplastic agent**
Immunotherapy, antineoplastic
▶Infusion of cintredekin besudotox◀
Interleukin therapy
Low-dose interleukin-2 [IL-2] therapy
Tumor vaccine

> **EXCLUDES**   high-dose infusion interleukin-2 [IL-2] (00.15)

AHA: 4Q, '03, 92; 2Q, '99, 8; 2Q, '98, 10; 4Q, '94, 51

99.29   **Injection or infusion of other therapeutic or prophylactic substance**

> **EXCLUDES**   administration of neuroprotective agent (99.75)
> immunization (99.31-99.59)
> injection of sclerosing agent into:
>   esophageal varices (42.33)
>   hemorrhoids (49.42)
>   veins (39.92)
> injection or infusion of:
>   human B-type natriuretic peptide (hBNP) (00.13)
>   nesiritide (00.13)
>   platelet inhibitor (99.20)
>   thrombolytic agent (99.10)

AHA: 2Q, '03, 10; 3Q, '02, 19, 24; 1Q, '01, 15; 2Q, '00, 14; 1Q, '00, 8, 18, 23; 4Q, '99, 17; 3Q, '99, 21; 4Q, '98, 83; 2Q, '98, 17, 18, 23, 24; 1Q, '98, 6; 2Q, '97, 11; 1Q, '97, 3; 4Q, '95, 67; 2Q, '95, 12; 4Q, '90, 14; 2Q, '90, 23; 2Q, '89, 17; 1Q, '88, 9; N-D, '87, 4; S-O, '87, 11

✓4ᵗʰ **99.3**   **Prophylactic vaccination and inoculation against certain bacterial diseases**
DEF: Administration of a killed bacteria suspension to produce immunity.

99.31   **Vaccination against cholera**

99.32   **Vaccination against typhoid and paratyphoid fever**
Administration of TAB vaccine

99.33   **Vaccination against tuberculosis**
Administration of BCG vaccine

99.34   **Vaccination against plague**

99.35   **Vaccination against tularemia**

99.36   **Administration of diphtheria toxoid**

> **EXCLUDES**   administration of:
> diphtheria antitoxin (99.58)
> diphtheria-tetanus-pertussis, combined (99.39)

99.37   **Vaccination against pertussis**

> **EXCLUDES**   administration of diphtheria-tetanus-pertussis, combined (99.39)

99.38   **Administration of tetanus toxoid**

> **EXCLUDES**   administration of:
> diphtheria-tetanus-pertussis, combined (99.39)
> tetanus antitoxin (99.56)

99.39   **Administration of diphtheria-tetanus-pertussis, combined**

Diagnostic and Therapeutic Procedures

99.4–99.83

✓4ᵗʰ **99.4 Prophylactic vaccination and inoculation against certain viral diseases**

DEF: Administration of a killed virus suspension to produce immunity.

99.41 Administration of poliomyelitis vaccine

99.42 Vaccination against smallpox

99.43 Vaccination against yellow fever

99.44 Vaccination against rabies

99.45 Vaccination against measles

> EXCLUDES   *administration of measles-mumps-rubella vaccine (99.48)*

99.46 Vaccination against mumps

> EXCLUDES   *administration of measles-mumps-rubella vaccine (99.48)*

99.47 Vaccination against rubella

> EXCLUDES   *administration of measles-mumps-rubella vaccine (99.48)*

99.48 Administration of measles-mumps-rubella vaccine

✓4ᵗʰ **99.5 Other vaccination and inoculation**

99.51 Prophylactic vaccination against the common cold

99.52 Prophylactic vaccination against influenza

99.53 Prophylactic vaccination against arthropod-borne viral encephalitis

99.54 Prophylactic vaccination against other arthropod-borne viral diseases

99.55 Prophylactic administration of vaccine against other diseases

> Vaccination against: Vaccination against:
> anthrax   Staphylococcus
> brucellosis   Streptococcus
> Rocky Mountain   typhus
>   spotted fever
>
> AHA: 2Q, '00, 9; 1Q, '94, 10

99.56 Administration of tetanus antitoxin

99.57 Administration of botulism antitoxin

99.58 Administration of other antitoxins

> Administration of:
> diphtheria antitoxin
> gas gangrene antitoxin
> scarlet fever antitoxin

99.59 Other vaccination and inoculation

> Vaccination NOS
>
> EXCLUDES   *injection of:*
> *gamma globulin (99.14)*
> *Rh immune globulin (99.11)*
> *immunization for:*
> *allergy (99.12)*
> *autoimmune disease (99.13)*

✓4ᵗʰ **99.6 Conversion of cardiac rhythm**

> EXCLUDES   *open chest cardiac:*
> *electric stimulation (37.91)*
> *massage (37.91)*

DEF: Correction of cardiac rhythm.

99.60 Cardiopulmonary resuscitation, not otherwise specified

> AHA: 1Q, '94, 16

99.61 Atrial cardioversion

> DEF: Application of electric shock to upper heart chamber to restore normal heart rhythm.

99.62 Other electric countershock of heart

> Cardioversion:
> NOS
> external
> Conversion to sinus rhythm
> Defibrillation
> External electrode stimulation

99.63 Closed chest cardiac massage

> Cardiac massage NOS
> Manual external cardiac massage
>
> DEF: Application of alternating manual pressure over breastbone to restore normal heart rhythm.

99.64 Carotid sinus stimulation

99.69 Other conversion of cardiac rhythm

> AHA: 4Q, '88, 11

✓4ᵗʰ **99.7 Therapeutic apheresis or other injection, administration, or infusion of other therapeutic or prophylactic substance**

99.71 Therapeutic plasmapheresis

> EXCLUDES   *extracorporeal immuno-adsorption [ECI] (99.76)*

99.72 Therapeutic leukopheresis

> Therapeutic leukocytapheresis

99.73 Therapeutic erythrocytapheresis

> Therapeutic erythropheresis
>
> AHA: 1Q, '94, 20

99.74 Therapeutic plateletpheresis

99.75 Administration of neuroprotective agent

> AHA: 4Q, '00, 68
>
> DEF: Direct application of neuroprotective agent (e.g., nimodipine) to miinimize ischemic injury by inhibiting toxic neurotransmitters, blocking free ions, removing free radicals, and causing vasodilation.

99.76 Extracorporeal immunoadsorption

> Removal of antibodies from plasma with protein A columns
>
> AHA: 4Q, '02, 112

99.77 Application or administration of adhesion barrier substance

> AHA: 4Q, '02, 113

99.78 Aquapheresis

> Plasma water removal
> Ultrafiltration [for water removal]
>
> EXCLUDES   *hemodiafiltration (39.95)*
> *hemodialysis (39.95)*
> *therapeutic plasmapheresis (99.71)*

99.79 Other

> Apheresis (harvest) of stem cells
>
> AHA: ▶1Q, '06, 12, 13;◀ 1Q, '05, 16; 4Q, '97, 55

✓4ᵗʰ **99.8 Miscellaneous physical procedures**

99.81 Hypothermia (central) (local)

> EXCLUDES   *gastric cooling (96.31)*
> *gastric freezing (96.32)*
> *that incidental to open heart surgery (39.62)*

99.82 Ultraviolet light therapy

> Actinotherapy

99.83 Other phototherapy

> Phototherapy of the newborn
>
> EXCLUDES   *extracorporeal photochemo-therapy (99.88)*
> *photocoagulation of retinal lesion (14.23-14.25, 14.33-14.35, 14.53-14.55)*
>
> AHA: 2Q, '89, 15
>
> DEF: Treating disease with light rays of various concentrations.

BI Bilateral Procedure   NC Non-covered Procedure   LC Limited Coverage Procedure   ▶◀ Revised Text   ● New Code   ▲ Revised Code Title

99.84   Isolation

    Isolation after contact with infectious disease

    Protection of individual from his
        surroundings

    Protection of surroundings from individual

99.85   Hyperthermia for treatment of cancer

    Hyperthermia (adjunct therapy) induced by
        microwave, ultrasound, low energy
        radio frequency, probes (interstitial),
        or other means in the treatment of
        cancer

    Code also any concurrent chemotherapy or
        radiation therapy

    AHA: 3Q, '96, 11; 3Q, '89, 17

**99.86   Non-invasive placement of bone growth
        stimulator**

    Transcutaneous (surface) placement of pads
        or patches for stimulation to aid bone
        healing

    EXCLUDES   *insertion of invasive or semi-
        invasive bone growth
        stimulators (device)
        (percutaneous
        electrodes) (78.90-78.99)*

99.88   Therapeutic photopheresis

    Extracorporeal photochemotherapy

    Extracorporeal photopheresis

    EXCLUDES   *other phototherapy (99.83)
        ultraviolet light therapy (99.82)*

    AHA: 2Q, '99, 7

    DEF: Extracorporeal photochemotherapy: Treating
    disease with drugs that react to ultraviolet radiation or
    sunlight.

√4ᵗʰ 99.9   Other miscellaneous procedures

99.91   Acupuncture for anesthesia

99.92   Other acupuncture

    EXCLUDES   *that with smouldering moxa
        (93.35)*

99.93   Rectal massage (for levator spasm)

99.94   Prostatic massage   ♂

99.95   Stretching of foreskin   ♂

99.96   Collection of sperm for artificial ♂
        insemination

99.97   Fitting of denture

99.98   Extraction of milk from lactating breast ♀

99.99   Other

    Leech therapy

Pharmacological Listings

Pharmacology Considerations

Medications are listed by classification and brand name for each of the chapters of ICD-9-CM. The list includes many of the common medications and should not be considered exhaustive. The pharmacology considerations that follow are presented as guidance only for the recognition of the link between implication of disease process and treatment.

Infectious and Parasitic Diseases (001-139)

AIDS Related Complex (ARC) Therapeutic Agents

Agenerase	Crixivan
Epivir	Fortovase
Hivid	Intron A
Invirase	Norvir
Pentam	Rescriptor
Retrovir	Rimactane
Roferon-A	Sustiva
Videx	Viracept
Vitravene	Zerit
Ziagen	Zovirax

Antibiotics

Achromycin-V	Amikin
Amoxicillin	Amoxil
Ampicillin	Ancef
Augmentin	Azactam
Bactrim	Bicillin
Biocef	Ceclor
Cefizox•	Cefobid
Cefotan	Ceftin
Chloromycetin	Cipro
Claforan	Cleocin
Duricef	E-Mycin
ERYC	Ery-Tab
Erythromycin	Factive
Floxin	Fortaz
Garamycin	Levaquin
Macrobid	Maxipime
Mefoxin	Minocin
Nebcin	Neo-fradin
PCE Dispertab	Penicillin G
Penicillin V	Pfizerpen
Pipracil	Primaxin
Proloprim	Septra
Spectrobid	Suprax
Synersid	Tazicef
Tazidime	Terramycin
Tetracycline HCl	Ticar
Timentin	Totacillin
Trimox	Trimpex
Unasyn	Unipen
Vancocin	Vibramycin
Vibra-Tabs	Wycillin
Zefazone	Zinacef
Zithromax	Zosyn
Zymar	

Antiparasitics

Antiminth	Aralen
Daraprim	Flagyl
G-well	Helidac
MepronnebuPent	Pentam 300
Penticarinat	Pin-X
Protostat	Vermox

Corticosteroids

Aristocort	Celestone
Cortastat	Cortef
Cortenema	Cortone Acetate
Dalalone	Decadron
Deltasone	Depo-Medrol
Florinef acetate	Hydeltrasol
Hydrocortisone	Hydrocortone
Medralone	Medrol
Orasone	Predalone
Prednisone	Prelone
Protocort	Solu-Cortef

Fungal Medications

Abelcet	AmBisome
Amphocin	Amphotec
Ancobon	Diflucan
Fulvicin P/G	Fungilin
Fungizone	Fungoid
Grifulvin	Grisactin
Gris-PEG	Lamisil
Lotrimin	Lotrisone
Monistat	Mycelex-G
Mycolog	Mycostatin
Nilstst	Nizoral
Spectazole	Sporanox

Tuberculosis Preparations

Capastat	INH Tablets
Lamprene	Laniazid
Myambutol	Mycobutin
Priftin	Pyrazinamide
Rifadin	Rifamate
Rimactane	Seromycin
Sodium P.A.S.	Streptomycin
Trecator-SC	

Viral Agents

Abreva	Agenerase
Combivir	Crixivan
Cytovene	Emtriva
Epivir	Famvir
Flumadine	Fortovase
Foscavir	Fuzeon
Herplex	Hepsera
Hivid	Invirase
Lexiva	Norvir
Relenza	Rescriptor
Retrovir	Reyataz
Sustiva	Symmetrel
Tamiflu	Valtrex
Videx	Viracept
Viramune	Virazole
Vistide	Vitravene
Zerit	Ziagen
Zovirax	

Neoplasms (140-239)

Adjunct

Anzemet	Arrestin
Compazine	Epogen
Ergamisol	Kytril
Leukine	Martinol
Metastron	Neumega
Neupogen	Procrit
Prokine	Quadramet
Reglan	Relcomide
Salagen	Sandostatin
Zinecard	Zofran

Androgen Inhibitor

Casodex	Eulexin
Lupron	Nilandron
Zoladex	

Antibiotic Derivatives

Adriamycin	Blenoxane
Cerubidine	Cosmegen
Doxorubicin	Idamycin
Mutamycin	Mithracin
Nipent	Novantrone
Pacis	Rubex
TheraCys	

Antiestrogen

Femara	Nolvadex

Antimetabolites

Adrucil	Cytarabine
Cytosar-U	Droxia
Efudex	Folex
Fludara	Fluoroplex
Fluorouracil	FUDR
Intron A	Leustatin
Methotrexate	Purinethol

Roferon-A	Thioguanine
Xeloda	

Cytotoxic Agents

Adriamycin	BiCNU
CeeNU	Cerubidine
Cytosar-U	Doxorubicin
Gemzar	Hexalen
Hydrea	Intron A
Matulane	Mutamycin
Myleran	Novantrone
Paraplatin	Platinol
Zanosar	

Hormones

Arimidex	Aromasin
Depo-Provera	Eligard
Emcyt	Estinyl
Estradurin	Fareston
Lupron	Megace
Stilphostrol	Teslac
Zoladex	

Nitrogen Mustard Derivatives

Alkeran	Cytoxan
Leukeran	Mustargen
Neosar	Thiotepa

Steroids and Combinations

Celestone Soluspan

Other

Camptosar	DTIC-Dome
Elspar	Etopophos
Iressa	Navelbine
Oncaspar	Oncovin
Phosphocol P32	Photofrin
Proleukin	Rituxan
Semzar	Taxol
Taxotere	TICE
Velban	Velcade
VePesid	Vesanoid
Vumon	

Endocrine, Nutritional and Metabolic Diseases and Immunity Disorders (240-279)

Acidifier and Alkalinizers

Ammonium chloride	Citrocarbonate
Sodium bicarbonate	Sodium lactate
Tham	

Antigout Agents

Anturane	Benemid
Colchicine	Probalan
Zyloprim	

Antilipemics

atorvastatin calcium	fluvastatin sodium
Lescol	Lipitor
lovastatin	Mevacor
Pravachol	pravastatin sodium
simvastatin	Tricor
Vytorin	Zetia
Zocor	

Antioxidants

Aquasol E	Calcium-D
Calcium Health Packs	Carotene-E
Carotene Health Packs	Glutathione
Performance Packs	Pure-E

Appetite Suppressants

Adipex-P	Adipost
Biphetamine	Bontril
Desoxyn	Didrex
Fastin	Ionamin
Mazanor	Meridia
Phentride	Plegine

Pondimin
Prelu-2
Sanorex
Tenuate

Diabetic Agents and Glucagon
Actos
Amaryl
Avandia
DiaBeta
Diabinese
Glucagon
Glucophage
Glucotrol
Glynase
Glyset
Humulin R
Iletin II
Lantus
Lispro (Humalog)
Micronase
Novolin
NovoLog
Prandin
Precose
Rezulin
Riomet
Ultralente
Velosulin

Electrolytes and Replacement Solutions
Calcium acetate
Calcium carbonate
Calcium chloride
Calcium citrate
Calcium gluconate
Calcium lactate
Calcium phosphate,
Calcium phosphate,
   dibasic
   tribasic
Dextran
Gendex
Hespan
Magnesium chloride
Magnesium sulfate
Phoslo
Potassium acetate
Potassium bicarbonate (K+ Care ET, Klor-Con/EF,
   K-Vescent)
Potassium chloride (Kaochlor, Kaon-Cl, Kato Powder, Kay
   Ciel, K-Lease, K-Lor, Klor-10%, Klor-Con, Klorvess,
   Klotrix, K-Lyte/Cl, K-Tab, Micro-K Extencaps,
   SK-Potassium Chloride, Slow-K, Ten-K)
Potassium gluconate (Glu-K, Kaon, Kayliker, K-G Elixir)
Slow-mag
Ringer's Injection

Hormones
Anadrol-50
Android
A.P.L.
Combipatch
Delatestryl
Depo-Provers
Estrace
Estraderm
Estratab
Estrovis
Factrel
Halotestin
Micronor
Norplant
Ogen
Ortho-Est
Ortho-Novum
Orvette
Pregnyl
premarin
Proscar
Provera
Testoderm
Testred

Parathyroid-like Agents
Aredia
Calcimar
Calderol
Cibacalcin
Didronel
E-Vista
Fosamax
Miacalcin
Osteocalcin
Rocaltrol
Salmonine

Pituitary Hormones
ACTH
Acthar
Cortrosyn
Diapid
Genotropin
Humatrope
Pegvisomant
Pitressin
Protropin
Somavert
Stimate

Thyroid Antagonists
Pima
Tapazole

Thyroid Hormones
Cytomel
Euthroid
Levothroid
Levoxine
Levoxyl
Triostat
Synthroid

Vitamins
Vitamin A
Vitamin B complex (including cyanocobalamin,
   hydroxocobalamin, folic acid, leucovorin calcium,
   niacin, niacinamide, pyridoxine hydrochloride,
   riboflavin, thiamine hydrochloride)
Vitamin C
Vitamin D (cholecalciferol, ergocalciferol)
Vitamin E
Vitamin K analogs (menadione/menadiol sodium
   diphosphate, phytonadione, sodium fluoride)
Trace elements (chromium, copper, iodine, manganese,
   selenium, zinc)

Blood and Blood-Forming Organs (280-289)
Anticoagulants
abciximab
Aggrastat
cilostazol
clopidrogrel bisulfate
eptifibatide
Integrilin
Plavix
Pletal
RepPro
Ticlid
ticlopidine hydrochloride
tirofiban hydrochloride

Coagulants
AlphaNine Coagulation Factor
Profilate OSD Antihemophilic Factor
Trasylol

Hematinics
Ferrous fumarate:
Femiron
Feostat
Hemocyte
Ircon
Nephro-Fer
Novofumar
Vitron-C

Ferrous gluconate:
Fergon
Feratab
Fer-Gen-Sol

Ferrous sulfate:
ED-IN-SOL
Fe50
Feosol
Fer-In-Sol
Fer-Iron
Slow Fe

Iron dextran:
DexFerrum
INFeD

Others
Konyne-HT Factor IX Complex   Nu-Iron
Monoclate-P Factor VIII:C, Antihemophilic Factor

Mental Disorders (290-319)
Central Nervous System Stimulants
Adderall XR
Atomoxetine HCl
Concerta
Cylert
Desoxyn
Dexedrine
Dopram
Methylin
Provigil
Ritalin
Strattera
Vivarin

Cerebral Metabolic Enhancer
Ergostat
Hydergine
Migranal

Alzheimer's Dementia Agents
Aricept
Cognex
Exelon
Namenda
Reminyl

Anti-anxiety
Atarax
Ativan
BuSpar
Libritabs
Librium
Miltown
Serax
Tranxene
Valium
Versed
Xanax

Anti-depressants
Anafranil
Asendin
Aventyl
Celexa
Desyrel
Effexor
Elavil
Lexapro
Nardil
Norpramin
Pamelor
Parnate
Paxil
Prozac
Remeron
Serzone
Sinequan
Surmontil
Tofranillbutrin
Trialodine
Wellbutrin
Zoloft

Anti-psychotics
Clozaril
Etrafon
Haldol
Loxitane
Mellaril
Navane
Orap
Prolixin
Risperdal
Serentil
Seroquel
Serpasil
Stelazine
Thorazine
Triavil
Trilafon
Zyprexa

Sedatives
Ambien
Dalmane

Diprivan
Mebaral
Nembutal
Precedex
ProSom
Restoril
Seconal SodiumSonata
Tuinal
Unisom

Other Psychotrophics
Antabuse
Cibalith-S
Eskalith
Lithane
Lithium Carbonate
Lithobid
Luvox
Meridia
Methadone
Zomig
Zyban

Nervous System and Sense Organs (320-389)
Antibiotics Central Nervous System Agents:
Amikin
Ancef
Cefizox
Fortaz
Garamycin
Kefurox
Nebcin
Rocephin
Tazidime

Anticonvulsants
Celontin
Cerebyx
Depakene
Depakote
Dilantin
Felbatol
Keppra
Klonopin
Lamictal
Mebaral
Mesantoin
Milontin
Mysoline
Neurontin
Peganone
Phenobarbital
Phenytoin
Phenurone
Tegretol
Tranxene
Tridione
Zarontin

Dopamine Receptor Agonist
Eldepryl
Mirapex
Parlodel
Permax
Requip
Sinemet
Stalevo
Symmetrel
Tasmar

Miscellaneous Ophthalmics
Alphagan
Betoptic
Emadine
Iopidine
Lacrisert
Lumigan
Opticrom
OptiPranolol
OPTIVAR
Propine
Timoptic
Trusopt
Zaditor

Migraine Agents
Amerge
Cafergot
Depakote
Ergostat
Imitrex
Inderal
Isocom
Maxalt
Midrin
Migranal
Relpax
Sansert
Wigraine
Zomig

Miotics
Carboptic
Miochol-E
Miostat
Pilocar
Pilostat
Phospholine Iodide

Mydriatics
AK-Dilate
AK-Nefrin
AK-Pentolate
Atropisol
Cyclogyl
Epifrin
Epinal
Eppy/N
Homatropine
Glaucon
Isopto Atropine
Isopto Frin
Isopto Homatropine
Isopto Hyoscine
Minims
Mydfrin
Mydriacyl

Ophthalmic Antiinfectives
AK-Tracin
Bleph-10 Liqifilm
Chloromycetin
Ciloxan
Garamycin
Ilotycin
Polymyxin B Sulfate
Oculflox
Sodium Sulamyd
Tobradex
Tobrex
Vigamox
Vira-A
Zymar

Ophthalmic Antiinflammatory Agents
Acular
Decadron Phosphate
Flarex
Fluor-Op
Maxidex
Ocufen
Voltarin

Otics

Augmentin	Auro-Dri
Cerumex	Chloromycetin Otic
Coly-Mycin S	Cortisporin
Cotrim	LazerSporin-C
Murine Ear	OticTridesilon
PediOtic	Septra

Parasympathomimetics

Duvoid	Evoxac
Mestinon	Prostigmin
Tensilon	Urecholine

Parkinsonism Agents

Akineton	Artane
Benztropine	Cogentin
Comtan	Dopar
Larodopa	Mirapex
Parlodel	Permax
Requip	Sinemet
Symmetrel	

Skeletal Muscle Relaxants

Dantrium	Flexeril
Lioresal	Vanadom
Zaraflex	

Vertigo Agents

Antivert	Vergon

Circulatory System (390-459)

Alpha Adrenoceptor Agonists

Aldomet	Catapres
Combipres	Wytensin

Alpha Receptor Blocking Agents

Cardura	Hytrin
Minipress	Regitine
Trandate	

Anginal Preparations

Calan	Cardia XT
Cardizem	Dilitrate-SR
Inderal	Isoptin
Isordil	Nitro-Bid
Nitro-Dur	Nitrodisc
Nitrogard	Nitrostat IV
Procardia	Sorbitrate
Transderm-Nitro	

Angiotensin Converting Enzyme Inhibitors

Accupril	Altace
Avapro	Capoten
Capozide	Cozaar
Lotensin	Mavik
Monopril	Prinivil
Univasc	Vasotec
Zestril	

Antihypertensives

Aldactazide	Aldactone
Aldomet	Apresoline
Atacard	Atenolol
Avapro	Benicar HCT
Calan	Capoten
Cardizem	Cardura
Catapres	Corlopam
Cozaar	Diuril
HydroDIURIL	Hyperstat
Hytrin	Hyzaar
Inderal	Isoptin
Levatol	Lopressor
Miniptress	Monopril
Procardia	Renese
Temex	Tenormin
Teveten	Vasotec
Wytensin	Zestric

Arrhythmia Medications

Betapace	Calan
Cardioquin	Cordarone
Inderal	Isoptin
Mexitil	Norpace
Procan	Pronestyl
Quinaglute	Rythmol
Tonocard	

Beta Blocking Agents

Blocadren	Cartrol
Coreg	Corgard
Corzide	Inderal
Kerlone	Levatol

Lopressor	Normodyne
Sectral	Tenoretic
Tenormin	Toprol XL
Trandate	Visken
Zebeta	

Calcium Channel Blockers

Adalat	Calan
Cardene	Cardizem
DynaCirc	Isoptin
Norvasc	Plendil
Posicor	Procardia
Sular	Vascor
Verelan	Cardiac Glycosides
Lanoxin (Digoxin)	

Diuretics

Aldactazide	Aldoril
Bumex	Combipres
Demadex	Diuril
Dyazide	Edecrin
Esidrix	Esimil
Furosemide	Lasix
Rauzide	Renese
Zaroxolyn	

Thrombolytic Enzymes

Abbokinase	Activase
Kabikinase	Retavase
Streptase	

Vasodilators, Cerebral

Pavabid	

Vasodilators, Coronary

Cardilate	Isordil
Nitro-Bid	Nitro-Dur
Nitrolingual Spray	Nitrostat IV
Pavabid	Peritrate
Sorbitrate	Transderm-Nitro

Vasodilators, Peripheral

Apresoline	Dibenzyline
Esimil	Hyperstat IV
Loniten	Pavabid

Respiratory System (460-519)

Allergy Relief Products

Antihist-1	Benadryl
Brexin	Bromphen
Clarinex	Dristan
Naldecon	Tavist
Trimeton	

Antibiotics

Achromycin	Amikin
Amoxicillin	Amoxil
Ampicillin	Ancef
Augmentin	Azactam
Bactrim	Biaxin
Bicillin	Ceclor
Cefizox	Cefobid
Cefotan	Ceftin
Cipro	Claforan
Duricef	Dynabec
E-Mycin	Ery-Tab
ERYC	Erythromycin
Factive	Floxin
Fortaz	Garamycin
Geocillin	Ilosone
Iotycin	Keflex
Keftab	Kefurox
Levaquin	Mandol
Mefoxin	Meropen
Mezlin	Minocin
Nebcin	Netromycin
PCE Dispertab	Penicillin G
Penicillin V	Pipracil
Primaxin	Raxar
Rocephin	Septra
Spectrobid	Suprax
Tazicef	Tazidime
Tetracycline HCl	Ticar
Timentin	Trovan
Wycillin	Zagam
Zefazone	Zinacef
Zithromax	

Antihistamines

Actifed	Allegra
Allerest	Atarax

Benadryl	Bromphen
Chlor-Trimeton	Claritin
Coricidin	Deconamine
Four-Way	Periactin
Tavist	Triaminic
Zyrtec	

Asthma Preparations

Accolate	AeroBid
Alupent	Aminophylline
Beclovent	Brethine
Bronkaid	Choledyl SA
Crolom	Dilor
Flovent	Intal
Maxair	Metaprel
Primatene	Proventil
Serevent	Singulair
TheoDur	Tilade
Tornalate	Vanceril
Ventolin	Zyflo

Bronchial Dilators

Accolate	Advair Diskus
Alupent	Aminophylline
Asbron G	Atrovent
Brethaire Inhaler	Bricanyl
Bronkephrine	Bronkometer
Combivent	Choledyl
Isuprel	Lufyllin
Marax	Maxair
Medihaler-Iso	Prez-D
Primatene	Proventil
Quadrinal	Quibron
Serevent	Singulair
Slo-bid	Tedral
Theolair	Tornalate
Ventolin	Xolair
Xopenex	Zyflo

Cold, Cough Preparations and Mucolytics

Calcidrine	Cheracol
Comtrex	Dimetapp
Dimetane	Entex
Guaifed	Humibid
Hycomine	Naldecon
Novahistine	Nucofed
Ornade	Quelidrine
Quibron	Robitussin
Rondec	Ru-Tuss
Rynatan	Rynatuss
Sine-Aid	Triaminic
Tuss-Ornade	Tussi-Organdin
Tussionex	

Corticosteroids

Aristocort	Celestone
Cortone Acetate	Deltasone
Depo-Medrol	Hydeltrasol
Hydrocortone	Prednisone
Solu-Cortef	Solu-Medrol

Nasal Preparations

Adrenalin Chloride	Afrin
Beconase	Decadron Phosphate
Dopram Injectable	Flonase
Nasacort	Nasalide
Nasarel	Otrivin
Privine	Respiratory Stimulants
Rhinocort	Turbinaire
Vancenase	

Respiratory Therapy Agents

Alupent	Arm-a-Med Isoetharine
Survanta	

Digestive System (520-579)

Anorectal Products

Analpram-HC	Proctofoam-HC
Rowasa	

Antacids

Alka-Seltzer	Amphojel
Basaljel	Di-Gel
Gaviscon	Maalox
Mylanta	Polycitra
Riopan	Tums

Antibiotics and Antibacterials

Amikin	Ancef
Azactam	Cefizox
Cefobid	Cefotan

Pharmacological Listing

Claforan	Fortaz
Furoxone	Kefzol
Mandol	Mefoxin
Nebcin	Netromycin
Pipracil	Primaxin
Tazicef	Tazidime
Ticar	Unasyn
Vancocin	Zefazone

Antispasmodics and Anticholinergics

Bentyl	Darabid
Donnatal	Levsin
Librax	Prilosec
Pro-Banthine	Quarzan
Reglan	Robinul

Antiulcer

cimetidine	esomeprazole magnesium
famotidine	iansoprazole
Nexium	omeprazole
Pepcid AC	Prevacid
Prilosec	ranitidine hydrochloride
Tagamet	Zantac

Corticosteroids

Alinia	Aristocort
Cortenema	Decadron
Deltasone	Depo-Medrol
Hydeltrasol	Hydrocortone
Prednisone	Solu-Cortef
Solu-Medrol	

Diarrhea Medications

Alinia	Arco-Lase Plus
Charcoal Plus	Donnagel
Furoxone	Kaopectate
Kapectolin	Imodium
Lomotil	Mitrolan
Motofen	Pepto-Bismol

Digestants

Cotazym	Donnazyme
Entozyme	Ku-Zyme
Lactaid	Pancrease
Pancreatin	Ultrase
Viokase	

Flatulence Relief

Flatulex	Gas-X
Kutrase	Mylicon
Phazyme	

Gallstone Dissolution Agent

Actigall Capsules

Gastric Acid Secretion Inhibitor

Axid	Cytotec
Prevacid	Zantac

Gastrointestinal Antigranulomatous Disease

Azulfidine Tablets, EN-tabs	Dipentum Capsules
Mesasal	Pentasa
Remicade	Rowasa

Nausea and Vertigo Medications

Aloxi	Anzeme
Anfernet	Antivert
Aprepitant	Bonine
Bucladin-S Softab	Compazine
Dramamine	Emend
Kytril	Marinol
Reglan	Tigan
Torecan	Vergon
Zofran	

Parasympatholytics

Bellergal-S	Bentyl
Cantil	Levsin
Robinul	

Genitourinary System (580-629)

Antibiotics

Achromycin	Ancef
Augmentin	Azactam
Azo Gantanol	Azo Gantrisin
Bactrim	Ceclor
Cefizox	Cefobid
Cefotan	Ceftin
Ceptaz	Cipro
Claforan	Duricef
E-Mycin	Ery-tab

Floxin	Fortaz
Garamycin	Keftab
Kefurox	Mefoxin
Mezlin	Monuril
Nebcin	Netromycin
Noroxin	PCE Dispertab
Penetrex	Primaxin
Rocephin	Septra
Sumycin	Suprax
Tazidime	Timentin
Unasyn	Zinacef

Gonadotropin Inhibitors

Antagon	Danocrine Capsules
Synarel Nasal Solution	

Hormones

Androgen and estrogen combinations:

Estratest	
Premarin with Methyltestosterone	
Premphase	Prempro

Estrogens:

Climara	Estrace
Estraderm	Estrofem
Femring	Levolet
Menest	Ogen
Premarin	Seasonale

Gonadotropin:

Lutrepulse	Pregnyl
Profasi	Synarel

Menotropins:

Humegon	Pergonal
Repronex	

Progesterone:

Cycrin	Provera

Progestogen:

Aygestin	Micronor

Urinary Tract Agents

Analgesics:

Pyridium	Rimso-50

Antibacterials:

Bactrim	Cipro
Furadantin	Gantanol
Gantrisin	Macrobid
Macrodantin	NegGram
Neosporin	Noroxin
Proloprim	Septra
Thiosulfil	Trimpex
Uroqid Acid No. 2	

Antispasmodics:

Cystospaz	Levsin
Oxytrol	Urised
Urispas	UroXatral

Vaginal Preparations

Antifungal agents:

Betadine Douche	Femstat
Gyne-Lotrimin	Monistat
Mycelex	Terazol
Vagistat	Yeast-X

Capsules, tablets:

Mycelex-G	Sultrin

Creams:

Amino-Cerv	Estrace
Mycostatin	Nystex
Premarin	Trysul

Inserts, suppositories:

Terazol	Vagisec Plus

Jellies, ointments:

Aci-Jel

Pregnancy, Childbirth, Puerperium (630-677)

Antibiotics

Amikin	Ancef
Azactam	Ceclor
Cefizox	Cefobid
Cefotan	Claforan
E-Mycin	Fortaz
Garamycin	Keftab
Kefzol	Mefoxin
Nebcin	PCE Dispertab
Primaxin	Rocephin
Tazidime	Ticar
Timentin	Trobicin
Unasyn	Zefazone
Zolicef	Zyvox

Antihypertensives

Adalat	Aldactazide
Aldactone	Aldomet
Apresoline	Calan
Cardizem	Catapres
Deponit	Diuril
Esidrix	Hydralazine
HydroDIURIL	Hygroton
Hyperstat	Hytrin
Inderal	Isoptin
Levatol	Lopressor
Midamor	Minipress
Minoxidil	Nitrostat
Procardia	Renese
Tenormin	Tridil
Vasotec	Wytensin

Diuretics

Aldactazide	AldactoneAldoril
Bumex	Demadex Diuril
Dyazide	
Dyrenium	Edecrin
Esidrix	Esimil
HydroDIURIL	Lasix
Lozol	Maxzide
Rauzide	Renese
Zaroxolyn	

Galactokinetic Agents

Syntocinon Nasal Spray

Nausea Medication

Antivert	Arrestin
Bonine	Compazine
Emetrol	Norzine
Tigan	Torecan

Oxytocics

Hemabate	Cervidil
Methergine	Oxytocin
Pitocin	Syntocinon

Uterine Relaxants

Yutopar

Skin and Subcutaneous Tissue (680-709)

Abradants

Ureacin

Acne Preparations

Accutane Tablets	Azelex
Benzac	Benzamycin
Cleocin	Clinda-Derm
Desquam	Emgel
Erycette	Novacet
Persa-Gel	Retin-A
Staticin	Sulfacet-R Acne
Theramycin Z	Xerac

Antibacterials, Antifungals and Combinations

Benzamycin	Fungi-Nail
Loprox	Lotrisone
Neosporin	Nizoral
Sporanox	

Antibiotics

Amikin	Ancef
Azactam	Bactroban
Ceclor	Cefizox
Cefobid	Cefotan
Ceftin	Cipro
Cubicin	Duricef
ERYC	Erythromycin

Floxin
Garamycin
Ilotycin
Keftab
Mandol
Mezlin
Pipracil
Rocephin
Spectrobid
Ticar
Ultracef
Zinacef

Furacin
Ilosone
Keflex
Kefzol
Mefoxin
Netromycin
Primaxin
Silvadene
Tazidime
Timentin
Zefazone

Antiinflammatory Agents

Aclovate
Cortisporin
Cyclocort
Diprolene
Halog
Lidex
Mantadil
Nutracort
Synalar
Topicort
Ultravate

Aristocort
Cutivate
Decadron
Elocon
Kenalog
Lotrisone
NeoDecadron
Synacort
Temovate
Tridesilon
Westcort

Corticosteroids

Amcort
Cortef
Depo-Medrol
Solu-Cortef

Celestone
Deltasone
Hydeltrasol
Solu-Medrol

Depigmenting Agents

Benoquin Cream
Eldoquin

Eldopaque

Dermatologicals

Dermatitis Herpetiformis:

Dapsone USP

Dermatitis Relief:

Decaspray
Florone
Locoid
Psorcon

Elidel
Hytone
Mytrex

Epidermal and Cellular Growth:

Lazer Cream

Fungicides:

Amphotec
BAZA Cream
Exelderm
Grisactin
Lamisil
Lotrimin
Mycelex
Mycostatin

Abelcet
Clioquinol
Fungoid Creme
Halotex
Loprox
Lotrisone
Mycolog-11
Spectazole

Keratolytics:

Adrucil
Keralyt Gel

Fluoroplex
Occlusal-HP

Pruritis Medications:

Alphatrex
Dermoplast
Eurax
Hytone
Locoid
Periactin
Psorcon

Betatrex
Eldecort
Florone
Hyzine-50
Mytrex
Pramosone
Vistaril

Psoriasis Agents:

Amevive
Cormax
DHS Tar
Drithocreme
Enbrel
Pentrax
Tazorac
Zetar

Anthra-Derm
Denorex
Dovonex
Dritho-Scalp
Hunira
Raptiva
Temovate

Steroids and Combinations:

Neo-Synalar
Synalar
Vanoxide-HC

Psorcon
Synemol
Vytone

Wart Removers:

Compound W
LazerFormalyde
Podocon-25
Sal-Plant Gel

Condylox
Occlusal
Sal-Acid Plasters
Trans-Plantar

Trans-Ver-Sal
Verrex
Viranol Gel

Verr-Canth
Verrusol

Musculoskeletal System and Connective Tissue (710-739)

Analgesics

Advil
Anaprox
Ansaid
Bufferin
Clinoril
Darvon
Disalcid
Easprin
Empirin/Codeine
Esgic
Feldene
Hydrocodone
Lortab/Lorcet
Medipren
Motrin
Naprosyn
Norgesic
Parafon Forte
Percocet
Phenaphen/Codeine
Salflex
Synalgos-DC
Talwin
Trilisate
Tylenol/Codeine
Vicodin

Anacin
Anexsia
Ascriptin
Butazolidin
Darvocet
Datril
Dolobid
Ecotrin
Equagesic
Exedrin
Flexeril
Indocin
Meclomen
Mono-Gesic
Nalfon
Norflex
Orudis
Ponstel
Percodan
Rufen
Sarapin
Talacen
Tolectin
Tylenol
Tylox
Wygesic

Antibiotics (Osteomyelitis Treatments)

Amikin
Cefizox
Cipro
Floxin
Garamycin
Keftab
Kefzol
Mefoxin
Pipracil
Timentin
Zinacef

Ancef
Cefotan
Clindamycin
Fortaz
Keflex
Kefurox
Mandol
Monocid
Rocephin
Vancocin

Antiinflammatory Agents, Steroids and Combinations

Aristocort
Celebrex
Decadron
Hydeltra-T.B.A.
Hydrocortone
Iodine
Medrol
Remicade

Bextra
Cortone
Deltasone Depo-Medrol
Hydeltrasol
Kenalog
Lexiva
Relafen
Voltren

Calcium Preparations

Calcium-D
Caltrate
Dical-D
Nephro-Calci
Phos-Ex

Calphosan
Citracal
Neo-Calglucon
Os-Cal
Posture

Muscle Relaxants

Actonel
Forteo
Parafon Forte
Robaxisal
Soma
Valrelease

Flexeril
Paraflex
Robaxin
Skelaxin
Valium

Osteoporosis Preparations

Aredia
Calcimar
Evista
Gerimed
Miacalcin

Boniva
Didronel
Fosamax
Lexiva

Congenital Anomalies (740-759)

A pharmacological reference list cannot be presented for this chapter because most conditions listed are treatable only by surgical methods and are not affected by medications.

Conditions in the Perinatal Period (760-779)

Antibiotics

Amoxcillin
Bicillin
Dicloxacillin
Fortaz
Kefzol
Mezlin
Rocephin
Tazicef
Ticar
Zithromax

Biaxin
Cloxacillin
E-Mycin
Garamycin
Mandol
Nebcin
Spectrobid
Tazidime
Vibramycin

Bronchodilators

Aerolate Jr.
Bronkephrine
Dilor
Quadrinal
Theolair

Asbron G
Choledyl
Proventil
Somophyllin
Ventolin

Corticosteroids

Aristocort
Cortone Acetate
Deltasone
Hydeltrasol
Solu-Cortef

Celeston
Decadron
Depo-Medrol
Prednisone
Solu-Medrol

Electrolytes

Infalyte
Pedialyte

Oralyte
Rehydralyte

Galactokinetics (Milk Flow Stimulants)

Syntocinon Nasal Spray

Galactorrhea (Lactation) Inhibitors

Parlodel

Neonatal Respiratory Distress Syndrome Agents

Exosurf
Survanta

Ophthalmic Ointments, Antibiotics

Ilotycin

Rh Hemolytic Disease-Related Agents

Gamulin Rh
HypRho-D Full Dose (for baby)
HypRho-D Mini-Dose (for mother)
Win Rho-SD   Gamulin Rh
HypRho-D Full Dose (for baby)
HypRho-D Mini-Dose (for mother)   Win Rho-SD

Uterine Contractants

Oxytocin

Vitamins

AquaMEPHYTON

Symptoms, Signs and Ill-Defined Conditions (780-799)

Analgesics

Acetaminophens and combinations:

Acetaminophen
Anexsia
Datril
Feverall
Midrin

Anacin—Aspirin-Free
Bufferin
Excedrin
Isocom
Tylenol

Aspirins:

Easprin
Forprin

Ecotrin

Aspirin combinations:

Anacin
Bufferin
Norgesic

Ascriptin A/D
Equagesic

Narcotics, synthetics and combinations:

Alfenta
Astramorph/PF
B&O Supprettes
Damason-P
Darvon
Dilaudid
Duramorph
Fioricet
Hydrocet
Levo-Dromoran
Lurline

Anexsia
Azdone
Dalgan
Darvocet-N
Demerol
Dolophine
Esgic
Fiorinal
Infumorph
Lortab
Mepergan

Methadone-HCl	MS-Contin
MSIR	Nubain
Numorphan	Oralet
Oramorph	Percocet
Percodan	Phenaphen/Codeine
Phrenilin	Roxanol
Roxicodone	Sedapap
Stadol	Sublimaze
Sufenta	Synalgos-DC
Talacen	Talwin-NX
Tylox	Vicodin

Nonsteroidal antiinflammatory drugs (NSAIDs):
Advil	Anaprox
Daypro	Duract
Feldene	Indocin
Lodine	Meclomen
Medipren	Motrin
Nalfon	Naprosyn
Nuprin	Orudis
Ponstel	Rufen
Tolectin	Toradol
Voltaren	

Other:
Alka-Seltzer	Dolobid
Empirin/Codeine	Mono-Gesic
Norflex	Parafon Forte
Salflex	Sarapin
Trilisate	

Antacids
Alka-Seltzer	Amphojel
Basaljel	Maalox
Mylanta	Riopan

Anticonvulsives
Depakane	Depakote
Dilantin	Jabatril
Lamictal	Nurontin
Phenobarbital	Tegretol
Topamax	

Antiflatulents and Antigas Medications
Flatulex	Kutrase
Mylicon	

Antipyretics
Acetaminophen	Ascriptin A/D
Feverall	PediaProfen
Rufen	Trilisate
Tylenol	

Antispasmodics and Anticholinergics
Arco-Lase	Bentyl
Cantil	Darabid
Donnatal	Kinesed
Kutrase	Levsin
Levsinex	Librax
Prilosec	Pro-Banthine
Quarzan	Robinul
Valpin-50	

Appetite Suppressants
Amphetamines:
Biphetamine	Desoxyn
Dexedrine	Didrex

Nonamphetamines:
Adipex-P	Bontril
Fastin	Ionamin
Plegine	Pondimin
Prelu-2	Redux
Sanorex	Tenuate

Digestives
Cotazym	Donnazyme
Ku-Zyme	Pancrease
Pancreatin	Viokase

Diuretics
Aldactazide	Aldactone
Bumex	Capozide
Corzide	Demadex
Diamox	Diulo
Diuril	Dyazide
Dyrenium	Edecrin
Enduron	Enduronyl
Esidrex	Exna
HydroDIURIL	Hydromox
Lasix	Lozol
Maxzide	Midamor

Moduretic	Naturetin
Oretic	Prinzide
Rauzide	Renese
Saluron	Thalitone
Vaseretic	Zestoretic

Nausea and Vertigo Agents
Aloxi	Antivert
Bonine	Compazine
Emend	Emetrol
Kytril	Norzine
Phenergan	Tigan
Torecan	Zofran

Sleep Aids
Ambien	Chloral hydrate
Dalmane	Doriden
Halcion	Restoril
Valmid	

Hypnotics:
Butisol	Mebaral
Phenobarbital	

Sedatives (barbiturates):
Benadryl	BufferinAF
Excedrin PM	Magonate
Mepergan	Phenergan
Tylenol PM	Unisom
Versed	

Sedatives (nonbarbiturates):
Eldertonic	Niferex
Nu-Iron	

Tonics
Inderal

Tremor Preparations
Eldertonic	Niferex
Nu-Iron	Inderal

Injury and Poisoning (800-999)
Agents Used in Poisonings
Amyl nitrate	Antilirium
Antizole	BAL
Benadryl	Desferal
Digibind	Ipecac Syrup
Narcan (Naloxone)	Penicillamine
Pralidoxime	Protopam Chloride
Revex	Romazicon
Sodium nitrite	

Analgesics
Acetaminophens and combinations:
Acetaminophen	Anexsia
Aspirin-Free Anacin	Excedrin
Feverall	Isocom
Midrin	Tylenol
Tylenol with codeine	

Aspirins:
Aspirin	Easprin
Ecotrin	

Aspirin combinations:
Anacin	Ascriptin A/D
Bufferin	Equagesic
Norgesic	

Narcotics, synthetics and combinations:
Alfenta	Anexsia
Astromorph PF	Azdone
B&O Supprettes	Dalgan
Damason-P	Darvocet-N
Darvon	Demerol
Dilaudid	Dolophine
Duramorph	Esgic
Fioricet	Fiorinal
Hydrocet	Infumorph
Levo-Dromoran	Lortab/Lorcet
Lurline	Mepergan
Methadone HCl	MS Contin
MSIR	Nubain
Numorphan	Oramorph
Percocet	Percodan
Phrenilin	Roxanol
Roxicodone	Sedapap
Stadol	Sublimaze
Sufenta	Synalgos-DC

Talacen	Talwin
Tegretol	Tylox
Vicodin	Wygesic
Zydone	

Nonsteroidal antiinflammatory drugs (NSAIDs):
Advil	Anaprox
Ansaid	Cataflam
Clinoril	Daypro
Feldene	Ibuprofen
Lodine	Meclamen
Medipren	Motrin
Nalfon	Naprosyn
Nuprin	Orudis
Ponstel	Relafen
Rufen	Tolectin
Toradol	Voltaren

Antibiotics
Achromycin	Amikin
Amoxicillin	Amoxil
Ancef	Augmentin
Azactam	Ceclor
Cefizox	Cefobid
Cefotan	Cipro
Claforan	Floxin
Garamycin	Keflex
Keftab	Kefurox
Kefzol	Mefoxin
Mezlin	Nebcin
Netromycin	Pipracil
Tazidime	Timentin
Zefazone	Zinacef

Anticoagulants
Calciparine	Coumadin
Dicumarol	Fragmin
Heparin Sodium	Lovenox
Organan	Panwarfin

Antihistamines
Allegra	Atarax/Vistaril
Benadryl	Chlor-Trimeton
Claritin	Dimetap
Extendryl	Hismanal
Optimine	Seldane
Tacaryl	Temaril
Zyrtec	

Antivertigo Medications
Antivert	Bonine
Bucladin-S	Meclizine
Vontrol	

Burn Agents
Americaine	Aquaphor
Butesin Picrate	Chloresium
Collagenase Santyl	Dermoplast
Eucerin	Nupercainal
Panafil	Prophyllin
Silvadine	Sween Cream
Tronothane	

Corticosteroids
Aristocort	Celestone
Decadron	Deltasone
Depo-Medrol	Hydeltrasol
Hydrocortone	Prednisone
Solu-Cortef	Solu-Medrol

Detoxifying Agents
Mesnex Injection

Skin Wound Preparations
Betadine	Debrisan
DuoDERM	

Wound Dressings
Aquaphor	Chloresium
Critic-Aid	Debrisan
DuoDERM	Granulex
Lazer	Panafil
SSD	

Diagnosis Code/MDC/DRG List

The following list provides the MDC and Medical DRG(s) to which the diagnosis code is assigned when listed as principal diagnosis with the exception of principal diagnoses in combination with secondary diagnoses causing assignment to MDC 24 or the presence of a secondary diagnosis causing assignment to MDC 25. Resources used to compile this list are the *3M Definitions Manual, Version 24.0* and Medicare Program; Changes to the Hospital Inpatient Prospective Payment System; Proposed Rule (*Federal Register*, April 25, 2006).

DX	MDC	DRG	DX	MDC	DRG	DX	MDC	DRG	DX	MDC	DRG	DX	MDC	DRG
Infectious and Parasitic			008.63	06	182-184	011.44	04	079-081	012.85	04	079-081	014.06	06	188-190
Diseases			008.64	06	182-184	011.45	04	079-081	012.86	04	079-081	014.80	06	188-190
001.0	06	182-184	008.65	06	182-184	011.46	04	079-081	013.00	01	020	014.81	06	188-190
001.1	06	182-184	008.66	06	182-184	011.50	04	079-081	013.01	01	020	014.82	06	188-190
001.9	06	182-184	008.67	06	182-184	011.51	04	079-081	013.02	01	020	014.83	06	188-190
002.0	18	423	008.69	06	182-184	011.52	04	079-081	013.03	01	020	014.84	06	188-190
002.1	18	423	008.8	06	182-184	011.53	04	079-081	013.04	01	020	014.85	06	188-190
002.2	18	423	009.0	06	182-184	011.54	04	079-081	013.05	01	020	014.86	06	188-190
002.3	18	423	009.1	06	182-184	011.55	04	079-081	013.06	01	020	015.00	08	238
002.9	18	423	009.2	06	182-184	011.56	04	079-081	013.10	01	020	015.01	08	238
003.0	06	182-184	009.3	06	182-184	011.60	04	079-081	013.11	01	020	015.02	08	238
003.1	18	416-417	010.00	04	079-081	011.61	04	079-081	013.12	01	020	015.03	08	238
003.20	18	423	010.01	04	079-081	011.62	04	079-081	013.13	01	020	015.04	08	238
003.21	01	020	010.02	04	079-081	011.63	04	079-081	013.14	01	020	015.05	08	238
003.22	04	079-081	010.03	04	079-081	011.64	04	079-081	013.15	01	020	015.06	08	238
003.23	08	242	010.04	04	079-081	011.65	04	079-081	013.16	01	020	015.10	08	242
003.24	08	238	010.05	04	079-081	011.66	04	079-081	013.20	01	020	015.11	08	242
003.29	18	423	010.06	04	079-081	011.70	04	079-081	013.21	01	020	015.12	08	242
003.8	18	423	010.10	04	079-081	011.71	04	079-081	013.22	01	020	015.13	08	242
003.9	18	423	010.11	04	079-081	011.72	04	079-081	013.23	01	020	015.14	08	242
004.0	06	182-184	010.12	04	079-081	011.73	04	079-081	013.24	01	020	015.15	08	242
004.1	06	182-184	010.13	04	079-081	011.74	04	079-081	013.25	01	020	015.16	08	242
004.2	06	182-184	010.14	04	079-081	011.75	04	079-081	013.26	01	020	015.20	08	242
004.3	06	182-184	010.15	04	079-081	011.76	04	079-081	013.30	01	020	015.21	08	242
004.8	06	182-184	010.16	04	079-081	011.80	04	079-081	013.31	01	020	015.22	08	242
004.9	06	182-184	010.80	04	079-081	011.81	04	079-081	013.32	01	020	015.23	08	242
005.0	06	182-184	010.81	04	079-081	011.82	04	079-081	013.33	01	020	015.24	08	242
005.1	18	423	010.82	04	079-081	011.83	04	079-081	013.34	01	020	015.25	08	242
005.2	06	182-184	010.83	04	079-081	011.84	04	079-081	013.35	01	020	015.26	08	242
005.3	06	182-184	010.84	04	079-081	011.85	04	079-081	013.36	01	020	015.50	08	238
005.4	06	182-184	010.85	04	079-081	011.86	04	079-081	013.40	01	020	015.51	08	238
005.81	06	182-184	010.86	04	079-081	011.90	04	079-081	013.41	01	020	015.52	08	238
005.89	06	182-184	010.90	04	079-081	011.91	04	079-081	013.42	01	020	015.53	08	238
005.9	06	182-184	010.91	04	079-081	011.92	04	079-081	013.43	01	020	015.54	08	238
006.0	06	182-184	010.92	04	079-081	011.93	04	079-081	013.44	01	020	015.55	08	238
006.1	06	182-184	010.93	04	079-081	011.94	04	079-081	013.45	01	020	015.56	08	238
006.2	06	182-184	010.94	04	079-081	011.95	04	079-081	013.46	01	020	015.60	03	073-074
006.3	07	205-206	010.95	04	079-081	011.96	04	079-081	013.50	01	020	015.61	03	073-074
006.4	04	079-081	010.96	04	079-081	012.00	04	079-081	013.51	01	020	015.62	03	073-074
006.5	01	020	011.00	04	079-081	012.01	04	079-081	013.52	01	020	015.63	03	073-074
006.6	09	283-284	011.01	04	079-081	012.02	04	079-081	013.53	01	020	015.64	03	073-074
006.8	18	423	011.02	04	079-081	012.03	04	079-081	013.54	01	020	015.65	03	073-074
006.9	18	423	011.03	04	079-081	012.04	04	079-081	013.55	01	020	015.66	03	073-074
007.0	06	182-184	011.04	04	079-081	012.05	04	079-081	013.56	01	020	015.70	08	238
007.1	06	182-184	011.05	04	079-081	012.06	04	079-081	013.60	01	020	015.71	08	238
007.2	06	182-184	011.06	04	079-081	012.10	04	079-081	013.61	01	020	015.72	08	238
007.3	06	182-184	011.10	04	079-081	012.11	04	079-081	013.62	01	020	015.73	08	238
007.4	06	182-184	011.11	04	079-081	012.12	04	079-081	013.63	01	020	015.74	08	238
007.5	06	182-184	011.12	04	079-081	012.13	04	079-081	013.64	01	020	015.75	08	238
007.8	06	182-184	011.13	04	079-081	012.14	04	079-081	013.65	01	020	015.76	08	238
007.9	06	182-184	011.14	04	079-081	012.15	04	079-081	013.66	01	020	015.80	08	242
008.00	06	182-184	011.15	04	079-081	012.16	04	079-081	013.80	01	020	015.81	08	242
008.01	06	182-184	011.16	04	079-081	012.20	04	079-081	013.81	01	020	015.82	08	242
008.02	06	182-184	011.20	04	079-081	012.21	04	079-081	013.82	01	020	015.83	08	242
008.03	06	182-184	011.21	04	079-081	012.22	04	079-081	013.83	01	020	015.84	08	242
008.04	06	182-184	011.22	04	079-081	012.23	04	079-081	013.84	01	020	015.85	08	242
008.09	06	182-184	011.23	04	079-081	012.24	04	079-081	013.85	01	020	015.86	08	242
008.1	06	182-184	011.24	04	079-081	012.25	04	079-081	013.86	01	020	015.90	08	242
008.2	06	182-184	011.25	04	079-081	012.26	04	079-081	013.90	01	020	015.91	08	242
008.3	06	182-184	011.26	04	079-081	012.30	03	073-074	013.91	01	020	015.92	08	242
008.41	06	182-184	011.30	04	079-081	012.31	03	073-074	013.92	01	020	015.93	08	242
008.42	06	182-184	011.31	04	079-081	012.32	03	073-074	013.93	01	020	015.94	08	242
008.43	06	182-184	011.32	04	079-081	012.33	03	073-074	013.94	01	020	015.95	08	242
008.44	06	182-184	011.33	04	079-081	012.34	03	073-074	013.95	01	020	015.96	08	242
008.45	06	182-184	011.34	04	079-081	012.35	03	073-074	013.96	01	020	016.00	11	320-322
008.46	06	182-184	011.35	04	079-081	012.36	03	073-074	014.00	06	188-190	016.01	11	320-322
008.47	06	182-184	011.36	04	079-081	012.80	04	079-081	014.01	06	188-190	016.02	11	320-322
008.49	06	182-184	011.40	04	079-081	012.81	04	079-081	014.02	06	188-190	016.03	11	320-322
008.5	06	182-184	011.41	04	079-081	012.82	04	079-081	014.03	06	188-190	016.04	11	320-322
008.61	06	182-184	011.42	04	079-081	012.83	04	079-081	014.04	06	188-190	016.05	11	320-322
008.62	06	182-184	011.43	04	079-081	012.84	04	079-081	014.05	06	188-190	016.06	11	320-322

DX	MDC	DRG	DX	MDC	DRG	DX	MDC	DRG	DX	MDC	DRG	DX	MDC	DRG
016.10	11	320-322	017.34	02	046-048	022.1	04	079-081	039.4	09	283-284	053.10	01	018-019
016.11	11	320-322	017.35	02	046-048	022.2	06	188-190	039.8	18	423	053.11	01	018-019
016.12	11	320-322	017.36	02	046-048	022.3	18	416-417	039.9	18	423	053.12	01	018-019
016.13	11	320-322	017.40	03	073-074	022.8	18	423	040.0	18	423	053.13	01	018-019
016.14	11	320-322	017.41	03	073-074	022.9	18	423	040.1	18	423	053.14	01	020
016.15	11	320-322	017.42	03	073-074	023.0	18	423	040.2	06	188-190	053.19	01	018-019
016.16	11	320-322	017.43	03	073-074	023.1	18	423	040.3	18	423	053.20	02	046-048
016.20	11	320-322	017.44	03	073-074	023.2	18	423	040.81	08	248	053.21	02	046-048
016.21	11	320-322	017.45	03	073-074	023.3	18	423	040.82	18	423	053.22	02	046-048
016.22	11	320-322	017.46	03	073-074	023.8	18	423	040.89	18	423	053.29	02	046-048
016.23	11	320-322	017.50	10	300-301	023.9	18	423	041.00	18	423	053.71	03	073-074
016.24	11	320-322	017.51	10	300-301	024	18	423	041.01	18	423	053.79	18	421-422
016.25	11	320-322	017.52	10	300-301	025	18	423	041.02	18	423	053.8	18	421-422
016.26	11	320-322	017.53	10	300-301	026.0	18	423	041.03	18	423	053.9	09	272-273
016.30	11	320-322	017.54	10	300-301	026.1	18	423	041.04	18	423	054.0	09	283-284
016.31	11	320-322	017.55	10	300-301	026.9	18	423	041.05	18	423	054.10	12	350
016.32	11	320-322	017.56	10	300-301	027.0	18	423	041.09	18	423	054.10	13	368
016.33	11	320-322	017.60	10	300-301	027.1	18	423	041.10	18	423	054.11	13	368
016.34	11	320-322	017.61	10	300-301	027.2	18	423	041.11	18	423	054.12	13	368
016.35	11	320-322	017.62	10	300-301	027.8	18	423	041.19	18	423	054.13	12	350
016.36	11	320-322	017.63	10	300-301	027.9	18	423	041.2	18	423	054.19	12	350
016.40	12	350	017.64	10	300-301	030.0	18	423	041.3	18	423	054.19	13	368
016.41	12	350	017.65	10	300-301	030.1	18	423	041.4	18	423	054.2	03	185-187
016.42	12	350	017.66	10	300-301	030.2	18	423	041.5	18	423	054.3	01	020
016.43	12	350	017.70	16	398-399	030.3	18	423	041.6	18	423	054.40	02	046-048
016.44	12	350	017.71	16	398-399	030.8	18	423	041.7	18	423	054.41	02	046-048
016.45	12	350	017.72	16	398-399	030.9	18	423	041.81	18	423	054.42	02	046-048
016.46	12	350	017.73	16	398-399	031.0	04	079-081	041.82	18	423	054.43	02	046-048
016.50	12	350	017.74	16	398-399	031.1	09	283-284	041.83	18	423	054.44	02	046-048
016.51	12	350	017.75	16	398-399	031.2	18	423	041.84	18	423	054.49	02	046-048
016.52	12	350	017.76	16	398-399	031.8	18	423	041.85	18	423	054.5	18	416-417
016.53	12	350	017.80	06	188-190	031.9	18	423	041.86	18	423	054.6	09	283-284
016.54	12	350	017.81	06	188-190	032.0	03	073-074	041.89	18	423	054.71	06	188-190
016.55	12	350	017.82	06	188-190	032.1	03	073-074	041.9	18	423	054.72	01	021
016.56	12	350	017.83	06	188-190	032.2	03	073-074	042	25	489-490	054.73	03	073-074
016.60	13	368	017.84	06	188-190	032.3	03	073-074	045.00	01	020	054.74	01	020
016.61	13	368	017.85	06	188-190	032.81	02	046-048	045.01	01	020	054.79	18	421-422
016.62	13	368	017.86	06	188-190	032.82	05	144-145	045.02	01	020	054.8	18	421-422
016.63	13	368	017.90	18	423	032.83	06	188-190	045.03	01	020	054.9	09	283-284
016.64	13	368	017.91	18	423	032.84	11	320-322	045.10	01	020	055.0	01	020
016.65	13	368	017.92	18	423	032.85	09	283-284	045.11	01	020	055.1	04	079-081
016.66	13	368	017.93	18	423	032.89	18	423	045.12	01	020	055.2	03	068-070
016.70	13	368	017.94	18	423	032.9	18	423	045.13	01	020	055.71	02	046-048
016.71	13	368	017.95	18	423	033.0	04	096-098	045.20	18	421-422	055.79	18	421-422
016.72	13	368	017.96	18	423	033.1	04	096-098	045.21	18	421-422	055.8	18	421-422
016.73	13	368	018.00	18	423	033.8	04	096-098	045.22	18	421-422	055.9	18	421-422
016.74	13	368	018.01	18	423	033.9	04	096-098	045.23	18	421-422	056.00	01	018-019
016.75	13	368	018.02	18	423	034.0	03	068-070	045.90	01	020	056.01	01	020
016.76	13	368	018.03	18	423	034.1	18	423	045.91	01	020	056.09	01	020
016.90	11	320-322	018.04	18	423	035	09	277-279	045.92	01	020	056.71	08	244-245
016.91	11	320-322	018.05	18	423	036.0	01	020	045.93	01	020	056.79	18	421-422
016.92	11	320-322	018.06	18	423	036.1	01	020	046.0	01	012	056.8	18	421-422
016.93	11	320-322	018.80	18	423	036.2	18	416-417	046.1	01	012	056.9	18	421-422
016.94	11	320-322	018.81	18	423	036.3	18	416-417	046.2	01	012	057.0	18	421-422
016.95	11	320-322	018.82	18	423	036.40	05	144-145	046.3	01	012	057.8	18	421-422
016.96	11	320-322	018.83	18	423	036.41	05	144-145	046.8	01	012	057.9	18	421-422
017.00	09	283-284	018.84	18	423	036.42	05	126	046.9	01	012	060.0	18	421-422
017.01	09	283-284	018.85	18	423	036.43	05	144-145	047.0	01	021	060.1	18	421-422
017.02	09	283-284	018.86	18	423	036.81	02	045	047.1	01	021	060.9	18	421-422
017.03	09	283-284	018.90	18	423	036.82	08	242	047.8	01	021	061	18	421-422
017.04	09	283-284	018.91	18	423	036.89	18	416-417	047.9	01	021	062.0	01	020
017.05	09	283-284	018.92	18	423	036.9	18	416-417	048	01	021	062.1	01	020
017.06	09	283-284	018.93	18	423	037	18	423	049.0	01	021	062.2	01	020
017.10	09	272-273	018.94	18	423	038.0	18	416-417	049.1	01	021	062.3	01	020
017.11	09	272-273	018.95	18	423	038.10	18	416-417	049.8	01	020	062.4	01	020
017.12	09	272-273	018.96	18	423	038.11	18	416-417	049.9	01	020	062.5	01	020
017.13	09	272-273	020.0	18	423	038.19	18	416-417	050.0	18	421-422	062.8	01	020
017.14	09	272-273	020.1	18	423	038.2	18	416-417	050.1	18	421-422	062.9	01	020
017.15	09	272-273	020.2	18	416-417	038.3	18	416-417	050.2	18	421-422	063.0	01	020
017.16	09	272-273	020.3	04	079-081	038.40	18	416-417	050.9	18	421-422	063.1	01	020
017.20	16	398-399	020.4	04	079-081	038.41	18	416-417	051.0	18	421-422	063.2	01	020
017.21	16	398-399	020.5	04	079-081	038.42	18	416-417	051.1	09	283-284	063.8	01	020
017.22	16	398-399	020.8	18	423	038.43	18	416-417	051.2	09	283-284	063.9	01	020
017.23	16	398-399	020.9	18	423	038.44	18	416-417	051.9	18	421-422	064	01	020
017.24	16	398-399	021.0	18	423	038.49	18	416-417	052.0	01	020	065.0	18	421-422
017.25	16	398-399	021.1	06	188-190	038.8	18	416-417	052.1	04	079-081	065.1	18	421-422
017.26	16	398-399	021.2	04	079-081	038.9	18	416-417	052.2	01	020	065.2	18	421-422
017.30	02	046-048	021.3	18	423	039.0	09	283-284	052.7	18	421-422	065.3	18	421-422
017.31	02	046-048	021.8	18	423	039.1	04	079-081	052.8	18	421-422	065.4	18	421-422
017.32	02	046-048	021.9	18	423	039.2	06	188-190	052.9	18	421-422	065.8	18	421-422
017.33	02	046-048	022.0	09	283-284	039.3	09	283-284	053.0	01	021	065.9	18	421-422

DX	MDC	DRG
066.0	18	421-422
066.1	18	421-422
066.2	01	020
066.3	18	421-422
066.40	18	421-422
066.41	18	421-422
066.42	18	421-422
066.49	18	421-422
066.8	18	421-422
066.9	18	421-422
070.0	07	205-206
070.71	07	205-206
070.1	07	205-206
070.20	07	205-206
070.21	07	205-206
070.22	07	205-206
070.23	07	205-206
070.30	07	205-206
070.31	07	205-206
070.32	07	205-206
070.33	07	205-206
070.41	07	205-206
070.42	07	205-206
070.43	07	205-206
070.44	07	205-206
070.49	07	205-206
070.51	07	205-206
070.52	07	205-206
070.53	07	205-206
070.54	07	205-206
070.59	07	205-206
070.6	07	205-206
070.70	07	205-206
070.71	07	205-206
070.9	07	205-206
071	01	020
072.0	12	350
072.1	01	021
072.2	01	020
072.3	07	204
072.71	07	205-206
072.72	01	018-019
072.79	18	421-422
072.8	18	421-422
072.9	18	421-422
073.0	04	079-081
073.7	18	421-422
073.8	18	421-422
073.9	18	421-422
074.0	03	068-070
074.1	04	089-091
074.20	05	144-145
074.21	05	144-145
074.22	05	135-137
074.23	05	144-145
074.3	18	421-422
074.8	18	421-422
075	18	421-422
076.0	02	046-048
076.1	02	046-048
076.9	02	046-048
077.0	02	046-048
077.1	02	046-048
077.2	02	046-048
077.3	02	046-048
077.4	02	046-048
077.8	02	046-048
077.98	02	046-048
077.99	02	046-048
078.0	09	283-284
078.10	09	283-284
078.11	09	283-284
078.19	09	283-284
078.2	18	421-422
078.3	16	398-399
078.4	18	421-422
078.5	18	421-422
078.6	11	320-322
078.7	18	421-422
078.81	01	034-035
078.82	06	182-184
078.88	18	421-422
078.89	18	421-422
079.0	18	421-422
079.1	18	421-422
079.2	18	421-422
079.3	18	421-422
079.4	18	421-422
079.50	18	421-422
079.51	18	421-422
079.52	18	421-422
079.53	18	421-422
079.59	18	421-422
079.6	18	421-422
079.81	18	421-422
079.88	18	421-422
079.89	18	421-422
079.98	18	421-422
079.99	18	421-422
080	18	423
081.0	18	423
081.1	18	423
081.2	18	423
081.9	18	423
082.0	18	423
082.1	18	423
082.2	18	423
082.3	18	423
082.40	18	423
082.41	18	423
082.49	18	423
082.8	18	423
082.9	18	423
083.0	18	423
083.1	18	423
083.2	18	423
083.8	18	423
083.9	18	423
084.0	18	423
084.1	18	423
084.2	18	423
084.3	18	423
084.4	18	423
084.5	18	423
084.6	18	423
084.7	18	423
084.8	18	423
084.9	18	423
085.0	18	423
085.1	09	283-284
085.2	09	283-284
085.3	09	283-284
085.4	09	283-284
085.5	09	283-284
085.9	18	423
086.0	05	144-145
086.1	18	423
086.2	18	423
086.3	18	423
086.4	18	423
086.5	18	423
086.9	18	423
087.0	18	423
087.1	18	423
087.9	18	423
088.0	18	423
088.81	18	423
088.82	18	423
088.89	18	423
088.9	18	423
090.0	18	423
090.1	18	423
090.2	18	423
090.3	02	046-048
090.40	01	020
090.41	01	020
090.42	01	020
090.49	01	020
090.5	18	423
090.6	18	423
090.7	18	423
090.9	18	423
091.0	12	350
091.0	13	368
091.1	06	188-190
091.2	18	423
091.3	09	283-284
091.4	16	398-399
091.50	02	046-048
091.51	02	046-048
091.52	02	046-048
091.61	08	238
091.62	07	205-206
091.69	06	188-190
091.7	18	423
091.81	01	020
091.82	09	283-284
091.89	18	423
091.9	18	423
092.0	18	423
092.9	18	423
093.0	05	135-137
093.1	05	135-137
093.20	05	126
093.21	05	135-137
093.22	05	135-137
093.23	05	135-137
093.24	05	135-137
093.81	05	144-145
093.82	05	144-145
093.89	05	144-145
093.9	05	144-145
094.0	01	012
094.1	01	012
094.2	01	020
094.3	01	020
094.81	01	020
094.82	01	012
094.83	02	046-048
094.84	02	046-048
094.85	01	012
094.86	03	073-074
094.87	01	034-035
094.89	01	012
094.9	01	012
095.0	02	046-048
095.1	04	079-081
095.2	06	188-190
095.3	07	205-206
095.4	11	320-322
095.5	08	238
095.6	08	248
095.7	08	248
095.8	18	423
095.9	18	423
096	18	423
097.0	18	423
097.1	18	423
097.9	18	423
098.0	12	350
098.0	13	368
098.10	12	350
098.10	13	368
098.11	11	320-322
098.12	12	350
098.13	12	350
098.14	12	350
098.15	13	368
098.16	13	368
098.17	13	368
098.19	12	350
098.19	13	368
098.2	12	350
098.2	13	368
098.30	11	320-322
098.31	11	320-322
098.32	12	350
098.33	12	350
098.34	12	350
098.35	13	368
098.36	13	368
098.37	13	368
098.39	12	350
098.39	13	368
098.40	02	046-048
098.41	02	046-048
098.42	02	046-048
098.43	02	046-048
098.49	02	046-048
098.50	08	242
098.51	08	242
098.52	08	242
098.53	08	238
098.59	08	242
098.6	03	068-070
098.7	06	188-190
098.81	02	046-048
098.82	01	020
098.83	05	144-145
098.84	05	126
098.85	05	144-145
098.86	06	188-190
098.89	18	423
099.0	12	350
099.0	13	368
099.1	12	350
099.1	13	368
099.2	12	350
099.2	13	368
099.3	08	240-241
099.40	12	350
099.40	13	368
099.41	12	350
099.41	13	368
099.49	12	350
099.49	13	368
099.50	12	350
099.50	13	368
099.51	03	068-070
099.52	06	188-190
099.53	12	350
099.53	13	368
099.54	11	320-322
099.55	12	350
099.55	13	368
099.56	06	188-190
099.59	12	350
099.59	13	368
099.8	12	350
099.8	13	368
099.9	12	350
099.9	13	368
100.0	18	423
100.81	01	020
100.89	01	020
100.9	18	423
101	03	068-070
102.0	09	283-284
102.1	09	283-284
102.2	09	283-284
102.3	09	283-284
102.4	09	283-284
102.5	03	073-074
102.6	08	242
102.7	18	423
102.8	18	423
102.9	18	423
103.0	09	283-284
103.1	09	283-284
103.2	18	423
103.3	09	283-284
103.9	18	423
104.0	18	423
104.8	18	423
104.9	18	423
110.0	09	283-284
110.1	09	283-284
110.2	09	283-284
110.3	09	283-284
110.4	09	283-284
110.5	09	283-284
110.6	09	283-284
110.8	09	283-284
110.9	09	283-284
111.0	09	283-284
111.1	09	283-284
111.2	09	283-284
111.3	09	283-284
111.8	09	283-284
111.9	09	283-284
112.0	03	185-187
112.1	13	368
112.2	12	350
112.2	13	368
112.3	09	283-284
112.4	04	079-081
112.5	18	423
112.81	05	126
112.82	03	073-074
112.83	01	020
112.84	06	182-184
112.85	06	182-184
112.89	18	423
112.9	18	423
114.0	04	079-081
114.1	09	283-284
114.2	01	020
114.3	18	423
114.4	04	079-081
114.5	04	079-081
114.9	18	423
115.00	18	423
115.01	01	020
115.02	02	046-048
115.03	05	144-145
115.04	05	126
115.05	04	079-081
115.09	18	423
115.10	18	423
115.11	01	020
115.12	02	046-048
115.13	05	144-145
115.14	05	126
115.15	04	079-081
115.19	18	423
115.90	18	423
115.91	01	020
115.92	02	046-048
115.93	05	144-145
115.94	05	126
115.95	04	079-081
115.99	18	423
116.0	18	423
116.1	18	423
116.2	18	423
117.0	18	423
117.1	18	423
117.2	18	423
117.3	18	423
117.4	18	423
117.5	18	423
117.6	18	423
117.7	18	423
117.8	18	423
117.9	18	423
118	18	423
120.0	11	320-322
120.1	07	205-206
120.2	18	423
120.3	09	283-284
120.8	18	423
120.9	18	423
121.0	07	205-206
121.1	07	205-206
121.2	04	079-081
121.3	07	205-206
121.4	07	205-206
121.5	18	423
121.6	18	423
121.8	18	423
121.9	18	423
122.0	07	205-206
122.1	04	079-081
122.2	10	300-301
122.3	18	423

DX ...MDC ..DRG	DX ...MDC ..DRG	DX ...MDC ..DRG	DX ...MDC ..DRG	DX ...MDC ..DRG
122.4 ...18 ..423	136.2 ...18 ..423	150.0 ...06 ..172-173	163.0 ...04 ..082	183.2 ...13 ..366-367
122.5 ...07 ..205-206	136.3 ...04 ..079-081	150.1 ...06 ..172-173	163.1 ...04 ..082	183.3 ...13 ..366-367
122.6 ...18 ..423	136.4 ...18 ..423	150.2 ...06 ..172-173	163.8 ...04 ..082	183.4 ...13 ..366-367
122.7 ...18 ..423	136.5 ...18 ..423	150.3 ...06 ..172-173	163.9 ...04 ..082	183.5 ...13 ..366-367
122.8 ...07 ..205-206	136.8 ...18 ..423	150.4 ...06 ..172-173	164.0 ...17 ..413-414	183.8 ...13 ..366-367
122.9 ...18 ..423	136.9 ...18 ..423	150.5 ...06 ..172-173	164.1 ...05 ..144-145	183.9 ...13 ..366-367
123.0 ...06 ..182-184	137.0 ...04 ..092-093	150.8 ...06 ..172-173	164.2 ...04 ..082	184.0 ...13 ..366-367
123.1 ...06 ..182-184	137.1 ...01 ..034-035	150.9 ...06 ..172-173	164.3 ...04 ..082	184.1 ...13 ..366-367
123.2 ...06 ..182-184	137.2 ...11 ..320-322	151.0 ...06 ..172-173	164.8 ...04 ..082	184.2 ...13 ..366-367
123.3 ...06 ..182-184	137.3 ...08 ..256	151.1 ...06 ..172-173	164.9 ...04 ..082	184.3 ...13 ..366-367
123.4 ...06 ..182-184	137.4 ...18 ..423	151.2 ...06 ..172-173	165.0 ...03 ..064	184.4 ...13 ..366-367
123.5 ...06 ..182-184	138 .....01 ..034-035	151.3 ...06 ..172-173	165.8 ...04 ..082	184.8 ...13 ..366-367
123.6 ...06 ..182-184	139.0 ...01 ..034-035	151.4 ...06 ..172-173	165.9 ...04 ..082	184.9 ...13 ..366-367
123.8 ...06 ..182-184	139.1 ...02 ..046-048	151.5 ...06 ..172-173	170.0 ...08 ..239	185 .....12 ..338,344,346-347
123.9 ...06 ..182-184	139.8 ...18 ..423	151.6 ...06 ..172-173	170.1 ...08 ..239	186.0 ...12 ..338,344,346-347
124 .....18 ..423	**Neoplasms**	151.8 ...06 ..172-173	170.2 ...08 ..239	186.9 ...12 ..338,344,346-347
125.0 ...18 ..423	140.0 ...03 ..064	151.9 ...06 ..172-173	170.3 ...08 ..239	187.1 ...12 ..338,344,346-347
125.1 ...18 ..423	140.1 ...03 ..064	152.0 ...06 ..172-173	170.4 ...08 ..239	187.2 ...12 ..338,344,346-347
125.2 ...18 ..423	140.3 ...03 ..064	152.1 ...06 ..172-173	170.5 ...08 ..239	187.3 ...12 ..338,344,346-347
125.3 ...18 ..423	140.4 ...03 ..064	152.2 ...06 ..172-173	170.6 ...08 ..239	187.4 ...12 ..338,344,346-347
125.4 ...18 ..423	140.5 ...03 ..064	152.3 ...06 ..172-173	170.7 ...08 ..239	187.5 ...12 ..338,344,346-347
125.5 ...18 ..423	140.6 ...03 ..064	152.8 ...06 ..172-173	170.8 ...08 ..239	187.6 ...12 ..338,344,346-347
125.6 ...18 ..423	140.8 ...03 ..064	152.9 ...06 ..172-173	170.9 ...08 ..239	187.7 ...12 ..338,344,346-347
125.7 ...18 ..423	140.9 ...03 ..064	153.0 ...06 ..172-173	171.0 ...08 ..239	187.8 ...12 ..338,344,346-347
125.9 ...18 ..423	141.0 ...03 ..064	153.1 ...06 ..172-173	171.2 ...08 ..239	187.9 ...12 ..338,344,346-347
126.0 ...06 ..182-184	141.1 ...03 ..064	153.2 ...06 ..172-173	171.3 ...08 ..239	188.0 ...11 ..318-319
126.1 ...06 ..182-184	141.2 ...03 ..064	153.3 ...06 ..172-173	171.4 ...08 ..239	188.1 ...11 ..318-319
126.2 ...06 ..182-184	141.3 ...03 ..064	153.4 ...06 ..172-173	171.5 ...08 ..239	188.2 ...11 ..318-319
126.3 ...06 ..182-184	141.4 ...03 ..064	153.5 ...06 ..164-165,172-173	171.6 ...08 ..239	188.3 ...11 ..318-319
126.8 ...06 ..182-184	141.5 ...03 ..064	153.6 ...06 ..172-173	171.7 ...08 ..239	188.4 ...11 ..318-319
126.9 ...06 ..182-184	141.6 ...03 ..064	153.7 ...06 ..172-173	171.8 ...08 ..239	188.5 ...11 ..318-319
127.0 ...06 ..182-184	141.8 ...03 ..064	153.8 ...06 ..172-173	171.9 ...08 ..239	188.6 ...11 ..318-319
127.1 ...06 ..182-184	141.9 ...03 ..064	153.9 ...06 ..172-173	172.0 ...09 ..272-273	188.7 ...11 ..318-319
127.2 ...06 ..182-184	142.0 ...03 ..064	154.0 ...06 ..172-173	172.1 ...02 ..046-048	188.8 ...11 ..318-319
127.3 ...06 ..182-184	142.1 ...03 ..064	154.1 ...06 ..172-173	172.2 ...09 ..272-273	188.9 ...11 ..318-319
127.4 ...06 ..182-184	142.2 ...03 ..064	154.2 ...06 ..172-173	172.3 ...09 ..272-273	189.0 ...11 ..318-319
127.5 ...06 ..182-184	142.8 ...03 ..064	154.3 ...06 ..172-173	172.4 ...09 ..272-273	189.1 ...11 ..318-319
127.6 ...06 ..182-184	142.9 ...03 ..064	154.8 ...06 ..172-173	172.5 ...09 ..272-273	189.2 ...11 ..318-319
127.7 ...06 ..182-184	143.0 ...03 ..064	155.0 ...07 ..199,203	172.6 ...09 ..272-273	189.3 ...11 ..318-319
127.8 ...18 ..423	143.1 ...03 ..064	155.1 ...07 ..199,203	172.7 ...09 ..272-273	189.4 ...11 ..318-319
127.9 ...06 ..182-184	143.8 ...03 ..064	155.2 ...07 ..199,203	172.8 ...09 ..272-273	189.8 ...11 ..318-319
128.0 ...18 ..423	143.9 ...03 ..064	156.0 ...07 ..199,203	172.9 ...09 ..272-273	189.9 ...11 ..318-319
128.1 ...18 ..423	144.0 ...03 ..064	156.1 ...07 ..199,203	173.0 ...09 ..283-284	190.0 ...02 ..046-048
128.8 ...18 ..423	144.1 ...03 ..064	156.2 ...07 ..199,203	173.1 ...02 ..046-048	190.1 ...02 ..046-048
128.9 ...18 ..423	144.8 ...03 ..064	156.8 ...07 ..199,203	173.2 ...09 ..283-284	190.2 ...02 ..046-048
129 .....06 ..182-184	144.9 ...03 ..064	156.9 ...07 ..199,203	173.3 ...09 ..283-284	190.3 ...02 ..046-048
130.0 ...01 ..020	145.0 ...03 ..064	157.0 ...07 ..199,203	173.4 ...09 ..283-284	190.4 ...02 ..046-048
130.1 ...02 ..046-048	145.1 ...03 ..064	157.1 ...07 ..199,203	173.5 ...09 ..283-284	190.5 ...02 ..046-048
130.2 ...02 ..046-048	145.2 ...03 ..064	157.2 ...07 ..199,203	173.6 ...09 ..283-284	190.6 ...02 ..046-048
130.3 ...05 ..144-145	145.3 ...03 ..064	157.3 ...07 ..199,203	173.7 ...09 ..283-284	190.7 ...02 ..046-048
130.4 ...04 ..079-081	145.4 ...03 ..064	157.4 ...07 ..199,203	173.8 ...09 ..283-284	190.8 ...02 ..046-048
130.5 ...07 ..205-206	145.5 ...03 ..064	157.8 ...07 ..199,203	173.9 ...09 ..283-284	190.9 ...02 ..046-048
130.7 ...18 ..423	145.6 ...03 ..064	157.9 ...07 ..199,203	174.0 ...09 ..274-275	191.0 ...01 ..010-011
130.8 ...18 ..423	145.8 ...03 ..064	158.0 ...17 ..413-414	174.1 ...09 ..274-275	191.1 ...01 ..010-011
130.9 ...18 ..423	145.9 ...03 ..064	158.8 ...06 ..172-173	174.2 ...09 ..274-275	191.2 ...01 ..010-011
131.00 ..12 ..350	146.0 ...03 ..064	158.9 ...06 ..172-173	174.3 ...09 ..274-275	191.3 ...01 ..010-011
131.00 ..13 ..368	146.1 ...03 ..064	159.0 ...06 ..172-173	174.4 ...09 ..274-275	191.4 ...01 ..010-011
131.01 ..13 ..368	146.2 ...03 ..064	159.1 ...17 ..400-404	174.5 ...09 ..274-275	191.5 ...01 ..010-011
131.02 ..12 ..350	146.3 ...03 ..064	159.8 ...06 ..172-173	174.6 ...09 ..274-275	191.6 ...01 ..010-011
131.02 ..13 ..368	146.4 ...03 ..064	159.9 ...06 ..172-173	174.8 ...09 ..274-275	191.7 ...01 ..010-011
131.03 ..12 ..350	146.5 ...03 ..064	160.0 ...03 ..064	174.9 ...09 ..274-275	191.8 ...01 ..010-011
131.09 ..12 ..350	146.6 ...03 ..064	160.1 ...03 ..064	175.0 ...09 ..274-275	191.9 ...01 ..010-011
131.09 ..13 ..368	146.7 ...03 ..064	160.2 ...03 ..064	175.9 ...09 ..274-275	192.0 ...01 ..010-011
131.8 ...18 ..423	146.8 ...03 ..064	160.3 ...03 ..064	176.0 ...09 ..283-284	192.1 ...01 ..010-011
131.9 ...18 ..423	146.9 ...03 ..064	160.4 ...03 ..064	176.1 ...09 ..283-284	192.2 ...01 ..010-011
132.0 ...09 ..283-284	147.0 ...03 ..064	160.5 ...03 ..064	176.2 ...03 ..064	192.3 ...01 ..010-011
132.1 ...09 ..283-284	147.1 ...03 ..064	160.8 ...03 ..064	176.3 ...06 ..172-173	192.8 ...01 ..010-011
132.2 ...09 ..283-284	147.2 ...03 ..064	160.9 ...03 ..064	176.4 ...04 ..082	192.9 ...01 ..010-011
132.3 ...09 ..283-284	147.3 ...03 ..064	161.0 ...03 ..064	176.5 ...17 ..401-404	193 .....10 ..300-301
132.9 ...09 ..283-284	147.8 ...03 ..064	161.1 ...03 ..064	176.8 ...09 ..283-284	194.0 ...10 ..300-301
133.0 ...09 ..283-284	147.9 ...03 ..064	161.2 ...03 ..064	176.9 ...09 ..283-284	194.1 ...10 ..300-301
133.8 ...09 ..283-284	148.0 ...03 ..064	161.3 ...03 ..064	179 .....13 ..366-367	194.3 ...10 ..300-301
133.9 ...09 ..283-284	148.1 ...03 ..064	161.8 ...03 ..064	180.0 ...13 ..366-367	194.4 ...01 ..010-011
134.0 ...09 ..283-284	148.2 ...03 ..064	161.9 ...03 ..064	180.1 ...13 ..366-367	194.5 ...01 ..010-011
134.1 ...09 ..283-284	148.3 ...03 ..064	162.0 ...04 ..082	180.8 ...13 ..366-367	194.6 ...01 ..010-011
134.2 ...09 ..283-284	148.8 ...03 ..064	162.2 ...04 ..082	180.9 ...13 ..366-367	194.8 ...10 ..300-301
134.8 ...09 ..283-284	148.9 ...03 ..064	162.3 ...04 ..082	181 .....13 ..366-367	194.9 ...10 ..300-301
134.9 ...09 ..283-284	149.0 ...03 ..064	162.4 ...04 ..082	182.0 ...13 ..366-367	195.0 ...03 ..064
135 .....04 ..092-093	149.1 ...03 ..064	162.5 ...04 ..082	182.1 ...13 ..366-367	195.1 ...04 ..082
136.0 ...18 ..423	149.8 ...03 ..064	162.8 ...04 ..082	182.8 ...13 ..366-367	195.2 ...06 ..172-173
136.1 ...08 ..240-241	149.9 ...03 ..064	162.9 ...04 ..082	183.0 ...13 ..366-367	195.3 ...12 ..346-347

DX	MDC	DRG
195.3	13	366-367
195.4	17	413-414
195.5	17	413-414
195.8	17	413-414
196.0	17	401-404
196.1	17	401-404
196.2	17	401-404
196.3	17	401-404
196.5	17	401-404
196.6	17	401-404
196.8	17	401-404
196.9	17	401-404
197.0	04	082
197.1	04	082
197.2	04	082
197.3	04	082
197.4	06	172-173
197.5	06	172-173
197.6	06	172-173
197.7	07	199,203
197.8	06	172-173
198.0	11	318-319
198.1	11	318-319
198.2	09	274-275
198.3	01	010-011
198.4	01	010-011
198.5	08	239
198.6	13	366-367
198.7	10	300-301
198.81	09	274-275
198.82	12	346-347
198.82	13	366-367
198.89	17	413-414
199.0	17	413-414
199.1	17	413-414
200.00	17	401-404
200.01	17	401-404
200.02	17	401-404
200.03	17	401-404
200.04	17	401-404
200.05	17	401-404
200.06	17	401-404
200.07	17	401-404
200.08	17	401-404
200.10	17	401-404
200.11	17	401-404
200.12	17	401-404
200.13	17	401-404
200.14	17	401-404
200.15	17	401-404
200.16	17	401-404
200.17	17	401-404
200.18	17	401-404
200.20	17	401-404
200.21	17	401-404
200.22	17	401-404
200.23	17	401-404
200.24	17	401-404
200.25	17	401-404
200.26	17	401-404
200.27	17	401-404
200.28	17	401-404
200.80	17	401-404
200.81	17	401-404
200.82	17	401-404
200.83	17	401-404
200.84	17	401-404
200.85	17	401-404
200.86	17	401-404
200.87	17	401-404
200.88	17	401-404
201.00	17	401-404
201.01	17	401-404
201.02	17	401-404
201.03	17	401-404
201.04	17	401-404
201.05	17	401-404
201.06	17	401-404
201.07	17	401-404
201.08	17	401-404
201.10	17	401-404
201.11	17	401-404
201.12	17	401-404
201.13	17	401-404
201.14	17	401-404
201.15	17	401-404
201.16	17	401-404
201.17	17	401-404
201.18	17	401-404
201.20	17	401-404
201.21	17	401-404
201.22	17	401-404
201.23	17	401-404
201.24	17	401-404
201.25	17	401-404
201.26	17	401-404
201.27	17	401-404
201.28	17	401-404
201.40	17	401-404
201.41	17	401-404
201.42	17	401-404
201.43	17	401-404
201.44	17	401-404
201.45	17	401-404
201.46	17	401-404
201.47	17	401-404
201.48	17	401-404
201.50	17	401-404
201.51	17	401-404
201.52	17	401-404
201.53	17	401-404
201.54	17	401-404
201.55	17	401-404
201.56	17	401-404
201.57	17	401-404
201.58	17	401-404
201.60	17	401-404
201.61	17	401-404
201.62	17	401-404
201.63	17	401-404
201.64	17	401-404
201.65	17	401-404
201.66	17	401-404
201.67	17	401-404
201.68	17	401-404
201.70	17	401-404
201.71	17	401-404
201.72	17	401-404
201.73	17	401-404
201.74	17	401-404
201.75	17	401-404
201.76	17	401-404
201.77	17	401-404
201.78	17	401-404
201.90	17	401-404
201.91	17	401-404
201.92	17	401-404
201.93	17	401-404
201.94	17	401-404
201.95	17	401-404
201.96	17	401-404
201.97	17	401-404
201.98	17	401-404
202.00	17	401-404
202.01	17	401-404
202.02	17	401-404
202.03	17	401-404
202.04	17	401-404
202.05	17	401-404
202.06	17	401-404
202.07	17	401-404
202.08	17	401-404
202.10	17	401-404
202.11	17	401-404
202.12	17	401-404
202.13	17	401-404
202.14	17	401-404
202.15	17	401-404
202.16	17	401-404
202.17	17	401-404
202.18	17	401-404
202.20	17	401-404
202.21	17	401-404
202.22	17	401-404
202.23	17	401-404
202.24	17	401-404
202.25	17	401-404
202.26	17	401-404
202.27	17	401-404
202.28	17	401-404
202.30	17	401-404
202.31	17	401-404
202.32	17	401-404
202.33	17	401-404
202.34	17	401-404
202.35	17	401-404
202.36	17	401-404
202.37	17	401-404
202.38	17	401-404
202.40	17	401-404
202.41	17	401-404
202.42	17	401-404
202.43	17	401-404
202.44	17	401-404
202.45	17	401-404
202.46	17	401-404
202.47	17	401-404
202.48	17	401-404
202.50	17	413-414
202.51	17	413-414
202.52	17	413-414
202.53	17	413-414
202.54	17	413-414
202.55	17	413-414
202.56	17	413-414
202.57	17	413-414
202.58	17	413-414
202.60	17	401-404
202.61	17	401-404
202.62	17	401-404
202.63	17	401-404
202.64	17	401-404
202.65	17	401-404
202.66	17	401-404
202.67	17	401-404
202.68	17	401-404
202.80	17	401-404
202.81	17	401-404
202.82	17	401-404
202.83	17	401-404
202.84	17	401-404
202.85	17	401-404
202.86	17	401-404
202.87	17	401-404
202.88	17	401-404
202.90	17	401-404
202.91	17	401-404
202.92	17	401-404
202.93	17	401-404
202.94	17	401-404
202.95	17	401-404
202.96	17	401-404
202.97	17	401-404
202.98	17	401-404
203.00	17	401-404
203.01	17	401-404
203.10	17	401-404
203.11	17	401-404
203.80	17	401-404
203.81	17	401-404
204.00	17	405,473
204.01	17	405,473
204.10	17	401-404
204.11	17	401-404
204.20	17	401-404
204.21	17	401-404
204.80	17	401-404
204.81	17	401-404
204.90	17	401-404
204.91	17	401-404
205.00	17	405,473
205.01	17	405,473
205.10	17	401-404
205.11	17	401-404
205.20	17	401-404
205.21	17	401-404
205.30	17	401-404
205.31	17	401-404
205.80	17	401-404
205.81	17	401-404
205.90	17	401-404
205.91	17	401-404
206.00	17	405,473
206.01	17	405,473
206.10	17	401-404
206.11	17	401-404
206.20	17	401-404
206.21	17	401-404
206.80	17	401-404
206.81	17	401-404
206.90	17	401-404
206.91	17	401-404
207.00	17	405,473
207.01	17	405,473
207.10	17	401-404
207.11	17	401-404
207.20	17	401-404
207.21	17	401-404
207.80	17	401-404
207.81	17	401-404
208.00	17	405,473
208.01	17	405,473
208.10	17	401-404
208.11	17	401-404
208.20	17	401-404
208.21	17	401-404
208.80	17	401-404
208.81	17	401-404
208.90	17	401-404
208.91	17	401-404
210.0	03	185-187
210.1	03	185-187
210.2	03	073-074
210.3	03	185-187
210.4	03	185-187
210.5	03	073-074
210.6	03	073-074
210.7	03	073-074
210.8	03	073-074
210.9	03	073-074
211.0	06	188-190
211.1	06	188-190
211.2	06	188-190
211.3	06	188-190
211.4	06	188-190
211.5	07	205-206
211.6	07	204
211.7	10	300-301
211.8	06	188-190
211.9	06	188-190
212.0	03	073-074
212.1	03	073-074
212.2	04	082
212.3	04	082
212.4	04	082
212.5	04	082
212.6	16	398-399
212.7	05	144-145
212.8	04	082
212.9	04	082
213.0	08	256
213.1	03	185-187
213.2	08	256
213.3	04	082
213.4	08	256
213.5	08	256
213.6	08	256
213.7	08	256
213.8	08	256
213.9	08	256
214.0	09	283-284
214.1	09	283-284
214.2	04	082
214.3	06	188-190
214.4	12	352
214.8	09	283-284
214.9	09	283-284
215.0	08	256
215.2	08	256
215.3	08	256
215.4	08	256
215.5	08	256
215.6	08	256
215.7	08	256
215.8	08	256
215.9	08	256
216.0	09	283-284
216.1	02	046-048
216.2	09	283-284
216.3	09	283-284
216.4	09	283-284
216.5	09	283-284
216.6	09	283-284
216.7	09	283-284
216.8	09	283-284
216.9	09	283-284
217	09	283-284
218.0	13	369
218.1	13	369
218.2	13	369
218.9	13	369
219.0	13	369
219.1	13	369
219.8	13	369
219.9	13	369
220	13	369
221.0	13	369
221.1	13	369
221.2	13	369
221.8	13	369
221.9	13	369
222.0	12	352
222.1	12	352
222.2	12	352
222.3	12	352
222.4	12	352
222.8	12	352
222.9	12	352
223.0	11	318-319
223.1	11	318-319
223.2	11	318-319
223.3	11	318-319
223.81	11	318-319
223.89	11	318-319
223.9	11	318-319
224.0	02	046-048
224.1	02	046-048
224.2	02	046-048
224.3	02	046-048
224.4	02	046-048
224.5	02	046-048
224.6	02	046-048
224.7	02	046-048
224.8	02	046-048
224.9	02	046-048
225.0	01	010-011
225.1	01	010-011
225.2	01	010-011
225.3	01	010-011
225.4	01	010-011
225.8	01	010-011
225.9	01	010-011
226	10	300-301
227.0	10	300-301
227.1	10	300-301
227.3	10	300-301
227.4	01	010-011
227.5	01	010-011
227.6	01	010-011
227.8	10	300-301
227.9	10	300-301
228.00	05	144-145
228.01	09	283-284
228.02	01	034-035
228.03	02	046-048

DX	MDC	DRG	DX	MDC	DRG	DX	MDC	DRG	DX	MDC	DRG	DX	MDC	DRG
228.04	06	182-184	238.6	17	401-404	250.43	11	331-333	259.1	10	300-301	274.81	08	244-245
228.09	05	144-145	238.71	16	398-399	250.50	02	046-048	259.2	10	300-301	274.82	08	244-245
228.1	16	398-399	238.72	16	395-396	250.51	02	046-048	259.3	10	300-301	274.89	08	244-245
229.0	16	398-399	238.73	16	395-396	250.52	02	046-048	259.4	10	300-301	274.9	08	244-245
229.8	17	413-414	238.74	16	395-396	250.53	02	046-048	259.5	10	300-301	275.0	10	299
229.9	17	413-414	238.75	16	395-396	250.60	01	018-019	259.8	10	300-301	275.1	10	299
230.0	03	064	238.76	17	403-404	250.61	01	018-019	259.9	10	300-301	275.2	10	296-298
230.1	06	172-173	238.79	17	403-404	250.62	01	018-019	260	10	296-298	275.3	10	299
230.2	06	172-173	238.8	17	413-414	250.63	01	018-019	261	10	296-298	275.40	10	296-298
230.3	06	172-173	238.9	17	413-414	250.70	05	130-131	262	10	296-298	275.41	10	296-298
230.4	06	172-173	239.0	06	172-173	250.71	05	130-131	263.0	10	296-298	275.42	10	296-298
230.5	06	172-173	239.1	04	082	250.72	05	130-131	263.1	10	296-298	275.49	10	296-298
230.6	06	172-173	239.2	08	256	250.73	05	130-131	263.2	10	296-298	275.8	10	299
230.7	06	172-173	239.3	09	276	250.80	10	294-295	263.8	10	296-298	275.9	10	299
230.8	07	199,203	239.4	11	318-319	250.81	10	294-295	263.9	10	296-298	276.0	10	296-298
230.9	06	172-173	239.5	11	318-319	250.82	10	294-295	264.0	02	046-048	276.1	10	296-298
231.0	03	064	239.6	01	010-011	250.83	10	294-295	264.1	02	046-048	276.2	10	296-298
231.1	04	082	239.7	10	300-301	250.90	10	294-295	264.2	02	046-048	276.3	10	296-298
231.2	04	082	239.8	17	413-414	250.91	10	294-295	264.3	02	046-048	276.4	10	296-298
231.8	04	082	239.9	17	413-414	250.92	10	294-295	264.4	02	046-048	276.50	10	296-298
231.9	04	082				250.93	10	294-295	264.5	02	046-048	276.51	10	296-298

Endocrine, Nutritional and Metabolic Diseases, and Immunity Disorders

DX	MDC	DRG	DX	MDC	DRG	DX	MDC	DRG
232.0	09	283-284	240.0	10	300-301	251.0	10	296-298
232.1	02	046-048	240.9	10	300-301	251.1	10	300-301
232.2	09	283-284	241.0	10	300-301	251.2	10	296-298
232.3	09	283-284	241.1	10	300-301	251.3	10	300-301
232.4	09	283-284	241.9	10	300-301	251.4	10	300-301
232.5	09	283-284	242.00	10	300-301	251.5	06	176
232.6	09	283-284	242.01	10	300-301	251.8	10	300-301
232.7	09	283-284	242.10	10	300-301	251.9	10	300-301
232.8	09	283-284	242.11	10	300-301	252.00	10	300-301
232.9	09	283-284	242.20	10	300-301	252.01	10	300-301
233.0	09	257-260,274-275	242.21	10	300-301	252.02	10	300-301
233.1	13	366-367	242.30	10	300-301	252.08	10	300-301
233.2	13	366-367	242.31	10	300-301	252.1	10	300-301
233.3	13	366-367	242.40	10	300-301	252.8	10	300-301
233.4	12	346-347	242.41	10	300-301	252.9	10	300-301
233.5	12	346-347	242.80	10	300-301	253.0	10	300-301
233.6	12	346-347	242.81	10	300-301	253.1	10	300-301
233.7	11	318-319	242.90	10	300-301	253.2	10	300-301
233.9	11	318-319	242.91	10	300-301	253.3	10	300-301
234.0	02	046-048	243	10	300-301	253.4	10	300-301
234.8	17	413-414	244.0	10	300-301	253.5	10	300-301
234.9	17	413-414	244.1	10	300-301	253.6	10	300-301
235.0	03	064	244.2	10	300-301	253.7	10	300-301
235.1	03	064	244.3	10	300-301	253.8	10	300-301
235.2	06	172-173	244.8	10	300-301	253.9	10	300-301
235.3	07	199,203	244.9	10	300-301	254.0	16	398-399
235.4	06	172-173	245.0	10	300-301	254.1	16	398-399
235.5	06	172-173	245.1	10	300-301	254.8	16	398-399
235.6	03	064	245.2	10	300-301	254.9	16	398-399
235.7	04	082	245.3	10	300-301	255.0	10	300-301
235.8	04	082	245.4	10	300-301	255.10	10	300-301
235.9	04	082	245.8	10	300-301	255.11	10	300-301
236.0	13	366-367	245.9	10	300-301	255.12	10	300-301
236.1	13	366-367	246.0	10	300-301	255.13	10	300-301
236.2	13	366-367	246.1	10	300-301	255.14	10	300-301
236.3	13	363,366-367	246.2	10	300-301	255.2	10	300-301
236.4	12	346-347	246.3	10	300-301	255.3	10	300-301
236.5	12	346-347	246.8	10	300-301	255.4	10	300-301
236.6	12	346-347	246.9	10	300-301	255.5	10	300-301
236.7	11	318-319	250.00	10	294-295	255.6	10	300-301
236.90	11	318-319	250.01	10	294-295	255.8	10	300-301
236.91	11	318-319	250.02	10	294-295	255.9	10	300-301
236.99	11	318-319	250.03	10	294-295	256.0	13	369
237.0	10	300-301	250.10	10	294-295	256.1	13	369
237.1	01	010-011	250.11	10	294-295	256.2	13	369
237.2	10	300-301	250.12	10	294-295	256.31	13	369
237.3	01	010-011	250.13	10	294-295	256.39	13	369
237.4	10	300-301	250.20	10	294-295	256.4	13	369
237.5	01	010-011	250.21	10	294-295	256.8	13	369
237.6	01	010-011	250.22	10	294-295	256.9	13	369
237.70	01	034-035	250.23	10	294-295	257.0	10	300-301
237.71	01	034-035	250.30	10	294-295	257.1	10	300-301
237.72	01	034-035	250.31	10	294-295	257.2	10	300-301
237.9	01	010-011	250.32	10	294-295	257.8	10	300-301
238.0	08	239	250.33	10	294-295	257.9	10	300-301
238.1	08	256	250.40	11	331-333	258.0	10	300-301
238.2	09	283-284	250.41	11	331-333	258.1	10	300-301
238.3	09	274-275	250.42	11	331-333	258.8	10	300-301
238.4	17	401-404				258.9	10	300-301
238.5	17	401-404				259.0	10	300-301

DX	MDC	DRG	DX	MDC	DRG
265.0	10	296-298	276.52	10	296-298
265.1	10	296-298	276.6	10	296-298
265.2	10	296-298	276.7	10	296-298
266.0	10	296-298	276.8	10	296-298
266.1	10	296-298	276.9	10	296-298
266.2	10	296-298	277.00	10	296-298
266.9	10	296-298	277.01	15	387,389
267	10	296-298	277.02	04	79, 80, 81
268.0	08	244-245	277.03	06	188-190
268.1	08	244-245	277.09	10	296-298
268.2	08	244-245	277.1	10	299
268.9	10	296-298	277.2	10	299
269.0	10	296-298	277.30	08	240-241
269.1	10	296-298	277.31	08	240-241
269.2	10	296-298	277.39	08	240-241
269.3	10	296-298	277.4	07	205-206
269.8	10	296-298	277.5	10	299
269.9	10	296-298	277.6	10	299
270.0	10	299	277.7	10	299
270.1	10	299	277.81	10	299
270.2	10	299	277.82	10	299
270.3	10	299	277.83	10	299
270.4	10	299	277.84	10	299
270.5	10	299	277.85	10	299
270.6	10	299	277.86	10	299
270.7	10	299	277.87	10	299
270.8	10	299	277.89	10	299
270.9	10	299	277.9	10	299
271.0	10	299	278.00	10	296-298
271.1	10	299	278.01	10	296-298
271.2	06	182-184	278.02	10	296-298
271.3	06	182-184	278.1	10	296-298
271.4	10	299	278.2	10	296-298
271.8	10	299	278.3	10	296-298
271.9	10	299	278.4	10	296-298
272.0	10	299	278.8	10	296-298
272.1	10	299	279.00	16	398-399
272.2	10	299	279.01	16	398-399
272.3	10	299	279.02	16	398-399
272.4	10	299	279.03	16	398-399
272.5	10	299	279.04	16	398-399
272.6	10	299	279.05	16	398-399
272.7	10	299	279.06	16	398-399
272.8	10	299	279.09	16	398-399
272.9	10	299	279.10	16	398-399
273.0	16	398-399	279.11	16	398-399
273.1	16	398-399	279.12	16	398-399
273.2	17	401-404	279.13	16	398-399
273.3	17	401-404	279.19	16	398-399
273.4	10	299	279.2	16	398-399
273.8	17	413-414	279.3	16	398-399
273.9	17	413-414	279.4	08	240-241
274.0	08	244-245	279.8	16	398-399
274.10	11	331-333	279.9	16	398-399
274.11	11	323-324			
274.19	11	331-333			

Diseases of the Blood and Blood Forming Organs

DX	MDC	DRG
280.0	16	395-396
280.1	16	395-396
280.8	16	395-396
280.9	16	395-396

DX	MDC	DRG	DX	MDC	DRG	DX	MDC	DRG	DX	MDC	DRG	DX	MDC	DRG
281.0	16	395-396	288.63	16	398-399	295.14	19	430	296.43	19	430	301.4	19	428
281.1	16	395-396	288.64	16	398-399	295.15	19	430	296.44	19	430	301.50	19	428
281.2	16	395-396	288.65	16	398-399	295.20	19	430	296.45	19	430	301.51	19	428
281.3	16	395-396	288.69	16	398-399	295.21	19	430	296.46	19	430	301.59	19	428
281.4	16	395-396	288.8	16	398-399	295.22	19	430	296.50	19	430	301.6	19	428
281.8	16	395-396	288.9	16	398-399	295.23	19	430	296.51	19	430	301.7	19	428
281.9	16	395-396	289.0	16	398-399	295.24	19	430	296.52	19	430	301.81	19	428
282.0	16	395-396	289.1	16	398-399	295.25	19	430	296.53	19	430	301.82	19	428
282.1	16	395-396	289.2	06	188-190	295.30	19	430	296.54	19	430	301.83	19	428
282.2	16	395-396	289.3	16	398-399	295.31	19	430	296.55	19	430	301.84	19	428
282.3	16	395-396	289.4	16	398-399	295.32	19	430	296.56	19	430	301.89	19	428
282.41	16	395-396	289.50	16	398-399	295.33	19	430	296.60	19	430	301.9	19	428
282.42	16	395-396	289.51	16	398-399	295.34	19	430	296.61	19	430	302.0	19	432
282.49	16	395-396	289.52	16	398-399	295.35	19	430	296.62	19	430	302.1	19	432
282.5	16	395-396	289.53	16	398-399	295.40	19	430	296.63	19	430	302.2	19	432
282.60	16	395-396	289.59	16	398-399	295.41	19	430	296.64	19	430	302.3	19	432
282.61	16	395-396	289.6	16	398-399	295.42	19	430	296.65	19	430	302.4	19	432
282.62	16	395-396	289.7	16	395-396	295.43	19	430	296.66	19	430	302.50	19	432
282.63	16	395-396	289.81	16	398-399	295.44	19	430	296.7	19	430	302.51	19	432
282.64	16	395-396	289.82	16	398-399	295.45	19	430	296.80	19	430	302.52	19	432
282.68	16	395-396	289.83	17	403-404	295.50	19	430	296.81	19	430	302.53	19	432
282.69	16	395-396	289.89	16	398-399	295.51	19	430	296.82	19	430	302.6	19	432
282.7	16	395-396	289.9	16	398-399	295.52	19	430	296.89	19	430	302.70	19	432
282.8	16	395-396				295.53	19	430	296.90	19	430	302.71	19	432
282.9	16	395-396	**Mental Disorders**			295.54	19	430	296.99	19	430	302.72	19	432
283.0	16	395-396	290.0	19	429	295.55	19	430	297.0	19	430	302.73	19	432
283.10	16	395-396	290.10	19	429	295.60	19	430	297.1	19	430	302.74	19	432
283.11	16	395-396	290.11	19	429	295.61	19	430	297.2	19	430	302.75	19	432
283.19	16	395-396	290.12	19	429	295.62	19	430	297.3	19	430	302.76	19	432
283.2	16	395-396	290.13	19	429	295.63	19	430	297.8	19	430	302.79	19	432
283.9	16	395-396	290.20	19	429	295.64	19	430	297.9	19	430	302.81	19	432
284.01	16	395-396	290.21	19	429	295.65	19	430	298.0	19	430	302.82	19	432
284.09	16	395-396	290.3	19	429	295.70	19	430	298.1	19	430	302.83	19	432
284.1	16	395-396	290.40	19	429	295.71	19	430	298.2	19	432	302.84	19	432
284.2	17	403-404	290.41	19	429	295.72	19	430	298.3	19	430	302.85	19	432
284.8	16	395-396	290.42	19	429	295.73	19	430	298.4	19	430	302.89	19	432
284.9	16	395-396	290.43	19	429	295.74	19	430	298.8	19	430	302.9	19	432
285.0	16	395-396	290.8	19	429	295.75	19	430	298.9	19	430	303.00	20	521-523
285.1	16	395-396	290.9	19	429	295.80	19	430	299.00	19	429	303.01	20	521-523
285.21	16	395-396	291.0	20	521-523	295.81	19	430	299.01	19	429	303.02	20	521-523
285.22	16	395-396	291.1	20	521-523	295.82	19	430	299.10	19	429	303.03	20	521-523
285.29	16	395-396	291.2	20	521-523	295.83	19	430	299.11	19	429	303.90	20	521-523
285.8	16	395-396	291.3	20	521-523	295.84	19	430	299.80	19	430	303.91	20	521-523
285.9	16	395-396	291.4	20	521-523	295.85	19	430	299.81	19	430	303.92	20	521-523
286.0	16	397	291.5	20	521-523	295.90	19	430	299.90	19	430	303.93	20	521-523
286.1	16	397	291.81	20	521-523	295.91	19	430	299.91	19	430	304.00	20	521-523
286.2	16	397	291.82	20	521-523	295.92	19	430	300.00	19	425	304.01	20	521-523
286.3	16	397	291.89	20	521-523	295.93	19	430	300.01	19	425	304.02	20	521-523
286.4	16	397	291.9	20	521-523	295.94	19	430	300.02	19	425	304.03	20	521-523
286.5	16	397	292.0	20	521-523	295.95	19	430	300.09	19	425	304.10	20	521-523
286.6	16	397	292.11	20	521-523	296.00	19	430	300.10	19	425	304.11	20	521-523
286.7	16	397	292.12	20	521-523	296.01	19	430	300.11	19	425	304.12	20	521-523
286.9	16	397	292.2	20	521-523	296.02	19	430	300.12	19	425	304.13	20	521-523
287.0	16	397	292.81	20	521-523	296.03	19	430	300.13	19	425	304.20	20	521-523
287.1	16	397	292.82	20	521-523	296.04	19	430	300.14	19	428	304.21	20	521-523
287.2	16	397	292.83	20	521-523	296.05	19	430	300.15	19	425	304.22	20	521-523
287.30	16	397	292.84	20	521-523	296.06	19	430	300.16	19	425	304.23	20	521-523
287.31	16	397	292.85	20	521-523	296.10	19	430	300.19	19	425	304.30	20	521-523
287.32	16	397	292.89	20	521-523	296.11	19	430	300.20	19	427	304.31	20	521-523
287.33	16	397	292.9	20	521-523	296.12	19	430	300.21	19	427	304.32	20	521-523
287.39	16	397	293.0	19	425	296.13	19	430	300.22	19	427	304.33	20	521-523
287.4	16	397	293.1	19	425	296.14	19	430	300.23	19	427	304.40	20	521-523
287.5	16	397	293.81	19	429	296.15	19	430	300.29	19	427	304.41	20	521-523
287.8	16	397	293.82	19	429	296.16	19	430	300.3	19	427	304.42	20	521-523
287.9	16	397	293.83	19	429	296.20	19	430	300.4	19	426	304.43	20	521-523
288.00	16	398-399	293.84	19	429	296.21	19	430	300.5	19	427	304.50	20	521-523
288.01	16	398-399	293.89	19	429	296.22	19	430	300.6	19	427	304.51	20	521-523
288.02	16	398-399	293.9	19	425	296.23	19	430	300.7	19	427	304.52	20	521-523
288.03	16	398-399	294.10	19	429	296.24	19	430	300.81	19	427	304.53	20	521-523
288.04	16	398-399	294.11	19	429	296.25	19	430	300.82	19	427	304.60	20	521-523
288.09	16	398-399	294.8	19	429	296.26	19	430	300.89	19	427	304.61	20	521-523
288.1	16	398-399	294.9	19	429	296.30	19	430	300.9	19	425	304.62	20	521-523
288.2	16	398-399	295.00	19	430	296.31	19	430	301.0	19	428	304.63	20	521-523
288.3	16	398-399	295.01	19	430	296.32	19	430	301.10	19	428	304.70	20	521-523
288.4	16	398-399	295.02	19	430	296.33	19	430	301.11	19	428	304.71	20	521-523
288.50	16	398-399	295.03	19	430	296.34	19	430	301.12	19	426	304.72	20	521-523
288.51	16	398-399	295.04	19	430	296.35	19	430	301.13	19	428	304.73	20	521-523
288.59	16	398-399	295.05	19	430	296.36	19	430	301.20	19	428	304.80	20	521-523
288.60	16	398-399	295.10	19	430	296.40	19	430	301.21	19	428	304.81	20	521-523
288.61	16	398-399	295.11	19	430	296.41	19	430	301.22	19	428	304.82	20	521-523
288.62	16	398-399	295.12	19	430	296.42	19	430	301.3	19	428	304.83	20	521-523
			295.13	19	430									

DX	MDC	DRG
304.90	.20	.521-523
304.91	.20	.521-523
304.92	.20	.521-523
304.93	.20	.521-523
305.00	.20	.521-523
305.01	.20	.521-523
305.02	.20	.521-523
305.03	.20	.521-523
305.1	.23	.467
305.20	.20	.521-523
305.21	.20	.521-523
305.22	.20	.521-523
305.23	.20	.521-523
305.30	.20	.521-523
305.31	.20	.521-523
305.32	.20	.521-523
305.33	.20	.521-523
305.40	.20	.521-523
305.41	.20	.521-523
305.42	.20	.521-523
305.43	.20	.521-523
305.50	.20	.521-523
305.51	.20	.521-523
305.52	.20	.521-523
305.53	.20	.521-523
305.60	.20	.521-523
305.61	.20	.521-523
305.62	.20	.521-523
305.63	.20	.521-523
305.70	.20	.521-523
305.71	.20	.521-523
305.72	.20	.521-523
305.73	.20	.521-523
305.80	.20	.521-523
305.81	.20	.521-523
305.82	.20	.521-523
305.83	.20	.521-523
305.90	.20	.521-523
305.91	.20	.521-523
305.92	.20	.521-523
305.93	.20	.521-523
306.0	.08	.248
306.1	.04	.101-102
306.2	.05	.144-145
306.3	.09	.283-284
306.4	.06	.182-184
306.50	.11	.331-333
306.51	.13	.369
306.52	.13	.369
306.53	.11	.331-333
306.59	.11	.331-333
306.6	.10	.300-301
306.7	.19	.427
306.8	.19	.432
306.9	.19	.427
307.0	.19	.432
307.1	.19	.428
307.20	.01	.034-035
307.21	.01	.034-035
307.22	.01	.034-035
307.23	.01	.034-035
307.3	.19	.432
307.40	.19	.432
307.41	.19	.432
307.42	.19	.432
307.43	.19	.432
307.44	.19	.432
307.45	.19	.432
307.46	.19	.432
307.47	.19	.432
307.48	.19	.432
307.49	.19	.432
307.50	.19	.432
307.51	.19	.432
307.52	.19	.431
307.53	.19	.427
307.54	.19	.432
307.59	.19	.432
307.6	.19	.431
307.7	.19	.431
307.80	.19	.427
307.81	.01	.024-026
307.89	.19	.427
307.9	.19	.427
308.0	.19	.425
308.1	.19	.425
308.2	.19	.425
308.3	.19	.425
308.4	.19	.425
308.9	.19	.425
309.0	.19	.426
309.1	.19	.426
309.21	.19	.427
309.22	.19	.427
309.23	.19	.427
309.24	.19	.427
309.28	.19	.427
309.29	.19	.427
309.3	.19	.427
309.4	.19	.427
309.81	.19	.427
309.82	.19	.427
309.83	.19	.427
309.89	.19	.427
309.9	.19	.427
310.0	.19	.429
310.1	.19	.429
310.2	.01	.024-026
310.8	.19	.429
310.9	.19	.429
311	.19	.426
312.00	.19	.431
312.01	.19	.431
312.02	.19	.431
312.03	.19	.431
312.10	.19	.431
312.11	.19	.431
312.12	.19	.431
312.13	.19	.431
312.20	.19	.431
312.21	.19	.431
312.22	.19	.431
312.23	.19	.431
312.30	.19	.431
312.31	.19	.428
312.32	.19	.428
312.33	.19	.431
312.34	.19	.428
312.35	.19	.428
312.39	.19	.428
312.4	.19	.431
312.81	.19	.431
312.82	.19	.431
312.89	.19	.431
312.9	.19	.431
313.0	.19	.427
313.1	.19	.427
313.21	.19	.431
313.22	.19	.431
313.23	.19	.431
313.3	.19	.431
313.81	.19	.431
313.82	.19	.431
313.83	.19	.431
313.89	.19	.431
313.9	.19	.431
314.00	.19	.431
314.01	.19	.431
314.1	.19	.431
314.2	.19	.431
314.8	.19	.431
314.9	.19	.431
315.00	.19	.431
315.01	.19	.431
315.02	.19	.431
315.09	.19	.431
315.1	.19	.431
315.2	.19	.431
315.31	.19	.431
315.32	.19	.431
315.39	.19	.431
315.4	.19	.431
315.5	.19	.431
315.8	.19	.431
315.9	.19	.431
316	.19	.429
317	.19	.429
318.0	.19	.429
318.1	.19	.429
318.2	.19	.429
319	.19	.429

Diseases of the Nervous System and Sense Organs

DX	MDC	DRG
320.0	.01	.020
320.1	.01	.020
320.2	.01	.020
320.3	.01	.020
320.7	.01	.020
320.81	.01	.020
320.82	.01	.020
320.89	.01	.020
320.9	.01	.020
321.0	.01	.020
321.1	.01	.020
321.2	.01	.020
321.3	.01	.020
321.4	.01	.020
321.8	.01	.020
322.0	.01	.020
322.1	.01	.020
322.2	.01	.020
322.9	.01	.020
323.01	.01	.020
323.02	.01	.020
323.1	.01	.020
323.2	.01	.020
323.41	.01	.020
323.42	.01	.020
323.51	.01	.020
323.52	.01	.020
323.61	.01	.020
323.62	.01	.020
323.63	.01	.020
323.71	.01	.034-035
323.72	.01	.034-035
323.81	.01	.020
323.82	.01	.020
323.9	.01	.020
324.0	.01	.020
324.1	.01	.020
324.9	.01	.020
325	.01	.034-035
326	.01	.034-035
327.00	.19	.432
327.01	.19	.432
327.02	.19	.432
327.09	.19	.432
327.10	.19	.432
327.11	.19	.432
327.12	.19	.432
327.13	.19	.432
327.14	.19	.432
327.15	.19	.432
327.19	.19	.432
327.20	.03	.073-074
327.21	.01	.034-035
327.22	.04	.099-100
327.23	.03	.073-074
327.24	.03	.073-074
327.25	.03	.073-074
327.26	.03	.073-074
327.27	.01	.034-035
327.29	.03	.073-074
327.30	.01	.034-035
327.31	.01	.034-035
327.32	.01	.034-035
327.33	.01	.034-035
327.34	.01	.034-035
327.35	.01	.034-035
327.36	.01	.034-035
327.37	.01	.034-035
327.39	.01	.034-035
327.40	.03	.073-074
327.41	.01	.034-035
327.42	.03	.073-074
327.43	.01	.034-035
327.44	.03	.073-074
327.49	.03	.073-074
327.51	.01	.034-035
327.52	.01	.034-035
327.53	.03	.073-074
327.59	.03	.073-074
327.8	.03	.073-074
330.0	.01	.012
330.1	.01	.012
330.2	.01	.012
330.3	.01	.012
330.8	.01	.012
330.9	.01	.012
331.0	.01	.012
331.11	.01	.012
331.19	.01	.012
331.2	.01	.012
331.3	.01	.012
331.4	.01	.012
331.7	.01	.012
331.81	.01	.034-035
331.82	.01	.012
331.83	.01	.012
331.89	.01	.012
331.9	.01	.012
332.0	.01	.012
332.1	.01	.012
333.0	.01	.012
333.1	.01	.034-035
333.2	.01	.034-035
333.3	.01	.034-035
333.4	.01	.012
333.5	.01	.012
333.6	.01	.012
333.71	.01	.012
333.72	.01	.034-035
333.79	.01	.034-035
333.81	.02	.046-048
333.82	.01	.034-035
333.83	.01	.034-035
333.84	.01	.034-035
333.85	.01	.034-035
333.89	.01	.034-035
333.90	.01	.012
333.91	.01	.034-035
333.92	.01	.034-035
333.93	.01	.034-035
333.99	.01	.012
334.0	.01	.013
334.1	.01	.013
334.2	.01	.013
334.3	.01	.013
334.4	.01	.013
334.8	.01	.013
334.9	.01	.013
335.0	.01	.012
335.10	.01	.012
335.11	.01	.012
335.19	.01	.012
335.20	.01	.012
335.21	.01	.012
335.22	.01	.012
335.23	.01	.012
335.24	.01	.012
335.29	.01	.012
335.8	.01	.012
335.9	.01	.012
336.0	.01	.012
336.1	.01	.034-035
336.2	.01	.034-035
336.3	.01	.034-035
336.8	.01	.034-035
336.9	.01	.034-035
337.0	.01	.018-019
337.1	.01	.018-019
337.20	.01	.018-019
337.21	.01	.018-019
337.22	.01	.018-019
337.29	.01	.018-019
337.3	.01	.018-019
337.9	.01	.018-019
338.0	.23	.463-464
338.11	.23	.463-464
338.12	.23	.463-464
338.18	.23	.463-464
338.19	.23	.463-464
338.21	.23	.463-464
338.22	.23	.463-464
338.28	.23	.463-464
338.29	.23	.463-464
338.3	.23	.463-464
338.4	.23	.463-464
340	.01	.013
341.0	.01	.013
341.1	.01	.013
341.20	.01	.020
341.21	.01	.020
341.22	.01	.020
341.8	.01	.013
341.9	.01	.013
342.00	.01	.012
342.01	.01	.012
342.02	.01	.012
342.10	.01	.012
342.11	.01	.012
342.12	.01	.012
342.80	.01	.012
342.81	.01	.012
342.82	.01	.012
342.90	.01	.012
342.91	.01	.012
342.92	.01	.012
343.0	.01	.009
343.1	.01	.009
343.2	.01	.009
343.3	.01	.034-035
343.4	.01	.009
343.8	.01	.034-035
343.9	.01	.034-035
344.00	.01	.009
344.01	.01	.009
344.02	.01	.009
344.03	.01	.009
344.04	.01	.009
344.09	.01	.009
344.1	.01	.009
344.2	.01	.009
344.30	.01	.034-035
344.31	.01	.034-035
344.32	.01	.034-035
344.40	.01	.034-035
344.41	.01	.034-035
344.42	.01	.034-035
344.5	.01	.034-035
344.60	.01	.018-019
344.61	.11	.331-333
344.81	.01	.034-035
344.89	.01	.034-035
344.9	.01	.034-035
345.00	.01	.024-026
345.01	.01	.024-026
345.10	.01	.024-026
345.11	.01	.024-026
345.2	.01	.024-026
345.3	.01	.024-026
345.40	.01	.024-026
345.41	.01	.024-026
345.50	.01	.024-026
345.51	.01	.024-026
345.60	.01	.024-026
345.61	.01	.024-026
345.70	.01	.024-026
345.71	.01	.024-026
345.80	.01	.024-026
345.81	.01	.024-026
345.90	.01	.024-026
345.91	.01	.024-026
346.00	.01	.024-026
346.01	.01	.024-026

DX ...MDC ..DRG	DX ...MDC ..DRG	DX ...MDC ..DRG	DX ...MDC ..DRG	DX ...MDC ..DRG
346.10 ..01 ..024-026	357.1 ...01 ..018-019	361.13 ..02 ..046-048	363.12 ..02 ..046-048	365.15 ..02 ..046-048
346.11 ..01 ..024-026	357.2 ...01 ..018-019	361.14 ..02 ..046-048	363.13 ..02 ..046-048	365.20 ..02 ..046-048
346.20 ..01 ..024-026	357.3 ...01 ..018-019	361.19 ..02 ..046-048	363.14 ..02 ..046-048	365.21 ..02 ..046-048
346.21 ..01 ..024-026	357.4 ...01 ..018-019	361.2 ..02 ..046-048	363.15 ..02 ..046-048	365.22 ..02 ..046-048
346.80 ..01 ..024-026	357.5 ...01 ..018-019	361.30 ..02 ..046-048	363.20 ..02 ..046-048	365.23 ..02 ..046-048
346.81 ..01 ..024-026	357.6 ...01 ..018-019	361.31 ..02 ..046-048	363.21 ..02 ..046-048	365.24 ..02 ..046-048
346.90 ..01 ..024-026	357.7 ...01 ..018-019	361.32 ..02 ..046-048	363.22 ..02 ..046-048	365.31 ..02 ..046-048
346.91 ..01 ..024-026	357.81 ..01 ..018-019	361.33 ..02 ..046-048	363.30 ..02 ..046-048	365.32 ..02 ..046-048
347.00 ..01 ..034-035	357.82 ..01 ..018-019	361.81 ..02 ..046-048	363.31 ..02 ..046-048	365.41 ..02 ..046-048
347.01 ..01 ..034-035	357.89 ..01 ..018-019	361.89 ..02 ..046-048	363.32 ..02 ..046-048	365.42 ..02 ..046-048
347.10 ..01 ..034-035	359.81 ..01 ..034-035	361.9 ..02 ..046-048	363.33 ..02 ..046-048	365.43 ..02 ..046-048
347.11 ..01 ..034-035	359.89 ..01 ..034-035	362.01 ..02 ..046-048	363.34 ..02 ..046-048	365.44 ..02 ..046-048
348.0 ..01 ..034-035	357.9 ...01 ..018-019	362.02 ..02 ..046-048	363.35 ..02 ..046-048	365.51 ..02 ..046-048
348.1 ..01 ..034-035	358.00 ..01 ..012	362.03 ..02 ..046-048	363.40 ..02 ..046-048	365.52 ..02 ..046-048
348.2 ..01 ..024-026	358.01 ..01 ..012	362.04 ..02 ..046-048	363.41 ..02 ..046-048	365.59 ..02 ..046-048
348.30 ..01 ..016-017	358.1 ...01 ..012	362.05 ..02 ..046-048	363.42 ..02 ..046-048	365.60 ..02 ..046-048
348.31 ..01 ..016-017	358.2 ...01 ..018-019	362.06 ..02 ..046-048	363.43 ..02 ..046-048	365.61 ..02 ..046-048
348.39 ..01 ..016-017	358.8 ...01 ..018-019	362.07 ..02 ..046-048	363.50 ..02 ..046-048	365.62 ..02 ..046-048
348.4 ..01 ..023	358.9 ...01 ..018-019	362.10 ..02 ..046-048	363.51 ..02 ..046-048	365.63 ..02 ..046-048
348.5 ..01 ..023	359.0 ...01 ..034-035	362.11 ..02 ..046-048	363.52 ..02 ..046-048	365.64 ..02 ..046-048
348.8 ..01 ..016-017	359.1 ...01 ..034-035	362.12 ..02 ..046-048	363.53 ..02 ..046-048	365.65 ..02 ..046-048
348.9 ..01 ..016-017	359.2 ...01 ..034-035	362.13 ..02 ..046-048	363.54 ..02 ..046-048	365.81 ..02 ..046-048
349.0 ..01 ..024-026	359.3 ...01 ..034-035	362.14 ..02 ..046-048	363.55 ..02 ..046-048	365.82 ..02 ..046-048
349.1 ..01 ..034-035	359.4 ...01 ..034-035	362.15 ..02 ..046-048	363.56 ..02 ..046-048	365.83 ..02 ..046-048
349.2 ..01 ..034-035	359.5 ...01 ..034-035	362.16 ..02 ..046-048	363.57 ..02 ..046-048	365.89 ..02 ..046-048
349.81 ..01 ..034-035	359.6 ...01 ..034-035	362.17 ..02 ..046-048	363.61 ..02 ..046-048	365.9 ..02 ..046-048
349.82 ..01 ..034-035	359.8 ...01 ..034-035	362.18 ..02 ..046-048	363.62 ..02 ..046-048	366.00 ..02 ..046-048
349.89 ..01 ..016-017	359.9 ...01 ..034-035	362.21 ..02 ..046-048	363.63 ..02 ..046-048	366.01 ..02 ..046-048
349.9 ..01 ..016-017	360.00 ..02 ..044	362.29 ..02 ..046-048	363.70 ..02 ..046-048	366.02 ..02 ..046-048
350.1 ...01 ..018-019	360.01 ..02 ..044	362.30 ..02 ..045	363.71 ..02 ..046-048	366.03 ..02 ..046-048
350.2 ...01 ..018-019	360.02 ..02 ..044	362.31 ..02 ..045	363.72 ..02 ..046-048	366.04 ..02 ..046-048
350.8 ...01 ..018-019	360.03 ..02 ..046-048	362.32 ..02 ..045	363.8 ...02 ..046-048	366.09 ..02 ..046-048
350.9 ...01 ..018-019	360.04 ..02 ..044	362.33 ..02 ..045	363.9 ...02 ..046-048	366.10 ..02 ..046-048
351.0 ...01 ..018-019	360.11 ..02 ..046-048	362.34 ..02 ..045	364.00 ..02 ..046-048	366.11 ..02 ..046-048
351.1 ...01 ..018-019	360.12 ..02 ..046-048	362.35 ..02 ..045	364.01 ..02 ..046-048	366.12 ..02 ..046-048
351.8 ...01 ..018-019	360.13 ..02 ..044	362.36 ..02 ..045	364.02 ..02 ..046-048	366.13 ..02 ..046-048
351.9 ...01 ..018-019	360.14 ..02 ..046-048	362.37 ..02 ..045	364.03 ..02 ..046-048	366.14 ..02 ..046-048
352.0 ...01 ..018-019	360.19 ..02 ..044	362.40 ..02 ..046-048	364.04 ..02 ..046-048	366.15 ..02 ..046-048
352.1 ...01 ..018-019	360.20 ..02 ..046-048	362.41 ..02 ..046-048	364.05 ..02 ..046-048	366.16 ..02 ..046-048
352.2 ...01 ..018-019	360.21 ..02 ..046-048	362.42 ..02 ..046-048	364.10 ..02 ..046-048	366.17 ..02 ..046-048
352.3 ...01 ..018-019	360.23 ..02 ..046-048	362.43 ..02 ..046-048	364.11 ..02 ..046-048	366.18 ..02 ..046-048
352.4 ...01 ..018-019	360.24 ..02 ..046-048	362.50 ..02 ..046-048	364.21 ..02 ..046-048	366.19 ..02 ..046-048
352.5 ...01 ..018-019	360.29 ..02 ..046-048	362.51 ..02 ..046-048	364.22 ..02 ..046-048	366.20 ..02 ..046-048
352.6 ...01 ..018-019	360.30 ..02 ..046-048	362.52 ..02 ..046-048	364.23 ..02 ..046-048	366.21 ..02 ..046-048
352.9 ...01 ..018-019	360.31 ..02 ..046-048	362.53 ..02 ..046-048	364.24 ..02 ..046-048	366.22 ..02 ..046-048
353.0 ...01 ..018-019	360.32 ..02 ..046-048	362.54 ..02 ..046-048	364.3 ...02 ..046-048	366.23 ..02 ..046-048
353.1 ...01 ..018-019	360.33 ..02 ..046-048	362.55 ..02 ..046-048	364.41 ..02 ..043	366.30 ..02 ..046-048
353.2 ...01 ..018-019	360.34 ..02 ..046-048	362.56 ..02 ..046-048	364.42 ..02 ..046-048	366.31 ..02 ..046-048
353.3 ...01 ..018-019	360.40 ..02 ..046-048	362.57 ..02 ..046-048	364.51 ..02 ..046-048	366.32 ..02 ..046-048
353.4 ...01 ..018-019	360.41 ..02 ..046-048	362.60 ..02 ..046-048	364.52 ..02 ..046-048	366.33 ..02 ..046-048
353.5 ...01 ..018-019	360.42 ..02 ..046-048	362.61 ..02 ..046-048	364.53 ..02 ..046-048	366.34 ..02 ..046-048
353.6 ...01 ..018-019	360.43 ..02 ..046-048	362.62 ..02 ..046-048	364.54 ..02 ..046-048	366.41 ..02 ..046-048
353.8 ...01 ..018-019	360.44 ..02 ..046-048	362.63 ..02 ..046-048	364.55 ..02 ..046-048	366.42 ..02 ..046-048
353.9 ...01 ..018-019	360.50 ..02 ..046-048	362.64 ..02 ..046-048	364.56 ..02 ..046-048	366.43 ..02 ..046-048
354.0 ...01 ..018-019	360.51 ..02 ..046-048	362.65 ..02 ..046-048	364.57 ..02 ..046-048	366.44 ..02 ..046-048
354.1 ...01 ..018-019	360.52 ..02 ..046-048	362.66 ..02 ..046-048	364.59 ..02 ..046-048	366.45 ..02 ..046-048
354.2 ...01 ..018-019	360.53 ..02 ..046-048	362.70 ..02 ..046-048	364.60 ..02 ..046-048	366.46 ..02 ..046-048
354.3 ...01 ..018-019	360.54 ..02 ..046-048	362.71 ..02 ..046-048	364.61 ..02 ..046-048	366.50 ..02 ..046-048
354.4 ...01 ..018-019	360.55 ..02 ..046-048	362.72 ..02 ..046-048	364.62 ..02 ..046-048	366.51 ..02 ..046-048
354.5 ...01 ..018-019	360.59 ..02 ..046-048	362.73 ..02 ..046-048	364.63 ..02 ..046-048	366.52 ..02 ..046-048
354.8 ...01 ..018-019	360.60 ..02 ..046-048	362.74 ..02 ..046-048	364.64 ..02 ..046-048	366.53 ..02 ..046-048
354.9 ...01 ..018-019	360.61 ..02 ..046-048	362.75 ..02 ..046-048	364.70 ..02 ..046-048	366.8 ...02 ..046-048
355.0 ...01 ..018-019	360.62 ..02 ..046-048	362.76 ..02 ..046-048	364.71 ..02 ..046-048	366.9 ...02 ..046-048
355.1 ...01 ..018-019	360.63 ..02 ..046-048	362.77 ..02 ..046-048	364.72 ..02 ..046-048	367.0 ...02 ..046-048
355.2 ...01 ..018-019	360.64 ..02 ..046-048	362.81 ..02 ..046-048	364.73 ..02 ..046-048	367.1 ...02 ..046-048
355.3 ...01 ..018-019	360.65 ..02 ..046-048	362.82 ..02 ..046-048	364.74 ..02 ..046-048	367.20 ..02 ..046-048
355.4 ...01 ..018-019	360.69 ..02 ..046-048	362.83 ..02 ..046-048	364.75 ..02 ..046-048	367.21 ..02 ..046-048
355.5 ...01 ..018-019	360.81 ..02 ..046-048	362.84 ..02 ..046-048	364.76 ..02 ..046-048	367.22 ..02 ..046-048
355.6 ...01 ..018-019	360.89 ..02 ..046-048	362.85 ..02 ..046-048	364.77 ..02 ..046-048	367.31 ..02 ..046-048
355.71 ..01 ..018-019	360.9 ...02 ..046-048	362.89 ..02 ..046-048	364.8 ...02 ..046-048	367.32 ..02 ..046-048
355.79 ..01 ..018-019	361.00 ..02 ..046-048	362.9 ...02 ..046-048	364.9 ...02 ..046-048	367.4 ...02 ..046-048
355.8 ...01 ..018-019	361.01 ..02 ..046-048	363.00 ..02 ..046-048	365.00 ..02 ..046-048	367.51 ..02 ..046-048
355.9 ...01 ..018-019	361.02 ..02 ..046-048	363.01 ..02 ..046-048	365.01 ..02 ..046-048	367.52 ..02 ..045
356.0 ...01 ..018-019	361.03 ..02 ..046-048	363.03 ..02 ..046-048	365.02 ..02 ..046-048	367.53 ..02 ..046-048
356.1 ...01 ..018-019	361.04 ..02 ..046-048	363.04 ..02 ..046-048	365.03 ..02 ..046-048	367.81 ..02 ..046-048
356.2 ...01 ..018-019	361.05 ..02 ..046-048	363.05 ..02 ..046-048	365.04 ..02 ..046-048	367.89 ..02 ..046-048
356.3 ...01 ..034-035	361.06 ..02 ..046-048	363.06 ..02 ..046-048	365.10 ..02 ..046-048	367.9 ...02 ..046-048
356.4 ...01 ..018-019	361.07 ..02 ..046-048	363.07 ..02 ..046-048	365.11 ..02 ..046-048	368.00 ..02 ..046-048
356.8 ...01 ..018-019	361.10 ..02 ..046-048	363.08 ..02 ..046-048	365.12 ..02 ..045	368.01 ..02 ..046-048
356.9 ...01 ..018-019	361.11 ..02 ..046-048	363.10 ..02 ..046-048	365.13 ..02 ..046-048	368.02 ..02 ..046-048
357.0 ...01 ..020	361.12 ..02 ..046-048	363.11 ..02 ..046-048	365.14 ..02 ..046-048	368.03 ..02 ..046-048

DX ...MDC ..DRG	DX ...MDC ..DRG	DX ...MDC ..DRG	DX ...MDC ..DRG	DX ...MDC ..DRG
368.10 ..02 ..046-048	370.02 ..02 ..046-048	371.9 ...02 ..046-048	374.41 ..02 ..046-048	376.52 ..02 ..046-048
368.11 ..02 ..045	370.03 ..02 ..044	372.00 ..02 ..046-048	374.43 ..02 ..046-048	376.6 ...02 ..046-048
368.12 ..02 ..045	370.04 ..02 ..044	372.01 ..02 ..046-048	374.44 ..02 ..046-048	376.81 ..02 ..046-048
368.13 ..02 ..046-048	370.05 ..02 ..044	372.02 ..02 ..046-048	374.45 ..02 ..045	376.82 ..02 ..045
368.14 ..02 ..046-048	370.06 ..02 ..044	372.03 ..02 ..046-048	374.46 ..02 ..046-048	376.89 ..02 ..046-048
368.15 ..02 ..046-048	370.07 ..02 ..046-048	372.04 ..02 ..046-048	374.50 ..02 ..046-048	376.9 ...02 ..046-048
368.16 ..02 ..046-048	370.20 ..02 ..046-048	372.05 ..02 ..046-048	374.51 ..09 ..283-284	377.00 ..01 ..034-035
368.2 ...02 ..045	370.21 ..02 ..046-048	372.10 ..02 ..046-048	374.52 ..02 ..046-048	377.01 ..01 ..034-035
368.30 ..02 ..046-048	370.22 ..02 ..046-048	372.11 ..02 ..046-048	374.53 ..02 ..046-048	377.02 ..02 ..046-048
368.31 ..02 ..046-048	370.23 ..02 ..046-048	372.12 ..02 ..046-048	374.54 ..02 ..046-048	377.03 ..02 ..046-048
368.32 ..02 ..046-048	370.24 ..02 ..046-048	372.13 ..02 ..046-048	374.55 ..02 ..046-048	377.04 ..01 ..034-035
368.33 ..02 ..046-048	370.31 ..02 ..046-048	372.14 ..02 ..046-048	374.56 ..02 ..046-048	377.10 ..02 ..045
368.34 ..02 ..046-048	370.32 ..02 ..046-048	372.15 ..02 ..046-048	374.81 ..02 ..046-048	377.11 ..02 ..045
368.40 ..02 ..045	370.33 ..02 ..046-048	372.20 ..02 ..046-048	374.82 ..02 ..046-048	377.12 ..02 ..045
368.41 ..02 ..045	370.34 ..02 ..046-048	372.21 ..02 ..046-048	374.83 ..02 ..046-048	377.13 ..02 ..046-048
368.42 ..02 ..046-048	370.35 ..02 ..046-048	372.22 ..02 ..046-048	374.84 ..02 ..046-048	377.14 ..02 ..046-048
368.43 ..02 ..045	370.40 ..02 ..046-048	372.30 ..02 ..046-048	374.85 ..02 ..046-048	377.15 ..02 ..045
368.44 ..02 ..045	370.44 ..02 ..046-048	372.31 ..02 ..046-048	374.86 ..02 ..046-048	377.16 ..02 ..045
368.45 ..02 ..045	370.49 ..02 ..046-048	372.33 ..02 ..046-048	374.87 ..02 ..046-048	377.21 ..02 ..045
368.46 ..02 ..045	370.50 ..02 ..046-048	372.39 ..02 ..046-048	374.89 ..02 ..046-048	377.22 ..02 ..046-048
368.47 ..02 ..045	370.52 ..02 ..046-048	372.40 ..02 ..046-048	374.9 ...02 ..046-048	377.23 ..02 ..046-048
368.51 ..02 ..046-048	370.54 ..02 ..046-048	372.41 ..02 ..046-048	375.00 ..02 ..046-048	377.24 ..02 ..045
368.52 ..02 ..046-048	370.55 ..02 ..044	372.42 ..02 ..046-048	375.01 ..02 ..044	377.30 ..02 ..045
368.53 ..02 ..046-048	370.59 ..02 ..046-048	372.43 ..02 ..046-048	375.02 ..02 ..044	377.31 ..02 ..045
368.54 ..02 ..046-048	370.60 ..02 ..046-048	372.44 ..02 ..046-048	375.03 ..02 ..046-048	377.32 ..02 ..045
368.55 ..02 ..045	370.61 ..02 ..046-048	372.45 ..02 ..046-048	375.11 ..02 ..046-048	377.33 ..02 ..045
368.59 ..02 ..046-048	370.62 ..02 ..046-048	372.50 ..02 ..046-048	375.12 ..02 ..046-048	377.34 ..02 ..045
368.60 ..02 ..046-048	370.63 ..02 ..046-048	372.51 ..02 ..046-048	375.13 ..02 ..046-048	377.39 ..02 ..045
368.61 ..02 ..046-048	370.64 ..02 ..046-048	372.52 ..02 ..046-048	375.14 ..02 ..046-048	377.41 ..02 ..045
368.62 ..02 ..046-048	370.8 ...02 ..046-048	372.53 ..02 ..046-048	375.15 ..02 ..046-048	377.42 ..02 ..045
368.63 ..02 ..046-048	370.9 ...02 ..046-048	372.54 ..02 ..046-048	375.16 ..02 ..046-048	377.43 ..02 ..045
368.69 ..02 ..046-048	371.00 ..02 ..046-048	372.55 ..02 ..046-048	375.20 ..02 ..046-048	377.49 ..02 ..045
368.8 ...02 ..046-048	371.01 ..02 ..046-048	372.56 ..02 ..046-048	375.21 ..02 ..046-048	377.51 ..01 ..034-035
368.9 ...02 ..046-048	371.02 ..02 ..046-048	372.61 ..02 ..046-048	375.22 ..02 ..046-048	377.52 ..01 ..034-035
369.00 ..02 ..046-048	371.03 ..02 ..046-048	372.62 ..02 ..046-048	375.30 ..02 ..046-048	377.53 ..01 ..034-035
369.01 ..02 ..046-048	371.04 ..02 ..046-048	372.63 ..02 ..046-048	375.31 ..02 ..044	377.54 ..01 ..034-035
369.02 ..02 ..046-048	371.05 ..02 ..046-048	372.64 ..02 ..046-048	375.32 ..02 ..044	377.61 ..01 ..034-035
369.03 ..02 ..046-048	371.10 ..02 ..046-048	372.71 ..02 ..046-048	375.33 ..02 ..046-048	377.62 ..01 ..034-035
369.04 ..02 ..046-048	371.11 ..02 ..046-048	372.72 ..02 ..046-048	375.41 ..02 ..046-048	377.63 ..01 ..034-035
369.05 ..02 ..046-048	371.12 ..02 ..046-048	372.73 ..02 ..046-048	375.42 ..02 ..046-048	377.71 ..01 ..034-035
369.06 ..02 ..046-048	371.13 ..02 ..046-048	372.74 ..02 ..046-048	375.43 ..02 ..046-048	377.72 ..01 ..034-035
369.07 ..02 ..046-048	371.14 ..02 ..046-048	372.75 ..02 ..046-048	375.51 ..02 ..046-048	377.73 ..01 ..034-035
369.08 ..02 ..046-048	371.15 ..02 ..046-048	372.81 ..02 ..046-048	375.52 ..02 ..046-048	377.75 ..01 ..034-035
369.10 ..02 ..046-048	371.16 ..02 ..046-048	327.89 ..02 ..046-048	375.53 ..02 ..046-048	377.9 ...01 ..034-035
369.11 ..02 ..046-048	371.20 ..02 ..046-048	372.9 ...02 ..046-048	375.54 ..02 ..046-048	378.00 ..02 ..046-048
369.12 ..02 ..046-048	371.21 ..02 ..046-048	373.00 ..02 ..046-048	375.55 ..02 ..046-048	378.01 ..02 ..046-048
369.13 ..02 ..046-048	371.22 ..02 ..046-048	373.01 ..02 ..046-048	375.56 ..02 ..046-048	378.02 ..02 ..046-048
369.14 ..02 ..046-048	371.23 ..02 ..046-048	373.02 ..02 ..046-048	375.57 ..02 ..046-048	378.03 ..02 ..046-048
369.15 ..02 ..046-048	371.24 ..02 ..046-048	373.11 ..02 ..046-048	375.61 ..02 ..046-048	378.04 ..02 ..046-048
369.16 ..02 ..046-048	371.30 ..02 ..046-048	373.12 ..02 ..046-048	375.69 ..02 ..046-048	378.05 ..02 ..046-048
369.17 ..02 ..046-048	371.31 ..02 ..046-048	373.13 ..02 ..046-048	375.81 ..02 ..046-048	378.06 ..02 ..046-048
369.18 ..02 ..046-048	371.32 ..02 ..046-048	373.2 ...02 ..046-048	375.89 ..02 ..046-048	378.07 ..02 ..046-048
369.20 ..02 ..046-048	371.33 ..02 ..046-048	373.31 ..02 ..046-048	375.9 ...02 ..046-048	378.08 ..02 ..046-048
369.21 ..02 ..046-048	371.40 ..02 ..046-048	373.32 ..02 ..046-048	376.00 ..02 ..046-048	378.10 ..02 ..046-048
369.22 ..02 ..046-048	371.41 ..02 ..046-048	373.33 ..02 ..046-048	376.01 ..02 ..044	378.11 ..02 ..046-048
369.23 ..02 ..046-048	371.42 ..02 ..046-048	373.34 ..02 ..046-048	376.02 ..02 ..044	378.12 ..02 ..046-048
369.24 ..02 ..046-048	371.43 ..02 ..046-048	373.4 ...02 ..046-048	376.03 ..02 ..044	378.13 ..02 ..046-048
369.25 ..02 ..046-048	371.44 ..02 ..046-048	373.5 ...02 ..046-048	376.04 ..02 ..044	378.14 ..02 ..046-048
369.3 ...02 ..046-048	371.45 ..02 ..046-048	373.6 ...02 ..046-048	376.10 ..02 ..046-048	378.15 ..02 ..046-048
369.4 ...02 ..046-048	371.46 ..02 ..046-048	373.8 ...02 ..046-048	376.11 ..02 ..046-048	378.16 ..02 ..046-048
369.60 ..02 ..046-048	371.48 ..02 ..046-048	373.9 ...02 ..046-048	376.12 ..02 ..046-048	378.17 ..02 ..046-048
369.61 ..02 ..046-048	371.49 ..02 ..046-048	374.00 ..02 ..046-048	376.13 ..02 ..046-048	378.18 ..02 ..046-048
369.62 ..02 ..046-048	371.50 ..02 ..046-048	374.01 ..02 ..046-048	376.21 ..02 ..046-048	378.20 ..02 ..046-048
369.63 ..02 ..046-048	371.51 ..02 ..046-048	374.02 ..02 ..046-048	376.22 ..02 ..046-048	378.21 ..02 ..046-048
369.64 ..02 ..046-048	371.52 ..02 ..046-048	374.03 ..02 ..046-048	376.30 ..02 ..046-048	378.22 ..02 ..046-048
369.65 ..02 ..046-048	371.53 ..02 ..046-048	374.04 ..02 ..046-048	376.31 ..02 ..046-048	378.23 ..02 ..046-048
369.66 ..02 ..046-048	371.54 ..02 ..046-048	374.05 ..02 ..046-048	376.32 ..02 ..046-048	378.24 ..02 ..046-048
369.67 ..02 ..046-048	371.55 ..02 ..046-048	374.10 ..02 ..046-048	376.33 ..02 ..046-048	378.30 ..02 ..046-048
369.68 ..02 ..046-048	371.56 ..02 ..046-048	374.11 ..02 ..046-048	376.34 ..02 ..045	378.31 ..02 ..046-048
369.69 ..02 ..046-048	371.57 ..02 ..046-048	374.12 ..02 ..046-048	376.35 ..02 ..045	378.32 ..02 ..046-048
369.70 ..02 ..046-048	371.58 ..02 ..046-048	374.13 ..02 ..046-048	376.36 ..02 ..045	378.33 ..02 ..046-048
369.71 ..02 ..046-048	371.60 ..02 ..046-048	374.14 ..02 ..046-048	376.40 ..02 ..046-048	378.34 ..02 ..046-048
369.72 ..02 ..046-048	371.61 ..02 ..046-048	374.20 ..02 ..046-048	376.41 ..02 ..046-048	378.35 ..02 ..046-048
369.73 ..02 ..046-048	371.62 ..02 ..046-048	374.21 ..02 ..046-048	376.42 ..02 ..046-048	378.40 ..02 ..046-048
369.74 ..02 ..046-048	371.70 ..02 ..046-048	374.22 ..02 ..046-048	376.43 ..02 ..046-048	378.41 ..02 ..046-048
369.75 ..02 ..046-048	371.71 ..02 ..046-048	374.23 ..02 ..046-048	376.44 ..02 ..046-048	378.42 ..02 ..046-048
369.76 ..02 ..046-048	371.72 ..02 ..046-048	374.30 ..02 ..045	376.45 ..02 ..046-048	378.43 ..02 ..046-048
369.8 ...02 ..046-048	371.73 ..02 ..046-048	374.31 ..02 ..045	376.46 ..02 ..046-048	378.44 ..02 ..046-048
369.9 ...02 ..046-048	371.81 ..02 ..046-048	374.32 ..02 ..045	376.47 ..02 ..046-048	378.45 ..02 ..046-048
370.00 ..02 ..044	371.82 ..02 ..046-048	374.33 ..02 ..046-048	376.50 ..02 ..046-048	378.50 ..02 ..045
370.01 ..02 ..046-048	371.89 ..02 ..046-048	374.34 ..02 ..046-048	376.51 ..02 ..046-048	378.51 ..02 ..045

DX ...MDC ..DRG	DX ...MDC ..DRG	DX ...MDC ..DRG	DX ...MDC ..DRG	DX ...MDC ..DRG
378.52 ..02 ..045	380.12 ..03 ..073-074	385.02 ..03 ..073-074	389.00 ..03 ..073-074	405.99 ..05 ..134
378.53 ..02 ..045	380.13 ..03 ..073-074	385.03 ..03 ..073-074	389.01 ..03 ..073-074	410.00 ..05 ..144-145
378.54 ..02 ..045	380.14 ..03 ..073-074	385.09 ..03 ..073-074	389.02 ..03 ..073-074	410.01 ..05 ..121-123
378.55 ..02 ..045	380.15 ..03 ..073-074	385.10 ..03 ..073-074	389.03 ..03 ..073-074	410.02 ..05 ..144-145
378.56 ..02 ..045	380.16 ..03 ..073-074	385.11 ..03 ..073-074	389.04 ..03 ..073-074	410.10 ..05 ..144-145
378.60 ..02 ..046-048	380.21 ..03 ..073-074	385.12 ..03 ..073-074	389.08 ..03 ..073-074	410.11 ..05 ..121-123
378.61 ..02 ..046-048	380.22 ..03 ..073-074	385.13 ..03 ..073-074	389.10 ..03 ..073-074	410.12 ..05 ..144-145
378.62 ..02 ..046-048	380.23 ..03 ..073-074	385.19 ..03 ..073-074	389.11 ..03 ..073-074	410.20 ..05 ..144-145
378.63 ..02 ..046-048	380.30 ..03 ..073-074	385.21 ..03 ..073-074	389.12 ..03 ..073-074	410.21 ..05 ..121-123
378.71 ..02 ..046-048	380.31 ..03 ..073-074	385.22 ..03 ..073-074	389.14 ..03 ..073-074	410.22 ..05 ..144-145
378.72 ..02 ..045	380.32 ..03 ..073-074	385.23 ..03 ..073-074	389.15 ..03 ..073-074	410.30 ..05 ..144-145
378.73 ..02 ..045	380.39 ..03 ..073-074	385.24 ..03 ..073-074	389.16 ..03 ..073-074	410.31 ..05 ..121-123
378.81 ..02 ..046-048	380.4 ...03 ..073-074	385.30 ..03 ..073-074	389.18 ..03 ..073-074	410.32 ..05 ..144-145
378.82 ..02 ..046-048	380.50 ..03 ..073-074	385.31 ..03 ..073-074	389.2 ...03 ..073-074	410.40 ..05 ..144-145
378.83 ..02 ..046-048	380.51 ..03 ..073-074	385.32 ..03 ..073-074	389.7 ...03 ..073-074	410.41 ..05 ..121-123
378.84 ..02 ..046-048	380.52 ..03 ..073-074	385.33 ..03 ..073-074	389.8 ...03 ..073-074	410.42 ..05 ..144-145
378.85 ..02 ..046-048	380.53 ..03 ..073-074	385.35 ..03 ..073-074	389.9 ...03 ..073-074	410.50 ..05 ..144-145
378.86 ..01 ..034-035	380.81 ..03 ..073-074	385.82 ..03 ..073-074		410.51 ..05 ..121-123
378.87 ..02 ..045	380.89 ..03 ..073-074	385.83 ..03 ..073-074	**Diseases of the Circulatory**	410.52 ..05 ..144-145
378.9 ...02 ..046-048	380.9 ...03 ..073-074	385.89 ..03 ..073-074	**System**	410.60 ..05 ..144-145
379.00 ..02 ..046-048	381.00 ..03 ..068-070	385.9 ...03 ..073-074	390 .....08 ..240-241	410.61 ..05 ..121-123
379.01 ..02 ..046-048	381.01 ..03 ..068-070	386.00 ..03 ..065	391.0 ...05 ..144-145	410.62 ..05 ..144-145
379.02 ..02 ..046-048	381.02 ..03 ..068-070	386.01 ..03 ..065	391.1 ...05 ..135-137	410.70 ..05 ..144-145
379.03 ..02 ..046-048	381.03 ..03 ..068-070	386.02 ..03 ..065	391.2 ...05 ..144-145	410.71 ..05 ..121-123
379.04 ..02 ..046-048	381.04 ..03 ..068-070	386.03 ..03 ..065	391.8 ...05 ..144-145	410.72 ..05 ..144-145
379.05 ..02 ..046-048	381.05 ..03 ..068-070	386.04 ..03 ..065	391.9 ...05 ..144-145	410.80 ..05 ..144-145
379.06 ..02 ..046-048	381.06 ..03 ..068-070	386.10 ..03 ..065	392.0 ...05 ..144-145	410.81 ..05 ..121-123
379.07 ..02 ..046-048	381.10 ..03 ..068-070	386.11 ..03 ..065	392.9 ...05 ..144-145	410.82 ..05 ..144-145
379.09 ..02 ..046-048	381.19 ..03 ..068-070	386.12 ..03 ..065	393 .....05 ..144-145	410.90 ..05 ..144-145
379.11 ..02 ..046-048	381.20 ..03 ..068-070	386.19 ..03 ..065	394.0 ...05 ..135-137	410.91 ..05 ..121-123
379.12 ..02 ..046-048	381.29 ..03 ..068-070	386.2 ...03 ..065	394.1 ...05 ..135-137	410.92 ..05 ..144-145
379.13 ..02 ..046-048	381.3 ...03 ..068-070	386.30 ..03 ..065	394.2 ...05 ..135-137	411.0 ...05 ..121,124,144-145
379.14 ..02 ..046-048	381.4 ...03 ..068-070	386.31 ..03 ..065	394.9 ...05 ..135-137	411.1 ...05 ..124,140
379.15 ..02 ..046-048	381.50 ..03 ..068-070	386.32 ..03 ..065	395.0 ...05 ..135-137	411.81 ..05 ..124,140
379.16 ..02 ..046-048	381.51 ..03 ..068-070	386.33 ..03 ..065	395.1 ...05 ..135-137	411.89 ..05 ..124,140
379.19 ..02 ..046-048	381.52 ..03 ..068-070	386.34 ..03 ..065	395.2 ...05 ..135-137	412. ...05 ..132-133
379.21 ..02 ..046-048	381.60 ..03 ..073-074	386.35 ..03 ..065	395.9 ...05 ..135-137	413.0 ...05 ..140
379.22 ..02 ..046-048	381.61 ..03 ..073-074	386.40 ..03 ..073-074	396.0 ...05 ..135-137	413.1 ...05 ..140
379.23 ..02 ..046-048	381.62 ..03 ..073-074	386.41 ..03 ..073-074	396.1 ...05 ..135-137	413.9 ...05 ..140
379.24 ..02 ..046-048	381.63 ..03 ..073-074	386.42 ..03 ..073-074	396.2 ...05 ..135-137	414.00 ..05 ..132-133
379.25 ..02 ..046-048	381.7 ...03 ..073-074	386.43 ..03 ..073-074	396.3 ...05 ..135-137	414.01 ..05 ..132-133
379.26 ..02 ..046-048	381.81 ..03 ..073-074	386.48 ..03 ..073-074	396.8 ...05 ..135-137	414.02 ..05 ..132-133
379.29 ..02 ..046-048	381.89 ..03 ..073-074	386.50 ..03 ..065	396.9 ...05 ..135-137	414.03 ..05 ..132-133
379.31 ..02 ..046-048	381.9 ...03 ..073-074	386.51 ..03 ..065	397.0 ...05 ..135-137	414.04 ..05 ..132-133
379.32 ..02 ..046-048	382.00 ..03 ..068-070	386.52 ..03 ..065	397.1 ...05 ..135-137	414.05 ..05 ..132-133
379.33 ..02 ..046-048	382.01 ..03 ..068-070	386.53 ..03 ..065	397.9 ...05 ..135-137	414.06 ..05 ..132-133
379.34 ..02 ..046-048	382.02 ..03 ..068-070	386.54 ..03 ..065	398.0 ...05 ..144-145	414.07 ..05 ..132-133
379.39 ..02 ..046-048	382.1 ...03 ..068-070	386.55 ..03 ..065	398.90 ..05 ..144-145	414.10 ..05 ..121,144-145
379.40 ..02 ..045	382.2 ...03 ..068-070	386.56 ..03 ..065	398.91 ..05 ..121,124, 127	414.11 ..05 ..121,144-145
379.41 ..02 ..045	382.3 ...03 ..068-070	386.58 ..03 ..065	398.99 ..05 ..144-145	414.12 ..05 ..121, 144-145
379.42 ..02 ..045	382.4 ...03 ..068-070	386.8 ...03 ..065	401.0 ...05 ..134	414.19 ..05 ..121,144-145
379.43 ..02 ..045	382.9 ...03 ..068-070	386.9 ...03 ..065	401.1 ...05 ..134	414.8 ...05 ..132-133
379.45 ..01 ..012	383.00 ..03 ..068-070	387.0 ...03 ..073-074	401.9 ...05 ..134	414.9 ...05 ..132-133
379.46 ..02 ..045	383.01 ..03 ..068-070	387.1 ...03 ..073-074	402.00 ..05 ..134	415.0 ...05 ..124,144-145
379.49 ..02 ..045	383.02 ..03 ..068-070	387.2 ...03 ..073-074	402.01 ..05 ..121,124,127,	415.11 ..04 ..078
379.50 ..02 ..045	383.1 ...03 ..068-070	387.8 ...03 ..073-074	402.10 ..05 ..134	415.19 ..04 ..078
379.51 ..02 ..046-048	383.20 ..03 ..068-070	387.9 ...03 ..073-074	402.11 ..05 ..121,124,127,	416.0 ...05 ..121,144-145
379.52 ..02 ..045	383.21 ..03 ..068-070	388.00 ..03 ..073-074	402.90 ..05 ..134	416.1 ...05 ..144-145
379.53 ..02 ..046-048	383.22 ..03 ..068-070	388.01 ..03 ..073-074	402.91 ..05 ..121,124,127,	416.8 ...05 ..144-145
379.54 ..02 ..045	383.30 ..03 ..073-074	388.02 ..03 ..073-074	403.00 ..11 ..331-333	416.9 ...05 ..144-145
379.55 ..02 ..045	383.31 ..03 ..073-074	388.10 ..03 ..073-074	403.01 ..11 ..316	417.0 ...05 ..144-145
379.56 ..02 ..046-048	383.32 ..03 ..073-074	388.11 ..03 ..073-074	403.10 ..11 ..331-333	417.1 ...05 ..144-145
379.57 ..02 ..045	383.33 ..03 ..073-074	388.12 ..03 ..073-074	403.11 ..11 ..316	417.8 ...05 ..144-145
379.58 ..02 ..045	383.81 ..03 ..073-074	388.2 ...03 ..073-074	403.90 ..11 ..331-333	417.9 ...05 ..144-145
379.59 ..02 ..046-048	383.89 ..03 ..073-074	388.30 ..03 ..073-074	403.91 ..11 ..316	420.0 ...05 ..124,144-145
379.60 ..02 ..046-048	383.9 ...03 ..068-070	388.31 ..03 ..073-074	404.00 ..05 ..134	420.90 ..05 ..124,144-145
379.61 ..02 ..046-048	384.00 ..03 ..068-070	388.32 ..03 ..073-074	404.01 ..05 ..121,124,127,	420.91 ..05 ..124,144-145
379.62 ..02 ..046-048	384.01 ..03 ..068-070	388.40 ..03 ..073-074	404.02 ..11 ..316	420.99 ..05 ..124,144-145
379.63 ..02 ..046-048	384.09 ..03 ..068-070	388.41 ..03 ..073-074	404.03 ..05 ..121,124,127,	421.0 ...05 ..124,126
379.8 ...02 ..046-048	384.1 ...03 ..068-070	388.42 ..03 ..073-074	404.10 ..05 ..134	421.1 ...05 ..124,126
379.90 ..02 ..046-048	384.20 ..03 ..073-074	388.43 ..03 ..073-074	404.11 ..05 ..121,124,127,	421.9 ...05 ..124,126
379.91 ..02 ..046-048	384.21 ..03 ..073-074	388.44 ..03 ..073-074	404.12 ..11 ..316	422.0 ...05 ..124,144-145
379.92 ..02 ..046-048	384.22 ..03 ..073-074	388.5 ...03 ..073-074	404.13 ..05 ..121,124,127,	422.90 ..05 ..124,144-145
379.93 ..02 ..046-048	384.23 ..03 ..073-074	388.60 ..03 ..073-074	404.90 ..05 ..134	422.91 ..05 ..124,144-145
379.99 ..02 ..046-048	384.24 ..03 ..073-074	388.61 ..01 ..034-035	404.91 ..05 ..121,124,127,	422.92 ..05 ..124,144-145
380.00 ..03 ..068-070	384.25 ..03 ..073-074	388.69 ..03 ..073-074	404.92 ..11 ..316	422.93 ..05 ..124,144-145
380.01 ..08 ..256	384.81 ..03 ..073-074	388.70 ..03 ..073-074	404.93 ..05 ..121,124,127,	422.99 ..05 ..124,144-145
380.02 ..08 ..256	384.82 ..03 ..073-074	388.71 ..03 ..073-074	405.01 ..05 ..134	423.0 ...05 ..124,144-145
380.03 ..08 ..256	384.9 ...03 ..073-074	388.72 ..03 ..073-074	405.09 ..05 ..134	423.1 ...05 ..144-145
380.10 ..03 ..073-074	385.00 ..03 ..073-074	388.8 ...03 ..073-074	405.11 ..05 ..134	423.2 ...05 ..144-145
380.11 ..03 ..073-074	385.01 ..03 ..073-074	388.9 ...03 ..073-074	405.19 ..05 ..134	423.8 ...05 ..144-145
			405.91 ..05 ..134	

DX	MDC	DRG
423.9	05	144-145
424.0	05	135-137
424.1	05	135-137
424.2	05	135-137
424.3	05	135-137
424.90	05	124,135-137
424.91	05	124,135-137
424.99	05	135-137
425.0	05	144-145
425.1	05	144-145
425.2	05	124,144-145
425.3	05	124,144-145
425.4	05	124,144-145
425.5	05	124,144-145
425.7	05	124,144-145
425.8	05	124,144-145
425.9	05	124,144-145
426.0	05	121,138-139
426.10	05	121,138-139
426.11	05	138-139
426.12	05	121,138-139
426.13	05	121,138-139
426.2	05	138-139
426.3	05	121,138-139
426.4	05	138-139
426.50	05	138-139
426.51	05	121,138-139
426.52	05	121,138-139
426.53	05	121,138-139
426.54	05	121,138-139
426.6	05	138-139
426.7	05	138-139
426.81	05	138-139
426.82	05	138-139
426.89	05	138-139
426.9	05	138-139
427.0	05	121,138-139
427.1	05	121,124,138-139
427.2	05	121,138-139
427.31	05	121,138-139
427.32	05	121,138-139
427.41	05	121,138-139
427.42	05	121,138-139
427.5	05	121,124,129
427.60	05	138-139
427.61	05	138-139
427.69	05	138-139
427.81	05	138-139
427.89	05	138-139
427.9	05	138-139
428.0	05	121,124,127
428.1	05	121,124,127
428.9	05	121,124,127
428.20	05	121, 124, 127
428.21	05	121, 124, 127
428.22	05	121, 124, 127
428.23	05	121, 124, 127
428.30	05	121, 124, 127
428.31	05	121, 124, 127
428.32	05	121, 124, 127
428.33	05	121, 124, 127
428.40	05	121, 124, 127
428.41	05	121, 124, 127
428.42	05	121, 124, 127
428.43	05	121, 124, 127
429.0	05	144-145
429.1	05	144-145
429.2	05	132-133
429.3	05	132-133
429.4	05	124,144-145
429.5	05	121,124,135-137
429.6	05	121,124,135-137
429.71	05	124,144-145
429.79	05	124,144-145
429.81	05	121,124,135-137
429.82	05	124,144-145
429.83	05	144-145
429.89	05	132-133
429.9	05	132-133
430	01	014
431	01	014
432.0	01	014
432.1	01	014
432.9	01	014
433.00	01	015
433.01	01	014
433.10	01	015
433.11	01	014
433.20	01	015
433.21	01	014
433.30	01	015
433.31	01	014
433.80	01	015
433.81	01	014
433.90	01	015
433.91	01	014
434.00	01	015
434.01	01	014
434.10	01	015
434.11	01	014
434.90	01	015
434.91	01	014
435.0	01	524
435.1	01	524
435.2	01	524
435.8	01	524
435.9	01	524
436	01	014
437.0	01	016-017
437.1	01	524
437.2	01	022
437.3	01	034-035
437.4	01	024-026
437.5	01	034-035
437.6	01	034-035
437.7	01	016-017
437.8	01	016-017
437.9	01	016-017
438.0	01	012
438.10	01	012
438.11	01	012
438.12	01	012
438.19	01	012
438.20	01	012
438.21	01	012
438.22	01	012
438.30	01	012
438.31	01	012
438.32	01	012
438.40	01	012
438.41	01	012
438.42	01	012
438.50	01	012
438.51	01	012
438.52	01	012
438.53	01	012
438.6	01	012
438.7	01	012
438.81	01	012
438.82	01	012
438.83	01	012
438.84	01	012
438.85	01	012
438.89	01	012
438.9	01	012
440.0	05	130-131
440.1	11	331-333
440.20	05	130-131
440.21	05	130-131
440.22	05	130-131
440.23	05	130-131
440.24	05	130-131
440.29	05	130-131
440.30	05	130-131
440.31	05	130-131
440.32	05	130-131
440.8	05	130-131
440.9	05	130-131
441.00	05	121,130-131
441.01	05	121,130-131
441.02	05	121,130-131
441.03	05	121,130-131
441.1	05	130-131
441.2	05	130-131
441.3	05	130-131
441.4	05	130-131
441.5	05	130-131
441.6	05	130-131
441.7	05	130-131
441.9	05	130-131
442.0	05	130-131
442.1	11	331-333
442.2	05	130-131
442.3	05	130-131
442.81	05	130-131
442.82	05	130-131
442.83	05	130-131
442.84	05	130-131
442.89	05	130-131
442.9	05	130-131
443.0	08	240-241
443.1	05	130-131
443.21	05	130-131
443.22	05	130-131
443.23	11	331-333
443.24	05	130-131
443.29	05	130-131
443.81	05	130-131
443.82	05	130-131
443.89	05	130-131
443.9	05	130-131
444.0	05	130-131
444.1	05	130-131
444.21	05	130-131
444.22	05	130-131
444.81	05	130-131
444.89	05	130-131
444.9	05	130-131
445.01	05	130-131
445.02	05	130-131
445.81	11	331-333
445.89	05	130-131
446.0	08	240-241
446.1	08	240-241
446.20	08	240-241
446.21	08	240-241
446.29	08	240-241
446.3	08	239
446.4	08	239
446.5	08	240-241
446.6	08	240-241
446.7	08	240-241
447.0	05	130-131
447.1	05	130-131
447.2	05	130-131
447.3	11	331-333
447.4	06	182-184
447.5	05	130-131
447.6	08	240-241
447.8	05	130-131
447.9	05	130-131
448.0	05	130-131
448.1	09	283-284
448.9	05	130-131
451.0	05	130-131
451.11	05	128
451.19	05	128
451.2	05	128
451.81	05	128
451.82	05	130-131
451.83	05	130-131
451.84	05	130-131
451.89	05	130-131
451.9	05	130-131
452	07	205-206
453.0	07	205-206
453.1	05	130-131
453.2	05	128
453.3	11	331-333
453.40	05	130-131
453.41	05	130-131
453.42	05	130-131
453.8	05	130-131
453.9	05	130-131
454.0	05	130-131
454.1	05	130-131
454.2	05	130-131
454.8	05	130-131
454.9	05	130-131
455.0	06	188-190
455.1	06	188-190
455.2	06	188-190
455.3	06	188-190
455.4	06	188-190
455.5	06	188-190
455.6	06	188-190
455.7	06	188-190
455.8	06	188-190
455.9	06	188-190
456.0	06	174-175
456.1	06	188-190
456.20	06	188-190
456.21	06	188-190
456.3	05	130-131
456.4	12	352
456.5	12	352
456.6	13	369
456.8	05	130-131
457.0	09	276
457.1	09	283-284
457.2	09	277-279
457.8	16	398-399
457.9	16	398-399
458.0	05	141-142
458.1	05	144-145
458.21	05	141-142
458.29	05	141-142
458.8	05	121,144-145
458.9	05	121,144-145
459.0	05	144-145
459.1	05	130-131
459.2	05	130-131
459.10	05	130-131
459.11	05	130-131
459.12	05	130-131
459.13	05	130-131
459.19	05	130-131
459.30	05	130-131
459.31	05	130-131
459.32	05	130-131
459.33	05	130-131
459.39	05	130-131
459.81	05	130-131
459.89	05	132-133
459.9	05	132-133

Diseases of the Respiratory System

DX	MDC	DRG
460	03	068-070
461.0	03	068-070
461.1	03	068-070
461.2	03	068-070
461.3	03	068-070
461.8	03	068-070
461.9	03	068-070
462	03	068-070
463	03	068-070
464.00	03	068-070
464.01	03	068.070
464.10	04	096-098
464.11	04	096-098
464.20	03	071
464.21	03	071
464.30	03	067
464.31	03	067
464.4	03	071
464.50	03	068-070
464.51	03	068-070
465.0	03	068-070
465.8	03	068-070
465.9	03	068-070
466.0	04	096-098
466.11	04	096-098
466.19	04	096-098
470	03	072
471.0	03	073-074
471.1	03	073-074
471.8	03	073-074
471.9	03	073-074
472.0	03	068-070
472.1	03	068-070
472.2	03	068-070
473.0	03	068-070
473.1	03	068-070
473.2	03	068-070
473.3	03	068-070
473.8	03	068-070
473.9	03	068-070
474.00	03	068-070
474.01	03	068-070
474.02	03	068-070
474.10	03	073-074
474.11	03	073-074
474.12	03	073-074
474.2	03	073-074
474.8	03	073-074
474.9	03	073-074
475	03	068-070
476.0	03	068-070
476.1	03	068-070
477.0	03	068-070
477.1	03	068-070
477.2	03	068-070
477.8	03	068-070
477.9	03	068-070
478.0	03	073-074
478.11	03	073-074
478.19	03	073-074
478.20	03	073-074
478.21	03	068-070
478.22	03	068-070
478.24	03	068-070
478.25	03	073-074
478.26	03	073-074
478.29	03	073-074
478.30	03	073-074
478.31	03	073-074
478.32	03	073-074
478.33	03	073-074
478.34	03	073-074
478.4	03	073-074
478.5	03	073-074
478.6	03	073-074
478.70	03	073-074
478.71	03	068-070
478.74	03	073-074
478.75	03	073-074
478.79	03	073-074
478.8	03	068-070
478.9	03	068-070
480.0	04	089-091
480.1	04	089-091
480.2	04	089-091
480.8	04	089-091
480.9	04	089-091
481	04	089-091
482.0	04	079-081
482.1	04	079-081
482.2	04	089-091
482.30	04	089-091
482.31	04	089-091
482.32	04	089-091
482.39	04	089-091
482.40	04	079-081
482.40	05	121
482.40	15	387,389,489
482.41	04	079-081
482.41	05	121
482.41	15	387,389
482.49	04	079-081
482.49	05	121
482.49	15	387,389
482.49	25	489
482.81	04	079-081
482.81	15	387,389

DX	MDC	DRG
482.81	.25	.489
482.82	.04	.079-081
482.82	.15	.387,389
482.82	.25	.489
482.83	.04	.079-081
482.83	.15	.387,389
482.83	.25	.489
482.84	.04	.079-081
482.89	.04	.079-081
482.89	.15	.387,389
482.89	.25	.489
482.9	.04	.089-091
483.0	.04	.089-091
483.1	.04	.089-091
483.1	.15	.387,389
483.8	.04	.089-091
484.1	.04	.079-081
484.3	.04	.079-081
484.5	.04	.079-081
484.6	.04	.079-081
484.7	.04	.079-081
484.8	.04	.079-081
485	.04	.089-091
486	.04	.089-091
487.0	.04	.089-091
487.1	.03	.068-070
487.8	.18	.421-422
490	.04	.096-098
491.0	.04	.096-098
491.1	.04	.088
491.20	.04	.088
491.21	.04	.088
491.22	.04	.088
491.8	.04	.088
491.9	.04	.088
492.0	.04	.088
492.8	.04	.088
493.00	.04	.096-098
493.01	.04	.096-098
493.02	.04	.096-098
493.10	.04	.096-098
493.11	.04	.096-098
493.12	.04	.096-098
493.20	.04	.088
493.21	.04	.088
493.22	.04	.088
493.81	.04	.096-098
493.82	.04	.096-098
493.90	.04	.096-098
493.91	.04	.096-098
493.92	.04	.096-098
494.0	.04	.088
494.1	.04	.088
495.0	.04	.092-093
495.1	.04	.092-093
495.2	.04	.092-093
495.3	.04	.092-093
495.4	.04	.092-093
495.5	.04	.092-093
495.6	.04	.092-093
495.7	.04	.092-093
495.8	.04	.092-093
495.9	.04	.092-093
496	.04	.088
500	.04	.092-093
501	.04	.092-093
502	.04	.092-093
503	.04	.092-093
504	.04	.092-093
505	.04	.092-093
506.0	.04	.101-102
506.1	.04	.087
506.2	.04	.101-102
506.3	.04	.101-102
506.4	.04	.088
506.9	.04	.088
507.0	.04	.079-081
507.1	.04	.079-081
507.8	.04	.079-081
508.0	.04	.101-102
508.1	.04	.092-093
508.8	.04	.101-102
508.9	.04	.101-102
510.0	.04	.079-081
510.9	.04	.079-081
511.0	.04	.089-091
511.1	.04	.079-081
511.8	.04	.085-086
511.9	.04	.085-086
512.0	.04	.094-095
512.8	.04	.094-095
513.0	.04	.079-081
513.1	.04	.079-081
514	.04	.087
515	.04	.092-093
516.0	.04	.092-093
516.1	.04	.092-093
516.2	.04	.092-093
516.3	.04	.092-093
516.8	.04	.092-093
516.9	.04	.092-093
517.1	.04	.092-093
517.2	.04	.092-093
517.3	.04	.092-093
517.8	.04	.092-093
518.0	.04	.101-102
518.1	.04	.094-095
518.2	.04	.101-102
518.3	.04	.092-093
518.4	.04	.087
518.5	.04	.087
518.6	.04	.092-093
518.7	.04	.101-102
518.81	.04	.087
518.82	.04	.099-100
518.83	.04	.087
518.84	.04	.087
518.84	.22	.506-507
518.89	.04	.101-102
519.00	.04	.101-102
519.0	.04	.101-102
519.02	.04	.101-102
519.09	.04	.101-102
519.11	.04	.096-098
519.19	.04	.096-098
519.2	.04	.079-081
519.3	.04	.101-102
519.4	.04	.101-102
519.8	.04	.101-102
519.9	.04	.101-102

Diseases of the Digestive System

DX	MDC	DRG
520.0	.03	.185-187
520.1	.03	.185-187
520.2	.03	.185-187
520.3	.03	.185-187
520.4	.03	.185-187
520.5	.03	.185-187
520.6	.03	.185-187
520.7	.03	.185-187
520.8	.03	.185-187
520.9	.03	.185-187
521.00	.03	.185-187
521.01	.03	.185-187
521.02	.03	.185-187
521.03	.03	.185-187
521.04	.03	.185-187
521.06	.03	.185-187
521.07	.03	.185-187
521.08	.03	.185-187
521.09	.03	.185-187
521.10	.03	.185-187
521.11	.03	.185-187
521.12	.03	.185-187
521.13	.03	.185-187
521.14	.03	.185-187
521.15	.03	.185-187
521.20	.03	.185-187
521.21	.03	.185-187
521.22	.03	.185-187
521.23	.03	.185-187
521.24	.03	.185-187
521.25	.03	.185-187
521.30	.03	.185-187
521.31	.03	.185-187
521.32	.03	.185-187
521.33	.03	.185-187
521.34	.03	.185-187
521.35	.03	.185-187
521.40	.03	.185-187
521.41	.03	.185-187
521.42	.03	.185-187
521.49	.03	.185-187
521.5	.03	.185-187
521.6	.03	.185-187
521.7	.03	.185-187
521.81	.03	.185-187
521.89	.03	.185-187
521.9	.03	.185-187
522.0	.03	.185-187
522.1	.03	.185-187
522.2	.03	.185-187
522.3	.03	.185-187
522.4	.03	.185-187
522.5	.03	.185-187
522.6	.03	.185-187
522.7	.03	.185-187
522.8	.03	.185-187
522.9	.03	.185-187
523.00	.03	.185-187
523.01	.03	.185-187
523.10	.03	.185-187
523.11	.03	.185-187
523.20	.03	.185-187
523.21	.03	.185-187
523.22	.03	.185-187
523.23	.03	.185-187
523.24	.03	.185-187
523.25	.03	.185-187
523.30	.03	.185-187
523.31	.03	.185-187
523.32	.03	.185-187
523.33	.03	.185-187
523.40	.03	.185-187
523.41	.03	.185-187
523.42	.03	.185-187
523.5	.03	.185-187
523.6	.03	.185-187
523.8	.03	.185-187
523.9	.03	.185-187
524.00	.03	.185-187
524.01	.03	.185-187
524.02	.03	.185-187
524.03	.03	.185-187
524.04	.03	.185-187
524.05	.03	.185-187
524.06	.03	.185-187
524.07	.03	.185-187
524.09	.03	.185-187
524.10	.03	.185-187
524.11	.03	.185-187
524.12	.03	.185-187
524.19	.03	.185-187
524.20	.03	.185-187
524.21	.03	.185-187
524.22	.03	.185-187
524.23	.03	.185-187
524.24	.03	.185-187
524.25	.03	.185-187
524.26	.03	.185-187
524.27	.03	.185-187
524.28	.03	.185-187
524.29	.03.	.185-187
524.30	.03	.185-187
524.31	.03	.185-187
524.32	.03	.185-187
524.33	.03	.185-187
524.34	.03	.185-187
524.35	.03	.185-187
524.36	.03	.185-187
524.37	.03	.185-187
524.39	.03	.185-187
524.4	.03	.185-187
524.50	.03	.185-187
524.51	.03	.185-187
524.52	.03	.185-187
524.53	.03	.185-187
524.54	.03	.185-187
524.55	.03	.185-187
524.56	.03	.185-187
524.57	.03	.185-187
524.59	.03	.185-187
524.60	.03	.185-187
524.61	.03	.185-187
524.62	.03	.185-187
524.63	.03	.185-187
524.64	.03	.185-187
524.69	.03	.185-187
524.70	.03	.185-187
524.71	.03	.185-187
524.72	.03	.185-187
524.73	.03	.185-187
524.74	.03	.185-187
524.75	.03	.185-187
524.76	.03	.185-187
524.79	.03	.185-187
524.81	.03	.185-187
524.82	.03	.185-187
524.89	.03	.185-187
524.9	.03	.185-187
525.0	.03	.185-187
525.10	.03	.185-187
525.11	.03	.185-187
525.12	.03	.185-187
525.13	.03	.185-187
525.19	.03	.185-187
525.20	.03	.185-187
525.21	.03	.185-187
525.22	.03	.185-187
525.23	.03	.185-187
525.24	.03	.185-187
525.25	.03	.185-187
525.26	.03	.185-187
525.3	.03	.185-187
525.40	.03	.185-187
525.41	.03	.185-187
525.42	.03	.185-187
525.43	.03	.185-187
525.44	.03	.185-187
525.50	.03	.185-187
525.51	.03	.185-187
525.52	.03	.185-187
525.53	.03	.185-187
525.54	.03	.185-187
525.60	.03	.185-187
525.61	.03	.185-187
525.62	.03	.185-187
525.63	.03	.185-187
525.64	.03	.185-187
525.65	.03	.185-187
525.66	.03	.185-187
525.67	.03	.185-187
525.69	.03	.185-187
525.8	.03	.185-187
525.9	.03	.185-187
526.0	.03	.185-187
526.1	.03	.185-187
526.2	.03	.185-187
526.3	.03	.185-187
526.4	.03	.185-187
526.5	.03	.185-187
526.61	.03	.185-187
526.62	.03	.185-187
526.63	.03	.185-187
526.69	.03	.185-187
526.81	.03	.185-187
526.89	.03	.185-187
526.9	.03	.185-187
527.0	.03	.073-074
527.1	.03	.073-074
527.2	.03	.073-074
527.3	.03	.073-074
527.4	.03	.073-074
527.5	.03	.073-074
527.6	.03	.073-074
527.7	.03	.073-074
527.8	.03	.073-074
527.9	.03	.073-074
528.00	.03	.185-187
528.01	.03	.185-187
528.02	.03	.185-187
528.09	.03	.185-187
528.1	.03	.185-187
528.2	.03	.185-187
528.3	.03	.185-187
528.4	.03	.185-187
528.5	.03	.185-187
528.6	.03	.185-187
528.71	.03	.185-187
528.72	.03	.185-187
528.79	.03	.185-187
528.8	.03	.185-187
528.9	.03	.185-187
529.0	.03	.185-187
529.1	.03	.185-187
529.2	.03	.185-187
529.3	.03	.185-187
529.4	.03	.185-187
529.5	.03	.185-187
529.6	.03	.185-187
529.8	.03	.185-187
529.9	.03	.185-187
530.0	.06	.182-184
530.10	.06	.182-184
530.11	.06	.182-184
530.12	.06	.182-184
530.19	.06	.182-184
530.20	.06	.176
530.21	.06	.176
530.3	.06	.182-184
530.4	.06	.182-184
530.5	.06	.182-184
530.6	.06	.182-184
530.7	.06	.174-175
530.81	.06	.182-184
530.82	.06	.174-175
530.83	.06	.182-184
530.84	.06	.182-184
530.85	.06	.176
530.86	.06	.188-190
530.87	.06	.188-190
530.89	.06	.182-184
530.9	.06	.182-184
531.00	.06	.174-175
531.01	.06	.174-175
531.10	.06	.176
531.11	.06	.176
531.20	.06	.174-175
531.21	.06	.174-175
531.30	.06	.177-178
531.31	.06	.176
531.40	.06	.174-175
531.41	.06	.174-175
531.50	.06	.176
531.51	.06	.176
531.60	.06	.174-175
531.61	.06	.174-175
531.70	.06	.177-178
531.71	.06	.176
531.90	.06	.177-178
531.91	.06	.176
532.00	.06	.174-175
532.01	.06	.174-175
532.10	.06	.176
532.11	.06	.176
532.20	.06	.174-175
532.21	.06	.174-175
532.30	.06	.177-178
532.31	.06	.176
532.40	.06	.174-175
532.41	.06	.174-175
532.50	.06	.176
532.51	.06	.176
532.60	.06	.174-175
532.61	.06	.174-175

DX	MDC	DRG
532.70	06	177-178
532.71	06	176
532.90	06	177-178
532.91	06	176
533.00	06	174-175
533.01	06	174-175
533.10	06	176
533.11	06	176
533.20	06	174-175
533.21	06	174-175
533.30	06	177-178
533.31	06	176
533.40	06	174-175
533.41	06	174-175
533.50	06	176
533.51	06	176
533.60	06	174-175
533.61	06	174-175
533.70	06	177-178
533.71	06	176
533.90	06	177-178
533.91	06	176
534.00	06	174-175
534.01	06	174-175
534.10	06	176
534.11	06	176
534.20	06	174-175
534.21	06	174-175
534.30	06	176
534.31	06	176
534.40	06	174-175
534.41	06	174-175
534.50	06	176
534.51	06	176
534.60	06	174-175
534.61	06	174-175
534.70	06	176
534.71	06	176
534.90	06	176
534.91	06	176
535.00	06	182-184
535.01	06	174-175
535.10	06	182-184
535.11	06	174-175
535.20	06	182-184
535.21	06	174-175
535.30	06	182-184
535.31	06	174-175
535.40	06	182-184
535.41	06	174-175
535.50	06	182-184
535.51	06	174-175
535.60	06	182-184
535.61	06	174-175
536.0	06	182-184
536.1	06	182-184
536.2	06	182-184
536.3	06	182-184
536.40	06	188-190
536.41	06	188-190
536.42	06	188-190
536.49	06	188-190
536.8	06	182-184
536.9	06	182-184
537.0	06	176
537.1	06	182-184
537.2	06	182-184
537.3	06	176
537.4	06	182-184
537.5	06	182-184
537.6	06	182-184
537.81	06	182-184
537.82	06	182-184
537.83	06	174-175
537.84	06	174-175
537.89	06	182-184
537.9	06	182-184
538	06	182-184
540.0	06	188-190
540.1	06	188-190
540.9	06	188-190
541	06	188-190
542	06	188-190
543.0	06	188-190
543.9	06	188-190
550.00	06	188-190
550.01	06	188-190
550.02	06	188-190
550.03	06	188-190
550.10	06	188-190
550.11	06	188-190
550.12	06	188-190
550.13	06	188-190
550.90	06	188-190
550.91	06	188-190
550.92	06	188-190
550.93	06	188-190
551.00	06	188-190
551.01	06	188-190
551.02	06	188-190
551.03	06	188-190
551.1	06	188-190
551.20	06	188-190
551.21	06	188-190
551.29	06	188-190
551.3	06	188-190
551.8	06	188-190
551.9	06	188-190
552.00	06	188-190
552.01	06	188-190
552.02	06	188-190
552.03	06	188-190
552.1	06	188-190
552.20	06	188-190
552.21	06	188-190
552.29	06	188-190
552.3	06	182-184
552.8	06	188-190
552.9	06	188-190
553.00	06	188-190
553.01	06	188-190
553.02	06	188-190
553.03	06	188-190
553.1	06	188-190
553.20	06	188-190
553.21	06	188-190
553.29	06	188-190
553.3	06	182-184
553.8	06	188-190
553.9	06	188-190
555.0	06	179
555.1	06	179
555.2	06	179
555.9	06	179
556.0	06	179
556.1	06	179
556.2	06	179
556.3	06	179
556.4	06	179
556.5	06	179
556.6	06	179
556.8	06	179
556.9	06	179
557.0	06	188-190
557.1	06	188-190
557.9	06	188-190
558.1	06	188-190
558.2	06	188-190
558.3	06	182-184
558.9	06	182-184
560.0	06	180-181
560.1	06	180-181
560.2	06	180-181
560.30	06	180-181
560.31	06	180-181
560.39	06	180-181
560.81	06	180-181
560.89	06	180-181
560.9	06	180-181
562.00	06	182-184
562.01	06	182-184
562.02	06	174-175
562.03	06	174-175
562.10	06	182-184
562.11	06	182-184
562.12	06	174-175
562.13	06	174-175
564.00	06	182-184
564.01	06	182-184
564.02	06	182-184
564.09	06	182-184
564.1	06	182-184
564.2	06	182-184
564.3	06	182-184
564.4	06	182-184
564.5	06	182-184
564.6	06	182-184
564.7	06	188-190
564.81	06	182-184
564.89	06	182-184
564.9	06	182-184
565.0	06	188-190
565.1	06	188-190
566	06	188-190
567.0	06	188-190
567.1	06	188-190
567.21	06	188-190
567.22	06	188-190
567.23	06	188-190
567.29	06	188-190
567.31	06	188-190
567.38	06	188-190
567.39	06	188-190
567.81	06	188-190
567.82	06	188-190
567.89	06	188-190
567.9	06	188-190
568.0	06	188-190
568.81	06	188-190
568.82	06	188-190
568.89	06	188-190
568.9	06	188-190
569.0	06	188-190
569.1	06	188-190
569.2	06	188-190
569.3	06	174-175
569.41	06	188-190
569.42	06	188-190
569.49	06	188-190
569.5	06	188-190
569.60	06	188-190
569.61	06	188-190
569.62	06	188-190
569.69	06	188-190
569.81	06	188-190
569.82	06	188-190
569.83	06	188-190
569.84	06	188-190
569.85	06	174-175
569.86	06	188-190
569.89	06	188-190
569.9	06	188-190
570	07	205-206
571.0	07	205-206
571.1	07	202
571.2	07	202
571.3	07	202
571.40	07	205-206
571.41	07	205-206
571.49	07	205-206
571.5	07	202
571.6	07	202
571.8	07	205-206
571.9	07	205-206
572.0	07	205-206
572.1	07	205-206
572.2	07	205-206
572.3	07	205-206
572.4	07	205-206
572.8	07	205-206
573.0	07	205-206
573.1	07	205-206
573.2	07	205-206
573.3	07	205-206
573.4	07	205-206
573.8	07	205-206
573.9	07	205-206
574.00	07	207-208
574.01	07	207-208
574.10	07	207-208
574.11	07	207-208
574.20	07	207-208
574.21	07	207-208
574.30	07	207-208
574.31	07	207-208
574.40	07	207-208
574.41	07	207-208
574.50	07	207-208
574.51	07	207-208
574.60	07	207-208
574.61	07	207-208
574.70	07	207-208
574.71	07	207-208
574.80	07	207-208
574.81	07	207-208
574.90	07	207-208
574.91	07	207-208
575.0	07	207-208
575.10	07	207-208
575.11	07	207-208
575.12	07	207-208
575.2	07	207-208
575.3	07	207-208
575.4	07	207-208
575.5	07	207-208
575.6	07	207-208
575.8	07	207-208
575.9	07	207-208
576.0	07	207-208
576.1	07	207-208
576.2	07	207-208
576.3	07	207-208
576.4	07	207-208
576.5	07	207-208
576.8	07	207-208
576.9	07	207-208
577.0	07	204
577.1	07	204
577.2	07	204
577.8	07	204
577.9	07	204
578.0	06	174-175
578.1	06	174-175
578.9	06	174-175
579.0	06	182-184
579.1	06	182-184
579.2	06	182-184
579.3	06	182-184
579.4	06	182-184
579.8	06	182-184
579.9	06	182-184

Diseases of the Genitourinary System

DX	MDC	DRG
580.0	11	331-333
580.4	11	331-333
580.81	11	331-333
580.89	11	331-333
580.9	11	331-333
581.0	11	331-333
581.1	11	331-333
581.2	11	331-333
581.3	11	331-333
581.81	11	331-333
581.89	11	331-333
581.9	11	331-333
582.0	11	331-333
582.1	11	331-333
582.2	11	331-333
582.4	11	331-333
582.81	11	331-333
582.89	11	331-333
582.9	11	331-333
583.0	11	331-333
583.1	11	331-333
583.2	11	331-333
583.4	11	331-333
583.6	11	331-333
583.7	11	331-333
583.81	11	331-333
583.89	11	331-333
583.9	11	331-333
584.5	11	316
584.6	11	316
584.7	11	316
584.8	11	316
584.9	11	316
585.1	11	315-316
585.2	11	315-316
585.3	11	315-316
585.4	11	315-316
585.5	11	315-316
585.6	11	315-316
585.9	11	315-316
586	11	316
587	11	331-333
588.0	11	331-333
588.1	11	331-333
588.81	11	331-333
588.89	11	331-333
588.9	11	331-333
589.0	11	331-333
589.1	11	331-333
589.9	11	331-333
590.0	11	320-322
590.01	11	320-322
590.10	11	320-322
590.11	11	320-322
590.2	11	320-322
590.3	11	320-322
590.80	11	320-322
590.81	11	320-322
590.9	11	320-322
591	11	323-324
592.0	11	323-324
592.1	11	323-324
592.9	11	323-324
593.0	11	331-333
593.1	11	331-333
593.2	11	331-333
593.3	11	320-322
593.4	11	323-324
593.5	11	323-324
593.6	11	331-333
593.70	11	331-333
593.71	11	331-333
593.72	11	331-333
593.73	11	331-333
593.81	11	331-333
593.82	11	331-333
593.89	11	331-333
593.9	11	331-333
594.0	11	331-333
594.1	11	323-324
594.2	11	323-324
594.8	11	323-324
594.9	11	323-324
595.0	11	320-322
595.1	11	320-322
595.2	11	320-322
595.3	11	320-322
595.4	11	320-322
595.81	11	320-322
595.82	11	331-333
595.89	11	320-322
595.9	11	320-322
596.0	11	331-333
596.1	11	331-333
596.2	11	331-333
596.3	11	331-333
596.4	11	331-333
596.51	11	331-333
596.52	11	331-333
596.53	11	331-333
596.54	11	331-333
596.55	11	331-333

DX ...MDC ..DRG	DX ...MDC ..DRG	DX ...MDC ..DRG	DX ...MDC ..DRG	DX ...MDC ..DRG
596.59 ..11 .331-333	608.22 ..12 .352	618.82 ..13 .369	626.8 ..13 .369	635.11 ..14 .380
596.6 ..11 .331-333	608.23 ..12 .352	618.83 ..13 .369	626.9 ..13 .369	635.12 ..14 .380
596.7 ..11 .331-333	608.24 ..12 .352	618.84 ..13 .369	627.0 ..13 .369	635.20 ..14 .380
596.8 ..11 .331-333	608.3 ..12 .352	618.89 ..13 .369	627.1 ..13 .369	635.21 ..14 .380
596.9 ..11 .331-333	608.4 ..12 .350	618.9 ..13 .369	627.2 ..13 .369	635.22 ..14 .380
597.0 ..11 .320-322	608.81 ..12 .352	619.0 ..13 .369	627.3 ..13 .369	635.30 ..14 .380
597.80 ..11 .320-322	608.82 ..12 .352	619.1 ..06 .188-190	627.4 ..13 .369	635.31 ..14 .380
597.81 ..11 .320-322	608.83 ..12 .352	619.2 ..13 .369	627.8 ..13 .369	635.32 ..14 .380
597.89 ..11 .320-322	608.84 ..12 .352	619.8 ..13 .369	627.9 ..13 .369	635.40 ..14 .380
598.00 ..11 .328-330	608.85 ..12 .352	619.9 ..13 .369	628.0 ..13 .369	635.41 ..14 .380
598.01 ..11 .328-330	608.86 ..12 .352	620.0 ..13 .369	628.1 ..13 .369	635.42 ..14 .380
598.1 ..11 .328-330	608.87 ..12 .352	620.1 ..13 .369	628.2 ..13 .369	635.50 ..14 .380
598.2 ..11 .328-330	608.89 ..12 .352	620.2 ..13 .369	628.3 ..13 .369	635.51 ..14 .380
598.8 ..11 .328-330	608.9 ..12 .352	620.3 ..13 .369	628.4 ..13 .369	635.52 ..14 .380
598.9 ..11 .328-330	610.0 ..09 .276	620.4 ..13 .369	628.8 ..13 .369	635.60 ..14 .380
599.0 ..11 .320-322	610.1 ..09 .276	620.5 ..13 .369	628.9 ..13 .369	635.61 ..14 .380
599.1 ..11 .331-333	610.2 ..09 .276	620.6 ..13 .369	629.0 ..13 .369	635.62 ..14 .380
599.2 ..11 .331-333	610.3 ..09 .276	620.7 ..13 .369	629.1 ..13 .369	635.70 ..14 .380
599.3 ..11 .331-333	610.4 ..09 .276	620.8 ..13 .369	629.20 ..13 .369	635.71 ..14 .380
599.4 ..11 .331-333	610.8 ..09 .276	620.9 ..13 .369	629.21 ..13 .369	635.72 ..14 .380
599.5 ..11 .331-333	610.9 ..09 .276	621.0 ..13 .369	629.22 ..13 .369	635.80 ..14 .380
599.60 ..11 .331-333	611.0 ..09 .276	621.1 ..13 .369	629.23 ..13 .369	635.81 ..14 .380
599.69 ..11 .331-333	611.1 ..09 .276	621.2 ..13 .369	629.29 ..13 .369	635.82 ..14 .380
599.7 ..11 .325-327	611.2 ..09 .276	621.30 ..13 .369	629.81 ..13 .368	635.90 ..14 .380
599.81 ..11 .331-333	611.3 ..09 .276	621.31 ..13 .369	629.89 ..13 .368	635.91 ..14 .380
599.82 ..11 .331-333	611.4 ..09 .276	621.32 ..13 .369	629.9 ..13 .369	635.92 ..14 .380
599.83 ..11 .331-333	611.5 ..09 .276	621.33 ..13 .369		636.00 ..14 .380
599.84 ..11 .331-333	611.6 ..09 .276	621.4 ..13 .369	**Complications of Pregnancy, Childbirth and the Puerperium**	636.01 ..14 .380
599.89 ..11 .331-333	611.71 ..09 .276	621.5 ..13 .369	630 .....14 .383-384	636.02 ..14 .380
599.9 ..11 .331-333	611.72 ..09 .276	621.6 ..13 .369	631 .....14 .383-384	636.10 ..14 .380
600.00 ..12 .348-349	611.79 ..09 .276	621.7 ..13 .369	632 .....14 .380	636.11 ..14 .380
600.01 ..12 .348-349	611.8 ..09 .276	621.8 ..13 .369	633.00 ..14 .378	636.12 ..14 .380
600.10 ..12 .348-349	611.9 ..09 .276	621.9 ..13 .369	633.01 ..14 .378	636.20 ..14 .380
600.11 ..12 .348-349	614.0 ..13 .368	622.0 ..13 .369	633.10 ..14 .378	636.21 ..14 .380
600.20 ..12 .348-349	614.1 ..13 .368	622.10 ..13 .369	633.11 ..14 .378	636.22 ..14 .380
600.21 ..12 .348-349	614.2 ..13 .368	622.11 ..13 .369	633.20 ..14 .378	636.30 ..14 .380
600.30 ..12 .348-349	614.3 ..13 .368	622.12 ..13 .369	633.21 ..14 .378	636.31 ..14 .380
600.31 ..12 .348-349	614.4 ..13 .368	622.2 ..13 .369	633.80 ..14 .378	636.32 ..14 .380
600.90 ..12 .348-349	614.5 ..13 .368	622.3 ..13 .369	633.81 ..14 .378	636.40 ..14 .380
600.91 ..12 .348-349	614.6 ..13 .368	622.4 ..13 .369	633.90 ..14 .378	636.41 ..14 .380
601.0 ..12 .350	614.7 ..13 .368	622.5 ..13 .369	633.91 ..14 .378	636.42 ..14 .380
601.1 ..12 .350	614.8 ..13 .368	622.6 ..13 .369	633.0 ..14 .378	636.50 ..14 .380
601.2 ..12 .350	614.9 ..13 .368	622.7 ..13 .369	633.1 ..14 .378	636.51 ..14 .380
601.3 ..12 .350	615.0 ..13 .368	622.8 ..13 .369	633.2 ..14 .378	636.52 ..14 .380
601.4 ..12 .350	615.1 ..13 .368	622.9 ..13 .369	633.8 ..14 .378	636.60 ..14 .380
601.8 ..12 .350	615.9 ..13 .368	623.0 ..13 .369	633.9 ..14 .378	636.61 ..14 .380
601.9 ..12 .350	616.0 ..13 .368	623.1 ..13 .369	634.00 ..14 .380	636.62 ..14 .380
602.0 ..12 .352	616.10 ..13 .368	623.2 ..13 .369	634.01 ..14 .380	636.70 ..14 .380
602.1 ..12 .352	616.11 ..13 .368	623.3 ..13 .369	634.02 ..14 .380	636.71 ..14 .380
602.2 ..12 .352	616.2 ..13 .369	623.4 ..13 .369	634.10 ..14 .380	636.72 ..14 .380
602.3 ..12 .352	616.3 ..13 .368	623.5 ..13 .369	634.11 ..14 .380	636.80 ..14 .380
602.8 ..12 .352	616.4 ..13 .368	623.6 ..13 .369	634.12 ..14 .380	636.81 ..14 .380
602.9 ..12 .352	616.50 ..13 .369	623.7 ..13 .369	634.20 ..14 .380	636.82 ..14 .380
603.0 ..12 .352	616.51 ..13 .369	623.8 ..13 .369	634.21 ..14 .380	636.90 ..14 .380
603.1 ..12 .350	616.81 ..13 .368	623.9 ..13 .369	634.22 ..14 .380	636.91 ..14 .380
603.8 ..12 .352	616.89 ..13 .368	624.0 ..13 .369	634.30 ..14 .380	636.92 ..14 .380
603.9 ..12 .352	616.9 ..13 .368	624.1 ..13 .369	634.31 ..14 .380	637.00 ..14 .380
604.0 ..12 .350	617.0 ..13 .369	624.2 ..13 .369	634.32 ..14 .380	637.01 ..14 .380
604.90 ..12 .350	617.1 ..13 .369	624.3 ..13 .369	634.40 ..14 .380	637.02 ..14 .380
604.91 ..12 .350	617.2 ..13 .369	624.4 ..13 .369	634.41 ..14 .380	637.10 ..14 .380
604.99 ..12 .350	617.3 ..13 .369	624.5 ..13 .369	634.42 ..14 .380	637.11 ..14 .380
605 .....12 .350	617.4 ..13 .369	624.6 ..13 .369	634.50 ..14 .380	637.12 ..14 .380
606.0 ..12 .352	617.5 ..06 .182-184	624.8 ..13 .369	634.51 ..14 .380	637.20 ..14 .380
606.1 ..12 .352	617.6 ..09 .283-284	624.9 ..13 .369	634.52 ..14 .380	637.21 ..14 .380
606.8 ..12 .352	617.8 ..13 .369	625.0 ..13 .369	634.60 ..14 .380	637.22 ..14 .380
606.9 ..12 .352	617.9 ..13 .369	625.1 ..13 .369	634.61 ..14 .380	637.30 ..14 .380
607.0 ..12 .352	618.00 ..13 .369	625.2 ..13 .369	634.62 ..14 .380	637.31 ..14 .380
607.1 ..12 .350	618.01 ..13 .369	625.3 ..13 .369	634.70 ..14 .380	637.32 ..14 .380
607.2 ..12 .350	618.02 ..13 .369	625.4 ..13 .369	634.71 ..14 .380	637.40 ..14 .380
607.3 ..12 .352	618.03 ..13 .369	625.5 ..13 .369	634.72 ..14 .380	637.41 ..14 .380
607.81 ..12 .350	618.04 ..13 .369	625.6 ..13 .369	634.80 ..14 .380	637.42 ..14 .380
607.82 ..12 .352	618.05 ..13 .369	625.8 ..13 .369	634.81 ..14 .380	637.51 ..14 .380
607.83 ..12 .352	618.09 ..13 .369	625.9 ..13 .369	634.82 ..14 .380	637.52 ..14 .380
607.84 ..12 .352	618.1 ..13 .369	626.0 ..13 .369	634.90 ..14 .380	637.60 ..14 .380
607.85 ..12 .352	618.2 ..13 .369	626.1 ..13 .369	634.91 ..14 .380	637.61 ..14 .380
607.89 ..12 .352	618.3 ..13 .369	626.2 ..13 .369	634.92 ..14 .380	637.62 ..14 .380
607.9 ..12 .352	618.4 ..13 .369	626.3 ..13 .369	635.00 ..14 .380	637.70 ..14 .380
608.0 ..12 .350	618.5 ..13 .369	626.4 ..13 .369	635.01 ..14 .380	637.71 ..14 .380
608.1 ..12 .352	618.6 ..13 .369	626.5 ..13 .369	635.02 ..14 .380	637.72 ..14 .380
608.20 ..12 .352	618.7 ..13 .369	626.6 ..13 .369	635.10 ..14 .380	637.80 ..14 .380
608.21 ..12 .352	618.81 ..13 .369	626.7 ..13 .369		

DX	MDC	DRG
637.81	14	380
637.82	14	380
637.90	14	380
637.91	14	380
637.92	14	380
638.0	14	380
638.1	14	380
638.2	14	380
638.3	14	380
638.4	14	380
638.5	14	380
638.6	14	380
638.7	14	380
638.8	14	380
638.9	14	380
639.0	14	376
639.1	14	376
639.2	14	376
639.3	14	376
639.4	14	376
639.5	14	376
639.6	14	376
639.8	14	376
639.9	14	376
640.00	14	379
640.01	14	372-373
640.03	14	379
640.80	14	379
640.81	14	372-373
640.83	14	379
640.90	14	379
640.91	14	372-373
640.93	14	379
641.00	14	469
641.01	14	372-373
641.03	14	383-384
641.10	14	469
641.11	14	372-373
641.13	14	383-384
641.20	14	469
641.21	14	372-373
641.23	14	383-384
641.30	14	469
641.31	14	372-373
641.33	14	383
641.80	14	469
641.81	14	372-373
641.83	14	383-384
641.90	14	469
641.91	14	372-373
641.93	14	383-384
642.00	14	469
642.01	14	372-373
642.02	14	372-373
642.03	14	383
642.04	14	376
642.10	14	469
642.11	14	372-373
642.12	14	372-373
642.13	14	383
642.14	14	376
642.20	14	469
642.21	14	372-373
642.22	14	372-373
642.23	14	383
642.24	14	376
642.30	14	469
642.31	14	372-373
642.32	14	372-373
642.33	14	383-384
642.34	14	376
642.40	14	469
642.41	14	372-373
642.42	14	372-373
642.43	14	383
642.44	14	376
642.50	14	469
642.51	14	372-373
642.52	14	372-373
642.53	14	383
642.54	14	376
642.60	14	469
642.61	14	372-373
642.62	14	372-373
642.63	14	383
642.64	14	376
642.70	14	469
642.71	14	372-373
642.72	14	372-373
642.73	14	383
642.74	14	376
642.90	14	469
642.91	14	372-373
642.92	14	372-373
642.93	14	383
642.94	14	376
643.00	14	469
643.01	14	372-373
643.03	14	383
643.10	14	469
643.11	14	372-373
643.13	14	383
643.20	14	469
643.21	14	372-373
643.23	14	383
643.80	14	469
643.81	14	372-373
643.83	14	383
643.90	14	469
643.91	14	372-373
643.93	14	383
644.00	14	379
644.03	14	379
644.10	14	382
644.13	14	382
644.20	14	383-384
644.21	14	372-373
645.10	14	469
645.11	14	372-373
645.13	14	383-384
645.20	14	469
645.21	14	372-373
645.23	14	383-384
646.00	14	372-373
646.01	14	372-373
646.03	14	383-384
646.10	14	469
646.11	14	372-373
646.12	14	372-373
646.13	14	383
646.14	14	376
646.20	14	469
646.21	14	372-373
646.22	14	372-373
646.23	14	383
646.24	14	376
646.30	14	469
646.31	14	372-373
646.33	14	383-384
646.40	14	469
646.41	14	372-373
646.42	14	372-373
646.43	14	383
646.44	14	376
646.50	14	469
646.51	14	372-373
646.52	14	372-373
646.53	14	383-384
646.54	14	376
646.60	14	469
646.61	14	372-373
646.62	14	372-373
646.63	14	383
646.64	14	376
646.70	14	469
646.71	14	372-373
646.73	14	383
646.80	14	469
646.81	14	372-373
646.82	14	372-373
646.83	14	383
646.84	14	376
646.90	14	469
646.91	14	372-373
646.93	14	383-384
647.00	14	469
647.01	14	372-373
647.02	14	372-373
647.03	14	383
647.04	14	376
647.10	14	469
647.11	14	372-373
647.12	14	372-373
647.13	14	383
647.14	14	376
647.20	14	469
647.21	14	372-373
647.22	14	372-373
647.23	14	383
647.24	14	376
647.30	14	469
647.31	14	372-373
647.32	14	372-373
647.33	14	383
647.34	14	376
647.40	14	469
647.41	14	372-373
647.42	14	372-373
647.43	14	383
647.44	14	376
647.50	14	469
647.51	14	372-373
647.52	14	372-373
647.53	14	383
647.54	14	376
647.60	14	469
647.61	14	372-373
647.62	14	372-373
647.63	14	383
647.64	14	376
647.80	14	469
647.81	14	372-373
647.82	14	372-373
647.83	14	383
647.84	14	376
647.90	14	469
647.91	14	372-373
647.92	14	372-373
647.93	14	383
647.94	14	376
648.00	14	469
648.01	14	372-373
648.02	14	372-373
648.03	14	383
648.04	14	376
648.10	14	469
648.11	14	372-373
648.12	14	372-373
648.13	14	383
648.14	14	376
648.20	14	469
648.21	14	372-373
648.22	14	372-373
648.23	14	383
648.24	14	376
648.30	14	469
648.31	14	372-373
648.32	14	372-373
648.33	14	383
648.34	14	376
648.40	14	469
648.41	14	372-373
648.42	14	372-373
648.43	14	383
648.44	14	376
648.50	14	469
648.51	14	372-373
648.52	14	372-373
648.53	14	383
648.54	14	376
648.60	14	469
648.61	14	372-373
648.62	14	372-373
648.63	14	383
648.64	14	376
648.70	14	469
648.71	14	372-373
648.72	14	370-375
648.73	14	383
648.74	14	376
648.80	14	469
648.81	14	372-373
648.82	14	372-373
648.83	14	383
648.84	14	376
648.90	14	469
648.91	14	372-373
648.92	14	372-373
648.93	14	383
648.94	14	376
649.00	14	469
649.01	14	372-373
649.02	14	372-373
649.03	14	383-384
649.04	14	376
649.10	14	469
649.11	14	372-373
649.12	14	372-373
649.13	14	383-384
649.14	14	376
649.20	14	469
649.21	14	372-373
649.22	14	372-373
649.23	14	383-384
649.24	14	376-377
649.30	14	469
649.31	14	372-373
649.32	14	372-373
649.33	14	383-384
649.34	14	376
649.40	14	469
649.41	14	372-373
649.42	14	372-373
649.43	14	383-384
649.44	14	376
649.50	14	469
649.51	14	372-373
649.53	14	383, 384
649.60	14	469
649.61	14	372-373
649.62	14	372-373
649.63	14	383-384
649.64	14	376
650	14	372-373
651.00	14	469
651.01	14	372-373
651.03	14	383-384
651.10	14	469
651.11	14	372-373
651.13	14	383-384
651.20	14	469
651.21	14	372-373
651.23	14	383-384
651.30	14	469
651.31	14	372-373
651.33	14	383-384
651.40	14	469
651.41	14	372-373
651.43	14	383-384
651.50	14	469
651.51	14	372-373
651.53	14	383-384
651.60	14	469
651.61	14	372-373
651.63	14	383-384
651.70	14	469
651.71	14	372-373
651.73	14	383-384
651.80	14	469
651.81	14	372-373
651.83	14	383-384
651.90	14	469
651.91	14	372-373
651.93	14	383-384
652.00	14	469
652.01	14	372-373
652.03	14	383-384
652.10	14	469
652.11	14	372-373
652.13	14	383-384
652.20	14	469
652.21	14	372-373
652.23	14	383-384
652.30	14	469
652.31	14	372-373
652.33	14	383-384
652.40	14	469
652.41	14	372-373
652.43	14	383-384
652.50	14	469
652.51	14	372-373
652.53	14	383-384
652.60	14	469
652.61	14	372-373
652.63	14	383-384
652.70	14	469
652.71	14	372-373
652.73	14	383-384
652.80	14	469
652.81	14	372-373
652.83	14	383-384
652.90	14	469
652.91	14	372-373
652.93	14	383-384
653.00	14	469
653.01	14	372-373
653.03	14	383-384
653.10	14	469
653.11	14	372-373
653.13	14	383-384
653.20	14	469
653.21	14	372-373
653.23	14	383-384
653.30	14	469
653.31	14	372-373
653.33	14	383-384
653.40	14	469
653.41	14	372-373
653.43	14	383-384
653.50	14	469
653.51	14	372-373
653.53	14	383-384
653.60	14	469
653.61	14	372-373
653.63	14	383-384
653.70	14	469
653.71	14	372-373
653.73	14	383-384
653.80	14	469
653.81	14	372-373
653.83	14	383-384
653.90	14	469
653.91	14	372-373
653.93	14	383-384
654.00	14	469
654.01	14	372-373
654.02	14	372-373
654.03	14	383-384
654.04	14	376
654.10	14	469
654.11	14	372-373
654.12	14	372-373
654.13	14	383-384
654.14	14	376
654.20	14	469
654.21	14	372-373
654.23	14	383-384
654.30	14	469
654.31	14	372-373
654.32	14	372-373
654.33	14	383-384
654.34	14	376
654.40	14	469
654.41	14	372-373
654.42	14	372-373

DX	MDC	DRG	DX	MDC	DRG	DX	MDC	DRG	DX	MDC	DRG	DX	MDC	DRG
654.43	14	383-384	656.80	14	469	660.70	14	372-373	664.50	14	372-373	668.90	14	372-373
654.44	14	376	656.81	14	372-373	660.71	14	372-373	664.51	14	372-373	668.91	14	372-373
654.50	14	469	656.83	14	383-384	660.73	14	383-384	664.54	14	376	668.92	14	372-373
654.51	14	372-373	656.90	14	469	660.80	14	372-373	664.80	14	372-373	668.93	14	383-384
654.52	14	372-373	656.91	14	372-373	660.81	14	372-373	664.81	14	372-373	668.94	14	376
654.53	14	383-384	656.93	14	383-384	660.83	14	383-384	664.84	14	376	669.00	14	372-373
654.54	14	376	657.00	14	469	660.90	14	372-373	664.90	14	372-373	669.01	14	372-373
654.60	14	469	657.01	14	372-373	660.91	14	372-373	664.91	14	372-373	669.02	14	372-373
654.61	14	372-373	657.03	14	383-384	660.93	14	383-384	664.94	14	376	669.03	14	383-384
654.62	14	372-373	658.00	14	469	661.00	14	372-373	665.00	14	372-373	669.04	14	376
654.63	14	383-384	658.01	14	372-373	661.01	14	372-373	665.01	14	372-373	669.10	14	372-373
654.64	14	376	658.03	14	383-384	661.03	14	383-384	665.03	14	383-384	669.11	14	372-373
654.70	14	469	658.10	14	372-373	661.10	14	372-373	665.10	14	372-373	669.12	14	372-373
654.71	14	372-373	658.11	14	372-373	661.11	14	372-373	665.11	14	372-373	669.13	14	383-384
654.72	14	372-373	658.13	14	383-384	661.13	14	383-384	665.20	14	372-373	669.14	14	376
654.73	14	383-384	658.20	14	372-373	661.20	14	372-373	665.22	14	372-373	669.20	14	372-373
654.74	14	376	658.21	14	372-373	661.21	14	372-373	665.24	14	376	669.21	14	372-373
654.80	14	469	658.23	14	383-384	661.23	14	383-384	665.30	14	372-373	669.22	14	372-373
654.81	14	372-373	658.30	14	372-373	661.30	14	372-373	665.31	14	372-373	669.23	14	383-384
654.82	14	372-373	658.31	14	372-373	661.31	14	372-373	665.34	14	376	669.24	14	376
654.83	14	383-384	658.33	14	383-384	661.33	14	383-384	665.40	14	372-373	669.30	14	372-373
654.84	14	376	658.40	14	372-373	661.40	14	372-373	665.41	14	372-373	669.32	14	372-373
654.90	14	469	658.41	14	372-373	661.41	14	372-373	665.44	14	376	669.34	14	376
654.91	14	372-373	658.43	14	383-384	661.43	14	383-384	665.50	14	372-373	669.40	14	372-373
654.92	14	372-373	658.80	14	469	661.90	14	372-373	665.51	14	372-373	669.41	14	372-373
654.93	14	383-384	658.81	14	372-373	661.91	14	372-373	665.54	14	376	669.42	14	372-373
654.94	14	376	658.83	14	383-384	661.93	14	383-384	665.60	14	372-373	669.44	14	376
655.00	14	469	658.90	14	469	662.00	14	372-373	665.61	14	372-373	669.50	14	372-373
655.01	14	372-373	658.91	14	372-373	662.01	14	372-373	665.64	14	376	669.51	14	372-373
655.03	14	383-384	658.93	14	383-384	662.03	14	383-384	665.70	14	372-373	669.60	14	372-373
655.10	14	469	659.00	14	372-373	662.10	14	372-373	665.71	14	372-373	669.61	14	372-373
655.11	14	372-373	659.01	14	372-373	662.11	14	372-373	665.72	14	372-373	669.70	14	372-373
655.13	14	383-384	659.03	14	383-384	662.13	14	383-384	665.74	14	376	669.71	14	372-373
655.20	14	469	659.10	14	372-373	662.20	14	372-373	665.80	14	372-373	669.80	14	372-373
655.21	14	372-373	659.11	14	372-373	662.21	14	372-373	665.81	14	372-373	669.81	14	372-373
655.23	14	383-384	659.13	14	383-384	662.23	14	383-384	665.82	14	372-373	669.82	14	372-373
655.30	14	469	659.20	14	372-373	662.30	14	372-373	665.83	14	383-384	669.83	14	383-384
655.31	14	372-373	659.21	14	372-373	662.31	14	372-373	665.84	14	376	669.84	14	376
655.33	14	383-384	659.23	14	383-384	662.33	14	383-384	665.90	14	372-373	669.90	14	372-373
655.40	14	469	659.30	14	372-373	663.00	14	372-373	665.91	14	372-373	669.91	14	372-373
655.41	14	372-373	659.31	14	372-373	663.01	14	372-373	665.92	14	372-373	669.92	14	372-373
655.43	14	383-384	659.33	14	383-384	663.03	14	383-384	665.93	14	383-384	669.93	14	383-384
655.50	14	469	659.40	14	469	663.10	14	372-373	665.94	14	376	669.94	14	376
655.51	14	372-373	659.41	14	372-373	663.11	14	372-373	666.00	14	469	670.00	14	469
655.53	14	383-384	659.43	14	383-384	663.13	14	383-384	666.02	14	372-373	670.02	14	372-373
655.60	14	469	659.50	14	372-373	663.20	14	372-373	666.04	14	376	670.04	14	376
655.61	14	372-373	659.51	14	372-373	663.21	14	372-373	666.10	14	469	671.00	14	469
655.63	14	383-384	659.53	14	383-384	663.23	14	383-384	666.12	14	372-373	671.01	14	372-373
655.70	14	469	659.60	14	372-373	663.30	14	372-373	666.14	14	376	671.02	14	372-373
655.71	14	372-373	659.61	14	372-373	663.31	14	372-373	666.20	14	469	671.03	14	383-384
655.73	14	383-384	659.63	14	383-384	663.33	14	383-384	666.22	14	372-373	671.04	14	376
655.80	14	469	659.70	14	372-373	663.40	14	372-373	666.24	14	376	671.10	14	469
655.81	14	372-373	659.71	14	372-373	663.41	14	372-373	666.30	14	469	671.11	14	372-373
655.83	14	383-384	659.73	14	383-384	663.43	14	383-384	666.32	14	372-373	671.12	14	372-373
655.90	14	469	659.80	14	372-373	663.50	14	372-373	666.34	14	376	671.13	14	383-384
655.91	14	372-373	659.81	14	372-373	663.51	14	372-373	667.00	14	469	671.14	14	376
655.93	14	383-384	659.83	14	383-384	663.53	14	383-384	667.02	14	372-373	671.20	14	469
656.00	14	469	659.90	14	372-373	663.60	14	372-373	667.04	14	376	671.21	14	372-373
656.01	14	372-373	659.91	14	372-373	663.61	14	372-373	667.10	14	469	671.22	14	372-373
656.03	14	383-384	659.93	14	383-384	663.63	14	383-384	667.12	14	372-373	671.23	14	383-384
656.10	14	469	660.00	14	372-373	663.80	14	372-373	667.14	14	376	671.24	14	376
656.11	14	372-373	660.01	14	372-373	663.81	14	372-373	668.00	14	372-373	671.30	14	469
656.13	14	383-384	660.03	14	383-384	663.83	14	383-384	668.01	14	372-373	671.31	14	372-373
656.20	14	469	660.10	14	372-373	663.90	14	372-373	668.02	14	372-373	671.33	14	383-384
656.21	14	372-373	660.11	14	372-373	663.91	14	372-373	668.03	14	383-384	671.40	14	469
656.23	14	383-384	660.13	14	383-384	663.93	14	383-384	668.04	14	376	671.42	14	372-373
656.30	14	372-373	660.20	14	372-373	664.00	14	372-373	668.10	14	372-373	671.44	14	376
656.31	14	372-373	660.21	14	372-373	664.01	14	372-373	668.11	14	372-373	671.50	14	469
656.33	14	383-384	660.23	14	383-384	664.04	14	376	668.12	14	372-373	671.51	14	372-373
656.40	14	372-373	660.30	14	372-373	664.10	14	372-373	668.13	14	383-384	671.52	14	372-373
656.41	14	372-373	660.31	14	372-373	664.11	14	372-373	668.14	14	376	671.53	14	383-384
656.43	14	383-384	660.33	14	383-384	664.14	14	376	668.20	14	372-373	671.54	14	376
656.50	14	469	660.40	14	372-373	664.20	14	372-373	668.21	14	372-373	671.80	14	469
656.51	14	372-373	660.41	14	372-373	664.21	14	372-373	668.22	14	372-373	671.81	14	372-373
656.53	14	383-384	660.43	14	383-384	664.24	14	376	668.23	14	383-384	671.82	14	372-373
656.60	14	469	660.50	14	372-373	664.30	14	372-373	668.24	14	376	671.83	14	383-384
656.61	14	372-373	660.51	14	372-373	664.31	14	372-373	668.80	14	372-373	671.84	14	376
656.63	14	383-384	660.53	14	383-384	664.34	14	376	668.81	14	372-373	671.90	14	469
656.70	14	469	660.60	14	372-373	664.40	14	372-373	668.82	14	372-373	671.91	14	372-373
656.71	14	372-373	660.61	14	372-373	664.41	14	372-373	668.83	14	383-384	671.92	14	372-373
656.73	14	383-384	660.63	14	383-384	664.44	14	376	668.84	14	376	671.93	14	383-384

DX	MDC	DRG
671.94	14	376
672.00	14	469
672.02	14	372-373
672.04	14	376
673.00	14	469
673.01	14	372-373
673.02	14	372-373
673.03	14	383-384
673.04	14	376
673.10	14	469
673.11	14	372-373
673.12	14	372-373
673.13	14	383-384
673.14	14	376
673.20	14	469
673.21	14	372-373
673.22	14	372-373
673.23	14	383-384
673.24	14	376
673.30	14	469
673.31	14	372-373
673.32	14	372-373
673.33	14	383-384
673.34	14	376
673.80	14	469
673.81	14	372-373
673.82	14	372-373
673.83	14	383-384
673.84	14	376
674.00	14	469
674.01	14	372-373
674.02	14	372-373
674.03	14	383-384
674.04	14	376
674.10	14	469
674.12	14	372-373
674.14	14	376
674.20	14	469
674.22	14	372-373
674.24	14	376
674.30	14	469
674.32	14	372-373
674.34	14	376
674.40	14	469
674.42	14	372-373
674.44	14	376
674.50	14	469
674.51	14	372-373
674.53	14	383-384
674.54	14	376
674.80	14	469
674.82	14	372-373
674.84	14	376
674.90	14	469
674.92	14	372-373
674.94	14	376
675.00	14	469
675.01	14	372-373
675.02	14	372-373
675.03	14	383-384
675.04	14	376
675.10	14	469
675.11	14	372-373
675.12	14	372-373
675.13	14	383-384
675.14	14	376
675.20	14	469
675.21	14	372-373
675.22	14	372-373
675.23	14	383-384
675.24	14	376
675.80	14	469
675.81	14	372-373
675.82	14	372-373
675.83	14	383-384
675.84	14	376
675.90	14	469
675.91	14	372-373
675.92	14	372-373
675.93	14	383-384
675.94	14	376
676.00	14	469
676.01	14	372-373
676.02	14	372-373
676.03	14	383-384
676.04	14	376
676.10	14	469
676.11	14	372-373
676.12	14	372-373
676.13	14	383-384
676.14	14	376
676.20	14	469
676.21	14	372-373
676.22	14	372-373
676.23	14	383-384
676.24	14	376
676.30	14	469
676.31	14	372-373
676.32	14	372-373
676.33	14	383-384
676.34	14	376
676.40	14	469
676.41	14	372-373
676.42	14	372-373
676.43	14	383-384
676.44	14	376
676.50	14	469
676.51	14	372-373
676.52	14	372-373
676.53	14	383-384
676.54	14	376
676.60	14	469
676.61	14	372-373
676.62	14	372-373
676.63	14	383-384
676.64	14	376
676.80	14	469
676.81	14	372-373
676.82	14	372-373
676.83	14	383-384
676.84	14	376
676.90	14	469
676.91	14	372-373
676.92	14	372-373
676.93	14	383-384
676.94	14	376
677	14	469

Diseases of the Skin and Subcutaneous Tissue

DX	MDC	DRG
680.0	09	277-279
680.1	09	277-279
680.2	09	277-279
680.3	09	277-279
680.4	09	277-279
680.5	09	277-279
680.6	09	277-279
680.7	09	277-279
680.8	09	277-279
680.9	09	277-279
681.00	09	277-279
681.01	09	277-279
681.02	09	277-279
681.10	09	277-279
681.11	09	277-279
681.9	09	277-279
682.0	09	277-279
682.1	09	277-279
682.2	09	277-279
682.3	09	277-279
682.4	09	277-279
682.5	09	277-279
682.6	09	277-279
682.7	09	277-279
682.8	09	277-279
682.9	09	277-279
683	16	398-399
684	09	277-279
685.0	09	277-279
685.1	09	277-279
686.00	09	277-279
686.01	09	277-279
686.09	09	277-279
686.1	09	277-279
686.8	09	277-279
686.9	09	277-279
690.10	09	283-284
690.11	09	283-284
690.12	09	283-284
690.18	09	283-284
690.8	09	283-284
691.0	09	283-284
691.8	09	283-284
692.0	09	283-284
692.1	09	283-284
692.2	09	283-284
692.3	09	283-284
692.4	09	283-284
692.5	09	283-284
692.6	09	283-284
692.70	09	283-284
692.71	09	283-284
692.72	09	283-284
692.73	09	283-284
692.74	09	283-284
692.75	09	283-284
692.76	09	283-284
692.77	09	283-284
692.79	09	283-284
692.81	09	283-284
692.82	09	283-284
692.83	09	283-284
692.84	09	283-284
692.89	09	283-284
692.9	09	283-284
693.0	09	283-284
693.1	09	283-284
693.8	09	283-284
693.9	09	283-284
694.0	09	283-284
694.1	09	283-284
694.2	09	283-284
694.3	09	283-284
694.4	09	272-273
694.5	09	272-273
694.60	09	272-273
694.61	02	046-048
694.8	09	272-273
694.9	09	272-273
695.0	09	272-273
695.1	09	272-273
695.2	09	272-273
695.3	09	283-284
695.4	09	272-273
695.81	09	272-273
695.89	09	283-284
695.9	09	283-284
696.0	08	240-241
696.1	09	272-273
696.2	09	272-273
696.3	09	283-284
696.4	09	283-284
696.5	09	283-284
696.8	09	283-284
697.0	09	283-284
697.1	09	283-284
697.8	09	283-284
697.9	09	283-284
698.0	09	283-284
698.1	12	352
698.1	13	368
698.2	09	283-284
698.3	09	283-284
698.4	09	283-284
698.8	09	283-284
698.9	09	283-284
700	09	283-284
701.0	09	283-284
701.1	09	283-284
701.2	09	283-284
701.3	09	283-284
701.4	09	283-284
701.5	09	283-284
701.8	09	283-284
701.9	09	283-284
702.0	09	283-284
702.11	09	283-284
702.19	09	283-284
702.8	09	283-284
703.0	09	283-284
703.8	09	283-284
703.9	09	283-284
704.00	09	283-284
704.01	09	283-284
704.02	09	283-284
704.09	09	283-284
704.1	09	283-284
704.2	09	283-284
704.3	09	283-284
704.8	09	283-284
704.9	09	283-284
705.0	09	283-284
705.1	09	283-284
705.21	09	283-284
705.22	09	283-284
705.81	09	283-284
705.82	09	283-284
705.83	09	283-284
705.89	09	283-284
705.9	09	283-284
706.0	09	283-284
706.1	09	283-284
706.2	09	283-284
706.3	09	283-284
706.8	09	283-284
706.9	09	283-284
707.00	09	271
707.01	09	271
707.02	09	271
707.03	09	271
707.04	09	271
707.05	09	271
707.06	09	271
707.07	09	271
707.09	09	271
707.10	09	271
707.11	09	271
707.12	09	271
707.13	09	271
707.14	09	271
707.15	09	271
707.19	09	271
707.8	09	271
707.9	09	271
708.0	09	283-284
708.1	09	283-284
708.2	09	283-284
708.3	09	283-284
708.4	09	283-284
708.5	09	283-284
708.8	09	283-284
708.9	09	283-284
709.00	09	283-284
709.01	09	283-284
709.09	09	283-284
709.1	09	283-284
709.2	09	283-284
709.3	09	283-284
709.4	09	283-284
709.8	09	283-284
709.9	09	283-284

Diseases of the Musculoskeletal System and Connective Tissue

DX	MDC	DRG
710.0	08	240-241
710.1	08	240-241
710.2	08	240-241
710.3	08	240-241
710.4	08	240-241
710.5	08	240-241
710.8	08	240-241
710.9	08	240-241
711.00	08	242
711.01	08	242
711.02	08	242
711.03	08	242
711.04	08	242
711.05	08	242
711.06	08	242,501-502
711.07	08	242
711.08	08	242
711.09	08	242
711.10	08	240-241
711.11	08	240-241
711.12	08	240-241
711.13	08	240-241
711.14	08	240-241
711.15	08	240-241
711.16	08	240-241
711.17	08	240-241
711.18	08	240-241
711.19	08	240-241
711.20	08	240-241
711.21	08	240-241
711.22	08	240-241
711.23	08	240-241
711.24	08	240-241
711.25	08	240-241
711.26	08	240-241
711.27	08	240-241
711.28	08	240-241
711.29	08	240-241
711.30	08	244-245
711.31	08	244-245
711.32	08	244-245
711.33	08	244-245
711.34	08	244-245
711.35	08	244-245
711.36	08	244-245
711.37	08	244-245
711.38	08	244-245
711.39	08	244-245
711.40	08	242
711.41	08	242
711.42	08	242
711.43	08	242
711.44	08	242
711.45	08	242
711.46	08	242
711.47	08	242
711.48	08	242
711.49	08	242
711.50	08	244-245
711.51	08	244-245
711.52	08	244-245
711.53	08	244-245
711.54	08	244-245
711.55	08	244-245
711.56	08	244-245
711.57	08	244-245
711.58	08	244-245
711.59	08	244-245
711.60	08	242
711.61	08	242
711.62	08	242
711.63	08	242
711.64	08	242
711.65	08	242
711.66	08	242
711.67	08	242
711.68	08	242
711.69	08	242
711.70	08	242
711.71	08	242
711.72	08	242
711.73	08	242
711.74	08	242
711.75	08	242
711.76	08	242
711.77	08	242
711.78	08	242
711.79	08	242
711.80	08	242
711.81	08	242
711.82	08	242
711.83	08	242

DX	MDC	DRG	DX	MDC	DRG	DX	MDC	DRG	DX	MDC	DRG	DX	MDC	DRG
711.84	.08	.242	714.33	.08	.240-241	716.35	.08	.244-245	718.09	.08	.256	719.00	.08	.256
711.85	.08	.242	714.4	.08	.244-245	716.36	.08	.244-245	718.10	.08	.256	719.01	.08	.256
711.86	.08	.242	714.81	.04	.092-093	716.37	.08	.244-245	718.11	.08	.256	719.02	.08	.256
711.87	.08	.242	714.89	.08	.240-241	716.38	.08	.244-245	718.12	.08	.256	719.03	.08	.256
711.88	.08	.242	714.9	.08	.244-245	716.39	.08	.244-245	718.13	.08	.256	719.04	.08	.256
711.89	.08	.242	715.00	.08	.244-245	716.40	.08	.246	718.14	.08	.256	719.05	.08	.256
711.90	.08	.242	715.04	.08	.244-245	716.41	.08	.246	718.15	.08	.256	719.06	.08	.256
711.91	.08	.242	715.09	.08	.244-245	716.42	.08	.246	718.17	.08	.256	719.07	.08	.256
711.92	.08	.242	715.10	.08	.244-245	716.43	.08	.246	718.18	.08	.256	719.08	.08	.256
711.93	.08	.242	715.11	.08	.244-245	716.44	.08	.246	718.19	.08	.256	719.09	.08	.256
711.94	.08	.242	715.12	.08	.244-245	716.45	.08	.246	718.20	.08	.250-252	719.10	.08	.244-245
711.95	.08	.242	715.13	.08	.244-245	716.46	.08	.246	718.21	.08	.253-255	719.11	.08	.244-245
711.96	.08	.242	715.14	.08	.244-245	716.47	.08	.246	718.22	.08	.253-255	719.12	.08	.244-245
711.97	.08	.242	715.15	.08	.244-245	716.48	.08	.246	718.23	.08	.250-252	719.13	.08	.244-245
711.98	.08	.242	715.16	.08	.244-245	716.49	.08	.246	718.24	.08	.250-252	719.14	.08	.244-245
711.99	.08	.242	715.17	.08	.244-245	716.50	.08	.246	718.25	.08	.256	719.15	.08	.244-245
712.10	.08	.244-245	715.18	.08	.244-245	716.51	.08	.246	718.26	.08	.253-255	719.16	.08	.244-245
712.11	.08	.244-245	715.20	.08	.244-245	716.52	.08	.246	718.27	.08	.253-255	719.17	.08	.244-245
712.12	.08	.244-245	715.21	.08	.244-245	716.53	.08	.246	718.28	.08	.256	719.18	.08	.244-245
712.13	.08	.244-245	715.22	.08	.244-245	716.54	.08	.246	718.29	.08	.256	719.19	.08	.244-245
712.14	.08	.244-245	715.23	.08	.244-245	716.55	.08	.246	718.30	.08	.256	719.20	.08	.244-245
712.15	.08	.244-245	715.24	.08	.244-245	716.56	.08	.246	718.31	.08	.253-255	719.21	.08	.244-245
712.16	.08	.244-245	715.25	.08	.244-245	716.57	.08	.246	718.32	.08	.253-255	719.22	.08	.244-245
712.17	.08	.244-245	715.26	.08	.244-245	716.58	.08	.246	718.33	.08	.250-252	719.23	.08	.244-245
712.18	.08	.244-245	715.27	.08	.244-245	716.59	.08	.246	718.34	.08	.250-252	719.24	.08	.244-245
712.19	.08	.244-245	715.28	.08	.244-245	716.60	.08	.246	718.35	.08	.256	719.25	.08	.244-245
712.20	.08	.244-245	715.30	.08	.244-245	716.61	.08	.246	718.36	.08	.253-255	719.26	.08	.244-245
712.21	.08	.244-245	715.31	.08	.244-245	716.62	.08	.246	718.37	.08	.253-255	719.27	.08	.244-245
712.22	.08	.244-245	715.32	.08	.244-245	716.63	.08	.246	718.38	.08	.256	719.28	.08	.244-245
712.23	.08	.244-245	715.33	.08	.244-245	716.64	.08	.246	718.39	.08	.256	719.29	.08	.244-245
712.24	.08	.244-245	715.34	.08	.244-245	716.65	.08	.246	718.40	.08	.256	719.30	.08	.244-245
712.25	.08	.244-245	715.35	.08	.244-245	716.66	.08	.246	718.41	.08	.256	719.31	.08	.244-245
712.26	.08	.244-245	715.36	.08	.244-245	716.67	.08	.246	718.42	.08	.256	719.32	.08	.244-245
712.27	.08	.244-245	715.37	.08	.244-245	716.68	.08	.246	718.43	.08	.256	719.33	.08	.244-245
712.28	.08	.244-245	715.38	.08	.244-245	716.80	.08	.246	718.44	.08	.256	719.34	.08	.244-245
712.29	.08	.244-245	715.80	.08	.244-245	716.81	.08	.246	718.45	.08	.256	719.35	.08	.244-245
712.30	.08	.244-245	715.89	.08	.244-245	716.82	.08	.246	718.46	.08	.256	719.36	.08	.244-245
712.31	.08	.244-245	715.90	.08	.244-245	716.83	.08	.246	718.47	.08	.256	719.37	.08	.244-245
712.32	.08	.244-245	715.91	.08	.244-245	716.84	.08	.246	718.48	.08	.256	719.38	.08	.244-245
712.33	.08	.244-245	715.92	.08	.244-245	716.85	.08	.246	718.49	.08	.256	719.39	.08	.244-245
712.34	.08	.244-245	715.93	.08	.244-245	716.86	.08	.246	718.50	.08	.244-245	719.40	.08	.247
712.35	.08	.244-245	715.94	.08	.244-245	716.87	.08	.246	718.51	.08	.244-245	719.41	.08	.247
712.36	.08	.244-245	715.95	.08	.244-245	716.88	.08	.246	718.52	.08	.244-245	719.42	.08	.247
712.37	.08	.244-245	715.96	.08	.244-245	716.89	.08	.246	718.53	.08	.244-245	719.43	.08	.247
712.38	.08	.244-245	715.97	.08	.244-245	716.90	.08	.246	718.54	.08	.244-245	719.44	.08	.247
712.39	.08	.244-245	715.98	.08	.244-245	716.91	.08	.246	718.55	.08	.244-245	719.45	.08	.247
712.80	.08	.244-245	716.00	.08	.244-245	716.92	.08	.246	718.56	.08	.244-245	719.46	.08	.247
712.81	.08	.244-245	716.01	.08	.244-245	716.93	.08	.246	718.57	.08	.244-245	719.47	.08	.247
712.82	.08	.244-245	716.02	.08	.244-245	716.94	.08	.246	718.58	.08	.244-245	719.48	.08	.247
712.83	.08	.244-245	716.03	.08	.244-245	716.95	.08	.246	718.59	.08	.244-245	719.49	.08	.247
712.84	.08	.244-245	716.04	.08	.244-245	716.96	.08	.246	718.60	.08	.256	719.50	.08	.247
712.85	.08	.244-245	716.05	.08	.244-245	716.97	.08	.246	718.65	.08	.256	719.51	.08	.247
712.86	.08	.244-245	716.06	.08	.244-245	716.98	.08	.246	718.70	.08	.256	719.52	.08	.247
712.87	.08	.244-245	716.07	.08	.244-245	716.99	.08	.246	718.71	.08	.256	719.53	.08	.247
712.88	.08	.244-245	716.08	.08	.244-245	717.0	.08	.253-255	718.72	.08	.256	719.54	.08	.247
712.89	.08	.244-245	716.09	.08	.244-245	717.1	.08	.253-255	718.73	.08	.256	719.55	.08	.247
712.90	.08	.244-245	716.10	.08	.244-245	717.2	.08	.253-255	718.74	.08	.256	719.56	.08	.247
712.91	.08	.244-245	716.11	.08	.244-245	717.3	.08	.253-255	718.75	.08	.256	719.57	.08	.247
712.92	.08	.244-245	716.12	.08	.244-245	717.40	.08	.253-255	718.76	.08	.256	719.58	.08	.247
712.93	.08	.244-245	716.13	.08	.244-245	717.41	.08	.253-255	718.77	.08	.256	719.59	.08	.247
712.94	.08	.244-245	716.14	.08	.244-245	717.42	.08	.253-255	718.78	.08	.256	719.60	.08	.247
712.95	.08	.244-245	716.15	.08	.244-245	717.43	.08	.253-255	718.79	.08	.256	719.61	.08	.247
712.96	.08	.244-245	716.16	.08	.244-245	717.49	.08	.253-255	718.80	.08	.256	719.62	.08	.247
712.97	.08	.244-245	716.17	.08	.244-245	717.5	.08	.253-255	718.81	.08	.256	719.63	.08	.247
712.98	.08	.244-245	716.18	.08	.244-245	717.6	.08	.256	718.82	.08	.256	719.64	.08	.247
712.99	.08	.244-245	716.19	.08	.244-245	717.7	.08	.253-255	718.83	.08	.256	719.65	.08	.247
713.0	.08	.244-245	716.20	.08	.244-245	717.81	.08	.253-255	718.84	.08	.256	719.66	.08	.247
713.1	.08	.244-245	716.21	.08	.244-245	717.82	.08	.253-255	718.85	.08	.256	719.67	.08	.247
713.2	.08	.244-245	716.22	.08	.244-245	717.83	.08	.253-255	718.86	.08	.256	719.68	.08	.247
713.3	.08	.244-245	716.23	.08	.244-245	717.84	.08	.253-255	718.87	.08	.256	719.69	.08	.247
713.4	.08	.244-245	716.24	.08	.244-245	717.85	.08	.253-255	718.88	.08	.256	719.7	.08	.247
713.5	.08	.244-245	716.25	.08	.244-245	717.89	.08	.253-255	718.89	.08	.256	719.80	.08	.247
713.6	.08	.244-245	716.26	.08	.244-245	717.9	.08	.253-255	718.90	.08	.256	719.81	.08	.247
713.7	.08	.244-245	716.27	.08	.244-245	718.00	.08	.256	718.91	.08	.256	719.82	.08	.247
713.8	.08	.244-245	716.28	.08	.244-245	718.01	.08	.253-255	718.92	.08	.256	719.83	.08	.247
714.0	.08	.240-241	716.29	.08	.244-245	718.02	.08	.253-255	718.93	.08	.256	719.84	.08	.247
714.1	.08	.240-241	716.30	.08	.244-245	718.03	.08	.250-252	718.94	.08	.256	719.85	.08	.247
714.2	.08	.240-241	716.31	.08	.244-245	718.04	.08	.250-252	718.95	.08	.256	719.86	.08	.247
714.30	.08	.240-241	716.32	.08	.244-245	718.05	.08	.256	718.97	.08	.256	719.87	.08	.247
714.31	.08	.240-241	716.33	.08	.244-245	718.07	.08	.253-255	718.98	.08	.256	719.88	.08	.247
714.32	.08	.240-241	716.34	.08	.244-245	718.08	.08	.256	718.99	.08	.256	719.89	.08	.247

DX	MDC	DRG	DX	MDC	DRG	DX	MDC	DRG	DX	MDC	DRG	DX	MDC	DRG
719.90	08	247	726.12	08	248	729.0	08	247	730.94	08	238	736.31	08	256
719.91	08	247	726.19	08	248	729.1	08	247	730.95	08	238	736.32	08	256
719.92	08	247	726.2	08	248	729.2	01	018-019	730.96	08	238	736.39	08	256
719.93	08	247	726.30	08	248	729.30	09	283-284	730.97	08	238	736.41	08	256
719.94	08	247	726.31	08	248	729.31	09	283-284	730.98	08	238	736.42	08	256
719.95	08	247	726.32	08	248	729.39	09	283-284	730.99	08	238	736.5	08	256
719.96	08	247	726.33	08	248	729.4	08	248	731.0	08	244-245	736.6	08	256
719.97	08	247	726.39	08	248	729.5	08	247	731.1	08	244-245	736.70	08	256
719.98	08	247	726.4	08	248	729.6	08	256	731.2	08	244-245	736.71	08	256
719.99	08	247	726.5	08	248	729.71	08	248	731.3	08	244-245	736.72	08	256
720.0	08	240-241	726.60	08	248	729.72	08	248	731.8	08	244-245	736.73	08	256
720.1	08	243	726.61	08	248	729.73	08	248	732.0	08	244-245	736.74	01	018-019
720.2	08	243	726.62	08	248	729.79	08	248	732.1	08	244-245	736.75	08	256
720.81	08	243	726.63	08	248	729.81	08	247	732.2	08	244-245	736.76	08	256
720.89	08	243	726.64	08	248	729.82	08	247	732.3	08	244-245	736.79	08	256
720.9	08	243	726.65	08	248	729.89	08	247	732.4	08	244-245	736.81	08	256
721.0	08	243	726.69	08	248	729.9	08	247	732.5	08	244-245	736.89	08	256
721.1	08	243	726.70	08	248	730.00	08	238	732.6	08	244-245	736.9	08	256
721.2	08	243	726.71	08	248	730.01	08	238	732.7	08	244-245	737.0	08	243
721.3	08	243	726.72	08	248	730.02	08	238	732.8	08	244-245	737.10	08	243
721.41	08	243	726.73	08	256	730.03	08	238	732.9	08	244-245	737.11	08	243
721.42	08	243	726.79	08	248	730.04	08	238	733.00	08	244-245	737.12	08	243
721.5	08	243	726.8	08	248	730.05	08	238	733.01	08	244-245	737.19	08	243
721.6	08	243	726.90	08	248	730.06	08	238	733.02	08	244-245	737.20	08	243
721.7	08	243	726.91	08	248	730.07	08	238	733.03	08	244-245	737.21	08	243
721.8	08	243	727.00	08	248	730.08	08	238	733.09	08	244-245	737.22	08	243
721.90	08	243	727.01	08	248	730.09	08	238	733.10	08	239	737.29	08	243
721.91	08	243	727.02	08	256	730.10	08	238	733.11	08	239	737.30	08	243
722.0	08	243	727.03	08	248	730.11	08	238	733.12	08	239	737.31	08	243
722.10	08	243	727.04	08	248	730.12	08	238	733.13	08	239	737.32	08	243
722.11	08	243	727.05	08	248	730.13	08	238	733.14	08	239	737.33	08	243
722.2	08	243	727.06	08	248	730.14	08	238	733.15	08	239	737.34	08	243
722.30	08	243	727.09	08	248	730.15	08	238	733.16	08	239	737.39	08	243
722.31	08	243	727.1	08	256	730.16	08	238	733.19	08	239	737.40	08	243
722.32	08	243	727.2	08	248	730.17	08	238	733.20	08	244-245	737.41	08	243
722.39	08	243	727.3	08	248	730.18	08	238	733.21	08	244-245	737.42	08	243
722.4	08	243	727.40	08	248	730.19	08	238	733.22	08	244-245	737.43	08	243
722.51	08	243	727.41	08	248	730.20	08	238	733.29	08	244-245	737.8	08	243
722.52	08	243	727.42	08	248	730.21	08	238	733.3	08	256	737.9	08	243
722.6	08	243	727.43	08	248	730.22	08	238	733.40	08	244-245	738.0	03	072
722.70	08	243	727.49	08	248	730.23	08	238	733.41	08	244-245	738.10	08	256
722.71	08	243	727.50	08	248	730.24	08	238	733.42	08	244-245	738.11	08	256
722.72	08	243	727.51	08	248	730.25	08	238	733.43	08	244-245	738.12	08	256
722.73	08	243	727.59	08	248	730.26	08	238	733.44	08	244-245	738.19	08	256
722.80	08	243	727.60	08	248	730.27	08	238	733.49	08	244-245	738.2	08	256
722.81	08	243	727.61	08	248	730.28	08	238	733.5	08	244-245	738.3	08	256
722.82	08	243	727.62	08	248	730.29	08	238	733.6	04	101-102	738.4	08	243
722.83	08	243	727.63	08	248	730.30	08	244-245	733.7	08	256	738.5	08	243
722.90	08	243	727.64	08	248	730.31	08	244-245	733.81	08	256	738.6	08	256
722.91	08	243	727.65	08	248	730.32	08	244-245	733.82	08	256	738.7	03	073-074
722.92	08	243	727.66	08	248	730.33	08	244-245	733.90	08	256	738.8	08	256
722.93	08	243	727.67	08	248	730.34	08	244-245	733.91	08	256	738.9	08	256
723.0	08	243	727.68	08	248	730.35	08	244-245	733.92	08	244-245	739.0	08	247
723.1	08	243	727.69	08	248	730.36	08	244-245	733.93	08	239	739.1	08	243
723.2	01	018-019	727.81	08	248	730.37	08	256	733.94	08	239	739.2	08	243
723.3	01	018-019	727.82	08	248	730.38	08	256	733.95	08	239	739.3	08	243
723.4	01	018-019	727.83	08	248	730.39	08	256	733.99	08	256	739	08	243
723.5	08	243	727.89	08	248	730.70	08	256	734	08	256	739.5	08	247
723.6	09	283-284	727.9	08	248	730.71	08	256	735.0	08	256	739.6	08	247
723.7	08	243	728.0	08	248	730.72	08	256	735.1	08	256	739.7	08	247
723.8	08	243	728.10	08	248	730.73	08	256	735.2	08	256	739.8	08	247
723.9	08	243	728.11	08	248	730.74	08	256	735.3	08	256	739.9	08	247
724.00	08	243	728.12	08	248	730.75	08	256	735.4	08	256			
724.01	08	243	728.13	08	248	730.76	08	256	735.5	08	256	**Congenital Anomalies**		
724.02	08	243	728.19	08	248	730.77	08	256	735.8	08	256	740.0	01	034-035
724.09	08	243	728.2	08	248	730.78	08	256	735.9	08	256	740.1	01	034-035
724.1	08	243	728.3	08	248	730.79	08	256	736.00	08	256	740.2	01	034-035
724.2	08	243	728.4	08	248	730.80	08	238	736.01	08	256	741.00	01	034-035
724.3	08	243	728.5	08	248	730.81	08	238	736.02	08	256	741.01	01	034-035
724.4	08	243	728.6	08	248	730.82	08	238	736.03	08	256	741.02	01	034-035
724.5	08	243	728.71	08	248	730.83	08	238	736.04	08	256	741.03	01	034-035
724.6	08	243	728.79	08	248	730.84	08	238	736.05	01	018-019	741.90	01	034-035
724.70	08	243	728.81	08	248	730.85	08	238	736.06	01	018-019	741.91	01	034-035
724.71	08	243	728.82	08	248	730.86	08	238	736.07	01	018-019	741.92	01	034-035
724.79	08	243	728.83	08	248	730.87	08	238	736.09	08	256	741.93	01	034-035
724.8	08	243	728.84	08	248	730.88	08	238	736.1	08	256	742.0	01	034-035
724.9	08	243	728.85	08	247	730.89	08	238	736.20	08	256	742.1	01	034-035
725.	08	240-241	728.87	08	247	730.90	08	238	736.21	08	256	742.2	01	034-035
726.0	08	248	728.88	08	248	730.91	08	238	736.22	08	256	742.3	01	034-035
726.10	08	248	728.89	08	248	730.92	08	238	736.29	08	256	742.4	01	034-035
726.11	08	248	728.9	08	248	730.93	08	238	736.30	08	256	742.51	01	034-035
												742.53	01	034-035

DX	MDC	DRG	DX	MDC	DRG	DX	MDC	DRG	DX	MDC	DRG	DX	MDC	DRG
742.59	.01	.034-035	745.3	.05	.135-137	750.11	.03	.185-187	754.0	.08	.256	756.12	.08	.243
742.8	.01	.034-035	745.4	.05	.135-137	750.12	.03	.185-187	754.1	.08	.256	756.13	.08	.243
742.9	.01	.034-035	745.5	.05	.135-137	750.13	.03	.185-187	754.2	.08	.256	756.14	.08	.243
743.00	.02	.046-048	745.60	.05	.135-137	750.15	.03	.185-187	754.30	.08	.256	756.15	.08	.243
743.03	.02	.046-048	745.61	.05	.135-137	750.16	.03	.185-187	754.31	.08	.256	756.16	.08	.256
743.06	.02	.046-048	745.69	.05	.135-137	750.19	.03	.185-187	754.32	.08	.256	756.17	.01	.034-035
743.10	.02	.046-048	745.7	.05	.135-137	750.21	.03	.073-074	754.33	.08	.256	756.19	.08	.243
743.11	.02	.046-048	745.8	.05	.135-137	750.22	.03	.073-074	754.35	.08	.256	756.2	.08	.256
743.12	.02	.046-048	745.9	.05	.135-137	750.23	.03	.073-074	754.40	.08	.256	756.3	.04	.101-102
743.20	.02	.046-048	746.00	.05	.135-137	750.24	.03	.073-074	754.41	.08	.253-255	756.4	.08	.256
743.21	.02	.046-048	746.01	.05	.135-137	750.25	.03	.185-187	754.42	.08	.256	756.50	.08	.256
743.22	.02	.046-048	746.02	.05	.135-137	750.26	.03	.185-187	754.43	.08	.256	756.51	.08	.256
743.30	.02	.046-048	746.09	.05	.135-137	750.27	.03	.073-074	754.44	.08	.256	756.52	.08	.256
743.31	.02	.046-048	746.1	.05	.135-137	750.29	.03	.073-074	754.50	.08	.256	756.53	.08	.256
743.32	.02	.046-048	746.2	.05	.135-137	750.3	.06	.188-190	754.51	.08	.256	756.54	.08	.256
743.33	.02	.046-048	746.3	.05	.135-137	750.4	.06	.188-190	754.52	.08	.256	756.55	.08	.256
743.34	.02	.046-048	746.4	.05	.135-137	750.5	.06	.188-190	754.53	.08	.256	756.56	.08	.256
743.35	.02	.046-048	746.5	.05	.135-137	750.6	.06	.188-190	754.59	.08	.256	756.59	.08	.256
743.36	.02	.046-048	746.6	.05	.135-137	750.7	.06	.188-190	754.60	.08	.256	756.6	.04	.101-102
743.37	.02	.046-048	746.7	.05	.135-137	750.8	.06	.188-190	754.61	.08	.256	756.70	.06	.188-190
743.39	.02	.046-048	746.81	.05	.135-137	750.9	.06	.188-190	754.62	.08	.256	756.71	.06	.188-190
743.41	.02	.046-048	746.82	.05	.135-137	751.0	.06	.176	754.69	.08	.256	756.79	.06	.188-190
743.42	.02	.046-048	746.83	.05	.135-137	751.1	.06	.188-190	754.70	.08	.256	756.81	.08	.256
743.43	.02	.046-048	746.84	.05	.135-137	751.2	.06	.188-190	754.71	.08	.256	756.82	.08	.256
743.44	.02	.046-048	746.85	.05	.135-137	751.3	.06	.188-190	754.79	.08	.256	756.83	.08	.256
743.45	.02	.046-048	746.86	.05	.138-139	751.4	.06	.188-190	754.81	.04	.101-102	756.89	.08	.256
743.46	.02	.046-048	746.87	.05	.135-137	751.5	.06	.188-190	754.82	.04	.101-102	756.9	.08	.256
743.47	.02	.046-048	746.89	.05	.135-137	751.60	.07	.207-208	754.89	.08	.256	757.0	.09	.283-284
743.48	.02	.046-048	746.9	.05	.135-137	751.61	.07	.207-208	755.00	.08	.256	757.1	.09	.283-284
743.49	.02	.046-048	747.0	.05	.135-137	751.62	.07	.205-206	755.01	.08	.256	757.2	.09	.283-284
743.51	.02	.046-048	747.10	.05	.135-137	751.69	.07	.205-206	755.02	.08	.256	757.31	.09	.283-284
743.52	.02	.046-048	747.11	.05	.135-137	751.7	.07	.204	755.10	.08	.256	757.32	.09	.283-284
743.53	.02	.046-048	747.20	.05	.135-137	751.8	.06	.188-190	755.11	.08	.256	757.33	.09	.283-284
743.54	.02	.046-048	747.21	.05	.135-137	751.9	.06	.188-190	755.12	.08	.256	757.39	.09	.283-284
743.55	.02	.046-048	747.22	.05	.135-137	752.0	.13	.369	755.13	.08	.256	757.4	.09	.283-284
743.56	.02	.046-048	747.29	.05	.135-137	752.10	.13	.369	755.14	.08	.256	757.5	.09	.283-284
743.57	.02	.046-048	747.3	.05	.135-137	752.11	.13	.369	755.20	.08	.256	757.6	.09	.276
743.58	.02	.046-048	747.40	.05	.135-137	752.19	.13	.369	755.21	.08	.256	757.8	.09	.283-284
743.59	.02	.046-048	747.41	.05	.135-137	752.2	.13	.369	755.22	.08	.256	757.9	.09	.283-284
743.61	.02	.046-048	747.42	.05	.135-137	752.3	.13	.369	755.23	.08	.256	758.0	.19	.429
743.62	.02	.046-048	747.49	.05	.135-137	752.40	.13	.369	755.24	.08	.256	758.1	.19	.429
743.63	.02	.046-048	747.5	.05	.130-131	752.41	.13	.369	755.25	.08	.256	758.2	.19	.429
743.64	.02	.046-048	747.60	.05	.130-131	752.42	.13	.369	755.26	.08	.256	758.31	.19	.429
743.65	.02	.046-048	747.61	.05	.130-131	752.49	.13	.369	755.27	.08	.256	758.32	.19	.429
743.66	.02	.046-048	747.62	.05	.130-131	752.51	.12	.352	755.28	.08	.256	758.33	.19	.429
743.69	.02	.046-048	747.63	.05	.130-131	752.52	.12	.352	755.29	.08	.256	758.39	.19	.429
743.8	.02	.046-048	747.64	.05	.130-131	752.61	.12	.352	755.30	.08	.256	758.4	.23	.467
743.9	.02	.046-048	747.69	.05	.130-131	752.62	.12	.352	755.31	.08	.256	758.5	.23	.467
744.00	.03	.073-074	747.81	.01	.034-035	752.63	.12	.352	755.32	.08	.256	758.6	.12	.352
744.01	.03	.073-074	747.83	.15	.387-389	752.64	.12	.352	755.33	.08	.256	758.6	.13	.369
744.02	.03	.073-074	747.89	.05	.130-131	752.65	.12	.352	755.34	.08	.256	758.7	.12	.352
744.03	.03	.073-074	747.9	.05	.130-131	752.69	.12	.352	755.35	.08	.256	758.8	.12	.352
744.04	.03	.073-074	748.00	.03	.073-074	752.7	.12	.352	755.36	.08	.256	758.81	.12	.352
744.05	.03	.073-074	748.1	.03	.073-074	752.7	.13	.369	755.37	.08	.256	758.81	.13	.369
744.09	.03	.073-074	748.2	.03	.073-074	752.81	.12	.352	755.38	.08	.256	758.89	.12	.352
744.1	.03	.073-074	748.3	.03	.073-074	752.89	.12	.352	755.39	.08	.256	758.89	.13	.369
744.21	.03	.073-074	748.4	.04	.101-102	752.8	.13	.369	755.4	.08	.256	758.9	.23	.467
744.22	.03	.073-074	748.5	.04	.101-102	752.9	.12	.352	755.50	.08	.256	759.0	.16	.398-399
744.23	.03	.073-074	748.60	.04	.101-102	752.9	.13	.369	755.51	.08	.256	759.1	.10	.300-301
744.24	.03	.073-074	748.61	.04	.088	753.0	.11	.331-333	755.52	.08	.256	759.2	.10	.300-301
744.29	.03	.073-074	748.69	.04	.101-102	753.10	.11	.331-333	755.53	.08	.256	759.3	.06	.188-190
744.3	.03	.073-074	748.8	.04	.101-102	753.11	.11	.331-333	755.54	.08	.256	759.4	.06	.188-190
744.41	.03	.073-074	748.9	.04	.101-102	753.12	.11	.331-333	755.55	.08	.256	759.5	.01	.034-035
744.42	.03	.073-074	749.00	.03	.185-187	753.13	.11	.331-333	755.56	.08	.256	759.6	.17	.413-414
744.43	.03	.073-074	749.01	.03	.185-187	753.14	.11	.331-333	755.57	.08	.256	759.7	.08	.256
744.46	.03	.073-074	749.02	.03	.185-187	753.15	.11	.331-333	755.58	.08	.256	759.81	.08	.256
744.47	.03	.073-074	749.03	.03	.185-187	753.16	.11	.331-333	755.59	.08	.256	759.82	.05	.135-137
744.49	.03	.073-074	749.04	.03	.185-187	753.17	.11	.331-333	755.60	.08	.256	759.83	.19	.429
744.5	.09	.283-284	749.10	.03	.185-187	753.19	.11	.331-333	755.61	.08	.256	759.89	.08	.256
744.81	.03	.185-187	749.11	.03	.185-187	753.20	.11	.331-333	755.62	.08	.256	759.9	.23	.467
744.82	.03	.185-187	749.12	.03	.185-187	753.21	.11	.331-333	755.63	.08	.256			
744.83	.03	.185-187	749.13	.03	.185-187	753.22	.11	.331-333	755.64	.08	.256			
744.84	.03	.185-187	749.14	.03	.185-187	753.23	.11	.331-333	755.65	.08	.256	**Certain Conditions Originating in the Perinatal Period**		
744.89	.03	.073-074	749.20	.03	.185-187	753.29	.11	.331-333	755.66	.08	.256			
744.9	.09	.283-284	749.21	.03	.185-187	753.3	.11	.331-333	755.67	.08	.256	760.0	.15	.390
745.0	.05	.135-137	749.22	.03	.185-187	753.4	.11	.331-333	755.69	.08	.256	760.1	.15	.390
745.10	.05	.135-137	749.23	.03	.185-187	753.5	.11	.331-333	755.8	.08	.256	760.2	.15	.390
745.11	.05	.135-137	749.24	.03	.185-187	753.6	.11	.331-333	755.9	.08	.256	760.3	.15	.390
745.12	.05	.135-137	749.25	.03	.185-187	753.7	.11	.331-333	756.0	.08	.256	760.4	.15	.390
745.19	.05	.135-137	750.0	.03	.185-187	753.8	.11	.331-333	756.10	.08	.243	760.5	.15	.390
745.2	.05	.135-137	750.10	.03	.185-187	753.9	.11	.331-333	756.11	.08	.243	760.6	.15	.390
												760.70	.15	.390

DX ...MDC ..DRG	DX ...MDC ..DRG	DX ...MDC ..DRG	DX ...MDC ..DRG	DX ...MDC ..DRG
760.71 ..15 .390	765.20 ..15 .391	772.5 ...15 .387,389	780.31 ..01 .024-026	784.99 ..03 .073-074
760.72 ..15 .390	765.21 ..15 .386	772.6 ...15 .390	780.31 ..15 .387, 389	785.0 ...05 .138-139
760.73 ..15 .390	765.22 ..15 .386	772.8 ...15 .390	780.32 ..01 .024-026	785.1 ...05 .138-139
760.74 ..15 .390	765.23 ..15 .386	772.9 ...15 .390	780.39 ..01 .024-026	785.2 ...05 .135-137
760.75 ..15 .390	765.24 ..15 .387-388	773.0 ...15 .390	780.39 ..15 .387, 389	785.3 ...05 .144-145
760.77 ..15 .390	765.25 ..15 .387-388	773.1 ...15 .390	780.4 ...03 .065	785.4 ...05 .130-131
760.78 ..15 .390	765.26 ..15 .387-388	773.2 ...15 .387,389	780.50 ..19 .432	785.50 ..05 .121,124,127
760.79 ..15 .390	765.27 ..15 .387-388	773.3 ...15 .387,389	780.51 ..01 .034-035	785.51 ..05 .121,124,127
760.8 ...15 .390	765.28 ..15 .387-388	773.4 ...15 .387,389	780.52 ..19 .432	785.52 ..05 .121,124,127
760.9 ...15 .390	765.29 ..15 .391	773.5 ...15 .387,389	780.53 ..01 .034-035	785.59 ..18 .416-417
761.0 ...15 .390	766.0 ...15 .391	774.0 ...15 .387,389	780.54 ..19 .432	785.6 ...16 .398-399
761.1 ...15 .390	766.1 ...15 .391	774.1 ...15 .387,389	780.55 ..19 .432	785.9 ...05 .144-145
761.2 ...15 .390	766.21 ..15 .391	774.2 ...15 .387,389	780.56 ..19 .432	786.00 ..04 .099-100
761.3 ...15 .390	766.22 ..15 .391	774.30 ..15 .387,389	780.57 ..01 .034-035	786.01 ..04 .099-100
761.4 ...15 .390	767.0 ...15 .387,389	774.31 ..15 .387,389	780.58 ..19 .432	786.02 ..04 .099-100
761.5 ...15 .390	767.11 ..15 .389	774.39 ..15 .387,389	780.59 ..19 .432	786.03 ..04 .099-100
761.6 ...15 .390	767.19 ..15 .391	774.4 ...15 .387,389	780.6 ...18 .419-420,422	786.03 ..25 .490
761.7 ...15 .390	767.2 ...15 .390	774.5 ...15 .387,389	780.71 ..23 .463-464	786.04 ..04 .099-100
761.8 ...15 .390	767.3 ...15 .390	774.6 ...15 .391	780.71 ..25 .490	786.04 ..25 .490
761.9 ...15 .390	767.4 ...15 .387,389	774.7 ...15 .387,389	780.79 ..23 .463-464	786.05 ..04 .099-100
762.0 ...15 .390	767.5 ...15 .390	775.0 ...15 .390	780.79 ..25 .490	786.05 ..25 .490
762.1 ...15 .390	767.6 ...15 .390	775.1 ...15 .387,389	780.8 ...09 .283-284	786.06 ..04 .099-100
762.2 ...15 .390	767.7 ...15 .387,389	775.2 ...15 .387,389	780.9 ...23 .463-464	786.06 ..25 .490
762.3 ...15 .390	767.8 ...15 .390	775.3 ...15 .387,389	780.91 ..23 .463-464	786.07 ..04 .099-100
762.4 ...15 .391	767.9 ...15 .390	775.4 ...15 .387,389	780.92 ..23 .463-464	786.07 ..25 .490
762.5 ...15 .391	768.0 ...15 .390	775.5 ...15 .387,389	780.93 ..23 .463-464	786.09 ..04 .099-100
762.6 ...15 .391	768.1 ...15 .390	775.6 ...15 .387,389	780.94 ..23 .463-464	786.1 ...04 .099-100
762.7 ...15 .390	768.2 ...15 .390	775.7 ...15 .387,389	780.95 ..23 .463-464	786.2 ...04 .099-100
762.8 ...15 .390	768.3 ...15 .390	775.8 ...15 .390	780.96 ..23 .463-464	786.3 ...04 .099-100
762.9 ...15 .390	768.4 ...15 .390	775.9 ...15 .390	780.97 ..23 .463-464	786.4 ...04 .099-100
763.0 ...15 .391	768.5 ...15 .387,389	776.0 ...15 .387,389	780.99 ..23 .463-464	786.50 ..05 .143
763.1 ...15 .391	768.6 ...15 .391	776.1 ...15 .387,389	781.0 ...01 .034-035	786.51 ..05 .143
763.2 ...15 .391	768.9 ...15 .390	776.2 ...15 .387,389	781.1 ...01 .034-035	786.52 ..04 .099-100
763.3 ...15 .391	769 ...15 .386	776.3 ...15 .387,389	781.2 ...01 .034-035	786.59 ..05 .143
763.4 ...15 .387,389	770.0 ...15 .387,389	776.4 ...15 .390	781.3 ...01 .034-035	786.6 ...04 .099-100
763.5 ...15 .390	770.10 ..15 .387,389	776.5 ...15 .390	781.4 ...01 .034-035	786.7 ...04 .099-100
763.6 ...15 .391	770.11 ..15 .387,389	776.6 ...15 .387,389	781.5 ...04 .101-102	786.8 ...04 .099-100
763.7 ...15 .390	770.12 ..15 .387,389	776.7 ...15 .390	781.6 ...01 .034-035	786.9 ...04 .099-100
763.81 ..15 .390	770.13 ..15 .387, 389	776.8 ...15 .390	781.7 ...10 .296-298	787.01 ..06 .182-184
763.82 ..15 .390	770.14 ..15 .387, 389	776.9 ...15 .390	781.91 ..01 .034-035	787.02 ..06 .182-184
763.83 ..15 .390	770.15 ..15 .387, 389	777.1 ...15 .387,389	781.92 ..01 .034-035	787.03 ..06 .182-184
763.84 ..15 .390	770.16 ..15 .387, 389	777.2 ...15 .387,389	781.93 ..08 .243	787.1 ...06 .182-184
763.89 ..15 .390	770.17 ..15 .387,389	777.3 ...15 .390	781.94 ..01 .034-035	787.2 ...06 .182-184
763.9 ...15 .391	770.18 ..15 .387,389	777.4 ...15 .390	781.99 ..01 .034-035	787.3 ...06 .182-184
764.00 ..15 .390	770.2 ...15 .387,389	777.5 ...15 .387,389	782.0 ...01 .034-035	787.4 ...06 .182-184
764.01 ..15 .390	770.3 ...15 .387,389	777.6 ...15 .387,389	782.1 ...09 .283-284	787.5 ...06 .182-184
764.02 ..15 .390	770.4 ...15 .387,389	777.8 ...15 .390	782.2 ...09 .283-284	787.6 ...06 .182-184
764.03 ..15 .390	770.5 ...15 .390	777.9 ...15 .390	782.3 ...23 .463-464	787.7 ...06 .182-184
764.04 ..15 .390	770.6 ...15 .390	778.0 ...15 .387,389	782.4 ...07 .205-206	787.9 ...06 .182-184
764.05 ..15 .390	770.7 ...04 .092-093	778.1 ...15 .390	782.5 ...23 .463-464	788.0 ...11 .323-324
764.06 ..15 .390	770.8 ...15 .387,389	778.2 ...15 .390	782.61 ..23 .463-464	788.1 ...11 .325-327
764.07 ..15 .390	770.81 ..15 .390	778.3 ...15 .390	782.62 ..23 .463-464	788.20 ..11 .325-327
764.08 ..15 .390	770.82 ..15 .390	778.4 ...15 .390	782.7 ...16 .397	788.21 ..11 .325-327
764.09 ..15 .391	770.83 ..15 .390	778.5 ...15 .390	782.8 ...09 .283-284	788.29 ..11 .325-327
764.10 ..15 .390	770.84 ..15 .387, 389	778.6 ...15 .390	782.9 ...09 .283-284	788.30 ..11 .325-327
764.11 ..15 .387,389	770.85 ..15 .387, 389	778.7 ...15 .390	783.0 ...10 .296-298	788.31 ..11 .325-327
764.12 ..15 .387,389	770.86 ..15 .387, 389	778.8 ...15 .391	783.1 ...10 .296-298	788.32 ..11 .325-327
764.13 ..15 .387,389	770.89 ..15 .390	778.9 ...15 .390	783.21 ..10 .296-298	788.33 ..11 .325-327
764.14 ..15 .387,389	770.9 ...15 .390	779.0 ...15 .387,389	783.22 ..10 .296-298	788.34 ..11 .325-327
764.15 ..15 .387,389	771.0 ...15 .387,389	779.1 ...15 .387,389	783.40 ..10 .296-298	788.35 ..11 .325-327
764.16 ..15 .387,389	771.1 ...15 .387,389	779.2 ...15 .387,389	783.41 ..10 .296-298	788.36 ..11 .325-327
764.17 ..15 .387,389	771.2 ...15 .387,389	779.3 ...15 .391	783.42 ..10 .296-298	788.37 ..11 .325-327
764.18 ..15 .387,389	771.3 ...15 .390	779.4 ...15 .387,389	783.43 ..10 .296-298	788.38 ..11 .325-327
764.19 ..15 .390	771.4 ...15 .387,389	779.5 ...15 .387,389	783.5 ...10 .296-298	788.39 ..11 .325-327
764.20 ..15 .390	771.5 ...15 .387,389	779.6 ...15 .390	783.6 ...10 .296-298	788.41 ..11 .325-327
764.21 ..15 .387,389	771.6 ...15 .390	779.7 ...01 .034-035	783.7 ...10 .296-298	788.42 ..11 .325-327
764.22 ..15 .387,389	771.7 ...15 .390	779.8 ...15 .390	783.9 ...10 .296-298	788.43 ..11 .325-327
764.23 ..15 .387,389	771.8 ...15 .387,389	779.81 ..15 .390	784.0 ...01 .024-026	788.5 ...11 .316
764.24 ..15 .387,389	771.81 ..15 .387, 389	779.82 ..15 .390	784.1 ...03 .073-074	788.61 ..11 .325-327
764.25 ..15 .387,389	771.82 ..15 .387, 389	779.83 ..15 .391	784.2 ...09 .283-284	788.62 ..11 .325-327
764.26 ..15 .387,389	771.83 ..15 .387, 389	779.84 ..15 .390	784.3 ...01 .034-035	788.63 ..11 .325-327
764.27 ..15 .387,389	771.89 ..15 .387, 389	779.89 ..15 .390	784.40 ..03 .073-074	788.64 ..11 .325-327
764.28 ..15 .387,389	772.0 ...15 .387,389	779.9 ...15 .390	784.41 ..03 .073-074	788.65 ..11 .325-327
764.29 ..15 .390	772.10 ..15 .387,389		784.49 ..03 .073-074	788.69 ..11 .325-327
764.90 ..15 .390	772.11 ..15 .387,389	**Symptoms, Signs and Ill-defined Conditions**	784.5 ...01 .034-035	788.7 ...11 .325-327
764.91 ..15 .390	772.12 ..15 .387,389	780.01 ..01 .023	784.60 ..19 .432	788.8 ...11 .325-327
764.92 ..15 .390	772.13 ..15 .387,389	780.02 ..19 .429	784.61 ..19 .431	788.9 ...11 .325-327
764.93 ..15 .390	772.14 ..15 .387,389	780.03 ..01 .023	784.69 ..19 .431	789.00 ..06 .182-184
765.17 ..15 .387-388	772.2 ...15 .387,389	780.09 ..01 .023	784.7 ...03 .066	789.01 ..06 .182-184
765.18 ..15 .387-388	772.3 ...15 .390	780.1 ...19 .425	784.8 ...03 .073-074	789.02 ..06 .182-184
765.19 ..15 .387-388	772.4 ...15 .387,389	780.2 ...05 .141-142	784.91 ..03 .073-074	789.03 ..06 .182-184

DX	MDC	DRG	DX	MDC	DRG	DX	MDC	DRG	DX	MDC	DRG	DX	MDC	DRG
789.04	06	182-184	794.13	02	046-048	800.23	01	027	801.24	01	027	802.39	03	185-187
789.05	06	182-184	794.14	02	046-048	800.24	01	027	801.25	01	027	802.4	03	185-187
789.06	06	182-184	794.15	03	073-074	800.25	01	027	801.26	01	027	802.5	03	185-187
789.07	06	182-184	794.16	03	073-074	800.26	01	027	801.29	01	027-030	802.6	02	046-048
789.09	06	182-184	794.17	08	256	800.29	01	027-030	801.30	01	027-030	802.7	02	046-048
789.1	07	205-206	794.19	01	034-035	800.30	01	027-030	801.31	01	027-030	802.8	08	256
789.2	16	398-399	794.2	04	101-102	800.31	01	027-030	801.32	01	027-030	802.9	08	256
789.30	06	182-184	794.30	05	144-145	800.32	01	027-030	801.33	01	027	803.00	01	027-030
789.31	06	182-184	794.31	05	144-145	800.33	01	027	801.34	01	027	803.01	01	027-030
789.32	06	182-184	794.39	05	144-145	800.34	01	027	801.35	01	027	803.02	01	027-030
789.33	06	182-184	794.4	11	325-327	800.35	01	027	801.36	01	027	803.03	01	027
789.34	06	182-184	794.5	10	300-301	800.36	01	027	801.39	01	027-030	803.04	01	027
789.35	06	182-184	794.6	10	300-301	800.39	01	027-030	801.40	01	027-030	803.05	01	027
789.36	06	182-184	794.7	10	300-301	800.40	01	027-030	801.41	01	027-030	803.06	01	027
789.37	06	182-184	794.8	07	205-206	800.41	01	027-030	801.42	01	027-030	803.09	01	027-030
789.39	06	182-184	794.9	11	325-327	800.42	01	027-030	801.43	01	027	803.10	01	027-030
789.40	06	182-184	795.00	13	369	800.43	01	027	801.44	01	027	803.11	01	027-030
789.41	06	182-184	795.01	13	369	800.44	01	027	801.45	01	027	803.12	01	027-030
789.42	06	182-184	795.02	13	369	800.45	01	027	801.46	01	027	803.13	01	027
789.43	06	182-184	795.03	13	369	800.46	01	027	801.49	01	027-030	803.14	01	027
789.44	06	182-184	795.04	13	369	800.49	01	027-030	801.50	01	027-030	803.15	01	027
789.45	06	182-184	795.05	13	369	800.50	01	027-030	801.51	01	027-030	803.16	01	027
789.46	06	182-184	795.06	13	369	800.51	01	027-030	801.52	01	027-030	803.19	01	027-030
789.47	06	182-184	795.08	13	369	800.52	01	027-030	801.53	01	027	803.20	01	027-030
789.49	06	182-184	795.09	13	369	800.53	01	027	801.54	01	027	803.21	01	027-030
789.5	23	463-464	795.1	04	082	800.54	01	027	801.55	01	027	803.22	01	027-030
789.9	06	182-184	795.2	23	467	800.55	01	027	801.56	01	027	803.23	01	027
790.01	16	395-396	795.3	18	423	800.56	01	027	801.59	01	027-030	803.24	01	027
790.09	16	395-396	795.31	18	423	800.59	01	027-030	801.60	01	027-030	803.25	01	027
790.1	23	463-464	795.39	18	423	800.60	01	027-030	801.61	01	027-030	803.26	01	027
790.21	10	296-298	795.4	23	463-464	800.61	01	027-030	801.62	01	027-030	803.29	01	027-030
790.22	10	296-298	795.5	04	079-081	800.62	01	027-030	801.63	01	027	803.30	01	027-030
790.29	10	296-298	795.6	08	240-241	800.63	01	027	801.64	01	027	803.31	01	027-030
790.3	20	521-523	795.71	16	398-399	800.64	01	027	801.65	01	027	803.32	01	027-030
790.4	23	463-464	795.79	16	398-399	800.65	01	027	801.66	01	027	803.33	01	027
790.5	23	463-464	795.81	23	463-464	800.66	01	027	801.69	01	027-030	803.34	01	027
790.6	23	463-464	795.82	23	463-464	800.69	01	027-030	801.70	01	027-030	803.35	01	027
790.7	18	416-417	795.89	23	463-464	800.70	01	027-030	801.71	01	027-030	803.36	01	027
790.8	18	421-422	796.0	21	454-455	800.71	01	027-030	801.72	01	027-030	803.39	01	027-030
790.91	23	463-464	796.1	01	034-035	800.72	01	027-030	801.73	01	027	803.40	01	027-030
790.92	23	463-464	796.2	05	144-145	800.73	01	027	801.74	01	027	803.41	01	027-030
790.93	23	463-464	796.3	05	144-145	800.74	01	027	801.75	01	027	803.42	01	027-030
790.94	23	463-464	796.4	23	463-464	800.75	01	027	801.76	01	027	803.43	01	027
790.95	23	463-464	796.5	14	383-384	800.76	01	027	801.79	01	027-030	803.44	01	027
790.99	23	463-464	796.6	23	463-464	800.79	01	027-030	801.80	01	027-030	803.45	01	027
791.0	11	325-327	796.9	23	463-464	800.80	01	027-030	801.81	01	027-030	803.46	01	027
791.1	11	325-327	797	19	429	800.81	01	027-030	801.82	01	027-030	803.49	01	027-030
791.2	11	325-327	798.0	01	034-035	800.82	01	027-030	801.83	01	027	803.50	01	027-030
791.3	23	463-464	798.1	05	129	800.83	01	027	801.84	01	027	803.51	01	027-030
791.4	07	205-206	798.2	05	129	800.84	01	027	801.85	01	027	803.52	01	027-030
791.5	10	294-295	798.9	23	467	800.85	01	027	801.86	01	027	803.53	01	027
791.6	10	296-298	799.01	4	101-102	800.86	01	027	801.89	01	027-030	803.54	01	027
791.7	11	325-327	799.02	4	101-102	800.89	01	027-030	801.90	01	027-030	803.55	01	027
791.9	11	325-327	799.1	04	101-102	800.90	01	027-030	801.91	01	027-030	803.56	01	027
792.0	01	034-035	799.2	19	425	800.91	01	027-030	801.92	01	027-030	803.59	01	027-030
792.1	06	182-184	799.3	23	463-464	800.92	01	027-030	801.93	01	027	803.60	01	027-030
792.2	12	352	799.4	23	463-464	800.93	01	027	801.94	01	027	803.61	01	027-030
792.3	14	383-384	799.81	23	467	800.94	01	027	801.95	01	027	803.62	01	027-030
792.4	03	073-074	799.89	23	467	800.95	01	027	801.96	01	027	803.63	01	027
792.5	23	463-464	799.9	23	467	800.96	01	027	801.99	01	027-030	803.64	01	027
792.9	23	463-464				800.99	01	027-030	802.0	03	072	803.65	01	027
793.0	01	034-035	**Injury and Poisoning**			801.00	01	027-030	802.1	03	072	803.66	01	027
793.1	04	099-100	800.00	01	027-030	801.01	01	027-030	802.20	03	185-187	803.69	01	027-030
793.2	05	132-133	800.01	01	027-030	801.02	01	027-030	802.21	03	185-187	803.70	01	027-030
793.3	07	207-208	800.02	01	027-030	801.03	01	027	802.22	03	185-187	803.71	01	027-030
793.4	06	182-184	800.03	01	027	801.04	01	027	802.23	03	185-187	803.72	01	027-030
793.5	11	325-327	800.04	01	027	801.05	01	027	802.24	03	185-187	803.73	01	027
793.6	06	182-184	800.05	01	027	801.06	01	027	802.25	03	185-187	803.74	01	027
793.7	08	256	800.06	01	027	801.09	01	027-030	802.26	03	185-187	803.75	01	027
793.80	09	276	800.09	01	027-030	801.10	01	027-030	802.27	03	185-187	803.76	01	027
793.81	09	276	800.10	01	027-030	801.11	01	027-030	802.28	03	185-187	803.79	01	027-030
793.89	09	276	800.11	01	027-030	801.12	01	027-030	802.29	03	185-187	803.80	01	027-030
793.91	23	463-464	800.12	01	027-030	801.13	01	027	802.30	03	185-187	803.81	01	027-030
793.99	23	463-464	800.13	01	027	801.14	01	027	802.31	03	185-187	803.82	01	027-030
794.00	01	034-035	800.14	01	027	801.15	01	027	802.32	03	185-187	803.83	01	027
794.01	01	034-035	800.15	01	027	801.16	01	027	802.33	03	185-187	803.84	01	027
794.02	01	034-035	800.16	01	027	801.19	01	027-030	802.34	03	185-187	803.85	01	027
794.09	01	034-035	800.19	01	027-030	801.20	01	027-030	802.35	03	185-187	803.86	01	027
794.10	01	034-035	800.20	01	027-030	801.21	01	027-030	802.36	03	185-187	803.89	01	027-030
794.11	02	046-048	800.21	01	027-030	801.22	01	027-030	802.37	03	185-187	803.90	01	027-030
794.12	02	046-048	800.22	01	027-030	801.23	01	027	802.38	03	185-187	803.91	01	027-030

DX . . .MDC . .DRG	DX . . .MDC . .DRG	DX . . .MDC . .DRG	DX . . .MDC . .DRG	DX . . .MDC . .DRG
803.92 . .01 . .027-030	804.93 . .01 . .027	806.8 . . .01 . .009	812.50 . .08 . .253-255	815.13 . .08 . .250-252
803.93 . .01 . .027	804.94 . .01 . .027	806.9 . . .01 . .009	812.51 . .08 . .253-255	815.14 . .08 . .250-252
803.94 . .01 . .027	804.95 . .01 . .027	807.00 . .04 . .101-102	812.52 . .08 . .253-255	815.19 . .08 . .250-252
803.95 . .01 . .027	804.96 . .01 . .027	807.01 . .04 . .101-102	812.53 . .08 . .253-255	816.00 . .08 . .250-252
803.96 . .01 . .027	804.99 . .01 . .027-030	807.02 . .04 . .101-102	812.54 . .08 . .253-255	816.01 . .08 . .250-252
803.99 . .01 . .027-030	805.00 . .08 . .243	807.03 . .04 . .083-084	812.59 . .08 . .253-255	816.02 . .08 . .250-252
804.00 . .01 . .027-030	805.01 . .08 . .243	807.04 . .04 . .083-084	813.00 . .08 . .250-252	816.03 . .08 . .250-252
804.01 . .01 . .027-030	805.02 . .08 . .243	807.05 . .04 . .083-084	813.01 . .08 . .250-252	816.10 . .08 . .250-252
804.02 . .01 . .027-030	805.03 . .08 . .243	807.06 . .04 . .083-084	813.02 . .08 . .250-252	816.11 . .08 . .250-252
804.03 . .01 . .027	805.04 . .08 . .243	807.07 . .04 . .083-084	813.03 . .08 . .250-252	816.12 . .08 . .250-252
804.04 . .01 . .027	805.05 . .08 . .243	807.08 . .04 . .083-084	813.04 . .08 . .250-252	816.13 . .08 . .250-252
804.05 . .01 . .027	805.06 . .08 . .243	807.09 . .04 . .083-084	813.05 . .08 . .250-252	817.0 . . .08 . .250-252
804.06 . .01 . .027	805.07 . .08 . .243	807.10 . .04 . .083-084	813.06 . .08 . .250-252	817.1 . . .08 . .250-252
804.09 . .01 . .027-030	805.08 . .08 . .243	807.11 . .04 . .083-084	813.07 . .08 . .250-252	818.0 . . .08 . .253-255
804.10 . .01 . .027-030	805.10 . .08 . .243	807.12 . .04 . .083-084	813.08 . .08 . .250-252	818.1 . . .08 . .253-255
804.11 . .01 . .027-030	805.11 . .08 . .243	807.13 . .04 . .083-084	813.10 . .08 . .250-252	819.0 . . .21 . .444-446
804.12 . .01 . .027-030	805.12 . .08 . .243	807.14 . .04 . .083-084	813.11 . .08 . .250-252	819.1 . . .21 . .444-446
804.13 . .01 . .027	805.13 . .08 . .243	807.15 . .04 . .083-084	813.12 . .08 . .250-252	820.00 . .08 . .236
804.14 . .01 . .027	805.14 . .08 . .243	807.16 . .04 . .083-084	813.13 . .08 . .250-252	820.01 . .08 . .236
804.15 . .01 . .027	805.15 . .08 . .243	807.17 . .04 . .083-084	813.14 . .08 . .250-252	820.02 . .08 . .236
804.16 . .01 . .027	805.16 . .08 . .243	807.18 . .04 . .083-084	813.15 . .08 . .250-252	820.03 . .08 . .236
804.19 . .01 . .027-030	805.17 . .08 . .243	807.19 . .04 . .083-084	813.16 . .08 . .250-252	820.09 . .08 . .236
804.20 . .01 . .027-030	805.18 . .08 . .243	807.2 . . .04 . .083-084	813.17 . .08 . .250-252	820.10 . .08 . .236
804.21 . .01 . .027-030	805.2 . . .08 . .243	807.3 . . .04 . .083-084	813.18 . .08 . .250-252	820.11 . .08 . .236
804.22 . .01 . .027-030	805.3 . . .08 . .243	807.4 . . .04 . .083-084	813.20 . .08 . .250-252	820.12 . .08 . .236
804.23 . .01 . .027	805.4 . . .08 . .243	807.5 . . .03 . .073-074	813.21 . .08 . .250-252	820.13 . .08 . .236
804.24 . .01 . .027	805.5 . . .08 . .243	807.6 . . .03 . .073-074	813.22 . .08 . .250-252	820.19 . .08 . .236
804.25 . .01 . .027	805.6 . . .08 . .243	808.0 . . .08 . .236	813.23 . .08 . .250-252	820.20 . .08 . .236
804.26 . .01 . .027	805.7 . . .08 . .243	808.1 . . .08 . .236	813.30 . .08 . .250-252	820.21 . .08 . .236
804.29 . .01 . .027-030	805.8 . . .08 . .243	808.2 . . .08 . .236	813.31 . .08 . .250-252	820.22 . .08 . .236
804.30 . .01 . .027-030	805.9 . . .08 . .243	808.3 . . .08 . .236	813.32 . .08 . .250 252	820.30 . .08 . .236
804.31 . .01 . .027-030	806.00 . .01 . .009	808.4 . . .08 . .236	813.33 . .08 . .250-252	820.31 . .08 . .236
804.32 . .01 . .027-030	806.01 . .01 . .009	808.42 . .08 . .236	813.40 . .08 . .250-252	820.32 . .08 . .236
804.33 . .01 . .027	806.02 . .01 . .009	808.43 . .08 . .236	813.41 . .08 . .250-252	820.8 . . .08 . .236
804.34 . .01 . .027	806.03 . .01 . .009	808.49 . .08 . .236	813.42 . .08 . .250-252	820.9 . . .08 . .236
804.35 . .01 . .027	806.04 . .01 . .009	808.51 . .08 . .236	813.43 . .08 . .250-252	821.00 . .08 . .235
804.36 . .01 . .027	806.05 . .01 . .009	808.52 . .08 . .236	813.44 . .08 . .250-252	821.01 . .08 . .235
804.39 . .01 . .027-030	806.06 . .01 . .009	808.53 . .08 . .236	813.45 . .08 . .250-252	821.10 . .08 . .235
804.40 . .01 . .027-030	806.07 . .01 . .009	808.59 . .08 . .236	813.45 . .24 . .487	821.11 . .08 . .235
804.41 . .01 . .027-030	806.08 . .01 . .009	808.8 . . .08 . .236	813.50 . .08 . .250-252	821.20 . .08 . .235
804.42 . .01 . .027-030	806.09 . .01 . .009	808.9 . . .08 . .236	813.51 . .08 . .250-252	821.21 . .08 . .235
804.43 . .01 . .027	806.10 . .01 . .009	809.0 . . .08 . .256	813.52 . .08 . .250-252	821.22 . .08 . .235
804.44 . .01 . .027	806.11 . .01 . .009	809.1 . . .08 . .256	813.53 . .08 . .250-252	821.23 . .08 . .235
804.45 . .01 . .027	806.12 . .01 . .009	810.00 . .08 . .253-255	813.54 . .08 . .250-252	821.29 . .08 . .235
804.46 . .01 . .027	806.13 . .01 . .009	810.01 . .08 . .253-255	813.80 . .08 . .250-252	821.30 . .08 . .235
804.49 . .01 . .027-030	806.14 . .01 . .009	810.02 . .08 . .253-255	813.81 . .08 . .250-252	821.31 . .08 . .235
804.50 . .01 . .027-030	806.15 . .01 . .009	810.03 . .08 . .253-255	813.82 . .08 . .250-252	821.32 . .08 . .235
804.51 . .01 . .027-030	806.16 . .01 . .009	810.10 . .08 . .253-255	813.83 . .08 . .250-252	821.33 . .08 . .235
804.52 . .01 . .027-030	806.17 . .01 . .009	810.11 . .08 . .253-255	813.90 . .08 . .250-252	821.39 . .08 . .235
804.53 . .01 . .027	806.18 . .01 . .009	810.12 . .08 . .253-255	813.91 . .08 . .250-252	822.0 . . .08 . .253-255
804.54 . .01 . .027	806.19 . .01 . .009	810.13 . .08 . .253-255	813.92 . .08 . .250-252	822.1 . . .08 . .253-255
804.55 . .01 . .027	806.20 . .01 . .009	811.00 . .08 . .253-255	813.93 . .08 . .250-252	823.00 . .08 . .253-255
804.56 . .01 . .027	806.21 . .01 . .009	811.01 . .08 . .253-255	814.00 . .08 . .250-252	823.01 . .08 . .253-255
804.59 . .01 . .027-030	806.22 . .01 . .009	811.02 . .08 . .253-255	814.01 . .08 . .250-252	823.02 . .08 . .253-255
804.60 . .01 . .027-030	806.23 . .01 . .009	811.03 . .08 . .253-255	814.02 . .08 . .250-252	823.10 . .08 . .253-255
804.61 . .01 . .027-030	806.24 . .01 . .009	811.09 . .08 . .256	814.03 . .08 . .250-252	823.11 . .08 . .253-255
804.62 . .01 . .027-030	806.25 . .01 . .009	811.10 . .08 . .253-255	814.04 . .08 . .250-252	823.12 . .08 . .253-255
804.63 . .01 . .027	806.26 . .01 . .009	811.11 . .08 . .253-255	814.05 . .08 . .250-252	823.20 . .08 . .253-255
804.64 . .01 . .027	806.27 . .01 . .009	811.12 . .08 . .253-255	814.06 . .08 . .250-252	823.21 . .08 . .253-255
804.65 . .01 . .027	806.28 . .01 . .009	811.13 . .08 . .253-255	814.07 . .08 . .250-252	823.22 . .08 . .253-255
804.66 . .01 . .027	806.29 . .01 . .009	811.19 . .08 . .256	814.08 . .08 . .250-252	823.30 . .08 . .253-255
804.69 . .01 . .027-030	806.30 . .01 . .009	812.00 . .08 . .253-255	814.09 . .08 . .250-252	823.31 . .08 . .253-255
804.70 . .01 . .027-030	806.31 . .01 . .009	812.01 . .08 . .253-255	814.10 . .08 . .250-252	823.32 . .08 . .253-255
804.71 . .01 . .027-030	806.32 . .01 . .009	812.02 . .08 . .253-255	814.11 . .08 . .250-252	823.40 . .08 . .253-255
804.72 . .01 . .027-030	806.33 . .01 . .009	812.03 . .08 . .253-255	814.12 . .08 . .250-252	823.41 . .08 . .253-255
804.73 . .01 . .027	806.34 . .01 . .009	812.09 . .08 . .253-255	814.13 . .08 . .250-252	823.42 . .08 . .253-255
804.74 . .01 . .027	806.35 . .01 . .009	812.10 . .08 . .253-255	814.14 . .08 . .250-252	823.80 . .08 . .253-255
804.75 . .01 . .027	806.36 . .01 . .009	812.11 . .08 . .253-255	814.15 . .08 . .250-252	823.81 . .08 . .253-255
804.76 . .01 . .027	806.37 . .01 . .009	812.12 . .08 . .253-255	814.16 . .08 . .250-252	823.82 . .08 . .253-255
804.79 . .01 . .027-030	806.38 . .01 . .009	812.13 . .08 . .253-255	814.17 . .08 . .250-252	823.90 . .08 . .253-255
804.80 . .01 . .027-030	806.39 . .01 . .009	812.19 . .08 . .253-255	814.18 . .08 . .250-252	823.91 . .08 . .253-255
804.81 . .01 . .027-030	806.4 . . .01 . .009	812.20 . .08 . .253-255	814.19 . .08 . .250-252	823.92 . .08 . .253-255
804.82 . .01 . .027-030	806.5 . . .01 . .009	812.21 . .08 . .253-255	815.00 . .08 . .250-252	824.0 . . .08 . .253-255
804.83 . .01 . .027	806.60 . .01 . .009	812.30 . .08 . .253-255	815.01 . .08 . .250-252	824.1 . . .08 . .253-255
804.84 . .01 . .027	806.61 . .01 . .009	812.31 . .08 . .253-255	815.02 . .08 . .250-252	824.2 . . .08 . .253-255
804.85 . .01 . .027	806.62 . .01 . .009	812.40 . .08 . .253-255	815.03 . .08 . .250-252	824.3 . . .08 . .253-255
804.86 . .01 . .027	806.69 . .01 . .009	812.41 . .08 . .253-255	815.04 . .08 . .250-252	824.4 . . .08 . .253-255
804.89 . .01 . .027-030	806.70 . .01 . .009	812.42 . .08 . .253-255	815.09 . .08 . .250-252	824.5 . . .08 . .253-255
804.90 . .01 . .027-030	806.71 . .01 . .009	812.43 . .08 . .253-255	815.10 . .08 . .250-252	824.6 . . .08 . .253-255
804.91 . .01 . .027-030	806.72 . .01 . .009	812.44 . .08 . .253-255	815.11 . .08 . .250-252	824.7 . . .08 . .253-255
804.92 . .01 . .027-030	806.79 . .01 . .009	812.49 . .08 . .253-255	815.12 . .08 . .250-252	824.8 . . .08 . .253-255

DX	MDC	DRG
824.9	08	253-255
825.0	08	253-255
825.1	08	253-255
825.20	08	250-252
825.21	08	250-252
825.22	08	250-252
825.23	08	250-252
825.24	08	250-252
825.25	08	250-252
825.29	08	250-252
825.30	08	250-252
825.31	08	250-252
825.32	08	250-252
825.33	08	250-252
825.34	08	250-252
825.35	08	250-252
825.39	08	250-252
826.0	08	250-252
826.1	08	250-252
827.0	08	253-255
827.1	08	253-255
828.0	21	444-446
828.1	21	444-446
829.0	08	250-252
829.1	08	250-252
830.0	03	185-187
830.1	03	185-187
831.00	08	253-255
831.01	08	253-255
831.02	08	253-255
831.03	08	253-255
831.04	08	253-255
831.09	08	253-255
831.10	08	253-255
831.11	08	253-255
831.12	08	253-255
831.13	08	253-255
831.14	08	253-255
831.19	08	253-255
832.00	08	253-255
832.01	08	253-255
832.02	08	253-255
832.03	08	253-255
832.04	08	253-255
832.09	08	253-255
832.10	08	253-255
832.11	08	253-255
832.12	08	253-255
832.13	08	253-255
832.14	08	253-255
832.19	08	253-255
833.00	08	250-252
833.01	08	250-252
833.02	08	250-252
833.03	08	250-252
833.04	08	250-252
833.05	08	250-252
833.09	08	250-252
833.10	08	250-252
833.11	08	250-252
833.12	08	250-252
833.13	08	250-252
833.14	08	250-252
833.15	08	250-252
833.19	08	250-252
834.00	08	250-252
834.01	08	250-252
834.02	08	250-252
834.10	08	250-252
834.11	08	250-252
834.12	08	250-252
835.00	08	237
835.01	08	237
835.02	08	237
835.03	08	237
835.10	08	237
835.11	08	237
835.12	08	237
835.13	08	237
836.0	08	253-255
836.1	08	253-255
836.2	08	253-255
836.3	08	253-255
836.4	08	253-255
836.50	08	253-255
836.51	08	253-255
836.52	08	253-255
836.53	08	253-255
836.54	08	253-255
836.59	08	253-255
836.60	08	253-255
836.61	08	253-255
836.62	08	253-255
836.63	08	253-255
836.64	08	253-255
836.69	08	253-255
837.0	08	253-255
837.1	08	253-255
838.00	08	250-252
838.01	08	250-252
838.02	08	250-252
838.03	08	250-252
838.04	08	250-252
838.05	08	250-252
838.06	08	250-252
838.09	08	250-252
838.10	08	250-252
838.11	08	250-252
838.12	08	250-252
838.13	08	250-252
838.14	08	250-252
838.15	08	250-252
838.16	08	250-252
838.19	08	250-252
839.00	08	243
839.01	08	243
839.02	08	243
839.03	08	243
839.04	08	243
839.05	08	243
839.06	08	243
839.07	08	243
839.08	08	243
839.10	08	243
839.11	08	243
839.12	08	243
839.13	08	243
839.14	08	243
839.15	08	243
839.16	08	243
839.17	08	243
839.18	08	243
839.20	08	243
839.21	08	243
839.30	08	243
839.31	08	243
839.40	08	243
839.41	08	243
839.42	08	243
839.49	08	243
839.50	08	243
839.51	08	243
839.52	08	243
839.59	08	243
839.61	04	083-084
839.69	08	250-252
839.71	04	083-084
839.79	08	250-252
839.8	08	250-252
839.9	08	250-252
840.0	08	253-255
840.1	08	253-255
840.2	08	253-255
840.3	08	253-255
840.4	08	253-255
840.5	08	253-255
840.6	08	253-255
840.7	08	253-255
840.8	08	253-255
840.9	08	253-255
841.0	08	250-252
841.1	08	250-252
841.2	08	250-252
841.3	08	250-252
841.8	08	250-252
841.9	08	250-252
842.00	08	250-252
842.01	08	250-252
842.02	08	250-252
842.09	08	250-252
842.10	08	250-252
842.11	08	250-252
842.12	08	250-252
842.13	08	250-252
842.19	08	250-252
843.0	08	237
843.1	08	237
843.8	08	237
843.9	08	237
844.0	08	253-255
844.1	08	253-255
844.2	08	253-255
844.3	08	253-255
844.8	08	253-255
844.9	08	253-255
845.00	08	253-255
845.01	08	253-255
845.02	08	253-255
845.03	08	253-255
845.09	08	253-255
845.10	08	250-252
845.11	08	250-252
845.12	08	250-252
845.13	08	250-252
845.19	08	250-252
846.0	08	243
846.1	08	243
846.2	08	243
846.3	08	243
846.8	08	243
846.9	08	243
847.0	08	243
847.1	08	243
847.2	08	243
847.3	08	243
847.4	08	243
847.9	08	243
848.0	08	256
848.1	03	185-187
848.2	08	256
848.3	04	101-102
848.40	04	101-102
848.41	04	101-102
848.42	04	101-102
848.49	04	101-102
848.5	08	237
848.8	08	250-252
848.9	08	250-252
850.0	01	031-033
850.11	01	031-033
850.12	01	031-033
850.2	01	031-033
850.3	01	031-033
850.4	01	031-033
850.5	01	031-033
850.9	01	031-033
851.00	01	027-030
851.01	01	027-030
851.02	01	027-030
851.03	01	027
851.04	01	027
851.05	01	027
851.06	01	027
851.09	01	027-030
851.10	01	027-030
851.11	01	027-030
851.12	01	027-030
851.13	01	027
851.14	01	027
851.15	01	027
851.16	01	027
851.19	01	027-030
851.20	01	027-030
851.21	01	027-030
851.22	01	027-030
851.23	01	027
851.24	01	027
851.25	01	027
851.26	01	027
851.29	01	027-030
851.30	01	027-030
851.31	01	027-030
851.32	01	027-030
851.33	01	027
851.34	01	027
851.35	01	027
851.36	01	027
851.39	01	027-030
851.40	01	027-030
851.41	01	027-030
851.42	01	027-030
851.43	01	027
851.44	01	027
851.45	01	027
851.46	01	027
851.49	01	027-030
851.50	01	027-030
851.51	01	027-030
851.52	01	027-030
851.53	01	027
851.54	01	027
851.55	01	027
851.56	01	027
851.59	01	027-030
851.60	01	027-030
851.61	01	027-030
851.62	01	027-030
851.63	01	027
851.64	01	027
851.65	01	027
851.66	01	027
851.69	01	027-030
851.70	01	027-030
851.71	01	027-030
851.72	01	027-030
851.73	01	027
851.74	01	027
851.75	01	027
851.76	01	027
851.79	01	027-030
851.80	01	027-030
851.81	01	027-030
851.82	01	027-030
851.83	01	027
851.84	01	027
851.85	01	027
851.86	01	027
851.89	01	027-030
851.90	01	027-030
851.91	01	027-030
851.92	01	027-030
851.93	01	027
851.94	01	027
851.95	01	027
851.96	01	027
851.99	01	027-030
852.00	01	027-030
852.01	01	027-030
852.02	01	027-030
852.03	01	027
852.04	01	027
852.05	01	027
852.06	01	027
852.09	01	027-030
852.10	01	027-030
852.11	01	027-030
852.12	01	027-030
852.13	01	027
852.14	01	027
852.15	01	027
852.16	01	027
852.19	01	027-030
852.20	01	027-030
852.21	01	027-030
852.22	01	027-030
852.23	01	027
852.24	01	027
852.25	01	027
852.26	01	027
852.29	01	027-030
852.30	01	027-030
852.31	01	027-030
852.32	01	027-030
852.33	01	027
852.34	01	027
852.35	01	027
852.36	01	027
852.39	01	027-030
852.40	01	027-030
852.41	01	027-030
852.42	01	027-030
852.43	01	027
852.44	01	027
852.45	01	027
852.46	01	027
852.49	01	027-030
852.50	01	027-030
852.51	01	027-030
852.52	01	027-030
852.53	01	027
852.54	01	027
852.55	01	027
852.56	01	027
852.59	01	027-030
853.00	01	027-030
853.01	01	027-030
853.02	01	027-030
853.03	01	027
853.04	01	027
853.05	01	027
853.06	01	027
853.09	01	027-030
853.10	01	027-030
853.11	01	027-030
853.12	01	027-030
853.13	01	027
853.14	01	027
853.15	01	027
853.16	01	027
853.19	01	027-030
854.00	01	027-030
854.01	01	027-030
854.02	01	027-030
854.03	01	027
854.04	01	027
854.05	01	027
854.06	01	027
854.09	01	027-030
854.10	01	027-030
854.11	01	027-030
854.12	01	027-030
854.13	01	027
854.14	01	027
854.15	01	027
854.16	01	027
854.19	01	027-030
860.0	04	094-095
860.1	04	094-095
860.2	04	094-095
860.3	04	094-095
860.4	04	094-095
860.5	04	094-095
861.00	05	144-145
861.01	05	144-145
861.02	05	144-145
861.03	05	144-145
861.10	05	144-145
861.11	05	144-145
861.12	05	144-145
861.13	05	144-145
861.20	04	101-102
861.21	04	101-102
861.22	04	083-084
861.30	04	101-102
861.31	04	101-102

DX	MDC	DRG	DX	MDC	DRG	DX	MDC	DRG	DX	MDC	DRG	DX	MDC	DRG
861.32	04	083-084	866.10	11	331-333	873.43	03	185-187	881.01	09	280-282	902.11	21	444-446
862.0	04	083-084	866.11	11	331-333	873.44	03	185-187	881.02	09	280-282	902.19	21	444-446
862.1	04	083-084	866.12	11	331-333	873.49	09	280-282	881.10	21	444-446	902.20	21	444-446
862.21	04	083-084	866.13	11	331-333	873.50	09	280-282	881.11	21	444-446	902.21	21	444-446
862.22	06	188-190	867.0	11	331-333	873.51	09	280-282	881.12	21	444-446	902.22	21	444-446
862.29	04	101-102	867.1	11	331-333	873.52	09	280-282	881.20	08	256	902.23	21	444-446
862.31	04	083-084	867.2	11	331-333	873.53	03	185-187	881.21	08	256	902.24	21	444-446
862.32	06	188-190	867.3	11	331-333	873.54	03	185-187	881.22	08	256	902.25	21	444-446
862.39	04	101-102	867.4	13	369	873.59	09	280-282	882.0	09	280-282	902.26	21	444-446
862.8	21	444-446	867.5	13	369	873.60	03	185-187	882.1	21	444-446	902.27	21	444-446
862.9	21	444-446	867.6	12	352	873.61	03	185-187	882.2	08	256	902.29	21	444-446
863.0	06	188-190	867.6	13	369	873.62	03	185-187	883.0	09	280-282	902.31	21	444-446
863.1	06	188-190	867.7	12	352	873.63	03	185-187	883.1	21	444-446	902.32	21	444-446
863.20	06	188-190	867.7	13	369	873.64	03	185-187	883.2	08	256	902.33	21	444-446
863.21	06	188-190	867.8	12	352	873.65	03	185-187	884.0	09	280-282	902.34	21	444-446
863.29	06	188-190	867.8	13	369	873.69	03	185-187	884.1	21	444-446	902.39	21	444-446
863.30	06	188-190	867.9	12	352	873.70	03	185-187	884.2	08	256	902.40	21	444-446
863.31	06	188-190	867.9	13	369	873.71	03	185-187	885.0	21	444-446	902.41	21	444-446
863.39	06	188-190	868.00	06	188-190	873.72	03	185-187	885.1	21	444-446	902.42	21	444-446
863.40	06	188-190	868.01	10	300-301	873.73	03	185-187	886.0	21	444-446	902.49	21	444-446
863.41	06	188-190	868.02	07	207-208	873.74	03	185-187	886.1	21	444-446	902.50	21	444-446
863.42	06	188-190	868.03	06	188-190	873.75	03	185-187	887.0	21	444-446	902.51	21	444-446
863.43	06	188-190	868.04	11	331-333	873.79	03	185-187	887.1	21	444-446	902.52	21	444-446
863.44	06	188-190	868.09	21	444-446	873.8	09	280-282	887.2	21	444-446	902.53	21	444-446
863.45	06	188-190	868.10	06	188-190	873.9	09	280-282	887.3	21	444-446	902.54	21	444-446
863.46	06	188-190	868.11	10	300-301	874.00	03	073-074	887.4	21	444-446	902.55	21	444-446
863.49	06	188-190	868.12	07	207-208	874.01	03	073-074	887.5	21	444-446	902.56	21	444-446
863.50	06	188-190	868.13	06	188-190	874.02	04	083-084	887.6	21	444-446	902.59	21	444-446
863.51	06	188-190	868.14	11	331-333	874.10	03	073-074	887.7	21	444-446	902.81	21	444-446
863.52	06	188-190	868.19	21	444-446	874.11	03	073-074	890.0	09	280-282	902.82	21	444-446
863.53	06	188-190	869.0	21	444-446	874.12	04	083-084	890.1	21	444-446	902.87	21	444-446
863.54	06	188-190	869.1	21	444-446	874.2	10	300-301	890.2	08	256	902.89	21	444-446
863.55	06	188-190	870.0	02	046-048	874.3	10	300-301	891.0	09	280-282	902.9	21	444-446
863.56	06	188-190	870.1	02	046-048	874.4	03	073-074	891.1	21	444-446	903.00	21	444-446
863.59	06	188-190	870.2	02	046-048	874.5	03	073-074	891.2	08	256	903.01	21	444-446
863.80	06	188-190	870.3	02	046-048	874.8	09	280-282	892.0	09	280-282	903.02	21	444-446
863.81	07	204	870.4	02	046-048	874.9	09	280-282	892.1	21	444-446	903.1	21	444-446
863.82	07	204	870.8	02	046-048	875.0	09	280-282	892.2	08	256	903.2	21	444-446
863.83	07	204	870.9	02	046-048	875.1	21	444-446	893.0	09	280-282	903.3	21	444-446
863.84	07	204	871.0	02	046-048	876.0	09	280-282	893.1	21	444-446	903.4	21	444-446
863.85	06	188-190	871.1	02	046-048	876.1	09	280-282	893.2	08	256	903.5	21	444-446
863.89	06	188-190	871.2	02	046-048	877.0	09	280-282	894.0	09	280-282	903.8	21	444-446
863.90	06	188-190	871.3	02	046-048	877.1	09	280-282	894.1	21	444-446	903.9	21	444-446
863.91	07	204	871.4	02	046-048	878.0	12	352	894.2	08	256	904.0	21	444-446
863.92	07	204	871.5	02	046-048	878.1	12	352	895.0	21	444-446	904.1	21	444-446
863.93	07	204	871.6	02	046-048	878.2	12	352	895.1	21	444-446	904.2	21	444-446
863.94	07	204	871.7	02	046-048	878.3	12	352	896.0	21	444-446	904.3	21	444-446
863.95	06	188-190	871.9	02	046-048	878.4	13	369	896.1	21	444-446	904.40	21	444-446
863.99	06	188-190	872.00	03	073-074	878.5	13	369	896.2	21	444-446	904.41	21	444-446
864.00	07	205-206	872.01	03	073-074	878.6	13	369	896.3	21	444-446	904.42	21	444-446
864.01	07	205-206	872.02	03	073-074	878.7	13	369	897.0	21	444-446	904.50	21	444-446
864.02	07	205-206	872.10	03	073-074	878.8	12	352	897.1	21	444-446	904.51	21	444-446
864.03	07	205-206	872.11	03	073-074	878.8	13	369	897.2	21	444-446	904.52	21	444-446
864.04	07	205-206	872.12	03	073-074	878.9	12	352	897.3	21	444-446	904.53	21	444-446
864.05	24	487	872.61	03	073-074	878.9	13	369	897.4	21	444-446	904.54	21	444-446
864.09	07	205-206	872.62	03	073-074	879.0	09	280-282	897.5	21	444-446	904.6	21	444-446
864.10	07	205-206	872.63	03	073-074	879.1	09	280-282	897.6	21	444-446	904.7	21	444-446
864.11	07	205-206	872.64	03	073-074	879.2	09	280-282	897.7	21	444-446	904.8	21	444-446
864.12	07	205-206	872.69	03	073-074	879.3	21	444-446	900.00	21	444-446	904.9	21	444-446
864.13	07	205-206	872.71	03	073-074	879.4	09	280-282	900.01	21	444-446	905.0	01	034-035
864.14	07	205-206	872.72	03	073-074	879.5	09	280-282	900.02	21	444-446	905.1	08	243
864.15	07	205-206	872.73	03	073-074	879.6	09	280-282	900.03	21	444-446	905.2	08	249
864.15	24	487	872.74	03	073-074	879.7	21	444-446	900.1	21	444-446	905.3	08	249
864.19	07	205-206	872.79	03	073-074	879.8	09	280-282	900.81	21	444-446	905.4	08	249
865.00	16	398-399	872.8	03	073-074	879.9	21	444-446	900.82	21	444-446	905.5	08	249
865.01	16	398-399	872.9	03	073-074	880.00	09	280-282	900.89	21	444-446	905.6	08	250-252
865.02	16	398-399	873.0	09	280-282	880.01	09	280-282	900.9	21	444-446	905.7	08	250-252
865.03	16	398-399	873.1	09	280-282	880.02	09	280-282	901.0	21	444-446	905.8	08	249
865.04	16	398-399	873.20	03	072	880.03	09	280-282	901.1	21	444-446	905.9	08	249
865.09	16	398-399	873.21	03	073-074	880.09	09	280-282	901.2	21	444-446	906.0	09	280-282
865.10	16	398-399	873.22	03	073-074	880.10	21	444-446	901.3	21	444-446	906.1	09	280-282
865.11	16	398-399	873.23	03	073-074	880.11	21	444-446	901.40	21	444-446	906.2	09	280-282
865.12	16	398-399	873.29	03	073-074	880.12	21	444-446	901.41	21	444-446	906.3	09	280-282
865.13	16	398-399	873.30	03	073-074	880.13	21	444-446	901.42	21	444-446	906.4	09	280-282
865.14	16	398-399	873.31	03	073-074	880.19	21	444-446	901.81	21	444-446	906.5	09	280-282
865.19	16	398-399	873.32	03	073-074	880.20	08	256	901.82	21	444-446	906.6	09	280-282
866.00	11	331-333	873.33	03	073-074	880.21	08	256	901.83	21	444-446	906.7	09	280-282
866.01	11	331-333	873.39	03	073-074	880.22	08	256	901.89	21	444-446	906.8	09	280-282
866.02	11	331-333	873.40	09	280-282	880.23	08	256	901.9	21	444-446	906.9	09	280-282
866.03	11	331-333	873.41	09	280-282	880.29	08	256	902.0	21	444-446	907.0	01	034-035
			873.42	09	280-282	881.00	09	280-282	902.10	21	444-446	907.1	01	034-035

DX ...MDC ..DRG	DX ...MDC ..DRG	DX ...MDC ..DRG	DX ...MDC ..DRG	DX ...MDC ..DRG
907.2 ...01 ..009	916.1 ...09 ..277-279	926.19 ..21 ..444-446	941.24 ..22 ..510-511	943.03 ..22 ..510-511
907.3 ...01 ..034-035	916.2 ...09 ..283-284	926.8 ...21 ..444-446	941.25 ..22 ..510-511	943.04 ..22 ..510-511
907.4 ...01 ..034-035	916.3 ...09 ..277-279	926.9 ...21 ..444-446	941.26 ..22 ..510-511	943.05 ..22 ..510-511
907.5 ...01 ..034-035	916.4 ...09 ..283-284	927.00 ..21 ..444-446	941.27 ..22 ..510-511	943.06 ..22 ..510-511
907.9 ...01 ..034-035	916.5 ...09 ..277-279	927.01 ..21 ..444-446	941.28 ..22 ..510-511	943.09 ..22 ..510-511
908.0 ...04 ..101-102	916.6 ...09 ..280-282	927.02 ..21 ..444-446	941.29 ..22 ..510-511	943.10 ..22 ..510-511
908.1 ...06 ..188-190	916.7 ...09 ..277-279	927.03 ..21 ..444-446	941.30 ..22 ..506-509	943.11 ..22 ..510-511
908.2 ...12 ..352	916.8 ...09 ..280-282	927.09 ..21 ..444-446	941.31 ..22 ..506-509	943.12 ..22 ..510-511
908.2 ...13 ..369	916.9 ...09 ..277-279	927.10 ..21 ..444-446	941.32 ..02 ..046-048	943.13 ..22 ..510-511
908.3 ...05 ..130-131	917.0 ...09 ..280-282	927.11 ..21 ..444-446	941.33 ..22 ..506-509	943.14 ..22 ..510-511
908.4 ...05 ..130-131	917.1 ...09 ..277-279	927.20 ..21 ..444-446	941.34 ..22 ..506-509	943.15 ..22 ..510-511
908.5 ..21 ..444-446	917.2 ...09 ..283-284	927.21 ..21 ..444-446	941.35 ..22 ..506-509	943.16 ..22 ..510-511
908.6 ...21 ..444-446	917.3 ...09 ..277-279	927.3 ...21 ..444-446	941.36 ..22 ..506-509	943.19 ..22 ..510-511
908.9 ...21 ..444-446	917.4 ...09 ..283-284	927.8 ...21 ..444-446	941.37 ..22 ..506-509	943.20 ..22 ..510-511
909.0 ...21 ..454-455	917.5 ...09 ..277-279	927.9 ...21 ..444-446	941.38 ..22 ..506-509	943.21 ..22 ..510-511
909.1 ...21 ..454-455	917.6 ...09 ..280-282	928.00 ..21 ..444-446	941.39 ..22 ..506-509	943.22 ..22 ..510-511
909.2 ...21 ..454-455	917.7 ...09 ..277-279	928.01 ..21 ..444-446	941.40 ..22 ..506-509	943.23 ..22 ..510-511
909.3 ...21 ..454-455	917.8 ...09 ..280-282	928.10 ..21 ..444-446	941.41 ..22 ..506-509	943.24 ..22 ..510-511
909.4 ...21 ..454-455	917.9 ...09 ..277-279	928.11 ..21 ..444-446	941.42 ..02 ..046-048	943.25 ..22 ..510-511
909.9 ...21 ..454-455	918.0 ...02 ..046-048	928.20 ..21 ..444-446	941.43 ..22 ..506-509	943.26 ..22 ..510-511
910.0 ...09 ..280-282	918.1 ...02 ..046-048	928.21 ..21 ..444-446	941.44 ..22 ..506-509	943.29 ..22 ..510-511
910.1 ...09 ..277-279	918.2 ...02 ..046-048	928.3 ...21 ..444-446	941.45 ..22 ..506-509	943.30 ..22 ..506-509
910.2 ...09 ..283-284	918.9 ...02 ..046-048	928.8 ...21 ..444-446	941.46 ..22 ..506-509	943.31 ..22 ..506-509
910.3 ...09 ..283-284	919.0 ...09 ..280-282	928.9 ...21 ..444-446	941.47 ..22 ..506-509	943.32 ..22 ..506-509
910.4 ...09 ..283-284	919.1 ...09 ..277-279	929.0 ...21 ..444-446	941.48 ..22 ..506-509	943.33 ..22 ..506-509
910.5 ...09 ..277-279	919.2 ...09 ..283-284	929.9 ...21 ..444-446	941.49 ..22 ..506-509	943.34 ..22 ..506-509
910.6 ...09 ..280-282	919.3 ...09 ..277-279	930.0 ...02 ..046-048	941.50 ..22 ..506-509	943.35 ..22 ..506-509
910.7 ...09 ..277-279	919.4 ...09 ..283-284	930.1 ...02 ..046-048	941.51 ..22 ..506-509	943.36 ..22 ..506-509
910.8 ...09 ..280-282	919.5 ...09 ..277-279	930.2 ...02 ..046-048	941.52 ..02 ..046-048	943.39 ..22 ..506-509
910.9 ...09 ..277-279	919.6 ...09 ..280-282	930.8 ...02 ..046-048	941.53 ..22 ..506-509	943.40 ..22 ..506-509
911.0 ...09 ..280-282	919.7 ...09 ..277-279	930.9 ...02 ..046-048	941.54 ..22 ..506-509	943.41 ..22 ..506-509
911.1 ...09 ..277-279	919.8 ...09 ..280-282	931 .....03 ..073-074	941.55 ..22 ..506-509	943.42 ..22 ..506-509
911.2 ...09 ..283-284	919.9 ...09 ..277-279	932 .....03 ..072	941.56 ..22 ..506-509	943.43 ..22 ..506-509
911.3 ...09 ..277-279	920. ...09 ..280-282	933.0 ...03 ..073-074	941.57 ..22 ..506-509	943.44 ..22 ..506-509
911.4 ...09 ..283-284	921.0 ...02 ..046-048	933.1 ...03 ..073-074	941.58 ..22 ..506-509	943.45 ..22 ..506-509
911.5 ...09 ..277-279	921.1 ...02 ..043	934.0 ...04 ..101-102	941.59 ..22 ..506-509	943.46 ..22 ..506-509
911.6 ...09 ..280-282	921.2 ...02 ..046-048	934.1 ...04 ..101-102	942.00 ..22 ..510-511	943.49 ..22 ..506-509
911.7 ...09 ..277-279	921.3 ...02 ..043	934.8 ...04 ..101-102	942.01 ..22 ..510-511	943.50 ..22 ..506-509
911.8 ...09 ..280-282	921.9 ...02 ..046-048	934.9 ...04 ..101-102	942.02 ..22 ..510-511	943.51 ..22 ..506-509
911.9 ...09 ..277-279	922.0 ...09 ..280-282	935.0 ...03 ..185-187	942.03 ..22 ..510-511	943.52 ..22 ..506-509
912.0 ...09 ..280-282	922.1 ...09 ..280-282	935.1 ...06 ..188-190	942.04 ..22 ..510-511	943.53 ..22 ..506-509
912.1 ...09 ..277-279	922.2 ...09 ..280-282	935.2 ...06 ..188-190	942.05 ..22 ..510-511	943.54 ..22 ..506-509
912.2 ...09 ..280-282	922.31 ..09 ..280-282	936 .....06 ..188-190	942.09 ..22 ..510-511	943.55 ..22 ..506-509
912.3 ...09 ..277-279	922.31 ..24 ..484-487	937 .....06 ..188-190	942.10 ..22 ..510-511	943.56 ..22 ..506-509
912.4 ...09 ..283-284	922.32 ..09 ..280-282	938 .....06 ..188-190	942.11 ..22 ..510-511	943.59 ..22 ..506-509
912.5 ...09 ..277-279	922.32 ..24 ..484-487	939.0 ...11 ..331-333	942.12 ..22 ..510-511	944.00 ..22 ..510-511
912.6 ...09 ..280-282	922.33 ..09 ..280-282	939.1 ...13 ..369	942.13 ..22 ..510-511	944.01 ..22 ..510-511
912.7 ...09 ..277-279	922.33 ..24 ..484-487	939.2 ...13 ..369	942.14 ..22 ..510-511	944.02 ..22 ..510-511
912.8 ...09 ..280-282	922.4 ...12 ..352	939.3 ...12 ..352	942.15 ..22 ..510-511	944.03 ..22 ..510-511
912.9 ...09 ..277-279	922.4 ...13 ..369	939.9 ...11 ..331-333	942.19 ..22 ..510-511	944.04 ..22 ..510-511
913.0 ...09 ..280-282	922.8 ...09 ..280-282	940.0 ...02 ..046-048	942.20 ..22 ..506-509	944.05 ..22 ..510-511
913.1 ...09 ..277-279	922.9 ...09 ..280-282	940.1 ...02 ..046-048	942.21 ..22 ..510-511	944.06 ..22 ..510-511
913.2 ...09 ..283-284	923.00 ..09 ..280-282	940.2 ...02 ..046-048	942.22 ..22 ..510-511	944.07 ..22 ..510-511
913.3 ...09 ..277-279	923.01 ..09 ..280-282	940.3 ...02 ..046-048	942.23 ..22 ..510-511	944.08 ..22 ..510-511
913.4 ...09 ..283-284	923.02 ..09 ..280-282	940.4 ...02 ..046-048	942.24 ..22 ..510-511	944.10 ..22 ..510-511
913.5 ...09 ..277-279	923.03 ..09 ..280-282	940.5 ...02 ..046-048	942.25 ..22 ..510-511	944.11 ..22 ..510-511
913.6 ...09 ..280-282	923.09 ..09 ..280-282	940.9 ...02 ..046-048	942.29 ..22 ..510-511	944.12 ..22 ..510-511
913.7 ...09 ..277-279	923.10 ..09 ..280-282	941.00 ..22 ..510-511	942.30 ..22 ..506-509	944.13 ..22 ..510-511
913.8 ...09 ..280-282	923.11 ..09 ..280-282	941.01 ..22 ..510-511	942.31 ..22 ..506-509	944.14 ..22 ..510-511
913.9 ...09 ..277-279	923.20 ..09 ..280-282	941.02 ..02 ..046-048	942.32 ..22 ..506-509	944.15 ..22 ..510-511
914.0 ...09 ..280-282	923.21 ..09 ..280-282	941.03 ..22 ..510-511	942.33 ..22 ..506-509	944.16 ..22 ..510-511
914.1 ...09 ..277-279	923.3 ...09 ..280-282	941.04 ..22 ..510-511	942.34 ..22 ..506-509	944.17 ..22 ..510-511
914.2 ...09 ..283-284	923.8 ...09 ..280-282	941.05 ..22 ..510-511	942.35 ..22 ..506-509	944.18 ..22 ..510-511
914.3 ...09 ..277-279	923.9 ...09 ..280-282	941.06 ..22 ..510-511	942.39 ..22 ..506-509	944.20 ..22 ..510-511
914.4 ...09 ..283-284	924.00 ..09 ..280-282	941.07 ..22 ..510-511	942.40 ..22 ..506-509	944.21 ..22 ..510-511
914.5 ...09 ..277-279	924.01 ..09 ..280-282	941.08 ..22 ..510-511	942.41 ..22 ..506-509	944.22 ..22 ..510-511
914.6 ...09 ..280-282	924.10 ..09 ..280-282	941.09 ..22 ..510-511	942.42 ..22 ..506-509	944.23 ..22 ..510-511
914.7 ...09 ..277-279	924.11 ..09 ..280-282	941.10 ..22 ..510-511	942.43 ..22 ..506-509	944.24 ..22 ..510-511
914.8 ...09 ..280-282	924.20 ..09 ..280-282	941.11 ..22 ..510-511	942.44 ..22 ..506-509	944.25 ..22 ..510-511
914.9 ...09 ..277-279	924.21 ..09 ..280-282	941.12 ..02 ..046-048	942.45 ..22 ..506-509	944.26 ..22 ..510-511
915.0 ...09 ..280-282	924.3 ...09 ..280-282	941.13 ..22 ..510-511	942.49 ..22 ..506-509	944.27 ..22 ..510-511
915.1 ...09 ..277-279	924.4 ...09 ..280-282	941.14 ..22 ..510-511	942.50 ..22 ..506-509	944.28 ..22 ..510-511
915.2 ...09 ..283-284	924.5 ...09 ..280-282	941.15 ..22 ..510-511	942.51 ..22 ..506-509	944.30 ..22 ..506-509
915.3 ...09 ..277-279	924.8 ...09 ..280-282	941.16 ..22 ..510-511	942.52 ..22 ..506-509	944.31 ..22 ..506-509
915.4 ...09 ..283-284	924.9 ...09 ..280-282	941.17 ..22 ..510-511	942.53 ..22 ..506-509	944.32 ..22 ..506-509
915.5 ...09 ..277-279	925.1 ...21 ..444-446	941.18 ..22 ..510-511	942.54 ..22 ..506-509	944.33 ..22 ..506-509
915.6 ...09 ..280-282	925.2 ...21 ..444-446	941.19 ..22 ..510-511	942.55 ..22 ..506-509	944.34 ..22 ..506-509
915.7 ...09 ..277-279	926.0 ...12 ..352	941.20 ..22 ..510-511	942.59 ..22 ..506-509	944.35 ..22 ..506-509
915.8 ...09 ..280-282	926.0 ...13 ..369	941.21 ..22 ..510-511	943.00 ..22 ..510-511	944.36 ..22 ..506-509
915.9 ...09 ..277-279	926.11 ..21 ..444-446	941.22 ..02 ..046-048	943.01 ..22 ..510-511	944.37 ..22 ..506-509
916.0 ...09 ..280-282	926.12 ..21 ..444-446	941.23 ..22 ..510-511	943.02 ..22 ..510-511	944.38 ..22 ..506-509

DX	MDC	DRG	DX	MDC	DRG	DX	MDC	DRG	DX	MDC	DRG	DX	MDC	DRG
944.40	.22	.506-509	948.11	.22	.506-509	952.07	.01	.009	960.0	.21	.449-451	968.7	.21	.449-451
944.41	.22	.506-509	948.20	.22	.510-511	952.08	.01	.009	960.1	.21	.449-451	968.9	.21	.449-451
944.42	.22	.506-509	948.21	.22	.504-505	952.09	.01	.009	960.2	.21	.449-451	969.0	.21	.449-451
944.43	.22	.506-509	948.22	.22	.504-505	952.10	.01	.009	960.3	.21	.449-451	969.1	.21	.449-451
944.44	.22	.506-509	948.30	.22	.510-511	952.11	.01	.009	960.4	.21	.449-451	969.2	.21	.449-451
944.45	.22	.506-509	948.31	.22	.504-505	952.12	.01	.009	960.5	.21	.449-451	969.3	.21	.449-451
944.46	.22	.506-509	948.32	.22	.504-505	952.13	.01	.009	960.6	.21	.449-451	969.4	.21	.449-451
944.47	.22	.506-509	948.33	.22	.504-505	952.14	.01	.009	960.7	.21	.449-451	969.5	.21	.449-451
944.48	.22	.506-509	948.40	.22	.510-511	952.15	.01	.009	960.8	.21	.449-451	969.6	.21	.449-451
944.50	.22	.506-509	948.41	.22	.506-509	952.16	.01	.009	960.9	.21	.449-451	969.7	.21	.449-451
944.51	.22	.506-509	948.42	.22	.504-505	952.17	.01	.009	961.0	.21	.449-451	969.8	.21	.449-451
944.52	.22	.506-509	948.43	.22	.504-505	952.18	.01	.009	961.1	.21	.449-451	969.9	.21	.449-451
944.53	.22	.506-509	948.44	.22	.504-505	952.19	.01	.009	961.2	.21	.449-451	970.0	.21	.449-451
944.54	.22	.506-509	948.50	.22	.510-511	952.2	.01	.009	961.3	.21	.449-451	970.1	.21	.449-451
944.55	.22	.506-509	948.51	.22	.504-505	952.3	.01	.009	961.4	.21	.449-451	970.8	.21	.449-451
944.56	.22	.506-509	948.52	.22	.504-505	952.4	.01	.009	961.5	.21	.449-451	970.9	.21	.449-451
944.57	.22	.506-509	948.53	.22	.504-505	952.8	.01	.009	961.6	.21	.449-451	971.0	.21	.449-451
944.58	.22	.506-509	948.54	.22	.504-505	952.9	.01	.009	961.7	.21	.449-451	971.1	.21	.449-451
945.00	.22	.510-511	948.55	.22	.504-505	953.0	.01	.018-019	961.8	.21	.449-451	971.2	.21	.449-451
945.01	.22	.510-511	948.60	.22	.510-511	953.1	.01	.018-019	961.9	.21	.449-451	971.3	.21	.449-451
945.02	.22	.510-511	948.61	.22	.504-505	953.2	.01	.018-019	962.0	.21	.449-451	971.9	.21	.449-451
945.03	.22	.510-511	948.62	.22	.504-505	953.3	.01	.018-019	962.1	.21	.449-451	972.0	.21	.449-451
945.04	.22	.510-511	948.63	.22	.504-505	953.4	.01	.018-019	962.2	.21	.449-451	972.1	.21	.449-451
945.05	.22	.510-511	948.64	.22	.504-505	953.5	.01	.018-019	962.3	.21	.449-451	972.2	.21	.449-451
945.06	.22	.510-511	948.65	.22	.504-505	953.8	.01	.018-019	962.4	.21	.449-451	972.3	.21	.449-451
945.09	.22	.510-511	948.66	.22	.504-505	953.9	.01	.018-019	962.5	.21	.449-451	972.4	.21	.449-451
945.10	.22	.510-511	948.70	.22	.510-511	954.0	.01	.018-019	962.6	.21	.449-451	972.5	.21	.449-451
945.11	.22	.510-511	948.71	.22	.504-505	954.1	.01	.018-019	962.7	.21	.449-451	972.6	.21	.449-451
945.12	.22	.510-511	948.72	.22	.504-505	954.8	.01	.018-019	962.8	.21	.449-451	972.7	.21	.449-451
945.13	.22	.510-511	948.73	.22	.504-505	954.9	.01	.018-019	962.9	.21	.449-451	972.8	.21	.449-451
945.14	.22	.510-511	948.74	.22	.504-505	955.0	.01	.018-019	963.0	.21	.449-451	972.9	.21	.449-451
945.15	.22	.510-511	948.75	.22	.504-505	955.1	.01	.018-019	963.1	.21	.449-451	973.0	.21	.449-451
945.16	.22	.510-511	948.76	.22	.504-505	955.2	.01	.018-019	963.2	.21	.449-451	973.1	.21	.449-451
945.19	.22	.510-511	948.77	.22	.504-505	955.3	.01	.018-019	963.3	.21	.449-451	973.2	.21	.449-451
945.20	.22	.510-511	948.80	.22	.510-511	955.4	.01	.018-019	963.4	.21	.449-451	973.3	.21	.449-451
945.21	.22	.510-511	948.81	.22	.504-505	955.5	.01	.018-019	963.5	.21	.449-451	973.4	.21	.449-451
945.22	.22	.510-511	948.82	.22	.504-505	955.6	.01	.018-019	963.8	.21	.449-451	973.5	.21	.449-451
945.23	.22	.510-511	948.83	.22	.504-505	955.7	.01	.018-019	963.9	.21	.449-451	973.6	.21	.449-451
945.24	.22	.510-511	948.84	.22	.504-505	955.8	.01	.018-019	964.0	.21	.449-451	973.8	.21	.449-451
945.25	.22	.510-511	948.85	.22	.504-505	955.9	.01	.018-019	964.1	.21	.449-451	973.9	.21	.449-451
945.26	.22	.510-511	948.86	.22	.504-505	956.0	.01	.018-019	964.2	.21	.449-451	974.0	.21	.449-451
945.29	.22	.510-511	948.87	.22	.504-505	956.1	.01	.018-019	964.3	.21	.449-451	974.1	.21	.449-451
945.30	.22	.506-509	948.88	.22	.504-505	956.2	.01	.018-019	964.4	.21	.449-451	974.2	.21	.449-451
945.31	.22	.506-509	948.90	.22	.510-511	956.3	.01	.018-019	964.5	.21	.449-451	974.3	.21	.449-451
945.32	.22	.506-509	948.91	.22	.504-505	956.4	.01	.018-019	964.6	.21	.449-451	974.4	.21	.449-451
945.33	.22	.506-509	948.92	.22	.504-505	956.5	.01	.018-019	964.7	.21	.449-451	974.5	.21	.449-451
945.34	.22	.506-509	948.93	.22	.504-505	956.8	.01	.018-019	964.8	.21	.449-451	974.6	.21	.449-451
945.35	.22	.506-509	948.94	.22	.504-505	956.9	.01	.018-019	964.9	.21	.449-451	974.7	.21	.449-451
945.36	.22	.506-509	948.95	.22	.504-505	957.0	.01	.018-019	965.00	.21	.449-451	975.0	.21	.449-451
945.39	.22	.506-509	948.96	.22	.504-505	957.1	.01	.018-019	965.01	.21	.449-451	975.1	.21	.449-451
945.40	.22	.506-509	948.97	.22	.504-505	957.8	.01	.018-019	965.02	.21	.449-451	975.2	.21	.449-451
945.41	.22	.506-509	948.98	.22	.504-505	957.9	.01	.018-019	965.09	.21	.449-451	975.3	.21	.449-451
945.42	.22	.506-509	948.99	.22	.504-505	958.0	.04	.078	965.1	.21	.449-451	975.4	.21	.449-451
945.43	.22	.506-509	949.0	.22	.510-511	958.1	.04	.078	965.4	.21	.449-451	975.5	.21	.449-451
945.44	.22	.506-509	949.1	.22	.510-511	958.2	.21	.454-455	965.5	.21	.449-451	975.6	.21	.449-451
945.45	.22	.506-509	949.2	.22	.510-511	958.3	.18	.418	965.61	.21	.449-451	975.7	.21	.449-451
945.46	.22	.506-509	949.3	.22	.506-509	958.4	.21	.454-455	965.69	.21	.449-451	975.8	.21	.449-451
945.49	.22	.506-509	949.4	.22	.506-509	958.5	.11	.316	965.7	.21	.449-451	976.0	.21	.449-451
945.50	.22	.506-509	949.5	.22	.506-509	958.6	.08	.256	965.8	.21	.449-451	976.1	.21	.449-451
945.51	.22	.506-509	950.0	.02	.046-048	958.7	.04	.094-095	965.9	.21	.449-451	976.2	.21	.449-451
945.52	.22	.506-509	950.1	.01	.034-035	958.8	.21	.454-455	966.0	.21	.449-451	976.3	.21	.449-451
945.53	.22	.506-509	950.2	.01	.034-035	958.90	.21	.454-455	966.1	.21	.449-451	976.4	.21	.449-451
945.54	.22	.506-509	950.3	.01	.034-035	958.91	.21	.454-455	966.2	.21	.449-451	976.5	.02	.046-048
945.55	.22	.506-509	950.9	.01	.034-035	958.92	.21	.454-455	966.3	.21	.449-451	976.6	.21	.449-451
945.56	.22	.506-509	951.0	.01	.018-019	958.93	.21	.454-455	966.4	.21	.449-451	976.7	.21	.449-451
945.59	.22	.506-509	951.1	.01	.018-019	958.99	.21	.454-455	967.0	.21	.449-451	976.8	.21	.449-451
946.0	.22	.510-511	951.2	.01	.018-019	959.01	.21	.444-446	967.1	.21	.449-451	976.9	.21	.449-451
946.1	.22	.510-511	951.3	.01	.018-019	959.09	.21	.444-446	967.2	.21	.449-451	977.0	.21	.449-451
946.2	.22	.510-511	951.4	.01	.018-019	959.11	.21	.444-446	967.3	.21	.449-451	977.1	.21	.449-451
946.3	.22	.506-509	951.5	.03	.073-074	959.12	.21	.444-446	967.4	.21	.449-451	977.2	.21	.449-451
946.4	.22	.506-509	951.6	.01	.018-019	959.13	.21	.444-446	967.5	.21	.449-451	977.3	.21	.449-451
946.5	.22	.506-509	951.7	.01	.018-019	959.14	.21	.444-446	967.6	.21	.449-451	977.4	.21	.449-451
947.0	.03	.073-074	951.8	.01	.018-019	959.19	.21	.444-446	967.8	.21	.449-451	977.8	.21	.449-451
947.1	.04	.101-102	951.9	.01	.018-019	959.2	.21	.444-446	967.9	.21	.449-451	977.9	.21	.449-451
947.2	.06	.188-190	952.00	.01	.009	959.3	.21	.444-446	968.0	.21	.449-451	978.0	.21	.449-451
947.3	.06	.188-190	952.01	.01	.009	959.4	.21	.444-446	968.1	.21	.449-451	978.1	.21	.449-451
947.4	.13	.369	952.02	.01	.009	959.5	.21	.444-446	968.2	.21	.449-451	978.2	.21	.449-451
947.8	.22	.510-511	952.03	.01	.009	959.6	.21	.444-446	968.3	.21	.449-451	978.3	.21	.449-451
947.9	.22	.510-511	952.04	.01	.009	959.7	.21	.444-446	968.4	.21	.449-451	978.4	.21	.449-451
948.00	.22	.510-511	952.05	.01	.009	959.8	.21	.444-446	968.5	.21	.449-451	978.5	.21	.449-451
948.10	.22	.510-511	952.06	.01	.009	959.9	.21	.444-446	968.6	.21	.449-451	978.6	.21	.449-451

DX ...MDC ..DRG	DX ...MDC ..DRG	DX ...MDC ..DRG	DX ...MDC ..DRG	DX ...MDC ..DRG
978.8 ...21 .449-451	992.4 ...21 .454-455	996.52 ..21 .452-453	998.89 ..21 .452-453	V06.4 ...23 .467
978.9 ...21 .449-451	992.5 ...21 .454-455	996.53 ..02 .046-048	998.9 ...21 .452-453	V06.8 ...23 .467
979.0 ...21 .449-451	992.6 ...21 .454-455	996.54 ..09 .276	999.0 ...18 .421-422	V06.9 ...23 .467
979.1 ...21 .449-451	992.7 ...21 .454-455	996.55 ..21 .452-453	999.1 ...04 .078	V07.0 ...23 .467
979.2 ...21 .449-451	992.8 ...21 .454-455	996.56 ..21 .452-453	999.2 ...05 .144-145	V07.1 ...23 .467
979.3 ...21 .449-451	992.9 ...21 .454-455	996.57 ..21 .452-453	999.3 ...18 .423	V07.2 ...23 .467
979.4 ...21 .449-451	993.0 ...03 .068-070	996.59 ..21 .452-453	999.4 ...21 .447-448	V07.31 ..23 .467
979.5 ...21 .449-451	993.1 ...03 .068-070	996.60 ..21 .452-453	999.5 ...21 .447-448	V07.39 ..23 .467
979.6 ...21 .449-451	993.2 ...21 .454-455	996.61 ..05 .144-145	999.6 ...16 .395-396	V07.4 ...23 .467
979.7 ...21 .449-451	993.3 ...21 .454-455	996.62 ..05 .144-145	999.7 ...16 .395-396	V07.8 ...23 .467
979.9 ...21 .449-451	993.4 ...21 .454-455	996.63 ..01 .034-035	999.8 ...16 .395-396	V07.9 ...23 .467
980.0 ...21 .449-451	993.8 ...21 .454-455	996.64 ..11 .331-333	999.9 ...21 .452	V10.00 ..17 .411-412
980.1 ...21 .449-451	993.9 ...21 .454-455	996.65 ..11 .331-333		V10.01 ..17 .411-412
980.2 ...21 .449-451	994.0 ...21 .454-455	996.66 ..08 .249	**Supplementary**	V10.02 ..17 .411-412
980.3 ...21 .449-451	994.1 ...21 .454-455	996.67 ..08 .249	**Classification of Factors**	V10.03 ..17 .411-412
980.8 ...21 .449-451	994.2 ...21 .454-455	996.68 ..21 .452-453	**Influencing Health Status**	V10.04 ..17 .411-412
980.9 ...21 .449-451	994.3 ...21 .454-455	996.69 ..21 .452-453	**and Contact with Health**	V10.05 ..17 .411-412
981 .....21 .449-451	994.4 ...21 .454-455	996.70 ..21 .452-453	**Services**	V10.06 ..17 .411-412
982.0 ...21 .449-451	994.5 ...21 .454-455	996.71 ..05 .144-145	V01.0 ...23 .467	V10.07 ..17 .411-412
982.1 ...21 .449-451	994.6 ...03 .065	996.72 ..05 .144-145	V01.1 ...23 .467	V10.09 ..17 .411-412
982.2 ...21 .449-451	994.7 ...21 .454-455	996.73 ..05 .144-145	V01.2 ...23 .467	V10.11 ..17 .411-412
982.3 ...21 .449-451	994.8 ...21 .454-455	996.74 ..05 .144-145	V01.3 ...23 .467	V10.12 ..17 .411-412
982.4 ...21 .449-451	994.9 ...21 .454-455	996.75 ..01 .034-035	V01.4 ...23 .467	V10.20 ..17 .411-412
982.8 ...21 .449-451	995.0 ...21 .447-448	996.76 ..11 .331-333	V01.5 ...23 .467	V10.21 ..17 .411-412
983.0 ...21 .449-451	995.1 ...21 .447-448	996.77 ..08 .249	V01.6 ...23 .467	V10.22 ..17 .411-412
983.1 ...21 .449-451	995.20 ..15 .387-389	996.78 ..08 .249	V01.71 ..23 .467	V10.29 ..17 .411-412
983.2 ...21 .449-451	995.20 ..21 .449-451	996.79 ..21 .452-453	V01.79 ..23 .467	V10.3 ...17 .411-412
983.9 ...21 .449-451	995.21 ..15 .387-389	996.80 ..21 .452-453	V01.81 ..15 .391	V10.40 ..17 .411-412
984.0 ...21 .449-451	995.21 ..21 .449-451	996.81 ..11 .331-333	V01.81 ..23 .467	V10.41 ..17 .411-412
984.1 ...21 .449-451	995.22 ..15 .387-389	996.82 ..07 .205-206	V01.83 ..23 .467	V10.42 ..17 .411-412
984.8 ...21 .449-451	995.22 ..21 .449-451	996.83 ..05 .144-145	V01.84 ..23 .467	V10.43 ..17 .411-412
984.9 ...21 .449-451	995.23 ..15 .387-389	996.84 ..04 .101-102	V01.89 ..15 .391	V10.44 ..17 .411-412
985.0 ...21 .449-451	995.23 ..21 .449-451	996.85 ..16 .398-399	V01.89 ..23 .467	V10.45 ..17 .411-412
985.1 ...21 .449-451	995.27 ..15 .387-389	996.86 ..07 .204	V01.9 ...23 .467	V10.46 ..17 .411-412
985.2 ...21 .449-451	995.27 ..21 .449-451	996.87 ..21 .452-453	V02.0 ...23 .467	V10.47 ..17 .411-412
985.3 ...21 .449-451	995.29 ..15 .387-389	996.89 ..21 .452-453	V02.1 ...23 .467	V10.48 ..17 .411-412
985.4 ...21 .449-451	995.29 ..21 .449-451	996.90 ..08 .249	V02.2 ...23 .467	V10.49 ..17 .411-412
985.5 ...21 .449-451	995.3 ...21 .447-448	996.91 ..08 .249	V02.3 ...23 .467	V10.50 ..17 .411-412
985.6 ...21 .449-451	995.4 ...21 .454-455	996.92 ..08 .249	V02.4 ...23 .467	V10.51 ..17 .411-412
985.8 ...21 .449-451	995.50 ..21 .454-455	996.93 ..08 .249	V02.51 ..23 .467	V10.52 ..17 .411-412
985.9 ...21 .449-451	995.51 ..21 .454-455	996.94 ..08 .249	V02.52 ..23 .467	V10.53 ..17 .411-412
986 .....21 .449-451	995.52 ..21 .454-455	996.95 ..08 .249	V02.59 ..23 .467	V10.59 ..17 .411-412
987.0 ...21 .449-451	995.53 ..21 .454-455	996.96 ..08 .249	V02.60 ..07 .205-206	V10.60 ..17 .411-412
987.1 ...21 .449-451	995.54 ..21 .454-455	996.99 ..08 .249	V02.61 ..07 .205-206	V10.61 ..17 .411-412
987.2 ...21 .449-451	995.55 ..21 .454-455	997.0 ...01 .034-035	V02.62 ..07 .205-206	V10.62 ..17 .411-412
987.3 ...21 .449-451	995.59 ..21 .454-455	997.1 ...05 .144-145	V02.69 ..07 .205-206	V10.63 ..17 .411-412
987.4 ...21 .449-451	995.7 ...21 .454-455	997.2 ...05 .130-131	V02.7 ...23 .467	V10.69 ..17 .411-412
987.5 ...21 .449-451	995.80 ..21 .454-455	997.3 ...04 .101-102	V02.8 ...23 .467	V10.71 ..17 .411-412
987.6 ...21 .449-451	995.81 ..21 .454-455	997.4 ...06 .188-190	V02.9 ...23 .467	V10.72 ..17 .411-412
987.7 ...21 .449-451	995.82 ..21 .454-455	997.5 ...11 .331-333	V03.0 ...23 .467	V10.79 ..17 .411-412
987.8 ...21 .449-451	995.83 ..21 .454-455	997.60 ..08 .256	V03.1 ...23 .467	V10.81 ..17 .411-412
987.9 ...21 .449-451	995.84 ..21 .454-455	997.61 ..08 .256	V03.2 ...23 .467	V10.82 ..17 .411-412
988.0 ...21 .449-451	995.85 ..21 .454-455	997.62 ..08 .256	V03.3 ...23 .467	V10.83 ..17 .411-412
988.1 ...21 .449-451	995.86 ..21 .454-455	997.69 ..08 .256	V03.4 ...23 .467	V10.84 ..17 .411-412
988.2 ...21 .449-451	995.89 ..21 .454-455	997.71 ..06 .188-190	V03.5 ...23 .467	V10.85 ..17 .411-412
988.8 ...21 .449-451	995.90 ..18 .416-417	997.71 ..15 .387, 389	V03.6 ...23 .467	V10.86 ..17 .411-412
988.9 ...21 .449-451	995.91 ..18 .416-417	997.72 ..11 .331-333	V03.7 ...23 .467	V10.87 ..17 .411-412
989.0 ...21 .449-451	995.92 ..18 .416-417	997.72 ..15 .387, 389	V03.81 ..23 .467	V10.88 ..17 .411-412
989.1 ...21 .449-451	995.93 ..18 .416-417	997.79 ..05 .130-131	V03.82 ..23 .467	V10.89 ..17 .411-412
989.2 ...21 .449-451	995.94 ..18 .416-417	997.79 ..15 .387, 389	V03.89 ..23 .467	V10.9 ...17 .411-412
989.3 ...21 .449-451	996.00 ..05 .144-145	997.9 ...21 .452-453	V03.9 ...23 .467	V11.0 ...23 .467
989.4 ...21 .449-451	996.01 ..05 .138-139	998.0 ...21 .452-453	V04.0 ...23 .467	V11.1 ...23 .467
989.5 ...21 .449-451	996.02 ..05 .135-137	998.11 ..15 .387, 389	V04.1 ...23 .467	V11.2 ...23 .467
989.6 ...21 .449-451	996.03 ..05 .144-145	998.11 ..21 .452-453	V04.2 ...23 .467	V11.3 ...23 .467
989.7 ...21 .449-451	996.09 ..05 .144-145	998.12 ..21 .452-453	V04.3 ...23 .467	V11.8 ...23 .467
989.8 ...21 .449-451	996.1 ...05 .144-145	998.13 ..15 .387, 389	V04.4 ...23 .467	V11.9 ...23 .467
989.9 ...21 .449-451	996.2 ...01 .034-035	998.13 ..21 .452-453	V04.5 ...23 .467	V12.00 ..23 .467
990 .....21 .454-455	996.30 ..11 .331-333	998.2 ...21 .452-453	V04.6 ...23 .467	V12.01 ..23 .467
991.0 ...21 .454-455	996.31 ..11 .331-333	998.3 ...21 .452-453	V04.7 ...23 .467	V12.02 ..23 .467
991.1 ...21 .454-455	996.32 ..13 .369	998.31 ..21 .452-453	V04.81 ..23 .467	V12.03 ..23 .467
991.2 ...21 .454-455	996.39 ..11 .331-333	998.32 ..21 .452-453	V04.82 ..23 .467	V12.09 ..23 .467
991.3 ...21 .454-455	996.40 ..08 .249	998.4 ...21 .452-453	V04.89 ..23 .467	V12.1 ...23 .467
991.4 ...21 .454-455	996.41 ..08 .249	998.51 ..15 .387, 389	V05.0 ...23 .467	V12.2 ...23 .467
991.5 ...21 .454-455	996.42 ..08 .249	998.51 ..18 .418	V05.1 ...23 .467	V12.3 ...23 .467
991.6 ...21 .454-455	996.43 ..08 .249	998.59 ..15 .387, 389	V05.2 ...23 .467	V12.40 ..23 .467
991.8 ...21 .454-455	996.44 ..08 .249	998.59 ..18 .418	V05.8 ...23 .467	V12.41 ..23 .467
991.9 ...21 .454-455	996.45 ..08 .249	998.6 ...21 .452-453	V05.9 ...23 .467	V12.42 ..23 .467
992.0 ...21 .454-455	996.46 ..08 .249	998.7 ...21 .452-453	V06.0 ...23 .467	V12.49 ..23 .467
992.1 ...21 .454-455	996.47 ..08 .249	998.81 ..21 .452-453	V06.1 ...23 .467	V12.5 ...23 .467
992.2 ...21 .454-455	996.49 ..08 .249	998.82 ..02 .046-048	V06.2 ...23 .467	V12.60 ..23 .467
992.3 ...21 .454-455	996.51 ..02 .046-048	998.83 ..21 .452-453	V06.3 ...23 .467	V12.61 ..23 .467

DX	MDC	DRG	DX	MDC	DRG	DX	MDC	DRG	DX	MDC	DRG	DX	MDC	DRG
V12.69	23	467	V18.2	23	467	V26.4	23	467	V42.1	05	144-145	V47.2	23	467
V12.70	23	467	V18.3	23	467	V26.51	23	467	V42.2	05	144-145	V47.3	23	467
V12.71	23	467	V18.4	23	467	V26.52	23	467	V42.3	09	283-284	V47.4	23	467
V12.72	23	467	V18.51	23	467	V26.8	23	467	V42.4	08	256	V47.5	23	467
V12.79	23	467	V18.59	23	467	V26.9	23	467	V42.5	02	046-048	V47.9	23	467
V13.00	23	467	V18.61	23	467	V27.0	23	467	V42.6	04	101-102	V48.0	23	467
V13.01	23	467	V18.69	23	467	V27.1	23	467	V42.7	07	205-206	V48.1	23	467
V13.02	23	467	V18.7	23	467	V27.2	23	467	V42.81	16	398-399	V48.2	23	467
V13.03	23	467	V18.8	23	467	V27.3	23	467	V42.82	16	398-399	V48.3	23	467
V13.09	23	467	V18.9	23	467	V27.4	23	467	V42.83	07	467	V48.4	23	467
V13.1	23	467	V19.0	23	467	V27.5	23	467	V42.84	07	467	V48.5	23	467
V13.2	23	467	V19.1	23	467	V27.6	23	467	V42.89	23	467	V48.6	23	467
V13.21	23	467	V19.2	23	467	V27.7	23	467	V42.9	23	467	V48.7	23	467
V13.29	23	467	V19.3	23	467	V27.9	23	467	V43.0	02	046-048	V48.8	23	467
V13.3	23	467	V19.4	23	467	V28.0	14	383-384	V43.1	02	046-048	V48.9	23	467
V13.4	23	467	V19.5	23	467	V28.1	14	383-384	V43.21	05	144-145	V49.0	23	467
V13.5	23	467	V19.6	23	467	V28.2	14	383-384	V43.22	05	144-145	V49.1	23	467
V13.61	23	467	V19.7	23	467	V28.3	23	467	V43.3	05	144-145	V49.2	23	467
V13.69	23	467	V19.8	23	467	V28.4	23	467	V43.4	05	144-145	V49.3	23	467
V13.7	23	467	V20.0	23	467	V28.5	23	467	V43.5	11	331-333	V49.4	23	467
V13.8	23	467	V20.1	23	467	V28.6	23	467	V43.60	08	256	V49.5	23	467
V13.9	23	467	V20.2	23	467	V28.8	23	467	V43.61	08	256	V49.81	23	467
V14.0	23	467	V21.0	23	467	V28.9	23	467	V43.62	08	256	V49.82	23	467
V14.1	23	467	V21.1	23	467	V29.0	23	467	V43.63	08	256	V49.83	23	467
V14.2	23	467	V21.2	23	467	V29.1	23	467	V43.64	08	256	V49.84	23	467
V14.3	23	467	V21.30	23	467	V29.2	23	467	V43.65	08	256	V49.89	23	467
V14.4	23	467	V21.31	23	467	V29.3	23	467	V43.66	08	256	V50.0	09	283-284
V14.5	23	467	V21.32	23	467	V29.8	23	467	V43.69	08	256	V50.1	09	283-284
V14.6	23	467	V21.33	23	467	V29.9	23	467	V43.7	08	256	V50.2	12	350
V14.7	23	467	V21.34	23	467	V30.00	15	391	V43.83	23	467	V50.3	23	467
V14.8	23	467	V21.35	23	467	V30.01	15	391	V43.89	23	467	V50.8	23	467
V14.9	23	467	V21.8	23	467	V30.1	15	391	V44.0	23	467	V50.9	23	467
V15.01	23	467	V21.9	23	467	V30.2	15	469	V44.1	23	467	V51	09	283-284
V15.02	23	467	V22.0	23	467	V31.00	15	391	V44.2	23	467	V52.0	08	249
V15.03	23	467	V22.1	23	467	V31.01	15	391	V44.3	23	467	V52.1	08	249
V15.04	23	467	V22.2	23	467	V31.1	15	391	V44.4	23	467	V52.2	23	467
V15.05	23	467	V23.0	14	469	V31.2	15	469	V44.50	23	467	V52.3	23	467
V15.06	23	467	V23.1	14	469	V32.00	15	391	V44.51	23	467	V52.4	23	467
V15.07	23	467	V23.2	14	469	V32.01	15	391	V44.52	23	467	V52.8	23	462
V15.08	23	467	V23.3	14	469	V32.1	15	391	V44.59	23	467	V52.9	23	462
V15.09	23	467	V23.41	14	469	V32.2	15	469	V44.6	23	467	V53.01	01	034-035
V15.1	23	467	V23.49	14	469	V33.00	15	391	V44.7	23	467	V53.02	01	034-035
V15.2	23	467	V23.5	14	469	V33.01	15	391	V44.8	23	467	V53.09	01	034-035
V15.3	23	467	V23.7	14	469	V33.1	15	391	V44.9	23	467	V53.1	23	467
V15.41	23	467	V23.81	14	469	V33.2	15	469	V45.00	23	467	V53.2	23	467
V15.42	23	467	V23.82	14	469	V34.00	15	391	V45.01	23	467	V53.31	05	144-145
V15.49	23	467	V23.83	14	469	V34.01	15	391	V45.02	23	467	V53.32	05	144-145
V15.5	23	467	V23.84	14	469	V34.1	15	391	V45.09	23	467	V53.39	05	144-145
V15.6	23	467	V23.89	14	469	V34.2	15	469	V45.1	23	467	V53.4	23	467
V15.7	23	467	V23.9	14	469	V35.00	15	391	V45.2	23	467	V53.5	06	188-190
V15.81	23	467	V24.0	14	376	V35.01	15	391	V45.3	23	467	V53.6	11	331-333
V15.88	23	467	V24.1	23	467	V35.1	15	391	V45.4	23	467	V53.7	08	249
V15.89	23	467	V24.2	23	467	V35.2	15	469	V45.51	23	467	V53.8	23	467
V15.9	23	467	V25.01	23	467	V36.00	15	391	V45.52	23	467	V53.90	23	467
V16.0	23	467	V25.02	23	467	V36.01	15	391	V45.59	23	467	V53.91	23	467
V16.1	23	467	V25.03	23	467	V36.1	15	391	V45.61	23	467	V53.99	23	467
V16.2	23	467	V25.09	23	467	V36.2	15	469	V45.69	23	467	V54.01	08	249
V16.3	23	467	V25.1	23	467	V37.00	15	391	V45.71	23	467	V54.02	08	249
V16.40	23	467	V25.2	12	351	V37.01	15	391	V45.72	23	467	V54.09	08	249
V16.41	23	467	V25.2	13	369	V37.1	15	391	V45.73	23	467	V54.8	08	249
V16.42	23	467	V25.3	13	369	V37.2	15	469	V45.74	11	331-333	V54.9	08	249
V16.43	23	467	V25.40	23	467	V39.00	15	391	V45.75	23	467	V54.10	08	249
V16.49	23	467	V25.41	23	467	V39.01	15	391	V45.76	04	101-102	V54.11	08	249
V16.51	23	467	V25.42	23	467	V39.1	15	391	V45.77	12	352	V54.12	08	249
V16.59	23	467	V25.43	23	467	V39.2	15	469	V45.78	02	046-048	V54.13	08	249
V16.6	23	467	V25.49	23	467	V40.0	23	467	V45.79	23	467	V54.14	08	249
V16.7	23	467	V25.5	23	467	V40.1	23	467	V45.81	23	467	V54.15	08	249
V16.8	23	467	V25.8	23	467	V40.2	23	467	V45.84	23	467	V54.16	08	249
V16.9	23	467	V25.9	23	467	V40.3	23	467	V45.85	23	467	V54.17	08	249
V17.0	23	467	V26.0	12	352	V40.9	23	467	V45.86	23	467	V54.19	08	249
V17.1	23	467	V26.0	13	369	V41.0	23	467	V45.89	23	467	V54.20	08	249
V17.2	23	467	V26.1	23	467	V41.1	23	467	V46.0	23	467	V54.21	08	249
V17.3	23	467	V26.21	23	467	V41.2	23	467	V46.11	23	467	V54.22	08	249
V17.4	23	467	V26.22	23	467	V41.3	23	467	V46.12	23	467	V54.23	08	249
V17.5	23	467	V26.29	23	467	V41.4	23	467	V46.13	23	467	V54.24	08	249
V17.6	23	467	V26.31	23	467	V41.5	23	467	V46.14	23	467	V54.25	08	249
V17.7	23	467	V26.32	23	467	V41.6	23	467	V46.2	23	467	V54.26	08	249
V17.81	23	467	V26.33	23	467	V41.7	23	467	V46.8	23	467	V54.27	08	249
V17.89	23	467	V26.34	23	467	V41.8	23	467	V46.9	23	467	V54.29	08	249
V18.0	23	467	V26.35	23	467	V41.9	23	467	V47.0	23	467	V54.81	08	249
V18.1	23	467	V26.39	23	467	V42.0	11	331-333	V47.1	23	467	V54.89	08	249

DX	MDC	DRG
V55.0	04	101-102
V55.1	06	188-190
V55.2	06	188-190
V55.3	06	188-190
V55.4	06	188-190
V55.5	11	331-333
V55.6	11	331-333
V55.7	13	369
V55.8	23	467
V55.9	23	467
V56.0	11	317
V56.2	11	317
V56.31	11	317
V56.32	11	317
V56.8	11	317
V57.0	23	467
V57.1	23	462
V57.21	23	462
V57.22	23	462
V57.3	23	462
V57.4	23	467
V57.81	23	467
V57.89	23	462
V57.9	23	462
V58.0	17	409
V58.11	17	410, 492
V58.12	17	410, 492
V58.2	23	467
V58.30	23	467
V58.31	23	467
V58.32	23	467
V58.41	23	465-466
V58.42	23	465-466
V58.43	23	465-466
V58.44	23	465-466
V58.49	23	465-466
V58.5	23	465-466
V58.62	23	465-466
V58.63	23	465-466
V58.64	23	465-466
V58.65	23	465-466
V58.66	23	465-466
V58.67	23	465-466
V58.71	23	465-466
V58.72	23	465-466
V58.73	23	465-466
V58.74	23	465-466
V58.75	23	465-466
V58.76	23	465-466
V58.77	23	465-466
V58.78	23	465-466
V58.81	23	465-466
V58.83	23	465-466
V58.89	23	465-466
V58.9	23	465-466
V59.0	23	467
V59.1	09	283-284
V59.2	08	256
V59.3	23	467
V59.4	11	331-333
V59.5	23	467
V59.70	23	467
V59.71	23	467
V59.72	23	467
V59.73	23	467
V59.74	23	467
V59.8	23	467
V59.9	23	467
V60.0	23	467
V60.1	23	467
V60.2	23	467
V60.3	23	467
V60.4	23	467
V60.5	23	467
V60.6	23	467
V60.8	23	467
V60.9	23	467
V61.0	23	467
V61.10	23	467
V61.11	23	467
V61.12	23	467
V61.20	23	467
V61.21	23	467
V61.22	23	467
V61.29	23	467
V61.3	23	467
V61.41	23	467
V61.49	23	467
V61.5	13	369
V61.6	14	383-384
V61.7	14	380
V61.8	23	467
V61.9	23	467
V62.0	23	467
V62.1	23	467
V62.2	23	467
V62.3	23	467
V62.4	23	467
V62.5	23	467
V62.6	23	467
V62.81	23	467
V62.82	23	467
V62.83	23	467
V62.84	19	425
V62.89	23	467
V62.9	23	467
V63.0	23	467
V63.1	23	467
V63.2	23	467
V63.8	23	467
V63.9	23	467
V64.00	23	467
V64.01	23	467
V64.02	23	467
V64.03	23	467
V64.04	23	467
V64.05	23	467
V64.06	23	467
V64.07	23	467
V64.08	23	467
V64.09	23	467
V64.1	23	467
V64.2	23	467
V64.3	23	467
V64.41	23	467
V64.42	23	467
V64.43	23	467
V65.0	23	467
V65.11	23	467
V65.19	23	467
V65.2	23	467
V65.3	23	467
V65.40	23	467
V65.41	23	467
V65.42	23	467
V65.43	23	467
V65.44	23	467
V65.45	23	467
V65.46	23	467
V65.5	23	467
V65.8	23	467
V65.9	23	467
V66.0	23	467
V66.1	23	467
V66.2	23	467
V66.3	23	467
V66.4	23	467
V66.5	23	467
V66.6	23	467
V66.7	23	467
V66.9	23	467
V67.00	23	465-466
V67.01	23	465-466
V67.09	23	465-466
V67.1	17	409
V67.2	17	410,492
V67.3	23	467
V67.4	23	465-466
V67.51	13	369
V67.59	23	467
V67.6	23	467
V67.9	23	467
V68.0	23	467
V68.1	23	467
V68.2	23	467
V68.81	23	467
V68.89	23	467
V68.9	23	467
V69.4	23	467
V69.5	23	467
V70.0	23	467
V70.1	23	467
V70.2	23	467
V70.3	23	467
V70.4	23	467
V70.5	23	467
V70.6	23	467
V70.7	23	467
V70.81	23	467
V70.89	23	467
V70.9	23	467
V71.01	19	425
V71.02	19	425
V71.09	19	432
V71.1	17	411-412
V71.2	04	079-081
V71.3	21	454-455
V71.4	21	454-455
V71.5	23	467
V71.6	21	454-455
V71.7	05	143
V71.81	23	467
V71.82	23	467
V71.83	23	467
V71.89	23	467
V71.9	23	467
V72.0	23	467
V72.11	23	467
V72.19	23	467
V72.2	23	467
V72.31	23	467
V72.32	23	467
V72.40	23	467
V72.41	23	467
V72.42	23	467
V72.5	23	467
V72.6	23	467
V72.7	23	467
V72.81	23	467
V72.82	23	467
V72.83	23	467
V72.84	23	467
V72.85	23	467
V72.86	23	467
V72.9	23	467
V73.0	23	467
V73.1	23	467
V73.2	23	467
V73.3	23	467
V73.4	23	467
V73.5	23	467
V73.6	23	467
V73.88	23	467
V73.89	23	467
V73.98	23	467
V73.99	23	467
V74.0	23	467
V74.1	23	467
V74.2	23	467
V74.3	23	467
V74.4	23	467
V74.5	23	467
V74.6	23	467
V74.8	23	467
V74.9	23	467
V75.0	23	467
V75.1	23	467
V75.2	23	467
V75.3	23	467
V75.4	23	467
V75.5	23	467
V75.6	23	467
V75.7	23	467
V75.8	23	467
V75.9	23	467
V76.0	23	467
V76.10	23	467
V76.11	23	467
V76.12	23	467
V76.19	23	467
V76.2	23	467
V76.3	23	467
V76.41	23	467
V76.42	23	467
V76.43	23	467
V76.44	23	467
V76.45	23	467
V76.46	23	467
V76.47	23	467
V76.49	23	467
V76.50	23	467
V76.51	23	467
V76.52	23	467
V76.81	23	467
V76.89	23	467
V76.9	23	467
V77.0	23	467
V77.1	23	467
V77.2	23	467
V77.3	23	467
V77.4	23	467
V77.5	23	467
V77.6	23	467
V77.7	23	467
V77.8	23	467
V77.91	23	467
V77.99	23	467
V78.0	23	467
V78.1	23	467
V78.2	23	467
V78.3	23	467
V78.8	23	467
V78.9	23	467
V79.0	23	467
V79.1	23	467
V79.2	23	467
V79.3	23	467
V79.8	23	467
V79.9	23	467
V80.0	23	467
V80.1	23	467
V80.2	23	467
V80.3	23	467
V81.0	23	467
V81.1	23	467
V81.2	23	467
V81.3	23	467
V81.4	23	467
V81.5	23	467
V81.6	23	467
V82.0	23	467
V82.1	23	467
V82.2	23	467
V82.3	23	467
V82.4	23	467
V82.5	23	467
V82.6	23	467
V82.71	23	467
V82.79	23	467
V82.81	23	467
V82.89	23	467
V82.9	23	467
V83.01	23	467
V83.02	23	467
V83.81	23	467
V83.89	23	467
V84.01	23	467
V84.02	23	467
V84.03	23	467
V84.04	23	467
V84.09	23	467
V84.8	23	467
V85.0	23	467
V85.1	23	467
V85.21	23	467
V85.22	23	467
V85.23	23	467
V85.24	23	467
V85.25	23	467
V85.30	23	467
V85.31	23	467
V85.32	23	467
V85.33	23	467
V85.34	23	467
V85.35	23	467
V85.36	23	467
V85.37	23	467
V85.38	23	467
V85.39	23	467
V85.4	10	296-298
V85.51	23	467
V85.52	23	467
V85.53	23	467
V85.54	23	467
V86.0	23	467
V86.1	23	467

Complication & Comorbidity (CC) Code List

The following is a standard list of conditions considered to be complications and comorbidities that when present as a secondary diagnosis may affect DRG assignment. An asterisk (*) indicates a code range is represented. **Note:** Not all new 2007 ICD-9-CM codes designated as CC were identified in time to be published in this edition. Please visit www.ingenixonline.com and click on the ICD-9, CPT® and HCPCS Alerts link under the Quick Access Resources menu to view these edits.

*008.4	094.1	176.5	261	295.04	304.40	359.0	*428
*011	094.2	189.0	262	295.10	304.41	359.1	429.4
*012.0	094.3	189.1	*263	295.11	304.42	377.00	429.5
*012.1	094.81	189.2	269.0	295.12	304.50	377.01	429.6
*013	094.87	*191	273.3	295.13	304.51	377.02	*429.7
*014	094.89	192.0	276.0	295.14	304.52	383.01	429.81
*016	094.9	192.1	276.1	295.21	304.60	383.30	429.82
*017.2	098.0	192.2	276.2	295.22	304.61	383.81	430
*017.3	*098.1	192.3	276.3	295.23	304.62	*394	431
*017.4	112.0	192.8	276.4	295.24	304.70	*395	432.0
*017.5	112.4	*196	*276.5	295.30	304.71	*396	432.1
*017.6	112.5	*197	276.6	295.31	304.72	*397	433.01
*017.7	112.81	*198	276.7	295.32	304.80	398.0	433.11
*017.8	112.82	199.0	276.9	295.33	304.81	398.91	433.21
*017.9	112.83	*200	*277.0	295.34	304.82	401.0	433.31
*018	112.84	*201	279.02	295.40	304.90	*402.0	433.81
031.0	112.85	*202	279.03	295.41	304.91	402.11	433.91
*036	114.0	*203	279.04	295.42	304.92	402.91	434.01
037	114.2	*204	279.05	295.43	305.00	*403.0	434.11
*038	114.3	*205	279.06	295.44	305.01	403.11	434.91
040.0	114.9	*206	279.09	295.60	305.02	403.91	436
040.82	115.00	*207	*279.1	295.61	305.30	*404.0	437.2
042	115.01	*208	279.2	295.62	305.31	404.11	437.4
046.2	115.02	*242	279.3	295.63	305.32	404.12	437.5
*052	115.03	250.01	279.4	295.64	305.40	404.13	437.6
053.0	115.04	250.02	279.8	295.70	305.41	404.91	440.24
*053.1	115.05	250.03	279.9	295.71	305.42	404.92	*441.0
053.79	*115.1	250.11	280.0	295.72	305.50	404.93	441.1
053.8	*115.9	250.12	281.4	295.73	305.51	405.01	441.3
054.3	116.0	250.13	281.8	295.74	305.52	405.09	441.5
054.5	116.1	250.21	*282.4	295.80	305.60	410.01	441.6
054.71	117.3	250.22	*282.6	295.81	305.61	410.11	*444
054.72	117.4	250.23	*283	295.82	305.62	410.21	*445
054.74	117.5	250.31	*284	295.83	305.70	410.31	446.0
054.79	117.6	250.32	285.0	295.84	305.71	410.41	*446.2
054.8	117.7	250.33	285.1	295.90	305.72	410.51	446.3
055.0	118	250.41	*286	295.91	305.90	410.61	446.4
055.1	130.0	250.42	*287	295.92	305.91	410.71	446.5
055.2	130.1	250.43	288.0	295.93	305.92	410.81	446.6
055.71	130.2	250.51	288.1	295.94	307.1	410.91	446.7
055.79	130.3	250.52	289.81	296.04	*320	*411	451.0
055.9	130.4	250.53	289.82	296.14	*321	*413	451.11
056.00	130.5	250.61	291.0	296.34	*322	*415	451.19
056.01	130.7	250.62	291.1	296.44	*324	416.0	451.2
056.09	130.8	250.63	291.2	296.54	325	*420	451.81
056.71	135	250.71	291.3	296.64	331.4	*421	452
056.79	136.3	250.72	291.4	298.0	*335	*422	*453
056.8	137.0	250.73	291.81	298.3	340	423.0	456.0
070.2	137.1	250.81	291.89	298.4	343.2	423.1	456.20
070.3	137.2	250.82	291.9	299.00	*344.0	423.2	459.0
070.4	138	250.83	292.0	299.10	345.01	*424	464.11
070.5	*150	250.91	292.11	299.80	345.10	*425	464.21
070.6	*151	250.92	292.12	299.90	345.11	426.0	464.31
*070.7	*152	250.93	292.2	303.00	345.2	426.12	475
070.9	*153	251.0	292.81	303.01	345.3	426.13	478.21
072.0	*154	251.3	292.82	303.02	345.41	426.53	478.22
072.1	*155	252.1	292.83	303.90	345.51	426.54	478.24
072.2	*156	253.2	292.84	303.91	345.61	426.6	*478.3
072.3	*157	253.5	292.89	303.92	345.71	426.7	480.3
072.71	162.2	254.1	292.9	304.00	345.81	426.81	481
072.72	162.3	255.0	293.81	304.01	345.91	426.89	*482
072.79	162.4	255.3	293.82	304.02	348.1	426.9	*483
072.8	162.5	255.4	293.83	304.10	349.1	427.0	*484
079.82	162.8	255.5	293.84	304.11	349.81	427.1	485
086.0	162.9	255.6	295.00	304.12	349.82	427.2	486
*090.4	*163	*258	295.01	304.20	357.0	*427.3	487.0
*093	*164	259.2	295.02	304.21	*358.0	*427.4	491.1
094.0	176.4	260	295.03	304.22	358.1	427.5	*491.2

491.8	*533.4	575.3	*644.1	*745.1	775.6	838.19	902.54
491.9	*533.5	575.4	*646.6	745.2	775.7	*839.0	902.59
492.8	*533.6	575.5	*646.7	745.3	776.0	*839.1	902.87
493.01	533.71	576.1	*647.3	745.4	776.1	*850	904.0
493.02	533.91	576.3	*647.4	745.60	776.2	*851	*925
493.11	*534.0	576.4	*648.0	745.69	776.3	*852	929.0
493.12	*534.1	577.0	*648.2	745.7	777.1	*853	*952
493.20	*534.2	577.2	*648.3	746.01	777.2	*854	*953
493.21	534.31	*578	*648.5	746.02	777.5	*860	958.0
493.22	*534.4	579.3	*648.6	746.1	777.6	861.01	958.1
493.91	*534.5	580.0	*659.3	746.2	778.0	861.02	958.2
493.92	*534.6	580.4	*665.0	746.3	779.0	861.03	958.3
494.1	534.71	*580.8	*665.1	746.4	779.1	*861.1	958.4
*495	534.91	580.9	666.32	746.5	779.3	861.22	958.5
496	535.01	*581	666.34	746.6	779.4	*861.3	958.7
506.0	535.11	583.4	*668	746.7	779.7	862.1	995.4
506.1	535.21	584.5	*669.1	746.81	780.01	*862.2	995.86
*507	535.31	584.6	*669.3	746.82	780.03	*862.3	*995.9
508.0	535.41	584.7	*670	746.83	780.1	862.9	*996.0
508.1	535.51	584.8	*671.2	746.84	780.31	863.1	996.1
510.0	535.61	584.9	*671.3	746.86	780.32	*863.3	996.2
510.9	536.1	*585	*671.4	*747.1	780.39	*863.5	996.30
511.1	*536.4	*590.1	*673	747.22	781.7	*863.9	996.39
511.8	537.0	590.2	*674.0	748.4	785.4	*864	*996.4
511.9	537.3	590.3	674.10	748.5	*785.5	*865	*996.5
*512	537.4	590.8	674.12	748.61	786.03	*866	*996.6
*513	537.83	590.9	*674.2	765.01	786.04	*867	*996.7
515	537.84	591	*674.5	765.02	786.3	*868	*996.8
*516	*540	592.1	675.10	765.03	788.20	*869	*996.9
517.1	*550.0	593.5	675.11	765.04	788.29	870.3	*997.0
517.2	*550.1	595.0	675.12	765.05	789.5	870.4	997.1
517.8	*551	595.1	*680	765.06	790.7	870.8	997.2
518.0	*552	595.2	682.0	765.07	791.1	870.9	997.3
518.1	557.0	595.4	682.1	765.08	791.3	871.0	997.4
518.4	558.1	*595.8	682.2	767.0	*799.0	871.1	997.5
518.5	558.2	595.9	682.3	767.11	799.1	871.2	997.62
518.6	*560	596.0	682.5	768.5	799.4	871.3	997.7
518.7	562.02	596.1	682.6	769	*800	871.4	997.99
518.81	562.03	596.2	682.7	770.0	*801	871.9	998.0
518.82	562.12	596.4	682.8	770.12	802.1	872.72	*998.1
518.83	562.13	596.6	682.9	770.14	*802.2	872.73	998.2
518.84	566	596.7	684	770.16	*802.3	872.74	*998.3
*519.0	*567	597.0	685.0	770.18	802.4	873.33	998.4
519.2	568.81	598.1	694.4	770.2	802.5	873.9	*998.5
527.3	569.3	598.2	694.5	770.3	802.6	*874.0	998.6
527.4	569.5	599.0	695.0	770.4	802.7	*874.1	998.7
528.3	*569.6	599.4	696.0	770.5	802.8	874.3	998.83
530.21	569.83	*599.6	*707.0	770.7	802.9	874.5	998.89
530.4	569.85	599.7	*707.1	770.84	*803	*875	998.9
530.7	569.86	601.0	710.0	770.86	*804	*887	999.1
530.82	570	601.2	710.1	771.0	*805	*896	999.2
530.84	571.2	601.3	710.3	771.1	*806	*897	999.3
530.86	571.49	602.1	710.4	771.3	807.04	*900	999.4
530.87	571.5	603.1	710.5	771.81	807.05	901.0	999.5
*531.0	571.6	604.0	710.8	771.83	807.06	901.1	999.6
*531.1	572.0	611.72	*711.0	*772.1	807.07	901.2	999.7
*531.2	572.1	614.0	*711.6	772.2	807.08	901.3	999.8
531.31	572.2	614.3	714.1	772.4	807.09	901.41	V23.7
*531.4	572.4	614.5	714.2	772.5	*807.1	901.42	*V23.8
*531.5	573.1	615.0	*714.3	773.0	807.2	901.83	V23.9
*531.6	573.2	616.3	*722.8	773.1	807.3	902.0	V42.0
531.71	573.3	616.4	723.4	773.2	807.4	*902.1	V42.1
531.91	573.4	620.7	723.5	773.3	807.5	902.20	V42.2
*532.0	*574.0	*634	728.0	773.4	807.6	902.22	V42.6
*532.1	*574.1	*639	728.86	774.0	808.0	902.23	V42.7
*532.2	574.21	*640	728.88	774.1	808.1	902.24	*V42.8
532.31	*574.3	*641.0	*730.0	774.2	808.2	902.25	*V43.2
*532.4	*574.4	*641.1	*730.8	*774.3	808.3	902.26	V45.1
*532.5	*574.5	*641.3	*730.9	774.4	808.43	902.27	*V46.1
*532.6	*574.6	*641.8	*733.1	774.5	808.49	902.29	V49.83
532.71	*574.7	*641.9	*733.8	774.7	*808.5	*902.3	
532.91	*574.8	*642.4	733.93	775.1	808.8	*902.4	
*533.0	*574.9	*642.5	733.94	775.2	808.9	902.50	
*533.1	575.0	*642.6	733.95	775.3	*820	902.51	
*533.2	575.12	*642.7	*741	775.4	*821.0	902.52	
533.31	575.2	*644.0	745.0	775.5	*821.1	902.53	

Valid Three-digit ICD-9-CM Codes

Three-digit ICD-9-CM codes are used to identify a condition or disease only when a fourth or fifth digit is not available. The following are the only ICD-9-CM codes that are valid without further specificity.

024 Glanders

025 Melioidosis

035 Erysipelas

037 Tetanus

042 Human immunodeficiency virus (HIV) disease

048 Other enterovirus diseases of central nervous system

061 Dengue

064 Viral encephalitis transmitted by other and unspecified arthropods

071 Rabies

075 Infectious mononucleosis

080 Louse-borne [epidemic] typhus

096 Late syphilis, latent

101 Vincent's angina

118 Opportunistic mycoses

124 Trichinosis

129 Intestinal parasitism, unspecified

135 Sarcoidosis

138 Late effects of acute poliomyelitis

179 Malignant neoplasm of uterus, part unspecified

181 Malignant neoplasm of placenta

185 Malignant neoplasm of prostate

193 Malignant neoplasm of thyroid gland

217 Benign neoplasm of breast

220 Benign neoplasm of ovary

226 Benign neoplasm of thyroid glands

243 Congenital hypothyroidism

260 Kwashiorkor

261 Nutritional marasmus

262 Other severe, protein-calorie malnutrition

267 Ascorbic acid deficiency

311 Depressive disorder, not elsewhere classified

316 Psychic factors associated with diseases classified elsewhere

317 Mild mental retardation

319 Unspecified mental retardation

325 Phlebitis and thrombophlebitis of intracranial venous sinuses

326 Late effects of intracranial abscess or pyogenic infection

340 Multiple sclerosis

390 Rheumatic fever without mention of heart involvement

393 Chronic rheumatic pericarditis

412 Old myocardial infarction

430 Subarachnoid hemorrhage

431 Intracerebral hemorrhage

436 Acute, but ill-defined, cerebrovascular disease

452 Portal vein thrombosis

460 Acute nasopharyngitis [common cold]

462 Acute pharyngitis

463 Acute tonsillitis

470 Deviated nasal septum

475 Peritonsillar abscess

481 Pneumococcal pneumonia [streptococcus pneumoniae pneumonia]

485 Bronchopneumonia, organism unspecified

486 Pneumonia, organism unspecified

490 Bronchitis, not specified as acute or chronic

496 Chronic airway obstruction, not elsewhere classified

500 Coal workers' pneumoconiosis

501 Asbestosis

502 Pneumoconiosis due to other silica or silicates

503 Pneumoconiosis due to other inorganic dust

504 Pneumoconopathy due to inhalation of other dust

505 Pneumoconiosis, unspecified

514 Pulmonary congestion and hypostasis

515 Postinflammatory pulmonary fibrosis

538 Gastrointestinal mucostitis (ulcerative)

541 Appendicitis, unqualified

542 Other appendicitis

566 Abscess of anal and rectal regions

570 Acute and subacute necrosis of liver

586 Renal failure, unspecified

587 Renal sclerosis, unspecified

591 Hydronephrosis

605 Redundant prepuce and phimosis

630 Hydatidiform mole

631 Other abnormal product of conception

632 Missed abortion

650 Normal delivery

677 Late effect of complication of pregnancy, childbirth, and the puerperium

683 Acute lymphadenitis

684 Impetigo

700 Corns and callosities

725 Polymyalgia rheumatica

734 Flat foot

769 Respiratory distress syndrome

797 Senility without mention of psychosis

920 Contusion of face, scalp, and neck except eye(s)

931 Foreign body in ear

932 Foreign body in nose

936 Foreign body in intestine and colon

937 Foreign body in anus and rectum

938 Foreign body in digestive system, unspecified

981 Toxic effect of petroleum products

986 Toxic effect of carbon monoxide

990 Effects of radiation, unspecified

V08 Asymptomatic HIV infection status

V51 Aftercare involving the use of plastic surgery